CHILTON'S

TRUCK and VAN SERVICE MANUAL

Editorial Director Alan F. Turner
Editor-In-Chief Kerry A. Freeman, S.A.E.
Managing Editor Dean F. Morgantini, S.A.E. □ **Managing Editor** John H. Weise, A.S.E., S.A.E.
Assistant Managing Editor David H. Lee, A.S.E., S.A.E.

Project Manager W. Calvin Settle, Jr., S.A.E.
Service Editors John M. Baxter, S.A.E., Lawrence C. Braun, S.A.E., A.S.C., Dennis Carroll, Nick D'Andrea, Carl Denny, A.S.E., Wayne A. Eiffes, A.S.E., S.A.E., Martin J. Gunther, Vincent Kershner, Robert McAnally, Michael A. Newsome, Michael J. Randazzo, Richard J. Rivele, S.A.E., Richard T. Smith, Anthony Tortorici, Ron Webb
Editorial Consultants Edward K. Shea, S.A.E., Stan Stephenson

Production Manager John J. Cantwell
Art & Production Coordinator Robin S. Miller
Supervisor Mechanical Paste-up Margaret A. Stoner
Mechanical Artists Cynthia Fiore, William Gaskins

National Sales Manager Albert M. Kushnerick □ **Assistant** Jacquelyn T. Powers
Regional Sales Managers Joseph Andrews, Jr., David Flaherty, James O. Callahan

OFFICERS
President Lawrence A. Fornasieri
Vice President & General Manager John P. Kushnerick

CHILTON BOOK COMPANY Chilton Way, Radnor, Pa. 19089
Manufactured in USA
ISBN 0-8019-7832-7 Library of Congress Catalog Card No. 82-71518
1234567890 7654321098

SAFETY NOTICE

Proper service and repair procedures are vital to the safe, reliable operation of all motor vehicles, as well as the personal safety of those performing repairs. This manual outlines procedures for servicing and repairing vehicles using safe effective methods. The procedures contain many NOTES, CAUTIONS and WARNINGS which should be followed along with standard safety procedures to eliminate the possibility of personal injury or improper service which could damage the vehicle or compromise its safety.

It is important to note that repair procedures and techniques, tools and parts for servicing motor vehicles, as well as the skill and experience of the individual performing the work vary widely. It is not possible to anticipate all of the conceivable ways or conditions under which vehicles may be serviced, or to provide cautions as to all of the possible hazards that may result. Standard and accepted safety precautions and equipment should be used when handling toxic or flammable fluids, and safety goggles or other protection should be used during cutting, grinding, chiseling, prying, or any other process that can cause material removal or projectiles.

Some procedures require the use of tools specially designed for a specific purpose. Before substituting another tool or procedure, you must be completely satisfied that neither your personal safety, nor the performance of the vehicle will be endangered.

PARTS LISTINGS

Part numbers listed in this reference are not recommendations by Chilton for any product by brand name. They are references that can be used with interchange manuals and aftermarket supplier catalogs to locate each brand supplier's discrete part number.

Although information in this manual is based on industry sources and is as complete as possible at the time of publication, the possibility exists that some car manufacturers made later changes which could not be included here. While striving for total accuracy, Chilton Book Company cannot assume responsibility for any errors, changes, or omissions that may occur in the compilation of this data.

Chevrolet/GMC

1

INDEX

BEFORE SERVICING, SEE THE SAFETY NOTICE AT THE FRONT OF THE BOOK

Chevrolet Trucks

Year	Model Designation	Model Name
1982	Stepside 6½	C10 Pick Up
	Stepside 6½ Scotsdale	C10 Pick Up
	Stepside 6½ Silverado	C10 Pick Up
	Fleetside 6½	C10 Pick Up
	Fleetside 6½ Scotsdale	C10 Pick Up
	Fleetside 6½ Silverado	C10 Pick Up
	Fleetside 8½	C10 Pick Up
	Fleetside 8½ Scotsdale	C10 Pick Up
	Fleetside 8½ Silverado	C10 Pick Up
	Suburban	C10 Pick Up
	Suburban Scotsdale	C10 Pick Up
	Suburban Silverado	C10 Pick Up
	Stepside 8	C20 Pick Up
	Stepside 8 Scotsdale	C20 Pick Up
	Stepside 8 Silverado	C20 Pick Up
	Fleetside 8	C20 Pick Up
	Fleetside 8 Scotsdale	C20 Pick Up
	Fleetside 8 Silverado	C20 Pick Up
	Fleetside Bonus Cab	C20 Pick Up
	Fleetside Bonus Cab Scotsdale	C20 Pick Up
	Fleetside Bonus Cab Silverado	C20 Pick Up
	Fleetside Crew Cab	C20 Pick Up
	Fleetside Crew Cab Scotsdale	C20 Pick Up
	Fleetside Crew Cab Silverado	C20 Pick Up
	Suburban	C20 Pick Up
	Suburban Scotsdale	C20 Pick Up
	Suburban Silverado	C20 Pick Up
	Stepside 8	C30 Pick Up
	Stepside 8 Scotsdale	C30 Pick Up
	Stepside 8 Silverado	C30 Pick Up
	Fleetside 8	C30 Pick Up
	Fleetside 8 Scotsdale	C30 Pick Up
	Fleetside 8 Silverado	C30 Pick Up
	Fleetside Bonus Cab	C30 Pick Up
	Fleetside Bonus Cab Scotsdale	C30 Pick Up
	Fleetside Bonus Cab Silverado	C30 Pick Up
	Fleetside Crew Cab	C30 Pick Up
	Fleetside Crew Cab Scotsdale	C30 Pick Up
	Fleetside Crew Cab Silverado	C30 Pick Up
	Suburban	C30 Pick Up
	Suburban Scotsdale	C30 Pick Up
	Suburban Silverado	C30 Pick Up
	S10	S10 Pick Up
	S10 Fleetside 6	S10 Pick Up
	S10 Fleetside 6 Durango	S10 Pick Up

Chevrolet Trucks

Year	Model Designation	Model Name
1982	S10 Fleetside 6 Sport	S10 Pick Up
	S10 Fleetside 6 Tahoe	S10 Pick Up
	S10 Fleetside 7½	S10 Pick Up
	S10 Fleetside 7½ Durango	S10 Pick Up
	S10 Fleetside 7½ Sport	S10 Pick Up
	S10 Fleetside 7½ Tahoe	S10 Pick Up
	Blazer	K10 Blazer
	Blazer Silverado	K10 Blazer
	Chevy Van	G10 Van
	Sportvan	G10 Van
	Bonaventure	G10 Van
	Beauville	G10 Van
	Chevy Van	G20 Van
	Sportvan	G20 Van
	Bonaventure	G20 Van
	Beauville	G20 Van
	Chevy Van	G30 Van
	Sportvan	G30 Van
	Bonaventure	G30 Van
	Beauville	G30 Van
1983	Stepside 6½	C10 Pick Up
	Stepside 6½ Scotsdale	C10 Pick Up
	Stepside 6½ Silverado	C10 Pick Up
	Fleetside 6½	C10 Pick Up
	Fleetside 6½ Scotsdale	C10 Pick Up
	Fleetside 6½ Silverado	C10 Pick Up
	Fleetside 8½	C10 Pick Up
	Fleetside 8½ Scotsdale	C10 Pick Up
	Fleetside 8½ Silverado	C10 Pick Up
	Suburban	C10 Pick Up
	Suburban Scotsdale	C10 Pick Up
	Suburban Silverado	C10 Pick Up
	Stepside 8	C20 Pick Up
	Stepside 8 Scotsdale	C20 Pick Up
	Stepside 8 Silverado	C20 Pick Up
	Fleetside 8	C20 Pick Up
	Fleetside 8 Scotsdale	C20 Pick Up
	Fleetside 8 Silverado	C20 Pick Up
	Fleetside Bonus Cab	C20 Pick Up
	Fleetside Bonus Cab Scotsdale	C20 Pick Up
	Fleetside Bonus Cab Silverado	C20 Pick Up
	Fleetside Crew Cab	C20 Pick Up
	Fleetside Crew Cab Scotsdale	C20 Pick Up
	Fleetside Crew Cab Silverado	C20 Pick Up
	Suburban	C20 Pick Up
	Suburban Scotsdale	C20 Pick Up

Chevrolet Trucks

Year	Model Designation	Model Name
1983	Suburban Silverado	C20 Pick Up
	Stepside 8	C30 Pick Up
	Stepside 8 Scotsdale	C30 Pick Up
	Stepside 8 Silverado	C30 Pick Up
	Fleetside 8	C30 Pick Up
	Fleetside 8 Scotsdale	C30 Pick Up
	Fleetside 8 Silverado	C30 Pick Up
	Fleetside Bonus Cab	C30 Pick Up
	Fleetside Bonus Cab Scotsdale	C30 Pick Up
	Fleetside Bonus Cab Silverado	C30 Pick Up
	Fleetside Crew Cab	C30 Pick Up
	Fleetside Crew Cab Scotsdale	C30 Pick Up
	Fleetside Crew Cab Silverado	C30 Pick Up
	Suburban	C30 Pick Up
	Suburban Scotsdale	C30 Pick Up
	Suburban Silverado	C30 Pick Up
	S10	S10 Pick Up
	S10 Fleetside 6	S10 Pick Up
	S10 Fleetside 6 Durango	S10 Pick Up
	S10 Fleetside 6 Sport	S10 Pick Up
	S10 Fleetside 6 Tahoe	S10 Pick Up
	S10 Fleetside 7½	S10 Pick Up
	S10 Fleetside 7½ Durango	S10 Pick Up
	S10 Fleetside 7½ Sport	S10 Pick Up
	S10 Fleetside 7½ Tahoe	S10 Pick Up
	S10 Fleetside Extra Cab	S10 Pick Up
	S10 Fleetside Extra Cab Durango	S10 Pick Up
	S10 Fleetside Extra Cab Sport	S10 Pick Up
	S10 Fleetside Extra Cab Tahoe	S10 Pick Up
	S10 Blazer	S10 Blazer
	S10 Blazer Tahoe	S10 Blazer
	S10 Blazer Sport	S10 Blazer
	Blazer	K10 Blazer
	Blazer Silverado	K10 Blazer
	Chevy Van	G10 Van
	Sportvan	G10 Van
	Bonaventure	G10 Van
	Beauville	G10 Van
	Chevy Van	G20 Van
	Sportvan	G20 Van
	Bonaventure	G20 Van
	Beauville	G20 Van
	Chevy Van	G30 Van
	Sportvan	G30 Van
	Bonaventure	G30 Van
	Beauville	G30 Van

Chevrolet Trucks

Year	Model Designation	Model Name
1984	Stepside 6½	C10 Pick Up
	Stepside 6½ Scotsdale	C10 Pick Up
	Stepside 6½ Silverado	C10 Pick Up
	Fleetside 6½	C10 Pick Up
	Fleetside 6½ Scotsdale	C10 Pick Up
	Fleetside 6½ Silverado	C10 Pick Up
	Fleetside 8½	C10 Pick Up
	Fleetside 8½ Scotsdale	C10 Pick Up
	Fleetside 8½ Silverado	C10 Pick Up
	Suburban	C10 Pick Up
	Suburban Scotsdale	C10 Pick Up
	Suburban Silverado	C10 Pick Up
	Stepside 8	C20 Pick Up
	Stepside 8 Scotsdale	C20 Pick Up
	Stepside 8 Silverado	C20 Pick Up
	Fleetside 8	C20 Pick Up
	Fleetside 8 Scotsdale	C20 Pick Up
	Fleetside 8 Silverado	C20 Pick Up
	Fleetside Bonus Cab	C20 Pick Up
	Fleetside Bonus Cab Scotsdale	C20 Pick Up
	Fleetside Bonus Cab Silverado	C20 Pick Up
	Fleetside Crew Cab	C20 Pick Up
	Fleetside Crew Cab Scotsdale	C20 Pick Up
	Fleetside Crew Cab Silverado	C20 Pick Up
	Suburban	C20 Pick Up
	Suburban Scotsdale	C20 Pick Up
	Suburban Silverado	C20 Pick Up
	Stepside 8	C30 Pick Up
	Stepside 8 Scotsdale	C30 Pick Up
	Stepside 8 Silverado	C30 Pick Up
	Fleetside 8	C30 Pick Up
	Fleetside 8 Scotsdale	C30 Pick Up
	Fleetside 8 Silverado	C30 Pick Up
	Fleetside Bonus Cab	C30 Pick Up
	Fleetside Bonus Cab Scotsdale	C30 Pick Up
	Fleetside Bonus Cab Silverado	C30 Pick Up
	Fleetside Crew Cab	C30 Pick Up
	Fleetside Crew Cab Scotsdale	C30 Pick Up
	Fleetside Crew Cab Silverado	C30 Pick Up
	Suburban	C30 Pick Up
	Suburban Scotsdale	C30 Pick Up
	Suburban Silverado	C30 Pick Up
	S10	S10 Pick Up
	S10 Fleetside 6	S10 Pick Up
	S10 Fleetside 6 Durango	S10 Pick Up
	S10 Fleetside 6 Sport	S10 Pick Up

Chevrolet Trucks

Year	Model Designation	Model Name
1984	S10 Fleetside 6 Tahoe	S10 Pick Up
	S10 Fleetside 7½	S10 Pick Up
	S10 Fleetside 7½ Durango	S10 Pick Up
	S10 Fleetside 7½ Sport	S10 Pick Up
	S10 Fleetside 7½ Tahoe	S10 Pick Up
	S10 Fleetside Extra Cab	S10 Pick Up
	S10 Fleetside Extra Cab Durango	S10 Pick Up
	S10 Fleetside Extra Cab Sport	S10 Pick Up
	S10 Fleetside Extra Cab Tahoe	S10 Pick Up
	S10 Blazer	S10 Blazer
	S10 Blazer Tahoe	S10 Blazer
	S10 Blazer Sport	S10 Blazer
	Blazer	K10 Blazer
	Blazer Silverado	K10 Blazer
	Chevy Van	G10 Van
	Sportvan	G10 Van
	Bonaventure	G10 Van
	Beauville	G10 Van
	Chevy Van	G20 Van
	Sportvan	G20 Van
	Bonaventure	G20 Van
	Beauville	G20 Van
	Chevy Van	G30 Van
	Sportvan	G30 Van
	Bonaventure	G30 Van
	Beauville	G30 Van
1985	Stepside 6½	C10 Pick Up
	Stepside 6½ Scotsdale	C10 Pick Up
	Stepside 6½ Silverado	C10 Pick Up
	Fleetside 6½	C10 Pick Up
	Fleetside 6½ Scotsdale	C10 Pick Up
	Fleetside 6½ Silverado	C10 Pick Up
	Fleetside 8½	C10 Pick Up
	Fleetside 8½ Scotsdale	C10 Pick Up
	Fleetside 8½ Silverado	C10 Pick Up
	Suburban	C10 Pick Up
	Suburban Scotsdale	C10 Pick Up
	Suburban Silverado	C10 Pick Up
	Stepside 8	C20 Pick Up
	Stepside 8 Scotsdale	C20 Pick Up
	Stepside 8 Silverado	C20 Pick Up
	Fleetside 8	C20 Pick Up
	Fleetside 8 Scotsdale	C20 Pick Up
	Fleetside 8 Silverado	C20 Pick Up
	Fleetside Bonus Cab	C20 Pick Up
	Fleetside Bonus Cab Scotsdale	C20 Pick Up

Chevrolet Trucks

Year	Model Designation	Model Name
1985	Fleetside Bonus Cab Silverado	C20 Pick Up
	Fleetside Crew Cab	C20 Pick Up
	Fleetside Crew Cab Scotsdale	C20 Pick Up
	Fleetside Crew Cab Silverado	C20 Pick Up
	Suburban	C20 Pick Up
	Suburban Scotsdale	C20 Pick Up
	Suburban Silverado	C20 Pick Up
	Stepside 8	C30 Pick Up
	Stepside 8 Scotsdale	C30 Pick Up
	Stepside 8 Silverado	C30 Pick Up
	Fleetside 8	C30 Pick Up
	Fleetside 8 Scotsdale	C30 Pick Up
	Fleetside 8 Silverado	C30 Pick Up
	Fleetside Bonus Cab	C30 Pick Up
	Fleetside Bonus Cab Scotsdale	C30 Pick Up
	Fleetside Bonus Cab Silverado	C30 Pick Up
	Fleetside Crew Cab	C30 Pick Up
	Fleetside Crew Cab Scotsdale	C30 Pick Up
	Fleetside Crew Cab Silverado	C30 Pick Up
	Suburban	C30 Pick Up
	Suburban Scotsdale	C30 Pick Up
	Suburban Silverado	C30 Pick Up
	S10	S10 Pick Up
	S10 Fleetside 6	S10 Pick Up
	S10 Fleetside 6 Durango	S10 Pick Up
	S10 Fleetside 6 Sport	S10 Pick Up
	S10 Fleetside 6 Tahoe	S10 Pick Up
	S10 Fleetside 7½	S10 Pick Up
	S10 Fleetside 7½ Durango	S10 Pick Up
	S10 Fleetside 7½ Sport	S10 Pick Up
	S10 Fleetside 7½ Tahoe	S10 Pick Up
	S10 Fleetside Extra Cab	S10 Pick Up
	S10 Fleetside Extra Cab Durango	S10 Pick Up
	S10 Fleetside Extra Cab Sport	S10 Pick Up
	S10 Fleetside Extra Cab Tahoe	S10 Pick Up
	S10 Blazer	S10 Blazer
	S10 Blazer Tahoe	S10 Blazer
	S10 Blazer Sport	S10 Blazer
	Blazer	K10 Blazer
	Blazer Silverado	K10 Blazer
	Chevy Van	G10 Van
	Sportvan	G10 Van
	Bonaventure	G10 Van
	Beauville	G10 Van
	Chevy Van	G20 Van
	Sportvan	G20 Van

Chevrolet Trucks

Year	Model Designation	Model Name
1985	Bonaventure	G20 Van
	Beauville	G20 Van
	Chevy Van	G30 Van
	Sportvan	G30 Van
	Bonaventure	G30 Van
	Beauville	G30 Van
	Cargo Van	Astro
	Van	Astro
	Van CS	Astro
	Van CL	Astro
1986	Stepside 6½	C10 Pick Up
	Stepside 6½ Scotsdale	C10 Pick Up
	Stepside 6½ Silverado	C10 Pick Up
	Fleetside 6½	C10 Pick Up
	Fleetside 6½ Scotsdale	C10 Pick Up
	Fleetside 6½ Silverado	C10 Pick Up
	Fleetside 8½	C10 Pick Up
	Fleetside 8½ Scotsdale	C10 Pick Up
	Fleetside 8½ Silverado	C10 Pick Up
	Suburban	C10 Pick Up
	Suburban Scotsdale	C10 Pick Up
	Suburban Silverado	C10 Pick Up
	Stepside 8	C20 Pick Up
	Stepside 8 Scotsdale	C20 Pick Up
	Stepside 8 Silverado	C20 Pick Up
	Fleetside 8	C20 Pick Up
	Fleetside 8 Scotsdale	C20 Pick Up
	Fleetside 8 Silverado	C20 Pick Up
	Fleetside Bonus Cab	C20 Pick Up
	Fleetside Bonus Cab Scotsdale	C20 Pick Up
	Fleetside Bonus Cab Silverado	C20 Pick Up
	Fleetside Crew Cab	C20 Pick Up
	Fleetside Crew Cab Scotsdale	C20 Pick Up
	Fleetside Crew Cab Silverado	C20 Pick Up
	Suburban	C20 Pick Up
	Suburban Scotsdale	C20 Pick Up
	Suburban Silverado	C20 Pick Up
	Stepside 8	C30 Pick Up
	Stepside 8 Scotsdale	C30 Pick Up
	Stepside 8 Silverado	C30 Pick Up
	Fleetside 8	C30 Pick Up
	Fleetside 8 Scotsdale	C30 Pick Up
	Fleetside 8 Silverado	C30 Pick Up
	Fleetside Bonus Cab	C30 Pick Up
	Fleetside Bonus Cab Scotsdale	C30 Pick Up
	Fleetside Bonus Cab Silverado	C30 Pick Up

Chevrolet Trucks

Year	Model Designation	Model Name
1986	Fleetside Crew Cab	C30 Pick Up
	Fleetside Crew Cab Scotsdale	C30 Pick Up
	Fleetside Crew Cab Silverado	C30 Pick Up
	Suburban	C30 Pick Up
	Suburban Scotsdale	C30 Pick Up
	Suburban Silverado	C30 Pick Up
	S10	S10 Pick Up
	S10 Fleetside EL	S10 Pick Up
	S10 Fleetside 6	S10 Pick Up
	S10 Fleetside 6 Durango	S10 Pick Up
	S10 Fleetside 6 Sport	S10 Pick Up
	S10 Fleetside 6 Tahoe	S10 Pick Up
	S10 Fleetside 7½	S10 Pick Up
	S10 Fleetside 7½ Durango	S10 Pick Up
	S10 Fleetside 7½ Sport	S10 Pick Up
	S10 Fleetside 7½ Tahoe	S10 Pick Up
	S10 Fleetside Extra Cab	S10 Pick Up
	S10 Fleetside Extra Cab Durango	S10 Pick Up
	S10 Fleetside Extra Cab Sport	S10 Pick Up
	S10 Fleetside Extra Cab Tahoe	S10 Pick Up
	S10 Blazer	S10 Blazer
	S10 Blazer Tahoe	S10 Blazer
	S10 Blazer Sport	S10 Blazer
	Blazer	K10 Blazer
	Blazer Silverado	K10 Blazer
	Chevy Van	G10 Van
	Sportvan	G10 Van
	Bonaventure	G10 Van
	Beauville	G10 Van
	Chevy Van	G20 Van
	Sportvan	G20 Van
	Bonaventure	G20 Van
	Beauville	G20 Van
	Chevy Van	G30 Van
	Sportvan	G30 Van
	Bonaventure	G30 Van
	Beauville	G30 Van
	Cargo Van	Astro
	Van	Astro
	Van CS	Astro
	Van CL	Astro
1987-88	Stepside 6½	R10 Pick Up
	Stepside 6½ Scotsdale	R10 Pick Up
	Stepside 6½ Silverado	R10 Pick Up
	Fleetside 6½	R10 Pick Up
	Fleetside 6½ Scotsdale	R10 Pick Up

Chevrolet Trucks

Year	Model Designation	Model Name
1987–88	Fleetside 6½ Silverado	R10 Pick Up
	Fleetside 8½	R10 Pick Up
	Fleetside 8½ Scotsdale	R10 Pick Up
	Fleetside 8½ Silverado	R10 Pick Up
	Suburban	R10 Pick Up
	Suburban Scotsdale	R10 Pick Up
	Suburban Silverado	R10 Pick Up
	Stepside 8	R20 Pick Up
	Stepside 8 Scotsdale	R20 Pick Up
	Stepside 8 Silverado	R20 Pick Up
	Fleetside 8	R20 Pick Up
	Fleetside 8 Scotsdale	R20 Pick Up
	Fleetside 8 Silverado	R20 Pick Up
	Fleetside Bonus Cab	R20 Pick Up
	Fleetside Bonus Cab Scotsdale	R20 Pick Up
	Fleetside Bonus Cab Silverado	R20 Pick Up
	Fleetside Crew Cab	R20 Pick Up
	Fleetside Crew Cab Scotsdale	R20 Pick Up
	Fleetside Crew Cab Silverado	R20 Pick Up
	Suburban	R20 Pick Up
	Suburban Scotsdale	R20 Pick Up
	Suburban Silverado	R20 Pick Up
	Stepside 8	R30 Pick Up
	Stepside 8 Scotsdale	R30 Pick Up
	Stepside 8 Silverado	R30 Pick Up
	Fleetside 8	R30 Pick Up
	Fleetside 8 Scotsdale	R30 Pick Up
	Fleetside 8 Silverado	R30 Pick Up
	Fleetside Bonus Cab	R30 Pick Up
	Fleetside Bonus Cab Scotsdale	R30 Pick Up
	Fleetside Bonus Cab Silverado	R30 Pick Up
	Fleetside Crew Cab	R30 Pick Up
	Fleetside Crew Cab Scotsdale	R30 Pick Up
	Fleetside Crew Cab Silverado	R30 Pick Up
	Suburban	R30 Pick Up
	Suburban Scotsdale	R30 Pick Up
	Suburban Silverado	R30 Pick Up
	S10	S10 Pick Up
	S10 Fleetside EL	S10 Pick Up
	S10 Fleetside 6	S10 Pick Up
	S10 Fleetside 6 Durango	S10 Pick Up
	S10 Fleetside 6 Sport	S10 Pick Up
	S10 Fleetside 6 Tahoe	S10 Pick Up
	S10 Fleetside 7½	S10 Pick Up
	S10 Fleetside 7½ Durango	S10 Pick Up
	S10 Fleetside 7½ Sport	S10 Pick Up

Chevrolet Trucks

Year	Model Designation	Model Name
1987–88	S10 Fleetside 7½ Tahoe	S10 Pick Up
	S10 Fleetside Extra Cab	S10 Pick Up
	S10 Fleetside Extra Cab Durango	S10 Pick Up
	S10 Fleetside Extra Cab Sport	S10 Pick Up
	S10 Fleetside Extra Cab Tahoe	S10 Pick Up
	S10 Blazer	S10 Blazer
	S10 Blazer Tahoe	S10 Blazer
	S10 Blazer Sport	S10 Blazer
	Blazer	K10 Blazer
	Blazer Silverado	K10 Blazer
	Chevy Van	G10 Van
	Sportvan	G10 Van
	Bonaventure	G10 Van
	Beauville	G10 Van
	Chevy Van	G20 Van
	Sportvan	G20 Van
	Bonaventure	G20 Van
	Beauville	G20 Van
	Chevy Van	G30 Van
	Sportvan	G30 Van
	Bonaventure	G30 Van
	Beauville	G30 Van
	Cargo Van	Astro
	Van	Astro
	Van CS	Astro
	Van CL	Astro
	Van CT	Astro

GMC TRUCKS

Year	Model Designation	Model Name
1982	Fenderside 6½	C1500 Pick Up
	Fenderside 6½ High Sierra	C1500 Pick Up
	Fenderside 6½ Sierra Classic	C1500 Pick Up
	Wideside 6½	C1500 Pick Up
	Wideside 6½ High Sierra	C1500 Pick Up
	Wideside 6½ Sierra Classic	C1500 Pick Up
	Wideside 8	C1500 Pick Up
	Wideside 8 High Sierra	C1500 Pick Up
	Wideside 8 Sierra Classic	C1500 Pick Up
	Suburban	C1500 Pick Up
	Suburban High Sierra	C1500 Pick Up
	Suburban Sierra Classic	C1500 Pick Up
	Fenderside 8	C2500 Pick Up

GMC TRUCKS

Year	Model Designation	Model Name
1982	Fenderside 8 High Sierra	C2500 Pick Up
	Fenderside 8 Sierra Classic	C2500 Pick Up
	Wideside 8	C2500 Pick Up
	Wideside 8 High Sierra	C2500 Pick Up
	Wideside 8 Sierra Classic	C2500 Pick Up
	Bonus Cab 8	C2500 Pick Up
	Bonus Cab 8 High Sierra	C2500 Pick Up
	Bonus Cab 8 Sierra Classic	C2500 Pick Up
	Crew Cab 8	C2500 Pick Up
	Crew Cab 8 High Sierra	C2500 Pick Up
	Crew Cab 8 Sierra Classic	C2500 Pick Up
	Suburban	C2500 Pick Up
	Suburban High Sierra	C2500 Pick Up
	Suburban Sierra Classic	C2500 Pick Up
	Fenderside 8	C3500 Pick Up
	Fenderside 8 High Sierra	C3500 Pick Up
	Fenderside 8 Sierra Classic	C3500 Pick Up
	Wideside 8	C3500 Pick Up
	Wideside 8 High Sierra	C3500 Pick Up
	Wideside 8 Sierra Classic	C3500 Pick Up
	Bonus Cab 8	C3500 Pick Up
	Bonus Cab 8 High Sierra	C3500 Pick Up
	Bonus Cab 8 Sierra Classic	C3500 Pick Up
	Crew Cab 8	C3500 Pick Up
	Crew Cab 8 High Sierra	C3500 Pick Up
	Crew Cab 8 Sierra Classic	C3500 Pick Up
	Suburban	C3500 Pick Up
	Suburban High Sierra	C3500 Pick Up
	Suburban Sierra Classic	C3500 Pick Up
	S15	S15 Pick Up
	S15 Wideside 6 High Sierra	S15 Pick Up
	S15 Wideside 6 Sierra Classic	S15 Pick Up
	S15 Wideside 6 Gypsy	S15 Pick Up
	S15 Wideside 7½ High Sierra	S15 Pick Up
	S15 Wideside 7½ Sierra Classic	S15 Pick Up
	S15 Wideside 7½ Gypsy	S15 Pick Up
	Jimmy	K15 Jimmy
	Jimmy Sierra Classic	K15 Jimmy
	GMC Van	G1500 Van
	Vandura	G1500 Van
	Rally	G1500 Van
	Rally Custom	G1500 Van
	Rally STX	G1500 Van
	GMC Van	G2500 Van
	Vandura	G2500 Van
	Rally	G2500 Van

GMC TRUCKS

Year	Model Designation	Model Name
1982	Rally Custom	G2500 Van
	Rally STX	G2500 Van
	GMC Van	G3500 Van
	Vandura	G3500 Van
	Rally	G3500 Van
	Rally Custom	G3500 Van
	Rally STX	G3500 Van
1983	Fenderside 6½	C1500 Pick Up
	Fenderside 6½ High Sierra	C1500 Pick Up
	Fenderside 6½ Sierra Classic	C1500 Pick Up
	Wideside 6½	C1500 Pick Up
	Wideside 6½ High Sierra	C1500 Pick Up
	Wideside 6½ Sierra Classic	C1500 Pick Up
	Wideside 8	C1500 Pick Up
	Wideside 8 High Sierra	C1500 Pick Up
	Wideside 8 Sierra Classic	C1500 Pick Up
	Suburban	C1500 Pick Up
	Suburban High Sierra	C1500 Pick Up
	Suburban Sierra Classic	C1500 Pick Up
	Fenderside 8	C2500 Pick Up
	Fenderside 8 High Sierra	C2500 Pick Up
	Fenderside 8 Sierra Classic	C2500 Pick Up
	Wideside 8	C2500 Pick Up
	Wideside 8 High Sierra	C2500 Pick Up
	Wideside 8 Sierra Classic	C2500 Pick Up
	Bonus Cab 8	C2500 Pick Up
	Bonus Cab 8 High Sierra	C2500 Pick Up
	Bonus Cab 8 Sierra Classic	C2500 Pick Up
	Crew Cab 8	C2500 Pick Up
	Crew Cab 8 High Sierra	C2500 Pick Up
	Crew Cab 8 Sierra Classic	C2500 Pick Up
	Suburban	C2500 Pick Up
	Suburban High Sierra	C2500 Pick Up
	Suburban Sierra Classic	C2500 Pick Up
	Fenderside 8	C3500 Pick Up
	Fenderside 8 High Sierra	C3500 Pick Up
	Fenderside 8 Sierra Classic	C3500 Pick Up
	Wideside 8	C3500 Pick Up
	Wideside 8 High Sierra	C3500 Pick Up
	Wideside 8 Sierra Classic	C3500 Pick Up
	Bonus Cab 8	C3500 Pick Up
	Bonus Cab 8 High Sierra	C3500 Pick Up
	Bonus Cab 8 Sierra Classic	C3500 Pick Up
	Crew Cab 8	C3500 Pick Up
	Crew Cab 8 High Sierra	C3500 Pick Up
	Crew Cab 8 Sierra Classic	C3500 Pick Up

GMC TRUCKS

Year	Model Designation	Model Name
1983	Suburban	C3500 Pick Up
	Suburban High Sierra	C3500 Pick Up
	Suburban Sierra Classic	C3500 Pick Up
	S15	S15 Pick Up
	S15 Wideside 6 High Sierra	S15 Pick Up
	S15 Wideside 6 Sierra Classic	S15 Pick Up
	S15 Wideside 6 Gypsy	S15 Pick Up
	S15 Wideside 7½ High Sierra	S15 Pick Up
	S15 Wideside 7½ Sierra Classic	S15 Pick Up
	S15 Wideside 7½ Gypsy	S15 Pick Up
	S15 Jimmy	S15 Jimmy
	S15 Jimmy Sierra Classic	S15 Jimmy
	S15 Jimmy Gypsy	S15 Jimmy
	Jimmy	K15 Jimmy
	Jimmy Sierra Classic	K15 Jimmy
	GMC Van	G1500 Van
	Vandura	G1500 Van
	Rally	G1500 Van
	Rally Custom	G1500 Van
	Rally STX	G1500 Van
	GMC Van	G2500 Van
	Vandura	G2500 Van
	Rally	G2500 Van
	Rally Custom	G2500 Van
	Rally STX	G2500 Van
	GMC Van	G3500 Van
	Vandura	G3500 Van
	Rally	G3500 Van
	Rally Custom	G3500 Van
	Rally STX	G3500 Van
1984	Fenderside 6½	C1500 Pick Up
	Fenderside 6½ High Sierra	C1500 Pick Up
	Fenderside 6½ Sierra Classic	C1500 Pick Up
	Wideside 6½	C1500 Pick Up
	Wideside 6½ High Sierra	C1500 Pick Up
	Wideside 6½ Sierra Classic	C1500 Pick Up
	Wideside 8	C1500 Pick Up
	Wideside 8 High Sierra	C1500 Pick Up
	Wideside 8 Sierra Classic	C1500 Pick Up
	Suburban	C1500 Pick Up
	Suburban High Sierra	C1500 Pick Up
	Suburban Sierra Classic	C1500 Pick Up
	Fenderside 8	C2500 Pick Up
	Fenderside 8 High Sierra	C2500 Pick Up
	Fenderside 8 Sierra Classic	C2500 Pick Up
	Wideside 8	C2500 Pick Up

GMC TRUCKS

Year	Model Designation	Model Name
1984	Wideside 8 High Sierra	C2500 Pick Up
	Wideside 8 Sierra Classic	C2500 Pick Up
	Bonus Cab 8	C2500 Pick Up
	Bonus Cab 8 High Sierra	C2500 Pick Up
	Bonus Cab 8 Sierra Classic	C2500 Pick Up
	Crew Cab 8	C2500 Pick Up
	Crew Cab 8 High Sierra	C2500 Pick Up
	Crew Cab 8 Sierra Classic	C2500 Pick Up
	Suburban	C2500 Pick Up
	Suburban High Sierra	C2500 Pick Up
	Suburban Sierra Classic	C2500 Pick Up
	Fenderside 8	C3500 Pick Up
	Fenderside 8 High Sierra	C3500 Pick Up
	Fenderside 8 Sierra Classic	C3500 Pick Up
	Wideside 8	C3500 Pick Up
	Wideside 8 High Sierra	C3500 Pick Up
	Wideside 8 Sierra Classic	C3500 Pick Up
	Bonus Cab 8	C3500 Pick Up
	Bonus Cab 8 High Sierra	C3500 Pick Up
	Bonus Cab 8 Sierra Classic	C3500 Pick Up
	Crew Cab 8	C3500 Pick Up
	Crew Cab 8 High Sierra	C3500 Pick Up
	Crew Cab 8 Sierra Classic	C3500 Pick Up
	Suburban	C3500 Pick Up
	Suburban High Sierra	C3500 Pick Up
	Suburban Sierra Classic	C3500 Pick Up
	S15	S15 Pick Up
	S15 Wideside 6 High Sierra	S15 Pick Up
	S15 Wideside 6 Sierra Classic	S15 Pick Up
	S15 Wideside 6 Gypsy	S15 Pick Up
	S15 Wideside 7½ High Sierra	S15 Pick Up
	S15 Wideside 7½ Sierra Classic	S15 Pick Up
	S15 Wideside 7½ Gypsy	S15 Pick Up
	S15 Jimmy	S15 Jimmy
	S15 Jimmy Sierra Classic	S15 Jimmy
	S15 Jimmy Gypsy	S15 Jimmy
	Jimmy	K15 Jimmy
	Jimmy Sierra Classic	K15 Jimmy
	GMC Van	G1500 Van
	Vandura	G1500 Van
	Rally	G1500 Van
	Rally Custom	G1500 Van
	Rally STX	G1500 Van
	GMC Van	G2500 Van
	Vandura	G2500 Van
	Rally	G2500 Van

GMC TRUCKS

Year	Model Designation	Model Name
1984	Rally Custom	G2500 Van
	Rally STX	G2500 Van
	GMC Van	G3500 Van
	Vandura	G3500 Van
	Rally	G3500 Van
	Rally Custom	G3500 Van
	Rally STX	G3500 Van
1985	Fenderside 6½	C1500 Pick Up
	Fenderside 6½ High Sierra	C1500 Pick Up
	Fenderside 6½ Sierra Classic	C1500 Pick Up
	Wideside 6½	C1500 Pick Up
	Wideside 6½ High Sierra	C1500 Pick Up
	Wideside 6½ Sierra Classic	C1500 Pick Up
	Wideside 8	C1500 Pick Up
	Wideside 8 High Sierra	C1500 Pick Up
	Wideside 8 Sierra Classic	C1500 Pick Up
	Suburban	C1500 Pick Up
	Suburban High Sierra	C1500 Pick Up
	Suburban Sierra Classic	C1500 Pick Up
	Fenderside 8	C2500 Pick Up
	Fenderside 8 High Sierra	C2500 Pick Up
	Fenderside 8 Sierra Classic	C2500 Pick Up
	Wideside 8	C2500 Pick Up
	Wideside 8 High Sierra	C2500 Pick Up
	Wideside 8 Sierra Classic	C2500 Pick Up
	Bonus Cab 8	C2500 Pick Up
	Bonus Cab 8 High Sierra	C2500 Pick Up
	Bonus Cab 8 Sierra Classic	C2500 Pick Up
	Crew Cab 8	C2500 Pick Up
	Crew Cab 8 High Sierra	C2500 Pick Up
	Crew Cab 8 Sierra Classic	C2500 Pick Up
	Suburban	C2500 Pick Up
	Suburban High Sierra	C2500 Pick Up
	Suburban Sierra Classic	C2500 Pick Up
	Fenderside 8	C3500 Pick Up
	Fenderside 8 High Sierra	C3500 Pick Up
	Fenderside 8 Sierra Classic	C3500 Pick Up
	Wideside 8	C3500 Pick Up
	Wideside 8 High Sierra	C3500 Pick Up
	Wideside 8 Sierra Classic	C3500 Pick Up
	Bonus Cab 8	C3500 Pick Up
	Bonus Cab 8 High Sierra	C3500 Pick Up
	Bonus Cab 8 Sierra Classic	C3500 Pick Up
	Crew Cab 8	C3500 Pick Up
	Crew Cab 8 High Sierra	C3500 Pick Up
	Crew Cab 8 Sierra Classic	C3500 Pick Up

GMC TRUCKS

Year	Model Designation	Model Name
1985	Suburban	C3500 Pick Up
	Suburban High Sierra	C3500 Pick Up
	Suburban Sierra Classic	C3500 Pick Up
	S15	S15 Pick Up
	S15 Wideside 6 High Sierra	S15 Pick Up
	S15 Wideside 6 Sierra Classic	S15 Pick Up
	S15 Wideside 6 Gypsy	S15 Pick Up
	S15 Wideside 7½ High Sierra	S15 Pick Up
	S15 Wideside 7½ Sierra Classic	S15 Pick Up
	S15 Wideside 7½ Gypsy	S15 Pick Up
	S15 Jimmy	S15 Jimmy
	S15 Jimmy Sierra Classic	S15 Jimmy
	S15 Jimmy Gypsy	S15 Jimmy
	Jimmy	K15 Jimmy
	Jimmy Sierra Classic	K15 Jimmy
	GMC Van	G1500 Van
	Vandura	G1500 Van
	Rally	G1500 Van
	Rally Custom	G1500 Van
	Rally STX	G1500 Van
	GMC Van	G2500 Van
	Vandura	G2500 Van
	Rally	G2500 Van
	Rally Custom	G2500 Van
	Rally STX	G2500 Van
	GMC Van	G3500 Van
	Vandura	G3500 Van
	Rally	G3500 Van
	Rally Custom	G3500 Van
	Rally STX	G3500 Van
	Cargo Van	Safari
	Van SL	Safari
	Van SLX	Safari
	Van SLE	Safari
1986	Fenderside 6½	C1500 Pick Up
	Fenderside 6½ High Sierra	C1500 Pick Up
	Fenderside 6½ Sierra Classic	C1500 Pick Up
	Wideside 6½	C1500 Pick Up
	Wideside 6½ High Sierra	C1500 Pick Up
	Wideside 6½ Sierra Classic	C1500 Pick Up
	Wideside 8	C1500 Pick Up
	Wideside 8 High Sierra	C1500 Pick Up
	Wideside 8 Sierra Classic	C1500 Pick Up
	Suburban	C1500 Pick Up
	Suburban High Sierra	C1500 Pick Up
	Suburban Sierra Classic	C1500 Pick Up

GMC TRUCKS

Year	Model Designation	Model Name
1986	Fenderside 8	C2500 Pick Up
	Fenderside 8 High Sierra	C2500 Pick Up
	Fenderside 8 Sierra Classic	C2500 Pick Up
	Wideside 8	C2500 Pick Up
	Wideside 8 High Sierra	C2500 Pick Up
	Wideside 8 Sierra Classic	C2500 Pick Up
	Bonus Cab 8	C2500 Pick Up
	Bonus Cab 8 High Sierra	C2500 Pick Up
	Bonus Cab 8 Sierra Classic	C2500 Pick Up
	Crew Cab 8	C2500 Pick Up
	Crew Cab 8 High Sierra	C2500 Pick Up
	Crew Cab 8 Sierra Classic	C2500 Pick Up
	Suburban	C2500 Pick Up
	Suburban High Sierra	C2500 Pick Up
	Suburban Sierra Classic	C2500 Pick Up
	Fenderside 8	C3500 Pick Up
	Fenderside 8 High Sierra	C3500 Pick Up
	Fenderside 8 Sierra Classic	C3500 Pick Up
	Wideside 8	C3500 Pick Up
	Wideside 8 High Sierra	C3500 Pick Up
	Wideside 8 Sierra Classic	C3500 Pick Up
	Bonus Cab 8	C3500 Pick Up
	Bonus Cab 8 High Sierra	C3500 Pick Up
	Bonus Cab 8 Sierra Classic	C3500 Pick Up
	Crew Cab 8	C3500 Pick Up
	Crew Cab 8 High Sierra	C3500 Pick Up
	Crew Cab 8 Sierra Classic	C3500 Pick Up
	Suburban	C3500 Pick Up
	Suburban High Sierra	C3500 Pick Up
	Suburban Sierra Classic	C3500 Pick Up
	S15 Special	S15 Pick Up
	S15 Wideside 6 High Sierra	S15 Pick Up
	S15 Wideside 6 Sierra Classic	S15 Pick Up
	S15 Wideside 6 Gypsy	S15 Pick Up
	S15 Wideside 7½ High Sierra	S15 Pick Up
	S15 Wideside 7½ Sierra Classic	S15 Pick Up
	S15 Wideside 7½ Gypsy	S15 Pick Up
	S15 Jimmy	S15 Jimmy
	S15 Jimmy Sierra Classic	S15 Jimmy
	S15 Jimmy Gypsy	S15 Jimmy
	Jimmy	K15 Jimmy
	Jimmy Sierra Classic	K15 Jimmy
	GMC Van	G1500 Van
	Vandura	G1500 Van
	Rally	G1500 Van
	Rally Custom	G1500 Van

GMC TRUCKS

Year	Model Designation	Model Name
1986	Rally STX	G1500 Van
	GMC Van	G2500 Van
	Vandura	G2500 Van
	Rally	G2500 Van
	Rally Custom	G2500 Van
	Rally STX	G2500 Van
	GMC Van	G3500 Van
	Vandura	G3500 Van
	Rally	G3500 Van
	Rally Custom	G3500 Van
	Rally STX	G3500 Van
	Cargo Van	Safari
	Van SL	Safari
	Van SLX	Safari
	Van SLE	Safari
1987-88	Fenderside 6½	C1500 Pick Up
	Fenderside 6½ High Sierra	C1500 Pick Up
	Fenderside 6½ Sierra Classic	C1500 Pick Up
	Wideside 6½	C1500 Pick Up
	Wideside 6½ High Sierra	C1500 Pick Up
	Wideside 6½ Sierra Classic	C1500 Pick Up
	Wideside 8	C1500 Pick Up
	Wideside 8 High Sierra	C1500 Pick Up
	Wideside 8 Sierra Classic	C1500 Pick Up
	Suburban	C1500 Pick Up
	Suburban High Sierra	C1500 Pick Up
	Suburban Sierra Classic	C1500 Pick Up
	Fenderside 8	C2500 Pick Up
	Fenderside 8 High Sierra	C2500 Pick Up
	Fenderside 8 Sierra Classic	C2500 Pick Up
	Wideside 8	C2500 Pick Up
	Wideside 8 High Sierra	C2500 Pick Up
	Wideside 8 Sierra Classic	C2500 Pick Up
	Bonus Cab 8	C2500 Pick Up
	Bonus Cab 8 High Sierra	C2500 Pick Up
	Bonus Cab 8 Sierra Classic	C2500 Pick Up
	Crew Cab 8	C2500 Pick Up
	Crew Cab 8 High Sierra	C2500 Pick Up
	Crew Cab 8 Sierra Classic	C2500 Pick Up
	Suburban	C2500 Pick Up
	Suburban High Sierra	C2500 Pick Up
	Suburban Sierra Classic	C2500 Pick Up
	Fenderside 8	C3500 Pick Up
	Fenderside 8 High Sierra	C3500 Pick Up
	Fenderside 8 Sierra Classic	C3500 Pick Up
	Wideside 8	C3500 Pick Up

GMC TRUCKS

Year	Model Designation	Model Name
1987-88	Wideside 8 High Sierra	C3500 Pick Up
	Wideside 8 Sierra Classic	C3500 Pick Up
	Bonus Cab 8	C3500 Pick Up
	Bonus Cab 8 High Sierra	C3500 Pick Up
	Bonus Cab 8 Sierra Classic	C3500 Pick Up
	Crew Cab 8	C3500 Pick Up
	Crew Cab 8 High Sierra	C3500 Pick Up
	Crew Cab 8 Sierra Classic	C3500 Pick Up
	Suburban	C3500 Pick Up
	Suburban High Sierra	C3500 Pick Up
	Suburban Sierra Classic	C3500 Pick Up
	S15 Special	S15 Pick Up
	S15 Wideside 6 High Sierra	S15 Pick Up
	S15 Wideside 6 Sierra Classic	S15 Pick Up
	S15 Wideside 6 Gypsy	S15 Pick Up
	S15 Wideside 7½ High Sierra	S15 Pick Up
	S15 Wideside 7½ Sierra Classic	S15 Pick Up
	S15 Wideside 7½ Gypsy	S15 Pick Up
	S15 Jimmy	S15 Jimmy
	S15 Jimmy Sierra Classic	S15 Jimmy
	S15 Jimmy Gypsy	S15 Jimmy
	Jimmy	K15 Jimmy

GMC TRUCKS

Year	Model Designation	Model Name
1987-88	Jimmy Sierra Classic	K15 Jimmy
	GMC Van	G1500 Van
	Vandura	G1500 Van
	Rally	G1500 Van
	Rally Custom	G1500 Van
	Rally STX	G1500 Van
	GMC Van	G2500 Van
	Vandura	G2500 Van
	Rally	G2500 Van
	Rally Custom	G2500 Van
	Rally STX	G2500 Van
	GMC Van	G3500 Van
	Vandura	G3500 Van
	Rally	G3500 Van
	Rally Custom	G3500 Van
	Rally STX	G3500 Van
	Cargo Van	Safari
	Van SL	Safari
	Van SLX	Safari
	Van SLE	Safari
	Van SLT	Safari

ENGINE IDENTIFICATION CODES BY VIN NUMBER

Engine Cu. In. (liter)	Cylinders	1982	1983	1984	1985	1986	1987	1988
119 (1.9)	4	A	A	A	A	—	—	—
121 (2.0)	4	—	Y	Y	—	—	—	—
135 (2.2)	4	—	S	S	S	S	—	—
151 (2.5)	4	—	—	—	E	E	E	E
173 (2.8)	6	B	B	B	B	B	—	—
173 (2.8)	6	—	—	—	—	R	R	R
252 (4.1)	6	D	D	D	—	—	—	—
260 (4.3)	6	—	—	—	N	N	—	—
260 (4.3)	6	—	—	—	—	Z	Z	Z
292 (4.8)	6	T	T	T	T	T	T	T
305 (5.0)	8	F	F	F	F	F	—	—
305 (5.0)	8	H	H	H	H	H	H	H
350 (5.7)	8	L	L	L	L	L	L	—
350 (5.7)	8	M	M	M	M	M	M	M
350 (5.7)	8	P	P	P	—	—	—	—

ENGINE IDENTIFICATION CODES BY VIN NUMBER

Engine Cu. In. (liter)	Cylinders	1982	1983	1984	1985	1986	1987	1988
350 (5.7)	8	—	—	—	—	—	K	K
380 (6.2)	8	C	C	C	C	C	C	C
380 (6.2)	8	J	J	J	J	J	J	J
454 (7.4)	8	W	W	W	W	W	W	—
454 (7.4)	8	—	—	—	—	—	N	N

GENERAL ENGINE SPECIFICATIONS

Year	VIN	No. Cylinder Displacement cu. in. (liter)	Fuel System type	Net Horsepower @ rpm	Net Torque @ rpm (ft. lbs.)	Bore × Stroke (in.)	Com-pression Ratio	Oil Pressure @ rpm
1982	A	4-119 (1.9)	Carb	82 @ 4600	101 @ 3000	3.43×3.23	8.4:1	55 ①
	B	6-173 (2.8)	Carb	115 @ 4800	150 @ 2100	3.56×3.04	8.5:1	40 ①
	D	6-252 (4.1)	Carb	110 @ 3600	195 @ 2000	3.88×3.53	8.3:1	50 ①
	T	6-292 (4.8)	Carb	115 @ 3400	215 @ 1600	3.88×4.12	8.0:1	50 ①
	F	8-305 (5.0)	Carb	150 @ 3800	240 @ 2400	3.74×3.48	8.5:1	45 ①
	H	8-305 (5.0)	Carb	165 @ 4400	240 @ 2000	3.74×3.48	9.0:1	45 ①
	L	8-350 (5.7)	Carb	165 @ 3800	275 @ 1600	4.00×3.48	8.3:1	45 ①
	M	8-350 (5.7)	Carb	185 @ 4000	285 @ 2400	4.00×3.48	8.3:1	45 ①
	P	8-350 (5.7)	Carb	155 @ 4000	240 @ 2800	4.00×3.48	8.3:1	45 ①
	C	8-380 (6.2)	Diesel	130 @ 3600	240 @ 2000	3.98×3.80	21.0:1	35 ①
	J	8-380 (6.2)	Diesel	135 @ 3600	240 @ 2000	3.98×3.80	21.0:1	35 ①
	W	8-454 (7.4)	Carb	240 @ 3800	375 @ 3200	4.25×4.00	8.0:1	40 ①
1983	A	4-119 (1.9)	Carb	82 @ 4600	101 @ 3000	3.43×3.23	8.4:1	55 ①
	Y	4-121 (2.0)	Carb	83 @ 4600	108 @ 2400	3.50×3.15	9.3:1	45 ①
	S	4-135 (2.2)	Diesel	62 @ 4300	96 @ 2200	3.46×3.62	21.0:1	60 ①
	B	6-173 (2.8)	Carb	115 @ 4800	150 @ 2100	3.56×3.04	8.5:1	40 ①
	D	6-252 (4.1)	Carb	110 @ 3600	195 @ 2000	3.88×3.53	8.3:1	50 ①
	T	6-292 (4.8)	Carb	115 @ 3400	215 @ 1600	3.88×4.12	8.0:1	50 ①
	F	8-305 (5.0)	Carb	150 @ 3800	240 @ 2400	3.74×3.48	8.5:1	45 ①
	H	8-305 (5.0)	Carb	165 @ 4400	240 @ 2000	3.74×3.48	9.0:1	45 ①
	L	8-350 (5.7)	Carb	165 @ 3800	275 @ 1600	4.00×3.48	8.3:1	45 ①
	M	8-350 (5.7)	Carb	185 @ 4000	285 @ 2400	4.00×3.48	8.3:1	45 ①
	P	8-350 (5.7)	Carb	155 @ 4000	240 @ 2800	4.00×3.48	8.3:1	45 ①
	C	8-380 (6.2)	Diesel	130 @ 3600	240 @ 2000	3.98×3.80	21.0:1	35 ①
	J	8-380 (6.2)	Diesel	135 @ 3600	240 @ 2000	3.98×3.80	21.0:1	35 ①
	W	8-454 (7.4)	Carb	240 @ 3800	375 @ 3200	4.25×4.00	8.0:1	40 ①
1984	A	4-119 (1.9)	Carb	82 @ 4600	101 @ 3000	3.43×3.23	8.4:1	55 ①
	Y	4-121 (2.0)	Carb	83 @ 4600	108 @ 2400	3.50×3.15	9.3:1	45 ①
	S	4-135 (2.2)	Diesel	62 @ 4300	96 @ 2200	3.46×3.62	21.0:1	60 ①
	B	6-173 (2.8)	Carb	115 @ 4800	150 @ 2100	3.56×3.04	8.5:1	40 ①
	D	6-252 (4.1)	Carb	110 @ 3600	195 @ 2000	3.88×3.53	8.3:1	50 ①
	T	6-292 (4.8)	Carb	115 @ 3400	215 @ 1600	3.88×4.12	8.0:1	50 ①
	F	8-305 (5.0)	Carb	150 @ 3800	240 @ 2400	3.74×3.48	8.5:1	45 ①

GENERAL ENGINE SPECIFICATIONS

Year	VIN	No. Cylinder Displacement cu. in. (liter)	Fuel System type	Net Horsepower @ rpm	Net Torque @ rpm (ft. lbs.)	Bore × Stroke (in.)	Com-pression Ratio	Oil Pressure @ rpm
1984	H	8-305 (5.0)	Carb	165 @ 4400	240 @ 2000	3.74×3.48	9.0:1	45 ①
	L	8-350 (5.7)	Carb	165 @ 3800	275 @ 1600	4.00×3.48	8.3:1	45 ①
	M	8-350 (5.7)	Carb	185 @ 4000	285 @ 2400	4.00×3.48	8.3:1	45 ①
	P	8-350 (5.7)	Carb	155 @ 4000	240 @ 2800	4.00×3.48	8.3:1	45 ①
	C	8-380 (6.2)	Diesel	130 @ 3600	240 @ 2000	3.98×3.80	21.0:1	35 ①
	J	8-380 (6.2)	Diesel	135 @ 3600	240 @ 2000	3.98×3.80	21.0:1	35 ①
	W	8-454 (7.4)	Carb	240 @ 3800	375 @ 3200	4.25×4.00	8.0:1	40 ①
1985	A	4-119 (1.9)	Carb	82 @ 4600	101 @ 3000	3.43×3.23	8.4:1	55 ①
	S	4-135 (2.2)	Diesel	62 @ 4300	96 @ 2200	3.46×3.62	21.0:1	60 ①
	E	4-151 (2.5)	F.I.	92 @ 4400	134 @ 2800	4.00×3.00	9.0:1	45 ①
	B	6-173 (2.8)	Carb	115 @ 4800	150 @ 2100	3.56×3.04	8.5:1	40 ①
	N	6-260 (4.3)	Carb	145 @ 4000	225 @ 2400	4.00×3.48	9.3:1	50 ①
	T	6-292 (4.8)	Carb	115 @ 3400	215 @ 1600	3.88×4.12	8.0:1	50 ①
	F	8-305 (5.0)	Carb	150 @ 3800	240 @ 2400	3.74×3.48	8.5:1	45 ①
	H	8-305 (5.0)	Carb	165 @ 4400	240 @ 2000	3.74×3.48	9.0:1	45 ①
	L	8-350 (5.7)	Carb	165 @ 3800	275 @ 1600	4.00×3.48	8.3:1	45 ①
	M	8-350 (5.7)	Carb	185 @ 4000	285 @ 2400	4.00×3.48	8.3:1	45 ①
	C	8-380 (6.2)	Diesel	130 @ 3600	240 @ 2000	3.98×3.80	21.0:1	35 ①
	J	8-380 (6.2)	Diesel	135 @ 3600	240 @ 2000	3.98×3.80	21.0:1	35 ①
	W	8-454 (7.4)	Carb	240 @ 3800	375 @ 3200	4.25×4.00	8.0:1	40 ①
1986	S	4-135 (2.2)	Diesel	62 @ 4300	96 @ 2200	3.46×3.62	21.0:1	60 ①
	E	4-151 (2.5)	F.I.	92 @ 4400	134 @ 2800	4.00×3.00	9.0:1	45 ①
	B	6-173 (2.8)	Carb	115 @ 4800	150 @ 2100	3.56×3.04	8.5:1	40 ①
	R	6-173 (2.8)	F.I.	125 @ 4800	150 @ 2200	3.50×2.99	8.5:1	50 ①
	N	6-260 (4.3)	Carb	145 @ 4000	225 @ 2400	4.00×3.48	8.3:1	50 ①
	Z	6-260 (4.3)	F.I.	145 @ 4000	230 @ 2400	4.00×3.48	9.3:1	35 ①
	T	6-292 (4.8)	Carb	115 @ 3400	215 @ 1600	3.88×4.12	8.0:1	50 ①
	F	8-305 (5.0)	Carb	150 @ 3800	240 @ 2400	3.74×3.48	8.5:1	45 ①
	H	8-305 (5.0)	Carb	165 @ 4400	240 @ 2000	3.75×3.48	9.0:1	45 ①
	L	8-350 (5.7)	Carb	165 @ 3800	275 @ 1600	4.00×3.48	8.3:1	45 ①
	M	8-350 (5.7)	Carb	185 @ 4000	285 @ 2400	4.00×3.48	8.3:1	45 ①
	C	8-380 (6.2)	Diesel	230 @ 3600	240 @ 2000	3.98×3.80	21.0:1	35 ①
	J	8-380 (6.2)	Diesel	135 @ 3600	240 @ 2000	3.98×3.80	21.0:1	35 ①
	W	8-454 (7.4)	Carb	240 @ 3800	375 @ 3200	4.25×4.00	8.0:1	40 ①
1987	E	4-151 (2.5)	F.I.	92 @ 4400	134 @ 2800	4.00×3.00	9.0:1	45 ①
	R	6-173 (2.8)	F.I.	125 @ 4800	150 @ 2200	3.56×3.04	8.5:1	50 ①
	Z	6-260 (4.3)	F.I.	145 @ 4000	230 @ 2400	4.00×3.48	9.3:1	35 ①
	T	6-292 (4.8)	Carb	115 @ 3400	215 @ 1600	3.88×4.12	8.0:1	50 ①
	H	8-305 (5.0)	F.I.	165 @ 4400	240 @ 2000	3.75×3.48	9.0:1	45 ①
	L	8-350 (5.7)	Carb	165 @ 3800	275 @ 1600	4.00×3.48	8.3:1	45 ①
	K	8-350 (5.7)	F.I.	—	—	4.00×3.48	8.5:1	45 ①
	M	8-350 (5.7)	Carb	185 @ 4000	285 @ 2400	4.00×3.48	8.3:1	45 ①
	C	8-380 (6.2)	Diesel	130 @ 3600	240 @ 2000	3.98×3.80	21.0:1	35 ①

GENERAL ENGINE SPECIFICATIONS

Year	VIN	No. Cylinder Displacement cu. in. (liter)	Fuel System type	Net Horsepower @ rpm	Net Torque @ rpm (ft. lbs.)	Bore × Stroke (in.)	Com-pression Ratio	Oil Pressure @ rpm
	J	8-380 (6.2)	Diesel	135 @ 3600	240 @ 2000	3.98×3.80	21.0:1	35 ①
	W	8-454 (2.4)	Carb	240 @ 3800	375 @ 3200	4.25×4.00	8.0:1	40 ①
	N	8-454 (7.4)	F.I.	—	—	4.25×4.00	8.0:1	40 ①
1988	E	4-151 (2.5)	F.I.	92 @ 4400	134 @ 2800	4.00×3.00	9.0:1	45 ①
	R	6-173 (2.8)	F.I.	125 @ 4800	150 @ 2200	3.56×3.04	8.5:1	50 ①
	Z	6-260 (4.3)	F.I.	145 @ 4000	230 @ 2400	4.00×3.48	9.3:1	35 ①
	T	6-292 (4.8)	Carb	115 @ 3400	215 @ 1600	3.88×4.12	8.0:1	50 ①
	H	8-305 (5.0)	F.I.	165 @ 4400	240 @ 2000	3.74×3.48	9.0:1	45 ①
	K	8-350 (5.7)	F.I.	—	—	4.00×3.48	8.5:1	45 ①
	M	8-350 (5.7)	Carb	185 @ 4000	285 @ 2400	4.00×3.48	8.3:1	45 ①
	C	8-380 (6.2)	Diesel	130 @ 3600	240 @ 2000	3.98×3.80	21.0:1	35 ①
	J	8-380 (6.2)	Diesel	135 @ 3600	240 @ 2000	3.98×3.80	21.0:1	35 ①
	N	8-454 (7.4)	F.I.	—	—	4.25×4.00	8.0:1	40 ①

F.I. = Fuel Injection
① At 2000 RPM

GASOLINE ENGINE TUNE-UP SPECIFICATIONS

Year	VIN	No. Cylinder Displacement cu. in. (liter)	Spark Plugs Type	Spark Plugs Gap (in.)	Ignition Timing (deg.) MT	Ignition Timing (deg.) AT	Com-pression Pressure (psi)	Fuel Pump (psi)	Idle Speed (rpm) MT	Idle Speed (rpm) AT	Valve Clearance In.	Valve Clearance Ex.
1982	A	4-119 (1.9)	R42XLS	.040	6	6	NA	3.0	800	900	.006	.010
	B	6-173 (2.8)	R42TS	.040	12	12	NA	7.0	1000	750	Hyd.	Hyd.
	D	6-252 (4.1)	R44T	.035	8	8	NA	4.5	850	750	Hyd.	Hyd.
	T	6-292 (4.8)	R44T	.035	8	8	NA	4.5	850	750	Hyd.	Hyd.
	F	8-305 (5.0)	R45TS	.045	4	4	NA	8.0	650	750	Hyd.	Hyd.
	H	8-305 (5.0)	R45TS	.045	4	4	NA	8.0	650	750	Hyd.	Hyd.
	L	8-350 (5.7)	R45TS	.045	4	4	NA	8.0	700	750	Hyd.	Hyd.
	M	8-350 (5.7)	R45TS	.045	4	4	NA	8.0	700	750	Hyd.	Hyd.
	P	8-350 (5.7)	R45TS	.045	4	4	NA	8.0	700	750	Hyd.	Hyd.
	W	8-454 (7.4)	R44T	.045	4	4	NA	5.0	700	750	Hyd.	Hyd.
1983	A	4-119 (1.9)	R42XLS	.040	6	6	NA	3.0	800	900	.006	.010
	Y	4-121 (2.0)	R42CTS	.035	12	12	NA	5.0	750	700	Hyd.	Hyd.
	B	6-173 (2.8)	R42TS	.040	16	16	NA	7.0	700	650	Hyd.	Hyd.
	D	6-252 (4.1)	R45TS	.045	8	8	NA	5.0	950	900	Hyd.	Hyd.
	T	6-292 (4.8)	R44T	.035	8	8	NA	5.0	700	700	Hyd.	Hyd.
	F	8-305 (5.0)	R45TS	.045	4	4	NA	8.0	700	700	Hyd.	Hyd.
	H	8-305 (5.0)	R45TS	.045	4	4	NA	8.0	700	700	Hyd.	Hyd.
	L	8-350 (5.7)	R45TS	.045	4	4	NA	8.0	700	700	Hyd.	Hyd.
	M	8-350 (5.7)	R45TS	.045	4	4	NA	8.0	700	700	Hyd.	Hyd.
	P	8-350 (5.7)	R45TS	.045	4	4	NA	8.0	700	700	Hyd.	Hyd.
	W	8-454 (7.4)	R44T	.045	4	4	NA	8.0	700	700	Hyd.	Hyd.

GASOLINE ENGINE TUNE-UP SPECIFICATIONS

Year	VIN	No. Cylinder Displacement cu. in. (liter)	Spark Plugs Type	Spark Plugs Gap (in.)	Ignition Timing (deg.) MT	Ignition Timing (deg.) AT	Compression Pressure (psi)	Fuel Pump (psi)	Idle Speed (rpm) MT	Idle Speed (rpm) AT	Valve Clearance In.	Valve Clearance Ex.
1984	A	4-119 (1.9)	R42XLS	.040	6	6	NA	3.0	800	900	.006	.010
	Y	4-121 (2.0)	R42CTS	.035	12	12	NA	5.0	750	700	Hyd.	Hyd.
	B	6-173 (2.8)	R42CTS	.040	16	16	NA	7.0	700	650	Hyd.	Hyd.
	D	6-252 (4.1)	R45TS	.045	8	8	NA	5.0	950	900	Hyd.	Hyd.
	T	6-292 (4.8)	R44T	.035	8	8	NA	5.0	700	700	Hyd.	Hyd.
	F	8-305 (5.0)	R45TS	.045	4	4	NA	8.0	700	700	Hyd.	Hyd.
	H	8-305 (5.0)	R45TS	.045	4	4	NA	8.0	700	700	Hyd.	Hyd.
	L	8-350 (5.7)	R45TS	.045	4	4	NA	8.0	700	700	Hyd.	Hyd.
	M	8-350 (5.7)	R45TS	.045	4	4	NA	8.0	700	700	Hyd.	Hyd.
	P	8-350 (5.7)	R45TS	.045	4	4	NA	8.0	700	700	Hyd.	Hyd.
	W	8-454 (7.4)	R44T	.045	4	4	NA	8.0	700	700	Hyd.	Hyd.
1985	A	4-119 (1.9)	R42XLS	.046	6	6	NA	3.0	800	900	.006	.010
	E	4-151 (2.5)	R43TSX	②	②	②	NA	5.0	①	①	Hyd.	Hyd.
	B	6-173 (2.8)	R42TS	.040	16	16	NA	7.0	700	650	Hyd.	Hyd.
	N	6-260 (4.3)	R43CTS	.040	②	②	NA	5.0	①	①	Hyd.	Hyd.
	T	6-292 (4.8)	R44T	.035	8	8	NA	5.0	700	700	Hyd.	Hyd.
	F	8-305 (5.0)	R45TS	.045	4	4	NA	8.0	700	700	Hyd.	Hyd.
	H	8-305 (5.0)	R45TS	.045	4	4	NA	8.0	700	700	Hyd.	Hyd.
	L	8-350 (5.7)	R45TS	.045	4	4	NA	8.0	700	700	Hyd.	Hyd.
	M	8-350 (5.7)	R45TS	.045	4	4	NA	8.0	700	700	Hyd.	Hyd.
	W	8-454 (7.4)	R44T	.045	4	4	NA	8.0	700	700	Hyd.	Hyd.
1986	E	4-151 (2.5)	R43TSX	②	②	②	NA	5.0	①	①	Hyd.	Hyd.
	B	6-173 (2.8)	R42TS	.040	16	16	NA	7.0	700	650	Hyd.	Hyd.
	R	6-173 (2.8)	R43LTSE	②	②	②	NA	34–40	①	①	Hyd.	Hyd.
	N	6-260 (4.3)	R43CTS	.040	②	②	NA	5.0	①	①	Hyd.	Hyd.
	Z	6-260 (4.3)	R43CTS	.040	0	0	NA	5.0	①	①	Hyd.	Hyd.
	T	6-292 (4.8)	R44T	.035	8	8	NA	5.0	700	700	Hyd.	Hyd.
	F	8-305 (5.0)	R45TS	.045	4	4	NA	8.0	700	700	Hyd.	Hyd.
	H	8-305 (5.0)	R45TS	.045	4	4	NA	8.0	700	700	Hyd.	Hyd.
	L	8-350 (5.7)	R45TS	.045	4	4	NA	8.0	700	700	Hyd.	Hyd.
	M	8-350 (5.7)	R45TS	.045	4	4	NA	8.0	700	700	Hyd.	Hyd.
	W	8-454 (7.4)	R44T	.045	4	4	NA	8.0	700	700	Hyd.	Hyd.
1987	E	4-151 (2.5)	R43TSX	②	②	②	NA	5.0	①	①	Hyd.	Hyd.
	R	6-173 (2.8)	R43LTSE	②	②	②	NA	34–40	①	①	Hyd.	Hyd.
	Z	6-260 (4.3)	R43CTS	.040	0	0	NA	5.0	①	①	Hyd.	Hyd.
	T	6-292 (4.8)	R44T	.035	8	8	NA	5.0	700	700	Hyd.	Hyd.
	H	8-305 (5.0)	R45TS	.045	4	4	NA	40–47③	700	700	Hyd.	Hyd.
	L	8-350 (5.7)	R45TS	.045	4	4	NA	34–46③	700	700	Hyd.	Hyd.
	M	8-350 (5.7)	R45TS	.045	4	4	NA	34–46③	700	700	Hyd.	Hyd.
	K	8-350 (5.7)	R45TS	.045	4	4	NA	34–46③	700	700	Hyd.	Hyd.
	W	8-454 (7.4)	44T	.045	4	4	NA	5.0	700	700	Hyd.	Hyd.
	N	8-454 (7.4)	44T	.045	4	4	NA	34–46③	700	700	Hyd.	Hyd.

GASOLINE ENGINE TUNE-UP SPECIFICATIONS

Year	VIN	No. Cylinder Displacement cu. in. (liter)	Spark Plugs Type	Spark Plugs Gap (in.)	Ignition Timing (deg.) MT	Ignition Timing (deg.) AT	Compression Pressure (psi)	Fuel Pump (psi)	Idle Speed (rpm) MT	Idle Speed (rpm) AT	Valve Clearance In.	Valve Clearance Ex.
1988	E	4-151 (2.5)	R43TSX	②	②	②	NA	5.0	①	①	Hyd.	Hyd.
	R	6-173 (2.8)	R43LTSE	②	②	②	NA	34–40	①	①	Hyd.	Hyd.
	Z	6-260 (4.3)	R43CTS	.040	0	0	NA	5.0	①	①	Hyd.	Hyd.
	T	6-292 (4.8)	R44T	.035	8	8	NA	5.0	700	700	Hyd.	Hyd.
	H	8-305 (5.0)	R45TS	.045	4	4	NA	40-47③	700	700	Hyd.	Hyd.
	M	8-350 (5.7)	R45TS	.045	4	4	NA	34-46③	700	700	Hyd.	Hyd.
	K	8-350 (5.7)	R45TS	.045	4	4	NA	34-46③	700	700	Hyd.	Hyd.
	N	8-454 (7.4)	R44T	.045	4	4	NA	34-46③	700	700	Hyd.	Hyd.

① Controlled By E.C.M.
② See Underhood Sticker
③ Fuel Injected

FIRING ORDERS

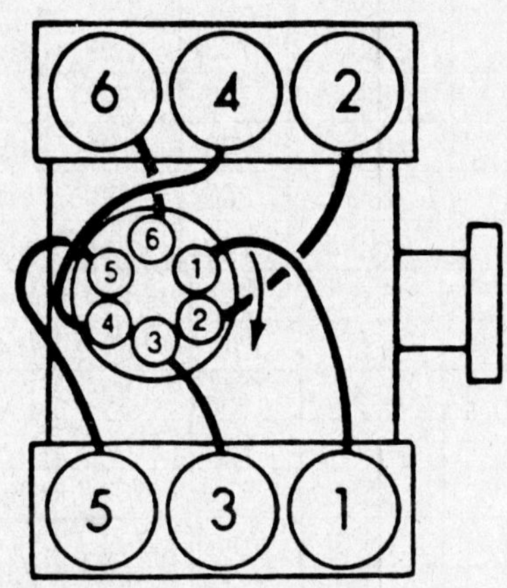

173 CID V6 engine
Firing order:1-2-3-4-5-6

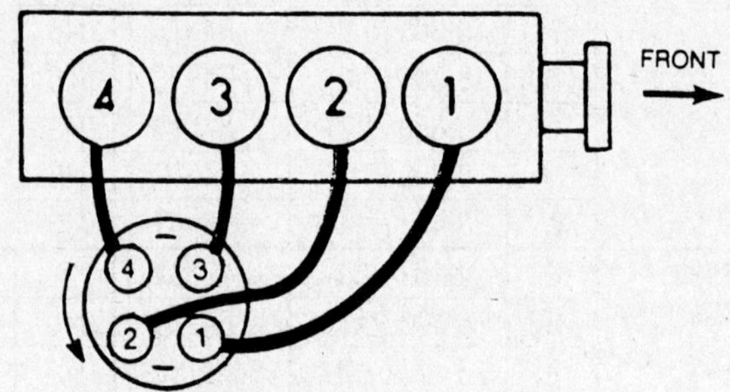

119 CID 4 cylinder
Firing order: 1-3-4-2

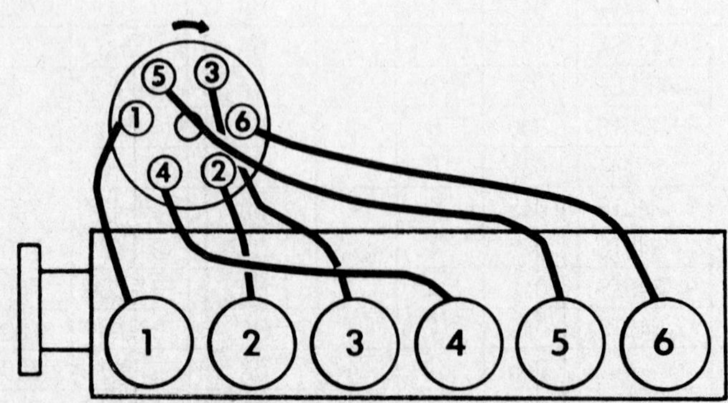

250 and 292 6-cylinder
Firing order: 1-5-3-6-2-4

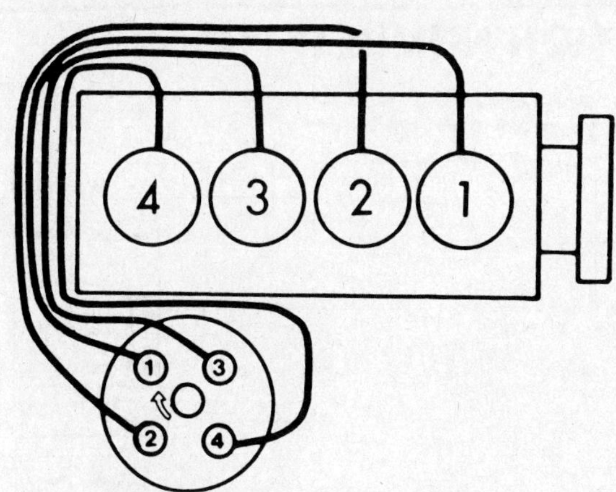

151-L4 Engine
Firing order: 1-3-4-2

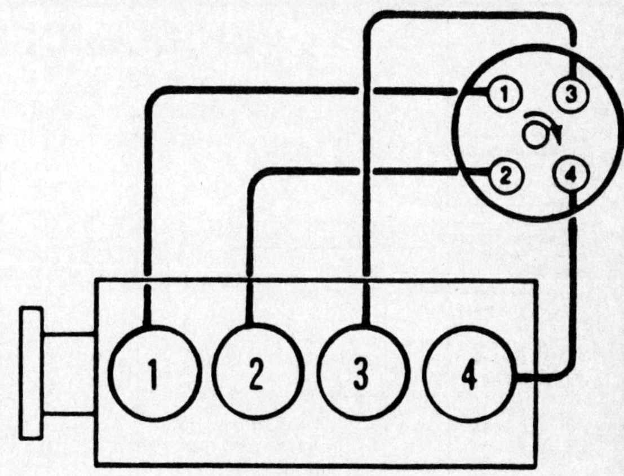

GM 122 (2.0L) 4 cylinder
Engine firing order: 1–3–4–2
Distributor rotation: clockwise

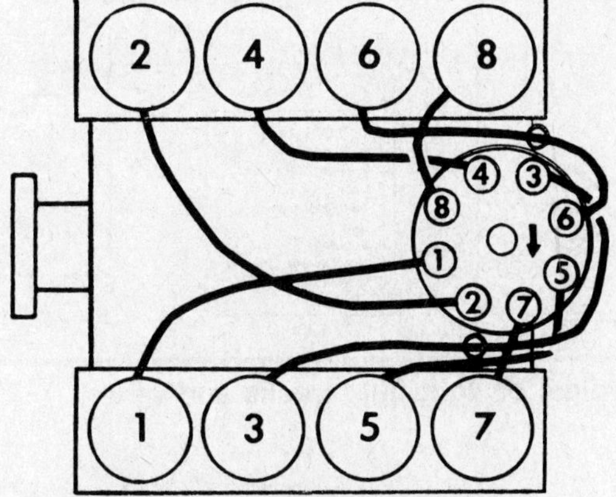

305,350, and 454 cu.in. engines
Firing order: 1-8-4-3-6-5-7-2

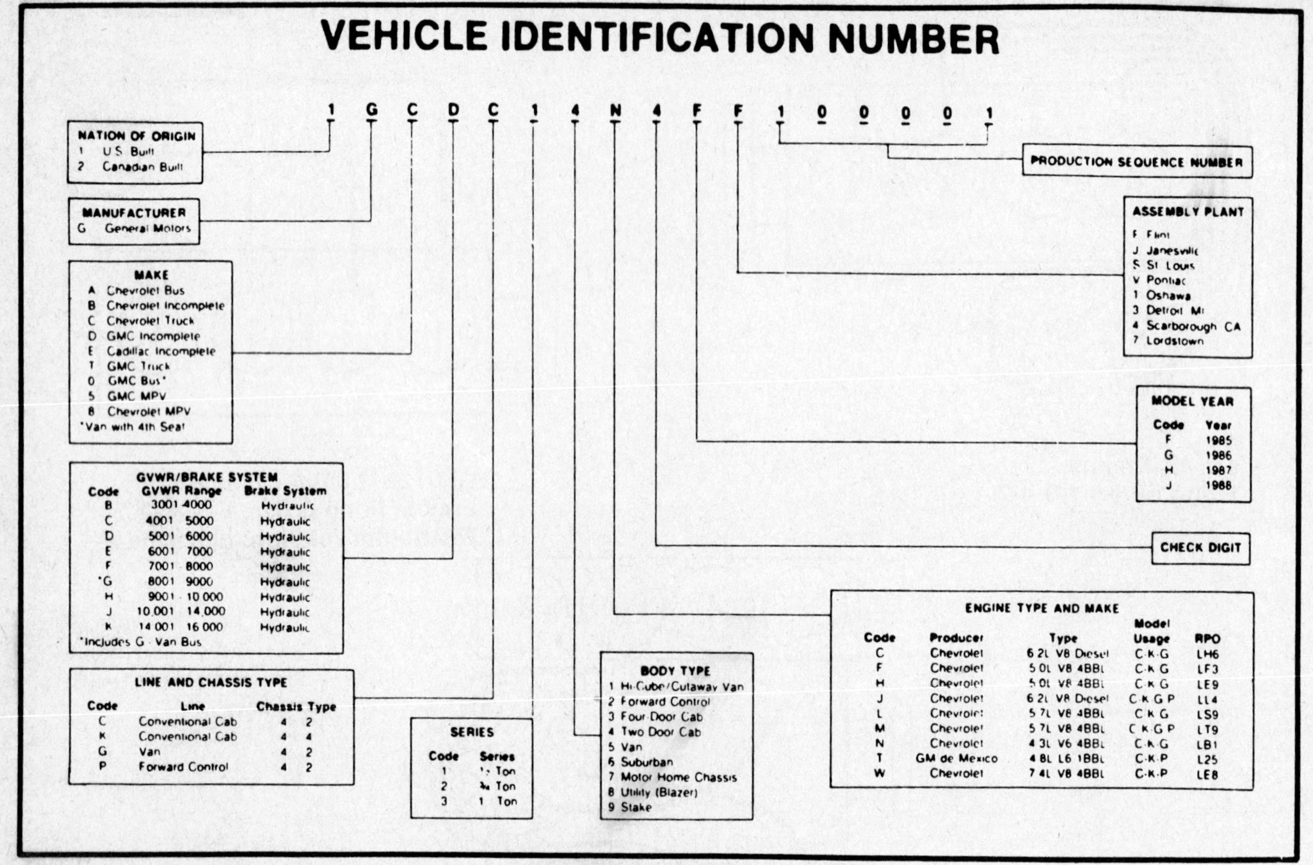

Vehicle Identification Number—Typical of light duty trucks and vans

CRANKSHAFT AND CONNECTING ROD SPECIFICATIONS

All measurements are given in inches.

			Crankshaft				Connecting Rod		
Year	VIN	No. Cylinder Displacement cu. in. (liter)	Main Brg. Journal Dia.	Main Brg. Oil Clearance	Shaft End-play	Thrust on No.	Journal Diameter	Oil Clearance	Side Clearance
1982	A	4-119 (1.9)	2.1555–2.2050	.0008–.0025	.0024–.0094	3	1.8799–1.9290	.0007–.0030	.0137 Max.
	B	6-173 (2.8)	2.4937–2.4946	.0017–.0030	.0020–.0070	3	1.9983–1.9993	.0014–.0035	.0063–.0173
	D	6-252 (4.1)	2.2979–2.2994	③	.0020–.0060	7	1.9990–2.0000	.0010–.0030	.0010–.0026
	T	6-292 (4.8)	2.2979–2.2994	③	.0020–.0060	7	2.0990–2.1000	.0010–.0030	.0010–.0026
	F	8-305 (5.0)	⑦	⑧	.0020–.0060	⑤	2.0988–2.0998	.0013–.0035	.0080–.0140
	H	8-305 (5.0)	⑦	⑧	.0020–.0060	⑤	2.0988–2.0998	.0013–.0035	.0080–.0140
	L	8-350 (5.7)	⑦	⑧	.0020–.0060	⑤	2.0988–2.0998	.0013–.0035	.0080–.0140
	M	8-350 (5.7)	⑦	⑧	.0020–.0060	⑤	2.0988–2.0998	.0013–.0035	.0080–.0140

CRANKSHAFT AND CONNECTING ROD SPECIFICATIONS

All measurements are given in inches.

Year	VIN	No. Cylinder Displacement cu. in. (liter)	Crankshaft Main Brg. Journal Dia.	Crankshaft Main Brg. Oil Clearance	Crankshaft Shaft End-play	Crankshaft Thrust on No.	Connecting Rod Journal Diameter	Connecting Rod Oil Clearance	Connecting Rod Side Clearance
1982	P	8-350 (5.7)	⑦	⑧	.0020–.0060	⑤	2.0988–2.0998	.0013–.0035	.0080–.0140
	C	8-380 (6.2)	2.9490–2.9500	⑪	—	3	2.3980–2.3990	.0017–.0039	—
	J	8-380 (6.2)	2.9490–2.9500	⑪	—	3	2.3980–2.3990	.0017–.0039	—
	W	8-454 (7.4)	⑨	⑩	.0060–.0100	5	2.1990–2.2000	.0009–.0025	.0130–.0230
1983	A	4-119 (1.9)	2.1555–2.2050	.0008–.0025	.0024–.0094	3	1.8799–1.9290	.0007–.0030	.0137 Max.
	Y	4-121 (2.0)	①	②	.0019–.0082	4	1.9983–1.9993	.0009–.0031	.0039–.0149
	S	4-135 (2.2)	2.3591–2.3594	.0011–.0033	.0020–.0080	3	2.0835–2.0839	.0016–.0047	—
	B	6-173 (2.8)	④	.0016–.0032	.0020–.0070	3	1.9983–1.9993	.0014–.0035	.0063–.0173
	D	6-252 (4.1)	2.2979–2.2994	③	.0020–.0060	7	1.9990–2.0000	.0010–.0030	.0010–.0026
	T	6-292 (4.8)	2.2979–2.2940	③	.0020–.0060	7	2.0990–2.1000	.0010–.0030	.0010–.0026
	F	8-305 (5.0)	⑦	⑧	.0020–.0060	5	2.0988–2.0998	.0013–.0035	.0080–.0140
	H	8-305 (5.0)	⑦	⑧	.0020–.0060	5	2.0988–2.0998	.0013–.0035	.0080–.0140
	L	8-350 (5.7)	⑦	⑧	.0020–.0060	5	2.0988–2.0998	.0013–.0035	.0080–.0140
	M	8-350 (5.7)	⑦	⑧	.0020–.0060	5	2.0988–2.0998	.0013–.0035	.0080–.0140
	P	8-350 (5.7)	⑦	⑧	.0020–.0060	5	2.0988–2.0998	.0013–.0035	.0080–.0140
	C	8-380 (6.2)	2.9490–2.9500	⑪	—	3	2.3980–2.3990	.0017–.0039	—
	J	8-380 (6.2)	2.9490–2.9500	⑪	—	3	2.3980–2.3990	.0017–.0039	—
	W	8-454 (7.4)	⑨	⑩	.0060–.0100	5	2.1990–2.2000	.0009–.0025	.0130–.0230
1984	A	4-119 (1.9)	2.1555–2.2050	.0008–.0025	.0024–.0094	3	1.8799–1.9290	.0007–.0030	.0137 Max.
	Y	4-121 (2.0)	①	②	.0019–.0082	4	1.9983–1.9993	.0009–.0031	.0039–.0149
	S	4-135 (2.2)	2.3591–2.3594	.0011–.0033	.0020–.0080	3	2.0835–2.0839	.0016–.0047	—
	B	6-173 (2.8)	④	.0016–.0032	.0020–.0070	3	1.9983–1.9993	.0014–.0035	.0063–.0173
	D	6-252 (4.1)	2.2979–2.2994	③	.0020–.0060	7	1.9990–2.0000	.0010–.0030	.0010–.0026
	T	6-292 (4.8)	2.2979–2.2994	③	.0020–.0060	7	2.0990–2.1000	.0010–.0030	.0010–.0026

CRANKSHAFT AND CONNECTING ROD SPECIFICATIONS

All measurements are given in inches.

Year	VIN	No. Cylinder Displacement cu. in. (liter)	Crankshaft: Main Brg. Journal Dia.	Crankshaft: Main Brg. Oil Clearance	Crankshaft: Shaft End-play	Crankshaft: Thrust on No.	Connecting Rod: Journal Diameter	Connecting Rod: Oil Clearance	Connecting Rod: Side Clearance
1984	F	8-305 (5.0)	⑦	⑧	.0020–.0060	5	2.0989–2.0998	.0013–.0035	.0080–.0140
	H	8-305 (5.0)	⑦	⑧	.0020–.0060	5	2.0989–2.0998	.0013–.0035	.0080–.0140
	L	8-350 (5.7)	⑦	⑧	.0020–.0060	5	2.0989–2.0998	.0013–.0035	.0080–.0140
	M	8-350 (5.7)	⑦	⑧	.0020–.0060	5	2.0989–2.0998	.0013–.0035	.0080–.0140
	P	8-350 (5.7)	⑦	⑧	.0020–.0060	5	2.0989–2.0998	.0013–.0035	.0080–.0140
	C	8-380 (6.2)	2.9490–2.9500	⑪	—	3	2.3980–2.3990	.0017–.0039	—
	J	8-380 (6.2)	2.9490–2.9500	⑪	—	3	2.3980–2.3990	.0017–.0039	—
	W	8-454 (7.4)	⑨	⑩	.0060–.0100	5	2.1990–2.2000	.0009–.0025	.0130–.0230
1985	A	4-119 (1.9)	2.1555–2.2050	.0008–.0025	.0024–.0094	3	1.8795–1.9290	.0007–.0030	.0317 Max.
	S	4-135 (2.2)	2.3591–2.3594	.0011–.0033	.0020–.0080	3	2.0835–2.0839	.0016–.0047	—
	E	4-151 (2.5)	2.3000	.0005–.0022	.0035–.0085	5	2.0000	.0005–.0026	.0060–.0220
	B	6-173 (2.8)	④	.0016–.0032	.0020–.0070	3	1.9983–1.9993	.0014–.0035	.0063–.0173
	N	6-260 (4.3)	⑤	⑥	.0020–.0060	3	2.2487–2.2497	.0020–.0030	.0070–.0150
	T	6-292 (4.8)	2.2979–2.2994	③	.0020–.0060	7	2.0990–2.1000	.0010–.0030	.0010–.0026
	F	8-305 (5.0)	⑦	⑧	.0020–.0060	5	2.0988–2.0998	.0013–.0035	.0080–.0140
	H	8-305 (5.0)	⑦	⑧	.0020–.0060	5	2.0988–2.0998	.0013–.0035	.0080–.0140
	L	8-350 (5.7)	⑦	⑧	.0020–.0060	5	2.0988–2.0998	.0013–.0035	.0080–.0140
	M	8-350 (5.7)	⑦	⑧	.0020–.0060	5	2.0988–2.0998	.0013–.0035	.0080–.0140
	C	8-380 (6.2)	2.9490–2.9500	⑪	—	3	2.3980–2.3990	.0017–.0039	—
	J	8-380 (6.2)	2.9490–2.9500	⑪	—	3	2.3980–2.3990	.0017–.0039	—
	W	8-454 (7.4)	⑨	⑩	.0060–.0100	5	2.1990–2.2000	.0009–.0025	.0130–.0230

CRANKSHAFT AND CONNECTING ROD SPECIFICATIONS

All measurements are given in inches.

Year	VIN	No. Cylinder Displacement cu. in. (liter)	Crankshaft				Connecting Rod		
			Main Brg. Journal Dia.	Main Brg. Oil Clearance	Shaft End-play	Thrust on No.	Journal Diameter	Oil Clearance	Side Clearance
1986	S	4-135 (2.2)	2.3591–2.3594	.0011–.0033	.0020–.0080	3	2.0835–2.0839	.0016–.0047	—
	E	4-151 (2.5)	2.3000	.0005–.0022	.0035–.0085	5	2.000	.0005–.0026	.0060–.0220
	B	6-173 (2.8)	④	.0016–.0032	.0020–.0070	3	1.9983–1.9993	.0014–.0035	.0063–.0173
	R	6-173 (2.8)	④	.0016–.0032	.0020–.0070	3	1.9983–1.9993	.0014–.0035	.0063–.0173
	N	6-260 (4.3)	⑤	⑥	.0020–.0060	4	2.2487–2.2497	.0020–.0030	.0070–.0150
	Z	6-260 (4.3)	⑤	⑥	.0020–.0060	4	2.2487–2.2497	.0020–.0030	.0070–.0150
	T	6-292 (4.8)	2.2979–2.2994	③	.0020–.0060	7	2.0990–2.1000	.0010–.0030	.0010–.0026
	F	8-305 (5.0)	⑦	⑧	.0020–	5	2.0988–2.0998	.0013–.0035	.0080–.0140
	H	8-305 (5.0)	⑦	⑧	.0020–	5	2.0988–2.0998	.0013–.0035	.0080–.0140
	L	8-350 (5.7)	⑦	⑧	.0020–	5	2.0988–2.0998	.0013–.0035	.0080–.0140
	M	8-350 (5.7)	⑦	⑧	.0020–	5	2.0988–2.0998	.0013–.0035	.0080–.0140
	C	8-380 (6.2)	2.9490–2.9500	⑪	—	3	2.3980–2.3990	.0017–.0039	—
	J	8-380 (6.2)	2.9490–2.9500	⑪	—	3	2.3980–2.3990	.0017–.0039	—
	W	8-454 (7.4)	⑨	⑩	.0060–.0100	5	2.1990–2.2000	.0009–.0025	.0130–.0230
1987	E	4-151 (2.5)	2.3000	.0005–.0022	.0035–.0085	5	2.0000	.0005–.0026	.0060–.0220
	R	6-173 (2.8)	④	.0016–.0032	.0020–.0070	3	1.9985–1.9993	.0014–.0035	.0063–.0173
	Z	6-260 (4.3)	⑤	⑥	.0020–.0060	4	2.2487–2.2497	.0020–.0030	.0070–.0150
	T	6-292 (4.8)	2.2979–2.2994	③	.0020–.0060	7	2.0990–2.1000	.0010–.0030	.0010–.0026
	H	8-305 (5.0)	⑦	⑧	.0020–.0060	5	2.0988–2.0998	.0013–.0035	.0080–.0140
	L	8-350 (5.7)	⑦	⑧	.0020–.0060	5	2.0988–2.0998	.0013–.0035	.0080–.0140
	K	8-350 (5.7)	⑦	⑧	.0020–.0060	5	2.0988–2.0998	.0013–.0035	.0080–.0140
	M	8-350 (5.7)	⑦	⑧	.0020–.0060	5	2.0988–2.0998	.0013–.0035	.0080–.0140
	C	8-380 (6.2)	2.9490–2.9500	⑪	—	3	2.3980–2.3990	.0017–.0039	—
	J	8-380 (6.2)	2.9490–2.9500	⑪	—	3	2.3980–2.3990	.0017–.0039	—

CRANKSHAFT AND CONNECTING ROD SPECIFICATIONS

All measurements are given in inches.

Year	VIN	No. Cylinder Displacement cu. in. (liter)	Crankshaft: Main Brg. Journal Dia.	Crankshaft: Main Brg. Oil Clearance	Crankshaft: Shaft End-play	Crankshaft: Thrust on No.	Connecting Rod: Journal Diameter	Connecting Rod: Oil Clearance	Connecting Rod: Side Clearance
1987	W	8-434 (7.4)	⑨	⑩	.0060–.0100	5	2.1990–2.2000	.0009–.0025	.0130–.0230
	N	8-454 (7.4)	⑨	⑩	.0060–.0100	5	2.1990–2.2000	.0009–.0025	.0130–.0230
1988	E	4-151 (2.5)	2.3000	.0005–.0022	.0035–.0085	5	2.0000	.0005–.0026	.0060–.0220
	R	6-173 (2.8)	④	.0016–.0032	.0020–.0070	3	1.9983–1.9993	.0014–.0035	.0063–.0173
	Z	6-260 (4.3)	⑤	⑥	.0020–.0060	4	2.2487–2.2497	.0020–.0030	.0070–.0150
	T	6-292 (4.8)	2.2979–2.2994	③	.0020–.0060	7	2.0990–2.1000	.0010–.0036	.0010–.0026
	H	8-305 (5.0)	⑦	⑧	.0020–.0060	5	2.0988–2.0998	.0013–.0035	.0080–.0014
	K	8-350 (5.7)	⑦	⑧	.0020–.0060	5	2.0988–2.0998	.0013–.0035	.0080–.0014
	M	8-350 (5.7)	⑦	⑧	.0020–.0060	5	2.0988–2.0998	.0013–.0035	.0080–.0014
	C	8-380 (6.2)	2.9490–2.9500	⑪	—	3	2.3480–2.3990	.0017–.0039	—
	J	8-380 (6.2)	2.9490–2.9500	⑪	—	3	2.3480–2.3990	.0017–.0039	—
	N	8-454 (2.4)	⑨	⑩	.0060–.0010	5	2.1990–2.2000	.0009–.0025	.0130–.0230

① 1-4 2.4944-2.4954
5 2.4936-2.4946
② 1-4 .0010-.0023
5 .0018-.0031
③ 1-6 .0010-.0024
7 .0016-.0035
④ 1-4 2.4937-2.4946
3 2.4930-2.4941
⑤ Front—2.4484-2.4493
Inter.—2.4481-2.4490
Rear—2.4479-2.4488
⑥ Front—.0010-.0015
Inter.—.0010-.0020
Rear—.0025-.0030
⑦ 1 2.4484-2.4493
2-4 2.4481-2.4490
5 2.4479-2.4488
⑧ 1 .0008-.0020
2-4 .0011-.0023
5 .0017-.0032
⑨ 1-4 2.7481-2.7490
5 2.7476-2.7486
⑩ 1-4 .0013-.0025
5 .0024-.0040
⑪ 1-4 .0017-.0032
5 .0022-.0037

VALVE SPECIFICATIONS

Year	VIN	No. Cylinder Displacement cu. in. (liter)	Seat Angle (deg.)	Face Angle (deg.)	Spring Test Pressure (lbs.)	Spring Installed Height (in.)	Stem-to-Guide Clearance (in.) Intake	Stem-to-Guide Clearance (in.) Exhaust	Stem Diameter (in.) Intake	Stem Diameter (in.) Exhaust
1982	A	4-119 (1.9)	45	45	①	②	.0009–.0022	.0015–.0032	.3102 ③	.3091 ③
	B	6-173 (2.8)	46	45	195 @ 1.81	1.57	.0010–.0027	.0010–.0027	.3410–.3420	.3410–.3420
	D	6-252 (4.1)	46	45	175 @ 1.26	1.66	.0010–.0027	.0015–.0032	.3410–.3417	.3410–.3417
	T	6-292 (4.8)	46	46	175 @ 1.26	1.66	.0010–.0027	.0015–.0032	.3410–.3417	.3410–.3417
	F	8-305 (5.0)	46	45	200 @ 1.25	1.70	.0010–.0027	.0010–.0027	.3410–.3417	.3410–.3417

VALVE SPECIFICATIONS

Year	VIN	No. Cylinder Displacement cu. in. (liter)	Seat Angle (deg.)	Face Angle (deg.)	Spring Test Pressure (lbs.)	Spring Installed Height (in.)	Stem-to-Guide Clearance (in.)		Stem Diameter (in.)	
							Intake	Exhaust	Intake	Exhaust
1982	H	8-305 (5.0)	46	45	200 @ 1.25	1.70	.0010–.0027	.0010–.0027	.3410–.3417	.3410–.3417
	L	8-350 (5.7)	46	45	200 @ 1.25	1.70	.0010–.0027	.0010–.0027	.3410–.3417	.3410–.3417
	M	8-350 (5.7)	46	45	200 @ 1.25	1.70	.0010–.0027	.0010–.0027	.3410–.3417	.3410–.3417
	P	8-350 (5.7)	46	45	200 @ 1.25	1.70	.0010–.0027	.0010–.0027	.3410–.3417	.3410–.3417
	C	8-380 (6.2)	46	45	230 @ 1.38	1.81	.0010–.0027	.0010–.0027	—	—
	J	8-380 (6.2)	46	45	230 @ 1.38	1.81	.0010–.0027	.0010–.0027	—	—
	W	8-454 (7.4)	46	45	220 @ 1.40	1.80	.0010–.0027	.0012–.0029	.3715–.3722	.3715–.3722
1983	A	4-119 (1.9)	45	45	①	②	.0009–.0022	.0015–.0032	.3102 ③	.3091 ③
	Y	4-121 (2.0)	46	45	182 @ 1.33	1.60	.0011–.0026	.0014–.0030	—	—
	S	4-135 (2.2)	45	45	④	⑤	.0015–.0027	.0025–.0037	.3140	.3140
	B	6-173 (2.8)	46	45	195 @ 1.81	1.57	.0010–.0027	.0010–.0027	.3410–.3420	.3410–.3420
	D	6-252 (4.1)	46	45	175 @ 1.26	1.66	.0010–.0027	.0015–.0032	.3410–.3417	.3410–.3417
	T	6-292 (4.8)	46	46	175 @ 1.26	1.66	.0010–.0027	.0015–.0032	.3410–.3417	.3410–.3417
	F	8-305 (5.0)	46	45	200 @ 1.25	1.70	.0010–.0027	.0010–.0027	.3410–.3417	.3410–.3417
	H	8-305 (5.0)	46	45	200 @ 1.25	1.70	.0010–.0027	.0010–.0027	.3410–.3417	.3410–.3417
	L	8-350 (5.7)	46	45	200 @ 1.25	1.70	.0010–.0027	.0010–.0027	.3410–.3417	.3410–.3417
	M	8-350 (5.7)	46	45	200 @ 1.25	1.70	.0010–.0027	.0010–.0027	.3410–.3417	.3410–.3417
	P	8-350 (5.7)	46	45	200 @ 1.25	1.70	.0010–.0027	.0010–.0027	.3410–.3417	.3410–.3417
	C	8-380 (6.2)	46	45	230 @ 1.38	1.81	.0010–.0027	.0010–.0027	—	—
	J	8-380 (6.2)	46	45	230 @ 1.38	1.81	.0010–.0027	.0010–.0027	—	—
	W	8-454 (7.4)	46	45	220 @ 1.40	1.80	.0010–.0027	.0012–.0029	.3715–.3722	.3715–.3722

VALVE SPECIFICATIONS

Year	VIN	No. Cylinder Displacement cu. in. (liter)	Seat Angle (deg.)	Face Angle (deg.)	Spring Test Pressure (lbs.)	Spring Installed Height (in.)	Stem-to-Guide Clearance (in.)		Stem Diameter (in.)	
							Intake	Exhaust	Intake	Exhaust
1984	A	4-119 (1.9)	45	45	55 @ 1.61	1.89	.0009–.0022	.0015–.0031	.3102 ③	.3091 ③
	Y	4-121 (2.0)	46	45	182 @ 1.33	1.60	.0011–.0026	.0014–.0030	—	—
	S	4-135 (2.2)	45	45	④	⑤	.0015–.0027	.0025–.0037	.3140	.3140
	B	6-173 (2.8)	46	45	195 @ 1.81	1.57	.0010–.0027	.0010–.0027	.3410–.3420	.3410–.3420
	D	6-252 (4.1)	46	45	175 @ 1.26	1.66	.0010–.0027	.0015–.0032	.3410–.3417	.3410–.3417
	T	6-292 (4.8)	46	46	175 @ 1.26	1.66	.0010–.0027	.0015–.0032	.3410–.3417	.3410–.3417
	F	8-305 (5.0)	46	45	200 @ 1.25	1.70	.0010–.0027	.0010–.0027	.3410–.3417	.3410–.3417
	H	8-305 (5.0)	46	45	200 @ 1.25	1.70	.0010–.0027	.0010–.0027	.3410–.3417	.3410–.3417
	L	8-350 (5.7)	46	45	200 @ 1.25	1.70	.0010–.0027	.0010–.0027	.3410–.3417	.3410–.3417
	M	8-350 (5.7)	46	45	200 @ 1.25	1.70	.0010–.0027	.0010–.0027	.3410–.3417	.3410–.3417
	P	8-350 (5.7)	46	45	200 @ 1.25	1.70	.0010–.0027	.0010–.0027	.3410–.3417	.3410–.3417
	C	8-380 (6.2)	46	45	230 @ 1.38	1.81	.0010–.0027	.0010–.0027	—	—
	J	8-380 (6.2)	46	45	230 @ 1.38	1.81	.0010–.0027	.0010–.0027	—	—
	W	8-454 (7.4)	46	45	220 @ 1.40	1.80	.0010–.0027	.0012–.0029	.3715–.3762	.3715–.3722
1985	A	4-119 (1.9)	45	45	55 @ 1.61	1.89	.0009–.0022	.0015–.0032	.3102 ③	.3091 ③
	S	4-135 (2.2)	45	45	④	⑤	.0015–.0027	.0025–.0037	.3140	.3140
	E	4-151 (2.5)	46	45	151 @ 1.25	1.66	.0010–.0027	⑥	.3418–.3425	.3418–.3425
	B	6-173 (2.8)	46	45	175 @ 1.26	1.66	.0010–.0027	.0010–.0027	.3410–.3420	.3410–.3420
	N	6-260 (4.3)	46	45	220 @ 1.25	1.70	.0010–.0027	.0010–.0027	.3410–.3417	.3410–.3417
	T	6-292 (4.8)	46	46	175 @ 1.26	1.66	.0010–.0027	.0015–.0032	.3410–.3417	.3410–.3417
	F	8-305 (5.0)	46	45	220 @ 1.25	1.70	.0010–.0027	.0010–.0027	.3410–.3417	.3410–.3417
	H	8-305 (5.0)	46	45	220 @ 1.25	1.70	.0010–.0027	.0010–.0027	.3410–.3417	.3410–.3417
	L	8-350 (5.7)	46	45	200 @ 1.25	1.70	.0010–.0027	.0010–.0027	.3410–.3417	.3410–.3417
	M	8-350 (5.7)	46	45	200 @ 1.25	1.70	.0010–.0027	.0010–.0027	.3410–.3417	.3410–.3417
	C	8-380 (6.2)	46	45	230 @ 1.38	1.81	.0010–.0027	.0010–.0027	—	—

VALVE SPECIFICATIONS

Year	VIN	No. Cylinder Displacement cu. In. (liter)	Seat Angle (deg.)	Face Angle (deg.)	Spring Test Pressure (lbs.)	Spring Installed Height (in.)	Stem-to-Guide Clearance (in.) Intake	Stem-to-Guide Clearance (in.) Exhaust	Stem Diameter (in.) Intake	Stem Diameter (in.) Exhaust
1985	J	8-380 (6.2)	46	45	230 @ 1.38	1.81	.0010–.0027	.0010–.0027	—	—
	W	8-454 (7.4)	46	45	220 @ 1.40	1.80	.0010–.0027	.0012–.0029	.3715–.3722	.3715–.3722
1986	S	4-135 (2.2)	45	45	④	⑤	.0015–.0027	.0025–.0037	.3140	.3140
	E	4-151 (2.5)	46	45	151 @ 1.25	1.66	.0010–.0027	⑥	.3418–.3425	.3418–.3425
	B	6-173 (2.8)	46	45	175 @ 1.26	1.66	.0010–.0027	.0010–.0027	.3410–.3420	.3410–.3420
	R	6-173 (2.8)	46	45	175 @ 1.26	1.66	.0010–.0027	.0010–.0027	.3410–.3420	.3410–.3420
	N	6-260 (4.3)	46	45	220 @ 1.25	1.70	.0010–.0027	.0010–.0027	.3410–.3417	.3410–.3417
	Z	6-260 (4.3)	46	45	220 @ 1.25	1.70	.0010–.0027	.0010–.0027	.3410–.3417	.3410–.3417
	T	6-292 (4.8)	46	46	175 @ 1.26	1.66	.0010–.0027	.0015–.0032	.3410–.3417	.3410–.3417
	F	8-305 (5.0)	46	45	220 @ 1.25	1.70	.0010–.0027	.0010–.0027	.3410–.3417	.3410–.3417
	H	8-305 (5.0)	46	45	200 @ 1.25	1.70	.0010–.0027	.0010–.0027	.3410–.3417	.3410–.3417
	L	8-350 (5.7)	46	45	200 @ 1.25	1.70	.0010–.0027	.0010–.0027	.3410–.3417	.3410–.3417
	M	8-350 (5.7)	46	45	200 @ 1.25	1.70	.0010–.0027	.0010–.0027	.3410–.3417	.3410–.3417
	C	8-380 (6.2)	46	45	230 @ 1.38	1.81	.0010–.0027	.0010–.0027	—	—
	J	8-380 (6.2)	46	45	230 @ 1.38	1.81	.0010–.0027	.0010–.0027	—	—
	W	8-454 (7.4)	46	45	220 @ 1.40	1.80	.0010–.0027	.0012–.0029	.3715–.3722	.3715–.3722
1987	E	4-151 (2.5)	46	45	151 @ 1.25	1.66	.0010–.0027	⑥	.3418–.3425	.3418–.3425
	R	6-173 (2.8)	46	45	175 @ 1.26	1.66	.0010–.0027	.0010–.0027	.3410–.3420	.3410–.3420
	Z	6-260 (4.3)	46	45	220 @ 1.25	1.70	.0010–.0027	.0010–.0027	.3410–.3417	.3410–.3417
	T	6-292 (4.8)	46	46	175 @ 1.26	1.66	.0010–.0027	.0015–.0032	.3410–.3417	.3410–.3417
	H	8-305 (5.0)	46	45	220 @ 1.25	1.70	.0010–.0027	.0010–.0027	.3410–.3417	.3410–.3417
	L	8-350 (5.7)	46	45	200 @ 1.25	1.70	.0010–.0027	.0010–.0027	.3410–.3417	.3410–.3417
	K	8-350 (5.7)	46	45	200 @ 1.25	1.70	.0010–.0027	.0010–.0027	.3410–.3417	.3410–.3417
	M	8-350 (5.7)	46	45	200 @ 1.25	1.70	.0010–.0027	.0010–.0027	.3410–.3417	.3410–.3417
	C	8-380 (6.2)	46	45	230 @ 1.38	1.81	.0010–.0027	.0010–.0027	—	—

VALVE SPECIFICATIONS

Year	VIN	No. Cylinder Displacement cu. in. (liter)	Seat Angle (deg.)	Face Angle (deg.)	Spring Test Pressure (lbs.)	Spring Installed Height (in.)	Stem-to-Guide Clearance (in.) Intake	Stem-to-Guide Clearance (in.) Exhaust	Stem Diameter (in.) Intake	Stem Diameter (in.) Exhaust
1987	J	8-380 (6.2)	46	45	230 @ 1.38	1.81	.0010–.0027	.0010–.0027	—	—
	W	8-454 (7.4)	46	45	220 @ 1.40	1.80	.0010–.0027	.0012–.0029	.3715–.3722	.3715–.3722
	N	8-454 (7.4)	46	45	220 @ 1.40	1.80	.0010–.0027	.0012–.0029	.3715–.3722	.3715–.3722
1988	E	4-151 (2.5)	46	45	151 @ 1.25	1.66	.0010–.0027	⑥	.3418–.3425	.3418–.3425
	R	6-173 (2.8)	46	45	175 @ 1.26	1.66	.0010–.0027	.0010–.0027	.3410–.3420	.3410–.3420
	Z	6-260 (4.3)	46	45	220 @ 1.25	1.70	.0010–.0027	.0010–.0027	.3410–.3417	.3410–.3417
	T	6-292 (4.8)	46	46	175 @ 1.26	1.66	.0010–.0027	.0015–.0032	.3410–.3417	.3410–.3417
	H	8-305 (5.0)	46	45	220 @ 1.25	1.70	.0010–.0027	.0010–.0027	.3410–.3417	.3410–.3417
	K	8-350 (5.7)	46	45	220 @ 1.25	1.70	.0010–.0027	.0010–.0027	.3410–.3417	.3410–.3417
	M	8-350 (5.7)	46	45	220 @ 1.25	1.70	.0010–.0027	.0010–.0027	.3410–.3417	.3410–.3417
	C	8-380 (6.2)	46	45	230 @ 1.38	1.81	.0010–.0027	.0010–.0027	—	—
	J	8-380 (6.2)	46	45	230 @ 1.38	1.81	.0010–.0027	.0010–.0027	—	—
	N	8-454 (7.4)	46	45	220 @ 1.40	1.80	.0010–.0027	.0012–.0029	.3715–.3722	.3715–.3722

① 19 @ 1.52 Inner
34 @ 1.61 Outer
② 1.78 Inner
1.84 Outer
③ Minimum
④ 13 @ 1.46 Inner
45 @ 1.54 Outer
⑤ 1.89 Inner
1.86 Outer
⑥ .0010–.0027 Top
.0020–.0037 Bottom

PISTON AND RING SPECIFICATIONS

Year	VIN	No. Cylinder Displacement cu. in. (liter)	Piston Clearance	Ring Gap Top Compression	Ring Gap Bottom Compression	Ring Gap Oil Control	Ring Side Clearance Top Compression	Ring Side Clearance Bottom Compression	Ring Side Clearance Oil Control
1982	A	4-119 (1.9)	.0018–.0026	.0140–.0200	.0140–.0200	.0080–.0350	.0059 Max.	.0059 Max.	.0059 Max.
	B	6-173 (2.8)	.0007–.0017	.0100–.0200	.0100–.0200	.0200–.0550	.0012–.0027	.0015–.0037	.0078 Max.
	D	6-252 (4.1)	.0010–.0020	.0100–.0200	.0100–.0200	.0150–.0550	.0012–.0027	.0012–.0032	.0050 Max.
	T	6-292 (4.8)	.0026–.0036	.0100–.0200	.0100–.0200	.0150–.0550	.0020–.0040	.0020–.0040	.0005–.0055
	F	8-305 (5.0)	.0007–.0017	.0100–.0200	.0100–.0250	.0150–.0550	.0012–.0032	.0012–.0032	.0020–.0070
	H	8-305 (5.0)	.0007–.0017	.0100–.0200	.0100–.0250	.0150–.0550	.0012–.0032	.0012–.0032	.0020–.0070

PISTON AND RING SPECIFICATIONS

Year	VIN	No. Cylinder Displacement cu. in. (liter)	Piston Clearance	Ring Gap			Ring Side Clearance		
				Top Compression	Bottom Compression	Oil Control	Top Compression	Bottom Compression	Oil Control
1982	L	8-350 (5.7)	.0007–.0017	.0100–.0200	.0130–.0250	.0150–.0550	.0012–.0032	.0012–.0032	.0020–.0070
	M	8-350 (5.7)	.0007–.0017	.0100–.0200	.0130–.0250	.0150–.0550	.0012–.0032	.0012–.0032	.0020–.0070
	P	8-350 (5.7)	.0007–.0017	.0100–.0200	.0130–.0250	.0150–.0550	.0012–.0032	.0012–.0032	.0020–.0070
	C	8-380 (6.2)	①	.0120–.0220	.0300–.0400	.0100–.0210	.0030–.0071	.0300–.0400	.0016–.0038
	J	8-380 (6.2)	①	.0120–.0220	.0300–.0400	.0100–.0210	.0030–.0071	.0300–.0400	.0016–.0038
	W	8-454 (7.4)	.0030–.0040	.0100–.0200	.0100–.0200	.0150–.0550	.0017–.0032	.0017–.0032	.0050–.0065
1983	A	4-119 (1.9)	.0018–.0026	.0140–.0200	.0140–.0200	.0080–.0350	.0059 Max.	.0059 Max.	.0059 Max.
	Y	4-121 (2.0)	.0006 .0016	.0100–.0200	.0100–.0200	.0150–.0550	.0012–.0027	.0012–.0027	.0078 Max.
	S	4-135 (2.2)	.0014–.0022	.0080	.0080	—	—	—	—
	B	6-173 (2.8)	.0007–.0017	.0100–.0200	.0100–.0200	.0200–.0550	.0012–.0027	.0015–.0037	.0078 Max.
	D	6-252 (4.1)	.0010–.0020	.0100–.0200	.0100–.0200	.0150–.0550	.0012–.0027	.0012–.0032	.0050 Max.
	T	6-292 (4.8)	.0026–.0036	.0100–.0200	.0100–.0200	.0150–.0550	.0120–.0027	.0020–.0040	.0005–.0055
	F	8-305 (5.0)	.0007–.0017	.0100–.0200	.0100–.0250	.0150–.0550	.0012–.0032	.0012–.0032	.0020–.0070
	H	8-305 (5.0)	.0007–.0017	.0100–.0200	.0100–.0250	.0150–.0550	.0012–.0032	.0012–.0032	.0020–.0070
	L	8-350 (5.7)	.0007–.0017	.0100–.0200	.0130–.0250	.0150–.0550	.0012–.0032	.0012–.0032	.0020–.0070
	M	8-350 (5.7)	.0007–.0017	.0100–.0200	.0130–.0250	.0150–.0550	.0012–.0032	.0012–.0032	.0020–.0070
	P	8-350 (5.7)	.0007–.0017	.0100–.0200	.0130–.0250	.0150–.0550	.0012–.0032	.0012–.0032	.0020–.0070
	C	8-380 (6.2)	①	.0120–.0220	.0300–.0400	.0100–.0210	.0030–.0071	.0300–.0400	.0016–.0038
	J	8-380 (6.2)	①	.0120–.0220	.0300–.0400	.0100–.0210	.0030–.0071	.0300–.0400	.0016–.0038
	W	8-454 (7.4)	.0030–.0040	.0100–.0200	.0100–.0200	.0150–.0550	.0017–.0032	.0017–.0032	.0050–.0065
1984	A	4-119 (1.9)	.0018–.0026	.0140–.0200	.0140–.0200	.0080–.0350	.0059 Max.	.0059 Max.	.0059 Max.
	Y	4-121 (2.0)	.0006–.0016	.0100–.0200	.0100–.0200	.0150–.0550	.0012–.0027	.0012–.0027	.0078– Max.
	S	4-135 (2.2)	.0014–.0022	.0080	.0080	—	—	—	—
	B	6-173 (2.8)	.0007–.0017	.0100–.0200	.0100–.0200	.0200–.0550	.0012–.0027	.0015–.0037	.0078 Max.
	D	6-252 (4.1)	.0010–.0020	.0100–.0200	.0100–.0200	.0150–.0550	.0012–.0027	.0012–.0032	.0050 Max.
	T	6-292 (4.8)	.0026–.0036	.0100–.0200	.0100–.0200	.0150–.0550	.0010–.0027	.0020–.0040	.0005–.0055

PISTON AND RING SPECIFICATIONS

Year	VIN	No. Cylinder Displacement cu. in. (liter)	Piston Clearance	Ring Gap Top Compression	Ring Gap Bottom Compression	Ring Gap Oil Control	Ring Side Clearance Top Compression	Ring Side Clearance Bottom Compression	Ring Side Clearance Oil Control
1984	F	8-305 (5.0)	.0007–.0017	.0100–.0200	.0100–.0250	.0150–.0550	.0012–.0032	.0012–.0032	.0020–.0070
	H	8-305 (5.0)	.0007–.0017	.0100–.0200	.0100–.0250	.0150–.0550	.0012–.0032	.0012–.0032	.0020–.0070
	L	8-350 (5.7)	.0007–.0017	.0100–.0200	.0130–.0250	.0150–.0550	.0012–.0032	.0012–.0032	.0020–.0070
	M	8-350 (5.7)	.0007–.0017	.0100–.0200	.0130–.0250	.0150–.0550	.0012–.0032	.0012–.0032	.0020–.0070
	P	8-350 (5.7)	.0007–.0017	.0100–.0200	.0130–.0250	.0150–.0550	.0012–.0032	.0012–.0032	.0020–.0070
	C	8-380 (6.2)	①	.0120–.0220	.0300–.0400	.0100–.0210	.0030–.0071	.0300–.0400	.0016–.0038
	J	8-380 (6.2)	①	.0120–.0220	.0300–.0400	.0100–.0210	.0030–.0071	.0300–.0400	.0016–.0038
	W	8-454 (7.4)	.0030–.0040	.0100–.0200	.0100–.0200	.0150–.0550	.0017–.0032	.0017–.0032	.0050–.0065
1985	N	4-119 (1.9)	.0018–.0026	.0140–.0200	.0140–.0200	.0080–.0350	.0059 Max.	.0059 Max.	.0059 Max.
	S	4-135 (2.2)	.0014–.0022	.0080	.0080	—	—	—	—
	E	4-151 (2.5)	.0014–.0022	.0100–.0220	.0100–.0270	.0150–.0550	.0015 .0030	.0015 .0030	—
	B	6-173 (2.8)	.0007–.0017	.0100–.0200	.0100–.0200	.0200–.0550	.0012–.0027	.0015–.0037	.0078–Max.
	N	6-260 (4.3)	.0007–.0017	.0100–.0250	.0100–.0250	.0150–.0550	.0012–.0032	.0012–.0032	.0020–.0070
	T	6-292 (4.8)	.0026–.0036	.0100–.0200	.0100–.0200	.0150–.0550	.0010–.0027	.0020–.0040	.0005–.0055
	F	8-305 (5.0)	.0007–.0017	.0100–.0200	.0100–.0250	.0150–.0550	.0012–.0032	.0012–.0032	.0020–.0070
	H	8-305 (5.0)	.0007–.0017	.0100–.0200	.0100–.0250	.0150–.0550	.0012–.0032	.0012–.0032	.0020–.0070
	L	8-350 (5.7)	.0007–.0017	.0100–.0200	.0130–.0250	.0150–.0550	.0012–.0032	.0012–.0032	.0020–.0070
	M	8-350 (5.7)	.0007–.0017	.0100–.0200	.0130–.0250	.0150–.0550	.0012–.0032	.0012–.0032	.0020–.0070
	C	8-380 (6.2)	①	.0120–.0220	.0300–.0400	.0100–.0210	.0030–.0071	.0300–.0400	.0016–.0038
	J	8-380 (6.2)	①	.0120–.0220	.0300–.0400	.0100–.0210	.0030–.0071	.0300–.0400	.0016–.0038
	W	8-454 (7.4)	.0030–.0040	.0100–.0200	.0100–.0200	.0150–.0550	.0017–.0032	.0017–.0032	.0050–.0065
1986	S	4-135 (2.2)	.0014–.0022	.0080	.0080	—	—	—	—
	E	4-151 (2.5)	.0014–.0017	.0100–.0220	.0100–.0270	.0150–.0550	.0015 .0030	.0015 .0030	—
	B	6-173 (2.8)	.0007–.0017	.0100–.0220	.0100–.0220	.0200–.0550	.0012–.0027	.0015–.0037	.0078 Max.
	R	6-173 (2.8)	.0007–.0017	.0100–.0220	.0100–.0220	.0200–.0550	.0012–.0027	.0015–.0037	.0078 Max.
	N	6-260 (4.3)	.0007–.0017	.0100–.0250	.0100–.0250	.0150–.0550	.0012–.0032	.0012–.0032	.0020–.0070

PISTON AND RING SPECIFICATIONS

(All measurements are given in inches)

Year	VIN	No. Cylinder Displacement cu. in. (liter)	Piston Clearance	Ring Gap Top Compression	Ring Gap Bottom Compression	Ring Gap Oil Control	Ring Side Clearance Top Compression	Ring Side Clearance Bottom Compression	Ring Side Clearance Oil Control
1986	Z	6-260 (4.3)	.0007–.0017	.0100–.0250	.0100–.0250	.0150–.0550	.0012–.0032	.0012–.0032	.0020–.0070
	T	6-292 (4.8)	.0026–.0036	.0100–.0200	.0100–.0200	.0150–.0550	.0010–.0027	.0020–.0040	.0005–.0055
	F	8-305 (5.0)	.0007–.0017	.0100–.0200	.0100–.0250	.0150–.0550	.0012–.0032	.0012–.0032	.0020–.0070
	H	8-305 (5.0)	.0007–.0017	.0100–.0200	.0100–.0250	.0150–.0550	.0012–.0032	.0012–.0032	.0020–.0070
	L	8-350 (5.7)	.0007–.0017	.0100–.0200	.0130–.0250	.0150–.0550	.0012–.0032	.0012–.0032	.0020–.0070
	M	8-350 (5.7)	.0007–.0017	.0100–.0200	.0130–.0250	.0150–.0550	.0012–.0032	.0012–.0032	.0020–.0070
	C	8-380 (6.2)	①	.0120–.0220	.0300–.0400	.0100–.0210	.0030–.0071	.0300–.0400	.0016–.0038
	J	8-380 (6.2)	①	.0120–.0220	.0300–.0400	.0100–.0210	.0030–.0071	.0300–.0400	.0016–.0038
	W	8-454 (7.4)	.0030–.0040	.0100–.0200	.0100–.0200	.0150–.0550	.0017–.0032	.0017–.0032	.0050–.0065
1987	E	4-151 (2.5)	.0014–.0022	.0100–.0220	.0100–.0270	.0150–.0550	.0015 .0030	.0150 .0030	—
	R	6-173 (2.8)	.0007–.0017	.0100–.0220	.0100–.0220	.0200–.0550	.0012–.0027	.0015–.0037	.0078–Max.
	Z	6-260 (4.3)	.0007–.0017	.0100–.0250	.0100–.0250	.0150–.0550	.0012–.0032	.0012–.0032	.0020–.0070
	T	6-292 (4.8)	.0026–.0036	.0100–.0200	.0100–.0200	.0150–.0550	.0010–.0027	.0020–.0040	.0005–.0055
	H	8-305 (5.0)	.0007–.0017	.0100–.0200	.0100–.0250	.0150–.0550	.0012–.0032	.0012–.0032	.0020–.0070
	L	8-350 (5.7)	.0007–.0017	.0100–.0200	.0130–.0250	.0150–.0550	.0012–.0032	.0012–.0032	.0020–.0070
	K	8-350 (5.7)	.0007–.0017	.0100–.0200	.0130–.0250	.0150–.0550	.0012–.0032	.0012–.0032	.0020–.0070
	M	8-350 (5.7)	.0007–.0017	.0100–.0200	.0130–.0250	.0150–.0550	.0012–.0032	.0012–.0032	.0020–.0070
	C	8-380 (6.2)	①	.0120–.0220	.0300–.0400	.0100–.0210	.0030–.0071	.0300–.0400	.0016–.0038
	J	8-380 (6.2)	①	.0120–.0220	.0300–.0400	.0100–.0210	.0030–.0071	.0300–.0400	.0016–.0038
	W	8-454 (7.4)	.0030–.0040	.0100–.0200	.0100–.0200	.0150–.0550	.0017–.0032	.0017–.0032	.0050–.0065
	N	8-454 (7.4)	.0030–.0040	.0100–.0200	.0100–.0200	.0150–.0550	.0017–.0032	.0017–.0032	.0050–.0065
1988	E	4-151 (2.5)	.0014–.0022	.0100–.0220	.0100–.0270	.0150–.0550	.0015–.0030	.0015–.0030	—
	R	6-173 (2.8)	.0007–.0017	.0100–.0220	.0100–.0220	.0200–.0550	.0012–.0027	.0015–.0037	.0078–Max.
	Z	6-260 (4.3)	.0007–.0017	.0100–.0250	.0100–.0250	.0150–.0550	.0012–.0032	.0012–.0032	.0020–.0070
	T	6-292 (4.8)	.0026–.0036	.0100–.0200	.0100–.0200	.0150–.0550	.0010–.0027	.0020–.0040	.0005–.0055
	H	8-305 (5.0)	.0007–.0017	.0100–.0200	.0100–.0250	.0150–.0550	.0012–.0032	.0012–.0032	.0020–.0070

PISTON AND RING SPECIFICATIONS

(All measurements are given in inches)

Year	VIN	No. Cylinder Displacement cu. in. (liter)	Piston Clearance	Ring Gap Top Compression	Ring Gap Bottom Compression	Ring Gap Oil Control	Ring Side Clearance Top Compression	Ring Side Clearance Bottom Compression	Ring Side Clearance Oil Control
1988	K	8-350 (5.7)	.0007–.0017	.0100–.0200	.0130–.0250	.0150–.0550	.0012–.0032	.0012–.0032	.0020–.0070
	M	8-350 (5.7)	.0007–.0017	.0100–.0200	.0130–.0250	.0150–.0550	.0012–.0032	.0012–.0032	.0020–.0070
	C	8-380 (6.2)	①	.0120–.0220	.0300–.0400	.0100–.0210	.0030–.0071	.0300–.0400	.0016–.0038
	J	8-380 (6.2)	①	.0120–.0220	.0300–.0400	.0100–.0210	.0030–.0071	.0300–.0400	.0016–.0038
	N	8-454 (7.4)	.0030–.0040	.0100–.0200	.0100–.0200	.0150–.0550	.0017–.0032	.0017–.0032	.0050–.0065

① Bohn Pistons 1-6—.089-.115mm
7-8—.102-.128mm
Zollner Pistons 1-6—.112-.138mm
7-8—.125-.151mm

TORQUE SPECIFICATIONS

Year	VIN	No. Cylinder Displacement cu. in. (liter)	Cylinder Head Bolts	Main Bearing Bolts	Rod Bearing Bolts	Crankshaft Pulley Bolts	Flywheel Bolts	Manifold Intake	Manifold Exhaust	Spark Plugs
1982	A	4-119 (1.9)	72	72	43	87	76	16	16	18–22
	B	6-173 (2.8)	70	70	35	75	50	22	25	7–15
	D	6-252 (4.1)	95 ②	65	35	—	60	30	30	17–27
	T	6-292 (4.8)	95 ②	65	35	60	60	30	30	17–27
	F	8-305 (5.0)	65	⑤	45	60	60	30	30	17–27
	H	8-305 (5.0)	65	⑤	45	60	60	30	30	17–27
	L	8-350 (5.7)	65	⑤	45	60	60	30	30	17–27
	M	8-350 (5.7)	65	⑤	45	60	60	30	30	17–27
	P	8-350 (5.7)	65	⑤	45	60	60	30	30	17–27
	C	8-380 (6.2)	③	④	48	151	60	31	25	—
	J	8-380 (6.2)	③	④	48	151	60	31	25	—
	W	8-454 (7.4)	80	110	50	85	65	30	20	17–27
1983	A	4-119 (1.9)	72	72	43	87	76	16	16	18–22
	Y	4-121 (2.0)	70	70	35	75	50	25	25	7–19
	S	4-135 (2.2)	①	120	60	130	70	15	15	—
	B	6-173 (2.8)	70	70	35	50	50	22	25	7–15
	D	6-252 (4.1)	95 ②	65	35	—	60	30	30	17–27
	T	6-292 (4.8)	95 ②	65	35	60	60	30	30	17–27
	F	8-305 (5.0)	65	⑤	45	60	60	30	30	17–27
	H	8-305 (5.0)	65	⑤	45	60	60	30	30	17–27
	L	8-350 (5.7)	65	⑤	45	60	60	30	30	17–27
	M	8-350 (5.7)	65	⑤	45	60	60	30	30	17–27
	P	8-350 (5.7)	65	⑤	45	60	60	30	30	17–27
	C	8-380 (6.2)	③	④	48	151	60	31	25	—
	J	8-380 (6.2)	③	④	48	151	60	31	25	—
	W	8-454 (7.4)	80	110	50	85	65	30	20	17–27

TORQUE SPECIFICATIONS

Year	VIN	No. Cylinder Displacement cu. in. (liter)	Cylinder Head Bolts	Main Bearing Bolts	Rod Bearing Bolts	Crankshaft Pulley Bolts	Flywheel Bolts	Manifold Intake	Manifold Exhaust	Spark Plugs
1984	A	4-119 (1.9)	72	72	43	87	76	16	16	18–22
	Y	4-121 (2.0)	70	70	35	75	50	25	25	7–19
	S	4-135 (2.2)	①	120	60	130	70	15	15	—
	B	6-173 (2.8)	70	70	35	50	50	22	25	7–15
	D	6-252 (4.1)	95 ②	65	35	—	60	30	30	17–27
	T	6-292 (4.8)	95 ②	65	35	60	60	30	30	17–27
	F	8-305 (5.0)	65	⑤	45	60	60	30	30	17–27
	H	8-305 (5.0)	65	⑤	45	60	60	30	30	17–27
	L	8-350 (5.7)	65	⑤	45	60	60	30	30	17–27
	M	8-350 (5.7)	65	⑤	45	60	60	30	30	17–27
	P	8-350 (5.7)	65	⑤	45	60	60	30	30	17–27
	C	8-380 (6.2)	③	④	48	151	60	31	25	—
	J	8-380 (6.2)	③	④	48	151	60	31	25	—
	W	8-454 (7.4)	80	110	50	85	65	30	20	17–27
1985	A	4-119 (1.9)	72	72	43	87	76	16	16	18–22
	S	4-135 (2.2)	①	120	60	130	70	15	15	—
	E	4-151 (2.5)	90	70	32	160	44	29	44	7–15
	B	6-173 (2.8)	70	70	35	50	50	22	25	7–15
	N	6-260 (4.3)	65	70	45	60	65	30	20	22
	T	6-292 (4.8)	95 ②	65	35	60	60	30	30	17–27
	F	8-305 (5.0)	65	⑤	45	60	60	30	30	17–27
	H	8-305 (5.0)	65	⑤	45	60	60	30	30	17–27
	L	8-350 (5.7)	65	⑤	45	60	60	30	30	17–27
	M	8-350 (5.7)	65	⑤	45	60	60	30	30	17–27
	C	8-380 (6.2)	③	④	48	151	60	31	25	—
	J	8-380 (6.2)	③	④	48	151	60	31	25	—
	W	8-454 (7.4)	80	110	50	85	65	30	20	17–27
1986	S	4-135 (2.2)	①	120	60	130	70	15	15	—
	E	4-151 (2.5)	90	70	32	160	44	29	44	7–15
	B	6-173 (2.8)	70	70	35	50	50	22	25	7–15
	R	6-173 (2.8)	70	70	35	50	50	22	25	7–15
	N	6-260 (4.3)	65	70	45	60	65	30	20	22
	Z	6-260 (4.3)	65	75	45	70	75	36	24	22
	T	6-292 (4.8)	95 ②	65	35	60	60	30	30	17–27
	F	8-305 (5.0)	65	⑤	45	60	60	30	30	17–27
	H	8-305 (5.0)	65	⑤	45	60	60	30	30	17–27
	L	8-350 (5.7)	65	⑤	45	60	60	30	30	17–27
	M	8-350 (5.7)	65	⑤	45	60	60	30	30	17–27
	C	8-380 (6.2)	③	④	48	151	60	31	25	—
	J	8-380 (6.2)	③	④	48	151	60	31	25	—
	W	8-454 (7.4)	80	110	50	85	65	30	20	17–27
1987	E	4-151 (2.5)	90	70	32	160	44	29	44	7–15
	R	6-173 (2.8)	70	70	35	50	50	22	25	7–15
	Z	6-260 (4.3)	65	75	45	70	75	36	24	22
	T	6-292 (4.8)	95 ②	65	35	60	60	30	30	17–27

TORQUE SPECIFICATIONS

Year	VIN	No. Cylinder Displacement cu. in. (liter)	Cylinder Head Bolts	Main Bearing Bolts	Rod Bearing Bolts	Crankshaft Pulley Bolts	Flywheel Bolts	Manifold Intake	Manifold Exhaust	Spark Plugs
1987	H	8-305 (5.0)	65	⑤	45	60	60	30	30	17–27
	L	8-350 (5.7)	65	⑤	45	60	60	30	30	17–27
	K	8-350 (5.7)	65	⑤	45	60	60	30	30	17–27
	M	8-350 (5.7)	65	⑤	45	60	60	30	30	17–27
	C	8-380 (6.2)	③	④	48	151	60	31	25	—
	J	8-380 (6.2)	③	④	48	151	60	31	25	—
	W	8-454 (7.4)	80	110	50	85	65	30	20	17–27
	N	8-454 (7.4)	80	110	50	85	65	30	20	17–27
1988	E	4-151 (2.5)	90	70	32	160	44	29	44	7–15
	R	6-173 (2.8)	70	70	35	50	50	22	25	7–15
	Z	6-260 (4.3)	65	75	45	70	75	36	24	22
	T	6-292 (4.8)	95 ②	65	35	60	60	30	30	17–27
	H	8-305 (5.0)	65	⑤	45	60	60	30	30	17–27
	K	8-350 (5.7)	65	⑤	45	60	60	30	30	17–27
	M	8-350 (5.7)	65	⑤	45	60	60	30	30	17–27
	C	8-380 (6.2)	③	④	48	151	60	31	25	—
	J	8-380 (6.2)	③	④	48	151	60	31	25	—
	N	8-454 (7.4)	80	110	50	85	65	30	20	17–27

① New Bolts—40-47 then 54-61
Used Bolts—61-69
② Left Front Bolt 85
③ 1st 20
2nd 50
3rd ¼ turn
④ Inner 111
Outer 110
⑤ 2, 3, 4 70
Others 80

CAPACITIES

Year	Model	No. Cylinder Displacement cu. in. (liter)	Engine Crankcase with Filter	Engine Crankcase without Filter	Transmission (pts.) 4-Spd	Transmission (pts.) 5-Spd	Transmission (pts.) Auto.	Drive Axle (pts.)	Fuel Tank (gal.)	Cooling System (qts.)
1982	A	4-119 (1.9)	4.0	4.0	①	4.0	②	3.5	13.0	9.5
	B	6-173 (2.8)	4.0	4.0	①	4.0	②	3.5	13.0 ⑥	12.0
	D	6-252 (4.1)	5.0	4.0	8.0	—	②	3.5 ⑧	17.5 ⑦	14.5
	T	6-292 (4.8)	5.0	4.0	8.0	—	②	3.5 ⑧	17.5 ⑦	15.0
	F	8-305 (5.0)	5.0	4.0	8.0	—	②	3.5 ⑧	22.0 ⑦	17.0
	H	8-305 (5.0)	5.0	4.0	8.0	—	②	3.5 ⑧	22.0 ⑦	17.0
	L	8-350 (5.7)	5.0	4.0	8.0	—	②	3.5 ⑧	22.0 ⑦	17.0
	M	8-350 (5.7)	5.0	4.0	8.0	—	②	3.5 ⑧	22.0 ⑦	17.0
	P	8-350 (5.7)	5.0	4.0	8.0	—	②	3.5 ⑧	22.0 ⑦	17.0
	C	8-380 (6.2)	7.0	7.0	8.0	—	②	3.5 ⑧	20.0 ⑦	25.5
	J	8-380 (6.2)	7.0	7.0	8.0	—	②	3.5 ⑧	20.0 ⑦	25.5
	W	8-454 (7.4)	7.0	6.0	8.0	—	②	3.5 ⑧	20.0 ⑦	24.5
1983	A	4-119 (1.9)	4.0	4.0	①	4.0	②	3.5 ③	13.0 ⑥	9.5
	Y	4-121 (2.0)	4.0	4.0	①	4.0	②	3.5 ③	13.0 ⑥	9.5
	S	4-135 (2.2)	5.5	5.0	①	4.0	②	3.5 ③	14.0 ⑥	12.0
	B	6-173 (2.8)	4.0	4.0	①	4.0	②	3.5 ③	13.0 ⑥	12.0

CAPACITIES

Year	Model	No. Cylinder Displacement cu. in. (liter)	Engine Crankcase with Filter	Engine Crankcase without Filter	Transmission (pts.) 4-Spd	Transmission (pts.) 5-Spd	Transmission (pts.) Auto.	Drive Axle (pts.)	Fuel Tank (gal.)	Cooling System (qts.)
1983	D	6-252 (4.1)	5.0	4.0	8.0	—	②	3.5 ⑧	17.5 ⑦	14.5
	T	6-292 (4.8)	5.0	4.0	8.0	—	②	3.5 ⑧	17.5 ⑦	15.0
	F	8-305 (5.0)	5.0	4.0	8.0	—	②	3.5 ⑧	22.0 ⑦	17.0
	H	8-305 (5.0)	5.0	4.0	8.0	—	②	3.5 ⑧	22.0 ⑦	17.0
	L	8-350 (5.7)	5.0	4.0	8.0	—	②	3.5 ⑧	22.0 ⑦	17.0
	M	8-350 (5.7)	5.0	4.0	8.0	—	②	3.5 ⑧	22.0 ⑦	17.0
	P	8-350 (5.7)	5.0	4.0	8.0	—	②	3.5 ⑧	22.0 ⑦	17.0
	C	8-380 (6.2)	7.0	7.0	8.0	—	②	3.5 ⑧	20.0 ⑦	25.5
	J	8-380 (6.2)	7.0	7.0	8.0	—	②	3.5 ⑧	20.0 ⑦	25.5
	W	8-454 (7.4)	7.0	6.0	8.0	—	②	3.5 ⑧	20.0 ⑦	24.5
1984	A	4-119 (1.9)	4.0	4.0	①	4.0	②	3.5 ③	13.0 ⑥	9.5
	Y	4-121 (2.0)	4.0	4.0	①	4.0	②	3.5 ③	13.0 ⑥	9.5
	S	4-135 (2.2)	5.5	5.0	①	4.0	②	3.5 ③	14.0 ⑥	12.0
	B	6-173 (2.8)	4.0	4.0	①	4.0	②	3.5 ③	13.0 ⑥	12.0
	D	8-252 (4.1)	5.0	4.0	8.0	—	②	3.5 ⑧	17.5 ⑦	14.5
	T	8-292 (4.8)	5.0	4.0	8.0	—	②	3.5 ⑧	17.5 ⑦	15.0
	F	8-305 (5.0)	5.0	4.0	8.0	—	②	3.5 ⑧	22.0 ⑦	17.0
	H	8-305 (5.0)	5.0	4.0	8.0	—	②	3.5 ⑧	22.0 ⑦	17.0
	L	8-350 (5.7)	5.0	4.0	8.0	—	②	3.5 ⑧	22.0 ⑦	17.0
	M	8-350 (5.7)	5.0	4.0	8.0	—	②	3.5 ⑧	22.0 ⑦	17.0
	P	8-350 (5.7)	5.0	4.0	8.0	—	②	3.5 ⑧	22.0 ⑦	17.0
	C	8-380 (6.2)	8.0	7.0	8.0	—	②	3.5 ⑧	20.0 ⑦	25.5
	J	8-380 (6.2)	8.0	7.0	8.0	—	②	3.5 ⑧	20.0 ⑦	25.5
	W	8-454 (7.4)	7.0	6.0	8.0	—	②	3.5 ⑧	20.0 ⑦	24.5
1985	A	4-119 (1.9)	4.0	4.0	①	4.0	②	3.5 ③	13.0 ⑥	9.5
	S	4-135 (2.2)	5.5	5.0	①	4.0	②	3.5 ③	14.0 ⑥	12.0
	E	4-151 (2.5)	4.0	3.0	①	4.0	②	4.0 ③	④	9.2 ⑤
	B	6-173 (2.8)	4.0	4.0	①	4.0	②	3.5 ③	13.0 ⑥	12.0
	N	6-260 (4.3)	5.0	4.0	①	4.0	②	4.0 ③	④	13.5 ⑤
	T	6-292 (4.8)	5.0	4.0	8.0	—	②	3.5 ⑧	17.5 ⑦	15.0
	F	8-305 (5.0)	5.0	4.0	8.0	—	②	3.5 ⑧	22.0 ⑦	17.0
	H	8-305 (5.0)	5.0	4.0	8.0	—	②	3.5 ⑧	22.0 ⑦	17.0
	L	8-350 (5.7)	5.0	4.0	8.0	—	②	3.5 ⑧	22.0 ⑦	17.0
	M	8-350 (5.7)	5.0	4.0	8.0	—	②	3.5 ⑧	22.0 ⑦	17.0
	C	8-380 (6.2)	7.0	7.0	8.0	—	②	3.5 ⑧	20.0 ⑦	25.5
	J	8-380 (6.2)	7.0	7.0	8.0	—	②	3.5 ⑧	20.0 ⑦	25.5
	W	8-454 (7.4)	7.0	6.0	8.0	—	②	3.5 ⑧	20.0 ⑦	24.5
1986	S	4-119 (1.9)	5.5	5.0	①	4.0	②	3.5 ③	14.0 ⑥	12.0
	E	4-151 (2.5)	4.0	3.0	①	4.0	②	4.0 ③	④	9.2 ⑤
	B	6-173 (2.8)	4.0	4.0	①	4.0	②	3.5 ③	13.0 ⑥	12.0
	R	6-173 (2.8)	4.0	4.0	①	4.0	②	3.5 ③	13.0 ⑥	12.0
	N	6-260 (4.3)	5.0	4.0	①	4.0	②	4.0 ③	④	13.5 ⑤
	Z	6-260 (4.3)	5.0	5.0	—	—	②	4.2 ⑧	22.0	14.0
	T	6-292 (4.8)	5.0	4.0	8.0	—	②	3.5 ⑧	17.5 ⑦	15.0
	F	8-305 (5.0)	5.0	4.0	8.0	—	②	3.5 ⑧	22.0 ⑦	17.0

CAPACITIES

Year	Model	No. Cylinder Displacement cu. in. (liter)	Engine Crankcase with Filter	Engine Crankcase without Filter	Transmission (pts.) 4-Spd	Transmission (pts.) 5-Spd	Transmission (pts.) Auto.	Drive Axle (pts.)	Fuel Tank (gal.)	Cooling System (qts.)
1986	H	8-305 (5.0)	5.0	4.0	8.0	—	②	3.5 ⑧	22.0 ⑦	17.0
	L	8-350 (5.7)	5.0	4.0	8.0	—	②	3.5 ⑧	22.0 ⑦	17.0
	M	8-350 (5.7)	5.0	4.0	8.0	—	②	3.5 ⑧	22.0 ⑦	17.0
	C	8-380 (6.2)	7.0	7.0	8.0	—	②	3.5 ⑧	20.0 ⑦	25.5
	J	8-380 (6.2)	7.0	7.0	8.0	—	②	3.5 ⑧	20.0 ⑦	25.5
	W	8-454 (7.4)	7.0	6.0	8.0	—	②	3.5 ⑧	20.0 ⑦	24.5
1987	E	4-151 (2.5)	4.0	3.0	①	4.0	②	4.0 ③	④	13.5 ⑤
	R	6-173 (2.8)	4.0	4.0	①	4.0	②	3.5 ③	13.0 ⑥	12.0
	Z	6-260 (4.3)	5.0	5.0	—	—	②	4.2 ⑧	22.0	14.0
	T	6-292 (4.8)	5.0	4.0	8.0	—	②	3.5 ⑧	17.5 ⑦	15.0
	H	8-305 (5.0)	5.0	4.0	8.0	—	②	3.5 ⑧	22.0 ⑦	17.0
	L	8-350 (5.7)	5.0	4.0	8.0	—	②	3.5 ⑧	22.0 ⑦	17.0
	K	8-350 (5.7)	5.0	4.0	8.0	—	②	3.5 ⑧	22.0 ⑦	17.0
	M	8-350 (5.7)	5.0	4.0	8.0	—	②	3.5 ⑧	22.0 ⑦	17.0
	C	8-380 (6.2)	7.0	7.0	8.0	—	②	3.5 ⑧	20.0 ⑦	25.5
	J	8-380 (6.2)	7.0	7.0	8.0	—	②	3.5 ⑧	20.0 ⑦	25.5
	W	8-454 (7.4)	7.0	6.0	8.0	—	②	3.5 ⑧	20.0 ⑦	24.5
	N	8-454 (7.4)	7.0	6.0	8.0	—	②	3.5 ⑧	20.0 ⑦	24.5
1988	E	4-151 (2.5)	4.0	3.0	①	4.0	②	4.0 ③	④	13.5 ⑤
	R	6-173 (2.8)	4.0	4.0	①	4.0	②	3.5 ③	13.0 ⑥	12.0
	Z	6-260 (4.3)	5.0	5.0	—	—	②	4.2 ⑧	22.0	14.0
	T	6-292 (4.8)	5.0	4.0	8.0	—	②	3.5 ⑧	17.5 ⑦	15.0
	H	8-305 (5.0)	5.0	4.0	⑧	—	②	3.5 ⑧	22.0 ⑦	17.0
	K	8-350 (5.7)	5.0	4.0	⑧	—	②	3.5 ⑧	22.0 ⑦	17.0
	M	8-350 (5.7)	5.0	4.0	⑧	—	②	3.5 ⑧	22.0 ⑦	17.0
	C	8-380 (6.2)	7.0	7.0	⑧	—	②	3.5 ⑧	20.0 ⑦	25.5
	J	8-380 (6.2)	7.0	7.0	⑧	—	②	3.5 ⑧	20.0 ⑦	25.5
	N	8-454 (7.4)	7.0	6.0	⑧	—	②	3.5 ⑧	20.0 ⑦	24.5

① 4.0 77mm Trans., 4.8 77.5 Trans.
② 7.0 200c, 10.0 700R4, 10.0 350, 12.0 400
③ 2.5 Front axle
④ 17.0 Astro/Safari, 13.0 except Blazer/Jimmy, 13.5 Blazer/Jimmy
⑤ 12.0 S Series
⑥ 20.0 S Series with optional tank
⑦ 20.0, 25.0 or 27.0 optional tank
⑧ 8½ Ring gear, all others refer to tag, 5.0 front axle

WHEEL ALIGNMENT
S-Series, Astro/Safari

Year	Model	Caster Range (deg.)	Caster Preferred Setting (deg.)	Camber Range (deg.)	Camber Preferred Setting (deg.)	Toe-in (in.)	Steering Axis Inclination (deg.)
1982	S Series (2WD)	1P–3P+1+3	2P	0–1 3/4P	13/16P	1/8P	NA
1983	S Series (2WD)	1P–3P+1+3	2P	0–1 3/4P	13/16P	1/8P	NA
	(4WD)	1P–3P	2P	0–1 3/4P	13/16P	1/8P	NA
1984	S Series (2WD)	1P–3P+1+3	2P	0–1 3/4P	13/16P	1/8P	NA
	(4WD)	1P–3P+1+3	2P	0–1 3/4P	13/16P	1/8P	NA
1985	S Series (2WD)	1P–3P+1+3	2P	0–1 3/4P	13/16P	1/8P	NA
	(4WD)	1P–3P+1+3	2P	0–1 3/4P	13/16P	1/8P	NA
	Astro/Safari	1 11/16P–3 11/16P	2 11/16P	1/8P–1 3/4P	15/16P	5/32P	NA
1986	S Series (2WD)	1P–3P	2P	0–1 3/4P	13/16P	1/8P	NA
	(4WD)	1P–3P	2P	0–1 3/4P	13/16P	1/8P	NA
	Astro/Safari	1 11/16P–3 11/16P	2 11/16P	1/8P–1 3/4P	15/16P	5/32P	NA
1987	S Series (2WD)	1P–3P	2P	0–1 3/4P	13/16P	1/8P	NA
	(4WD)	1P–3P	2P	0–1 3/4P	13/16P	1/8P	NA
	Astro/Safari	1 11/16P–3 11/16P	2 11/16P	1/8P–1 3/4P	15/16P	5/32P	NA
1988	S Series (2WD)	1P–3P	2P	0–1 3/4P	13/16P	1/8P	NA
	(4WD)	1P–3P	2P	0–1 3/4P	13/16P	1/8P	NA
	Astro/Safari	1 11/16P–3 11/16P	2 11/16P	1/8P–1 3/4P	15/16P	5/32P	NA

WHEEL ALIGNMENT
Except S-Series, Astro/Safari

	Vehicle Identification		Caster @ Height Measurement (Degs.) Suspension Height Measurement (M)							Camber (Degrees)				
Year	Chevrolet Model	GMC Model	1 1/2	2	2 1/2	3	3 1/2	3 3/4	4	Min.	Pref.	Max.	Toe-In (Inches)	Toe-In (Deg.)
1982-88	C,R-10	C,R-1500	—	—	3 5/8	3 1/8	2 5/8	2 3/8	2	0	11/16	1 3/8	3/16 ± 1/8	3/8 ± 1/4
	C,R-20, 30	C,R-2500, 3500	—	—	1 1/2	15/16	5/16	1/8	0	1/2N	1/4	1	3/16 ± 1/8	3/8 ± 1/4
1982-84	K-10, 20	K-1500, 2500	—	—	8	8	8	8	8	5/16	1	1 11/16	3/16 ± 1/8	3/8 ± 1/4
	K-30	K-3500	—	—	8	8	8	8	8	3/16N	1/2	1 3/16	3/16 ± 1/8	3/8 ± 1/4
1985-88	K,V-10, 20, 30	K,V-1500, 2500, 3500	—	—	8	8	8	8	8	3/4	1 1/2	2	0 ± 1/8	0 ± 1/4
1982-85	G-10, 20	G-1500, 2500	3 1/2	3 1/8	2 11/16	2 3/8	2 1/8	1 15/16	1 7/8	3/16N	1/2	1 3/16	3/16 ± 1/8	3/8 ± 1/4
	G-30	G-3500	2 7/8	2 3/16	1 5/8	1	1/2	3/16	0	1/2N	3/16	7/8	3/16 ± 1/8	3/8 ± 1/4
1986-88	G-10, 20	G-1500, 2500	3 3/8	3	2 11/16	2 5/16	2	1 13/16	1 11/16	1/4N	1/2	1 1/4	3/16 ± 1/8	3/8 ± 1/4
	G-30	G-3500	3 1/8	2 11/16	2 1/8	1 1/2	1	11/16	1/2	1/2N	1/4	1	3/16 ± 1/8	3/8 ± 1/4
1982-85	P-10 P20, 30	P-1500 P-2500, 3500	—	—	2 5/16	1 11/16	1 3/16	15/16	5/8	1/2N	3/16	7/8	3/16 ± 1/8	3/8 ± 1/4
1986-88	P20, 30 exc. I-Beam	P2500, 3500 exc. I-Beam	—	—	2 5/16	1 11/16	1 3/16	15/16	5/8	1/2N	1/4	1	3/16 ± 1/8	3/8 ± 1/4
	w/I-Beam	w/I-Beam	5	5	5	5	5	5	5		1 1/2		1/16 ± 1/8	1/8 ± 1/4
1982-84	P-30 Motor Home	P-3500 Motor Home	—	—	5 1/2	5	4 3/8	4 1/8	3 7/8	1/2N	3/16	7/8	5/16 ± 1/8	5/8 ± 1/4
1985	P-30 Motor Home	P-3500 Motor Home	—	—	5 1/2	5	4 3/8	4 1/8	3 7/8	1/2N	3/16	7/8	1/4 ± 1/8	1/2 ± 1/4

WHEEL ALIGNMENT
Except S-Series, Astro/Safari

Year	Vehicle Identification Chevrolet Model	GMC Model	Caster @ Height Measurement (Degs.) Suspension Height Measurement (M) 1 1/2	2	2 1/2	3	3 1/2	3 3/4	4	Camber (Degrees) Min.	Pref.	Max.	Toe-In (Inches)	Toe-In (Deg.)
1986–88	P-30 Motor Home exc. I-Beam	P-3500 Motor Home exc. I-Beam	—	—	5 1/2	5	4 3/8	4 1/8	3 13/16	1/2N	1/4	1	3/16 ± 1/8	3/8 ± 1/4
	w/I-Beam	w/I-Beam	5	5	5	5	5	5	5		1 1/2		1/16 ± 1/8	1/8 ± 1/4

NOTE: With vehicle level, measure frame angle with a bubble protractor. Record the suspension height measurement.

a. Subtract an up-in-rear frame angle from a positive caster specification.

b. Subtract a down-in-rear frame angle from a negative caster specification.

c. Add an up-in-rear frame angle to a negative caster specification.

d. Add a down-in-rear frame angle to a positive caster specification.

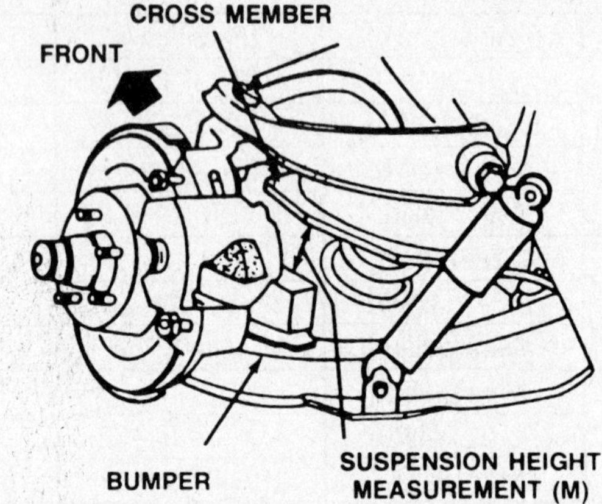

ENGINE ELECTRICAL

Alternator

Removal and Installation

1. Disconnect the negative battery cable. Disconnect the electrical connectors at the alternator.
2. Remove the necessary components in order to gain access to the alternator assembly. On Astro/Safari, remove the upper radiator fan shroud.
3. Remove the alternator belt. Remove the alternator retaining bolts. Remove the alternator from the vehicle.
4. Installation is the reverse of the removal procedure. Adjust the alternator belt, as required.

Starter

OVERHAUL

Refer to the Electrical Section as required.

Removal and Installation

1. Disconnect the negative battery cable. As required, raise and support the vehicle safely.
2. Remove the flywheel cover. Remove the exhaust crossover pipe, as required.
3. Disconnect the electrical wiring harness and battery leads at solenoid terminals.
4. Remove the starter mounting bolts and retaining nuts. Remove the starter assembly from the vehicle.
5. Installation is the reverse of the removal procedure. Install any shims that were removed with the starter.

Distributor

Removal and Installation

1. Disconnect the negative battery cable.
2. Remove all necessary components in order to gain access to the distributor assembly.
3. Disconnect the distributor electrical connectors. If equipped, disconnect the vacuum line. Mark and remove the spark plug wires.
4. Remove the distributor cap. Position the engine at TDC. Matchmark the rotor and the distributor body. Matchmark the distributor assembly and the engine block.
5. Remove the distributor retaining bolt. Carefully remove the distributor from the vehicle.

NOTE: As the distributor is removed from the engine, the rotor will turn counterclockwise. Observe and mark the start and finish rotation of the rotor. When reinstalling, position the rotor at the last mark and set the distributor into the engine. As the distributor drops into place, the rotor should turn to its original position, providing the engine crankshaft had not been rotated with the distributor out.

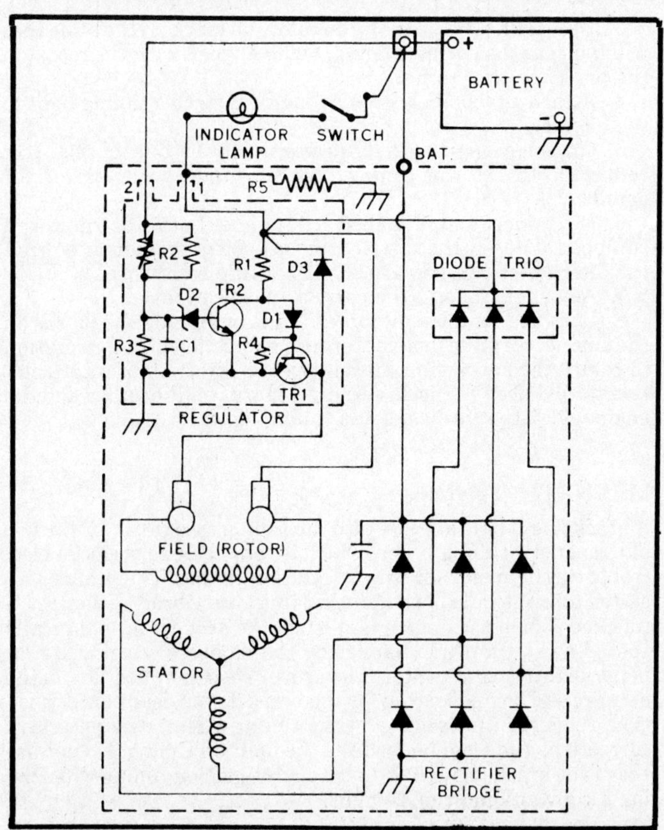

Schematic of internal regulator and alternator electrical circuits—typical of 10-SI, 15-SI and 27-SI alternator series

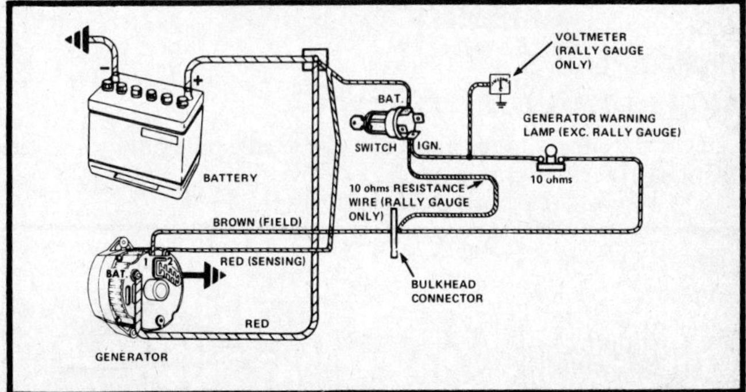

Schematic of typical SI charging system with either indicator light or rally gauge

6. Installation is the reverse of the removal procedure.

TIMING LIGHT AND TACHOMETER CONNECTIONS

Connect the timing light per manufacturers instructions to the engine. Be sure to time the engine on No.1 cylinder. Connect the tachometer to the engine per manufacturers instructions. If the vehicle is equipped with a diesel engine, a special timing light and a digital tachometer must be used. Some engines incorporate a bracket and hole which are cast into the timing case cover for the use of a magnetic timing probe, which is connected to a special electronic timing meter for precise ignition timing. If using this type of timing equipment, be sure to follow the manufacturers instructions.

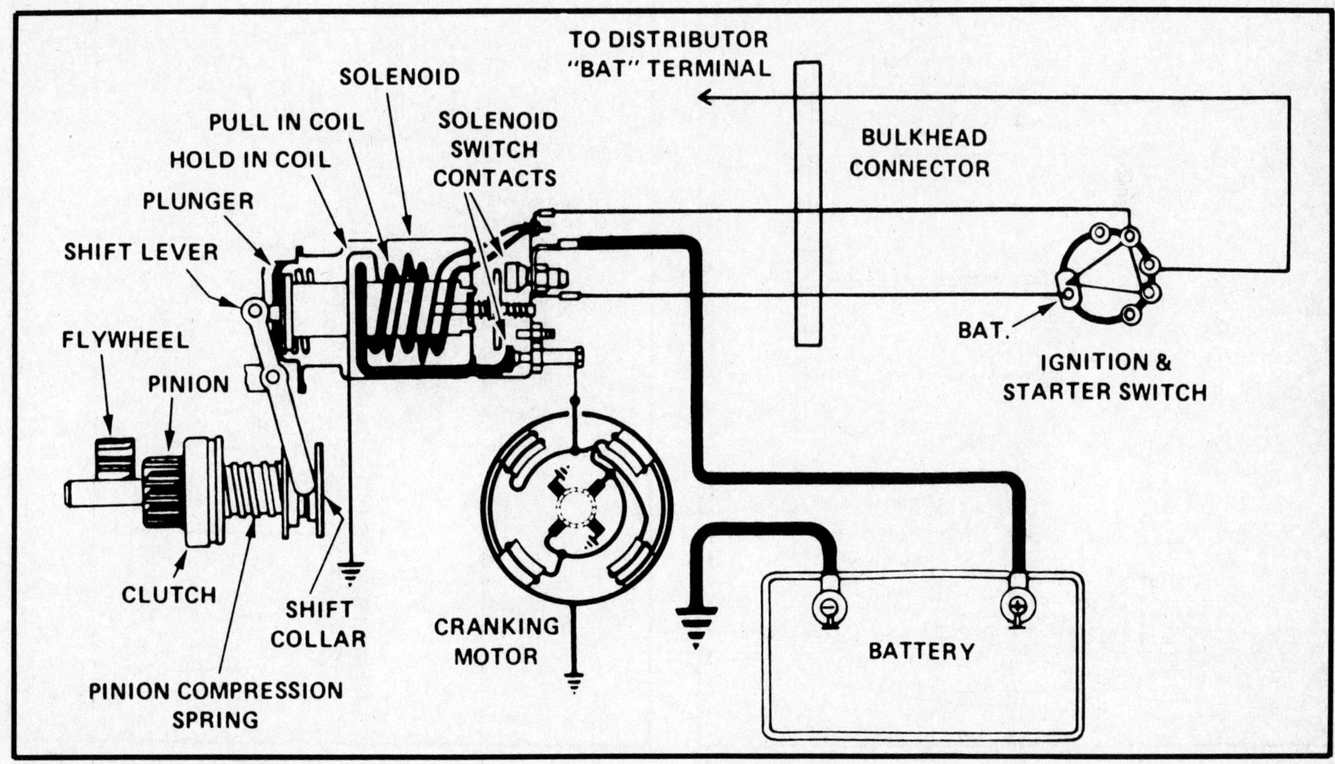

Typical cranking circuit

IGNITION TIMING

Procedure

EXCEPT MAGNETIC TIMING

1. Locate the timing marks on the crankshaft pulley and the front of the timing case cover.
2. Clean off the timing marks.

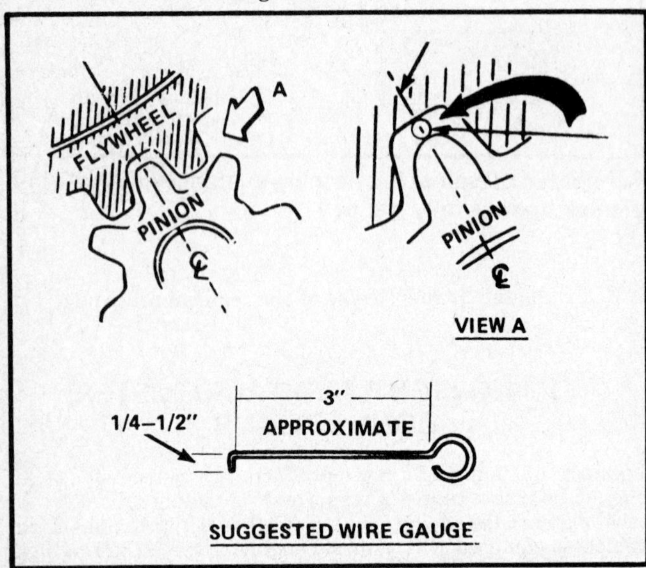

Flywheel to starter pinion clearance during starter installation

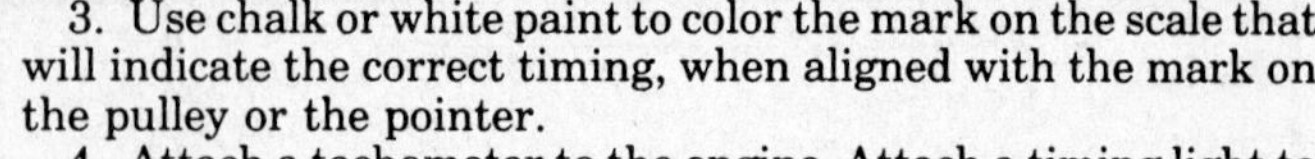

3. Use chalk or white paint to color the mark on the scale that will indicate the correct timing, when aligned with the mark on the pulley or the pointer.
4. Attach a tachometer to the engine. Attach a timing light to the engine.
5. On some engines, it is necessary to disconnect the EST connector to set the timing. See the underhood sticker for details.
6. Disconnect and plug the vacuum lines to the distributor, if equipped. Loosen the distributor lockbolt just enough so that the distributor can be turned with a little resistance.
7. Adjust the idle to the correct specification.
8. With the timing light aimed at the pulley and the marks on the engine, turn the distributor in the direction of rotor rotation to retard the spark, and in the opposite direction of rotor rotation to advance the spark. Align the marks on the pulley and the engine with the flashes of the timing light.

MAGNETIC TIMING

A bracket and hole are cast into the timing case cover for the use of a magnetic timing probe, which is connected to a special electronic timing meter for precise ignition timing. The probe is inserted into the hole of the bracket until the vibration damper is touched. When the engine is started, the probe is automatically spaced away from the damper by the dampers eccentricity, or being slightly out of center. The probe senses a milled slot on the damper and compensating for the brackets top dead center position, registers the reading on the timing meter. Any necessary corrections can then be made to the ignition timing. Do not use the probe bracket and hole to check the ignition timing when using a conventional timing light.

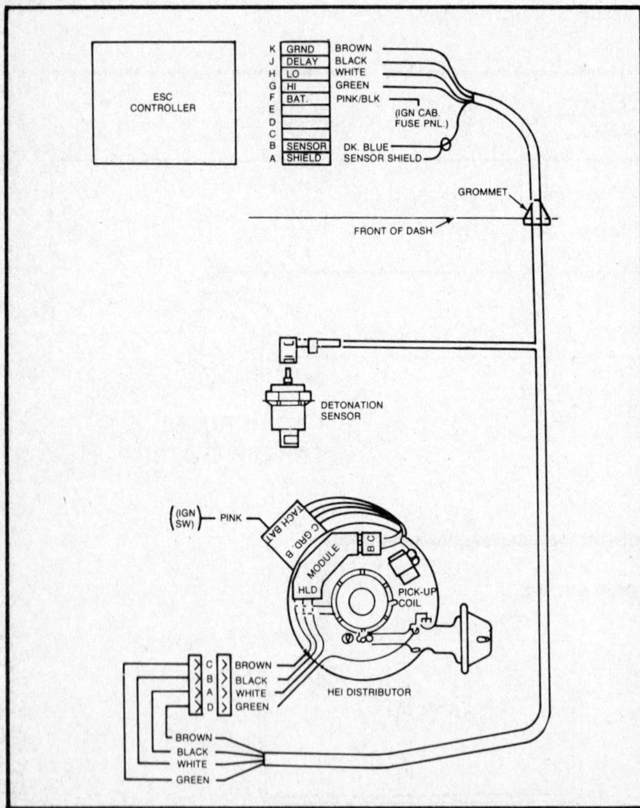

Typical electronic spark control wiring schematic

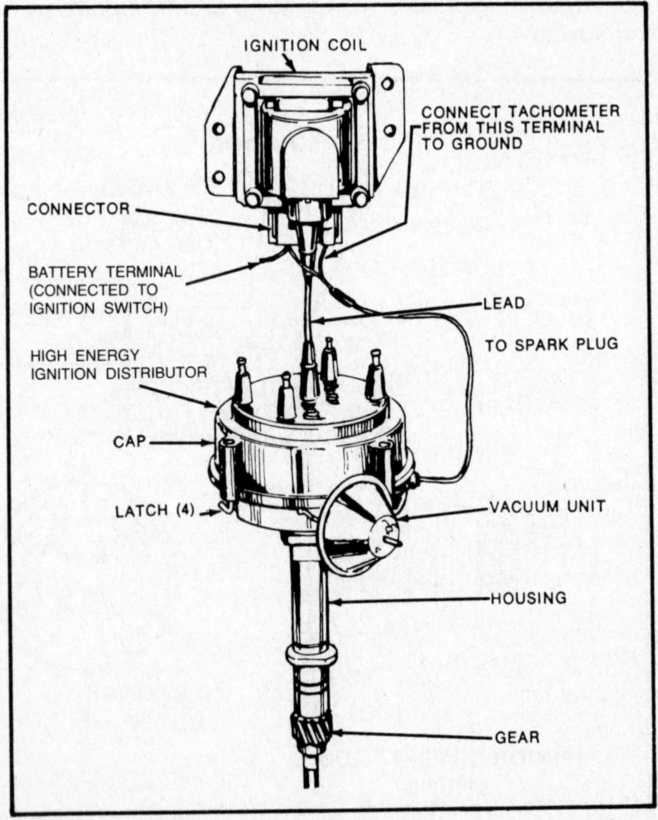

HEI distributor with vacuum advance

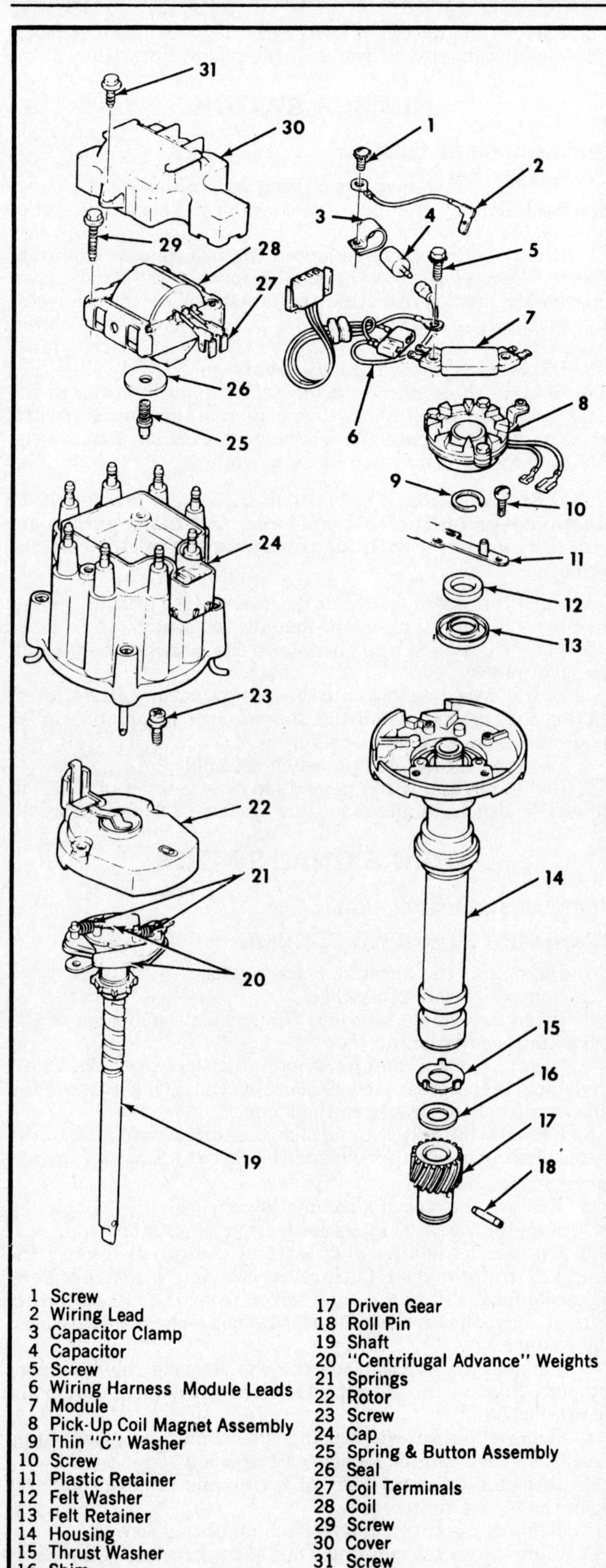

HEI distributor without vacuum advance—V8 engine—typical

Electrical Controls

IGNITION SWITCH

Removal and Installation

1. Disconnect the negative battery cable. If equipped, remove the lower trim panel.
2. Remove the steering column retaining bolts. Lower the steering column assembly to gain access to the switch retaining screws. Extreme care is necessary to prevent damage to the collapsible column.
3. Make sure the switch is in the LOCK position. If the lock cylinder is out, pull the switch rod up to the stop, then go down one detent.
4. Remove the electrical connections from the switch. Remove the switch retaining screws. Remove the switch from the column.
5. Installation is the reverse of the removal procedure. Before installation, make sure the switch is in the LOCK position. Install the switch using the original screws. Use of screws that are too long could prevent the column from collapsing on impact.

HEADLIGHT SWITCH

Removal and Installation

S SERIES (1982–83)

1. Disconnect the negative battery cable. Pull the switch control knob to the ON position.
2. Remove the lower trim plate, as required. Reach up from under the dash assembly and release the shaft retainer button while pulling on the switch control knob.
3. Remove the headlight switch trim plate retaining screws. Remove the switch trim plate.
4. Remove the headlight switch retaining nut. Disconnect the switch electrical connections. Remove the switch from the vehicle.
5. Installation is the reverse of the removal procedure.

S SERIES (1984–85)

1. Disconnect the negative battery cable. Remove the lower trim panel. Remove the hood release handle to instrument panel retaining screws.
2. Remove the lower steering column trim cover. If equipped, remove the cruise control module which is located behind the instrument panel. Remove the delay wiper switch knob and locknut.
3. Pull the switch control knob to the ON position. Reach up from under the dash assembly and release the shaft retainer button while pulling on the switch control knob.
4. Depress the lock tabs and remove the parking brake release handle. Disconnect the parking brake cable.
5. Remove the headlight switch bezel. Disconnect the electrical connectors from the switch. Remove the switch from the vehicle.
6. Installation is the reverse of the removal procedure.

S SERIES (1986–88)

1. Disconnect the negative battery cable. As required, remove the lower instrument panel trim assembly.
2. Remove the headlight switch assembly retaining screws. Disconnect the electrical connections from the headlight switch assembly.
3. Remove the headlight switch assembly from the vehicle.
4. Installation is the reverse of the removal procedure.

ASTRO/SAFARI

1. Disconnect the negative battery cable. As required, remove the lower steering column cover to instrument panel retaining screws.

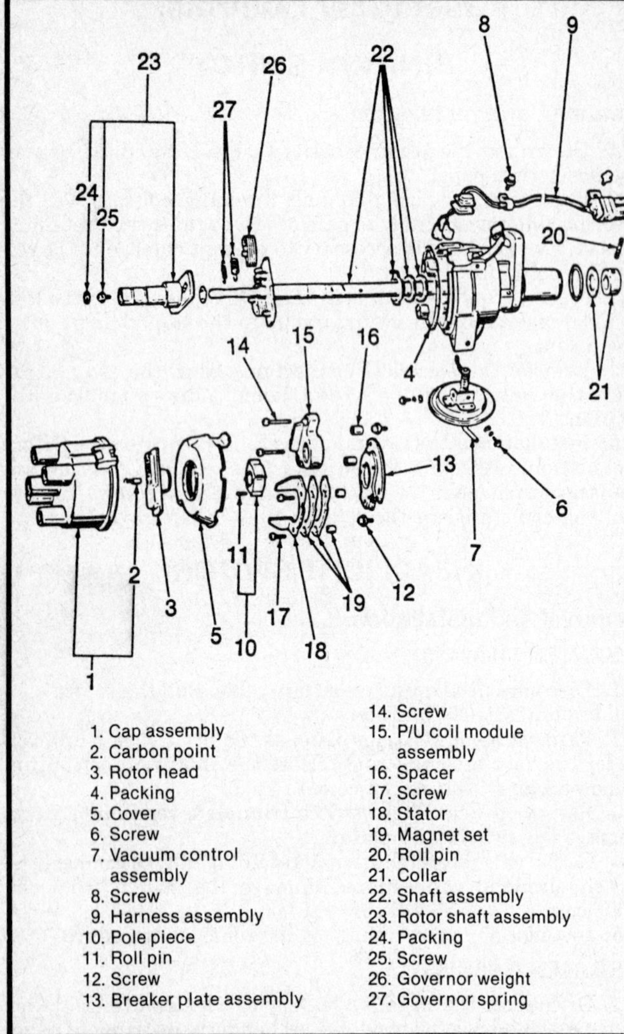

Exploded view of typical four cylinder distributor

2. Remove the instrument cluster trim panel. Pull the headlight switch assembly forward and disconnect the electrical connectors from the back of the switch.
3. Remove the switch assembly from the cluster trim plate.
4. Installation is the reverse of the removal procedure.

PICK UP (1982–87), BLAZER/JIMMY, SUBURBAN AND VAN

1. Disconnect the negative battery cable. Pull the switch control knob to the ON position.
2. Remove the lower trim plate, as required. Reach up from under the dash assembly and release the shaft retainer button while pulling on the switch control knob.
3. Remove the headlight switch trim plate retaining screws. Remove the switch trim plate.
4. Remove the headlight switch retaining nut. Disconnect the switch electrical connections. Remove the switch from the vehicle.
5. Installation is the reverse of the removal procedure.

PICK UP (1988)

1. Disconnect the negative battery cable. Remove the instrument panel trim plate.
2. Remove the switch assembly retaining screws. Pull the switch forward and disconnect the electrical connections.
3. Remove the headlight switch assembly from the vehicle.
4. Installation is the reverse of the removal procedure.

DIMMER SWITCH

Removal and Installation

1. Disconnect the negative battery cable. Remove the steering wheel. Remove the turn signal switch and position it out of the way.
2. It may be necessary to loosen the two column mounting nuts and remove the four bracket to mast jacket screws, then separate the bracket from the mast jacket to allow the connector clip on the ignition switch to be pulled out of the column assembly.
3. Disconnect the switch lower connector.
4. Remove the screws attaching the column housing to the mast jacket. Be sure to note the position of the dimmer switch actuator rod for reassembly in the same position. Remove the column housing and switch as an assembly.

NOTE: The tilt and travel columns have a removable plastic cover on the column housing. This provides access to the switch without removing the entire column housing.

5. Turn the assembly upside down and use a drift to remove the pivot pin from the switch. Remove the switch.
6. Place the switch into position in the housing, then install the pivot pin.
7. Position the housing onto the mast jacket and attach by installing the screws. Install the dimmer switch actuator rod as required. Check switch operation.
8. Reconnect lower end of switch assembly.
9. Install remaining components in reverse order of removal. Be sure to attach column mounting bracket in original position.

TURN SIGNAL SWITCH

Removal and Installation

STANDARD STEERING COLUMN

1. Disconnect the negative battery cable.
2. Remove the steering wheel.
3. Insert a suitable tool into the lockplate and remove the lockplate cover assembly.
4. Install a spring compressor onto the steering shaft. Tighten the tool to compress the lockplate and the spring. Remove the snapring from the groove in the shaft.
5. Remove the lockplate and slide the turn signal cam and the upper bearing preload spring and the thrust washer off the upper steering shaft.
6. Remove the steering column lower cover.
7. Remove the turn signal lever from the column.
8. On vehicles equipped with cruise control, disconnect the cruise control wire from the harness near the bottom of the column. Remove the harness protector from the cruise control wire. Remove the turn signal lever. Do not remove the wire from the column.
9. Remove the vertical bolts at the steering column upper support. Remove the shim packs. Keep the shims in order for reinstallation.
10. Remove the screws securing the column upper mounting bracket to the column. Remove the bracket.
11. Disconnect the turn signal wiring and remove the wires from the plastic protector.
12. Remove the turn signal switch mounting screws.
13. Slide the switch connector out of the bracket on the steering column.
14. If the switch is known to be bad, cut the wires and discard the switch. Before cutting the wires, verify that the wire codes are the same. Tape the connector of the new switch to the old

wires, and pull the new harness down through the steering column while removing the old wires.

15. If the original switch is to be reused, wrap tape around the wire and connector and pull the harness up through the column. It may be helpful to attach a length of wire to the harness connector before pulling it up through the column to facilitate installation.

16. After freeing the switch wiring protector from its mounting, pull the turn signal switch straight up and remove the switch, switch harness, and the connector from the column.

17. Installation is the reverse of the removal procedure.

TILT STEERING COLUMN

1. Disconnect the negative battery cable. Remove the steering wheel.
2. Remove the rubber sleeve bumper from the steering shaft.
3. Remove the plastic retainer and disengage the tabs on the retainer from the C-ring.
4. Compress the upper steering shaft preload spring with a spring compressor and remove the C-ring. When installing the spring compressor, pull the upper shaft up about one inch and turn the ignition to the lock position to hold the shaft in place.
5. Remove the spring compressor and remove the upper steering shaft lock plate, horn contact carrier and the preload spring.
6. Remove the steering column lower cover. Unscrew and remove the turn signal lever.
7. If equipped with cruise control, disconnect the cruise control wire from the harness near the bottom of the steering column. Slide the protector off the cruise control wire. Remove the lever attaching screw and carefully pull the lever out enough to allow the removal of the turn signal switch.
8. Remove the nuts and shim packs from the upper column support. Keep the shims together as a unit for reinstallation.
9. Remove the bracket from the steering column by removing the two attaching screws from each side.
10. Disconnect the turn signal wiring harness and remove the wires from the plastic protector.
11. Remove the turn signal switch retaining screws and pull the switch up out of the steering column.
12. If the switch is to be replaced, cut the wires from the switch and tape the new switch connector to the old wires. Verify that the wire codes are the same, before cutting the wires. Carefully pull the new harness down through the column as the old wires are removed.
13. If the old switch is to be reused, tape the connector to the wires and carefully pull the harness up out of the column.
14. Feed the wiring harness down through the steering column to replace the old switch.
15. Secure the switch in the steering column.
16. Install the upper shaft preload spring.
17. Install the lock plate and carrier assembly. Make sure that the flat on the lower end of the steering shaft is pointing up and that the small plastic tab on the carrier is up or nearest the top of the column. The flat surface of the lock plate must be installed facing down against the turn signal switch.
18. Install the spring compressor, compress the preload spring and lock plate and install the C-ring with the wide side toward the keyway.
19. Remove the spring compressor and install the plastic retainer on the C-ring.
20. Install the rubber sleeve bumper over the steering shaft and install the steering wheel.
21. Install the turn signal lever. If the vehicle is equipped with cruise control, secure the lever to the switch with the retaining screw and install the wiring harness.
22. Remove the tape from the end of the harness and connect the switch and cruise control, if so equipped, to the wire harness.
23. Cover both harnesses with the plastic protector and position it to the column. The turn signal connector slides on the tabs of the column.
24. Position the steering column upper bracket over the turn signal switch harness plastic protector.
25. Install the mounting bracket nuts and shims in their original positions.
26. Install the steering column lower cover.

WINDSHIELD WIPER SWITCH

Removal and Installation

COLUMN MOUNTED

1. Disconnect the negative battery cable. Remove the steering wheel. Remove the turn signal switch.
2. It may be necessary to loosen the two column mounting nuts and remove the four bracket to mast jacket screws, then separate the bracket from the mast jacket to allow the connector clip on the ignition switch to be pulled out of the column assembly.
3. Disconnect the washer/wiper switch lower connector.
4. Remove the screws attaching the column housing to the mast jacket. Be sure to note the position of the dimmer switch actuator rod for reassembly in the same position. Remove the column housing and switch as an assembly.

NOTE: Some tilt columns have a removable plastic cover on the column housing. This provides access to the wiper switch without removing the entire column housing.

5. Turn the assembly upside down and use a drift to remove the pivot pin from the washer/wiper switch. Remove the switch.
6. Place the switch into position in the housing, then install the pivot pin.
7. Position the housing onto the mast jacket and attach by installing the screws. Install the dimmer switch actuator rod in the same position as noted earlier. Check switch operation.
8. Reconnect lower end of switch assembly.
9. Install remaining components in reverse order of removal. Be sure to attach column mounting bracket in original position.

DASH MOUNTED

1. Disconnect the negative battery cable.
2. Remove all required trim and instrument panel bezels in order to remove the switch.
3. Disconnect the electrical connectors from the switch assembly.
4. Remove the switch retaining screws. Remove the switch.
5. Installation is the reverse of removal.

WINDSHIELD WIPER MOTOR

Removal and Installation

1. Disconnect the negative battery cable.
2. Remove the cowl screen, as required.
3. Loosen the transmission drive link to crank arm retaining bolts. Remove the drive link from the motor crank arm.
4. Disconnect the electrical wiring and the washer hoses from the motor assembly.
5. Remove the motor retaining screws. Remove the windshield wiper motor while guiding the crank arm through the hole.
6. Installation is the reverse of the removal procedure. The motor must be in the park position before assembling the crank arm to the drive link.

WINDSHIELD WIPER LINKAGE

Removal and Installation

1. Disconnect the negative battery cable. As required, remove the cowl vent screen.

2. Remove the right and left wiper arm and blade assemblies.
3. Loosen but do not remove, the attaching nuts securing the transmission drive links to the motor crank arm.
4. Disconnect the transmission drive link from the motor crank arm.
5. Remove the wiper transmission to body attaching screws.
6. Remove the wiper transmission and linkage by guiding it through the plenum chamber opening or to the left side under the dash panel extension.
7. Installation is the reverse of the removal procedure.

INSTRUMENT CLUSTER

Removal and Installation

1. Disconnect the negative battery cable. Remove the steering column lower cover screws. Remove the cover. As required, remove all accessories in order to remove the cluster assembly.
2. If equipped with automatic transmission, disconnect the shift indicator cable from the steering column. Remove the steering column to instrument panel screws.
3. As required, lower the steering column. Use extreme care when lowering the steering column in order to prevent damage to column assembly.
4. Remove the screws and the snap in fasteners from the perimeter of the instrument cluster housing.
5. Pull the cluster assembly forward and disconnect the speedometer cable and the electrical connectors, as necessary. Be sure to keep fingers and other foreign objects away from the circuit board pins.
6. Remove the instrument cluster assembly from the vehicle.
7. Installation is the reverse of the removal procedure.

COOLING AND HEATING SYSTEM

Water Pump

S SERIES

Removal and Installation

119 CID (1.9L) ENGINE

1. Disconnect the negative battery cable. Remove the bolts holding the lower cover. Remove the cover. Drain the cooling system.
2. On vehicles without air conditioning, remove the four nuts retaining the engine fan. Remove the fan assembly.
3. On vehicles equipped with air condition, remove the air pump and alternator mounting bolts. Remove the fan and air pump drive belt by pivoting the air pump and alternator in toward the engine. Remove the bolts retaining the fan and pulley, remove the fan together with the fan pulley and air pump drive pulley. Remove the retaining bolts attaching the fan set plate and fan pulley. Remove the set plate and pulley.
4. Remove the water pump retaining bolts. Remove the pump assembly from the engine.
5. Installation is the reverse of the removal procedure. Use a new gasket or RTV sealant, as required.
6. Before installation. clean the mounting surface on water pump and engine block.

121 CID (2.0L) ENGINE

1. Disconnect the negative battery cable. Drain the cooling system. Remove the drive belts.
2. Remove all the necessary components in order to gain access to the water pump retaining bolts.
3. Remove the water pump mounting bolts. Remove the water pump from the engine.
4. Installation is the reverse of the removal procedure. Use a new gasket or RTV sealant, as required.
5. Before installation. clean the mounting surface on water pump and engine block.

151 CID (2.5L) ENGINE

1. Disconnect the negative battery cable. Remove the necessary accessory drive belts. Drain the cooling system.
2. Remove the upper fan shroud. Remove the fan and pump pulley. Remove the radiator hose and heater hoses.
3. Remove the water pump retaining bolts. Remove the water pump from the engine.
4. Installation is the reverse of the removal procedure. Use a new gasket or RTV sealant, as required.
5. Before installation. clean the mounting surface on water pump and engine block.

173 CID (2.8L) ENGINE

1. Disconnect the negative battery cable. Drain the coolant. Remove the fan shroud, as necessary. Remove the drive belts. Remove the fan and pulley assembly.
2. Remove the necessary components in order to gain access to the water pump retaining bolts.
3. Remove the water pump retaining bolts. Remove the water pump assembly from the engine.
4. Installation is the reverse of the removal procedure. Use a new gasket or RTV sealant, as required.
5. Before installation. clean the mounting surface on water pump and engine block.

ASTRO/SAFARI

Removal and Installation

1. Disconnect the negative battery cable. Drain the coolant. Remove the fan shroud, as necessary. Remove the drive belts. Remove the fan and pulley assembly.
2. Remove the necessary components in order to gain access to the water pump retaining bolts.
3. Remove the water pump retaining bolts. Remove the water pump assembly from the engine.
4. Installation is the reverse of the removal procedure. Use a new gasket or RTV sealant, as required.
5. Before installation. clean the mounting surface on water pump and engine block.

PICK UP, BLAZER/JIMMY, SUBURBAN AND VAN

Removal and Installation

1. Disconnect the negative battery cable. Drain the cooling system. Remove the drive belts. If necessary, remove the alternator bracket.
2. As required, remove the fan shroud. Remove the fan and pulley assembly.
3. Remove the lower radiator hose and the heater hose from the water pump. On 7.4L engine, remove the bypass hose.
4. Remove the water pump retaining bolts. Remove the water pump from the engine.
5. Installation is the reverse of the removal procedure. Use a new gasket or RTV sealant, as required.

6. Before installation. clean the mounting surface on water pump and engine block.

Thermostat

Removal and Installation

1. Disconnect the negative battery cable. Drain the cooling system.
2. Remove the necessary components in order to gain access to the thermostat housing retaining bolts.
3. Remove the top radiator hose and the bypass hose, as required. Disconnect the electrical connection on the housing, as required.
4. Remove the thermostat housing retaining bolts. Remove the thermostat housing from the engine.
5. Installation is the reverse of the removal procedure. Be sure to use a new gasket or RTV sealant, as required.

Heater Core

WITHOUT AIR CONDITIONING

Removal and Installation

S SERIES

1. Disconnect the negative battery. Drain the cooling system.
2. Remove and plug the heater hoses Remove the radio suppression strap.
3. Remove the heater core cover retaining screws. Remove the cover from under the dash.
4. Remove the heater core retainers at each end of the heater core. Remove the heater core assembly.
5. To install, position the heater core and install the retainers at each end of the core.
6. Install the heater core cover and install the retaining screws.
7. Install the radio suppression cable. Install the heater hoses.
8. Connect the negative battery cable. Fill the cooling system.

ASTRO/SAFARI

1. Disconnect the negative battery cable. Drain the engine coolant.
2. Remove the engine coolant bottle. Remove the two bolts from the windshield washer bottle and position the bottle out of the way.
3. Remove and plug the heater hoses at the heater core.
4. Remove the instrument panel lower right filler panel. Remove the air distributor duct.
5. It may be necessary to remove the engine cover for additional clearance. Remove the heater assembly retaining nuts. Remove the air duct assembly.
6. Remove the heater assembly from the vehicle.
7. Remove the heater core cover plate retaining screws. Remove the heater core.
8. Installation is the reverse of the removal procedure.

PICK UP (1982–87), BLAZER/JIMMY AND SUBURBAN

1. Disconnect the negative battery cable. Drain the cooling system. Remove and plug the heater hoses.
2. Remove the retaining nuts from the distributor duct assembly that protrudes into the engine compartment.
3. Remove the glove box and door assembly. Disconnect the air defrost and temperature door cables.
4. Remove the floor outlets. Remove the defroster duct to heater distributor duct screw.
5. Remove the heater distributor to dash panel screws, pull the assembly rearward to gain access to the wiring harness and disconnect all connectors attached to the unit.
6. Remove the heater distributor from the vehicle.
7. Remove the heater core retaining straps. Remove the core from the case.
9. Installation is the reverse of the removal procedure.

PICK UP (1988)

1. Disconnect the negative battery cable. Drain the cooling system. Disconnect and plug the heater hoses.
2. Remove the coolant bottle. Disconnect the antenna cable at the mast. Disconnect the electrical wiring harness from the computer.
3. Remove the computer and its bracket. Remove the kick pad. Remove the right side lower dash panel bolt and nut.
4. Remove the heater case retaining bolts. Remove the heater case from the vehicle. It may be necessary to raise the dash for additional working clearance.
5. Remove the heater case retaining bolts. Remove the heater core from the heater case.
6. Installation is the reverse of the removal procedure.

VAN

1. Disconnect the negative battery cable.
2. Remove the coolant recovery tank and position it out of the way.
3. Drain the cooling system. Remove and plug the heater hoses.
4. Remove the heater distributor duct to distributor case attaching screws and distributor duct to engine cover screw. Remove the duct.
5. Remove the engine housing cover.
6. Remove the instrument panel attaching screws at the windshield Remove all the lower screws and right lower instrument panel support bracket at the door pillar and engine housing.
7. Lower the steering column. Raise and support the right side of the instrument panel.
8. Remove the screw attaching the defroster duct to the distributor case and the two screws attaching the distributor to the heater case.
9. Disconnect the temperature door cable and fold the cable back for access.
10. Remove the three retaining nuts on the engine compartment side of the distributor case and one screw from the passenger compartment side.
11. Remove the heater core and the heater distributor as an assembly. It will be necessary to tilt the case assembly rearward at the top while lifting up until the core tubes clear the dash opening.
12. Remove the heater core retaining strap screws. Remove the core.
13. Remove the core to case and case to dash panel sealer and renew as required.
14. Installation is the reverse of the removal procedure.

WITH AIR CONDITIONING

Removal and Installation

S SERIES

1. Disconnect the negative battery cable.
2. Drain the cooling system.
3. Remove and plug the heater hoses at the heater core.
4. Remove the heater core cover attaching screws and remove the cover.
5. Remove the four screw retainers at the end of the heater core.
6. Remove the core from under the dash assembly.
7. Installation is the reverse of the removal procedure.

ASTRO/SAFARI

1. Disconnect the negative battery cable. Drain the engine coolant.

2. Remove the engine coolant bottle. Remove the two bolts from the windshield washer bottle and position it to the side. Remove and plug the heater hoses at the heater core.
3. Remove the instrument panel lower right filler panel. Remove the air distributor duct. Remove the engine cover as needed.
4. Remove the air duct. Remove vacuum lines and control cables as required.
5. Remove the heater core assembly retaining screws. Remove the heater core assembly from the vehicle.
6. Remove the heater core cover plate. Remove the heater core.
7. Installation is the reverse of the removal procedure.

PICK UP (1982–87), BLAZER/JIMMY AND SUBURBAN

1. Disconnect the negative battery cable.
2. Drain the cooling system. Remove and plug the heater hoses at the heater core.
3. Remove the glove box and door as an assembly.
4. Remove the center duct to selector duct and instrument panel screws. Remove the center lower and center upper ducts.
5. Disconnect the bowden cable at the temperature door.
6. Remove the retaining nuts from the three selector duct studs projecting through the dash panel.
7. Remove the selector duct to dash panel screws from inside the vehicle.
8. Pull the selector duct assembly rearward until the core tubes clear the dash panel. Lower the selector assembly far enough to gain access to all vacuum and electrical harnesses.
9. Disconnect the vacuum and electrical harness and remove the selector duct assembly.
10. Remove the core mounting strap. Remove the core assembly.
11. Installation is the reverse of the removal procedure.

PICK UP (1988)

1. Disconnect the negative battery cable. Drain the cooling system.
2. As required, properly discharge the air condition system. Disconnect and plug the evaporator lines.
3. Remove the coolant overflow tank. Disconnect and plug the heater hoses. Disconnect all electrical connectors.
4. Remove the heater case bottom plate retaining screws. Remove the bottom plate.
5. Remove the heater core retaining bracket and screws. Remove the heater core from its mounting.
6. Installation is the reverse of the removal procedure.

VAN

1. Disconnect the negative battery cable.
2. Remove the engine comer from inside the vehicle.
3. Remove the steering column to instrument panel attaching bolts and lower the steering column.
4. Remove the upper and lower instrument panel attaching screws and the radio support bracket attaching screw.
5. Raise and support the right side of the instrument panel.
6. Remove the right lower instrument panel support bracket.
7. Remove the recirculating air door vacuum actuator and plate.
8. Disconnect the temperature cable and vacuum hoses at the distributor case.
9. Remove the heater distributor duct and retaining screws.
10. Remove the two defroster duct to dash panel attaching screws, located below the windshield.
11. From the engine compartment, remove and plug the heater hoses.
12. Remove the three retaining nuts holding the heater core case to the dash panel and the one screw at the lower right corner on the inside.
13. Remove the distributor housing from the vehicle.
14. Remove the gasket, exposing the case half retaining screws. Remove the screws, separate the case and remove the heater core.
15. Installation is the reverse of the removal procedure.

Blower Motor

WITHOUT AIR CONDITIONING

Removal and Installation

S SERIES

1. Disconnect the negative battery cable.
2. Disconnect the blower motor wiring connector.
3. Remove the blower motor attaching screws.
4. Remove the blower motor from the blower housing. Separate the wheel from the motor assembly, as required.
5. Installation is in the reverse of the removal procedure.

ASTRO/SAFARI

1. Disconnect the negative battery cable. Disconnect the electrical connections at the blower motor assembly.
2. Remove the engine coolant bottle. Remove the two bolts from the windshield washer bottle and position the bottle out of the way.
3. Remove the blower motor retaining screws. Remove the blower motor from the vehicle. Separate the wheel from the motor assembly, as required.
4. Installation is the reverse of the removal procedure.

PICK UP, BLAZER/JIMMY, SUBURBAN AND VAN

1. Disconnect the negative battery cable.
2. if necessary, remove the coolant recovery tank. Remove the power antenna, if equipped.
3. Remove the power lead from the blower motor assembly. Remove the five retaining screws and remove the blower motor from the housing.
4. Separate the wheel and motor assembly as required.
5. Installation is the reverse of the removal procedure. Renew the blower motor flange sealer, as required.

WITH AIR CONDITIONING

Removal and Installation

S SERIES

1. Disconnect the battery ground cable.
2. Remove the vacuum tank assembly, if required. Disconnect the blower motor electrical connections.
3. Remove the blower motor attaching screws. Remove the blower motor from the vehicle.
4. Installation is the reverse of the removal procedure.

ASTRO/SAFARI

1. Disconnect the negative battery cable.
2. Remove the engine coolant bottle. Remove the two bolts from the windshield washer bottle and position the assembly out of the way.
3. Disconnect the electrical connections from the heater blower assembly. Remove the blower motor relay bracket, as required.
4. Remove the blower motor retaining screws. Remove the heater motor from the vehicle.
5. Installation is the reverse of the removal procedure. Transfer the blower motor squirrel cage, as required. Upon installation align the motor assembly with the alignment pin.

PICK UP, BLAZER/JIMMY AND SUBURBAN

1. Disconnect the negative battery cable.
2. Disconnect the blower motor electrical wire and the ground wire.

3. Disconnect the blower motor cooling tube.
4. Remove the blower to case retaining screws. Remove the blower motor assembly.
5. Installation is the reverse of the removal procedure.

VAN

1. Disconnect the negative battery cable.
2. Vehicles equipped with a diesel engine have extra insulation around the blower motor and evaporator core. The parking lamp may have to be removed along with the coolant recovery tank. Remove the retaining screws and remove the insulation through the hood opening.
3. Remove the coolant recovery tank. Remove the power antenna, if equipped.
4. Disconnect the blower motor electrical connector.
5. Remove the retaining screws from the blower motor to housing. Remove the blower motor.
6. Installation is the reverse of the removal procedure. Replace the sealer on the motor flange as required.

FUEL SYSTEM

Refer to the Unit Overhaul Section as required.

Carburetor

Removal and Installation

1. Disconnect the negative battery cable. Properly relieve the fuel pump pressure. Remove the air cleaner.
2. Disconnect and plug the fuel lines. Disconnect the necessary vacuum lines and electrical connections.
3. Disconnect the accelerator linkage. Disconnect the transmission linkage, as required.
4. Remove the carburetor retaining bolts. Remove the carburetor and gasket from the engine.
5. Installation is the reverse of the removal procedure. Be sure to use a new carburetor base gasket.

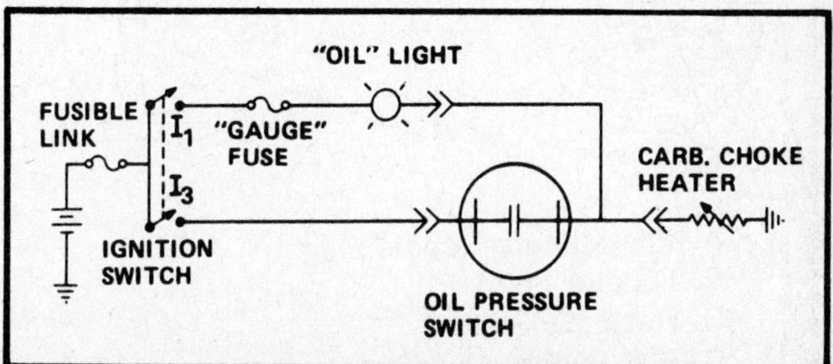

Electric choke heater wiring schematic

Adjustments

IDLE MIXTURE LIGHT DUTY EMISSION VEHICLES

Idle mixture needles were preset and sealed at the factory. Idle mixture should only be adjusted during major carburetor overhaul, throttle body replacement or if high emissions are determined by inspection.

Because of sealed idle mixture needles, the idle mixture checking procedure requires artificial enrichment by adding propane. Adjusting mixture by other than the following method may violate government regulations.

1. Set the parking brake and block the drive wheels. Start the engine and allow it to reach normal operating temperature. Turn air conditioning off, if equipped.
2. Disconnect and plug the hoses as indicated by the underhood emission control label.
3. Connect a tachometer to the engine according to manufacturers instructions.
4. Disconnect the vacuum advance and set the timing according to the emission control label. Reconnect the vacuum advance hose.
5. Set the carburetor idle speed to specification.
6. Disconnect the cranckcase ventilation tube from the air cleaner assembly.
7. Insert the propane enrichment tool hose with the rubber stopper into the into the crankcase ventilation tube opening in the air cleaner. The propane cartridge must be kept in a vertical position.
8. With the engine idling in drive (neutral for manual transmissions), slowly open the propane control valve while pressing the button. Continue to add propane until the engine speed drops due to over richness.
9. If the enriched idle speed is within the enriched idle specification, the mixture is correct. Go to Step 18.

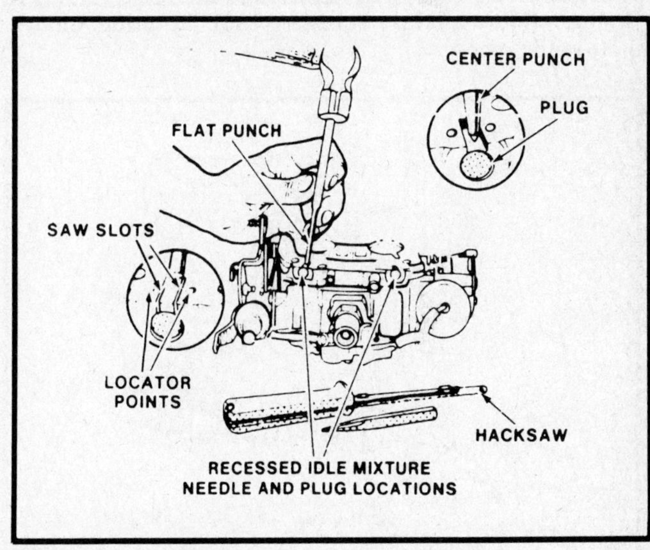

Removing idle mixture screws—1984-86 light duty emission vehicles

10. If the enriched idle speed is not within specification, remove the idle mixture needles:
    a. Remove the carburetor from the engine.
    b. Invert the carburetor and drain the fuel.
    c. Place the carburetor onto a holding fixture.
    d. Using a hacksaw or other suitable tool, make two parallel cuts in the throttle body, one on each side of the locator point by each idle mixture needle plug. Cut down to the steel plug, but not more than ⅛ in. beyond the locator point.
    e. Place a flat punch at a point near the ends of the saw marks. Hold the punch at a 45° angle and drive it into the

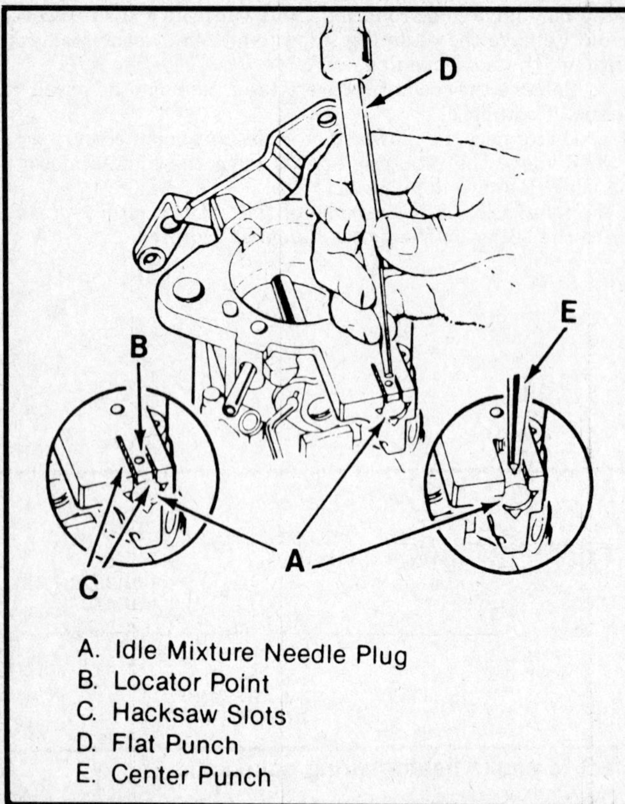

Removing idle mixture screws—1987 light duty emission vehicles

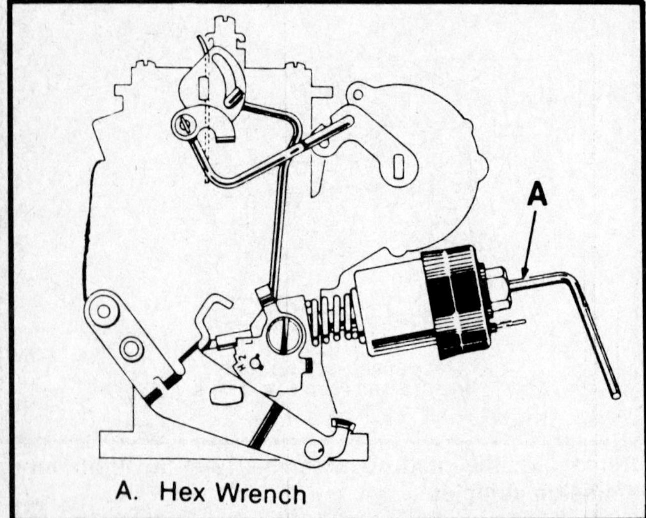

Light duty emission vehicles base idle adjustment

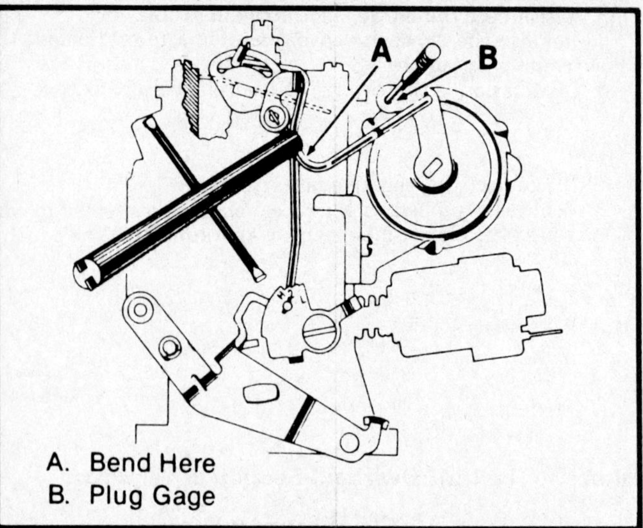

Light duty emission vehicles choke coil lever adjustment

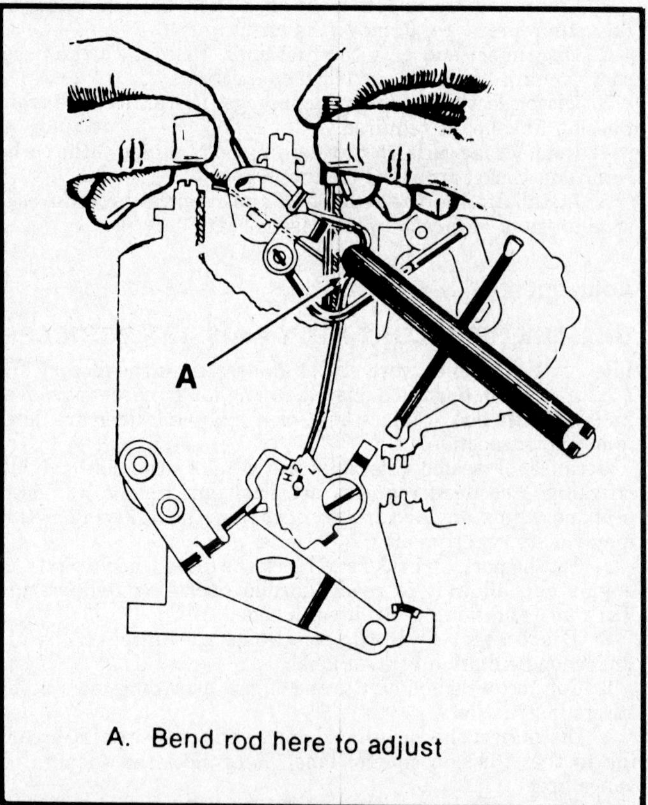

Light duty emission vehicles choke rod adjustment

throttle body until the casting brakes away, exposing the steel plug.

f. Hold a center punch vertically and drive it into the steel plug. Remove the plug from the casing and all loose particles.

g. Repeat the procedure for the other plug.

11. Install the carburetor on the engine.
12. Using tool J-29030-B or equivalent, lightly seat the mixture needles, then back out equally, just enough to run the engine.
13. Place the transmission in drive (automatic) or neutral (manual).
14. Back each needle out (richen $^1/_8$ turn at a time) until maximum idle speed is obtained. Set the idle speed to the enriched idle specification.
15. Turn each mixture needle ($^1/_8$ turn at a time) until idle speed reaches specification.
16. Recheck the enriched speed using the propane method. If not within specification, repeat the procedure from Step 12.

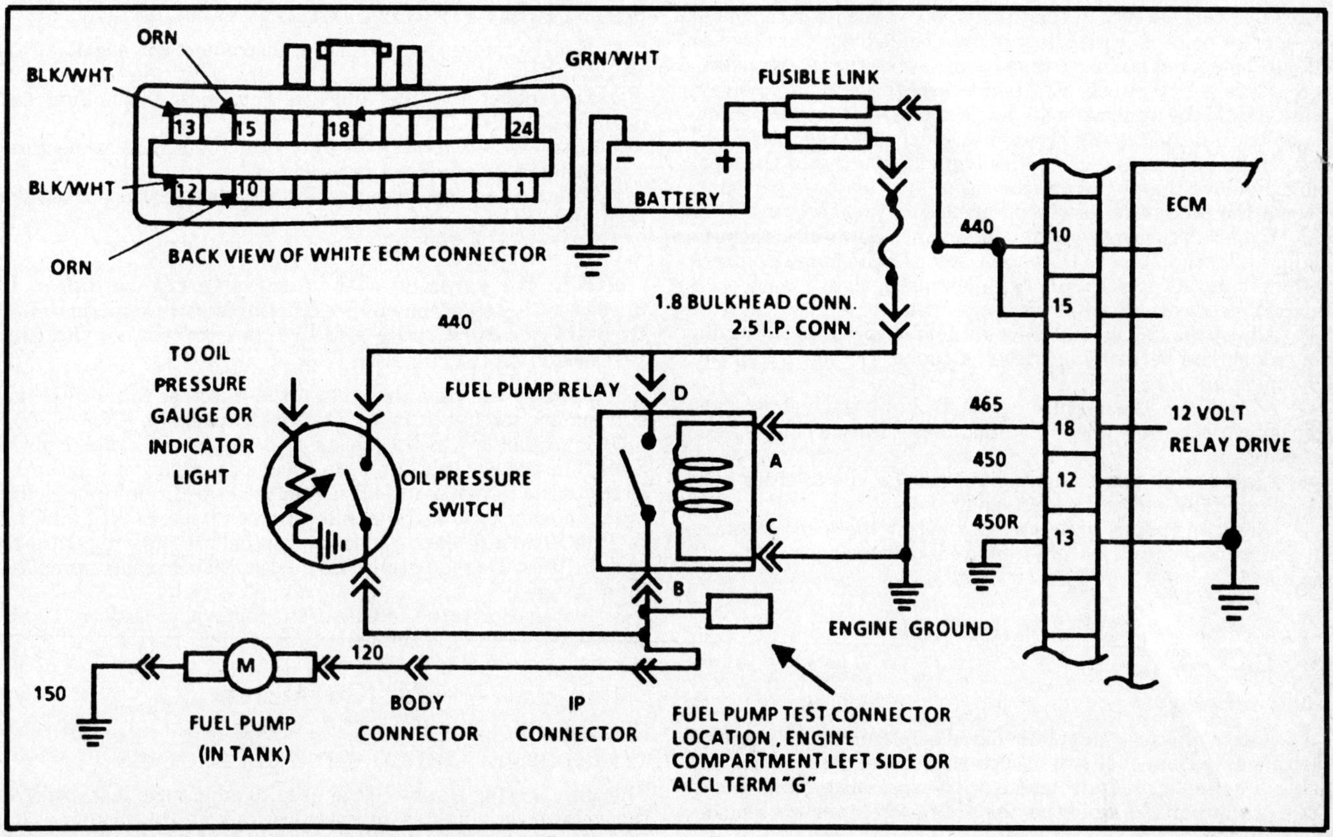

Electrical schematic of 2.5L engine with TBI system

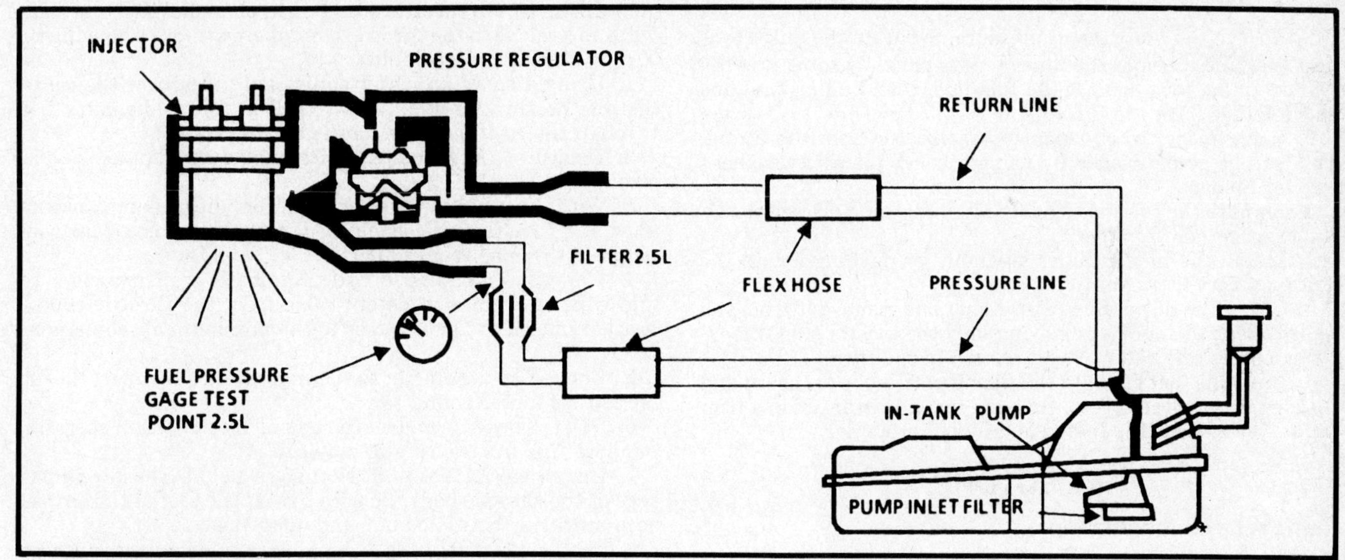

Fuel system diagram, 2.5L engine with TBI system

17. After all adjustments are made, seal the idle mixture needles using RTV sealer or equivalent.
18. Check and adjust the fast idle, if necessary.
19. Turn the engine off. Remove the propane tool. Connect the crankcase ventilation tube. Unplug and reconnect any vacuum hoses that were removed. Install the air cleaner.

IDLE MIXTURE HEAVY DUTY EMISSION VEHICLES

Idle mixture needles were preset and sealed at the factory. Idle mixture should only be adjusted during major carburetor overhaul, throttle body replacement or if high emissions are determined by inspection.

This adjustment should be performed with the engine at normal operating temperature, parking brake engaged, transmission in Park or Neutral and the drive wheels blocked.

1. Remove the air cleaner.
2. Remove the carburetor from the vehicle and place in a suitable holding fixture. Using a hacksaw or other suitable tool,

make two parallel cuts in the throttle body, one on each side of the locator point by each idle mixture needle plug. Cut down to the steel plug, but not more than ⅛ in. beyond the locator point.

3. Place a flat punch at a point near the ends of the saw marks. Hold the punch at a 45° angle and drive it into the throttle body until the casting brakes away, exposing the steel plug.

4. Hold a center punch vertically and drive it into the steel plug. Remove the plug from the casing and all loose particles. Repeat the procedure for the other plug.

5. Install the carburetor on the engine. Connect a vacuum gauge and tachometer to the engine according to manufacturers instructions. As a preliminary adjustment, lightly seat each mixture needle and back it out two turns.

6. Adjust the idle speed screw to the idle speed specification. Engine should be running with the choke wide open and the transmission in neutral.

7. Adjust each idle mixture needle to obtain the highest rpm. Repeat until the best idle is obtained. Reset the curb idle speed, if necessary.

8. After completing adjustments, seal the idle mixture needles using RTV sealant or equivalent.

9. Check and adjust, if necessary, the fast idle speed. Remove all gauges and reconnect any removed vacuum lines. Turn off engine.

FUEL INJECTION

Relieve Pressure

Fuel system pressure must be relieved before disconnecting any fuel lines. Release fuel system pressure at the test connection using a suitable pressure gauge with a pressure bleed valve. Take precautions to avoid the risk of fire whenever working on or around any open fuel system.

Quick Disconnect Fitting

1. Relieve the fuel system pressure. Separate the quick connect fuel line tubes at the inner fender panel by squeezing the two retaining tabs against the fuel line, then pulling the tube and retainer from the fitting.

2. Remove the two O-rings and the spacer from the fitting. This can be accomplished by using a heavy piece of wire bent into an L-shape.

3. Remove the retainer from the fuel tube and discard the O-rings, spacer and retainer.

4. Install the new retainer assembly by pushing it into the quick connect fitting until it clicks.

5. Grasp the disposable plastic plug and remove it from the replacement fitting. By removing only the plastic plug, the O-rings, spacer and retainer will remain in the fitting.

6. Push the fuel line into the fitting until a click is heard and the connection is complete. Give the fuel line connection a firm tug to verify that it is seated and locked properly.

INJECTORS

Removal and Installation

THROTTLE BODY INJECTION

1. Relieve the fuel pump pressure. Disconnect the negative battery cable. Remove the air cleaner assembly.

2. Remove the fuel injector wire. Remove the fuel injector retainer clip screws. Remove the fuel injector retainer clip.

3. Using a small pair of pliers, gently grasp the center collar of the injector, between the electrical terminals, and carefully remove the injector using a lifting twisting motion.

4. Discard the upper and lower O-rings. Note that the back up ring fits over the upper O-ring.

5. Installation is the reverse of the removal procedure. Lubricate both O-rings with light oil before installation.

MULTI PORT FUEL INJECTION

1. Relieve fuel system pressure. Disconnect the negative battery cable.

2. Disconnect the fuel lines at the ends of the fuel rail assembly.

3. Mark and disconnect the injector wire harness connectors.

4. Remove the fuel rail retaining bolts.

5. Disconnect the vacuum line from the fuel pressure regulator.

6. Remove the fuel rail assembly from the engine.

NOTE: On vehicles with automatic transmission, it may be necessary to remove the automatic transmission throttle pressure cable and bracket to remove the fuel rail assembly.

7. Remove the clips that retain the injectors to the fuel rail and remove the injectors. An O-ring kit (part No. PN 8983 503 637) is available which consists of 6 brown seals and 7 black seals. The brown seals fit on the injector tip area and seal the injector to the intake manifold. The black seals fit on the rail end of the injector to to seal the injector when it is installed into the fuel rail. The last black seal is for the fuel pressure regulator to seal the pressure regulator to the fuel rail. These seals cannot be interchanged.

8. Installation is the reverse of the removal procedure. Tighten the fuel rail mounting bolts to 20 ft. lbs.

ADJUSTMENT

Idle Speed

121 CID (2.0L) AND 151 CID (2.5L) ENGINES

The throttle stop screw that is used to adjust the idle speed of the vehicle, is adjusted to specifications at the factory. The throttle stop screw is then covered with a steel plug to prevent the unnecessary readjustment in the field. If it is necessary to gain access to the throttle stop screw, the following procedure will allow access to the throttle stop screw without removing the TBI unit from the manifold.

1. Using a small punch or equivalent mark over the center line of the throttle stop screw. Drill a $\frac{5}{32}$ in. diameter hole through the casting of the hardened steel plug.

2. Using a $\frac{1}{16}$ in. diameter punch or equivalent punch out the steel plug.

3. With the vehicle in the park position, the parking brake applied and the drive wheels blocked, remove the air cleaner and plug the thermac vacuum port.

4. On vehicles equipped with automatic transmsission, remove the transmission detent cable from the throttle control bracket in order to gain access to the minimum air adjustment screw.

5. Connect a tachometer to the engine and disconnect the idle air control motor connector.

6. Start the engine and let the engine reach normal operating temperature and the rpm to stabilize.

7. Install special tool J-33047 or equivalent in the idle air passage of the throttle body. Be sure to seat the tool in the air passage until it is bottomed our and no air leaks exist.

8. On the 121 CID (2.0L) engine it may be necessary to remove the air cleaner insulator in order to install the special tool.

9. On the 151 CID (2.5L) engine, use a #20 torx head bit or equivalent, turn the throttle stop screws until the rpm is within specification.

10. On the 121 CID (2.0L) engine, install the insulator bolts with 0.079 in. or thicker washers under each bolt head. Adjust the idle to specification. Remove the bolts and washers.

11. If removed install the isolator. Install the transmission detent cable, as required.

12. Shut down the engine and remove the special tool or equivalent from the throttle body.

13. Reconnect the idle air control motor connector and seal the

hole drilled through the throttle body housing with silicone sealant or equivalent.

14. Check the throttle position sensor voltage as required. Install the air cleaner and thermac vacuum line.

EXCEPT 121 CID (2.0L) AND 151 CID (2.5L) ENGINES

1. Remove the air cleaner, adapter and gaskets. Discard the gaskets. Plug any vacuum line ports, as necessary.
2. Leave the idle air control (IAC) valve connected and ground the diagnostic terminal (ALDL connector).
3. Turn the ignition switch to the on position, do not start the engine. Wait for at least 30 seconds (this allows the IAC valve pintle to extend and seat in the throttle body).
4. With the ignition switch still in the on position, disconnect IAC electrical connector.
5. Remove the ground from the diagnostic terminal and start the engine. Let the engine reach normal operating temperature.
6. Apply the parking brake and block the drive wheels. Remove the plug from the idle stop screw by piercing it first with a suitable tool, then applying leverage to the tool to lift the plug out.
7. With the engine in the proper shifter selector range adjust the idle stop screw to secification.
8. Turn the ignition off and reconnect the IAC valve connector. Unplug any plugged vacuum line ports and install the air cleaner, adapter and new gaskets.

CONTROLLED IDLE SPEED
1987 and 1988 Model Year Trucks

Engine	Transmission	Gear (D/N)	Idle Speed (rpm)	IAC Counts ④	Open/Closed Loop ⑤
2.5L	Man.	N	900 (S/T) 800 (M)	5–20	CL
	Auto.	D	800 (S) 650 (T) 750 (M)	15–40	CL
2.8L	Man.	N	800	5–20	OL
	Auto.	D	800	5–30	OL
4.3L	Man.	N	500–550	2–12	CL
	Auto.	D	500–550	10–25	CL
	Auto. ①	D	500–550	2–20	CL
5.0L	Man.	N	600	5–30	OL
	Auto.	D	500	5–30	OL
	Auto. ②	D	550	5–30	CL
5.7L	Man.	N	600	5–30	OL
(under 8500 GVW)	Auto.	D	500	5–30	OL
5.7L	Man.	N	650	5–30	
(over 8500 GVW)	Man. ③	N	600	5–30	OL
	Auto.	D	550	5–30	OL
7.4L	Man.	N	800	5–30	OL
	Auto.	D	750	5–30	OL

① 4.3L S series.
② 3 speed Auto in a C10 Pickup w/.Fed. emissions and no AIR system.
③ G van or Suburban with a single catalytic converter.
④ Add 2 counts for engines with less than 500 miles. Add 2 counts for every 1000 ft. above sea level (4.3L and V8). Add 1 count for every 1000 ft. above sea level (2.5L and 2.8L).
⑤ Let engine idle until proper fuel control status (open/closed loop) is reached.

MINIMUM IDLE AIR RATE
1987 and 1988 Model Year Trucks

Engine	Transmission	Gear (D/N)	Engine Speed (rpm)	Open/Closed Loop ③
2.5L	Man.	N	600±50	CL
	Auto.	N	500±50	CL
2.8L	Man.	N	700±50	OL
	Auto.	N	700±50	OL

MINIMUM IDLE AIR RATE
1987 and 1988 Model Year Trucks

Engine	Transmission	Gear (D/N)	Engine Speed (rpm)	Open/Closed Loop ③
4.3L	Man.	N	450±50	CL
	Auto.	D	400±50	CL
	Auto. ①	N	475±50	CL
5.0L	Man.	N	500±25	OL
	Auto.	D	425±25	OL
	Auto. ②	D	425±25	CL
5.7L (under 8500 GVW)	Man.	N	500±25	OL
	Auto.	D	425±25	OL
5.7L (over 8500 GVW)	Man.	N	550±25	CL
	Auto.	D	450±25	CL
7.4L	Man.	N	700±25	OL
	Auto.	D	700±25	OL

① 4.3L S series.
② 5.0L without AIR system.
③ Let engine idle until Open/Closed Loop is reached.

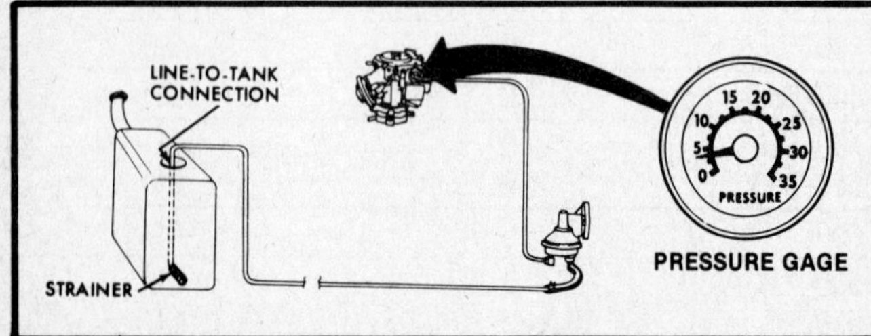

Pressure test of mechanical fuel pump

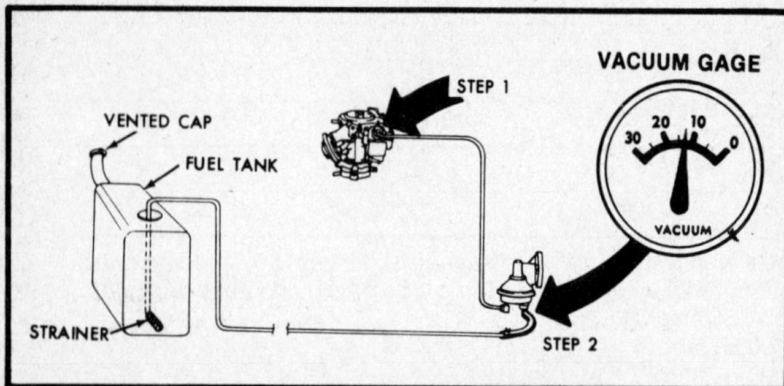

Vacuum test of mechanical fuel pump

Fuel Pump

MECHANICAL

Removal and Installation

1. Properly relieve the fuel pump pressure. Disconnect the negative battery cable. Remove the necessary components in order to gain access to the fuel pump retaining bolts.

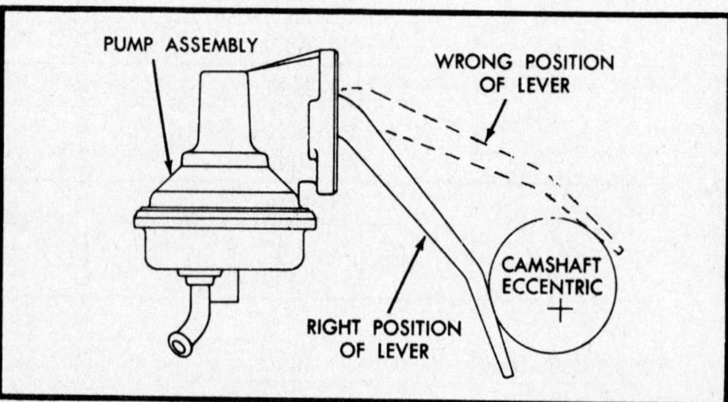

Fuel pump installation

2. Disconnect and cap the fuel lines. Remove the fuel pump retaining bolts. Remove the fuel pump from the vehicle.
3. On vehicles so equipped, be sure that the fuel pump push rod remains in position.
4. Installation is the reverse of the removal procedure. Be sure to use a new gasket.

ELECTRICAL

Removal and Installation

1. Properly relieve the fuel pump pressure. Disconnect the negative battery cable.
2. Disconnect and cap the fuel lines. Disconnect the electrical connector. As required, remove the fuel tank from the vehicle.
3. Remove the fuel pump retaining assembly. Remove the fuel pump from the vehicle.
4. Installation is the reverse of the removal procedure. Be sure to use a new gasket or rubber O-ring, as required.

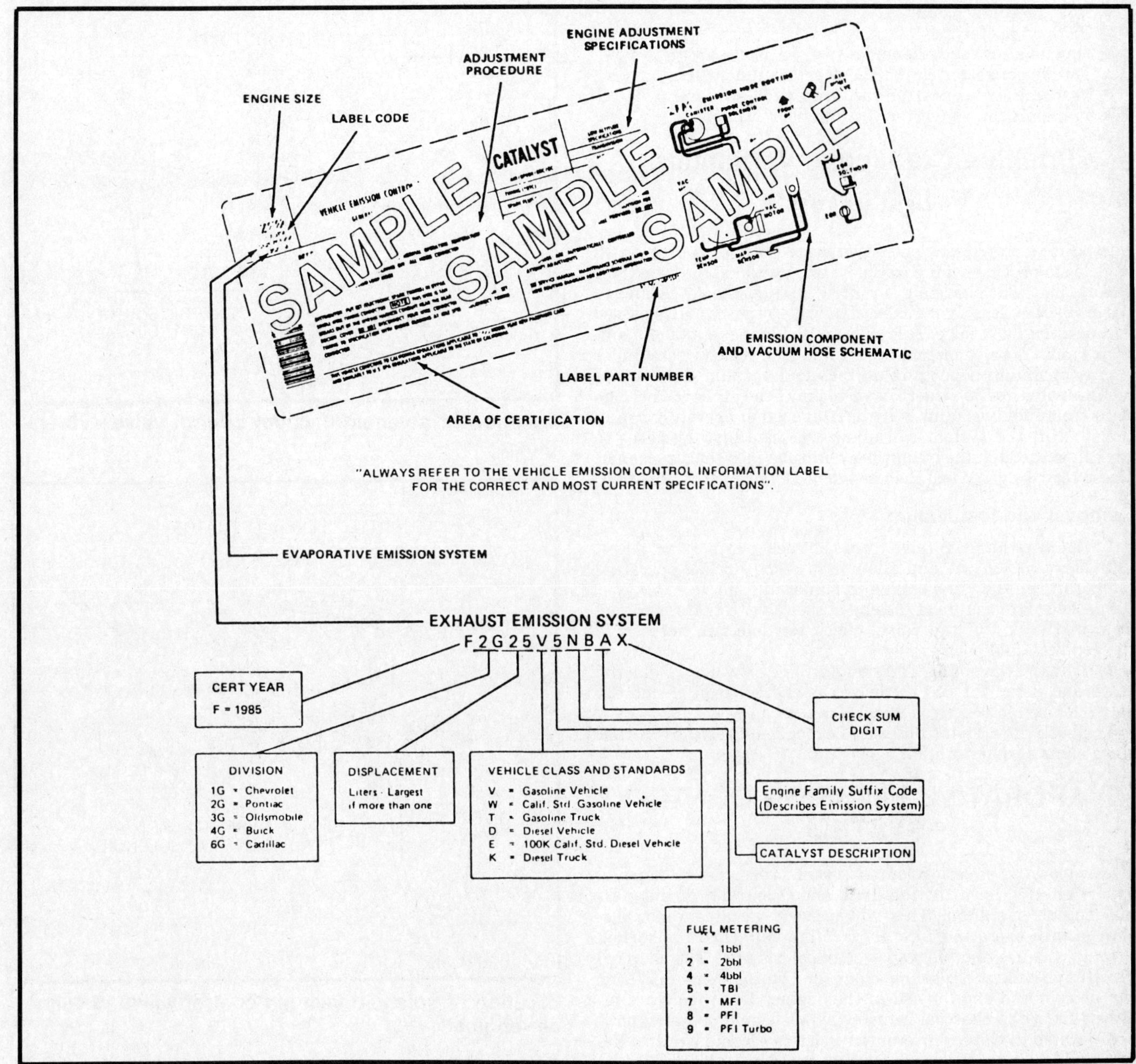

Typical Emission information label and decoding examples

EMISSION CONTROLS

- Catalytic converter
- Positive crankcase ventilation (PCV)
- Thermostatic air cleaner (THERMAC)
- Exhaust gas recirculation (EGR)
- Early fuel evaporation (EFE)
- Air injector reactor (AIR)
- Evaporative emission control (EEC)
- Computer command control (CCC)
- Backpressure exhaust gas recirculation
- Emissions calibrated carburetor
- Emissions calibrated distributor
- Charcoal canister
- Canister control valve
- Canister purge thermal vacuum switch
- Deceleration mixture control valve
- Deceleration valve
- EGR backpressure transducer
- EGR thermal vacuum switch
- EGR vacuum bleed solenoid
- EGR solenoid

- Hot idle compensator
- Oxidizing catalyst
- Slow idle fuel cut solenoid
- Torque converter clutch thermal vacuum switch
- Transmission converter vacuum switch
- Transmission converter vacuum delay valve

Positive Crankcase Ventilation

PCV VALVE

The positive crankcase ventilation system (PCV) is used on all vehicles to provide a more complete evacuation of the crankcase vapors. Outside vehicle air is routed through the air cleaner to the crankcase. It is then mixed with blow-by gases and is passed through the PCV valve. It is then routed into the intake manifold. The PCV valve meters the air flow rate which varies under engine operation depending on manifold vacuum. In order to maintain idle quality, the PCV valve limits the air flow when the intake manifold vacuum is high. If abnormal operating conditions occur, the system will allow excessive blow-by gases to back flow through the crankcase vent tube into the air cleaner. These blow-by gases will then be burned by normal combustion.

Removal and Installation

1. Remove the PCV valve from the rocker arm cover.
2. Start the engine and allow it to reach normal operating temperature. Allow the engine to run at idle speed.
3. Check for vacuum at the end of the valve. If there is no vacuum at the end of the valve, check for defective hoses or a clogged manifold port.
4. Turn off the engine and remove the PCV valve. Shake the valve and listen for the rattle of the check needle inside the valve. If no rattle is present, replace the valve.
5. Check the systems hoses and clamps and replace any that show signs of deterioration.

EVAPORATIVE EMISSION CONTROL SYSTEM

The evaporative emission control system is designed to trap fuel vapors emitted from the fuel tank and carburetor during normal engine operation. This will prevent gasoline vapor discharge into the atmosphere. Gasoline vapors are absorbed through the use of a fuel vapor charcoal canister. The charcoal canister absorbs the gasoline vapors and stores them until they can be removed and burned in the engine. The vapors are removed from the charcoal canister by a solenoid operated bowl vent located in the carburetor. In order to accomplish this, the fuel tank requires a non vented fuel cap. A vent located in the fuel tank, high enough above the fuel, will allow the vent to be in fuel vapors all the time. Another vent pipe is connected directly to the charcoal canister, where excess vapor is stored. From the fuel charcoal canister, the vapors are routed to the PCV system. This will allow the vapors to be burned during engine operation.

CHARCOAL CANISTER

This fuel vapor canister is used to store and absorb fuel vapors from the carburetor bowl and fuel tank. The canister purge valve is an integral part of the vapor canister. The valve consists of a housing and tube molded into the canister cover, valve assembly, diaphragm, diaphragm and valve spring. The diaphragm cover has a built in control vacuum signal tube.

While the engine is idling, spring tension holds the purge valve closed. Only a small amount of fuel vapor can be drawn from the canister. This is accomplished through a small calibrated constant bleed hole which leads from the charcoal to the tube marked PCV. This will allow purge of the canister through

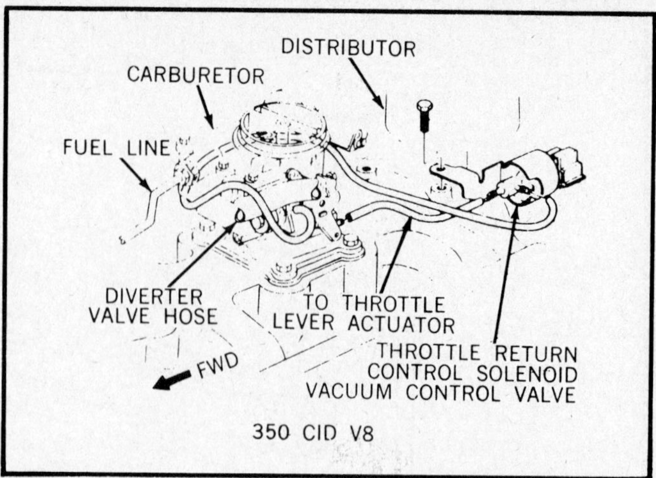

Location of solenoid vacuum control valve—V8 engines

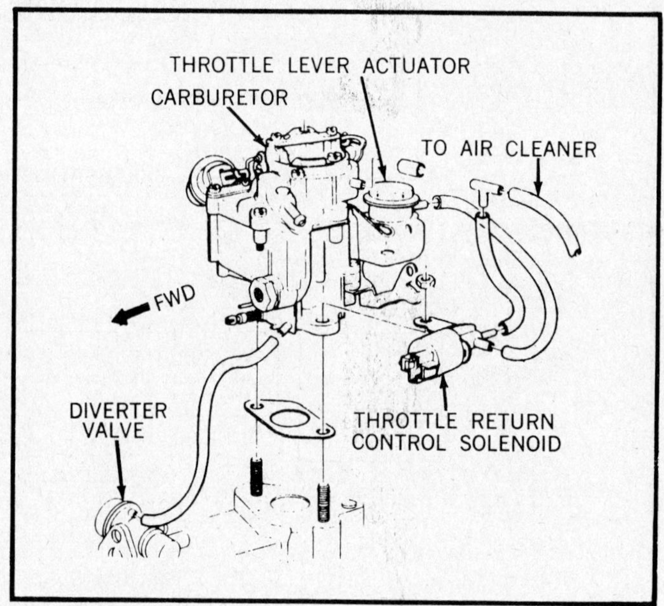

Location of solenoid vacuum control valve—6 cylinder engine

the PCV hose during engine idle. A replaceable filter is used on the bottom of the canister which prevents contaminants from entering the charcoal canister. Part of normal servicing requires that the filter element be replaced.

AUXILIARY VAPOR CANISTER

Vehicles equipped with dual fuel tanks are also equipped with an auxiliary fuel vapor canister. It is added to the primary canister. On the bottom of the auxiliary canister is a hose which connects to the primary canister's purge air inlet.

Vapor overflowing from the primary canister is stored in the auxiliary canister. During the purge, vapor flows through the auxiliary canister, the primary canister and into the intake manifold for burning during combustion.

System Test

1. Apply a length of hose to the PCV tube of the purge valve

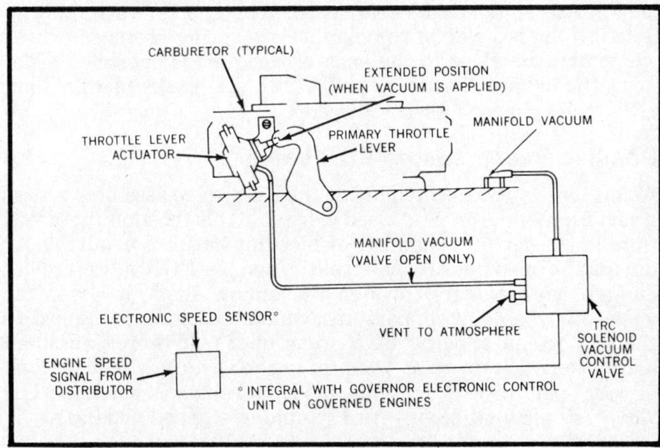

Throttle return control system

assembly (lower tube), and try to blow air through it. Little or no air should pass into the charcoal canister.

NOTE: If the vehicle is equipped with constant purge, a small amount of air will pass into the canister.

2. Using a vacuum pump, apply vacuum (15 in. Hg. or 51 kPa) through the control vacuum signal tube to the purge valve diaphragm. If the diaphragm does not hold vacuum for at least 20 seconds the diaphragm is leaking. Replace the charcoal canister.

3. If the diaphragm holds vacuum, attempt to blow air through the hose connected to the PCV tube while vacuum is still being applied. An increase of air should be observed. If no air increase is noted, the charcoal canister must be replaced.

Removal and Installation

1. Disconnect the negative battery cable.
2. Remove the necessary components in order to gain access to the charcoal canister.
3. Tag and disconnect the hoses from the canister.
4. Remove the charcoal canister retaining nut.
5. Remove the canister from the vehicle.
6. Installation is the reverse of the removal procedure. Refer to the vehicle emission control label, located in the engine compartment for proper routing of the vacuum hoses.

AUXILLARY VAPOR CANISTER

Removal and Installation

1. Disconnect the negative battery cable.
2. Tag and disconnect the hoses from the auxiliary canister.
3. Remove the retaining screw from the auxiliary canister bracket.
4. Remove the canister from the vehicle.
5. Installation is the reverse of the removal procedure.

Exhaust Emission Control System

Thermostatic Air Cleaner

Fresh air supplied to the air cleaner comes either from the normal snorkel, or a tube which is connected to the exhaust manifold. A door in the snorkel regulates the source of incoming air so that the engine always takes in warm air. The snorkel door may be controlled in a number of ways, but most are vacuum operated. The vacuum operated models use a thermostatic bi-metal switch inside the air cleaner that bleeds off vacuum as the engine warms up, and regulates the position of the air door. On certain vehicles, the snorkel is connected to a tube which is routed to the front of the vehicle in order to take in cooler air from outside the engine compartment. A vacuum diaphragm motor, which is built into the air cleaner snorkel, moves the damper door to admit hot air from the exhaust manifold, outside air or a combination of both.

A temperature sensor, located inside the air cleaner reacts to air intake temperature and controls the amount of vacuum the engine receives. When the outside temperature is below approximately 86 ° F. (30 ° C.), the sensor allows vacuum to the motor and the damper door will shut off outside air to the engine, allowing only heated air from the exhaust manifold to enter the air cleaner.

When the temperature is above 131 ° F. (55 ° C.), the damper door opens allowing only outside air to enter the air cleaner. When the outside temperature is between these two readings, the damper door opens partially allowing a combination of outside and heated air to enter the air cleaner. Incorrect TAC operation can result in warm up hesitation, lack of power or sluggishness on a hot engine.

System Service

1. Inspect the system to verify that all hoses and heat tube are connected properly. Inspect for kinked or rotted hoses.
2. Inspect the air cleaner element for proper gasket seal.
3. When the air cleaner assembly is installed, the damper door should be open.
4. Start the engine. when the engine is first started, the damper door should close off any outside air.
5. If the TAC system fails to operate properly perform the vacuum motor check. If the complaint is a drivability problem, perform the temperature sensor check.

TEMPERATURE SENSOR

System Service

1. The test must be performed with the air cleaner temperature below 86 ° F. (30 ° C.). If the engine is warm, place a temperature sensing probe as close as possible to the temperature sensor. allow the engine to cool until it reaches the above temperature.
2. Start the engine and observe the damper door. It should move to close off any outside air.
3. When the damper door starts to open, remove the air cleaner cover and read the temperature sensing probe. It should read approximately 131 ° (55 ° C.). If not, replace the temperature sensor.

Removal and Installation

1. Remove the air cleaner assembly from the vehicle.
2. Tag and disconnect the vacuum hoses from the temperature sensor.
3. Reposition the tabs on the temperature sensor retaining clip.
4. Remove the clip and sensor from the air cleaner. Take note of the sensor position for ease of reinstallation.

5. Installation is the reverse of the removal procedure.

VACUUM MOTOR

System Service

1. With the engine off, disconnect the vacuum hose at the vacuum diaphragm motor.
2. Apply about 7 in. Hg. of vacuum to the vacuum diaphragm motor. The damper door should completely block the outside air out. If not, check to be sure that the linkage is installed correctly.
3. With vacuum still applied, trap the vacuum in the vacuum diaphragm motor assembly by bending the hose. The damper door should remain closed, if not replace the vacuum motor assembly.
4. If the vacuum motor proves to be good, check all hoses and connections and if they are good, replace the temperature sensor.

CATALYTIC CONVERTER

The catalytic converter is mounted in the engine exhaust stream and works as a gas reactor in which its major function is to speed up the heat producing chemical reaction between the exhaust gas components, in order to reduce the air pollutants in the engine exhaust. The converter produces CO_2 and water when operating. The catalyst material is either a ceramic substance or pellets which are coated with a base of alumina and then impregnated with catalytically active metals. It is the surface of the catalyst material that controls the heat producing chemical reaction.

System Service

1. Raise and support the vehicle safely.
2. Inspect the catalytic converter protector for any damage. If any part of the protector is dented to the extent that it contacts the converter, replace it.
3. Check the heat insulator for adequate clearance between the converter and the heat insulator. Repair or replace any damaged components.

Removal and Installation

1. Raise the vehicle and support safely.
2. Making sure that the catalytic converter is cool, remove the air suction pipe.
3. Remove the retaining bolts at the front and the rear of the converter.
4. Remove the catalytic converter from the vehicle.
5. Installation is the reverse of the removal procedure. Lower the vehicle, start the engine and check for exhaust leaks.

EXHAUST GAS RECIRCULATION SYSTEM

The EGR system is used to reduce the oxide of nitrogen emission levels caused by high combustion temperatures. This is accomplished by reducing the combustion temperatures. The EGR valve is mounted on the intake manifold. It is opened by manifold vacuum to allow exhaust gas to flow into the intake manifold. The exhaust gas then moves along with the air/fuel mixture, into the combustion chamber. If too much exhaust gas enters, combustion will not occur. Because of this, very little exhaust gas is allowed to pass through the valve. The EGR valve will open once the engine reaches normal operating conditions and above idle speed. The EGR system is turned off on vehicles equipped with transmission converter clutch (TCC) when the TCC is on. The EGR system may or may not be tied in with the ECM. There are three basic types of systems.

Ported EGR Valve

This valve is controlled by a flexible diaphragm. It is spring loaded in order to hold the valve closed. When ported vacuum is applied to the top side of the diaphragm, spring pressure is overcome and the valve in the exhaust gas port is opened. This allows the exhaust gas to be pulled into the intake manifold and enter the cylinders for combustion.

Positive Backpressure EGR Valve

An air bleed valve, located inside the EGR valve assembly acts as a vacuum regulator. The bleed valve controls the amount of vacuum in the vacuum chamber by bleeding vacuum to outside air during the open phase of the cycle. When the EGR valve receives enough backpressure through the hollow shaft, it closes the valve. At this point, maximum available vacuum is applied to the diaphragm and the EGR valve opens. If there is a small amount of vacuum or no vacuum in the vacuum chamber such as wide open throttle or at idle, the EGR valve will not open. The valve will also not open with the engine stopped or idling.

Negative Backpressure EGR Valve

The negative backpressure EGR valve is similar to the positive backpressure EGR valve except that the bleed valve spring is moved from above the diaphragm to below, and the valve is normally closed. The negative backpressure valve varies the amount of exhaust gas flow into the manifold depending on manifold vacuum and variations in exhaust back pressure. The diaphragm on the valve has an internal air bleed hole which is held closed by a small spring when there is no exhaust backpressure. Engine vacuum opens the EGR valve against the pressure of a spring. When manifold vacuum combines with negative exhaust back pressure, the vacuum bleed hole opens and the EGR valve closes. This valve will open if vacuum is applied with the engine not running.

EGR Valve Identification

Positive backpressure EGR valves will have a "P" stamped on the top side of the valve after the part number. Negative backpressure EGR valves will have a "N" stamped on the top side of the valve after the part number. Port EGR valves have no identification stamped after the part number.

AIR INJECTION REACTION SYSTEM

The AIR system is used to reduce carbon monoxide (CO) and hydrocarbon (HC) exhaust emissions. On cold engine start up, the system will also help to heat up the catalytic converter more quickly. With faster catalytic converter heat up, the exhaust gas burning process is accelerated.

The system incorporates a dual bed converter. It consists of a two way catalyst, which controls HC and CO emissions and a three way catalyst, which controls HC, CO and NOx exhaust emissions. Both the two and three way catalyst are encased in one unit. A pipe connects the two converters to allow air to be injected into the second converter. Injected air into the second converter, helps to increase the CO and HC burning process. The system may or may not be controlled by the ECM.

Operation Without ECM

A belt driven air pump supplies compressed air through a centrifugal filter fan to a diverter valve. During normal operation, this valve allows air to go to the exhaust manifolds or ports. At high engine speeds, air directed to the air cleaner/silencer. During engine deceleration, when there is a rise in the manifold vacuum signal, air is directed to the air cleaner/silencer.

The system is equipped with check valves, which prevents the back flow of exhaust gases into the air pump in the event of an exhaust backfire or pump drive belt failure.

Operation With ECM

A belt driven air pump supplies air through a centrifugal filter fan to the electric air control valve. This valve directs the air to either the engine exhaust manifold ports or to the air cleaner. When the engine is cold or in the wide open throttle position, the ECM energizes the solenoid on the valve and air is directed to the exhaust manifold ports.

As the coolant temperature increases, the solenpoid is de-energized and air goes into the air cleaner which also acts as a silencer. At higher engine speeds, air is directed to the air cleaner through a pressure relief valve even though the solenoid may be energized.

During engine deceleration, when there is a rise in the manifold vacuum signal, air is directed to the air cleaner. A check valve on either side of the engine prevents back flow of exhaust gases into the air pump if there is an exhaust backfire or pump drive belt failure.

Air Pump Operation

The air injection reaction system is controlled by an air pump, check valve, a control valve and the necessary tubing. The belt driven air pump, located on the front of the engine, supplies air to the system. A centrifugal fan at the front of the pump, separates any foreign material from the air to be injected. Air then flows from the pump through the control valve, which is ECM controlled, to the check valve. The check valve will prevent any back flow of exhaust gases into the pump in the event of pump drive belt failure or vehicle backfire.

Computer Command Control System

The computer command control system is used to control emissions by close regulation of the air/fuel ratio and by the use of a three way catalytic converter which lowers the level of oxides of nitrogen, hydrocarbons and carbon monoxide.

The major components are an exhaust gas oxygen sensor, an electronic control module, an electronically controlled air/fuel ratio carburetor and a three way catalytic converter.

In order to maintain good idle and driveability under all driving conditions input signals are used to modify the computer output signal. These input signals are supplied by the engine temperature sensor, the vacuum control switches, the throttle position switch, the map sensor and the barometer pressure sensor.

MAJOR COMPONENTS AND OPERATION

Electronic Control Module

The electronic control module monitors the voltage output of the oxygen sensor along with information from other input signals. This is done to generate a control signal to the carburetor solenoid assembly. This control signal is continually cycling the solenoid between on, which is lean command, and off, which is rich command. When the solenoid is energized it pulls down a metering rod which reduces fuel flow. When the solenoid is denerigized the spring loaded metering rod returns to the up position and fuel flow increases. The amount of time that this assembly functions is based on input voltage from the oxygen sensor.

On some engines the electronic control module also controls the electronic spark control timing system and the electronic module retard system. This system has the capability to retard the engine timing ten degrees during certain engine operations. During other engine operations the module functions the same as the regular HEI module. The "R" terminal on the module is connected to the electronic control module and the retard function is accomplished by an internal ground. The timing retard is ten degrees only when the engine coolant temperature is between 66 degrees F. and 130 degrees F. and with the throttle opening position below 45 percent and engine speed above 400 rpm.

TACHOMETER SIGNAL TO COMPUTER

The computer monitors the engine crankshaft position signal in order to determine engine rpm. This signal is generated as a pulse from the HEI distributor. The tachometer signal comes from the tach terminal of the distributor. A tachometer signal filter is located between the distributor and the computer in order to reduce interference from the radio. A tachometer cannot be connected in line between the tach filter and the computer, if it is the computer may not receive the tach signal. The presence of the tach signal from the distributor can be determined by connecting a tachometer to the distributor tach terminal.

ENGINE COOLANT SENSOR

The engine coolant temperature sensor, which is located in the engine block, sends the electronic control module information on engine temperature. This information can be used to vary the air/fuel ratio as the coolant temperature varies with time during a cold start. It also accomplishes various switching functions at different temperatures and provides a switch point for hot temperature light indication and spark advance.

This sensor has a connector which allows the ground return lead to surround the signal lead. This design provides an interference shield to prevent high voltage in the spark plug wires from affecting the sensor signal to the computer.

EXHAUST OXYGEN SENSOR

The oxygen sensor is located in the exhaust manifold. Its function is to compare oxygen content in the exhaust stream to the oxygen content in the outside air. This shows that there is a passage from the top of the oxygen sensor to the inner chamber that allows outside air to enter the system. When servicing the sensor do not plug or restrict this chamber.

A rich exhaust stream is low in oxygen content and will cause the sensor to send a rich signal of about one volt to the computer. A lean exhaust stream will result in a lean signal of less than half a volt being sent to the computer.

As the sensor temperature increases during engine warm up the sensor voltage also increases. Because of the minimum voltage required to operate is half a volt the computer will not use the oxygen sensor signal until the temperature reaches about 600 ° F. to operate the sensor

THROTTLE POSITION SENSOR

This sensor is located in the carburetor body and is actuated by the accelerator pump lever. The stem of the sensor projects up through the air horn, contacting the underside of the lever. As the throttle valves are opened, the pump lever presses down proportionately on the sensor, thus indicating throttle position.

The throttle position sensor changes the voltage in circuit E (reference voltage) to G (voltage input to the computer) as the sensor shaft moves up or down. This is similar to the operation of the gas tank gauge sending unit, except that the throttle position sensor permits the computer to read throttle position.

BAROMETRIC PRESSURE SENSOR

The barometric pressure sensor provides a voltage to the computer to allow ambient pressure compensation of the controlled functions. This unit senses ambient barometric pressure and provides information to the computer on atmospheric pressure changes due to weather and/or altitude. The computer uses this information to adjust the air/fuel ratio. The sensor is mounted under the instrument panel near the right hand air condition outlet and is electronically connected to the computer. The atmospheric opening is covered by a foam filter.

MIXTURE CONTROL SOLENOID

The mixture control solenoid actuates two spring loaded rods that control fuel flow to the idle and main metering circuits of the carburetor. Energizing the solenoid lowers the metering rod into the main metering jet. This makes the air-fuel mixture in the carburetor leaner. The Varajet carburetor has a solenoid operated fuel control valve.

The mixture control solenoid changes the air/fuel ratio by allowing more or less fuel to flow through the carburetor. When no electrical signal is applied to the solenoid, maximum fuel flows to the idle and main metering circuits. When an electrical signal is applied to the solenoid, the mixture is leaned.

COMPUTER COMMAND CONTROL SYSTEM CARBURETORS

Three types of Rochester carburetors are used for system applications. The Varajet is a two barrel, staged opening carburetor. The Quadrajet is a four barrel nonstaged carburetor, essentially the primary side of a Quadrajet. The metering rods and an idle bleed valve are connected to a 12 volt mixture control solenoid. The model E2SE carburetor, used with the computer command control system, is a controlled air/fuel ratio carburetor of a two barrel, two stage down draft design with the primary bore smaller in size than the secondary bore. Air/fuel ratio control is accomplished with a solenoid controlled on/off fuel valve which supplements the preset flow of fuel which supplies the idle and main metering systems. The solenoid on/off cycle is controlled by a 12 volt signal from the computer. The solenoid also controls the amount of air bled into the idle system. The air bleed valve and fuel control valve work together so that the fuel valve is closed when the air bleed valve is open, resulting in a leaner air/fuel mixture. Enrichment occurs when the fuel valve is opened and air bleed valve closed.

The Quadrajet Dualjet arrangement is such that the level of metering is dependent on the positioning of rods in the orifices. The Varajet system is different in that it features a non-moving part main system for lean mixtures and a supplemental system to provide for rich mixture.

AIR FLOW CONTROL SYSTEMS

Two types of air systems are used on computer command control engines, the pulse air injection reactor (PAIR) and the belt drive air pump (AIR). Both types are controlled by the computer through solenoid valves. The pair system uses an on/off solenoid which is open during cold operation and wide open throttle (WOT). Air is injected into the exhaust ports when the solenoid valves are open.

AIR MANAGEMENT SYSTEM

The computer controlled solenoid can divert air during any desired operating mode. The valves diverting the switching the air flow are the air diverter valve and the air select valve. With the air divert valve, a rapid increase of engine manifold vacuum diverts air to the air cleaner and high air system pressure is diverted to the air cleaner. The air select valve switches air between the catalytic converter and exhaust ports.

DISTRIBUTOR HEI MODULE

The computer will control the module above 200 rpm by applying a voltage to the bypass line and signaling terminal E. Current loss at terminals R or B will cause the distributor (HEI) module to take over. Loss of terminal E electonic spark timing will cause the engine to stop assuming bypass voltage is present.If the engine is equipped with electronic spark control, the computer electronic spark timing line would go to the electronic spark control distributor. The electronic spark control delay output would go to the HEI electronic spark timing input.

ELECTRONIC SPARK TIMING

Electronic spark timing is a computer controlled system that has all the engine spark timing information stored in memory. At various engine operating conditions as determined by rpm and manifold pressure, the system determines the proper spark advance. It then produces the firing signal at the desired cranckshaft position. Other parameters, such as coolant temperature and barometric pressure, can be sensed and this information used to modify, as appropriate, the spark advance number from the table. The system provides a much more flexible and accurate spark timing control than the conventional centrifugal and vacuum advance mechanisms in the distributor.

VACUUM SENSORS

The vacuum sensors measure changes in manifold pressure and provides this information to the ECM. The pressure changes reflect need for adjustments in air/fuel mixture, spark timing (EST) and other controlled operations to maintain good vehicle performance under various driving conditions.

VEHICLE SPEED SENSORS

The vehicle speed sensor is mounted behind the speedometer in the instrument cluster. It provides a series of pulses to the ECM which are used to determine vehicle speed.

Closed Loop Emissions System

The closed loop emission control system consists of an Air Injection Reactor (AIR) System, (ECM controlled), an Exhaust Gas Recirculation (EGR) System, a Thermostatically Controlled Air (TCA) Induction System, a Positive Crankcase Ventilation (PCV) System, an Evaporative Emission Control system (ECS) and a Closed Loop emission control system.

The closed loop emission control is a system that precisely controls the air/fuel ratio near a balanced point that allows the use of a three way catalyst to reduce oxides of nitrogen and oxidize hydrocarbons and carbon monoxide. The essential components are an exhaust gas oxygen sensor, and electric control module (ECM), a vacuum controller with duty solenoid, a control air fuel ratio carburetor and a three way catalytic converter. The closed loop emission control system is an electronically controlled exhaust emissions system. The major components are, an oxygen sensor, and electronic control module, a vacuum controller and catalytic converter.

This system features a CHECK ENGINE fault lamp on the instrument panel which will light in case of a system malfunction and will remain illuminated as long as the engine runs with the malfunction uncorrected. This same lamp, through an integral diagnostic system, will aid a technician in locating the cause of the light.

OXYGEN SENSOR

The oxygen sensor used in the closed loop control system consists of a closed end zirconia sensor placed in the engine exhaust gas stream. This sensor is mounted in the exhaust manifold. The sensor generates a voltage which varies with the oxygen content in the exhaust gas stream. As oxygen content rises, (lean mixture) voltage falls, and as oxygen content falls, (rich mixture) voltage rises.

ELECTRONIC CONTROL MODULE

The ECM generates a control signal to the vacuum controller solenoid which controls carburetor air /fuel ratio through vacuum signals. This control signal is continuously cycling the solenoid between on and off time as a function of the input voltages from the sensors. The control signal generated by the ECM is selected from four operational modes. Mode number one is, no signal to vacuum controller solenoid. Mode number two is enrichment mode A is a fixed preprogrammed duty cycle to vacuum controlled solenoid. Mode number three open loop mode, which is a fixed preprogrammed duty cycle to vacuum controller. Mode number four closed loop mode, which is a calculated duty cycle, is generated based on oxygen sensor and other sensor outputs. During closed loop operation, the ECM monitors the voltage output of the oxygen sensor. When the exhaust is lean, the oxygen sensor voltage is low and the ECM commands a richer mixture. When the exhaust is rich, the oxygen sensor voltage is higher and the ECM commands a leaner mixture.

The ECM also stores in memory the current duty cycle being used for either idle or off idle condition. When the ECM sees a change from idle condition (as signaled by the vacuum switch) to off idle condition, it immediately steps to the duty cycle last recorded for optimum operation. From then on, while at that engine operating condition, the system uses the basic controls as previously described.

The ECM sends a signal to control the slow cut solenoid valve incorporated in the carburetor. The ECM senses the coasting condition by means of the signals from the transmission gear position, clutch pedal position switch and idle position switch, it opens the circuit to the slow cut solenoid valve when the engine speed is above the speed specified, causing the fuel flow to the carburetor to be shut down. The circuit to the slow cut solenoid valve is cut off only at the time when the following four conditions exist simultaneously. Condition one, the transmission is not in neutral position (M/T), or in either neutral or park position (A/T). Condition two, the clutch is engaged (M/T). Condition three, the accelerator is at idle position. Condition four, the engine speed exceeds the limit of the specified speed.

VACUUM CONTROLLER

The vacuum controller converts the electrical signals from the electronic control module into vacuum signals by means of the vacuum control solenoid. The vacuum signals operate the fuel control actuators in the carburetor, thereby controlling the air/fuel ratios. This vacuum controller consists of a vacuum regulator and a vacuum control solenoid. The vacuum regulator regulates the inconstant vacuum from the intake manifold to the constant vacuum needed to control the actuators. The vacuum control solenoid, controlled by the ECM, uses the vacuum from the vacuum regulator to operate the fuel control actuators in the carburetor.

TEMPERATURE SWITCH

The temperature switch is a bimetal disc snap action type and this switch sends engine coolant temperature information to the ECM. This temperature information is used as one of the inputs to determine when the system is ready to enter the closed loop mode of operation. The information from this switch is also used as the inputs to determine the secondary air injection.

CATALYTIC CONVERTER

The three way catalytic converter reduces oxides of nitrogen which oxidizes hydrocarbons and carbon monoxide. To maintain high conversion efficiency, it is necessary to closely control the air fuel ratio near 14.7 to 1.

TROUBLE DIAGNOSIS

The closed loop emission control system has a self diagnostic system. When there is an indication of a fault in the system, a CHECK ENGINE lamp on the instrument panel will remain on when the engine is running.

The system requires the following tools and equipment in order to diagnosis and repair any malfunctions that may occur. A tachometer, either a crankshaft harmonic balance revolution pickup type of electronic coil trigger signal pickup type. A dwellmeter that is used to indicate the performance conditions of the idle or off idle circuit. Connect the positive lead of dwellmeter to the bright green connector in the wiring harness and the negative lead to ground. Place a meter on four cylinder scale. The scale on the meter will show the change from idle condition to off idle condition. A vacuum gauge which is used to monitor manifold engine vacuum. A vacuum pump which is used to check pressure or vacuum sensors and vacuum operated valves. A voltmeter and ohmmeter which must be digital to measure voltage and ohm for circuits. A set of jumper wires to bypass a circuit and to insert between special connectors to permit access to the connector terminals for circuit checking. A test light and various connector tools or tool J-28742 for the removal of terminals on weather pack connectors.

ACTIVATING DIAGNOSTICS

1. Start engine.
2. Locate diagnostic terminal tape on system harness near ECM.
3. Connect terminals together and note CHECK ENGINE light.
4. If a trouble code is stored in system the light will begin to flash a two digit code.
3. An example is Code 24. To indicate this code the light would flash twice and there would be a short pause and then it would flash four times, them there will be a longer pause and this code would repeat three times.
4. If there is more than one trouble code stored, the system starts with the lowest code number followed by the next highest code number. The next higher code will flash three times and if there are no additional codes, the system will repeat the cycle.

EGR VALVE

Removal and Installation

1. Disconnect EGR pipe from adaptor. Disconnect EGR valve vacuum hose at valve.
2. Remove bolts holding EGR valve on manifold adapter and remove valve.
3. Clean EGR mounting surface. Install replacement EGR valve using new gasket. Connect EGR pipe.

BACK PRESSURE TRANSDUCER

Removal and Installation

1. Remove back pressure transducer from clamp bracket.
2. Remove hoses from transducer.
3. Reverse procedure to install transducer.

EFE HEATER

Removal and Installation

1. Remove air cleaner. Disconnect all electrical, vacuum, and fuel connections from carburetor.
2. Disconnect EFE Heater electrical connector. Remove carburetor. Replace EFI heater insulator assembly.
3. Reinstall carburetor. Reconnect EFI Heater electrical connection.

4. Reconnect electrical, vacuum and fuel connections to carburetor. Replace air cleaner. Start engine and check for vacuum leaks.

EFE TEMPERATURE SWITCH

Removal and Installation

1. Drain coolant below level of engine coolant outlet housing.
2. Disconnect electrical connector. Remove the switch.
3. Apply a soft setting sealant uniformly on replacement switch threads. No sealant should be applied to sensor of switch.
4. Install switch and tighten to 10 ft. lbs. Connect electrical connector. Add coolant as required.

EFE RELAY

Removal and Installation

1. Disconnect battery ground. Disconnect electrical connector at relay.
2. Remove bolts holding relay and remove relay.
3. Installation is the reverse of the removal procedure.

AIR INJECTION PUMP

Removal and Installation

1. Remove air pump drive belt from air pump pulley.
2. Disconnect hose from air switching valve.
3. Remove attaching bolts from engine mount and jack up mount.
4. Remove air pump mounting bolts and remove air pump and air switching valve.
5. Remove air switching valve from air pump.
6. Reverse procedure to install.

AIR SWITCHING VALVE

Removal and Installation

If the air switching valve is normal, the secondary continues to blow out from the valve for a few seconds when the accelerator pedal is depressed all the way to the floor and released quickly. If the secondary air continues to blow out for more than 5 seconds, replace air switching valve. Remove hoses from air switching valve. Remove mounting hardware and remove valve. Reverse procedure to install.

CHECK VALVE

Removal and Installation

1. Release clamp and disconnect air hose from check valve.
2. Unscrew check valve from air injection pipe.
3. Reverse procedure to install.

VACUUM SWITCHING VALVE

Removal and Installation

1. Disconnect electrical connector.
2. Remove hoses from valve.
3. Remove vacuum switching valve.
4. Reverse procedure to install valve.

ELECTRONIC CONTROL MODULE

Removal and Installation

The ECM is located on the passenger side, under the instrument panel. Do not replace the ECM unless diagnostic procedures have determined it to be malfunctioning.

TEMPERATURE SWITCH

Removal and Installation

1. Disconnect electrical connection at temperature switch.
2. Remove temperature switch.
3. Install switch and tighten to 72 inch lbs.
4. Connect electrical connector.

VACUUM CONTROLLER

Removal and Installation

1. Disconnect electrical connector.
2. Disconnect vacuum hoses from vacuum regulator and solenoid.
3. Remove vacuum controller.
4. Reverse procedure for installation.

IDLE AND WOT VACUUM SWITCH

Removal and Installation

1. Disconnect electrical connector.
2. Disconnect vacuum hoses from sensors.
3. Remove idle and WOT vacuum switch.
4. Reverse procedure for installation.

OXYGEN SENSOR

NOTE: Oxygen sensor uses a permanently attached pigtail and connector. This pigtail should not be removed from the oxygen sensor. Damage or removal of pigtail or connector could affect proper operation of the oxygen sensor. Care must be taken when handling an oxygen senor in order to preserve the efficiency. The inline electrical connector and louvered end must be kept free of grease or other contaminants. Do not use cleaning solvents of any type.

Removal and Installation

Oxygen sensor may be difficult to remove when engine temperature is below 120°F. Excessive force may damage threads on exhaust manifold or exhaust pipe. Disconnect electrical connector and any attaching hardware. Remove oxygen sensor. A new oxygen sensor is precoated with antiseize compound, but if same oxygen sensor is being installed, coat threads of oxygen sensor with antiseize compound P/N 5613695, or equivalent. Install the sensor and torque to 30 ft. lbs.

ENGINE MECHANICAL

Refer to the Unit Overhaul Section for Overhaul Procedures.

Engine

S SERIES

Removal and Installation

119 CID (1.9L) AND 151 CID (2.5L) ENGINES

1. Disconnect the negative battery cable. Matchmark and remove the hood. Drain the cooling system. Disconnect and plug the transmission oil cooler lines, if equipped.
2. Remove the air cleaner assembly and vacuum hoses. Mark the vacuum hoses for reinstallation. Remove the air condition compressor and position it to the side, if equipped.
3. Disconnect all hoses, tubing and electrical leads from the engine and mark them for reinstallation. Remove the power steering pump, if equipped and lay aside.
4. Remove the radiator. Remove the fan assembly. Disconnect the exhaust pipe from the exhaust manifold. Disconnect the oxygen sensor wire. Properly relieve the fuel pump pressure. Disconnect and plug the fuel line hoses.
5. Raise the vehicle and support it safely. Drain the engine oil.
6. If equipped with a manual transmission, remove the clutch return spring and cable. If equipped, remove the skid plate. Remove the strut rods on two wheel drive vehicles.
7. Remove the starter. Remove the flywheel cover pan. Remove the crossmember and disconnect the transmission cooler lines, as required.
8. Remove flexplate to converter retaining bolts, if equipped with auto transmission. Remove the bell housing bolts and support the transmission.
9. Lift the engine slightly and remove the engine mount nuts. Make certain that all lines, hoses, wires and cables have been disconnected from the engine and the frame.
10. Lower the vehicle. Properly support the transmission. Using the proper lifting equipment, remove the engine from the vehicle.
11. Installation is the reverse of the removal procedure.

121 CID (2.0L) ENGINE

1. Disconnect the negative battery cable. Remove the air cleaner assembly. Matchmark and remove the hood. If equipped, remove the power steering pump and position it to the side.
2. Drain the radiator. Remove the radiator hoses. Disconnect and plug the transmission oil cooler lines, if equipped. Remove the radiator. Remove the fan assembly. If equipped, remove the air condition compressor and position it to the side.
3. Disconnect the heater hoses from the engine. Disconnect all electrical wiring from the engine assembly. Disconnect all the necessary vacuum lines in order to remove the engine.
4. Disconnect the accelerator cable from the carburetor. Properly relieve the fuel pump pressure. Disconnect and cap the fuel line at the fuel pump.
5. Raise and support the vehicle safely. Drain the engine oil. Disconnect the exhaust pipe at the exhaust manifold. If equipped with manual transmission, remove the clutch bell crank.
6. Remove the motor mount through bolts. Remove the left side body mount bolts and air dam bolts.
7. Raise the body of the vehicle to gain access to the upper bell housing bolts. Remove the bolts. Lower the vehicle body and remove the dust cover.
8. Lower the vehicle. Properly support the transmission assembly. Using the proper lifting equipment, remove the engine from the vehicle.
11. Installation is the reverse of the removal procedure.

135 CID (2.2L) ENGINE

1.Disconnect the battery cables. Remove the battery. As required, remove the battery cables. Matchmark and remove the hood. 2.Disconnect the exhaust pipe at the manifold. Remove the power steering reservoir. Remove the upper fan shroud. Disconnect and plug the transmission oil cooler lines, if equipped.

3.Remove the under cover. Drain the cooling system. Disconnect the radiator hoses. Remove the radiator. Remove the fan and the lower fan shroud.

4. Disconnect the heater hoses at the engine. Remove the PCV valve at the cylinder head. Remove the air cleaner assembly.
5. Properly discharge the air condition system and remove the compressor. Properly cap the lines to avoid damage. Disconnect the power steering pump from the engine.
6. Disconnect and tag all electrical wires and vacuum hoses in order to remove the engine. Disconnect the accelerator control cable from the injection pump.
7. Remove the starter from the engine. Properly relieve the fuel pump pressure. Disconnect and plug the fuel hoses at the injection pump.
8. Remove the shifter boot and the shifter. Raise the vehicle and support safely. Drain the engine oil. Remove the right side motor mount through bolt.
9. Disconnect the lower clutch cable. Disconnect the clutch bellcrank at the frame. Disconnect the back-up light switch wires and the speedometer cable at the transmission.
10. Remove the driveshaft. Remove the transmission mount nut. Properly support the transmission. Remove the transmission crossmember.
11. Remove the transmission to bell housing bolts. Carefully remove the transmission. Remove the bell housing to engine bolts. Remove the bellhousing.
12. Lower the vehicle. Disconnect the upper clutch cable and remove the bellcrank.
13. Properly install a lifting device to the engine. Remove the left side motor mount through bolt. Carefully remove the engine from the vehicle.
14. Installation is the reverse of the removal procedure.

173 CID (2.8L) ENGINE WITH TWO WHEEL DRIVE

1. Disconnect the negative battery cable. Matchmark and remove the hood.
2. Drain the cooling system. Disconnect the radiator hoses. Disconnect and plug the transmission oil cooler lines at the radiator, if equipped. Remove the radiator. Remove the fan assembly.
3. Disconnect the heater hoses. Remove the air cleaner. Disconnect the vacuum hoses and the necessary electrical wires in order to remove the engine.
4. Disconnect the throttle cable. Disconnect the cruise control cable, as required. Remove the distributor cap. Disconnect the air condition comprerssor, if equipped. Disconnect the power steering pump, if equipped.
5. Raise and support the vehicle safely. Drain the engine oil. Remove the catalytic converter to exhaust pipe bolts. Remove the exhaust manifolds from both sides.
6. Remove the strut rods at the bell housing. Remove the flywheel cover. Remove the torque converter bolts, if equipped with automatic transmission.
7. Disconnect the shield from the rear of the catalytic converter. Remove the converter hanger at the exhaust pipe.
8. Remove the lower fan shroud. Properly relieve the fuel

pump pressure. Disconnect and plug the fuel hoses at the fuel pump. Remove the two outer air dam bolts. Remove the left side body mount bolts.

9. Properly raise the vehicle body. Remove the bellhousing bolts. Remove the motor mount through bolts. Lower the vehicle body. Lower the vehicle.

10. Properly support the transmission assembly. Using the proper engine lifting equipment, carefully remove the engine from the vehicle.

11. Installation is the reverse of the removal procedure.

173 CID (2.8L) ENGINE WITH FOUR WHEEL DRIVE AND MANUAL TRANSMISSION

1. Matchmark and remove the hood. Disconnect and remove the battery. Remove the air cleaner assembly.

2. Drain the cooling system. Remove the upper fan shroud. Remove the radiator hoses. Remove the radiator. Remove the fan assembly.

3. Remove the air condition compressor and position it to the side, if equipped. Remove the power steering pump and position it to the side, if equipped.

4. Properly relieve the fuel pump pressure. Disconnect and plug the fuel lines. Disconnect the vacuum hoses and the necessary electrical wires in order to remove the engine.

5. Disconnect the accelerator cable. Disconnect the cruise control cable, if equipped. Disconnect the heater hoses at the engine.

6. Disconnect the negative ground strap at the bulkhead. Disconnect the engine wiring harness at the bulkhead connector, if necessary. Remove the main feed wire at the bulkhead.

7. Remove the lower fan shroud. Remove the distributor cap. Remove the diverter valve.

8. Remove the shifter boot, transfer case shifter and the transmission shift lever assembly.

9. Raise the vehicle and support it safely. Remove the front skid plate, the rear skid plate and the front splash shield.

10. Drain the transfer case, transmission and engine oil. Remove the rear driveshaft. Disconnect the speedometer cable.

11. Disconnect the front driveshaft at the transfer case. Disconnect the shift linkage and vacuum hoses at the transfer case.

12. Disconnect the parking brake cable. Remove the rear transmission mount. Remove the catalytic converter bracket.

13. Properly support the transfer case and remove the case bolts. Remove the transfer case from the vehicle. Remove the crossmember.

14. Disconnect the back-up light wire and clip. Remove the clutch slave cylinder retaining bolts. Remove the cylinder and position it to the side.

15. Remove the transmission retaining bolts. Remove the transmission from the vehicle. Remove the clutch release bearing. Remove the inspection cover.

16. Remove the left side body mount bolts. Loosen the left hand radiator support bolt. Properly raise the left side of the body and support it safely.

17. Remove the bellhousing assembly from the engine. Lower the vehicle body. Disconnect the exhaust at the catalytic converter and manifold. Disconnect the clutch cross shaft at the frame.

18. Remove the starter. Remove the engine mount bolts. Lower the vehicle.

19. Properly support the transmission assembly. Using the proper engine lifting equipment, carefully remove the engine from the vehicle.

20. Installation is the reverse of the removal procedure.

173 CID (2.8L) ENGINE WITH FOUR WHEEL DRIVE AND AUTOMATIC TRANSMISSION

1. Matchmark and remove the hood. Remove the battery. Raise and support the vehicle safely.

2. On Blazer/Jimmy, remove the body mounts. Remove the front air dam end bolts.

3. Raise the body from the frame enough to gain access to the top transmission bolts. Remove the bolts. Lower the body. Remove the remaining transmission to engine mounting bolts.

4. Remove the rear crossmember bolts. Remove the crossmember. Disconnect the exhaust at the manifold and disconnect the catalytic converter hanger.

5. Remove the torque converter cover bolts and remove the cover. Disconnect the front driveshaft at the front differential.

6. Disconnect the oil cooler lines at the engine retaining clips. Remove the engine mount bolts. Remove the flexplate to torque converter bolts.

7. Remove the front splash shield and the lower fan shroud bolts.

8. Lower the vehicle. Drain the cooling system. Remove the upper fan shroud. Disconnect the radiator hoses. Disconnect and plug the transmission oil cooler lines. Remove the radiator. Remove the fan assembly.

9. Remove the air cleaner assembly. If equipped with air condition, remove the compressor and position it to the side. If equipped with power steering, remove the pump and position it to the side.

10. Properly relieve the fuel pump pressure. Disconect and plug the fuel lines. Disconnect and plug the necessary vacuum lines, wires and emission hoses. Disconnect the accelerator and TV cable. Disconnect the cruise control cable, if equipped.

11. Properly support the transmission assembly. Using the proper engine lifting equipment, carefully remove the engine from the vehicle.

12. Installation is the reverse of the removal procedure.

ASTRO/SAFARI

Removal and Installation

151 CID (2.5L) ENGINE

1. Disconnect and remove the battery. Remove the engine cover. As necessary, remove the hood.

2. Drain the radiator. Remove the headlamp bezel. Remove the grille.

3. Remove the radiator lower panel. Remove the radiator support brace and the lower tie bar. Remove the cross brace and the hood latch assembly.

4. Remove the upper core support. Disconnect the radiator hoses at the radiator. Remove the radiator filler panels. Remove the radiator and fan shroud as an assembly.

5. Disconnect the engine wiring harness at the bulkhead connector. Disconnect the wiring harness at the ECM and pull through the bulkhead.

6. Disconnect the heater hoses at the heater core. Disconnect the accelerator cable. Disconnect the battery ground strap at the cylinder head.

7. Disconnect the canister purge hose. Remove the air cleaner assembly.

8. Raise the vehicle and support it safely. Disconnect the exhaust pipe at the manifold. Disconnect the wiring harness at the transmission and frame.

9. Remove the starter. Remove the flywheel shield. Drain the engine oil.

10. Properly relieve the fuel pump pressure. Disconnect and plug the fuel hoses. Remove the engine mount through bolts. Remove the bell housing bolts.

11. Lower the vehicle. Remove the oil filler neck. Remove the thermostat outlet.

12. Install a suitable engine lifting device, properly support the transmission. Carefully remove the engine from the vehicle.

13. Installation is the reverse of the removal procedure.

260 CID (4.3L) ENGINE

1. Disconnect and remove the battery. As necessary, remove the hood. Drain the cooling system. Raise and support the vehicle safely. Drain the engine oil and remove the filter.

2. Disconnect the exhaust pipes at the manifolds. Disconnect the strut rods at the flywheel inspection cover. Remove the torque converter bolts. Remove the starter.

3. Disconnect the necessary electrical wires. Disconnect and plug the fuel hoses. Disconnect the lower transmission cooler line at the radiator.

4. Disconnect the lower engine oil cooler line at the radiator. Remove the lower fan shroud bolts. Remove the engine mount bolts. Remove the bell housing bolts.

5. Lower the vehicle. Remove the headlamp bezel and the grille assembly. Remove the radiator lower close out panel.

6. Remove the radiator support brace and the lower tie bar. Remove the hood latch assembly. Disconnect the master cylinder and position it aside.

7. Remove the upper fan shroud and the upper radiator core support. Disconnect the radiator hose at the radiator. Disconnect the upper transmission oil cooler line and the upper engine oil cooler line from the radiator. Remove the radiator.

8. Discharge the air condition system. Remove the radiator filler panels. Remove the engine cover. Remove the air condition brace at the rear of the compressor.

9. Disconnect air condition hose at the accumulator. Remove the air condition compressor and bracket. Remove the power steering pump.

10. Disconnect the necessary vacuum hoses and wiring harness at the bulkhead. Remove the right kick panel and disconnect the harness at the ESC module. Push the harness through the bulkhead.

11. Remove the distributor cap. Remove the air condition accumulator assembly. Properly relieve the fuel pump pressure. Disconnect and plug the fuel lines.

12. As required, remove the diverter valve and horn and the AIR check valves. Disconnect the transmission dipstick tube. remove the heater hose at the heater core.

13. Install a suitable engine lifting device and properly support the transmission. Carefully remove the engine from the vehicle.

14. Installation is the reverse of the removal procedure.

PICK UP, BLAZER/JIMMY AND SUBURBAN

Removal and Installation

252 CID (4.1L) AND 292 CID (4.8L) ENGINES

1. Disconnect the negative battery cable. Remove the battery, as required. Matchmark and remove the hood. Drain the cooling system.

2. Disconnect the accelerator cable from the carburetor throttle lever. As required, remove the detent cable from the throttle lever.

3. Remove air cleaner assembly. Disconnect all necessary electrical wiring from the engine. Disconnect all necessary vacuum hoses from the engine.

4. Remove the radiator hoses from the radiator. Remove the heater hoses from the engine. Remove the radiator. Remove the fan assembly and water pump pulley.

5. Properly relieve the fuel pump pressure. Disconnect and plug the fuel line at the fuel pump.

6. Raise the vehicle and support it safely. Drain the engine oil. Remove the starter. Remove the flywheel cover. Disconnect the exhaust pipe from the exhaust manifold.

7. Properly support the engine and remove the engine mount through bolts. If equipped with an automatic transmission, remove the flex plate bolts. If equipped with four wheel drive, remove the strut rods at the engine mounts. Remove the bell housing to engine retaining bolts.

8. Properly support the transmission assembly. Using the proper lifting device, carefully remove the engine from the vehicle.

9. Installation is the reverse of the removal procedure.

EXCEPT 380 CID (6.2L) ENGINE

1. Matchmark and remove the hood. Disconnect the negative battery cable. As required, remove the battery. Drain the cooling system.

2. Remove the air cleaner assembly. Remove the fan assembly and the water pump pulley.

3. Disconnect the upper and lower radiator hoses at the engine. Disconnect the heater hoses at the engine. If equipped with automatic transmission, disconnect the cooler lines at the radiator. Remove the radiator and shroud assembly.

4. Disconnect the accelerator linkage. As required, disconnect the detent cable. If equipped with air condition, remove the compressor and position it aside.

5. If equipped with power steering, remove the pump from the engine and position it aside. Remove the engine wiring harness from the engine components.

6. Properly relieve the fuel line pressure. Disconnect the fuel line at the engine. Disconnect all necessary vacuum lines.

7. Raise the vehicle and support it safely. Drain the engine oil. Disconnect the exhaust pipe from the exhaust manifold.

8. On four wheel drive vehicles equipped with automatic transmission, remove the strut rods from the engine mounts. Remove the flywheel conver.

9. Disconnect the wiring along the right pan rail and the gas gauge wire. Remove the starter. If equipped with automatic transmission, remove the converter to flex plate attaching bolts.

10. Properly support the transmission. Remove the bell housing to engine bolts, leaving one or more loosely to support the weight of the asssembly. Remove the lower engine mount bracket to frame bolts. Lower the vehicle.

11. Attach a lifting device to the engine, remove the remaining bell housing bolts. Carefully remove the engine from the vehicle.

12. Installation is the reverse of the removal procedure.

380 CID (6.2L) ENGINE

1. Remove the hood. Disconnect the batteries and remove them from the vehicle.

2. Raise the vehicle and support it safely. Drain the engine oil.

3. Remove the flywheel cover. Disconnect the torque converter from the flexplate. Disconnect the exhaust pipes from the manifolds.

4. Remove the starter bolts. Remove the transmission bell housing to engine bolts, leaving one or more loosely to prevent separation.

5. Remove the engine mount bolts. Disconnect the block heaters, remove the wiring harness, transmission oil cooler lines and the front battery cable clamp at the oil pan.

6. Properly relieve the fuel pump pressure. Disconnect and plug the fuel lines and the oil cooler lines at the engine block. Remove the lower fan shroud bolts.

7. Lower the vehicle. Drain the engine coolant. Remove the air cleaner assembly. Disconnect the ground cable from the alternator bracket. Disconnect the alternator wires and clips.

8. Disconnect the TPS, EGR–EPR and the fuel cut-off at the injection pump. Remove the harness from the clips at the rocker covers and disconnect the glow plugs.

9. Disconnect the EGR–EPR solenoids, glow plugs, controller, temperature sender and move the harness aside. Disconnect the ground strap on the left side.

10. Remove the fan assembly. Remove the upper radiator hoses at the engine. Remove the fan shroud.

11. Remove the power steering pump and belt. Remove the reservoir and lay the pump and reservoir aside. If equipped with air condition, remove the compressor and position it to aside.

12. Disconnect the vacuum lines at the cruise servo and accelerator cable at the injection pump. Disconnect the heater hoses and the oil cooler lines at the engine.

13. Disconnect the lower radiator hose, the oil cooler lines, the

heater hose, the automatic transmission cooler lines and the overflow hose at the radiator.

14. Remove the upper radiator cover. Remove the radiator. Remove the detent cable.

15. Install an engine lifting device, remove the loose bolts in the bell housing. Properly support the transmission. Carefully remove the engine from the vehicle.

17. Installation is the reverse of the removal procedure.

VAN

Removal and Installation

252 CID (4.1L) AND 292 CID (4.8L) ENGINES

1. Disconnect the battery cables and remove the battery. As required, remove the hood.
2. Drain the cooling system. Remove the engine cover. Remove the air cleaner assembly.
3. If equipped with air condition, evacuate the system and remove the compressor.
4. Disconnect the accelerator linkage. Properly relieve the fuel line pressure. If equipped with a carburetor, remove it.
5. Remove the grille and the cross brace. Remove the windshield washer and the air condition vacuum reservoir.
6. Remove the radiator hoses from the radiator. Remove the radiator to radiator support attaching brackets. Remove the transmission cooling lines from the radiator, if equipped. Remove the radiator.
7. If equipped with air condition, remove the condensor. Remove the heater hoses from the engine. Disconnect the wiring harness from the engine components.
8. Raise the vehicle and support it safely. Remove the fuel line from the engine. Drain the engine oil. Remove the driveshaft.
9. Remove the exhaust pipe from the manifold. Disconnect the speedometer cable. Remove the linkage from the transmission.
10. Remove the transmission crossmember mount bolts. If equipped with manual transmission, disconnect the clutch linkage and remove the clutch cross shaft. Remove the engine through bolts.
11. Lower the vehicle. Properly support the transmission. Install a lifting device to the engine assembly.
12. Raise the engine slightly and remove the right hand engine mount from the engine.
13. Carefully remove the engine and the transmission assembly from the vehicle.
14. Installation is the reverse of the removal procedure.

EXCEPT 380 CID (6.2L) ENGINE

1. Disconnect the battery and remove it. As required, remove the hood.
2. Remove the glove box. Remove the engine cover. Drain the engine coolant.
3. Remove the outside air duct and the power steering reservoir bracket. Disconnect the hood release cable.
4. Remove the upper fan shroud bolts. Disconnect the overflow hoses. Disconnect the transmission cooler lines. Disconnect the radiator hoses. Remove the radiator.
5. Remove the upper fan shroud. Remove the fan assembly. Remove the air cleaner assembly. If equipped, remove the cruise control servo.
6. Disconnect the brake vacuum line. Disconnect the accelerator and T.V. cables.
7. Properly relieve the fuel line pressure. If equipped with a carburetor, disconnect the fuel line and remove the carburetor. If equipped with fuel injection, remove the TBI unit.
8. Remove the distributor cap. Remove the diverter valve assembly. Disconnect the coolant hose at the intake manifold. Disconnect the PCV valve.
9. Disconnect the necessary vacuum lines, the necessary wiring and harness connectors from the components.
10. Properly discharge the air condition system and remove the compressor. Disconnect the upper half of the engine dipstick tube. Remove the oil filler tube. Remove the transmission dipstick tube. Disconnect the accelerator cable at the dipstick.
11. Disconnect and plug the fuel line hoses. Disconnect the power steering pump. Remove the air condition idler pulley.
12. Remove the headlamp bezels and the grille. Remove the upper radiator support. Remove the lower fan shroud and the lower filler panel. Remove hood latch support. Remove the air condition condenser.
13. Raise and support the vehicle safely. Drain the engine oil. Disconnect the exhaust pipes at the manifolds.
14. Disconnect the strut rods at the flywheel cover. Remove the cover. Remove the starter assembly.
15. Disconnect the necessary wires from engine and transmission assembly. Remove the driveshaft.
16. Remove the transmission crossmember mount bolts. If equipped with manual transmission, disconnect the clutch linkage and remove the clutch cross shaft. Remove the engine through bolts.
17. Lower the vehicle. Properly support the transmission. Install a lifting device to the engine assembly.
18. Raise the engine slightly and remove the right hand engine mount from the engine.
19. Carefully remove the engine and the transmission assembly from the vehicle.
20. Installation is the reverse of the removal procedure.

380 CID (6.2L) ENGINE

1. Disconnect the batteries and remove them from the vehicle. Remove the engine cover. As required, remove the hood.
2. Remove the headlamp bezels and the grille. Remove the front bumper assembly, along with the lower valence panel.
3. Remove the hood latch. Remove the coolant recovery bottle. Remove the upper fan shroud and the upper tie bar.
4. If equipped with air condition, properly discharge the system. Remove the condenser. Drain the engine coolant. Disconnect the transmission and engine oil cooler lines at the radiator.
5. Disconnect the upper and lower radiator hoses at the radiator. Remove the radiator from the vehicle. Remove the fan assembly.
6. Properly relieve the fuel line pressure. Remove the fuel injection pump from the engine.
7. Raise and support the vehicle safely. Disconnect the exhaust pipe at the manifold. Remove the converter inspection cover. Remove the flex plate to torque converter retaining bolts.
8. Remove the engine mount through bolts. Disconnect the block heater at the element and disconnect the ground wire to block.
9. Remove the bell housing to engine bolts. Remove the starter assembly. Lower the vehicle.
10. If equipped with cruise control, remove the cruise control transducer. If equipped with air condition discharge the system and remove the compressor.
11. Remove the power steering pump and position it aside. Remove the oil fill tube upper bracket and the glow plug relay. Disconnect the oil pressure sender electrical connector.
12. Remove the air cleaner resonator and bracket. Remove the transmission fill tube nut. Disconnect the heater, radiator and bypass hoses at the crossover. Disconnect the fuel lines at the fuel pump.
13. Install a lifting device to the engine and carefully remove the engine from the vehicle. A lifting device adapter, part number J-33888, is available to connect a common lifting device to the engine.
14. Installation is the reverse of the removal procedure.

Intake Manifold

S SERIES

Removal and Installation

119 CID (1.9L) ENGINE

1. Disconnect the negative battery cable. Remove the air cleaner assembly. Remove the EGR pipe clamp bolt at the rear of the cylinder head.
2. Raise and support the vehicle safely. Remove the EGR pipe from the intake and exhaust manifolds. Remove the EGR valve and bracket assembly from the intake manifold.
3. Lower the vehicle. Drain the cooling system. Remove the upper coolant hoses from the manifold.
4. Disconnect the accelerator linkage, vacuum lines and electrical wiring. Properly relieve the fuel line pressure. Disconnect the fuel line from the intake manifold.
5. Remove the intake manifold retaining nuts. Remove the manifold from the cylinder head.
6. Remove the lower heater hose while holding the manifold away from the engine. Remove the manifold from the vehicle.
7. Installation is the reverse of the removal procedure.

121 CID (2.0) ENGINE

1. Disconnect the negative battery cable. Remove the air cleaner. Drain the cooling system.
2. Tag and disconnect all necessary vacuum lines and wires. Remove the idler pulley, as required.
3. Remove the AIR drive belt. If equipped with power steering, remove the drive belt. Remove the pump and position it to the side.
4. Remove the AIR bracket to intake manifold bolt. Remove the air pump pulley. If equipped with power steering, remove the AIR pump thru bolt and then the power steering adjusting bracket.
5. Loosen the lower bolt on the air pump mounting bracket so that the bracket will rotate.
6. Properly relieve the fuel line pressure. Disconnect the fuel line at the carburetor. Disconnect the carburetor linkage. Remove the carburetor. Lift off the EFE heater grid.
7. Remove the distributor.
8. Remove the intake manifold retaining nuts. Remove the intake manifold. Make sure to disconnect the heater hose and condenser from the bottom of the intake manifold before you lift it all the way out.
9. Installation is the reverse of the removal procedure.

151 CID (2.5L) ENGINE

1. Disconnect the negative battery cable. Remove the air cleaner assembly.
2. Drain the cooling system. Disconnect the vacuum pipe rail at the exhaust and thermostat housing.
3. Disconnect the electrical and vacuum connections, as required. Disconnect the accelerator cable at the TBI unit.
4. Properly relieve the fuel line pressure. Disconnect and plug the fuel lines at the intake manifold. Disconnect the heater hoses at the intake manifold.
5. Remove the alternator bracket retaining bolts. Remove the alternator and position it aside. Remove the ignition coil.
6. Remove the intake manifold retaining bolts. Remove the intake manifold.
7. Installation is the reverse of the removal procedure.

173 CID (2.8L) ENGINE

1. Disconnect the nagative battery cable. Drain the cooling system. If equipped, remove the AIR pump and bracket.
2. Remove the distributor. Remove the heater and radiator hoses from the intake manifold. Remove the power brake vacuum hose.
3. Disconnect and label all vacuum hoses. Remove the EFE

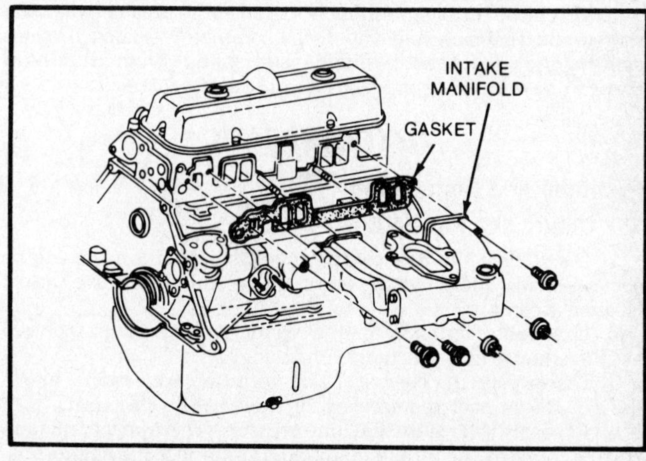

Removing intake manifold—typical 4 cylinder

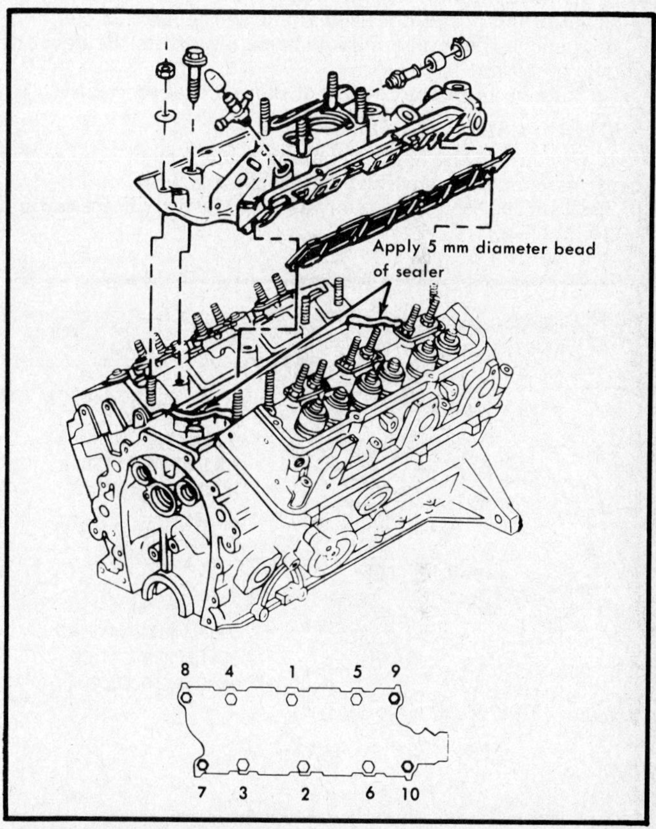

Intake manifold installation—173 CID V6 engine

pipe from the rear of the manifold. Remove the accelerator linkage. Properly relieve the fuel pump pressure. Disconnect and plug the fuel line.

4. As required, remove the TBI unit. Remove the intake manifold retaining bolts. Remove the intake manifold from the engine.
5. Installation is the reverse of the removal procedure. The gaskets are marked for right and left side installation. Do not interchange them. Clean the sealing surface of the engine block and apply a $^3/_{16}$ in. bead of silicone sealer to each ridge.
6. Install the new gaskets onto the heads. The gaskets will have to be cut slightly to fit past the center pushrods. Do not cut any more material than necessary. Hold the gaskets in place by extending the ridge bead of sealer ¼ in. onto the gasket ends.

7. When the intake manifold is installed the area between the ridges and the manifold should be completely sealed. Do not over torque the intake manifold, as it is made from aluminum and can be warped or cracked with excessive force.

ASTRO/SAFARI

Removal and Installation

151 CID.(2.5L) ENGINE

1. Disconnect the negative battery cable. Remove the engine cover assembly. Remove the glove box assembly. Remove the air cleaner assembly.
2. Drain the cooling system. Disconnect the vacuum pipe rail at the exhaust and thermostat housing.
3. Disconnect the electrical and vacuum connections, as required. Disconnect the accelerator cable at the TBI unit.
4. Properly relieve the fuel line pressure. Disconnect and plug the fuel lines at the intake manifold. Disconnect the heater hoses at the intake manifold.
5. Remove the alternator bracket retaining bolts. Remove the alternator and position it aside. Remove the ignition coil.
6. Remove the intake manifold retaining bolts. Remove the intake manifold.
7. Installation is the reverse of the removal procedure.

260 CID (4.3L) ENGINE

1. Disconnect the negative battery cable. Remove the engine cover assembly. Remove the air cleaner assembly.
2. Drain the cooling systemr. Remove the distributor cap and ignition wires.

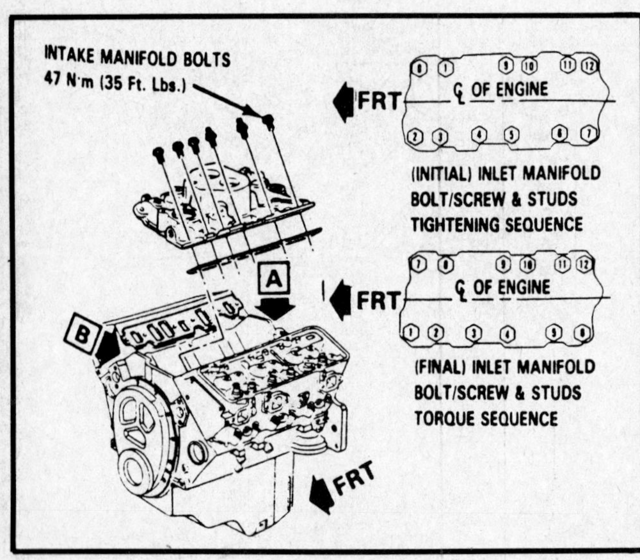

Intake manifold torque sequence for 4.3L engine

3. Disconnect the ESC connector and remove the distributor.
4. Remove the detent and accelerator cables. If equipped, remove the air condition compressor rear brace.
5. Remove the transmission and engine oil filler tubes at the alternator brace. Remove the cruise control transducer, if equipped.
6. If equipped, remove the air condition idler pulley at the alternator brace. Remove the alternator brace.
7. Properly relieve the fuel line pressure. Disconnect the fuel lines. Remove the necessary vacuum hoses and electrical wires.
8. Remove the AIR hoses and brackets. If necessary, remove the upper radiator hose. Remove the heater hose at the manifold. As required, remove the carburetor. As required remove the TBI unit.

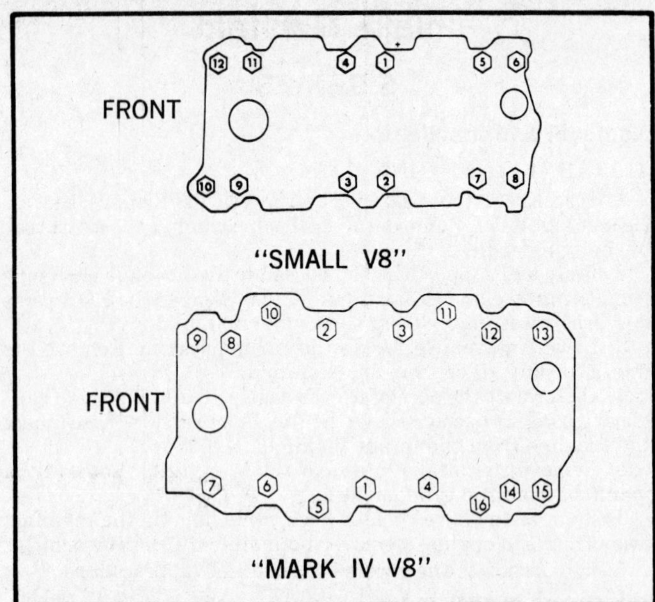

Intake manifold—bolt torquing sequence

9. Remove the intake manifold retaining bolts. Remove the intake manifold from the engine.
10. Installation is the reverse of the removal procedure. Be sure to apply a $^3/_{16}$ in. bead of RTV sealant to the front and rear sealing surfaces of the engine block. Extend the bead about ½ in. up each cylinder head in order to seal and retain the gaskets in position.

PICK UP, BLAZER/JIMMY, SUBURBAN AND VAN

Removal and Installation

EXCEPT 252 CID (4.1L) AND 292 CID (4.8L) ENGINES

1. Disconnect the negative battery cable. On Van, remove the engine cover. Drain the radiator. Remove the top hose at thermostat housing and the bypass or heater hoses.
2. Remove the air cleaner assembly. Remove oil fill tube and cap. Remove the distributor. As required, position the air condition compressor to the side.
3. Properly relieve the fuel system pressure. Disconnect the fuel line. Disconnect all vacuum hoses, throttle linkage, choke connections and the crankcase ventilation valve. Disconnect all electrical connections.
4. Remove the carburetor, if necessary. Remove the TBI unit, if necessary.
5. Remove the intake manifold retaining bolts. Remove the intake manifold from the engine.
6. Installation is the reverse of the removal procedure. On all engines except 454 CID (7.4L), be sure to apply a $^3/_{16}$ in. bead of RTV sealant to the front and rear sealing surfaces of the engine block. Extend the bead about ½ in. up each cylinder head in order to seal and retain the gaskets in position.

Exhaust Manifold

S SERIES

Removal and Installation

119 CID (1.9L) ENGINE

1. Disconnect the negative battery cable. Remove the air cleaner assembly.

2. Remove the EGR pipe clamp bolt at the rear of the cylinder head.
3. Raise and support the vehicle safely. Remove the EGR pipe from the intake and exhaust manifolds.
4. Separate the exhaust pipe from the manifold. Remove the manifold shield and remove the heat stove.
5. Remove the manifold retaining nuts. Remove the manifold from the engine.
6. Installation is the reverse of the removal procedure.

121 CID (2.0) ENGINE

1. Disconnect the negative battery cable. Remove the air cleaner assembly. Remove the exhaust manifold shield.
2. Raise and support the vehicle safely. Disconnect the exhaust pipe at the manifold. Lower the vehicle.
3. Disconnect the air management to check valve hose and remove the bracket. Disconnect the oxygen sensor lead wire.
4. Remove the alternator belt. Remove the alternator adjusting bolts, loosen the pivot bolt and pivot the alternator upward. Remove the alternator brace and the AIR pipes bracket bolt.
5. Remove the manifold retaining bolts. Remove the exhaust manifold from the engine. The manifold should be removed with the AIR plumbing as an assembly.
6. Installation is the reverse of the removal procedure.

151 CID (2.5L) ENGINE

1. Disconnect the negative battery cable. Remove the exhaust stove pipe at the manifold. Disconnect the oxygen sensor wire.
2. Raise and safely support the vehicle. Disconnect the exhaust pipe at the exhaust manifold. Remove the rear air condition compressor bracket.
3. Remove the exhaust manifold retaining bolts. Remove the manifold from the engine.
4. Installation is the reverse of the removal procedure.

173 CID (2.8L) ENGINE

1. Disconnect the negative battery cable. Disconnect the exhaust pipe from the manifold.
2. Raise and support the vehicle safely. Remove the rear manifold retaining bolts.
3. Remove the air management hoses and electrical connections. Lower the vehicle.
4. If equipped, remove the power steering bracket when removing the left manifold.
5. Remove the remaining manifold attaching bolts. Remove the manifold from the engine.
6. Installation is the reverse of the removal procedure.

ASTRO/SAFARI

Removal and Installation

151 CID.(2.5L) ENGINE

1. Disconnect the negative battery cable. Remove the glove box and the engine cover assembly.
2. Remove the exhaust stove pipe at the manifold. Disconnect the oxygen sensor wire.
3. Raise and safely support the vehicle. Disconnect the exhaust pipe at the exhaust manifold. Remove the rear air condition compressor bracket.
4. Remove the exhaust manifold retaining bolts. Remove the manifold from the engine.
5. Installation is the reverse of the removal procedure.

260 CID (4.3L) ENGINE

1. Disconnect the negative battery cable. Remove the engine cover. Raise and support the vehicle safely.
2. Disconnect the exhaust pipes from the exhaust manifolds. Lower the vehicle.
3. To remove the right manifold, disconnect the heat stove pipe and the dipstick tube bracket.

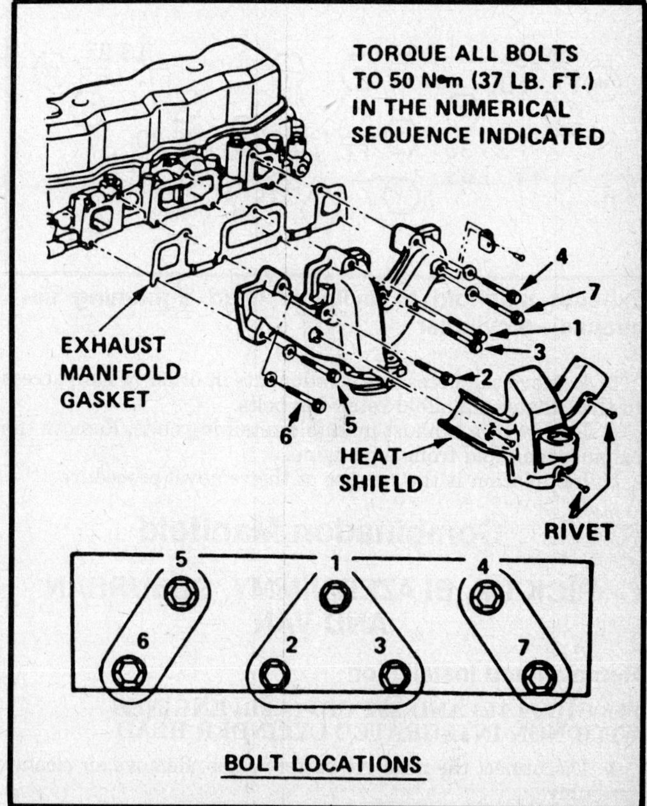

Exhaust manifold bolt torque sequence for 2.5L engine

4. To remove the left manifold, disconnect the oxygen sensor wire. Disconnect the power steering bracket at the manifold, if equipped. Disconnect the alternator bracket at the manifold.
5. Remove the AIR hoses at the check valve. Remove the exhaust manifold retaining bolts. Remove the manifold from the engine.
6. Installation is the reverse of the removal procedure.

PICK UP, BLAZER/JIMMY, SUBURBAN AND VAN

Removal and Installation

252 CID (4.1L) AND 292 CID (4.8L) ENGINES WITH INTEGRATED CYLINDER HEAD

1. Disconnect the negative battery cable.Remove the air cleaner assembly.
2. If equipped, remove the power steering pump and the AIR pump assemblies. Remove the PAIR pipes.
3. Raise and support the vehicle safely. Disconnect the exhaust pipe at the manifold. Disconnect the catalytic converter bracket at the transmission mounr. Lower the vehicle.
4. Remove the exhaust manifold retaining bolts. Remove the exhaust manifold from the engine.
5. Installation is the reverse of the removal procedure.

EXCEPT 252 CID (4.1L) AND 292 CID (4.8L) ENGINES

1. Disconnect the negative battery cable. On Van, remove the engine cover and glove box, as required.
2. Raise and support the vehicle safely. Disconnect the exhaust manifolds at the exhaust pipe. Lower the vehicle. As required, remove the spark plugs.

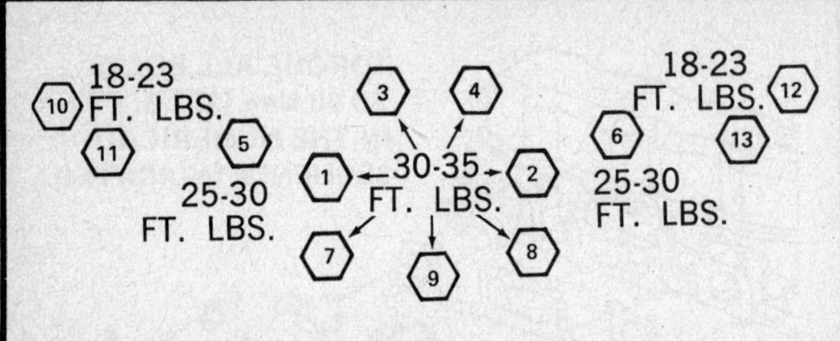

Exhaust manifold to cylinder head tightening sequence – 6 cylinder

3. Remove the necessary components in order to gain access to the exhaust manifold retaining bolts.
4. Remove the exhaust manifold retaining bolts. Remove the exhaust manifold from the engine.
5. Installation is the reverse of the removal procedure.

Combination Manifold

PICK UP, BLAZER/JIMMY, SUBURBAN AND VAN

Removal and Installation

252 CID (4.1L) AND 292 CID (4.8L) ENGINES WITH NON INTEGRATED CYLINDER HEAD

1. Disconnect the negative battery cable. Remove air cleaner assembly.
2. Disconnect throttle controls, rods, linkage and return spring.
3. Disconnect the necessary vacuum lines and electrical connections. Properly relieve the fuel system pressure. Disconnect the fuel line.
4. Disconnect the crankcase ventilation valve, vacuum brake or transmission spark control hoses, as necessary.
5. Remove the carburetor. Remove oil filter support bracket and position the filter aside, if equipped. Disconnect exhaust pipe at the flange.
6. Remove the combination manifold retaining bolts and clamps. Remove the manifold assembly.
7. Installation is the reverse of the removal procedure. As required, use new gaskets.

Cylinder Head

S SERIES

Removal and Installation

119 CID (1.9L) ENGINE

1. Disconnect the negative battery cable. Remove the cam cover. Remove the EGR pipe clamp bolt at rear of cylinder head.
2. Raise and support the vehicle safely. Disconnect the exhaust pipe at the exhaust manifold. Lower vehicle.
3. Drain the cooling system. Disconnect the heater hoses at the intake manifold and at the front of the cylinder head.
4. Remove air condition compressor and the power steering pump and position them aside.
5. Disconnect accelerator linkage. Properly relieve the fuel pump pressure. Disconnect the fuel line. Disconnect all necessary electrical connections, spark plug wires and vacuum lines.
6. Rotate the camshaft until number four cylinder is in the firing position. Remove the distributor cap and matchmark the rotor to the housing. Remove the distributor. Remove the fuel pump.

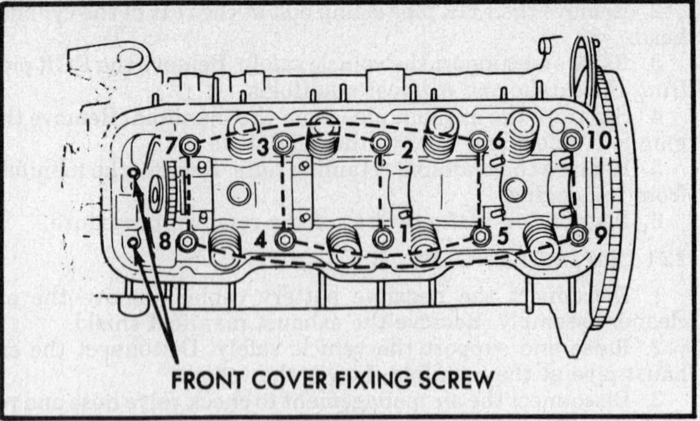

1.9 liter head bolt torque sequence

7. Lock the shoe on the automatic adjuster in the fully retracted position by depressing the adjuster lock lever with a suitable tool.
8. Remove the timing sprocket to camshaft bolt. Remove the sprocket and the fuel pump drive cam from the camshaft. Keep the sprocket on the chain damper and tensioner. Do not remove the sprocket from the chain.
9. Disconnect the air hose and check valve at air manifold. Remove cylinder head to timing cover bolts.
10. Remove the cylinder head bolts using tool J-24239-01. Remove the bolts in progressional sequence, beginning with the outer bolts. Remove the cylinder head along with the intake and exhaust manifold as an assembly.
11. Installation is the reverse of the removal procedure. Be sure that the cylinder bolt threads in the block and threads on the bolts are cleaned, as dirt will affect bolt torque.
12. Position the new gasket over the dowel pins with "TOP" side of gasket up. Torque the cylinder head bolts a little at a time, to specification, and in the proper sequence.

121 CID (2.0L) ENGINE

1. Disconnect the negative battery cable. Drain the engine coolant. Remove the air cleaner assembly.
2. Raise and support the vehicle safely. Remove the exhaust shield. Disconnect the exhaust pipe. Remove the heater hose from the intake manifold. Lower the vehicle.
3. Unscrew the mounting bolts and remove the engine lift bracket, including the air management assembly.
4. Remove the distributor. Disconnect the vacuum manifold at the alternator bracket. Tag and disconnect the remaining vacuum lines at the intake manifold and thermostat.
5. Remove the air management pipe at the exhaust check valve. Disconnect the accelerator linkage and remove the linkage bracket.
6. Tag and disconnect all necessary electrical wires. Remove the upper radiator hose at the thermostat. Remove the bolt attaching the dipstick tube and hot water bracket.
7. Remove the idler pulley. Remove the AIR and power steering pump drive belts. Remove the AIR bracket to intake manifold bolt.
8. If equipped with power steering, remove the air pump pulley, the AIR thru bolt and the power steering adjusting bracket.
9. Loosen the AIR mounting bracket lower bolt so that the bracket will rotate. Properly relieve the fuel pump pressure. Disconnect and plug the fuel line.
10. Remove the alternator. Remove the alternator brace and the upper mounting bracket. Remove the cylinder head cover. Remove the rocker arms and push rods.
11. Remove the cylinder head retaining bolts. Remove the cylinder head along with the intake and exhaust manifolds as an assembly.

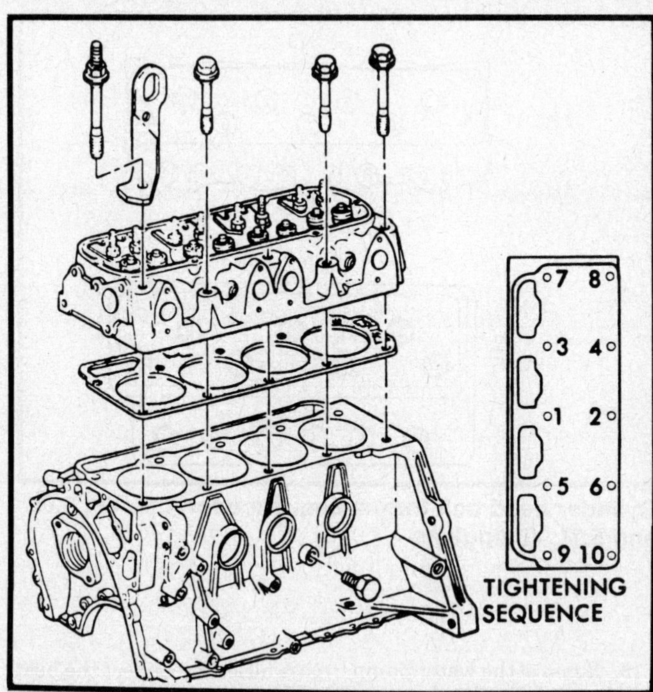

Cylinder head bolt torque sequence 121 CID (2.0L) engine

12. Installation is the reverse of the removal procedure. Be sure that the cylinder bolt threads in the block and threads on the bolts are cleaned, as dirt will affect bolt torque. Position the new gasket over the dowel pins. Torque the cylinder head bolts a little at a time, to specification, and in the proper sequence.

151 CID (2.5L) ENGINE

1. Disconnect the negative battery cable. Drain the cooling system. Remove the air cleaner assembly.
2. Remove the air condition compressor and position it to the side. Remove the rocker arm cover. Remove the rocker arms and pushrods. Keep them in order for reinstallation.
3. Properly relieve the fuel system pressure. Disconnect the fuel line from the TBI unit. Disconnect all necessary electrical and vacuum lines.
4. Disconnect the accelerator cable, the cruise control cable and the TVS cables. Remove the alternator and brackets.
5. Remove the water pump bypass hose. Disconnect the heater hoses at the intake manifold. Remove the upper radiator hose.
6. Disconnect the exhaust pipe from the exhaust manifold. Remove the fuel filter and filter brackets at the rear of the cylinder head assembly.
7. Remove the coil wire and spark plug wires. Disconnect the oxygen sensor electrical wire.
8. Remove the cylinder head retaining bolts. Remove the cylinder head along with the intake and exhaust manifold assembly.
9. Installation is the reverse of the removal procedure. Be sure that the cylinder bolt threads in the block and threads on the bolts are cleaned, as dirt will affect bolt torque.

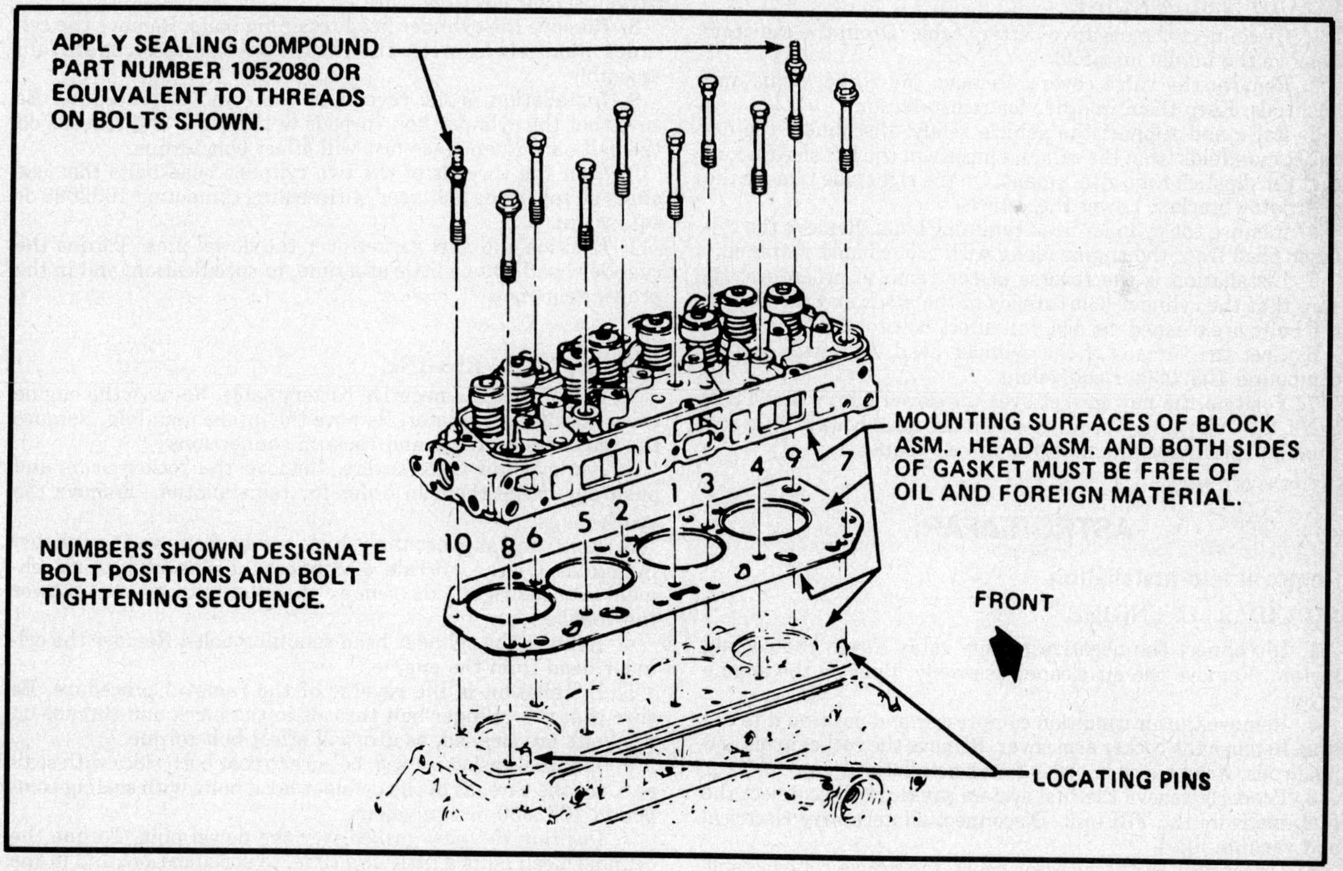

APPLY SEALING COMPOUND PART NUMBER 1052080 OR EQUIVALENT TO THREADS ON BOLTS SHOWN.

MOUNTING SURFACES OF BLOCK ASM., HEAD ASM. AND BOTH SIDES OF GASKET MUST BE FREE OF OIL AND FOREIGN MATERIAL.

NUMBERS SHOWN DESIGNATE BOLT POSITIONS AND BOLT TIGHTENING SEQUENCE.

10 8 6 5 2 1 3 4 9 7

FRONT

LOCATING PINS

Cylinder head bolt torque sequence for 2.5L engine

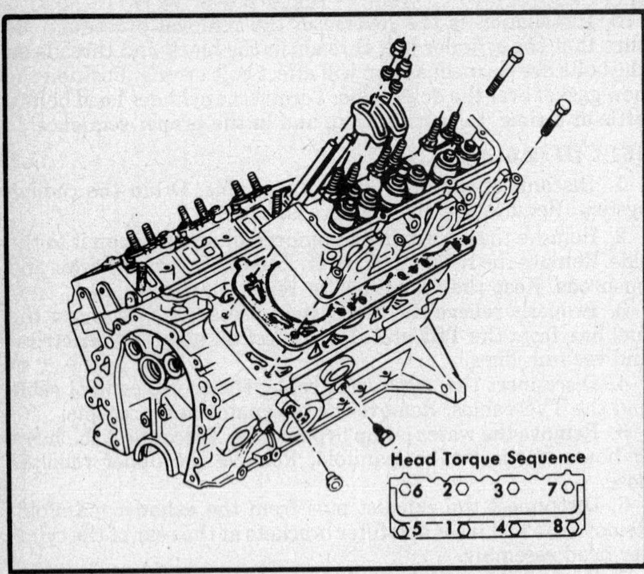

Cylinder head installation—173 CID V6 engine

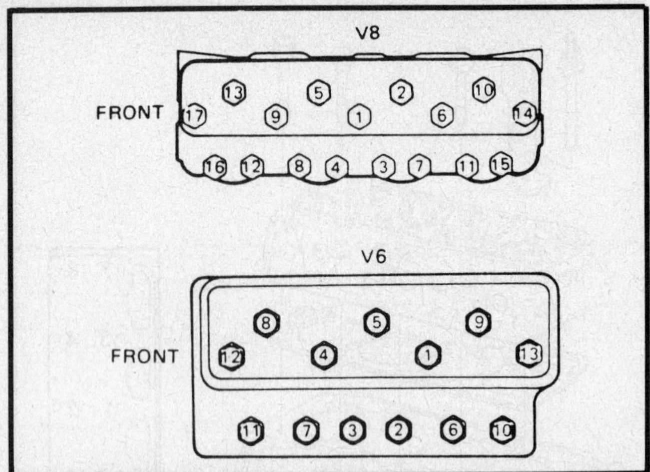

Cylinder head bolt torque sequence for 4.3L V6, 5.0L and 5.7L V8 engines

10. Coat the threads of the two cylinder head bolts that use studs on top of the bolt head with sealing compound 1052080 or equivalent.

11. Position the new gasket over the dowel pins. Torque the cylinder head bolts a little at a time, to specification, and in the proper sequence.

173 CID (2.8L) ENGINE

1. Disconnect the negative battery cable. Drain the radiator. Remove the intake manifold.
2. Remove the valve covers. Remove the rocker arms and pushrods. Keep them in order for reinstallation.
3. Raise and support the vehicle safely. Disconnect the exhaust manifolds from the exhaust pipes. On the left side disconnect the dipstick tube attachment. On the right side remove the alternator bracket. Lower the vehicle.
4. Remove the cylinder head retaining bolts. Remove the cylinder head from the engine along with the exhaust manifold.
5. Installation is the reverse of the removal procedure. Be sure that the cylinder bolt threads in the block and threads on the bolts are cleaned, as dirt will affect bolt torque.
6. Coat the threads of the cylinder head bolts with sealing compound 1052080 or equivalent.
7. Position the new gasket over the dowel pins with "THIS SIDE UP" showing. Torque the cylinder head bolts a little at a time, to specification, and in the proper sequence.

ASTRO/SAFARI

Removal and Installation

151 CID (2.5L) ENGINE

1. Disconnect the negative battery cable. Drain the cooling system. Remove the air cleaner assembly. Remove the engine cover.
2. Remove the air condition compressor and position it to the side. Remove the rocker arm cover. Remove the rocker arms and pushrods. Keep them in order for reinstallation.
3. Properly relieve the fuel system pressure. Disconnect the fuel line from the TBI unit. Disconnect all necessary electrical and vacuum lines.
4. Disconnect the accelerator cable, the cruise control cable and the TVS cables. Remove the alternator and brackets.
5. Remove the water pump bypass hose. Disconnect the heater hoses at the intake manifold. Remove the upper radiator hose.
6. Disconnect the exhaust pipe from the exhaust manifold. Remove the fuel filter and filter brackets at the rear of the cylinder head assembly.
7. Remove the coil wire and spark plug wires. Disconnect the oxygen sensor electrical wire.
8. Remove the cylinder head retaining bolts. Remove the cylinder head along with the intake and exhaust manifold assembly.
9. Installation is the reverse of the removal procedure. Be sure that the cylinder bolt threads in the block and threads on the bolts are cleaned, as dirt will affect bolt torque.
10. Coat the threads of the two cylinder head bolts that use studs on top of the bolt head with sealing compound 1052080 or equivalent.
11. Position the new gasket over the dowel pins. Torque the cylinder head bolts a little at a time, to specification, and in the proper sequence.

260 CID (4.3L) ENGINE

1. Disconnect the negative battery cable. Remove the engine cover. Drain the radiator. Remove the intake manifold. Remove the required electrical and vacuum connections.
2. Remove the valve covers. Remove the rocker arms and pushrods. Keep them in order for reinstallation. Remove the spark plugs.
3. Raise and support the vehicle safely. Remove the exhaust manifolds. On the left side, disconnect the dipstick tube attachment. On the right side, remove the alternator bracket. Lower the vehicle.
4. Remove the cylinder head retaining bolts. Remove the cylinder head from the engine.
5. Installation is the reverse of the removal procedure. Be sure that the cylinder bolt threads in the block and threads on the bolts are cleaned, as dirt will affect bolt torque.
6. If a steel gasket is used, be sure to coat both sides with sealer. Coat the threads of the cylinder head bolts with sealing compound 1052080 or equivalent.
7. Position the new gasket over the dowel pins. Torque the cylinder head bolts a little at a time, to specification, and in the proper sequence.

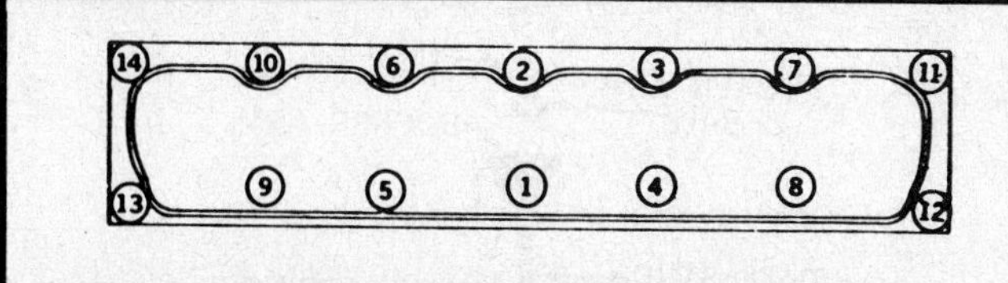

Cylinder head bolt torque sequence 252 CID (4.1L) and 292 CID (4.8L) engines

PICK UP, BLAZER/JIMMY, SUBURBAN AND VAN

Removal and Installation

252 CID (4.1L) AND 292 CID (4.8L) ENGINES

1. Disconnect the negative battery cable. Drain cooling system. Remove air cleaner assembly.
2. Properly relieve the fuel pump pressure. Disconnect the fuel line at the carburetor. Disconnect the accelerator and transmission linkages. Disconnect all required electrical and vacuum lines.
3. Remove the combination manifold assembly retaining bolts. Remove the combination manifold from the engine.
4. Remove the valve cover. Remove the rocker arms and pushrods. Keep them in order for reinstallation.
5. If equipped, disconnect the AIR injection hose at the check valve. Disconnect the upper radiator hose at the thermostat housing. Remove the battery ground strap.
6. Remove the cylinder head retaining bolts. Remove the cylinder head from the engine.
7. Installation is the reverse of the removal procedure. Be sure that the cylinder bolt threads in the block and threads on the bolts are cleaned, as dirt will affect bolt torque.
8. Coat the threads of the cylinder head bolts with sealing compound 1052080 or equivalent.
9. Position the new gasket over the dowel pins. Torque the cylinder head bolts a little at a time, to specification, and in the proper sequence.

EXCEPT 252 CID (4.1L) AND 292 CID (4.8L) ENGINES

1. Disconnect the negative battery cable. Drain the cooling system. On Van, remove the engine cover. Remove intake manifold.
2. Remove the exhaust manifolds. Remove the necessary components in order to gain access to the cylinder head retaining bolts.
3. Remove the valve covers. Remove the rocker arms and pushrods. Keep them in order for reinstallation. As required, remove the spark plugs.
4. Remove the cylinder head retaining bolts. Remove the cylinder head from the engine.
5. Installation is the reverse of the removal procedure. Be sure that the cylinder bolt threads in the block and threads on the bolts are cleaned, as dirt will affect bolt torque.
6. If a steel gasket is used, coat both sides of the gasket with sealer. Coat the threads of the cylinder head bolts with sealing compound 1052080 or equivalent.
7. Position the new gasket over the dowel pins. Torque the cylinder head bolts a little at a time, to specification, and in the proper sequence.

Rocker Arm

Removal and Installation

1. Disconnect the negative battery cable. On Vans, remove the engine cover.

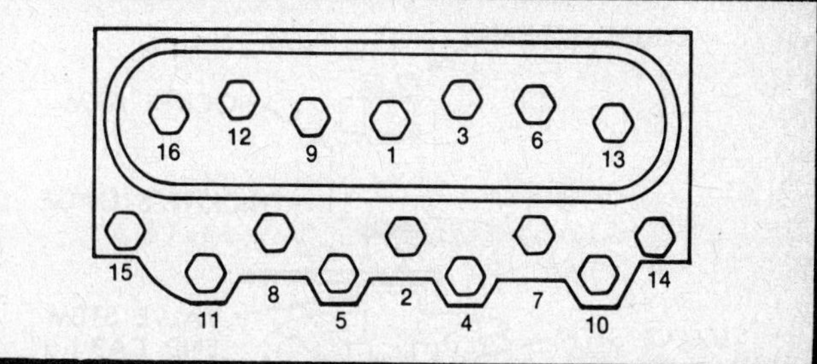

Cylinder head bolt torque sequence 454 CID (7.4L) engine

2. Remove all the necessary components in order to gain access to the engine valve covers. As required, properly relieve the fuel system pressure before disconnecting any fuel lines.
3. Remove the valve cover retaining bolts. Remove the valve cover from the engine.
4. Remove the rocker arm assemblies. Keep them in order for reinstallation.
5. Installation is the reverse of the removal procedure. Be sure to use new gaskets or RTV sealant, as necessary.

Valve Arrangement

119 CID (1.9L) AND 121 (2.0L) ENGINES

E–I–I–E–E–I–I–E

151 CID (2.5L) ENGINE

I–E–I–E–E–I–E–I

173 CID (2.8L) ENGINE

E–I–I–E–I–E

252 CID (4.1L) AND 292 (4.8L) ENGINES

E–I–I–E–E–I–I–E–E–I–I–E

260 CID (4.3L) ENGINE

Left Side E–I–E–I–I–E
Right Side E–I–I–E–I–E

V8 EXCEPT 454 CID (7.4L) ENGINE

E–I–I–E–E–I–I–E

454 CID (7.4L) ENGINE

E–I–E–I–E–I–E–I

Valve Adjustment Procedure

119 CID (1.9L) ENGINE

1. Disconnect the negative battery cable. Remove the valve cover. Check the rocker arm shaft bracket nuts for looseness and retighten as necessary.
2. Bring either the No. 1 or No. 4 piston to top dead center on the compression stroke.
3. Hold the crankshaft in above position and adjust the clearance of the required valves. Measurement should be taken at the clearance between rocker arm and valve stem.
4. Turn crankshaft one full turn and adjust clearance of remaining valves.
5. Valve clearance specification is 0.006 in. for the intake valves and 0.010 in. for the exhaust valves.

EXCEPT 119 CID (1.9L) ENGINE

1. Run engine until normal operating temperature is reached. Remove the rocker cover.
2. Reduce engine idle as low as possible. Back off the rocker arm adjusting nut until the rocker arm starts to clatter, then turn nut down slowly until the clatter stops. This is zero lash position.

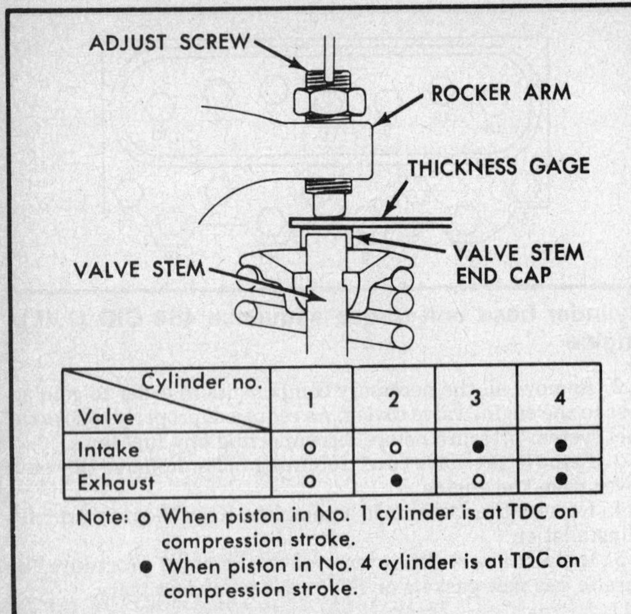

Valve \ Cylinder no.	1	2	3	4
Intake	o	o	●	●
Exhaust	o	●	o	●

Note: o When piston in No. 1 cylinder is at TDC on compression stroke.
● When piston in No. 4 cylinder is at TDC on compression stroke.

1.9 liter valve adjustment sequence

3. Turn the adjusting nut down 1/4 turn and pause 10 seconds until the engine runs smoothly. Repeat the operation until one full turn is reached. This must be done slowly and in stages to allow the lifter to adjust itself in order to prevent the possibility of internal interference or bent push rods.

Timing Gears and Chain

CRANKSHAFT PULLEY

Removal and Installation

1. Disconnect the negative battery cable. Remove the engine drive belts and pulley. Remove all necessary components in order to gain access to the crankshaft pulley bolt.
2. As required, raise the vehicle and support it safely. Remove the crankshaft pully retaining bolt.
3. Remove the crankshaft pulley from the engine, using the proper removal tool.
4. Installation is the reverse of the removal procedure.

TIMING COVER AND OIL SEAL

Removal and Installation

1. Disconnect the negative battery cable. Remove the crankshaft vibration damper. Remove the necessary components in order to gain access to the front cover assembly.

NOTE: At this point it is possible to remove the oil seal from the timing cover without removing the cover from the engine. However it is recommemded that the cover be removed to insure against seal leakage.

2. As required, remove the water pump. Remove the timing cover retaining bolts. Remove the timing cover from the engine. On some engines it will be necessary to remove the oil pan before removing the timing cover.
3. Pry old seal out of its housing. Be careful not to bend the cover.
4. Installation is the reverse of the removal procedure. Coat the new seal with clean engine oil before installation. If the front was removed, be sure to use a new gasket or RTV sealant as required.

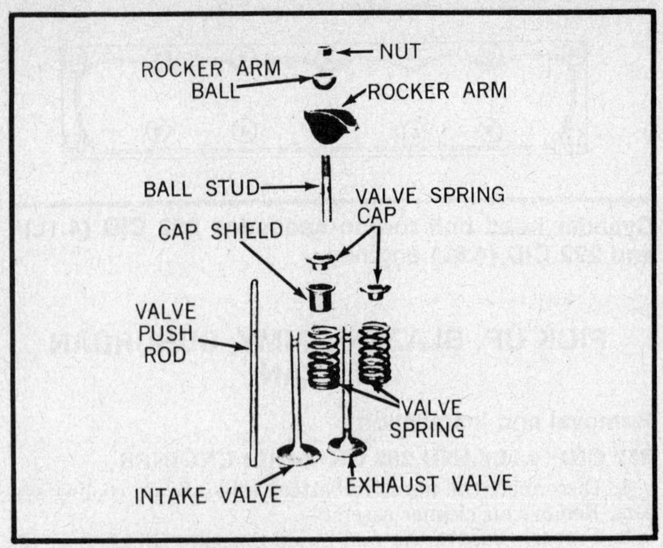

Valve system—V8 engines

TIMING CHAIN AND GEAR

Removal and Installation

119 CID. (1.9L) ENGINE

1. Disconnect the negative battery cable. Remove all the necessary components in order to gain access to the timing cover bolts. Remove the timing cover.
2. Lock the shoe on the automatic adjuster in the fully retracted position by depressing the shoe with a pry bar tool and turning the adjuster lock lever towards the engine block.
3. Remove the timing chain from the crankshaft sprocket. Check the timing sprockets for wear or damage. If crankshaft sprocket must be replaced, remove sprocket and pinion gear from crankshaft using tool J–25031 or equivalent. Check the timing chain for wear or damage, replace as necessary.
4. Remove the attaching bolt and remove the automatic chain adjuster. Check that the shoe becomes locked when the shoe is pushed in with the lock lever released. Check that the lock is released when the shoe is pushed in. The adjuster assembly must be replaced if the rack teeth are found to be worn excessively.
5. Remove the "E" clip and remove the chain tensioner. Check the tensioner for wear or damage, replace as necessary.
6. Inspect the tensioner pin for wear or damage. If replacement is necessary, remove pin from the cylinder block using locking pliers. Lubricate the new pin of the tensioner with clean engine oil. Start the pin in the block, place the tensioner over the appropriate pin. Place the "E" clip on the pin and then tap the pin into the block until the clip just clears the tensioner. Check the tensioner and adjuster for freedom of rotation on the pins.
6. Inspect the guide for wear or damage and a plugged lower oil jet. If replacement or cleaning is necessary, remove the guide bolts, guide and oil jet. Install a new guide and upper attaching bolt. Install the lower oil jet and bolt so that the oil port is pointed toward crankshaft.
7. Install the timing sprocket and pinion gear (groove side toward front cover). Align the key grooves with the key on the crankshaft and then drive it into position using tool J–26587.
8. Turn the crankshaft so that the key is turned toward the cylinder head side (#1 and #4 pistons at top dead center).
9. Install the timing chain by aligning the mark plate on the chain with the mark on crankshaft timing sprocket. The side of the chain with the mark plate is on the front side and the side of chain with the most links between mark plates is on the chain

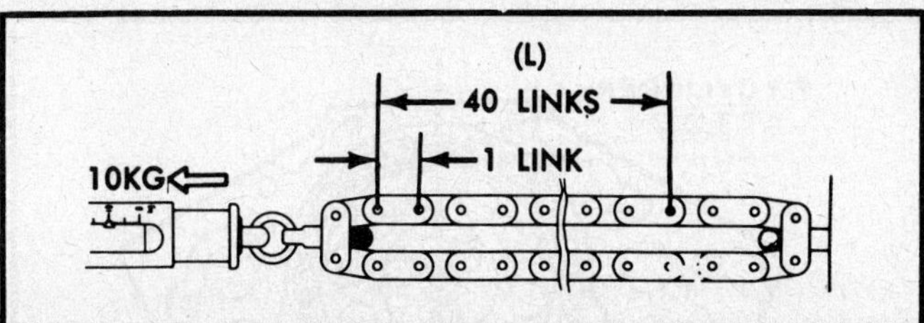

Check timing chain for wear—4 cyl 119 cu.in. shown

Depressing lock lever, 1.9L engine

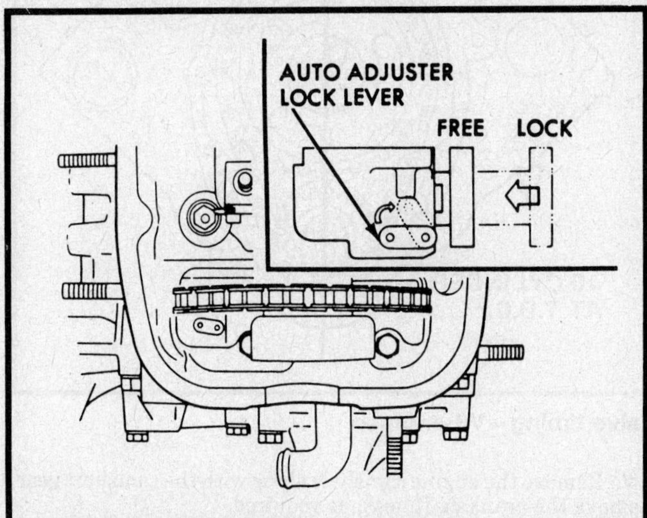

Locking the chain adapter, 1.9L engine

guide side. Keep the timing chain engaged with the camshaft timing sprocket until the camshaft timing sprocket is installed on camshaft.

10. Install the camshaft timing sprocket so that the marked side of the sprocket faces forward and so that the triangular mark aligns with the chain mark plate.

11. Install the automatic chain adjuster. Release the lock by depressing the shoe on the adjuster by hand. Check to make certain that the chain is properly tensioned when the lock is released.

12. Continue the installation in the reverse order of the removal procedure.

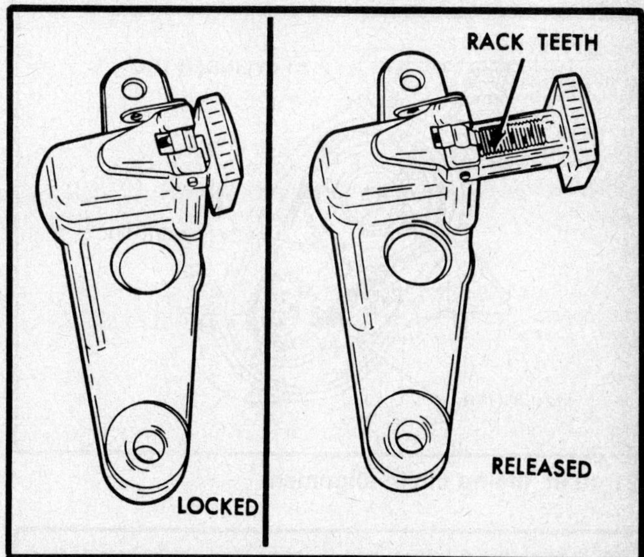

Timing chain adjuster—1.9L engine

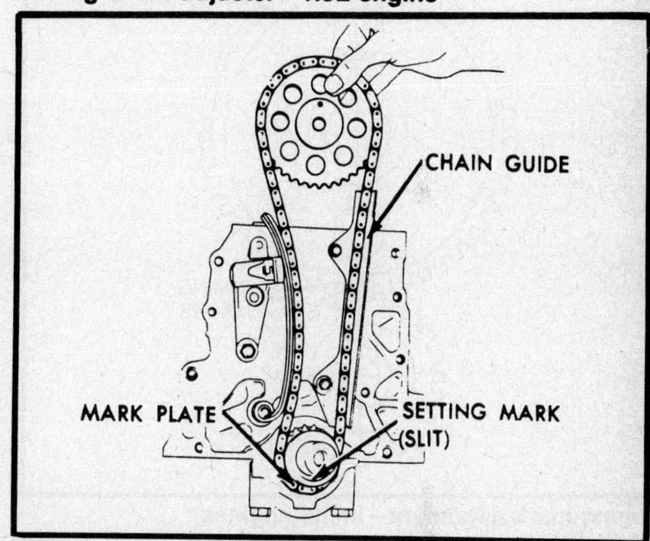

Timing chain guide, tensioner and adjuster, 1.9L engine

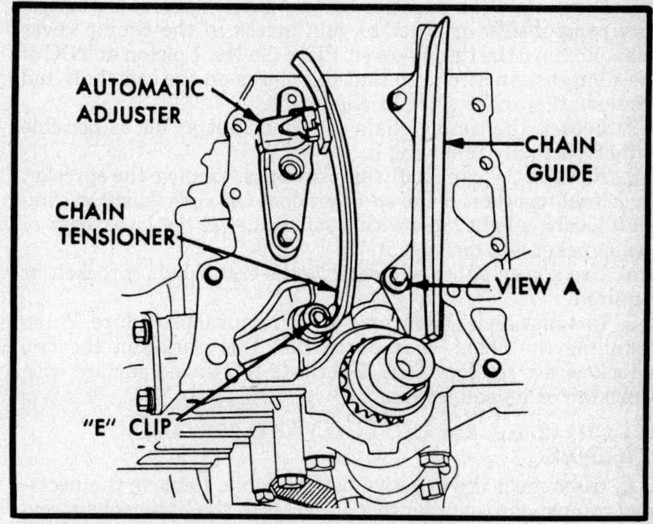

Alignment of timing chain, 1.9L engine

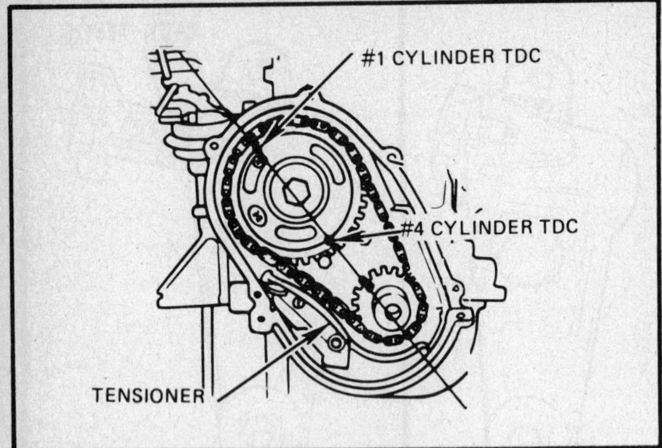

121 cu.in. timing chain alignment

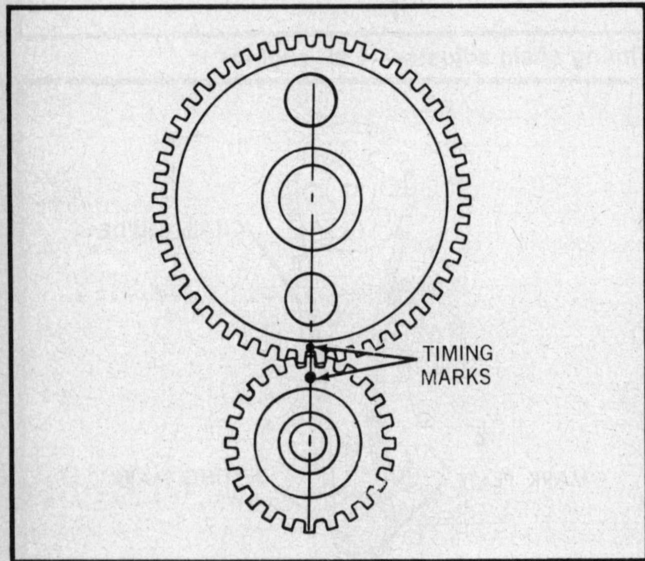

Timing mark alignment—inline engines

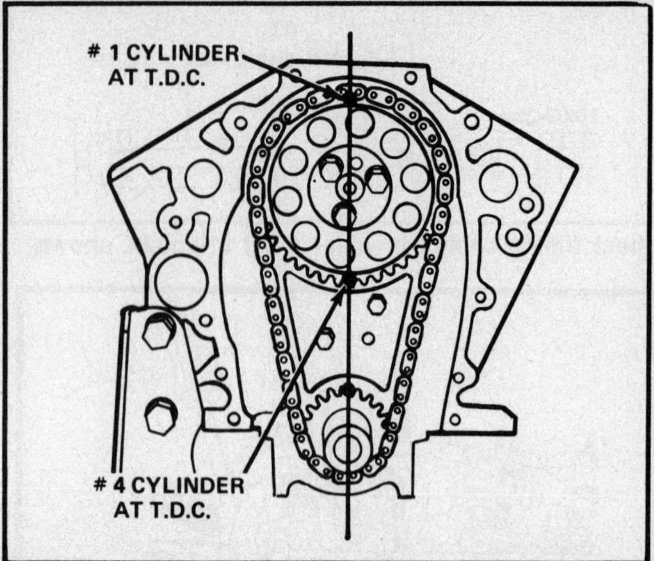

Camshaft sprocket alignment marks—typical of V6 engines

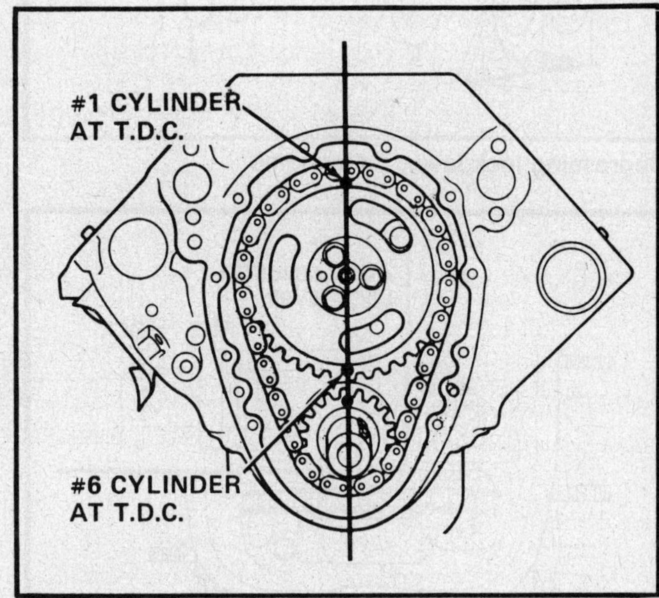

Valve timing—V8 engines

121 CID. (2.0L) ENGINE

1. Disconnect the negative battery cable. Remove the necessary components in order to gain access to the timing cover bolts. Remove the timing cover. Place the No. 1 piston at TDC of the compression stroke so that the marks on the camshaft and crankshaft sprockets are in alignment.
2. Loosen the timing chain tensioner nut as far as possible without actually removing it.
3. Remove the camshaft sprocket bolts. Remove the sprocket and chain together. If the sprocket does not slide from the camshaft easily, a light blow with a soft mallet at the lower edge of the sprocket will dislodge it.
4. Use a gear puller and remove the crankshaft sprocket, as required.
5. Installation is the reverse of the removal procedure. When installing the chain, make sure that the marks on the two sprockets are in alignment. Lubricate the thrust surface with Molykote or its equivalent.

151 CID (2.5L), 252 CID (4.1L) AND 292 (4.8L) ENGINES

1. Disconnect the negative battery cable. Remove the necessary components in order to gain access to the timing chain cover. Remove the timing chain cover.
2. Remove the engine camshaft along with the camshaft gear. Remove the crankshaft gear, as required.
3. Properly press the camshaft gear from the cam assembly.
4. Installation is the reverse of the removal procedure.

EXCEPT 119 CID. (1.9L), 121 CID. (2.0L) 151 CID (2.5L), 252 CID (4.1L) AND 292 (4.8L) ENGINES

1. Disconnect the negative battery cable. Remove the necessary components in order to gain access to the timing chain cover. Remove the timing chain cover assembly. On some engines it will be necessary to remove the oil pan before removing the timing cover.
2. Crank the engine until the marks punched on both sprockets are closest to one another and in line between the shaft centers.
3. Remove the bolts that hold the camshaft sprocket to the

camshaft. This sprocket is a light press fit on the camshaft and will come off readily. It is located by a dowel.

4. Remove the timing chain. Using the proper tools remove the crankshaft sprocket, as required.

5. Installation is the reverse of the removal procedure. After the sprockets are in place, turn the engine two full revolutions to make certain that the timing marks are in correct alignment between the shaft centers.

VALVE TIMING PROCEDURE

1. Remove the rocker arm covers.

2. Turn the crankshaft so that the crankshaft pulley timing mark is at the "O" mark on the pointer and the No. 1 cylinder is ready to fire.

3. To verify that number one cylinder is on its firing stroke, rotate the crankshaft counterclockwise $\frac{1}{8}$ of a turn before TDC and then rotate the crankshaft clockwise slowly through the TDC position, while observing the valves and rocker arms on the companion cylinder of number one. As the crankshaft is rotated, the exhaust valve will be ending its closing stroke, while the intake valve will just begin to open. This indicates that number one cylinder is on its firing stroke.

4. Companion cylinders are as follows:

four cylinder engines with firing order 1–3–4–2
Cylinders 1 and 4
Cylinders 3 and 2

2.8L V6 Engine with firing order 1–2–3–4–5–6
Cylinders 1 and 4
Cylinders 2 and 5
Cylinders 3 and 6

4.3L V6 Engine with firing order 1–6–5–4–3–2
Cylinders 1 and 4
Cylinders 6 and 3
Cylinders 5 and 2

Inline 6 cylinder Engines with firing order 1–5–3–6–2–4
Cylinders 1 and 6
Cylinders 5 and 2
Cylinders 3 and 4

V8 Engines with firing order 1–8–4–3–6–5–7–2
Cylinders 1 and 6
Cylinders 8 and 5
Cylinders 4 and 7
Cylinders 3 and 2

5. If the exhaust or intake valves on the companion cylinder do not open and close as outlined in Step 3 when the crankshaft pulley is moved through TDC, the camshaft is out of time, or that cylinder is on its firing stroke- observe valve action on its comparison cylinder.which is usually caused by either stripped gears or a stretched timing chain.

6. Verification of which cylinder is in its firing position can be made by observing the distributor rotor and its positioning towards either number one cylinder or its companion cylinder. Should the crankshaft and camshaft timing be correct and the distributor rotor incorrect, indications of a distributor gear or shaft malfunction would be indicated.

7. To verify valve timing, turn the crankshaft 180 degrees and repeat Steps 2 and 3.

Camshaft

S SERIES

Removal and Installation

119 CID (1.9L) ENGINE

1. Disconnect the negative battery cable. Remove cam cover.

2. Rotate camshaft until No.4 cylinder is in firing position. Remove the distributor cap and mark rotor to housing position.

3. Remove the distributor. Remove the fuel pump.

4. Lock the shoe on the automatic adjuster in the fully retracted position by depressing the adjuster lock lever in the proper direction. After locking the automatic adjuster, check that the chain is in a free state.

5. Remove the timing sprocket to camshaft bolt and remove the sprocket and fuel pump drive cam from the camshaft. Keep the timing sprocket on the chain damper and tensioner without removing the chain from the sprocket.

6. Remove the rocker arm assembly. Remove the camshaft assembly from the engine.

7. Installation is the reverse of the removal procedure. Before installing the camshaft apply a generous amount of clean engine oil to the camshaft and journals of cylinder head.

121 CID (2.0L) ENGINE

1. Disconnect the negative battery cable. Drain the cooling system. Remove the radiator.

2. Remove the valve cover. Remove the rocker arm assemblies and pushrods. Keep them in order for reinstallation. Remove the valve lifters. Keep them in order for reinstallation.

3. Remove the front cover. Remove the distributor. Remove the fuel pump and the fuel pump pushrod. Remove the timing chain and sprocket.

4. Carefully pull the camshaft from the block. Be sure that the camshaft lobes do not contact the bearings.

5. Installation is the reverse of the removal procedure. Before installation, lubricate the camshaft journals with clean engine oil. Lubricate the lobes with Molykote or the equivalent.

151 CID (2.5L) ENGINE

1. Disconnect the negative battery cable. Drain the cooling system. Remove the radiator.

2. Remove the engine side cover. Remove the air cleaner assembly. Remove the EGR valve.

3. Disconnect the power steering reservoir and position it to the side. Remove the drive belts and pulleys. Remove the upper fan shroud. Remove the front cover.

4. Rotate the crankshaft until the timing marks are in alignment. Remove the distributor assembly. Remove the oil pump driveshaft cover and driveshaft.

5. Remove the rocker cover. Remove the rockers and pushrods. Keep them in order for reinstallation. Remove the valve lifters. Keep them in order for reinstallation.

6. If equipped with air condition, it may be necessary to reposition the condenser in order to withdraw the camshaft from the engine. If the condenser must be removed, properly discharge the system before condenser removal.

7. As required, remove the headlight bezel and grille assembly.

8. Remove the camshaft thrust plate bolts. Carefully remove the camshaft from the vehicle.

9. Installation is the reverse of the removal procedure. Before installation, lubricate the camshaft journals with clean engine oil. Lubricate the lobes with Molykote or the equivalent.

173 CID (2.8L) ENGINE

1. Disconnect the negative battery cable. Drain the cooling system. Remove the radiator. On some vehicles it will be necessary to remove the grille and headlight bezel assembly. Remove the intake manifold.

2. If equipped with air condition, it may be necessary to reposition the condenser in order to withdraw the camshaft from the engine. If the condenser must be removed, properly discharge the system before condenser removal.

3. Remove the rocker cover. Remove the rockers and pushrods. Keep them in order for reinstallation. Remove the valve lifters. Keep them in order for reinstallation.

4. Remove the engine front cover. As required, remove the

fuel pump and the fuel pump pushrod. Remove the timing chain and camshaft sprocket.

5. Carefully remove the camshaft from the engine.

6. Installation is the reverse of the removal procedure. Before installation, lubricate the camshaft journals with clean engine oil. Lubricate the lobes with Molykote or the equivalent.

ASTRO/SAFARI

Removal and Installation

151 CID (2.5L) ENGINE

1. Disconnect the negative battery cable. Remove the engine cover. Drain the cooling system. Remove the radiator.

2. Remove the engine side cover. Remove the air cleaner assembly. Remove the EGR valve.

3. Disconnect the power steering reservoir and position it to the side. Remove the drive belts and pulleys. Remove the upper fan shroud. Remove the front cover.

4. Rotate the crankshaft until the timing marks are in alignment. Remove the distributor assembly. Remove the oil pump driveshaft cover and driveshaft.

5. Remove the rocker cover. Remove the rockers and pushrods. Keep them in order for reinstallation. Remove the valve lifters. Keep them in order for reinstallation.

6. If equipped with air condition, it may be necessary to reposition the condenser in order to withdraw the camshaft from the engine. If the condenser must be removed, properly discharge the system before condenser removal.

7. As required, remove the headlight bezel and grille assembly.

8. Remove the camshaft thrust plate bolts. Carefully remove the camshaft from the vehicle.

9. Installation is the reverse of the removal procedure. Before installation lubricate the camshaft journals with clean engine oil. Lubricate the lobes with Molykote or the equivalent.

260 CID (4.3L) ENGINE

1. Disconnect the negative battery cable. Drain the cooling system. Remove the radiator. On some vehicles it will be necessary to remove the grille and headlight bezel assembly. Remove the intake manifold.

2. If equipped with air condition, it may be necessary to reposition the condenser in order to withdraw the camshaft from the engine. If the condenser must be removed, properly discharge the system before condenser removal.

3. Remove the rocker cover. Remove the rockers and pushrods. Keep them in order for reinstallation. Remove the valve lifters. Keep them in order for reinstallation.

4. Remove the engine front cover. As required, remove the fuel pump and the fuel pump pushrod. Remove the timing chain and camshaft sprocket.

5. Carefully remove the camshaft from the engine.

6. Installation is the reverse of the removal procedure. Before installation lubricate the camshaft journals with clean engine oil. Lubricate the lobes with Molykote or the equivalent.

PICK UP, BLAZER/JIMMY, SUBURBAN AND VAN

Removal and Installation

252 CID (4.1L) AND 292 CID (4.8L) ENGINES

1. Disconnect the negative battery cable. Remove the engine from the vehicle.

2. Remove the rocker cover. Remove the rockers and pushrods. Keep them in order for reinstallation. Remove the valve lifters. Keep them in order for reinstallation.

3. Remove the fuel pump. Remove the front cover assembly. Remove the timing chain and camshaft sprocket.

4. Remove the camshaft to thrust plate retaining bolts. Carefully remove the camshaft from the engine.

5. Installation is the reverse of the removal procedure. Before installation lubricate the camshaft journals with clean engine oil. Lubricate the lobes with Molykote or the equivalent.

EXCEPT 252 CID (4.1L) AND 292 (4.8L) ENGINES

1. Disconnect the negative battery cable. On Vans, remove the engine cover. Drain the cooling system. Remove the radiator. On some vehicles it will be necessary to remove the grille and headlight bezel assembly. Remove the intake manifold.

2. If equipped with air condition, it may be necessary to reposition the condenser in order to withdraw the camshaft from the engine. If the condenser must be removed, properly discharge the system before condenser removal.

3. Remove the rocker cover. Remove the rockers and pushrods. Keep them in order for reinstallation. Remove the valve lifters. Keep them in order for reinstallation.

4. Remove the engine front cover. As required, remove the fuel pump and the fuel pump pushrod. Remove the timing chain and camshaft sprocket.

5. Carefully remove the camshaft from the engine.

6. Installation is the reverse of the removal procedure. Before installation lubricate the camshaft journals with clean engine oil. Lubricate the lobes with Molykote or the equivalent.

Piston and Connecting Rods

IDENTIFICATION

ENGINES

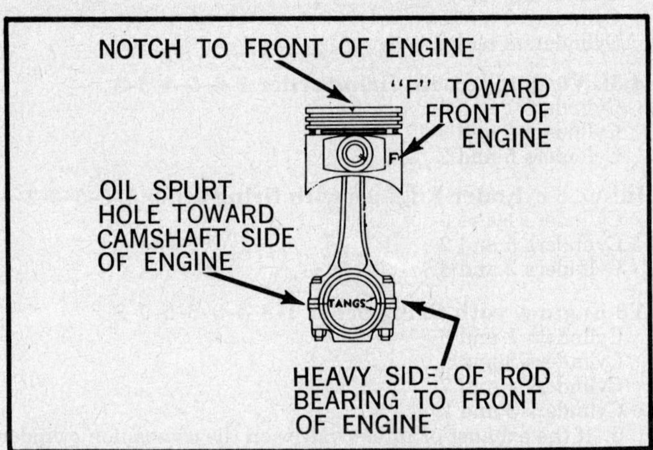

Correct relationship of piston and rod on 250 engine

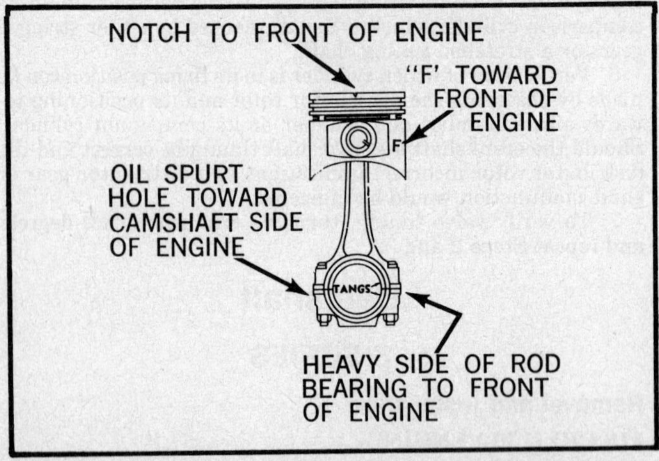

Correct relationship of piston and rod on 292 engines

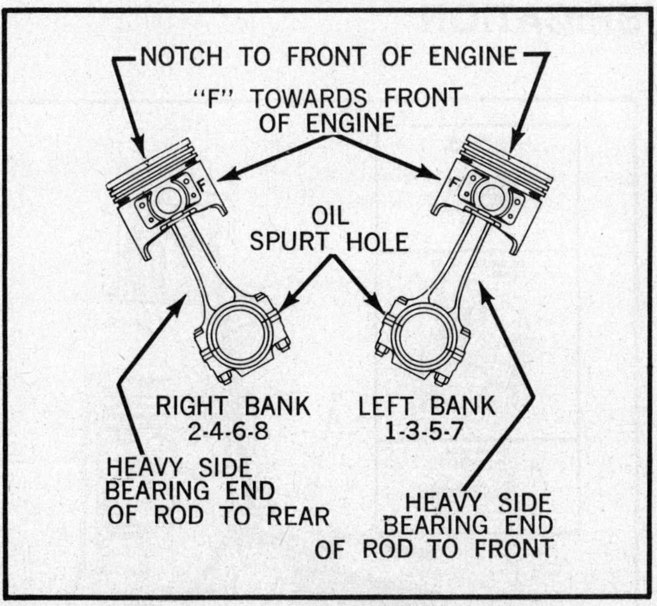

Correct relationship of piston and rod on 305 and 350 engines

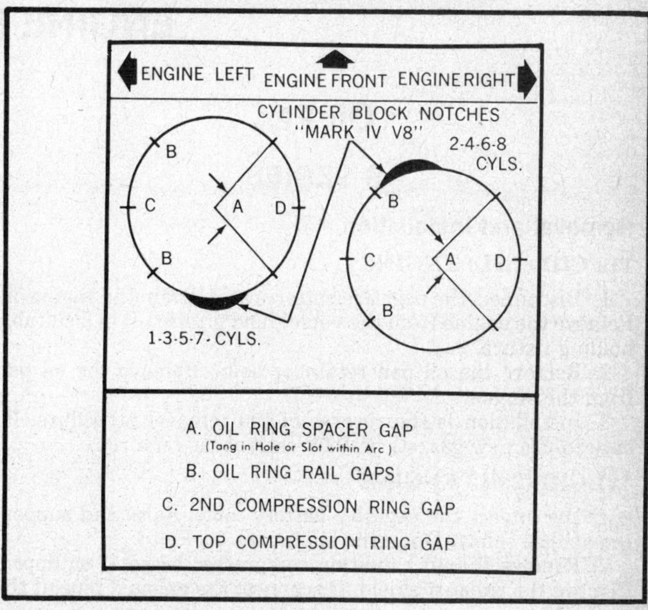

Ring gap location – V8 – typical

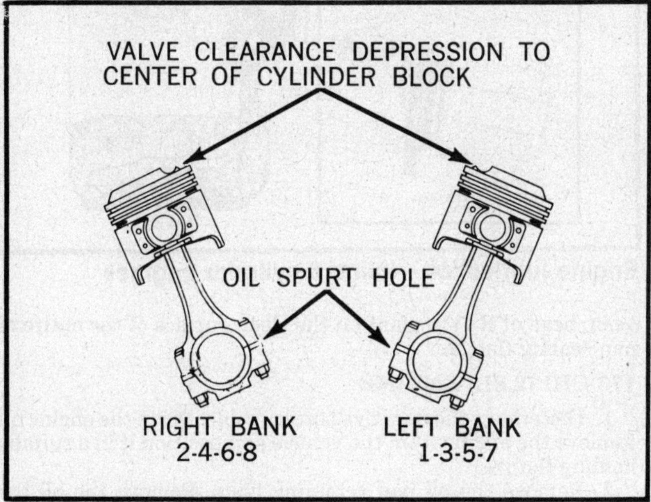

Correct relationship of piston and rod 454 CID (7.4L) engine

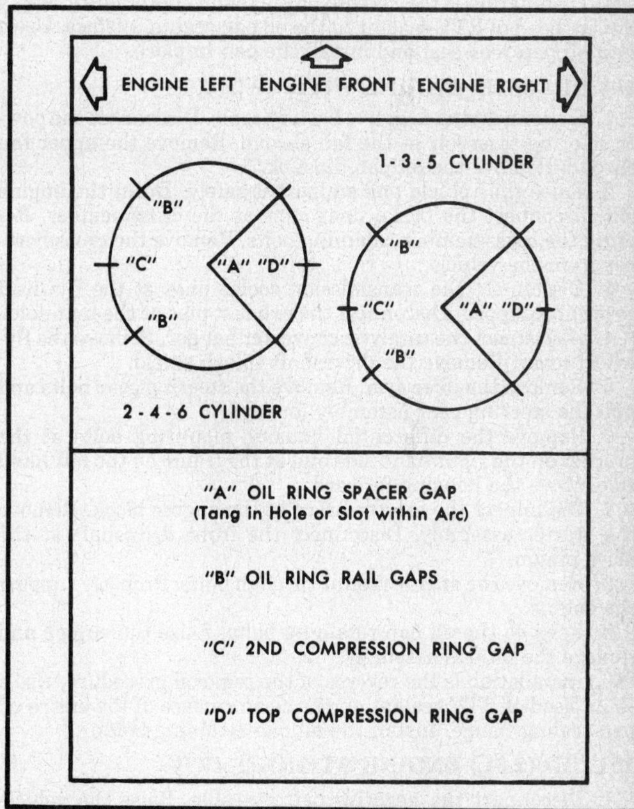

Piston ring gap locations – V6 engine

ENGINE LUBRICATION

Oil Pan

S SERIES

Removal and Installation

119 CID (1.9L) ENGINE

1. Disconnect the negative battery cable. Drain the engine oil. Remove the engine from the vehicle and position it in a suitable holding fixture.
2. Remove the oil pan retaining bolts. Remove the oil pan from the engine.
3. Installation is the reverse of the removal procedure. Be sure to use new gaskets or RTV sealant, as required.

121 CID (2.0L) ENGINE

1. Disconnect the negative battery cable. Raise and support the vehicle safely. Drain the engine oil.
2. Remove the air condition compressor brace, if equipped. Remove the exhaust shield. Disconnect the exhaust pipe at the manifold.
3. Remove the starter. Remove the flywheel cover. Remove the oil pan retaining bolts. Remove the oil pan from the engine.
4. Installation is the reverse of the removal procedure. Apply a ⅛ in. bead of RTV sealant to the oil pan sealing surface. Use a new oil pan rear seal and install the pan in place.

151 CID (2.5L) ENGINE WITH 4WD

1. Disconnect the negative battery cable. Disconnect the power steering reservoir at the fan shroud. Remove the upper fan shroud. Remove the oil pan dipstick.
2. Raise the vehicle and support it safely. Drain the engine oil. Disconnect the brake lines clips at the crossmember. Remove the crossmember retaining bolts. Remove the crossmember from the vehicle.
3. Disconnect the transmission cooler lines at the flywheel cover, if equipped. Disconnect the exhaust pipe at the manifold.
4. Disconnect the catalytic converter hanger. Remove the flywheel cover. Remove the driveshaft splash shield.
5. Remove the idler arm. Remove the steering gear bolts and pull the steering gear assembly forward.
6. Remove the differential housing mounting bolts at the bracket on the right hand side and at the frame on the left hand side. Move the housing forward.
7. Disconnect the starter brace at the engine block. Remove the starter assembly. Disconnect the front driveshaft at the drive pinion.
8. Remove the engine mount through bolts. Properly support the engine.
9. Remove the oil pan retaining bolts. Raise the engine and remove the oil pan assembly.
10. Installation is the reverse of the removal procedure. Use a ⅛ in. bead of RTV sealant on the clean surface of the entire oil pan sealing flange. Install the oil pan retaining bolts.

151 CID (2.5L) ENGINE WITHOUT 4WD

1. Disconnect the negative battery cable. Raise the vehicle and support it safely. Drain the engine oil.
2. Remove the strut rods. Remove the torque converter cover. Disconnect the exhaust pipe at the catalytic converter hanger. Disconnect the exhaust pipe at the manifold.
3. Disconnect the starter brace at the engine block. remove the starter assembly. Disconnect the oil cooler lines at the oil pan.
4. Remove the oil pan retaining bolts. Remove the oil pan from the engine.
5. Installation is the reverse of the removal procedure. Use a ⅛ in. bead of RTV sealant on the clean surface of the entire oil pan sealing flange.

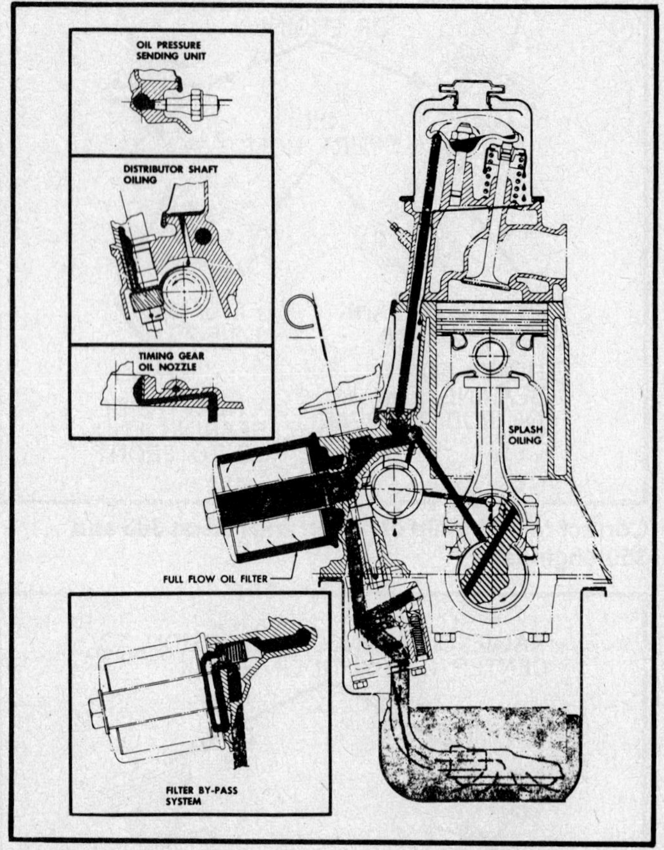

Engine lubrication – inline 6 cylinder engines

173 CID (2.8L) ENGINE

1. Disconnect the negative battery cable. Drain the engine oil. Remove the engine from the vehicle and position it in a suitable holding fixture.
2. Remove the oil pan retaining bolts. Remove the oil pan from the engine.
3. Installation is the reverse of the removal procedure. Be sure to use new gaskets or RTV sealant, as required.
4. If using RTV sealant, run a ⅛ in. bead of sealer along the entire sealing surface of the pan.

ASTRO/SAFARI

Removal and Installation

151 CID (2.5L) ENGINE

1. Disconnect the negative battery cable. Remove the engine cover. Raise the vehicle and support it safely. Drain the engine oil.
2. Remove the strut rods. Remove the torque converter cover. Disconnect the exhaust pipe at the catalytic converter hanger. Disconnect the exhaust pipe at the manifold.
3. Disconnect the starter brace at the engine block. remove the starter assembly. Disconnect the oil cooler lines at the oil pan.
4. Remove the oil pan retaining bolts. Remove the oil pan from the engine.

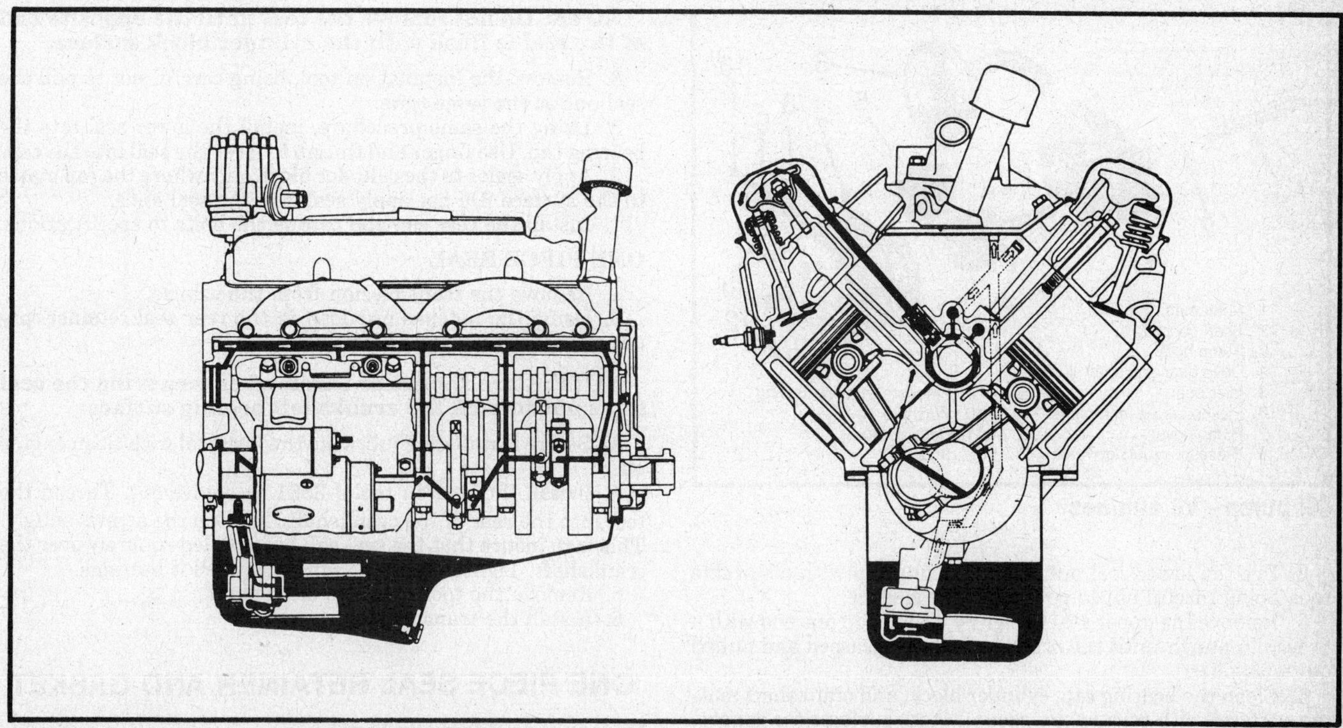

Engine lubrication—305, 350 cu.in. engines

5. Installation is the reverse of the removal procedure. Use a ⅛ in. bead of RTV sealant on the clean surface of the entire oil pan sealing flange.

260 CID (4.3L) ENGINE

1. Disconnect the negative battery cable. Raise the vehicle and support it safely. Drain the engine oil.
2. Disconnect the exhaust pipes at the manifolds. Remove the engine strut rods at the flywheel cover.
3. Remove the flywheel cover. Remove the starter assembly. Remove the engine mount trim bolts. Properly raise the engine to gain working clearance.
4. Remove the oil pan retaining bolts. Remove the oil pan from the vehicle.
5. Installation is the reverse of the removal procedure. Be sure to use new gaskets or RTV sealant, as required.

PICK UP, BLAZER/JIMMY, SUBURBAN AND VAN

Removal and Installation

252 CID (4.1L) AND 292 (4.8L) ENGINES

1. Disconnect the negative battery cable. Raise the vehicle and support it safely. Drain the engine oil.
2. Remove the flywheel cover. Remove the starter assembly.
3. Remove the engine mount through bolts from the engine front mounts. Raise the engine enough to remove the oil pan.
4. Remove the oil pan retaining bolts. Remove the oil pan from the engine.
5. Installation is the reverse of the removal procedure. Use new gaskets or RTV sealant, as required.

EXCEPT 252 CID (4.1L) AND 292 (4.8L) ENGINES

1. Disconnect the negative battery cable. Remove the air cleaner assembly, as required. Remove the distributor cap, if necessary.
2. Raise the vehicle and support it safely. Drain the engine oil. Remove the flywheel cover. Remove the starter assembly.
3. On some vehicles equipped with V6 engine, remove the strut rods at the flywheel cover, as necessary.
4. On 4wd vehicles with automatic transmission, remove the strut rods at the engine mounts.
5. On vehicles equipped with gauges, remove the oil pressure line from the side of the engine block to avoid damage when raising the engine. As necessary, remove the oil filter.
6. Properly raise the engine to gain clearance in order to remove the oil pan. Remove the oil pan retaining bolts. Remove the oil pan from the engine.
6. Installation is the reverse of the removal procedure. Use new gaskets or RTV sealant, as required.

Oil Pump

Removal and Installation

1. Disconnect the negative battery cable. Remove the oil pan.
2. On some engines it will be necessary to first remove the oil suction pipe at the housing, be sure not to disturb the screen on the pick up pipe.
3. If equipped,remove the oil pan baffle assembly.
4. Remove the oil pump mounting bolts. Remove the oil pump from the engine.
5. Installation is the reverse of the removal procedure. The pump should slide easily into place, if not, remove and relocate the slot. Pack the oil pump gear cavity with petroleum jelly, prior to installation.

Rear Main Bearing Oil Seal

Removal and Installation

EXCEPT ONE PIECE SEAL

1. Remove the oil pan. Remove the oil pump where required. Remove the rear main bearing cap.

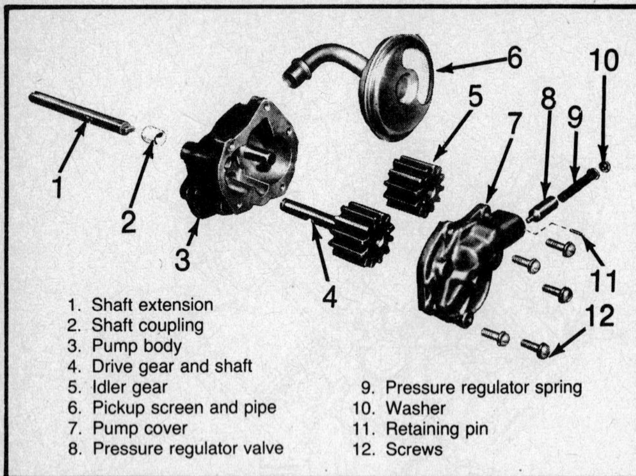

Oil pump—V8 engines

2. Pry the lower seal out of the bearing cap with a suitable tool, being careful not to gouge the cap surface.
3. Remove the upper seal by lightly tapping on one end with a brass pin punch until the other end can be grasped and pulled out with pliers.
4. Clean the bearing cap, cylinder block, and crankshaft mating surfaces with solvent. Inspect all these surfaces for gouges, nicks, and burrs.
5. Apply light engine oil on the seal lips and bead, but keep the seal ends clean.
6. Insert the tip of the installation tool between the crankshaft and the seal of the cylinder block. Place the seal between the crankshaft and the seal of the cylinder block. Place the seal between the tip of the tool and the crankshaft, so that the bead contacts the tip of the tool.
7. Be sure that the seal lip is facing the front of the engine, and work the seal around the crankshaft, using the installation tool to protect the seal from the corner of the cylinder block.

NOTE: Do not remove the tool until the opposite end of the seal is flush with the cylinder block surface.

8. Remove the installation tool, being careful not to pull the seal out at the same time.
9. Using the same procedure, install the lower seal into the bearing cap. Use finger and thumb to lever the seal into the cap.
10. Apply sealer to the cylinder block only where the cap mates to the surface. Do not apply sealer to the seal ends.
11. Install the rear cap and torque the bolts to specifications.

ONE PIECE SEAL

1. Remove the transmission from the vehicle.
2. Using the notches provided in the rear seal retainer, pry out the seal using the proper tool.

NOTE: Care should be taken when removing the seal so as not to nick the crankshaft sealing surface.

3. Before installation lubricate the new seal with clean engine oil.
4. Install the seal on tool J-3561 or equivalent. Thread the tool into the rear of the crankshaft. Tighten the screws snugly. This is to insure that the seal will be installed squarely over the crankshaft. Tighten the tool wing nut until it bottoms.
5. Remove the tool from the crankshaft.
6. Install the transmission.

ONE PIECE SEAL RETAINER AND GASKET

Removal and Installation

1. Remove the transmission from the vehicle.
2. Remove the oil pan bolts. Lower the oil pan.
3. Remove the retainer and seal assembly.
4. Remove the gasket.

NOTE: Whenever the retainer is removed a new retainer gasket and rear main seal must be installed.

5. Installation is the reverse of the removal procedure. Once the oil pan has been installed, the new rear main oil seal can be installed.

FRONT SUSPENSION

I-Beam Axle

Removal and Installation

P SERIES

1. Raise and support the vehicle safely. Support the axle to relieve tension on the springs. Remove the tire and wheel assembly.
2. Remove the steering arm, steering knuckle and spindle assembly.
3. Remove the shock absorber to axle retaining bolts. Remove the stabilizer link from the stabilizer bar. Use tool J-6627-A to seperate the stabilizer bar from the stabilizer link.
4. Remove the stabilizer link from the axle. Remove the spring retaining bolts. Remove the spring. Remove the steering damper from the axle.
5. Lower the floor jack and remove the axle assembly from the vehicle.
6. Installation is the reverse of the removal procedure.

Coil Spring

Removal and Installation

S SERIES 2WD

1. Raise and support the vehicle safely. Remove the shock absorber lower retaining screws.
2. Push the shock absorber through the control arm and into the spring.
3. With the vehicle supported so that the control arms hang free, install tool J-23028. Secure the tool using a suitable jack.
4. Remove the stabilizer to lower control arm attachment. Raise the jack and remove the tension on the lower control arm bolts.
5. Install a safety chain around the spring and through the lower control arm. Remove the lower control arm rear bolt, than remove the other retaining bolt.
6. Lower the jack and allow the lower control arm to hang free. Remove the spring assembly from the vehicle.

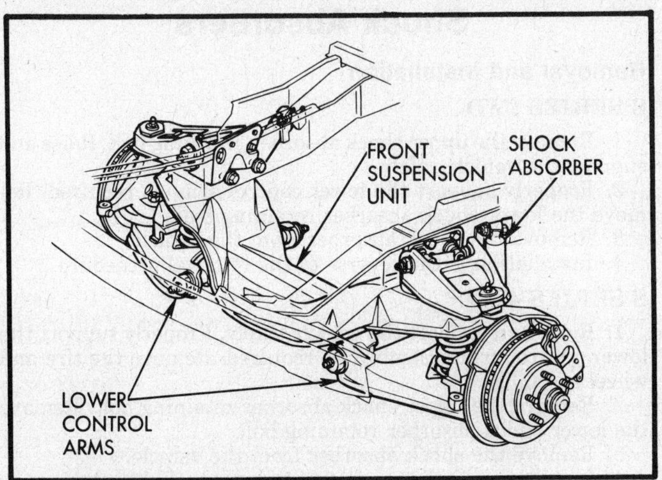

Coil spring suspension

7. Installation is the reverse of the removal procedure. When positioning the spring in the lower control arm, be sure that the spring insulator is in the proper position before lifting the control arm in place.
8. Check and adjust front alignment, as required.

ASTRO/SAFARI

1. Raise and support the vehicle safely. Remove the shock absorber lower retaining screws.
2. Push the shock absorber through the control arm and into the spring.
3. With the vehicle supported so that the control arms hang free, install tool J-23028. Secure the tool using a suitable jack.
4. Remove the stabilizer to lower control arm attachment. Raise the jack and remove the tension on the lower control arm bolts.
5. Install a safety chain around the spring and through the lower control arm. Remove the lower control arm rear bolt, than remove the other retaining bolt.
6. Lower the jack and allow the lower control arm to hang free. Remove the spring assembly from the vehicle.
7. Installation is the reverse of the removal procedure. When positioning the spring in the lower control arm, be sure that the spring insulator is in the proper position before lifting the control arm in place.
8. Check and adjust front alignment, as required.

PICK UP (1982-87), BLAZER/JIMMY, SUBURBAN AND VAN 2WD

1. Raise and support the vehicle safely. Remove the shock absorber lower retaining screws and push the shock absorber to the side..
2. With the vehicle supported so that the control arms hang free, install tool J-23028. Secure the tool using a suitable jack. Install a safety chain around the spring and through the lower control arm.
4. Raise the jack and remove the tension on the lower control cross shaft. Remove the bolts securing the cross shaft to the crossmember.
5. Lower the jack and allow the lower control arm to hang free. Remove the spring assembly from the vehicle.
6. Installation is the reverse of the removal procedure. When positioning the spring in the lower control arm, be sure that the spring insulator is in the proper position before lifting the control arm in place.
7. Check and adjust front alignment, as required.

PICK UP (1988) 2WD

1. Raise and support the vehicle safely. Allow the control arms to hang free. Remove the tire and wheel assembly. Remove the shock absorber assembly, as required.
2. With the vehicle supported so that the control arms hang free, install tool J-23028. Secure the tool using a suitable jack. Install a safety chain around the spring and through the lower control arm.
3. Remove the stabilizer shaft from the lower control arm. Raise the jack and remove the tension on the lower control arm bolts.
4. Remove the lower control arm rear bolt, than remove the other retaining bolt.
5. Lower the jack and allow the lower control arm to hang free. Remove the spring assembly from the vehicle.
6. Installation is the reverse of the removal procedure. When positioning the spring in the lower control arm, be sure that the spring insulator is in the proper position before lifting the control arm in place.
7. Check and adjust front alignment, as required.

Leaf Spring

Removal and Installation

PICK UP (1982-87), BLAZER/JIMMY AND SUBURBAN 4WD

1. Raise and support the vehicle safely. Relieve the tension from the spring by positioning a suitable lifting device under the axle assembly.
2. Remove the shackle upper retaining bolt. Remove the front spring eye bolt.
3. Remove the spring to axle U bolt nuts. Remove the spring, lower plate and spring pads.
4. Installation is the reverse of the removal procedure.
5. Check and adjust front alignment, as required.

P SERIES WITH I-BEAM SUSPENSION

1. Raise and support the vehicle safely. Support the axle to relieve tension on the springs. Remove the tire and wheel assembly.
2. Remove the shock absorber to axle retaining bolts. Remove the stabilizer link from the stabilizer bar. Use tool J-6627-A to separate the stabilizer bar from the stabilizer link.
3. Remove the stabilizer link from the axle. Remove the spring retaining bolts. Remove the leaf spring from the vehicle.
4. Installation is the reverse of the removal procedure.
5. Check and adjust front alignment, as required.

Torsion Bar

Removal and Installation

S SERIES 4WD

1. Raise and support the vehicle safely.
2. Using tool J-22517-C, remove the torsion bar adjusting screw, record the number of turns on the adjusting bolt for reinstallation.
3. Remove the support retainer retaining bolts.
4. Slide the torsion bar forward in the lower control arm until the torsion bar clears the support. Pull down on the bar and remove it from the control arm.
5. Remove the required components and remove the torsion bar from the vehicle.
6. Installation is the reverse of the removal procedure. The gap between the torsion bar and the support assembly should not exceed 6.0mm.
5. Check and adjust front alignment, as required.

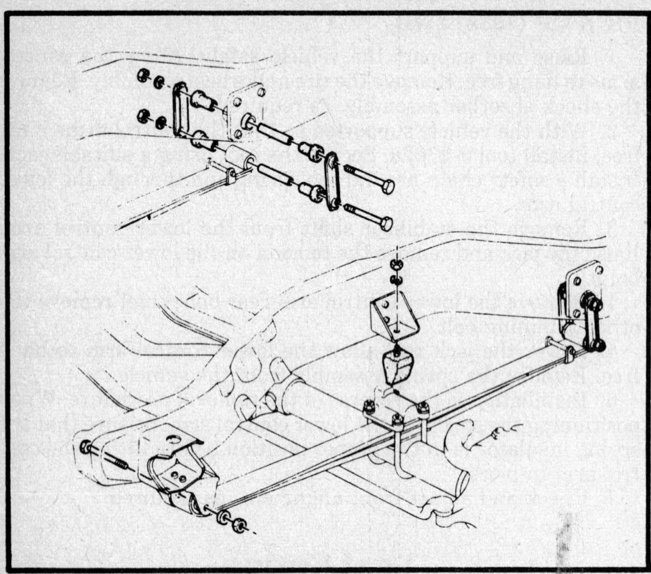

Spring assembly—front drive axle

TIGHTENING SEQUENCE

1. INSTALL ALL FOUR NUTS TO UNIFORM ENGAGEMENT ON U-BOLTS TO RETAIN AND POSITION ANCHOR POSITION (PERPENDICULAR TO PLATE IN DESIGN AXIS OF U-BOLTS).
2. TORQUE NUTS IN POSITIONS 1 AND 3 TO 10-25 FT. LBS.
3. TORQUE ALL NUTS TO FULL TORQUE IN FOLLOWING SEQUENCE: 2-4-1-3

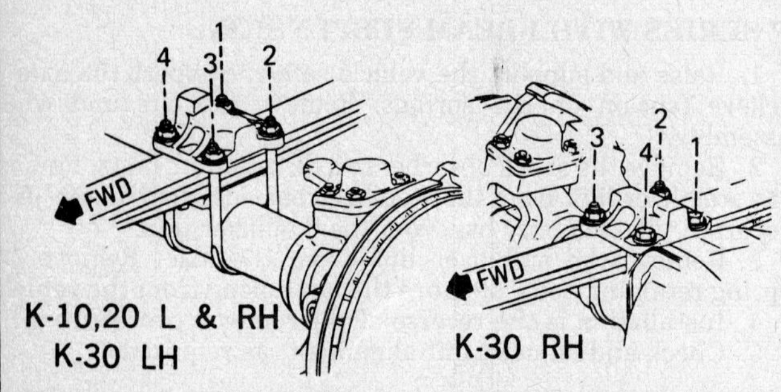

U-bolt tightening sequence—front drive axle

PICK UP (1988) 4WD

1. Raise and support the vehicle safely.
2. As required use tool J-22517-C, to remove the torsion bar adjusting screw. Record the number of turns on the adjusting bolt for reinstallation.
3. Remove the support retainer retaining bolts.
4. Slide the torsion bar forward in the lower control arm until the torsion bar clears the support. Pull down on the bar and remove it from the control arm.
5. Remove the required components and remove the torsion bar from the vehicle.
6. Installation is the reverse of the removal procedure. The gap between the torsion bar adjusting arm and the support assembly should not exceed 1.3 in.
7. Check and adjust front alignment, as required.

Shock Absorbers

Removal and Installation

S SERIES 2WD

1. Remove the upper shock absorber retaining bolt. Raise and support the vehicle safely.
2. Properly support the lower control arm, as required. Remove the lower shock absorber retaining bolt.
3. Remove the shock absorber from the vehicle.
4. Installation is the reverse of the removal procedure.

S SERIES 4WD

1. Raise and support the vehicle safely. Properly support the lower control arm assembly, as required. Remove the tire and wheel assembly.
2. Remove the upper shock absorber retaining bolt. Remove the lower shock absorber retaining bolt.
3. Remove the shock absorber from the vehicle.
4. Installation is the reverse of the removal procedure.

ASTRO/SAFARI

1. Remove the upper shock absorber retaining bolt. Raise and support the vehicle safely.
2. Properly support the lower control arm, as required. Remove the lower shock absorber retaining bolt.
3. Remove the shock absorber from the vehicle.
4. Installation is the reverse of the removal procedure.

PICK UP (1982-87), BLAZER/JIMMY, SUBURBAN AND VAN

1. Raise and support the vehicle safely. Properly support the lower control arm assembly, as required. Remove the tire and wheel assembly.
2. Remove the upper shock absorber retaining bolt. Remove the lower shock absorber retaining bolt. Vehicles equipped with quad shocks have a spacer between them.
3. Remove the shock absorber from the vehicle.
4. Installation is the reverse of the removal procedure.

PICK UP (1988) 2WD

1. Remove the upper shock absorber retaining bolt. Raise and support the vehicle safely.
2. Properly support the lower control arm, as required. Remove the lower shock absorber retaining bolt.
3. Remove the shock absorber from the vehicle.
4. Installation is the reverse of the removal procedure.

PICK UP (1988) 4WD

1. Raise and support the vehicle safely. Properly support the lower control arm assembly, as required. Remove the tire and wheel assembly.
2. Remove the upper shock absorber retaining bolt. Remove the lower shock absorber retaining bolt. Vehicles equipped with quad shocks have a spacer between them.
3. Remove the shock absorber from the vehicle.
4. Installation is the reverse of the removal procedure.

Upper Control Arm

Removal and Installation

S SERIES

1. Note and record the amount of shims. These shims must be installed in the same location as removed. Remove the nuts and the shims.
2. Raise and support the vehicle safely. Properly support the lower control arm, using the necessary equipment. The control arm must be supported so that the spring and the control arm remain intact.
3. Remove the tire and wheel assembly. Loosen the upper ball

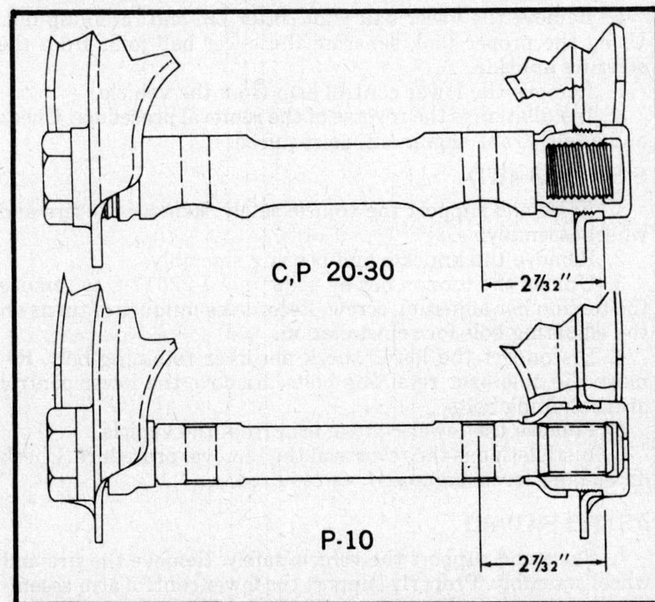

Correctly positioned upper control arm steel bushings

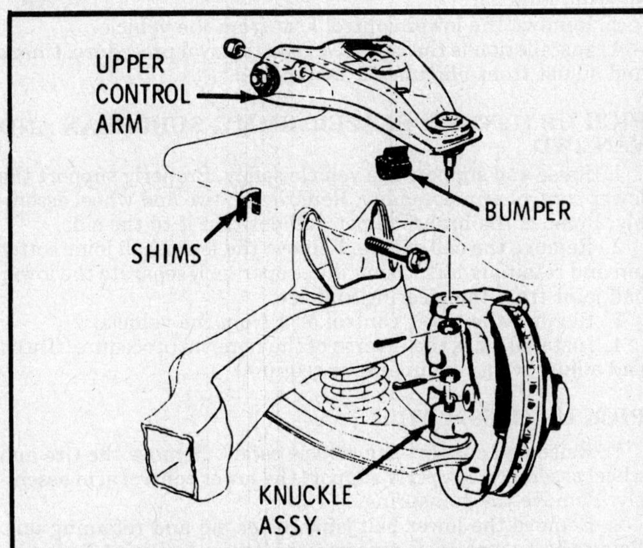

Upper control arm assembly on S-series

joint from the steering knuckle, using the proper tool. Support the hub assembly.

4. Remove the upper control arm retaining bolts. Remove the upper control arm from the vehicle.

5. Installation is the reverse of the removal procedure. Check and adjust front alignment, as required.

ASTRO/SAFARI

1. Note and record the amount of shims. These shims must be installed in the same location as removed. Remove the nuts and the shims.

2. Raise and support the vehicle safely. Properly support the lower control arm, using the necessary equipment. The control arm must be supported so that the spring and the control arm remain intact.

3. Remove the tire and wheel assembly. Loosen the upper ball joint from the steering knuckle, using the proper tool. Support the hub assembly.

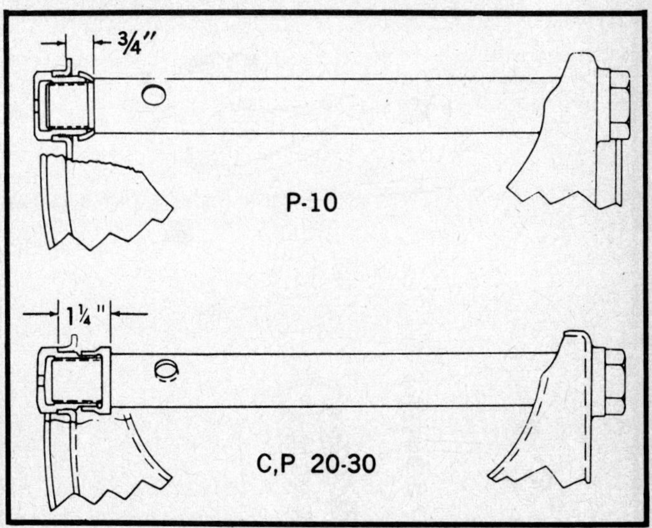

Correctly positioned lower control arm steel bushings

4. Remove the upper control arm retaining bolts. Remove the upper control arm from the vehicle.

5. Installation is the reverse of the removal procedure. Check and adjust front alignment, as required.

PICK UP (1982-87), BLAZER/JIMMY, SUBURBAN AND VAN 2WD

1. Note and record the amount of shims. These shims must be installed in the same location as removed. Remove the nuts and the shims.

2. Raise and support the vehicle safely. Properly support the lower control arm, using the necessary equipment. The control arm must be supported so that the spring and the control arm remain intact.

3. Remove the tire and wheel assembly. Remove the brake caliper assembly and position it to the side. Loosen the upper ball joint from the steering knuckle, using the proper tool. Support the hub assembly.

4. Remove the upper control arm retaining bolts. Remove the upper control arm from the vehicle.

5. Installation is the reverse of the removal procedure. Check and adjust front alignment, as required.

PICK UP (1988)

1. Disconnect the negative battery cable. Remove the air cleaner assembly, as necessary.

2. Raise and support the vehicle safely. Support the lower control arm, using the proper equipment. The control arm must be supported so that the spring and the control arm remain intact.

3. Remove the tire and wheel assembly. Remove the brake hose and position it out of the way. Disconnect the upper ball joint from the steering knuckle.

4. Remove the upper control arm retaining bolts. Note the amount and location of any shims, for reinstallation.

5. Remove the upper control arm from the vehicle.

6. Installation is the reverse of the removal procedure. Check and adjust front alignment, as required.

Lower Control Arm

Removal and Installation

S SERIES 2WD

1. Raise and support the vehicle safely. Remove the tire and wheel assembly. Properly support the lower control arm assembly. Remove the coil spring.

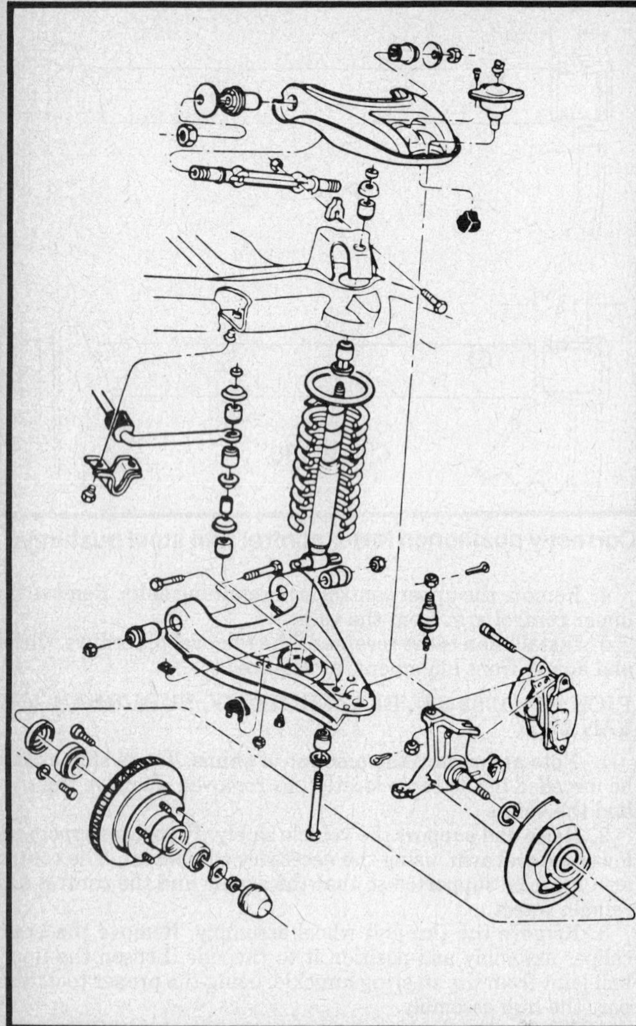

Exploded view of front suspension components, S series (2WD) and Astro van models

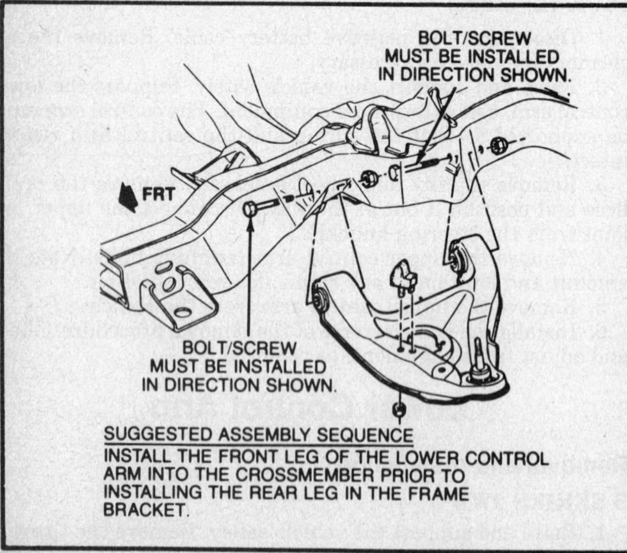
BOLT/SCREW
MUST BE INSTALLED
IN DIRECTION SHOWN.
FRT
BOLT/SCREW
MUST BE INSTALLED
IN DIRECTION SHOWN.
SUGGESTED ASSEMBLY SEQUENCE
INSTALL THE FRONT LEG OF THE LOWER CONTROL ARM INTO THE CROSSMEMBER PRIOR TO INSTALLING THE REAR LEG IN THE FRAME BRACKET.

Lower control arm assembly on S-series

2. Remove the lower ball joint cotter pin and retaining nut. Using the proper tool, separate the lower ball joint from the steering knuckle.
3. Remove the lower control arm from the vehicle.
4. Installation is the reverse of the removal procedure. Check and adjust front alignment, as required.

S SERIES 4WD

1. Raise and support the vehicle safely. Remove the tire and wheel assembly.
2. Remove the knuckle and bearing assembly.
3. Unload the torsion bar by using tool J-22517-C to remove the torsion bar adjusting screw. Record the number of turns on the adjusting bolt for reinstallation.
4. Disconnect the lower shock absorber retaining bolt. Remove the stabilizer retaining bolts. Remove the lower control arm retaining bolts.
5. Remove the lower control arm from the vehicle.
6. Installation is the reverse of the removal procedure. Check and adjust front alignment, as required.

ASTRO/SAFARI

1. Raise and support the vehicle safely. Remove the tire and wheel assembly. Properly support the lower control arm assembly. Remove the coil spring.
2. Remove the lower ball joint cotter pin and retaining nut. Using the proper tool, separate the lower ball joint from the steering knuckle.
3. Remove the lower control arm from the vehicle.
4. Installation is the reverse of the removal procedure. Check and adjust front alignment, as required.

PICK UP (1982-87), BLAZER/JIMMY, SUBURBAN AND VAN 2WD

1. Raise and support the vehicle safely. Properly support the lower control arm assembly. Remove the tire and wheel assembly. Remove the brake caliper and position it to the side.
2. Remove the coil spring. Remove the lower ball joint cotter pin and retaining nut. Using the proper tool, separate the lower ball joint from the steering knuckle.
3. Remove the lower control arm from the vehicle.
4. Installation is the reverse of the removal procedure. Check and adjust front alignment, as required.

PICK UP (1988) 2WD

1. Raise and support the vehicle safely. Remove the tire and wheel assembly. Properly support the lower control arm assembly. Remove the coil spring.
2. Remove the lower ball joint cotter pin and retaining nut. Using the proper tool, seperate the lower ball joint from the steering knuckle.
3. Remove the lower control arm from the vehicle.
4. Installation is the reverse of the removal procedure. Check and adjust front alignment, as required.

PICK UP (1988) 4WD

1. Raise and support the vehicle safely. Remove the tire and wheel assembly.
2. Unload the torsion bar by using tool J-22517-C to remove the torsion bar adjusting screw. Record the number of turns on the adjusting bolt for reinstallation.
3. Remove the stabilizer bar retaining bolts. Disconnect the lower shock absorber retaining bolt and position the shock absorber ou of the way.
4. Properly support the lower control arm. Separate the ball joint from the steering knuckle, using the proper tool.
5. Remove the lower control arm to fram retaining bolts. Remove the lower control arm from the vehicle.
6. Installation is the reverse of the removal procedure. Check and adjust front alignment, as required.

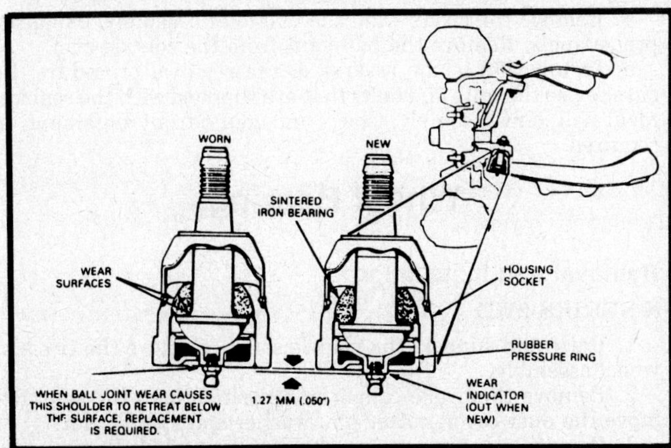

Ball joint wear indicators

Ball Joints

UPPER BALL JOINT

Removal and Installation

S SERIES

1. Raise and support the vehicle safely. Properly support the lower control arm, using the necessary equipment. The control arm must be supported so that the spring and the control arm remain intact.
2. Remove the tire and wheel assembly. As required, remove the brake caliper and position it to the side.
3. Remove the cotter pin and the upper ball joint retaining bolt. Using the proper tool separate the upper joint from its mounting. Support the knuckle assembly so that its weight will not damage the brake hose.
4. Remove the rivets from the ball joint assembly, using the proper tools. Remove the ball joint from the upper control arm.
5. Installation is the reverse of the removal procedure. Be sure to use the nuts and bolts that are supplied with the replacement ball joint assembly. Check and adjust front alignment, as required.

ASTRO/SAFARI

1. Raise and support the vehicle safely. Properly support the lower control arm, using the necessary equipment. The control arm must be supported so that the spring and the control arm remain intact.
2. Remove the tire and wheel assembly. As required, remove the brake caliper and position it to the side.
3. Remove the cotter pin and the upper ball joint retaining bolt. Using the proper tool separate the upper joint from its mounting. Support the knuckle assembly so that its weight will not damage the brake hose.
4. Remove the rivets from the ball joint assembly, using the proper tools. Remove the ball joint from the upper control arm.
5. Installation is the reverse of the removal procedure. Be sure to use the nuts and bolts that are supplied with the replacement ball joint assembly. Check and adjust front alignment, as required.

PICK UP (1982-87), BLAZER/JIMMY, SUBURBAN AND VAN 2WD

1. Raise and support the vehicle safely. Properly support the lower control arm, using the necessary equipment. The control arm must be supported so that the spring and the control arm remain intact.
2. Remove the tire and wheel assembly. Remove the brake caliper and position it to the side.
3. Remove the cotter pin and the upper ball joint retaining bolt. Using the proper tool separate the upper joint from its mounting. Support the knuckle assembly so that its weight will not damage the brake hose.
4. Remove the rivets from the ball joint assembly, using the proper tools. Remove the ball joint from the upper control arm.
5. Installation is the reverse of the removal procedure. Be sure to use the nuts and bolts that are supplied with the replacement ball joint assembly. Check and adjust front alignment, as required.

PICK UP (1982-87), BLAZER/JIMMY AND SUBURBAN 4WD

1. Raise and support the vehicle safely. Remove the tire and wheel assembly.
2. Remove the hub and rotor assembly. Remove the spindle.
3. Remove the steering knuckle assembly. If removing the left axle yoke ball joints, remove the steering arm. Position the steering knuckle assembly in a suitable vise.
4. The lower ball joint must be removed before service can be performed on the upper ball joint. first. Press the lower ball joint from the knuckle assembly, using the proper tools.
5. Press the upper ball joint from the knuckle assembly, using the proper tools.
6. Installation is the reverse of the removal procedure. Check and adjust front alignment, as required.

PICK UP (1988)

1. Raise and support the vehicle safely. Properly support the lower control arm, using the necessary equipment. The control arm must be supported so that the spring and the control arm remain intact.
2. Remove the tire and wheel assembly. Remove the brake caliper and position it to the side.
3. Remove the cotter pin and the upper ball joint retaining bolt. Using the proper tool separate the upper joint from its mounting. Support the knuckle assembly so that its weight will not damage the brake hose.
4. Remove the rivets from the ball joint assembly, using the proper tools. Remove the ball joint from the upper control arm.
5. Installation is the reverse of the removal procedure. Be sure to use the nuts and bolts that are supplied with the replacement ball joint assembly. Check and adjust front alignment, as required.

LOWER BALL JOINT

Removal and Installation

S SERIES 2WD

1. Raise and support the vehicle safely. Properly support the lower control arm, using the necessary equipment. The control arm must be supported so that the spring and the control arm remain intact.
2. Remove the tire and wheel assembly. As required, remove the brake caliper and position it to the side.
3. Remove the cotter pin and the lower ball joint retaining bolt. Using the proper tool separate the ball joint from its mounting. Support the knuckle assembly so that its weight will not damage the brake hose.
4. Press the ball joint out of the lower control arm, using the proper tools.
5. Installation is the reverse of the removal procedure. Check and adjust front alignment, as required.

S SERIES 4WD

1. Raise and support the vehicle safely. Properly support the lower control arm, using the necessary equipment. The control arm must be supported so that the spring and the control arm remain intact.

2. Remove the tire and wheel assembly. As required, remove the brake caliper and position it to the side.

3. Remove the cotter pin and the lower ball joint retaining bolt. Using the proper tool separate the ball joint from its mounting. Support the knuckle assembly so that its weight will not damage the brake hose.

4. Remove the rivets from the ball joint assembly, using the proper tools. Remove the ball joint from the control arm.

5. Installation is the reverse of the removal procedure. Be sure to use the nuts and bolts that are supplied with the replacement ball joint assembly. Check and adjust front alignment, as required.

ASTRO/SAFARI

1. Raise and support the vehicle safely. Properly support the lower control arm, using the necessary equipment. The control arm must be supported so that the spring and the control arm remain intact.

2. Remove the tire and wheel assembly. As required, remove the brake caliper and position it to the side.

3. Remove the cotter pin and the lower ball joint retaining bolt. Using the proper tool separate the ball joint from its mounting. Support the knuckle assembly so that its weight will not damage the brake hose.

4. Press the ball joint out of the lower control arm, using the proper tools.

5. Installation is the reverse of the removal procedure. Check and adjust front alignment, as required.

PICK UP (1982-87), BLAZER/JIMMY, SUBURBAN AND VAN 2WD

1. Raise and support the vehicle safely. Properly support the lower control arm, using the necessary equipment. The control arm must be supported so that the spring and the control arm remain intact.

2. Remove the tire and wheel assembly. As required, remove the brake caliper and position it to the side.

3. Remove the cotter pin and the lower ball joint retaining bolt. Using the proper tool separate the ball joint from its mounting. Support the knuckle assembly so that its weight will not damage the brake hose.

4. Press the ball joint out of the lower control arm, using the proper tools.

5. Installation is the reverse of the removal procedure. Check and adjust front alignment, as required.

PICK UP (1982-87), BLAZER/JIMMY AND SUBURBAN 4WD

1. Raise and support the vehicle safely. Remove the tire and wheel assembly.

2. Remove the hub and rotor assembly. Remove the spindle.

3. Remove the steering knuckle assembly. If removing the left axle yoke ball joints, remove the steering arm.

4. Position the steering knuckle assembly in a suitable vise. Press the lower ball joint from the knuckle assembly, using the proper tools.

5. Installation is the reverse of the removal procedure. Check front alignment, as required.

PICK UP (1988)

1. Raise and support the vehicle safely. Properly support the lower control arm, using the necessary equipment. The control arm must be supported so that the spring and the control arm remain intact.

2. Remove the tire and wheel assembly. As required, remove the brake caliper and position it to the side.

3. Remove the cotter pin and the lower ball joint retaining bolt. Using the proper tool separate the ball joint from its mounting. Support the knuckle assembly so that its weight will not damage the brake hose.

4. Remove the rivets from the ball joint assembly, using the proper tools. Remove the ball joint from the control arm.

5. Installation is the reverse of the removal procedure. Be sure to use the nuts and bolts that are supplied with the replacement ball joint assembly. Check and adjust front alignment, as required.

Wheel Bearings

Removal and Installation

S SERIES 2WD

1. Raise and support the vehicle safely. Remove the tire and wheel assembly.

2. Remove the brake caliper and position it to the side. Remove the dust cover, cotter pin, washer and spindle nut.

3. Remove the outer wheel bearing assembly. Remove the brake rotor. Remove the inner wheel bearing assembly.

4. Installation is the reverse of the removal procedure. When installing new bearings, be sure to install new bearing races inside the rotor, using the proper removal and installation tools.

5. Pack new bearings with the proper grade and type wheel bearing grease. Adjust wheel bearings, as required.

ASTRO/SAFARI

1. Raise and support the vehicle safely. Remove the tire and wheel assembly.

2. Remove the brake caliper and position it to the side. Remove the dust cover, cotter pin, washer and spindle nut.

3. Remove the outer wheel bearing assembly. Remove the brake rotor. Remove the inner wheel bearing assembly.

4. Installation is the reverse of the removal procedure. When installing new bearings, be sure to install new bearing races inside the rotor, using the proper removal and installation tools.

5. Pack new bearings with the proper grade and type wheel bearing grease. Adjust wheel bearings, as required.

PICK UP, BLAZER/JIMMY, SUBURBAN AND VAN 2WD

1. Raise and support the vehicle safely. Remove the tire and wheel assembly.

2. Remove the brake caliper and position it to the side. Remove the dust cover, cotter pin, washer and spindle nut.

3. Remove the outer wheel bearing assembly. Remove the brake rotor. Remove the inner wheel bearing assembly.

4. Installation is the reverse of the removal procedure. When installing new bearings be sure to install new bearing races inside the rotor, using the proper removal and installation tools.

5. Pack new bearings, with the proper grade and type wheel bearing grease. Adjust wheel bearings, as required.

PICK UP (1982-87), BLAZER/JIMMY AND SUBURBAN 4WD

1. Raise and support the vehicle safely. Remove the tire and wheel assembly.

2. Remove the brake caliper. Remove the locking hub assembly.

3. Remove the hub and rotor assembly along with the outer wheel bearing assembly. Remove the inner wheel bearing assembly.

4. Installation is the reverse of the removal procedure. When installing new bearings be sure to install new bearing races inside the rotor, using the proper removal and installation tools.

5. Pack new bearings, with the proper grade and type wheel bearing grease. Adjust wheel bearings, as required.

Adjustment

EXCEPT 4WD

1. Raise and support the vehicle safely. Remove the dust cap and cotter pin.

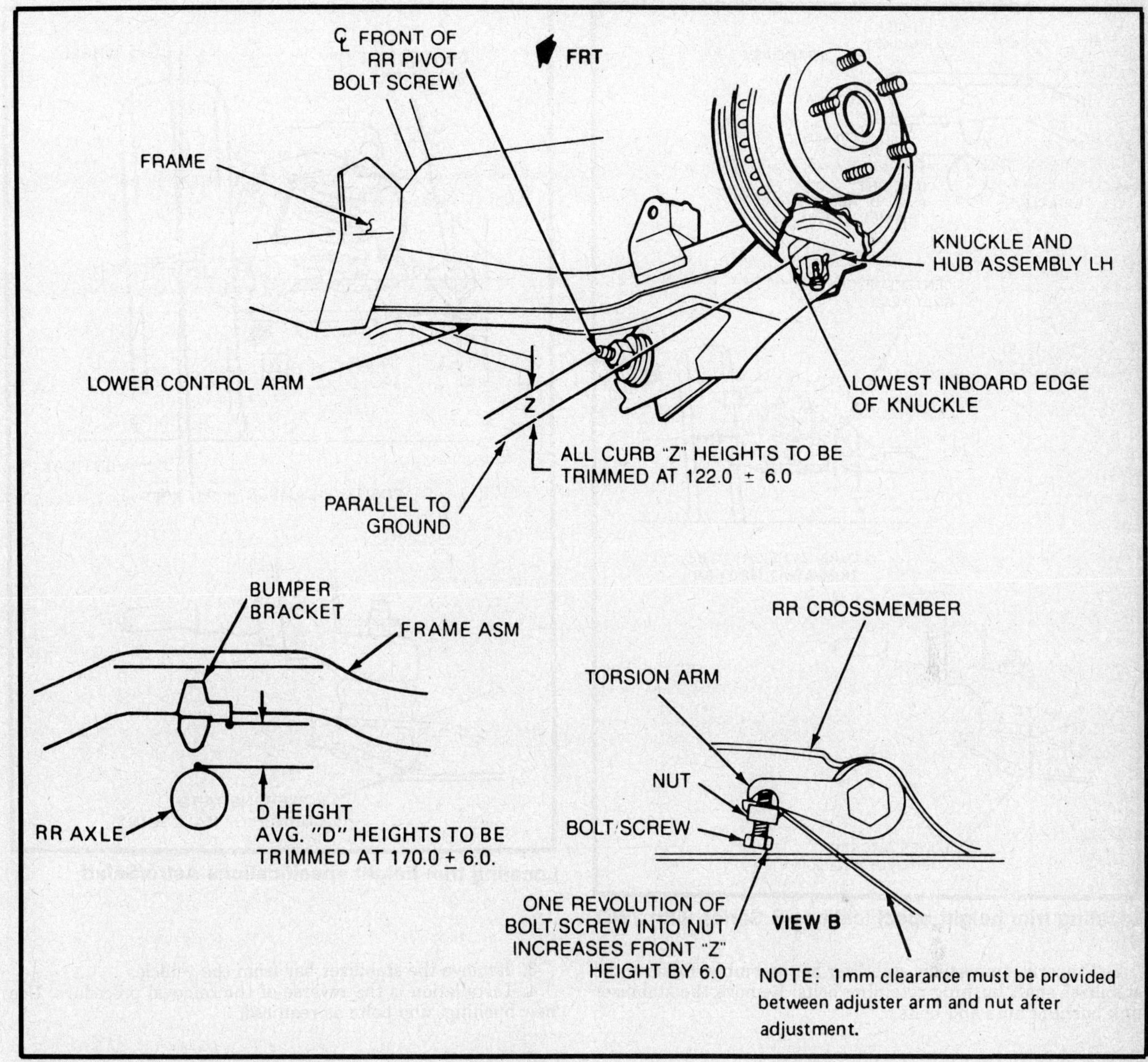

Locating trim height specifications S Series with 4WD

2. Tighten the spindle nut to 12 ft. lbs. while turning the tire and wheel assembly. Back off the nut to the just loose position.
3. Hand tighten the spindle nut. Loosen the nut until the cotter pin can be installed in the spindle slot.
4. End play should be 0.001–0.005 in. (P Series vehicles with I-Beam suspension 0.0005–0.008 in.).

4WD

1. Raise and support the vehicle safely. Remove the locking hub assembly, lock nut and ring.
2. Torque the adjusting nut to 50 ft. lbs. while rotating the hub and rotor assembly. Back off the adjusting nut and retighten.
3. If the vehicle is equipped with automatic hubs, torque the adjusting nut to 35 ft. lbs. while rotating the wheel assembly. Back off the adjusting nut a maximum of $^3/_8$ turn.
4. If the vehicle is equipped with manual hubs, torque the adjusting nut to 50 ft. lbs. while rotating the wheel assembly. Back off the adjusting nut to free the bearing.
5. Install the ring and locknut. The tang on the inside diameter of the ring must pass onto the slot on the spindle. The hole in the ring must align with the pin on the locknut. Move the adjustment nut to align the pin.
6. The endplay in the hub and rotor assembly should be 0.001–0.010 in.
7. Install the locking hub assembly.

Stabilizer Bar

Removal and Installation

1. Raise and support the vehicle safely. As required, remove the tire and wheel assemblies.

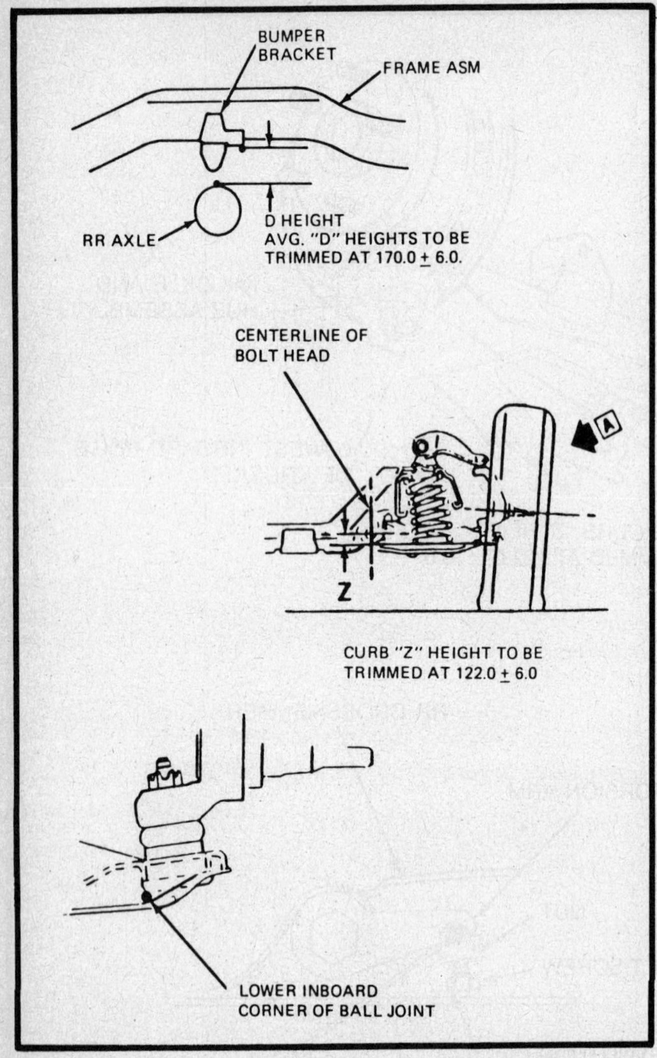

Locating trim height specifications S Series with 2WD

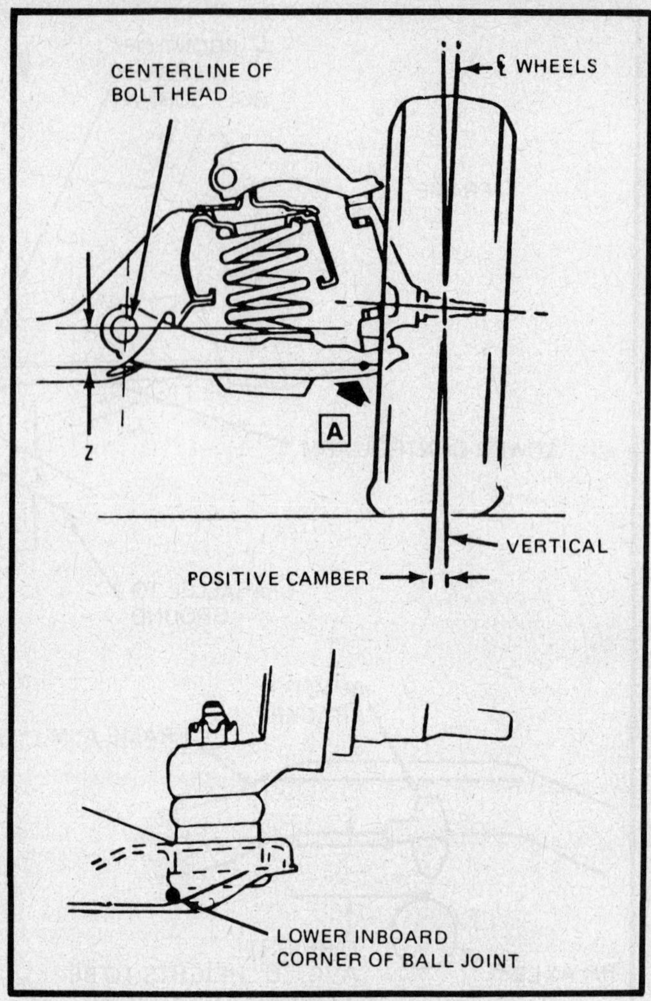

Locating trim height specifications Astro/Safari

2. Properly support the stabilizer bar assembly. Remove the stabilizer shaft bushing retaining bolts. Remove the stabilizer link bushing nuts and bolts.

3. Remove the stabilizer bar from the vehicle.

4. Installation is the reverse of the removal procedure. Use new bushings and bolts as required.

STEERING GEAR AND LINKAGE

Refer to the Unit Overhaul Section for Overhaul Procedures.

Manual Steering Gear

Removal and Installation

1. Disconnect the negative battery cable. Raise and support the vehicle safely. Position the wheels in the straight position. Be sure that the steering wheel is in the right position.

2. If equipped, remove the steering gear coupling shield. Remove the steering gear coupling bolt. On some vehicles it may be necessary to separate the coupling at the two flange bolts.

3. Matchmark the pitman arm to the steering gear. Remove the pitman arm retaining nut and washer. Using the proper tool, separate the pitman arm from the steering gear assembly.

4. Remove the steering gear retaining bolts. Remove the steering gear from the vehicle.

5. Installation is the reverse of the removal procedure.

Power Steering Gear

Removal and Installation

1. Disconnect the negative battery cable. Raise and support the vehicle safely. Position the wheels in the straight position. Be sure that the steering wheel is in the right position.

2. Disconnect and cap the fluid lines.

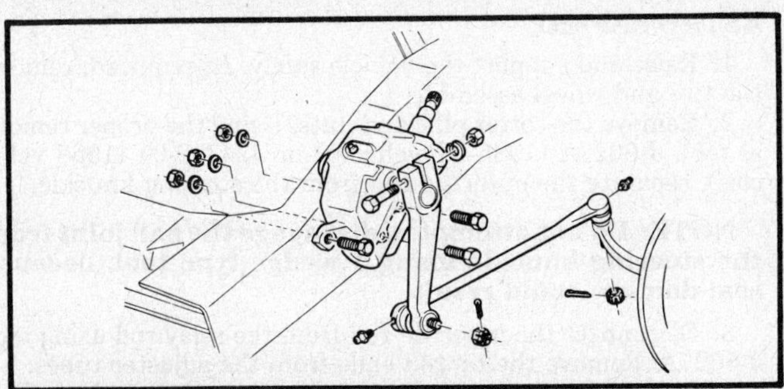
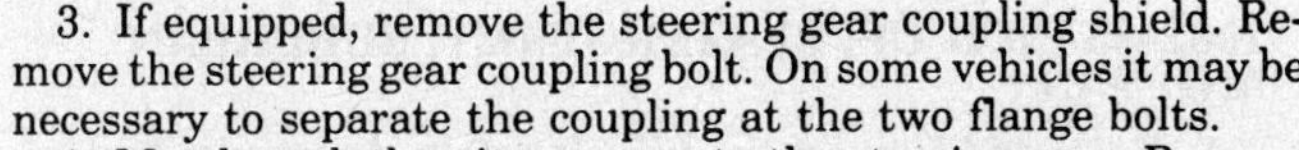
Manually operated steering gear – P models

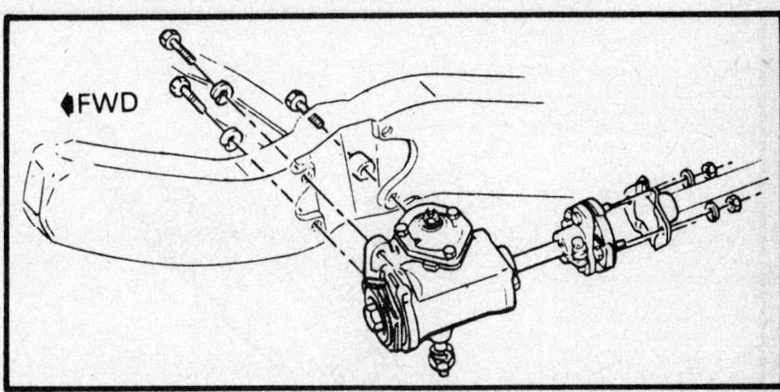

Manually operated steering gear – C and K models

3. If equipped, remove the steering gear coupling shield. Remove the steering gear coupling bolt. On some vehicles it may be necessary to separate the coupling at the two flange bolts.
4. Matchmark the pitman arm to the steering gear. Remove the pitman arm retaining nut and washer. Using the proper tool, separate the pitman arm from the steering gear assembly.
5. Remove the steering gear retaining bolts. Remove the steering gear from the vehicle.
6. Installation is the reverse of the removal procedure. As required, bleed the power steering system.

Power Steering Pump

Removal and Installation

1. Disconnect the negative battery cable. Disconnect and cap the power steering pump hoses. Loosen the tensioner assembly, if equipped. Remove the power steering pump drive belt.
2. Remove the necessary components in order to gain access to the pump retaining bolts.
3. As required, remove the power steering pump pulley using tool J-25034-B.
4. Remove the pump mounting bolts. Remove the pump from the vehicle.
5. Installation is the reverse of the removal procedure. Bleed the power steering system, as required.

Bleeding System

1. Fill the reservoir to the proper level and allow the fluid to stand for at least two minutes.
2. Operate the engine for at least one minute. Check and add fluid, as required. Repeat until the fluid level remains constant.
3. Raise a support the vehicle safely. Run the engine and increase the idle speed to about 1500 rpm.
4. Turn the steering wheel from right to left, contacting the steering stops only lightly. Check and add fluid, as required.
5. Lower the vehicle. Turn the wheels from full right to full left. Check and add fluid, as required.
6. Repeat as necessary until all air is bled from the system. If, after repeated attempts to bleed the system, air is still present in the fluid (fluid is foamy), check the system for leaks.

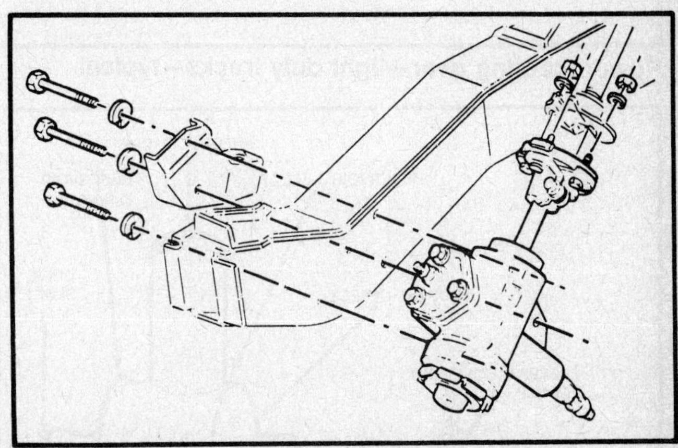
Manually operated steering gear – G models

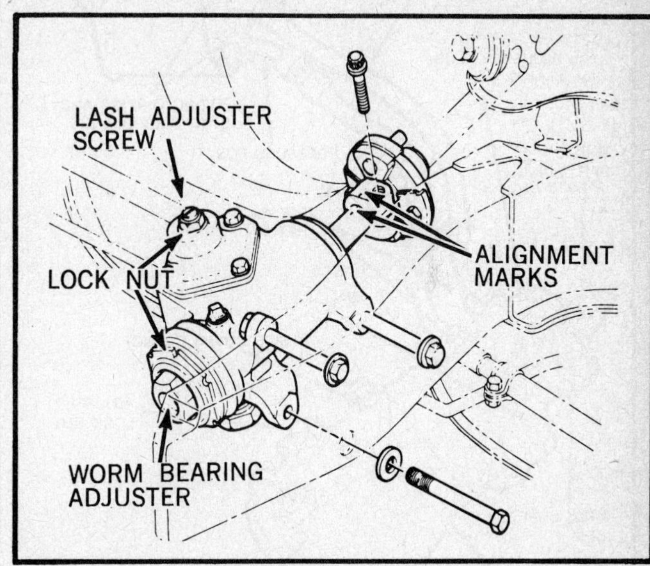

Steering gear adjustments – typical

Tie Rods

Removal and Installation

S SERIES

1. Raise and support the vehicle safely. As required, remove the tire and wheel assembly.
2. Remove the cotter pins and nuts. Using the proper removal tool, J-6627A, separate the outer tie rod from the steering knuckle.

NOTE: Do not attempt to disengage the ball joint from the steering knuckle using a wedge type tool, because seal damage could result.

3. Disconnect the inner tie rod from the relay rod using tool J-6627A. Remove the tie rod ends from the adjuster tubes.
4. Installation is the reverse of the removal procedure. The number of threads on both the inner and outer tie rod ends must be equal within three threads.
5. Adjust the front alignment, as required.

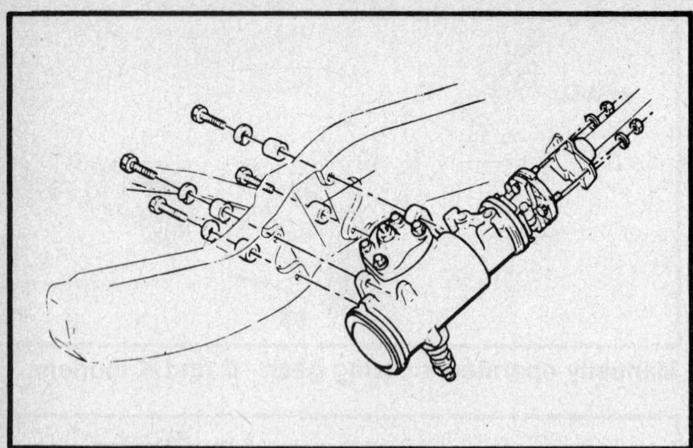

Power steering gear – light duty trucks – typical

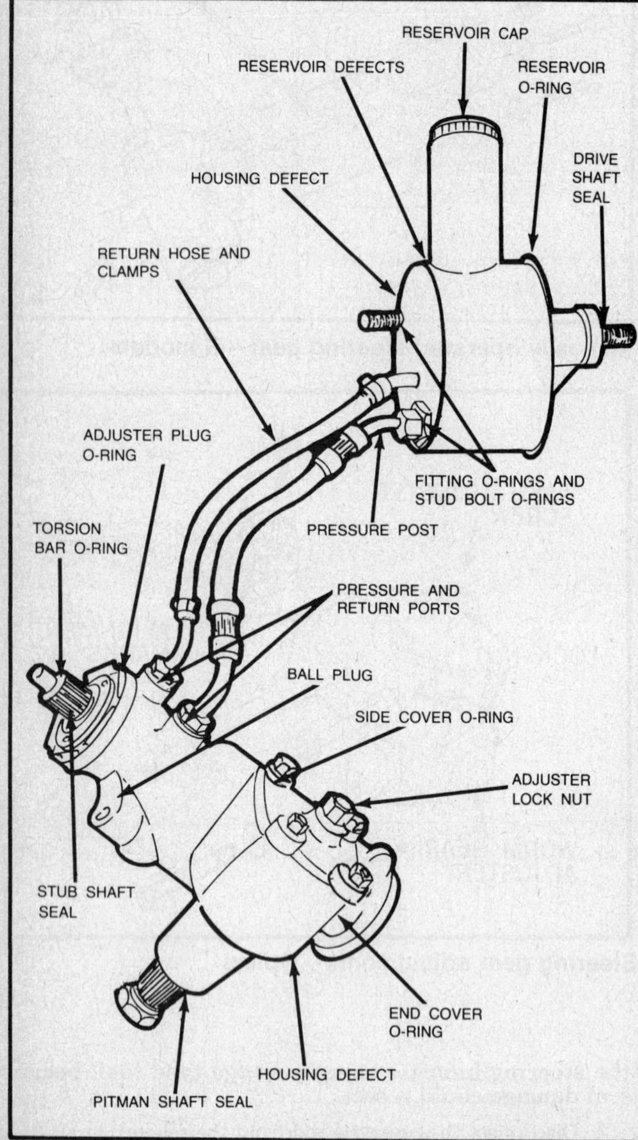

Potential leakage areas – light duty power steering system

ASTRO/SAFARI

1. Raise and support the vehicle safely. As required, remove the tire and wheel assembly.
2. Remove the cotter pins and nuts. Using the proper removal tool, J-6627A (1985–87 vehicles) or J24319-01 (1988 vehicles), separate the outer tie rod from the steering knuckle.

NOTE: Do not attempt to disengage the ball joint from the steering knuckle using a wedge type tool, because seal damage could result.

3. Disconnect the inner tie rod from the relay rod using tool J-6627A. Remove the tie rod ends from the adjuster tubes.
4. Installation is the reverse of the removal procedure. The number of threads on both the inner and outer tie rod ends must be equal within three threads.
5. Adjust the front alignment, as required.

1982–85 PICK UP, BLAZER/JIMMY, SUBURBAN AND VAN

1. Raise and support the vehicle safely. As required, remove the tire and wheel assembly.
2. Remove the cotter pins and nuts. Using the proper removal tool, separate the outer tie rod from the steering knuckle.
3. Disconnect the inner tie rod from the relay rod using the proper tool. Remove the tie rod ends from the adjuster tubes.
4. Installation is the reverse of the removal procedure. Adjust the front alignment, as required.

1986–88 PICK UP, BLAZER/JIMMY, SUBURBAN AND VAN (TYPE ONE)

1. Raise and support the vehicle safely. As required, remove the tire and wheel assembly.
2. Remove the cotter pins and nuts. Using the proper removal tool, J-6627A, separate the outer tie rod from the steering knuckle.

NOTE: Do not attempt to disengage the ball joint from the steering knuckle using a wedge type tool, because seal damage could result.

3. Disconnect the inner tie rod from the relay rod using tool J-6627A. Remove the tie rod ends from the adjuster tubes.
4. Installation is the reverse of the removal procedure. The number of threads on both the inner and outer tie rod ends must be equal within three threads.
5. Adjust the front alignment, as required.

1986–88 PICK UP, BLAZER/JIMMY, SUBURBAN AND VAN (TYPE TWO)

1. Raise and support the vehicle safely. As required, remove the tire and wheel assembly.
2. Remove the cotter pins and nuts from the rod assembly. Disconnect the shock absorber from the tir rod assembly.
3. Using the proper removal tool, J-6627A, separate the outer tie rod from the steering knuckle.

NOTE: Do not attempt to disengage the ball joint from the steering knuckle using a wedge type tool, because seal damage could result.

4. Disconnect the tie rod end bodies. Count the number of turns needed to remove the end bodies. Remove the tie rod ends from the adjuster tibe.
5. For reinstallation note the position of the adjuster tube and the direction from which the bolts are installed.
6. Installation is the reverse of the removal procedure. The number of threads on both the inner and outer tie rod ends must be equal within three threads.
7. Adjust the front alignment, as required.

BRAKE SYSTEM

Refer to the Unit Overhaul Section for Overhaul Procedures.

Master Cylinder

Removal and Installation

1. Disconnect the negative battery cable. Disconnect any electrical connections from the master cylinder, as required. Disconnect and plug the fluid lines.
2. If equipped with power brakes, remove the master cylinder to power booster retaining bolts. Remove the RAWL control module assembly, if equipped.
3. If equipped with manual brakes, remove the master cylinder pushrod from the brake pedal. Remove the RAWL control module assembly, if equipped.
4. Remove the master cylinder from the vehicle. If equipped with power brakes remove the vacuum booster pushrod.
5. Installation is the reverse of the removal procedure. Bench bleed the master cylinder prior to installation. If equipped with power brakes be sure to install the vacuum booster pushrod. Bleed the system, as required.

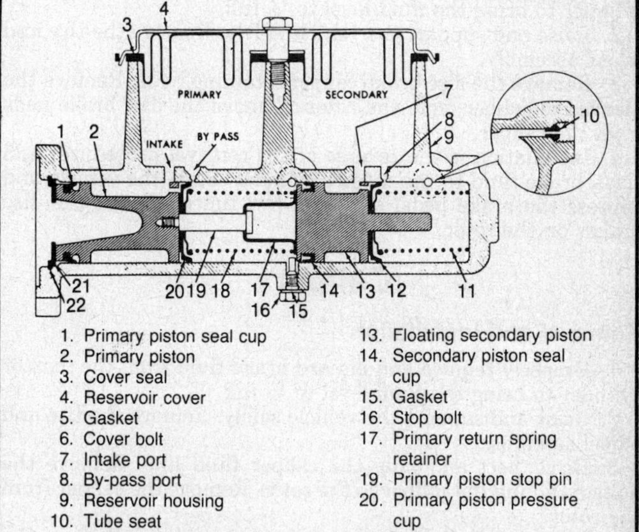

1. Primary piston seal cup
2. Primary piston
3. Cover seal
4. Reservoir cover
5. Gasket
6. Cover bolt
7. Intake port
8. By-pass port
9. Reservoir housing
10. Tube seat
11. Secondary piston return spring
12. Secondary piston pressure cup
13. Floating secondary piston
14. Secondary piston seal cup
15. Gasket
16. Stop bolt
17. Primary return spring retainer
19. Primary piston stop pin
20. Primary piston pressure cup
21. Stop plate
22. Retainer ring

Typical split system master cylinder

BLEEDING

Procedure

NOTE: The manufacturer specifically advises that pressure bleeding equipment be use to properly bleed the hydraulic brake system. This equipment must be of the diaphragm type.

1. Be certain that the brake fluid in the bleeder equipment is at the operating level.
2. Remove all dirt from the top of the master cylinder and remove the cylinder cover and rubber diaphragm.
3. Attach a brake bleeder adapter tool for the frame mounted boosters to the master cylinder.
4. Connect a hose from the bleeder equipment to the bleeder adapter and open the release valve on the bleeder equipment.

NOTE: The combination valve must be held in the open position while bleeding. Install tool, J-23709 or equivalent with the open slot under the mounting bolt and pushing in on the pin in the end of the valve.

5. Bleed the brakes in the following order. Right rear, left rear, right front and left front.
6. Fill a transparent container with a sufficient amount of brake fluid to ensure that the submerged end of the bleeder hose will remain below the surface of the fluid.
7. Place a brake bleeder wrench over the first bleeder valve and install one end of the bleeder hose over the valve.
8. Place the loose end of the bleeder hose in the container of brake fluid. Make sure that the hose end remains submerged in the brake fluid.
9. Open the bleeder valve by turning the bleeder wrench ¾ turn counterclockwise and allow fluid to flow until no air is seen in the fluid.
10. Close the bleeder valve tightly and proceed in the same manner with the remaining bleeder valves until there is no longer any air in the brake system.
11. Disconnect the brake bleeder equipment from the adapter at the master cylinder and remove the adapter from the master cylinder.
12. Fill the master cylinder reservoir to within ¼ in. of the top rim.

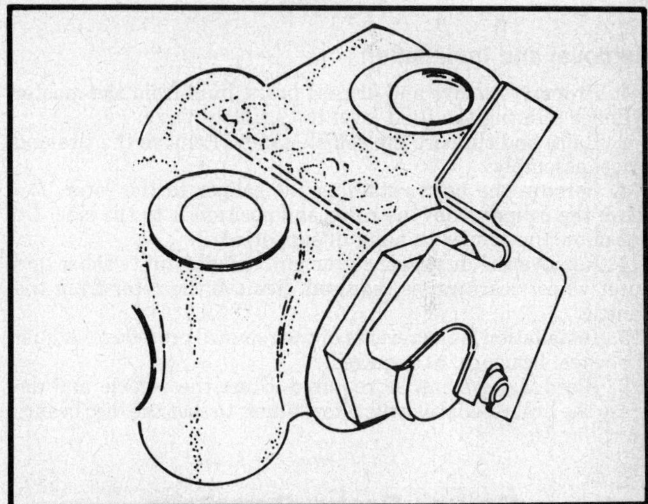

Typical metering valve assembly positioned in the open position with proper tool

Wheel Cylinder

Removal and Installation

1. Raise and support the vehicle safely. Remove the tire and wheel assembly. Remove the brake drum.
2. Remove the brake shoe assembly. Disconnect and plug the wheel cylinder fluid line.
3. Remove the wheel cylinder retaining bolts or clip. Remove the wheel cylinder from the vehicle.
4. Installation is the reverse of the removal procedure. Bleed the system, as required.

Disc Brakes

Removal and Installation

1. Properly remove and discard brake fluid from the master cylinder to bring the fluid level to $\frac{1}{3}$ full.
2. Raise and support the vehicle safely. Remove the tire and wheel assembly.
3. Remove the disc brake caliper retaining bolts. Remove the disc brake caliper from the rotor. Remove the disc brake pads from the caliper.
4. Installation is the reverse of the removal procedure. Add clean brake fluid to the master cylinder. Start the vehicle and depress the brake pedal slowly, a few times, to seat the disc brakes on the rotor.

Calipers

Removal and Installation

1. Properly remove and discard brake fluid from the master cylinder to bring the fluid level to $\frac{1}{3}$ full.
2. Raise and support the vehicle safely. Remove the tire and wheel assembly.
3. Disconnect and plug the caliper fluid line. Remove the bolts retaining the caliper to the rotor. Remove the caliper from the rotor.
4. Remove the disc brake pads from the caliper. Remove the disc brake pad retaining clips from inside the caliper.
5. Installation is the reverse of the removal procedure. If the brake hose was removed, be sure to position it properly or damage will result. Bleed the system, as required.

Rotors

Removal and Installation

1. Properly remove and discard brake fluid from the master cylinder to bring the fluid level to $\frac{1}{3}$ full.
2. Raise and support the vehicle safely. Remove the tire and wheel assembly.
3. Remove the bolts retaining the caliper to the rotor. Remove the caliper from the rotor and position it to the side. Do not allow the caliper to hang unsupported.
4. Remove the dust cap, cotter pin, spindle nut, washer and outer wheel bearings, as required. Remove the rotor from the vehicle.
5. Installation is the reverse of the removal procedure. Adjust the wheel bearings, as required.
6. Bleed the system, as required. Start the vehicle and depress the brake pedal slowly, a few times, to seat the disc brakes on the rotor.

Power Brake Boosters

Removal and Installation

VACUUM

1. Disconnect the negative battery cable. Do not disconnect the master cylinder fluid lines, unless there is a clearance problem. Remove the master cylinder and position it to the side.
2. Remove the vacuum booster pushrod. Disconnect the vacuum hose from the booster assembly.
3. From inside the vehicle, remove the mounting studs which secure the vacuum booster to the fire wall.
4. Pull the booster away from the cowl and remove it from the vehicle.
5. Installation is the reverse of the removal procedure. Be sure to properly install the vacuum booster pushrod. Bleed the system, as required.

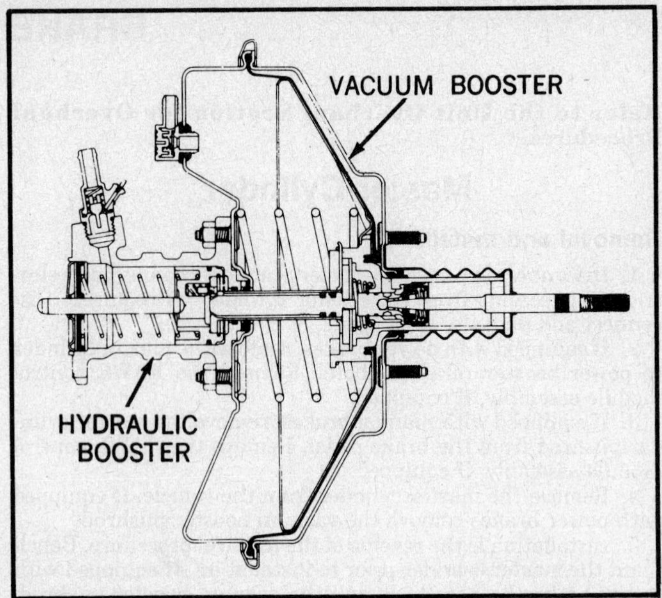

Dual power booster

HYDRAULIC

1. Disconnect the negative battery cable. Do not disconnect the master cylinder fluid lines, unless there is a clearance problem. Remove the master cylinder and position it to the side.
2. Disconnect and plug the fluid lines from the hydro boost assembly. Depending upon the vehicle, remove the pushrod from the brake pedal assembly inside the vehicle or from the bracket assembly on the firewall.
3. From inside the vehicle, remove the mounting studs which secure the hydro boost to the fire wall.
4. Pull the booster away from the cowl and remove it from the vehicle.
5. Installation is the reverse of the removal procedure. Bleed the brake system, as required.
6. To bleed the hydro boost system, fill the power steering pump to the proper level. Allow the fluid to remain undisturbed for a few minutes.
7. Start the engine and add fluid until the level is constant with the engine running.
8. Raise and support the vehicle safely. Start the engine and turn the wheels from stop to stop, add fluid as required. Turn the engine off and lower the vehicle.
9. Start the engine and depress the brake pedal several times while rotating the steering wheel from stop to stop. Turn the engine off and pump the brake pedal four or five times.
10. If the power steering fluid is extremely foamy, allow the vehicle to sit for a short time and then perform step nine again.

Stop Light Switch

Removal and Installation

1. Disconnect the negative battery cable. Remove the under dash trim panel.
2. Disconnect the switch electrical connections. Remove the switch assembly from its mounting.
3. Installation is the reverse of the removal procedure. Adjust the switch, as required.

Adjustment

1. Depress the brake pedal and press the switch in until it is firmly seated in its mounting.

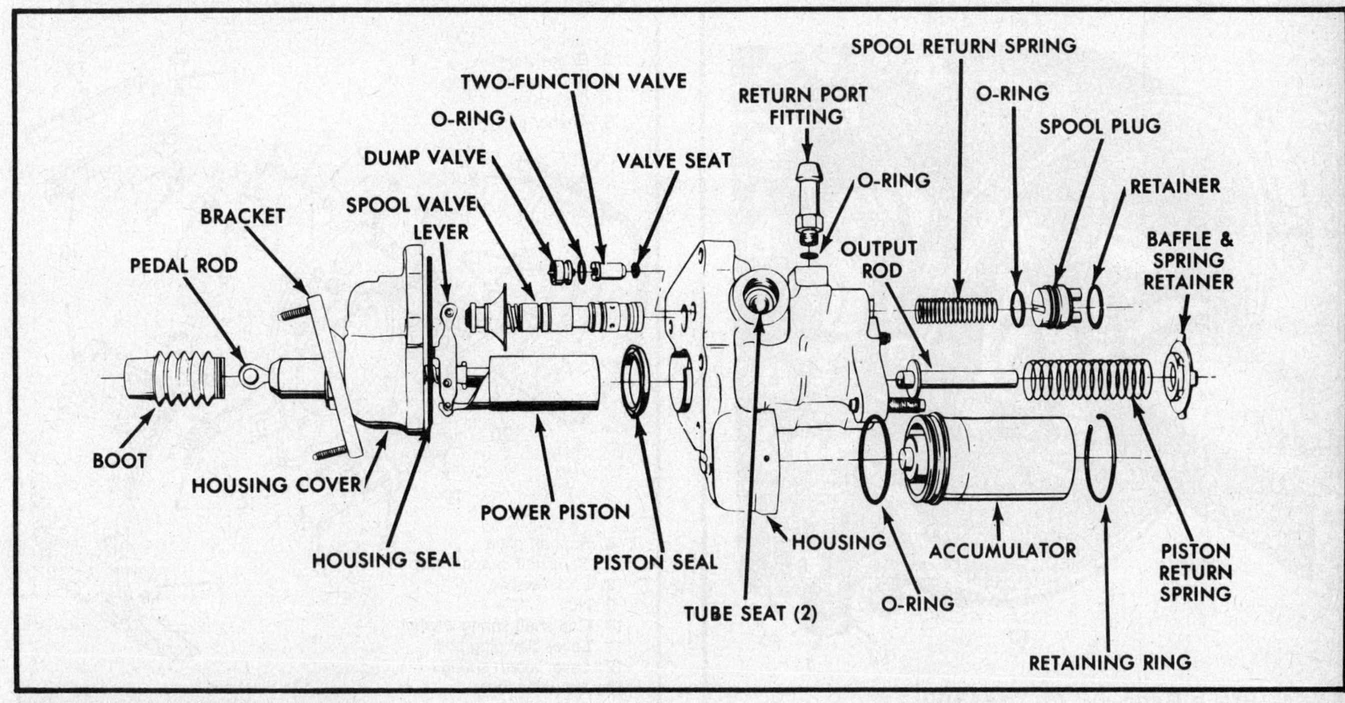

Typical hydro-boost assembly

2. Pull the brake pedal against the pedal stop until the switch does not make any noise.
3. Electrical contact should be made when the brake pedal is depressed from its fully released position.

Parking Brake

Adjustment

S SERIES, ASTRO/SAFARI

1. Raise and support the vehicle safely. Loosen the equalizer nut. Some vehicles may require the removal of the cable guide on the equalizer.
2. Set the parking brake pedal two clicks (2WD vehicles) and three clicks (4WD vehicles).
3. Tighten the equalizer nut until the rear wheels will not rotate without excessive force in the forward motion.
4. Back off the equalizer nut until there is light drag when the wheels are rotated in the forward motion.
5. If removed, install the cable guide. Release the parking brake. Rotate the rear wheels in the forward motion. There should be no brake drag.

PICK UP (1982–87), BLAZER/JIMMY, SUBURBAN AND VAN (FOOT PEDAL TYPE)

1. Raise and support the vehicle safely. Loosen the equalizer nut.
2. Set the parking brake pedal four clicks. Tighten the equalizer nut until the rear wheels will not rotate without excessive force in the forward motion.
3. Back off the equalizer nut until there is light drag when the wheels are rotated in the forward motion.
4. Release the parking brake. Rotate the rear wheels in the forward motion. There should be no brake drag.

PICK UP (1982–87), BLAZER/JIMMY, SUBURBAN AND VAN (LEVER TYPE)

1. Raise and support the vehicle safely. Turn the adjusting knob on the parking brake lever counterclockwise until it stops.
2. Apply the parking brake. Loosen the equalizer nut.
3. Tighten the equalizer nut until light drag is felt while rotating the rear wheels in the forward motion.
4. Adjust the knob on the parking brake lever until a definite snap over center is felt.
5. Release the parking brake. Rotate the rear wheels in the forward motion. There should be no brake drag.

PICK UP (1982–87), BLAZER/JIMMY, SUBURBAN AND VAN (DRIVESHAFT TYPE)

1. Raise and support the vehicle safely. Remove the clevis pin connecting the pull rod and the relay lever.
2. Rotate the brake drum to align the access hole with the adjusting screw. If the vehicle is equipped with manual transmission the access hole is located at the bottom of the backing plate. If the vehicle is equipped with automatic transmission the access hole is located at the top of the shoe.
3. For first time adjustment it will be necessary to remove the driveshaft and the drum in order to remove the lanced area from the drum and clean out the metal shavings.
4. Adjust the screw until the drum cannot be rotated by hand. Back off the adjusting screw ten notches, the drum should rotate freely.
5. Position the parking brake lever in the fully released position. Take up the slack in the cable to overcome spring tension.
6. Adjust the clevis of the pull rod to align with the hole in the relay lever. Install the clevis pin. Install a new cover in the drum access hole.

PICK UP (1988)

1. Raise and support the vehicle safely. Matchmark the wheel to the axle flange. Remove the tire and wheel assembly.
2. Matchmark the drum to the axle flange. Remove the brake drum.
3. Using tool J-21177A, or equivalent, measure and record the brake drum inside diameter.
4. Turn the adjuster nut and adjust the shoe and lining to a diameter 0.010–0.020 inch less than the measured inside diameter of the brake drum.
5. Be sure that the stops on the parking brake levers are

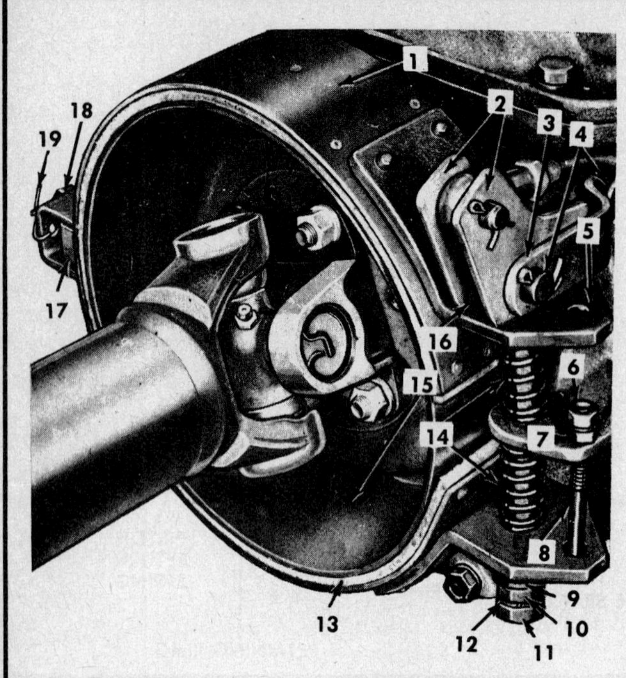

1. Brake Band
2. Cams
3. Links
4. Clevis Pins
5. Cam Shoe
6. Nut
7. Adjusting Nut
8. Locating Bolt
9. Washer
10. Adjusting Nut
11. Nut
12. Washer
13. Brake Linings
14. Release Springs
15. Brake Drum
16. Adjusting Bolt
17. Anchor Bar
18. Anchor Screw
19. Wire

Contracting band (external) parking brake

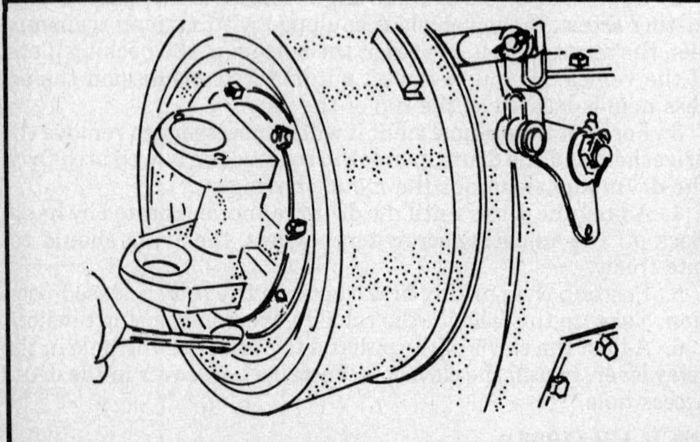

Internal expanding type adjustment

against the edge of the brake shoe web. If not, loosen the parking brake cable adjustment.

6. Tighten the parking brake cable at the adjuster nut until the lever stops begin to move off of the shoe webs. Loosen the adjustment nut until the lever stops move back, barely touching the shoe webs. The final clearance between the stops and either web should be 0.5mm.

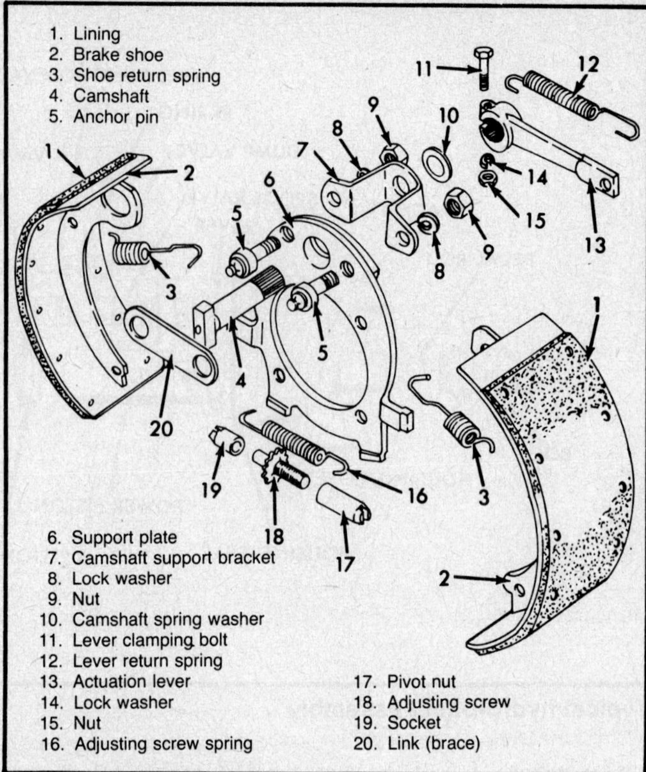

Internal expanding type brake

7. Install the drums and wheels. Align the assemblies with the matchmarks made during removal.
8. Apply and release the service brake pedal 30–35 times using normal pedal force. Pause about one second between each pedal application.
9. Depress the parking brake six clicks. Check the rear wheels they should not rotate.
10. Release the parking brake lever. Check for free wheel rotation.

Removal and Installation

1982–85 S SERIES (FRONT CABLE)

1. Raise and support the vehicle safely. Loosen the adjuster nut and disconnect the front cable from the connector.
2. Compress the retainer fingers and loosen the assembly at the frame. Remove the supports.
3. Lower the vehicle. Remove the windshield washer bottle.
4. Disconnect the cable from the parking brake pedal, compress the retainer fingers. Remove the cable from the vehicle.
5. Installation is the reverse of the removal procedure. Adjust the parking brake.

1982–85 S SERIES (CENTER CABLE)

1. Raise and support the vehicle safely. Remove the adjuster nut at the equalizer. Pull the cable from the equalizer.
2. Disconnect the cable at the retainers. Remove the cable from the vehicle.
3. Installation is the reverse of the removal procedure. Adjust the parking brake.

1982–85 S SERIES (REAR CABLE)

1. Raise and support the vehicle safely. Remove the tire and wheel assembly. Remove the brake drum.
2. Loosen the equalizer and disconnect the cable at the center retainer.

3. Compress the plastic retainer fingers and remove the retainer from the frame bracket.
4. Remove the rear brake shoe assembly. Disconnect the parking brake cable. Remove the cable from the frame and from the brake backing plate.
5. Installation is the reverse of the removal procedure. Adjust the rear brakes, as required. Adjust the parking brake.

1986–88 S SERIES (FRONT CABLE)

1. Raise and support the vehicle safely. Loosen the adjuster nut and disconnect the front cable from the connector.
2. Compress the retainer fingers and loosen the assembly at the frame. Remove the supports.
3. Lower the vehicle. As required, remove dash trim panels to gain access to the parking brake pedal assembly.
4. Disconnect the cable from the parking brake pedal, compress the retainer fingers. Remove the cable from the vehicle.
5. Installation is the reverse of the removal procedure. Adjust the parking brake.

1986–88 S SERIES (REAR CABLE)

1. Raise and support the vehicle safely. Remove the tire and wheel assembly. Remove the brake drum.
2. Loosen the equalizer and disconnect the cable at the center retainer.
3. Compress the plastic retainer fingers and remove the retainer from the frame bracket.
4. Remove the rear brake shoe assembly. Disconnect the parking brake cable. Remove the cable from the frame and from the brake backing plate.
5. Installation is the reverse of the removal procedure. Adjust the rear brakes, as required. Adjust the parking brake.

ASTRO/SAFARI (FRONT CABLE)

1. Raise and support the vehicle safely. Loosen the adjuster nut and disconnect the front cable from the connector.
2. Compress the retainer fingers and loosen the assembly at the frame. Remove the supports.
3. Lower the vehicle. As required, remove the fuse box cover.
4. Disconnect the cable from the parking brake pedal, compress the retainer fingers. Remove the cable from the vehicle.
5. Installation is the reverse of the removal procedure. Adjust the parking brake.

ASTRO/SAFARI (REAR CABLE)

1. Raise and support the vehicle safely. Remove the tire and wheel assembly. Remove the brake drum.
2. Loosen the equalizer and disconnect the cable at the center retainer.
3. Compress the plastic retainer fingers and remove the retainer from the frame bracket.
4. Remove the rear brake shoe assembly. Disconnect the parking brake cable. Remove the cable from the frame and from the brake backing plate.
5. Installation is the reverse of the removal procedure. Adjust the rear brakes, as required. Adjust the parking brake.

PICK UP, BLAZER/JIMMY, SUBURBAN AND VAN (FRONT CABLE)

1. Raise and support the vehicle safely. Loosen the adjuster nut and disconnect the front cable from the connector.
2. Compress the retainer fingers and loosen the assembly at the frame. Remove the supports. Lower the vehicle.
3. Disconnect the cable from the parking brake pedal, compress the retainer fingers. Remove the cable from the vehicle.
4. Installation is the reverse of the removal procedure. Adjust the parking brake.

PICK UP, BLAZER/JIMMY, SUBURBAN AND VAN (CENTER CABLE)

1. Raise and support the vehicle safely.
2. Remove the nut from the equalizer assembly. Remove the front connector. Remove the rear connector.
3. Remove the cable from the vehicle.
4. Installation is the reverse of the removal procedure. Adjust the parking brake.

PICK UP, BLAZER/JIMMY, SUBURBAN AND VAN (REAR CABLE)

1. Raise and support the vehicle safely. Remove the tire and wheel assembly. Remove the brake drum.
2. Loosen the equalizer and disconnect the cable at the center retainer.
3. Compress the plastic retainer fingers and remove the retainer from the frame bracket.
4. Remove the rear brake shoe assembly. Disconnect the parking brake cable. Remove the cable from the frame and from the brake backing plate.
5. Installation is the reverse of the removal procedure. Adjust the rear brakes, as required. Adjust the parking brake.

CLUTCH

Clutch Assembly

Removal and Installation

S SERIES AND ASTRO/SAFARI

1. Disconnect the negative battery cable. Raise and support the vehicle safely. Remove the transmission. As required, remove the flywheel cover.
2. Remove the slave cylinder retaining bolts. Remove the slave cylinder from its mounting. On 1982–85 S Series, remove the left body mounting bolts. Loosen the radiator support bolt.
3. On 1982–85 S Series, raise and support the vehicle on the left side to gain clearance in order to remove the upper bell housing retaining bolts. Remove the bolts.
4. Remove the bell housing retaining bolts. Remove the bell housing from the vehicle.
5. Slide the clutch fork from the ball stud. Inspect the ball stud and replace as required.
6. Install the clutch removal tool and support the clutch assembly. Matchmark the clutch and pressure plate for reassembly.
7. Loosen the clutch plate retaining bolts slowly and evenly one at a time until all pressure is released from the pressure plate assembly.
8. Remove the clutch, pressure plate and removal tool from the vehicle. Check the flywheel for damage, repair or replace, as required.
9. Installation is the reverse of the removal procedure. Adjust the clutch, as required. Bleed hydraulic system, as required.

PICK UP, BLAZER/JIMMY, SUBURBAN AND VAN

1. Disconnect the negative battery cable. Raise and support

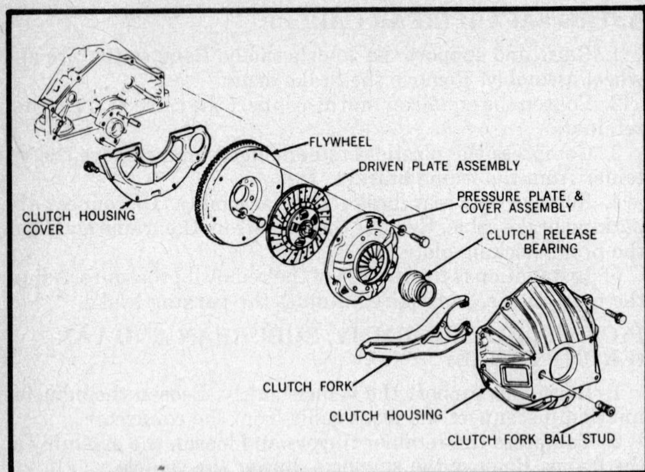

Clutch system components

the vehicle safely. Remove the transmission. As required, remove the flywheel cover.

2. If equipped, remove the slave cylinder retaining bolts and remove the slave cylinder from its mounting.
3. If equipped, remove the adjusting spring, pull back spring and retaining springs.
4. Remove the bell housing retaining bolts. Remove the bell housing from the vehicle.
5. Slide the clutch fork from the ball stud. Inspect the ball stud and replace as required.
6. Install the clutch removal tool and support the clutch assembly. Matchmark the clutch and pressure plate for reassembly.
7. Loosen the clutch plate retaining bolts slowly and evenly one at a time until all pressure is released from the pressure plate assembly.
8. Remove the clutch, pressure plate and removal tool from the vehicle. Check the flywheel for damage, repair or replace, as required.
9. Installation is the reverse of the removal procedure. Adjust the clutch, as required. Bleed hydraulic system, as required.

Adjustment

PICK UP (1982–87), BLAZER/JIMMY AND SUBURBAN

1. Disconnect the return spring at the clutch fork.
2. Rotate the clutch lever and shaft assembly until the clutch pedal is firmly against the rubber bumper on the brake pedal bracket.
3. Push the outer end of the clutch fork rearward until the release bearing just contacts the pressure plate fingers or levers.
4. Loosen the locknut and adjust the rod length so that the swevil slips freely into the gauge hole. Increase the pushrod length until all lash is removed from the system.
5. Remove the swivel from the gauge hole and insert it into the lower hole on the lever.
6. Install the two washers and the cotter pin. Tighten the locknut, but do not to change the pushrod length.
7. Install the return spring. Check the pedal for proper clearance, it should be 1 $^3/_8$–1$^5/_8$ in. for all except P Series and 1¼–1½ in. for P Series.
8. If not within specification, repeat the procedure.

VAN

1. Disconnect the clutch fork return spring at the clutch fork.
2. Loosen the pushrod nut and back it off from the swivel about ½ in.
3. Hold the clutch fork pushrod against the fork in order to move the release bearing against the clutch fingers. The pushrod will slide through the swivel at the cross shaft.
4. Adjust the other pushrod nut to obtain approximately ¼ in. clearance between the second nut and the swivel.
5. Release the pushrod, connect the return spring and tighten the first nut to lock the swivel against the second nut.
6. Check the pedal for proper clearance, it should be 1¼–1½ in. If not within specification, repeat the procedure.

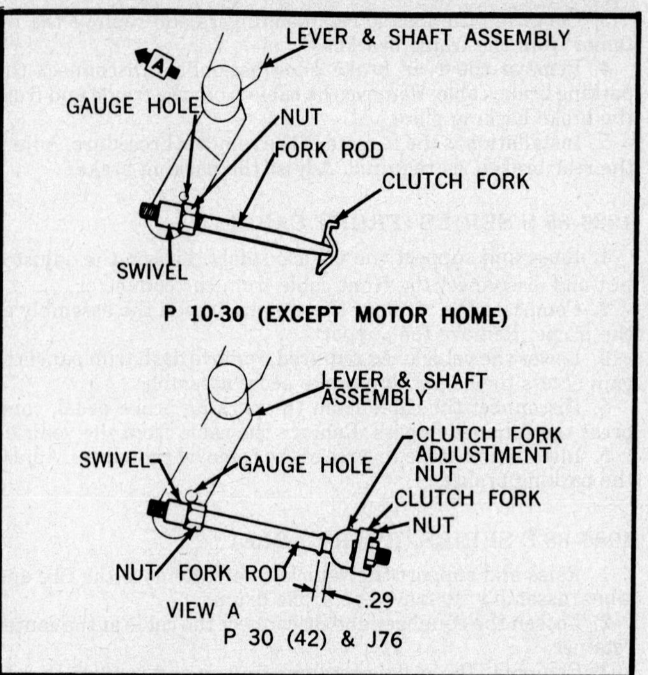

Free pedal travel – P models

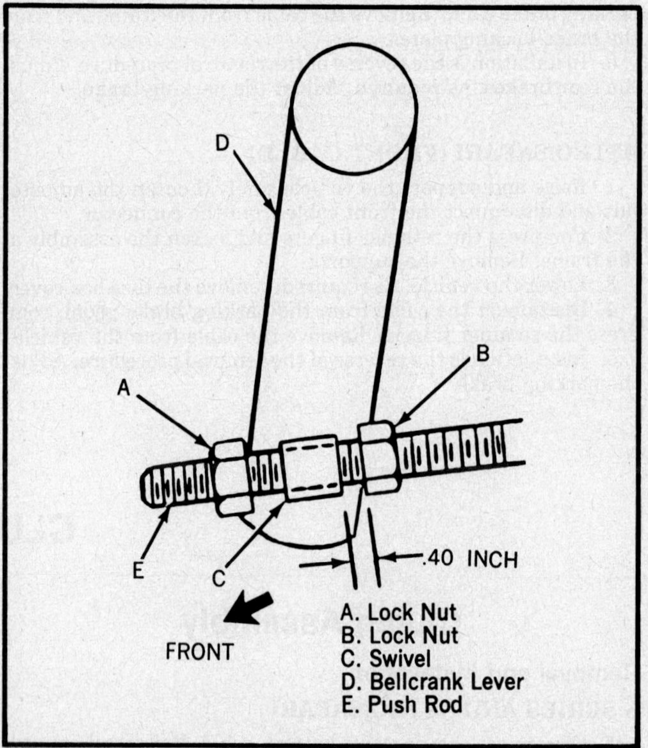

Clutch linkage adjustment

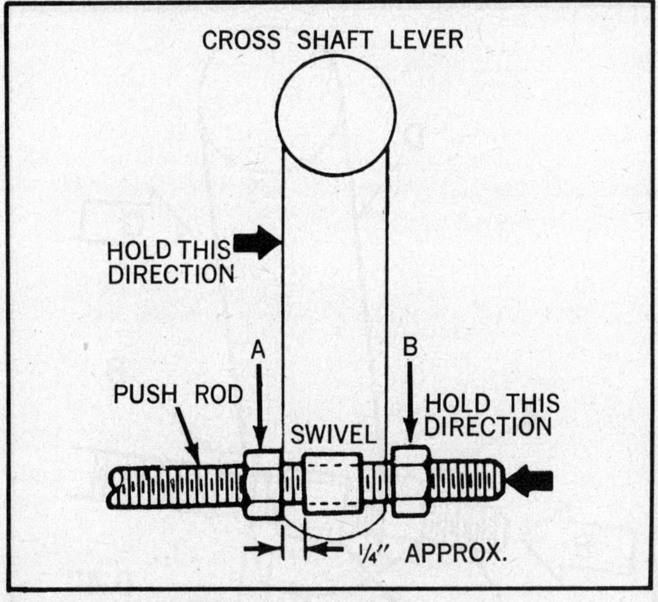

Free travel adjustment – G models

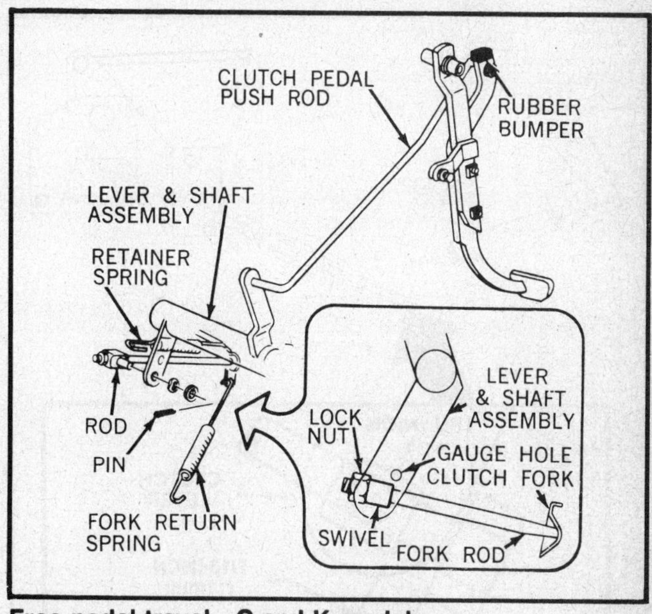

Free pedal travel – C and K models

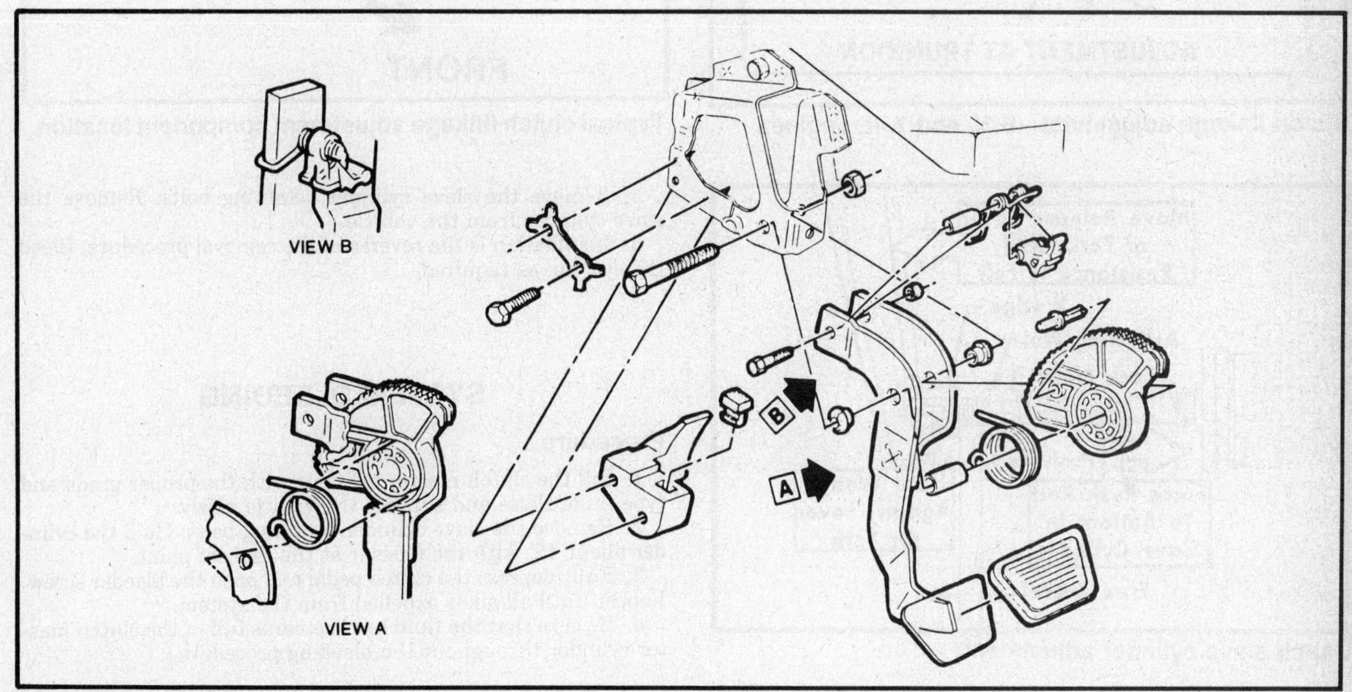

Self-adjusting clutch mechanism

MASTER CYLINDER

Removal and Installation

1. Disconnect the negative battery cable. Remove the under dash hush panel. Remove the lower steering column cover, as required. Remove the left side air condition duct work, as required.
2. Disconnect the pushrod from the clutch pedal. Disconnect the clutch master cylinder retaining nuts.
3. Disconnect and plug the reservoir hose at the clutch master cylinder assembly.
4. Disconnect and plug the fluid line to the slave cylinder at the clutch master clyinder assembly.
5. Remove the clutch master cylinder from the vehicle.
6. Installation is the reverse of the removal procedure. Bleed the system, as required.

SLAVE CYLINDER

Removal and Installation

1. Disconnect the negative battery cable.
2. Raise and support the vehicle safely. Disconnect and plug the fluid line at the slave cylinder.

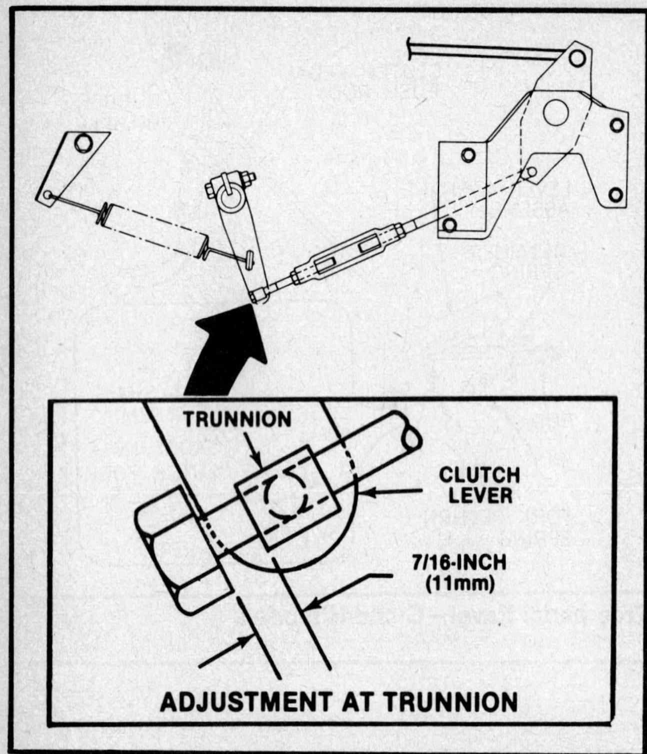

Clutch linkage adjustment – 6.2L and 7.4L engines

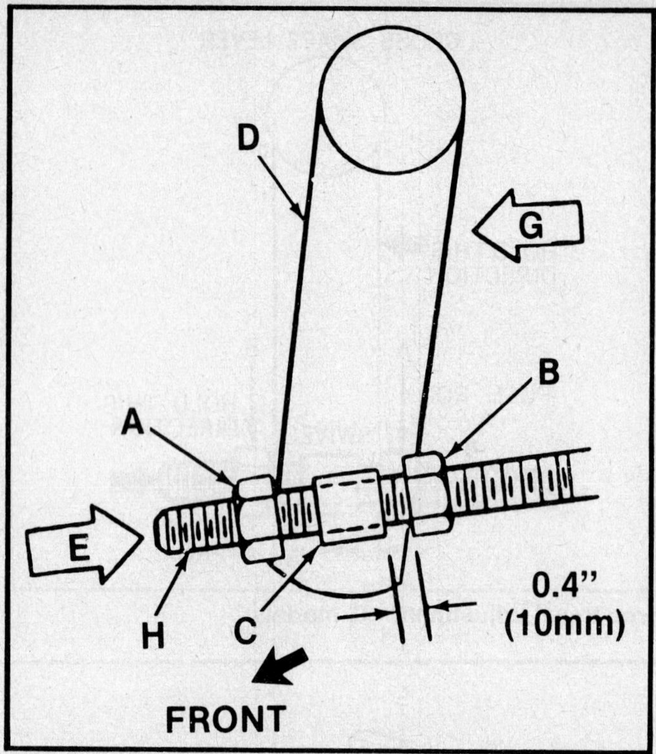

Typical clutch linkage adjustment component location

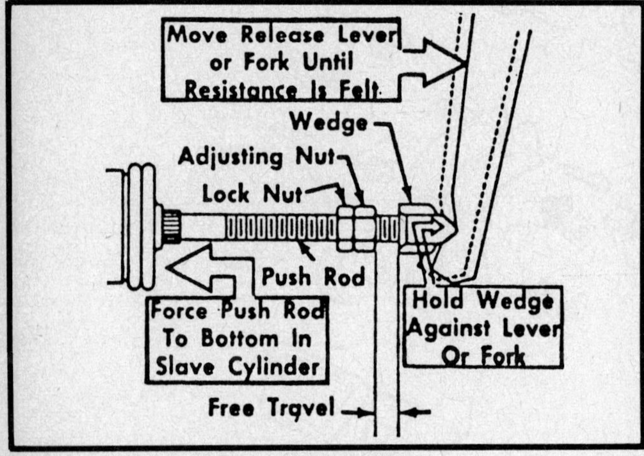

Clutch slave cylinder adjustment

3. Remove the slave cylinder retaining bolts. Remove the slave cylinder from the vehicle.
4. Installation is the reverse of the removal procedure. Bleed the system, as required.

SYSTEM BLEEDING

Procedure

1. Fill the clutch master cylinder with the proper grade and type fluid. Raise and support the vehicle safely.
2. Remove the slave cylinder retaining bolts. Hold the cylinder about 45° with the bleeder at the highest point.
3. Fully depress the clutch pedal and open the bleeder screw. Repeat until all air is expelled from the system.
4. Be sure that the fluid level remains full in the clutch master cylinder throughout the bleeding procedure.

MANUAL TRANSMISSION

Refer to the Unit Overhaul Section for Overhaul Procedures.

Manual Transmission Assembly

Removal and Installation

S SERIES AND ASTRO/SAFARI

1. Disconnect the negative battery cable. As required, on four speed transmission, remove the upper starter mounting screw.
2. Shift the transmission into neutral and remove the shift lever boot. Raise and support the vehicle safely. Drain the fluid.
3. Remove the shift lever assembly. If equipped, remove the parking brake lever and controls. Remove the driveshaft. If equipped, drain and remove the transfer case.
4. Disconnect the speedometer cable at the transmission. Disconnect all electrical wires, as required.
5. Disconnect and remove exhaust components, as required. Properly support the transmission assembly. Remove the clutch slave cylinder from its mounting.

6. Remove the transmission assembly retaining bolts. Remove the transmission crossmember retaining bolts. Remove the transmission mount retaining bolts. Remove the crossmember from the vehicle.
7. As required, on four speed transmission, remove the lower starter bolt and starter assembly. Properly support the clutch release bearing.
8. As required, on vehicles equipped with four speed transmission, remove the left body mounting bolts and loosen the radiator support screw. Raise and support the left side of the vehicle.
9. Properly support the engine assembly. Carefully remove the transmission assembly from the vehicle.
10. Installation is the reverse of the removal procedure. Fill the transmission with the proper grade and type fluid. A djust linkages, as required.

PICK UP, BLAZER/JIMMY, SUBURBAN AND VAN

1. Disconnect the negative battery cable. As required, remove the shift control lever and boot assembly.
2. If the vehicle is equipped with a five speed transmisiion, remove the shift tower and seal. Be sure to properly cover the opening.
3. Raise and support the vehicle safely. Drain the transmission fluid. Remove the driveshaft.
4. If equipped, drain and remove the transfer case from the vehicle. Remove the parking brake and controls, as required.
5. Disconnect and remove all required exhasut components. Disconnect all electrical connectors from the transmission assembly. Disconnect the speedometer cable, if equipped.
6. Remove the clutch slave cylinder and position it to the side, if equipped. Disconnect or remove clutch linkage, as required.
7. If the vehicle is equipped with a five speed transmission, remove the flywheel cover. Properly support the transmission assembly.
8. Remove the crossmember retaining bolts. Remove the transmission mount retaining bolts. Remove the crossmember from the vehicle.
9. Remove the transmission retaining bolts. If the vehicle is equipped with the 117mm four speed transmission, remove the top transmission bolts and install guide pin tool J-1126. Support the clutch release bearing.
10. Properly support the engine assembly. Carefully remove the transmission assembly from the vehicle.
11. Installation is the reverse of the removal procedure. Fill the transmission with the proper grade and type fluid. As adjust linkages, as required.

Linkage

Adjustment

PICK UP (1982–87), BLAZER/JIMMY, SUBURBAN AND VAN

1. Disconnect the negative battery cable. Raise and support the vehicle safely.
2. Loosen the linkage rod retaining nuts. Move the shift control lever into the neutral position.

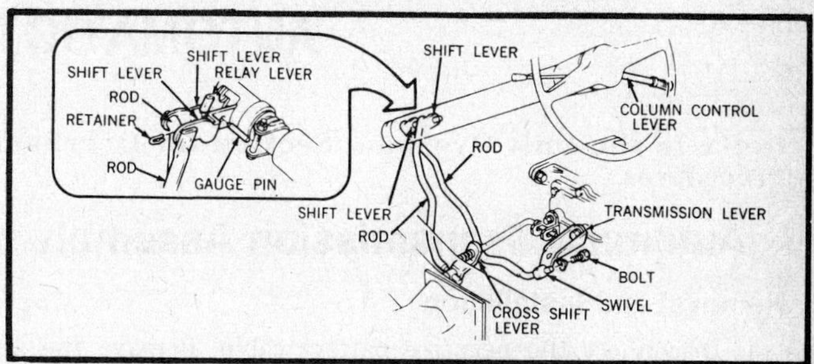

Column shift linkage – C and K models

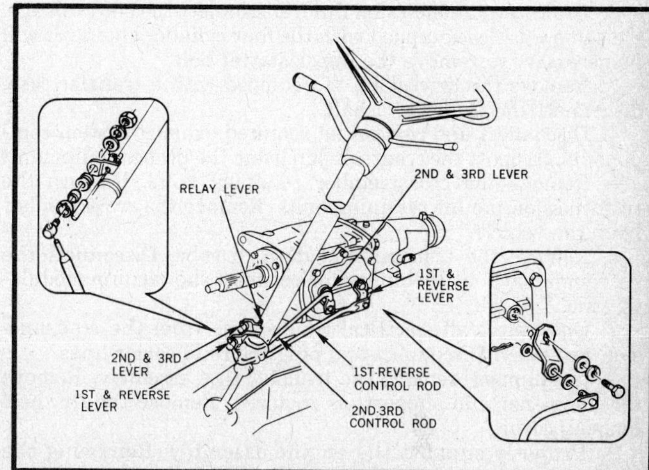

Column shift linkage – G models

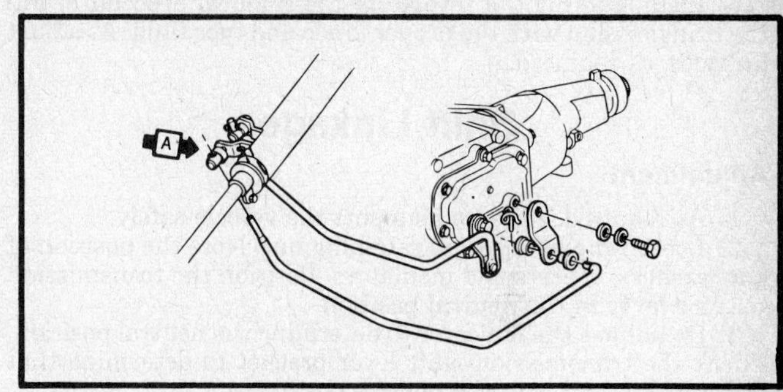

Column shift linkage – P models

3. Move the remaining levers into there neutral positions. Position a 0.249–0.250 gauge pin through the control levers.
4. Hold the shift rods tightly into their swivels and tighten the linkage rod retaining nuts.
5. Remove the gauge pin. Lubricate the shift control assembly. Check for proper operation.

AUTOMATIC TRANSMISSION

Refer to the Unit Overhaul Section for Overhaul Procedures.

Automatic Transmission Assembly

Removal and Installation

1. Disconnect the negative battery cable. Remove the air cleaner assembly. Disconnect the throttle valve cable and the throttle linkage. Raise and support the vehicle safely.
2. Drain the transmission fluid. Disconnect the shift linkage. On some vehicles equipped with the four cylinder engine, it will be necessary to remove the upper starter bolt.
3. Remove the driveshaft. If equipped with a transfer case, disconnect the front driveshaft.
4. Disconnect and remove all required exhaust system components. Support the transmission using the proper equipment.
5. Remove the crossmember retaining bolts. Remove the transmission mount retaining bolts. Remove the crossmember from the vehicle.
6. Remove the transmission dipstick tube. Disconnect the speedometer cable. If equipped, disconnect the vacuum modulator line.
7. Disconnect all electrical connections from the transmission assembly. Disconnect and plug the fluid cooler lines.
8. If equipped, remove the transfer case assembly. Remove the dampener and support, as required. Remove the flywheel housing cover.
9. Properly support the engine assembly. Removing the transmission to engine retaining bolts. Carefully remove the automatic transmission from the vehicle.
10. Installation is the reverse of the removal procedure. Fill the transmission with the proper grade and type fluid. As adjust linkages, as required.

Shift Linkage

Adjustment

1. As required, raise and support the vehicle safely.
2. Loosen the linkage rod retaining nut. Note the position of any washers, spacers and insulators. Position the transmission selector lever in the neutral position.
3. Do not use the indicator to determine the neutral position. Check the transmission shift lever bracket to determine that the transmission is in the neutral position.
3 Hold the selector rod and tighten the swivel to 17 ft. lbs. Position the selector lever in the park detent.
4. Check the adjustment. The selector lever must go into all positions. The engine must only start in the park or neutral position. Align the selector indicator, as required.

Modulator

Removal and installation

1. Disconnect the negative battery cable. Raise and support the vehicle safely.
2. Remove the vacuum line from the modulator. Remove the vacuum modulator retaining bolt.
3. Remove the modulator from the vehicle.
4. Installation is the reverse of the removal procedure. Be sure to check and add fluid, as required.

Detent Cable

Removal and Installation

1. Disconnect the negative battery cable. Remove the air cleaner assembly.

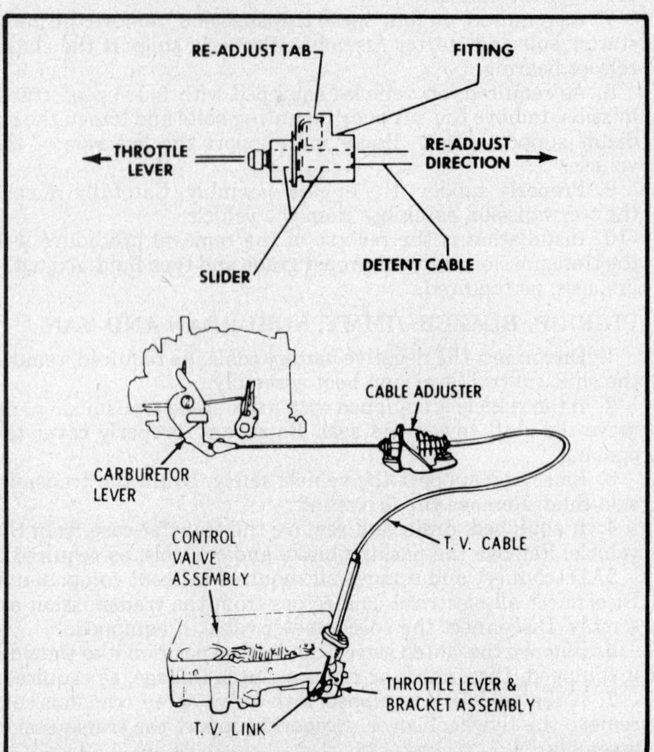

Throttle valve cable adjustment point

2. Disconnect the cable assembly from its mounting on the engine.
3. As required, raise and support the vehicle safely. Drain the transmission fluid, as required. Remove the cable retaining bolt on the transmission.
4. Pull the cable upward slowly and disconnect it from the linkage rod. Remove the cable from the vehicle.
5. Installation is the reverse of the removal procedure. Use a new detent cable seal. Adjust the cable, as required. Add transmission fluid, as necessary.

Adjustment

1. As required, remove the air cleaner assembly.
2. Depress and hold down the metal readjust tab at the engine end of the throttle valve cable.
3. Move the slider until it stops against the fitting. Release the readjustment tab.
4. Rotate the throttle lever to its full travel position. The slider must move toward the lever when the lever is rotated to its full travel position.
5. Check for proper operation. When the engine is cold, the cable may appear to be functioning properly, check the cable when the engine is hot.
6. Road test the vehicle and correct any problem, as necessary.

Neutral Start Switch

Removal and Installation

S SERIES AND ASTRO/SAFARI

These vehicles incorporate a mechanical neutral start system. The system relies on a mechanical block rather than the starter

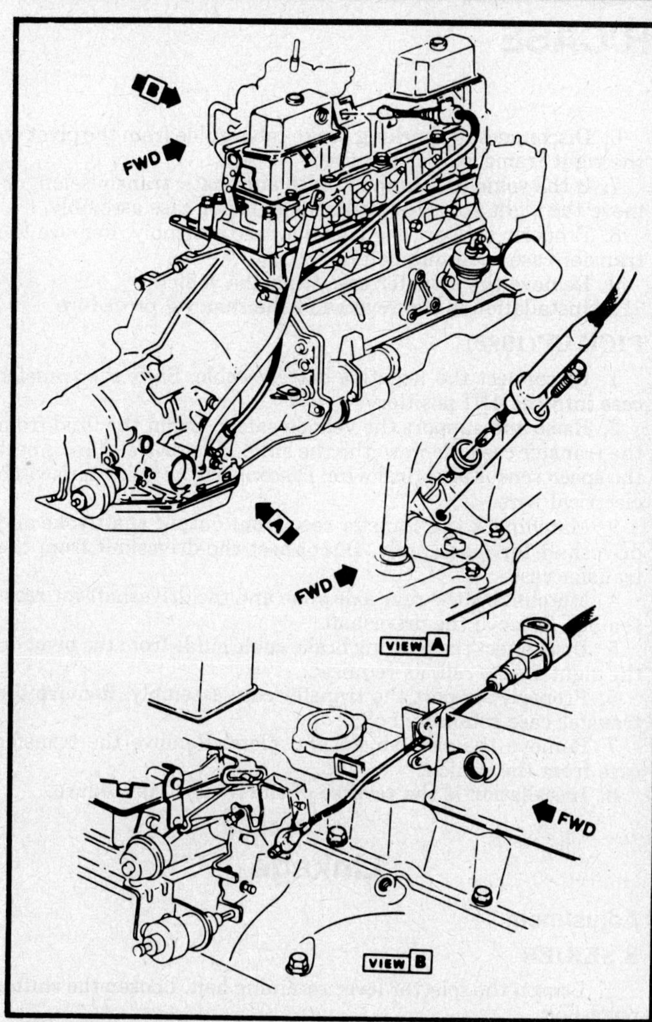

Detent cable adjustment – in-line engines

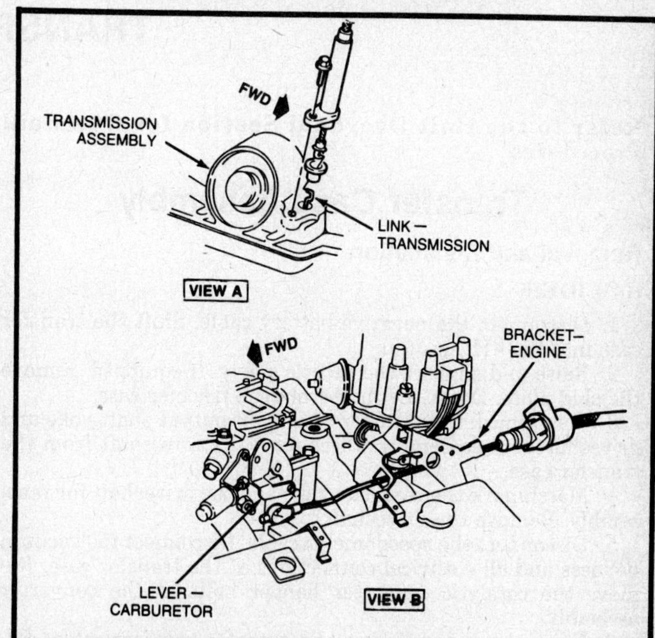

Detent cable adjustment – V8 engines

safety switch to prevent starting the engine in other than the park or neutral positions.

PICK UP, BLAZER/JIMMY AND SUBURBAN

1. Disconnect the negative battery cable. Remove the under dash hush panel, as required.
2. Disconnect the electrical connector at the switch assembly.
3. Remove the switch retaining screws. Remove the switch assembly from the vehicle.
4. Installation is the reverse of the removal procedure. Adjust the switch, as required.

VAN

1. Disconnect the negative battery cable. raise and support the vehicle safely.
2. Disconnect the electrical connector from the switch assembly.
3. Remove the switch mounting bracket retaining bolts. Remove the switch from the transmission.
4. Installation is the reverse of the removal procedure. Adjust the switch, as required.

Adjustment

1. Loosen the switch retaining screws. Position the selector lever in the neutral position.
2. Install the proper size alignment tool.
3. Tighten the switch retaining screws. Check for proper operation.

Oil Pan

Removal and Installation

1. Disconnect the negative battery cable. Raise and support the vehicle safely. If equipped, remove the drain plug and drain the fluid.
2. Remove the fluid pan retaining bolts. Be careful when separating the pan from the transmission case.
3. Installation is the reverse of the removal procedure. Be sure to use a new pan gasket or RTV sealant, as necessary.

Fluid and Filter

Replacement

1. Disconnect the negative battery cable. Raise and support the vehicle safely. If equipped, remove the drain plug and drain the fluid.
2. Remove the fluid pan retaining bolts. Be careful when separating the pan from the transmission case.
3. Remove the transmission filter retaining bolt or clip. Remove the filter from the valve body.
4. Installation is the reverse of the removal procedure. Be sure to use a new pan gasket or RTV sealant, as necessary.

TRANSFER CASE

Refer to the Unit Overhaul Section for Overhaul Procedures.

Transfer Case Assembly

Removal and Installation

S SERIES

1. Disconnect the negative battery cable. Shift the transfer case into the 4HI position.
2. Raise and support the vehicle safely. If equipped, remove the skid plate. Drain the fluid from the transfer case.
3. Matchmark the transfer case front output shaft yoke and driveshaft for reassembly. Disconnect the driveshaft from the transfer case.
4. Matchmark the rear axle yoke and the driveshaft for reassembly. Remove the driveshaft.
5. Disconnect the speedometer cable. Disconnect the vacuum harness and all electrical connections at the transfer case. Remove the catalytic converter hanger bolts at the converter assembly.
6. Raise the transmission and transfer case assembly. Remove the transmission mount retaining bolts. Remove the mount and the catalytic converter hanger. Lower the transmission and transfer case assembly.
7. Properly support the transfer case assembly. Remove the transfer case retaining bolts.
8. On vehicles equipped with automatic transmission, it will be necessary to remove the shift lever bracket mounting bolts from the transfer case adapter in order to remove the upper left transfer case retaining bolt.
9. Separate the transfer case from its mounting and remove it from the vehicle.
10. Installation is the reverse of the removal procedure.

PICK UP (1982–87), BLAZER/JIMMY AND SUBURBAN (MODEL205)

1. Disconnect the negative battery cable. Raise and support the vehicle safely.
2. Drain the fluid from the transfer case. Disconnect the speedometer cable. Remove the skid plate and the crossmember supports, as required.
3. Matchmark the transfer case front output shaft yoke and driveshaft for reassembly. Disconnect the driveshaft from the transfer case.
4. Matchmark the rear axle yoke and the driveshaft for reassembly. Remove the driveshaft. Disconnect the shift lever rod from the shift rail link.
5. Properly support the transfer case assembly. Remove the transfer case retaining bolts.
6. Remove the transfer case from the vehicle.
7. Installation is the reverse of the removal procedure.

PICK UP (1982–87), BLAZER/JIMMY AND SUBURBAN (MODEL208)

1. Disconnect the negative battery cable. Shift the transfer case into the 4HI position.
2. Raise and support the vehicle safely. Drain the fluid from the transfer case. Remove the cotter pin from the shift lever swivel.
3. Matchmark the transfer case front output shaft yoke and driveshaft for reassembly. Disconnect the driveshaft from the transfer case.
4. Matchmark the rear axle yoke and the driveshaft for reassembly. Remove the driveshaft.
5. Disconnect the speedometer cable. Disconnect the vacuum harness and all electrical connections at the transfer case.
6. Disconnect the parking brake cable guide from the pivot on the right frame rail, as required.
7. If the vehicle is equipped with automatic transmission, remove the right strut rod from the transfer case assembly.
8. Properly support the transfer case assembly. Remove the transfer case retaining bolts.
9. Remove the transfer case from the vehicle.
10. Installation is the reverse of the removal procedure.

PICK UP(1988)

1. Disconnect the negative battery cable. Shift the transfer case into the 4HI position.
2. Raise and support the vehicle safely. Drain the fluid from the transfer case. Remove the the shift lever swivel. Disconnect the speed sensor electrical wire. Disconnect the indicator switch electrical wire.
3. Matchmark the transfer case front output shaft yoke and driveshaft for reassembly. Disconnect the driveshaft from the transfer case.
4. Matchmark the rear axle yoke and the driveshaft for reassembly. Remove the driveshaft.
5. Disconnect the parking brake cable guide from the pivot on the right frame rail, as required.
6. Properly support the transfer case assembly. Remove the transfer case retaining bolts.
7. Remove the skid shield and plate. Remove the transfer case from the vehicle.
8. Installation is the reverse of the removal procedure.

Linkage

Adjustment

S SERIES

1. Loosen the selector lever retaining bolt. Loosen the shifter pivot bolt.
2. Shift the transfer case into the 4HI position. Remove the console assembly. Raise the shifter boot out of the way.
3. Install a $^5/_{16}$ in. gauge pin through the shifter and into the bracket. Install a service bolt at the transfer case shift lever. This will lock the transfer case in the 4HI position.
4. Tighten the selector lever retaining bolt 25–35 ft. lbs. Tighten the shifter pivot bolt 88–103 ft. lbs.
5. Remove the service bolt. Remove the gauge pin. Install removed parts.
6. Check for proper operation.

PICK UP (1982–87), BLAZER/JIMMY AND SUBURBAN (MODEL208)

1. Position the transfer case lever in the 4HI detent. Push the lower shift lever forward to the 4HI stop.
2. Install the swivel rod in the shift lever hole. Hang a 0.200 in. gauge rod behind the swivel
3. Install the rear rod nut against the gauge with the shifter against the 4HI stop.
4. Remove the gauge tool. Push the rear of the swivel rearward against the nut.
5. Tighten the front rod nut against the swivel. Check for proper operation.

PICK UP(1988)

1. Raise and support the vehicle safely. Remove the swivel from the transfer case shift lever.
2. Turn the swivel inward or outward to determine the correct shift detent.
3. Reinstall the swivel to the shift lever.

DRIVE LINES AND UNIVERSAL JOINTS

Drive Lines

Removal and Installation

ONE PIECE

1. Raise and support the vehicle safely.
2. If equipped, remove the skid plate.
3. Matchmark the front yoke of the driveshaft to the transmission. Matchmark the rear of the driveshaft to the differential housing.
4. Remove the bolts and retainers from the rear of the driveshaft. Remove the driveshaft from the vehicle.
5. Installation is the reverse of the removal procedure. Be sure to add transmission fluid, as required.

TWO PIECE

1. Raise and support the vehicle safely.
2. As required, remove the skid plate.

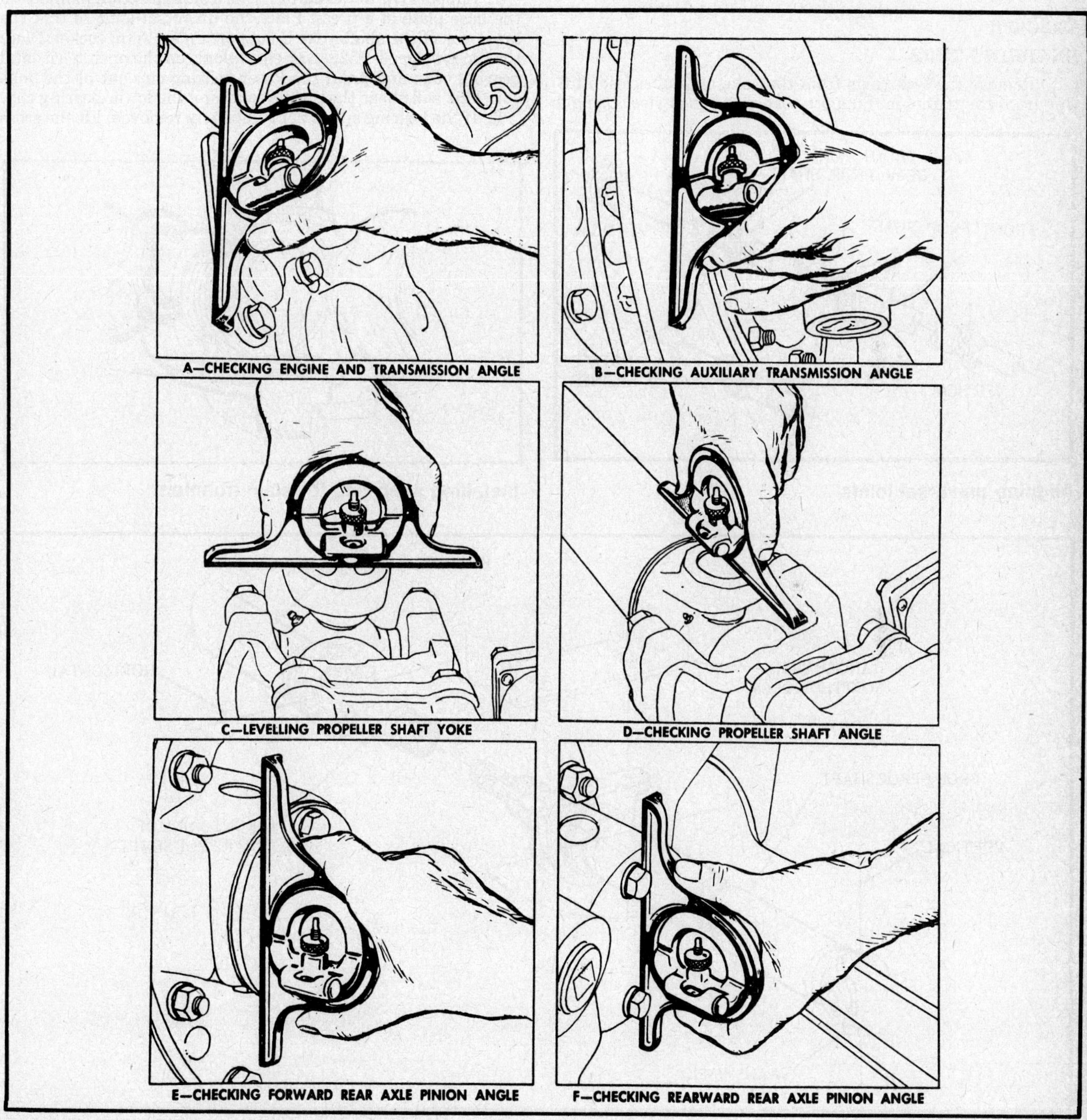

A—CHECKING ENGINE AND TRANSMISSION ANGLE
B—CHECKING AUXILIARY TRANSMISSION ANGLE
C—LEVELLING PROPELLER SHAFT YOKE
D—CHECKING PROPELLER SHAFT ANGLE
E—CHECKING FORWARD REAR AXLE PINION ANGLE
F—CHECKING REARWARD REAR AXLE PINION ANGLE

Method of checking drive line angles—typical

3. Matchmark the front yoke of the driveshaft to the transmission. Matchmark the rear of the driveshaft to the differential housing.

4. Remove the center bearing bolts and washers. Remove the center bearing.

5. Remove the front driveshaft. Remove the rear driveshaft bolts and retainers. Remove the rear driveshaft.

6. Installation is the reverse of the removal procedure. When installing the center bearing, be sure to align it 90° to the driveshaft center lines. Be sure to add transmission fluid, as required.

Universal Joints

Overhaul

SNAPRING TYPE

1. Remove the lock rings from the yoke and lubrication fitting from the trunnion. Support yoke in a bench vise. Using a soft drift and hammer, drive on one trunnion bearing to drive the opposite bearing from yoke.

2. The bearing cap cannot be driven completely out. Grasp the cap in the vise and work it out. Support the other side of yoke and drive the other bearing cap from the yoke and removeit. Remove the trunnion from the driveshaft yoke.

3. If equipped with a sliding sleeve, remove the trunnion bearings from the sleeve yoke in the same manner. Remove the seal retainer from the end of the sleeve and pull seal and the washer from the retainer.

4. Assembly is the reverse of the disassembly procedure.

PLASTIC RETAINING RING TYPE

1. Support the driveshaft in a horizontal position in line with the base plate of a press. Place the universal joint so that the lower ear of the shaft yoke is support on a 1⅛ in. socket. Place the cross press, J–9522–3 or equivalent, on the open horizontal bearing cups and press the lower bearing cup out of the yoke ear. This will shear the plastic retaining the lower bearing cup.

2. If the bearing cup is not completely removed, lift the cross

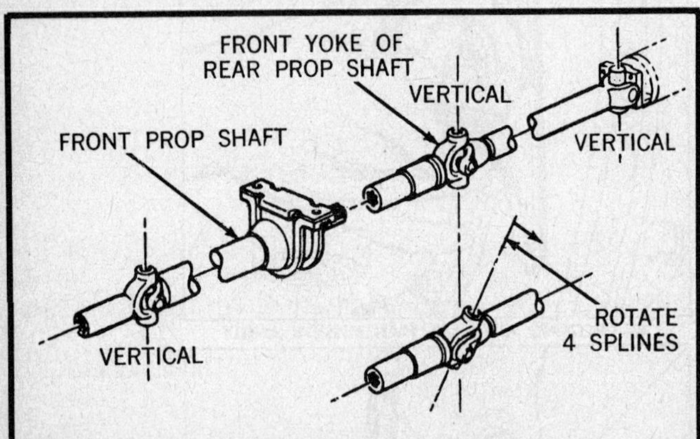

Aligning universal joints

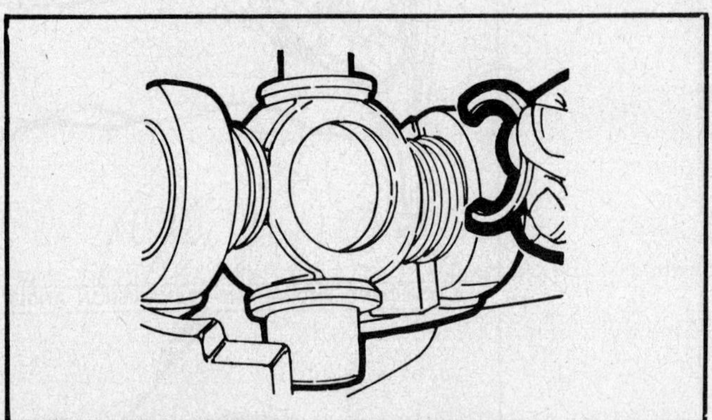

Installing snap ring to retain trunnion

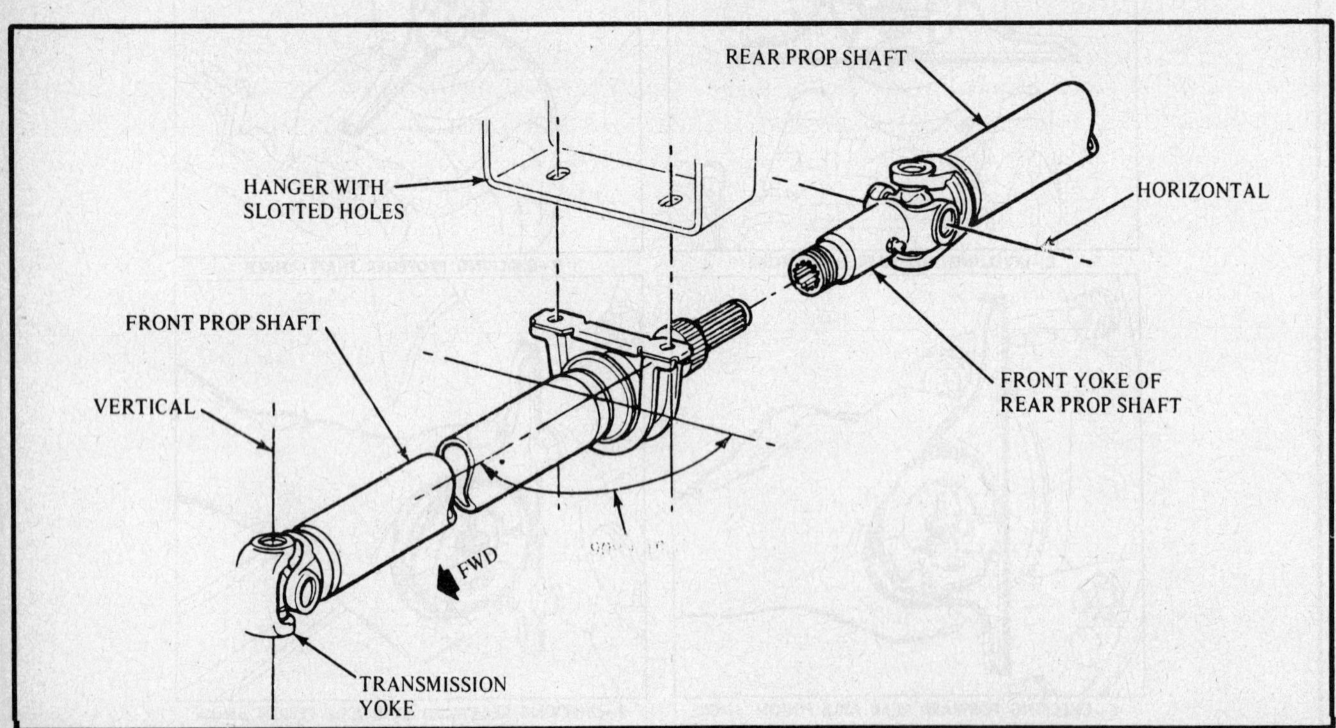

Center bearing support installation, typical

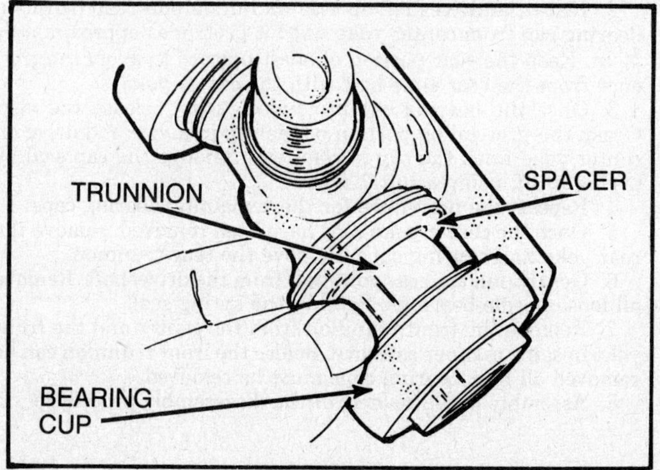

Using spacer to remove bearing cup – plastic retaining ring type

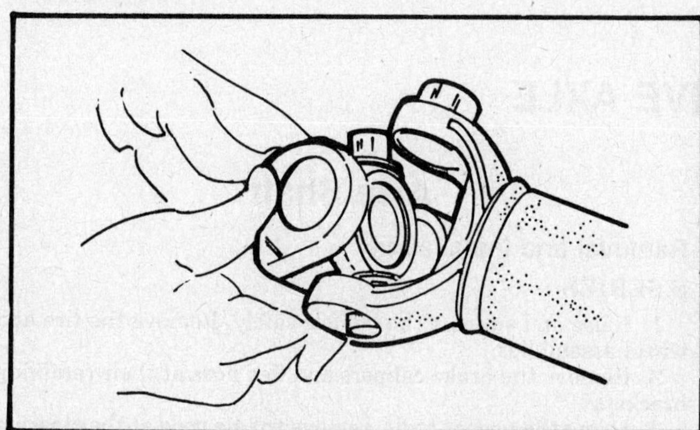
Installing trunnion into yoke – plastic retaining ring type

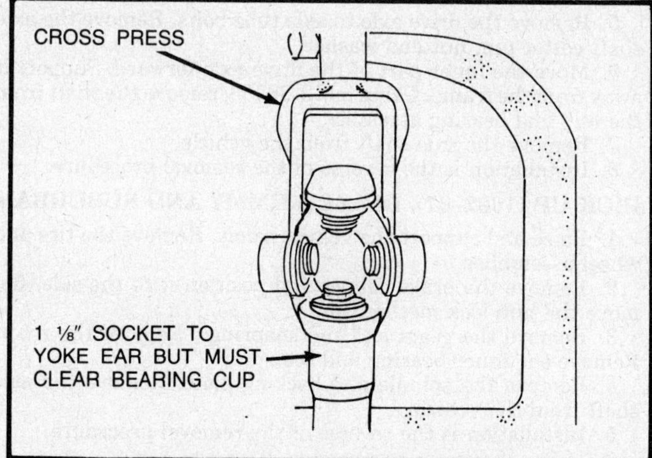

Pressing out bearing cup – plastic retaining ring type

and insert spacer J–9522–5 or equivalent, between the seal and bearing cup being removed. Complete the removal of the bearing cup, by pressing it out of the yoke.

3. Rotate the driveshaft, shear the opposite plastic retainer and press the opposite bearing cup out of the yoke as before, using spacer J–9522.

4. Disengage the cross from the yoke and remove.

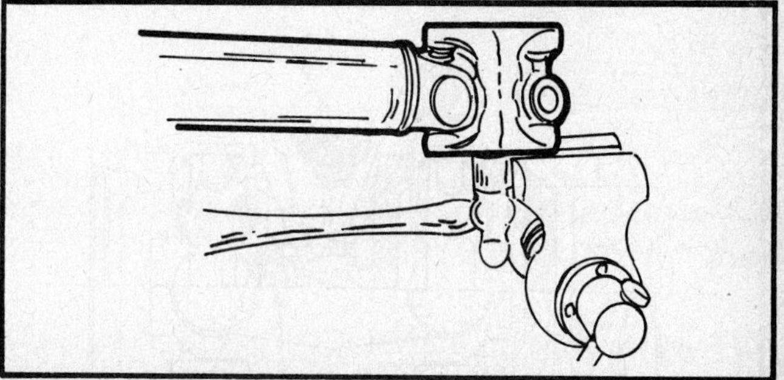
Driving yoke away from bearing cup

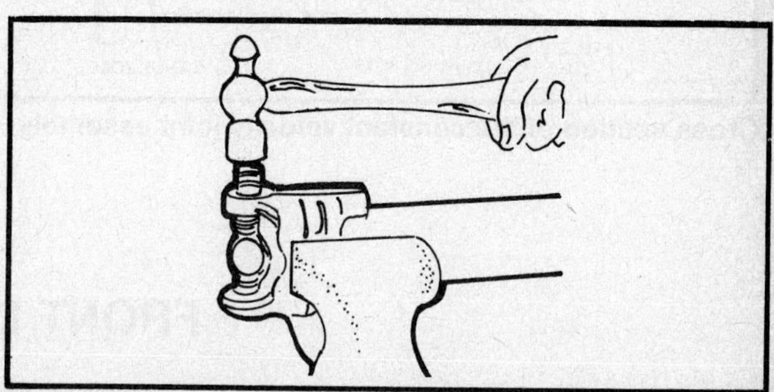
Driving out constant velocity joint bearing cups

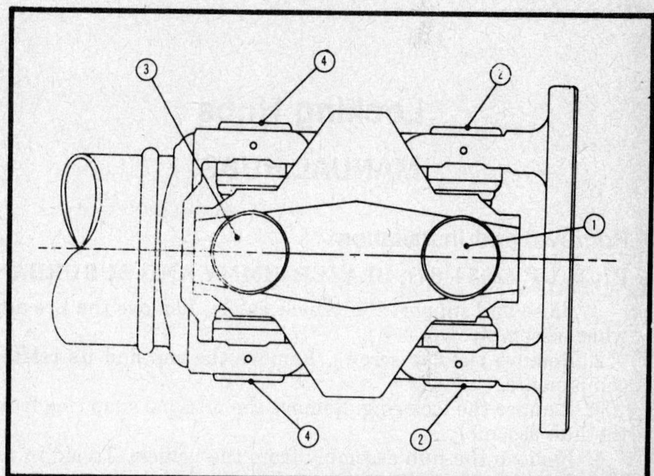

Constant velocity joint bearing cap removal sequence

NOTE: Production universal joints cannot be reassembled. There are no bearing retainer grooves in production bearing cups. Discard all universal joint parts removed.

5. Remove the remains of the sheared plastic bearing retainer from the ears of the yoke. This will aid in reassembly of the service joint bearing cups. It usually is easier to remove plastic if a small pin or punch is first driven through the injection holes.

6. If the front universal joint is being serviced, remove the pair of bearing cups from the slip yoke in the same manner.

7. Assembly is the reverse of the disassembly procedure.

CONSTANT VELOCITY JOINT

1. Remove the front driveshaft from vehicle. Remove the rear trunnion snaprings from center yoke. Remove the grease fitting.

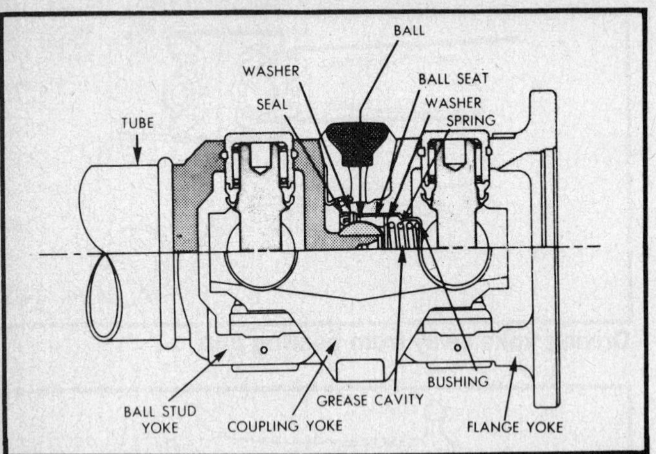

Cross section of the constant velocity joint assembly

2. Place the driveshaft in vise and drive one rear trunnion bearing cap from center yoke until it protrudes approximately $^3/_8$ in. Keep the rear portion of shaft upward to avoid interference from the rear yoke half with the center yoke.
3. Once the bearing cap protrudes $^3/_8$ in., release the vise. Grasp the protruding portion of the cap in a vise and drive on center yoke until the cap is removed. Remove the cap seal by prying it off, using a suitable tool.
4. Repeat, the procedure for the remaining bearing caps.
5. Once the center yoke caps have been removed, remove the rear yoke half bearing caps. Remove the rear trunnion.
6. Gently pull the rear yoke half from the driveshaft. Remove all loose needle bearings. Remove the spring seal.
7. Remove the front trunnion from the center and the front yoke in same manner as above. Before the front trunnion can be removed all four bearing caps must be removed.
8. Assembly is the reverse of the disassembly procedure.

FRONT DRIVE AXLE

Refer to the Unit Overhaul Section for Overhaul Procedures.

Locking Hubs

MANUAL HUBS

Removal and Installation

PICK UP (1982–87), BLAZER/JIMMY AND SUBURBAN

1. Raise and support the vehicle safely. Remove the tire and wheel assembly.
2. Remove the cap screws. Remove the cap and its related components.
3. Remove the lock ring. Remove the internal snap ring from the hub assembly.
4. Remove the hub assembly from the vehicle. To aid in removal, loosely thread two screws into the hub body perimeter. Use the screws to withdraw the hub from its mounting.
5. Installation is the reverse of the removal procedure.

AUTOMATIC HUBS

Removal and Installation

PICK UP (1982–87), BLAZER/JIMMY AND SUBURBAN

1. Raise and support the vehicle safely. Remove the tire and wheel assembly.
2. Remove the screws and O ring seals. Remove the cover. Remove the spring.
3. Remove the complete bearing assembly. Remove the seal.
4. Remove the keeper from the outer clutch housing. Depress the ring to release the locking unit. Using the proper tool, remove the ring.
5. Remove the locking unit from the hub assembly. To aid in removal, loosely thread two screws into the hub body perimeter. Use the screws to withdraw the hub from its mounting.
6. Installation is the reverse of the removal procedure.

Axle Shaft

Removal and Installation

S SERIES

1. Raise and support the vehicle safely. Remove the tire and wheel assemblies.
2. Remove the brake calipers and flex hose at their retaining brackets.
3. Using the proper tools, remove the tie rods at the steering knuckles.
4. Remove the lower shock absorber retaining bolts and move the shock absorbers out of the way. As required, remove the skid plate.
5. Remove the drive axle to axle tube bolts. Remove the axle shaft cotter pin, nut and washer.
6. Move the inner part of the drive axle forward. Support it away from the frame. Using tool J-28733, remove the shaft from the hub and bearing assembly.
7. Remove the axle shaft from the vehicle.
8. Installation is the reverse of the removal procedure.

PICK UP (1982–87), BLAZER/JIMMY AND SUBURBAN

1. Raise and support the vehicle safely. Remove the tire and wheel assemblies.
2. Remove the brake caliper and position it to the side. Remove the hub lock mechanism.
3. Remove the gears and the snaprings. Remove the rotor. Remove the inner bearing and seal.
4. Remove the spindle and backing plate. Remove the axle shaft from the vehicle.
5. Installation is the reverse of the removal procedure.

PICK UP (1988)

1. Raise and support the vehicle safely. Remove the tire and wheel assemblies.
2. Remove the brake calipers and flex hoses at their retaining brackets.
3. Using the proper tools, remove the tie rods at the steering knuckles.
4. Remove the lower shock absorber retaining bolts and move the shock absorbers out of the way. Remove the skid plate.

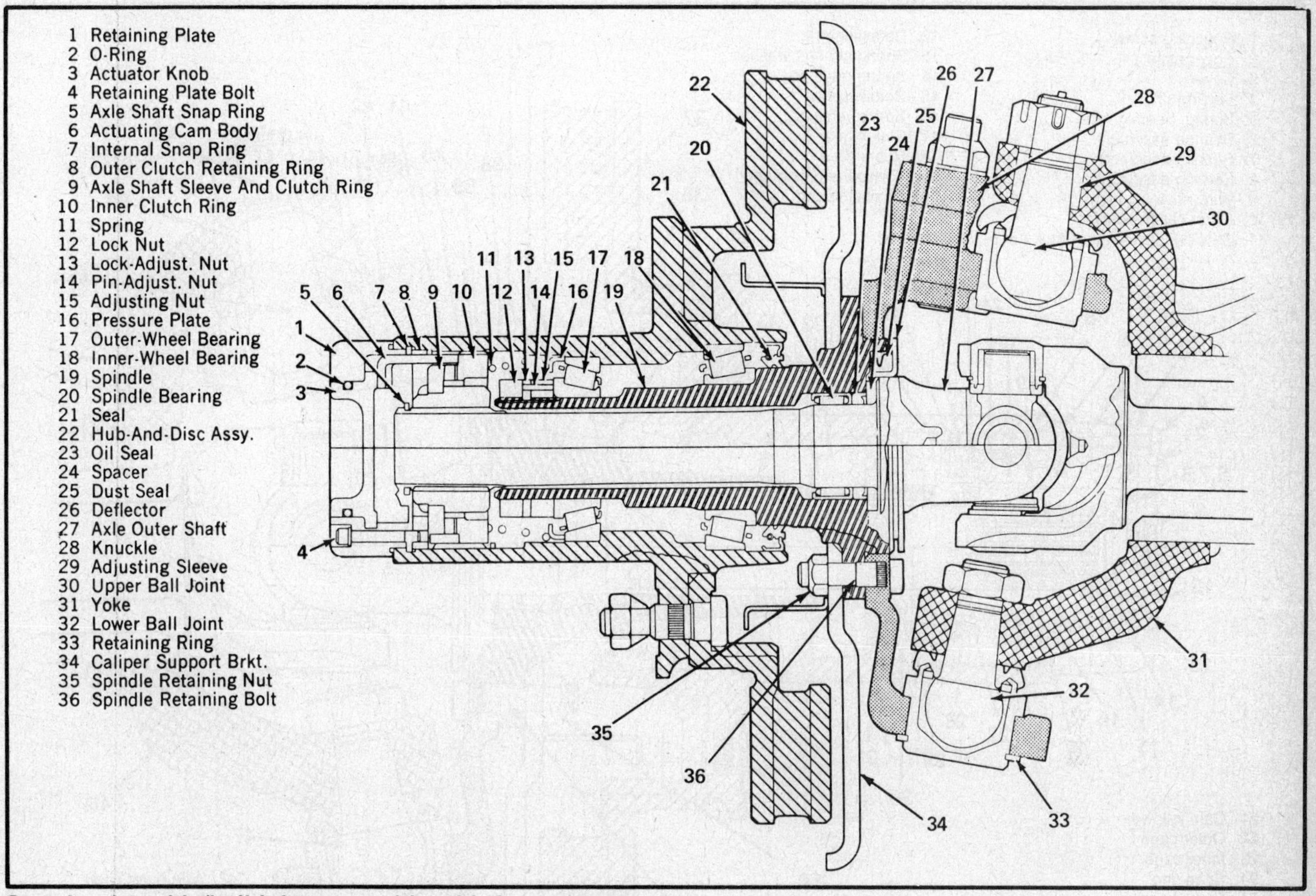

1 Retaining Plate
2 O-Ring
3 Actuator Knob
4 Retaining Plate Bolt
5 Axle Shaft Snap Ring
6 Actuating Cam Body
7 Internal Snap Ring
8 Outer Clutch Retaining Ring
9 Axle Shaft Sleeve And Clutch Ring
10 Inner Clutch Ring
11 Spring
12 Lock Nut
13 Lock-Adjust. Nut
14 Pin-Adjust. Nut
15 Adjusting Nut
16 Pressure Plate
17 Outer-Wheel Bearing
18 Inner-Wheel Bearing
19 Spindle
20 Spindle Bearing
21 Seal
22 Hub-And-Disc Assy.
23 Oil Seal
24 Spacer
25 Dust Seal
26 Deflector
27 Axle Outer Shaft
28 Knuckle
29 Adjusting Sleeve
30 Upper Ball Joint
31 Yoke
32 Lower Ball Joint
33 Retaining Ring
34 Caliper Support Brkt.
35 Spindle Retaining Nut
36 Spindle Retaining Bolt

Steering knuckle/ball joint assembly with free-wheeling hub

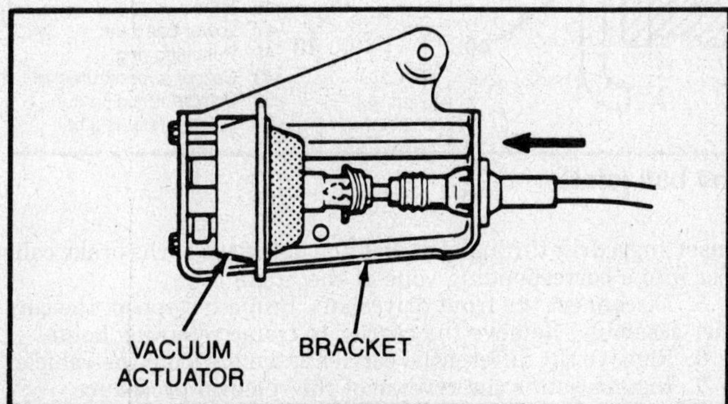

Cable-to-vacuum actuator attachment

5. Remove the drive axle to axle tube bolts. Remove the axle shaft cotter pin, nut and washer.
6. Move the inner part of the drive axle forward. Support it away from the frame. Using tool J-28733, remove the shaft from the hub and bearing assembly.
7. Remove the axle shaft from the vehicle.
8. Installation is the reverse of the removal procedure.

Axle Shaft Seal

Removal and Installation

PICK UP (1982–87), BLAZER/JIMMY AND SUBURBAN

1. Raise and support the vehicle safely. Remove the tire and wheel assemblies.
2. Remove the brake caliper and position it to the side. Remove the hub lock mechanism.
3. Remove the gears and the snaprings. Remove the rotor. Remove the inner bearing and seal.
4. Remove the spindle and backing plate. Remove the axle shaft from the vehicle.
5. Remove the axle shaft seal from its mounting.
6. Installation is the reverse of the removal procedure.

Axle Housing

Removal and Installation

S SERIES

1. Raise and support the vehicle safely. Remove the tube and shaft assembly.
2. Remove the bolt securing the steering stabilizer to the frame. Remove the idle arm retaining bolts.
3. Push the steering linkage toward the front of the vehicle. Remove the axle vent hose from the carrier fitting.
4. Disconnect the left hand drive axle shaft from the carrier by removing the retaining bolts. Keep the axle from turning by inserting a drift through the opening in the top of the brake caliper into a corresponding vane of the brake rotor.
5. Disconnect the front driveshaft. Properly support the carrier assembly. Remove ther carrier to frame retaining bolts..
6. Remove the differential carrier assembly from the vehicle.
7. Installation is the reverse of the removal procedure.

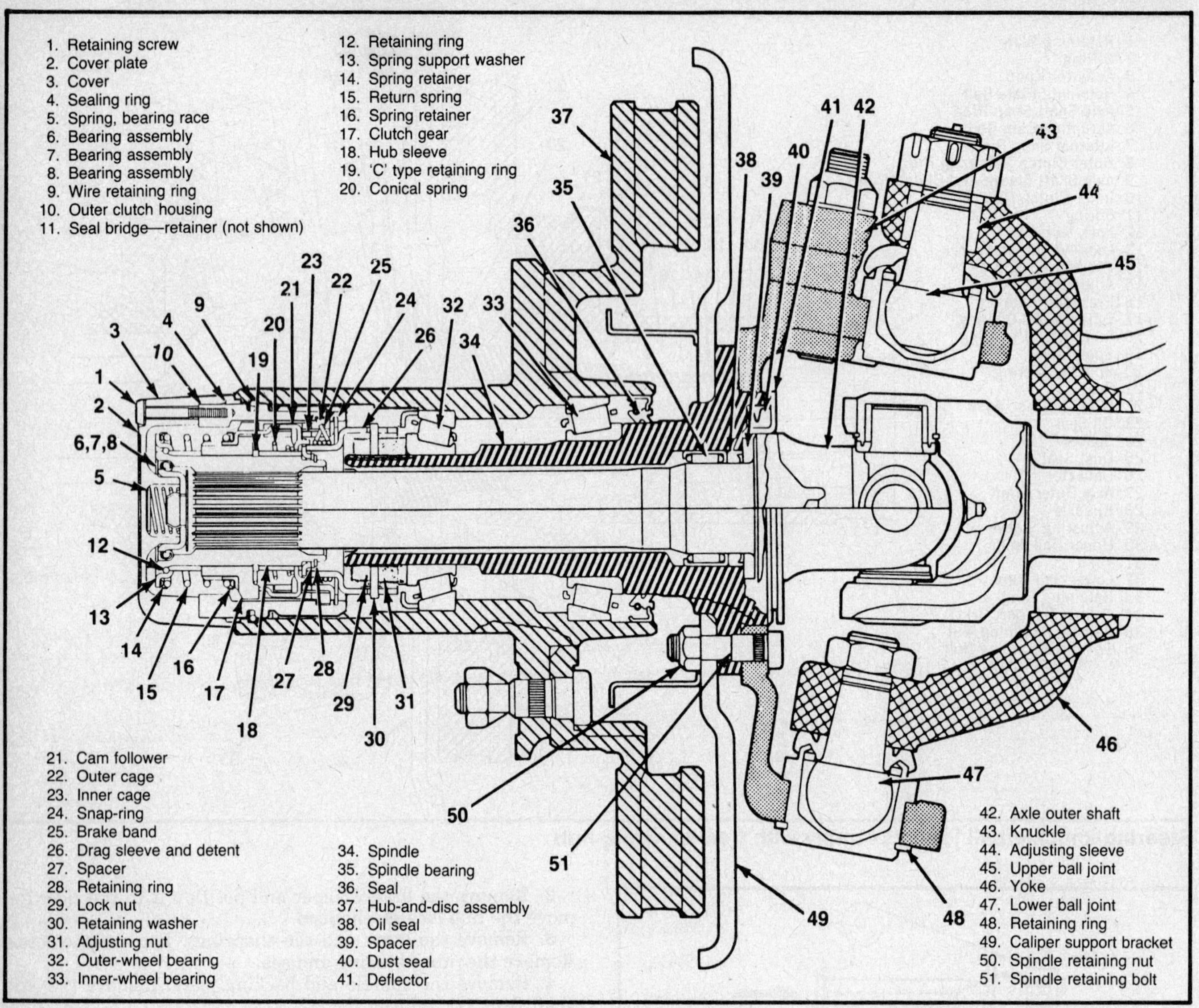

Typical front axle assembly with automatic locking hubs and ball joints

PICK UP (1982–87), BLAZER/JIMMY AND SUBURBAN

1. Raise and support the vehicle safely. Remove the driveshaft.
2. Disconnect the connecting rod from the steering arm. Disconnect the brake caliper and properly position it to the side.
3. Disconnect the shock absorbers from the axle brackets. As required, remove the front stabilizer bar.
4. Disconnect the axle vent tube clip at the differential housing. Properly support the axle assembly using a suitable jack.
5. Remove the U bolts from the axle and separate the axle from the springs. Remove the axle assembly from the vehicle.
6. Installation is the reverse of the removal procedure.

PICK UP (1988)

1. Raise and support the vehicle safely. Remove the tube and shaft assembly.
2. Remove the bolt securing the steering stabilizer to the frame. Remove the idle arm retaining bolts.
3. Push the steering linkage toward the front of the vehicle. Remove the axle vent hose from the carrier fitting.
4. Disconnect the left hand drive axle shaft from the carrier by removing the retaining bolts. Keep the axle from turning by inserting a drift through the opening in the top of the brake caliper into a corresponding vane of the brake rotor.
5. Disconnect the front driveshaft. Properly support the carrier assembly. Remove the carrier to frame retaining bolts.
6. Remove the differential carrier assembly from the vehicle.
7. Installation is the reverse of the removal procedure.

Tube and Shaft Assembly

Removal and Installation

S Series

1. Disconnect the negative battery cable. Disconnect the shift cable from the vacuum actuator by disengaging the locking spring. Then push the actuator diaphragm in to release the cable.
2. Unlock the steering wheel at the steering column so that the linkage is free to move. Raise and support the vehicle safely. Remove the tire and wheel assembly.

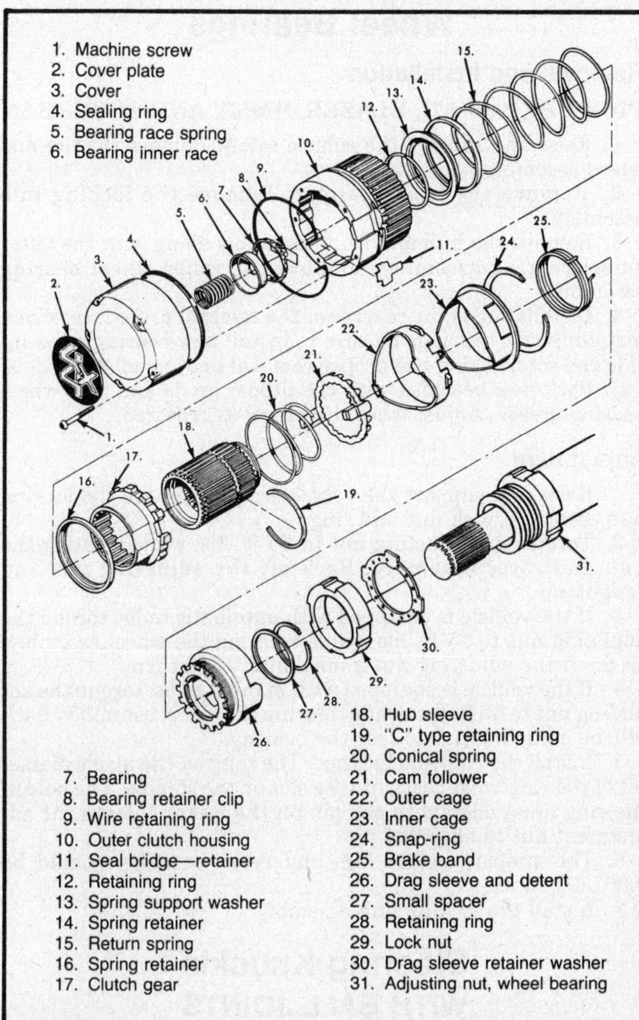

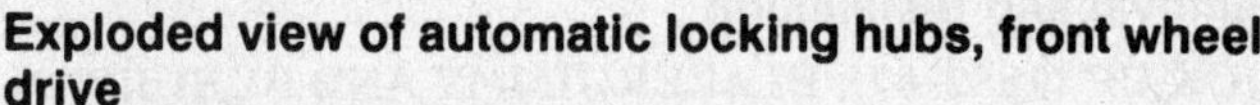
Exploded view of automatic locking hubs, front wheel drive

3. Remove the engine drive belt shield. If equipped, remove the skid plate.
4. Place a support under the right hand lower control arm and disconnect the right hand upper ball joint. Remove the support so that the control arm will hang free.
5. Disconnect the right hand drive axle shaft from the tube assembly by removing the retaining bolts. Keep the axle from turning by inserting a drift through the opening on top of the brake caliper and into a corresponding vane of the brake rotor.
6. Disconnect the four wheel drive indicator light electrical connection from the switch.
7. Remove the bolts securing the cable and the switch housing to the carrier and pull the housing away to gain access to the cable locking spring. Do not unscrew the cable coupling nut unless cable is being replaced.
8. Disconnect the cable from the shift fork shaft by lifting the spring over the slot in the shift fork. Remove two bolts securing the tube bracket to the frame.
9. Remove the remaining two upper bolts securing the tube assembly to carrier.
10. Remove the tube assembly by working it around the drive axle. Be careful not to allow sleeve, thrust washers, connector and output shaft to fall out of the carrier or be damaged when removing the tube.
11. Installation is the reverse of the removal procedure.

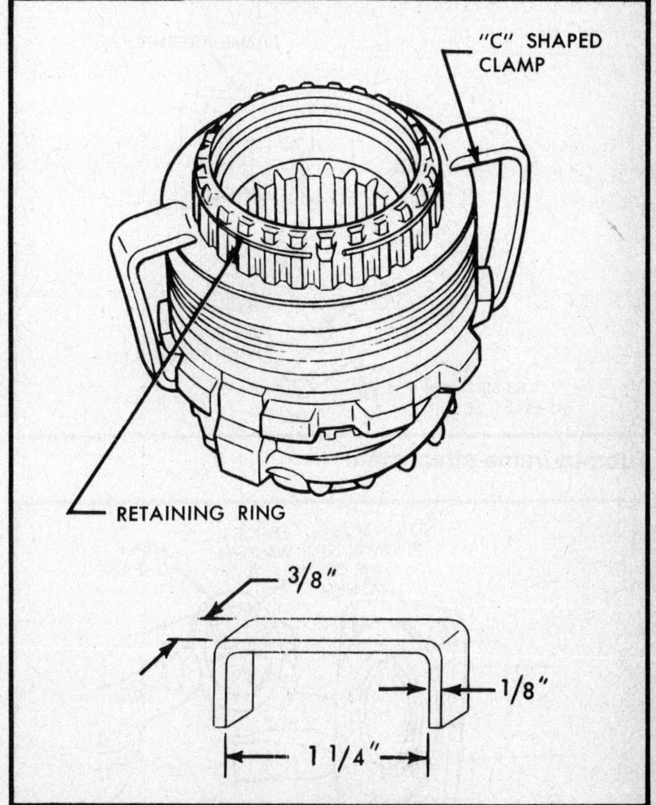

Fabricated "C" shaped clamps

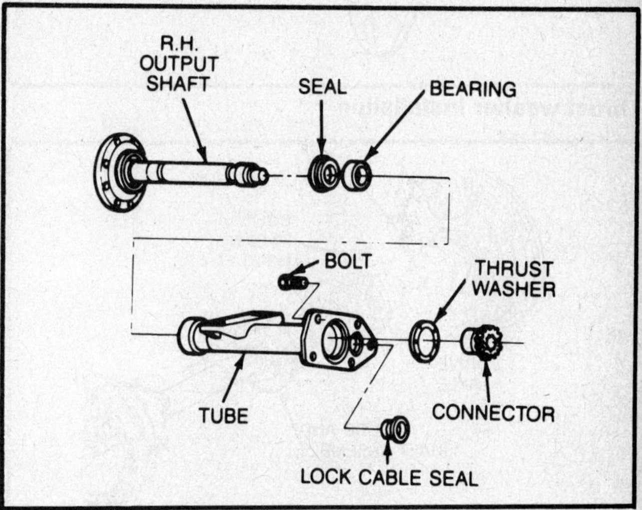

Right side output shaft and tube

Shift Cable

Removal and Installation

S Series

1. Disengage the shift cable from the vacuum actuator by disengaging the locking spring. Push the actuator diaphragm in to release the cable. Squeeze the two locking fingers of the cable with a pliers, then pull the cable out of of the bracket hole.
2. Raise the vehicle and remove the bolts securing the cable

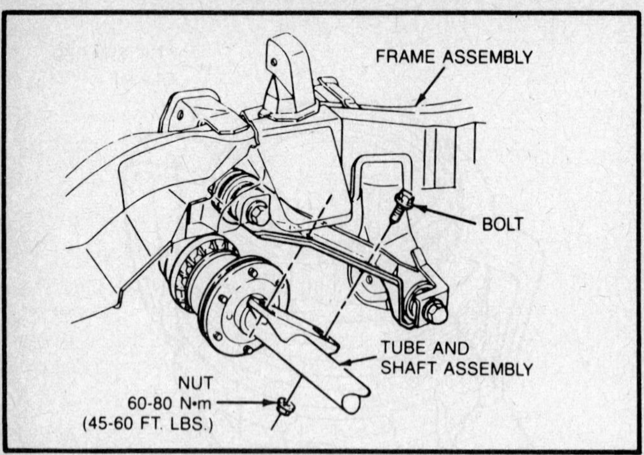

Tube-to-frame attachment

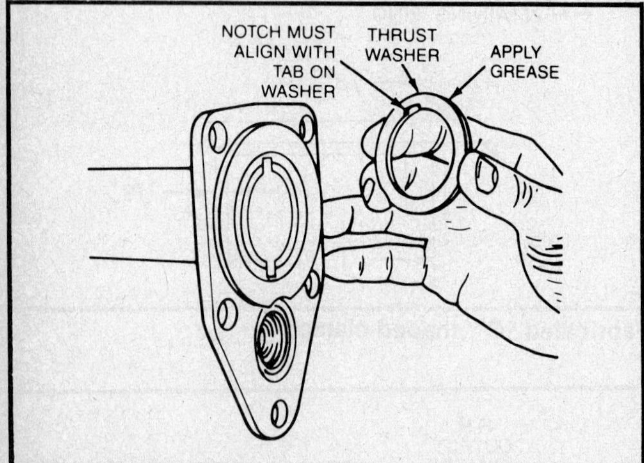

Thrust washer installation

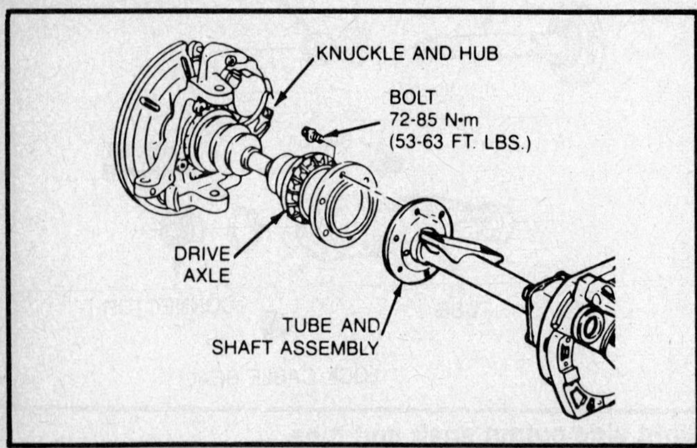

Drive axle bolts

and the switch housing to the carrier. Pull the housing away to gain access to the cable locking spring. Disconnect the cable from the shift fork shaft by lifting the spring over the slot in the shift fork.

3. Unscrew the cable from the housing. Remove the cable from the vehicle.

4. Installation is the reverse of the removal procedure. Check for proper cable operation.

Wheel Bearings

Removal and Installation

PICK UP (1982–87), BLAZER/JIMMY AND SUBURBAN

1. Raise and support the vehicle safely. Remove the tire and wheel assembly.
2. Remove the brake caliper. Remove the locking hub assembly.
3. Remove the hub and rotor assembly along with the outer wheel bearing assembly. Remove the inner wheel bearing assembly.
4. Installation is the reverse of the removal procedure. When installing new bearings be sure to install new bearing races inside the rotor, using the proper removal and installation tools.
5. Pack new bearings with the proper grade and type wheel bearing grease. Adjust wheel bearings, as required.

Adjustment

1. Raise and support the vehicle safely. Remove the locking hub assembly, lock nut and ring.
2. Torque the adjusting nut to 50 ft. lbs. while rotating the hub and rotor assembly. Back off the adjusting nut and retighten.
3. If the vehicle is equipped with automatic hubs, torque the adjusting nut to 35 ft. lbs. while rotating the wheel assembly. Back off the adjusting nut a maximum of $^3/_8$ turn.
4. If the vehicle is equipped with manual hubs, torque the adjusting nut to 50 ft. lbs. while rotating the wheel assembly. Back off the adjusting nut to free the bearing.
5. Install the ring and locknut. The tang on the inside diameter of the ring must pass onto the slot on the spindle. The hole in the ring must align with the pin on the locknut. Move the adjustment nut to align the pin.
6. The endplay in the hub and rotor assembly should be 0.001–0.010 in.
7. Install the locking hub assembly.

Steering Knuckle

WITH BALL JOINTS

Removal and Installation

PICK UP (1982–87), BLAZER/JIMMY AND SUBURBAN

1. With the spindle and axle removed, disconnect the tie rod end from the steering arm.
2. If necessary for working clearance, remove the steering arm from the knuckle. If the steering arm is removed, discard the three self locking nuts and replace them with new self locking nuts upon assembly.
3. Remove the upper and lower ball joint retaining nuts. The upper ball joint stud and nut have a cotter pin retainer, while the lower ball point stud and nut have none.
4. Using the proper wedge type tool, separate the lower ball joint stud from the knuckle. Repeat this operation for the upper ball joint stud.
5. Remove the snapring retainer from the lower ball joint. Using the proper tools, press the lower ball joint from the knuckle. The lower ball joint must be removed before any service can be performed on the upper ball joint.
6. Using the proper tool, press the upper ball joint from the knuckle. Replacement of the knuckle can be accomplished at this point in the disassembly.
7. Installation is the reverse of the removal procedure.

WITH KING PINS

Removal and Installation

PICK UP (1982–87), BLAZER/JIMMY AND SUBURBAN

1. Remove the hub and spindle assembly. It may be necessary

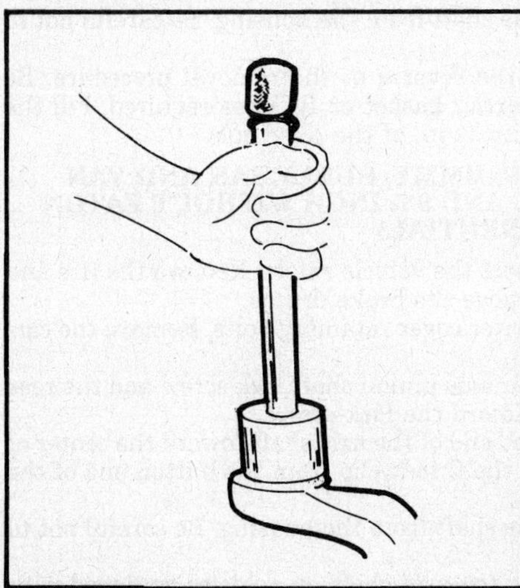
Installing oil seal—front drive yoke w/king pins

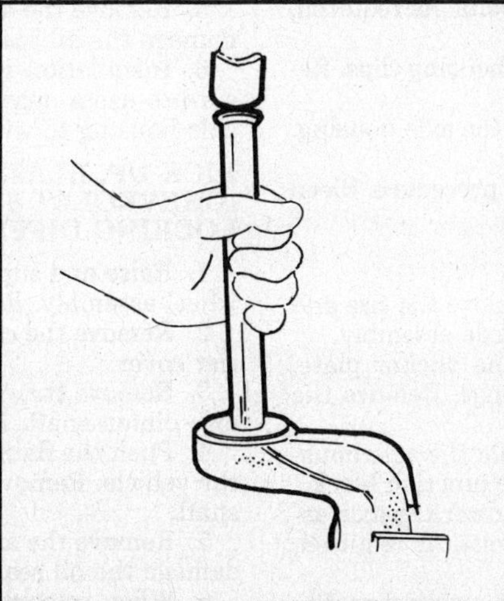
Installing grease retainer—front drive yoke w/king pins

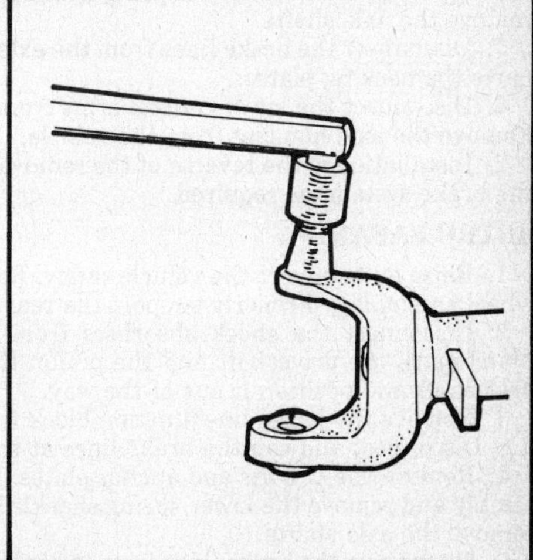
Installing upper king pin—front drive axle

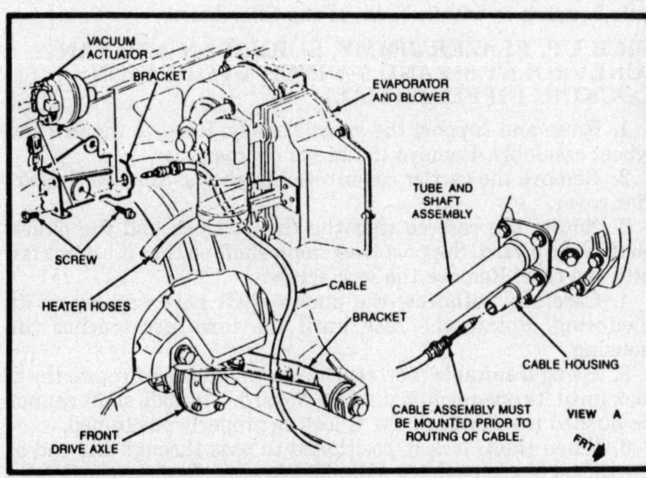

Vacuum actuator assembly

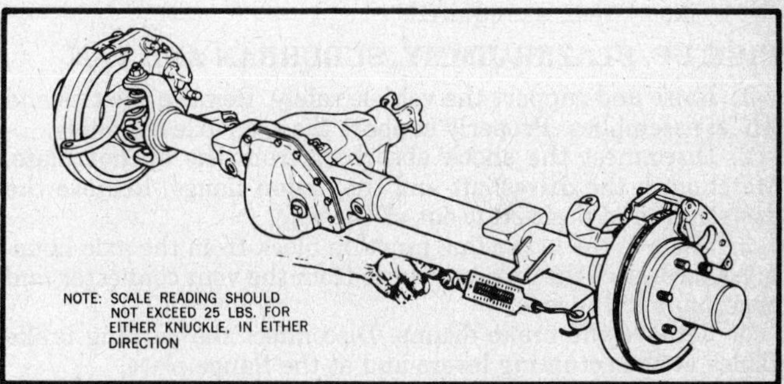

Checking front drive axle ball joint adjustment

to tap lightly on the spindle with a rawhide hammer in order to free it from the knuckle.

2. Remove the four cap nuts from the upper king pin. Spring pressure will force the cap up. Remove the cap, spring and gasket. Discard the gasket.

3. Remove the four cap screws from the lower king pin bearing. Remove the cap and the lower king pin. Remove the upper king pin bushing.

4. Remove the knuckle from the yoke. Remove the king pin felt seal.

5. Remove the upper king pin from the yoke using a breaker bar and any suitable adapter designed to fit the king pin. Considerable force will be required to remove the king pin from the yoke as the king pin is originally torqued to 500–600 ft. lbs

6. Remove the lower king pin bearing cup, cone, grease retainer and seal. Discard the seal. Discard the grease retainer if damaged.

7. Installation is the reverse of the removal procedure. Torque the upper king pin to 500–600 ft. lbs.

REAR DRIVE AXLE

Refer to the Unit Overhaul Section for Overhaul Procedures.

Axle Housing Assembly

Removal and Installation

S SERIES

1. Raise and support the vehicle safely. Remove the tire and wheel assemblies. Properly support the rear axle assembly.

2. Disconnect the shock absorbers from the anchor plate. Matchmark the driveshaft and the pinion flange. Remove the driveshaft and position it out of the way.

3. Remove the brake line junction block from the axle housing. Disconnect and cap the brake lines at the junction block.

4. Remove the U bolts and anchor plates. Lower the axle as-

sembly and remove the lower spring shackle bolts. As required, remove the axle shafts.

5. Disconnect the brake lines from the axle housing clips. Remove the backing plates.

6. Disconnect the lower control arms from the axle housing. Remove the axle housing from the vehicle.

7. Installation is the reverse of the removal procedure. Bleed the brake system, as required.

ASTRO/SAFARI

1. Raise and support the vehicle safely. Remove the tire and wheel assemblies. Properly support the rear axle assembly.

2. Disconnect the shock absorbers from the anchor plate. Matchmark the driveshaft and the pinion flange. Remove the driveshaft and position it out of the way.

3. Remove the brake line junction block from the axle housing. Disconnect and cap the brake lines at the junction block.

4. Remove the U bolts and anchor plates. Lower the axle assembly and remove the lower spring shackle bolts. As required, remove the axle shafts.

5. Disconnect the brake lines from the axle housing clips. Remove the backing plates.

6. Disconnect the lower control arms from the axle housing. Remove the axle housing from the vehicle.

7. Installation is the reverse of the removal procedure. Bleed the brake system, as required.

PICK UP, BLAZER/JIMMY, SUBURBAN AND VAN

1. Raise and support the vehicle safely. Remove the tire and wheel assemblies. Properly support the rear axle assembly.

2. Disconnect the shock absorbers from the anchor plate. Matchmark the driveshaft and the pinion flange. Remove the driveshaft and position it out of the way.

3. Remove the brake line junction block from the axle housing. Disconnect the axle vent hose from the vent connector and position it to the side.

4. Remove the brake drums. Disconnect the parking brake cables at the actuating levers and at the flange plate.

5. Remove the U bolts and anchor plates. Remove the axle housing from the vehicle.

8. Installation is the reverse of the removal procedure.

Axle Shaft

Removal and Installation

S SERIES

1. Raise and support the vehicle safely. Remove the tire and wheel assembly. Drain the lubricant.

2. Remove the carrier cover retaining bolts. Remove the carrier cover.

3. Remove the rear axle pinion shaft lock screw and the rear axle pinion shaft. Discard the lock screw.

4. Push the flanged end of the axle shaft toward the center of the vehicle. Remove the C lock clip from the button end of the shaft.

5. Remove the axle shaft from the housing. Be careful not to damage the oil seal.

6. Installation is the reverse of the removal procedure. Be sure to use a new carrier gasket or RTV, as required. Fill the axle housing to within 3/8 in. of the filler hole.

ASTRO/SAFARI

1. Raise and support the vehicle safely. Remove the tire and wheel assembly. Remove the brake drums. Drain the lubricant.

2. Remove the carrier cover retaining bolts. Remove the carrier cover.

3. Remove the rear axle pinion shaft lock screw and the rear axle pinion shaft. Discard the lock screw.

4. Push the flanged end of the axle shaft toward the center of the vehicle. Remove the C lock clip from the button end of the shaft.

5. Remove the axle shaft from the housing. Be careful not to damage the oil seal.

6. Installation is the reverse of the removal procedure. Be sure to use a new carrier gasket or RTV, as required. Fill the axle housing to within 3/8 in. of the filler hole.

PICK UP, BLAZER/JIMMY, SUBURBAN AND VAN (CHEVROLET 8½ AND 9½ INCH WITHOUT EATON LOCKING DIFFERENTIAL)

1. Raise and support the vehicle safely. Remove the tire and wheel assembly. Remove the brake drums.

2. Remove the carrier cover retaining bolts. Remove the carrier cover.

3. Remove the rear axle pinion shaft lock screw and the rear axle pinion shaft. Discard the lock screw.

4. Push the flanged end of the axle shaft toward the center of the vehicle. Remove the C lock clip from the button end of the shaft.

5. Remove the axle shaft from the housing. Be careful not to damage the oil seal.

6. When removing the axle shaft on vehicles equipped with the 9½ inch ring gear, be sure that the thrust washer in the differential case does not slide out.

7. Installation is the reverse of the removal procedure. Be sure to use a new carrier gasket or RTV, as required. Fill the axle housing to within 3/8 in. of the filler hole.

PICK UP, BLAZER/JIMMY, SUBURBAN AND VAN (CHEVROLET 8½ AND 9½ INCH WITH EATON LOCKING DIFFERENTIAL)

1. Raise and support the vehicle safely. Remove the tire and wheel assembly. Remove the brake drums.

2. Remove the carrier cover retaining bolts. Remove the carrier cover.

3. Rotate the case so that the thrust block and the pinion shaft are upward. Support the pinion shaft so that it cannot fall into the case. Remove the lock screw.

4. Carefully withdraw the pinion shaft part way out of its mounting. Rotate the case until the case just touches the housing.

5. Using a suitable tool, reach into the case and rotate the C lock until its open points directly inward. The axle shaft cannot be pushed inward until the C lock is properly positioned.

6. When the C lock is positioned to pass through the end of the thrust block, push the axle shaft inward. Remove the C lock.

7. Remove the axle shaft from the vehicle.

8. Installation is the reverse of the removal procedure. Be sure to use a new carrier gasket or RTV, as required. Fill the axle housing to within 3/8 in. of the filler hole.

PICK UP, BLAZER/JIMMY, SUBURBAN AND VAN (CHEVROLET 10½ AND DANA 9¾ AND 10½ INCH)

1. Raise and support the vehicle safely. Remove the tire and wheel assembly.

2. Remove the bolts that retain the axle shaft flange to the wheel hub.

3. Tap the flange with a suitable hammer and loosen the axle shaft.

4. Twist the shaft assembly and remove it from the axle tube.

5. Installation is the reverse of the removal procedure.

6. Place a new gasket or apply RTV sealant over the axle shaft. Position the shaft in the housing so that the shaft splines enter the differential side gear.

PICK UP, BLAZER/JIMMY, SUBURBAN AND VAN (ROCKWELL 12 INCH)

1. Raise and support the vehicle safely. As required, remove the tire and wheel assembly.

2. Install tool J-8177 into the tapped hole on the axle flange. Using a slide hammer, remove the axle shaft from its mounting.

3. Installation is the reverse of the removal procedure. Be

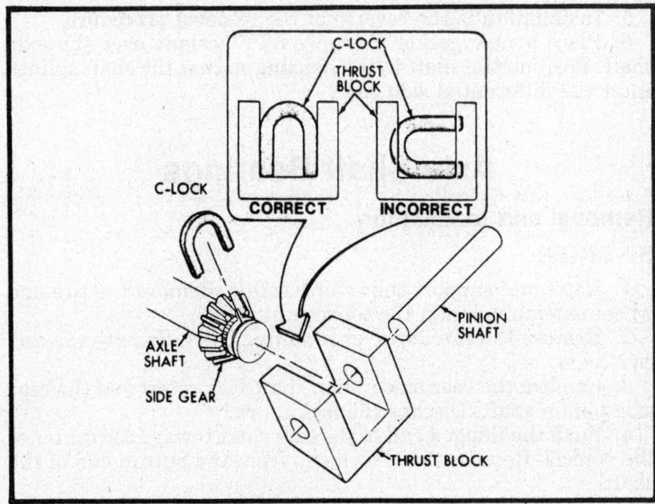

Correct "C" lock position

sure that the flange splines index into the hub splines. Tap the shaft into position.

Pinion Seal

Removal and Installation

S SERIES

1. Raise and support the vehicle safely. Matchmark the driveshaft and the pinion flange.
2. Disconnect the driveshaft from the rear differential. Position the driveshaft out of the way.
3. Mark the position of the pinion flange, pinion shaft and nut. Using tool J-8614-01 or equivalent, remove the pinion flange nut and washer.
4. Remove the pinion flange. Position a drain pan under the assembly to catch any excess lubricant.
5. Using the proper tool, remove the seal from its mounting.
6. Installation is the reverse of the removal procedure. Be sure to replace any lost lubricant.

ASTRO/SAFARI

1. Raise and support the vehicle safely. Matchmark the driveshaft and the pinion flange.
2. Disconnect the driveshaft from the rear differential. Position the driveshaft out of the way.
3. Mark the position of the pinion flange, pinion shaft and nut. Using tool J-8614-01 or equivalent, remove the pinion flange nut and washer.
4. Remove the pinion flange. Position a drain pan under the assembly to catch any excess lubricant.
5. Using the proper tool, remove the seal from its mounting.
6. Installation is the reverse of the removal procedure. Be sure to replace any lost lubricant.

PICK UP, BLAZER/JIMMY, SUBURBAN AND VAN

1. Raise and support the vehicle safely. Matchmark the driveshaft and the pinion flange.
2. Disconnect the driveshaft from the rear differential. Position the driveshaft out of the way.
3. Mark the position of the pinion flange, pinion shaft and nut. Using the proper flange removal tools, remove the pinion flange nut and washer.
4. Remove the pinion flange. Position a drain pan under the assembly to catch any excess lubricant.
5. Using the proper tool, remove the seal from its mounting.
6. Installation is the reverse of the removal procedure. Be sure to replace any lost lubricant.

Removing lock nut—typical

Axle Shaft Seal

Removal and Installation

S SERIES

1. Raise and support the vehicle safely. Remove the tire and wheel assembly. Drain the lubricant.
2. Remove the carrier cover retaining bolts. Remove the carrier cover.
3. Remove the rear axle pinion shaft lock screw and the rear axle pinion shaft. Discard the lock screw.
4. Push the flanged end of the axle shaft toward the center of the vehicle. Remove the C lock clip from the button end of the shaft.
5. Remove the axle shaft from the housing.
6. Using the proper seal removal tool, remove the seal from its mounting.
7. Installation is the reverse of the removal procedure. Be sure to use a new carrier gasket or RTV, as required. Fill the axle housing to within 3⁄8 in. of the filler hole.

ASTRO/SAFARI

1. Raise and support the vehicle safely. Remove the tire and wheel assembly. Drain the lubricant.
2. Remove the carrier cover retaining bolts. Remove the carrier cover.
3. Remove the rear axle pinion shaft lock screw and the rear axle pinion shaft. Discard the lock screw.
4. Push the flanged end of the axle shaft toward the center of the vehicle. Remove the C lock clip from the button end of the shaft.
5. Remove the axle shaft from the housing.
6. Using the proper seal removal tool, remove the seal from its mounting.
7. Installation is the reverse of the removal procedure. Be sure to use a new carrier gasket or RTV, as required. Fill the axle housing to within 3⁄8 in. of the filler hole.

PICK UP, BLAZER/JIMMY, SUBURBAN AND VAN (CHEVROLET 8½ AND 9½ INCH)

1. Raise and support the vehicle safely. Remove the tire and wheel assembly. Remove the brake drum.
2. Remove the carrier cover retaining bolts. Remove the carrier cover.
3. Remove the rear axle pinion shaft lock screw and the rear axle pinion shaft. Discard the lock screw.
4. Push the flanged end of the axle shaft toward the center of the vehicle. Remove the C lock clip from the button end of the shaft.
5. Remove the axle shaft from the housing.
6. When removing the axle shaft on vehicles equipped with

the 9½ inch ring gear, be sure that the thrust washer in the differential case does not slide out.

7. Using the proper removal tool, remove the seal from its mounting.

8. Installation is the reverse of the removal procedure. Be sure to use a new carrier gasket or RTV, as required. Fill the axle housing to within 3/8 in. of the filler hole.

PICK UP, BLAZER/JIMMY, SUBURBAN AND VAN (CHEVROLET 10½ AND DANA 9¾ AND 10½ INCH)

1. Raise and support the vehicle safely. Remove the tire and wheel assembly.
2. Remove the bolts that retain the axle shaft flange to the wheel hub.
3. Tap the flange with a suitable hammer and loosen the axle shaft.
4. Twist the shaft assembly and remove it from the axle tube. Remove the oil seal from its mounting.

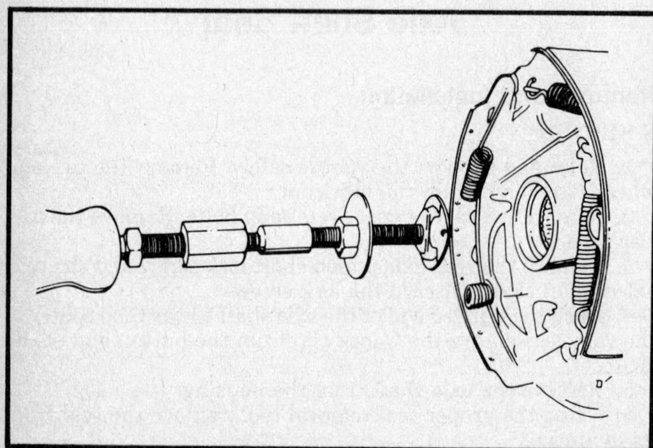

Bearing and oil seal removal

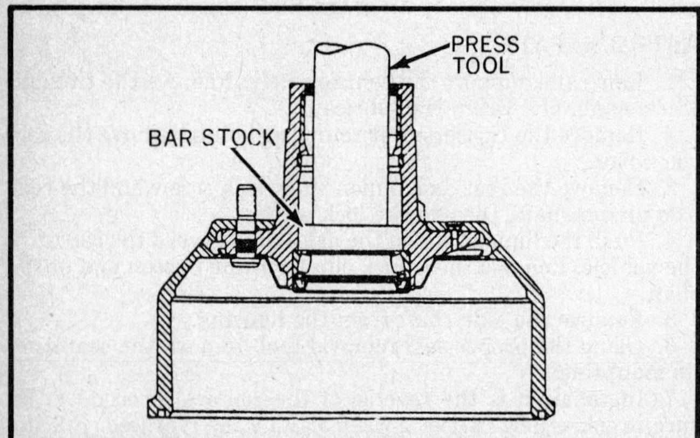

Removing hub inner bearing cup

5. Installation is the reverse of the removal procedure.
6. Place a new gasket or apply RTV sealant over the axle shaft. Position the shaft in the housing so that the shaft splines enter the differential side gear.

Axle Shaft Bearings

Removal and Installation

S SERIES

1. Raise and support the vehicle safely. Remove the tire and wheel assembly. Drain the lubricant.
2. Remove the carrier cover retaining bolts. Remove the carrier cover.
3. Remove the rear axle pinion shaft lock screw and the rear axle pinion shaft. Discard the lock screw.
4. Push the flanged end of the axle shaft toward the center of the vehicle. Remove the C lock clip from the button end of the shaft.
5. Remove the axle shaft from the housing. Using the proper seal removal tool, remove the seal from its mounting.
6. Install tool J-23689 into the bore and position it behind the bearing so that the tangs on the tool engage the bearing outer race.
7. Using a slide hammer, remove the bearing from its mounting.
8. Installation is the reverse of the removal procedure. Be sure to use a new carrier gasket or RTV, as required. Fill the axle housing to within 3/8 in. of the filler hole.

ASTRO/SAFARI

1. Raise and support the vehicle safely. Remove the tire and wheel assembly. Drain the lubricant.
2. Remove the carrier cover retaining bolts. Remove the carrier cover.
3. Remove the rear axle pinion shaft lock screw and the rear axle pinion shaft. Discard the lock screw.
4. Push the flanged end of the axle shaft toward the center of the vehicle. Remove the C lock clip from the button end of the shaft.
5. Remove the axle shaft from the housing. Using the proper seal removal tool, remove the seal from its mounting.
6. Install tool J-23689 into the bore and position it behind the bearing so that the tangs on the tool engage the bearing outer race.
7. Using a slide hammer, remove the bearing from its mounting.
8. Installation is the reverse of the removal procedure. Be sure to use a new carrier gasket or RTV, as required. Fill the axle housing to within 3/8 in. of the filler hole.

PICK UP, BLAZER/JIMMY, SUBURBAN AND VAN (CHEVROLET 8½ AND 9½ INCH)

1. Raise and support the vehicle safely. Remove the tire and wheel assembly. Remove the brake drum.
2. Remove the carrier cover retaining bolts. Remove the carrier cover.

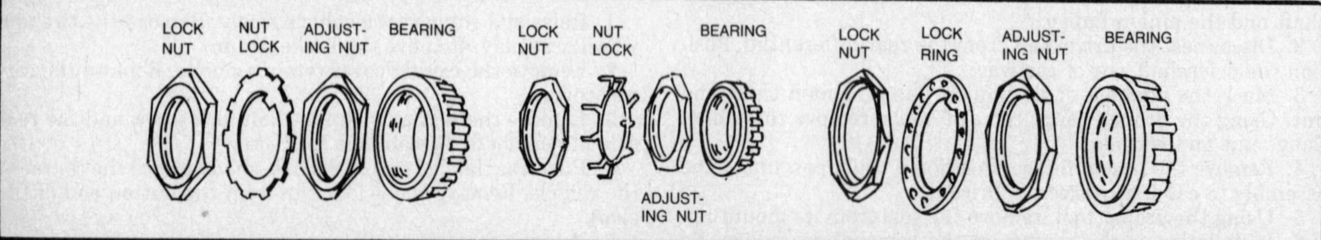

Typical lock types used on rear axle bearing nuts—full floating axle system

3. Remove the rear axle pinion shaft lock screw and the rear axle pinion shaft. Discard the lock screw.
4. Push the flanged end of the axle shaft toward the center of the vehicle. Remove the C lock clip from the button end of the shaft.
5. Remove the axle shaft from the housing.
6. When removing the axle shaft on vehicles equipped with the 9½ inch ring gear, be sure that the thrust washer in the differential case does not slide out.
7. Using the proper removal tool, remove the seal from its mounting.
8. Insert tool J-23689 into the bore so that the tool grasps behind the bearing. Slide the washer against the outside of the seal. Turn the nut finger tight. Using a slide hammer remove the bearing and seal.
9. On vehicles equipped with the 9½ inch ring gear, use tool J-29712. Insert the tool into the axle tube so that it grasps behind the bearing. Center the receiver on the axle tube and tighten the nut. Back off the nut and remove the bearing and seal from the tool.
10. Installation is the reverse of the removal procedure. Be sure to use a new carrier gasket or RTV, as required. Fill the axle housing to within ⅜ in. of the filler hole.

PICK UP, BLAZER/JIMMY, SUBURBAN AND VAN (CHEVROLET 10½ AND DANA 9¾ AND 10½ INCH)

1. Raise and support the vehicle safely. Remove the tire and wheel assembly.
2. Remove the bolts that retain the axle shaft flange to the wheel hub.
3. Tap the flange with a suitable hammer and loosen the axle shaft.
4. Twist the shaft assembly and remove it from the axle tube. Remove the oil seal from its mounting.
5. Using a hammer and a long drift pin, knock the inner bearing, cup and oil seal from the hub assembly.
6. Using a snap ring pliers, remove the outer bearing. Using tool J-24426 and J-8092, drive the outter bearing and cup from the hub assembly.
7. Installation is the reverse of the removal procedure.
8. Place a new gasket or apply RTV sealant over the axle shaft. Position the shaft in the housing so that the shaft splines enter the differential side gear.

Differential Carrier

Removal and Installation

PICK UP, BLAZER/JIMMY, SUBURBAN AND VAN (DANA 9¾ AND 10½ INCH)

1. Raise and support the vehicle safely. Allow the rear axle assembly to hang freely. Remove the tire and wheel assemblies. Drain the lubricant.
2. Remove the axle shaft to hub retaining nuts. Rap the axle shaft to loosen it from the hub. Remove the shafts.
3. Remove the cap screws and lock washers retaining the cover to the carrier. Remove the carrier cover and gasket.
4. Mark one side of the carrier and matching cap for reassembly in the same position. Remove the bearing caps.
5. Using a spreader tool and a dial indicator gauge, spread the carrier assembly to a maximum of .015 in.
6. Remove the dial indicator tool. Use a prybar and remove the differential case from the carrier.
7. Record the dimension and location of the side bearing shims. Remove the spreader tool.
8. Installation is the reverse of the removal procedure.

PICK UP, BLAZER/JIMMY, SUBURBAN AND VAN (ROCKWELL 12 INCH)

1. As required, raise and support the vehicle safely. Drain the lubricant.
2. Remove the axle shaft from the drive unit and housing. Disconnect the universal at the pinion shaft.
3. Remove the carrier to housing stud nuts and washers. Loosen the two top nuts and leave the studs to prevent the carrier from falling.
4. Break the carrier loose from the axle housing using the proper hammer.
5. Installation is the reverse of the removal procedure.

REAR SUSPENSION

Leaf Spring

Removal and Installation

S SERIES

1. Raise and support the vehicle safely. Properly support the rear axle assembly to relieve tension on the springs.
2. Remove the shock absorber. Remove the U bolt nuts, washers, anchor plate and U bolt.
3. Remove the shackle to frame bolt, washers and nut. Remove the spring assembly to front bracket nut, washers and bolt.
4. Remove the spring assembly from the vehicle. As required, separate the spring from the shackle.
5. Installation is the reverse of the removal procedure.

ASTRO/SAFARI

1. Raise and support the vehicle safely. Properly support the rear axle assembly to relieve tension on the springs.
2. Remove the shock absorber. Remove the U bolt nuts, washers, anchor plate and U bolt.
3. Remove the shackle to frame bolt, washers and nut. Remove the spring assembly to front bracket nut, washers and bolt.
4. Remove the spring assembly from the vehicle. As required, separate the spring from the shackle.
5. Installation is the reverse of the removal procedure.

PICK UP (1982–87), BLAZER/JIMMY, SUBURBAN AND VAN

1. Raise and support the vehicle safely. Properly support the rear axle assembly to relieve tension on the springs.
2. If equipped, remove the stabilizer bar. Loosen, but do not remove the spring to shackle nut and bolt.
3. Remove the nut and bolt securing the shackle to the rear hanger. Remove the nut and bolt securing the leaf spring to the front hanger.
4. Remove the leaf spring from the front hanger. Remove the nut and bolt securing the shackle to the leaf spring. Remove the shackle.
5. Remove the nuts and washers holding the spring to the

frame. If equipped, remove the rear stabilizer anchor plate, spacers, shims and auxiliary spring.

6. Remove the U bolts from the assembly. Remove the leaf spring from the vehicle.

7. Installation is the reverse of the removal procedure.

PICK UP (1988)

1. Raise and support the vehicle safely. Properly support the rear axle assembly to relieve tension on the springs.

2. Remove the shock absorber. Remove the U bolt nuts, washers, anchor plate and U bolt.

3. Remove the shackle to frame bolt, washers and nut. Remove the spring assembly to front bracket nut, washers and bolt.

4. Remove the spring assembly from the vehicle. As required, separate the spring from the shackle.

5. Installation is the reverse of the removal procedure.

Shock Absorbers

Removal and Installation

1. Raise and support the vehicle safely. Properly support the rear axle assembly. On Astro/Safari remove the parking brake bracket from the right shock absorber.

2. Remove the upper shock absorber retaining bolt. Remove the lower shock absorber bolt.

3. Remove the shock absorber from the vehicle.

4. Installation is the reverse of the removal procedure.

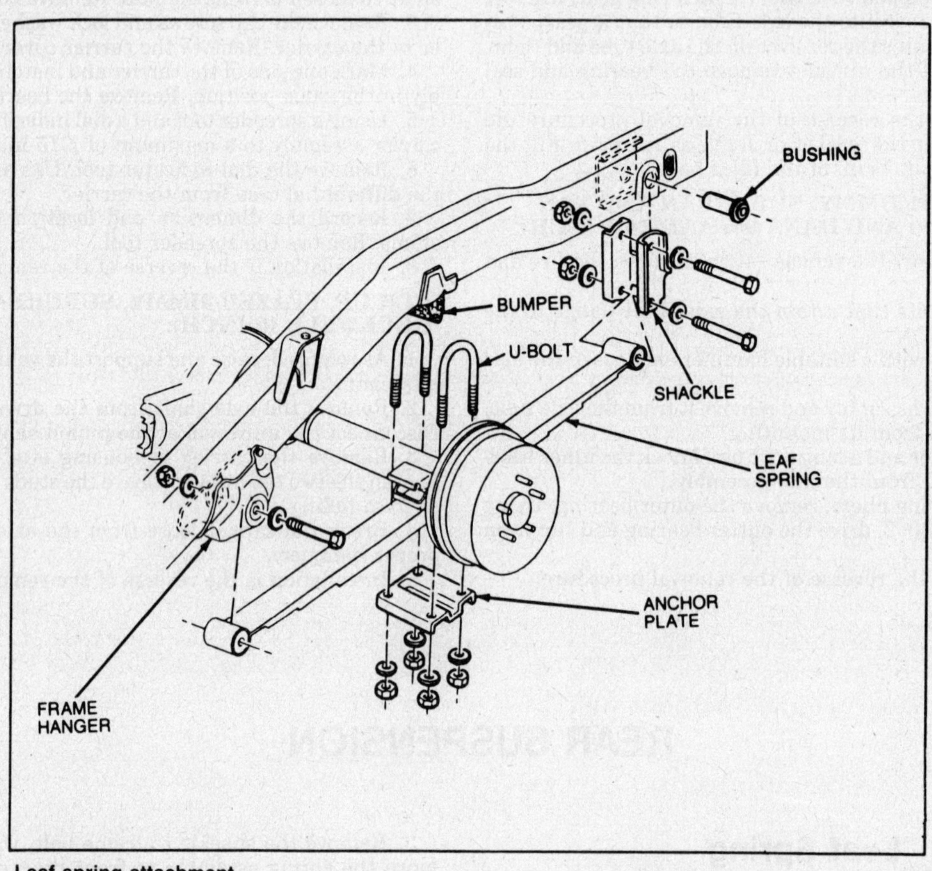

Leaf spring attachment

Dodge/Plymouth 2

INDEX

BEFORE SERVICING, SEE THE SAFETY NOTICE AT THE FRONT OF THE BOOK

DODGE/PLYMOUTH TRUCKS

ENGINE IDENTIFICATION CODES

The (V.I.N.) vehicle identificaton number consists of 17 digits. The number plate is located on the upper left corner of the instrument panel, near the windshield. The engine identification number will be the 8th digit (letter) from the left.

ENGINE IDENTIFICATION CODES BY VIN NUMBER
Dodge Trucks and Vans

Engine Cu. In. (liter)	Cylinders	1982	1983	1984	1985	1986	1987	1988
105 (1.7)	4	A	B	—	—	—	—	—
135 (2.2)	4	B	C	C	C	C	C	C
135 (2.2) T①	4	C	—	E	—	—	—	—
135 (2.2) EFI②	4	—	—	D	—	—	—	—
153 (2.5)	4	—	—	—	—	—	—	K
156 (2.6)	4	D	G	G	G	G	G	—
225 (3.7) 1bbl	6	E	J	H	H	H	H	H
225 (3.7) 2bbl	6	W	—	—	—	—	—	—
238.5 (3.9)	V6	—	—	—	—	—	M	M
181 (3.0)	V6	—	—	—	—	—	—	3
318 (5.2) 2bbl	V8	P	T	T	T	T	T	T
318 (5.2) 4bbl	V8	R	U	—	—	—	—	—
360 (5.9) 2bbl	V8	S	V	—	—	—	—	—
360 (5.9) 4bbl	V8	T	W	W	W	W	W	W
360 (5.9) 4bbl③	V8	U	I	I	I	I	I	I

① T: Turbocharged
② EFI: Electronic Fuel Injection
③ California

MODEL IDENTIFICATION
Dodge/Plymouth Trucks

Year	Model Designation	Model Name
1982	B150 ½ Ton Wagon	Dodge Van
	B150 ½ Ton Mini Ram Wagon	Dodge Van
	B150 ½ Ton Van	Dodge Van
	B150 ½ Ton Long Range Ram Van	Dodge Van
	PB150 ½ Ton Voyager	Plymouth Van
	PB250 ¾ Ton Voyager	Plymouth Van
	PB350 1 Ton Voyager	Plymouth Van
	B250 ¾ Ton Mini Ram Wagon	Dodge Van
	B250 ¾ Ton Wagon	Dodge Van
	B250 ¾ Ton Van	Dodge Van
	D150 ½ Ton Club Cab LB	Dodge Pickup
	D150 ½ Ton Ram Miser	Dodge Pickup
	D150 ½ Ton Ram Miser LB	Dodge Pickup
	D150 ½ Ton Sweptline	Dodge Pickup
	D150 ½ Ton Sweptline LB	Dodge Pickup

MODEL IDENTIFICATION
Dodge/Plymouth Trucks

Year	Model Designation	Model Name
1982	D150 ½ Ton Utiline	Dodge Pickup
	D150 ½ Ton Utiline LB	Dodge Pickup
	D250 ¾ Ton Club Cab LB	Dodge Pickup
	D250 ¾ Ton Sweptline LB	Dodge Pickup
	D250 ¾ Ton Utiline LB	Dodge Pickup
	Ramcharger Utility	Dodge Pickup
1983	B150 ½ Ton Wagon	Dodge Van
	B150 ½ Ton Mini Ram Wagon	Dodge Van
	B150 ½ Ton Van	Dodge Van
	B150 ½ Ton Long Range Ram Van	Dodge Van
	PB150 ½ Ton Voyager	Plymouth Van
	PB250 ¾ Ton Voyager	Plymouth Van
	PB350 1 Ton Voyager	Plymouth Van
	B250 ¾ Ton Wagon	Dodge Van
	B250 ¾ Ton Van	Dodge Van

MODEL IDENTIFICATION
Dodge/Plymouth Trucks

Year	Model Designation	Model Name
1983	D150 ½ Ton Ram Miser	Dodge Pickup
	D150 ½ Ton Ram Miser LB	Dodge Pickup
	D150 ½ Ton Sweptline	Dodge Pickup
	D150 ½ Ton Sweptline LB	Dodge Pickup
	D150 ½ Ton Utiline	Dodge Pickup
	D150 ½ Ton Utiline LB	Dodge Pickup
	D250 ¾ Ton Sweptline LB	Dodge Pickup
	D250 ¾ Ton Utiline LB	Dodge Pickup
	Ramcharger Utility	Dodge Pickup
1984	B150 ½ Ton Wagon	Dodge Van
	B150 ½ Ton Value Wagon	Dodge Van
	B150 ½ Ton Van	Dodge Van
	B150 ½ Ton Long Range Ram Van	Dodge Van
	B250 ¾ Ton Wagon	Dodge Van
	B250 ¾ Ton Van	Dodge Van
	Caravan	Dodge FWD Van
	Caravan SE	Dodge FWD Van
	Caravan LE	Dodge FWD Van
	Voyager	Plymouth FWD Van
	Voyager SE	Plymouth FWD Van
	Voyager LE	Plymouth FWD Van
	D100 ½ Ton Sweptline	Dodge Pickup
	D100 ½ Ton Sweptline LB	Dodge Pickup
	D150 ½ Ton Ram Miser	Dodge Pickup
	D150 ½ Ton Ram Miser LB	Dodge Pickup
	D150 ½ Ton Sweptline	Dodge Pickup
	D150 ½ Ton Sweptline LB	Dodge Pickup
	D150 ½ Ton Utiline	Dodge Pickup
	D150 ½ Ton Utiline LB	Dodge Pickup
	D250 ¾ Ton Sweptline LB	Dodge Pickup
	D250 ¾ Ton Utiline LB	Dodge Pickup
	Ramcharger Utility	Dodge Pickup
1985	B150 ½ Ton Wagon	Dodge Van
	B150 ½ Ton Value Wagon	Dodge Van
	B150 ½ Ton Van	Dodge Van
	B150 ½ Ton Long Range Ram Van	Dodge Van
	B250 ¾ Ton Wagon	Dodge Van
	B250 ¾ Ton Van	Dodge Van
	Caravan	Dodge FWD Van
	Caravan SE	Dodge FWD Van

MODEL IDENTIFICATION
Dodge/Plymouth Trucks

Year	Model Designation	Model Name
1985	Caravan LE	Dodge FWD Van
	Voyager	Plymouth FWD Van
	Voyager SE	Plymouth FWD Van
	Voyager LE	Plymouth FWD Van
	D100 ½ Ton Sweptline	Dodge Pickup
	D100 ½ Ton Sweptline LB	Dodge Pickup
	D150 ½ Ton Ram Miser	Dodge Pickup
	D150 ½ Ton Ram Miser LB	Dodge Pickup
	D150 ½ Ton Sweptline	Dodge Pickup
	D150 ½ Ton Sweptline LB	Dodge Pickup
	D150 ½ Ton Utiline	Dodge Pickup
	D150 ½ Ton Utiline LB	Dodge Pickup
	D250 ¾ Ton Sweptline LB	Dodge Pickup
	D250 ¾ Ton Utiline LB	Dodge Pickup
	Ramcharger Utility	Dodge Pickup
1986	B150 ½ Ton Wagon	Dodge Van
	B150 ½ Ton Value Wagon	Dodge Van
	B150 ½ Ton Van	Dodge Van
	B150 ½ Ton Long Range Ram Van	Dodge Van
	B250 ¾ Ton Wagon	Dodge Van
	B250 ¾ Ton Van	Dodge Van
	Caravan	Dodge FWD Van
	Caravan SE	Dodge FWD Van
	Caravan LE	Dodge FWD Van
	Voyager	Plymouth FWD Van
	Voyager SE	Plymouth FWD Van
	Voyager LE	Plymouth FWD Van
	D100 ½ Ton Sweptline	Dodge Pickup
	D100 ½ Ton Sweptline LB	Dodge Pickup
	D150 ½ Ton Ram Miser	Dodge Pickup
	D150 ½ Ton Ram Miser LB	Dodge Pickup
	D150 ½ Ton Sweptline	Dodge Pickup
	D150 ½ Ton Sweptline LB	Dodge Pickup
	D250 ¾ Ton Sweptline LB	Dodge Pickup
	Ramcharger Utility	Dodge Pickup
1987–88	B150 ½ Ton Wagon	Dodge Van
	B150 ½ Ton Value Wagon	Dodge Van
	B150 ½ Ton Van	Dodge Van

MODEL IDENTIFICATION
Dodge/Plymouth Trucks

Year	Model Designation	Model Name
1987–88	B150 ½ Ton Long Range Ram Van	Dodge Van
	B250 ¾ Ton Wagon	Dodge Van
	B250 ¾ Ton Van	Dodge Van
	Caravan	Dodge FWD Van
	Caravan SE	Dodge FWD Van
	Caravan LE	Dodge FWD Van
	Dakota ½ Ton Sweptline	Dodge Pickup
	Dakota ½ Ton Sweptline S	Dodge Pickup
	Dakota ½ Ton Sweptline LB	Dodge Pickup
	Voyager	Plymouth FWD Van
	Voyager SE	Plymouth FWD Van

MODEL IDENTIFICATION
Dodge/Plymouth Trucks

Year	Model Designation	Model Name
1987-88	Voyager LE	Plymouth FWD Van
	D100 ½ Ton Sweptline	Dodge Pickup
	D100 ½ Ton Sweptline LB	Dodge Pickup
	D150 ½ Ton Ram Miser	Dodge Pickup
	D150 ½ Ton Ram Miser LB	Dodge Pickup
	D150 ½ Ton Sweptline	Dodge Pickup
	D150 ½ Ton Sweptline LB	Dodge Pickup
	D250 ¾ Ton Sweptline LB	Dodge Pickup
	Ramcharger Utility	Dodge Pickup

LB = Long Bed

GASOLINE ENGINE TUNE-UP SPECIFICATIONS

Year	VIN	No. Cylinder Displacement cu. in. (liter)	Spark Plugs Type	Spark Plugs Gap (in.)	Ignition Timing (deg.) MT	Ignition Timing (deg.) AT	Compression Pressure (psi)	Fuel Pump (psi)	Idle Speed (rpm) MT	Idle Speed (rpm) AT	Valve Clearance (in.) In.	Valve Clearance (in.) Ex.
1982	B	4–135 (2.2)	65PR	.035	12B	12B	130–150	4.5–6.0	850	900	.012	.012
	D	4–156 (2.6)	65PR	.041②	–	12B	149	4.5–6.0	–	800	Hyd.	Hyd.
	E	6–225 (3.7)	560PR	.035	12B	16B	100	3.5–5.0	③	③	Hyd.	Hyd.
	W	6–225 (3.7)	560PR	.035	12B	16B	100	3.5–5.0	750	750	Hyd.	Hyd.
	P	8–318 (5.2)	64PR	.035	10B	16B	100	5.0–7.0	650	650	Hyd.	Hyd.
	R	8–318 (5.2)	64PR	.035	12B	12B	100	5.0–7.0	750	750	Hyd.	Hyd.
	S	8–360 (5.9)	64PR	.035	–	4B	100	5.0–7.0	600	625	Hyd.	Hyd.
	T	8–360 (5.9)	64PR	.035	–	4B	100	5.0–7.0	750	750	Hyd.	Hyd.
	U	8–360 (5.9)	64PR	.035	–	4B	100	5.0–7.0	700	700	Hyd.	Hyd.
1983	C	4–135 (2.2)	65PR	.035	12B	20B	130–150	4.5–6.0	850	900	Hyd.	Hyd.
	G	4–156 (2.6)	65PR	.041②	–	12B	149	4.5–6.0	–	800	Hyd.	Hyd.
	J	6–225 (3.7)	560PR	.035	12B	16B	100	3.5–5.0	③	③	Hyd.	Hyd.
	T	8–318 (5.2)	64PR	.035	10B	16B	100	5.0–7.0	650	650	Hyd.	Hyd.
	U	8–318 (5.2)	64PR	.035	12B	12B	100	5.0–7.0	750	750	Hyd.	Hyd.
	V	8–360 (5.9)	64PR	.035	–	4B	100	5.0–7.0	600	625	Hyd.	Hyd.
	W	8–360 (5.9)	64PR	.035	–	4B	100	5.0–7.0	750	750	Hyd.	Hyd.
	I	8–360 (5.9)	64PR	.035	–	4B	100	5.0–7.0	700	700	Hyd.	Hyd.
1984	C	4–135 (2.2)	65PR	.035	12B	12B	130–150	4.5–6.0	850	900	Hyd.	Hyd.
	G	4–156 (2.6)	65PR	.041②	–	12B	149	4.5–6.0	–	800	Hyd.	Hyd.
	H	6–225 (3.7)	560PR	.035	12B	16B	100	3.5–5.0	③	③	Hyd.	Hyd.
	T	8–318 (5.2)	64PR	.035	10B	16B	100	5.0–7.0	650	650	Hyd.	Hyd.
	W	8–360 (5.9)	64PR	.035	–	4B	100	5.0–7.0	750	750	Hyd.	Hyd.
	I	8–360 (5.9)	64PR	.035	–	4B	100	5.0–7.0	700	700	Hyd.	Hyd.

GASOLINE ENGINE TUNE-UP SPECIFICATIONS

Year	VIN	No. Cylinder Displacement cu. in. (liter)	Spark Plugs Type	Spark Plugs Gap (in.)	Ignition Timing (deg.) MT	Ignition Timing (deg.) AT	Compression Pressure (psi)	Fuel Pump (psi)	Idle Speed (rpm) MT	Idle Speed (rpm) AT	Valve Clearance (in.) In.	Valve Clearance (in.) Ex.
1985	C	4–135 (2.2)	65PR	.035	12B	12B	130–150	4.5–6.0	850	900	Hyd.	Hyd.
	G	4–156 (2.6)	65PR	.041②	–	12B	149	4.5–6.0	–	800	Hyd.	Hyd.
	H	6–225 (3.7)	560PR	.035	12B	16B	100	3.5–5.0	③	③	Hyd.	Hyd.
	T	8–318 (5.2)	64PR	.035	10B	16B	100	5.0–7.0	650	650	Hyd.	Hyd.
	W	8–360 (5.9)	64PR	.035	–	4B	100	5.0–7.0	750	750	Hyd.	Hyd.
	I	8–360 (5.9)	64PR	.035	–	4B	100	5.0–7.0	700	700	Hyd.	Hyd.
1986	C	4–135 (2.2)	65PR	.035	12B	12B	130–150	4.5–6.0	800	900	Hyd.	Hyd.
	G	4–156 (2.6)	65PR	.041②	–	12B	149	4.5–6.0	–	800	Hyd.	Hyd.
	H	6–225 (3.7)	560PR	.035	12B	16B	100	3.5–5.0	③	③	Hyd.	Hyd.
	T	8–318 (5.2)	64PR	.035	10B	16B	100	5.0–7.0	650	650	Hyd.	Hyd.
	W	8–360 (5.9)	64PR	.035	–	4B	100	5.0–7.0	750	750	Hyd.	Hyd.
	I	8–360 (5.9)	64PR	.035	–	4B	100	5.0–7.0	700	700	Hyd.	Hyd.
1987	C	4–135 (2.2)	65PR	.035	12B	12B	130–150	4.5–6.0	800	900	Hyd.	Hyd.
	G	4–156 (2.6)	65PR	.041②	–	12B	149	4.5–6.0	–	800	Hyd.	Hyd.
	H	6–225 (3.7)	560PR	.035	12B	16B	100	3.5–5.0	③	③	Hyd.	Hyd.
	M	6–238 (3.0)	RN12YC	.035	7B	7B	100	NA	720	700	Hyd.	Hyd.
	T	8–318 (5.2)	64PR	.035	10B	16B	100	5.0–7.0	650	650	Hyd.	Hyd.
	W	8–360 (5.9)	64PR	.035	–	4B	100	5.0–7.0	750	750	Hyd.	Hyd.
	I	8–360 (5.9)	64PR	.035	–	4B	100	5.0–7.0	700	700	Hyd.	Hyd.
1988	C	4–135 (2.2)	65PR	.035	12B	12B	130–150	4.5–6.0	800	900	Hyd.	Hyd.
	K	4–153 (2.5)	RN12YC	.035	12B	12B	100	14.5	850	850	Hyd.	Hyd.
	3	6–181 (3.0)	RN11YC4	.041	–	12B	178⑤	48	–	④	Hyd.	Hyd.
	M	6–238 (3.0)	RN12YC	.035	7B	7B	100	NA	720	700	Hyd.	Hyd.
	T	8–318 (5.2)	64PR	.035	10B	16B	100	5.0–7.0	650	650	Hyd.	Hyd.
	W	8–360 (5.9)	64PR	.035	–	4B	100	5.0–7.0	750	750	Hyd.	Hyd.
	I	8–360 (5.9)	64PR	.035	–	4B	100	5.0–7.0	700	700	Hyd.	Hyd.

① Use the specifications on the vehicle emission control label

② Canada: .030

③ Federal: 600
Cailifornia: 800
Canada: 725

④ 700 in Drive
800 in Neutral

⑤ At 250 rpm

GENERAL ENGINE SPECIFICATIONS

Year	VIN	No. Cylinder Displacement cu. in. (liter)	Fuel System Type	Net Horsepower @ rpm	Net Torque @ rpm (ft.lbs.)	Bore × Stroke (in.)	Com-pression Ratio	Oil Pressure @ 2000 rpm
1982	B	4–135 (2.2)	2bbl	84 @ 4800	111 @ 2400	3.44 × 3.62	8.5:1	60–90
	D	4–156 (2.6)	2bbl	92 @ 4500	131 @ 2500	3.59 × 3.86	8.2:1	56
	E	6–225 (3.7)	1bbl	90 @ 3600	160 @ 1600	3.40 × 4.12	8.4:1	35–65
	W	6–225 (3.7)	2bbl	90 @ 3600	160 @ 1600	3.40 × 4.12	8.4:1	35–65
	P	8–318 (5.2)	2bbl	120 @ 3600	245 @ 1600	3.91 × 3.31	8.5:1	35–65
	R	8–318 (5.2)	4bbl	155 @ 4000	240 @ 2000	3.91 × 3.31	8.5:1	35–65
	S	8–360 (5.9)	2bbl	130 @ 3200	255 @ 2000	4.00 × 3.58	8.4:1	35–65
	T	8–360 (5.9)	4bbl	185 @ 4000	275 @ 2000	4.00 × 3.58	8.0:1	35–65
	U	8–360 (5.9)	4bbl	185 @ 4000	275 @ 2000	4.00 × 3.58	8.0:1	35–65
1983	C	4–135 (2.2)	2bbl	84 @ 4800	111 @ 2400	3.44 × 3.62	8.5:1	60–90
	G	4–156 (2.6)	2bbl	92 @ 4500	131 @ 2500	3.59 × 3.86	8.2:1	56
	J	6–225 (3.7)	1bbl	90 @ 3600	160 @ 1600	3.40 × 4.12	8.4:1	35–65
	T	8–318 (5.2)	2bbl	120 @ 3600	245 @ 1600	3.91 × 3.31	8.5:1	35–65
	U	8–318 (5.2)	4bbl	155 @ 4000	240 @ 2000	3.91 × 3.31	8.5:1	35–65
	V	8–360 (5.9)	2bbl	130 @ 3200	255 @ 2000	4.00 × 3.58	8.4:1	35–65
	W	8–360 (5.9)	4bbl	185 @ 4000	275 @ 2000	4.00 × 3.58	8.0:1	35–65
	I	8–360 (5.9)	4bbl	185 @ 4000	275 @ 2000	4.00 × 3.58	8.0:1	35–65
1984	C	4–135 (2.2)	2bbl	84 @ 4800	111 @ 2400	3.44 × 3.62	8.5:1	60–90
	G	4–156 (2.6)	2bbl	92 @ 4500	131 @ 2500	3.59 × 3.86	8.2:1	56
	H	6–225 (3.7)	1bbl	90 @ 3600	160 @ 1600	3.40 × 4.12	8.4:1	35–65
	T	8–318 (5.2)	2bbl	120 @ 3600	245 @ 1600	3.91 × 3.31	8.5:1	35–65
	W	8–360 (5.9)	4bbl	185 @ 4000	275 @ 2000	4.00 × 3.58	8.0:1	35–65
	I	8–360 (5.9)	4bbl	185 @ 4000	275 @ 2000	4.00 × 3.58	8.0:1	35–65
1985	C	4–135 (2.2)	2bbl	84 @ 4800	111 @ 2400	3.44 × 3.62	9.5:1	60–90
	G	4–156 (2.6)	2bbl	92 @ 4500	131 @ 2500	3.59 × 3.86	8.7:1	56
	H	6–225 (3.7)	1bbl	90 @ 3600	160 @ 1600	3.40 × 4.12	8.4:1	35–65
	T	8–318 (5.2)	2bbl	120 @ 3600	245 @ 1600	3.91 × 3.31	9.0:1	35–65
	W	8–360 (5.9)	4bbl	120 @ 3600	245 @ 1600	4.00 × 3.58	8.0:1	35–65
	I	8–360 (5.9)	4bbl	185 @ 4000	275 @ 2000	4.00 × 3.58	8.0:1	35–65
1986	C	4–135 (2.2)	2bbl	84 @ 4800	111 @ 2400	3.44 × 3.62	9.5:1	60–90
	G	4–156 (2.6)	2bbl	92 @ 4500	131 @ 2500	3.59 × 3.86	8.7:1	56
	H	6–225 (3.7)	1bbl	90 @ 3600	160 @ 1600	3.40 × 4.12	8.4:1	35–65
	T	8–318 (5.2)	2bbl	120 @ 3600	245 @ 1600	3.91 × 3.31	9.0:1	35–65
	W	8–360 (5.9)	4bbl	120 @ 3600	245 @ 1600	4.00 × 3.58	8.5:1	35–65
	I	8–360 (5.9)	4bbl	185 @ 4000	275 @ 2000	4.00 × 3.58	8.0:1	35–65
1987	C	4–135 (2.2)	2bbl	84 @ 4800	111 @ 2400	3.44 × 3.62	9.5:1	60–90
	G	4–156 (2.6)	2bbl	92 @ 4500	131 @ 2500	3.59 × 3.86	8.7:1	56

GENERAL ENGINE SPECIFICATIONS

Year	VIN	No. Cylinder Displacement cu. in. (liter)	Fuel System Type	Net Horsepower @ rpm	Net Torque @ rpm (ft.lbs.)	Bore × Stroke (in.)	Com-pression Ratio	Oil Pressure @ 2000 rpm
1987	H	6–225 (3.7)	1bbl	90 @ 3600	160 @ 1600	3.40 × 4.12	8.4:1	35–65
	M	6–238 (3.0)	2bbl	125 @ 4000	195 @ 2000	3.40 × 4.12	8.4:1	30–70①
	T	8–318 (5.2)	2bbl	120 @ 3600	245 @ 1600	3.91 × 3.31	9.0:1	35–65
	W	8–360 (5.9)	4bbl	120 @ 3600	245 @ 1600	4.00 × 3.58	8.5:1	30–80
	I	8–360 (5.9)	4bbl	185 @ 4000	275 @ 2000	4.00 × 3.58	8.0:1	35–65
1988	C	4–135 (2.2)	2bbl	84 @ 4800	111 @ 2400	3.44 × 3.62	9.5:1	60–90
	K	4–153 (2.5)	EFI	96 @ 4400	133 @ 2800	3.45 × 4.09	8.0:1	35–65
	3	6–181 (3.0)	EFI	140 @ 4800	170 @ 2800	3.59 × 2.99	8.8:1	30–80
	M	6–238 (3.0)	2bbl	125 @ 4000	195 @ 2000	3.40 × 4.12	8.4:1	30–70①
	T	8–318 (5.2)	2bbl	120 @ 3600	245 @ 1600	3.91 × 3.31	9.0:1	35–65
	W	8–360 (5.9)	4bbl	120 @ 3600	245 @ 1600	4.00 × 3.58	8.5:1	30–80
	I	8–360 (5.9)	4bbl	185 @ 4000	275 @ 2000	4.00 × 3.58	8.0:1	35–65

① at 3000 rpm

FIRING ORDERS

NOTE: To avoid confusion, always replace spark plug wires one at a time.

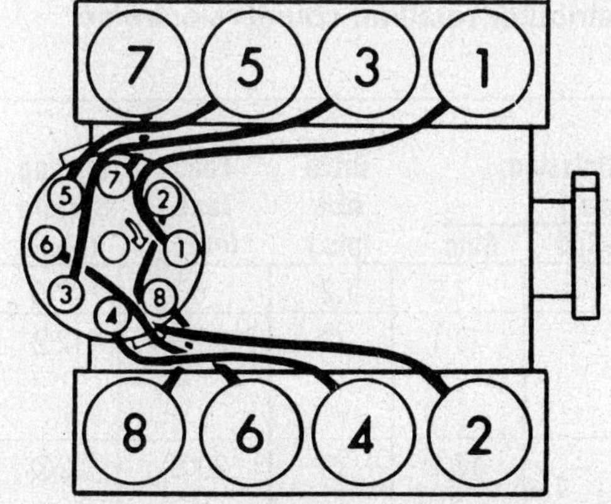

Chrysler 318 cu. in. V8 (5.2L)
Firing order: 1-8-4-3-6-5-7-2
Distributor rotation: clockwise

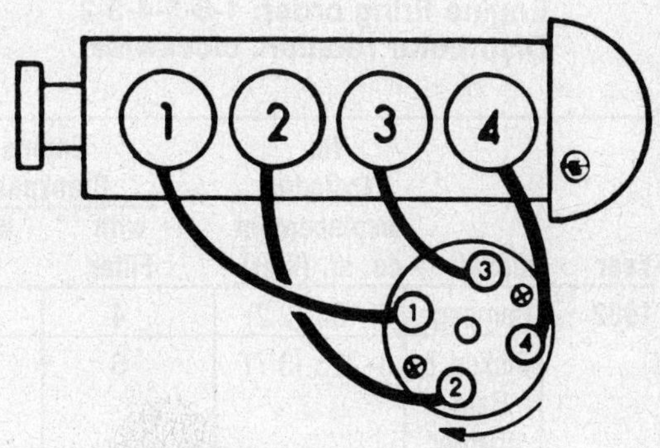

Chrysler 105 cu. in. 4 cyl (1.7L)
Firing order: 1-3-4-2
Distributor rotation: clockwise

FIRING ORDERS

NOTE: To avoid confusion, always replace spark plug wires one at a time.

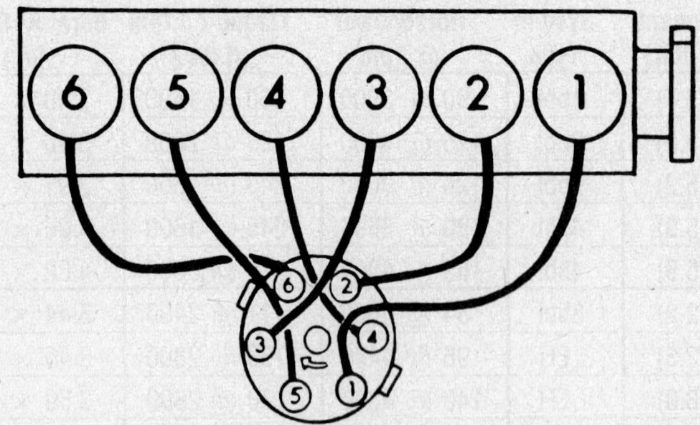

Chrysler 225 cu. in. 6 cyl (3.7L)
Firing order: 1-5-3-6-2-4
Distributor rotation: clockwise

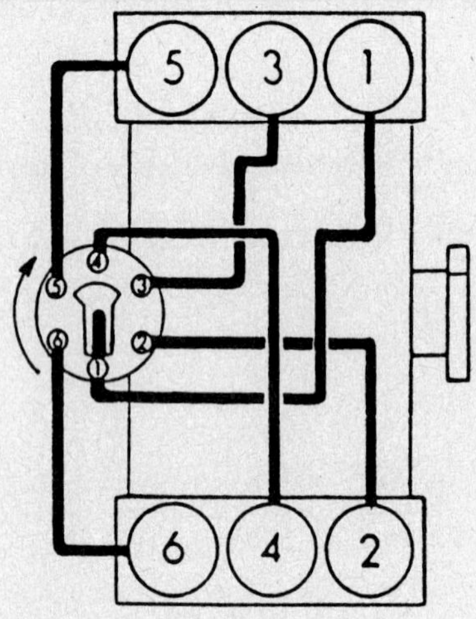

Chrysler Corp. 3.9L, V6
Engine firing order: 1-6-5-4-3-2
Distributor rotation: clockwise

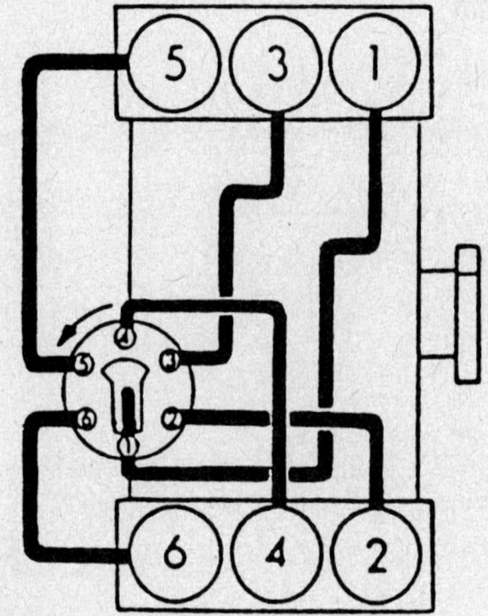

Chrysler Corp. 3.0L, V6
Engine firing order: 1-2-3-4-5-6
Distributor rotation: counterclockwise

CAPACITIES

Year	Model	No. Cylinder Displacement cu. in. (liter)	Engine Crankcase with Filter	Engine Crankcase without Filter	Transmission (pts.) 4-Spd	5-Spd	Auto.	Drive Axle (pts.)	Fuel Tank (gal.)	Cooling System (qts.)
1982	Rampage	4–135 (2.2)	4	4	⑥	9	7.5	1.2	13	7.0
	Pickup & Ram-charger	6–225 (3.7)	6	5	7①	–	17.1	②	20③	12④
	Pickup & Ram-charger	8–318 (5.2)	6	5	7①	–	17.1	②	20③	12④
	Pickup Ram-charger	8–360 (5.9)	6	5	7①	–	17.1	②	20③	14.5

CAPACITIES

Year	Model	No. Cylinder Displacement cu. in. (liter)	Engine Crankcase with Filter	Engine Crankcase without Filter	Transmission (pts.) 4-Spd	Transmission (pts.) 5-Spd	Transmission (pts.) Auto.	Drive Axle (pts.)	Fuel Tank (gal.)	Cooling System (qts.)
1982	Vans & Wagons	6–225 (3.7)	6	5	7.5	–	16.6	②	22⑤	12④
	Vans & Wagons	8–318 (5.2)	6	5	7.5	–	16.6	②	22⑤	16④
	Vans & Wagons	8–360 (5.9)	6	5	7.5	–	16.6	②	22⑤	14.5④
1983	Rampage	4–135 (2.2)	4	4	⑥	9	⑦	–	13⑧	9.0
	Pickup & Ram-charger	6–225 (3.7)	6	5	7①	–	17.1	②	20③	12④
	Pickup & Ram-charger	8–318 (5.2)	6	5	7①	–	17.1	②	20③	12④
	Pickup & Ram-charger	8–360 (5.9)	6	5	7①	–	17.1	②	20③	14.5
	Van & Wagon	6–225 (3.7)	6	5	7.5	–	16.6	②	22⑤	12④
	Van & Wagon	8–318 (5.2)	6	5	7.5	–	16.6	②	22⑤	16④
	Van & Wagon	8–360 (5.9)	6	5	7.5	–	16.6	②	22⑤	14.5④
1984	Rampage	4–135 (2.2)	4	4	8	9	⑦	–	13⑧	9.0
	Mini Van	4–135 (2.2)	4	4	8	–	⑦	–	15⑨	8.5
	Mini Van	4–156 (2.6)	5	5	–	9	⑦	–	15⑨	9.5
	Pickup & Ram-charger	6–225 (3.7)	6	5	7①	–	17.1	②	20③	12④
	Pickup & Ram-charger	8–318 (5.2)	6	5	7①	–	17.1	②	20③	12④
	Pickup & Ram-charger	8–360 (5.9)	6	5	7①	–	17.1	②	20③	14.5
	Van & Wagon	6–225 (3.7)	6	5	7.5	–	8	②	22⑤	12④
	Van & Wagon	8–318 (5.2)	6	5	7.5	–	8	②	22⑤	16④
	Van & Wagon	8–360 (5.9)	6	5	7.5	–	8	②	22⑤	14.5④
1985	Mini Van	4–135 (2.2)	4	4	8	–	⑦	–	15⑨	8.5
	Mini Van	4–156 (2.6)	5	5	–	9	⑦	–	15⑨	9.5
	Pickup & Ram-charger	6–225 (3.7)	6	5	7①	–	17.1⑩	②	20③	12④

CAPACITIES

Year	Model	No. Cylinder Displacement cu. in. (liter)	Engine Crankcase with Filter	Engine Crankcase without Filter	Transmission (pts.) 4-Spd	5-Spd	Auto.	Drive Axle (pts.)	Fuel Tank (gal.)	Cooling System (qts.)
1985	Pickup & Ram-charger	8–318 (5.2)	6	5	7①	–	17.1⑩	②	20③	12④
	Pickup & Ram-charger	8–360 (5.9)	6	5	7①	–	17.1⑩	②	20③	14.5
	Van & Wagon	6–225 (3.7)	6	5	7.5	–	8	②	22⑤	12④
	Van & Wagon	8–318 (5.2)	6	5	7.5	–	8	②	22⑤	16④
	Van & Wagon	8–360 (5.9)	6	5	7.5	–	8	②	22⑤	14.5④
1986	Mini Van	4–135 (2.2)	4	4	8	–	⑦	–	15⑨	8.5
	Mini Van	4–156 (2.6)	5	5	–	9	⑦	–	15⑨	9.5
	Pickup & Ram-charger	6–225 (3.7)	6	5	7①	–	17.1⑩	②	20③	12④
	Pickup & Ram-charger	8–318 (5.2)	6	5	7①	–	17.1⑩	②	20③	12④
	Pickup & Ram-charger	8–360 (5.9)	6	5	7①	–	17.1⑩	②	20③	14.5
	Van & Wagon	6–225 (3.7)	6	5	7.5	–	8	②	22⑤	12④
	Van & Wagon	8–318 (5.2)	6	5	7.5	–	8	②	22⑤	16④
	Van & Wagon	8–360 (5.9)	6	5	7.5	–	8	②	22⑤	14.5④
1987	Mini Van	4–135 (2.2)	4	4	8	–	⑦	–	15⑨	8.5
	Mini Van	4–156 (2.6)	5	5	–	9	⑦	–	15⑨	9.5
	Dakota	4–135 (2.2)	5	5	–	4	17	⑪	15⑫	14
	Dakota	6–238 (3.9)	4	4	–	4	16	⑪	15⑫	9.8
	Pickup & Ram-charger	6–225 (3.7)	6	5	7①	–	17.1⑩	②	20③	12④
	Pickup & Ram-charger	8–318 (5.2)	6	5	7①	–	17.1⑩	②	20③	12④
	Pickup & Ram-charger	8–360 (5.9)	6	5	7①	–	17.1⑩	②	20③	14.5
	Van & Wagon	6–225 (3.7)	6	5	7.5	–	8	②	22⑤	12④
	Van & Wagon	8–318 (5.2)	6	5	7.5	–	8	②	22⑤	16④

CAPACITIES

Year	Model	No. Cylinder Displacement cu. in. (liter)	Engine Crankcase with Filter	Engine Crankcase without Filter	Transmission (pts.) 4-Spd	Transmission (pts.) 5-Spd	Transmission (pts.) Auto.	Drive Axle (pts.)	Fuel Tank (gal.)	Cooling System (qts.)
1987	Van & Wagon	8–360 (5.9)	6	5	7.5	—	8	②	22⑤	14.5④
1988	Mini Van	4–135 (2.2)	4	4	8	—	⑦	—	15⑨	8.5
	Mini Van	4–156 (2.6)	5	5	—	9	⑦	—	15⑨	9.5
	Dakota	4–135 (2.2)	5	5	—	4	17	⑪	15⑫	14
	Dakota	6–238 (3.9)	4	4	—	4	16			
	15⑫	9.8								
	Pickup & Ram-charger	6–225 (3.7)	6	5	7①	—	17.1⑩	②	20③	12④
	Pickup & Ram-charger	8–318 (5.2)	6	5	7①	—	17.1⑩	②	20③	12④
	Pickup & Ram-charger	8–360 (5.9)	6	5	7①	—	17.1⑩	②	20③	14.5
	Van & Wagon	6–225 (3.7)	6	5	7.5	—	8	②	22⑤	12④
	Van & Wagon	8–318 (5.2)	6	5	7.5	—	8	②	22⑤	16④
	Van & Wagon	8–360 (5.9)	6	5	7.5	—	8	②	22⑤	14.5④

①With overdrive: 7.5 pints
②Chrysler: 4.5 pints
Spicer 9.75 in.: 6 pints
Spicer 10.5 in.: 6.5 pints
③Optional fuel tank: 30 gallons
Sport Utility: 35 gallons
④Add one quart for H.D. or A/C
⑤Optional fuel tank: 36 gallons
⑥With A–412 transmission: 6 pints
With A–460 transmission: 8 pints
⑦Except Fleet: 18 pints
Fleet: 19 pints
⑧With EFI: 14 gallons
⑨Optional fuel tank: 20 gallons
⑩With A–727 transmission: 7.7 pints
⑪With 7.25 in.: 2.5 pints
With 8.25 in.: 4.4 pints
4 Wheel Drive front axle: 2.6 pints
⑫Optional fuel tank: 22 gallons

CRANKSHAFT AND CONNECTING ROD SPECIFICATIONS

All measurements are given in inches.

Year	VIN	No. Cylinder Displacement cu. in. (liter)	Crankshaft Main Brg. Journal Dia.	Crankshaft Main Brg. Oil Clearance	Crankshaft Shaft End-play	Crankshaft Thrust on No.	Connecting Rod Journal Diameter	Connecting Rod Oil Clearance	Connecting Rod Side Clearance
1982	A	4–105 (1.7)	2.1244–2.1236	.0008–.0030	.003–.007	3	1.8087–1.8094	.0011–.0034	.014
	B	4–135 (2.2)	2.3620–2.3630	.0003–.0031	.002–.007	3	1.9680–1.9690	.0008–.0034	.005–.013
	D	4–156 (2.6)	2.3622	.0008–.0028	.002–.007	3	2.0866	.0008–.0028	.004–.010

CRANKSHAFT AND CONNECTING ROD SPECIFICATIONS

All measurements are given in inches.

		No. Cylinder	Crankshaft				Connecting Rod		
Year	VIN	Displacement cu. in. (liter)	Main Brg. Journal Dia.	Main Brg. Oil Clearance	Shaft End-play	Thrust on No.	Journal Diameter	Oil Clearance	Side Clearance
1982	E	6–225 (3.7)	2.7495–2.7505	.0010–.0025	.0035–.0095	3	2.1865–2.1875	.0010–.0022	.001–.002
	P	8–318 (5.2)	2.4995–2.5005	.0005–.0020 ①	.002–.007	3	2.1240–2.1250	.0005–.0022	.006–.014
	P	8–360 (5.9)	2.8095–2.8105	.0005–.0020 ①	.002–.009	3	2.1240–2.1250	.0005–.0022	.006–.014
1983	B	4–105 (1.7)	2.1244–2.1236	.0008–.0030	.003–.007	3	1.8087–1.8094	.0011–.0034	.014
	C	4–135 (2.2)	2.3620–2.3630	.0003–.0031	.002–.007	3	1.9680–1.9690	.0008–.0034	.005–.013
	G	4–156 (2.6)	2.3622	.0008–.0028	.002–.007	3	2.0866	.0008–.0028	.004–.010
	J	6–225 (3.7)	2.7495–2.7505	.0010–.0025	.0035–.0095	3	2.1865–2.1875	.0010–.0022	.001–.002
	T	8–318 (5.2)	2.4995–2.5005	.0005–.0020 ①	.002–.007	3	2.1240–2.1250	.0005–.0022	.006–.014
	V	8–360 (5.9)	2.8095–2.8105	.0005–.0020 ①	.002–.009	3	2.1240–2.1250	.0005–.0022	.006–.014
1984	C	4–135 (2.2)	2.3620–2.3630	.0003–.0031	.002–.007	3	1.9680–1.9690	.0008–.0034	.005–.013
	G	4–156 (2.6)	2.3622	.0008–.0028	.002–.007	3	2.0866	.0008–.0028	.004–.010
	H	6–225 (3.7)	2.7495–2.7505	.0010–.0025	.0035–.0095	3	2.1865–2.1875	.0010–.0022	.001–.002
	T	8–318 (5.2)	2.4995–2.5005	.0005–.0020 ①	.002–.007	3	2.1240–2.1250	.0005–.0022	.006–.014
	W	8–360 (5.9)	2.8095–2.8105	.0005–.0020 ①	.002–.009	3	2.1240–2.1250	.0005–.0022	.006–.014
1985	C	4–135 (2.2)	2.3620–2.3630	.0003–.0031	.002–.007	3	1.9680–1.9690	.0008–.0034	.005–.013
	G	4–156 (2.6)	2.3622	.0008–.0028	.002–.007	3	2.0866	.0008–.0028	.004–.010
	H	6–225 (3.7)	2.7495–2.7505	.0010–.0025	.0035–.0095	3	2.1865–2.1875	.0010–.0022	.001–.002
	T	8–318 (5.2)	2.4995–2.5005	.0005–.0020 ①	.002–.007	3	2.1240–2.1250	.0005–.0022	.006–.014

CRANKSHAFT AND CONNECTING ROD SPECIFICATIONS

All measurements are given in inches.

Year	VIN	No. Cylinder Displacement cu. in. (liter)	Crankshaft: Main Brg. Journal Dia.	Crankshaft: Main Brg. Oil Clearance	Crankshaft: Shaft End-play	Crankshaft: Thrust on No.	Connecting Rod: Journal Diameter	Connecting Rod: Oil Clearance	Connecting Rod: Side Clearance
1985	W	8-360 (5.9)	2.8095–2.8105	.0005–.0020 ①	.002–.009	3	2.1240–2.1250	.0005–.0022	.006–.014
1986	C	4-135 (2.2)	2.3620–2.3630	.0003–.0031	.002–.007	3	1.9680–1.9690	.0008–.0034	.005–.013
	G	4-156 (2.6)	2.3622	.0008–.0028	.002–.007	3	2.0866	.0008–.0028	.004–.010
	H	6-225 (3.7)	2.7495–2.7505	.0010–.0025	.0035–.0095	3	2.1865–2.1875	.0010–.0022	.001–.002
	T	8-318 (5.2)	2.4995–2.5005	.0005–.0020 ①	.002–.007	3	2.1240–2.1250	.0005–.0022	.006–.014
	W	8-360 (5.9)	2.8095–2.8105	.0005–.0020 ①	.002–.009	3	2.1240–2.1250	.0005–.0022	.006–.014
1987	C	4-135 (2.2)	2.3620–2.3630	.0003–.0031	.002–.007	3	1.9680–1.9690	.0008–.0034	.005–.013
	G	4-156 (2.6)	2.3622	.0008–.0028	.002–.007	3	2.0866	.0008–.0028	.004–.010
	H	6-225 (3.7)	2.7495–2.7505	.0010–.0025	.0035–.0095	3	2.1865–2.1875	.0010–.0022	.001–.002
	M	6-238 (3.9)	2.4995–2.5005	.0005–.0020 ①	.002–.007	2	2.1240–2.1250	.0005–.0022	.006–.014
	T	8-318 (5.2)	2.4995–2.5005	.0005–.0020 ①	.002–.007	3	2.1240–2.1250	.0005–.0022	.006–.014
	W	8-360 (5.9)	2.8095–2.8105	.0005–.0020 ①	.002–.009	3	2.1240–2.1250	.0005–.0022	.006–.014
1988	C	4-135 (2.2)	2.3620–2.3630	.0003–.0031	.002–.007	3	1.9680–1.9690	.0008–.0034	.005–.013
	K	4-153 (2.6)	2.3620–2.3630	.0004–.0028	.002–.007	3	1.9680–1.9690	.0008–.0034②	.004–.005
	H	6-225 (3.7)	2.7495–2.7505	.0010–.0025	.0035–.0095	3	2.1865–2.1875	.0010–.0022	.013–.002
	M	6-238 (3.9)	2.4995–2.5005	.0005–.0020 ①	.002–.007	2	2.1240–2.1250	.0005–.0022	.006–.014
	3	6-181 (3.0)	2.3610–2.3632	.0006–.0020	.002–.010	3	NA	NA	NA
	T	8-318 (5.2)	2.4995–2.5005	.0005–.0020 ①	.002–.007	3	2.1240–2.1250	.0005–.0022	.006–.014

CRANKSHAFT AND CONNECTING ROD SPECIFICATIONS

All measurements are given in inches.

Year	VIN	No. Cylinder Displacement cu. in. (liter)	Crankshaft: Main Brg. Journal Dia.	Crankshaft: Main Brg. Oil Clearance	Crankshaft: Shaft End-play	Crankshaft: Thrust on No.	Connecting Rod: Journal Diameter	Connecting Rod: Oil Clearance	Connecting Rod: Side Clearance
1988	W	8–360 (5.9)	2.8095–2.8105	.0005–.0020 ①	.002–.009	3	2.1240–2.1250	.0005–.0022	.006–.014

① .0005–.0015 on No. 1 cylinder
② Turbocharged Engine: .0008–.0031

VALVE SPECIFICATIONS

Year	VIN	No. Cylinder Displacement cu. in. (liter)	Seat Angle (deg.)	Face Angle (deg.)	Spring Test Pressure (lbs.)	Spring Installed Height (in.)	Stem-to-Guide Clearance (in.) Intake	Stem-to-Guide Clearance (in.) Exhaust	Stem Diameter (in.) Intake	Stem Diameter (in.) Exhaust
1982	A	4–105 (1.7)	45	①	②	③	.002–.003	.002–.003	.3140	.3130
	B	4–135 (2.2)	45	45	175	1.65	.001–.003	.002–.004	.312–.313	.311–.312
	D	4–156 (2.6)	45	45	61	1.59	.0012–.0024	.0020–.0035	.315	.315
	E	6–225 (3.7)	45	A	137–150	$1^{11}/_{16}$	.001–.003	.003–.004	.372–.373	.371–.372
	P	8–318 (5.2)	45	45	④	⑤	.001–.003	.002–.004	.372–.373	.371–.372
	T	8–360 (5.9)	45	45	④	⑤	.001–.003	.002–.004	.372–.373	.371–.372
1983	B	4–105 (1.7)	45	①	②	③	.002–.003	.002–.003	.3140	.3130
	C	4–135 (2.2)	45	45	175	1.65	.001–.003	.002–.004	.312–.313	.311–.312
	G	4–156 (2.6)	45	45	61	1.59	.0012–.0024	.0020–.0035	.315	.315
	J	6–225 (3.7)	45	A	137–150	$1^{11}/_{16}$	.001–.003	.003–.004	.372–.373	.371–.372
	T	8–318 (5.2)	45	45	④	⑤	.001–.003	.002–.004	.372–.373	.371–.372
	W	8–360 (5.9)	45	45	④	⑤	.001–.003	.002–.004	.372–.373	.371–.372
1984	C	4–135 (2.2)	45	45	175	1.65	.001–.003	.002–.004	.312–.313	.311–.312
	G	4–156 (2.6)	45	45	61	1.59	.0012–.0024	.0020–.0035	.315	.315
	H	6–225 (3.7)	45	A	137–150	$1^{11}/_{16}$	.001–.003	.003–.004	.372–.373	.371–.372
	T	8–318 (5.2)	45	45	④	⑤	.001–.003	.002–.004	.372–.373	.371–.372

VALVE SPECIFICATIONS

Year	VIN	No. Cylinder Displacement cu. in. (liter)	Seat Angle (deg.)	Face Angle (deg.)	Spring Test Pressure (lbs.)	Spring Installed Height (in.)	Stem-to-Guide Clearance (in.) Intake	Stem-to-Guide Clearance (in.) Exhaust	Stem Diameter (in.) Intake	Stem Diameter (in.) Exhaust
1984	W	8-360 (5.9)	45	45	④	⑤	.001-.003	.002-.004	.372-.373	.371-.372
1985	C	4-135 (2.2)	45	45	175	1.65	.001-.003	.002-.004	.312-.313	.311-.312
	G	4-156 (2.6)	45	45	61	1.59	.0012-.0024	.0020-.0035	.315	.315
	H	6-225 (3.7)	45	A	137-150	1 11/16	.001-.003	.003-.004	.372-.373	.371-.372
	T	8-318 (5.2)	45	45	④	⑤	.001-.003	.002-.004	.372-.373	.371-.372
	W	8-360 (5.9)	45	45	④	⑤	.001-.003	.002-.004	.372-.373	.371-.372
1986	C	4-135 (2.2)	45	45	175	1.65	.001-.003	.002-.004	.312-.313	.311-.312
	G	4-156 (2.6)	45	45	61	1.59	.0012-.0024	.0020-.0035	.315	.315
	H	6-225 (3.7)	45	A	137-150	1 11/16	.001-.003	.003-.004	.372-.373	.371-.372
	T	8-318 (5.2)	45	45	④	⑤	.001-.003	.002-.004	.372-.373	.371-.372
	W	8-360 (5.9)	45	45	④	⑤	.001-.003	.002-.004	.372-.373	.371-.372
1987	C	4-135 (2.2)	45	45	165	2.39	.0009-.0026	.0030-.0035	.312-.313	.311-.312
	G	4-156 (2.6)	45	45	61	1.59	.0012-.0024	.0020-.0035	.315	.315
	H	6-225 (3.7)	45	A	137-150	1 11/16	.001-.003	.003-.004	.372-.373	.371-.372
	M	6-238 (3.9)	44	45	—	1.988	.001-.002	.0019-.0030	.313-.314	.3120-.3125
	T	8-318 (5.2)	45	45	④	⑤	.001-.003	.002-.004	.372-.373	.371-.372
	W	8-360 (5.9)	45	45	④	⑤	.001-.003	.002-.004	.372-.373	.371-.372
1988	C	4-135 (2.2)	45	45	165	2.39	.0009-.0026	.0030-.0047	.312-.313	.311-.312
	K	4-153 (2.5)	—	—	165	2.39	.0009-.0026	.0030-.0047	—	—
	M	6-238 (3.9)	44	45	—	1.988	.001-.002	.0019-.0030	.313-.314	.3120-.3125
	3	6-181 (3.0)	44	45	73	1.988	.001-.002	.0019-.0030	.313-.314	.3120-.3125
	T	8-318 (5.2)	45	45	④	⑤	.001-.003	.002-.004	.372-.373	.371-.372

VALVE SPECIFICATIONS

Year	VIN	No. Cylinder Displacement cu. in. (liter)	Seat Angle (deg.)	Face Angle (deg.)	Spring Test Pressure (lbs.)	Spring Installed Height (in.)	Stem-to-Guide Clearance (in.)		Stem Diameter (in.)	
							Intake	Exhaust	Intake	Exhaust
1988	W	8–360 (5.9)	45	45	④	⑤	.001–.003	.002–.004	.372–.373	.371–.372

① Intake 45°; Exhaust 43°
② Outer 101; Inner 49
③ Outer 1.28; Inner 1.13
④ Intake 170–184; Exhaust 181–197
⑤ Intake 1 $^{11}/_{16}$; Exhaust 1 $^{33}/_{64}$

PISTON AND RING SPECIFICATIONS

All measurments are given in inches.

Year	VIN	No. Cylinder Displacement cu. in. (liter)	Piston Clearance	Ring Gap			Ring Side Clearance		
				Top Compression	Bottom Compression	Oil Control	Top Compression	Bottom Compression	Oil Control
1982	B	4–135 (2.2)	.0005–.0015	.011–.012	.011–.021	.016–.055	.0016–.0028	.0008–.0020	.0008–.0020
	D	4–156 (2.6)	.0008–.0016	.010–.018	.010–.018	.0078–.0350	.0015–.0031	.0015–.0037	—
	E	6–225 (3.7)	.0015	.010–.020	.010–.020	.015–.055	.0015–.0030	.0015–.0030	.0002–.0050
	P	8–318 (5.2)	.0015	.010–.020	.010–.020	.015–.055	.0015–.0030	.0015–.0030	.0002–.0050
	T	8–360 (5.9)	.0015	.010–.020	.010–.020	.015–.055	.0015–.0030	.0015–.0030	.0002–.0050
1983	C	4–135 (2.2)	.0005–.0015	.011–.012	.011–.021	.016–.055	.0016–.0028	.0008–.0020	.0008–.0020
	G	4–156 (2.6)	.0008–.0016	.010–.018	.010–.018	.0078–.0350	.0015–.0031	.0015–.0037	—
	J	6–225 (3.7)	.0015	.010–.020	.010–.020	.015–.055	.0015–.0030	.0015–.0030	.0002–.0050
	T	8–318 (5.2)	.0015	.010–.020	.010–.020	.015–.055	.0015–.0030	.0015–.0030	.0002–.0050
	W	8–360 (5.9)	.0015	.010–.020	.010–.020	.015–.055	.0015–.0030	.0015–.0030	.0002–.0050
1984	C	4–135 (2.2)	.0005–.0015	.011–.012	.011–.021	.016–.055	.0016–.0028	.0008–.0020	.0008–.0020
	G	4–156 (2.6)	.0008–.0016	.010–.018	.010–.018	.0078–.0350	.0015–.0031	.0015–.0037	—
	H	6–225 (3.7)	.0015	.010–.020	.010–.020	.015–.055	.0015–.0030	.0015–.0030	.0002–.0050
	T	8–318 (5.2)	.0015	.010–.020	.010–.020	.015–.055	.0015–.0030	.0015–.0030	.0002–.0050
	W	8–360 (5.9)	.0015	.010–.020	.010–.020	.015–.055	.0015–.0030	.0015–.0030	.0002–.0050

PISTON AND RING SPECIFICATIONS

All measurments are given in inches.

Year	VIN	No. Cylinder Displacement cu. in. (liter)	Piston Clearance	Ring Gap			Ring Side Clearance		
				Top Compression	Bottom Compression	Oil Control	Top Compression	Bottom Compression	Oil Control
1985	C	4–135 (2.2)	.0005–.0015	.011–.012	.011–.021	.016–.055	.0016–.0028	.0008–.0020	.0008–.0020
	G	4–156 (2.6)	.0008–.0016	.010–.018	.010–.018	.0078–.0350	.0015–.0031	.0015–.0037	–
	H	6–225 (3.7)	.0015	.010–.020	.010–.020	.015–.055	.0015–.0030	.0015–.0030	.0002–.0050
	T	8–318 (5.2)	.0015	.010–.020	.010–.020	.015–.055	.0015–.0030	.0015–.0030	.0002–.0050
	W	8–360 (5.9)	.0015	.010–.020	.010–.020	.015–.055	.0015–.0030	.0015–.0030	.0002–.0050
1986	C	4–135 (2.2)	.0005–.0015	.011–.012	.011–.021	.016–.055	.0016–.0028	.0008–.0020	.0008–.0020
	G	4–156 (2.6)	.0008–.0016	.010–.018	.010–.018	.0078–.0350	.0015–.0031	.0015–.0037	–
	H	6–225 (3.7)	.0015	.010–.020	.010–.020	.015–.055	.0015–.0030	.0015–.0030	.0002–.0050
	T	8–318 (5.2)	.0015	.010–.020	.010–.020	.015–.055	.0015–.0030	.0015–.0030	.0002–.0050
	W	8–360 (5.9)	.0015	.010–.020	.010–.020	.015–.055	.0015–.0030	.0015–.0030	.0002–.0050
1987	C	4–135 (2.2)	.0005–.0015	.011–.012	.011–.021	.016–.055	.0016–.0028	.0008–.0020	.0008–.0020
	G	4–156 (2.6)	.0008–.0016	.010–.018	.010–.018	.0078–.0350	.0015–.0031	.0015–.0037	–
	H	6–225 (3.7)	.0015	.010–.020	.010–.020	.015–.055	.0015–.0030	.0015–.0030	.0002–.0050
	M	6–239 (3.9)	.0005–.0015	.010–.020	.010–.020	.015–.055	.0015–.0030	.0015–.0030	.0002–.0050
	T	8–318 (5.2)	.0015	.010–.020	.010–.020	.015–.055	.0015–.0030	.0015–.0030	.0002–.0050
	W	8–360 (5.9)	.0015	.010–.020	.010–.020	.015–.055	.0015–.0030	.0015–.0030	.0002–.0050
1988	C	4–135 (2.2)	.0005–.0015	.011–.012	.011–.021	.016–.055	.0016–.0028	.0008–.0020	.0008–.0020
	K	6–239 (3.9)	.0005–.0015	.011–.021	.011–.021	.015–.055	.0015–.0031	.0015–.0037	–
	M	6–239 (3.9)	.0005–.0015	.010–.020	.010–.020	.015–.055	.0015–.0030	.0015–.0030	.0002–.0050
	3	6–181 (3.0)	.0008–.0015	.012–.018	.010–.016	.012–.035	.0020–.0035	.0008–.0020	–
	T	8–318 (5.2)	.0015	.010–.020	.010–.020	.015–.055	.0015–.0030	.0015–.0030	.0002–.0050
	W	8–360 (5.9)	.0015	.010–.020	.010–.020	.015–.055	.0015–.0030	.0015–.0030	.0002–.0050

TORQUE SPECIFICATIONS

All readings in ft. lbs.

Year	VIN	No. Cylinder Displacement cu. in. (liter)	Cylinder Head Bolts	Main Bearing Bolts	Rod Bearing Bolts	Crankshaft Pulley Bolts	Flywheel Bolts	Manifold		Spark Plugs
								Intake	Exhaust	
1982	B	4-135 (2.2)	45(1)	30(2)	40(2)	50	65(3)	17	17	26
	D	4-156 (2.6)	69	58	34	87	(4)	12.5	12.5	18
	E	6-225 (3.7)	70	85	45	(5)	55	(6)	10	10
	P	8-318 (5.2)	105	85	45	100	55	40	(7)	30
	T	8-360 (5.9)	105	85	45	100	55	40	(7)	30
1983	C	4-135 (2.2)	45(1)	30(2)	40(2)	50	65(3)	17	17	26
	G	4-156 (2.6)	69	58	34	87	(4)	12.5	12.5	18
	J	6-225 (3.7)	70	85	45	(5)	55	(6)	10	10
	T	8-318 (5.2)	105	85	45	100	55	40	(7)	30
	W	8-360 (5.9)	105	85	45	100	55	40	(7)	30
1984	C	4-135 (2.2)	45(1)	30(2)	40(2)	50	65(3)	17	17	26
	G	4-156 (2.6)	69	58	34	87	(4)	12.5	12.5	18
	H	6-225 (3.7)	70	85	45	(5)	55	(6)	10	10
	T	8-318 (5.2)	105	85	45	100	55	40	(7)	30
	W	8-360 (5.9)	105	85	45	100	55	40	(7)	30
1985	C	4-135 (2.2)	45(1)	30(2)	40(2)	50	65(3)	17	17	26
	G	4-156 (2.6)	69	58	34	87	(4)	12.5	12.5	18
	H	6-225 (3.7)	70	85	45	(5)	55	(6)	10	10
	T	8-318 (5.2)	105	85	45	100	55	40	(7)	30
	W	8-360 (5.9)	105	85	45	100	55	40	(7)	30
1986	C	4-135 (2.2)	45(1)	30(2)	40(2)	50	65(3)	17	17	26
	G	4-156 (2.6)	69	58	34	87	(4)	12.5	12.5	18
	H	6-225 (3.7)	70	85	45	(5)	55	(6)	10	10
	T	8-318 (5.2)	105	85	45	100	55	40	(7)	30
	W	8-360 (5.9)	105	85	45	100	55	40	(7)	30
1987	C	4-135 (2.2)	45(1)	30(2)	40(2)	50	65(3)	17	17	26
	G	4-156 (2.6)	69	58	34	87	(4)	12.5	12.5	18
	H	6-225 (3.7)	70	85	45	(5)	55	(6)	10	10
	M	6-238 (3.7)	105	85	45	135	55	45	(7)	30
	T	8-318 (5.2)	105	85	45	100	55	40	(7)	30
	W	8-360 (5.9)	105	85	45	100	55	40	(7)	30
1988	C	4-135 (2.2)	45(1)	30(2)	40(2)	50	65(3)	17	17	26
	K	4-153 (2.5)	(8)	30(2)	40(2)	50	70	17	17	26
	M	6-238 (3.7)	105	85	45	135	55	45	(7)	30
	3	6-181 (3.0)	70	60	38	110	70	–	–	–

TORQUE SPECIFICATIONS

All readings in ft. lbs.

Year	VIN	No. Cylinder Displacement cu. in. (liter)	Cylinder Head Bolts	Main Bearing Bolts	Rod Bearing Bolts	Crankshaft Pulley Bolts	Flywheel Bolts	Manifold		Spark Plugs
								Intake	Exhaust	
1988	T	8–318 (5.2)	105	85	45	100	55	40	⑦	30
	W	8–360 (5.9)	105	85	45	100	55	40	⑦	30

① Tighten in four Steps:
1st Step: 30 ft. lbs.
2nd Step: 45 ft. lbs.
3rd Step: 45 ft. lbs.
4th Step: Turn the bolts 90° additional

② Plus 90° turn

③ Manual Transmission

④ With A–404 Transmission: 50 ft. lbs.
With A–413 Transmission: 65 ft. lbs.
With A–470 Transmission: 100 ft. lbs.

⑤ Press Fit

⑥ Bolt 17; Nut 20

⑦ Screw 20; Nut 15

⑧ Tighten in four Steps:
1st Step: 45 ft. lbs.
2nd Step: 65 ft. lbs.
3rd Step: 65 ft. lbs.
4th Step: Turn the bolts 90° additional

WHEEL ALIGNMENT

Year	Model	Caster		Camber		Toe-in (in.)	Steering Axis Inclination (deg.)
		Range (deg.)	Preferred Setting (deg.)	Range (deg.)	Preferred Setting (deg.)		
1982	D–100, 150, 200 D–250, 300, 350 Ramcharger 4 × 2	½N–1½P	½P	0–1P	¼P	⅛P	8½
	W–150, 200, Ramcharger 4 × 4, W–250①, 300, 350 B–100, 200, 300	—	3P	—	1½P	0	8½
	PB–100, 200, 300	1¼P–3¼P	2½P	¼N–1P	⅜P	⅛P	—
1983	D–100, 150, 200 D–250, 300, 350 Ramcharger 4 × 2	½N–1½P	½P	0–1P	¼P	⅛P	8½
	W–150, 200, Ramcharger 4 × 4, W–250①, 300, 350 B–100, 200, 300	—	3P	—	1½P	0	8½
	PB–100, 200, 300	1¼P–3¾P	2½P	¼N–1P	⅜P	⅛P	—
1984	D–150, 250, 350 Ramcharger 4 × 2	½N–1½P	½P	0–1P	¼P	⅛P	8½
	W–150, 250, 350 Ramcharger 4 × 4, B–100, 200, 300	—	3P	—	1½P	0	8½
	PB–100, 200, 300	1¼P–3¾P	2½P	¼N–1P	⅜P	⅛P	—
	Mini Vans (Front)	—	⅜P	¼N–¾P	5/16P	1/16P	—
	Mini Vans (Rear)	—	—	1⅛N–⅛N	½N	0	—
1985	D–150, 250, 350 Ramcharger 4 × 2	½N–1½P	½P	0–1P	¼P	⅛P	8½
	W–150, 250, 350 Ramcharger 4 × 4, B–100, 200, 300	—	3P	—	1½P	0	8½

WHEEL ALIGNMENT

Year	Model	Caster Range (deg.)	Caster Preferred Setting (deg.)	Camber Range (deg.)	Camber Preferred Setting (deg.)	Toe-in (in.)	Steering Axis Inclination (deg.)
1985	PB-100, 200, 300	1 1/4P–3 3/4P	2 1/2P	1/4N–1P	3/8P	1/8P	—
	Mini Vans (Front)	—	3/8P	1/4N–3/4P	5/16P	1/16P	—
	Mini Vans (Rear)	—	—	1 1/8N–1/8N	1/2N	0	—
1986	D-150, 250, 350 Ramcharger 4×2	1/2N–1 1/2P	1/2P	0–1P	1/4P	1/8P	8 1/2
	W-150, 250, 350 Ramcharger 4×4, B-100, 200, 300	—	3P	—	1 1/2P	0	8 1/2
	PB-100, 200, 300	1 1/4P–3 3/4P	2 1/2P	1/4N–1P	3/8P	1/8P	—
	Mini Vans (Front)	—	3/8P	1/4N–3/4P	5/16P	1/16P	—
	Mini Vans (Rear)	—	—	1 3/8N–1/4N	13/16N	0	—
1987–88	D-150, 250, 350 Ramcharger 4×2	1/2N–1 1/2P	1/2P	0–1P	1/4P	1/8P	8 1/2
	W-150, 250, 350 Ramcharger 4×4, B-100, 200, 300	—	3P	—	1 1/2P	0	8 1/2
	PB-100, 200, 300	1 1/4P–3 3/4P	2 1/2P	1/4N–1P	3/8P	1/8P	—
	Mini Vans (Front)	—	3/8P	1/4N–3/4P	5/16P	1/16P	—
	Mini Vans (Rear)	—	—	1 3/8N–1/4N	13/16N	0	—
	Dakota (Front)	1/2P–2 1/2P	1 1/2P	0–1P	1/2P	1/8P	—
	Dakota (Rear)	—	—	1/16P–3/32P	1/32P	1/32P	—

ENGINE ELECTRICAL

Alternator

Removal and Installation

1. Disconnect battery ground cable at the negative terminal.
2. Disconnect alternator output BAT and field FLD leads and disconnect ground wire.
3. Loosen the alternator adjusting bolt and swing the alternator in towards the engine. Disconnect the alternator drive belt.
4. Remove the alternator mounting bolts and remove the alternator from the vehicle from the vehicle.
5. Installation is the reverse of the removal procedure.
6. Start engine and observe alternator operation.
7. Test current output.

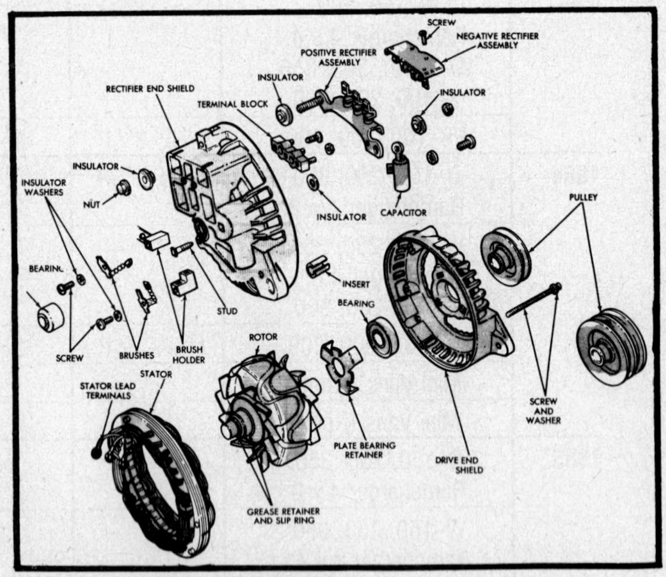

Exploded view of alternator

Voltage Regulator

ELECTRONIC VOLTAGE REGULATOR

Removal and Installation

1. Release the spring clips and pull off the regulator wiring plug.
2. Unbolt and remove the regulator.

3. Installation is the reverse of removal. Be sure that the spring clips engage the wiring plug.

Adjustment

The electronic voltage regulator has no moving parts and no adjustments are possible.

Starter

Removal and Installation

Note: The following is a general procedure on starter removal and installation. Change the procedure accordingly.

1. Disconnect the battery ground cable.
2. Remove the cable at the starter. Remove the heat shield clamp and heat shield if equipped.
3. If the solenoid is mounted on the starter, disconnect the wires at the solenoid terminals.
4. Remove the starter to flywheel housing mounting bolts. Remove automatic transmission oil cooler tube bracket off the stud if necessary. Remove the starter and removable seal, if so equipped.
5. Before installing the starter, make sure the starter and flywheel housing mounting surfaces are free of dirt and oil. These surfaces must be clean.
6. Install the starter to flywheel housing removable seal, if so equipped.
7. Position the starter to the flywheel housing and, if necessary, install the automatic transmission oil cooler bracket. Install mounting bolts. Tighten securely.

NOTE: When tightening the mounting bolt and nut on the starter, hold the starter away from the engine for correct alignment.

8. If the solenoid is mounted on the starter, connect the wires to the solenoid terminals.
9. Connect the cable to the starter terminal.
10. Connect the battery ground cable and test operation of the starter for proper engine cranking.

OVERHAUL

For starter motor overhaul procedures see the Electrical section in the Unit Repair Section.

Distributor

Removal and Installation

1. Disconnect the distributor lead wire at the connector.
2. Disconnect vacuum hose at distributor or vacuum controller.
3. On the Holley distributor, disconnect tachometer drive and governor inlet and outlet lines.
4. Unfasten distributor cap retaining clips and remove distributor cap.
5. Scribe a line on the distributor housing and engine block to indicate positioning of the rotor and housing.
6. Remove distributor holdown clamp or screw.
7. Carefully lift out distributor assembly.

NOTE: Do not disturb engine position.

8. If the crankshaft has not been rotated, install distributor into block with the rotor and body aligned to the previously scribed marks. Make sure O-ring seal is in groove of shank.

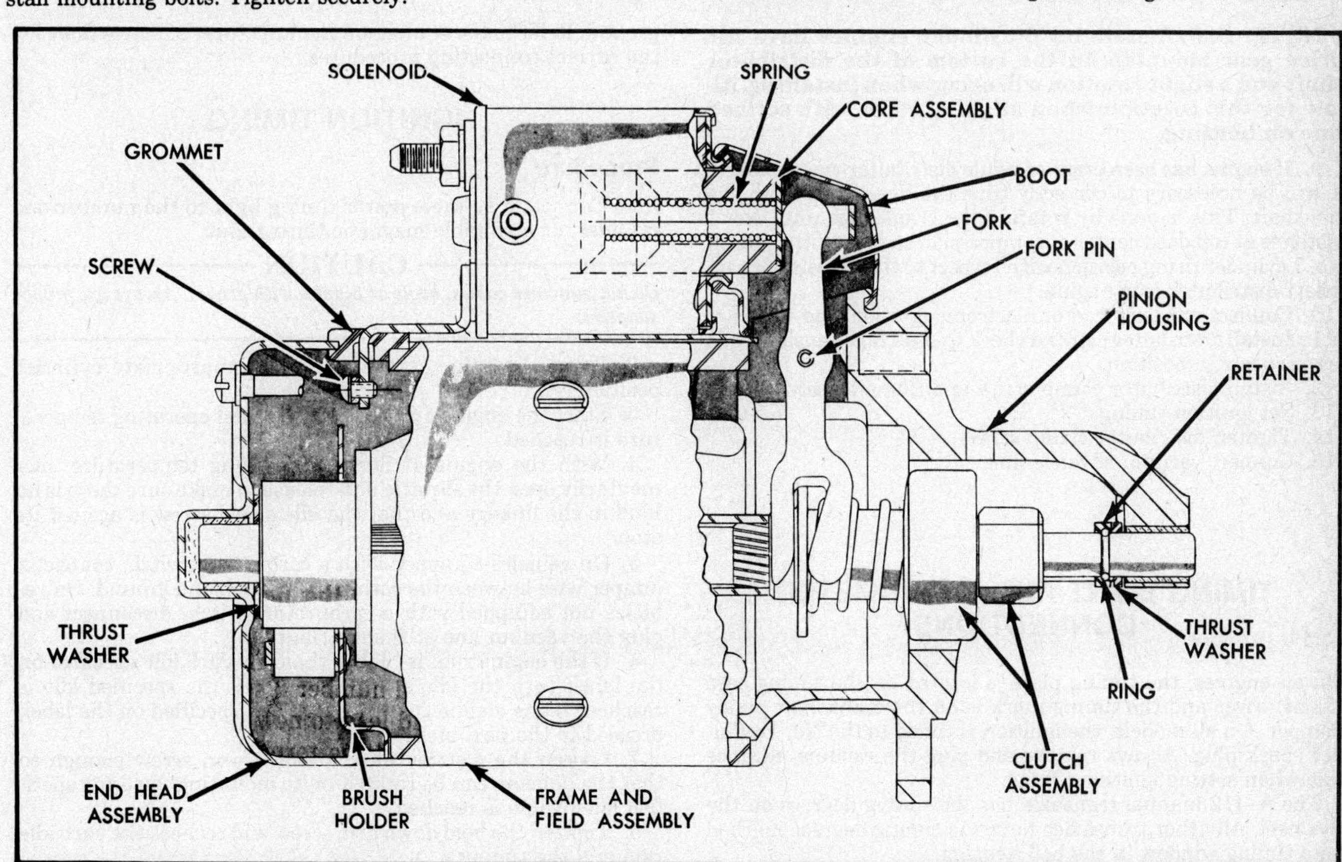

Starter motor (direct drive type)

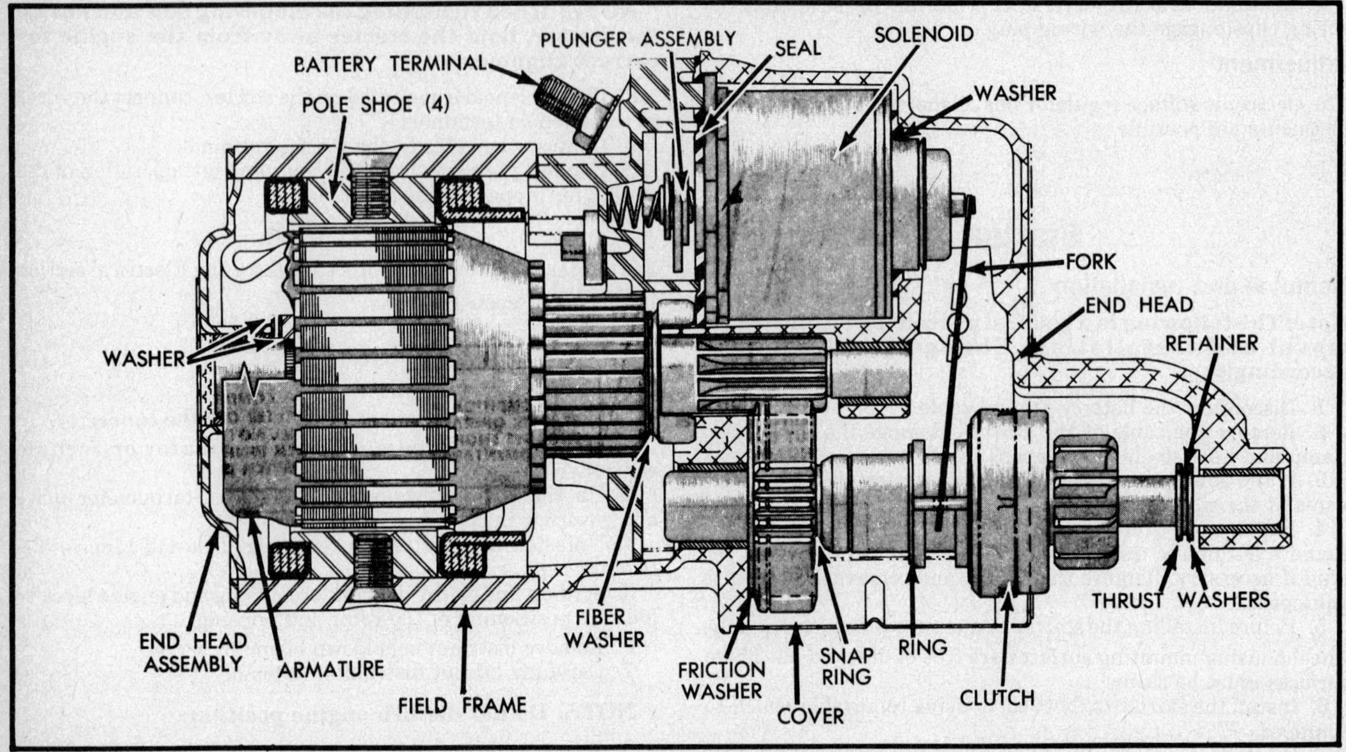

Starter motor (reduction gear type)

NOTE: Distributors on 6 cylinder engines have the drive gear mounted on the bottom of the distributor shaft and a slight rotation will occur when installing. Allow for this rotation when aligning rotor with scribed line on housing.

9. If engine has been cranked while distributor was removed, it will be necessary to correctly time the distributor with the camshaft. This is done by rotating the crankshaft until No. 1 piston is at top dead center of compression stroke. With rotor in No. 1 cylinder firing position with respect to the distributor cap, insert distributor into engine.
10. Connect primary lead or electronic ignition lead wire.
11. Install distributor cap and check that all high tension leads are securely in position.
12. Install distributor clamp screw and clamp loosely.
13. Set ignition timing.
14. Tighten distributor clamp screw.
15. Connect vacuum advance line.

TIMING LIGHT AND TACHOMETER CONNECTIONS

On all engines, the timing plate is located on the timing case (front) cover and the timing mark is on the crankshaft pulley damper. On all models, the ignition is timed to the No. 1 cylinder spark plug. Always remove and plug the vacuum advance line when setting ignition timing.

The A–412 manual transaxle has the timing degrees on the flywheel. All other transaxles have the timing degrees marked on a timing window in the bell housing.

Connect the red lead of the test tachometer unit to the negative primary terminal of the coil and the black lead to a good ground. Refer to the equipment manufacturer's instructions for the correct connecting procedures.

IGNITION TIMING

Procedure

1. Connect a suitable power timing light to the number one cylinder, or a suitable magnetic timing unit.

CAUTION

Do not puncture cables, boots or nipples with probes. Always use proper adapters.

2. Turn the selector switch to the appropriate cylinder position.
3. Start the engine and run until normal operating temperature is reached.
4. With the engine at normal operating temperature, momentarily open the throttle and release to make sure there is no bind in the linkage and that the idle speed screw is against its stop.
5. On vehicles equipped with a carburetor switch, connect a jumper wire between the carburetor switch and ground. On vehicles not equipped with a carburetor switch, disconnect and plug the vacuum line at the distributor.
6. If the engine rpm is higher than the curb idle specified on the label, turn the idle speed screw until the specified idle is reached. If the engine rpm is lower than specified on the label, proceed to the next step.
7. Loosen the distributor hold down arm screw enough so that the housing can be rotated in its mounting until the specified label value is reached.
8. Tighten the hold down arm screw and recheck the curb idle rpm and the timing.
9. Turn off the engine. Unplug and reconnect the vacuum lines. Remove the jumper wire, if installed, the tachometer.

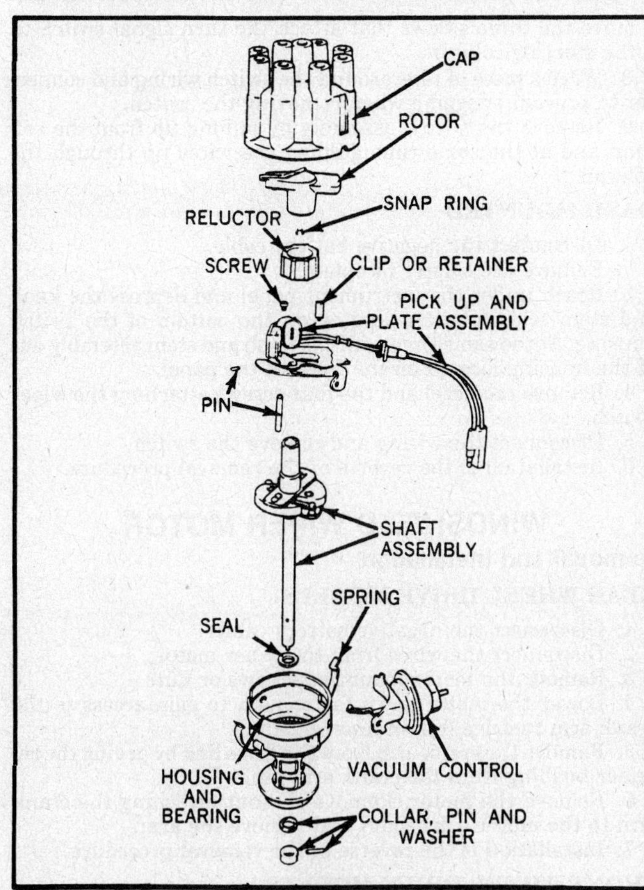

V8 electronic ignition distributor

Electrical Controls

IGNITION SWITCH

Removal and Installation

1. Remove the lower steering column cover. On the front wheel drive models, remove the left lower instrument panel cover.
2. If equipped with automatic transmission, position the gear selector into drive and disconnect the indicator cable.
3. On the front wheel drive models, remove the lower panel reinforcement.
4. Remove the five nuts securing the steering column to the support bracket and lower the column.
5. Disconnect the electrical connector from the ignition switch. Position the lock cylinder into the LOCK position.
6. Tape the ignition switch rod to the steering column to prevent the rod from falling out of the lock cylinder assembly.
7. Remove the two screws from the ignition switch and remove the switch.
8. Installation is the reverse of the removal procedure.

HEADLIGHT SWITCH

Removal and Installation

1. Disconnect the negative battery cable.
2. Remove the headlamp switch trim bezel and the steering column cover.
3. Remove the knob and stem by depressing the button on the switch and pulling the knob and stem from the switch.
4. Remove the switch bezel and pull the assembly rearward to disconnect the wiring.

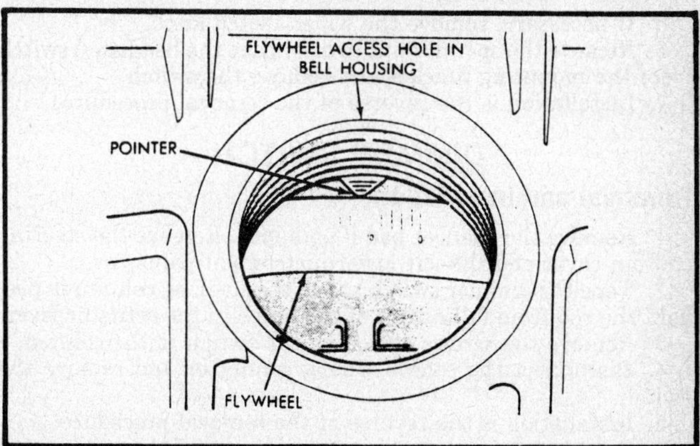

Manual A-412 transaxle timing mark location on 1.7L engine

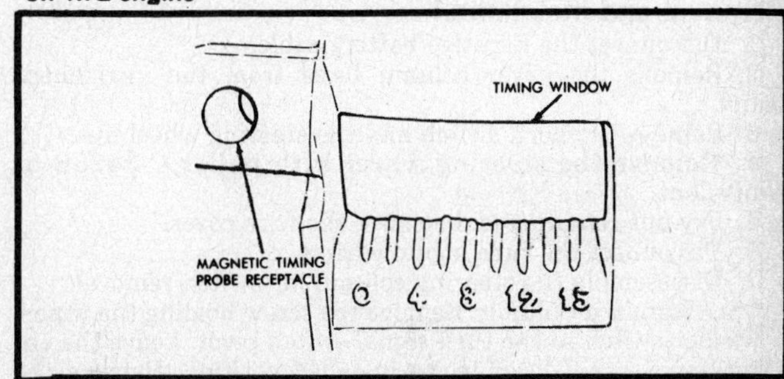

135 (2.2L) timing mark location

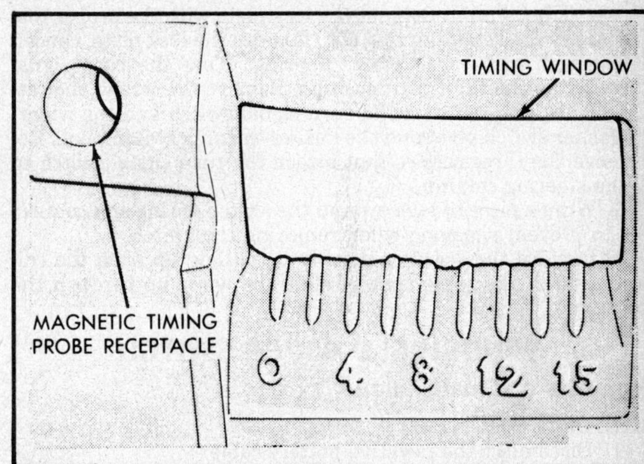

All manual transaxle except A-412—timing mark location

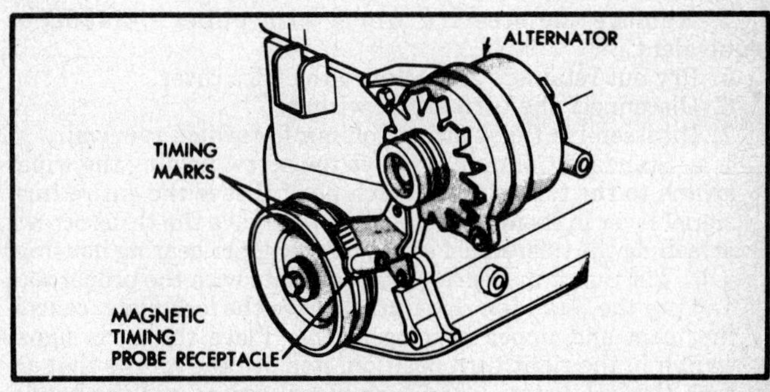

155.9 (2.6L) timing mark location

5. If necessary, remove the wiper switch knob.
6. Remove the spanner nut to disengage the headlamp switch from the mounting bracket and remove the switch.
7. Installation is the reverse of the removal procedure.

DIMMER SWITCH

Removal and Installation

1. Remove the silencer pad if equipped. Remove the steering column cover and the left lower instrument panel cover.
2. Tape the dimmer switch rod to the steering column to prevent the rod from falling out of the notch in the actuator lever.
3. Remove the screws attaching the switch to the column.
4. Disconnect the switch wiring connector and remove the switch.
5. Installation is the reverse of the removal procedure.

TURN SIGNAL SWITCH

Removal and Installation

1. Disconnect the negative battery cable.
2. Remove the lower column bezel from the instrument panel.
3. Remove the horn switch and the steering wheel nut.
4. Remove the steering wheel with puller C-3428B or equivalent.
5. Pry out retainers and remove the wire cover.
6. Disconnect the turn signal wiring.
7. Disassemble the steering column for switch removal.
   a. Standard Column: Remove the screw holding the wiper-washer switch to the turn signal switch pivot. Leave the entire turn signal lever in its installed position. Remove the three screws attaching the turn signal switch to the upper bearing housing.
   b. Tilt Column: Depress the lock plate with the proper tool and pry the retaining ring out. Remove the lock plate, cancelling cam and upper bearing spring. Place the turn signal switch in the right turn position. Remove the screws that attach the link between the turn signal switch and the wiper-washer switch pivot and the hazard warning switch knob. Remove the three screws that attach the turn signal switch to the steering column.
8. Wrap a piece of tape around the switch wiring and connector to prevent snagging when removing the switch.
9. Remove the switch assembly by pulling up from the column and at the same time guiding the wires up through the column.

WINDSHIELD WIPER SWITCH

Removal and Installation

COLUMN MOUNTED

1. Disconnect the negative battery cable.
2. Remove the lower column bezel from the instrument panel.
3. Remove the horn switch and the steering wheel nut.
4. Remove the steering wheel with puller C-3428B or equivalent.
5. Pry out retainers and remove the wire cover.
6. Disconnect the turn signal wiring.
7. Disassemble the steering column for switch removal.
   a. Standard Column: Remove the screw holding the wiper switch to the turn signal switch pivot. Leave the entire turn signal lever in its installed position. Remove the three screws attaching the turn signal switch to the upper bearing housing.
   b. Tilt Column: Depress the lock plate with the proper tool and pry the retaining ring out. Remove the lock plate, cancelling cam and upper bearing spring. Place the turn signal switch in the right turn position. Remove the screws that attach the link between the turn signal switch and the wiper-washer switch pivot and the hazard warning switch knob. Remove the three screws that attach the turn signal switch to the steering column.
8. Wrap a piece of tape around the switch wiring and connector to prevent snagging when removing the switch.
9. Remove the switch assembly by pulling up from the column and at the same time guiding the wires up through the column.

DASH MOUNTED

1. Disconnect the negative battery cable.
2. Remove the cluster faceplate.
3. Reach under the instrument panel and depress the knob and stem release button located on the bottom of the switch housing. At the same time, pull the knob and stem assembly out of the housing located on the front of the panel.
4. Remove the bezel and the four screws attaching the wiper switch.
5. Disconnect the wiring and remove the switch.
6. Installation is the reverse of the removal procedure.

WINDSHIELD WIPER MOTOR

Removal and Installation

REAR WHEEL DRIVE MODELS

1. Disconnect the negative battery cable.
2. Disconnect the wires from the wiper motor.
3. Remove the motor mounting screws or nuts.
4. Lower the motor down far enough to gain access to the crank arm to drive link retainer bushing.
5. Remove the crank arm from the drive link by prying the retainer bushing from the crank arm pin.
6. Remove the motor. Remove the nut attaching the crank arm to the motor drive shaft and remove the arm.
7. Installation is the reverse of the removal procedure.

FRONT WHEEL DRIVE MODELS

NOTE: On the front wheel drive models, the wiper motor and the linkage are serviced as one assembly.

1. Disconnect the negative battery cable.
2. Remove the windshield wiper arms.
3. Open the hood and remove the cowl top plenum grille and the chamber plastic screen.
4. Remove the hose connectors and the wiper pivot retaining screws. Push the pivots down into the plenum chamber.
5. Remove the nut from the output shaft and remove the linkage assembly.
6. Disconnect the wiper motor wiring harness.
7. Remove the mounting screw and nuts and remove the motor.
8. Installation is the reverse of the removal procedure.

WINDSHIELD WIPER LINKAGE

Removal and Installation

NOTE: On the front wheel drive models, the linkage is serviced with the windshield wiper motor.

1. Remove the wiper motor and the wiper arms.
2. Remove the cowl cover grille.
3. Reach through the access hole to disconnect the linkage.
4. Remove the linkage assembly through the access hole.
5. To install the linkage, reverse the removal procedure.

INSTRUMENT CLUSTER

Removal and Installation

PICK UP AND RAMCHARGER

1. Remove the faceplate and the lower steering column cover.
2. Disconnect the PRND21 actuator cable from the steering column.

3. Loosen the heater and A/C control. Pull rearward to clear the cluster housing.
4. Remove the screws that retain the cluster and pull the cluster rearward.
5. Disconnect the three connectors near the speedometer cable.
6. Remove the EMR and gate open lamp sockets and remove the cluster.
7. Installation is the reverse of the removal procedure.

DAKOTA

1. Remove the silencer pad, if equipped and the steering column cover.
2. Remove the cluster bezel.
3. If equipped with automatic transmission, put the gearshift lever in the Drive position. Remove the retaining clip and disconnect the gearshift indicator cable at the steering column.
4. Remove the cluster to instrument panel screws.
5. Pull the cluster rearward and disconnect the wiring and the speedometer cable.
6. Move the cluster past the steering wheel to remove.
7. Installation is the reverse of the removal procedure.

VANS AND WAGONS

1. Disconnect the negative battery cable.
2. Remove the screws that fasten the hood and bezel assembly. Pull the bezel off of the upper retaining clips.
3. Remove the cluster screws. Pull the cluster out far enough to disconnect the speedometer cable by pushing the spring clip towards the cluster.
4. Remove the right and left printed circuit board multiple connectors and the connector near the speedometer cable.
5. Remove the cluster assembly.
6. Installation is the reverse of the removal procedure.

RAM VAN, CARAVAN AND VOYAGER

1. Disconnect the negative battery cable.
2. Remove the instrument cluster bezel.
3. On vehicles equipped with automatic transmission, remove the instrument panel lower left cover and disconnect the shift indicator wire.
4. Remove the screws attaching the cluster to the instrument panel.
5. Disconnect the speedometer cable at the speedometer.
6. Disconnect the cluster wiring and remove the cluster past the right side of the steering column.
7. Installation is the reverse of the removal procedure.

SPEEDOMETER

Removal and Installation

1. Disconnect the negative battery cable.
2. Remove the cluster, bezel and mask.
3. Remove the speedometer mounting screws.
4. Disconnect the speedometer cable and remove the speedometer.
5. Installation is the reverse of the removal procedure.

COOLING AND HEATING SYSTEM

Water Pump

Removal and Installation

6 CYL AND V8 ENGINES

1. Drain the cooling system and remove the fan belt and fan shroud. Remove the radiator.
2. Unscrew fan blade bolts and remove fan blade, spacers and bolts as an assembly.

NOTE: Silicone drive fans must be kept in their normal attitude. If the shaft points down, silicone fluid will contaminate the fan drive bearing.

3. Position the 6 cylinder lower clamp in the center of the bypass hose. Disconnect or remove heater and radiator hoses.
4. Remove water pump retaining bolts and remove water pump assembly.

NOTE: On air conditioned equipped vehicles with V8 engines, the compressor clutch assembly and the front mounting brackets may have to be removed to allow for the removal of the water pump assembly.

5. Install a new by-pass hose, if necessary, with clamps positioned in the center of the hose.
6. Use a new gasket and install water pump. Install and tighten pump retaining bolts to 30 ft. lbs. Position and tighten bypass hose clamps. Install the heater and radiator hoses.
7. Install fan blade, spacer and bolt assembly. Start all bolts, then tighten to 15–18 ft. lbs.
8. Install fan belt and adjust belt tension. Fill cooling system. Start the engine and check for leaks.

4–2.2L ENGINE

1. Drain cooling system.
2. Remove upper radiator hose.
3. Remove air conditioning compressor from engine brackets and set aside. Do not discharge the system.
4. Remove alternator and lay aside.
5. Remove water pump by disconnecting lower radiator hose, bypass hose and four water pump to engine attaching bolts.
6. Installation is the reverse of the removal procedure.
7. Tighten top water pump bolts to 250 inch lbs. (30 Nm) and the lower bolt to 50 ft. lbs. (68 Nm).

4–2.5L ENGINE

1. Drain the cooling system.
2. On vehicles without A/C, remove the alternator and the mounting bracket.
3. Vehicles with A/C, remove the compressor and the alternator from the solid mount bracket and set aside. Do not discharge the system.
4. Vehicles equipped with A/C, use the following procedure to remove the solid mount accessory bracket.
   a. Remove the five side mounting bolts.
   b. Remove the front mounting nut and the front bolt.
   c. Slide the bracket away from the engine and off of the front stud. The front mounting bolt and spacer will be removed with the bracket.
   d. Replace the front mounting bolt in the front of the engine to prevent further coolant loss.
5. Disconnect the lower radiator and heater hoses.
6. Remove the four screws holding the water pump to the engine and remove the pump.

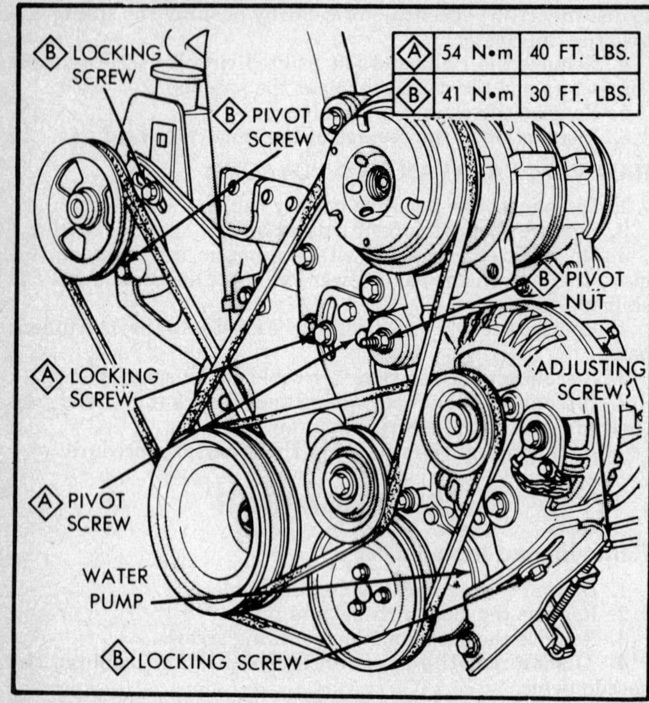

Accessory drive belt arrangement on the 2.2L engine

7. Installation is the reverse of the removal procedure. Tighten the water pump top three screws to 250 inch lbs. (30 Nm). Tighten the lower screw to 50 ft. lbs. (68 Nm).

8. To install the solid mount bracket, use the following procedure.

a. Install the spacer and the bracket on the front mounting stud and slide the bracket over the timing belt cover and into position.

b. Install the front mounting nut and all bolts hand tight.

CAUTION

Bolts must be tightened in sequence and to specified torque as follows.

c. Tighten the rear inner bolt to 30 inch lbs. (30 Nm).

d. Tighten the front bolt and nut to 40 ft. lbs. (54 Nm).

e. Tighten the rear inner bolt to 40 ft. lbs. (54 Nm).

f. Tighten the front inner bolt and the lower outer bolt to 40 ft. lbs. (54 Nm).

g. Tighten the two top bolts to 40 ft. lbs. (54 Nm).

h. Install the alternator and the compressor and tighten the compressor mounting bolts to 40 ft. lbs. (54 Nm).

V6-3.0L ENGINE

1. Drain the cooling system.
2. Remove the A/C compressor mounting bolts and set the compressor aside. Remove the mounting bracket.
3. Remove the adjustable drive belt tensioner from block and engine mounting bracket.
4. Remove the steering pump/alternator automatic belt tensioner.
5. Remove the steering pump mounting screws and lay the pump aside.
6. Remove the water pump mounting bolts.
7. Separate the water pump from the water inlet pipe and remove.
8. Installation is the reverse of the removal procedure.
9. Use a new O-ring on the water inlet pipe and torque the pump to block mounting bolts to 20 ft. lbs. (27 Nm).

4-2.6L ENGINE

1. Drain cooling system.
2. Remove the radiator hose, bypass hose and heater hose from the water pump.
3. Remove the drive pulley shield.
4. Remove the locking screw and pivot screws.
5. Remove the drive belt and lift off the water pump.
6. Installation is the reverse of the removal procedure.

Thermostat

Removal and Installation

1. Drain the cooling system down to the thermostat level or below.
2. Remove the thermostat housing bolts and the housing.
3. Remove the thermostat and discard the gasket. Clean both gasket sealing surfaces.
4. Installation is the reverse of the removal procedure. Use a new gasket dipped in clean water. Tighten bolts to specifications.

Heater Core

WITH AIR CONDITIONING

Removal and Installation

MINI VANS

1. Disconnect the negative battery cable. Discharge the A/C system. Drain the cooling system.
2. Remove the steering column cover which is secured to the lower portion of the instrument panel with seven screws.
3. Remove the lower reinforcement under the steering column. Remove the right side cowl and sill trim. Remove the bolt holding the right side instrument panel to the right cowl.
4. Loosen the two brackets supporting the lower edge to the evaporator unit housing. Remove the instrument panel trim covering mid reinforcement. Remove the retaining screws from the right side to center of the steering column.
5. Disconnect the source vacuum line at the brake booster and the vacuum line at the water valve.
6. Remove and plug the heater hoses.
7. Disconnect the "H" valve connection at the valve. Remove the four retaining nuts from the package mounting studs.
8. Disconnect the blower motor wiring, resistor wiring and the temperature control cable.
9. Disconnect the hanger strap from the package and bend rearward.
10. Pull the right side of the instrument panel rearward until it reaches the passengers seat.
11. Pull the evaporator unit housing assembly rearward from the dash panel and remove it from the vehicle.
12. To disassemble the evaporator housing assembly, remove the retaining screws from the cover. Remove the cover and the temperature control.
13. Remove the retaining screw from the heater core and remove the core from the housing assembly.
14. Installation is the reverse of the removal procedure. Evacuate and recharge the system. Check the system for proper operation.

PICK UP AND RAMCHARGER

1. Disconnect the negative battery cable. Discharge the air condition system. Drain the cooling system. Disconnect and plug the heater hoses and the refrigerant lines.
2. Remove the condensation tube from the housing.
3. If equipped, move the transfer case and gear shift levers away from the instrument panel.
4. If equipped, remove the right side cowl trim panel. Remove the glove box and swing it out from the bottom.

5. Remove the structural brace from the through hole in the glove box opening. Remove the ash tray.
6. Remove the right lower half of the reinforcement by removing the retaining screws holding it to the instrument panel and to the cowl side trim panel.
7. Disconnect the radio ground strap, if equipped. Remove the center distribution duct. Remove the floor air distribution duct.
8. Disconnect the temperature control cable from the assembly through the hole in the glove box. Position it out of the way.
9. Disconnect the vacuum lines from the extension on the control unit. Unclip the vacuum lines from the defroster duct.
10. Remove the wiring connector from the resistor block. Remove the blower motor electrical connector from the engine side of the assembly.
11. Disconnect all vacuum lines. Remove the assembly retaining nuts.
12. Remove the screw that retains the assembly to the cowl side of the sheetmetal.
13. Remove the assembly. The plastic instrument panel may have to be flexed outward to gain clearance.
14. Remove the evaporator case cover retaining screws. Remove the heater core retaining screws. Remove the heater core from its mounting.
15. Installation is the reverse of the removal procedure. Evacuate and recharge the A/C system. Check the system for proper operation.

VANS

1. Disconnect the negative battery cable. Discharge the A/C system. Drain the cooling system. Disconnect and cap the refrigerant lines and the heater hose lines.
3. Disconnect the refrigerant plumbing from the "H" valve. Remove the two screws from the filter drier bracket and swing the plumbing out of the way towards the center of the vehicle.
4. Remove the temperature control cable from the evaporator housing.
5. Working from inside the vehicle, remove the glove box, spot cooler bezel and the appearance shield.
6. Working through the glove box opening and under the instrument panel, remove the screws and nuts attaching the evaporator core housing to the dash panel.
7. Remove the two screws from the flange connection to the blower housing. Separate the evaporator core housing from the blower housing.
8. Carefully remove the evaporator core housing from the vehicle.
9. Remove the cover from the housing and remove the screw retaining the strap to heater core. Remove the heater core.
10. Installation is the reverse of the removal procedure. Evacuate and recharge the system. Check the system for proper operation.

DAKOTA

1. Disconnect the negative battery cable. Discharge the A/C system. Remove the evaporator unit housing assembly.
2. Locate and remove the retaining nut from the blend air door pivot shaft. Remove the crank arm from the pivot shaft.
3. Disconnect the vacuum lines from the defrost and panel mode vacuum actuators. Position them out of the way.
4. Remove the three evaporator cover retaining screws that go upward at the defroster outlet chamber.
5. Remove the two evaporator cover retaining screws that go upward at the air inlet plenum.
6. Remove the eleven evaporator unit housing cover screws that go downward into the housing. Lift the cover from the assembly.
7. Remove the heater core retaining screws. Remove the heater core from its mounting.
8. Installation is the reverse of the removal procedure. Evacuate and recharge the system. Check the system for proper operation.

Heater Core

WITHOUT AIR CONDITIONING

MINI VANS

1. Disconnect the negative battery cable. Drain the cooling system.
2. Remove the steering column cover which is secured to the lower portion of the instrument panel with seven screws.
3. Remove the lower reinforcement under the steering column. Remove the right side cowl and sill trim. Remove the bolt holding the right side instrument panel to the right cowl.
4. Loosen the two brackets supporting the lower edge to the heater housing. Remove the instrument panel trim covering and reinforcement. Remove the retaining screws from the right side to center of the steering column.
5. Disconnect the source vacuum line at the brake booster. Disconnect the vacuum line at the water valve, if equipped.
6. Clamp off the heater hoses before the core and remove the hoses from the core tubes. Plug the hose ends and the core tubes to prevent spillage of coolant.
7. Disconnect the blower motor wiring, resistor wiring and the temperature control cable. Disconnect the hanger strap from the package and bend rearward.
8. Pull the right side of the instrument panel rearward until it reaches the passenger seat.
9. Pull the heater core assembly rearward from the dash panel and remove it from the vehicle.
10. Disassemble the heater core assembly by removing the retaining screws from the cover. Remove the cover and the temperature control rod.
11. Remove the retaining screw from the heater core and remove the core from the housing assembly.
12. Installation is the reverse of the removal procedure.

PICK UP AND RAMCHARGER WITH STANDARD HEATER ASSEMBLY

1. Disconnect the negative battery cable.
2. Drain the cooling system. Remove and plug the heater core hoses.
3. Remove the right side cowl trim panel, if equipped. Remove the glove box assembly. Swing out from the bottom to avoid catches and stops. Remove the structural brace through the glovebox opening.
4. Remove the right half of the instrument panel lower reinforcement. Disconnect the ground strap.
5. Disconnect the control cables from the heater housing. Disconnect the blower motor wires on the engine side. Remove the wires from the resistor block.
6. Remove the retaining screw between the package to cowl side sheet metal.
7. Remove the heater housing retaining nuts on the engine side of the heater assembly. Remove the heater housing assembly from under the dash.
8. Remove the heater housing retaining screws and the mode door crank. Separate the cover from the housing.
9. Carefully lift the heater core from the heater housing.
10. The blower motor can be removed from the housing, if required.
11. Installation is the reverse of the removal procedure.

PICK UP AND RAMCHARGER WITH BI-LEVEL HEATER ASSEMBLY

1. Disconnect the negative battery cable.
2. Drain the coolant. Remove and plug the heater hoses.
3. Remove the drain tube from the housing. As required, move the transfer case and/or gear shift levers away from the instrument panel.

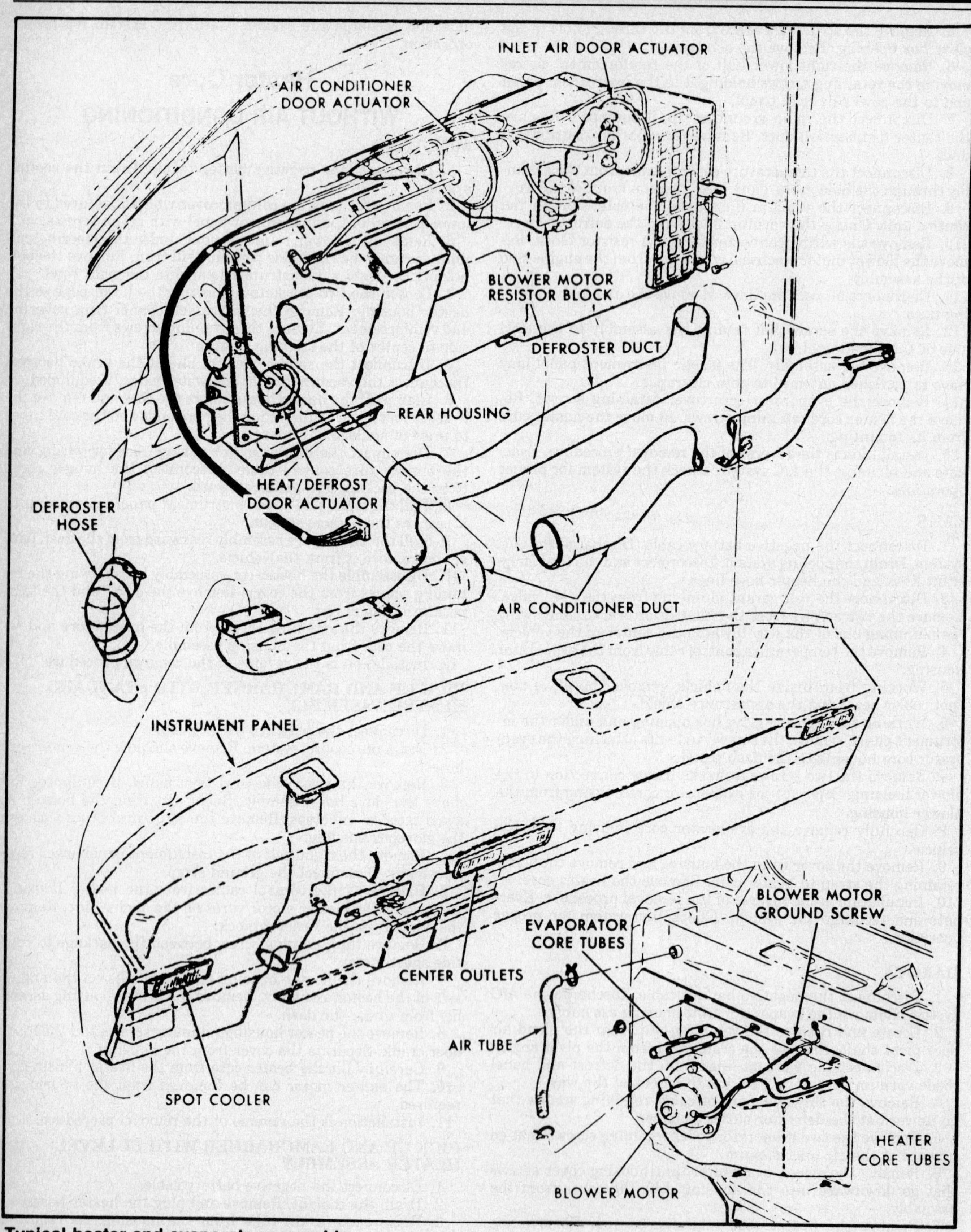

Typical heater and evaporator assembly

4. Remove the glove box and swing out from the bottom to avoid catch and stops.
5. Remove the structural brace from behind the glove box area.
6. Remove the ash tray. Remove the right half of the lower reinforcement. Disconnect the radio ground strap.
7. Remove the center air distribution duct by removing the instrument panel center brace. Remove the right kick pad and the right instrument panel pivot bolt.
8. Remove the instrument panel cluster assembly. Disconnect the shift lever cable. Lower the steering column. Remove the steering column studs.
9. Remove the radio assembly. Remove the scoop connecting the heater unit to the center distribution duct.
10. Remove the duct mounting screws and remove the center distribution duct by pulling the bottom of the instrument panel out and dropping the duct out.
11. Disconnect the temperature control cable from the heater unit and move it out of the way.
12. Disconnect the vacuum lines from the extension on the control unit and unclip the vacuum lines from the defroster duct.
13. Remove the wiring from the resistor block and remove the blower motor connector on the engine side. Disconnect the vacuum lines on the engine side.
14. Be sure the gromment is free from the dash panel and pull the carpet back for clearance.
15. Remove the engine side retaining nuts. Remove the retaining screw that retains the package to the cowl side sheet metal.
16. Remove the heater assembly. The instrument panel may have to be flexed outward to allow the assembly to be removed.
17. The heater unit must be separated to gain access to the heater core.
18. Carefully remove the heater core.
19. Installation is the reverse of the removal procedure. Be sure all seals are in place and all retaining screws and nuts are properly installed.

VANS

1. Disconnect the negative battery cable.
2. Drain the cooling system. Disconnect and plug the heater hoses.
3. Disconnect the temperature control cable from the heater core cover and the blend door crank. Disconnect the vent cable.
4. Disconnect the blower motor feed wire and the ground wire connector.
5. Remove the screws retaining the heater assembly to the side cowl and the nuts fastening the heater assembly to the dash panel.
6. Lift the heater unit from the vehicle.
7. Remove the back plate and remove the screws holding the heater core cover to the heater housing. Lift the cover from the housing.
8. Remove the retaining screws from the heater core and remove the core from the heater housing.
9. Installation is the reverse of the removal procedure.

DAKOTA

1. Disconnect the negative battery cable. Remove the heater unit housing from the vehicle.
2. Remove the heater unit top cover.
3. Remove the the nut from the bottom of the blend air door pivot shaft. Lift the blend air door from the heater unit housing.
4. Remove the heater core from the housing.
5. Installation is the reverse of the removal procedure.

Blower Motor

WITH AIR CONDITIONING

Removal and Installation

MINI VANS

1. Disconnect the negative battery cable. If required, remove the evaporator assembly from the vehicle.
2. Remove the screw retaining the vacuum harness and feed the harness assembly through the hole in the cover.
3. Remove the screws from the cover. Remove the cover along with the temperature door.
4. Remove the nut and lever from the door shaft in order to remove the temperature door from the cover.
5. Remove the blower motor retaining screws. Remove the sound helmet, blower motor and wheel assembly.
6. Remove the blower motor wheel from the blower motor assembly as required.
7. Installation is the reverse of the removal procedure. Evacuate and recharge the system. Check for proper system operation.

PICK UP AND RAMCHARGER

1. Disconnect the negative battery cable.
2. Disconnect the blower motor electrical connector and the ground wire.
3. Remove the retaining screws to separate the blower motor plate from the housing.
4. Remove the blower motor assembly. Separate the fan from the motor shaft as required.
5. The blower motor can be removed from the plate after the fan wheel is removed.
6. Installation is the reverse of the removal procedure. Be sure the gasket or sealer has no breaks for proper sealing.

VANS

1. Disconnect the negative battery cable.
2. Remove the top half of the shroud and move out of the way. Top right screw on the shroud of a six cylinder engine is hidden behind the discharge line muffler.
3. Disconnect the electrical connection to the blower motor.
4. Remove the motor cooling tube and the three retaining bolts holding the blower motor to the blower housing.
5. Pull the refrigerant lines inboard and upward while pulling the blower motor assembly from the housing.
6. The blower motor can then be repaired or replaced, as required.
7. Rubber adhesive should be applied to the blower mounting plate gasket seal during the installation. The installation is the reverse of the removal procedure.

DAKOTA

1. Disconnect the negative battery cable. If required, remove the evaporator unit housing from the vehicle.
2. Remove the two evaporator unit housing cover retaining screws going upward from the plenum intake.
3. Remove the five retaining screws from the recirculating air housing. Separate the housing from the evaporator unit.
4. Disconnect the blower motor vent tube from the rear of the evaporator unit housing. Remove the three retaining screws from the blower motor and wheel assembly mounting. Remove the assembly from the heater unit.
5. Remove the spring type retaining ring from the center of the blower motor. Remove the blower motor wheel from the blower motor assembly.
6. Installation is the reverse of the removal procedure.

Blower Motor

WITHOUT AIR CONDITIONING

MINI VANS

1. Disconnect the negative battery cable. If required, remove the heater unit housing from the vehicle.
2. Disconnect the electrical connectors from the blower motor assembly. Remove the blower motor retaining screws.
3. Remove the blower motor from its mounting.
4. Installation is the reverse of the removal procedure.

PICK UP AND RAMCHARGER

1. Disconnect the negative battery cable.
2. Disconnect the blower motor feed wire connector and ground wire.
3. Remove the retaining screws to separate the blower motor plate from the heater housing.
4. Remove the blower motor assembly and separate the fan from the motor shaft by removing the retaining clip.
5. The motor can be removed from the plate after the fan wheel is removed.
6. The installation is the reverse of the removal procedure. Be sure the gasket or sealer has no breaks for proper adhesion.

VANS AND WAGONS

1. Disconnect the negative battery cable.
2. Disconnect the blower motor electrical wire and the ground wire.
3. Remove the screws fastening the back plate to the heater housing assembly. Remove the blower motor assembly.
4. Installation is the reverse of the removal procedure.

DAKOTA

1. Disconnect the negative battery cable. If required, remove the heater unit housing from the vehicle.
2. Remove the two heater unit cover retaining screws going upward from the plenum intake.
3. Remove the five retaining screws from the recirculating air housing. Separate the housing from the heater unit.
4. Disconnect the blower motor vent tube from the rear of the heater housing. Remove the three retaining screws from the blower motor and wheel assembly mounting. Remove the assembly from the heater unit.
5. Remove the spring type retaining ring from the center of the blower motor. Remove the blower motor wheel from the blower motor assembly.
6. Installation is the reverse of the removal procedure.

Cooling Fans

Testing

Lift the end of the thermostatic coil from the slot and rotate it counterclockwise until a stop is felt. The gap between the end of the coil and the clip on the housing should be approximately ½ inch (12 mm). Replace the drive unit if the shaft does not rotate with the coil. After testing, reinstall the end of the coil in the slot in the housing.

Removal and Installation

6 CYL AND V8 ENGINES

1. Disconnect the negative battery cable.
2. Disconnect the fusible link in the engine compartment and drain the coolant partially.
3. Remove the upper hose from the radiator and the upper half of the fan shroud.
4. Loosen the fan belt and remove the fan and fluid drive assembly from the water pump.
5. Remove the fan from the fluid drive.
6. Installation is the reverse of the removal procedure.

4 CYL

1. Disconnect the negative battery cable.
2. Disconnect the electric motor lead.
3. Remove the fan, motor and shroud as an assembly from the radiator support.
4. Bench support the motor and the motor shaft while removing the fan retaining clip to remove the fan.
5. Installation is the reverse of the removal procedure.

FUEL SYSTEM

Carburetor

Removal and Installation

1. Disconnect the negative battery cable.
2. Remove the air cleaner. On the 2.6L engine, remove the air intake housing from the air horn.
3. Remove the fuel tank pressure-vacuum filler cap. The tank could be under a small amount of pressure.
4. Disconnect and plug the fuel lines. Use two wrenches to avoid twisting the fuel line. A container is also useful to catch any fuel which spills from the lines.
5. Disconnect the throttle and choke linkage and all wiring.
6. Tag and disconnect any vacuum lines preventing access to the carburetor mounting bolts.
7. Remove the mounting bolts.
8. Carefully remove the carburetor from the engine and carry it in a level position to a clean work place.
9. Installation is the reverse of the removal procedure.

IDLE SPEED AND MIXTURE

Adjustment

1. Check the ignition timing and adjust if necessary.
2. Disconnect and plug the vacuum hoses at the EGR valve and the vapor canister.
3. Remove the PCV valve from the cylinder head cover and allow the valve to draw underhood air.
4. Ground the carburetor switch with a jumper wire.
5. On vehicles not equipped with a Spark Control Computer, disconnect and plug the vacuum hose from the carburetor at the heated air temperature sensor and at the OSAC valve and remove the air cleaner.
6. Start the engine and run until normal operating temperature is reached.
7. If the engine rpm is not correct, turn the idle speed screw on the solenoid to obtain the correct rpm.
8. On vehicles equipped with an O^2 feedback, disconnect the engine harness lead from the O^2 sensor and ground it.
9. Remove and plug the vacuum hose at the transducer on the Spark Control Computer. Connect an auxiliary vacuum supply to the transducer and set at 16 inches of vacuum.
10. Allow the engine to run for two minutes to allow the effect of disconnecting the O^2 sensor.
11. If the idle rpm is not correct, turn the screw on the solenoid to obtain the correct rpm.
12. Turn the engine off and reconnect all hoses and electrical connections.

Fuel Injection

Relieve Pressure

1. Loosen the gas cap to release any in tank pressure.
2. Remove the wiring harness connector from the injector.
3. Ground one injector terminal with a jumper. Connect a

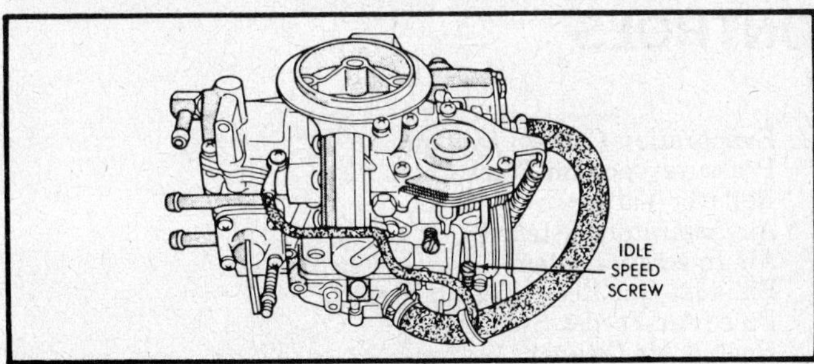

Idle speed adjusting – 155.9 (2.6L) engines

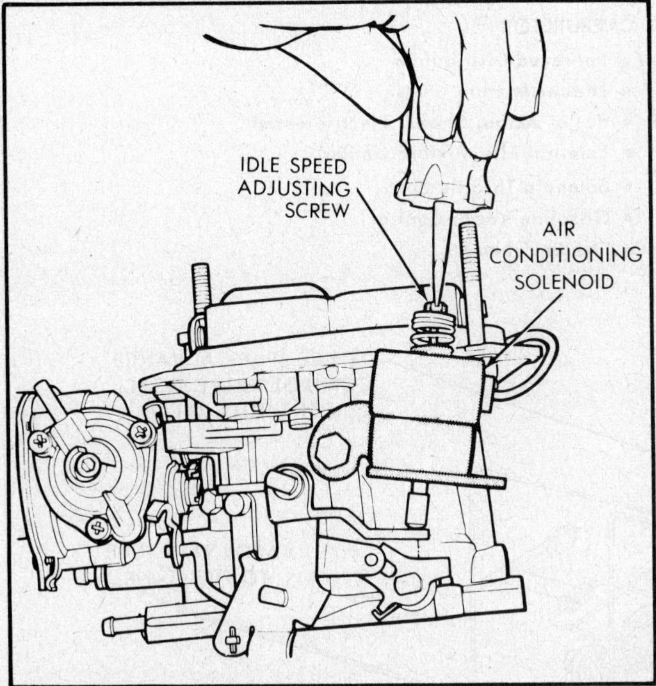

Rampage idle speed adjustment

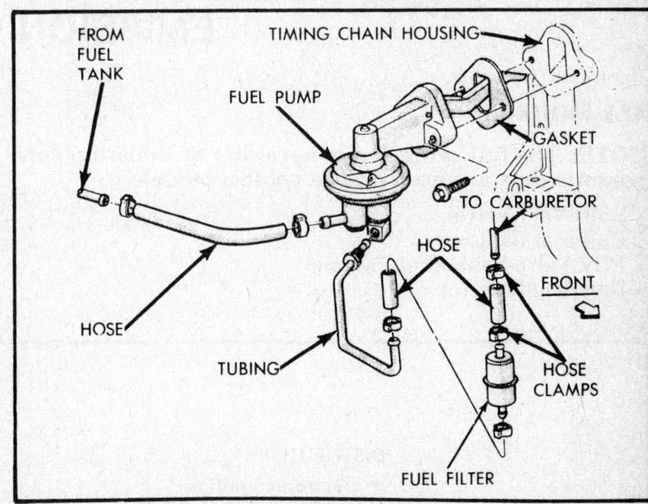

318 and 360 engine fuel pump details

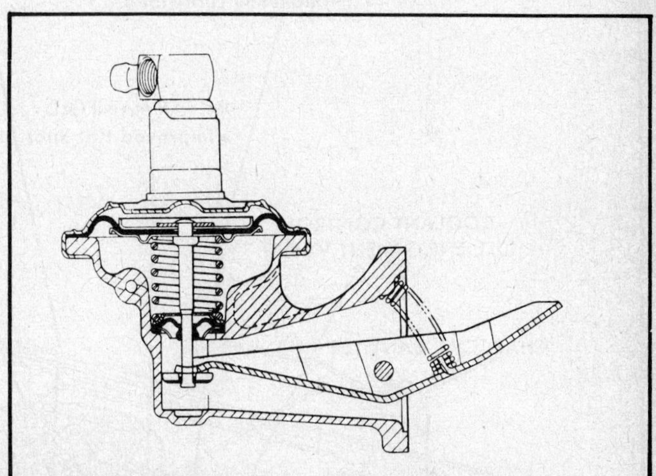
Fuel pump 6 cylinder

jumper wire to the second terminal and touch the positive battery post for no longer than 10 seconds.

4. Remove the jumper wires and continue servicing the fuel system.

INJECTORS

Removal and Installation

1. Disconnect the negative battery cable.
2. Remove the air cleaner and release the fuel system pressure.
3. Remove the fuel pressure regulator.
4. Remove the torx screw holding down the injector cap.
5. Lift the top off the injector using the slots provided.
6. Pry the injector from the pod using the hole provided in the front of the electrical connector.
7. Installation is the reverse of the removal procedure. The injector and the cap are keyed for installation.

Fuel Pump

MECHANICAL

Removal and Installation

1. Disconnect the fuel lines from the inlet and output sides of the fuel pump.
2. Plug these lines to prevent gasoline from leaking out.
3. Unbolt the retaining bolts from the fuel pump and remove the fuel pump from the engine.
4. Remove the old gasket from the engine and/or fuel pump.
5. Clean all mounting surfaces.
6. Installation is the reverse of the removal procedure. The 2.2L engine will require the use of 2 gaskets.

ELECTRIC

Removal and Installation

1. Remove the fuel tank from the vehicle.
2. Using a hammer and a nonmetallic punch, tap the lock ring counterclockwise to release the pump.
3. Pull the pump assembly partway out of the tank until the return line hose connection is visible at the intake end of the pump.
4. Disconnect the fuel fitting by pressing the ears together.
5. Remove the pump from the tank with the O-ring seal.
6. Installation is the reverse of the removal procedure. Use a new seal, pump inlet filter and inlet seal.

EMISSION CONTROLS

ALL MODELS

NOTE: The following is a general list of Emission components that are used on the vehicle models.

Bowl Vent Valve
Charcoal Canister
PCV Valve Ventilation System
Damping Canister
Evaporation Control System
Pressure Vacuum Filler Cap
Rollover Valve
Air Aspirator System
Air Injection System
Exhaust Gas Recirculation System
Pulse Air Feeder System
Heated Air Cleaner

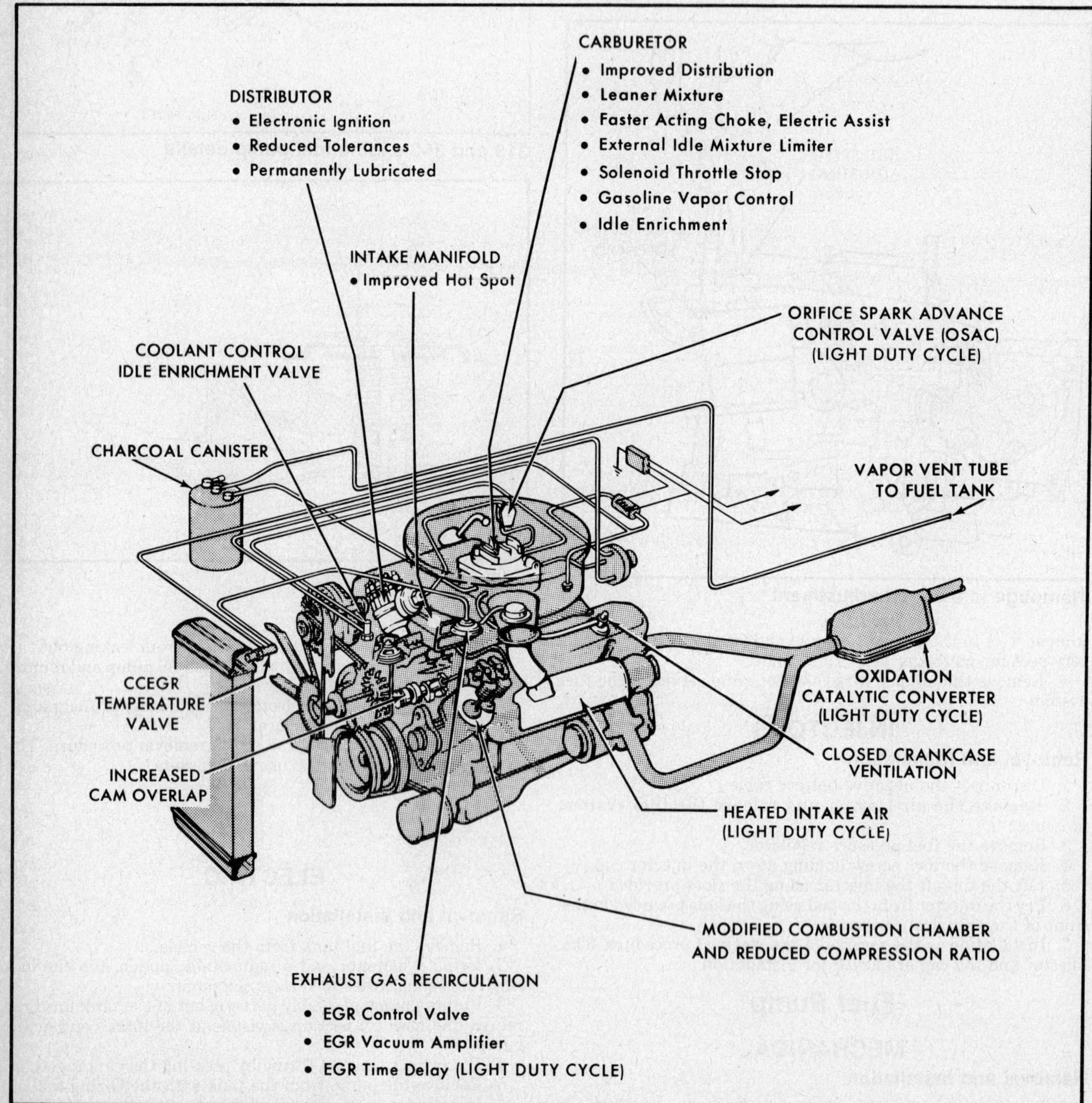

Typical vehicle emission controls

Emission Calibrated Carburetor
Emission Calibrated Distributor
Catalytic Converter
Fresh Air Intake
Electric Choke

Crankcase Emission Control System

PCV SYSTEM

All vehicles are equipped with a closed crankcase ventilation system. The system consists of a PCV valve mounted on the cylinder head cover, with a hose extending from the valve to the base of the carburetor. A closed engine oil inlet air cleaner with a hose connecting it to the carburetor air cleaner housing provides a source of air to the system. The ventilation system operates by manifold vacuum, which is air drawn from the carburetor air cleaner through the crankcase air cleaner and into the engine crankcase. It is then circulated through the engine and drawn out through the PCV valve hose and into a passage at the base of the carburetor where it becomes part of the air/fuel mixture. It is then drawn into the combustion chamber where it is burned and expelled with the exhaust gases.

System Service

1. With the engine running remove the valve from its mounting. A hissing sound should be heard and vacuum should be felt from the inlet side of the valve.
2. Reinstall the valve. Remove the crankcase inlet air cleaner. Loosley hold a piece of stiff paper over the opening in the rocker cover. Allow one minute for the crankcase pressure to reduce itself. The paper should then suck itself against the rocker cover with noticeable force. Replace the inlet air cleaner in the rocker cover.
3. With the engine stopped remove the PCV valve. Shake the valve, a clicking sound should be heard indicating that the valve is not stuck.
4. If the valve fails any of the above tests, it should be replaced.

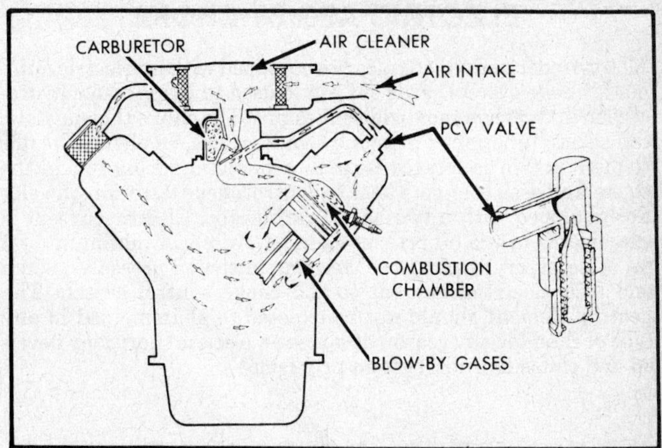

Closed crankcase ventilation system

Evaporative Emission Control System

EVAPORATION CONTROL SYSTEM

The function of the evaporation control system is to prevent the emission of gas vapors from the fuel tank and carburetor to be expelled into the atmosphere. When fuel evaporates in the gas tank or the carburetor float chamber the vapors pass through the vent hoses to the charcoal canister where they are stored until they can be drawn into the intake manifold when the engine is running. All vehicles are equipped with the charcoal canister for the storage of fuel vapors. The fuel bowls of all carburetors are vented to the charcoal canister.

System Service

The charcoal canister itself is a non-serviceable component. The only service required for the system is to replace the filter pad on the bottom of the canister. The filter requires replacement every 12 months or 12,000 miles. If the vehicle is driven under severe conditions, the filter should be replaced more often.

DUAL CANISTER

Some vehicles use a dual canister system. When fuel evaporates in the carburetor float chamber, the vapors pass through the vent hoses to the primary canister where they are stored until they can be drawn into the intake manifold when the engine is running. A vacuum source, located at the base of the carburetor, governs vapor flow to the engine. The fuel tank is vented through a vapor vent tube assembly. A tube from the vent tube assembly leads to the primary or secondary canister where evaporated fuel vapors are stored until they can be drawn into the intake manifold while the engine is running. Fuel vapors are purged from the canisters through a vacuum connection on the carburetor, which uses the throttle valve of the carburetor as a purge valve. Fuel vapors are purged through the positive crankcase ventilation hose to the carburetor, using a vacuum signal from the distributor vacuum hose, which in turn opens the canister purge system.

DAMPING CANISTER

2.6L ENGINE

The damping canister is a purge control device and does not store carburetor bowl or fuel tank vapor. It is isolated from these vapor sources by the closed purge control valve. This canister is connected to the purge line in series with the primary canister and the intake manifold port. The canister cushions the effect of a sudden release of fuel rich vapors when the purge control valve is signaled to open. These fuel vapors are momentarily held then gradually phased into the intake manifold.

ROLLOVER VALVE

All vehicles are equipped with a rollover valve to prevent fuel leakage in the event of vehicle rollover. The valve is mounted on the top of the fuel tank.

BOWL VENT VALVE

The bowl vent valve is connected to the carburetor fuel bowl, the charcoal canister and the air pump discharge. When the engine is not running there is no air pump pressure applied there is a direct connection between the fuel bowl and the canister. When the engine is shut down, the valve air pressure bleeds down and the fuel bowl is allowed to vent into the canister.

PRESSURE VACUUM GAS FILLER CAP

The gas tank is sealed with a specially designed gas cap which incorporates a pressure vacuum relief valve. The relief valve inside the cap operates as a safety feature to prevent excessive pressure or vacuum in the gas tank which can be caused by a malfunction in the system or damage to the vent lines. When repairing or removing the fuel lines, be sure to remove the gas cap.

ELECTRIC ASSIST CHOKE

All 6 cylinder and V8 engines are equipped with an electric automatic choke system. This system is used to help reduce hydrocarbon and carbon monoxide emissions. The choke thermostatic coil spring functions on engine temperature. An electric heater element which is located next to a bi-metal spring inside the choke well assists engine heat to control choke duration on vehicles equipped with a two barrel carburetor. Electric current is supplied from the oil pressure sender switch. A minimum of 4 psi is necessary to close the contacts in the oil pressure switch and feed electrical current to the choke control switch. The heating element should not be exposed to or immersed in any type of fluid for any reason at all, as an electric short may develop and cause ignition system problems.

Exhaust Emission Control System

HEATED INLET AIR SYSTEM

ALL EXCEPT 2.6L ENGINE

All vehicle engines are equipped with carburetor air preheaters. This component is part of the air cleaner and controls the temperature of the air entering the carburetor when ambient temperatures are low. By maintaining this temperature, the carburetor can be calibrated much leaner to reduce emissions, to improve engine warm up characteristics and to minimize carburetor icing. The heated air system is a two circuit flow system. When air temperature is 15 degrees or more above control temperature, there will be air flow through the outside air inlet. When air temperature is below the control temperature, there will be air flow through both circuits after the engine has been started and the exhaust manifold starts to give off heat. The colder the air the greater the flow of air through the heat stove, and the warmer the air the greater the flow through the snorkel. The quality of air through each circuit is controlled by a heat control door in the snorkel to maintain a predetermined temperature at the temperature sensor, which is mounted inside the air cleaner assembly. The modulation of the induction air temperature is performed by intake manifold vacuum, a temperature sensor and a vacuum diaphragm. The diaphragm operates the heat control door in the snorkel. With the vacuum diaphragm opposed by a spring, temperature modulation will occur only at road load throttle conditions or when the intake manifold vacuum is above the operating vacuum of the vacuum diaphragm.

2.6L ENGINE

These engines are equipped with a temperature regulated air cleaner which improves engine warm up characteristics and helps to minimize carburetor icing. This air cleaner has a door inside the snorkel to modulate the temperature of the air entering the carburetor. The door is controlled by a vacuum motor and a bi-metal temperature sensor combination system which reacts to intake manifold vacuum and the temperature inside the air horn. When the bi-metal senses the inside air horn temperature at or below 86 degrees F. the air bleed valve portion of the temperature sensor remains closed. Intake manifold vacuum is applied to the vacuum motor which opens the air control door to let the pre hea ted air flow through the heat cowl and air duct into the air cleaner. When the bi-metal sensor senses the inside the air horn temperature at or above 86 degrees F. the air bleed valve portion of the temperature sensor is fully open, this allows the intake air to go directly to the carburetor through the outside air duct, closing the heated air duct regardless of the intake manifold vacuum. At intermediate temperatures the air entering the carburetor is a blend of outside air and pre heated air as regulated by the bi-metal sensor controlling the degree of opening on the air control door.

THERMOSTATIC CHOKE SYSTEM

All 6 cylinder and V8 engines over 6,000 GVW are equipped with a thermostatic choke. This choke is non-adjustable and uses engine heat only to position the choke valve.

DUAL SNORKEL AIR CLEANER
3.7L, 5.2L AND 5.9L ENGINES

The dual snorkel air cleaner system is the same as the thermo-

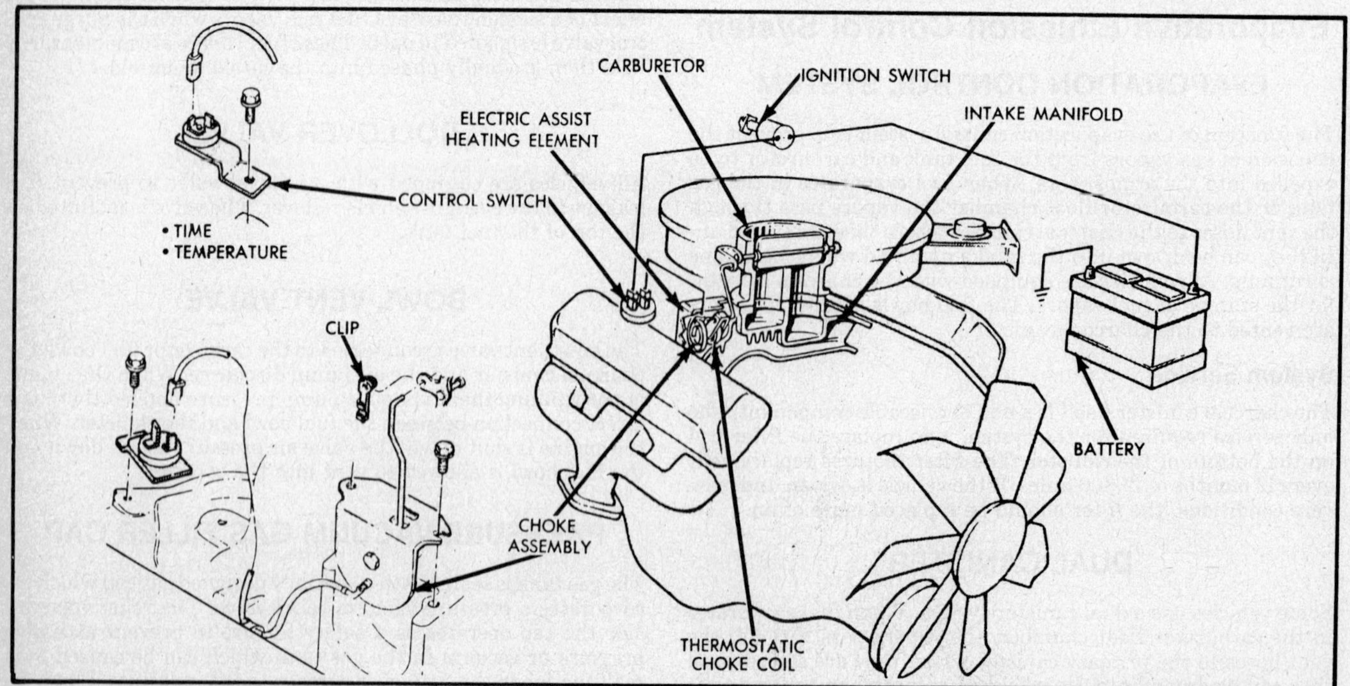

Electric assist choke system

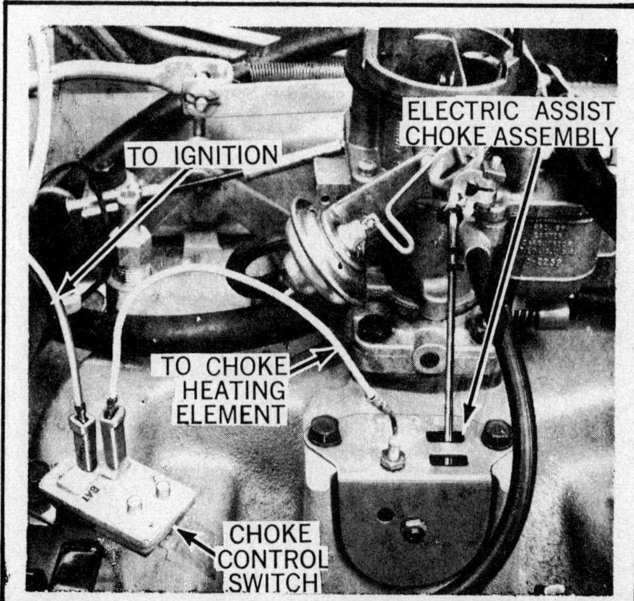

Typical electric choke system

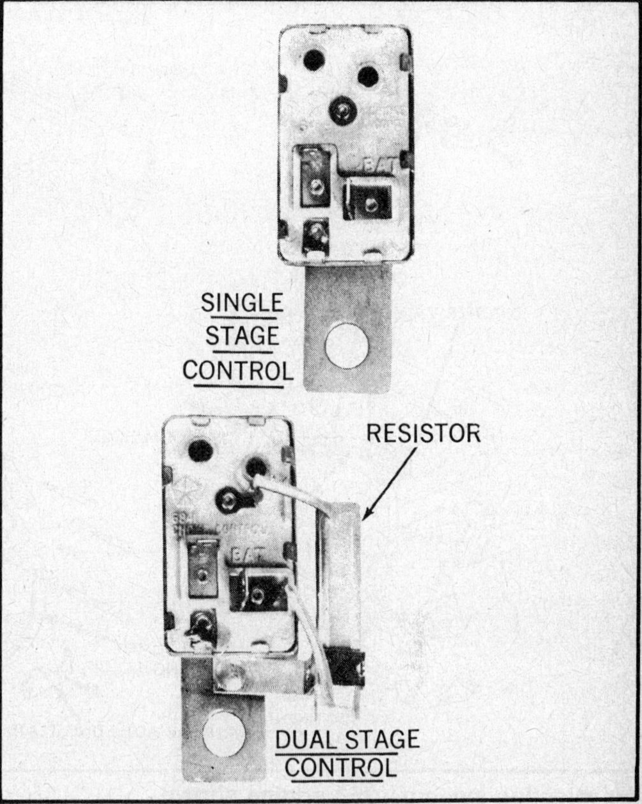

Two types of electric choke controls

static choke system with the exception that on full throttle accelerations, both snorkels are open when the vacuum drops below 5 in. Hg. Also the non-heated snorkel is connected to manifold vacuum through a tee in the vacuum hose between the carburetor and the sensor.

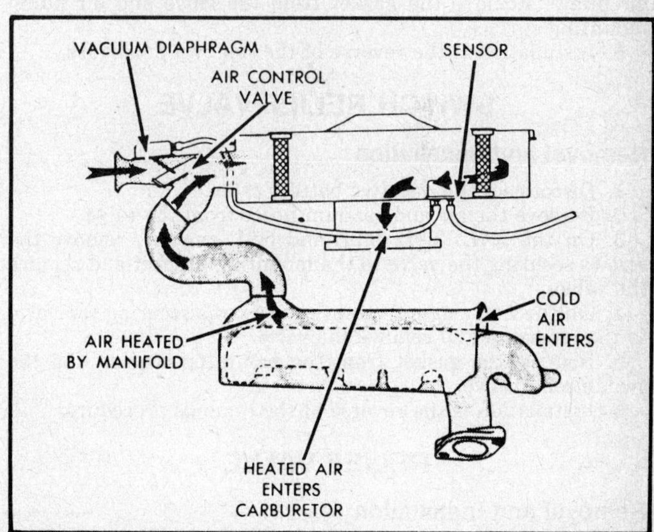

Heated air inlet system

(EGR) EXHAUST GAS RECIRCULATION VALVE

Removal and Installation

1. Disconnect the vacuum line to the EGR valve.
2. Remove the two bolts from the intake manifold.
3. Remove the EGR valve from the manifold.
4. Discard the gasket and clean the mating surfaces.
5. Installation is the reverse of the removal procedure.

Air Injection System

An exhaust port air injection system is used on all vehicles to reduce carbon monoxide and hydrocarbons. This system adds a controlled amount of air to the exhaust gases, causing oxidation of the gases and reduction of an appreciable amount of the carbon monoxide and hydrocarbons in the exhaust stream. The system on all engines, except the 2.6L engine, an air switching valve is incorporated in the system. The system has been designed so that the air injection will not interfere with the ability of the EGR system to control emissions and on vehicles equipped with an oxygen sensor, to insure proper air fuel distribution for maximum fuel economy. Air is injected into the base of the exhaust manifold for a short time during engine warm up causing an oxidation of the exhaust gases. Once the vehicle has warmed up, the air flow is switched to a point in the three way catalyst between the reduction and oxidation catalysts where it enhances the oxidation catalyst reaction, thereby reducing the amounts of carbon monoxide and hydrocarbons in the exhaust. The switching function is controlled by a vacuum solenoid or the CVSCO valve. Some vehicles also incorporate a coolant temperature sensor which is located in the water passage. The function of this sensor is to monitor engine temperature. The sensor signals the computer when to operate the air switching system and the spark advance system. This system consists of a belt driven air pump, a switch/relief valve, rubber hoses and check valve tube assemblies.

AIR PUMP

Removal and Installation

1. Disconnect the negative battery cable.
2. Remove the air hoses from the air pump. Remove the air and vacuum hoses from the diverter valve or switch/relief valve.
3. Remove the air pump drive pulley shield from the engine.
4. Loosen the air pump pivot and adjusting bolts. Remove the air pump drive belt.
5. Remove the diverter valve or switch/relief valve from the

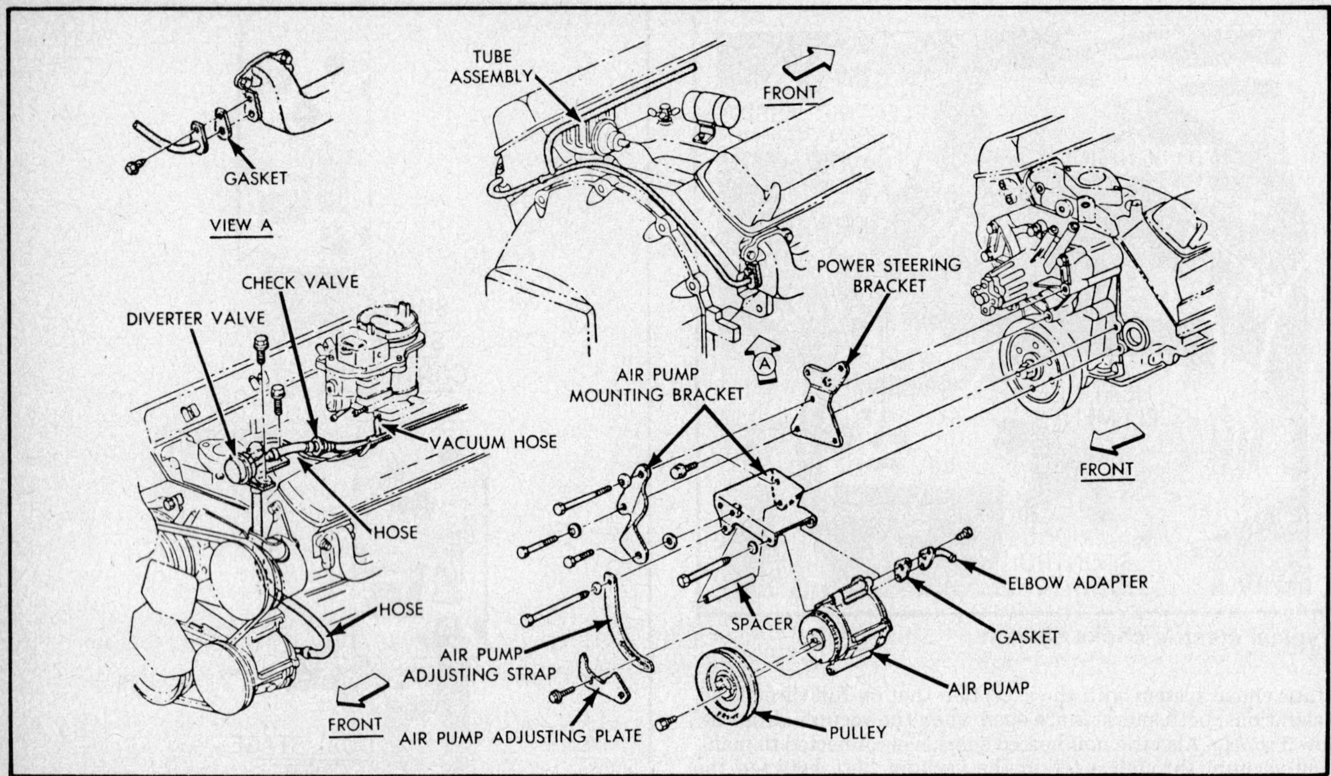

Air injection system – 360 engine shown

air pump. Remove the gasket from the valve and air pump mounting surface.

6. Installation is the reverse of the removal procedure.

SWITCH RELIEF VALVE

Removal and Installation

1. Disconnect the negative battery cable.
2. Remove the air and vacuum hoses from the valve.
3. On the 3.7L, 3.9L, 5.2L and 5.9L engines, remove the screws securing the valve to the mounting bracket and remove the valve.
4. On the 2.2L engine, remove the screws securing the valve to the air pump and remove the valve.
5. Remove the gasket from the mounting surface and the switch/relief valve.
6. Installation is the reverse of the removal procedure.

RELIEF VALVE

Removal and Installation

1. Disconnect the negative battery cable.
2. Remove the screws securing the valve to the air pump. Remove the valve.
3. Remove the gasket from the valve and the air pump mounting surfaces.
4. Installation is the reverse of the removal procedure.

CHECK VALVE

Removal and Installation

1. Disconnect the negative battery cable.
2. Release the clamp and disconnect the air hose from the valve inlet.
3. Remove the tube nut securing the injection tube to the exhaust manifold or catalyst.
4. On the 2.2L engine, loosen the starter motor attaching bolt.Remove the injection tube from the engine.
5. Remove the catalyst injection tube attaching tube from the catalyst flange. Remove the injection tube from the exhaust system.
6. Installation is the reverse of the removal procedure.

DIVERTER VALVE

Removal and Installation

3.7L, 5.2L AND 5.9L ENGINES

1. Disconnect the negative battery cable.
2. Remove the air and the vacuum hoses from the diverter valve.
3. Remove the screws securing the diverter valve to the mounting flange. Remove the valve from the vehicle.
4. Remove the gasket material from the valve and its mounting surface.
5. Installation is the reverse of the removal procedure.

POWER HEAT CONTROL VALVE

Removal and Installation

3.7L, 3.9L, 5.2L AND 5.9L ENGINES

1. Disconnect the negative battery cable.
2. Disconnect the exhaust pipe at the exhaust manifold.
3. Disconnect the vacuum line from the power heat control valve.
4. Remove the power heat control valve.
5. Installation is the reverse of the removal.

Air Aspiration System

Some vehicles are equipped with an air aspiration system. This system uses an air aspiration valve, which uses exhaust pressure pulsation to draw fresh air from the air cleaner into the exhaust system. This component reduces carbon monoxide and to a lessor degree, hydrocarbon emissions. The aspirator valve works most effectively at idle and slightly off idle, where the negative pulses are the strongest. The valve remains closed at higher engine speeds.

ASPIRATOR VALVE

Removal and Installation

1. Disconnect the negative battery cable.
2. Disconnect the air hose from the aspirator valve inlet.
3. Unscrew the valve assembly from the tube.
4. Installation is the reverse of the removal procedure.

ASPIRATOR TUBE ASSEMBLY

Removal and Installation

1. Disconnect the negative battery cable.
2. Disconnect the air hose from the aspirator valve inlet assembly.
3. Remove the screws securing the tube assembly to the exhaust manifold. On the 2.6L engine, remove the screw from the aspirator tube bracket.
4. Remove the aspirator tube assembly from the vehicle.
5. Installation is the reverse of the removal procedure.

Pulse Air Feeder System

Removal and Installation

1. Disconnect the negative battery cable.
2. Remove the screw and air deflector duct from the right side of the radiator.
3. Remove the carburetor protector shield.
4. Remove the oil dipstick. Remove the oil dipstick tube.
5. Remove the three pulse air feeder mounting tubes.
6. Raise and support the vehicle safely. Disconnect the hoses from the pulse air feeder. Remove the component from the vehicle.
7. Installation is the reverse of the removal procedure.

Feedback Carburetor System

This system is basically an emissions control system which uses an electronic signal, generated by an exhaust gas oxygen sensor, to precisely control the air fuel mixture ratio in the carburetor. This inturn allows the engine to produce exhaust gases of the proper composition to permit the use of a three way catalyst. The three way catalyst is designed to convert the three exhaust pollutants, hydrocarbons, carbon monoxide and oxides of nitrogen into harmless substances. There are two operating modes in the electronic feedback carburetor (EFC) system. These operating modes are Open Loop which is air/fuel ratio and is controlled by information programmed into the computer by the manufacturer. Closed Loop which is air/fuel ratio that is varied by the computer, based on information supplied by the oxygen sensor and other sensors.

When the engine is cold, the system will be operating in the open loop mode. During this time, the air fuel ratio will be fixed at a richer level. This time will allow proper engine warm up. Also during this time time period, the air injection stream coming from the air injection pump, will be injected upstream in the exhaust manifold.

System Service

1. Using a suitable tachometer, maintain an engine speed of 1500 rpm. Disconnect the oxygen feedback solenoid connector from the solenoid. The average engine speed should increase a minimum of 50 rpm.
2. Reconnect the feedback solenoid connector. The engine speed should decrease or return to 1500 rpm.
3. Disconnect the 12 pin connector at the fuel control computer. Connect a ground to the harness connector pin 15. The engine speed should decrease a minimum of 50 rpm.
4. If the engine speed does not change accordingly, service the carburetor and check for air leaks.

OXYGEN SENSOR

Removal and Installation

1. Disconnect the negative battery cable. Disconnect the engine harness lead from the oxygen sensor.

NOTE: Be careful when removing the wiring harness from the oxygen sensor, so that no pulling force is placed on the sensor wire. The bullet connector is to be disconnected four inches from the sensor. Use care in working around the sensor because the manifold will be extremely hot.

2. Remove the oxygen sensor using tool C-4589 or equivalent. When the sensor is removed, the exhaust manifold threads must be cleaned with a 18mm x 1.5 x 6E tap.
3. If the same sensor is to be reinstalled, the sensor threads must be coated with a suitable antisieze compound.
4. New sensors are packaged with compound on the threads and no additional compound is needed . Torque the oxygen sensor to 20 ft. lbs.

ORIFICE SPARK ADVANCE CONTROL (OSAC)

The OSAC system is used to control NO. The system controls the amount of vacuum supplied to the vacuum advance mechanism of the distributor.

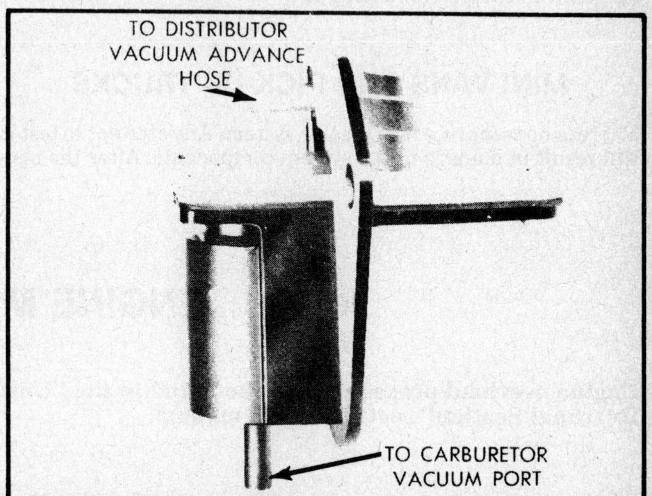

OSAC valve

Reset Maintenance Lamp

ALL EQUIPPED WITH EFA/EFC SYSTEM

Procedure

The EFA/EFC (Electronic Spark Advance/Electronic Fuel Control) is programmed to monitor several different systems. If a problem is detected often enough to indicate a problem, its fault

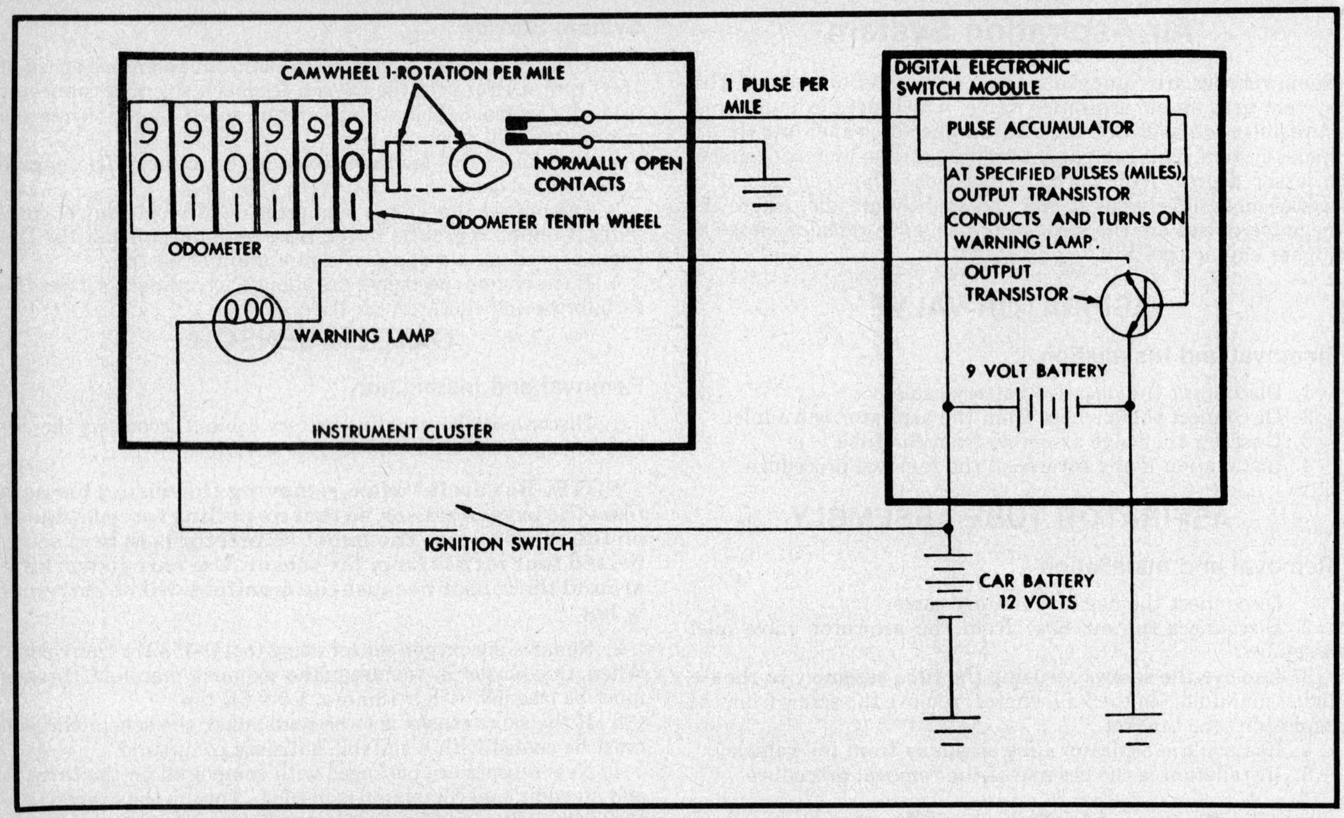

Maintenance lamp electrical schematic

code is stored in the computer for future display. If the problem is repaired or ceases to exist, the computer cancels the code after 20 to 40 ignition key on/off cycles. The memory can also be cleared by disconnecting the computer 14-way connector for one minute and then reconnecting it.

MINI VANS AND PICK-UP TRUCKS

There is no test procedure for this system. Any attempt to test it will result in damage to the system components. After the necessary maintenance has been completed, reset the system module as follows.

1. Slide the module off its bracket (located in the lower left cluster area to the right of the steering column, behind the instrument panel). Leave the vehicle battery connected and the module wires connected.
2. Remove the module battery cover and remove the 9 volt battery.
3. Reset the module by inserting a small rod or blade into the hole in the module case to close the switch.
4. Replace the 9 volt battery with a new 9 volt battery. Slide the module back into its bracket.

ENGINE MECHANICAL

Engine overhaul procedures can be found in the "Unit Overhaul Section" section of this manual.

Engine

Removal and Installation

FRONT WHEEL DRIVE

1. Disconnect the negative battery cable.
2. Scribe the hood hinge outlines on the hood and remove the hood.
3. Drain the cooling system and remove the hoses from the radiator and the engine.
4. Remove the radiator and cooling fan assembly. Disconnect all electrical connections.
5. Remove the air cleaner, duct and hose assembly. Label vacuum hoses for reinstallation identification.
6. Remove the A/C compressor and mounting brackets. Leave the hoses attached and position the compressor out of the way.
7. Remove the power steering pump and brackets. Leave the hoses attached and position the pump out of the way.
8. Remove the oil filter. Disconnect the fuel lines, accelerator linkage, heater hoses and air pump hoses.
9. Remove the alternator. Disconnect the exhaust pipe from the exhaust manifold.
10. On models equipped with manual transaxle, disconnect the clutch cable from the throwout bearing arm.
11. On models equipped with automatic transaxle, mark the

flex plate to torque converter. Remove the screws holding the converter to the flex plate. Attach a C-clamp on the front bottom of the housing to prevent the torque converter from coming out.

12. Remove the lower transaxle case lower cover.
13. Remove the starter motor. Install a suitable jack under the transaxle assembly.
14. Install an engine lifting sling and attach to a chain hoist. Remove the lifting chain slack. Raise transmission jack until contact is made with the transaxle.
15. Remove the inner right side splash shield if necessary in order to gain working clearance. Remove the engine ground to chassis bonding strap.
16. Remove the transaxle to engine mounting bolts.
17. Remove the "through" nut(s) and bolt(s) from the front engine mount and anti-roll struts. Remove the left mount through bolt or insulator mounting bolts. Raise or lower the engine slightly with the chain hoist to relieve pressure on the through bolts.
18. Raise engine, separate from the transaxle and remove from vehicle.
19. Installation is the reverse of the removal procedure.

REAR WHEEL DRIVE

1. Mark the hood hinge outlines on the hood and remove the hood.
2. Disconnect the negative battery cable. Remove the oil dipstick.
3. Raise the vehicle and remove the exhaust crossover pipe.
4. Drain the coolant from the radiator and engine block. Drain the engine oil.
5. Remove the inspection cover from the transmission. Remove the engine to transmission strut.
6. Remove the engine oil pan. It may be necessary to turn the crankshaft to clear the front of the oil pan.
7. Remove the oil pump and pickup tube assembly.
8. Remove the flywheel to torque converter bolts. On vehicles equipped with a manual transmission, remove the transmission and the clutch housing.
9. Remove the starter. Remove the lower transmission bell housing bolts.
10. Remove the engine mount lower nuts.
11. Lower the vehicle and remove the engine cover, air cleaner and carburetor.
12. If equipped with A/C, discharge the system and disconnect the condenser lines.

NOTE: Seal all openings in the A/C lines to prevent dirt and moisture from entering the system.

13. If necessary, remove the fan shroud and the windshield washer and the coolant reserve tank.
14. Remove the front bumper, grille and support brace. Disconnect both radiator hoses and remove the radiator and support brace as a unit.
15. Remove the power steering and air pumps with the hoses attached and lay them aside.
16. Tag and disconnect the throttle linkage, heater and vacuum hoses and all electrical connections to the ignition, alternator and all other electrical connections.
17. Remove the alternator, fan, pulley and drive belts.
18. Remove and plug the inlet line to the fuel pump.
19. On V8s, remove the intake manifold and left exhaust manifold.
20. Remove the spark plug wires and the distributor cap.
21. Attach lifting fixture to the engine. If equipped with an automatic transmission, support the transmission.
22. Remove the upper bell housing bolts.
23. Remove the engine from the engine compartment. On vans and wagons remove the engine from the front of the vehicle.
24. Installation is the reverse of removal. Check all fluid levels and perform all tune-up adjustments.

Intake Manifold

Removal and Installation

V6 AND V8 ENGINES EXCEPT 3.0L V6

1. Drain cooling system and disconnect battery.
2. Remove alternator, carburetor air cleaner and fuel line.
3. Disconnect accelerator linkage.
4. Remove vacuum control between carburetor and distributor.
5. Remove the distributor cap and wires.
6. Disconnect coil wires, temperature sending unit wire, heater hoses and bypass hose.
7. Remove intake manifold, ignition coil and carburetor as an assembly.
8. Installation is the reverse of the above procedure. Tighten the intake manifold to head bolts from center alternating out.

3.0L V6 ENGINE

1. Disconnect the negative battery cable.
2. Drain the cooling system.
3. Release the fuel system pressure.
4. Remove the air cleaner to throttle body hose.
5. Remove the throttle cable and the transaxle kickdown linkage.
6. Remove the (AIS) and the (TPS) wiring connectors from the throttle body.
7. Remove the vacuum hose harness from the throttle body.
8. Remove the EGR tube flange from the intake plenum.
9. Remove the wiring connectors from the charge and coolant temperature sensor.

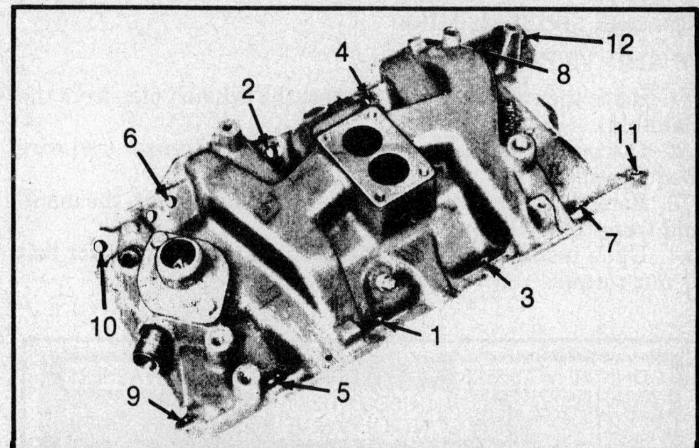

V8 intake manifold tightening sequence

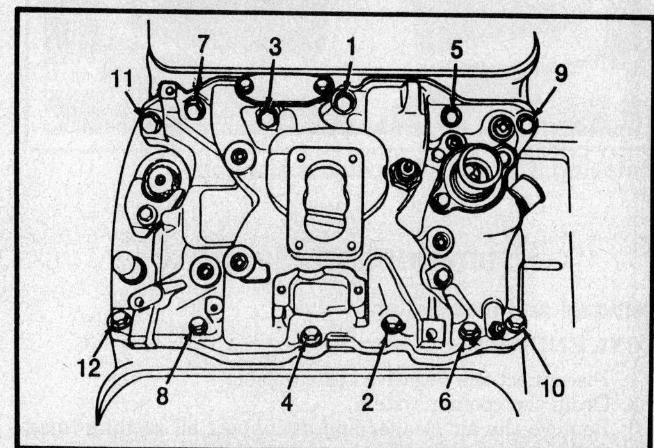

3.9L V6 Intake manifold bolt tightening sequence

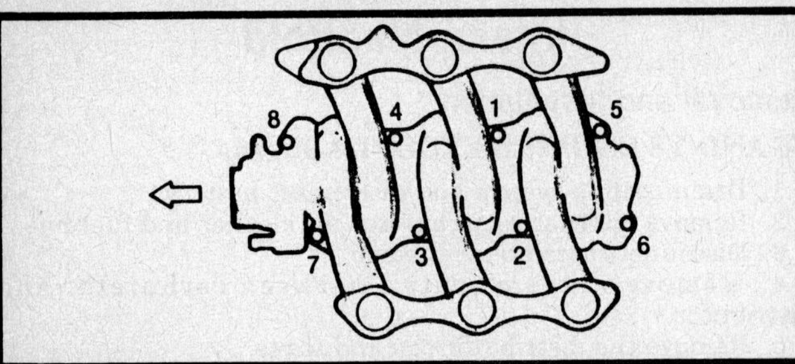

3.0L V6 Intake (cross) manifold nut tightening sequence

10. Remove the vacuum connections from the air intake plenum.
11. Remove the fuel hoses from the fuel rail.
12. Remove the 8 fasteners and the air intake plenum. Cover the intake manifold.
13. Remove the vacuum hoses from the fuel rail and the pressure regulator.
14. Disconnect the fuel injector wiring harness from the engine wiring harness.
15. Remove the pressure regulator from the rail and remove the rail from the intake manifold.
16. Remove the radiator and the heater hoses.
17. Remove the 8 nuts and remove the intake manifold.
18. Installation is the reverse of the removal procedure.

Exhaust Manifold

Removal and Installation

V6 AND V8 ENGINES

1. Raise the vehicle and disconnect the exhaust pipe from the manifold.
2. Disconnect the EGR tube and the oxygen sensor lead wire if equipped.
3. Remove the bolts, nuts and washers and remove the manifold from the cylinder head.
4. Upon installation, refer to the specification tables for bolt or nut torque.

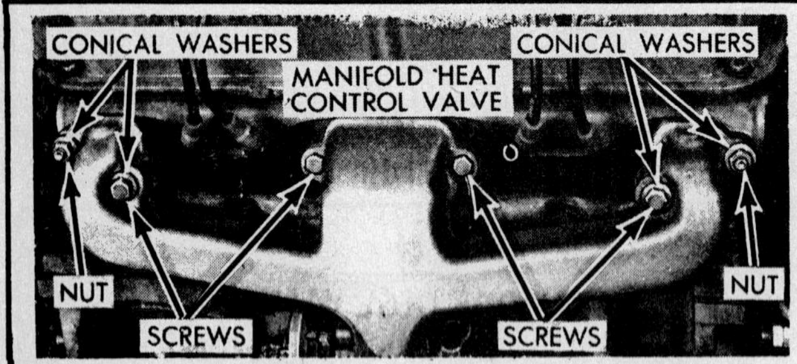

Installing 318 and 360 exhaust manifold

Combination Manifold

Removal and Installation

4 CYL ENGINES

1. Disconnect the negative battery cable.
2. Drain the cooling system.
3. Remove the air cleaner and disconnect all vacuum lines, electrical wiring and fuel lines.
4. Remove the throttle linkage.
5. Remove the power steering and air pump brackets and belts.
6. Remove the power brake vacuum hose from the intake manifold.
7. Remove the water hoses from the water crossover.
8. If equipped with an air pump, remove the diverter valve and disconnect the air injection tube from the exhaust manifold.
9. Raise the vehicle and remove the exhaust pipe from the manifold.
10. Remove the EGR tube.
11. Remove the intake manifold support bracket and the retaining screws.
12. Lower the vehicle and remove the intake manifold.
13. Remove the exhaust manifold retaining nuts and remove the manifold.
14. Installation is the reverse of the removal procedure. Use a new gasket and tighten the nuts or bolts from the center out.

6 CYL 3.7L ENGINE

1. Disconnect all vacuum lines from the air cleaner and the carburetor and remove the air cleaner.
2. Remove the carburetor air heater.
3. Disconnect the fuel line, automatic choke rod and throttle linkage from the carburetor. Remove the carburetor.
4. Disconnect the exhaust pipe at the exhaust manifold.
5. Remove the nuts and washers attaching the manifold assembly to the cylinder head and remove the manifold.
6. Remove the three screws securing the intake to the exhaust manifold and seperate the manifolds.

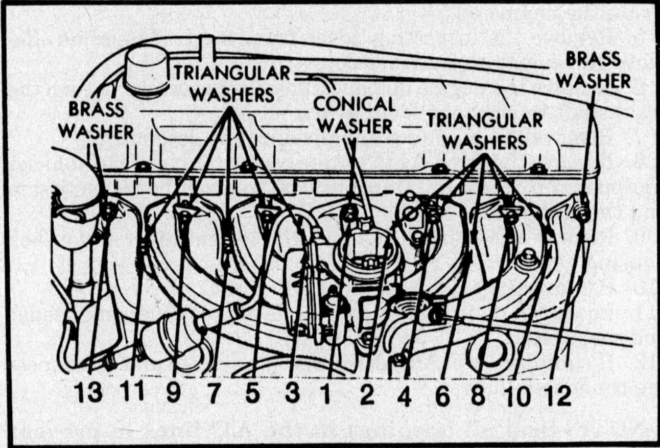

Six cylinder manifold nut tightening sequence

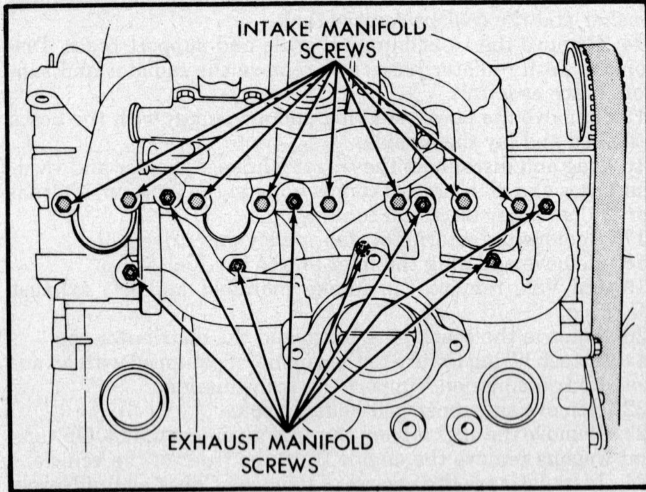

Rampage 2.2L intake and exhaust attaching points

7. To install, use a new gasket between the manifolds and install the screws but do not tighten at this time.
8. Install a new gasket between the manifold and cylinder head. Place the manifold assembly in position on the cylinder head.
9. Tighten the intake to exhaust manifold stud nut first, then the two screws to 260 inch lbs. (31 Nm).
10. Tighten the manifold to cylinder head nuts to 120 inch lbs. (14 Nm).

Cylinder Head

Removal and Installation

4 CYL 2.6L ENGINE

1. Disconnect the negative battery cable.
2. Drain cooling system. Remove the upper radiator hose and disconnect the heater hoses.
3. Disconnect spark plug wires and remove the distributor.
4. Remove the carburetor to valve cover bracket.
5. Remove the fuel lines and the pump.
6. Remove the cylinder head cover.
7. Disconnect accelerator linkage.
8. Remove the water pump belt and pulley.
9. Turn the crankshaft until the number 1 piston is at TDC.
10. Matchmark the timing chain with the timing mark on the camshaft sprocket.
11. Remove the camshaft sprocket with the distributor drive gear.
12. Disconnect the air feeder hoses.
13. Disconnect the power steering pump and set it aside.
14. Remove the ground wire and the dipstick tube.
15. Remove the exhaust manifold shield and seperate the manifold from the converter.
16. Remove the cylinder head bolts in the correct sequence and remove the head.
17. Installation is the reverse of the removal procedure. Tighten the cylinder head bolts in sequence to 34 ft. lbs. (40 Nm).
18. Follow the sequence a second time and torque the bolts to 69 ft. lbs. (94 Nm).

4 CYL 2.2L AND 2.5L ENGINES

1. Disconnect the dipstick tube from the thermoatat housing and rotate the bracket from the stud.
2. Remove the solid mount compressor bracket if equipped.
3. Remove the cylinder head bolts in sequence and remove the head.
4. Installation is the reverse of the removal procedure.
5. Tighten the head bolts in sequence using the following four steps.
   a. All to 45 ft. lbs. (61 Nm)
   b. All to 65 ft. lbs. (88 Nm)
   c. All again to 65 ft. lbs. (88 Nm)
   d. Plus ¼ turn more.

NOTE: Bolt torque after ¼ turn should be over 90 ft. lbs.. If not replace the bolt.

6 CYL 3.7L ENGINE

1. Drain cooling system.
2. Remove air cleaner and fuel line.
3. Remove vacuum line at carburetor and distributor.
4. Disconnect accelerator linkage.
5. Disconnect spark plug wires by pulling boot straight out in line with plugs.
6. Disconnect heater hose and by-pass hose clamp.
7. Disconnect temperature sending wire.
8. Disconnect exhaust pipe at exhaust manifold flange. Disconnect diverter valve vacuum line on engines with air pump.
9. Remove intake and exhaust manifolds.
10. Remove closed vent system (PCV) and rocker cover.
11. Remove rocker shaft assembly.
12. Remove pushrods in sequence and mark them in such a way that they may be put back into their original positions.
13. Remove head bolts.
14. Remove spark plugs.
15. To install, clean all gasket surfaces of cylinder block and cylinder head and install spark plugs.
16. Install cylinder head attaching bolts. Tighten all bolts in sequence starting at the top center to 35 ft. lbs. (47 Nm).
17. Repeat the procedure, retightening all cylinder head bolts to 70 ft. lbs. (95 Nm).

V6 3.0L ENGINE

1. Remove the air cleaner assembly.
2. Disconnect the battery and relocate the spark plug wires.
3. Remove all vacuum connections.
4. Remove the rocker arm cover.

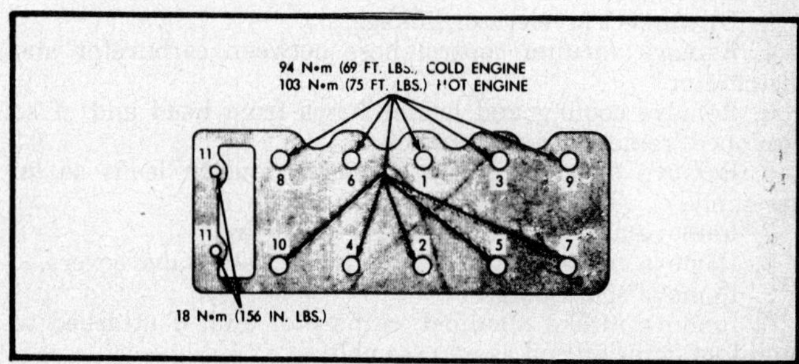

Cylinder head torque sequence – 155.9 (2.6L) engine

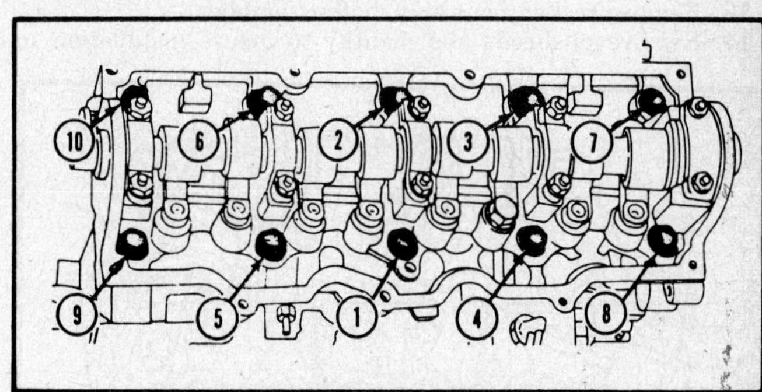

Rampage 2.2L cylinder head bolt tightening sequence

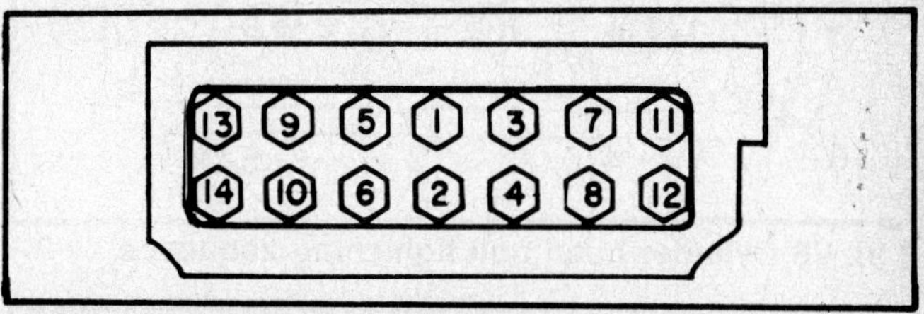

6-cylinder head bolt tightening sequences

5. Remove the accessory drive belts.
6. Remove the A/C compressor mounting bracket screws and lay the compressor aside.
7. Remove the compressor mounting bracket and the adjustable drive belt tensioner.
8. Remove the steering pump/alternator automatic belt tensioner.

9. Remove the steering pump to engine mounting screws and lay the pump aside.
10. Remove the timing belt cover, timing belt and the camshaft sprockets.
11. Install auto lash adjuster retainers MO998443 on rocker arms.
12. Remove the distributor extension.
13. Remove the rocker arms, shafts and bearing cap as an assembly.
14. Remove the upper intake manifold assembly.
15. Remove the distributor.
16. Remove the exhaust manifolds and crossover.
17. Remove the cylinder head bolts in sequence and remove the head.
18. Installation is the reverse of the removal procedure. Tighten the cylinder head bolts in two or three steps and finally to the specified torque of 70 ft. lbs. (95 Nm).

V6 3.9L AND V8 ENGINES

1. Drain cooling system and disconnect battery.
2. Remove alternator, air cleaner and fuel line.
3. Disconnect accelerator linkage.
4. Remove vacuum control hose between carburetor and distributor.
5. Remove cooling and heater hoses from head and, if so equipped, remove air compressor.
6. Remove distributor cap and high tension leads as an assembly.
7. Remove heat indicator sending unit wire.
8. Remove crankcase ventilation system and valve covers.
9. Remove spark plugs.
10. Remove intake manifold, carburetor and, if attached to manifold, ignition coil as an assembly.
11. Remove tappet chamber cover.
12. Remove exhaust manifolds.
13. Remove rocker arms and shaft assemblies.
14. Remove pushrods and identify to insure installation in original location.
15. Remove cylinder head bolts and cylinder heads.
16. Installation is the reverse of the removal procedure. Tighten bolts in sequence, first to 50 ft. lbs. (68 Nm) then in sequence again to 105 ft. lbs. (143 Nm).

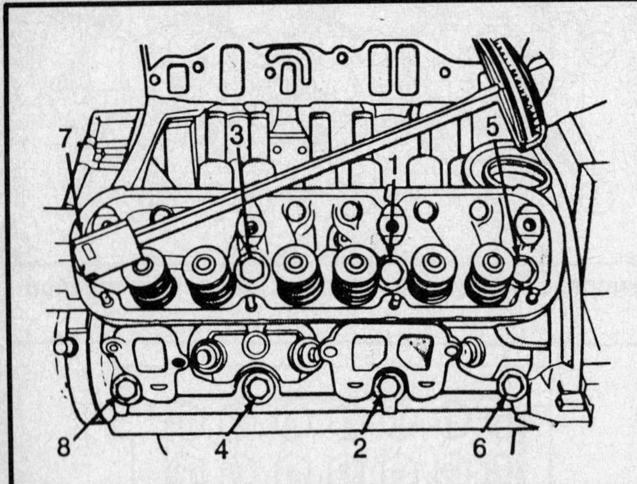

3.9L V6 Cylinder head bolt tightening sequence

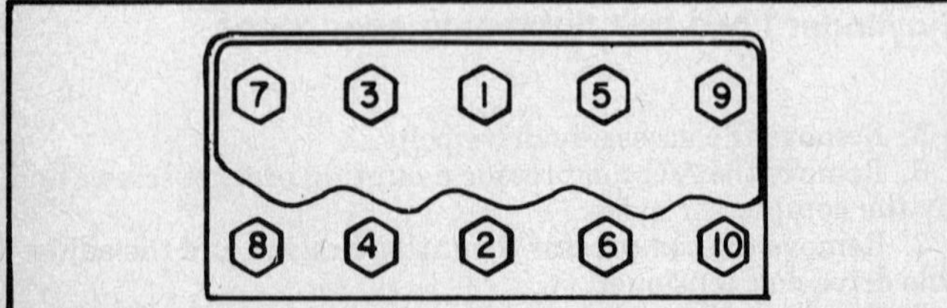

Cylinder head tightening sequence—360 and smaller V8

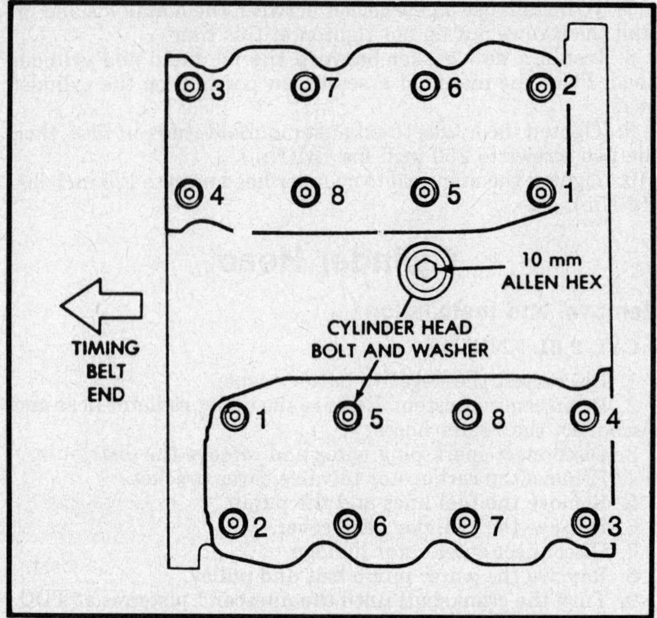

3.0L V6 Cylinder head bolt removal sequence

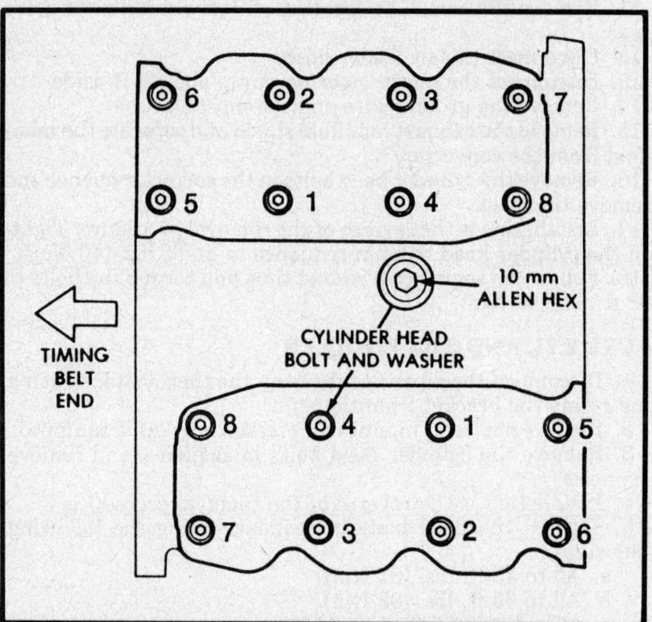

3.0L V6 Cylinder head bolt tightening sequence

Rocker Arm and Shaft

Removal and Installation

4 CYL 2.2L AND 2.5L ENGINE

CAUTION

When depressing the valve spring with Chrysler tool 4682, or the equivalent, the valve locks can become dislocated. Check and make sure both locks are fully seated in the valve grooves and retainer.

1. Remove the valve cover.
2. Rotate the camshaft until the lobe base is on the rocker arm that is to be removed.
3. Slightly depress the valve spring using Chrysler tool 4682 or equivalent. Slide the rocker off the lash adjuster and valve tip and remove. Label the rocker arms for position identification. Proceed to next rocker arm and repeat Step 2 and 3. Install in reverse order. Check the valve keys, be sure they are not dislocated.

4 CYL 2.6L ENGINE

1. Turn the engine until No. 1 piston is at TDC (top dead center) of the compression stroke. Remove the distributor cap and confirm that the rotor tip is pointed at the No. 1 plug wire location. Disconnect the negative battery cable. Remove the distributor.
2. Remove the water pump cover (upper shield) and valve cover.
3. Confirm that No. 1 piston is at TDC of the compression stroke. Take white paint and mark the timing chain in line with the camshaft sprocket timing mark.
4. Remove the camshaft sprocket bolt, distributor drive gear and sprocket with chain meshed. Secure sprocket and chain in holder.
5. Loosen the camshaft bearing bracket and rocker arm assembly mounting bolts. Start at each end and work toward the center. Do not remove the retaining bolts. When all retaining bolts are loose, lift assembly from the cylinder head.
6. Remove the bolts from the camshaft bearing caps and remove the rocket shafts and arms. Keep all parts in order. Note the way the rocker shafts, rocker arms, springs and wave washers are mounted, the left shaft has 12 oil holes which face down. The right shaft has 4 oil holes that face down.
7. Lubricate all parts and assemble in reverse order. Secure the assembled shafts in position with retaining bolts through the cam bearing caps and install on head.

6 CYL 3.7L ENGINE

1. Remove the closed ventilation system.
2. Remove the evaporative control system.
3. Remove the valve cover with its gasket.
4. Turn out the rocker arm and shaft assembly securing bolts and remove the rocker arm and shaft.
5. Reverse the above for installation. The oil hole on the end of the shaft must be on the top and point toward the front of the engine to provide proper lubrication to the rocker arms. The special bolt goes to the rear. Torque the rocker arm bolts to 25 ft. lbs. and adjust the valves.

V6 AND V8 ENGINES

1. Disconnect the spark plug wires.
2. Disconnect the closed ventilation and evaporative control system.
3. Remove the valve covers with their gaskets.

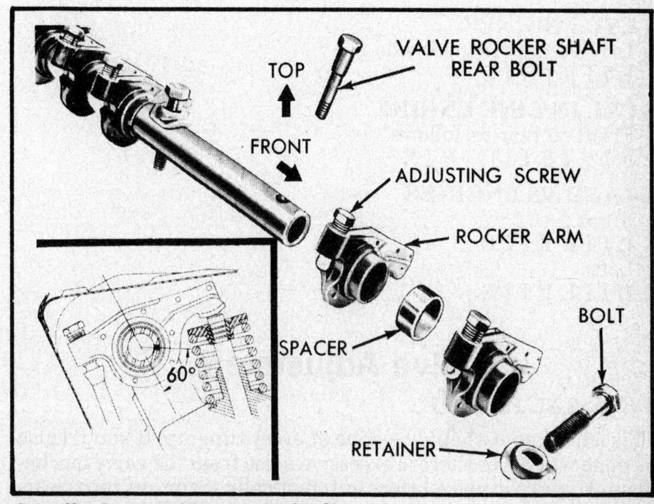

6 cylinder rocker arm shaft

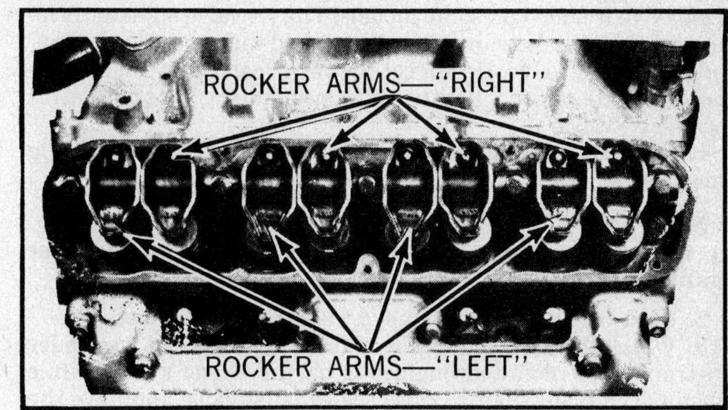

Proper rocker arm location on shaft

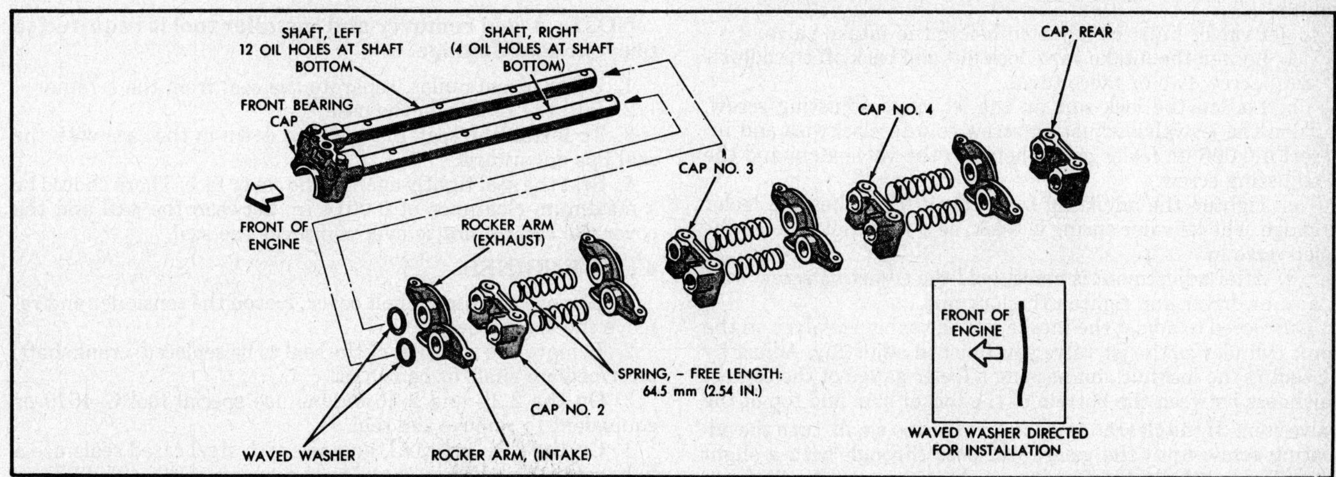

155.9 (2.6L) engine – rocker arm and shaft assembly

4. Remove the rocker shaft bolts and retainers and lift off the rocker arm assembly.

5. Reverse the above procedure to install. The notch on the end of both rocker shafts should point to the engine centerline and toward the front of the engine on the left cylinder head, or toward the rear on the right cylinder head. Torque the rocker shaft bolts to 200 inch lbs. (23 Nm).

Valve Arrangement

4 CYL ENGINES

Drivers to passenger side
E I E I I E I E

6 CYL IN LINE ENGINE

Front to rear as follows
E I E I E I I E I E I E

V6 AND V8 ENGINES

Right
E I I E E I I E
Left
E I I E E I I E

Valve Adjustment

4 CYL 2.6L ENGINE

This adjustment should be done at every tune-up. It should also be done whenever there is excessive noise from the valve mechanism. Hydraulic valve lifters automatically maintain zero clearance. After engine reassembly, these lifters adjust themselves as soon as engine oil pressure builds up.

A jet valve is added on some models. The jet valve adjuster is located on the intake valve rocker arm and must be adjusted before the intake valve. Do not set the valve lash closer than specified in an attempt to quiet the valve mechanism. This will result in burned valve.

1. Start the engine and allow it to reach normal operating temperature.

NOTE: Do not run the engine with the rocker arm cover removed, oil will be sprayed onto the hot exhaust manifold.

2. Shut off engine and remove the rocker arm cover.
3. Watch the valve operation on No. 1 cylinder (No. 1 cylinder on transverse mounted engines is on the driver's side) while turning the crankshaft to close the exhaust valve and have the intake valve just begin to open. This places the No. 4 cylinder on TDC of its firing stroke and permits the adjustment of the valves.
4. Jet valves must be adjusted before the intake valve.
   a. Loosen the intake valve lock nut and back off the adjustment screw two or more turns.
   b. Loosen the lock nut on the jet valve adjusting screw. Turn the jet valve adjusting screw counterclockwise and insert a 0.006 in. feeler gauge between the valve stem and the adjusting screw.
   c. Tighten the adjusting screw until it touches the feeler gauge. The jet valve spring is weak, be careful not to force the jet valve in.
   d. After adjustment is made, hold the adjusting screw with a screwdriver and tighten the lock nut.
5. Proceed to adjust the intake and the exhaust valves on the same cylinder as the jet valve you finished adjusting. Adjust by loosening the locknut and passing a feeler gauge of the correct thickness between the bottom of the rocker arm and top of the valve stem. If the clearance is too great or too small, turn the adjusting screw until the gauge will pass through with a slight drag. Tighten the locknut and proceed to the next valve. Refer to the chart in Step 3 for the adjusting sequence.

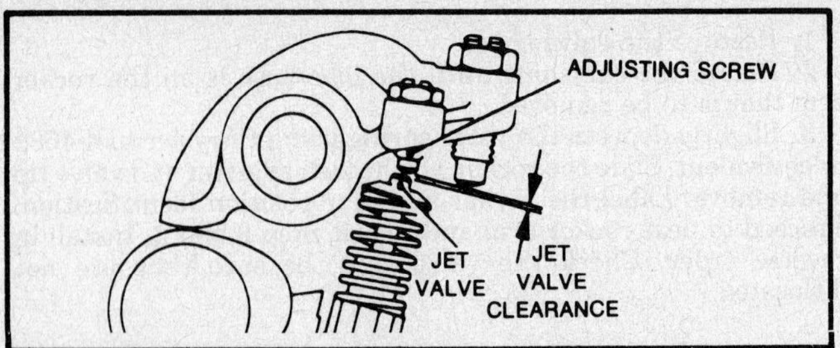

Adjusting the jet valve on 155.9 (2.6L) engines

Exhaust Valve Closing	Adjust
No. 1 cylinder	No. 4 cylinder valves
No. 2 cylinder	No. 3 cylinder valves
No. 3 cylinder	No. 2 cylinder valves
No. 4 cylinder	No. 1 cylinder valves

Timing Gears and/or Chain

CRANKSHAFT PULLEY

Removal and Installation

The crankshaft sprocket is located by a key on the shaft and is retained by a bolt. To remove the pulley, first remove the timing belt cover and belt and then use the following procedure.

NOTE: When removing the crankshaft pulley, don't remove the four socket head bolts which retain the outer belt pulley to the timing belt pulley.

1. Remove the center bolt.
2. Gently pry the pulley off the shaft.
3. If the pulley is stubborn in coming off, use a gear puller. Don't hammer on the pulley.
4. Remove the pulley and key.
5. Install the pulley in the reverse order of removal.
6. Tighten the center bolt to 58 ft. lbs.
7. Install the timing belt, check valve timing, tension belt, and install the cover.

TIMING COVER OIL SEAL

Removal and Installation

EXCEPT 4 CYLINDER ENGINES

NOTE: A seal remover and installer tool is required to prevent seal damage.

1. Using a seal puller, separate the seal from the retainer.
2. Pull the seal from the case.
3. To install the seal, place it face down in the case with the seal lips downward.
4. Seat the seal tightly against the cover face. There should be a maximum clearance of 0.0014 in. between the seal and the cover. Be careful not to over-compress the seal.

4 CYL ENGINES

1. Remove the timing belt cover, loosen the tensioner and remove the timing belt.
2. Remove the sprocket of the seal to be replaced; crankshaft, intermediate shaft or camshaft.
3. On the 2.2L and 2.5L engine use special tool C-4679 or equivalent to remove the seal.
4. On the 2.2L and 2.5L engines with steel cased seals use a light coat of Loctite® stud and bearing mount (P/N 4057987), or equivalent. If the seal is rubber cased, use a solution of soap and

water to lubricate it for installation. Install the seals with special tool C-4680 or equivalent.

5. Install the timing belt and adjust the tension.
6. Install the timing belt cover and all related components.

TIMING CHAIN AND GEARS

Removal and Installation

4 CYL 2.2L AND 2.5L ENGINE

1. Remove the timing belt cover.
2. Place a jack under the engine with a piece of wood separating it from the jacking point.
3. Remove the right engine mounting bolt and raise the engine slightly. Be sure the engine is supported securely.
4. Loosen the belt tensioner and remove the timing belt.
5. Turn the crankshaft until the dot mark on the sprocket is at about two o'clock. Turn the intermediate shaft sprocket until the dot mark is at about eight o'clock. Line up the crankshaft and intermediate sprocket marks.
6. Turn the camshaft until the arrows on the mounting hub are in line with the front (no. 1) camshaft retaining cap flat spots. The small hole in the camshaft sprocket must be at the top and be in a vertical center line with the engine.
7. Install the timing belt. Adjust and tighten the belt tensioner.
8. Adjust the tensioner by turning the large tensioner hex to the right. Tension should be correct when the belt can be twisted 90° with the thumb and the forefinger, midway between the camshaft and the intermediate sprocket.
9. Complete the belt installation by reversing the removal steps.

NOTE: After applying the belt tensioner, rotate the engine two complete revolutions and recheck the timing marks for alignment.

4 CYL 2.6L ENGINE

1. Bring the engine to No. 1 piston at TDC (Top Dead Center) of the compression stroke.
2. Disconnect the negative battery cable. Remove the air cleaner assembly.
3. Remove the alternator drive belt. Tag and disconnect the spark plug wires from the plugs, free wires from supports. Remove the distributor with cap and wires attached.
4. Remove the air conditioner compressor drive belt. Remove the compressor and mounting brackets, with lines attached; and position out of the way.
5. Remove the power steering drive belt. Remove the power steering pump and brackets, with lines attached and position out of the way.
6. Raise and support the front of the vehicle on jackstands.
7. Remove the right front inner splash shield. Drain the engine oil. Remove the crankshaft pulley.
8. Place a floor jack under the engine with a piece of wood mounted between jack and lifting point.

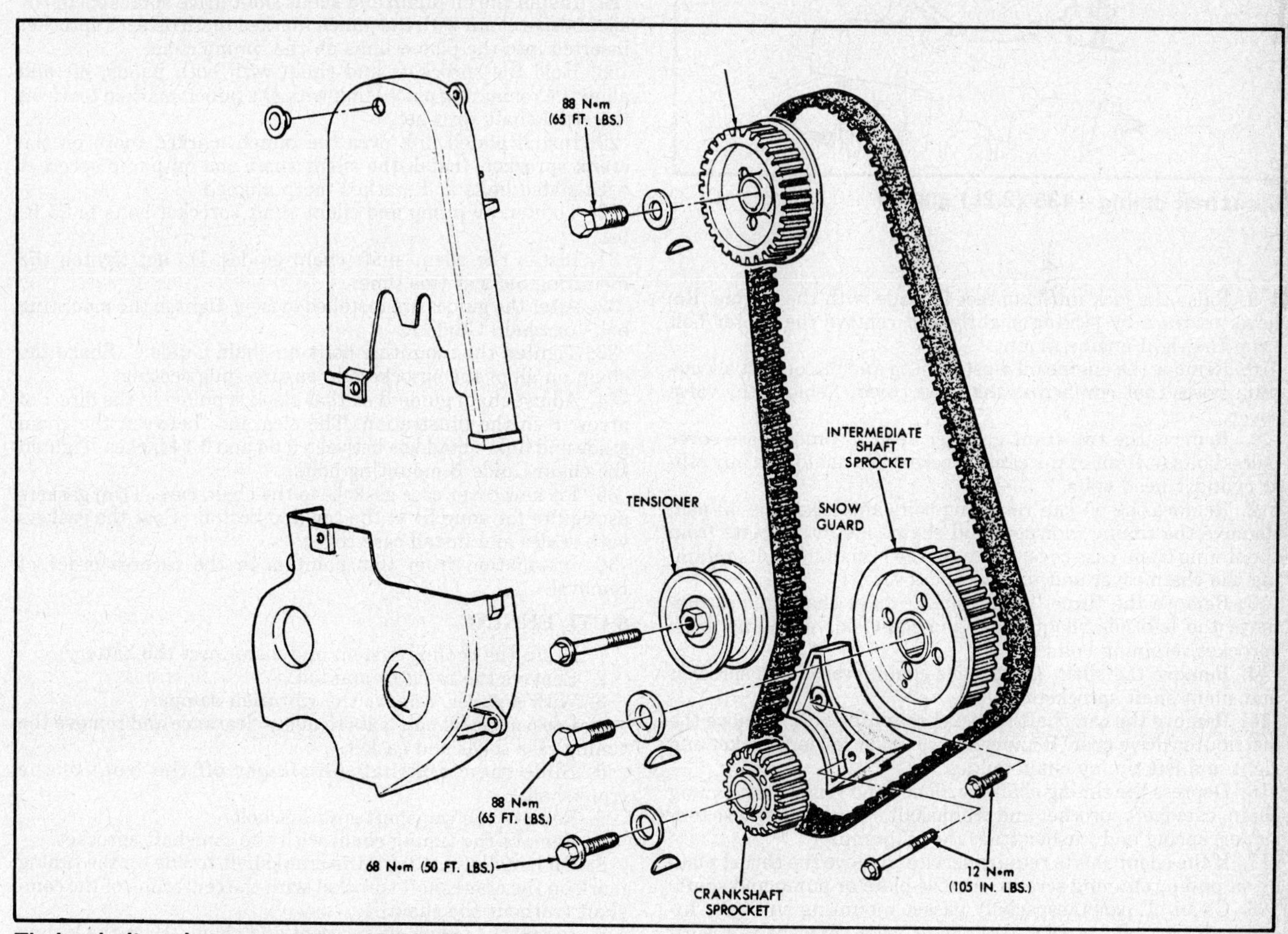

Timing belt and components—135 (2.2L) engine

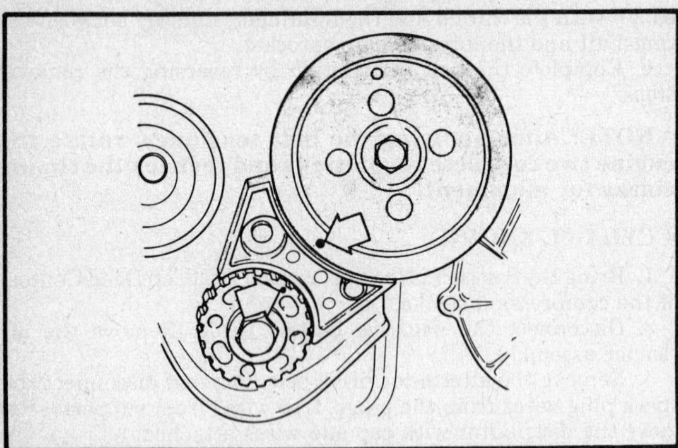
Crankshaft and intermediate shaft timing alignment—135 (2.2L) engine

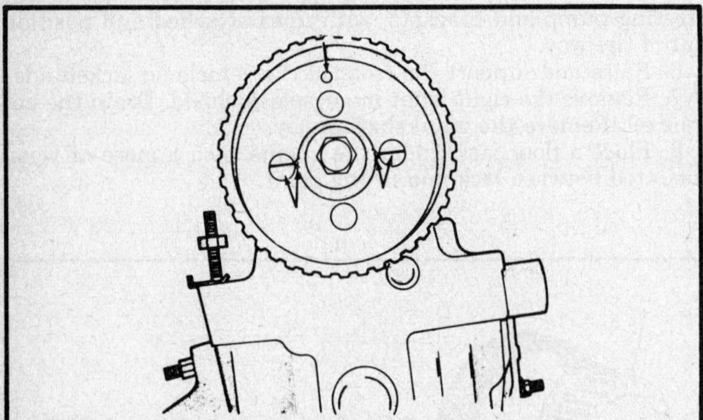
Camshaft timing—135 (2.2L) engine

9. Raise the jack until contact is made with the engine. Relieve pressure by jacking slightly and remove the center bolt from the right engine mount.
10. Remove the engine oil dipstick. Tag and disconnect all vacuum hoses that run across the valve cover. Remove the valve cover.
11. Remove the two front cylinder head to timing case cover bolts (bolts in front of the cam sprocket). Do not loosen any other cylinder head bolts.
12. Remove the oil pan retaining bolts and lower the oil pan. Remove the timing indicator and engine mounting plate from the timing chain case cover. Remove the remaining bolts retaining the chain cover and remove the cover.
13. Remove the three "silent shaft" drive chain guides. Remove the left side silent shaft and right side oil pump drive sprocket retaining bolts.
14. Remove the silent shaft drive chain, crankshaft sprocket and silent shaft sprockets.
15. Remove the camshaft sprocket retaining bolt. Remove the distributor drive gear. Remove the sprocket holder bracket and right and left timing chain guides.
16. Depress the timing chain tensioner and remove the timing chain, camshaft sprocket and crankshaft sprocket. Remove tensioner, spring and washer from the oil pump.
17. If the silent shafts require service, remove the thrust plate or oil pump retaining screws, remove plate or pump and shaft.
18. Clean all parts, especially gasket mounting surfaces. Inspect all parts for cracks, damage or wear. Replace the worn parts as necessary.
19. Install the left side silent shaft and thrust plate with a new O-ring. Tighten the retaining bolts to 71 inch lbs.
20. Install the right side silent shaft, prime the oil pump with fresh oil and install. Tighten the retaining bolts to 71 inch lbs.

NOTE: Use bolts without heads to act as guides when installing the silent shaft thrust plate or oil pump. When plate or pump is installed, remove the guide bolts and install regular bolts.

21. Verify that No. 1 piston is at TDC on the compression stroke (keyway at approx. 3 o'clock). Make sure the dowel pin hole on the front of the camshaft is in the vertical position at 12 o'clock.
22. Install the cam sprocket holder. Install the right and left chain guides. Install the tensioner spring, washer and shoe on the oil pump body.
23. Position the crankshaft and camshaft sprockets on the timing chain with timing marks aligned. The crank and camshaft sprockets have a punch mark on one gear tooth. The timing chain is equipped with two plated links. The marked tooth on each gear should be installed in the plated link.
24. Using both hands, lift the gears and chain with marks aligned. Slide the gears onto their respective shafts with dowel hole and keyway in proper position. Verify gear marks and plated links are aligned.
25. Install the dowel pin, distributor drive gear and sprocket bolt on the camshaft. Torque bolt to 40 ft. lbs.
26. Install the silent shaft chain drive sprocket on the crankshaft.
27. Install the oil pump and silent shaft drive sprockets in the silent drive chain with the punch marked tooth on each sprocket inserted into the plated links on the timing chain.
28. Hold the sprockets and chain with both hands, lift and align the remaining plated link with the punch marked tooth on the crankshaft sprocket.
29. Install plated link over the punch marked tooth on the crank sprocket. Install the silent shaft and oil pump sprocket with plated links and marked tooth aligned.
30. Tighten oil pump and silent shaft sprocket bolts to 25 ft. lbs.
31. Install the silent shaft chain guides. Do not tighten the mounting bolts at this time.
32. After the guides are installed loosely, tighten the mounting bolts on chain Guide A.
33. Tighten the mounting bolts on chain Guide C. Shake the chain on all of the sprockets to ensure snug seating.
34. Adjust chain guide B so that slack is pulled in the direct of arrow F in the illustration. The clearance between the chain guide and links should be between 0.04 and 0.14 inches. Tighten the chain Guide B mounting bolts.
35. Fit new cover case gaskets to the chain case. Trim gaskets as require for snug fit at the top and bottom. Coat the gaskets with sealer and install case cover.
36. Installation from this point is in the reverse order of removal.

6 CYL ENGINE

1. Drain the cooling system and disconnect the battery.
2. Remove the radiator and fan.
3. With a puller, remove the vibration damper.
4. Loosen the oil pan bolts to allow clearance and remove the timing case cover and gasket.
5. Slide the crankshaft oil slinger off the front of the crankshaft.
6. Remove the camshaft sprocket bolt.
7. Remove the timing chain with the camshaft sprocket.
8. On installation: Turn the crankshaft to line up the timing mark on the crankshaft sprocket with the centerline of the camshaft (without the chain).
9. Install the camshaft sprocket and chain. Align the timing marks.

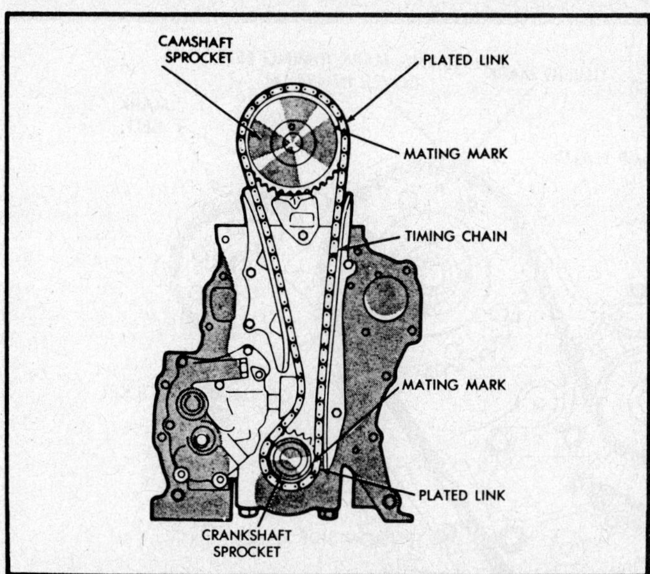

Timing gears and chain alignment – 155.9 (2.6L) engine

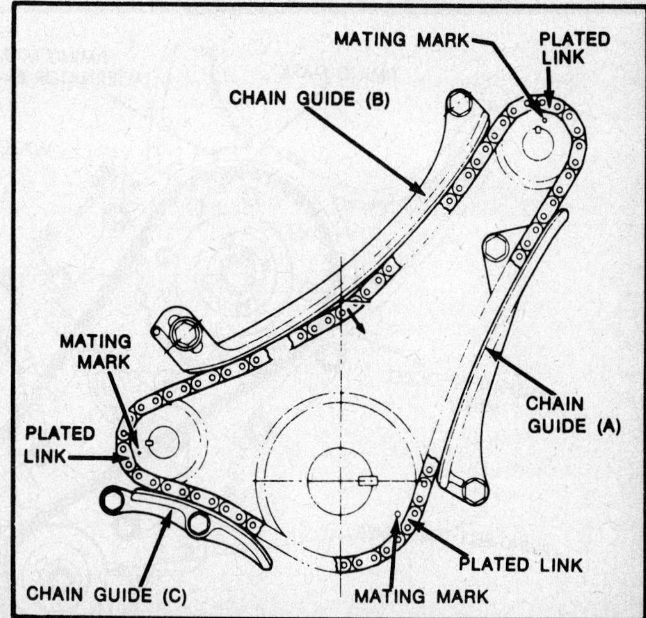

"Silent Shaft" balance system timing mark alignment – 155.9 (2.6L) engine

10. Torque the camshaft sprocket bolt to 35 ft. lbs.
11. Replace the oil slinger.
12. Reinstall the timing case cover with a new gasket and torque the bolts to 17 ft. lbs. Retighten the engine oil pan to 17 ft. lbs.
13. Press the vibration damper back on.
14. Replace the radiator and hoses.
15. Refill the cooling system.

V6 AND V8 ENGINES

1. Disconnect the battery and drain the cooling system. Remove the radiator.
2. Remove the vibration damper pulley. Unbolt and remove the vibration damper with a puller. On 318 CID and 360 CID engines, remove the fuel lines and fuel pump, then loosen the oil pan bolts and remove the front bolt on each side.
3. Remove the timing gear cover and the crankshaft oil slinger.
4. On 318 and 360 CID engines, remove the camshaft sprocket lockbolt, securing cup washer and fuel pump eccentric. Remove the timing chain with both sprockets.
5. To begin the installation procedure, place the camshaft and crankshaft sprockets on a flat surface with the timing indicators on an imaginary centerline through both sprocket bores. Place the timing chain around both sprockets. Be sure that the timing marks are in alignment.

CAUTION

When installing the timing chain, have an assistant support the camshaft with a suitable tool to prevent it from contacting the plug in the rear of the engine block. Remove the distributor and the oil pump/distributor drive gear. Position the suitable tool against the rear side of the cam gear and be careful not to damage the cam lobes.

6. Turn the crankshaft and camshaft to align them with the keyway location in the crankshaft sprocket and the keyway or dowel hole in the camshaft sprocket.
7. Lift the sprockets and timing chain while keeping the sprockets tight against the chain in the correct position. Slide both sprockets evenly onto their respective shafts.
8. Use a straightedge to measure the alignment of the sprocket timing marks. They must be perfectly aligned.
9. On 318 and 360 CID engines, install the fuel pump eccentric, cup washer and camshaft sprocket lockbolt and torque to

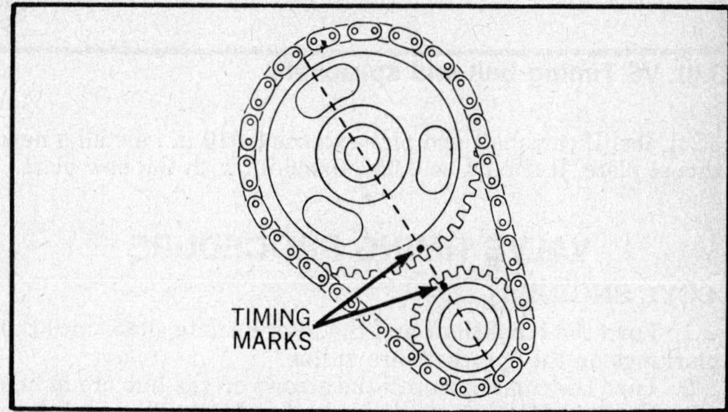

Alignment of timing gear marks – 6 cylinder

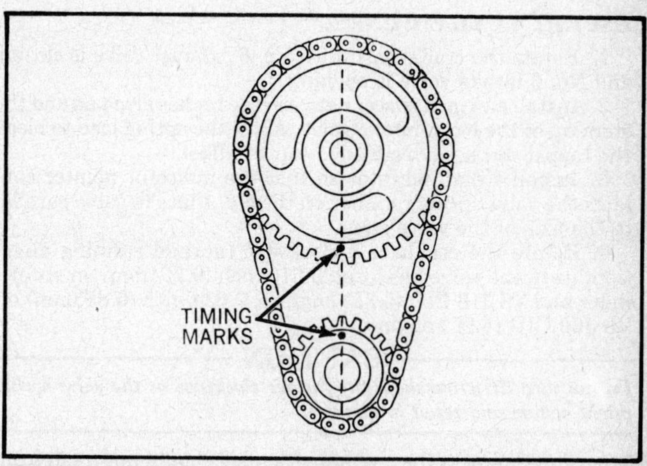

Alignment of timing gear marks – V8 engines

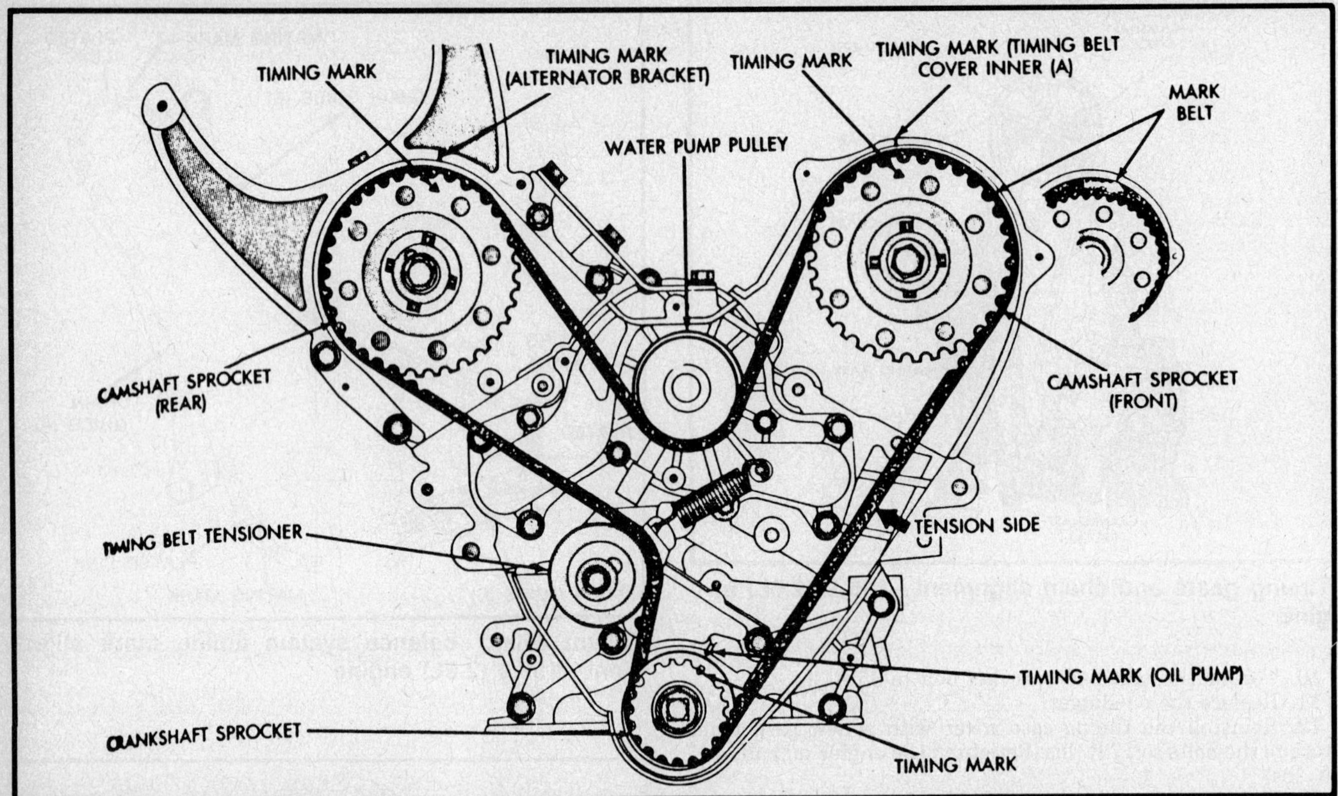

3.0L V6 Timing belt and sprockets

35 ft. lbs. If camshaft end play exceeds 0.010 in., install a new thrust plate. It should be 0.002–0.006 in. with the new plate.

VALVE TIMING PROCEDURE

4 CYL ENGINES

1. Turn the crankshaft and the intermediate shaft until the markings on the sprockets are in line.
2. Turn the camshaft until the arrows on the hub are in line with No. 1 camshaft cap to cylinder head line. The small hole must be in vertical center line.
3. Install the timing belt.
4. Rotate the crankshaft two full revolutions and recheck the timing.

EXCEPT 4 CYL ENGINES

1. Rotate the crankshaft until No. 6 exhaust valve is closing and No. 6 intake valve is opening.
2. Install a 1/4 inch spacer between the rocker arm pad and the stem tip of the No. 1 intake valve. Allow the spring load to bleed the tappet down, giving a solid tappet effect.
3. Install a dial indicator so that the indicator pointer contacts the valve spring retainer on the No. 1 intake valve parallel to the axis of the valve stem.
4. Rotate the crankshaft clockwise (normal running direction) until the valve has lifted 0.010 inch (0.254mm) on six cylinder and V8 318 CID (5.2L) engines, 0.034 inch (0.863mm) on V8 360 CID (5.9L) engine.

CAUTION

Do not turn the crankshaft any further clockwise as the valve spring might bottom and result in damage.

5. The timing of the crankshaft pulley should now read from 10 degrees BTDC to 2 degrees ATDC on all except six cylinder

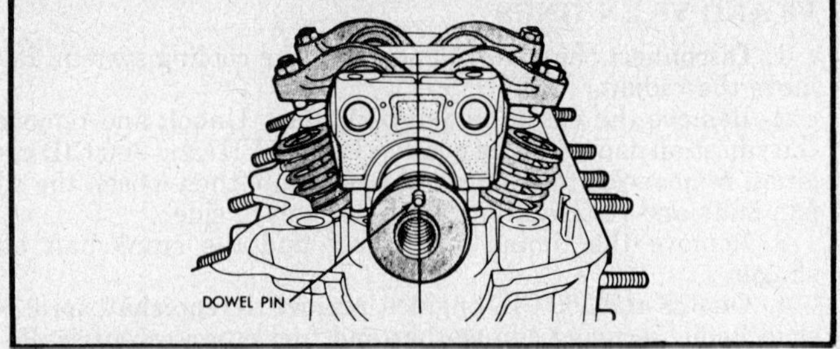

Camshaft alignment – 155.9 (2.6L) engine

225 CID (3.7L) engine. It should read 12 degrees BTDC to dead center on the 225 CID (3.7L) engine. Remove the spacer.

NOTE: If the reading is not within specified limits, inspect the sprocket index marks, inspect the timing chain for wear and inspect the accuracy of the "DC" mark on the timing indicator.

Camshaft

Removal and Installation

4 CYL ENGINES

1. Remove the valve cover.
2. Remove the timing belt covers, loosen the tensioner and remove the timing belt.
3. Remove the camshaft sprocket and use special tool C-4679 or equivalent to remove the camshaft seal.
4. Mark the rocker arms for re-installation in the same position.

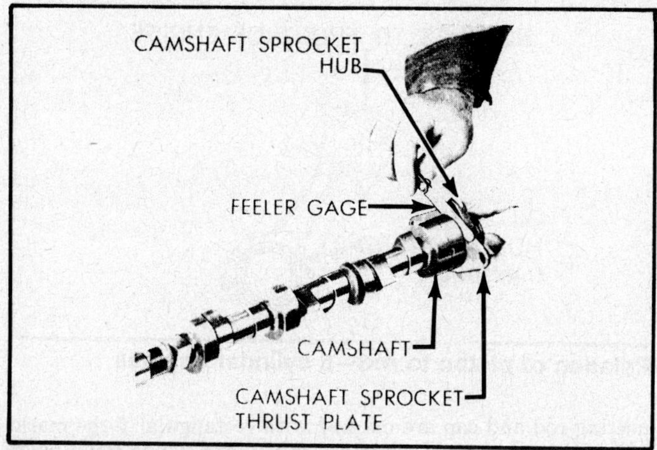

Measuring camshaft end play

5. Loosen the bearing caps a little at a time on each cap, but do not remove the nuts.
6. Use a soft mallet to break the camshaft free.
7. Remove the nuts evenly a little at a time from each cap.

NOTE: Cocking the camshaft during removal or installation could cause damage to the cam or bearing thrust surfaces.

8. Check the bearing cap oil holes for blockage.
9. Align the bearing caps in sequence with No. 1 at the timing belt end and No. 5 at the transmission end of the head. The arrows on the caps No. 1, 2, 3 and 4 must point in the direction of the timing belt.
10. Apply anaerobic form-in-place gasket sealer to No. 1 and No. 5 bearing caps. Install the bearing caps before installing the camshaft seals.
11. Install the camshaft seal using tool C-4680 or equivalent. Install the timing belt and cover.
12. Install the related front of engine components. Install the valve cover using a new gasket.

6 CYL 225 CID (3.7L) ENGINE

1. Remove the cylinder head, timing gear cover, camshaft sprocket and timing chain.
2. Remove the valve tappets, keeping them in order to ensure installation in their original locations.
3. Remove the crankshaft sprocket.
4. Remove the distributor and oil pump.
5. Remove the fuel pump.
6. Install a long bolt into the front of the camshaft to facilitate its removal.
7. Remove the camshaft, being careful not to damage the cam bearings with the cam lobes.
8. Prior to installation, lubricate the camshaft lobes and bearing journals. It is recommended that 1 pt. of crankcase conditioner be added to the initial crankcase oil fill.
9. Install the camshaft in the engine block. From this point, reverse the removal procedure.

V6 AND V8 ENGINES

1. Remove the intake manifold, cylinder head covers, rocker arm assemblies, push rods and valve tappets, keeping them in order to insure the installation in their original locations.
2. Remove the timing gear cover, the camshaft and crankshaft sprockets and the timing chain.
3. Remove the distributor and lift out the oil pump and distributor driveshaft.
4. Remove the camshaft thrust plate.
5. Install a long bolt into the front of the camshaft and remove the camshaft, being careful not to damage the cam bearings with the cam lobes.

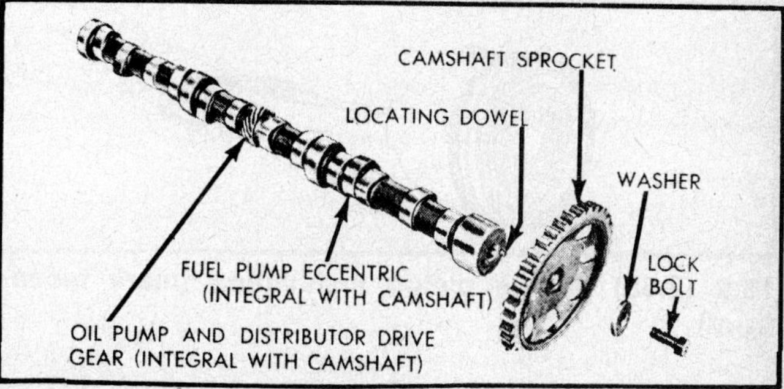

Camshaft – 6 cylinder engines

6. Prior to installation, lubricate the camshaft lobes and bearing journals. It is recommended that 1 pt. of Crankcase Conditioner be added to the initial crankcase oil fill. Insert the camshaft into the engine block within 2 in. of its final position in the block.
7. Have an assistant support the camshaft with a suitable tool to prevent the camshaft from contacting the plug in the rear of the engine block. Position the tool against the rear side of the cam gear and be careful not to damage the cam lobes.
8. Replace the camshaft thrust plate. If camshaft end play exceeds 0.010 in., install a new thrust plate. It should be 0.002-0.006 in. with the new plate.
9. Install the timing chain and sprockets, timing gear cover, and pulley.
10. Install the tappets, pushrods, rocker arms and cylinder head covers. Install fuel pump, if removed.
11. Install the distributor and oil pump driveshaft. Install the distributor.
12. After starting the engine, adjust the ignition timing.

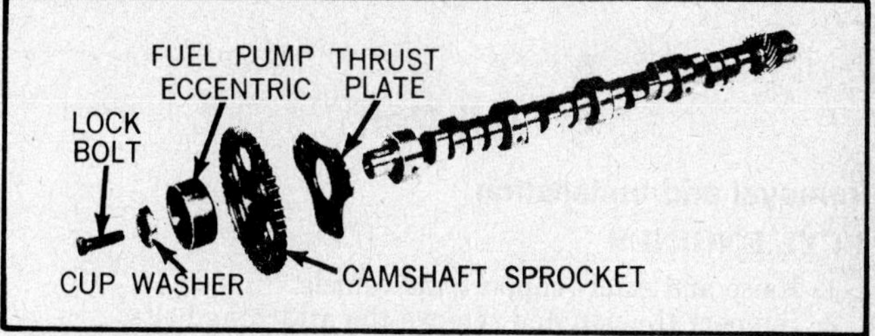

Typical V8 camshaft and sprocket assembly – 318/360 shown

Pistons and Connecting Rods

4 CYL ENGINES

The piston crown is marked with an arrow which must point toward the drive belt end of the engine when installed. The con-

135 (2.2L) engine piston installation

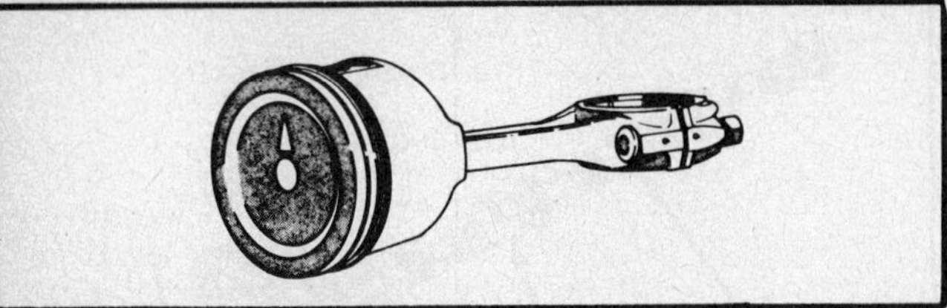

15.9 (2.6L) engine piston installation (mark faces front)

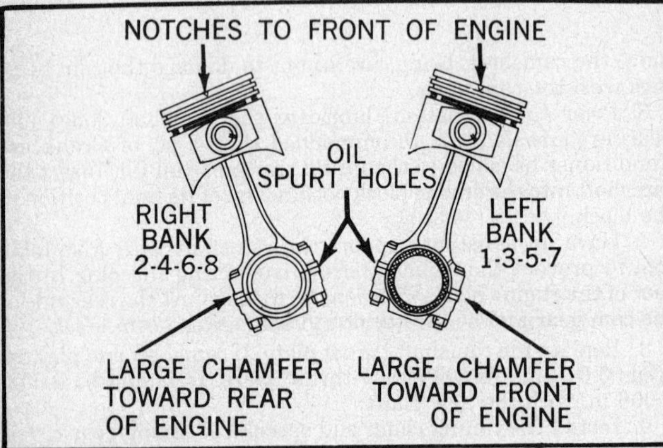

Relation of piston to rod—V8 engines

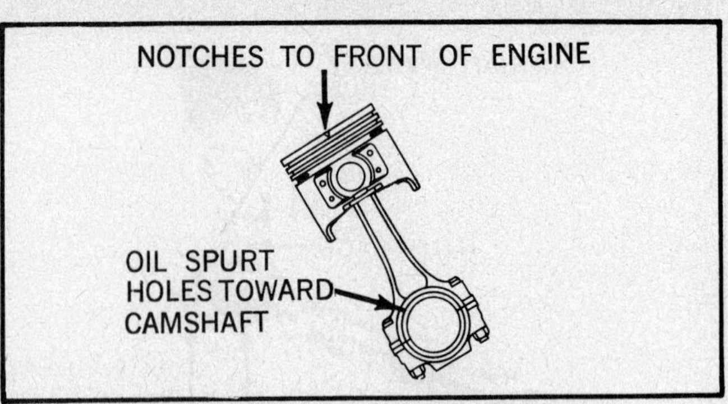

Relation of piston to rod—6 cylinder engines

necting rod and cap are marked with rectangular forge marks which must be mated when assembled and which must be on the intermediate shaft side of the engine when installed.

6 AND 8 CYL ENGINES

The notch on the top of each piston must face the front of the engine. To position the connecting rod correctly, the oil squirt hole should point to the right-side on all six-cylinder engines. On all V8 engines, the larger chamfer of the lower connecting rod bore must face to the rear on the right bank and to the front on the left bank.

Connecting Rod and Main Bearings

Detailed procedures for fitting main and rod bearings can be found in the Engine Overhaul Section.

ENGINE LUBRICATION

Oil Pan

Removal and Installation

4 CYL ENGINES

1. Raise and safely support the vehicle.
2. Support the pan and remove the attaching bolts.
3. Lower the pan and discard the gaskets.
4. Clean all gasket surfaces thoroughly and install the pan using gasket sealer and a new gasket.
5. Torque the pan bolts to 7 ft. lbs.
6. Refill the pan, start the engine and check for leaks.

6 CYL VANS AND WAGONS

1. Disconnect the battery and remove the dipstick.
2. Remove the engine cover and remove the starter and air cleaner.
3. Raise the vehicle and support safely. Drain the crankcase oil.
4. Install an engine support as described under "Engine Removal."
5. Disconnect and tie out of the way: driveshaft, transmission linkage and exhaust pipe at the manifold.
6. Remove the clutch torque shaft (if equipped) and the oil cooler lines (if equipped).
7. Disconnect the speedometer cable and electrical connections to the transmission.
8. Remove the support bracket, inspection plate and drive plate-to-converter attaching screws if equipped.
9. Remove the bolts which attach the transmission to the clutch housing. Carefully work the transmission and converter rearward off the engine dowels and disengage the converter hub from the end of the crankshaft if so equipped. Remove the transmission.
10. Support the rear of the engine and raise it two inches.
11. Remove the oil pan attaching bolts. Positioning the crankshaft so that the counterweights will clear the pan, rotate the pan to the steering gear side and remove it. The pump pickup tube may have to be turned for clearance.
12. Installation is the reverse of removal. Make sure that the pickup screen contacts the bottom of the pan. Fill the engine with oil and check for leaks.

V6, V8 VANS AND WAGONS

1. Disconnect the battery ground cable. Remove the dipstick and tube, engine cover and air cleaner.
2. Disconnect the throttle linkage at the rear of the engine and the clutch or automatic transmission linkage.
3. Raise the engine slightly and support it with the device described under "Engine Removal".
4. Raise the vehicle and drain the oil. Remove the starter.
5. Remove the driveshaft and engine rear support.
6. Remove the transmission from the van. Remove the automatic transmission with the filler tube installed and the torque converter separated from the drive plate.
7. Remove the clutch assembly and flywheel (or driveplate) from the crankshaft.
8. Raise the engine about 2 in.
9. Rotate the crankshaft so that the counterweights will clear the oil pan. Maximum clearance is with the notch in the crank-

shaft flange at the 3 o'clock position. Remove the oil pan. It will be necessary to reach inside the oil pan and turn the oil pick-up tube and strainer slightly to the right to clear the pan.

10. Installation is the reverse of removal. Be sure to check all fluid levels and be sure that there are no leaks.

TWO WHEEL DRIVE PICKUP

1. Disconnect the negative battery cable. Remove the oil dipstick.
2. Raise and support the vehicle safely.
3. Drain the oil from the vehicle.
4. Remove the torque converter or clutch housing brace.
5. Remove the exhaust pipe, if necessary, in order to gain working clearance.
6. Remove the oil pan bolts and remove the pan.
7. Installation is the reverse of removal.

FOUR WHEEL DRIVE PICKUP

1. Raise the vehicle and support safely.
2. Remove the two front engine mounting bolts.
3. Remove the left-side support, connecting the converter housing and cylinder block.
4. Raise the engine approximately 2 in.
5. Drain oil.
6. Remove the oil pan bolts, lower pan down and to the rear. (Do not turn oil pickup out of position).

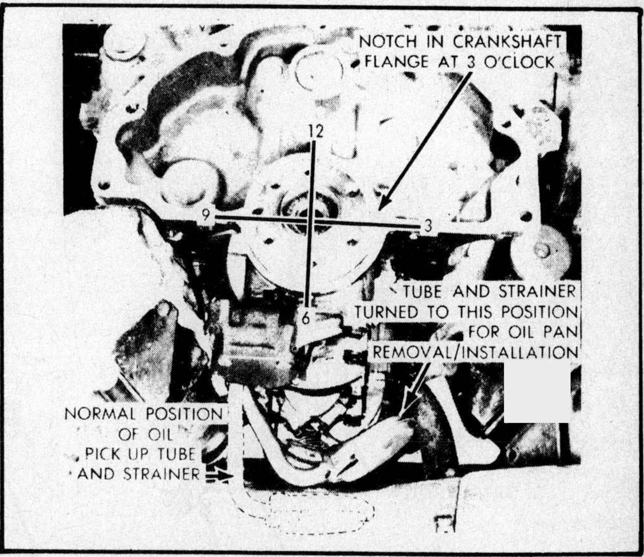

The crankshaft and oil pick up tube positioned for oil pan removal and installation

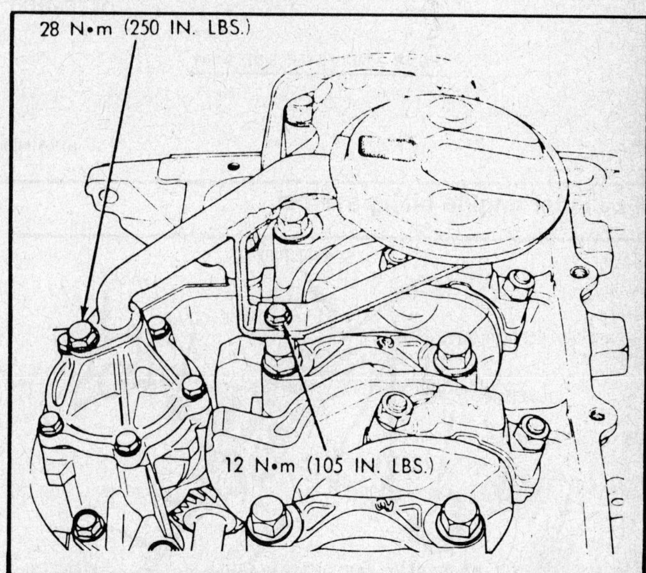

Rampage 2.2L oil pick up

Oil Pump

Removal and Installation

4 CYL ENGINES

1. Disconnect the negative battery cable.
2. Raise and support the vehicle safely. Drain the engine oil and remove the oil pan and gasket.
3. Remove the hex head retaining bolts from the oil pump assembly.
4. Pull the pump assembly down from the engine.
5. Installation is the reverse of the removal procedure. Pump indexing is not required.

6–225 CID 3.7L ENGINE

The rotor type oil pump is externally mounted on the rear right-hand (camshaft) side of the engine and is gear driven (helical) from the camshaft. The oil filter screws into the pump body.

1. Remove oil pump mounting bolts and remove pump and filter assembly from engine.
2. Disassemble the oil pump (drive gear must be pressed off) and inspect the following clearances: maximum cover wear is 0.0015″; outer rotor to body maximum clearance is 0.014″; maximum clearance between rotors is 0.010″. Inspect the pressure relief valve for scoring and free operation. Relief valve spring should have a free length of $2^1/_4$ in.
3. Install new oil seal rings between cover and body, tightening cover attaching bolts to 95 inch lbs.
4. Install oil pump to engine block using a new gasket and tightening mounting bolts to 200 inch lbs.

V6 AND V8 ENGINES

NOTE: It is necessary to remove the oil pan and to remove the oil pump from the rear main bearing cap to service the oil pump.

1. Drain the engine oil and remove the oil pan.
2. Remove the oil pump mounting bolts and remove the oil pump from the rear main bearing cap.
3. To remove the relief valve, drill a $^1/_8$ in. hole into the relief valve retainer cap and insert a self-threading sheet metal screw into the cap. Clamp the screw into a vise and while supporting the oil pump, remove the cap by tapping the pump body using a soft hammer. Discard the retainer cap and remove the spring and the relief valve.
4. Remove the oil pump cover and lockwashers and lift off the cover. Discard the oil ring seal. Remove the pump rotor and shaft and lift out the outer rotor.

NOTE: Wash all parts in solvent and inspect for damage or wear. The mating surfaces of the oil pump cover should be smooth. Replace the pump assembly if this is not the case.

5. Lay a straight edge across the pump cover surface and if a 0.0015 in. feeler gauge can be inserted between the cover and the straight edge, the pump assembly should be replaced. Measure the thickness and the diameter of the outer rotor. If the outer rotor thickness measures 0.825 in. or less or if the diameter is 2.469 in. or less, replace the outer rotor. If the inner rotor measures 0.825 in. or less, then the inner rotor and shaft assembly must be replaced.

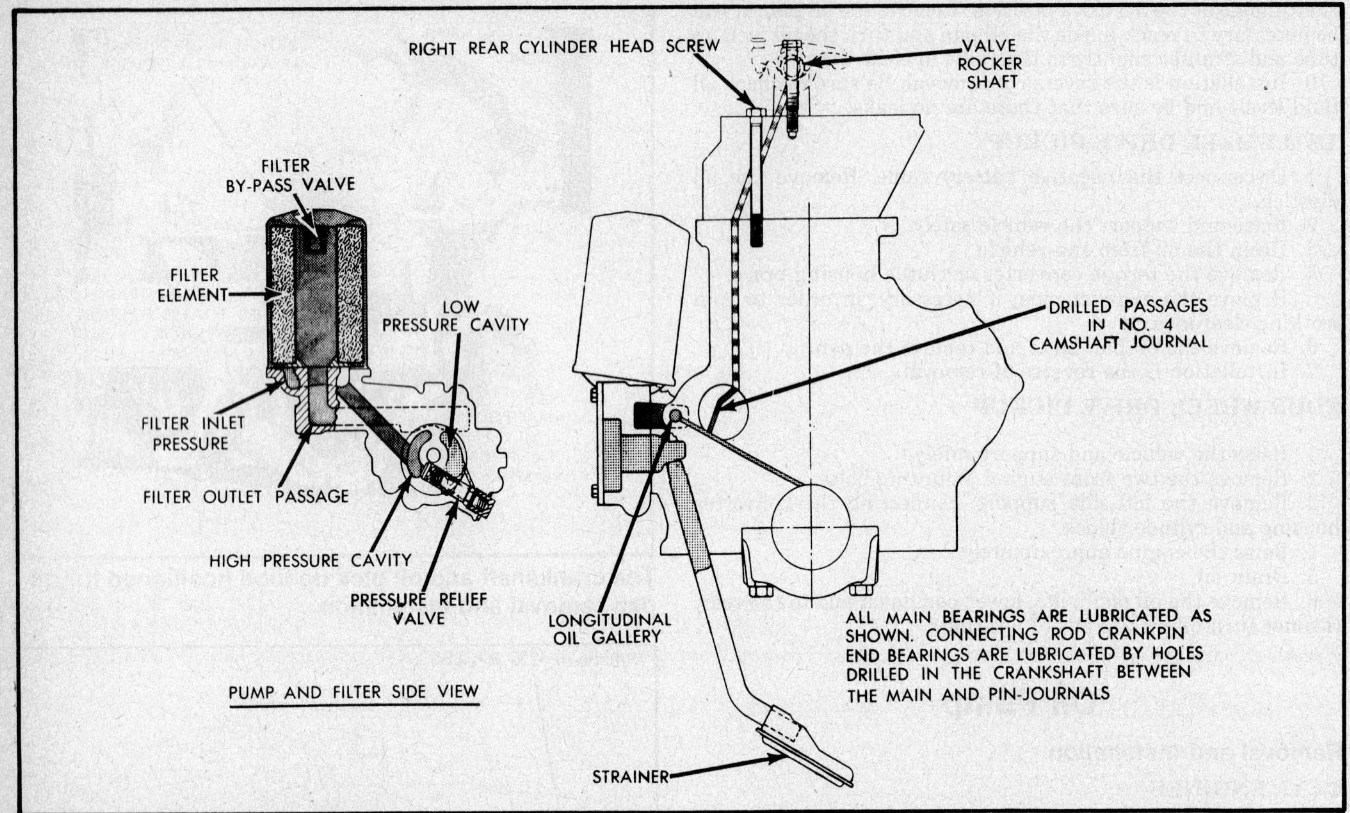

6 cylinder engine oiling system

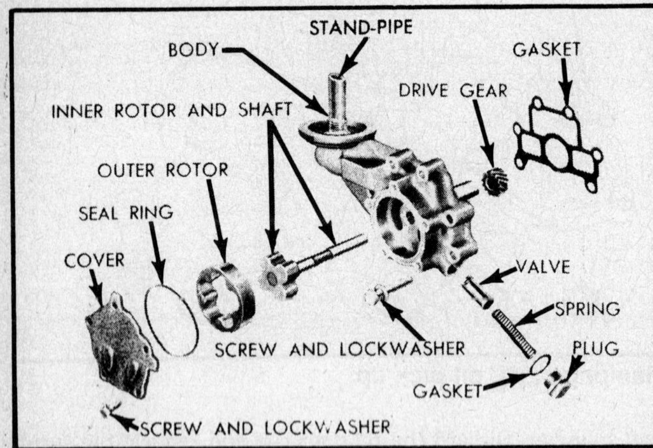

6 cylinder oil pump

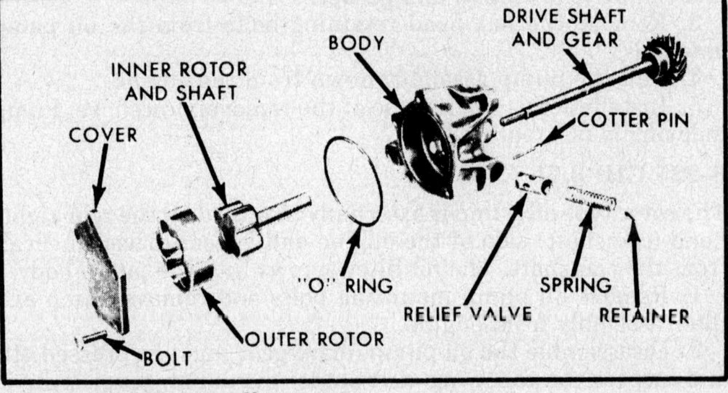

318 and 360 V8 oil pump

6. Slide the outer rotor into the pump body, do this by pressing it to one side and measure the clearance between the rotor and the pump body. If the measurement is 0.014 in. or more, replace the oil pump assembly. Install the inner rotor and shaft into the pump body. If the clearance between the inner and outer rotors is 0.010 in. or more, replace the shaft and both rotors.

7. Place a straight edge across the face of the pump, between the bolt holes. If a feeler gauge of 0.004 in. or more can be inserted between the rotors and the straight edge, replace the pump assembly.

8. Inspect the oil pressure relief valve plunger for scoring and free operation in its bore. Small marks may be removed with 400-grit wet or dry sandpaper.

9. The relief valve spring has a free length of 2–2⅞ in. Replace the spring if it fails to meet this specification.

10. To install, assemble the oil pump, using new parts as required. Tighten the cover bolts to 95 inch lbs.

11. Prime the oil pump before installation by filling the rotor cavity with engine oil. Install the oil pump on the engine and tighten attaching bolts to 30 ft. lbs.

12. Continue the installation in the reverse order of the removal.

13. Fill the engine with the proper grade motor oil. Start the engine and check for leaks.

Clearance Checking

1. Check the end play with a straight edge and feeler gauge. Check end-play to a minimum of 0.001 in. and a maximum of 0.006 in.

2. Check the outer pump rotor for a maximum thickness of 0.825 in. and a minimum outer diameter of 2.469 in.

3. Check between the inner and outer rotors, with a feeler gauge for a maximum of 0.010 in. of clearance.

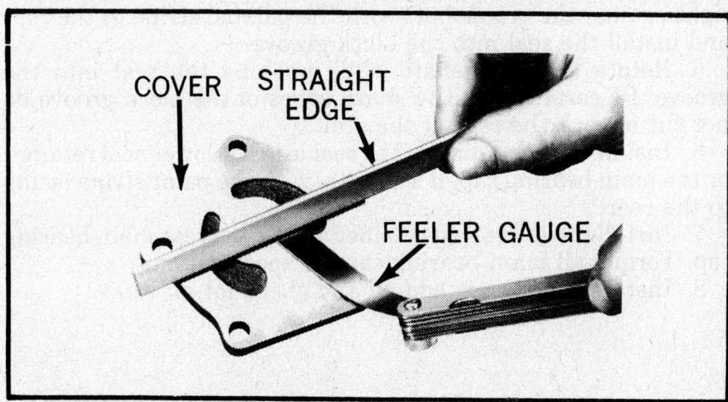

Measuring oil pump cover wear—typical

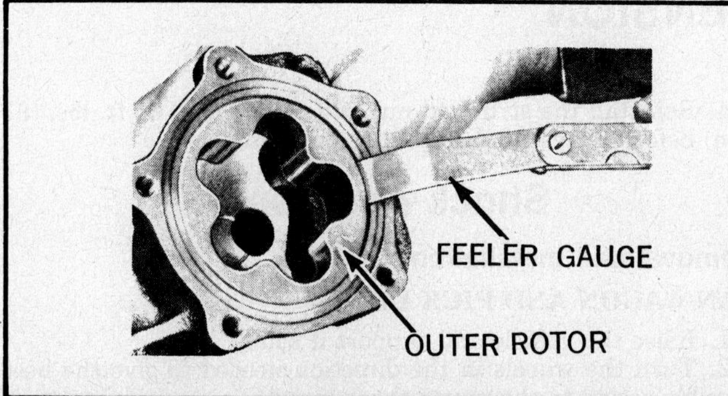

Measuring the outer rotor clearance—typical

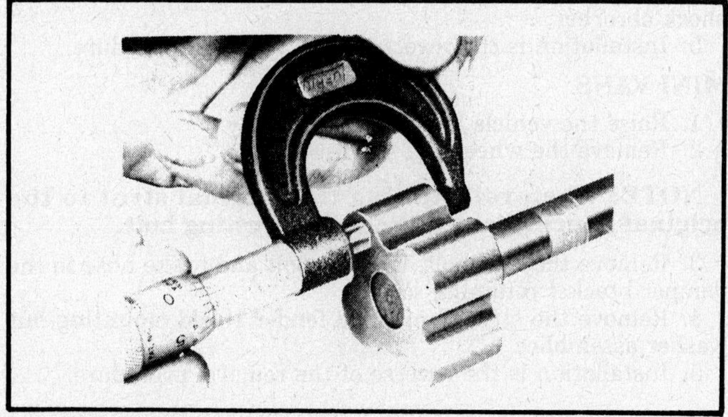

Measuring the inner rotor clearance—typical

4. Check between the outer rotor and pump body, with a feeler gauge for a maximum clearance of 0.014 in.

Rear Main Bearing Oil Seal

Removal and Installation

4 CYL ENGINES

The rear main seal is located in a housing on the rear of the block. To replace the seal, it is necessary to remove the engine.

1. Remove the transaxle and flywheel. Before running the transaxle, align the dimple on the flywheel with the pointer on the flywheel housing. The transaxle will not mate with the engine during installation unless this alignment is observed.
2. Very carefully, pry the old seal out of the support ring.
3. Coat the new seal with clean engine oil and press it into place with a flat piece of metal. Take great care not to scratch the seal or crankshaft.
4. Install the flywheel and transaxle.

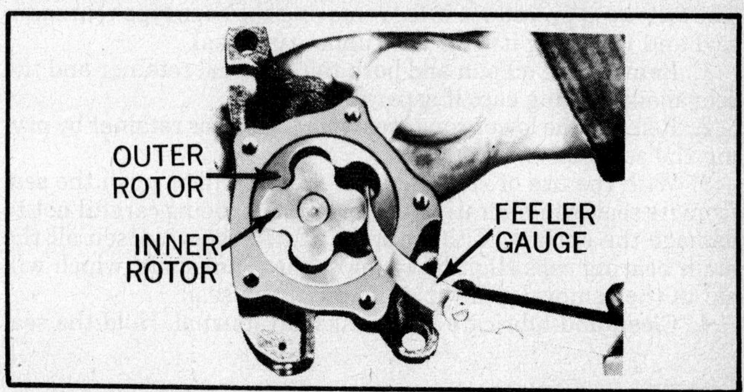

Measuring the clearance between the rotors—typical

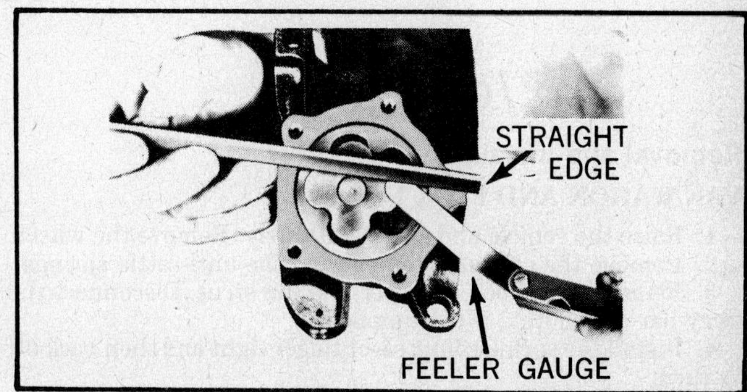

Measuring the clearance over the rotors—typical

TOOL

Rampage 2.2L rear oil seal installation

6 CYL AND V8 ENGINES

Service replacement seals are of the split rubber type composition. This type of seal makes it possible to replace the upper rear seal without removing the crankshaft. The seal must be used as an upper and lower set and cannot be used with the rope type seal.

NOTE: Rope type seals are included in overhaul gasket sets, for use when the crankshaft has been removed, on all engines, except the 360 V8, which uses only the composition seal.

The following procedure is for removing the rope type rear main seal and replacing it with the rubber type seal.

1. Remove the oil pan and both the rear seal retainer and the rear main bearing cap, if separate.
2. Remove the lower rope seal from the cap or retainer by prying the seal out of the groove.
3. With the use of suitable tools, either pull or push the seal from its seal, while rotating the crankshaft, being careful not to damage the surface of the journal. If necessary, loosen all the main bearing caps slightly, to lower the crankshaft, which will aid in the removal and replacement of the seal.
4. Clean and lubricate the crankshaft journal. Hold the seal tight against the crankshaft with the painted stripe to the rear and install the seal into the block groove.
5. Rotate the crankshaft while pushing the seal into the groove. Be careful that the sharp edges of the block groove do not cut or nick the rear of the seal.
6. Install the lower half of the seal into the lower seal retainer or the main bearing cap, if separate, with the paint stripe facing to the rear.
7. Install the lower seal retainer and/or the rear main bearing cap. Torque all main bearing caps to specifications.
8. Install the oil pan, add oil and check for oil leaks.

FRONT SUSPENSION

Coil Springs

Removal and Installation

VAN/WAGON AND PICK UP

1. Raise the vehicle and support it safely. Remove the wheel.
2. Remove the caliper retainers and the anti-rattle springs.
3. Remove the shock absorber and the strut. Disconnect the sway bar at the link, if so equipped.
4. Install the spring compressor finger tight and then back off ½ turn.
5. Remove the cotter pins and ball joint nuts. Install ball joint breaker tool C3564A, or equivalent and lock securely against the lower stud.
6. Spread the tool enough to place the lower stud under pressure, then strike the steering knuckle with a hammer to loosen the stud.
7. Remove the ball joint breaker tool. Loosen the coil spring compressor until all tension is relieved from the spring.
8. Remove the coil spring compressor and the spring.
9. Installation is the reverse of the removal procedure. Tighten the ball joint nuts to 135 ft. lbs. (189 Nm).

DAKOTA

1. Raise the vehicle and support it safely.
2. Remove the shock absorber and loosely install spring compressor tool DD1278 or its equivalent.
3. Disconnect the sway bar end link assembly from the control arm.
4. Support the control arm below the frame and remove the mounting bolts from the frame.
5. Lower the control arm until the tension on the coil spring is relieved. Remove the compressor tool and the coil spring.
6. Installation is the reverse of the removal procedure. Tighten the control arm mounting bolt front nut to 130 ft. lbs. (176 Nm) and the rear nut to 80 ft. lbs. (108 Nm).

MINI VANS

1. Use a coil spring compressor (strut type) to compress the coil spring.
2. Hold the strut rod while removing the strut rod.
3. Remove the strut damper mount assembly and the coil spring.

NOTE: If both strut springs are to be removed and reinstalled, mark them so they can be returned to their original position.

CAUTION

If Chrysler special tool spring compressor tool L-4514 is used, do not open the tool jaws beyond 9 ¼ in. (230mm).

4. Reinstall the strut rod nut and torque it to 60 ft. lbs. (81 Nm) before releasing the spring compressor.

Shock Absorbers

Removal and Installation

VAN/WAGON AND PICK UP

1. Raise the vehicle and support it safely.
2. Turn the wheels in the direction needed to give the best possible access to the upper shock mount.
3. Remove the upper nut and retainer.
4. Remove the two lower mounting bolts and remove the shock absorber.
5. Installation is the reverse of the removal procedure.

MINI VANS

1. Raise the vehicle and support it safely.
2. Remove the wheel and tire assembly.

NOTE: When reinstalling the original strut to the original knuckle, mark the cam adjusting bolt.

3. Remove the cam bolt, knuckle bolt and brake hose to the damper bracket retaining screw.
4. Remove the strut damper to fender shield mounting nut washer assemblies.
5. Installation is the reverse of the removal procedure.

Upper Control Arm

Removal and Installation

NOTE: Any time the control arm is removed, it is necessary to align the front end.

1. Raise the vehicle and support it safely.
2. Remove the wheel.
3. Remove the shock absorber and shock absorber upper bushing and sleeve.
4. Install a spring compressor and tighten it finger-tight.
5. Remove the cotter pins and ball joint nuts.
6. Install a ball joint breaker and turn the threaded portion of the tool, locking it securely against the upper stud. Spread the tool enough to place the upper ball joint under pressure and strike the steering knuckle sharply to loosen the stud. Do not attempt to remove the stud from the steering knuckle with the tool.
7. Remove the tool.
8. Remove the eccentric pivot bolts, after making their relative positions in the control arm.

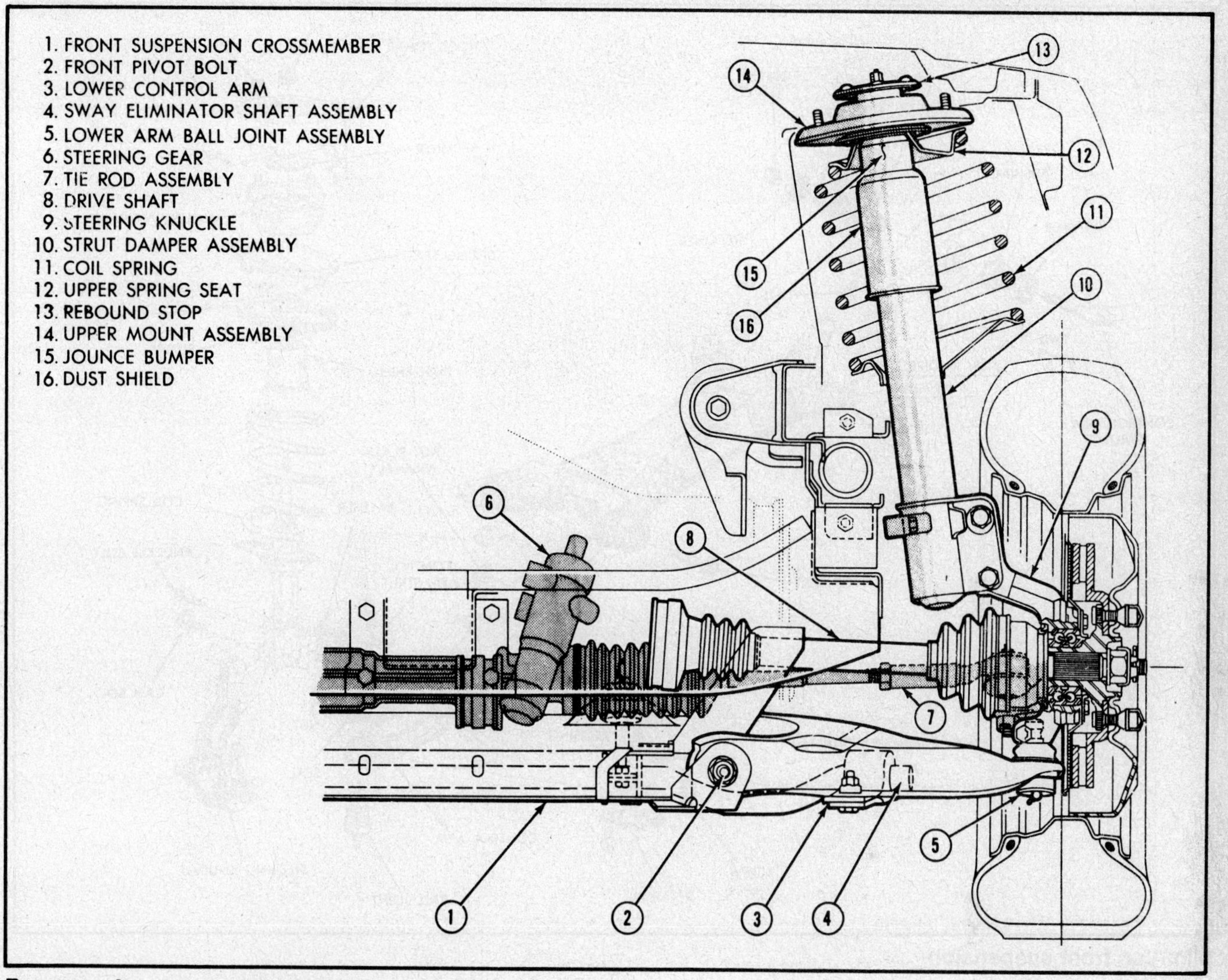

1. FRONT SUSPENSION CROSSMEMBER
2. FRONT PIVOT BOLT
3. LOWER CONTROL ARM
4. SWAY ELIMINATOR SHAFT ASSEMBLY
5. LOWER ARM BALL JOINT ASSEMBLY
6. STEERING GEAR
7. TIE ROD ASSEMBLY
8. DRIVE SHAFT
9. STEERING KNUCKLE
10. STRUT DAMPER ASSEMBLY
11. COIL SPRING
12. UPPER SPRING SEAT
13. REBOUND STOP
14. UPPER MOUNT ASSEMBLY
15. JOUNCE BUMPER
16. DUST SHIELD

Rampage front suspension—front wheel drive with struts

FRONT ADJUSTING BOLT
REAR ADJUSTING BOLT
CASTER
+
+
CAMBER
FRONT
SIDE

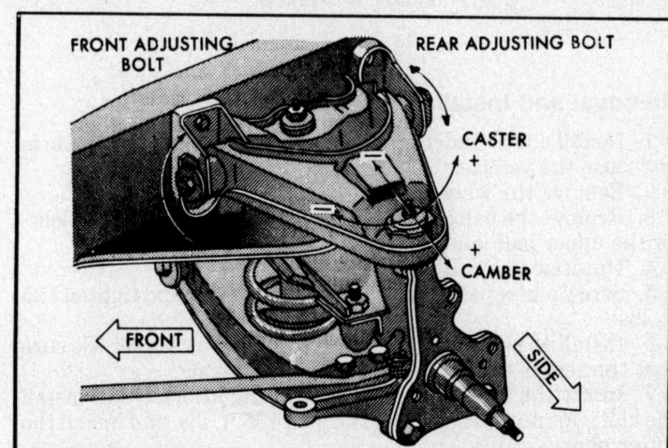

Independent front suspension alignment points

9. Remove the upper control arm.
10. Installation is the reverse of removal. Tighten the ball joint nuts to 135 ft. lbs. Tighten the eccentric pivot bolts to 70 ft. lbs.
11. Adjust the caster and camber.

Lower Control Arm

Removal and Installation

REAR WHEEL DRIVE

1. Follow the procedure outlined under "Coil Spring Removal and Installation."
2. Remove the mounting bolt from the crossmember.
3. Remove the lower control arm from the vehicle.
4. Installation is the reverse of removal.

FRONT WHEEL DRIVE

1. Raise the vehicle and support it safely.
2. Remove the front inner pivot through bolt and the rear stub strut nut, retainer and bushing.
3. Remove the ball joint to steering knuckle clamp bolt and separate the stud from the steering knuckle.

CAUTION

Pulling the steering knuckle out from the vehicle after releasing it from the ball joint can seperate the inner C/V joint.

4. Remove the sway bar to control arm end bushing retainer nuts and rotate the control arm over the sway bar. Remove the stub strut retainer.

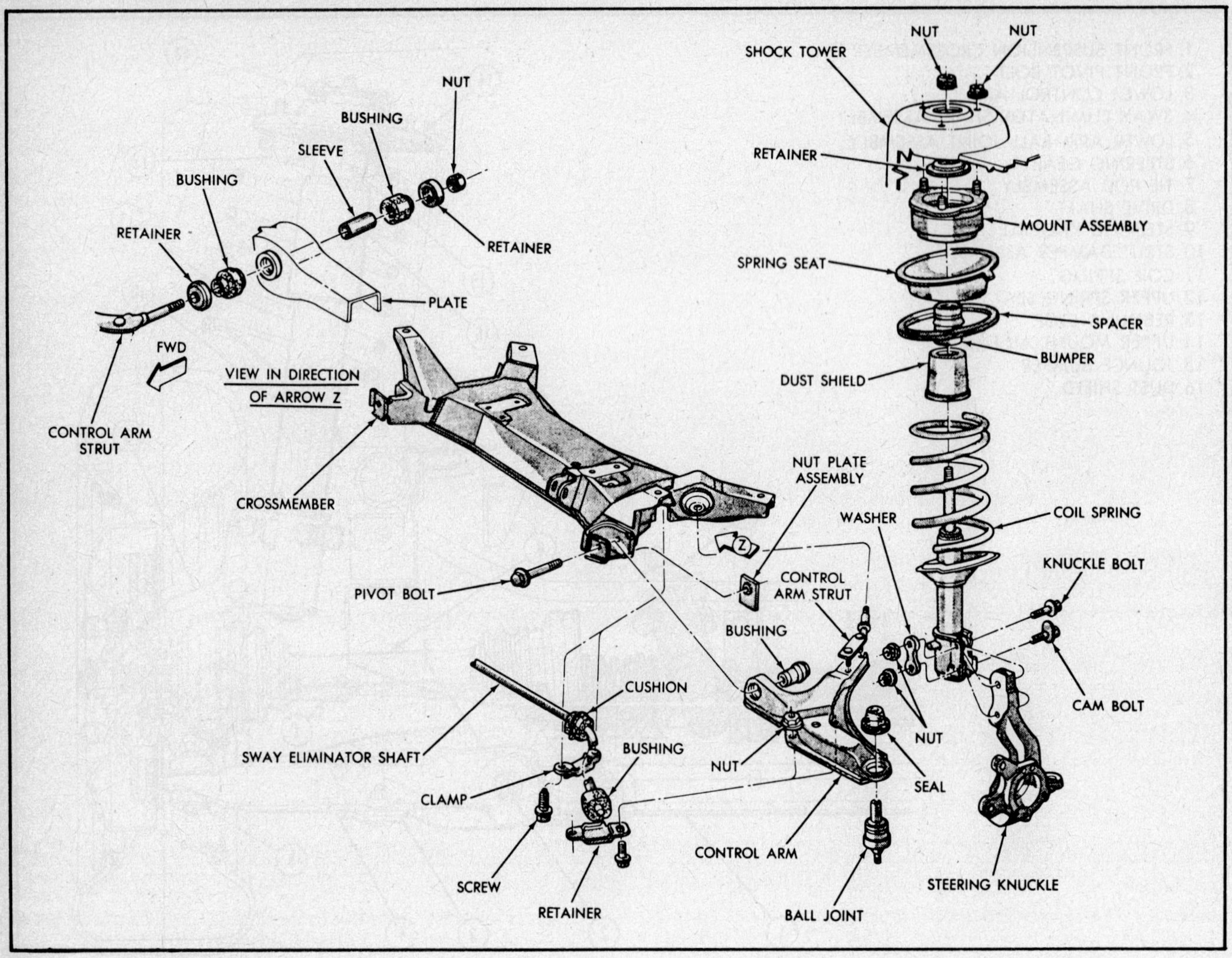

NUT
NUT
SHOCK TOWER
NUT
BUSHING
SLEEVE
BUSHING
RETAINER
RETAINER
PLATE
RETAINER
MOUNT ASSEMBLY
SPRING SEAT
SPACER
BUMPER
DUST SHIELD
FWD
VIEW IN DIRECTION OF ARROW Z
CONTROL ARM STRUT
CROSSMEMBER
NUT PLATE ASSEMBLY
WASHER
COIL SPRING
KNUCKLE BOLT
PIVOT BOLT
CONTROL ARM STRUT
BUSHING
CUSHION
CAM BOLT
NUT
SWAY ELIMINATOR SHAFT
BUSHING
NUT
SEAL
CLAMP
CONTROL ARM
STEERING KNUCKLE
SCREW
RETAINER
BALL JOINT

Mini-Van front suspension

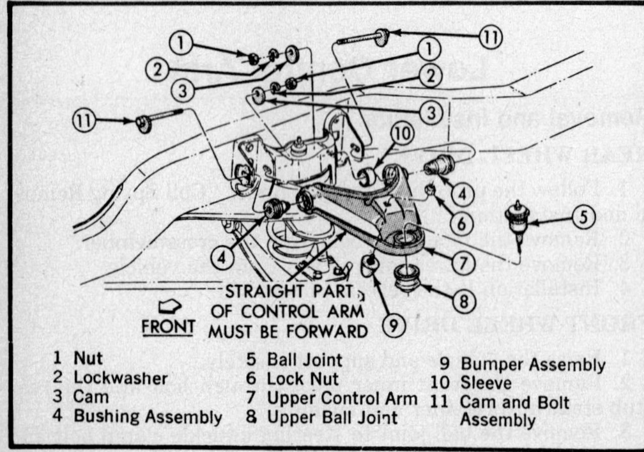

Upper control arm details

5. Installation is the reverse of the removal procedure. Tighten the ball joint clamp bolt to 70 ft. lbs. (95 Nm). Tighten the end bushing retainer bolts to 25 ft. lbs. (34 Nm).
6. Lower the vehicle and tighten the front pivot bolt to 105 ft. lbs. (142 Nm). Tighten the stub strut nut to 70 ft. lbs. (95 Nm).

Ball Joints

UPPER

Removal and Installation

1. Install a jack under the outer end of the lower control arm and raise the vehicle.
2. Remove the wheel.
3. Remove the ball joint nuts. Using a ball joint breaker, loosen the upper ball joint.
4. Unscrew the ball joint from the control arm.
5. Screw a new ball joint into the control arm and tighten 125 ft. lbs.
6. Install the new ball joint seal, using a 2 in. socket. Be sure that the seal is seated on the ball joint housing.
7. Insert the ball joint into the steering knuckle and install the ball joint nuts. Tighten the nuts to 135 ft. lbs. and install the cotter pins.
8. Install the wheel and lower the truck to the ground.

LOWER

1. Follow the procedure under "Coil Spring Removal".
2. Remove the ball joint seal.

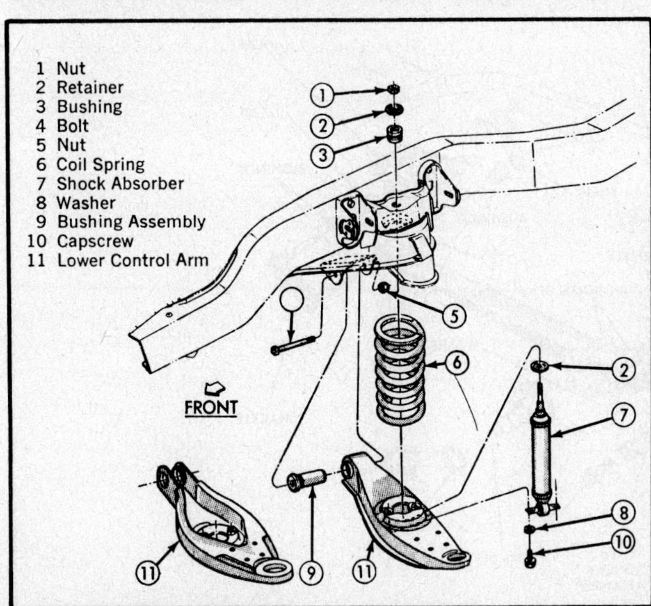

Lower control details

3. Using an arbor press and a sleeve, press the ball joint from the control arm.
4. Installation is the reverse of removal. Be sure that the ball joint is fully seated. Install a new ball joint seal.
5. Install the lower control arm. Be sure to install the ball joint cotter pins.

Wheel Bearings

Removal and Installation

FRONT WHEEL BEARINGS, FOUR WHEEL DRIVE

1. Block brake pedal in the up position.
2. Raise vehicle and support safely.
3. Remove wheel and tire assembly.
4. Remove allen screw holding caliper to adapter.
5. Tap adapter lock and spring from between caliper and adapter.
6. Carefully separate caliper from adapter. Hang caliper out of the way. Inner brake shoe will remain on adapter.

NOTE: Do not allow caliper to hang or be supported by hydraulic brake hose.

7. Remove hub cap. Remove snap ring.
8. Remove flange nuts and lockwashers. Remove drive flange and discard gasket, or remove locking hub if so equipped.
9. Straighten tang on lock ring and remove outer lock nut, lock ring, inner lock nut and outer bearing. Carefully slide hub and rotor assembly from spindle.
10. Remove oil seal and inner bearing from hub.
11. Clean bearings and interior of hub, removing all old grease.
12. If bearings and cups are to be replaced. Remove cups from the hub with a brass drift or use suitable remover.
13. Replace bearing cups with a suitable installer.
14. Install inner bearing in grease coated hub and install new seal with a seal installer tool. Exercise extreme care not to damage seals when installing.
15. Carefully install hub and rotor assembly onto grease coated spindle. Install outer bearing and inner lock nut.
16. Tighten to 50 ft. lbs. (68 Nm) to seat bearings, back off lock nut and retighten to 30 to 40 ft. lbs. (41 to 54 Nm) while rotating hub and rotor. Back nut off 135° to 150°. Assemble lock ring and outer lock nut. Tighten lock nut to 65 ft. lbs. (88 Nm) minimum. Bend one tang of lock ring over inner lock nut and one tang of lock ring over outer lock nut. Final bearing end play to be 0.001 to 0.010 inch (0.025 to 0.254mm).
17. Install new gasket on hub. Install drive flange, lockwashers and nuts. Tighten to 30 to 40 ft. lbs. Install snap ring. Install hub cap, or install locking hub if equipped.
18. Carefully position caliper onto adapter. Position adapter lock and spring between caliper and adapter and tap into position. Install allen screw and tighten to 12 to 18 ft. lbs. (16-24 Nm).
19. Install wheel and tire assembly. Tighten nuts to 75 ft. lbs. (102 Nm).

FRONT WHEEL BEARINGS, FRONT WHEEL DRIVE

1. Remove the cotter pin, lock nut and spring washer.
2. Loosen the hub nut with the vehicle on the floor and the brakes applied.
3. Raise the vehicle and support it safely. Remove the wheel assembly.
4. Remove the hub nut. Disconnect the tie rod end from the steering arm with tool C3894A, or its equivalent.
5. Disconnect the brake hose retainer from the strut damper.
6. Remove the clamp bolt that secures the ball joint stud into the steering knuckle. Remove the brake caliper adaptor screws and support the caliper.
7. Remove the rotor. Separate the ball joint stud from the knuckle and pull the knuckle out and away from the drive shaft.
8. Remove the bearing from the hub with tool kit C4811, or its equivalent. Remove the three screws and bearing retainer from the knuckle.
9. Pry the bearing seal from the machined recess in the knuckle. Discard the bearing and seal.
10. Press the new bearing into the knuckle with the "RED seal on the bearing positioned outboard towards the bearing retainer.
11. Install a new seal and bearing retainer, torquing the retainer screws to 20 ft. lbs. (27 Nm).
12. Press the hub into the bearing and position a new seal in the recess. Press into place.
13. When installing the hub nut to the axle shaft, apply the brakes and tighten the hub nut to 180 ft. lbs. (245 Nm).
14. Install the spring washer, nut lock and cotter pin.

FRONT WHEEL BEARINGS, REAR WHEEL DRIVE

1. Raise and support the vehicle safely.
2. Remove the wheel and caliper assembly. Suspend the caliper from the body with a wire hook to avoid strain on the brake hose.
3. Remove the grease cap, cotter pin, nut lock, nut, thrust washer and outer wheel bearing.
4. Pull the disc and hub from the spindle.
5. After bearing repacking or replacement, install the disc and hub assembly onto the spindle.
6. Install the outer bearing, thrust washer and nut.
7. While rotating the disc and hub, tighten the adjusting nut to 90 inch lbs. on the D and W 150–350 models and to 240–300 inch lbs. on the RWD vans and wagons.
8. After backing off the adjusting nut to release all preload, adjust the nut finger tight.
9. Position the locknut on the nut, with one pair of slots in line with the cotter pin hole. Install and lock the cotter pin.
10. Put light coating of grease in the grease cap and install. Complete the operation with the installation of the wheel assembly and removal of the supports.

Alignment

Procedure

1. Inflate all tires to recommended pressure. Check for un-

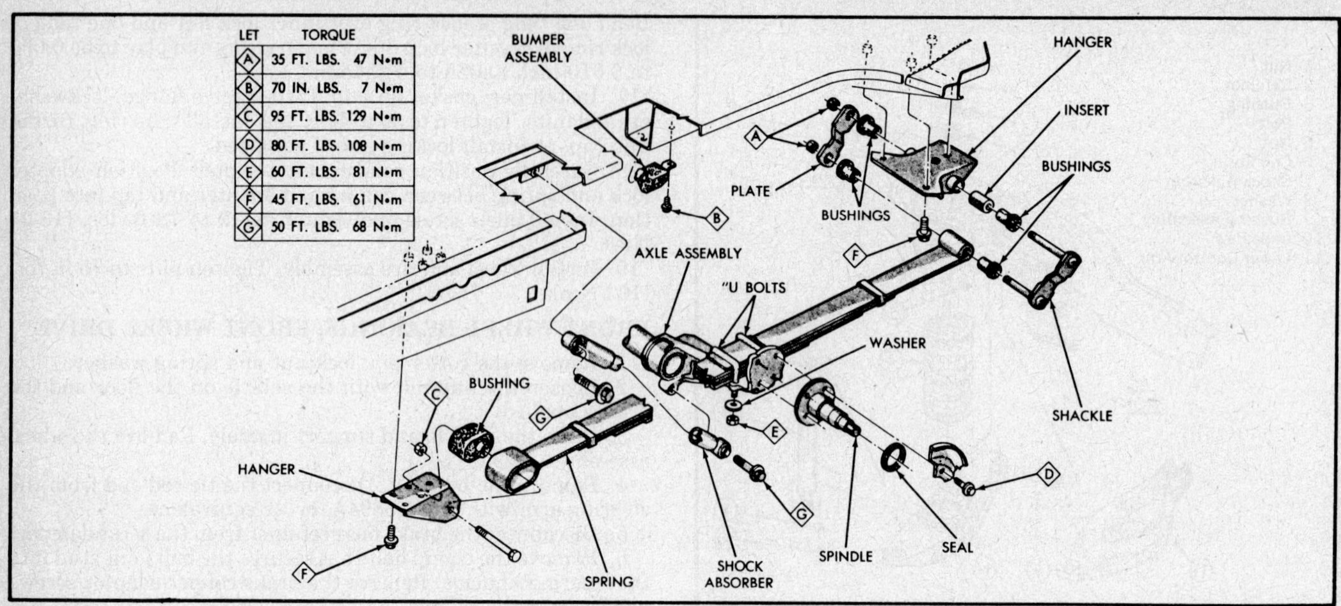

Mini-Van rear suspension

balance conditions. All tires should be the same size and in good condition.

2. Check and adjust the front wheel bearings.
3. Inspect the ball joints and all linkage pivot points for excessive looseness.
4. Check the shock absorbers for leaks. Jounce the vehicle to determine if the shocks have proper control.
5. Check the steering gear for roughness, binding or sticking condition and adjust as necessary.
6. Check the rear springs for cracks or broken leaves. Measure height differential between right and left sides of the vehicle.
7. The vehicle should be level with full tank of gas and no luggage or passenger load.
8. Remove all dirt from the exposed threads of the cam adjusting bolts.
9. Record the initial camber and caster readings before loosening the cam bolt nuts.
10. The camber setting should be held as close as possible to the preferred setting. Caster should be held as nearly equal as possible on both wheels.
11. The toe setting should be the final operation of the alignment. The front wheels must be straight ahead and the steering wheel centered. Make the toe-in adjustment by turning both tie rod sleeves an equal amount.

Stabilizer Bar

Removal and Installation

1. Disconnect the bar at each end link.
2. Remove the bolts from the frame mounting brackets.
3. Lower the bar assembly from the vehicle.
4. Installation is the reverse of the removal procedure.

STEERING GEAR AND LINKAGE

For steering gear overhaul procedures, refer to the Unit Overhaul Section.

Steering Gear

Removal and Installation

REAR WHEEL DRIVE

1. Remove the two bolts from the wormshaft coupling.
2. Remove the steering arm from the steering gear using tool C-4150 or its equivalent.
3. If equipped with power steering, disconnect the pressure and the return hoses.
4. Remove the steering gear from the frame bolts and remove from the vehicle.
5. Installation is the reverse of the removal procedure.

FRONT WHEEL DRIVE

1. Raise the vehicle and support it safely. Remove the front wheels.
2. Remove the tie rod ends using suitable puller.
3. Remove the anti-rotational link from the crossmember, if so equipped.
4. Remove the front crossmember attaching bolts and lower the crossmember so that the gear can be disconnected from the column.
5. Remove the splash shields and the boot seal shields.
6. Remove the bolts attaching the gear to the crossmember and remove the gear.
7. Installation is the reverse of the removal procedure. Tighten the crossmember bolts to 90 ft. lbs. (122 Nm).

CAUTION

Proper torque of the crossmember bolts is very important.

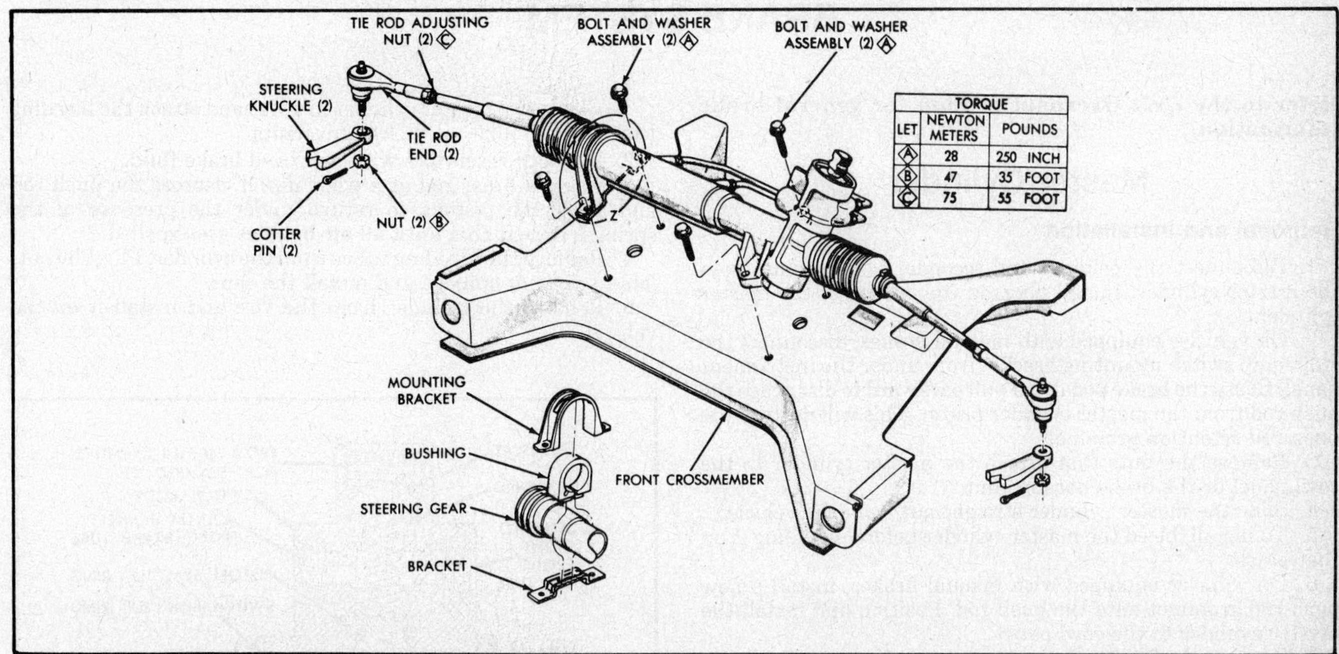

TORQUE		
LET	NEWTON METERS	POUNDS
A	28	250 INCH
B	47	35 FOOT
C	75	55 FOOT

Typical steering assembly mounting – Mini-Van

RACK AND PINION TYPE

1. Remove the tie rod ends using a suitable puller. The lower universal joint is removed with the steering gear.
2. If equipped with power steering, remove the tubes to the pump.
3. Disconnect the tie rod ends from the steering knuckles.
4. Remove the bolts attaching the gear to the front crossmember and remove the gear from the vehicle.

Power Steering Pump

Removal and Installation

REAR WHEEL DRIVE

1. Disconnect the power steering hoses from the pump.
2. Remove the adjusting bolt and slip off the belt.
3. Support the pump, remove the mounting bolts and lift out the pump.
4. Installation is the reverse of removal. Adjust the belt to specifications.

FRONT WHEEL DRIVE

1. Disconnect the vapor separator hose from the carburetor and two wires from the air conditioning clutch cycling switch.
2. Remove the drive belt adjustment locking screw from the front of the pump and the end hose bracket nut.
3. Raise the vehicle and support it safely. Disconnect the return hose from the gear tube and drain the oil from the pump through the open end of the hose.
4. Remove the right side splash shield that protects the drive belts.
5. Disconnect both hoses from the pump. Remove the lower stud nut and pivot screw from the pump.
6. Lower the vehicle and remove the belt from the pulley.
7. Move the pump rearward to clear the mounting bracket and remove the adjustment bracket.

Model 553 Saginaw steering gear

8. Rotate the pump clockwise so that the pump pulley faces the rear of the vehicle and pull upwards to remove the pump.
9. Installation is the reverse of the removal procedure.

Tie Rods

1. Raise the vehicle and support it safely.
2. Remove the cotter pin and nut from the tie rod end.
3. Install the tie rod end puller tool C-3894-A, or its equivalent. Apply sufficient pressure with tool to free tie rod end from knuckle arm or center link.
4. Loosen the tie rod sleeve clamping bolt and unscrew the tie rod end.
5. Installation is the reverse of the removal procedure.

BRAKE SYSTEM

Refer to the Unit Overhaul Section for general brake information.

Master Cylinder

Removal and Installation

1. Disconnect the primary and secondary brake lines from the master cylinder. Install plugs in the outlets of the master cylinder.
2. On vehicles equipped with manual brakes, disconnect the stop lamp switch mounting bracket from under the instrument panel. Grasp the brake pedal and pull backward to disengage the push rod from the master cylinder piston. This will destroy the push rod retention grommet.
3. Remove the nuts that attach the master cylinder to the cowl panel or the brake booster unit.
4. Slide the master cylinder straight out from the vehicle.
5. To install, bleed the master cylinder before installing it on the vehicle.
6. On vehicles equipped with manual brakes, install a new push rod grommet onto the push rod. Position and install the master cylinder to the cowl panel.
7. Connect the front and rear brake lines. From under the instrument panel, moisten the push rod grommet with a drop of water, align the push rod with the master cylinder piston and using the brake pedal, apply pressure to fully seat the push rod into the piston.
8. On vehicles equipped with power brakes, position the master cylinder to the power brake unit and install. Connect the front and rear brake lines.
9. Bleed the brake system, being sure that the proper fluid level in the master cylinder is maintained.

BLEEDING

NOTE: Before installing the master cylinder on the vehicle, it must be bled on the bench.

1. Clamp the master cylinder in a vise and attach the bleeding tubes tool C-4029, or their equivalents.
2. Fill both reservoirs with approved brake fluid.
3. Using a brass rod or a wood dowel, depress the push rod and allow the pistons to return under the pressure of the springs. Repeat this until all air bubbles are expelled.
4. Remove the bleeding tubes from the cylinder. Plug the outlets to prevent spillage and install the caps.
5. Remove the cylinder from the vise and install it on the vehicle.

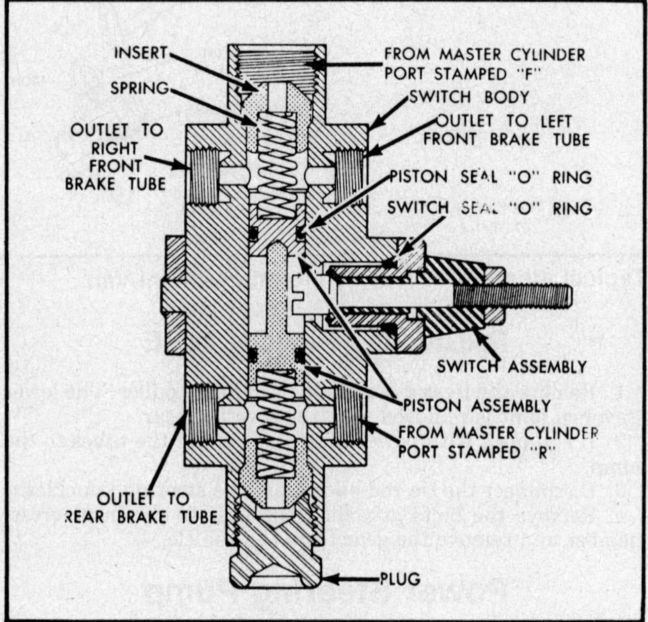

Dual brake system safety switch

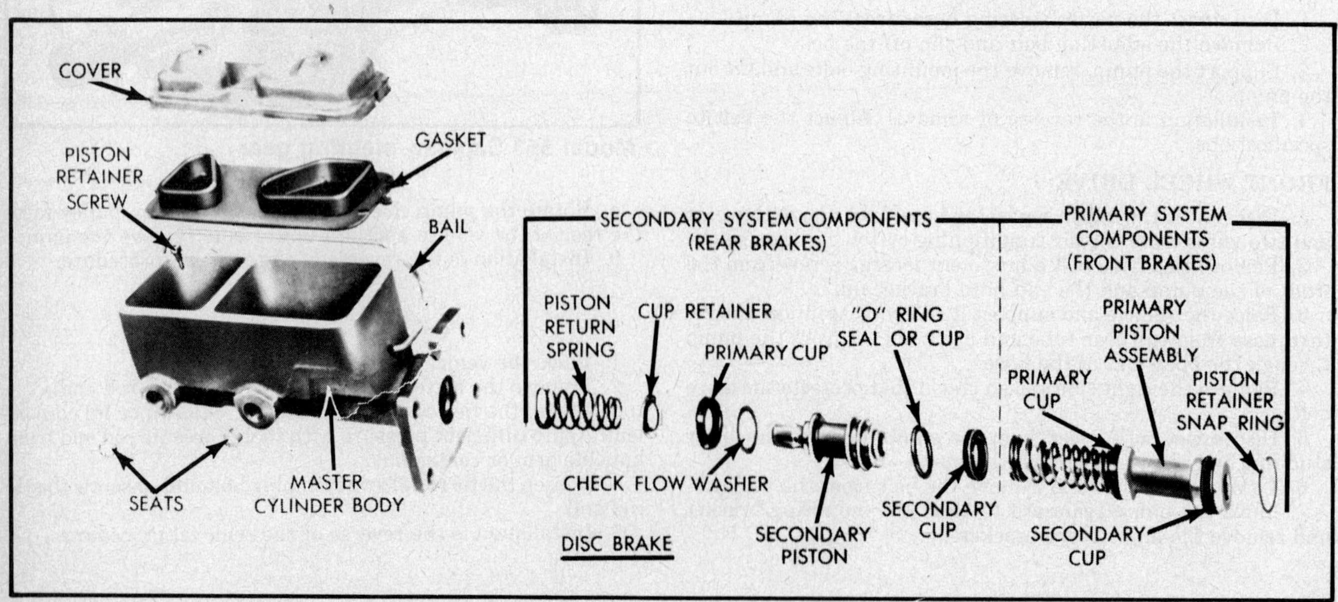

Exploded view of typical tandem master cylinder

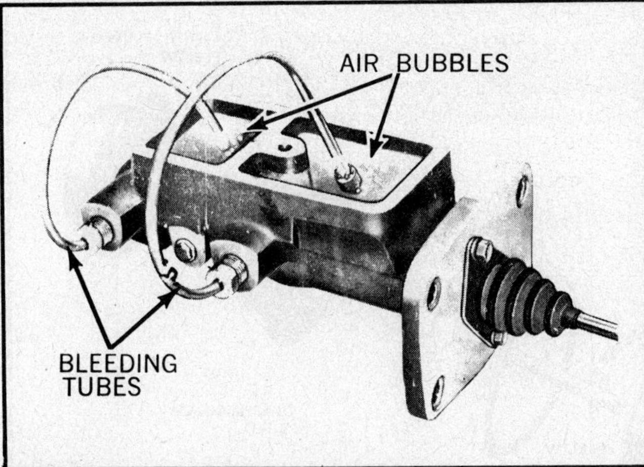

Bleeding dual master cylinder

Wheel Cylinder

Removal and Installation

NOTE: In case of a leak, replace the brake shoes if soaked with grease or brake fluid.

1. Remove the wheel, drum and brake shoes.
2. Disconnect the brake hose from the brake tube at the frame bracket for front wheels and disconnect the brake tube from the wheel cylinder for the rear wheels.
3. Remove the wheel cylinder attaching bolts and slide the cylinder from the brake support plate.
4. Installation is the reverse of the removal procedure. Overhaul or replace the cylinder as required.

Disc Brakes

Removal and Installation

1. Raise the vehicle and support it safely.
2. Remove the front wheel and tire assembly.
3. Remove the caliper retaining clips and the anti-rattle springs.
4. Remove the caliper from the disc by sliding the caliper assembly out and away from the disc.
5. Remove the outboard shoe by prying between the shoe and the caliper fingers.
6. Remove the inboard shoe by pulling the shoe away from the piston.

NOTE: Do not let the caliper hang on the brake hose.

Calipers

Removal and Installation

1. Raise the vehicle and support it safely. Remove the front wheel and tire assembly.
2. Disconnect the flexible brake hose from the tube at the caliper. Plug the connector to prevent loss of fluid.
3. Remove the retaining screw, clip and anti-rattle spring that attach the caliper to the adapter.
4. Slide the caliper out and away from the disc.
5. Installation is the reverse of the removal procedure.

Rotors

Removal and Installation

1. Raise the vehicle and support it safely. Remove the tire and wheel assembly.
2. Remove the caliper assembly and suspend it from a wire hook to avoid strain on the flexible brake hose.
3. On front wheel drive models, remove the rotor from the drive flange studs.
4. On rear wheel drive models, remove the grease cap, cotter pin, nut lock, nut thrust washer and outer wheel bearing. Remove the rotor from the spindle.
5. Installation is the reverse of the removal procedure.

Power Brake Booster

Removal and Installation

IN-LINE MOUNTED

1. Disconnect the vacuum hose from the check valve.
2. Remove the master cylinder to booster mounting nuts.
3. From under the instrument panel, position a small awl between the center tang on the retainer clip and the pin in the brake pedal.
4. Rotate the awl enough to allow the tang to pass over the end of the pin and pull the retainer clip from the pin.
5. Remove the mounting nuts and slide the booster away from the dash panel.
6. Installation is the reverse of the removal procedure.

TRANSVERSE MOUNTED

1. Remove the vacuum hose from the check valve.
2. Remove the master cylinder to booster mounting nuts.
3. Remove the booster push rod to bellcrank attaching bolt.
4. Remove the mounting nuts from the mounting plate and remove the booster.
5. Installation is the reverse of the removal procedure.

Stop Light Switch

The stop lamp switch and mounting bracket are attached to the brake pedal bracket. The switch is actuated by the brake pedal blade.

Adjustment

WITHOUT SPEED CONTROL

1. Loosen the switch to pedal bracket attaching screw and slide the assembly away from the pedal blade.
2. Push the brake pedal down and allow it to return to the free position.
3. Place the proper spacer gauge on the brake pedal.
4. Slide the switch toward the pedal blade until the plunger is fully depressed against the spacer gauge without moving the pedal.
5. Retighten the switch bracket screw to 82 inch lbs. (9 Nm).
6. Remove the spacer and check that the switch does not prevent full pedal return.

WITH SPEED CONTROL

1. Push the switch through the clip in the mounting bracket until the switch is seated against the bracket. The brake pedal will move forward slightly.
2. Pull back on the brake pedal as far as it will go. The switch will ratchet backwards to the correct position and no further adjustment is required.

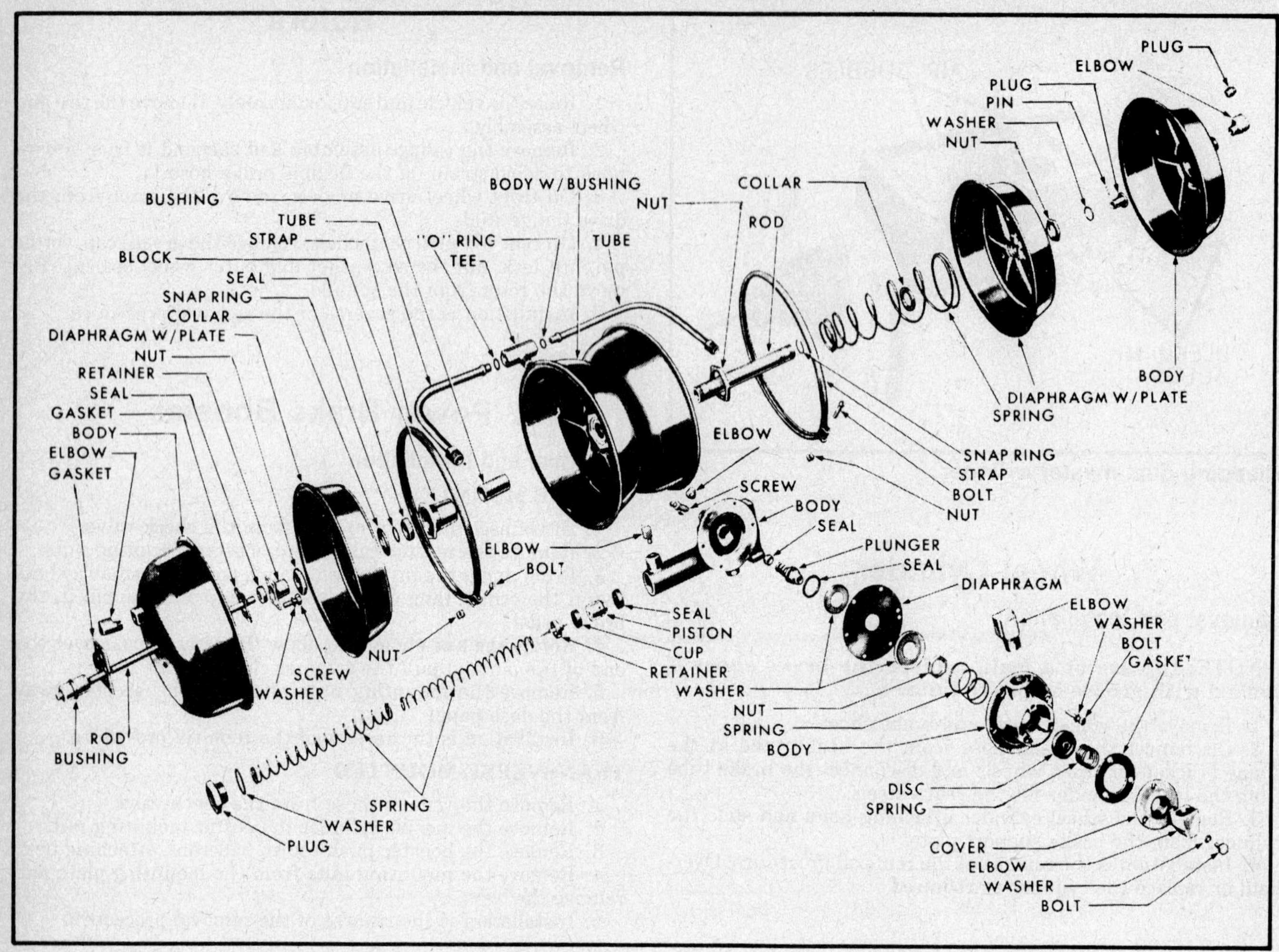

Exploded view of double diaphragm power brake unit

Parking Brake

Removal and Installation

FRONT CABLE

1. Raise the vehicle and support it safely.
2. Remove the adjusting nut at the link. Remove the cable retaining clips.
3. Remove the cable and housing from the mounting bracket.
4. Remove the cable housing anchor clip at the parking brake lever and remove the cable.
5. Installation is the reverse of the removal procedure.

INTERMEDIATE CABLE

1. Remove the adjusting nut at the adjusting link.
2. Disengage the rear end of the cable from the ratio lever or the cable equalizer and remove.
3. On the Dakota model, remove the adjuster hook from the frame rail. Disconnect both the front and rear cables from the intermediate cable and pull it forward through the frame guides.
4. Installation is the reverse of the removal procedure.

REAR CABLE

1. Raise the vehicle and support it safely. Remove the rear wheels.
2. Remove the brake drums from the rear axle.
3. On all models except B350 Van, remove the brake shoe return spring, retaining springs and the strut and spring from the support plate.
4. Disconnect the cable from the operating arm.
5. Compress the retainers on the end of the cable housing and remove the cables from the support plate.
6. Disconnect the cables from the connector and adjuster then remove the cables.
7. Installation is the reverse of the removal procedure.

CLUTCH

Clutch Assembly

Removal and Installation

ALL MODELS-EXCEPT FRONT WHEEL DRIVE

1. Raise the vehicle and support safely.
2. Support the engine on a suitable jack.
3. Remove the crossmember, if necessary.
4. Remove the transmission. Remove the transfer case, if equipped.
5. Remove the clutch housing pan, if equipped.
6. Remove the clutch fork, clutch bearing and sleeve assembly, if not removed from the transmission.
7. Mark the position of the clutch cover and flywheel. Remove the clutch cover retaining bolts, loosening them evenly so as not to distort the clutch cover.
8. Pull the pressure plate assembly clear of the flywheel and, while supporting the pressure plate, slide the clutch disc from between the flywheel and the pressure plate.
9. To install, clean all working surfaces of the flywheel and pressure plate.
10. Grease radius at the back of the bushing.
11. Rotate the clutch cover and pressure plate assembly for maximum clearance between flywheel and frame crossmember if crossmember was not removed during clutch removal.
12. Tilt top edge of clutch cover and pressure plate assembly back and move it up into the clutch housing. Support clutch cover and pressure plate assembly and slide clutch disc into position.
13. Position clutch disc and plate against flywheel and insert spare transmission main drive gear shaft or clutch installing tool through clutch disc hub and into main drive bearing.
14. Rotate clutch cover until the punch marks on cover and flywheel line up.

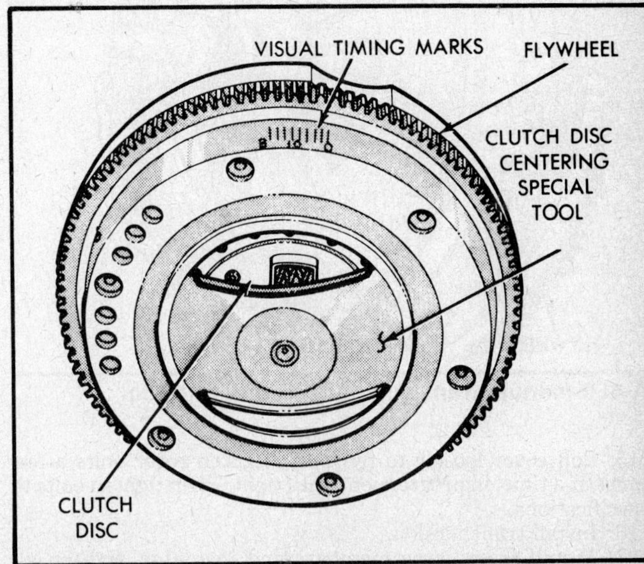

A-412 manual transaxle clutch centering tool

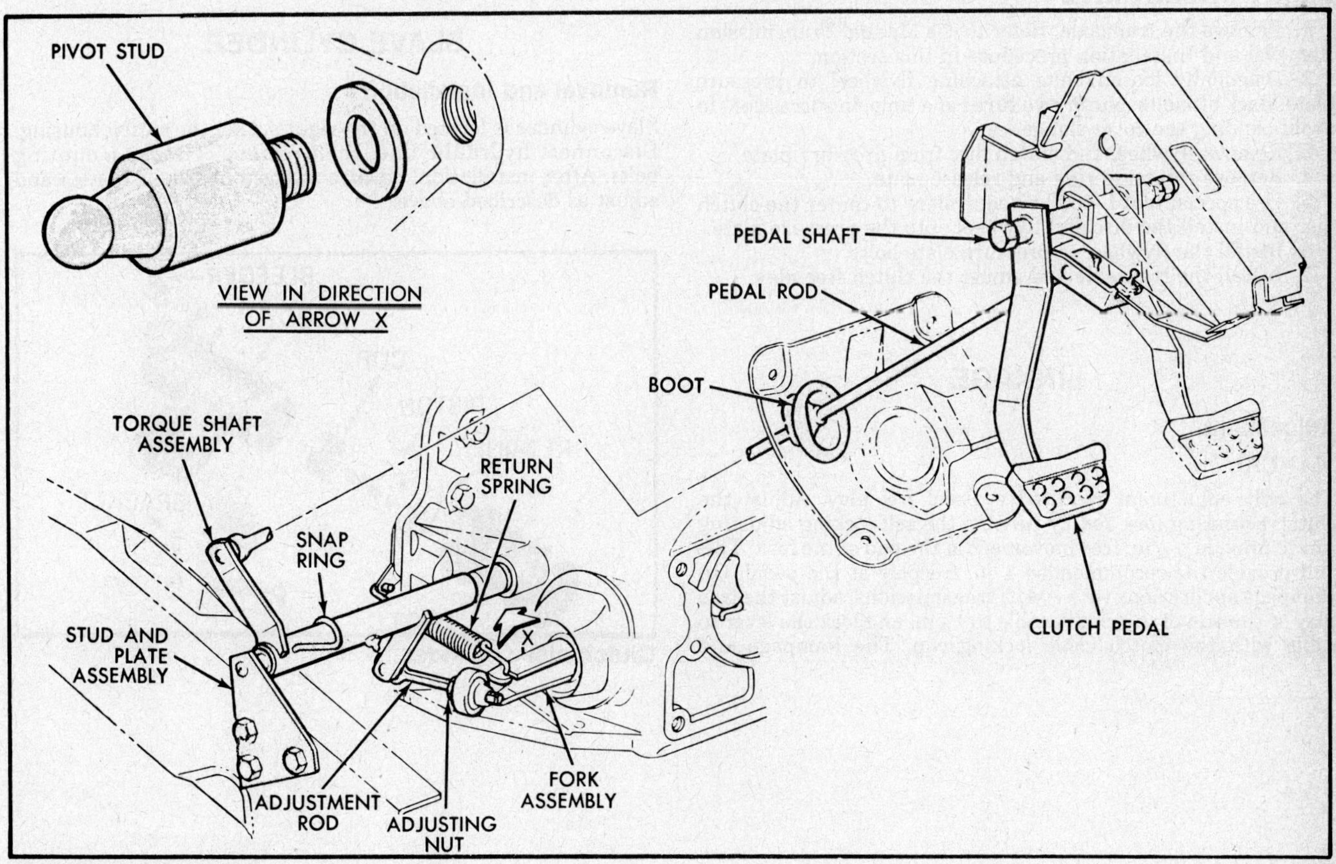

Typical clutch linkage

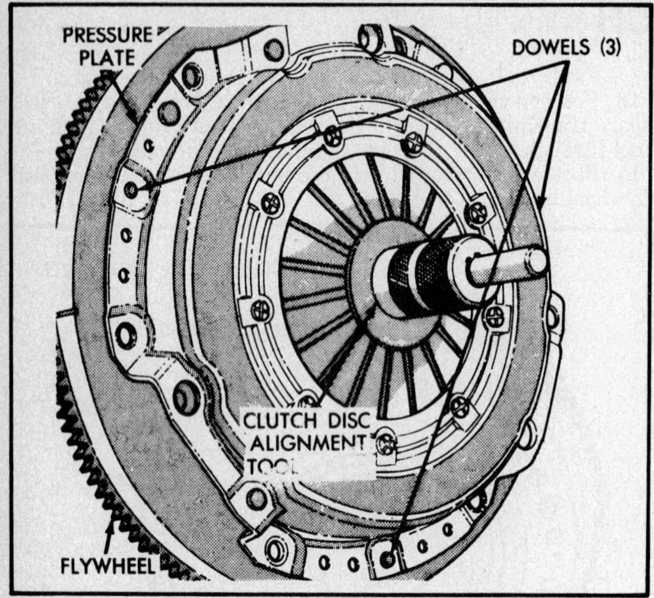

A-460 manual transaxle clutch centering tool

15. Bolt cover loosely to flywheel. Tighten cover bolts a few turns at a time, in progression, until tight. Then tighten bolts to specifications.
16. Install transmission.
17. Install frame crossmembers and insulator, tighten all bolts.

FRONT WHEEL DRIVE

1. Remove the tranxaxle. Refer to the Manual Transmission Removal and Installation procedure in this section.
2. Diagonally loosen bolts attaching flywheel to pressure plate. Back off bolts, one or two turns at a time, in succession, to avoid bending the cover flange.
3. Remove flywheel and clutch disc from pressure plate.
4. Remove retaining ring and release plate.
5. Use special tool L-4533 or equivalent to center the clutch disc and install the disc and flywheel onto the pressure plate.
6. Install the flywheel to pressure plate bolts.
7. Install the transaxle and adjust the clutch free play.

LINKAGE

Adjustment

MANUAL

The only adjustment required is pedal free-play. Adjust the clutch actuating fork rod by turning the self-locking adjusting nut to provide $^3/_{32}$ in. free movement at the end of the fork. This will provide the recommended 1 in. freeplay at the pedal. On Rampage applications with A-412 transmissions, adjust the free play at the end of the clutch cable to $^1/_4$ in. and lock the lever to cable with the clutch cable locking clip. The Rampage and

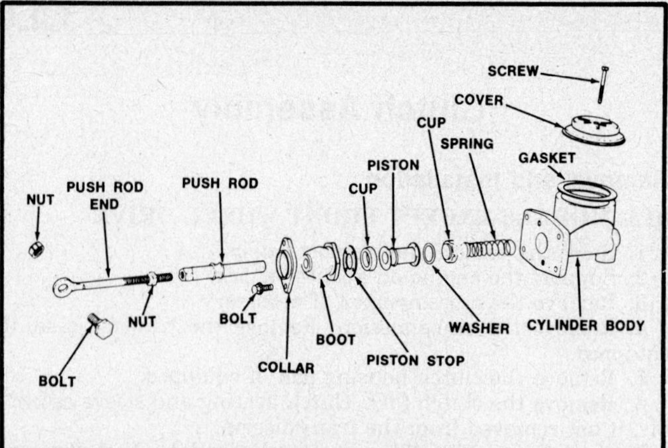

Exploded view of clutch master cylinder

Scamp A-460, A-465 and A-525 transmissions have automatic clutch linkage adjustment.

MASTER CYLINDER

Removal and Installation

1. Remove pedal return spring.
2. Disconnect push rod end at clutch pedal and hydraulic fluid line at master cylinder.
3. Unbolt master cylinder from firewall.
4. Installation is the reverse of the above procedure. Adjust master cylinder push rod to 0.010 in. free play. Bleed hydraulic system.

SLAVE CYLINDER

Removal and Installation

Slave cylinder is located on the right side of the clutch housing. Disconnect hydraulic line, then remove cylinder mounting bolts. After installation, be sure to bleed hydraulic system and adjust as described above.

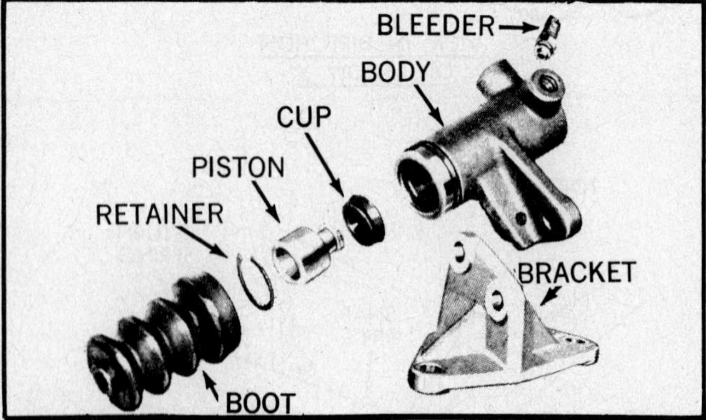

Clutch slave cylinder

MANUAL TRANSMISSION

For Manual Transmission overhaul procedures refer to the Unit Overhaul Section.

Manual Transmission

Removal and Installation

2WD MODELS

1. Shift transmission into any gear.
2. Disconnect universal joint and loosen yoke retaining nut.
3. Disconnect parking brake (if so equipped) and speedometer cables at transmission.
4. Remove lever retainer by pressing down, rotating retainer counterclockwise slightly, then releasing.
5. Remove lever and its springs and washers.
6. Support the rear of the engine and remove the crossmember. Remove transmission to clutch bell housing retaining bolts and pull transmission rearward until drive pinion clears clutch, then remove transmission.
7. To install, place $^1/_2$ teaspoon of short fibre grease in pinion shaft pilot bushing, taking care not to get any grease on flywheel face.
8. Align clutch disc and backing plate with a spare drive pinion shaft or clutch aligning tool, then carefully install transmission.
9. Install transmission to bell housing bolts, tightening to 50 ft. lbs. torque. Replace the crossmember.
10. Install gear shift lever, shift into any gear and tighten yoke nut to 95-105 ft. lbs. torque.
11. Install universal joint, speedometer cable and brake cable.
12. Adjust clutch.
13. Install transmission drain plug and fill transmission with lubricant.
14. Road test.

4WD MODELS

1. Raise and support the truck.
2. Remove the skid plate, if any.
3. Disconnect the speedometer cable.
4. Disconnect and match-mark the front and rear driveshafts. Suspend each shaft from a convenient place; do not allow them to hang free.
5. Disconnect the shift rods at the transfer case. On 4-speed transmissions, remove the shift lever retainer by pressing down and turning it counterclockwise. Remove the shift lever springs and washers.
6. Remove the rear driveshaft. Matchmark the driveshaft and rear U-joints before removing the driveshaft.
7. Support the transfer case.
8. Remove the extension-to-transfer case mounting bolts.
9. Move the transfer case rearward to disengage the front input shaft spline.
10. Lower and remove the transfer case.
11. Disconnect the back-up light switch.
12. Support the engine.
13. Support the transmission.
14. Remove the transmission crossmember.
15. Remove the transmission-to-clutch housing bolts.
16. Slide the transmission rearward until the mainshaft clears the clutch disc.
17. Lower and remove the transmission.
18. Installation is the reverse of removal. The transmission pilot bushing in the end of the crankshaft requires high-temperature grease. Multipurpose grease should be used. Do not lubricate the end of the mainshaft, clutch splines, or clutch release levers. Adjust the gearshift linkage on 3-speed transmissions.

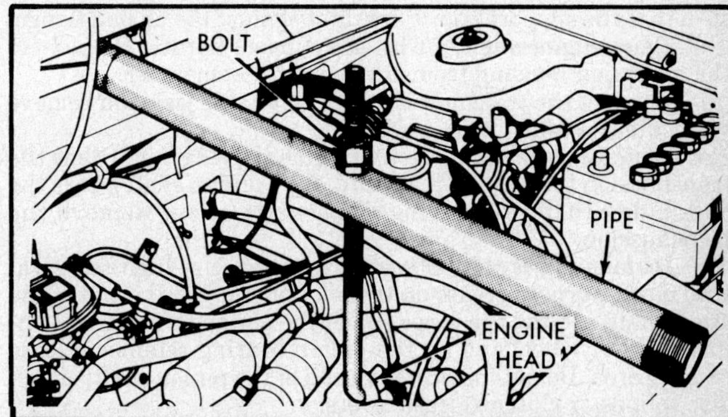

Locally fabricated engine support fixture—A-412 transaxle removal

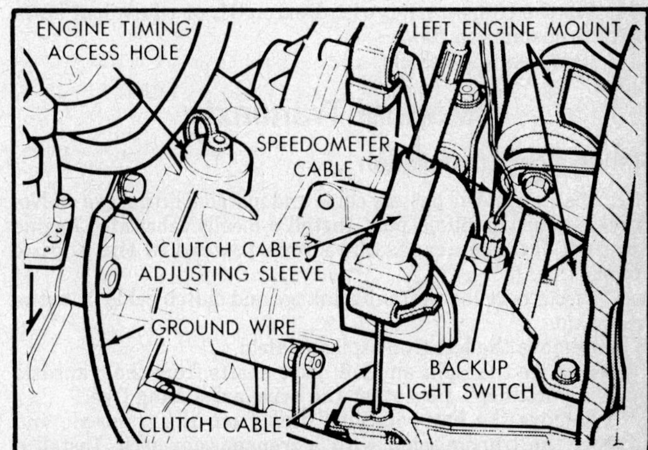

A-412 transaxle removal—engine compartment components to be removed

Locally fabricated engine support fixture—A-460 transaxle removal

OVERDRIVE, FOUR SPEED

1. Disconnect the negative battery cable.
2. Remove the retaining screws from the floor pan boot and slide the boot up and off the shift lever.
3. Remove the shift lever, retaining clips, washers and control rods from the shift unit.
4. Remove the two bolts and washers which secure the shift unit to mounting plate on the extension housing and remove the unit.

5. Drain the fluid from the transmission.
6. Disconnect the speedometer cable and backup light switch leads.
8. Install engine support fixture C-3487-A, or equivalent. Be sure that the support points are tight against the oil pan flange.
9. Raise engine slightly with the support fixture. Disconnect the extension housing from the center crossmember.
10. Support the transmission with a suitable jack and remove the center crossmember.
11. Remove the transmission to clutch housing bolts. Slide the transmission toward the rear until drive pinion shaft clears the clutch disc, before lowering the transmission. Remove the transmission.
12. Installation is the reverse of removal. Use high temperature multi-purpose grease on the pilot bushing in the end of the crankshaft, around the inner end of the pinion shaft pilot bushing in the flywheel and on the pinion bearing retainer release bearing area. Do not lubricate the end of the pinion shaft, clutch disc splines or clutch release levers.
13. Torque the clutch housing bolts to 50 ft. lbs. (68 Nm). Tighten the crossmember bolts to 30 ft. lbs. (41 Nm). Torque engine and transmission mounts to 50 ft. lbs. (68 Nm).
14. Fill the transmission with Dexron®II, or equivalent automatic transmission fluid.
15. Road test the vehicle.

Manual Transaxle

Removal and Installation

1. Disconnect the battery cable and install a lifting eye on No. 4 cyl exhaust manifold bolt. Install a locally fabricated engine support fixture across the shock towers in the engine compartment.
2. Disconnect the gearshift linkage and clutch cable from the transaxle.
3. Remove the left front splash shield.
4. Remove the right and left drive shafts from the transaxle and support them. Do not let the drive axles hang free.
5. Remove the anti-rotational link from the transaxle and support the transmission with a transmission jack. Install a chain around the jack and transmission for safety.
6. Remove the speedometer adaptor and pinion from the transaxle.
7. Remove the engine mount from the front crossmember and the front mount insulator through bolt. Remove the upper ball housing bolts.
8. Remove the left engine mount and remove the lower bell housing bolts.
9. Pry the transaxle away from the engine and lower the assembly from the vehicle.
10. Installation is the reverse of removal. Refill the transaxle with Dexron®II or equivalent automatic transmission fluid. Adjust the clutch free play and transmission linkage.
11. Torque the engine mounting bolts to 40 ft. lbs. (54 Nm). Torque the transmission to cylinder block bolts to 70 ft. lbs. (95 Nm). Torque the hub nut to 180 ft. lbs. (245 Nm) and torque the lug nuts to 80 ft. lbs. (108 Nm).

Linkage

Adjustment

REAR WHEEL DRIVE

1. Install the shift lever aligning tool to hold the levers in the neutral crossover position.
2. With all rods removed from the transmission shift levers, place the levers in the neutral detent positions.
3. Rotate the threaded shift rods to make the length exactly right to enter the transmission levers.
4. Replace all washers and clips. Remove the aligning tool and test the shifting action.

FRONT WHEEL DRIVE

1. Working over the left front fender, remove the lock pin from the transaxle selector shaft housing.
2. Reverse the lock pin (so the long end is down) and insert the pin into the same threaded hole while pushing the selector shaft into the selector housing. This operation locks the selector shaft in the 1-2 neutral position.
3. Raise the vehicle on a hoist and loosen the clamp bolt that secures the gearshift tube to the gearshift connector.
4. Check to see that the gearshift connector slides and turns freely in the gearshift tube.
5. Position the shifter mechanism connector assembly so that the isolator is contacting the upstanding flange and the rib on the isolator is aligned for and aft with the hole in the blockout bracket. Hold the connector isolator in this position while tightening the clamp bolt on the gearshift tube to 14.1 ft. lbs. (19 Nm).

NOTE: No significant force should be exerted upward on the linkage, while tightening the clamp.

6. Remove the lock pin from the selector shaft housing and reinstall it in a reversed position. Torque the lock pin to 8.4 ft. lbs. (12 Nm).
7. Check the first to reverse shifting and for the blockout into reverse.

AUTOMATIC TRANSMISSION

For overhaul procedures, refer to Chilton's Automatic Transmission Manual.

Automatic Transmission

Removal

1. Remove the transmission and converter as an assembly; otherwise the coverter drive plate, pump bushing and oil seal will be damaged. The drive plate will not support a load. Therefore, none of the weight of the transmission should be allowed to rest on the plate during removal. Remove the transfer case, as necessary.
2. Attach a remote control starter switch to the starter solenoid so the engine can be rotated from under the vehicle.
3. Disconnect high tension cable from the ignition coil.
4. Remove cover plate from in front of the converter assembly to provide access to the converter drain plug and mounting bolts.
5. Rotate engine to bring drain plug to "6 o'clock" position. Drain the converter and transmission.
6. Mark converter and drive plate to aid in reassembly.
7. Rotate the engine with the remote control switch to locate two converter to drive plate bolts at 5 and 7 o'clock positions. Remove the two bolts, rotate engine again and remove the other two bolts.
8. Disconnect battery ground cable. Remove engine to transmission struts, if necessary. The exhaust system on some models may have to be dropped.

9. Remove the starter.
10. Remove wire from the neutral starting switch.
11. Remove gearshift cable or rod from the transmission and the lever.
12. Disconnect the throttle rod from left side of transmission.
13. Disconnect the oil cooler lines at transmission and remove the oil filler tube. Disconnect the speedometer cable.
14. Disconnect the driveshaft.
15. Install engine support fixture to hold up the rear of the engine.
16. Raise transmission slightly with jack to relieve load and remove support bracket or crossmember. Remove all bell housing bolts and carefully work transmission and converter rearward off engine dowels and disengage converter hub from end of crankshaft.

CAUTION

Attach a small C-clamp to edge of bell housing to hold converter in place during transmission removal; otherwise the front pump bushing might be damaged.

Installation

NOTE: Install transmission and converter as an assembly. The drive plate will not support a load. Do not allow weight of transmission to rest on the plate during installation.

1. Rotate pump rotors until the rotor lugs are vertical.
2. Carefully slide converter assembly over input shaft and reaction shaft. Make sure converter impeller shaft slots are also vertical and fully engaged front pump inner rotor lugs.
3. Use a "C" clamp on edge of converter housing to hold converter in place during transmission installation.
4. Converter drive plate should be free of distortion and drive plate to crankshaft bolts tightened to 55 ft. lbs. torque.
5. Using a jack, position transmission and converter assembly in alignment with engine.
6. Rotate converter so mark on converter (made during removal) will align with mark on drive plate. The offset holes in plate are located next to the $^1/_8$ in. hole in inner circle of the plate. A stamped "V" mark identified the offset hole in converter front cover. Carefully work transmission assembly forward over engine block dowels with converter hub entering the crankshaft opening.
7. Install converter housing to engine bolts and tighten to 28 ft. lbs.
8. Install the two lower drive plate to converter bolts and tighten to 270 inch lbs. torque.
9. Install engine to transmission struts, if required. Install starting motor and connect battery ground cable.
10. Rotate engine and install two remaining drive plate to converter bolts.
11. Install crossmember and tighten attaching bolts to 90 ft. lbs. torque. Lower transmission so that extension housing is aligned and rests on the rear mount. Install bolts and tighten to 40 ft. lbs. torque.
12. Remove transmission jack and engine support fixture, then install tie-bars under the transmission.
13. Replace the driveshaft.
14. Connect oil coolerlines, install oil filler tube and connect the speedometer cable.
15. Connect gearshift cable or rod and torqueshaft assembly to the transmission case to the lever.
16. Connect throttle rod to the lever at left side of transmission bell housing.
17. Connect wire to back-up and neutral starting switch.
18. Install cover plate in front of the converter assembly.
19. Refill transmission with fluid.
20. Adjust throttle and shift linkage.

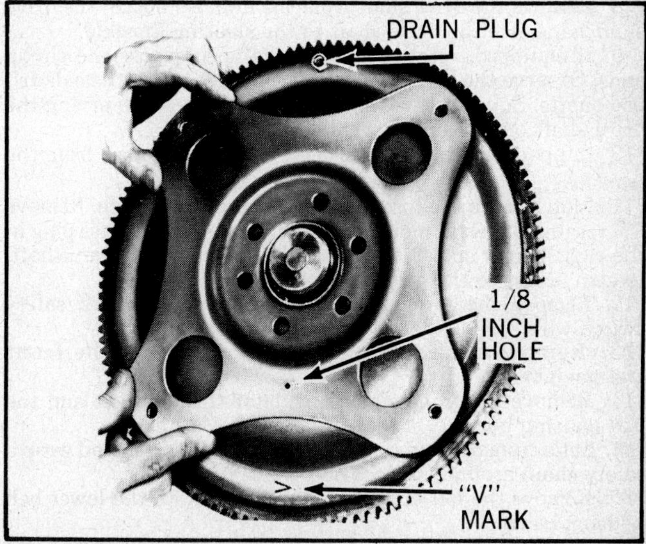

Converter and drive plate markings typical

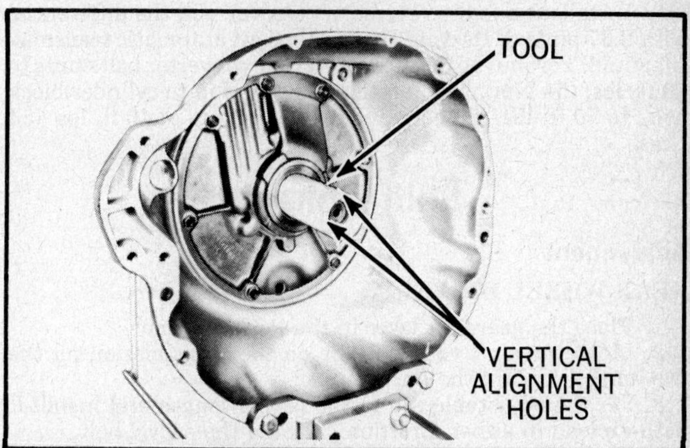

Aligning the pump rotors

Automatic Transaxle

Removal and Installation

The transaxle removal does not require engine removal. The transaxle and converter must be removed as an assembly. Leaving the weight of the transaxle on the drive plate during removal or installation could damage the plate. Leaving the converter with the engine, could damage the drive plate, pump bushing or oil seal.

1. Disconnect the negative battery cable.
2. Disconnect the throttle and shift linkage from the transaxle.
3. Loosen the hub nut on both front wheels (vehicle on the floor and brakes applied).
4. Raise the vehicle and remove the front wheels.
5. Remove the left fender well splash shield

NOTE: If the axle shafts are held in the differential by circlips, drain the differential and remove the cover. If the axles are retained by spring pressure the differential cover need not be removed.

6. Remove the speedometer adaptor, cable and pinion.
7. Remove the front sway bar and the lower ball joint to steering knuckle bolts. Pry the ball joints from the steering knuckles.

8. Remove the drive shaft from the hub. Do not let the drive shaft hang. Tie the drive shaft to the steering knuckle.

9. If equipped, rotate the drive shafts to expose the circlip ends. Observe the flat surface on the inner ends of the axle tripod shafts. Squeeze the circlip ends together, while prying the drive shaft out of the side gear.

10. Support both ends of the drive shaft and remove from the transaxle.

11. Match mark the torque converter and drive plate. Remove the torque converter mounting bolts. Remove the access plug in the right fender splash shield, to rotate the engine crankshaft, to gain access to the torque converter bolts.

12. Remove the lower cooler tube and neutral/park safety switch wire.

13. Remove the engine mount bracket from the front crossmember.

14. Remove the front mount insulator through bolt and the bell housing bolts.

15. Set a transmission jack under the transmission and wrap a safety chain around the jack and transmission.

16. Remove the left engine mount and remove the lower bell housing bolts.

17. Pry the transaxle and converter away from the engine and lower the assembly from the vehicle.

18. Installation is the reverse of removal. Fill the differential with 2.37 pints of Dexron®II or equivalent automatic transmission fluid. Torque the flex plate to torque converter bolts/nuts to 40 ft. lbs. (54 Nm). Tighten the transmission to cylinder block bolts to 70 ft. lbs. (95 Nm) and motor mounts to 40 ft. lbs. (54 Nm).

Shift Linkage

Adjustment

REAR WHEEL DRIVE

1. Place the gearshift lever in the Park position.

2. Move the shift control lever on the transmission all the way to the rear (in the Park detent).

3. Set the adjustable rod to the proper length and install it with no load in either direction. Tighten the swivel bolt.

4. The shift linkage must be free of binding and be positive in all positions. Make sure that the engine can start only when the gearshift lever is in the Park or Neutral position. Be sure that the gearshift lever will not jump into an unwanted gear.

FRONT WHEEL DRIVE

1. Place the gearshift lever in the "P" (PARK) position and loosen the adjusting bolt.

2. Pull the shift lever by hand all the way to the front detent position (PARK) with a load of 10 pounds. While maintaining the 10 pounds of pull on the shift lever, tighten the lock nut bolt to 7.5 ft. lbs. (10 Nm).

3. Check for proper adjustment as follows:

a. The detent position for neutral and drive should be within limits of the hand lever gate stops.

b. Key starting must occur only when the shift lever is in park or neutral.

Band Adjustments

KICKDOWN BAND

The kickdown band adjusting screw is located on the left-hand side of the transmission case near the throttle lever shaft (top front of the transaxle case).

Procedure

1. Loosen the locknut and back off about five turns. Be sure that the adjusting screw is free in the case.

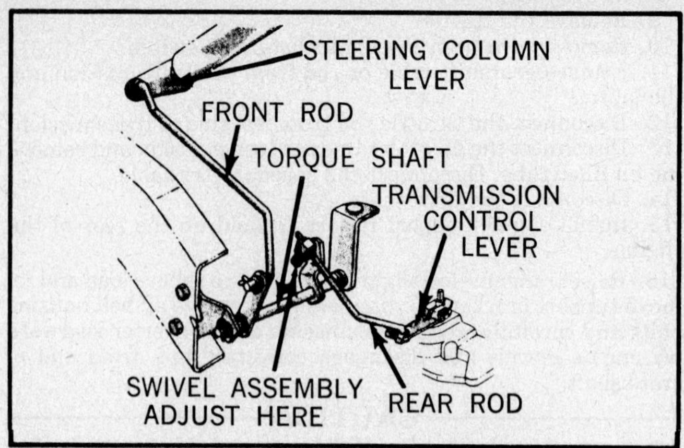

Typical Loadflite® transmission shift linkage

2. Torque the adjusting screw to 72 inch lbs. (8.1 Nm).

3. Back off the adjusting screw 2 turns. On 6 cylinder and V8 engines, back off $2^1/_2$ turns. On V8 van and wagon and A-345 four speed, back off 2 turns. On Rampage transaxle A-404, back off 3 turns and on the Rampage A-413, A-470, back off $2^3/_4$ turns. Hold the adjusting screw and torque the locknut to 35 ft. lbs. (47 Nm).

LOW AND REVERSE BAND

Drain the transmission and remove the oil pan to gain access to the low and reverse band adjusting screw. If the A-404 band is worn, it must be replaced. The loadflite and A-413, A-470 transaxle are adjustable.

Procedure

1. Remove the skid plate equipped and drain the transmission. Remove the transmission pan.

2. Loosen the band adjusting screw locknut and back it off about five turns.

3. On Loadflite, torque the adjusting screw to 72 inch lbs. On the Rampage A-413 and A-470, torque the adjusting screw to 41 inch lbs. (5 Nm).

4. Back off the adjusting screw 2 turns on the Loadflite and $3^1/_2$ turns on the A-413, A-470 transaxles.

5. Torque the Loadflite locknut to 30 ft. lbs. (40.7 Nm). Torque the A-413, A-470 locknut to 20 ft. lbs. (27.1 Nm).

6. Using a new gasket, install the pan and torque the pan bolts to 150 inch lbs. Refill the transmission with Dexron®II automatic transmission fluid.

THROTTLE LINKAGE

Adjustment

REAR WHEEL DRIVE

1. Perform adjustment with the vehicle at normal operating temperature.

2. Raise the vehicle and support it safely.

3. Adjustment is made at the transmission throttle lever. Loosen the adjustment swivel lock screw.

4. Hold the transmission lever firmly forward against its internal stop and tighten the swivel lock screw to 100 inch lbs. (11 Nm).

5. Linkage backlash is automatically removed by the preload spring.

6. Lower the vehicle. Test the linkage freedom of operation by moving the throttle rod rearward, releasing it to confirm it will return fully forward.

FRONT WHEEL DRIVE

1. Perform the transaxle throttle pressure cable adjustment with the engine at normal operating temperature.
2. Loosen the cable mounting bracket lock screw. The bracket should be positioned with both alignment tabs touching the transaxle cast surface.
3. Tighten the lock screw to 105 inch lbs. (12 Nm). Release the cross-lock on the cable assembly.
4. Move the throttle control lever fully clockwise against its internal stop and press the the cross-lock downward into locked position. Throttle cable backlash was automatically removed.
5. Test the cable freedom of operation by moving the throttle lever forward and release it to return fully rearward.

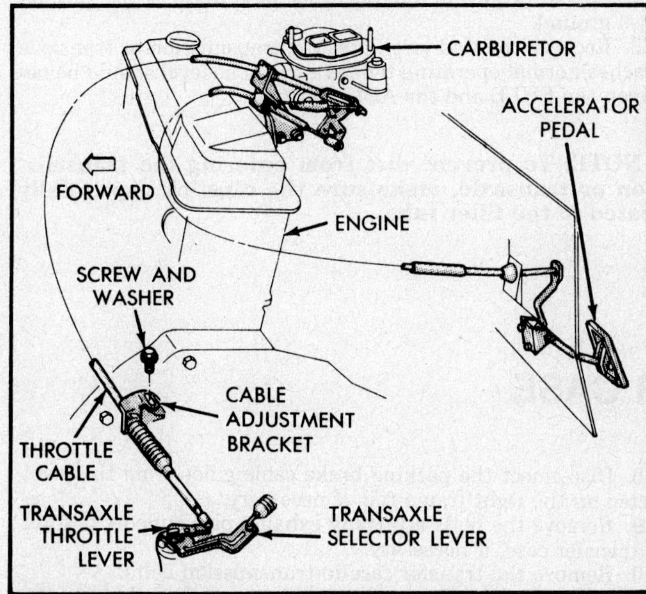

Rampage automatic transmission throttle control—typical

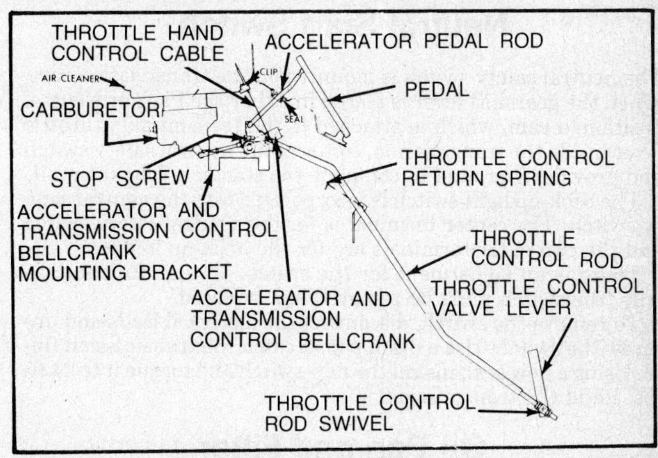

Throttle linkage assembly—typical

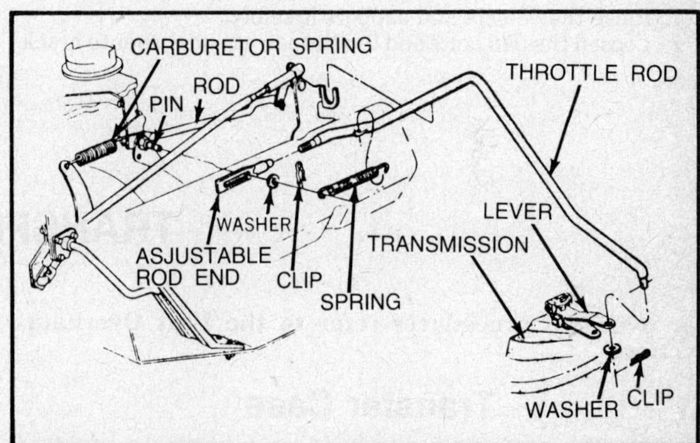

Typical Loadflite® transmission kickdown throttle linkage—V8

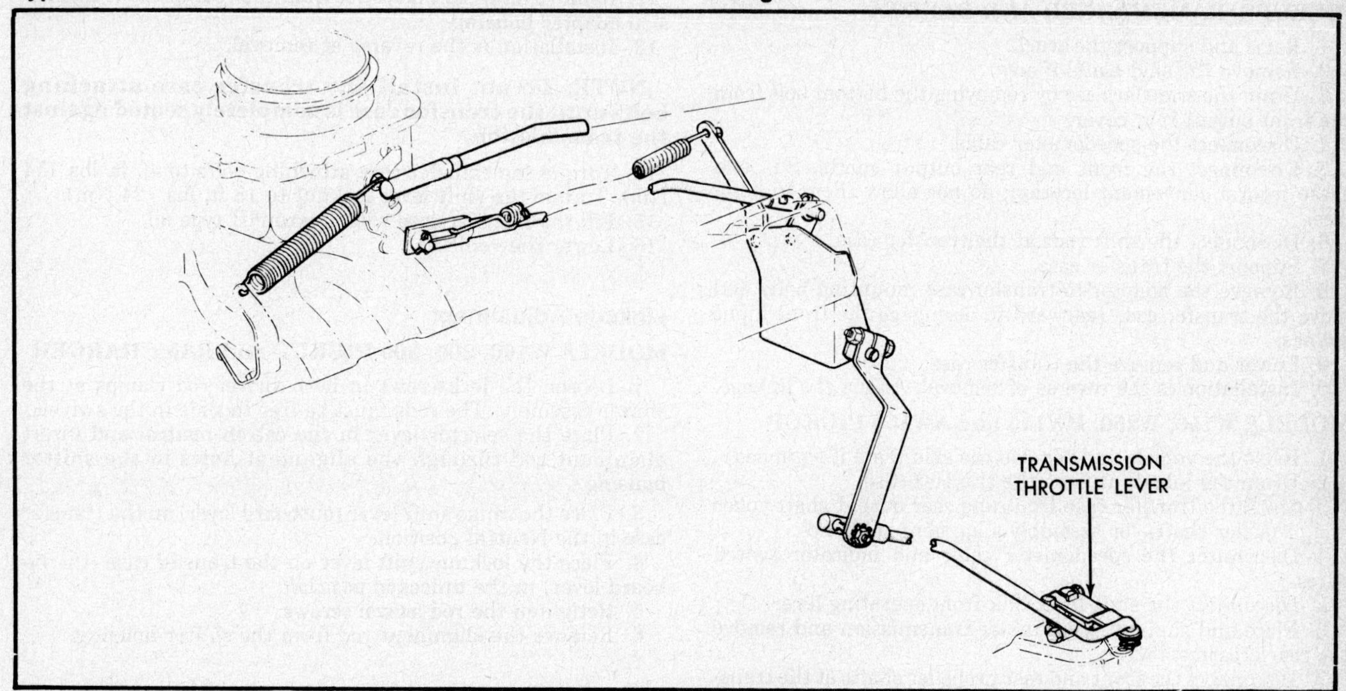

Loadflite® transmission kickdown throttle linkage—V8 conventional truck

Neutral Start Switch

The neutral safety switch is mounted on the transmission case. When the gearshift lever is placed in either the Park or Neutral position, a cam, which is attached to the transmission throttle lever inside the transmission, contacts the neutral safety switch and provides a ground to complete the starter solenoid circuit.

The back-up light switch is incorporated into the neutral safety switch. The center terminal is for the neutral safety switch and the two outer terminals are for the back-up lamps.

There is no adjustment for the switch. If a malfunction occurs, the switch must be removed and replaced.

To remove the switch, disconnect the electrical leads and unscrew the switch. Use a drain pan to catch the transmission fluid. Using a new seal, install the new switch and torque it to 24 ft. lbs. Refill the transmission.

Oil Pan and Filter

Removal and Installation

1. Raise the vehicle and support it safely.
2. Loosen the pan bolts and tap the pan at one corner to break it loose allowing the fluid to drain, then remove the oil pan.
3. Install a new filter on the bottom of the valve body and tighten the retaining screws to 35 inch lbs. (4 Nm). On a transaxle, tighten the retaining screws to 40 inch lbs. (5 Nm).
4. Clean the oil pan and the magnet. Reinstall the oil pan using a new gasket and torque the bolts to 150 inch lbs. (17 Nm). On a transaxle, use R.T.V. sealant and tighten the pan bolts to 165 inch lbs. (19 Nm).
5. Pour four quarts of Automatic Transmission Fluid through the dipstick opening.
6. Start the engine and allow it to idle for at least two minutes, then move the selector lever through each position, ending in Park or Neutral.
7. Add sufficient fluid to bring the level to the ADD mark on level ground.
8. Recheck the flud level after the transmission or transaxle reaches normal operating temperature. The level should be between the FULL and the ADD mark.

NOTE: To prevent dirt from entering the transmission or transaxle, make sure the dipstick cap is fully seated in the filler tube.

TRANSFER CASE

For overhaul procedures refer to the Unit Overhaul Section.

Transfer Case

Removal and Installation

MODELS W250, W350, W450, W100, W200 AND W300 PICKUPS, RAMCHARGER AND DAKOTA

1. Raise and support the truck.
2. Remove the skid plate, if any.
3. Drain the transfer case by removing the bottom bolt from the front output rear cover.
4. Disconnect the speedometer cable.
5. Disconnect the front and rear output shafts. Suspend these from a convenient location; do not allow them to hang free.
6. Disconnect the shift rods at the transfer case.
7. Support the transfer case.
8. Remove the adaptor-to-transfer case mounting bolts and move the transfer case rearward to disengage the front input splines.
9. Lower and remove the transfer case.
10. Installation is the reverse of removal. Adjust the linkage.

MODELS W150, W250, PW150 and AW150 PICKUP

1. Raise the vehicle and remove the skid plate if equipped.
2. Drain the lubricant from the transfer case.
3. Mark the transfer case front and rear output shaft yokes and propeller shafts for assembly alignment reference.
4. Disconnect the speedometer cable and indicator switch wires.
5. Disconnect the shift lever link from operating lever.
6. Place and support stand under transmission and remove the rear crossmember.
7. Disconnect the front and rear propeller shafts at the transfer case yokes. Secure shafts to frame rails with wire. Do not allow shafts to hang.
8. Disconnect the parking brake cable guide from the pivot locted on the right frame rail, if necessary.
9. Remove the bolts attaching exhaust pipe support bracket to transfer case, if necessary.
10. Remove the transfer case-to-transmission bolts.
11. Move the transfer case assembly rearward until free of the transmission output shaft and remove assembly.
12. Remove all gasket material from the rear of the transmission adapter housing.
13. Installation is the reverse of removal.

NOTE: Do not install any transfer case attaching bolts until the transfer case is completely seated against the transmission.

14. Torque the transfer case attaching bolts to 40 ft. lbs. (54 Nm). Torque the shift lever locknut to 18 ft. lbs. (24 Nm).
15. Fill the transfer case with Dexron®II type oil.
16. Lower the vehicle.

Linkage Adjustment

MODELS W100, 200, 300 PICKUP and RAMCHARGER

1. Loosen the lockscrews in both swivel rod clamps at the shifter assembly. The rods must be free to slide in the swivels.
2. Place the selector lever in the cab in neutral and insert alignment rod through the alignment holes in the shifter housing.
3. Place the range shift lever (outboard lever) on the transfer case in the Neutral position.
4. Place the locknut shift lever on the transfer case (the inboard lever) in the unlocked position.
5. Retighten the rod swivel screws.
6. Remove the alignment rod from the shifter housing.

NOTE: The W250, W350, W450, W150, PW 150 and AW150 shift linkage is not adjustable.

DRIVE LINES AND UNIVERSAL JOINTS

Drive Lines

FRONT SHAFT

Removal and Installation

1. Slide the propeller shaft with the front yoke from the transmission output shaft.
2. When no leakage is evident at the sliding yoke seal, do not disturb it.
3. Protect the machined surface of the yoke for damage after the propeller shaft has been removed.
4. Reverse the procedure for installation.

CENTER BEARING AND SHAFT

Removal and Installation

1. Mark the parts for reassembly and remove the propeller shafts.
2. Place the front shaft in a vise and pull the bearing support and insulator from the bearing.
3. Bend the slinger away from the bearing with a hammer to obtain clearance to install the bearing puller.
4. Remove the bearing with the puller and remove the slinger.

REAR SHAFT

Removal and Installation

1. Mark the propeller shaft and the pinion flange for the correct reinstallation in the same position.
2. Remove the two universal joint roller and bushing clamps from the rear axle drive pinion flange.

NOTE: The propeller shaft should not be allowed to drop or hang loose from either joint during removal.

3. Reverse the procedure to install.

Universal Joints

Removal and Installation

LOCK RING AND THE SNAP-RING TYPE

The lockring and the snap-ring type universal joints are basically the same, except for the locations of the retainers. The lockring retainers hold the bearing cups in the yoke by being installed in a machined groove on the bearing cup, which is located on the inner side of the yoke when the joint is assembled.

The snap-ring type retainer holds the bearing cup in the yoke by being installed in a machined groove in the upper area of the bearing bore of the yoke.

The disassembly and assembly are as follows:

1. Hammer the bushings (roller cups) slightly inward to relieve pressure on the retainers. Remove the retainers.
2. Place the yoke in a vise with a socket bigger than the bushing on one side and one smaller than the bushing on the other side.
3. Apply pressure, forcing one bushing out into the larger socket.
4. Reverse the vise and socket arrangement to remove the other bushing and the cross.

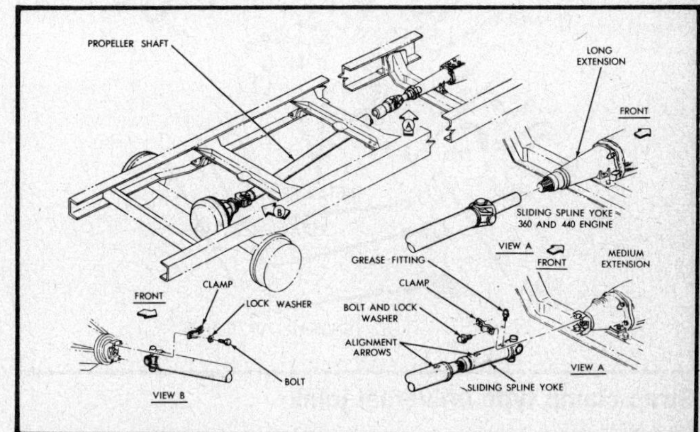

Single section driveshaft

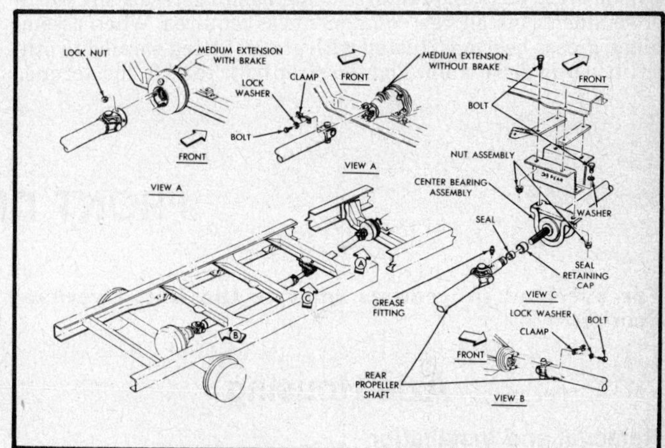

Two-section driveshaft

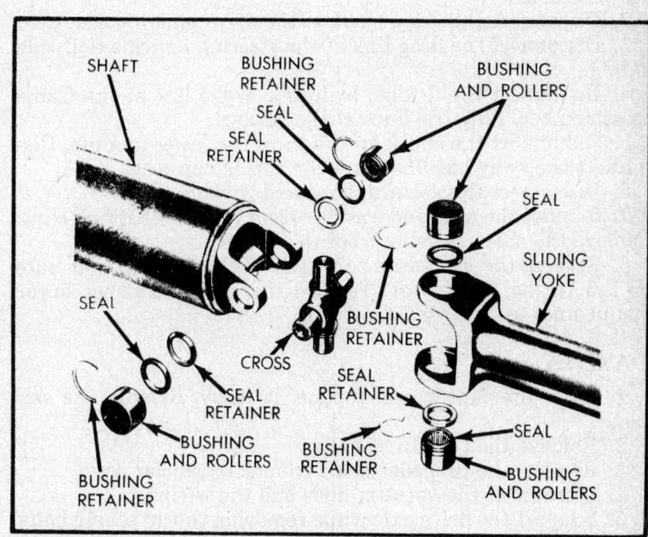

Lock ring type universal joint

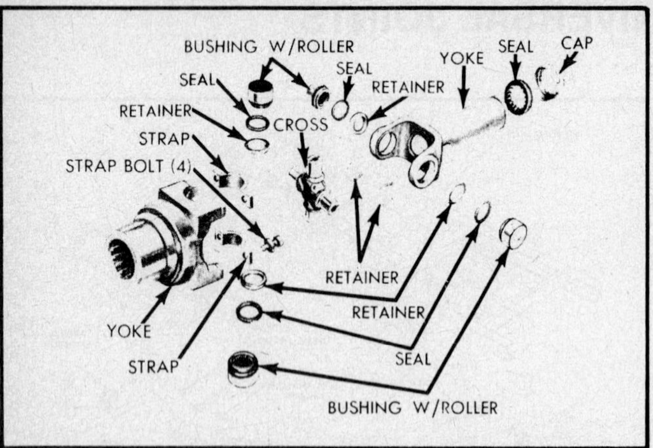

Strap clamp type universal joint

5. On installation, press the new bushings in just far enough to install the retainer.

STRAP CLAMP TYPE (REAR AXLE YOKE)

Unbolt strap bolts and remove straps, bushings, seals and washer retainers. Install new components as required. When assembling, grease bearings. Install with grease fitting parallel to other fittings in drive train. Tighten strap bolts to 20 ft. lbs. torque.

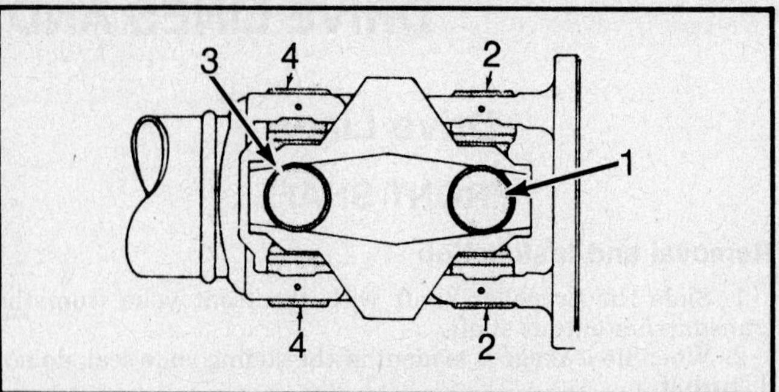

Constant velocity joint bearing cup removal sequence

CONSTANT VELOCITY U-JOINT

Removal and Installation

This is the double universal joint used in the front driveshaft on four-wheel drive models. These are disassembled in the same way as the snap-ring type U-joint. Original equipment U-joints are held together by plastic retainers which shear when pressed out. The bearing cups in the center part of the joint should be pressed out before those in the yoke. Original equipment constant velocity joints cannot be reassembled. Replacement part kits have bearing cups with grooves for retaining rings.

FRONT DRIVE AXLE

For overhaul procedures refer to the Unit Overhaul Section.

Axle Housing

Removal and Installation

EXCEPT DAKOTA

1. Block the brake pedal in the up position. Raise and support the vehicle safely.
2. Disconnect the drive shaft at the drive pinion yoke.
3. Disconnect the drag link at the steering knuckle (left side only).
4. Disconnect the flexible hydraulic brake line at the frame crossmember. Plug the lines at the fittings.
5. Disconnect the shock absorbers at the lower mounts. Disconnect the sway bar link from the spring clip plate.
6. Disconnect the vacuum lines and wiring.
7. Remove the nuts and washers from the U-bolt spring clips. Remove the axle assembly from the vehicle.
8. Reverse the procedure to install. Tighten the U-bolt nuts to 110 ft. lbs. (149 Nm). Tighten the shock absorber lower mount nuts to 55 ft. lbs. (75 Nm).

DAKOTA

1. Raise the vehicle and support it safely. Remove the skid plate.
2. Remove the C/V driveshafts.
3. Remove the propeller shaft from the transfer case.
4. Disconnect the vacuum lines and the wiring.
5. Support the drive axle while removing the attaching bolts.
6. Lower the unit and removing it from the vehicle.
7. Reverse the procedure for installation.

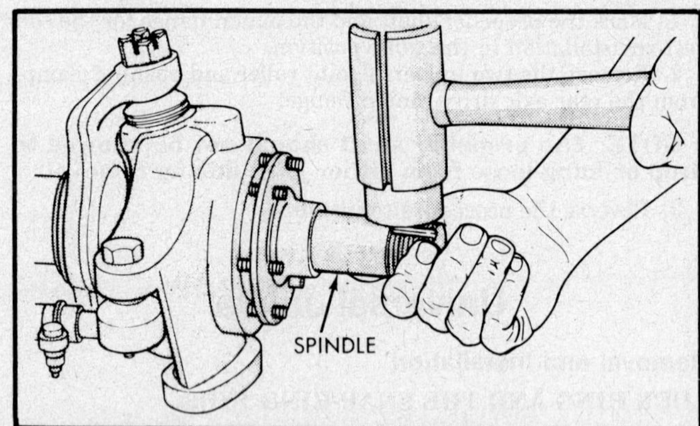

Removing spindle from steering knuckle

Locking Hubs

Removal and Installation

1. Turn the switch knob to the engage position.
2. Apply pressure to the face of the shift knob and remove the three screws nearest to the flange.
3. With an outward pull, remove the shift knob from the mounting base.
4. Remove the snap-ring from the axle shaft.
5. Remove the capscrews and lockwashers from the mounting base flange.
6. Seperate and remove the locking hub from the rotor hub.
7. Reverse the procedure for installation. Tighten the capscrews to 30–40 ft. lbs. (41–54 Nm).

Axle Shaft

MODEL 44FBJ (W/O LOCKING HUBS)

Removal and Installation

1. Remove wheel cover. Remove cotter key and loosen outer axle shaft nut.
2. Raise vehicle and support safely. Remove wheel and tire assembly.

Removing or installing spindle and splash shield

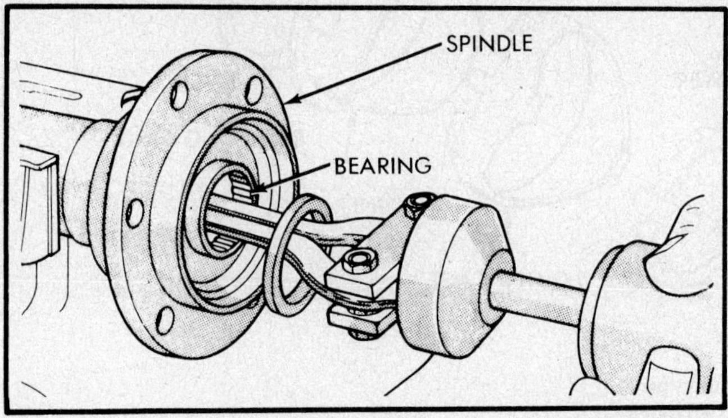

Removing needle bearing from the spindle assembly

3. Remove caliper retainer and anti-rattle spring assemblies. Remove caliper from disc by sliding out and away from disc. Hang caliper out of the way. Remove inboard shoe.

NOTE: Do not allow caliper to hang or be supported by hydraulic brake hose. Support the brake caliper using wire or other suitable device.

4. Remove outer axle shaft nut and washer.
5. Through hole in rotor assembly, remove retainer bolts. Position Puller Tool over wheel studs and install wheel nuts. Tighten main screw of tool to remove hub, rotor, bearings, retainer and outer seal as an assembly.
6. Remove wheel nuts and Puller from hub and rotor assembly.
7. Remove the brake caliper adapter from the knuckle.
8. Position a pry bar behind the inner axle shaft yoke and push the bearings out of the knuckle.
9. Remove the O-ring from the knuckle (if so equipped) and discard.
10. Carefully remove the axle shaft assembly. Remove seal and slinger from shaft.
11. Reverse the procedure for installation. Install brake dust shield (if removed), tighten mounting bolts to 160 inch lbs. (18 Nm).

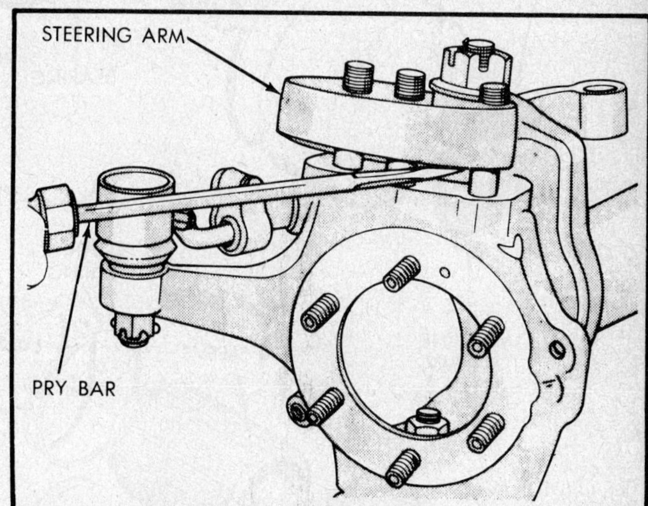

Removing steering knuckle arm

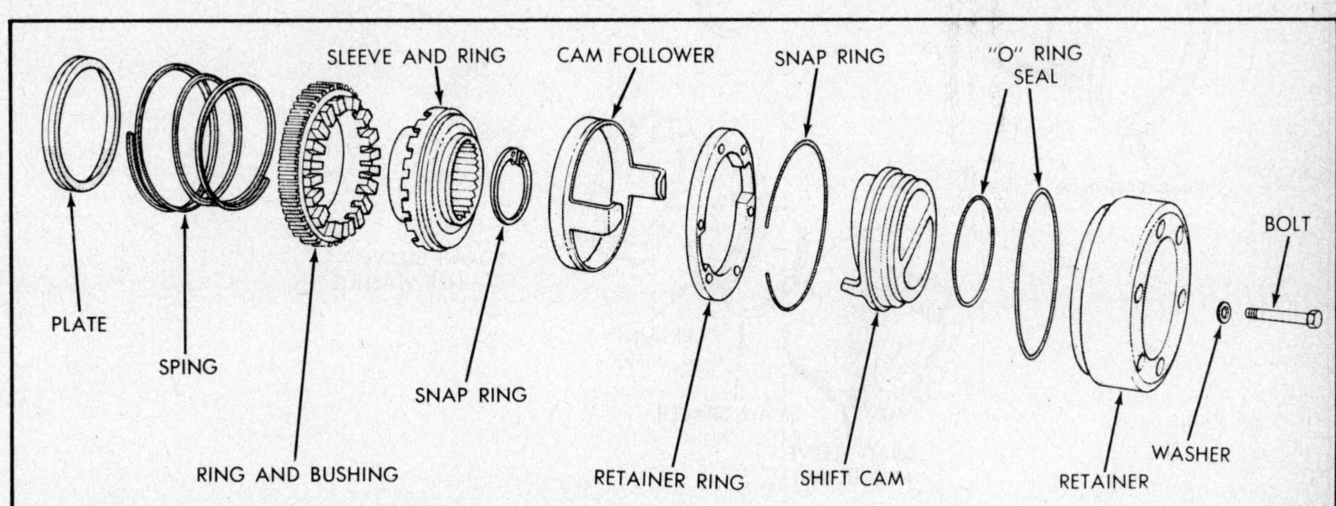

Exploded view of locking hub assembly

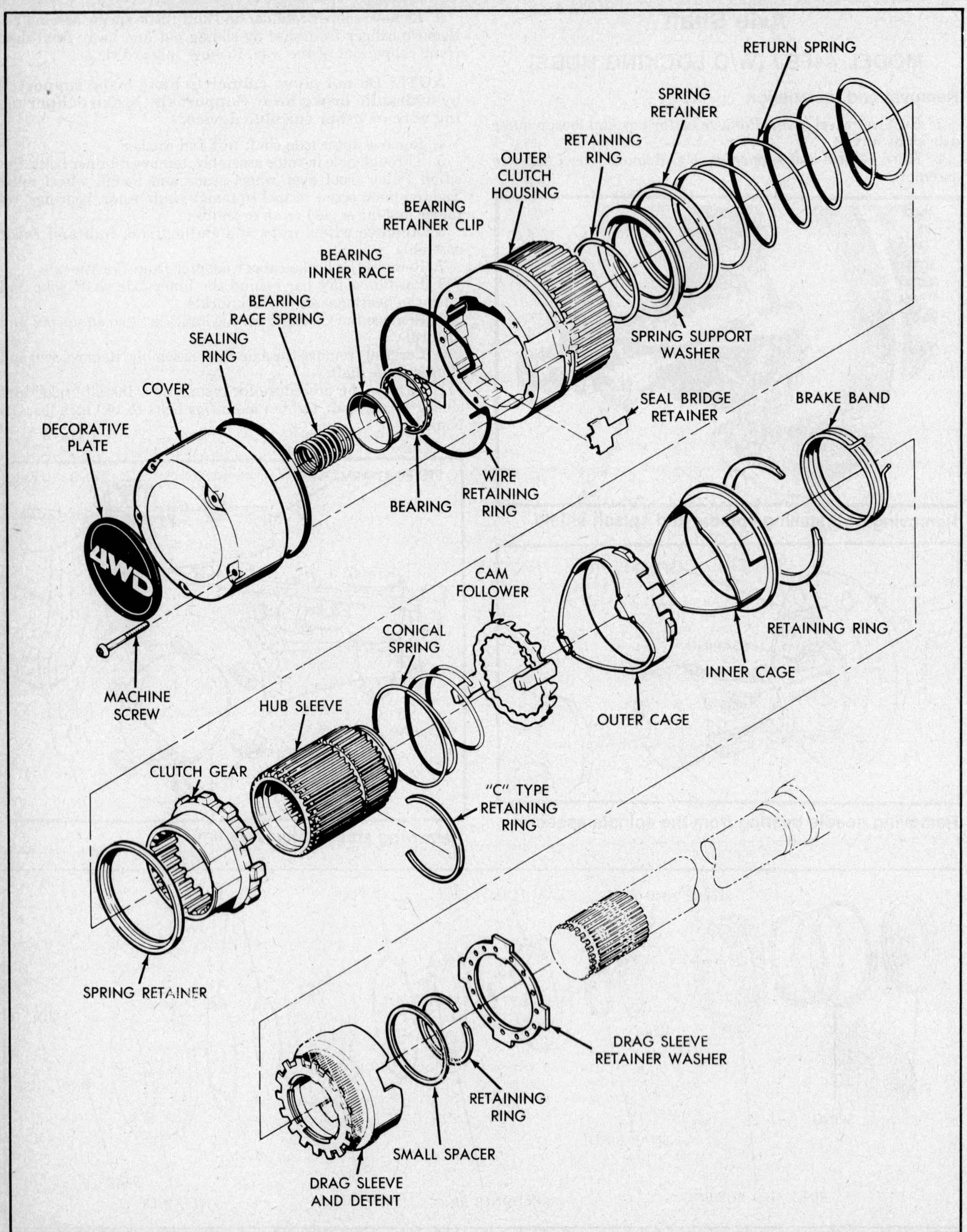
RETURN SPRING
SPRING RETAINER
RETAINING RING
OUTER CLUTCH HOUSING
BEARING RETAINER CLIP
BEARING INNER RACE
BEARING RACE SPRING
SEALING RING
COVER
DECORATIVE PLATE
4WD
SPRING SUPPORT WASHER
SEAL BRIDGE RETAINER
BRAKE BAND
WIRE RETAINING RING
BEARING
CAM FOLLOWER
CONICAL SPRING
RETAINING RING
INNER CAGE
OUTER CAGE
MACHINE SCREW
HUB SLEEVE
CLUTCH GEAR
"C" TYPE RETAINING RING
SPRING RETAINER
DRAG SLEEVE RETAINER WASHER
RETAINING RING
SMALL SPACER
DRAG SLEEVE AND DETENT

Exploded view of Automatic locking hub

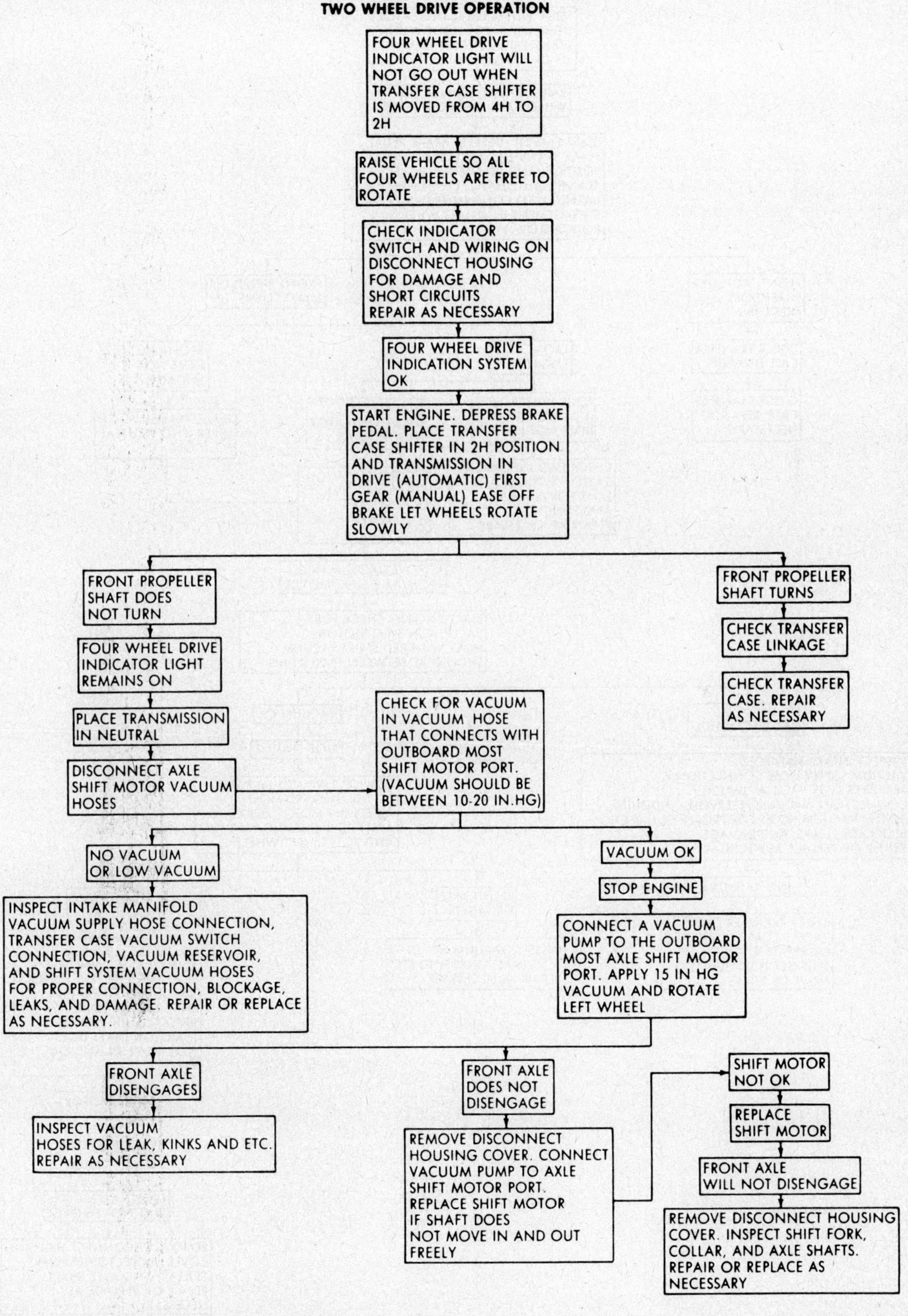
DISCONNECT AXLE DIAGNOSIS CHART
TWO WHEEL DRIVE OPERATION
FOUR WHEEL DRIVE INDICATOR LIGHT WILL NOT GO OUT WHEN TRANSFER CASE SHIFTER IS MOVED FROM 4H TO 2H
RAISE VEHICLE SO ALL FOUR WHEELS ARE FREE TO ROTATE
CHECK INDICATOR SWITCH AND WIRING ON DISCONNECT HOUSING FOR DAMAGE AND SHORT CIRCUITS REPAIR AS NECESSARY
FOUR WHEEL DRIVE INDICATION SYSTEM OK
START ENGINE. DEPRESS BRAKE PEDAL. PLACE TRANSFER CASE SHIFTER IN 2H POSITION AND TRANSMISSION IN DRIVE (AUTOMATIC) FIRST GEAR (MANUAL) EASE OFF BRAKE LET WHEELS ROTATE SLOWLY
FRONT PROPELLER SHAFT DOES NOT TURN
FOUR WHEEL DRIVE INDICATOR LIGHT REMAINS ON
PLACE TRANSMISSION IN NEUTRAL
DISCONNECT AXLE SHIFT MOTOR VACUUM HOSES
CHECK FOR VACUUM IN VACUUM HOSE THAT CONNECTS WITH OUTBOARD MOST SHIFT MOTOR PORT. (VACUUM SHOULD BE BETWEEN 10-20 IN.HG)
FRONT PROPELLER SHAFT TURNS
CHECK TRANSFER CASE LINKAGE
CHECK TRANSFER CASE. REPAIR AS NECESSARY
NO VACUUM OR LOW VACUUM
INSPECT INTAKE MANIFOLD VACUUM SUPPLY HOSE CONNECTION, TRANSFER CASE VACUUM SWITCH CONNECTION, VACUUM RESERVOIR, AND SHIFT SYSTEM VACUUM HOSES FOR PROPER CONNECTION, BLOCKAGE, LEAKS, AND DAMAGE. REPAIR OR REPLACE AS NECESSARY.
VACUUM OK
STOP ENGINE
CONNECT A VACUUM PUMP TO THE OUTBOARD MOST AXLE SHIFT MOTOR PORT. APPLY 15 IN HG VACUUM AND ROTATE LEFT WHEEL
FRONT AXLE DISENGAGES
INSPECT VACUUM HOSES FOR LEAK, KINKS AND ETC. REPAIR AS NECESSARY
FRONT AXLE DOES NOT DISENGAGE
REMOVE DISCONNECT HOUSING COVER. CONNECT VACUUM PUMP TO AXLE SHIFT MOTOR PORT. REPLACE SHIFT MOTOR IF SHAFT DOES NOT MOVE IN AND OUT FREELY
SHIFT MOTOR NOT OK
REPLACE SHIFT MOTOR
FRONT AXLE WILL NOT DISENGAGE
REMOVE DISCONNECT HOUSING COVER. INSPECT SHIFT FORK, COLLAR, AND AXLE SHAFTS. REPAIR OR REPLACE AS NECESSARY

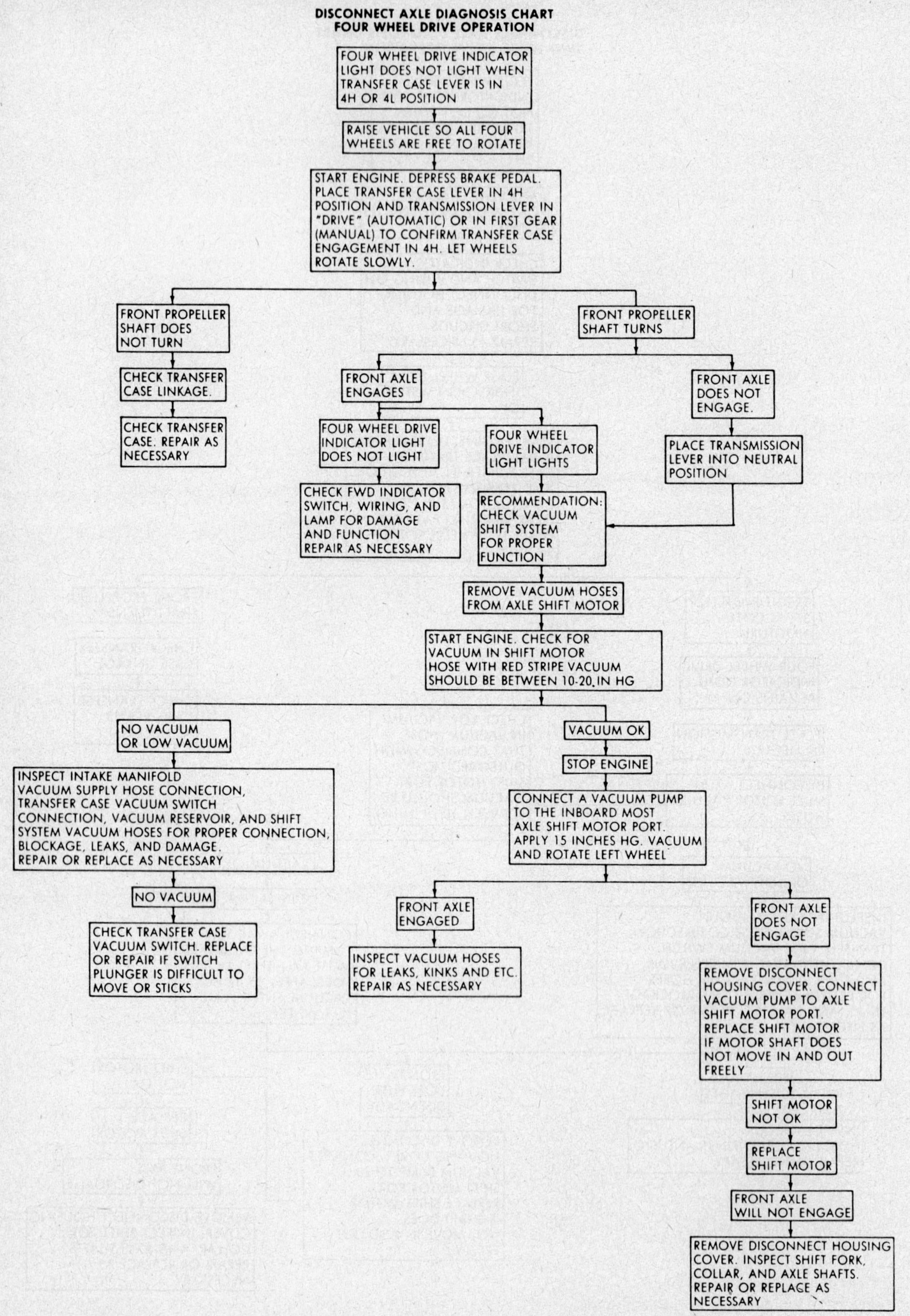
DISCONNECT AXLE DIAGNOSIS CHART
FOUR WHEEL DRIVE OPERATION
FOUR WHEEL DRIVE INDICATOR LIGHT DOES NOT LIGHT WHEN TRANSFER CASE LEVER IS IN 4H OR 4L POSITION
RAISE VEHICLE SO ALL FOUR WHEELS ARE FREE TO ROTATE
START ENGINE. DEPRESS BRAKE PEDAL. PLACE TRANSFER CASE LEVER IN 4H POSITION AND TRANSMISSION LEVER IN "DRIVE" (AUTOMATIC) OR IN FIRST GEAR (MANUAL) TO CONFIRM TRANSFER CASE ENGAGEMENT IN 4H. LET WHEELS ROTATE SLOWLY.
FRONT PROPELLER SHAFT DOES NOT TURN
CHECK TRANSFER CASE LINKAGE.
CHECK TRANSFER CASE. REPAIR AS NECESSARY
FRONT PROPELLER SHAFT TURNS
FRONT AXLE ENGAGES
FOUR WHEEL DRIVE INDICATOR LIGHT DOES NOT LIGHT
CHECK FWD INDICATOR SWITCH, WIRING, AND LAMP FOR DAMAGE AND FUNCTION REPAIR AS NECESSARY
FOUR WHEEL DRIVE INDICATOR LIGHT LIGHTS
RECOMMENDATION: CHECK VACUUM SHIFT SYSTEM FOR PROPER FUNCTION
FRONT AXLE DOES NOT ENGAGE.
PLACE TRANSMISSION LEVER INTO NEUTRAL POSITION
REMOVE VACUUM HOSES FROM AXLE SHIFT MOTOR
START ENGINE. CHECK FOR VACUUM IN SHIFT MOTOR HOSE WITH RED STRIPE VACUUM SHOULD BE BETWEEN 10-20 IN HG
NO VACUUM OR LOW VACUUM
INSPECT INTAKE MANIFOLD VACUUM SUPPLY HOSE CONNECTION, TRANSFER CASE VACUUM SWITCH CONNECTION, VACUUM RESERVOIR, AND SHIFT SYSTEM VACUUM HOSES FOR PROPER CONNECTION, BLOCKAGE, LEAKS, AND DAMAGE. REPAIR OR REPLACE AS NECESSARY
NO VACUUM
CHECK TRANSFER CASE VACUUM SWITCH. REPLACE OR REPAIR IF SWITCH PLUNGER IS DIFFICULT TO MOVE OR STICKS
VACUUM OK
STOP ENGINE
CONNECT A VACUUM PUMP TO THE INBOARD MOST AXLE SHIFT MOTOR PORT. APPLY 15 INCHES HG. VACUUM AND ROTATE LEFT WHEEL
FRONT AXLE ENGAGED
INSPECT VACUUM HOSES FOR LEAKS, KINKS AND ETC. REPAIR AS NECESSARY
FRONT AXLE DOES NOT ENGAGE
REMOVE DISCONNECT HOUSING COVER. CONNECT VACUUM PUMP TO AXLE SHIFT MOTOR PORT. REPLACE SHIFT MOTOR IF MOTOR SHAFT DOES NOT MOVE IN AND OUT FREELY
SHIFT MOTOR NOT OK
REPLACE SHIFT MOTOR
FRONT AXLE WILL NOT ENGAGE
REMOVE DISCONNECT HOUSING COVER. INSPECT SHIFT FORK, COLLAR, AND AXLE SHAFTS. REPAIR OR REPLACE AS NECESSARY

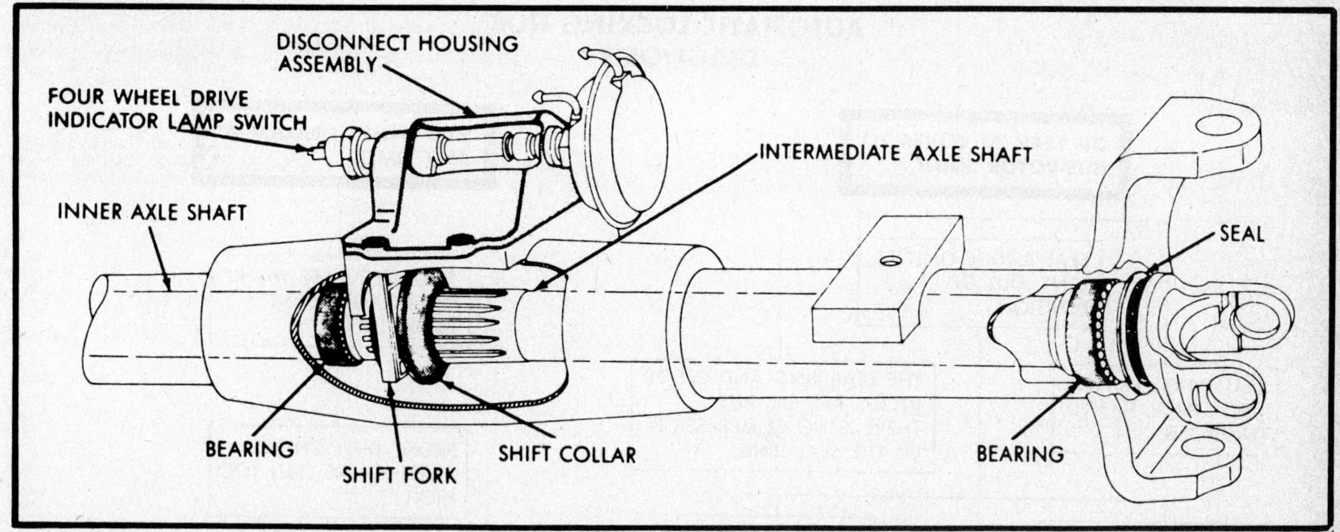

Disconnect Axle Housing Assembly

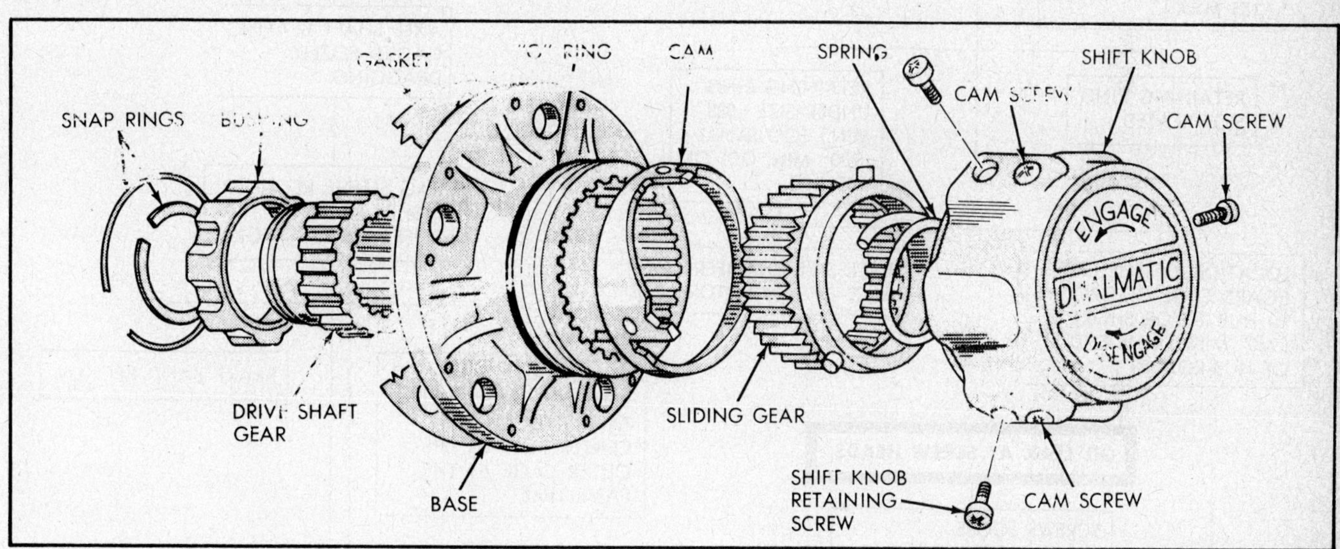

Exploded view of Dualmatic locking hubs

MODEL 44FBJ (WITH LOCKING HUBS) AND MODEL 44–8FD (RIGHT SIDE)

Removal and Installation

1. Remove locking hub assembly.
2. Raise vehicle and support safely. Remove wheel and tire assembly.
3. Remove caliper retainer and anti-rattle spring assemblies. Remove caliper from disc by sliding out and away from disc. Hang caliper out of the way. Remove inboard shoe.

NOTE: Do not allow caliper to hang or be supported by hydraulic brake hose. Support the brake caliper using a length of wire or other suitable device.

4. Remove outer axle shaft lock nut washer and nut.
5. Remove rotor and bearing assembly.
6. Remove six nuts which fasten splash shield and spindle to knuckle.
7. Remove splash shield and spindle.
8. Remove the brake caliper adaptor from the knuckle.
9. Carefully remove the axle shaft assembly. Remove seal and stone shield (if equipped) from shaft.
10. Installation is the reverse of the removal procedure.

MODEL 44–8FD (LEFT SIDE)

Removal and Installation

1. Raise the vehicle and support it safely. Remove the tire and wheel assembly.
2. Remove the caliper from the rotor and support it out of the way.
3. Remove the rotor and the inboard brake pad.
4. Remove the splash shield and the spindle.
5. Disconnect the vacuum lines and the switch wiring.
6. Remove the housing cover and the shield.
7. Remove the intermediate axle shaft and remove the bearing from it.
8. Push the inner axle shaft toward the center of the vehicle and remove the C-lock from the recessed groove on the shaft and remove the shaft.
9. Reverse the procedure for installation.

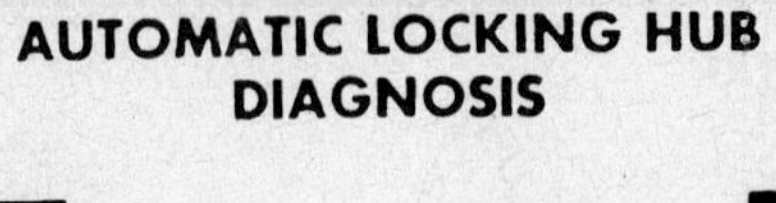

AUTOMATIC LOCKING HUB DIAGNOSIS

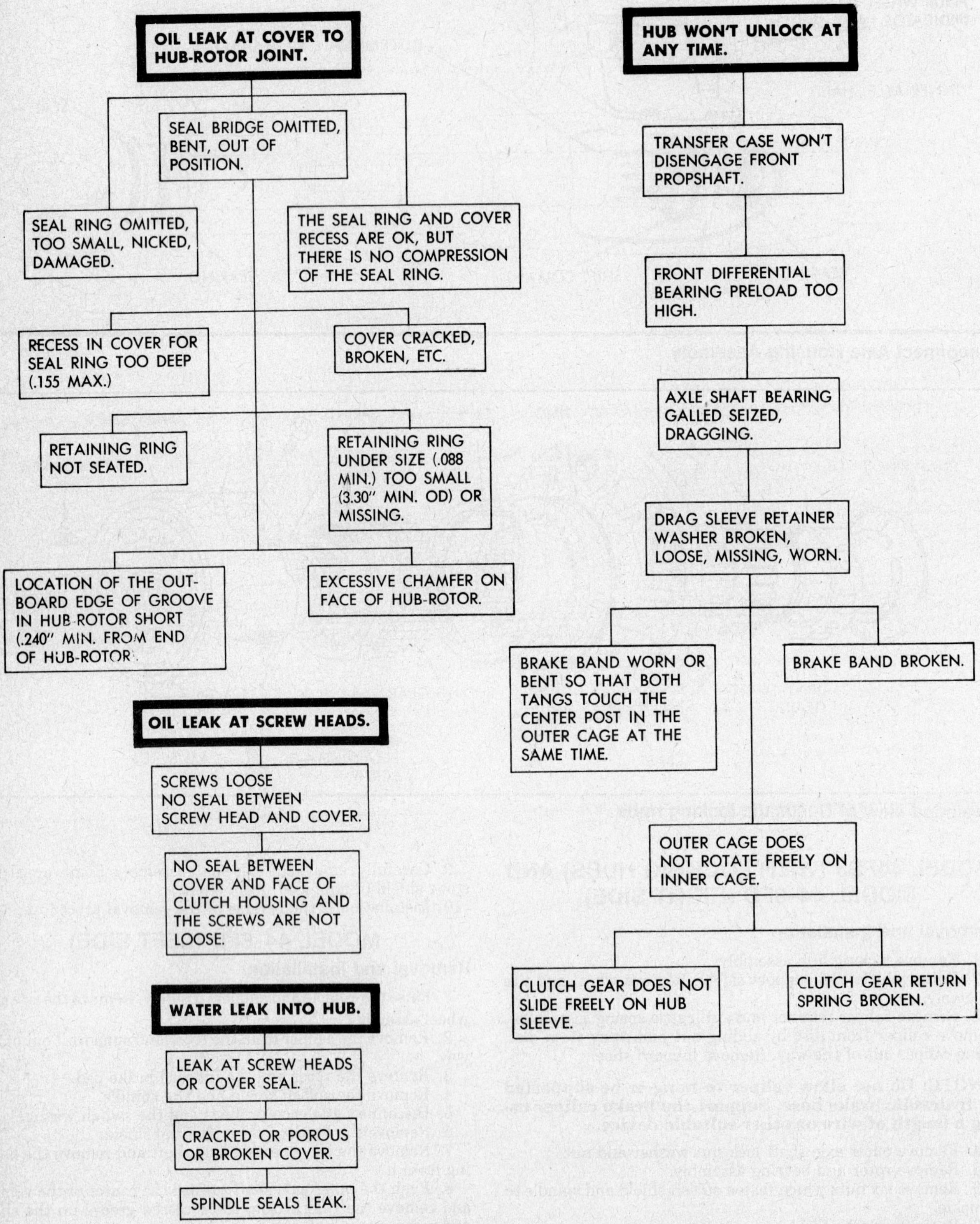

OIL LEAK AT COVER TO HUB-ROTOR JOINT.

- SEAL BRIDGE OMITTED, BENT, OUT OF POSITION.
- SEAL RING OMITTED, TOO SMALL, NICKED, DAMAGED.
- THE SEAL RING AND COVER RECESS ARE OK, BUT THERE IS NO COMPRESSION OF THE SEAL RING.
  - RECESS IN COVER FOR SEAL RING TOO DEEP (.155 MAX.)
  - COVER CRACKED, BROKEN, ETC.
  - RETAINING RING NOT SEATED.
  - RETAINING RING UNDER SIZE (.088 MIN.) TOO SMALL (3.30" MIN. OD) OR MISSING.
  - LOCATION OF THE OUT-BOARD EDGE OF GROOVE IN HUB-ROTOR SHORT (.240" MIN. FROM END OF HUB-ROTOR).
  - EXCESSIVE CHAMFER ON FACE OF HUB-ROTOR.

OIL LEAK AT SCREW HEADS.

- SCREWS LOOSE NO SEAL BETWEEN SCREW HEAD AND COVER.
- NO SEAL BETWEEN COVER AND FACE OF CLUTCH HOUSING AND THE SCREWS ARE NOT LOOSE.

WATER LEAK INTO HUB.

- LEAK AT SCREW HEADS OR COVER SEAL.
- CRACKED OR POROUS OR BROKEN COVER.
- SPINDLE SEALS LEAK.

HUB WON'T UNLOCK AT ANY TIME.

- TRANSFER CASE WON'T DISENGAGE FRONT PROPSHAFT.
- FRONT DIFFERENTIAL BEARING PRELOAD TOO HIGH.
- AXLE SHAFT BEARING GALLED SEIZED, DRAGGING.
- DRAG SLEEVE RETAINER WASHER BROKEN, LOOSE, MISSING, WORN.
- BRAKE BAND WORN OR BENT SO THAT BOTH TANGS TOUCH THE CENTER POST IN THE OUTER CAGE AT THE SAME TIME.
- BRAKE BAND BROKEN.
- OUTER CAGE DOES NOT ROTATE FREELY ON INNER CAGE.
  - CLUTCH GEAR DOES NOT SLIDE FREELY ON HUB SLEEVE.
  - CLUTCH GEAR RETURN SPRING BROKEN.

AUTOMATIC LOCKING HUB DIAGNOSIS

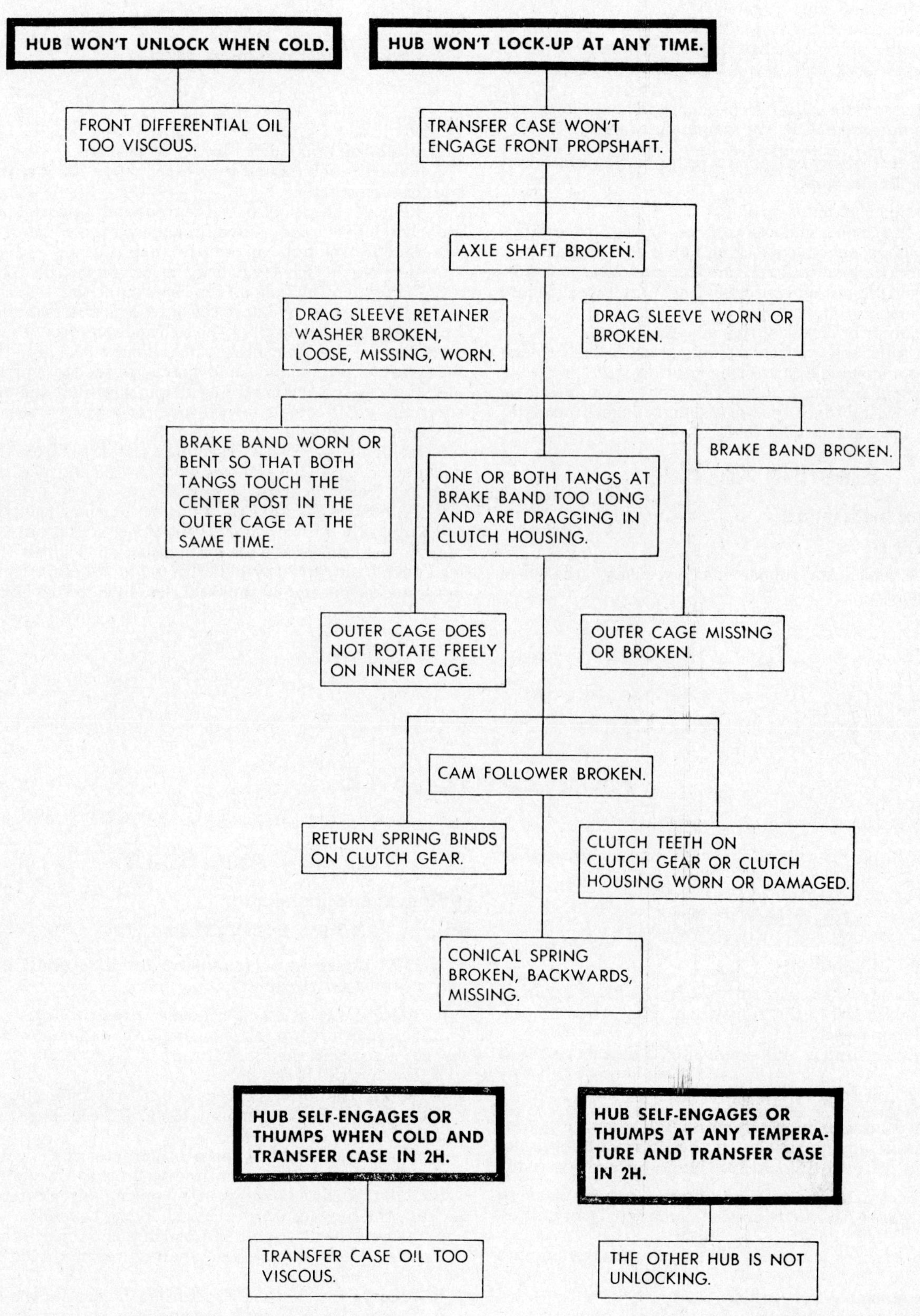

MODEL 60

Removal and Installation

1. Block brake pedal in the up position.
2. Raise vehicle and support safely.
3. Remove wheel and tire assembly.
4. Remove allen screw holding caliper to adapter.
5. Tap adapter lock and spring from between caliper and adapter.
6. Carefully separate caliper from adapter. Hang caliper out of the way. Inner brake shoe will remain on adapter.

NOTE: Do not allow caliper to hang or be supported by hydraulic brake hose.

7. Remove hub cap and snap ring.
8. Remove flange nuts and lockwashers. Remove drive flange and discard gasket, or remove locking hub if so equipped.
9. Straighten tang on lock ring and remove outer lock nut, lock ring, inner lock nut and outer bearing. Carefully slide hub and rotor assembly from spindle.
10. Remove inner brake shoe from adapter.
11. Remove nuts and washers holding brake splash shield, brake adapter and spindle to steering knuckle.
12. Remove spindle from knuckle. Slide inner and outer axle shaft complete with bronze spacer, seal and slinger from axle.
13. Reverse the procedure for installation.

Steering Knuckle

Removal and Installation

MODEL 44–8FD

1. Raise the vehicle and support it safely. Remove the wheel and tire assembly.
2. Remove the caliper and support it out of the way.
3. Remove the inboard brake pad and the rotor.
4. Remove the caliper adapter from the knuckle.
5. Remove the six torque nuts from the spindle to steering knuckle attaching bolts.
6. Remove the splash shield. Hit the spindle lightly to break it free from the steering knuckle.
7. Reverse the procedure to install.

MODEL 60

1. Block the brake pedal in the up position.
2. Raise the vehicle and wupport it safely. Remove the wheel and tire assembly.
3. Remove the caliper from the rotor and support it out of the way. The inner brake pad will remain on the adapter.
4. Remove the hub cap and the snap ring.
5. Remove the drive flange or the locking hub if so equipped.
6. Straighten the tang on the lock ring. Using tool DD-1241-JD, or its equivalent, remove the outer lock nut, lock ring, inner lock and outer bearing. Slide the hub and rotor from the spindle.
7. Remove the inner brake shoe. Remove the nuts that hold the splash shield, adapter and spindle to the steering knuckle.
8. Remove the spindle from the knuckle. Slide the inner and outer axle shaft complete with the bronze spacer, seal and the slinger from the axle.
9. Using tool C-3894-A, disconnect the tie rod from the steering knuckle. On the left side use tool C-4150 and disconnect the drag link from the knuckle arm.
10. To remove the knuckle from the housing, swing it out at the bottom then lift up and off the upper socket pin.
11. Reverse the procedure for installation. Tighten the steering knuckle nuts to 70 to 90 ft. lbs. (95 to 122 Nm). Tighten the upper socket pin to 500 to 600 ft. lbs. (668 to 813 Nm).

REAR DRIVE AXLE

See the Unit Repair Section for overhaul procedures for rear axles.

Axle Housing

Removal and Installation

1. Raise vehicle and support safely at front of rear springs.
2. Block brake pedal in the up position.
3. Remove rear wheels.
4. Disconnect hydraulic brake hose at "T" fitting or at each wheel.
5. Disconnect parking brake cable.

NOTE: To insure proper drive line balance when reassembling, make scribe marks on the driveshaft universal joint and differential pinion flange before removal.

6. Disconnect driveshaft at rear universal joint bearing clamps and secure with wire to prevent damage to front universal joint.
7. Disconnect shock absorbers and remove rear spring nuts and U-bolts.
8. Remove assembly from vehicle.
9. To install, reverse the removal procedure.

Axle Shaft

Removal and Installation

$8^1/_4$, $8^3/_8$ AND $9^1/_4$ INCH AXLES

NOTE: There is no provision for axle shaft end-play adjustment on these axles.

1. Raise the vehicle and remove the rear wheels.
2. Clean all dirt from the housing cover and remove the housing cover to drain the lubricant.
3. Remove the brake drum.
4. Rotate the differential case until the differential pinion shaft lockscrew can be removed. Remove the lockscrew and pinion shaft.
5. Push the axle shafts toward the center of the vehicle and remove the C-locks from the grooves on the axle shafts.
6. Pull the axle shafts from the housing, being careful not to damage the bearing which remains in the housing.
7. Inspect the axle shaft and bearings and replace any doubtful parts. Whenever the axle shaft is replaced, the bearings should also be replaced.
8. Remove the axle shaft seal from the bore in the housing.
9. Remove the axle shaft bearing from the housing.

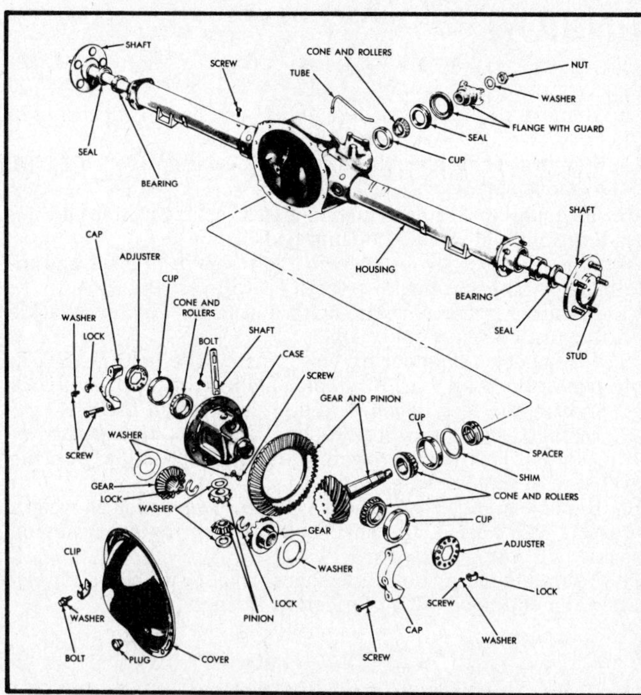

8$^3/_8$ inch rear axle, the 9¼ inch is similar

10. Check the bearing shoulder in the axle housing for imperfections and should be corrected.
11. Clean the axle shaft bearing cavity.
12. Install the axle shaft bearing seal. It should be seated beyond the end of the flange face.
14. Insert the axle shaft, making sure that the splines do not damage the seal. Be sure that the splines are properly engaged with the differential side gear splines.
15. Install the C-locks in the grooves on the axle shafts. Pull the shafts outward so that the C-locks seat in the counterbore of the differential side gears.
16. Install the differential pinion shaft through the case and pinions. Install the lockscrew and secure it in position.
17. Install the cover and a new gasket.

NOTE: Replacement gaskets may not be available for differential covers. In this case, the use of a gel type nonsticking sealant is recommended.

Be sure that the rear axle ratio identification tag is replaced under one of the cover bolts. Refill the axle with the specified lubricant to $^1/_2$ in. below the filler plug hole. Do not overfill.

18. Install the brake drum and wheel.
19. Lower the vehicle to the ground and test the operation of the brakes.

60, 60M AND 70 AXLES

1. Raise the vehicle and support it safely. Remove the wheel and tire assembly.
2. Remove the axle shaft flange nuts and lockwashers.
3. Tap the axle shafts in the center of the flange with a hammer to free the dowels. Remove the tapered dowels and the axle shafts.
4. Reverse the procedure for installation.

Pinion Seal

Removal and Installation

1. Raise the vehicle and support it safely. Make scribe marks on the drive shaft and the drive pinion flange for proper installation. Remove the drive shaft.
2. Remove the rear wheel and brake drums to prevent any drag.
3. Using an inch lbs. torque wrench, measure the pinion bearing preload by rotating the pinion with the handle of the wrench floating. Read the torque while the handle of the wrench is moving through several complete revolutions.

NOTE: The preload measurement is very important for reassembling.

4. Fold the companion flange and remove the drive pinion nut and Belleville washer.
5. Remove the companion flange, using tool C-452, or its equivalent. Lower the rear of the vehicle to prevent fluid loss.
6. Using a seal remover tool, remove the seal from the carrier and clean the seat.
7. The outside diameter of the seal is precoated with a special sealer so no sealing compound is required for installing. The seal is properly installed when the flange contacts the housing flange face.
8. Install the companion flange and the washer with the convex side out.
9. Tighten the pinion nut to 210 ft. lbs. (285 Nm). Rotate the pinion a few revolutions to properly seat the bearing rollers.
10. Using an inch lbs. torque wrench, measure the pinion bearing preload. Continue tightening the nut until the preload is at the original setting.

NOTE: The preload should not be more than 10 inch lbs. (1 Nm) over the original setting.

Differential Carrier

Removal and Installation

1. Raise the vehicle and support it safely. Remove the wheels and the brake drums.
2. Mark the drive shaft and the pinion flange before removal. Remove the drive shaft.
3. Remove the housing cover and drain the lubricant.
4. Turn the differential case to make the pinion lock screw accessible. Remove the lock screw and shaft.
5. Push both axle shafts toward the center of the vehicle and remove the C-locks from the recessed groove of the axle shaft. Remove the axle shafts from the housing.
6. Position a pinch bar between the left side of the axle housing and the differential case flange. Using a prying motion, determine if side play is present. There should be no side play.
7. Mount a dial indicator on the pilot stud and load the stem lightly with plunger at right angles to back face of the drive gear. Turn the drive gear a few complete revolutions and read the dial indicator. The reading should be no more than 0.005 in. (.13 mm).
8. Loosen and remove the pedestal cap bolts and remove the differential case from the carrier and tube assembly.
9. Inspect parts and record all measurements. Reverse the procedure for installation.

Wheel Bearings

For removal and installation procedures, refer to axle shaft removal and installation.

REAR SUSPENSION

Shock absorbers

Removal and Installation

1. Remove the bolts retaining the shock absorber to the frame/bracket and axle/spring housing.

NOTE: On some 4WD models, it will be necessary to remove the lower bracket bolt, loosen the upper bolt and rotate the bracket until the shock absorber clears the upper bolt to remove it.

2. Remove the shock absorber from the vehicle. Remove the necessary brackets and install onto the replacement units, as required.
3. The installation of the shock absorber is the reverse of the removal procedure.

Leaf Spring

Removal and Installation

1. Raise rear of truck until weight is removed from springs, wheels just touching the floor.

NOTE: Truck must be lifted by jack or hoist under frame side rail at crossmember behind the axle, being careful not to bend flange of side rail.

2. Place stands under side frame members as a safety precaution.
3. Remove nuts, lockwashers and U-bolts securing spring to axle.
4. Remove spring shackle bolts, shackle and spring front bolt, then remove spring.
5. To install, position spring on axle so spring center bolt enters locating hole in axle housing pad.
6. Line up spring front eye with bolt hole in bracket and install spring bolt and nut.
7. Install the rear shackle, bolts and nuts. Tighten shackle bolt nut until slack is taken up.
8. On headless type spring bolts, install the bolts with lock bolt groove lined up with lock bolt hole in bracket. Install lock bolt and tighten lock bolt nut. Install lubrication fittings.
9. Install U-bolts, new lockwashers and nuts, tightening until nuts push lockwashers against axle. Align auxiliary spring parallel with main spring.
10. Remove stands from under vehicle, lower truck so weight is resting on wheels. Tighten U-bolt nuts, spring eye nuts and shackle bolt nuts.
11. Lubricate spring bolts and shackle bolts with chassis lubricant when equipped with lubrication fittings.

Auxiliary Springs

For removal and installation procedures refer to the leaf spring removal and installation procedure. They are used on the following models, D150, D250, D350, W250 and W350.

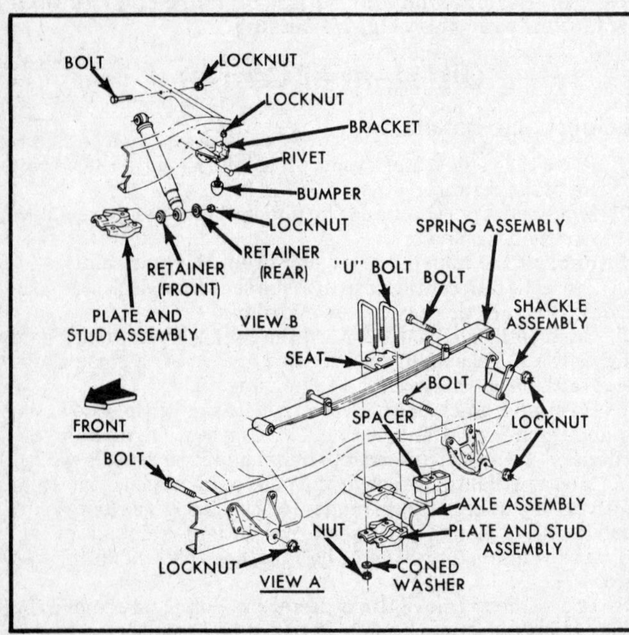

Rear suspension Ramcharger and Trail Duster

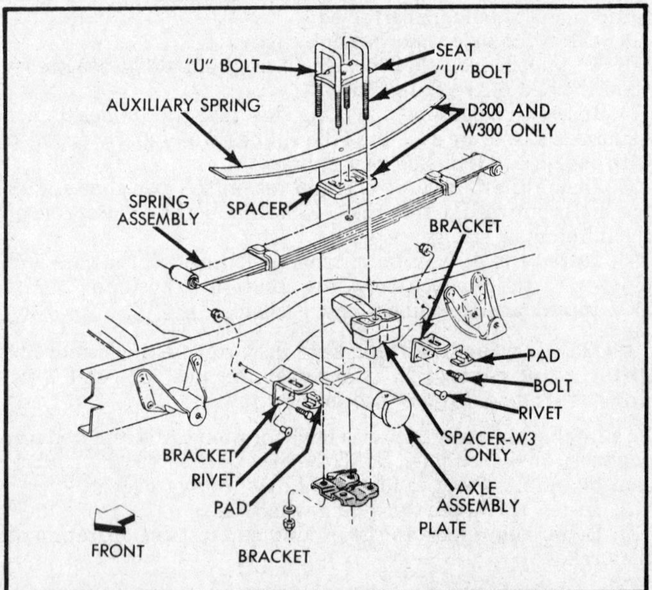

Rear suspension—W200, W300 and D300 shown

Ford 3

INDEX

BEFORE SERVICING, SEE THE SAFETY NOTICE AT THE FRONT OF THE BOOK

MODEL IDENTIFICATION
Ford Trucks

Year	Model Designation	Model Name
1983	Bronco Wagon	Bronco
	Bronco XLT	Bronco
	Bronco XLS	Bronco
	Club Wagon E150	Club Wagon
	Club Wagon E250	Club Wagon
	Super Wagon S250	Club Wagon
	Super Wagon S350	Club Wagon
	E100 Cargo Van	Econoline E100
	E100 Window Van	Econoline E100
	E100 Display Van	Econoline E100
	E150 Cargo Van	Econoline E150
	E150 Window Van	Econoline E150
	E150 Display Van	Econoline E150
	E150 Super Cargo Van	Econoline E150
	E150 Super Window Van	Econoline E150
	E150 Super Display Van	Econoline E150
	E250 Cargo Van	Econoline E250
	E250 Window Van	Econoline E250
	E250 Display Van	Econoline E250
	E250 Super Cargo Van	Econoline E250
	E250 Super Window Van	Econoline E250
	E250 Super Display Van	Econoline E250
	E350 Cargo Van	Econoline E350
	E350 Window Van	Econoline E350
	E350 Display Van	Econoline E350
	E350 Super Cargo Van	Econoline E350
	E350 Super Window Van	Econoline E350
	E350 Super Display Van	Econoline E350
	E350 Cutaway Van	Econoline E350
	E350 Parcel Delivery Van	Econoline E350
	F100 Flareside 6½ ft.	F100 Custom
	F100 Styleside 6¾ ft.	F100 Custom
	F100 Styleside 8 ft.	F100 Custom
	F150 Flareside 6¾ ft.	F150 Custom
	F150 Styleside 6¾ ft.	F150 Custom
	F150 Styleside 8 ft.	F150 Custom
	F150 Styleside Supercab	F150 Custom
	F250 Chassis & Cab	F250 Custom
	F250 Styleside 8 ft.	F250 Custom
	F250 Styleside Supercab	F250 Custom
	F350 Chassis & Cab	F350 Custom
	F350 Styleside 8 ft.	F350 Custom
	F350 Styleside Crew Cab	F350 Custom
1984	Bronco Wagon	Bronco
	Bronco XLT	Bronco

MODEL IDENTIFICATION
Ford Trucks

Year	Model Designation	Model Name
1984	Bronco II Wagon	Bronco II
	Bronco II XLT	Bronco II
	Bronco II XLS	Bronco II
	Bronco II Eddie Bauer	Bronco II
	Club Wagon E150	Club Wagon
	Club Wagon E250	Club Wagon
	Super Wagon S250	Club Wagon
	Super Wagon S350	Club Wagon
	E150 Cargo Van	Econoline E150
	E150 Window Van	Econoline E150
	E150 Display Van	Econoline E150
	E150 Super Cargo Van	Econoline E150
	E150 Super Window Van	Econoline E150
	E150 Super Display Van	Econoline E150
	E250 Cargo Van	Econoline E250
	E250 Window Van	Econoline E250
	E250 Display Van	Econoline E250
	E250 Super Cargo Van	Econoline E250
	E250 Super Window Van	Econoline E250
	E350 Super Display Van	Econoline E350
	E350 Cargo Van	Econoline E350
	E350 Window Van	Econoline E350
	E350 Display Van	Econoline E350
	E350 Super Cargo Van	Econoline E350
	E350 Super Window Van	Econoline E350
	E350 Super Display Van	Econoline E350
	E350 Cutaway Van	Econoline E350
	E350 Parcel Delivery Van	Econoline E350
	F150 Flareside 6½ ft.	F150 Custom
	F150 Styleside 6½ ft.	F150 Custom
	F150 Styleside 8 ft.	F150 Custom
	F150 Styleside Supercab 6½ ft.	F150 Custom
	F150 Styleside Supercab 8 ft.	F150 Custom
	F250 Chassis & Cab	F250 Custom
	F250 Styleside 8 ft.	F250 Custom
	F250 Styleside Supercab	F250 Custom
	F350 Chassis & Cab	F350 Custom
	F350 Styleside 8 ft.	F350 Custom
	F350 Styleside Crew Cab	F350 Custom
1985	Bronco Wagon	Bronco
	Bronco XLT	Bronco
	Bronco Eddie Bauer	Bronco
	Bronco II Wagon	Bronco II
	Bronco II XLT	Bronco II
	Bronco II XLS	Bronco II

MODEL IDENTIFICATION
Ford Trucks

Year	Model Designation	Model Name
1985	Bronco II Eddie Bauer	Bronco II
	Club Wagon E150	Club Wagon
	Club Wagon E250	Club Wagon
	Super Wagon S350	Club Wagon
	E150 Cargo Van	Econoline E150
	E150 Window Van	Econoline E150
	E150 Display Van	Econoline E150
	E150 Super Cargo Van	Econoline E150
	E150 Super Window Van	Econoline E150
	E250 Cargo Van	Econoline E250
	E250 Window Van	Econoline E250
	E250 Display Van	Econoline E250
	E250 Super Cargo Van	Econoline E250
	E250 Super Window Van	Econoline E250
	E350 Cargo Van	Econoline E350
	E350 Window Van	Econoline E350
	E350 Display Van	Econoline E350
	E350 Super Cargo Van	Econoline E350
	E350 Super Window Van	Econoline E350
	E350 Cutaway Van	Econoline E350
	F150 Flareside 6½ ft.	F150 Custom
	F150 Styleside 6½ ft.	F150 Custom
	F150 Styleside 8 ft.	F150 Custom
	F150 Styleside Supercab 6½ ft.	F150 Custom
	F150 Styleside Supercab 8 ft.	F150 Custom
	F250 Chassis & Cab	F250 Custom
	F250 Styleside 8 ft.	F250 Custom
	F250 Styleside Supercab	F250 Custom
	F350 Chassis & Cab	F350 Custom
	F350 Styleside 8 ft.	F350 Custom
	F350 Chassis & Cab (161 W.B.)	F350 Custom
	F350 Styleside Crew Cab	F350 Custom
	Ranger Styleside	Ranger
	Ranger Styleside S	Ranger
	Ranger Styleside LB	Ranger
1986	Aerostar Cargo Van	Aerostar
	Aerostar Wagon	Aerostar
	Aerostar Window Van	Aerostar
	Bronco Wagon	Bronco
	Bronco XLT	Bronco
	Bronco Eddie Bauer	Bronco
	Bronco II Wagon	Bronco II
	Bronco II XLT	Bronco II
	Bronco II Eddie Bauer	Bronco II
	Club Wagon E150	Club Wagon

MODEL IDENTIFICATION
Ford Trucks

Year	Model Designation	Model Name
1986	Club Wagon E250	Club Wagon
	Super Wagon S350	Club Wagon
	E150 Cargo Van	Econoline E150
	E150 Window Van	Econoline E150
	E150 Super Cargo Van	Econoline E150
	E150 Super Window Van	Econoline E150
	E250 Cargo Van	Econoline E250
	E250 Window Van	Econoline E250
	E250 Super Cargo Van	Econoline E250
	E350 Cargo Van	Econoline E350
	E350 Window Van	Econoline E350
	E350 Display Van	Econoline E350
	E350 Super Cargo Van	Econoline E350
	E350 Super Window Van	Econoline E350
	E350 Cutaway Van	Econoline E350
	F150 Flareside 6½ ft.	F150 Custom
	F150 Styleside 6½ ft.	F150 Custom
	F150 Styleside 8 ft.	F150 Custom
	F150 Styleside Supercab 6½ ft.	F150 Custom
	F150 Styleside Supercab 8 ft.	F150 Custom
	F250 Styleside 8 ft.	F250 Custom
	F250 Styleside Supercab	F250 Custom
	F350 Chassis & Cab	F350 Custom
	F350 Styleside 8 ft.	F350 Custom
	F350 Chassis & Cab (137 W.B.)	F350 Custom
	F350 Chassis & Cab (161 W.B.)	F350 Custom
	F350 Styleside Crew Cab	F350 Custom
	Ranger Styleside	Ranger
	Ranger Styleside S	Ranger
	Ranger Styleside LB	Ranger
	Ranger Supercab	Ranger
1987-88	Aerostar Cargo Van	Aerostar
	Aerostar Wagon	Aerostar
	Aerostar Window Van	Aerostar
	Bronco Wagon	Bronco
	Bronco XLT	Bronco
	Bronco Eddie Bauer	Bronco
	Bronco II Wagon	Bronco II
	Bronco II XLT	Bronco II
	Bronco II Eddie Bauer	Bronco II
	Club Wagon E150	Club Wagon
	Club Wagon E250	Club Wagon
	E150 Cargo Van	Econoline E150
	E150 Window Van	Econoline E150
	E250 Cargo Van	Econoline E250

MODEL IDENTIFICATION
Ford Trucks

Year	Model Designation	Model Name
1987–88	E250 Window Van	Econoline E250
	F150 Flareside 6½ ft.	F150 Custom
	F150 Styleside 6½ ft.	F150 Custom
	F150 Styleside 8 ft.	F150 Custom
	F150 Styleside Supercab 6½ ft.	F150 Custom
	F150 Styleside Supercab 8 ft.	F150 Custom

MODEL IDENTIFICATION
Ford Trucks

Year	Model Designation	Model Name
1987–88	F250 Styleside 8 ft.	F250 Custom
	F250 Styleside Supercab	F250 Custom
	Ranger Styleside	Ranger
	Ranger Styleside S	Ranger
	Ranger Styleside LB	Ranger
	Ranger Supercab	Ranger

ENGINE IDENTIFICATION CODES BY VIN NUMBER

Engine Cu. In. (liter)	Cylinders	1982	1983	1984	1985	1986	1987	1988
122 (2.0)	4	—	—	K	K	C	C	C
134 (2.2) ⑤	4	—		3	—	—	—	—
140 (2.3)	4	—	—	Z	Z	A	A	A
140 (2.3) ①	4	—	—	—	—	E	E	E
171 (2.8)	V6	—	—	S	—	S	S	S
177 (2.9)	V6	—	—	—	—	T	T	T
183 (3.0)	V6	—	—	—	—	U	U	U
232 (3.8)	V6	3	3	—	—	—	—	—
255 (4.2)	V8	D	—	—	—	—	—	—
300 (4.9)	6	E	Y	Y	Y	Y	Y	Y
302 (5.0)	V8	F	F	F	F	—	—	—
302 (5.0) ②	V8	—	—	—	N	N	N	N
351 (5.8)	V8	W	G	G	G	—	—	—
351 (5.8) ③	V8	—	—	—	H	H	H	H
400 (6.6)	V8	Z	—	—	—	—	—	—
421 (6.9) ④	V8	—	I	I	I	I	I	I
460 (7.5)	V8	L	L	L	L	L	L	L

① Mitsubishi Diesel (Turbo)
② E.F.I.
③ 4 BBL.
④ International Harvester (Diesel)
⑤ Diesel

GENERAL ENGINE SPECIFICATIONS

Year	VIN	No. Cylinder Displacement cu. in. (liter)	Fuel System Type	Net Horsepower @ rpm	Net Torque @ rpm (ft. lbs.)	Bore × Stroke (in.)	Com-pression Ratio	Oil Pressure @ rpm
1982	3	6 232 (3.8)	2 bbl.	112 @ 4000	175 @ 2600	3.81 × 3.39	8.6:1	56 @ 2500
	D	8 255 (4.2)	2 bbl.	111 @ 3400	194 @ 1600	3.68 × 3.00	8.2:1	50 @ 2000
	E	6 300 (4.9)	1 bbl.	120 @ 3400	229 @ 1400	4.00 × 3.98	8.0:1	50 @ 2000
	F	8 302 (5.0)	2 bbl.	135 @ 3600	239 @ 1900	4.00 × 3.00	8.4:1	50 @ 2000
	W	8 351 (5.8)	2 bbl.	⑤	⑥	4.00 × 3.50	8.3:1	52 @ 2000
	Z	8 400 (6.6)	2 bbl.	153 @ 3200	296 @ 1600	4.00 × 4.00	8.0:1	62 @ 2000
	L	8 460 (7.5)	4 bbl.	212 @ 4000	339 @ 2400	4.36 × 3.85	8.0:1	52 @ 2000
1983	3	6 232 (3.8)	2 bbl.	112 @ 4000	175 @ 2600	3.81 × 3.39	8.6:1	56 @ 2500
	Y	6 300 (4.9)	1 bbl.	120 @ 3400	229 @ 1400	4.00 × 3.98	8.0:1	50 @ 2000
	F	8 302 (5.0)	2 bbl.	135 @ 3600	239 @ 1900	4.00 × 3.00	8.4:1	50 @ 2000
	G	8 351 (5.8)	2 bbl.	⑦	⑧	4.00 × 3.50	8.3:1	52 @ 2000
	I	8 420 (6.9)	Diesel	161 @ 3300	307 @ 1800	4.00 × 4.18	20.7:1	50 @ 2000
	L	8 460 (7.5)	4 bbl.	202 @ 4000	331 @ 2200	4.36 × 3.85	8.0:1	52 @ 2000

GENERAL ENGINE SPECIFICATIONS

Year	VIN	No. Cylinder Displacement cu. in. (liter)	Fuel System Type	Net Horsepower @ rpm	Net Torque @ rpm (ft. lbs.)	Bore × Stroke (in.)	Com-pression Ratio	Oil Pressure @ rpm
1984	K	4 122 (2.0)	1 bbl.	73 @ 4000	107 @ 2406	3.52 × 3.13	9.0:1	50 @ 2000
	Z	4 140 (2.3)	1 bbl.	79 @ 3800 ①	124 @ 2400 ②	3.78 × 3.13	9.0:1	50 @ 2000
	S	6 173 (2.8)	2 bbl.	115 @ 4600	150 @ 2600	3.66 × 2.70	8.7:1	50 @ 2000
	Y	6 300 (4.9)	1 bbl.	120 @ 3400	229 @ 1400	4.00 × 3.98	8.0:1	50 @ 2000
	F	8 302 (5.0)	2 bbl.	135 @ 3600	239 @ 1900	4.00 × 3.00	8.4:1	50 @ 2000
	G	8 351 (5.8)	2 bbl.	160 @ 3200	280 @ 2000	4.00 × 3.50	8.3:1	52 @ 2000
	I	8 420 (6.9)	Diesel	NA	NA	4.00 × 4.18	20.7:1	50 @ 2000
	L	8 460 (7.5)	4 bbl.	220 @ 4000	360 @ 2600	4.36 × 3.85	8.0:1	52 @ 2000
1985	K	4 122 (2.0)	1 bbl.	73 @ 4000	107 @ 2400	3.52 × 3.13	9.0:1	50 @ 2000
	Z	4 140 (2.3)	EFI	79 @ 3800 ①	124 @ 2800 ②	3.78 × 3.13	9.0:1	50 @ 2000
	Y	6 300 (4.9)	1 bbl.	120 @ 3000	260 @ 1400	4.36 × 3.85	8.0:1	50 @ 2000
	F	8 302 (5.0)	2 bbl.	135 @ 3600	239 @ 1900	4.00 × 3.00	8.4:1	50 @ 2000
	N	8 302 (5.0)	EFI	NA	NA	4.00 × 3.00	8.4:1	50 @ 2000
	G	8 351 (5.8)	2 bbl.	160 @ 3200	280 @ 2000	4.00 × 3.50	8.3:1	52 @ 2000
	H	8 351 (5.8)	4 bbl.	210 @ 4000	305 @ 2800	4.00 × 3.50	8.3:1	52 @ 2000
	I	8 420 (6.9)	Diesel	NA	NA	4.00 × 4.18	20.7:1	50 @ 2000
	L	8 460 (7.5)	4 bbl.	220 @ 4000 ①	360 @ 2600	4.36 × 3.85	8.0:1	52 @ 2000
1986	C	4 122 (2.0)	1 bbl	73 @ 4000 ①	107 @ 2400	3.52 × 3.13	9.0:1	50 @ 2000
	A	4 140 (2.3)	EFI	90 @ 4000	130 @ 1800	3.78 × 3.13	9.0:1	50 @ 2000
	E	4 140 (2.3)	Diesel	86 @ 4200	134 @ 2000	3.59 × 3.54	21.0:1	11.4 @ Idle
	S	6 173 (2.8)	2 bbl.	115 @ 4600	150 @ 2600	3.65 × 2.70	8.7:1	50 @ 2000
	T	6 177 (2.9)	EFI	140 @ 4600	170 @ 2600	3.66 × 2.83	9.0:1	50 @ 2000
	U	6 182 (3.0)	EFI	145 @ 4800	165 @ 3600	3.50 × 3.14	9.3:1	50 @ 2500
	Y	6 300 (4.9)	1 bbl.	125 @ 3200	245 @ 1800	4.00 × 3.98	8.0:1	50 @ 2000
	N	8 302 (5.0)	EFI	150 @ 3600	249 @ 2600	4.00 × 3.00	8.4:1	50 @ 2000
	H	8 351 (5.8)	4 bbl.	210 @ 4000	304 @ 2800	4.00 × 3.50	8.3:1	52 @ 2000
	I	8 420 (6.9)	Diesel	NA	NA	4.00 × 4.18	20.7:1	50 @ 2000
	L	8 460 (7.5)	4 bbl.	226 @ 4400	365 @ 2800	4.36 × 3.85	8.0:1	52 @ 2000
1987-88	C	4 122 (2.0)	2 bbl.	80 @ 4200	106 @ 2600	3.52 × 3.13	9.0:1	50 @ 2000
	A	4 140 (2.3)	EFI	90 @ 4000 ③	134 @ 2000 ④	3.78 × 3.13	9.5:1	50 @ 2000
	E	4 140 (2.3)	Diesel	86 @ 4200	134 @ 2000	3.59 × 3.54	21.0:1	11.4 @ Idle
	T	6 177 (2.9)	EFI	140 @ 4600	170 @ 2600	3.66 × 2.83	9.0:1	50 @ 2000
	U	6 183 (3.0)	EFI	145 @ 4800	165 @ 3600	3.50 × 3.14	9.3:1	50 @ 2500
	Y	6 300 (4.9)	EFI	150 @ 3400	260 @ 2000	4.00 × 3.98	8.8:1	50 @ 2000
	N	8 302 (5.0)	EFI	185 @ 3800	270 @ 2400	4.00 × 3.00	9.0:1	50 @ 2000
	H	8 351 (5.8)	4 bbl.	190 @ 4000	285 @ 2600	4.00 × 3.50	8.3:1	52 @ 2000
	I	8 420 (6.9)	Diesel	170 @ 3300	315 @ 1400	4.00 × 4.18	21.5:1	55 @ 2000
	L	8 460 (7.5)	4 bbl.	245 @ 4200	380 @ 2600	4.36 × 3.85	8.0:1	48 @ 2000

① Auto Trans. 82 @ 4200
② Auto Trans. 126 @ 2200
③ Aerostar 88 @ 4000
④ Aerostar 132 @ 2200
⑤ E-150-250 exc. Calif., 144 @ 3200; E-250-350, 157 @ 3400; Bronco, F-150-250 & F-250 under 8500 lbs. exc. Calif., 136 @ 3000; Bronco, F-150-250, E-150-250 & F-250 under 8500 lbs. Calif., 139 & 3200; F-250 over 8500 lbs. & F-350, 142 @ 3400.
⑥ E-100-250 exc. Calif., 269 @ 1200; E-250-350, 271 @ 2400; Bronco, F-150-250 & F-250 under 8500 lbs. exc. Calif., 262 @ 1600; Bronco, F-150-250, E-150-250 & F-250 under 8500 lbs. Calif., 279 @ 1400; F-250 over 8500 lbs. & F-350, 251 @ 2400.
⑦ Bronco & F-150-250 under 8500 lbs., 139 @ 3200; F-250 over 8500 lbs. & F-350, 147 @ 3200; E-100-150 & E-250 van, 145 @ 3200; E-250 wagon & E-350, 150 @ 3200.

GENERAL ENGINE SPECIFICATIONS

⑥ Bronco, F-150 & F-250 under 8500 lbs., 278 @ 1400; F-250 over 8500 lbs. & F-350, 276 @ 2000; E-100-150 & E-250 van, 270 @ 1400; E-250 wagon & E-350, 279 @ 2000.

GASOLINE ENGINE TUNE-UP SPECIFICATIONS

Year	VIN	No. Cylinder Displacement cu. in. (liter)	Spark Plugs Type	Spark Plugs Gap (in.)	Ignition Timing (deg.) MT	Ignition Timing (deg.) AT	Compression Pressure (psi)	Fuel Pump (psi)	Idle Speed (rpm) MT	Idle Speed (rpm) AT	Valve Clearance In.	Valve Clearance Ex.
1982	3	6 232 (3.8)	AGSP-52	.044	10	12	NA	6–8	650	550	.0008–.0025	.0018–.0035
	D	8 255 (4.2)	ASF-42	.044	8	8	NA	6–8	750	625	.0010–.0027	.0015–.0032
	E	6 300 (4.9)	BSF-42	.044	①	①	NA	5–7	①	①	.0010–.0027	.0010–.0027
	F	8 302 (5.0)	ASF-42	.044	①	①	NA	6–8	700	575	.0010–.0027	.0015–.0032
	W	8 351 (5.8)	ASF-42	.044	8	8	NA	6–8	700	650	.0010–.0027	.0015–.0032
	Z	8 400 (6.6)	ASF-52	.044	6	6	NA	6–8	600	500	.0010–.0027	.0015–.0032
	L	8 460 (7.5)	ASF-42	.044	—	8	NA	6–8	—	650	.0010–.0027	.0015–.0027
1983	3	6 232 (3.8)	AGSP-52	.044	10	12	NA	6–8	650	550	.0008–.0025	.0018–.0035
	Y	8 300 (4.9)	BSF-42	.044	①	①	NA	5–7	①	①	.0010–.0027	.0010–.0027
	F	8 302 (5.0)	ASF-42	.044	①	①	NA	6–8	700	575	.0010–.0027	.0015–.0032
	G	8 351 (5.8)	ASF-42	.044	8	8	NA	6–8	700	650	.0010–.0027	.0015–.0032
	L	8 460 (7.5)	ASF-42	.044	8	8	NA	6–8	800	600	.0010–.0027	.0010–.0027
1984	K	4 122 (2.0)	AWSF-42	.034	8	8	NA	5–7	800	800	.0010–.0027	.0015–.0032
	Z	4 140 (2.3)	AWSF-44	.044	①	①	NA	5–7	850	850	.0010–.0027	.0015–.0032
	S	6 171 (2.8)	AWSF-42	.044	10	10	NA	39	②	②	.0008–.0025	.0018–.0025
	Y	6 300 (4.9)	BSF-42	.044	①	①	NA	5–7	①	①	.0010–.0027	.0010–.0027
	F	8 302 (5.0)	ASF-42	.044	①	①	NA	6–8	700	575	.0010–.0027	.0015–.0032
	G	8 351 (5.8)	ASF-42	.044	8	8	NA	6–8	700	650	.0010–.0027	.0015–.0032
	L	8 460 (7.5)	ASF-42	.044	8	8	NA	6–8	800	600	.0010–.0027	.0010–.0027
1985	K	4 122 (2.0)	AWSF-42	.034	8	8	NA	5–7	800	800	.0010–.0027	.0015–.0032
	Z	4 140 (2.3)	AWSF-44	.044	①	①	NA	5–7	850	850	.0010–.0027	.0015–.0032

GASOLINE ENGINE TUNE-UP SPECIFICATIONS (Continued)

Year	VIN	No. Cylinder Displacement cu. in. (liter)	Spark Plugs Type	Spark Plugs Gap (in.)	Ignition Timing (deg.) MT	Ignition Timing (deg.) AT	Compression Pressure (psi)	Fuel Pump (psi)	Idle Speed (rpm) MT	Idle Speed (rpm) AT	Valve Clearance In.	Valve Clearance Ex.
1985	Y	6 300 (4.9)	BSF-42	.044	10	10	NA	5–7	650	600	.0010–.0027	.0010–.0027
	F	8 302 (5.0)	ASF-42	.044	10	10	NA	6–8	—	575	.0010–.0027	.0015–.0032
	N	8 302 (5.0)	ASF-32C	.044	①	①	NA	35–45	②	②	.0010–.0027	.0015–.0032
	G	8 351 (5.8)	ASF-32C	.044	①	①	NA	6–8	650	650	.0010–.0027	.0015–.0032
	H	8 351 (5.8)	ASF-42	.044	10	10	NA	35–45	700	700	.0010–.0027	.0015–.0032
	L	8 460 (7.5)	ASF-42	.044	8	8	NA	6–8	800	650	.0010–.0027	.0010–.0027
1986	C	4 122 (2.0)	AWSF-52C	.044	6	6	NA	39	②	②	.0010–.0027	.0015–.0032
	A	4 140 (2.3)	AWSF-44C	.044	10	10	NA	39	②	②	.0010–.0027	.0015–.0032
	S	6 171 (2.8)	AWSF-42C	.046	10	10	NA	39	②	②	.0008–.0025	.0018–.0025
	T	6 177 (2.9)	AWSF-42C	.044	10	10	NA	39	②	②	.0008–.0025	.0018–.0035
	Y	6 300 (4.9)	BSF-42	.044	10	10	NA	5–7	650	600	.0010–.0027	.0010–.0027
	N	8 302 (5.0)	ASF-32C	.044	10	10	NA	35–45	②	②	.0010–.0027	.0015–.0032
	H	8 351 (5.8)	ASF-32C	.044	10	10	NA	35–45	650	650	.0010–.0027	.0015–.0032
	L	8 460 (7.5)	ASF-42	.044	8	8	NA	6–8	800	650	.0010–.0027	.0010–.0027
1987–88	C	4 122 (2.0)	AWSF-52C	.044	6	6	NA	5–7	②	②	.0010–.0027	.0015–.0032
	A	4 140 (2.3)	AWSF-44C	.044	10	10	NA	39	②	②	.0010–.0027	.0015–.0032
	S	6 171 (2.8)	AWSF-42C	.046	10	10	NA	39	②	②	.0008–.0025	.0018–.0025
	T	6 177 (2.9)	AWSF-42C	.044	10	10	NA	39	②	②	.0008–.0025	.0018–.0035
	U	6 183 (3.0)	AWSF-32P	.044	10	10	NA	35–45	②	②	.0010–.0027	.0015–.0032
	Y	6 300 (4.9)	BSF-44C	.044	10	10	NA	5–7	②	②	.0010–.0027	.0010–.0027
	N	8 302 (5.0)	ASF-42C	.044	10	10	NA	35–45	②	②	.0010–.0027	.0015–.0032
	H	8 351 (5.8)	ASF-32C	.044	10	10	NA	6–8	—	650	.0010–.0027	.0015–.0032
	L	8 460 (7.5)	ASF-42	.044	8	8	NA	6–8	800	650	.0010–.0027	.0010–.0027

① See Underhood Sticker
② Not Adjustable

FIRING ORDERS

NOTE: To avoid confusion, always replace spark plug wires one at a time.

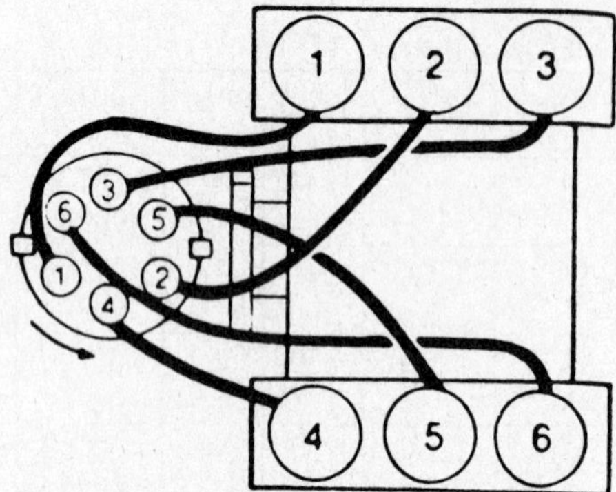

171 (2.9L) and 232 (3.8L) V6 engine
Firing order: 1-4-2-5-3-6
Distributor rotation: counterclockwise

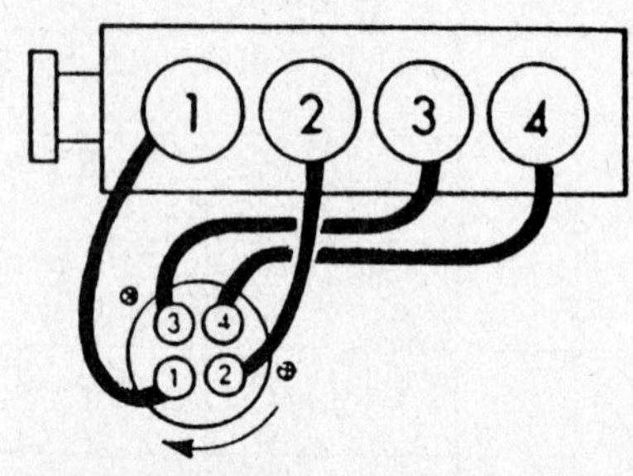

122 (2.0L) and 140 (2.3L) 4 cylinder
Engine firing order: 1-3-4-2
Distributor rotation: clockwise

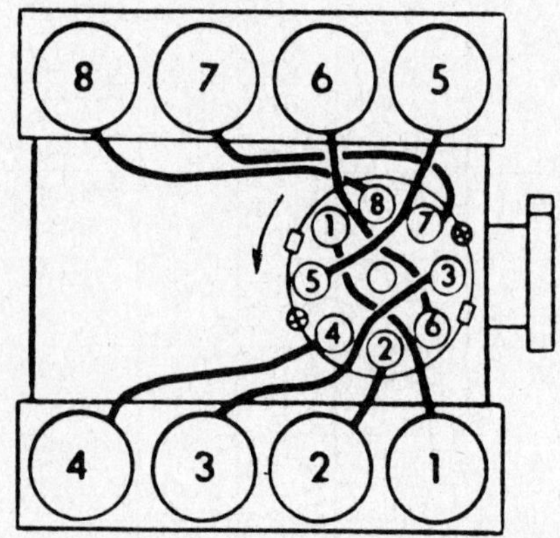

255 (4.2L), 302 (5.0L) exc. HO and 460 (7.5L) V8 engine
Firing order: 1-5-4-2-6-3-7-8
Distributor rotation: counterclockwise

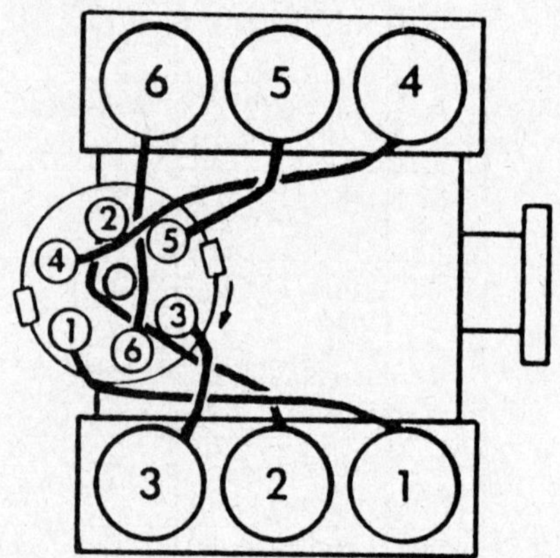

173 (2.8L) and 181 (3.0L) V6 engine
Firing order: 1-4-2-5-3-6
Distributor rotation: clockwise

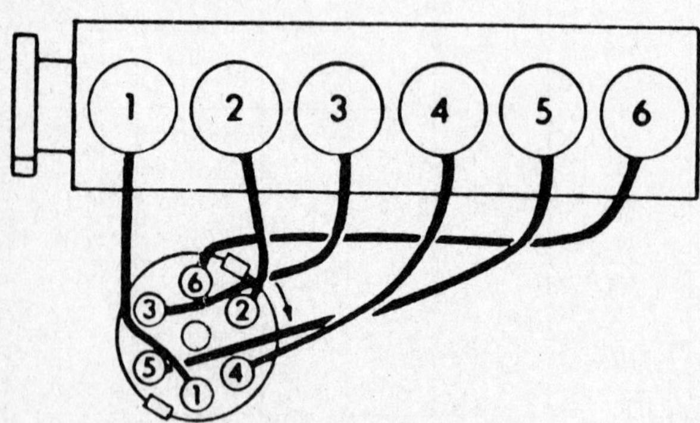

300 (4.9L) 6 cylinder engine
Firing order: 1-5-3-6-2-4
Distributor rotation: clockwise

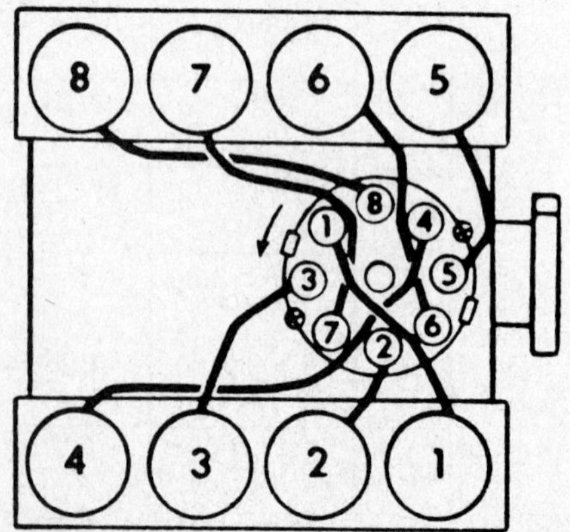

302 (5.0L) HO, 351 (5.8L) and 400 (6.6L) V8 engine
Firing order: 1-3-7-2-6-5-4-8
Distributor rotation: counterclockwise

CAPACITIES

Year	Model	No. Cylinder Displacement cu. in. (liter)	Engine Crankcase with Filter	Engine Crankcase without Filter	Transmission (pts.) 4-Spd	Transmission (pts.) 5-Spd	Transmission (pts.) Auto.	Drive Axle (pts.)	Fuel Tank (gal.)	Cooling System (qts.) ⑮
1982	Bronco	6 300 (4.9)	6	5	①	—	27	6.5	25	14
		8 302 (5.0)	6	5	①	—	27	6.5	16.5	14
		8 351 (5.8)	6	5	①	—	27	6.5	25	16
	E100-350	6 300 (4.9)	6	5	①	—	23	6	22.1 ②	20
	E100-250	8 302 (5.0)	6	5	4.5	—	23	6	22.1 ②	18
	E100-350	8 351 (5.8)	6	5	4.5	—	23	6	22.1 ②	21
	E250-350	8 400 (6.6)	6	5	4.5	—	23	6	22.1 ②	21
	E350	8 460 (7.5)	6	5	4.5	—	23	6	22.1 ②	28
	F100	6 232 (3.8)	6	5	①	—	③	6.5	19	11
	F100	8 255 (4.2)	6	5	①	—	③	6.5	19	14
	F100-350	6 300 (4.9)	6	5	①	—	③	6.5	25	14
	F100-350	8 302 (5.0)	6	5	①	—	③	6.5	19	14
	F150-350	8 351 (5.8)	6	5	①	—	③	6.5	19	16
	F250-350	8 400 (6.6)	6	5	①	—	③	6.5	19	16
1983	Bronco	6 300 (4.9)	6	5	①	—	27	5.5	25	14
		8 302 (5.0)	6	5	①	—	27	5.5	25	14
		8 351 (5.8)	6	5	①	—	27	5.5	25	16
	E100-350	6 300 (4.9)	6	5	4.5	—	23	6	22.1 ②	20
		8 302 (5.0)	6	5	4.5	—	23	6	22.1 ②	④
		8 351 (5.8)	6	5	4.5	—	23	6	22.1 ②	⑤
	E250-350	8 460 (7.5)	6	5	4.5	—	23	6	22.1 ②	28
	F100	6 232 (3.8)	6	5	①	—	③	6.5	16.5	12
	F100-350	6 300 (4.9)	6	5	①	—	23	6.5	25	14
	F100-250	8 302 (5.0)	6	5	4.5	—	23	6	25	14
	F100-350	8 351 (5.8)	6	5	4.5	—	23	6	25	16
	F250-350	8 420 (6.9)	10	9	4.5	—	23	6	25	31
		8 460 (7.5)	6	5	4.5	—	23	6	25	17.5
1984	Bronco	6 300 (4.9)	6	5	①	—	27	5.5	32	14
		8 302 (5.0)	6	5	①	—	27	5.5	32	14
		8 351 (5.8)	6	5	①	—	27	5.5	32	16
	E150-350	6 300 (4.9)	6	5	4.5	—	23	6	22.1 ②	17.5
		8 302 (5.0)	6	5	4.5	—	24	6	22.1 ②	⑥
		8 351 (5.8)	6	5	4.5	—	24	6	22.1 ②	⑤
	E250-350	8 460 (7.5)	6	5	4.5	—	24	6	22.1 ②	28
	F150-350	6 300 (4.9)	6	5	①	—	23	6.5	25	14
		8 302 (5.0)	6	5	①	—	③	6.5	25	14
		8 351 (5.8)	6	5	4.5	—	23	6	25	16
	F250-350	8 420 (6.9)	10	9	4.5	—	23	6	25	31
		8 460 (7.5)	6	5	4.5	—	23	6	25	17.5
	Bronco II & Ranger	4 122 (2.0)	5	4	3	3	16	⑦	15	7
		4 134 (2.2)	6.5	5.5	3.2	3	—	⑦	15	11
		4 140 (2.3)	6	5	3	3	16	⑦	15	7.2
		6 171 (2.8)	5	4	3	3	16	⑦⑧	15 ⑨	7.8

CAPACITIES (Continued)

Year	Model	No. Cylinder Displacement cu. in. (liter)	Engine Crankcase with Filter	Engine Crankcase without Filter	Transmission (pts.) 4-Spd	Transmission (pts.) 5-Spd	Transmission (pts.) Auto.	Drive Axle (pts.)	Fuel Tank (gal.)	Cooling System (qts.) ⑮
1985	Bronco	6 300 (4.9)	6	5	7 ⑩	—	27	5.5	32	14
		8 302 (5.0)	6	5	7 ⑩	—	27	5.5	32	14
		8 351 (5.8)	6	5	7 ⑩	—	27	5.5	32	15
	E150-350	6 300 (4.9)	6	5	7 ⑩	—	24	6 ⑪	22.1 ②	17.5
		8 302 (5.0)	6	5	7 ⑩	—	24	6 ⑪	22.1 ②	⑥
		8 351 (5.8)	6	5	7 ⑩	—	24	6 ⑪	22.1 ②	⑤
	E250-350	8 420 (6.9)	10	9	7 ⑩	—	24	6 ⑪	22.1 ②	31
		8 460 (7.5)	6	5	7 ⑩	—	24	6 ⑪	22.1 ②	28
	F150-350	6 300 (4.9)	6	5	7 ⑩	—	24	6 ⑪	25	14
	F150-250	8 302 (5.0)	6	5	7 ⑩	—	24	6 ⑪	25	14
	F150-350	8 351 (5.8)	6	5	7 ⑩	—	24 ⑫	6 ⑪	25	15
	F250-350	8 420 (6.9)	10	9	7 ⑩	—	24	6 ⑪	22.1 ②	31
	F150-350	8 460 (7.5)	6	5	7 ⑩	—	24 ⑫	6 ⑪	25	16
	Bronco II & Ranger	4 122 (2.0)	5	4	—	⑬	18	⑦	15	7.8
		4 140 (2.3)	6.5	5.5	—	⑬	18	⑦	15	7.2
		4 140 (2.3)	6.8	6.8	3.1	—	—	⑦⑧	15 ⑨	13
		6 171 (2.8)	5	4	3	3	16	⑦⑧	15 ⑨	7.8
1986	Bronco	6 300 (4.9)	6	5	7 ⑩	—	27	5.5	32	14
		8 302 (5.0)	6	5	7 ⑩	—	27	5.5	32	14
		8 351 (5.8)	6	5	7 ⑩	—	27	5.5	32	15
	E150-350	6 300 (4.9)	6	5	7 ⑩	—	24	6 ⑪	22.1 ②	17.5
		8 302 (5.0)	6	5	7 ⑩	—	24	6 ⑪	22.1 ②	⑥
		8 351 (5.8)	6	5	7 ⑩	—	24	6 ⑪	22.1 ②	⑤
	E250-350	8 420 (6.9)	10	9	7 ⑩	—	24	6 ⑪	22.1 ②	31
		8 460 (7.5)	6	5	7 ⑩	—	24	6 ⑪	22.1 ②	28
	F150-350	6 300 (4.9)	6	5	7 ⑩	—	24	6 ⑪	25	14
	F150-250	8 302 (5.0)	6	5	7 ⑩	—	24	6 ⑪	25	14
	F150-350	8 351 (5.8)	6	5	7 ⑩	—	24 ⑫	6 ⑪	25	15
	F250-350	8 420 (6.9)	10	9	7 ⑩	—	24	6 ⑪	22.1 ②	31
	F150-350	8 460 (7.5)	6	5	7 ⑩	—	24 ⑫	6 ⑪	25	16
	Bronco II & Ranger	4 122 (2.0)	5	4	—	⑬	18	⑦	15	7.8
		4 140 (2.3)	6.5	5.5	—	⑬	18	⑦	15	7.2
		4 140 (2.3)	6.8	6.8	3.1	—	—	⑦⑧	15 ⑨	13
		6 171 (2.8)	5	4	3	3	16	⑦⑧	15 ⑨	7.8
	Aerostar	4 140 (2.3)	5	5	—	3	19	5	17	⑭
		6 171 (2.8)	5	4	—	3	19	5	17	8

CAPACITIES (Continued)

Year	Model	No. Cylinder Displacement cu. in. (liter)	Engine Crankcase with Filter	Engine Crankcase without Filter	Transmission (pts.) 4-Spd	Transmission (pts.) 5-Spd	Transmission (pts.) Auto.	Drive Axle (pts.)	Fuel Tank (gal.)	Cooling System (qts.) ⑮
1987-88	Bronco	6 300 (4.9)	6	5	7 ⑩	—	27	5.5	32	14
		8 302 (5.0)	6	5	7 ⑩	—	27	5.5	32	14
		8 351 (5.8)	6	5	7 ⑩	—	27	5.5	32	15
	E150-350	6 300 (4.9)	6	5	7 ⑩	—	24	6 ⑪	22.1 ②	17.5
		8 302 (5.0)	6	5	7 ⑩	—	24	6 ⑪	22.1 ②	⑥
		8 351 (5.8)	6	5	7 ⑩	—	24	6 ⑪	22.1 ②	⑤
	E250-350	8 420 (6.9)	10	9	7 ⑩	—	24	6 ⑪	22.1 ②	31
		8 460 (7.5)	6	5	7 ⑩	—	24	6 ⑪	22.1 ②	28
	F150-350	6 300 (4.9)	6	5	7 ⑩	—	24	6 ⑪	25	14
	F150-250	8 302 (5.0)	6	5	7 ⑩	—	24	6 ⑪	25	14
	F150-350	8 351 (5.8)	6	5	7 ⑩	—	24 ⑫	6 ⑪	25	15
	F250-350	8 420 (6.9)	10	9	7 ⑩	—	24	6 ⑪	22.1 ②	31
	F150-350	8 460 (7.5)	6	5	7 ⑩	—	24 ⑫	6 ⑪	25	16
	Bronco II & Ranger	4 122 (2.0)	5	4	—	⑬	18	⑦	15	7.8
		4 140 (2.3)	6.5	5.5	—	⑬	18	⑦	15	7.2
		4 140 (2.3)	6.8	6.8	3.1	—	—	⑦⑧	15 ⑨	13
		6 171 (2.8)	5	4	3	3	16	⑦⑧	15 ⑨	7.8
	Aerostar	4 140 (2.3)	5	5	—	3	19	5	17	⑭
		6 171 (2.8)	5	4	—	3	19	5	17	8
		6 183 (3.0)	5	4	—	3	19	5	17	8

① New Process Model 7 pts.
4 sp. overdrive 4.5 pts.
② E100-150 w/124″ W.B. 18
③ C5—22 pts.
C6—24 pts.
Overdrive 24 pts.
4x4 models 25 pts.
④ Man. Trans. 15
Auto. Trans. 17½
⑤ Man. Trans. 15
Auto. Trans. 21
⑥ Manual Trans. 17½
Auto. Trans. 18½
⑦ 6¾″ Ring gear 3 pts.
7½″ Ring gear 5 pts.
⑧ Bronco II w/7½″ Ring gear 5.5 pts.
⑨ Bronco II—23 gals.
⑩ Ford Overdrive 4.5 pts.
⑪ Heavy Duty 7.5 pts.
⑫ 4x4 models—27 pts.
⑬ Mazda Trans. 3 pts.
Mitzubishi Trans. 4.8 pts.
⑭ w/Manual—6.8
w/Automatic—7.6
⑮ w/Air Conditioning

CRANKSHAFT AND CONNECTING ROD SPECIFICATIONS

All measurements are given in inches.

Year	VIN	No. Cylinder Displacement cu. in. (liter)	Crankshaft				Connecting Rod		
			Main Brg. Journal Dia.	Main Brg. Oil Clearance	Shaft End-play	Thrust on No.	Journal Diameter	Oil Clearance	Side Clearance
1982	3	6 232 (3.8)	2.5190	.0009–.0027	.004–.008	3	2.3107	.0009–.0027	.004–.011
	D	8 255 (4.2)	2.2490	.0005–① .0024	.004–.008	3	2.1232	.0008–.0025	.010–.020
	E	6 300 (4.9)	2.3982–2.3990	.0009–.0028	.004–.008	5	2.1228–2.1236	.0009–.0027	.006–.013
	F	8 302 (5.0)	2.2482–2.2490	.0005–② .0015	.004–.008	3	2.1228–2.1236	.0010–.0015	.010–.020
	W	8 351 (5.8)	2.2994–3.0002	.0008–③ .0015	.004–.008	3	2.3103–2.3111	.0008–.0026	.010–.020
	Z	8 400 (6.6)	2.9994–3.0002	.0008–.0025	.004–.008	3	2.3103–2.3111	.0008–.0025	.010–.020
	L	8 460 (7.5)	2.9994–3.0002	.0008–.0015	.004–.008	3	2.4992–2.5000	.0008–.0015	.010–.020
1983	3	6 232 (3.8)	2.5190–	.0009–.0027	.004–.008	3	2.3107–	.0009–.0027	.004–.011
	Y	6 300 (4.9)	2.3982–2.3990	.0009–.0028	.004–.008	5	2.1228–2.1236	.0009–.0027	.006–.013
	F	8 302 (5.0)	2.2482–2.2490	.0005–② .0015	.004–.008	3	2.1228–2.1236	.0010–.0015	.010–.020
	G	8 351 (5.8)	2.2994–3.0002	.0008–③ .0015	.004–.008	3	2.3103–2.3111	.0008–.0026	.010–.020
	I	8 420 (6.9)	3.1228–3.1236	.0018–.0036	.001–.009	—	2.6905–2.6910	.0011–.0026	.008–.020
	L	8 460 (7.5)	2.9994–3.0002	.0008–.0015	.004–.008	3	2.4992–2.5000	.0008–.0015	.010–.020
1984	K	4 122 (2.0)	2.3982–2.3990	.0008–.0015	.004–.008	3	2.0472	.0008–.0015	.0035–.0105
	3	4 134 (2.2)	2.5586–2.5596	.0016–.0036	.0040–.0080	—	2.0861–2.0871	.0014–.0032	.0094–.0134
	Z	4 140 (2.3)	2.3982–2.3990	.0008–.0015	.004–.008	3	2.0472	.0008–.0015	.0035–.0105
	S	6 173 (2.8)	2.2441	.0008–.0015	.012	3	2.1260	.0006–.0016	.004–.011
	Y	6 300 (4.9)	2.3982 2.3990	.0009–.0028	.004 .008	5	2.1228–2.1236	.0009–.0027	.006–.013
	F	8 302 (5.0)	2.2482 2.2490	.0005–② .0015	.004 .008	3	2.1228–2.1236	.0010–.0015	.010–.020
	G	8 351 (5.8)	2.2994 3.0002	.0008–③ .0015	.004 .008	3	2.3103–2.3111	.0008–.0026	.010–.020
	I	8 420 (6.9)	3.1228 3.1236	.0018–.0036	.001–.009	—	2.6905–2.6910	.0011–.0026	.008–.020
	L	8 460 (7.5)	2.9994 3.0002	.0008–.0015	.004–.008	3	2.4992–2.5000	.0008–.0015	.010–.020

CRANKSHAFT AND CONNECTING ROD SPECIFICATIONS

All measurements are given in inches.

Year	VIN	No. Cylinder Displacement cu. in. (liter)	Crankshaft Main Brg. Journal Dia.	Crankshaft Main Brg. Oil Clearance	Crankshaft Shaft End-play	Crankshaft Thrust on No.	Connecting Rod Journal Diameter	Connecting Rod Oil Clearance	Connecting Rod Side Clearance
1985	K	4 122 (2.0)	2.3982 2.3990	.0008– .0015	.004– .008	3	2.0472	.0008– .0015	.0035– .0105
	Z	4 140 (2.3)	2.3982 2.3990	.0008– .0015	.004– .008	3	2.0472	.0008– .0015	.0035– .0105
	Y	6 300 (4.9)	2.3982 2.3990	.0009– .0028	.004– .008	5	2.1228– 2.1236	.0009– .0027	.006– .013
	F&N	8 302 (5.0)	2.2482 2.2490	.0005–② .0015	.004– .008	3	2.1228– 2.1236	.0010– .0015	.010– .020
	G&H	8 351 (5.8)	2.2994 3.0002	.0008–③ .0015	.004– .008	3	2.3103– 2.3111	.0008– .0026	.010– .020
	I	8 420 (6.9)	3.1228 3.1236	.0018– .0036	.001– .009	—	2.6905– 2.6910	.0011– .0026	.008– .020
	L	8 460 (7.5)	2.9994 3.0002	.0008– .0015	.004– .008	3	2.4992– 2.5000	.0008– .0015	.010– .020
1986	C	4 122 (2.0)	2.3982 2.3990	.0008– .0015	.004– .008	3	2.0472	.0008– .0015	.0035– .0105
	A	4 140 (2.3)	2.3982 2.3990	.0008– .0015	.004– .008	3	2.0472	.0008– .0015	.0035– .0105
	E	4 140 (2.3) ④	2.598	.0008– .0020	.0008– .0020	3	2.087	.0008– .0024	.0008– .0020
	S	6 173 (2.8)	2.2441	.0008– .0015	.012	3	2.1260	.0006– .0016	.004– .011
	T	6 177 (2.9)	2.2433 2.2441	.0008– .0015	.0040 .0080	3	2.1252– 2.1260	.0006– .0016	.004– .011
	U	6 182 (3.0)	2.5190 2.5198	.001– .0014	.004 .008	3	2.1253– 2.1261	.001– .0014	.006– .014
	Y	6 300 (4.9)	2.3982 2.3990	.0009– .0028	.004– .008	5	2.1228– 2.1236	.0009– .0027	.006– .013
	N	8 302 (5.0)	2.2482 2.2490	.0008– .0015	.004– .008	3	2.1228– 2.1236	.0008– .0015	.010– .020
	H	8 351 (5.8)	2.2994 3.0002	.0008– .0015	.004– .008	3	2.3103– 2.3111	.0008– .0026	.010– .020
	I	8 420 (6.9)	3.1228– 3.1236	.0018– .0036	.001– .009	—	2.6905– 2.6910	.0011– .0026	.008– .020
	L	8 460 (7.5)	2.9994– 3.0002	.0008– .0015	.004– .008	3	2.4992– 2.5000	.0008– .0015	.010– .020

CRANKSHAFT AND CONNECTING ROD SPECIFICATIONS

All measurements are given in inches.

Year	VIN	No. Cylinder Displacement cu. in. (liter)	Crankshaft				Connecting Rod		
			Main Brg. Journal Dia.	Main Brg. Oil Clearance	Shaft End-play	Thrust on No.	Journal Diameter	Oil Clearance	Side Clearance
1987-88	C	4 122 (2.0)	2.3982–2.3990	.0008–.0015	.004–.008	3	2.0472–	.0008–.0015	.0035–.0105
	A	4 140 (2.3)	2.3982–2.3990	.0008–.0015	.004–.008	3	2.0472	.0008–.0015	.0035–.0105
	E	4 140 (2.3) ④	2.598	.0008–.0020	.0008–.0020	3	2.087	.0008–.0024	.0008–.0020
	S	6 173 (2.8)	2.2441	.0008–.0015	.012	3	2.1260	.0006–.0016	.004–.011
	T	6 177 (2.9)	2.2433–2.2441	.0008–.0015	.0040–.0080	3	2.1252–2.1260	.0006–.0016	.004–.011
	U	6 182 (3.0)	2.5190–2.5198	.001–.0014	.004–.008	3	2.1253–2.1261	.001–.0014	.006–.014
	Y	6 300 (4.9)	2.3982–2.3990	.0009–.0028	.004–.008	5	2.1228–2.1236	.0009–.0027	.006–.013
	N	8 302 (5.0)	2.2482–2.2490	.0008–.0015	.004–.008	3	2.1228–2.1236	.0008–.0015	.010–.020
	H	8 351 (5.8)	2.2994–3.0002	.0008–.0015	.004–.008	3	2.3103–2.3111	.0008–.0026	.010–.020
	I	8 420 (6.9)	3.1228–3.1236	.0018–.0036	.001–.009	—	2.6905–2.6910	.0011–.0026	.008–.020
	L	8 460 (7.5)	2.9994–3.0002	.0008–.0015	.004–.008	3	2.4992–2.5000	.0008–.0015	.010–.020

① No. 1 .0001–.0020
② No. 2 .0001–.0015
③ No. 1 .0005–.0015
④ Diesel engine

VALVE SPECIFICATIONS

Year	VIN	No. Cylinder Displacement cu. in. (liter)	Seat Angle (deg.)	Face Angle (deg.)	Spring Test Pressure (lbs.)	Spring Installed Height (in.)	Stem-to-Guide Clearance (in.)		Stem Diameter (in.)	
							Intake	Exhaust	Intake	Exhaust
1982	3	6 232 (3.8)	45	44	215	1.70–1.78	.0010–.0025	.0015–.0032	.3432	.3415
	D	8 255 (4.2)	45	46	①	②	.0010–.0027	.0010–.0027	.3420	.3415
	E	6 300 (4.9)	45	44	③	④	.0010–.0027	.0010–.0027	.3420	.3420
	F	8 302 (5.0)	45	44	⑤	②	.0010–.0027	.0015–.0032	.3420	.3415
	W	8 351 (5.8)	45	44	200	⑥	.0010–.0027	.0015–.0032	.3420	.3415
	Z	8 400 (6.6)	45	44	226	⑦	.0010–.0027	.0015–.0032	.3420	.3415
	L	8 460 (7.5)	45	44	229	1 13/16	.0010–.0027	.0010–.0027	.3420	.3420

VALVE SPECIFICATIONS

Year	VIN	No. Cylinder Displacement cu. in. (liter)	Seat Angle (deg.)	Face Angle (deg.)	Spring Test Pressure (lbs.)	Spring Installed Height (in.)	Stem-to-Guide Clearance (in.)		Stem Diameter (in.)	
							Intake	Exhaust	Intake	Exhaust
1983	3	6 232 (3.8)	45	44	215	1.70–1.78	.0010–.0025	.0015–.0032	.3432	.3415
	Y	6 300 (4.9)	45	44	③	④	.0010–.0027	.0010–.0027	.3420	.3420
	F	8 302 (5.0)	45	44	⑤	②	.0010–.0027	.0015–.0032	.3420	.3415
	G	8 351 (5.8)	45	44	200	⑥	.0010–.0027	.0015–.0032	.3420	.3415
	I	8 420 (6.9)	⑧	⑧	60	—	.0012–.0029	.0012–.0029	.3720	.3720
	L	8 460 (7.5)	45	44	229	1 13/16	.0010–.0027	.0010–.0027	.3420	.3420
1984	K	4 122 (2.0)	45	44	149	1.49	.0010–.0027	.0015–.0032	.3420	.3415
	3	4 134 (2.2)	⑨	⑨	⑩	⑪	.0015–.0046	.0020–.0051	.3150	.3150
	Z	4 140 (2.3)	45	44	149	1.56	.0010–.0027	.0015–.0032	.3420	.3415
	S	6 171 (2.8)	45	44	144	1.60	.0008–.0025	.0018–.0035	.3163	.3133
	Y	6 300 (4.9)	45	44	③	④	.0010–.0027	.0010–.0027	.3420	.3420
	F	8 302 (5.0)	45	44	⑤	②	.0010–.0027	.0015–.0032	.3420	.3415
	G	8 351 (5.8)	45	44	200	⑥	.0010–.0027	.0015–.0032	.3420	.3415
	I	8 420 (6.9)	⑧	⑧	60	—	.0012–.0029	.0012–.0029	.3720	.3720
	L	8 460 (7.5)	45	44	229	1 13/16	.0010–.0027	.0010–.0027	.3420	.3420
1985	K	4 122 (2.0)	45	44	149	1.49	.0010–.0027	.0015–.0032	.3420	.3415
	Z	4 140 (2.3)	45	44	149	1.49	.0010–.0027	.0015–.0032	.3420	.3415
	Y	6 300 (4.9)	45	44	175	⑫	.0010–.0027	.0010–.0027	.3420	.3420
	F&N	8 302 (5.0)	45	44	⑤	②	.0010–.0027	.0015–.0032	.3420	.3415
	G&H	8 351 (5.8)	45	44	200	⑥	.0010–.0027	.0015–.0032	.3420	.3415
	I	8 420 (6.9)	⑧	⑧	60	—	.0012–.0029	.0012–.0029	.3720	.3720
	L	8 460 (7.5)	45	44	229	1 13/16	.0010–.0027	.0010–.0027	.3420	.3420

VALVE SPECIFICATIONS

Year	VIN	No. Cylinder Displacement cu. in. (liter)	Seat Angle (deg.)	Face Angle (deg.)	Spring Test Pressure (lbs.)	Spring Installed Height (in.)	Stem-to-Guide Clearance (in.) Intake	Stem-to-Guide Clearance (in.) Exhaust	Stem Diameter (in.) Intake	Stem Diameter (in.) Exhaust
1986	C	4 122 (2.0)	45	44	149	1.49	.0010–.0027	.0015–.0032	.3420	.3415
	A	4 140 (2.3)	45	44	149	1.49	.0010–.0027	.0015–.0032	.3420	.3415
	E	4 140 (2.3) ⑬	45	44	149	1.49	.0010–.0027	.0015–.0032	.3420	.3415
	S	6 171 (2.8)	45	44	144	1.60	.0008–.0025	.0018–.0035	.3163	.3133
	T	6 177 (2.9)	45	44	144	1.58	.0008–.0025	.0018–.0035	.3163	.3133
	U	6 183 (3.0)	45	44	185	1.85	.0010–.0027	.0015–.0032	.3135	.3125
	Y	6 300 (4.9)	45	44	175	⑫	.0010–.0027	.0010–.0027	.3420	.3415
	N	8 302 (5.0)	45	44	⑤	②	.0010–.0027	.0015–.0032	.3420	.3415
	H	8 351 (5.8)	45	44	200	⑥	.0010–.0027	.0015–.0032	.3420	.3415
	I	8 420 (6.9)	⑧	⑧	60	—	.0012–.0029	.0012–.0029	.3720	.3720
	L	8 460 (7.5)	45	44	229	1 13/16	.0010–.0027	.0010–.0027	.3420	.3420
1987-88	C	4 122 (2.0)	45	44	149	1.49	.0010–.0027	.0015–.0032	.3420	.3415
	A	4 140 (2.3)	45	44	149	1.49	.0010–.0027	.0015–.0032	.3420	.3415
	E	4 140 (2.3) ⑬	45	44	149	1.49	.0010–.0027	.0015–.0032	.3420	.3415
	S	6 171 (2.8)	45	44	144	1.60	.0008–.0025	.0018–.0035	.3163	.3133
	T	6 177 (2.9)	45	44	144	1.58	.0008–.0025	.0018–.0035	.3163	.3133
	U	6 183 (3.0)	45	44	185	1.85	.0010–.0027	.0015–.0032	.3135	.3125
	Y	6 300 (4.9)	45	44	175	⑫	.0010–.0027	.0010–.0027	.3420	.3415
	N	8 302 (5.0)	45	44	⑤	②	.0010–.0027	.0015–.0032	.3420	.3415
	H	8 351 (5.8)	45	44	200	⑥	.0010–.0027	.0015–.0032	.3420	.3415
	I	8 420 (6.9)	⑧	⑧	60	—	.0012–.0029	.0012–.0029	.3720	.3720
	L	8 460 (7.5)	45	44	229	1 13/16	.0010–.0027	.0010–.0027	.3420	.3420

① Intake 202
Exhaust 200
② Intake 1 11/16
Exhaust 1 19/32
③ Intake 197
Exhaust 192
④ Intake 1 45/64
Exhaust 1 37/64
⑤ Intake 204
Exhaust 200
⑥ Intake 1 25/32
Exhaust 1 19/32
⑦ Intake 1 53/64
Exhaust 1 45/64
⑧ Intake 30
Exhaust 37.5
⑨ Intake 45
Exhaust 30
⑩ Inner spring 28
Outer spring 40
⑪ Inner spring 1.488
Outer spring 1.587
⑫ Intake 1.64
Exhaust 1.47
⑬ Diesel Engine

PISTON AND RING SPECIFICATIONS

All measurements are given in inches.

Year	VIN	No. Cylinder Displacement cu. in. (liter)	Piston Clearance	Ring Gap			Ring Side Clearance		
				Top Compression	Bottom Compression	Oil Control	Top Compression	Bottom Compression	Oil Control
1982	3	6 232 (3.8)	.0014–.0022	.0100–.0200	.0100–.0200	.0150–.0550	.0020–.0040	.0020–.0040	Snug
	D	8 255 (4.2)	.0014–.0024	.0100–.0200	.0100–.0200	.0150–.0550	.0020–.0040	.0020–.0040	Snug
	E	6 300 (4.9)	.0014–.0022	.0100–.0200	.0100–.0200	.0100–.0350	.0019–.0036	.0020–.0040	Snug
	F	8 302 (5.0)	.0018–.0026	.0100–.0200	.0100–.0200	.0150–.0350	.0020–.0040	.0020–.0040	Snug
	W	8 351 (5.8)	.0022–.0030	.0100–.0200	.0100–.0200	.0150–.0350	.0019–.0036	.0020–.0040	Snug
	Z	8 400 (6.6)	.0014–.0022	.0100–.0200	.0100–.0200	.0150–.0350	.0019–.0036	.0020–.0040	Snug
	L	8 460 (7.5)	.0022–.0300	.0100–.0200	.0100–.0200	.0100–.0350	.0019–.0036	.0020–.0040	Snug
1983	3	6 232 (3.8)	.0014–.0022	.0100–.0200	.0100–.0200	.0150–.0550	.0020–.0040	.0020–.0040	Snug
	Y	6 300 (4.9)	.0014–.0022	.0100–.0200	.0100–.0200	.0100–.0350	.0019–.0036	.0020–.0040	Snug
	F	8 302 (5.0)	.0018–.0026	.0100–.0200	.0100–.0200	.0150–.0350	.0020–.0040	.0020–.0040	Snug
	G	8 351 (5.8)	.0022–.0030	.0100–.0200	.0100–.0200	.0150–.0350	.0019–.0036	.0020–.0040	Snug
	I	8 420 (6.9)	.0055–.0075	.0140–.0240	.0100–.0240	.0600–.0700	.0020–.0040	.0020–.0040	.0010–.0030
	L	8 460 (7.5)	.0014–.0022	.0100–.0200	.0100–.0200	.0150–.0350	.0019–.0036	.0020–.0040	Snug
1984	K	4 122 (2.0)	.0014–.0022	.0100–.0200	.0100–.0200	.0150–.0550	.0020–.0040	.0020–.0040	Snug
	3	4 134 (2.2)	.0021–.0031	.0157–.0217	.0118–.0157	.0138–.0217	.0020–.0035	.0016–.0031	.0012–.0028
	Z	4 140 (2.3)	.0014–.0022	.0100–.0200	.0100–.0200	.0150–.0550	.0020–.0040	.0020–.0040	Snug
	S	6 171 (2.8)	.0011–.0019	.0150–.0230	.0150–.0230	.0150–.0550	.0020–.0033	.0020–.0033	Snug
	Y	6 300 (4.9)	.0014–.0022	.0100–.0200	.0100–.0200	.0100–.0350	.0019–.0036	.0020–.0040	Snug
	F	8 302 (5.0)	.0018–.0026	.0100–.0200	.0100–.0200	.0150–.0350	.0020–.0040	.0020–.0040	Snug
	G	8 351 (5.8)	.0022–.0030	.0100–.0200	.0100–.0200	.0150–.0350	.0019–.0036	.0020–.0040	Snug
	I	8 420 (6.9)	.0055–.0075	.0140–.0240	.0100–.0240	.0600–.0700	.0020–.0040	.0020–.0040	.0010–.0030
	L	8 460 (7.5)	.0014–.0022	.0100–.0200	.0100–.0200	.0150–.0350	.0019–.0036	.0020–.0040	Snug

PISTON AND RING SPECIFICATIONS

All measurements are given in inches.

Year	VIN	No. Cylinder Displacement cu. in. (liter)	Piston Clearance	Ring Gap Top Compression	Ring Gap Bottom Compression	Ring Gap Oil Control	Ring Side Clearance Top Compression	Ring Side Clearance Bottom Compression	Ring Side Clearance Oil Control
1985	K	4 122 (2.0)	.0014–.0022	.0100–.0200	.0100–.0200	.0150–.0550	.0020–.0040	.0020–.0040	Snug
	Z	4 140 (2.3)	.0014–.0022	.0100–.0200	.0100–.0200	.0150–.0550	.0020–.0040	.0020–.0040	Snug
	Y	6 300 (4.9)	.0014–.0022	.0100–.0200	.0100–.0200	.0100–.0350	.0019–.0036	.0020–.0040	Snug
	F&N	8 302 (5.0)	.0018–.0026	.0100–.0200	.0100–.0200	.0150–.0350	.0020–.0040	.0020–.0040	Snug
	G&H	8 351 (5.8)	.0022–.0030	.0100–.0200	.0100–.0200	.0150–.0350	.0019–.0036	.0020–.0040	Snug
	I	8 420 (6.9)	.0055–.0075	.0140–.0240	.0100–.0240	.0600–.0700	.0020–.0040	.0020–.0040	.0010–.0030
	L	8 460 (7.5)	.0014–.0022	.0100–.0200	.0100–.0200	.0150–.0350	.0019–.0036	.0020–.0040	Snug
1986	C	4 122 (2.0)	.0014–.0022	.0100–.0200	.0100–.0200	.0150–.0550	.0020–.0040	.0020–.0040	Snug
	A	4 140 (2.3)	.0014–.0022	.0100–.0200	.0100–.0200	.0150–.0550	.0020–.0040	.0020–.0040	Snug
	E	4 140 (2.3) ①	.0016–.0024	.0100–.0160	.0100–.0160	.0100–.0180	.0010–.0020	.0010–.0030	.0010–.0030
	S	6 171 (2.8)	.0011–.0019	.0150–.0230	.0150–.0230	.0150–.0550	.0020–.0033	.0020–.0033	Snug
	T	6 177 (2.9)	.0011–.0019	.0150–.0230	.0150–.0230	.0150–.0550	.0020–.0033	.0020–.0033	Snug
	U	6 183 (3.0)	.0012–.0023	.0100–.0200	.0100–.0200	.0100–.0490	.0016–.0037	.0016–.0037	Snug
	Y	6 300 (4.9)	.0014–.0022	.0100–.0200	.0100–.0200	.0100–.0350	.0019–.0036	.0020–.0040	Snug
	N	8 302 (5.0)	.0018–.0026	.0100–.0200	.0100–.0200	.0150–.0350	.0020–.0040	.0020–.0040	Snug
	H	8 351 (5.8)	.0022–.0030	.0100–.0200	.0100–.0200	.0150–.0350	.0019–.0036	.0020–.0040	Snug
	I	8 420 (6.9)	.0055–.0075	.0140–.0240	.0100–.0240	.0600–.0700	.0020–.0040	.0020–.0040	.0010–.0030
	L	8 460 (7.5)	.0014–.0022	.0100–.0200	.0100–.0200	.0150–.0350	.0019–.0036	.0020–.0040	Snug

PISTON AND RING SPECIFICATIONS

All measurements are given in inches.

Year	VIN	No. Cylinder Displacement cu. in. (liter)	Piston Clearance	Ring Gap			Ring Side Clearance		
				Top Compression	Bottom Compression	Oil Control	Top Compression	Bottom Compression	Oil Control
1987-88	C	4 122 (2.0)	.0014–.0022	.0100–.0200	.0100–.0200	.0150–.0550	.0020–.0040	.0020–.0040	Snug
	A	4 140 (2.3)	.0014–.0022	.0100–.0200	.0100–.0200	.0150–.0550	.0020–.0040	.0020–.0040	Snug
	E	4 140 (2.3) ①	.0016–.0024	.0100–.0160	.0100–.0160	.0100–.0180	.0010–.0020	.0010–.0030	.0010–.0030
	S	6 171 (2.8)	.0011–.0019	.0150–.0230	.0150–.0230	.0150–.0550	.0020–.0033	.0020–.0033	Snug
	T	6 177 (2.9)	.0011–.0019	.0150–.0230	.0150–.0230	.0150–.0550	.0020–.0033	.0020–.0033	Snug
	U	6 183 (3.0)	.0012–.0023	.0100–.0200	.0100–.0200	.0100–.0490	.0016–.0037	.0016–.0037	Snug
	Y	6 300 (4.9)	.0014–.0022	.0100–.0200	.0100–.0200	.0100–.0350	.0019–.0036	.0020–.0040	Snug
	N	8 302 (5.0)	.0018–.0026	.0100–.0200	.0100–.0200	.0150–.0350	.0020–.0040	.0020–.0040	Snug
	H	8 351 (5.8)	.0022–.0030	.0100–.0200	.0100–.0200	.0150–.0350	.0019–.0036	.0020–.0040	Snug
	I	8 420 (6.9)	.0055–.0075	.0140–.0240	.0100–.0240	.0600–.0700	.0020–.0040	.0020–.0040	.0010–.0030
	L	8 460 (7.5)	.0014–.0022	.0100–.0200	.0100–.0200	.0150–.0350	.0019–.0036	.0020–.0040	Snug

① Diesel Engine

TORQUE SPECIFICATIONS

All readings in ft. lbs.

Year	VIN	No. Cylinder Displacement cu. in. (liter)	Cylinder Head Bolts	Main Bearing Bolts	Rod Bearing Bolts	Crankshaft Pulley Bolts	Flywheel Bolts	Manifold		Spark Plugs
								Intake	Exhaust	
1982	3	6 232 (3.8)	74 ①	65–81	31–36	93–121	54–64	18–20	15–22	17–22
	D	8 255 (4.2)	65–72 ②	60–70	19–24	70–90	75–85	23–35	18–24	10–15
	E	6 300 (4.9)	85 ③	60–70	40–45	130–150	75–85	22–32	22–32	10–15
	F	8 302 (5.0)	65–72 ②	60–70	40–45	70–90	75–85	23–35	18–24	10–15
	W	8 351 (5.8)	105–112 ④	95–105	40–45	70–90	75–85	23–35	18–24	10–15
	Z	8 400 (6.6)	⑤	95–105	40–45	70–90	75–85	22–32	18–24	10–15
	L	8 460 (7.5)	⑥	95–105	45–50	70–90	75–85	22–32	28–33	5–10
1983	3	6 232 (3.8)	74 ①	65–81	31–36	93–121	54–64	18–20	15–22	17–22
	Y	6 300 (4.9)	85 ③	60–70	40–45	130–150	75–85	22–32	22–32	10–15
	F	8 302 (5.0)	65–72 ②	60–70	40–45	70–90	75–85	23–35	18–24	10–15
	G	8 351 (5.8)	105–112 ④	95–105	40–45	70–90	75–85	23–35	18–24	10–15
	I	8 420 (6.9)	⑦	⑧	⑨	90	38	NA	30	—
	L	8 460 (7.5)	⑥	95–105	45–50	70–90	75–85	22–32	28–33	5–10
1984	K	4 122 (2.0)	⑩	⑩	⑫	100–120	56–64	⑫	⑬	5–10
	Z	4 140 (2.3)	⑩	⑩	⑫	100–120	56–64	⑫	⑬	5–10
	3	4 134 (2.2)	80–85	80–85	50–54	253–289	95–137	12–17	17–20	—
	S	6 173 (2.8)	⑭	65–75	19–24	85–96	47–52	⑮	20–30	18–28
	Y	6 300 (4.9)	85 ③	60–70	40–45	130–150	75–85	22–32	22–32	10–15
	F	8 302 (5.0)	65–72 ②	60–70	40–45	70–90	75–85	23–35	18–24	10–15
	G	8 351 (5.8)	105–112 ④	95–105	40–45	70–90	75–85	23–35	18–24	10–15
	I	8 420 (6.9)	⑦	⑧	⑨	90	38	NA	30	—
	L	8 460 (7.5)	⑥	95–105	45–50	70–90	75–85	22–32	28–33	5–10
1985	K	4 122 (2.0)	⑩	⑩	⑪	100–120	56–64	⑫	⑬	5–10
	Z	4 140 (2.3)	⑩	⑩	⑪	100–120	56–64	⑫	⑬	5–10
	Y	6 300 (4.9)	85 ③	60–70	40–45	130–150	75–85	22–32	22–32	10–15
	F&N	8 302 (5.0)	65–72 ②	60–70	40–45	70–90	75–85	23–35	18–24	10–15
	G&H	8 351 (5.8)	105–112 ④	95–105	40–45	70–90	75–85	23–35	18–24	10–15
	I	8 420 (6.9)	⑦	⑧	⑨	90	38	NA	30	—
	L	8 460 (7.5)	⑥	95–105	45–50	70–90	75–85	22–32	28–33	5–10
1986	C	4 122 (2.0)	⑩	⑩	⑪	100–120	56–64	⑫	⑬	5–10
	A	4 140 (2.3)	⑩	⑩	⑪	100–120	56–64	⑫	⑬	5–10
	E	4 140 (2.3)	⑯	55–61	33–34	123–137	94–101	11–14	11–14	—
	S	6 173 (2.8)	⑮	65–75	19–24	85–96	47–52	⑮	20–30	18–28
	T	6 179 (2.9)	⑱	65–75	19–24	85–96	47–52	⑮	20–30	18–28
	Y	6 300 (4.9)	85 ③	60–70	40–45	130–150	75–85	22–32	22–32	10–15
	N	8 302 (5.0)	65–72 ②	60–70	40–45	70–90	75–85	23–35	18–24	10–15
	H	8 351 (5.8)	105–112 ④	95–105	40–45	70–90	75–85	23–35	18–24	10–15
	I	8 420 (6.9)	⑦	⑧	⑨	90	38	NA	30	—
	L	8 460 (7.5)	⑥	95–105	45–50	70–90	75–85	22–32	28–33	5–10

TORQUE SPECIFICATIONS

All readings in ft. lbs.

Year	VIN	No. Cylinder Displacement cu. in. (liter)	Cylinder Head Bolts	Main Bearing Bolts	Rod Bearing Bolts	Crankshaft Pulley Bolts	Flywheel Bolts	Manifold Intake	Manifold Exhaust	Spark Plugs
1987-88	C	4 122 (2.0)	⑩	⑩	⑪	100-120	56-64	⑫	⑬	5-10
	A	4 140 (2.3)	⑩	⑪	⑪	100-120	56-64	⑫	⑬	5-10
	E	4 140 (2.3)	⑯	55-61	33-34	123-137	94-101	11-14	11-14	—
	S	6 173 (2.8)	⑭	65-75	19-24	85-96	47-52	⑮	20-30	18-28
	T	6 179 (2.9)	⑰	65-75	19-24	85-96	47-52	⑮	20-30	18-28
	U	6 183 (3.0)	⑱	65-81	⑲	141-169	54-64	⑳	NA	5-11
	Y	6 300 (4.9)	85 ③	60-70	40-45	130-150	75-85	22-32	22-32	10-15
	N	8 302 (5.0)	65-72 ②	60-70	40-45	70-90	75-85	23-35	18-24	10-15
	H	8 351 (5.8)	105-112 ④	95-105	40-45	70-90	75-85	23-35	18-24	10-15
	I	8 420 (6.9)	⑦	⑧	⑨	90	38	NA	30	—
	L	8 460 (7.5)	⑥	95-105	45-50	70-90	75-85	22-32	28-33	5-10

① Torque in 4 steps
a. 47
b. 55
c. 63
d. 74
back off 2-3 turns and repeat.

② Torque in 2 steps
a. 55-65
b. 65-72

③ Torque in 3 steps
a. 55
b. 60
c. 85

④ Torque in 3 steps
a. 85
b. 95
c. 105-112

⑤ Torque in 2 steps
a. 75
b. 95-105

⑥ Torque in 3 steps
a. 80
b. 110
c. 130-140

⑦ Torque in 2 steps
a. 43
b. 60

⑧ Torque in 2 steps
a. 75
b. 95

⑨ Torque in 2 steps
a. 38
b. 46-51

⑩ Torque in 2 steps
a. 50-60
b. 80-90

⑪ Torque in 2 steps
a. 25-30
b. 30-36

⑫ Torque in 2 steps
a. 5-7
b. 14-21 non turbo
13-18 turbo

⑬ Torque in 2 steps
a. 5-7
b. 16-23

⑭ Torque in 3 steps
a. 29-40
b. 40-51
c. 70-85

⑮ Hand start and snug
Then 4 steps
a. 3-6
b. 6-11
c. 11-15
d. 15-18

⑯ Cold 76-83
Hot 84-90

⑰ 3 steps
a. 22
b. 51-55
c. Then turn 90°

⑱ Torque in 2 steps
a. 48-54
b. 63-80

⑲ 3 steps
a. 20-28
b. Back off a minimum of 2 revolutions
c. 20-25

⑳ 2 steps
a. 11
b. 18

WHEEL ALIGNMENT

Year	Model	Ride Height Min.	Ride Height Max.	Caster (Degrees) Min.	Caster (Degrees) Max.	Camber (Degrees) Min.	Camber (Degrees) Max.	Toe-in (in.)	Toe-in (in.)
1982	F-150, Bronco (4 × 4)	2 3/4	3 1/4	6	9	−2 1/2	−1/4	1/32	1/16
		3 1/4	3 1/2	5	8	−1 3/4	1/2	1/32	1/16
		3 1/2	4	4	7	−3/4	1 1/2	1/32	1/16
		4	4 1/4	3	6	0	2 1/4	1/32	1/16
		4 1/4	4 3/4	2	5	1	3 1/4	1/32	1/16
		4 3/4	5	1	4	1 3/4	4	1/32	1/16
	E-100, 150	3 1/4	3 1/2	6 1/4	8	−1 3/4	−1/4	1/32	1/16
		3 1/2	3 3/4	5 3/4	7 1/4	−1 1/2	1/4	1/32	1/16
		3 3/4	4	5	6 3/4	−1	3/4	1/32	1/16
		4	4 1/4	4 1/2	5 3/4	−1/2	1 1/4	1/32	1/16
		4 1/4	4 1/2	4	5 1/2	0	1 3/4	1/32	1/16
		4 1/2	4 3/4	3 1/4	4 1/2	1/2	2 1/4	1/32	1/16
		4 3/4	5	2 1/2	4	1	2 3/4	1/32	1/16
		5	5 1/4	2	3 1/4	1 1/2	3 1/4	1/32	1/16
		5 1/4	5 1/2	1 1/2	2 3/4	2	3 3/4	1/32	1/16
	E-250, 350	3 1/4	3 1/2	9	10 1/2	−1 3/4	−1/4	1/32	1/16
		3 1/2	3 3/4	8 1/2	9 3/4	−1 1/2	1/4	1/32	1/16
		3 3/4	4	7 7/8	9	−1	3/4	1/32	1/16
		4	4 1/4	7 1/8	8 1/2	−1/2	1 1/4	1/32	1/16
		4 1/4	4 1/2	6 1/2	7 3/4	0	1 3/4	1/32	1/16
		4 1/2	4 3/4	5 3/4	7	1/2	2 1/4	1/32	1/16
		4 3/4	5	5 1/4	6 1/2	1	2 3/4	1/32	1/16
		5	5 1/4	4 5/8	6	1 1/2	3 1/4	1/32	1/16
		5 1/4	5 1/2	4	5 1/2	2	3 3/4	1/32	1/16
	F-250, 350 (4 × 4)	4 3/4	5	3	5	4 3/4	5	1/32	1/16
		5	5 1/2	3 1/8	5 1/8	−1 3/4	3/4	1/32	1/16
		5 1/2	6	3 1/8	5 1/8	−3/4	1 3/4	1/32	1/16
		6	6 1/4	3 1/4	5 1/4	1/4	2 3/4	1/32	1/16
		6 1/4	6 3/4	3 3/8	5 3/8	1 1/4	4	1/32	1/16
		6 3/4	7	3 1/2	5 1/2	2 1/2	5	1/32	1/16
	F-100, F-150 (4 × 2)	2 1/4	2 3/4	6	10	−3	−1/2	1/32	1/16
		2 3/4	3 1/4	5	9	−2	1/2	1/32	1/16
		3 1/4	3 1/2	4	8	−1 1/4	1 1/4	1/32	1/16
		3 1/2	4	3	7	−1/4	2 1/4	1/32	1/16
		4	4 1/4	2	6	1/2	3	1/32	1/16
		4 1/4	4 3/4	1	5	1 1/2	4	1/32	1/16
	F-250, 350 (4 × 2)	2	2 1/4	5 3/4	9	−2 1/2	0	1/32	1/16
		2 1/4	2 3/4	4 3/4	8	−1 1/2	1	1/32	1/16
		2 1/4	3 1/4	3 3/4	7	−1/4	1 3/4	1/32	1/16
		3 1/4	3 3/4	2 3/4	6	1/4	2 3/4	1/32	1/16
		3 1/2	4	1 3/4	5	1	3 1/2	1/32	1/16
		4	4 1/4	3/4	4	2	4 1/2	1/32	1/16

WHEEL ALIGNMENT

Year	Model	Ride Height Min.	Ride Height Max.	Caster (Degrees) Min.	Caster (Degrees) Max.	Camber (Degrees) Min.	Camber (Degrees) Max.	Toe-in (in.)	Toe-in (in.)
1983	F-150,	3 1/4	3 1/2	6	7	−1 1/2	3/4	1/32	1/16
	Bronco	3 1/2	4	5	6	−3/4	1 3/4	1/32	1/16
		4	4 1/4	4	5	1/4	2 3/4	1/32	1/16
		4 1/4	4 3/4	3	4	1 1/4	3 1/2	1/32	1/16
	F-250,	5	5 1/2	3 1/16	5 1/8	−1 3/4	3/4	1/32	1/16
	350	5 1/2	6	3 1/8	5 1/4	−3/4	1 3/4	1/32	1/16
	(4 × 4)	6	6 1/4	3 1/4	5 3/8	1/4	3	1/32	1/16
		6 1/4	6 3/4	3 3/8	5 1/2	1 1/2	4	1/32	1/16
		6 3/4	7	3 1/2	5 1/2	2 1/2	4 1/4	1/32	1/16
	F-100,	2 3/4	3 1/4	5 1/2	7 1/2	−1 1/2	3/4	1/32	1/16
	150	3 1/4	3 1/2	5	6	−3/4	1 1/2	1/32	1/16
	(4 × 2)	3 1/2	4	4 1/4	5 1/4	1/4	2 1/2	1/32	1/16
		4	4 1/4	3 1/4	4 1/4	1	3 1/2	1/32	1/16
		4 1/4	4 3/4	2 1/2	3 1/2	2	4 1/2	1/32	1/16
	F-250,	2 1/2	2 3/4	5 1/2	7	−1/2	1/2	1/32	1/16
	350	2 3/4	3 1/4	5	6	−1/2	1 1/2	1/32	1/16
	(4 × 2)	3 1/4	3 1/2	4	5	1/4	2 1/4	1/32	1/16
		3 1/2	4	3	4	1	3	1/32	1/16
		4	4 1/4	—	—	2	3 1/2	1/32	1/16
	E-100,	3 3/4	4	—	—	−3/4	3/4	1/32	1/16
	150	4	4 1/2	4 1/2	5 1/4	−5/8	1 5/8	1/32	1/16
		4 1/2	5	3 1/4	4	3/8	2 5/8	1/32	1/16
		5	5 1/2	2	2 3/4	1 1/4	3 5/8	1/32	1/16
		5 1/2	5 3/4	3/4	2 1/4	2 1/4	4 1/8	1/32	1/16
	E-250,	3 3/4	4	—	—	−5/8	7/8	1/32	1/16
	350	4	4 1/2	7 1/4	8	−1/2	1 7/8	1/32	1/16
		4 1/2	5	6	6 3/4	1/2	2 7/8	1/32	1/16
		5	5 1/2	4 3/4	5 1/2	1 1/2	3 7/8	1/32	1/16
		5 1/2	5 3/4	3 1/4	4	2 1/2	4 3/8	1/32	1/16
1984–88	F-150,	3 1/4	3 1/2	6	8	−1 3/4	−1/4	1/32	1/16
	Bronco	3 1/2	3 3/4	5	7	−3/4	3/4	1/32	1/16
	(4 × 4)	4	4 1/4	4	6	1/4	1 3/4	1/32	1/16
		4 1/4	4 1/2	3	5	1 1/4	2 3/4	1/32	1/16
	F-250, 350	5	5 1/4	3	5	−1 3/4	−1/4	1/32	1/16
	(4 × 4)	5 1/2	5 3/4	3 1/8	5 1/8	−3/4	3/4	1/32	1/16
	exc.	6	6 1/4	3 1/4	5 1/4	1/2	2	1/32	1/16
	Monobeam	6 1/4	6 1/2	3 3/8	5 3/8	1 1/2	3	1/32	1/16
	Susp.	6 3/4	7	3 1/2	5 1/2	2 1/2	4	1/32	1/16
	F-150	3 1/4	3 1/2	5	7	−3/4	3/4	1/32	1/16
	(4 × 2)	3 1/2	4	4	6	−1/4	1 1/4	1/32	1/16
		4	4 1/4	3 1/4	5 1/4	1/2	2	1/32	1/16
		4 1/4	4 3/4	2 1/2	4 1/2	2	3 1/2	1/32	1/16
		4 3/4	5	1 1/2	3 1/2	3	4 1/2	1/32	1/16

WHEEL ALIGNMENT

Year	Model	Ride Height		Caster (Degrees)		Camber (Degrees)		Toe-in (in.)	Toe-in (in.)
		Min.	Max.	Min.	Max.	Min.	Max.		
1984	F250, 350 (4 × 2)	2 1/2	2 3/4	5	7	−3/4	3/4	1/32	1/16
		2 3/4	3	4	6	1/4	1 3/4	1/32	1/16
		3 1/4	3 1/2	3 1/4	5 1/4	1	2 5/8	1/32	1/16
		3 3/4	4	2 1/2	4 1/2	2	3 1/2	1/32	1/16
		4	4 1/4	1 1/2	3 1/2	3	4 1/2	1/32	1/16
1985	F-250, 350 (4 × 2)	2 1/2	2 3/4	5 1/4	7 1/4	−1	1/2	3/32	3/16
		2 3/4	3	5	7	−1/2	3/4	3/32	3/16
		3 1/4	3 1/2	4 1/2	6 1/2	−1/8	1 1/4	3/32	3/16
		3 3/4	4	4	6	1/2	1 3/4	3/32	3/16
		4	4 1/4	3 1/2	5 1/2	3/4	2 1/4	3/32	3/16
1984	E-150	3 1/2	3 3/4	—	—	—	—	1/32	1/16
		4	4 1/4	4 5/8	6 1/4	−3/4	1/2	1/32	1/16
		4 1/2	4 3/4	3 1/4	5 1/4	1/2	1 3/4	1/32	1/16
		5	5 1/4	2	4	1 1/2	2 3/4	1/32	1/16
		5 1/2	5 3/4	1/4	2 1/4	2 3/8	3 5/8	1/32	1/16
1984–88	E-250, 350	3 1/4	3 1/2	—	—	—	—	1/32	1/16
		3 3/4	4	7 5/8	9 5/8	−3/4	1/2	1/32	1/16
		4 1/4	4 1/2	6 1/4	8 1/4	1/4	1 1/2	1/32	1/16
		4 3/4	5	5	7	1 1/4	2 1/2	1/32	1/16
		5 1/4	5 1/2	3 3/4	5 3/4	2 1/4	3 1/2	1/32	1/16
1985–88	E-150	3 1/2	3 3/4	—	—	—	—	1/32	1/16
		4	4 1/2	7 1/2	9 1/2	−1 1/4	1/4	1/32	1/16
		4 1/2	5	6 1/4	8 1/4	−1/8	1 1/4	1/32	1/16
		5	5 1/2	5	7	7/8	2 1/4	1/32	1/16
		5 1/2	5 3/4	3 1/4	5 1/4	1 3/4	3 1/4	1/32	1/16
1986	F-250, 350 (4 × 2)	3	3 1/4	5 1/2	7 1/2	−1	0	3/32	3/16
		3 1/4	3 1/2	5	7	−1/2	1/2	3/32	3/16
		3 1/2	3 3/4	4 1/4	6 1/4	1/2	1 1/2	3/32	3/16
		3 3/4	4	3 1/2	5 1/2	3/4	1 3/4	3/32	3/16
		4	4 1/4	2 3/4	4 3/4	1 1/2	2 1/2	3/32	3/16
1987–88	F-250, 350 (4 × 2)	3 1/4	3 1/2	5 3/4	7 3/4	−1	1/2	3/32	3/16
		3 3/4	4	4 1/2	6 1/2	1/4	1 3/4	3/32	3/16
		4 1/4	4 1/2	3 1/4	5 1/4	1 1/2	3	3/32	3/16
		4 3/4	5	2 1/4	4 1/4	2 1/2	4	3/32	3/16
		5 1/4	5 3/4	1	3	3 3/4	5 1/4	3/32	3/16
1986–88	F-350 (4 × 4) w/Mono Beam Susp.	4 3/4	4 3/4	5	5	1 1/2	1 1/2	1/32	1/16

WHEEL ALIGNMENT

Year	Model	Ride Height Min.	Ride Height Max.	Caster (Degrees) Min.	Caster (Degrees) Max.	Camber (Degrees) Min.	Camber (Degrees) Max.	Toe-in (in.)	Toe-in (in.)
1983	Ranger, (4 × 2)	2 3/4	3 1/4	4 1/2	7	−1	1	1/32	1/16
		3 1/4	3 1/2	4	6 1/2	−1/2	1 3/4	1/32	1/16
		3 1/2	4	3 3/8	5 7/8	0	2 3/8	1/32	1/16
		4	4 1/4	2 5/8	5 1/8	3/4	3	1/32	1/16
		4 1/4	4 3/4	2	4 1/2	1 1/2	3 3/4	1/32	1/16
	Ranger, (4 × 4)	2 3/4	3 1/4	5	8	−1	1/2	1/32	1/16
		3 1/4	3 1/2	4	7	0	1 1/2	1/32	1/16
		3 1/2	4	3	6	1/2	2	1/32	1/16
		4	4 1/4	2 1/2	5 1/2	1 1/4	2 3/4	1/32	1/16
		4 1/4	4 3/4	1 3/4	5	2	3 3/4	1/32	1/16
1984-88	Ranger, (4 × 2) w/Forged Axle	3 1/4	3 1/2	5 1/4	8 1/4	−2	−1/2	1/32	1/16
		3 1/2	3 3/4	4 1/2	7 1/2	−1 5/8	1/8	1/32	1/16
		3 3/4	4	3 1/2	6 1/2	−1/2	1	1/32	1/16
		4	4 1/4	3	6	1/4	1 3/4	1/32	1/16
		4 1/2	4 3/4	1 7/8	4 7/8	1 1/4	2 3/4	1/32	1/16
	w/Stamped Axle	3	3 1/4	5 1/4	8 1/4	−2	−1/2	1/32	1/16
		3 1/4	3 1/2	4 1/2	7 1/2	−1 5/8	1/8	1/32	1/16
		3 1/2	3 3/4	3 1/2	6 1/2	−1/2	1	1/32	1/16
		3 3/4	4	3	6	1/4	1 3/4	1/32	1/16
		4 1/4	4 1/2	1 7/8	4 7/8	1 1/4	2 3/4	1/32	1/16
1984-88	Ranger (exc. STX) & Bronco II (4 × 4)	2 3/4	3	5 1/2	8 1/2	−2	−1/2	1/32	1/16
		3 1/4	3 1/2	4	7	−1	1/2	1/32	1/16
		3 1/2	3 3/4	3	6	0	1 1/2	1/32	1/16
		4	4 1/4	2	5	1	2 1/2	1/32	1/16
		4 1/4	4 1/2	1	4	2	3 1/2	1/32	1/16
1987-88	Ranger, (4 × 4) STX	4 1/4	4 1/2	5 1/2	8 1/2	−2	−1/2	1/32	1/16
		4 1/2	5	4	7	−1	1/2	1/32	1/16
		5	5 1/4	3	6	0	1 1/2	1/32	1/16
		5 1/4	5 3/4	2	5	1	2 1/2	1/32	1/16
		5 3/4	6	1	4	2	3 1/2	1/32	1/16
1986-88	Aerostar	—	—	3	5	−5/16	11/16	1/32	1/16

ENGINE ELECTRICAL

Alternator

Removal and Installation

1. Disconnect battery ground cable.
2. Loosen the alternator mounting bolts and remove the adjustment arm to alternator attaching bolt.
3. Remove the electrical connectors from the alternator. The stator and field connectors are of the push-on type and should be pulled straight off to prevent damage to the terminal studs.
4. Disengage the alternator belt.
5. Remove the alternator mounting bolt and alternator.
6. Installation is the reverse of the removal procedure.

Voltage Regulator

EXTERNAL

NOTE: If vehicle is equipped with an electric choke, be sure to disconnect electric choke wire from starter terminal of the alternator when working on the charging system. Check electric choke wire for a ground condition. Removing the connector from an ungrounded regulator with the ignition switch on will destroy the regulator.

Removal and Installation

1. Disconnect the battery ground cable.
2. Remove the regulator mounting screws.
3. Disconnect the regulator from the wiring harness.
4. Installation is the reverse of the removal procedure.

Adjustment

These regulators are 100 percent solid state, consisting of transistors, diodes and resistors. They are calibrated and preset by the manufacturer. No readjustment is required or possible on these units.

INTEGRAL

Removal and Installation

1. Disconnect the battery ground cable.
2. Disconnect the wire harness attachments to the alternator/regulator assembly. Pull the two connectors straight out.
3. Loosen the alternator pivot. Remove the adjustment arm bolt from the alternator.
4. Disengage the drive belt from the alternator pulley.
5. Remove the pivot bolt and the alternator/regulator assembly.
6. Remove the fan shield if so equipped.
7. Installation is the reverse of the removal procedure.

Adjustment

The regulator automatically adjusts the alternator field current to maintain the alternator output voltage within prescribed limits to correctly charge the battery. The alternator is self current limiting.

Starter

For complete diagnostic and overhaul procedures for starter motor, see "Starters" in the Unit Repair Section.

Removal and Installation

1. Disconnect the negative battery cable.
2. Raise the vehicle and support it safely.
3. Disconnect starter cable at the starter terminal.

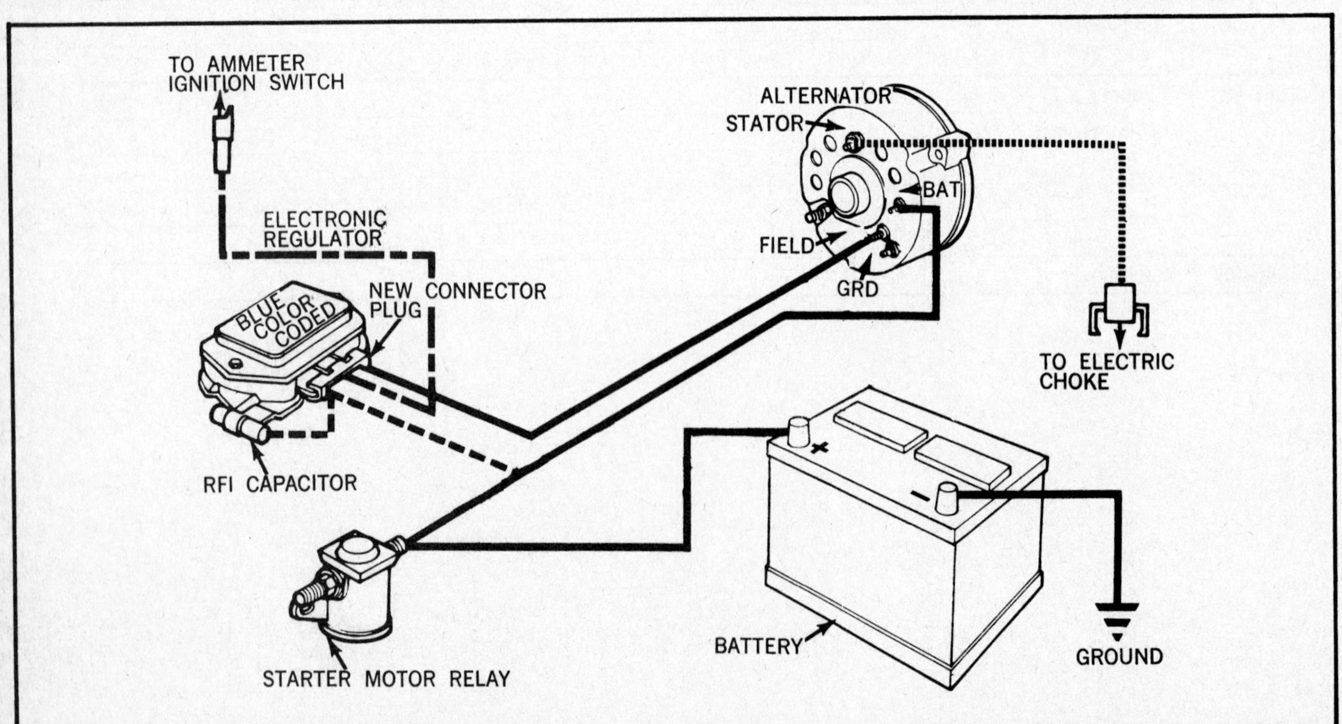

Electronic regulator and ammeter circuitry

3. Remove the starter mounting bolts.
4. Remove the starter assembly.
5. Installation is the reverse of the removal procedure.
6. Position the starter assembly to the flywheel housing and start the mounting bolts.
7. Snug all the bolts while holding the starter squarely against its mounting surface and fully inserted into the pilot hole. Tighten the bolts to 15–20 ft. lbs. (21–27 Nm).

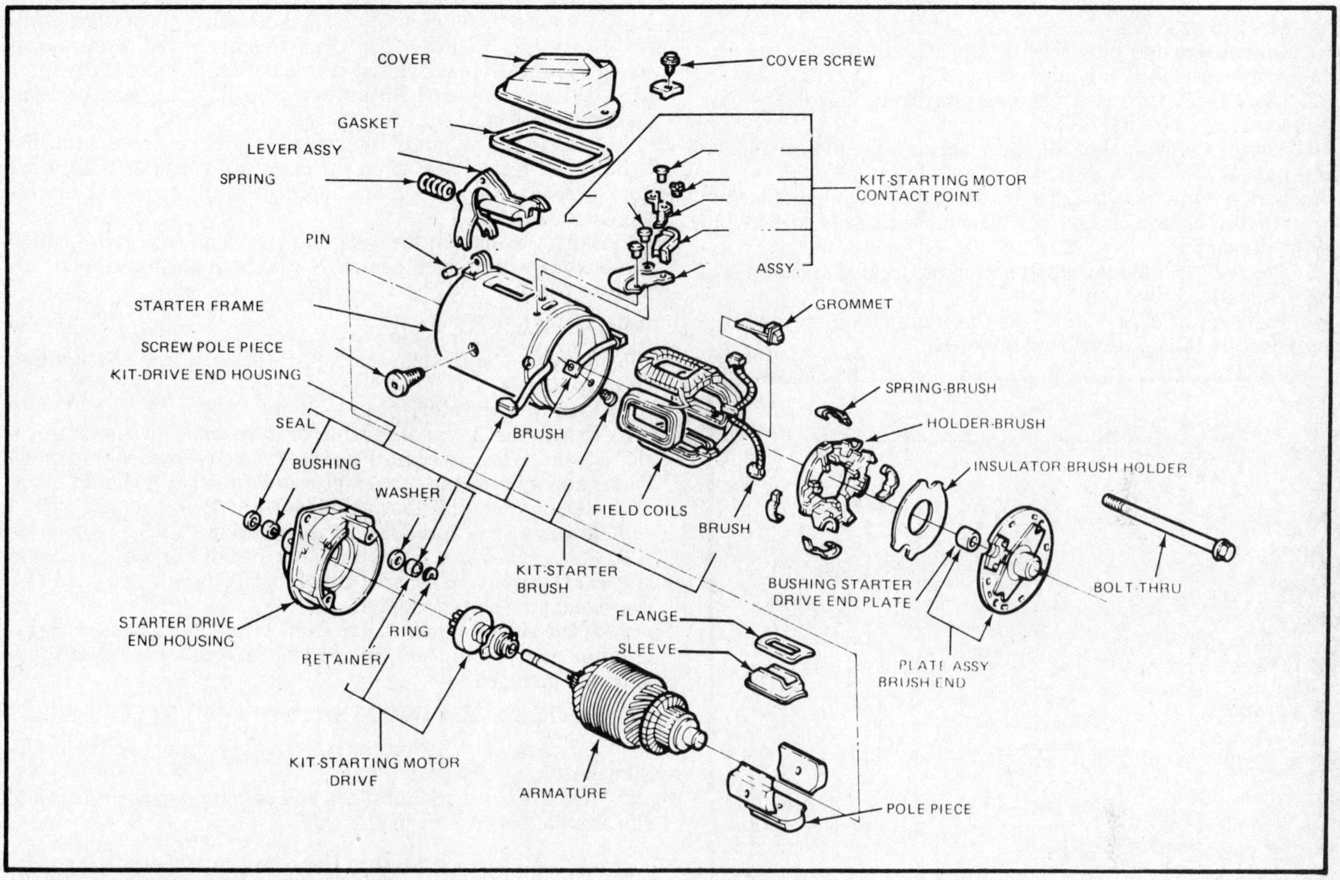

Disassembled view of Autolite starter

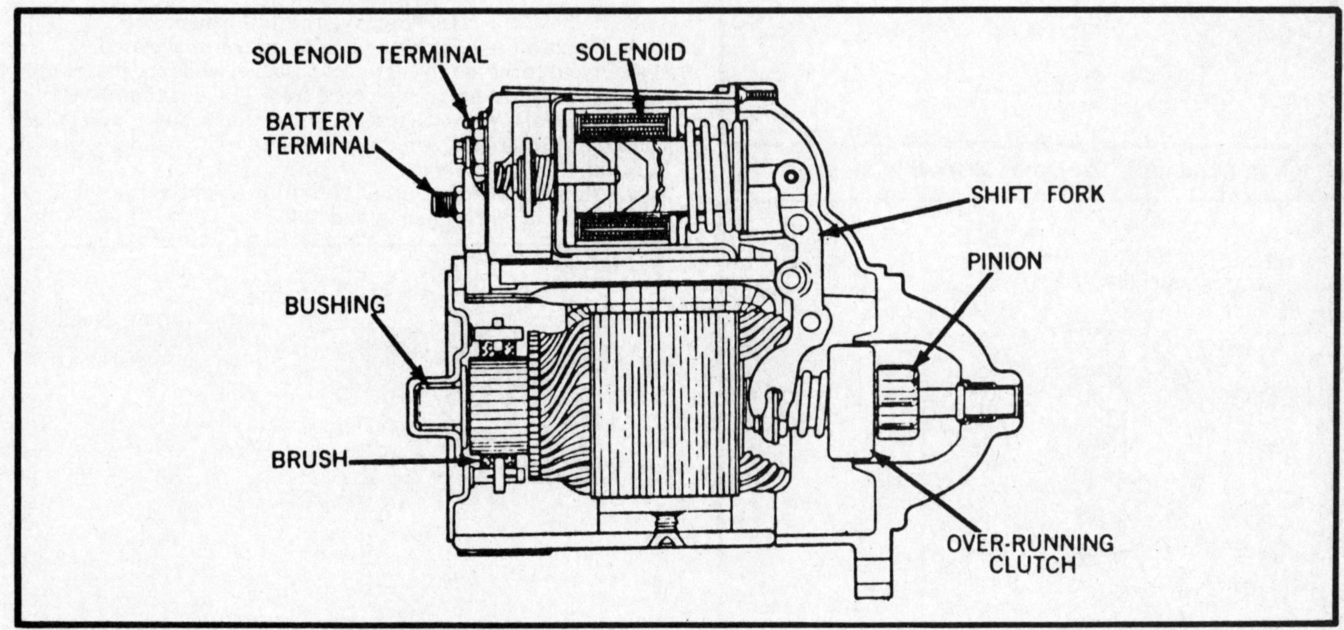

Cross section of solenoid actuated starter

Distributor

Removal and Installation

DURASPARK II

1. Remove the distributor cap and position the cap and ignition wires to the side.
2. Disconnect and plug the vacuum hoses from the vacuum diaphragm assembly, if equipped.
3. Disconnect the wire harness plug from the distributor connector.
4. Rotate the engine to align the stator pole and any armature pole.
5. Scribe a mark on the distributor body and engine block to indicate the position of the rotor tip and position of the distributor in the engine.
6. Remove the holddown bolt and clamp located at the base of the distributor.
7. Remove the distributor from the engine. Do not rotate the engine while the distributor is removed.

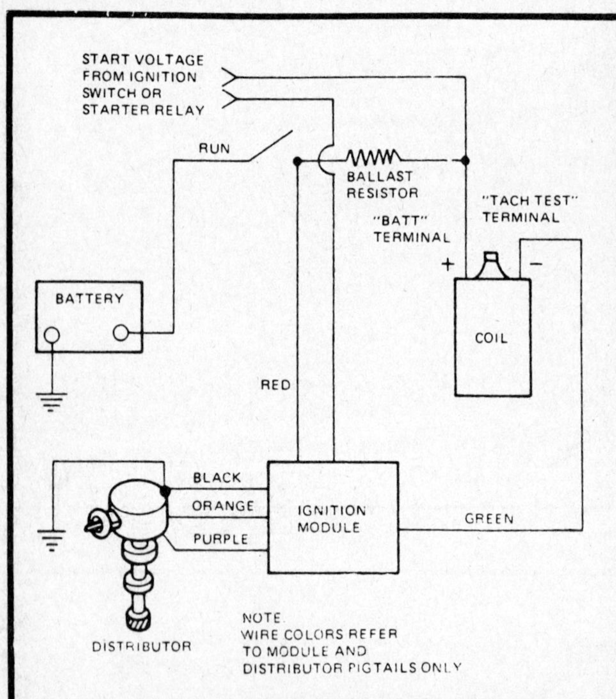

Ignition schematic for Dura Spark II system

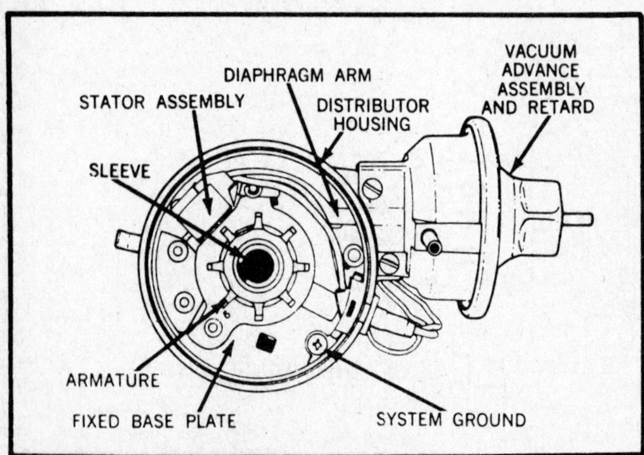

Electronic ignition distributor

8. To install position the distributor in the engine with the rotor aligned to the marks made on the distributor, or to the place the rotor pointed when the distributor was removed.
9. Install the mounting bolt and clamp, but do not tighten so the distributor can be turned for ignition timing purposes.
10. If the engine was rotated while the distributor was removed, rotate the engine (in normal direction of rotation) until No. 1 piston is on TDC (Top Dead Center) of the compression stroke. The TDC mark on the crankshaft pulley and the pointer should align. Rotor tip pointing at No. 1 spark plug wire position on distributor cap.
11. Engage the oil pump intermediate shaft and insert the distributor until fully seated on the engine, if the distributor does not fully seat, turn the engine slightly to fully engage the intermediate shaft.
12. Turn the distributor a slight bit more (if required) to align the stator (pick-up coil) assembly pole with an (the closest) armature pole.

DURASPARK III

1. Remove the distributor cap. Position it and the ignition wires aside.
2. Remove the rotor.
3. Rotate the engine until the No. 1 piston is on the compression stroke. The distributor sleeve groove (when looking down from the top) and the cap adaptor alignment slot should align.
4. Remove the distributor holddown bolt and clamp.
5. Reverse the procedure for installation.
6. Make sure when positioning the distributor that the slot in the distributor base will engage the block tab and the sleeve/adaptor slots are aligned.
7. If the sleeve/adapter slots cannot be aligned, raise the distributor and rotate the shaft to engage a different gear tooth with the cam gear.

TFI (THICK FILM INTEGRATED) IV SYSTEM

1. Disconnect the primary wiring connector from the distributor.
2. Remove the distributor cap and adapter and position it and the attached wires out of the way.

NOTE: Before removing the distributor cap, mark the position of the No. 1 wire tower on the distributor base for installation purposes.

3. Remove the rotor. Remove the TFI connector.
4. Remove the distributor holddown bolt and clamp.
5. Avoid turning the engine, if possible, while the distributor is removed. If the engine is turned from TDC position, TDC timing marks will have to be reset before the distributor is installed.
6. The stator and armature or vane switch should also be aligned.
7. After the distributor has been fully seated on the block, install the hold down bracket and bolt.

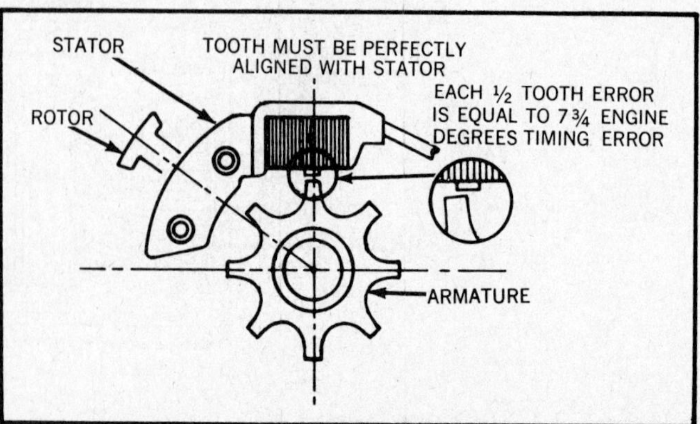

Electronic ignition static timing position

TACHOMETER CONNECTION

The solid state ignition coil connector allows a tachometer test lead with an alligator-type clip to be connected to the DEC (Distributor Electronic Control) terminal without removing the connector. When the engine rpm must be checked, install the tachometer alligator clip into the "TACH TEST" cavity. If the coil connector must be removed, grasp the wires and pull horizontally until it disconnects from the terminals.

IGNITION TIMING

Procedure

EEC IV AND TFI

On models equipped with EEC IV, all ignition timing is controlled by the EEC IV module. Initial ignition timing is not adjustable and no attempt at adjustment should be made. Models equipped with the TFI IV ignition system do not require ignition timing as routine maintenance, since the system adjusts itself.

The connection between the EEC IV microprocessor and the Thick Film Integrated (TFI) ignition module is called the SPOUT circuit. SPOUT simply means "spark out" since a signal carried to the TFI shuts off the coil and produces a spark for firing the spark plugs. A description of the system operation to control spark and advance follows.

1. The TFI IV module sends a voltage signal to the PIP (Profile Ignition Pickup) sensor, part of the Hall Effect assembly inside the distributor.
2. The PIP sensor then provides crankshaft position information and sends this signal back to the TFI module.
3. The TFI module sends the information to the EEC IV module and the required spark timing need is calculated.
4. The required timing information goes back to the TFI module through electrical circuitry (the SPOUT) and the primary circuit to the coil is turned off, causing secondary voltage to be produced and the spark plug to be fired at the precise time.
5. The TFI module also determines dwell and limits primary circuit to a safe value. If there is an open in the SPOUT signal wire, the TFI module will use the PIP sensor to provide spark; but the engine will only run at basic timing setting.
6. To check basic timing, the SPOUT wire must be disconnected. An inline connector is provided on the "yellow with a green dot" or a "black" single SPOUT wire. The wire is located between the distributor and engine harness. With the wire disconnected, the TFI module is locked into no advance and basic timing may be checked and adjusted if necessary.

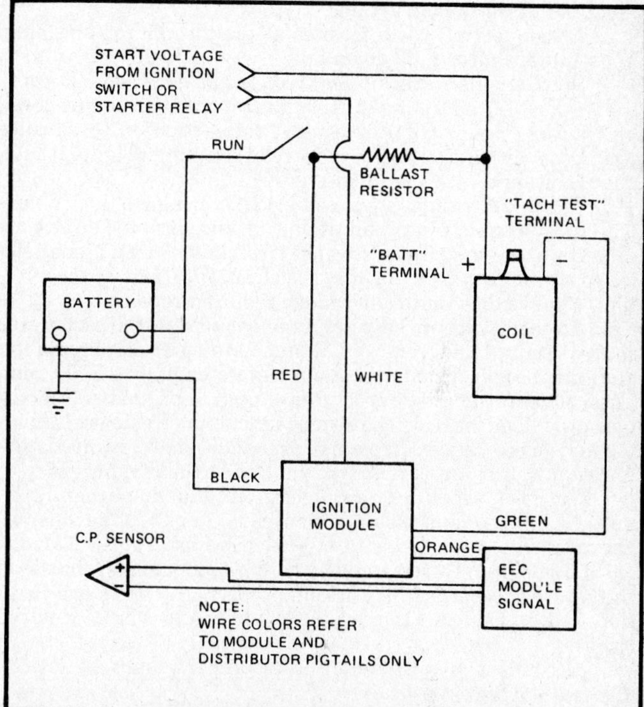

Ignition schematic for Dura III—ECC system

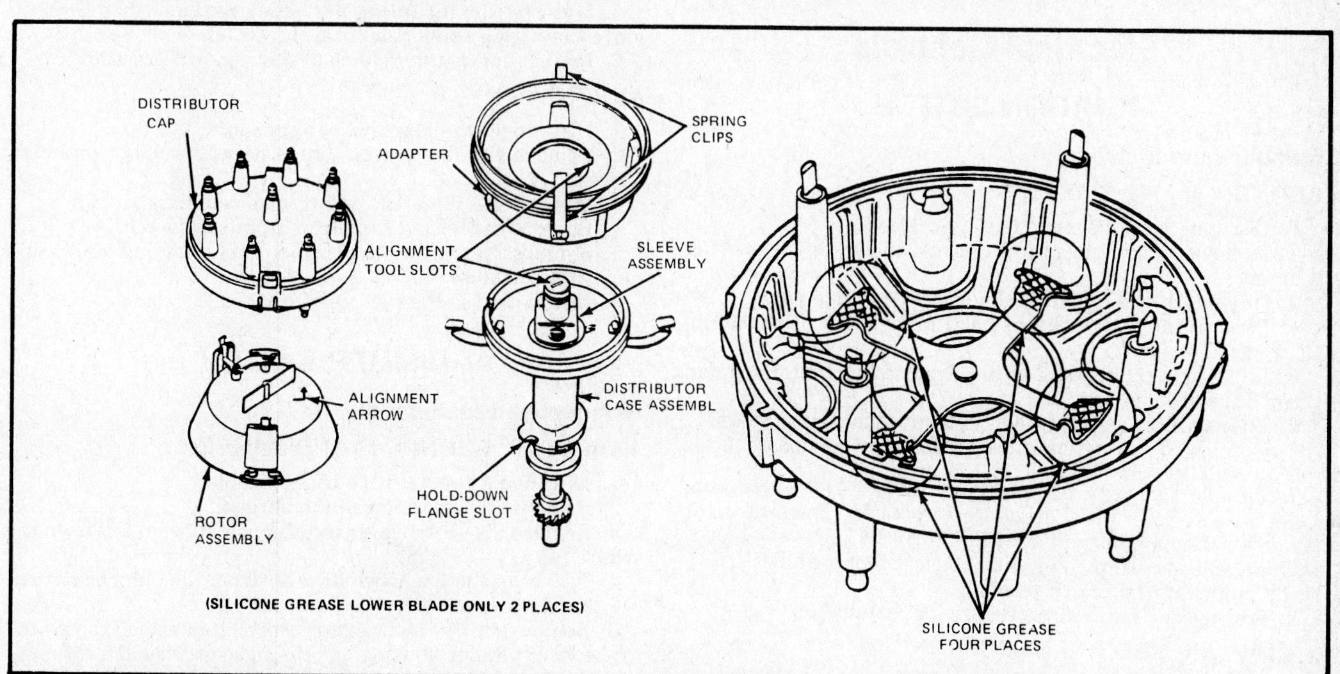

Bi-level distributor cap and rotor—Dura Spark III and ECC system

MONOLITHIC TIMING

The monolithic timing receptacle was made standard on all engines, while still retaining the conventional timing method. The monolithic system employs a timing receptacle designed to accept an electronic probe that is connected to a digital read-out meter. The receptacle is located in the front of the engine, so the probe is next to the balancer pulley. To time the engine with the monolithic timing equipment, follow the procedure below.

1. Install monolithic timing equipment to engine as per manufacturerer's instructions.
2. Disconnect all vacuum lines at the distributor and plug. Loosen distributor hold-down bolt.
3. Start engine warm up and reduce idle speed to 600 rpm.
4. Adjust initial timing to specification noted on engine decal, by rotating the distributor against rotor rotation to advance timing or with rotor rotation to retard timing. Tighten hold-down bolt, and recheck engine timing.
5. Check centrifugal advance by accelerating engine (in neutral) to 2500 rpm. If ignition timing advance is noted during acceleration, the centrifugal advance mechanism is functional. Refer to the engine decal for this specification. If out of specification, remove distributor and make required repairs.
6. To check vacuum advance, unplug and reinstall carburetor source vacuum line (removed in Step 2) to outer diaphragm (on dual diaphragm distributors). Accelerate engine to 2500 rpm. Total advance should be greater now than in prior step (centrifugal only) if advance mechanism is functional. Remove distributor and make required repairs if no additional advance is observed and vacuum is noted at the line to the diaphragm.
7. To check vacuum retard operation (dual diaphragm) connect the intake manifold line (removed in Step 2) to the inner diaphragm side of the distributor. With the engine at normal idle, a 6 or 12 degree retard should be noted, depending on shuttle, if the retard mechanism is working properly. If the retard function is not evident, remove distributor and make required repairs.
8. Reconnect all distributor lines properly and check curb idle, reset if necessary.
9. Remove engine tachometer and monolithic timing equipment.

Electrical Controls

IGNITION SWITCH

Removal and Installation

BRONCO, E AND F SERIES

1. Disconnect the negative battery cable.
2. Remove the steering column shroud and lower the steering column.
3. Disconnect the switch wiring at the multiple plug.
4. Remove the two nuts that hold the switch to the steering column.
5. Lift the switch upward to disengage the actuator rod and remove the switch.
6. To install the switch, the locking mechanism at the top of the column and the switch must be in the LOCK position for correct adjustment.
7. To hold the parts of the column in the LOCK position, move the shift lever into Park (with automatic transmission) or Reverse (with manual transmission), turn the key to the LOCK position and remove the key. New replacement switches are already pinned in the LOCK position.
8. Reverse the removal procedure for installation.

AEROSTAR, BRONCO II AND RANGER

1. Rotate the lock cylinder to the LOCK position. Disconnect the negative battery cable.
2. If equipped with tilt column, remove the steering wheel and the tilt lever.
3. Remove the upper extension shroud by squeezing it at the top and bottom positions and popping it free of the retaining plate at the right.
4. Remove the two trim shroud halves. Disconnect the ignition switch electrical connector.
5. Drill out the break off head bolts connecting the switch to the lock cylinder housing by using a $^1/_8$ inch drill. Remove the two bolts.
6. Disengage the ignition switch from the actuator pin.
7. To install, rotate the ignition key to the RUN position and align the holes in the switch casting base with the holes in the lock cylinder housing.
8. Install the new break off head bolts and tighten until the heads shear off. Connect the electrical connector to the ignition switch and install the steering column trim shrouds.
9. Reconnect the negative battery cable and check the switch for proper operation.

HEADLIGHT SWITCH

Removal and Installation

BRONCO AND F SERIES

1. Disconnect the negative battery cable.
2. Remove the wiper/washer and headlamp switch knobs using a hook tool to release each knob lock tab.
3. Remove the fog lamp switch knob if so equipped.
4. Remove the steering column shroud and the cluster finish panel.
5. Remove the switch from the instrument panel then the wiring connector from the switch.
6. Installation is the reverse of the removal procedure.

BRONCO II, E SERIES AND RANGER

1. Disconnect the negative battery cable.
2. Pull the headlamp switch knob to the full On position. Depress the shaft release button and remove the knob and shaft assembly.
3. Remove the instrument panel finish panel.
4. Unscrew the mounting nut. Remove the switch, then remove the wiring connector from the switch.
5. Installation is the reverse of the removal procedure.

AEROSTAR

1. Disconnect the negative battery cable.
2. Remove the five cluster finish panel assembly retaining screws.
3. Remove the three left control pad retaining screws.
4. Remove the wiring connector from the switch.
5. Remove the two switch to control pod retaining screws and remove the switch.
6. Installation is the reverse of removal.

DIMMER SWITCH

Removal and Installation

AEROSTAR, BRONCO II AND RANGER

1. Disconnect the negative battery cable.
2. Remove the steering column shroud.
3. Remove the switch lever by pulling it straight out from the switch.
4. Peel back the foam switch cover from the dimmer switch.
5. Disconnect the electrical connectors.
6. Remove the two self tapping screws that attach the switch to the lock cylinder housing and disengage the switch from the housing.
7. For installation reverse the removal procedure.

TURN SIGNAL SWITCH

Removal and Installation

BRONCO, E AND F SERIES

1. Disconnect the negative battery cable.
2. Remove the horn switch.
3. Remove the steering wheel.
4. Unscrew the turn signal switch lever from the steering column.
5. Remove the steering column shroud and the opening cover.
6. Disconnect the switch wiring connector.
7. Remove the screws that secure the switch to the column.
8. Vehicles equipped with a fixed column, remove the switch by lifting it out of the column and guiding the connector plug through the opening in the shift socket. On E series with automatic transmission, also remove the PRNDL lamp assembly from the shift socket.
9. Vehicles equipped with a tilt column require disassembly of the turn signal switch harness plug before removing the switch from the column. On E series with automatic transmission, remove the PRNDL lamp wire from the turn signal switch harness sheath.
10. Reverse the procedure for installation.

AEROSTAR, BRONCO II AND RANGER

1. Disconnect the negative battery cable.
2. Remove the steering column shroud.
3. Remove the switch lever by pulling it straight out from the switch.
4. Peel back the foam sight shield from the turn signal switch.
5. Disconnect the electrical connectors.
6. Remove the two self tapping screws that attach the switch to the lock cylinder housing and disengage the switch from the housing.
7. For installation reverse the removal procedure.

WINDSHIELD/WIPER SWITCH

Removal and Installation

BRONCO AND F SERIES

1. Disconnect the negative battery cable.
2. Remove the wiper switch knob and bezel.
3. Pull out the switch from under the instrument panel.
4. Disconnect the plug connector from the switch and remove the switch.
5. Reverse the procedure for installation.

E SERIES

1. Disconnect the negative battery cable.
2. Remove the windshield wiper switch knob.
3. Remove the ignition switch bezel.
4. Remove the headlamp switch knob and shaft by pulling the switch to the On position. Depress the button on the top of the switch and pull the knob and shaft out.
5. Remove the two screws at the bottom of the finish panel, then pry the two upper retainers away from the instrument panel.
6. Disconnect the connector from the switch.
7. Remove the attaching screws and remove the switch.
8. Reverse the procedure for installation.

BRONCO II AND RANGER

NOTE: The switch handle is an integral part of the switch and cannot be removed seperately.

1. Disconnect the negative battery cable.
2. Remove the trim shrouds.
3. Disconnect the electrical connector.
4. Peel back the foam sight shield.
5. Remove the two screws holding the switch and remove the switch.
6. Installation is the reverse of the removal procedure.

AEROSTAR

NOTE: The switch handle is an integral part of the switch and cannot be removed seperately.

1. Disconnect the negative battery cable.
2. Remove the cluster finish panel five retaining screws.
3. Remove the three left control pod retaining screws.
4. Remove the wiring connector from the switch.
5. Remove the two lamp switch to control pod retaining screws and remove the switch.
6. Installation is the reverse of the removal procedure.

WINDSHIELD/WIPER MOTOR

Removal and Installation

BRONCO E AND F SERIES

NOTE: The wiper motor is not serviceable. It must be replaced as a complete assembly.

1. Disconnect the negative battery cable.
2. On E series, remove the fuse panel and bracket assembly.
3. Remove both wiper arm and blade assemblies.
4. Disconnect the washer nozzle hose and remove the cowl grille assembly.
5. Remove the wiper linkage clip from the motor output arm.
6. Disconnect the motor wiring connector.
7. Remove the three attaching screws and remove the motor.
8. Installation is the reverse of removal procedure.

AEROSTAR, BRONCO II AND RANGER

1. Turn the wiper switch on. Turn the ignition switch on until the blades are straight up. Then turn the ignition switch off to keep them there.
3. Disconnect the wiper motor wiring connector.
4. Remove the RH wiper arm and blade. On the Aerostar, remove both wiper arms and the cowl grille.
5. Disconnect the negative battery cable.
6. Remove the RH pivot nut and allow the linkage to drop into the cowl.
7. Remove the linkage access cover, located on the RH side of the dash panel near the wiper motor.
8. Reach through the access cover opening and unsnap the wiper motor clip.
9. Push the clip away from the linkage until it clears the crank pin, then push it off of the linkage.
10. Remove the wiper linkage from the motor crank pin.
11. Remove the three attaching screws and remove the motor.
12. Installation is the reverse of the removal procedure.

WINDSHIELD/WIPER LINKAGE

Removal and Installation

BRONCO, E AND F SERIES

1. Disconnect the negative battery cable.
2. Remove the wiper blade and arm assemblies from the pivot shaft.
3. Disconnect the washer hose and remove the cowl grille assembly.
4. Remove the wiper linkage clip from the motor output arm and pull the linkage from the arm.
5. Remove the body to cowl panel screws and remove the linkage and pivot shaft assembly. On the Bronco and the F series,

the LH and the RH pivots and linkage are independent and can be serviced separately.

6. Reverse the procedure for installation.

AEROSTAR, BRONCO II AND RANGER

1. Follow the Wiper Motor Removal and Installation procedure.
2. On the Bronco II and the Ranger, if the LH linkage is to be serviced use the following procedure:
   a. Remove the LH wiper arm and blade assembly.
   b. Remove the LH linkage access cover.
   c. Remove the pivot nut.
   d. Lower the linkage and slide it out through the LH access opening.
3. Installation is the reverse of the removal procedure.

INSTRUMENT CLUSTER

Removal and Installation

BRONCO AND F SERIES

1. Disconnect the negative battery cable.
2. Remove the wiper/washer knob using a hook tool to release each knob lock tab.
3. Remove the knob from the headlamp switch. Remove the fog lamp switch knob, if so equipped.
4. Remove the steering column shroud.
5. If equipped with an automatic transmission, remove the loop on the indicator cable assembly from the retainer pin. Open the cable retaining clips. Remove the screw from the cable bracket and slide the bracket out of the slot in the tube.
6. Remove the cluster finish panel assembly.
7. Remove the four cluster attaching screws and disconnect the speedometer cable.
8. Disconnect the wire connector from the printed circuit.
9. Disconnect the 4WD indicator light, if so equipped and remove the cluster.
10. Installation is the reverse of the removal procedure.

BRONCO II, E SERIES AND RANGER

1. Disconnect the negative battery cable.
2. Remove the steering column shroud.
3. If equipped with a tilt steering column, loosen the bolts which attach the column to the band support to provide sufficient clearance for cluster removal.
4. Remove the seven cluster to panel retaining screws.
5. Position the cluster away from the panel to disconnect the speedometer cable.
6. Disconnect the harness connector plug from the printed circuit and remove the cluster assembly.
7. Reverse the procedure for installation.

AEROSTAR

1. Disconnect the negative battery cable.
2. Remove the cluster housing.
3. Remove the four cluster mounting screws.
4. Disconnect the wiring harness connectors from the printed circuit.
5. Disconnect the speedometer cable and remove the cluster assembly.
6. If equipped with an electronic cluster, pull the top toward the steering wheel. Reach behind the cluster and unplug the three connectors. Swing the bottom of the cluster out and remove it.
7. Installation is the reverse of the removal procedure.

SPEEDOMETER

Removal and Installation

1. Remove the instrument cluster.
2. Remove the lens and mask from the cluster.
3. Remove the two speedometer attaching screws and remove the speedometer cable.
4. Remove the speedometer.
5. Reverse the procedure for installation.

COOLING AND HEATING SYSTEM

Water Pump

Removal and Installation

122 CID (2.0L) AND 140 CID (2.3L) 4 CYLINDER ENGINES

1. Disconnect the negative battery cable. Drain the cooling system. Loosen and remove the drive belt.
2. Remove the two bolts that retain the fan shroud and position the shroud back over the fan.
3. Remove the four bolts that retain the cooling fan. Remove the fan and shroud.
4. Loosen and remove the power steering and A/C compressor drive belts.
5. Remove the water pump pulley and the vent hose to the emissions canister.
6. Remove the heater hose at the water pump.
7. Remove the cam belt cover. Remove the lower radiator hose from the water pump.
8. Remove the water pump mounting bolts and the water pump. Clean all gasket mounting surfaces.
9. Install the water pump in the reverse order of removal. Coat the threads of the mounting bolts with sealer before installation.

173 CID (2.8L) V6 ENGINE

1. Disconnect the negative battery cable. Drain the cooling system.
2. Loosen and remove drive belts. Remove pump pulley. Disconnect all the water hoses from the water pump and thermostat housing.
3. Remove the radiator shroud (if necessary) and cooling fan and clutch assembly. The fan clutch assembly mounting nut is equipped with a left hand thread, remove by turning clockwise.
4. Remove the mounting bolts and water pump, water inlet and thermostat housing as an assembly.
5. Clean all gasket mounting surfaces. Transfer parts to the new pump.
6. Install the water pump in the reverse order of removal.

177 CID (2.9L) V6 ENGINE

1. Disconnect the negative battery cable. Drain the cooling system.
2. Remove the lower radiator hose and the heater return hose from the pump.
3. Remove the fan and clutch assembly.
4. Loosen the alternator mounting bolts and remove the belt. If equipped with A/C, remove the alternator and the bracket.

5. Remove the water pump pulley.
6. Remove the water pump attaching bolts and remove the pump assembly.
7. Installation is the reverse of removal.

183 CID (3.0L) V6 ENGINE

1. Disconnect the negative battery cable. Drain the cooling system.
2. Loosen the accessory drive belt idler and remove the belts.
3. Remove the two nuts and one bolt attaching the idler bracket to the engine.
4. Disconnect the heater hose at the water pump.
5. Remove the four pulley to pump hub bolts. The pulley will remain loose on the hub due to insufficient clearance between the body and the pump restricting removal.
6. Remove the eleven water pump to engine attaching bolts and remove the pump.
7. Installation is the reverse of removal.

232 CID (3.8L) V6 ENGINE

1. Disconnect the negative battery cable. Drain the cooling system.
2. Remove the air cleaner and duct assembly.
3. Remove drive belts and pump pulley. Remove the fan shroud and cooling fan/clutch assembly.
4. Remove the power steering pump with mounting brackets and hoses attached. Position out of the way.
5. Remove the A/C compressor front mounting bracket. Leave the compressor in place.
6. Disconnect the by-pass hose from the water pump. Disconnect the heater and radiator hose at the water pump.
7. Remove the mounting bolts and the water pump.
8. Clean all gasket mounting surfaces. Installation is in the reverse order of removal.

300 CID (4.9L) 6 CYLINDER ENGINE

1. Disconnect the negative battery cable. Drain cooling system.
2. Disconnect radiator lower hose and heater hose at the water pump.
3. Remove fan belt, fan and water pump pulley. Remove the air pump and alternator belts.
4. On vehicles equipped with air compressors, remove the air compressor belt as required.
5. Remove water pump retaining bolts, then remove pump and gasket.
6. To install, clean gasket surfaces of pump body and engine block.
7. If a new water pump is being installed, remove the fittings from the old pump and install them on the new pump.
8. Coat new gasket with water-resistant sealer on both sides and install gasket and pump on engine. Tighten mounting bolts securely.
9. Install water pump pulley, fan and fan belt, adjusting fan belt tension.
10. If so equipped, install air compressor belt.
11. Connect radiator and heater hoses.
12. Fill cooling system and operate engine to bleed air. Check for leaks and recheck coolant level.

255 CID (4.2L), 302 CID (5.0L), 351W CID (5.8L) V8 ENGINES

1. Disconnect the negative battery cable. Drain the cooling system.
2. Remove the bolts securing the fan shroud to the radiator, if so equipped, and position the shroud over the fan.
3. Disconnect the lower radiator hose, heater hose and bypass hose at the water pump. Remove the drive belts, fan, fan spacer and pulley. Remove the fan shroud, if so equipped.
4. Loosen the alternator pivot bolt and the bolt attaching the alternator adjusting arm to the water pump.
5. Remove the bolts securing the water pump to the timing chain cover and remove the water pump.
6. Install the water pump in the reverse order of removal, using a new gasket.

400 CID (6.6L), 460 CID (7.5L) V8 ENGINES

1. Disconnect the negative battery cable. Drain the cooling system and remove the fan shroud attaching bolts.
2. Remove the fan assembly attaching screws and remove the shroud and fan.
3. Loosen the power steering pump attaching bolts.
4. If the vehicle is equipped with air conditioning, loosen the compressor attaching bolts, and remove the air conditioning compressor and power steering pump drive belts.
5. Loosen the alternator pivot bolt. Remove the two attaching bolts and spacer. Remove the drive belt, then rotate the bracket out of the way.
6. Remove the three air conditioning compressor attaching bolts and secure the compressor out of the way.
7. Remove the power steering pump attaching bolts and position the pump to one side.
8. Remove the air conditioner bracket attaching bolts and remove the bracket.
9. Disconnect the lower radiator hose and heater hose from the water pump.
10. Loosen the by-pass hose clamp at the water pump.
11. Remove the remaining water pump attaching bolts and remove the pump from the front cover. Remove the separator plate from the pump. Discard the gaskets.
12. Remove all gasket material from all of the mating surfaces.
13. Install the water pump in the reverse order of removal, using a new gasket and waterproof sealer. When the water pump is first positioned to the front cover of the engine, install only those bolts not used to secure the air conditioner and alternator brackets.

Thermostat

Removal and Installation

1. Drain the radiator so that the coolant level is below the thermostat.
2. If equipped with a V8 engine, disconnect the bypass hoses at the water pump and the intake manifold. Remove the bypass tube.
3. Remove the water outlet housing attaching bolts and pull the housing away from the engine to gain access to the thermostat.
4. Installation is the reverse of removal.

Heater Core

WITH AIR CONDITIONING

Removal and Installation

E SERIES

1. Disconnect the resistor electrical leads on the front of the blower cover inside the vehicle. Detach the vacuum line from the vacuum motor. Remove the blower cover.
2. Remove the nut and push washer from the air door shaft. Remove the control cable from the bracket and the air door shaft.
3. Remove the blower motor housing and the air door housing.
4. Drain the coolant and detach the heater hoses.
5. Remove the heater core retaining brackets. Remove the core and seal assembly.
6. Reverse the procedure for installation.

BRONCO AND F SERIES

1. Disconnect the negative battery cable. Disconnect the heater hoses from the heater core tubes and plug the hoses.
2. Remove the glove compartment liner.
3. Remove eight screws attaching the heater core cover to the plenum and remove the cover.
4. Remove the heater core from the plenum, taking care not to spill coolant from the core.
5. Installation is the reverse of removal.

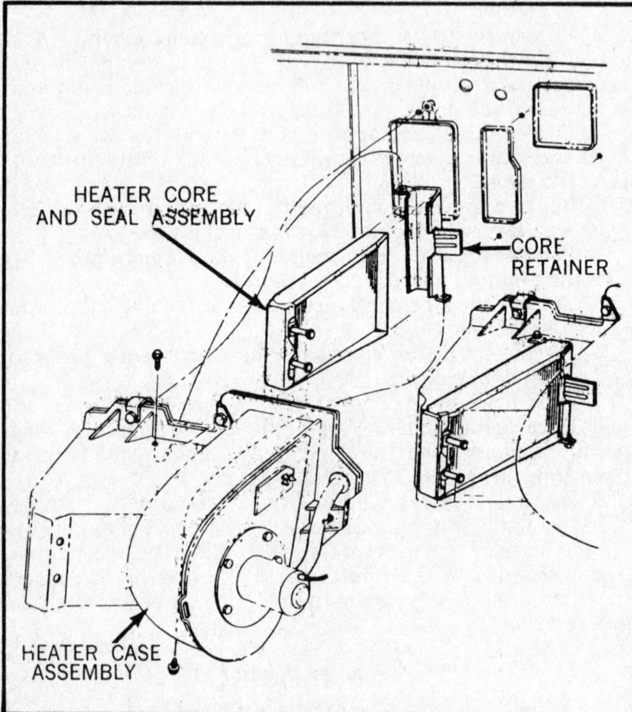

Econoline heater installation—typical

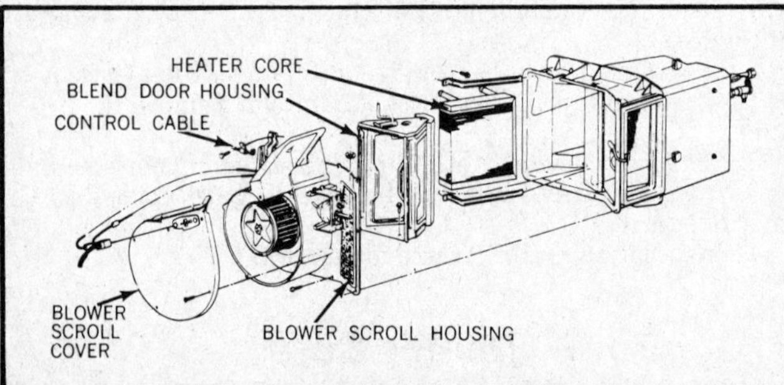

Econoline with A/C heater core installation—typical

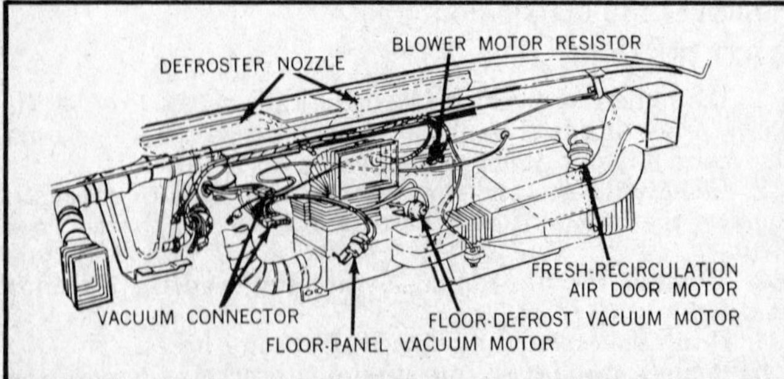

F-100-350 and Bronco heater-A/C installation—typical

AEROSTAR, BRONCO II AND RANGER

1. Disconnect the negative battery cable. Allow the engine to cool down completely. Drain the cooling system to a point that is below the heater hoses.
2. Disconnect the heater hoses from the heater core tubes. Plug the core tubes.
3. From under the dash, remove the screws that attach the access cover to the plenum assembly. Remove the access cover.
4. Pull the core down and out of the plenum assembly.
5. Install in the reverse order. Fill cooling system, start the engine and check for leaks.

WITHOUT AIR CONDITIONING

Removal and Installation

E SERIES

1. Drain the coolant; remove the battery.
2. Disconnect the resistor wiring harness and the orange blower motor lead. Remove the ground wire screw from the firewall.
3. Detach the heater hoses and the plastic hose retaining strap.
4. Remove the five mounting screws inside the vehicle.
5. Remove the heater assembly.
6. Cut the seal at the top and bottom edge of the core retainer. Remove the two screws and the retainer. Slide the core and seal out of the case.
7. Reverse the procedure for installation.

BRONCO AND F SERIES WITH COMFORT VENT HEATERS

1. Disconnect the negative battery cable. Disconnect the heater hoses from the heater core tubes and plug the hoses.
2. Remove the glove compartment liner.
3. Remove two spring clips attaching the heater core cover to the plenum along the top edge of the heater core cover.
4. Remove eight screws attaching the heater core cover to the plenum and remove the cover.
5. Remove the heater core from the plenum taking care not to spill coolant from the core.
6. Install the heater core in the plenum.
7. Install the heater core cover screws and spring clips along the top edge of the cover.
8. Install the glove compartment liner.
9. Connect the heater hoses to the heater core. Tighten the hose clamps.
10. Add coolant to raise the coolant level to specification.
11. Check the system for proper operation and for coolant leaks.

BRONCO AND F SERIES WITH STANDARD & HIGH OUTPUT HEATERS

1. Disconnect the negative battery cable. Disconnect the temperature cable from the temperature blend door and the mounting bracket on top of the heater case.
2. Disconnect the wires from the blower motor resistor and the blower motor.
3. Disconnect the heater hoses from the heater core and plug the hoses.
4. Working under the instrument panel, remove two nuts retaining the left end of the heater case and the right end of the plenum to the dash panel.
5. In the engine compartment, remove one screw attaching the top center of the heater to the dash panel.
6. Remove two screws attaching the right end of the heater case to the dash panel, and remove the heater case from the vehicle.
7. Remove nine screws and one bolt and nut attaching the heater housing plate to the heater case, and remove the heater housing plate.

8. Remove three screws attaching the heater core frame to the heater case and remove the frame.
9. Remove the heater core and seal from the heater case.
10. Position the heater core and seal in the heater case.
11. Install the heater core frame.
12. Position the heater housing plate on the heater case and install the nine screws and one bolt and nut.
13. Position the heater case to the dash panel and install the three attaching screws.
14. Working in the passenger compartment, install two nuts to retain the heater case and plenum right end to the dash panel.
15. Connect the heater hoses to the heater core. Tighten the hose clamps.
16. Connect the wires to the blower motor resistor assembly.
17. Connect the blower motor wires.
18. Position (slide) the self adjusting clip on the temperature cable to a position approximately one inch from the cable end loop.
19. Snap the temperature cable on the cable mounting bracket of the heater case. Then, position the self adjusting clip on the door crank arm.
20. Adjust the temperature cable.
21. Check the system for proper operation.

AEROSTAR, BRONCO II AND RANGER

1. Disconnect the negative battery cable. Allow the engine to cool down completely. Drain the cooling system to a point that is below the heater hoses.
2. Disconnect the heater hoses from the heater core tubes. Plug the core tubes.
3. From under the dash, remove the screws that attach the access cover to the plenum assembly. Remove the access cover.
4. Pull the core down and out of the plenum assembly.
5. Install in the reverse order. Fill cooling system, start the engine and check for leaks.

Blower Motor

WITH AIR CONDITIONING

Removal and Installation

E SERIES

1. Disconnect the electrical leads from the resistor on the front face of the A/C blower scroll cover. Remove the scroll cover.
2. Push the wiring grommet forward out of the hole in the blower housing.
3. Remove the four screws from the blower motor mounting plate.
4. Remove the motor and wheel assembly.
5. Installation is the reverse of removal.

BRONCO AND F SERIES

1. Disconnect the motor connector.
2. Disconnect the air cooling tube from the motor.
3. Remove the four mounting plate screws and remove the motor and wheel assembly from the blower housing.
4. Installation is the reverse of removal.

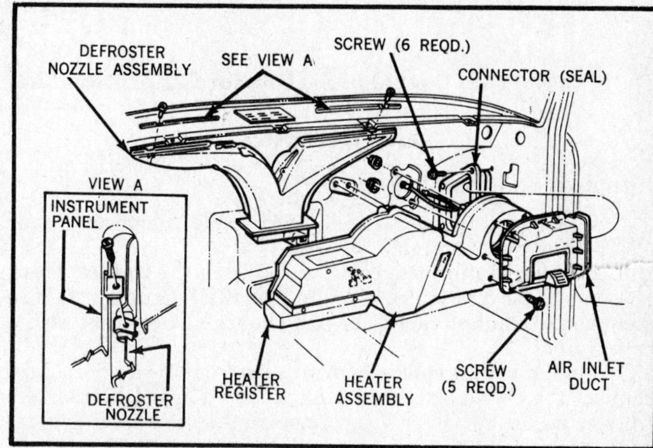

F-100-350 heater installation

AEROSTAR, BRONCO II AND RANGER

1. Disconnect the negative battery cable.
2. In the engine compartment, disconnect the wire harness connection from the motor by pushing down on the tab while pulling the connector off at the motor.
3. Remove the solenoid box cover, if so equipped.
4. Remove the air cleaner or the air inlet duct as necessary.
5. Disconnect the cooling tube from the blower motor.
6. Remove the four mounting plate screws and remove the motor and wheel assembly from the blower housing.
7. Installation is the reverse of removal.

WITHOUT AIR CONDITIONING

Removal and Installation

E SERIES

1. Disconnect the lead wire (orange/black) at the wiring harness.
2. Remove the ground wire (black) mounting from the dash panel.
3. Remove the three mounting plate screws and remove the motor and wheel assembly.
4. Install in reverse order.

ALL EXCEPT E SERIES

1. Disconnect the negative battery cable.
2. On California vehicles, remove the emission module forward of the blower motor.
3. On Aerostar, remove the air cleaner and duct as necessary. Remove the vacuum reservoir from the blower.
4. Disconnect the wire harness connection from the motor by pushing down on the tab while pulling the connector off at the motor.
5. Disconnect the cooling tube from the blower motor.
6. Remove the three mounting plate screws.
7. Holding the cooling tube aside, pull the motor and wheel assembly from the blower housing.
8. Installation is the reverse of removal.

FUEL SYSTEM

Refer to the Unit Overhaul Section for Calibration List.

Carburetor

Removal and Installation

1. Disconnect the negative battery cable. Remove the air cleaner and duct assembly.
2. Remove the throttle cable or rod from the throttle lever. Disconnect the distributor vacuum line, EGR vacuum line, if so equipped, the inline fuel filter and the choke heat tube at the carburetor.
3. Disconnect the choke clean air tube from the air horn. Disconnect the choke actuating cable, if so equipped. Disconnect the electric choke wire at the connector, if so equipped. Disconnect the governor throttle control lines and governor wire connector at the carburetor, if so equipped.
4. Remove the carburetor retaining nuts, then remove the carburetor. Remove the carburetor mounting gasket, spacer (if so equipped), and the lower gasket from the intake manifold.
5. Installation is the reverse of the removal procedure. Adjust the carburetor to specification, as required.

Idle Speed Adjustment

122 CID (2.0L) AND 140 CID (2.3L) ENGINES W/YFA–IV AND YFA–IV FB CARBURETORS

1. Block the wheels and apply the parking brake. Place the transmission in Neutral or Park.
2. Bring the engine to normal operating temperature.
3. Turn OFF the ignition key and place the A/C selector in the OFF position.
4. Disconnect the vacuum hose at the EGR valve and plug it.
5. Place the fast idle RPM adjusting screw on the specified step of the fast idle cam (see the underhood sticker).
6. Start the engine without touching the accelerator pedal check/adjust the fast idle RPM to specifications.
7. Reconnect the EGR vacuum hose.
8. Place the transmission in the specified position (see the underhood sticker) and check/adjust the curb idle RPM.
9. If adjustment is required, turn the hex head adjustment at the rear of the TSP housing.

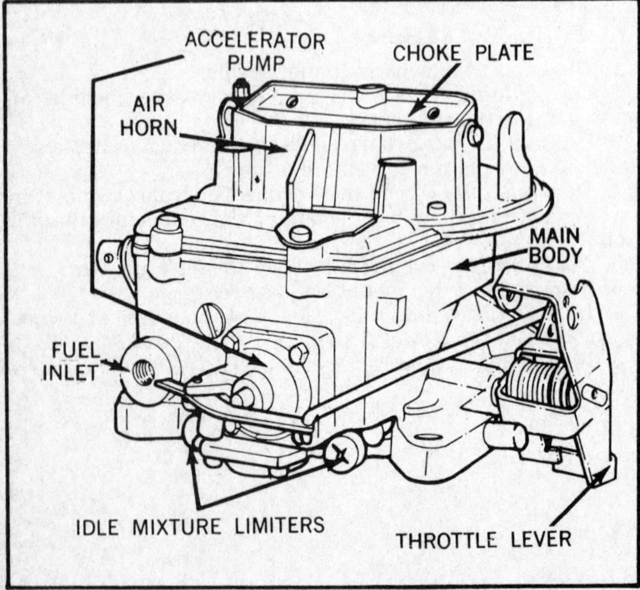

Motorcraft 2100 2 bbl (manual choke) component locations

10. If curb idle RPM adjustment was required and the carburetor is equipped with a dashpot, adjust the dashpot clearance as follows:
    a. Turn the key to the ON position.
    b. Open the throttle to allow the TSP solenoid plunger to extend to the curb idle position.
    c. Collapse the dashpot plunger to the maximum extent. Measure the clearance between the tip of the plunger and the extension pad on the throttle vent lever.
    d. If required, adjust to specifications and tighten the dashpot locknut
11. If curb idle adjustment was required, check/adjust the bowl vent setting as follows:
    a. Turn ignition key to the On position to activate the TSP (engine not running). Open throttle to allow the TSP solenoid plunger to extend to the curb idle position.
    b. Secure the choke plate in the wide open position.
    c. Open throttle so that the throttle vent lever does not touch the bowl vent rod. Close the throttle to the idle set position and measure the travel of the fuel bowl vent rod from the open throttle position.
    d. Travel of the bowl vent rod should be within specification (0.100 to 0.150 in.).
    e. If out of specification, bend the throttle vent lever at notch to obtain required travel.
10. Remove all test equipment and reinstall air cleaner assembly. Tighten the holddown bolt to specification.

300 CID (4.4L) ENGINE WITH YFA IV AND YFA IV FB CARBURETOR

1. Block the wheels and apply the parking brake. Position the transmission selector lever in park or neutral.
2. Bring engine to normal operating temperature.
3. Place A/C Heat Selector to Off position.
4. Place transmission in specified gear.
5. Check/adjust curb idle RPM:
    a. TSP-dashpot. Insure that TSP is activated using a $^3/_8$ in. open end wrench, adjust curb idle RPM by rotating the nut directly behind the dashpot housing.
    b. Adjust curb idle RPM by turning the idle RPM speed screw.
    c. Front mounted TSP (Note same as A/C kicker on all other calibrations) insure that TSP is activated. After loosening lock nut, adjust curb idle RPM by rotating TSP solenoid until specified RPM is obtained. Tighten locknut.

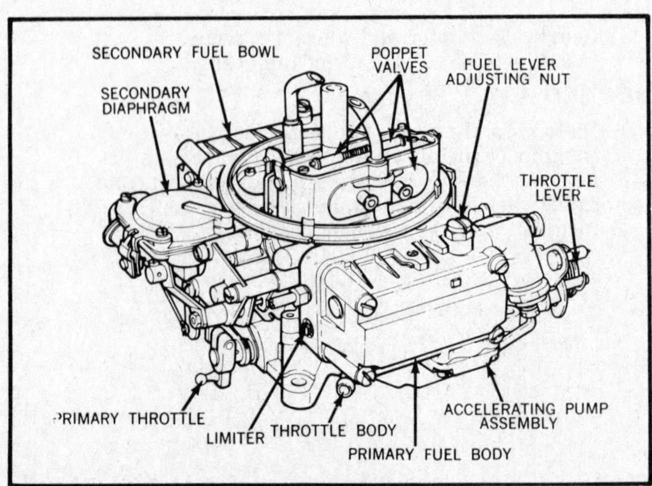

Holley 4 bbl component locations

6. Check/adjust anti-diesel (TSP-Off). Manually collapse the TSP by rotating the carb throttle shaft lever until the TSP-Off adjusting screw contacts the carburetor body. If adjustment is required, turn the TSP-Off adjusting screw while holding the lever adjustment screw against the stop.
7. Place the transmission in Neutral or Park. Rev the engine momentarily. Place the transmission in specified position and recheck curb idle rpm. Readjust if required.
8. Check/adjust dashpot clearance to 0.120 ± 0.030.
9. If a final curb idle speed adjustment is required, the bowl vent setting must be checked as follows:
   a. Stop the engine and turn the ignition key to the On position, so that the TSP dashpot or TSP is activated but the engine is not running (where applicable). Secure the choke plate in the wide-open position.
   b. Open the throttle, so that the throttle vent lever does not touch the fuel bowl vent rod.
   c. Close the throttle, and measure the travel of the fuel bowl vent rod from the open throttle position. Travel of the fuel bowl vent rod should be within 0.100 to 0.150 in.
   d. If out of specification, bend the throttle vent lever to obtain the required travel.
   e. Remove all test equipment, and tighten the air cleaner holddown bolt to specification.
10. Whenever it is required to adjust engine idle speed by more than 50 rpm, the adjustment screw on the AOD linkage lever at the carburetor should also be readjusted.

173 CID (2.8L), 232 CID (3.8L) & 302 CID (5.0L) ENGINES WITH 2150 2VFB (FEEDBACK) CARBURETOR

1. Set parking brake and block wheels.
2. Put the transmission in Park.
3. Bring the engine to normal operating temperature.
4. Disconnect the electric connector on the EVAP purge solenoid.
5. Disconnect and plug the vacuum hose to the VOTM kicker.
6. Place the transmission in Drive position.
7. Check/adjust curb idle rpm, if adjustment is required:
   a. Use the curb idle speed screw.
   b. Use the saddle bracket adjusting screw.
8. Place the transmission in Neutral or Park. Rev the engine momentarily. Place the transmission in Drive position and recheck curb idle rpm. Readjust if required.
9. Remove the plug from the vacuum hose to the VOTM kicker and reconnect.
10. Reconnect the electrical connector on the EVAP purge solenoid.

302 CID (5.0L)ENGINE WITH 2150 2V (NON-FEEDBACK) CARBURETOR

1. Set parking brake and block wheels.
2. Place the transmission in Neutral or Park.
3. Bring engine to normal operating temperature.
4. Place A/C Heat selector to Off position.
5. Disconnect and plug vacuum hose to thermactor air bypass valve.
6. Place the transmission in specified gear.
7. Check curb idle rpm. Adjust to specification:
   a. Using the curb idle rpm speed screw.
   b. Using the saddle bracket adjusting screw.
8. Place the transmission in Neutral or Park. Rev the engine momentarily. Place the transmission in specified position, and recheck curb idle rpm. Readjust if required.
9. Remove plug from vacuum hose to thermactor air bypass valve and reconnect.
10. Whenever it is required to adjust engine idle speed by more than 50 rpm, the adjustment screw on the AOD linkage lever at the carburetor should also be readjusted.

351 CID (5.8L) ENGINE WITH 2150 2V CARBURETOR

1. Block the wheels and apply the parking brake. Position the transmission selector lever in park or neutral.
2. Bring the engine to normal operating temperature.
3. Disconnect purge hose on canister side of evaporator purge solenoid. Check to ensure that purge vacuum is present (solenoid has opened and will require 3- to 5-minute wait after starting engine followed by a short time at part-throttle). Reconnect purge hose.
4. Disconnect and plug the vacuum hose to the VOTM kicker.
5. Place the transmission in specified position.
6. Check/adjust curb idle rpm. If adjustment is required proceed as follows:
   a. Use the curb idle speed screw.
   b. Use the saddle bracket adjusting screw (ensure curb idle speed screw is not touching throttle shaft lever).
7. Place the transmission in Neutral or Park. Rev the engine momentarily. Place the transmission in specified position and recheck curb idle rpm. Readjust if required.
8. Check/adjust throttle position sensor (TPS).
9. Remove the plug from the vacuum hose to the VOTM kicker and reconnect.
10. Apply a slight pressure on top of the nylon nut located on the accelerator pump to take up the linkage clearance.
11. Turn the nylon nut on the accelerator pump rod clockwise until a 0.010 ± 0.005 clearance is obtained between the top of the accelerator pump and the pump lever.
12. Turn the accelerator pump rod nut one turn counterclockwise to set the lever lash preload.
13. If curb idle adjustment exceeds 50 rpm, adjust automatic transmission TV linkage.

302 CID (5.0L) AND 351 CID (5.8L) ENGINES (CANADA) WITH 2150 2V CARBURETOR

1. Place the transmission in Neutral or Park.
2. Bring engine to normal operating temperature.
3. Place A/C Heat Selector to Off position.
4. Place the transmission in specified gear.
5. Check curb idle rpm. Adjust to specification:
   a. Using the curb idle speed screw.
   b. Using the hex head on the rear of the solenoid or the saddle bracket adjustment screw.
6. Place the transmission in Neutral or Park. Rev the engine momentarily. Place the transmission in specified position and recheck curb idle rpm. Readjust if required.
7. TSP-Off: With transmission in specified gear, collapse the solenoid plunger and set specified TSP-Off speed on the speed screw.
8. Disconnect vacuum hose to decel throttle control modulator and plug (if so equipped).
9. Connect a slave vacuum from manifold vacuum to the decel throttle control modulator (if so equipped).
10. Check/adjust decel throttle control rpm. Adjust if necessary.
11. Remove slave vacuum hose.
12. Remove plug from decel throttle control modulator hose and reconnect.

460 CID (7.5L) ENGINE

1. Block the wheels and apply parking brake.
2. Run engine until normal operating temperature is reached.
3. Place the vehicle in Park or Neutral, A/C in Off position, and set parking brake.
4. Remove air cleaner.
5. Disconnect and plug decel throttle control kicker diaphragm vacuum hose.
6. Connect a slave vacuum hose from an engine manifold vacuum source to the decel throttle control kicker.
7. Run engine at approximately 2500 rpm for 15-seconds, then release the throttle.

8. If decel throttle control rpm is not within ± 50 rpm of specification, adjust the kicker.
9. Disconnect the slave vacuum hose and allow engine to return to curb idle.
10. Adjust curb idle, if necessary, using the curb idle adjusting screw.
11. Rev the engine momentarily, recheck curb idle and adjust if necessary.
12. Reconnect the decel throttle control vacuum hose to the diaphragm.
13. Reinstall the air cleaner.

Idle Mixture Adjustment

PROPANE ENRICHMENT METHOD

NOTE: Remove the air cleaner when necessary to perform adjustments.

1. Bring the engine to normal operation temperature and connect a tachometer.

NOTE: If vehicle is equipped with the Dura Spark II ignition system, be sure to use a tachometer rated for this type of ignition system.

2. Disconnect the evaporative emission purge hose from the air cleaner. Disconnect the PCV closure hose from the air cleaner and plug the hose.
3. Adjust the curb idle speed to specifications on engine decal.

NOTE: With the transmission in neutral, run the engine at 2500 rpm for 15 seconds before each speed check. The idle speed must be adjusted with the air cleaner in place.

4. If vehicle is equipped with Thermactor System, revise the dump valve vacuum hoses as follows:
   a. For dump valves with two vacuum fittings, disconnect and plug the hose(s).
   b. For dump valves with one fitting, remove the hose at the dump valve and plug it. Connect a slave hose from the dump valve vacuum fitting to an intake manifold vacuum fitting.
5. Place the special gas tool into the air cleaner evaporative purge nipple. With the engine idling, slowly open the propane valve until the engine speed reaches a maximum and then begins to drop. Note the maximum speed increase. If the speed will not drop, check the bottle gas supply. If necessary, repeat the operation with a new bottle gas supply.
   a. If the speed increase is within specifications, but not zero rpm, proceed to Step 6. If the speed increase is zero and minus specification is zero, proceed to Step 5d.
   b. If the speed increase is higher than specification; enrich the mixture without propane by turning the mixture limiter screws counterclockwise in equal amounts until the rpm increases as necessary. Example: If the increase was 80 rpm and the desired reset is 50 rpm, the mixture screws should be richened to attain a 30 rpm increase. Repeat Steps 3 and 5.
   c. If the speed increase is lower than specifications proceed as follows; lean the mixture without propane by turning the mixture screws clockwise in equal amounts until the rpm decreases as necessary. Example: If the increase was zero rpm and the desired reset increase is 20 rpm, the mixture screws should be leaned to attain a 20 rpm decrease. Repeat Steps 3 and 5.
   d. If the speed increase is zero rpm and the minimum speed gain specification is zero, perform the following speed drop test; Turn the mixture limiters counterclockwise to the maximum rich position. (If the limiters have been removed, do not enrich; assume the mixture screws are already set at the maximum rich position.) Lean the idle fuel mixture by turning the screws clockwise equally as specified. Note the drop in engine rpm.
   e. If the speed drop is equal to or greater than the specified minimum speed drop, return the mixture limiters to the maximum rich position or the mixture screws to the "assumed" maximum rich position. If the engine speed before mixture adjustment was 650 rpm and the speed drop specification is 100 rpm minimum, proceed to Step 6 if the engine speed drops to at least 550 rpm or stalls.
   f. If the speed drop is less than the specified minimum speed drop, leave the mixture limiters or screws in the adjusted position and repeat Steps 3 and 5.
6. If the idle limiters were removed, install new blue service limiters at the maximum rich stop. Check the speed increase after installation of the limiters to be certain that the settings were not disturbed. If the setting is within specification, proceed to Step 7, if not correct as required.
7. Remove the gas tool from the nipple and connect all system components that were removed.
8. Set the curb idle speed to specification if Step 3 required an idle speed adjustment.
9. Turn off the engine and disconnect the tachometer. Every time propane is administered, place the transmission in the range specified on the engine decal. Remove the limiter caps with appropriate tool if required.

OPTIMUM IDLE METHOD

NOTE: This alternate method is to be used only when propane enrichment equipment is not available. Remove the air cleaner when necessary to perform adjustments.

1. Bring the engine to normal operation temperature and connect a tachometer.

NOTE: If vehicle is equipped with the Dura Spark II Ignition System, be sure to use a tachometer rated for this type of ignition system.

2. Disconnect the evaorative emission purge hose from the air cleaner.
3. If vehicle is equipped with Thermactor System, revise the dump valve vacuum hoses as follows:
   a. For dump valves with two vacuum fittings, disconnect and plug the hose(s).
   b. For dump valves with one fitting, remove the hose at the dump valve and plug it. Connect a slave hose from the dump valve vacuum fitting to an intake manifold vacuum fitting.
4. Remove the idle mixture limiter.
5. With the transmission in neutral, run the engine at 2500 rpm for 15 seconds.
6. Block the wheels or apply the brake. With the transmission in drive for automatic and neutral for manual, adjust the idle to curb idle rpm plus the optimum idle speed range rpm (if the specified optimum idle speed range is zero rpm, simply adjust to the curb idle rpm).
7. With the transmission in drive for automatic and neutral for manual, adjust the idle mixture screws to the maximum idle rpm, leaving the screws in the leanest position that will maintain this "maximum idle rpm."
8. Repeat Steps 5, 6 and 7 until further adjustment of the idle mixture screws does not increase the idle rpm.
9. If the specified optimum idle speed rpm is zero proceed to Step 11. Otherwise proceed to the next step.
10. With the transmission in drive for automatic and neutral for manual, turn the mixture screws equally in the lean direction until the curb idle rpm is obtained.
11. Install new blue service limiter caps at the maximum rich stops. Check the idle speed to insure that the limiter cap installation did not disturb the setting. Correct if necessary.
12. Turn off the engine, disconnect the tachometer, reinstall the system components, and make sure that the air cleaner attaching nut is tight.

FUEL INJECTION

Relieve Pressure

If the fuel charging assembly is mounted to the engine, remove the fuel filler cap and release the pressure from the system by opening the pressure relief valve on the fuel line in the upper RH corner of the engine compartartment.

NOTE: The cap on the relief valve must be removd.

INJECTORS

Removal and Installation

1. Disconnect the negative battery cable.
2. Remove the fuel tank at tank pressure.
3. Release the pressure from the fuel system.
4. Remove the upper intake manifold as follows:
   a. Disconnect the electrical connectors at the air bypass valve, throttle position sensor and EGR position sensor.
   b. Disconnect the throttle linkage at the throttle ball and the AOD transmission linkage from the throttle body.
   c. Disconnect all vacuum lines to the upper intake, EGR valve and the fuel pressure regulator.
   d. Disconnect the PCV system hose from the rear of the upper manifold.
   e. Remove the two canister purge lines and the water heater lines from the fittings on the throttle body.
   f. Disconnect the EGR tube from the valve by removing the flange nut.
   g. Remove the six upper intake manifold retaining bolts and remove it and the throttle body as an assembly.
5. Remove the fuel supply manifold as follows:
   a. Disconnect the fuel chassis inlet and outlet fuel hoses from the fuel supply manifold.
   b. Disconnect the fuel supply and the return line connections.
   c. Remove the four manifold retaining bolts. Disengage the manifold from the injectors and remove it.
6. Remove the electrical harness connectors from the injectors and remove the injectors.
7. Installation is the reverse of the removal procedure.

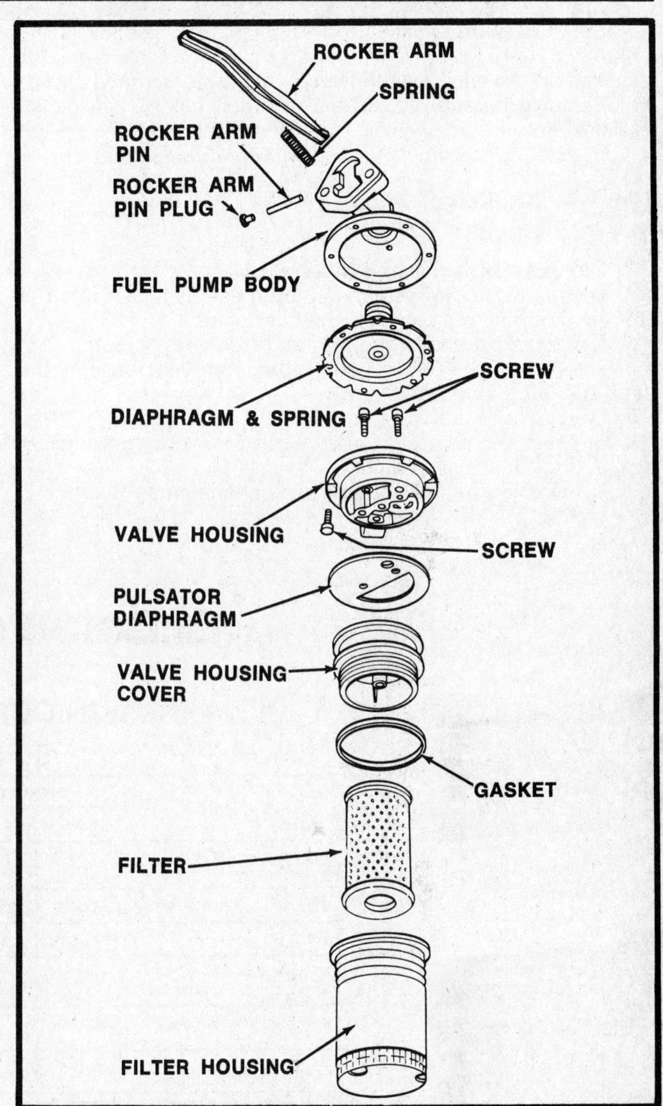

Typical mechanical fuel pump

Fuel Pump

MECHANICAL

Removal and Installation

1. Loosen the threaded connections and then retighten them snugly. Do not remove the lines at this time.
2. Loosen the mounting bolts about two turns and loosen the fuel pump from the engine.
3. Rotate the engine until the fuel pump cam lobe is near its low position.
4. Disconnect the fuel pump inlet, outlet and vapor return line, if so equipped.
5. Remove the fuel pump attaching bolts and remove the fuel pump and gasket.
6. Installation is the reverse of removal.

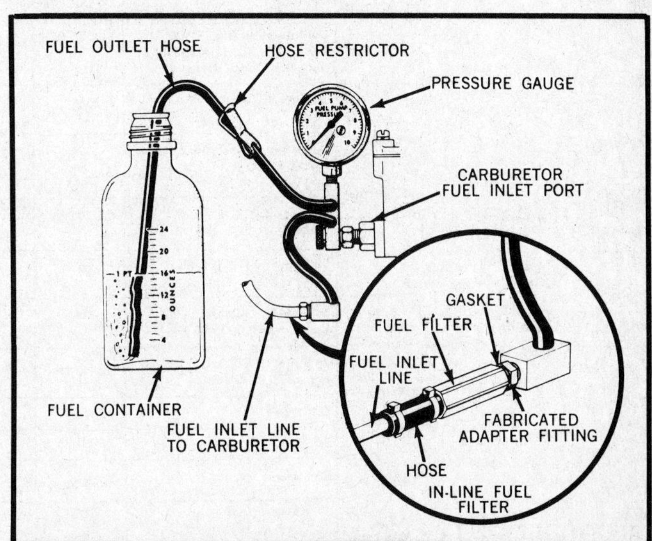

Testing mechanical fuel pump

ELECTRIC

Two electric pumps are used on injected models; a low pressure boost pump mounted in the gas tank and a high pressure pump mounted on the vehicle frame. Models equipped with the 7.5L engine use a single low pressure pump mounted in the gas tank. On injected models the low pressure pump is used to provide pressurized fuel to the inlet of the high pressure pump and helps prevent noise and heating problems. The externally mounted high pressure pump is capable of supplying 15.9 gallons of fuel an hour. System pressure is controlled by a pressure regulator mounted on the engine. On internal fuel tank mounted pumps tank removal is required. Frame mounted models can be accessed from under the vehicle. Prior to servicing release system pressure (see proceeding Fuel Supply Manifold details).

Removal and Installation

IN-TANK PUMP

1. Disconnect the negative battery cable.
2. Depressurize the system and drain as much gas from the tank by pumping out through the filler neck.
3. Raise the back of the vehicle and safely support it.
4. Disconnect the fuel supply, return and vent lines at the right and left side of the frame.
5. Disconnect the wiring harness to the fuel pump.
6. Support the gas tank, loosen and remove the mounting straps. Remove the gas tank.
7. Disconnect the lines and harness at the pump flange.
8. Clean the outside of the mounting flange and retaining ring. Turn the fuel pump lock ring counterclockwise and remove.
9. Remove the fuel pump.
10. Clean the mount faces. Put a light coat of grease on the mounting sufaces and on the new sealing ring. Install the new fuel pump.
11. Installation is in the reverse order of removal. Fill the tank with at least 10 gals. of gas. Turn the ignition key ON for three seconds. Repeat 6 or 7 times until the fuel system is pressurized. Check for any fitting leaks. Start the engine and check for leaks.

EXTERNAL PUMP

1. Disconnect the negative battery cable.
2. Depressurize the fuel system.
3. Raise and support the rear of the vehicle safely.
4. Disconnect the inlet and outlet fuel lines.
5. Remove the pump from the mounting bracket.
7. Install in reverse order, make sure the pump is indexed correctly in the mounting bracket insulator.

EMISSION CONTROLS

1982 EMISSION CONTROLS APPLICATION
50 States

ENGINE	USAGE	CATALYST		CARBURETOR		EEC	EGR	THERM-ACTOR AIR	IGNITION
		TYPE	LOCATION	MFG	MODEL				
4.9L (300 CID)	49 States (under 8500 lbs. GVW)	COC	UB	Carter	YFA-1V	No.	BP	CT	DS-II
	Altitude	COC	UB	Carter	YFA-iV	No	BP	CT	UIC
	49S, F-100 (only)	COC&TWC	UB LOC	Carter	YFA-1V FBC	MCU	BP	MTA	UIC
	50 States (over 8500 lbs. GVW)	NA	NO	Carter	YFA-1V	No	Ported	CT	DS-II
	California (under β500 lbs.	COC&TWC	UB LOC	Carter	YFA-1V FBC	MCU	BP	MTA	DS-II
4.2L (255 CID)	49 States (F-100)	COC	UB	Ford	2150-2V	No	BP	CT	DS-II
5.0L (302 CID)	49 States (Bronco, F-100, F-200, E-100 and E-250) under 8500 lbs. GVW	COC	UB	Ford	2150-2V	No	BP	CT	DS-II
	Altitude	COC	UB	Ford	2150-2V	No	BP	CT	UIC
	California (Bronco, F-100, 150, F-250, E-100, 150 & E-250) under 8500 lbs. GVW	COC&TWC	UB LOC	Ford	7200-VV	EEC-III	Sonic-Cooler	MTA	DS-II
5.8L (351W CID)	49 States (E-100, E-250) under 8500 lbs. GVW	COC	UB	Ford	2150-2V	No	BP	CT	DS-II
	California (Bronco, F-150, F-250, E-150 and E-250 under 8500 lbs. GVW)	COC & TWC	UB	Ford	7200-VV	EEC-III	Sonic-Cooler	MTA	DS-II
	50 States F-150 & 250 under 8500 lbs.	COC&TWC	UB	Ford	7200VV	EEC-III	Sonic Cooler	MTA	DS-II
	50 States E&F-250 & 350 over 8500 lbs.	NA	NA	Ford	2150-2V	No	BP	CT	DS-II
6.6L (400 CID)	50 States (F-350 and E-250, E-350 over 8500 lbs GVW)	NA	NA	Ford	2150-2V	No	BP	CT	DS-II
7.5L (460 CID)	49 States (E-350 and E-250 over 8500 lbs GVW)	NA	NA	Holley	4180C-4V	No	Ported	CT	DS-II
6.1L (370 CID)	50 States	NA	NA	Holley	2300EG-2V	No	Ported	CT	DS-II
	50 States	NA	NA	Holley	4180EG-4V	No	Ported	CT	DS-II
7.0L (429 CID)	50 States	NA	NA	Holley	4180EG-4V	No	Ported	CT	DS-II
3.8L (230 CID)	49 States F-100	COC	UB	Ford	2150-2V	No	BP	CT	UIC, Man. DS-II, Auto.

1982 EMISSION CONTROLS APPLICATION
Canada

ENGINE	USAGE	CATALYST		CARBURETOR		EEC	EGR	THERMACTOR AIR	IGNITION
		TYPE	LOCATION	MFG	MODEL				
4.9L (300 CID)	Bronco, F-Series, E-Series w/Catalyst	COC	UB	Carter	YFA-1V	No	BP	CT	DS-II
	Altitude	COC	UB	Carter	YFA-1V	No	BP	CT	UIC
	F-150-F-350 4x2, F-150 4x4 and E-150-E350 w/Leaded Fuel	None		Carter	YFA-1V	No	None	None	DS-II
4.2L (255 CID)	F-100 w/Catalyst	COC	UB	Ford	2150-2V	No	BP	CT	DS-II
5.0L (302 CID)	Bronco, F-100-F-250 4x2, F-150-F-250 4x4, E-100-E250 under 8,500 # GVW	COC	UB	Ford	2150-2V	No	BP	CT	DS-II
	Altitude	COC	UB	Ford	2150-2V	No	BP	CT	UIC
	F-150 4x2, F-150-F-250 4x4, E-150-E-250 6-8,500 lbs. GVW w/Leaded Fuel	None		Ford	2150-2V	No	BP	None	DS-II
5.8L (351W CID)	E-100-E-250 w/Catalyst	COC	UB	Ford	2150-2V	No	BP	CT	DS-II
	E & F 150, 250, 350 over 6000 lbs GVW w/Leaded Fuel	None		Ford	2150-2V	No	No		DS-II
4.9L	F-100 (only)	COC&TWC	UB	Carter	YFA-1V FBC	MCU	BP	MTA	UIC
6.6L (400 CID)	Bronco, F-250-F350 4x2, F150-F350 4x4, E-250-E-350 w/Leaded Fuel	None		Ford	2150-2V	No	BP	CT	DS-II
7.5L (460 CID)	E-250-E-350 w/Leaded Fuel	None		Holley	4180C-4V	No	Ported	CT	DS-II
6.1L (370 CID)	Medium Trucks	None		Holley	2300EG-2V	No	Ported	CT	DS-II
	Medium Trucks	None		Holley	4180EG-4V	No	Ported	CT	DS-II
7.0L (429 CID)	Medium Trucks	None		Holley	4150EG-4V	No	Ported	CT	DS-II

ABBREVIATIONS:

NA = Not Applicable
COC = Conventional Oxidation Catalyst
TWC = Three-Way Catalyst
EEC-III = Electronic Engine Control (System III)
FBC = Feedback Carburetor
EFI = Electronic Fuel Injection
MCU = Microprocessor Control Unit
EGR = Exhaust Gas Recirculation
MTA = Managed Thermactor Air
CT = Conventional Thermactor
BP = Back-Pressure
TB = Toe Board
UB = Underbody
FM = Flange Mounted (to Exhaust Manifold)
M/T = Manual Transmission
A/T = Automatic Transmission
MFG = Manufacturer
DBUB = Dual Brick Underbody
DS-II = Duraspark II
DS-III = Duraspark III
TFI = Thick Film Ignition
UIC = Universal Integrated Circuit

1983 EMISSION CONTROLS APPLICATION
50 States

ENGINE	USAGE	CATALYST TYPE	CATALYST LOCATION	CARBURETOR MFG	CARBURETOR MODEL	EEC	EGR	THERM-ACTOR AIR	IGNI-TION
2.0L	49 States (Ranger)	COC&TWC	UB	Carter	YFA-1V	MCU	BP	CT	DS-II
2.3L	50 States	COC&TWC	UB	Carter	YFA-1V, FB	MCU	BP	CT	DS-II
	Altitude	COC	UB	Carter	YFA-1V	No	BP	CT*	UIC
3.8L (230 CID)	49 States F-100	COC	UB	Ford	2150-2V	No	BP	CT	UIC, Man. DS-II, Auto.
4.9L (300 CID)	49 States (under 8500 lbs. GVW)	COC	UB	Carter	YFA-1V	No	BP	CT	DS-II
	Altitude	COC	UB	Carter	YFA-1V	No	BP	CT	UIC
	49S, F-100 (only)	COC&TWC LOC	UB	Carter	YFA-1V FBC	MCU	BP	MTA	UIC
	50 States (over 8500 lbs. GVW)	NA	NO	Carter	YFA-1V	No	Ported	CT	DS-II
	California (under 8500 lbs. GVW)	COC&TWC	UB LOC	Carter	YFA-1V FBC	MCU	BP	MTA	UIC
5.0L (302 CID)	49 States (Bronco, F-100-150, F-250, E-100-150-250 under 8500 lbs. GVW)	COC	UB	Ford	2150A-2V FB	No	BP	CT	DS-II
	Altitude	COC	UB	Ford	2150A-2V**	No	BP	CT	UIC
	California (Bronco, F-100, 150, F-250, E-100, 150 & E-250 under 8500 lbs. GVW)	COC&TWC	UB	Ford	2150A-2V F.B.	EEC-III	Sonic-Cooler	MTA	DS-III
5.8L (351W CID)	49 States (E-100, E-250 under 8500 lbs. GVW)	COC	UB	Ford	2150-2V	No	BP	CT	DS-II
	50 States (F-150,-250 & Bronco under 8500 lbs. GVW)	COC&TWC	UB	Ford	7200VV	EEC-III	Sonic-Cooler	MTA	DS-III
	49 States (E&F-250 & 350 over 8500 lbs. GVW)	NA	NA	Ford	2150-2V	No	BP	CT	DS-II
7.5L (460 CID)	49 States (E-350 and E-250 over 8500 lbs. GVW)	NA	NA	Holley	4180C-4V	No	Ported	CT	DS-II
6.1L (370 CID)	50 States	NA	NA	Holley	2300EG-2V	No	Ported	CT	DS-II
	50 States	NA	NA	Holley	4190EG-4V	No	Ported	CT	DS-II
7.0L (429 CID)	50 States	NA	NA	Holley	4190EG-4V	No	Ported	CT	DS-II
5.8L	Altitude (Bronco, F-150/250)	COC	UB	Ford	7200-VV	EEC-III	Sonic-Cooler	MTA	DS-III
	Altitude (E-150/250)	COC	UB	Ford	2150-2V	No	BP	CT	DS-II

*No Diverter Valve.
**Integral gradient altitude components.

ABBREVIATIONS:

NA = Not Applicable
COC = Conventional Oxidation Catalyst
TWC = Three-Way Catalyst
EEC-IV = Electronic Engine Control (System IV)
FBC = Feedback Carburetor
EFI = Electronic Fuel Injection
CFI = Central Fuel Injection

DS-II = Duraspark II
TFI = Thick Film Ignition
UIC = Universal Integrated Circuit
HO = High Output
S.V.O. = Special Vehicle Operation
MTX = Manual Transaxle
ATX = Automatic Transaxle
MCU = Microprocessor Control Unit
EGR = Exhaust Gas Recirculation
MTA = Managed Thermactor Air
PA = Pulse Air
CT = Conventional Thermactor

BP = Backpressure
BVT = Backpressure Variable Transducer
SBUB = Single Brick Underbody
TB = Toe Board
UB = Underbody
MT = Manual Transmission
AT = Automatic Transmission
MFG = Manufacturer
DBUB = Dual Brick Underbody

1983 EMISSION CONTROLS APPLICATION
Canada

ENGINE	USAGE	CATALYST		CARBURETOR		EEC	EGR	THERMACTOR AIR	IGNITION
		TYPE	LOCATION	MFG	MODEL				
2.0L	Ranger	COC+TWC	UB	Carter	YFA-1V	MCU	BP	CT	DS-II
2.3L	Ranger	COC+TWC	UB	Carter	YFA-1V	MCU	BP	CT	DS-II
4.9L (300 CID)	Bronco, F-Series, E-Series w/Catalyst	COC	UB	Carter	YFA-1V	No	BP	CT	DS-II
	Altitude	COC	UB	Carter	YFA-1V	No	BP	CT	UIC
	F-150-F-350 4x2, F-150 4x4 and E-150-E-350 w/Leaded Fuel	None		Carter	YFA-1V	No	None	None	DS-II
4.9L	F-100 (only)	COC&TWC LOC	UB	Carter	YFA-1V FBC	MCU	BP	MTA	UIC
5.0L (302 CID)	Bronco, F-100-F-250 4x2, F-150-F-250 4x4, E-100-E250 under 8500 lbs. GVW	COC	UB	Ford	2150-2V	No	BP	CT	DS-II
	Altitude	COC	UB	Ford	2150-2V	No	BP	CT	UIC
	F-150-F-250 4x2, F-150-F-250 4x4, Bronco, E-150-E-250 6-8500 lbs. GVW w/Leaded Fuel	None		Ford	2150-2V	No	BP	None	DS-II
5.8L (351W CID)	E-100-E-150-E-250 w/Catalyst	COC	UB	Ford	2150-2V	No	BP	CT	DS-II
	E & F-150, 250, 350, Bronco over 6000 lbs. GVW w/Leaded Fuel	None		Ford	2150-2V	No	None	None	DS-II
7.5L (460 CID)	E-250-E-350 w/Leaded Fuel	None		Holley	4180C-4V	No	Ported	CT	DS-II
6.1L (370 CID)	Medium Trucks	None		Holley	2300EG-2V	No	Ported	CT	DS-II
	Medium Trucks	None		Holley	4190EG-4V	No	Ported	CT	DS-II
7.0L (429 CID)	Medium Trucks	None		Holley	4190EG-4V	No	Ported	CT	DS-II

ABBREVIATIONS:
NA = Not Applicable
COC = Conventional Oxidation Catalyst
TWC = Three-Way Catalyst
EEC-IV = Electronic Engine Control (System IV)
FBC = Feedback Carburetor
EFI = Electronic Fuel Injection
CFI = Central Fuel Injection
MCU = Microprocessor Control Unit
EGR = Exhaust Gas Recirculation
MTA = Managed Thermactor Air
PA = Pulse Air
CT = Conventional Thermactor
BP = Backpressure
BVT = Backpressure Variable Transducer
SBUB = Single Brick Underbody
TB = Toe Board
UB = Underbody
M/T = Manual Transmission
A/T = Automatic Transmission
MFG = Manufacturer
DBUB = Dual Brick Underbody
DS-II = Duraspark II
TFI = Thick Film Ignition
UIC = Universal Integrated Circuit
HO = High Output
S.V.O. = Special Vehicle Operation
MTX = Manual Transaxle
ATX = Automatic Transaxle

1984 EMISSION CONTROLS APPLICATION
50 States

ENGINE	USAGE	CATALYST TYPE	CATALYST LOCATION	CARBURETOR MFG	CARBURETOR MODEL	EEC	EGR	THERM-ACTOR AIR	IGNI-TION
2.0L	49 States (Ranger)	COC & TWC	UB	Carter	YFA-1V, F.B.	MCU	BP	CT	DS-II
2.3L	50 States	COC & TWC	UB	Carter	YFA-IV, FB	MCU	BP	CT	DS-II
	Altitude	COC	UB	Carter	YFA-1V	No	BP	CT*	UIC
2.8L	50 States & Altitude Ranger/Bronco II	TWC & COC	DBUB	Ford	2150A-2V F.B.	EEC-IV	Sonic	MTA	TFI-IV
4.9L (300 CID)	50 States (over 8500 lbs. GVW)	NA	NA	Carter	YFA-1V	No	Ported	CT	DS-II
	50 States (under 8500 lbs. GVW)	COC & TWC	UB	Carter	YFA-1V F.B.	EEC-IV	BP	MTA	TFI-IV
5.0L (302 CID)	49 States (Bronco F-150, F-250, E-150-250 under 8500 lbs. GVW)	COC & TWC	UB	Ford	2150A-2V	No	BP	MTA	DS-II
	Altitude	COC & TWC	UB	Ford	2150A-2V**	No	BP	MTA	UIC
	California (Bronco, F-150, F-250, E-150 & E-250 under 8500 lbs. GVW)	COC & TWC	UB	Ford	2150A-2V F.B.	EEC-IV	Sonic-Cooler	MTA	TFI-IV
5.8L (351W CID)	50 States (E-100, E-250 under 8500 lbs. GVW)	COC & TWC	UB	Ford	2150A-2V F.B.	EEC-IV	Sonic-Cooler	MTA	TFI-IV
	50 States (F-150-250 & Bronco under 8500 lbs. GVW)	COC & TWC	UB	Ford	2150A-2V F.B.	EEC-IV	Sonic-Cooler	MTA	TFI-IV
	49 States (E & F-250 & 350 over 8500 lbs. GVW)	NA	NA	Ford	2150-2V	No	BP	CT	DS-II
7.5L (460 CID)	49 States (E-350 and E-250 over 8500 lbs. GVW)	NA	NA	Holley	4180C-4V	No	Ported	CT	DS-II
6.1L (370 CID)	50 States	NA	NA	Holley	2300EG-2V	No	Ported	CT	DS-II
	50 States	NA	NA	Holley	4190EG-4V	No	Ported	CT	DS-II
7.0L (429 CID)	50 States	NA	NA	Holley	4190EG-4V	No	Ported	CT	DS-II
5.8L	Altitude (Bronco, F-150/250) Auto only	COC & TWC	UB	Ford	2150A-2V F.B.	EEC-IV	Sonic-Cooler	MTA	TFI-IV

*No Diverter Valve.
**Integral gradient altitude components.

ABBREVIATIONS:

NA = Not Applicable
COC = Conventional Oxidation Catalyst
TWC = Three-Way Catalyst
EEC-IV = Electronic Engine Control (System IV)
FBC = Feedback Carburetor
EFI = Electronic Fuel Injection
CFI = Central Fuel Injection
MCU = Microprocessor Control Unit
EGR = Exhaust Gas Recirculation
MTA = Managed Thermactor Air
PA = Pulse Air
CT = Conventional Thermactor
BP = Backpressure
BVT = Backpressure Variable Transducer
SBUB = Single Brick Underbody
TB = Toe Board
UB = Underbody
M/T = Manual Transmission
A/T = Automatic Transmission
MFG = Manufacturer
DBUB = Dual Brick Underbody
DS-II = Duraspark II
TFI = Thick Film Ignition
UIC = Universal Integrated Circuit
HO = High Output
S.V.O. = Special Vehicle Operation
MTX = Manual Transaxle
ATX = Automatic Transaxle

1984 EMISSION CONTROLS APPLICATION
Canada

ENGINE	USAGE	CATALYST TYPE	CATALYST LOCATION	CARBURETOR MFG	CARBURETOR MODEL	EEC	EGR	THERMACTOR AIR	IGNITION
2.0L	Ranger	COC & TWC	UB	Carter	YFA-IV, FB	MCU	BP	CT	DS-II
2.3L	Ranger	COC & TWC	UB	Carter	YFA-IV, FB	MCU	BP	CT	DS-II
2.8L	Ranger/Bronco II	COC & TWC	DBUB	Ford	2150A-2V F.B.	EEC-IV	Sonic	MTA	TFI-IV
4.9L (300 CID)	Bronco, F-Series, E-Series w/ Catalyst	COC & TWC	UB	Carter	YFA-IV FB	EEC-IV	BP	MTA	TFI-IV
	F-150-F-350 4x2, F-150 4x4 and E-150-E-350 w/Leaded Fuel	None		Carter	YFA-IV	No	None	None	DS-II
5.0L (302 CID)	Bronco, F-150-F-250 4x2, F-150-F-250 4x4, E-150 E-250 under 8500 lbs. GVW	COC & TWC	UB	Ford	2150A-2V	No	BP	MTA	DS-II
	Altitude	COC & TWC	UB	Ford	2150-A-2V**	No	BP	MTA	UIC
	F-150 — F-250 4x2, F-150 — F-250 4x4, Bronco, E-150 — E-250 6- 8500 lbs. GVW w/ Leaded Fuel	None		Ford	2150-2V	No	None	None	DS-II
5.8L (351W CID)	E & F-150, 250, 350, Bronco over 6000 lbs. GVW w/Leaded Fuel	None		Ford	2150-2V	No	None	None	DS-II
7.5L (460 CID)	E-250-E-350 w/Leaded Fuel	None		Holley	4180C-4V	No	Ported	CT	DS-II
6.1L (370 CID)	Medium Trucks	None		Holley	2300EG-2V	No	Ported	CT	DS-II
	Medium Trucks	None		Holley	4190EG-4V	No	Ported	CT	DS-II
7.0L (429 CID)	Medium Trucks	None		Holley	4190EG-4V	No	Ported	CT	DS-II

**Integral Gradient Altitude Components

ABBREVIATIONS:

NA = Not Applicable
COC = Conventional Oxidation Catalyst
TWC = Three-Way Catalyst
EEC-IV = Electronic Engine Control (System IV)
FBC = Feedback Carburetor
EFI = Electronic Fuel Injection
CFI = Central Fuel Injection
MCU = Microprocessor Control Unit
EGR = Exhaust Gas Recirculation
MTA = Managed Thermactor Air
PA = Pulse Air
CT = Conventional Thermactor
BP = Backpressure
BVT = Backpressure Variable Transducer
SBUB = Single Brick Underbody
TB = Toe Board
UB = Underbody
M/T = Manual Transmission
A/T = Automatic Transmission
MFG = Manufacturer
DBUB = Dual Brick Underbody
DS-II = Duraspark II
TFI = Thick Film Ignition
UIC = Universal Integrated Circuit
HO = High Output
S.V.O. = Special Vehicle Operation
MTX = Manual Transaxle
ATX = Automatic Transaxle

1985 EMISSION CONTROLS APPLICATION
50 States

ENGINE	VEHICLE APPLICATION	CATALYST(S) TYPE	CATALYST(S) LOCATION	FUEL SYSTEM MFG	FUEL SYSTEM TYPE	ELECTRONIC ENGINE CONTROL	EGR CONTROL	THERM-ACTOR SYSTEM	IGNITION SYSTEM
2.0L	Ranger (49 States)	COC	UB	Carter	YFA-1V Carburetor	None	Ported	CT	DS-II
2.3L	Ranger/Aerostar (49 States & Altitude)	TWC	UB	Bosch/ Ford	EFI	EEC-IV	Sonic	None	TFI-IV
	Ranger/Aerostar (California)	TWC & TWC	DBUB	Bosch/ Ford	EFI	EEC-IV	Sonic	None	TFI-IV
2.8L	Ranger/Bronco II	COC & TWC	DBUB	Ford	2150A-2V FBC Carburetor	EEC-IV	Sonic	MTA	TFI-IV
	Aerostar	COC & TWC	SBUB (2)	Ford	2150A-2V FBC Carburetor	EEC-IV	Sonic	MTA	TFI-IV
4.9L	Bronco/E-Series/F-Series	COC & TWC	UB	Carter	YFA-1V FBC Carburetor	EEC-IV	BP	MTA	TFI-IV
5.0L	Bronco/E-Series/F-Series	COC & TWC	UB	Ford	2150A-2V FBC Carburetor	EEC-IV	Sonic	MTA	TFI-IV
	Bronco/F-Series (1985¼)	COC & TWC	UB	Bosch/ Ford	EFI	EEC-IV	Sonic	MTA	TFI-IV
5.8L	Bronco/E-Series/F-Series (49 States-A/T)	COC & TWC	UB	Holley	4180-C Carburetor	None	Ported/BP	MTA	DS-II
	Bronco/E-Series/F-Series (Altitude-A/T)	COC & TWC	UB	Holley	4180-C Carburetor	None	Ported	MTA	UIC
	F-Series (49 States-M/T)	COC & TWC	UB	Ford	2150A-2V FBC Carburetor	EEC-IV	Sonic	MTA	TFI-IV
	F-Series (Altitude-M/T)	COC & TWC	UB	Ford	2150A-2V FBC Carburetor	EEC-IV	Sonic	MTA	TFI-IV
	Bronco/E-Series/F-Series (California-A/T)	COC & TWC	UB	Ford	2150A-2V FBC Carburetor	EEC-IV	Sonic-Cooler	MTA	TFI-IV

ABBREVIATIONS:

NA = Not Applicable
COC = Conventional Oxidation Catalyst
TWC = Three-Way Catalyst
EEC-IV = Electronic Engine Control (System IV)
FBC = Feedback Carburetor
EFI = Electronic Fuel Injection
CFI = Central Fuel Injection
MCU = Microprocessor Control Unit
EGR = Exhaust Gas Recirculation
MTA = Managed Thermactor Air
PA = Pulse Air
CT = Conventional Thermactor
BP = Backpressure
BVT = Backpressure Variable Transducer
SBUB = Single Brick Underbody
TB = Toe Board
UB = Underbody
M/T = Manual Transmission
A/T = Automatic Transmission
MFG = Manufacturer
DBUB = Dual Brick Underbody
DS-II = Duraspark II
TFI = Thick Film Ignition
UIC = Universal Integrated Circuit
HO = High Output
S.V.O. = Special Vehicle Operation
MTX = Manual Transaxle
ATX = Automatic Transaxle

1985 EMISSION CONTROLS APPLICATION
Canada

ENGINE	VEHICLE APPLICATION	CATALYST(S) TYPE	CATALYST(S) LOCATION	FUEL SYSTEM MFG	FUEL SYSTEM TYPE	ELECTRONIC ENGINE CONTROL	EGR CONTROL	THERMACTOR SYSTEM	IGNITION SYSTEM
2.0L	Ranger	COC	UB	Carter	YFA-IV Carburetor	None	Ported	CT	DS-II
2.3L	Ranger/Aerostar	TWC	UB	Bosch/ Ford	EFI	EEC-IV	Sonic	None	TFI-IV
2.8L	Ranger/Bronco II	COC & TWC	DBUB	Ford	2150A-2V FBC Carburetor	EEC-IV	Sonic	MTA	TFI-IV
	Aerostar	COC & TWC	SBUB (2)	Ford	2150A-2V FBC Carburetor	EEC-IV	Sonic	MTA	TFI-IV
4.9L	Bronco/E-Series/F-Series	COC & TWC	UB	Carter	YFA-IV FBC Carburetor	EEC-IV	BP	MTA	TFI-IV
	E-Series/F-Series (with leaded fuel)	None		Carter	YF-IV Carburetor	None	None	None	DS-II
5.0L	Bronco/E-Series/F-Series	COC & TWC	UB	Ford	2150A-2V FBC	EEC-IV	Sonic	MTA	TFI-IV
	Bronco/F-Series (1985½)	COC & TWC	UB	Bosch/ Ford	EFI	EEC-IV	Sonic	MTA	TFI-IV
5.8L	Bronco/E-Series/F-Series (A/T)	COC & TWC	UB	Holley	4180C-4V Carburetor	None	Ported/BP	MTA	DS-II
	F-Series (M/T)	COC & TWC	UB	Ford	2150A FBC Carburetor	EEC-IV	Ported	MTA	TFI-IV
	Bronco/E-Series/F-Series (A/T)	None	N/A	Ford	2150-2V	None	Ported	None	DS-II

ABBREVIATIONS:
NA = Not Applicable
COC = Conventional Oxidation Catalyst
TWC = Three-Way Catalyst
EEC-IV = Electronic Engine Control (System IV)
FBC = Feedback Carburetor
EFI = Electronic Fuel Injection
CFI = Central Fuel Injection
MCU = Microprocessor Control Unit
EGR = Exhaust Gas Recirculation
MTA = Managed Thermactor Air
PA = Pulse Air
CT = Conventional Thermactor
BP = Backpressure
BVT = Backpressure Variable Transducer
SBUB = Single Brick Underbody
TB = Toe Board
UB = Underbody
M/T = Manual Transmission
A/T = Automatic Transmission
MFG = Manufacturer
DBUB = Dual Brick Underbody
DS-II = Duraspark II
TFI = Thick Film Ignition
UIC = Universal Integrated Circuit
HO = High Output
S.V.O. = Special Vehicle Operation
MTX = Manual Transaxle
ATX = Automatic Transaxle

1986 EMISSION CONTROLS APPLICATION
50 States and Canada

Engine	Vehicle Application	Catalyst(s) Type	Catalyst(s) Location	Fuel System Type, Mfg	Electronic Eng Ctrl	EGR System	Thermactor System	Ignition System	Idle Speed Control
2.0L OHC	Ranger (49 States)	COC	UB	YFA-2V NFB, Carter	None	Ported	CT	DS-II	DCM
2.3L OHC	Ranger/Bronco II Aerostar (49 States)	COC	UB	EFI	EEC-IV	ELEC	None	TFI-IV	BPA
	Ranger/Bronco II (Calif)	TWC	DBUB	EFI	EEC-IV	ELEC	None	TFI-IV	BPA
	Aerostar (Calif.)	TWC	(2) SBUB	EFI	EEC-IV	ELEC	None	TFI-IV	BPA
2.8L	Aerostar	COC & COC	DBUB	2150A-2V FBC, Ford	EEC-IV	ELEC	MTA	TFI-IV	DCM
2.9L	Ranger/Bronco II	COC & TWC	DBUB	EFI	EEC-IV	PFE	None	TFI-IV	BPA
3.0L	Aerostar	TWC TWC	UB #1 UB #2	EFI	EEC-IV	PFE	None	TFI-IV	BPA
4.9L	E-Series/F-Series Bronco	TWC COC	UB #1 UB #2	YFA-1V FBC, Carter	EEC-IV	IBP	MTA	TFI-IV	DCM
5.0L	E-Series/F-Series Bronco	TWC TWC	UB #1 UB #2	EFI	EEC-IV	ELEC	MTA/ AM1, AM2	TFI-IV	BPA
5.8L	E-Series/F-Series Bronco (49 States)	TWC COC	UB #1 UB #2	4180-C Holley	None	IBP	MTA	DS-II	None
7.5L	E-Series/F-Series	None	NA	4180C-4V Holley	None	Ported	CT	DS-II	None

ABBREVIATIONS:

COC = Conventional Oxidation Catalyst
TWC = Three-Way Catalyst
UB = Underbody
DBUB = Dual Brick Underbody
SBUB = Single Brick Underbody
MFG = Manufacturer
NFB = Non-Feedback Carburetor
FBC = Feedback Carburetor
EFI = Electronic Fuel Injection
EGR = Exhaust Gas Recirculation
ELEC = Electronic Valve
IBP = Integral Backpressure
EEC-IV = Electronic Engine Control (System-IV)
PFE = Pressure Feedback Electronic
CT = Conventional Thermactor
MTA = Managed Thermactor Air
AM(1), (2) = Air Management (1), (2)
DS-II = Duraspark II
TFI = Thick Film Ignition
BPA = Bypass Air
DCM = D. C. Motor

1987-88 EMISSION CONTROLS APPLICATION
50 States and Canada

Engine	Vehicle Application	Catalyst(s)		Fuel System Type, Mfg	Electronic Eng Ctrl	EGR System	Secondary Air System	Ignition System	Idle Speed Control
		Type	Location						
2.0L OHC	Ranger (49 States)	TWC COC	DBUB	Aisan Y NFB	None	Ported	CT	DS-II	DCM
2.3L OHC	Ranger Aerostar (49 States)	TWC	UB	EFI	EEC-IV	EEGR	None	TFI-IV	BPA
	Ranger (Calif)	TWC TWC	DBUB	EFI	EEC-IV	EEGR	None	TFI-IV	BPA
	Aerostar (Calif.)	TWC TWC	(2) SBUB	EFI	EEC-IV	EEGR	None	TFI-IV	BPA
2.9L	Ranger/Bronco II	TWC TWC	(2) SBUB	EFI	EEC-IV	PFE	None	TFI-IV	BPA
3.0L	Aerostar	TWC TWC	(2) SBUB	EFI	EEC-IV	None	None	TFI-IV	BPA
4.9L	E-Series F-Series Bronco	TWC (2) COC	UB #1 UB #2	EFI	EEC-IV	EEGR	MTA AM1, AM2	TFI-IV	BPA
5.0L	E-Series/F-Series Bronco	TWC (2) COC	UB #1 UB #2	EFI	EEC-IV	EEGR	MTA AM1, AM2	TFI-IV	BPA
5.8L	E-Series F-Series Bronco	TWC (2) COC	UB #1 UB #2	4180-C-4V NFB, Holley	None	IBP	MTA	DS-II	None
7.5L	E-Series F-Series	None	NA	4180C-4V Holley	None	Ported	MTA	DS-II	None
7.5L	E-Series/F-Series 1987-1/2	(4) REDOX	UB	EFI	EEC-IV	EEGR	MTA	TFI-IV	BPA

ABBREVIATIONS:

AM (1), AM(2) = Air Management (1), (2)
BPA = Bypass Air
COC = Conventional Oxidation Catalyst
CT = Conventional Thermactor
DBUB = Dual Brick Underbody
DCM = D.C. Motor
DS-II = Duraspark II
EEC-IV = Electronic Engine Control (System-IV)
EEGR = Electronic EGR Valve (Sonic)
EFI = Electronic Fuel Injection
EGR = Exhaust Gas Recirculation
IBP = Integral Backpressure
Mfg = Manufacturer
MTA = Managed Thermactor Air
NA = Not Applicable
NFB = Non-Feedback Carburetor
PFE = Pressure Feedback Electronic
REDOX = Reduction-Oxidation
SBUB = Single Brick Underbody
TFI = Thick Film Ignition
TWC = Three-Way Catalyst
UB = Underbody

Crankcase Emission Control System

The crankcase emission control equipment consists of a positive crankcase ventilation (PCV) valve, a crankcase air filter that is vented to the air cleaner, and the hoses that connect the equipment.

When the engine is running, a small amount of the gases formed in the combustion chamber leak by the piston rings and enter the crankcase. The PCV system pulls these gases back into the intake manifold allowing fresh air to flow into the crankcase through the filter and filler cap. For service to the PCV system, refer to the Emission Control in the Unit Repair section.

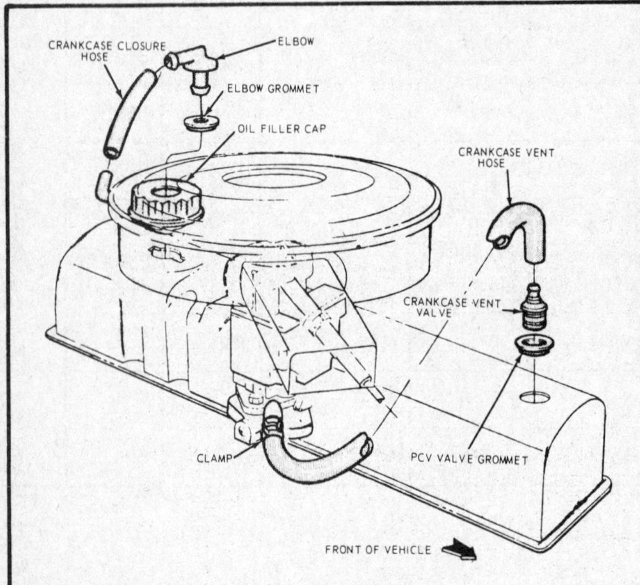

Closed crankcase ventilation system

EVAPORATIVE EMISSION CONTROL SYSTEM

The evaporative emission control system consists of a sealed fuel tank, a vapor controlling orifice valve located in the top of the fuel tank, a pressure/vacuum relief fuel cap, and a carbon canister. This system is designed to limit the fuel vapors released into the atmosphere.

The open orifice valve is used to control the flow of fuel vapor and to minimize the amount of liquid gasoline entering the fuel vapor delivery line. The delivery line conducts the vapor forward to the carbon canister where the vapor is stored. During normal driving, the engine compartment mounted canister is purged of the fuel vapor by means of a hose connected to the air cleaner assembly. The vapors are drawn into the engine's induction system. The fuel cap is sealed and contains a vacuum and pressure relief valve. The vacuum valve relieves tank vacuum caused by consumption or cooling and the pressure relief valve prevents excessive fuel tank pressurization due to any system component failure or operation extremes.

Exhaust Emission Control System

CATALYTIC CONVERTER

The catalytic converter is a muffler type device installed in the vehicles exhaust system which contains a chemical catalyst. When the hot exhaust gas passes over and through the catalyst, it heats up to a high temperature and the chemical reaction which occurs breaks down the exhaust into harmless elements.

EXHAUST GAS RECIRCULATION (EGR) SYSTEM

In this system, a vacuum-operated EGR flow valve is attached to the carburetor spacer (except on the 302 V8). A passage in the carburetor spacer mates with a hole in the mounting face of the

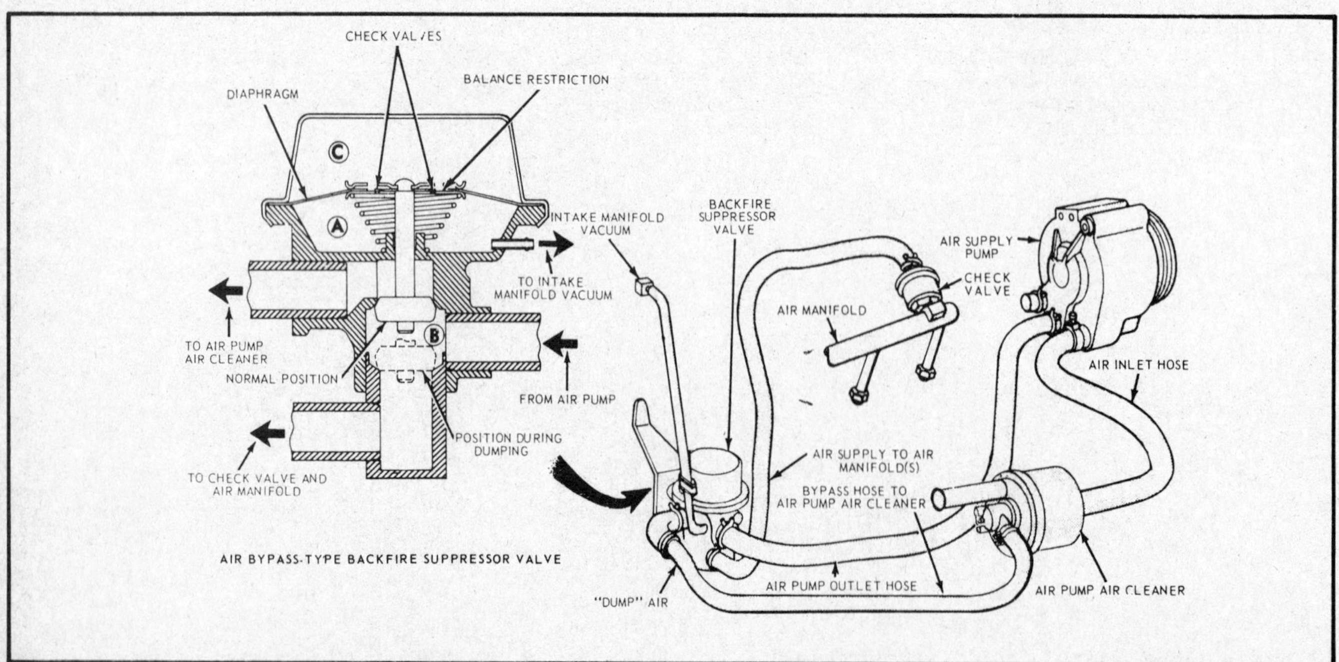

Thermactor exhaust emission control system

DIAPHRAGM
SEAT
BLACK CAP
DUMP VALVE
FILTER
RESTRICTOR IN BODY PORT (D8EE-AA ONLY)
VACUUM SIGNAL
THERMACTOR VACUUM VENT VALVE
CHECK VALVE
RESTRICTOR
SEAT
NATURAL CAP
DUMP VALVE
FILTER
DIAPHRAGM
VACUUM SIGNAL
TO DISTRIBUTOR (BODY PORT)
DISTRIBUTOR VACUUM VENT VALVE

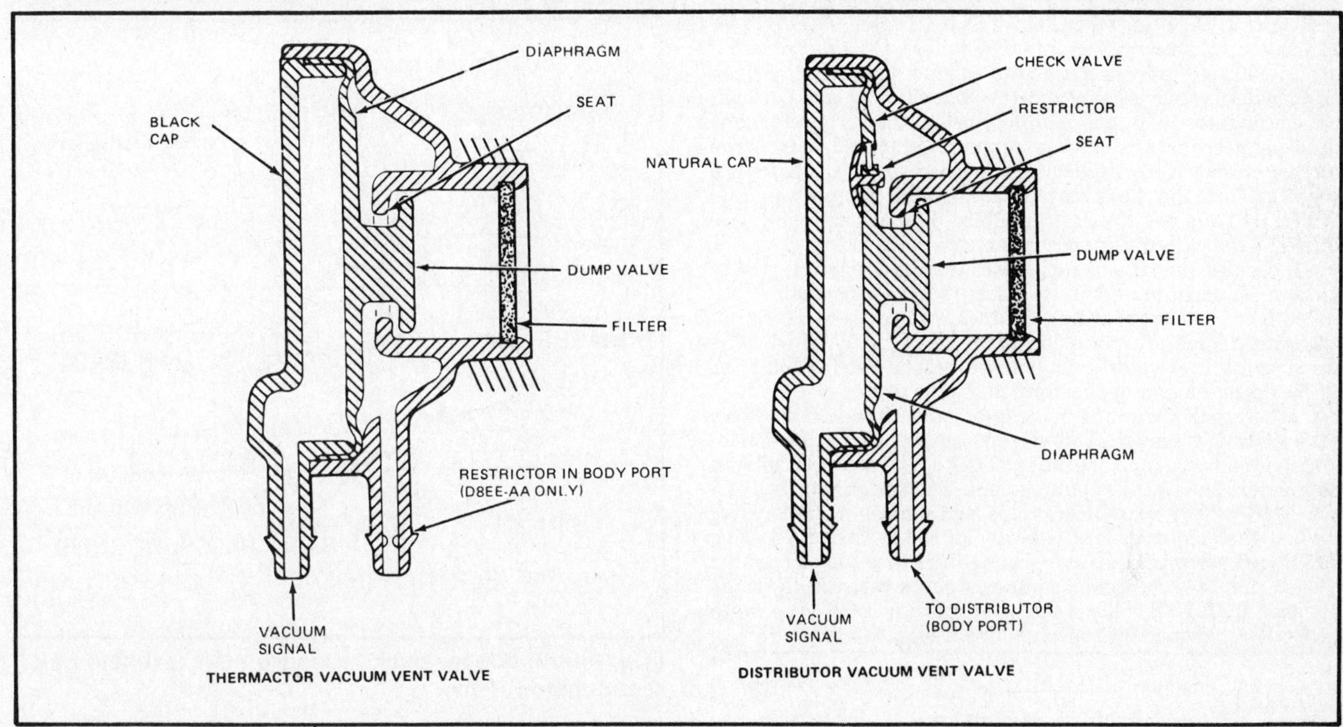

Typical spark delay valves (SDV)—two types illustrated

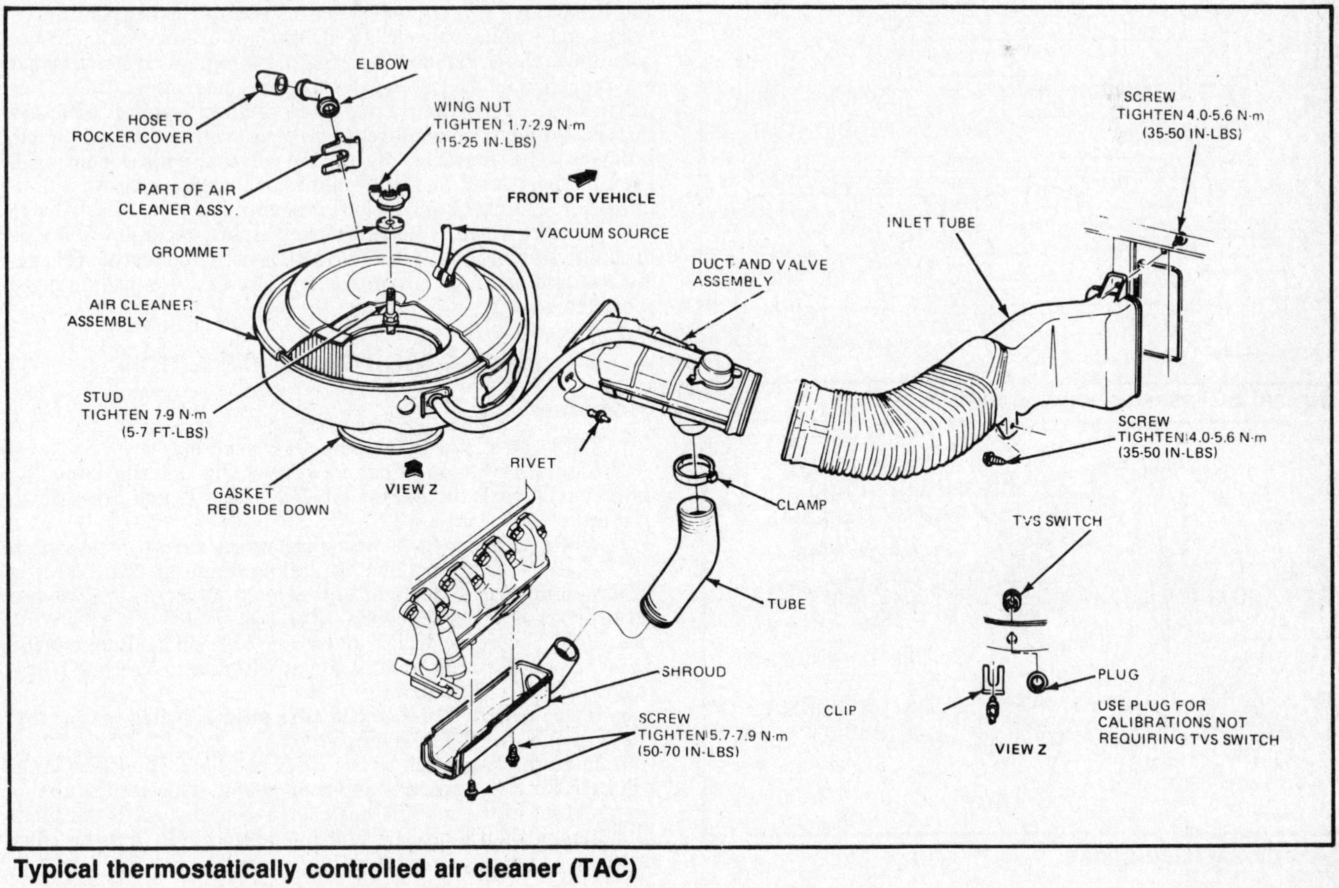

ELBOW
HOSE TO ROCKER COVER
WING NUT TIGHTEN 1.7-2.9 N·m (15-25 IN-LBS)
PART OF AIR CLEANER ASSY.
FRONT OF VEHICLE
GROMMET
VACUUM SOURCE
AIR CLEANER ASSEMBLY
DUCT AND VALVE ASSEMBLY
INLET TUBE
SCREW TIGHTEN 4.0-5.6 N·m (35-50 IN-LBS)
STUD TIGHTEN 7-9 N·m (5-7 FT-LBS)
GASKET RED SIDE DOWN
VIEW Z
RIVET
CLAMP
SCREW TIGHTEN 4.0-5.6 N·m (35-50 IN-LBS)
TVS SWITCH
TUBE
SHROUD
SCREW TIGHTEN 5.7-7.9 N·m (50-70 IN-LBS)
CLIP
PLUG
USE PLUG FOR CALIBRATIONS NOT REQUIRING TVS SWITCH
VIEW Z

Typical thermostatically controlled air cleaner (TAC)

EGR valve or the intake manifold. The EGR valve on the 302 V8 is located on the rear of the intake manifold. On all engines except the 302 V8, the system allows exhaust gases to flow from the exhaust crossover, through the control valve and through the spacer into the intake manifold below the carburetor. For those engines where exhaust gases cannot be picked up from the exhaust crossover (6 cylinder) as described above, the gases are picked up from the choke stove located on the exhaust manifold or directly from the exhaust manifold. The exhaust gases are routed to the carburetor spacer through steel tubing.

The vacuum signal which operates the EGR valve originates at the EGR vacuum port in the carburetor. This signal is controlled by at least one, and sometimes, two series of valves.

A water temperature sensing valve (the EGR PVS) which is closed until the water temperature reaches either 60°F or 125°F, depending on application, is always used.

Another system working in conjunction with the EGR system is the EGR/CSC system. This system regulates both the distributor spark advance and operation of the EGR valve according to the temperature of the engine coolant. The system consists of a 95°F EGR valve, a spark delay valve, and a vacuum check valve.

When the engine coolant is below 82°F, the EGR PVS valve admits carburetor EGR port vacuum directly to the distributor advance diaphragm through a one-way check valve. At the same time, the EGR PVS valve shuts off carburetor EGR vacuum to the EGR valve and transmission diaphragm.

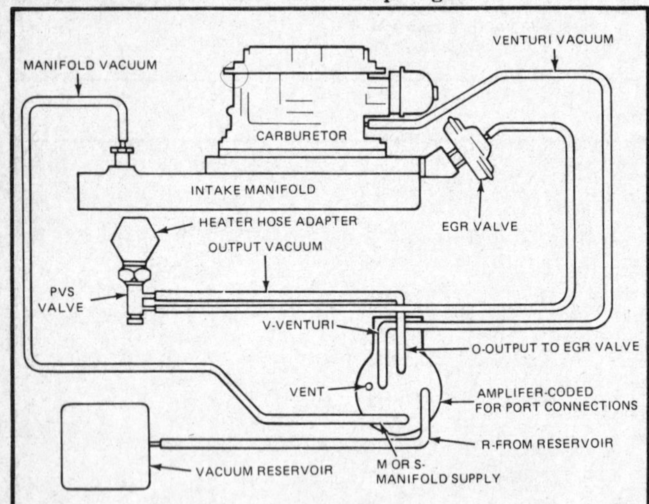

Typical EGR system components

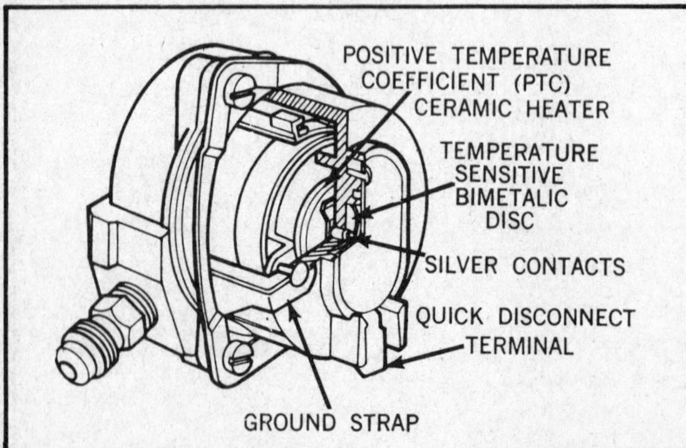

Electric assisted choke

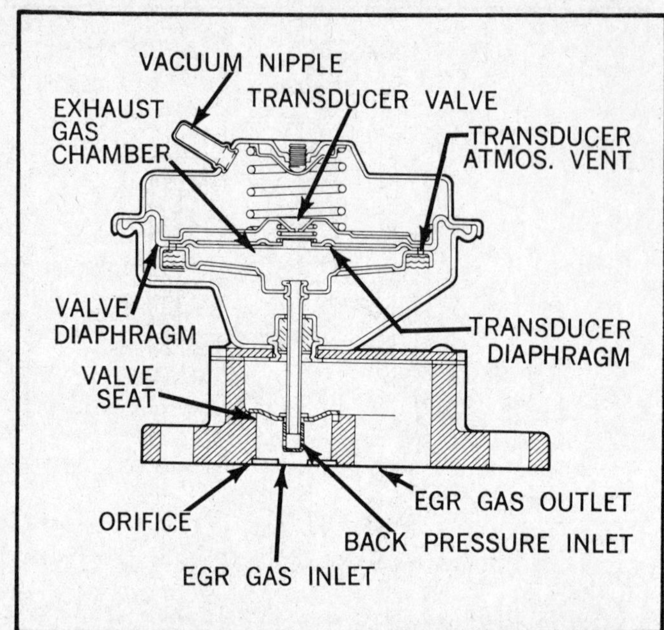

Integral transducer back pressure EGR (exhaust gas recirculation) valve

When the engine coolant temperature is above 95°F, the EGR PVS valve is actuated and directs carburetor EGR vacuum to the EGR valve and transmission instead of the distributor.

The spark delay valve (SDV) delays carburetor spark advance vacuum to the distributor advance diaphragm by restricting the vacuum through the SDV valve for a predetermined time. During normal acceleration, little or no vacuum is admitted to the distributor advance diaphragm until acceleration is completed, because of the time delay of the SDV valve, and the re-routing of the EGR port vacuum, if the engine coolant temperature is 95°F or higher. The check valve blocks vacuum from the SDV valve to the EGR PVS valve so that carburetor spark vacuum will not be dissipated when the EGR PVS valve is actuated above 95°F. increases and the increase in coolant circulation and fan speed cools the engine.

Reset Maintenance Lamp

Procedure

1. Turn the key switch to the OFF position.
2. Lightly push a Phillips screwdriver through the .2 inch diameter hole with the sticker labeled 'RESET' and press down and hold.
3. While pressing the screwdriver down, turn the keyswitch to the RUN position. The Emission Maintenance Warning (EMW) lamp will then light and remain lit for as long as the screwdriver is pressed down.
4. Hold the screwdriver down for 5 seconds. Remove the screwdriver. The lamp should go out within 2 to 5 seconds indicating a reset has occurred.
5. If the lamp does not go out, turn the keyswitch to the OFF position and use the following step.
6. Turn the keyswitch to the RUN position. The EMW lamp will light for 2 to 5 seconds and then go out. This verifies that a proper reset of the module has been accomplished. If the lamp remains on, then a proper reset has not occured and the reset procedure should be repeated.

ENGINE MECHANICAL

For overhaul procedures, refer to the Unit Overhaul Section.

Engine

BRONCO AND F SERIES

Removal and Installation

300 CID (4.9L) ENGINE

1. Drain the cooling system and the crankcase. Remove the hood and the air cleaner. Disconnect the negative battery cable.
2. Disconnect the heater hose from the water pump and coolant outlet housing.
3. Disconnect the flexible fuel line from the fuel pump. Remove the throttle body inlet tubes (if so equipped).
4. Remove the air conditioner compressor and the condenser.
5. Remove the radiator. Remove the fan, water pump pulley, and fan belt.
6. Disconnect the accelerator cable at the carburetor or throttle body. Remove the throttle return spring.
7. On vehicles equipped with power brakes, disconnect the brake booster vacuum hose at the intake manifold. On vehicles with automatic transmissions, disconnect the transmission kickdown rod at the bellcrank assembly or the cable at the throttle body.
7. Disconnect the exhaust pipe from the exhaust manifold.
8. Disconnect the body ground strap and the battery ground cable from the engine. Disconnect the Electronic Engine Control (EEC) harness from all sensors (if so equipped).
9. Disconnect the engine wiring harness at the ignition coil, the coolant temperature sending unit, and the oil pressure sending unit. Position the wiring harness out of the way.
10. Remove the alternator mounting bolts and position the alternator out of the way.
11. On a vehicle equipped with power steering, remove the power steering pump from the mounting brackets and move it to one side, leaving the lines attached.
12. If equipped with an air compressor, bleed the air system and disconnect the two air pressure lines at the compressor.
13. Raise and safely support the vehicle. Remove the starter and automatic transmission filler tube bracket, if so equipped. Also, remove the rear engine plate upper right bolt.
14. On manual transmission equipped vehicles, remove the flywheel housing lower attaching bolts and disconnect the clutch return spring.
15. On automatic transmission equipped vehicles, remove the converter housing access cover assembly and remove the flywheel-to-converter attaching nuts. Secure the converter in the housing. Remove the transmission oil cooler lines from the retaining clip at the engine. Remove the lower converter housing-to-engine attaching bolts.
16. Remove the nut from each of the two front engine mounts.
17. Lower the vehicle and position a jack under the transmission and support it. Remove the remaining bellhousing-to-engine attaching bolts.
18. Attach the engine lifting device and raise the engine slightly and carefully pull it from the transmission. Lift the engine out of the vehicle.
19. Installation is the reverse of the removal procedure.
20. Torque all bolts to specifications. Fill the cooling system. Fill the crankcase.
21. Start the engine and check for leaks. Bleed the cooling system. Adjust the clutch pedal free-play or the automatic transmission control linkage.

232 CID (3.8L) V6 AND V8 ENGINES

1. Drain the cooling system and crankcase. Remove the hood.
2. Disconnect the battery, negative cable first, and alternator cables from the cylinder block.
3. Remove the air cleaner and intake duct assembly, plus the crankcase ventilation hose.
4. Disconnect the upper and lower radiator hoses, and, if so equipped, the automatic transmission oil cooler lines.
5. Discharge the A/C system and remove the condensor.
6. Remove the fan shroud and lay it over the fan. Remove the radiator and fan, shroud, fan, spacer, pulley, and belt.
7. Disconnect the alternator leads and the alternator adjusting bolts. Allow the alternator to swing down out of the way.
8. Disconnect the oil pressure sending unit lead from the sending unit.
9. Disconnect the fuel tank-to-pump fuel line at the fuel pump and plug the line. For EFI, disconnect the chassis fuel line quick disconnects at the fuel rails.
10. Disconnect the accelerator linkage. Disconnect the speed control linkages. Disconnect the automatic transmission kickdown rod and remove the return spring, if so equipped.
11. Disconnect the power brake booster vacuum hose.
12. For EFI, after disconnecting the accelerator and the T.V.cable from the throttle body, disconnect the throttle bracket from the upper intake manifold and swing out of the way with the cables still attached to the bracket.
13. Disconnect the heater hoses from the water pump and intake manifold. Disconnect the temperature sending unit wire from the sending unit.
14. Remove the upper bellhousing-to-engine attaching bolts.
15. Disconnect the primary wire from the coil. Remove the wiring harness from the left rocker arm cover and position the wires out of the way. Disconnect the ground strap from the cylinder block.
16. Raise the front of the vehicle and disconnect the starter cable from the starter. Remove the starter.
17. Disconnect the exhaust pipe from the exhaust manifolds.
18. Disconnect the engine mounts from the brackets on the frame.
19. On vehicles with automatic transmissions, remove the converter inspection plate and remove the torque converter-to-flywheel attaching bolts.
20. Remove the remaining bellhousing-to-engine attaching bolts.
21. Lower the vehicle and support the transmission with a jack.
22. Install an engine lifting device.
22. Raise the engine slightly and carefully pull it out from the transmission. Lift the engine out of the engine compartment.
21. Install the engine in the reverse order of removal. Make sure that the dowels in the engine block engage the holes in the bellhousing through the rear cover plate.

460 CID (7.5L) V8 ENGINE

1. Remove the hood.
2. Drain the cooling system, the radiator and the cylinder block.
3. Disconnect the negative battery cable and remove the air cleaner assembly.
4. Disconnect the upper and lower radiator hoses and the transmission oil cooler lines from the radiator.
5. Remove the fan shroud from the radiator and remove the fan from the water pump. Remove the fan and shroud from the engine compartment.
6. Remove the upper support and remove the radiator.
7. If the vehicle is equipped with air conditioning, remove the compressor from the engine and position it out of the way. If the compressor must be removed completely, loosen the air conditioning service valves (disconnect) carefully to discharge the air conditioning system. Remove the compressor.

8. Remove the power steering pump from the engine, if so equipped, and position it to one side. Do not disconnect the fluid lines.
9. Disconnect the fuel pump inlet line from the pump and plug the line.
10. Remove the alternator drive belts and disconnect the alternator from the engine, positioning it aside.
11. Disconnect the ground cable from the right front corner of the engine.
12. Disconnect the heater hoses.
13. Remove the transmission fluid filler tube attaching bolt from the right-side valve cover and position the tube out of the way.
14. Disconnect all vacuum lines at the rear of the intake manifold.
15. Disconnect the speed control cable at the carburetor, if so equipped. Disconnect the accelerator rod and the transmission kickdown rod and secure them out of the way.
16. Disconnect the engine wiring harness at the connector on the fire wall.
17. Raise and support the vehicle safely. Disconnect the exhaust pipes at the exhaust manifolds.
18. Disconnect the starter cable and remove the starter. Bring the starter forward and rotate the solenoid outward to remove the assembly.
19. Remove the access cover from the converter housing and remove the flywheel-to-converter attaching nuts. Remove the lower converter housing-to-engine attaching bolts.
20. Remove the engine mount through-bolts attaching the rubber insulators to the frame brackets.
21. Lower the vehicle and place a jack under the transmission to support it.
22. Remove the converter housing-to-engine block attaching bolts (left-side).
23. Disconnect the coil wire and remove the coil and bracket assembly from the intake manifold.
24. Attach the engine lifting device and carefully lift the engine from the engine compartment.
25. Install the engine in the reverse order of removal.

420 CID (6.9L) DIESEL ENGINE

1. Disconnect battery ground cables from both batteries.
2. Scribe alignment marks at hood hinges and remove hood.
3. Drain cooling system.
4. Remove air cleaner and intake duct assembly. Install intake manifold cover over air intake opening.
5. Remove radiator fan shroud halves.
6. Remove fan and clutch assembly. Left-hand thread. Remove by turning nut clockwise.
7. Disconnect radiator upper and lower hoses from radiator.
8. Disconnect automatic transmission oil cooler lines at radiator, if so equipped.
9. Remove radiator.
10. Loosen A/C compressor, if so equipped, and remove drive belt.
11. Remove A/C compressor from its mounting, if so equipped, and position it on radiator upper support.
12. Loosen power steering pump and remove drive belt. Remove power steering pump and position out of the way on left side of engine compartment.
13. Disconnect fuel supply line heater and alternator wires at alternator. Disconnect oil pressure sending unit wire at sending unit. Remove oil pressure sender from dash panel and lay on engine.
14. Disconnect accelerator cable from injection pump. Disconnect speed control cable from injection pump, if so equipped. Remove accelerator cable bracket with cables attached, from intake manifold and position out of the way.
15. Disconnect transmission kick down rod from injection pump, if so equipped. Disconnect main wiring harness connector from right side of engine. Disconnect engine ground strap from rear of engine. Disconnect fuel return hose from left rear of engine.
16. Remove two upper transmission-to-engine attaching bolts.
17. Disconnect heater hoses from water pump and right cylinder head. Disconnect water temperature sender wire from sender on left front of engine block. Disconnect water temperature overheat light switch wire from switch on top of left cylinder head. Position wires out of the way.
18. Raise and safely support the vehicle.
19. Disconnect both battery ground cables from lower front of engine.
20. Disconnect and cap fuel inlet line at fuel supply pump.
21. Disconnect starter cables at starter motor.
22. Disconnect muffler inlet pipe at exhaust manifold.
23. Disconnect engine insulators from No. 1 crossmember. Remove flywheel inspection plate. Remove four converter-to-flywheel attaching nuts, if so equipped. Lower vehicle.
24. Support transmission with a floor jack. Remove four lower transmission to engine attaching bolts.
25. Attach engine lifting sling, and chain hoist. Raise engine high enough to clear number one crossmember and pull forward.
26. Rotate the front of the engine approximately 45 degrees to the left and lift it out of the engine compartment.
27. When installing the engine; lower engine into engine compartment. Use care not to damage windshield wiper motor when installing engine in vehicle.
28. Start transmission main shaft into clutch disc. It may be necessary to adjust position of transmission in relation to engine if main shaft binds or will not enter clutch disc. If engine hangs up after main shaft enters clutch disc, rotate crankshaft slowly (transmission in gear) until mainshaft splines mesh with clutch disc splines. Align convertor to flywheel studs, if so equipped.
29. Lower into engine insulator brackets on number one crossmember.
30. Install four lower transmission to engine attaching bolts and tighten. Remove engine lifting sling. Raise and safely support the vehicle.
31. Install four converter to flywheel attaching nuts, if so equipped. Install flywheel inspection plate.
32. Install engine insulator support to crossmember bracket attaching nuts and washers. Connect muffler inlet pipes to exhaust manifolds. Connect both battery ground cables to the lower front of the engine. Connect starter cables to starter. Install fuel pump inlet line on fuel pump. Lower vehicle.
33. Connect water temperature sender wire to sender on left front of engine block. Connect wire to water temperature overheat light switch on top of left cylinder head. Install heater hoses on right cylinder head and water pump and tighten clamps.
34. Connect engine ground strap at rear of engine. Connect fuel return hose at left rear of engine. Connect transmission kickdown rod, if so equipped.
35. Install accelerator cable bracket on intake manifold. Connect accelerator cable to injection pump. Connect speed control cable, if so equipped, to injection pump.
36. Install oil pressure sender on dash panel. Connect oil pressure gauge sender wire to oil pressure sender.
37. Connect fuel supply line heater and alternator wires to alternator.
38. Install power steering pump and drive belt. Do not adjust belt at this time.
39. Install A/C compressor and drive belt. Adjust A/C compressor and power steering pump drive belts.
40. Install radiator. Connect automatic transmission oil cooler lines at radiator, if so equipped. Connect upper and lower radiator hoses to radiator and tighten hose clamps. Fill and bleed the cooling system.
41. Install fan and clutch assembly. Turn nut counterclockwise to tighten.
42. Install radiator fan shroud halves.

43. Remove intake manifold cover, and install air cleaner. Install intake duct assembly.
44. Install hood using scribe marks drawn on hood at removal.
45. Connect battery ground cables at both batteries. Check the engine oil level and fill as needed with the specified type and grade of oil. Run engine and check for fuel, oil and coolant leaks.

E SERIES

Removal and Installation

300 CID (4.9L) ENGINE

1. Take off the engine cover, drain the coolant, remove the air cleaner and disconnect the battery.
2. Remove the bumper, grille and gravel deflector.
3. Detach the upper radiator hose at the engine. Remove the alternator splash shield and detach the lower hose at the radiator. Remove the radiator and shroud, if equipped.
4. Disconnect the engine heater hoses and the alternator wires. Remove the power steering pump and support.
5. Disconnect and plug the fuel line at the pump.
6. Disconnect the Electronic Engine Control (EEC) harness from all sensors, if so equipped.
7. Detach from the engine: distributor and gauge sending unit wires, brake booster hose, accelerator cable and bracket.
8. Disconnect the automatic transmission kickdown linkage at the bellcrank. With fuel injection, disconnect the cable at the throttle body.
9. Remove the exhaust manifold heat deflector and unbolt the pipe from the manifold.
10. Disconnect the automatic transmission vacuum line from the intake manifold and from the junction. Remove the transmission dipstick tube support bolt at the intake manifold.
11. Remove the upper engine-to-transmission bolts.
12. Remove the starter. Remove the flywheel inspection cover. Remove the four automatic transmission torque converter nuts, then remove the front engine support nuts. Remove the oil filter.
13. Remove the rest of the transmission-to-engine fasteners, then lift the engine out from the engine compartment with a floor crane.
14. Installation is the reverse of the removal procedure.

232 CID (3.8L) V6 AND V8 ENGINES EXCEPT DIESEL

1. Take off the engine cover, drain the coolant, remove the air cleaner, and disconnect the battery. Remove the bumper, grille, and gravel deflector. Remove the upper grille support bracket, hood lock support, and air conditioning condenser upper mounting brackets.
2. With air conditioning, the system must be discharged to remove the condenser. Disconnect the lines at the compressor.
3. Remove the accelerator cable bracket and the heater hoses. Detach the radiator hoses and the automatic transmission cooler lines, if any. Remove the fan shroud, fan, and radiator.
4. Pivot the alternator in and detach the wires.
5. Remove the air cleaner, duct and valve, exhaust manifold shroud, and flex tube.
6. Disconnect the automatic transmission shift rod.
7. Disconnect the fuel and choke lines, detach the vacuum lines, and remove the carburetor and spacer.
8. Remove the oil filter. Detach the exhaust pipe from the manifold. Unbolt the automatic transmission tube bracket from the cylinder head. Remove the starter.
9. Remove the engine mount bolts. With automatic, remove the converter inspection cover and unbolt the converter from the flex plate.
10. Unbolt the engine ground cable and support the transmission.
11. Remove the power steering front bracket. Detach only one vacuum line at the rear of the intake manifold. Disconnect the engine wiring loom. Remove the speed control servo from the manifold. Detach the compressor clutch wire.
12. Install a lifting bracket and attach a floor crane. Remove the transmission-to-engine bolts, making sure the transmission is supported. Remove the engine.
13. Installation is the reverse of the removal procedure.

420 CID (6.9L) DIESEL ENGINE

1. Remove the engine cover.
2. Disconnect battery ground cables from both batteries.
3. Drain cooling system.
4. Remove the front bumper, grille assembly and gravel deflector.
5. Remove the speed control servo bracket and position out of the way.
6. Mark the location and remove the hood latch and cable assembly from the grille upper support bracket. Remove the upper support bracket.
7. Disconnect the A/C lines from the condensor and remove the condensor.
8. Disconnect automatic transmission oil cooler lines at radiator, if so equipped.
9. Remove the radiator cooling fan and clutch. Remove the shroud.
10. Disconnect radiator upper and lower hoses from radiator. Remove radiator.
11. Loosen A/C compressor, if so equipped, and remove drive belt.
12. Remove A/C compressor from its mounting, if so equipped, and position it on radiator upper support.
13. Loosen power steering pump and remove drive belt. Remove power steering pump and position out of the way on left side of engine compartment.
14. Disconnect fuel supply line heater and alternator wires at alternator. Disconnect oil pressure sending unit wire at sending unit. Remove oil pressure sender from dash panel and lay on engine.
15. Disconnect accelerator cable from injection pump. Disconnect speed control cable from injection pump, if so equipped. Remove accelerator cable bracket with cables attached, from intake manifold and position out of the way.
16. Disconnect transmission kick down rod from injection pump, if so equipped. Disconnect main wiring harness connector from right side of engine. Disconnect engine ground strap from rear of engine. Disconnect fuel return hose from left rear of engine.
17. Remove two upper transmission-to-engine attaching bolts.
18. Disconnect heater hoses from water pump and right cylinder head. Disconnect water temperature sender wire from sender on left front of engine block. Disconnect water temperature overheat light switch wire from switch on top of left cylinder head. Position wires out of the way.
19. Raise and safely support the vehicle.
20. Disconnect and cap fuel inlet line at fuel supply pump.
21. Disconnect starter cables at starter motor.
22. Disconnect muffler inlet pipe at exhaust manifold.
23. Disconnect engine insulators from No. 1 crossmember. Remove flywheel inspection plate. Remove four converter-to-flywheel attaching nuts, if so equipped. Lower vehicle.
24. Support transmission with a floor jack. Remove four lower transmission to engine attaching bolts.
25. Attach engine lifting sling, and chain hoist. Raise engine high enough to clear number one crossmember and pull forward.
26. Rotate the front of the engine approximately 45 degrees to the left and lift it out of the engine compartment.
27. Reverse the order to install the engine.

BRONCO II AND RANGER

Removal and Installation

122 CID (2.0L) AND 140 CID (2.3L) ENGINES

1. Raise the hood and install protective fender covers. Drain the coolant from the radiator. Remove the air cleaner and duct assembly.
2. Disconnect the battery ground cable at the engine and disconnect the battery positive cable at the battery and set aside.
3. Mark the location of the hood hinges and remove the hood.
4. Disconnect the upper and lower radiator hoses from the engine. Remove the radiator shroud screws. Remove the radiator upper supports.
5. Remove engine fan and shroud assembly. Then remove the radiator. Remove the oil fill cap.
6. Disconnect the coil primary wire at the coil. Disconnect the oil pressure and the water temperature sending unit wires from the sending units.
7. Disconnect the alternator wire from the alternator, the starter cable from the starter and the accelerator cable from the carburetor. If so equipped, disconnect the transmission kickdown rod.
8. If so equipped, remove the A/C compressor from the mounting bracket and position it out of the way, leaving the refrigerant lines attached.
9. Disconnect the power brake vacuum hose. Disconnect the chassis fuel line from the fuel pump. Disconnect the heater hoses from the engine.
10. Remove the engine mount nuts. Raise and safely support the vehicle.
11. Drain engine oil from the crankcase. Remove the starter motor.
12. Disconnect the muffler exhaust inlet pipe at the exhaust manifold.
13. Remove the dust cover (manual transmission) or converter inspection plate (automatic transmission).
14. On vehicles with a manual transmission, remove the flywheel housing cover lower attaching bolts. On vehicles with automatic transmissions, remove the converter-to-flywheel bolts, then remove the converter housing lower attaching bolts.
15. Remove clutch slave cylinder (manual transmission). Lower the vehicle.
16. Support the transmission and flywheel or converter housing with a jack.
17. Remove the flywheel housing or converter housing upper attaching bolts.
18. Attach the engine lifting hooks to the existing lifting brackets. Carefully, so as not to damage any components, lift the engine out of the vehicle.
19. Installation is the reverse of the removal procedure.

179 CID (2.9L) V6 ENGINE

1. Disconnect the battery ground cable and drain the cooling system.
2. Remove the hood after scribing hinge positions. Remove the air cleaner and intake duct assembly.
3. Remove or disconnect thermactors system parts that will interfere with removal or installation of the engine.
4. Disconnect the radiator upper and lower hoses at the radiator. Remove the fan shroud attaching bolts and position the shroud over the fan. Remove the radiator and shroud.
5. Remove the alternator and bracket. Position the alternator out of the way. Disconnect the alternator ground wire from the cylinder block.
6. Remove A/C compressor and power steering and position out of way, if so equipped.
7. Disconnect the heater hoses at the block and water pump.
8. Remove the ground wires from the cylinder block.
9. Disconnect the fuel tank to fuel pump fuel line at the fuel pump. Plug the fuel tank line.
10. Disconnect the throttle cable linkage at the carburetor and intake manifold.
11. Disconnect the primary wires from the ignition coil. Disconnect the brake booster vacuum hose. Disconnect the wiring from the oil pressure and engine coolant temperature senders.
12. Raise and support the vehicle safely. Disconnect the muffler inlet pipes at the exhaust manifolds.
13. Disconnect the starter cable and remove the starter.
14. Remove the engine front support to crossmember attaching nuts or through bolts.
15. If equipped with automatic transmission, remove the converter inspection cover and disconnect the flywheel from the converter.
16. Remove the kickdown rod. Remove the converter housing to cylinder block bolts and the adapter plate to converter housing bolt.
17. On vehicles equipped with a manual transmission, remove the clutch linkage. Lower the vehicle.
18. Attach engine lifting sling and hoist to lifting brackets at exhaust manifolds.
19. Position a jack under the transmission. Raise the engine slightly and carefully pull it from the transmission. Carefully lift the engine out of the engine compartment so that the rear cover plate is not bent or components damaged.
20. Reverse the procedure for installation.

134 CID (2.2L) DIESEL ENGINE

1. Open hood and install protective fender covers. Mark location of hood hinges and remove hood.
2. Disconnect battery ground cables from both batteries. Disconnect battery ground cables at engine.
3. Drain coolant from radiator.
4. Disconnect air intake hose from air cleaner and intake manifold.
5. Disconnect upper and lower radiator hoses from engine. Remove engine cooling fan. Remove radiator shroud screws. Remove radiator upper supports and remove radiator and shroud.
6. Disconnect radio ground strap, if so equipped.
7. Remove No. 2 glow plug relay from dash, with harness attached, and lay on engine.
8. Disconnect engine wiring harness at main connector located on left fender apron. Disconnect starter cable from starter.
9. Disconnect accelerator cable and speed control cable, if so equipped, from injection pump.
10. Remove cold start cable from injection pump.
11. Discharge A/C system and remove A/C refrigerant lines and position out of the way.
12. Remove pressure and return hoses from power steering pump, if so equipped.
13. Disconnect vacuum fitting from vacuum pump and position fitting and vacuum hoses out of the way.
14. Disconnect and cap fuel inlet line at fuel line heater and fuel return line at injection pump.
15. Disconnect heater hoses from engine.
16. Loosen engine insulator nuts. Raise and support the vehicle safely.
17. Drain engine oil from oil pan and remove primary oil filter.
18. Disconnect oil pressure sender hose from oil filter mounting adapter.
19. Disconnect muffler inlet pipe at exhaust manifold.
20. Remove bottom engine insulator nuts. Remove transmission bolts. Lower vehicle. Attach engine lifting sling and chain hoist.
21. Carefully lift engine out of vehicle to avoid damage to components.
22. Installation is the reverse of the removal procedure.

140 CID (2.3L) TURBO DIESEL ENGINE

1. Mark the location of the hood hinges and remove the hood.
2. Disconnect the negative battery cables from both batteries and at the engine.

3. Drain the engine coolant.
4. Remove the crankcase breather hose at the rocker cover.
5. Remove the intake hose between the air cleaner and the turbocharger.
6. Remove the A/C compressor and position it out of the way.
7. Disconnect the heater hoses from the heater core.
8. Remove the cooling fan. Disconnect the radiator hoses and remove the radiator.
9. Disconnect the electrical connector and the fuel supply line at the fuel conditioner. Disconnect the fuel return line and the throttle cable at the injection pump.
10. Disconnect the vacuum lines at the pump fitting.
11. Disconnect the engine harness from the chassis harness at the alternator bracket.
12. Disconnect the wires from the glow plug bus bar.
13. Disconnect the starter motor wiring and remove the starter.
14. Raise the vehicle and support it safely. Remove the RH wheel and the RH inner fender.
15. Disconnect the oil pressure switch wire.
16. Disconnect the oil filter lines at the oil filter adapter.
17. Remove the nuts attaching the engine mounts to the brackets.
18. Disconnect the muffler inlet pipe from the turbo exhaust outlet pipe.
19. Disconnect the power steering pump hoses at the pump.
20. Disconnect the clutch servo hydraulic line at the clutch housing and position it out of the way.
21. Remove the transmission attaching bolts, except the top two.
22. Lower the vehicle. Attach an engine lifting hoist to the lifting brackets.
23. Remove the top two transmission bolts and remove the engine from the vehicle.
24. Installation is the reverse of the removal procedure.

AEROSTAR

Removal and Installation

140 CID (2.3L) ENGINE

1. Raise the hood. Drain the coolant from the radiator. Remove the air cleaner and duct assembly.
2. Disconnect the battery ground cable.
3. Disconnect the upper and lower radiator hoses from the engine. Remove the radiator shroud screws.
4. Remove engine fan and shroud assembly. Then remove the radiator. Remove the oil fill cap.
5. Disconnect the coil primary wire at the coil. Disconnect the oil pressure and the water temperature sending unit wires from the sending units.
6. Disconnect the alternator wire from the alternator, the starter cable from the starter and the accelerator cable from the carburetor. If so equipped, disconnect the transmission kickdown rod.
7. If so equipped, remove the A/C compressor from the mounting bracket and position it out of the way, leaving the refrigerant lines attached.
8. Disconnect the power brake vacuum hose. Disconnect the chassis fuel line from the fuel pump. Disconnect the heater hoses from the engine.
9. Remove the engine mount nuts. Raise and safely support the vehicle.
10. Drain engine oil from the crankcase. Remove the starter motor.
11. Disconnect the muffler exhaust inlet pipe at the exhaust manifold.
12. Remove the dust cover (manual transmission) or converter inspection plate (automatic transmission).
13. On vehicles with a manual transmission, remove the flywheel housing cover lower attaching bolts. On vehicles with automatic transmissions, remove the converter-to-flywheel bolts, then remove the converter housing lower attaching bolts.
14. Remove clutch slave cylinder (manual transmission). Lower the vehicle.
15. Support the transmission and flywheel or converter housing with a jack.
16. Remove the flywheel housing or converter housing upper attaching bolts.
17. Attach the engine lifting hooks to the existing lifting brackets. Carefully, so as not to damage any components, lift the engine out of the vehicle.
18. Installation is the reverse of the removal procedure.

171 CID (2.8L) AND 183 CID (3.0L) V6 ENGINES

1. Disconnect the battery ground cable and drain the cooling system.
2. Remove the air cleaner and intake duct assembly.
3. Remove or disconnect thermactors system parts that will interfere with removal or installation of the engine.
4. Disconnect the radiator upper and lower hoses at the radiator. Remove the fan shroud attaching bolts and position the shroud over the fan. Remove the radiator and shroud.
5. Remove the alternator and bracket. Position the alternator out of the way. Disconnect the alternator ground wire from the cylinder block.
6. Remove A/C compressor and power steering and position out of way, if so equipped.
7. Disconnect the heater hoses at the block and water pump.
8. Remove the ground wires from the cylinder block.
9. Disconnect the fuel tank to fuel pump fuel line at the fuel pump. Plug the fuel tank line.
10. Disconnect the throttle cable linkage at the carburetor and intake manifold.
11. Disconnect the primary wires from the ignition coil. Disconnect the brake booster vacuum hose. Disconnect the wiring from the oil pressure and engine coolant temperature senders.
12. Raise and support the vehicle safely. Disconnect the muffler inlet pipes at the exhaust manifolds.
13. Disconnect the starter cable and remove the starter.
14. Remove the engine front support to crossmember attaching nuts or through bolts.
15. If equipped with automatic transmission, remove the converter inspection cover and disconnect the flywheel from the converter.
16. Remove the kickdown rod. Remove the converter housing to cylinder block bolts and the adapter plate to converter housing bolt.
17. On vehicles equipped with a manual transmission, remove the clutch linkage. Lower the vehicle.
18. Attach engine lifting sling and hoist to lifting brackets at exhaust manifolds.
19. Position a jack under the transmission. Raise the engine slightly and carefully pull it from the transmission. Carefully lift the engine out of the engine compartment so that the rear cover plate is not bent or components damaged.
20. Reverse the procedure for installation.

Intake Manifold

Removal and Installation

122 CID (2.0L) AND 140 CID (2.3L) ENGINES

1. Drain the cooling system. Remove the air cleaner and duct assembly. Disconnect the negative battery cable.
2. Disconnect the accelerator cable, vacuum hoses (as required) and the hot water hose at the manifold fitting. Be sure to identify all vacuum hoses for proper reinstallation.
3. Remove the engine oil dipstick. Disconnect the heat tube at the EGR (exhaust gas recirculation) valve. Disconnect the fuel line at the carburetor fuel fitting.

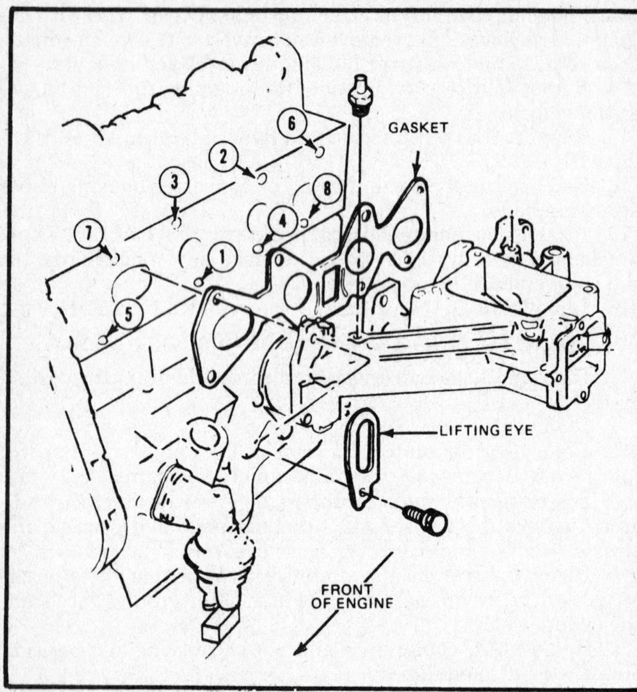

122(2.0L) and 140(2.3L) intake manifold bolt tightening sequence

4. Remove the dipstick retaining bolt from the intake manifold.
5. Disconnect and remove the PCV at the engine and intake manifold.
6. Remove the distributor cap and position the cap and wires out of the way, after removing the plastic plug connector from the valve cover.
7. Remove the intake manifold retaining bolts. Remove the manifold from the engine.
8. Clean all gasket mounting surfaces.
9. Install a new mounting gasket and intake manifold on the engine. Torque the bolts in proper sequence. The rest of the installation procedure is in the reverse order of removal.

173 CID (2.8L) AND 177 CID (2.9L) V6 ENGINES

1. Drain the cooling system. Remove the air cleaner and duct assembly.
2. Disconnect the negative battery cable. Disconnect the accelerator cable from the carburetor linkage.
3. Disconnect and remove the upper radiator hose. Disconnect and remove the bypass hose from the intake manifold and thermostat housing.
4. Remove the distributor cap and spark plug wires as an assembly. Turn the engine till No. 1 piston is at TDC (top dead center) on the compression stroke. Remove the distributor.
5. Remove any vacuum lines and controls that will interfere with the intake manifold removal. Label all hoses for identification.
6. Remove both valve covers. Remove the manifold mounting nuts and bolts. Remove the manifold. Tap the manifold lightly with a plastic mallet (if necessary) to break the gasket seal.
7. Remove all old gasket material and sealing compound from the mounting surfaces.
8. Apply sealing compound to the joining surfaces. Place the intake mounting gasket into position. Make sure that the tab on the right bank head gasket fits into the cutout of the manifold gasket. Apply sealing compound to the intake manifold bolt bosses and install the intake manifold. Tighten the mounting nuts and bolts in the proper torque sequence.
9. Install the distributor and the rest of the removed components in reverse order.
10. Refill the cooling system, start the engine and check for coolant or oil leaks.
11. Check idle RPM and ignition timing. Adjust if necessary.

183 CID (3.0L) V6 ENGINE

1. Disconnect the negative battery cable.
2. Drain the engine cooling system.
3. Remove the throttle body. Disconnect the fuel lines.
4. Remove the fuel injector wiring harness from the engine.
5. Disconnect the upper radiator hose and the water outlet heater hose.
6. Remove the distributor. Remove the rocker arm covers.

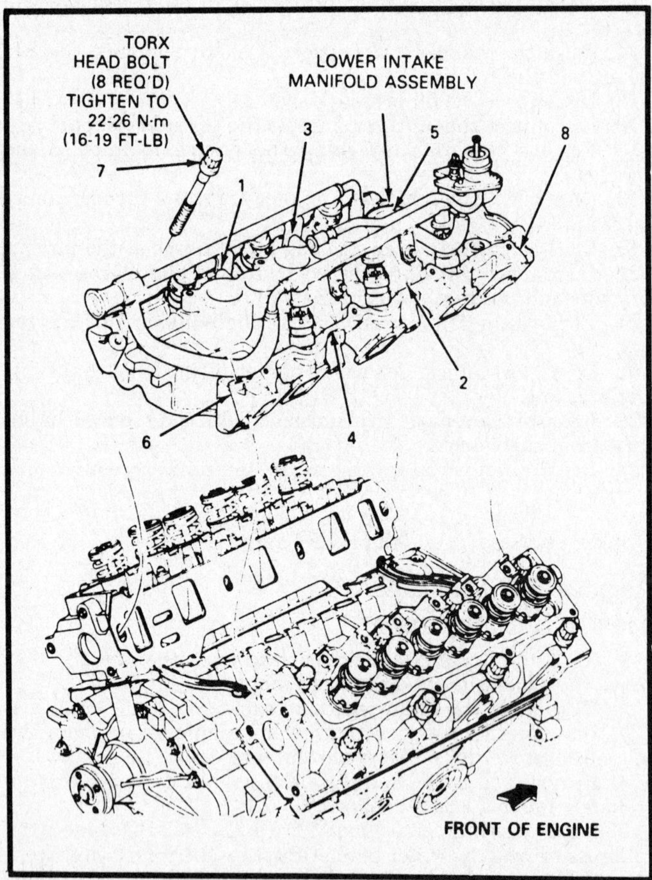

Intake manifold bolt tightening sequence 183 CID (3.0L) V6

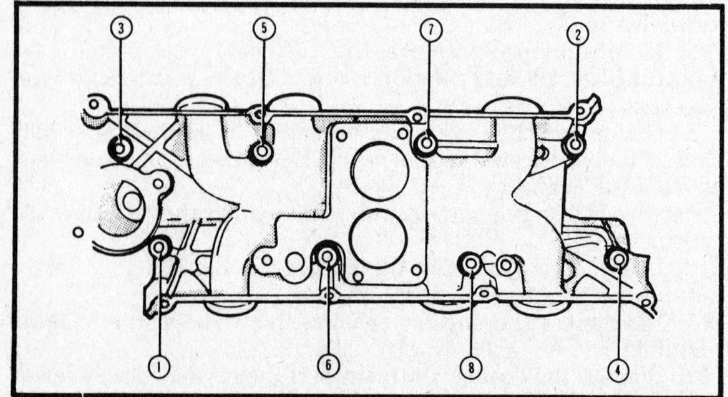

173(2.8L) V6 intake manifold bolt tightening sequence

7. Remove the intake manifold attaching bolts and studs. The manifold can be removed with fuel rails and injectors in place.
8. Reverse the procedure for installation. Lightly oil all attaching bolts and stud threads before installation.

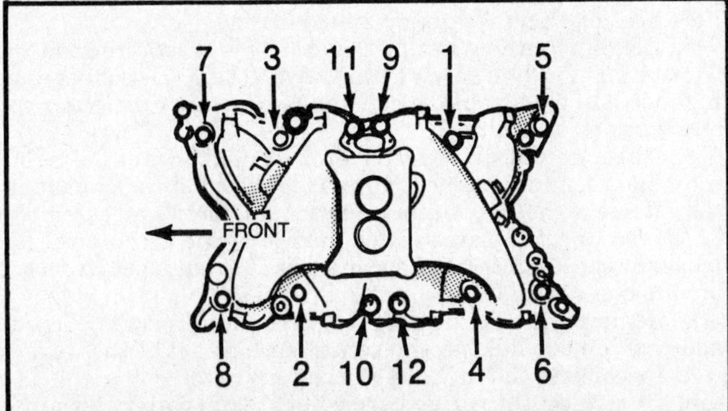

Silicone rubber sealer application on intake manifold seal—351M and 400 V8 engines

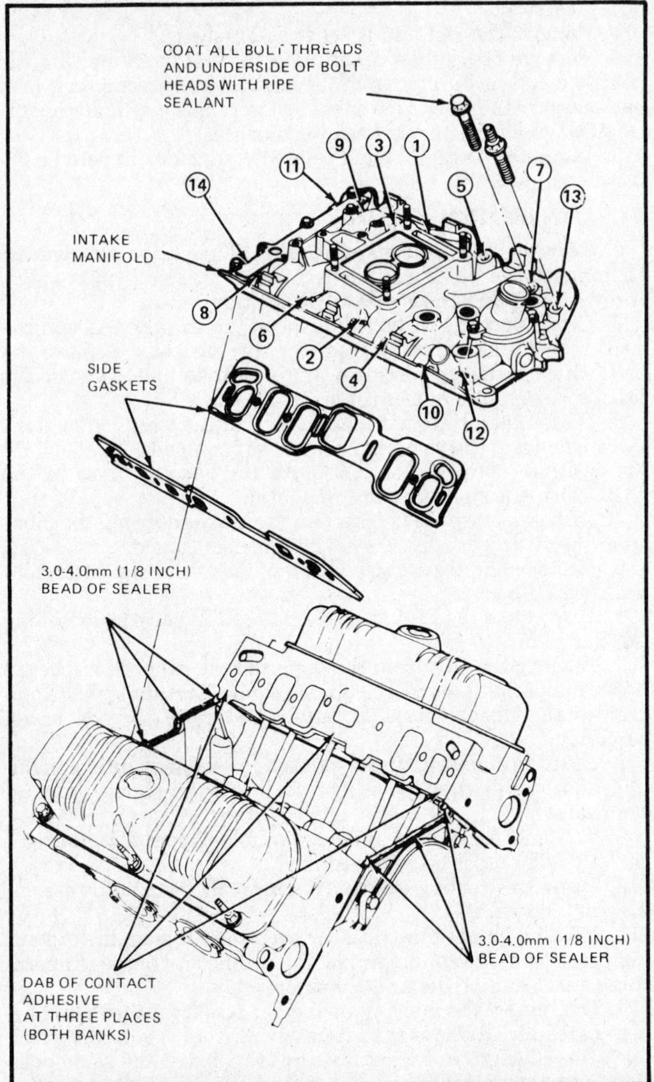

Installation of intake manifold (torque sequence numbered)—232 CID engine

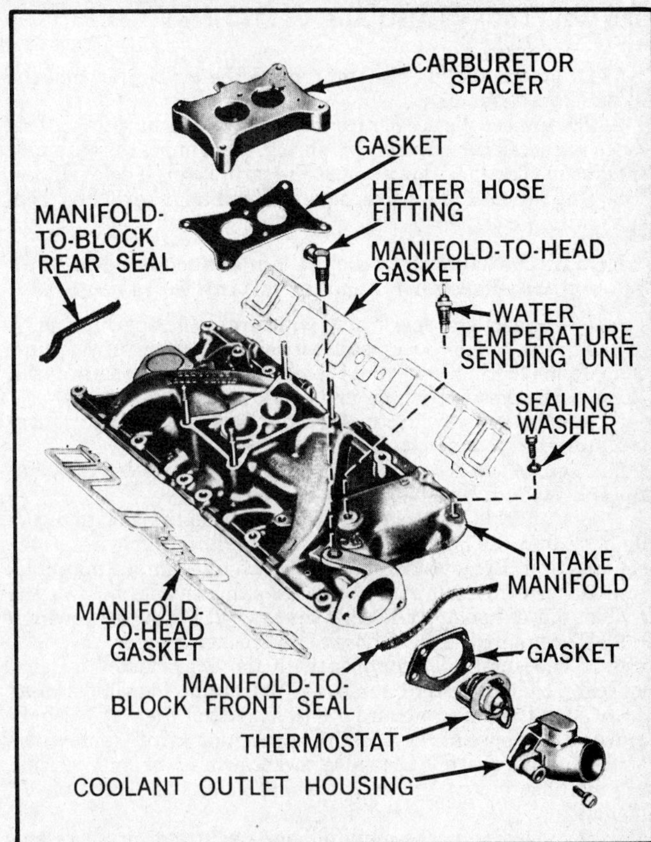

Intake manifold—302 and 351 V8

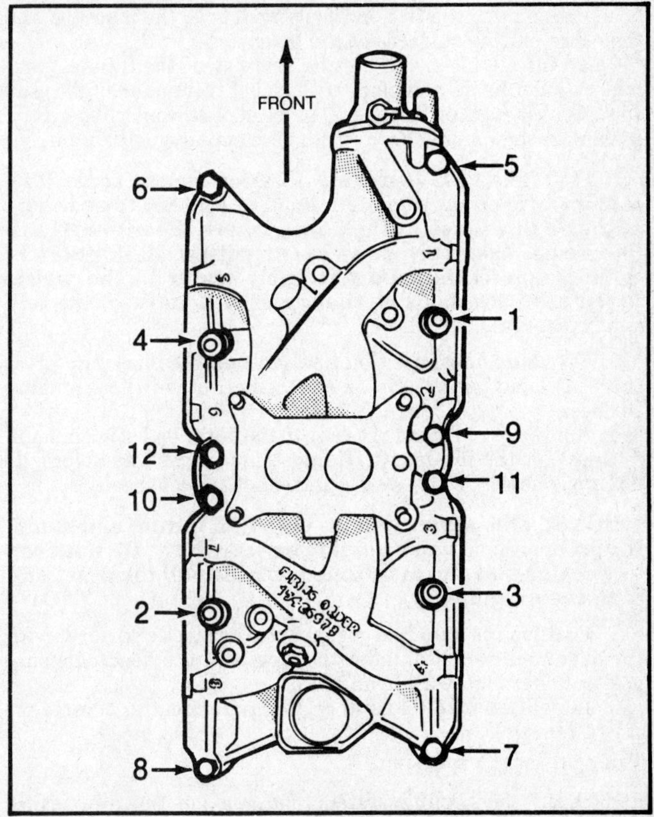

Intake manifold torque sequence—302 V8

232 CID (3.8L) V6 AND ALL V8 ENGINES, EXCEPT 460 CID (7.5L)

1. Drain the cooling system, remove the air cleaner and the intake duct assembly.
2. Disconnect the accelerator rod from the carburetor and remove the accelerator retracting spring. Disconnect the automatic transmission kick-down rod at the carburetor, if so equipped.
3. Disconnect the high tension lead and all other wires from the ignition coil.

NOTE: Distributor removal is not necessary on 3.8L V6 engines, disregard steps pretaining to its removal.

4. Disconnect the spark plug wires from the spark plugs by grasping the rubber boots and twisting and pulling at the same time. Remove the wires from the brackets on the rocker covers. Remove the distributor cap and spark plug wire assembly.
5. Remove the carburetor fuel inlet line and the distributor vacuum line from the carburetor.
6. Remove the distributor lockbolt and remove the distributor and vacuum line, as required.
7. Disconnect the upper radiator hose from the coolant outlet housing and the water temperature sending unit wire at the sending unit. Remove the heater hose from the intake manifold.
8. Loosen the clamp on the water pump bypass hose at the coolant outlet housing and slide the hose off the outlet housing.
9. Disconnect the PCV hose at the rocker cover.
10. If the engine is equipped with the Thermactor exhaust emission control system, remove the air pump to cylinder head air hose at the air pump and position it out of the way. Also remove the air hose at the backfire suppressor valve. Remove the air hose bracket from the valve rocker arm cover and position the air hose out of the way. Remove EGR valve tube on V6 models.
11. Remove the intake manifold and carburetor as an assembly. It may be necessary to pry the intake manifold from the cylinder head. Remove all traces of the intake manifold to cylinder head gaskets and the two end seals from both the manifold and the other mating surfaces of the engine.
12. To install, clean the mating surfaces of the intake manifold, cylinder heads and block with laquer thinner or similar solvent. On V8 engines, apply a ⅛ in. bead of silicone rubber RTV sealant at the points shown in the accompanying diagram.

NOTE: The 3.8L V6 engine does not use end seals. RTV sealant is used. Apply ⅛ in. bead of sealant to each end of the engine block at the points where the intake manifold rests. Assembly must occur within 15 minutes of sealant application. Do not apply sealer to the waffle portions of the seals as the sealer will rupture the end seal material.

13. On V8 engines, position new seals on the block and press the seal locating extensions into the holes in the mating surfaces.
14. Apply a $^1/_{16}$ in. bead of sealer to the outer end of each manifold seal for the full length of the seal (4 places). As before, do not apply sealer to the waffle portion of the end seals.

NOTE: This sealer sets in about 15 minutes, depending on brand, so work quickly but carefully. Do not drop any sealer into the manifold cavity. It will form, set and plug the oil gallery.

15. Position the manifold gasket onto the block and heads with the alignment notches under the dowels in the heads. Be sure gasket holes align with head holes.
16. Install the manifold and related equipment in reverse order of removal.

460 CID (7.5L) ENGINE

1. Drain the cooling system and remove the air cleaner assembly.
2. Disconnect the upper radiator hose at the engine.
3. Disconnect the heater hoses at the intake manifold and the water pump. Position them out of the way. Loosen the water pump by-pass hose clamp at the intake manifold.
4. Disconnect the PCV valve and hose at right valve cover. Disconnect all of the vacuum lines at the rear of the intake manifold and tag them for proper reinstallation.
5. Disconnect the wires at the spark plugs, and remove the wires from the brackets on the valve covers. Disconnect the high-tension wire from the coil and remove the distributor cap and wires as an assembly.
6. Disconnect all of the distributor vacuum lines at the carburetor and vacuum control valve and tag them for proper installation. Remove the distributor and vacuum lines as an assembly.
7. Disconnect the accelerator linkage at the carburetor. Remove the speed control linkage bracket, if so equipped, from the manifold and carburetor.
8. Remove the bolts holding the accelerator linkage bellcrank and position the linkage and return springs out of the way.
9. Disconnect the fuel line at the carburetor.
10. Disconnect the wiring harness at the coil battery terminal, engine temperature sending unit, oil pressure sending unit, and other connections as necessary. Disconnect the wiring harness from the clips at the left valve cover and position the harness out of the way.
11. Remove the coil and bracket assembly.
12. Remove the intake manifold attaching bolts and lift the manifold and carburetor from the engine as an assembly. It may be necessary to pry the manifold away from the cylinder heads. Do not damage the gasket sealing surfaces.
13. Install the manifold and related equipment in reverse order of removal.

FUEL INJECTED ENGINE

1. To remove the upper manifold: Remove the air cleaner. Disconnect the electrical connectors at the air bypass valve, throttle position sensor and EGR position sensor.
2. Disconnect the throttle linkage at the throttle ball and the AOD transmission linkage from the throttle body. Remove the bolts that secure the bracket to the intake and position the bracket and cables out of the way.
3. Disconnect the upper manifold vacuum fitting connections by removing all the vacuum lines at the vacuum tree (label lines for position identification). Remove the vacuum lines to the EGR valve and fuel pressure regulator.
4. Disconnect the PCV system by disconnecting the hose from the fitting at the rear of the upper manifold.
5. Remove the two canister purge lines from the fittings at the throttle body.
6. Disconnect the EGR tube from the EGR valve by loosening the flange nut.
7. Remove the bolt from the upper intake support bracket to upper manifold. Remove the upper manifold retaining bolts and remove the upper intake manifold and throttle body as an assembly.
8. Position a new mounting gasket on the lower intake manifold and install the upper manifold in the reverse order of removal.
9. To remove the lower intake manifold: Upper manifold and throttle body must be removed first.
10. Drain the cooling system. Remove the distributor assembly, cap and wires.
11. Disconnect the electrical connectors at the engine coolant temperature sensor and sending unit, at the air charge temperature sensor and at the knock sensor.
13. Disconnect the injector wiring harness from the main harness assembly. Remove the ground wire from the intake manifold stud. The ground wire must be installed at the same position it was removed from.
14. Disconnect the fuel supply and return lines from the fuel rails.

15. Remove the upper radiator hose from the thermostat housing. Remove the bypass hose. Remove the heater outlet hose at the intake manifold.

16. Remove the air cleaner mounting bracket. Remove the intake manifold mounting bolts and studs. Pay attention to the location of the bolts and studs for reinstallation. Remove the lower intake manifold assembly.

17. Installation is the reverse of the removal procedure.

Exhaust Manifold

Removal and Installation

122 CID (2.0L) AND 140 CID (2.3L) ENGINES

1. Remove the air cleaner and duct assembly. Disconnect the negative battery cable.
2. Remove the EGR line at the exhaust manifold. Loosen the EGR tube. Remove the check valve at the exhaust manifold and disconnect the hose at the end of the air by-pass valve.
3. Remove the bracket attaching the heater hoses to the valve cover. Disconnect the exhaust pipe from the exhaust manifold.
4. Remove the exhaust manifold mounting bolts/nuts and remove the manifold.
5. Install the exhaust manifold in the reverse order.

173 CID (2.8L) V6 AND 179 CID (2.9L) V6 ENGINES

1. Disconnect the negative battery cable. Remove the air cleaner and duct assembly.
2. Remove the left side heat shroud from the exhaust manifold. Remove any thermactor system parts that will interfere with manifold removal. Disconnect the choke heat tube at the carburetor.
3. Disconnect the exhaust pipes from the exhaust manifolds. Remove the mounting nuts from exhaust manifold studs. Remove the exhaust manifolds.
4. Install in the reverse order using new exhaust pipe to manifold gaskets.

183 CID (3.0L) V6 ENGINE

1. The following steps are for removal of the LH manifold.
   a. Remove the dipstick tube support bracket.
   b. Remove the power steering pump pressure and return hoses.
   c. Remove the manifold to exhaust pipe attaching nuts.
   d. Remove the exhaust manifold attaching bolts and remove the manifold.
2. The following steps are for removal of the RH manifold.
   a. Remove the heater hose support bracket.
   b. Disconnect the heater hoses.
   c. Remove the manifold to exhaust pipe attaching nuts.
   d. Remove the manifold attaching bolts and remove the manifold.
3. Install the manifolds in the reverse order of removal.

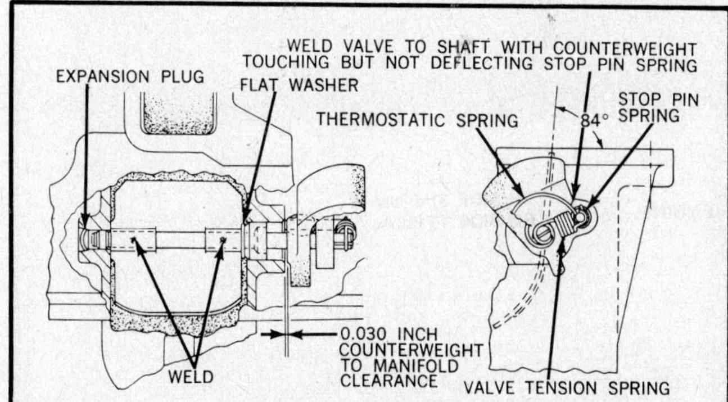

Exhaust valve plate position and counterweight clearance

232 CID (3.8L) AND ALL V8 ENGINES

1. Remove the air cleaner if the manifold being removed has the carburetor heat stove attached to it. On 351 and 400 engines, remove the oil filter.
2. Remove the dipstick tube bracket bolt/nut on the 302 V8. On 351 and 400 V8 vehicles with a column mounted automatic transmission lever, disconnect the selector lever cross-shaft for clearance. Disconnect the EGO sensor, if equipped.
3. Remove any of the thermactor parts that will interfere with the manifold removal.
4. Disconnect the exhaust pipe or catalytic converter from the exhaust manifold. Remove and discard the donut gasket.
5. Disconnect the EGR downtube. Remove the exhaust manifold attaching screws and remove the manifold from the cylinder head.

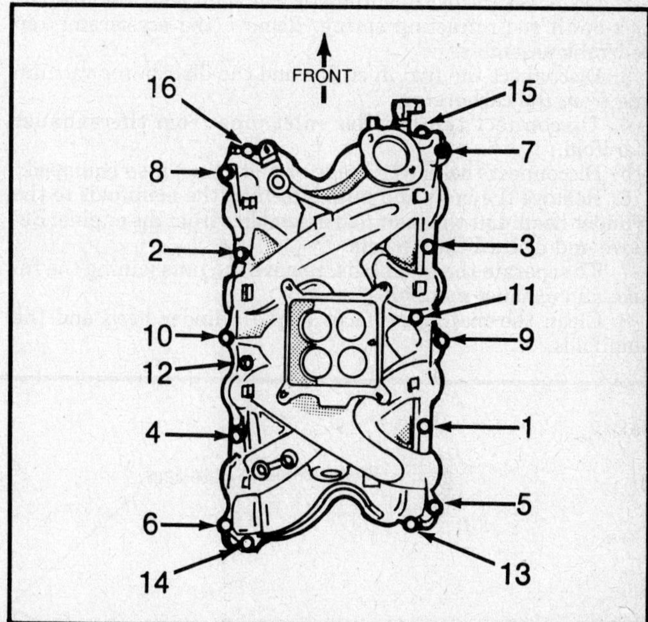

Intake manifold torque sequence – 370, 429 and 460 V8

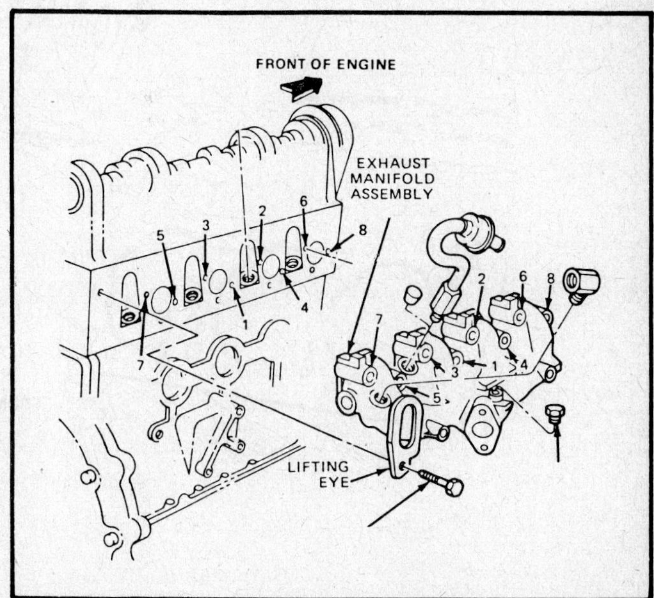

Cylinder head bolt tightening sequence – 6 cylinder 300 engine

6. Install the exhaust manifold in the reverse order of removal. Apply a light coat of graphite grease to the mating surface of the manifold. Install and tighten the attaching bolts, starting from the center and working to both ends alternately. Tighten to the proper specifications.

Combination Manifold

Removal and Installation

300 CID (4.9L) ENGINE

1. Remove the air cleaner. Disconnect the choke cable at the carburetor. Disconnect the accelerator cable or rod at the carburetor. Remove the accelerator retracting spring.
2. On a vehicle with automatic transmission, remove the kick-down rod-retracting spring. Remove the accelerator rod bellcrank assembly.
3. Disconnect the fuel inlet line and the distributor vacuum line from the carburetor.
4. Disconnect the muffler inlet pipe from the exhaust manifold.
5. Disconnect the power brake vacuum line, if so equipped.
6. Remove the bolts and nuts attaching the manifolds to the cylinder head. Lift the manifold assemblies from the engine. Remove and discard the gaskets.
7. To separate the manifolds, remove the nuts joining the intake and exhaust manifolds.
8. Clean the mating surfaces of the cylinder head and the manifolds.
9. If the intake and exhaust manifolds have been separated, coat the mating surfaces lightly with graphite grease and place the exhaust manifold over the studs on the intake manifold. Install the lockwashers and nuts. Tighten them finger tight.
10. Install a new intake manifold gasket.
11. Coat the mating surfaces lightly with graphite grease. Place the manifold assemblies in position against the cylinder head. Make sure that the gaskets have not become dislodged. Install the attaching washers, bolts and nuts. Tighten the attaching nuts and bolts in the proper sequence to 26 ft. lbs. If the intake and exhaust manifolds were separated, tighten the nuts joining them.

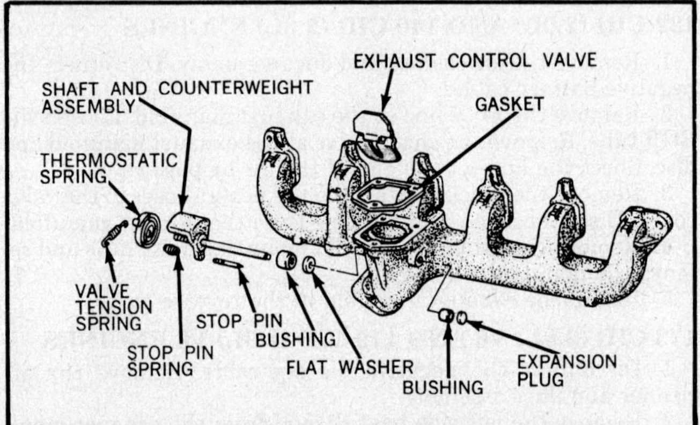

Exhaust control valve assembly – 300 engine

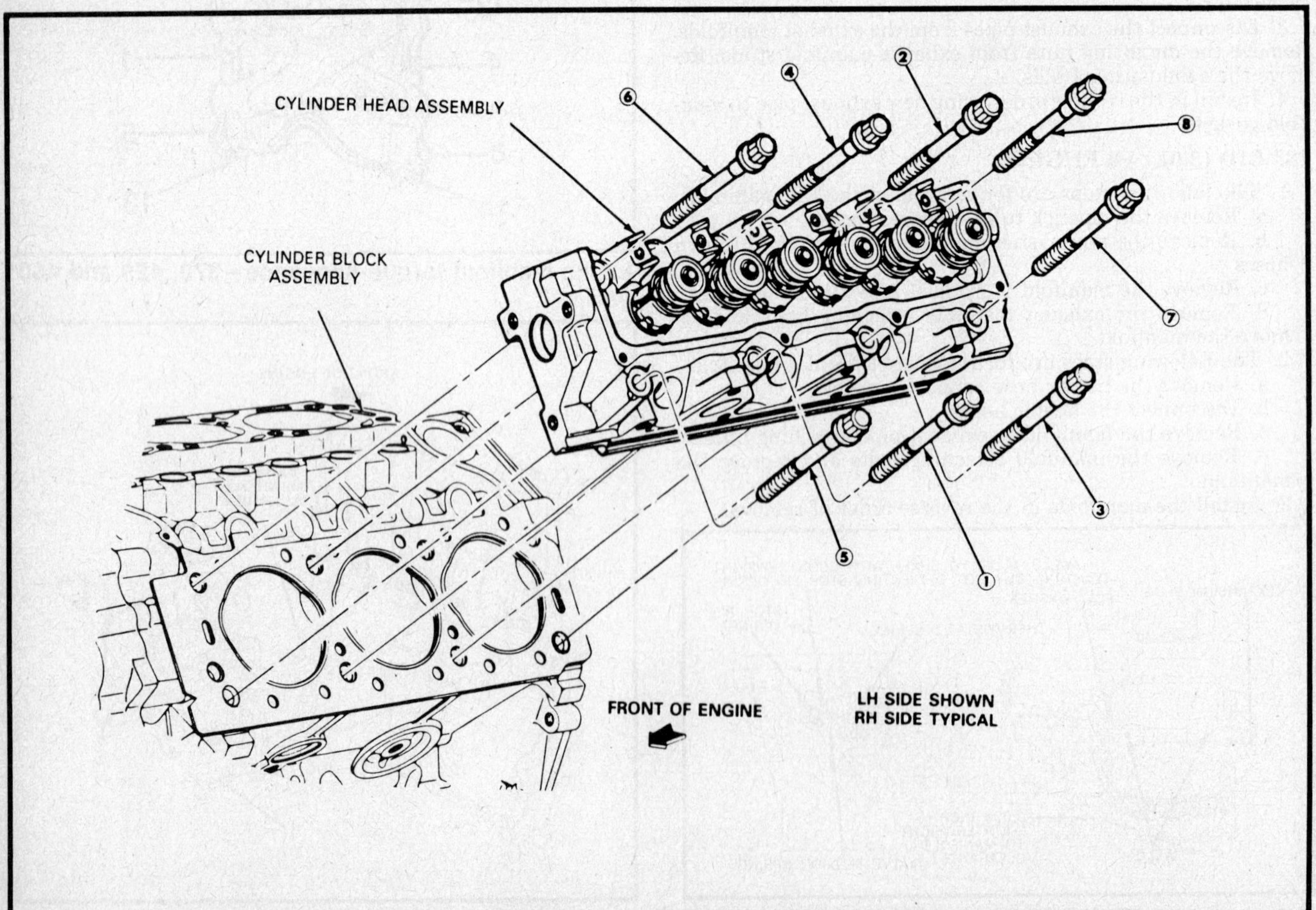

Cylinder head bolt tightening sequence 183 CID (3.0L) V6

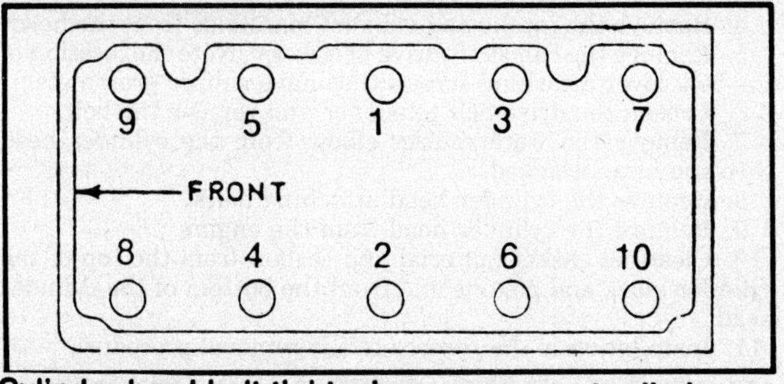

9 5 1 3 7
FRONT
8 4 2 6 10
Cylinder head bolt tightening sequence - 4 cylinder engines

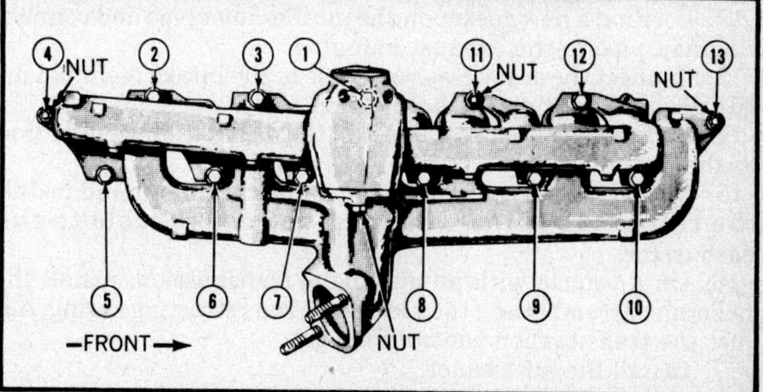

4 NUT
2
3
1
11 NUT
12
NUT 13
5
6
7
8
9
10
FRONT
NUT
Manifold tightening sequence – 300 engine

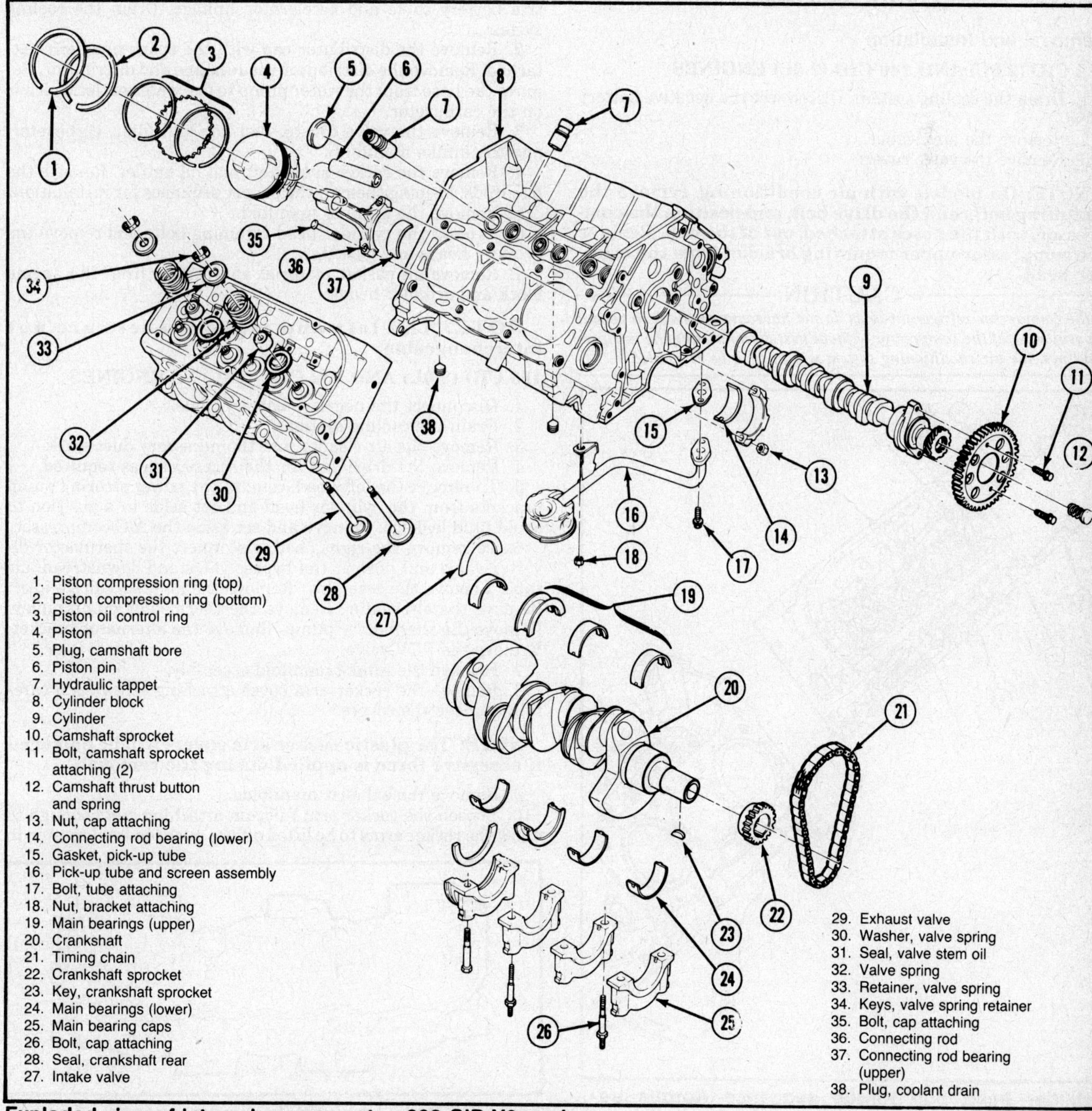

1. Piston compression ring (top)
2. Piston compression ring (bottom)
3. Piston oil control ring
4. Piston
5. Plug, camshaft bore
6. Piston pin
7. Hydraulic tappet
8. Cylinder block
9. Cylinder
10. Camshaft sprocket
11. Bolt, camshaft sprocket attaching (2)
12. Camshaft thrust button and spring
13. Nut, cap attaching
14. Connecting rod bearing (lower)
15. Gasket, pick-up tube
16. Pick-up tube and screen assembly
17. Bolt, tube attaching
18. Nut, bracket attaching
19. Main bearings (upper)
20. Crankshaft
21. Timing chain
22. Crankshaft sprocket
23. Key, crankshaft sprocket
24. Main bearings (lower)
25. Main bearing caps
26. Bolt, cap attaching
28. Seal, crankshaft rear
27. Intake valve
29. Exhaust valve
30. Washer, valve spring
31. Seal, valve stem oil
32. Valve spring
33. Retainer, valve spring
34. Keys, valve spring retainer
35. Bolt, cap attaching
36. Connecting rod
37. Connecting rod bearing (upper)
38. Plug, coolant drain
Exploded view of internal components – 232 CID V6 engine

12. Position a new gasket on the muffler inlet pipe and connect the inlet pipe to the exhaust manifold.
13. Connect the crankcase vent hose to the intake manifold inlet tube and position the hose clamp.
14. Connect the fuel inlet line and the distributor vacuum line to the carburetor.
15. Connect the accelerator cable to the carburetor and install the retracting spring. Connect the choke cable to the carburetor.
16. On a vehicle with an automatic transmission, install the bellcrank assembly and the kick-down rod retracting spring. Adjust the transmission control linkage.
17. Install the air cleaner.

Cylinder Head

Removal and Installation

122 CID (2.0L) AND 140 CID (2.3L) ENGINES

1. Drain the cooling system. Disconnect the negative battery cable.
2. Remove the air cleaner.
3. Remove the valve cover.

NOTE: On models with air conditioning, remove the mounting bolts and the drive belt, and position the compressor, with the hoses attached, out of the way. Remove the compressor upper mounting bracket from the cylinder head.

CAUTION

If the compressor refrigerant lines do not have enough slack to permit repositioning of the compressor without first disconnecting the refrigerant lines, the air conditioning system will have to be evacuated.

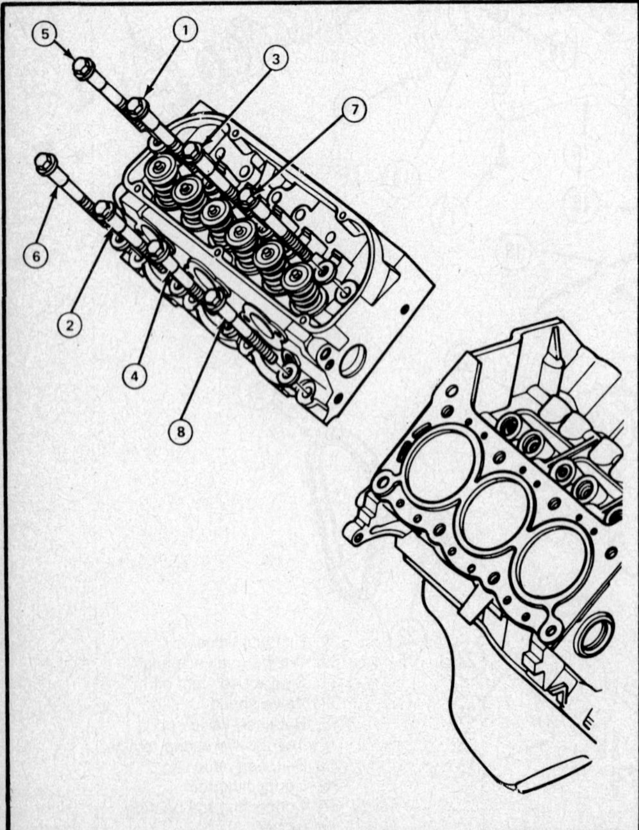

Cylinder head bolt torque sequence (torque sequence numbered)—232 CID V6 engine

4. Remove the intake and exhaust manifolds from the head.
5. Remove the camshaft drive belt cover. Note the location of the belt cover attaching screws that have rubber grommets.
6. Loosen the drive belt tensioner and remove the belt.
7. Remove the water outlet elbow from the cylinder head with the hose attached.
8. Remove the cylinder head attaching bolts.
9. Remove the cylinder head from the engine.
10. Clean all gasket material and carbon from the top of the cylinder block and pistons and from the bottom of the cylinder head.
11. Installation is the reverse of the removal procedure.

173 CID (2.8L) V6 AND 179 CID (2.9L) V6 ENGINES

1. Remove the air cleaner assembly and disconnect the negative battery cable and accelerator linkage. Drain the cooling system.
2. Remove the distributor cap with the spark plug wires attached. Remove the distributor vacuum line and distributor. Remove the hose from the water pump to the water outlet which is on the carburetor.
3. Remove the valve covers, fuel line and filter, carburetor, and the intake manifold.
4. Remove the rocker arm shaft and oil baffles. Remove the pushrods, keeping them in the proper sequence for installation.
5. Remove the exhaust manifold.
6. Remove the cylinder head retaining bolts and remove the cylinder heads and gaskets.
7. Remove all gasket material and carbon from the engine block and cylinder heads.

NOTE: The left and right gaskets are not interchangeable.

183 CID (3.0L) AND 232 CID (3.8L) V6 ENGINES

1. Disconnect the negative battery cable.
2. Drain the cooling system.
3. Remove the air cleaner and the necessary duct work.
4. Remove the drive belt for the accessories as required.
5. To remove the left head, remove the power steering pump brackets from the cylinder head and set aside in a position to avoid fluid leakage. Remove and set aside the A/C compressor.
6. To remove the right head, disconnect the thermactor diverter valve and hose at the bypass valve and downstream air tube. Remove the assembly. Remove the accessory drive idler. Remove the alternator. Remove the thermactor pump pulley. Remove the thermactor pump. Remove the alternator bracket. Remove the PCV valve.
7. Remove the intake manifold assembly.
8. Remove the rocker arm cover attaching screws and carefully remove the covers.

NOTE: The plastic rocker arm covers will be damaged if excessive force is applied during the removal.

9. Remove the exhaust manifolds.
10. Loosen the rocker arm fulcrum attaching bolts enough to allow the rocker arms to be lifted off the pushrods and rotated to

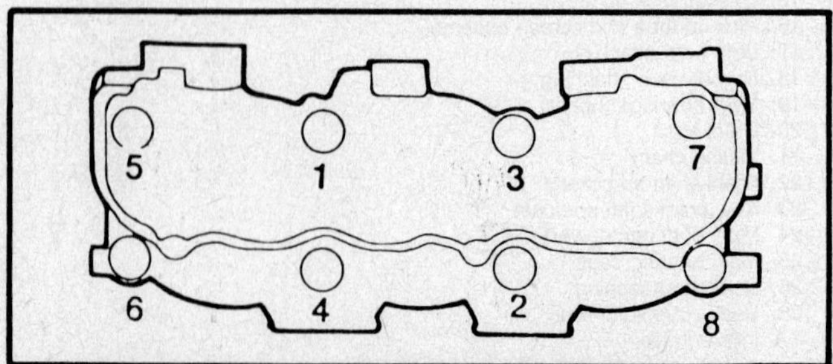

163(2.8L) V6 head bolt tightening sequence

one side. Remove the pushrods, keeping them in order to facilitate easier reassembly.

11. Remove the cylinder head attaching bolts and carefully remove the cylinder head from the engine block.

12. To reassemble the cylinder heads to the engine block, reverse the removal procedures. Use new gaskets during the reassembly, along with new cylinder head bolts to assure a leak tight assembly.

300 CID (4.9L) ENGINE

1. Drain the cooling system. Remove the air cleaner. Remove the oil filler tube. Disconnect the negative battery cable.
2. Disconnect the muffler inlet pipe at the exhaust manifold. Pull the muffler inlet pipe down. Remove the gasket.
3. Disconnect the accelerator rod or cable retracting spring. Disconnect the choke control cable if applicable and the accelerator rod at the carburetor.
4. Disconnect the transmission kickdown rod. Disconnect the accelerator linkage at the bellcrank assembly.
5. Disconnect the fuel inlet line at the fuel filter hose and the distributor vacuum line at the carburetor. Disconnect other vacuum lines as necessary for accessibility and identify them for proper connection.
6. Remove the radiator upper hose at the coolant outlet housing.
7. Disconnect the distributor vacuum line at the distributor. Disconnect the carburetor fuel inlet line at the fuel pump. Remove the lines as an assembly.
8. Disconnect the spark plug wires at the spark plugs and the temperature sending unit wire at the sending unit.
9. Grasp the PCV vent hose near the PCV valve and pull the valve out of the grommet in the valve rocker arm cover. Disconnect the PCV vent hose at the hose fitting in the intake manifold spacer and remove the vent hose and PCV valve.
10. Disconnect the carburetor air vent tube and remove the valve rocker arm cover.
11. Remove the valve rocker arm shaft assembly. Remove the pushrods in sequence so that they can be identified and reinstalled in their original positions.
12. Remove the cylinder head bolts and remove the cylinder head. Do not pry between the cylinder head and the block as the gasket surfaces may be damaged.
13. Installation is the reverse of the removal procedure.

V8 ENGINES, EXCEPT 460 CID (7.5L)

1. Disconnect the negative battery cable. Remove the intake manifold and carburetor as an assembly.
2. Remove rocker arm cover.
3. To remove right cylinder head, loosen alternator adjusting arm bolt and remove the alternator mounting bracket bolt and spacer. Swing alternator down out of the way. On some vehicles it may be necessary to remove the coil and air cleaner inlet duct from the right head. To remove left cylinder head, remove accelerator shaft fastening bolts at the front of the head. On some later models, it may be necessary to remove the air conditioning compressor bracket.
4. Disconnect exhaust pipe from the manifold.
5. Loosen rocker arm stud nuts and twist rocker arms so that the pushrods may be removed. Identify the pushrods when removing so that they may be reinstalled in their original locations.
6. Remove the cylinder head retaining bolts and remove the assembly from the vehicle.
7. To install, clean all gasket surfaces of block, head and rocker cover. Position new head gasket over the dowels onto the block (do use sealer on this composition gasket). Install the cylinder head on the engine block.
8. Install head bolts and tighten in three steps: first to 50 ft. lbs., then to 60 ft. lbs., and finally to 65–72 ft. lbs. Tighten in the proper sequence for each step.
9. Clean pushrods, blowing out oil passage, and check them for straightness. Lubricate pushrod ends, valve stem tips and rocker arm cups, fulcrum sets and followers. Install pushrods in their original positions, install exhaust stem caps and install rocker arms. Adjust the valve clearance.
10. Connect the exhaust pipe to the manifold, using new gasket and torque nuts to 25–35 ft. lbs.
11. On right cylinder head, position the alternator and install the attaching bolt and spacer, ignition coil and air cleaner inlet duct. Adjust drive belt tension. On left cylinder head, install accelerator shaft assembly, and air conditioning compressor bracket.
12. Install rocker cover using new gasket and tightening cover bolts to 3–5 ft. lbs.
13. Install intake manifold and carburetor assembly.
14. Install the thermactor air supply assembly where necessary.

460 CID (7.5L) ENGINE

1. Disconnect the negative battery cable. Remove the intake manifold and carburetor as an assembly.
2. Disconnect the exhaust pipe from the exhaust manifold. Some applications may require the removal of the exhaust manifold at the cylinder heads.
3. Loosen the air conditioning compressor drive belt, if so equipped.
4. Loosen the alternator attaching bolts and remove the bolt attaching the alternator bracket to the right cylinder head.
5. Disconnect the air conditioning compressor from the engine and move it aside, out of the way. Do not discharge the air conditioning system, if possible.
6. Remove the bolts securing the power steering reservoir bracket to the left cylinder head. Position the reservoir and bracket out of the way. Remove air brake and thermactor brackets as necessary.
7. Remove the valve rocker arm covers. Remove the rocker arm bolts, rocker arms, oil deflectors, fulcrums, and pushrods in sequence so that they can be reinstalled in their original positions.
8. Remove the cylinder head bolts and lift the head and exhaust manifold off the engine. If necessary, pry at the forward corners of the cylinder head against the casting bosses provided on the cylinder block. Do not damage the gasket mating surfaces of the cylinder head and block by prying against them.
9. Remove all gasket material from the cylinder head and block. Clean all gasket material from the mating surfaces of the intake manifold. If the exhaust manifold was removed, clean the

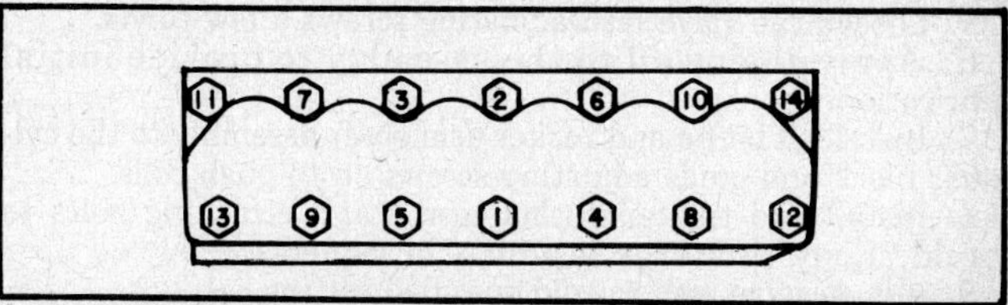

Cylinder head bolt tightening sequence—6 cylinder 300 engine

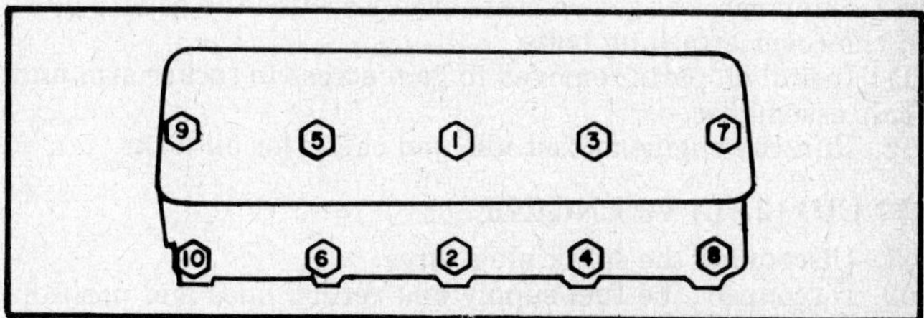

Cylinder head bolt tightening sequence—all V8 engines

mating surfaces of the cylinder head exhaust port areas and install the exhaust manifold.

10. Position the two long cylinder head bolts in the two rear lower bolt holes of the left cylinder head. Place a long cylinder head bolt in the rear lower bolt hole of the right cylinder head. Use rubber bands to keep the bolts in position until the cylinder heads are installed on the cylinder block.

11. Position new cylinder head gaskets on the cylinder block dowels. Do not apply sealer to the gaskets, heads, or block.

12. Place the cylinder heads on the block, guiding the exhaust pipe connections. Install the remaining cylinder head bolts. The longer bolts go in the lower row of holes.

13. Tighten all the cylinder head attaching bolts in the proper sequence in three stages: 75 ft. lbs., 105 ft. lbs., and finally, to 135 ft. lbs. When this procedure is used, it is not necessary to retorque the heads after extended use.

Rocker Arm and Shaft

Removal and Installation

122 CID (2.0L) AND 140 CID (2.3L) ENGINES

NOTE: A special tool is required to compress the lash adjuster.

1. Remove the valve cover and associated parts as required.
2. Rotate the camshaft so that the base circle of the cam is against the cam follower you intend to remove.
3. Remove the retaining spring from the cam follower, if so equipped.
4. Using special tool T74P-6565-B or a valve spring compressor tool, collapse the lash adjuster and/or depress the valve spring, as necessary and slide the cam follower over the lash adjuster and out from under the camshaft.
5. Install the cam follower in the reverse order of removal. Make sure that the lash adjuster is collapsed and released before rotating the cam shaft.

173 CID (2.8L) V6 ENGINE

1. Remove spark plug wires from the spark plugs.
2. Remove throttle linkage to carburetor if it interferes with removal operation.
3. Remove rocker arm cover attaching screws. Tap rocker arm cover lightly to break gasket seal. Lift off rocker arm cover.
4. Remove rocker arm shaft stand retaining bolts by loosening the bolts two turns at a time, in sequence. Lift off rocker arm and shaft assembly and oil baffle.
5. Loosen the valve lash adjusting screws a few turns.
6. Apply engine oil to the assembly to provide initial lubrication.
7. Install oil baffle and rocker arm shaft assembly to the cylinder block and guide adjusting screws on to push rods.
8. Install and tighten rocker arm stand attaching bolts to specifications, two turns at a time, in sequence.
9. Adjust valve lash to cold specified setting.
10. Clean the valve rocker arm cover and cylinder head gasket surfaces. Coat one side of a new gasket with an oil-resistant sealer and lay cemented side of gasket on the cover. Install the cover, making sure the gasket seats evenly around the head. Tighten the cover attaching bolts.
11. Install all parts removed to gain access to rocker arm and shaft assemblies.
12. Run the engine at fast idle and check for oil leaks.

177 CID (2.9L) V6 ENGINE

1. Disconnect the spark plug wires.
2. Disconnect the fuel supply and return lines and position out of the way.
3. Remove the LH lifting eye on vehicles equipped with A/C.
4. Remove the PCV valve hose and breather.
5. Remove the rocker arm attaching screws and the load distribution washers. Ensure the washers are installed in their original position.
6. Tap the rocker arm cover to break the seal and remove the covers.
7. Remove the rocker arm shaft stand attaching bolts by loosening the bolts two turns at a time, in sequence.
8. Lift off the rocker arm and shaft assembly and the oil baffle.
9. Reverse the removal procedure to install. Apply SF type engine oil to the assembly to provide initial lubrication.

300 CID (4.9L) ENGINE

1. Disconnect the inlet air hose at the oil fill cap. Remove the air cleaner.
2. Disconnect the accelerator cable at the carburetor. Remove the cable retracting spring. Remove the accelerator cable bracket from the cylinder head and position the cable and bracket assembly out of the way.
3. Remove the PCV valve from the valve rocker arm cover. Remove the cover bolts and remove the valve rocker arm cover.
4. Remove the valve rocker arm stud nut, fulcrum seat and rocker arm. Inspect the rocker arm cover bolts for worn or damaged seals under the bolt heads and replace as necessary. If it is necessary to remove a rocker arm stud, Tool T79T-6527-A is available. A 0.006 oversize reamer T62F-6527-B3 or equivalent and a 0.015 inch oversize reamer T62F-6527-B5 or equivalent are available. For 0.010 inch oversize studs, use reamer T66P-6527-B or equivalent. To press in replacement studs, use stud replacer T79T-6527-B or equivalent. Rocker arm studs that are broken or have damaged threads may be replaced with standard studs. Loose studs in the head may be replaced with 0.006, 0.010 or 0.015 inch oversize studs which are available for service.
5. Standard and oversize studs can be identified by measuring the stud diameter within 1 $^1/_8$ in. from the pilot enl of the stud. The stud diameters are:
   a. 0.006 oversize – – 0.3774–0.7781
   b. 0.010 oversize – – 0.3814–0.3821
   c. 0.015 oversize – – 0.3864–0.3871
6. When going from a standard size rocker arm stud to a 0.010 or 0.015 inch oversize stud, always use the 0.006 inch oversize reamer before finish reaming with the 0.010 or 0.015 inch oversize reamer.

183 CID (3.0L) V6 AND ALL V8 ENGINES

1. Remove air cleaner and intake duct assembly.

122, 140-4 cyl.
E-I-E-I-E-I-E-I

300 6-cyl.
E-I-E-I-E-I-E-I-E-I-E-I

173-V6
RT I-E-I-E-E-I
LT I-E-E-I-E-I

232-V6
RT I-E-I-E-I-E
LT E-I-E-I-E-I

302, 351, 400, 460-V8
RT I-E-I-E-I-E-I-E-I-E
LT E-I-E-I-E-I-E-I-E-I

Valve arrangements

2. Remove crankcase ventilation hose from rocker cover. Remove the coil and the solenoid brackets.
3. For removal of the RH rocker cover, remove the lifting eye and the thermactor tube.
4. Remove the oil filler pipe hose from the LH rocker arm cover, if so equipped.
5. Disconnect spark plug leads and remove leads from bracket on the valve rocker cover.
6. Remove the vacuum harness and the electrical connectors to the vacuum solenoids mounted on the rocker arm covers and position out of the way.
7. Disconnect the choke tubes at the carburetor and position out of the way.
8. Disconnect the evaporative system hoses from the canister and position out of the way.
9. Remove the thermactor air supply hose.
10. Remove the rocker cover bolts and remove the covers.
11. Remove the valve rocker arm bolt, fulcrum seat and rocker arm.
12. For installation, reverse the removal procedure. Install the fulcrum guide, valve rocker arm, fulcrum seat and bolt. Tighten to 18–25 ft. lbs. (25–32 Nm).

Valve Adjustment Procedure

173 CID (2.8L) ENGINE

1. With engine cold and valve covers removed, place a finger on the adjusting screw of the intake valve rocker arm for cylinder No. 5. Valve arrangement, from front to rear, on the left bank is I(intake)-E(exhaust)I-E-E-I-E-I; on the right it is I-E-I-E-E-I.

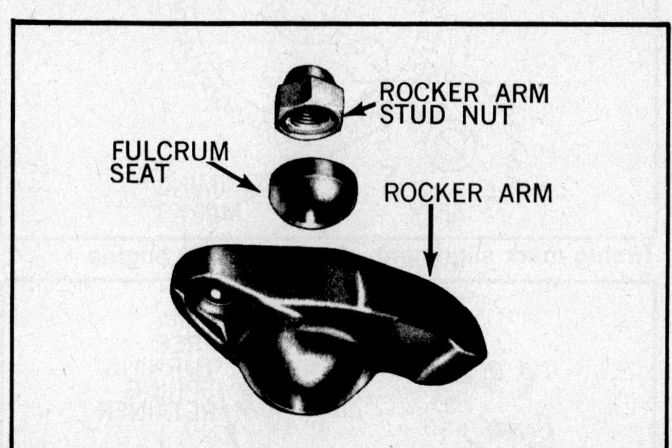

Stud/nut type rocker arm

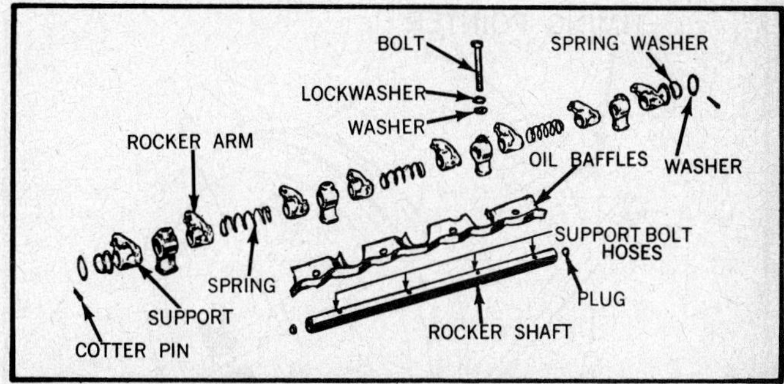

Valve rocker arm shaft assembly V8-typical

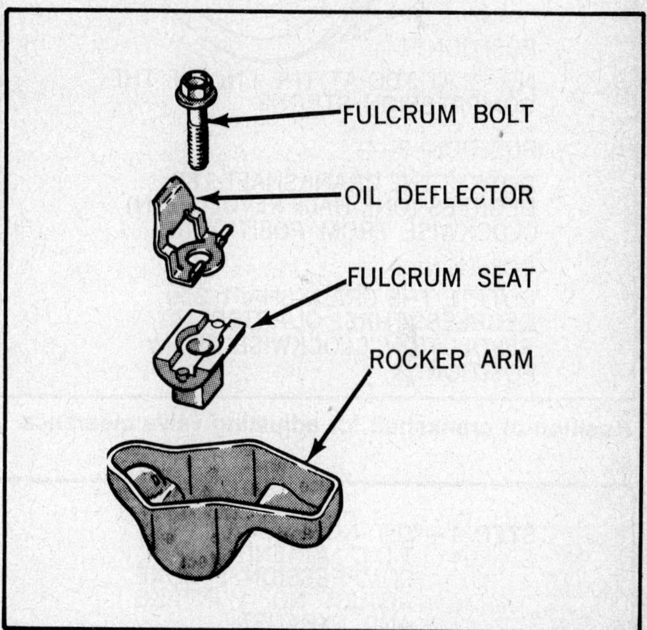

Bolt and fulcrum rocker arm

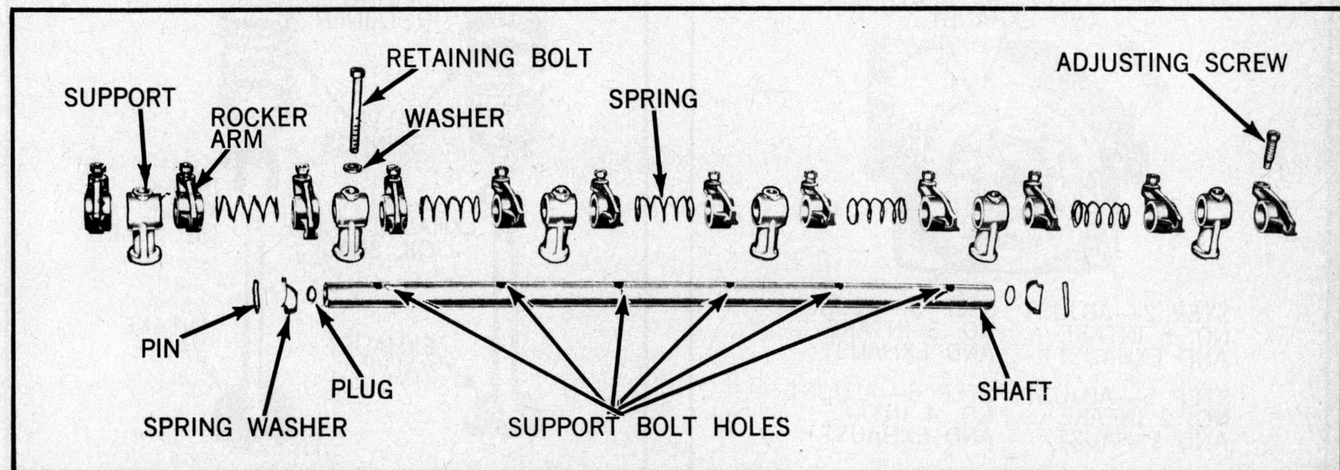

Rocker arm shaft assembly – 6 cylinder – typical

WITH NO. 1 AT TDC AT THE END OF THE COMPRESSION STROKE MAKE A CHALK MARK AT POINTS 2 AND 3 APPROXIMATELY 90 DEGREES APART.

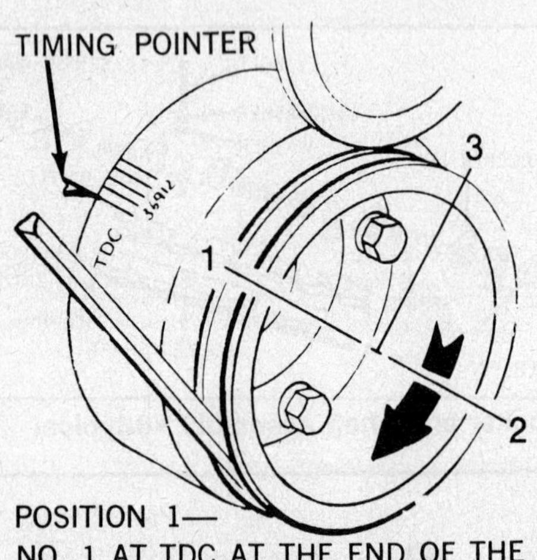

POSITION 1—
NO. 1 AT TDC AT THE END OF THE COMPRESSION STROKE

POSITION 2—
ROTATE THE CRANKSHAFT 180 DEGREES (ONE HALF REVOLUTION) CLOCKWISE FROM POSITION 1

POSITION 3—
ROTATE THE CRANKSHAFT 270 DEGREES (THREE QUARTER REVOLUTION CLOCKWISE FROM POSITION 2

Position of crankshaft for adjusting valve clearance

STEP 1—SET NO. 1 PISTON ON T.D.C. AT END OF COMPRESSION STROKE ADJUST NO. 1 INTAKE AND EXHAUST

STEP 4—ADJUST NO. 6 INTAKE AND EXHAUST

STEP 2—ADJUST NO. 5 INTAKE AND EXHAUST

STEP 3—ADJUST NO. 3 INTAKE AND EXHAUST

STEP 5—ADJUST NO. 2 INTAKE AND EXHAUST

STEP 6—ADJUST NO. 4 INTAKE AND EXHAUST

6-cylinder preliminary valve adjustment

2. Use a remote starter switch to bump the engine over until you can just feel the valve begin to open. The cam is now in position to adjust the intake and exhaust valves on the No. 1 cylinder.

3. Adjust the No. 1 intake valve so that a 0.014 in. feeler gauge has a slight drag, while a 0.015 in. feeler gauge is a tight fit. To decrease lash, turn the adjusting screw clockwise; to increase lash, turn the adjusting screw counterclockwise. There are no lockbolts to tighten as the adjusting screws are self-tightening.

CAUTION

Do not use a step-type, "go-no go" feeler gauge. When checking lash, you must insert the feeler gauge and move it parallel with the crankshaft. Do not move it in and out perpendicular with the crankshaft as this will give an erroneous feel which will result in overtightened valves.

11. Adjust the exhaust valve the same way so that an 0.016 in. feeler gauge has a slight drag, while a 0.017 in. gauge is a tight fit.

12. The rest of the valves are adjusted in the same way, in their firing order (1–4–2–5–3–6), by positioning the cam according to the valve adjusting chart.

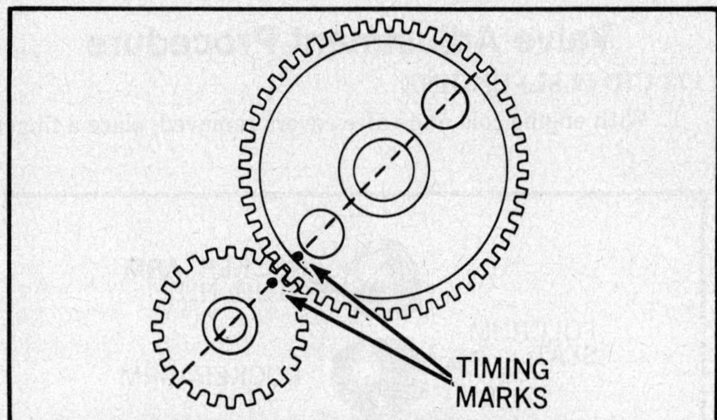

Timing mark alignment—6-cylinder 300 engine

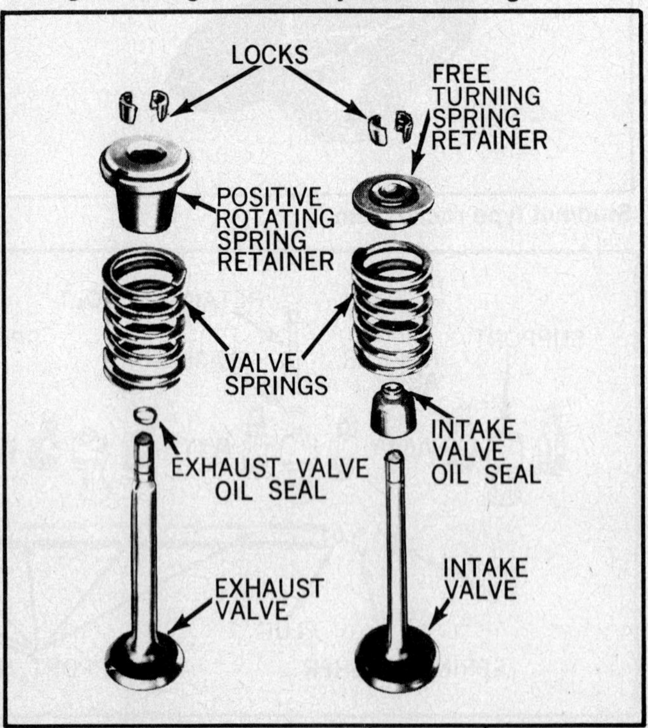

Typical valve layout

177 CID (2.9L) V6 ENGINE

1. On the cylinder to be adjusted, position the cams so that the tappets are on the base circle.

2. Loosen the adjusting screws until a lash between the roller arm pad and the valve tip end can be noticed.

3. Screw in the adjustment screws until the roller arms slightly touch the valves.

4. To achieve the nominal working position of the plunger, turn in the adjusting screw 1.5 turns.

232 CID (3.8L) ENGINE

1. Rotate the crankshaft to place each tappet on the heel (base circle) of the camshaft lobe. As each tappet is located on the base of the lobe, torque the fulcrum attaching bolt to 62–132 inch lbs.

NOTE: The fulcrums must be seated in the cylinder head and the pushrods must be seated in the rocker arm sockets, prior to the final tightening.

300 CID (4.9L) ENGINE

1. Crank the engine until the TDC mark on the crankshaft damper is aligned with timing pointer on the cylinder front cover.

2. Scribe a mark on the damper at this point.

3. Scribe two more marks on the damper, each equally spaced from the first mark.

4. With the engine on TDC of the compression stroke, back off the rocker arm adjusting nut until there is end-play in the pushrod. Tighten the adjusting nut until all clearance is removed, then tighten the adjusting nut one additional turn. To determine when all clearance is removed from the rocker arm, turn the pushrod with the fingers. When the pushrod can no longer be turned, all clearance has been removed.

5. Repeat this procedure for each valve, turning the crankshaft $\frac{1}{3}$ turn to the next mark each time and following the engine firing order of 1–5–3–6–2–4.

V8 ENGINES

1. Install an auxiliary starter switch. Crank the engine with the ignition switch OFF until No. 1 piston is on TDC after the compression stroke.

2. With the crankshaft in the positions designated in Steps 5, 6 and 7, position a hydraulic tappet compressor tool on the rocker arm.

3. Slowly apply pressure to bleed down the hydraulic tappet until the plunger is completely bottomed. Hold the tappet in this position and check the available clearance between the rocker arm and the valve stem tip with a feeler gauge.

4. If the clearance is less than specification, install a shorter push rod. If clearance is greater than specification, install a longer push rod.

5. With the No. 1 piston on TDC at the end of the compression stroke, Position 1 on the crankshaft pulley, check the following valves:

302 and 460 CID engines
No. 1 intake
No. 1 exhaust
No. 7 intake
No. 5 exhaust
No. 8 intake
No. 4 exhaust

351 and 400 CID engines
No. 1 intake
No. 1 exhaust
No. 4 intake
No. 3 exhaust
No. 8 intake
No. 6 exhaust

6. After these valves have been checked, rotate the crankshaft to Position 2 and check the following valves:

302 and 460 CID engines
No. 5 intake
No. 2 exhaust
No. 4 intake
No. 6 exhaust

351 and 400 CID engines
No. 3 intake
No. 2 exhaust
No. 7 intake
No. 6 exhaust

7. After these valves have been checked, rotate the crankshaft to Position 3 and check the following valves:

302 and 460 CID engines
No. 2 intake
No. 7 exhaust
No. 3 intake
No. 3 exhaust
No. 6 intake
No. 8 exhaust

351 and 400 CID engines
No. 2 intake
No. 4 exhaust
No. 5 intake
No. 5 exhaust
No. 6 intake
No. 8 exhaust

Timing Gears and/or Chain

122 CID (2.0L) AND 140 CID (2.3L) ENGINES

The front seal has been designed so that it is not necessary to remove the front cover with the engine in the chassis. The front cover, camshaft and the auxiliary shaft seals are replaced in the same manner with the same tools after the respective gear has been removed. To remove the cam and the auxiliary shaft sprockets, use tool T74P-6256-B or equivalent. To remove the crankshaft sprocket, use tool T74P-6306-A or equivalent. All of the seals are removed with tool T74P-6700-B.

CRANKSHAFT PULLEY

Removal and Installation

171 CID (2.8L) AND 177 CID (2.9L) V6 ENGINES

1. Drain the cooling system and the crankcase.

2. Remove the oil pan and the radiator.

3. Remove the front cover and water pump, drive belt and camshaft timing gear.

4. Use pulley remover T71P-19703-B and shaft protector T71P-7137-H to remove the crankshaft gear.

5. To install the gear align the keyway in the gear with the key. Then slide the gear onto the shaft until it seats tight against the spacer.

183 CID (3.0L) V6 ENGINE

1. Remove the crankshaft pulley, damper and front cover assemblies.

2. Cover the oil pan opening to prevent dirt from entering.

3. Rotate the crankshaft until the No. 1 piston is at TDC on the compression stroke and the timing marks are aligned.

4. Remove the camshaft sprocket attaching bolts and washer. Slide both sprockets and timing chain forward and remove as an assembly.

5. Reverse the procedure for installation.

300 CID (4.9L) ENGINE

1. Bring the engine to No. 1 piston at TDC (top dead center) on the compression stroke. Drain the cooling system. Disconnect negative battery cable.
2. Remove the radiator and shroud.
3. Remove the alternator adjusting arm bolt, loosen the drive belt and swing the alternator arm aside. Remove the fan, drive belts and pulleys.
4. Remove the screw and washer from the end of the crankshaft. Remove the crankshaft damper.
5. Remove the front oil pan and front cover attaching screws.

NOTE: Be careful not to get foreign material in the crankcase during service work, or the crankcase oil will have to be changed.

6. Remove the cylinder front cover and discard the gasket.
7. Remove the camshaft and crankshaft gears using a suitable puller. Install the new gears, camshaft first using Ford tool T65L6306A or the equivalent. Do not hammer on the gears. Install the crankshaft gear over the drive key and install with tool. Verify that the timing marks on both gears are aligned. Install the crankshaft oil slinger.

Timing Cover Oil Seal

Removal and Installation

171 CID (2.8L) AND 177 (2.9L) V6 ENGINES

NOTE: It is not necessary to remove the front cover for this operation.

1. Drain the coolant and remove the radiator.
2. Remove the crankshaft pulley and the water pump drive belt.
3. Remove the front cover oil seal with tool 1175-AC or equivalent and impact slide hammer T59L-100-B or equivalent.
4. Installation is the reverse of removal. Coat the new front seal with heavy SF engine oil before installing.

183 CID (3.0L) V6 ENGINE

1. Loosen the accessory drive belts.
2. Disengage the belt and remove the crankshaft pulley.
3. Remove the damper from the crankshaft using tool T58P-6316-D and T82L-6316-B or equivalent.
4. Pry the seal from the timing cover with a flat bladed tool. Use care to prevent damage to the front cover and the crankshaft.
5. Installation is the reverse of removal. Lubricate the seal lip with clean engine oil before installing.

232 CID (3.8L) V6 ENGINE, 302 CID (5.0L) AND 351 CID (5.8L) V8 ENGINES

1. Remove the fan clutch assembly and the shroud.
2. Loosen the accessory drive belts.
3. Raise the vehicle.
4. Disengage the accessory drive belt and remove the crankshaft pulley.
5. Remove the crankshaft damper using tool T58P-6316-D and T82L-6316-B or equivalent.
6. Pry the seal from the front cover using care to prevent damage to front cover and the crankshaft.
7. Installation is the reverse of the removal procedure. Lubricate the seal lip with clean engine oil before installing.

TIMING CHAIN AND/OR GEAR

Removal and Installation

232 CID (3.8L) ENGINE

1. Bring the number one piston to TDC of the compression stroke. Drain the cooling system.
2. Disconnect the cable from the battery negative terminal.
3. Remove the air cleaner assembly and air intake duct.
4. Remove the fan shroud attaching screws. Remove the fan/clutch assembly attaching bolts.
5. Remove the fan/clutch assembly and shroud.
6. Loosen the accessory drive belt idler. Remove the drive belt and water pump pulley.
7. If equipped with power steering, remove the pump mounting brackets' attaching bolts.
8. If equipped with air conditioning, remove the compressor front support bracket. Leave the compressor in place.
9. Disconnect the coolant by-pass hose at the water pump.
10. Disconnect the heater hose at the water pump.
11. Disconnect the radiator upper hose at the thermostat housing.
12. Disconnect the coil wire from the distributor cap and remove the cap with the secondary wires attached.
13. Remove the distributor hold down clamp and lift the distributor out of the front cover.
14. Raise the vehicle and support safely.
15. Remove the crankshaft damper.
16. Remove the fuel pump crash shield (if so equipped).
17. Disconnect the fuel pump to carburetor fuel line at the fuel pump.
18. Remove the fuel pump attaching bolts. Pull the pump out of the front cover and lay the pump aside with flexible line attached.
19. Remove the oil filter.
20. Disconnect the radiator lower hose at the water pump.
21. Remove the oil pan.

NOTE: The front cover cannot be removed without lowering the oil pan.

22. Lower the vehicle.
23. Remove the front cover attaching bolts. It is not necessary to remove the water pump.

NOTE: Do not overlook the cover attaching bolt located behind the oil filter adapter. The front cover will break if pried upon and all attaching bolts are not removed.

24. Remove the ignition timing indicator.
25. Remove the front cover and water pump as an assembly.
26. Remove the cover gasket and discard.
27. Remove the camshaft thrust button and spring from the end of the camshaft.
28. Remove the camshaft sprocket attaching bolts.
29. Remove the camshaft sprocket, crankshaft sprocket and the timing chain.
30. Installation is the reverse of the removal procedure. Lubricate the timing chain with clean engine oil before installing.

255 CID (4.2L), 302 CID (5.0L) AND 351 CID (5.8L) V8 ENGINES, EXCEPT IN E SERIES

1. Bring the engine to No. 1 cylinder at TDC (top dead center) on the compression stroke. Disconnect the negative battery cable. Drain the cooling system.
2. Remove the fan shroud to radiator attaching bolts. Position the shroud over the fan.
3. Disconnect the radiator lower hose, heater hose and bypass hose at the water pump. Remove the drive belts, fan, fan spacer, and pulley.
4. Remove the fan shroud.
5. Loosen the alternator pivot bolt and bolt attaching the alternator adjusting arm to the water pump.
6. Remove the crankshaft pulley from the crankshaft vibration damper. Remove the damper attaching bolt and washer. Install a puller on the vibration damper and remove the damper.
7. Disconnect the fuel pump outlet line from the fuel pump.

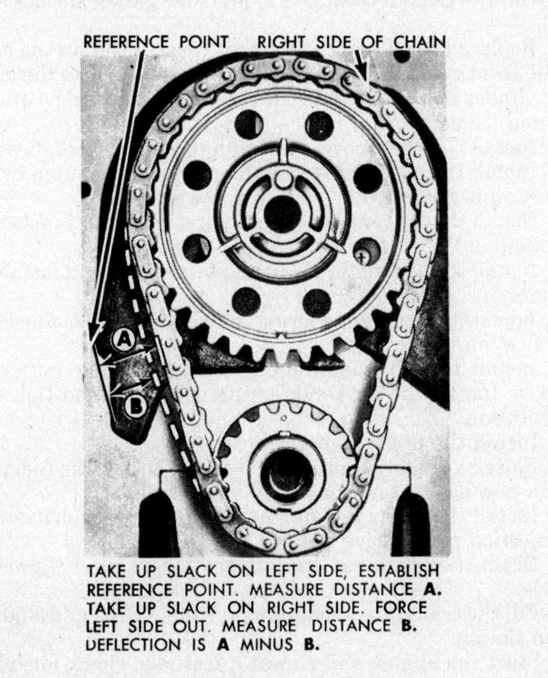

REFERENCE POINT
RIGHT SIDE OF CHAIN
A
B
TAKE UP SLACK ON LEFT SIDE, ESTABLISH REFERENCE POINT. MEASURE DISTANCE A. TAKE UP SLACK ON RIGHT SIDE. FORCE LEFT SIDE OUT. MEASURE DISTANCE B. DEFLECTION IS A MINUS B.

Checking timing chain deflection except—232 CID V-6 engine

Remove the fuel pump to one side with the flexible fuel line still attached.

8. Remove the oil dipstick and the bolt attaching the dipstick to the exhaust manifold.

9. Remove the oil pan to cylinder front cover attaching bolts. Use a knife with a thin blade to cut the oil pan gasket flush with the cylinder block face prior to separating the cover from the cylinder block. Remove the cylinder front cover and water pump as an assembly.

10. Discard the cylinder front cover gasket. Remove the crankshaft front oil slinger.

11. Check the timing chain deflection. The method for checking timing chain deflection is outlined at the end of this section. If the deflection exceeds specification, replace the chain and sprockets as follows:

a. Crank the engine until the timing marks on the sprockets are correctly aligned.

b. Remove the camshaft sprocket capscrew, washers, and fuel pump eccentric. Slide both sprockets and the timing chain forward and remove the chain and sprockets as an assembly.

c. Position the sprockets and timing chain on the camshaft. Be sure that the timing marks are properly aligned.

d. Install the fuel pump, eccentric, washers, and camshaft sprocket capscrew. Tighten the capscrew to specification.

12. Install the crankshaft front oil slinger.

13. Clean the cylinder front cover, oil pan and block gasket surfaces. Clean the oil pan gasket surface where the oil pan and front cover fasten.

14. Install a new crankshaft front oil seal.

15. Lubricate the timing chain and fuel pump eccentric with a heavy engine oil.

16. Coat the gasket surface of the oil pan with sealer, then cut and position the required sections of a new gasket on the oil pan and apply sealer at the corners. Install the pan seal as required. Coat the gasket surfaces of the block and cover with sealer, and position a new gasket on the block.

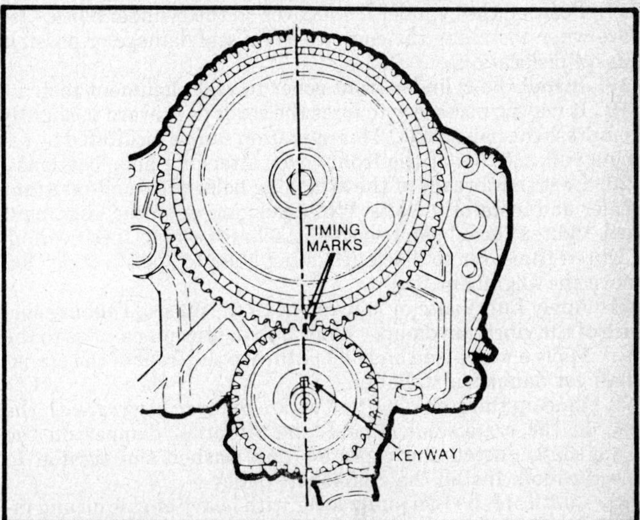

173(2.3L) V6 timing mark alignment

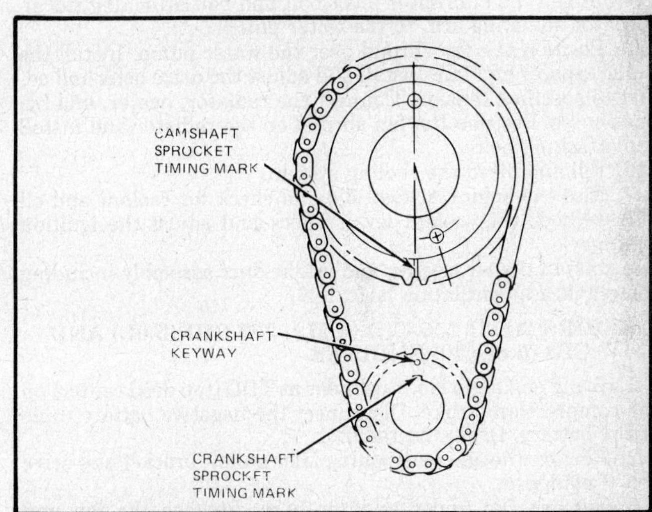

Alignment of timing gears—232 CID V-6 engine

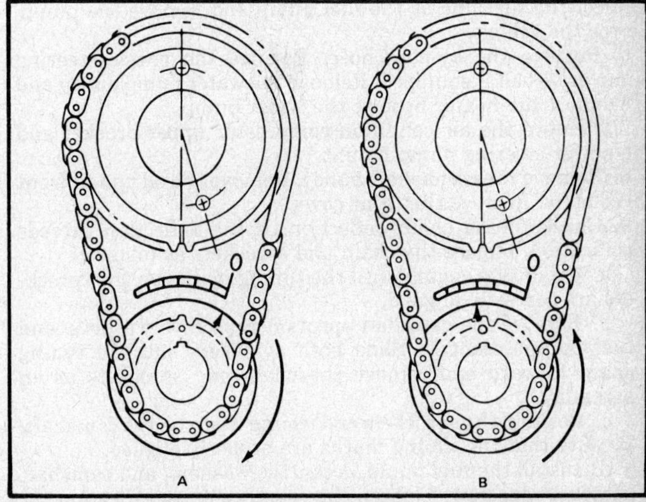

Checking timing chain deflection—232 CID V-6 engine

17. Position the cylinder front cover on the cylinder block. Use care when installing the cover to avoid seal damage or possible gasket dislocation.
18. Install the cylinder front cover to seal alignment tool.
19. It may be necessary to force the cover downward to slightly compress the pan gasket. This operation can be facilitated by using a suitable tool at the front cover attaching hole locations.
20. Coat the threads of the attaching bolts with a oil-resistant sealer and install the bolts. While pushing in on the alignment tool, tighten the oil pan to cover attaching bolts to specification. Tighten the cover to block attaching bolts to specification. Remove the alignment tool.
21. Apply Lubriplate or equivalent to the oil seal rubbing surface of the vibration damper inner hub to prevent damage to the seal. Apply a white lead and oil mixture to the front of the crankshaft for damper installation.
22. Line up the crankshaft vibration damper keyway with the key on the crankshaft. Install the vibration damper on the crankshaft. Install the capscrew and washer and tighten to specification. Install the crankshaft pulley.
23. Lubricate the fuel pump lever with heavy engine oil and install the pump using a new gasket. Connect the fuel pump outlet pipe.
24. Install the alternator pivot bolt and bolt attaching the alternator adjusting arm to the water pump.
25. Position the fan shroud over the water pump. Install the pulley, spacer and fan. Install and adjust the drive belts and adjust to specified tension. Connect the radiator, heater, and by-pass hoses. Position the fan shroud on the radiator and install the attaching bolts.
26. Fill and bleed the cooling system.
27. Run the engine at fast idle and check for coolant and oil leaks. Check the coolant level. Check and adjust the ignition timing.
28. Install the air cleaner and intake duct assembly including the crankcase ventilation hose.

E SERIES WITH 255 CID (4.2L), 302 CID (5.0L) AND 351W CID (5.8L) V8 ENGINES

1. Bring engine to No. 1 cylinder at TDC (top dead center) on the compression stroke. Disconnect the negative battery cable at the battery. Drain the radiator.
2. Remove the air conditioning idler pulley, bracket and drive belt if equipped.
3. Remove the upper radiator hose. Remove the fan and shroud as an assembly. Raise and support the vehicle safely.
4. Loosen the thermactor and alternator drive belts.
5. Disconnect the lower radiator hose at the water pump. Disconnect the fuel line at the fuel pump and remove the pump. Lower the vehicle.
6. Remove the by-pass hose. Remove the power steering pump drive belt if equipped. Remove the water pump pulley and disconnect the heater hose at the water pump.
7. Remove the air condition compressor upper bracket and the power steering pump mount.
8. Remove the crankshaft pulley. Remove the oil pan to front cover bolts. Remove the front cover.
9. Check timing chain deflection. If the deflection exceeds specification, replace the chain and sprockets as follows:
   a. Crank the engine until the timing marks on the sprockets are correctly aligned.
   b. Remove the camshaft sprocket capscrew, washers, and fuel pump eccentric. Slide both sprockets and the timing chain forward and remove the chain and sprockets as an assembly.
   c. Position the sprockets and timing chain on the camshaft. Be sure that the timing marks are properly aligned.
   d. Install the fuel pump, eccentric, washers, and camshaft sprocket capscrew. Tighten the capscrew to specification.
10. Clean the front cover, fuel pump, and damper. Lubricate the crankshaft front seal. Clean the gasket surface at the pan and trim the gasket. Clean the front cover gasket surface at the block.
11. Replace the oil seal in the front cover. Position the gasket on the front cylinder cover. Apply a silicone sealer to the oil pan and cylinder block junction. Cut the pan gasket and position on pan and front cover.
12. Install the front cover, fuel pump, and crankshaft pulley.
13. Install the power steering pump and water pump by-pass hose. Connect the heater hose at the water pump.
14. Install the air conditioning compressor upper bracket, water pump pulley and power steering drive belt.
15. Install the alternator belt, thermactor belt, and fan/shroud assembly.
16. Adjust the power steering pump drive belt tension to specification.
17. Install the air conditioning drive belt idler pulley and bracket. Install the air conditioning drive belt and tighten to specification.
18. Install the upper radiator hose.
19. Raise and safely support the vehicle. Install the fuel pump with a new gasket and connect the fuel line.
20. Install the lower radiator hose. Adjust the alternator and air injection pump drive belts to specified tension.
21. Drain the crankcase and replace the oil filter. Lower the vehicle.
22. Fill the crankcase and cooling system. Check and adjust ignition timing.
23. Start the engine and run at a fast idle, check for oil and coolant leaks.

400 CID (6.6L) V8 ENGINE

1. Bring the engine to No. 1 piston at TDC (top dead center) on the compression stroke. Drain the cooling system and disconnect the battery.
2. Remove the fan shroud attaching bolts and move the shroud to the rear.
3. Remove the fan and spacer from the water pump shaft.
4. Remove the air conditioner compressor drive belt lower idler pulley and the compressor mount to water pump bracket.
5. Loosen the alternator and power steering pump and remove the drive belts.
6. Remove the water pump pulley.
7. Remove the alternator and power steering pump brackets from the water pump and position them out of the way.
8. Disconnect the lower radiator and heater hose from the water pump.
9. Remove the crankshaft pulley from the crankshaft vibration damper. Remove the vibration damper attaching screw. Install a puller and remove the damper.
10. Remove the timing pointer.
11. Remove the bolts attaching the front cylinder cover to the cylinder block. Remove the front cover and water pump assembly.
12. Disconnect the fuel pump outlet line from the pump. Remove the fuel pump attaching bolts and lay the pump to one side with the flexible line still attached.
13. Discard the cylinder front cover gasket and oil pan seal.
14. Check the timing chain deflection, as outlined at the end of this section.
15. If the timing chain deflection exceeds specification, proceed as follows:
   a. Crank the engine until the timing marks on the sprockets are aligned.
   b. Remove the camshaft sprocket capscrew, washer, and two piece fuel pump eccentric. Slide both sprockets and the timing chain forward, and remove them as an assembly.
   c. Position the sprockets and timing chain on the camshaft and crankshaft. Be certain that the timing marks on the sprockets are correctly aligned.
   d. Install the two piece fuel pump eccentric, washers, and camshaft sprocket capscrew. Tighten the camshaft capscrew

to specification. Make sure that the outer fuel pump eccentric sleeve rotates freely.

16. Coat a new fuel pump gasket with oil resistant sealer and position the fuel pump and gasket on the cylinder block with the fuel pump arm resting on the eccentric outer sleeve. Install the pump attaching bolt and nut and tighten to specification. Connect the fuel pump outlet line.

17. Remove the front crankshaft seal from the front cover. Clean the cylinder front cover and the engine block gasket surfaces.

18. Coat the gasket surfaces of the block and cover with sealer, and position a new gasket on the cylinder block alignment dowels.

19. Position the cylinder front cover and water pump assembly on the cylinder block alignment dowels.

20. Coat the threads of the attaching bolts with an oil resistant sealer and install the timing pointer and attaching bolts. Tighten the bolts to specifications.

21. Install the front cover oil seal into the cylinder front cover.

22. Apply Lubriplate® or its equivalent to the oil seal rubbing surface of the vibration damper inner hub to prevent damage to the seal. Apply a white lead and oil mixture to the front of the crankshaft for damper installation.

23. Line up the crankshaft vibration damper keyway with the key on the crankshaft. Install the vibration damper on the crankshaft by pressing on with appropriate tool. Install the capscrew and washer, tighten to specification. Install the crankshaft pulley.

24. Connect the heater hose and the lower radiator hose to the water pump.

25. Install the air conditioner compressor to water pump bracket and lower idler pulley.

26. Position the alternator bracket and power steering pump bracket on the water pump and install the bolts.

27. Position the water pump pulley on the water pump shaft and install the drive belts.

28. Place the fan shroud over the pulley, and install the fan and spacer.

29. Position the fan shroud over the radiator and install the attaching bolts.

30. Adjust the drive belts to specification.

31. Raise and support the vehicle safely. Remove the oil pan and install new gaskets and seals.

32. Lower the vehicle. Fill the crankcase. Fill and bleed the cooling system. Connect the battery cable.

33. Operate the engine until normal operating temperature has been reached and check for oil or coolant leaks.

460 CID (7.5L) V8 ENGINE

1. Bring the engine to No. 1 piston at TDC (top dead center) on the compression stroke. Drain the cooling system and crankcase.

2. Remove the radiator shroud and fan.

3. Disconnect the upper and lower radiator hoses, and the automatic transmission oil cooler lines from the radiator.

4. Remove the radiator upper support and remove the radiator.

5. Loosen the alternator attaching bolts and air conditioning compressor idler pulley and remove the drive belts with the water pump pulley. Remove the bolts attaching the compressor support to the water pump and remove the bracket (support), if so equipped.

6. Remove the crankshaft pulley from the vibration damper. Remove the bolt and washer attaching the crankshaft damper and remove the damper with a puller. Remove the Woodruff key from the crankshaft.

7. Loosen the by-pass hose at the water pump, and disconnect the heater return tube at the water pump.

8. Disconnect and plug the fuel inlet and outlet lines at the fuel pump, and remove the fuel pump.

9. Remove the bolts attaching the front cover to the cylinder block. Cut the oil pan seal flush with the cylinder block face with a thin knife blade prior to separating the cover from the cylinder block. Remove the cover and water pump as an assembly. Discard the front cover gasket and oil pan seal.

10. Transfer the water pump if a new cover is going to be installed. Clean all of the gasket sealing surfaces on both the front cover and the cylinder block.

11. Check the timing chain deflection. If timing chain deflection exceeds specification, proceed as follows:

a. Crank the engine until the timing marks on the sprockets are aligned.

b. Remove the camshaft sprocket capscrew, washer, and two piece fuel pump eccentric. Slide both sprockets and the timing chain forward, and remove them as an assembly.

c. Position the sprockets and timing chain on the camshaft and crankshaft. Be certain that the timing marks on the sprockets are correctly aligned.

d. Install the two piece fuel pump eccentric, washers, and camshaft sprocket capscrew. Tighten the camshaft capscrew to specification.

12. Coat the gasket surface of the oil pan with sealer. Cut and position the required sections of a new seal on the oil pan. Apply sealer to the corners.

13. Coat the gasket surfaces of the cylinder block and cover with sealer and position the new gasket on the block.

14. Position the front cover on the cylinder block. Use care not to damage the seal and gasket or mislocate them.

15. Coat the front cover attaching screws with sealer and install them.

Checking timing gear backlash

Checking camshaft gear runout

NOTE: It may be necessary to force the front cover downward to compress the oil pan seal in order to install the front cover attaching bolts. Use a drift to engage the cover screw holes through the cover and pry downward.

16. Assemble and install the remaining components in the reverse order of removal. Tighten the front cover bolts to 15–20 ft. lbs., the water pump attaching screws to 12–15 ft. lbs., the crankshaft damper to 70–90 ft. lbs., the crankshaft pulley to 35–50 ft. lbs., fuel pump to 19–27 ft. lbs., the oil pan bolts to 9–11 ft. lbs. for the $^5/_{16}$ in. screws and to 7–9 ft. lbs. for the $^1/_4$ in. screws, and the alternator pivot bolt to 45–57 ft. lbs.

VALVE TIMING PROCEDURE

122 CID (2.0L) AND 140 CID (2.3L) ENGINES

1. Remove the timing belt outer cover.
2. If the belt timing is incorrect, loosen the belt tensioner adjustment screw. Place camshaft belt tension adjusting tool T74P-6254-A on the tension spring rollpin and retract the belt tensioner. Tighten the adjustment screw to hold the tensioner in the retracted position.
3. Remove the crankshaft pulley and belt guide.
4. Position the crankshaft and the camshaft sprockets so that the timing marks index with the timing pointers.
5. Remove the distributor cap and set the distributor rotor to No. 1 firing position by turning the auxiliary shaft.
6. Install the timing belt over the crankshaft sprocket and then counterclockwise over the auxiliary and camshaft sprockets.
7. Loosen the tensioner adjustment bolt and allow the tensioner to move against the belt. To ensure the belt does not jump time during rotation, remove the spark plugs.
8. Rotate the crankshaft two complete turns in normal rotation to remove the slack from the belt. Tighten the tensioner adjustment and pivot bolts to specifications.

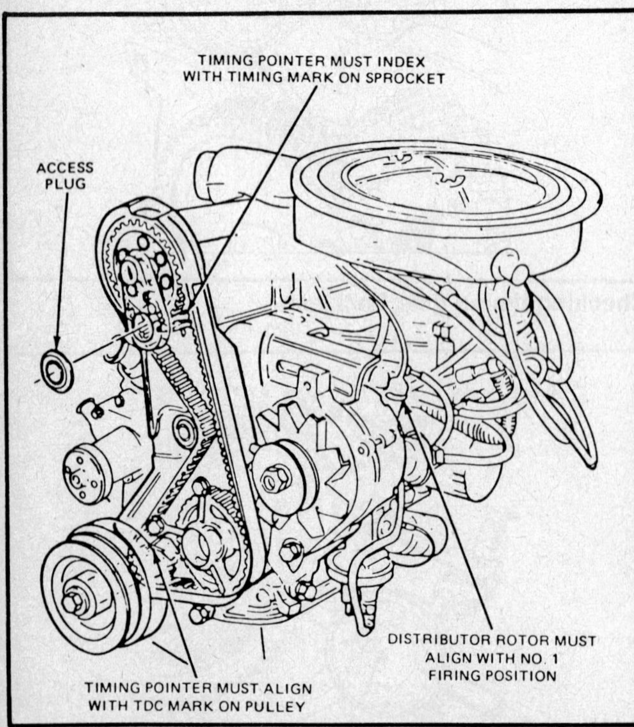

Timing mark alignment—122(2.0L) and 140(2.3L) engines

Camshaft

Removal and Installation

122 CID (2.0L) AND 140 CID (2.3L) ENGINES

NOTE: The following procedure covers camshaft removal and installation with the cylinder head on or off the engine. If the cylinder head has been removed start at Step 9.

1. Drain the cooling system. Remove the air cleaner assembly and disconnect the negative battery cable.
2. Remove the spark plug wires from the plugs, disconnect the retainer from the valve cover and position the wires out of the way. Disconnect rubber vacuum lines as necessary.
3. Remove all drive belts. Remove the alternator mounting bracket-to-cylinder head mounting bolts, position bracket and alternator out of the way.
4. Disconnect and remove the upper radiator hose. Disconnect the radiator shroud.
5. Remove the fan blades and water pump pulley and fan shroud. Remove cam belt and valve covers.
6. Align engine timing marks at TDC. Remove cam drive belt.
7. Raise and support the front of the vehicle safely. Remove the front motor mount bolts. Disconnect the lower radiator hose from the radiator. Disconnect and plug the automatic transmission cooler lines.
8. Position a piece of wood on a floor jack and raise the engine carefully as far as it will go. Place blocks of wood between the engine mounts and crossmember pedestals.
9. Remove the rocker arms.
10. Remove the camshaft drive gear and belt guide using a suitable puller. Remove the front oil seal with a sheet metal screw and slide hammer.
11. Remove the camshaft retainer located on the rear mounting stand by unbolting the two bolts.
12. Remove the camshaft by carefully withdrawing toward the front of the engine. Caution should be used to prevent damage to cam bearings, lobes and journals.
13. Check the camshaft journals and lobes for wear. Inspect the cam bearings, replace as required. The cylinder head must be removed for new bearings to be installed.
14. Cam installation is in the reverse order of removal.

NOTE: Coat the camshaft with heavy SF oil before sliding it into the cylinder head. Install a new front seal. Apply a coat of sealer or teflon tape to the cam drive gear bolt before installation.

CAUTION

After any procedure requiring removal of the rocker arms, each lash adjuster must be fully collapsed after assembly, then released. This must be done before the camshaft is turned.

173 CID (2.8L) AND 177 CID (2.9L) V6 ENGINES

1. Disconnect the negative battery cable from the battery. Drain the coolant and remove the radiator, fan, spacer, water pump pulley and the drive belt.
2. Remove the distributor cap with spark plug wires as an assembly. Remove the distributor vacuum line, distributor, alternator, thermactor, rocker arm covers, fuel line and filter, carburetor, EGR tube, and intake manifold. Remove the spark plug wire boots.
3. Drain the crankcase. Remove the rocker arm and the shaft assemblies. Lift out the pushrods and place in a marked rack so they can be reinstalled in the same location.
4. Remove the oil pan.
5. Remove the drive sprocket attaching bolt and slide the sprocket off the end of the shaft.
6. Remove the engine front cover and water pump as an assembly.

7. Remove the camshaft gear retaining bolt and slide the gear off the camshaft.
8. Remove the camshaft thrust plate and the screws.
9. Remove the valve lifters.
10. Carefully pull the camshaft from the block, avoiding any damage to the camshaft bearings. Remove the camshaft gear key and spacer ring.
11. Oil the camshaft journals with gear oil or assembly lube and apply it to the cam lobes.
12. Install the camshaft in the block, carefully avoiding damage to the bearing surfaces.
13. Install the spacer ring with the chamfered side toward the camshaft. Insert the camshaft key and install the thrust plate so that it covers the main oil gallery. Torque the attaching screws to specifications.
14. Check the camshaft for the specified end-play. The spacer ring and thrust plate are available in two thicknesses to permit adjusting the end-play.
15. Turn the camshaft and the crankshaft as necessary to align the timing marks and install the camshaft gear. Install the retaining washer and bolt and tighten to specifications.
16. Install the valve lifters to their original locations.
17. Install the engine front cover and water pump as an assembly.
18. Install the belt drive pulley and secure with washer and retaining bolt. Tighten the bolt to specifications.
19. Install the oil pan.
20. Apply a light grease to both ends of the pushrods. Install the valve pushrods in their original locations. Continue the installation in the reverse order of the removal procedure.

181 CID (3.0L) V6 ENGINE

1. Drain the cooling system, fuel system and the crankcase.
2. Remove the engine from the vehicle.
3. Remove the timing cover. Remove the intake manifold.
4. Remove the valve lifters. If they are stuck in the bores from excessive varnish, use puller tool T70L-6500-A to remove them.
5. Check the camshaft end play. If it is excessive, replace the thrust plate.
6. Remove the timing chain and the sprockets.
7. Remove the camshaft thrust plate. Remove the camshaft by pulling it toward the front of the engine. Avoid damaging the bearings journals and the lobes.
8. Installation is the reverse of the removal procedure. Lubricate the camshaft journals and lobes and the valve lifters with heavy engine oil (SAE 50) before installation.

300 CID (4.9L) ENGINE

1. Drain the cooling system. Disconnect the negative battery cable. Remove the radiator shroud and radiator. On some models, it may be necessary to remove the grille and radiator support for necessary clearance.
2. Remove the front cover.
3. Remove air cleaner and crankcase vent tube at the rocker cover.
4. Disconnect accelerator cable, choke cable and hand throttle cable (if so equipped). Remove accelerator cable retracting spring.
5. If applicable, remove air compressor and power steering belts.
6. Disconnect oil filler hose from rocker cover.
7. Remove distributor cap and wiring as an assembly, then disconnect vacuum line and primary wire and remove distributor.
8. Remove fuel pump.
9. Remove valve rocker cover, loosen rocker arm stud nuts and move rocker arms to one side. Remove push rods, identifying each so that they may be installed in their original locations.
10. Remove push rod cover and valve lifters, identifying the position of each.

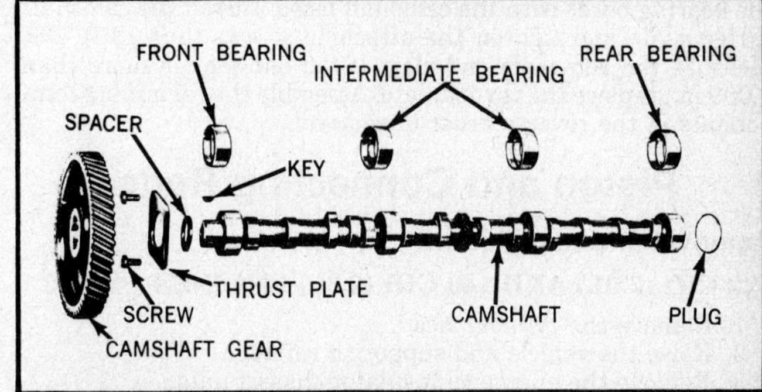

Camshaft 6-cylinder—300 engine

11. Turn crankshaft to align timing marks, remove camshaft thrust plate bolts and carefully pull camshaft and gear from block. Metal camshaft gear (300 HD) is bolted onto camshaft and fiber gear (300 LD) is pressed on and must be removed with an arbor press.
12. To install camshaft, oil journals and apply Lubriplate to lobes, then carefully install camshaft, spacer, thrustplate and gear as an assembly, making sure timing marks are aligned, then tightening thrustplate bolts to 19–20 ft. lbs. Do not rotate crankshaft until distributor is installed.

232 CID (3.8L) V6 AND ALL V8 ENGINES

1. Disconnect the negative battery cable. Remove all required components to gain access to the intake manifold. Remove the intake manifold and valley pan, if so equipped. On Econolines, remove the grill.
2. Remove the rocker covers and either remove the rocker arm shafts or loosen the rockers on their pivots. Remove the push rods. The push rods must be reinstalled in their original positions.
3. Remove the valve lifters in sequence with a magnet. They must be replaced in their original positions.
4. Remove the timing gear cover and timing chain and sprockets.
5. In addition to the radiator and air conditioning condenser, if so equipped, it may be necessary to remove the front grille assembly and the hood lock assembly to gain the necessary clearance to slide the camshaft out the front of the engine.
6. Remove the camshaft thrust plate attaching screws and carefully slide the camshaft out of its bearing bores. Use extra caution not to scratch the bearing journals with the camshaft lobes.
7. Install the camshaft in the reverse order of removal. Coat the camshaft with engine oil liberally before installing it. Slide the camshaft into the engine very carefully so as not to scratch

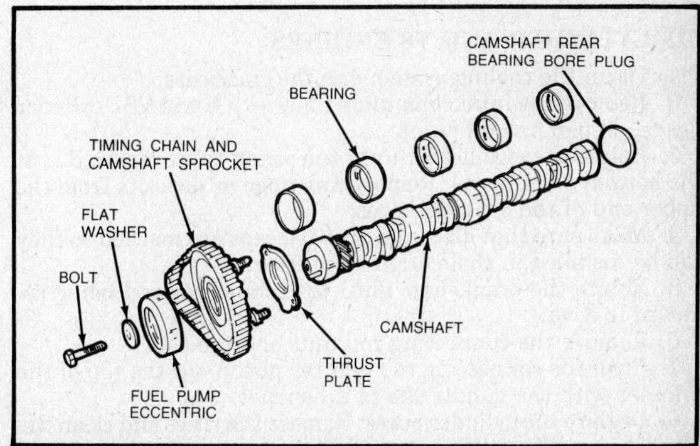

Typical camshaft—V8 engines

the bearing bores with the camshaft lobes. Install the camshaft thrust plate and tighten the attaching screws to 9–12 ft. lbs. Measure the camshaft end-play. If the end-play is more than 0.009 in., replace the thrust plate. Assemble the remaining components in the reverse order of removal.

Piston and Connecting Rods

Removal and Installation

122 CID (2.0L) AND 140 CID (2.3L) ENGINES

1. Remove the cylinder head.
2. Raise the vehicle and support it safely.
3. Remove the engine to insulator chassis nuts.
4. Remove the starter.
5. Raise the engine as high as it will go. Place blocks of wood between the mounts and the chassis brackets and remove the jack.
6. Remove the oil pan from the vehicle. Clean the gasket surface at the cylinder block.
7. Remove the pickup tube and screen assembly.
8. Remove the connecting rod cap and bearing. Push the pistons up into the cylinder bores. Lower the vehicle.
9. Remove the pistons from the bores. Deglaze the cylinder bores. Remove the rings and clean the ring grooves. Clean the carbon from the pistons. Reverse the order for installation.

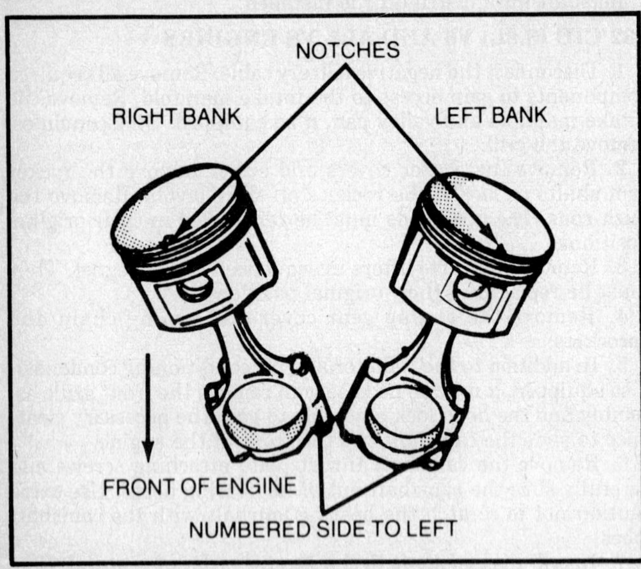

Piston installation – 173(2.8L) V6 engine

SIX CYLINDER AND V8 ENGINES

1. Drain the cooling system and the crankcase.
2. Remove the intake manifold (only on V6 and V8), cylinder heads, oil pan and oil pump.
3. Rotate the crankshaft until the piston to be removed is at the bottom of its travel. Remove any ridge or deposits from the upper end of the cylinder bores.
4. Make sure that all connecting rod caps are marked so they can be installed in their original positions.
5. Rotate the crankshaft until the connecting rod being removed is down.
6. Remove the connecting rod nuts and the cap.
7. Push the connecting rod and the piston out the top of the cylinder with the handle end of a hammer.
8. Deglaze the cylinder bores. Remove the rings and clean the ring grooves. Clean the carbon from the pistons. Reverse the order for installation.

Connecting Rod and Main Bearings

Service procedures for connecting rod and main bearings can be found in the Unit Overhaul Section.

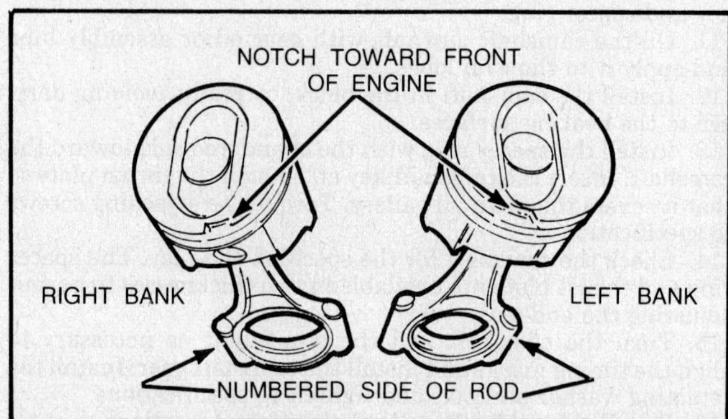

Piston and rod relationship – 370, 429, and 460 V8 engines

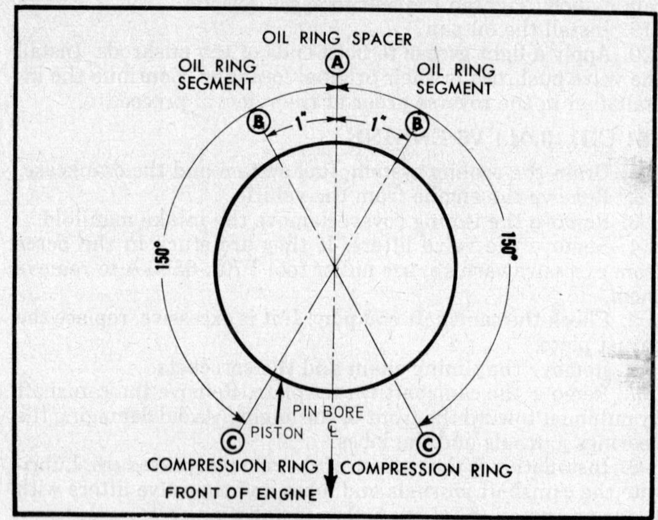

Piston ring gap spacing

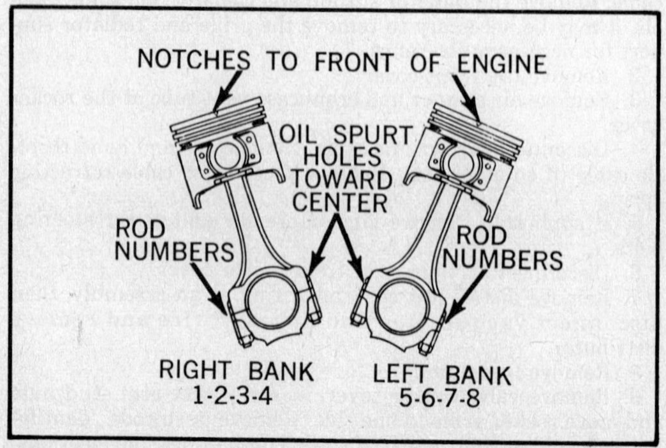

Piston-to-rod relationship – 302 and 351M V8, V6 similar

ENGINE LUBRICATION

Oil Pan

Removal and Installation

122 CID (2.0L) AND 140 CID (2.3L) ENGINES

1. Disconnect the negative battery cable.
2. Remove air cleaner assembly. Remove oil dipstick. Remove engine mount retaining nuts.
3. Remove oil cooler lines at the radiator, if so equipped. Remove (2) bolts retaining the fan shroud to the radiator and remove shroud.
4. Remove radiator retaining bolts (automatic only). Position radiator upward and wire to the hood (automatic only).
5. Raise and safely support the vehicle.
6. Drain oil from crankcase.
7. Remove starter cable from starter and remove starter.
8. Disconnect the exhaust manifold tube to the inlet pipe bracket at the thermactor check valve.
9. Remove transmission mount retaining nuts to the crossmember.
10. Remove bellcrank from converter housing (automatic only).
11. Remove oil cooler lines from retainer at the block (automatic only).
12. Remove front crossmember (automatic only).
13. Disconnect right front lower shock absorber mount (manual only).
14. Position jack under engine, raise and block with a piece of wood approximately 2 ½ in. high. Remove jack.
15. Position jack under the transmission and raise slightly (automatic only).
16. Remove oil pan retaining bolts, lower pan to the chassis. Remove oil pump drive and pick up tube assembly.
17. Remove oil pan (out the front for automatic only) (out the rear for manual only).
18. Installation is the reverse of the removal procedure.

173 CID (2.8L) AND 179 CID (2.9L) V6 ENGINES

1. Disconnect negative battery cable. Remove carburetor air cleaner assembly.
2. Remove fan shroud and position over fan.
3. Remove distributor cap, position forward of dash panel. Remove distributor and cover bore opening.
4. Remove nuts attaching engine front insulators to cross member. Remove engine oil dipstick tube.
5. Raise vehicle and safely support on jackstands.
6. Drain engine crankcase. Remove transmission fluid filler tube and plug pan hole (auto trans. only).
7. Remove engine oil filter element. Disconnect muffler inlet pipe(s).
8. Disconnect oil cooler bracket and lower (if so equipped). Remove starter motor.
9. Position out of way, transmission oil cooler lines (if so equipped). Disconnect front stabilizer bar and position forward.
10. Position jack under engine and raise engine maximum height (until it touches dash panel) and install wooden blocks between front insulator mounts and #2 crossmember.
11. Lower engine onto blocks and remove jack.
12. Remove oil pan attaching bolts. Lower oil pan assembly.
13. Remove oil pump and pickup tube assembly (attached to bearing cap) and lower into oil pan. Remove oil pan assembly.
14. Installation is the reverse of the removal procedure.

183 CID (3.0L) V6 ENGINE

1. Disconnect the negative battery cable.
2. Remove the oil level dipstick. Raise the vehicle and support it safely.
3. If equipped with an oil level sensor, remove the retaining clip at the sensor. Remove the electrical connector from the sensor.
4. Drain the crankcase. Remove the starter motor.
5. Remove the flywheel dust cover from the converter housing.
6. Loosen the transmission bolts and slide the transmission ¼ in. (6.35 mm).
7. Remove the oil pan attaching bolts and remove the pan.
8. Installation is the reverse of removal.

F SERIES WITH 300 CID (4.9L) ENGINE

1. Drain the crankcase.
2. On the F-100–250, also drain the cooling system.
3. Remove radiator from F-100–250 vehicles.
4. Raise and support the vehicle safely. Disconnect and remove the starter.
5. On F-100–250, remove engine front support insulator to support bracket nuts and washers. Use a transmission jack to raise the front of the engine, then install blocks (1 in. thick) between the front support insulators and support brackets. Lower engine onto blocks and remove jack.
6. Remove the attaching bolts and oil pan. It may be necessary to remove the oil pump inlet tube and screen assembly in order to free the pan.
7. Remove the rear main bearing cap and front cover seals. Clean out the seal grooves and all gasket surfaces.
8. Apply oil resistant sealer in the spaces between the rear main bearing cap and the block. Install new rear cap seal, then apply a bead of sealer to the tapered ends of the seal.
9. Install the pan in the reverse order of removal.

E SERIES WITH 300 CID (4.9L) ENGINE

1. Remove the engine cover. Remove the air cleaner and the carburetor.
2. If equipped with air conditioning, discharge the system and remove the compressor.
3. If the vehicle is an E-350, disconnect the thermactor check valve inlet hose and remove the check valve. Remove the EGR valve.
4. Remove the radiator hoses. Unbolt the fan shroud and position on the fan. If equipped with automatic transmission, disconnect the cooler lines and remove the oil filler tube.
5. Remove exhaust inlet pipe to manifold nuts. Raise and support the vehicle safely. Disconnect and plug fuel pump inlet line. Remove the starter. Remove alternator splash shield and front engine support nuts.
6. Remove the power steering return line clip which is located in front of the No. 1 crossmember.

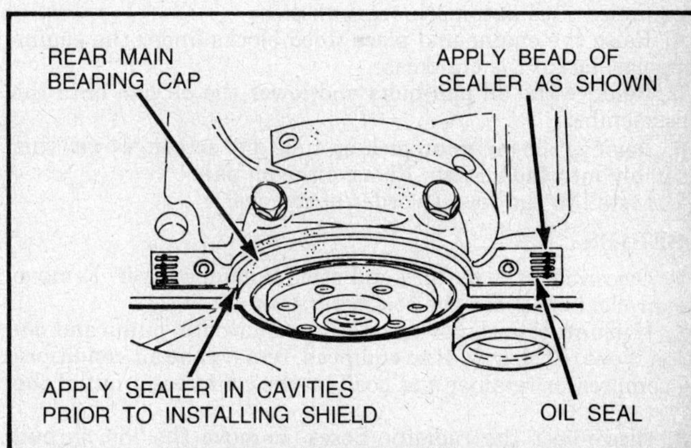

Installing oil pan seal—300 engine

7. Raise the engine and place 3 in. blocks under the engine mounts. Remove the oil pan dipstick tube.

8. Remove the oil pan bolts and remove the oil pan. Remove the pickup tube and screen from the oil pump.

9. Installation is the reverse of the removal procedure.

232 CID (3.8L) V6 ENGINE

1. Disconnect the cable from the battery negative cable.
2. Remove the air cleaner and duct assembly.
3. Remove the bolts attaching the fan shroud to the radiator and position the shroud over the fan.
4. Remove the engine oil dipstick.
5. Raise and support the vehicle safely. Drain the engine oil and replace the drain plug.
6. Remove the oil filter.
7. Disconnect the muffler inlet pipes from the exhaust manifolds. Remove the clamp attaching inlet pipe to converter pipe and remove inlet pipe from vehicle.
8. Disconnect the transmission shift linkage at the transmission.
9. Disconnect the transmission cooler lines at the radiator if so equipped.
10. Remove the nuts attaching the engine supports to the chassis brackets.
11. Raise the engine as high as possible, and place wood blocks between the engine supports and the chassis brackets. Remove the jack.
12. Remove the oil pan attaching bolts and drop the oil pan. Remove the oil pick-up and tube assembly and let them lay in the oil pan. Remove the oil pan from the vehicle.
13. Installation is the reverse of the removal procedure.

BRONCO W/302 CID (5.0L) OR 351W CID (5.8L) V8 ENGINES

1. Remove the air cleaner and duct assembly. Remove the oil dipstick tube. Drain the engine oil.
2. Remove the oil pan bolts and remove the oil pan.
3. To install, clean the oil pan and the cylinder block of all old gasket material. Position a new oil pan gasket and end seals to the cylinder block.
4. Clean and install the oil pump pick-up tube and screen assembly, if removed.
5. Install the oil pan to the cylinder block. Install the oil dipstick tube, air cleaner and duct assembly.
6. Fill the crankcase with the proper oil. Start the engine and check for leaks.

F-SERIES

1. Remove the oil dipstick. Remove the bolts attaching the fan shroud to the radiator and position the shroud over the fan.
2. Remove the nuts and lockwashers attaching the engine support insulators to the chassis bracket.
3. Disconnect the oil cooler line at the left side of the radiator, if equipped with automatic transmission.
4. Raise the engine and place wood blocks under the engine supports. Drain the crankcase.
5. Remove the oil pan bolts and lower the oil pan onto the crossmember.
6. Remove the oil pump pick-up tube and screen. Lower this assembly into the oil pan. Remove the oil pan.
7. Install in the reverse order of removal.

E SERIES

1. Disconnect the battery and remove engine cover. Remove the air cleaner. Drain the cooling system.
2. If equipped with power steering remove the pump and position it out of the way. If so equipped, remove the air conditioning compressor retainer and position the compressor out of the way.
3. Disconnect the radiator hoses. Remove the fan shroud bolts and oil filler tube. Remove the oil dipstick bolt. Raise the vehicle on a hoist.
4. Remove the alternator splash shield. If equipped, disconnect the automatic transmission cooler lines at the radiator.
5. Disconnect and plug the fuel line at the fuel pump. Remove the engine mount nuts. Drain the engine oil. Remove the dipstick tube. Disconnect the muffler inlet pipe from the exhaust manifolds.
6. If equipped, remove the automatic transmission dipstick and tube. Disconnect the manual linkage at the transmission. Remove the center driveshaft support and remove the driveshaft from the transmission.
7. Place a transmission jack under the oil pan and insert a wooden block between the pan and jack.

NOTE: The engine and transmission assembly will pivot around the rear engine mount. The engine assembly must be raised four inches (measured from the front motor mounts). The engine must remain centered in the engine compartment to obtain this much lift.

8. Raise the engine and transmission assembly. Insert wooden blocks to support the engine in its uppermost position.
9. Remove the oil pan bolts and lower the oil pan. Unbolt the oil pump and the oil pick-up tube and lay them in the oil pan. Remove the oil pan from the vehicle. The oil pump must be removed along with the removal of the oil pan.
10. Installation is the reverse of the removal procedure.

400 CID (6.6L) V8 ENGINES

1. Remove the oil dipstick. Remove the fan shroud bolts and position the shroud over the fan.
2. Raise and support the vehicle safely. Drain the crankcase. Disconnect the starter cable and remove the starter.
3. Place a jack and a wood block under the oil pan and support the engine. Remove the engine front support through bolts.
4. Raise the engine and place wood blocks between the engine supports and the chassis brackets. Remove the jack.
5. If equipped with an automatic transmission, position the oil cooler lines out of the way.
6. Remove the oil pan attaching bolts and remove the oil pan.
7. Install in the reverse order of removal.

460 CID (7.5L) V8 ENGINE, EXCEPT IN E SERIES

1. Disconnect the battery ground cable. Disconnect the radiator shroud and position it over the fan.
2. Raise and support the vehicle. Drain the crankcase. Remove the oil filter.
3. Remove the through bolt from each engine support. Place a floor jack under the front edge of the oil pan, with a block of wood between the jack and the oil pan. Raise the engine just high enough to insert 1 $^1/_4$ in. blocks of wood between the insulators and the brackets. Remove the floor jack.
4. Remove the oil pan bolts and remove the oil pan. It may be necessary to rotate the crankshaft to provide clearance between the pan and the crankshaft counterweights.
5. Installation is the reverse of removal.

E SERIES WITH 460 CID (7.5L) V8 ENGINE

1. Remove the engine cover, disconnect the battery and drain the cooling system.
2. Remove the air cleaner assembly. Disconnect the throttle and transmission linkage at the carburetor. Disconnect the power brake vacuum lines.
3. Disconnect the fuel line, choke lines and remove the carburetor air cleaner adaptor from the carburetor.
4. Disconnect the radiator hoses. If equipped, disconnect the oil cooler lines. Remove the fan assembly and remove the radiator. If equipped, remove the power steering pump and position it aside.
5. Remove the front engine mount attaching bolts. Remove the engine oil dipstick tube from the exhaust manifold. Remove the oil filler tube and bracket.

6. If so equipped, rotate the air conditioning lines (at the rear of the compressor) down to clear the dash (or remove them).
7. Raise and support the vehicle safely. Drain the crankcase and remove the oil filter.
8. Remove the muffler inlet pipe assembly. Disconnect the manual and kickdown linkage from the transmission. Remove the driveshaft and coupling shaft assembly. Remove the transmission tube assembly.
9. Remove the dipstick and tube from the oil pan. Place a transmission jack under the engine oil pan. Insert a wood block between the jack surface and the oil pan. Jack the engine upward, pivoting on the rear mount until the transmission contacts the floor. Block the engine in position. The engine must remain centralized to obtain the maximum height. The engine must be raised four inches at the mounts to remove the oil pan.
10. Remove the oil pan bolts and lower the oil pan. Remove the oil pump and pick up tube attachments and drop them into the oil pan. Remove the oil pan rearward from the vehicle.

NOTE: The oil pump must be removed when removing the oil pan.

11. Installation is the reverse of the removal procedure.

Oil Pump

Removal and Installation

ALL ENGINES EXCEPT 232 CID (3.8L) V6 ENGINE

1. Remove the oil pan.
2. Remove the oil pump mounting bolts and remove the oil pump from the cylinder block.
3. To install, prime the pump by filling the inlet port with engine oil. Rotate the pump shaft to distribute oil within the pump body. Install the distributor intermediate shaft in the oil pump rotor shaft.
4. Insert the intermediate shaft into the distributor shaft hex bore. Make certain that the intermediate shaft is properly seated. Do not force the pump into position if it will not seat readily. The intermediate shaft hex may be misaligned with the distributor shaft. To align, rotate the intermediate shaft until it can be seated.
5. Secure the oil pump to the cylinder block and tighten the bolts. Install the oil pan and other related parts.

232 CID (3.8L) V6 ENGINE

1. If necessary remove the oil filter.
2. Remove the oil pump cover attaching bolts and remove the cover.
3. Lift the pump gears of the pocket in the front cover.

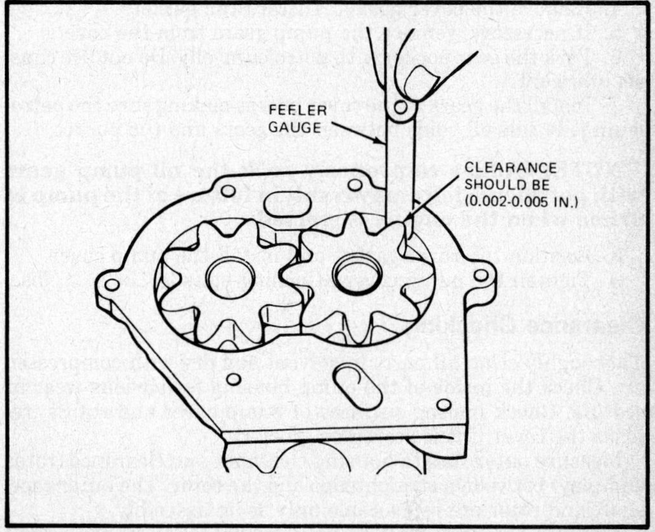

Oil pump side clearance check—232 CID V-6 engine

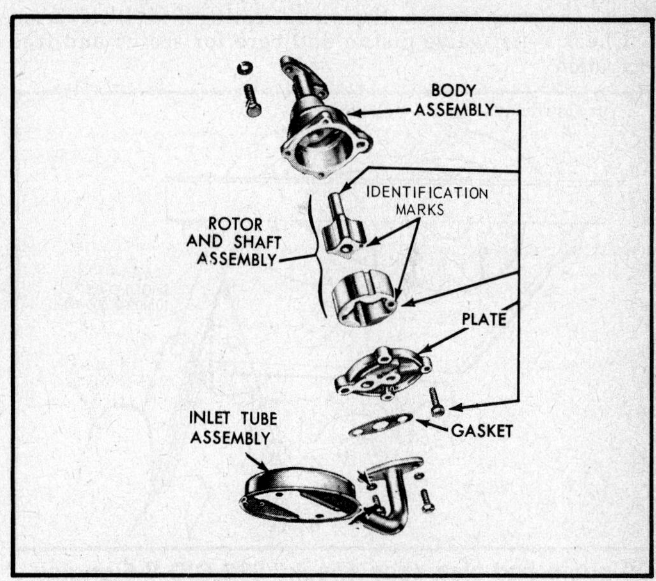

Oil pump assembly—232 CID V-6 engine rear

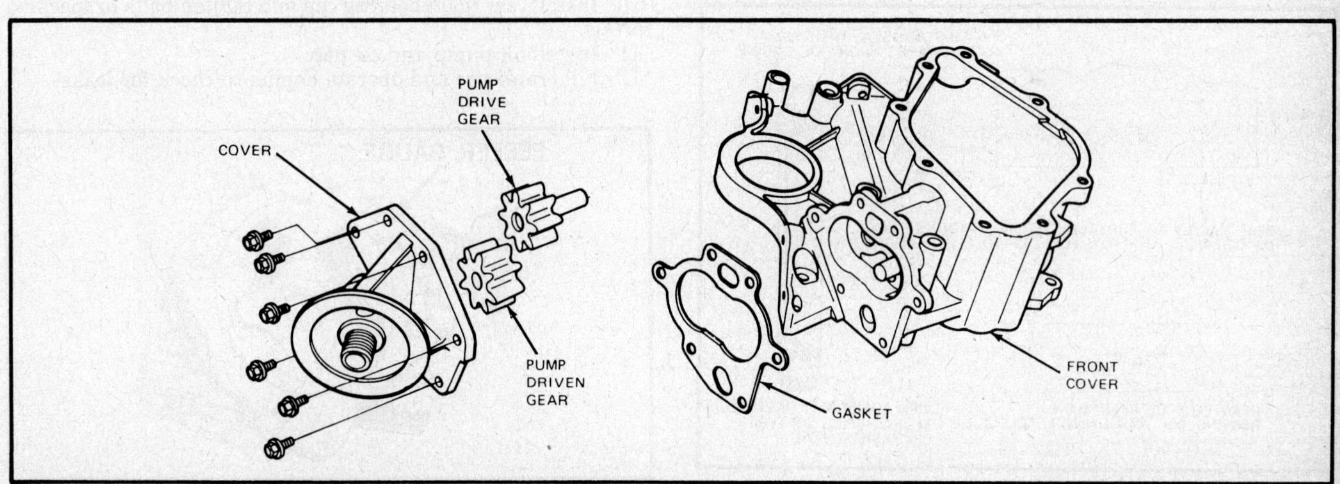

Typical oil pump assembly

4. Remove the cover gasket. Discard the gasket.
5. If necessary, remove the pump gears from the cover.
6. Pack the gear pocket with petroleum jelly. Do not use chassis lubricant.
7. Install the gears in the cover pocket making sure the petroleum jelly fills all voids between the gears and the pocket.

NOTE: Failure to properly pack the oil pump gears with petroleum jelly may result in failure of the pump to prime when the engine is started.

8. Position the cover gasket and install the pump cover.
9. Tighten the pump cover attaching bolts to 18–22 ft. lbs.

Clearance Checking

Thoroughly clean all parts in solvent and dry with compressed air. Check the inside of the pump housing for obvious wear or scoring. Check mating surfaces of pump cover and rotors, replace the cover if it is scored or grooved.

Measure outer race to housing clearance and clearance (rotor end-play) between a straightedge and the rotor. The outer race, shaft and rotor are replaceable only as an assembly.

Measure the driveshaft to housing clearance by comparing shaft OD to housing bearing ID.

Inspect relief valve spring for collapsed or worn condition. Check the pring tension. Replace the spring if weak or worn.

Check relief valve piston and bore for scores and free operation.

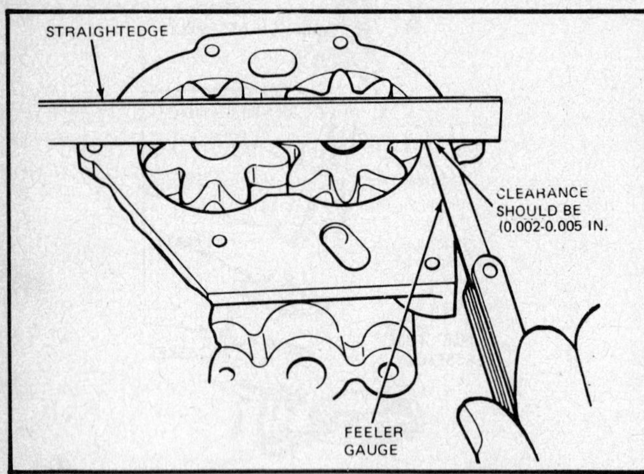

Oil pump and clearance check—232 CID V-6 engine gear

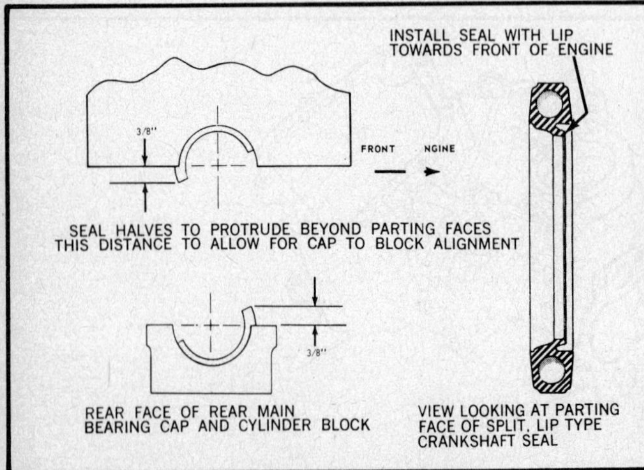

Crankshaft rear oil seal installation

Rear Main Oil Seal

Removal and Installation

ONE PIECE SEAL

1. Remove the transmission, clutch assembly or converter and flywheel.
2. Lower the oil pan if necessary for working room.
3. Use an awl to punch two small holes on opposite sides of the seal just above the split between the main bearing cap and engine block. Install a sheet metal screw in each hole. Use two small pry bars and pry evenly on both screws using two small blocks of wood as a fulcrum point for the pry bars. Use caution throughout to avoid scratching or damage to the oil seal mounting surfaces.
4. When the seal has been removed, clean the mounting recess.
5. Coat the seal and block mounting surfaces with oil. Apply white lube to the contact surface of the seal and crankshaft. Start the seal into the mounting recess and install with seal mounting tool.
6. Install the remaining components in the reverse.

SPLIT SEAL

Remove the oil pan. In some cases it may be necessary to remove the oil pump pick-up and screen or the whole pump assembly.

1. Loosen all main bearing caps, lowering the crankshaft slightly, but not more than $\frac{1}{32}$ in.
2. Remove the rear main bearing cap.
3. Remove the seal halves from cap and block. Use a seal removing tool on the block half or install a small metal screw in one end so that the seal may be pulled out.

NOTE: Do not damage or scratch the crankshaft seal surfaces.

4. If so equipped, remove the oil seal retaining pin from the bearing cap.
5. Thoroughly clean seal grooves in block and cap with brush and solvent.
6. Dip seal halves in engine oil.
7. Carefully install upper half of seal with the lip facing toward the front of the engine until $\frac{3}{8}$ in. is left protruding below parting surface. Be careful not to scrape seal.
8. Tighten all but the rear main bearing caps to specified torque.
9. Install lower seal half in the rear main bearing cap with the lip facing toward the front of the engine. Apply a light coat of oil-resistant sealer to the rear of the top mating surface of the cap. Do not apply sealer to the area forward of the side seal groove.
10. Install rear main bearing cap and tighten bolts to specified torque.
11. Install oil pump and oil pan.
12. Fill crankcase and operate engine to check for leaks.

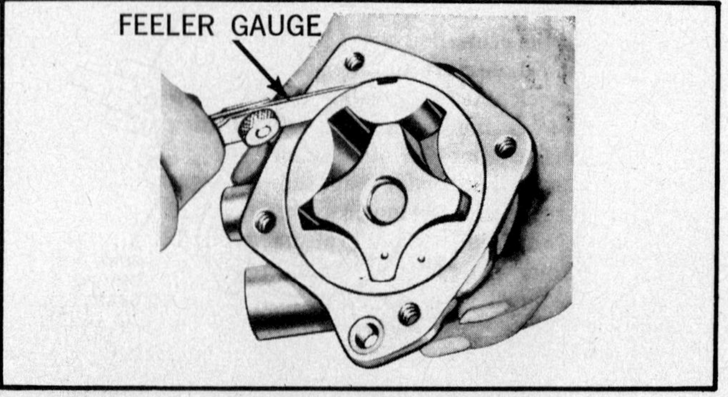

Checking outer race-to-housing clearance

FRONT SUSPENSION

Twin I—Beam Axle

Removal and Installation

1. Remove the front wheel spindle, the front spring, and the stabilizer bar (if so equipped).
2. Remove the spring lower seat from the radius arm, and then remove the bolt and nut that attaches the stabilizer bar bracket and radius arm the front axle.
3. Remove the axle to frame pivot bracket bolt and nut.
4. To install, position the axle to the frame pivot bracket and install the bolt and nut finger tight.
5. Position the opposite end of the of the axle to the radius arm, install the attaching bolt from underneath through the bracket, the radius arm and the axle. Install the nut and tighten to 120–150 ft. lbs. (163–203 Nm).
6. Install the spring lower seat on the radius arm so that the hole in the seat indexes over the arm to axle bolt. Install the front spring.
7. Install the front wheel spindle.

NOTE: Lower the vehicle on its wheels or support the vehicle on the front springs prior to tightening the axle pivot bolt and nut.

8. Tighten the axle to frame pivot bracket bolt to specified torque.

Coil Spring

Removal and Installation

ALL EXCEPT AEROSTAR

1. Raise the front of the vehicle and support it safely. Also put a jack under the axle.
2. Disconnect the shock absorber from the lower bracket.
3. Remove the spring lower retainer attaching nuts from inside of the spring coil and remove the retainer.
4. Remove the spring upper retainer attaching screws and remove the retainer.
5. Slowly lower the axle and remove the spring.
6. Installation is the reverse of the removal procedure. Tighten all bolts to specifications.

AEROSTAR

1. Place the steering wheel and the steering system in the "on center" position.
2. Raise the vehicle and support it safely. Remove the wheel assembly.
3. Disconnect the stabilizer link bolt from the lower arm.
4. Remove the two bolts attaching the shock to the lower arm. Remove the upper nut and washer and remove the shock.
5. Remove the steering center link from the pitman arm.
6. Using spring compressor tool D78P-5310-A, install one plate with the pivot ball seat facing downward into the coils of the spring. Rotate the plate so that it is flush with the upper surface of the lower arm.
7. Install the other plate with the pivot ball seat facing upward into the coils of the spring. Insert the upper ball nut through the coils of the spring, so that the nut rests in the upper plate.
8. Insert the compression rod into the opening in the lower arm, through the upper and lower plate and upper ball nut. Insert the securing pin through the upper ball nut and the compression rod.
9. Loosen the lower arm pivot bolts. Remove the cotter pin and loosen but do not remove the nut attaching the lower ball joint to the spindle. Loosen the lower ball joint. Support the lower control arm and remove the ball joint nut. Lower the control arm and remove the spring.
10. Reverse the removal procedure for installation.

Leaf Spring

Removal and Installation

F 250 AND 350 4WD

1. Raise the vehicle frame until the weight is off the front spring and the wheels stil touching the floor.
2. Disconnect the lower end of the shock absorber from the U-bolt spacer. Remove the U-bolts, cap and the spacer.
3. On vehicles equipped with a Dana Model 60 Monobeam axle, remove the two bolts that retain the tracking bar to the right spring cap and tracking bar mounting bracket.
4. Remove the nut from the hanger bolt retaining the springat the rear. Drive out the hanger bolt.
5. Remove the nut connecting the front shackle and the spring eye. Drive out the shackle bolt and remove the spring.
6. Installation is the reverse of the removal procedure.

King Pin and Bushings

Removal and Installation

1. Raise and support the vehicle safely.
2. Remove the wheel and tire.
3. Remove the caliper key retaining screw. Drive out the caliper support key and spring with brass drift and hammer. Remove the caliper from the spindle by pushing the caliper downward against the spindle assembly and rotating the upper end of the caliper upward and out of the spindle assembly. It is not necessary to disconnect the brake fluid hose. Wire the caliper to a suspension part to remove the weight of the caliper from the hose. Disconnect the steering linkage from the spindle arm.
4. Disconnect the steering linkage from the integral spindle and spindle arm.
5. Remove the nut and lockwasher from the locking pin, and remove the locking pin.
6. Remove the upper and lower spindle bolt plugs, and drive the spindle bolt out from the top of the axle. Remove the spindle and bearing. Knock out the seal
7. Make sure that the spindle bolt hole in the axle is free of nicks, burrs and dirt. Install a new seal and coat the spindle bolt bushings and bolt hole with oil.
8. Place the spindle in position on the axle.
9. Pack the spindle thrust bearing with chassis lubricant and insert the bearing into the spindle with the open end of the bearing seal facing down into the spindle.
10. Install the spindle pin in the spindle with the locking pin notch in the spindle bolt aligned with the locking pin hole in the axle. Drive the spindle bolt through the axle from the top side until the spindle bolt locking pin notch is aligned with the locking pin hole.
11. Install a new locking pin. Install the locking pin lockwasher and nut. Tighten the nut to 40–55 ft. lbs. Install the spindle bolt plugs at the top and bottom of the spindle bolt.
12. Position the caliper on the spindle assembly. Be careful to prevent tearing or cutting of the piston boot as the caliper is slipped over the inner brake pad. Use a suitable tool to hold the upper machined surface of the caliper against the surface of the spindle. Install the caliper support spring and key. Drive the key and spring into position with a soft hammer. Install the key retaining screw and tighten the nut to 50–70 ft. lbs. advancing the nut as necessary to install the cotter pin.
13. Install the wheel.
14. Grease the spindle assembly with a grease gun.

15. Check and adjust, if necessary, the toe-in adjustment.

Shock Absorbers

Removal and Installation

BRONCO, E AND F SERIES

1. Insert a wrench from the rear side of the spring upper seat to hold the shock absorber upper retaining nut.
2. Loosen the stud by turning the hex provided on the exposed (lower) part of the stud and remove the nut.
3. Disconnect the lower end of the shock absorber from the lower bracket by removing the nut and bolt.
4. Compress the shock absorber and remove it from the vehicle.
5. Installation is the reverse of the removal procedure.

F 250 AND 350 4WD

1. Remove the nut and bolt that retains the shock absorber to the upper shock bracket.
2. Disconnect the lower end of the shock absorber from the U-bolt plate.
3. Compress the shock absorber and remove it.
4. Reverse the removal procedure for installation.

AEROSTAR, BRONCO II AND RANGER

1. Remove the nut and the washer that attaches the shock absorber to the spring seat.
2. Remove the nut and bolt that retain the shock absorber to the radius arm and lower shock bracket.
3. Slightly compress the shock and remove it from the vehicle.
4. On Aerostar, remove the two bolts retaining the shock absorber to the bottom of the lower control arm. Remove the shock through the lower control arm.
5. Installation is the reverse of the removal procedure.

Upper Control Arm

Removal and Installation

AEROSTAR

1. Place the steering wheel and the steering system in the "on-center" position.
2. Raise the vehicle and support it safely under the body rails.
3. Remove the spindle. Remove the cowl drain bracket and the bolt retainer plate.
4. Mark the position of the control arm mounting brackets on the flat plate.
5. Remove the bolt and washer retaining the front bracket to the flat plate.
6. From beneath the rail, remove the three nuts from the bolts retaining the two upper control arm mounting brackets to the body rail.
7. Remove the three long bolts retaining the mounting brackets to the body rail by rotating the upper control arm out of position in order to remove the bolts.
8. Remove the upper control arm, upper ball joint and mounting bracket assembly and flat plate from the vehicle.
9. Installation is the reverse of the removal procedure.

Lower Control Arm

Removal and Installation

AEROSTAR

1. Place the steering and the steering system in the "on-center" position.
2. Raise the vehicle and support it safely under the frame.
3. Remove the coil spring.
4. Remove the bolts and nuts retaining the control arm to the No.1 crossmember. Remove the lower control arm.
5. Install in the reverse order of removal.

Ball Joints

Removal and Installation

BRONCO II, F SERIES AND RANGER

1. Remove the spindle. Remove the snap ring from the ball joints.
2. Assemble the C-frame tool (T74P-4635-C) and reciever cup tool (D81T-3010-A) on the upper ball joint.
3. Turn the forcing screw clockwise until the ball joint is removed from the axle.
4. Use the same procedure on the lower ball joint.

NOTE: Always remove the upper ball joint first. Do not heat the ball joint or the axle to aid in removal.

5. Installation is the reverse of the removal procedure. The lower ball joint must be installed first.

AEROSTAR

The control arms and the ball joints are only serviced as assemblies. Refer to the Upper or Lower Control Arm Removal and Installation procedures.

Wheel Bearings

Removal and Installation

1. Raise the vehicle until the tire clears the floor. Support the vehicle safely and remove the wheel.
2. Remove the brake caliper and wire it to the underbody to prevent damage to the brake hose.
3. Remove the grease cap, cotter pin, retainer adjusting nut and washer. Remove the outer bearing.
4. Pull the hub and rotor off the spindle. Remove and discard the grease seal.
5. Remove the inner bearing from the hub. Remove all traces of old lubricant from the bearings, hub and spindle with solvent and dry thoroughly.

NOTE: Do not spin the bearings dry with compressed air.

6. Inspect the bearing races for scratches, pits or cracks. If the races are worn or damaged, remove them with a drift.
7. If the inner or outer bearing races were removed, replace them in the hub with the proper tool and driver handle T80T-4000-W. The cups will be properly seated when they are fully bottomed.
8. Replace the grease retainer. Pack the inside of the hub with lithium base grease, High Temperature Multi-Purpose Long Life Lubricant. Fill the hub until the grease is flush with the inside diameters of both bearing races.
9. Pack the bearings with wheel bearing grease, working as much lubricant as possible between the rollers and the cages.
10. For installation reverse the removal procedure.

Adjustments

REAR DRIVE MODELS

1. Raise the vehicle until the tire clears the floor and support it safely.
2. Remove the wheel cover and the grease cap from the hub. Remove the cotter pin and the lock nut. Loosen the adjusting nut three turns.
3. Remove the caliper. While rotating the wheel, tighten the adjusting nut to 17–25 ft. lbs. (23–34 Nm) to seat the bearings.
4. On E and F series, back off the adjusting nut ⅛ turn and

install the retainer and new cotter pin without additional movement of the adjusting nut.

5. On Aerostar, Bronco II and Ranger, loosen the adjusting nut ½ turn then retighten to 18–20 inch lbs. (2.0–2.3 Nm).

6. Check the wheel rotation. Reinstall the grease cap and the wheel cover.

FRONT DRIVE MODELS

1. Raise the vehicle and support it safely.
2. For Bronco and F series with Dana 44IFS front axle, use the following:
   a. Remove the hub lock assembly.
   b. Using a torque wrench and a lock nut wrench, apply inward pressure to unlock the adjusting nut locking splines and turn the nut clockwise to tighten to 50–60 ft. lbs. (68–81 Nm) while rotqting the wheel back and forth.
   c. Apply inward pressure to the lock nut wrench to disengage the adjusting nut locking splines and back off the adjusting nut 90°.
   d. Retighten the adjusting nut to 15 ft. lbs. (20 Nm). Remove the tools and install the hub lock.
3. For F series with Dana 501IFS and Dana 60 Monobeam front axle, use the following:
   a. Remove the hub lock assembly.
   b. Remove the outer locknut and lockwasher.
   c. Using a locknut wrench, tighten the inner locknut to 50 ft. lbs. (68 Nm) to seat the bearing.
   d. Back off the inner locknut and retighten to 31–39 ft. lbs. (41–54 Nm).
   e. While rotating the wheel, back off the locknut 135°–150°. Install the lockwasher. Install the outer locknut and tighten to 160–205 ft. lbs. (217–278 Nm). Install the hub locks.

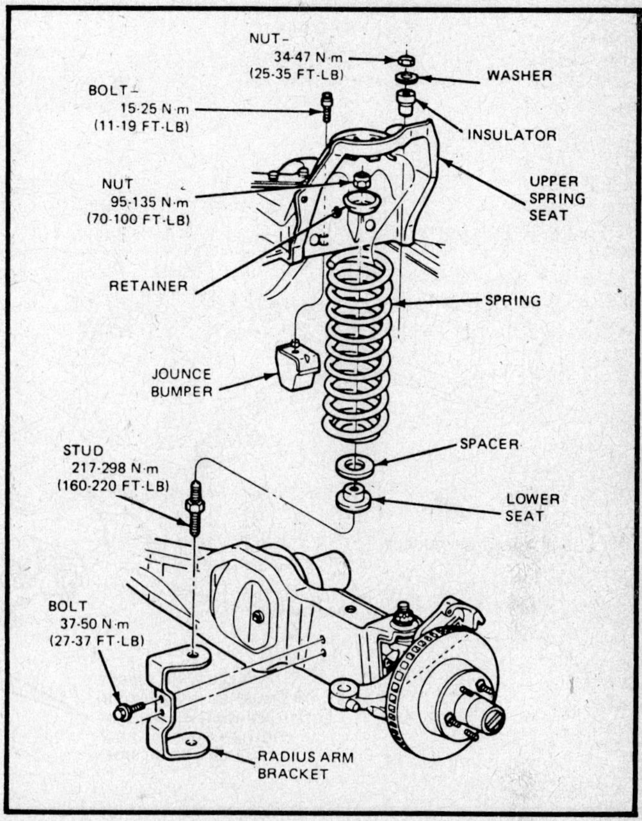

Coil spring and related components—Ranger and Bronco II

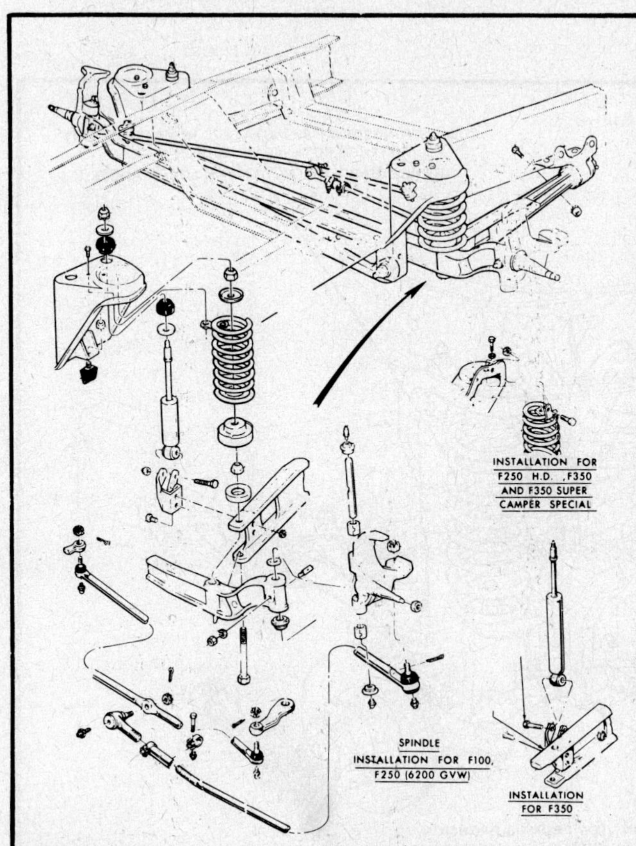

Exploded view of twin I-beam front axle—F-100-350 shown

4. Bronco II and Ranger with Manual Locking Hubs, use the following procedure:
   a. Remove the wheel. Remove the retainer washers from the lug nut studs and remove the locking hub assembly from the spindle.
   b. Remove the snap ring from the end of the spindle shaft. Remove the axle shaft spacer, needle thrust bearing and the bearing spacer.
   c. Remove the outer wheel bearing locknut and the washer from the spindle.
   d. Loosen the inner wheel bearing locknut and then tighten to 35 ft. lbs. (47 Nm) to seat the bearings.
   e. Spin the rotor and back off the inner locknut ¼ turn. Retighten the inner locknut to 16 inch lbs. (1.8 Nm).
   f. Install the lockwasher and the outer wheel bearing lock nut and tighten to 150 ft. lbs. (203 Nm).
5. Bronco II and Ranger with Automatic Locking Hubs, use the following procedure:
   a. Remove the wheel assembly. Remove the retainer washers from the lug nut studs and remove the locking hub assembly from the spindle. Remove the snap ring from the end of the end of the spindle shaft.
   b. Remove the axle shaft spacer, needle thrust bearing and the bearing spacer.
   c. Pull the plastic cam assembly off the wheel bearing adjusting nut and remove the thrust washer and needle thrust bearing from the adjusting nut.
   d. Loosen the wheel bearing adjusting nut from the spindle. While rotating the hub and rotor, tighten the wheel bearing adjusting nut to 35 ft. lbs. (47 Nm) to seat the bearings.
   e. Spin the rotor and back off the nut ¼ turn. Retighten the nut to 16 inch lbs. (1.8 Nm).
   f. Install the locking hub assembly in the reverse order of removal.

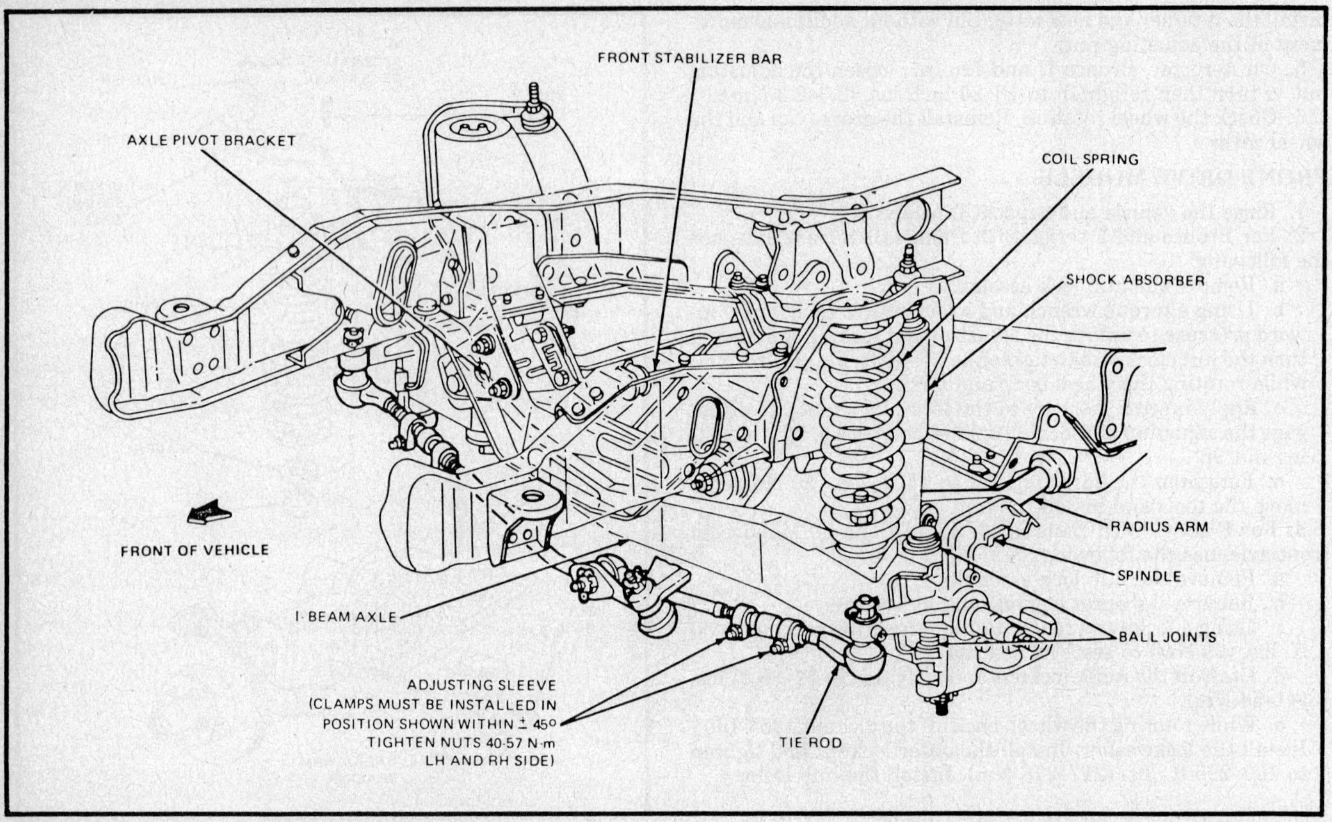

Front suspension—Ranger and Bronco II (2 × 4)

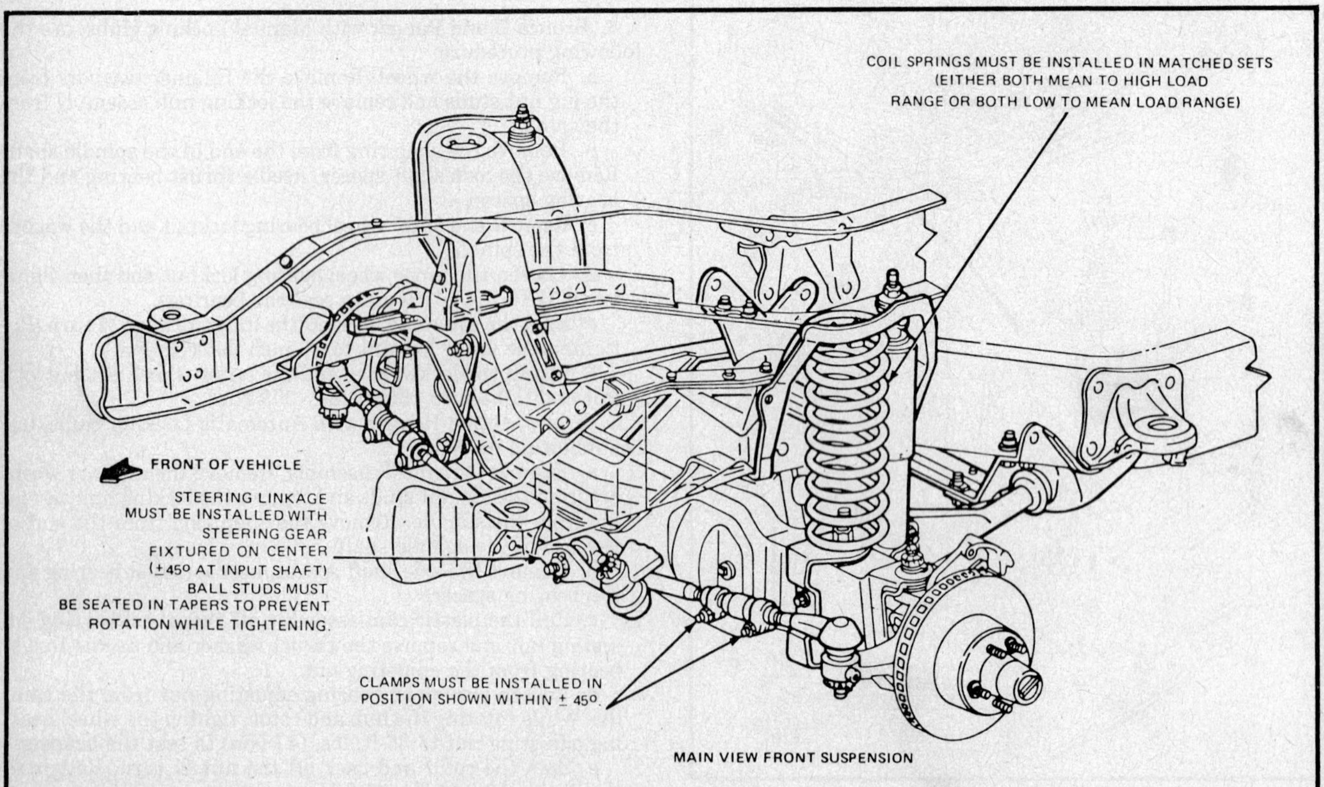

Front suspension—Ranger and Bronco II (4 × 4)

Stabilizer Bar

Removal and Installation

E AND F SERIES EXCEPT 4WD

1. Disconnect the left and right ends of the bar from the link assembly attached to the I-Beam bracket.
2. Disconnect the retainer bolts and remove the stabilizer bar.
3. Disconnect the link assemblies by looosening the right and left locknuts from their I-Beam brackets.
4. Install in the reverse order of removal.

NOTE: The link must be installed with the bend facing forward on E series. On F series, right and left link assemblies are stamped with an "R" or an "L" to identify them.

BRONCO AND F 150 4WD

1. Disconnect the stabilizer bar from the connecting links. Remove the nuts and bolts of the stabilizer bar retainer.
2. Remove the insulator assembly. To remove the mounting bracket, the coil spring must be removed. The stud does not have to be removed.
3. To reinstall the mounting bracket, locate the casting so that the locating tang is positioned in the radius arm notch or quad shock bracket notch.
4. Reinstall the stabilizer bar in the reverse order of removal.

F 250 4WD

1. Remove the bolts, washers and the nuts securing the links to the spring seat caps. If equipped with a Dana Model 60 Monobeam front axle, the links are secured to the mounting brackets.
2. Disconnect the links from the stabilizer bar and remove them.
3. Remove the retainers from the mounting bracket. Remove the stabilizer bar.
4. Installation is the reverse of the removal procedure.

BRONCO II

1. Remove the bolts and the retainers from the center and the right hand end of the stabilizer bar.
2. Disconnect the stabilizer bar from the stabilizer link.
3. Remove the stabilizer bar and bushings.
4. Installation is the reverse of removal.

RANGER

1. Remove the nuts and U-bolts retaining the lower shock bracket/stabilizer bar bushing to the radius arm.
2. Remove the retainers and remove the stabilizer bar and bushing.
3. Install in the reverse order of removal.

AEROSTAR

1. Remove the nuts retaining the stabilizer bar to the lower control arm link.
2. Remove the insulators and disconnect the bar from the links. If required, remove the links from the lower control arm.
3. Remove the bolts retaining the bar mounting bracket to the frame and remove the stabilizer bar.
4. Install in the reverse order of removal.

STEERING GEAR AND LINKAGE

For steering gear overhaul procedures, refer to the Unit Overhaul Section.

Manual Steering Gear

Removal and Installation

1. Raise the vehicle and support it safely with the front wheels in the straight ahead position.
2. On all except E series, disengage the flex coupling shield from the steering gear input shaft shield and slide it up the intermediate shaft.
3. Disconnect the flex coupling from the steering shaft flange by removing the two attaching nuts.
4. On E and F series, disconnect the drag link from the sector shaft pitman arm.
5. Remove the pitman arm from the gear sector shaft using proper pulling tools.

NOTE: Do not hammer on the end of the sector shaft or the tool, this will damage the steering gear.

6. While supporting the steering gear, disconnect it from the frame side rail. Lower the gear assembly from the vehicle.
7. Install in the reverse order of removal. Before installing the gear, rotate the input shaft from stop to stop counting the total number of turns. Then turn back exactly half way, placing the gear on center. Make sure that the flat on the gear input shaft is facing straight up and aligns with the flat on the flex coupling.

Adjustment

PRELOAD AND MESHLOAD – IN VEHICLE

1. Make sure that the steering column is properly aligned and that the intermediate shaft flex coupling is not distorted.
2. Disconnect the pitman arm at the ball stud.
3. Lubricate the wormshaft seal with a drop of automatic transmission fluid.

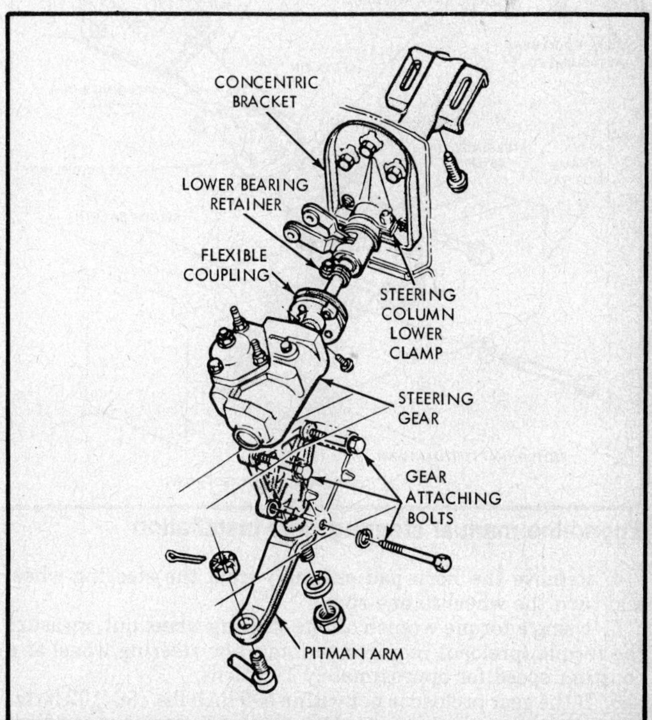

Steering gear installation – F-100, 250 and 350 (4 × 2)

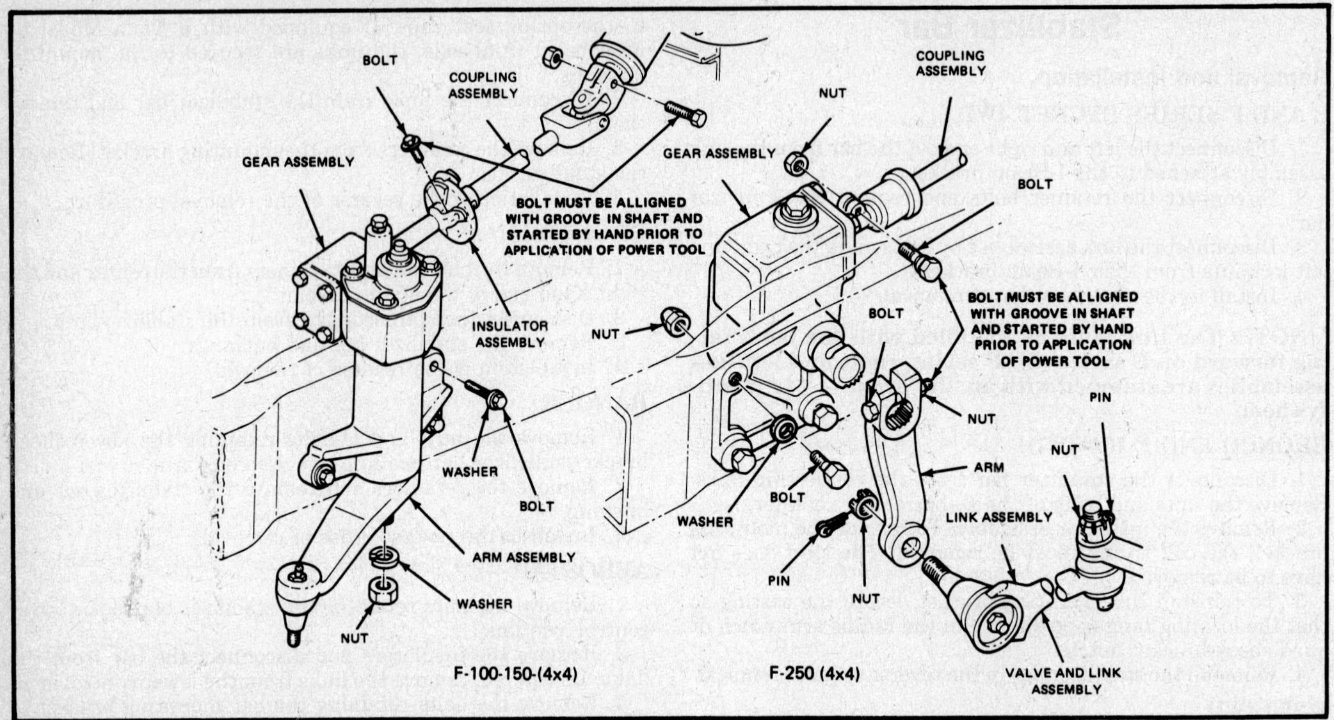

F-100, F-150 and F-250 manual steering gear installation

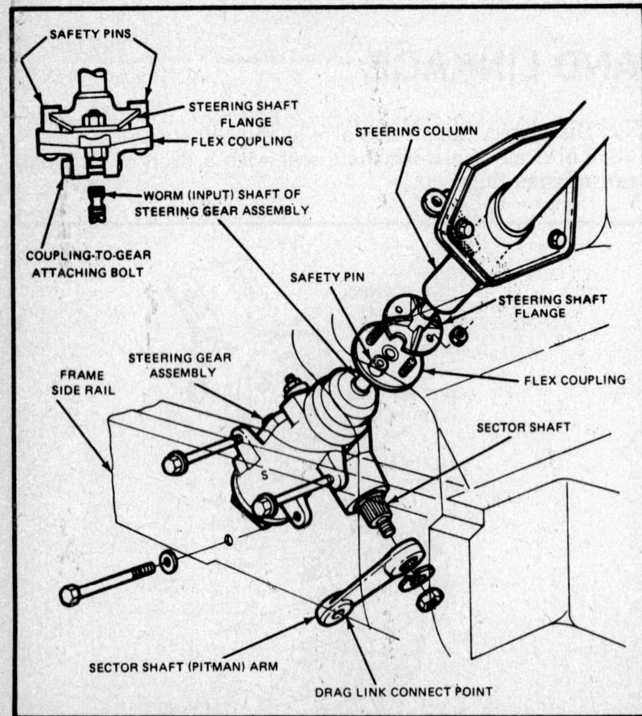

Econoline manual steering gear installation

4. Remove the horn pad assembly from the steering wheel and turn the wheel to one stop.

5. Using a torque wrench on the steering wheel nut, measure the torque (preload) required to rotate the steering wheel at a constant speed for approximately 1½ turns.

6. If the gear preload is not within 5–9 inch lbs. (56–102 Ncm) the preload must be readjusted. Gear must be removed to adjust worm preload.

7. With the torque wrench still on the steering wheel nut, observe the highest reading (meshload) by rotating the steering shaft 90° either way across center. The meshload must be within 9–14 inch lbs. (102–158 Ncm) and at least 2 inch lbs. (23 Ncm) over the preload.

8. If adjustment is required, turn the sector shaft adjusting screw. Hold the screw and tighten the locknut to 25 ft. lbs. (34 Nm)

Manual Rack and Pinion

Removal and Installation

1. Raise the vehicle and support it safely with the front wheels in the straight ahead position.

2. To center the steering gear, rotate the input shaft from stop to stop counting the total number of turns. Then turn back exactly half way placing the gear on center.

3. Remove the bolt retaining the intermediate steering column shaft to the steering gear pinion. Separate the shaft from the pinion.

4. Separate the tie rod ends from the spindle arms using a pitman arm puller.

5. Support the steering gear and disconnect it from the crossmember. Remove the gear from the vehicle.

6. Installation is the reverse of the removal procedure.

Power Steering Gear

Removal and Installation

1. Disconnect the pressure and return lines from the gear. Plug the lines and the ports in the gear to prevent entry of dirt.

2. If equipped, remove the splash shield from the flex coupling. Disconnect the flex coupling at the steering gear.

3. Raise the vehicle and support it safely. Remove the pitman arm from the sector shaft.

4. Support the steering gear and remove the attaching bolts. Work the steering gear free from the flex coupling and remove the gear from the vehicle.

5. Install in the reverse order of removal procedure.

Adjustment

1. Make sure that the steering column is correctly aligned.
2. Disconnect the steering linkage from the pitman arm on the steering gear. Remove the horn pad.
3. Disconnect the fluid reservoir return line and cap the reservoir return line tube. Place the end of the return line in a clean container and turn the steering wheel back and forth several times to empty the steering gear.
4. Turn the steering wheel nut with an inch pound torque wrench slowly. Find the torque required at $\frac{1}{2}$ turn off right and left stops, $\frac{1}{2}$ turn off center both right and left, and over-center (full turn). The over-center torque should be 4–6 inch lbs. more than the end readings, but the total over-center torque must not exceed 14 inch lbs.

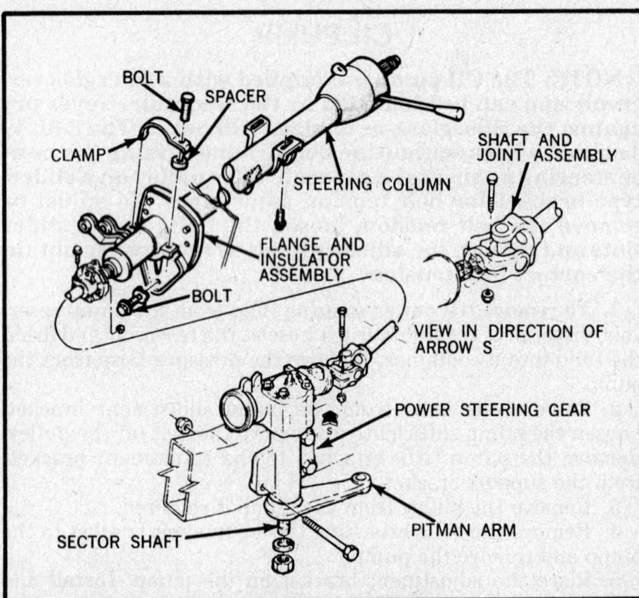

Bronco power steering gear installation

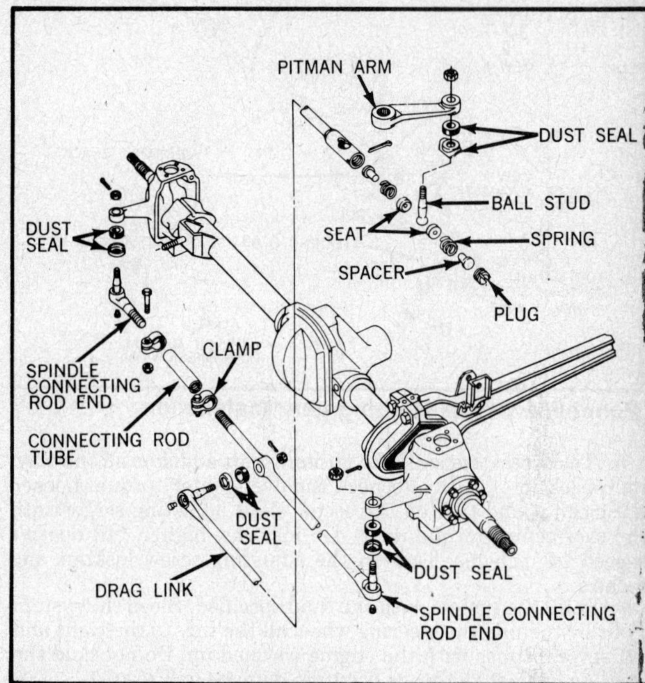

Steering linkage – F-100 and (4 x 4) Bronco

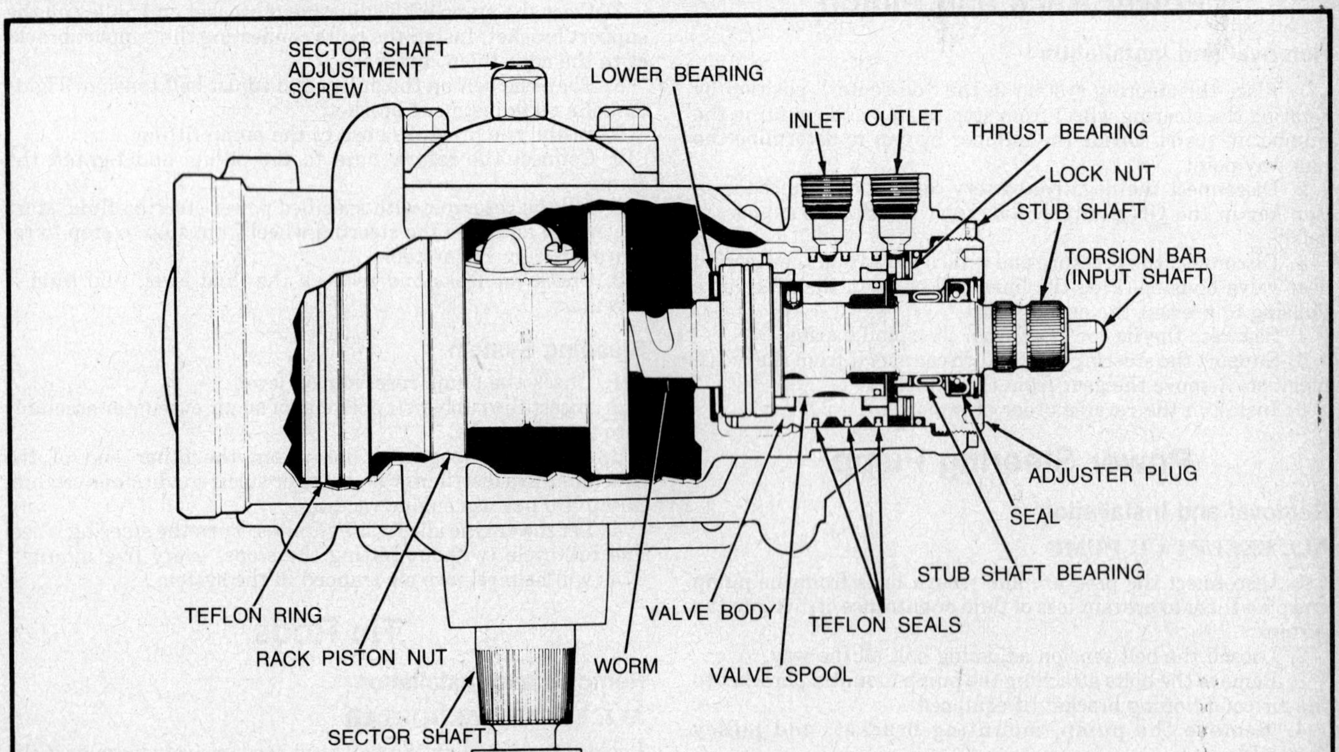

Ford integral power steering gear

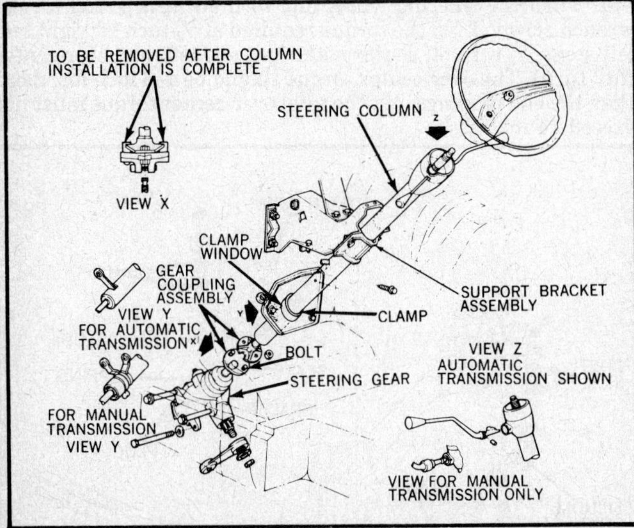

Econoline power steering gear installation

5. To correct, back off the pitman shaft adjuster all the way, then back in ½ turn. Recheck the over-center torque. Loosen the locknut and tighten the sector shaft adjusting screw until the over-center torque reads 4–6 inch lbs. higher, but doesn't exceed 14 inch lbs. Tighten the adjusting screw locknut and recheck.
6. Refill the system with the fluid specified. Bleed the system of air by turning the steering wheel all the way to the right and left several times with the engine warmed up. Do not hold the steering against the stops or pump damage will result.

Power Rack and Pinion

Removal and Installation

1. Place the steering system in the "on-center" position by rotating the steering wheel from stop to stop and counting the number of turns. Divide the number by two to determine the half way point.
2. Disconnect the negative battery cable and leave the ignition key in the ON position. Raise the vehicle and support it safely.
3. Disconnect the pressure and return lines from the steering gear valve housing. Plug the lines and ports in the gear valve housing to prevent the entry of dirt.
4. Separate the tie rod ends from the spindle arms.
5. Support the steering gear and disconnect it from the crossmember. Remove the gear from the vehicle.
6. Install in the reverse order of removal.

Power Steering Pump

Removal and Installation

ALL EXCEPT CII PUMP

1. Disconnect the pressure and return lines from the pump and plug them to prevent loss of fluid or entrance of dirt into the system.
2. Loosen the belt tension adjusting bolt all the way.
3. Remove the bolts attaching the pump mounting bracket to the air conditioning bracket (if equipped).
4. Remove the pump, mounting bracket, and pulley asssembly.
5. Install the pump, bracket and pulley assembly and loosely attach the bolts that secure the pump mounting bracket to the air conditioning bracket (if equipped).
6. Install the drive belts on the pulley.
7. Loosely install the belt tension adjusting nut.
8. Pry between the pump adjustment bracket and the engine block until correct tension is achieved. While still holding this tension, tighten the adjusting bolt.
9. Tighten all attaching bolts.
10. Connect the pressure and return lines to the pump.
11. Fill the reservoir with power steering fluid. Bleed the air from the system by turning the steering wheel from left to right several times. Inspect for leaks.

CII PUMP

NOTE: The CII pump is equipped with a fiberglas reservoir and can be identified by the reservoir. Never pry against the fiberglass, as damage will occur. The 3.8L V-6 engine with a serpentine belt driving driving the power steering pump uses a separate idler pulley on a slider-type bracket for belt tension adjustment. To adjust or remove the belt tension, loosen the bolts in the slider slots and tighten the adjusting belt as required to obtain the correct belt tension.

1. To remove the power steering fluid from the pump reservoir, disconnect the fluid return hose at the reservoir and drain the fluid into a container. Remove the pressure hose from the pump.
2. Remove the bolts from the pump adjustment bracket. Loosen the pump sufficiently to remove the belt off the pulley. Remove the pump (still attached to the adjustment bracket) from the support bracket.
3. Remove the pulley from the pump if required.
4. Remove the bolts attaching the adjustment bracket to the pump and remove the pump.
5. Place the adjustment bracket on the pump. Install and tighten the bolts to specification.
6. Install the pulley on the pump if removed.
7. Place the pump with adjustment bracket and pulley on the support bracket. Install the bolts connecting the support bracket to the adjustment bracket.
8. Place the belt on the pulley and adjust belt tension. Tighten bolts on adjustment bracket.
9. Install the pressure hose to the pump fitting.
10. Connect the return hose to the pump, and tighten the clamp.
11. Fill the reservoir with specified power steering fluid, start the engine and turn the steering wheel from stop to stop to remove air from the system.
12. Check for leaks and recheck the fluid level. Add fluid if necessary.

Bleeding System

1. Check the pump reservoir oil level.
2. Insert the rubber stopper end of an air evacuator assembly into the filler tube.
3. Connect a length of hose from the other end of the evacuator to a distributor machine or an air conditioner vacuum pump. Do not use engine vacuum.
4. Let the engine idle for 15 minutes. Turn the steering wheel one full cycle (without hitting the stops) every five minutes. This will help remove air trapped in the system.

Tie Rods

Removal and Installation

ALL EXCEPT AEROSTAR

Replace the drag link if a ball stud is excessively loose or if the drag link is bent. Do not attempt to straighten a drag link. Replace the connecting rod if the ball stud is excessively loose, if the connecting rod is bent or if the threads are stripped. Do not attempt to straighten connecting rod. After installing a connect-

ing rod or adjusting toe-in, check to insure that the adjustment sleeve clamps are correctly positioned.

1. Remove the cotter pins and nuts from the drag link, ball studs and from the right connecting rod ball stud.
2. Remove the right connecting rod ball stud from the drag link.
3. Remove the drag link ball studs from the spindle and the Pitman arm.
4. Position the new drag link, ball studs in the spindle, and Pitman arm and install nuts.
5. Position the right connecting rod ball stud in the drag link and install nut.
6. Tighten the nuts to 50–75 ft. lbs. and install the cotter pins.
7. Remove the cotter pin and nut from the connecting rod.
8. Remove the ball stud from the mating part.
9. Loosen the clamp bolt and turn the rod out of the adjustment sleeve. Count the number of turns for approximate position when installing.
10. Lubricate the threads of the new connecting rod, and turn it into the adjustment sleeve to about the same distance the old rods were installed. This will provide an approximate toe-in setting. Position the connecting rod ball studs in the spindle arms.
11. Install the nuts on to the connecting rod ball studs, tighten the nut to 50–75 ft. lbs. and install the cotter pin.
12. Check the toe-in and adjust, if necessary. After checking or adjusting toe-in, center the adjustment sleeve clamps between the locating nibs, position the clamps and tighten the nuts to 29–41 ft. lbs.

AEROSTAR

1. Place the steering wheel and the front wheels in the "on-center" position.
2. Separate the tie rod assembly from the spindle arm.
3. Hold the tie rod with a wrench and loosen the tie rod jam nut.
4. Mark the exact position of the tie rod end on the tie rod threads. Grip the tie rod with a pair of pliers and remove the tie rod end from the tie rod.
5. Install in the reverse order of removal.

BRAKE SYSTEM

For brake system overhaul service, refer to the Unit Overhaul Section.

Master Cylinder

Removal and Installation

1. If stoplight switch is mounted on the master cylinder, disconnect wires.
2. On dash-mounted master cylinders, disconnect the dust boot from the rear of the master cylinder at the dash panel. If the boot is connected to the master cylinder only, leave it in place.
3. Disconnect the hydraulic line(s) from the master cylinder.
4. Disconnect the brake pedal pushrod.
5. Remove the master cylinder retaining bolts. Remove the master cylinder from the vehicle.
6. Installation is the reverse of the removal procedure.

BLEEDING

Procedure

1. Support the master cylinder body in a soft-jawed vise, and fill both reservoirs with extra heavy duty brake fluid.
2. Loosely install plugs in the front and rear outlet ports. Depress the primary piston several times until air bubbles no longer appear in the brake fluid.

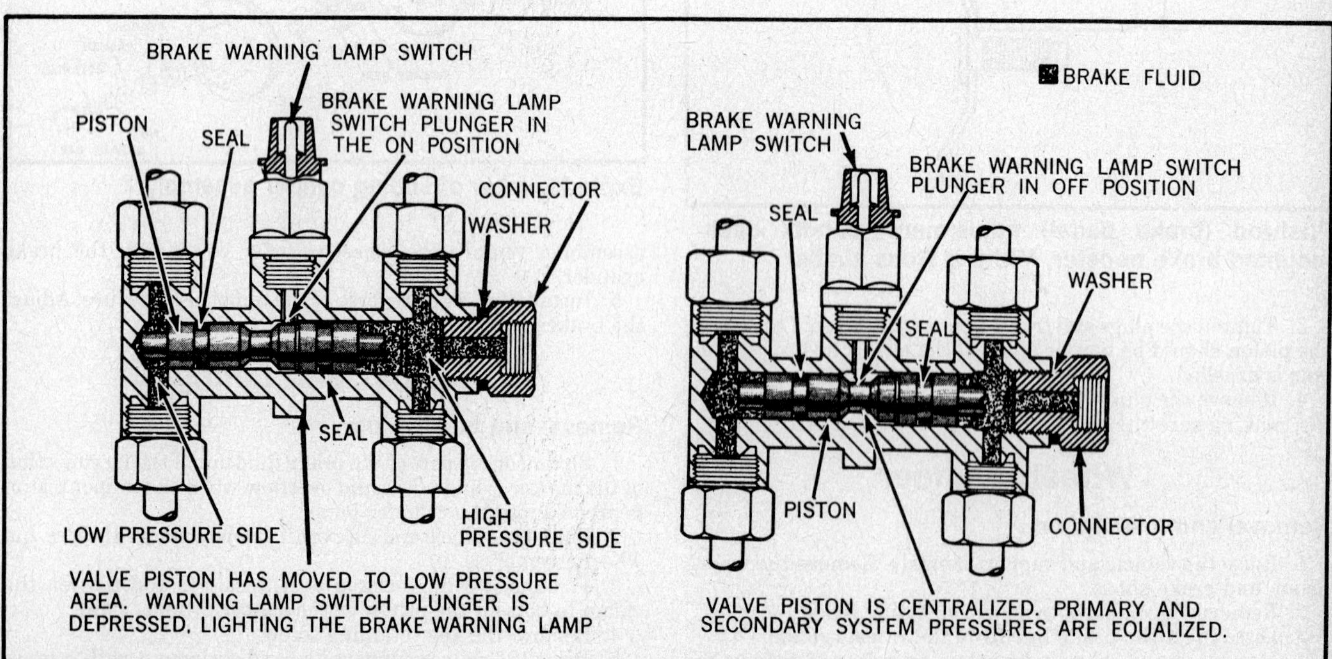

Brake differential valve—100-400 series

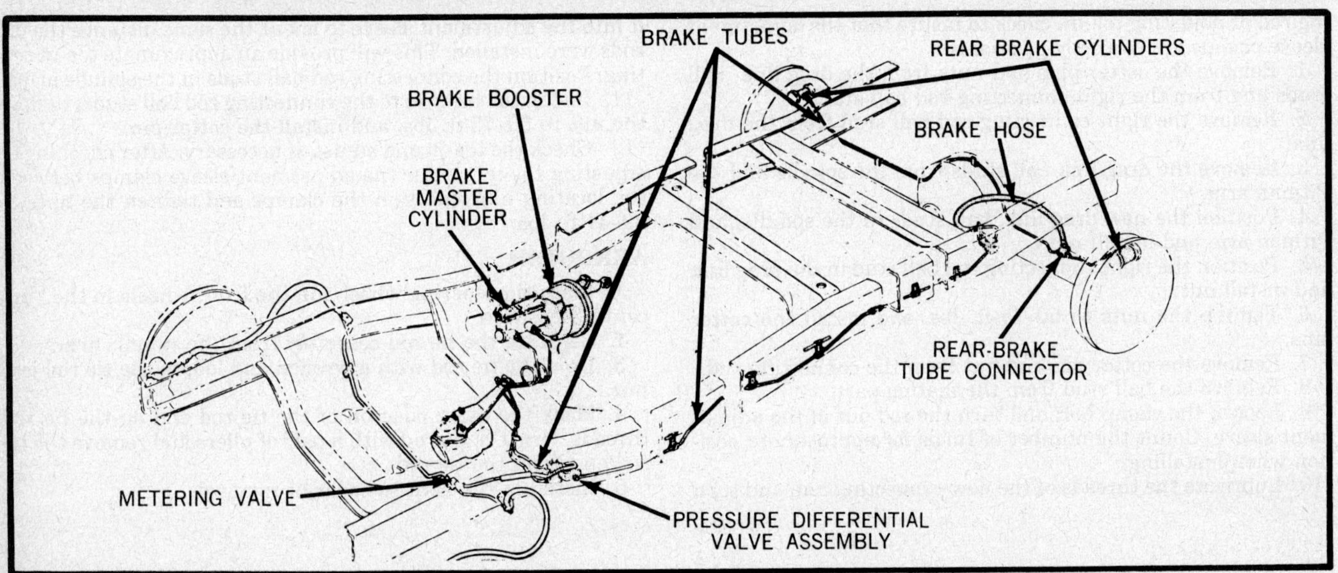

Disc brake system

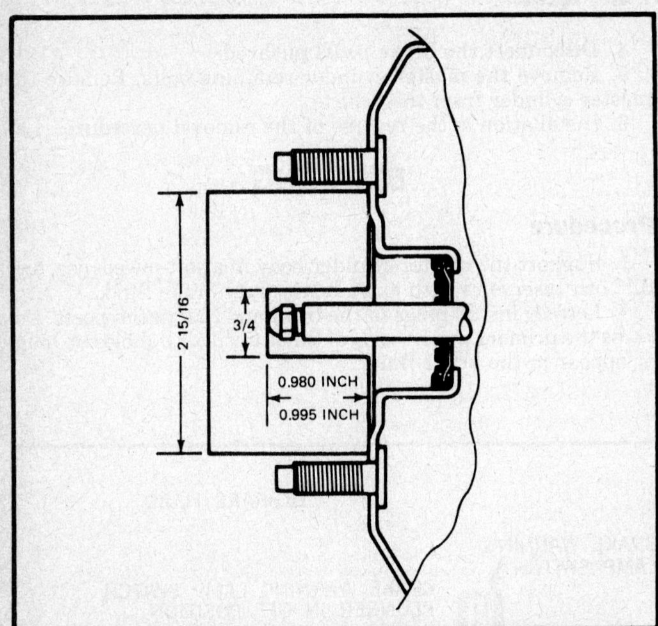

Pushrod (brake pedal) adjustment—Bendix dash mounted brake booster, Midland Ross similar

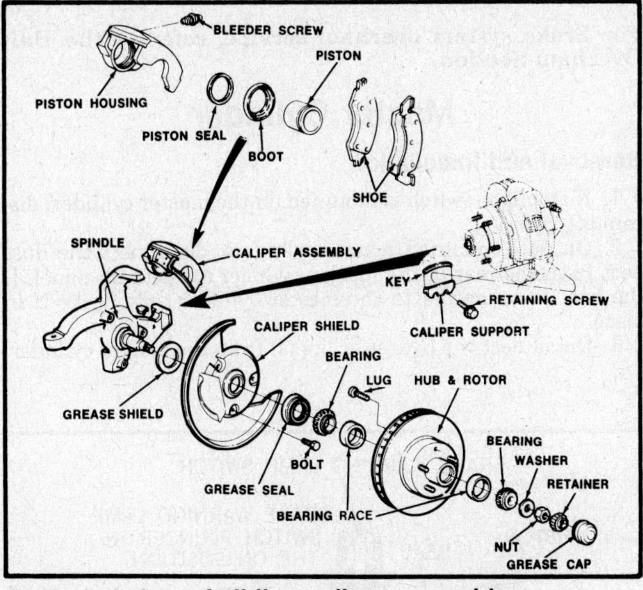

Exploded view of sliding caliper assembly

3. Tighten the plugs and try to depress the piston. Depressing the piston should be harder after all the air in the brake reservoir is expelled.

4. Remove the plugs. Install the cover and diaphragm assembly, making sure the cover retainer is tightened securely.

Wheel Cylinder

Removal and Installation

1. Raise the vehicle and support it safely. Remove the wheel, drum, and brake shoes.
2. Remove the cylinder to shoe connecting links.
3. Disconnect the brake line from the wheel cylinder.
4. Remove the wheel cylinder retaining bolts and remove the cylinder from the brake backing plate. On two-cylinder brake assemblies remove the wheel cylinder cover with the brake cylinder.
5. Installation is the reverse of the removal procedure. Adjust the brakes and bleed the system as required.

Caliper and Lining

Removal and Installation

1. Siphon or dip part of the brake fluid out of the large section of the master cylinder to avoid overflow when the caliper piston is pressed into the cylinder bore.
2. Raise the vehicle and support it safely. Remove the tire and wheel assembly.
3. Position a 8 in. C-clamp on the caliper and tighten the clamp to bottom the piston in the caliper cylinder bore.
4. Remove the key retaining screw.
5. Drive the caliper support key and spring out with a brass rod and light hammer.

6. Disconnect the brake hose from the inlet port. Cap the hose and inlet port to prevent fluid leakage.
7. Remove the caliper from the spindle assembly by pushing it downward against the spindle and rotating the upper end upward out of the spindle assembly.
8. Remove the outer shoe and lining from the caliper. Remove the inner shoe and lining from the spindle assembly. Remove the shoe anti-rattle clip from the lower shoe abutment surface on the spindle assembly.
9. Thoroughly clean the areas of the caliper and spindle assembly that come in contact during the sliding action of the caliper.
10. Installation is the reverse of the removal procedure. Use new components as required. Bleed the system as required.

Rotors

Removal and Installation

1. Raise the front of the vehicle and support it safely. Remove the wheel.
2. Remove the caliper assembly from the rotor and support it out of the way with wire.
3. Remove the dust cap, cotter pin, nut, washer and outer bearing and remove the rotor from the spindle.
4. On 4WD vehicles, the locking hub assembly must also be removed.
5. Install in the reverse order of removal.

Power Brake Boosters

Removal and Installation

1. Disconnect the negative battery cable. Remove retaining nuts and master cylinder from booster.
2. Loosen hose clamp and remove manifold vacuum hose from booster.
3. From inside the cab, remove the attaching bolt, nut and plastic bushings and disconnect the booster pushrod from the brake pedal.
4. Remove nuts that retain the booster mounting bracket to the dash panel.
5. Remove the booster assembly from engine compartment.
6. To install, mount the booster and bracket assembly to the engine side of the dash panel by sliding the bracket mounting bolts and valve operating rod in through the holes in the dash panel.
7. From inside the cab, install the booster mounting bracket to dash panel retaining nuts.
8. Position the master cylinder to the booster assembly and install the retaining nuts.
9. Connect the manifold vacuum hose to the booster and secure with clamp.
10. From inside the cab connect the booster valve operating rod to the brake pedal with the attaching bolt, nut and plastic bushings.
11. Start engine and check operation of the brake system.

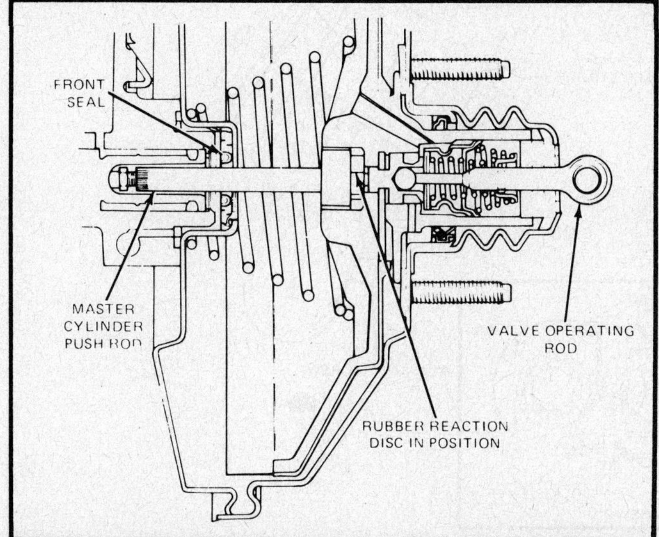

Single diaphragm vacuum booster cross section

Brake Pedal Adjustment

1. Remove the master cylinder.
2. Fabricate a gauge and place it against the master cylinder mounting surface on the booster body.
3. Adjust the push rod screw until the end of the screw just touches the inner edge of the slot in the gauge.
4. Install the master cylinder.

Stop Light Switch

The switch should be checked on vehicles with dragging or lock-

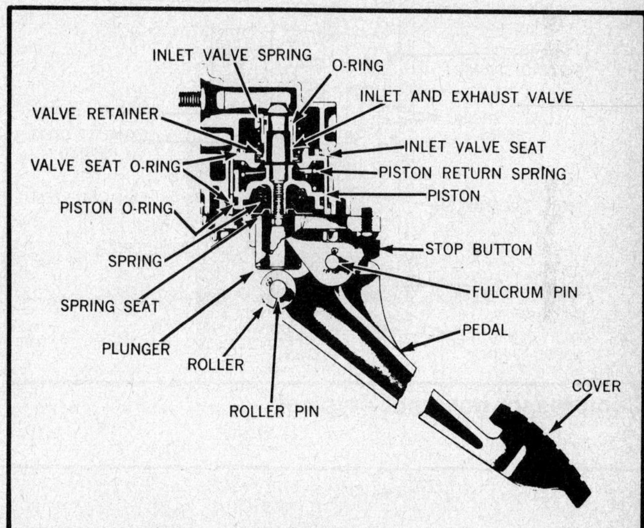

Foot control valve—typical

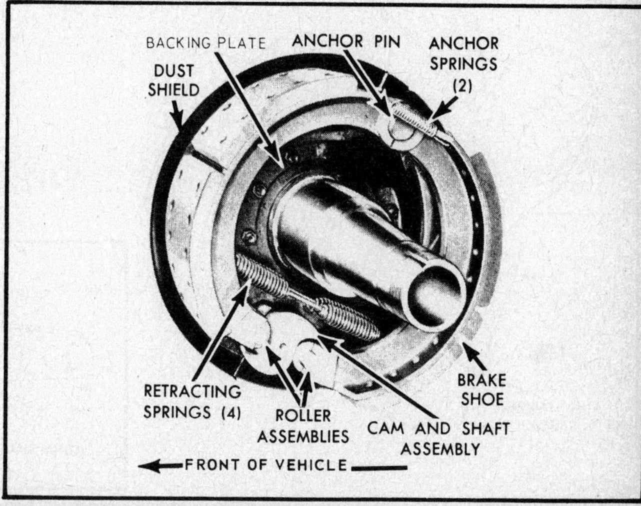

Cam type brake assembly (rear)

ing brakes. An improperly positioned stop light switch may restrict the brake pedal from returning to its non applied position and prevent the brake fluid from returning to the master cylinder reservoir which can cause dragging or locked brakes.

Check switch for proper seating by pulling the brake pedal with no more than 25 lbs. force, which will seat the switch properly and may relieve these conditions.

When installing a new stop light switch be sure to insert the switch into the retainer on the brake pedal by pushing the switch rearward until it bottoms in the brake switch bracket. Then manually pull the brake pedal rearward against stop to set switch in proper position.

Adjustment

Install the switch into the pedal bracket as far as possible and pull the pedal to its extreme return position to properly set the stop lamp switch assembly.

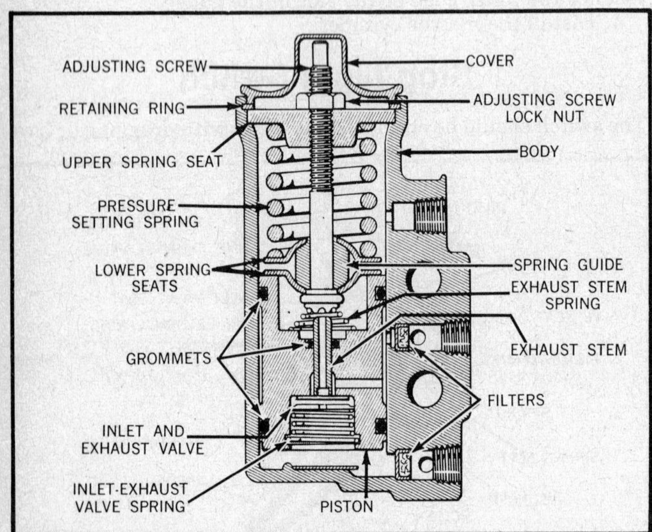

Compressor governor—typical

Parking Brake Cables

ALL EXCEPT AEROSTAR

Removal and Installation

EQUALIZER TO CONTROL ASSEMBLY

1. Raise the vehicle and support it safely.
2. Back off the equalizer nut and remove slug of front cable from the tension limiter.
3. Remove the parking brake cable from the bracket or crossmember. Lower the vehicle.
4. Remove the forward ball end of the parking brake cable from the control clevis.

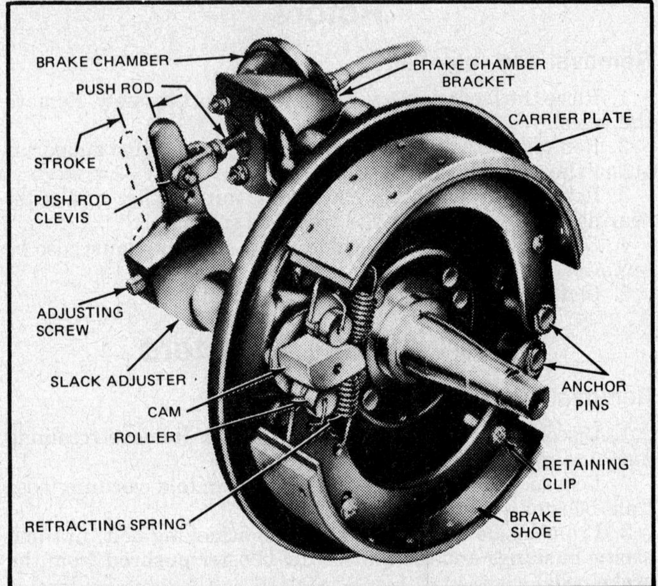

Cam type brake assembly (front) showing slack adjuster adjustment

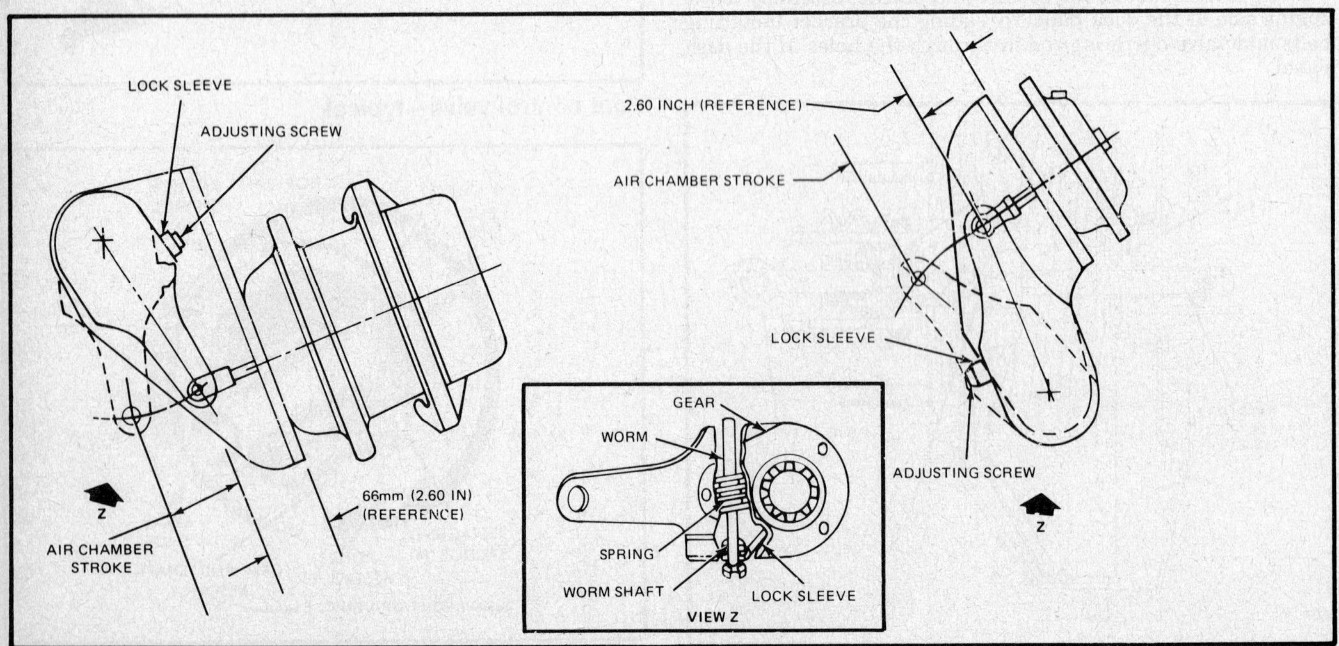

Slack adjuster brake preliminary adjustment

5. Remove the cable from the control by compressing the conduit end fitting prongs.
6. Using a cord attached to the control lever end of the cable, remove the cable from the vehicle.
7. Install in the reverse order of removal.

EQUALIZER TO REAR WHEEL

1. Raise the vehicle and support it safely.
2. Remove the wheel, tension limiter and brake drum.
3. Remove the lock nut on the threaded rod and disconnect the cable from the equalizer.
4. Working on the wheel side, compress the prongs on the cable retainer so they can pass through the hole in the brake backing plate.

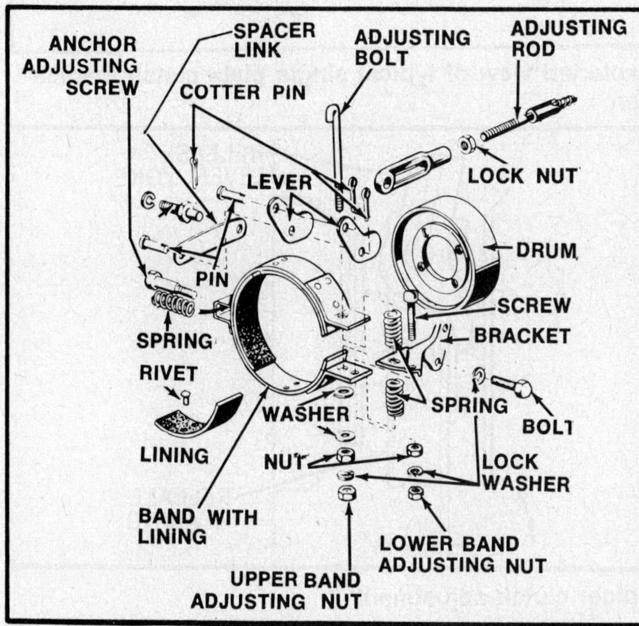

Exploded view of external band type parking brake

5. With the spring tension off of the parking brake lever, lift the cable out of the slot in the lever and remove the cable through the brake backing plate hole.
6. Install in the reverse order of removal.

AEROSTAR

Removal and Installation

1. Place the control in the released position and insert the lock pin in the control assembly.
2. Disconnect the rear parking brake cables from the equalizer. Remove the equalizer from the front cable.
3. Remove the cover from the underbody reinforcemnet bracket.
4. Remove the cable anchor pin from the pivot hole in the control ratchet plate. Guide the front cable from the control.
5. Compress the retainer fingers of the front cable and push the retainer rearward through the hole.
6. Compress the retainer fingers on the rear crossmember and remove the retainer from the rear crossmember.
7. Pull the cable ends through the crossmember and remove the cable.
8. Install in the reverse order of removal.

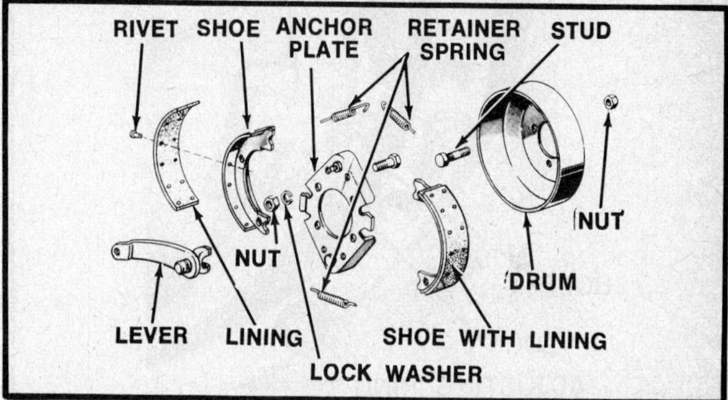

Exploded view of internal shoe type parking brake

CLUTCH

Clutch Assembly

HYDRAULIC/MANUAL

Removal and Installation

1. Disconnect the release lever retracting spring and pushrod at the lever.
2. If so equipped, remove the slave cylinder attaching bolts.
3. Remove the transmission.
4. If there is no dust cover on the flywheel housing remove the starter. Remove the release lever and bearing and remove the housing.
5. If the flywheel housing has a dust cover, remove it with the housing. Remove the release lever and bearing from the clutch housing. Mark the pressure plate and cover assembly and the flywheel, so that the parts can be reinstalled in the same position.
6. Loosen the pressure plate attaching bolts evenly until the springs are loose then remove the bolts, pressure plate assembly and clutch disc. Do not remove the pilot bushing unless it is to be replaced.
7. To install, position the disc on the flywheel and install a pilot tool or spare transmission spline shaft.
8. Install the pressure plate assembly over the aligning tool and align the marks made during removal. Install the retaining bolts, tightening securely.
9. Remove pilot tool and apply a light coat of lithium-base grease to the hub splines of the clutch disc.
10. Apply lithium-base grease to the sides of the driving lugs.
11. Position throwout bearing and bearing hub on the release lever and install release lever on the trunnion in the flywheel housing.
12. Apply a light film of lithium-base grease to the release lever fingers and to the lever trunnion or fulcrum. Fill the angular groove of the release bearing hub with grease.
13. If removed, install the flywheel housing, tightening bolts securely.
14. Install the starter motor if it was removed.
15. Apply a light film of lithium-base grease to the transmission front bearing retainer and install the transmission assembly on the clutch housing, tightening attaching bolts securely.
16. Install the slave cylinder, if applicable.
17. Adjust the clutch linkage and install the clutch housing dust cover.

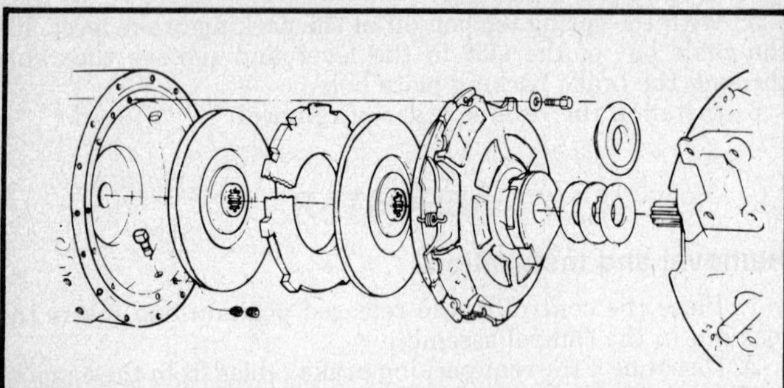

Exploded view of 14 and 15½ double disc clutch, typical installation

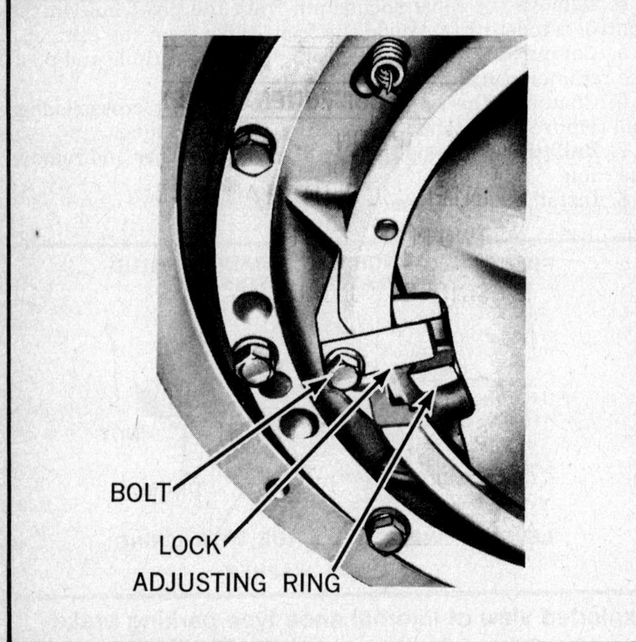

Internal clutch adjustment

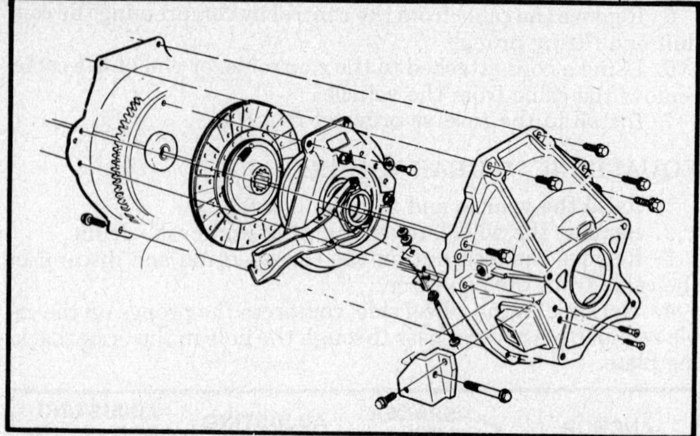

Exploded view of typical single plate clutch installation

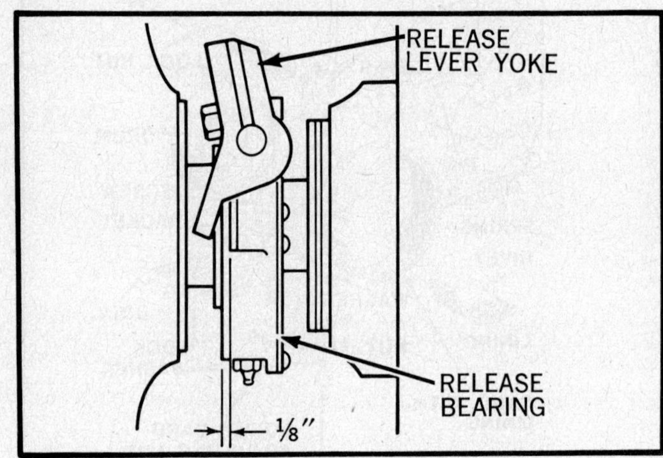

Spicer clutch adjustment

LINKAGE

Adjustment

MANUAL

1. Measure the distance from the clutch pedal pad to the steering wheel rim. Depress the pedal until the free travel between the release bearing and the pressure plate is taken up. The distance between the two measurements is the free travel. If the free travel measurement is less than ½ inch (12.7mm) or more than 2 inches (50.8mm), the clutch linkage must be adjusted.
2. Remove the retracting spring. Loosen the two jam nuts on the release rod and back off both nuts several turns.
3. Slide the release rod extension against the release lever. Push the release rod forward against the equalizer bar lever to eliminate all free play from the system.
4. Insert a 0.135 in. thick guage between the jam nut and the rod extension. Tighten the first jam nut finger tight against the gauge. Tighten the second jam nut finger tight against the first jam nut then tighten it to 15–20 ft. lbs. (21–27 Nm).
5. Recheck the pedal free travel.

HYDRAULIC

The hydraulic clutch system provides automatic adjustment. No adjustment of clutch linkage or pedal position is required.

MASTER CYLINDER

Removal and Installation

1. Disconnect the master cylinder push rod by prying the retainer bushing and the push rod off the shaft.
2. Remove the master cylinder and reservoir from the engine compartment.
3. Remove the tubing to the slave cylinder and plug the lines to prevent entry of dirt.
4. Install in the reverse order of removal.

SLAVE CYLINDER

Removal and Installation

BRONCO, E AND F SERIES

NOTE: Prior to any vehicle service that requires removal of the slave cylinder, the master cylinder push rod must be disconnected from the clutch pedal. If not disconnected, permanent damage to the slave cylinder will occur if the clutch pedal is depressed while the slave cylinder is disconnected.

1. On the 420 CID (6.9L Diesel) and the 460 CID (7.5L V8) engines, lift the two retaining tabs of the slave cylinder retaining bracket. Disengage the tabs from the bell housing lugs and slide outward to remove.
2. On the 300 CID (4.9L Six Cyl.) and other V8 engines, re-

move the C-clip from the slave cylinder. Disengage the push rod from the release lever as the slave cylinder is removed.

3. Install in the reverse order.

AEROSTAR, BRONCO II AND RANGER

1. Remove the transmission from the vehicle.
2. Remove the clutch housing from the transmission.
3. Remove the slave cylinder from the transmission input shaft.
4. Install in the reverse order of removal.

MANUAL TRANSMISSION

For overhaul service procedures, refer to the Unit Overhaul Section.

Manual Transmission Assembly

FORD 3.03 THREE SPEED

Removal and Installation

BRONCO

1. Shift the transfer case into Neutral.
2. Remove the bolts attaching the fan shroud to the radiator support, if so equipped.
3. Raise and support the vehicle safely.
4. Support the transfer case shield with a jack and remove the bolts that attach the shield to the frame side rails. Remove the shield.
5. Drain the transmission and transfer case lubricant. To drain the transmission lubricant, remove the lower extension housing-to-transmission bolt.
6. Disconnect the front and rear driveshafts at the transfer case.
7. Disconnect the speedometer cable at the transfer case.
8. Disconnect the T.R.S. switch, if so equipped.
9. **Disconnect the shift rods from the transmission shift levers. Place the First-Reverse gear shift lever into the first gear position and insert the fabricated tool. The tool consists of a length of rod, the same diameter as the holes in the shift levers, which is bent in such a way to fit in the holes in the two shift levers and hold them in the position stated above. More important, this tool will prevent the input shaft roller bearings from dropping into the transmission and output shaft. This tool is a must when performing this operation.**
10. Support the engine with a jack.
11. Remove the two cotter pins, bolts, washers, plate and insulators that secure the crossmember to the transfer case adapter.
12. Remove the crossmember-to-frame side support attaching bolts.
13. Position a transmission jack under the transfer case and remove the upper insulators from the crossmember. Remove the crossmember.
14. Roll back the boot enclosing the transfer case shift linkage. Remove the threaded cap holding the shift lever assembly to the shift bracket. Remove the shift lever assembly.
15. Remove the two lower bolts attaching the transmission to the flywheel housing.
16. Reposition the transmission jack under the transmission and secure it with a chain.
17. Remove the two upper bolts securing the transmission to the flywheel housing. Move the transmission and transfer case rearward and downward out of the vehicle.
18. Move the assembly to a bench and remove the transfer case-to-transmission attaching bolts.
19. Slide the transmission assembly off the transfer case.
20. To install, position the transfer case to the transmission. Apply an oil-resistant sealer to the bolt threads and install the attaching bolts. Tighten to 42–50 ft. lbs.
21. Position the transmission and transfer case on a transmission jack and secure them with a chain.
22. Raise the transmission and transfer case assembly into position and install the transmission case to the flywheel housing.
23. Install the two upper and two lower transmission attaching bolts and torque them to 37–42 ft. lbs.
24. Position the transfer case shift lever and install the threaded cap to the shift bracket. Reposition the rubber boot.
25. Raise the transmission and transfer case high enough to provide clearance for installing the crossmember. Position the upper insulators to the crossmember and install the crossmember-to-frame side support attaching bolts.
26. Align the bolt holes in the transfer case adapter with those in the crossmember, then lower the transmission and remove the jack.
27. Install the crossmember-to-transfer case adapter bolts, nuts, insulators, plates and washers. Tighten the nuts and secure them with cotter pins.
28. Remove the engine jack.
29. Remove the fabricated tool and connect each shift rod to its respective lever on the transmission. Adjust the linkage.
30. Connect the speedometer cable.
31. Connect the T.R.S. switch, if so equipped.
32. Install the front and rear driveshafts to the transfer case.
33. Fill the transmission and transfer case to the bottom of the filler hole with the recommended lubricant.
34. Position the transfer case shield to the frame side rails and install the attaching bolts.
35. Lower the vehicle.
36. Install the fan shroud, if so equipped.
37. Check the operation of the transfer case and the transmission shift linkage.

E SERIES

1. Raise and support the vehicle safely. Drain the lubricant from the transmission by removing the drain plug if the vehicle is so equipped. For models without drain plugs, remove the lower extension housing-to-transmission bolt.
2. Disconnect the driveshaft from the flange at the transmission. Secure the front end of the driveshaft out of the way with lock wire.
3. Disconnect the speedometer cable from the extension housing and disconnect the gear shift rods from the transmission shift levers. Remove the wire to the TCS switch if so equipped.
4. Position a transmission jack under the transmission. Secure the transmission to the jack.
5. Raise the transmission slightly and remove the four bolts retaining the transmission support crossmember to the frame side rails. Remove the bolt retaining the transmission extension housing to the crossmember.
6. Remove the four transmission-to-flywheel housing bolts.
7. Position engine support bar (tool T65E-6000-J) to the frame.
8. Lower the transmission.
9. To install, make certain that the machined surfaces of the transmission case and the flywheel housing are free of dirt, paint and burrs.
10. Install a guide pin in each lower mounting bolt hole.

11. Start the input shaft through the release bearing. Align the splines on the input shaft with the splines in the clutch disc. Move the transmission forward on the guide pins until the input shaft pilot enters the bearing or bushing in the crankshaft. If the transmission front bearing retainer binds up on the clutch release bearing hub, work the release bearing lever until the hub slides onto the transmission front bearing retainer. Install the two transmission-to-flywheel housing upper mounting bolts and lockwashers. Remove the two guide pins and install the lower mounting bolts and lockwashers.
12. Raise the jack slightly and remove the engine support bar.
13. Position the support crossmember on the frame side rails and install the retaining bolts. Install the extension housing-to-crossmember retaining bolt.
14. Connect the gear shift rods and the speedometer cable.
15. Install the driveshaft and torque the attaching bolts to specification.
16. Fill the transmission to the bottom of the filler hole with the recommended lubricant.
17. Adjust the clutch pedal free travel and shift linkage as required.

F SERIES

1. Raise and support the vehicle safely. Support the engine with a jack and wood block placed under the oil pan.
2. Drain the transmission lubricant by removing the drain plug if the vehicle is so equipped. For models without drain plugs, remove the lower extension housing-to-transmission bolt.
3. Position a transmission jack under the transmission.
4. Disconnect the gear shift linkage at the transmission.
5. If the vehicle has a four-wheel drive, remove the transfer case shift lever bracket from the transmission.
6. On the Warner T-85N model, disconnect the solenoid and governor wires at the connectors near the solenoid. Remove the overdrive wiring harness from its clip on the transmission. Disconnect the overdrive cable.
7. Disconnect the speedometer cable. Disconnect the driveshaft from the transmission.
8. Remove the transmission-to-clutch housing attaching bolts.
9. Move transmission to the rear until the input shaft clears the clutch housing and lower the transmission. Do not depress the clutch pedal while the transmission is removed.
10. Before installing the transmission, apply a light film of lubricant to the clutch disc splines, release bearing inner hub surfaces, release lever fulcrum and fork and the transmission front bearing retainer. Exercise care to avoid contaminating the clutch disc with excessive grease.
11. Place the transmission on a transmission jack. Raise the transmission until the input shaft splines are in line with the clutch disc splines. The clutch release bearing and hub must be properly positioned in the release lever fork.
12. Install a guide stud in each lower clutch housing-to-transmission case mounting bolt and align the splines on the input shaft with the splines on the clutch disc.
13. Slide the transmission forward on the guide studs until it contacts the clutch housing.
14. Install the two transmission to flywheel housing upper mounting bolts and nuts. Remove the two guide studs and install the lower mounting bolts.
15. Connect the speedometer cable and the driven gear.
16. Install the driveshaft.
17. Connect each shift rod to its respective lever on the transmission.
18. If the vehicle is equipped with four-wheel drive, install the four-wheel drive shaft bracket.
19. Fill the transmission to the proper level with an approved lubricant.
20. Adjust the clutch pedal free travel and shift linkage as required.

WARNER T 18 AND T 19 FOUR SPEED

Removal and Installation

EXCEPT 4 × 4 WITH T 18 TRANSMISSION AND 4 × 2 WITH T 19B TRANSMISSION

1. Disconnect the back-up light switch located at the rear of the gearshift housing cover.
2. Remove the rubber boot, floor mat, and the body floor pan cover, and remove the transmission shift lever. Remove the weather pad and pad retainer.
3. Raise and support the vehicle safely. Position a transmission jack under the transmission and disconnect the speedometer cable.
4. If the vehicle is equipped with band-type parking brake, disconnect the brake cable clevis at the cam. Remove the brake cable conduit clamp.
5. Remove the front U-joint flange attaching bolts. Remove the bolts that attach the coupling shaft center support to the crossmember and wire the coupling shaft and driveshaft to one side. Remove the transmission rear support, as required.
6. Remove the transmission attaching bolts.
7. Move the transmission to the rear until the input shaft clears the clutch housing, and lower the transmission.

NOTE: Before installing the transmission, apply a light film of lubricant to the clutch disc splines, release bearing inner hub surfaces, release lever fulcrum and fork, and the transmission front bearing retainer. Care must be exercised to avoid excessive grease from contaminating the clutch disc.

8. Place the transmission on a transmission jack, and raise the transmission until the input shaft splines are aligned with the clutch disc splines. The clutch release bearing and hub must be properly positioned in the release lever fork.
9. Install guide studs in the clutch housing and slide the transmission forward on the guide studs until it is in position on the clutch housing. Install the attaching bolts and nuts. Remove the guide studs and install the two lower attaching bolts.
10. Connect the speedometer cable and driven gear and parking brake clevis. Install the brake cable conduit clamp, and shift linkage.
11. Install the bolts attaching the coupling shaft center support to the crossmember.
12. Install the bolts attaching the front U-joint flange to the transmission output shaft flange. Install the transmission rear support, if removed.
13. Connect the back-up light switch.
14. Install the shift lever and lubricate the spherical ball seat with lubricant.
15. Install the weather pad and pad retainer. Install the floor pan cover, floor mat and boot.

4 × 4 (WITH T 18 TRANSMISSION)

1. Open the door and cover seat. Remove the shift knobs. Remove the transmission shift lever boot assembly.
2. Remove the screws holding the floor mat. Remove the screws holding the access cover to the floor pan. Place the shift lever in reverse and remove the cover.
3. Remove the insulator and the dust cover. Remove the transfer case shift lever. Remove the bolts holding the shift cover and the gasket.
4. Cover the shift cover opening to protect the transmission from dirt during the removal procedure.
5. Raise and support the vehicle safely. Drain the transmission.
6. Disconnect the front and the rear driveshaft from the transfer case and wire them out of the way. Remove the cotter pin that holds the shift link in place and remove the shift link.
7. Remove the speedometer cable from the transfer case. Position a transmission jack under the transfer case. Remove the

bolts holding the transfer case to the transmission and remove the transfer case from the vehicle.

8. Remove the bolts that hold the rear support bracket to the transmission.

9. Position a transmission jack under the transmission and remove the rear support bracket and brace. Remove the bolts that hold the transmission to the bell housing and remove the transmission.

10. To install, place the transmission on a transmission jack and install it in the vehicle. Install two guide pins in the bell housing top holes, to guide the transmission in place.

11. Install the two lower bolts, remove the guide pins and install the upper two bolts.

12. Continue the installation in the reverse order of the removal. Fill the transfer case and the transmission with lubricant. Lower the vehicle.

4 × 2 (WITH T 19B TRANSMISSION)

1. Remove the floor mat, and the body floor pan cover, and remove the gearshift lever shift ball and boot as an assembly. Remove the weather pad.

2. Raise and support the vehicle safely. Position a suitable jack under the transmission, and disconnect the speedometer cable.

3. Disconnect the back-up lamp switch located at the rear of the gear shift housing cover.

4. Disconnect the drive shaft or coupling shaft and clutch linkage from the transmission and wire it to one side.

5. Remove the transmission rear insulator and lower retainer. Remove the crossmember. Remove the transmission attaching bolts.

6. Move the transmission to the rear until the in shaft clears the clutch housing. Lower transmission.

7. Place the transmission on a suitable jack install guide studs in the clutch housing and raise the transmission until the input shaft splines are aligned with the clutch disc splines. The clutch release bearing and hub must be properly positioned in the release lever fork.

8. Slide the transmission forward on the guide stud until it is in position on the clutch housing. Install the attaching bolts and tighten them to 45–50 ft. lbs. Remove the guide studs and install the lower attaching bolts.

9. Install the crossmember. Position the insulator and retainer between the transmission and crossmember. Install bolts and tighten to 45–60 ft. lbs. Install the nut retaining the insulator and retainer to crossmember. Tighten to 50–70 ft. lbs.

10. Connect the speedometer cable and driven gear and clutch linkage.

11. Install the bolts attaching the front U-joint of the coupling shaft to the transmission output shaft flange. Install the transmission rear support and upper and lower absorbers. Connect the back-up lamp switch.

12. Install the shift lever, boot and shift ball as and assembly and lubricate the spherical ball seat with Multi-Purpose Long-Life Lubricant C1AZ-1959 (ESA-M1C75-B) or equivalent.

13. Install the weather pad. Install the floor pan cover and floor mat.

FOUR SPEED OVERDRIVE TRANSMISSION

Removal and Installation

1. Raise and support the vehicle safely. Mark the driveshaft so that it may be installed in the same position. Disconnect the driveshaft from the U-joint flange. Slide the driveshaft off the transmission output shaft and install the extension housing seal installation tool into the extension housing to prevent the transmission lubricant from leaking out.

2. Disconnect the speedometer cable at the extension housing. Remove the retaining clips, flat washers, and spring washers that secure the shift rods to the shift levers. Remove the bolts connecting the shift control to the transmission extension housing. Remove the nut connecting the shift control to the transmission case.

NOTE: A '6' or '8' is stamped on the transmission extension housing by the shift control plate bolt holes. The '6' and '8' refer to either a 6 or 8 cylinder engine application. The shift control plate bolts must be placed in the right holes for proper plate positioning dependent upon the engine used in the vehicle.

3. Remove the rear transmission support connecting bolts attaching the support on the crossmember to the transmission extension housing. Support the engine with a transmission jack and remove the extension housing-to-engine rear support attaching bolts.

4. Raise the rear of the engine high enough to relieve the weight from the crossmember. Remove the bolts retaining the crossmember to the frame side supports and remove the crossmember.

5. Support the transmission on a jack and remove the transmission-to-flywheel housing bolts. Move the transmission and the jack rearward until the transmission input shaft clears the flywheel housing. Lower the engine enough to obtain clearance for transmission removal and remove the unit.

NOTE: Do not depress the clutch pedal while the transmission is removed.

6. To install, make sure that the mounting surfaces of the transmission and the flywheel housing are free of dirt, paint, and burrs. Install two guide pins in the flywheel housing lower mounting bolt holes. Move the transmission forward on the guide pins until the input shaft splines enter the clutch hub splines and the case is positioned against the flywheel housing.

7. Install the two upper transmission mounting bolts, remove the guide pins and install the lower mounting bolts.

8. Continue the installation in the reverse order of the removal.

9. Fill the transmission to the proper level with lubricant. Lower the vehicle. Check the shift and crossover motion for full shift engagement and smooth crossover operation.

FOUR SPEED TRANSMISSION

Removal and Installation

RANGER AND BRONCO II

1. Place the gearshift lever in neutral. Remove the boot retainer screws. Remove the bolts attaching the retainer cover to the gearshift lever retainer. Disconnect the clutch master cylinder push rod from the clutch pedal.

2. Pull the gearshift lever assembly, shim and bushing straight up and away from the gearshift lever retainer. Cover the shift tower opening in the extension housing with a cloth.

3. Disconnect the clutch hydraulic system master clyinder push rod from the clutch pedal.

4. Open the hood and disconnect the negative battery cable from the battery terminal.

5. Raise and safely support the vehicle. Disconnect the driveshaft at the rear axle. Pull the driveshaft rearward and disconnect from the transmission. Install a suitable plug in the extension housing to prevent lubricant leakage.

6. Remove the clutch housing dust shield and slave cylinder and secure it at one side.

7. Remove the speedometer cable from the extension housing or from the speed control sensor, if so equipped.

8. Disconnect the starter motor and back-up lamp switch wires. Place a jack under the engine, protecting the oil pan with a wood block.

NOTE: If the vehicle is equipped with four wheel drive, remove the transfer case.

9. Remove the starter. Position a suitable jack under the transmission assembly. Remove the bolts attaching the transmission to the engine rear plate. Remove the nuts and bolts attaching the transmission mount and damper to the crossmember.
10. Remove the nuts attaching the crossmember to the frame side rails and remove the crossmember.
11. Lower the engine jack. Work the clutch housing off the locating dowels and slide the transmission rearward until the input shaft spline clears the clutch disc. Remove the transmission from the vehicle.
13. Make sure that the machined mating surfaces and the locating dowels on the engine rear plate are free of burrs, dirt or paint. Check the mating face of the clutch housing and the locating dowel holes for burrs, dirt or paint. Mount the transmission on a suitable jack. Position it under the vehicle and start the input shaft into the clutch disc. Align the splines on the input shaft with the splines in the clutch disc. Move the transmission forward and carefully seat the clutch housing on the locating dowels of the engine rear plate. The engine plate dowels must not shave or burr the clutch housing dowel holes.
14. Install the bolts that attach the clutch housing to the engine rear plate. Remove the transmission jack.
15. Install the starter motor.
16. Raise the engine and install the rear crossmember and attaching nuts and washers.
17. Install the bolts, nuts and washers attaching the transmission mount and damper to the crossmember. Remove the engine jack.

NOTE: On four wheel drive units install the transfer case.

18. Insert the driveshaft into the transmission extension housing and install the center bearing attaching nuts, washers and lockwashers.
19. Connect the driveshaft to the rear axle drive flange.
20. Connect the starter and back-up lamp switch wires. Install the clutch slave cylinder and dust shield on the clutch housing. Install the speedometer cable.
21. Check the transmission fluid level at the fill plug. Fill with specified lubricant, if necessary. Lower the vehicle.
22. Open the hood and connect the negative battery cable to the battery terminal.
23. Re-connect the clutch master cylinder push rod to the clutch pedal.
24. Remove the cloth from the shift tower opening in the extension housing. Avoid getting dirt inside the transmission.
25. Position the gearshift lever assembly straight up above the gearshift lever retainer, then insert the gearshift in the retainer. Install the bolts attaching the retainer cover to the gearshift lever retainer.
26. Install the cover boot with the retainer screws.

FIVE SPEED OVERDRIVE AND FIVE SPEED TRANSMISSION

Removal and Installation

AEROSTAR, BRONCO II AND RANGER

1. Place the gearshift lever in neutral. Remove the boot retainer screws. Remove the bolts attaching the retainer cover to the gearshift lever retainer. Disconnect the clutch master cylinder push rod from the clutch pedal.
2. Pull the gearshift lever assembly, shim and bushing straight up and away from the gearshift lever retainer. Cover the shift tower opening in the extension housing with a cloth.
3. Disconnect the clutch hydraulic system master cylinder push rod from the clutch pedal.
4. Open the hood and disconnect the negative battery cable from the battery terminal.
5. Raise and safely support the vehicle. Disconnect the driveshaft at the rear. Pull the driveshaft rearward and disconnect from the transmission. Install a suitable plug in the extension housing to prevent lubricant leakage.
6. Remove the clutch housing dust shield and slave cylinder and secure it at one side.
7. Remove the speedometer cable from the extension housing.
8. Disconnect the starter motor and back-up lamp switch wires.
9. Place a jack under the engine, protecting the oil pan with a wood block.

NOTE: If vehicle is four wheel drive, remove the transfer case.

10. Remove the starter motor. Position a suitable jack under the transmission.
11. Remove the bolts, lockwashers and flat washers attaching the transmission to the engine rear plate.
12. Remove the nuts and bolts attaching the transmission mount and damper to the crossmember.
13. Remove the nuts attaching the crossmember to the frame side rails and remove the crossmember.
14. Lower the engine jack. Work the clutch housing off the locating dowels and slide the transmission rearward until the input shaft spline clears the clutch disc. Remove the transmission from the vehicle.
15. Installation is the reverse of removal.

NEW PROCESS 435 FOUR SPEED

Removal and Installation

1. If equipped, remove the rubber boot and floor mat.
2. If necessary, remove the floor pan transmission cover plate. It may be necessary first to remove the seat assembly.
3. Disconnect the back-up light switch located in the rear of the gearshift housing cover.
4. Raise and support the vehicle safely. Position a transmission jack under the transmission, and disconnect the speedometer cable.
5. Disconnect the parking brake lever from its linkage, and remove the gearshift housing. On a C-Series, disconnect parking brake cable and bracket at the transmission.
6. Disconnect the driveshaft. Remove the bolts that attach the coupling shaft center support to the cross-member and wire the coupling shaft and driveshaft to one side. If equipped, remove the transfer case. Remove the transmission rear support as required.
7. Remove the two transmission upper mounting nuts at the clutch housing.
8. Remove the transmission attaching bolts at the clutch housing, and remove the transmission.
9. Before installing the transmission, apply a light film of lubricant to the clutch disc splines, release bearing inner hub surfaces, release lever fulcrum and fork, and the transmission front bearing retainer. Care must be exercised to avoid excessive grease from contaminating the clutch disc.
10. Place the transmission on a transmission jack, and raise the transmission until the input shaft splines are aligned with the clutch disc splines. The clutch release bearing and hub must be properly positioned in the release lever fork.
11. Install guide studs in the clutch housing and slide the transmission forward on the guide studs until it is in position on the clutch housing. Install the attaching bolts and nuts. Remove the guide studs and install the two lower attaching bolts.
12. Install the bolts attaching the coupling shaft center support to the crossmember.
13. Connect the driveshaft and the speedometer cable. Install transmission rear support, if removed. Install transfer case, if removed.

14. Connect the parking brake to the transmission.
15. Connect the back-up light switch.
16. If equipped, install the weather pad, the pad retainer and the transmission cover plate. Install the seat assembly, if it was removed.

Linkage

FORD 3.03 THREE SPEED, EXCEPT VANS

Adjustment

1. Place the shifter in the Neutral position and insert a gauge pin ($^3/_{16}$ in. diameter) through the steering column shift levers and the locating hole in the spacer.
2. If the shift rods at the transmission are equipped with threaded sleeves, adjust the sleeves so that they enter the shift levers on the transmission easily with the shift levers in the Neutral position. Now lengthen the rods seven turns of the sleeves and insert them into the shift levers.
3. If the shift rods, are slotted, loosen the attaching nut, make sure that the transmission shift levers are in the Neutral position, then retighten the attaching nuts.
4. Remove the gauge pin and check the operation of the shift linkage.

FOUR SPEED OVERDRIVE W/EXTERNAL LINKAGE, EXCEPT VANS

Adjustment

1. Attach the shift rods to the levers.
2. Rotate the output shaft to determine that the transmission is in neutral.
3. Insert an alignment pin into the shift control assembly alignment hole.
4. Attach the slotted end of the shift rods over the flats of the studs in the shift control assembly.
5. Install the locknuts and remove the alignment pin.

VANS WITH FORD 3.03 THREE SPEED TRANSMISSION

Adjustment

1. Place the gearshift lever in the Neutral position.
2. Loosen the adjustment nuts on the transmission shift levers sufficiently to allow the shift rods to slide freely on the transmission shift levers.
3. Insert a $^3/_{16}$ in. rod through the pilot hole in the shift tube mounting bracket until it enters the adjustment hole of both the upper and lower shift lever.
4. Place the transmission shift levers in the Neutral position and tighten the adjustment nuts on the transmission shift levers.
5. Remove the $^1/_4$ in. rod from the pilot hole, and check the operation of the gearshift lever in all gear positions.

VANS WITH FOUR SPEED OVERDRIVE TRANSMISSION W/EXTERNAL LINKAGE

Adjustment

1. Disconnect the 3 shift rods from the shifter assembly.
2. Insert a 0.25 in. diameter pin through the alignment hole in the shifter assembly. Make sure the levers are in the neutral position.
3. Align the 3 transmission levers as follows: forward lever (3rd–4th lever) in the mid-position (neutral), rearward lever (1st–2nd lever) in the mid-position (neutral), and middle lever (reverse lever) rotate counterclockwise to the neutral position.
4. Rotate the output shaft to assure that the transmission is in neutral.
5. Attach the slotted end of the shift rods over the slots of the studs in the shifter assembly. Install and tighten the locknuts to 15–20 ft. lbs.
6. Remove the alignment pin. Check for proper operation.

AUTOMATIC TRANSMISSION

For complete overhaul procedures, see Chilton's Automatic Transmission Manual.

C5 AUTOMATIC TRANSMISSION

Removal and Installation

1. Raise and support the vehicle safely. Disconnect the transmission fluid filler tube from the pan. Drain the transmission fluid.
2. At the front lower edge of the converter housing, remove the cover attaching bolts and remove the dust cover. Remove the splash shield at the control levers.
3. Remove the drive shaft or coupling shaft. Remove the converter drain plug. Allow the converter to drain and install the drain plug.
4. Disconnect the oil cooler lines from the transmission.
5. Disconnect the manual and downshift linkage rods from the transmission control levers.
6. Remove the speedometer gear from the extension housing.
7. Remove the four converter to flywheel attaching nuts. Disconnect the starter cable. Remove the three starter to converter housing attaching bolts. Remove the starter.
8. Disconnect the vacuum line from the diaphragm unit and the vacuum line retaining clip.
9. Position the transmission jack to support the transmission. Install the safety chain to hold the transmission on the jack.
10. Remove the two engine rear support crossmember-to-frame attaching bolts.
11. Remove the two engine rear support-to-extension housing attaching bolts.
12. Raise the transmission and remove the rear support. Remove the six converter housing-to-engine attaching bolts.
13. Move the transmission away from the engine. Lower the transmission and remove it from under the vehicle.
14. To install, secure the transmission on a transmission jack. Align the transmission with the engine and move it into place, using care not to damage the flywheel and the converter pilot.

NOTE: The converter must rest squarely against the flywheel. This indicates that the converter pilot is not binding in the crankshaft.

15. Install the six converter housing-to-engine attaching bolts. Install the converter-to-flywheel attaching nuts.
16. Install the rear support. Install the rear support-to-extension housing attaching bolts.
17. Position the starter into the converter housing and install the three attaching bolts. Install the starter cable.

18. Remove the transmission jack.
19. Connect the transmission filler tube to the transmission pan. Connect the oil coolers lines to the transmission.
20. Install the speedometer driven gear in the extension housing.
21. Connect the transmission linkage rods to the transmission control levers.

NOTE: When making transmission control attachments, new retaining rings and grommets should be used.

22. Install the driveshaft or coupling shaft.
23. Install the vacuum line in the retaining clip. Connect the vacuum line to the diaphragm unit.
24. At the front lower area of the converter housing, install the lower cover and the control lever dust shield. Install the attaching bolts.
25. Secure the fluid filler tube to the pan.
26. Lower the vehicle.
27. Fill the transmission to the proper level.
28. Raise the vehicle and check for transmission fluid leakage. Lower the vehicle and adjust the throttle and manual linkage.

C6 AUTOMATIC TRANSMISSION

Removal and Installation

BRONCO AND F SERIES

1. Raise and support the vehicle safely.
2. Remove the two upper converter housing-to-engine bolts.
3. Remove the bolt securing the fluid filler tube to the engine cylinder head.
4. Drain the fluid from the transmission and converter.
5. Disconnect the coupling shaft or driveshaft from the transmission companion flange and position it out of the way.
6. Disconnect the speedometer cable from the bearing retainer.
7. Disconnect the throttle and manual linkage rods from the levers at the transmission.
8. Disconnect the oil cooler lines from the transmission.
9. Remove the vacuum hose from the vacuum unit. Remove the vacuum line retaining clip.
10. Disconnect the cable from the terminal on the starter motor. Remove the three attaching bolts and remove the starter motor.
11. Remove the four flywheel attaching nuts. Place a wrench on the crankshaft pulley attaching bolt to turn the converter to gain access to the nuts.
12. On F-150–F-250 (4 × 4) and Bronco remove the transfer case, if equipped.
13. Remove the two engine rear support crossmember-to-frame attaching bolts.
14. Remove the two engine rear support-to-extension housing attaching bolts.
15. Remove the eight bolts securing the No. 2 crossmember to the frame side rails.
16. Raise the transmission with a transmission jack and remove both crossmembers.
17. Secure the transmission to the jack with the safety chain.
18. Remove the remaining converter housing-to-engine attaching bolts.
19. Move the transmission away from the engine. Lower the transmission and remove it from under the vehicle.
20. To install, tighten the converter drain plug. Position the converter on the transmission making sure the converter drive flats are fully engaged in the pump gear.
21. With the converter properly installed, place the transmission on the jack. Secure the unit to the jack with a chain.
22. Rotate the converter so that studs and drain plug are in alignment with those in the flywheel.
23. Move the transmission toward the cylinder block until they are in contact.

NOTE: The converter must rest squarely against the flywheel. This indicates that the converter pilot is not binding in the engine crankshaft.

24. Install the converter housing-to-engine bolts.
25. Remove the transmission jack safety chain from around the transmission.
26. Position the No. 2 crossmember to the frame side rails. Install the attaching bolts.
27. If equipped, install the transfer case.
28. Position the engine rear support crossmember to the frame side rails. Install the rear support to extension housing mounting bolts.
29. Lower the transmission and remove the jack.
30. Secure the engine rear support crossmember to the frame side rails with the attaching bolts.
31. Connect the vacuum line to the vacuum diaphragm making sure that the metal tube is secured in the retaining clip.
32. Connect the oil cooler lines to the transmission.
33. Connect the throttle and manual linkage rods to their respective levers on the transmission.
34. Connect the speedometer cable to the bearing retainer.
35. Secure the starter motor in place with the attaching bolts. Connect the cable to the terminal on the starter.
36. Install a new O-ring on the lower end of the transmission filler tube and insert the tube in the case.
37. Secure the converter-to-flywheel attaching nuts. Use a wrench on the crankshaft pulley attaching nut to rotate the flywheel. Do not use a wrench on the converter attaching nuts to rotate it.
38. Install the converter housing dust shield and secure it with the attaching bolts.
39. Connect the coupling shaft driveshaft.
40. Adjust the shift linkage.
41. Lower the vehicle. Then install the two upper converter housing-to-engine bolts.
42. Position the transmission fluid filler tube to the cylinder head and secure with the attaching bolt.
43. Fill the transmission to the correct level with the specified lubricant. Start the engine and shift the transmission through all ranges, then re-check the fluid level.

E SERIES

1. Remove the engine cover from inside the vehicle.
2. Disconnect the neutral start wires at the plug connector.
3. If the vehicle is equipped witha V8 engine, remove the flexhose from the air cleaner heat tube.
4. Remove the upper converter housing to engine attaching bolts. Remove the bolt securing the filler tube to the engine.
5. Raise the vehicle and support it safely.
6. Drain the transmission fluid pan loosening the bolts from the rear first and work toward the frontof the pan.
7. Remove the converter cover from the flywheel housing.
8. Remove the coverter to flywheel attaching nuts. Use a wrench on the crankshaft pulley bolt to turn the converter to gain access to the nuts then turn the converter to gain access to the drain plug and drain the converter.
9. Disconnect the driveshaft. Remove the fluid filler tube.
10. Disconnect the starter cable at the starter and remove the starter from the converter housing.
11. Disconnect the cooler lines from the transmission. Disconnect the vacuum line from the modulator.
12. Remove the speedometer driven gear from the extension housing.
13. Disconnect the manual and downshift linkage rods or cable from the control levers.
14. Support the engine. Position a jack under the transmission. Install the safety chain to hold the transmisson.

15. Remove the bolts and nuts securing the rear mount to the crossmember. Disconnect the crossmember from the side rails. Raise the transmission with the jack and remove the crossmember.
16. Remove the remaining converter housing to engine attaching bolts. Lower the jack and remove the converter and transmission assembly from under the vehicle.
17. Install in the reverse order of removal.

C3 AUTOMATIC TRANSMISSION

Removal and Installation

1. Raise and support the vehicle safely. Place a drain pan under the transmission fluid pan. Starting at the rear of the pan and working toward the front, loosen the attaching bolts and allow the fluid to drain. Then remove all of the pan attaching bolts except two at the front, to allow the fluid to further drain. After all the fluid has drained, install two bolts on the rear side of the pan to temporarily hold it in place.
2. Remove the converter drain plug access cover and adapter plate bolts from the lower end of the converter housing.
3. Remove the four flywheel to converter attaching nuts. Crank the engine to turn the converter to gain access to the nuts, using a wrench on the crankshaft pulley attaching bolt. On belt driven overhead camshaft engines, never turn the engine backwards.
4. Crank the engine until the converter drain plug is accessible and remove the plug. Place a drain pan under the converter to catch the fluid. After all the fluid has been drained from the converter, reinstall the plug and tighten to 20–30 ft. lbs. Remove the driveshaft. Install cover, plastic bag etc. over end of extension housing.
5. Remove the speedometer cable from the extension housing. Disconnect the shift rod at the transmission manual lever. Disconnect the downshift rod at the transmission downshift lever.
6. Remove the starter-to-converter housing attaching bolts and position the starter out of the way.
7. Disconnect the neutral start switch wires from the switch. Remove the vacuum line from the transmission vacuum modulator.
8. Position a suitable jack under the transmission and raise it slightly.
9. Remove the engine rear support-to-crossmember bolts. Remove the crossmember-to-frame side support attaching bolts and remove the crossmember insulator and support and damper.
10. Lower the jack under the transmission and allow the transmission to hang.
11. Position a jack to the front of the engine and raise the engine to gain access to the two upper converter housing-to-engine attaching bolts.
12. Disconnect the oil cooler lines at the transmission. Plug all openings to keep out dirt.
13. Remove the lower converter housing-to-engine attaching bolts. Remove the transmission filler tube.
14. Secure the transmission to the jack with a safety chain.
15. Remove the two upper converter housing-to-engine attaching bolts. Move the transmission to the rear and down to remove it from under the vehicle.
16. Position the converter to the transmission making sure the converter hub is fully engaged in the pump. With the converter properly installed, place the transmission on the jack and secure with safety chain.
17. Rotate the converter so the drive studs and drain plug are in alignment with their holes in the flywheel. With the transmission mounted on a transmission jack, move the converter and transmission assembly forward into position being careful not to damage the flywheel and the converter pilot.
18. Install the two upper converter housing-to-engine attaching bolts and tighten to 28–38 ft. lbs.
19. Remove the safety chain from the transmission. Insert the filler tube in the stub tube and secure it to the cylinder block with the attaching bolt. Tighten the bolt to 28–38 ft. lbs. If the stub tube is loosened or dislodged, it should be replaced. Install the oil cooler lines in the retaining clip at the cylinder block. Connect the lines to the transmission case.
20. Remove the jack supporting the front of the engine. Raise the transmission. Position the crossmember, insulator and support and damper to the frame side supports and install the attaching bolts. Tighten the bolts to 20–30 ft. lbs.
21. Lower the transmission and install the rear engine support-to-crossmember nut. Tighten the bolt to 60–80 ft. lbs.
22. Remove the transmission jack. Install the vacuum hose on the transmission vacuum unit. Install the vacuum line into the retaining clip.
23. Connect the neutral start switch plug to the switch. Install the starter and tighten the attaching bolts to 15–20 ft. lbs.
24. Install the four flywheel-to-converter attaching nuts.
25. Install the converter drain plug access cover and adaptor plate bolts. Tighten the bolts to 12–16 ft. lbs.
26. Connect the muffler inlet pipe to the exhaust manifold.
27. Connect the transmission shift rod to the manual lever. Connect the downshift rod to the downshift lever.
28. Connect the speedometer cable to the extension housing. Install the driveshaft. Tighten the companion flange U-bolt attaching nuts to 70–95 ft. lbs.
29. Adjust the manual and downshift linkage as required.
30. Lower the vehicle. Fill the transmission to the proper level with the specified fluid.

AUTOMATIC OVERDRIVE

Removal and Installation

1. Raise the vehicle and support it safely.
2. Place the drain pan under the transmission fluid pan. Starting at the rear of the pan and working toward the front, loosen the attaching bolts and allow the fluid to drain. Finally remove all of the pan attaching bolts except two at the front, to allow the fluid to further drain. With fluid drained, install two bolts on the rear side of the pan to temporarily hold it in place.
3. Remove the converter drain plug access cover from the lower end of the converter housing.
4. Remove the converter-to-flywheel attaching nuts. Place a wrench on the crankshaft pulley attaching bolt to turn the converter to gain access to the nuts.
5. Place a drain pan under the converter to catch the fluid. With the wrench on the crankshaft pulley attaching bolt, turn the converter to gain access to the converter drain plug and remove the plug. After the fluid has been drained, reinstall the plug.
6. Disconnect the driveshaft from the rear axle and slide shaft rearward from the transmission. Install a seal installation tool in the extension housing to prevent fluid leakage.
7. Disconnect the cable from the terminal on the starter motor. Remove the three attaching bolts and remove the starter motor. Disconnect the neutral start switch wires at the plug connector.
8. Remove the rear mount-to-crossmember attaching bolts and the two crossmember-to-frame attaching bolts.
9. Remove the two engine rear support-to-extension housing attaching bolts.
10. Disconnect the TV linkage rod from the transmission TV lever. Disconnect the manual rod from the transmission manual lever at the transmission.
11. Remove the two bolts securing the bellcrank bracket to the converter housing.
12. Raise the transmission with a transmission jack to provide clearance to remove the crossmember. Remove the rear mount

from the crossmember and remove the crossmember from the side supports.

13. Lower the transmission to gain access to the oil cooler lines.
14. Disconnect each oil line from the fittings on the transmission.
15. Disconnect the speedometer cable from the extension housing.
16. Remove the bolt that secures the transmission fluid filler tube to the cylinder block. Lift the filler tube and the dipstick from the transmission.
17. Secure the transmission to the jack with the chain.
18. Remove the converter housing-to-cylinder block attaching bolts.
19. Carefully move the transmission and converter assembly away from the engine and, at the same time, lower the jack to clear the underside of the vehicle.
20. Remove the converter and mount the transmission in a holding fixture.
21. Tighten the converter drain plug.
22. Position the converter on the transmission, making sure the converter drive flats are fully engaged in the pump gear by rotating the converter.
23. With the converter properly installed, place the transmission on the jack. Secure the transmission to the jack with a chain.
24. Rotate the converter until the studs and drain plug are in alignment with the holes in the flywheel.
25. Move the converter and transmission assembly forward into position, using care not to damage the flywheel and the converter pilot. The converter must rest squarely against the flywheel. This indicates that the converter pilot is not binding in the engine crankshaft.
26. Install and tighten the converter housing-to-engine attaching bolts to 40–50 ft. lbs.
27. Remove the safety chain from around the transmission.
28. Install a new O-ring on the lower end of the transmission filler tube. Insert the tube in the transmission case and secure the tube to the engine with the attaching bolt.
29. Connect the speedometer cable to the extension housing.
30. Connect the oil cooler lines to the right side of transmission case.
31. Position the crossmember on the side supports. Position the rear mount on the crossmember and install the attaching bolt and nut.
32. Secure the engine rear support to the extension housing and tighten the bolts to 16–20 ft. lbs.
33. Lower the transmission and remove the jack.

A4LD AUTOMATIC TRANSMISSION

Removal and Installation

1. Raise the vehicle and support it safely.
2. Drain the transmission fluid pan. Loosen the bolts starting at the rear of the pan and working toward the front.
3. Remove the converter access cover from the bottom of the engine oil pan on 4 cylinder engines and from the right side on 6 cylinder engines.
4. Remove the four flywheel to converter attaching nuts. Rotate the crankshaft pulley clockwise (as viewed from the front) to gain access to each of the nuts.
5. Scribe a mark indexing the driveshaft to the rear axle flange. Remove the driveshaft.
6. Remove the speedometer cable from the extension housing.
7. Disconnect the shift rod at the transmission manual lever. Remove the kickdown cable from the ball stud lever.
8. Depress the tab on the retainer and remove the kickdown cable from the bracket.
9. Remove the starter from the covnerter housing.
10. Disconnect the neutral start switch wires and the converter clutch solenoid connector. Disconnect the vacuum line from the modulator.
11. Remove the filler tube. Position a jack under the transmission and remove the rear mount to crossmember nut. Remove the crossmember to frame side rail attaching bolts. Raise the transmission and remove the crossmember.
12. Disconnect the oil cooler lines at the transmisslion. Plug the openings to keep dirt out.
13. Remove the converter housing to engine attaching bolts.
14. Move the transmission to the rear so that it disengages the dowl pins and the converter disengages the flywheel. Lower the transmission from the vehicle.
15. Install in the reverse order of removal.

Shift Linkage

Adjustment

BRONCO, E AND F SERIES

1. Position the selector lever in the Drive (D) position for C5 and C6 transmissions and in the Overdrive position for AOD transmissions. Hold it against the stop by applying an eight pound weight to the selector lever knob.
2. Loosen the shift rod adjusting nut at the bell housing.
3. Shift the manual lever at the transmission into the Drive (D) or Overdrive position, by moving the lever all the way rearward, then forward two detents.
4. With the selector lever and the manual lever in position, tighten the nut at the bell housing to 12–18 ft. lbs. (17–24 Nm).
5. Remove the eight pound wieght from the steering column selector lever knob.
6. Check the selector lever in all detent positions with engine running to ensure correct adjustment.

BRONCO II AND RANGER

1. Position the selector lever in the Drive (D) position and loosen the trunnion bolt.
2. Position the manual lever in the Drive (D) by moving the bell crank lever all the way rearward, then forward four detents.
3. With the floor shifter selector lever and manual lever in the Drive (D) position, apply light forward pressure to the floor shifter lower arm while tightening the trunnion bolt to 13–23 ft.lbs. (18–31 Nm).

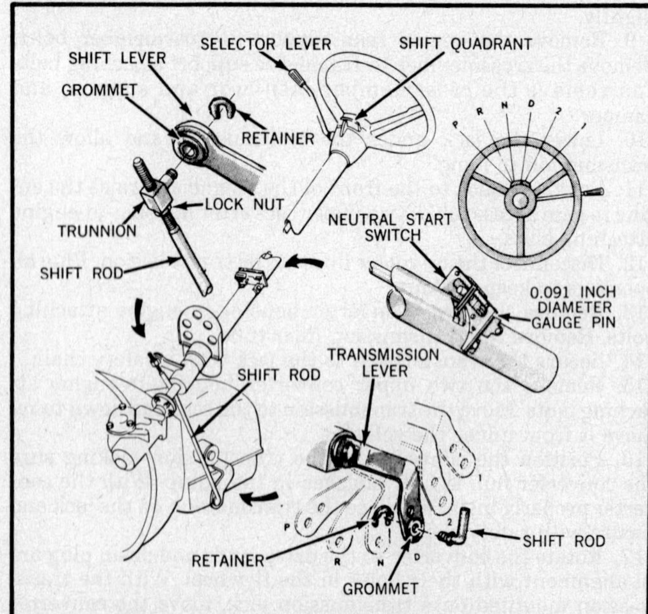

Manual linkage adjustment F-100-250-350

4. Check the selector lever in all detent positions with engine running to ensure correct adjustment.

AEROSTAR

1. Place the shift lever in the Overdrive position.
2. From below the vehicle, loosen the adjustment screw on the shift cable and remove the end fitting from the manual lever ball stud.
3. Position the manual lever in the Overdrive position by moving the lever all the way rearward, then three detents forward.
4. Hold the shift lever against the rear stop. Connect the cable end fitting to the manual lever.
5. Tighten the adjustment screw to 45–60 inch lbs. (5–7 Nm).
6. Check the selector lever in all detent positions with engine running to ensure correct adjustment.

Band Adjustments

LOW/REVERSE BAND

C5 TRANSMISSION

1. Raise and support the vehicle safely. Clean all dirt from around the band adjusting screw and remove and discard the locknut.
2. Install a new locknut on the adjusting screw. Using a torque wrench, tighten the adjusting screw to 10 ft. lbs.
3. Back off the adjusting screw exactly 3 full turns.
4. Hold the adjusting screw steady and tighten the locknut to 35–45 ft. lbs.

INTERMEDIATE

C5 AND C6 TRANSMISSION

1. Raise and support the vehicle safely. Clean adjusting screw, apply penetrating lubricant and remove and discard locknut.
2. Install a new locknut (loosely) and torque adjusting screw to 10 ft. lbs., then back off 1 3/4 turns.
3. Hold adjusting screw and tighten locknut.

FRONT

C3 TRANSMISSION

1. Remove the downshift rod from the transmission downshift lever. Clean all of the dirt away from the band adjusting nut and screw area. Remove and discard the locknut.
2. Tighten the adjusting screw to 10 ft. lbs. Back off the adjusting screw exactly two turns.

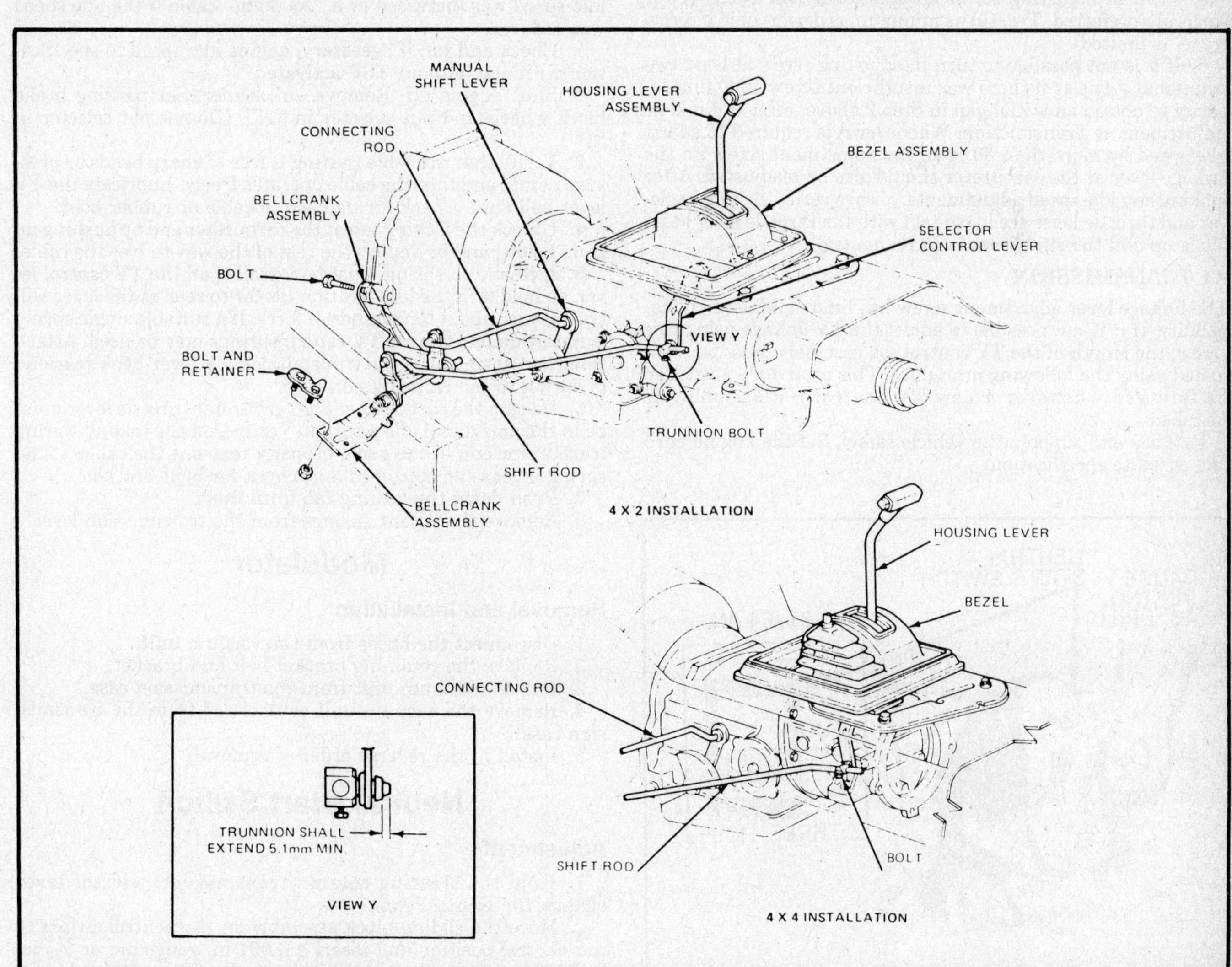

Floor shift controls—C5 automatic transmission

3. Install a new locknut, hold the adjusting screw in position and tighten the locknut to 35–45 ft. lbs. Install the downshift rod.

Throttle Linkage

AUTOMATIC OVERDRIVE

Adjustment

CARBURETOR W/ROD LINKAGE

The TV control linkage may be adjusted at the carburetor using the following procedure:

1. Check that engine idle speed is set at specification.
2. De-cam the fast idle cam on the carburetor so that the throttle lever is at its idle stop. Place shift lever in N (neutral), set park brake (engine off).
3. Backout linkage lever adjusting screw all the way (screw end is flush with lever face).
4. Turn in adjusting screw until a thin shim (0.005 inch max.) or piece of writing paper fits snugly between end of screw and throttle lever. To eliminate effect of friction, push linkage lever forward (tending to close gap) and release before checking clearance between end of screw and throttle lever. Do not apply any load on levers with tools or hands while checking gap.
5. Turn in adjusting screw an additional four turns (Four turns are preferred. Two turns minimum is permissible if screw travel is limited).
6. If it is not possible to turn in adjusting screw at least two additional turns or if there was insufficient screw adjusting capacity to obtain an initial gap in Step 2 above, refer to Linkage Adjustment at Transmission. Whenever it is required to adjust idle speed by more than 50 rpm, the adjustment screw on the linkage lever at the carburetor should also be readjusted. After making any idle speed adjustments, always verify the linkage lever and throttle lever are in contact with the throttle lever at its idle stop and the shift lever is in N (neutral).

AT TRANSMISSION

The linkage lever adjustment screw has limited adjustment capability. If it is not possible to adjust the TV linkage using this screw, the length of the TV control rod assembly must be readjusted using the following procedure. This procedure must also be followed whenever a new TV control rod assembly is installed.

1. Raise and support the vehicle safely. Set the engine curb idle speed to specification.

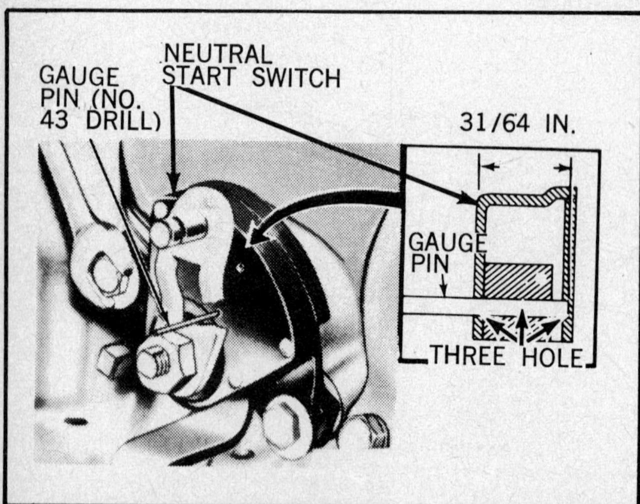

Neutral safety switch adjustment

2. With engine off de-cam the fast idle cam on the carburetor so that the throttle lever is against the idle stop. Place shift lever in Neutral and set park brake (engine off).
3. Set the linkage lever adjustment screw at its approximately mid-range.
4. If a new TV control rod assembly is being installed. Connect the rod to the linkage lever at the carburetor.
5. Using a 13 mm box end wrench, loosen the bolt on the sliding trunnion block on the TV control rod assembly.
6. Remove any corrosion from the control rod and freeup the trunnion block so that it slides freely on the control rod. Insert pin into transmission lever grommet.
7. Push up on the lower end of the control rod to insure that the linkage lever at carburetor is firmly against the throttle lever. Release force on rod. Rod must stay up.
8. Push the TV control lever on the transmission up against its internal stop with a firm force (approximately 5 pounds) and tighten the bolt on the trunnion block. Do not relax force on lever until it is tightened.
9. Lower the vehicle and verify that the throttle lever is still against the idle stop. If not, repeat Steps 2 through 9.

ADJUSTMENT W/CABLE

Whenever it is required to adjust the idle speed by more than 150 RPM, the TV control cable should be readjusted. Failure to do so may result in the symptoms due to a "to short" cable if the idle speed was increased or a "too long" cable if the idle speed was reduced.

1. Check and set, if necessary, engine idle speed to specification with and without TSP activated.
2. Shut engine off. Remove air cleaner. Set parking brake block wheels and put selector in "N". (Do not put selector in "P").
3. Verify that the cable routing is free of sharp bends or pressure points and that the cable operates freely. Lubricate the TV lever ball stud. Check for damage to cable or rubber boot.
4. Unlock the locking tab at the carburetor end by pushing up from below, and prying up the rest of the way to free the cable.
5. A retention spring must be installed on the TV control lever, to hold it in the idle position (as far to rear as the lever will travel) with about ten pounds of force. If a suitable single spring is not available, two V8 TV return springs may be used. Attach retention spring(s) to the transmission TV lever hook rear end of spring to the transmission case.
6. De-cam the carburetor. The carburetor throttle lever must be in the anti-diesel idle position. Verify that the take-up spring (carburetor end of the cable properly tensions the cable. If the spring is loose or bottomed out, check for bent brackets.
7. Push down the locking tab until flush.
8. Remove the detent springs from the transmission lever.

Modulator

Removal and Installation

1. Disconnect the hoses from the vacuum unit.
2. Remove the retaining bracket bolt and bracket.
3. Pull the vacuum unit from the transmission case.
4. Remove the vacuum unit control rod from the transmission case.
5. Install in the reverse order of removal.

Neutral Start Switch

Adjustment

1. Hold the steering column transmission selector lever against the Neutral stop.
2. Move the sliding block assembly on the neutral switch to the neutral position and insert a 0.091 in. gauge pin or $^3/_{32}$ in. drill in the alignment hole on the terminal side of the switch.
3. Move the switch assembly housing so that the sliding block

contacts the actuating pin lever. Secure the switch to the outer tube of the steering column and remove the gauge pin.

4. Check the operation of the switch. The engine should only start in Neutral and Park.

Oil Pan

Removal and Installation

1. Raise the vehicle and support it safely.
2. Place a drain pan under the transmission oil pan. Loosen the bolts starting from the rear and working forward.
3. Let the fluid drain out of one corner of the pan. Remove the bolts and the pan. Clean the mating surfaces of the pan and the transmission case.
4. Install in the reverse order ov removal.

Fluid and Filter

Replacement

1. Remove the oil pan.
2. Remove the screws retaining the filter to the transmission. Remove the filter and the gasket.
3. Install a new filter with the gasket in place. Install the pan and gasket.
4. Before starting the vehicle, fill with four quarts of transmission fluid.
5. Lower the vehicle. Run the engine till it reaches normal operating temperature. Move the gear shift selector lever through all the gears and back to Park (P) position.
6. Recheck the fluid level. Fill to the correct Hot level.

TRANSFER CASES

For transfer case overhaul procedures, see the Unit Repair section.

Transfer Case

Removal and Installation

NEW PROCESS MODEL 208

1. Raise the vehicle and support it safely. Drain the fluid from the transfer case.
2. Disconnect the four wheel drive indicator switch wire connector at the transfer case.
3. Disconnect the speedometer driven gear from the transfer case rear bearing retainer.
4. Remove the nut retaining the transmission shift lever assembly to the transfer case.
5. Remove the skid plate from the frame, if so equipped.
6. Remove the heat shield from the frame.
7. Support the transfer case with a transmission jack or equivalent.
8. Disconnect the front driveshaft from the front output shaft yoke.
9. Disconnect the rear driveshaft from the rear output shaft yoke.
10. Remove the bolts retaining the transfer case to the transmission adapter.
11. Lower the transfer case from the vehicle.
12. When installing place a new gasket between the transfer case and the adapter.
13. Raise the transfer case with a transmission jack so the transmission output shaft aligns with the splined transfer case input shaft.
14. Install the bolts retaining the case to the adapter.
15. Connect the rear driveshaft to the rear output shaft yoke.
16. Connect the front driveshaft to the front output yoke.
17. Remove the transmission jack from the transfer case.
18. Position the heat shield to the frame crossmember and mounting lug to the transfer case and install and tighten the bolts and screw.
19. Install the skid plate to the frame.
20. Install the shift lever to the transfer case and tighten the retaining nut.
21. Install the speedometer driven gear to the transfer case.
22. Connect the four wheel drive indicator switch wire to the transfer case.
23. Install the drain plug. Remove the filler plug and install six pints of Dexron® II or equivalent type transmission fluid.
24. Lower the vehicle.

BORG WARNER MODEL 1345

1. Raise the vehicle and support it safely.
2. Drain the fluid from the transfer case.
3. Disconnect the four wheel drive indicator switch wire connector at the transfer case.
4. Remove the skid plate from the frame, if so equipped.
5. Disconnect the front driveshaft from the front output yoke.
6. Disconnect the rear driveshaft from the rear output shaft yoke.
7. Disconnect the speedometer driven gear from the transfer case rear bearing retainer.
8. Remove the retaining rings and shift rod from the transfer case shift lever.
9. Disconnect the vent hose from the transfer case.
10. Remove the heat shield from the frame.
11. Support the transfer case with a transmission jack.
12. Remove the bolts retaining the transfer case to the transmission adapter.
13. Lower the transfer case from the vehicle.
14. When installing place a new gasket between the transfer case and the adapter.
15. Raise the transfer case with the transmission jack so that the transmission output shaft aligns with the splined transfer case input shaft. Install the bolts retaining the transfer case to the adapter.
16. Remove the transmission jack from the transfer case.
17. Connect the rear driveshaft to the rear output shaft yoke.
18. Install the shift lever to the transfer case and install the retaining nut.
19. Connect the speedometer driven gear to the transfer case.
20. Connect the four wheel drive indicator switch wire connector at the transfer case.
21. Connect the front driveshaft to the front output yoke.
22. Position the heat shield to the frame crossmember and the mounting lug on the transfer case. Install and tighten the retaining bolts.
23. Install the skid plate to the frame.
24. Install the drain plug. Remove the filler plug and install six pints of Dexron® II type transmission fluid or equivalent.
25. Lower the vehicle.

BORG WARNER MODEL 1350

1. Raise and safely support the vehicle. Remove the skid plate from the frame.
2. Place a drain pan under transfer case, remove the drain plug and drain fluid from the transfer case.

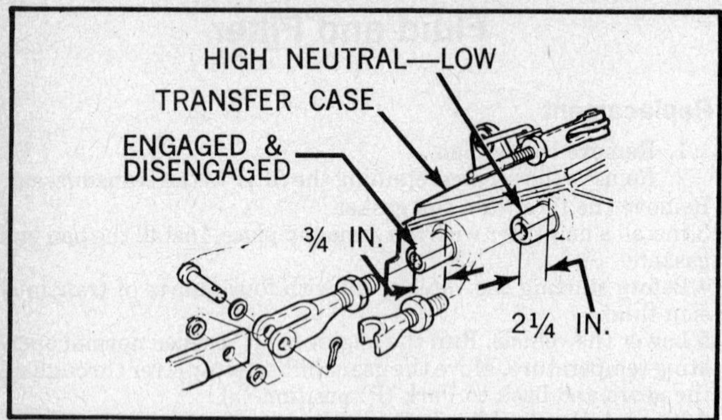

Transfer case control lever rod and shift lever rod

3. Disconnect the four-wheel drive indicator switch wire connector at the transfer case.
4. Disconnect the front driveshaft from the axle input yoke.
5. Loosen the clamp retaining the front driveshaft boot to the transfer case, and pull the driveshaft and front boot assembly out of the transfer case front output shaft.
6. Disconnect the rear driveshaft from the transfer case output shaft yoke.
7. Disconnect the speedometer driven gear from the transfer case rear cover. Disconnect the vent hose from the control lever.
8. Loosen or remove the large bolt and the small bolt retaining the shifter to the extension housing. Pull on the control lever until the bushing slides off the transfer case shift lever pin. If necessary, unscrew the shift lever from the control lever. Remove the heat shield from the transfer case.

NOTE: The catalytic converter is located beside the heat shield. Be careful when working around the catalytic converter because of the extremely high temperatures generated by the converter.

9. Support the transfer case with a suitable jack. Remove the five bolts retaining the transfer case to the transmission and the extension housing.
10. Slide the transfer case rearward off the transmission output shaft and lower the transfer case from the vehicle. Remove the gasket from between the transfer case and extension housing.
11. Place a new gasket between the transfer case and the extension housing.
12. Raise the transfer case with a suitable jack so that the transmission output shaft aligns with the splined transfer case input shaft. Slide the transfer case forward onto the transmission output shaft and onto the dowel pin. Install the five bolts retaining the transfer case to the extension housing. Tighten bolts to 23–35 ft. lbs.
13. Remove the transmission jack from the transfer case.
14. Install the heat shield on the transfer case. Tighten the bolts to 27–37 ft. lbs.
15. Move the control lever until the bushing is in position over the transfer case shift lever pin. Install and hand start the attaching bolts. First, tighten the large bolt retaining the shifter to the extension housing to 70–90 ft. lbs., then the small bolt to 31–42 ft. lbs.

NOTE: Always tighten the large bolt retaining the shifter to the extension housing before tightening the small bolt.

16. Install the vent assembly so the white marking on the hose is in position in the notch in the shifter.

NOTE: The upper end of the vent hose should be two inches above the top of the shifter and positioned inside of the shift lever boot.

17. Connect the speedometer driven gear to the transfer case rear cover. Tighten the screw to 20–25 inch lbs.
18. Connect the rear driveshaft to the transfer case output shaft yoke. Tighten the bolts to 12–15 ft. lbs.
19. Clean the transfer case front output shaft female splines. Apply 5–8 grams of multi-purpose long-life lubricant, or equivalent to the splines. Insert the front driveshaft male spline.
20. Connect the front driveshaft to the axle input yoke. Tighten the bolts to 12–15 ft. lbs.
21. Push the driveshaft boot to engage the external groove on the transfer case front output shaft. Secure with a clamp.
22. Connect the four-wheel drive indicator switch wire connector at the transfer case.
23. Install the drain plug and tighten to 14–22 ft. lbs. Remove the fill plug and install 3 pints of DEXRON®II, automatic transmission fluid, or equivalent. Install fill plug and tighten to 14–22 ft. lbs.
24. Install the skid plate to frame. Tighten nuts and bolts to 22–30 ft. lbs.
25. Lower the vehicle.

BORG WARNER MODEL 1356 ELECTRONIC

1. Raise the vehicle and support it safely.
2. Remove the nuts, bolts and skid plate from the frame, if so equipped.
3. Remove the plug and drain the fluid from the transfer case.
4. Remove the wire connector from the feed wire harness at the rear of the transfer case.
5. Disconnect the front driveshaft from the front output shaft yoke.
6. Disconnect the rear driveshaft from the transfer case rear output shaft yoke.
7. Disconnect the speedometer driven gear from the transfer case rear cover.
8. Disconnect the vent hose from the mounting bracket.
9. Support the transfer case with a jack. Remove the six bolts retaining the transfer case to the transmission and the extension housing.
10. Slide the transfer case rearward off the transmission output shaft and lower the transfer case from the vehicle.
11. Install in the reverse order of removal.

BORG WARNER MODEL 1359

1. Raise the vehicle and support it safely.
2. Disconnect the rear driveshaft from the transfer case output shaft flange.
3. Disconnect the speedometer cable from the transfer case rear cover.
4. Support the transfer case with a jack. Remove the five bolts retaining the case to the transmission extension housing.
5. Slide the transfer case rearward off the transmission output shaft and lower the transfer case from the vehicle.
6. Install in the reverse order of removal.

Linkage

Adjustment

MODEL 1350

1. Raise the shift boot to expose the top surface of the cam plate.
2. Loosen the two bolts on the control lever approximately two turns. Move the transfer shift lever to the 4L position.
3. Move the cam plate rearward until the bottom chamfered corner of the neutral lug just contacts the forward right edge of the shift lever.
4. Hold the cam plate in this position and tighten the two control lever bolts to specifications.
5. Move the in cab shift lever to all shift positions to check the positive engagement.
6. Install the shift boot assembly.

DRIVE LINES AND UNIVERSAL JOINTS

Drive Lines

NOTE: Mark the relationship of the rear driveshaft yoke and axle pinion flange before disassembly, to maintain driveline balance. If a vibration should exist, the driveshaft should be disconnected from the axle, rotated 180 degrees and re-installed.

SINGLE SNAP RING U-JOINT TYPE

Removal and Installation

1. Disconnect the driveshaft from the rear axle flange.
2. If vehicle has a coupling shaft, slide the driveshaft off the coupling splines.
3. Working from the center support nearest to the rear of the vehicle, remove the two attaching bolts and support the bearing.
4. On a vehicle with more than one coupling shaft, disconnect the rear shaft from the front one.
5. Remove the remaining center support attaching bolts and support the bearing.
6. Remove the transmission coupling shaft flange attaching nuts and remove the shaft and center bearing(s) as an assembly.
7. Thoroughly clean all driveshaft components before installing.
8. To install, connect the front flange or joint to the transmission flange.
9. Secure the center bearing to the frame bracket, tightening the bracket attaching bolts securely.
10. If vehicle has more than one coupling shaft, connect the rear shaft to the forward one, then install the remaining center support.
11. Connect the rear universal to the rear axle flange, tightening nuts or bolts securely.
12. Be sure all driveshaft and coupling shaft yokes are in phase.

DOUBLE CARDAN U-JOINT TYPE

Removal and Installation

1. To remove the front or rear driveshaft, disconnect the double cardan joint from the flange at the transfer case.
2. Disconnect the single U-joint from the flange at the axle. Remove the driveshaft.
3. To install, position the single U-joint end of the driveshaft to the axle, before the cardan end. Install and tighten all U-bolts, nuts, bolts and lockwashers.

ONE PIECE DRIVESHAFT MODELS

Removal and Installation

1. If the alignment marks are not visible, mark the relationship of the rear drive shaft yoke and the drive pinion flange of the axle in line with the drive shaft so that they may be re-installed in the same position.
2. Disconnect the rear U-joint from the companion flange. Wrap tape around the loose bearing caps to prevent them from falling off the spider. Pull the driveshaft toward the rear of the vehicle until the slip yoke clears the transmission extension housing and the seal. Install the appropriate tool in the housing to prevent the lubricant or fluid from leaking.
3. To install, reverse the removal procedure, taking note that if either the rubber seal on the output shaft or the seal in the end of the transmission extension housing is damaged it must be replaced. Also if the lugs on the axle pinion flange are shaved or distorted so that the bearings slide, replace the flange.
4. Install the U-bolts and torque the nuts to 8–15 ft. lbs.

CENTER BEARING

Removal and Installation

1. Remove the driveshafts.
2. Remove the two center support bearing attaching bolts and remove the assembly from the vehicle.
3. Do not immerse the sealed bearing in any type of cleaning fluid. Wipe the bearing and cushion clean with a cloth dampened with cleaning fluid.
4. Check the bearing for wear or rough action by rotating the inner race while holding the outer race. If wear or roughness is evident, replace the bearing. Examine the rubber cushion for evidence of hardening, cracking, or deterioration. Replace it if it is damaged in any way.
5. Place the bearing in the rubber support and the rubber support in the U-shaped support and install the bearing in the reverse order of removal.

U-Joints

SINGLE SNAP RING TYPE U-JOINT AND DOUBLE CARDAN TYPE U-JOINT

Disassembly and Assembly

1. Mark the position of the spiders, the center yoke, and the centering socket as related to the stud yoke which is welded to the front of the driveshaft tube. The spiders must be assembled with the bosses in their original positions to provide proper clearance.
2. Remove the snap-rings that secure the bearings in the front of the center yoke.
3. Position the driveshaft in a vise so that the bearing caps that are pressed into the center yoke can be pressed or driven out with a drift and hammer. Do this for all of the spiders.
4. Clean all the serviceable parts in cleaning solvent. If you are using a repair kit, install all of the parts supplied with the kit.

NOTE: If the driveshaft is damaged in any way, replace the complete driveshaft to insure a balanced assembly.

5. Assemble the U-joints in the reverse order of disassembly.

BEARING CAP AND BOLT TYPE U-JOINT

Disassembly and Assembly

1. Remove the cap screws attaching the bearing caps to the U-joint flange and yoke. Remove the bearing caps and bearings from the spider.
2. Remove the grease seals and retainers from the spider.

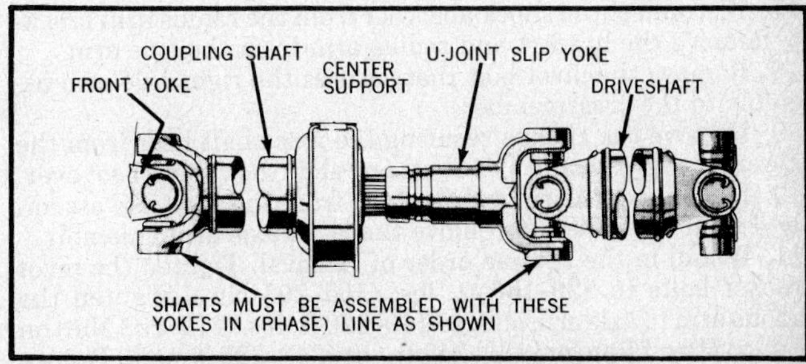

Drive shaft components—132 in. wheelbase

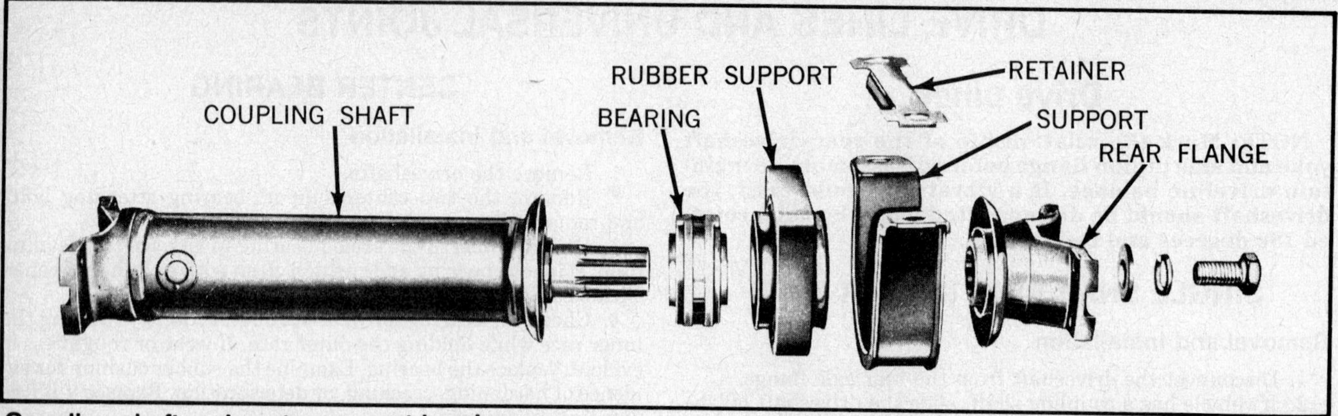

Coupling shaft and center support bearings

3. Clean the assembly thoroughly and check for damage or wear.
4. Pack the recess in the spider with the proper grade of grease.
5. Install the grease seals on the spider.
6. Position the needle bearings in the bearing cap, then position the caps on the spider. Place the spider in the yokes, and then install the bearing caps.
7. Lubricate the U-joints with the proper grade of grease.

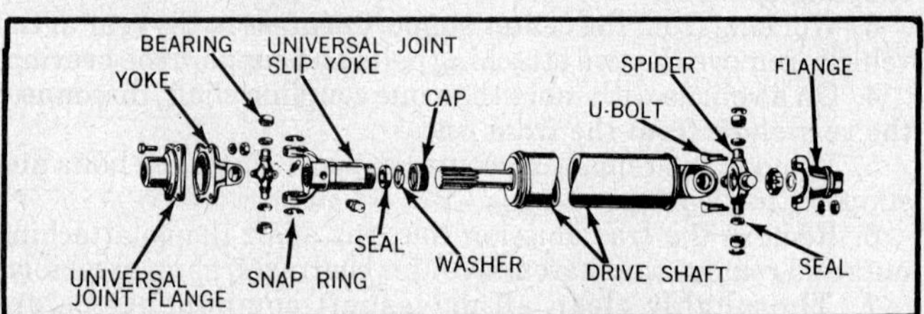

Drive shaft components—115 in. wheelbase

FRONT DRIVE AXLE

For overhaul procedures, refer to the Unit Overhaul Section.

Axle Housing

Removal and Installation

DANA MODELS 28, 44 AND 50

1. Raise the vehicle and support it safely under the radius arm brackets.
2. Disconnect the driveshaft from the front axle yoke. Remove the front wheels.
3. Remove the disc brake calipers and support them on a frame rail.
4. Disconnect the steering linkage from the spindle.
5. On the Bronco and F 150 series, position a jack under the axle arm and slightly compress the coil spring. Remove the nut that retains the lower part of the spring to the axle arm. Lower the jack and remove the coil spring, spacer, seat and stud.
6. On the F 250 and 350 series, position a jack under the axle and remove the two U-bolts that secure the shock absorber mounting plate and leaf springs to the tube and yoke assembly.
7. Disconnect the shock absorber from the radius arm bracket. Remove the bracket and radius arm from the axle arm.
8. Remove the pivot bolt that secures the right axle arm assembly to the crossmember.
9. Remove the clamps securing the axle shaft boot from the axle shaft slip yoke and axle shaft and slide the rubber boot over.
10. Disconnect the right driveshaft from the slip yoke assembly. Lower the jack and remove the right axle arm assembly.
11. Install in the reverse order of removal. Tighten the pivot bracket bolts to 120–150 ft. lbs. (163–203 Nm). Tighten the radous arm to axle arm stud to 160–220 ft. lbs. (217–298 Nm) on Bronco II and Ranger, 180–240 ft. lbs (245–325 Nm) on Bronco and F series. Tighten the coil spring retainer nut to 70-100 ft. lbs. (95–135 Nm) on Bronco II and Ranger, 30–70 ft. lbs. (41–94 Nm) on Bronco and F series. Tighten the tie rod to ball joint nut to 50–75 ft. lbs. (68–101 Nm). On the F 250 and 350 with leaf springs, tighten the two U-bolts to 85–120 ft. lbs. (116–162 Nm).

DANA MODEL 60 MONOBEAM

1. Raise the vehicle and support it safely. Remove the front wheels from the vehicle. Remove the hubs.
2. Remove the brake calipers from the rotors.
3. Disconnect the stabilizer links from the stabilizer bar.
4. Seperate the spindle connecting rods from the steering knuckles, using a pitman arm puller of equivalent. Wire the steering linkage to the spring.
5. Remove the two U-bolts from the U-joint flange and disconnect the axle from the front pinion flange. Wire the driveshaft to the frame.
6. Disconnect the vent tube at the axle housing and plug the fitting.
7. On the right side of the vehicle, disconnect the tracking bar from the spring cap.
8. Support the vehicle under the front leaf springs between the front axle leaf spring and the rear mounting shackle.
9. Support the axle under the differential carrier with a jack. Remove the U-bolts and nuts securing the axle to the spring. Lower the axle from the vehicle.
10. Installation is the reverse of the removal procedure.

Locking Hubs

Removal and Installaton

WITHOUT FREE-RUNNING HUBS EXCEPT RANGER AND BRONCO II

1. Raise and support the vehicle safely.

2. Remove the front hub grease cap and driving hub snap-ring.

3. Remove the splined driving hub and the pressure spring. This may require slight prying with a suitable tool.

4. Remove the wheel bearing locknut, lockring, and adjusting nut.

5. Remove the caliper assembly.

6. Pack the inside of the hub with wheel bearing grease. Add grease to the hub until the grease is flush with the inside diameter of the bearing cup.

7. Carefully position the hub assembly onto the spindle. Be careful not to damage the new seal. Install the caliper and adjust the wheel bearings.

WITH FREE-RUNNING HUB EXCEPT RANGER AND BRONCO II

1. Raise the vehicle and support it safely. Remove the tire and wheel assembly.

2. To remove hub, first separate cap assembly from body assembly by removing the six (6) socket head capscrews from the cap assembly and slip apart.

3. Remove snap-ring (retainer ring) from the end of the axle shaft.

4. Remove the lock ring seated in the groove of the wheel hub. The body assembly will now slide out of the wheel hub. If necessary, use an appropriate puller to remove the body assembly.

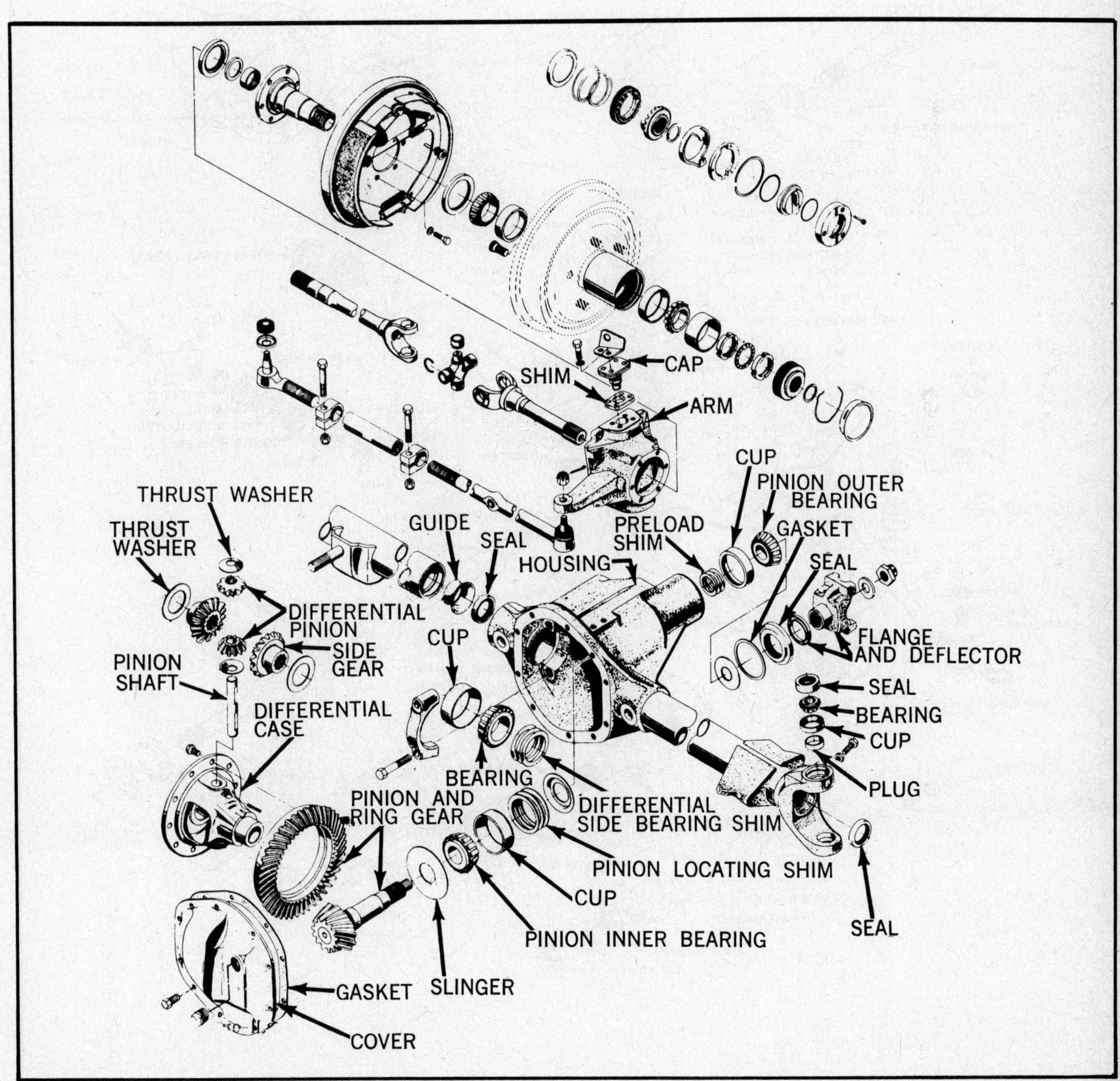

Front drive axle – F-100 and F-150

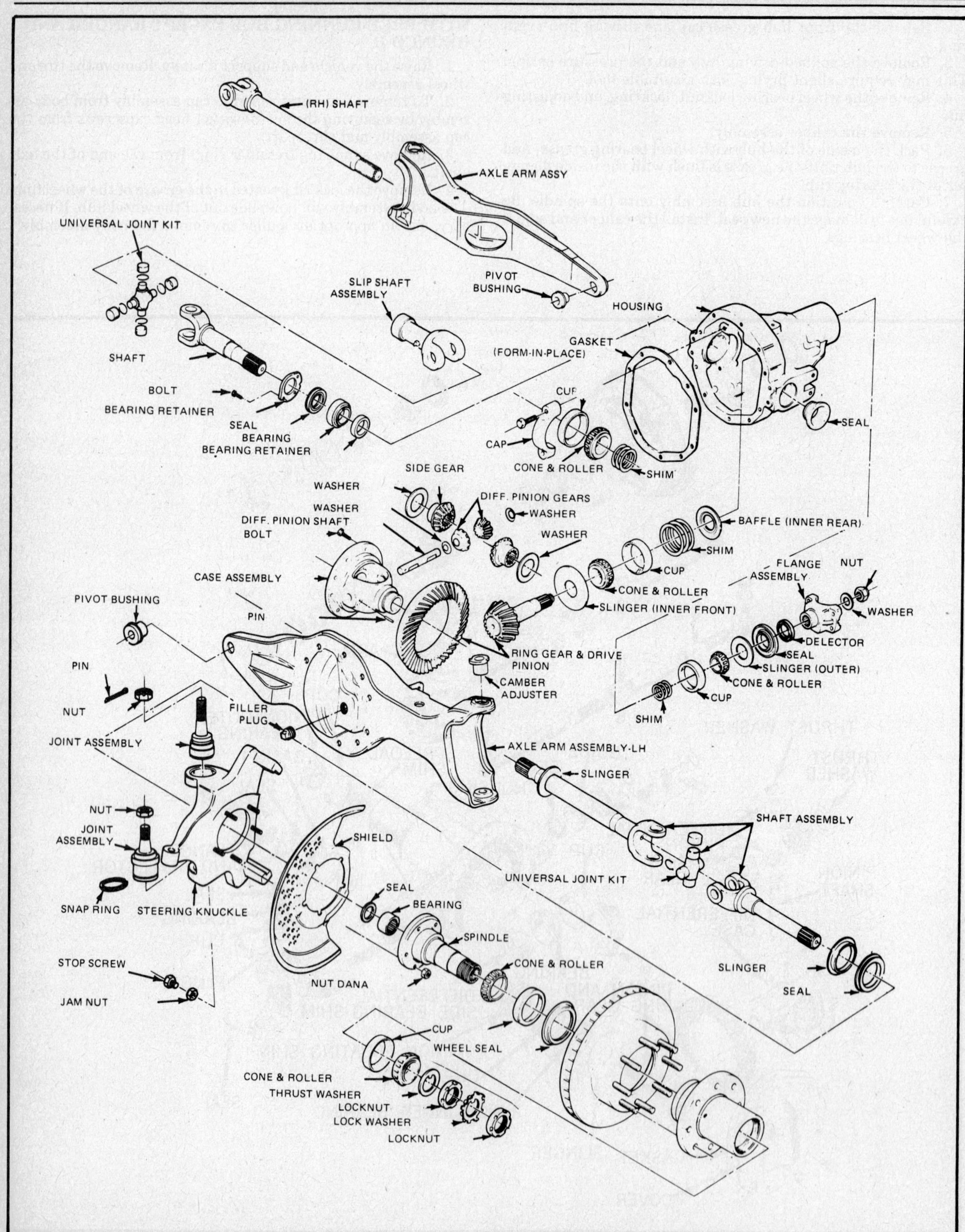

Exploded view of Dana 50 IFS front driving axle—typical of 44 IFS and H/D models

5. Install hub in reverse order of removal. Torque socket head capscrews to 30–35 inch lbs

AUTOMATIC LOCKING HUBS, EXCEPT RANGER AND BRONCO II

1. Raise the vehicle and support it safely. Remove the wheel and tire.
2. Remove capscrews and remove hub cap assembly from spindle. Remove capscrew from end of axle shaft.
3. Remove lock ring seated in the groove of the wheel hub with a knife blade or with a small sharp awl with the tip bent in the shape of a hook.
4. Remove body assembly from spindle. If body assembly does not slide out easily, use an appropriate puller.
5. Unscrew all three sets in the spindle locknut until the heads are flush with the edge of the locknut. Remove outer spindle locknut with automatic hub lock nut wrench.
6. Reinstall in reverse order of removal. Tighten the outer spindle locknut to 15–20 ft. lbs. with automatic hub lock nut wrench. Tighten down all three set screws. Firmly push in body assembly until the friction shoes are on top of the spindle outer locknut.
7. Install capscrew into the axle shaft and tighten to 35–50 ft. lbs.
8. Place cap on spindle and install capscrews. Tighten to 35–50 inch lbs Turn dial firmly from stop to stop, causing the dialing mechanism to engage the body spline.

NOTE: Be sure both hub dials are in the same position; "AUTO" or "LOCK."

RANGER AND BRONCO II, EXCEPT WITH AUTOMATIC LOCKING HUBS

1. Raise and support the vehicle safely.
2. Remove the wheel lug nuts and remove the wheel and tire assembly.
3. Remove the retainer washers from the lug nut studs and remove the manual locking hub assembly. To remove the interal hub lock assembly from the outer body assembly, remove the outer lock ring seated in the hub body groove. The internal assembly, spring and clutch gear will now slide out of the hub body.

NOTE: Do not remove the screw from the plastic dial.

4. Rebuild the hub assembly in the reverse order of disassembly.
5. Install the manual locking hub assembly over the spindle and place the retainer washers on the lug nut studs.

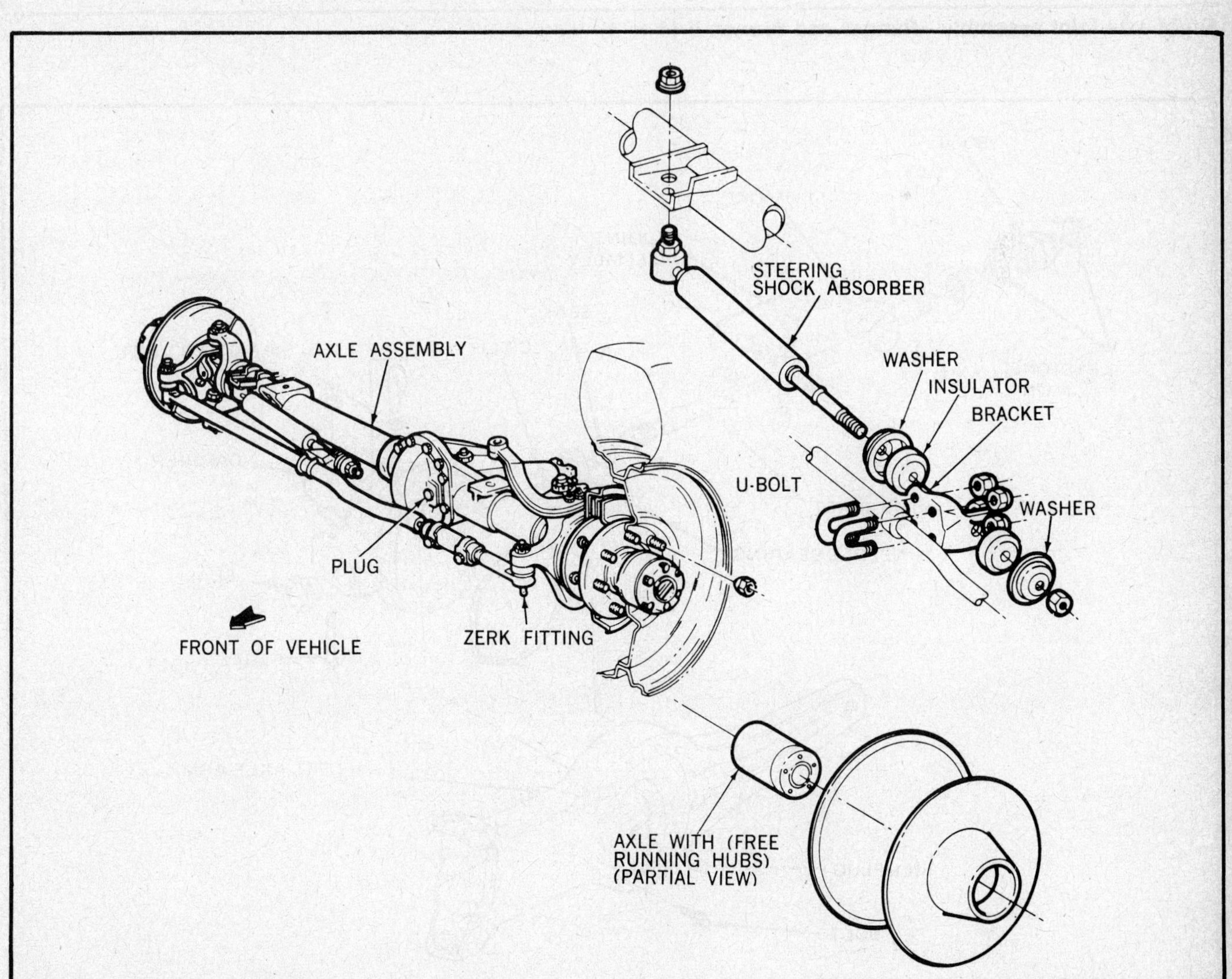

Front axle assembly – F-250 (4 × 4) – typical

SEAL
RIGHT AXLE ARM
KEYSTONE CLAMP
SLIP YOKE AND
STUB SHAFT
RIGHT SHAFT AND
JOINT ASSEMBLY
RUBBER BOOT
LEFT AXLE ARM

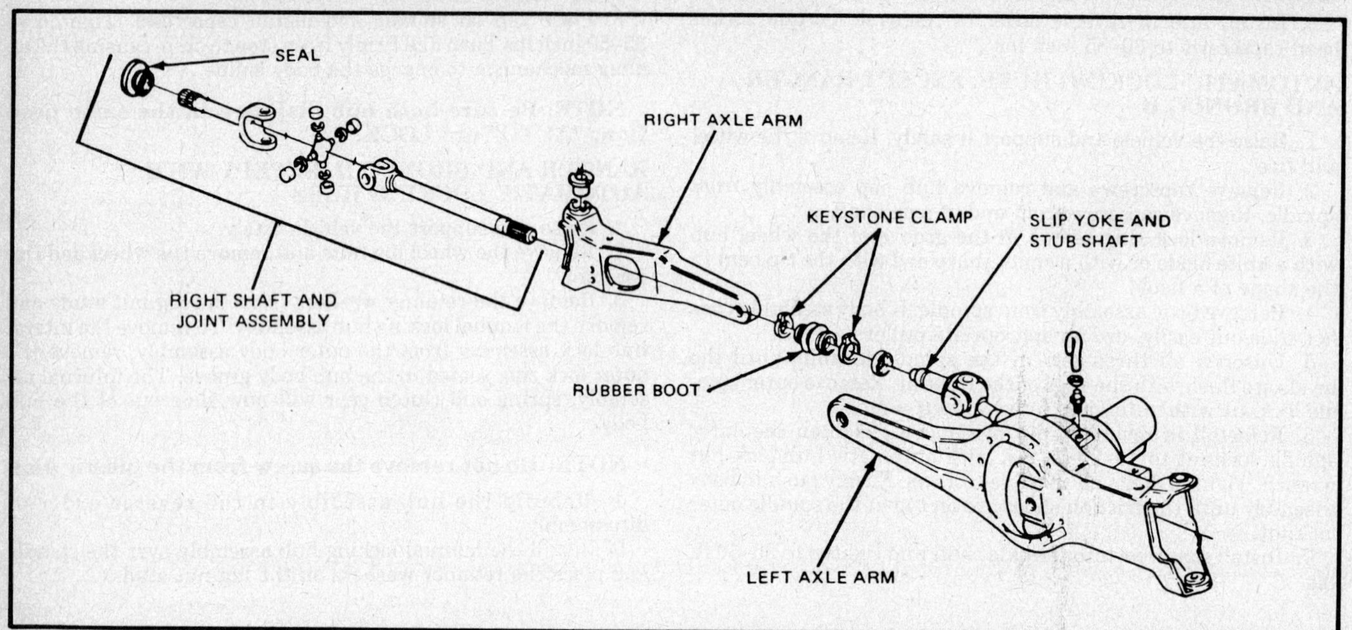

Right axle joint assembly—Ranger and Bronco II (4 × 4)

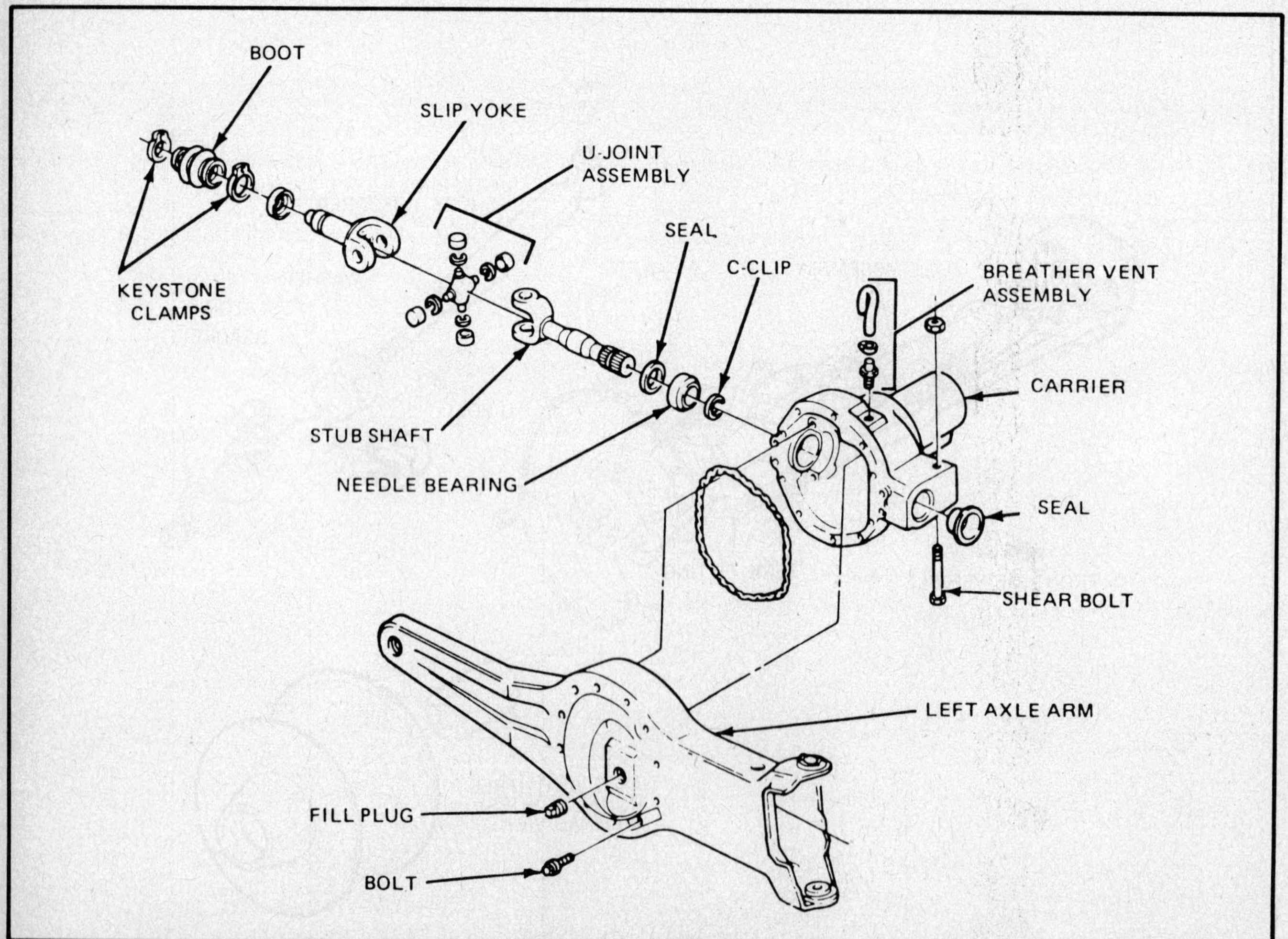

BOOT
SLIP YOKE
U-JOINT
ASSEMBLY
SEAL
KEYSTONE
CLAMPS
C-CLIP
BREATHER VENT
ASSEMBLY
CARRIER
STUB SHAFT
NEEDLE BEARING
SEAL
SHEAR BOLT
LEFT AXLE ARM
FILL PLUG
BOLT

Carrier assembly and related components—Ranger and Bronco II

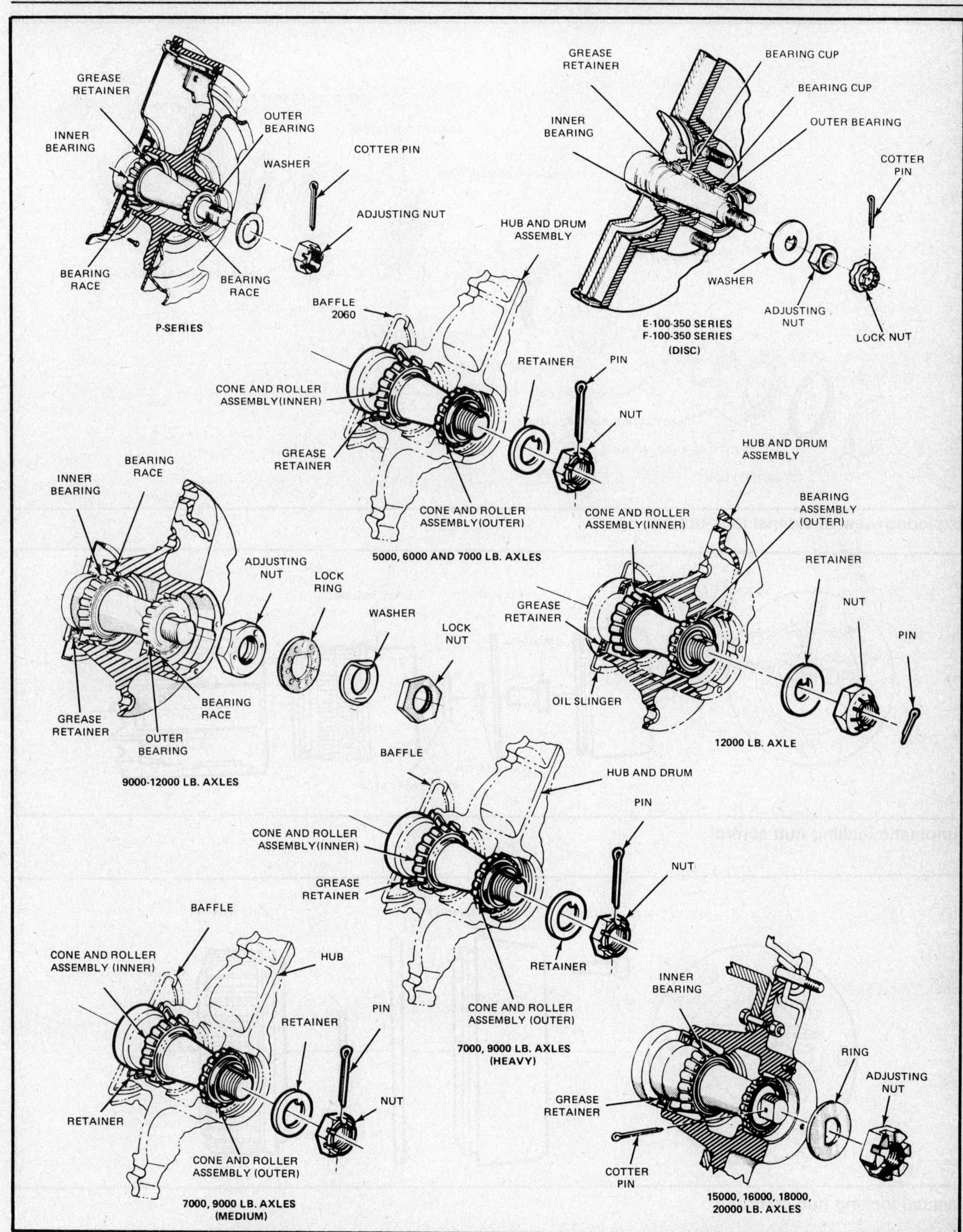

Front hubs, bearings and locking components—varied axles

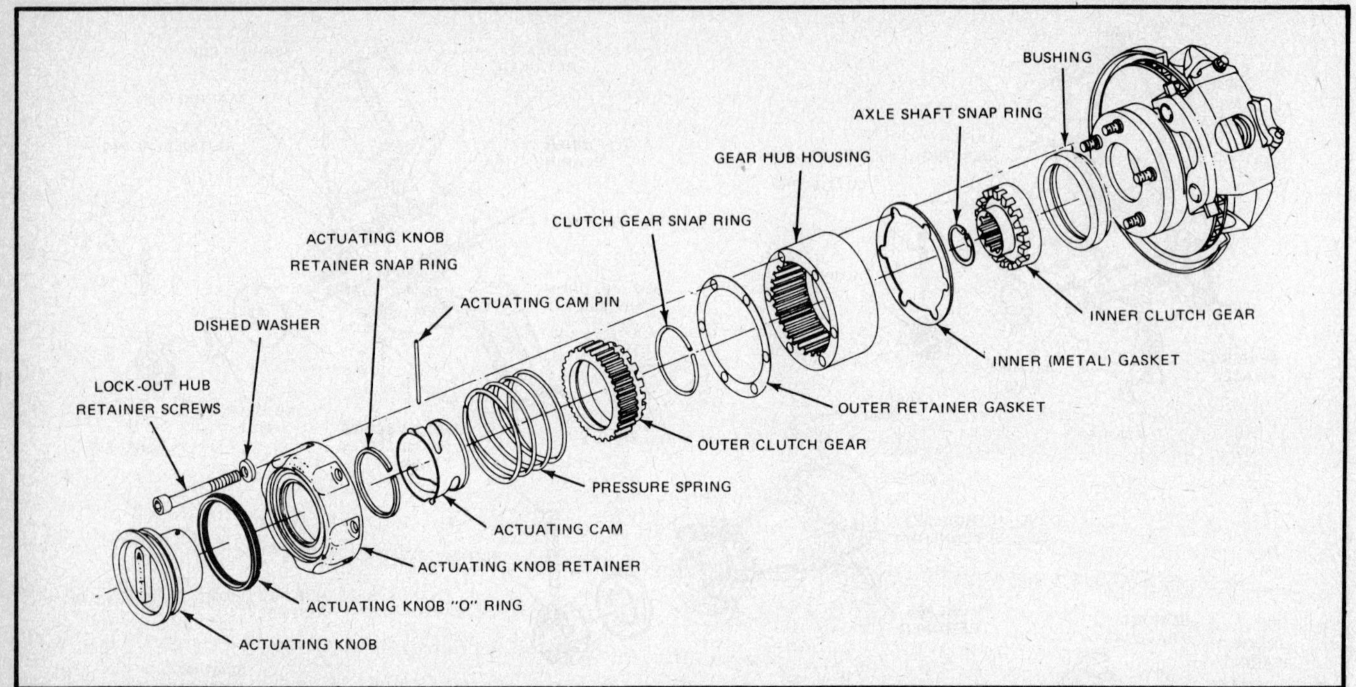

Exploded view of extenal lock-out hub

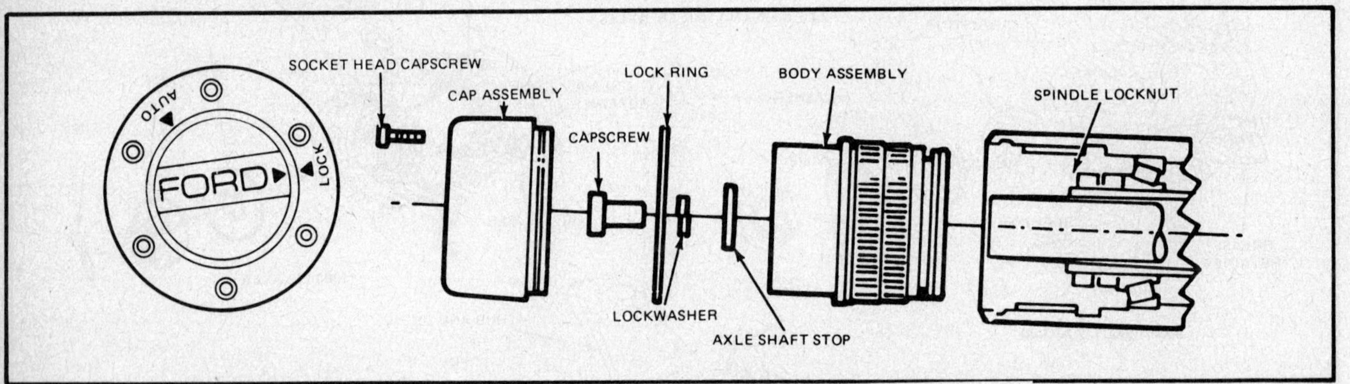

Automatic locking hub control

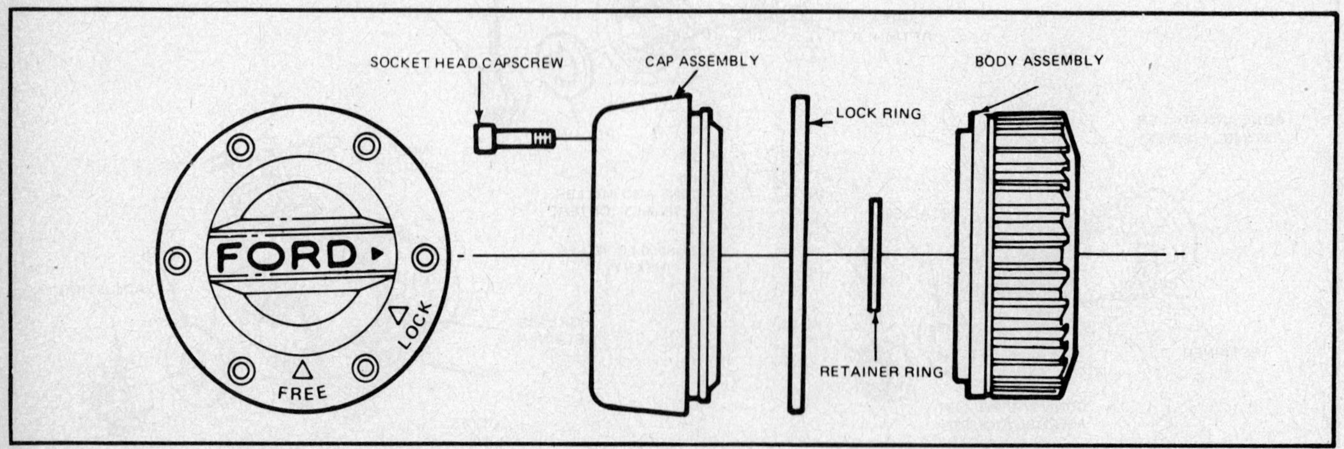

Manual locking hub control

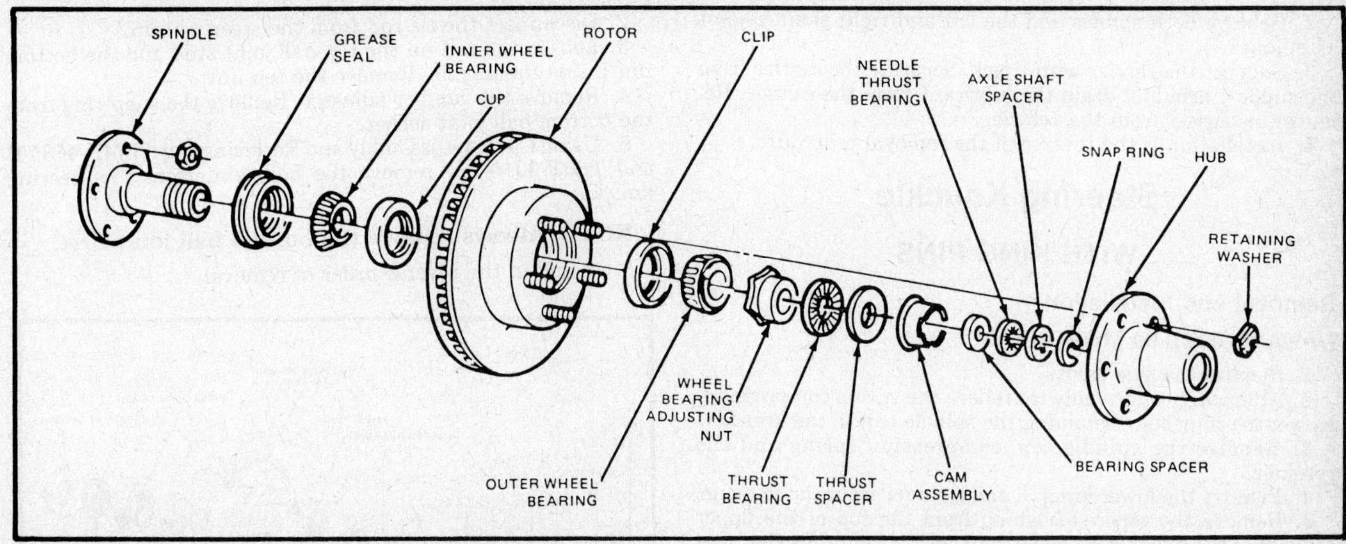

Automatic locking hubs – Ranger and Bronco II

6. Install the wheel and tire assembly. Install the lug nuts and tighten to 85–115 ft. lb.

RANGER AND BRONCO II WITH AUTOMATIC LOCKING HUBS.

1. Raise and support the vehicle safely. Remove the wheel lug nuts and remove the wheel and tire assembly.
2. Remove the retainer washers from the lug nut studs and remove the automatic locking hub assembly from the spindle.
3. Remove the snap ring from the end of the spindle shaft.
4. Remove the axle shaft spacer, needle thrust bearing and the bearing spacer. Being careful not to damage the plastic moving cam, pull the cam assembly off the wheel bearing adjusting nut and remove the thrust washer and needle thrust bearing from the adjusting nut.
5. Loosen the wheel bearing adjusting nut from the spindle using a 2 $^3/_8$ in. hex socket tool.
6. While rotating the hub and rotor assembly, tighten the wheel bearing adjusting nut to 35 ft. lbs. to seat the bearings, then back off the nut $^1/_4$ turn (90°).
7. Retighten the adjusting nut to 16 inch lb. using a torque wrench. Align the closest hole in the wheel bearing adjusting nut with the center of the spindle keyway slot. Advance the nut to the next hole if required.
8. Install the locknut needle bearing and thrust washer in the order of removal and push or press the cam assembly onto the locknut by lining up the key in the fixed cam with the spindle keyway.
9. Install the bearing thrust washer, needle thrust bearing and axle shaft spacer. Clip the snap ring onto the end of the spindle.
10. Install the automatic locking hub assembly over the spindle by lining up the three legs in the hub assembly with three pockets in the cam assembly. Install the retainer washers.
11. Install the wheel and tire assembly. Install and tighten lugnuts to 85–115 ft. lbs.
12. Final end play of the wheel on the spindle should be 0.001–0.003 in.

Axle Shaft, Seal and Bearings

Removal and Installation

DANA MODEL 28

1. Raise the front of the vehicle and support it safely. Remove the front wheel.
2. Remove the disc brake caliper and wire it to the frame.
3. Remove the hub locks, wheel bearings and lock nuts.
4. Remove the rotor and the outer wheel bearing.
5. Remove the grease seal and the inner wheel bearing from the rotor. Remove the inner and the outer races from the rotor.
6. Remove the spindle from the steering knuckle. Remove the splash shield.
7. On the right side of the vehicle, remove the shaft and joint by pulling the assembly out of the carrier. On the right side of the carrier, remove the clamp from the shaft and joint.
8. Slide the rubber boot onto the stub shaft and pull the shaft and joint from the splines of the stub shaft.
9. If required remove the needle bearing from the spindle and remove the seal from the shaft.
10. Install in the reverse order of removal. Pack the bearing with Multi-purpose Long Life Lubricant. Also pack the thrust face of the seal in the spindle bore and the V-seal on the axle shaft with lubricant.

DANA MODELS 44, 50 AND 60 MONOBEAM

1. Raise the front of the vehicle and support it safely. Remove the front wheel.
2. Remove the disc brake caliper and wire it to the frame.
3. Remove the cap from the hub body. Remove the snap ring that retains the axle shaft in the hub body.
4. Remove the lock ring seated in the groove of the hub body. Remove the body from the hub.
5. Remove the outer locknut, lockwasher and the inner locknut from the spindle. Remove the hub and rotor.
6. Remove the nuts retaining the spindle to the knuckle. Remove the splash shield and the caliper support from the knuckle.
7. Pull the axle shaft out of the steering knuckle. If required remove the caged needle bearing from the spindle and remove the seal.
8. Install in the reverse order of removal. Pack the bearing with Multi-purpose Long Life Lubricant. Also pack the thrust face of the seal in the spindle bore and the V-seal on the axle shaft with lubricant.

Differential Carrier

Removal and Installation

DANA MODEL 28

1. Disconnect the driveshaft from the yoke. Wire the driveshaft out of the way.

2. Remove both splines and the left and right shaft U-joint assemblies.
3. Support the carrier with a jack. Separate the carrier from the support arm and drain the lubricant from the carrier. Remove the carrier from the vehicle.
4. Installation is the reverse of the removal procedure.

Steering Knuckle

WITH KING PINS

Removal and Installation

DANA MODEL 60 MONOBEAM

1. Remove the axle shaft.
2. Alternately and evenly (to relieve the spring compression) loosen the four bolts retaining the spindle cap to the knuckle.
3. Remove the spindle cap, compression spring and the retainer.
4. Remove the lower kingpin and retainer from the knuckle.
5. Remove the tapered bushing from the top of the upper kingpin in the knuckle. Remove the knuckle from the axle yoke.
6. Remove the upper kingpin from the axle yoke.
7. Press the lower kingpin grease retainer, bearing, race and seal from the axle yoke lower bore.
8. Install in the reverse order of removal.

WITH BALL JOINTS

Removal and Installation

DANA MODELS 28, 44 AND 50

1. Remove the spindle and the shaft and joint assembly.
2. Disconnect the tie rod from the steering arm.
3. Loosen the nut on the top ball joint stud and the bottom nut inside the knucle. Remove the top nut.
4. Remove the camber adjuster. Remove the snap ring from the bottom ball joint socket.
5. Using C Frame assembly and Recieving Cup (T74P-4635-C and T80T-3010-A4) remove the ball joint from the steering knuckle.

NOTE: Always remove the bottom ball joint first.

6. Install in the reverse order of removal.

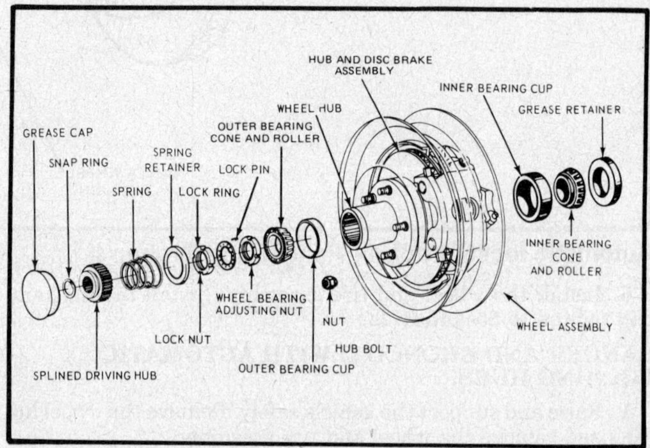

Front hub and wheel bearing components, front wheel drive – typical

REAR DRIVE AXLE

For overhaul procedures, refer to the Unit Overhaul Section.

Axle Housing

E 250 AND 350

Removal and Installation

DANA INTEGRAL CARRIER AXLE

1. Loosen the wheel stud nuts and the axle shaft retaining bolts.
2. Disconnect the rear shock absorbers from the spring seat caps. Then raise the rear end of the vehicle frame until the weight is off the rear springs. Place safety stands under the frame in this position.
3. Disconnect the flexible hydraulic line at the frame and disconnect the axle vent hose at the axle connection.
4. Disconnect the parking brake cable (if so equipped) at the equalizer, and remove the cables from the cable support brackets.
5. Disconnect the driveshaft from the rear U-joint flange.
6. Remove the nuts from the spring clips (U-bolts), and remove the spring seat caps.
7. Roll the axle from under the vehicle, and drain the lubricant. Remove the wheels. Mount the axle in a work stand.
8. Installation is the reverse of the removal procedure.

BRONCO, E 150, F 250 LIGHT DUTY AND F250/350 REGULAR AND CHASSIS CAB

Removal and Installation

FORD INTEGRAL CARRIER 8.8 AND 10.25 INCH RING GEAR

1. Raise the vehicle and support it safely.
2. Remove the cover an drain the lubricant.
3. Remove both rear wheels and remove the drums.
4. Remove the nuts that attach the wheel bearing retainers to the axle housing. Pull the axle shafts out.
5. Remove the vent hose from the vent tube then remove the vent from the axle housing.
6. Remove the brake backing plate and wire it to the frame rail. Remove both seals.
7. Disengage the brake line from the clips that retain the line to the axle housing.
8. Remove the hydraulic brake T-fitting from the axle housing.
9. Mark the driveshaft end yoke and the axle U-joint flange for proper reassembly. Remove the driveshaft.
10. Support the rear axle housing on a jack, then remove the spring clip U-bolt nuts. Remove the U-bolts and plates.
11. Disconnect the lower shock absorber studs from the mounting brackets on the axle housing.

12. Lower the axle housing and remove it from under the vehicle.
13. Installation is the reverse of the removal procedure.

BRONCO, E 150 ANDF 150

Removal and Installation

FORD REMOVABLE CARRIER 9.0 INCH RING GEAR

1. Remove the carrier from the axle housing.
2. Raise the vehicle and support it safely.
3. Remove the vent hose from the vent tube then remove the vent from the axle housing.
4. Remove the brake backing plate and wire it to the frame rail. Remove both seals.
5. Disengage the brake line from the clips that retain the line to the axle housing.
6. Remove the hydraulic brake T-fitting from the axle housing.
7. Mark the driveshaft end yoke and the axle U-joint flange for proper reassembly. Remove the driveshaft.
8. Support the rear axle housing on a jack, then remove the spring clip U-bolt nuts. Remove the U-bolts and plates.
9. Disconnect the lower shock absorber studs from the mounting brackets on the axle housing.
10. Lower the axle housing and remove it from under the vehicle.
11. Installation is the reverse of the removal procedure.

BRONCO II AND RANGER

Removal and Installation

INTEGRAL CARRIER 6¾ AND 7½ RING GEAR

1. Raise the vehicle and support it safely under the rear frame member.
2. Remove the cover an drain the lubricant.
3. Remove both rear wheels and remove the drums.
4. Working through the hole in the axle shaft flange, remove the nuts that attach the wheel bearing retainers to the axle housing. Pull the axle shafts out.
5. Remove the vent hose from the vent tube then remove the vent from the axle housing.
6. Remove the brake backing plate and wire it to the frame rail. Remove both seals.
7. Disengage the brake line from the clips that retain the line to the axle housing.
8. Remove the hydraulic brake T-fitting from the axle housing.
9. Mark the driveshaft end yoke and the axle U-joint flange for proper reassembly. Remove the driveshaft.
10. Support the rear axle housing on a jack, then remove the spring clip U-bolt nuts. Remove the U-bolts and plates.
11. Disconnect the lower shock absorber studs from the mounting brackets on the axle housing.
12. Lower the axle housing and remove it from under the vehicle.
13. Installation is the reverse of the removal procedure.

AEROSTAR

Removal and Installation

INTEGRAL CARRIER 7½ INCH RING GEAR

1. Raise the vehicle and support it safely under the frame rear lift points or the rear bumper support brackets.
2. Release the parking brake cable tension by pulling rearward on the front cable. Clamp the cable behind the crossmember to release the tension on the rear cables.
3. Remove the cables from the equalizer. Pull the cables through the rear crossmember.
4. Mark the drive shaft to the rear axle for correct installation. Remove the driveshaft. Remove the wheels from the brake drums.
5. Disconnect the brake lines at the master cylinder rear tube.
6. Disconnect the shock absorbers from the lower control arm.
7. Lower the axle until the springs are no longer under compression. Remove the coil springs.
8. Raise the axle to the normal load position and disconnect the control arms at the axle. Remove the upper control arm from the axle.
9. Mark the position of the cam adjuster in the axle bushing. Lower the axle from the vehicle.
10. Install in the reverse order of removal.

Axle Shaft

Removal and Installation

FORD REMOVABLE CARRIER

1. Raise and support the vehicle and remove the wheel/tire assembly from the brake drum.
2. Remove the nuts which secure the brake drum to the axle flange, then remove the drum from the flange.
3. Working through the hole provided in each axle shaft flange, remove the nuts which secure the wheel bearing retainer plate.
4. Using an axle puller, pull the axle shaft assembly out of the axle housing.

NOTE: The brake backing plate must not be dislodged. Install one nut to hold the plate in place after the axle shaft is removed.

5. If the axle has ball bearings: Loosen the bearing retainer ring by nicking it in several places with a cold chisel, then slide it off the axle shaft. On models equipped with a thick retaining ring, drill a ¼ in. to ½ in. hole part way through the ring, then break it with a cold chisel. A hydraulic press is needed to press the bearing off and to press the new one on. Press the new bearing and the new retainer ring on separately. Use a slide hammer to pull the old seal out of the axle housing. Carefully drive the new seal evenly into the axle housing, preferably with a seal driver tool.
6. If the axle has tapered roller bearings, use a slide hammer to remove the bearing cup from the axle housing. Drill a ¼–½ in. hole part way through the bearing retainer ring, then break it with a cold chisel. A hydraulic press is needed to press the bearing off and remove the seal. Press on the new seal and bearing, then the new retainer ring. Do not press the bearing and ring on together. Put the cup on the bearing, not in the housing, and lubricate the outer diameter of the cup and seal.
7. With ball bearings: Place a new gasket between the housing flange and backing plate. Carefully slide the axle shaft into place. Turn the shaft to start the splines into the side gear and push it in.
8. With tapered roller bearing: Move the seal out toward the axle shaft flange so there is at least $^{3}/_{32}$ in. between the edge of the outer seal and the bearing cup, to prevent snagging on installation. Carefully slide the axle shaft into place. Turn the shaft to start the splines into the side gear and push it in.
9. Install the bearing retainer plate.
10. Replace the brake drum and the wheel and tire.

DANA INTEGRAL CARRIER

1. Remove the lockbolts and lockwashers which hold the axle flange to the hub and and drum assembly.

NOTE: It is not necessary to raise the vehicle to remove the axle shafts.

2. Carefully slide the axle shaft out of the axle housing.
3. Clean the mating surfaces of the axle flange and the hub and drum assembly.
4. Position a new gasket on the axle flange and carefully slide the axle shaft into the axle housing. When the splined end of the axle shaft reaches the side gear, gently rotate the shaft until it is inserted into the side gear.
5. Position the gasket between the axle flange and the hub and drum and install the lockbolts and lockwashers.

FORD INTEGRAL CARRIER

1. Raise the vehicle and support it safely.
2. Remove the wheels and tires from the brake drums.
3. Place a drain pan under the housing and drain the lubricant by loosening the housing cover.
4. Remove the locks securing the brake drums to the axle shaft flanges and remove the drums.
5. Remove the housing cover and gasket, if used.
7. Working through the opening in the differential case, remove the side gear pinion shaft lockbolt and the side gear pinion shaft.
8. Push the axle shafts inward and remove the C-locks from the inner end of the axle shafts. Temporarily replace the shaft and lockbolt to retain the differential gears in position.
9. Remove the axle shafts with a slide hammer. Be sure the seal is not damaged by the splines on the axle shaft.
10. Remove the bearing and oil seal from the housing. Both the seal and bearing can be removed with a slide hammer. Two types of bearings are used on some axles, one requiring a press fit and the other a loose fit. A loose fitting bearing does not necessarily indicate excessive wear.
11. Inspect the axle shaft housing and axle shafts for burrs or other irregularities. Replace any work or damaged parts. A light yellow color on the bearing journal of the axle shaft is normal, and does not require replacement of the axle shaft. Slight pitting and wear is also normal.
12. Lightly coat the wheel bearing rollers with axle lubricant. Install the bearings in the axle housing until the bearing seats firmly against the shoulder.
13. Wipe all lubricant from the oil seal bore, before installing the seal.
14. Inspect the original seals for wear. If necessary, these may be replaced with new seals, which are prepacked with lubricant and do not require soaking.
15. Install the oil seal.
16. Remove the lockbolt and pinion shaft. Carefully slide the axle shafts into place. Be careful that you do not damage the seal with the splined end of the axle shaft. Engage the splined end of the shaft with the differential side gears.
17. Install the axle shaft C-locks on the inner end of the axle shafts and seat the C-locks in the counterbore of the differential side gears.
18. Rotate the differential pinion gears until the differential pinion shaft can be installed. Install the differential pinion shaft lockbolt. Tighten to 15–22 ft. lbs.
19. Install the brake drum on the axle shaft flange.
20. Install the wheel and tire on the brake drum and tighten the attaching nuts.

Pinion Seal

Removal and Installation

1. Raise the vehicle and support it safely.
2. Remove the wheels and the brake drums.
3. Mark the driveshaft axle end flange and the axle companion flange for correct installation. Remove the driveshaft.
4. Using an inch pound torque wrench on the pinion nut, record the torque required for rotation of the pinion through several revolutions.
5. Remove the pinion nut. Mark the companion flange in relation to the pinion for reinstallation.
6. Remove the rear axle companion flange. To remove the seal, pry it out of the carrier.
7. Install in the reverse order.

Differential Carrier

Removal and Installation

FORD REMOVABLE CARRIER

1. Raise the vehicle and support it safely. Remove the two rear wheel and tire assemblies.
2. Remove the two brake drums (3 Tinnerman nuts at each drum) from the axle shaft flange studs. If difficulty is experienced in removing the drums, back off the brake shoes.
3. Working through the hole provided in each axle shaft flange, remove the nuts that secure the rear wheel bearing retainer plate. Pull each axle shaft assembly out of the axle housing using axle shaft remover, Tool 4235-C. Care must be exercised to prevent damage to oil seal, if so equipped. Any roughing or cutting of the seal element during removal or installation can result in early seal failure. Install a nut on one of the brake carrier plate attaching bolts to hold the plate to the axle housing after the shaft has been removed. Whenever a rear axle shaft is replaced, the wheel bearing oil seals must be replaced. Remove the seals with tool 1175-AB.
4. Make scribe marks on the driveshaft end yoke and the axle U-joint flange to insure proper position at assembly. Disconnect the driveshaft at the rear axle U-joint, remove the driveshaft from the transmission extension housing. Install oil seal replacer tool T57P-7657-A in the housing to prevent transmission leakage.
5. Place a drain pan under the carrier and housing, remove the carrier attaching nuts, and drain the axle. Remove the carrier assembly from the axle housing.
6. Synthetic wheel bearing seals must not be cleaned, soaked or washed in cleaning solvent. Clean the axle housing and shafts using kerosene and swabs. To avoid contamination of the grease in the sealed ball bearings, do not allow any quantity of solvent

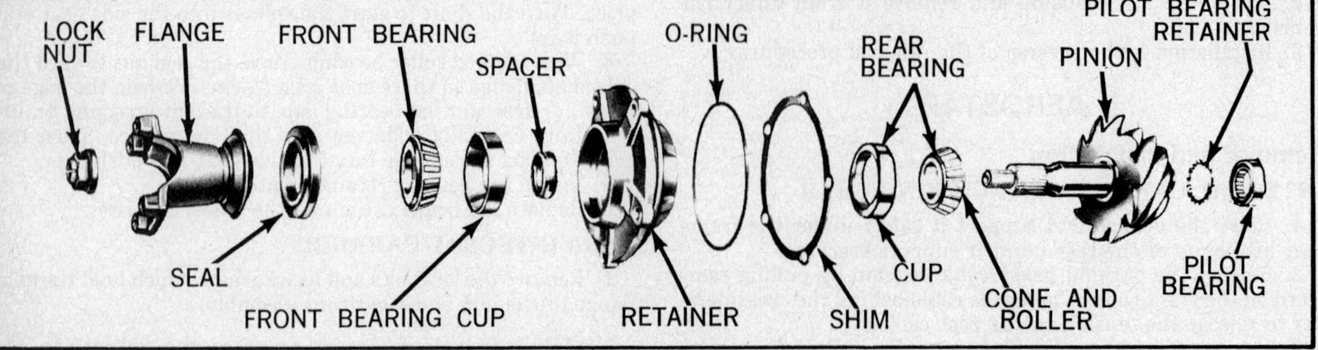

Pinion and bearing retainer components—typical

directly on the wheel bearings. Clean the matting surfaces of the axle housing and carrier.

7. Position the differential carrier on the studs in the axle housing using a new gasket between carrier and housing. Install the carrier-to-housing attaching nuts.

8. Remove the oil seal replacer tool from the transmission extension housing. Position the driveshaft so that the front U-joint slip yoke splines to the transmission output shaft.

9. Connect the driveshaft to the axle U-joint flange, aligning the scribe marks made on the driveshaft end yoke and the axle U-joint flange during the removal procedure. Install the U-bolts and nuts and torque to specifications.

10. Wipe a small amount of an oil-resistant sealer on the outer edge of each seal before it is installed. Do not put any of the sealer on the sealing lip. Install the oil seals in the ends of the rear axle housing with the special tool.

11. Install the two axle shaft assemblies in the axle housing. Care must be exercised to prevent damage to the oil seals. The shorter shaft goes into the left side of the housing. When installing an axle shaft, place a new gasket between the housing flange and the brake backing plate, and carefully slide the axle shaft into the housing so that the rough forging of the shaft will not damage the oil seal. Start the axle splines into the differential side gear, and push the shaft in until the bearing bottoms in the housing.

12. Install the bearing retainer plates on the attaching bolts on the axle housing flanges. Install and tighten the nuts on the bolts.

13. Install the two rear brake drums and the drum attaching nuts.

14. Install the rear wheel and tire assemblies.

15. If the rear brake shoes were backed off, adjust the brakes.

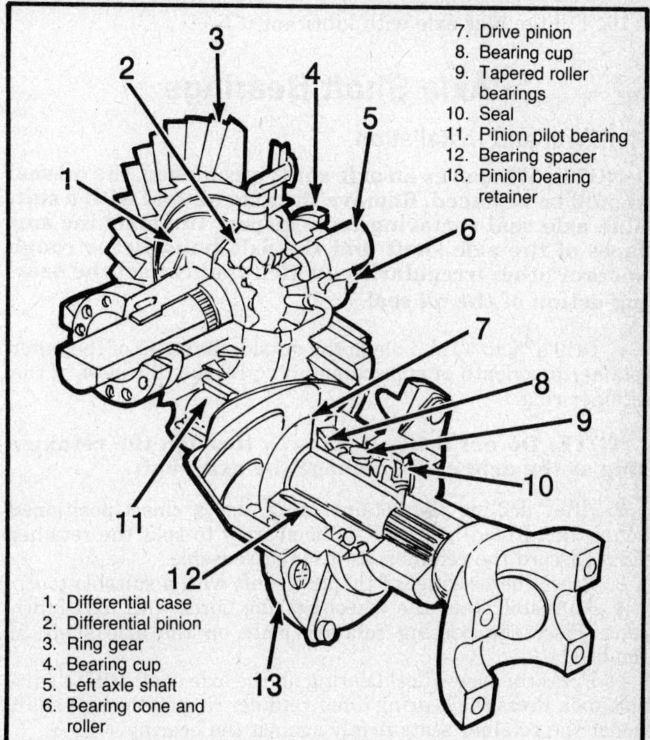

Ford banjo (removeable carrier) type differential

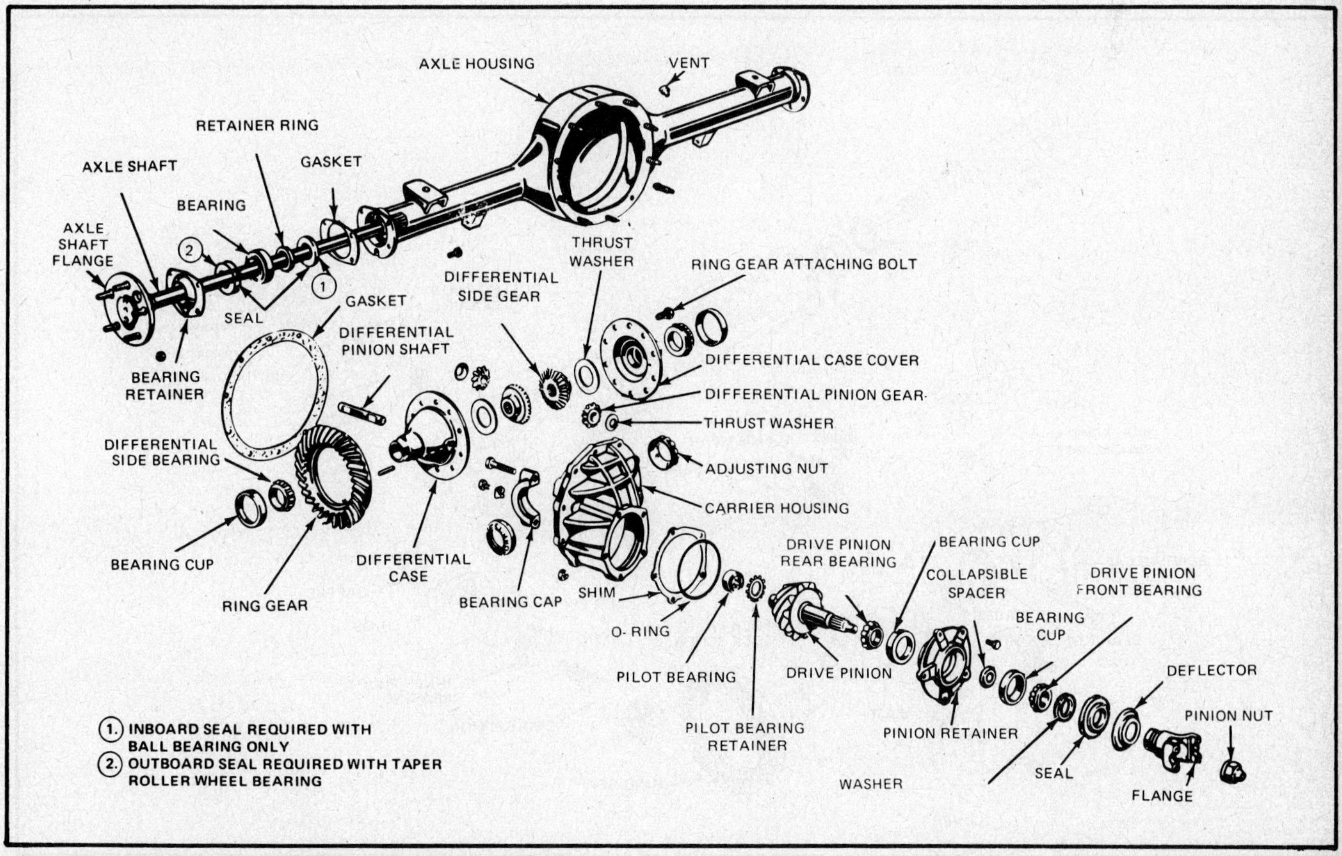

Exploded view of Ford banjo type differential

16. Fill the rear axle with lubricant.

Axle Shaft Bearings

Removal and Installation

NOTE: Whenever an axle shaft is removed, the oil seal should be replaced. Remove the axle oil seal with a suitable axle seal removing tool. Inspect the machine surfaces of the axle shaft and the axle housing for rough spots or other irregularities which could affect the bearing action of the oil seal.

1. Drill a $^1/_4$ to $^1/_2$ in. hole in the outside diameter of the inner retainer to a depth of approximately $^3/_4$ in. the thickness of the retainer ring.

NOTE: Do not drill all the way through the retainer ring as the drill could damage the axle shaft.

2. After drilling the retainer ring, use a chisel positioned across the drilled hole and strike sharply to split the retainer ring. Discard the retainer, as it is not reusable.
3. Press the bearing off the axle shaft with a suitable tool.
4. To install, coat the wheel bearing bores with axle lubricant. Place the bearing retainer plate on the axle shaft, if removed.
5. Press the new wheel bearing on the axle shaft with a suitable tool. Press the bearing inner retainer ring on the axle shaft under the retainer seats firmly against the bearing.

NOTE: Do not attempt to press both the bearing and the inner retainer ring on the axle shaft at the same time.

Rear Wheel Bearings

Removal and Installation

The wheel bearings on the full floating rear axle are packed with wheel bearing grease. Axle lubricant can also flow into the wheel hubs and bearings, however, wheel bearing grease is the primary lubricant. The wheel bearing grease provides lubrication until the axle lubricant reaches the bearings during normal operation.

1. Set the parking brake and loosen the axle shaft bolts.
2. Raise the rear wheels off the floor and place jackstands under the rear axle housing so that the axle is parallel with the floor.
3. Remove the axle shaft bolts.
4. Remove the axle shaft and gaskets.
5. With the axle shaft removed, remove the gasket from the axle shaft flange studs.
6. Bend the lockwasher tab away from the locknut, and then remove the locknut, lockwasher, and the adjusting nut.
7. Remove the outer bearing cone and pull the wheel straight off the axle.
8. With a piece of hardwood which will just clear the outer bearing cup, drive the inner bearing cone and inner seal out of the wheel hub.
9. Wash all the old grease or axle lubricant out of the wheel hub, using a suitable solvent.
10. Wash the bearing cups and rollers and inspect them for pitting, galling, and uneven wear patterns. Inspect the roller for end wear.
11. If the bearing cups are to be replaced, drive them out with a drift. Install the new cups with a block of wood and hammer or press them in.
12. If the bearing cups are properly seated, a 0.0015 in. feeler

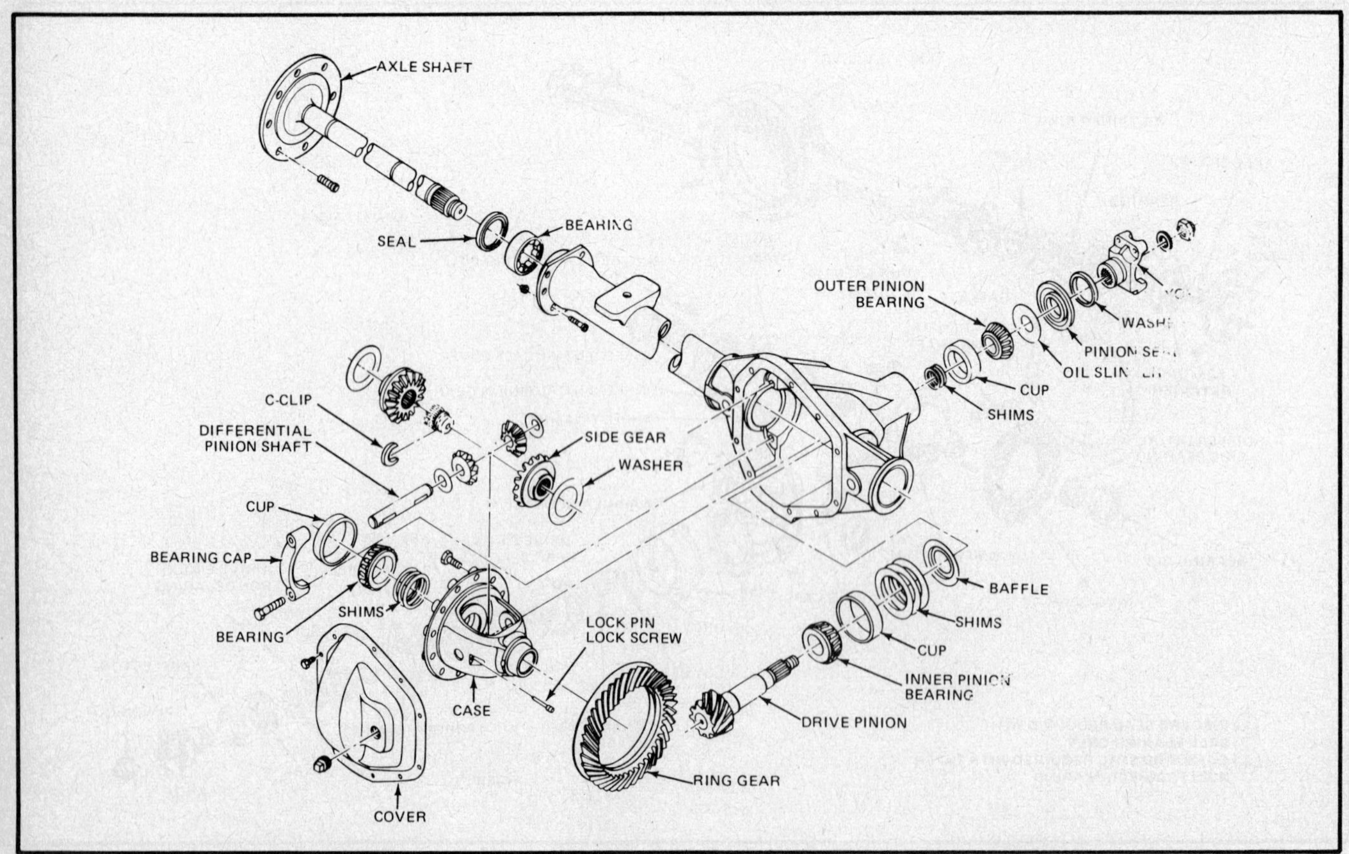

Ford integral carrier differential

gauge will not fit between the cup and the wheel hub.

13. Pack each bearing cone and roller with a bearing packer or in the manner previously outlined for the front wheel bearings on 2WD trucks.
14. Place the inner bearing cone and roller assembly in the wheel hub. Install a new inner seal in the hub.
15. Install the wheel.
16. Install and tighten the bearing adjusting nut to 50–80 ft. lbs. while rotating the wheel.
17. Back off (loosen) the adjusting nut $^3/_8$ of a turn.
18. Apply axle lube to a new lockwasher and install it with the smooth side out.
19. Install the locknut and tighten it to 90–110 ft. lbs. The wheel must rotate freely after the locknut is tightened. The wheel end-play should be within 0.001–0.010 in.
20. Bend two lockwasher tabs inward over an adjusting nut flat and two lockwasher tabs outward over the locknut flat.
21. Install the axle shaft, gasket, lockbolts, and washers. Tighten the bolts to 40–50 ft. lbs.
22. Adjust the brakes, if necessary.

REAR SUSPENSION

Shock Absorber

Removal and Installation

AEROSTAR, BRONCO AND E SERIES

1. Raise the vehicle and support it safely.
2. Remove the shock absorber lower attaching nut and bolt, and swing the lower end free of the mounting bracket on the axle housing.
3. Remove the attaching nut from the upper mounting stud, and remove the shock absorber.
4. To install, position the shock absorber with the rubber bushings and steel washers to the upper mounting bolt.
5. Swing the lower end of the shock absorber into the mounting bracket on the axle housing. Install the attaching washers, mounting bolt, and self-locking nut.
6. Install the self-locking nut on the upper mounting bolt.
7. Lower the vehicle.

BRONCO II, F SERIES AND RANGER

1. Remove the self-locking nut, steel washer, and rubber bushings at the upper and lower ends of the shock absorber.
2. Remove the unit from the vehicle.
3. To install, position the shock absorber on the mounting brackets with the large diameter at the top.
4. Install the rubber bushing, steel washer, and self-locking nut.

Coil Spring

Removal and Installation

AEROSTAR

1. Raise the vehicle and support it safely.
2. Place jack stands on the frame rear lift points or under the rear bumper support brackets.
3. Disconnect the shock absorber from the axle mount on the lower control arm and disconnect it from the axle bracket.
4. Lower the rear axle until the coil springs are no longer under compression.
5. Disconnect the lower retainer from the control arm. Disconnect the upper retainer and spring from the frame.
6. Remove the spring, retainers and insulators.
7. Install in the reverse order of removal.

Leaf Spring

Removal and Installation

E SERIES

1. Raise the rear end of the vehicle and support the chassis with safety stands. Support the rear axle with a floor jack or hoist.
2. Disconnect the lower end of the shock absorber from the bracket on the axle housing.
3. Remove the two spring clips (U-bolts) and the spring clip cap.
4. Lower the axle and remove the spring front bolt from the hanger.
5. Remove the two attaching bolts from the rear of the spring. Remove the spring and the shackle.
6. Assemble the upper end of the shackle to the spring with the attaching bolt.
7. Connect the front of the spring to the front bracket with the attaching bolt.
8. Assemble the spring and shackle to the rear bracket with the attaching bolt.
9. Place the spring clip plate over the head of the center bolt.
10. Raise the axle with a jack and guiding it so that the center bolt enters the pilot hole in the pad on the axle housing.
11. Install the spring clips, cap and attaching nuts. Tighten the nuts snugly.
12. Connect the lower end of the shock absorber to the lower bracket.
13. Tighten the spring front mounting bolt and nut, the rear shackle nuts and spring clip nuts.
14. Remove the safety stands and lower the vehicle.

F SERIES 2WD AND RANGER/BRONCO II

1. Raise the vehicle frame, until the weight is off the rear spring, with the tires still touching the floor.
2. Remove the nuts from the spring U-bolts and drive the U-bolts from the U-bolt plate. If so equipped, remove the auxiliary spring and the spacer.
3. Remove the spring-to-bracket nut and bolt at the front of the spring.
4. Remove the shackle upper and lower nuts and bolts at the rear of the spring. Remove the spring and shackle assembly from the rear shackle bracket.
5. If the bushings in the spring or shackle are worn or damaged, replace them.
6. To install, position the spring in the shackle, and install the upper shackle-to-spring bolt and nut with the bolt head facing outboard.
7. Position the front end of the spring in the bracket and install. Position the shackle in the rear bracket and install.
8. Position the spring on top of the axle with the spring tie bolt centered in the hole provided in the seat. If equipped, install the auxiliary spring and spacer.
9. Install the spring U-bolt plate and nuts. Lower the vehicle. Tighten the spring U-bolt nuts. Tighten the front spring bolt and nut and the rear shackle bolts and nuts.

BRONCO

1. Raise the vehicle by the axles and install safety stands under the frame.

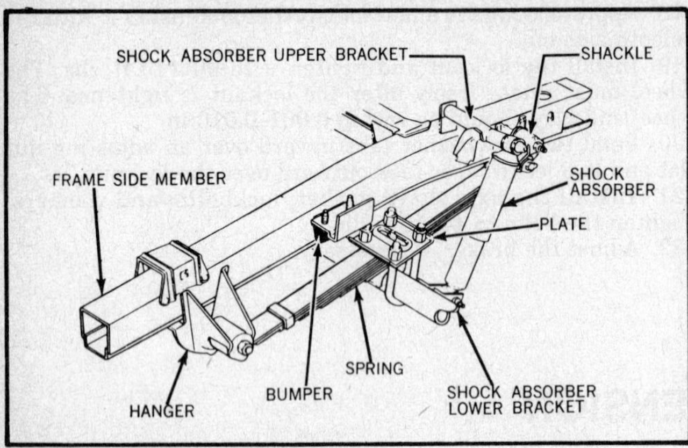

Rear suspension—Bronco

2. Disconnect the shock absorber from the axle.
3. Remove the U-bolt attaching nuts and remove the two U-bolts and the spring clip plate.
4. Lower the axle to relieve spring tension and remove the nut from the spring front attaching bolt.
5. Remove the spring front attaching bolt from the spring and hanger with a drift.
6. Remove the nut from the shackle to hanger attaching bolt and drive the bolt from the shackle and hanger with a drift and remove the spring from the vehicle.
7. Remove the nut from the spring rear attaching bolt. Drive the bolt out of the spring and shackle with a drift.
8. Position the shackle (closed section facing toward front of vehicle) to the spring rear eye and install the bolt and nut.
9. Position the spring front eye and bushing to the spring front hanger, and install the attaching bolt and nut.
10. Position the spring rear eye and bushing to the shackle, and install the attaching bolt and nut.
11. Raise the axle to the spring and install the U-bolts (when an axle cap is not used, the U-bolt shank should contact the leaf edges) and spring clip plate. Align the spring leaves.
12. Tighten the U-bolt nuts and the spring front and rear attaching bolt nuts. The U-bolts should contact the spring assembly edges or axle seat.
13. Connect the shock absorber to the axle and tighten the nut.
14. Remove the safety stands and lower the vehicle.

F SERIES 4WD

1. Raise the vehicle frame until the weight is off the rear springs with the wheels still touching the floor.
2. Remove the nuts from the spring U-bolts.
3. Drive the U-bolts out of the shock absorber lower bracket and the spring cap and remove the U-bolts.
4. Remove the spacer from the top of the spring.
5. If equipped with auxiliary springs, remove the auxiliary spring and spacer.
6. Remove the shackle to bracket bolt and nut from the rear of the spring.
7. Remove the spring-to-hanger bolt and nut from the front of the spring and remove the spring.
8. Remove the shackle-to-spring bolt and nut and remove the shackle from the spring.
9. Position the shackle to the spring and install the attaching bolt and nut. The bolt must be installed so the nut is away from the frame.
10. Position the spring to the spring front hanger and install the attaching bolt and nut.
11. Position the shackle to the bracket and install the attaching bolt and nut.
12. Align the spring toe bolt with the pilot hole in the axle spring seat and, if so equipped, install the auxiliary spring and spacer.
13. Position the spacer on top of the spring and install the U-bolts over the spacer, spring and axle.
14. Position the spring cap and shock lower bracket to the axle and U-bolts. Install the U-bolt attaching nuts.
15. Lower the vehicle and tighten the front spring bracket bolt and nut and the rear shackle bolts and nuts.

Control Arms and Links

UPPER CONTROL ARM

Removal and Installation

AEROSTAR

1. Raise the vehicle and support it safely. Place jack stands under the frame rear lift points or under the rear bumper support brackets.
2. Place jack stands on the frame rear lift points or under the rear bumper support brackets.
3. Disconnect the shock absorber from the axle mount on the lower control arm and disconnect it from the axle bracket.
4. Lower the rear axle until the coil springs are no longer under compression.
5. Disconnect the lower retainer from the control arm. Disconnect the upper retainer and spring from the frame.
6. Rotate the upper control arm to disengage it from the body bracket.
7. Disconnect the control arm from the left frame bracket.
8. Remove the outer insulator and spacer and remove the control arm from the bracket.
9. Install in the reverse order of removal.

LOWER CONTROL ARM

Removal and Installation

AEROSTAR

1. Raise the vehicle and support it safely. Place jack stands under the frame rear lift points or under the rear bumper support brackets.
2. Disconnect the shock absorber from the axle bracket. Swing the lower end of the shock free of the axle bracket.
3. Lower the rear axle until the coil springs are no longer under compression.
4. Disconnect the lower retainer from the control arm. Remove the insulator from the arm.
5. Remove the bolt and nut retaining the lower control arm to the axle housing.
6. Disconnect the lower control arm from the frame bracket. Remove the lower control arm.
7. Install in the reverse order of removal.

Jeep 4

INDEX

BEFORE SERVICING, SEE THE SAFETY NOTICE AT THE FRONT OF THE BOOK

ENGINE IDENTIFICATION CODES BY VIN NUMBER
Jeep Trucks

Engine Cu. In. (liter)	Cylinders	1982	1983	1984	1985	1986	1987	1988
126 (2.0)	4	—	—	—	—	B	B	B
150 (2.5)	4	—	U	U	U	U	U	U
150 (2.5)	4	—	—	—	H	H	H	H
151 (2.5)	4	B	B	—	—	—	—	—
173 (2.8)	6	—	—	W	W	W	W	W
243 (4.0)	6	—	—	—	—	—	—	M
258 (4.2)	6	C	C	C	C	C	C	C
360 (5.9)	8	N	N	N	N	N	N	N

MODEL IDENTIFICATION
All Models

	Model Designation	Model Name
1983	CJ5	CJ5
	CJ5 Renagade	CJ5
	CJ5 Laredo	CJ5
	CJ5 Limited	CJ5
	CJ7	CJ7
	CJ7 Renagade	CJ7
	CJ7 Laredo	CJ7
	CJ7 Limited	CJ7
	Scrambler	Scrambler
	Scrambler Renegade	Scrambler
	Scrambler Laredo	Scrambler
	Scrambler Limited	Scrambler
	Scrambler SR Sport	Scrambler
	Scrambler SL Sport	Scrambler
	J10 Pickup	J10
	J10 Pioneer	J10
	J10 Honcho	J10
	J10 Laredo	J10
	J20 Pickup	J20
	J20 Pioneer	J20
	J20 Honcho	J20
	J20 Laredo	J20
	Wagoneer	Wagoneer
	Wagoneer Brougham	Wagoneer
	Wagonner Limited	Wagoneer
	Cherokee	Cherokee
	Cherokee Chief	Cherokee
	Cherokee Laredo	Cherokee
	Cherokee Pioneer	Cherokee
	Grand Wagoneer	Grand Wagoneer
1984	CJ7	CJ7
	CJ7 Renagade	CJ7
	CJ7 Laredo	CJ7
	Scrambler	Scrambler
	Scrambler Renegade	Scrambler
	Scrambler Laredo	Scrambler
	Scrambler SR Sport	Scrambler
	Scrambler SL Sport	Scrambler
	J10 Pickup	J10
	J10 Pioneer	J10

MODEL IDENTIFICATION
All Models

	Model Designation	Model Name
	J10 Laredo	J10
	J20 Pickup	J20
	J20 Pioneer	J20
	J20 Laredo	J20
	Wagoneer	Wagoneer
	Wagonner Limited	Wagoneer
	Cherokee	Cherokee
	Cherokee Chief	Cherokee
	Cherokee Laredo	Cherokee
	Cherokee Pioneer	Cherokee
	Grand Wagoneer	Grand Wagoneer
1985	CJ7	CJ7
	CJ7 Renagade	CJ7
	CJ7 Laredo	CJ7
	Scrambler	Scrambler
	Scrambler Renegade	Scrambler
	Scrambler Laredo	Scrambler
	J10 Pickup	J10
	J10 Pioneer	J10
	J20 Pickup	J20
	J20 Pioneer	J20
	Wagoneer	Wagoneer
	Wagonner Limited	Wagoneer
	Cherokee	Cherokee
	Cherokee Chief	Cherokee
	Cherokee Laredo	Cherokee
	Cherokee Pioneer	Cherokee
	Grand Wagoneer	Grand Wagoneer
1986	CJ7	CJ7
	CJ7 Renagade	CJ7
	CJ7 Laredo	CJ7
	J10 Pickup	J10
	J10 Pioneer	J10
	J20 Pickup	J20
	J20 Pioneer	J20
	Wagoneer	Wagoneer
	Wagonner Limited	Wagoneer
	Cherokee	Cherokee
	Cherokee Chief	Cherokee
	Cherokee Laredo	Cherokee

MODEL IDENTIFICATION
All Models

Year	Model Designation	Model Name
	Cherokee Pioneer	Cherokee
	Grand Wagoneer	Grand Wagoneer
	Comanche Pickup	Comanche
	Comanche X	Comanche
	Comanche XLS	Comanche
1987-88	J10 Pickup	J10
	J10 Pioneer	J10
	J20 Pickup	J20
	J20 Pioneer	J20
	Wagoneer	Wagoneer
	Wagonner Limited	Wagoneer
	Cherokee	Cherokee

MODEL IDENTIFICATION
All Models

Year	Model Designation	Model Name
	Cherokee Chief	Cherokee
	Cherokee Laredo	Cherokee
	Cherokee Pioneer	Cherokee
	Grand Wagoneer	Grand Wagoneer
	Comanche Pickup	Comanche
	Comanche LB	Comanche
	Comanche Pioneer	Comanche
	Comanche Chief	Comanche
	Comanche Laredo	Comanche
	Wrangler	Wrangler
	Wrangler S	Wrangler
	Wrangler Laredo	Wrangler

GENERAL ENGINE SPECIFICATIONS

Year	VIN	No. Cylinder Displacement cu. in. (liter)	Fuel System Type	Net Horsepower @ rpm	Net Torque @ rpm (ft.lbs.)	Bore × Stroke (iA.)	Com-pression Ratio	Oil Pressure @ 2000 rpm
1982	B	4-151 (2.5)	Carb.	87 @ 4400	128 @ 2400	4.000 × 3.000	8.3:1	38
	C	6-258 (4.2)	Carb.	110 @ 3200	210 @ 1800	3.750 × 3.895	8.0:1	37
	A	8-360 (5.9)	Carb.	175 @ 4000	285 @ 2900	4.080 × 3.440	8.25:1	37
1983	U	4-150 (2.5)	Carb.	83 @ 4200	116 @ 2600	3.876 × 3.188	9.2:1	40
	B	4-151 (2.5)	Carb.	87 @ 4400	128 @ 2400	4.000 × 3.000	8.3:1	38
	C	6-258 (4.2)	Carb.	110 @ 3200	210 @ 1800	3.750 × 3.895	8.0:1	37
	A	8-360 (5.9)	Carb.	175 @ 4000	285 @ 2900	4.080 × 3.440	8.25:1	37
1984	U	4-150 (2.5)	Carb.	83 @ 4200	116 @ 2600	3.876 × 3.188	9.2:1	40
	W	6-173 (2.8)	Carb.	110 @ 4800	148 @ 2000	3.500 × 2.990	8.5:1	45
	C	6-258 (4.2)	Carb.	110 @ 3200	210 @ 1800	3.750 × 3.895	8.0:1	37
	A	8-360 (5.9)	Carb.	175 @ 4000	285 @ 2900	4.080 × 3.440	8.25:1	37
1985	B	4-126 (2.0)	Diesel	NA	NA	3.358 × 3.503	21.5:1	46
	U	4-150 (2.5)	Carb.	83 @ 4200	116 @ 2600	3.876 × 3.188	9.2:1	40
	H	4-150 (2.5)	TBI	83 @ 4200	116 @ 2600	3.876 × 3.188	9.2:1	40
	W	6-173 (2.8)	Carb.	110 @ 4800	148 @ 2000	3.500 × 2.990	8.5:1	45
	C	6-258 (4.2)	Carb.	110 @ 3200	210 @ 1800	3.750 × 3.895	8.0:1	37
	A	8-360 (5.9)	Carb.	175 @ 4000	285 @ 2900	4.080 × 3.440	8.25:1	37
1986	B	4-126 (2.0)	Diesel	NA	NA	3.358 × 3.503	21.5:1	46
	U	4-150 (2.5)	Carb.	83 @ 4200	116 @ 2600	3.876 × 3.188	9.2:1	40
	H	4-150 (2.5)	TBI	83 @ 4200	116 @ 2600	3.876 × 3.188	9.2:1	40
	W	6-173 (2.8)	Carb.	110 @ 4800	148 @ 2000	3.500 × 2.990	8.5:1	45
	C	6-258 (4.2)	Carb.	110 @ 3200	210 @ 1800	3.750 × 3.895	8.0:1	37
	A	8-360 (5.9)	Carb.	175 @ 4000	285 @ 2900	4.080 × 3.440	8.25:1	37

GENERAL ENGINE SPECIFICATIONS

Year	VIN	No. Cylinder Displacement cu. in. (liter)	Fuel System Type	Net Horsepower @ rpm	Net Torque @ rpm (ft.lbs.)	Bore × Stroke (in.)	Com-pression Ratio	Oil Pressure @ 2000 rpm
1987-88	B	4-126 (2.0)	Diesel	NA	NA	3.358 × 3.503	21.5:1	46
	U	4-150 (2.5)	Carb.	83 @ 4200	116 @ 2600	3.876 × 3.188	9.2:1	40
	H	4-150 (2.5)	TBI	83 @ 4200	116 @ 2600	3.876 × 3.188	9.2:1	40
	W	6-173 (2.8)	Carb.	110 @ 4800	148 @ 2000	3.500 × 2.990	8.5:1	45
	M	6-243 (4.0)	MPI	173 @ 4500	220 @ 2500	3.8750 × 3.876	9.2:1	37
	C	6-258 (4.2)	Carb.	110 @ 3200	210 @ 1800	3.750 × 3.895	9.2:1	37
	A	8-360 (5.9)	Carb.	175 @ 4000	285 @ 2900	4.080 × 3.440	8.25:1	37

GASOLINE ENGINE TUNE-UP SPECIFICATIONS

Year	VIN	No. Cylinder Displacement cu. in. (liter)	Spark Plugs Type	Spark Plugs Gap (in.)	Ignition Timing (deg.) ① MT	Ignition Timing (deg.) ① AT	Com-pression Pressure (psi)	Fuel Pump (psi)	Idle Speed (rpm) MT	Idle Speed (rpm) AT	Valve Clearance In.	Valve Clearance Ex.
1982	B	4-151 (2.5)	RBL13Y6	.060	14	14	NA	4-5.75	500	650	Hyd.	Hyd.
	C	6-258 (4.2)	N-13L	.035	8	8	NA	4-5	700	600	Hyd.	Hyd.
	N	8-360 (5.9)	N-12Y	.035	8	8	NA	5-6.50	800	600	Hyd.	Hyd.
1983	U	4-150 (2.5)	RFN14LY	.035	12	12	NA	6.50-8	750	750	Hyd.	Hyd.
	B	4-151 (2.5)	R44T5X	.060	10	12	NA	6.50-8	900	700	Hyd.	Hyd.
	C	6-258 (4.2)	RFN14LY	.035	8②	8	NA	4-5	700	600	Hyd.	Hyd.
	N	8-360 (5.9)	RN12Y	.035	8	8	NA	5-6	800	600	Hyd.	Hyd.
1984	U	4-150 (2.5)	RFN14LY	.035	12	12	NA	6.5-8	750	750	Hyd.	Hyd.
	W	6-173 (2.8)	RUT2YC	.040	10	10	NA	5-7	750	750	⑥	⑥
	C	6-258 (4.2)	RFN14LY	.035	8②	8	NA	4-5	700	600	Hyd.	Hyd.
	N	8-360 (5.9)	RN12Y	.035	8	8	NA	5-6	800	600	Hyd.	Hyd.
1985	U	4-150 (2.5)	RFN14LY	.035	12	12	NA	6.5-8	750	750	Hyd.	Hyd.
	H	4-150 (2.5)	RC12LYC	.035	12	12	NA	6.5-8	750	750	Hyd.	Hyd.
	W	6-173 (2.8)	RUT2YC	.040	10	10	NA	5-7	750	750	⑥	⑥
	C	6-258 (4.2)	RFN14LY	.035	8	12	NA	4-5	700	600	Hyd.	Hyd.
	N	8-360 (5.9)	RN12Y	.035	8	8	NA	5-6	800	600	Hyd.	Hyd.
1986	U	4-150 (2.5)	RFN14LY	.035	12	12	NA	6.5-8	750	750	Hyd.	Hyd.
	H	4-150 (2.5)	RC12LYC	.035	12	12	NA	6.5-8	750	750	Hyd.	Hyd.
	W	6-173 (2.8)	RUT2YC	.040	10	10	NA	5-7	750	750	⑥	⑥
	C	6-258 (4.2)	RFN14LY	.035	8	12	NA	4-5	700	600	Hyd.	Hyd.
	N	8-360 (5.9)	RN12Y	.035	8	8	NA	5-6	800	600	Hyd.	Hyd.

GASOLINE ENGINE TUNE-UP SPECIFICATIONS

Year	VIN	No. Cylinder Displacement cu. in. (liter)	Spark Plugs Type	Spark Plugs Gap (in.)	Ignition Timing (deg.) ① MT	Ignition Timing (deg.) ① AT	Compression Pressure (psi)	Fuel Pump (psi)	Idle Speed (rpm) MT	Idle Speed (rpm) AT	Valve Clearance In.	Valve Clearance Ex.
1987-88	U	4-150 (2.5)	RFN14LY	.035	12	12	NA	6.5-8	750	750	Hyd.	Hyd.
	H	4-150 (2.5)	RC12LYC	.035	⑤	⑤	NA	6.5-8	NA	NA	Hyd.	Hyd.
	W	6-173 (2.8)	RUT2YC	.040	10	10	NA	5-7	750	750	⑥	⑥
	M	6-243 (4.0)	NA	NA	NA	NA	NA	NA	NA	NA	Hyd.	Hyd.
	C	6-258 (4.2)	RFN14LY	.035	9③	9③	NA	4-5	700	600	Hyd.	Hyd.
	N	8-360 (5.9)	RN12LY	.035	12④	12④	NA	5-6	600	500	Hyd.	Hyd.

① BTDC
② Calif.—CJ6
③ at 1600 RPM; High altitude 16 @ 1600 RPM
④ at 600 RPM; High altitude 16 @ 600 RPM
⑤ Not adjustable
⑥ Hydraulic—Turn Rocker arm stud nut until all lash is gone, then tighten 1½ turns more

FIRING ORDERS

NOTE: To avoid confusion, always replace spark plug wires one at a time.

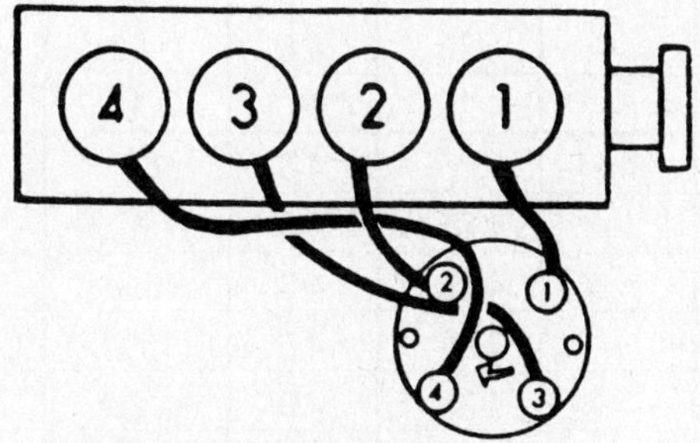

AMC 151 CID 4-cyl
Engine firing order: 1-3-4-2
Distributor rotation: clockwise

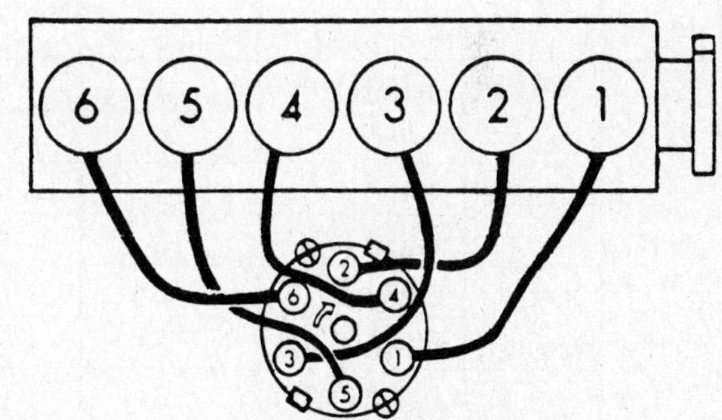

6 cylinder engines
Firing order:1-5-3-6-2-4

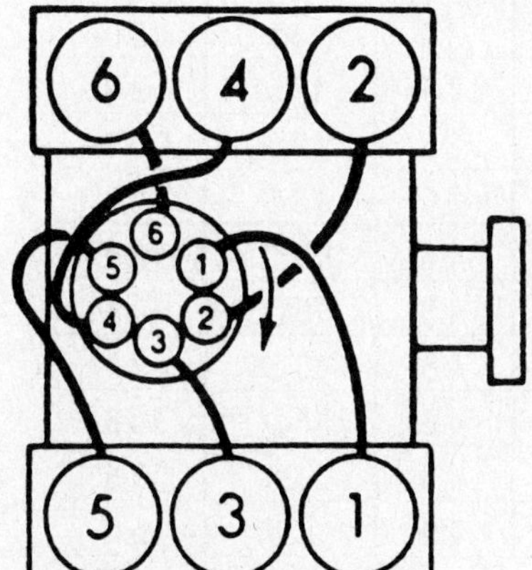

173 V6 (2.8L)
Engine firing order: 1-2-3-4-5-6
Distributor rotation: clockwise

②

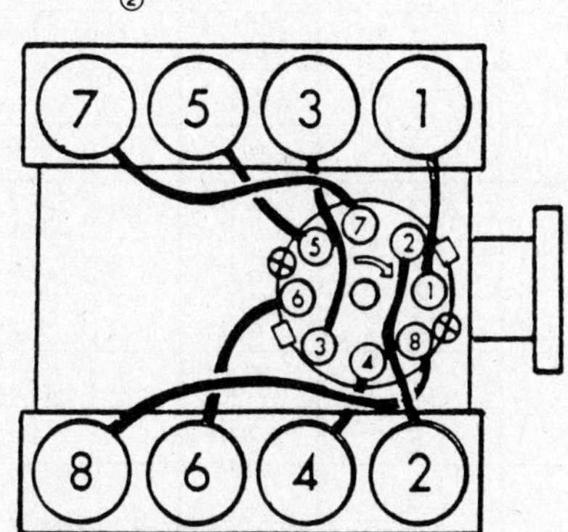

V8 engines
Firing order: 1-8-4-3-6-5-7-2

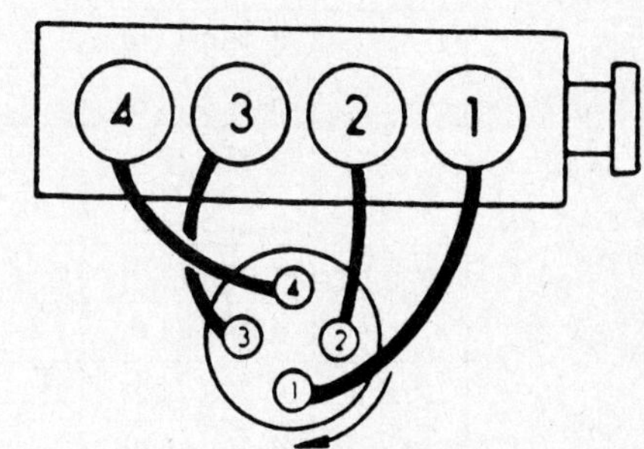

AMC 150 4cyl
Engine firing order: 1-3-4-2
Distributor rotation- Clockwise

CAPACITIES

Year	Model	No. Cylinder Displacement cu. in. (liter)	Engine Crankcase with Filter	Engine Crankcase without Filter	Transmission (pts.) 4-Spd	Transmission (pts.) 5-Spd	Transmission (pts.) Auto.	Drive Axle (pts.)	Fuel Tank (gal.)	Cooling System (qts.)
1982	CJ	4-150 (2.5)	4	4	4.0	4.5	—	4.8	15③	9.0
		4-151 (2.5)	3	3	4.0	4.5	—	4.8	15③	8.0
		6-258 (4.2)	4	5	3.5	4.5	4.25	4.8	15③	10.5
	Scrambler	4-150 (2.5)	4	4	4.0	4.5	—	4.8	15③	9.0
		4-151 (2.5)	3	3	4.0	4.5	—	4.8	15C	8.0
		6-258 (4.20	4	5	3.5	4.5	4.25	4.8	15③	10.5
	Grand	6-258 (4.2)	4	4	3.5	4.5	4.25	4.8	20	10.5
	Wagoneer	8-360 (5.9)	4	5	3.5	—	4.25	4.8	20	14.0
	Truck	6-258 (4.2)	4	5	3.5	4.5	4.25	4.8	18	10.5
		8-360 (5.9)	4	5	3.5①	—	4.25	4.8①	18	14.0
1983	CJ	4-150 (2.5)	4	4	4.0	4.5	—	4.8	15③	9.0
		6-258 (4.2)	6	6	4.0	4.5	4.25	4.8	15③	10.5
	Scrambler	4-150 (2.5)	4	4	4.0	4.5	—	4.8	15③	9.0
		6-258 (4.20	6	6	4.0	4.5	4.25	4.8	15③	10.5
	Grand	6-258 (4.2)	6	6	3.5	—	4.25	4.8	20	10.5
	Wagoneer	8-360 (5.9)	5	5	—	—	4.25	4.8	20	15.0
	Truck	6-258 (4.2)	6	6	3.5	—	4.25	4.8	18	10.5
		8-360 (5.9)	5	5	3.5	—	4.25	4.8①	18	15.0
1984	CJ	4-150 (2.5)	4	4	4.0	4.5	4.25	4.8	15③	9.0
		6-258 (4.2)	6	6	3.5	—	4.25	4.8	15③	10.5
	Scrambler	4-150 (2.5)	4	4	4.0	4.5	4.25	4.8	15③	9.0
		6-258 (4.2)	6	6	3.5	—	4.25	4.8	15③	10.5
	Grand	6-258 (4.2)	6	6	3.5	—	4.25	4.8	20	10.5
	Wagoneer	8-360 (5.9)	5	5	—	—	4.25	4.8	20	15.0
	Truck	6-258 (4.2)	6	6	3.5	—	4.25	4.8	18	10.5
		8-360 (5.9)	5	5	—	—	4.25	4.8①	18	15.0
	Cherokee	4-150 (2.5)	4	4	4.0④	4.5⑤	6.5	2.5	13.5	10.0
		6-173 (2.8)	4	4	4.0④	4.5⑤	6.5	2.5	13.5	12.0
	Wagoneer	4-126 (2.0)	6.3	6.3	4.0④	4.5⑤	6.5	2.5	13.5	9.0
		4-150 (2.5)	4	4	4.0④	4.5⑤	6.5	2.5	13.5	10.0
		6-173 (2.8)	4	4	4.0④	4.5⑤	6.5	2.5	13.5	12.0
1985	CJ	4-150 (2.5)	4	4	4.0	4.5	4.25	4.8	15③	9.0
		6-258 (4.2)	6	6	3.5	4.5	4.25	4.8	15③	10.5
	Scrambler	4-150 (2.5)	4	4	4.0	4.5	4.25	4.8	15③	9.0
		6-258 (4.2)	6	6	3.5	—	4.25	4.8	15③	10.5
	Grand	6-258 (4.2)	6	6	3.5	—	4.25	4.8	20	10.5
	Wagoneer	8-360 (5.9)	5	5	—	—	4.25	4.8	20	15.0

CAPACITIES

Year	Model	No. Cylinder Displacement cu. in. (liter)	Engine Crankcase with Filter	Engine Crankcase without Filter	Transmission (pts.) 4-Spd	Transmission (pts.) 5-Spd	Transmission (pts.) Auto.	Drive Axle (pts.)	Fuel Tank (gal.)	Cooling System (qts.)
	Truck	6-258 (4.2)	6	6	3.5	–	4.25	4.8	18	10.5
		8-360 (5.9)	5	5	–	–	4.25	4.8①	18	15.0
	Cherokee	4-126 (2.0)	6.3	6.3	4.0④	4.5③	6.5	2.5	13.5	9.0
		4-150 (2.5)	4	4	4.0④	4.5③	6.5	2.5	13.5	9.0
	Wagoneer	4-126 (2.0)	6.3	6.3	4.0④	4.5③	6.5	2.5	13.5	9.0
		4-150 (2.5)	4	4	4.0④	4.5③	6.5	2.5	13.5	9.0
		6-258 (4.2)	4	4	4.0④	4.5③	6.5	2.5	13.5	9.0
1986	CJ	4–150 (2.5)	4	4	4.0	4.5	4.25	4.8	15③	9.0
		6–258 (4.2)	6	6	3.5	–	4.25	4.8	15③	10.5
	Scrambler	4–150 (2.5)	4	4	4.0	4.5	4.25	4.8	15③	9.0
		6–258 (4.2)	6	6	3.5	–	4.25	4.8	15③	10.5
	Grand Wagoneer	6-258 (4.2)	6	6	3.5	–	4.25	4.8	20	10.5
		8-360 (5.9)	5	5	–	–	4.25	4.8	20	15.0
	Truck	6-258 (4.2)	6	6	3.5	–	4.25	4.8	18	10.5
		8-360 (5.9)	5	5	–	–	4.25	4.8①	18	15.0
	Cherokee	4-126 (2.0)	6.3	6.3	4.0④	4.5③	6.5	2.5	13.5	9.0
		4-150 (2.5)	4	4	4.0④	4.5③	6.5	2.5	13.5	9.0
		6-173 (2.5)	4	4	4.0④	4.5③	6.5	2.5	13.5	9.0
	Wagoneer	4-126 (2.0)	6.3	6.3	4.0④	4.5③	6.5	2.5	13.5	9.0
		4-150 (2.5)	4	4	4.0④	4.5③	6.5	2.5	13.5	9.0
		6-258 (4.2)	4	4	4.0④	4.5③	6.5	2.5	13.5	9.0
	Comanche	4-126 (2.0)	6.3	6.3	4.0④	4.5③	6.5	2.5	13.5	9.0
		4-150 (2.5)	4	4	4.0④	4.5③	6.5	2.5	13.5	9.0
		6-173 (2.5)	4	4	4.0④	4.5③	6.5	2.5	13.5	9.0
1987–88	Wrangler	4–150 (2.5)	4	4	4.0	4.5	4.25	4.8	15③	9.0
		6–243 (4.0)	6	6	3.5	–	4.25	4.8	15③	10.5
		6–258 (4.2)	6	6	3.5	–	4.25	4.8	15③	10.5
	Grand Wagoneer	6-258 (4.2)	6	6	3.5	–	4.25	4.8	20	10.5
		8-360 (5.9)	5	5	–	–	4.25	4.8	20	15.0
	Truck	6-258 (4.2)	6	6	3.5	–	4.25	4.8	18	10.5
		8-360 (5.9)	5	5	–	–	4.25	4.8①	18	15.0
	Cherokee	4-126 (2.0)	6.3	6.3	4.0④	4.5③	6.5	2.5	13.5	9.0
		4-150 (2.5)	4	4	4.0④	4.5③	6.5	2.5	13.5	9.0
		6-173 (2.5)	4	4	4.0④	4.5③	6.5	2.5	13.5	9.0
	Wagoneer	4-126 (2.0)	6.3	6.3	4.0④	4.5③	6.5	2.5	13.5	9.0
		4-150 (2.5)	4	4	4.0④	4.5③	6.5	2.5	13.5	9.0
		6-173 (2.8)	4	4	4.0④	4.5③	6.5	2.5	13.5	9.0

CAPACITIES

Year	Model	No. Cylinder Displacement cu. in. (liter)	Engine Crankcase with Filter	Engine Crankcase without Filter	Transmission (pts.) 4-Spd	Transmission (pts.) 5-Spd	Transmission (pts.) Auto.	Drive Axle (pts.)	Fuel Tank (gal.)	Cooling System (qts.)
	Comanche	4-126 (2.0)	6.3	6.3	4.0④	4.5⑤	6.5	2.5	13.5	9.0
		4-150 (2.5)	4	4	4.0④	4.5⑤	6.5	2.5	13.5	9.0
		6-173 (2.5)	4	4	4.0④	4.5⑤	6.5	2.5	13.5	9.0

① J20 Series: 6
② Rear
③ 20 Gallon optional fuel tank
④ Borg Warner Asian: 7.5
⑤ Borg Warner Asian: 7.0

CRANKSHAFT AND CONNECTING ROD SPECIFICATIONS

All measurements are given in inches.

Year	VIN	No. Cylinder Displacement cu. in. (liter)	Crankshaft Main Brg. Journal Dia.	Crankshaft Main Brg. Oil Clearance	Crankshaft Shaft End-play	Crankshaft Thrust on No.	Connecting Rod Journal Diameter	Connecting Rod Oil Clearance	Connecting Rod Side Clearance
1982	B	4–151 (2.5)	2.2988	.0005–.0022	.0035–.0085	5	1.8690	.0007–.0027	.006–.022
	C	6–258 (4.2)	2.4986–2.5001	.0010–.0020	.0015–.0065	3	2.0934–2.0955	.0010–.0020	.005–.014
	N	8–360 (5.9)	2.7474–2.7489 ①	.0010–.0020 ②	.003–.008	3	2.0934–2.0955	.0010–.0030	.006–.018
1983	U	4–150 (2.5)	2.4996–2.5001	.0001–.0025	.0015–.0065	2	2.0934–2.0955	.0010–.0030	.010–.019
	B	4–151 (2.5)	2.2988	.0005–.0022	.0035–.0085	5	1.8690	.0007–.0027	.006–.022
	C	6–258 (4.2)	2.4986–2.5001	.0010–.0020	.0015–.0065	3	2.0934–2.0955	.0010–.0020	.005–.014
	N	8–360 (5.9)	2.7474–2.7489 ①	.0010–.0020 ②	.003–.008	3	2.0934–2.0955	.0010–.0030	.006–.018
1984	U	4–150 (2.5)	2.4996–2.5001	.0001–.0025	.0015–.0065	2	2.0934–2.0955	.0010–.0030	.010–.019
	W	6–173 (2.8)	2.4940	.0017–.0030	.0020–.0067	3	1.9980	.0014–.0032	.0063–.0173
	C	6–258 (4.2)	2.4986–2.5001	.0010–.0020	.0015–.0065	3	2.0934–2.0955	.0010–.0020	.005–.014
	N	8–360 (5.9)	2.7474–2.7489 ①	.0010–.0020 ②	.003–.008	3	2.0934–2.0955	.0010–.0030	.006–.018

CRANKSHAFT AND CONNECTING ROD SPECIFICATIONS

All measurements are given in inches.

			Crankshaft				Connecting Rod		
Year	VIN	No. Cylinder Displacement cu. in. (liter)	Main Brg. Journal Dia.	Main Brg. Oil Clearance	Shaft End-play	Thrust on No.	Journal Diameter	Oil Clearance	Side Clearance
1985	U	4–150 (2.5)	2.4996–2.5001	.0001–.0025	.0015–.0065	2	2.0934–2.0955	.0010–.0030	.010–.019
	H	4–150 (2.5)	2.4996–2.5001	.0001–.0025	.0015–.0065	2	2.0934–2.0955	.0010–.0030	.010–.019
	W	6–173 (2.8)	2.4940	.0017–.0030	.0020–.0067	3	1.9980	.0014–.0032	.0063–.0173
	C	6–258 (4.2)	2.4986–2.5001	.0010–.0020	.0015–.0065	3	2.0934–2.0955	.0010–.0020	.005–.014
	N	8–360 (5.9)	2.7474–2.7489 ①	.0010–.0020 ②	.003–.008	3	2.0934–2.0955	.0010–.0030	.006–.018
1986	U	4–150 (2.5)	2.4996–2.5001	.0001–.0025	.0015–.0065	2	2.0934–2.0955	.0010–.0030	.010–.019
	H	4–150 (2.5)	2.4996–2.5001	.0001–.0025	.0015–.0065	2	2.0934–2.0955	.0010–.0030	.010–.019
	W	6–173 (2.8)	2.4940	.0017–.0030	.0020–.0067	3	1.9980	.0014–.0032	.0063–.0173
	C	6–258 (4.2)	2.4986–2.5001	.0010–.0020	.0015–.0065	3	2.0934–2.0955	.0010–.0020	.005–.014
	N	8–360 (5.9)	2.7474–2.7489 ①	.0010–.0020 ②	.003–.008	3	2.0934–2.0955	.0010–.0030	.006–.018
1987–88	U	4–150 (2.5)	2.4996–2.5001	.0001–.0025	.0015–.0065	2	2.0934–2.0955	.0010–.0030	.010–.019
	H	4–150 (2.5)	2.4996–2.5001	.0001–.0025	.0015–.0065	2	2.0934–2.0955	.0010–.0030	.010–.019
	W	6–173 (2.8)	2.4940	.0017–.0030	.0020–.0067	3	1.9980	.0014–.0032	.0063–.0173
	M	6–243 (4.0)	2.4996–2.5001	.0010–.0025	.0015–.0065	3	2.2085–2.2090	.0010–.0030	.010–.019
	C	6–258 (4.2)	2.4986–2.5001	.0010–.0020	.0015–.0065	3	2.0934–2.0955	.0010–.0020	.005–.014
	N	8–360 (5.9)	2.7474–2.7489 ①	.0010–.0020 ②	.003–.008 .008	3	2.0934–2.0955 2.0955	.0010–.0030 .0030	.006–.018 .018

① No. 5: 2.7464–2.7479
② No. 5: .0020–.0030

VALVE SPECIFICATIONS

Year	VIN	No. Cylinder Displacement cu. in. (liter)	Seat Angle (deg.)	Face Angle (deg.)	Spring Test Pressure (lbs.)	Spring Installed Height (in.)	Stem-to-Guide Clearance (in.)		Stem Diameter (in.)	
							Intake	Exhaust	Intake	Exhaust
1982	B	4-151 (2.5)	46	45	82 @ 1.66	1 21/32	.0010–.0027	.0010–.0027	.3422	.3422
	C	6-258 (4.2)	44.5①	44②	100 @ 1 13/16	2 5/64	.0010–.0030	.0010–.0030	.3720	.3720
	N	8-360 (5.9)	44.5①	44②	84 @ 1 13/16	2 5/64	.0010–.0030	.0010–.0030	.3720	.3720
1983	U	4-150 (2.5)	45	44	212 @ 1.20	1.82	.0010–.0030	.0010–.0030	.3412	.3412
	B	4-151 (2.5)	46	45	82 @ 1.66	1 21/32	.0010–.0027	.0010–.0027	.3422	.3422
	C	6-258 (4.2)	44.5①	44②	100 @ 1 13/16	2 5/64	.0010–.0030	.0010–.0030	.3720	.3720
	N	8-360 (5.9)	44.5①	44②	84 @ 1 13/16	2 5/64	.0010–.0030	.0010–.0030	.3720	.3720
1984	U	4-150 (2.5)	45	44	212 @ 1.20	1.82	.0010–.0030	.0010–.0030	.3412	.3412
	W	6-173 (2.8)	46	45	195 @ 1.18	1.57	.0010–.0027	.0010–.0027	.3416	.3416
	C	6-258 (4.2)	44.5①	44②	100 @ 1 13/16	2 5/64	.0010–.0030	.0010–.0030	.3720	.3720
	N	8-360 (5.9)	44.5①	44②	84 @ 1 13/16	2 5/64	.0010–.0030	.0010–.0030	.3720	.3720
1985	U	4-150 (2.5)	45	44	212 @ 1.20	1.82	.0010–.0030	.0010–.0030	.3412	.3412
	H	4-150 (2.5)	45	44	212 @ 1.20	1.82	.0010–.0030	.0010–.0030	.3412	.3412
	W	6-173 (2.8)	46	45	195 @ 1.18	1.57	.0010–.0027	.0010–.0027	.3416	.3416
	C	6-258 (4.2)	44.5①	44②	100 @ 1 13/16	2 5/64	.0010–.0030	.0010–.0030	.3720	.3720
	N	8-360 (5.9)	44.5①	44②	84 @ 1 13/16	2 5/64	.0010–.0030	.0010–.0030	.3720	.3720
1986	U	4-150 (2.5)	45	44	212 @ 1.20	1.82	.0010–.0030	.0010–.0030	.3412	.3412
	H	4-150 (2.5)	45	44	212 @ 1.20	1.82	.0010–.0030	.0010–.0030	.3412	.3412
	W	6-173 (2.8)	46	45	195 @ 1.18	1.57	.0010–.0027	.0010–.0027	.3416	.3416
	C	6-258 (4.2)	44.5①	44②	100 @ 1 13/16	2 5/64	.0010–.0030	.0010–.0030	.3720	.3720
	N	8-360 (5.9)	44.5①	44②	84 @ 1 13/16	2 5/64	.0010–.0030	.0010–.0030	.3720	.3720

VALVE SPECIFICATIONS

Year	VIN	No. Cylinder Displacement cu. in. (liter)	Seat Angle (deg.)	Face Angle (deg.)	Spring Test Pressure (lbs.)	Spring Installed Height (in.)	Stem-to-Guide Clearance (in.) Intake	Stem-to-Guide Clearance (in.) Exhaust	Stem Diameter (in.) Intake	Stem Diameter (in.) Exhaust
1987–88	U	4–150 (2.5)	45	44	212 @ 1.20	1.82	.0010–.0030	.0010–.0030	.3412	.3412
	H	4–150 (2.5)	45	44	212 @ 1.20	1.82	.0010–.0030	.0010–.0030	.3412	.3412
	W	6–173 (2.8)	46	45	195 @ 1.18	1.57	.0010–.0027	.0010–.0027	.3416	.3416
	M	6–243 (4.0)	44.5	45	188 @ 1.41	1.82	.0010–.0030	.0010–.0030	.3720	.3720
	C	6–258 (4.2)	44.5①	44②	100 @ 1 13/16	2 5/64	.0010–.0030	.0010–.0030	.3720	.3720
	N	8–360 (5.9)	44.5①	44②	84 @ 1 13/16	2 5/64	.0010–.0030	.0010–.0030	.3720	.3720

① Exhaust; Intake 30°
② Exhaust; Intake 29°

PISTON AND RING SPECIFICATIONS

All measurments are given in inches.

Year	VIN	No. Cylinder Displacement cu. in. (liter)	Piston Clearance	Ring Gap Top Compression	Ring Gap Bottom Compression	Ring Gap Oil Control	Ring Side Clearance Top Compression	Ring Side Clearance Bottom Compression	Ring Side Clearance Oil Control
1982	B	4–151 (2.5)	.0025–.0033	.010–.020	.010–.020	.010–.020	.0025–.0033	.0025–.0033	.0025–.0033
	C	6–258 (4.2)	.0009–.0017	.010–.020	.010–.020	.010–.025	.0015–.0030	.0015–.0030	.001–.008
	N	8–360 (5.9)	.0012–.0020	.010–.020	.010–.020	.015–.045	.0015–.0035	.0015–.0035	.001–.007
1983	U	4–150 (2.5)	.0009–.0017	.010–.020	.010–.020	.010–.025	.0017–.0032	.0017–.0032	.001–.008
	B	4–151 (2.5)	.0025–.0033	.010–.020	.010–.020	.010–.020	.0025–.0033	.0025–.0033	.0025–.0033
	C	6–258 (4.2)	.0009–.0017	.010–.020	.010–.020	.010–.025	.0015–.0030	.0015–.0030	.001–.008
	N	8–360 (5.9)	.0012–.0020	.010–.020	.010–.020	.015–.045	.0015–.0035	.0015–.0035	.001–.007
1984	U	4–150 (2.5)	.0009–.0017	.010–.020	.010–.020	.010–.025	.0017–.0032	.0017–.0032	.001–.008
	W	6–173 (2.8)	.0017–.0027	.010–.020	.010–.020	.020–.055	.0012–.0028	.0016–.0037	.0078 Max.
	C	6–258 (4.2)	.0009–.0017	.010–.020	.010–.020	.010–.025	.0015–.0030	.0015–.0030	.001–.008
	N	8–360 (5.9)	.0012–.0020	.010–.020	.010–.020	.015–.045	.0015–.0035	.0015–.0035	.001–.007

PISTON AND RING SPECIFICATIONS

All measurments are given in inches.

		No. Cylinder		Ring Gap			Ring Side Clearance		
Year	VIN	Displacement cu. in. (liter)	Piston Clearance	Top Compression	Bottom Compression	Oil Control	Top Compression	Bottom Compression	Oil Control
1985	U	4–150 (2.5)	.0009–.0017	.010–.020	.010–.020	.010–.025	.0017–.0032	.0017–.0032	.001–.008
	H	4–150 (2.5)	.0009–.0017	.010–.020	.010–.020	.010–.025	.0017–.0032	.0017–.0032	.001–.008
	W	6–173 (2.8)	.0017–.0027	.010–.020	.010–.020	.020–.055	.0012–.0028	.0016–.0037	.0078 Max.
	C	6–258 (4.2)	.0009–.0017	.010–.020	.010–.020	.010–.025	.0015–.0030	.0015–.0030	.001–.008
	N	8–360 (5.9)	.0012–.0020	.010–.020	.010–.020	.015–.045	.0015–.0035	.0015–.0035	.001–.007
1986	U	4–150 (2.5)	.0009–.0017	.010–.020	.010–.020	.010–.025	.0017–.0032	.0017–.0032	.001–.008
	H	4–150 (2.5)	.0009–.0017	.010–.020	.010–.020	.010–.025	.0017–.0032	.0017–.0032	.001–.008
	W	6–173 (2.8)	.0017–.0027	.010–.020	.010–.020	.020–.055	.0012–.0028	.0016–.0037	.0078 Max.
	C	6–258 (4.2)	.0009–.0017	.010–.020	.010–.020	.010–.025	.0015–.0030	.0015–.0030	.001–.008
	N	8–360 (5.9)	.0012–.0020	.010–.020	.010–.020	.015–.045	.0015–.0035	.0015–.0035	.001–.007
1987–88	U	4–150 (2.5)	.0009–.0017	.010–.020	.010–.020	.010–.025	.0017–.0032	.0017–.0032	.001–.008
	H	4–150 (2.5)	.0009–.0017	.010–.020	.010–.020	.010–.025	.0017–.0032	.0017–.0032	.001–.008
	W	6–173 (2.8)	.0017–.0027	.010–.020	.010–.020	.020–.055	.0012–.0028	.0016–.0037	.0078 Max.
	M	6–243 (4.0)	.0009–.0017	.010–.020	.010–.020	.010–.025	.0017–.0032	.0017–.0032	.001–.008
	C	6–258 (4.2)	.0009–.0017	.010–.020	.010–.020	.010–.025	.0015–.0030	.0015–.0030	.001–.008
	N	8–360 (5.9)	.0012–.0020	.010–.020	.010–.020	.015–.045	.0015–.0035	.0015–.0035	.001–.007

TORQUE SPECIFICATIONS

All readings in ft. lbs.

Year	VIN	No. Cylinder Displacement cu. in. (liter)	Cylinder Head Bolts	Main Bearing Bolts	Rod Bearing Bolts	Crankshaft Pulley Bolts	Flywheel Bolts	Manifold Intake	Manifold Exhaust	Spark Plugs
1982	B	4-151 (2.5)	95	65	30	160	55	40	25	28
	C	6-258 (4.2)	105	80	28	75	95	23	25	28
	N	8-360 (5.9)	110	100	33	90	95	43	25	28
1983	U	4-150 (2.5)	85	80	33	85	65	23	23	28
	B	4-151 (2.5)	95	65	30	160	55	40	25	28
	C	6-258 (4.2)	105	80	28	75	95	23	25	28
	N	8-360 (5.9)	110	100	33	90	95	43	25	28
1984	U	4-150 (2.5)	85	80	33	85	65	23	23	28
	W	6-173 (2.8)	70	70	35	75	50	23	25	15
	C	6-258 (4.2)	105	80	28	75	95	23	25	28
	N	8-360 (5.9)	110	100	33	90	95	43	25	28
1985	B	4-126 (2.0)	①	69	48	96	44	NA	NA	–
	U	4-150 (2.5)	85	80	33	85	65	23	23	28
	H	4-150 (2.5)	85	80	33	85	65	23	23	28
	W	6-173 (2.8)	70	70	35	75	50	23	25	15
	C	6-258 (4.2)	105	80	28	75	95	23	25	28
	N	8-360 (5.9)	110	100	33	90	95	43	25	28
1986	B	4-126 (2.0)	①	69	48	96	44	NA	NA	–
	U	4-150 (2.5)	85	80	33	85	65	23	23	28
	H	4-150 (2.5)	85	80	33	85	65	23	23	28
	W	6-173 (2.8)	70	70	35	75	50	23	25	15
	C	6-258 (4.2)	105	80	28	75	95	23	25	28
	N	8-360 (5.9)	110	100	33	90	95	43	25	28
1987-88	B	4-126 (2.0)	①	69	48	96	44	NA	NA	–
	U	4-150 (2.5)	85	80	33	85	65	23	23	28
	H	4-150 (2.5)	85	80	33	85	65	23	23	28
	W	6-173 (2.8)	70	70	35	75	50	23	25	15
	M	6-243 (4.0)	70	70	37	75	50	23	25	15
	C	6-258 (4.2)	105	80	28	75	95	23	25	28
	N	8-360 (5.9)	110	100	33	90	95	43	25	28

① 1st step: 22 ft. lbs.
2nd step: 37 ft. lbs.
3rd step: 50–70 ft. lbs.
4th step: 70–77 ft. lbs.

WHEEL ALIGNMENT

Year	Model	Caster Range (deg.)	Caster Preferred Setting (deg.)	Camber Range (deg.)	Camber Preferred Setting (deg.)	Toe-in (in.)	Steering Axis Inclination (deg.)
1982	CJ	6P–7P	6P	0–½P	0	$^3/_{64}$P–$^3/_{32}$P	8½
	Scrambler	6P–7P	6P	0–½P	0	$^3/_{64}$P–$^3/_{32}$P	8½
	Grand Wagoneer	4P–5P	4P	0–½P	0	$^3/_{64}$P–$^3/_{32}$P	8½
	Truck	4P–5P	4P	0–½P	0	$^3/_{64}$P–$^3/_{32}$P	8½
1983	CJ	6P–7P	6P	0–½P	0	$^3/_{64}$P–$^3/_{32}$P	8½
	Scrambler	6P–7P	6P	0–½P	0	$^3/_{64}$P–$^3/_{32}$P	8½
	Grand Wagoneer	4P–5P	4P	0–½P	0	$^3/_{64}$P–$^3/_{32}$P	8½
	Truck	4P–5P	4P	0–½P	0	$^3/_{64}$P–$^3/_{32}$P	8½
1984	CJ	6P–7P	6P	0–½P	0	$^3/_{64}$P–$^3/_{32}$P	8½
	Scrambler	6P–7P	6P	0–½P	0	$^3/_{64}$P–$^3/_{32}$P	8½
	Grand Wagoneer	4P–5P	4P	0–½P	0	$^3/_{64}$P–$^3/_{32}$P	8½
	Truck	4P–5P	4P	0–½P	0	$^3/_{64}$P–$^3/_{32}$P	8½
	Cherokee	7P–8P	7½P	½N–½P	0	$^1/_{16}$P	NA
	Wagoneer	7P–8P	7½P	½N–½P	0	$^1/_{16}$P	NA
1985	CJ	6P–7P	6P	0–½P	0	$^3/_{64}$P–$^3/_{32}$P	8½
	Scrambler	6P–7P	6P	0–½P	0	$^3/_{64}$P–$^3/_{32}$P	8½
	Grand Wagoneer	4P–5P	4P	0–½P	0	$^3/_{64}$P–$^3/_{32}$P	8½
	Truck	4P–5P	4P	0–½P	0	$^3/_{64}$P–$^3/_{32}$P	8½
	Cherokee	7P–8P	7½P	½N–½P	0	$^1/_{16}$P	NA
	Wagoneer	7P–8P	7½P	½N–½P	0	$^1/_{16}$P	NA
1986	CJ	NA	6P	NA	0	$^3/_{16}$P	10
	Grand Wagoneer	3P–5P	4P	½N–½P	0	$^3/_{64}$P–$^3/_{32}$P	8½
	Truck	3P–5P	4P	½N–½P	0	$^3/_{64}$P–$^3/_{32}$P	8½
	Cherokee	7P–8P	7½P	½N–½P	0	$^1/_{16}$P	NA
	Wagoneer	7P–8P	7½P	½N–½P	0	$^1/_{16}$P	NA
	Comanche	7P–8P	7½P	½N–½P	0	$^1/_{16}$P	NA
1987–88	Wrangler①	7½P–8½P	8P	NA	—	NA	NA
	Wrangler②	6P–7P	6½P	NA	—	NA	NA
	Grand Wagoneer	3P–5P	4P	½N–½P	0	$^3/_{64}$P–$^3/_{32}$P	8½
	Truck	3P–5P	4P	½N–½P	0	$^3/_{64}$P–$^3/_{32}$P	8½
	Cherokee	7P–8P	7½P	½N–½P	0	$^1/_{16}$P	NA
	Wagoneer	7P–8P	7½P	½N–½P	0	$^1/_{16}$P	NA
	Comanche	7P–8P	7½P	½N–½P	0	$^1/_{16}$P	NA

① With manual transmission
② With automatic transmission

ENGINE ELECTRICAL

Alternator

Removal and Installation

1. Disconnect the negative battery cable. Remove all necessary components in order to gain access to the alternator assembly. On some vehicles it may be easier to raise and support the vehicle safely and remove the alternator from underneath the vehicle.
2. Remove the wire terminals attached to the rear of the alternator.
3. Loosen the bolt holding the adjusting bar and the pivot bolt at the opposite side of the alternator.
4. Move the alternator inward to relieve the belt tension and remove the belt.
5. Remove the adjusting bar and pivot bolts and remove the alternator from the engine.
6. Installation is the reverse of the removal procedure.
7. When installing the belt, adjust to allow ½ in. deflection on thelongest run between the pulleys.

Starter

OVERHAUL

Refer to the Electrical Unit Repair section for starter test and overhaul procedures.

Removal and Installation

1. Disconnect the negative battery cable. On some vehicles the transmission oil filler tube may have to be removed to gain access to the starter assembly.
2. If necessary, raise the vehicle to gain working clearance. Remove all necessary components in order to gain access to the starter assembly.
3. Remove the positive battery lead from the starter or solenoid. Remove remaining wires as necessary.
4. Remove the starter retaining bolts. Remove the starter from the vehicle.
5. Installation is the reverse of the removal procedure.

Distributor

Removal and Installation

1. Disconnect the negative battery cable. Remove all necessary components in order to gain access to the distributor assembly.
2. Remove the distributor cap and wires. Remove all electrical connections and vacuum lines as required.
3. Note the position of the rotor in relation to the base. Scribe a mark on the base of the distributor and on the engine block to facilitate reinstallation. Align the marks with the direction the metal tip of the rotor is pointing.
4. Remove the bolt that holds the distributor to the engine.

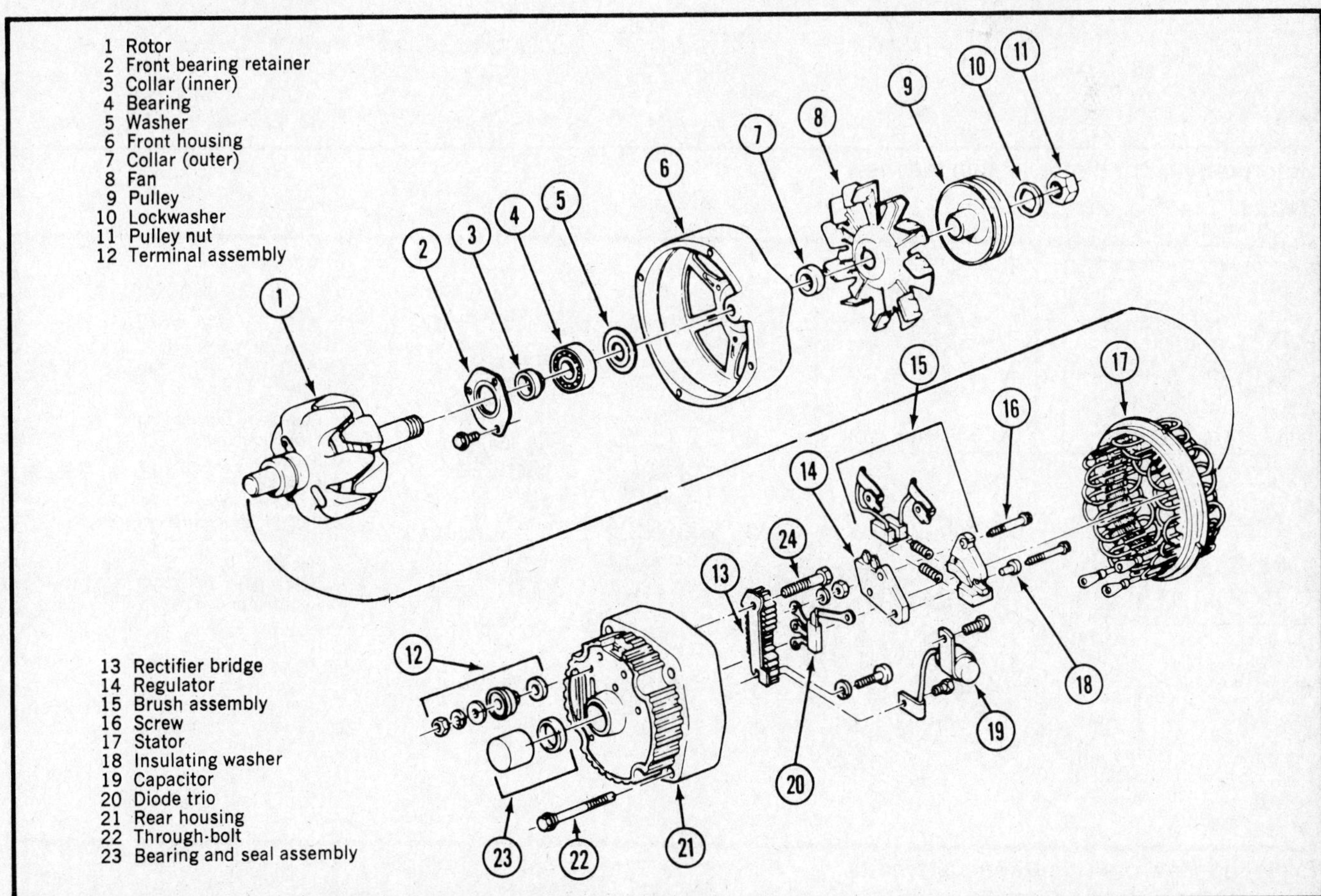

Exploded view of Delco alternator with mini regulator

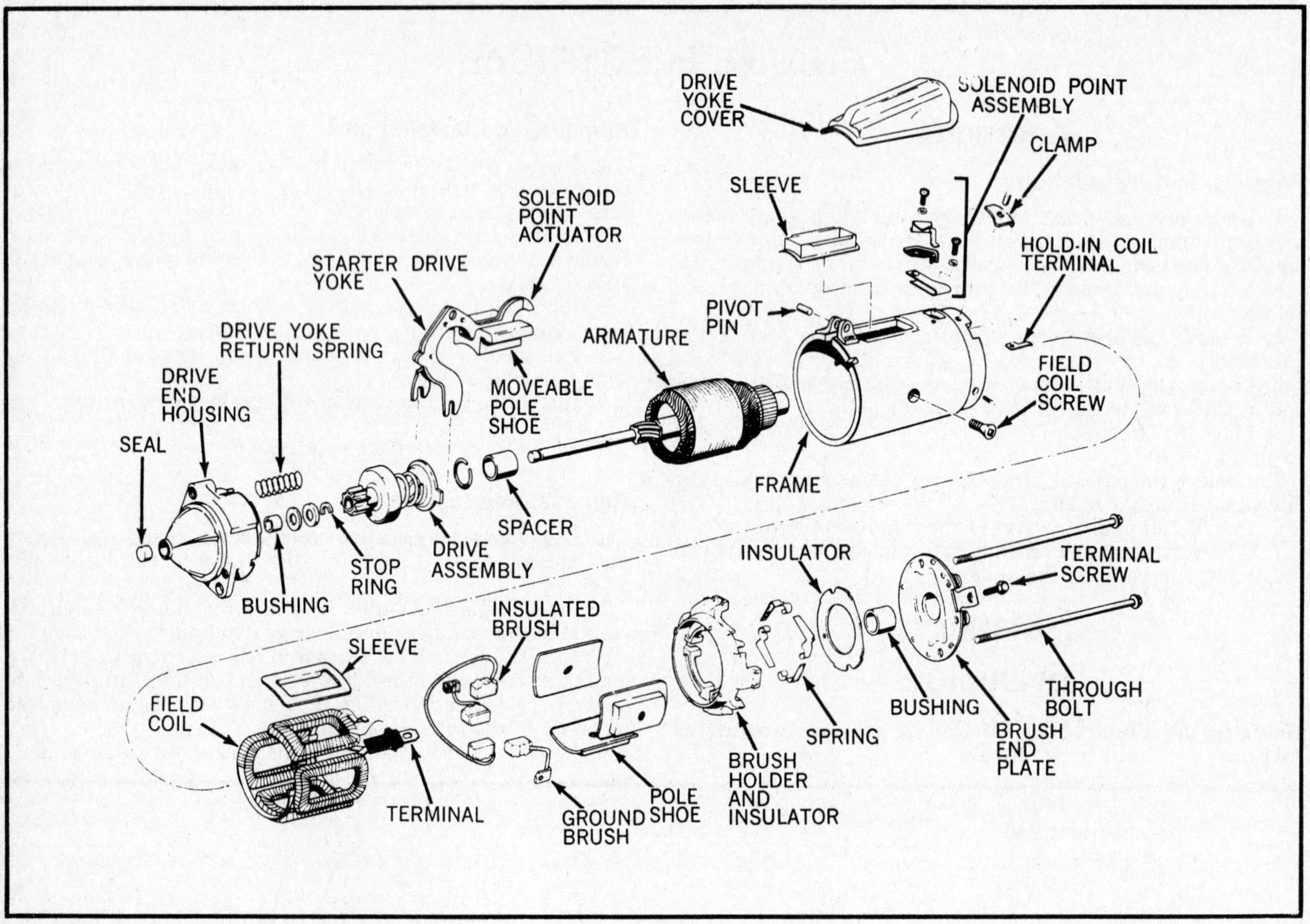

DRIVE YOKE COVER
SOLENOID POINT ASSEMBLY
CLAMP
SLEEVE
SOLENOID POINT ACTUATOR
HOLD-IN COIL TERMINAL
STARTER DRIVE YOKE
PIVOT PIN
DRIVE YOKE RETURN SPRING
ARMATURE
FIELD COIL SCREW
DRIVE END HOUSING
MOVEABLE POLE SHOE
SEAL
FRAME
SPACER
DRIVE ASSEMBLY
STOP RING
BUSHING
INSULATOR
TERMINAL SCREW
INSULATED BRUSH
SLEEVE
THROUGH BOLT
FIELD COIL
BUSHING
SPRING
BRUSH END PLATE
BRUSH HOLDER AND INSULATOR
POLE SHOE
TERMINAL
GROUND BRUSH

Motorcraft starter motor—exploded view

60 AMP REGULATOR
70 AMP REGULATOR
1
2
3
4
5
6
7
8
9
10
1. Pulley and fan assembly
2. Front housing
3. Stator
4. Bearing
5. Rear housing
6. Slip ring end frame cover
7. Rotor
8. Race
9. Rear lug
10. Rectifier bridge

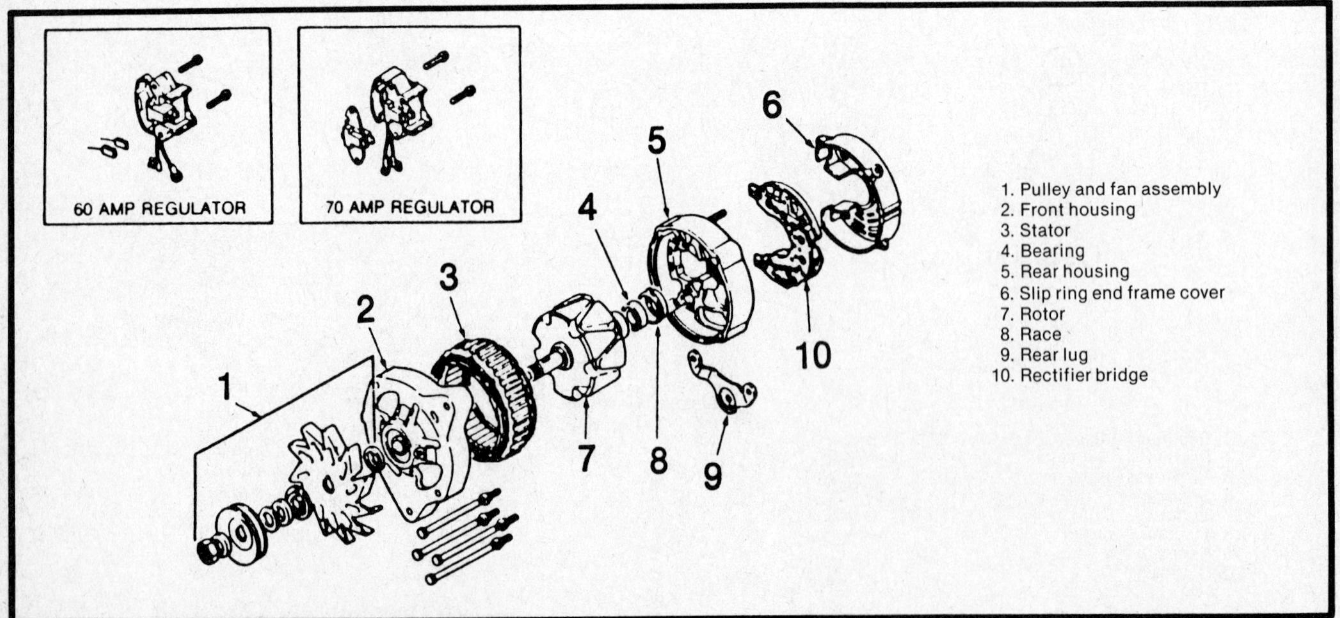

Exploded view of Paris-Rhone alternator

1. Bushing
2. Screw
3. Shield
4. Solenoid switch
5. Retainer
6. Stop ring
7. Bushing
8. Overrunnig clutch drive
9. Fork
10. Bearing pedestal
11. Sealing rubber
12. Planetary gear system
13. Armature
14. Stator Frame
15. Bush holder
16. Gasket
17. Commutator end shield
18. Bushing
19. Seal ring
20. Shim
21. Shim
22. Retaining washer
23. Closure cap
24. Hexagon-screw
25. Screw

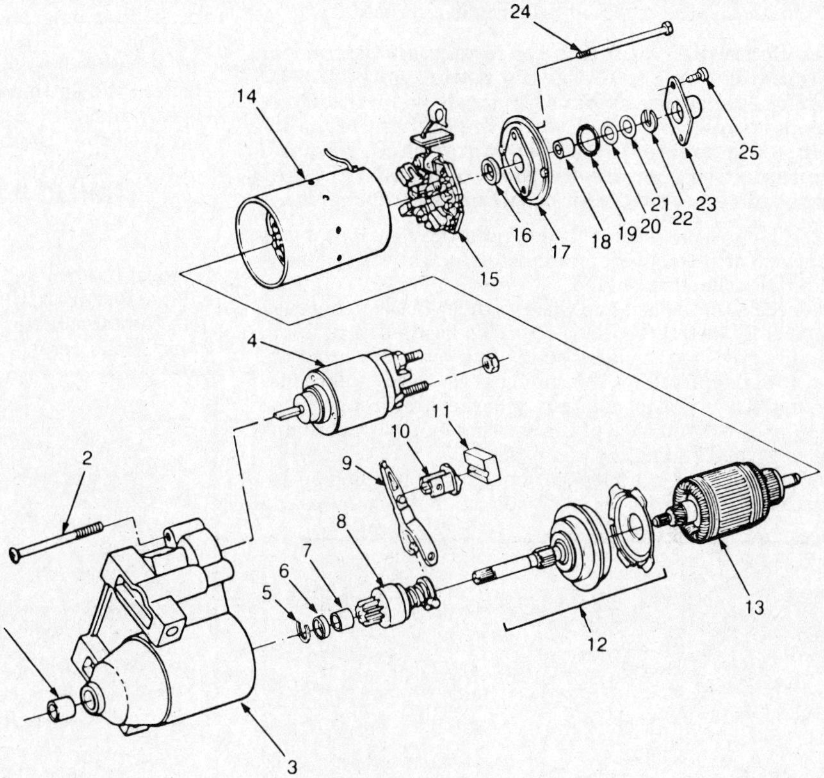

Bosch starter motor—exploded view

1. End housing bushing
2. Drive-end housing
3. Spacer
4. Pad
5. Solenoid plate
6. Solenoid
7. Pinion shift yoke
8. Support plate
9. Support plate bushing
10. Field winding and pole shoe sets (4)
11. Pole shoe screw (4)
12. Armature housing
13. Grommet
14. Brush set (4)

15. Brush spring (4)
16. Brush holder
17. Cap
18. Brush holder bushing
19. Through bolts (4)
20. Armature brake assembly
21. Armature
22. Starter drive pinion
23. Drive pinion stop
24. Shift yoke pivot pins
25. Shift yoke axle

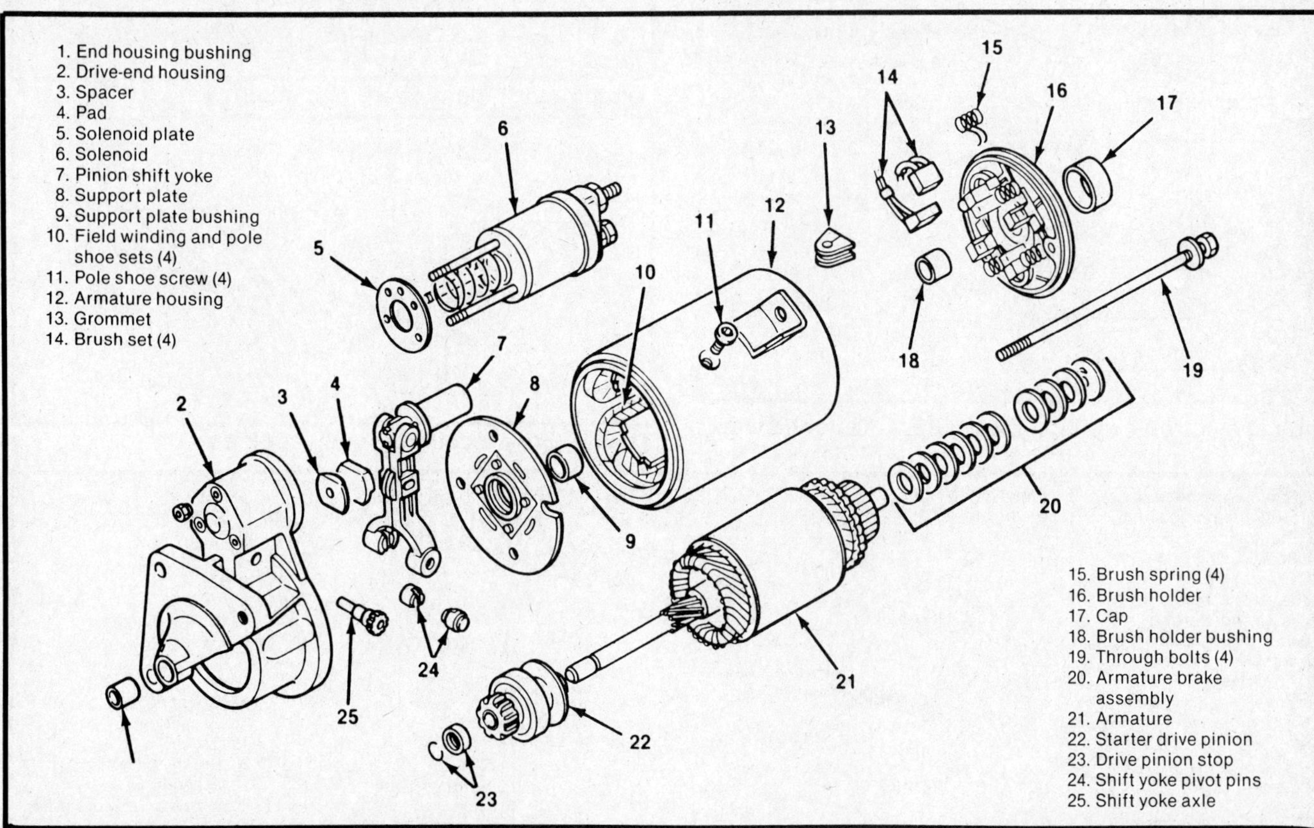

Paris-Rhone starter motor—exploded view

5. Lift the distributor assembly from the engine.
6. Installation is the reverse of the removal procedure.

NOTE: Some distributors have a gear on the end of the distributor shaft and a gear on the end of the oil pump drive, these gears have to mesh with the same teeth as originally installed when the distributor is inserted into the engine. If the distributor shaft gear and the oil pump drive gear are one tooth off from what they are supposed to be, the engine will not run correctly.

7. If the engine has been turned while the distributor has been removed, or if the marks were not drawn, it will be necessary to initially time the engine.
8. It is necessary to place the No. 1 cylinder in the firing position to correctly install the distributor. To locate this position, some engines have marks placed on the flywheel while other engines have marks placed on the timing gear covers and crankshaft pulleys. The flywheel marks may be viewed through a covered opening directly in back of the starting motor by loosening the hole cover and sliding it to one side.
9. Remove the No. 1 cylinder spark plug. Turn the engine until the piston in No. 1 cylinder is moving up on the compression stroke. This can be determined by placing your thumb over the spark plug hole and feeling the air being forced out of the cylinder.
10. Install the distributor, when the distributor shaft has reached the bottom of the hole, move the rotor back and forth slightly until the drive gears of the distributor and cam mesh and until the distributor assembly slides down into place.

1. Distributor cap
2. Rotor
3. Dust shield
4. Trigger wheel
5. Felt wick
6. Sensor assembly
7. Shaft assembly
8. Housing
9. Vacuum control
10. Shim
11. Drive gear
12. Pin

Typical electronic ignition distributor—exploded view

TIMING LIGHT AND TACHOMETER CONNECTIONS

Connect the timing light per manufacturers instructions to the engine. Be sure to time the engine on number one cylinder. Connect the tachometer to the engine per manufacturers instructions. If the vehicle is equipped with a diesel engine, a special

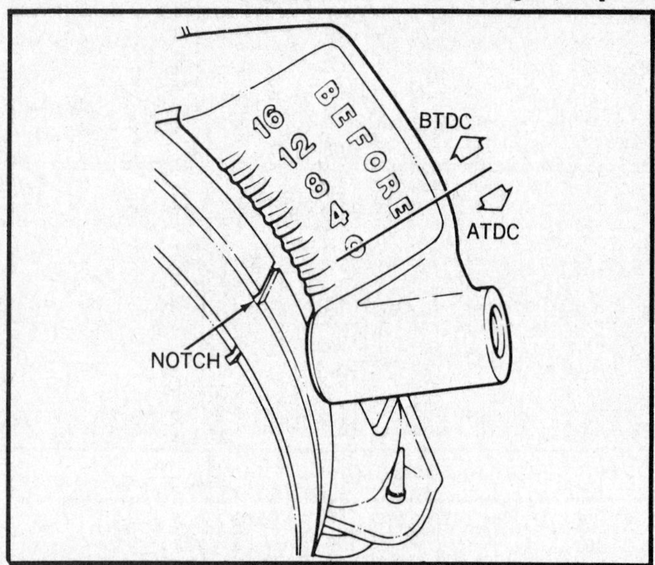

Timing mark location—6 cyl. engines

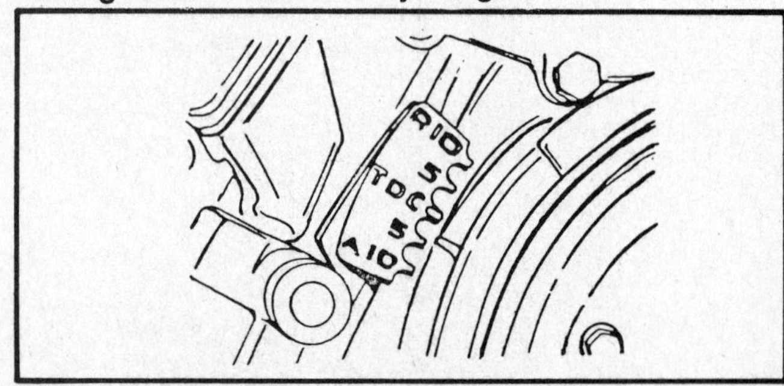

Timing mark location—8 cyl. engines

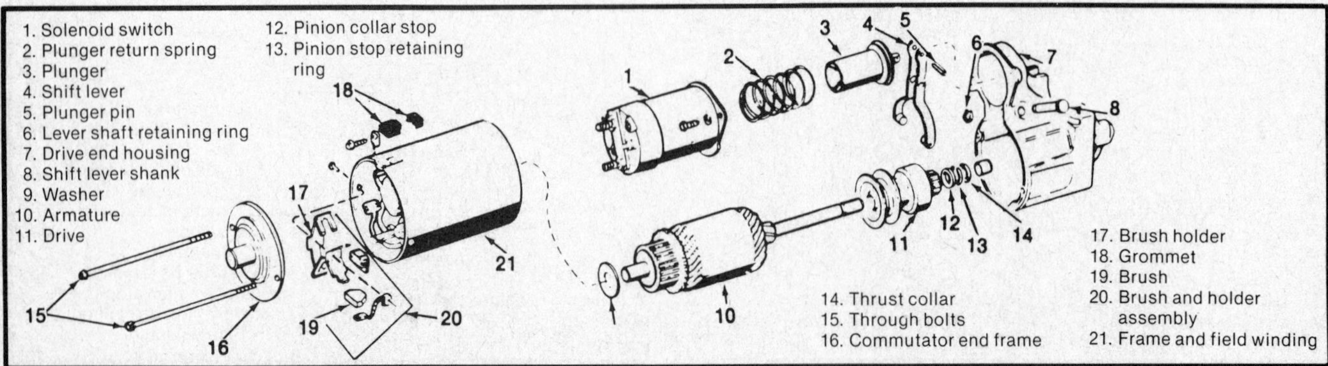

Delco starter motor—exploded view

timing light and a digital tachometer must be used. Some engines incorporate a bracket and hole which are cast into the timing case cover for the use of a magnetic timing probe, which is connected to a special electronic timing meter for precise ignition timing. If using this type of timing equipment, be sure to follow the manufacturers instructions.

IGNITION TIMING

Procedure

EXCEPT MAGNETIC TIMING

1. Locate the timing marks on the crankshaft pulley and the front of the timing case cover.
2. Clean off the timing marks.
3. Use chalk or white paint to color the mark on the scale that will indicate the correct timing, when aligned with the mark on the pulley or the pointer.
4. Attach a tachometer to the engine.
5. Attach a timing light to the engine.
6. Disconnect and plug the vacuum lines to the distributor, if equipped. Loosen the distributor lockbolt just enough so that the distributor can be turned with a little resistance.
7. Adjust the idle to the correct specification.
8. With the timing light aimed at the pulley and the marks on the engine, turn the distributor in the direction of rotor rotation to retard the spark, and in the opposite direction of rotor rotation to advance the spark. Align the marks on the pulley and the engine with the flashes of the timing light.

MAGNETIC TIMING

A bracket and hole are cast into the timing case cover for the use of a magnetic timing probe, which is connected to a special electronic timing meter for precise ignition timing. The probe is inserted into the hole of the bracket until the vibration damper is touched. When the engine is started, the probe is automatically spaced away from the damper by the dampers eccentricity, or being slightly out of center. The probe senses a milled slot on the damper and compensating for the brackets top dead center position, registers the reading on the timing meter. Any necessary corrections can then be made to the ignition timing. Do not use the probe bracket and hole to check the ignition timing when using a conventional timing light.

Electrical Controls

IGNITION SWITCH

Removal and Installation

1. Disconnect the negative battery cable. Position the key lock in the Off/Lock position.
2. Remove the lower trim panel, as required. Remove the ignition switch retaining screws.
3. Disconnect the ignition switch from the remote rod. Disconnect the electrical connectors from the switch assembly.
4. Remove the ignition switch from the vehicle.
5. With the actuator rod disconnected, position the switch to its mounting.
6. If the vehicle is equipped with a standard steering column, move the slider of the switch to the extreme left (accessory position). The left side of the ignition switch is toward the steering wheel.
7. If the vehicle is equipped with a tilt steering column move the slider of the switch to the extreme right (accessory position). The right side of the ignition switch is downward from the steering wheel.
8. Position the actuator rod in the slider hole. Install the switch to the steering column. Be sure not to move the slider out of the detent.
9. Hold the ignition key in the accessory detent position and push the switch assembly down the steering column in order to remove the slack in the actuator rod.
10. Connect the switch electrical connectors. Check the switch for proper operation. Install the trim panel, as required.

HEADLIGHT SWITCH

Removal and Installation

1. Disconnect the negative battery cable.
2. Pull the light switch control knob out as far as it will go. As required, remove the instrument panel trim plate.
3. From under the dash depress the headlight switch shaft retainer button. Pull the shaft along with the knob from the headlight switch assembly.
4. Remove the headlight switch retaining nut. Disconnect the electrical connector from the switch.
5. Remove the headlight switch from the vehicle.
6. Installation is the reverse of the removal procedure.

DIMMER SWITCH

Removal and Installation

1. Disconnect the negative battery cable.
2. As required, remove the instrument panel lower trim panel.
3. Remove the steering column to instrument panel retaining bolts. Lower the steering column as necessary to gain access to the dimmer switch assembly.
4. Properly secure the actuator rod to the steering column. Disconnect any electrical connections from the switch.
5. Remove the switch retaining screws. Pull the switch assembly from the actuator rod. Remove the assembly from the vehicle.
6. Installation is the reverse of the removal procedure.
7. To adjust the switch, depress the assembly slightly and insert a $^{3}/_{32}$ inch drill bit into the switch gauge adjusting hole. Move the switch toward the steering wheel. Once the slack is removed from the actuator rod tighten the switch retaining screws. Remove the drill bit.
8. Check the switch for proper operation.

TURN SIGNAL SWITCH

Removal and Installation

1. Disconnect the negative battery cable. Disconnect and tape the electrical harness connector from its mounting on the lower part of the steering column.
2. Remove the horn pad. Remove the steering wheel. Remove the lockplate cover.
3. Using the proper tools, compress the lockplate and remove the snapring.
4. Remove the lockplate tool, lockplate, canceling cam and upper bearing preload spring.
5. Position the turn signal lever in the right turn position. Remove the signal lever. Remove the hazzard button. Remove the wiring harness protector, if equipped.
6. Remove the turn signal switch retaining screws. Carefully pull the turn signal switch assembly upward and out of the steering column.
7. Installation is the reverse of the removal procedure.

WINDSHIELD WIPER SWITCH

Removal and Installation

COLUMN MOUNTED

1. Disconnect the negative battery cable. Disconnect and tape the electrical harness connector from its mounting on the lower part of the steering column.

2. Remove the horn pad. Remove the steering wheel. Remove the lockplate cover.
3. Using the proper tools, compress the lockplate and remove the snapring.
4. Remove the lockplate tool, lockplate, canceling cam and upper bearing preload spring.
5. Position the combination lever in the right turn position. Remove the combination lever retaining screws.
6. Carefully pull the combination lever assembly upward and out of the steering column.
7. Installation is the reverse of the removal procedure.

DASH MOUNTED

1. Disconnect the negative battery cable. Remove the switch knob.
2. On CJ7 and Scrambler equipped with air condition, remove the retaining screws attaching the evaporator assembly to the instrument panel. Lower the evaporator assembly.
3. Remove the nut from the switch assembly. Push the switch rearward. Disconnect the switch electrical connectors. Remove the switch from the vehicle.
4. Installation is the reverse of the removal procedure.

WINDSHIELD WIPER MOTOR

Removal and Installation

CJ, SCRAMBLER AND WRANGLER

1. Disconnect the negative battery cable. Remove the necessary hard or soft top components from the windshield frame.
2. Remove the left and right windshield holddown knobs and fold the shield forward.
3. Remove the left access hole cover. Disconnect the drive link from the left wiper pivot. Disconnect the wiper motor harness from the switch.
4. Remove the wiper motor retaining screws. Remove the wiper motor from the vehicle.
5. Installation is the reverse of the removal procedure.

GRAND WAGONEER, CHEROKEE AND TRUCK

1. Disconnect the negative battery cable.
2. Remove the screws attaching the motor adapter plate to the dash panel.
3. Separate the wiper wiring harness connector at the wiper motor.
4. Pull the motor and the linkage out of the opening to expose the drive link to crank stud retaining clip.
5. Raise up the lock tab of the clip and slide the clip off of the stud.
6. Remove the wiper motor from the vehicle.
7. Installation is the reverse of the removal procedure.

WAGONEER, CHEROKEE AND COMANCHE

1. Disconnect the negative battery cable.
2. Remove the wiper arm assemblies. Remove the cowl and trim panel.
3. Disconnect the washer hose. Remove the cowl mounting bracket attaching bolts and the pivot pin attaching screws.
4. Disconnect the wiring harness and remove the assembly. The motor is protected by a rubber case, care should be used as not to damage this protective coat.
5. Installation is the reverse of the removal procedure.

WINDSHIELD WIPER LINKAGE

Removal and Installation

CJ, SCRAMBLER AND WRANGLER

1. Remove the wiper arms.
2. Remove the nuts attaching the pivots to the windshield frame.
3. Remove the necessary components from the top of the windshield frame.
4. Remove the windshield holddown knobs and fold the windshield forward.
5. Remove the access hole covers on both sides of the windshield.
6. Disconnect the wiper motor drive link from the left wiper pivot.
7. Remove the wiper pivot shafts and linkage from the access hole.
8. Installation is the reverse of the removal procedure.

GRAND WAGONEER, CHEROKEE AND TRUCK WITHOUT AC

1. Remove the wiper arms and pivot shaft nuts, washers, escutcheons and gaskets.
2. Disconnect the drive arm from the motor crank.
3. Remove individual links where necessary, to remove the pivot shaft bodies without excessive interference.
4. Installation is the reverse of the removal procedure.

GRAND WAGONEER, CHEROKEE AND TRUCK WITH AC

1. Disconnect the negative battery cable.
2. Remove the wiper arms and pivot shaft nuts, washers, escutcheons and gaskets.
3. Remove the instrument cluster. Remove the left defroster duct.
4. Disconnect the drive arm from the motor crank.
5. Lower the glove box in order to gain access to the right linkage clip. Remove the linkage clip.
6. Remove the screws attaching the left pivot shaft body. Remove the left pivot shaft body and linkage assembly through the instrument cluster opening.
7. Installation is the reverse of the removal procedure.

INSTRUMENT CLUSTER

Removal and Installation

CJ AND SCRAMBLER

1. Disconnect the negative battery cable.
2. Disconnect the speedometer cable from the back of the speedometer.
3. Remove the instrument cluster attaching screws and pull the cluster forward.
4. Disconnect the instrument cluster electrical connectors. Remove the cluster from the vehicle.
5. Installation is the reverse of the removal procedure.

WRANGLER

1. Disconnect the negative battery cable.
2. Remove the dash panel trim plate.
3. Remove the speedometer assembly retaining screws.
4. Pull the speedometer forward. Disconnect the electrical connectors, as required. Disconnect the speedometer cable.
5. Remove the speedometer from the vehicle.
6. Installation is the reverse of the removal procedure.

WAGONEER, CHEROKEE, GRAND WAGONEER AND TRUCK

1. Disconnect the negative battery. Remove the cluster retaining screws.
2. Disconnect the speedometer cable.
3. Disconnect the cluster terminal pin plug. Disconnect the four terminal connector.
4. Mark the electrical connectors and hoses, disconnect them and the blend door air cable.
6. Remove the heater control panel lamps. Disconnect the heater temperature control wire from the lever. Remove the cluster.

7. Installation is the reverse of the removal procedure.

WAGONEER, CHEROKEE AND COMANCHE

1. Disconnect the negative battery cable.
2. Remove the instrument panel bezel screws and lift off the bezel. The bezel unsnaps.
3. Remove the cigar lighter housing screws.
4. Remove the rocker switch housing screws.
5. Remove the cluster screws.
6. Disconnect the speedometer cable, pull the cluster out slowly and disconnect the electrical connectors at the cluster back. Remove the cluster.
7. Installation is the reverse of the removal procedure.

SPEEDOMETER CABLE

Removal and Installation

1. Disconnect the negative battery cable.
2. If equipped, remove the under dash trim panel. Reach up behind the center of the speedometer head and disconnect the cable from the speedometer head.
3. The cable core can now be pulled from the cable assembly.
4. If the core is broken, detach the other end of the cable assembly and pull out the broken end of the cable.
5. Installation is the reverse of the removal procedure. When installing the cable, apply a very small amount of speedometer cable graphite lubricant.

COOLING AND HEATING SYSTEM

Water Pump

Removal and Installation

NOTE: Some vehicles are equipped with a serpentine drive belt and have a reverse rotating water pump coupled with a viscous fan drive assembly. The components are identified by the words REVERSE stamped on the cover of the viscous drive and on the inner side of the fan. The word REV is also cast into the body of the water pump.

4-151 CID (2.5L) ENGINE

1. Disconnect the negative battery cable. Drain the coolant. Remove the necessary components in order to gain access to the water pump retaining bolts.
2. Loosen the alternator and remove the fan belt. Remove the power steering and air conditioning belts, if so equipped.
3. Remove the fan, spacer, and water pump pulley. Remove the heater hose and the lower radiator hose at the pump.
4. Remove the water pump retaining bolts. Remove the water pump from the vehicle.
5. Installation is the reverse of the removal procedure.

4-150 CID (2.5L), 6-243 CID (4.0L) AND 6-258 CID (4.2L) ENGINES

1. Disconnect the negative battery cable. Drain the cooling system.
2. Remove the necessary components in order to gain access to the water pump retaining bolts. Disconnect the radiator and heater hoses from the water pump.
3. Loosen the alternator adjustment strap screw, upper pivot bolt and remove the drive belt.
4. If the vehicle is equipped with a radiator shroud, separate the shroud from the radiator to facilitate removal and installation of the cooling fan and hub.

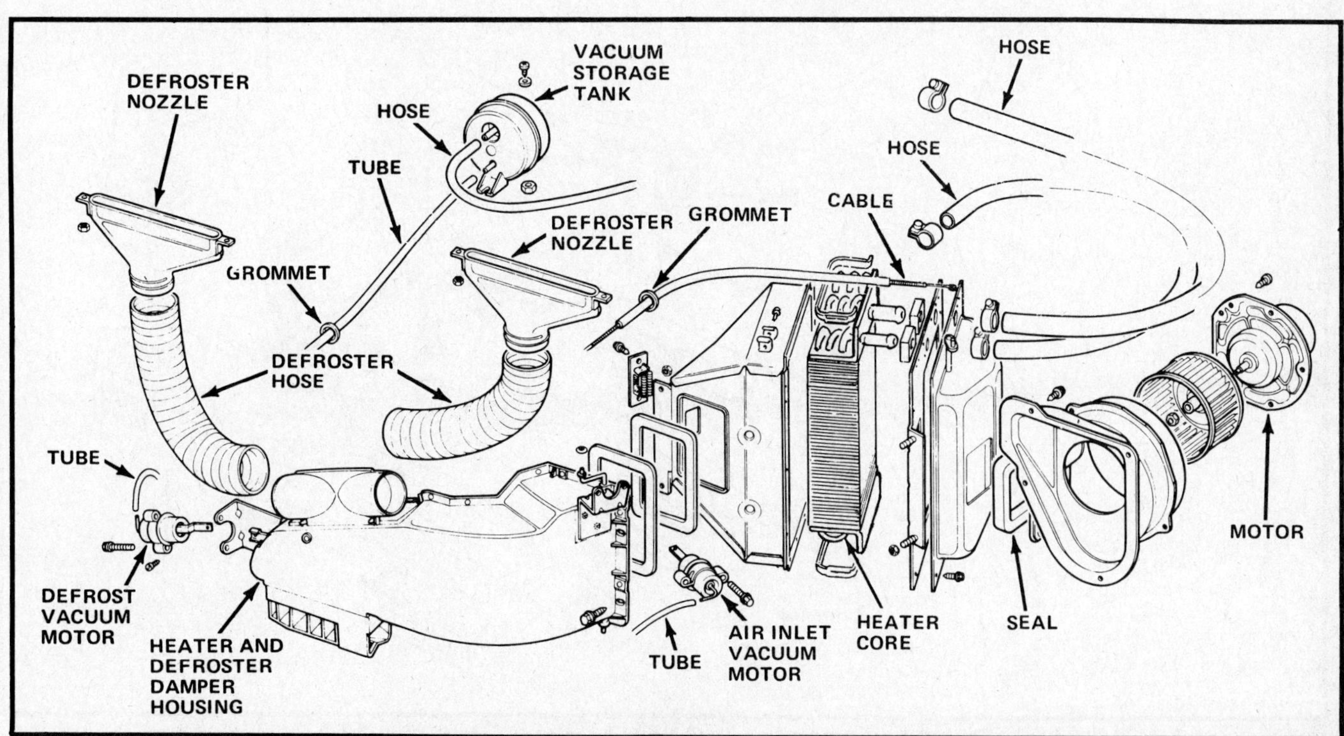

Heater defroster assembly—Cherokee and Wagoneer

5. Remove the cooling fan and hub assembly. Remove air conditioning intermediate idler pulley and mounting bracket, if equipped. Remove the power steering pump front mounting bracket, if equipped.

6. Remove the water pump retaining bolts. Remove the water pump from the vehicle.

7. Installation is the reverse of the removal procedure. Be sure to use a new gasket, as required.

V6–173 CID (2.8L) AND V8–360 CID (5.9L) ENGINES

1. Disconnect the negative battery cable. Drain the cooling system.

2. Remove the necessary components in order to gain access to the water pump retaining bolts.

3. Disconnect the upper radiator hose at the radiator. Loosen the drive belts. Remove the fan and hub assembly.

4. Separate the radiator shroud from the radiator, if equipped. If the vehicle is equipped with a viscous fan, remove the fan assembly and shroud all at the same time. Do not unbolt the fan blades.

5. Some vehicles equipped with air conditioning, install a double nut on the air conditioning compressor bracket to water pump stud and remove the stud. Removal of this stud eliminates removing the compressor mounting bracket.

6. Remove the alternator and mounting bracket assembly and place it aside. Do not disconnect the alternator wires.

7. Remove the two nuts attaching the power steering pump to the rear half of the pump mounting bracket, if equipped.

8. Remove the two bolts attaching the front half of the bracket to the rear half.

9. Remove the remaining upper bolt from the inner air pump support brace, loosen the lower bolt and drop the brace away from the power steering front bracket.

10. Remove the front half of the power steering bracket from the water pump mounting stud. Disconnect the heater hose, bypass hose, and lower radiator hose at the water pump.

11. Remove the water pump retaining bolts. Remove the water pump from the vehicle.

12. Installation is the reverse of the removal procedure. Be sure to use a new gasket, as required.

THERMOSTAT

Removal and Installation

1. Disconnect the negative battery cable. Drain the cooling system.

2. Remove the thermostat housing retaining bolts. On some vehicles it may be necessary to remove the upper radiator hose for manuverability.

3. Remove the thermostat and gasket from the vehicle.

4. Installation is the reverse of the removal procedure. Be sure to use a new gasket, as required.

Heater Core

Removal and Installation

CJ, SCRAMBLER AND WRANGLER

1. Disconnect the negative battery cable. Drain the radiator.

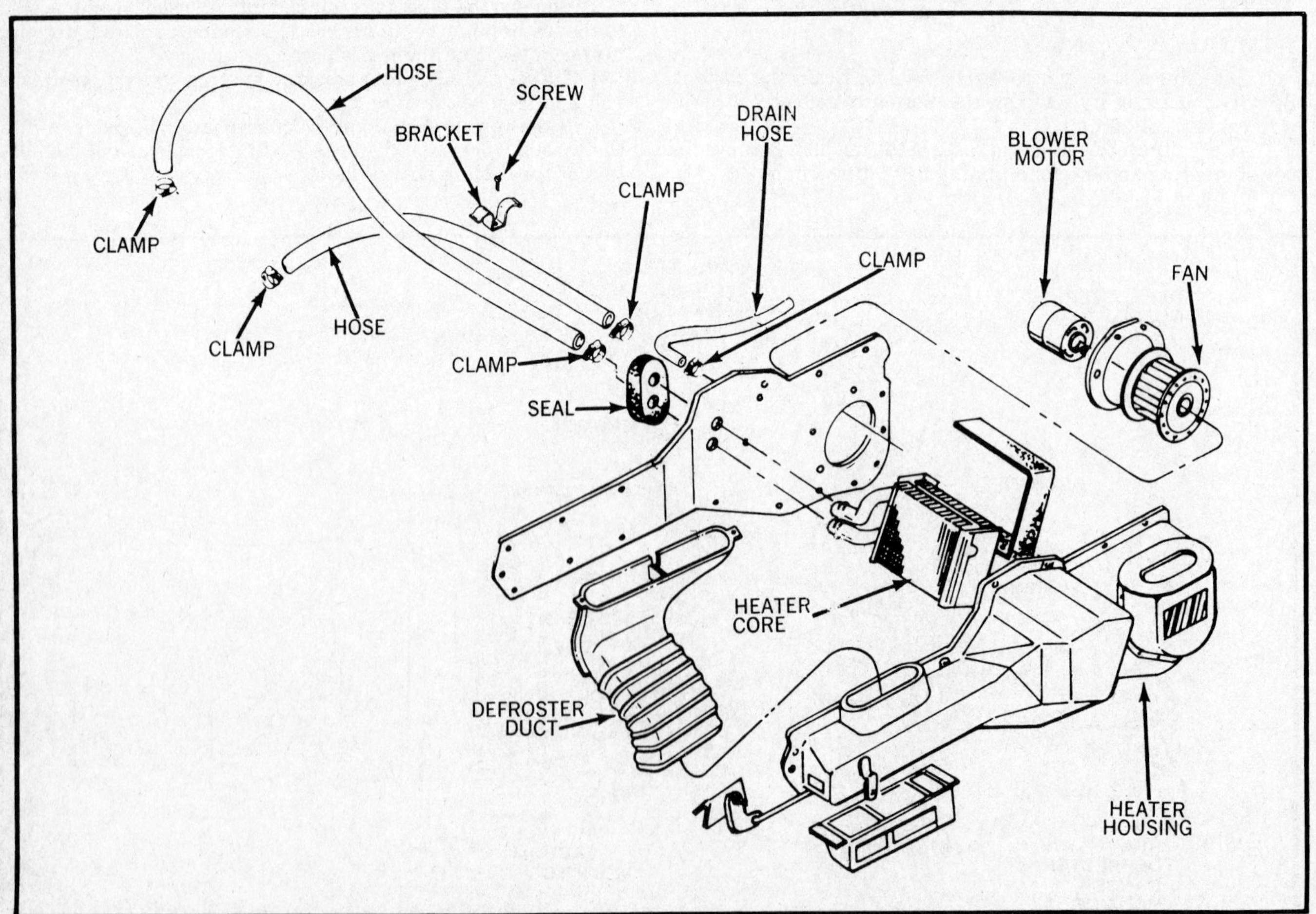

Heater and defroster assembly—CJ models

2. Disconnect the heater hoses. Disconnect the damper door control cables. Disconnect the blower motor wire.
3. Disconnect the defroster duct. Remove the heater core housing retaining nuts from inside the engine compartment.
4. Remove the heater core housing assembly from the vehicle.
5. Remove the heater core from the housing.
6. Installation is the reverse of the removal procedure.

CHEROKEE, WAGONEER AND COMANCHE

1. Disconnect the negative battery cable. Drain the radiator.
2. Disconnect the heater hoses at the heater core.
3. Remove the heater/evaporator housing.
4. Remove the heater core retaining screws. Remove the heater core from the vehicle.
5. Installation is the reverse of the removal procedure.

GRAND WAGONEER AND TRUCK

1. Disconnect the negative battery cable. Drain the radiator.
2. Disconnect the temperature control cable from the blend air door.
3. Disconnect the heater hoses at the heater core. Disconnect the blower motor resistor wires.
4. Remove the heater/evaporator housing retaining bolts. Remove the heater/evaporator housing from the vehicle.
5. Separate the housing and remove the heater core.
6. Installation is the reverse of the removal procedure.

Heater Core Housing

Removal and Installation

CHEROKEE, WAGONEER AND COMANCHE WITHOUT AC

1. Disconnect the negative battery cable. Drain the cooling system. Remove the left kick panel and remove the instrument panel retaining bolt. Remove the right and left "A" pillar trim.
2. Remove the defroster bezel retaining screws along the top of the assembly. Remove the bezel Remove the instrument panel retaining screws.
3. Lower the steering column. Pull the instrument panel about three inches from the dash panel.
4. Remove the defroster duct retaining screws. Remove the defroster duct and disconnect the hoses.
5. Disconnect the vacuum hoses from the heater core housing vacuum motors.
6. Remove the heater housing retaining nuts from inside the engine compartment. Remove the heater housing assembly from the vehicle.
7. Installation is the reverse of the removal procedure.

Blower Motor

Removal and Installation

CJ, SCRAMBLER AND WRANGLER WITHOUT AC

1. Disconnect the negative battery cable. Drain the radiator.
2. Disconnect the heater hoses. Disconnect the damper door control cables. Disconnect the blower motor wire.
3. Disconnect the defroster duct. Remove the heater core housing retaining nuts from inside the engine compartment.
4. Remove the heater core housing assembly from the vehicle.
5. Remove the blower motor to heater housing attaching bolts. Remove the heater motor assembly.
6. Installation is the reverse of the removal procedure.

CJ, SCRAMBLER AND WRANGLER WITH AC

NOTE: It is not necessary to discharge the air condition system in order to replace the blower motor assembly. The evaporator housing must be lowered in order to gain access to the blower motor assembly retaining screws.

1. Disconnect the negative battery cable.
2. Remove the evaporator housing to instrument panel retaining screws. Remove the the evaporator housing mounting bracket screw.
3. Lower the evaporator housing to gain access to the blower motor retaining screws. Remove the blower motor retaining screws. Remove the blower motor from the vehicle.
4. Installation is the reverse of the removal procedure.

COMANCHE, CHEROKEE AND WAGONEER

1. Disconnect the negative battery cable. Disconnect the electrical connections from the blower motor.
2. Remove the blower motor attaching screws. Remove the motor from the vehicle.
3. Installation is the reverse of the removal procedure.

GRAND WAGONEER AND TRUCK WITHOUT AC

1. Disconnect the negative battery cable. Disconnect the electrical connections from the blower motor.
2. Remove the blower motor attaching screws. Remove the motor from the vehicle.
3. Installation is the reverse of the removal procedure.

GRAND WAGONEER AND TRUCK WITH AC

NOTE: It is not necessary to discharge the air condition system in order to replace the blower motor assembly. The evaporator housing must be lowered in order to gain access to the blower motor assembly retaining screws.

1. Disconnect the negative battery cable.
2. Remove the evaporator housing to instrument panel retaining screws. Remove the the evaporator housing mounting bracket screw.
3. Lower the evaporator housing to gain access to the blower motor retaining screws. Remove the blower motor retaining screws. Remove the blower motor from the vehicle.
4. Installation is the reverse of the removal procedure.

FUEL SYSTEM

Carburetor

Removal and Installation

1. Disconnect the negative battery cable. Remove the air cleaner assembly.
2. Remove the necessary components in order to gain access to the carburetor retaining bolts. Disconnect and plug the fuel line. Disconnect all electrical connectors, as required.
3. Disconnect the accelerator linkage. Disconnect the automatic transmission linkage, as required.
4. Remove the carburetor retaining bolts. Remove the carburetor from the vehicle.
5. Installation is the reverse of the removal procedure. Be sure to use a new carburetor base gasket.

IDLE SPEED AND MIXTURE

Adjustments 1982 Vehicles

NOTE: Idle mixture screws on these carburetors are sealed with plugs or dowel pins. A mixture adjustment must be undertaken only when the carburetor is overhauled, the throttle body replaced, or the engine does not meet required emission standards.

EXCEPT SIX CYLINDER ENGINE

1. Position the transmission selector lever in neutral (manual transmission) or drive (automatic transmission).
2. Properly connect a tachometer to the engine. Start the engine and allow it to reach normal operating temperature.
3. If the idle is not within specification, turn the curb idle adjustment screw to obtain specified curb idle rpm.
4. Engines using the 2SE, E2SE or 2150 carburetor, turn the nut on the solenoid plunger or the hex screw on the solenoid carriage to obtain specified idle rpm. Tighten the locknut, if equipped.
5. Disconnect the solenoid wire connector. Adjust the curb idle screw to obtain 500 rpm idle speed. Connect the solenoid wire connector.
6. If equipped with a 2150 carburetor, place the throttle at the curb idle position, fully depress the dashpot stem and measure the clearance between the stem and the throttle lever. Clearance should be 0.032 in. Adjust it by loosening the locknut and turning the dashpot.

SIX CYLINDER ENGINE

1. Position the transmission selector lever in neutral (manual transmission) or drive (automatic transmission).
2. Properly connect a tachometer to the engine. Start the engine and allow it to reach normal operating temperature.
3. If the idle is not within specification, turn the curb idle adjustment screw to obtain specified curb idle rpm.
4. Disconnect the vacuum hose from the vacuum actuator and holding solenoid wire connector. Adjust the curb idle speed adjustment screw to specification, as required.
5. Apply a direct source of vacuum to the vacuum actuator. Turn the vacuum actuator adjustment screw on the throttle lever until the specified rpm is obtained (900 rpm for manual transmission, and 800 rpm for automatic transmission).
6. Disconnect the manifold vacuum source from vacuum actuator. With a jumper wire apply battery voltage to energize the holding solenoid. Turn the air condition on, if equipped.
7. The throttle must be opened manually to allow the solvac throttle positioner to be extended. With the solvac throttle positioner extended, idle speed should be 650 rpm for automatic transmission vehicles and 750 rpm for manual transmission vehicles.
8. If the idle speed is not within specification, adjust the solvac to obtain the proper rpm. Remove the jumper wire from the solvac holding solenoid wire connector. Connect the solvac holding solenoid wire connector. Connect the original hose to vacuum actuator.

Idle Speed Adjustment 1983–88 Vehicles

NOTE: The idle speed adjustments for the 2.5L TBI and 4.0L MPI engines are controlled by the electronic control unit. The idle speed is not adjustable on these engines.

4-150 CID (2.5L) ENGINE WITH YFA CARBURETOR, TRC (ANTI-DIESEL) AND CEC SYSTEM

The TRC (anti-diesel) adjustment screw is statically set at ¾ of turn from the throttle valve closed position during the factory assembly and does not normally require readjustment. Should this adjustment be required, turn the adjustment screw counterclockwise to the throttle plate closed position and then turn the screw clockwise ¾ turn.

To adjust the solevac actuator, proceed as follows;

1. Connect a tachometer to the ignition coil tach wire connector.
2. Place the transmission in the neutral position and depress the parking brake.
3. Start the engine and allow it to reach normal operating temperature.
4. Connect an external vacuum source to the solevac vacuum actuator and apply 10–15 in. Hg. Plug the engine vacuum hose.
5. Adjust the vacuum actuator to specification.
6. Remove the vacuum source from the vacuum actuator and retain the plug in the vacuum hose from the engine.
7. Adjust the curb idle speed to specification.
8. Stop the engine and connect the engine vacuum hose to the vacuum actuator.
9. Remove the tachometer from the engine.

6-258 CID (4.2L) ENGINE WITH MODEL BBD CARBURETOR AND CEC SYSTEM

1. Run the engine until normal operating temperature is reached. Connect a tachometer to the ignition coil negative terminal. The carburetor choke and intake manifold heater must be off. This occurs when the engine coolant heats to approximately 160°F.
2. Remove the vacuum hose to the solevac vacuum actuator unit. Plug the vacuum hose. Disconnect the holding solenoid wire connector.
3. Adjust the curb idle speed screw to specification.
4. Apply a direct source of vacuum to the vacuum actuator, using a hand vacuum pump or its equivalent. When the solevac throttle positioner is fully extended, turn the vacuum actuator adjustment screw on the throttler lever until the specified engine rpm is obtained. Disconnect the vacuum source from the vacuum actuator.
5. With a jumper wire, apply battery voltage to energize the holding solenoid. The holding wire connector can be installed and either the rear window defroster or the air conditioner (with the compressor clutch wire disconnected) can be turned on to energize the holding solenoid.
6. Hold the throttle open manually to allow the throttle positioner to fully extend. Without the vacuum actuator, the throttle must be opened manually to allow the solevac throttle positioner to fully extend.
7. If the holding solenoid idle speed is not within specifications, adjust the idle using the ¼ in. hexheaded adjustment screw on the end of the solevac unit.
8. Disconnect the jumper wire from the solevac solenoid wire connector, if used. Connect the wire connector to the solevac unit, if not connected. Install the original vacuum hose to the vacuum actuator.
9. Remove the tachometer and if disconnected, connect the compressor clutch wire.

V6-173 CID (2.8L) ENGINE WITH 2SE CARBURETOR

1. Connect a tachometer to the ignition coil negative terminal or to the pigtail wire connector above the heater blower motor.
2. Disconnect the plug the vacuum hose at the distributor vacuum advance.
3. If necessary, adjust the ignition timing with the engine speed at or below specifications.
4. Reconnect the vacuum hose to the distributor vacuum advance unit.
5. Disconnect the deceleration valve hose and canister purge hose. Plug the hose and remove the air cleaner assembly.
6. If equipped with air conditioning, turn the control switch to the ON position and open the throttle momentarily to insure the solenoid armature is fully extended. Adjust the solenoid idle speed adjusting screw to obtain the specified engine curb idle

speed rpm. Turn the air condition control switch to the OFF position.

7. If not equipped with air conditioning, adjust the engine idle speed rpm with the solenoid idle speed adjusting screw. Disconnect the solenoid wire and adjust the curb idle.

8. Install the air cleaner assembly. Connect all hoses and other connections.

V6–173 CID (2.8L) ENGINE WITH E2SE CARBURETOR

NOTE: Some 1985–88 California models with the V6 engine, are equipped with a 2200 hour engine timer. The timer activates a solenoid to control operation of the carburetor secondary vacuum brake after 2200 hours of vehicle operation. The timer is not a serviceable component and must not be disassembled. In the event of a timer malfunction, the complete engine wiring harness must be replaced

1. Connect a tachometer to the ignition system. Start the engine and operate to normal operating temperature.
2. Turn off all accessories. Position manual transmission vehicles in neutral and the automatic transmission vehicles in drive with the parking brake locked and the wheels chocked.
3. Adjust the curb idle speed adjusting screw to obtain the specified rpm of 700.
4. Disconnect the vacuum hose from the idle kick actuator and connect an outside vacuum source to the actuator. Apply 15 in. Hg. of vacuum to the actuator.
5. Adjust the actuator hexhead adjustment screw to 1200 rpms with the selector lever in the neutral position.
6. Stop the engine, remove the tachometer and vacuum pump. Install the vacuum hose to the actuator.

V8–360 CID (5.9L) ENGINE WITH 2150 CARBURETOR

NOTE: If the vehicle is equipped with automatic transmission, lock the parking brake, chock the wheels and place the selector lever in drive before adjusting the idle speed.

1. Connect a tachometer to the ignition coil negative terminal.
2. Start the engine and allow it to reach normal operating temperature.
3. Turn the hexhead adjustment screw on the solenoid carriage to obtain the correct engine speed.
4. Disconnect the solenoid wire connector and adjust the curb idle speed screw to specification.
5. Reconnect the solenoid wire connector and stop the engine.
6. If equipped with a dashpot, position the throttle at the curb idle position and depress the dashpot stem.
7. Measure the clearance between the stem and the throttle lever. A clearance of 0.032 in. should exist.
8. Adjust the clearance as required by loosening the locknut and turning the dashpot until the correct clearance is obtained. Tighten the dashpot locknut.

Idle Mixture Adjustment 1983–88 Vehicles

4–150 CID (2.5L) ENGINE WITH YFA CARBURETOR AND CEC SYSTEM

The idle mixture is preset at the time of manufacture and should normally not require readjustment. To prevent easy access to the idle mixture screw, a tamper resistant plug is set into the carburetor assembly to cover the screw. Should adjustment be required due to system diagnosis, contamination, replacement of components or tampering, the following procedure may be used to bring the adjustment into compliance with specifications.

1. Connect a tachometer to the tach terminal of the ignition coil wire connector and a dwell meter to the mixture solenoid test terminals in the diagnosis connector (D2–14 and D2–7) and adjust the dwell meter to the 6 cylinder scale.
2. If the idle mixture screw tamper resistant plug has not been removed, the carburetor must be removed from the engine for access to the plug. With the carburetor off the engine, invert the carburetor and place it in a suitable holding device and remove the plug by drilling a ⅛ in. hole in the center, installing a self tapping screw and pulling the plug from the carburetor.
3. Reinstall the carburetor on the engine, connect all lines and wires.
4. Place the transmission in the neutral position and apply the parking brake.
5. Disconnect and plug the canister purge vacuum hose at the charcoal canister.
6. Start the engine and operate at fast idle speed to bring the engine and coolant to normal operating temperature, thus allowing the CEC (feedback) system to operate in the closed loop mode of operation.
7. Return the engine to idle speed and adjust the carburetor for an idle speed 700 rpm for automatic transmission vehicles in drive and 750 rpm in neutral for manual transmission vehicles.
8. Adjust the idle mixture screw to obtain an average dwell reading of between 25 and 35 degrees, with 30 degrees preferred.
9. If the dwell is too low, turn the idle mixture screw counterclockwise. If the dwell is too high, turn the idle mixture screw clockwise. Allow time for the system to react and stabilize after each movement of the adjusting screw. The feedback system is very sensitive to adjustments.
10. Observe the final dwell indication with the adjusting tool removed. If the specified dwell cannot be obtained by adjustment, inspect the carburetor idle circuits for air leaks, restrictions and etc. Do any necessary repairs.
11. When the adjustment is complete, connect the canister purge hose and adjust the idle speed to specifications.
12. Stop the engine and remove the tachometer and dwell meter. Plug the idle mixture adjusting screw openings. Install the gasket and the air cleaner assembly on the carburetor.

6–258 CID (4.2L) ENGINE WITH BBD CARBURETOR AND CEC SYSTEM

The idle mixture adjustment should only be performed if the adjustment screws were removed during a carburetor overhaul procedure. When the carburetor is mounted to the engine, it must be removed to gain access to the dowel pin locations, whose removal must be accomplished before any adjustment of the mixture screws can be made.

1. Connect a tachometer to the engine. Run the engine until normal operating temperature is reached.
2. Set the parking brake firmly and chock the wheels. Position the gear selector in the neutral for manual transmission and in drive for automatic transmission. Adjust the idle speed.
3. Adjust the idle mixture screws clockwise (lean) until a loss of engine rpm is noted. Idle drop specification is 50 rpm for both automatic and manual transmission.
4. Turn the idle mixture screws counterclockwise (rich) until the highest engine rpm indication is obtained.

NOTE: Do not turn the screws any further than the point at which the highest engine rpm is first obtained. This is referred to as best lean mixture. The engine idle speed will increase above the curb idle speed by an amount that corresponds approximately to the idle drop specifications listed on the Emission Information Label.

5. Turn the mixture screws clockwise (lean) to obtain the specified drop in engine rpm. Turn both mixture screws in small, equal amounts until the specified idle drop is achieved.
6. If the final engine rpm differs more than 30 rpm plus or minus from the original curb idle rpm, adjust the curb idle speed to specifications and repeat the mixture adjustment procedure.

7. Install the dowel pins after completing the idle mixture adjustment. Use care not to disturb the mixture screw positions. It is necessary to remove the carburetor to gain access to the dowel pin locations. After the carburetor has been reinstalled, again check the idle speed specifications and correct as required.

V6–173 CID (2.8L) ENGINE WITH E2SE CARBURETOR (FEEDBACK TYPE)

1. Remove the carburetor from the engine and remove the tamper resistant plug in order to gain access to the idle mixture adjusting screw.
2. Modify special Kent Moore tool J–29030-B or its equivalent, by grinding ⅛ in off the rear and ¼ in off the front of the tool. Place the modified tool onto the idle mixture adjusting screw.
3. Turn the idle mixture screw in until it is lightly seated and back out four turns. If the seal in the air horn concealing the idle air bleed has been removed, replace the air horn. If the seal is still in place, do not remove the seal.
4. Remove the vent stack screen assembly to gain access to the lean mixture screw.
5. Turn the lean mixture screw in until lightly bottomed and then back out 2½ turns. Some resistance should be felt. If not, remove the screw and inspect for the presence of the spring.
6. Install the carburetor on the engine with the modified tool installed on the mixture adjusting screw. Do not install the air cleaner and gasket.

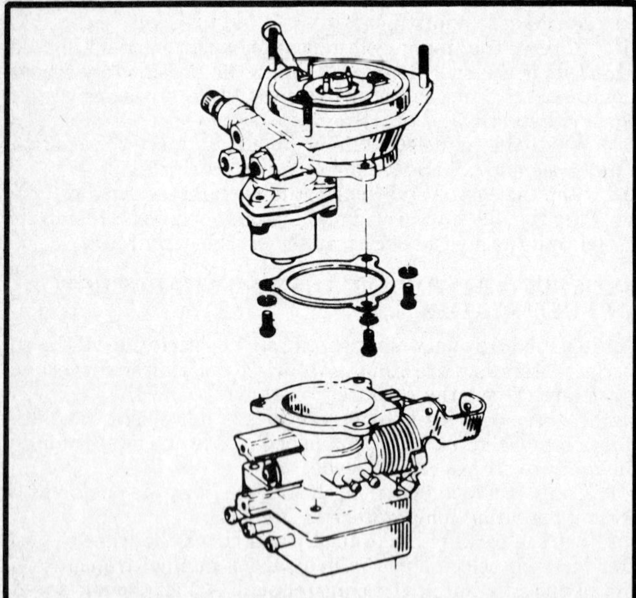

Fuel body assembly-exploded view

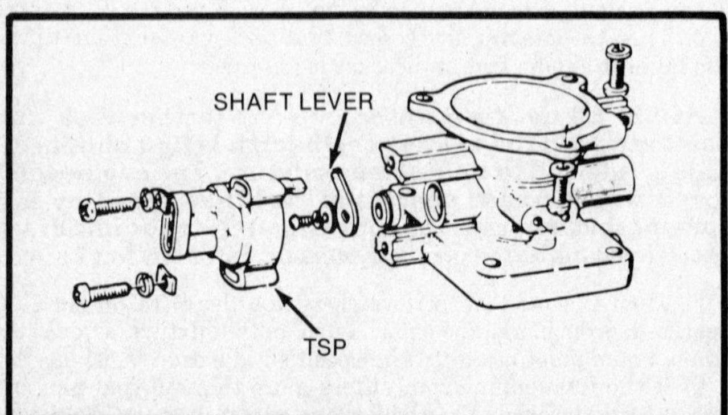

Throttle position sensor assembly

7. Disconnect the bowl vent line at the carburetor, disconnect the EGR valve hose and the canister purge hose at the carburetor. Cap the carburetor ports.
8. Refer to the vehicle emission control information label diagram, located under the vehicle hood, and locate the hose from port 'D' on the carburetor to the temperature sensor and the secondary vacuum break thermal vacuum switch.
9. Disconnect the hose at the temperature sensor on the air cleanser and plug the hose.
10. Connect a dwell meter positive probe to the mixture control solenoid dwell test wire with a green connection.
11. Connect the negative probe to ground and set the meter at the 6 cylinder scale position.
12. Connect a tachometer to the ignition system, set the parking brake and chock the wheels.
13. Place the transmission in park for automatic or neutral for manual.
14. Start and operate the engine until normal operating temperature is reached and the electronic engine control system is in the closed loop mode of operation.
15. Operate the engine at 3000 rpm and adjust the lean mixture screw slowly in small increments, allowing time for the dwell to stabilize after turning the screw to obtain an average dwell of 35 degrees.
16. If the dwell is too low, back the screw out and if too high, turn the screw in. If unable to adjust to specifications, inspect the main metering system for leaks, restriction, etc.
17. Return the engine to idle speed. Allow the engine to stabilize before the dwell is recorded.
18. Adjust the idle mixture screw with the modified tool J–29030-A or its equivalent, to obtain an average dwell of 25 degrees. If the dwell is too high, turn the screw in and if the dwell is too low, back the screw out. Allow time for the dwell to stabilize after each adjustment, because the adjustment is very sensitive. If unable to adjust to specifications, check for idle system air or vacuum leaks and restrictions.

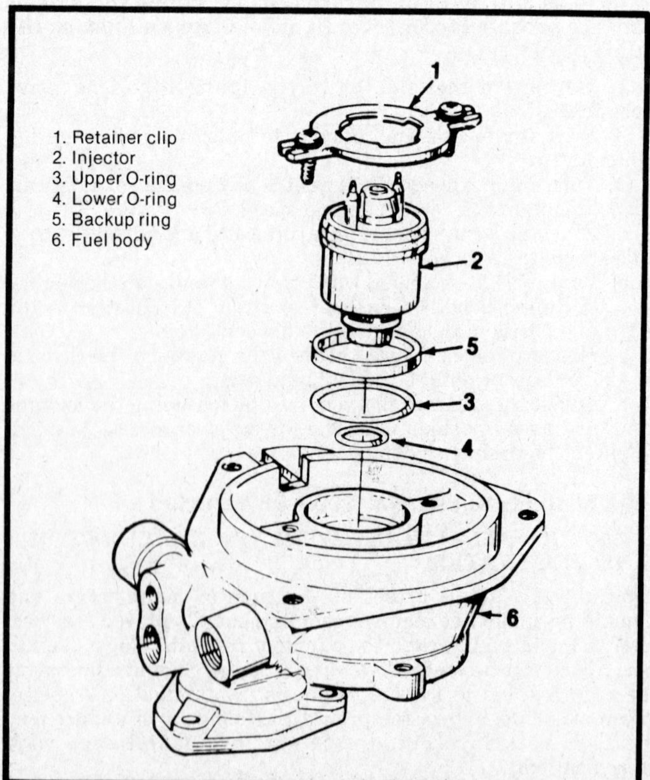

Fuel injector and related components

NOTE: The mixture control solenoid dwell is an indication of the ratio of ON to OFF time. The dwell of the mixture control solenoid is used to determine the calibration and is sensitive to changes in the fuel mixture caused by heat, air leaks, etc. While the engine is idling, it is normal for the dwell to increase and decrease fairly constant over a relativity narrow range, such as 5 degrees. However, it may occasionally vary as much as 10–15 degrees momentarily because of temporary mixture changes. The dwell specified is the average of the most consistant variations. The engine must be allowed to stabilize its self for a few minutes after returning the engine to idle in order to obtain a correct average.

19. Disconnect the mixture control solenoid and check for and engine speed change of at least 50 rpm. If the rpm does not change enough, inspect the idle air bleed circuit for restrictions, leaks, etc.
20. Increase the engine speed to 3000 rpm and operate for a few minutes. Note the dwell which should be varying with an average indications of 35 degrees.
21. If the average dwell is not at 25 degrees, adjust the lean mixture screw.
22. After adjusting the lean mixture screw, adjust the idle mixture screw to obtain 25 degrees dwell.
23. If at an average dwell of 25 degrees, remove the carburetor from the engine, remove the modified tool J-29030-A or equivalent from the idle mixture screw and seal the access hole.
24. Install the carburetor, connect all disconnected components and install the vent screen. Verify the idle speed is within specifications.

V8-360 CID (5.9L) ENGINE WITH 2150 CARBURETOR

NOTE: The idle mixture adjustment screws are concealed by tamper resistant caps. The idle mixture should be adjusted only if the mixture adjustment screws were removed or altered during major carburetor overhaul or tampering.

1. Connect a tachometer to the engine.
2. Start the engine and allow it to reach normal operating temperature.
3. Set the parking brake and chock the wheels. Position the automatic transmission in the drive detent.
4. Be sure choke is completely off and the idle speed is set to specifications.
5. Turn the idle mixture adjusting screws clockwise (leaner) until a perceptible loss of engine speed is noted on the tachometer.
6. Turn the idle mixture adjusting screws counterclockwise (richer) until the highest engine speed is obtained.
7. This position of the idle mixture adjusting screws is referred to as the lean best idle.
8. Turn both idle mixture adjusting screws clockwise in small, equal amounts until the specified idle speed drop is noted on the tachometer.

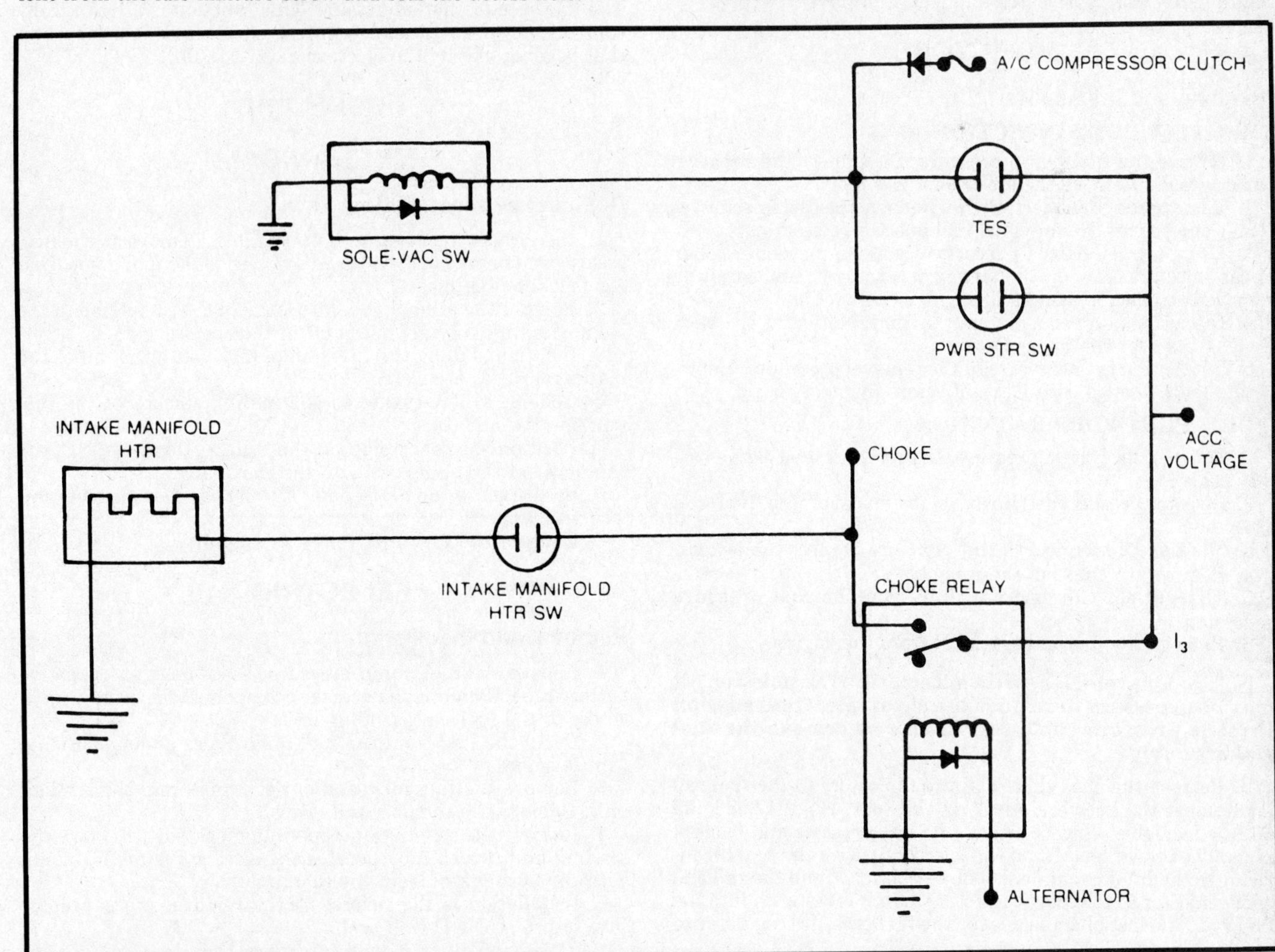

SOLE-VAC wiring schematic

Fuel Injection

Relieve Pressure

Fuel system pressure must be relieved before disconnecting any fuel lines. Release fuel system pressure at the test connection using a suitable pressure gauge with a pressure bleed valve. Take precautions to avoid the risk of fire whenever working on or around any open fuel system.

Quick Disconnect Fitting

1. Relieve the fuel system pressure. Separate the quick connect fuel line tubes at the inner fender panel by squeezing the two retaining tabs against the fuel line, then pulling the tube and retainer from the fitting.
2. Remove the two O-rings and the spacer from the fitting. This can be accomplished by using a heavy piece of wire bent into an L-shape.
3. Remove the retainer from the fuel tube and discard the O-rings, spacer and retainer.
4. Install the new retainer assembly by pushing it into the quick connect fitting until it clicks.
5. Grasp the disposable plastic plug and remove it from the replacement fitting. By removing only the plastic plug, the O-rings, spacer and retainer will remain in the fitting.
6. Push the fuel line into the fitting until a click is heard and the connection is complete. Give the fuel line connection a firm tug to verify that it is seated and locked properly.

INJECTORS

Removal and Installation

THROTTLE BODY INJECTION

1. Relieve the fuel pump pressure. Disconnect the negative battery cable. Remove the air cleaner assembly.
2. Remove the fuel injector wire. Remove the fuel injector retainer clip screws. Remove the fuel injector retainer clip.
3. Using a small pair of pliers, gently grasp the center collar of the injector, between the electrical terminals, and carefully remove the injector using a lifting twisting motion.
4. Discard the upper and lower O-rings. Note that the back up ring fits over the upper O-ring.
5. Installation is the reverse of the removal procedure. Lubricate both O-rings with light oil before installation.

MULTI PORT FUEL INJECTION

1. Relieve fuel system pressure. Disconnect the negative battery cable.
2. Disconnect the fuel lines at the ends of the fuel rail assembly.
3. Mark and disconnect the injector wire harness connectors.
4. Remove the fuel rail retaining bolts.
5. Disconnect the vacuum line from the fuel pressure regulator.
6. Remove the fuel rail assembly from the engine.

NOTE: On vehicles with automatic transmission, it may be necessary to remove the automatic transmission throttle pressure cable and bracke to remove the fuel rail assembly.

7. Remove the clips that retain the injectors to the fuel rail and remove the injectors. An O-ring kit (part No. PN 8983 503 637) is available which consists of 6 brown seals and 7 black seals. The brown seals fit on the injector tip area and seal the injector to the intake manifold. The black seals fit on the rail end of the injector to to seal the injector when it is installed into the fuel rail. The last black seal is for the fuel pressure regulator to seal the pressure regulator to the fuel rail. These seals cannot be interchanged.
8. Installation is the reverse of the removal procedure. Tighten the fuel rail mounting bolts to 20 ft. lbs.

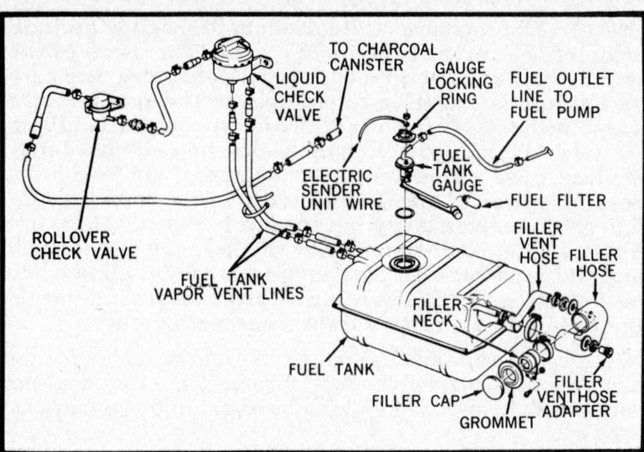

Typical fuel tank and vent lines

Idle Speed Adjustment

The idle speed is not adjustable. This function is electronically controlled by the vehicles computer system. It functions on data that is generated by the electronic control unit.

Fuel Pump

MECHANICAL

Removal and Installation

1. Disconnect the negative battery cable. Remove all the necessary components in order to gain access to the fuel pump. Disconnect the fuel lines.
2. Remove the attaching bolts that hold the fuel pump to the engine and lift the fuel pump off of the engine.
3. Before installing the fuel pump, make sure that all of the mating surfaces are clean.
4. Cement a new gasket to the mating surface of the fuel pump.
5. Position the fuel pump on the cylinder block so that the cam lever of the pump rests on the camshaft.
6. Secure the pump to the engine with the retaining bolts and lock washers.
7. Connect the fuel lines to the fuel pump.

ELECTRIC

Removal and Installation

1. Relieve the fuel pump pressure. Disconnect the negative battery cable. Remove all necessary components in order to gain access to the fuel tank sending unit.
2. Drain the fuel from the fuel tank. Raise and support the vehicle safely.
3. Remove the fuel inlet and outlet hoses from the sending unit. Remove the sending unit wires.
4. Remove the sending unit retaining lock ring. Remove the sending unit, which incorporates the electric fuel pump, along with the O-ring seal from the fuel tank.
5. Installation is the reverse of the removal procedure. Be sure to use a new O-ring seal.

EMISSION CONTROLS

4–150 (2.5) AND 4–151 CID (2.5L)
Emission Calibrated Carburetor
Emission Calibrated Distributor
Computerized Emission Control System (CEC)
Pulse Air Injection
Air Control Valve (upstream)
Air Control Valve (downstream)
Pulse Air Check Valve (upstream)
Pulse Air Check Valve (downstream)
Air Switch Solenoid
Catalytic Converter
Coolant Temperature Switch
EGR Valve
EGR/TVS Switch
Canister Purge/EGR CTO Valve
TAC System
TAC TVS Switch
TAC Delay Valve and Check Valve
Ignition CTO Valve
Ignition Electronic Spark Retard
Carburetor Vent to Canister
Electric Choke
SOLE-VAC Idle Control
Thermal Electric Switch
Oxygen Sensor
Microprocessor
Vacuum Switch Assembly
Positive Crankcase Valve (PCV)
Control Valve
Coolant Temperature Switch
Knock Sensor

6–243 CID (4.0L) AND 6–258 CID (4.2L)
Emission Calibrated Carburetor
Emission Calibrated Distributor
Computerized Emission Control system (CEC)
Pulse Air Injection
Air Control Valve (upstream)
Air Control Valve (downstream)
Pulse Air Check Valve (upstream)
Pulse Air Check Valve (downstream)
Air Switch Solenoid
Catalytic Converter
Coolant Temperature Switch (intake manifold heater)
EGR Valve
EGR/TVS Switch
Canister Purge – EGR/CTO Valve
TAC System
TAC Delay Valve and Check Valve
Ignition CTO Valve
Ignition Electronic Spark Retard
Ignition Delay Valve (dual reverse delay)
Carburetor Vent to Canister
Electric Choke
SOLE-VAC Idle Control
Thermal Electric Switch
Oxygen Sensor
Decel Valve
Microprocessor
Vacuum Switch Assembly
Positive Crankcase Valve (PCV)
PCV Solenoid
Coolant Temperature Switch
Knock Sensor
Decel Valve
Multi-Port Injection System (4.0L engine only)

V6–173 CID (2.8L)
Emission Calibrated Carburetor
Emission Calibrated Distributor
Positive Crankcase Valve (PCV)
Catalytic Converter
TAC System
Vapor Control, Canister Storage
Canister Purge Solenoid
EGR Valve
EGR/TVS Switch
Early Fuel Evaporation (EFE)
EFE Solenoid
Electric Choke
Electronic Spark Control
Oxygen Sensor
Computer Control Command System (C–3)
Air Induction Reaction System (AIR)
Air Management Valve
Deceleration Valve
Electric EFE Grid And Relay
Vacuum Check Valve

V8–360 CID (5.9L)
Emission Calibrated Carburetor
Emission Calibrated Distributor
Air Injection
Air Control Valve
Diverter Valve
Catalytic Converter
EGR Valve
EGR/TVS
EGR/CTO Valve Temperature
TAC System
TAC/TVS
TAC Delay Valve (reverse delay) and check valve
Vacuum Advance CTO Valve Temperature
Vacuum Advance Delay Valve
HD Vacuum Advance CTO Valve Temperature
Carburetor Vent to Canister
Electric Choke
SOLE-VAC Idle Control
Throttle Solenoid
Microprocessor
Vacuum Switch Assembly
Positive Crankcase Ventilation Valve (PCV)

Crankcase Emission Control System

POSITIVE CRANKCASE VENTILATION SYSTEM (PCV)

The PCV System functions to prevent crankcase vapors from entering the atmosphere. Filtered air is routed to the crankcase, the vapors drawn out and routed into the intake manifold to be burned along with the air/fuel mixture. Should the crankcase vapors exceed the flow capacity of the PCV valve, the air flow in the system reverses and the vapors are drawn through the air cleaner element and into the carburetor to be burned along with the air/fuel mixture.

On vehicles equipped with the Computerized Emission Control (CEC) Fuel Feedback system, a PCV valve solenoid is installed in the PCV hose to close the crankcase ventilation system when the engine is operating at idle speed. The antidieseling relay system, if equipped, is used to momentarily energize the PCV solenoid when the ignition key is turned off, to prevent air from entering the intake manifold below the throttle plates of the carburetor, thus preventing engine dieseling.

Valve Functional Test

Test the PCV valve with the engine at normal idle speed. The engine intake vacuum must be at least 14 in. Hg. to check the correct flow rate of the PCV valve. When determining engine vacuum level, connect a vacuum gauge to a centrally located fitting on the intake manifold.

Valve Flow Rate Test

With a low vacuum level, it may be necessary to load the engine while testing the flow rate. Replace the valve if the flow rate is not within specification.

If the engine manifold vacuum is 6–15 in. Hg., the air flow is .0–.2 cfm. If the engine manifold vacuum is 11–6 in. Hg., the air flow is .9–2.0 cfm. If the engine manifold vacuum is 5–3 in. Hg., the air flow is 1.5–2.5 cfm.

Evaporative Emission Control System

VAPOR STORAGE CANISTER

The fuel vapor canister is filled with activated charcoal granules, which absorb the fuel vapors that enter the canister. When the engine is started, the fuel vapors are metered into the induction system, along with the air/fuel mixture.

ROLLOVER CHECK VALVE

In the event of an automobile rollover, the rollover check valve prevents the loss of fuel through the vent hose or pipe.

CARBURETOR BOWL VAPOR VENT

The carburetor external bowl fuel vapor vent provides an outlet for the fuel vapors when the engine is not in the operating mode, to prevent the vapors from entering the atmosphere.

FUEL TANK CAP

The filler cap incorporates a pressure and vacuum relief valve that is closed during normal operation. The valve is calibrated to open when the pressure is in excess of 0.8 psi or a vacuum in excess of 0.1 in. Hg. develops in the fuel tank. As the pressure or vacuum is relieved, the valve returns to its normally closed position. In the event of a vehicle rollover, the fuel filler cap provides additional protection from spilled fuel.

FUEL RETURN SYSTEM

To reduce the possibility of high temperature fuel vapor problems, some engines may be equipped with a fuel return system. This system consists of a hose connecting the fuel filter to the fuel tank, through a third nipple on the filter. The fuel filter must be positioned with the third nipple on the top of the filter during its installation. During normal operation, a small amount of fuel returns to the tank, rather than entering the carburetor bowl. A one way check valve is positioned in the return line, at the filter or the hose, to prevent fuel from returning to the carburetor through the fuel return line.

Exhaust Emission Control System

THERMOSTATICALLY CONTROLLED AIR CLEANER (TAC)

The Thermostatically Controlled Air Cleaner (TAC) System provides heated air for the carburetor during engine warm up. The TAC system is comprised of a heat stove that partically encloses the exhaust manifold, a heated air tube, a special air cleaner assembly equipped with a thermal switch, a reverse delay valve, a check valve, a vacuum motor and an air valve assembly. The air cleaner snorkel duct is equipped with spring loaded trap door to close off the air flow to the carburetor when the engine is inoperative. A reverse delay valve is used to provide approximately 100 seconds delay before the trap door is allowed to close.

Testing

AIR VALVE VACUUM MOTOR

1. With the engine off, remove the ambient air duct at the air cleaner and observe the position of the air valve. It should be fully open to the incoming ambient air (Heat in the OFF position).
2. Start the engine and observe the position of the air valve. It should be fully closed to incoming ambient air (Heat in the ON position).
3. Depress the throttle rapidly (½–¾ position) and release. The air valve should briefly remain stationary and then move toward the heat OFF position and back to heat ON position.
4. Loosely attach the ambient air duct to the air cleaner and warm the engine to normal operating temperature.
5. Remove the ambient air duct and observe the air valve. It should be either fully open to ambient air or at a mixture position that provides the correct inlet air temperature to the carburetor. Reconnect the duct to the air cleaner.
6. If the air valve does not function as described, inspect for mechanical binding in the snorkel, vacuum hoses being disconnected, air leaks at the vacuum motor, thermal switch, reverse delay valve, check valve, intake manifold or defective vacuum hoses.
7. If the air valve manually operates freely and no hose disconnections or air leaks are detected, connect a hose from a vacuum source (engine or pump) directly to the vacuum motor and apply vacuum.
8. If the air valve closes, either the thermal switch, reverse delay valve or the check valve is defective and must be replaced. If the air valve does not close, replace the vacuum motor.

THERMAL SWITCH

1. Disconnect the vacuum hoses from the thermal switch. Connect the vacuum pump and vacuum gauge to the switch.
2. Apply a minimum of 14 in. Hg. vacuum to the switch. With the switch below 40°F., vacuum should be held.
3. With the switch heated above 55°F., the air vent valve should open and the vacuum should drop to zero. Replace the switch, if defective.
4. The temperature values listed above are only nominal switching values and can vary from switch to switch by a few or more degrees, plus or minus.

TRAP DOOR

1. With the engine off, remove the air cleaner cover and observe the position of the trapdoor, which should be closed.
2. Remove the vacuum hose from the intake manifold vacuum source and apply an external vacuum of approximately 2–4 in. Hg. The trap door should open.
3. If the vacuum hose is not defective, remove the reverse delay valve, join the vacuum hose with an adapter and retest. If the door opens, replace the reverse delay valve.
4. If the door does not open, apply vacuum directly to the vacuum motor on the air cleaner intake snorkel duct. If the door still does not open, inspect for binding or distortion and adjust as required. If the door opens, inspect the hoses for obstructions, cracks and kinks. Correct as necessary.
5. Replace the motor if the door swings freely.

REVERSE DELAY VALVE

1. Remove the vacuum hose from the yellow end of the valve and apply an external sourced vacuum of approximately 2–4 in. Hg.
2. With the aid of an elapsed time indicator, note the time re-

quired for the atmospheric pressure to pass through the valve and eliminate the vacuum.

3. Replace the valve if the time required to eliminate the vacuum is less than 4.5 seconds or more than 13.2 seconds.

4. When installing a replacement reverse delay valve, always position the yellow end of the valve toward the trapdoor vacuum motor.

EXHAUST GAS RECIRCULATION SYSTEM (EGR)

The EGR system is designed to lower the temperature of the burning air/fuel mixture in the combustion chamber by having metered amounts of exhaust gas redirected into the combustion chamber to dilute the air/fuel mixture. The EGR system consists of a diaphragm activated exhaust flow control valve (EGR valve), coolant temperature override (CTO) valve, thermal vacuum switch (TVS) and connecting hoses.

Do not disconnect the vacuum hose or cause the EGR valve to become inoperative for an extended period of time because the resulting preignition could cause piston burning and scuffing to occur.

Testing

VALVE OPENING

1. With the engine at normal operating temperature and running at curb idle speed, rapidly open and close the throttle to allow the engine speed to attain 1500 rpm.

2. A distinct movement should be noticed in the EGR control valve diaphragm. If the diaphragm does not move, probable causes are as follows.

3. Faulty vacuum hose to the EGR valve. Defective EGR valve diaphragm. Defective back pressure sensor diaphragm. Vacuum hose leakage.

4. Repair or replace defective components, as required.

VALVE CLOSING

1. With the engine at normal operating temperature and the engine running at curb idle speed, use a protective device or cover and manually depress the EGR valve diaphragm.

2. This should cause an immediate drop in engine rpm and indicate that the EGR valve is sealing, thus preventing the flow of the exhaust gas into the intake manifold.

3. If there is no change in the engine rpm and the engine is idling properly, exhaust gases are not entering the intake manifold.

4. The probable malfunction is a restricted passage between the EGR valve and the intake manifold.

5. If the engine idles improperly and the rpm is not greatly affected by depressing the EGR valve diaphragm, the EGR valve is not preventing the flow of exhaust gases into the intake manifold, which is usually indictative of a faulty or carboned EGR valve.

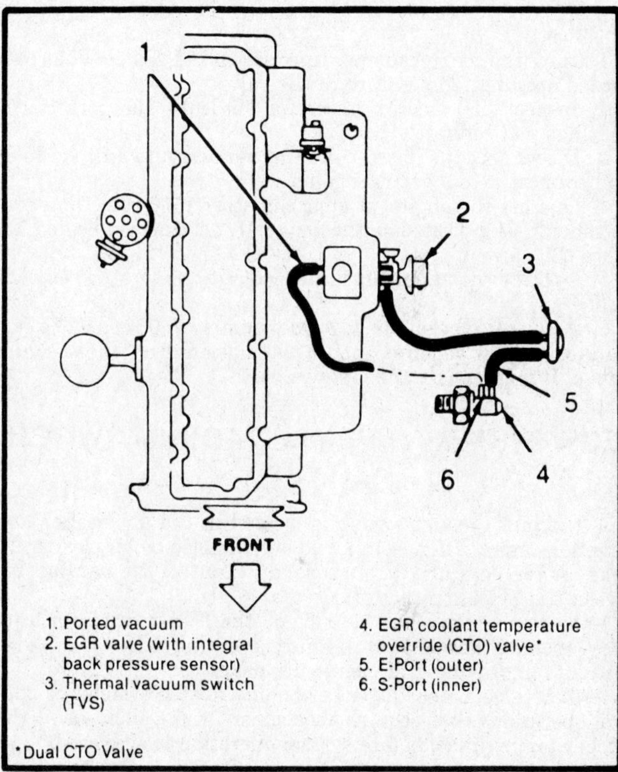

Typical EGR system—6 cylinder engine

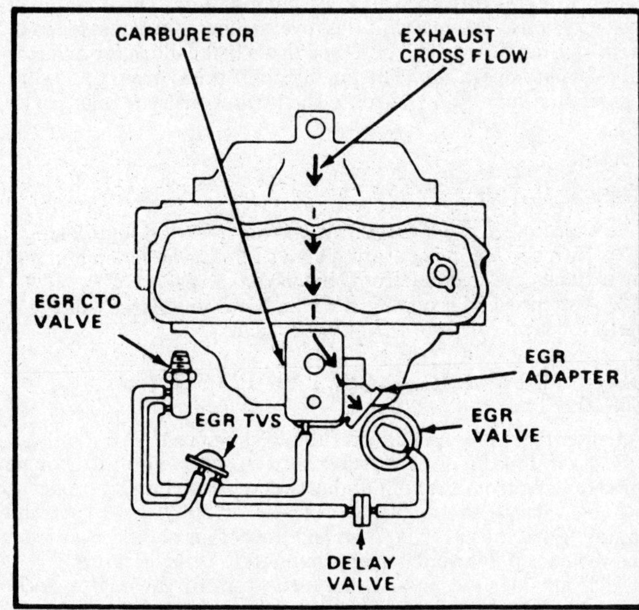

Typical EGR system—4 cylinder engine

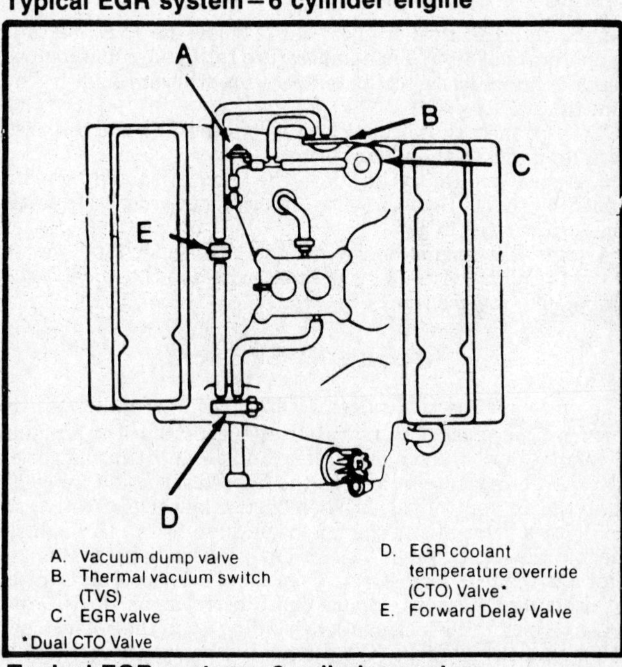

Typical EGR system—8 cylinder engine

EGR SYSTEM COOLANT TEMPERATURE OVERRIDE VALVE (CTO)

The EGR System CTO valve is located in the coolant passage at the left side of the intake manifold and is also used for distributor vacuum advance control. When the coolant temperature is below the calibrated rating of the CTO valve, there is no vacuum applied to the EGR valve. The valve starts to open at approximately 115°F.

Testing

1. Have the coolant temperature at least 10°F. below the calibrated opening temperature of the valve.
2. Inspect the vacuum hoses for air leaks and correct the routings and connections.
3. Disconnect the hose at the thermal vacuum switch (TVS) and connect it to a vacuum gauge.
4. Operate the engine at approximately 1500 rpm. No vacuum should be indicated on the gauge. If vacuum is indicated, replace the valve.
5. Operate the engine until the coolant temperature exceeds 115°F.
6. Accelerate the engine to approximately 1500 rpm. The carburetor ported vacuum should be indicated on the vacuum gauge. If not, replace the CTO valve.

EGR SYSTEM THERMAL VACUUM SWITCH (TVS)

The thermal vacuum switch is located in the air cleaner and functions as an off/on switch and is controlled by air cleaner intake air temperature. It purpose is to control the vacuum between the EGR and the CTO systems.

At air temperature below 40–55°F., the TVS prevents vacuum from opening the EGR valve, thus preventing EGR valve operation and improving cold engine driveability.

A TVS valve is used for other engine related systems to control operations that require air cleaner intake air to be at the proper temperature before system operation is activated.

Testing

1. Cool the air cleaner intake air to below the TVS calibrated temperature of 40°F. The temperature ratings are nominal values and the actual switching temperature will vary slightly from unit to unit.
2. Disconnect the vacuum hoses from the TVS and connect a vacuum pump to the inner port.
3. Apply vacuum to the TVS. The vacuum should be maintained by the TVS check valve. If the vacuum leaks from the line, replace the TVS.
4. Start the engine and warm the air cleaner intake air to above the 55°F. Vacuum should not be held in the line. If vacuum is held, replace the TVS.

PULSE AIR SYSTEM

The pulse air injection system utilizes the alternating positive and negative exhaust pressure pulsations instead of an air pump to inject air into the exhaust system and produce exhaust gas oxidation. The air enters through the filtered side of the air cleaner to the air control valve. When opened by the air switch, the air control valve allows the air to continue to and through the air injection check valve. The air enters the exhaust system, either upstream or downstream from the check valve, air is injected either into the front exhaust pipe (upstream) or into the catalytic converter (downstream), depending upon the engine operating conditions. The CEC system micro computer unit (MCU) controls the switching operation.

This system may contain any or all of the following major components.

An air injection check valve, which is a one way reed valve that is opened and closed by the negative and positive exhaust pressure pulsations. During the negative exhaust pulse (low Pressure), atmospheric pressure opens the check valve and forces air into the exhaust system. Being a one way valve, the valve reed prevents exhaust from being forced back through the valve during the positive exhaust pressure pulsations (high pressure).

An air control valve, that controls the supply of filtered air routed to the air injection check valve. The valve is opened and closed by the air switch solenoid.

An air switch solenoid, that controls the air control valve by switching the vacuum on and off. The solenoid is controlled by the micro computer unit (MCU).

A vacuum storage tank, which stores engine vacuum in a reservoir tank until released by the air switch solenoid.

A micro computer init (MCU), that switches air either upstream or downstream, depending upon the engine operating conditions, by energizing and de-energizing the air switch solenoids.

AIR PUMP INJECTION SYSTEM

The air pump air injection system incorporates a belt driven air pump, a vacuum controlled diverter valve, two air injection manifolds with check valves and the necessary connecting hoses. This system provides for air injection into the exhaust manifold and into the air cleaner assembly.

This system may contain any or all of the following major components.

An air pump, which is designed for long life and is serviced only by replacement. Do not disassemble the air pump for any reason since the internal components are not servicable.

A diverter valve, which has two outlets, one for each air injection manifold. The valve momentarily diverts air pump output from the manifolds and vents it to the atmosphere during rapid engine deceleration. The valve also functions as a pressure release valve for excessive air pump output.

The air injection manifolds distribute the air via the diverter valve , to each of the exhaust manifold inlet ports. A check valve, incorporating a stainless steel spring plunger and an asbestos seat, is integral with each air injection manifold. The function of the check valve is to prevent the reverse flow of exhaust gases to the air pump during the pump or drive belt failure, or diverter valve bypass operation. The air injection tubes are mounted to the exhaust manifold and route the airflow into the inlet ports.

Testing

CHECK VALVE

1. Disconnect the air hoses at the air injection manifolds.
2. With the engine operating above idle speed, listen and feel for exhaust gas leakage from the check valves.
3. A slight leakage of air is normal, however, a large leakage is cause for replacement of the check valve.

DIVERTER VALVE, EXCEPT V6–173 CID (2.8L) ENGINE

1. Start the engine and operate at idle speed.
2. Examine the diverter valve vent to ascertain if little or no air is flowing from the vent, indicating it is functioning properly.
3. Accelerate the engine to a speed of 2000–3000 rpm and rapidly close the throttle. A strong flow of air should pass from the diverter valve vent for approximately three seconds.
4. If air does not pass through the vent or the engine backfires, be sure the vacuum hose has vacuum and there is no air leakage.

NOTE: The diverter valve diverts and vents air pump output when the manifold vacuum of 20 in. Hg. or more is applied to the diaphragm. The valve also vents the air when the air pump output exceeds 5 psi.

5. Slowly accelerate the engine to between 2500 and 3500 rpm. Air should begin to flow from the diverter valve vent.
6. If vacuum is present at the valve and it does not perform as described, replace the valve assembly.

DIVERTER VALVE V6–173 CID (2.8L) ENGINE, EXCEPT CALIFORNIA VEHICLES

1. Bring the engine to normal operating temperature.
2. Remove the air cleaner cover.
3. Disconnect the lower vacuum hose from the diverter valve. The air pump air should now be directed to the air cleaner.
4. Connect the vacuum hose to the valve and the air pump air should be directed to the exhaust manifolds.
5. If air is not diverted when the vacuum hose is disconnected, check the vacuum source and ensure there is vacuum. If vacuum is present, replace the diverter valve.

DIVERTER VALVE V6–173 CID (2.8L) ENGINE CALIFORNIA VEHICLES

This type valve is a combination of an electrical diverter valve and a vacuum switching valve. The diverter valve solenoid is controlled directly by the electronic control module so that air is diverted to the air cleaner when the solenoid is deenergized at the following specified times.

1. Engine not operating (electrical control).
2. First five seconds of any start up of the engine (electrical control).
3. High electrical load on the engine control system.
4. Closed throttle deceleration (vacuum control).

CATALYTIC CONVERTER

Dual bed monolithic type or pellet type catalytic converters are used. The monolithic type is not serviceable, but the pellets can be replaced in the pellet type. The stainless steel converter body is designed to last the life of the automobile, but excessive heat can cause premature converter failure. Although the excessive heat would be contained in the converter, the cause of the overheating would not be the fault of the converter, but from an outside source. A defective fuel system, air injection system or ignition system malfunction that permits unburned fuel to enter the converter will usually be the cause. If the converter is heat damaged, the cause must be located and repaired before a new converter is installed.

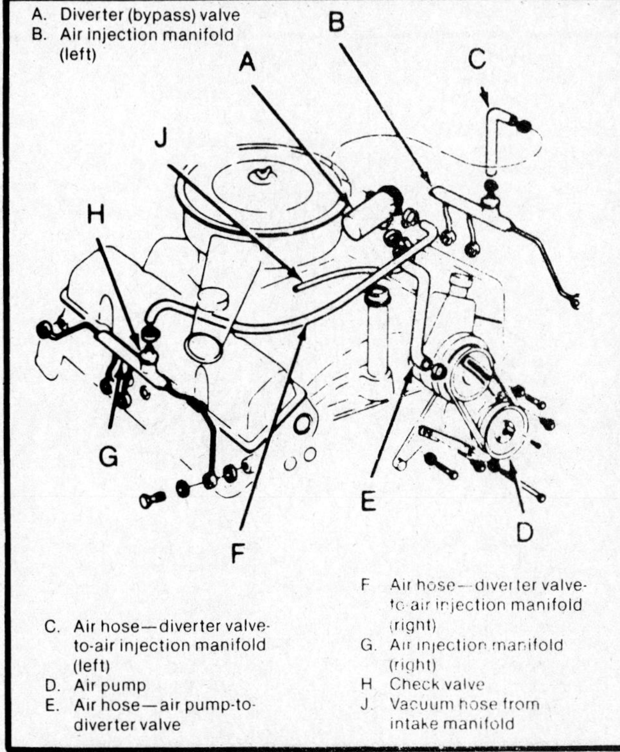

Air injection system and related components

RESTRICTED EXHAUST SYSTEM

A partically restricted or blocked exhaust system usually results in loss of power or backfire up through the carburetor. The system would have to be visually inspected to ascertain if a mechanical blockage exists.

Testing

1. If the system appears visually to be intact, connect a vacuum gauge to the intake manifold.

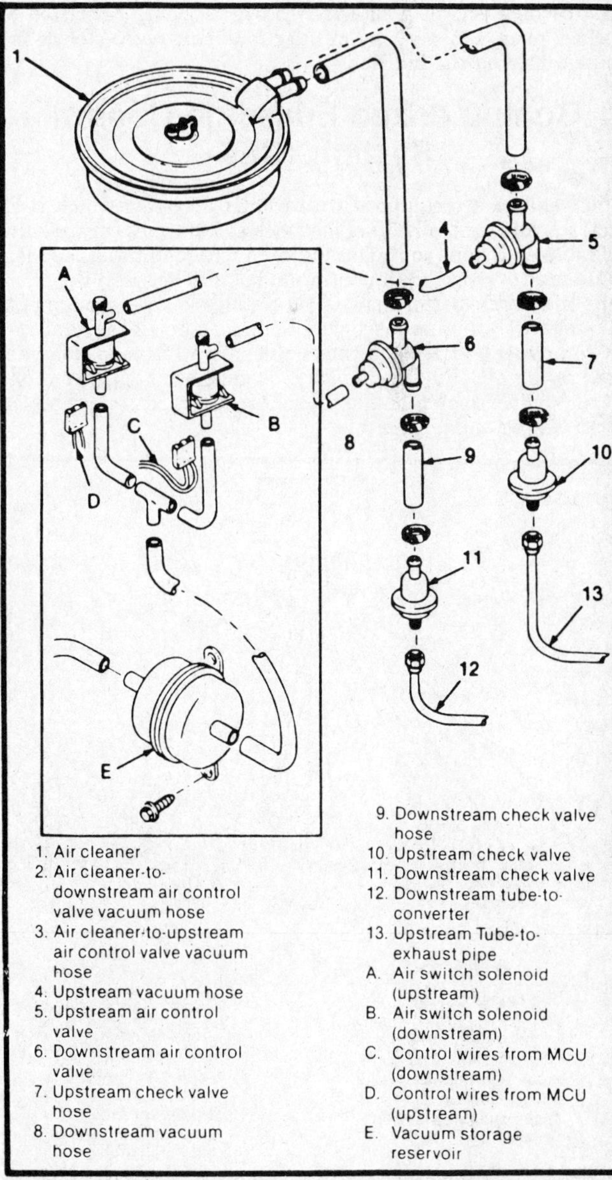

Pulse air system and related components

2. Connect a tachometer to the engine to register rpm.
3. Start the engine and observe the vacuum gauge. The gauge should indicate a vacuum of 16–21 in. Hg.
4. Increase the engine speed to 2000 rpm and observe the vacuum gauge.
5. The vacuum will decrease when the speed is increased rapidly, but should stabilize at 16–21 in. Hg. and remain constant.
6. If the vacuum remains below 16 in. Hg., the exhaust system is restricted or blocked. Stop the engine and disconnect the exhaust pipe at the manifold.
7. Start the engine and increase the engine speed to 2000 rpm. Observe the vacuum gauge.
8. If the vacuum stabilizes at 16–21 in. Hg., the restriction or blockage is either in the exhaust pipe, catalytic converter, muffler or tail pipe.
9. If the vacuum stabilizes below 16 in. Hg., the exhaust manifold is restricted.
10. Each section of the exhaust system can be checked by the process of elimination, by removing and installing each component and operating the engine in the manner previously described, while observing the vacuum reading.
11. In the event of a catalytic converter being restricted or blocked, always inspect the muffler to ensure converter debris has not entered the muffler.

Computerized Emission Control System (CEC)

Some vehicles are equipped with the CEC system which is an electronically controlled fuel feedback system that controls undesirable emissions to the atmosphere and maintains the ideal air/fuel ratio to provide an optimum balance between the emissions and engine performance. The system uses a micro computer unit (MCU), numerous signal input sensors and several output components. Based on the engine operating conditions, relayed to the MCU by input sensor signals, the MCU generates output signals to provide the proper air/fuel mixture, proper ignition timing and engine idle speed.

MCU

1. Coolant temperature switch
2. Thermal electric switch
3. Four- and Ten-inch Hg vacuum switches
4. Oxygen sensor
5. Wide open throttle (WOT) switch
6. Knock sensor
7. Distributor
8. Stepper motor
9. Idle relay
10. Sole-vac throttle positioner
11. Upstream and downstream solenoids
12. PCV solenoid

CEC components used on 4–150 CID engine

The system operates in either of two modes, the closed loop mode or the open loop mode. Closed loop is when the air/fuel ratio is varied, according to the oxygen content tin the exhaust gases. In the open loop mode, the air/fuel ratio is predetermined by the MCU for a number of engine operating conditions, such as engine start-up, cold engine operation, or wide open throttle (WOT) position. When the engine is started, the MCU then determines in which mode of operation , (closed or open loop), the engine should be operating. The MCU determines this by monitoring the input signals from the various input components, such as the air and coolant temperature information, engine rpm information and vacuum levels.

The MCU operates the system in the open loop mode based on a priority rating for the various predetermined engine operating conditions. It continues to operate the system and the MCU output components in the open loop mode until such time as a closed loop mode of operation is indicated. At this time, the MCU shifts the operation to the closed loop mode. Based on the oxygen content in the exhaust gases, and other inputs, it continues to operate the system in the closed loop mode, constantly varying the air/fuel ratio to maintain the optimum 14.7:1 ratio.

The engine operating conditions are constantly being monitored by the MCU and any changes that occur during the engine operation are quickly detected by the MCU, which places the system back in the appropriate open mode of operation.

Computer Comand Control (CCC)

Some vehicles equipped with a V6 engine, have a self diagnostic system with a CHECK ENGINE light mounted in the instrument panel cluster.

The self diagnostic system detects the troubles most likely to occur. The diagnostic system illuminates the CHECK ENGINE light when a trouble is detected. When a jumper wire is connected between trouble code TEST terminals 6 and 7 of the 15 terminal diagnostic connector, the CHECK ENGINE light will flash a trouble code or codes that indicate the trouble area.

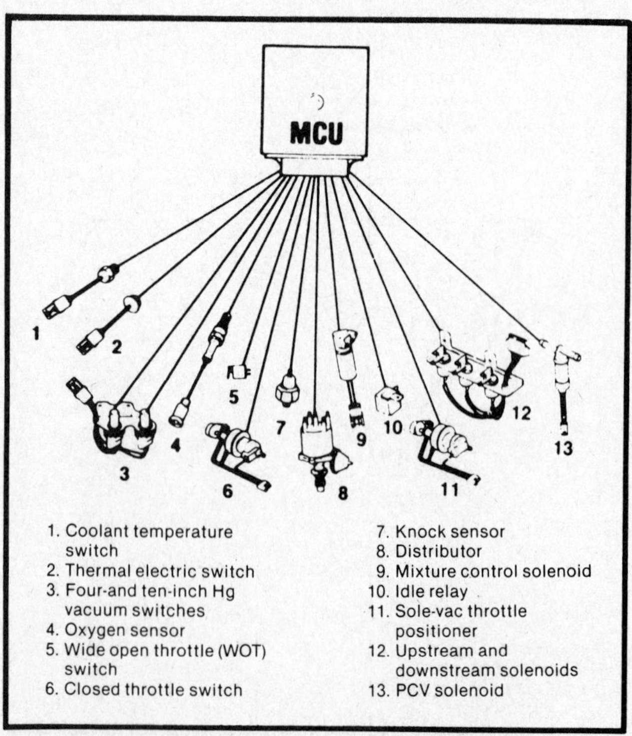

CEC components used on 6–285CID engine

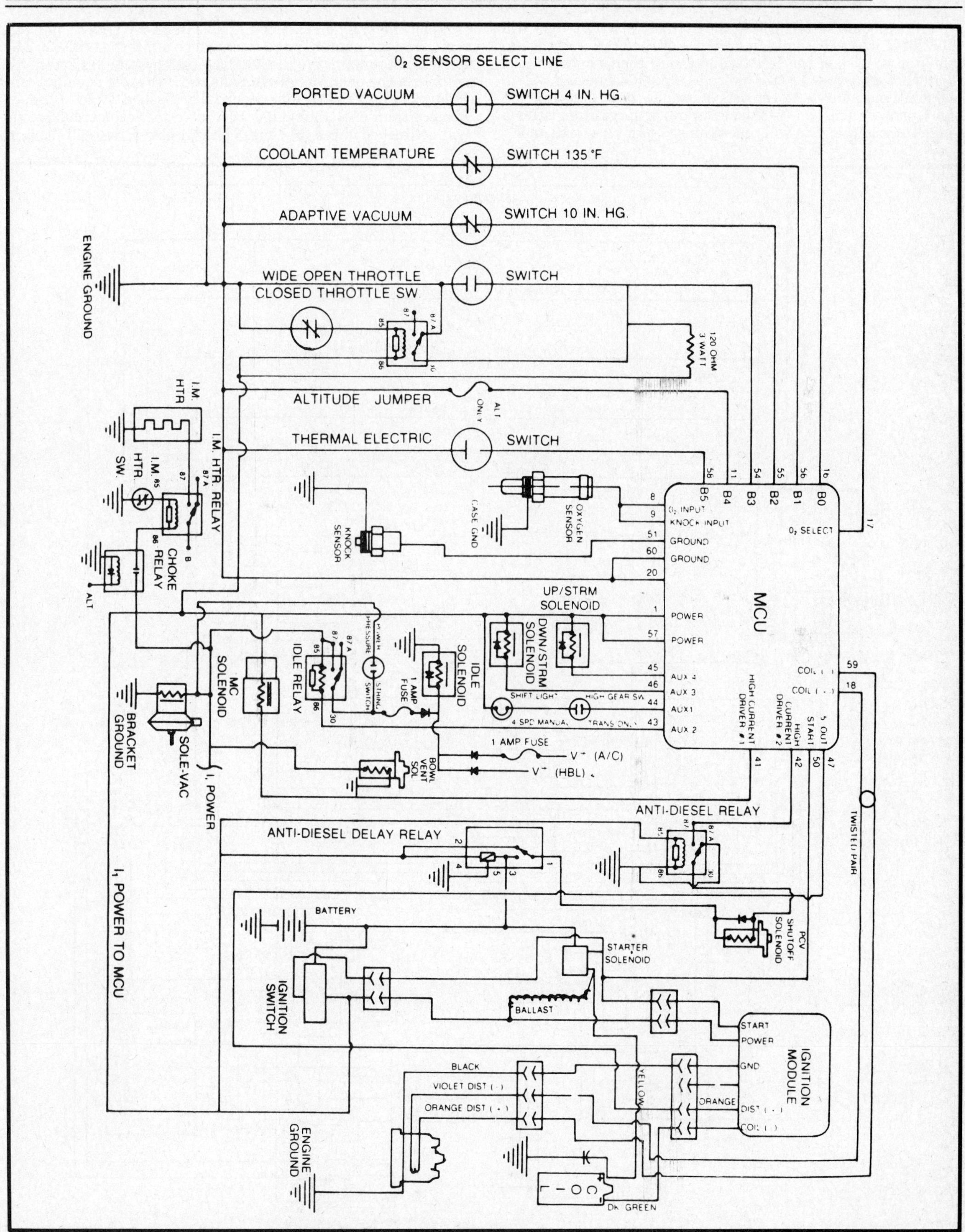

CEC system electrical schematic—4-150 CID engine

For a bulb and system check, the CHECK ENGINE light will illuminate when the ignition switch is turned ON and the engine not started. If the test terminals are then grounded, the light will flash a code 12 that indicates the self diagnostic system is operational. A code 12 consists of one (1) flash, followed by a short pause, then two (2) flashes in quick succession. After a longer pause, the code will repeat its self two (2) more times.

When the engine is started, the CHECK ENGINE light will remain on momentarily and then will go off. If the CHECK ENGINE light remains on, the self diagnostic system has detected a trouble in the operational components. If the test terminals are then grounded, the trouble code will be flashed three (3) times. If more than one trouble has been detected, each trouble code will be flashed three (3) times. The trouble codes will flash in

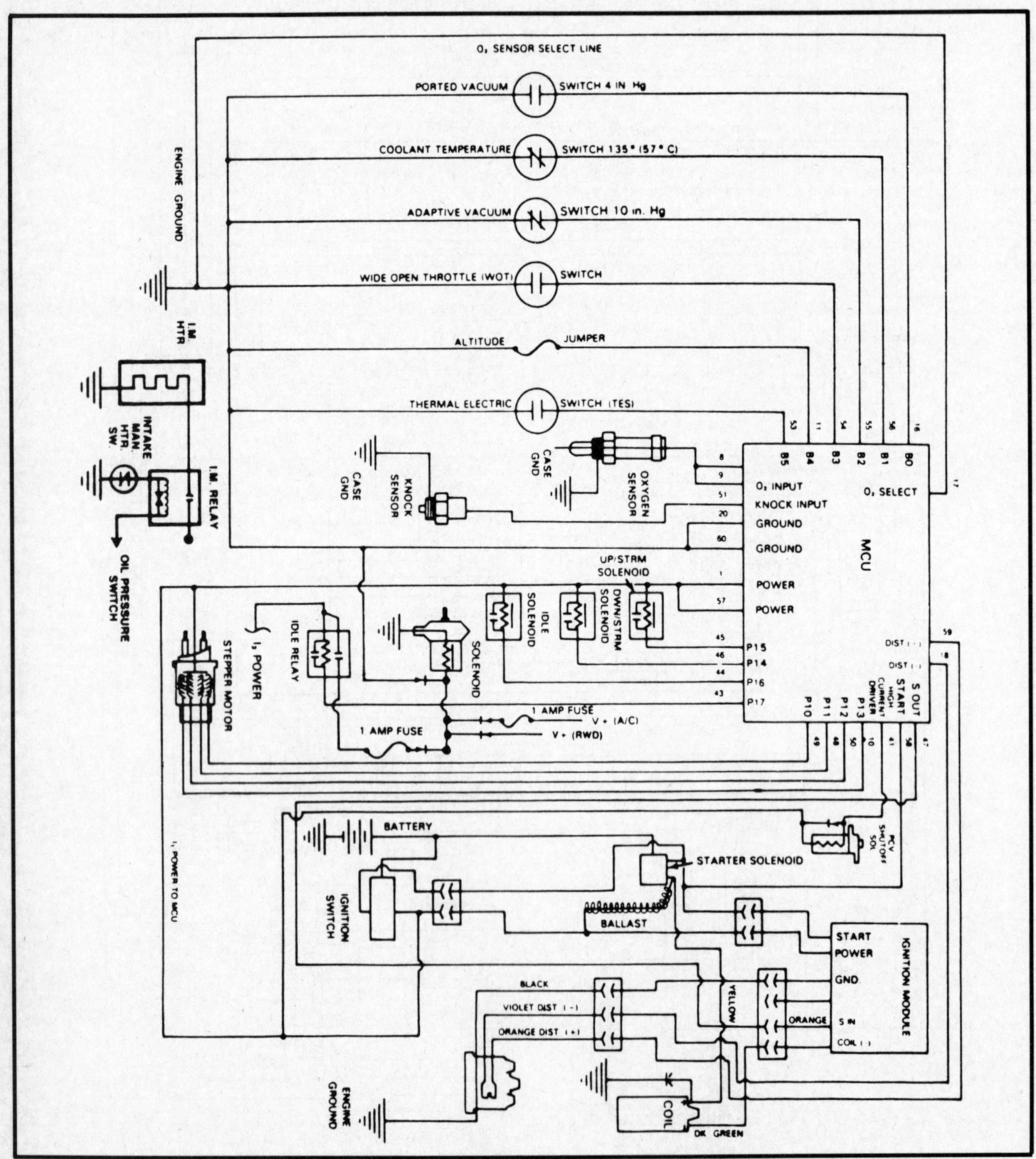

CEC system electrical schematic—4-258 CID engine

numeric order (lowest number code first). The trouble code series will repeat as long as the test terminals are grounded.

A trouble code indicates a trouble in a particular circuit or component. Trouble code 14, for example, indicates a trouble in the coolant sensor circuit, which includes the coolant sensor, connector, harness and the ECM.

The absence of a code does not mean a system is trouble free, because the self-diagnostic system does not detect all possible troubles. To determine if their is a system problem, a system performance test is necessary. This test is made when the CHECK ENGINE light and the self diagnostic system do not indicate a problem, but the system is suspected because no other reason can be found for the complaint.

When a problem develops in the feedback system, the CHECK ENGINE light will illuminate and a trouble code will be stored in the ECM memory. If the fault is intermittent, the CHECK ENGINE light will be turned off after ten (10) seconds when the problem ceases. However, the trouble code will be retained in the ECM memory until the battery voltage to the ECM is removed. To accomplish this, remove the negative battery cable for at least ten (10) seconds to erase all stored trouble codes.

The system should be considered as a possible source of trouble for engine performance, fuel economy and exhaust emission complaints, only after normal engine diagnosis has been completed. In many cases, the feedback system has been blamed for engine performance problems, when only simple, basic engine problems have been the cause. The system performance test verifies the system is functioning correctly and each step should be followed completely. Do not skip steps in order to short cut the tests.

TROUBLE CODE IDENTIFICATION

NOTE: The trouble code will be flashed on the CHECK ENGINE light only if a trouble exist that pertains to the following codes. Any codes stored in the ECM from a problem that has ceased to exist, will be erased from the ECM memory after fifty (50) engine starts.

1. Trouble Code 12 – No distributor reference pulses to the ECM. This code is not stored in memory and will only flash while the trouble exists. This is a normal code with the ignition ON and the engine not operating.
2. Trouble Code 13 – Refers to oxygen sensor circuit. The engine must operate up to five (5) minutes at part throttle , under road load, before this code will appear.
3. Trouble Code 14 – Coolant sensor circuit has short circuit. The engine must operate up to five (5) minutes before this code will appear.
4. Trouble Code 15 – Coolant sensor circuit has open circuit. The engine must operate up to five (5) minutes before this code will appear.
5. Trouble Code 21 – Throttle positioner sensor circuit problem. The engine must operate up to twenty five (25) seconds at specified curb idle speed before this code will appear.
6. Trouble Code 23 – The Mixture control solenoid has a short circuit to ground or an open circuit.
7. Trouble Code 34 – Vacuum sensor circuit problem. The engine must operate up to five (5) minutes at the specified curb idle speed before this code will appear.
8. Trouble Code 41 – No distributor reference pulses to the ECM at the specified engine manifold vacuum. This code will be stored in the ECM memory.
9. Trouble Code 42 – Electronic Spark Timing (EST) bypass circuit or EST circuit has short circuit to ground or an open circuit.
10. Trouble Code 44 – Lean exhaust indication. The engine must operate up to five (5) minutes, be in closed loop operation mode and at part throttle before this code will appear.
11. Trouble Code 44 and 45 at the same time – Indicates a faulty oxygen sensor.
12. Trouble Code 45 – Rich exhaust indication. The engine must operate up to five (5) minutes, be in closed loop and at part throttle before this code will appear.
13. Trouble Code 51 – Faulty calibration unit (PROM) or installed improperly. It requires up to thirty (30) seconds before this code will appear.
14. Trouble Code 54 – Mixture Control solenoid circuit has a short circuit and/or a faulty ECM.
15. Trouble Code 55 – Voltage reference has short circuit to ground (terminal 21), a faulty oxygen sensor or ECM.

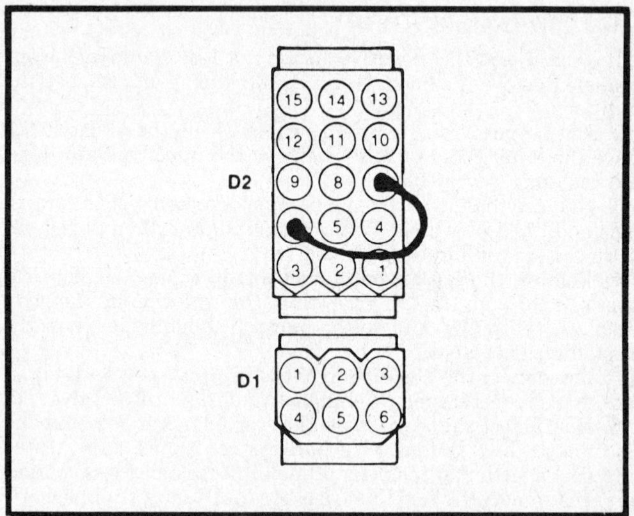

C-3 check engine malfunction light jumper wire installation

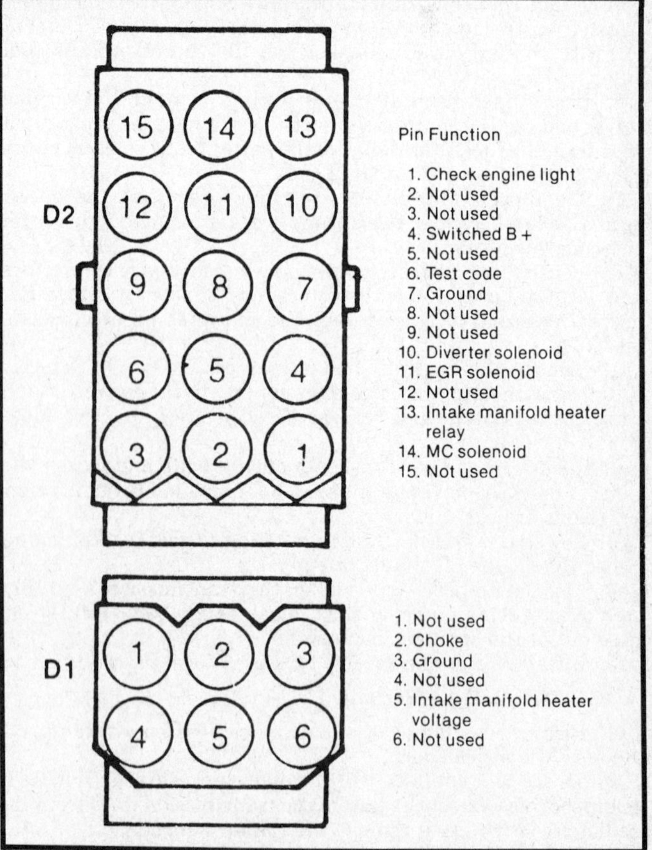

C-3 diagnostic connector

ENGINE MECHANICAL

Refer to the Unit Overhaul Section for Overhaul Procedures.

Engine

Removal and Installation

4–150 CID (2.5L) ENGINE

1. Disconnect the negative battery cable. Remove the air cleaner. Remove the hood. Drain the engine oil and remove the oil filter.
2. Discharge the air condition system. Drain the radiator. Remove the lower radiator hose. Remove the upper radiator hose and coolant recovery hose.
3. Remove the fan shroud. If equipped, disconnect the transmission fluid cooler lines. Remove the radiator. If equipped, remove the air condition condenser.
4. Remove the fan assembly and install a $\frac{5}{16}$ × ½ in. SAE capscrew through the fan pulley into the water pump flange to maintain the pulley and water pump in alignment when the crankshaft is rotated.
5. Disconnect the heater hoses. Disconnect the throttle linkages, cruise control cable, if equipped and the throttle valve rod.
6. Disconnect the wires from the starter motor solenoid and disconnect CEC system wire harness connector. If equipped with fuel injection, disconnect all fuel injection harness connectors. Disconnect the fuel line from the fuel pump, after properly relieving the fuel pump pressure.
7. If equipped with fuel injection, disconnect the quick connect fuel lines at the inner fender panel by squeezing the two retaining tabs against the fuel tube. Pull the fuel tube and the retainer from the quick connect fitting. Disconnect the TDC sensor wire connection. Disconnect the fuel line from the fuel pump.
8. If equipped with air conditioning, remove the service valves and cap the compressor ports. Disconnect the fuel return hose from the fuel filter. Remove the power brake vacuum check valve from the booster, if equipped.
9. If equipped with power steering, disconnect the hoses, drain the pump and cap the fittings in order to prevent dirt from entering the system.
10. Identify, tag and disconnect all necessary wire connectors and vacuum hoses. Raise the vehicle and support it safely. Remove the starter. Disconnect the exhaust pipe from the manifold.
11. Remove the flywheel housing access cover. On vehicles equipped with automatic transmission, mark the converter and drive plate location and remove the converter to drive plate bolts.
12. Remove the upper flywheel housing bolts and loosen the bottom bolts. Remove the engine mount cushion to engine compartment bracket bolts.
13. Lower the vehicle. Attach a lifting device to the engine. Raise the engine off the front supports.
14. Place a support stand under the transmission assembly. Remove the remaining transmission assembly bolts. Lift the engine out of the engine compartment.
15. Installation is the reverse of the removal procedure.

4–151 CID (2.5L) ENGINE

1. Disconnect the negative battery cable. Remove the hood. Remove the air cleaner.
2. Drain the coolant. Disconnect the radiator hoses. If equipped, disconnect the automatic transmission lines from the radiator. As required, remove the radiator shroud.
3. Remove the radiator. Remove the fan and spacer.
4. Remove and set aside the power steering pump and belt. Do not disconnect any of the hydraulic lines.
5. Properly discharge the air condition system. Remove the condenser and receiver assembly.
6. Noting their positions, disconnect all wires, lines, linkages, and hoses from the engine. Drain the oil and remove the oil filter.
7. Remove both engine front support cushion to frame retaining nuts. Disconnect the exhaust pipe at the support bracket and the manifold.
8. Support the engine with lifting equipment. Remove the front support cushion and bracket assemblies from the engine.
9. Remove the transfer case lever boot, the floor mat and the transmission access cover.
10. If equipped with automatic transmission, remove the upper bolts holding the bellhousing to the engine adapter plate. If equipped with manual transmission, remove the upper bolts holding the clutch housing to the engine.
11. Remove the starter.
12. On automatic transmission, remove the two adapter plate inspection covers. Mark the relationship of the converter to the flex plate and remove the converter to flex plate bolts. Remove the rest of the bolts holding the bellhousing to the adapter plate. On manual transmission, remove the clutch housing lower cover and the rest of the bolts holding the clutch housing to the engine.
13. Properly support the transmission. Remove the engine by pulling it forward and upward.
14. Installation is the reverse of the removal procedure.

V6–173 CID (2.8L) ENGINE

1. Disconnect the negative battery cable. Remove the air cleaner. Remove the hood.
2. Properly discharge the air condition system. Drain the radiator. Remove the lower radiator hose. Remove the upper radiator hose and coolant recovery hose.
3. Remove the fan shroud. If equipped, disconnect the transmission fluid cooler lines. Remove the radiator. If equipped, remove the air condition condenser.
4. Remove the fan assembly. Remove the heater hoses. Disconnect the throttle linkage, including the cruise control cable and automatic transmission throttle valve cable. Remove the power brake booster hose.
5. Identify, mark and disconnect the necessary wire connectors and vacuum hoses. Remove the power steering pump assembly and position it to the side.
6. Disconnect the fuel line at the fuel pump. Disconnect the hoses from the air condition compressor, if equipped.
7. Raise and support the vehicle safely. Remove the exhaust pipes from the exhaust manifold. Disconnect the exhaust pipe at the catalytic converter flange and allow the exhaust pipe to drop out of the way.
8. Remove the flywheel/converter housing access cover. Remove the torque converter bolts. Disconnect the wires at the starter.
9. Remove the flywheel/converter housing bolts. Lower the vehicle. Place a support under the transmission.
10. Remove the air pump and hose from the bracket. Attach an engine lifting device to the engine. Remove the engine mount through bolts. Disconnect the ground strap at the rear of the left cylinder head.
11. Remove the engine from the engine compartment.
12. Installation is the reverse of the removal procedure.

6–243 CID (4.0L) AND 6–258 CID (4.2L) ENGINES

1. Remove the hood. Disconnect the negative battery cable. Remove the air cleaner.
2. Drain the coolant. Disconnect the radiator hoses. Disconnect automatic transmission lines from the radiator, if

equipped. If there is a radiator shroud, remove it. Remove the radiator.

3. Remove the fan assembly and install a $^5/_{16}$ × ½ in. SAE capscrew through the fan pulley into the water pump flange to maintain the pulley and water pump in alignment when the crankshaft is rotated.

4. Remove and set aside the power steering pump and belt. Do not disconnect the hydraulic lines. If equipped, remove the power brake vacuum check valve from the booster.

5. Properly discharge the air condition system. Remove the condenser and receiver assembly. Disconnect all wires, lines, linkage, and hoses from the engine.

6. Disconnect and plug the fuel lines. If equipped with fuel injection, properly relieve the fuel pump pressure before disconnect the fuel lines.

7. Raise and support the vehicle safely. Drain the oil and remove the filter. Remove the starter. Remove the engine ground strap.

8. Remove both engine front support cushion to frame retaining nuts. Disconnect the exhaust pipe at the support bracket and the manifold. Support the engine with the lifting equipment.

9. Remove the front support cushion and bracket assemblies from the engine.

10. Remove the flywheel housing access cover. On vehicles equipped with automatic transmission, mark the converter and drive plate location and remove the converter to drive plate bolts.

11. Remove the upper flywheel housing bolts and loosen the bottom bolts. Remove the engine mount cushion to engine compartment bracket bolts.

12. Lower the vehicle. Attach a lifting device to the engine. Raise the engine off the front supports. Position a suitable stand under the transmission housing. Remove the remaining transmission housing bolts.

13. Lift the engine out of the engine compartment.

14. Installation is the reverse of the removal procedure.

126 (2.1) ENGINE

1. Disconnect the battery cables and remove the battery. Remove the hood. If equipped, remove the skid plate.

2. Drain the radiator. Remove the air cleaner assembly. If equipped, properly discharge the air condition system.

3. Disconnect the radiator hoses and remove the "E" clip from the bottom of the radiator.

4. Raise and support the vehicle safely. If the vehicle is equipped with automatic transmission disconnect the oil cooler lines at the radiator.

5. Remove the splash shield from the oil pan. Lower the vehicle. Loosen the radiator shroud and remove the radiator fan assembly. Remove the shroud and the splash shield.

6. Remove the radiator and the condenser assembly from the vehicle. Remove the inner cooler.

7. Remove the exhaust shield from the manifold. Drain the engine oil. Disconnect the hoses at the remote oil filter. Remove the oil filter.

8. Tag and disconnect all vacuum hoses and electrical connections. Properly relieve the fuel pump pressure. Disconnect and plug the fuel inlet and outlet lines at the fuel pump. If equipped with automatic transmission, remove the left motor mount through bolt retaining nut.

9. Remove the motor mount retaining bolts. Disconnect the accelerator cable. Raise and support the vehicle safely.

10. Disconnect the power steering hoses at the power steering pump. Disconnect the exhaust pipe at the exhaust manifold. Remove the motor mount retaining nuts.

11. Properly support the engine. Remove the left motor mount bolts, automatic transmission equipped vehicles, remove the left motor mount. Remove the starter.

12. If the vehicle is equipped with automatic transmission, mark and remove the converter to drive plate bolts through the starter opening. Install the left motor mount and retaining bolts finger tight. Install the motor mount cushion through bolt. Remove the engine support.

13. Remove the transmission to engine retaining bolts. Lower the vehicle. Remove the remaining engine to transmission retaining bolts.

14. Remove the power steering pump from the engine. Remove the oil separator and disconnect the hoses. Disconnect the heater hoses.

15. Remove the remaining engine to transmission retaining bolts. Remove the reference pressure regulator from the dash panel.

16. Install the engine lifting device. Properly position a suitable stand under the transmission.

17. Remove the engine from the vehicle.

18. Installation is the reverse of the removal procedure.

V8-360 CID (5.9L) ENGINE

1. Disconnect the negative battery cable. Remove the battery and the battery tray. Remove the hood. Remove the air cleaner assembly.

2. Drain the radiator. Remove the upper and lower radiator hoses. If equipped with automatic transmission, disconnect the cooler lines. Remove the radiator. Remove the fan assembly.

3. If equipped with power steering remove the pump and lay it aside. Do not disconnect the hoses from the pump. If equipped with air condition, properly discharge the system.

4. Remove the heater core housing and charcoal canister from the firewall as required. If equipped, remove cruise command vacuum servo bellows and mounting bracket as a complete assembly.

5. On some CJ models it may be necessary to remove the left front support cushion and bracket from cylinder block.

6. Disconnect all wires, lines linkage, and hoses which are connected to the engine.

7. If equipped with automatic transmission, disconnect the transmission filler tube bracket from the right cylinder head. Do not remove the filler tube from the transmission.

8. Remove both engine front support cushion to frame retaining nuts. Support the weight of the engine with a lifting device.

9. On some vehicles, it will be necessary to remove the transfer case shift lever boot, floor and transmission access cover.

10. Remove the upper bolts which secure the transmission bellhousing to the engine adapter plate on vehicles equipped with automatic transmission. If equipped with manual transmission, remove the upper bolts which secure the clutch housing to the engine.

11. Disconnect the exhaust pipes at the exhaust manifolds and support bracket. Remove the starter motor. Support the transmission with a floor jack.

12. If equipped with automatic transmission, remove the two engine adapter plate inspection covers. Mark the assembled position of the converter and flex plate and remove the converter to flex plate cap screws. Remove the remaining bolts which secure the transmission bellhousing to the engine adapter plate.

13. If equipped with manual transmission, remove the clutch housing lower cover and the remaining bolts which secure the clutch housing to the engine.

14. Remove the engine by pulling upward and forward. If equipped with power brakes, care must be taken to avoid damaging the power unit while removing the engine.

15. Installation is the reverse of the removal procedure.

Intake Manifold

Removal and Installation

4-150 CID (2.5L) ENGINE

1. Disconnect the negative battery cable. Drain the radiator. Remove the air cleaner.

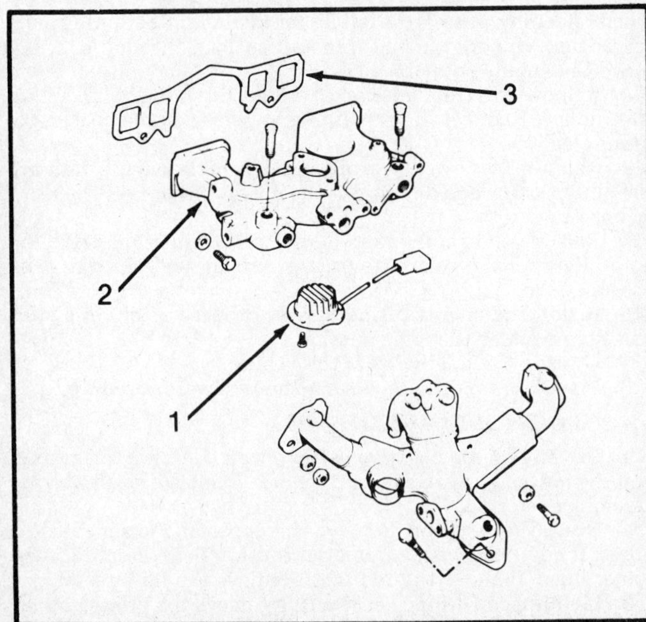

4-150 intake/exhaust manifold with electric fuel heater

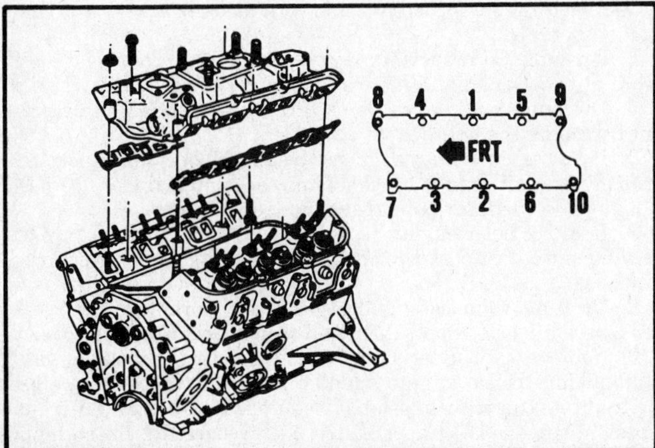

V6-173 intake manifold and torque sequence for attaching bolts

2. If equipped with fuel injection, relieve the fuel pump pressure. Disconnect the fuel pipe. Remove the carburetor or the throttle body, as required.

3. Disconnect the coolant hoses from the intake manifold. Disconnect the throttle cable from the bellcrank.

4. Disconnect the PCV valve vacuum hose from the intake manifold. If equipped, remove the vacuum advance CTO valve vacuum hoses.

5. Disconnect the system coolant temperature sender wire connector. Disconnect the air temperature sensor wire, if equipped. Disconnect the vacuum hose from the EGR valve.

6. On vehicles equipped with power steering remove the power steering pump and its mounting bracket. Do not detach the power steering pump hoses.

7. Disconnect the intake manifold electric heater wire connector, as required. Disconnect the throttle valve linkage, if equipped with automatic transmission. Disconnect the EGR valve tube from the intake manifold.

8. Remove the intake manifold retaining bolts. Remove the intake manifold from the vehicle.

9. Installation is the reverse of the removal procedure. Before installation, clean the mating surfaces of the manifold and cylinder head. Be sure to use a new gasket, as required. Be sure to properly torque the manifold retaining bolts.

4-151 CID (2.5L) ENGINE

1. Disconnect the negative battery cable. Remove air cleaner and PCV valve hose. Drain cooling system. Tag and remove vacuum hoses.

2. Disconnect fuel pipe and electrical wire connections from the carburetor. Disconnect carburetor throttle linkage. Remove carburetor.

3. Remove bellcrank and throttle linkage brackets and move to one side for clearance.

4. Remove the heater hose at the intake manifold. Remove the alternator. Note the position of the spacers for installation.

5. Remove the intake manifold retaining bolts. Remove the intake manifold from the vehicle.

6. Installation is the reverse of the removal procedure. Before installation, clean the mating surfaces of the manifold and cylinder head. Be sure to use a new gasket, as required. Be sure to properly torque the manifold retaining bolts.

V6-173 CID (2.8L) ENGINE

1. Disconnect the negative battery cable. Drain the radiator.

2. If equipped with air condition disconnect the compressor and move it to on side. Disconnect the spark plugs wires at the spark plugs. Disconnect the wires at the ignition coil. If equipped, remove the air pump and bracket.

3. Remove the distributor cap. Mark the position of the ignition rotor in relation to the distributor body. Remove the distributor.

4. Remove the EGR valve. Remove the air hose. Disconnect the charcoal canister hoses. Remove the pipe bracket from the left cylinder head, if equipped.

5. Remove the diverter valve. Remove the power brake vacuum hose. Remove the heater and radiator hoses from the intake manifold.

6. Disconnect and label the vacuum hoses. If equipped, remove the EFE pipe from the rear of the manifold. Disconnect the coolant temperature switches.

7. Remove the carburetor linkage. Disconnect and plug the fuel line.

8. Remove the manifold retaining bolts. Remove the intake manifold from the vehicle.

9. Installation is the reverse of the removal procedure. Before installation, clean the mating surfaces of the manifold and cylinder head. Be sure to use a new gasket. Be sure to properly torque the manifold retaining bolts.

NOTE: The gaskets are marked for right and left side installation. Do not interchange them. Clean the sealing surface of the engine block, and apply a $^{3}/_{16}$ in. bead of silicone sealer to each ridge. Install the new gaskets onto the heads. The gaskets will have to be cut slightly to fit past the center pushrods. Do not cut any more material than necessary. Hold the gaskets in place by extending the ridge bead of sealer ¼ in. onto the gasket ends.

V8-360 CID (5.9L) ENGINE

1. Disconnect the negative battery cable. Drain the coolant from the radiator.

2. Remove the air cleaner assembly. Disconnect the spark plug wires.

3. Disconnect the upper radiator hose and the bypass hose from the intake manifold. Disconnect the heater hose from the rear of the manifold.

4. Disconnect the ignition coil bracket and lay the coil aside. If equipped, disconnect the TCS solenoid vacuum valve from the right side valve cover.

5. Disconnect all lines, hoses, linkages and wires from the carburetor and intake manifold and TCS components as required. Remove the carburetor.

6. Disconnect the air delivery hoses at the air distribution manifolds. Disconnect the air pump diverter valve and lay the valve and the bracket assembly, including the hoses, forward of the engine.

7. Remove the intake manifold retaining bolts. Remove the intake manifold from the vehicle.

8. Installation is the reverse of the removal procedure. Before installation, clean the mating surfaces of the manifold and cylinder head. Be sure to use a new gasket, as required. Be sure to properly torque the manifold retaining bolts.

Exhaust Manifold

Removal and Installation

4-150 CID (2.5L) ENGINE

1. Disconnect the negative battery cable. Remove the intake manifold.

2. Disconnect the EGR valve tube. Disconnect the exhaust pipe from the exhaust manifold. Disconnect the oxygen sensor wire connector.

3. Remove the exhaust manifold retaining bolts. Remove the exhaust manifold from the vehicle.

4. Installation is the reverse of the removal procedure. Be sure to use a new gasket, as required. Torque the bolts to specification.

4-151 CID (2.5L) ENGINE

1. Disconnect the negative battery cable. Remove air cleaner and heated air tube. Remove engine oil dipstick tube attaching bolt. Remove oxygen sensor, if equipped.

2. Raise the vehicle and support it safely. Disconnect the exhaust pipe from the exhaust manifold. Lower the vehicle.

3. Remove the exhaust manifold retaining bolts. Remove manifold and gasket from the vehicle.

4. Installation is the reverse of the removal procedure. Be sure to use a new gasket, as required. Torque the bolts to specification.

V6-173 CID (2.8L) ENGINE

1. Disconnect the negative battery cable. Remove the air cleaner. Remove the carburetor heat stove pipe. Remove the air supply plumbing from the exhaust manifold.

2. Raise and support the vehicle safely. Unbolt and remove the exhaust pipe at the manifold. Lowewr the vehicle.

3. As required, remove the spark plug wires from the plugs. Remove the cruise control servo from the right inner fender panel, if equipped.

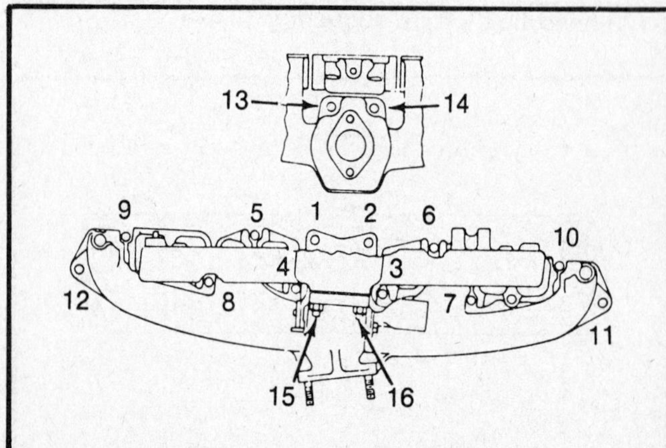

Intake/exhaust manifold torque sequence – 6 cyl.

4. If removing the right manifold, remove the air supply pipes from the manifold. Remove the pulsair bracket bolt from the rocker cover, if equipped, then remove the pipe assembly.

5. Remove the manifold retaining bolts. Remove the manifold from the vehicle.

6. Installation is the reverse of the removal procedure. Be sure to use a new gasket, as required. Torque the bolts to specification.

V8-360 CID (5.9L) ENGINE

1. Disconnect the negative battery cable. Disconnect the spark plug wires. Disconnect the air delivery hose at the distribution manifold.

2. Remove the air distribution manifold and the injection tubes. Disconnect the exhaust pipe at the manifold.

3. Remove the exhaust manifold retaining bolts along with the spark plug shields. Remove the exhaust manifold from the vehicle.

4. Installation is the reverse of the removal procedure. Be sure to use a new gasket, as required. Torque the bolts to specification.

Combination Manifold

Removal and Installation

6-243 CID (4.0L) AND 6-258 CID (4.2L) ENGINES

1. Disconnect the negative battery cable. Remove the air cleaner. Remove the carburetor. If equiupped with fuel injection, properly relieve the fuel pressure. Remove the throttle body assembly.

2. Disconnect the accelerator cable from the accelerator bellcrank. Disconnect the PCV vacuum hose from the intake manifold. Remove the vacuum advance CTO valve vacuum hoses as required.

3. Disconnect the distributor vacuum hose and electrical wires at the TCS solenoid vacuum valves. If equipped, disconnect the CEC system coolant temperature sender wire connector on the intake manifold.

4. Remove the TCS solenoid vacuum valve and bracket from the intake manifold. In some cases it might not be necessary to remove the TCS unit.

5. Disconnect the EGR valve and back pressure sensor hoses. If equipped, disconnect the electric heater wire connector.

6. Remove the power steering mounting bracket and pump and set it aside without disconnecting the hoses. Remove air pump, if equipped.

7. Remove the EGR valve and backpressure sensor. If equipped, remove air conditioning drive belt idler assembly from cylinder head.

8. Disconnect the exhaust pipe from the manifold flange. If equipped with automatic transmission disconnect the throttle valve linkage.

9. Remove the manifold retaining bolts. Separate the intake manifold and exhaust manifold from the engine as an assembly.

10. If either manifold is to be replaced, they should be separated at the heat riser area.

11. Installation is the reverse of the removal procedure. Be sure to use a new gasket, as required. Torque the bolts to specification.

Cylinder Head

Removal and Installation

4-150 CID (2.5L) ENGINE

1. Disconnect the negative battery cable. Drain the coolant. Disconnect the hoses at the thermostat housing. Remove the air cleaner.

2. Remove the valve cover. Remove the rocker arms, bridge and pivot assemblies. Remove the push rods. Retain the push

rods, bridge, pivot and rocker arms in the same order as removed to facilitate installation in the original positions.

3. Disconnect the power steering pump bracket. Set the pump and bracket aside. Do not disconnect the hoses.

4. Remove the intake and exhaust manifolds from the cylinder head.

5. If equipped with air conditioning, remove the air conditioner compressor drive belt. Loosen the alternator drive belt. Remove the air condition compressor/alternator bracket to cylinder head mounting screw.

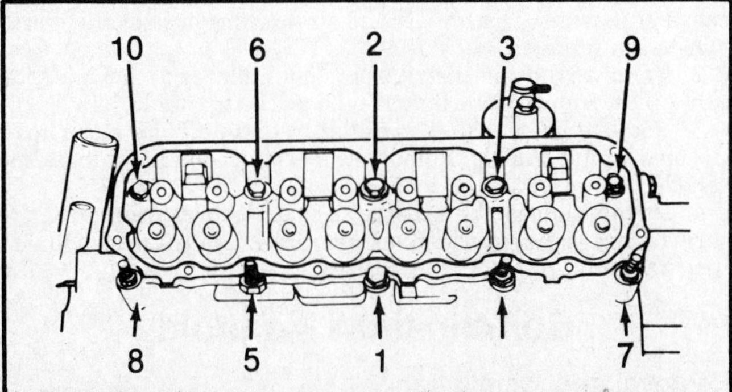

4-150 cylinder head torque sequence

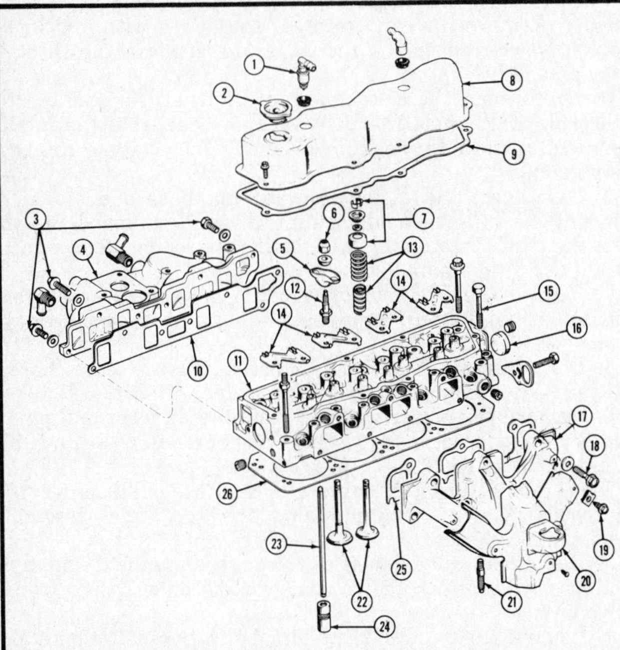

Exploded view of the cylinder head assembly—151 four cylinder

NOTE: The serpentine drive belt tension is released by loosening the alternator.

6. Remove the bolts from the air condition compressor, if equipped and alternator mounting bracket. Position the compressor to the side.

7. Disconnect the ignition wires and remove the spark plugs. Disconnect the temperature sending unit wire connector.

8. Remove the cylinder head bolts. Remove the cylinder head and gasket from the vehicle.

9. Thoroughly clean the machined surfaces of the cylinder head and block. Remove all gasket material and cement.

10. Installation is the reverse of the removal procedure. Apply an even coat of sealing compound, or equivalent, to both sides of the replacement cylinder head gasket and position the gasket on the cylinder block with the word TOP facing upward.

11. Coat the threads of the stud bolt in the number eight sequence position with Permatex sealant or equivalent. Torque to 75 ft. lbs.

NOTE: Do not apply sealing compound to the cylinder head and block machined surfaces. Do not allow the sealing compound to enter the cylinder bores.

12. Torque the head bolts to 85 ft. lbs. in the proper sequence.

4-151 CID (2.5L) ENGINE

1. Disconnect the negative battery cable. Drain the cooling system. Disconnect the hoses at the thermostat housing.

2. Remove the valve cover. Remove the rocker arm assembly and pushrods. The pushrods and rockers must be replaced in their original positions.

3. Remove the intake and exhaust manifolds from the cylinder head.

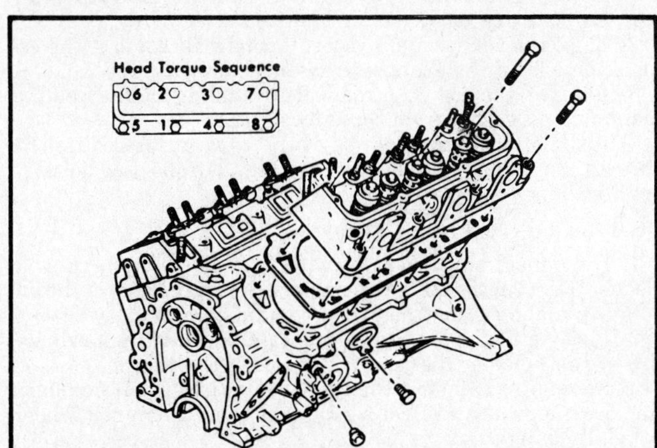

6-173 head bolt torque sequence

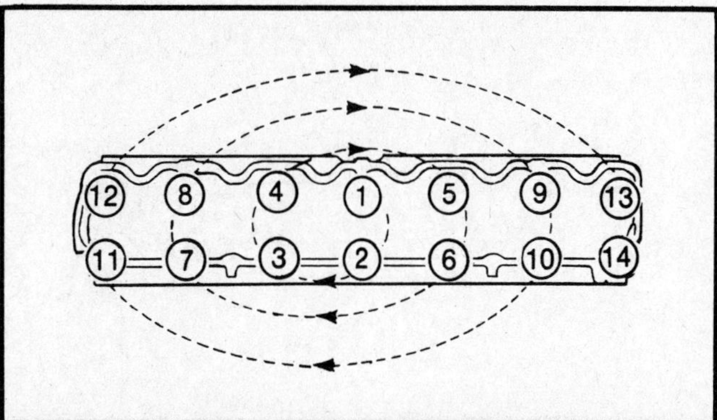

Cylinder head bolt tightening sequence—6 cyl.

4. Disconnect the spark plug wires and remove the spark plugs to avoid damaging them.
5. Remove air conditioning drive belt idler bracket from cylinder head. Loosen alternator belt and remove bracket to head mounting screw. Remove compressor mounting bracket and set the unit aside.
6. Disconnect the temperature sending unit wire, ignition coil and bracket assembly and battery ground cable from the engine.
7. Remove the cylinder head bolts. Remove the cylinder head and gasket from the vehicle..
8. Installation is the reverse of the removal procedure. Tighten the cylinder head bolts to the specified torque, in the proper sequence.

V6–173 CID (2.8L) ENGINE

1. Disconnect the negative battery cable. Raise and support the vehicle safely. Disconnect the exhaust pipe from the exhaust manifold. Lower the vehicle.
2. Drain the coolant. Remove the intake manifold. Remove the exhaust manifold.
3. If equipped, remove the powewr steering pump and bracket. On the left head remove the dipstick tube.
4. On the right head remove the cruise control servo bracket, if equipped. Remove the alternator and air pump bracket assembly, as required.
5. Loosen the rocker arm bolts and remove the pushrods. Keep the pushrods in the same order as removed.
6. Remove the cylinder head bolts in stages and in the reverse order of the tightening sequence. Remove the cylinder head from the vehicle.
7. Installation is the reverse of the removal procedure. The words "This side Up" on the new cylinder head gasket should face upward. Coat the cylinder head bolts with sealer and torque to specifications.

6–243 CID (4.0L) AND 6–258 CID (4.2L) ENGINES

1. Disconnect the negative battery cable. Drain the cooling system. Disconnect the hoses at the thermostat housing. Remove the air cleaner.
2. Remove the valve cover, rocker arm assembly, and pushrods. The pushrods and rockers must be replaced in their original positions.
3. Disconnect the power steering pump and bracket from the cylinder head. Lay the assembly aside and do not disconnect the power steering pump hoses.
4. Disconnect the spark plug wires and remove the spark plugs to avoid damaging them.
5. Remove the intake and exhaust manifold from the cylinder head.
6. Remove the air conditioning drive belt idler bracket from cylinder head. Loosen alternator belt and remove bracket to head mounting screw. Remove compressor mounting bracket and set the unit aside.

NOTE: On vehicles so equipped, the serpentine drive belt tension is released by loosening the alternator.

7. Disconnect the temperature sending unit wire, ignition coil and bracket assembly and battery ground cable from the engine.
8. Remove the cylinder head bolts. Remove the cylinder head and gasket from the block.
9. Installation is the reverse of the removal procedure. Tighten the cylinder head bolts to specification and in the proper sequence.

V8–360 CID (5.9L) ENGINE

1. Disconnect the negative battery cable. Drain the cooling system.
2. When removing the right cylinder head, it may be necessary to remove the heater core housing from the firewall.

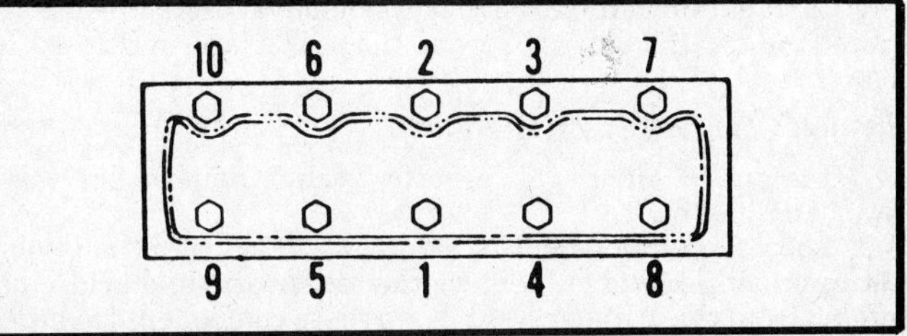

Cylinder head torque sequence—151 four cylinder engine

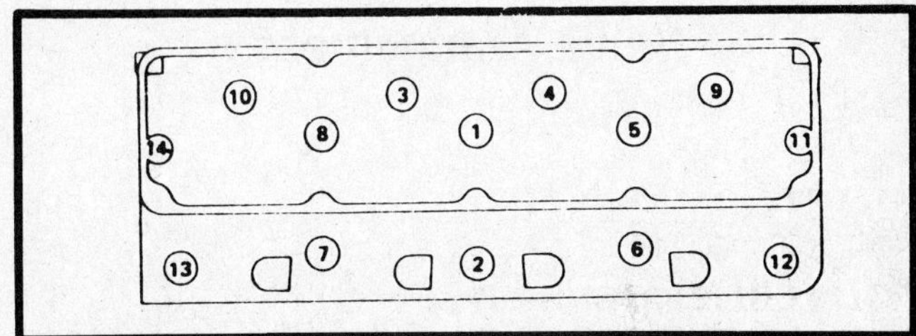

Cylinder head torque sequence—V8 engine

3. Remove the valve cover. Remove the rocker arm assemblies and push rods. The valve train components must be replaced in their original positions. Remove the spark plugs to avoid damaging them.
4. Remove the intake manifold. Remove the exhaust manifolds. Loosen all of the drive belts.
5. Disconnect negative battery cable at cylinder head. Remove air conditioning compressor mount bracket and alternator support brace from cylinder head.
6. Disconnect the air pump and power steering pump brackets from the cylinder head.
7. Remove the cylinder head bolts. Remove the cylinder head from the vehicle.
8. Installation is the reverse of the removal procedure. Apply an even coat of sealing compound to both sides of the new head gasket only. Wire brush the cylinder head bolts, then lightly oil them prior to installation. First, tighten all bolts to 80 ft. lbs., then tighten them to the specified torque and in the correct tightening sequence.

Rocker Arm and Shaft

Removal and Installation

4–150 CID (2.5L), 6–243 CID (4.0L) AND 6–258 CID (4.2L) ENGINES

1. Disconnect the negative battery cable. Remove the valve cover.
2. Remove the two capscrews at each bridge and pivot assembly.
3. Remove the bridges, pivots and rocker arms. Keep them in order as they must be installed in the same position as they were removed.
4. Installation is the reverse of the removal procedure. Torque the capscrews to 19 ft. lbs. Be sure to use new gaskets or RTV sealant as required.

4–151 CID (2.5L) AND V6–173 CID (2.8L) ENGINES

1. Disconnect the negative battery cable. Remove the valve cover and gasket. Remove the rocker arm nut and ball.
2. Lift the rocker arm off the rocker arm stud, always keep the rocker arm, nut and ball together and always assemble them on the same stud.
3. Remove the pushrod from its bore. Make sure the pushrods are always installed in the same bore with the same end in the block.

4. Installation is the reverse of the removal procedure. As required, adjust the valves. Torque the rocker arm nut to 20 ft. lbs.

V8–360 CID (5.9L) ENGINE

1. Disconnect the negative battery cable. Remove the valve cover and gasket.
2. Loosen the bridged pivot capscrews a turn at a time, so as not to break the bridge. Remove the rocker arm and bridge assembly from the cylinder head. Keep these components in order and reinstall them in the same position as removed.
3. Installation is the reverse of the removal procedure. Torque the capscrews to 19 ft. lbs.

Valve Arangement

4–150 CID (2.5L) ENGINE

E–I–I–E–E–I–I–E

4–151 CID (2.5L) ENGINE

I–E–I–E–E–I–E–I

V6–173 CID (2.8L) ENGINE

RIGHT E–I–I–E–I–E
LEFT E–I–I–E–I–E

6–243 CID (4.0L) AND 6–258 CID (4.2L) ENGINES

E–I–I–E–I–E–E–I–E–I–I–E

V8–360 CID (5.9L) ENGINE

RIGHT E–I–I–E–E–I–I–E
LEFT E–I–I–E–E–I–I–E

Valve Adjustment Procedure

V6–173 CID (2.8L) ENGINE

Tighten the rocker arm nut until it just touches the valve stem. Rotate the engine until number one piston is at TDC of the compression stroke. The "0" on the timing scale should be aligned with the timing pointer and the rotor should be at the number one spark plug tower of the distributor cap. The following valves can now be adjusted. Exhaust valves – 1–2–3, Intake valves – 1–5–6. Turn the adjusting nut until it backs off the stem slightly, then tighten until it just touches the stem. Then turn the nut one and one-half turns more to center the tappet plunger. Rotate the engine one complete revolution more. This will bring number four piston to TDC on the compression stroke. At this point the following valves should be adjusted. Exhaust valves – 4–5–6, Intake valves – 2–3–4.

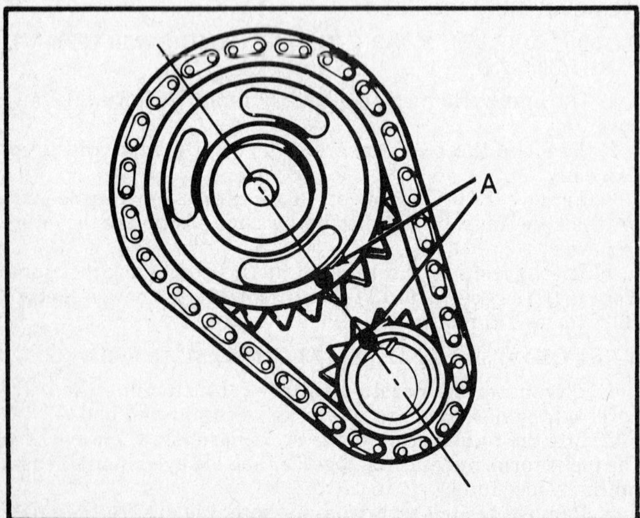

4-150 timing mark alignment

Timing Gears and Chain

CRANKSHAFT PULLEY

Removal and Installation

1. Disconnect the negative battery cable. Remove the fan shroud, as required. Remove drive belts from pulley.
2. Remove the retaining bolts and separate the pulley from the vibration damper.
3. Remove the vibration damper retaining bolt from the crankshaft end, if used.
4. Using a vibration damper puller, remove the damper from the crankshaft.
5. Installation is the reverse of the removal procedure. Upon installation, align the key slot of the pulley hub to the crankshaft key. Torque the retaining bolts to specifications.

TIMING COVER OIL SEAL

Removal and Installation

4–150 CID (2.5L) ENGINE

1. Disconnect the negative battery cable. Remove the radiator fan shroud, if equipped.
2. Remove the vibration pulley and damper assembly. Remove the fan and hub assembly.
3. If equipped, remove the air condition compressor. Remove the alternator bracket assembly from the cylinder head and position it aside.
4. Remove the oil pan to timing case cover retaining bolts, and the cover to cylinder block bolts.
5. Remove the timing case cover, front seal and gasket from the engine block.
6. Upon installation, cut off the oil pan side gasket end tabs and the oil pan front seal tabs flush with the front face of the cylinder block and remove the gasket tabs.
7. Using new gaskets as required complete the installation in the reverse order of the removal procedure.

4–151 CID (2.5L) ENGINE

1. Disconnect the negative battery cable. Remove the fan and spacer. Loosen the two lower cover retaining screws.
2. Remove the top cover retaining screw and nut and remove the cover, lifting it until the slots clear the lower screws.
3. To install, position the cover, lowering it until the slots are over the lower screws. Tighten the lower screws finger tight.
4. Install the upper screw and nut, then tighten all four screws to 50 inch lbs. Install the spacer and fan, tightening the bolts to 20 ft. lbs.

V6–173 CID (2.8L) ENGINE

1. Disconnect the negative battery cable. Remove the drive belts.
2. Remove the radiator fan shroud. Remove the fan and pulley assembly.
3. If the vehicle is equipped with air condition, remove the compressor from the mounting bracket. Remove the mounting bracket.
4. Drain the cooling system. Remove the water pump. Remove the vibration damper.

NOTE: On some vehicles the outer ring (weight) of the harmonic balancer is bonded to the hub with rubber. The balancer must be removed with a puller which acts on the inner hub only. Pulling on the outer portion of the balancer will break the rubber bond or destroy the tuning of the torsional damper.

5. Disconnect the lower radiator hose and heater hose.
6. Remove timing gear cover retaining screws. Remove the cover and gasket.
7. Clean all the gasket mounting surfaces on the front cover and block. Apply a continuous $^3/_{32}$ in. bead of sealer to front cover sealing surface and around coolant passage ports and central bolt holes.
8. Apply a bead of silicone sealer to the oil pan to cylinder block joint. Install a centering tool in the crankcase snout hole in the front cover and install the cover.
9. Install the front cover bolts finger tight, remove the centering tool and tighten the cover bolts. Install the harmonic balancer, pulley, water pump, belts, and all other parts.

NOTE: Breakage may occur if the balancer is hammered back onto the crankshaft. A press or special installation tool is necessary.

6-243 CID (4.0L) AND 258 CID (4.3) ENGINES

1. Disconnect the negative battery cable. Remove the drive belts, engine fan and hub assembly, the accessory pulley and vibration damper. Remove the air condition compressor and alternator bracket assembly.
2. Remove the oil pan to timing chain cover screws and the screws that attach the cover to the block.
3. Raise the timing chain cover just high enough to detach the retaining nibs of the oil pan neoprene seal from the bottom side of the cover. This must be done to prevent pulling the seal end tabs away from the tongues of the oil pan gaskets which would cause a leak.
4. Remove the timing chain cover and gasket from the engine.
5. Using the proper tool cut off the oil pan seal end tabs flush with the front face of the cylinder block and remove the seal. Clean the timing chain cover, oil pan, and cylinder block surfaces.
6. Remove the crankshaft oil seal from the timing chain cover.
7. Installation is the reverse of the removal procedure. It will be necessary to cut the same amount from the end tabs of a new oil pan seal as was cut from the original seal, before installing the new gasket. Be sure to use gasket sealer on both sides of the timing cover gasket.

V8-360 CID (5.9L) ENGINE

1. Disconnect the negative battery cable. Drain the cooling system. Disconnect the radiator hoses and the bypass hose.
2. Remove all of the drive belts and the fan and spacer assembly. Remove air conditioning compressor and bracket assembly from the engine, if equipped. Do not disconnect air conditioning hoses.
3. Remove the alternator and the front portion of the alternator bracket as an assembly. Disconnect the heater hose.
4. Remove the power steering pump and air pump, along with the mounting bracket as an assembly. Do not disconnect the power steering hoses.
5. Remove the distributor cap and note the position of the rotor. Remove the distributor. Remove the fuel pump. Remove the vibration damper and pulley.
6. Remove the two front oil pan bolts and the bolts which secure the timing chain cover to the engine block. The timing gear cover retaining bolts vary in length and must be installed in the same locations from which they were removed.
7. Remove the cover by pulling forward until it is free of the locating dowel pins. Remove the oil slinger. Clean the gasket surface of the cover and the engine block.
8. Pry out the original seal from inside the timing chain cover and clean the seal bore. Drive the new seal into place from the inside with a block of wood until it contacts the outer flange of the cover. Apply a light film of motor oil to the lips of the new seal.

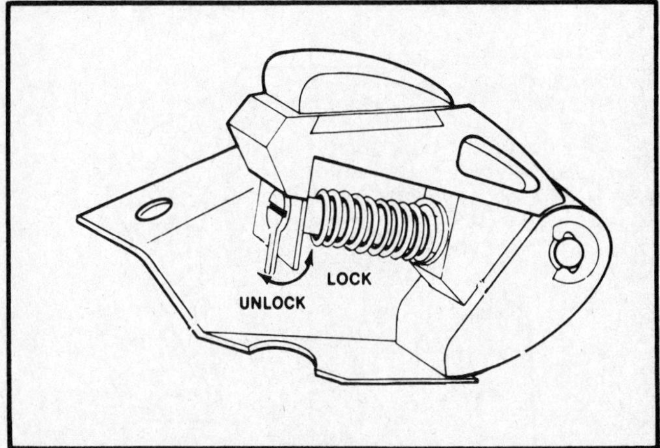

4-150 timing chain tensioner

9. Before reinstalling the timing gear cover, remove the lower locating dowel pin from the engine block. The pin is required for correct alignment of the cover and must either be reused or a replacement dowel pin installed after the cover is in position.
10. Cut both sides of the oil pan gasket flush with the engine block with a razor blade. Trim a new gasket to correspond to the amount cut off at the oil pan.
11. Apply sealer to both sides of the new gasket and install the gasket on the timing case cover. Install the new front oil pan seal.
12. Align the tongues of the new oil pan gasket pieces with the oil pan seal and cement them into place on the cover. Apply a bead of sealer to the cutoff edges of the original oil pan gaskets.
13. Place the timing case cover into position and install the front oil pan bolts. Tighten the bolts slowly and evenly until the cover aligns with the upper locating dowel.
14. Install the lower dowel through the cover and drive it into the corresponding hole in the engine block. Install the cover retaining bolts in the same locations from which they were removed, tightened to 25 ft. lbs.
15. Assemble the remaining components in the reverse order of the removal procedure.

TIMING CHAIN AND GEAR

Removal and Installation

4-150 CID (2.5L) ENGINE

1. Disconnect the negative battery cable. Remove the timing case cover.
2. Rotate the crankshaft until the zero timing mark on the crankshaft sprocket is closest to and on center line with the mark on the cam sprocket.
3. Remove the oil slinger from the crankshaft. Remove the camshaft retaining bolt and remove the sprockets and chain as an assembly.
4. Installation is the reverse of the removal procedure. Be sure to turn the tensioner lever to the unlock (down) position and pull the tensioner block toward the tensioner lever to compress the spring. Then, hold the block and turn the tensioner lever to the lock (up) position.

4-151 CID (2.5L) ENGINE

1. Disconnect the negative battery cable. Remove the camshaft from the vehicle.
2. The camshaft gear is pressed onto the camshaft. Using a press remove the old gear.
3. With the old gear pressed off, position the gear spacer ring and the thrust plate over the end of the camshaft. Install the woodruff key and position the new cam gear on the camshaft. Press the assembly in place.

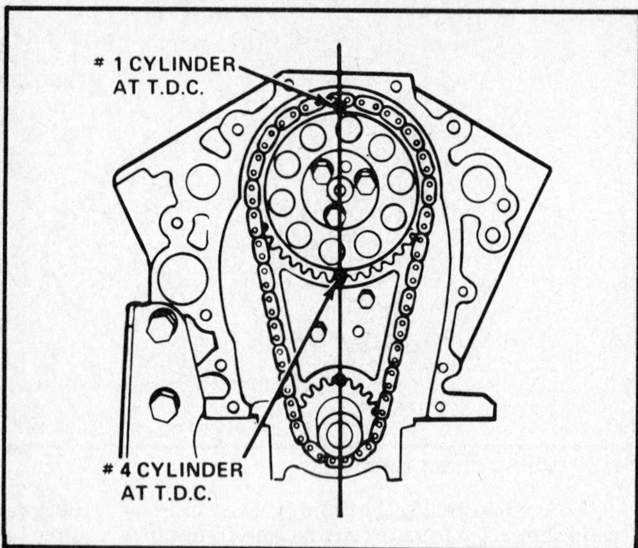

6-173 timing mark alignment

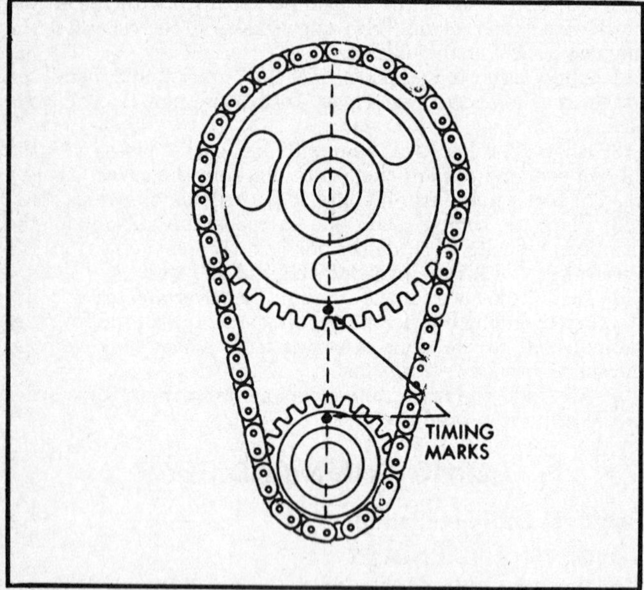

Alignment of timing chain sprockets—V8

4. The end clearance of the thrust plate must be 0.0015–0.0050 in. If not within specification, replace the spacer ring. If the specification is greater than 0.0050 in. replace the thrust plate.

5. Install the camshaft.

V6–173 CID (2.8L) ENGINE

1. Disconnect the negative battery cable. Remove the timing cover. Position the engine until the marks punched on both sprockets are closest to one another and in line between the shaft centers.

2. Remove the three bolts that hold the camshaft sprocket to the camshaft. This sprocket is a light press fit on the camshaft and is located by a dowel. The chain comes off with the camshaft sprocket. A gear puller may be required to remove the camshaft sprocket.

3. Without disturbing the position of the engine, mount the new crank sprocket on the shaft, then mount the chain over the camshaft sprocket. Arrange the camshaft sprocket in such a way that the timing marks will line up between the shaft centers and the camshaft locating dowel will enter the dowel hole in the cam sprocket.

4. Place the cam sprocket, with its chain mounted over it, in position on the front of the camshaft and pull up with the three bolts that hold it to the camshaft.

5. After the sprockets are in place, turn the engine two full revolutions to make certain that the timing marks are in correct alignment between the shaft centers.

6. Continue the installation in the reverse order of the removal procedure.

6–243 CID (4.0L) AND 6–258 CID (4.2L) ENGINES

1. Disconnect the negative battery cable. Remove the drive belts. Remove the engine fan and hub assembly and the accessory pulley. Remove the vibration damper.

2. Remove the timing chain cover. Remove the oil seal from the timing chain cover. Remove the camshaft sprocket retaining bolt and washer.

3. Rotate the crankshaft until the timing mark on the crankshaft sprocket is closest to and in a center line with the timing pointer of the camshaft sprocket.

4. Remove the crankshaft sprocket, camshaft sprocket and timing chain as an assembly. Disassemble the chain and sprockets.

5. Assemble the timing chain, crankshaft sprocket and camshaft sprocket with the timing marks aligned. Install the assembly to the crankshaft and the camshaft.

6. Install the camshaft sprocket retaining bolt and washer and tighten to 45–55 ft. lbs. Install the timing chain cover and a new oil seal.

7. Install the vibration damper, torque the retaining bolt to 80 ft. lbs. Continue the installation in the reverse order of the removal procedure.

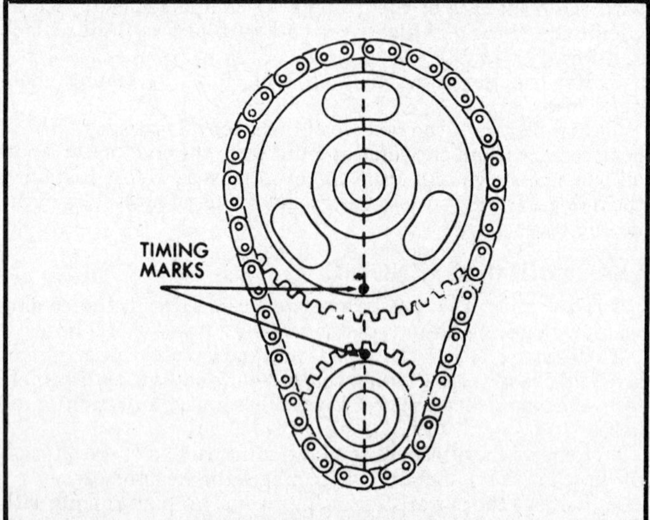

Alignment of timing chain sprockets—6 cyl.

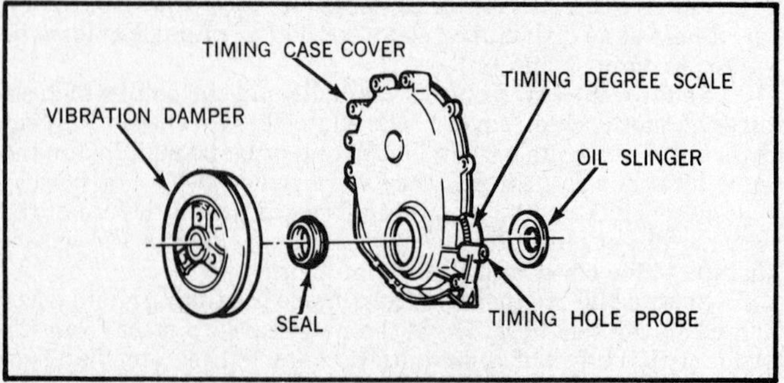

Timing case cover—6 cyl. engine

V8-360 CID (5.9L) ENGINE

1. Disconnect the negative battery cable. Remove the timing chain cover and gasket. Remove the crankshaft oil slinger.
2. Remove the camshaft sprocket retaining bolt and washer, distributor drive gear and fuel pump eccentric.
3. Rotate the crankshaft until the timing mark on the crankshaft sprocket is adjacent to, and on a center line with, the timing mark on the camshaft sprocket.
4. Remove the crankshaft sprocket, camshaft sprocket and timing chain as an assembly. Disassemble the chain and sprockets.
5. Assemble the timing chain, crankshaft sprocket and camshaft sprocket with the timing marks on both sprockets aligned. Install the assembly to the crankshaft and the camshaft.
6. Install the fuel pump eccentric. The fuel pump eccentric must be installed with the stamped word "REAR" facing the camshaft sprocket.
7. Install the distributor drive gear, washer and retaining bolt. Tighten the bolt to 25–35 ft. lbs.
8. Install the crankshaft oil slinger. Install the timing chain cover using a new gasket and oil seal.

VALVE TIMING PROCEDURE

EXCEPT 4-151 CID (2.5L) AND V6-173 CID (2.8L) ENGINES

1. Disconnect the negative battery cable. Remove the ignition wires. Remove the spark plugs.
2. Remove the valve cover. Remove the bridge and pivot assembly and the rocker arms from the number one cylinder.
3. Rotate the crankshaft until number six piston (number four piston on 4-150 CID (2.5L) engine) is at TDC on the compression stroke. Rotate the crankshaft counterclockwise, as viewed from the front of the engine, 90°.
4. Install a dial indicator gauge on the end of the number one cylinder intake valve push rod. Set the indicator gauge to zero.
5. Rotate the crankshaft clockwise, as viewed from the front of the engine, until the indicator gauge reads .016 in. (6-243 CID (4.0L) and 6-258 CID (4.2L) engines) or .020 in. (V8-360 CID (5.9L) engine) or .012 in. (4-150 CID (2.5L) engine) lift.
6. The timing mark on the vibration damper should be aligned with the TDC mark on the timing degree scale.
7. If the mark is more than ½ in. from TDC in either direction, valve timing is incorrect.

Camshaft

Removal and Installation

4-150 CID (2.5L) ENGINE

1. Disconnect the negative battery cable. Drain the cooling system.
2. Remove the shroud and the radiator. If equipped with air condition remove the condenser. Remove the fan and water pump pulley.
3. Remove the valve cover. Remove the rocker arms and pushrods. Remove the distributor. Remove the spark plugs. Remove the fuel pump.
4. Remove the rocker arms, bridges and pivots, and pushrods. Be sure to keep these components in order for reinstallation.
5. Remove the valve lifters from the cylinder head using tool J-21884 or equivalent. Remove the timing case cover. Remove the timing chain and sprockets.
6. If the cam appears to have been rubbing against the timing case cover, examine the oil pressure relief holes in the rear cam journal to be sure that they are free of debris.
7. Carefully remove the camshaft from the engine.
8. Installation is the reverse of the removal procedure.

4-151 CID (2.5L) ENGINE

1. Disconnect the negative battery cable. Drain the cooling system.
2. Remove the shroud and the radiator. If equipped with air condition it may be necessary to remove the condenser. Remove the fan and water pump pulley.
3. Remove the valve cover, rocker arms, and pushrods. Remove the distributor.
4. Remove the spark plugs and fuel pump. Remove the pushrod cover and gasket, then remove the lifters.
5. Remove the crankshaft hub and timing gear cover. Remove the two camshaft thrust plate screws by working through the holes in the gear.
6. Remove the camshaft and gear assembly by pulling it through the front of the block.
7. Installation is the reverse of the removal procedure.Make sure that the camshaft surfaces are dust free and lubed with oil. Torque the thrust plate screws to 75 inch lbs.

V6-173 CID (2.8L) ENGINE

1. Disconnect the negative battery cable. Drain the cooling system.
2. Remove the radiator. If equipped with air condition, carefully discharge the system and remove the condenser. Remove the intake manifold. Remove the valve lifters. Remove fuel pump and fuel pump pushrod.
3. Remove the timing cover. Remove the camshaft sprocket bolts, sprocket and timing chain.
4. Install two bolts into the camshaft bolt holes and pull the camshaft from the block.
5. Installation is the reverse of the removal procedure.

6-243 CID (4.0L) AND 6-258 CID (4.2L) ENGINES

1. Disconnect the negative battery cable. Drain the cooling system. Remove the radiator.
2. If equipped, carefully discharge the air condition system and remove the condenser and receiver assembly.
3. Remove the fuel pump. Remove the distributor. Remove the ignition wires. Remove the valve cover. As required, remove the front bumper and grille assembly.
4. Remove the rocker arms, bridged pivot assemblies and pushrods. Be sure to replace these parts in the same order as removed.
5. Remove cylinder head and gasket. Remove the valve lifters. Remove timing case cover. Remove timing chain and sprockets.
6. Carefully remove the camshaft from the vehicle..
7. Installation is the reverse of removal.

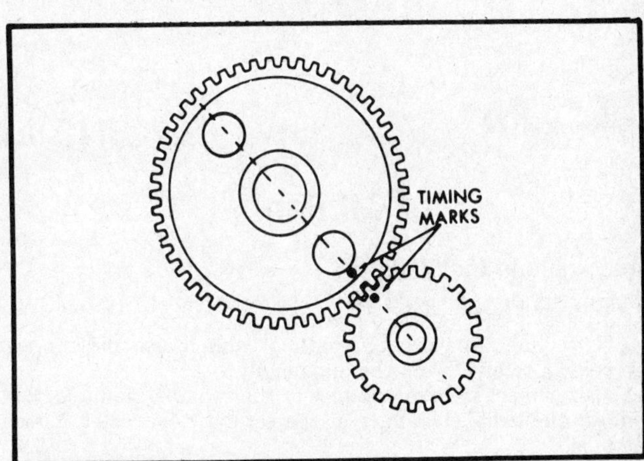

151 engine timing mark alignment

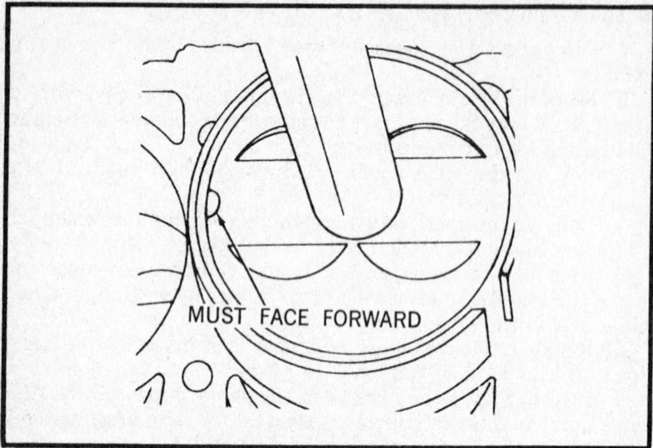

Piston installation—all engines

V8-360 CID (5.9L) ENGINE

1. Disconnect the negative battery cable. Drain the cooling system. Remove the radiator. Remove the drive belts, fan, and hub assembly.
2. If equipped, carefully discharge the air condition system and remove the condenser and receiver assembly. Remove the front bumper, grill and hood latch support bracket as required.
3. Remove the fuel pump. Remove the distributor. Remove the ignition wires.
4. Remove the valve cover. Remove rocker arms, bridged pivot assemblies and pushrods. Be sure to replace these parts in the same order as removed.
5. Remove the intake manifold. Remove the valve lifters.
6. Remove timing case cover. Remove distributor drive gear and fuel pump eccentric from the camshaft. Remove timing chain and sprockets.
7. Carefully remove the camshaft from the vehicle.
8. Installation is the reverse of the removal procedure. When installing the fuel pump eccentric it must be positioned with the word "REAR" facing the camshaft sprocket.

Pistons and Connecting Rods

IDENTIFICATION

EXCEPT 4-151 CID (2.5L) AND V6-173 CID (2.8L) ENGINES

The connecting rod caps are stamped with the number of the cylinder to which they belong. Replace them in there original positions. The numbered sides and squirt hole must face the camshaft when assembled in the six cylinder engine. The numbered sides must face out on the V8-360 CID (5.9L) engine when assembled.

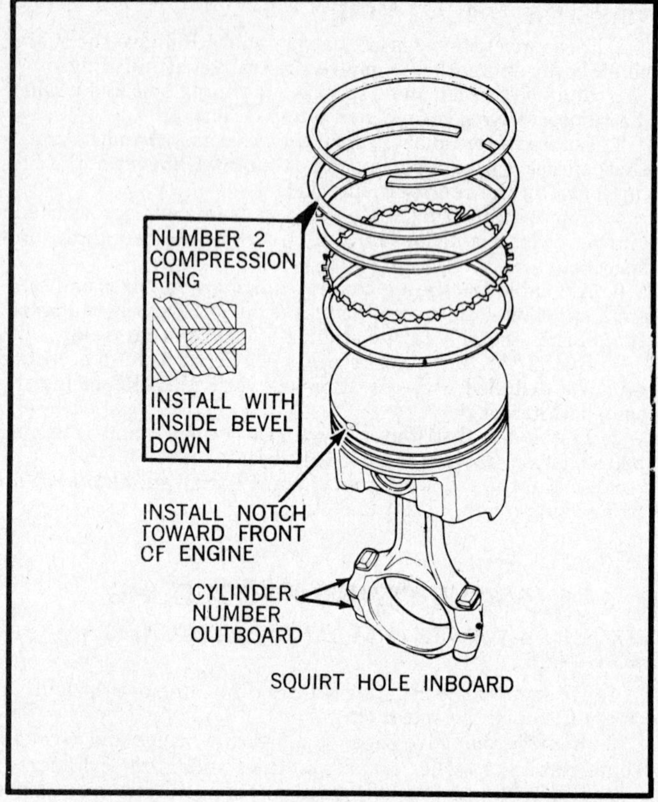

Engine piston and connecting rod assembly—V8

4-151 CID (2.5L) ENGINE

The letter "F" or the notches in the edge of the piston, goes toward the front of the engine. The notch on the connecting rod should be opposite the notch on the piston.

V6-173 CID (2.8L) ENGINE

There is a machined hole or a cast notch "E" in the top of all pistons to indicate proper installation. The piston assemblies should always be installed with the hole or notch toward the front of the engine.

ENGINE LUBRICATION

Oil Pan

Removal and Installation

4-150 CID (2.5L) ENGINE

1. Disconnect the negative battery cable. Raise and support the vehicle safely. Drain the engine oil.
2. Disconnect the exhaust pipe at the exhaust manifold. Disconnect the exhaust hanger at the catalytic converter. Lower the pipe.
3. Remove the starter. Remove the torque converter housing access cover.
4. Remove the oil pan retaining bolts. Remove the oil pan from the vehicle.
5. Installation is the reverse of the removal procedure.

4-151 CID (2.5L) ENGINE

1. Disconnect the negative battery cable. Raise and support the vehicle safely. Drain the engine oil. Remove the starter.
2. On some vehicles it may be necessary to position a jack under the transmission housing. Disconnect the right engine support cushion bracket from the block and raise the engine to allow clearance for oil pan removal.
3. Remove the oil pan retaining bolts. Remove the oil pan, front and rear neoprene seals and side gaskets.

4. Installation is the reverse of the removal procedure.

V6–173 CID (2.8L) ENGINE

1. Disconnect the negative battery cable. Disconnect the right exhaust pipe at the manifold.
2. Raise and support the vehicle safely. Drain the engine oil. Disconnect the left exhaust pipe at the manifold.
3. Remove the flywheel access cover. Remove the starter.
4. Disconnect the exhaust pipe at the converter and lower it so that the Y portion rests on the upper control arms.
5. Remove the oil pan retaining bolts. Remove the oil pan from the vehicle.
6. Installation is the reverse of the removal procedure. Apply RTV sealant in a ⅛ in. bead on the pan lip.

6–243 CID (4.0L) AND 6–258 CID (4.2L) ENGINE

1. Disconnect the negative battery cable. Raise and support the vehicle safely. Drain the engine oil. Remove the flywheel cover access housing. Remove the starter.
2. On some vehicles it may be necessary to place a jack under the transmission housing. Disconnect right engine support cushion bracket from the block and raise the engine to allow clearance for oil pan removal.
3. Remove the oil pasn retaining bolts. Remove the oil pan from the vehicle.
4. Installation is the reverse of the removal procedure.

V8–360 CID (5.9L) ENGINE

1. Disconnect the negative batttery cable. Raise and support the vehicle safely. Drain the engine oil. Remove the converter housing access cover. Remove the starter.
2. On some vehicles it may be necessary to remove the frame cross bar and automatic transmission lines.
3. If required, cut the corner of engine mount on right side to provide clearance for pan removal.
4. If equipped with manual transmission, bend the tabs down on dust shield.
5. Remove oil pan retaining bolts. Remove the oil pan from the vehicle.
6. Installation is the reverse of the removal procedure.

Oil Pump

Removal and Installation

EXCEPT V8–360 CID (5.9L) ENGINE

1. Disconnect the negative battery cable. Raise and support the vehicle safely. Drain the engine oil. Remove the oil pan.
2. Remove the oil pump retaining screws, oil pump, and gasket from the engine block.
3. Remove the cover retaining screws, cover, and gasket from the pump body.
4. Measure the gear end clearance between the gears and the face of the oil pump body.
5. Measure the gear lobe clearance to the pump body sides.
6. Remove the gears and shaft from the body.
7. Remove the cotter pin, spring retainer, spring, and oil pressure relief valve from the pump body.
8. Repair or replace defective components as required.
9. Installation is the reverse of the removal procedure. Be sure to use new gaskets and seals as required. Fill the pump gear cavity with petroleum jelly prior to the installation of the pump cover, to insure self priming.

V8–360 CID (5.9L) ENGINE

1. Disconnect the negative battery cable. Drain the engine oil. Remove the engine oil filter.
2. Remove the engine oil pump cover from the timing chain cover. Remove the oil pump gears and shaft.
3. Remove the oil pressure relief valve from the body.
4. Inspect the gears for abnormal wear, chips, looseness on the shafts, galling, and scoring.
5. Inspect the cover and cavity for breaks, cracks, distortion, and abnormal wear.

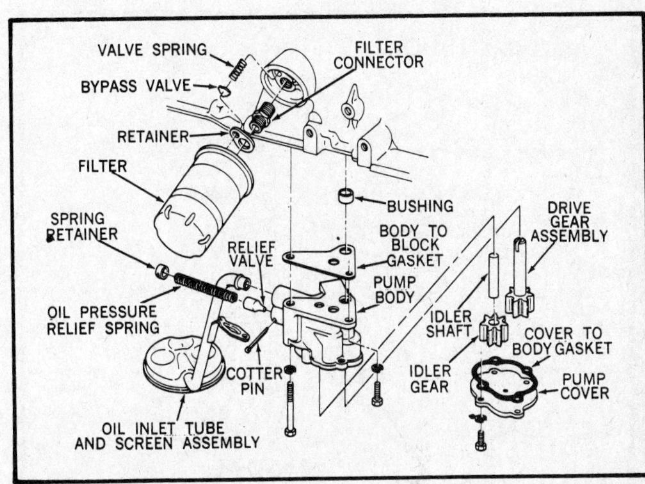

Oil pump assembly—6 cyl.

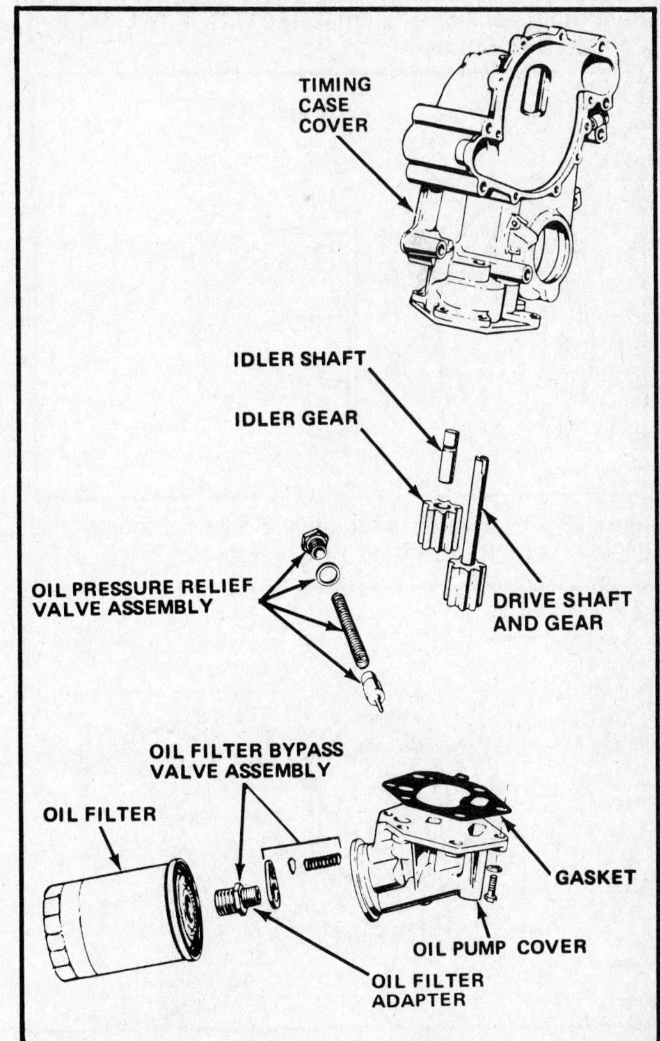

Oil pump assembly—V8

6. Install the gears into the pump cavity, and with the use of a straight edge and feeler gauge, check the gear to housing clearance.

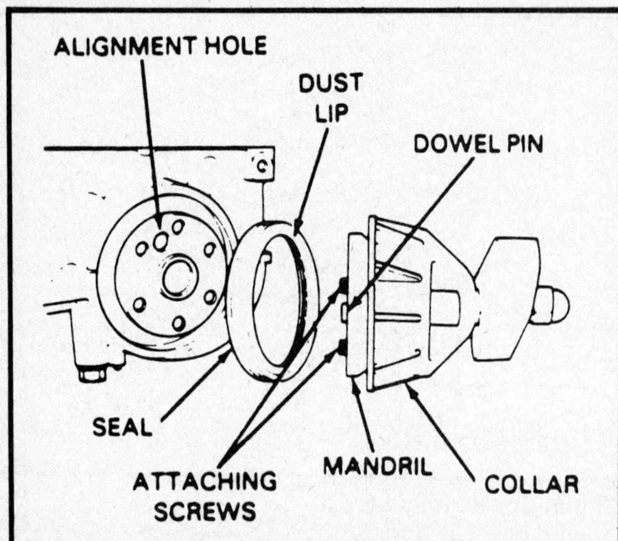

Rear main seal installation 4–150 CID, 4–151 CID and V6–173 CID engines

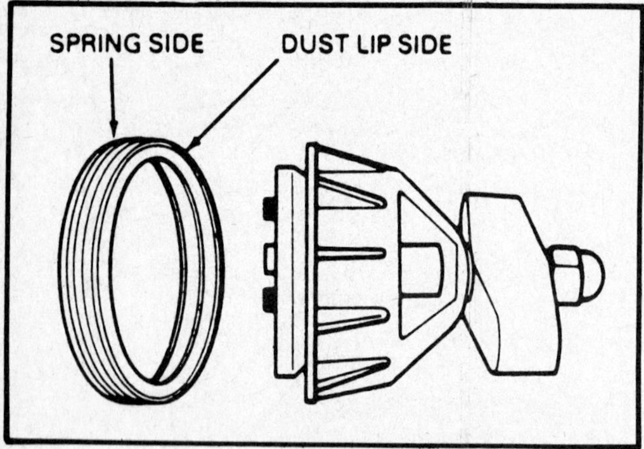

Installing rear main seal on installation tool 4–150 CID, 4–151 CID and 4–173 CID engines

Removing rear main seal 4–150 CID, 4–151 CID and V6–173 CID engines

7. If the clearances measure out of the allowable span, the timing chain cover and gears should be replaced.

8. Installation is the reverse of the removal procedure. be sure to use new gaskets and seals as required.

9. Be sure to fill the pump gear cavity with petroleum jelly prior to the installation of the pump cover, to insure self priming.

Rear Main Bearing Oil Seal

Removal and Installation

4–150 CID (2.5L), 4–151 CID (2.5L) AND V6–173 CID (2.8L) ENGINES

1. Disconnect the negative battery cable. Raise and support the vehicle safely.
2. Remove the transmission assembly. Remove the engine flywheel.
3. Remove the seal from the crankshaft flange by prying around the flange, using a suitable tool.
4. Before installing the seal coat it with clean engine oil. Insert the seal into place and gently tap it flush with the cylinder block using a soft rubber mallet.
5. Continue the installation in the reverse order of the removal procedure.

6–243 CID (4.0L), 6–258 CID (4.2L) AND 360 (5.0) ENGINES

1. Disconnect the negative battery cable. Raise and support the vehicle safely.
2. Remove the transmission. Remove the flywheel from the engine. Remove the oil pan.
3. Remove the rear main bearing cap. Remove the lower rear main bearing oil seal.
4. Loosen the reamaining main bearings. Tap the upper half of the seal with a brass drift until it protrudes out far enough to pull it out from around the crankshaft.
5. Before installation coat the rear main seal with clean engine oil. Insert the top half of the seal into the engine block and around the crankshaft. The seal lip must face inward toward the front of the engine.
6. Coat both sides of the lower seal with RTV sealant. Coat the outer curved surface of the lower seal with liquid soap.
7. Position the lower seal into the main bearing cap recess and seat it firmly.
8. Coat both chamfered edges on the bearing cap with RTV sealant. Do not apply sealant to the engine block to bearing cap mating surface. Install the rear main bearing cap and torque to specification.
9. Continue the installation in the reverse order of the removal procedure.

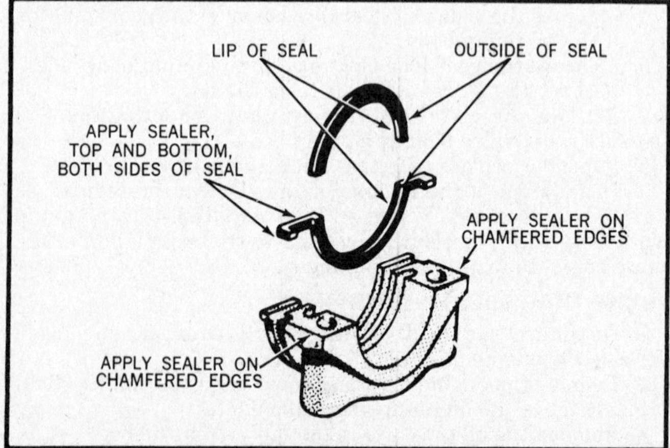

Rear main seal installation—all engines

FRONT SUSPENSION

Front Axle Assembly

Removal and Installation

EXCEPT WAGONEER, WRANGLER, CHEROKEE AND COMANCHE

1. Raise and support the vehicle safely. Remove the tire and wheel assembly.
2. Index the propeller shaft to the differential yoke for the proper alignment upon installation. Disconnect the propeller shaft at the axle yoke and secure the shaft to the frame rail.
3. Disconnect the steering linkage from the steering knuckles. Disconnect the shock absorbers at the axle housing.
4. If the vehicle is equipped with a stabilizer bar, remove the nuts attaching the stabilizer bar connecting links to the spring tie plates.
5. On vehicles equipped with sway bar, remove nuts attaching sway bar connecting links to spring tie plates.
6. Disconnect the breather tube from the axle housing. Disconnect the stabilizer bar link bolts at the spring clips.
7. Remove the brake calipers, hub and rotor, and the brake shield.
8. Remove the U-bolts and the tie plates.
9. Support the assembly using a suitable jack. Loosen the nuts securing the rear shackles, but do not remove the bolts.
10. Remove the front spring shackle bolts. Lower the springs to the floor.
11. Pull the jack and axle housing from underneath the vehicle.
12. Installation is the reverse of the removal procedure. Check the front end alignment, as required.

WAGONEER, CHEROKEE AND COMANCHE

1. Raise and support the vehicle safely.
2. Remove the wheels, calipers and rotors.
3. Disconnect all vacuum hoses at the axle.
4. Mark the relation between the front driveshaft and yoke.
5. Disconnect the stabilizer bar, rod and center link, front driveshaft, shock absorbers, steering damper, track bar.
6. Position a suitable jack under the axle. Disconnect the upper and lower control arms at the axle assembly. Remove the assembly from the vehicle..
8. Installation is the reverse of the removal procedure. Discard the U-joint straps new replacement straps must be used whenever the straps are removed.

WRANGLER

1. Raise and support the vehicle safely. Remove the tire and wheel assembly.
2. Remove the calipers and position them to the side. Remove the rotors.
3. Disconnect the vacuum harness from the shift motor and the vent hose from the axle housing.
4. Disconnect the center link at the right side of the tie rod. Disconnect the shock absorbers at the axle assembly.
5. Disconnect the steering damper. Disconnect the track bar at the axle assembly.
6. Loosen the stabilizer bar links at the stabilizer bar. Disconnect the stabilizer bar links from the spring tie plates.
7. Loosen the bolts retaining the front springs to the frame brackets. Loosen the bolts retaining the front springs to the shackles.
8. Support the axle using a suitable jack. Remove the spring U-bolts and tie plates.
9. Raise the jack enough to relieve the axle weight from the springs. Remove the front shackle bolts. Lower the assembly to the floor.
10. Installation is the reverse of the removal procedure.

Spring

COIL SPRING

Removal and Installation

1. Disconnect the negative battery cable. Raise the vehicle and support it safely. Remove the tire and wheel assembly.
2. Matchmark and disconnect the front driveshaft. Disconnect the lower control arm at the axle.
3. Disconnect the track bar at the frame. Position a suitable jack under the axle.
4. Disconnect the stabilizer bar. Disconnect the shock absorbers. Disconnect the center link at the pitman arm.
5. Lower the axle to the floor. Loosen the spring retainer. Remove the spring from the vehicle.
6. Installation is the reverse of the removal procedure.

LEAF SPRING

Removal and Installation

1. Disconnect the negative battery cable. Raise the vehicle and support it safely.
2. Position a suitable jack under the axle. Raise the axle to relieve the springs of the axle weight.
3. If equipped, disconnect the stabilizer bar. Remove the spring U-bolts and tie plates.
4. Remove the bolt attaching the spring front eye to the shackle. Remove the bolt attaching the spring rear eye to the shackle.
5. Remove the spring from its mounting.
6. Installation is the reverse of the removal procedure.

Shock Absorbers

Removal and Installation

1. Disconnect the negative battery cable. Raise the vehicle and support it safely.
2. As required, properly support the axle assembly. Remove the upper shock absorber retaining bolt. Remove the lower shock absorber retaining bolts.
3. Remove the shock absorber from the vehicle.
4. Installation is the reverse of the removal procedure.

Ball Joints

Inspection

EXCEPT WRANGLER, WAGONEER, CHEROKEE AND COMANCHE

1. Unlock the steering column. Raise and support the vehicle safely. Remove the front tire and wheel assemblies.
2. If equipped, disconnect the steering damper at the tie rod.
3. On CJ and Scrambler, disconnect the steering connecting rod at the right side of the steering knuckle.
4. On Grand Wagoneer and Truck, disconnect the steering connecting rod at the right side of the tie rod.
5. Remove the cotter pin and nut that retains the tie rod to the right side of the steering knuckle. Rotate both steering knuckles several times from the right side of the vehicle.
6. Position a torque wrench to the right tie rod retaining nut. The torque wrench must be positioned perpendicular to the arm.
7. Rotate the steering knuckles slowly and steadily through a complete arc. Measure the torque required to rotate the knuckles. If less than 25 ft. lbs., turning effort is normal. Check for other problems.

8. If greater than 25 ft. lbs., disconnect the tie rod from both steering knuckles. Install a ½X1 in. bolt, washer and nut into the tie rod mounting hole in each of the steering knuckles.

9. Rotate the steering knuckles slowly and steadily through a complete arc. Measure the torque required to rotate the knuckles. If less than 10 ft. lbs., turning effort is within specification. Check for damaged or tight tie rod ends.

UPPER BALL JOINT

Removal and Installation

CJ AND SCRAMBLER

1. Disconnect the negative battery cable. raise and support the vehicle safely.

2. Remove the steering knuckle from the vehicle. Position the assembly in a suitable holding fixture with the upper ball stud pointing downward.

3. Remove both arms from tool J-25215. Place button J-25211-3 on the upper ball stud. Install adapter tool J-25211-4 on the nut end of the puller screw so that the adapter shoulder faces the nut end of the screw.

4. Insert the nut end of the puller screw through the upper ball stud hole in the knuckle. Hold the adapter and the frame against the knuckle.

5. Remove the lower ball stud from the knuckle.

6. Installation is the reverse of the removal procedure. Check and adjust alignment, as required.

GRAND WAGONEER AND TRUCK

1. Disconnect the negative battery cable. raise and support the vehicle safely.

2. Remove the steering knuckle from the vehicle. Position the assembly in a suitable holding fixture with the upper ball stud pointing downward.

3. Remove both arms from tool J-25215. Place button J-25211-3 on the upper ball stud.

4. Thread the puller frame halfway onto the puller screw. Insert the nut end of the screw through the lower ball stud hole in the steering knuckle. Position the puller frame against the knuckle and the puller screw against tool J-25211.

5. Tighten the puller screw and press the upper ball stud out of the steering knuckle.

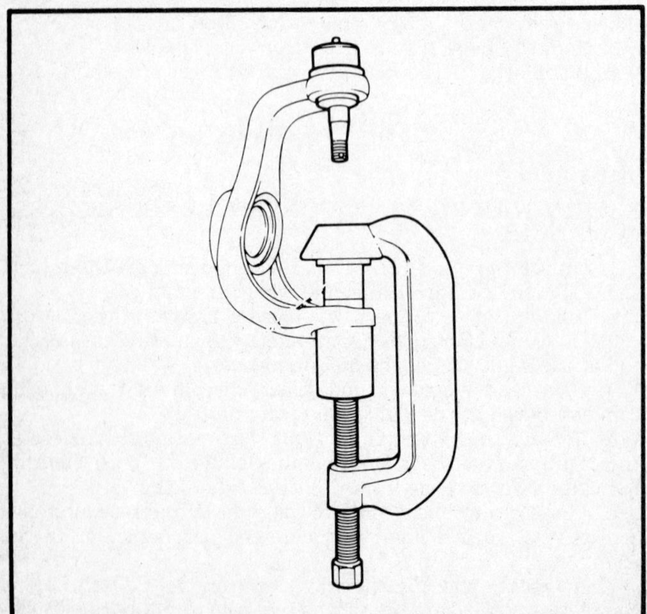

Lower ball joint removal

6. Installation is the reverse of the removal procedure. Check and adjust alignment, as required.

WRANGLER, WAGONEER, CHEROKEE AND COMANCHE

1. Disconnect the negative battery cable. Raise and support the vehicle safely. Remove the steering knuckle from the vehicle.

2. Position the receiver tool over the top of the ball joint. Set the adapter tool in a C-clamp and position the clamp so that tightening the clamp screw will remove the ball joint.

3. Remove the basll joint from the assembly.

4. Installation is the reverse of the removal procedure. Check and adjust alignment, as required.

LOWER BALL JOINT

Removal and Installation

CJ, SCRAMBLER, GRAND WAGONEER AND TRUCK

1. Disconnect the negative battery cable. Raise and support the vehicle safely.

2. Remove the steering knuckle from the vehicle. Position the assembly in a suitable holding fixture with the upper ball stud pointing downward.

3. Attach tool J-2511-1, or equivalent to the spindle mating surface of the knuckle assembly. Position tool J-25211-3 on the lower ball stud.

4. Assemble and install the puller on the steering knuckle. Hook one arm of the puller in the plate of tool J-25211-1 and the opposite arm of the tool in the steering knuckle.

5. Tighten the puller screw to press the lower stud out of the knuckle. Remove the tools from the knuckle.

6. Installation is the reverse of the removal procedure. Check and adjust front end alignment, as required.

WRANGLER, WAGONEER, CHEROKEE AND COMANCHE

1. Disconnect the negative battery cable. Raise and support the vehicle safely.

2. Remove the steering knuckle from the vehicle. Position the assembly in a suitable holding fixture with the upper ball stud pointing downward.

3. Use a Cclamp, with the receiver tool and the adapter tool to force out the ball joint.

4. Installation is the reverse of the removal procedure. Check and adjust front end alignment, as required.

Wheel Bearings

Adjustment

CJ AND SCRAMBLER

1. Raise and support the vehicle safely.

2. Remove the bolts attaching the front hub to the hub rotor. Remove the hub body and gasket.

3. Remove the snapring from the axle shaft and remove the hub clutch assembly.

4. Straighten the lip of the outer lock nut tabbed washer. Remove the outer locknut and tabbed washer.

5. Loosen and then tighten the inner locknut to 50 ft. lbs. Rotate the wheel while tightening the nut to seat the bearing properly.

6. Back off the inner locknut about ⅙ of a turn while rotating the wheel. The wheel must rotate freely.

7. Install the tabbed washer and the outer locknut.

8. Torque the outer locknut to 50 ft. lbs.

9. Recheck the bearing adjustment. The wheel must rotate freely. Correct as required.

GRAND WAGONEER AND TRUCK

1. Raise and support the vehicle safely.
2. If the vehicle is not equipped with front hubs, remove the wheel cover and hubcap. Remove the drive gear snapring. Remove the drive gear, pressure spring and spring cup.
3. If the vehicle is equipped with front hubs, Remove the socket head screws from the hub body and remove the body from the hub clutch assembly. Remove the large retaining ring from the hub. Remove the small retaining ring from the axle shaft. Remove the hub and clutch assembly. Remove the outer locknut and lock washer.
4. Seat the bearings by loosening and then tightening them to 50 ft. lbs. Back off the inner locknut about $\frac{1}{6}$ of a turn while rotating the wheel.
5. Install the lock washer. Align one of the lock washer holes with the peg on the inner locknut and install the washer on the nut.
6. Install and torque the outer locknut to 50 ft. lbs. Recheck the bearing adjustment. Correct as required.
7. On vehicles without front hubs, The spring cup must be installed so the recessed side faces the bearing and the flat side faces the pressure spring. The pressure spring should contact the flat side of the cup only.

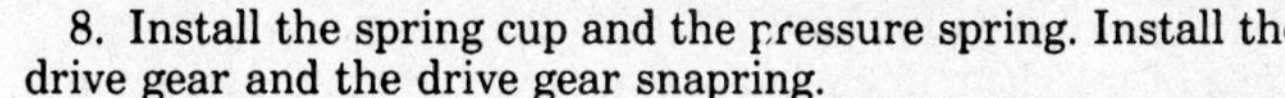

8. Install the spring cup and the pressure spring. Install the drive gear and the drive gear snapring.
9. If the vehicle is equipped with front hubs, Install the clutch assembly. Install the small retaining ring on the axle shaft. Install the large retaining ring on the hub.
10. Install the hub body on the hub clutch. Install the socket head screws in the hub and torque them to 30 inch lbs.

WRANGLER, CHEROKEE, WAGONEER AND COMANCHE (TYPE ONE)

1. Raise and support the vehicle safely. Remove the tire and wheel. Remove the disc brake caliper as required. Remove the cotter pin, locknut and axle hub nut.

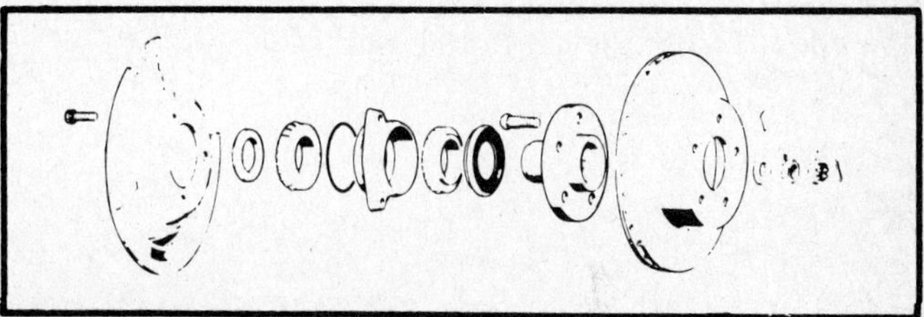

Wheel bearing assembly, type two

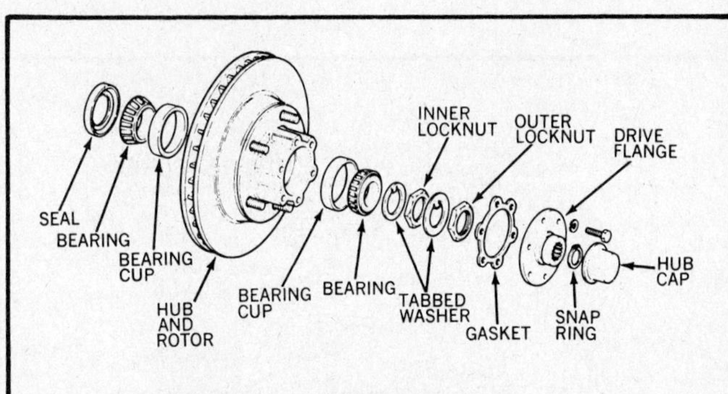

Wheel bearing assembly, type one

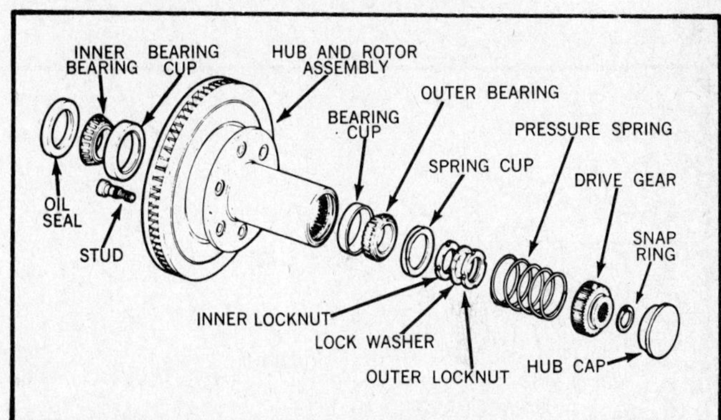

Wheel bearing assembly-Cherokee and Wagoneer

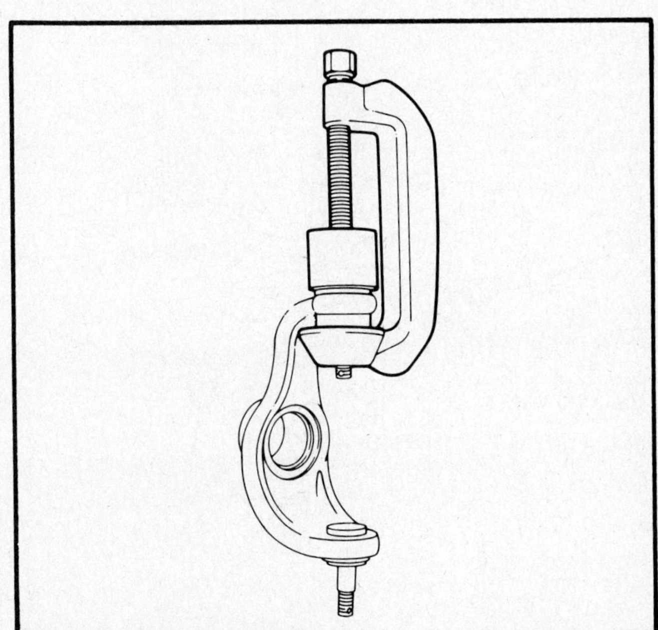

Upper ball joint removal

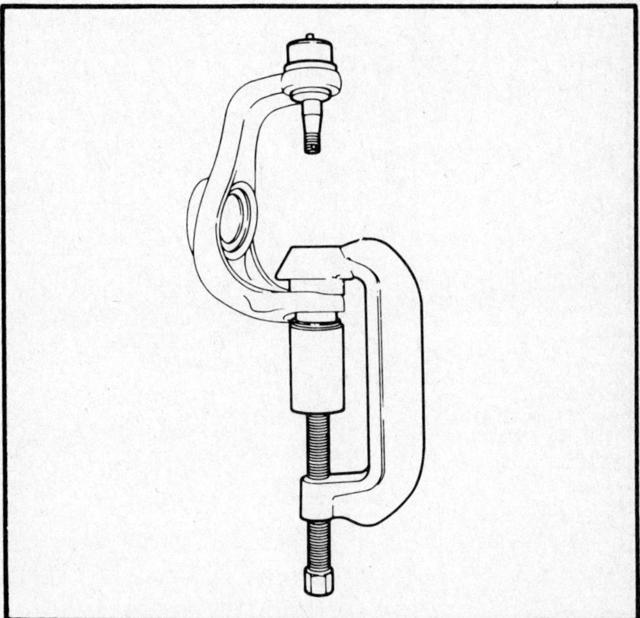

Lower ball joint installation

2. Tighten the hub bolts to 75 ft. lbs.

3. Install the hub washer and nut and tighten the hub nut to 175 ft. lbs. Install the locknut and new cotter pins.

4. Install the caliper, if removed. Install the wheel. Lower the vehicle.

CHEROKEE, WAGONEER AND COMANCHE (TYPE TWO)

1. Raise and support the vehicle safely. Remove the tire and wheel. Remove the caliper, as required.

2. Remove the grease cap, cotter pin and nut retainer.

3. Tighten the spindle nut to 25 ft. lbs. while rotating the rotor.

4. Loosen the spindle nut about one half turn while rotating the wheel. Torque the nut to 19 ft. lbs.

5. Install any removed components.

Procedures

Camber, on vehicles equipped with a solid axle, is set at the factory and cannot be adjusted.

Caster, on vehicles equipped with a solid axle, may be adjusted by installing new front end components or caster shims between the axle pad and the springs.

To adjust toe in on CJ, Scrambler, Grand Wagoneer and Truck, position the wheels straight ahead with the steering gear also in the straight ahead driving position. Turn both tie rod adjusting sleeves an equal amount until the toe in setting is obtained.

To adjust the toe in on Wrangler,Cherokee, Wagoneer and Comanche, Add or subtract shims at the rear of the lower control arms, as needed.

STEERING GEAR AND LINKAGE

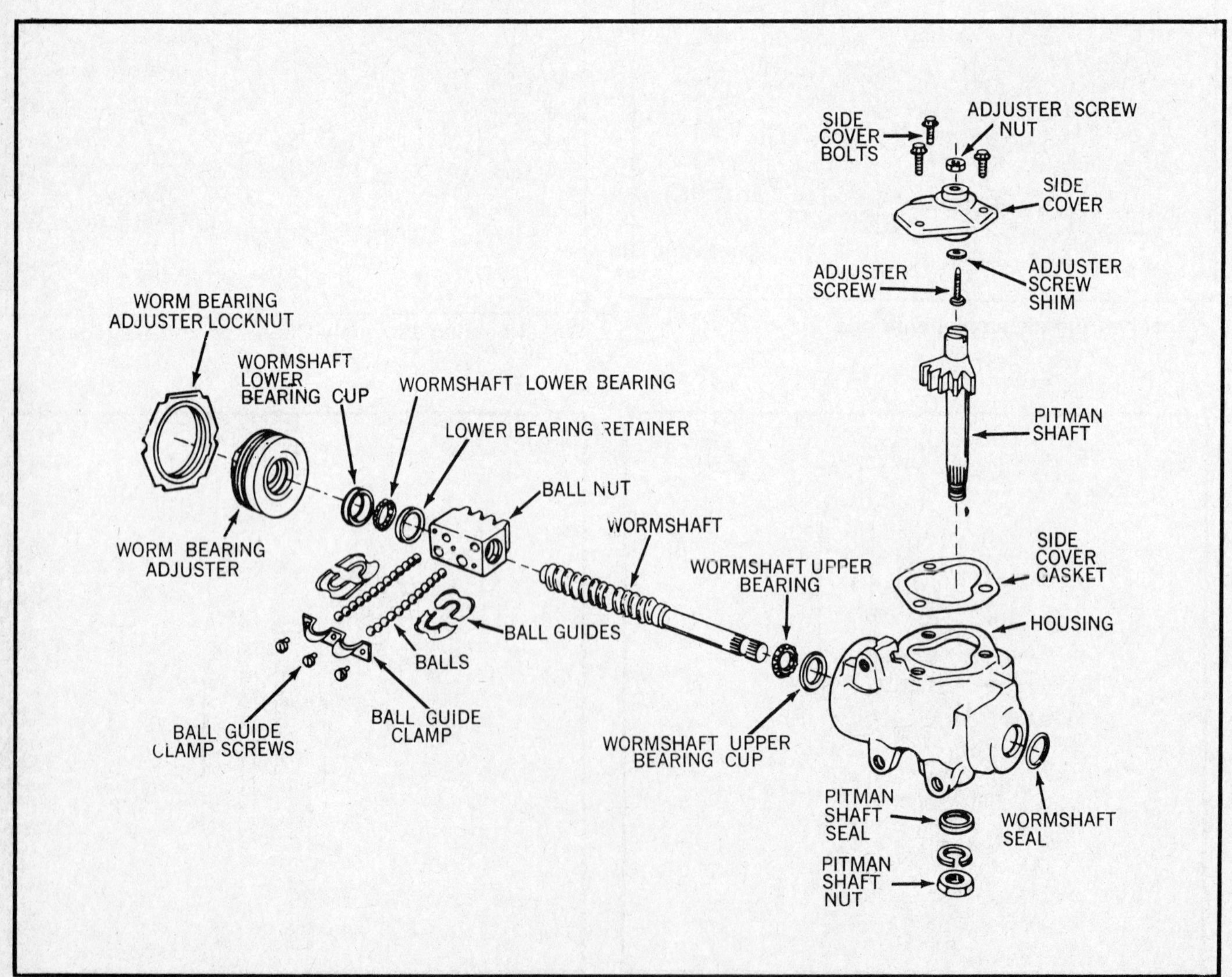

Manual steering gear—typical

Refer to the Unit Repair section for overhaul procedures.

Manual Steering Gear

Removal and Installation

CJ, SCRAMBLER, GRAND WAGONEER AND TRUCK

1. Disconnect the negative battery cable. Raise and support the vehicle safely. Remove the intermediate shaft to wormshaft coupling clamp bolt and disconnect the intermediate shaft.
2. Remove the pitman arm nut and lockwasher. Using a puller, remove the pitman arm from the shaft.
3. On some vehicles, raise the left side of the vehicle slightly to relieve tension on the left front spring and rest the frame on a jackstand. Remove the steering gear lower bracket to frame bolts.
4. Remove the bolts attaching the steering gear upper bracket to the crossmember. Remove the steering gear from the vehicle.
5. Installation is the reverse of the removal procedure. Loctite 271® or similar material must be applied to all attaching bolt threads prior to installation.
6. The steering gear may produce a slight roughness which can be eliminated by turning the steering wheel full left and right 10–15 times.

WAGONEER, CHEROKEE, COMANCHE AND WRANGLER

1. Disconnect the negative battery cable. Disconnnect the steering shaft from the gear.
2. Raise and support the vehicle safely. Disconnect the center link from the pitman arm. Remove the front stabilizer bar.
3. Remove the pitman arm nut, mark the relation between the arm and shaft, and using a puller, pull the pitman arm from the shaft.
4. Remove the steering gear attaching bolts. Remove the steering gear from the vehicle.
5. Installation is the reverse of the removal procedure.

Power Steering Gear

Removal and Installation

CJ, SCRAMBLER, GRAND WAGONEER AND TRUCK

1. Disconnect the negative battery cable. Raise and support the vehicle safely. Remove the intermediate shaft to wormshaft coupling clamp bolt and disconnect the intermediate shaft.
2. Disconnect and plug the fluid lines at the steering gear assembly. Remove the pitman arm nut and lockwasher. Using a puller, remove the pitman arm from the shaft.
3. On some vehicles, raise the left side of the vehicle slightly to relieve tension on the left front spring and rest the frame on a jackstand. Remove the steering gear lower bracket to frame bolts.
4. Remove the bolts attaching the steering gear upper bracket to the crossmember. Remove the steering gear from the vehicle.
5. Installation is the reverse of the removal procedure. Loctite 271® or similar material must be applied to all attaching bolt threads prior to installation. Fill the power steering pump with fluid. Bleed the system, as required.
6. The steering gear may produce a slight roughness which can be eliminated by turning the steering wheel full left and right 10–15 times.

WAGONEER, CHEROKEE, COMANCHE AND WRANGLER

1. Disconnect the negative battery cable. Disconnnect the steering shaft from the gear.
2. Raise and support the vehicle safely. Disconnect the center link from the pitman arm. Remove the front stabilizer bar. Disconnect and plug the fluid lines at the steering gear.
3. Remove the pitman arm nut, mark the relation between the arm and shaft, and using a puller, pull the pitman arm from the shaft.
4. Remove the steering gear attaching bolts. Remove the steering gear from the vehicle.
5. Installation is the reverse of the removal procedure. Fill the power steering pump with fluid. Bleed the system, as required.

Power Steering Pump

Removal and Installation

1. Disconnect the negative battery cable. Remove all the necessary components in order to gain access to the power steering pump retaining bolts.
2. Remove the pump drive belt tension adjusting bolt. Disconnect the belt from the pump.
3. Disconnect the return and pressure hoses from the pump. Cover the hose connector and union on the pump and open ends of the hoses to avoid the entrance of dirt.
4. On some engines, it will be necessary to, remove the front bracket from the engine. Remove the two nuts which secure the rear of the pump to the bracket, and the two bolts which secure the front of the pump to the bracket. Remove the pump from the vehicle.
5. Installation is the reverse of the removal procedure. Adjust the drive belt tension. Fill the pump reservoir to the correct level.
6. Start the engine and wait for at least three minutes before turning the steering wheel. Check the level frequently during this time.
7. Slowly turn the steering wheel through its entire range a few times with the engine running. Recheck the level and inspect for possible leaks.
8. If air becomes trapped in the fluid, the pump may become noisy until all of the air is out. This may take some time since trapped air does not bleed out rapidly.

Tie Rods

Removal and Installation

1. Disconnect the negative battery cable. Raise and support the vehicle safely. Remove the cotter pins and retaining nuts at both ends of the tie rod and from the end of the connecting rod where it attaches to the tie rod.
2. Remove the nut attaching the steering damper push rod to the tie rod bracket and move the damper aside.
3. Remove the tie rod ends from the steering arms and connecting rod. It may be necessary to use a puller on some vehicles.
4. Count the number of threads showing on the tie rod before removing the ends, as a guide to installation.
5. Loosen the adjusting tube clamp bolts and unthread the ends.
6. Installation is the reverse of removal. Adjust toein, if necessary.

LOCK NUT
SIDE COVER
GASKET
ADJUSTING SCREW
PITMAN SHAFT
HOSE CONNECTOR SEAT
POPPET CHECK VALVE
HOSE CONNECTOR SEAT
SPRING
WORM SHAFT
STUB SHAFT
SEAL RINGS (3)
DAMPER O-RING
ADJUSTER PLUG LOCK NUT
SPOOL VALVE
BACKUP O-RING (3)
VALVE BODY
BALL RETURN GUIDE HALVES
CLAMP
RACK PISTON
RETAINING RING
HOUSING END PLUG
RACE
O-RING
THRUST BEARING
RACE
BEARING
RACES
BEARING RETAINER
RETAINING RING
BALL BEARINGS (24)
GEAR HOUSING
SPACER
DUST SEAL
THRUST BEARING
BACKUP O-RING
O-RING
OIL SEAL
RACK PISTON SEAL RING
O-RING
RACK PISTON END PLUG
OIL SEALS
NEEDLE BEARING
ADJUSTER PLUG
WASHERS
RETAINING RING
PITMAN ARM NUT

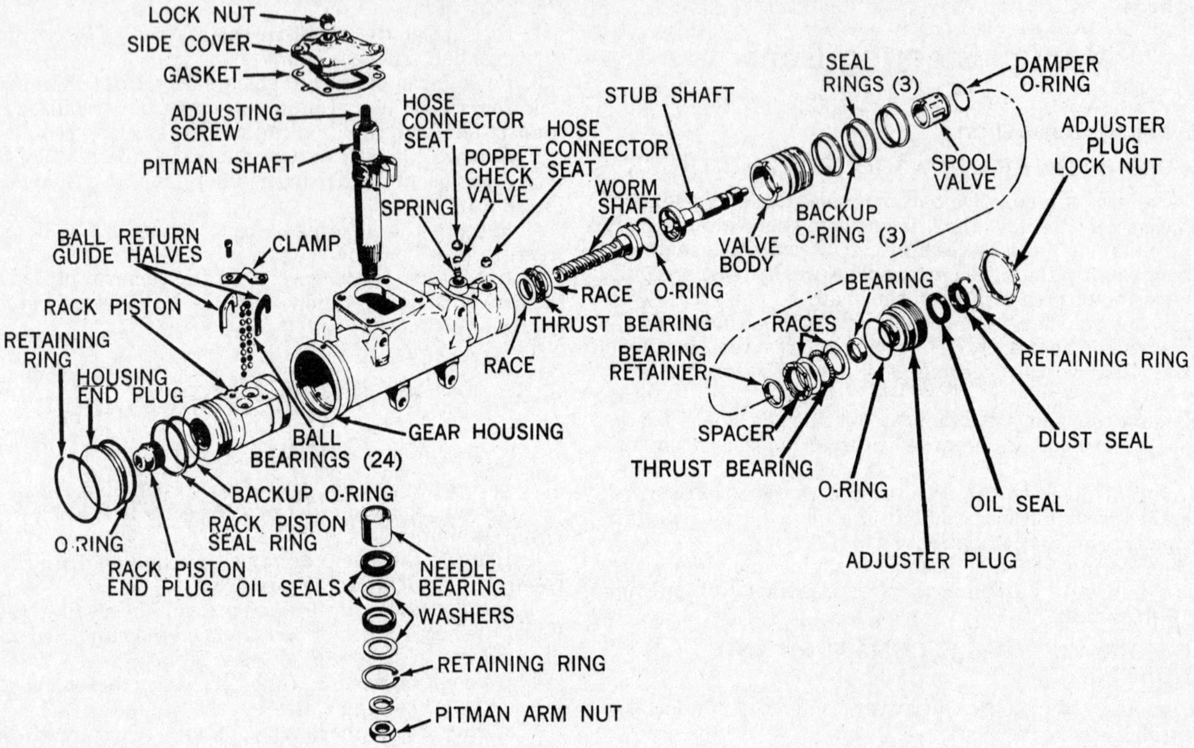

Power steering gear assembly—typical

CAP
MOUNTING STUD
RESERVOIR
RETAINING RING
RETAINING RING
UNION FITTING
PRESSURE PLATE
PUMP RING
VANE
DOWEL PIN(2)
MOUNTING STUD O-RING
THRUST PLATE
SEAL
PUMP BODY
PUMP SHAFT SEAL
O-RING
O-RING
MOUNTING STUD
END PLATE
SPRING
VALVE SPRING
FLOW CONTROL VALVE
PUMP SHAFT
MOUNTING STUD O-RING

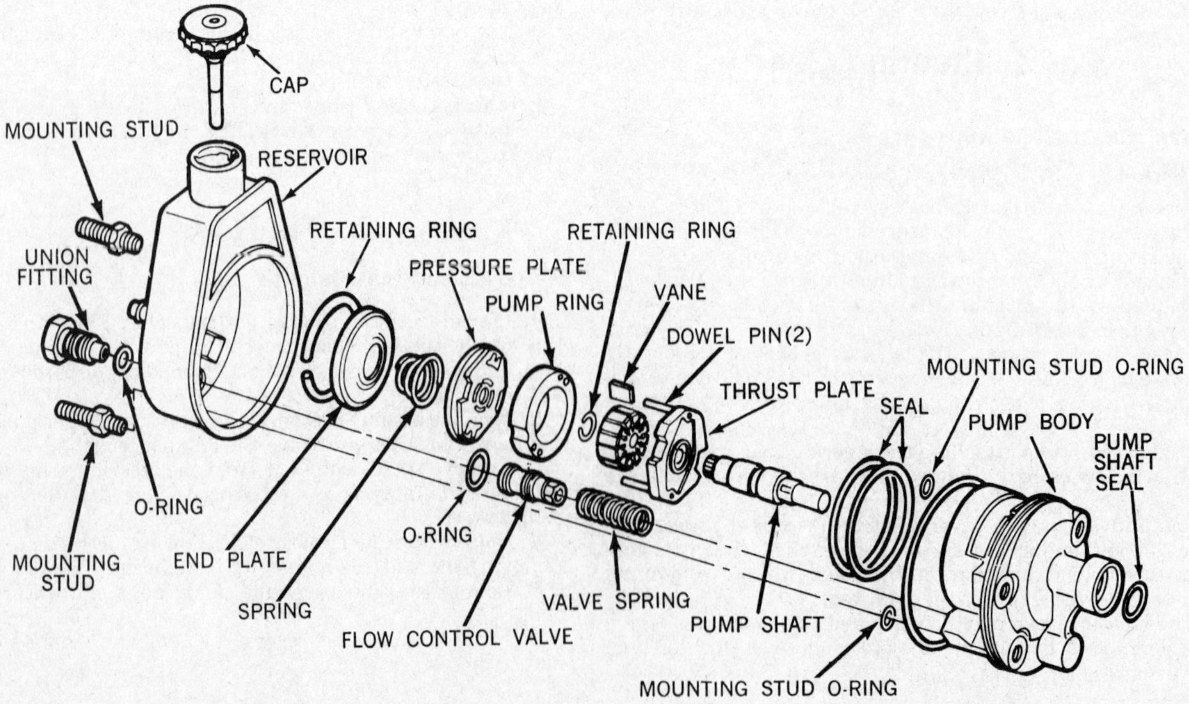

Power steering pump—typical

BRAKE SYSTEM

Refer to the Unit Repair section for overhaul procedures.

Master Cylinder

Removal and Installation

1. Disconnect the negative battery cable. Disconnect and plug the brake lines at the master cylinder.
2. Disconnect the master cylinder push rod at the brake pedal on vehicles with manual brakes.
3. Remove all attaching bolts and nuts and lift the master cylinder from the vehicle.
4. Installation is the reverse of the removal procedure. Bleed the hydraulic system, as required.

BLEEDING

Procedure

NOTE: On some vehicles, a combination differential and proportioning valve is used in the braking system. It is attached to the inner side of the left frame rail. When bleeding the brakes, the metering section of the valve must be held open. Loosen the front mounting bolt of the valve and insert tool J-23709 or J-26869, or its fabricated equivalent, under the bolt. Push in on the metering valve stem to open it and retighten the bolt to hold the tool in place. When the bleeding operation is complete, remove the tool.

1. Clean all dirt from around the master cylinder filler cap. Remove the cap and fill the master cylinder with the proper grade and type brake fluid.
2. If a bleeder tank is being used follow the manufacturers instructions.
3. Clean dirt from the bleeder connections at the calipers and wheel cylinders.
4. Attach the bleeder hose and fixture to the right rear wheel cylinder bleeder screw and place the end of the tube in a glass jar, filled with brake fluid.
5. Open the bleeder valve. Have and assistant depress the brake pedal slowly to the floor and then slowly release it.
6. Continue this operation until all air is expelled from the system. When the bubbles cease to appear at the end of the bleeder hose, close the bleeder valve.
7. Check the level of brake fluid in the master cylinder and refill as needed before going to the next wheel. Never reuse old brake fluid.
8. Repeat Steps 4–7 on the left rear wheel than the right front wheel and finally the left front wheel.

Wheel Cylinder

Removal and Installation

1. Raise and support the vehicle safely. Remove the brake drums. Remove the brake shoes. Disconnect the brake line.
2. Remove the wheel cylinder mounting bolts. Remove the wheel cylinder from the brake backing plate.
3. Installation is the reverse of the removal procedure. Bleed the system.

Disc Brakes

Removal and Installation

1. Remove approximately $^2/_3$ of the brake fluid from the master cylinder. Raise and support the vehicle safely. Remove the tire and wheel assembly.
2. Remove the caliper retaining bolts. Remove the brake caliper assembly from the rotor and position it to the side.
3. Carefully remove the disc brake linings from the caliper.
4. Installation is the reverse of the removal procedure. Be sure to use the proper tools to compress the caliper piston into its bore.
5. Bleed the brake system, as required.

Calipers

Removal and Installation

1. Raise and support the vehicle safely. Remove the tire and wheel assembly.
2. Disconnect the brake line fitting at the caliper assembly. Place a drain pan under the fluid line to contain the used brake fluid.
3. Remove the caliper retaining bolts. Remove the caliper from the vehicle.
4. Installation is the reverse of the removal procedure. Bleed the brake system.

Rotors

Removal and Installation

COMANCHE

1. Raise and support the vwehicle safely. Remove the tire and wheel assembly.
2. Remove the caliper and position it to the side.
3. Remove the grease cap, cotter pin, nut retainer, adjusting nut and thrust washer from the spindle.
4. Remove the hub and rotor from the vehicle.
5. Installation is the reverse of the removal procedure.

COMANCHE, WRANGLER, WAGONEER AND CHEROKEE

1. Raise and support the vwehicle safely. Remove the tire and wheel assembly.
2. Remove the caliper and position it to the side.
3. Remove the rotor from the vehicle.
4. Installation is the reverse of the removal procedure.

CJ AND SCRAMBLER

1. Raise and support the vwehicle safely. Remove the tire and wheel assembly.
2. Remove the caliper and position it to the side.
3. Remove the bolts retaining the hub body to the hub clutch. Remove the hub body.
4. Remove the retaining ring from the axle shaft. Remove the hub clutch and bearing assembly. Straighten the lip of the outer locknut retaining washer.
5. Remove the outer locknut and retaining washer. Remove the inner locknut and retaining washer.
6. Remove the hub and rotor assembly from the vehicle.
7. Installation is the reverse of the removal procedure.

GRAND WAGONEER AND TRUCK

1. Raise and support the vwehicle safely. Remove the tire and wheel assembly.
2. Remove the caliper and position it to the side.
3. On vehicles without front hubs, remove the rotor hub cap. Then remove the drive gear snap ring, the drive gear, the pressure spring and the spring cup.
4. On vehicles with front hubs, remove the socket head screws that retain the hub body to the hub clutch and remove the body from the clutch. Then remove the large and small hub retaining rings and the hub clutch from the axle shaft.

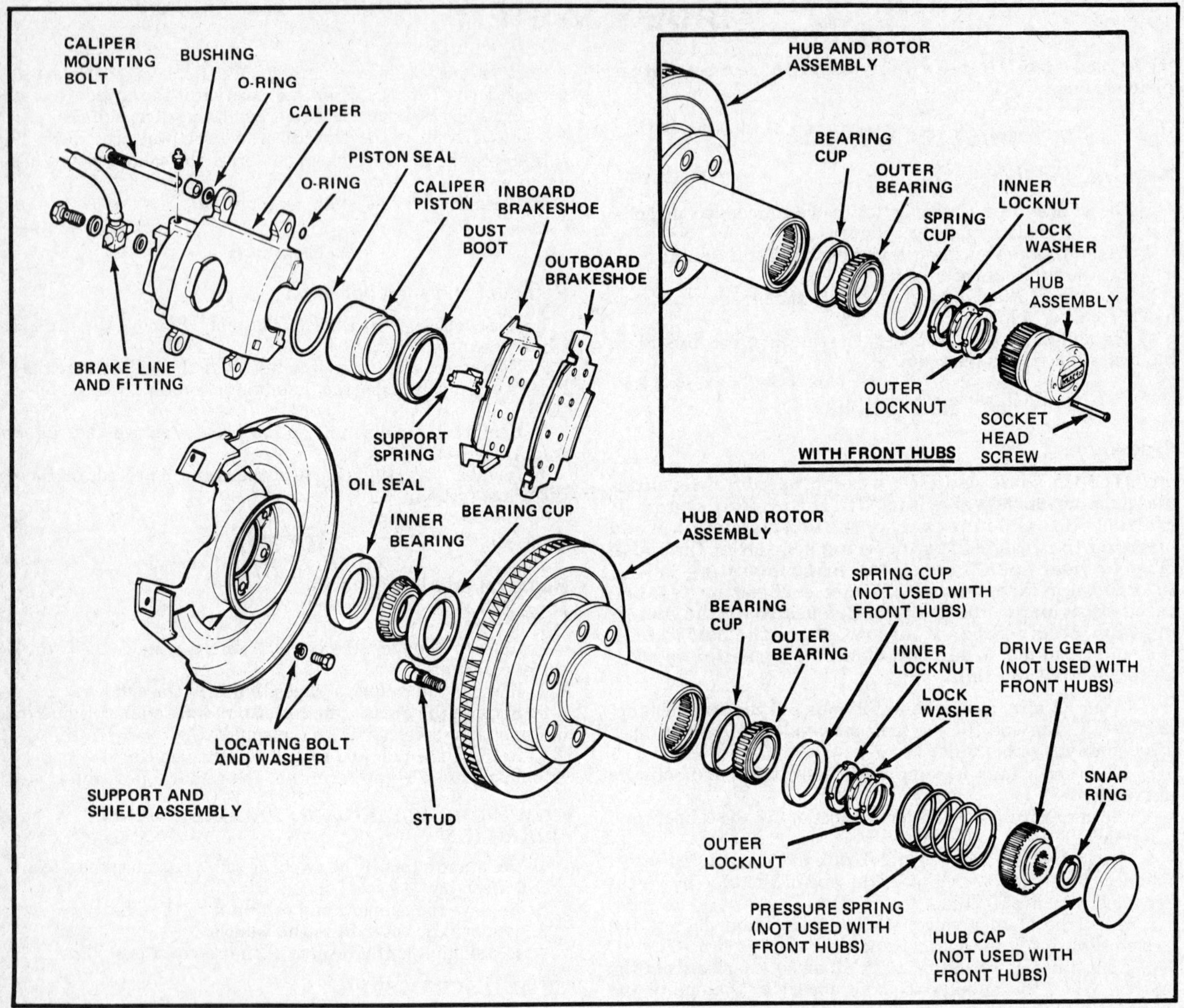

Typical disc brake assembly

5. Remove the wheel bearing outer and inner locknuts and retaining washers using tool J-6893-D.
6. Remove the rotor from the vehicle.
7. Installation is the reverse of the removal procedure.

Power Brake Booster

Removal and Installation

1. Disconnect the negative battery cable. Remove the under dash trim panel, if equipped.
2. Disconnect brake pedal pushrod at brake pedal. Disconnect vacuum hose from booster check valve.
3. Remove attaching nuts and separate master cylinder from brake booster. Do not disconnect brake lines at master cylinder.
4. If equipped, remove the bolts holding power unit bellcrank to dash panel and remove power unit and bellcrank as one assembly.
5. Remove the bolts retaining the power unit to the dash panel. Remove the unit from the vehicle.
6. Installation is the reverse of the removal procedure. When replacing the power brake unit, use the pushrod that is supplied with the new unit, as it has been correctly gauged and preset to the new unit.

Stop Light Switch

Removal and Installation

1. Disconnect the negative battery cable. Remove the under dash trim panel, if equipped.
2. On some vehicles equipped with air condition it may be necessary to remove the screws retaining the evaporator housing to the instrument panel to gain access for service.
3. Disconnect the stop light electrical connections. Remove the switch assembly from its mounting on the brake pedal support bracket.
4. Installation is the reverse of the removal procedure.

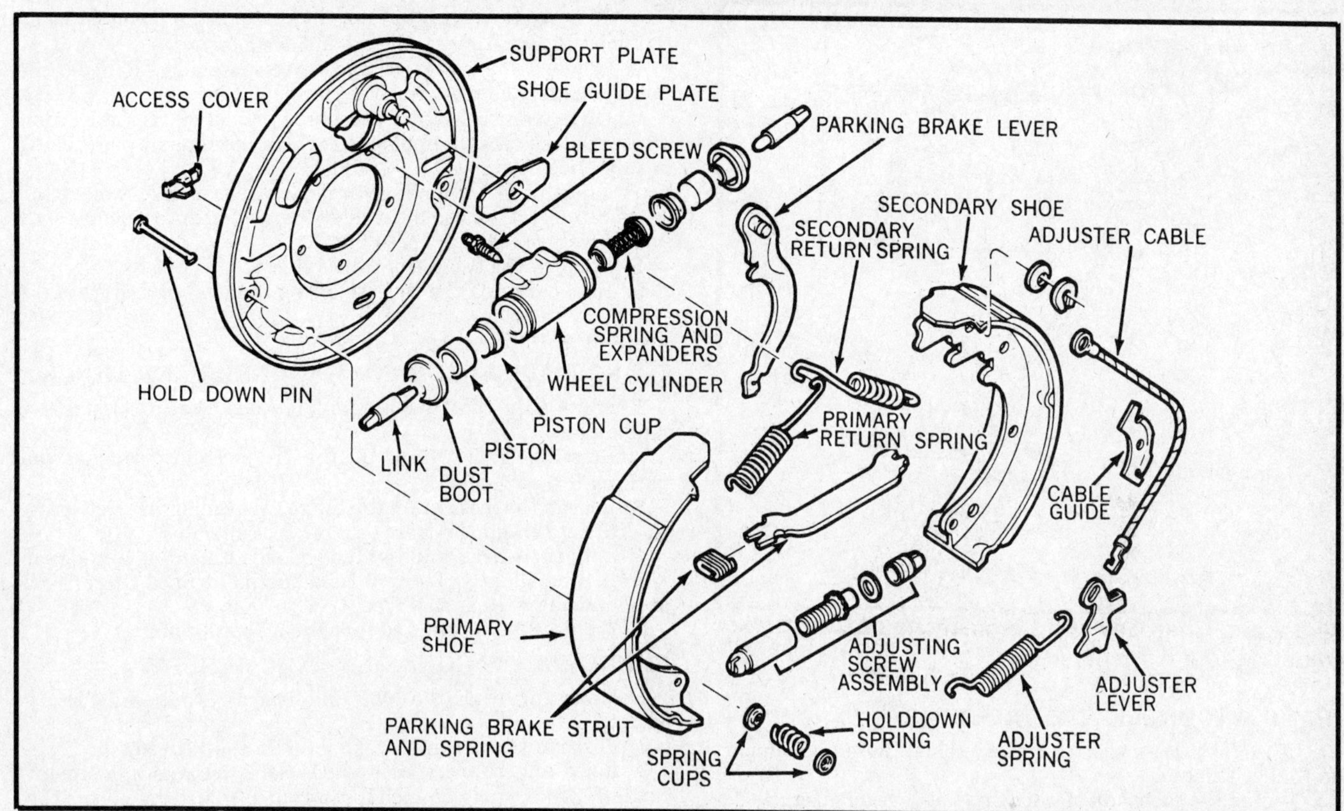

Drum brake assembly—CJ models

Adjustment

1. Remove the under dash trim panel, if equipped. On some vehicles equipped with air condition it may be necessary to remove the screws retaining the evaporator housing to the instrument panel to gain access for service.
2. Hold the brake pedal in the applied position.
3. Push the stop light switch through the mounting bracket until it stops against the brake pedal bracket. Release the pedal to set the switch in the proper position.
4. Check the position of the switch. The switch plunger should be in the ON position and the brake lights should light after a brake pedal travel of 3/8–5/8 in.

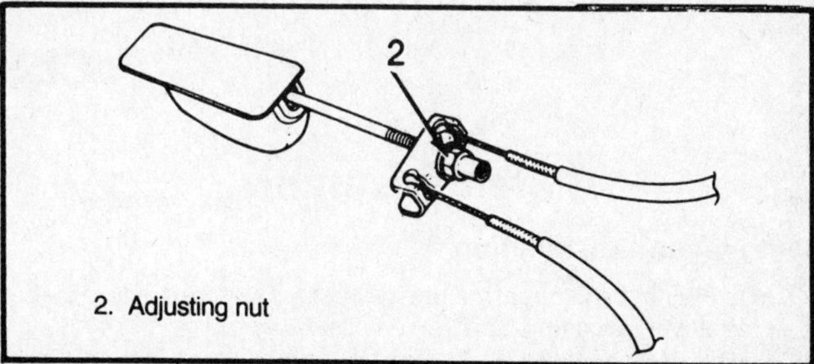

Wagoneer, Cherokee and Commanche parking brake adjusting nut

Parking Brake

FRONT CABLE

Removal and Installation

EXCEPT COMANCHE, WAGONEER AND CHEROKEE

1. Disconnect the negative battery cable. Raise and support the vehicle safely.
2. Remove the equalizer from the front cable. As required, remove the clip retaining the cable to the rear crossmember. Lower the vehicle.
3. Disconnect the front cable return spring at the parking brake lever assembly, if equipped.
4. Roll the carpet back and remove the front cable ferrule to parking brake lever assembly retaining clip.
5. Disengage the cable end from the parking brake lever assembly. Remove the front cable from the vehicle.
6. Installation is the reverse of the removal procedure. As required, adjust the parking brake.

REAR CABLE

Removal and Installation

EXCEPT COMANCHE, WAGONEER, CHEROKEE, GRAND WAGONEER AND TRUCK

1. Disconnect the negative battery cable. Raise and support the vehicle safely.
2. Loosen the cable adjuster nuts at the equalizer. Remove the clamps and cotter pin retaining the rear cable to the equalizer. Remove the cable from the equalizer.
3. Disconnect the rear cable locating spring. Disconnect the cable to frame retaining clip.
4. Remove the rear tire and wheel assembly. Remove the brake drum. Remove the brake linings.
5. Compress the lock tabs that hold the cable in the support plate, using a small hose clamp. Remove the cable from the vehicle.
6. Installation is the reverse of the removal procedure.

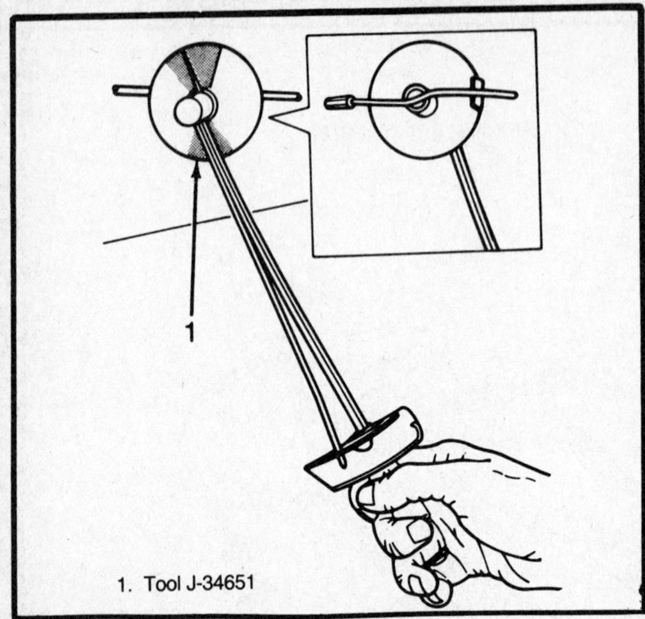

Wagoneer, Cherokee and Commanche parking brake adjusting tool

GRAND WAGONEER AND TRUCK

1. Disconnect the negative battery cable. Raise and support the vehicle safely.
2. Loosen the cable adjuster locknuts at the equalizer. Disengage the cable from the connector attached to the center cable.
3. If the left cable is being removed, the skid tank fuel plate must be removed.
4. Remove the clip retaining the cable in the frame bracket. Unhook the locating spring from the cable.
5. Remove the rear tire and wheel assembly. Remove the brake drum. Remove the brake linings.
6. On all vehicles except those with model 60 rear axle, compress the lock tabs that hold the cable in the support plate, using a small hose clamp.
7. On vehicles equipped with model 60 rear axle, remove the bolts retaining the cable through the plate until the cable lock tabs engage in the support plate.
8. Remove the cable from the vehicle.
9. Installation is the reverse of the removal procedure.

Adjustment

CJ, SCRAMBLER, GRAND WAGONEER AND TRUCK

1. Make sure that the hydraulic brakes are in satisfactory adjustment.
2. Raise the rear wheels off the ground and disengage the parking brake pedal.
3. Loosen the locknut on the brake cable adjusting rod, located directly behind the frame center crossmember.
4. Spin the wheels and tighten the adjustment until the rear wheels drag slightly. Loosen the adjustment until there is no drag and the wheels spin freely.
5. Tighten the locknut to lock the adjusting nut.

CHEROKEE, WAGONEER AND COMANCHE

1. Make sure that the hydraulic brakes are in satisfactory adjustment.
2. Position the parking brake lever in the fifth notch.
3. Raise and support the vehicle safely. Using adjustment gauge J–34651 apply 55 inch lbs. torque . Adjust the nut on the equalizer so that the gauge pointer is in the blue band.
4. Fully apply and release the parking brake lever five times. Recheck the adjustment.

CLUTCH

Clutch Assembly

Removal and Installation

1. Disconnect the negative battery cable. As required, remove the shift lever boot and shift lever assembly.
2. Raise the vehicle and support it safely. Properly support the engine assembly. Remove the transmission. If equipped, remove the transfer case.
3. If equipped, remove the slave cylinder to clutch housing bolts. Disengage the slave cylinder pushrod from the throwout lever and position the assembly out of the way.
4. Remove the starter, as required. Remove the throwout bearing. Unbolt and remove the clutch housing.
5. Mark the position of the clutch pressure plate and remove the pressure plate bolts evenly, a little at a time in rotation. Remove the clutch disc and pressure plate from the vehicle.
6. If equipped with a pilot bushing lubricating wick, remove it from its bore in the crankshaft.
7. Installation is the reverse of the removal procedure. If equipped with a lubricating wick dip it in clean engine oil before installation.

LINKAGE

NOTE: Some vehicles are equipped with a hydraulic clutch which is not adjustable.

1. Lift the pedal up against the stop.
2. Raise and support the vehicle safely. Loosen and release the rod adjuster jam nut.
3. Turn the release rod adjuster in or out to obtain the proper adjustment. Adjust the pedal free play to about one in. Tighten the jam nut.

Master Cylinder

Removal and Installation

1. Disconnect the negative battery cable. Disconnect the hydraulic line at the cylinder. Cap the hydraulic line to prevent dirt from entering.
2. Remove the cotter pin and washer securing the clutch pushrod to the pedal arm.
3. Remove the master cylinder retaining bolts. Remove the master cylinder from the vehicle.
4. Installation is the reverse of the removal procedure.

SLAVE CYLINDER

Removal and Installation

1. Disconnect the negative battery cable. Disconnect the hydraulic line at the cylinder.
2. Remove the bolts attaching the cylinder to the clutch cover housing. On 4–151 CID (2.5L) engine, remove the throwout lever to pushrod retaining spring.
3. Remove the cylinder retaining bolts. Remove the cylinder from the vehicle. Cap the hydraulic line.
4. Installation is the reverse of the removal procedure.

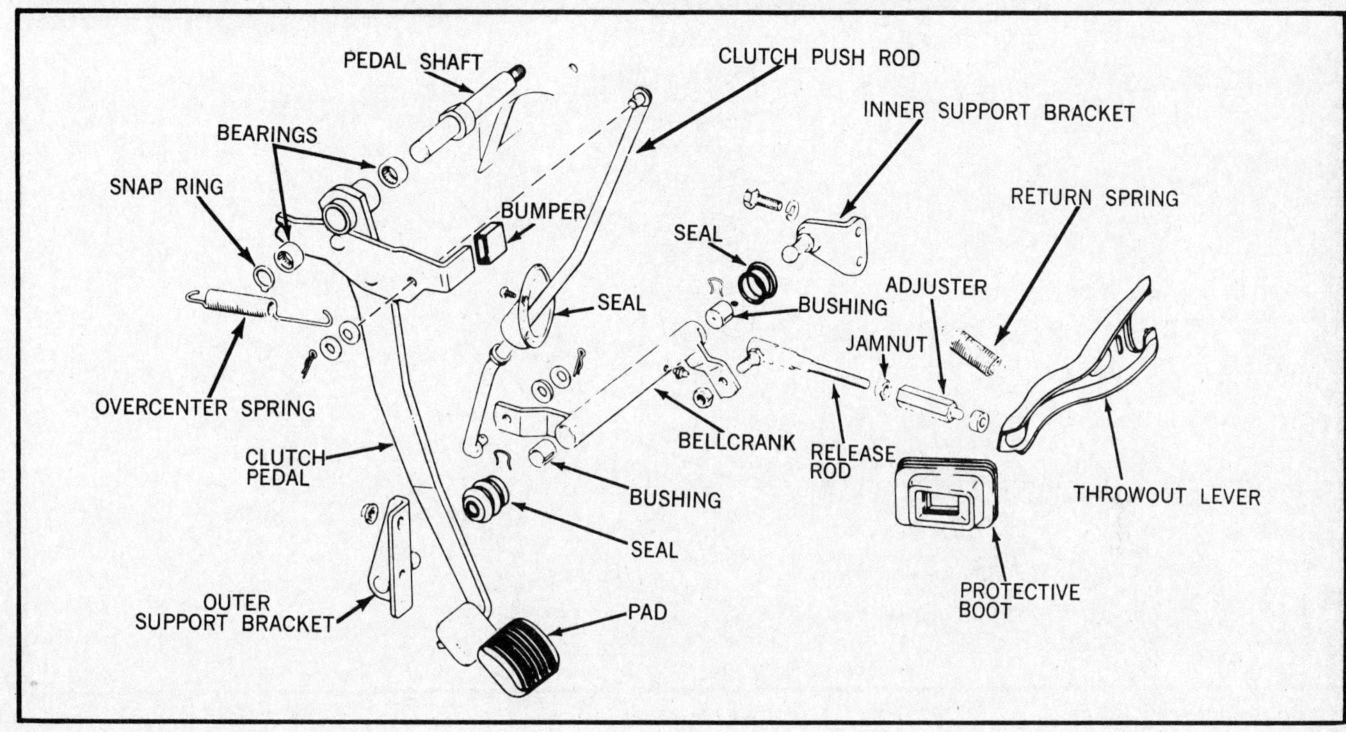

Clutch linkage – CJ model

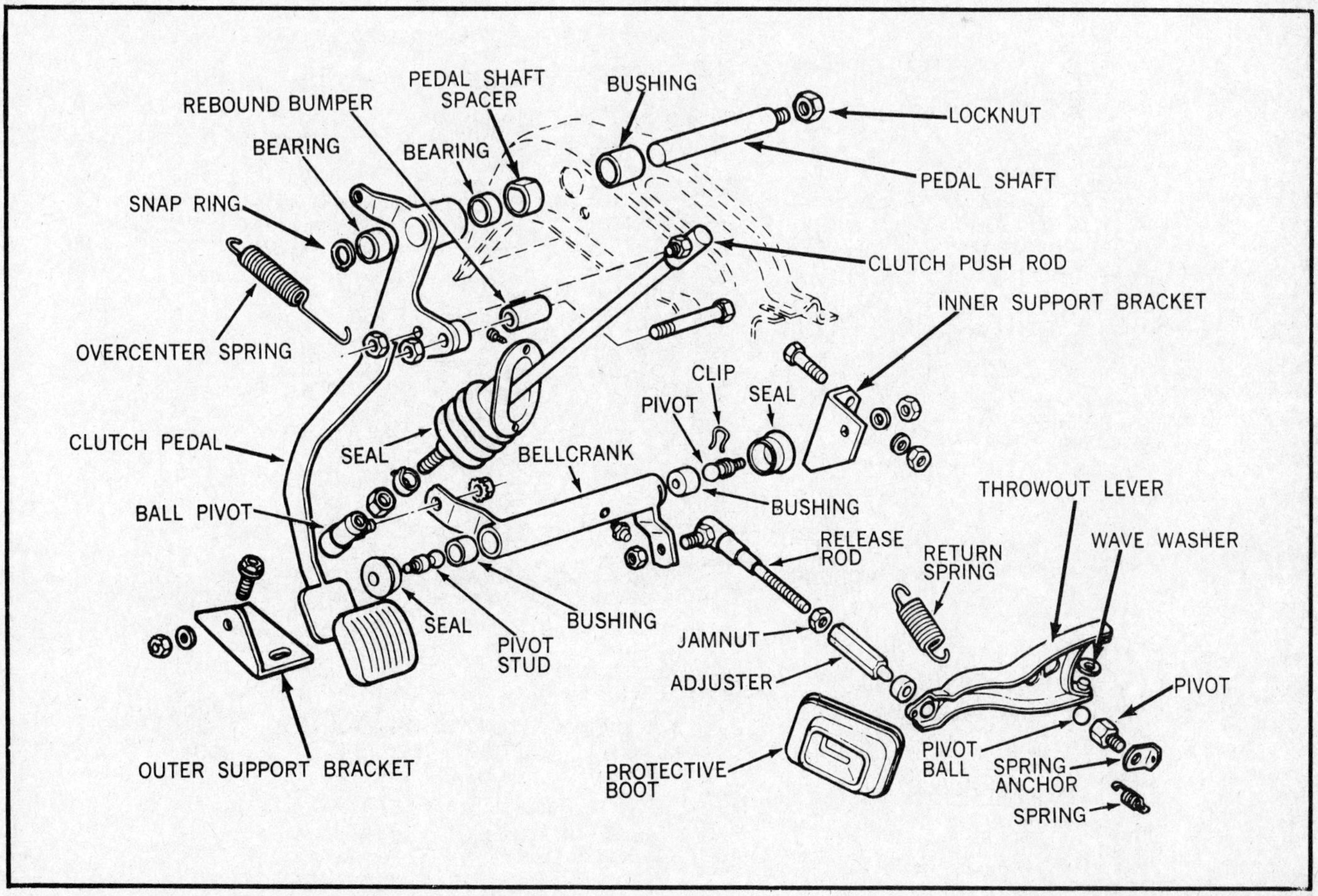

Clutch linkage – Cherokee model

OUTER COVER
RESERVOIR CAP
CAP SEAL
CLUTCH CYLINDER
STEM TIP SEAL
VALVE STEM
SPRING WASHER
SPRING RETAINER
VALVE SPRING
VALVE STEM RETAINER
PLUNGER SEAL
PLUNGER
RETAINING SNAP RING
PUSH ROD
RETAINING WASHER
SEAL
DUST BOOT

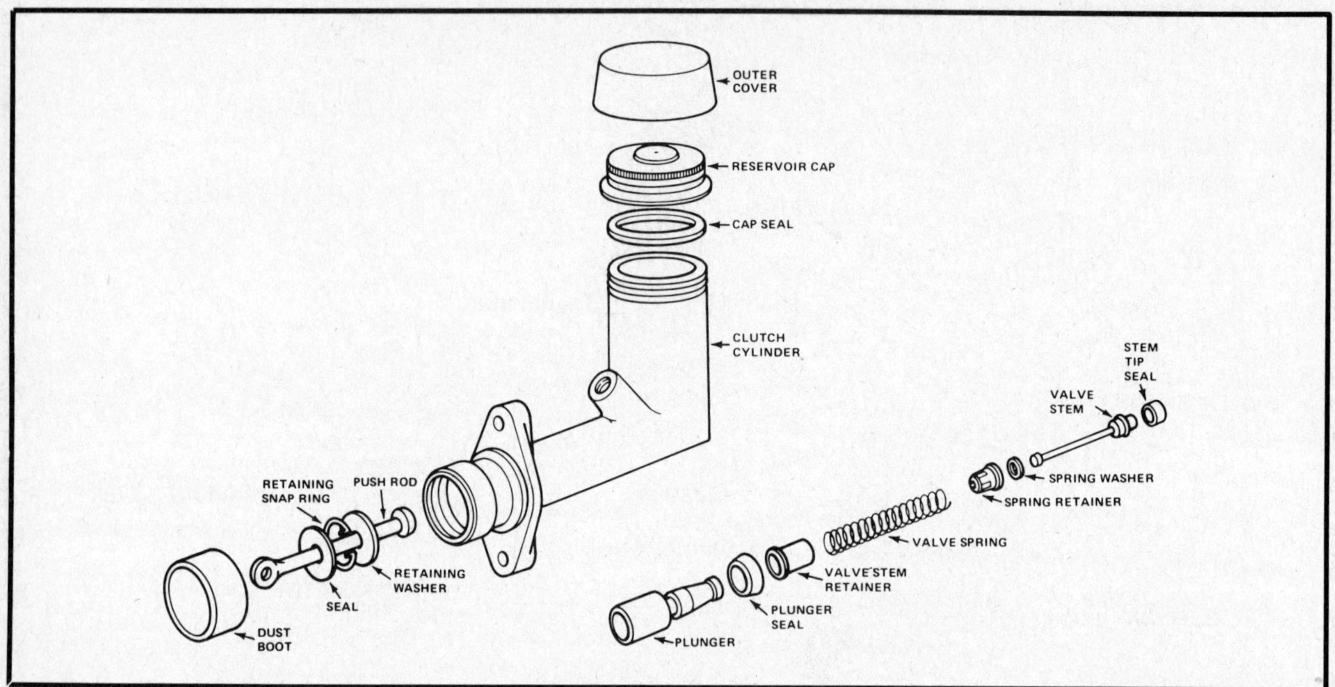

Clutch master cylinder

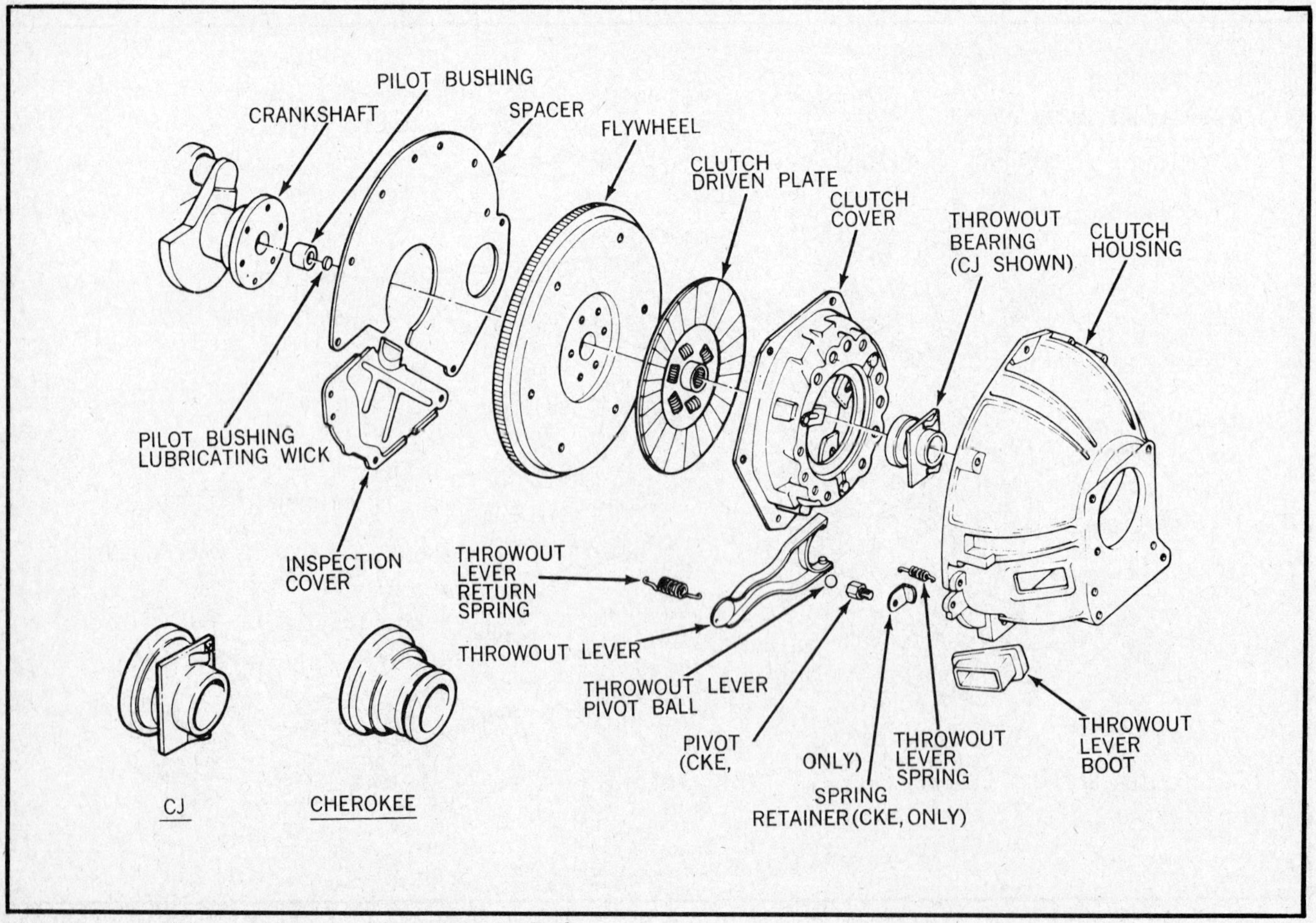

PILOT BUSHING
CRANKSHAFT
SPACER
FLYWHEEL
CLUTCH DRIVEN PLATE
CLUTCH COVER
THROWOUT BEARING (CJ SHOWN)
CLUTCH HOUSING
PILOT BUSHING LUBRICATING WICK
INSPECTION COVER
THROWOUT LEVER RETURN SPRING
THROWOUT LEVER
THROWOUT LEVER PIVOT BALL
PIVOT (CKE, ONLY)
THROWOUT LEVER SPRING
SPRING RETAINER (CKE, ONLY)
THROWOUT LEVER BOOT
CJ
CHEROKEE

Clutch assembly and throw out bearing—typical

MANUAL TRANSMISSION

Refer to the Unit Repair section for overhaul procedures.

Manual Transmission

Removal and Installation

CJ, SCRAMBLER, GRAND WAGONEER AND TRUCK

1. Disconnect the negative battery cable. Remove the shift level knobs, trim rings and bolts.
2. As required, remove the bolts attaching the transmission shift lever housing to the transmission. Remove the lever and the housing.
3. If the vehicle is equipped with the T176 transmission press and turn the transmission shift lever retainer counterclockwise to release the lever. Remove the lever, boot, spring and seat as an assembly.
4. Raise the vehicle and support it safely.
5. Mark the rear propeller shaft and the transfer case yoke for reassembly. Disconnect the rear propeller shaft at the transfer case yoke. Move the shaft aside and secure it out of the way.
6. Support the rear of the engine by placing a support under the clutch housing.
7. Remove the nuts and bolts attaching the rear crossmember to the frame rails and rear support cushion. Remove the rear crossmember from the vehicle.
8. Disconnect the speedometer cable, back-up light switch, four wheel drive indicator switch wire and the transfer case vent hose at the transfer case assembly.
9. Mark the front propeller shaft and the transfer case yoke for reassembly. Disconnect the front propeller shaft from the transfer case yoke. Move the shaft to the side and position it out of the way.
10. On all transmissions except the T176 transmission in the Grand Wagoneer and Truck, remove the transfer case shift lever as follows. Remove the shift lever retaining nut. Remove the cotter pins that retain the shift control link pins in the shift rods and remove the pins. Remove the shifter shaft and disengage the shift lever from the shift control links. Slide the lever upward in the boot in order to move the lever out of the way.
11. If the vehicle is a Grand Wagoneer or Truck equipped with the T176 transmission, remove the cotter pin and washers that connect the link to the shift lever and disconnect the link from the shift lever.
12. Support the transmission and transfer case assembly.
13. Remove the bolts attaching to the clutch housing. Remove the transmission and transfer case assembly. Remove the bolts attaching the transfer case to the transmission and remove the transmission.
14. Installation is the reverse of the removal procedure. Be sure to fill the transmission and transfer case with the proper grade and type lubricant.

CHEROKEE, WAGONEER AND COMANCHE

1. Disconnect the negative battery cable. Raise the shift lever boot and remove the upper part of the console. Remove the lower part of the console.
2. Remove the inner boot. Remove the shift lever using tool J–34635. Raise and support the vehicle safely.
3. Drain the transmission. Drain the transfer case, if equipped. Mark the relation between the rear driveshaft and the transmission output yoke. Remove the driveshaft.
4. If the vehicle is equipped with a transfer case, position a support stand under the transfer case in order to support the weight of both the transmission and the transfer case assembly.
5. If the vehicle is not equipped with a transfer case, position a support under the transmission assembly in order to support the weight of the transmission.
6. Remove the nuts and bolts attaching the rear crossmember to the frame rails and rear support cushion. Remove the rear crossmember. Disconnect the speedometer cable, backup light switch. If equipped, disconnect the transfer case vent hose.
7. Disconnect the transfer case vacuum hoses and linkage. Remove the clutch slave cylinder.
9. If equipped, mark the front propeller shaft and transfer case yoke for reinstallation. Move the shaft aside and secure it out of the way.
10. Properly support the transmission and the transfer case as required. Remove the transmission to engine mounting bolts and move the assembly re¬rward and lower it from the vehicle.
11. If the vehicle is equipped with a transfer case remove the transfer case to transmission retaining bolts and seperate the two units.
12. Installation is the reverse of the removal procedure. Be sure to fill the transmission and transfer case with the proper grade and type lubricant.

WRANGLER

1. Disconnect the negative battery cable. Remove the shift knpb and locknut from the transmission and the transfer case shift levers.
2. Remove the screws retaining the transmission and transfer case shift lever boots. Remove both boots.
3. Remove the transmission shift tower dust boot. Remove the transmission shift lever and stub shaft. Press the stub shaft retainer downward.
4. Rotate the retainer counterclockwise to release it from the lugs in the shift tower. Then lift the retainer, or remove the snapring, stub shaft and shift lever up and out of the shift tower. Do not remove the shift lever from the stub shaft.
5. Raise and support the vehicle safely. Drain the transmission and transfer case lubricant.
6. Matchmark the rear propeller shaft and remove it. Position a suitable stand under the transfer case to support the transmission and transfer case assembly.
7. Remove the rear crossmember retaining bolts. Remove the rear crossmember from the vehicle. Matchmark the front propeller shaft and remove it.
8. Disconnect the speedometer cable. Disconnect the back up light electrical connections. Disconnect the transmission and transfer case vent hoses.
9. Disconnect the master cylinder fluid line from the drivers side of the slave cylinder housing.
10. Position a suitable lifting fixture under the transmission and transfer case assembly. Secure the assembly to the lifting fixture.
11. Remove the bolts that retain the clutch housing to the engine. Remove the transmission and transfer case assembly from the vehicle.
12. Remove the bolts that retain the transmission to the transfer case and seperate the components.
13. Remove the slave cylinder and throwout bearing. Remove the clutch housing from the transmission.
14. Installation is the reverse of the removal procedure. Be sure to fill the transmission and transfer case with the proper grade and type lubricant.

Linkage

Adjustment

The shift lever is connected to the transfer case shift rails through rods and nonadjustable links, therefore external adjustments are not possible.

AUTOMATIC TRANSMISSION

Refer to Chilton's Automatic Transmission Manual for overhaul procedures.

Automatic Transmission

Removal and Installation

CJ, SCRAMBLER, GRAND WAGONEER AND TRUCK

1. Disconnect the negative battery cable. Disconnect the fan shroud, if equipped. Disconnect the transmission oil fill tube top bracket.
2. Raise the vehicle and support it safely. Remove the inspection cover from the lower part of the converter housing.
3. Remove the oil filler tube and dipstick. Remove the starter.
4. Mark the driveshafts and yokes for position. Disconnect the driveshafts from the transfer case yokes. Secure the shafts to the frame with wire so they are out of the way.
5. On V8 engines, disconnect the exhaust pipes at the exhaust manifolds and remove them as required, to gain working clearance. Drain the transfer case lubricant and transmission fluid.
6. Disconnect the speedometer cable, gearshift linkage, throttle linkage and the wires to the neutral safety switch.
7. Mark the converter drive plate and converter for location reference. Remove the bolts that attach the converter to the drive plate.
8. Properly support the transmission and transfer case assembly on a suitable jack. Be sure the transmission assembly is firmly chained or secured for removal.
9. Remove the rear crossmember. Lower the transmission slightly and disconnect the oil cooler lines. Remove the bolts that mount the transmission to the engine.
10. Move the transmission and converter back and away from the engine. Make sure the converter breaks loose from the drive plate and is firmly mounted on the transmission.
11. Hold the converter in position and lower the transmission assembly until the converter housing clears the engine. Remove the transmission and transfer case assembly from the vehicle. Remove the transfer case from the transmission.
12. Installation is in the reverse of the removal procedure. Be sure to line up the marks on the converter and drive plate when reinstalling. Fill the transmission and the transfer case with the proper grade and type fluid.

TWO WHEEL DRIVE
CHEROKEE, WAGONEER AND COMANCHE

1. Disconnect the negative battery cable. Raise and support the vehicle safely.
2. Mark the rear propeller shaft and yoke for reassembly. Disconnect and remove the rear propeller shaft.
3. Remove the torque converter inspection cover. Mark the converter drive plate and converter assembly for reassembly.
4. Remove the bolts attaching the torque converter to the flex plate. Properly support the transmission assembly.
5. Remove the bolts attaching the rear crossmember to the transmission side rail. Disconnect the exhaust pipe at the catalytic converter.
6. Lower the transmission slightly in order to disconnect the fluid cooler lines.
7. Disconnect the backup light switch wire and the speedometer cable. Disconnect the transmission linkage.
8. Remove the bolts attaching the transmission assembly to the engine. Move the transmission assembly and the torque converter rearward to clear the crankshaft.
9. Carefully lower the transmission assembly from the vehicle.
10. Installation is the reverse of the removal procedure.

FOUR WHEEL DRIVE
CHEROKEE, WAGONEER AND COMANCHE

1. Disconnect the negative battery cable. Raise and support the vehicle safely.
2. Mark the rear propeller shaft and yoke for reassembly. Disconnect and remove the rear propeller shaft.
3. Remove the torque converter inspection cover. Mark the converter drive plate and converter assembly for reassembly.
4. Remove the bolts attaching the torque converter to the flex plate. Properly support the transmission assembly.

NOTE: If the vehicle is equipped with a diesel engine, remove the left motor mount and starter in order to gain access to the torque converter drive plate bolts through the starter opening.

5. Remove the bolts attaching the rear crossmember to the transmission side rail. Disconnect the exhaust pipe at the catalytic converter.
6. Lower the transmission slightly in order to disconnect the fluid cooler lines. Mark the front propeller shaft assembly for reinstallation. Disconnect the propeller shaft at the transfer case and secure the assembly out of the way.
7. Disconnect the backup light switch wire and the speedometer cable. Disconnect the transfer case and the transmission linkage. Disconnect the vacuum lines and the vent hose.
8. Remove the bolts attaching the transmission assembly to the engine. Move the transmission assembly and the torque converter rearward to clear the crankshaft.
9. Carefully lower the transmission assembly from the vehicle. Remove the transfer case retaining bolts from the transmission assembly.
10. Installation is the reverse of the removal procedure.

WRANGLER

1. Disconnect the negative battery cable. Remove the fan shroud retaining screws. Disconnect the transmission fill tube upper bracket.
2. Raise and support the vehicle safely. Remove the torque converter cover. Remove the transmission fill tube. As required, remove the starter.
3. Matchmark the front and rear driveshafts and remove them. Disconnect the transmission gearshift and throttle linkage.
4. Disconnect the transfer case vent and vacuum hoses and the neutral safety switch wires.
5. Matchmark the torque converter to drive plate. Remove the torque converter retaining bolts.
6. Support the transmission using the proper equipment. Remove the rear crossmember retaining bolts. Remove the crossmember from the vehicle.
7. Drain the transfer case lubricant. Disconnect the speedometer cable. Disconnect and plug the fluid lines at the transmission assembly. Disconnect the transfer case shift linkage.
8. Properly support the transmission and transfer case assembly. Properly support the engine under the rear main.
9. Remove the transmission to engine block retaining bolts. Carefully remove the transmission and the transfer case from the vehicle.
10. Separate the transmission from the transfer case.
11. Installation is the reverse of the removal procedure. Be sure to fill the transmission and the transfer case with the proper grade and type lubricant.

Shift Linkage

Adjustment

1. Raise and safely support the vehicle.

2. Loosen the shift rod trunnion jamnuts.
3. Remove the lockpin that retains the shift rod trunnion to the bell crank. Disengage the trunnion and shift rod at the bell crank.
4. Place the gear shift lever in the park position and lock the steering column.
5. Move the transmission lever rearward into the park detent. Be sure the lever is as far rearward as it will go.
6. Check the engagement of the park detent by trying to rotate the driveshaft with the rear wheels off of the ground. The shaft will not rotate if the park detent is engaged.
7. Adjust the trunnion until it will fit in the bell crank arm freely. Tighten the jamnuts. Install the lock pin.
8. Check engine starting in park and neutral, be sure it will not start in any other gear.

Band Adjustments

FRONT

Procedure

The front band adjusting screw is located on the left side of the transmission case just above the manual valve and throttle control levers.

1. Raise and safely support the vehicle.
2. Loosen the adjusting screw locknut and back if off five turns.
3. Check the adjusting screw to make sure it turns freely, lubricate it if necessary.
4. Tighten the adjusting screw to 36 inch lbs.
5. Back of the adjusting screw two turns. Tighten the locknut. Do not allow the adjusting screw to turn when tightening the locknut.

REAR

Procedure

1. Raise and safely support the vehicle.
2. Drain the transmission fluid. Remove the transmission oil pan.
3. The adjusting screw is located on the right rear side above the rear side edge of the filter.
4. Loosen the locknut. Tighten the adjusting screw to 41 inch lbs. Back off the adjusting screw four turns on models 904 through 1983 and 7 turns on 904 in 1984 and later vehicles, four turns on 999, and two turns on model 727. Hold the adjusting screw so that it will not turn and tighten the locknut.
5. Install the transmission oil pan using a new gasket.

Throttle Linkage

Adjustment

4–151 CID (2.5L) ENGINE

1. Remove the air cleaner. Remove the spark plug wire holder from the throttle cable bracket and move the holder and wires aside. Raise and support the vehicle safely.
2. Hold the throttle control lever rearward against its stop. Hook one end of a spare spring to the lever and hook the oposite end to any convenient point. This will hold the lever in position.
3. Lower the vehicle. Block the choke open and move the carburetor linkage completely off the fast idle cam.
4. On vehicles without air conditioning, turn the ignition to ON to energize the solenoid.
5. Unlock the throttle control cable by releasing the T shaped adjuster clamp on the cable by lifting it upward, using a suitable tool.
6. Grasp the outer sheath of the cable and move the cable and sheath forward to remove any load on the cable bell crank.
7. Adjust the cable by removing the cable and sheath rearward until there is no play at all between the plastic cable and the bell crank ball.
8. When play has been eliminated, lock the cable by pressing the T shaped clamp downward until it snaps into place.
9. Turn the ignition off. Install all parts and remove the spare spring.

4–150 CID (2.5L) ENGINE WITH CARBURETOR

1. Disconnect the throttle control rod spring at the carburetor.
2. Raise and support the vehicle safely.
3. Use the throttle control rod spring to hold the transmission throttle control lever forward against its stop.
4. Hook one end of a spring on the throttle control lever and the other end of the spring on the throttle linkage bellcrank bracket, which is attached to the torque converter housing.
5. Lower the vehicle. Block the choke in the open position. Set the carburetor throttle off the fast idle cam.
6. Turn the ignition key to the ON position in order to energize the solenoid.
7. Open the throttle halfway to allow the solenoid to lock. Return the carburetor to the idle position.
8. Loosen the retaining bolt on the throttle control adjusting link. Do not remove the spring clip and nylon washer.
9. Pull the end of the link to eliminate lash. Tighten the retaining bolt. Turn the ignition to the OFF position.
10. Raise and support the vehicle safely. Remove the throttle control rod spring from the linkage. Lower the vehicle. Install the spring on the throttle control rod.

4–151 CID (2.5L) ENGINE WITH FUEL INJECTION

NOTE: An idle speed assembly exerciser box is required in order to make this adjustment. The purpose of this special tool is to bypass the idle speed motor.

1. Be sure that the vehicle ignition key is in the OFF position. Raise and support the vehicle safely.
2. Hook one end of a spring on the throttle control lever and the other end of the spring on the throttle linkage bellcrank bracket, which is attached to the torque converter housing. Lower the vehicle.
3. Disconnect the idle speed actuator motor wire harness and connect the idle speed assembly exerciser box. Upon connection, the adjustment light should turn off and the ready light should turn on.
4. Loosen the retaining bolt on the throttle control adjusting link. Pull the end of the link in order to eliminate lash and tighten the link retaining bolt.
5. Press the extend button on the idle speed assembly exerciser box until the idle speed actuator motor ratchets.
6. Disconnect the idle speed assembly exerciser box and reconnect the idle speed actuator motor wiring harness.
7. Raise and safely support the vehicle. Remove the spring from the linkage. Lower the vehicle.

V6–173 CID (2.8L) ENGINE

1. Remove the air cleaner assembly. Raise and support the vehicle safely.
2. Hold the throttle control lever rearward against its stop. Use a spring to hold the lever. Hook one end of the spring to the lever and the other end to a convenient mounting point.
3. Lower the vehicle. Block the choke open and set the carburetor linkage off of the fast idle cam.
4. Unlock the throttle control cable by releasing the T-shaped cable adjuster clamp. Release the clamp by lifting it upward using a suitable tool.
5. Grasp the cable outer sheath and move the cable and sheath forward, this will remove any cable load on the throttle cable bellcrank.

6. Adjust the cable by moving the cable and sheath rearward until there is zero lash between the plastic cable end and the bellcrank ball.

7. When this has been accomplished, lock the cable by pressing the T-shaped adjuster clamp downward.

8. Install the air cleaner assembly. Raise and support the vehicle safely. Remove the spring from its mounting. Lower the vehicle.

6–258 CID (4.2L) ENGINE

1. Disconnect the throttle control rod spring at the carburetor. Raise and support the vehicle safely.

2. Use the throttle control rod spring to hold the throttle control lever forward against its stop, by hooking one end of the spring on the throttle control lever and the other end on the throttle linkage bell crank bracket which is attached to the transmission housing.

3. Block the choke plate open and move the throttle linkage off the fast idle cam.

4. On carburetors equipped with a throttle operated solenoid valve, turn the ignition ON to energize the solenoid, then open the throttle halfway to allow the solenoid to lock and return the carburetor to the idle position.

5. Loosen the retaining bolt on the throttle control adjusting link. Do not remove the spring clip and nylon washer.

6. Pull on the end of the link to eliminate play and tighten the retaining bolt.

7. Remove the throttle control rod spring and install it on the control rod.

V8–360 CID (5.9L) ENGINE

1. Disconnect the throttle control rod spring at the carburetor. Raise and support the vehicle safely.

2. Use the throttle control rod spring to hold the transmission throttle valve control lever against its stop.

3. Block the choke plate open and make sure the throttle linkage is off the fast idle cam.

4. On carburetors equipped with a throttle operated solenoid valve, turn the ignition to ON to energize the solenoid. Then turn the throttle halfway to allow the solenoid to lock and return the carburetor to idle.

5. Loosen the retaining bolt on the throttle control rod adjuster link. Remove the spring clip and move the nylon washer to the rear of the link.

6. Push on the end of the link to eliminate play and tighten the link retaining bolt. Install the nylon washer and spring clip.

8. Remove the throttle control rod spring and install it in its intended position.

Neutral Start Switch

Removal and Installation

1. Raise and support the vehicle safely. Remove the wiring connector from the switch. Test for continuity between the center terminal pin and the transmission case. Continuity should exist only when the transmission control is in park or neutral.

2. If test shows that the switch is defective, check the gearshift linkage adjustment before replacing the switch.

3. Remove the switch from the transmission. A certain amount of fluid will leak out when the switch is removed, have a container ready to catch the fluid.

4. Move the gearshift lever to park and neutral positions. Inspect the switch operating lever fingers and manual lever and shaft for proper alignment with the switch opening in the transmission case.

5. Install a new switch and seal into the transmission case. Tighten to 24 ft. lbs. Test for continuity.

6. Lower the vehicle and correct the transmission fluid level.

Adjustment

The neutral safety switch is located on the side of the transmission by the manual linkage. It is an electrical switch that is thread mounted. The neutral starting section of the switch is contained in the center terminal of the three terminal switch. The other terminals control the backup lights.

Oil Pan

Removal and Installation

1. Raise the vehicle and support it safely.

2. Position a drain pan under the transmission and remove the oil pan bolts, except the four corner ones.

3. Loosen the corner bolts and pry the oil pan loose from the transmission case.

4. Allow the oil to drain from the corners of the oil pan, while tilting the pan to remove as much oil as possible.

5. Carefully remove the corner bolts. Remove the oil pan and gasket from the vehicle.

6. Installation is the reverse of the removal procedure. Fill the transmission assembly with the proper grade and type automatic transmission fluid.

Fluid and Filter

Replacement

1. Raise the vehicle and support it safely.

2. Position a drain pan under the transmission and remove the oil pan bolts, except the four corner ones.

3. Loosen the corner bolts and pry the oil pan loose from the transmission case.

4. Allow the oil to drain from the corners of the oil pan, while tilting the pan to remove as much oil as possible.

5. Carefully remove the corner bolts. Remove the oil pan and gasket from the vehicle.

6. Unbolt and remove the filter assembly.

7. Installation is the reverse of the removal procedure. Be sure to use a new transmission filter. Fill the transmission assembly with the proper grade and type automatic transmission fluid.

TRANSFER CASE

Refer to the Unit Overhaul Section.

Transfer Case

Removal and Installation

MODEL 20

1. Disconnect the negative battery cable. Remove shift lever knob, boot and shift lever.
2. Remove floor covering and remove transmission access cover from floorpan.
3. Drain lubricant from transfer case. On CJ models drain the transmission also.
4. If equipped, disconnect torque reaction bracket from crossmember. Disconnect speedometer at transfer case.
5. On CJ models, place support stand under clutch housing to support engine and transmission, and remove rear crossmember.
6. Disconnect front and rear driveshafts at transfer case, making sure to mark shaft yokes for assembly.
7. On Cherokee and Truck models, disconnect parking brake cable at equalizer and exhaust pipe support bracket at transfer case.
8. Remove bolts attaching transfer case to transmission and remove transfer case from the vehicle. One transfer case attaching bolt must be removed from front end of the case. This bolt is located at the bottom right corner of the transmission.
9. Prior to installation position a new gasket on the transmission. Shift the transfer case into 4WD low and install the case assembly on the guide bolts.
10. Rotate the transfer case output shaft until the transmission main shaft gear engages the rear output shaft gear of the transfer case.
11. Slide the transfer case forward until the two units mate flush. Install one upper bolt, remove the dowel guide bolts and install the remaining bolts. Torque to 30 ft. lbs.
12. Connect the speedometer cable and parking brake cable. Install the propeller shafts after aligning the indexing marks. Fill the unit with gear lube, and lower the vehicle. Install the transfer case shift lever, boot, and knob.

MODEL 207

1. Shift the unit into 4–High. Disconnect the negative battery cable. Raise and support the vehicle safely. Drain the lubricant from the case.
2. Mark the rear axle yoke and driveshaft for reference. Remove the rear driveshaft. Disconnect the speedometer cable, vacuum hoses and vent hose from the case.
3. Raise the transmission and transfer case slightly. Remove the crossmember attaching bolts. Remove the crossmember.
4. Mark the front driveshaft and transfer case flange for reference. Disconnect the front driveshaft from the transfer case.
5. Disconnect the shift lever linkage at the case. Remove the shift lever bracket bolts.
6. Support the transfer case safely. Remove the attaching bolts and lower the case from the vehicle.
7. Installation is the reverse of the removal procedure.

MODEL 208

1. Disconnect the negative battery cable. Raise and safely support the vehicle safely. Drain the lubricant from the transfer case.
2. Disconnect the speedometer cable and indicator switch wires. Disconnect the transfer case shift lever link at the operating lever.Support the rear of the transmission and remove the rear crossmember.
3. Mark the transfer case front and rear output shaft yokes and driveshafts for assembly alignment reference.
4. Disconnect the front and rear driveshafts at the transfer case yokes. Secure the shafts to the frame rails with wires to keep them out of the way.
5. Disconnect the parking brake cable guide from the pivot located on the right frame rail, if necessary.
6. Remove the bolts that attach the exhaust pipe support bracket to transfer case, if necessary.
7. Remove the bolts that attach the transfer case to the transmission. Move the transfer case assembly rearward until it is free of the transmission output shaft. Remove and lower the transfer case.
8. Installation is in the reverse order of removal. Torque the transfer case mounting bolts to 40 ft. lbs.

MODEL 219

1. Disconnect the negative battery cable. Raise and support the vehicle safely.
2. Remove reduction unit on Cherokee, Wagoneer, and Truck models, if equipped.
3. Index the marks on the front and rear yokes and propeller shafts for proper alignment during assembly.
4. Disconnect both the front and rear propeller shafts. On CJ7 models, place support stand under transmission and remove crossmember.
5. Mark the vacuum diaphragm control for identification during the assembly, and then disconnect the vacuum hoses, wiring, and speedometer cable.
6. Disconnect the parking brake cable guide from the pivot on the right frame side.
7. Remove the two front side transfer case to transmission bolts and install a guide bolt into the upper hole. Remove the two rear side bolts, holding the transfer case to the transmission, and install a guide bolt into the upper hole.
8. Move the transfer case rearward until the unit is free of the transmission output shaft and guide pins. Lower the assembly to the floor.
9. Remove all gasket material from the rear of the transmission. Install a new gasket on the rear of the transmission.
10. Install the guide bolts in the upper transmission adapter and transfer case, if they were removed.
11. Raise the transfer case, engage the guide bolts, and move the case assembly forward to the transmission. Make sure a flush fit is achieved.
12. If necessary, rotate the transfer case rear output shaft yoke until the drive hub splines align with the transmission output shaft.

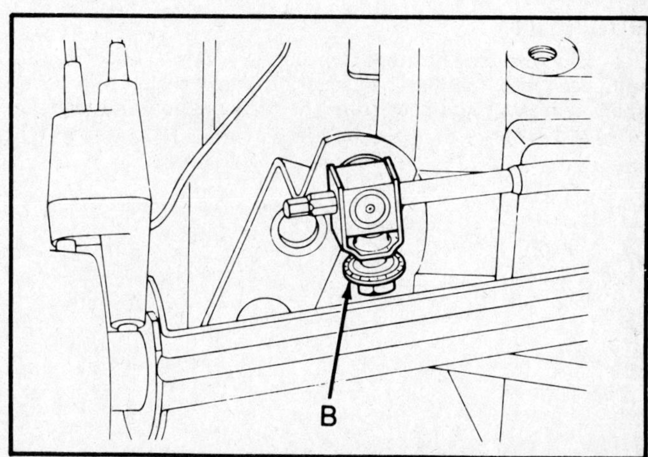

B is the adjusting point on the 229

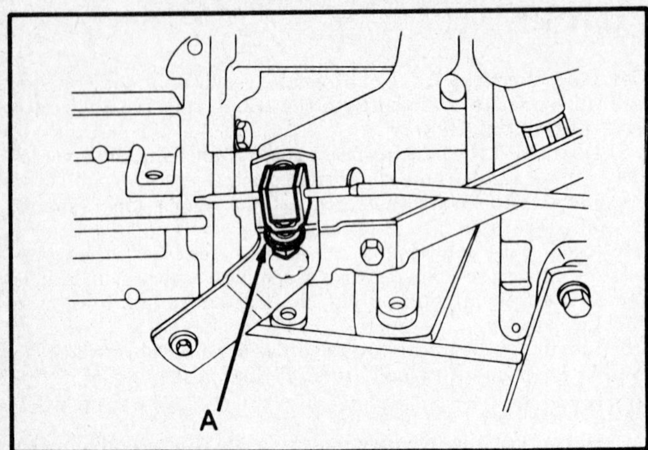

A is the adjusting point on the 207

13. Install front and rear attaching bolts and remove the guide bolts during this operation. Attach the exhaust pipe bracket support, if removed.

14. Align the propeller shaft and indexing marks on the yokes and attach the propeller shafts. Connect the speedometer cable, wiring, and vacuum hoses.

15. Connect the parking brake cable guide to the pivot bracket on the right frame side. Install the specified lubricant, and lower the vehicle.

MODEL 228 AND 229

1. Disconnect the negative battery cable. Raise and support the vehicle safely. Drain the lubricant from the transfer case.
2. Disconnect the speedometer cable and vent hose. Disconnect the transfer case shift lever link at the operating lever.
3. Support the weight of the transmission safely. Remove the rear crossmember.
4. Mark the relation of the front and rear driveshafts with their yokes for reference. Disconnect the front and rear driveshafts at the yokes.
5. Disconnect the shift motor vacuum hoses. Disconnect the transfer case shift linkage.
6. Properly support the transfer case. Remove the transfer case to transmission bolts.Move the transfer case rearward and lower it from the vehicle.
7. Installation is the reverse of removal. Do not install any mounting bolts until all parts are aligned. Make sure that all splined shafts mesh properly before tightening bolts. Torque the transfer case to transmission bolts to 40 ft. lb. and the driveshaft yoke nuts to 10 ft. lb.

MODEL 300

1. Disconnect the negative battery cable. On vehicles equipped with manual transmission remove the shift lever knob, trim ring and boot from the transmission and transfer case shift levers.
2. Remove the floor covering and remove the transmission access cover from the floorpan. Raise and safely support the vehicle. Drain the lubricant from the transfer case.
3. Support the engine and transmission under the clutch bell housing and remove the rear crossmember. Mark the transfer case front and rear yokes and driveshafts for assembly alignment reference.
4. Disconnect the front and rear driveshafts at the transfer case. Secure the shafts out of the way. Disconnect the speedometer cable at the transfer case.
5. Disconnect the parking brake cable at the equalizer and the exhaust pipe support bracket at the transfer case to gain any needed clearance.
6. Remove the bolts mounting the transfer case to the transmission. Remove the transfer case from the vehicle.
7. Installation is in the reverse order of removal. The transfer case should be shifted into the 4L position before installation. Rotate the output shaft yoke until the transmission output shaft gear engages the transfer case input shaft. Torque the mounting bolts to 30 ft. lbs.

Linkage

Adjustment

The shifter rails of the transfer case lever assembly connect to the shifter rails of the transfer case either directly or through nonadjustable links on vehicles with manual transmissions. An adjustable trunnion is provided on the lower shift rod to provide desired adjustment on vehicles equipped with automatic transmission. The linkage should be lubricated periodically.

QUADRA-TRAC®

Since the Quadra-Trac® system is a full time 4WD system, and is constantly engaged in 4WD, there is no shift linkage as such. There are two features which can be operated manually concerning the transfer case, they are the Lock-Out feature and the engagement of the optional Low Range Reduction Unit.

Since the Lock-Out feature is a vacuum actuated unit, there are no external adjustments that can be made other than making sure that all vacuum lines are in place, connected and not damaged in any way.

The Low Range Reduction Unit is actuated by a shift cable and can be adjusted in the following manner.

1. Loosen the nut which clamps the cable to the shift lever pivot. Be sure that the cable can move freely in the pivot.
2. Move the reduction shift lever to the most rearward detent position, the Hi-Range position.
3. Push the Low Range lever inward until it stops. Pull the Low Range lever out slightly, no more than $\frac{1}{16}$ in.
4. Tighten the cable clamp nut at the reduction unit shift lever. This applies to the Quadra-Trac transfer case equipped with a reduction unit.

DRIVE LINES AND UNIVERSAL JOINTS

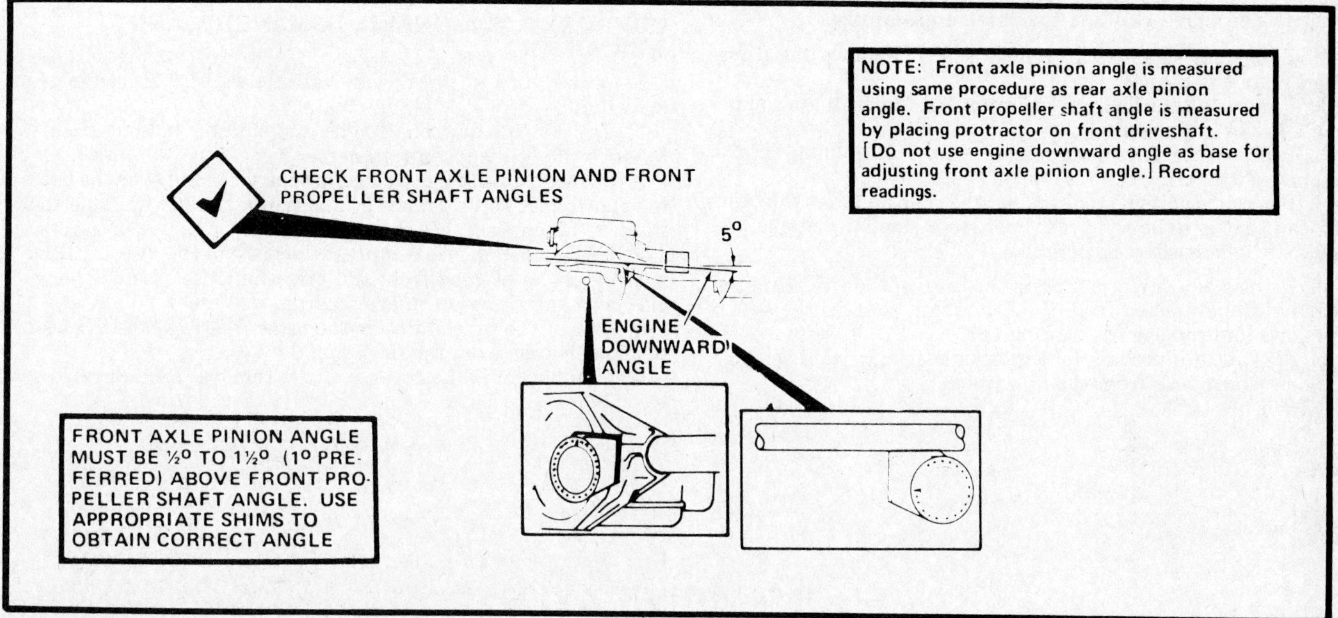

NOTE: Front axle pinion angle is measured using same procedure as rear axle pinion angle. Front propeller shaft angle is measured by placing protractor on front driveshaft. [Do not use engine downward angle as base for adjusting front axle pinion angle.] Record readings.
CHECK FRONT AXLE PINION AND FRONT PROPELLER SHAFT ANGLES
5°
ENGINE DOWNWARD ANGLE
FRONT AXLE PINION ANGLE MUST BE ½° TO 1½° (1° PREFERRED) ABOVE FRONT PROPELLER SHAFT ANGLE. USE APPROPRIATE SHIMS TO OBTAIN CORRECT ANGLE

Checking drive shaft angle and alignment

Drive Lines

FRONT

Removal and Installation

CJ AND SCRAMBLER

1. Raise and support the vehicle safely.
2. Mark the driveshaft yokes, transfer case output shaft yoke and axle yoke for rinstallation
3. Disconnect the driveshaft at the axle. Disconnect the driveshaft at the transfer case. Remove the assembly from the vehicle.
4. Installation is the reverse of the removal procedure.

WAGONEER, CHEROKEE AND COMANCHE

1. Position the transmission selector lever in the neutral position. Raise and support the vehicle safely.
2. Mark the driveshaft yoke and the axle yokes for reinstallation.
3. On Command Trac equipped vehicles, disconnect the driveshaft at the axle. On Selec Trac equipped vehicles, disconnect the driveshaft at the axle and at the transfer case.
4. Remove the driveshaft assembly from the vehicle.
5. Installation is the reverse of the removal procedure.

REAR

Removal and Installation

CJ, SCRAMBLER, GRAND WAGONEER, TRUCK

1. Raise and support the vehicle safely.
2. Mark the driveshaft yokes, transfer case output shaft yoke and axle yoke for rinstallation
3. Disconnect the driveshaft at the axle. Disconnect the driveshaft at the transfer case. Remove the assembly from the vehicle.
4. Installation is the reverse of the removal procedure.

WRANGLER

1. Raise and support the vehicle safely.
2. Mark the driveshaft yoke and the axle yokes for reinstallation.
3. Remove the U-joint clamp strap bolts. Disconnect the driveshaft from the axle yoke. Discard the clamps, do not reuse them.
4. Slide the slip yoke out of the transfer case. Remove the driveshaft from the vehicle.
5. Installation is the reverse of the removal procedure.

Universal Joints

Removal and Installation

CJ, SCRAMBLER, GRAND WAGONEER AND TRUCK WITH SINGLE CARDAN JOINT

1. Raise and support the vehicle safely. Remove the driveshaft from the vehicle.
2. If the slip yoke universal joint is being replaced mark the slip yoke and the driveshaft for reassembly.. Remove the slip yoke from the driveshaft.
3. Remove the loose bearing caps from the spider. Apply penerating oil to the bearing caps seated in the driveshaft yoke.
4. Mount the assembly in a vise. Do not clamp the driveshaft tube in the vise, clamp only the forged portion of the assembly in the vise. Do not overtighten the vise jaws.
5. Remove the bearing cap retainers. Reposition the driveshaft so that the yoke is supported on the jaws of the vise.
6. Tap the end of one bearing cap until the opposite bearing cap is driven out of the yoke.
7. Reposition the assembly in the vise. Tap the exposed end of the spider to drive the remaining bearing cap out of the yoke. Remove the spider from the yoke.
8. Installation is the reverse of the removal procedure.

CJ, SCRAMBLER, GRAND WAGONEER AND TRUCK WITH DOUBLER CARDAN JOINT

NOTE: The socket yoke, ball, spring, needle bearings, retainer and thrust washers are serviced as an assembly. Do not disassemble these components. If any one part is defective replace the entire assembly.

1. Raise and support the vehicle safely. Remove the driveshaft from the vehicle.
2. Remove all the bearing cap retainers. Mark all the components to aid in reassembly.
3. Position the driveshaft yoke in a suitable holding fixture. Remove the bearing cap retainers.
4. Position a suitable tool against the yoke and over the bearing cap that is to be removed. Position a smaller suitable tool against the opposite bearing cap.
5. Using a bench vise compress the jaws, of the vise, until the bearing cap is pressed from the driveshaft. Release the bench vise jaws and remove the bearing cap.
6. Repeat the procedure for the other bearing caps. Disengage the driveshaft yoke from the link yoke.
7. Repeat the above procedure for the other spider assembly. Remove the front spider from the yoke.
8. Installation is the reverse of the removal procedure.

CHEROKEE, WAGONEER, COMANCHE, AND WRANGLER

1. Raise and support the vehicle safely. Remove the driveshaft.
2. Position the driveshaft yoke in a suitable holding fixture. Remove the bearing cap retainers.
3. Position a suitable tool against the yoke and over the bearing cap that is to be removed. Position a smaller suitable tool against the opposite bearing cap.
4. Using a bench vise compress the jaws, of the vise, until the bearing cap is pressed from the driveshaft. Release the bench vise jaws and remove the bearing cap.
5. Repeat the procedure for the other bearing caps. Remove the spider joint from the driveshaft.
6. Installation is the reverse of the removal procedure.

FRONT DRIVE AXLE

Refer to the Unit Overhaul Section.

Locking Hubs

The front drive hubs that are used on the CJ, Scrambler, Grand Wagoneer and Truck are serviced as either a complete assembly or a sub assembly, such as the hub body or hub clutch assembly. Do not attempt to disassemble these units. If the entire hub assembly or subassembly has to be replaced it must be replaced as a complete unit.

Removal and Installation

CJ AND SCRAMBLER

1. Remove the bolts and the tabbed lockwashers that attach the hub body to the axle hub. Save the bolts and the washer.
2. Remove the hub body and gasket. Discard the gasket. Do not turn the hub control dial once the hub body has been removed.
3. Remove the retaining ring from the axle shaft. Remove the hub clutch and bearing assembly.
4. Clean and inspect the components for wear and damage. Replace defective components as required.
5. Installation is the reverse of the removal procedure.
6. Turn the control hub dials to the 4X2 position and rotate the wheels. They should rotate freely, if not check the hub installation. Be sure that the controls are in the fully engaged position.

GRAND WAGONEER AND TRUCK

1. Remove the socket head screws from the hub body assembly. Remove the large retaining ring from the axle hub. Remove the small retaining ring from the axle shaft.
2. Remove the hub and clutch assembly. Clean and inspect the components for wear and damage. Replace defective components as required.
3. Installation is the reverse of the removal procedure.
4. Turn both controls to the FREE position and rotate the wheels. They must rotate freely, if they drag check the hub installation. Be sure that the control dials are in the fully engaged position.

Axle Shaft

Removal and Installation

CJ AND SCRAMBLER

1. Raise and support the vehicle safely. Remove the disc brake caliper.

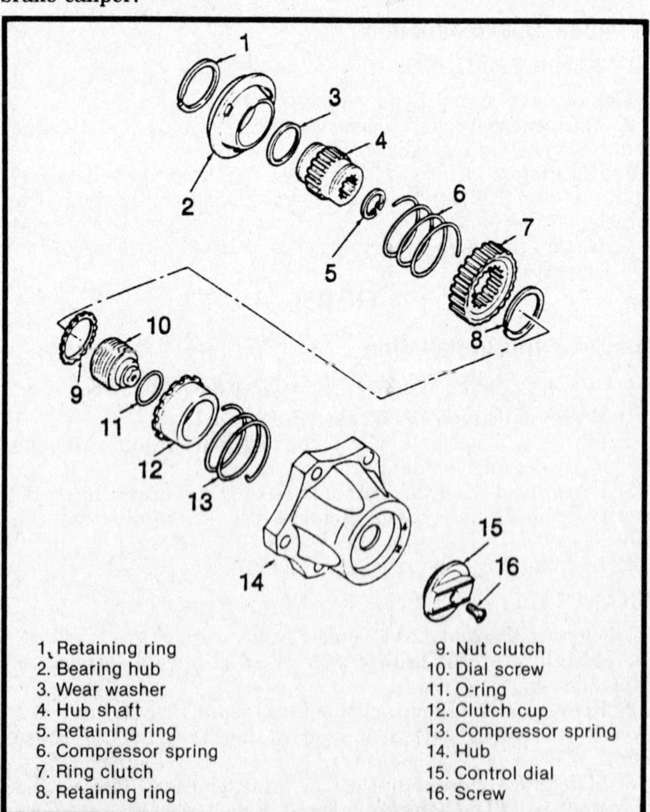

Front drive hubs—CJ and Scrambler

2. Remove the bolts that retain the front hub to the axle. Remove the hub body and gasket.
3. Remove the retaining ring from the axle shaft. Remove the hub clutch and bearing assembly from the axle. Straighten the lip of the lock washer.
4. Using tool J-25103 remove the outer locknut, lock washer, inner locknut and tabbed washer.
5. Remove the outer bearing. Remove the disc brake rotor. Remove the disc brake caliper adapter and splash shield.
6. Remove the axle spindle. Remove the axle shaft and the universal joint assembly from the vehicle.
7. Installation is the reverse of the removal procedure.

GRAND WAGONEER AND TRUCK

1. Raise and support the vehicle safely. Remove the disc brake caliper.
2. On vehicles without front hubs, remove the rotor hub cap. Remove the axle shaft snapring, drive gear, pressure spring and spring retainer.
3. On vehicles with front hubs, Remove the socket head screws from the hub body. Remove the body and the large retaining ring. Remove the small retaining ring from the axle shaft. Remove the hub clutch assembly from the axle.
4. Using tool J-6893-03, remove the outer locknut, washer and inner locknut. Remove the rotor, along with the spring retainer and outer bearing.
5. Remove the nuts and bolts that retain the spindle and support shield. Remove both components. Remove the axle shaft from the vehicle.
6. Installation is the reverse of the removal procedure. Adjust the wheel bearings, as required.

WRANGLER, WAGONEER, CHEROKEE AND COMANCHE

1. Raise and support the vehicle safely. Remove the wheel and tire assembly. Remove the brake caliper and rotor.
2. Remove the cotter pin, nutlock and axle hub nut. Remove the hub to knuckle retaining bolts.
3. Remove the hub assembly and splash shield from the steering knuckle. Remove the left side axle shaft from the vehicle.
4. Disconnect the vacuum harness from the shift motor. Remove the shift motor housing and the shift motor from the axle.
5. Remove the right side axle shaft from the vehicle.
6. Installation is the reverse of the removal procedure.

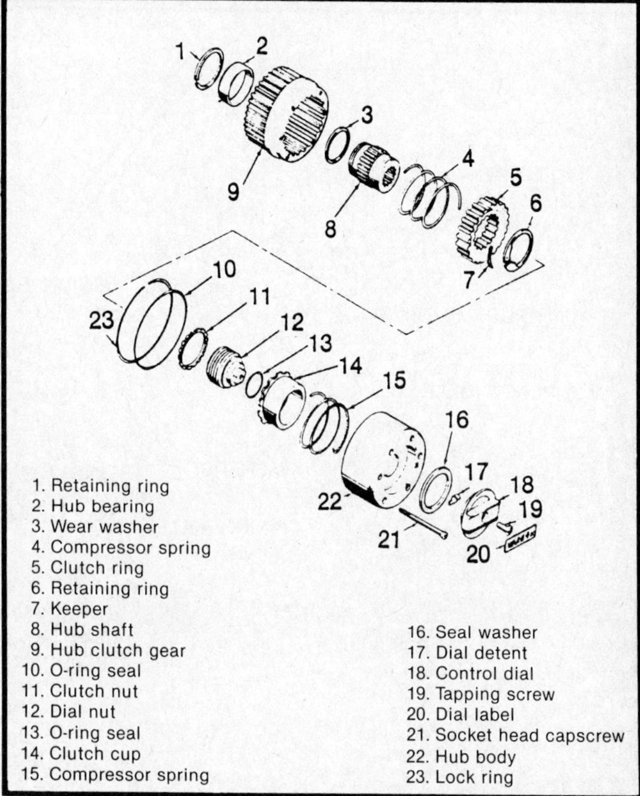

Front drive hubs – Grand Wagoneer and Truck

Axle Shaft Seal

Removal and Installation

CJ, SCRAMBLER, GRAND WAGONEER AND TRUCK

1. .Raise and support the vehicle safely. Remove the axle shaft from the vehicle.
2. Remove the seal from the axle shaft. Remove the bronze thrust washer. Replace the washer, as required.
3. Install the washer with the chamfered side toward the axle shaft seal. Install the axle seal with the seal lip facing the spindle.
4. Pack wheel bearing lubricant around the thrust face of the shaft and seal. Fill the area of the spindle with wheel bearing lubricant.
5. Install the axle shaft.

Differential Carrier

Removal and Installation

CJ, SCRAMBLER GRAND WAGONEER AND TRUCK

1. Raise and support the vehicle safely. Drain the lubricant. Remove the axle shafts.
2. Lower the right spring. Remove the front shock absorber at the tie plate. Remove the stabilizer bar connecting link to the tie plate retaining nut. Remove the U-bolts and the tie plate.
3. Loosen the nuts retaining the rear spring shackle to the spring. Properly support the axle housing.
4. Remove the bolts retaining the spring shackle to the spring. Lower the spring.
5. Remove the axle housing cover. Mark the differential bearing caps for alignment during the assembly. Loosen the bearing cap bolts but do not remove.
6. Install an axle housing spreader tool on the axle housing and secure with the holddown clamps. Mount a dial indicator on the axle housing to measure the amount of spread. Zero the indicator dial.
7. Spread the axle housing no more than 0.020 in. Remove the differential bearing caps and the dial indicator from the housing. Using two pry bars, remove the differential carrier from the axle housing.
8. Remove the spreader tool from the housing as soon as the differential carrier is removed to avoid the possibility of the axle housing taking a set.
9. To install, position the axle housing spreader tool on the axle housing and secure it in place with the holddown clamps. Install a dial indicator and center the dial.
10. Spread the axle housing to a maximum of 0.020 in.. Remove the dial indicator. Lubricate the differential side bearings and install the differential carrier in the axle housing.
11. Complete the assembly in the reverse of the removal procedure.

WRANGLER, CHEROKEE AND WAGONEER

1. Raise and support the vehicle safely. Remove the axle housing cover. Drain the lubricant.
2. Mark the propeller shaft and the axle yoke for reassembly. Remove the propeller shaft from the vehicle.
3. Remove the tire and wheel assembly. Remove the calipers, rotors, hubs, shift motor and housing. Remove the axle shafts.

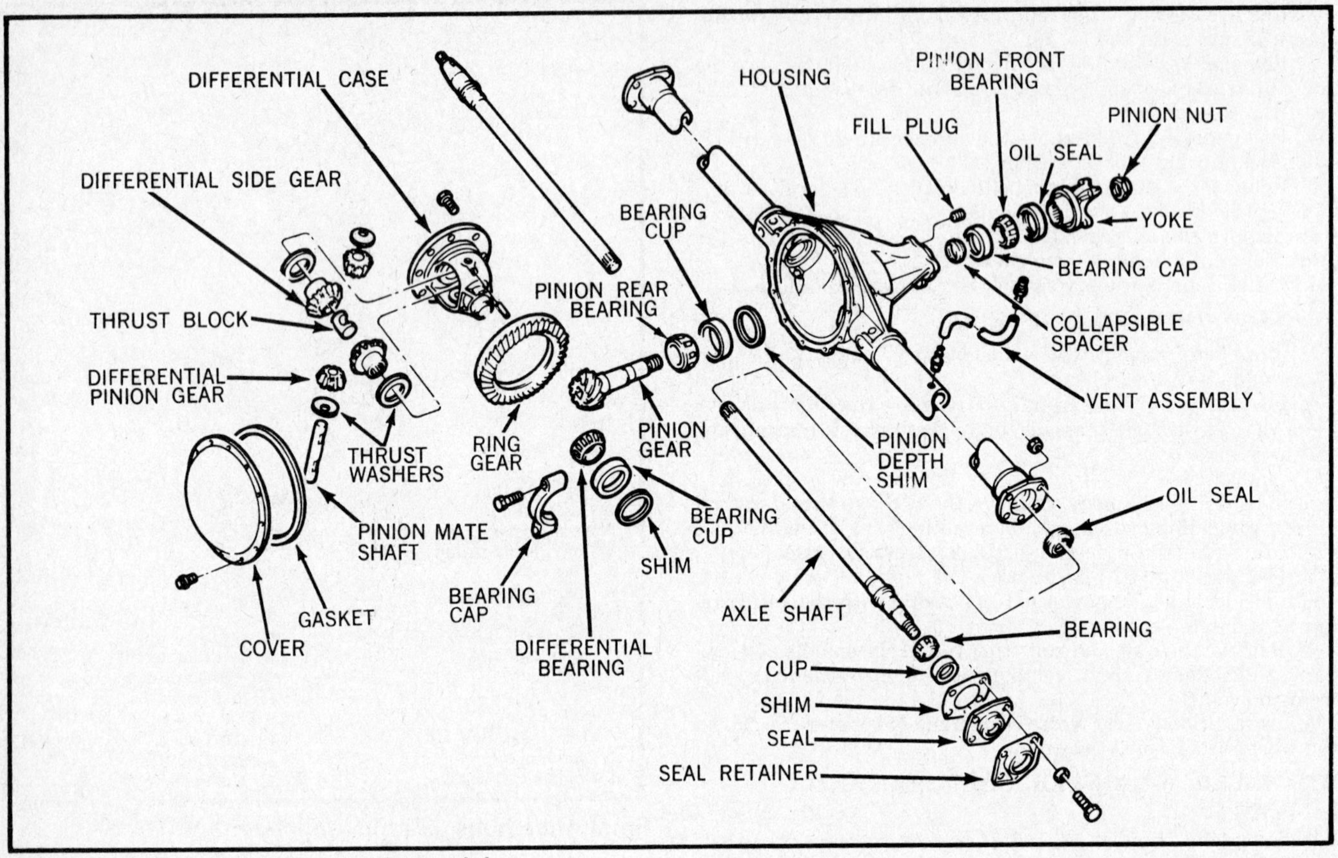

Tapered shaft axle assembly—CJ model

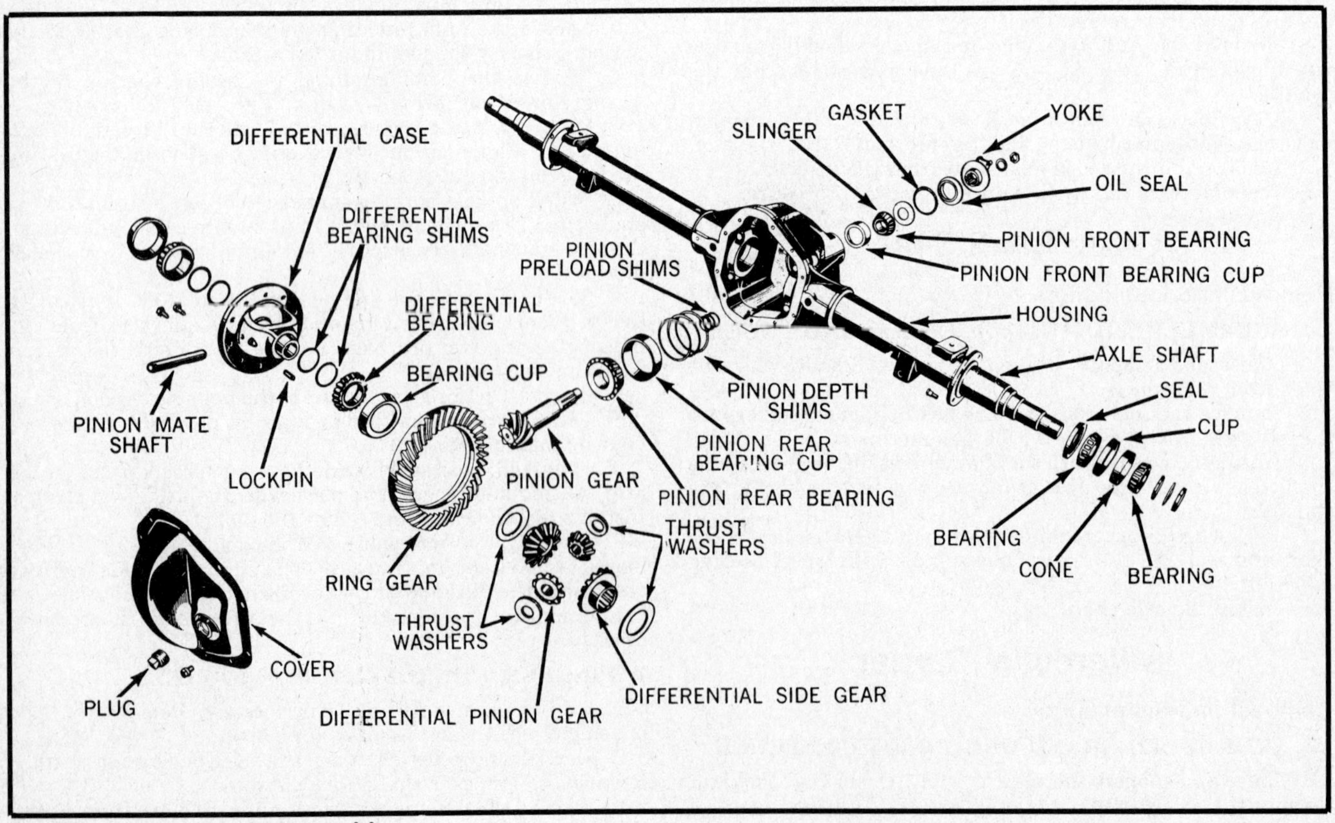

Full Floating rear axle assembly

4. Remove the intermediate shaft retaining clip. Disengage the shaft from the differential.
5. Mark the differential bearing caps for alignment during the assembly. Loosen the bearing cap bolts but do not remove.
6. Disconnect the tie rod from the left steering knuckle. Disconnect the track bar from the frame rail bracket.
7. Install an axle housing spreader tool on the axle housing and secure with the holddown clamps. Mount a dial indicator on the axle housing to measure the amount of spread. Zero the indicator dial.
8. Spread the axle housing no more than 0.010 in for Wrangler and 0.020 in for Cherokee and Wagoneer. Remove the differential bearing caps and the dial indicator from the housing. Using two pry bars, remove the differential carrier from the axle housing.
9. Remove the spreader tool from the housing as soon as the differential carrier is removed to avoid the possibility of the axle housing taking a set.
10. To install, position the axle housing spreader tool on the axle housing and secure it in place with the holddown clamps. Install a dial indicator and center the dial.
11. Complete the assembly in the reverse of the removal procedure.

Axle Shaft Bearings

Removal and Installation

CJ, SCRAMBLER, GRAND WAGONEER AND TRUCK

1. Raise and support the vehicle safely. Remove the spindle assembly.
2. The roller bearing is located in the spindle flange bore. Use the proper bearing removal tool to remove the needle bearing from the spindle bore.
3. Installation is the reverse of the removal procedure.

Steering Knuckle

Removal and Installation

CJ, SCRAMBLER, GRAND WAGONEER AND TRUCK

1. Raise and support the vehicle safely. Remove the axle shaft.
2. Disconnect the tie rod end at the steering knuckle arm. Remove the lower ball joint jamnut. Discard the jamnut.
3. Remove the cotter pin from the upper ball joint. Loosen the stud nut until the top edge of the nut is flush with the top of the stud.

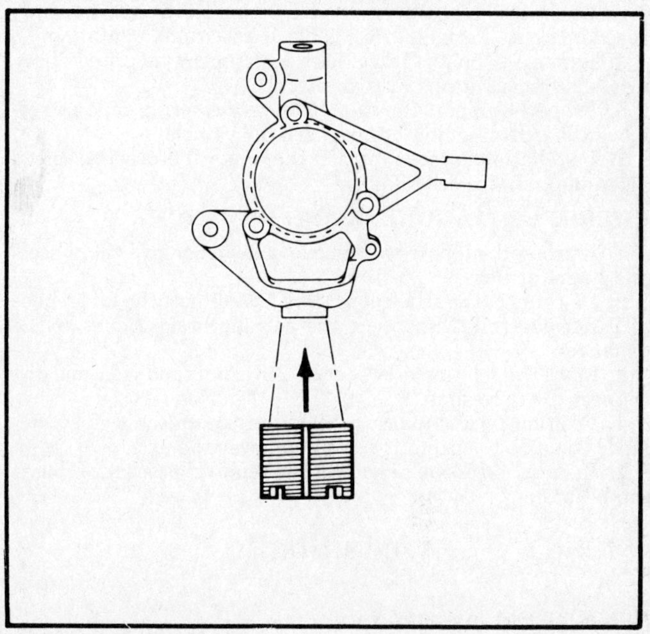

Split retaining ring

4. Using the proper tool, unseat the upper and lower ball joints. Remove the upper ball joint and steering knuckle from the vehicle.
5. Using tool J-23447, remove the upper ball joint split ring seat from the knuckle assembly.
6. Installation is the reverse of the removal procedure.

WRANGLER, CHEROKEE AND WAGONEER

1. Raise and support the vehicle safely. Remove the axle shaft. Remove the caliper anchor plate from the steering knuckle.
2. Remove the knuckle to ball joint cotter pins and retaining nuts. Tap the knuckle using a brass hammer and remove it from the vehicle.
3. Using tool J-23447, remove the split ring seat from the knuckle assembly.
4. Installation is the reverse of the removal procedure.
5. Using tool J-23447, install the split ring seat to a depth of 0.206 in. in the bottom ball joint bore of the steering knuckle assembly.

REAR DRIVE AXLE

Refer to the Unit Overhaul Section.

Axle Housing

Removal and Installation

CJ AND SCRAMBLER

1. Remove the cotter pins from the axle shaft nuts. Remove the axle shaft nuts. Raise the vehicle and support it safely.
2. Remove the rear wheels. Remove the brake drum retaining screws. Remove the brake drums.
3. Remove the axle hub using tool J–25109–01 or equivalent. Disconnect the brake lines at the wheel cylinders. Remove the support plates, oil seals and retainers and the end play shims. Axle shaft end play shims are installed on the left side of the axle only.
4. Remove the axle shafts using tool J–2498 or equivalent. Drain the lubricant and remove the axle housing cover. Disconnect the parking brake cables at the equalizer.
5. Mark the propeller shaft for reinstallation. Disconnect the shaft at the axle yoke.
6. Disconnect the flexible brake hose at the body floorpan bracket. Disconnect the vent hose at the axle tube.
7. Properly support the rear axle assembly. Remove the spring U-bolts, spring plates and spring clip plate, if the vehicle is equipped with a stabilizer bar.
8. Remove the rear axle from the vehicle.
9. Installation is the reverse of the removal procedure.

WRANGLER, GRAND WAGONEER AND TRUCK

1. Raise the vehicle and support it safely. Remove the rear wheels.
2. Place an indexing mark on the rear yoke and propeller shaft, and disconnect the shaft. If equipped, disconnect the track bar at the axle bracket and the vent tube at the axle.
3. Disconnect the shock absorbers from the axle tubes. Dis-

connect the brake hose from the tee fitting on the axle housing. Disconnect the parking brake cable at the frame mounting.

4. Remove U-bolts. On vehicles with spring mounted above axle, disconnect spring at rear shackle.
5. Properly support the axle. Remove the spring clips and remove the axle assembly from under the vehicle.
6. Installation is the reverse of the removal procedure. Bleed and adjust brakes accordingly.

CHEROKEE, WAGONEER AND COMANCHE

1. Raise and support the vehicle safely. Remove the wheels and brake drums.
2. Disconnect the shock absorbers. Disconnect the brake hose at the frame rail. Disconnect the parking brake cables at the equalizer.
3. Mark the relation between the driveshaft and yoke and disconnect the driveshaft.
4. Position a jack under the axle to take up the weight. Remove the axle to spring U-bolts and lower the axle.
5. Installation is the reverse of the removal procedure. Bleed the brakes.

Axle Shaft

Removal and Installation

CJ AND SCRAMBLER

1. Remove the cotter pins from the axle shaft nuts. Remove the axle shaft nuts. Raise the vehicle and support it safely.
2. Remove the rear wheels. Remove the brake drum retaining screws. Remove the brake drums.
3. Remove the axle hub using tool J–25109–01 or equivalent. Disconnect the brake lines at the wheel cylinders. Remove the support plates, oil seals and retainers and the end play shims. Axle shaft end play shims are installed on the left side of the axle only.
4. Remove the axle shafts using tool J–2498 or equivalent.
5. Installation is the reverse of the removal procedure. On vehicles equipped with a Trac Loc differential, do not rotate the differential gears unless both axles are in position. If one shaft is removed and the other shaft rotated, the side gear splines will become misaligned and prevent installation of the replacement shaft.

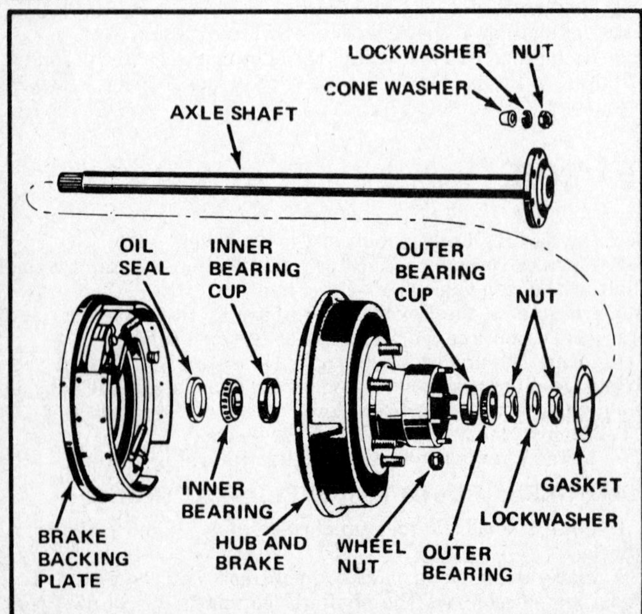

Axle shaft and wheel attaching parts—full floating axle

WRANGLER, GRAND WAGONEER, TRUCK EXCEPT FULL FLOATING AXLE SHAFT

1. Raise and support the vehicle safely. Remove the wheels. Remove the brake drum.
2. Remove the nuts attaching the support plate and retainer to the axle tube flange using the access hole in the axle shaft flange.
3. Position adapter tool J–21579, or equivalent and a slide hammer on the axle shaft flange. Remove the axle shaft from the rear axle assembly.
4. If the cup portion of the wheel bearing assembly remains in the axle assembly, remove it using tool J–2619–01 or J–26941.
5. Installation is the reverse of the removal procedure.

GRAND WAGONEER, TRUCK WITH FULL FLOATING AXLE SHAFT

It is not necessary to raise the rear wheels in order to remove the rear axle shaft on full floating rear axles.

1. Remove the axle flange nuts, lock washers and split washers retaining the axle shaft flange.
2. Remove the axle shaft from the axle housing.
3. Clean the axle flange mating area on the hub and axle, removing all old gasket material.
4. Install a new flange gasket onto the hub studs.
5. Insert the axle shaft into the housing. It may be necessary to rotate the axle shaft to align the shaft splines with the differential gear splines and the flange attaching holes with the hub studs.
6. Install the split washers, lockwashers and flange nuts. Tighten the nuts securely.

WAGONEER, CHEROKEE AND COMANCHE

1. Raise and support the vehicle safely.
2. Remove the wheel, brake drum and brake support retaining nuts.
3. Pull the axle with a slide hammer.
4. Installation is the reverse of removal. Clean the bore in the axle housing and apply a thin coat of grease to the outer diameter of the bearing cup. Tighten the brake support nuts alternately and evenly to seat the bearing cup rib ring.

Pinion Seal

Removal and Installation

SEMI-FLOATING AXLE WITH TAPERED SHAFT

1. Raise and support the vehicle safely. Remove the rear wheels and brake drums. Mark the driveshaft and yoke for reassembly and disconnect the driveshaft from the rear yoke.

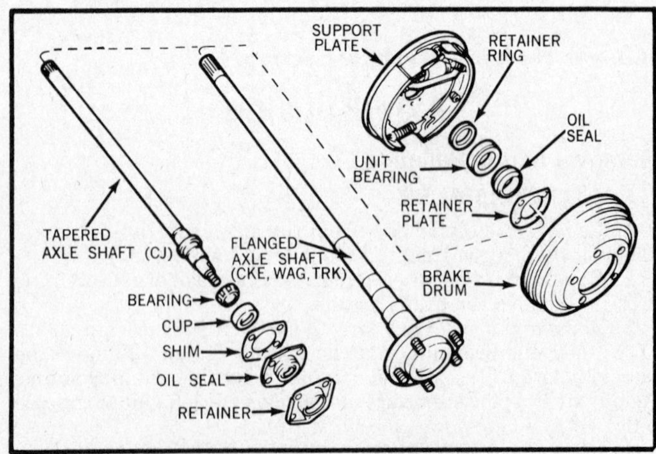

Typical flanged and tapered assemblies

2. With a socket on the pinion nut and an in. lb. torque wrench, rotate the drive pinion several revolutions. Check and record the torque required to turn the drive pinion.

3. Remove the pinion nut. Use a flange holding tool to hold the flange while removing the pinion nut. Discard the pinion nut.

4. Mark the yoke and the drive pinion shaft for reassembly reference. Remove the rear yoke with a puller.

5. Inspect the seal surface of the yoke and replace it with a new one if the seal surface is pitted, grooved, or otherwise damaged.

6. Remove the pinion oil seal. Before installing the new seal, coat the lip of the seal with rear axle lubricant.

7. Install the seal, driving it into place with the proper driving tool. Install the yoke on the pinion shaft. Align the marks made on the pinion shaft and yoke during disassembly.

8. Install a new pinion nut. Tighten nut until endplay is removed from the pinion bearing. Do not overtighten.

9. Check the torque required to turn the drive pinion. The pinion must be turned several revolutions to obatin an accurate reading.

10. Tighten the pinion nut to obtain the torque reading observed during disassembly (Step 3) plus 5 inch lbs. Tighten the nut minutely each time, to avoid overtightening. Do not loosen and then retighten the nut.

11. If the desired torque is exceeded, a new collapsible pinion spacer sleeve must be installed and the pinion gear preload reset. Refer to the Unit Repair section and Overhaul procedures for this operation.

12. Install the driveshaft, aligning the index marks made during disassembly. Install the rear brake drums and wheels.

SEMI-FLOATING AND FULL-FLOATING AXLES WITH FLANGE SHAFT

1. Raise and support the vehicle safely. Mark the driveshaft and yoke for reference during assembly and disconnect the driveshaft at the yoke.

2. Remove the pinion shaft nut and washer. Remove the yoke from the pinion shaft, using a puller. Remove the pinion shaft oil seal. Install the new seal with a suitable driver.

4. Install the pinion shaft washer and nut. Tighten the nut to 210 ft. lbs. on the semi-floating axles and 260 ft. lbs. on the full-floating axles.

5. Align the index marks on the driveshaft and yoke and install the driveshaft. Tighten the attaching bolts or nuts to 16 ft. lbs.

6. Remove the supports and lower the vehicle.

Axle Shaft Seal

Removal and Installation

1. Raise and support the vehicle safely. Remove the axle shaft and bearing assembly.

2. Remove the outer seal and the guide plate from the shaft. Remove the inner seal from the bore in the axle flange.

3. To install lubricate the replacement seal with wheel bearing lubricant. Using tool J-9431 install the inner seal.

4. Install the replacement guide plate and the seal on the shaft. Install the original seal retainer and the outer seal on the shaft.

5. Install the wheel bearing and a replacement bearing retainer ring on the shaft.

6. Properly install the axle shaft.

Differential Carrier

Removal and Installation

1. Raise the vehicle and support it safely. Remove the wheels and drums. Remove the axle shafts.

2. Drain the axle housing lubricant. Remove the axle housing cover. Mark the differential bearing caps for alignment during the assembly. Loosen the bearing cap bolts but do not remove.

3. Install an axle housing spreader tool on the axle housing and secure with the holddown clamps. Mount a dial indicator on the axle housing to measure the amount of spread. Zero the indicator dial.

4. Spread the axle housing no more than 0.020 in. Remove the differential bearing caps and the dial indicator from the housing. Using two pry bars, remove the differential carrier from the axle housing.

5. Remove the spreader tool from the housing as soon as the differential carrier is removed to avoid the possibility of the axle housing taking a set.

6. To install, position the axle housing spreader tool on the axle housing and secure it in place with the holddown clamps. Install a dial indicator and center the dial.

7. Spread the axle housing to a maximum of 0.020 in.. Remove the dial indicator. Lubricate the differential side bearings and install the differential carrier in the axle housing.

8. Prior shim fitting and bearing preload should be accomplished before differential carrier installation. Tap the unit in place with a soft faced hammer. Remove the axle housing spreader tool.

9. Install the bearing caps in their proper place and torque to 40 ft. lbs. on model 30 rear axle and to 80 ft. lbs. on models 44 and 60.

10. Install a dial indicator and recheck the ring gear backlash at two points. Correct as necessary. Complete the assembly in the reverse of the removal procedure.

Axle Shaft Bearings

Removal and Installation

CJ, SCRAMBLER, GRAND WAGONEER AND TRUCK

1. Raise and support the vehicle safely. Remove the axle shaft from the vehicle.
2. Using a combination puller, remove the bearing from the axle shaft.
3. The new bearing can be installed with the use of a combination puller, or with the use of a length of pipe, fitted to the diameter of the inner bearing race, and slipped over the axle end to contact and drive the bearing to its seat on the axle shaft.
4. Lubricate the bearing with wheel bearing grease, making sure the grease fills the cavities between the bearing rollers.
5. Continue the instakllation in the reverse order of the removal procedure.

WRANGLER, WAGONEER, CHEROKEE AND COMANCHE

1. Raise and support the vehicle safely. Remove the axle shaft. Position the axle shaft in a vise.

2. Remove the retaining ring by drilling a ¼ in. hole about ¾ of the way through the ring, then using a cold chisel over the hole, split the ring.

3. Remove the bearing with an arbor press, discard the seal and remove the retainer plate.

4. Installation is the reverse of removal. The new bearing must be pressed on. Make sure it is squarely seated.

REAR SUSPENSION

Leaf Spring

Removal and Installation

EXCEPT WRANGLER, WAGONEER, CHEROKEE AND COMANCHE MOUNTED BELOW THE AXLE

1. Raise the vehicle and support the axle.
2. Disconnect the shock absorber and stabilizer bar, if so equipped.
3. Remove the U-bolts and tie plates.
4. Disconnect the front and rear ends of the spring and remove the spring.
5. The spring can be disassembled by removing the spring rebound clips and the center bolt.
6. Installation is the reverse of the removal procedure.

EXCEPT WRANGLER, WAGONEER, CHEROKEE AND COMANCHE MOUNTED ABOVE THE AXLE

1. Raise the vehicle and support the frame ahead of the axle.
2. If the left side spring is being removed, remove the fuel tank skid plate.
3. Remove the wheel.
4. Disconnect the shock absorber.
5. Remove the tie plate U-bolts and the tie plate. Remove the bolt attaching the spring rear eye to the spring shackle.
6. Remove the bolt attaching the spring front eye to the spring hanger on the frame rail.
7. Remove the spring from the vehicle.
8. Installation is the reverse of the removal procedure.

WRANGLER, WAGONEER, CHEROKEE AND COMANCHE

1. Raise and support the vehicle safely.
2. Raise the axle assembly to relieve the weight.
3. Remove the wheel. Remove the shock absorber at the axle.
4. If equipped, disconnect the stabilizer bar links and the spring tie plate.
5. Remove the spring tie plate U-bolt and the spring tie plate. Remove the rear eye to spring shackle bolt and the front eye to bracket bolt.
6. Lower the spring from the vehicle.
7. Installation is the reverse of the removal procedure.

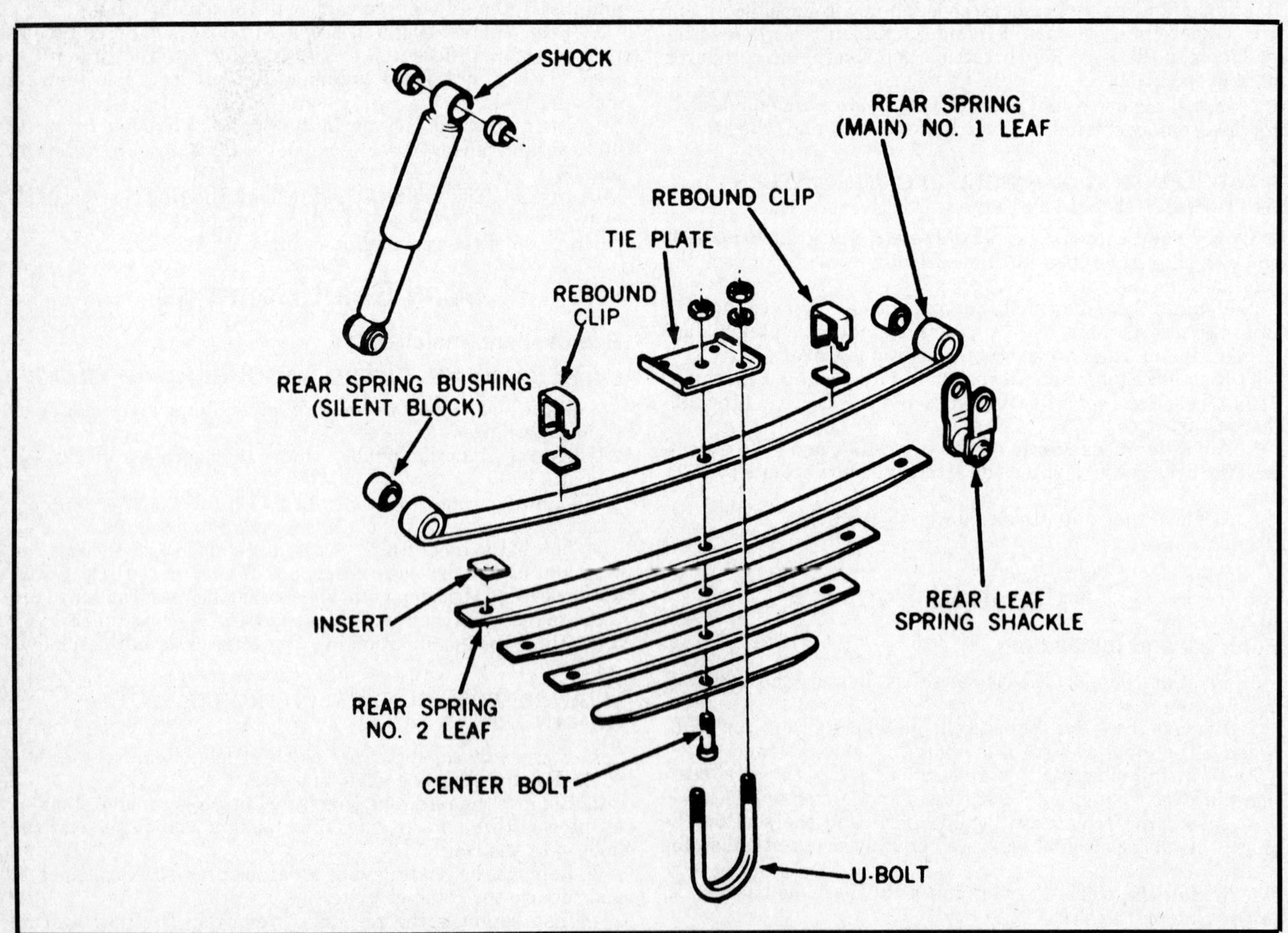

Typical rear spring and attaching parts

Electrical System
Domestic Trucks

INDEX

Alternators and Regulators

Electronic Ignition Systems

Starter Motors

ELECTRICAL DIAGNOSIS

To satisfy the growing trend toward organized engine diagnosis and tune-up, the following gauge and meter hook-ups, as well as diagnosis procedures are covered. It should be noted that the most sophisticated tune-up and diagnostic benches are no more complex then the basic gauges and meters in common, everyday use. Therefore, to understand gauge and meter hook-ups, their applications and procedure, is to be equipped with the know how to perform the most exacting diagnosis.

KNOW YOUR INSTRUMENTS

Ohmmeter

An ohmmeter is used to measure electrical resistance in a unit or circuit. The ohmmeter has a self-contained power supply. In use, it is connected across (or in parallel with) the terminals of the unit being tested.

Ammeter

An ammeter is used to measure current (amount of electricity) flowing through a unit, or circuit. Ammeters are always connected in the line (in series) with the unit or circuit being tested.

Voltmeter

A voltmeter is used to measure voltage (electrical pressure) pushing the current through a unit, or circuit. The meter is connected across the terminals of the unit being tested.

Alternators and Regulators

IS IT THE ALTERNATOR OR THE VOLTAGE REGULATOR?

The first step in diagnosing troubles of the charging system, is to identify the source of failure. Does the fault lie in the alternator or the regulator? The next move depends upon preference or necessity; either repair or replace the offending unit.

It is just as easy to separate an alternator, electrically, from the AC regulator as it is to separate its counterpart, the DC generator from its regular.

AC generator output is controlled by the amount of current supplied to the field circuit of the system.

Unlike the DC generator, an AC generator is capable of pro-

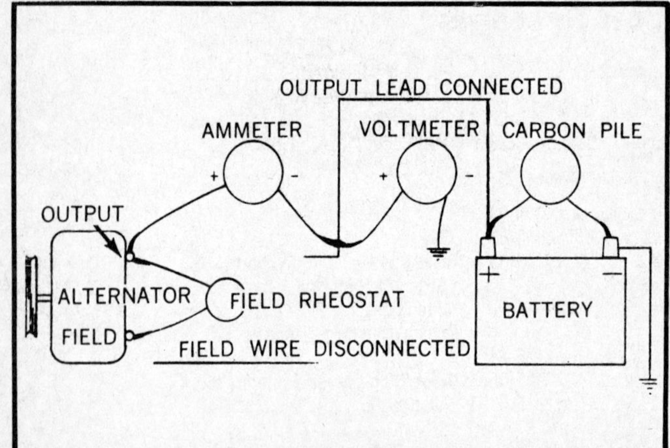

Checking current output of the charging system—typical

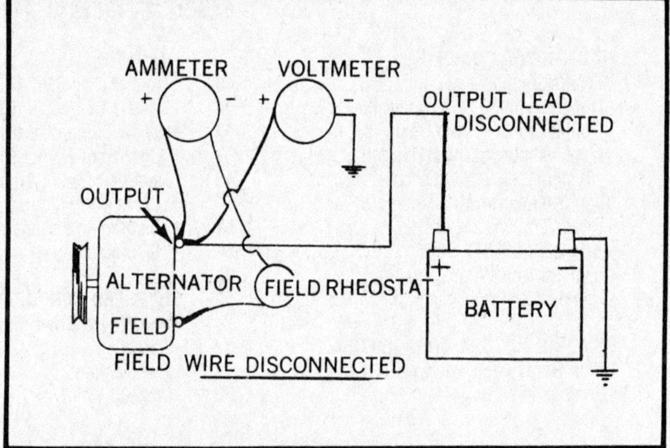

Checking current field draw—typical

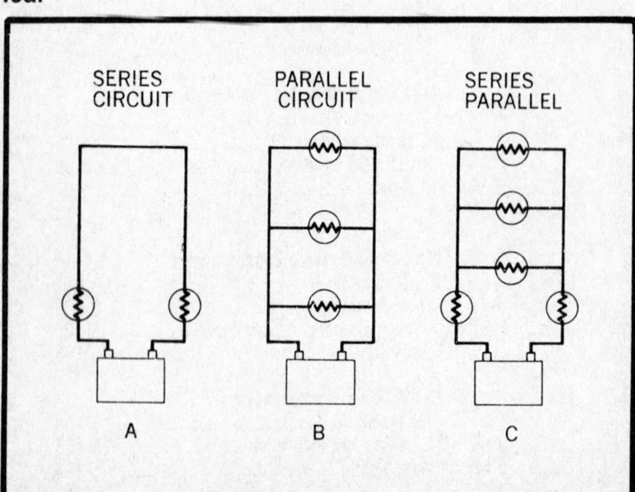

Basic electrical circuits

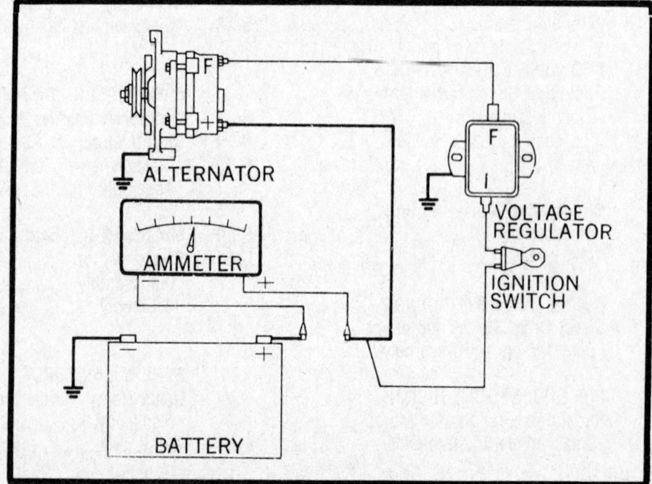

Ammeter connected in series circuits

ducing substantial current at idle speed. Higher maximum output is also a possibility. This presents a potential danger when testing. As a precaution, a field rheostat should be used in the field circuit when making the following isolation test. The field rheostat permits positive control of the amount of current allowed to pass through the field circuit during the isolation test. Unregulated alternator capacity could ruin the unit.

NOTE: Most manufacturers of precision gauges offer special test connectors, in sets, that will adapt to the leads and connections of any AC charging system.

ALTERNATOR TEST PLANS

The following is a procedure pattern for testing the various alternators and their control systems. There are certain precautionary measures that apply to alternator tests in general. These items are listed in detail to avoid repetition when testing each make of alternator and to encourage a habit of good test procedure.

1. Check alternator drive belt for condition and tension.
2. Disconnect battery cables, check physical, chemical and electrical condition of battery.
3. Be absolutely sure of polarity before connecting any battery for starting.
4. Never use a battery charger to start the engine.
5. Disconnect both battery cables when making a battery recharge hook-up.
6. Be sure of polarity hook-up when using a booster battery for starting.
7. Never ground the alternator output or battery terminal.
8. Never ground the field circuit between alternator and regulator.
9. Never run any alternator on an open circuit with the field energized.
10. Never try to polarize an alternator, unless directed by the alternator manufacturer.
11. Do not attempt to "motor" an alternator.
12. The regulator cover must be in place when taking voltage limiter readings.
13. The ignition switch must be in off position when removing or installing the regulator cover.
14. Use insulated tools only to make adjustments to the regulator.
15. When making engine idle speed adjustments, always consider potential load factors that influence engine rpm. To compensate for electrical load, switch on the lights, radio, heater, air conditioner, etc.

Diagnosis

1. Low or no charging such as:
   a. Blown fuse.
   b. Broken or loose fan belt.
   c. Voltage regulator not working.
   d. Brushes sticking.
   e. Slip ring dirty.
   f. Open circuit.
   g. Bad wiring connections.
   h. Bad diode rectifier.
   i. High resistance in charging circuit.
   j. Voltage regulator needs adjusting.
   k. Grounded stator.
   l. May be open rectifiers (check all three phases.).
   m. If rectifiers are found blown or open, check capacitor.
2. Noisy unit, such as:
   a. Damaged rotor bearing.
   b. Poor alignment of unit.
   c. Broken or loose belt.
   d. Open diode rectifiers.
3. Regulator points burnt or stuck, such as:
   a. Regulator set too high.
   b. Poor ground connections.
   c. Shorted generator field.
   d. Regulator air gap incorrect.

Chrysler Corp.

NOTE: All models use Chrysler built alternators with external regulators except some 1984–88 Ram Van, Caravan and Voyager models which use a Mitsubishi built alternator with a internal regulator.

CHRYSLER ISOLATED FIELD ALTERNATOR (ELECTRONIC REGULATOR)

The Chrysler isolated field alternator derives its name from its construction. Both of the brushes are insulated from ground and there is no heat sink connection, thereby isolating the internal field.

TROUBLESHOOTING

Fusible Links

Chrysler Corporation trucks have a single fusible link which is connected between the starter relay and the junction block.

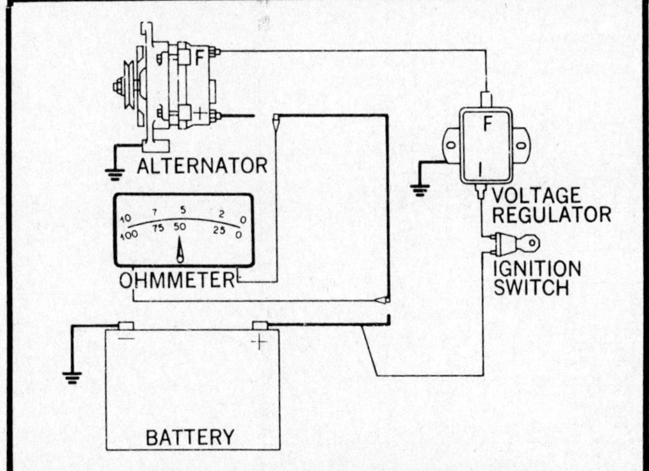

Ohmmeter connected to test wire resistance

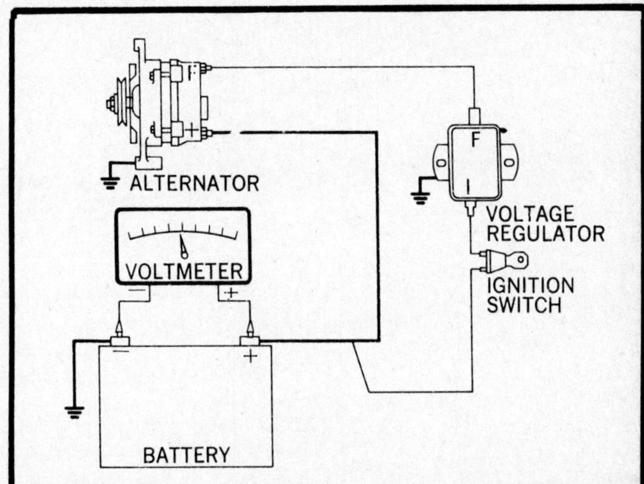

Voltmeter connected in parallel circuits

Failure of this link will cause all electrical systems to stop functioning.

Charging System Operation

NOTE: If the current indicator is to give an accurate reading, the battery cables must be of the same gauge and length as the original equipment.

1. With the engine running and all electrical systems off, place a current indicator over the positive battery cable.
2. If a charge of about 5 amps is recorded, the charging system is working. If a draw of about 5 amps is recorded the system is not working. The needle moves toward the battery when a charge condition is indicated and away from the battery when a draw condition is indicated. If a draw is indicated, proceed to the next testing procedure. If an overcharge of 10–15 amps is indicated, check for faulty regulator.

Ignition Switch to Regulator Circuit Check

1. Disconnect the regulator wires at the regulator.
2. Turn the key on but do not start the engine.
3. Using a voltmeter or test light, check for voltage across the I and F terminals. If there is current present, the circuit is good. If there is no current, check for bad connections, a bad ballast resistor, a bad ammeter, broken wires, or bad ground at the alternator or voltage regulator. Also, check for voltage from the I wire to ground; current should be present. Check for voltage from the F terminal to ground; current should not be present.

Isolation Test

1. Disconnect, at the alternator, the wire that runs between one of the alternator field connections and the voltage regulator.
2. Run a jumper wire from the disconnected alternator terminal to ground.
3. Connect a voltmeter to the battery. The positive voltmeter lead connects to the positive battery terminal and the negative lead goes to the negative terminal. Record the reading.
4. Make sure that all electrical systems are turned off. Start the engine. Do not race the engine.
5. Gradually raise engine speed to 1500-2000. There should be an increase of one or two volts on the voltmeter. If this is true, the alternator is good and the voltage regulator should be repaired. If there is no voltage increase, the alternator is faulty.

Charging Circuit Resistance Test

The purpose of this test is to determine the amount of "voltage drop" between the alternator output terminal wire and the battery.

1. Disconnect the battery ground cable at the "BAT" lead at the alternator output terminal.
2. Connect an ammeter with a scale to 10 amps in series between the alternator "BAT" terminal and the disconnected "BAT" wire.
3. Connect the positive lead of a voltmeter to the disconnected "BAT" wire. Connect the negative lead of the voltmeter to the negative post of the battery.
4. Disconnect the green colored regulator field wire from the alternator. Connect a jumper lead from the alternator field terminal to ground.
5. Connect a tachometer to the engine and reconnect the battery ground cable.
6. Connect a variable carbon pile rheostat to the battery cables. Be sure the carbon pile is in the "OPEN" or "OFF" position before connecting the leads to the battery terminals.
7. Start the engine and operate at an idle.
8. Adjust the engine speed and carbon pile to maintain a flow of 20 amperes in the circuit. Observe the voltmeter reading which should not exceed 0.7 volts.
9. If a higher voltage reading is indicated, inspect, clean and tighten all connections in the charging system.
10. If necessary, a voltage drop test can be done at each connection until the excessive resistance is located.
11. If the charging system resistance is within specifications, reduce the engine speed, turn off the carbon pile rheostat and stop the engine. Remove battery ground cable.
12. Remove the test instruments from the electrical system and reconnect the charging system wiring. Reconnect the battery ground cable.

Current Output Test

This test determines if the alternator is capable of delivering its rated current output.

1. Disconnect the battery ground cable and the "BAT" lead wire at the alternator output terminal.
2. Connect an ammeter in series between the alternator output terminal and the disconnected "BAT" lead wire.

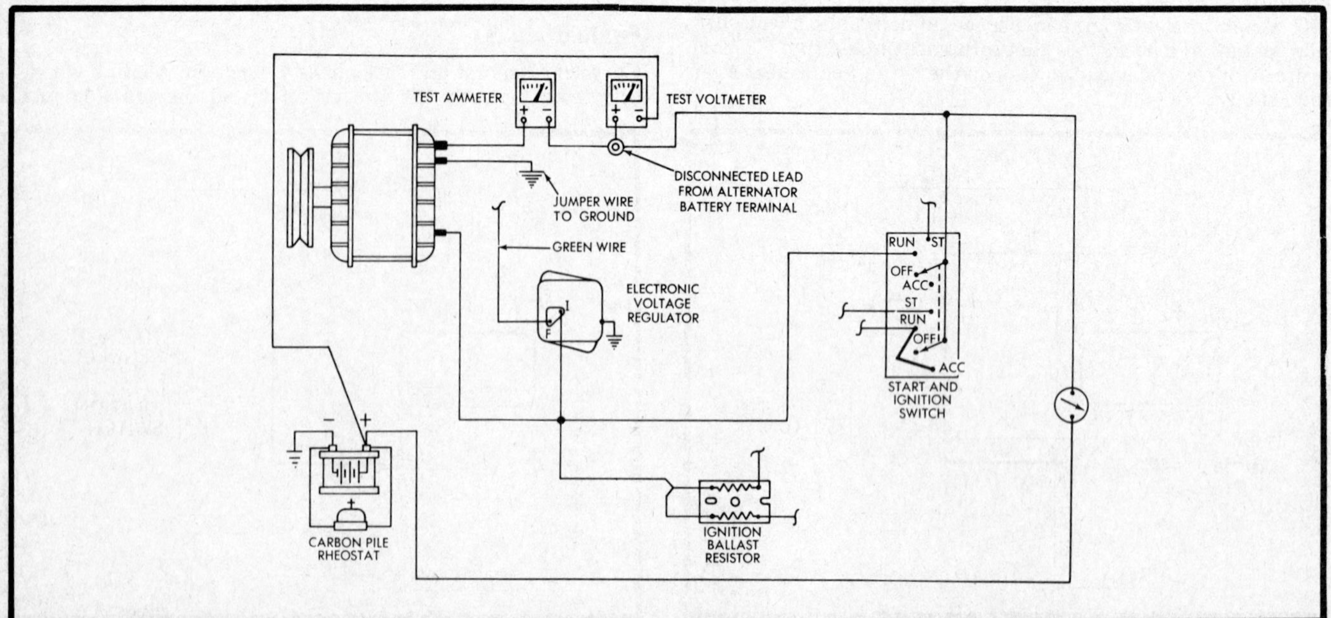

Charging circuit resistance test

NOTE: The ammeter must have a scale of 100 amps.

3. Connect the positive lead of a voltmeter to the output terminal of the alternator and the negative lead to a good ground.
4. Disconnect the green colored wire at the voltage regulator and connect a jumper wire from the alternator field terminal to ground.
5. Connect a tachometer to the engine and reconnect the battery ground wire.
6. Connect a variable carbon pile rheostat between the positive and negative battery cables.

NOTE: Be sure the rheostat control is in the "OPEN" or "OFF" position before connecting the leads to the battery cables.

7. Start the engine and operate at idle. Adjust the carbon pile rheostat control and the engine speed in increments until the voltmeter reading is 15 volts (13 volts for the 100 and 117 amp alternators) and the engine speed is 1250 rpm (900 rpm for the 100 and 117 amp alternators). Do not allow the voltage to rise to 16 volts.
8. The ammeter readings must be within specification.

NOTE: If measured at the battery, current output will be approximately 5 amperes lower than specified.

9. If the readings are less than specified, the alternator should be removed and checked during a bench test.
10. After the current output test is completed, reduce the engine speed, turn the carbon pile rheostat off and then stop the engine.
11. Disconnect the battery ground cable, remove the ammeter, voltmeter and carbon pile. Remove the jumper wire from the field terminal and reconnect the green colored wire to the alternator field terminal.
12. Reconnect the battery cable, if no further testing is to be done to the charging circuit.

Rotor Field Coil Draw Test

1. If on the vehicle, remove the drive belt and wiring connections from the alternator.
2. Connect a jumper wire from the negative terminal of the battery to one of the field terminals of the alternator.
3. Connect the test ammeter positive lead to the other field terminal of the alternator and the negative ammeter lead to the positive battery terminal.
4. Connect a jumper wire between the alternator end shield and the battery negative terminal.
5. Slowly rotate the alternator pulley by hand and observe the ammeter reading.
6. The field coil draw should be 4.5 to 6.5 amperes at 12 volts (4.75 to 6.0 amperes at 12 volts if vehicle is equipped with a 100 or 117 amp alternator).
7. A low rotor coil draw is an indication of high resistance in the field coil draw indicates an open rotor or defective brushes.
8. Remove the test equipment and jumper leads.

Current Rating	Identification	Current Output
41 amp	Red or violet tag	40 amps min.
60 amp	Blue, natural or yellow	57 amps min.
100, 117 amp	Yellow	72 amps min.

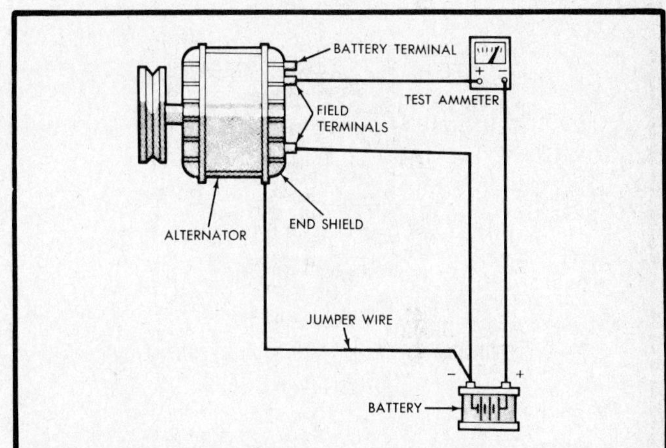

Rotor field coil current draw test

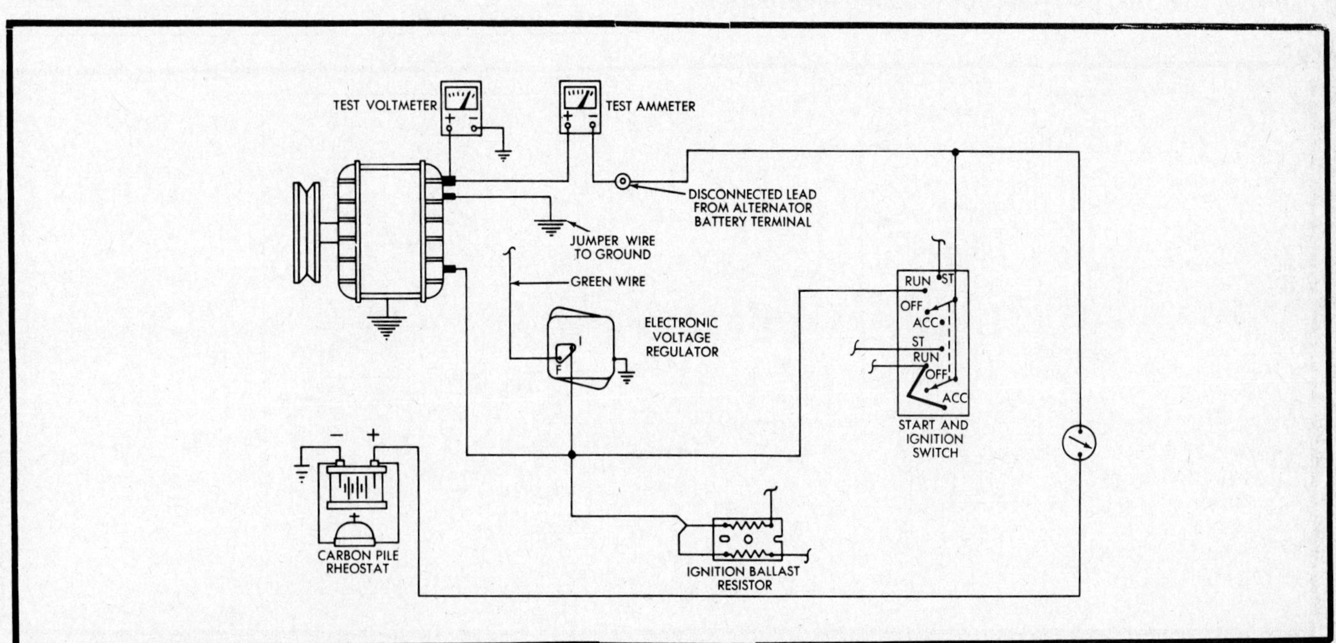

Current output test

Electronic Voltage Regulator Test

1. Make sure battery terminals are clean and battery is charged.
2. Connect the positive lead of a test voltmeter to ignition Terminal No. 1 of the ballast resistor.
3. Connect the negative voltmeter lead to a good body ground.
4. Start engine and allow it to idle at 1250 rpm, all lights and accessories turned off. Voltage should be within specification.
5. If the voltage regulator is below specification, check the following:
   a. Voltage regulator; ground check voltage drop between regulator cover and ground.
   b. Harness wiring; disconnect regulator plug (ignition switch off), then turn on ignition switch and check for battery voltage at the terminals having the red and green leads. Wiring harness must be disconnected from the regulator when checking individual leads. If no voltage is present in either lead, the problem is in the truck wiring or alternator field.

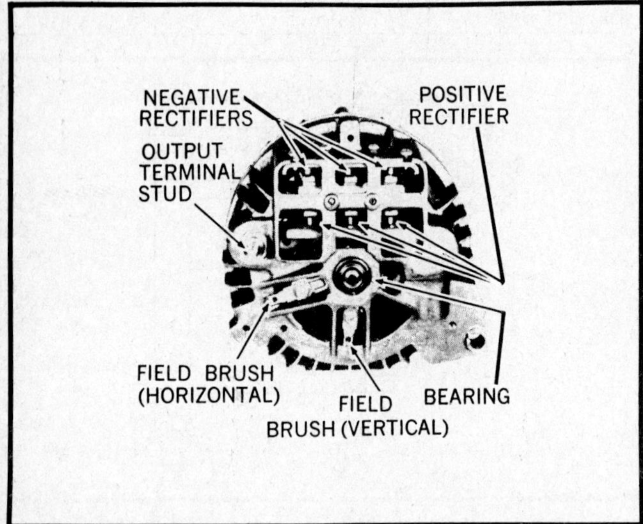

View of rear housing—except 100 amp alternator

6. If Step 5 tests showed no malfunctions, install a new regulator and repeat Step 4.
7. If voltage is above specifications (Step 4), or fluctuates, check the following:
   a. Ground between regulator and body and between body and engine.
   b. Ignition switch circuit between switch and regulator.
8. If voltage is still more than $^1/_2$ volt above specifications, install a new regulator and repeat Step 4.

CHRYSLER OVERHAUL AND INTERNAL TESTING

Alternator disassembly, repair and assembly procedures are basically the same for all Chrysler built alternators. Certain variations in design, or production modifications, could require slightly different procedures that should be obvious upon inspection of the unit being serviced.

Disassembly

NOTE: To prevent damage to the brush assemblies (100 and 117 amp), they should be removed before proceeding with the disassembly of the alternator. The brushes are mounted in a plastic holder that positions the brushes vertically against the slip rings.

1. Remove the retaining screw, flat washer, nylon washer and field terminal and carefully lift the plastic holder containing the spring and brush assembly from the end housing.
2. The ground brush (40 and 60 amp) is positioned horizontally against the slip ring and is retained in the holder that is integral with the end housing. Remove the retaining screw and lift the clip, spring and brush assembly from the end housing. The stator is laminated, don't burr the stator or end housings.

Ambient Temp. ¼ in. from Regulator	Voltage
20°F.	14.9 to 15.9
80°F.	13.9 to 14.6
140°F.	13.3 to 13.9
Above 140°F.	Less Than 13.6

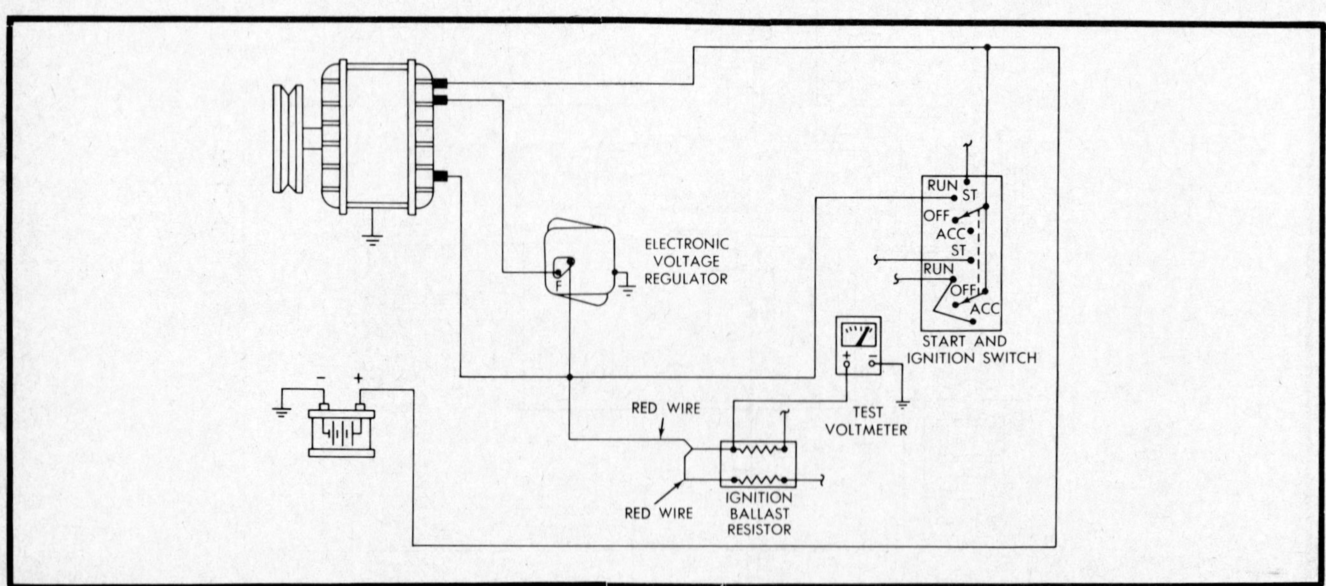

Voltage regulator test

3. Remove the through bolts and pry between the stator and drive end housing with a suitable tool. Carefully separate the drive end housing, pulley and rotor assembly from the stator and rectifier housing assembly.

4. The pulley is an interference fit on the rotor shaft. Remove with a puller and special adapters.

5. Remove the three nuts and washers and, while supporting the end frame, tap the rotor shaft with a plastic hammer and separate the rotor and end housing.

6. The drive end ball bearing is an interference fit with the rotor shaft. Remove the baring with puller and adapters.

NOTE: Further dismantling of the rotor is not advisable, as the remainder of the rotor assembly is not serviced separately.

7. Remove the DC output terminal nuts and washers and remove terminal screw and inside capacitor (on units so equipped).

8. Remove the insulator.

NOTE: Positive rectifiers are pressed into the heat sink and negative rectifiers in the end housing. When removing the rectifiers, it is necessary to support the end housing and/or heat sink to prevent damage to these castings. Another caution is in order relative to diode rectifiers. Don't subject them to unnecessary jolting. Heavy vibration or shock may ruin them.

9. Cut rectifier wire at point of crimp. Support rectifier housing. The factory tool is cut away and slotted to fit over the wires and around the bosses in the housing. Be sure that the bore of the tool completely surrounds the rectifier, then press the rectifier out of the housing.

NOTE: The roller bearing in the rectifier end frame is a press fit. To protect the end housing it is necessary to support the housing with a tool when pressing out the bearing.

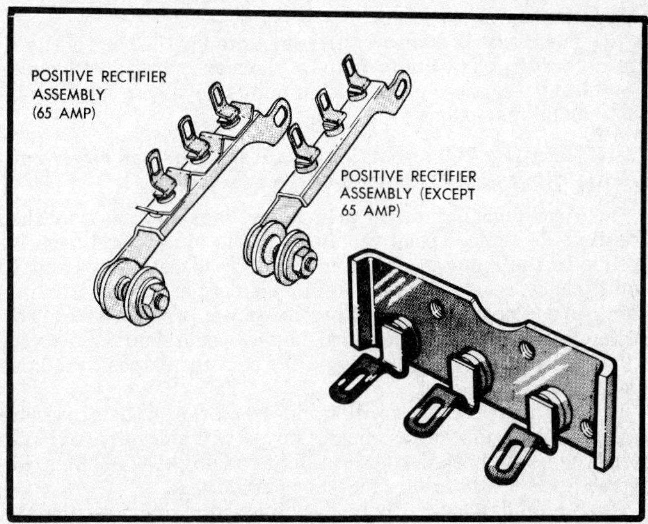

Chrysler charging system positive and negative rectifier identification

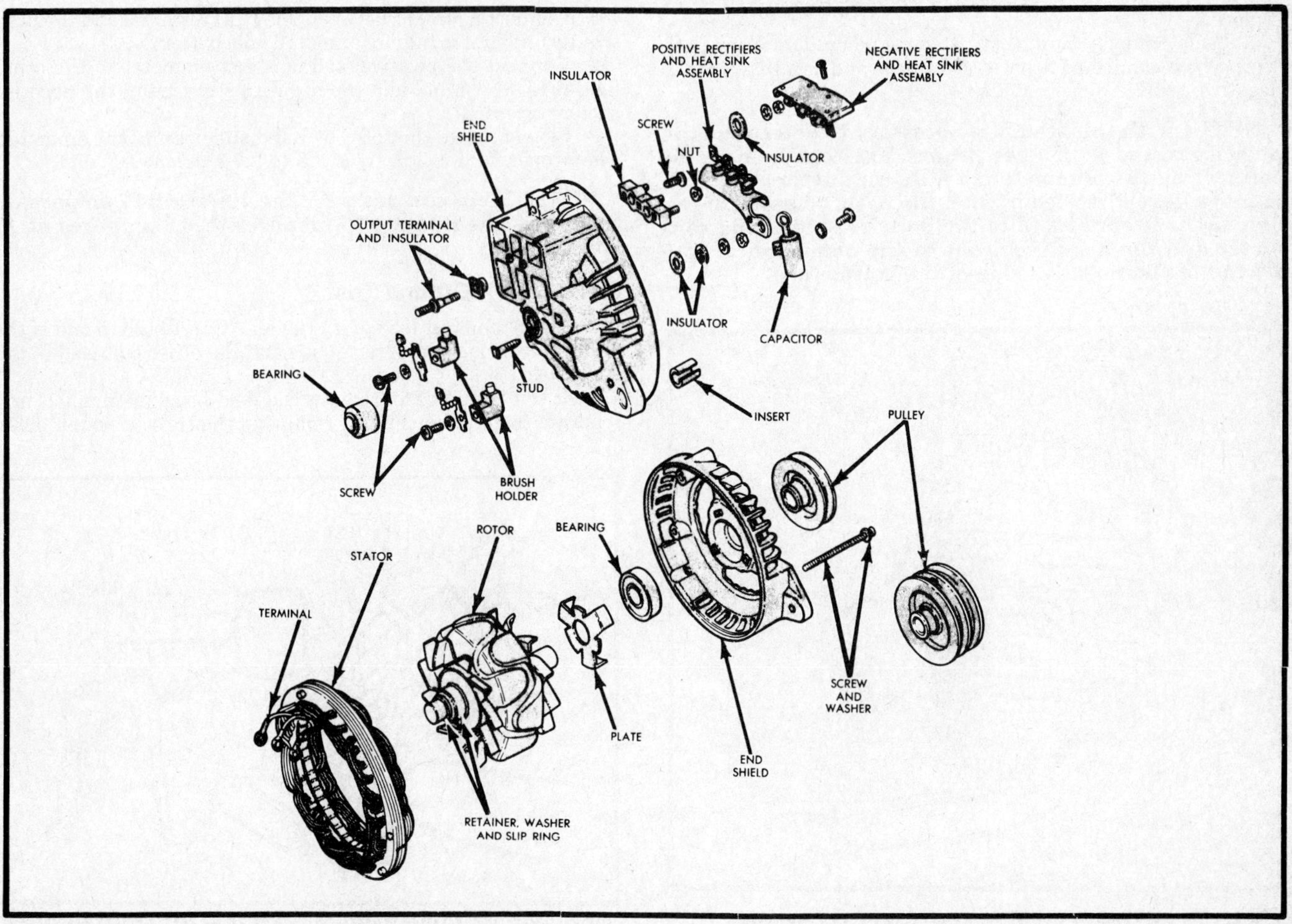

Typical Chrysler alternator—exploded view

BENCH TESTS

Testing Silicone Diode Rectifiers With Ohmmeter

**PREFERRED METHOD
(RECTIFIERS OPEN IN ALL THREE PHASES)**

1. Disassembly the alternator and separate the wires at the Y-connection of the stator.
2. There are six doide rectifiers mounted in the back of the alternator (40 and 60 amp). Three of them are marked with a plus (+) and three are marked with a minus (-). These marks indicate diode case polarity.

NOTE: The 100 and 117 amp alternator has twelve silicone diodes. Six positive and six negative.

3. To test, set ohmmeter to its lowest range. If case is marked positive (+), place positives meter probe to case and negative probe to the diode lead. Meter should read between 4 and 10 ohms. Now, reverse leads of ohmmeter, connecting negative meter probe to positive case and positive meter probe to wire of rectifier. Set meter on a high range. Meter needle should move very little, if any (infinite reading). Do this to all positive diode rectifiers.
4. The diode rectifiers with minus (-) marks on their cases are checked the same way as above. Only now the negative ohmmeter probe is connected to the case for a reading of 4–10 ohms. Reverse leads as above for the other part to test.
5. If a reading of 4–10 ohms is obtained in one direction and no reading (infinity) is read on the ohmmeter in the other direction, diode rectifiers are good. If either infinity or a low resistance is obtained in both directions on a rectifier, it must be replaced.
6. If meter reads more than 10 ohms when ohmmeter positive probe is connected to positive on diode and negative probe to negative, replace diode rectifier.

NOTE: With this test, it is necessary to determine the polarity of the ohmmeter probes. This can be done by connecting the ohmmeter to a DC voltmeter. The voltmeter will read up-scale when the positive probe of the ohmmeter is connected to the positive side of the voltmeter and the negative probe of the ohmmeter is connected to the negative side of the voltmeter.

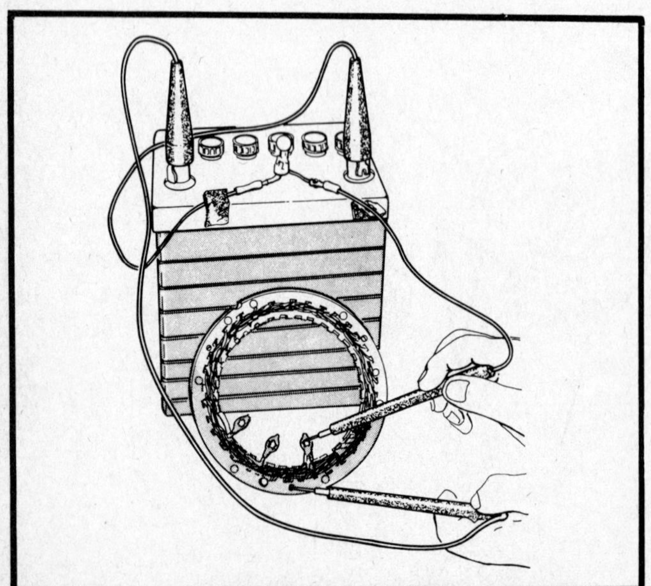

Chrysler charging system stator test for ground

ALTERNATE METHOD (TEST LIGHT)

1. Be sure that the lead from the center of the diode rectifiers is disconnected.
2. To test rectifiers with plus (+ — case, touch positive probe of tester to case and minus (-) probe to lead wire of rectifier. Bulb should light if rectifier is good. If bulb does not light, replace rectifier.
3. Now reserve tester probe connections to rectifier. Bulb should not light. If bulb does light, replace rectifier.
4. For testing minus (-) marked cases, follow above procedure, except that now bulb should light with negative probe of tester touching rectifier case and positive probe touching lead wire.
5. Rectifier is good if the bulb lights when tester probes are connect one way and does not light when tester connections are reversed.
6. Rectifier must be replaced if the bulb does not light either way. Also, replace rectifier if bulb lights both ways.

NOTE: The usual cause of an open or blown diode or rectifier is a defective capacitor or a battery that has been installed in reverse polarity. If the battery is installed properly and the diodes are open, test the capacitor.

The capacitor capacities are: Int. installed (158 microfarad min). Ext. installed (5 microfarad min).

ALTERNATOR BENCH TESTS

Field Coil Draw

1. Connect a jumper between one FLD terminal and the positive terminal of a fully charged 12 volt battery.
2. Connect the positive lead of a test ammeter to the other field (FLD) terminal and the negative test lead to the negative battery terminal.
3. Slowly rotate the rotor by hand and observe the ammeter. The proper field coil draw is 2.3 to 2.7 amps at 12 volts.

NOTE: Field coil draw for the 100 and 117 ampere alternators should be 4.75 amperes to 6.0 amperes at 12 volts.

Field Circuit Ground Test

1. Touch one test lead of a 110 volt AC test bulb to one of the alternator brush (field) terminals and the other test lead to the end shield.
2. If the lamp lights, remove the field brush assemblies and separate the end housing by removing the three through bolts.

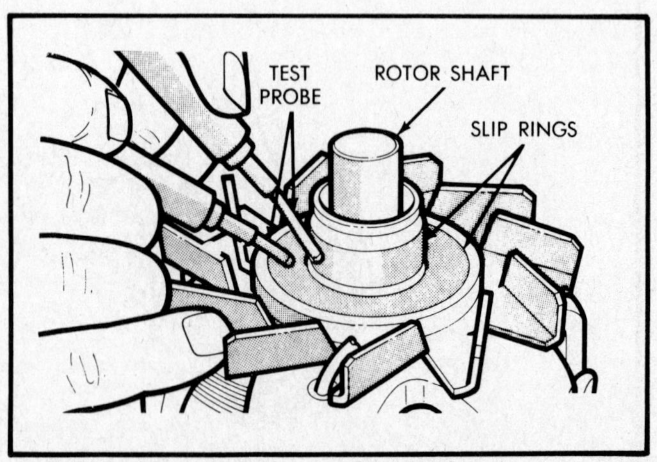

Chrysler charging system rotor test for short or open circuits

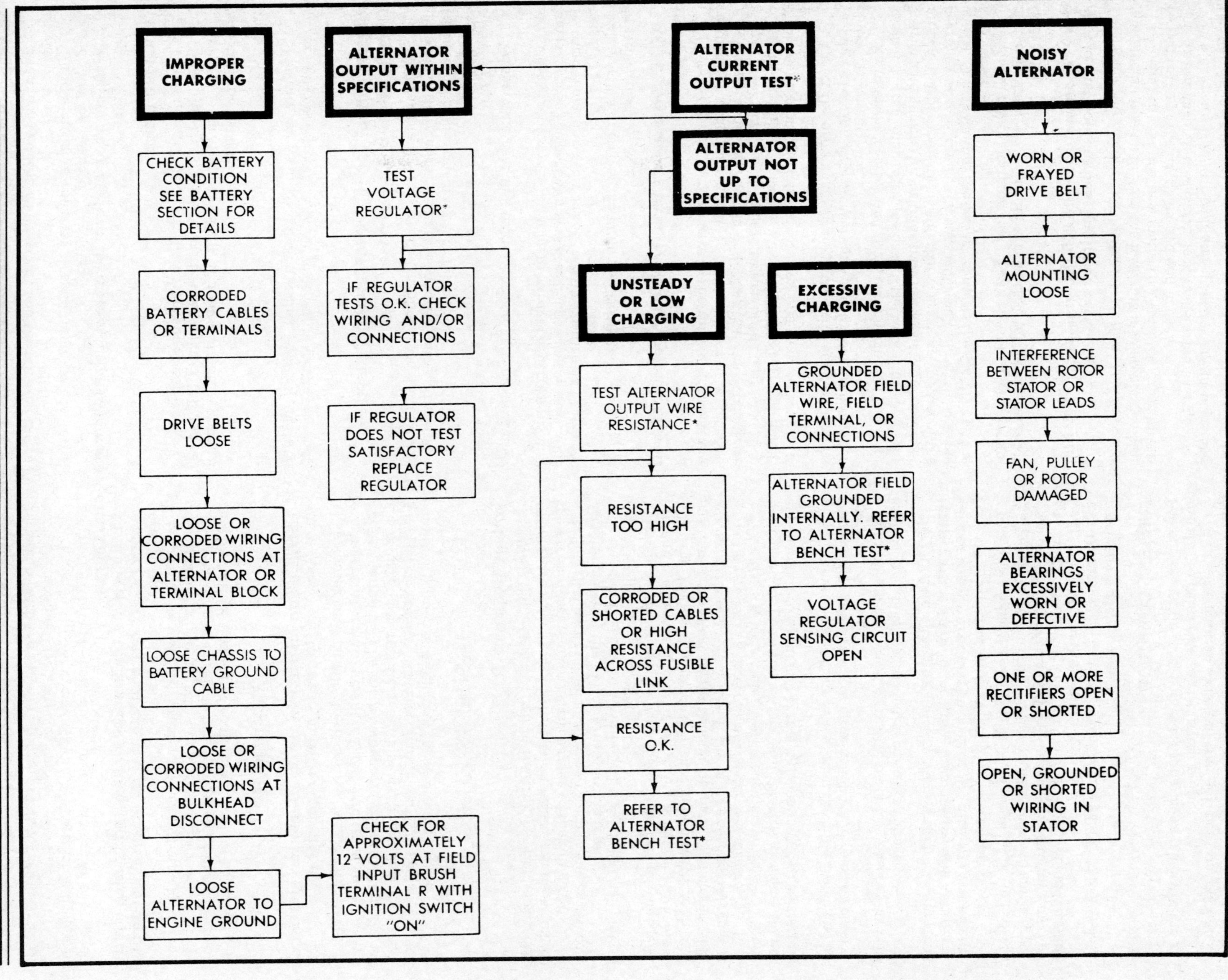

Mitsubishi alternator and electronic voltage regulator diagnosis

3. Place one test lead on a slip ring and the other on the end shield.
4. If the lamp lights, the rotor assembly is grounded internally and must be replaced.
5. If the lamp does not light, the cause of the problem was a grounded brush.

Grounded Stator

1. Disconnect the diode rectifiers from the stator leads.
2. Test from stator leads to stator core, using a 110 volt test lamp. Test lamp should not light. If it does, stator is grounded and must be replaced.

Low Output

1. Perform Steps 1, 2 and 3 (rectifier open in all three phases). If the rectifiers are found to be within specifications, replace the stator assembly.

Current Output Too High (No Control) Caused by Open Rectifier or Open Phase

1. Perform Steps 1, 2 and 3 (rectifier open in all three phases). If the rectifier tests satisfactorily, inspect the stator connections before replacing the stator.

Assembly

1. Support the heat sink or rectifier end housing or circular plate.
2. Check rectifier identification to be sure the correct rectifier is being used. The part numbers are stamped on the case of the rectifier. They are also marked, red for positive and black for negative.
3. Start the new rectifier into the casting and press it in squarely.

NOTE: Do not start rectifier with a hammer or it will be ruined.

4. Crimp the new rectifier wire to the wires disconnected at removal, or solder (using a heat sink with rosin core solder).
5. Support the end housing on tool so that the notch in the support tool will clear the raised section of the heat sink, then press the bearing into position with tool SP-3381, or equivalent. New bearings are prelubricated, additional lubrication is not required.
6. Insert the drive end bearing in the drive end housing and install the bearing plate, washers and nuts to hold the bearing in place.
7. Position the bearing and drive end housing on the rotor shaft and, while supporting the base of the rotor shaft, press the bearing and housing in position on the rotor shaft with an arbor press and arbor tool. Be careful that there is no cocking of the bearing at installation, or damage will result. Press the bearing on the rotor shaft until the bearing contacts the shoulder on the rotor shaft.
8. Install pulley on rotor shaft. Shaft of rotor must be supported so that all pressing force is on the pulley hub and rotor shaft.

NOTE: Do not exceed 6,800 lbs. pressure. Pulley hub should just contact bearing inner race.

9. Some alternators will be found to have the capacitor mounted internally. Be sure the heat sink insulator is in place.
10. Install the output terminal screw with the capacitor attached through the heat sink and end housing.
11. Install insulating washers, lockwashers and locknuts.
12. Make sure the heat sink and insulator are in place and tighten the locknut.
13. Position the stator on the rectifier end housing. Be sure that all of the rectifier connectors and phase leads are free of interference with the rotor fan blades and that the capacitor (internally mounted) lead has clearance.
14. Position the rotor assembly in the rectifier end housing. Align the through bolt holes in the stator with both end housings.
15. Enter stator shaft in the rectifier end housing bearing, compress stator and both end housings manually and install through bolts, washers and nuts.
16. Install the insulated brush and terminal attaching screw.
17. Install the ground screw and attaching screw.
18. Rotate pulley slowly to be sure the rotor fan blades do not hit the rectifier and stator connectors.

MITSUBISHI

NOTE: The Mitsubishi built alternator is used on some Ram Van, Caravan and Voyager models.

This integrated circuit alternator has fifteen built-in rectifiers, that convert A.C. current into D.C. current at the alternator battery terminal. The main components of the alternator are the rotor, stator, rectifiers, end shields, pulley, fan and capacitor. The electronic voltage regulator is very compact and is built into the rectifier end shield of the alternator.

TROUBLSHOOTING

Voltage Regulator Test

1. With the ignition switch in the OFF position, disconnect the positive cable from the battery and place a knife switch on the battery post and connect the cable to the knife switch.
2. Install the leads from an ammeter to the knife switch connectors and open the switch to battery current.
3. Connect the leads of a voltmeter between the L terminal of the alternator and a good ground.
4. The voltage reading should be 0 volts. Should voltage be present, a defective alternator or wiring is indicated.
5. If no voltage is present, turn the ignition switch to the ON position. The voltage present should be lower than battery voltage, by about one volt or less. If the voltage reading is higher or at battery voltage, a defective alternator is indicated.
6. Connect a tachometer to the engine and close the knife switch, mounted on the battery post. Start the engine. Do not apply any starting current through the ammeter when starting the engine. The ammeter can be ruined.
7. After the engine is operating, open the knife switch and increase the engine speed to approximately 2500 rpm and observe the ammeter reading.
8. If the ammeter reading is 10 amps or less, observe the voltage reading. This reading is the charging voltage.

NOTE: The charging voltage varies with the ambient temperature. It is necessary to measure the temperature of the air around the rear of the alternator and correct the charging voltage reading as required.

9. If the ammeter reading is more than 10 amps, continue to charge the battery until the reading falls under 10 amps, or replace the battery with a fully charged one. An alternate method is to limit the charging circuit by connecting a ¼ ohm (25 watt) resistor in series with the battery.
10. Disconnect all test equipment, remove knife switch and reinstall the battery positive cable.

CURRENT OUTPUT TEST

The purpose of this test is to determine the capability of the alternator to deliver its rated current output.

1. With the ignition switch in the OFF position, disconnect the battery ground cable.
2. Disconnect the Bat lead wire from the terminal of the alternator.

3. Connect a 0–100 scaled ammeter in series, between the Bat terminal and the Bat lead wire.

4. Connect the positive lead of a voltmeter to the Bat terminal of the alternator and ground the negative lead.

5. Disconnect the green field wire (to voltage regulator) at the alternator.

6. Connect a tachometer to the engine and reconnect the negative battery cable.

7. Connect a carbon pile rheostat between the battery terminals. Be sure the carbon pile is in the Open or Off position before connecting the leads.

8. Start the engine and operate at idle.

9. Adjust the carbon pile and accelerate the engine to the specified speed and measure the output current. The current should be within specifications. Do not allow the voltage to increase over 16 volts.

10. The ammeter reading must be within the specified limits. If not the alternator should be removed and bench tested.

11. After the tests, disconnect the test equipment from the components.

DISASSEMBLED ALTERNATOR TESTS

Rotor Assembly

1. Check the outside circumference of the slip ring for dirtiness and roughness. Clean or polish with fine sandpaper, if required. A badly roughened slip ring or a slip ring worn down beyond the service limit should be replaced.

VOLTAGE CHART	
Charging voltage	14.4 ± 0.3V at 20°C (68°F)
Temperature compensation gradient	−0.7 to .13V/10°C (50°F)

2. Check for continuity between the field coil and slip ring. If there is no continuity, the field coil is defective. Replace the rotor assembly.

3. Check for continuity between the slip ring and shaft (or core). If there is continuity, it means that the coil or slip ring is grounded. Replace the rotor assembly.

Stator Assembly

Check for continuity between the leads of the stator coil. If there is no continuity the stator coil is defective. Replace the stator assembly.

Rectifier Assembly

POSITIVE (+) HEAT SINK ASSEMBLY

Check for continuity between the positive (+) heat sink and stator coil lead connection terminal with a continuity tester. If there is continuity in both directions the diode is short circuited. Replace the rectifier assembly.

NEGATIVE (-) HEAT SINK ASSEMBLY

Check for continuity between the negative (-) heat sink and sta-

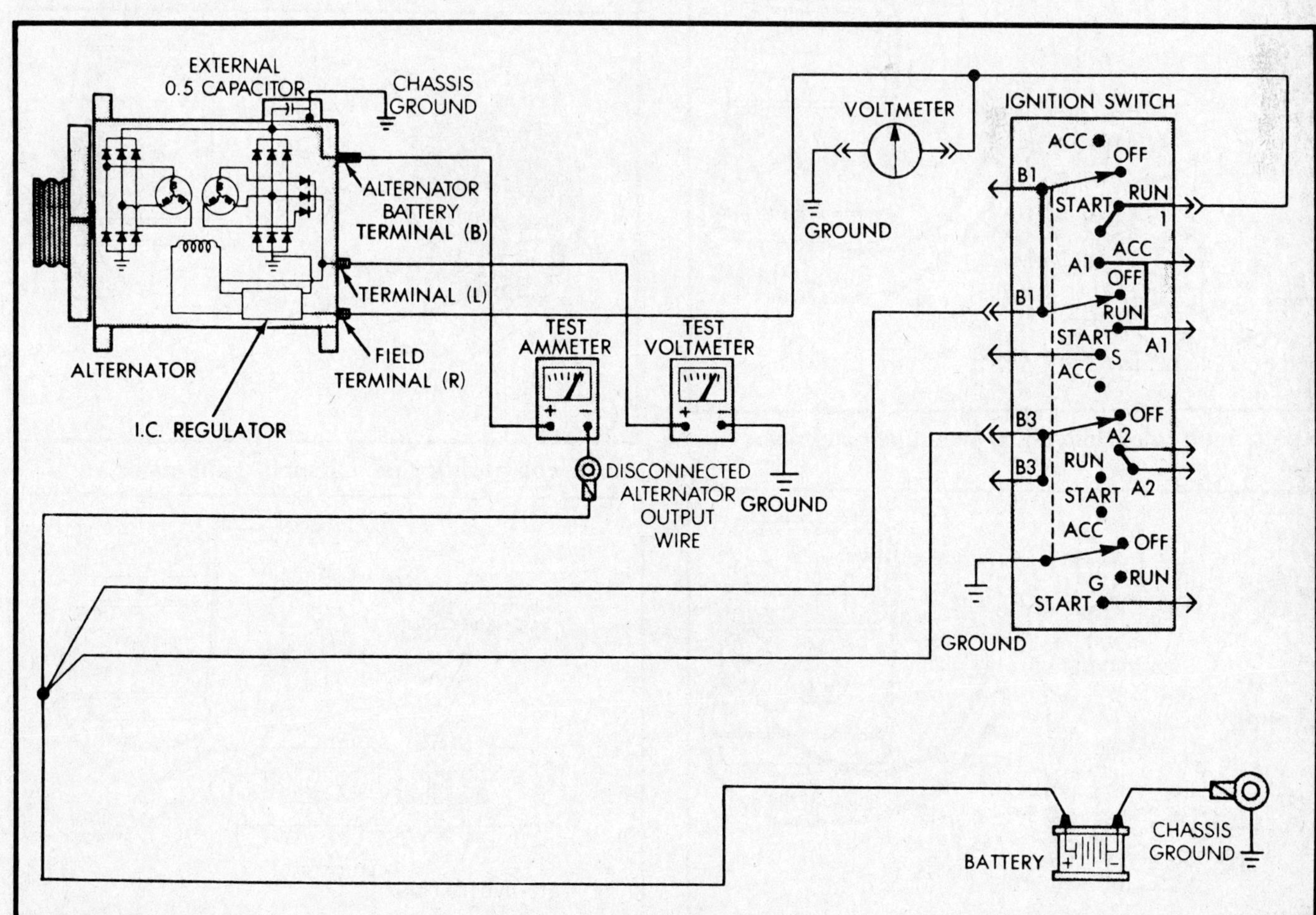

Mitsubishi Voltage regulator test

tor coil lead connection terminal. If there is continuity in both directions the diode is short circuited. Replace the rectifier assembly.

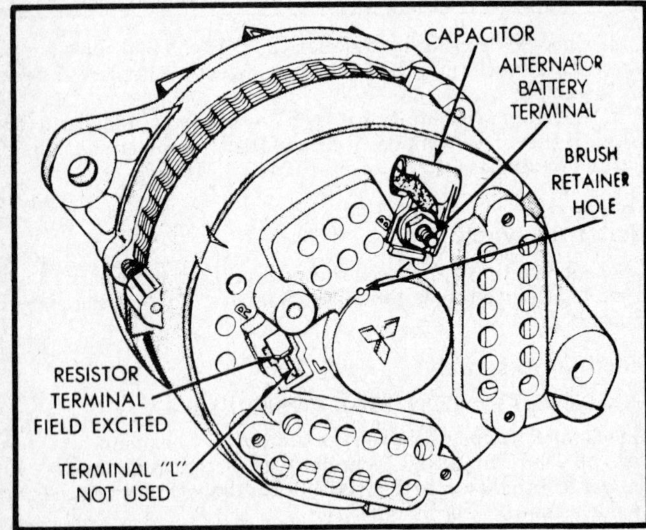

Mitsubishi alternator terminals

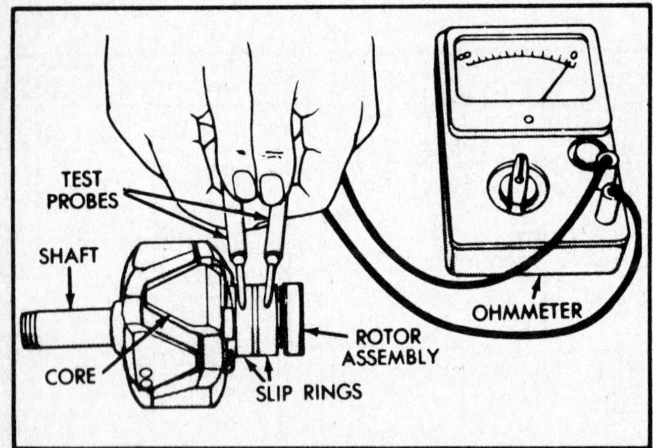

Testing the rotor field coils, Mitsubishi alternator

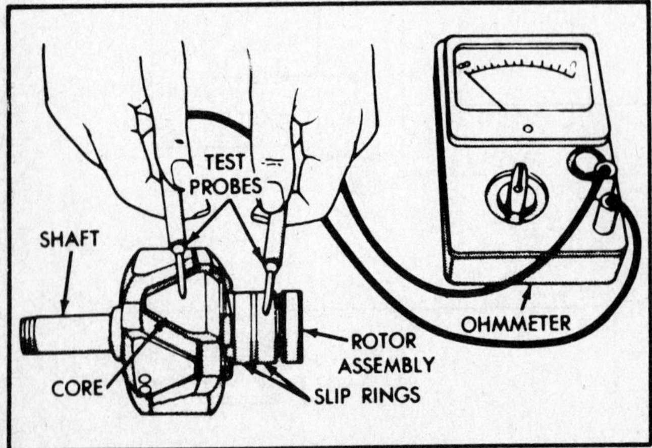

Testing the rotor for ground, Mitsubishi alternator

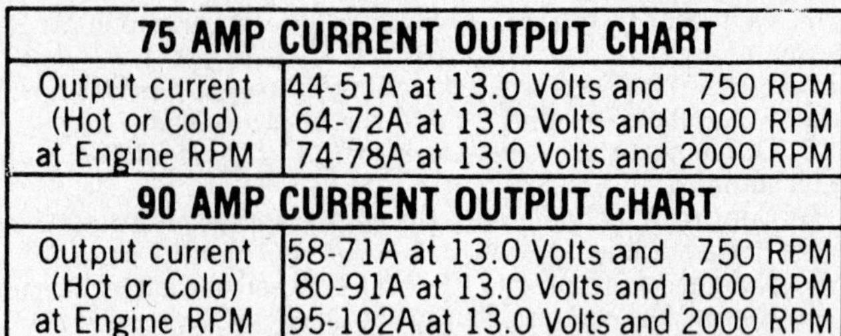

75 AMP CURRENT OUTPUT CHART	
Output current (Hot or Cold) at Engine RPM	44-51A at 13.0 Volts and 750 RPM 64-72A at 13.0 Volts and 1000 RPM 74-78A at 13.0 Volts and 2000 RPM

90 AMP CURRENT OUTPUT CHART	
Output current (Hot or Cold) at Engine RPM	58-71A at 13.0 Volts and 750 RPM 80-91A at 13.0 Volts and 1000 RPM 95-102A at 13.0 Volts and 2000 RPM

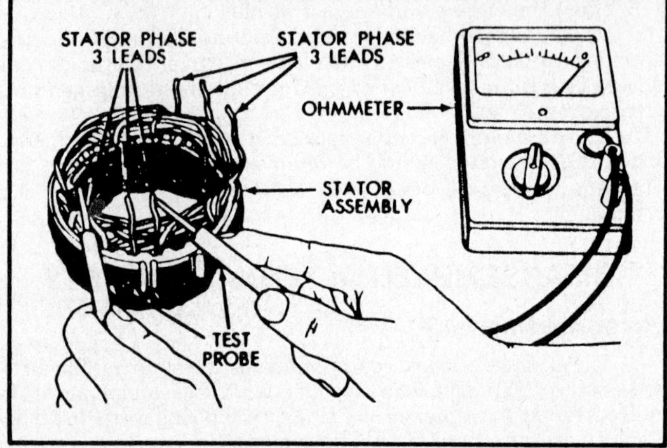

Stator coil continuity test, Mitsubishi alternator

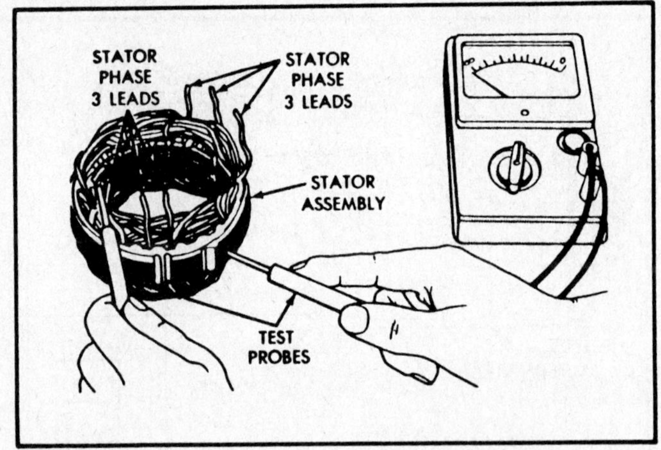

Stator coil ground test, Mitsubishi alternator

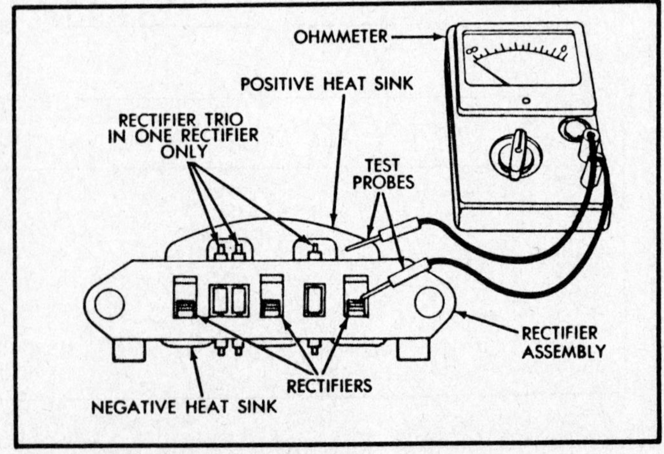

Testing the positive rectifiers, Mitsubishi alternator

Rectifier Trio Test

Using a circuit tester check the three diodes for continuity in both directions. If there is either continuity or an open circuit in both directions the diode is defective. Replace the rectifier assembly.

Disassembly

1. Place the alternator in a vise or similar holding fixture, mark the body components and remove the three through body bolts.
2. Pry between the stator and the drive end shield and carefully separate the drive end plate, the pulley and the rotor assembly from the stator and rectifier end shield assembly.
3. Carefully clamp the rotor and remove the pulley nut from the end of the shaft. Remove the pulley, the pulley fan, the pulley fan spacer and the alternator drive end shield from the rotor shaft.
4. The front bearing can be removed from the front drive housing by the removal of the dust seals, front and rear, the three bearing retainer screws, the retainer, exposing the bearing so that it can be tapped from the drive housing.
5. To remove the stator assembly. The six stator leads must be unsoldered from the rectifiers, as per the manufacturer's recommendation.
6. Remove the rectifiers from the stator end shield housing.
7. Remove the brush holder and regulator retaining screw.
8. Remove the Bat terminal retaining nut and remove the capacitor from the terminal.
9. Remove the regulator and rectifier assembly. Unsolder one rectifier to regulator assembly and remove the other rectifier assembly by sliding the battery stud out of the regulator.
10. Inspect the rotor bearing surface for scores and make the necessary off vehicle test on the electrical components.

Assembly

1. The assembly of the alternator is the reverse of the removal procedure. Certain steps must be performed as the alternator is assembled.

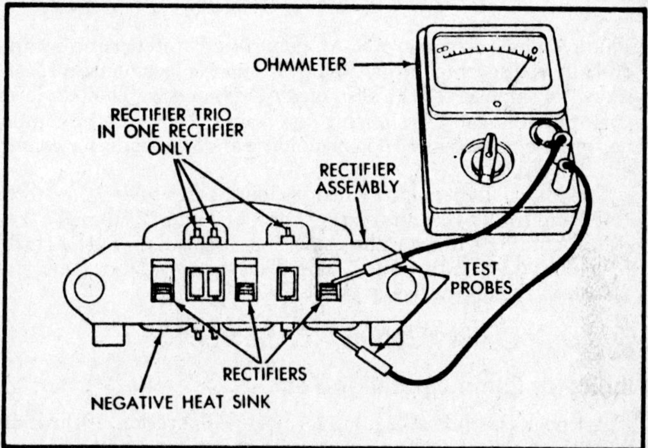

Testing the negative rectifiers, Mitsubishi alternator

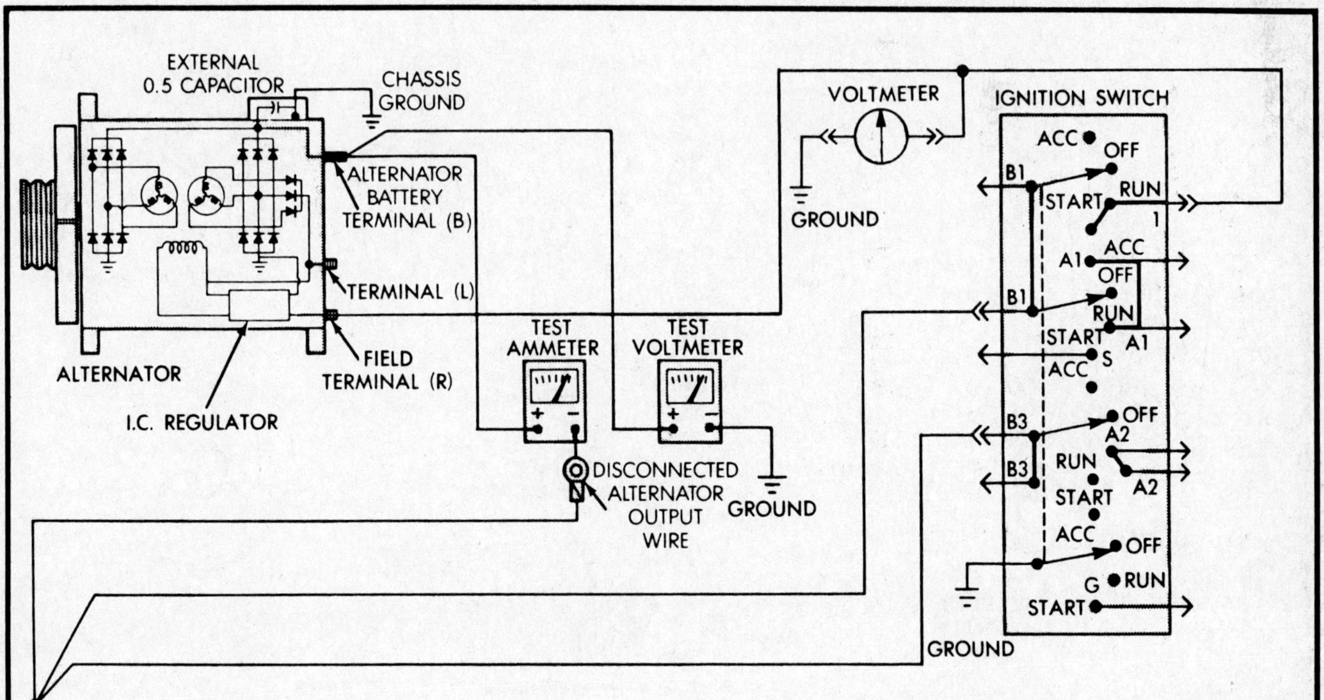

Mitsubishi current output test

2. Install the seals in the front and in the rear of the front bearing with the angled lip away from the bearing.

3. Push the brushes into the brush holder and insert a wire to hold them in the raised position. Install the rotor and remove the holding wire.

General Motors Corp.

DELCOTRON 10-SI, 12-SI, 15-SI, 17-SI, 27-SI TYPE 100

This system is an integrated AC generating system containing a built in voltage regulator. Removal and replacement is essentially the same as for the standard AC generator. The regulator is mounted inside the slip ring end frame. All regulator components are enclosed in an epoxy molding and the regulator cannot be adjusted.

The internal alternator wiring is identical between the 10-SI, 15-SI and the 27-SI units, except the 10-SI and 12-SI uses a "Y" stator winding while a Delta stator winding is used in the 15-SI, 17-SI and 27-SI alternators. The disassembly and assembly of the units remain basically the same.

DIAGNOSTIC TESTING

Indicator Lamp Operation Test

1. Check the indicator lamp for normal operation. If the indicator lamp operates properly, refer to the undercharged battery test. If the indicator lamp does not operate properly, proceed accordingly.

2. Switch off, lamp on. Unplug the connector from the generator No. 1 and No. 2 terminals. If the lamp stays on, there is a short between these two leads. If the lamp goes out, replace the rectifier bridge.

3. Switch on, lamp off, engine stopped. This condition can be caused by the defects listed above or by an open in the circuit. To determine where an open exists proceed as follows. Check for a blown fuse, or fusible link, a burned out bulb, defective bulb socket, or an open in No. 1 lead circuit between generator and ignition switch. If no defects have been found proceed to undercharged battery test.

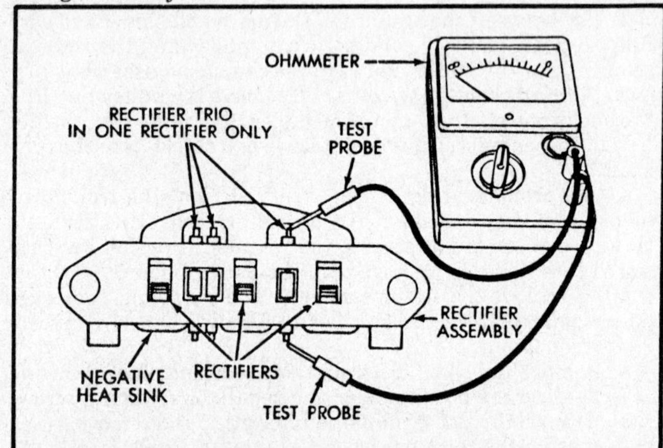

Rectifier trio test, Mitsubishi alternator

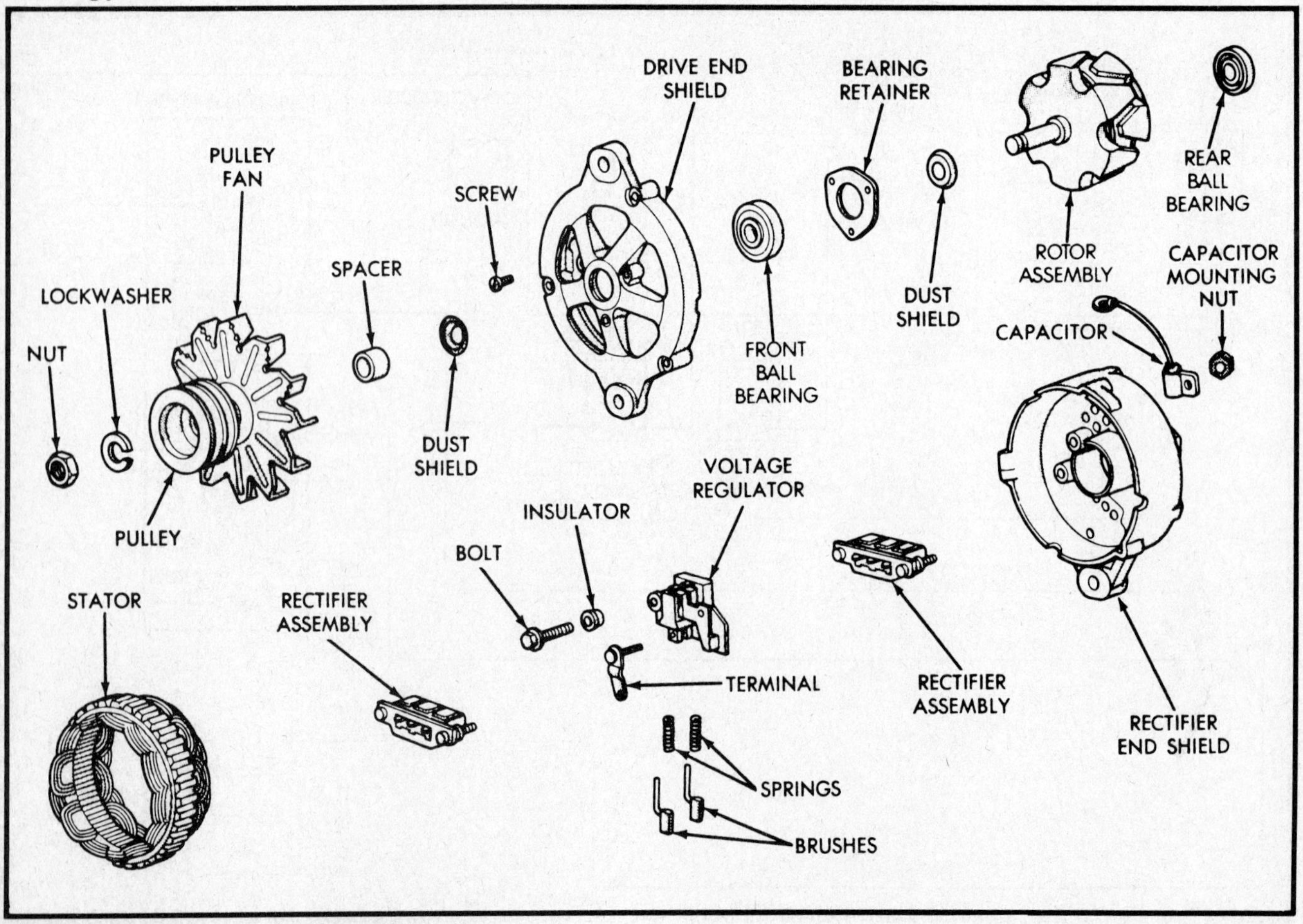

Disassembled view of the Mitsubishi alternator

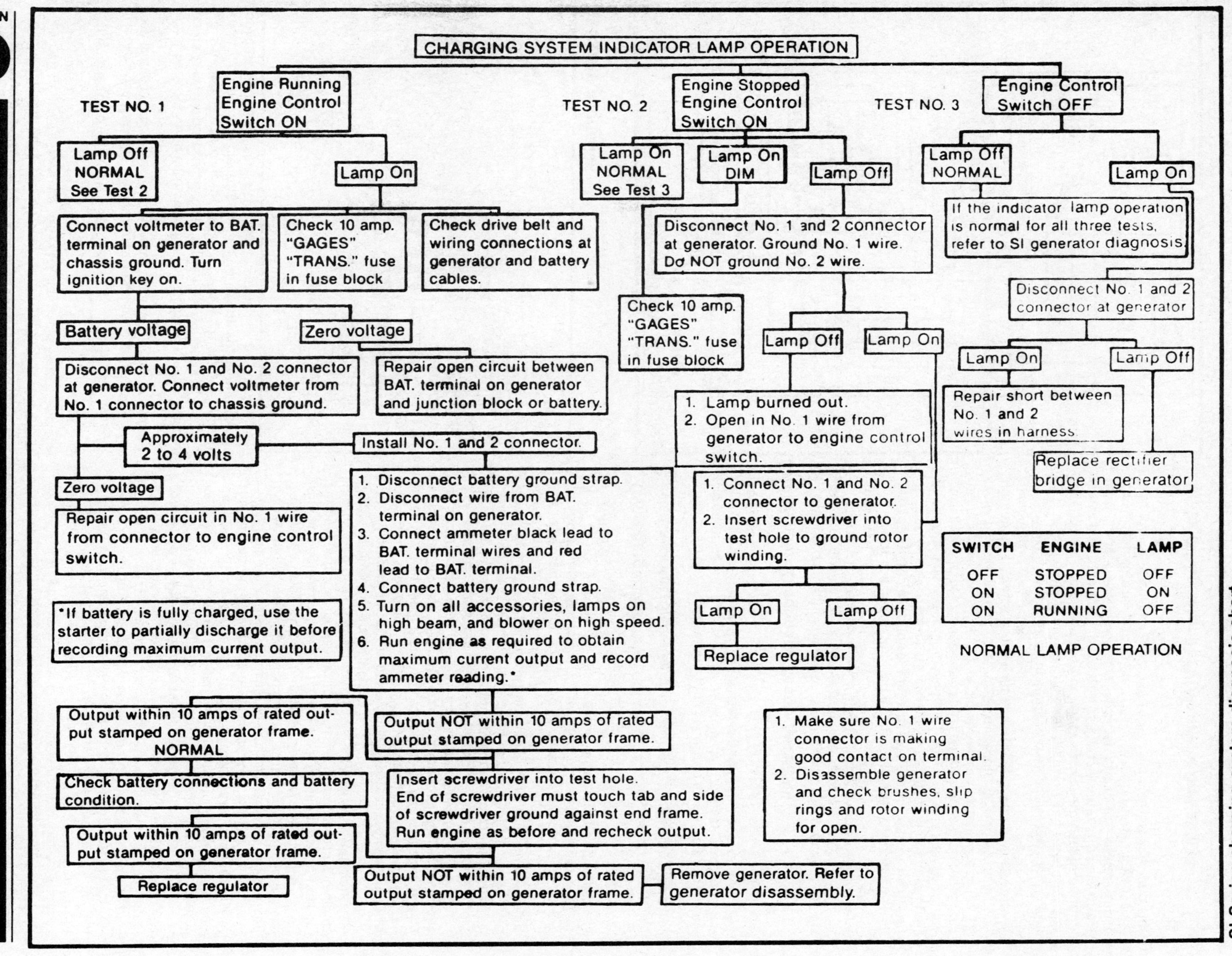

SI Series charging system diagnosis chart

4. Switch on, lamp on, engine running. Check for a blown fuse, (where used), between indicator lamp and switch and also in A/C circuit.

Undercharged Battery Test

1. Be sure that the undercharged battery condition has not been caused by accessories that have been left on for an extended period of time.
2. Check the alternator belt for proper belt tension. Inspect the battery for physical defects replace as required.
3. Inspect the wiring for defects. Check all connections for proper contact and cleanliness, including the slip connectors at the generator and baulkhead connections.

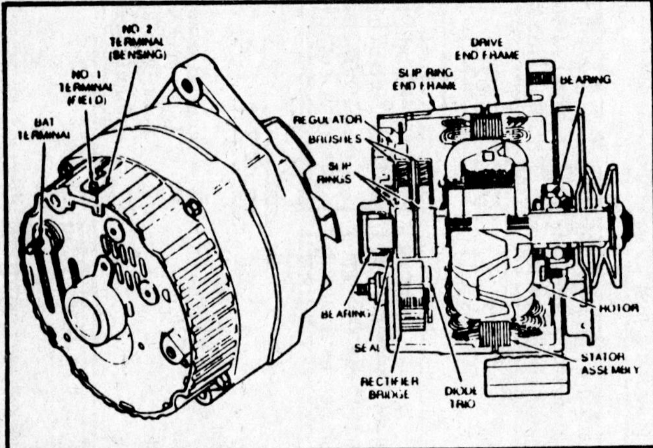

SI Series alternator

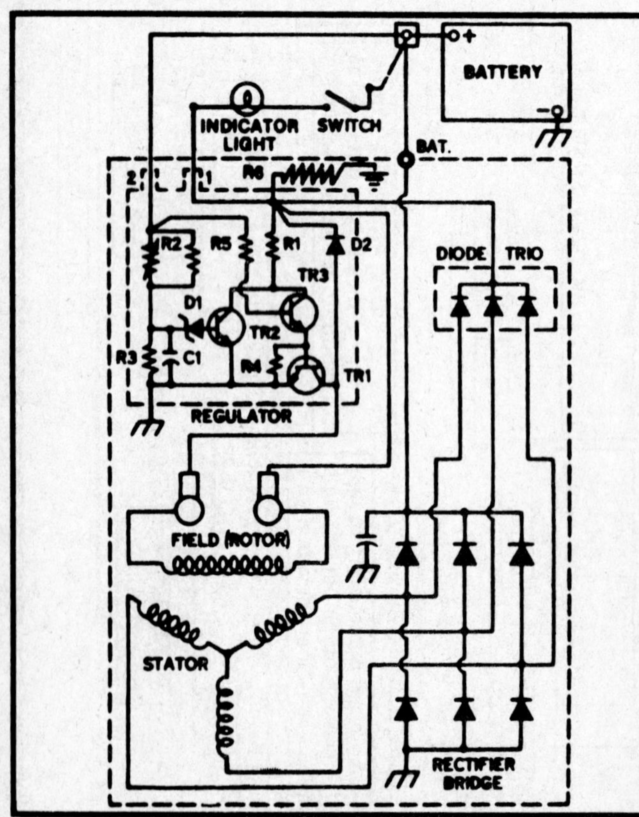

SI Series alternator schematic

4. With ignition switch ON and all wiring harness leads connected, connect a voltmeter from the generator Bat terminal to ground, from the generator No. 1 terminal to ground and from the generator No. 2 terminal to ground. A zero reading indicates an open between voltmeter connection and battery.
5. Delcotron alternators have a built in feature which prevents overcharge and accessory damage by preventing the alternator from turning on if there is an open in the wiring harness connected to the No. 2 alternator terminal.
6. If Steps 1 through 5 check out okay, check the alternator as follows. Disconnect negative battery cable. Connect an ammeter or alternator tester in the circuit at the Bat terminal of the alternator. Reconnect negative battery cable.
7. Turn on radio, windshield wipers, lights high beam and blower motor on high speed. Connect a carbon pile across the battery (or use alternator tester). Operate engine about 2000 rpm and adjust carbon pile as required, to obtain maximum current output. If ampere output is within 10 amperes of rated output as stamped on generator frame, alternator is not defective. Recheck Steps 1 through 5.
8. If ampere output is not within 10 percent of rated output, determine if test hole is accessible. Ground the field winding by inserting a suitable tool into the test hole. Tab is within ¾ inch of casting surface. Do not force suitable tool deeper than one inch into end frame to avoid damaging alternator.
9. Operate engine at moderate speed as required and adjust carbon pile as required to obtain maximum current output.
10. If output is within 10 amperes of rated output, check field winding, diode trio and rectifier bridge. Test regulator with an approved regulator tested.
11. If output is not within 10 amperes of rated output, check the field winding, diode trio, rectifier bridge and stator. If test hole is not accessible, disassemble alternator and repair as required.

Overcharged Battery Test

1. Check the condition of the battery before any testing is done.
2. If an obvious overcharging condition exists, remove the alternator from the vehicle and check the field windings for grounds or shorts. If defective, replace the rotor. Test the regulator.

Alternator Diagnostic Tester (J-26290)

This special diagnostic tester is designed to determine if the alternator should be removed from the vehicle.

1. Install tester J-26290 according to manufacturers instructions.
2. With the engine off and all lights and accessories off, test the alternator as follows. Light flashes, go to Step 3. Light on, indicates fault in tester which should be replaced. Light off, pull plug from generator. One flashing light, indicates that the alternator should be removed and the rectifier bridge replaced. Light off,indicates faulty tester or no voltage to tester. Check for 12 volts at #2 terminal of harness connector. Repair wiring or terminals if 12 volts is not available. Replace tester if 12 volts is available.
3. With the engine at fast idle and all accessories and lights off, test the alternator as follows. Light off indicates that the charging system good, do not remove alternator. Light on indicates a component failure within the alternator. Remove alternator and check diode trio, rectifier bridge and stator. Light flashing indicates a problem within the alternator. Remove alternator and check regulator, rotor field coil, brushes and slip rings.

Voltage Regulator Test (Alternator on Vehicle)

1. Connect a battery charger and a voltmeter to the battery.
2. Turn the ignition on and slowly increase the charge rate.

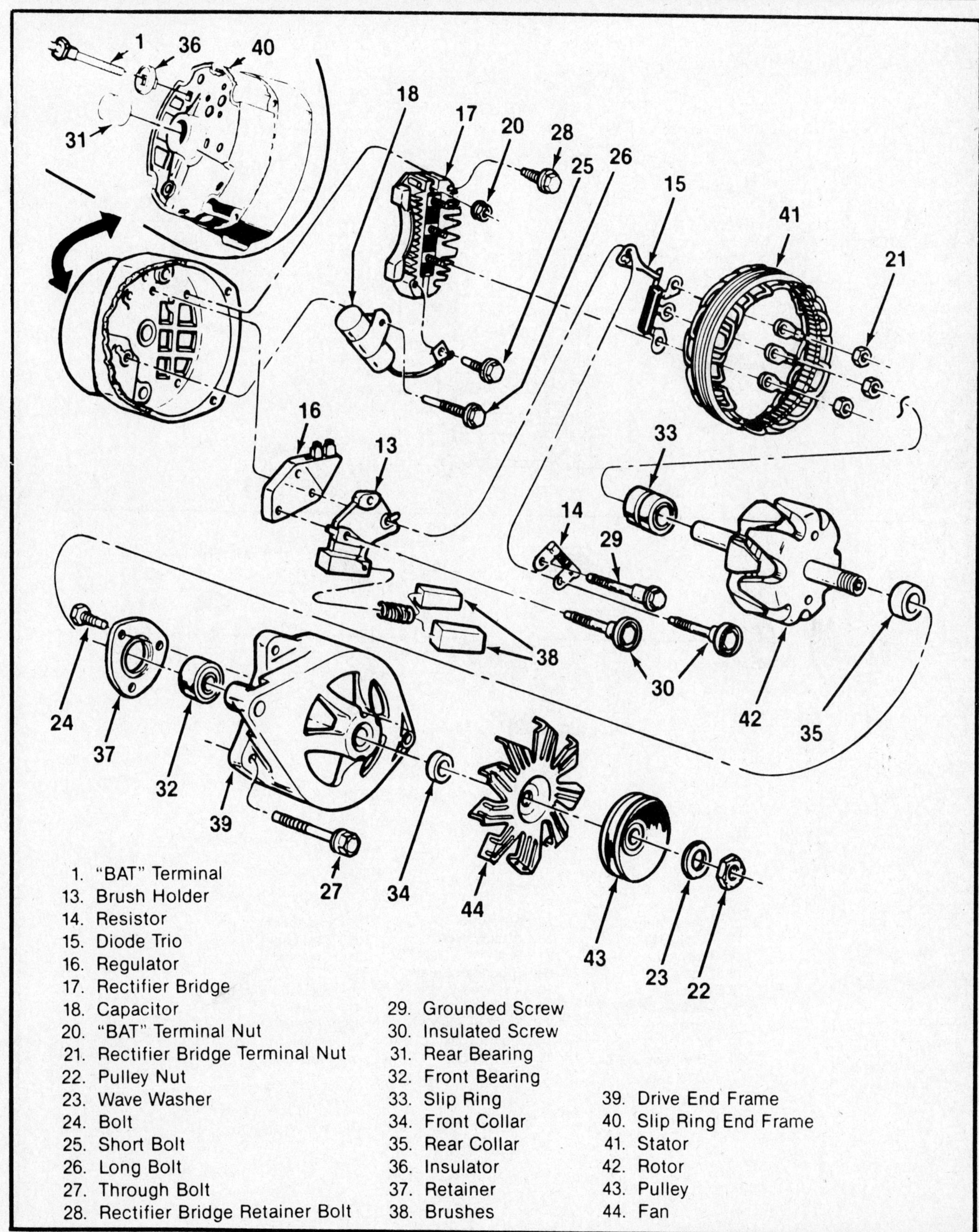
1
36
40
31
18
17
20
28
25
26
15
41
21
16
13
33
14
29
38
30
42
35
24
37
32
39
27
34
44
43
23
22
1. "BAT" Terminal
13. Brush Holder
14. Resistor
15. Diode Trio
16. Regulator
17. Rectifier Bridge
18. Capacitor
20. "BAT" Terminal Nut
21. Rectifier Bridge Terminal Nut
22. Pulley Nut
23. Wave Washer
24. Bolt
25. Short Bolt
26. Long Bolt
27. Through Bolt
28. Rectifier Bridge Retainer Bolt
29. Grounded Screw
30. Insulated Screw
31. Rear Bearing
32. Front Bearing
33. Slip Ring
34. Front Collar
35. Rear Collar
36. Insulator
37. Retainer
38. Brushes
39. Drive End Frame
40. Slip Ring End Frame
41. Stator
42. Rotor
43. Pulley
44. Fan

17SI Series alternator, exploded view

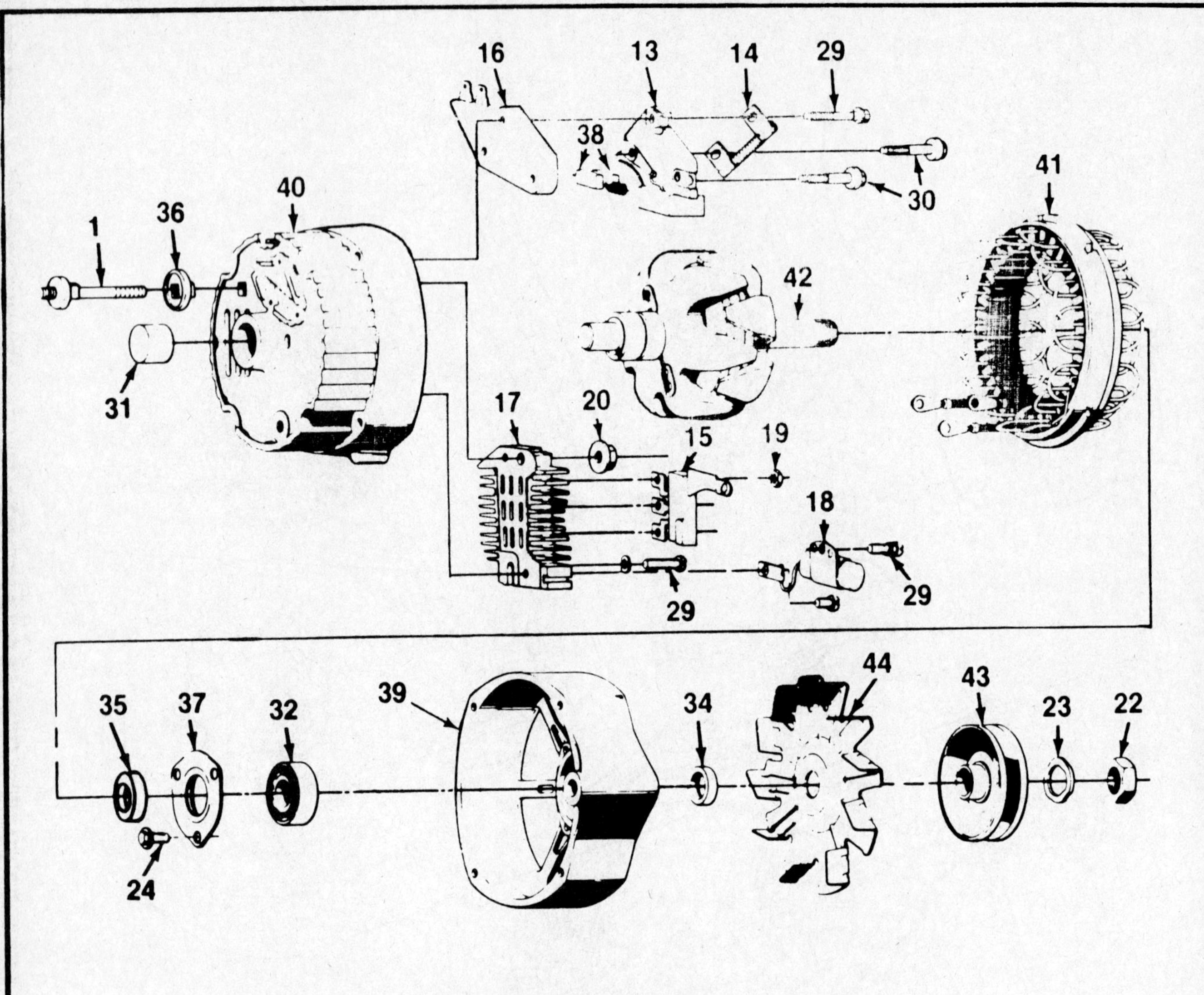

1. "Bat" Terminal
13. Brush Holder
14. Resistor
15. Diode Trio
16. Regulator
17. Rectifier Bridge
18. Capacitor
19. Nut
20. "Bat" Terminal Nut
22. Pulley Nut
23. Washer
24. Bolt
29. Grounded Screw
30. Insulated Screw
31. Rear Bearing
32. Front Bearing
34. Front Collar
35. Rear Collar
36. Insulator
37. Retainer
38. Brushes
39. Drive End Frame
40. Slip Ring End Frame
41. Stator
42. Rotor
43. Pulley
44. Fan

12SI alternator, exploded view

The alternator light in the vehicle will dim at the voltage regulator setting. Voltage regulator setting should be 13.5–16.0 volts. This test works if the rotor setting is good, even if the stator rectifier bridge or diode trio is bad.

Voltage Regulator Test (Alternator off Vehicle)

1. Remove the alternator from the vehicle.
2. Disassemble the alternator and remove the voltage regualtor.
3. Connect a voltmeter and a fast charger to a 12 volt battery. Connect a test light to the regulator and observe the battery polarity.
4. The test light should light.
5. Turn on the fast charger and slowly increase the charge rate. Observe the voltmeter, the light should go out at the voltage regualtor setting. The voltage regulator setting specification is 13.5–16.0 volts.

Alternator Bench Test

1. Remove the alternator from the vehicle. Position the unit in a suitable test stand.
2. Connect the alternator in series, but leave the carbon pile disconnected.

NOTE: Ground polarity of the battery must be the same as the alternator. Be sure to use a fully charged battery and a ten ohm resistor rated at six watts or more between the alternator No. 1 terminal and the battery.

3. Increase the alternator speed slowly and observe the voltage.
4. If the voltage is uncontrolled with speed and increases above 15.5 volts on a 12 volt system, or 31 volts on a 24 volt system, test regulator with an approved regulator tester and check field winding. If voltage is below 15.5 volts on a 12 volt system, or 31 volts on a 24 volt system, connect the carbon pile.

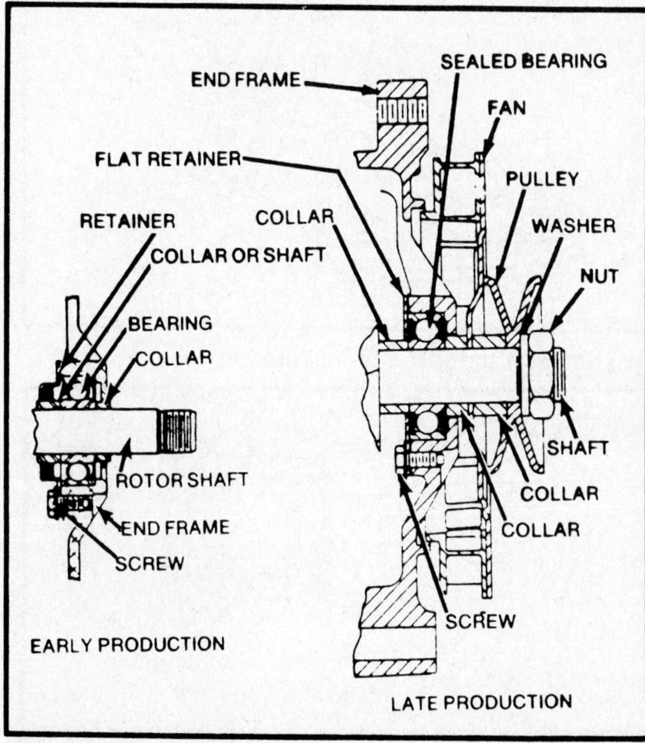

SI Series alternator, side view showing early and late bearing components

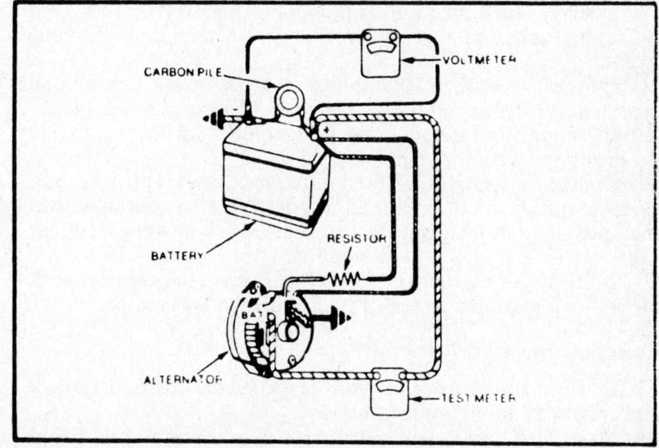

SI Series alternator bench test hook-up

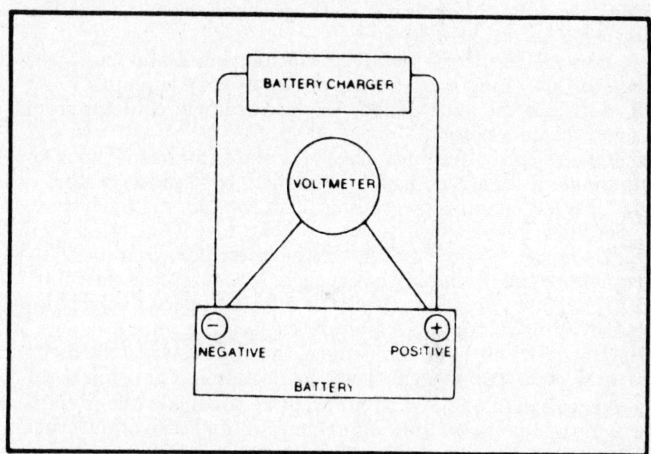

SI Series alternator voltage regulator test (on vehicle)

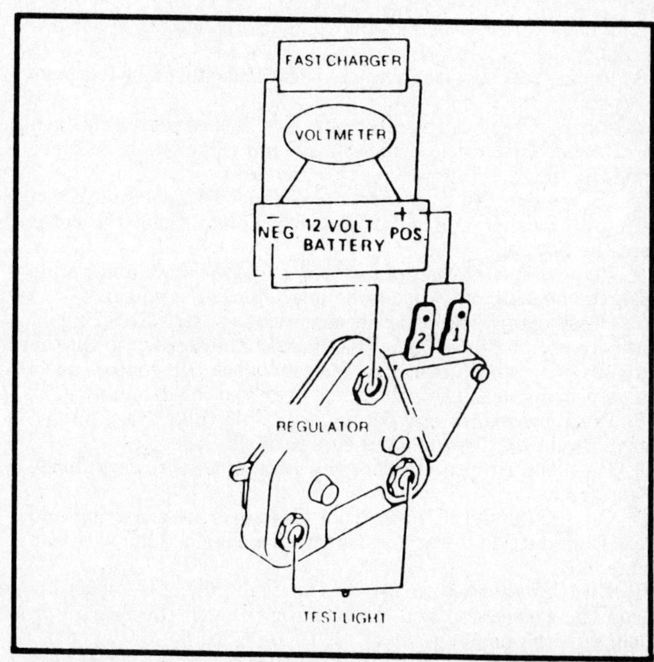

SI Series alternator voltage regulator test (off vehicle)

5. Operate the alternator at moderate speed as required and adjust the carbon pile as required to obtain maximum current output.

6. If output is within 10 amperes of rated output as stamped on alternator frame, alternator is good. If output is not within 10 amperes of rated output, keep battery loaded with carbon pile and ground alternator field.

7. Operate alternator at moderate speed and adjust carbon pile as required to obtain maximum output. If output is within 10 amperes of rated output, test regulator with an approved regulator tester and check field winding.

9. If output is not within 10 amperes of rated output, check the field winding, diode trio, rectifier bridge and stator.

Disassembly and Assembly

1. Remove the alternator from the vehicle. Position the assembly in a suitable holding fixture.

2. Make scribe marks on the alternator case end frames to aid in reassembly.

3. Remove the four through bolts that retain the assembly together. Separate the drive end frame assembly from the rectifier end frame assembly.

4. Remove the three rectifier attaching nuts and the three regulator attaching screws from the end frame assembly.

5. Separate the stator, diode trio and voltage regulator from the end frame assembly.

6. On the 10SI alternator, check the stator for opens using an ohmmeter. If high readings are obtained, replace the stator.

7. Check the stator for grounds, using an ohmmeter. If readings are low, replace the stator.

8. Using an ohmmeter, check the rotor for grounds. The ohmmeter reading should be very high. If not, replace the rotor.

9. Using an ohmmeter, check the rotor for opens. If the ohmmeter reading is not 2.4–3.5 ohms, replace the rotor.

10. To check the diode trio connect the ohmmeter to the diode trio and then reverse the lead connections. The ohmmeter should read high and low. If not, replace the diode trio. Repeat the same test between the single connector and each of the other connectors.

11. Check rectifier bridge with ohmmeter connected from grounded heat sink to flat metal on terminal. Reverse leads. If both readings are the same replace rectifier bridge.

12. Repeat test between grounded heat sink and other two flat metal clips.

13. Repeat test between insulated heat sink and three flat metal clips.

14. Clean or replace the alternator brushes as required. Position the brushes in the brush holder and retain them in place using the brush retainer wire or equivalent.

15. To remove the rotor and drive end bearing, remove the shaft nut, washer and pulley, fan and collar. Push the rotor from the housing.

16. Remove the retainer plate from inside the drive end frame. Push the bearing out. Clean or replace parts as required.

17. Press against the outer bearing race to push the bearing in. On early production alternators, it will be necessary to fill the bearing cavity with lubricant. Late production alternators use a sealed bearing and lubricant is not required for assembly.

18. Press rotor into end frame. Assemble collar, fan, pulley, washer and nut. Torque shaft nut 40–60 ft. lbs.

19. Push slip ring end bearing out from outside toward inside of end frame.

20. On 10SI and 15SI, place flat plate over new bearing and press from outside toward inside until bearing is flush with end frame.

21. On 15SI alternators, use the thin wall tube in the space between the grease cup and the housing to push the bearing in flush with the housing.

22. Assemble brush holder, regulator, resistor, diode trio, rectifier bridge and stator to slip ring end frame.

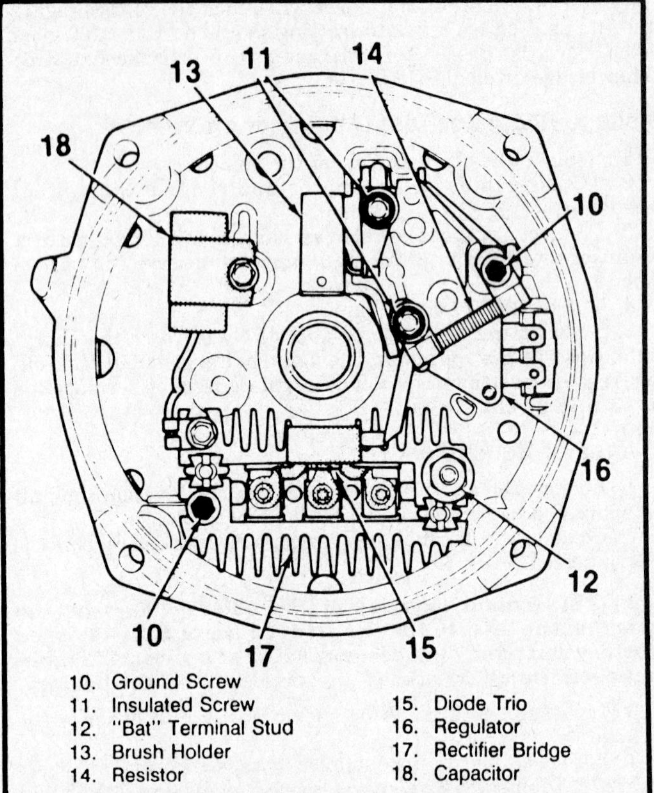

12SI Series alternator end frame and related components

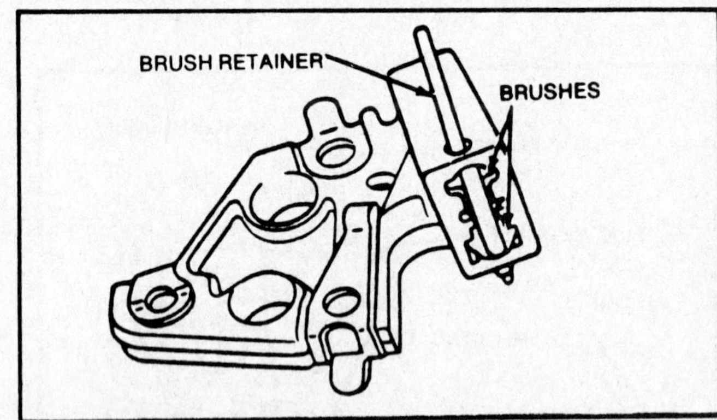

SI Series alternator brush installation

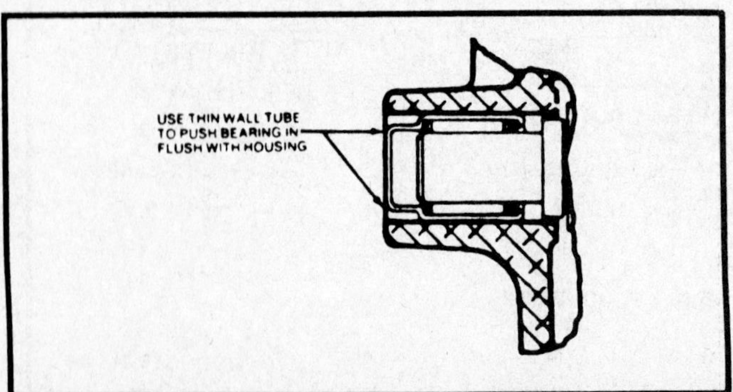

15 SI Series alternator rectifier end bearing installation

23. Assemble end frames together with through bolts. Remove brush retainer wire.

Delcotron CS-130

This alternator has an internal regulator, but does not have a diode trio. The delta stator, rectifier bridge and rotor with slip rings brushes are electrically similar to the other alternators.

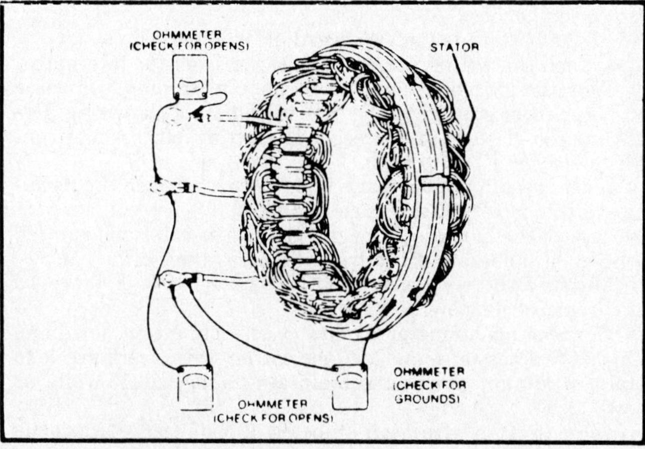

SI Series alternator stator test

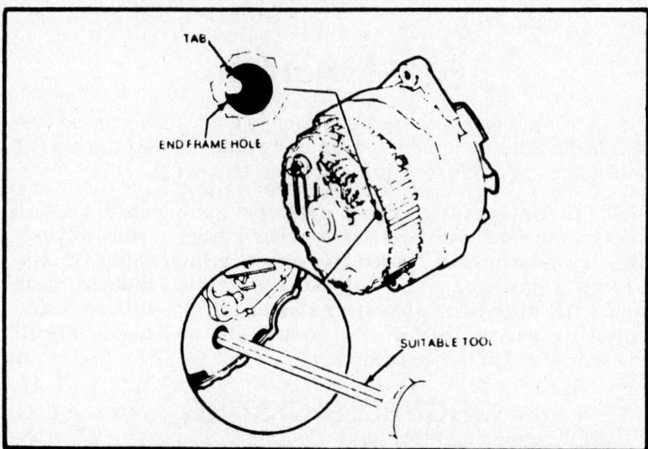

SI Series alternator-if a test hole is accessible, ground the field winding by inserting a suitable tool into the test hole (max. of 1 in.)

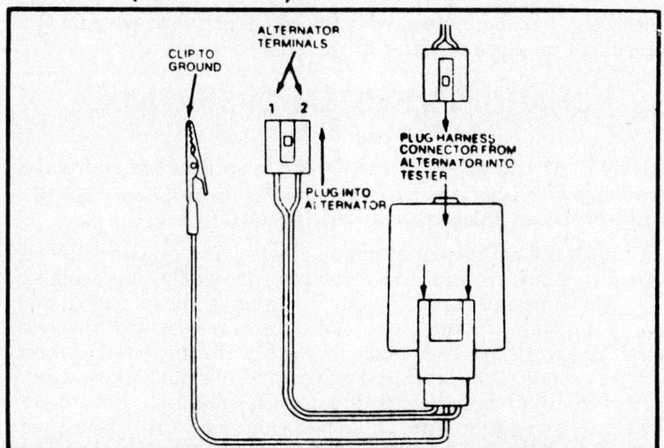

SI Series alternator diagnostic tester (J-26290)

The regulator voltage setting varies with temperature and limits system voltage by controlling rotor field current. The regulator has four terminals, "P","L","I" and "S". The "L" and"I" terminals serve to turn on the regualtor and allow the field current to flow when the switch is closed. The "I" terminal may be connected directly to the switch, or through a resistor. The "I" circuit may be used with or without the "L" circuit; that is, with or without anything connected to the "L"circuit. The use of "P", "L" and "S" terminals is optional.

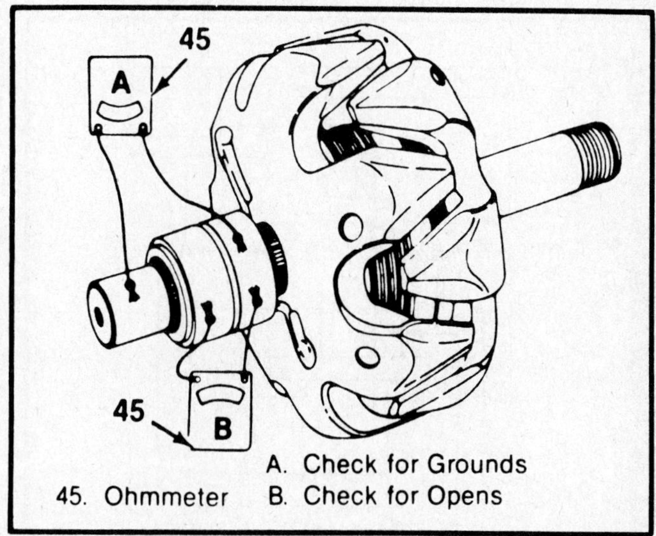

SI Series alternator rotor test

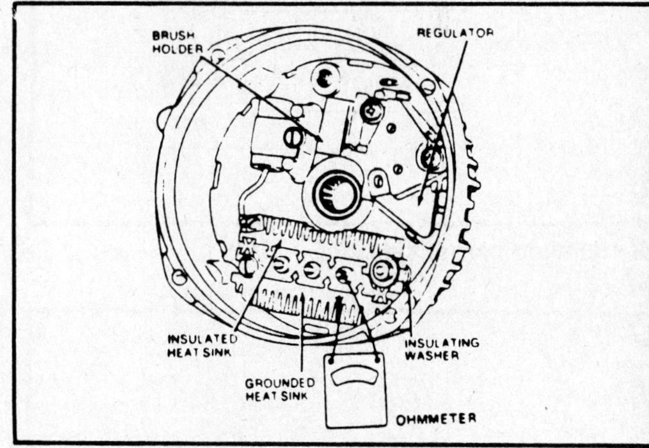

SI Series alternator rectifier bridge test

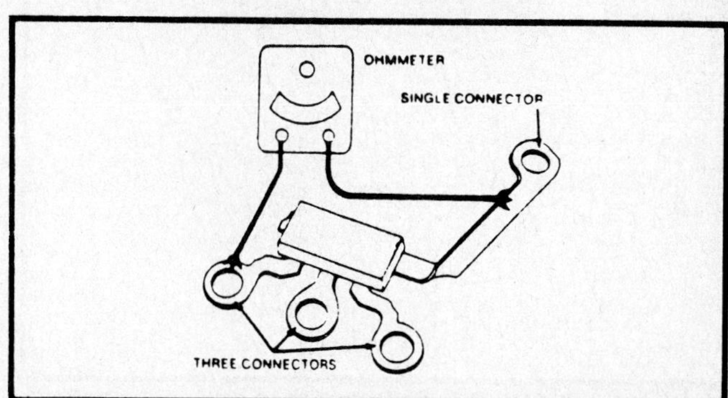

SI Series alternator diode trio test

DIAGNOSTIC TEST

NOTE: The CS-130 alternator is not serviceable and must be replaced, if found to be defective.

1. Check the belt for wear and tension.
2. For vehicles without a charge indicator lamp, proceed to step 5.
3. With the engine control switch on and the engine stopped, the lamp should be on. If not, detach the wiring harness at the alternator and ground the "L" terminal lead.

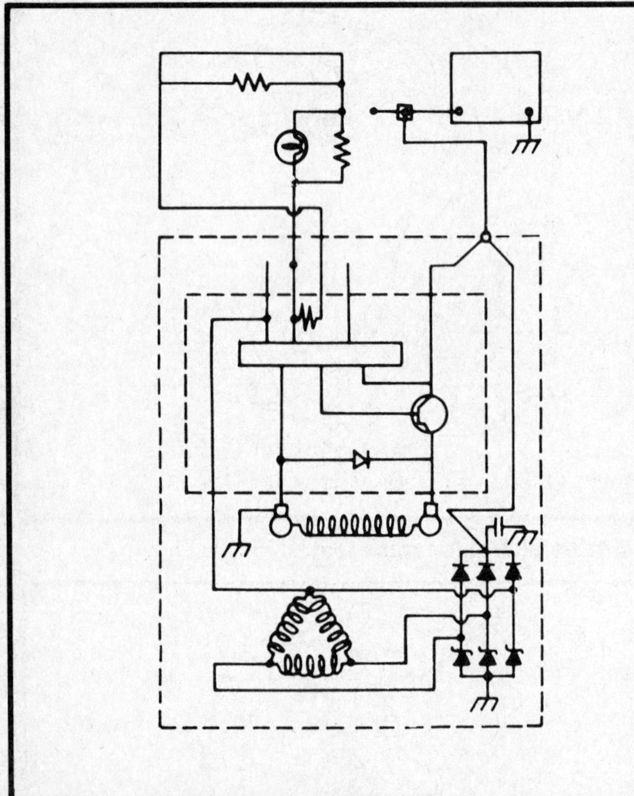

CS-130 alternator schematic

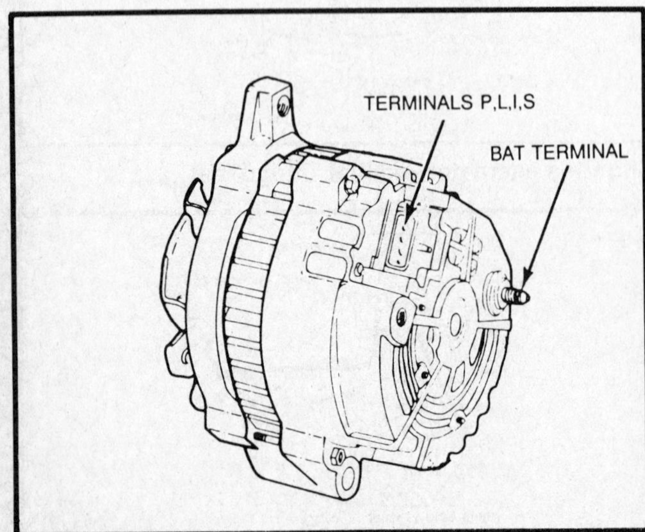

CS-130 alternator

- If the the lamp lights, replace the alternator.
- If the lamp does not light, locate the open circuit between the grounding lead and the engine control switch. the lamp may be open.

4. With the switch on and the engine running at moderate speed, the lamp should be off. If not, detach the wiring harness at the alternator.

- If the the lamp goes out, replace the generator.
- If the lamp stays on, check for a grounded "L" terminal wire in the harness.

If the battery is undercharged or overcharged:

Detach the wiring harness connector from the alternator.

With the switch on and the engine not running, connect a voltmeter from ground to the "L" terminal in the wiring harness and the "I" terminal, if used. The wiring harness may connect to either "I" or to both.

- A zero reading indicates an open circuit between the terminal and the battery. Correct as required.
- Connect the harness connector to the generator and run the engine at moderate speed with the accessories off.
- Measure the voltage across the battery. If it is above 16 volts, replace the generator.
- Connect an ammeter at the generator output terminal, turn on the accessories and load the battery with a carbon pile to obtain maximum amperage. Maintain voltage at 13 volts or above.

If the output is within 15 amperes of the rated output, the generator is OK.

If the output is not within 15 amperes of the rated output, replace the generator.

Ford-Motorcraft

The Ford-Motorcraft charging system is a negative ground system. It includes an alternator, an electronic regulator, a charge indicator or an ammeter and a storage battery.

NOTE: Late model Ford systems have replaced the electro mechanical regulator with either a non adjustable transistorized regulator or an adjustable transistorized regulator. The adjustable transistorized unit used with high output systems has a single, voltage limit adjusting screw under the cover. Do not use a metal screwdriver for adjustment.

TROUBLESHOOTING

NOTE: See the "Alternator Test Plans" section before proceeding further.

Fusible Links

Check the fusible link located between the starter relay and the alternator. Replace the link if it is burned or open.

CHARGING SYSTEM OPERATION

NOTE: If the current indicator is to give an accurate reading, the battery cables must be of the same gauge and length as the original equipment.

1. With the engine running and all electrical systems turned off, place a current indicator over the positive battery cable.
2. If a charge of about 5 amps is recorded, the charging system is working. If a draw of about 5 amps is recorded, the system is not working. The needle moves toward the battery when a charge condition is indicated and away from the battery when a draw condition is indicated. If a draw is indicated, continue to the next testing procedure. If an overcharge of 10 to 15 amps is indicated, check for a faulty regulator or a bad ground at the regulator or the alternator.

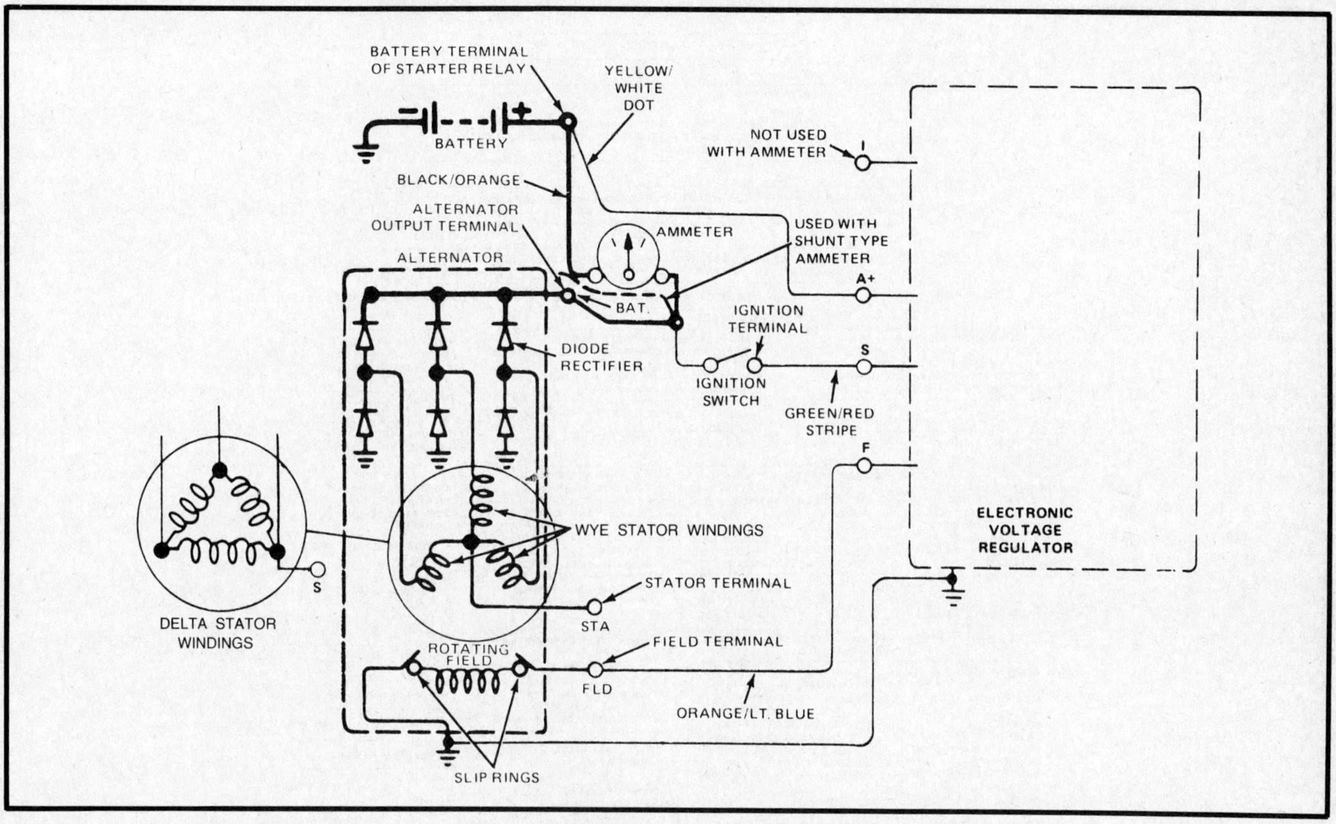

BATTERY TERMINAL OF STARTER RELAY
YELLOW/ WHITE DOT
BATTERY
NOT USED WITH AMMETER
I
BLACK/ORANGE
ALTERNATOR OUTPUT TERMINAL
AMMETER
USED WITH SHUNT TYPE AMMETER
A+
ALTERNATOR
BAT.
IGNITION TERMINAL
DIODE RECTIFIER
S
IGNITION SWITCH
GREEN/RED STRIPE
F
ELECTRONIC VOLTAGE REGULATOR
WYE STATOR WINDINGS
S
DELTA STATOR WINDINGS
STATOR TERMINAL
STA
ROTATING FIELD
FIELD TERMINAL
FLD
ORANGE/LT. BLUE
SLIP RINGS

Rear terminal alternator charging system schematic with ammeter—typical of side terminal alternators

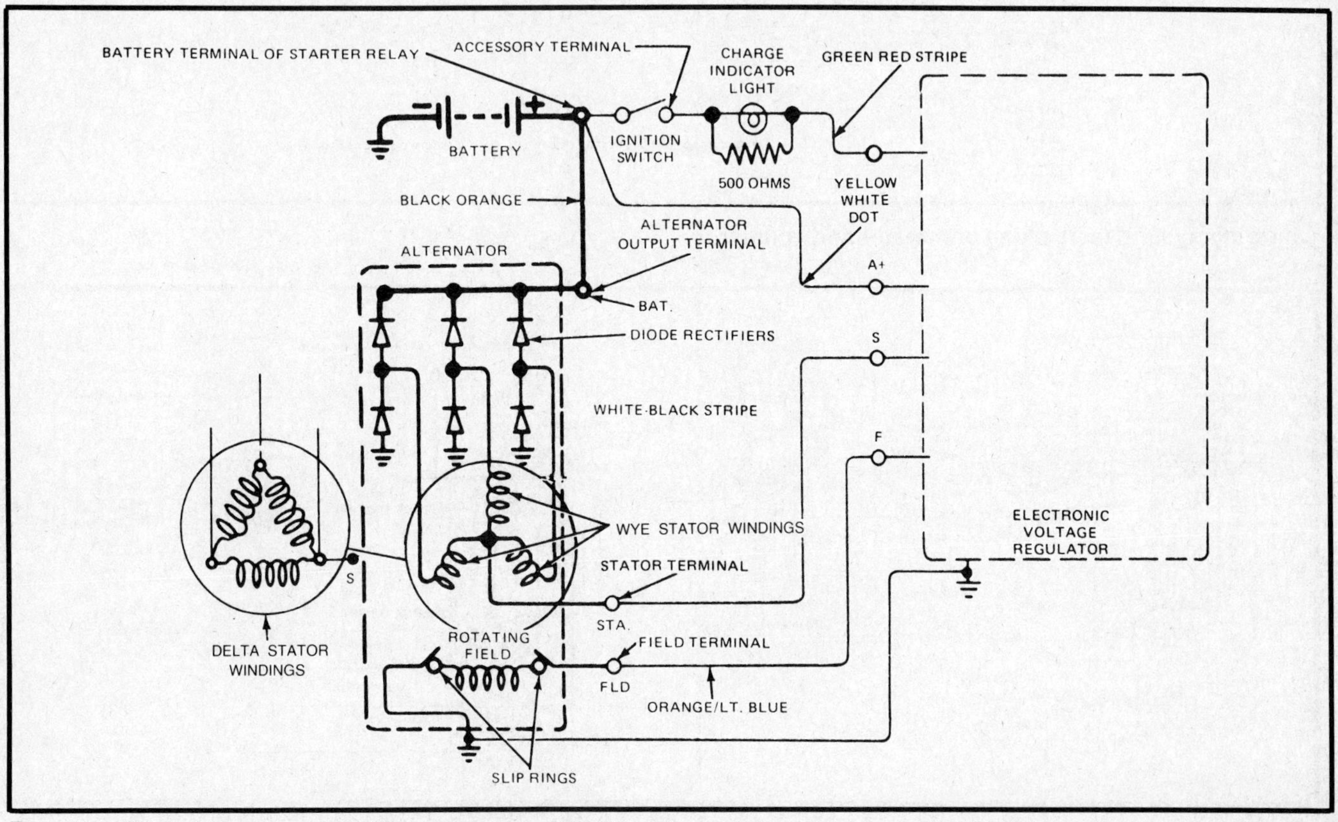

BATTERY TERMINAL OF STARTER RELAY
ACCESSORY TERMINAL
CHARGE INDICATOR LIGHT
GREEN RED STRIPE
BATTERY
IGNITION SWITCH
500 OHMS
YELLOW WHITE DOT
BLACK ORANGE
ALTERNATOR OUTPUT TERMINAL
ALTERNATOR
A+
BAT.
DIODE RECTIFIERS
S
WHITE-BLACK STRIPE
F
WYE STATOR WINDINGS
ELECTRONIC VOLTAGE REGULATOR
S
STATOR TERMINAL
STA.
DELTA STATOR WINDINGS
ROTATING FIELD
FIELD TERMINAL
FLD
ORANGE/LT. BLUE
SLIP RINGS

Rear terminal alternator charging system schematic with indicator light—typical of side terminal alternators

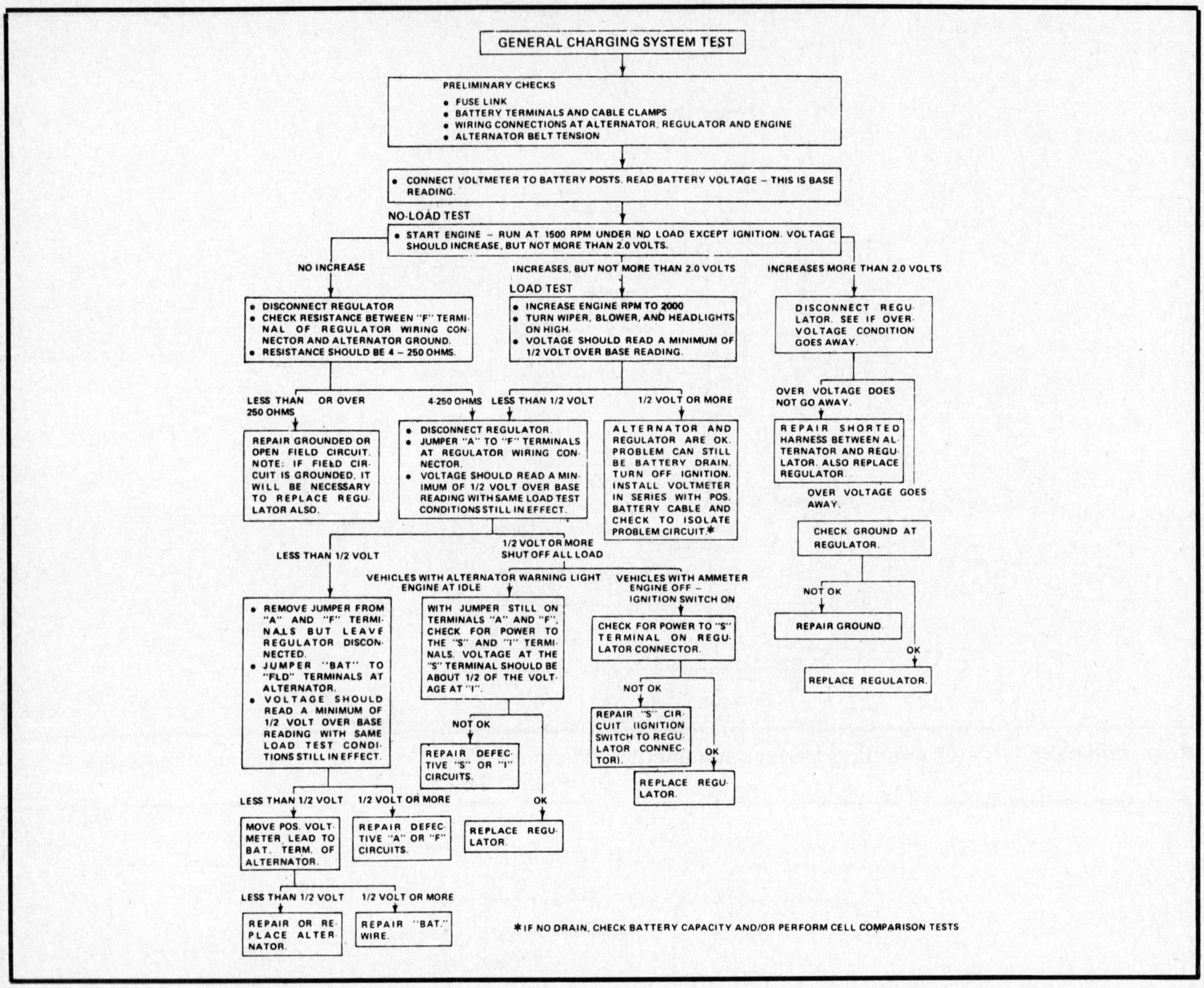

GENERAL CHARGING SYSTEM TEST

PRELIMINARY CHECKS
- FUSE LINK
- BATTERY TERMINALS AND CABLE CLAMPS
- WIRING CONNECTIONS AT ALTERNATOR, REGULATOR AND ENGINE
- ALTERNATOR BELT TENSION

- CONNECT VOLTMETER TO BATTERY POSTS. READ BATTERY VOLTAGE – THIS IS BASE READING.

NO-LOAD TEST
- START ENGINE – RUN AT 1500 RPM UNDER NO LOAD EXCEPT IGNITION. VOLTAGE SHOULD INCREASE, BUT NOT MORE THAN 2.0 VOLTS.

NO INCREASE
- DISCONNECT REGULATOR
- CHECK RESISTANCE BETWEEN "F" TERMINAL OF REGULATOR WIRING CONNECTOR AND ALTERNATOR GROUND.
- RESISTANCE SHOULD BE 4 – 250 OHMS.

LESS THAN OR OVER 250 OHMS

REPAIR GROUNDED OR OPEN FIELD CIRCUIT. NOTE: IF FIELD CIRCUIT IS GROUNDED, IT WILL BE NECESSARY TO REPLACE REGULATOR ALSO.

4-250 OHMS
- DISCONNECT REGULATOR.
- JUMPER "A" TO "F" TERMINALS AT REGULATOR WIRING CONNECTOR.
- VOLTAGE SHOULD READ A MINIMUM OF 1/2 VOLT OVER BASE READING WITH SAME LOAD TEST CONDITIONS STILL IN EFFECT.

LESS THAN 1/2 VOLT
- REMOVE JUMPER FROM "A" AND "F" TERMINALS BUT LEAVE REGULATOR DISCONNECTED.
- JUMPER "BAT" TO "FLD" TERMINALS AT ALTERNATOR.
- VOLTAGE SHOULD READ A MINIMUM OF 1/2 VOLT OVER BASE READING WITH SAME LOAD TEST CONDITIONS STILL IN EFFECT.

LESS THAN 1/2 VOLT
MOVE POS. VOLTMETER LEAD TO BAT. TERM. OF ALTERNATOR.

LESS THAN 1/2 VOLT
REPAIR OR REPLACE ALTERNATOR.

1/2 VOLT OR MORE
REPAIR "BAT." WIRE.

1/2 VOLT OR MORE
REPAIR DEFECTIVE "A" OR "F" CIRCUITS.

1/2 VOLT OR MORE
SHUT OFF ALL LOAD

VEHICLES WITH ALTERNATOR WARNING LIGHT ENGINE AT IDLE
WITH JUMPER STILL ON TERMINALS "A" AND "F", CHECK FOR POWER TO THE "S" AND "I" TERMINALS. VOLTAGE AT THE "S" TERMINAL SHOULD BE ABOUT 1/2 OF THE VOLTAGE AT "I".

NOT OK
REPAIR DEFECTIVE "S" OR "I" CIRCUITS.

OK
REPLACE REGULATOR.

VEHICLES WITH AMMETER ENGINE OFF – IGNITION SWITCH ON
CHECK FOR POWER TO "S" TERMINAL ON REGULATOR CONNECTOR.

NOT OK
REPAIR "S" CIRCUIT (IGNITION SWITCH TO REGULATOR CONNECTOR).

OK
REPLACE REGULATOR.

INCREASES, BUT NOT MORE THAN 2.0 VOLTS

LOAD TEST
- INCREASE ENGINE RPM TO 2000
- TURN WIPER, BLOWER, AND HEADLIGHTS ON HIGH.
- VOLTAGE SHOULD READ A MINIMUM OF 1/2 VOLT OVER BASE READING.

LESS THAN 1/2 VOLT (see "DISCONNECT REGULATOR. JUMPER "A" TO "F" TERMINALS" above)

1/2 VOLT OR MORE
ALTERNATOR AND REGULATOR ARE OK. PROBLEM CAN STILL BE BATTERY DRAIN. TURN OFF IGNITION. INSTALL VOLTMETER IN SERIES WITH POS. BATTERY CABLE AND CHECK TO ISOLATE PROBLEM CIRCUIT.*

INCREASES MORE THAN 2.0 VOLTS
DISCONNECT REGULATOR. SEE IF OVER-VOLTAGE CONDITION GOES AWAY.

OVER VOLTAGE DOES NOT GO AWAY.
REPAIR SHORTED HARNESS BETWEEN ALTERNATOR AND REGULATOR. ALSO REPLACE REGULATOR.

OVER VOLTAGE GOES AWAY.
CHECK GROUND AT REGULATOR.

NOT OK
REPAIR GROUND.

OK
REPLACE REGULATOR.

*IF NO DRAIN, CHECK BATTERY CAPACITY AND/OR PERFORM CELL COMPARISON TESTS

Charging system tests using ohmmeter and voltmeter

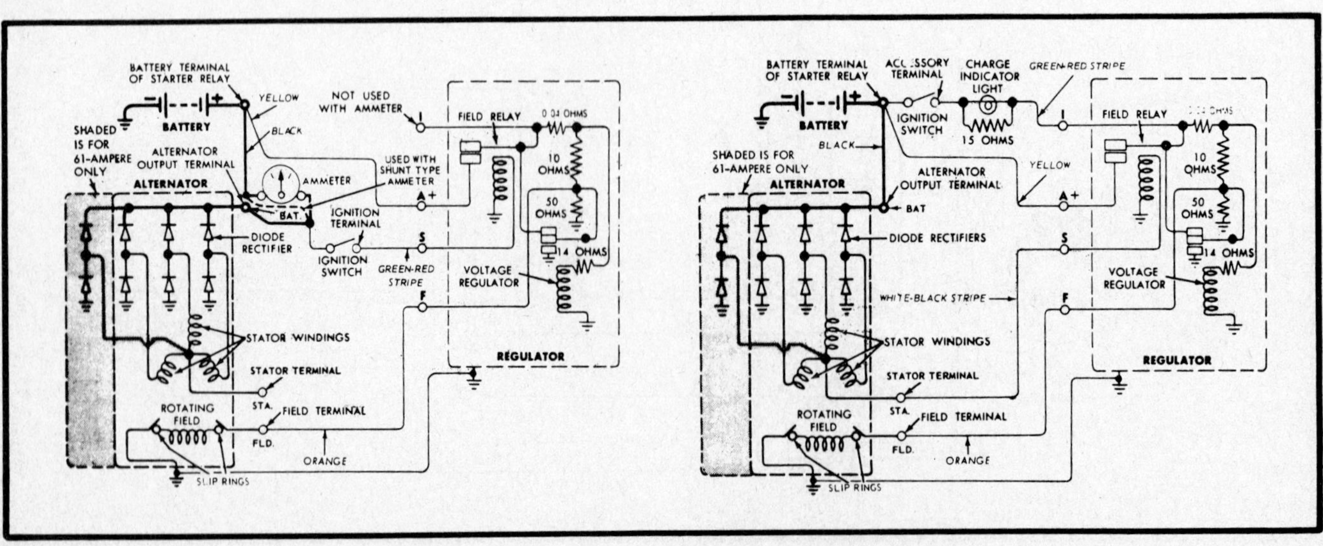

Charging system schematic with electro mechanical regulator and charging light

Testing the Ignition Switch to Regulator Circuit

1. Disconnect the regulator wiring harness from the regulator.
2. Turn on the key. Using a test light or voltmeter, check for voltage between the I wire and ground. Check for voltage between the A wire and ground. If voltage is present at this part of the system, the circuit is ok. If there is no voltage at the I wire, check for a burned out charge indicator bulb, a burned out resistor, or a break or short in the wiring. If there is no voltage present at the A wire, check for a bad connection at the starter relay or a break or short in the wire.

Isolation Test

This test determines whether the regulator or the alternator is faulty, after the rest of the circuit is found to be in good working order.

1. Disconnect the regulator wiring harness from the regulator.
2. Connect a jumper wire from the A wire to the F wire in the wiring harness plug.
3. Connect a voltmeter to the battery. The positive voltmeter lead goes to the positive terminal and the negative lead to the negative terminal. Record the reading on the voltmeter.

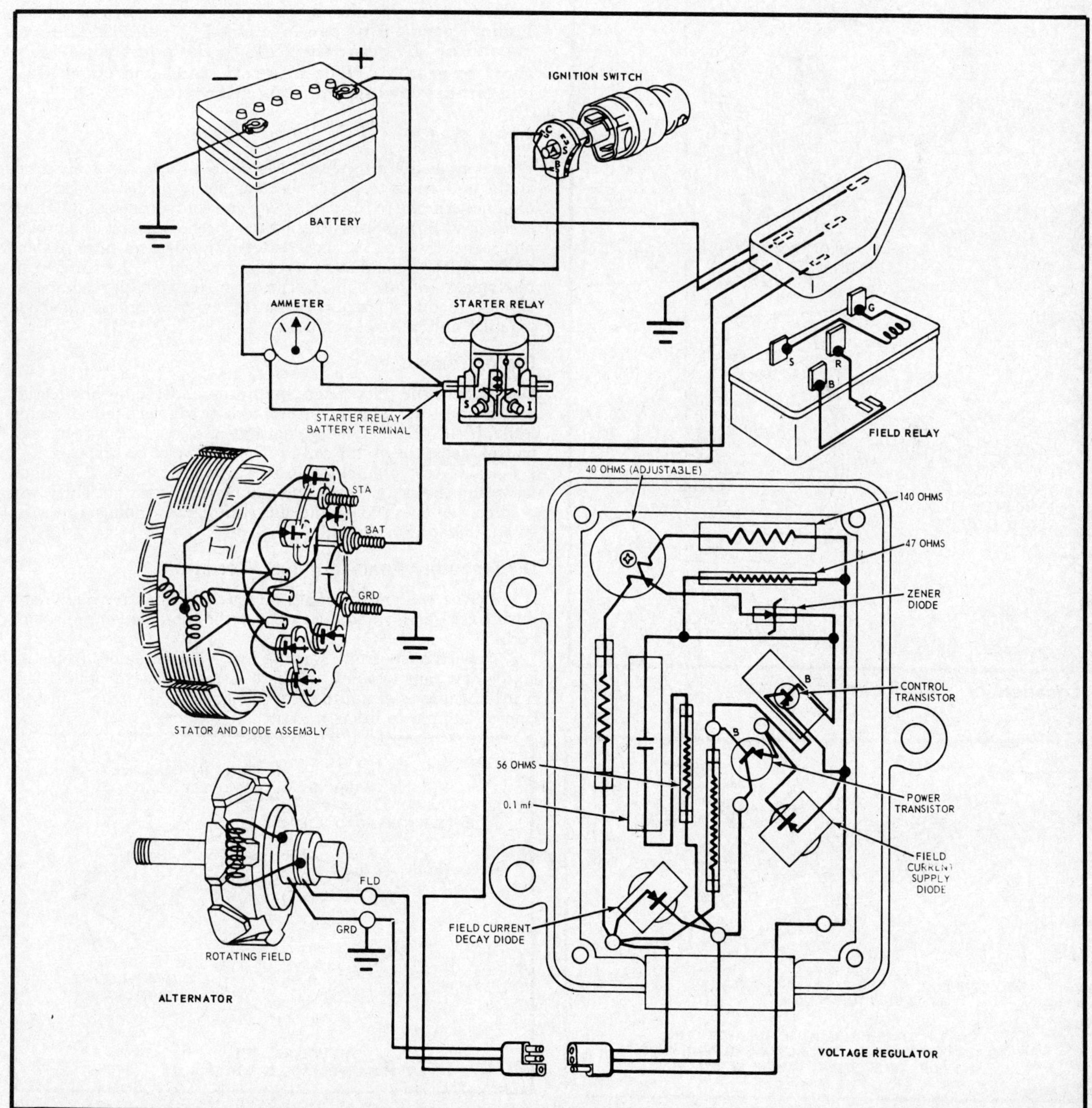

Charging system schematic with transistor regulator and ammeter

4. Turn off all of the electrical systems and start the engine. Do not race the engine.

5. Gradually increase engine speed between 1500 and 2000 rpm. The voltmeter reading should increase above the previously recorded battery voltage reading by at least one to two volts. If there is no increase, the alternator is not working correctly. If there is an increase, the voltage regulator is operating, but if it is adjustable, may need to be adjusted to its proper setting.

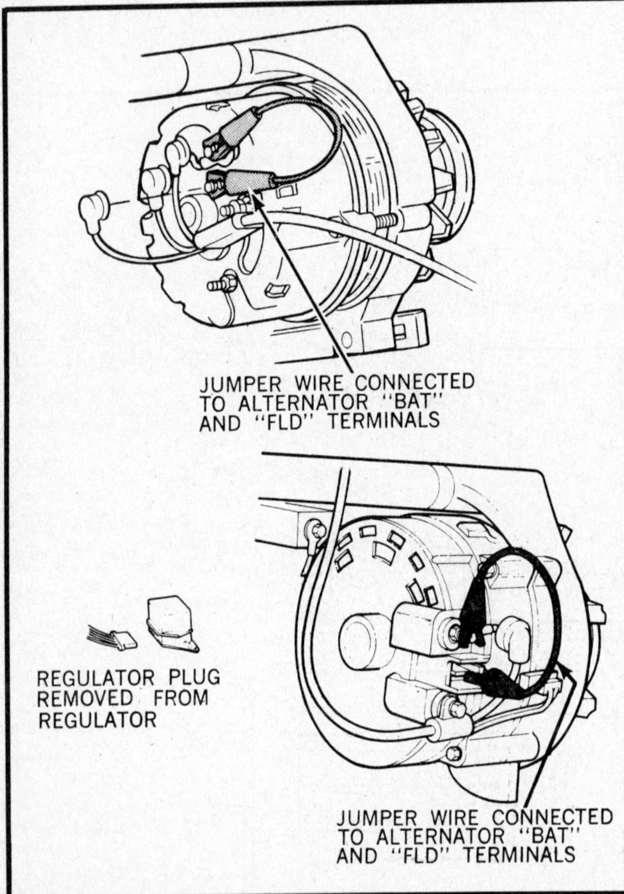

Location for jumper wire circuit tests

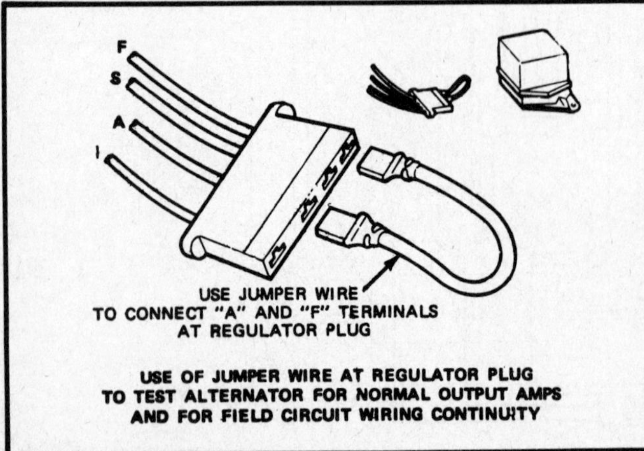

F
S
A
I
USE JUMPER WIRE
TO CONNECT "A" AND "F" TERMINALS
AT REGULATOR PLUG
USE OF JUMPER WIRE AT REGULATOR PLUG
TO TEST ALTERNATOR FOR NORMAL OUTPUT AMPS
AND FOR FIELD CIRCUIT WIRING CONTINUITY

Isolation test jumper wire

Current Draw Test

1. Remove the alternator from the vehicle. Connect a test ammeter between the alternator frame and the positive post of a 12 volt test battery.

2. Connect a jumper wire between the negative test battery post and the alternator field terminal.

3. Observe the ammeter. Little or no current flow indicates high brush resistance, open field windings, or high winding resistance. Current in excess of specifications (approximately 2.9 amps. for most models) indicates shorted or grounded field windings, or brush leads touching.

NOTE: Sometimes the alternator produces current output at low engine speeds, but ceases to put out at higher speeds. This can be caused by centrifugal force expanding the rotor windings to the point where they short to ground. Place in a test stand and check field current draw while spinning alternator.

Diode Tests

Disassemble the alternator. Disconnect diode assembly from stator and make tests. To test one set of diodes, contact one ohmmeter probe to the diode plate and contact each of the three stator lead terminals with the other probe. Reverse the probes and repeat the test. All six tests (eight for 61 amp autolite eight diode models) should show a reading of about 6 ohms in one direction and infinite ohms in the other. If two high readings, or two low readings, are obtained after reversing probes the diode is faulty and must be replaced.

Stator Tests

Disassemble the stator from the alternator assembly and rectifiers. Connect test ohmmeter probes between each pair of stator leads. If the ohmmeter does not indicate equally between each pair of leads, the stator coil is open and must be replaced.

Connect test ohmmeter probes between one of the stator leads and the stator core. The ohmmeter should not show any reading. If it does show continuity, the stator winding is grounded and must be replaced.

Disassembly Rear Terminal Alternators

1. Scribe the end housings and stator frame for alignment during reassembly and then remove the three housing through bolts.

2. Separate the front housing and rotor assembly from the stator and rear housing. If there is resistance in pulling the front housing free, tap the front housing lightly with a plastic tipped hammer to break it loose.

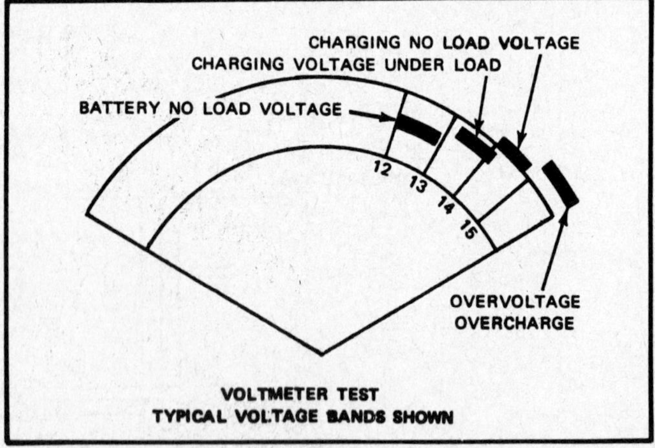

Voltmeter reading during isolation test

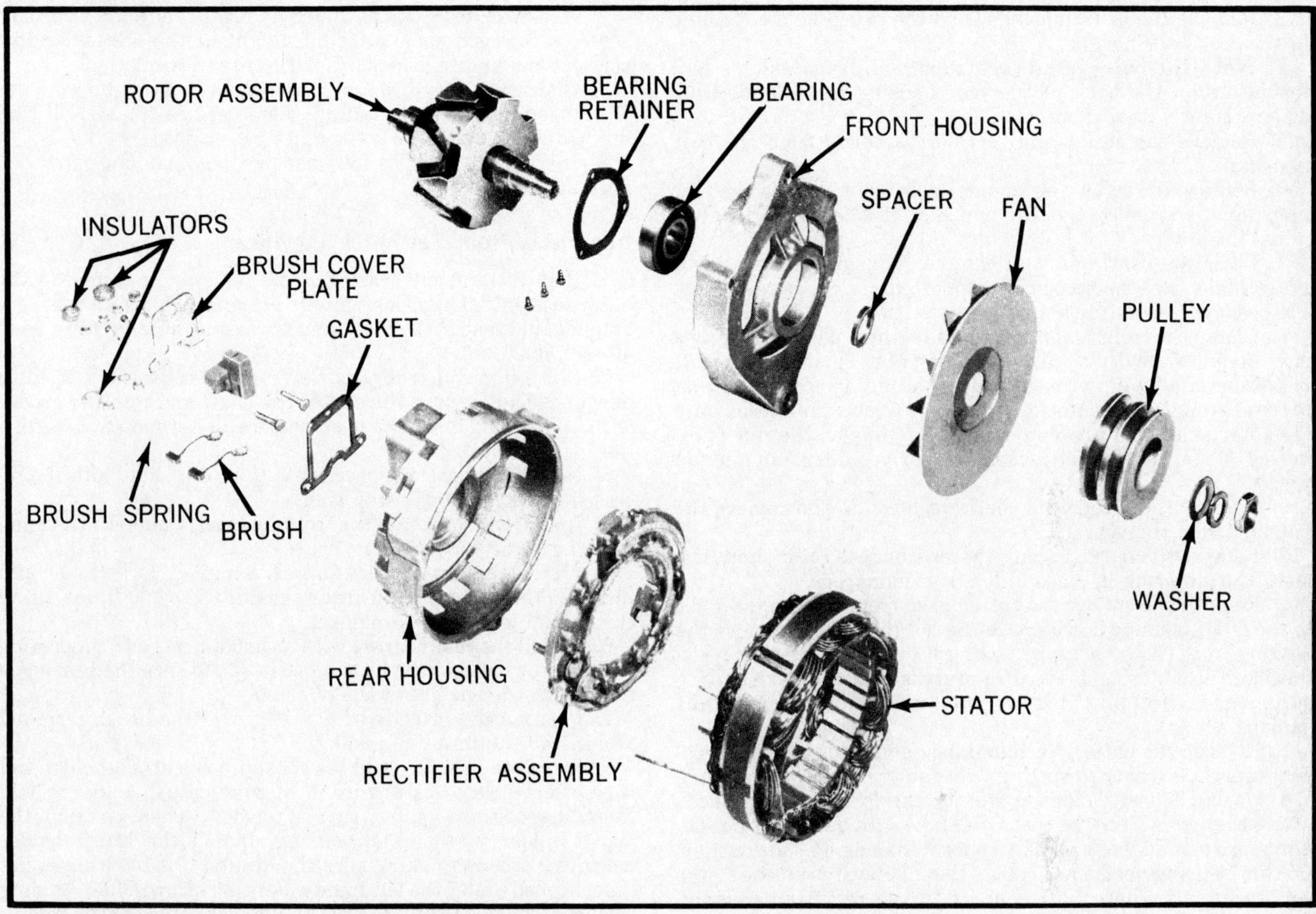

Rear terminal alternator—typical exploded view

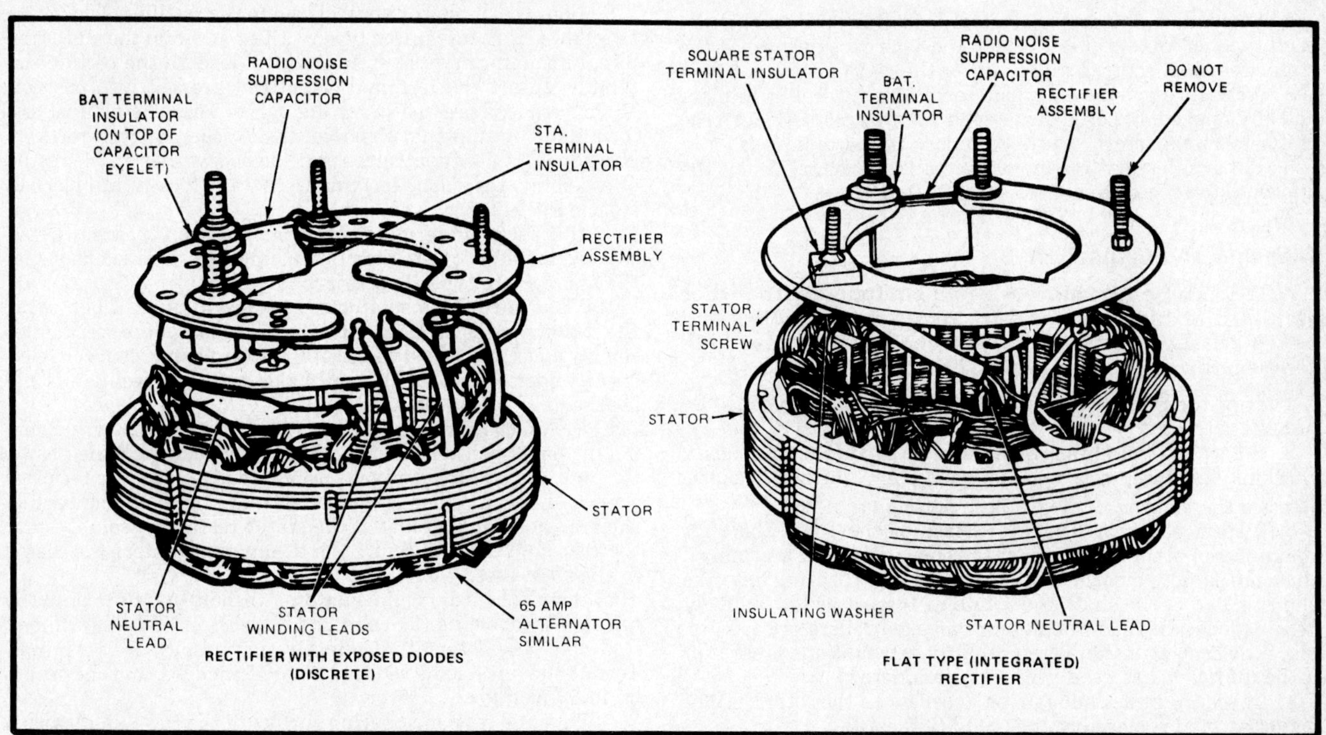

Typical stator and rectifier assemblies

3. Remove the brush springs from the brush holder, located in the rear housing.

4. Note the colors and locations of nuts, washers and insulators on the back of the rear housing for reconnection. Then, remove all of them.

5. Remove the stator and rectifier assembly from the rear housing.

6. Remove the screws attaching the brush holder to the rear housing; then remove the brush holder, brushes and brush terminal insulator.

7. Press the bearing out of the rear housing with an arbor press. Make sure the housing is supported as close as possible to the bearing boss to prevent damage to it.

8. Clamp the front housing in a vise equipped with protective jaws. Remove the drive pulley retaining nut. This requires a $^5/_{16}$ in. socket and $^3/_4$ in. wrench to drive it and a special tool that passes through the center of the socket wrench and locks onto the rotor shaft and prevents it from turning as the nut is removed. Then, remove the lockwasher, drive pulley, fan and fan spacer.

9. Remove the rotor from the front housing and remove the housing from the vise.

10. Remove the front bearing spacer from the rotor shaft, but leave the stop ring in place unless it is damaged.

11. Remove the screws that attach the front bearing retainer to the front housing and remove the retainer. Then remove the bearing from the housing by sliding it out, or, if there is resistance, using an arbor press. If a press is needed, make sure to support the housing close to the bearing boss to prevent damage.

12. Remove the battery terminal insulator and radio suppression capacitor from the rectifier assembly.

13. Use a 100 watt soldering iron to unsolder the stator leads where they connect to the rectifier. Make sure the iron is hot before starting and work quickly to avoid damaging the rectifier. Do this by using needle nose pliers to pull upwards on the stator lead terminals where they connect to the rectifier assembly. Once each connector comes loose, shake the molten solder from it.

14. Disconnect the stator neutral lead from the rectifier of each type as follows. Flat, integrated type rectifier, press the stator terminal screw straight out of the rectifier. Do not turn the screw during removal or the serrations holding it in place will be damaged. Exposed diode, separate type rectifier, turn the stator terminal screw $^1/_4$ turn to unlock it and remove it.

20. If it is necessary to remove the ground terminal, follow the appropriate procedure above.

Cleaning and Inspection

NOTE: These alternators come equipped with either standard or high temperature rectifier assemblies and bearings. High temperature alternators must use high temperature parts or failure will occur.

1. Wipe the rotor, stator and bearings with a clean cloth. Do not use solvent.

2. Rotate the front bearing on the drive end of the rotor shaft, checking for noise, looseness, roughness, or lubricant leakage. Replace the bearing if any of these defects are noted.

3. Inspect the rear bearing surface of the rotor shaft for roughness or severe chatter marks; replace the rotor assembly if the shaft is not smooth. Then, place the rear bearing onto the slip ring end of the shaft and rotate it. Inspect as for the front bearing, checking additionally for damaged rollers or cage. Replace the bearing if there are any of these conditions present or if the lubricant has been lost or contaminated.

4. Check the pulley and fan for looseness on the rotor shaft or distortion and replace if either condition exists.

5. Inspect both halves of the housing for cracks, especially in webbed areas and replace as necessary.

6. Check all leads on the stator and rotor for loose or broken soldered connections and for burned insulation. Resolder poor connections and replace parts with burned insulation.

7. Check the slip rings for nicks and surface roughness. Turn the rings to as small as 1.22 in. diameter, if necessary. If they are badly damaged, the rotor must be replaced.

8. Inspect the brushes for wear beyond $^1/_4$ in. and replace as necessary.

Assembly Rear Terminal Alternators

1. Install the front bearing in its housing, pressing on the outer race only. Then, position the bearing retainer on the front housing and install the attaching screws, torquing screws 25 to 40 inch lbs.

2. If the stop ring was removed from the rotor shaft, install a new one. Slide it over the end of the shaft and into the groove without opening it with snap ring pliers, or permanent deformation will result.

3. Install the bearing spacer onto the rotor shaft with the recessed side against the stop ring.

4. Install the rotor into the front housing. Clamp the housing in a vise.

5. Install the fan spacer, fan, drive pulley, lockwasher and nut onto the rotor shaft. Torque the nut 60 to 100 ft. lbs. using the special tool used in removal.

6. Install the rear bearing with an arbor press and supporting the housing close to the bearing boss. Make sure the bearing is flush with the surface of the housing.

7. Position the brush wiring eyelet over the brush terminal and install the terminal insulator.

8. Install the springs and brushes into the brush holder and then insert a piece of stiff wire through the brush holder to hold them in position against spring tension. Then position the brush holder in the rear housing. Install the brush holder mounting screws, making sure the ground brush wiring eyelet is positioned under the left hand mounting screw. Then, holding the brush holder firmly against the housing, torque the retaining screws 17 to 25 inch lbs.

9. Connect the stator neutral lead to the rectifier of each type as follows. Flat, integrated type rectifier, position the stator terminal insulator and the stator neutral lead on the rectifier assembly. Insert the terminal screw and press it into position. Make sure it is pressed in far enough to keep the neutral lead terminal from moving. Exposed diode, separate type rectifier, position the stator neutral lead and dished washer on the rectifier assembly. Insert the terminal screw and lock it into place by rotating it $^1/_4$ turn.

10. If the ground terminal was removed from the rectifier assembly, install it by pressing or turning it as outlined above for the appropriate type of rectifier.

11. Make sure the insulator sleeves are in place. Then, wrap the stator winding leads around the terminals of the rectifier assembly and solder them with a 100 watt iron and rosin core electrical solder. Work quickly to make sure the rectifier is not overheated.

12. Install the radio suppression capacitor and battery terminal insulator to the rectifier assembly. Then, install the insulator onto the stator terminal screw. Finally, align the terminal screws on the rectifier assembly with the holes on the back of the rear housing and install the stator rectifier assembly in to the rear housing. Make sure the terminal insulators are seated in their recesses.

13. Install the external insulators, washers and nuts onto the terminals, following the color code. Black on "STA" terminal, Red on "BAT" terminal and Orange on "FLD" terminal. Torque the nut for the red lead 30 to 55 inch lbs. and the others 25 to 35 inch lbs.

14. Wipe the rear end bearing surface of the rotor shaft with a clean, lint-free rag. Then, remove the rotor and front housing assembly from the vise. Finally, position the rear housing and

stator assembly over the rotor and align the scribe marks made during disassembly. Make sure the machined portion of the stator core is seated in the stop in both end housings. Install the through bolts.

15. Remove the wire holding the brushes in a retracted position.

Disassembly Side Terminal Alternator

1. Mark the front and rear housings and the stator for reassembly in the same positions. Then, remove the four housing through bolts. Without separating the rear housing and stator, pull the front housing and rotor from the assembly. Slots are provided in the front housing to help pry it away from the stator.

2. Remove the drive pulley nut with a $^{5}/_{16}$ in. socket and $^{3}/_{4}$ in. wrench to drive it and a special tool that passes through the center of the socket to hold the shaft in place. Remove the lockwasher, pulley, fan and fan spacer from the rotor shaft. Finally, pull the rotor and shaft from the front housing and remove the rotor shaft spacer.

3. Remove the three screws retaining the bearing to the front housing. If the bearing shows either wear or loss of lubricant, press it out of the housing, being sure to support the housing close to the bearing boss to prevent damage to it.

4. Unsolder and disengage the three stator leads from the rectifier. Use a hot iron and work quickly to avoid overheating it. Then, lift the stator from the rear housing.

5. Quickly unsolder and disengage the brush holder lead from the rectifier.

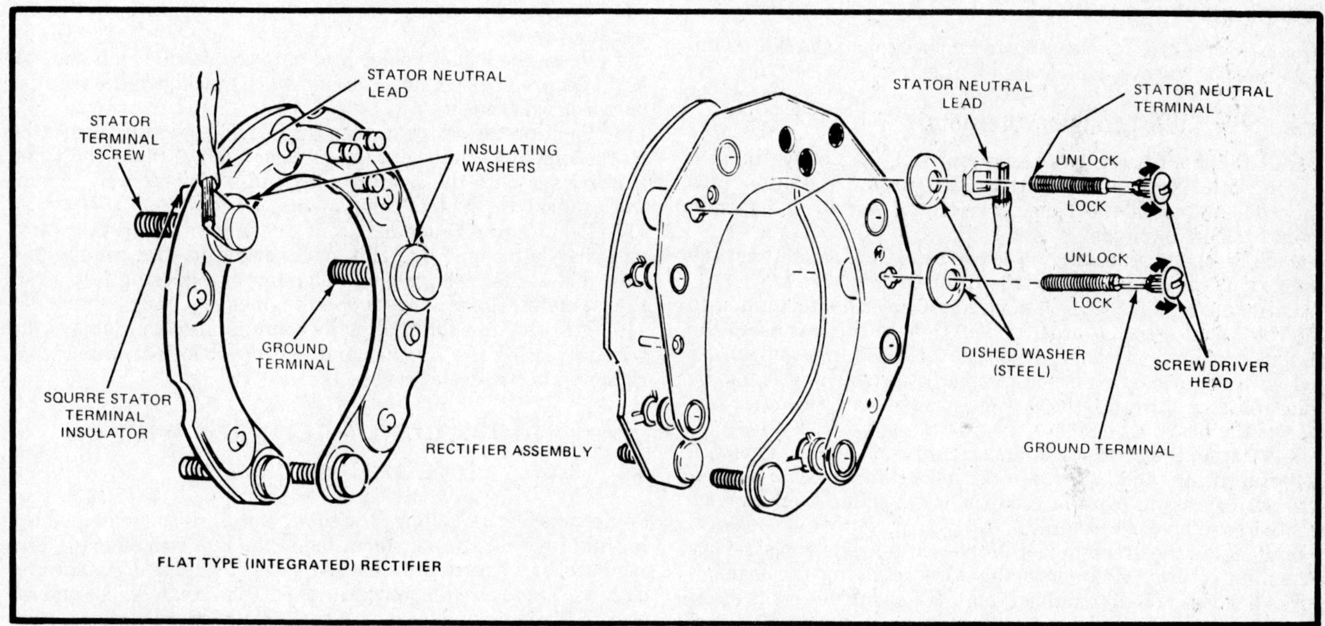

Typical rectifier assemblies

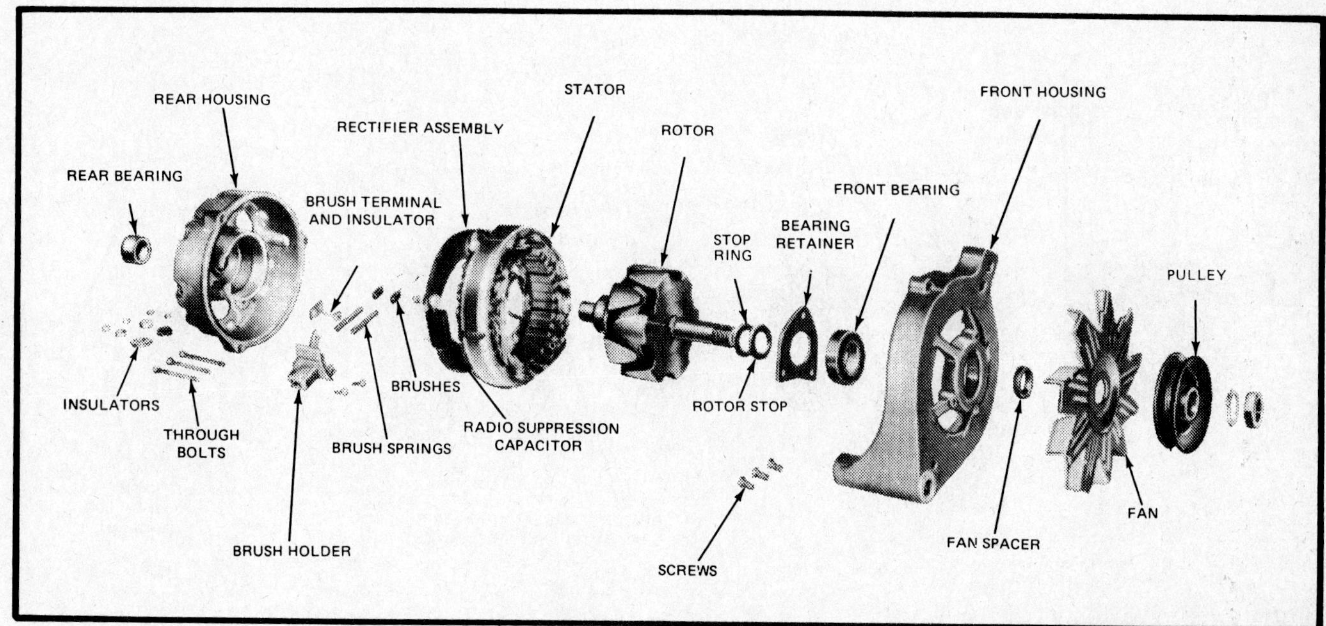

Exploded view of a rear terminal alternator

6. Remove the screw attaching the capacitor lead to the rectifier. Then, remove the four screws attaching the rectifier to the rear housing. Finally, remove the two terminal nuts and insulator from the outside of the housing and remove the rectifier.
7. Remove the two screws attaching the brush holder to the housing and remove the brushes and holder. Remove the two rectifier insulators from the housing bosses.
8. Remove any sealing compound from the rear housing and brush holder.
9. Remove the screw attaching the capacitor to the rear housing and remove the capacitor.
10. Inspect the rear bearing for excessive wear, damage, or loss of lubricant and, if necessary press it out, supporting the housing close to the bearing boss to prevent damage to it.

Cleaning and Inspection

See the procedures for cleaning and inspection of the side terminal alternator above, which are identical.

Assembly Side Terminal Alternators

1. If the front bearing is being replaced, first press the new bearing into the housing, putting pressure on the outer race only. Then, install the bearing retaining screws and torque them to 25–40 inch lbs.
2. Place the inner spacer on to the rotor shaft and insert the rotor shaft into the center of the front bearing.
3. Install the fan spacer, fan, pulley, lockwasher and nut onto the rotor shaft, in that order. Then, tighten the nut using the socket, open end wrench and special tool used in removal.
4. If the rear bearing is being replaced, press a new one in by the outer face only until the rear face is flush with the outer surface of the bearing boss.
5. Position the brush terminal on the brush holder. Then, install the springs and brushes in the holder and insert a piece of stiff wire across in front of the brushes to retain them in a retracted position for assembly.
6. Position the brush holder in the rear housing and start the attaching screws. Make sure the wire retaining the brushes sticks out far enough to pull it from the housing after the alternator is assembled. Poke any sealer that may be present out of the pin hole in the housing. Then, hold the brush holder firmly toward the brush enclosure opening while tightening the attaching screws. Finally, reseal the crack between the brush holder and the brush cavity in the rear housing with a body sealer. Don't use a silicone sealant.
7. Position the capacitor in the rear housing and start install the attaching screw.
8. Place the two rectifier bosses in the housing.
9. Place the insulator on the larger ("BAT") terminal of the rectifier and position the rectifier in the rear housing. Place the outside insulator on the "BAT" terminal. Install the nuts on both "BAT" and "GRD" terminals finger tight.
10. Start the four rectifier attaching screws. Then, tighten the "BAT" terminal nut to 35–50 inch lbs. and the "GRD" nut to 25–30 inch lbs. These nuts are located on the outside of the housing. Finally, tighten the four rectifier attaching screws to 40–50 inch lbs.
11. Connect the capacitor lead to the rectifier with the attaching screw.
12. Press the brush holder lead onto the rectifier pin and solder it securely. Use a hot iron and work quickly so the rectifier does not overheat.
13. Position the stator in the rear housing, aligning the scribe marks made at the beginning of disassembly. Press the three stator leads onto the rectifier pins and solder securely. Again, work quickly to protect components.
14. Position the rotor and front housing into/onto the stator and rear housing. Align the marks made in disassembly and then install the through bolts. Tighten two opposing bolts first; then, tighten the other two opposing bolts.
15. Test the unit for binding by spinning the fan. Remove the wire retracting the brushes and seal the hole with waterproof cement. Do not use a silicone sealer.

Motorcraft Alternator with Integral Regulator

Some vehicles are equipped with an Motorcraft alternator having an integral regulator mounted to the rear end housing. The regulator is a hybrid unit featuring use of solid state integrated circuits. These circuits may consist of transistors, diodes and resistors. The unusual feature of this type of micro-electronic circuit is that the entire circuit is within a silicone crystal approximately $\frac{1}{8}$ in. square. Because of the small size of the circuit, it is

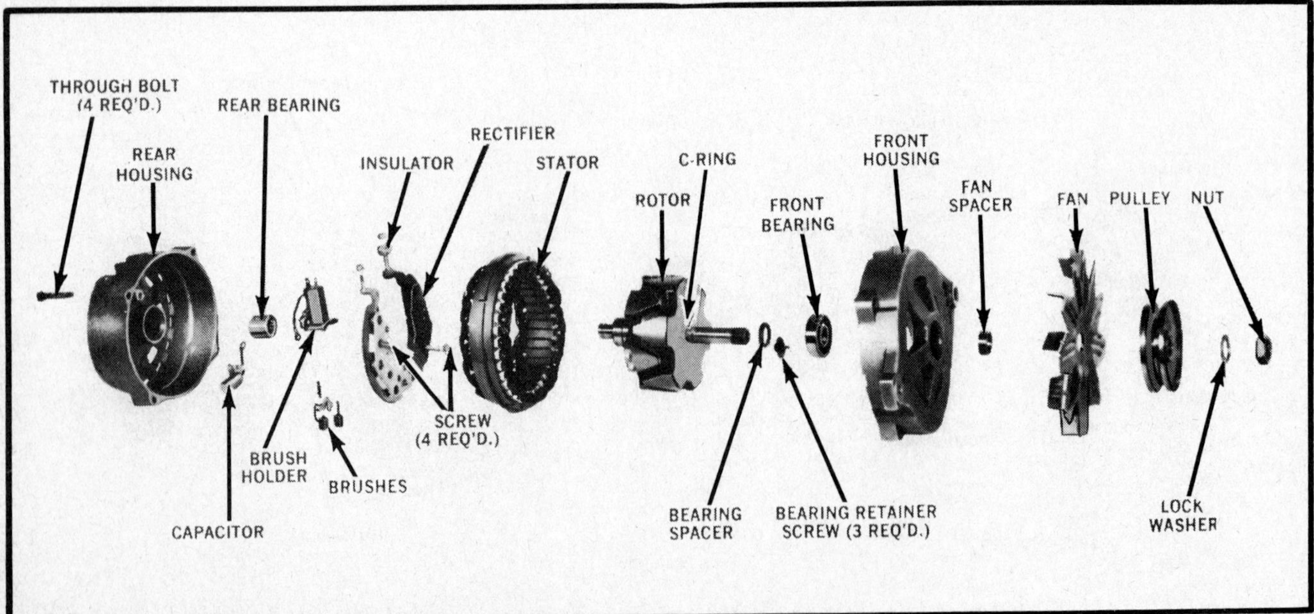

Side terminal alternator—typical exploded view

not repairable or adjustable and must be replaced as a unit if found to be defective. It should be noted that the size of the regulator housing is dictated only by the fact that some means of connecting the regulator to the alternator is necessary. Overhaul is the same as for other Motorcraft alternators.

TROUBLESHOOTING

NOTE: See the "Alternator Test Plans" section before proceeding further.

Fusible Links

Check the fusible link located between the starter relay and the alternator. Replace the link if it is burned or open.

Output Test

1. Place transmission in Neutral or Park.
2. Remove the positive battery cable and install a battery adapter switch in the line.
3. Attach one lead of a test voltmeter to the negative battery post and the other test lead to the circuit side of the adapter switch.
4. Connect a test ammeter to each side of the adapter switch, so that charging current will go through the ammeter when the switch is opened.
5. Connect a jumper wire between the alternator frame and the integral regulator field terminal (cover plug removed).
6. Close adapter switch, start engine and open adapter switch.
7. Running engine at 2000 rpm, observe voltmeter and ammeter. At 15 volts indicated, the ammeter should read 50 to 57 amps. If so and there is still a no-charge condition, the regulator is probably faulty and must be replaced. An output 2 to 8 amps. below 50 amps. usually indicates an open diode rectifier, while an output 10 to 15 amps. below minimum specifications usually indicates a shorted diode. An alternator with a shorted diode usually will whine at idle speed.

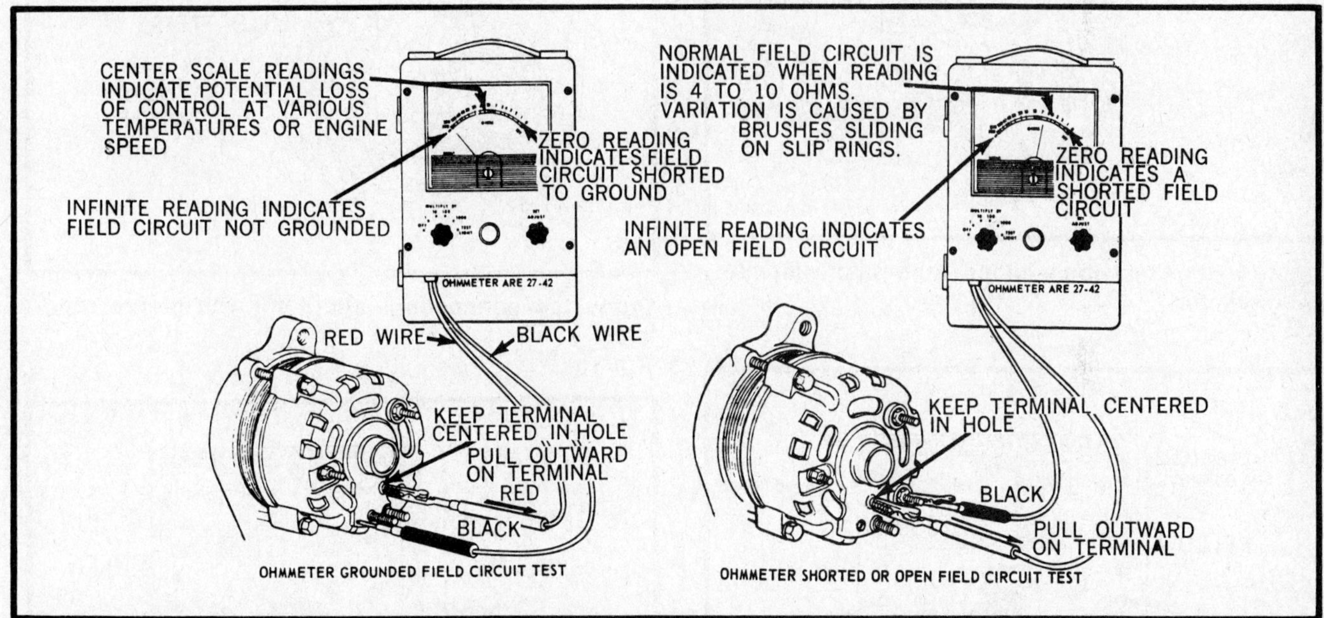

Field circuit test connection with ohmmeter—alternator with integral regulator

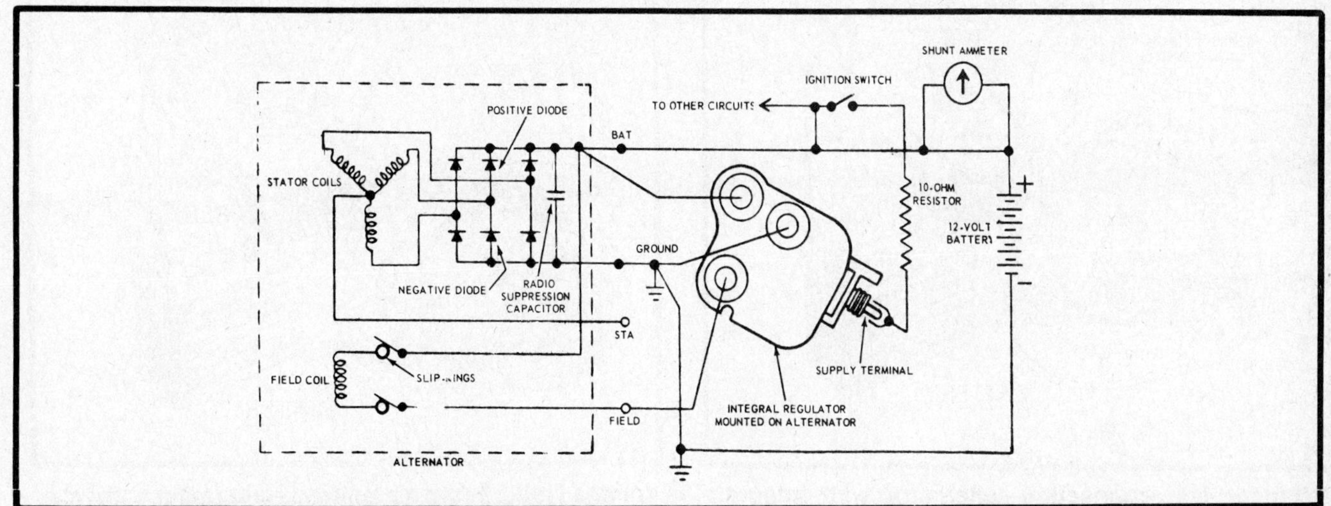

Charging system schematic with integral regulator

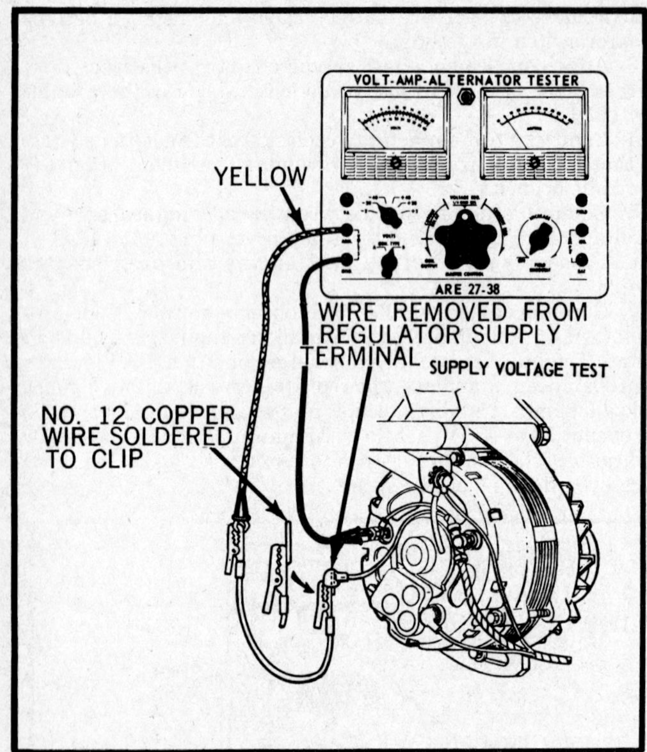

Supply voltage test connections—alternator with integral regulator

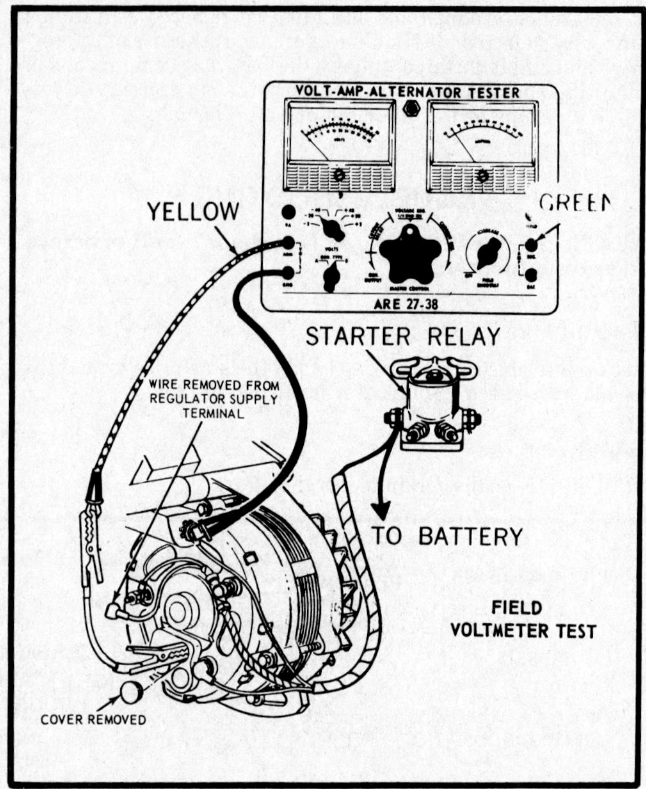

Output test connection—alternator with integral regulator

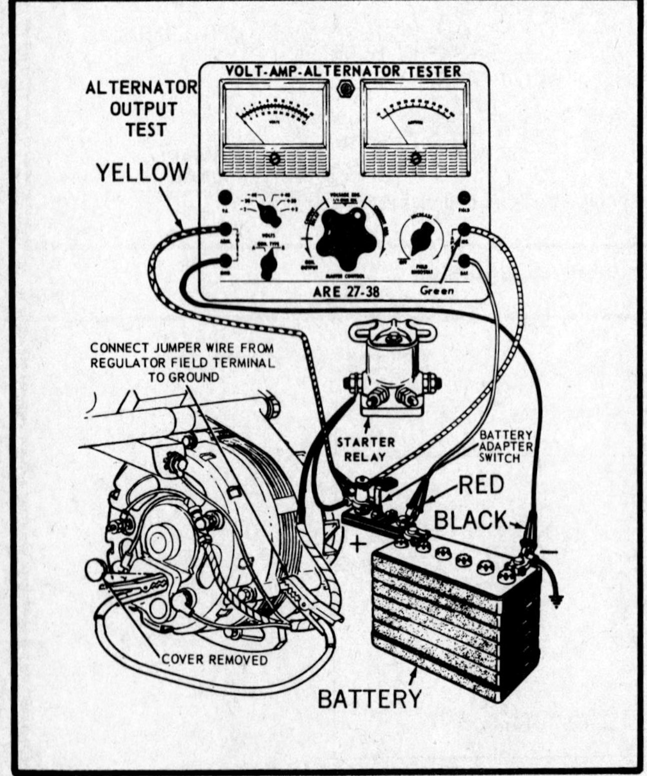

Voltmeter test connection—alternator with integral regulator

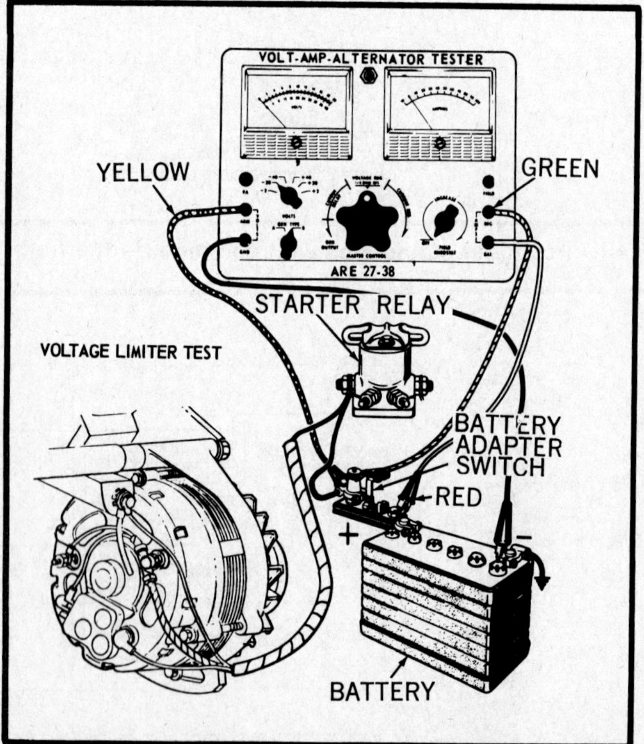

Voltage limiter test connections—alternator with integral regulator

Field Test (Voltmeter)

1. Turn ignition switch to OFF position.
2. Remove wire from regulator supply terminal.
3. Remove cover plug from regulator field terminal and connect one test voltmeter lead to this terminal. A $^1/_4$ ohm resistor should be in the circuit.
4. Connect the other test voltmeter lead to a good engine ground.
5. The voltmeter should read 12 volts. If no voltage is present, the field circuit is open or grounded.
6. If voltmeter reads more than 1 volt, but still less than battery voltage, there is probably a partial ground in the alternator field circuit and the circuit should be checked with an ohmmeter.

Field Test (Ohmmeter)

1. Disconnect battery ground cable, remove alternator from the vehicle.
2. Remove the regulator from the alternator.
3. Perform the ohmmeter test. If any of the tests indicate a field circuit problem, disassemble the alternator to further isolate the trouble. Connect each ohmmeter probe to a slip ring. Resistance should be 4 to 5 ohms. A higher reading indicates a damaged slip ring soldered connection or a broken wire. A lower reading indicates a shorted wire or slip ring assembly.
4. Connect one ohmmeter probe to a slip ring and the other probe to the rotor shaft. Any reading other than infinite ohms indicates a short to ground. If neither of these tests (A and B) isolates the trouble, the brushes or brush assembly are the probable cause.

Voltage Limiter Test

1. Check the battery specific gravity. If it is not at least 1230, charge the battery or install a charged battery for the test.
2. Make sure all lights and accessories are turned off, including such items as dome lights.
3. Make the test connections.
4. Place transmission in Neutral or Park, close battery adapter switch and start the engine.
5. Open the battery adapter switch and operate engine at 2000 rpm for 5 minutes. The voltmeter should read 13.3 to 15.3 volts.
6. If voltage does not rise above 12 volts, perform a regulator supply voltage test to determine whether or not the regulator is getting voltage from the battery. Before replacing a regulator, check the wiring of the entire charging system for shorts, opens, or high resistance connections.

Regulator Supply Voltage Test

The regulator is "turned on" by the application of battery voltage through a 10 ohm resistor wire. If the supply circuit is defective, the regulator will not function and the alternator will not put out current.

1. Connect a 12 volt test light or voltmeter between the regulator supply lead and ground.
2. Turn on the ignition switch. The test light should glow or the voltmeter indicate. If not, the supply circuit should be checked back to the battery, especially the resistance wire.

Overhaul

The overhaul procedures for the alternator are the same as for the Ford Autolite electro mechanical alternator.

Jeep

DELCOTRON 10-SI, 12-SI, 15-SI TYPE 100

The 1982-1988 Jeep vehicles use Delco-Remy alternators with the exception of the Cherokee and Wagoneer 70 Series turbo-diesel engines. These engines use Paris-Rhone alternators. The standard equipment alternators used on Jeep vehicles are rated at 42 amps and the optional, heavy-duty alternators are rated at 56, 66, 78, and 85 amps.

The charging system is an integrated AC generating system containing a built in voltage regulator. Removal and replacement is essentially the same as for the standard AC generator. The regulator is mounted inside the slip ring end frame. All regulator components are enclosed in an epoxy molding and the regulator cannot be adjusted.

The internal alternator wiring is identical between the 10-SI, 15-SI units, except the 10-SI and 12-SI use the "Y"stator wind-

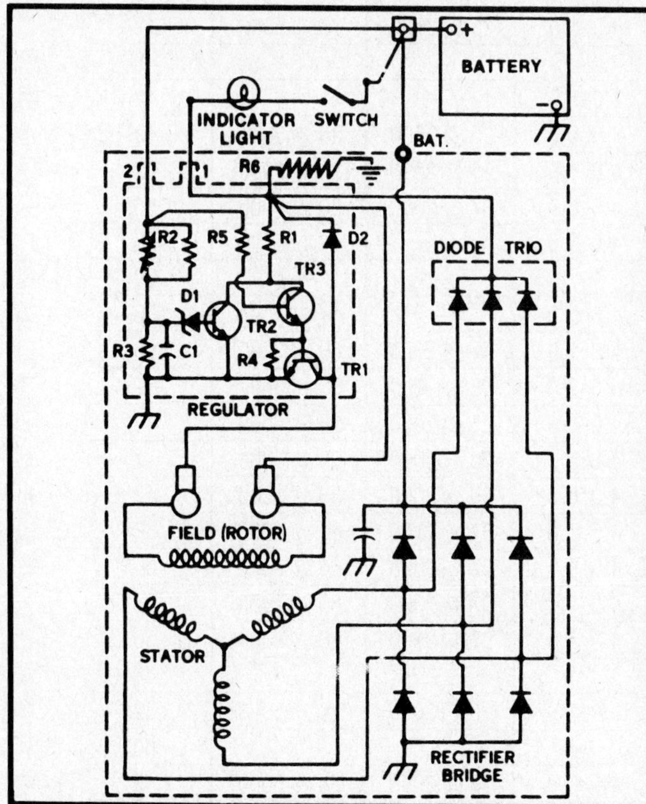

SI Series alternator schematic

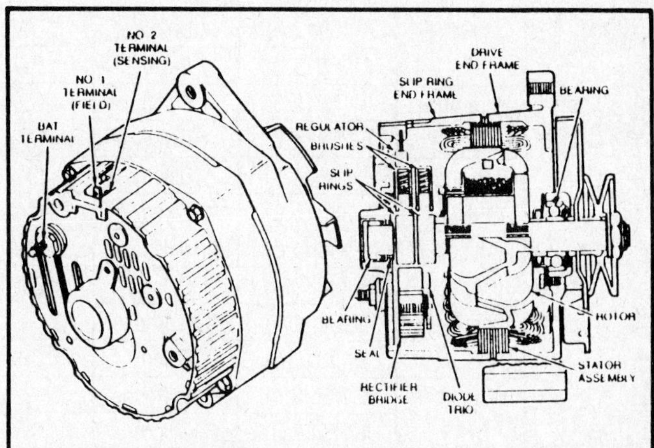

SI Series alternator

ALTERNATOR SPECIFICATIONS
Jeep

Year	Model	No. Cylinder Displacement cu in. (liter)	MFR	Rotation (Viewing Drive End)	Current @ 12 Volts Amps	Cold Output Amps @ min. rpm	Cold Output Amps @ max. rpm	Hot Output Amps
1982	CJ	4-151 (2.5)	Delco	—	4.0–5.0	—	—	42
		6-258 (4.2)	Delco	CW	4.0–5.0	—	—	42
	Scrambler	4-151 (2.5)	Delco	CW	4.0–5.0	—	—	42
		6-258 (4.2)	Delco	CW	4.0–5.0	—	—	42
	Wagoneer, Cherokee	6-258 (4.2)	Delco	CW	4.0–5.0	—	—	42
		8-360 (5.9)	Delco	CW	4.0–5.0	—	—	42
	Truck	6-258 (4.2)	Delco	CW	4.0–5.0	—	—	42
		8.360 (5.9)	Delco	CW	4.0–5.0	—	—	42
1983	CJ	4-151 (2.5)	Delco	CW	4.0–5.0	25 @ 2000	38 @ 5000	42
		6-258 (4.2)	Delco	CW	4.0–5.0	37 @ 2000	60 @ 7000	56
	Scrambler	4-151 (2.5)	Delco	CW	4.0–5.0	25 @ 2000	38 @ 5000	42
		6-258 (4.2)	Delco	CW	4.0–5.0	37 @ 2000	60 @ 7000	56
	Wagoneer, Cherokee	6-258 (4.2)	Delco	CW	4.0–5.0	25 @ 2000	60 @ 7000	42
		8-360 (5.9)	Delco	CW	4.0–5.0	25 @ 2000	60 @ 7000	42
	Truck	6-258 (4.2)	Delco	CW	4.5–5.0	37 @ 2000	60 @ 7000	42
		8-360 (5.9)	Delco	CW	4.5–5.0	37 @ 2000	60 @ 7000	42
1984	CJ	4-150 (2.5)	Delco	CW	4.0–5.0	25 @ 2000	38 @ 5000	42
		6-258 (4.2)	Delco	CW	4.0–5.0	25 @ 2000	38 @ 5000	42
	Scrambler	4-150 (2.5)	Delco	CW	4.0–5.0	25 @ 2000	38 @ 5000	42
		6-258 (4.2)	Delco	CW	4.0–5.0	25 @ 2000	38 @ 5000	42
	Grand Wagoneer	6-258 (4.2)	Delco	CW	4.0–5.0	—	—	42
		8-360 (5.9)	Delco	CW	4.0–5.0	—	—	42
	Truck	6-258 (4.2)	Delco	CW	4.0–5.0	25 @ 2000	38 @ 5000	42
		8-360 (5.9)	Delco	CW	4.0–5.0	25 @ 2000	38 @ 5000	42
	Cherokee	4-150 (2.5)	Delco	CW	4.5–5.0	37 @ 2000	60 @ 7000	56
		6-173 (2.8)	Delco	CW	4.0–5.0	—	—	56
	Wagoneer	4-126 (2.0)	Paris Rhone	—	—	—	—	60
		4-150 (2.5)	Delco	CW	4.5–5.0	—	—	56
		6-173 (2.8)	Delco	CW	4.0–5.0	37 @ 2000	60 @ 7000	56
1985	CJ	4-150 (2.5)	Delco	CW	4.0–5.0	25 @ 2000	38 @ 5000	42
		6-258 (4.2)	Delco	CW	4.0–5.0	25 @ 2000	38 @ 5000	42
	Scrambler	4-150 (2.5)	Delco	CW	4.0–5.0	25 @ 2000	38 @ 5000	42
		6-258 (4.2)	Delco	CW	4.0–5.0	25 @ 2000	38 @ 5000	42
	Grand Wagoneer	6-258 (4.2)	Delco	CW	4.5–5.0	37 @ 2000	60 @ 7000	56
		8-360 (5.9)	Delco	CW	4.5–5.0	37 @ 2000	60 @ 7000	56
	Truck	6-258 (4.2)	Delco	CW	4.5–5.0	37 @ 2000	60 @ 7000	56
		8-360 (5.9)	Delco	CW	4.5–5.0	37 @ 2000	60 @ 7000	56
	Cherokee	4-126 (2.0)	Paris Rhone	—	—	—	—	60
		4-150 (2.5)	Delco	CW	4.0–5.0	25 @ 2000	38 @ 5000	42
	Wagoneer	4-126 (2.0)	Paris Rhone	—	—	—	—	60
		4-150 (2.5)	Delco	CW	4.0–5.0	25 @ 2000	38 @ 5000	42

ALTERNATOR SPECIFICATIONS
Jeep

Year	Model	No. Cylinder Displacement cu in. (liter)	MFR	Rotation (Viewing Drive End)	Current @ 12 Volts Amps	Cold Output Amps @ min. rpm	Cold Output Amps @ max. rpm	Hot Output Amps
1986	CJ	4-150 (2.5)	Delco	CW	4.0–5.0	—	—	56
		6-258 (4.2)	Delco	CW	4.0–5.0	—	—	42
	Scrambler	4-150 (2.5)	Delco	CW	4.0–5.0	—	—	56
		6-258 (4.2)	Delco	CW	4.0–5.0	—	—	42
	Grand Wagoneer	6-258 (4.2)	Delco	CW	4.0–5.0	—	—	42
		8-360 (5.9)	Delco	CW	4.0–5.0	—	—	42
	Truck	6-258 (4.2)	Delco	CW	4.0–5.0	—	—	42
		8-360 (5.9)	Delco	CW	4.0–5.0	—	—	42
	Cherokee	4-126 (2.0)	Paris Rhone	—	—	—	—	60
		4-150 (2.5)	Delco	CW	4.0–5.0	—	—	56
		6-173 (2.5)	Delco	CW	4.0–5.0	—	—	56
	Wagoneer	4-126 (2.0)	Paris Rhone	—	—	—	—	60
		4-150 (2.5)	Delco	CW	4.0–5.0	—	—	56
		6-258 (4.2)	Delco	CW	4.0–5.0	—	—	42
	Comanche	4-126 (2.0)	Paris Rhone	—	—	—	—	60
		4-150 (2.5)	Delco	CW	4.0–5.0	—	—	56
		6-173 (2.5)	Delco	CW	4.0–5.0	—	—	56
1987-88	Wrangler	4-150 (2.5)	Delco	CW	4.0–5.0	—	—	56
		6-258 (4.2)	Delco	CW	4.0–5.0	—	—	56
	Grand Wagoneer	6-258 (4.2)	Delco	CW	4.0–5.0	—	—	56
		8-360 (5.9)	Delco	—	—	—	—	—
	Truck	6-258 (4.2)	Delco	CW	4.0–5.0	—	—	56
		8-360 (5.9)	Delco	—	—	—	—	—
	Cherokee	4-126 (2.0)	Paris Rhone	—	—	—	—	60
		4-150 (2.5)	Delco	—	—	—	—	61
		6-243 (4.0)	Delco	—	—	—	—	61
	Wagoneer	4-126 (2.0)	Paris Rhone	—	—	—	—	60
		4-150 (2.5)	Delco	—	—	—	—	61
		6-243 (4.0)	Delco	—	—	—	—	61
	Comanche	4-126 (2.0)	Paris Rhone	—	—	—	—	60
		4-150 (2.5)	Delco	—	—	—	—	61
		6-243 (4.0)	Delco	—	—	—	—	61

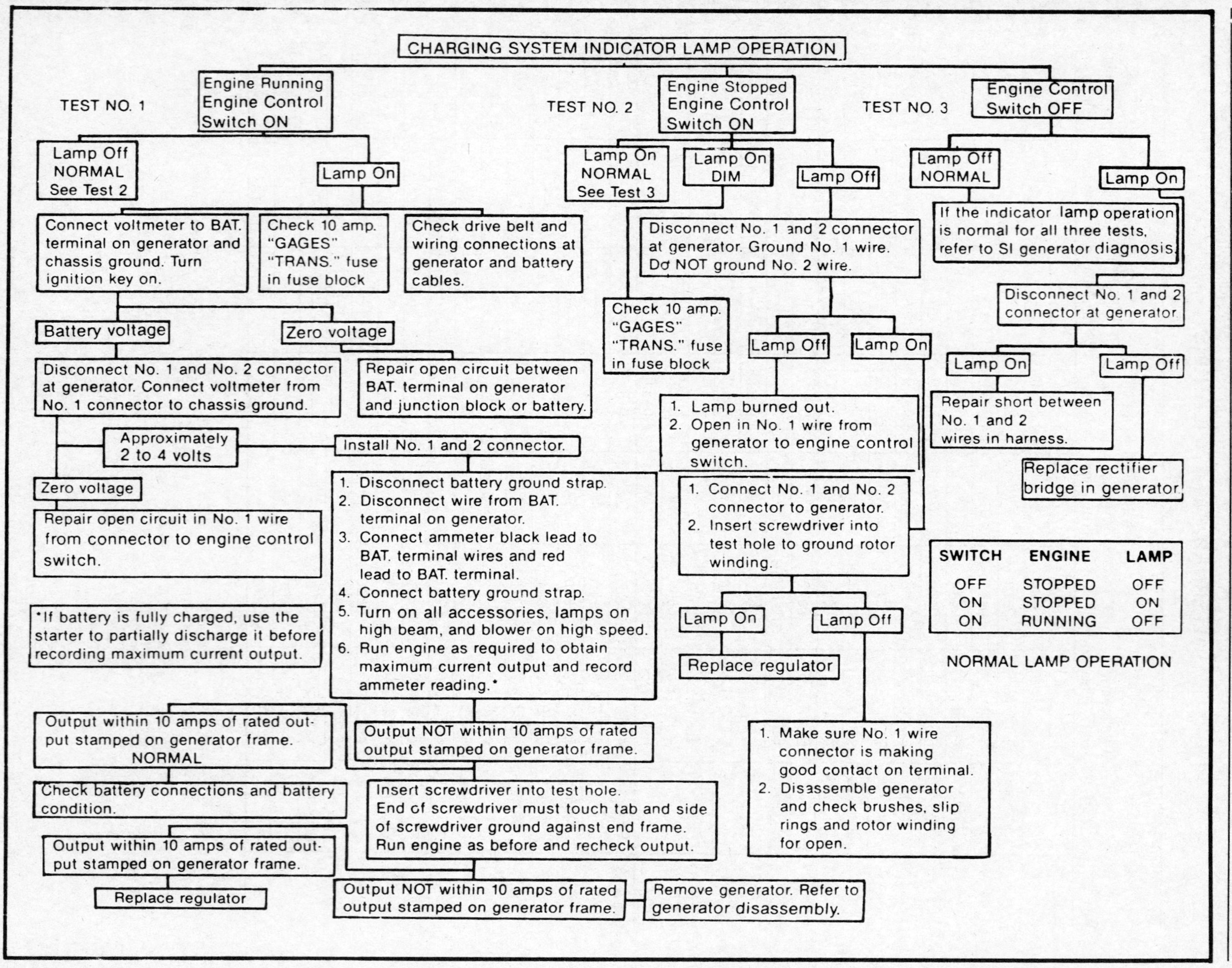

SI Series charging system diagnosis chart

ings while a Delta stator winding is used in the 15-SI alternators. The disassembly and assembly of the units remain basically the same.

DIAGNOSTIC TESTING

Indicator Lamp Operation Test

1. Check the indicator lamp for normal operation. If the indicator lamp operates properly, refer to the undercharged battery test. If the indicator lamp does not operate properly, proceed with the following tests.
2. Switch off, lamp on. Unplug the connector from the generator No. 1 and No. 2 terminals. If the lamp stays on, there is a short between these two leads. If the lamp goes out, replace the rectifier bridge.
3. Switch on, lamp off, engine stopped. This condition can be caused by the defects listed above or by an open in the circuit. To determine where an open exists, proceed as follows. Check for a blown fuse, or fusible link, a burned out bulb, defective bulb socket, or an open in No. 1 lead circuit between generator and ignition switch. If no defects have been found, proceed to undercharged battery test.
4. Switch on, lamp on, engine running. Check for a blown fuse, (where used), between indicator lamp, ignition switch and also in A/C circuit.

Undercharged Battery Test

1. Be sure that the undercharged battery condition has not been caused by accessories that have been left on for an extended period of time.
2. Check the alternator belt for proper belt tension. Inspect the battery for physical defects. Replace as required.
3. Inspect the wiring for defects. Check all connections for proper contact and cleanliness, including the slip connectors at the generator and bulkhead connections.
4. With ignition switch ON and all wiring harness leads connected, connect a voltmeter from the generator Bat terminal to ground, from the generator No. 1 terminal to ground and from the generator No. 2 terminal to ground. A zero reading indicates an open between voltmeter connection and battery.
5. Delcotron alternators have a built in feature which prevents overcharge and accessory damage by preventing the alternator from turning on if there is an open in the wiring harness connected to the No. 2 alternator terminal.
6. If Steps 1 through 5 check out okay, inspect the alternator as follows. Disconnect negative battery cable. Connect an ammeter or alternator tester in the circuit at the Bat terminal of the alternator. Reconnect negative battery cable.
7. Turn on radio, windshield wipers, lights (high beam) and blower motor on high speed. Connect a carbon pile across the battery (or use alternator tester). Operate engine about 2000 rpm and adjust carbon pile as required, to obtain maximum current output. If ampere output is within 10 amperes of rated output as stamped on generator frame, alternator is not defective. Recheck Steps 1 through 5.
8. If ampere output is not within 10 percent of rated output, determine if test hole is accessible. Ground the field winding by inserting a suitable tool into the test hole. Tab is within ¾ inch of casting surface. Do not force suitable tool deeper than one inch into end frame to avoid damaging alternator.
9. Operate engine at moderate speed as required and adjust carbon pile as required to obtain maximum current output.
10. If output is within 10 amperes of rated output, check field winding, diode trio and rectifier bridge. Test regulator with an approved regulator tested.
11. If output is not within 10 amperes of rated output, check the field winding, diode trio, rectifier bridge and stator. If test hole is not accessible, disassemble alternator and repair as required.

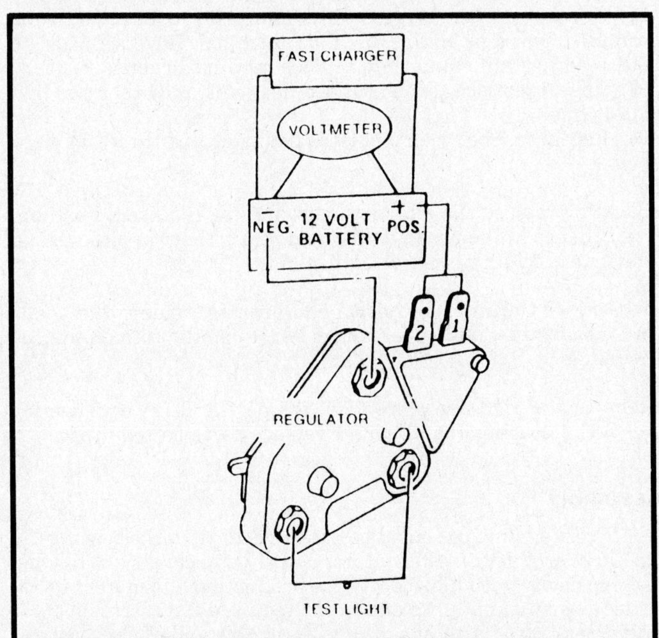

SI Series alternator voltage regulator test (off vehicle)

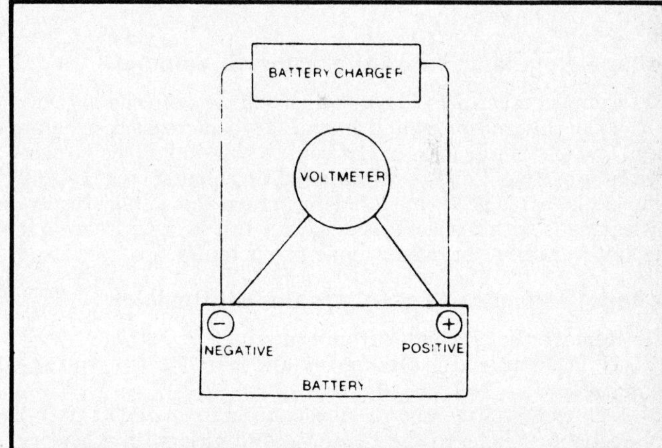

SI Series alternator voltage regulator test (on vehicle)

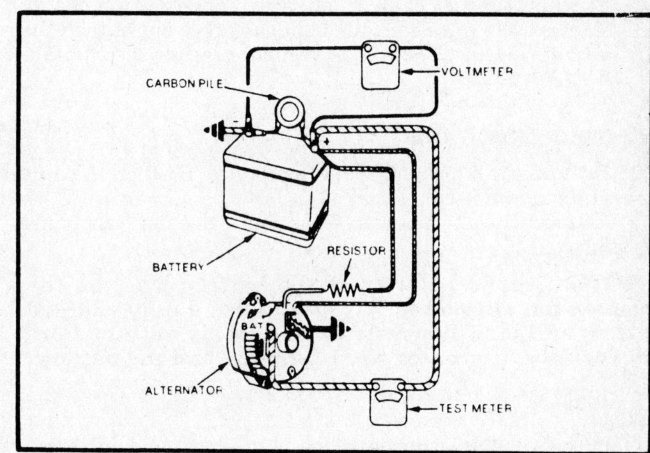

SI Series alternator bench test hook-up

Overcharged Battery Test

1. Check the condition of the battery before any testing is done.
2. If an obvious overcharging condition exists, remove the alternator from the vehicle and check the field windings for grounds or shorts. If defective, replace the rotor. Test the regulator.

Alternator Diagnostic Tester (J-26290)

This special diagnostic tester is designed to determine if the alternator should be removed from the vehicle.

1. Install tester J-26290 according to manufacturers instructions.
2. With the engine off and all lights and accessories off, test the alternator as follows. Light flashes, go to Step 3. Light on, indicates fault in tester which should be replaced. Light off, pull plug from generator. One flashing light, indicates that the alternator should be removed and the rectifier bridge replaced. Light off,indicates faulty tester or no voltage to tester. Check for 12 volts at #2 terminal of harness connector. Repair wiring or terminals if 12 volts is not available. Replace tester if 12 volts is available.
3. With the engine at fast idle and all accessories and lights off, test the alternator as follows. Light off indicates that the charging system good, do not remove alternator. Light on indicates a component failure within the alternator. Remove alternator and check diode trio, rectifier bridge and stator. Light flashing indicates a problem within the alternator. Remove alternator and check regulator, rotor field coil, brushes and slip rings.

Voltage Regulator Test (Alternator on Vehicle)

1. Connect a battery charger and a voltmeter to the battery.
2. Turn the ignition switch on and slowly increase the charge rate. The alternator light in the vehicle will dim at the voltage regulator setting. Voltage regulator setting should be 13.5–16.0 volts. This test is performed to determine if the voltage regulator setting is within specifications. This test is accurate even if the stator rectifier bridge or diode trio is faulty.

Voltage Regulator Test (Alternator off Vehicle)

1. Remove the alternator from the vehicle.
2. Disassemble the alternator and remove the voltage regualtor.
3. Connect a voltmeter and a fast charger to a 12 volt battery. Connect a test light to the regulator and observe the battery polarity.
4. The test light should light.
5. Turn on the fast charger and slowly increase the charge rate. Observe the voltmeter, the light should go out at the voltage regulator setting. The voltage regulator setting specification is 13.5–16.0 volts.

Alternator Bench Test

1. Remove the alternator from the vehicle. Position the unit in a suitable test stand.
2. Connect the alternator in series, but leave the carbon pile disconnected.

NOTE: Ground polarity of the battery must be the same as the alternator. Be sure to use a fully charged battery and a ten ohm resistor rated at six watts or more between the alternator No. 1 terminal and the battery.

3. Increase the alternator speed slowly and observe the voltage.
4. If the voltage is uncontrolled with speed and increases above 15.5 volts on a 12 volt system, or 31 volts on a 24 volt system, test regulator with an approved regulator tester and check field winding. If voltage is below 15.5 volts on a 12 volt system, or 31 volts on a 24 volt system, connect the carbon pile.
5. Operate the alternator at moderate speed as required and adjust the carbon pile as required to obtain maximum current output.
6. If output is within 10 amperes of rated output as stamped on alternator frame, alternator is good. If output is not within 10 amperes of rated output, keep battery loaded with carbon pile and ground alternator field.
7. Operate alternator at moderate speed and adjust carbon pile as required to obtain maximum output. If output is within 10 amperes of rated output, test regulator with an approved regulator tester and check field winding.
9. If output is not within 10 amperes of rated output, check the field winding, diode trio, rectifier bridge and stator.

Disassembly

1. Remove the alternator from the vehicle. Position the assembly in a suitable holding fixture.
2. Make scribe marks on the alternator case end frames to aid in reassembly.
3. Remove the four through bolts that retain the assembly together. Separate the drive end frame assembly from the rectifier end frame assembly.
4. Remove the three rectifier attaching nuts and the three regulator attaching screws from the end frame assembly.
5. Separate the stator, diode trio and voltage regulator from the end frame assembly.
6. On the 10SI alternator, check the stator for opens using an ohmmeter. If high readings are obtained, replace the stator.
7. Check the stator for grounds, using an ohmmeter. If readings are low, replace the stator.
8. Using an ohmmeter, check the rotor for grounds. The ohmmeter reading should be very high. If not, replace the rotor.
9. Using an ohmmeter, check the rotor for opens. If the ohmmeter reading is not 2.4–3.5 ohms, replace the rotor.
10. To check the diode trio connect the ohmmeter to the diode trio and then reverse the lead connections. The ohmmeter should read high and low. If not, replace the diode trio. Repeat the same test between the single connector and each of the other connectors.
11. Check rectifier bridge with ohmmeter connected from grounded heat sink to flat metal on terminal. Reverse leads. If both readings are equal then replace rectifier bridge.
12. Repeat test between grounded heat sink and other two flat metal clips.
13. Repeat test between insulated heat sink and three flat metal clips.
14. Clean or replace the alternator brushes as required. Position the brushes in the brush holder and retain them in place using the brush retainer wire or equivalent.
15. To remove the rotor and drive end bearing, remove the shaft nut, washer and pulley, fan and collar. Push the rotor from the housing.
16. Remove the retainer plate from inside the drive end frame. Push the bearing out. Clean or replace parts as required.

Assembly

1. Press against the outer bearing race to push the bearing in. On early production alternators, it will be necessary to fill the bearing cavity with lubricant. Late production alternators use a sealed bearing and lubricant is not required for assembly.
2. Press rotor into end frame. Assemble collar, fan, pulley, washer and nut. Torque shaft nut 40–60 ft. lbs.
3. Push slip ring end bearing out from outside toward inside of end frame.

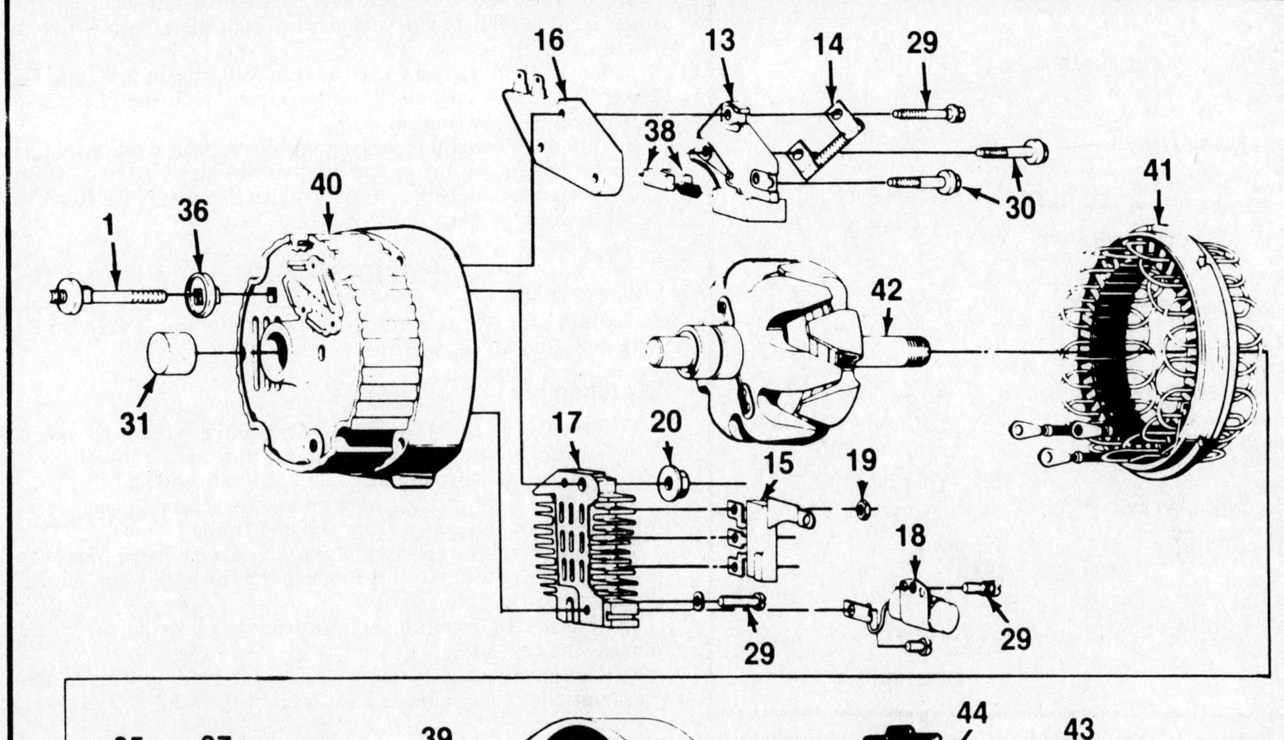

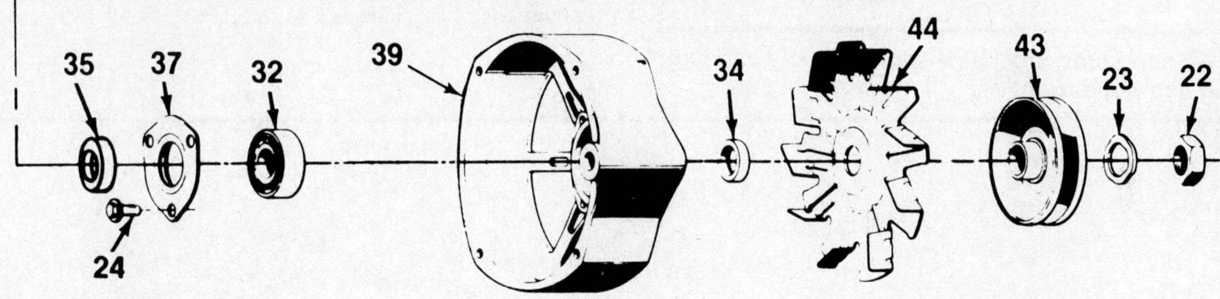

1. "Bat" Terminal
13. Brush Holder
14. Resistor
15. Diode Trio
16. Regulator
17. Rectifier Bridge
18. Capacitor
19. Nut
20. "Bat" Terminal Nut
22. Pulley Nut
23. Washer
24. Bolt
29. Grounded Screw
30. Insulated Screw
31. Rear Bearing
32. Front Bearing
34. Front Collar
35. Rear Collar
36. Insulator
37. Retainer
38. Brushes
39. Drive End Frame
40. Slip Ring End Frame
41. Stator
42. Rotor
43. Pulley
44. Fan

12SI alternator, exploded view

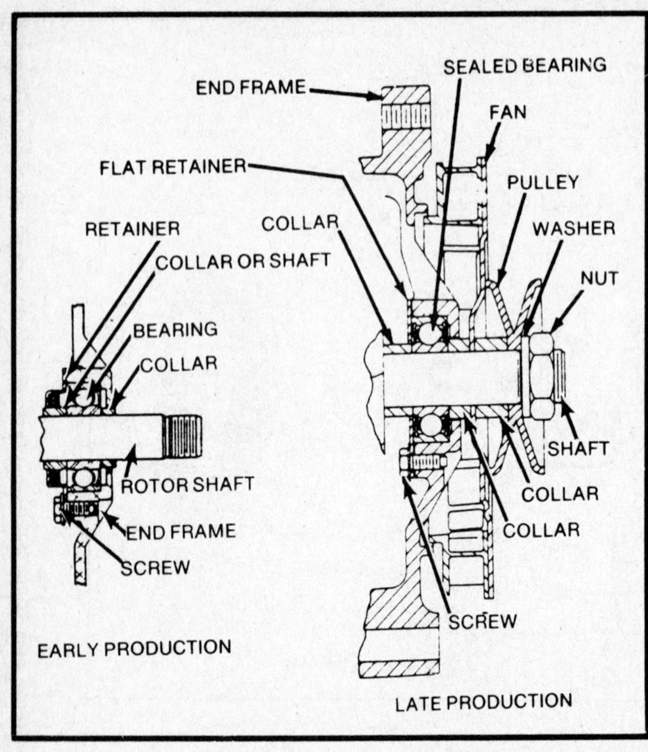

SI Series alternator, side view showing early and late bearing components

4. On 10SI and 15SI, place flat plate over new bearing and press from outside toward inside until bearing is flush with end frame.
5. On 15SI alternators, use the thin wall tube in the space between the grease cup and the housing to push the bearing in flush with the housing.
6. Assemble brush holder, regulator, resistor, diode trio, rectifier bridge and stator to slip ring end frame.
7. Assemble end frames together with through bolts. Remove brush retainer wire.

Paris Rhone

This alternator features an integral regulator and is rated at 60 amp and 70 amp capacities.

Disassembly

1. Remove the brush holder and regulator retaining screws.
2. Scribe a mark on the end frames to facilate reassembly.
3. Remove the through bolts and separate the end frames.
4. Remove the nuts, washers and diode assembly then carefully withdraw the stator from the end frame.
5. Position the rotor assembly in a vice with wood blocks to prevent damage to the rotor. Remove the the pulley and fan assembly from the rotor shaft.
6. Remove the retaining screws from the bearing cover and remove the cover.
7. Position the end frame in a suitable holding fixture and press out the rotor shaft and rotor shaft.

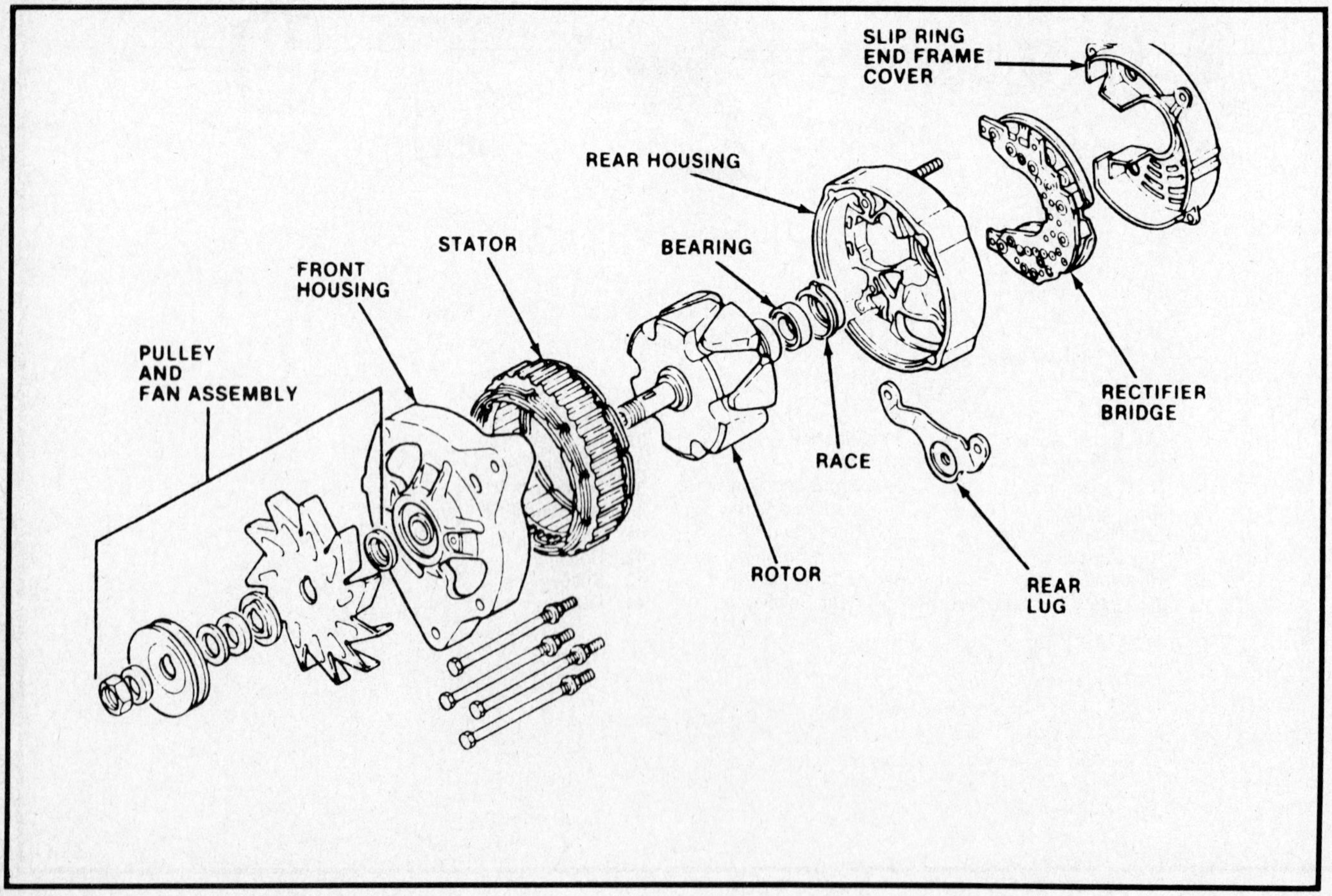

Paris-Rhone Turbo Diesel Alternator

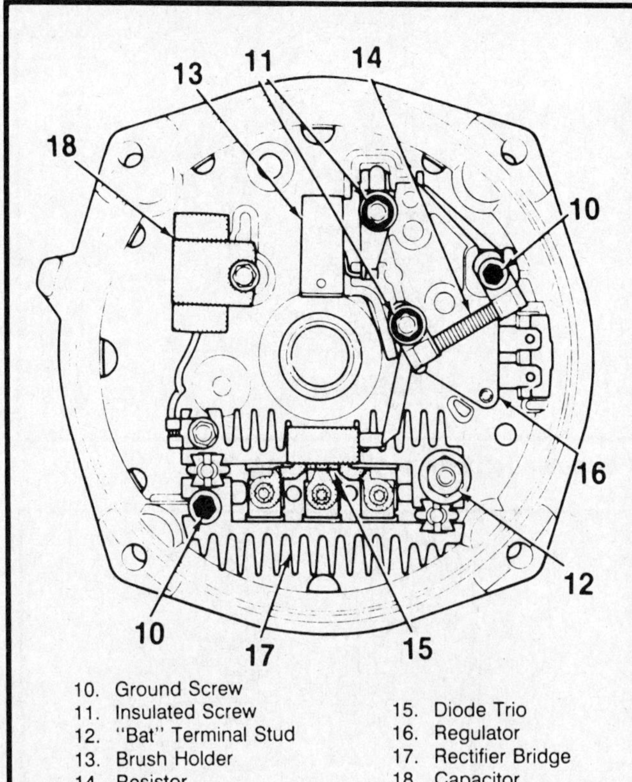

12SI Series alternator end frame and related components

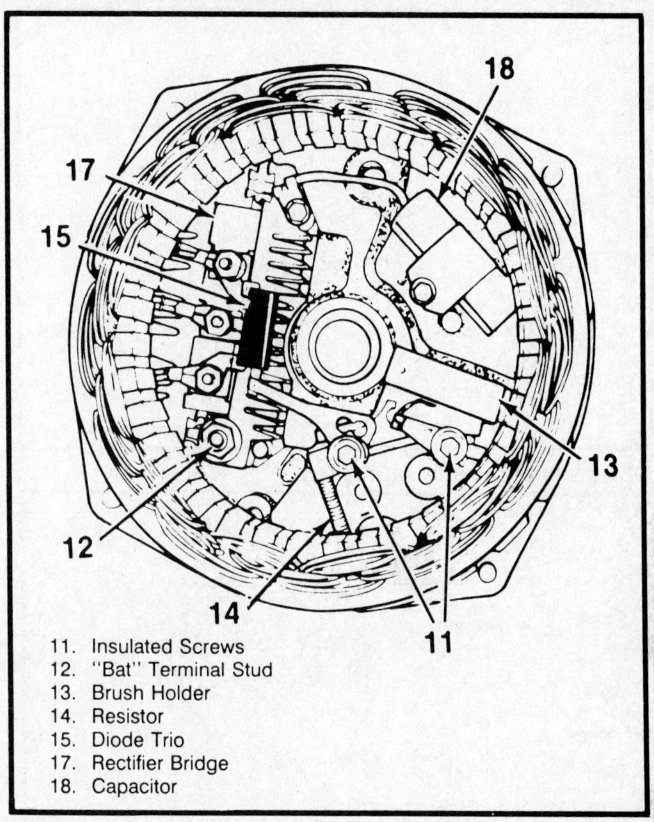

17SI Series alternator end frame and related components

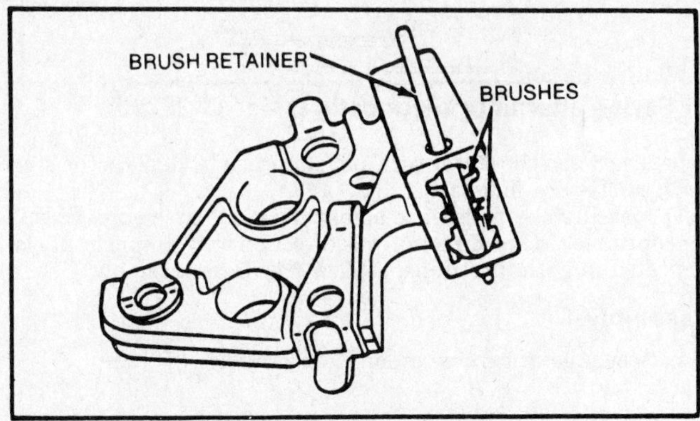

SI Series alternator brush installation

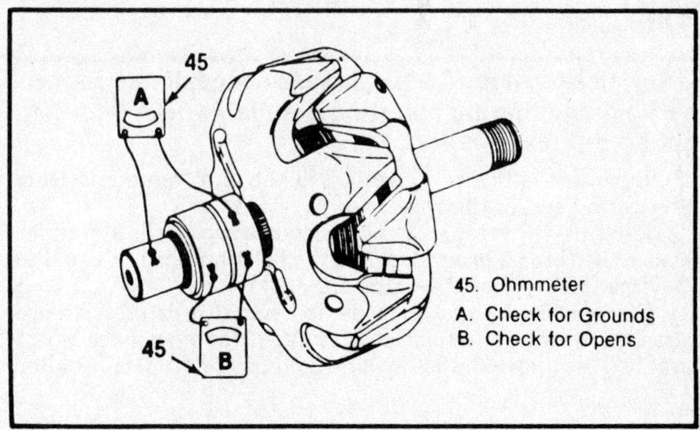

SI Series alternator rotor test

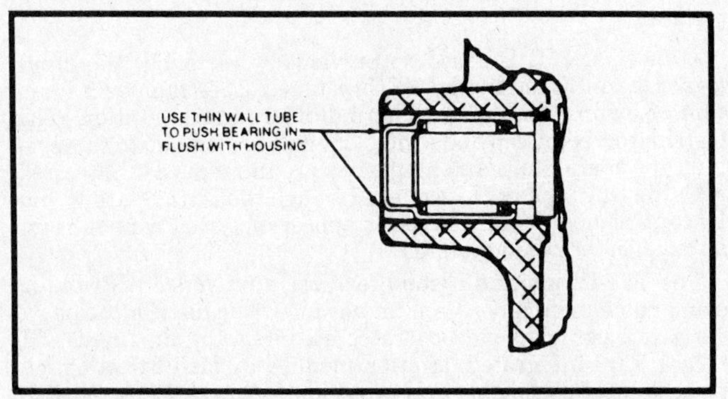

15 SI Series alternator rectifier end bearing installation

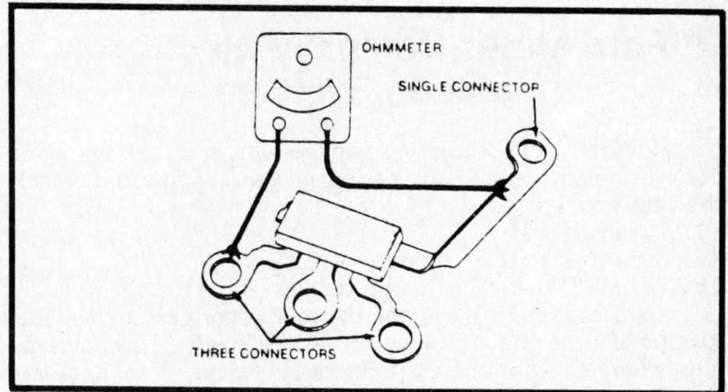

SI Series alternator diode trio test

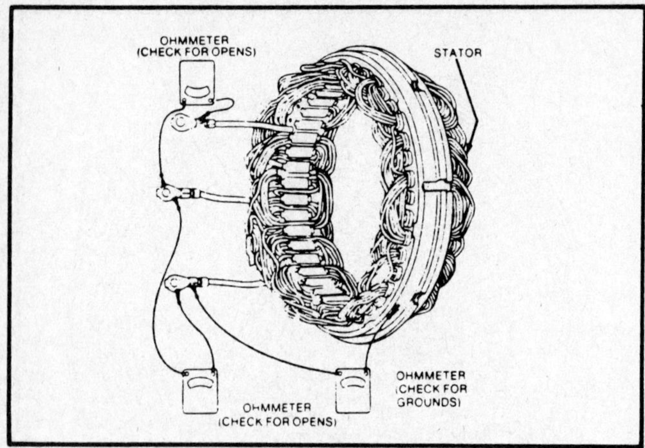

SI Series alternator stator test

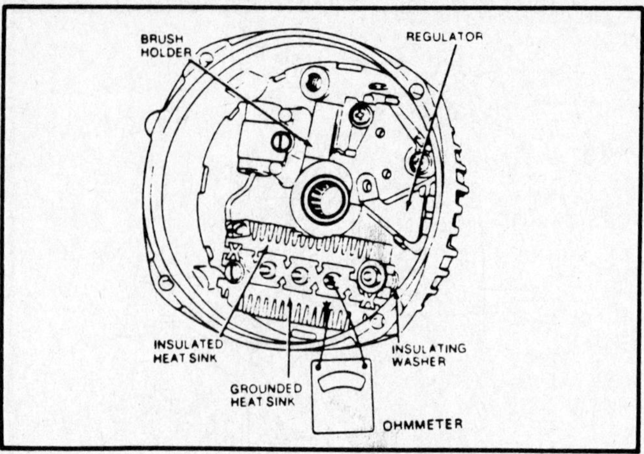

SI Series alternator rectifier bridge test

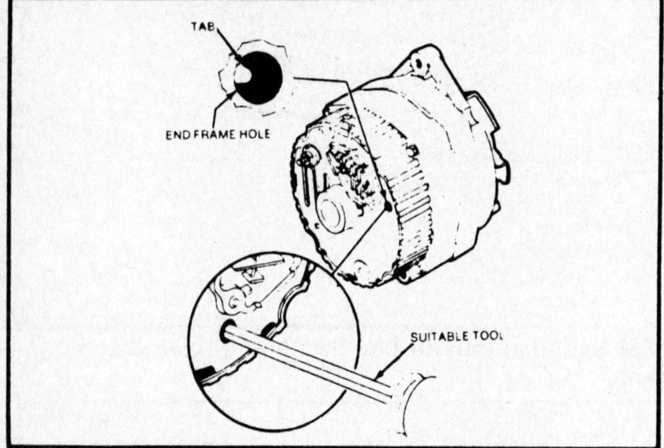

SI Series alternator-If a test hole is accessible, ground the field winding by inserting a suitable tool into the test hole (max. of 1 in.)

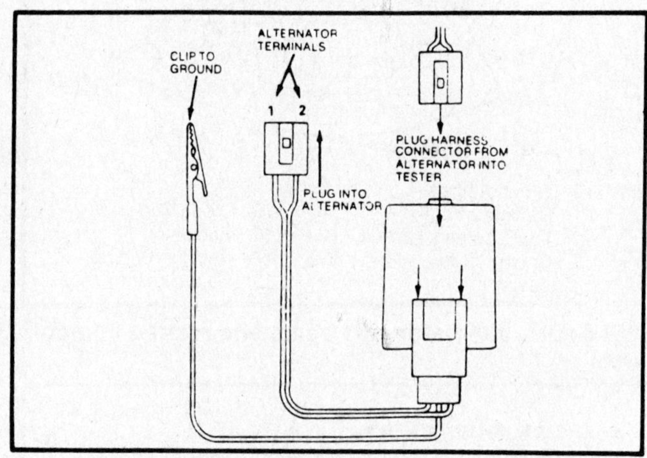

SI Series alternator diagnostic tester (J-26290)

8. Remove the bearing installed in the end frame and from the slip ring end of the rotor.

9. Measure the rotor winding resistance across the slip rings. Replace the rotor if grounded or if the resistance is not equal to 3.2 ohms (60 amp) or 2.4 ohms (70 amp).

10. Disconnect the stator leads and measure the resistance across the windings. Replace the stator if the resistance is not equal to 0.1 ohms (60 amp) or 0.082 ohms (70 amp). Check for shorts between the stator core and stator leads. Replace the stator if shorts are indicated.

11. Measure the resistance across the diode assembly. Check for continuity in one direction one direction only. If continuity is indicated in both directions, replace the diode assembly.

Assembly

1. Assemble in reverse order of disassmbly.

ELECTRONIC IGNITION SYSTEMS

Ford Motor Company Electronic Ignition Systems

Three different electronic ignition systems are used on Ford Motor Company vehicles, depending on year, engine and model. The three systems are:

1. Dura Spark II
2. Dura Spark III
3. TFI-IV (Thick Film Integrated)

On the Dura Spark II system, the coil is energized for the full amount of time that the ignition switch is ON. Keep this in mind when servicing the Dura Spark II system, as the ignition system could inadvertently "fire" while performing ignition system services (such as distributor cap removal) while the ignition is ON.

Dura Spark III is based on previous systems, but the input signal is controlled by the EEC system, rather than as a function of engine timing and distributor armature position. The distributor, rotor cap and control module are unique to this system; the spark plugs and plug wires are the same as those used with the Dura Spark II system. Although the Dura Spark II and III control modules are similar in appearance, they cannot be interchanged between systems.

The TFI-IV ignition system features a universal distributor using no centrifugal or vacuum advance. The distributor has a die cast base which incorporates an integrally mounted TFI (Thick Film Integrated) ignition module, a "Hall Effect" vane switch stator asasembly and provision for fixed octane adjustment. The TFI system uses an E-Core ignition coil in lieu of the Dura Spark coil. No distributor calibration is required and initial timing is not a normal adjustment, since advance etc. is controlled by the EEC-IV system.

GENERAL TESTING

Ignition Coil Test

The ignition coil must be diagnosed separately from the rest of the ignition system.

1. Primary resistance is measured between the two primary (low voltage) coil terminals, with the coil connector disconnected and the ignition switch off. Primary resistance must be 1.13–1.23 ohms for the Dura Spark II. For TFI systems, the primary resistance should be 0.3–1.0 ohms.
2. On Dura Spark ignitions, the secondary resistance is measured between the BATT and high voltage (secondary) terminals of the ignition coil with the ignition off and the wiring from the coil disconnected. Secondary resistance must be 7700–9300 ohms on Dura Spark II systems. For TFI systems, the primary resistance should be 8000–11500 ohms.
3. If resistance tests are okay, but the coil is still suspected, test the coil on a coil tester by following the test equipment manufacturer's instructions for a standard coil. If the reading differs from the original test, check for a defective harness.

Resistance Wire Test

Replace the resistance wire if it doesn't show a resistance of 1.05–1.15 for Dura Spark II. Resistance wire isn't used on TFI systems.

Spark Plug Wire Resistance

Resistance on these wires must not exceed 5000 ohms per inch. To properly measure this, remove the wires from the plugs and remove the distributor cap. Measure the resistance through the distributor cap at that end. Do not pierce any ignition wire for any reason. Measure only from the two ends.

NOTE: Silicone grease must be reapplied to the spark plug wires whenever they are removed. When removing the wires from the spark plugs, a special tool should be used. Do not pull on the wires. Grasp and twist the boot to remove the wire. Whenever the high tension wires are removed from the plugs, coil, or distributor, silicone grease must be applied to the boot before reconnection. Use a clean small screwdriver blade to coat the entire interior surface with Ford silicone grease D7AZ-19A331-A, Dow Corning #111, or General Electric G-627.

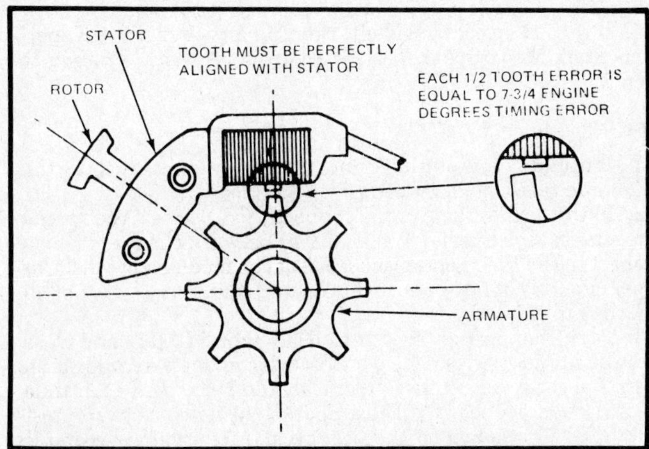

Breakerless armature alignment in relationship with ignition timing

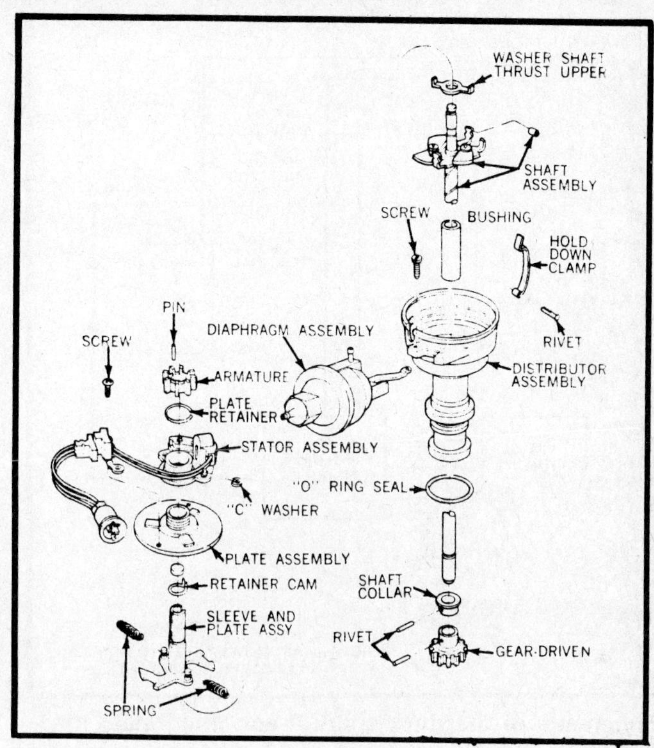

Eight cylinder breakerless distributor—exploded view

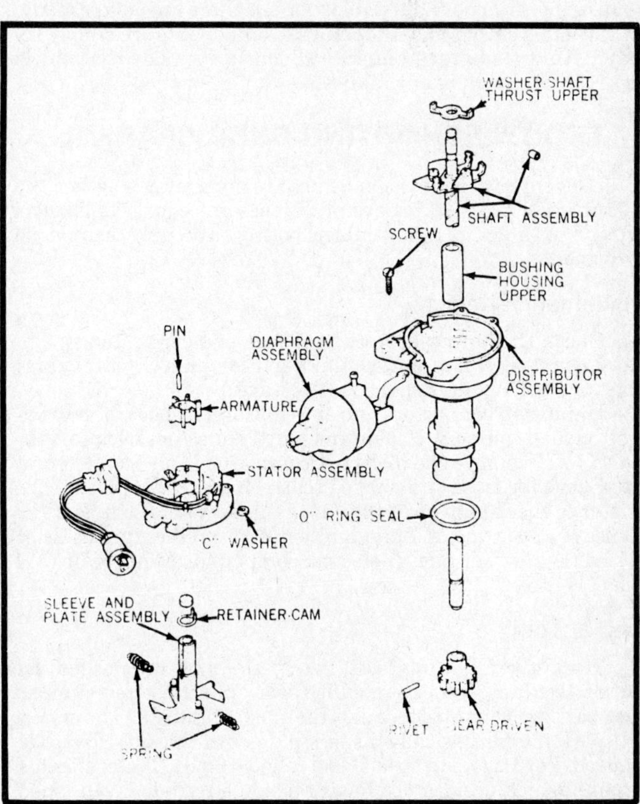

Six cylinder breakerless distributor—exploded view

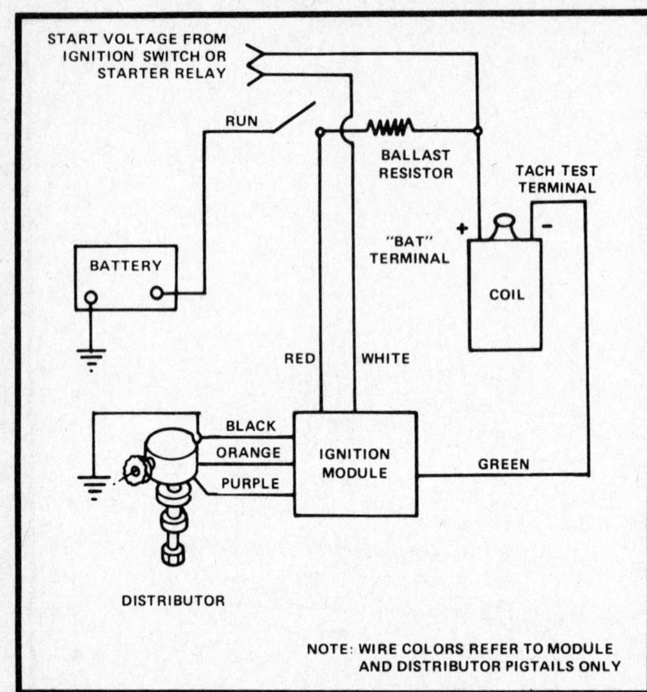

Schematic of the dura spark II and solid state ignitions

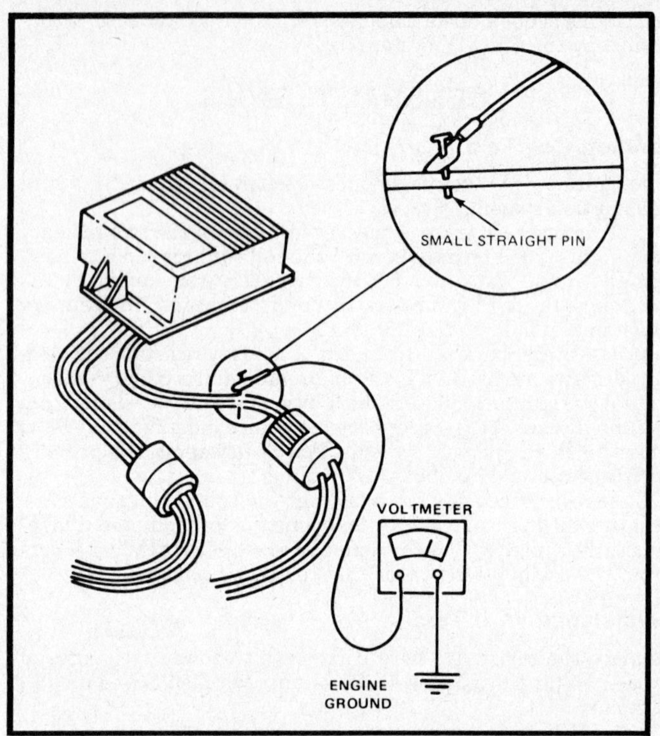

Measuring battery voltage using a straight pin

Adjustments

The air gap between the armature and magnetic pick-up coil in the distributor is not adjustable, nor are there any adjustments for the amplifier module. Inoperative components are simply replaced. Any attempt to connect components outside the vehicle may result in component failure.

TROUBLESHOOTING DURA SPARK II

The following procedures can be used to determine whether the ignition system is working or not. If these procedures fail to correct the problem, a full troubleshooting procedure should be performed.

Preliminary Checks

1. Check the battery's state of charge and connections.
2. Inspect all wires and connections for breaks, cuts, abrasions, or burn spots. Repair as necessary.
3. Unplug all connectors one at a time and inspect for corroded or burned contacts. Repair and plug connectors back together. DO NOT remove the dielectric compound in the connectors.
4. Check for loose or damaged spark plug or coil wires. A wire resistance check is given at the end of this section. If the boots or nipples are removed on 8mm ignition wires, reline the inside of each with new silicone di-electric compound (Motorcraft WA 10).

Special Tools

To perform the following tests, two special tools are needed; an ignition test jumper and a modified spark plug. The test jumper must be used when performing the following tests. The modified spark plug is basically a spark plug with the side electrode removed. Ford makes a special tool called a Spark Tester for this purpose, which besides not having a side electrode is equipped with a spring clip so that it can be grounded to engine metal. It is recommended that the Spark Tester be used as there is less chance of being shocked.

Run Mode Spark Test

NOTE: The wire colors given here are the main colors of the wires, not the dots or hashmarks.

STEP 1

1. Remove the distributor cap and rotor from the distributor.
2. With the ignition OFF, turn the engine over by hand until one of the teeth on the distributor armature aligns with the magnet in the pick-up coil.
3. Remove the coil wire from the distributor cap. Install the modified spark plug (see Special Tools, above) in the coil wire terminal and using heavy gloves and insulated pliers, hold the spark plug shell against the engine block.
4. Turn the ignition to RUN (not START) and tap the distributor body with a screwdriver handle. There should be a spark at the modified spark plug or at the coil wire terminal.
5. If a good spark is evident, the primary circuit is OK: perform Start Mode Spark Test. If there is no spark, proceed to Step 2.

STEP 2

1. Unplug the module connector(s) which contain(s) the green and black module leads.
2. In the harness side of the connector(s) , connect the special test jumper (see Special Tools, above) between the leads which connect to the green and black leads of the module pig tails. Use paper clips on connector socket holes to make contact. Do not allow clips to ground.
3. Turn the ignition switch to RUN (not START) and close the test jumper switch. Leave closed for about 1 second, then open. Repeat several times. There should be a spark each time the switch is opened. On Dura Spark I systems, close the test switch for 10 seconds on the first cycle. After that, 1 second is adequate.
4. If there is no spark, the problem is probably in the primary circuit through the ignition switch, the coil, the green lead or

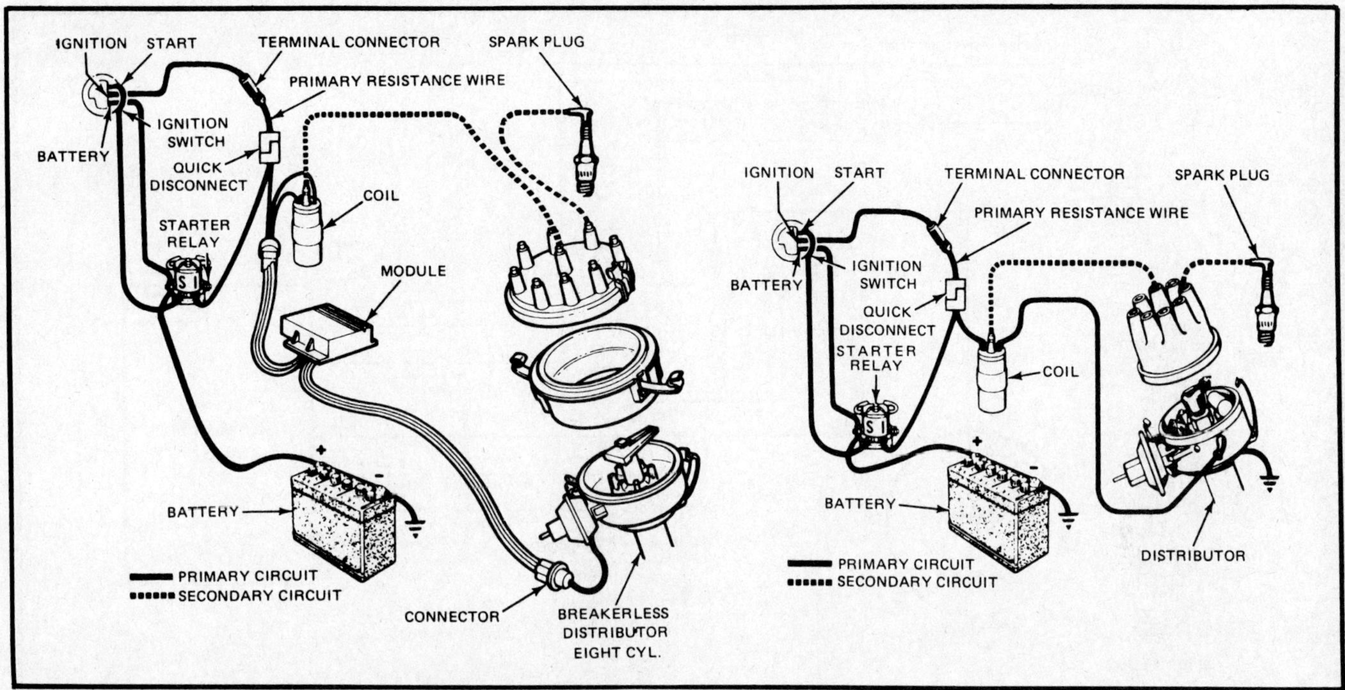

Circuit roundings for breakerless ignition systems

the black lead, or the ground connection in the distributor: perform Step 3. If there is a spark, the primary circuit wiring and coil are probably OK. The problem is probably in the distributor pick-up, the module red wire, or the module: perform Step 6.

STEP 3

1. Disconnect the test jumper lead from the black lead and connect it to a good ground. Turn the test jumper switch on and off several times as in Step 2.
2. If there is no spark, the problem is probably in the green lead, the coil, or the coil feed circuit: perform Step 5.
3. If there is spark, the problem is probably in the black lead or the distributor ground connection: perform Step 4.

STEP 4

Connect an ohmmeter between the black lead and ground. With the meter on its lowest scale, there should be no measurable resistance in the circuit. If there is resistance, check the distributor ground connection and the black lead from the module. Repair as necessary, remove the ohmmeter, plug in all connections and repeat Step 1. If there is no resistance, the primary ground wiring is OK: perform Step 6.

STEP 5

Disconnect the test jumper from the green lead and ground and connect it between the TACH-TEST terminal of the coil and a good ground on the engine. With the ignition switch in the RUN position, turn the jumper switch on. Hold it on for about 1 second and then turn it off as in Step 2. Repeat several times. There should be a spark each time the switch is turned off. If there is no spark, the problem is probably in the primary circuit running through the ignition switch to the coil BAT terminal, or in the coil itself. Check coil resistance (test given later in this section), and check the coil for internal shorts or opens. Check the coil feed circuit for opens, shorts or high resistance. Repair as necessary, reconnect all connectors and repeat Step 1. If there is spark, the coil and its feed circuit are OK. The problem could be in the green lead between the coil and the module. Check for open or short, repair as necessary, reconnect all connectors and repeat Step 1.

STEP 6

To perform this step, a voltmeter which is not combined with a dwell meter is needed. The slight needle oscillations ($\frac{1}{2}$ V) may not be detectable on the combined voltmeter/dwell meter unit.

1. Connect a voltmeter between the orange and purple leads on the harness side of the module connectors.

CAUTION

On the catalytic converter equipped cars, disconnect the air supply line between the Thermactor by-pass valve and the manifold before cranking the engine with the ignition off. This will prevent damage to the catalytic converter. After testing, run the engine for at least 3 minutes before reconnecting the by-pass valve, to clear excess fuel from the exhaust system.

2. Set the voltmeter on it lowest scale and crank the engine. The meter needle should oscillate slightly (about $\frac{1}{2}$ volt). If the meter does not oscillate, check the circuit through the magnetic pick-up in the distributor for open, shorts, shorts to ground and resistance. Resistance between the orange and purple leads should be 400–1000 ohms and between each lead and ground should be more than 70,000 ohms. Repair as necessary, reconnect all connectors and repeat Step 1. If the meter oscillates, the problem is probably in the power feed to the module (red wire) or in the module itself: proceed to Step 7.

STEP 7

1. Remove all meters and jumpers and plug in all connectors.
2. Turn the ignition switch to the RUN position and measure voltage between the battery positive terminal and engine ground. It should be 12 volts.
3. Measure voltage between the red lead of the module and engine ground. To make this measurement, it will be necessary to pierce the red wire with a straight pin and connect the voltmeter to the straight pin and to ground. DO NOT ALLOW THE STRAIGHT PIN TO GROUND ITSELF.
4. The two readings should be within one volt of each other. If not within one volt, the problem is in the power feed to the red lead. Check for shorts, open, or high resistance and correct as

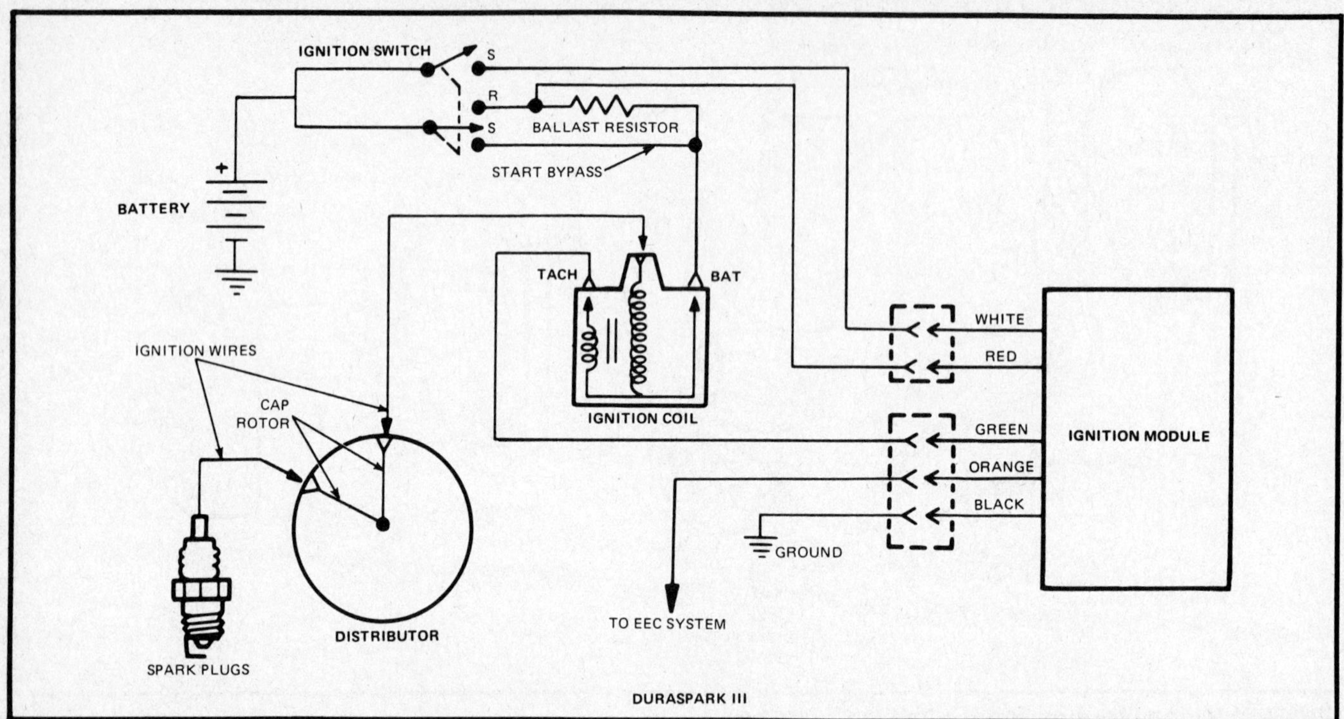

Wiring diagram for dura spark III ignition system

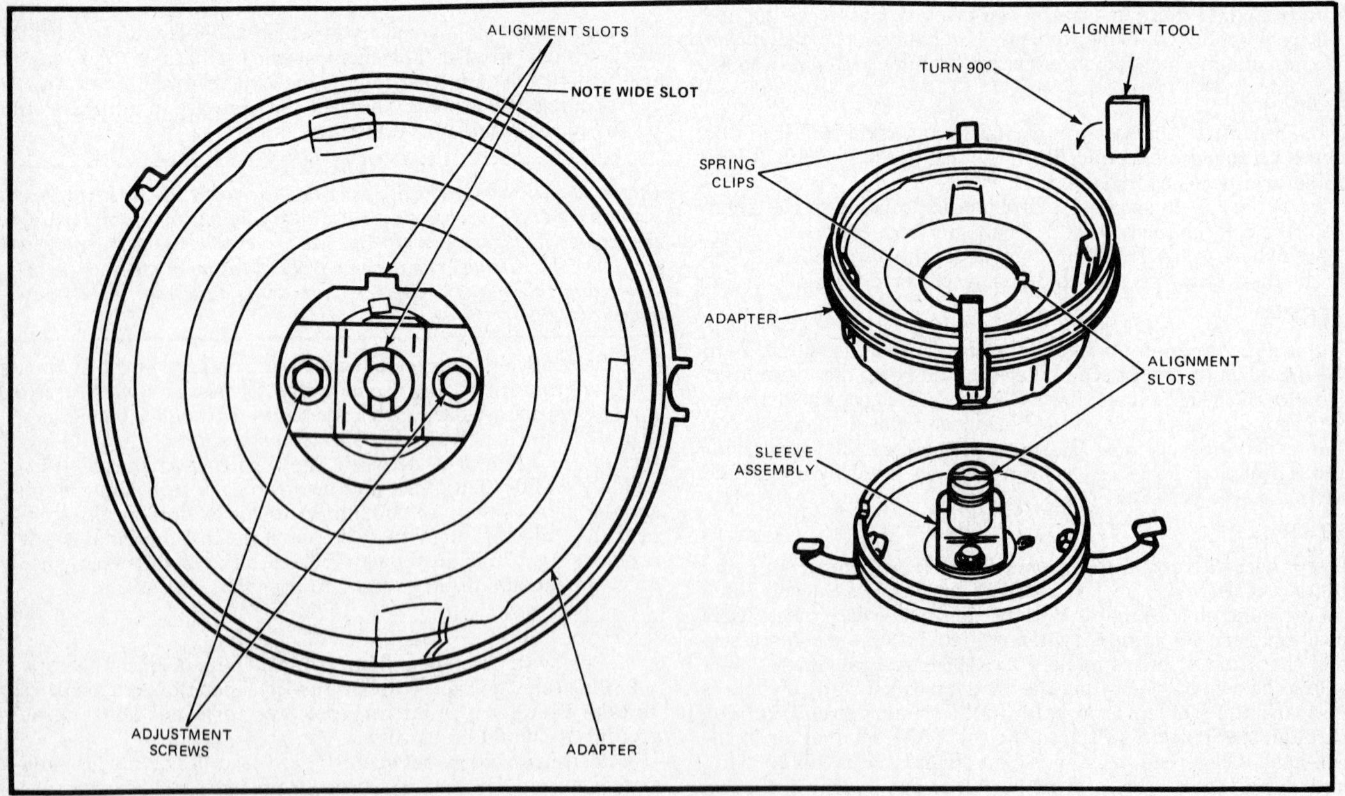

Rotor alignment—dura spark III

necessary. After repairs, repeat Step 1. If the readings are within one volt, the problem is probably in the module. Replace with a good module and repeat Step 1. If this corrects the problem, reconnect the old module and repeat Step 1. If problem returns, permanently install the new module.

Start Mode Spark Test

NOTE: The wire colors given here are the main colors of the wires, not the dots or hashmarks.

1. Remove the coil wire from the distributor cap. Install the modified spark plug mentioned under "Special Tools" in the coil wire and ground it to engine metal either by its spring clip (Spark Tester) or by holding the spark plug shell against the engine block with insulated pliers.

NOTE: See "CAUTION" under Step 6 of "Run Mode Spark Test", above.

2. Have an assistant crank the engine using the ignition switch and check for spark. If there is good spark, the problem is probably in the distributor cap, rotor, ignition cables or spark plugs. If there is no spark, proceed to Step 3.
3. Measure the battery voltage. Next, measure the voltage at the white wire of the module while cranking the engine. To make this measurement, it will be necessary to pierce the white wire with a straight pin and connect the voltmeter to the straight pin and to ground. DO NOT ALLOW THE STRAIGHT PIN TO GROUND ITSELF. The battery voltage and the voltage at the white wire should be within 1 volt of each other. If the readings are not within 1 volt of each other, check and repair the feed through the ignition switch to the white wire. Recheck for spark (Step 1). If the readings are within 1 volt of each other, or if there is still no spark after power feed to white wire is repaired, proceed to Step 4.
4. Measure the coil BAT terminal voltage while cranking the engine. The reading should be within 1 volt of battery voltage. If the readings are not within 1 volt of each other, check and repair the feed through the ignition switch to the coil. If the readings are within 1 volt of each other, the problem is probably in the ignition module. Substitute another module and repeat test for spark (Step 1).

TROUBLESHOOTING DURA SPARK III

This system is used in conjunction with EEC III (an Electronic Engine Control System) that controls spark advance in response to various engine sensors. On 3.8L V6 engines, the distributor is only slightly modified from the Dura Spark II model. The distributor stator provides the signal that, on Dura Spark II systems, caused the ignition module to interrupt the primary circuit; on this system, however, the EEC microprocessor determines the actual instant at which spark occurs. This means that the centrifugal and vacuum advance systems on the distributor are disabled and the microprocessor determines vacuum and centrifugal advance curves.

On V8 engines, the distributor stator assembly is replaced by a crankshaft position sensor; thus, the distributor consists only of the mechanical shaft and housing and the high tension cap and rotor. On these engines, the distributor has a fixed position in relation to the engine and it is the rotor position, rather than distributor position that is adjustable. In all other respects, the system resembles the Dura Spark II.

Rotor Alignment V8 Engines with Dura Spark III

1. Remove the distributor cap, noting the approximate location of the high tension wire going to No. 1 cylinder. Rotate the engine until No. 1 cylinder firing position is being approached by the rotor and the engine nears 0 degrees TDC. Remove the rotor and position a distributor alignment tool so that when the alignment slots reach an aligned position, the tool will slip into place.

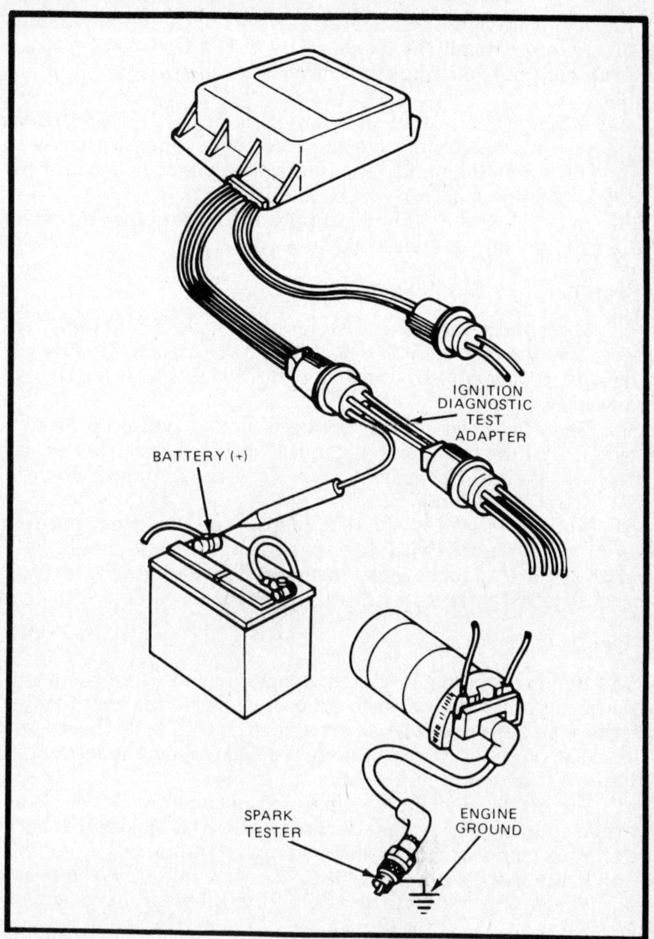

Connecting dura spark III test adapter

2. Turn the engine very slowly until the tool just slips into the alignment slots and then stop rotating the engine. Read the position of the timing mark on the vibration damper. If it is between 4 degrees Before Top Center and 4 degrees After Top Center, the rotor alignment meets specification. In this case, remove the tool and reposition the rotor and cap. If the timing mark is outside these limits, proceed with the Steps that follow.
3. Remove the alignment tool. Rotate the engine until the timing marks align at 0 degrees, TDC.
4. Loosen the two sleeve assembly adjustment screws. Then, rotate the sleeve assembly until the alignment tool can be inserted. With the tool in position, tighten the adjusting screws. Then, remove the tool and install the rotor and cap.

PRELIMINARY CHECKOUT

NOTE: When making these tests, make sure to follow wiring back to the module for color coding purposes. All instrument checks for wiring integrity should be accompanied by visual inspection and by wiggling of connectors to check for either bad insulation or loose connections.

Begin troubleshooting by inspecting all vacuum hoses and both high tension and wiring harness wiring for proper routing and secure connections. Check also for damaged insulation and burned connectors.

Make sure the battery is fully charged and turn off all accessories before starting tests. The procedure requires the following equipment.

1. A precise volt/ohmmeter, preferably with digital readout.
2. A commercially available spark tester that can replace a spark plug in the circuit and provide visible evidence of a hot spark.
3. A diagnostic test adapter designed for the Dura Spark III system. This must plug into the three wire connector going to the ignition module and apply voltage to the right module circuit for testing it directly from the battery.
4. A 12 volt test light and a supply of straight pins for testing the voltage and resistance in the wiring.

Test 1

1. Disconnect the three-wire ignition module connector. Inspect the connector for damage, dirt, or corrosion. If none are present, proceed with Step 2 otherwise, make repairs as necessary.
2. Install the test adapter between the two halves of the connector. Pull the coil high tension lead out of the distributor, install and ground the spark tester. Turn the ignition switch to the "RUN" position.
3. Touch the lead to the test adapter to the battery positive terminal while observing the spark tester. There should be a spark as the lead touches the terminal. Test repeatedly. If spark occurs consistently, go to Test 2.Otherwise, see Test 4.

Test 2

1. Remove the diagnostic test adapter from the ignition module circuit and reconnect the connector. Leave the spark tester in place and observe it while cranking the engine. If there is no spark, go on to test three. If there is spark, follow the rest of the Steps in this test.
2. Inspect the distributor cap, rotor and adapter for cracks or carbon tracking and replace parts as necessary. Make sure there is silicone compound to protect the tip of the rotor.
3. If the inspections above do not reveal and cure the problem, check the distributor rotor alignment and correct as necessary.

Test 3

1. If the starter relay has an "I" terminal, disconnect the cable from the starter relay to the starter motor.
2. If it has no "I" terminal, disconnect the wire to the "S" terminal of the relay.
3. Insert a straight pin through the center of the white wire leading to the ignition module. Make sure it does not contact any ground.
4. Measure the voltage existing between the positive and negative battery terminals.
5. Connect the VOM negative lead to a good engine ground. Use a pin to get a connection to the white wire going to the ignition module (without grounding the pin). Connect the positive lead to the VOM to the pin. Finally, turn the ignition switch to the START position and read the voltage while wiggling the wiring.
6. Connect the positive lead of the VOM to the BATT terminal of the ignition coil and with the ignition switch in the START position, repeat the test.
7. If either reading was less than 90 percent of battery voltage, refer to a wiring diagram and repair wiring and connectors in the faulty circuit. Otherwise, replace the ignition switch.
8. Remove the straight pin and reconnect the wiring to the starter relay. If the required repairs do not resolve the problem, or if both circuits passed the test, proceed to Test 4.

Test 4

1. Connect a test lamp between the TACH terminal of the ignition coil and a ground on the engine. Connect the diagnostic test adapter into the ignition system as in the first test. Turn the ignition switch to the "RUN" position.
2. Touch the test lead for the adapter to the battery positive terminal repeatedly while observing the test light.
3. Remove the diagnostic connector and test light and reconnect the three-prong connector. If the light flashes consistently, go to Test 5; if not, go to Test 6.

Test 5

1. Disconnect the coil high tension wire and connector. Inspect the wire and connector for a burned appearance and replace parts as necessary. Inspect the coil for cracks or carbon tracking in the high tension connector and replace it if necessary.
2. Test the high tension lead with an ohmmeter by removing it and connecting the meter to either end. Resistance should be 5,000 ohms per inch or less. If resistance is too high, replace the wire.
3. Measure the coil secondary circuit resistance by connecting the ohmmeter between the coil BATT terminal and the high voltage connector. Resistance must be between 7700 ohms and 10500 ohms. If resistance is either above or below this range, replace the coil.
4. Replace or reconnect parts as necessary.

Test 6

1. If the starter relay has an "I" terminal, disconnect the cable from the relay to the starter motor. If there is no "I" terminal on the relay, disconnect the wire to the "S" terminal of the relay. Insert straight pins into the centers of the red and white module wires. DO NOT GROUND. Measure the exact voltage by connecting the voltmeter between the positive and negative battery terminals.
2. Connect the voltmeter negative lead between the base of the distributor and the pin passing through the red lead. Turn the ignition switch to the "RUN" position. Measure the voltage while wiggling the wiring.
3. Connect the voltmeter positive lead over to the pin running through the white wire. Turn the ignition switch to the START position and read the voltage while wiggling the wiring.
4. Repeat the step above, but with the positive lead attached to the BATT terminal on the ignition coil to test the ballast resistor bypass. Turn the ignition switch off, remove the straight pins and reconnect the starter wiring.
5. If the voltage was more than 90 percent of battery voltage, inspect the wiring harness for faulty circuits and repair as necessary. Replace the ignition switch, or replace the radio interference capacitor on the coil as necessary until the system can pass the test.

Test 7

1. Attach the negative lead of the voltmeter to an engine ground and the positive lead to the BATT terminal on the coil.
2. With the ignition switch in the RUN position, measure the voltage.
3. Turn the ignition switch off and remove the voltmeter leads. If the voltage is 6 to 8 volts, proceed to Test 8; if it is less than 6 volts or greater than 8 volts, proceed to Test 9.

Test 8

1. Disconnect the ignition module three wire connector and the connector at the coil for the wire from the ignition module. Repair or replace bad connectors as necessary.
2. Connect an ohmmeter between an engine ground (-) and the TACH terminal of the coil. Reconnect module and coil connectors. If resistance is greater than one ohm, replace the module. If it is one ohm or less, just inspect the wiring harness between the module and coil to make sure there are no wiring problems.

Test 9

1. Disconnect the ignition coil primary connectors. Measure

coil primary resistance by connecting an ohmmeter between the BATT and TACH terminals. Disconnect the ohmmeter and reconnect connectors.

2. If resistance is between .8 and 1.6 ohms, proceed to Test 10. If resistance is less than or greater than specification, replace the coil.

Test 10

1. Insert a straight pin into the green wire at the module without grounding it.
2. Attach the negative lead of the voltmeter to an engine ground. Then, turn the ignition switch on and measure the voltage, first at the straight pin in the green wire and then at the TACH terminal of the ignition coil. If the difference in voltage is more than 5 volts, inspect and repair the green module to coil wire as necessary. If it is less than 0.5 volts, but more than 1.5, proceed to Test 12. If it is 1.5 volts or less, proceed to the test of the ballast resitor, Test 11.
3. Turn the ignition off and remove the leads and straight pin.

Test 11

1. Disconnect the two wire connector to the ignition module. Repair any defects in the connectors. Disconnect the coil primary connector.
2. Use an ohmmeter to measure resistance of the circuit between the BATT terminal of the ignition coil connector and the wiring harness connector mating with the red wire from the module. In both cases, measure on the wiring harness side, not at the coil or at the wire leading to the module.
3. If the resistance is 0.8 to 1.6 ohms, replace the ignition module. If it is less than 0.8 or greater than 1.6 ohms, replace the ballast resistor.
4. Remove the ohmmeter and reconnect connectors as necessary.

Test 12

1. Insert a straight pin into the black wire at the ignition module without grounding it.
2. Connect a voltmeter between the pin and an engine ground, with the positive lead at the pin. Turn the ignition switch to RUN position.
3. If the voltage read is less than 0.5 volt, replace the ignition module. If it is greater than 5 volts, proceed to the final test for further diagnosis of problems in the ground circuit.
4. Turn the ignition switch off, remove the voltmeter connectors and remove the straight pin.

Test 13

1. Disconnect the threewire connector to the module. Connect an ohmmeter between an engine ground and the harness side terminal mating with the black wire from the module. Read the resistance while wiggling the harness.
2. If resistance is less than one ohm, look for a problem in the wiring harness connectors and the module black wire. The problem is either intermittent or not in the ignition system. If resistance is greater than one ohm, inspect the harness and connectors between the module and ground connection. Repair wiring as necessary, disconnect the ohmmeter and reconnect the connector.

THICK FILM INTEGRATED (TFI—IV) IGNITION SYSTEM

The TFI-IV ignition system is used on 1983–85 Ranger and the 1984–85 Bronco II with the 2.8L V6, 1986–88 Ranger and Bronco II with the 2.3L 4 cylinder, 2.9L V6 engines and the 1986–88 Aerostar with the 2.3L 4 cylinder, 2.8L V6 and 3.0L V6 engines. TFI-IV is also used on some 1986–88 Broncos, Econolines and F Series pick-up models, depending on the engine calibration number. This system uses a universal distributor design which is gear driven and has a diecast base that incorporates an integrally mounted TFI-IV ignition module. The distributor also uses a "Hall Effect" vane switch stator assembly and has a provision for fixed octane adjustment. The new design eliminates the conventional centrifugal and vacuum advance mechanisms.

Distributor Identification

The distributor assembly can be identified by the part number information printed on a decal attached to the side of the distributor base.

NOTE: No distributor calibration is required and it is not normally necessary to adjust initial timing.

1. The new cap, adapter and rotor are designed for use with the new universal distributor.
2. The spark plug is a 14mm standard reach, tapered seat design.
3. The ignition module is a Thick Film Integrated design. The module is contained in moulded thermo plastic and is mounted on the distributor base. The TFI-IV module features a "push start" mode. This will allow "push starting" of the vehicle if it becomes necessary.
4. The TFI-IV system uses an "E-Core" ignition coil, which replaces the oil-filled design used with previous ignition systems.

Adjustments

Provisions have been incorporated into the Universal Distributor to allow fixed adjustment capability for octane needs. The adjustment is accomplished by replacing the standard 0° rod located in the distributor bowl with either a 3° or a 6° retard rod, which is released for service only through prior factory authorization.

NOTE: Except for the cap, adapter, rotor, TFI module, O-ring and octane rod, no other distributor assembly parts are replaceable. There is no calibration required with the universal distributor.

TROUBLESHOOTING THE TFI—IV SYSTEM

NOTE: After performing any test which requires piercing a wire with a straight pin, remove the straight pin and seal the holes in the wire with silicone sealer.

Ignition Coil Secondary Voltage

1. Disconnect the secondary (high voltage) coil wire from the distributor cap and install a spark tester (see Special Tools, located with the Dura Spark Troubleshooting) between the coil wire and ground.
2. Crank the engine. A good, strong spark should be noted at the spark tester. If spark is noted, but the engine will not start, check the spark plugs, spark plug wiring and fuel system. If there is no spark at the tester: Check the ignition coil secondary wire resistance; it should be no more than 5000 ohms per inch. Inspect the ignition coil for damage and/or carbon tracking. With the distributor cap removed, verify that the distributor shaft turns with the engine; if it does not, repair the engine as required. If the fault was not found proceed to the next test.

Ignition Coil Primary Circuit Switching.

1. Insert a small straight pin in the wire which runs from the coil negative (-) terminal to the TFI module, about one inch from the module.

CAUTION

The pin must not touch ground.

2. Connect a 12VDC test lamp between the straight pin and an engine ground.

3. Crank the engine, noting the operation of the test lamp. If the test lamp flashes, proceed to the next test. If the test lamp lights but does not flash, proceed to the Wiring Harness test. If the test lamp does not light at all, proceed to the Primary Circuit Continuity test.

Ignition Coil Resistance

Refer to the General Testing for an explanation of the resistance tests. Replace the ignition coil if the resistance is out of the specification range.

Wiring Harness

1. Disconnect the wiring harness connector from the TFI module; the connector tabs must be PUSHED to disengage the connector. Inspect the connector for damage, dirt and corrosion.

2. Attach the negative lead of a voltmeter to the base of the distributor. Attach the other voltmeter lead to a small straight pin. With the ignition switch in the RUN position, insert the straight pin into the No. 1 terminal of the TFI module connector. Note the voltage reading. With the ignition switch in the RUN position, move the straight pin to the No. 2 connector terminal. Again, note the voltage reading. Move the straight pin to the No. 3 connector terminal, then turn the ignition switch to the START position. Note the voltage reading then turn the ignition OFF.

3. The voltage readings should all be at least 90% of the available battery voltage. If the readings are okay, proceed to the Stator Assembly and Module test. If any reading is less than 90% of the battery voltage, inspect the wiring, connectors and/or ignition switch for defects. If the voltage is low only at the No. 1 terminal, proceed to the ignition coil primary voltage test.

Stator Assembly and Module

1. Remove the distributor from the engine.
2. Remove the TFI module from the distributor.
3. Inspect the distributor terminals, ground screw and stator wiring for damage. Repair as necessary.
4. Measure the resistance of the stator assembly, using an ohmmeter. If the ohmmeter reading is 800–975 ohms, the stator is okay, but the TFI module must be replaced. If the ohmmeter reading is less than 800 ohms or more than 975 ohms; the TFI module is okay, but the stator module must be replaced.
5. Repair as necessary and reinstall the TFI module and the distributor.

Primary Circuit Continuity

This test is performed in the same manner as the previous Wiring Harness test, but only the No. 1 terminal conductor is tested (ignition switch in RUN position). If the voltage is less than 90% of the available battery voltage, proceed to the coil primary voltage test.

Ignition Coil Primary Voltage

1. Attach the negative lead of a voltmeter to the distributor base.

2. Turn the ignition switch ON and connect the positive voltmeter lead to the negative (-) ignition coil terminal. Note the voltage reading and turn the ignition OFF. If the voltmeter reading is less than 90% of the available battery voltage, inspect the wiring between the ignition module and the negative (-) coil terminal, then proceed to the next test, which follows.

Ignition Coil Supply Voltage

1. Attach the negative lead of a voltmeter to the distributor base.

2. Turn the ignition switch ON and connect the positive voltmeter lead to the positive (+) ignition coil terminal Note the voltage reading, then turn the ignition OFF. If the voltage reading is at least 90% of the battery voltage, yet the engine will still not run; first, check the ignition coil connector and terminals for corrosion, dirt and/or damage; second, replace the ignition switch if the connectors and terminal are okay.

3. Connect any remaining wiring.

DISTRIBUTOR CAP, ADAPTER AND ROTOR

Removal

1. Remove the secondary wires.
2. Unclip the distributor cap and lift straight off the distributor.
3. Loosen the adapter attaching screws and remove the adapter.
4. Loosen the screw attaching the rotor to the distributor and remove the cap, if necessary.

Installation

1. If previously removed, position the distributor rotor with the square and round locator pins matched to the rotor mounting plate. Tighten the screws 2.1 to 2.9 ft. lbs.
2. Install adapter in position and tighten attaching screws 2.1 to 2.9 ft. lbs.
3. Install the cap, noting the square alignment locator and fasten the clips.
4. Install secondary wires, noting correct locations on the distributor cap.

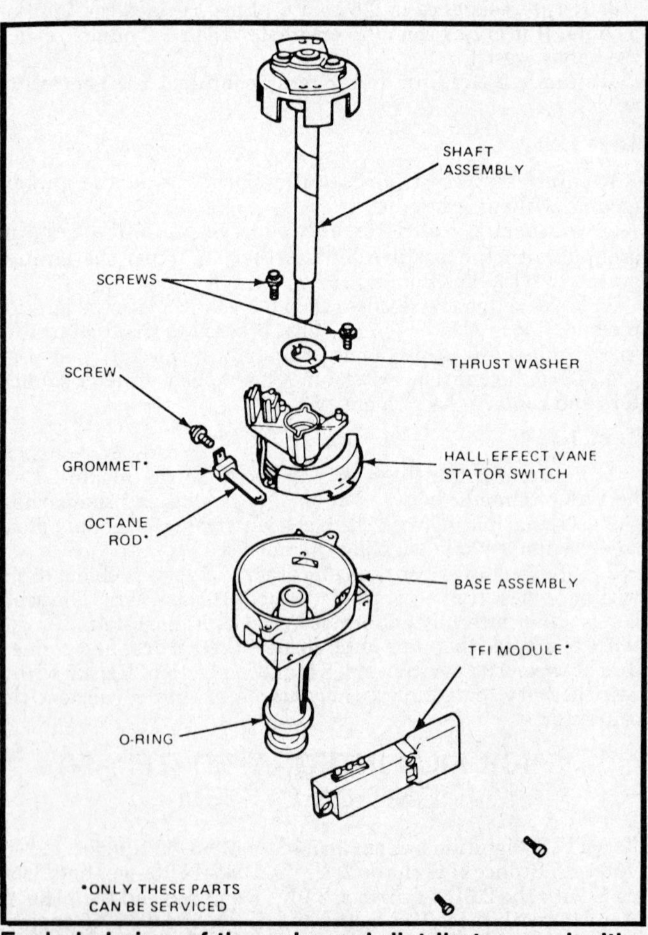

Exploded view of the universal distributor used with TFI ignition systems

TFI IGNITION MODULE

Removal

1. Remove distributor cap and adapter. Position it and the attached wires aside so as not to interfere with the work area.
2. Remove TFI harness connector.
3. Remove distributor from engine using security type distributor hold down bolt Tool T82L-12270-A, or equivalent.
4. Place removed distributor on work bench. Remove the two TFI module attachment screws.
5. Pull right side of module down the distributor mounting flange and then back up to disengage module terminals for connector in distributor base. The module may then be pulled toward flange and away from the distributor.

NOTE: Do not attempt to lift module from mounting surface prior to moving entire TFI module toward distributor flange as the pins at the distributor/module connector will break.

Installation

1. Coat the metal base plate of the TFI ignition module with silicone compound, approximately $1/32$ in. thick. Use D7AZ-19A331-A or equivalent grease.
2. Place TFI module on distributor base mounting flange.
3. Carefully position TFI module assembly toward distributor bowl and engage securely the three distributor connector pins.
4. Install the two TFI module mounting screws and tighten them 9 to 16 inch lbs.
5. Install distributor on engine.
6. Install distributor cap and adapter and tighten adapter mounting screws.
7. Install TFI harness connector.
8. Using an induction timing lamp, verify engine timing per engine decal.

OCTANE ROD

Removal

1. Remove cap, adapter and rotor.
2. Remove the octane rod 4mm retaining screw.
3. Slide the octane rod grommet out to a point where the rod can be disengaged from the stator retaining post and remove the octane rod. Retain the grommet for use with the new octane rod.

Installation

1. Install the grommet on the new octane rod.
2. Install the octane rod into the distributor, making sure it engages the stator retaining post.
3. Install the retaining screw and tighten to 15–35 inch lbs.
4. Install the rotor, adapter and cap. Tighten rotor and adapter attaching screws.

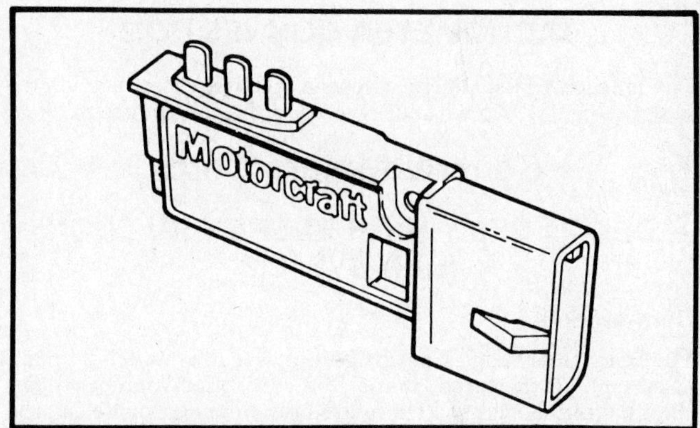

TFI ignition module—type IV

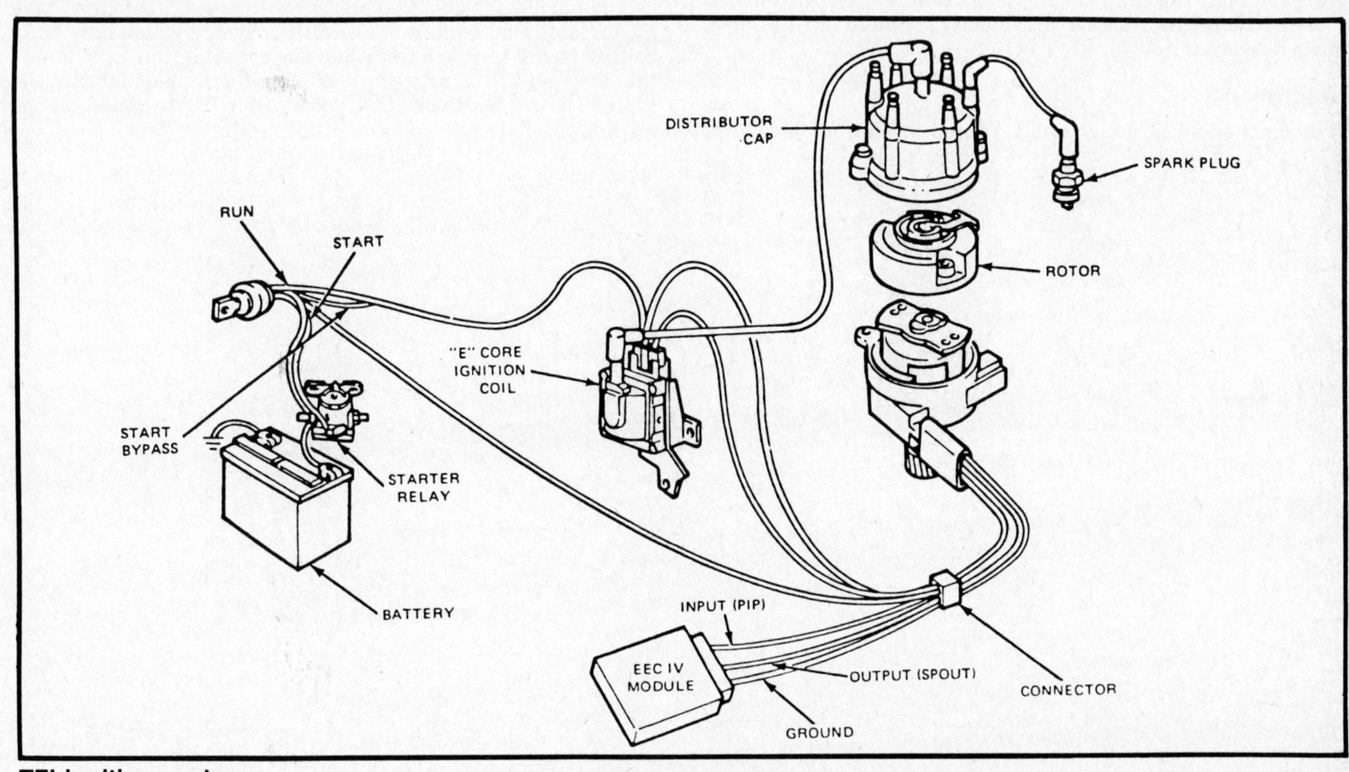

TFI ignition system

HIGH TENSION WIRES

Whenever a high tension wire is removed for any reason from a spark plug, coil or distributor cap or a new high tension wire is installed, silicone dielectric compound D1AZ-19A331-A or equivalent must be applied to the boot before it is reconnected. Using a small clean tool, coat the entire interior surface of the boot with Motorcraft silicone dielectric compound D7AZ-19A331-A or equivalent.

Insert each wire on the proper terminal of the distributor cap. Be sure the wires are all the way down over their terminals. The No. 1 terminal is identified on the cap. Install the wires starting with No. 1. The firing order is 1-4-2-5-3-6 clockwise.

Remove the wire retaining brackets from the old high tension wire set and install them on thc new set in the same relative position. Install the wires in the brackets on the valve rocker arm covers. Connect the wires to the proper spark plugs. Install the coil wire.

TACHOMETER CONNECTION

The ignition coil connector allows a tachometer connection using an alligator clip without removing the coil connector.

General Motors Corp.

DELCO REMY HIGH ENERGY IGNITION (HEI) SYSTEM

Components

The Delco Remy High Energy Ignition (HEI) System is a breakerless, pulse triggered, transistor controlled, inductive discharge ignition system. There are only nine external electrical connections; the ignition switch feed wire and the eight spark plug leads. On all 1982–86 V8 engines, 1986 vehicles equipped with a 4.3L engine and all 1987–88 vehicles equipped with Throttle Body Injection (TBI), the ignition coil is located within the distributor cap, connecting directly to the rotor. All others have a separate coil.

Operation

The magnetic pick up assembly located inside the distributor contains a permanent magnet, a pole piece with internal teeth, and a pick-up coil. When the teeth of the rotating timer core and pole piece align, an induced voltage in the pick-up coil signals the electronic module to open the coil primary circuit. As the primary current decreases, a high voltage is induced in the secondary windings of the ignition coil, directing a spark through the rotor and high voltage leads to fire the spark plugs. The dwell period is automatically controlled by the electronic module and is increased with increasing engine rpm. The HEI System features a longer spark duration which is instrumental in firing lean and EGR diluted fuel/air mixtures. The condenser (capacitor) located within the HEI distributor is provided for noise (static) suppression purposes only and is not a regularly replaced ignition system component.

Some 1983 and later engines use an Electronic Spark Timing (EST) distributor. This unit replaces vacuum and centrifugal advance units with an electronic actuator. A vacuum sensor provides manifold vacuum information and a reference pulse is generated by a pulse generator located near the engine vibration damper. These signals are fed to an Electronic Control Module which, in turn, sends a signal to the EST distributor for ignition timing determination.

Some 1983 and later 5.0L V8 engines and 1986 and later 4.3L engines also use an Electronic Spark Control (ESC) which responds to engine detonation with retardation of ignition timing. An engine block mounted sensor detects the presence of vibration generated by detonation and signals the ESC controller to process the signal and adjust the timing via the actuator on the distributor. The system gradually retards the spark until detonation has disappeared. A failed sensor would produce occasional detonation.

These ESC equipped engines also have a "tip in" vacuum switch. When the throttle is suddenly opened and manifold vacuum is suddenly decreased, the switch contacts close to send a signal to the ESC controller to arbitrarily retard the spark to prevent knock. Thus, if the engine knocks for a very short time after a rapid opening of the throttle, this switch may be at fault.

Some 1986–88 vehicles equipped with the 2.5L engines have distributors that contain a Hall Effect Switch which provides a voltage signal to thje ECM when the rotating iron vane blocks the magnetic flux between the permanent magnet and the switch circuit. On these distributors, the "R" terminal on the module inside the distributor is not used.

HEI DIAGNOSIS CHART 1980-82

Intermittent Operation or Miss

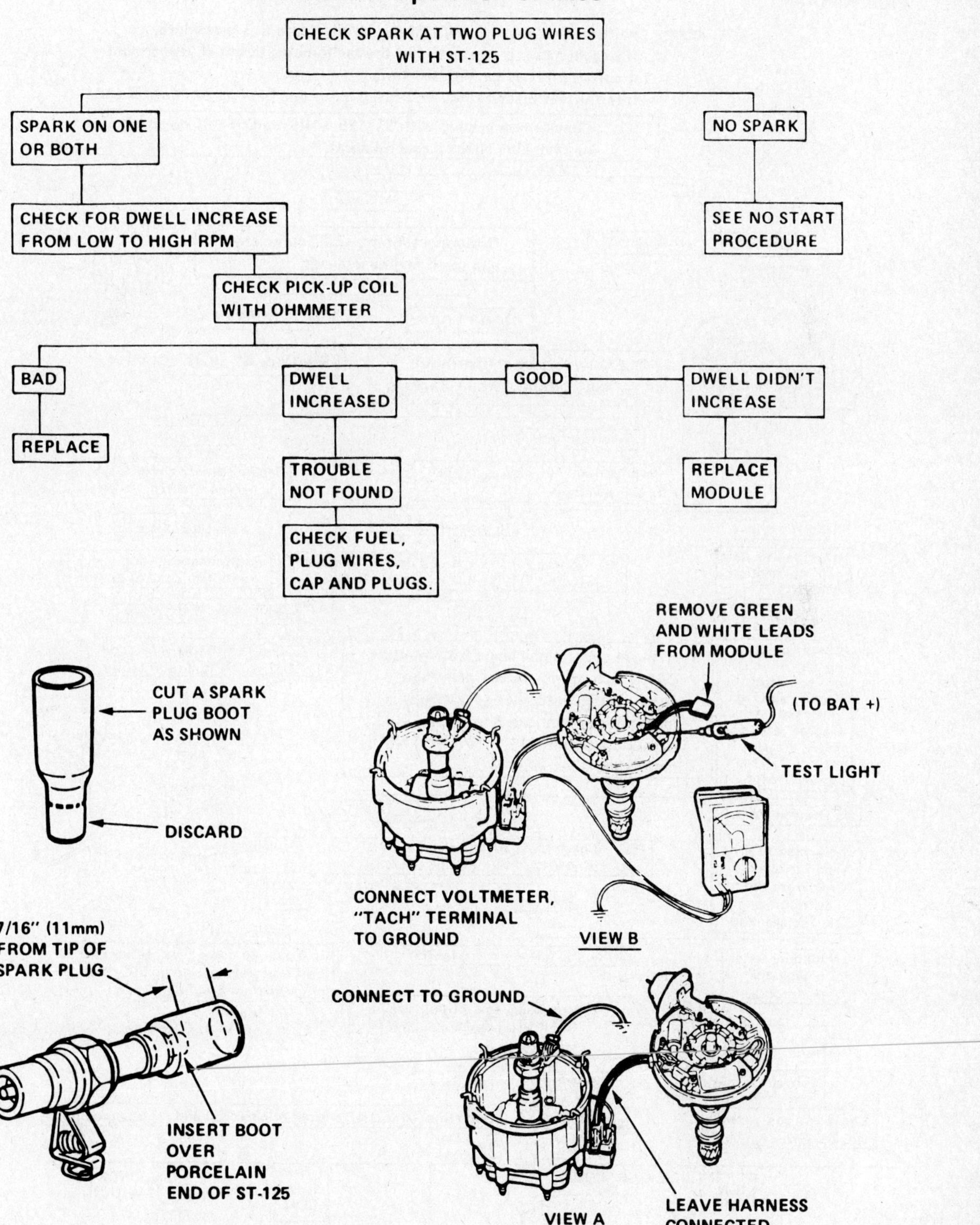
CHECK SPARK AT TWO PLUG WIRES WITH ST-125
SPARK ON ONE OR BOTH
NO SPARK
CHECK FOR DWELL INCREASE FROM LOW TO HIGH RPM
SEE NO START PROCEDURE
CHECK PICK-UP COIL WITH OHMMETER
BAD
DWELL INCREASED
GOOD
DWELL DIDN'T INCREASE
REPLACE
TROUBLE NOT FOUND
REPLACE MODULE
CHECK FUEL, PLUG WIRES, CAP AND PLUGS.
REMOVE GREEN AND WHITE LEADS FROM MODULE
(TO BAT +)
TEST LIGHT
CUT A SPARK PLUG BOOT AS SHOWN
DISCARD
CONNECT VOLTMETER, "TACH" TERMINAL TO GROUND
VIEW B
7/16" (11mm) FROM TIP OF SPARK PLUG
CONNECT TO GROUND
INSERT BOOT OVER PORCELAIN END OF ST-125
VIEW A
LEAVE HARNESS CONNECTED

HEI DIAGNOSIS CHART 1983 AND LATER
Engine Cranks, But Will Not Start

PRELIMINARY

NOTE: Perform Diagnostic Circuit Check before using this procedure.
If a tachometer is connected to the tachometer terminal, disconnect it before proceeding with the test.
Intermittent no start may be caused by wrong pick-up or ignition coil.

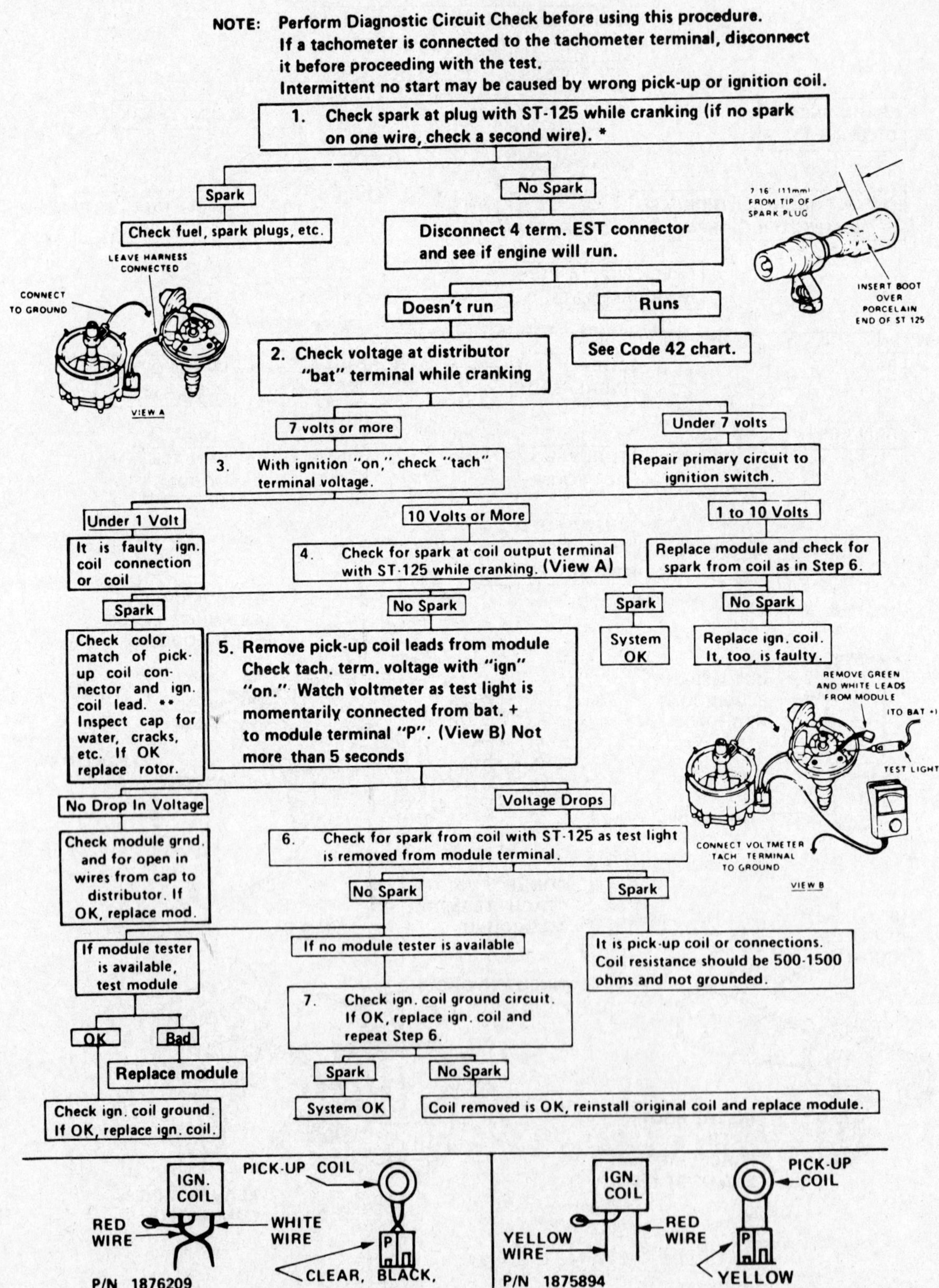
1. Check spark at plug with ST-125 while cranking (if no spark on one wire, check a second wire). *
Spark
Check fuel, spark plugs, etc.
No Spark
Disconnect 4 term. EST connector and see if engine will run.
7/16" (11mm) FROM TIP OF SPARK PLUG
INSERT BOOT OVER PORCELAIN END OF ST 125
LEAVE HARNESS CONNECTED
CONNECT TO GROUND
VIEW A
Doesn't run
Runs
See Code 42 chart.
2. Check voltage at distributor "bat" terminal while cranking
7 volts or more
Under 7 volts
Repair primary circuit to ignition switch.
3. With ignition "on," check "tach" terminal voltage.
Under 1 Volt
It is faulty ign. coil connection or coil
10 Volts or More
4. Check for spark at coil output terminal with ST-125 while cranking. (View A)
1 to 10 Volts
Replace module and check for spark from coil as in Step 6.
Spark
System OK
No Spark
Replace ign. coil. It, too, is faulty.
Spark
Check color match of pick-up coil connector and ign. coil lead. ** Inspect cap for water, cracks, etc. If OK replace rotor.
No Spark
5. Remove pick-up coil leads from module Check tach. term. voltage with "ign" "on." Watch voltmeter as test light is momentarily connected from bat. + to module terminal "P". (View B) Not more than 5 seconds
REMOVE GREEN AND WHITE LEADS FROM MODULE
(TO BAT +)
TEST LIGHT
CONNECT VOLTMETER TACH TERMINAL TO GROUND
VIEW B
No Drop In Voltage
Check module grnd. and for open in wires from cap to distributor. If OK, replace mod.
Voltage Drops
6. Check for spark from coil with ST-125 as test light is removed from module terminal.
No Spark
Spark
It is pick-up coil or connections. Coil resistance should be 500-1500 ohms and not grounded.
If module tester is available, test module
If no module tester is available
OK
Bad
Replace module
Check ign. coil ground. If OK, replace ign. coil.
7. Check ign. coil ground circuit. If OK, replace ign. coil and repeat Step 6.
Spark
System OK
No Spark
Coil removed is OK, reinstall original coil and replace module.
IGN. COIL
PICK-UP COIL
RED WIRE
WHITE WIRE
P
CLEAR, BLACK,
P/N 1876209
IGN. COIL
PICK-UP COIL
YELLOW WIRE
RED WIRE
P
YELLOW
P/N 1875894

* A few sparks and then nothing, is considered no spark.

HEI DIAGNOSIS CHART 1983 AND LATER
Continued

TROUBLE CODE 42
BYPASS OR EST PROBLEM

If vehicle will not start and run, check for grounded EST wire to ECM terminal "12." (Grounded and open EST circuit on 5.0L VIN "Y".)

A 1981 HEI module can cause a Code 42.

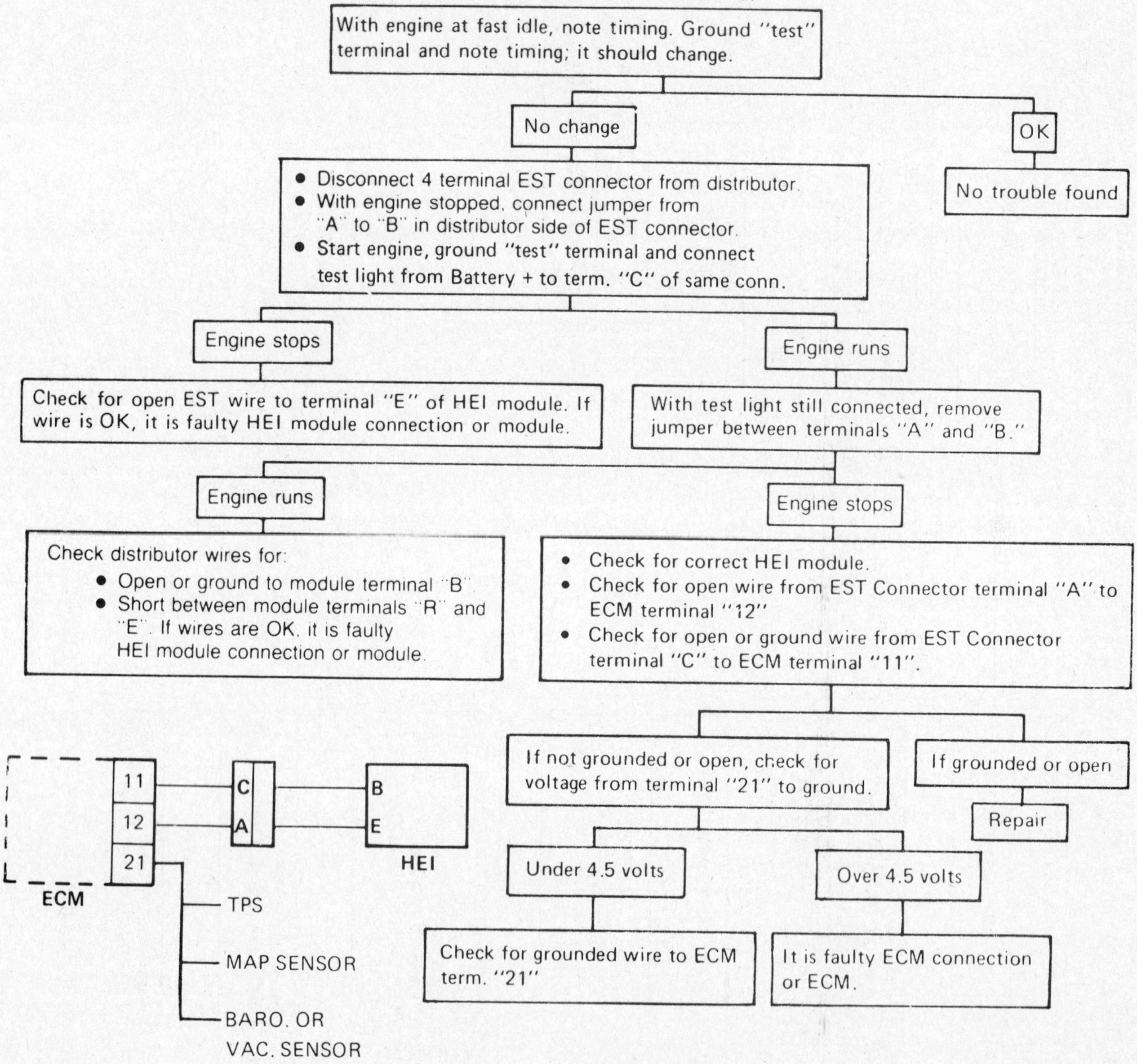

With engine at fast idle, note timing. Ground "test" terminal and note timing; it should change.

- **OK** → No trouble found
- **No change** →
  - Disconnect 4 terminal EST connector from distributor.
  - With engine stopped, connect jumper from "A" to "B" in distributor side of EST connector.
  - Start engine, ground "test" terminal and connect test light from Battery + to term. "C" of same conn.

  - **Engine stops** → Check for open EST wire to terminal "E" of HEI module. If wire is OK, it is faulty HEI module connection or module.
  - **Engine runs** → With test light still connected, remove jumper between terminals "A" and "B."
    - **Engine runs** → Check distributor wires for:
      - Open or ground to module terminal "B".
      - Short between module terminals "R" and "E". If wires are OK, it is faulty HEI module connection or module.
    - **Engine stops** →
      - Check for correct HEI module.
      - Check for open wire from EST Connector terminal "A" to ECM terminal "12"
      - Check for open or ground wire from EST Connector terminal "C" to ECM terminal "11".

      - **If grounded or open** → Repair
      - **If not grounded or open, check for voltage from terminal "21" to ground.**
        - **Under 4.5 volts** → Check for grounded wire to ECM term. "21"
        - **Over 4.5 volts** → It is faulty ECM connection or ECM.

ESC SYSTEMS DIAGNOSIS

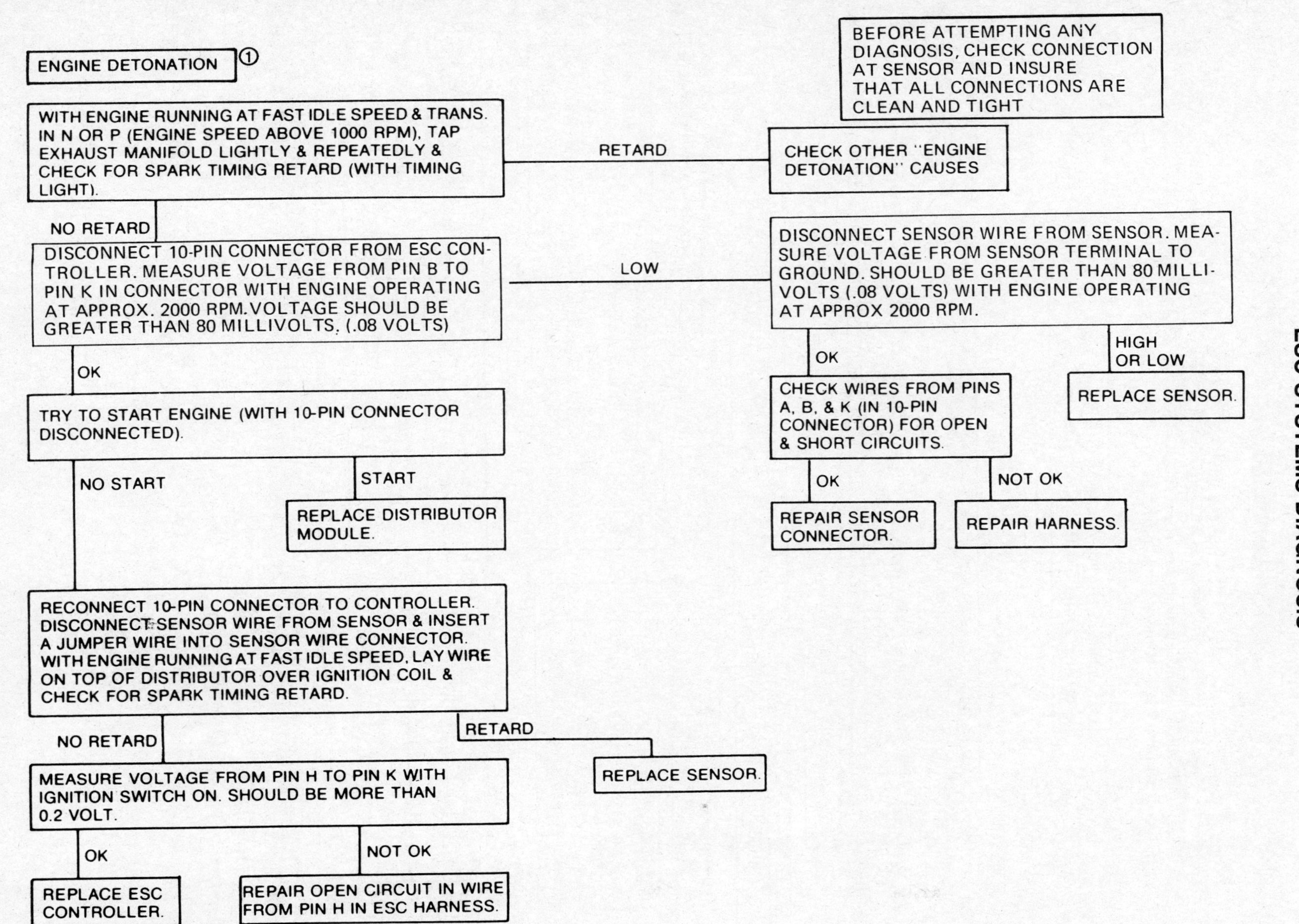
ENGINE DETONATION ①
WITH ENGINE RUNNING AT FAST IDLE SPEED & TRANS. IN N OR P (ENGINE SPEED ABOVE 1000 RPM), TAP EXHAUST MANIFOLD LIGHTLY & REPEATEDLY & CHECK FOR SPARK TIMING RETARD (WITH TIMING LIGHT).
RETARD
BEFORE ATTEMPTING ANY DIAGNOSIS, CHECK CONNECTION AT SENSOR AND INSURE THAT ALL CONNECTIONS ARE CLEAN AND TIGHT
CHECK OTHER "ENGINE DETONATION" CAUSES
NO RETARD
DISCONNECT 10-PIN CONNECTOR FROM ESC CONTROLLER. MEASURE VOLTAGE FROM PIN B TO PIN K IN CONNECTOR WITH ENGINE OPERATING AT APPROX. 2000 RPM. VOLTAGE SHOULD BE GREATER THAN 80 MILLIVOLTS, (.08 VOLTS)
LOW
DISCONNECT SENSOR WIRE FROM SENSOR. MEASURE VOLTAGE FROM SENSOR TERMINAL TO GROUND. SHOULD BE GREATER THAN 80 MILLIVOLTS (.08 VOLTS) WITH ENGINE OPERATING AT APPROX 2000 RPM.
OK
CHECK WIRES FROM PINS A, B, & K (IN 10-PIN CONNECTOR) FOR OPEN & SHORT CIRCUITS.
HIGH OR LOW
REPLACE SENSOR.
OK
REPAIR SENSOR CONNECTOR.
NOT OK
REPAIR HARNESS.
OK
TRY TO START ENGINE (WITH 10-PIN CONNECTOR DISCONNECTED).
START
REPLACE DISTRIBUTOR MODULE.
NO START
RECONNECT 10-PIN CONNECTOR TO CONTROLLER. DISCONNECT SENSOR WIRE FROM SENSOR & INSERT A JUMPER WIRE INTO SENSOR WIRE CONNECTOR. WITH ENGINE RUNNING AT FAST IDLE SPEED, LAY WIRE ON TOP OF DISTRIBUTOR OVER IGNITION COIL & CHECK FOR SPARK TIMING RETARD.
RETARD
REPLACE SENSOR.
NO RETARD
MEASURE VOLTAGE FROM PIN H TO PIN K WITH IGNITION SWITCH ON. SHOULD BE MORE THAN 0.2 VOLT.
OK
REPLACE ESC CONTROLLER.
NOT OK
REPAIR OPEN CIRCUIT IN WIRE FROM PIN H IN ESC HARNESS.
① SOME OCCASIONAL TRACE-TO-LIGHT DETONATION IS ACCEPTABLE.

ESC SYSTEM DIAGNOSIS

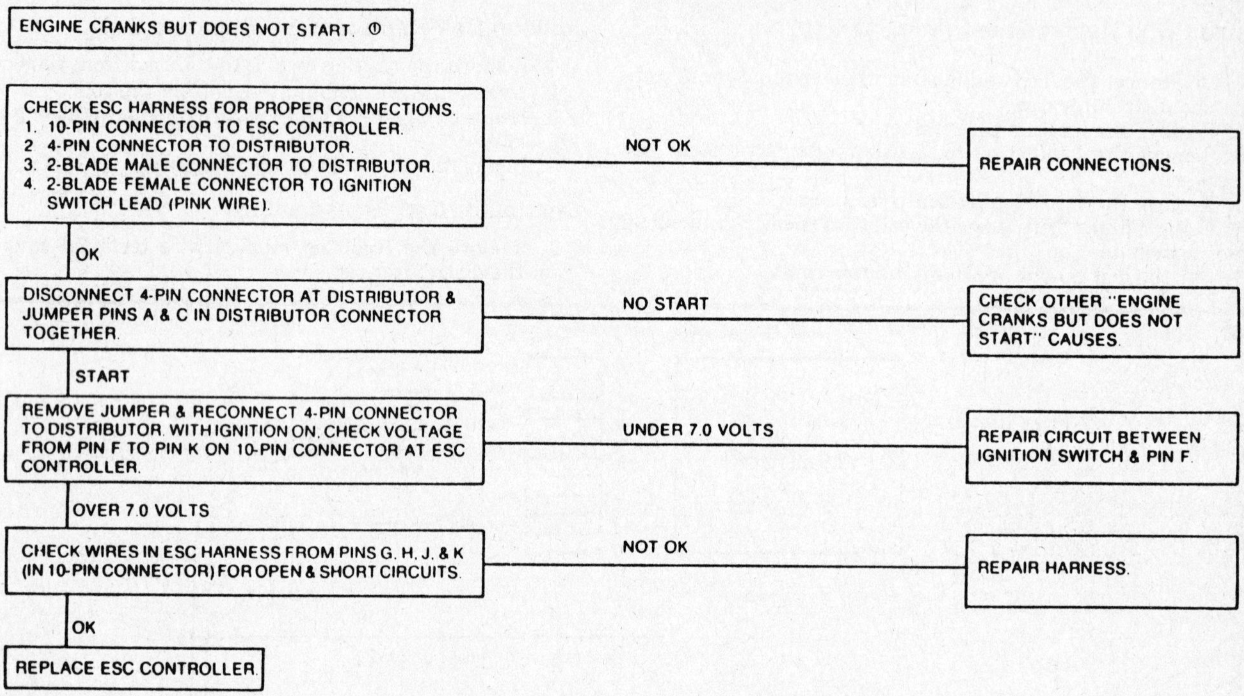

ENGINE CRANKS BUT DOES NOT START. ①

CHECK ESC HARNESS FOR PROPER CONNECTIONS.
1. 10-PIN CONNECTOR TO ESC CONTROLLER.
2. 4-PIN CONNECTOR TO DISTRIBUTOR.
3. 2-BLADE MALE CONNECTOR TO DISTRIBUTOR.
4. 2-BLADE FEMALE CONNECTOR TO IGNITION SWITCH LEAD (PINK WIRE).

- NOT OK → REPAIR CONNECTIONS.
- OK → DISCONNECT 4-PIN CONNECTOR AT DISTRIBUTOR & JUMPER PINS A & C IN DISTRIBUTOR CONNECTOR TOGETHER.
  - NO START → CHECK OTHER "ENGINE CRANKS BUT DOES NOT START" CAUSES.
  - START → REMOVE JUMPER & RECONNECT 4-PIN CONNECTOR TO DISTRIBUTOR. WITH IGNITION ON, CHECK VOLTAGE FROM PIN F TO PIN K ON 10-PIN CONNECTOR AT ESC CONTROLLER.
    - UNDER 7.0 VOLTS → REPAIR CIRCUIT BETWEEN IGNITION SWITCH & PIN F.
    - OVER 7.0 VOLTS → CHECK WIRES IN ESC HARNESS FROM PINS G, H, J, & K (IN 10-PIN CONNECTOR) FOR OPEN & SHORT CIRCUITS.
      - NOT OK → REPAIR HARNESS.
      - OK → REPLACE ESC CONTROLLER.

ESC SYSTEM DIAGNOSIS

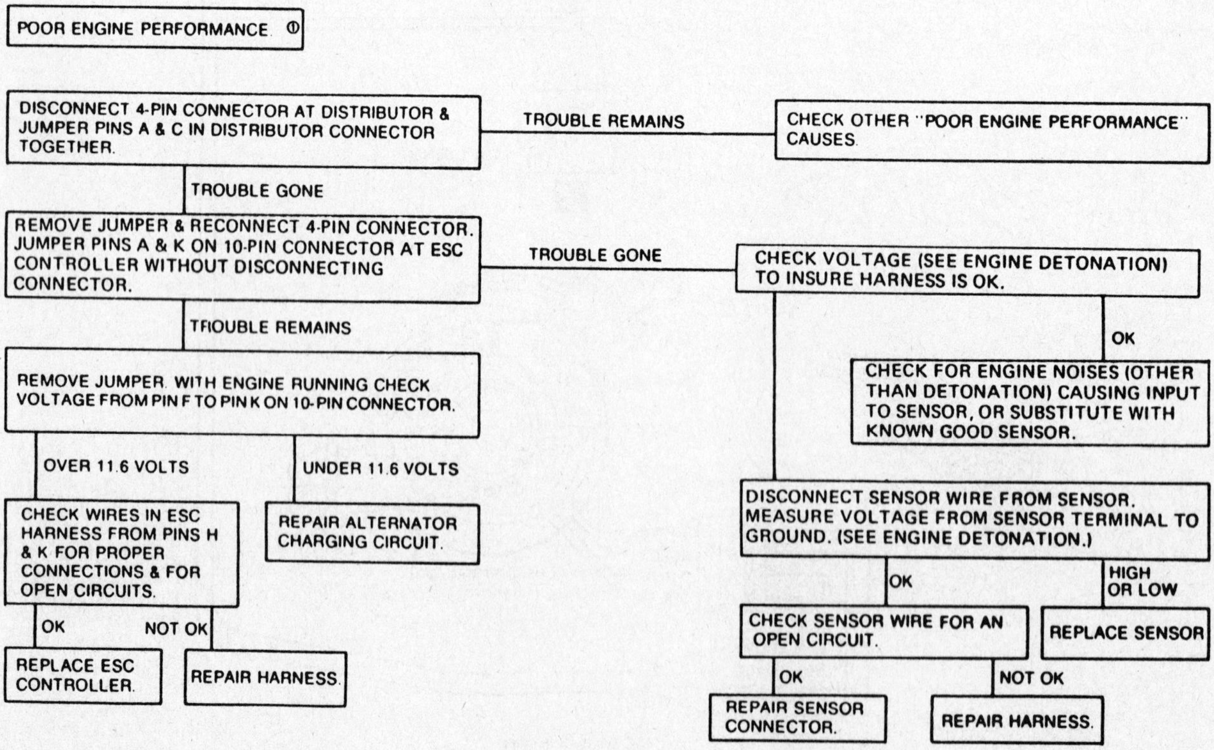

POOR ENGINE PERFORMANCE. ①

DISCONNECT 4-PIN CONNECTOR AT DISTRIBUTOR & JUMPER PINS A & C IN DISTRIBUTOR CONNECTOR TOGETHER.

- TROUBLE REMAINS → CHECK OTHER "POOR ENGINE PERFORMANCE" CAUSES.
- TROUBLE GONE → REMOVE JUMPER & RECONNECT 4-PIN CONNECTOR. JUMPER PINS A & K ON 10-PIN CONNECTOR AT ESC CONTROLLER WITHOUT DISCONNECTING CONNECTOR.
  - TROUBLE GONE → CHECK VOLTAGE (SEE ENGINE DETONATION) TO INSURE HARNESS IS OK.
    - OK → CHECK FOR ENGINE NOISES (OTHER THAN DETONATION) CAUSING INPUT TO SENSOR, OR SUBSTITUTE WITH KNOWN GOOD SENSOR.
    - → DISCONNECT SENSOR WIRE FROM SENSOR. MEASURE VOLTAGE FROM SENSOR TERMINAL TO GROUND. (SEE ENGINE DETONATION.)
      - HIGH OR LOW → REPLACE SENSOR.
      - OK → CHECK SENSOR WIRE FOR AN OPEN CIRCUIT.
        - OK → REPAIR SENSOR CONNECTOR.
        - NOT OK → REPAIR HARNESS.
  - TROUBLE REMAINS → REMOVE JUMPER. WITH ENGINE RUNNING CHECK VOLTAGE FROM PIN F TO PIN K ON 10-PIN CONNECTOR.
    - UNDER 11.6 VOLTS → REPAIR ALTERNATOR CHARGING CIRCUIT.
    - OVER 11.6 VOLTS → CHECK WIRES IN ESC HARNESS FROM PINS H & K FOR PROPER CONNECTIONS & FOR OPEN CIRCUITS.
      - OK → REPLACE ESC CONTROLLER.
      - NOT OK → REPAIR HARNESS.

MAJOR REPAIR OPERATIONS (DISTRIBUTOR IN ENGINE)

Ignition Coil Replacement (Integral Coil)

1. Disconnect the feed and module wire terminal connectors from the distributor cap.
2. Remove the ignition set retainer.
3. Remove the 4 coil cover to distributor cap screws and the coil cover.
4. Remove the 4 coil to distributor cap screws.
5. Using a blunt drift, press the coil wire spade terminals up out of distributor cap.
6. Lift the coil up out of the distributor cap.
7. Remove and clean the coil spring, rubber seal washer and coil cavity of the distributor cap.
8. Reverse the above procedures to install.

Ignition Coil Replacement (Separate Coil)

1. Remove the ignition switch to coil lead from the coil.
2. Unfasten the distributor leads from the coil.
3. Remove the screws which secure the coil to the engine and lift it off.
4. Installation is the reverse of removal.

Distributor Cap Replacement

1. Remove the feed and module wire terminal connectors from the distributor cap.

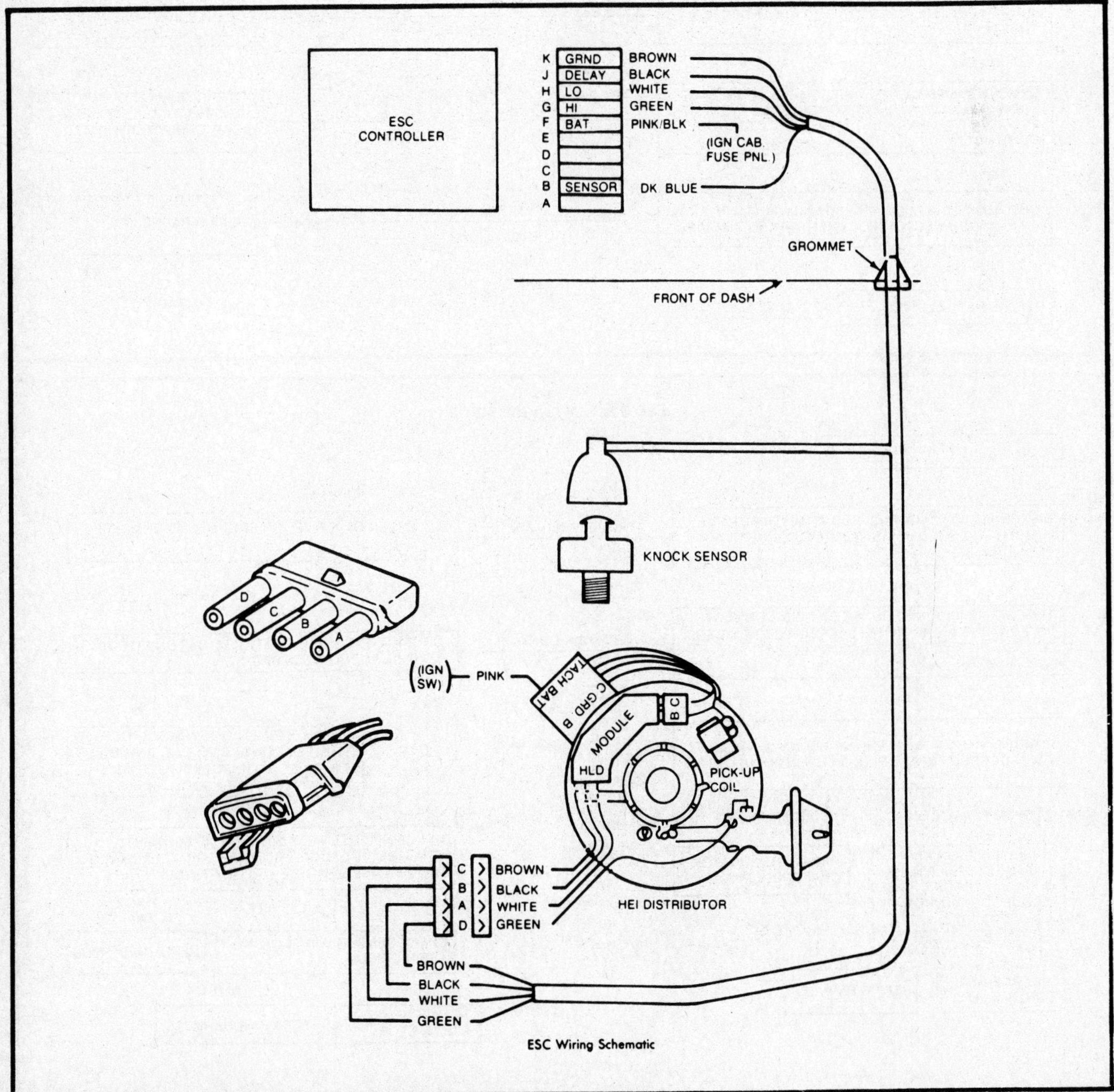

ESC Wiring Schematic

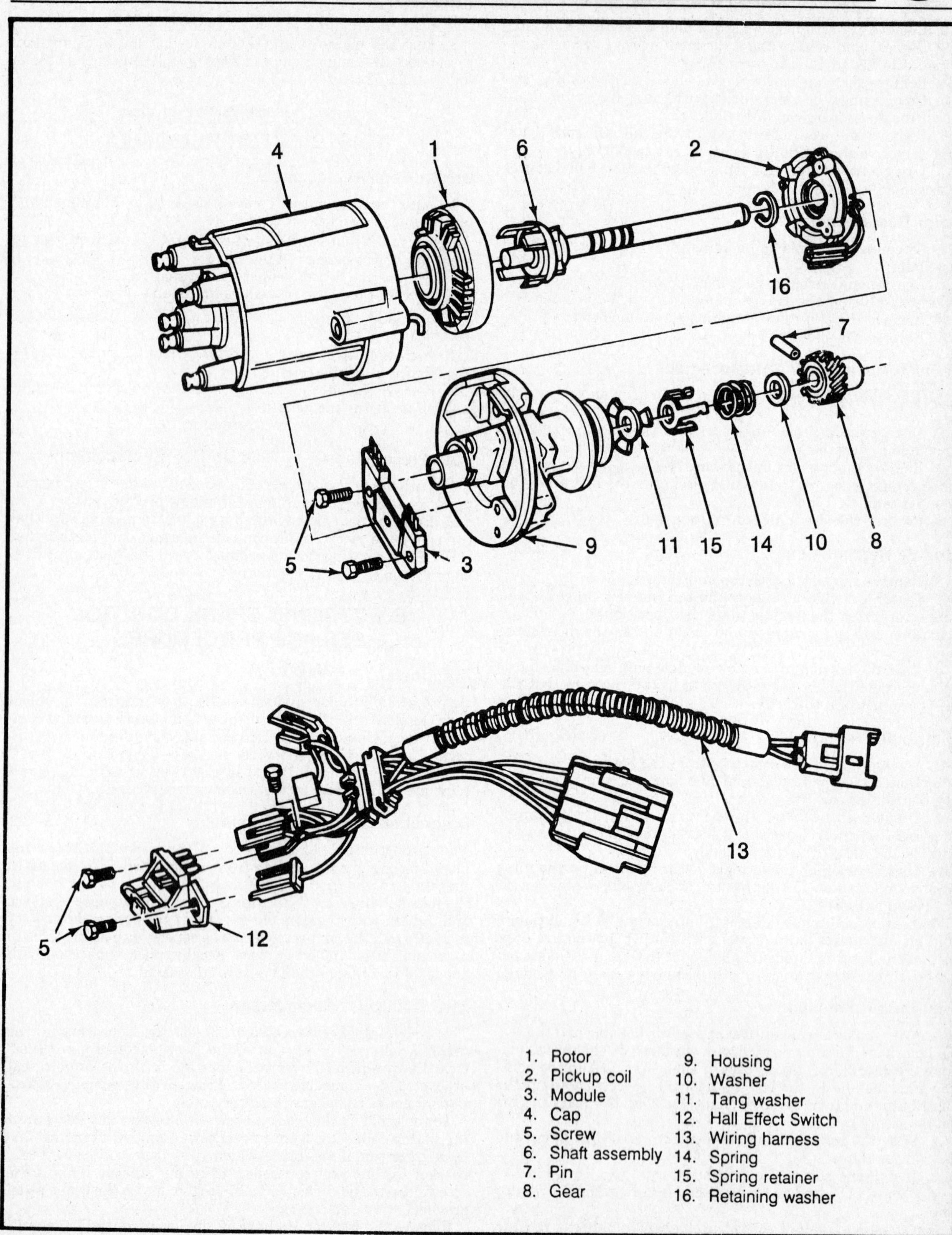

Seperate coil distributor (without sealed module connector)—exploded view

2. Remove the retainer and spark plug wires from the cap.
3. Depress and release the 4 distributor cap to housing retainers and lift off the cap assembly.
4. Remove the 4 coil cover screws and cover (V8 only).
5. Using a finger or a blunt drift, push the spade terminals up out of the distributor cap (V8 only).
6. Remove all 4 coil screws and lift the coil, coil spring and rubber seal washer out of the cap coil cavity (V8 only).
7. Using a new distributor cap, reverse the above procedures to assemble.

Rotor Replacement

1. Disconnect the feed and module wire connectors from the distributor.
2. Depress and release the 4 distributor cap to housing retainers and lift off the cap assembly.
3. Remove the two rotor attaching screws and rotor.
4. Reverse the above procedure to install.

Vacuum Advance Unit Replacement

1. Remove the distributor cap and rotor as previously described.
2. Disconnect the vacuum hose from the vacuum advance unit. Remove the module.
3. Remove the two vacuum advance retaining screws, pull the advance unit outward, rotate and disengage the operating rod from its tang.
4. Reverse the above procedure to install.

Module Replacement

1. Remove the distributor cap and rotor.
2. Disconnect the harness connector and pick-up coil spade connectors from the module (note their positions).
3. Remove the two screws and module from the distributor housing.
4. Coat the bottom of the new module with dielectric lubricant. Reverse the above procedure to install. Be sure that the leads are installed correctly.

Distributor Removal

1. Disconnect the ground cable from the battery.
2. Disconnect the feed and module terminal connectors from the distributor cap.
3. Disconnect the hose at the vacuum advance, if so equipped.
4. Depress and release the 4 distributor cap to housing retainers and lift off the cap assembly.
5. Using crayon or chalk, make locating marks on the rotor and module and on the distributor housing and engine for installation purposes.
6. Loosen and remove the distributor clamp bolt and clamp, and lift distributor out of the engine. Noting the relative position of the rotor and module alignment marks, make a second mark on the rotor to align it with the one mark on the module.

Distributor Installation

1. With a new O-ring on the distributor housing and the second mark on the rotor aligned with the mark on the module, install the distributor, taking care to align the mark on the housing with the one on the engine. It may be necessary to lift the distributor and turn the rotor slightly to align the gears and the oil pump driveshaft.
2. With the respective marks aligned, install the clamp and bolt finger tight.
3. Install and secure the distributor cap.
4. Connect the feed and module connectors to the distributor cap.
5. Connect a timing light to the engine and plug the vacuum hose.
6. Connect the ground cable to the battery.
7. Start the engine and set the timing.
8. Turn the engine off and tighten the distributor clamp bolt. Disconnect the timing light and unplug and connect the hose to the vacuum advance.

SERVICE PROCEDURES (DISTRIBUTOR REMOVED)

Driven Gear Replacement

1. With the distributor removed, use a ⅛ in. pin punch and tap out the driven gear roll pin.
2. Hold the rotor end of shaft and rotate the driven gear to shear any burrs in the roll pin hole.
3. Remove the driven gear from the shaft.
4. Reverse the above procedure to install.

Mainshaft Replacement

1. With the driven gear and rotor removed, gently pull the mainshaft out of the housing.
2. Remove the advance springs, weights and slide the weight base plate off the mainshaft.
3. Reverse the above procedure to install.

Pole Piece, Magnet or Pick Up Coil Replacement

1. With the mainshaft out of its housing, remove the 3 retaining screws, pole piece and magnet and/or pick up coil.
2. Reverse the removal procedure to install making sure that the pole piece teeth do not contact the timer core teeth by installing and rotating the mainshaft. Loosen the 3 screws and realign the pole piece as necessary.

ELECTRONIC SPARK CONTROL SERVICE PROCEDURES

Diagnosis

Before attempting to find an electrical or electronic problem with the Electronic Spark Control or Computer Command Control System, check that all electrical and vacuum connectors are securely connected. Otherwise, needless diagnostic or repair time may be expended. If no bad electrical or vacuum connections are found, refer to the accompanying charts.

Detonation Sensor Replacement

The detonation sensor is located on the lower portion of the block on the right side, just in front of the starter. To replace it, first unlatch and then pull off the connector. Apply a wrench to the flats and unscrew the sensor. Screw the new sensor in place and tighten with the wrench. Reconnect the connector and try to gently pull the connector from the sensor with slight force to make sure it is latched in place. Finally, push it back on with about 10 lb. of force to make sure it's seated.

ESC Controller Replacement

The ESC Controller is located on the mounting bracket for the brake pedal, just to the right of the steering column, on all except the van models, where the location is on the drivers seat bracket. On all models, before disconnecting wiring connections, remove the negative battery cable.

To replace it on the truck models, first release and disconnect the wiring connector from underneath. Remove the screw fastening the top of the brace which runs from the brake pedal bracket to the lower controller mounting bracket. This is the screw nearest the firewall accessible from inside the brake pedal bracket.

Remove the two screws holding the lower controller mounting bracket and lower brace in place and remove the lower bracket, brace and controller.

1. Vaccum unit
2. Rotor
3. Pickup coil assembly
4. Module
5. Cover
6. Ground strap
7. Ignition coil assembly
8. Seal
9. Cap
10. Resistor
11. Screw
12. Shaft assembly
13. Pin
14. Terminal block
15. Gear
16. Housing
17. Washer
18. Bolt
19. Tang washer

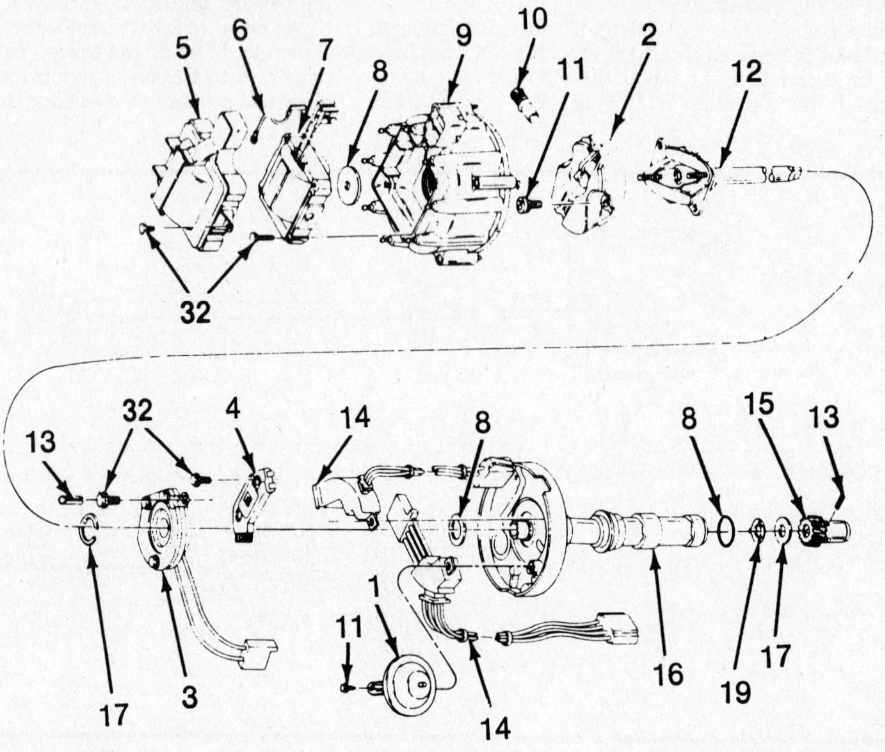

Integral coil distributor—exploded view

1. Rotor
2. Pickup coil
3. Module
4. Cap
5. Screw
6. Shaft assembly
7. Pin
8. Gear
9. Housing
10. Retainer
11. Shield
12. Spring
13. Spring retainer

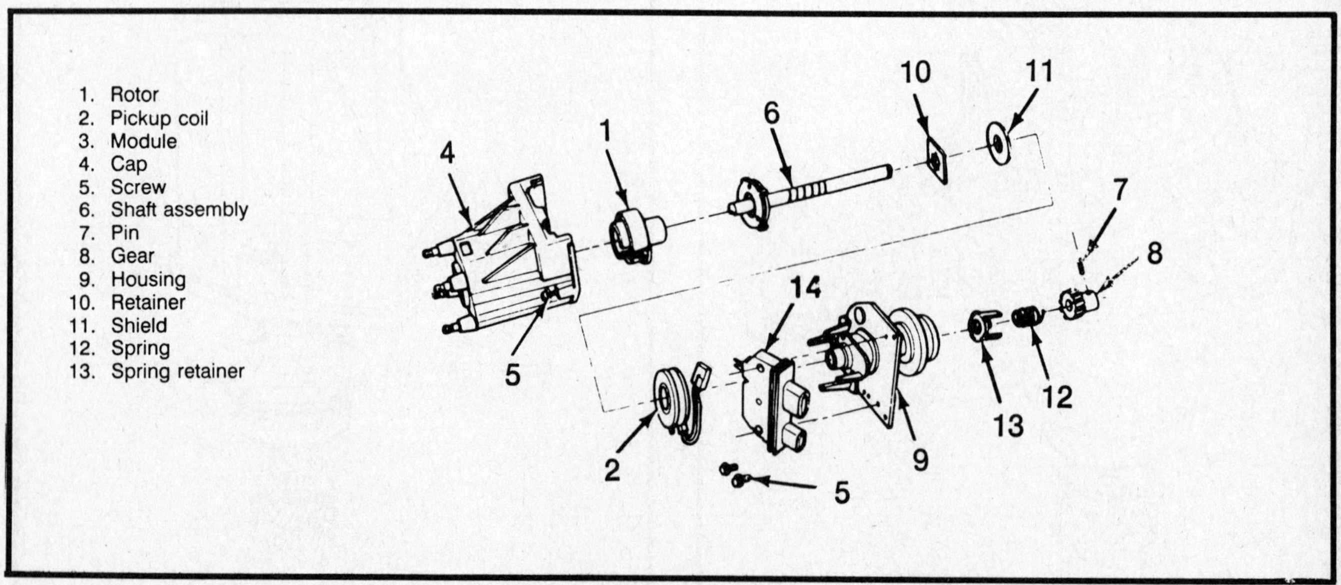

Seperate coil distributor (with sealed module connector exc. 8 cyl.)—exploded view

To remove the control module from the vans is a simple matter of disconnecting the wires and removing the attaching bolts. To install, reverse the procedure.

To install, first position the controller with the connection at the bottom and tabs facing away from the steering column. Slide the controller unit up under the tab at the top of its mounting bracket. Put the lower controller mounting bracket in position and install its rear screw. Position the brace so that its lower screw hole lines up with the open screw hole in the lower mounting bracket and its upper screw hole lines up with that in the brake pedal bracket. Install the screw which fastens the lower controller bracket and brace. Install the screw fastening the upper brace to the pedal mounting bracket. Finally, connect the electrical connector, checking that it locks securely.

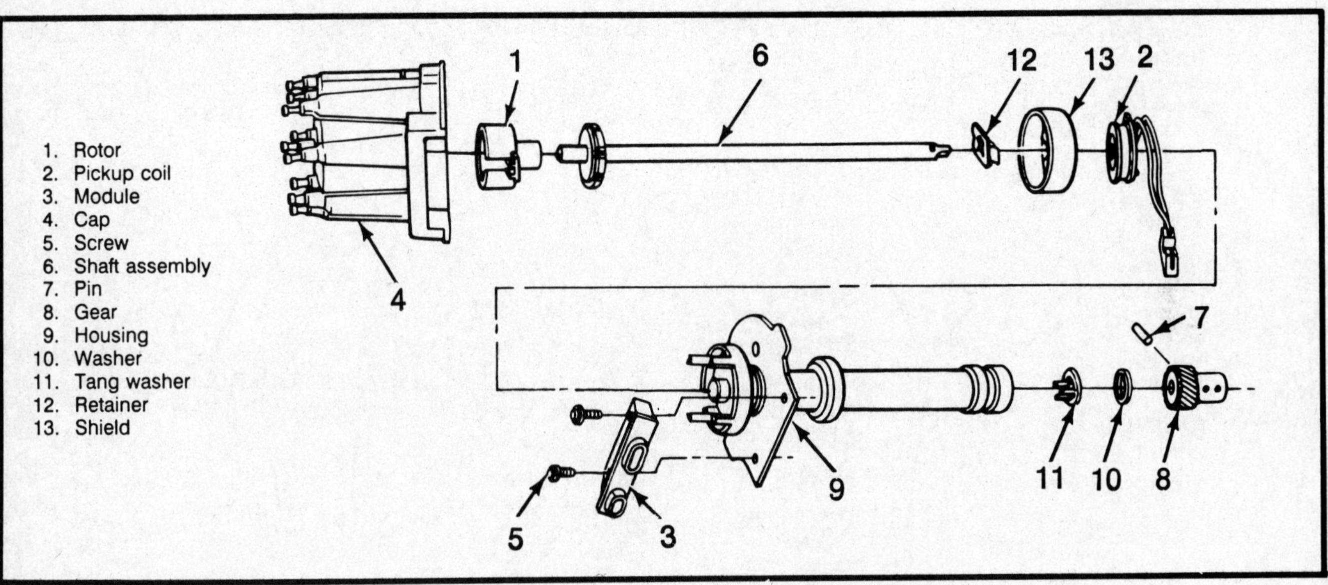

Seperate coil distributor (with sealed module connector 8 cyl.)—exploded view

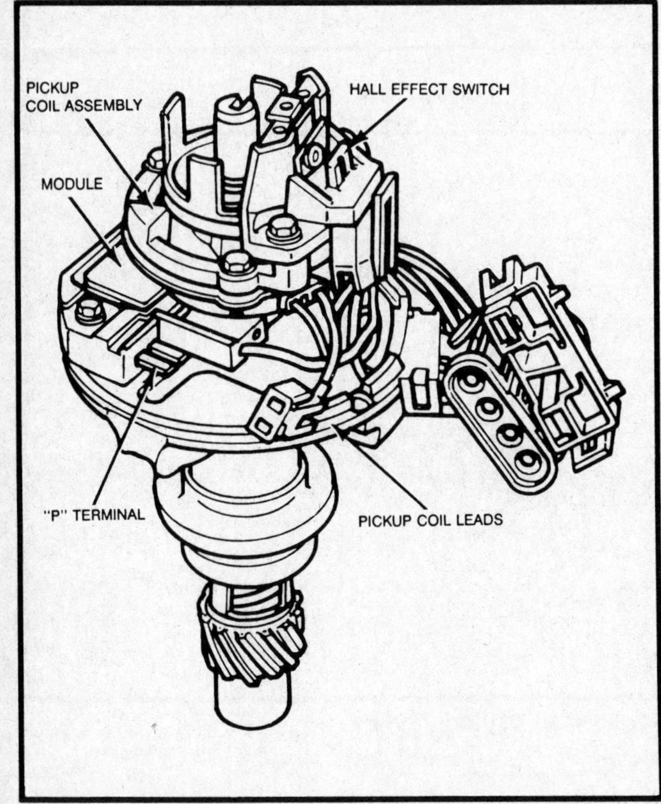

Typical HEI/EST distributor with Hall Effect Switch

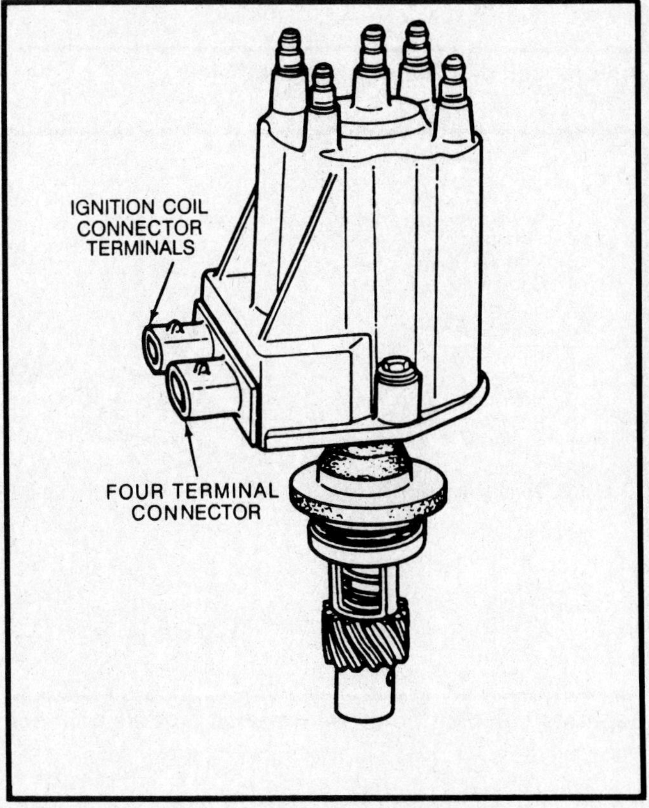

Typical HEI/EST distributor with separate coil

DISTRIBUTOR 4 CYL. 1.9L ENGINE (1982–85)

Disassembly

1. Remove the cap, rotor and the packing which seals the cap at the bottom.
2. Remove the reluctor cover by squeezing together the fastening tangs and pulling it out.
3. Remove the vacuum advance unit's mounting screws and remove the unit from the distributor.
4. Remove the screw which attaches the wiring harness clip to the side of the distributor and remove the clip. Disconnect the two connectors from the breaker plate. Slide the harness sealing grommet up and out of the side of the distributor and remove the harness.
5. Using the proper toole, remove the reluctor from the rotor shaft.
6. Remove the breaker plate mounting screws and remove the breaker plate assembly.
7. Remove the screws fastening the module to the breaker plate and remove module from the breaker plate.
8. Drive the roll pin out of the shaft with a hammer and punch. This refers to the roll pin in the collar keeping the shaft in the housing.
9. Remove the distributor shaft from the housing.
10. Slide the O-ring off the shaft. Then, remove the screw from the top of the shaft, this screw retains the governor shaft.
11. Scribe the relationship between the governor shaft and rotor shaft to maintain the offset in the governor shaft after reassembly. Then, remove the governor shaft.
12. Remove the governor weights and springs from the governor shaft assembly.

Inspection

All parts may be washed except for the inner surface of the vacuum advance unit. Inspect the cap for cracks and carbon tracks and contact wear. Inspect the rotor for wear at the center and outer contacts. Apply vacuum to the vacuum advance unit and then seal off the vacuum source. The unit should shown only negligible leakage.

Assembly

1. Assemble in reverse order. When installing the governor springs, make sure the hooks of smaller springs are positioned below those of the larger springs on the posts.
2. Make sure the offset of the end of the governor shaft is correct by aligning scribe marks.
3. Use a new roll pin to fasten the collar which retains the mainshaft.
4. Twist and release the governor shaft to check that centrifugal advance will respond to changes in engine speed. The mechanism should return fully when released.
5. Measure the air gap between the pole piece and the stator with a feeler gauge. Adjust if necessary until it is 0.12 to 0.20 in.

DISTRIBUTORS WITH INTEGRAL COILS

Disassembly

1. Disconnect the wiring harness connector from the ignition coil terminal connector.
2. Remove the cap by unlatching the four spring latches.
3. Remove the coil cover attaching bolts and remove the cover from the cap.
4. Remove the four coil attaching bolts.
5. Using needle nose pliers, disconnect the coil wires from the connector housing.
6. Remove the coil and wiring from the cap.
7. Remove the arc seal and the ground wire from the cap.
8. Remove the two bolts holding the rotor to the shaft and remove the rotor.
9. Remove the two bolts holding the Hall Effect switch to the housing, if so equipped.
10. Mark the shaft and driven gear so they can be aligned for reassembly, then drive out the roll pin with a small punch.
11. Remove the driven gear on the six cylinder engine and the driven gear, shim washer and thrust washer on the eight cylinder engine.
12. Remove the timer core shaft from the housing.

NOTE: Distributors for non-EST ignition systems have centrifugal advance weights and springs which are part of the shaft assembly and are not servicable.

13. Disconnect the four wire conncetor from the pick-up coil connector on distributors with ESC.
14. Disconnect the pick-up connector from the module.
15. Remove the screw holding the capacitor to the housing and remove the capacitor, wiring harness connector and module from the housing.
16. Disconnect the connector from the module.
17. Remove the magnetic shield, if so equipped.
18. Remove the thin washer, then remove the pick-up coil, assembly.

NOTE: The pick-up coil is serviced only as an assembly. Do not disassemble.

19. Remove the vacuum unit, if so equipped or the plastic retainer and two bolts

Inspection

All parts may be washed except for the inner surface of the vacuum advance unit. Inspect the cap for cracks and carbon tracks and contact wear. Inspect the rotor for wear at the center and outer contacts.

Assembly

1. Installation is the reverse of removal with the following precautions:

- When installing the pick-up coil assembly into the housing make sure to position the assembly over the pin on the vacuum unit or retainer and secure with a C-washer. If the arm of the assembly is not properly installed on the pin, the arm can float and cause the ignition timing to vary.
- When installing the module, coat the module terminals with a thin coat of petroleum jelly to prevent future oxidation.
- It is very important to coat the bottom of the module and the module rest pad in the housing with silicone grease or an equivalent heat transfer substance. Failure to do so could cause heat damage to the module.

DISTRIBUTORS WITH SEPARATE COILS (EXCEPT 4 CYL. 1.9L ENGINE)

Disassembly

1. On distributors with sealed module connectors, remove the cap by removing the retaining screws and washers.
2. On distributors without sealed module connectors, remove the cap by unlatching the spring latches.
3. Place marks on the rotor and shaft assembly to help line up the rotor during assembly, then remove the rotor.
4. On distributors without sealed module connectors, which may be equipped with a Hall Effect switch, the switch can be removed by removing the two retaining bolts and lifting away the locking tab of the connector to the switch.
5. Mark the shaft and driven gear so they can be aligned for reassembly, then drive out the roll pin with a small punch.
6. Remove the driven gear, washer or spring and the spring retainer and tang washer.

7. On distributors with sealed module connectors, remove the shaft with the pole piece and plate from the housing and pry the retainer from the housing. Remove the shield
8. On distributors without sealed module connectors, remove the shaft from the housing, then remove the "C" washer from inside the pick-up coil assembly.
9. Disconnect the pick-up coil connector from the module by by lifting away the locking tab of the connector, then remove the pick-up coil.
10. Remove the module by removing the two screws retaining it to the housing.

Inspection

Inspect the cap for cracks and carbon tracks and contact wear. Inspect the rotor for wear at the center and outer contacts. Check the shaft for shaft-to-bushing looseness. Insert the shaft in the housing. If the shaft wobbles, replace the shaft and/or housing.

Assembly

1. Installation is the reverse of removal with the following precautions:

- When installing the pick-up coil assembly into the housing make sure to position the tab on the bottom of the coil into the anchor hole in the housing.
- When installing the module, coat the module terminals with a thin coat of petroleum jelly to prevent future oxidation.
- It is very important to coat the bottom of the module and the module rest pad in the housing with silicone grease or an equivalent heat transfer substance. Failure to do so could cause heat damage to the module.
- When installing the Hall Effect Switch on models so equipped, the teeth on the shaft should rotate between the back plate and the magnet of the switch without touching.

Chrysler Corp. Electronic Ignition

REAR WHEEL DRIVE MODELS

The electronic ignition system on these models consits of a battery, ignition switch, ignition resister, control unit, coil, single or dual pick-up distributor, spark plugs and a dual pickup start-run relay on some models.

OPERATION

The ignition primary circuit is connected from the battery, through the ignition switch, through the primary side of the ignition coil, to the control unit where it is grounded. The secondary circuit is the same as in conventional ignition systems: the secondary side of the coil, the coil wire to the distributor, the rotor, the spark plug wires and the spark plugs.

The magnetic pulse distributor is also connected to the control unit. As the distributor shaft rotates, the distributor reluctor turns past the pick-up unit. As the reluctor turns past the pick-up unit, each of the eight teeth on the reluctor pass near the pick-up unit once during each distributor revolution (two crankshaft revolutions since the distributor runs at one-half crankshaft speed). As the reluctor teeth move close to the pick-up unit, the magnetic rotating reluctor induces voltage into the magnetic pick-up unit. This voltage pulse is sent to the ignition control unit from the magnetic pick-up unit. When the pulse enters the control unit, it signals the control unit to interrupt the ignition primary circuit. This causes the primary circuit to collapse and begins the induction of the magnetic lines of force from the primary side of the coil into the secondary side of the coil. This induction provides the required voltage to fire the spark plugs.

The advantages of this system are that the transistors in the control unit can make and break the primary ignition circuit much faster than conventional ignition points can and higher primary voltage can be utilized, since this system can be made to handle higher voltage without adverse effects, whereas ignition breaker points cannot. The quicker switching time of this system allows longer coil primary circuit saturation time and longer induction time when the primary circuit collapses. This increased time allows the primary circuit to build up more current and the secondary circuit to discharge more current.

TROUBLESHOOTING ELECTRONIC IGNITION SYSTEM

Chrysler Corporation has an Electronic Ignition System Tester to be used when checking the system. However, many shops are not able to obtain this equipment, so an alternate method has been developed. The system may be tested using a voltmeter with a scale of 20 volts and an ohmmeter with a scale of 20,000 ohms. When the ignition system is suspected of malfunctions, first inspect all wires for cracks and check all the connections at the components for tightness, then proceed with the diagnosis charts which follow.

PICK UP COIL

Replacement

1. Remove the distributor from the engine.
2. Using the proper tool, pry the reluctor off the shaft from the bottom. Be careful not to damage the teeth on the reluctor.
3. Unfasten the vacuum advance to distributor housing screws. Remove the vacuum unit, after disconnecting the arm from the upper plate.
4. Unfasten the pickup coil wires from the distributor housing.
5. Unfasten the two screws which secure the lower plate to the distributor housing. Lift out the lower plate together with the upper plate and pickup coil.
6. Separate the upper and lower plates by depressing the retaining clip on the underside of the plate and slide it away from the stud. The pickup coil will come off with the upper plate as they cannot be separated. They must be serviced as an assembly.
7. Installation is the reverse of removal. Place a small amount of distributor grease on the support pins on the lower plate.

Air Gap Adjustment

1. Align one reluctor tooth with the pickup coil tooth.
2. Loosen the pickup coil hold down screw.
3. Insert a 0.006 in. nonmagnetic feeler gauge between the reluctor tooth and the pickup coil tooth.
4. Adjust the air gap so that contact is made between the reluctor tooth, the feeler gauge and the pick-up coil tooth.
5. Tighten the hold down screw.
6. Remove the feeler gauge. No force should be required in removing the feeler gauge.
7. Check the air gap with a 0.008 in. feeler gauge. A 0.008 in. feeler gauge should not fit into the air gap. Do not force the gauge into the air gap.
8. Apply vacuum to the vacuum unit and rotate the governor shaft. The pickup pole should not hit the reluctor teeth. The gap was not properly adjusted if any hitting occurs. If hitting occurs on only one side of the reluctor, the distributor shaft is probably bent and the governor and shaft assembly should be replaced.

FRONT WHEEL DRIVE MODELS

2.2 ENGINE

The Electronic Fuel Control System used on these engines consist of a Spark Control Computer, various sensors and a specially calibrated carburetor.

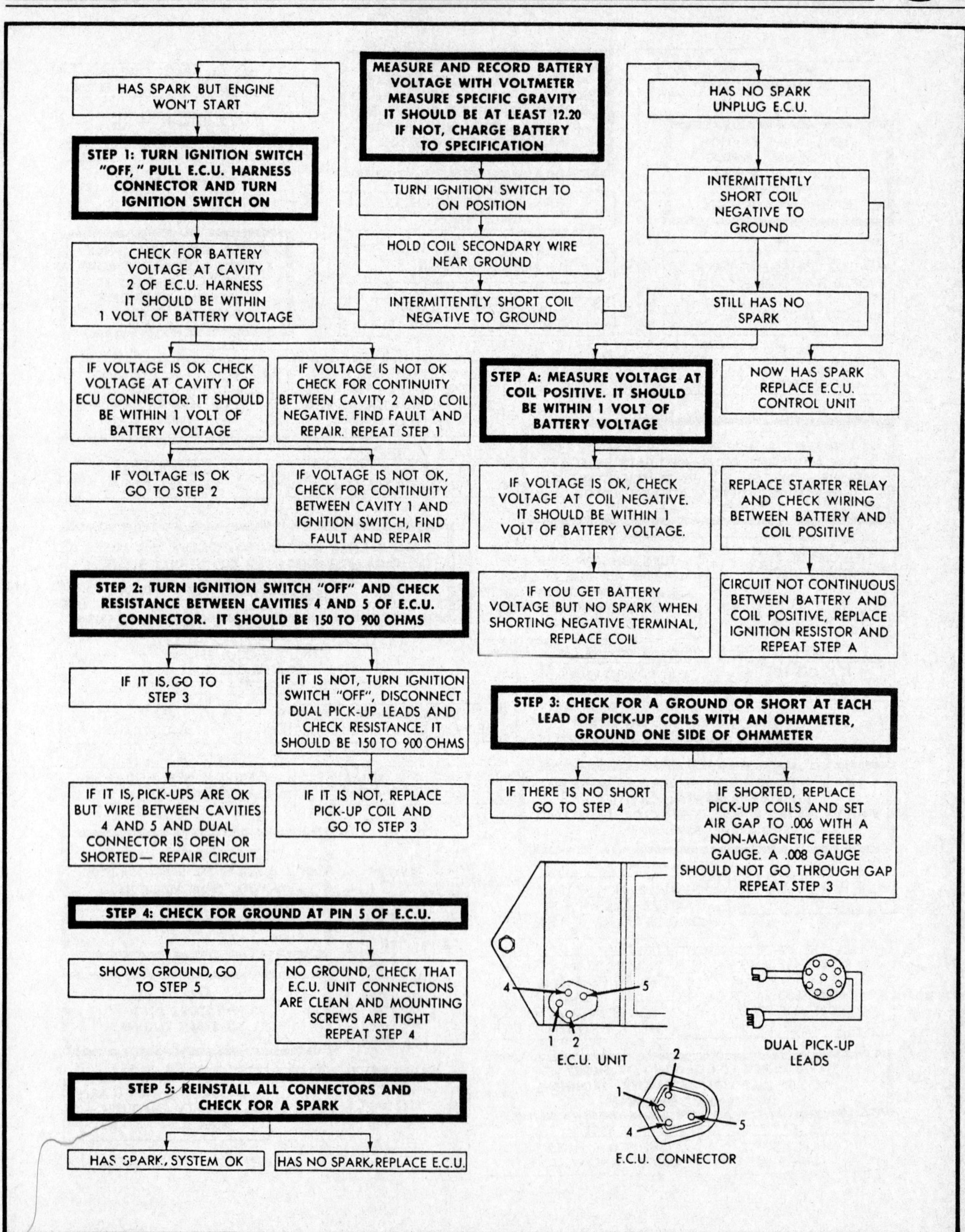

MEASURE AND RECORD BATTERY VOLTAGE WITH VOLTMETER MEASURE SPECIFIC GRAVITY IT SHOULD BE AT LEAST 12.20 IF NOT, CHARGE BATTERY TO SPECIFICATION
TURN IGNITION SWITCH TO ON POSITION
HOLD COIL SECONDARY WIRE NEAR GROUND
INTERMITTENTLY SHORT COIL NEGATIVE TO GROUND
HAS SPARK BUT ENGINE WON'T START
STEP 1: TURN IGNITION SWITCH "OFF," PULL E.C.U. HARNESS CONNECTOR AND TURN IGNITION SWITCH ON
CHECK FOR BATTERY VOLTAGE AT CAVITY 2 OF E.C.U. HARNESS IT SHOULD BE WITHIN 1 VOLT OF BATTERY VOLTAGE
IF VOLTAGE IS OK CHECK VOLTAGE AT CAVITY 1 OF ECU CONNECTOR. IT SHOULD BE WITHIN 1 VOLT OF BATTERY VOLTAGE
IF VOLTAGE IS NOT OK CHECK FOR CONTINUITY BETWEEN CAVITY 2 AND COIL NEGATIVE. FIND FAULT AND REPAIR. REPEAT STEP 1
IF VOLTAGE IS OK GO TO STEP 2
IF VOLTAGE IS NOT OK, CHECK FOR CONTINUITY BETWEEN CAVITY 1 AND IGNITION SWITCH, FIND FAULT AND REPAIR
STEP 2: TURN IGNITION SWITCH "OFF" AND CHECK RESISTANCE BETWEEN CAVITIES 4 AND 5 OF E.C.U. CONNECTOR. IT SHOULD BE 150 TO 900 OHMS
IF IT IS, GO TO STEP 3
IF IT IS NOT, TURN IGNITION SWITCH "OFF", DISCONNECT DUAL PICK-UP LEADS AND CHECK RESISTANCE. IT SHOULD BE 150 TO 900 OHMS
IF IT IS, PICK-UPS ARE OK BUT WIRE BETWEEN CAVITIES 4 AND 5 AND DUAL CONNECTOR IS OPEN OR SHORTED— REPAIR CIRCUIT
IF IT IS NOT, REPLACE PICK-UP COIL AND GO TO STEP 3
STEP 4: CHECK FOR GROUND AT PIN 5 OF E.C.U.
SHOWS GROUND, GO TO STEP 5
NO GROUND, CHECK THAT E.C.U. UNIT CONNECTIONS ARE CLEAN AND MOUNTING SCREWS ARE TIGHT REPEAT STEP 4
STEP 5: REINSTALL ALL CONNECTORS AND CHECK FOR A SPARK
HAS SPARK, SYSTEM OK
HAS NO SPARK, REPLACE E.C.U.
HAS NO SPARK UNPLUG E.C.U.
INTERMITTENTLY SHORT COIL NEGATIVE TO GROUND
STILL HAS NO SPARK
NOW HAS SPARK REPLACE E.C.U. CONTROL UNIT
STEP A: MEASURE VOLTAGE AT COIL POSITIVE. IT SHOULD BE WITHIN 1 VOLT OF BATTERY VOLTAGE
IF VOLTAGE IS OK, CHECK VOLTAGE AT COIL NEGATIVE. IT SHOULD BE WITHIN 1 VOLT OF BATTERY VOLTAGE.
REPLACE STARTER RELAY AND CHECK WIRING BETWEEN BATTERY AND COIL POSITIVE
IF YOU GET BATTERY VOLTAGE BUT NO SPARK WHEN SHORTING NEGATIVE TERMINAL, REPLACE COIL
CIRCUIT NOT CONTINUOUS BETWEEN BATTERY AND COIL POSITIVE, REPLACE IGNITION RESISTOR AND REPEAT STEP A
STEP 3: CHECK FOR A GROUND OR SHORT AT EACH LEAD OF PICK-UP COILS WITH AN OHMMETER, GROUND ONE SIDE OF OHMMETER
IF THERE IS NO SHORT GO TO STEP 4
IF SHORTED, REPLACE PICK-UP COILS AND SET AIR GAP TO .006 WITH A NON-MAGNETIC FEELER GAUGE. A .008 GAUGE SHOULD NOT GO THROUGH GAP REPEAT STEP 3
4
5
1 2
E.C.U. UNIT
DUAL PICK-UP LEADS
2
1
4
5
E.C.U. CONNECTOR

Electronic Ignition system diagnosis—Rear wheel drive models

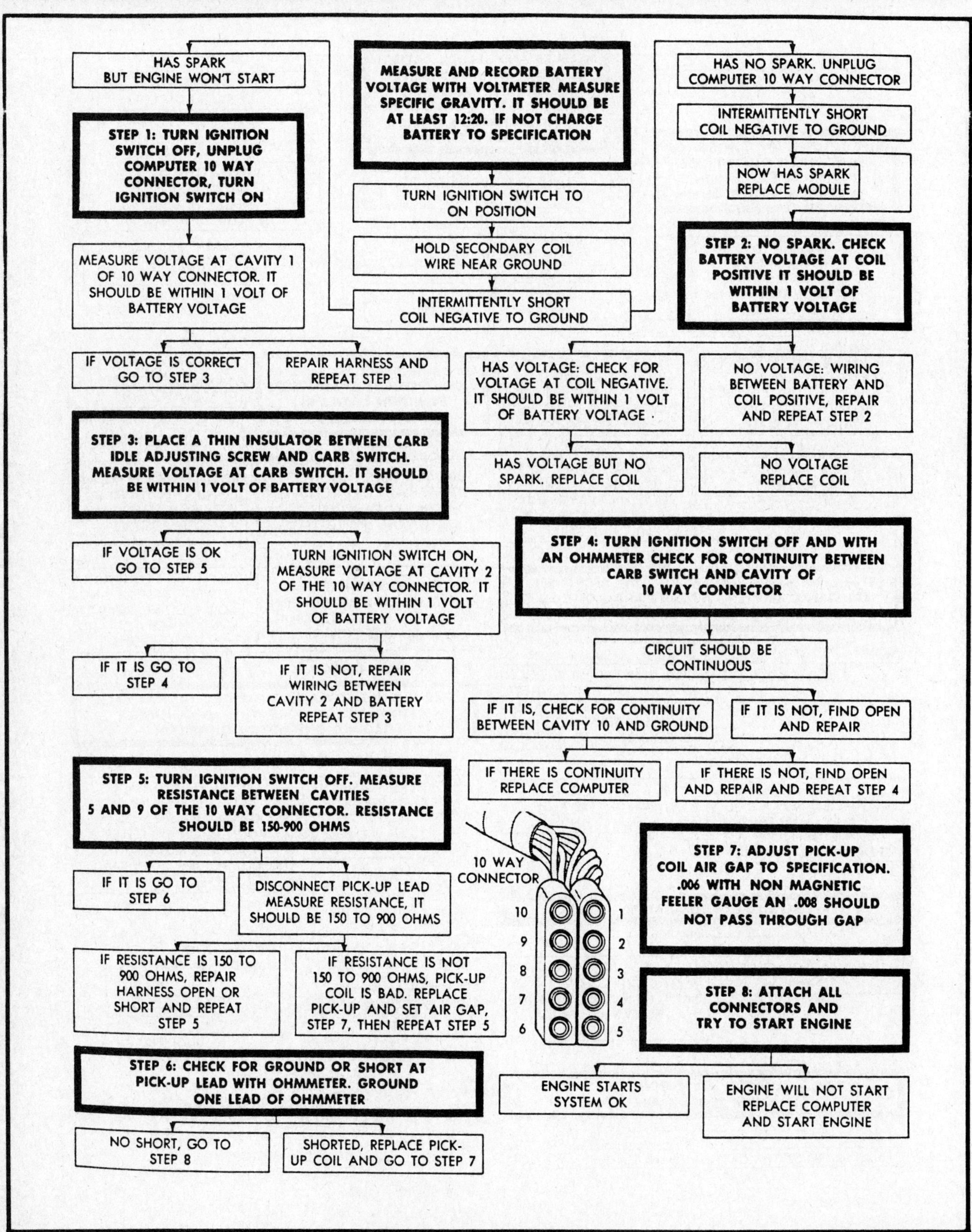
HAS SPARK BUT ENGINE WON'T START
STEP 1: TURN IGNITION SWITCH OFF, UNPLUG COMPUTER 10 WAY CONNECTOR, TURN IGNITION SWITCH ON
MEASURE VOLTAGE AT CAVITY 1 OF 10 WAY CONNECTOR. IT SHOULD BE WITHIN 1 VOLT OF BATTERY VOLTAGE
IF VOLTAGE IS CORRECT GO TO STEP 3
REPAIR HARNESS AND REPEAT STEP 1
STEP 3: PLACE A THIN INSULATOR BETWEEN CARB IDLE ADJUSTING SCREW AND CARB SWITCH. MEASURE VOLTAGE AT CARB SWITCH. IT SHOULD BE WITHIN 1 VOLT OF BATTERY VOLTAGE
IF VOLTAGE IS OK GO TO STEP 5
TURN IGNITION SWITCH ON, MEASURE VOLTAGE AT CAVITY 2 OF THE 10 WAY CONNECTOR. IT SHOULD BE WITHIN 1 VOLT OF BATTERY VOLTAGE
IF IT IS GO TO STEP 4
IF IT IS NOT, REPAIR WIRING BETWEEN CAVITY 2 AND BATTERY REPEAT STEP 3
STEP 5: TURN IGNITION SWITCH OFF. MEASURE RESISTANCE BETWEEN CAVITIES 5 AND 9 OF THE 10 WAY CONNECTOR. RESISTANCE SHOULD BE 150-900 OHMS
IF IT IS GO TO STEP 6
DISCONNECT PICK-UP LEAD MEASURE RESISTANCE, IT SHOULD BE 150 TO 900 OHMS
IF RESISTANCE IS 150 TO 900 OHMS, REPAIR HARNESS OPEN OR SHORT AND REPEAT STEP 5
IF RESISTANCE IS NOT 150 TO 900 OHMS, PICK-UP COIL IS BAD. REPLACE PICK-UP AND SET AIR GAP, STEP 7, THEN REPEAT STEP 5
STEP 6: CHECK FOR GROUND OR SHORT AT PICK-UP LEAD WITH OHMMETER. GROUND ONE LEAD OF OHMMETER
NO SHORT, GO TO STEP 8
SHORTED, REPLACE PICK-UP COIL AND GO TO STEP 7
MEASURE AND RECORD BATTERY VOLTAGE WITH VOLTMETER MEASURE SPECIFIC GRAVITY. IT SHOULD BE AT LEAST 12:20. IF NOT CHARGE BATTERY TO SPECIFICATION
TURN IGNITION SWITCH TO ON POSITION
HOLD SECONDARY COIL WIRE NEAR GROUND
INTERMITTENTLY SHORT COIL NEGATIVE TO GROUND
HAS NO SPARK. UNPLUG COMPUTER 10 WAY CONNECTOR
INTERMITTENTLY SHORT COIL NEGATIVE TO GROUND
NOW HAS SPARK REPLACE MODULE
STEP 2: NO SPARK. CHECK BATTERY VOLTAGE AT COIL POSITIVE IT SHOULD BE WITHIN 1 VOLT OF BATTERY VOLTAGE
HAS VOLTAGE: CHECK FOR VOLTAGE AT COIL NEGATIVE. IT SHOULD BE WITHIN 1 VOLT OF BATTERY VOLTAGE
NO VOLTAGE: WIRING BETWEEN BATTERY AND COIL POSITIVE, REPAIR AND REPEAT STEP 2
HAS VOLTAGE BUT NO SPARK. REPLACE COIL
NO VOLTAGE REPLACE COIL
STEP 4: TURN IGNITION SWITCH OFF AND WITH AN OHMMETER CHECK FOR CONTINUITY BETWEEN CARB SWITCH AND CAVITY OF 10 WAY CONNECTOR
CIRCUIT SHOULD BE CONTINUOUS
IF IT IS, CHECK FOR CONTINUITY BETWEEN CAVITY 10 AND GROUND
IF IT IS NOT, FIND OPEN AND REPAIR
IF THERE IS CONTINUITY REPLACE COMPUTER
IF THERE IS NOT, FIND OPEN AND REPAIR AND REPEAT STEP 4
10 WAY CONNECTOR
10
9
8
7
6
1
2
3
4
5
STEP 7: ADJUST PICK-UP COIL AIR GAP TO SPECIFICATION. .006 WITH NON MAGNETIC FEELER GAUGE AN .008 SHOULD NOT PASS THROUGH GAP
STEP 8: ATTACH ALL CONNECTORS AND TRY TO START ENGINE
ENGINE STARTS SYSTEM OK
ENGINE WILL NOT START REPLACE COMPUTER AND START ENGINE

Electronic Spark Control System diagnosis (Single pickup distributors)

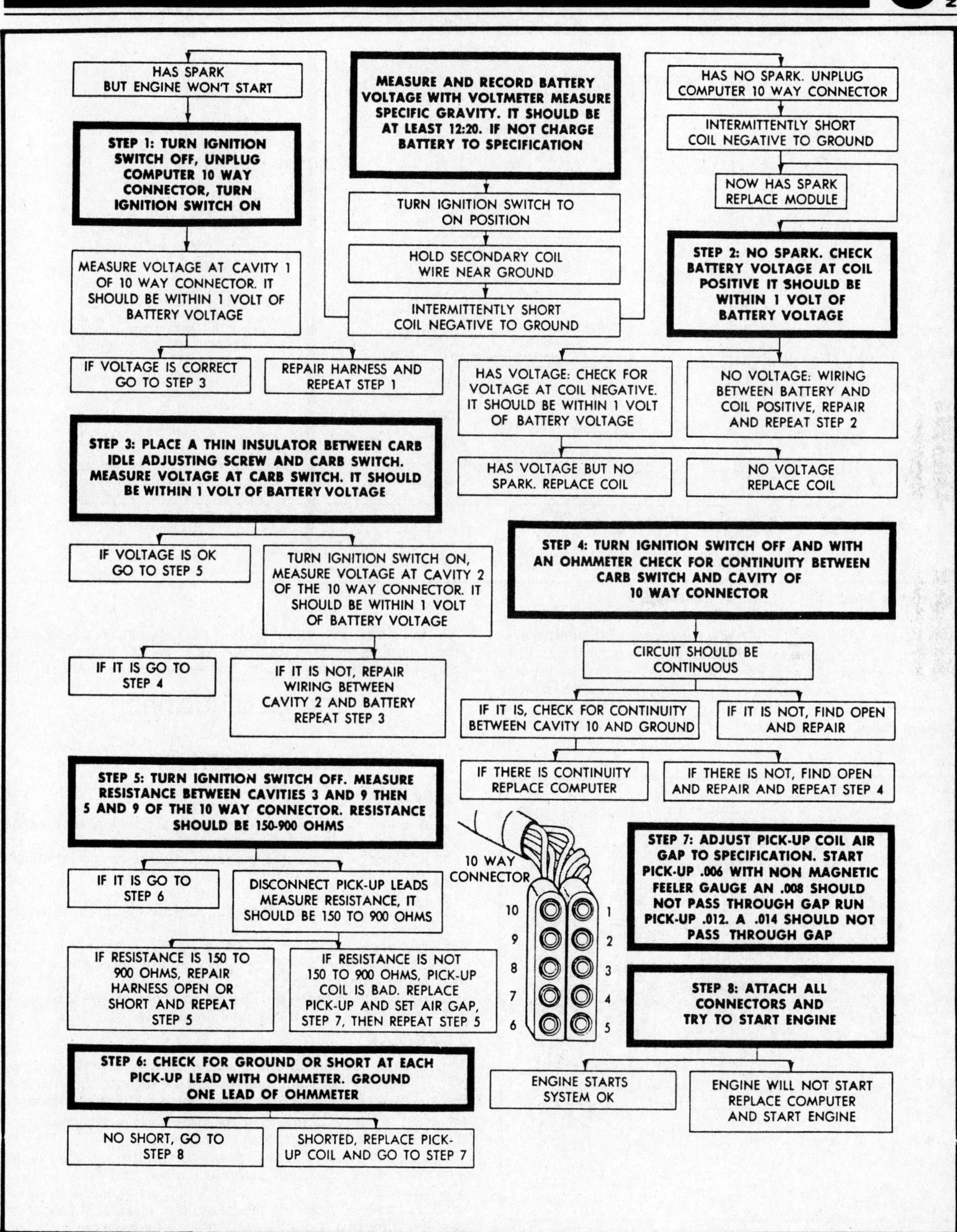

HAS SPARK BUT ENGINE WON'T START
STEP 1: TURN IGNITION SWITCH OFF, UNPLUG COMPUTER 10 WAY CONNECTOR, TURN IGNITION SWITCH ON
MEASURE VOLTAGE AT CAVITY 1 OF 10 WAY CONNECTOR. IT SHOULD BE WITHIN 1 VOLT OF BATTERY VOLTAGE
IF VOLTAGE IS CORRECT GO TO STEP 3
REPAIR HARNESS AND REPEAT STEP 1
STEP 3: PLACE A THIN INSULATOR BETWEEN CARB IDLE ADJUSTING SCREW AND CARB SWITCH. MEASURE VOLTAGE AT CARB SWITCH. IT SHOULD BE WITHIN 1 VOLT OF BATTERY VOLTAGE
IF VOLTAGE IS OK GO TO STEP 5
TURN IGNITION SWITCH ON, MEASURE VOLTAGE AT CAVITY 2 OF THE 10 WAY CONNECTOR. IT SHOULD BE WITHIN 1 VOLT OF BATTERY VOLTAGE
IF IT IS GO TO STEP 4
IF IT IS NOT, REPAIR WIRING BETWEEN CAVITY 2 AND BATTERY REPEAT STEP 3
STEP 5: TURN IGNITION SWITCH OFF. MEASURE RESISTANCE BETWEEN CAVITIES 3 AND 9 THEN 5 AND 9 OF THE 10 WAY CONNECTOR. RESISTANCE SHOULD BE 150-900 OHMS
IF IT IS GO TO STEP 6
DISCONNECT PICK-UP LEADS MEASURE RESISTANCE, IT SHOULD BE 150 TO 900 OHMS
IF RESISTANCE IS 150 TO 900 OHMS, REPAIR HARNESS OPEN OR SHORT AND REPEAT STEP 5
IF RESISTANCE IS NOT 150 TO 900 OHMS, PICK-UP COIL IS BAD. REPLACE PICK-UP AND SET AIR GAP, STEP 7, THEN REPEAT STEP 5
STEP 6: CHECK FOR GROUND OR SHORT AT EACH PICK-UP LEAD WITH OHMMETER. GROUND ONE LEAD OF OHMMETER
NO SHORT, GO TO STEP 8
SHORTED, REPLACE PICK-UP COIL AND GO TO STEP 7
MEASURE AND RECORD BATTERY VOLTAGE WITH VOLTMETER MEASURE SPECIFIC GRAVITY. IT SHOULD BE AT LEAST 12:20. IF NOT CHARGE BATTERY TO SPECIFICATION
TURN IGNITION SWITCH TO ON POSITION
HOLD SECONDARY COIL WIRE NEAR GROUND
INTERMITTENTLY SHORT COIL NEGATIVE TO GROUND
HAS NO SPARK. UNPLUG COMPUTER 10 WAY CONNECTOR
INTERMITTENTLY SHORT COIL NEGATIVE TO GROUND
NOW HAS SPARK REPLACE MODULE
STEP 2: NO SPARK. CHECK BATTERY VOLTAGE AT COIL POSITIVE IT SHOULD BE WITHIN 1 VOLT OF BATTERY VOLTAGE
HAS VOLTAGE: CHECK FOR VOLTAGE AT COIL NEGATIVE. IT SHOULD BE WITHIN 1 VOLT OF BATTERY VOLTAGE
NO VOLTAGE: WIRING BETWEEN BATTERY AND COIL POSITIVE, REPAIR AND REPEAT STEP 2
HAS VOLTAGE BUT NO SPARK. REPLACE COIL
NO VOLTAGE REPLACE COIL
STEP 4: TURN IGNITION SWITCH OFF AND WITH AN OHMMETER CHECK FOR CONTINUITY BETWEEN CARB SWITCH AND CAVITY OF 10 WAY CONNECTOR
CIRCUIT SHOULD BE CONTINUOUS
IF IT IS, CHECK FOR CONTINUITY BETWEEN CAVITY 10 AND GROUND
IF IT IS NOT, FIND OPEN AND REPAIR
IF THERE IS CONTINUITY REPLACE COMPUTER
IF THERE IS NOT, FIND OPEN AND REPAIR AND REPEAT STEP 4
10 WAY CONNECTOR
10
9
8
7
6
1
2
3
4
5
STEP 7: ADJUST PICK-UP COIL AIR GAP TO SPECIFICATION. START PICK-UP .006 WITH NON MAGNETIC FEELER GAUGE AN .008 SHOULD NOT PASS THROUGH GAP RUN PICK-UP .012. A .014 SHOULD NOT PASS THROUGH GAP
STEP 8: ATTACH ALL CONNECTORS AND TRY TO START ENGINE
ENGINE STARTS SYSTEM OK
ENGINE WILL NOT START REPLACE COMPUTER AND START ENGINE

Electronic Spark Control System diagnosis (Dual pickup distributors)

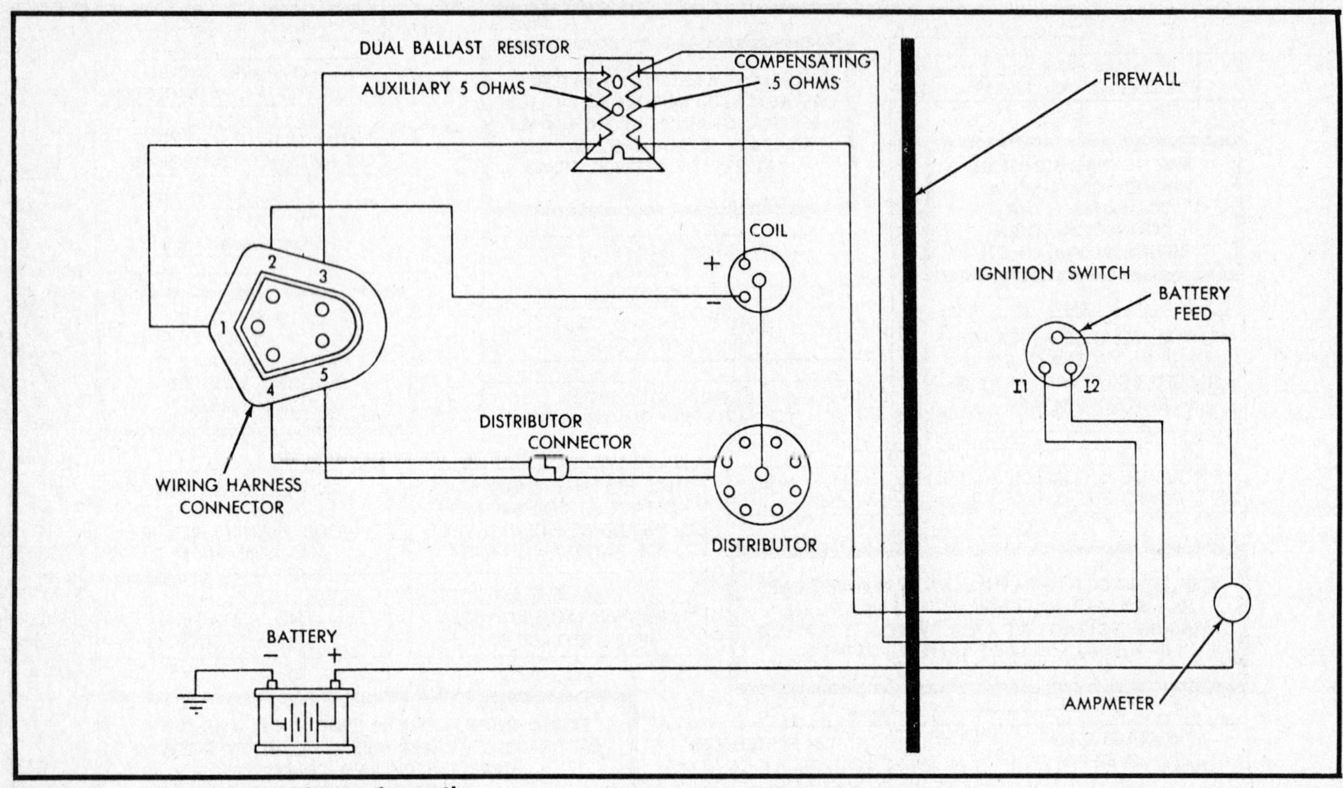

Chrysler electronic ignition schematic

The Spark Control Computer is the center of the entire system. It gives the capibility of igniting the fuel mixture according to different modes of engine operation by delivering an infinite amount of variable advance curves. The computer determines the exact instant when ignition is required; and then signals the ignition coil to produce the electrical impulses which fire the spark plugs.

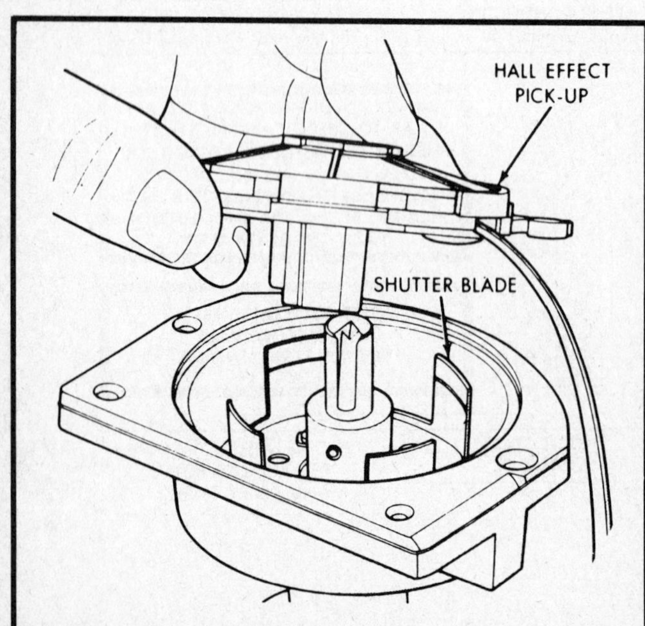

Hall Effect pick-up removal—2.2 engine

A Hall Effect Pickup, located in the distributor on these engines, supplies the basic timing signal to the computer. Also, the computer can determine from this signal engine speed (RPM)

TROUBLESHOOTING

HALL EFFECT PICKUP

Replacement

1. Remove the splash shield retaining screws and remove the splash shield.
2. Loosen the distributor cap retaining screws and lift off the distributor cap.
3. Remove the rotor from the shaft.
4. Remove the Hall Effect Pickup assembly from the distributor housing.
5. When placing the Hall Effect Pickup assembly into the housing make sure the lead retainer is in the locating hole properly before attaching the distributor cap.
6. Install the rotor with the ESA stamped on the top.
7. Install the cap and the shield assembly.

2.6 ENGINE

This system consists of the battery, ignition switch, ignition coil, IC igniter (electronic control unit), built into the distributor, spark plugs and intercomponent wiring. Primary current is switched by the IC ignitor in response to timing signals produced by a distributor magnetic pickup.

The distributor consists of a power distributing section, signal generator, IC igniter, advance mechanism and drive section. The signal generator is a small size magneto generator which produces signal for driving the IC ignitor. The distributor operates by using this signal as an ignition timing signal.

The distributor is equipped with both centrifugal and vacuum advance mechanisms.

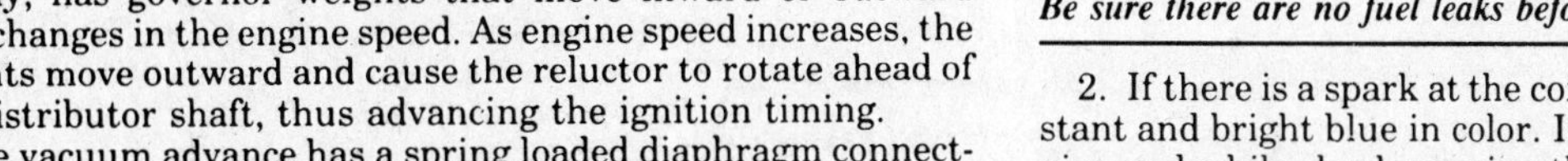

A centrifugal advance mechanism, located below the rotor assembly, has governor weights that move inward or outward with changes in the engine speed. As engine speed increases, the weights move outward and cause the reluctor to rotate ahead of the distributor shaft, thus advancing the ignition timing.

The vacuum advance has a spring loaded diaphragm connected to the breaker assembly. The diaphragm is actuated against the spring pressure by carburetor vacuum pressure. When the vacuum increases, the diaphragm causes the movable breaker assembly to pivot in a direction opposite to distributor rotation, advancing the ignition timing

TROUBLESHOOTING

Procedure

1. Remove the high voltage cable from the center tower of the distributor and hold the end of the cable at a point $^3/_{16}$–$^3/_8$ in. away from a good engine ground. In this condition, crank the engine with the starter and look for a spark at the coil high voltage cable.

CAUTION

Be sure there are no fuel leaks before performing this test.

2. If there is a spark at the coil secondary wire it must be constant and bright blue in color. If it is, continue to crank the engine and while slowly moving the the coil secondary wire away from the ground, look for arching at the coil tower. If arcing occurs replace the coil. If the spark is weak or not constant or there is no spark, proceed to stap 3.

If the spark is good or there is no arcing at the coil tower the ignition system is producing the necessary high secondary voltage. However, make sure that this voltage is getting to the spark plugs by checking the distributor rotor, cap, spark plug wires and spark plugs. If they are OK then the igniton syastem is not the rearson why the engine will not start. It will be necessary to check the fuel system and engine mechanical items.

3. Turn the ignition switch on and measure the voltage at the negative coil terminal. The voltage should be the same as battery voltage. If it is 3 volts or less the IC distributor is defective. If there is no voltage check for an open circuit in the coil or wiring

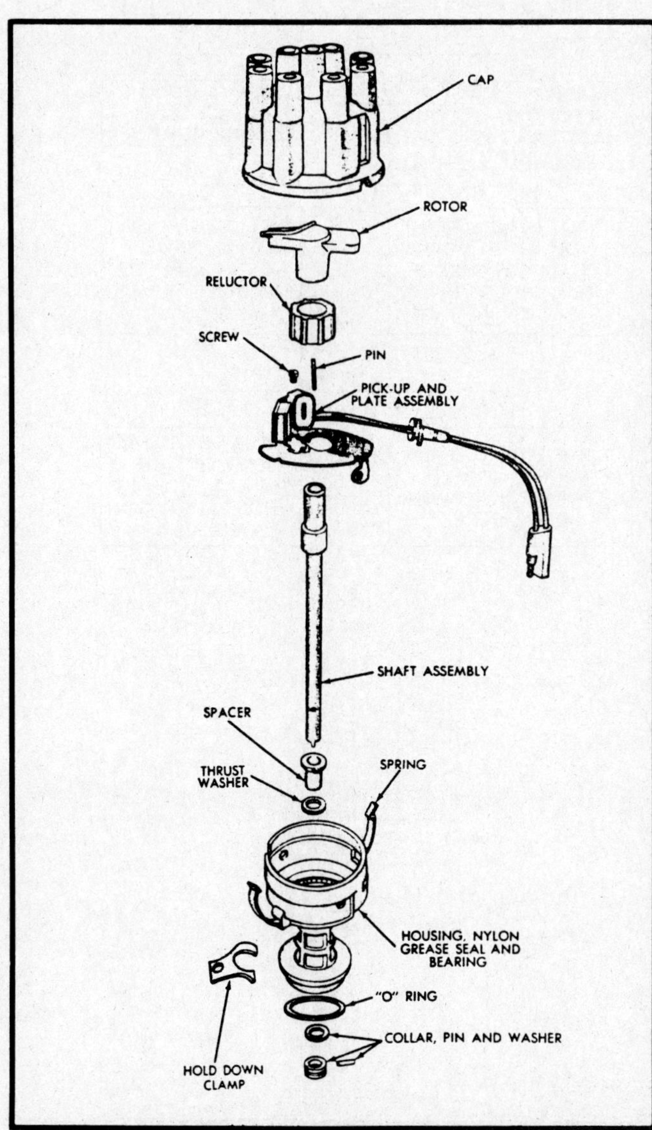

Typical eight cylinder ESA distributor – Exploded view

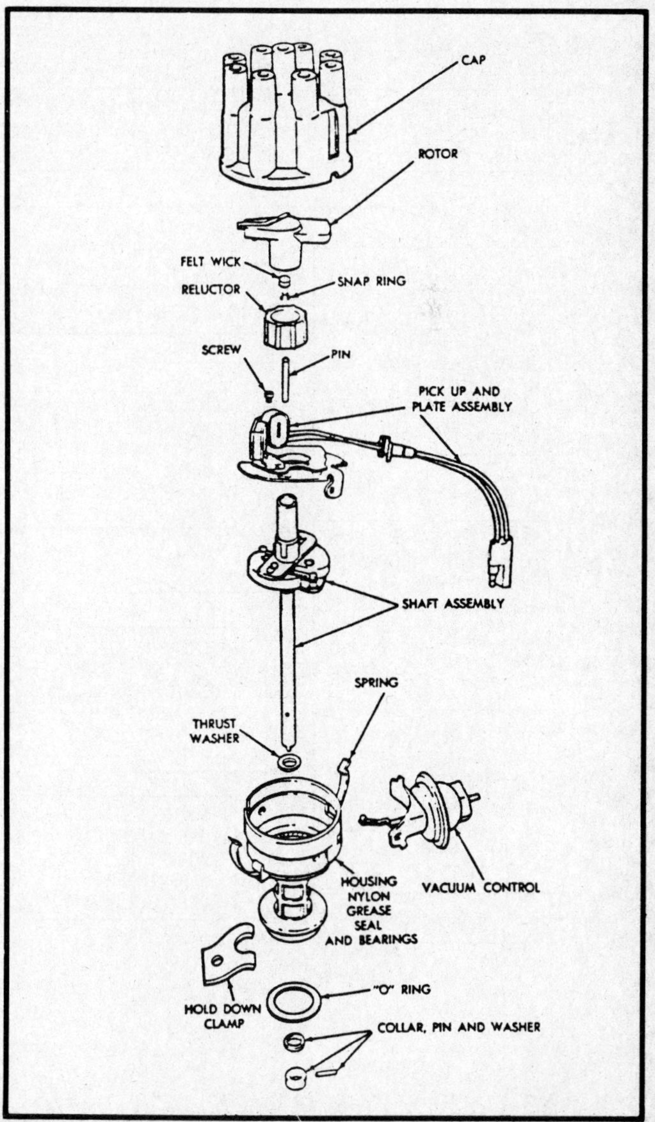

Exploded view of the eight cylinder ECU distributor – Single pickup shown

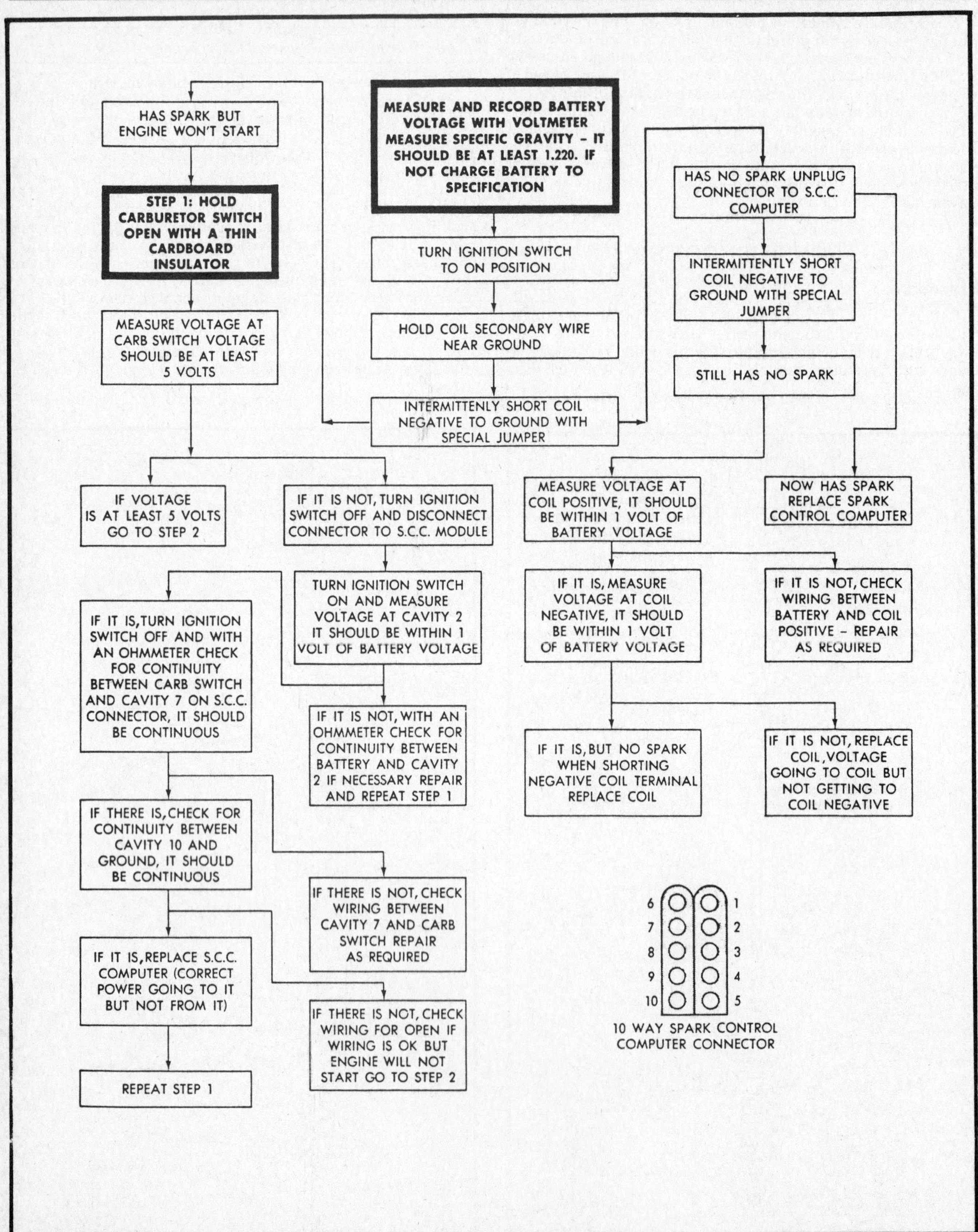
HAS SPARK BUT ENGINE WON'T START
STEP 1: HOLD CARBURETOR SWITCH OPEN WITH A THIN CARDBOARD INSULATOR
MEASURE VOLTAGE AT CARB SWITCH VOLTAGE SHOULD BE AT LEAST 5 VOLTS
IF VOLTAGE IS AT LEAST 5 VOLTS GO TO STEP 2
IF IT IS NOT, TURN IGNITION SWITCH OFF AND DISCONNECT CONNECTOR TO S.C.C. MODULE
TURN IGNITION SWITCH ON AND MEASURE VOLTAGE AT CAVITY 2 IT SHOULD BE WITHIN 1 VOLT OF BATTERY VOLTAGE
IF IT IS, TURN IGNITION SWITCH OFF AND WITH AN OHMMETER CHECK FOR CONTINUITY BETWEEN CARB SWITCH AND CAVITY 7 ON S.C.C. CONNECTOR, IT SHOULD BE CONTINUOUS
IF IT IS NOT, WITH AN OHMMETER CHECK FOR CONTINUITY BETWEEN BATTERY AND CAVITY 2 IF NECESSARY REPAIR AND REPEAT STEP 1
IF THERE IS, CHECK FOR CONTINUITY BETWEEN CAVITY 10 AND GROUND, IT SHOULD BE CONTINUOUS
IF THERE IS NOT, CHECK WIRING BETWEEN CAVITY 7 AND CARB SWITCH REPAIR AS REQUIRED
IF IT IS, REPLACE S.C.C. COMPUTER (CORRECT POWER GOING TO IT BUT NOT FROM IT)
IF THERE IS NOT, CHECK WIRING FOR OPEN IF WIRING IS OK BUT ENGINE WILL NOT START GO TO STEP 2
REPEAT STEP 1
MEASURE AND RECORD BATTERY VOLTAGE WITH VOLTMETER MEASURE SPECIFIC GRAVITY – IT SHOULD BE AT LEAST 1.220. IF NOT CHARGE BATTERY TO SPECIFICATION
TURN IGNITION SWITCH TO ON POSITION
HOLD COIL SECONDARY WIRE NEAR GROUND
INTERMITTENLY SHORT COIL NEGATIVE TO GROUND WITH SPECIAL JUMPER
HAS NO SPARK UNPLUG CONNECTOR TO S.C.C. COMPUTER
INTERMITTENTLY SHORT COIL NEGATIVE TO GROUND WITH SPECIAL JUMPER
STILL HAS NO SPARK
NOW HAS SPARK REPLACE SPARK CONTROL COMPUTER
MEASURE VOLTAGE AT COIL POSITIVE, IT SHOULD BE WITHIN 1 VOLT OF BATTERY VOLTAGE
IF IT IS, MEASURE VOLTAGE AT COIL NEGATIVE, IT SHOULD BE WITHIN 1 VOLT OF BATTERY VOLTAGE
IF IT IS NOT, CHECK WIRING BETWEEN BATTERY AND COIL POSITIVE – REPAIR AS REQUIRED
IF IT IS, BUT NO SPARK WHEN SHORTING NEGATIVE COIL TERMINAL REPLACE COIL
IF IT IS NOT, REPLACE COIL, VOLTAGE GOING TO COIL BUT NOT GETTING TO COIL NEGATIVE
6 1
7 2
8 3
9 4
10 5
10 WAY SPARK CONTROL COMPUTER CONNECTOR

Hall Effect Electronic Advance System diagnosis—Part 1 of 2

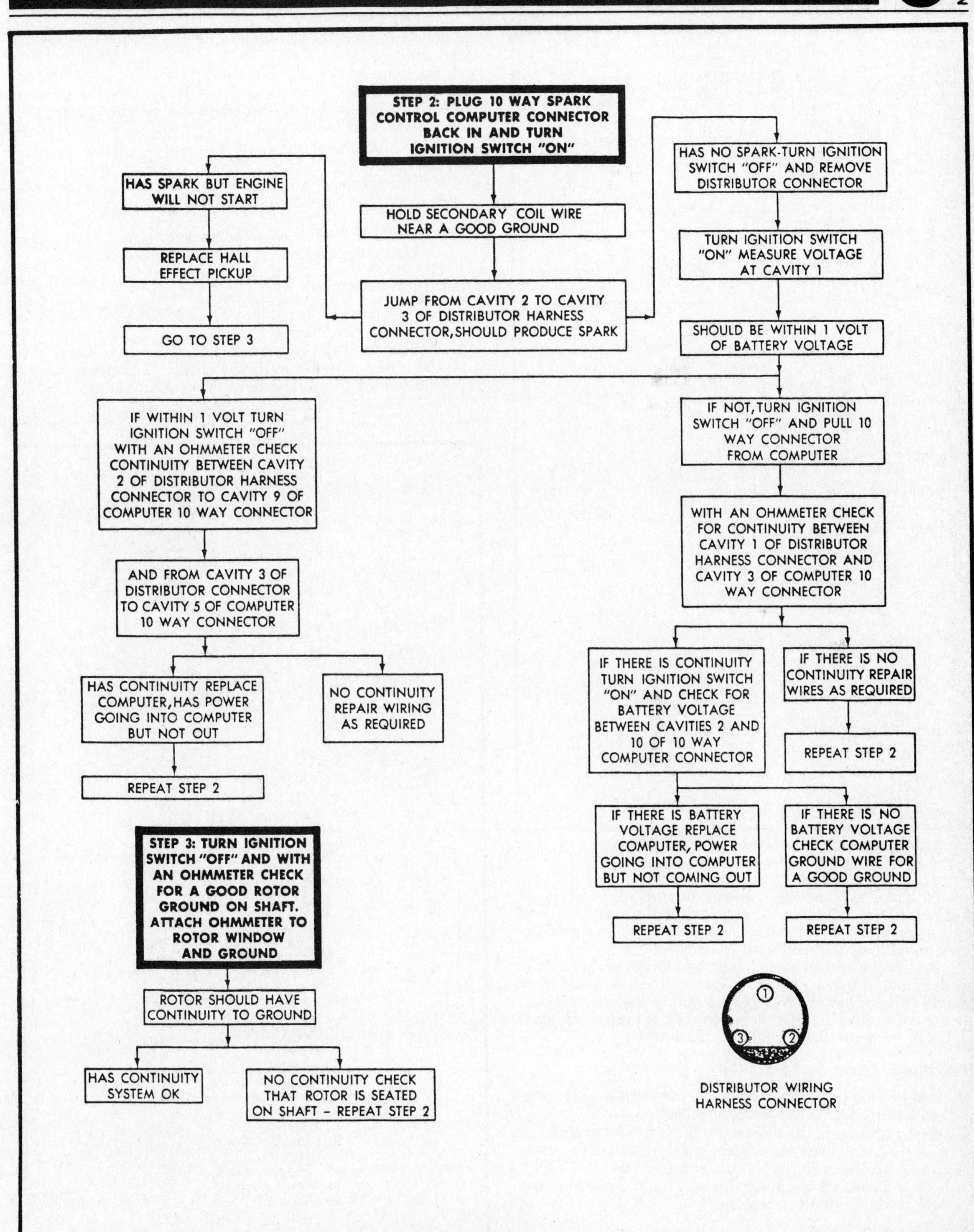
STEP 2: PLUG 10 WAY SPARK CONTROL COMPUTER CONNECTOR BACK IN AND TURN IGNITION SWITCH "ON"
HOLD SECONDARY COIL WIRE NEAR A GOOD GROUND
JUMP FROM CAVITY 2 TO CAVITY 3 OF DISTRIBUTOR HARNESS CONNECTOR, SHOULD PRODUCE SPARK
HAS SPARK BUT ENGINE WILL NOT START
REPLACE HALL EFFECT PICKUP
GO TO STEP 3
HAS NO SPARK-TURN IGNITION SWITCH "OFF" AND REMOVE DISTRIBUTOR CONNECTOR
TURN IGNITION SWITCH "ON" MEASURE VOLTAGE AT CAVITY 1
SHOULD BE WITHIN 1 VOLT OF BATTERY VOLTAGE
IF WITHIN 1 VOLT TURN IGNITION SWITCH "OFF" WITH AN OHMMETER CHECK CONTINUITY BETWEEN CAVITY 2 OF DISTRIBUTOR HARNESS CONNECTOR TO CAVITY 9 OF COMPUTER 10 WAY CONNECTOR
AND FROM CAVITY 3 OF DISTRIBUTOR CONNECTOR TO CAVITY 5 OF COMPUTER 10 WAY CONNECTOR
HAS CONTINUITY REPLACE COMPUTER, HAS POWER GOING INTO COMPUTER BUT NOT OUT
NO CONTINUITY REPAIR WIRING AS REQUIRED
REPEAT STEP 2
IF NOT, TURN IGNITION SWITCH "OFF" AND PULL 10 WAY CONNECTOR FROM COMPUTER
WITH AN OHMMETER CHECK FOR CONTINUITY BETWEEN CAVITY 1 OF DISTRIBUTOR HARNESS CONNECTOR AND CAVITY 3 OF COMPUTER 10 WAY CONNECTOR
IF THERE IS CONTINUITY TURN IGNITION SWITCH "ON" AND CHECK FOR BATTERY VOLTAGE BETWEEN CAVITIES 2 AND 10 OF 10 WAY COMPUTER CONNECTOR
IF THERE IS NO CONTINUITY REPAIR WIRES AS REQUIRED
REPEAT STEP 2
IF THERE IS BATTERY VOLTAGE REPLACE COMPUTER, POWER GOING INTO COMPUTER BUT NOT COMING OUT
IF THERE IS NO BATTERY VOLTAGE CHECK COMPUTER GROUND WIRE FOR A GOOD GROUND
REPEAT STEP 2
REPEAT STEP 2
STEP 3: TURN IGNITION SWITCH "OFF" AND WITH AN OHMMETER CHECK FOR A GOOD ROTOR GROUND ON SHAFT. ATTACH OHMMETER TO ROTOR WINDOW AND GROUND
ROTOR SHOULD HAVE CONTINUITY TO GROUND
HAS CONTINUITY SYSTEM OK
NO CONTINUITY CHECK THAT ROTOR IS SEATED ON SHAFT - REPEAT STEP 2
1
2
3
DISTRIBUTOR WIRING HARNESS CONNECTOR

Hall Effect Electronic Advance System diagnosis—Part 2 of 2

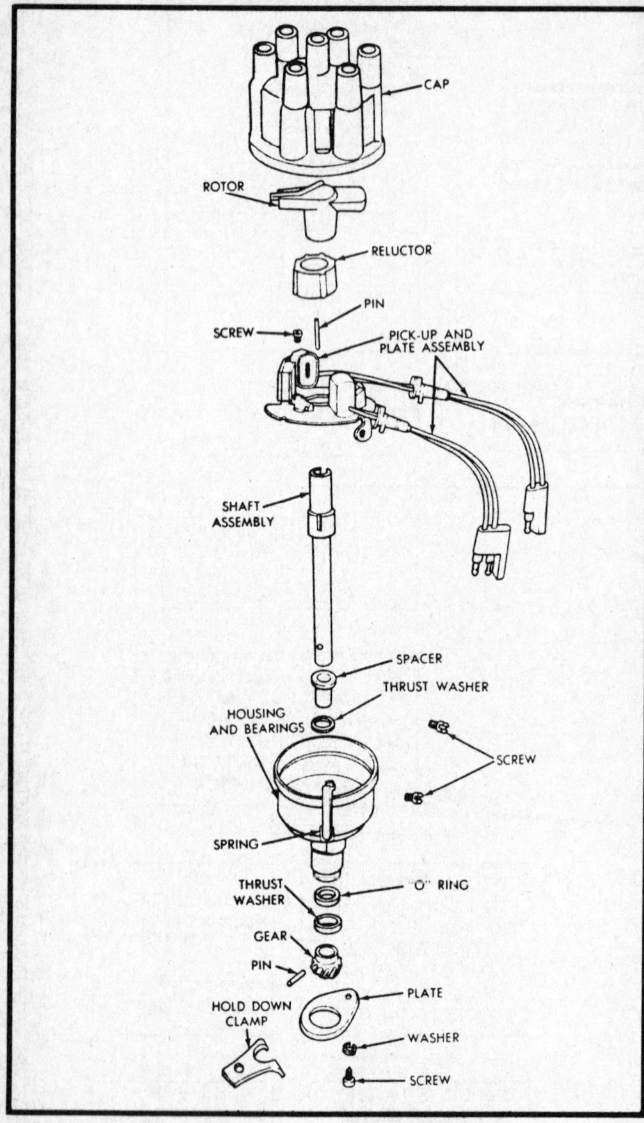

Exploded view of the six cylinder distributor

4. With the key on, use a special jumper wire and touch momemtarily the negative (-) terminal of the coil to ground while holding the the coil secondary wire ¼ in. from a good engine ground. A spark should be obtained.

5. If no spark was obtained, check for voltage at the positive (+) terminal of the coil with the key on. Voltage should be at least 12 volts or battery voltage. If proper voltage is obtained, the coil is defective and should be replaced. If proper voltage is not obtained, check the wiring and connections.

Centrifugal Advance Test

1. Run the engine at idle and remove the vacuum hose (non-stripped hose) from the vacuum controller.

2. Slowly accelerate the engine to check for advance.

a. Excessive advance could be a deteriorated governor spring. A broken spring will cause abrupt advance.

b. Insufficient advance or no advance could be the governor weight or cam in faulty operation.

Vacuum Advance Test

1. Set the engine speed at 2,500 rpm. Check for advance by disconnecting and then reconnecting the vacum hose at the distributor.

2. For more precise determination of weather the vacuum advance mechanism is operating properly, remove the vacuum hose from the distributor and connect a vacuum pump, tool No.C-4207, or equivalent.

3. Run the engine at idle and slowly apply apply vacuum pressure to check for advance.

a. Excessive advance could be a deteriorated or sagging vacuum controller spring. A broken spring will cause abrupt advance.

b. Insufficient advance or no advance could be a breaker plate in faulty operation or a broken diaphragm.

Distributor Overhaul

1. Remove the two distributor cap mounting screws and remove the distributor cap.

2. Remove the two rotor screws and remove the rotor.

3. Use a box or socket wrench and remove the governor assembly retaining bolt and remove the governor assembly.

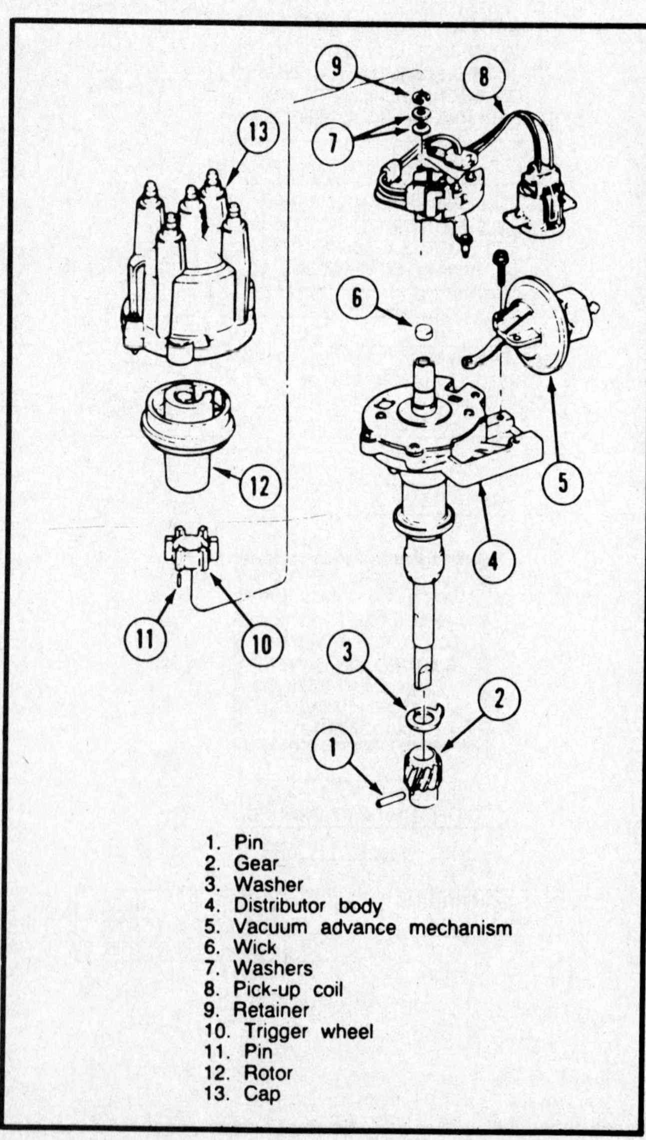

Exploded view of the 4-150 distributor—1984-86

NOTE: The two springs of the governor are built to different specifications. Each spring must be installed in its own position. Make note of this for reassembly.

4. Remove the wire clamp screw and remove the clamp.
5. Remove the two pick-up coil and IC igniter tightening screws and remove the pick-up coil and IC igniter simultaneously.
6. Remove the two governor vacuum chamber screws and remove the governor vacuum chamber.
7. Remove the two breaker assembly screws and remove the breaker assembly. Keep the breaker assembly clean.
8. Remove the two bearing retainer plate screws and remove the bearing retainer.
9. Make alignment marks on the gear and shaft for reassembly.
10. Drive out the distributor drive gear pin with a punch and remove the drive gear.
11. Remove the distributor shaft and bearing assembly.
12. Remove the distributor housing seal.
13. Remove the two governor springs.

NOTE: The two springs of the governor are built to different specifications. Each spring must be installed in its own position. Make note of this for reassembly.

14. Remove the governor centrifugal plate and the governor weight.
15. Installation is the reverse of removal.

Jeep

AMERICAN MOTORS SOLID STATE IGNITION (SSI) SYSTEM

This AMC Solid State Ignition (SSI) is standard equipment on all 1982 and later American Motors built engines used in Jeeps, except the 1987 4–150.

The system consists of a sensor and toothed trigger wheel inside the distributor and a permanently sealed electronic control unit which determines dwell, in addition to the coil, ignition wires and spark plugs.

The trigger wheel rotates on the distributor shaft. As one of its teeth nears the sensor magnet, the magnetic field shifts toward the tooth. When the tooth and sensor are aligned, the magnetic field is shifted to its maximum, signaling the electronic control unit to switch off the coil primary current. This starts an electronic timer inside the control unit, which allows the primary current to remain off only long enough for the spark plug to fire. The timer adjusts the amount of time primary current is off according to conditions, thus automatically adjusting dwell. There is also a special circuit within the control unit to detect and ignore spurious signals. Spark timing is adjusted by both mechanical (centrifugal) and vacuum advance.

A wire of 1.35Ω resistance is spliced into the ignition feed to reduce voltage to the coil during running conditions. The resistance wire is bypassed when the engine is being started so that

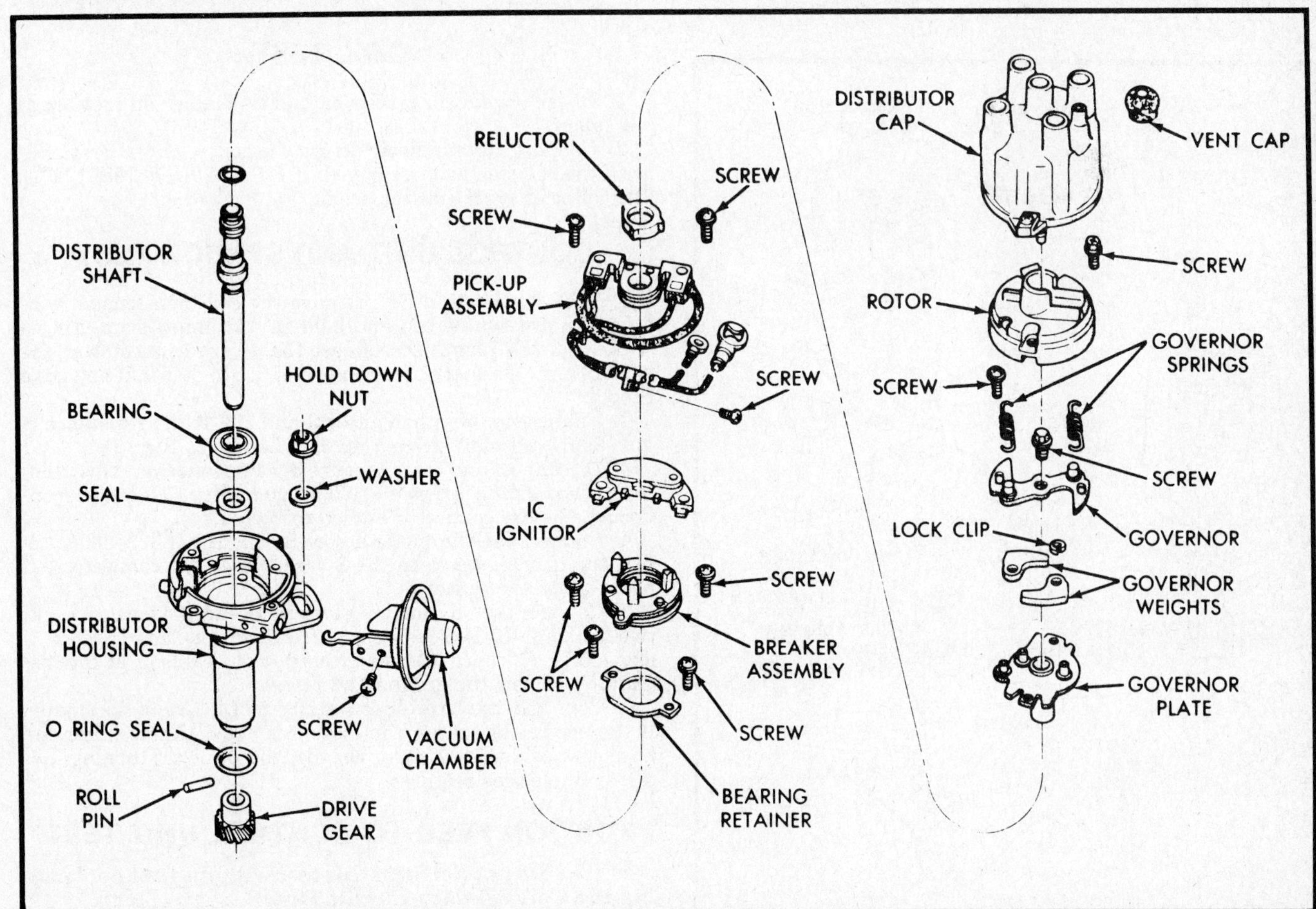

Exploded view of the 2.6 engine distributor

full battery voltage may be supplied to the coil. Bypass is accomplished by the I-terminal on the solenoid.

SECONDARY CIRCUIT TEST

1. Disconnect the coil wire from the center of the distributor cap.

NOTE: Twist the rubber boot slightly in either direction, then grasp the boot and pull straight up. Do not pull on the wire and do not use pliers.

2. Hold the wire ½" (12.7mm) from a ground with a pair of insulated pliers and a heavy glove. As the engine is cranked, watch for a spark.

3. If a spark appears, reconnect the coil wire. Remove the wire from one spark plug and test for a spark as above.

CAUTION

Do not remove the spark plug wires from cylinder 3 on the 4–150, or cylinder 1 or 5 on a 1982 and later 6–258, or cylinders 3 or 4 of an 8–360, when performing this test, as sensor damage could occur.

3. If a spark occurs, the problem is in the fuel system or ignition timing. If no spark occurs, check for a defective rotor, cap, or spark plug wires.

4. If no spark occurs from the coil wire in Step 2, test the coil wire resistance with an ohmmeter. It should be 7,700–9,300Ω at +75°F (24°C) or 12,000Ω maximum at +93°F (34°C).

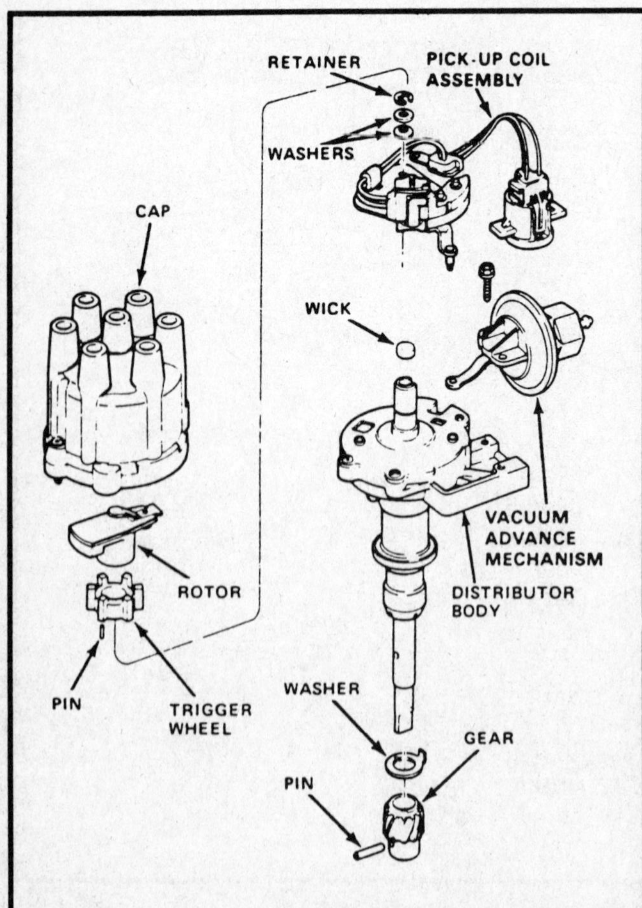

Exploded view of the SSI distributor—6 cyl shown V8 similar

COIL PRIMARY CIRCUIT TEST

1. Turn the ignition On. Connect a multitester to the coil positive (+) terminal and a ground. If the voltage is 5.5–6.5 volts, go to Step 2. If above 7 volts, go to Step 4. If below 5.5 volts, disconnect the condenser lead and measure. If the voltage is now 5.5–6.5 volts, replace the condenser. If not, go to Step 6.

2. With the multitester connected as in Step 1, read the voltage with the engine cranking. If battery voltage is indicated, the circuit is okay. If not, go to Step 3.

3. Check for a short or open in the starter solenoid I-terminal wire. Check the solenoid for proper operation.

4. Disconnect the wire from the starter solenoid I-terminal, with the ignition ON and the multitester connected as in Step 1. If the voltage drops to 5.5–6.5 volts, replace the solenoid. If not, connect a jumper between the coil negative (–) terminal and a ground. If the voltage drops to 5.5–6.5 volts, go to Step 5. If not, repair the resistance wire.

5. Check for continuity between the coil (–) terminal and D4, and D1 to ground. If the continuity is okay, replace the control unit. If not, check for an open wire and go back to Step 2.

6. Turn ignition OFF. Connect an ohmmeter between the + coil terminal and dash connector AV. If above 1.40Ω, repair the resistance wire.

7. With the ignition OFF, connect the ohmmeter between connector AV and ignition switch terminal 11. If less than 0.1 ohm, replace the ignition switch or repair the wire, whichever is the cause. If above 0.1 ohm, check connections and check for defective wiring.

COIL TEST

1. Check the coil for cracks, carbon tracks, etc. and replace as necessary.

2. Connect an ohmmeter across the coil + and – terminals, with the coil connector removed. If 1.13–1.23Ω @ 75°F (24°C), the coil is okay. If not, replace it.

CONTROL UNIT AND SENSOR TEST

1. With the ignition ON, remove the coil high tension wire from the distributor cap and hold ½" (12.7mm) from ground with insulated pliers. Disconnect the 4-wire connector at the control unit. If a spark occurs (normal), go to Step 2. If not, go to Step 5.

2. Connect an ohmmeter to D2 and D3. If the resistance is 400–800Ω (normal), go to Step 6. If not, go to Step 3.

3. Disconnect and reconnect the 3-wire connector at distributor. If the reading is now 400–800Ω, go to Step 6. If not, disconnect the 3-wire connector and go to Step 4.

4. Connect the ohmmeter across B2 and B3. If 300–800Ω, repair the harness between the 3-wire and 4-wire connectors. If not, replace the sensor.

5. Connect the ohmmeter between D1 and the battery negative terminal. If the reading is 0 (0.002 or less), go to Step 2. If above 0.002Ω, there is a bad ground in the cable or at the distributor. Repair the ground and retest.

6. Connect a multitester across D2 and D3. Crank the engine. If the needle fluctuates, the system is okay. If not, either the trigger wheel is defective, or the distributor is not turning. Repair or replace as required.

IGNITION FEED TO CONTROL UNIT TEST

NOTE: Do not perform this test without first performing the Coil Primary Circuit Test.

1. With the ignition ON, unplug the 2-wire connector at the module. Connect a multitester between F2 and ground. If the reading is battery voltage, replace the control unit and go to Step 3. If not, go to Step 2.

2. Repair the cause of the voltage reduction: either the ignition switch or a corroded dash connector. Check for a spark at the coil wire. If okay, stop. If not, replace the control unit and check for proper operation.

3. Reconnect the 2-wire connector at the control unit and unplug the 4-wire connector at the control unit. Connect an ammeter between C1 and ground. If it reads 0.9–1.1 amps, the system is okay. If not, replace the module.

AMERICAN MOTORS SOLID STATE (RENIX) IGNITION SYSTEM

Jeep with 1987 4-150 engine

These engines are equipped with electronically controlled fuel injection. Therefore, the electronic ignition system is different from that used on carbureted engines.

The system consists of:

- A solid state ignition control module (ICM)
- An electronic control module (ECU)
- A forty tooth rotor in the distributor
- TDC sensor mounted at the rear of the engine on the flywheel housing

The control module consists of a solid state ignition circuit and an integrated ignition coil each of which can be removed and serviced separately. Spark timing control is determined by the ignition control module. Signals from the ECU relay information about engine load and other driving conditions to both the ICM and fuel injection system electronic control components.

Electrical feed to the ICM is through terminal A of connector 1. Electrical feed occurs only when the ignition switch is in the START and RUN positions. Terminal B of connector 1 is grounded at the engine oil dipstick bracket, along with the ECU ground wire and the 0_2 sensor ground.

DIAGNOSIS

Primary System

Primary system diagnosis is made through the diagnostic connector, using the appropriate diagnostic computer. Primary circuit tests are made at (D1–2) B+ after ignition; tachometer voltage is at D1–1; vehicle ground is at D1–3.

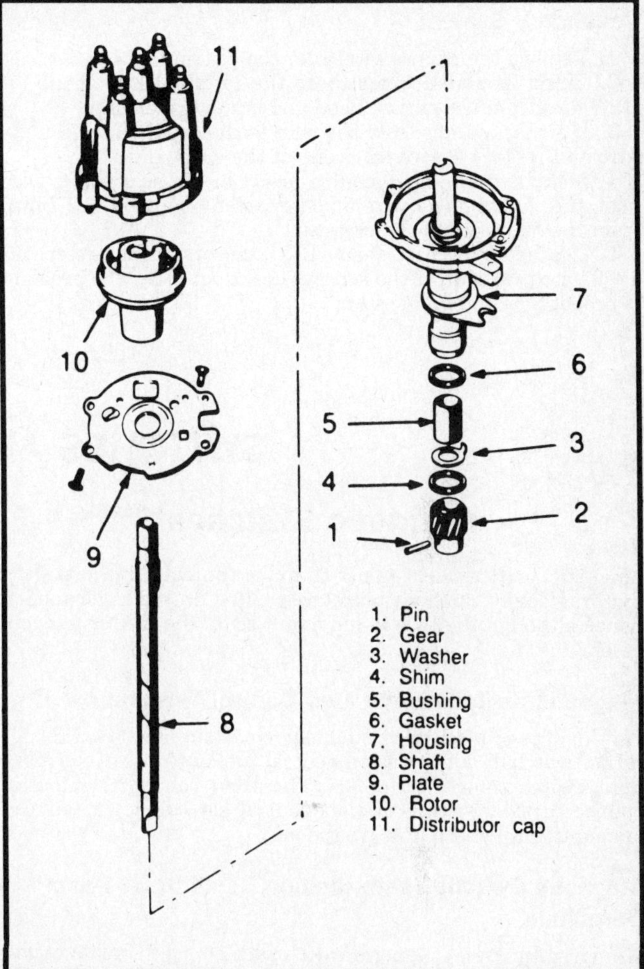

Exploded view of the 4-150 distributor—1987-88

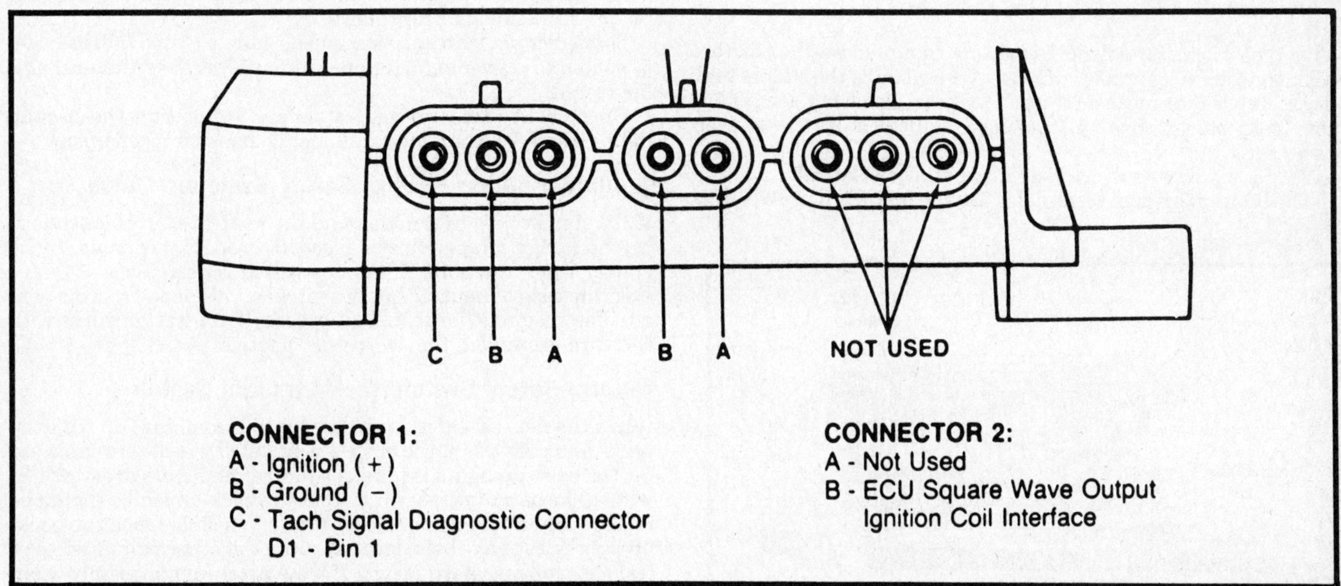

4-150 ignition control module—1987-88

Secondary System

1. Remove the center wire from the distributor cap.
2. Using insulated pliers, hold the terminal end about ½" (12.7mm) from the engine head and crank the engine.
3. If a spark jumps from the wire to the head, reconnect the wire and remove a wire from one of the spark plugs.
4. Make a metal extension to insert in the spark plug wire boot and, holding the wire and extension about ½" (12.7mm) from the head, crank the engine.
5. If a spark occurs, check ECU sensors using tester MS 1700, or equivalent. If the sensors check out okay, the problem is probably in the fuel system.
6. If no spark occurs, The rotor, distributor cap or spark plug wires are defective.

DELCO HIGH ENERGY IGNITION (HEI) SYSTEM

The General Motors HEI system is a pulse triggered, transistor controlled, inductive discharge ignition system. The entire HEI system is contained within the distributor cap. This system was used in Jeep vehicles equipped with the 4-151 and V6 173 engines.

Refer to the General Motors section for testing and overhaul.

SWITCHES AND SOLENOIDS

Magnetic Switches

Magnetic switches serve only to make contact for the starter motor. Usually, such switches are located on the inner fender panel, although they are found mounted on the starter in a few cases.

Magnetic Switches with Two Control Terminals

On this type of magnetic switch current is supplied from the ignition switch or transmission neutral button to one of the magnetic switch control terminals. The other control terminal is connected to the transmission neutral safety switch (on the transmission) where it is grounded.

Magnetic Switches with Ignition Resistor By-Pass Terminals

All normally use a magnetic switch with a single control terminal. The second terminal is an ignition resistor by-pass terminal.

SOLENOIDS WITHOUT RELAYS

This type of starter solenoid is always mounted on the starter. Makes electrical contact for the starter and pulls the starter and drive clutch into mesh with the flywheel. The Chrysler reduction gear starter has this solenoid embodied in the starter housing.

There is only one control terminal on the solenoid.

The ignition by-pass terminal is usually marked R or IGN, if it is used.

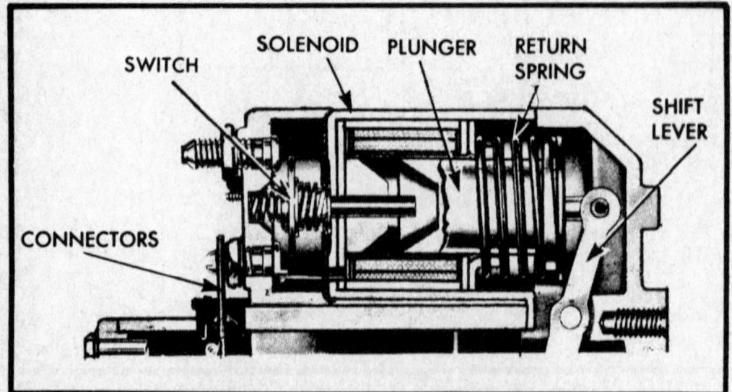

Starter solenoid mounted on starter motor

WITH SEPARATE RELAYS

The solenoid itself is always mounted on the starter. In addition to making contact for the starter, it also pulls the starter drive clutch gear into mesh with the flywheel. A single control terminal is used on the solenoid itself. The relay is usually found mounted to the inner fender panel or on the firewall.

WITH BUILT-IN RELAYS

These units are always mounted on the starter and are connected, through linkage, to the starter drive clutch. The relay portion is a square box built into and integral with the front end of the solenoid assembly.

NEUTRAL SAFETY SWITCHES

The purpose of the neutral safety switch is to prevent the starter from cranking the engine except when the transmission is in neutral or park.

On some trucks, the neutral safety switch is located on the transmission. It serves to ground the solenoid or magnetic switch, whichever is used.

On other trucks, the neutral safety switch is located either at the bottom of the steering column (where it contacts the shift mechanism), on the steering column, underneath the dash, or on the shift linkage (console).

Some manual transmission models have a clutch linkage safety switch to prevent starter operation unless the clutch pedal is depressed.

On most trucks, the neutral safety switch and the backup light switch are combined into a single switch mechanism.

Troubleshooting Neutral Safety Switches Quick Test

If the starter fails to function and the neutral safety switch is to be checked, a jumper can be placed across its terminals. If the starter then functions the safety switch is defective.

In the case of neutral safety switches with one wire, this wire must be grounded for testing purposes. If the starter works with the wire grounded, the switch is defective.

Neutral Safety Switch/Back-Up Light Switch

When the neutral safety switch is built in combination with the back-up light switch, the easiest way to tell which terminals are for the back-up lights is to take a jumper and cross every pair of wires. The pair of wires which light the back-up lamps should be ignored when testing the neutral safety switch. Once the back-up light wires have been located, jump the other pair of wires to test the neutral safety switch. If the starter functions only when the jumper is placed across these two wires, the neutral safety switch is defective or requires adjustment.

STARTING SYSTEMS

Starter Motor Testing

TESTING THE STARTER CIRCUIT

The starter circuit should be divided and tested in four separate phases:

1. Cranking voltage check
2. Amperage draw
3. Voltage drop on grounded side
4. Voltage drop on battery side

NOTE: The battery must be in good condition for this test to have significance. To accurately check battery condition, use equipment designed to measure its capacity under a load. Instructions accompanying the equipment should be followed.

Cranking Voltage

Connect voltmeter leads to prods tapped into the battery posts (observe polarity and reverse meter leads if necessary). Remove the high tension wire from the distributor cap and ground it to prevent starting. With electronic ignition, disconnect the control box harness from the distributor. Now, turn the key. Observe both voltmeter reading and cranking speed. The cranking speed should be even and at a satisfactory rate of speed, with a voltmeter reading of at least 9.6 volts for 12 volt systems.

Amperage Draw

The amount of current the starter motor draws is usually (but not always) associated with the mechanical problems involved in cranking the engine. (Mechanical trouble in the engine, frozen or worn starter parts, misaligned starter or starter components, etc.) Because starter motor amperage draw is directly influenced by anything restricting the free turning of the engine, or starter, it is important that the engine and all components be at operating temperatures.

To measure starter current draw, remove the high tension wire from the center of the distributor cap and ground it. With electronic ignition, disconnect the control box harness from the distributor. A very simple and inexpensive starter current indicator is available at auto stores. This indicator is an induction type gauge and shows, without disconnecting any wires, starter current draw.

Place the yoke of the meter directly over the insulated starter supply cable (cable must be straight for a minimum of 2 in.). Close the starter switch for about 20 seconds, watch the meter dial and record the average reading. If the indicator swings in the wrong direction, reverse the position of the meter.

The cranking amperage draw can vary from 150 to 400 amperes, depending on the engine size, engine compression and starter type.

NOTE: When starter specifications are not available, average starter draw amperage can be derived from testing a like starter unit, known to be operating satisfactorily.

More accurate but complex equipment is available from many manufacturers. This equipment consists of a combination voltmeter, ammeter and carbon pile rheostat. When using this equipment, follow the equipment manufacturer's procedures and recommendations.

High amperage and lazy performance would suggest an excessively tight engine, friction in the starter or starter drive, grounded starter field or armature.

Normal amperage and lazy performance suggest high resistance, or possibly poor connections somewhere in the starter circuit.

Low amperage and lazy or no performance suggest battery condition poor, bad cables or connections along the line.

Voltage Drop on Grounded Side

With a voltmeter on the 3 volt scale, without disconnecting any wires, connect negative test lead of the voltmeter to a prod secured in the grounded battery post. The positive test lead is connected to a cleaned, bare metal portion of the starter motor housing. Close the starter switch and note the voltmeter reading. If the reading is the same as battery reading, the ground circuit is open somewhere between the battery and the starter. In many cases the reading will be very small. The reading shown will indicate voltage drop (loss) between battery ground post and starter housing. The drop should not exceed 0.2 volt. If the voltage drop is above the specified amount, the next step is to isolate and correct the cause. It can be a bad cable or connection anywhere in the battery-to-starter ground circuit. A check of this type should progress along the various points of possible trouble, between the battery ground post and the starter motor housing, until the trouble spot has been located.

Voltage Drop on Battery Side

Bad starter cranking may result from poor connections or faulty components of the battery or hot phase of the starter motor circuit. To check this phase of the circuit, without disconnecting

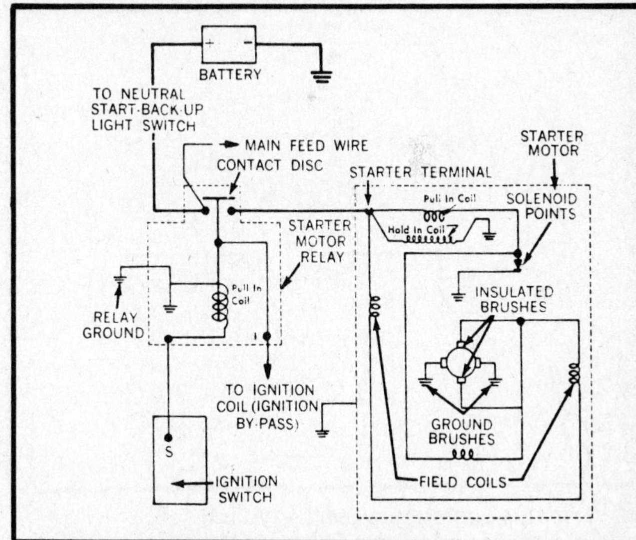

Positive engagement starter circuits

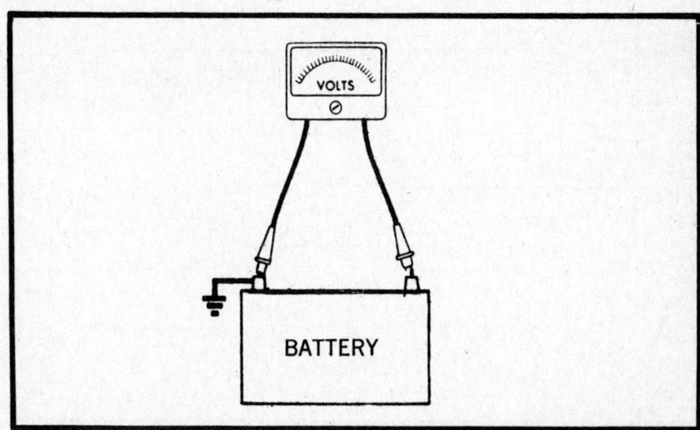

Voltmeter attached to battery for cranking voltage test

any wires, connect one lead of a voltmeter to a prod secured in the hot post of the battery and the other voltmeter lead to the field terminal of the starting motor. The meter should be set to the 16–20 volt scale. Before closing the starter switch, the voltmeter reading will be that of the battery. After closing the starter switch, change the selector on the voltmeter to the 3 volt scale. With a jumper wire between the relay battery terminal and the relay starter switch terminal, crank the engine. If the starting motor cranks the engine, the relay (solenoid) is operating.

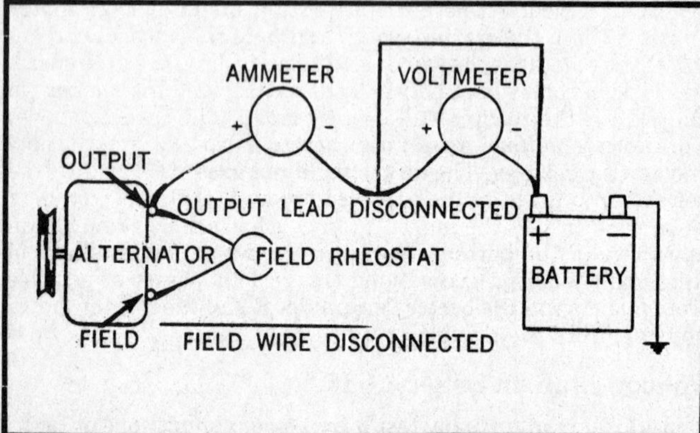

Checking charging system resistance—typical

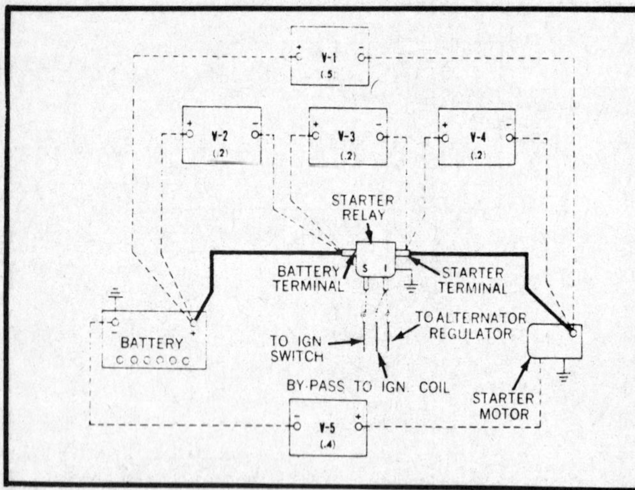

Starter cable resistance tests—typical

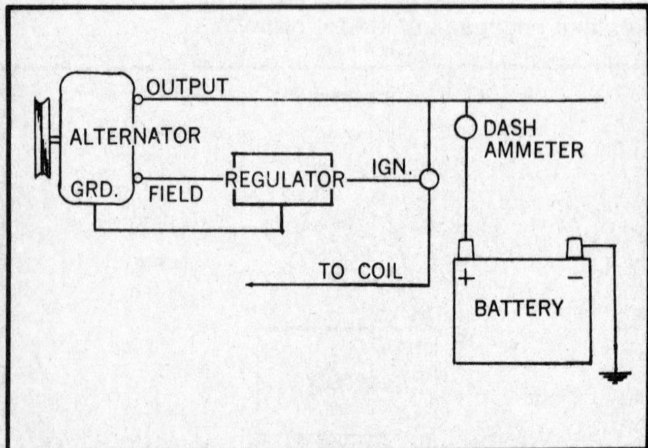

Alternator system with ammeter in the circuit

While the engine is being cranked, watch the voltmeter. It should not register more than 0.5 volt. If more than this, check each part of the circuit for voltage drop to isolate the trouble, (high resistance).

Without disturbing the voltmeter-to-battery hook-up, move the free voltmeter lead to the battery terminal of the relay (solenoid) and crank the engine. The voltmeter should show no more than 0.1 volt.

If this reading is correct, move the same voltmeter lead to the starting motor terminal of the relay (solenoid). While the engine is being cranked, the voltmeter should show no more than 0.3 volt. If it does, the trouble lies in the relay.

If the reading is correct, the trouble is in the cable or connections between the relay and the starting motor.

DIAGNOSIS

STARTER WON'T START ENGINE

1. Dead battery.
2. Open starter circuit, such as:
   a. Broken or loose battery cables.
   b. Inoperative starter motor solenoid.
   c. Broken or loose wire from starter switch to solenoid.
   d. Poor solenoid or starter ground.
   e. Bad starter switch.
3. Defective starter internal circuit, such as:
   a. Dirty or burned commutator.
   b. Stuck, worn or broken brushes.
   c. Open or shorted armature.
   d. Open or grounded fields.
4. Starter motor mechanical faults, such as:
   a. Jammed armature end bearings.
   b. Bad bearings, allowing armature to rub fields.
   c. Bent shaft.
   d. Broken starter housing.
   e. Bad starter worm or drive mechanism.
   f. Bad starter drive or flywheel driven gear.
5. Engine hard or impossible to crank such as:
   a. Hydrostatic lock, water in combustion chamber.
   b. Crankshaft seizing in bearings.
   c. Piston or ring seizing.
   d. Bent or broken connecting rod.
   e. Seizing of connecting rod bearing.
   f. Flywheel jammed or broken.
6. Starter spins free, won't engage such as:
   a. Sticking or broken drive mechanism.

Chrysler Corp.

REDUCTION GEAR STARTER MOTOR

The housing is die-cast aluminum. A 3.5 to 1 reduction, combined with the starter to ring gear ratio, results in a total gear reduction of about 45 to 1.

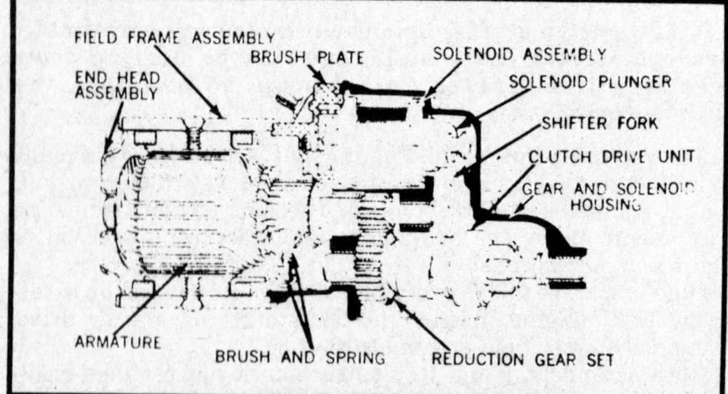

Reduction gear starter—cross section

NOTE: The high-pitched sound is caused by the higher starter speed.

The positive shift solenoid is enclosed in the starter housing and is energized through the ignition switch. When ignition switch is turned to start, the solenoid plunger engages drive gear through a shifting fork. At the completion of travel, the plunger closes a switch to revolve the starter.

The tension of the spring-type shifting prevents a butt-tooth lock up and motor will not start before total shift.

An overrunning clutch prevents motor damage if key is held on after engine starts.

No lubrication is required due to Oilite bearings.

Disassembly

1. Support assembly in a vise equipped with soft jaws. Do not clamp. Care must be used not to distort or damage the die cast aluminum.
2. Remove the through-bolts and the end housing.
3. Carefully pull the armature up and out of the gear housing and the starter frame and field assembly. Remove the steel and fiber thrust washer.

NOTE: On eight cylinder engines, the starting motors have the wire of the shunt field coil soldered to the brush terminal. Six cylinder engines have the four coils in series and do not have a wire soldered to the brush terminal. One pair of brushes is connected to this terminal. The other pair of brushes is attached to the series field coils by means of a terminal screw. Carefully pull the frame and field assembly up just enough to expose the terminal screw and the solder connection of the shunt field at the brush terminal. Place two wood blocks between the starter frame and starter gear housing to facilitate removal of the terminal screw and unsoldering of the shunt field wire at the brush terminal.

4. Support the brush terminal with a finger behind terminal and remove screw.

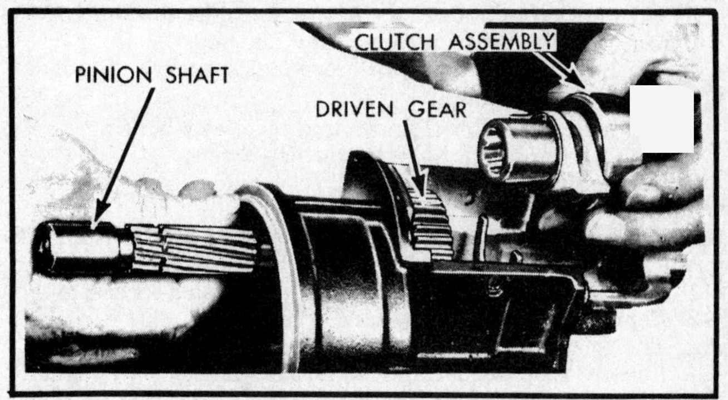

Removing clutch assembly

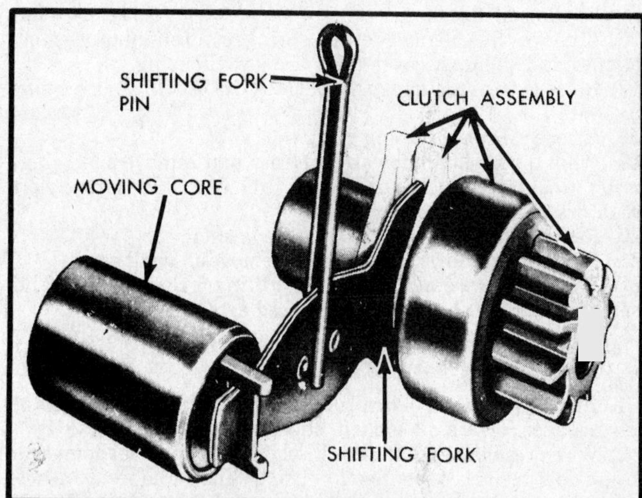

Shift fork and clutch arrangement

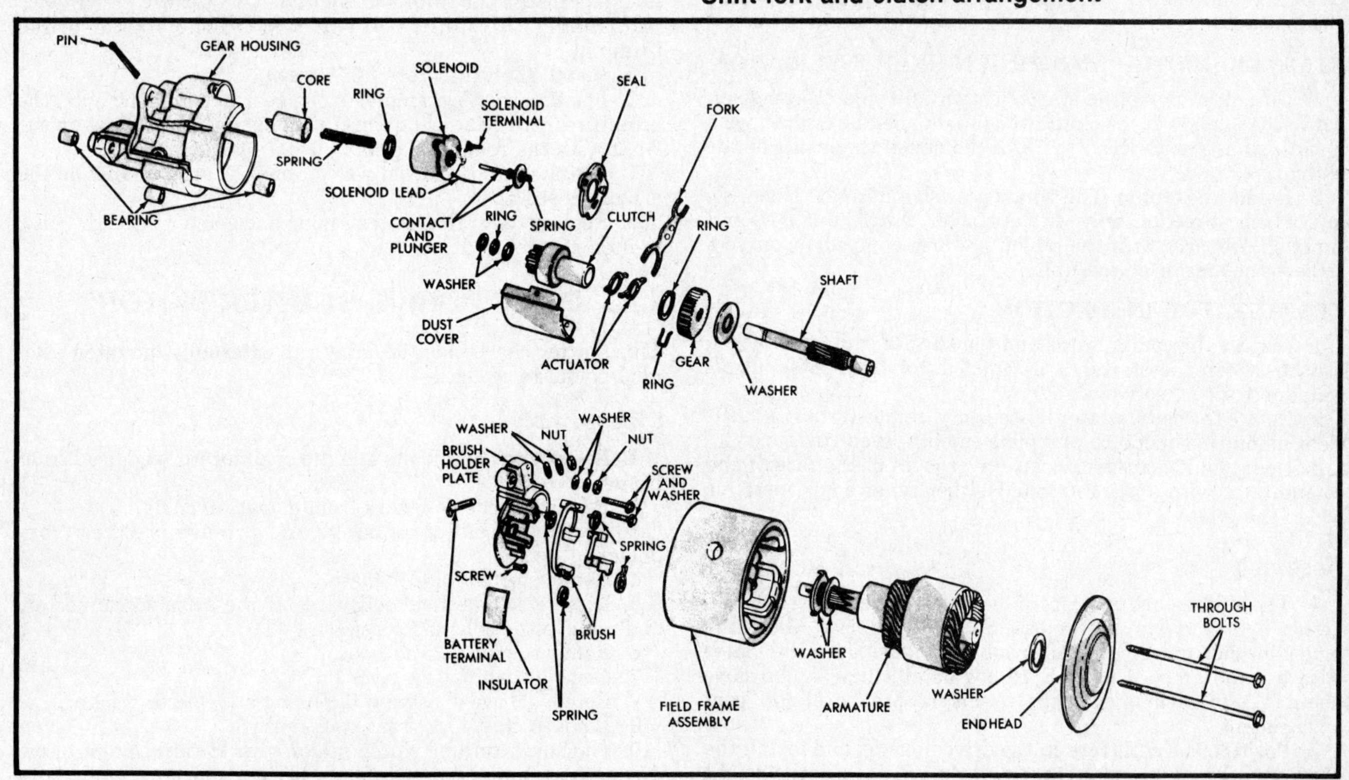

Reduction gear starter–exploded view

5. On eight cylinder engine starters, unsolder the shunt field coil lead from the brush terminal and housing.
6. The brush holder plate with terminal, contact and brushes is serviced as an assembly.
7. Clean all old sealer from around plate and housing.
8. Remove the brush holder attaching screw.
9. On the shunt type, unsolder the solenoid winding from the brush terminal.
10. Remove $^{11}/_{32}$ in. nut, washer and insulator from solenoid terminal.
11. Remove brush holder plate with brushes as an assembly.
12. Remove gear housing ground screw.
13. The solenoid assembly can be removed from the well.
14. Remove nut, washer and seal from starter battery terminal and remove terminal from plate.
15. Remove solenoid contact and plunger from solenoid and remove the coil sleeve.
16. Remove the solenoid return spring, coil retaining washer, retainer and the dust cover from the gear housing.
17. Release the snap-ring that locates the driven gear on pinion shaft.
18. Release front retaining ring.
19. Push pinion shaft toward the rear and remove snap-ring, thrust washers, clutch and pinion and two shift fork nylon actuators.
20. Remove driven gear and friction washer.
21. Pull shifting fork forward and remove moving core.
22. Remove fork retainer pin and shifting fork assembly. The gear housing with bushings is serviced as an assembly.

REPLACEMENT OF BRUSHES

1. Brushes that are worn more than one-half the length of new brushes, or are oil-soaked, should be replaced.
2. When resoldering the shunt field and solenoid lead, make a strong, low-resistance connection using a high-temperature solder and resin flux. Do not use acid or acid-core solder. Do not break the shunt field wire units when removing and installing the brushes.

STARTER CLUTCH AND PINION GEAR INSPECTION

1. Do not immerse the starter clutch unit in a cleaning solvent. The outside of the clutch and pinion must be cleaned with a cloth so as not to wash the lubricant from the inside of the clutch.
2. Rotate the pinion. The pinion gear should rotate smoothly and in one direction only. If the starter clutch unit does not function properly, or if the pinion is worn, chipped, or burred, replace the starter clutch unit.

COMMUTATOR INSPECTION

1. Inspect the commutator and the surface contacted by the brushes when the starter is assembled, for flat spots, out-of-roundness, or excessive wear.
2. Reface the commutator if necessary, removing only a sufficient amount of metal to provide a smooth, even surface.
3. Using light pressure, clean the grooves of the face of the commutator with a pointed tool. Neither remove any metal or widen the grooves.

Assembly

1. The shifter fork consists of two spring steel plates held together by two rivets. Before assembling the starter, check the plates for side movement. After lubricating between the plates with a small amount of SAE 10 engine oil, they should have about $^{1}/_{16}$ in. side movement to insure proper pinion gear engagement.
2. Position the shift fork in the drive housing and install the shifting fork retainer pin. One tip of the pin should be straight and the other bent at a 15 degree angle away from the housing. The fork and retainer pin should operate freely after bending the tip of the pin.
3. Install the solenoid moving core and engage the shifting fork.
4. Place the pinion shaft into the drive housing and install the friction washer and drive gear.
5. Install the clutch and pinion assembly, thrust washer and retaining washer.
6. Engage the shifting fork with the clutch actuators.

CAUTION

The friction washer must be positioned on the shoulder of the splines of the pinion shaft before the driven gear is positioned.

7. Install the driven gear snap-ring.
8. Install the pinion shaft retaining ring.
9. The starter solenoid return spring can now be inserted in the moveable core.
10. Install the solenoid contact plunger assembly into the solenoid and reform the double wires so they can be curved around the contactor. This will allow the terminal stud to enter the brush holder properly.

CAUTION

The contactor must not touch these double wires after assembly is complete.

11. Assemble the battery terminal stud in the brush holder.
12. Position the seal on the brush holder plate.
13. Run the solenoid lead wire through the hole in the brush holder and attach the solenoid stud, insulating washers, flat washer and nut.
14. Wrap the solenoid lead wire tightly around the brush terminal post and solder it.
15. Fix the brush holder to the solenoid attaching screws.
16. Gently lower the solenoid coil and brush plate into the gear housing.
17. Position the brush plate assembly into the starter gear housing, install the nuts and tighten.
18. Solder the shunt coil lead wire to the starter brush terminal.
19. Install the brush terminal screw.
20. Position the field frame on the gear housing and start the armature into the housing, carefully engaging the splines on the shaft with the reduction gear by rotating the armature.
21. Install the fiber thrust washer and the steel washer on the armature shaft.
22. Replace the starter end housing and starter through-bolts; tighten securely.

DIRECT DRIVE STARTER MOTOR

This starter can be identified by the externally mounted solenoid bolted to the case.

Disassembly

1. Remove through bolts and tap commutator end head from frame.
2. Remove thrust washers from armature shaft.
3. Lift brush holder springs and remove brushes from holders.
4. Remove brush holder plate.
5. Disconnect the field coil wires at the solenoid connector, and remove the solenoid screws.
6. Remove solenoid and boot.
7. Drive out shift fork pivot pin.
8. Remove drive end pinion housing and spacer washer.
9. Remove shift fork from starter drive.
10. Slide overrunning clutch pinion gear toward commutator, drive stop retainer toward clutch pinion gear and remove the snap ring.

11. Remove overrunning clutch drive from armature shaft.
12. If field coils are good, stop disassembly at this point. If field coils must be replaced, remove ground brushes terminal screw and remove brushes, terminal and shunt wire. Remove pole shoe screws, using the proper tools. Remove field coils.
13. Replacement of the brushes, inspection of the starter clutch and pinion and inspection of the commutator procedures are the same as the reduction gear starter procedures.

Assembly

1. Install field coils into frame, if removed.
2. Lubricate armature shaft and splines with engine oil.
3. Install starter drive, stop retainer, lock ring and spacer washer.
4. Install shift fork, with narrow leg of fork toward commutator.
5. Install pinion housing onto armature shaft, indexing shift fork with slot in housing.
6. Install shift fork pivot pin.
7. With clutch drive, shift fork and pinion housing assembled onto the armature, slide armature into frame until pinion housing indexes with slot.
8. Install solenoid and boot, tightening bolts to 60-70 in. lbs.
9. Connect field coil wires to solenoid connector, making sure they do not touch frame.
10. Install brush holder plate, indexing tang in frame hole.
11. Place brushes in holders, making sure field coil wires do not interfere.
12. Install thrust washers on commutator end of armature shaft to obtain a maximum of 0.010 in. end play.
13. Install commutator end head and through-bolts. Tighten bolts 40 to 50 in. lbs.
14. Measure drive gear pinion clearance; it should be $^1/_8$ in. Adjust by moving solenoid fore and aft as required.

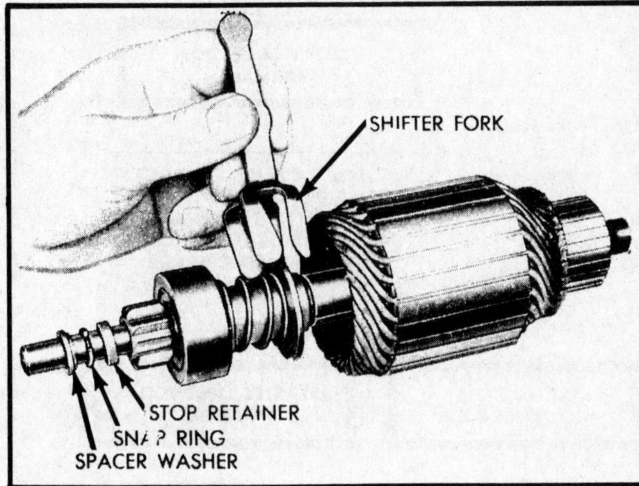

Removing shift fork

BOSCH AND NIPPONDENSO DIRECT DRIVE STARTER 1984–85 W/2.2L ENGINE

Disassembly and Assembly

1. Position the assembly in the proper holding fixture. Disconnect the field coil wire from the solenoid terminal.

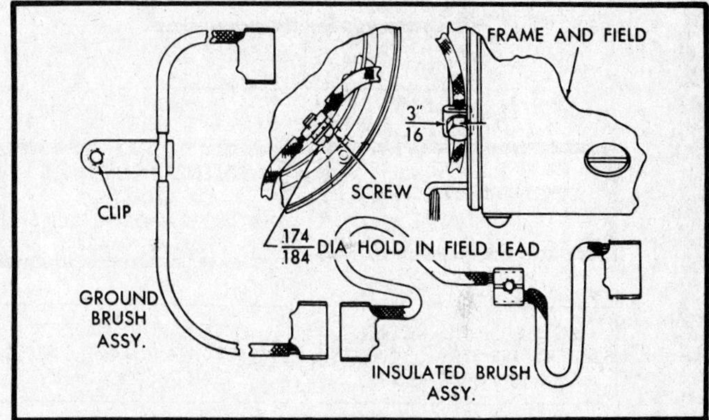

Brush lead arrangement – Chrysler direct drive starter

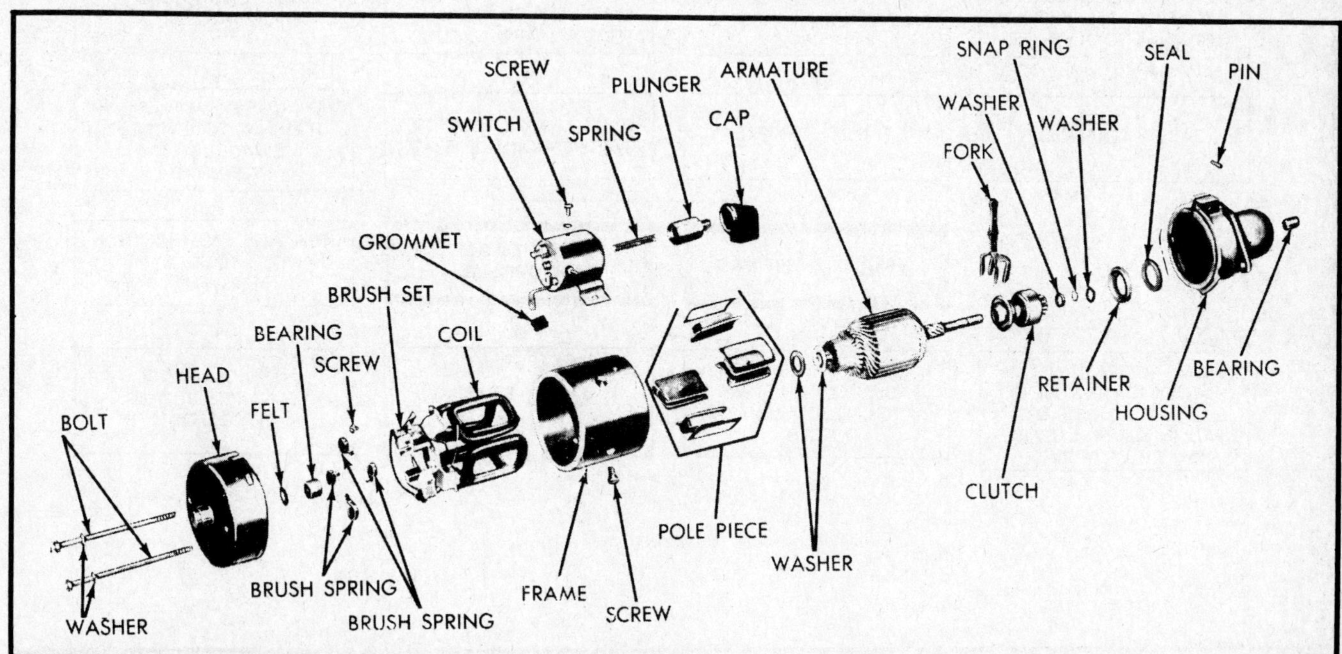

Chrysler direct drive starter – exploded view

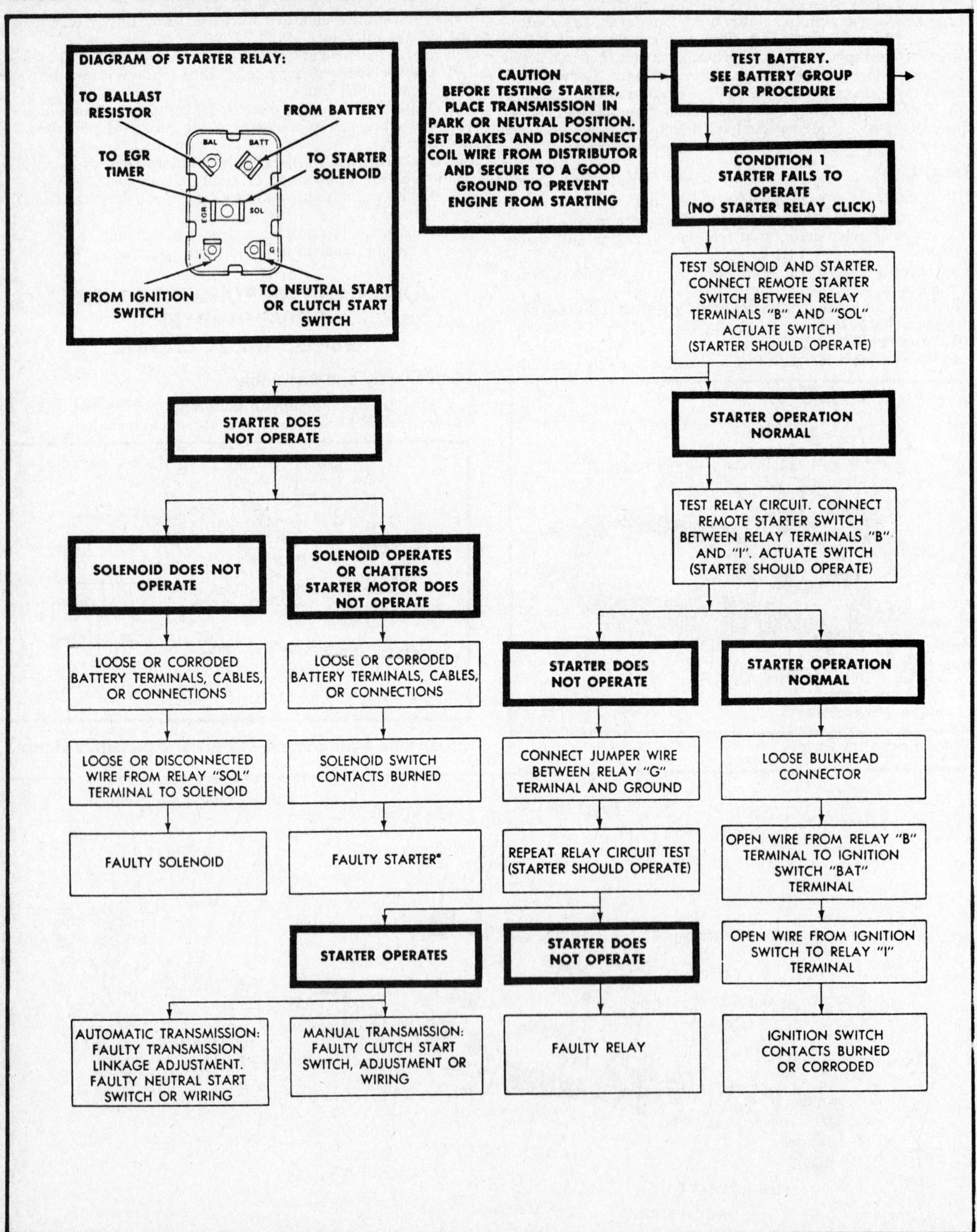

Reduction gear starter troubleshooting—Part 1 of 2

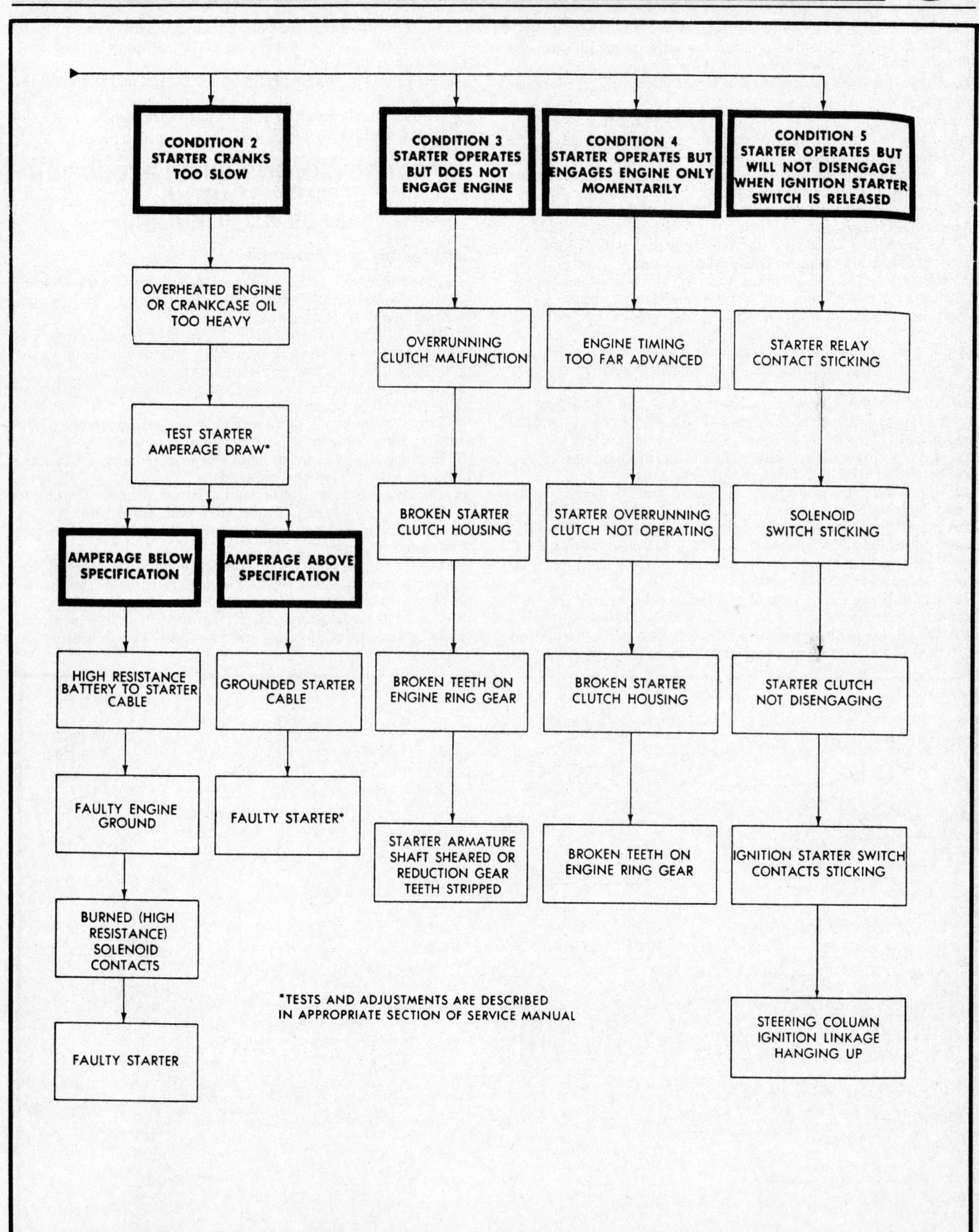

Reduction gear starter troubleshooting—Part 2 of 2

2. Remove the solenoid mounting screws (and the solenoid Bosch automatic transmission) and work the solenoid (plunger Bosch automatic transmission) off the shift fork.

3. On Nippondenso units, remove the bearing cover, armature shaft lock, washer, spring and seal.

4. On Bosch units, remove the two screws holding down the end shield bearing cap and remove the cap and washers.

5. Remove the through bolts and the commutator end frame cover. Remove the two brushes and the brush plate. Slide the field frame off over the armature.

6. Take out the shift lever pivot bolt. Take off the rubber gasket and metal plate.

7. For the Bosch (automatic transmission) and all Nippondenso units, remove the armature assembly and shift lever from the drive end housing. For the Bosch (manual transmission), press the stop collar off the snapring, remove the snapring, remove the clutch assembly and remove the drive end housing from the armature.

8. For all except the Bosch (manual transmission), press the stop collar off the snapring then remove the snapring, stop collar and clutch.

9. Brushes that are worn more than one half the length of new brushes, or are oil soaked should be replaced. New brushes are $^{11}/_{16}$ inch long.

10. Do not immerse the starter clutch unit in cleaning solvent. Solvent will wash the lubricant from the clutch.

11. Place the drive unit on the armature shaft and while holding the armature rotate the pinion. The drive pinion should rotate smoothly in one direction only. The pinion may not rotate easily but as long as it rotates smoothly it is in good condition. If the clutch unit does not function properly or if the pinion is worn, chipped or burred replace the unit.

12. Assembly is the reverse of the disassembly procedure. Lubricate the armature shaft and splines with SAE 10 or 30 W oil.

13. On all except the Bosch (manual transmission), install the clutch, stop collar, lock ring and shaft fork on the armature. On the Bosch (manual transmission), install the drive end housing on the armature, then install the clutch, stop collar and snap ring on the armature.

14. On all except the Bosch (manual transmission), install the armature assembly and shift fork in the drive end housing. On Bosch units install the shim and armature shaft lock. Check the end play, it should be 0.002–0.021 in.

NIPPONDENSO/MITSUBISHI REDUCTION GEAR STARTER 1984-88 W/2.6L ENGINE

Disassembly and Assembly

1. Position the assembly in a suitable holding fixture. Disconnect the wire terminal from the field coil stud and move the rubber shield away from the wire end.

2. Remove the two through bolts from the end frame. Remove the two screws from the end of the frame cap. Remove the upper left solenoid screw and remove the wire retainer.

3. Remove the end shield. Remove the two field frame brushes from the brush plate.

4. Remove the brush plate and slide the armature out of the field frame and remove the field frame.

5. Remove the two screws from the gear housing and remove the gear housing from the solenoid.

6. Remove the clutch rollers and retainer. Remove the pinion and clutch. Remove the solenoid steel ball and spring.

7. Remove the solenoid cover screws, the solenoid cover and the solenoid plunger.

8. Do not immerse parts in cleaning solvent. Immersing the field frame and coil assembly and armature will damage insulation. Wipe these parts with a cloth only.

9. Do not immerse drive unit in cleaning solvent. Drive clutch is prelubricated at the factory and solvent will wash lubrication from clutch.

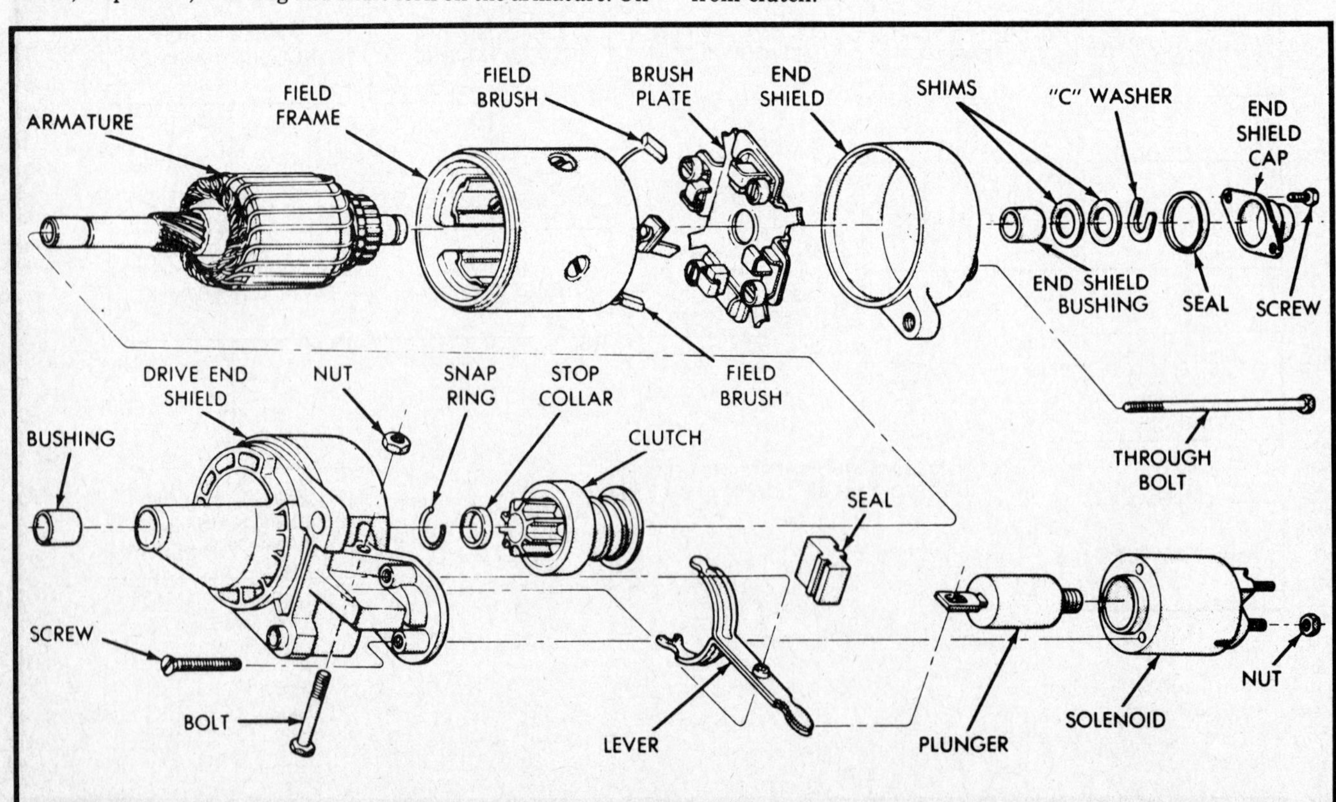

Exploded view of the Bosch starter—1984-85 with 2.2L engine

10. The drive unit may be cleaned with a brush moistened with cleaning solvent and wiped dry with a cloth. Brushes that are worn more than ½ the length of new brush, or are oil soaked, should be replaced.

11. Field brushes are serviced as part of the field and frame assembly. Ground brushes and all springs come as part of the brush plate assembly.

12. The assembly is the reverse of the disassembly procedure.

BOSCH REDUCTION GEAR STARTER 1986–88 W/2.5L ENGINE

Disassembly and Assembly

1. Position the assembly in a suitable holding fixture. Remove the field terminal nut. Remove the field terminal. Remove the field washer.

2. Remove the solenoid mounting screws. Work the solenoid off of the shift fork and remove the solenoid from the starter.

3. Remove the two starter end shield bushing cap screws. Remove the starter end shield bushing cap. Remove the end shield bushing and C washer.

4. Remove the starter end shield bushing washer. Remove the starter end shield bushing seal.

5. Remove the two starter through bolts. Remove the starter end shield. Remove the brush plate.

6. Slide the field frame off of the starter and over the armature. Remove the armature assembly from the drive end housing.

7. Remove the rubber seal from the drive end housing. Remove the starter drive gear train.

8. Remove the dust plate. Press the stop collar off the snapring using the proper tool. Loosen the snap ring using snapring pliers.

9. Remove the output shaft snapring. Remove the clutch stop ring collar. Remove the clutch assembly from the starter.

10. Remove the clutch shift lever bushing. Remove the clutch shift lever. Position a suitable tool and remove the C clip retainer.

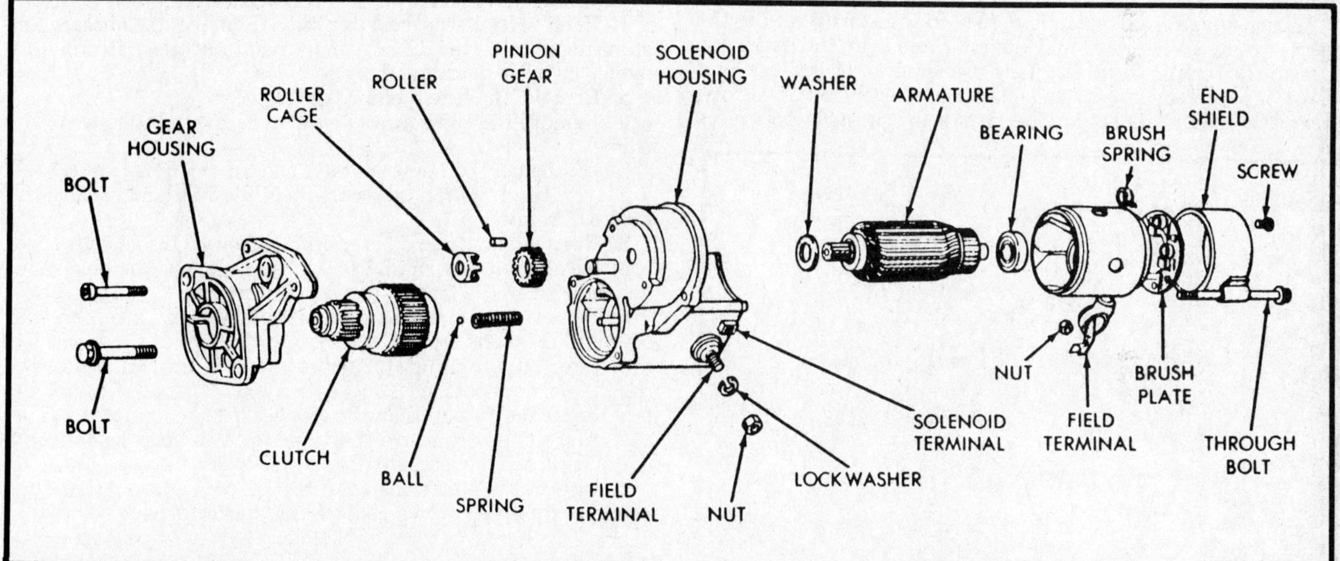

Exploded view of the Nippondenso/Mitsubishi starter – 1984-88 with 2.6L engine

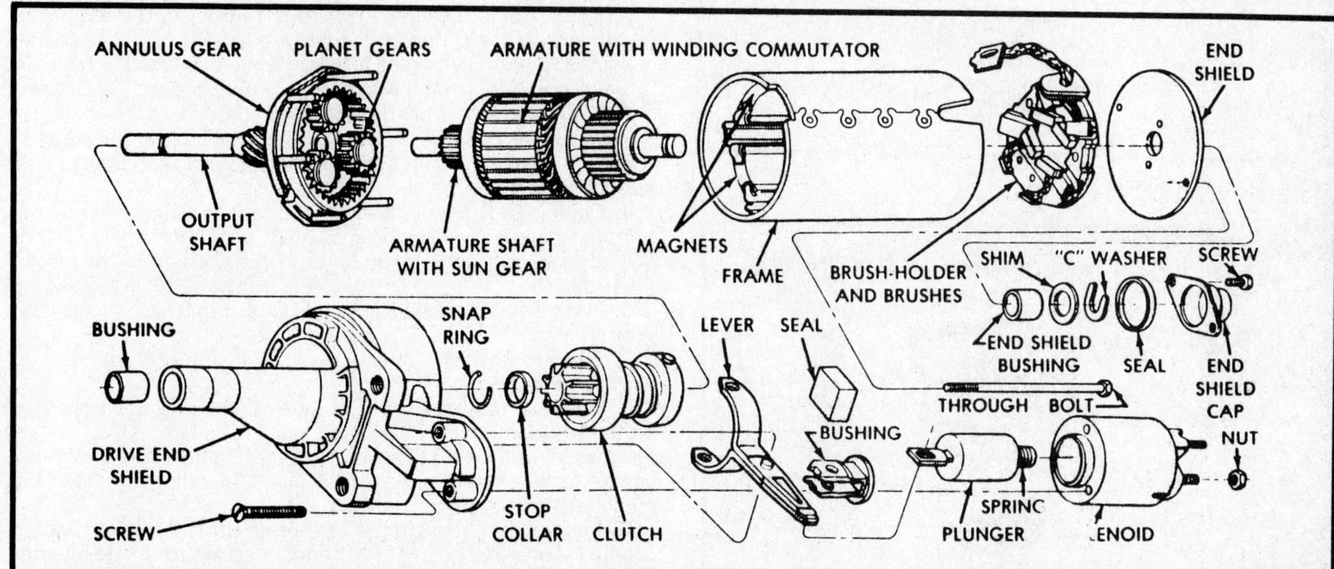

Exploded view of the Bosch starter – 1986-88 with 2.5L engine

11. Remove the retaining washer. Remove the sun and the planetary gears from the annulus gear,

12. Assembly is the reverse of the disassembly procedure. Replace all defective components as required.

Ford Motor Co.

MOTORCRAFT POSITIVE ENGAGEMENT STARTER MOTOR

This starting motor is a series parallel wound, four pole, four brush unit. It is equipped with an overrunning clutch drive pinion, which is engaged with the flywheel ring gear by an actuating lever, operated by a movable pole piece. This pole piece is hinged to the starter frame and can drop into position through an opening in the frame.

Three conventional field coils are located at three pole piece positions. The fourth field coil is designed to serve also as an engaging coil and a hold in coil for the operation of the drive pinion.

When the ignition switch is turned to the start position, the starter relay is energized and current flows from the battery to the starter motor terminal. This prime surge of current first flows through the starter engaging coil, creating a very strong magnetic field. This magnetism draws the movable pole piece down toward the starter frame, which then causes the lever attached to it to move the starter pinion into engagement with the flywheel ring gear.

When the movable pole shoe is fully seated, it opens the field coil, grounding contacts and the starter is then in normal operation. A holding coil is used to hold the movable pole shoe in the fully seated position during the engine cranking operation.

Vehicles equipped with automatic transmissions have a starter neutral switch circuit control. This is to prevent operation of the starter if the selector lever is not in Neutral or Park.

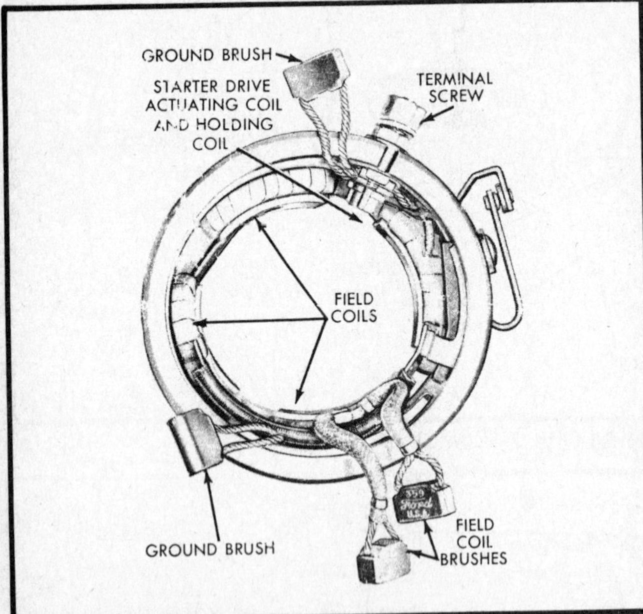

Field coil assembly

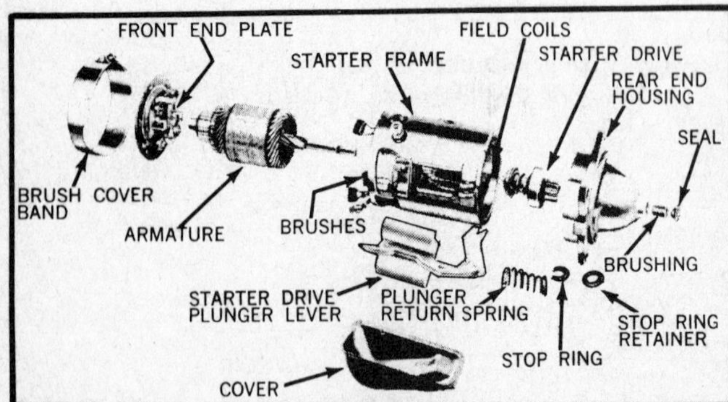

Starter motor—exploded view

Disassembly

1. Remove brush cover band and starter drive gear actuating lever cover. Observe the brush lead locations for reassembly, then remove the brushes from their holders. Factory brush length is $\frac{1}{2}$ in., wear limit is $\frac{1}{4}$ in.
2. Remove the through bolts, starter drive gear housing and the drive gear actuating lever return spring.
3. Remove the pivot pin retaining the starter gear actuating lever and remove the lever and the armature.
4. Remove the stop ring retainer. Remove and discard the stop ring holding the drive gear to the armature shaft; then remove the drive gear assembly.
5. Remove the brush end plate.
6. Remove the two screws holding the ground brushes to the frame.
7. On the field coil that operates the starter drive gear actuating lever, bend the tab up on the field retainer and remove the field coil retainer.
8. Remove the three coil retaining screws. Unsolder the field coil leads from the terminal screw, then remove the pole shoes and coils from the frame (use a 300 watt iron).
9. Remove the starter terminal nut, washer, insulator and terminal from the starter frame.
10. Check the commutator for runnout. If the commutator is rough, has flat spots, or is more then 0.005 in. out of round, reface the commutator. Clean the grooves in the commutator face.
11. Inspect the armature shaft and the two bearings for scoring and excessive wear. Replace if necessary.
12. Inspect the starter drive. If the gear teeth are pitted, broken, or excessively worn, replace the starter drive.

Assembly

1. Install starter terminal, insulator, washers and retaining nut in the frame. (Be sure to position the slot in the screw perpendicular to the frame end surface.)
2. Position coils and pole pieces, with the coil leads in the terminal screw slot, then install the retaining screws. As the pole screws are tightened, strike the frame several sharp hammer blows to align the pole shoes. Tighten, then stake the screws.
3. Install solenoid coil and retainer and bend the tabs to hold the coils to the frame.
4. Solder the field coils and solenoid wire to the starter terminal, using rosin core solder and a 300 watt iron.
5. Check for continuity and ground connections in the assembled coils.
6. Position the solenoid coil ground terminal over the nearest ground screw hole.
7. Position the ground brushes to the starter frame and install retaining screws.
8. Position the brush end plate to the frame, with the end plate boss in the frame slot.
9. Lightly lubricate the armature shaft splines and install the starter drive gear assembly in the shaft. Install a new retaining stop ring and stop ring retainer.
10. Position the fiber thrust washer on the commutator end of the armature shaft, then position the armature in the starter frame.
11. Position the starter drive gear actuating lever to the frame

and starter drive assembly and install the pivot pin. Fill drive gear housing bore ¼ full of grease.

12. Position the drive actuating lever return spring and the drive gear housing to the frame, then install and tighten the through bolts. Do not pinch brush leads between brush plate and frame. Be sure that the stop ring retainer is properly seated in the drive housing.

13. Install the brushes in the brush holders and center the brush springs on the brushes.

14. Position the drive gear actuating lever cover on the starter and install the brush cover band with a new gasket.

15. Check starter no load amperage draw.

MOTORCRAFT SOLENOID ACTUATED STARTER MOTOR

This starter motor is a four brush, four field, four pole wound unit. The frame encloses a wound armature, which is supported at the drive end by caged needle bearings and at the commutator end by a sintered copper bushing. The four pole shoes are retained to the frame by one pole screw apiece and on each pole shoe is wound a ribbon type field coil connected in series parallel.

The solenoid is mounted to a flange on the starter drive housing, which encloses the entire shift mechanism and solenoid plunger. The solenoid utilizes two windings, a pull in winding and a hold in winding.

Disassembly

1. Disconnect the copper strap from the solenoid starter terminal, remove the remaining screws and remove the solenoid.

2. Loosen the retaining screw and slide the brush cover band back far enough to gain access to the brushes.

3. Remove the brushes from their holders, then remove the through-bolts and separate the drive end housing from the frame and brush end plate. Factory brush length is ½ in., wear limit ¼ in.

4. Remove the solenoid plunger and shift fork. These two items can be separated from each other by removing the roll pin.

5. Remove the armature and drive assembly from the frame. Remove the drive stop ring and slide the drive off the armature shaft.

6. Remove the drive stop ring retainer from the drive housing.

7. Inspection of the commutator, armature and bearings and pinion gear procedures is the same as the positive engagement starter procedures.

Assembly

1. Lubricate the armature shaft splines, then install drive assembly and a new stop ring.

2. Lubricate shift lever pivot pin, then position solenoid plunger and shift lever assembly in the drive housing.

3. Place a new retainer in the drive housing. Apply a small amount of Lubricant to the drive end of the armature shaft, then place armature and drive assembly into the drive housing, indexing the shift lever tangs with the drive assembly.

4. Apply a small amount of Lubricant to the commutator end of the armature shaft, then position the frame and field assembly to the drive housing.

5. Position the brush plate assembly to the frame, making sure it properly indexes. Install through bolts and tighten 45 to 85 inch lbs.

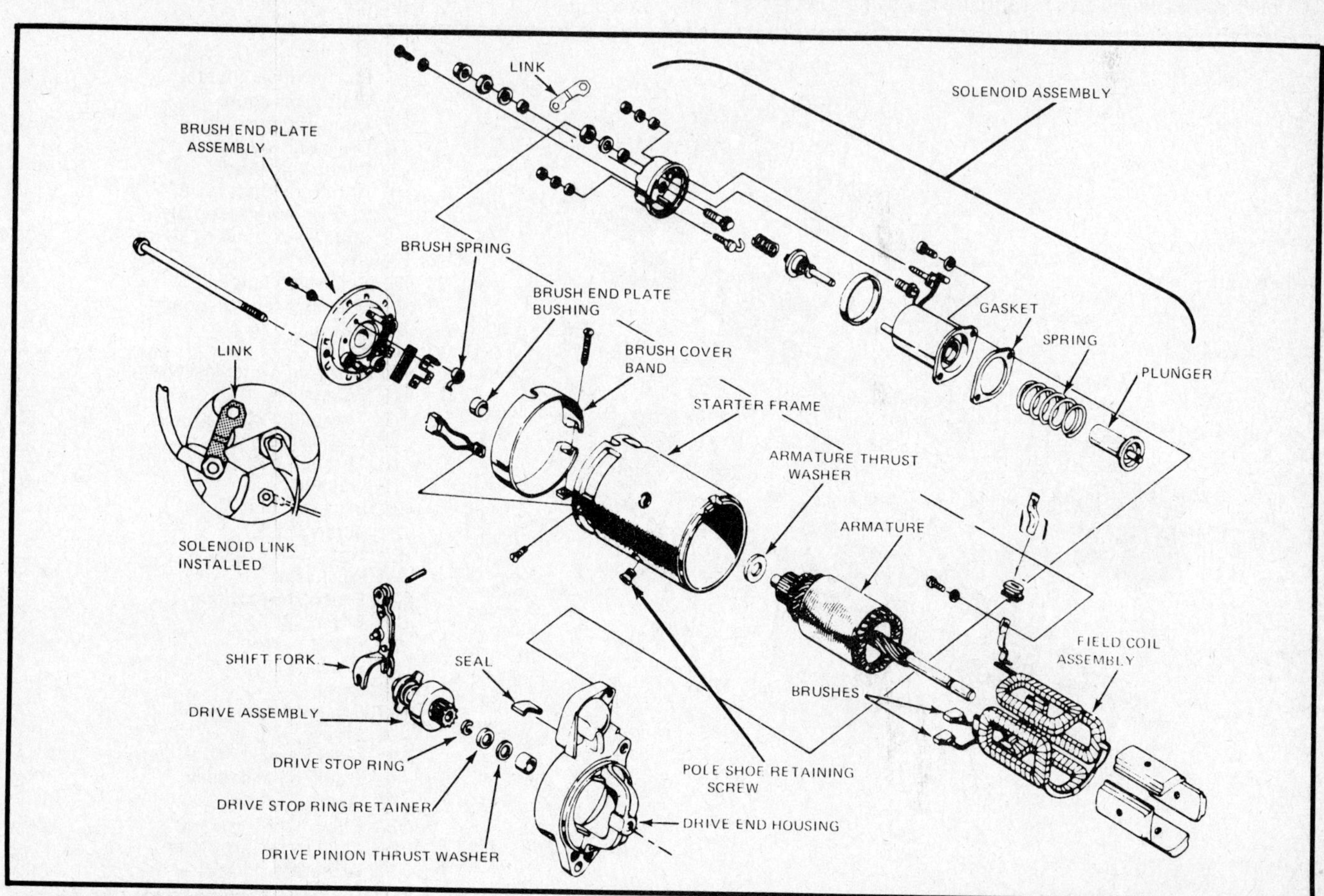

Ford Solenoid starter motor

6. Install brushes into their holders and make sure leads are not touching any interior starter components.

7. Place the rubber gasket between the solenoid mount and the frame solenoid mount and the frame surface.

8. Place the starter solenoid in position with metal gasket and spring, install heat shield (if so equipped) and install solenoid screws.

9. Connect copper strap and install cover band.

General Motors Corp.

DELCO REMY STARTER MOTOR

There are many different versions of the Delco Remy starter, depending upon application. In general, six cylinder engines use a unit having four field coils in series between the terminal and armature. Standard V8 engines use, depending on displacement, one of three types: one has two field coils in series with the armature and parallel to each other; another has two field coils in parallel between the field terminal and ground and another has three field coils in series with the armature and one field connected between the motor terminal and ground. Heavy duty starter motors, such as used on some of the largest General Motors high output engines have series compound windings. The relatively recent 20MT, 25MT and 27MT starters are used with diesels only. They differ from the others mainly in the use of a center bearing. Most repair procedures are generally similar for them, too. Where additional procedures are required for the center bearing, they will be noted.

In spite of these differences, all Delco Remy starters are disassembled and assembled in essentially the same manner.

Disassembly

1. Disconnect the field coil connectors from the motor solenoid terminal. Remove the solenoid mounting screws. Rotate the solenoid 90 degrees and remove it along with the plunger return spring. On models so equipped, remove solenoid mounting screws.

2. Remove the through bolts.

3. Remove the commutator end frame. On diesel starters only, remove the insulator. On all starters, remove the washer, field frame assembly and armature assembly from the drive housing. On diesel starters, the armature remains in the drive end frame.

4. On diesel starters only, remove the shift lever pivot bolt. On the 25MT only, remove the center bearing screws and remove the drive gear housing from the armature shaft. The shift lever/plunger assembly can now be separated from the starter clutch.

5. Remove the overrunning clutch from the armature shaft as follows. Slide the two piece thrust collar off the end of the armature shaft. Slide a standard $\frac{1}{2}$ in. pipe coupling or other spacer onto the shaft so that the end of the coupling butts against the edge of the retainer. Tap the end of the coupling with a hammer, driving retainer towards armature end of snap ring. Remove snap ring from its groove in the shaft using pliers. Slide retainer and clutch from armature shaft. On diesel starters, also remove the fiber washer and center bearing.

6. On all starters, except 5MT, remove the pivot pin which holds the brush holder and one insulated and one grounded brush in place. Remove the brush spring. On the 5MT starter, remove the brush holder from the brush support. Remove the screw from the brush holder and separate the brush and holder.

7. On models so equipped, separate solenoid from lever housing.

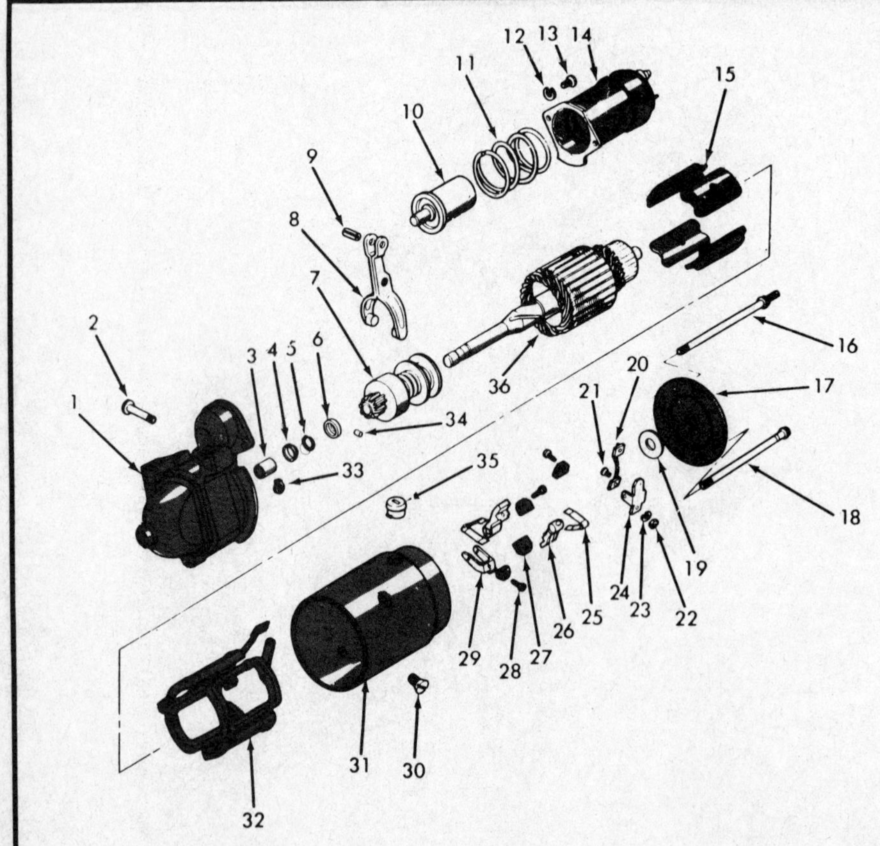

Delco starter—exploded view

Cleaning and Inspection

1. Clean parts with a rag, but do not immerse the parts in a solvent. Immersion in a solvent will dissolve the grease that is packed in the clutch mechanism and damage the armature and field coil insulation.

2. Test overrunning clutch action. The pinion should turn freely in the overrunning direction and must not slip in the cranking direction. Check pinion teeth to see that they have not been chipped, cracked, or excessively worn. Replace the unit if necessary.

3. Inspect the armature commutator. If the commutator is rough or out of round, it should be turned down.

4. Some starter motor models use a molded armature commutator design and no attempt to undercut the insulation should be made or serious damage may result to the commutator.

Assembly

1. Install brushes into holders. Install solenoid, if so equipped.

2. Assemble insulated and grounded brush holder together using the V-spring and position the assembled unit on the support pin. Push holders and spring to bottom of support and rotate spring to engage the slot in support. Attach ground wire to grounded brush and field lead wire to insulated brush, then repeat for other brush sets.

3. Assemble overrunning clutch to armature shaft as follows. Lubricate drive end of shaft with silicone lubricant. On diesel starters, install the center bearing assembly with the bearing facing the armature winding. Then, slide the clutch assembly onto the armature shaft with the pinion facing outward. Slide

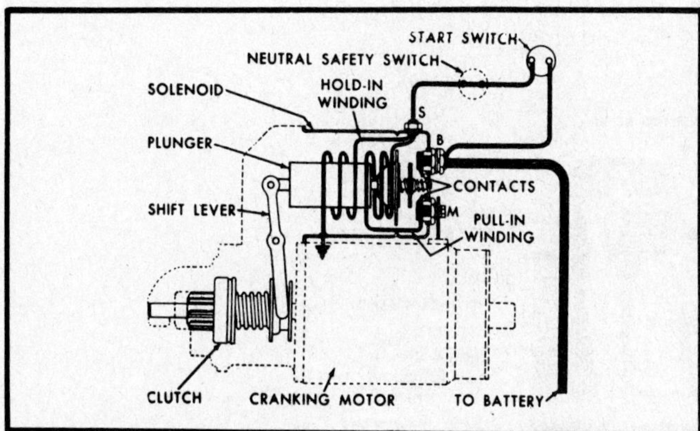

Delco solenoid windings

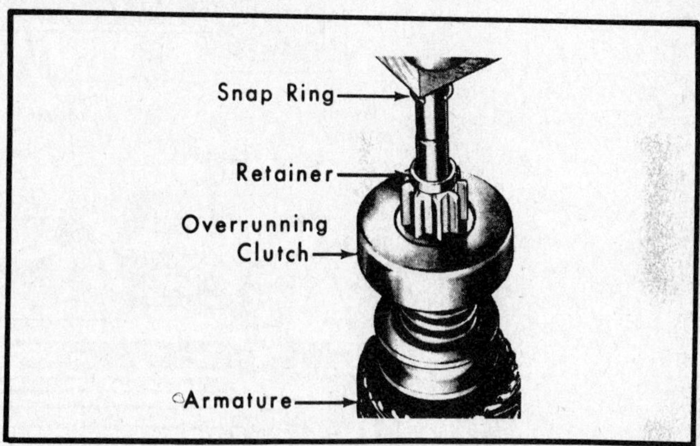

Brush holder removal procedure–delco starters

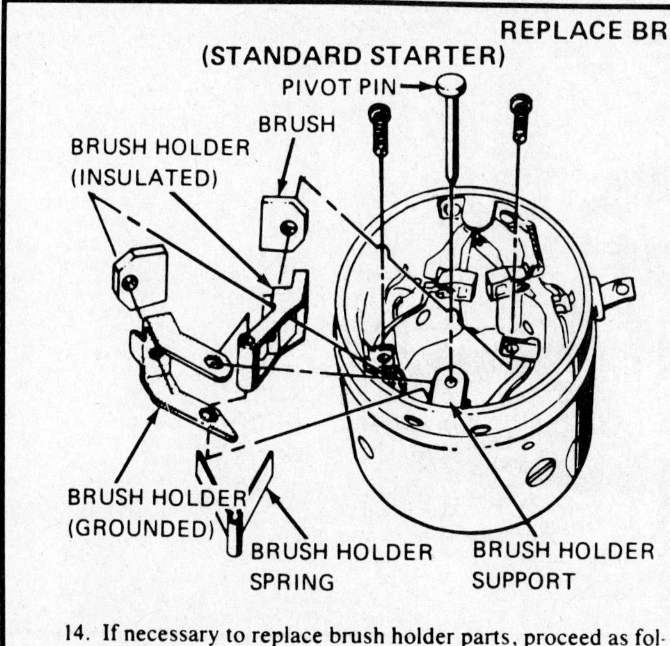

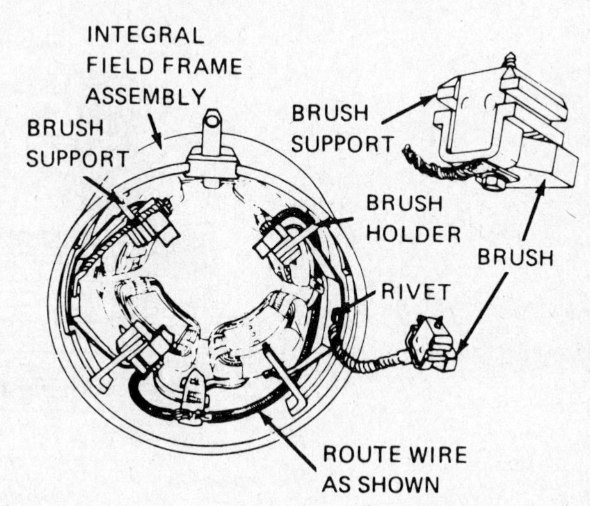

14. If necessary to replace brush holder parts, proceed as follows:

a. Remove brush holder pivot pin which positions one insulated and one grounded brush.

b. Remove brush spring.

c. Replace brushes as necessary.

a. Remove brush holder from brush support.

b. Remove screw from brush holder and separate brush and holder.

c. Inspect brush holder for wear or damage.

d. Replace brushes and/or holders as necessary.

Removing armature snap ring–delco starter

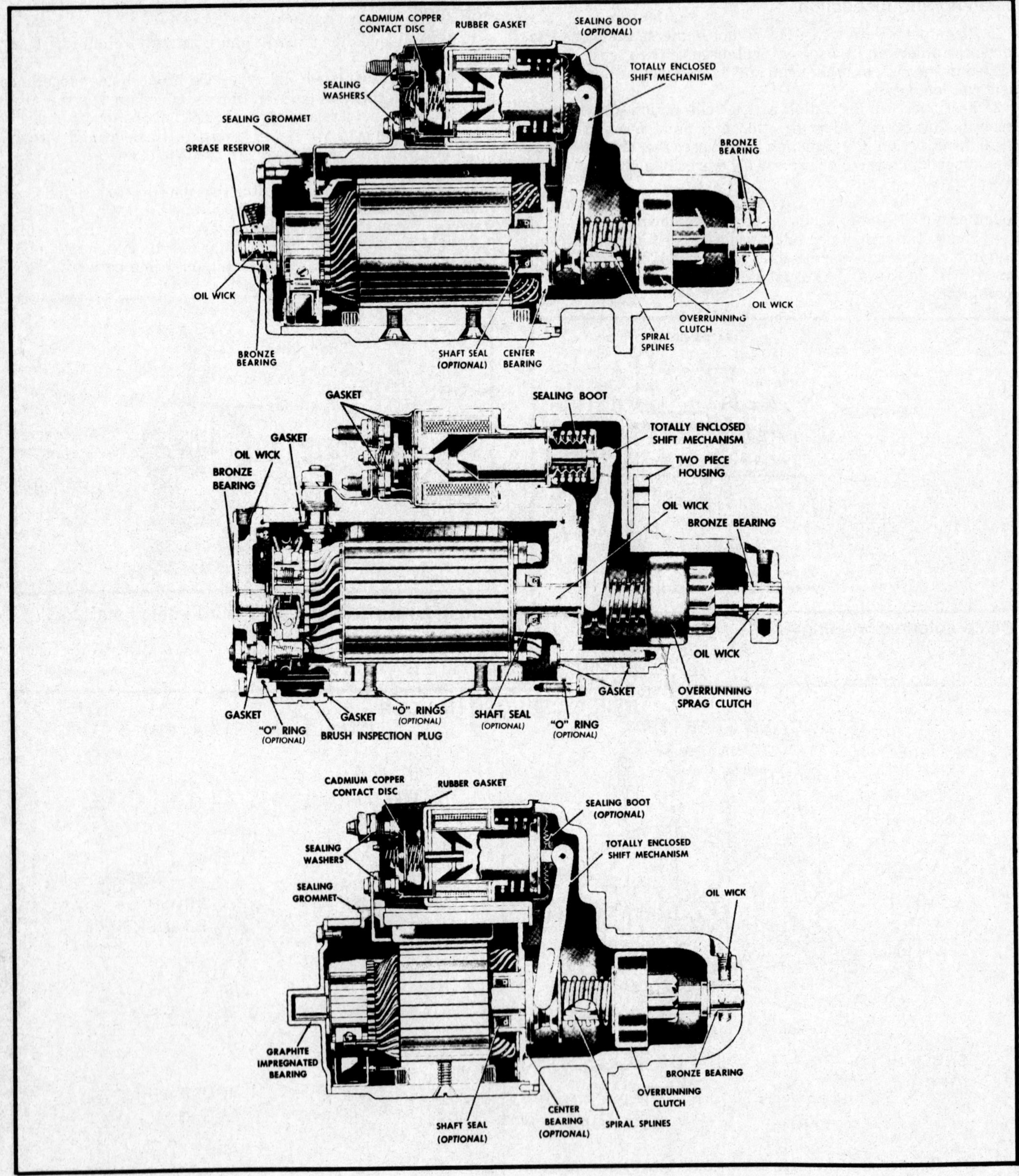

Typical delco starters

retainer onto shaft with cupped surface facing away from pinion. Stand armature up on a wood surface, commutator downwards. Position snap ring on upper end of shaft and drive it onto shaft with a small block of wood and a hammer. Slide snap ring into groove. Install thrust collar onto shaft with shoulder next to snap ring. With retainer on one side of snap ring and thrust collar on the other side, squeeze together with two sets of pliers until ring seats in retainer. On models without thrust collar, use a washer. Remember to remove washer before continuing.

4. Lubricate drive end bushing with silicone lubricant, then slide armature and clutch assembly into place, at the same time engaging shift lever with clutch. On non-diesel starters, the shift lever may be installed in the drive gear housing first. On the 25MT diesel starter only, install the center bearing screws and the shift lever pivot bolt. Tighten all securely.

5. Position field frame over armature and apply sealer (silicone) between frame and solenoid case. Position frame against drive housing, making sure brushes are not damaged in the process.

6. Lubricate the commutator end bushing with silicone lubricant. Place a leather brake washer on the armature shaft of gas engine starters. Place an insulator on the shaft of diesel engine starters. Slide the commutator end frame onto the shaft. Install the through bolts, making sure they pass through the bolt holes in the insulator on diesel starters. Install the through bolts and tighten to 65 inch lbs.

7. Reconnect field coil connector(s) to the solenoid motor terminal. Install solenoid mounting screws, if so equipped.

8. Check pinion clearance; it should be 0.010 to 0.140 in. on all models.

JEEP

1982-1988 Jeep vehicles use Bosch, Delco-Remy, and Motorcraft starters with the exception of Cherokee and Wagoneer 70 Series turbo-diesel engines. These engines use Paris-Rhone starters.

Bosch Reduction Gear Starter

Disassembly

1986-1988 W/2.5L ENGINE

CAUTION

When performing disassembly procedures, do not stike the thin wall stator frame with a hammer or any other instrument. Do not clamp the thin wall stator frame in the jaws of a vise. This may result in damage to the permanent magnets and the stator housing. The starter may be clamped by the mounting flange only.

1. Position the starter motor assembly in a suitable holding fixture, ensuring that it is secured by the mounting flange only. Remove the field terminal nut. Remove the field coil wire (Terminal 45) from the solenoid switch terminal post. Remove the field washer.

2. Remove the solenoid switch mounting screws. Disengage the solenoid switch from the fork lever and withdraw the solenoid switch with the armature and return spring from the housing.

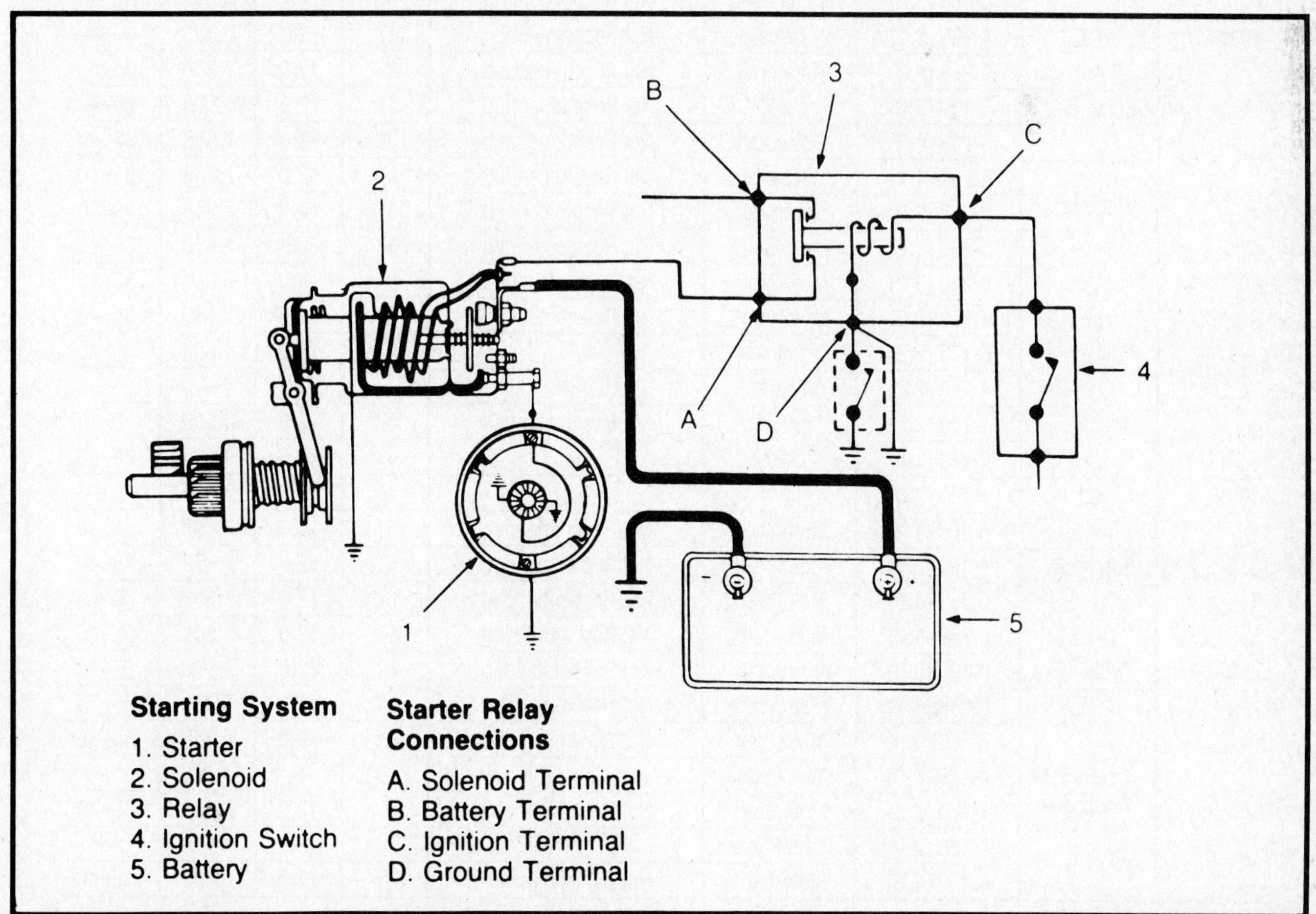

Bosch Starter Motor Simplified Circuit

STARTER SPECIFICATIONS
Jeep

Year	Model	No. Cylinder Displacement cu. in. (liter)	MFR	Lock Test Amps	Lock Test Volts	Lock Test Torque (ft-lb)	No-Load Test Amps	No-Load Test Volts	No-Load Test RPM	Brush Spring Tension (oz.)
1982	CJ	4-151 (2.5)	Delco	—	—	—	58	9.0	9,450	—
		6-258 (4.2)	Motorcraft	Not Recommended			67	12.0	7,868	35–40
	Scrambler	4-151 (2.5)	Delco	—	—	—	58	9.0	9,450	—
		6-258 (4.2)	Motorcraft	Not Recommended			67	12.0	7,868	35–40
	Wagoneer, Cherokee	6-258 (4.2)	Motorcraft	Not Recommended			67	12.0	7,868	35–40
		8-360 (5.9)	Motorcraft	Not Recommended			67	12.0	7,868	35–40
	Truck	6-258 (4.2)	Motorcraft	Not Recommended			67	12.0	7,868	35–40
		8-360 (5.9)	Motorcraft	Not Recommended			67	12.0	7,868	35–40
1983	CJ	4-151 (2.5)	Delco	—	—	—	58	9.0	9,450	35–40
		6-258 (4.2)	Motorcraft	Not Recommended			67	12.0	7,868	35–40
	Scrambler	4-151 (2.5)	Delco	—	—	—	58	9.0	9,450	35–40
		6-258 (4.2)	Motorcraft	Not Recommended			67	12.0	7,868	35–40
	Cherokee, Wagoneer	6-258 (4.2)	Motorcraft	Not Recommended			67	12.0	7,868	35–40
		8-360 (5.9)	Motorcraft	Not Recommended			67	12.0	7,868	35–40
	Truck	6-258 (4.2)	Motorcraft	Not Recommended			67	12.0	7,868	35–40
		8-360 (5.9)	Motorcraft	Not Recommended			67	12.0	7,868	35–40
1984	CJ	4-150 (2.5)	Delco	Not Recommended			67	12.0	8,500	30–40
		6-258 (4.2)	Motorcraft	Not Recommended			67	12.0	7,868	35–40
	Scrambler	4-150 (2.5)	Delco	Not Recommended			67	12.0	8,500	30–40
		6-258 (4.2)	Motorcraft	Not Recommended			67	12.0	7,868	35–40
	Grand Wagoneer	6-258 (4.2)	Motorcraft	Not Recommended			67	12.0	7,868	35–40
		8-360 (5.9)	Motorcraft	Not Recommended			67	12.0	7,868	35–40
	Truck	6-258 (4.2)	Motorcraft	Not Recommended			67	12.0	7,868	35–40
		8-360 (5.9)	Motorcraft	Not Recommended			67	12.0	7,868	35–40
	Cherokee Wagoneer	4-150 (2.5)	Motorcraft	Not Recommended			67	12.0	7,868	35–40
		6-173 (2.8)	Delco	—	—	—	67	12.0	8,500	30–40
		4-126 (2.0)	Bosch	—	—	—	—	—	—	—
		4-150 (2.5)	Delco	Not Recommended			67	12.0	8,500	30–40
		6-173 (2.8)	Delco	—	—	—	67	12.0	9,500	30–40
1985	CJ	4-150 (2.5)	Bosch	120	9.6	—	75	12.5	2,900	—
		6-258 (4.2)	Motorcraft	Not Recommended			67	12.0	7,868	35–40
	Scrambler	4-150 (2.5)	Motorcraft	Not Recommended			67	12.0	7,868	35–40
		6-258 (4.2)	Motorcraft	Not Recommended			67	12.0	7,868	35–40
	Grand Wagoneer	6-258 (4.2)	Motorcraft	Not Recommended			67	12.0	7,868	35–40
		8-360 (5.9)	Motorcraft	Not Recommended			67	12.0	7,868	35–40
	Truck	6-258 (4.2)	Motorcraft	Not Recommended			67	12.0	7,868	35–40
		8-360 (5.9)	Motorcraft	Not Recommended			67	12.0	7,868	35–40
	Cherokee Wagoneer	4-126 (2.0)	Paris Rhone	—	—	—	—	—	—	—
		4-150 (2.5)	Motorcraft	Not Recommended			67	12.0	7,868	35–40
		4-126 (2.0)	Paris Rhone	—	—	—	—	—	—	—
		4-150 (2.5)	Motorcraft	Not Recommended			67	12.0	7,868	35–40

STARTER SPECIFICATIONS
Jeep

Year	Model	No. Cylinder Displacement cu. in. (liter)	MFR	Lock Test Amps	Lock Test Volts	Lock Test Torque (ft-lb)	No-Load Test Amps	No-Load Test Volts	No-Load Test RPM	Brush Spring Tension (oz.)
1986	CJ	4-150 (2.5)	Motorcraft	Not Recommended			67	12.0	7,868	35–40
		6-258 (4.2)	Motorcraft	Not Recommended			67	12.0	7,868	35–40
	Scrambler	4-150 (2.5)	Motorcraft	Not Recommended			67	12.0	7,868	35–40
		6-258 (4.2)	Motorcraft	Not Recommended			67	12.0	7,868	35–40
	Grand Wagoneer	6-258 (4.2)	Motorcraft	Not Recommended			67	12.0	7,868	35–40
		8-360 (5.9)	Motorcraft	Not Recommended			67	12.0	7,868	35–40
	Truck	6-258 (4.2)	Motorcraft	Not Recommended			67	12.0	7,868	35–40
		8-360 (5.9)	Motorcraft	Not Recommended			67	12.0	7,868	35–40
	Cherokee	4-126 (2.0)	Paris Rhone	—	—	—	—	—	—	—
		4-150 (2.5)	Motorcraft	Not Recommended			67	12.0	7,868	35–40
		6-173 (2.5)	Delco	Not Recommended			58	12.0	9,500	30–40
	Wagoneer	4-126 (2.0)	Paris Rhone	—	—	—	—	—	—	—
		4-150 (2.5)	Motorcraft	Not Recommended			67	12.0	7,868	35–40
	Comanche	4-126 (2.0)	Paris Rhone	—	—	—	—	—	—	—
		4-150 (2.5)	Motorcraft	Not Recommended			67	12.0	7,868	35–40
		6-173 (2.5)	Delco	Not Recommended			58	12.0	9,500	30–40
1987–88	Wrangler	4-150 (2.5)	Bosch	120	9.6	N.A.	75	12.5	2,900	—
		6-258 (4.2)	Motorcraft	Not Recommended			67	12.0	7,868	35–40
	Grand Wagoneer	6-258 (4.2)	Motorcraft	Not Recommended			67	12.0	7,868	35–40
		8-360 (5.9)	Delco	—	—	—	—	—	—	—
	Truck	6-258 (4.2)	Motorcraft	Not Recommended			67	12.0	7,868	35–40
		8-360 (5.9)	Delco	—	—	—	—	—	—	—
	Cherokee	4-126 (2.0)	Paris Rhone	—	—	—	—	—	—	—
		4-150 (2.5)	Bosch	120	9.6	N.A.	75	12.5	2,900	—
		6-243 (4.0)	Delco	—	—	—	—	—	—	—
	Wagoneer	4-126 (2.0)	Paris Rhone	—	—	—	—	—	—	—
		4-150 (2.5)	Bosch	12.0	9.6	—	75	12.5	2,900	—
		6-243 (4.0)	Delco	—	—	—	—	—	—	—
	Comanche	4-126 (2.0)	Paris Rhone	—	—	—	—	—	—	—
		4-150 (2.5)	Bosch	12.0	9.6	—	—	—	—	—
		6-243 (4.0)	Delco	—	—	—	—	—	—	—

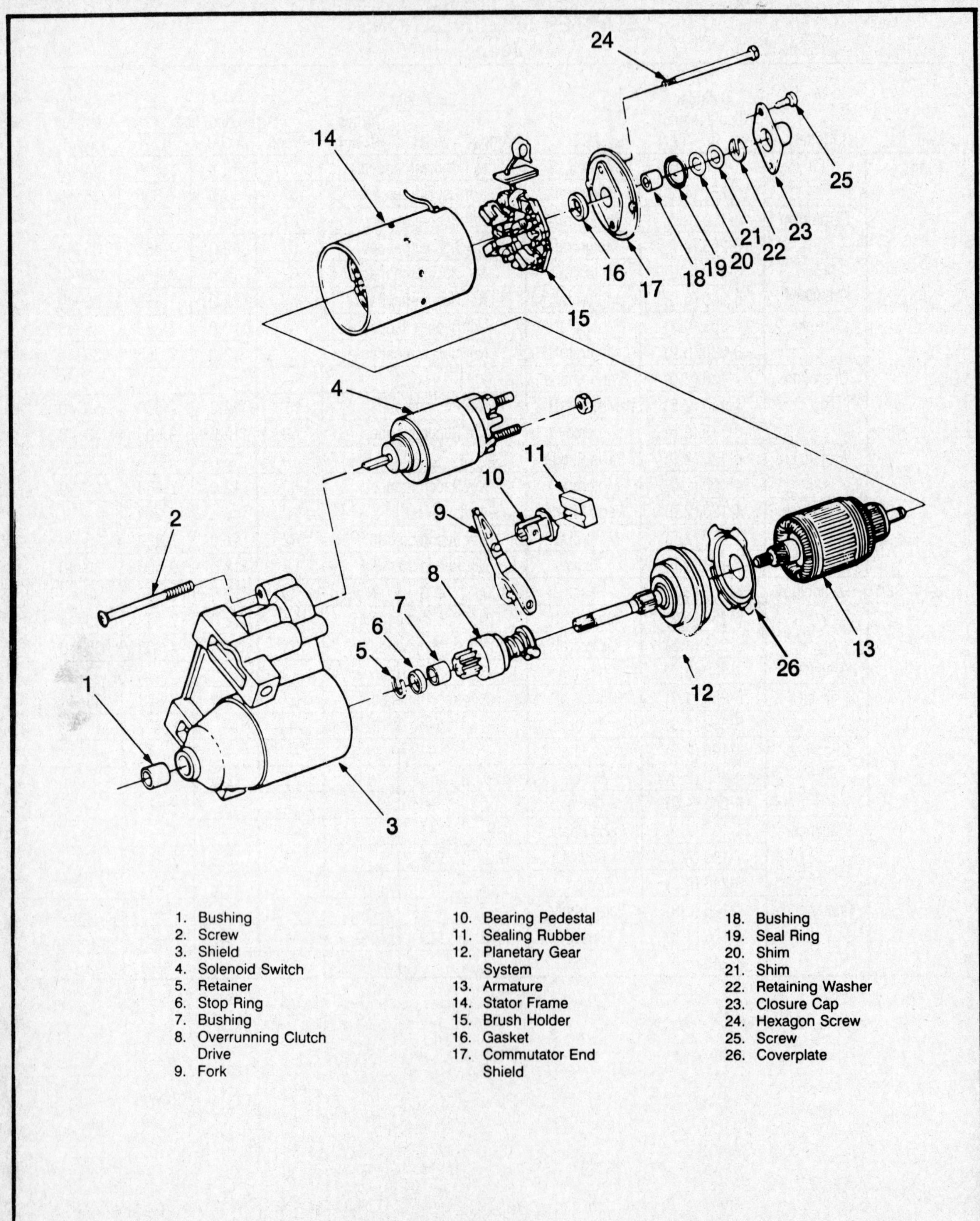

Exploded view of the Bosch starter—1986 with 2.5L engine

3. Loosen the closure cap screws, but do not remove them.

4. Remove the hexagon screws that attach the stator frame to shield housing. Remove the stator frame with the cover plate, armature and commutator end shield.

5. Remove the cover plate from the surface of the drive end bearing ring gear. Carefully press the armature with the commutator end shield out of the stator frame. At the same time, push out terminal 45 with the sealing rubber.

6. Remove the closure cap screws and remove the closure cap from the commutator end shield. Remove the retaining washer and shims from the armature shaft and remove the commutator end shield.

7. Using the proper tool, remove the brush plate from the armature shaft.

8. Remove the sealing rubber from the bearing pedestal. Remove the planetary gear system with the overruning clutch and fork assembly from the drive end shield. Mount both assemblies onto a suitable mounting base in the verticle position.

9. Using the proper tool, drive the stop ring down the input shaft.

10. With snapring pliers, separate the ends of the retainer far enough to allow removal from the drive shaft without damage. If necessary, carefully remove any burrs or nicks from the drive shaft, otherwise damage to the drive bushing may occur.

Cleaning and Inspection

1. The armature windings, overrunning clutch, and relay must be cleaned with compressed air and a clean dry rag. Other parts, such as screws and the armature shaft may be cleaned with cleaning solvent. Inspect all parts, seals, bushings, and gaskets for wear and damage. Replace all worn parts as required.

2. Inspect the stator frame and permanent magnets for damage. Do not remove the magnets from the stator frame. If the stator frame or magnets are damaged, then replace the stator frame.

3. Loosen and remove the retainer from the planetary gear drive. Remove the ring gear from the drive shaft. Inspect the ring gear for cracks and wear. Check the bushings in the ring gear for excessive play, out of roundness and wear by moving the drive shaft from side to side. Check the drive shaft bushing in the drive end shield and commutator end shield with the proper tool. Inspect the drive shaft in the ring gear for wear or damage. Replace the shaft and ring gear, if worn.

4. Inspect the fork lever and bearing pedestal for damage, replace if necessary. Inspect the bearing bushing in the overrunning clutch for wear. Replace the overrunning clutch, if the bearing bushing is worn.

5. Remove and inspect the carbon brushes for excessive wear. The length of a new brush is 11/16 in.. If the existing brushes are worn more than 1/2 the length of a new brush, or they are oil soaked, replace the existing brushes.

6. Place the drive unit on the armature shaft and support the armature by hand. Grasp the armature and rotate the drive pinion. The drive pinion should rotate smoothly in one direction only. Some resistance may be encountered when rotating the drive pinion; however, as long as the rotation is smooth then the drive unit is in good operating condition. If the clutch unit does not function properly or if the pinion is worn, chipped or burred, then replace the unit.

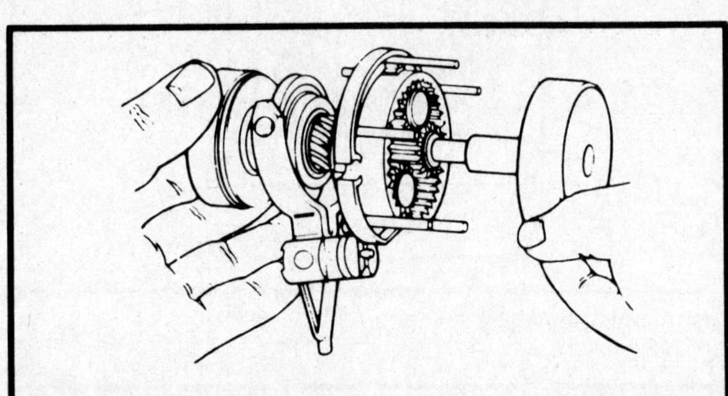

Removal of the overrunning clutch and planetary gear system

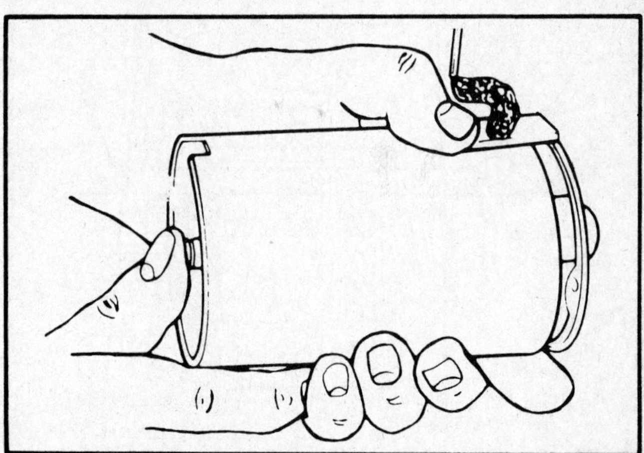

Removal of the armature

Component	Dimension	
Carbon Brushes	Minimum Length – 8mm (0.314-in)	
Ring/Pinion Clearance	0.2-0.3mm (0.78-0.118-in)	
Backlash (Meshed Ring and Pinion)	0.3-0.6mm (0.118-0.236-in)	
Commutator Diameter	**MAXIMUM** 2.3mm (1.27-in)	**MINIMUM** 31.2mm (1.23-in)
Out of Round: Commutator	0.03mm (0.001-in)	
Armature (Core)	0.08mm (0.003-in)	
Armature End Play	0.05mm (0.002-in)	

Specifications Chart

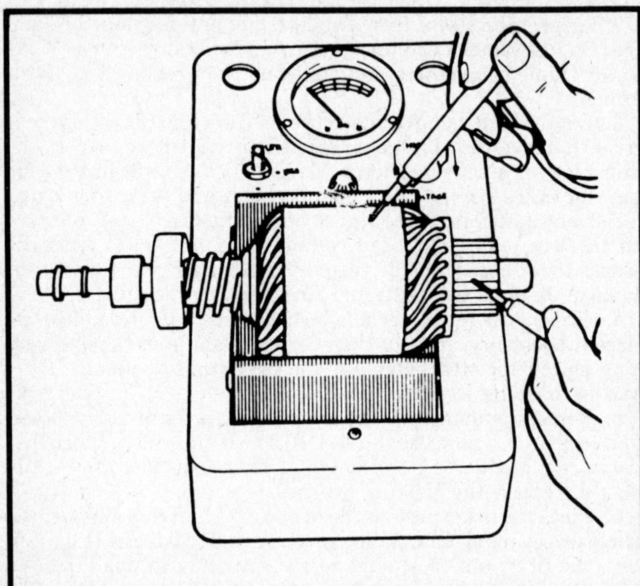
Armature ground test

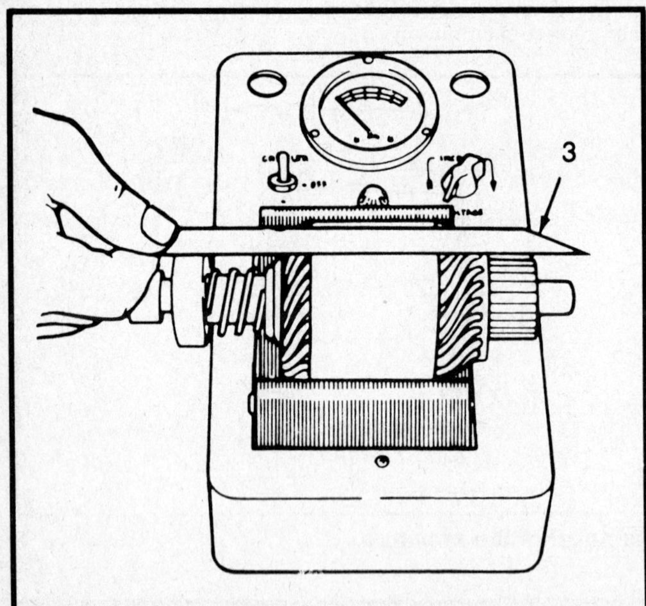

Armature short test

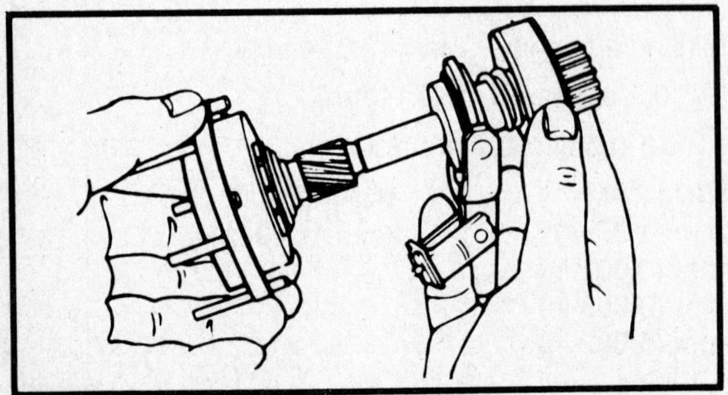
Assembly of the overrunning clutch and planetary gear system

TESTING ALTERNATOR COMPONENTS

Armature Ground Test

1. Position the armature in the growler jaws and turn the power switch to the Test position.
2. Touch one test probe to the armature core (1). Touch the other test probe to each commutator bar (2), one at a time and observe the test lamp. The test lamp should not light. If the test lamp lights on any bar, the armature has a short circuit to ground and must be replaced.

Armature Short Test

CAUTION

Never operate the growler with the power switch in the Test position without the armature in the growler jaws.

1. Place the armature in the growler jaws and turn the power switch to the Growler position.

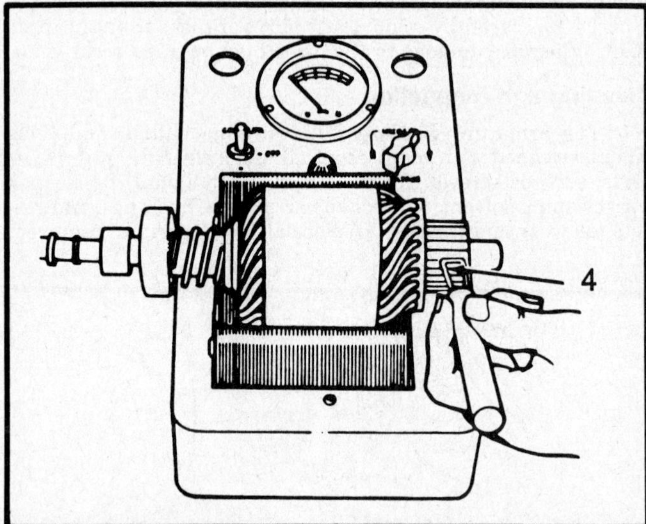

Armature balance test

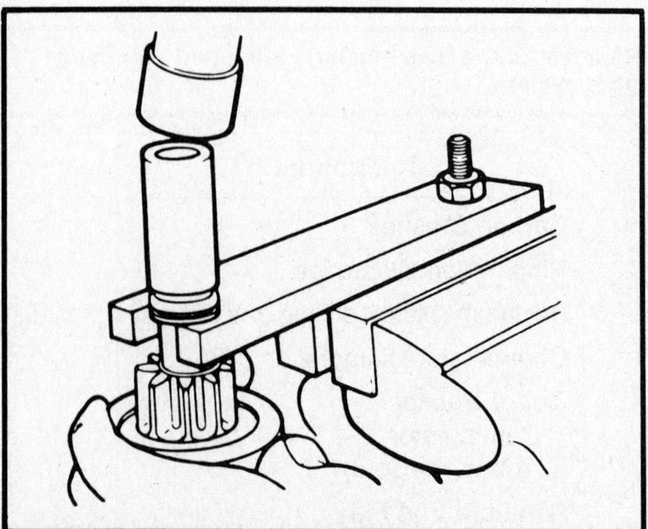
Seating the stop ring

2. Hold the steel blade parallel to and touching, the armature core (3). Slowly rotate the armature one or more revolutions in the growler jaws. If the steel blade vibrates at any one area of the core, the windings have a short circuit and the armature must be replaced.

Armature Balance Test

1. Place the armature in the growler jaws and turn the power switch to the Growler position.
2. Place the contact fingers of the meter test probe (4) across adjacent commutator bars at the side of the commutator.
3. Adjust the voltage control until the pointer indicates the highest voltage on the scale.
4. Test each commutator bar until all bars have been tested. Zero voltage across any pair indicates a short circuit and requires that the armature be replaced.

Armature Runout Test

1.Check that the armature runout is within the range shown on the specifications chart. If the runout is not within tolerance, then replace the armature.

Assembly

1. Place a light film of 20W SAE oil onto the surface of the overrunning clutch pinion bearing surface.

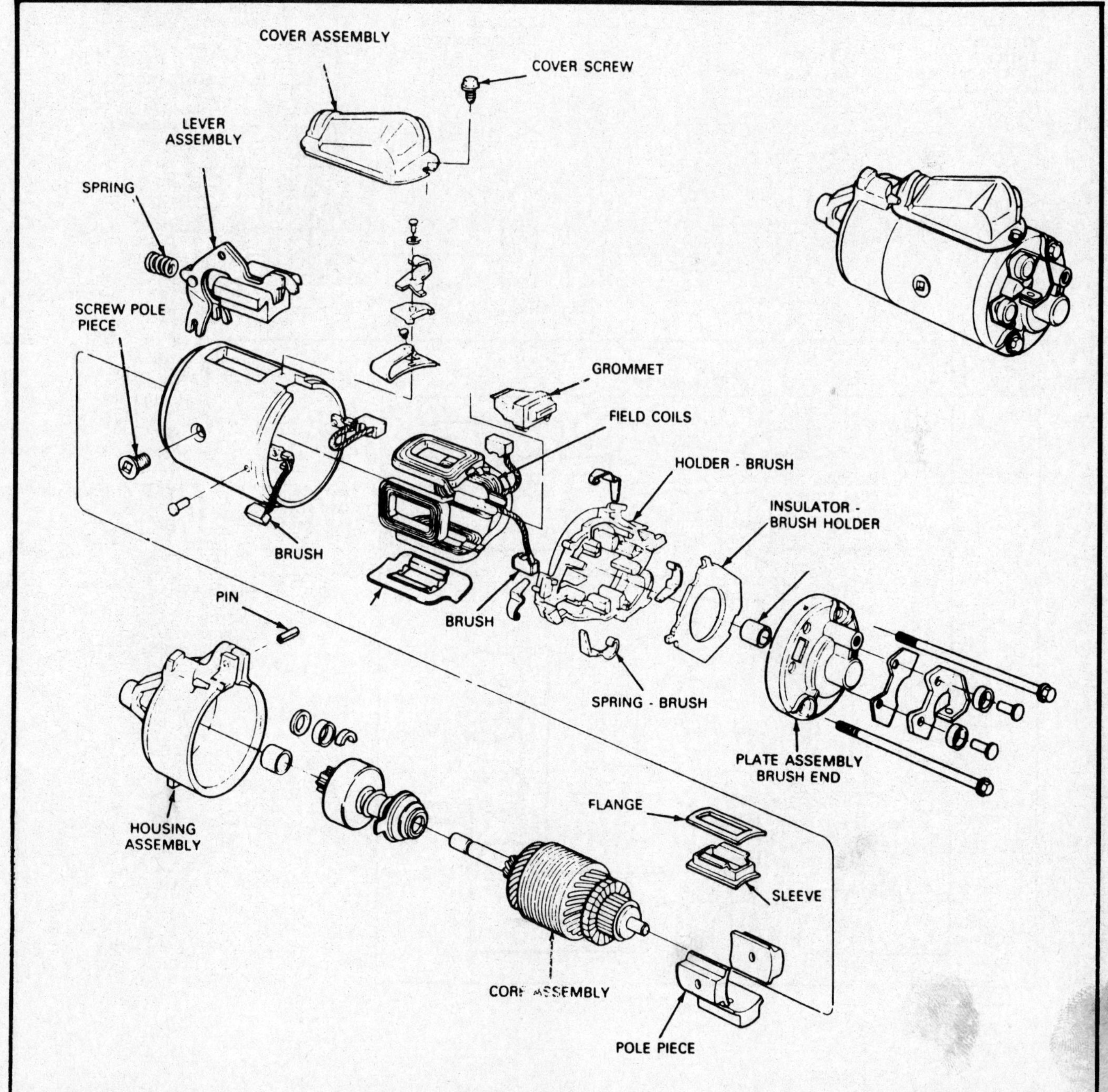

Exploded view of the Motorcraft positive engagement starter motor

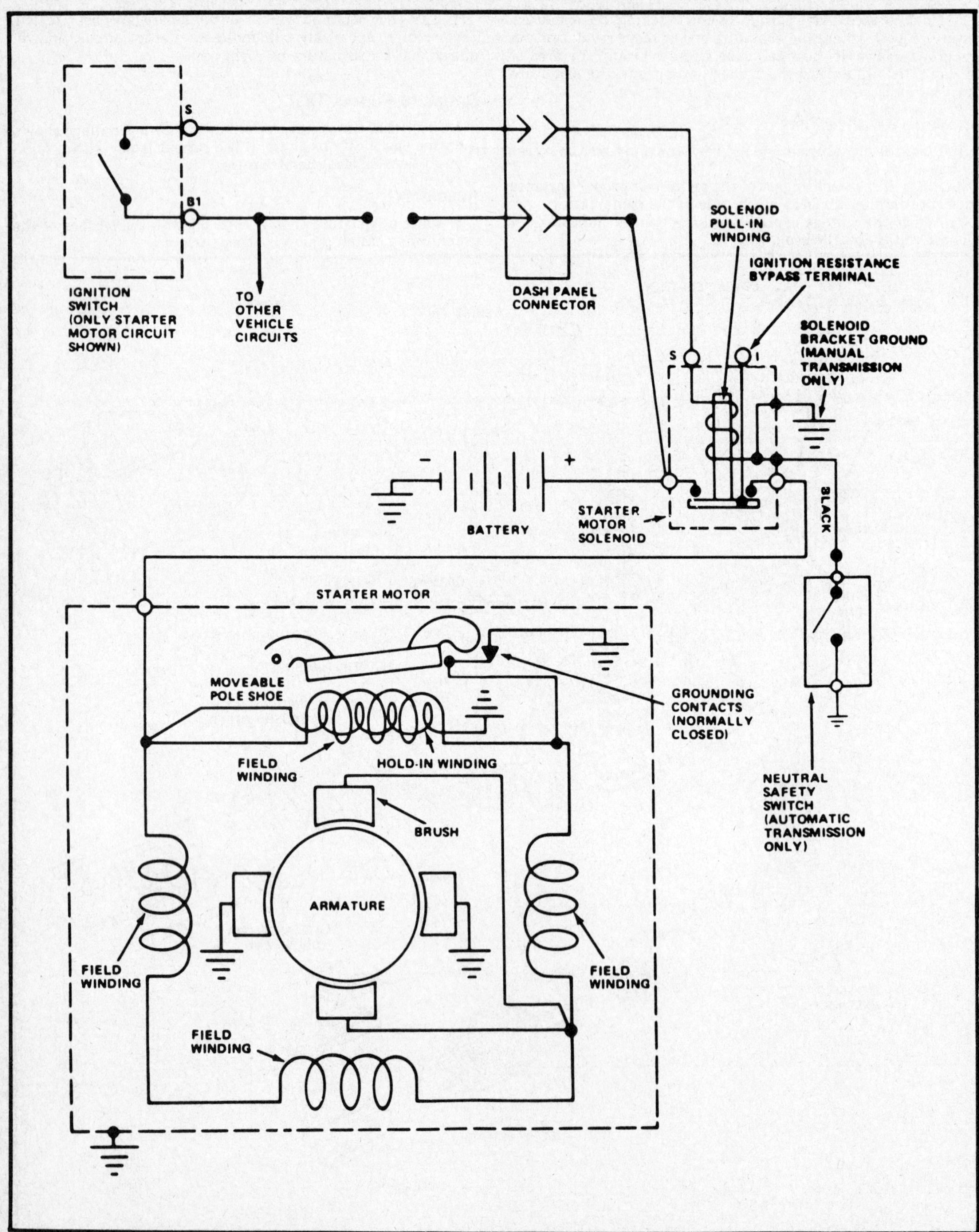

Motorcraft starter motor simplified circuit

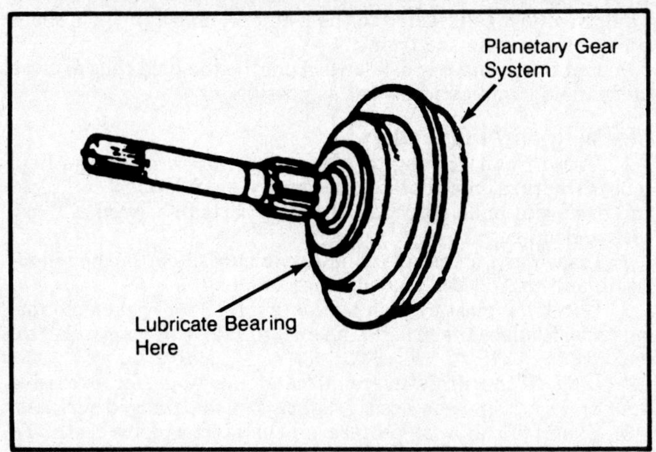

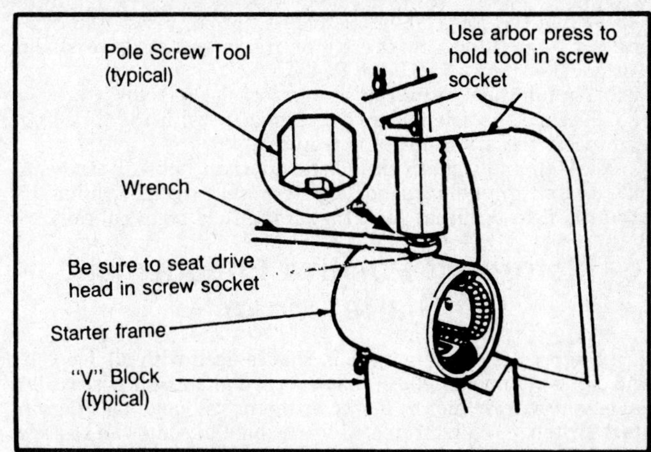

Pole shoe screw removal

2. Lightly grease the planetary gear spiral spline with Lubriplate grease.
3. Slide the overrunning clutch with the fork lever and bearing pedestal onto the drive shaft.
4. Slide the stop ring onto the armature shaft

CAUTION

When installing the retainer, be careful not to scratch the armature shaft.

5. With snapring pliers, separate the ends of the retainer and carefully install onto the groove in the armature shaft.
6. Using the proper tool, seat the stop ring.
7. The planetary gear bearing is located forward of the planetary gears. Lubricate this bearing thoroughly, but lightly, with 20W SAE oil.
8. Insert the planetary gear train with the the pinion, overrunning clutch, fork lever, and bearing pedestal into the drive housing.
9. Install the rubber seal onto the pedestal bearing.
10. Position and install the cover plate on the surface of the ring gear, ensuring that the recess in the cover plate mates with the lug machined in the surface of the ring gear.
11. Using the proper tool, position the brush plate onto the end of the commutator shaft. Slide the brush plate over the commutator, ensuring that the brush holders are properly seated in the anchor point. After the are properly seated, remove the tool.
12. Place a light coat of 20W SAE oil onto the felt ring gasket and install the gasket on the commutator end of the armature shaft.
13. Place a light coat of Lithium-based lubricant onto the commutator end shield bushing and install the bushing onto the armature shaft.
14. Slide the commutator end shield onto the armature shaft.
15. Set the armature endplay by installing one shim and the retaining washer. After installing the shim, check the endplay with the appropriate feeler gauges. The endplay should be within the range of 0.002-0.016 in. Should additional shims be required, three different sizes are available: 0.004 in., 0.047 in. and 0.055 in..
16. After setting the armature endplay, place a light coat of lubricant onto the retaining washer.
17. Position the seal ring against the commutator end shield and place the closure cap into installation position.
18. Install the closure cap screws far enough to hold the closure cap into place, but do not tighten at this time.
19. Support the stator frame by hand and slide the armature with the brush plate and commutator end shield carefully into the stator frame, ensuring that a sufficient gap is left to allow installation of the rubber seal.
20. Install the rubber seal onto Terminal 45 and slide the rubber seal into the groove of the stator frame.
21. With moderate force, rotate the pinion gear until the armature spline meshes evenly with the planetary gears.

NOTE: When positioning the stator frame ensure that the groove in the stator frame is aligned with and fits into the sealing rubber of the bearing pedestal.

22. Rotate the commutator end shield until the groove on the commutator end shield is aligned with the sealing rubber on the bearing pedestal.

Positive Engagement Starter Motor				Starter Brushes				
Dia. mm (Inches)	Current Draw Under Normal Load (Amps)	Normal Engine Cranking Speed (rpm)	Current Draw No. Load (Amps)	Mfg. Length mm (Inches)	Wear Limit mm (Inches)	Spring Tension kg (Ounces)	Through Bolt Torque N·m (In-lbs)	Mounting Bolt Torque N·m (ft-lbs)
101.60 (4)	150-200	180-250	70	12.2 (0.50)	6.35 (0.25)	1.134 (40)	6.21-8.47 (55-75)	21-27 (15-20)
114.30 (4.5)	150-180	150-290	80	12.2 (0.50)	6.35 (0.25)	1.134 (40)	6.21-8.47 (55-75)	21-27 (15-20)
Maximum Commutator runout is 0.1270mm (0.005 inch). Maximum starting circuit voltage drop (battery positive terminal to starter terminal) at normal engine temperature is 0.5 volt.								

Specifications Chart

23. When the proper alignment is achieved, install the hexagon screws that attach the stator frame to the drive shield. Torque the screws to 2.0-2.6 ft. lbs.
24. Torque the closure cap screws to 1.0-1.5 ft. lbs..
25. Engage the solenoid switch armature with the fork lever and insert the armature return spring.
26. Install and tighten the solenoid switch housing screws.
27. Install the field washer and terminal wire (Terminal 45) onto the field terminal post. Install the field terminal nut.

Motorcraft Positive Engagement Starter Motor

The Motorcraft starting system, that is used with all Jeep six- and eight- cylinder engines, consists of a lightweight positive engagement starter motor, a starter motor solenoid, an ignition/start switch, circuits protected by fusible links and the battery. Vehicles equipped with an automatic transmission also have a neutral safety switch to prevent operation of the starter if the selector lever is not in the Neutral or Park position. The Motorcraft starter motor has a moveable pole shoe and appropriate linkage to engage the drive mechanism. Inside the drive assembly, an overrunning clutch prevents the starter motor from being driven by the ring gear.

Disassembly

1. Remove the cover screw, cover, and through bolts.
2. Withdraw the pivot pin that retains the starter gear plunger lever. Remove the plunger lever, starter drive end housing and lever return spring.
3. Remove the stop ring retainer. Remove and discard the the stop ring that retains the starter drive gear to the end of the armature shaft. Remove the starter drive gear assembly.
4. Remove the brush end plate and insulator assembly.
5. Remove the brushes from the plastic brush holder and lift out the brush holder. Note location of brush holder with respect to the end terminal.
6. Remove the two screws or copper rivets that attach the ground brushes to the frame.
7. Locate the field coil that operates the starter drive gear actuating lever. Bend the edges on the retaining sleeve of this field coil and remove the sleeve and retainer.
8. Position the starter frame in an arbor press and remove the three coil retaining screws. Cut the field coil connection at the switch post lead and remove the small diameter ground wire from the upper tab riveted to the frame. Remove the pole shoes and the coils from the frame.
9. Cut the positive brush leads from the the field coils as close to the field connenction point as possible.

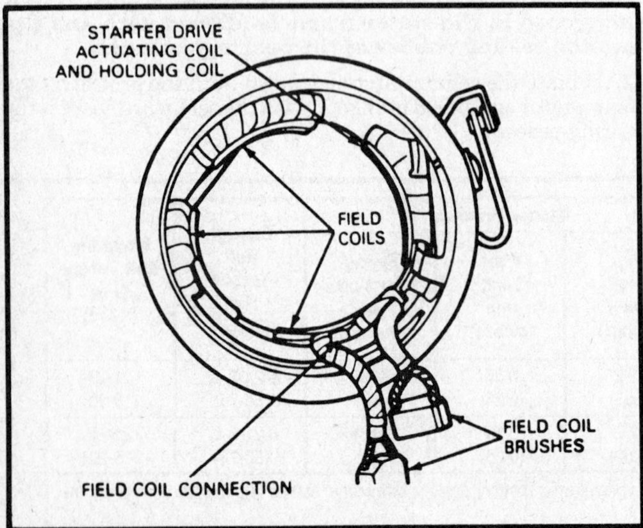

Cleaning and Inspection

1. Use a clean dry rag or compressed air to clean the field coils, armature, commutator, armature shaft, brush end plate and drive end housing. Wash all other parts in solvent and dry with a clean rag.
2. Inspect the armature windings for broken or burned insulation and unsoldered or open connections.
3. Check the plastic brush holder for cracks or broken mounting pads. Replace the brushes if worn to 1/4 in. in length or if oil soaked.
4. Inspect the armature shaft and bushings for excessive wear and scoring. If necessary, lightly polish damaged surfaces.
5. Examine the wear pattern on the starter drive teeth. To eliminate premature starter and ring gear failure, the pinion teeth must penetrate to a depth greater than one-half the ring gear tooth depth.
6. Examine the starter drive gear for milled, pitted or broken teeth. Replace the starter drive if necessary.
7. Inspect the overrunning clutch by grasping and rotating the pinion gear. The pinion gear should rotate smoothly and freely in the clockwise direction and lock in the counter-clockwise direction. Replace if necessary.

TESTING ALTERNATOR COMPONENTS

Hold-In Coil Winding Resistance Test

1. Insert a piece of paper (1) between the contact points to insulate them.
2. With an ohmmeter, measure the resistance between the S-terminal (2) and the starter motor frame. This will determine the resistance of the hold-in coil winding.
3. The resistance should be within the range of 2.0-3.5 ohms. If the resistance is not within this range, replace the field winding assembly.

Solenoid Contact Point Connection Test

1. With an ohmmeter, measure the resistance through solder joint (3). This will determine the integrity of the solder joint at the contacts.
2. A resistance reading greater than zero ohms indicates that the joint is faulty and must be repaired. If repair is required, resolder the joint.

Insulated Brush Connection Test

1. With an ohmmeter, measure the resistance through the solder joint by touching the test probes to the brush (4) and to the copper test bar (3). This will determine the integrity of the solder joint between the the insulated brush braided wire and the field windings.
2. A resistance reading greater than zero ohms indicates that the joint is faulty and must be repaired. If repair is required, resolder the joint.

Field Winding Terminal To Brush Continuity Test

1. Insert a piece of paper (6) between the contact points to insulate them.
2. Touch the test probes to the field winding terminal (7) and to the insulated brush (8). This will determine the integrity of all the field winding solder joints.
3. A resistance reading greater than zero ohms indicates that one or more of the field winding solder joints is faulty. Test each solder joint to identify the faulty joint(s). If repair is required, resolder the joint(s).

Terminal Bracket Insulation Test

1. With an ohmmeter, measure the resistance between the bracket and the cap. This will determine if the terminal bracket is properly insulated from the end cap.
2. If the resistance is less than infinite, then the end cap is faulty and must be replaced.

Armature Ground Test

1. Position the armature in the growler jaws and turn the power switch to the Test position.
2. Touch one test probe to the armature core (1). Touch the other test probe to each commutator bar (2) one at a time and observe the test lamp. The test lamp should not light. If the test lamp lights on any bar, the armature has a short circuit to ground and must be replaced.

Armature Short Test

CAUTION

Never operate the growler with the power switch in the Test position without the armature in the growler jaws.

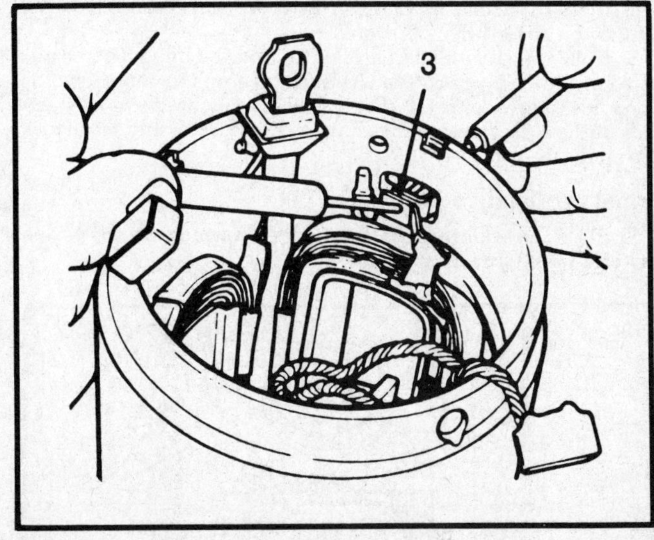

Insulated brush-connection test

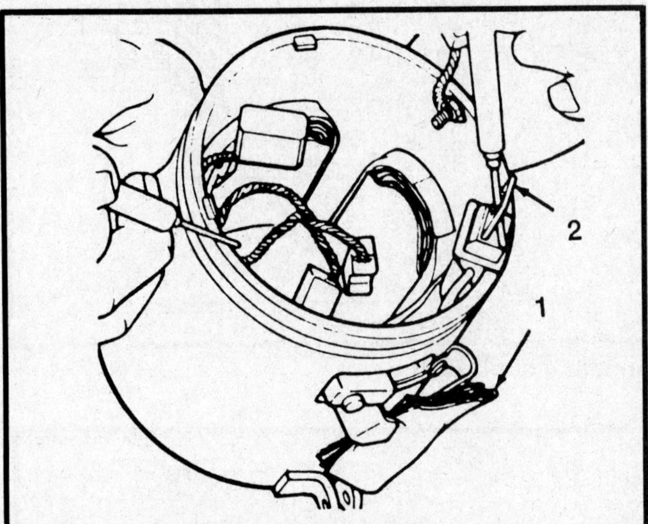

Hold-in coil winding-resistance test

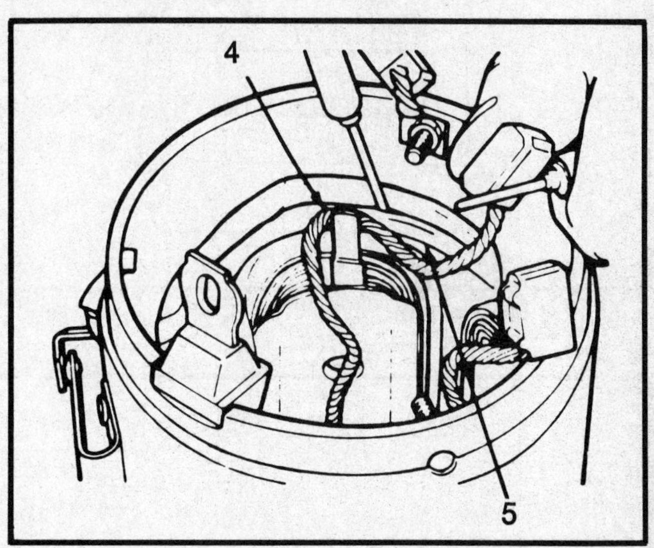

Field winding-terminal to brush continuity test

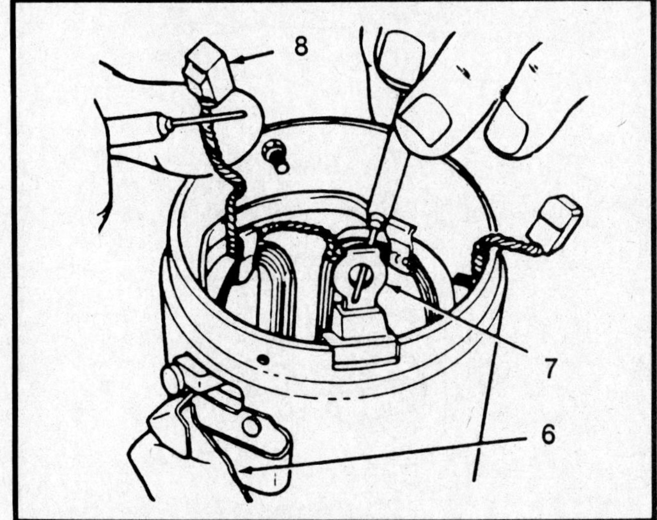

Solenoid Contact-Point Connection test

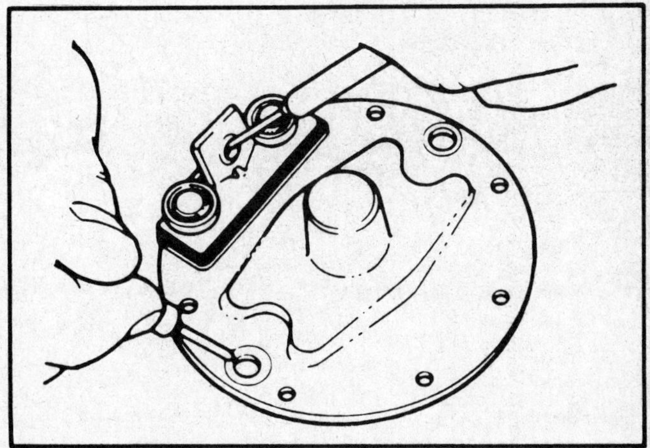

Terminal bracket insulation test

1. Place the armature in the growler jaws and turn the power switch to the Growler position.

2. Hold the steel blade parallel to, and touching, the armature core (3). Slowly rotate the armature one or more revolutions in the growler jaws. If the steel blade vibrates at any one area of the core, the windings have a short circuit and the armature must be replaced.

Armature Balance Test

1. Place the armature in the growler jaws and turn the power switch to the Growler position.

2. Place the contact fingers of the meter test probe (4) across adjacent commutator bars at the side of the commutator.

3. Adjust the voltage control until the pointer indicates the highest voltage on the scale.

4. Test each commutator bar until all bars have been tested. Zero voltage across any pair indicates a short circuit and requires that the armature be replaced.

Armature Runout Test

1. Lightly polish the commutator with commutator cloth prior to measuring runout. Do not use emory cloth.

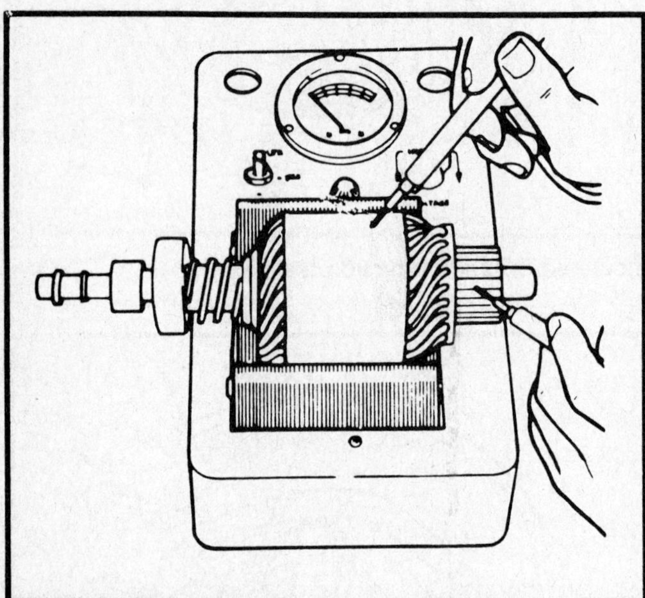

Armature ground test

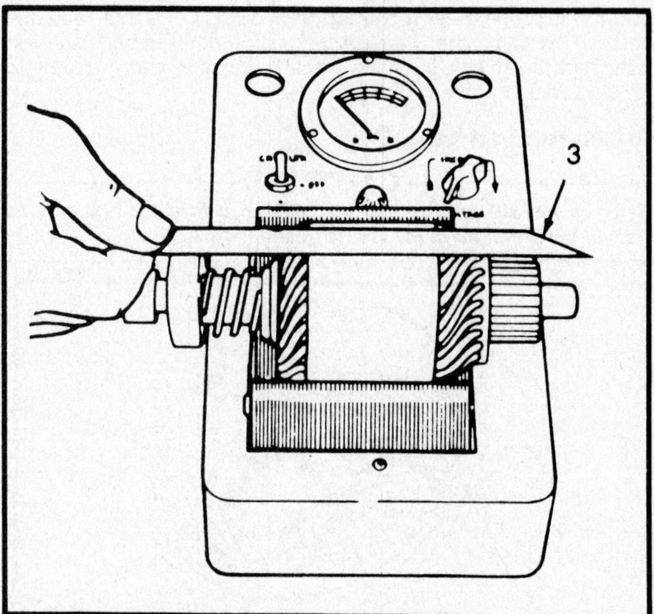

Armature short test

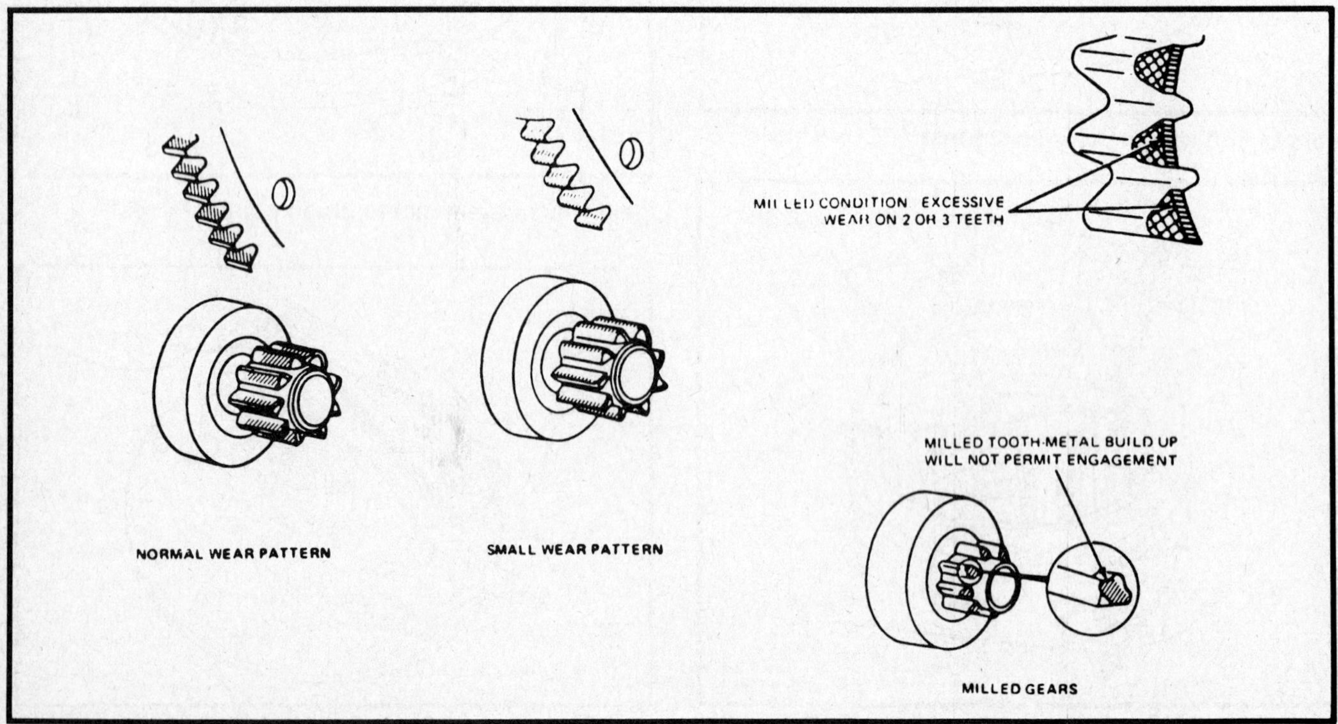

Pinion and ring gear wear patterns

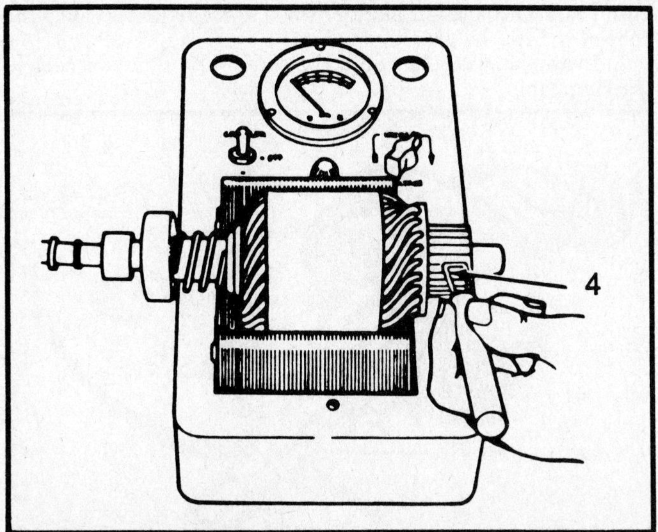

Armature balance test

2. Measure the commutator runnout. If the commutator is greater than 0.005 in. out-of-round or has insulation protruding from between the bars, turn it down on a lathe.

Assembly

1. Position three coils and pole pieces into the stator frame interior and support by hand. Install the pole piece screws.
2. Tighten the pole piece screws evenly and at regular intervals, tap the frame lightly with a soft-faced mallet. This will facilitate the alignment of the screws and the pole pieces.
3. Repeat procedures in step 3. until the screws are securely fastened and the pole pieces are in proper alignment.
4. Install the remaining coil and retainer and bend the tabs to secure the coils to the frame.
5. Solder the field coils and solenoid wire to the starter terminal.
6. Check for continuity and grounds in the assembled coils.
7. Ground the coil, that is located in the area of the retaining sleeve, by positioning the small diameter wire leading from the coil under the copper tab, held by the rivet attaching the contact to the frame.
8. Attach the ground brushes to the starter frame with the screws or rivets.
9. Apply a thin coating of Lubriplate or equivalent to the armature shaft splines. Install the starter motor drive gear assembly to the armature shaft and install a new retaining stop ring. Install a new stop retainer.
10. Install the armature assembly into the starter frame.
11. Fill the drive end housing bearing bore $\frac{1}{4}$ in. with lubricant. Position the starter drive gear plunger lever to the frame and starter drive assembly.
12. Position the starter drive plunger lever return spring and the drive end housing to the frame.
13. Install the brush holder and insert the brushes and springs into their respective positons. Position and install the brush holder insulator.

NOTE: When installing the end plate,do not to pinch or crimp the brush leads.

14. Position the end plate to the frame ensuring that the plate locater is aligned with the frame slot. Install the thru-bolts and torque them to 55-75 inch lbs.. Install the pivot pin.
15. Thoroughly clean the sealing surface of the lever cover to remove any traces of existing gasket material. Apply rubber gasket compound or equivalent to the sealing surface of the lever cover. Position the lever cover on the frame and secure with the attaching screw.

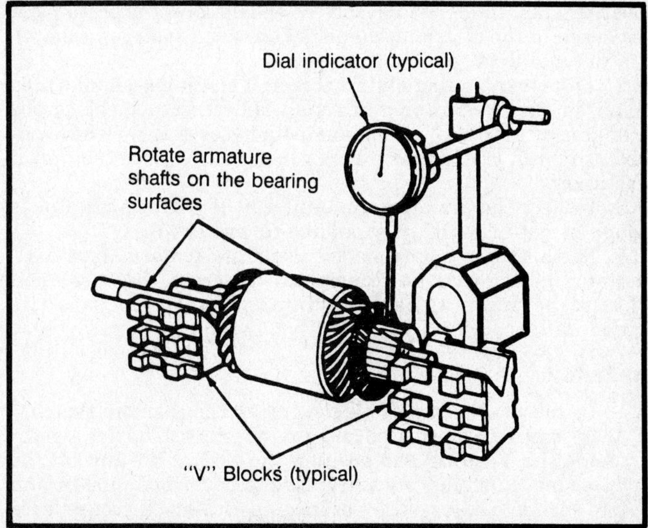

Commutator runout check

16. Check the starter no-load current draw.

Delco Remy Starter Motor

The Delco-Remy starter system consists of the starter motor, relay, ignition/start switch, battery and associated electrical wiring. Automobiles equipped with an automatic transmission incorporate a neutral safety switch that provides a ground for the starter motor relay when the selector lever is in either the Neutral or Park position. If equipped with a manual transmission, a jumper wire attached to back-up lamp connector provides a ground for the starter motor relay.
The field windings are permanently mounted in the motor frame. The number of field windings used varies according to starter model type and engine displacement. In the basic circuit, the solenoid is energized when the ignition starting switch is closed. The resulting plunger and shift lever movement causes the pinion gear to engage the flywheel (or drive plate) ring gear while closing the solenoid main contacts; therefore initiating engine cranking. When the engine starts, the pinion gear overrun clutch protects the armature from excessive speed until the switch is opened, at which time the return spring disengages the pinion gear.

Disassembly

1. Disconnect the field winding connection from the solenoid switch terminal.
2. Remove the through-bolts.
3. Remove the commutator and field frame assembly.
4. Remove the solenoid and shift lever assembly from the drive end housing.
5.Withdraw the armature assembly from the drive end housing.
6. Remove the thrust collar from the armature shaft.
7. To remove the pinion stop retainer ring, position a $\frac{1}{4}$ in. pipe coupling onto the armature shaft and flush against the retainer. Strike the coupling with a hammer to drive the retainer toward the armature core and away from the snap ring.
8. With snap ring pliers, separate and remove the snap ring from the groove in the armature shaft.
9. Remove the overrunning clutch from the armature shaft.
10. Remove the brush holder from the brush support. Remove the screw from the brush holder and separate the brush and holder.

CLEANING AND INSPECTION

1. Do not immerse the parts in solvent. Clean all parts with a

clean dry rag. Immersion in solvent will dissolve the grease that is packed in the clutch mechanism and cause damage to the armature and field coil insulation.

2. Test overrunning clutch action. The pinion should turn freely in the overrunning direction and must not slip in the cranking direction. Check pinion teeth to see that they have not been chipped, cracked, or excessively worn. Replace the unit if necessary.

3. Inspect the armature commutator. If the commutator is rough or out of round, it should be turned down.

4. Some starter motor models use a molded armature commutator design and no attempt to undercut the insulation should be made as serious damage may result to the commutator.

Assembly

1. Install brushes into holders. Install the solenoid switch.
2. Assemble the insulated and grounded brush holder together using the V-spring and position the assembled unit on the support pin. Push holders and spring to bottom of support and rotate spring to engage the slot in support. Attach ground wire to grounded brush and field lead wire to insulated brush, then repeat for remaining brush sets.
3. Assemble overrunning clutch to armature shaft as follows. Lubricate drive end of shaft with silicone lubricant.
4. Slide the clutch assembly onto the armature shaft with the pinion facing outward.
5. Slide the retainer onto the shaft with cupped surface facing away from pinion.
6. Stand the armature on a wood surface, commutator downwards. Position snap ring on upper end of the shaft and drive it onto shaft with a small block of wood and a hammer. Slide the snap ring into the groove.
7. Install thrust collar onto the shaft with shoulder next to the snap ring.

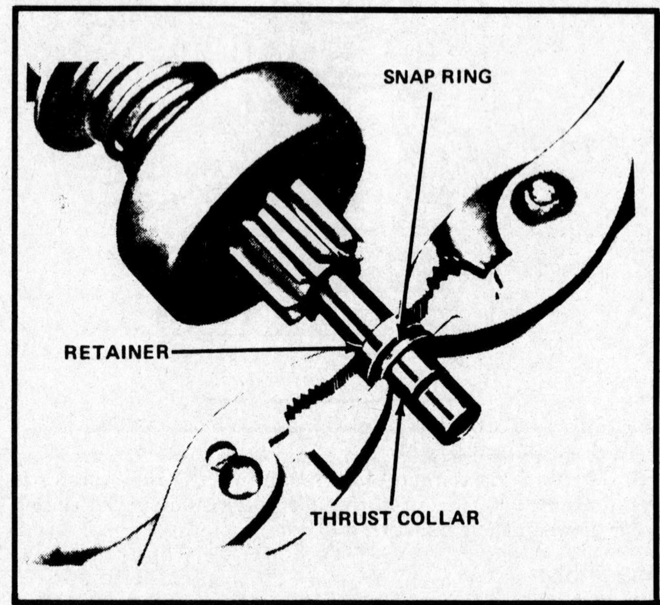

Installing the retainer

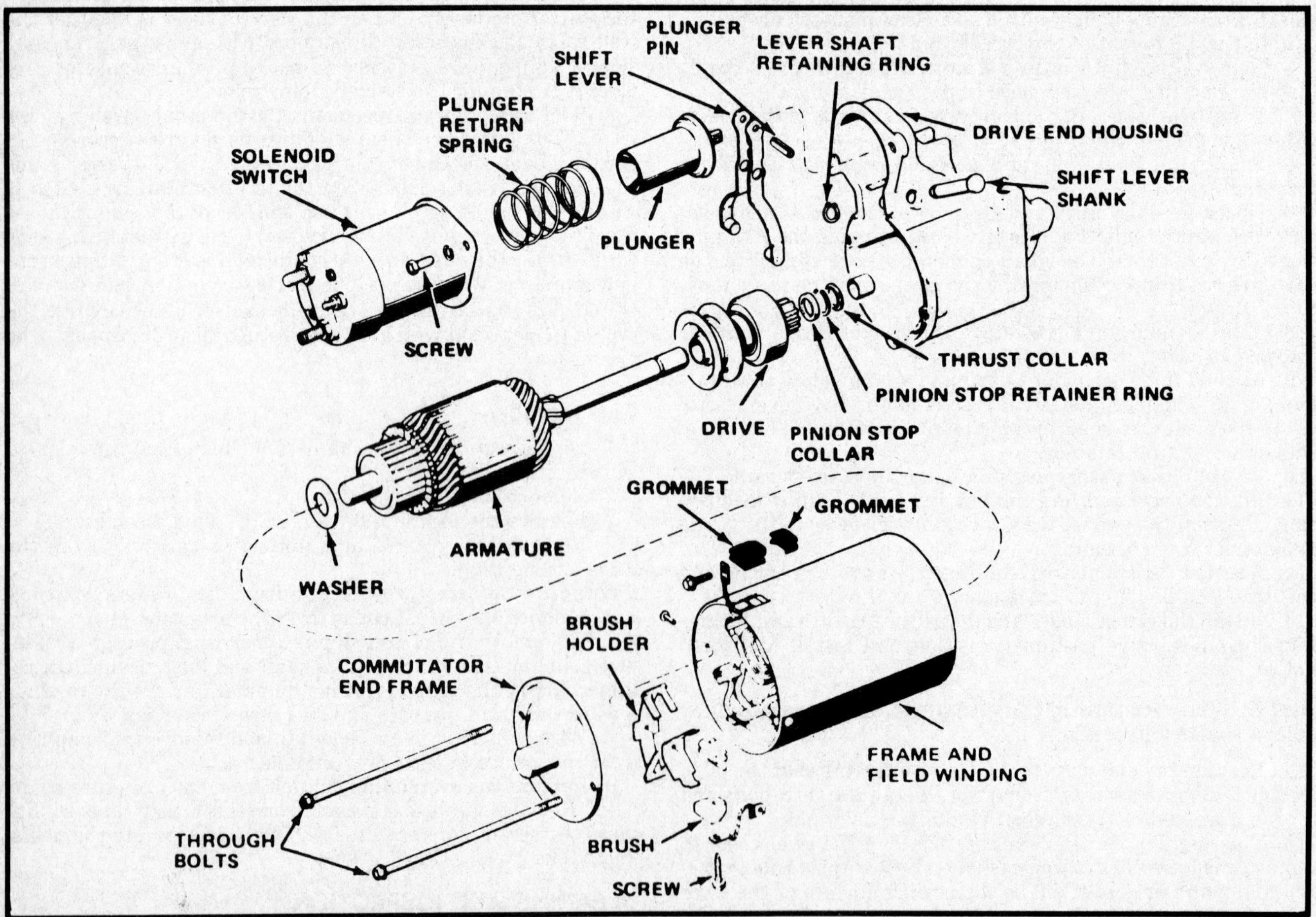

Exploded view of the Delco-Remy 5MT starter motor

8. With retainer on one side of snap ring and thrust collar on the other side, squeeze together with two sets of pliers until the snap ring seats in retainer. On models without thrust collar, use a washer. Remember to remove washer before continuing.

9. Lubricate drive end bushing with silicone lubricant, then slide the armature and clutch assembly into place, at the same time engaging the shift lever with clutch. Tighten all screws securely.

10. Position field frame over armature and apply sealer (silicone) between frame and solenoid case. Position frame against drive housing, making sure brushes are not damaged in the process.

11. Lubricate the commutator end bushing with silicone lubricant. Place a leather brake washer on the armature shaft (commutator end). Slide the commutator end frame onto the shaft. Install the through bolts and tighten to 65 inch lbs.

12. Reconnect field coil connector(s) to the solenoid motor terminal. Install solenoid mounting screws, if so equipped.

13. Check pinion clearance; it should be 0.010 to 0.140 in. on all models.

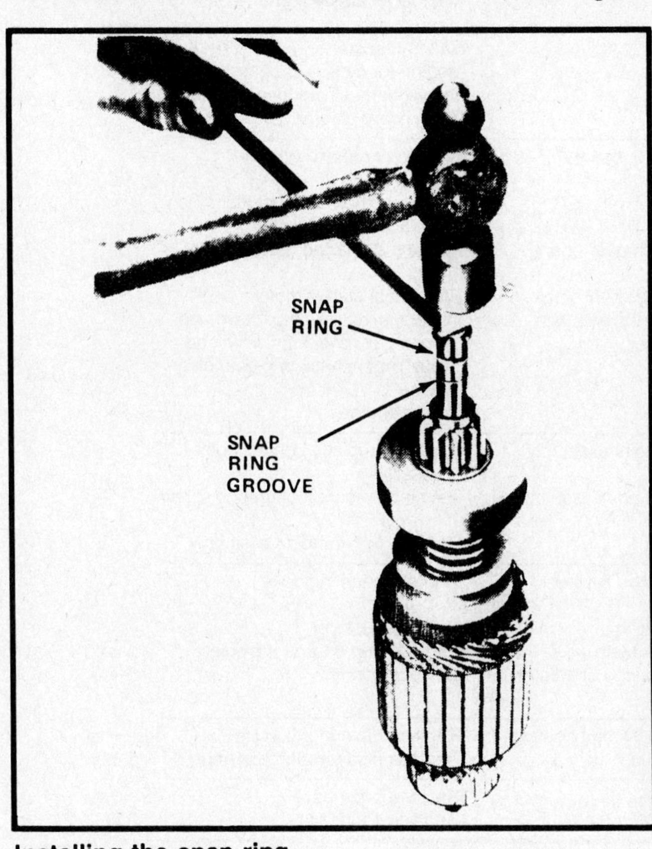

Installing the snap ring

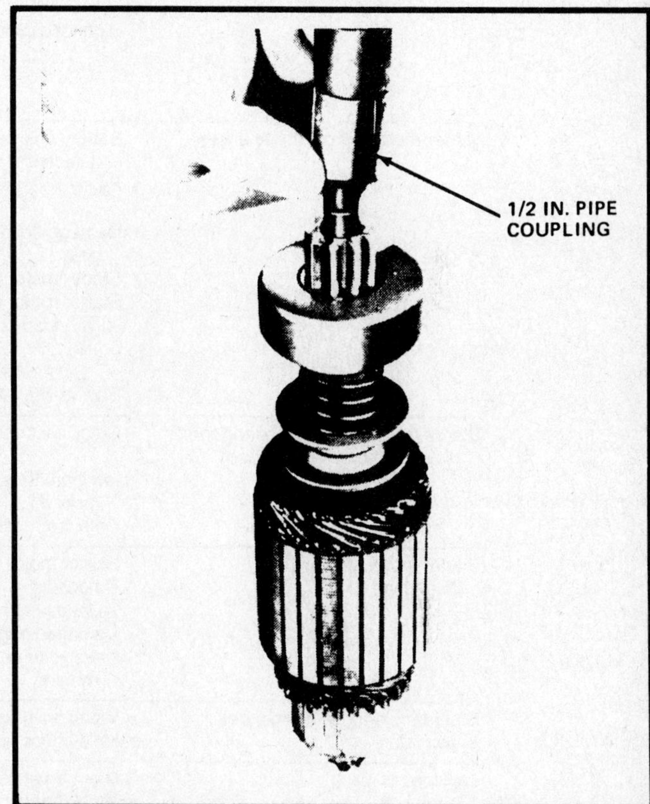

Removal of the retainer

Troubleshooting Basic Starting System Problems

Problem	Cause	Solution
Starter motor rotates engine slowly	· Battery charge low or battery defective · Defective circuit between battery and starter motor · Low load current · High load current	· Charge or replace battery · Clean and tighten, or replace cables · Bench-test starter motor. Inspect for worn brushes and weak brush springs. · Bench-test starter motor. Check engine for friction, drag or coolant in cylinders. Check ring gear-to-pinion gear clearance.
Starter motor will not rotate engine	· Battery charge low or battery defective · Faulty solenoid · Damage drive pinion gear or ring gear · Starter motor engagement weak · Starter motor rotates slowly with high load current · Engine seized	· Charge or replace battery · Check solenoid ground. Repair or replace as necessary. · Replace damaged gear(s) · Bench-test starter motor · Inspect drive yoke pull-down and point gap, check for worn end bushings, check ring gear clearance · Repair engine
Starter motor drive will not engage (solenoid known to be good)	· Defective contact point assembly · Inadequate contact point assembly ground · Defective hold-in coil	· Repair or replace contact point assembly · Repair connection at ground screw · Replace field winding assembly
Starter motor drive will not disengage	· Starter motor loose on flywheel housing · Worn drive end busing · Damaged ring gear teeth · Drive yoke return spring broken or missing	· Tighten mounting bolts · Replace bushing · Replace ring gear or driveplate · Replace spring
Starter motor drive disengages prematurely	· Weak drive assembly thrust spring · Hold-in coil defective	· Replace drive mechanism · Replace field winding assembly
Low load current	· Worn brushes · Weak brush springs	· Replace brushes · Replace springs

Brakes
Domestic Trucks

INDEX

DOMESTIC LIGHT TRUCKS 1982-87

Year, Make, Model	Brake Shoe* Minimum Lining Thickness	Brake Drum Diameter Standard Size	Brake Drum Diameter Machine To	Brake Pad Minimum Lining Thickness	Brake Rotor Min. Thickness Machine To	Brake Rotor Min. Thickness Discard At	Brake Rotor Variation From Parallelism	Brake Rotor Runout T.I.R.	DESIGN	Caliper Mounting Bolts Torque (ft-lbs)	Caliper Bridge, Pin or Key Bolts Torque (ft-lbs)	Wheel Lugs or Nuts Torque (ft-lbs)	Wheel Bearing Setting STEP 1 Tighten Spindle Nut (ft-lbs)	Wheel Bearing Setting STEP 2 Back Off Retorque (in-lbs)	Wheel Bearing Setting STEP 3 Lock, or Back Off and Lock
AMERICAN MOTORS—JEEP															
82-86 CJ, Scrambler	.030*	10.000	10.060	.062	—	.815	.001	.005	1	—	30	75	50	Skip	1/6 Turn
82-87 (Full Size) Cherokee, Wagoneer, J-10	.030*	11.000	11.060	.062	—	1.215	.001	.005	4	35	30	75	50	Skip	1/6 Turn
82-87 J-20	.030*	12.000	12.060	.062	—	1.215	.001	.005	4	35	30	75■	50	Skip	1/6 Turn
84-87 (Sportwagon) Cherokee, Wagoneer, Comanche	.030	10.000	10.060	.030	—	.815	—	.004	1	77	25-35	75	•	•	•
87 Wrangler	.030	10.000	10.060	.030	—	.815	—	.004	1	77	25-35	75	•	•	•

* .030″ over rivet head, if bonded lining use .062″
■ J20 (8400 GVW) 130 ft/lbs.
• torque hub bolts to 75 ft/lbs., torque hub nut to 175 ft/lbs.

Year, Make, Model	Brake Shoe* Minimum Lining Thickness	Brake Drum Diameter Standard Size	Brake Drum Diameter Machine To	Brake Pad Minimum Lining Thickness	Brake Rotor Min. Thickness Machine To	Brake Rotor Min. Thickness Discard At	Brake Rotor Variation From Parallelism	Brake Rotor Runout T.I.R.	DESIGN	Caliper Mounting Bolts Torque (ft-lbs)	Caliper Bridge, Pin or Key Bolts Torque (ft-lbs)	Wheel Lugs or Nuts Torque (ft-lbs)	Wheel Bearing Setting STEP 1 Tighten Spindle Nut (ft-lbs)	Wheel Bearing Setting STEP 2 Back Off Retorque (in-lbs)	Wheel Bearing Setting STEP 3 Lock, or Back Off and Lock
CHRYSLER CORP.—DODGE, PLYMOUTH															
82-83 D100/150 exc. w/9 1/4″ R. axle	.030	10.000	10.060	.030	1.220	1.190	.0005	.004	5	110	17	105	8	Handtight	Step 2
82-85 B100/150, PB100/150															
w/10″ rear brakes	.030	10.000	10.060	.030	1.220	1.190	.0005	.004	5	95-125	14-22	85-125	30-40	Handtight	Step 2
w/11″ rear brakes	.030	11.000	11.060	.030	1.220	1.190	.0005	.004	5	95-125	14-22	85-125	30-40	Handtight	Step 2
82-83 B200/250, PB200/250	.030	10.000	10.060	.030	1.220	1.190	.0005	.004	5	95-125	14-22	85-125	30-40	Handtight	Step 2
82-83 Ramcharger, Trail Duster															
4 x 2	.030	10.000	10.060	.030	1.220	1.190	.0005	.004	5	110	17	105	8	Handtight	Step 2
4 x 4	.030	10.000	10.060	.030	1.220	1.190	.001	.005	5	150	17	105	50	360-480	1/3 Turn
82-83 W150/W100	.030	10.000	10.060	.030	1.220	1.190	.001	.005	5	150	17	105	50	360-480	1/3 Turn
82-85 B300/350, CB 300/350, PB300/350															
w/3600 lb. F.A.	.030	12.000	12.060	.030	1.220	1.190	.0005	.004	4	95-125■	14-22	85-125	30-40	Handtight	Step 2
w/4000 lb. F.A.	.030	12.000	12.060	.030	1.160	1.130	.0005	.004	5	95-125■	14-22	175-225	30-40	Handtight	Step 2
82-87 D200/250 w/4000 lb. F.A., D300/350	.030	12.000	12.060	.030	1.160	1.130	.001	.005	5	160	17	105•	8	Handtight	Step 2
82-87 W200/250 Exc. w/Spicer 60	.030	12.000	12.060	.030	1.160	1.130	.001	.005	5	150	17	105	50	360-480	1/3 Turn
82-87 W200/250 w/Spicer 60, W300/350	.030	12.000	12.060	.030	1.160	1.130	.001	.005	21	160	15	105•	50	360-480	1/3 Turn
82-87 D200/250 w/3300 lb. F.A.	.030	12.000	12.060	.030	1.220	1.190	.001	.005	5	110	17	105	8	Handtight	Step 2
82 Rampage	.030	7.780	7.900	.030	.461	.431	.0005	.004	8	70-100	25-40	85	20-25	Handtight	Step 2

DOMESTIC LIGHT TRUCKS 1982-87

Year Make, Model	Brake Shoe* Minimum Lining Thickness	Brake Drum Diameter Standard Size	Brake Drum Diameter Machine To	Brake Pad Minimum Lining Thickness	Brake Rotor Min. Thickness Machine To	Brake Rotor Min. Thickness Discard At	Brake Rotor Variation From Parallelism	Brake Rotor Runout T.I.R.	DESIGN	Caliper Mounting Bolts Torque (ft-lbs)	Caliper Bridge, Pin or Key Bolts Torque (ft-lbs)	Wheel Lugs or Nuts Torque (ft-lbs)	Wheel Bearing Setting STEP 1 Tighten Spindle Nut (ft-lbs)	Wheel Bearing Setting STEP 2 Back Off Retorque (in-lbs)	Wheel Bearing Setting STEP 3 Lock, or Back Off and Lock
83-84 Rampage, Scamp	.030	7.874	7.904	.030	.461	.431	.0005	.004	8	130-190	25-35	80††	20-25	Handtight	Step 2
84-85 B250, PB250	.030	11.000	11.060	.030	1.220	1.190	.0005	.004	5	95-125	14-22	85-125	30-40	Handtight	Step 2
84-87 Caravan, Mini Ram Van, Voyager	.030	9.000	9.060	.030*	.833	.803	.0005	.005	8	130-190	25-35	95	20-25	Handtight	Step 2
84-87 Ramcharger 4 x 2	.030	11.000	11.060	.030	1.220	1.190	.0005	.004	5	110	17	105	8	Handtight	Step 2
4 x 4	.030	11.000	11.060	.030	1.220	1.190	.001	.005	5	150	17	105	50	360-480	1/3 Turn
84-87 D150	.030	11.000	11.060	.030	1.220	1.190	.0005	.004	5	110	17	105	8	Handtight	Step 2
84-87 W150	.030	11.000	11.060	.030	1.220	1.190	.001	.005	2	150	17	105	50	360-480	1/3 Turn
86-87 B150, B250	.030	11.000	11.060	.125▲	1.210	1.180	.0005	.004	5	95-125	15	85-110	30-40	Handtight	Step 2
87 Dakota 4x2															
w/9" rear brks.	.030	9.000	9.060	.030	.841	.811	.0005	.004	8	95-125	18-26	85	30-40	Handtight	Step 2
w/10" rear brks.	.030	10.000	10.060	.030	.841	.811	.0005	.004	8	95-125	18-26	85	30-40	Handtight	Step 2
87 Dakota 4x4															
w/9" rear brks.	.030	9.000	9.060	.030	.841	.811	.0005	.004	51	—	18-26	85		Not Adjustable	
w/10" rear brks.	.030	10.000	10.060	.030	.841	.811	.0005	.004	51	—	18-26	85		Not Adjustable	
87 B350 w/3600 lb. F.A.	.030	12.000	12.060	.125▲	1.210	1.180	.0005	.004	5	95-125■	15	85-110	30-40	Handtight	Step 2
w/4000 lb. F.A.	.030	12.000	12.060	.125▲	1.155	1.125	.0005	.004	5	95-125■	15	175-225+	30-40	Handtight	Step 2

• 5/8" whl. stud (82-87) 200 ft/lbs.
■ 5/8" bolt 140-180 ft/lbs.
† 2 or 5
+ w/cone type nut; w/flanged 300-350 ft/lbs.
* .030" over rivet head; if bonded lining, use .062".
†† 1984-95 ft/lbs.
▲ 1987 combined shoe & lining thickness .3125

DOMESTIC LIGHT TRUCKS 1982–87

Year, Make, Model	Brake Shoe* Minimum Lining Thickness	Brake Drum Diameter Standard Size	Brake Drum Diameter Machine To	Brake Pad Minimum Lining Thickness	Brake Rotor Min. Thickness Machine To	Brake Rotor Min. Thickness Discard At	Brake Rotor Variation From Parallelism	Brake Rotor Runout T.I.R.	DESIGN	Caliper Mounting Bolts Torque (ft-lbs)	Caliper Bridge, Pin or Key Bolts Torque (ft-lbs)	Wheel Lugs or Nuts Torque (ft-lbs)	Wheel Bearing Setting STEP 1 Tighten Spindle Nut (ft-lbs)	STEP 2 Back Off Retorque (in-lbs)	STEP 3 Lock, or Back Off and Lock
FORD MOTOR CO.															
82–85 F100, F150, E100, E150	.030	11.031	11.091	.030	—	1.120	.0007	.003	1	—	12–20	90	22–25	Skip	1/8 Turn
82–85 F250 (6900 GVW std.)	.030	12.000	12.060	.030	—	1.120	.0007	.003	1	—	12–20	90	22–25	Skip	1/8 Turn
82–85 F250 (6900 GVW H.D.), F350, E250, E350	.030	12.000	12.060	.030	—	1.180	.0007	.003	19	74–102	12–20 ★	90■	22–25	Skip	1/8 Turn
82–83 F100 w/46–4900 GVW	.030	10.000	10.060	.030	—	.810	.0005	.003	1	—	12–20	90	22–25	Skip	1/8 Turn
82 F250 (4x4)	.030	12.000	12.060	.030	—	1.180	.0007	.003	19	74–102	12–20 ★	90	50	Skip	90°
82 F350 (4x4)	.030	12.000	12.060	.030	—	1.180	.0007	.003	19	74–102	12–20 ★	90■	50	372–468	135°/150°
82–85 Bronco	.030	11.031	11.091	.030	—	1.120	.0007	.003	1	74–102	12–20	90	50	Skip	45°
82–85 F100, F150, F250 w/Dana 44IFS Front Axle (4x4)	.030	11.031	11.091	.030	—	1.120	.0007	.003	1	74–102	12–20	90	50	Skip	45°
83–85 F250 Exc. Dana 44IFS Front Axle (4x4), F350 (4x4)	.030	12.000	12.060	.030	—	1.180	.0007	.003	19	74–102	12–20 ★	100■	50	372–468	135°/150°
83–87 Ranger, 4x2, Bronco II 4x2	.030	9.000	9.060	.030	—	.810	.001 +	.003	59	—	32–47††	85–115	17–25	10–15	Step 2
83–87 Bronco II 4x4, Ranger 4x4	.030	9.000	9.060	.030	—	.810	.001 +	.003	59	—	—	85–115	35	90°	16 in/lbs.
86–87 E/F150, Bronco															
(4x2)	.030	11.031	11.091	.030	—	1.120	.0005‡	.003	1	—	—	100†	22–25	Skip	1/8 Turn
(4x4)	.030	11.031	11.091	.030	—	1.120	.0007▲	.005▲	1	—	—	100†	70	90°•	15 ft/lbs
86–87 E/F250, 350 (4x2)															
w/Single Rear Wheels	.030	12.000	12.060	.030	—	1.180	.0007	.003	19	—	—	140	22–25	Skip	1/8 Turn
w/Dual Rear Wheels	.030	12.000	12.060	.030	—	1.180	.001	.005▲	19	—	—	140	22–25	Skip	1/8 Turn
86–87 F250, 350 (4x4)															
w/Dana 44IFS axle	.030	12.000	12.060	.030	—	1.180	.001	.005	19	—	—	140	70	90°•	15 ft/lbs.
exc./Dana 44IFS axle	.030	12.000	12.060	.030	—	1.180	.001	.005	19	—	—	140	50	372–468	135°/150°
86–87 Aerostar w/9″ rear brakes	.030	9.000	9.060	.030	.980	.810	.001	.003	59	—	—	85–115	17–25	18–20	Skip
w/10″ rear brakes	.030	10.000	10.060	.030	.980	.810	.001	.003	59	—	—	85–115	17–25	18–20	Skip

★ Caliper bridge bolt 155–185 ft/lbs.
■ (1985) 140 ft/lbs. 350 w/single rear whls. (82–84) 145 ft/lbs., (82–84) 220 ft/lbs.
• 1986 45°
† 1986 90 ft/lbs.
‡ 1986 .0007
▲ 1986 .001
▲ 1986 .010
†† 1983 only.
+ 1987 .0005

DOMESTIC LIGHT TRUCKS 1982–87

Year, Make, Model	Brake Shoe* Minimum Lining Thickness	Brake Drum Diameter Standard Size	Brake Drum Diameter Machine To	Brake Pad Minimum Lining Thickness	Brake Rotor Min. Thickness Machine To	Brake Rotor Min. Thickness Discard At	Brake Rotor Variation From Parallelism	Brake Rotor Runout T.I.R.	DESIGN	Caliper Mounting Bolts Torque (ft-lbs)	Caliper Bridge, Pin or Key Bolts Torque (ft-lbs)	Wheel Lugs or Nuts Torque (ft-lbs)	Wheel Bearing Setting STEP 1 Tighten Spindle Nut (ft-lbs)	Wheel Bearing Setting STEP 2 Back Off Retorque (in-lbs)	Wheel Bearing Setting STEP 3 Lock, or Back Off and Lock
GENERAL MOTORS CORP.															
82 Blazer, Jimmy (4x2)	.062	11.150	11.210	.030	1.230	1.215	.0005	.004	4	—	35	75–100	12	Handtight	1/2 Flat
(4x4)	.062	11.150	11.210	.030	1.230	1.215	.0005	.004	4	—	35	70–90	50	420	3/8 Turn
82–87 Suburban, C,G,R, 10/15															
w/1.0" rotor.															
w/11" brakes	.062	11.000	11.060	.030	.980	.965	.0005	.004	4	—	35	75–100	12	Handtight	1/2 Flat
w/11 1/8" rear brakes	.062	11.150	11.210	.030	.980	.965	.0005	.004	4	—	35	75–100	12	Handtight	1/2 Flat
w/1.25" rotor															
w/11" rear brakes	.062	11.000	11.060	.030	1.230	1.215	.0005	.004	4	—	35	75–100	12	Handtight	1/2 Flat
w/11 1/8" rear brakes	.062	11.150	11.210	.030	1.230	1.215	.0005	.004	4	—	35	75–100	12	Handtight	1/2 Flat
82–87 Suburban, C,G,R, 20/25, 30/35 under 8600 GVW															
w/11 1/8" rear brakes	.062	11.150	11.210	.030	1.230	1.215	.0005	.004	4	—	35	90–120□	12	Handtight	1/2 Flat
w/13" rear brakes	.062	13.000	13.060	.030	1.230	1.215	.0005	.004	4	—	35	90–120□	12	Handtight	1/2 Flat
82–87 C,G,R 30/35 over 8600 GVW	.062	13.000	13.060	.030	1.480	1.465	.0005	.004	4	—	10–15	90–120•	12	Handtight	1/2 Flat
82–87 K,V 10/15, 20/25															
w/11 1/8" rear brakes	.062	11.150	11.210	.030	1.230	1.215	.0005	.004	4	—	35	70–90■	50	420+	3/8 Turn
w/13" rear brakes	.062	13.000	13.060	.030	1.230	1.215	.0005	.004	4	—	35	70–90■	50	420+	3/8 Turn
82–87 K,V 30/35	.062	13.000	13.060	.030	1.480	1.465	.0005	.004	4	—	35	90–120•	50	420+	3/8 Turn
82–87 S,T 10/15	.062	9.500	9.560	.030	.980	.965	.0005	.004	4	—	21–37	80†	12★	Handtight	1/2 Flat
83–87 Blazer, Jimmy (S, T Series)	.062	9.500	9.560	.030	.980	.965	.0005	.004	4	—	21–37	80†	12★	Handtight	1/2 Flat
83–87 Blazer, Jimmy (K, V Series)	.062	11.150	11.210	.030	1.230	1.215	.0005	.004	4	—	21–35	70–90■	50	420+	3/8 Turn
85–87 Astro Van	.030	9.500	9.560	.030	.980	.965	.0005	.004	4	—	30–45	90	12	Handtight	1/2 Flat

+ w/Auto hub shown; w/Manual 600 in/lbs.
□ G 20/25, K,V 10/15 is 75–100 ft/lbs.
• w/8 bolt whl. 110–140 ft/lbs., w/10 bolt whl. 130–200 ft/lbs.
■ Blazer, Jimmy, K,V 10/15 w/Alum. wheels 100 ft/lbs., K,V 20/25 is 90–120 ft/lbs.
† 1987–90 ft/lbs., 1983–86 4x2 std. shown, 4x2 & 4x4 w/1/2" bolt; 100 ft/lbs.
★ 4x2 only, 4x4 non adjustable

HYDRAULIC BRAKE SYSTEM TROUBLE DIAGNOSIS

Condition	Possible Cause	Correction
Insufficient brakes	1. Improper brake adjustment.	1. Adjust brakes.
	2. Worn lining.	2. Replace brake lining and adjust brakes.
	3. Sticking brakes.	3. Lubricate brake pivots and support platforms.
	4. Brake valve pressure low.	4. Inspect for leaks and obstructed brake lines.
	5. Slack adjuster to diaphragm rod not adjusted properly.	5. Adjust slack adjuster.
	6. Master cylinder low on brake fluid.	6. Fill master cylinder and inspect for leaks.
Brakes apply slowly	1. Improper brake adjustment or lack of lubrication.	1. Adjust brakes and lubricate linkage.
	2. Low air pressure.	2. Check belt tension and compressor for output. Adjust as necessary.
	3. Brake valve delivery pressure low.	3. Check valve pressure and clean or replace as necessary.
	4. Excessive leakage with brakes applied.	4. Inspect all fittings and lines for leaks and repair as necessary.
	5. Restriction in brake line or hose.	5. Clean or replace brake line or hose.
Spongy pedal	1. Air in hydraulic system.	1. Fill and bleed hydraulic system.
	2. Swollen rubber parts due to contaminated brake fluid.	2. Clean hydraulic system and recondition wheel cylinders and master cylinder.
	3. Improper brake shoe adjustment.	3. Adjust brakes.
	4. Brake fluid with low boiling point.	4. Flush hydraulic system and refill with proper brake fluid.
	5. Brake drums ground excessively.	5. Replace brake drums.
Erratic brakes	1. Linings soaked with grease or brake fluid.	1. Correct the leak and replace brake lining.
	2. Primary and secondary shoes mounted in wrong position.	2. Match the primary and secondary shoes and mount in proper position.
Chattering brakes	1. Improper adjustment of brake shoes.	1. Adjust brakes.
	2. Loose front wheel bearings.	2. Clean, pack and adjust wheel bearings.
	3. Hard spots in brake drums.	3. Grind or replace brake drums.
	4. Out-of-round brake drums.	4. Grind or replace brake drums.
	5. Grease or brake fluid on lining.	5. Correct leak and replace brake lining.
Squealing brakes	1. Incorrect lining.	1. Install correct lining.
	2. Distorted brakedrum.	2. Grind or replace brake drum.
	3. Bent brake support plate.	3. Replace brake support plate.
	4. Bent brake shoes.	4. Replace brake shoes.
	5. Foreign material embedded in brake lining.	5. Replace brake shoes.
	6. Dust or dirt in brake drum.	6. Use compressed air and blow out drums and support plate and shoes.
	7. Shoes dragging on support plate.	7. Sand support plate platforms and lubricate.
	8. Loose support plate.	8. Tighten support plate attaching nuts.
	9. Loose anchor bolts.	9. Tighten anchor bolts.
	10. Loose lining on brake shoes or improperly ground lining.	10. Replace brake shoes and cam-grind lining.
Brakes fading	1. Improper brake adjustment.	1. Adjust brakes correctly.
	2. Improper brake lining.	2. Replace brake lining.
	3. Improper type of brake fluid.	3. Drain, flush and refill hydraulic system.
	4. Brake drums ground excessively.	4. Replace brake drums.
Dragging brakes	1. Improper brake adjustment.	1. Correct adjust brakes.
	2. Distorted cylinder cups.	2. Recondition or replace cylinder.
	3. Brake shoe seized on anchor bolt.	3. Clean and lubricate anchor bolt.
	4. Broken brake shoe return spring.	4. Replace brake shoe return spring.
	5. Loose anchor bolt.	5. Adjust and tighten anchor bolt.
	6. Distorted brake shoe.	6. Replace defective brake shoes.
	7. Loose wheel bearings.	7. Lubricate and adjust wheel bearings.

HYDRAULIC BRAKE SYSTEM TROUBLE DIAGNOSIS

Condition	Possible Cause	Correction
Dragging brakes	8. Obstruction in brake line. 9. Swollen cups in wheel cylinder or master cylinder. 10. Master cylinder linkage improperly adjusted.	8. Clean or replace brake line. 9. Recondition wheel or master cylinder. 10. Correctly adjust master cylinder linkage.
Hard pedal	1. Incorrect brake lining. 2. Incorrect brake adjustment. 3. Frozen brake pedal linkage. 4. Restricted brake line or hose.	1. Install matched brake lining. 2. Adjust brakes and check fluid. 3. Free up and lubricate brake linkage. 4. Clean out or replace brake line hose.
Wheel locks	1. Loose or torn brake lining. 2. Incorrect wheel bearing adjustment. 3. Wheel cylinder cups sticking. 4. Saturated brake lining.	1. Replace brake lining. 2. Clean, pack and adjust wheel bearings. 3. Recondition or replace the wheel cylinder. 4. Reline front, rear or all four brakes.
Brakes fade (high speed)	1. Improper brake adjustment. 2. Distorted or out of round brake drums. 3. Overheated brake drums. 4. Incorrect brake fluid (low boiling temperature). 5. Saturated brake lining.	1. Adjust brakes and check fluid. 2. Grind or replace the drums. 3. Inspect for dragging brakes. 4. Drain flush and refill and bleed the hydraulic brake system. 5. Reline brakes as necessary.

HYDRAULIC SYSTEM SERVICE

Basic Hydraulic System

The hydraulic system controls the braking operation and consists of a master cylinder, hydraulic lines and hoses, control valves and calipers and/or wheel cylinders. When the brake pedal is depressed, the master cylinder forces brake fluid to the calipers and/or cylinders, via lines and hoses. Sliding rubber seals contain the fluid and prevent leakage.

Return springs in the master cylinder help the brake pedal return to the original unapplied position. Check valves (in most cases) regulate the return flow of the fluid to the master cylinder. Other valves, such as the metering valve, proportioning valve, or combination valve, regulate the flow of fluid to the caliper/wheel cylinder, to achieve efficient braking.

Single Braking Systems

On single brake systems, the master cylinder has only one piston which operates all of the wheel cylinders. The single brake system is confined to over the road vehicles above 10000 lbs. GVW, industrial and construction equipment.

Dual Braking Systems

The "dual"system differs from the "single" system by employing a "tandem" master cylinder, essentially two master cylinders (usually) formed by aligning two separate pistons and fluid reservoirs into one cylinder bore. Dual brake lines "split" the calipers and/or wheel cylinders into two groups, each actuated by a separate master cylinder piston. In event of failure of one of the "dual" systems, the other should provide enough braking power to safely stop the vehicle. The dual system usually includes a red warning light on the instrument panel which is activated by a pressure differential valve. The valve is sensitive to any loss of hydraulic pressure that might result from a braking failure on either side of the system.

Light trucks are equipped with either a front/rear wheel "split" or a diagonally "split" system. On front/rear systems, the front wheels are connected to one circuit while the rear wheels are connected to the other circuit. Diagonally split systems have diagonally opposite wheels connected to each circuit. Medium and heavy trucks may use the front/rear split or, if equipped with two wheel cylinders per wheel, each circuit will operate one cylinder per wheel.

General Information

Servicing the hydraulic brake system is chiefly a matter of adjustments, replacement of worn or damaged parts and correcting the damage caused by grit, dirt or contaminated brake fluid. Always make sure the brake system is clean and tightly sealed when a brake job is completed and that only approved heavy duty brake fluid is used.

The approved heavy duty type brake fluid retains the correct consistency throughout the widest range of temperature variation, will not affect rubber cups, helps protect the metal parts of the brake system against failure and assures long trouble free brake operation.

Never use brake fluid from a container that has been used for any other liquid. Mineral oil, alcohol, antifreeze, or cleaning solvents, even in very small quantities, will contaminate brake fluid. Contaminated brake fluid will cause piston cups and the valve(s) in the master cylinder to swell or deteriorate.

Brake adjustment is required after installation of new or relined brake shoes. Adjustment is also necessary whenever excessive travel of pedal is needed to start braking action.

LOW PEDAL

Normal brake lining wear reduces pedal reserve. Low pedal reserve may also be caused by the lack of brake fluid in the master cylinder. The wear condition may be compensated for by a minor brake adjustment. Check fluid level in master cylinder and add as required.

FLUID LOSS

If the master cylinder requires constant addition of hydraulic fluid, fluid may be leaking past the piston cups in the master cylinder or brake cylinders, the hydraulic lines; hoses or connections may be loose or broken. Loose connections should be tightened, or other necessary repairs or parts replacement made and the hydraulic brake system bled.

FLUID CONTAMINATION

To determine if contamination exists in the brake fluid, as indicated by swollen, deteriorated rubber cups, the following tests can be made.

Place a small amount of the drained brake fluid into a small clear glass bottle. Separation of the fluid into distinct layers will indicate mineral oil content. Be safe and discard old brake fluid that has been bled from the system. Fluid drained from the bleeding operation may contain dirt particles or other contamination and should not be reused.

BRAKE ADJUSTMENT

Self adjusting brakes usually do not require manual adjustment but in the event of a brake reline it may be advisable to make the initial adjustment manually to speed up adjusting time.

AUTOMATIC ADJUSTER CHECK

Raise and safely support the vehicle, have a helper in the driver's seat to apply brakes. Remove the plug from the adjustment slot to observe adjuster star wheel. Then, to exclude possibility of maximum adjustment which is, the adjuster refuses to operate because the closest possible adjustment has been reached; the star wheel should be backed off approximately 30 notches. It will be necessary to hold adjuster lever away from star wheel to allow backing off of the adjustment.

Spin the wheel and brake drum in reverse direction and apply brakes vigorously. This will provide the necessary inertia to cause the secondary brake shoe to leave the anchor. The wrap up effect will move the secondary shoe, and a cable or link will pull the adjuster lever away from the starwheel teeth. Upon release of brake pedal, the lever should snap back in position, turning star wheel. Thus, a definite rotation of adjuster star wheel can be observed if automatic adjuster is working properly. If by the described procedure one or more automatic adjusters do not function properly, the respective drum must be removed for adjuster servicing.

HYDRAULIC LINE REPAIR

Steel tubing is used in the hydraulic lines between the master cylinder and the front brake tube connector, and between the rear brake tube connector and the rear brake cylinders. Flexible hoses connect the brake tube to the front brake cylinders or calipers and to the rear brake tube connector.

When replacing hydraulic brake tubing, hoses, or connectors, tighten all connections securely. After replacement, bleed the brake system at the wheel cylinders or calipers and at the booster, if equipped with a bleeder screw.

BRAKE TUBE

If a section of the brake tube becomes damaged, the entire section should be replaced with tubing of the same type, size, shape, and length. Copper tubing should not be used in the hydraulic system. When bending brake tubing to fit the frame or rearaxle contours, be careful not to kink or crack the tube.

All brake tubing should be double flared to provide good leak proof connections. Always clean the inside of a new brake tube with clean isopropyl alcohol.

BRAKE HOSE

A flexible brake hose should be replaced if it shows signs of softening, cracking, or other damage.

When installing a new brake hose, position the hose to avoid contact with other vehicle components.

Hydraulic Control Valves

PRESSURE DIFFERENTIAL VALVE

Also known as a "warning valve", "dash-lamp valve" or "system effectiveness indicator". The valve activates a panel warning lamp in event of pressure loss failure. As pressure fails in one "split" system, the other system's normal pressure causes a piston in the switch to compress a spring and move until an electrical circuit is completed lighting the dash lamp. On some vehicles the spring balanced piston automatically recenters when the brake pedal is released, thus flashing the warning lamp only during brake application. On other vehicles the lamp will stay on until the cause of pressure loss is corrected.

Valves (pressure differential, metering or proportioning) may be located separately, but are usually part of a combination valve. On some brake systems the valve and switch are part of the master cylinder.

Resetting Valves

The pressure differential valve on many vehicles (equipped with a combination valve) will re-center automatically upon brake application after repairs to the system are completed. Other systems require manual resetting. Repair system as required, open a bleeder screw in the half of the system that did not fail. Turn on the ignition to light the warning lamp and slowly depress the brake pedal until the lamp goes out. If too much pressure is applied the piston will go to the other side and the procedure will have to be reversed by opening a bleeder screw in the opposite half of the system.

METERING VALVE

Often used on vehicles equipped with front disc and rear drum brakes, the metering valve improves braking balance during light brake applications by preventing application of the front disc brakes until pressure is built-up in the hydraulic system. The built up hydraulic pressure overcomes the tension of the rear brake shoe return springs. Thus, when the front brake pads contact the rotor the rear brakes shoes move outward to contact the brake drum at the same time.

The metering valve should be inspected whenever the brakes are serviced. A slight amount of moisture inside the boot does not indicate a defective valve, however a great deal of fluid indicates a worn valve and replacement is indicated. Make sure to install the brake lines in the correct ports when installing a new valve, crossed lines will cause the rear brakes to drag.

If a pressure bleeder is used to bleed a hydraulic system that includes a metering valve, the valve stem (inside the boot on some valves) must either be pushed in or pulled out, depending upon the type of valve. Never apply excessive pressure that might damage the valve. Never use a solid block or clamp to force the valve open. If the valve must be blocked, rig the stem with a yieldable spring load and take care not to exert more than normal pressure.

If the brakes are to be bled manually using the brake pedal,

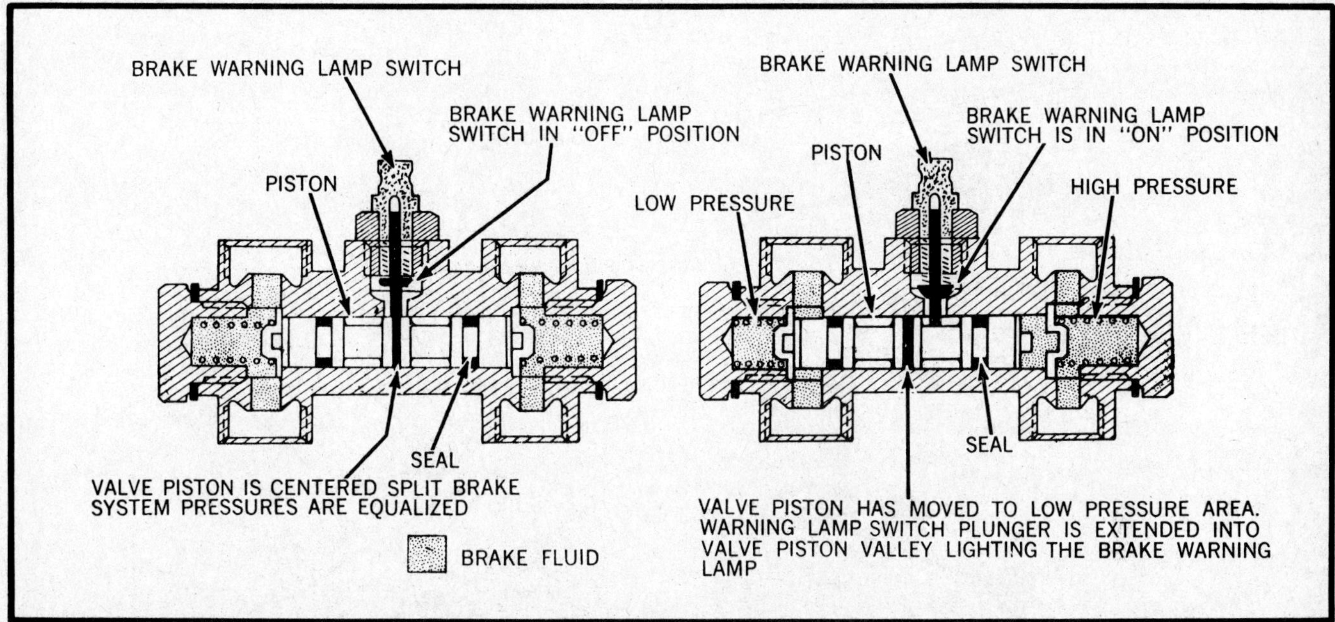

Differential valve system with split hydraulic brakes

the pressure developed is sufficient to overcome the metering valve and the stem need not be pushed in or pulled out.

PROPORTIONING VALVE

Used on vehicles equipped with front disc and rear drum brakes, the proportioning valve is installed in the line(s) to the rear drum brakes, and in a split system, below the pressure differential valve. By reducing pressure to the rear drum brakes, the valve helps to prevent premature lock-up during severe brake application and provides better braking balance.

Whenever the brakes are serviced, the valve should be inspected. To check valve operation, install hydraulic gauges ahead and behind the valve and determine that it has an operative transition point above which rear brake pressure is proportioned. If the valve is leaking replacement is required. Make sure the valve port marked "R" is connected to the rear brake line(s).

COMBINATION VALVE

A valve combining two or three functions (metering, proportioning, and/or brake warning) may be used. The combination valve is usually mounted under the hood close to the master cylinder, where the brake lines can be easily routed to the front and rear wheels. The combination valve is a non-serviceable unit, and if found to be malfunctioning, must be replaced as a unit.

Master Cylinder Service

CLEANING AND INSPECTION

Thoroughly clean the master cylinder and any other parts to be reused in clean alcohol. DO NOT USE PETROLEUM PRODUCTS FOR CLEANING. If the bore is not badly scored, rusted or corroded, it is possible to rebuild the master cylinder in some cases. A slight bit of honing is permissible to clean up and smooth out the bore. A master cylinder rebuilding kit and fresh fluid should be used. If the cylinder bore is badly pitted or corroded, or if it has been rebuilt before, the master cylinder should be replaced with a new one. Do not hone or repair a scratched or pitted bore of an aluminum master cylinder. Replace the master cylinder. Be sure to note the relative positions of all the parts, paying particular attention to the way the rubber cups are facing. Lubricate all new rubber parts with brake fluid or brake system assembly lubricant.

Cast Iron Bore Cleanup

Crocus cloth or an approved cylinder hone should be used to remove lightly pitted, scored, or corroded areas from the bore. Brake fluid can be used as a lubricant while honing lightly. The master cylinder should be replaced if it cannot be cleaned up readily. After using the crocus cloth or a hone, the master cylinder should be thoroughly washed in clean alcohol or brake fluid to remove all dust and grit. If alcohol is used, dry parts thoroughly before reinstalling. Other solvents should not be used. Check the clearance between the bore wall and the piston (primary piston of a dual system master cylinder) it should be as follows. If a narrow $1/8$ in. to $1/4$ in. wide. If a 0.006 in. feeler gauge can be inserted between the wall and a new piston, the clearance is excessive, and the master cylinder should be replaced. The maximum clearance allowed for units containing pistons without replenishing holes is 0.009 in.

Aluminum Bore Cleanup

Inspect the bore for scoring, corrosion and pitting. If the bore is scored or badly pitted and corroded the assembly should be replaced. Under no conditions should the bore be cleaned with an abrasive material. This will remove the wear and corrosion resistant anodized surface. Clean the bore with a clean piece of cloth around a wooden dowel and wash thoroughly with alcohol. Do not confuse bore discoloration or staining with corrosion.

Quick Take Up (GMC)

Disassembly and Assembly

1. Depress the primary piston and remove the snapring.
2. Remove the primary and secondary pistons and return springs from the cylinder bore.
3. Disassemble the secondary piston.
4. Inspect the master cylinder bore. If it is corroded, replace the master cylinder. Never use abrasives on the bore.

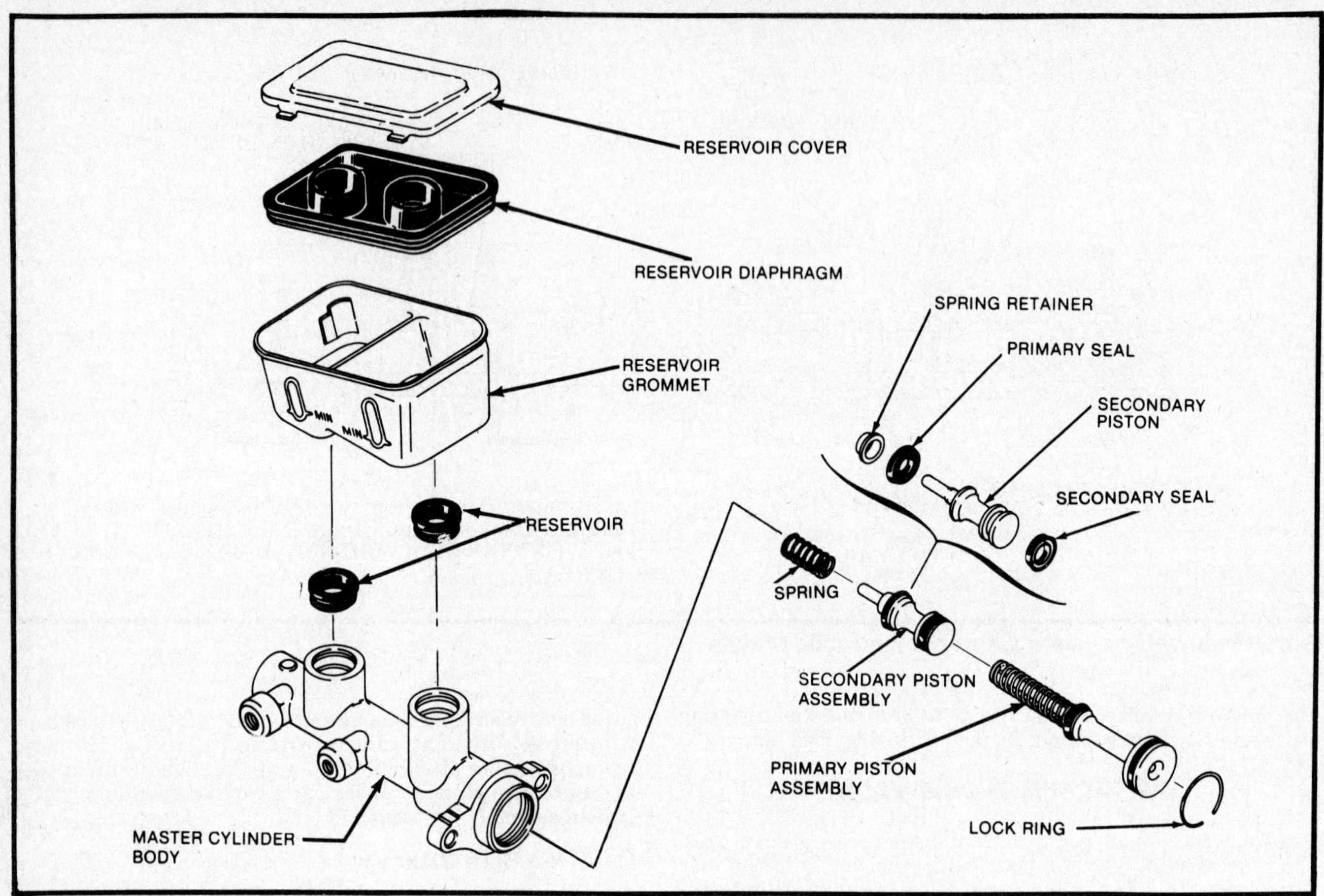

Quick take up master cylinder

NOTE: Always lubricate parts with clean, fresh brake fluid before assembly.

5. Install new seals on the secondary piston.
6. Install the spring and secondary piston into the cylinder.
7. Install the primary piston, depress and install the snapring.

Bendix Mini-Master

Disassembly and Assembly

1. Remove the reservoir cover and diaphragm, and drain the fluid from the reservoir.
2. Remove the four bolts that secure the body to the reservoir using special tool J–25085 or equivalent.

NOTE: Do not remove the two small filters from the inside of the reservoir unless they are damaged and are to be replaced.

3. Remove the small O-ring and the two compensating valve seals from the recessed areas on the bottom side of the reservoir.
4. Depress the primary piston using a tool with a smooth round end. Then remove the compensating valve poppets and the compensating valve springs from the compensating valve ports in the master cylinder body.
5. Remove the snapring at the end of the master cylinder bore. Then release the piston and remove the primary and secondary piston assemblies from the cylinder bore. It may be necessary to plug the front compensating valve port to remove the secondary piston assembly.
6. Lubricate the secondary piston assembly and the master cylinder bore with clean brake fluid.
7. Assemble the secondary spring (shorter of the two springs) in the open end of the secondary piston actuator, and assemble the piston return spring (longer spring) on the projection at the rear of the secondary piston.
8. Insert the secondary piston assembly, actuator end first, into the master cylinder bore and press the assembly to the bottom of the bore.
9. Lubricate the primary piston assembly with clean brake fluid. Insert the primary piston assembly, actuator end first, into the bore.
10. Place the snapring over a smooth round ended tool and depress the pistons in the bore.
11. Assemble the retaining ring in the groove in the cylinder bore.
12. Assemble the compensating valve seals and the small O-ring seal in the recesses on the bottom of the reservoir. Be sure that all seals are fully seated.
13. While holding the pistons depressed, assemble the compensating valve springs and the compensating valve poppets in the compensating valve ports.
14. Holding the pistons compressed, position the reservoir on the master cylinder body and secure it with the four mounting bolts. Torque the bolts 12–15 ft. lbs.

Bendix Tandem

Disassembly

1. Clean the outside of the master cylinder assembly. Remove the residual pressure valves.

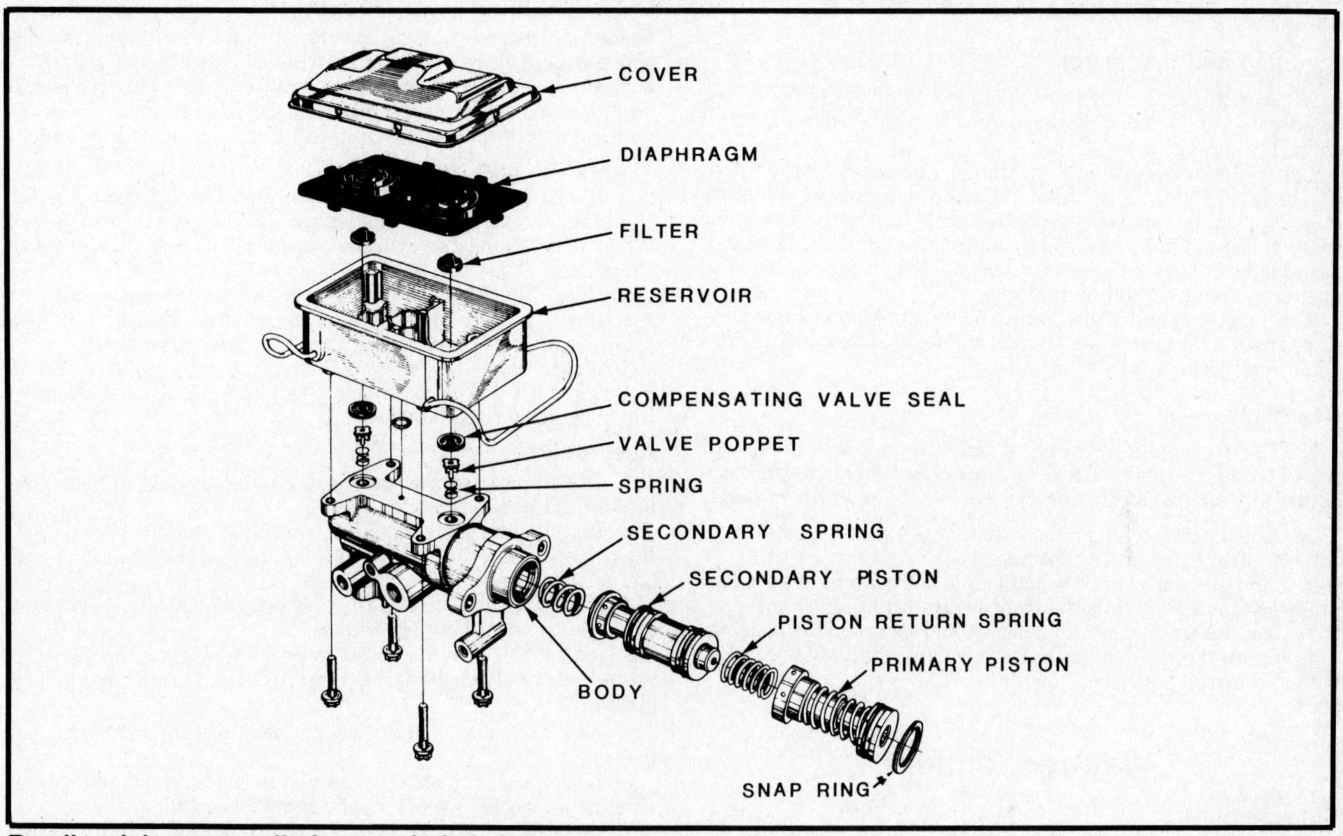

COVER
DIAPHRAGM
FILTER
RESERVOIR
COMPENSATING VALVE SEAL
VALVE POPPET
SPRING
SECONDARY SPRING
SECONDARY PISTON
PISTON RETURN SPRING
PRIMARY PISTON
BODY
SNAP RING

Bendix mini master cylinder—exploded view

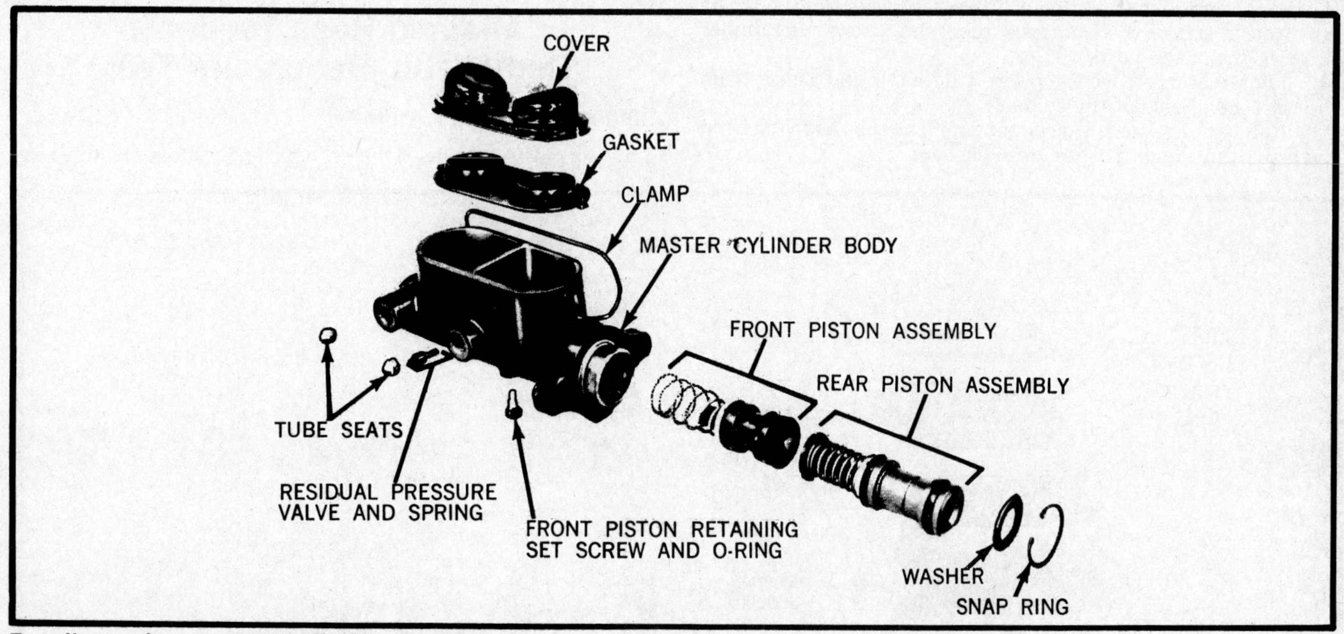

Bendix tandem master cylinder—exploded view

2. Remove the tube seats by installing easy outs firmly into the seats. Tap lightly with a hammer to loosen, remove seats.
3. Slide clamp off master cylinder cover and remove the cover and its gasket. Drain the brake fluid from the master cylinder.
4. Remove the snapring from the open end of the cylinder with snap ring pliers. Remove the washer from cylinder bore.
5. Remove the front piston retaining screw. Carefully remove the rear piston assembly.

6. Remove the front piston assembly.

Cleaning and Inspection

1. Clean all parts with a suitable solvent and dry with filtered compressed air. Wash cylinder bore with clean brake fluid and check for damage or wear.
2. If cylinder bore is lightly scratched or shows slight corrosion it can be cleaned with crocus cloth. Heavier scratches or corrosion can be removed by honing, providing that diameter of cylinder bore is not increased by more than 0.002 in. If master cylinder bore does not clean up at 0.002 in. when honed, the master cylinder should be replaced.
3. If master cylinder pistons are badly scored or corroded, replace them with new ones. All caps and seals should be replaced when rebuilding a master cylinder.

Assembly

NOTE: Before assembly of master cylinder, dip all parts in clean brake fluid and place on clean paper. Assembling master cylinder dry can damage rubber seals.

1. Coat master cylinder bore with brake fluid and carefully slide the front piston into cylinder body.
2. Slide the rear piston assembly into the cylinder bore. Compress pistons and install the front piston retaining screw.
3. Position washer in cylinder bore and secure with snapring.
4. Install the residual pressure valve and spring in the outlet port and install tube seats firmly.

Wagner Tandem

Disassembly

1. Clean the outside of the master cylinder. Remove the cylinder cover screw or spring retaining clip. Lift off the cover and the diaphragm gasket and pour off excess brake fluid. Use the push rod to stroke the cylinder forcing fluid from the cylinder through the outlet ports.
2. Loosen and remove the piston stop screw and gasket from the right hand side of the cylinder.
3. Pull back the push rod boot and remove the snap-ring from the groove in the end of the cylinder bore.
4. Remove the push rod and stop plate from the internal parts from the master cylinder. Remove the internal parts from the master cylinder. If the parts will not slide out apply air pressure at the secondary outlet port. If after applying air, parts still do not move easily, check bore carefully for extensive damage which may eliminate possibility of rebuilding master cylinder.

Inspection and Repair

1. Clean all parts in clean brake fluid. Inspect the parts for chipping, excessive wear or damage. Replace them as required. When using a master cylinder repair kit, install all the parts supplied.
2. Check all recesses, openings and internal passages to be sure they are open and free of foreign matter. Passages may be probed with soft copper wire, 0.020 in. OD, or smaller.
3. Minor scratches or blemishes in the cylinder bore can be removed with crocus cloth or a clean up hone. Do not oversize the bore more than 0.007 in.

Assembly

1. Dip all parts except the master cylinder in clean hydraulic brake fluid of the specified type.
2. Install the rear rubber cup on the secondary piston with the cup lip facing the rear. All other cups face the front or closed end of the cylinder.
3. Assemble and install the secondary piston spring, front cup, and the secondary piston.
4. Install the piston stop screw and gasket, making sure the screw enters the cylinder behind the rear of the secondary piston.
5. Assemble and install the primary piston and push rod parts.
6. Locate the stop plate in the seat in the bore and engage the snap ring into the groove at the rear of the cylinder.
7. Install the push rod boot onto the push rod and the groove of the cylinder housing.
8. Bleed the master cylinder.

Midland-Ross Tandem (Removable Reservoirs Type)

Disassembly and Assembly

1. Clean the outside of the cylinder and remove the filler cap

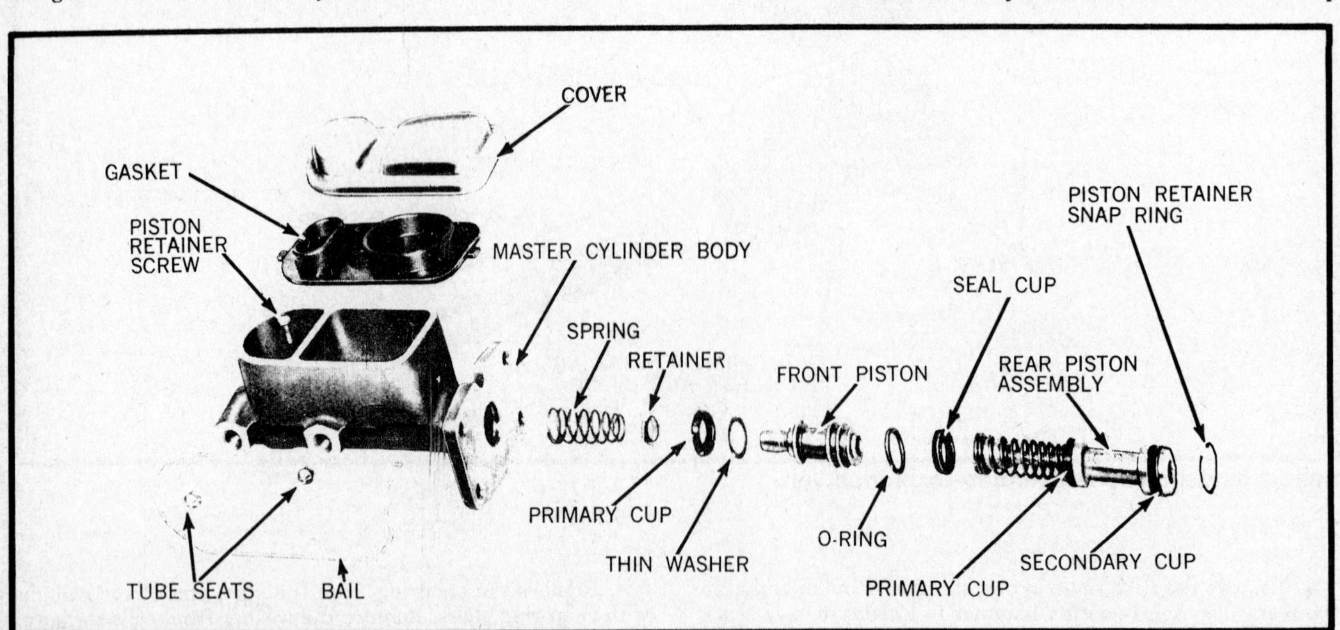

Chrysler tandem master cylinder—exploded view

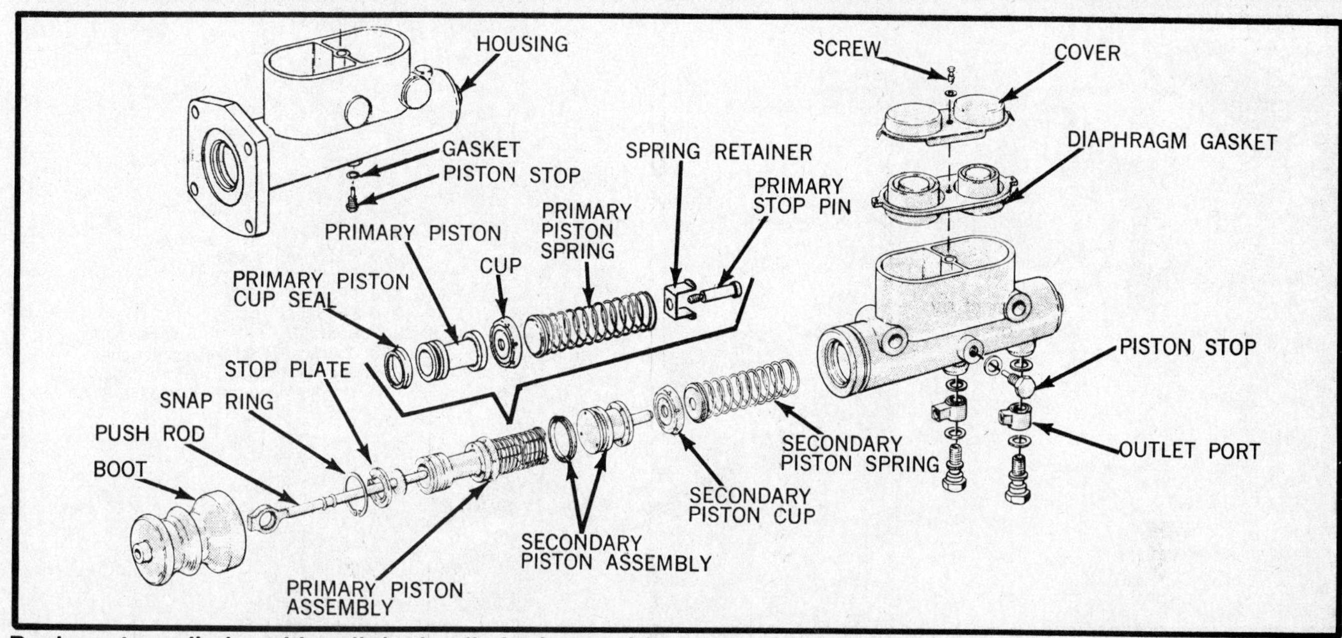

Dual master cylinder with split hydraulic brakes and frame mounted booster

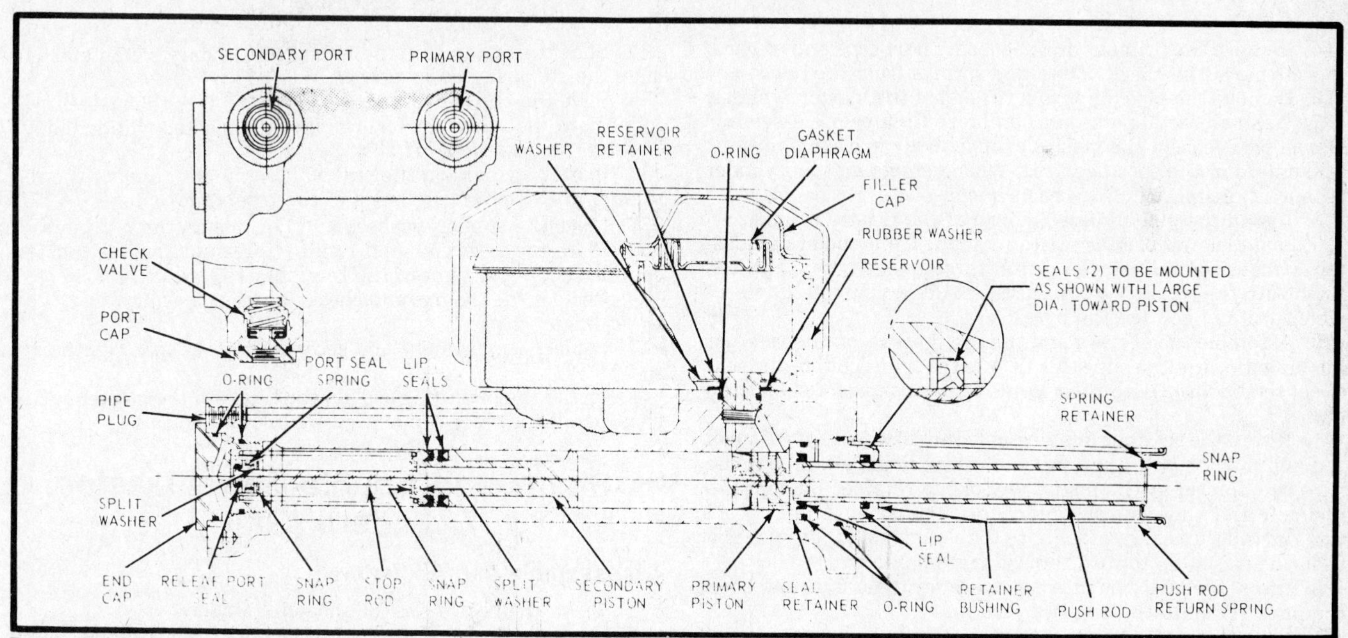

Dual master cylinder with Midland Ross dash mounted booster

and gasket (diaphragm). Pour out any brake fluid that may remain the reservoir. Stroke the push rod serveral times to remove fluid from the cylinder bore.

2. Remove the reservoir retainers, washers, and reservoir from the master cylinder body.

3. Remove the two rubber washers from the reservoir and the two O-rings from the reservoir retainers.

4. Remove the snapring, spring retainer and push rod spring.

5. Unscrew the retainer bushing counterclockwise and remove the push rod, retainer bushing, seal retainer and primary piston from the master cylinder.

6. Remove the primary piston from the push rod and discard it.

7. Remove the seal retainer, and retainer bushing from the push rod. Remove the two lip seals and two O-rings from the retainer bushing.

8. Unscrew the end cap counterclockwise and remove the end cap and secondary piston assembly from the master cylinder.

9. Remove the snapring from the secondary piston and remove the piston and return spring from the end cap and stop rod assembly.

10. Remove the two lip seals from the piston.

11. Remove the snapring from the end cap and remove the secondary piston stop rod, relief port seal spring, the two snaprings and the two split washers from the end cap.

12. Remove the relief port seal from the secondary piston stop rod.

13. Remove the O-rings from the end cap.

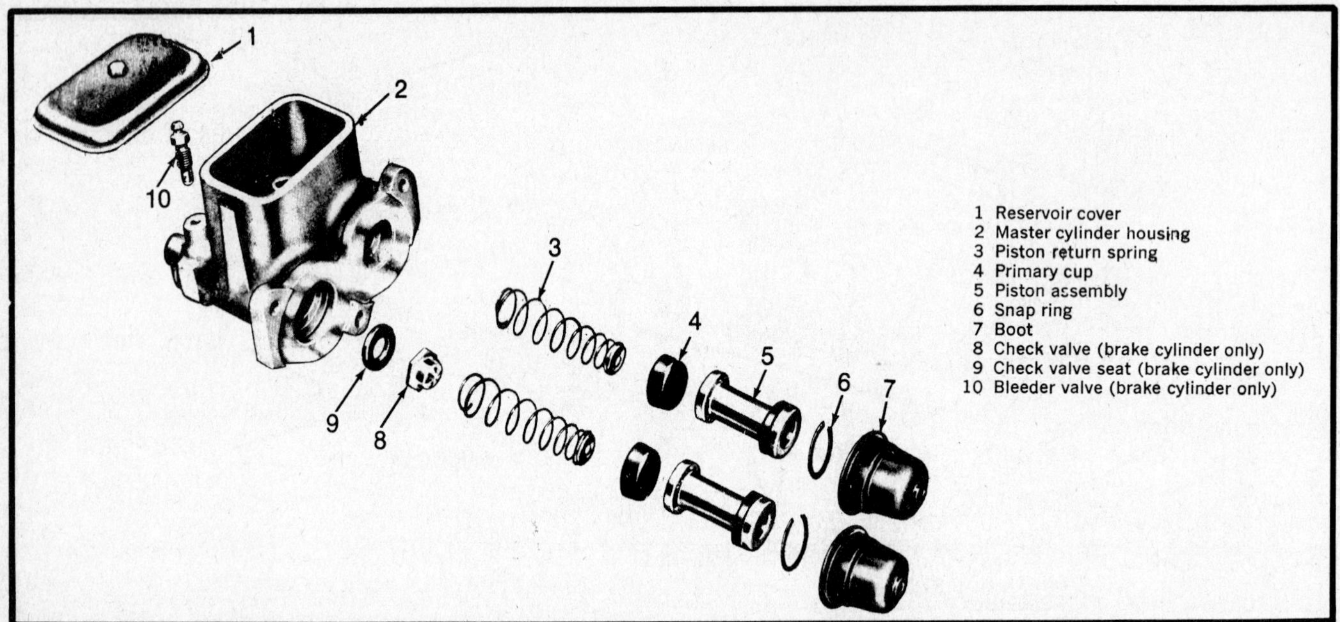

Dual reservoir master cylinder

14. Remove the primary and secondary port caps and discard.
15. Remove the check valves and springs from the ports.
16. Remove the pipe plug from the end of the master cylinder.
17. Wash all metal parts in clean brake fluid before assembly. Dip all parts except the master cylinder body in clean hydraulic brake fluid of the specified type. When using a master cylinder repair kit, install all of the parts supplied.
18. Install the pipe plug in the end of the master cylinder.
19. Install a new primary piston into the front end of the master cylinder bore. Push the piston through the bore until it is flush with the retainer bushing recess. Use a nonmetallic object which will not scratch the bore.
20. Assemble the O-rings and the two lip seals on the retainer bushing. Be sure the slip seals fit into the undercuts in the center of the bushing with their large diameters toward the piston end.
21. Install the retainer bushing onto the closed end of the push rod and push it onto the push rod approximately half way. Be sure the lip seal at the piston end of the retainer bushing remains in the undercut portion of the retainer bushing.
22. Install the seal retainer onto the closed end of the push rod with the raised lip toward the retainer bushing.
23. Insert the push rod into the master cylinder bore and hook the push rod onto the primary piston.
24. Slide the seal retainer into the recess in the master cylinder bore.
25. Screw the retainer bushing into the master cylinder body and tighten 15–20 ft. lbs.
26. Install the push spring with the large end toward the master cylinder and install the spring retainer and snapring.
27. Install the O-rings on the end can.
28. Install the relief port seal on the secondary piston stop rod.
29. Place the port seal spring, split washer (largest of two), and snapring (largest of two) on the piston stop rod.
30. Slide the assembly into the end cap and engage the snapring into its groove.
31. Install the lip seals on the secondary piston with the large diameters facing outward.
32. Place the secondary piston return spring on the end cap assembly.
33. Compress the spring and place the remaining snapring and split washer on the piston stop rod.
34. Slide the piston stop rod into the secondary piston and engage the snap-ring in its groove.
35. Slide the end cap and piston assembly into the master cylinder bore and screw the end cap into the master cylinder body. Tighten the cap 15–20 ft. lbs.
36. Install washers on the reservoir retainer and place the retainers in the mounting holes of the reservoir.
37. Place the rubber washers and O-rings on the retainers.
38. Place the reservoir and retainer assembly on the master cylinder body and tighten the retainers 15 to 20 ft. lbs.
39. Replace the springs and check valves in the output ports of the cylinder.
40. Replace the primary and secondary port caps. Tighten 15 to 20 ft. lbs.
41. Install the mounting seal on the flange of the master cylinder. Install the filler cap and gasket (diaphragm).

Single and Double Barrel Master Cylinders (GMC)

Disassembly and Assembly

1. Clean the outside of the master cylinder.
2. Remove the snapring from the groove in the cylinder bore.
3. Remove the washer (stop plate) from the clutch bore.
4. Remove the piston assembly, primary cup, return spring and retainer assembly, check valve, and the check valve seat from the brake cylinder bore.
5. Remove the piston assembly, primary cup, and return spring and retainer assembly from the clutch cylinder bore.
6. Remove the cover and the bleeder screw valve from the housing.
7. Thoroughly clean all parts with brake fluid.
8. Check the clearance between the piston and the cylinder wall. It should be within 0.001 in. to 0.005 in.
9. Coat all internal parts with brake fluid.
10. Install the parts in the brake cylinder bore. Install the check valve seat and then the check valve in the cylinder bore. Install the short return spring in the bore with the large diameter end of the spring over the check valve.
11. Install the primary cup in the cylinder bore with the lip of

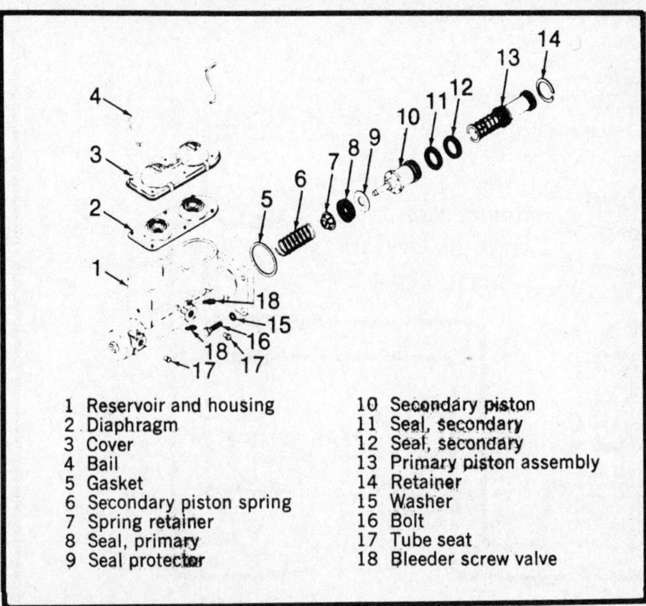

Split system master cylinder

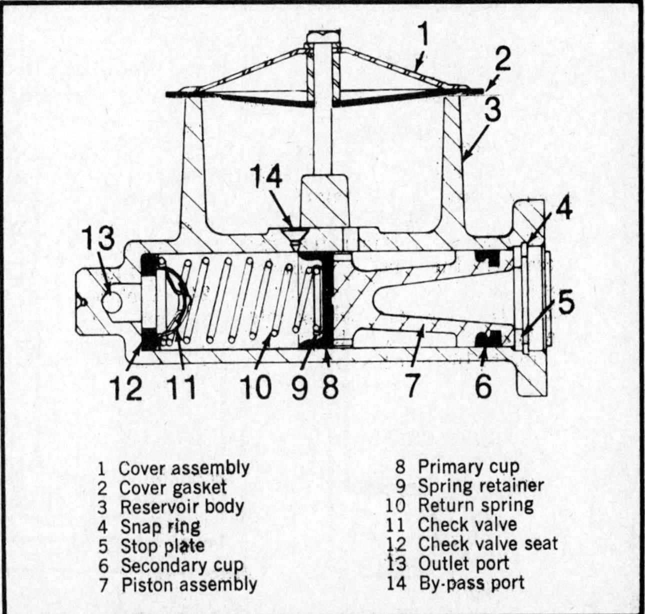

Single reservoir master cylinder

the cup toward the outlet end. Make sure the end of the return spring seats inside the cup.

12. Insert the piston and secondary cup assembly into the cylinder bore with the open end of the piston toward the open end of the cylinder bore.

14. Press all parts into the cylinder bore and install the washer (stop plate) if used and the snapring.

15. Install the parts in the clutch cylinder bore. Install the long return spring with the large diameter end first in the cylinder bore. Install the primary cup with the lip of the cup toward the outlet end.

16. Insert the piston and secondary cup into the cylinder bore, with the open end of the piston toward the open end of the cylinder. Press all parts into the cylinder bore and install the washer (stop plate) if used and the snapring.

17. Install the cover and the bleeder screw.

Split System Tandem (GMC)

Disassembly and Assembly

1. Remove the cover and reservoir seal.
2. Remove the retaining ring from the groove in the end of the cylinder of the cylinder bore.
3. Remove all parts from the cylinder bore.
4. Remove the bleeder screw valves.
5. Clean all parts in clean brake fluid.
6. Leave a coating of brake fluid on all internal parts and install parts in the cylinder bore using new rubber seals.
7. Install retainer ring and bleeder screws.

Bleeding Brakes

BENCH BLEEDING PROCEDURES

Bench bleed the master cylinder before installation. In order to expel air trapped in the cylinder, tandem master cylinders must be bench bled before they are installed on the vehicle. Bench bleeding reduces the possibility of air getting in the brake lines. Follow this simple procedure for bench bleeding:

1. Route two shortened brake lines from the outlet connection(s) into the fluid reservoir(s), below the normal fluid level.
2. Fill the reservoir(s) with fresh brake fluid and pump the cylinder until air bubbles no longer appear in the reservoir. If the cylinder does not have a check valve at the outlet port, use a clean piece of rubber or plastic, or the end of your finger to close off the end of the tubing during the back stroke. Otherwise, the fluid will merely pump back and forth in the tubing.
3. When all air has been purged from the master cylinder, bend the tubes up out of the fluid, and remove them. Refill the cylinder and securely install the master cylinder cap.
4. Install the master cylinder on the vehicle. Attach the lines, but do not tighten the tube connection.
5. Force out any air that might have been trapped in the connection by slowly depressing the pedal several times. Tighten the nut slightly before releasing pedal, and loosen before depressing each time. Catch the fluid in a rag to avoid damaging car finish. DO NOT BOTTOM THE PISTON. Tighten the connections when air bubbles are no longer present in the fluid. Make sure the master cylinder is adequately filled with brake fluid.

MANUAL BLEEDING

NOTE: See below for GM "Quick Take-Up" cylinder bleeding sequence

Bleed the longest line first on the individual system (i.e. front/rear split or diagonally front wheel, opposite side rear wheel split. If a single system, the right rear is usually the longest.) being serviced. During the complete bleeding operation, do not allow the reservoir to run dry. Keep the master cylinder reservoirs filled with the specified brake fluid. Never use brake fluid that has been drained from the hydraulic system.

1. Bleed the master cylinder at the outlet port side of the system being serviced.

NOTE: On a master cylinder without bleed screws, loosen the master cylinder to hydraulic line nut. Operate the brake pedal slowly until the brake fluid at the outlet connection is free of bubbles, then tighten the tube nut to the specified torque. Do not use the secondary piston stop screw located on the bottom of the master cylinder to bleed the brake system. Loosening or removing this screw could result in damage to the secondary piston or stop screw. Operate the brake pedal slowly

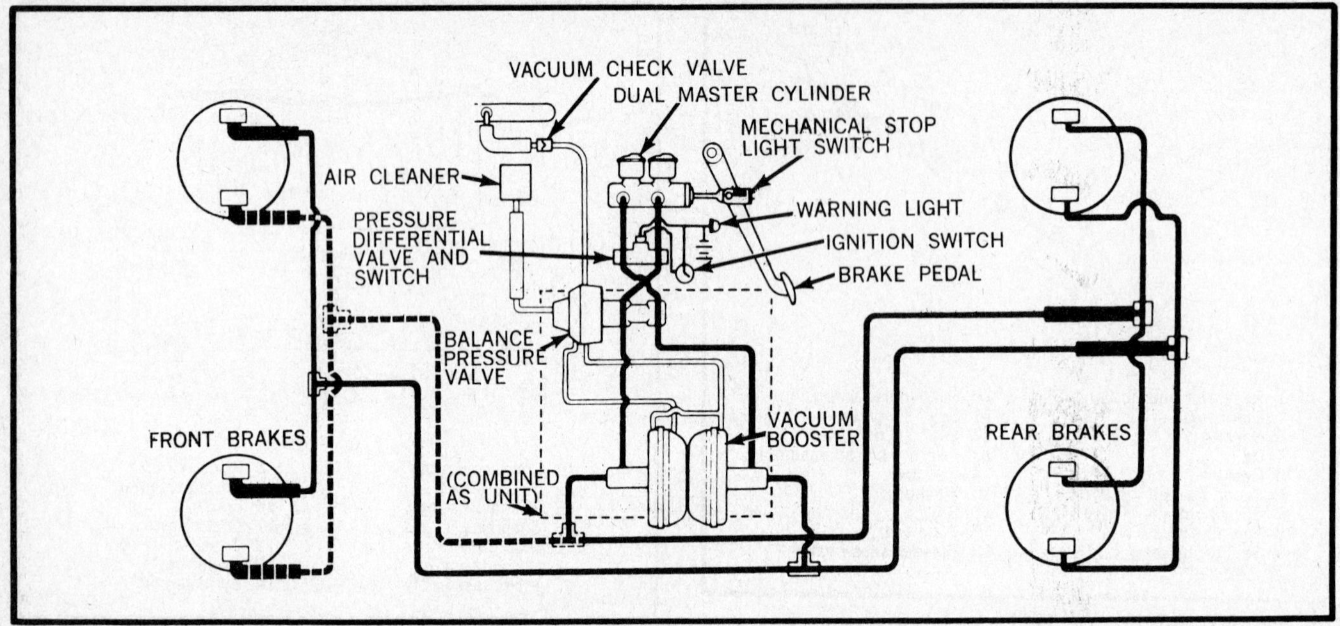

Split hydraulic brake system with frame mounted booster

until the brake fluid at the outlet connection is free of air bubbles, then tighten the bleed screw.

2. Position a suitable size (usually $^3/_8$ in.) box wrench on the bleeder fitting on the cylinder or caliper to be bled. Attach a rubber drain tube to the bleeder fitting. The end of the tube should fit snugly around the bleeder fitting.
3. Submerge the free end of the tube in a container partially filled with clean brake fluid, and loosen the bleeder fitting approximately $^3/_4$ turn.
4. Push the brake pedal down slowly thru its full travel. Close the bleeder fitting, then return the pedal to the full released position. Repeat this operation until air bubbles cease to appear at the submerged end of the bleeder tube.
5. When the fluid is completely free of air bubbles, close the bleeder fitting and remove the bleeder tube.
6. Repeat this procedure at the brake cylinder or caliper on the other side of the split system. Refill the master cylinder reservoir after each cylinder or caliper is bled. When the bleeding is complete, the master cylinder fluid level should be filled to within $^1/_4$ in. from the top of the reservoirs.
7. Centralize the pressure differential valve.

GM QUICK TAKE UP MASTER CYLINDER

Special procedures are required to manually bleed the quick take-up brake system used on some General Motors vehicles. Bleed the master cylinder first. Disconnect the left front brake line at the master cylinder, and fill the master cylinder until fluid flows from the port. Catch fluid in a rag and don't allow fluid or rag to contact car finish. Connect the line and tighten fitting.

Depress the brake pedal one time slowly and hold. Loosen same brake line fitting to purge air from the system. Retighten the fitting and release the brake pedal slowly. Wait 15 seconds. Then repeat the sequence, including the 15 second wait until all air is removed. Next bleed the right front connection in the same way as the left front.

Bleed the wheel cylinders and calipers only after you are sure that all the air has been removed from the master cylinder. Follow the specified RR, LF, LR, RF sequence and depress the brake pedal slowly one time before opening bleeder screw to release air. Tighten screw, slowly release pedal, and wait 15 seconds. Repeat all steps, including the 15 second delay until all air has been removed from the system. Rapid pumping of this system moves the secondary master cylinder piston down the bore in a manner that makes it difficult to bleed the left front/right rear part of the system.

SURGE BLEEDING

This method includes both manual and pressure bleeding, and deliberately creates a churning (higher pressure) turbulence in wheel cylinders so that any remaining air can be drawn off in the form of aerated fluid. It is important to remove all possible air before surging, this method is never used unless the routine manual or pressure bleeding method proves inadequate.

1. Bleed the brakes at all wheels in a usual manner.
2. At each wheel cylinder, in turn, open the bleeder screw and press the brake pedal down sharply several times. Close the bleeder screw. The action creates a turbulence in each cylinder, forcing out practically all of the remaining trapped air.

NOTE: After bleeding the brake system, road test to insure proper operation of the braking system.

BLEEDING THE POWER BRAKE UNIT

On power booster equipped vehicles, the engine should be turned off and the power system purged of vacuum or compressed air by depressing the brake pedal several times. After bleeding the master cylinder, bleed the power brake unit (if equipped with a bleeder screw).

Pressure multiplying type power units often have bleeder screws to remove the air trapped within the unit. If the unit has more that one bleeder screw, bleed the one at the pressure (main) cylinder first and the control valve second. When bleeding, manually close the bleeder screw before the pedal is allowed to back stroke each time.

Wheel Cylinders and Calipers

DRUM BRAKE WHEEL CYLINDER

The wheel cylinder performs in response to the master cylinder.

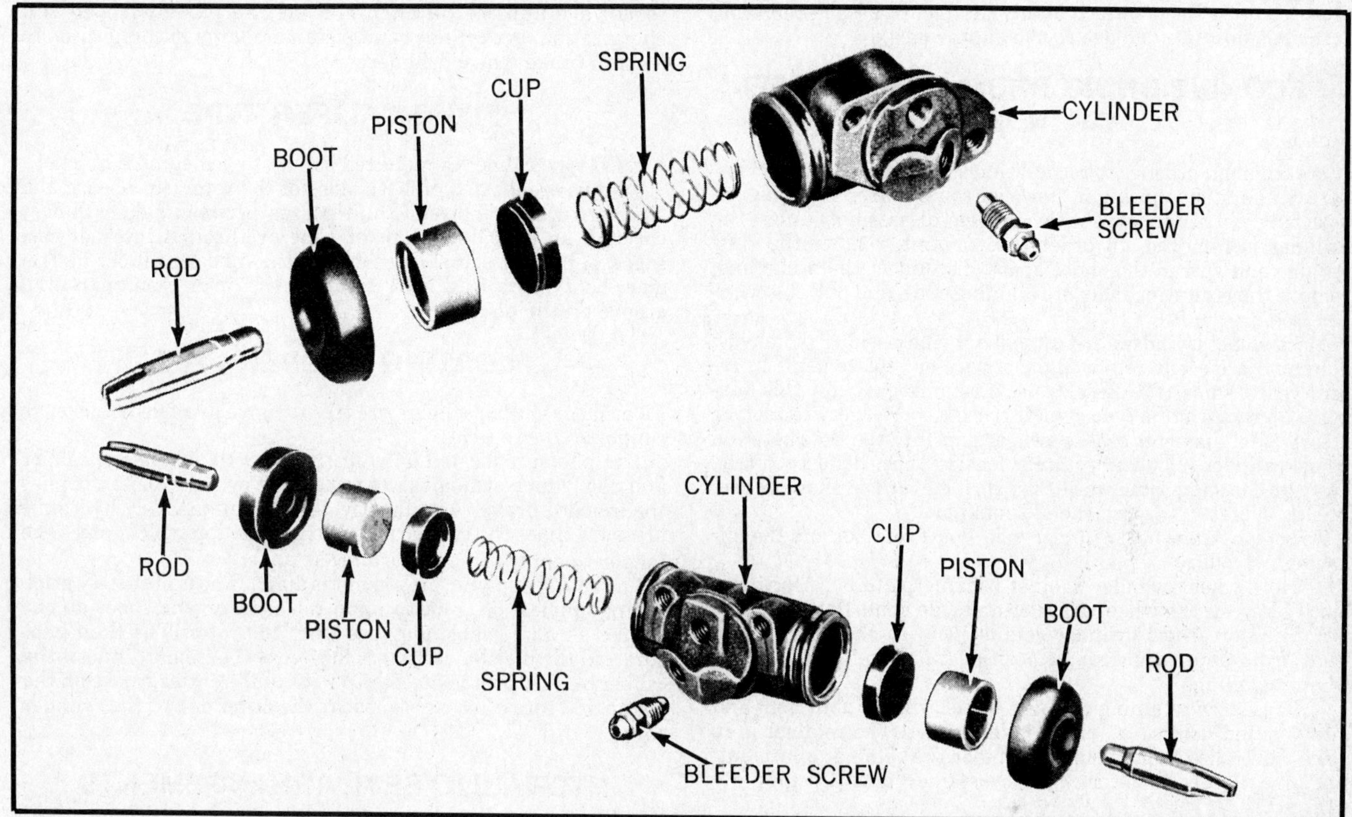

Typical wheel cylinder—exploded view

It receives fluid from the hydraulic hose through its inlet port. As the pressure increases the wheel cylinder cups and pistons are forced apart. As a result, the hydraulic pressure is converted into mechanical force acting on the brake shoes. The wheel cylinder size may vary from front to rear. The variation in wheel cylinder size (diameter) is one of the factors controlling the distribution of braking force in a vehicle. Larger diameter wheel cylinders are normally specified for the front brakes of front engine passenger cars equipped with drum brakes. Bleeder screws are provided to remove air or vapor trapped in the system.

Three types of wheel cylinders are normally used with drum brakes.

Single Piston or "Single-end" Type

A single piston wheel cylinder has only one cup, piston, and dust boot and spring. It may also contain a cup filler or cup expander.

Double Piston or "Double-end" Straight Bore Type

The double piston, straight bore type is most commonly used. This type carries two opposed pistons, two cups and two boots.

Double Piston or "Double-end" Step Bore Type

This type is used on some of the non-servo brakes and has the same components as the straight bore type. Two different sized dust boots, cups, and pistons are used. Opposed pistons of different diameters exert different amounts of force.

SERVICE PROCEDURES

Wheel cylinders may need reconditioning or replacement whenever the brake shoes are replaced or when required to correct a leak condition. On many designs, the wheel cylinders can be disassembled without removing them from the backing plate. On some designs, however, the cylinder is mounted in an indention in the backing plate or a cylinder piston stop is welded to the backing plate. When servicing brakes of this type, the cylinder must be removed from the backing plate before being disassembled.

Diagnostic Inspection and Cleaning

Leaks which coat the boot and the cylinder with fluid, or result in a dropped reservoir fluid level, or dampen and stain the brake linings are dangerous. Such leaks can cause the brakes to "grab" or fail and should be immediately corrected. A leakage, not immediately apparent, can be detected by pulling back the cylinder boot. A small amount of fluid seepage dampening the interior of the boot is normal, however a dripping boot is not. Unless other conditions causing a brake to pull, grab, or drag becomes obvious, the wheel cylinder is a suspect and should be included in general reconditioning.

Cylinder binding may be caused by rust, deposits, grime, or swollen cups due to fluid contamination, or by a cup wedged into an excessive piston clearance. If the clearance between the pistons and the bore wall exceeds allowable values, a condition called "heel drag" may exist. It can result in rapid cup wear and can cause the pistons to retract very slowly when the brakes are released.

A ring of a hard, crystal like substance is sometimes noticed in the cylinder bore where the piston stops after the brakes are released.

Some front wheel cylinders have a baffle located between the opposed pistons. The baffle contains a small hole which causes the cylinder to act as a fluid shock absorber damping servo brake shoes as they become energized. These cylinders cannot be honed and should be replaced if the bore is pitted or corroded.

Hydraulic system parts should not be allowed to come in contact with oil or grease, neither should those be handled with greasy hands. Even a trace of any petroleum based product is sufficient to cause damage to the rubber parts.

RECONDITIONING DRUM BRAKE WHEEL CYLINDERS

It is a common practice to recondition a drum brake wheel cylinder without dismounting it, however some brakes are equipped with external piston stops which prevent disassembly unless the cylinder is removed. In order to dismount, remove the shoe springs and spread the shoes apart, disconnect the brake line, remove the mounting bolts or retaining clips, and pull the cylinder free.

Most wheel cylinders are attached to the backing plate with bolts and are easily removed for service or replacement. In recent years, some GM vehicles use a retaining clip for this purpose. To remove this type cylinder, use a special service tool, or insert $\frac{1}{8}$ in. diameter or less awls or pins into the slots between wheel cylinder pilot and retainer locking tabs. Bend both tabs away at the same time until tabs spring over the shoulder, releasing cylinder. Discard the old retainer.

To replace the wheel cylinder, use a new retainer and the following procedure.

1. Hold wheel cylinder against backing plate by inserting a block between the wheel cylinder and axle shaft flange.
2. Position wheel cylinder retainer clip so the tabs will be away from and in horizontal position with the backing plate when installing.
3. Press new retaining clip over wheel cylinder abutment and into position using 1 $\frac{1}{8}$ in. 12 point socket. The retainer is in place when the tabs are snapped under the retainer abutment. Examine closely to be sure both retainer tabs are properly engaged.

Another variation of retainer clip is used on some imported vehicles. The retainer usually consists of two or three separate pieces which when slid together will lock themselves and the wheel cylinder in place. The retainers can be carefully removed without incurring damage which allows them to be reused. If they are damaged or corroded, however, they must be replaced.

Pull the protective dust boots off the cylinder. Internal parts should slide out, or be picked out easily. Parts can be driven out with a wooden dowel, or blown out at low pressure by applying compressed air to the fluid inlet port. Parts which cannot be removed easily indicate they are damaged beyond repair and the cylinder should be replaced.

Clean the cylinder and the parts in alcohol and/or brake fluid. (Do not use gasoline or other petroleum based products.) Use only lint free wiping cloths. Crocus cloth can be used to clean minute scratches, signs of rust, corrosion or discoloration from the cylinder bore and pistons. Slide the cloth in a circular rather than a lengthwise motion. A clean up hone may be used. After a cylinder has been honed, inspect it for excessive piston clearance and remove any burrs formed on the edge of fluid intake or bleeder screw ports.

NOTE: Do not rebuild aluminum cylinders. A cylinder that does not clean up at 0.002 in. should be discarded and a new cylinder installed. (Black stains on the cylinder walls are caused by the piston cups and will do no harm.)

Assemble the cylinder with the internal parts, making sure that the cylinder wall is wet with brake fluid. Insert the cups and pistons from each end of a double end cylinder; do not slide them through the cylinder. Cup lips should always face inward.

Disc Brake Caliper

An integral part of the caliper, the caliper bore(s) contains the piston(s) that direct thrust against the brake pads supported within the caliper. Since all braking forces (pad application force) are applied on each side of the rotor with no self energization, the cylinder and piston are large in comparison to a drum brake wheel cylinder.

FIXED CALIPER TYPE

A fixed type caliper is mounted solidly to the spindle bracket.

Pistons are located on both sides of the rotor, in inboard and outboard caliper halves. Fluid passes between caliper halves through an external crossover tube or through internal passages. A bleeder screw is located in the inboard caliper half. A dust boot protecting each cylinder fits in a circumferential groove on the piston.

FLOATING CALIPER TYPE

Floating or sliding calipers are free to move in a fixed bracket or support.

The piston is located only on the inboard side of the caliper housing, which straddles the rotor. The cylinder piston applies the inboard brake shoe directly, and simultaneously hydraulic pressure slides the caliper in a clamping action which forces the caliper to apply the outboard brake shoe.

The actual applying movement is small. The unit merely grips during application, relaxes upon release, and the shoes do not retract an appreciable distance from the rotor. The fluid inlet port and the bleeder screw are located n the inboard side of the caliper. A dust boot is fitted into a circumferential groove on the piston and into a recess at or near the outer end of the cylinder bore.

HYDRAULIC SEAL ARRANGEMENTS

Seal arrangements at the caliper pistons vary depending upon the brake manufacturer. Three makes of fixed caliper brakes, Bendix, Budd, and Delco-Moraine, use a ring seal which fits in a circumferential groove on the piston.

A fixed seal is now commonly used in brake calipers. During the very small applying movement of the piston, the elasticity of the fixed seal permits some deflection in the cylinder groove. The seal deflects as the brakes are applied and relaxes as the brakes are released, retracting the piston a small amount. Some GM types have a rolling seal that retracts the piston slightly further to reduce pad rubbing friction.

A scratched piston, nicked seal, or a sludge or varnish deposit which lifts the sealing edge away from the piston will cause a fluid leak. A serious leak could develop if calipers are not reconditioned when new pads are installed. Then dust and road grime, gradually accumulating behind the dust boot, could be carried into the seal when the piston is shoved inward to accommodate new thick linings. Old seals may have taken a "set," thus preventing proper seating in the retainer groove and on the piston. Therefore, when reconditioning calipers, new seals should be installed.

Service Procedures

Before servicing, syphon or syringe about $\frac{2}{3}$ of the fluid from the master cylinder reservoir do not allow the, fluid level to fall below the cylinder intake port. To prevent a gravity loss of fluid, plug the brake line after disconnecting from the caliper. To recondition, remove the caliper from the vehicle, allow the unit to drain, and remove the brake shoes. For benchwork, clamp the caliper housing in a soft jaw vice. On fixed-caliper types, remove the bridge bolts and separate the caliper into halves. Remove the sealing O-rings at cross-over points, if the unit has internal fluid passages across the halves.

Whenever required, use special tools to remove pistons, dust boots, and seals. If compressed air is used, apply it gradually, gently ease the pistons from the cylinders, and trap them in a

clean cloth; do not allow them to pop out. Take care to avoid pinching hands or fingers.

While removing stroking type seals and boots, work lip of boot from the groove in the caliper. After the boot is free, pull the piston, and strip the seal and boot from the piston.

While removing fixed position (rectangular ring) seals and boots, pull the piston through the boot. Do not use a metal tool which would scratch the piston. Use a small pointed wooden or plastic tool to lift the boots and seals from the grooves in the cylinder bore.

Cleaning, Inspection, and Installation

Use only alcohol and/or brake fluid and a lint free wiping cloth to clean the caliper and parts. Other solvents should not be used. Blow out passages with compressed air. Always wear eye protection when using compressed air or cleaning calipers.

To correct minor imperfections in the cylinder bore, polish with a fine grade of crocus cloth working in a circular rather than a lengthwise motion. Do not use any form of abrasive on a plated piston. Discard a piston which is pitted or has signs of plating wear.

Inspect the new seal. It should lie flat and be round. If it has suffered a distorted "set" during its shelf life, do not use it. Lubricate the cylinder wall and parts with brake fluid.

While installing stroking type seals and boots, stretch the boot and the seal over the piston and seat them in position.

Use special alignment tools for inserting lip cup seals. Be sure the seal does not twist or roll.

Where the boot lip is retained inside the cylinder bore the following method works well.

1. Lubricate bottom inside edge of piston and brake seal in caliper with brake fluid.
2. Pull boot over bottom end of piston so that boot is positioned on bottom of piston with lip about ¼ in. up from bottom end.
3. Hold piston suspended over bore.
4. Insert back boot lip into groove in caliper.
5. Then tuck the sides of boot into groove and work forward until only one bulge remains.
6. Tuck the final bulge into front of the groove.
7. Then push the piston carefully through the seal and boot to the bottom of the bore. The inside of the boot should slide on the piston and come to rest in the boot groove.
8. If the boot lip is retained outside the cylinder bore, first stretch boot over the piston and seat it in its groove, then press the piston through the seal. Fully depress the piston. You'll need 50 to 100 pounds force to fasten the boot lip in place. On some designs, it is necessary to use a wooden drift or a special tool to seat the metal boot in the caliper counterbore below the face of the caliper.

INSTALLING FIXED CALIPER BRIDGE BOLTS

If the caliper contains internal fluid cross-over passages, be sure to install the new O-ring seals at joints. Install high tensile strength bridge bolts on the mated caliper halves. Never replace the bridge bolts with ordinary standard hardware bolts.

Brake Disc (Rotor)

ROTOR RUNOUT

Manufacturers differ widely on permissible runout, but too much can sometimes be felt as a pulsation at the brake pedal. A wobble pump effect is created when a rotor is not perfectly smooth and the pad hits the high spots forcing fluid back into the master cylinder. This alternating pressure causes a pulsating feeling which can be felt at the pedal when the brakes are applied. This excessive runout also causes the brakes to be out of adjustment because disc brakes are self adjusting, they are designed so that the pads drag on the rotor at all times and therefore automatically compensate for wear. To check the actual runout of the rotor, first tighten the wheel spindle nut to a snug bearing adjustment, end play removed. Fasten a dial indicator on the suspension at a convenient place so that the indicator stylus contacts the rotor face approximately one in. from its outer edge. Set the dial at zero. Check the total indictor reading while turning the rotor one full revolution. If the rotor is warped beyond the runout specification, it is likely that it can be successfully remachined.

Lateral Runout: A wobbly movement of the rotor from side to side at it rotates. Excessive lateral runout causes the rotor faces to knock bac the disc pads and can result in chatter, excessive pedal travel, pumping or fighting pedal and vibration during the breaking action.

Parallelism (lack of): Refers to the amount of variation in the thickness of the rotor. Excessive variation can cause pedal vibration or fight, front end vibrations and possible "grab" during the braking action; a condition comparable to an "out-of-round brake drum." Check parallelism with a micrometer, "mike" the thickness at eight or more equally spaced points, equally distant from the outer edge of the rotor, preferrably at mid-points of the braking surface. Parallelism then is the amount of variation between maximum and minimum measurements.

Surface of Micro-inch finish, flatness, smoothness: Different from parallelism, these terms refer to the degree of perfection of the flat surface on each side of the rotor, that is, the minute hills, valleys and swirls inherent in machining the surface. In a visual inspection, the remachined surface should have a fine ground polish with, at most, only a faint trace of nondirectional swirls.

Disc Brake Surface Refinishing

To meet mandated brake system performance requirements, semi-metallic brake linings have been used for several years in some vehicle applications. In order to maintain the proper performance, it is important to correctly service these semi-metallic brake components as outlined in the following procedures.

Service Recommendations

1. Semi-metallic linings should be replaced with semi-metallic service linings, equal to the original equipment specifications.
2. Routine replacement of the disc pads does not require rotor refinishing, unless damage or extreme wear to the rotor has occurred.
3. Rotor refinishing should only be required if non-parallelism, excessive runout, rotor damage or scoring of the rotor surface has occurred.
4. If refinishing is necessary, the semi-metallic brake pads require a micro- inch surface refinish like new vehicle rotor specifications (10–50 micro-inches with non-directional swirl patterns).
5. The recommended procedure for obtaining this finish is outlined in the following chart.
6. When refinishing brake rotors for semi-metallic linings, the following is important;

ROTOR REFINISHING

Procedure	Rough Cut	Finish Cut
Spindle Speed	150 RPM	150 RPM
Depth of Cut Per Side	.005″	.002″
Tool Cross Feed Per Rev.	.006″.010″	.002″ Max.
Vibration Dampener	Yes	Yes
Swirl Pattern-120 GRIT	No	Yes

a. The brake lathe must be in good working order and have the capability to produce the intended surface finish.

b. Use the correct tool feed and arbor speeds. Too fast a speed or too deep a cut can result in a rough finish.

c. Cutting tools must be sharp.

d. Adapters must be clean and free of nicks.

e. Lathe finish cuts should be further improved and made non-directional by dressing the rotor surface with a sanding disc power tool, such as AMMCO model 8350 Safe Swirl Disc Rotor Grinder or its equivalaent.

f. Rotor surfaces are to be refinished to 10–50 micro-inches.

7. To become familiar with the required surface finish, drag the fingernail over the surface of a new rotor from parts stock or on a new vehicle. If your brake equipment cannot produce this smooth-a-finish when correctly used, contact the equipment manufacturer for corrective instructions.

8. When installing new rotors from service stock, do not refinish the surface as these parts are to the recommended finish. It also is not required to refinish a rotor on a vehicle which has a smooth finish.

Drum Brake Service

Basic Service

CAUTION

Do not blow the brake dust out of the drums with compressed air or lung power; always use a damp cloth, a vacuum unit and soft brush to gather the dust particles into a container for disposal. Use a nose/mouth protective cover Brake linings contain asbestos, a known cancer causing substance. Dispose of the residue safely.

NOTE: Never work on a vehicle supported only by a jack. Use a hydraulic lift and/or jack stands to support the vehicle safely.

Check For Leaks

Press the brake pedal to ensure that there are no leaks in the hydraulic system. If the pedal does not remain hard and drops to the end of its pedal travel, an internal or external fluid leakage is indicated in the master cylinder, hoses, wheel cylinders, or brake calipers. When performing this test, the engine should be running, if equipped with power brakes. With power brakes, it is normal for the pedal to drop slightly when the engine starts. If the pedal continues to drop, a leak in the system is indicated.

Drum Inspection

Check the drums for any cracks, scores, grooves, or out-of-round conditions. Slight scores can be removed with fine emery cloth, while extensive scoring requires machining the drum on a suitable drum lathe.

If the friction surface of the brake drum is scored or otherwise damaged beyond the allowable machining specification, it will require replacement. After machining, the drum diameter must not exceed the diameter specification cast on the drum or 0.060 in. (1.5mm) over the original nominal diameter. Carefully look for signs of grease, oil or brake fluid on the drum assembly and repair as required.

Rebuild the Wheel Cylinders

It is always a good practice to rebuild or replace the wheel cylinder when relining the brakes. This helps to assure a properly operating brake system and to prevent premature leakage of brake fluid past the cups and piston seals.

Clean and Lubricate

With the brake parts off, clean the backing plate with a damp cloth to avoid raising any asbestos dust and dispose of the rag after use. Clean any rust with a wire brush. File smooth any ridges or rough edges on the contact points of the backing plate. Lubricate the contact points with an approved brake lubricant. Clean and lightly lubricate the adjuster threads and screw the adjuster all the way together to facilitate reassembly of the brake components. If the wheel bearings are available, wash in solvent and repack with lubricant. Check the backing plate retaining bolts for tightness.

Reassemble And Install The Brake Shoes

Reassemble the brake shoes in the reverse order of their removal. Make sure all parts are in their proper position and that both brake shoes are properly positioned at either end of the adjuster assembly. Also, both brake shoes should correctly engage the wheel cylinder push rod and parking brake links, if equipped. With the brake shoes and components in position, measure the inside of the drum diameter and adjust the brake shoes to match the diameter with a brake shoe pre-set measuring tool. Install the brake drum and make final brake adjustment, as required. Install the remaining components and torque to specifications.

BLEED AND ROAD TEST

Bleed the air from the hydraulic system to insure a high, hard pedal and road test the vehicle. Self-adjusting mechanisms are activated by the application of the brake pedal when the vehicle is driven in reverse, driven forward or when the parking brake is applied. Be sure the road test course includes enough stops, enough traveling in reverse, and the use of the parking brake assembly, to allow the self adjusters to perform the proper adjustment on all wheels.

DRUM BRAKE SERVICE

Wagner

TWIN ACTION TYPE

Twin-action brake is a four-anchor type. Brake shoes are self-centering in operation, and both shoes are self-energizing in both forward and reverse.

Two wheel cylinders are mounted on opposite sides of the backing plate. One brake shoe is mounted above wheel cylinders and one below. Sliding pivot type anchor is used at front end of upper shoe and at rear end of lower shoe. Adjustable anchor is used at front end of lower shoe and at rear end of upper shoe. Four shoe return springs hold shoe ends firmly against anchors when brakes are released.

Anchor brackets are steel forgings, attached to flange on axle housing in conjunction with the backing plate. At adjustable anchor end of each shoe, shoe web bears against flat head of adjusting screw which threads into anchor bracket. The adjusting screw heads are notched and are rotated for brake adjustment through access holes in backing plate. A lock spring which fits over anchor bracket holds adjusting screw in position.

The brake backing plate has six machined bearing surfaces, three for each shoe, against which the inner edge of each shoe bears. Two brake shoe guide bolts are riveted to backing plate and extend through holes in center of brake shoe web. Shoes are retained on guide bolts by flat washers, nuts, and cotter pins.

Wheel cylinder push rods make contact between wheel cylinder pistons and brake shoes.

Inner edge of brake drum has a groove which fits over a flange on the edge of backing plate, forming a seal against the entrance of dirt and mud.

TWIN-ACTION TYPE REAR BRAKE

Brake Shoe Removal

1. Remove brake drums.

NOTE: If brake drums are worn severely, it may be necessary to retract the adjusting screws.

2. Remove the brake shoe pull back springs.

NOTE: Since wheel cylinder piston stops are incorporated in the anchor brackets, it is not necessary to install wheel cylinder clamps when the brake shoes are removed.

3. Loosen the adjusting lever cam cap screw, and while holding the star wheel end of the adjusting lever past the star wheel, remove the cap screw and cam.
4. Remove the brake shoe hold down springs and pins by compressing the spring and, at the same time, pushing the pin back through the flange plate toward the tool. Then, keeping the spring compressed, remove the lock (C-washer) from the pin with a magnet.
5. Lift off the brake shoe and self-adjuster lever as an assembly.
6. The self-adjuster lever can now be removed from the brake shoe by removing the hold-down spring and pin. Remove lever return spring also.

NOTE: The adjusting lever, override spring and pivot are an assembly. It is not recommended that they be disassembled for service purposes unless they are broken. It is much easier to assemble and disassemble the brake leaving them intact.

7. Thread the adjusting screw out of the brake shoe anchor and remove and discard the friction spring.
8. Clean all dirt out of brake drum. Inspect drums for roughness, scoring or out-of-round. Replace or recondition drums as necessary.
9. Carefully pull lower edges of wheel cylinder boots away from cylinders. If brake fluid flows out, overhaul of the wheel cylinders is necessary.

NOTE: A slight amount of fluid is nearly always present and acts as a lubricant for the piston.

10. Inspect flange plate for oil leakage past axle shaft oil seals. Install seals if necessary.

Brake Shoe Installation

1. Put a light film of lubricant on shoe bearing surfaces of brake flange plate and on threads of adjusting screw.
2. Thread adjusting screw completely into anchor without friction spring to be sure threads are clean and screw turns easily. Then remove screws, position a new friction spring on screw and reinstall in anchor.
3. Assemble self-adjuster assembly and lever return spring to brake shoe and position adjusting lever link on adjusting lever pivot.
4. Position hold-down pins in flange plate.
5. Install brake shoe and self-adjuster assemblies onto hold down pins. Insert ends of shoes in wheel cylinder push rods and legs of friction springs.

NOTE: Make sure the toe of the shoe is against the adjusting screw.

6. Install cup, spring and retainer on end of hold-down pin. With spring compressed, push the hold-down pin back through the flange plate toward the tool and install the lock on the pin.
7. Install brake shoe return springs.
8. Holding the star wheel end of the adjusting lever as far as possible past the star wheel, position the adjusting lever cam into the adjusting lever link and assemble with cap screw.
9. Check the brake shoes for being centered by measuring the

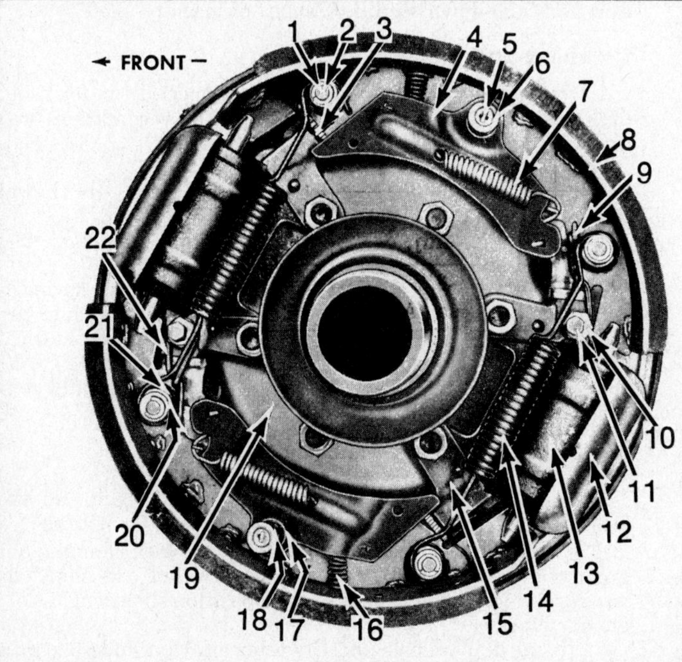

1. Hold-down pin spring lock
2. Hold-down pin
3. Adjusting screw
4. Adjusting lever
5. Adjuting lever pin spring
6. Hold-down spring cup
7. Lever override spring
8. Brake shoe and lining
9. Adjusting lever pivot
10. Adjusting lever cam
11. Adjusting lever bolt
12. Wheel cylinder shield
13. Wheel cylinder
14. Brake shoe return spring
15. Brake shoe anchor
16. Lever return spring
17. Adjusting lever pin sleeve
18. Hold-down spring
19. Brake backing plate
20. Hold-down pin retainer
21. Hold-down pin spring
22. Adjusting lever link

Twin action self adjusting brakes

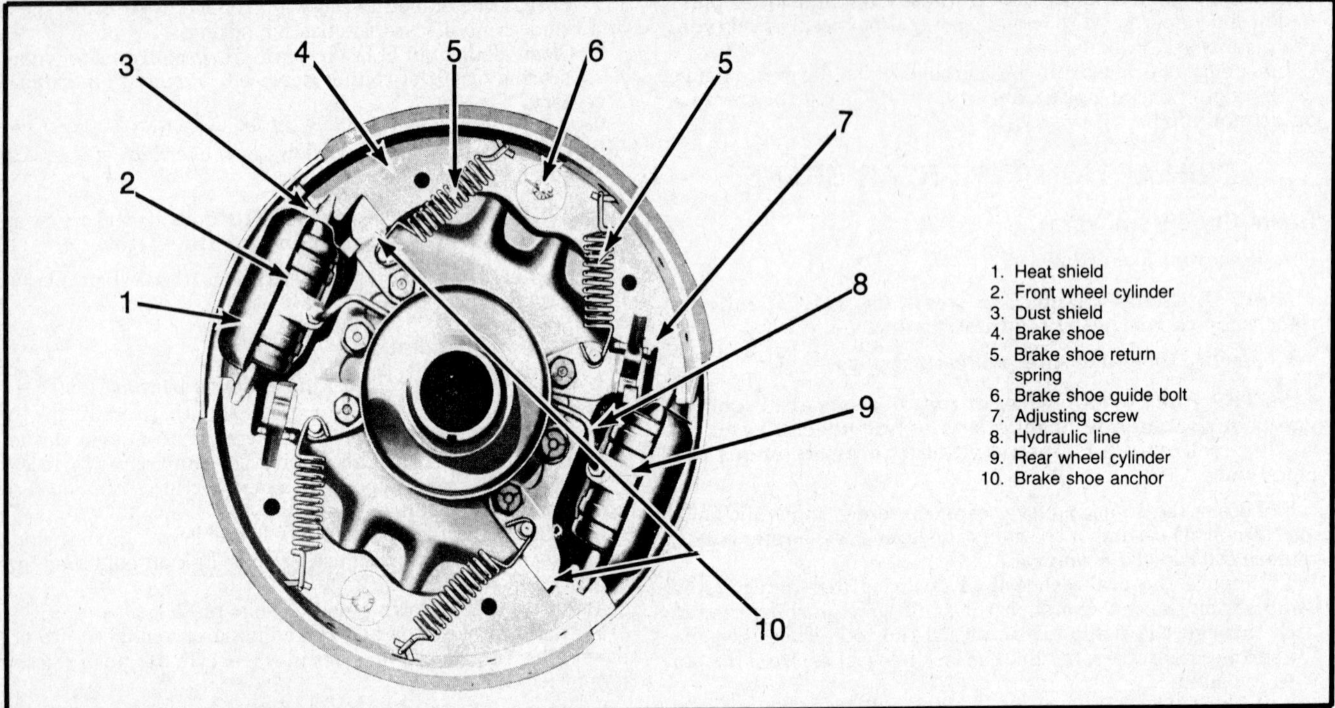

Twin action type brake installed

distance from the lining surface to the edge of the flange plate. To center the shoes, tap the upper or lower end of the shoes with a plastic mallet until the distances at each end become equal.

10. Locate the adjusting lever 0.020–0.039 in. above the outside diameter of the adjusting screw thread by loosening the cap screw and turning the adjusting cam.

NOTE: To determine 0.020–0.039 in., turn the adjusting screw 2 full turns out from the fully retracted position. Hold a 0.060 in. wire gauge at a 90° angle with the star wheel edge of the adjusting lever. Turn the adjusting cam until the adjusting lever and threaded area on the adjusting screw just touch the wire.

11. Secure the adjusting cam cap screw and retract the adjusting screw.
12. Install brake drums and wheels.
13. Adjust the brakes by making several forward and reverse stops until a satisfactory brake pedal height results.

Wagner

TYPE F

Two identical brake shoes are arranged on backing plate so that their toes are diagonally opposite. Two single-end wheel cylinders are arranged so that each cylinder is mounted between the toe of one shoe and the heel of the other. The two wheel cylinder pistons apply an equal amount of force to the toe of each shoe. Each cylinder casting is shaped to provide an anchor block for the brake shoe heel.

Each shoe is adjusted by means of an eccentric cam which contacts a pin pressed into brake shoe web. Each cam is attached to the backing plate by a cam and shoe guide stud which protrudes through a slot in the shoe web and, in conjunction with flat washers and C-washers, also serves as a shoe hold-down. Two return springs are connected between the shoes, one at each toe and heel.

With vehicle moving forward, both shoes are forward acting (primary shoes), self-energizing in forward direction of drum rotation. With vehicle in reverse, both shoes are reverse acting since neither is self-energized in the reverse direction of drum rotation.

Brake Shoe Removal

1. Remove both brake shoe return springs, using brake spring pliers.
2. Remove C-washer and flat washer from each adjusting cam and hold-down stud. Lift shoes off backing plate.

Cleaning and Inspection

1. Clean all dirt out of brake drum. Inspect drum for roughness, scoring, or out-of-round. Replace or recondition brake drum as necessary.
2. Inspect wheel bearings and oil seals.
3. Check backing plate attaching bolts to make sure they are tight. Clean all dirt off backing plate.
4. Inspect brake shoe return springs. If broken, cracked, or weakened, replace with new springs.
5. Check cam and shoe guide stud and friction spring on backing plate for corrosion or binding. Cam stud should turn easily with a wrench but should not be loose. If frozen, lubricate with kerosene or penetrating oil and work free.
6. Examine brake shoe linings for wear. Lining should be replaced if worn down close to rivet heads.

Brake Shoe Installation

1. Install anti-rattle spring washer on each cam and shoe guide stud, pronged side facing adjusting cam.
2. Place shoe assembly on backing plate with cam and shoe guide stud inserted through hole in shoe web; locate shoe toe in wheel cylinder piston shoe guide and position shoe heel in slot in anchor block.
3. Install flat washer and C-washer on cam and shoe guide stud. Crimp ends of C-washer together.
4. After installing both shoes, install brake shoe return

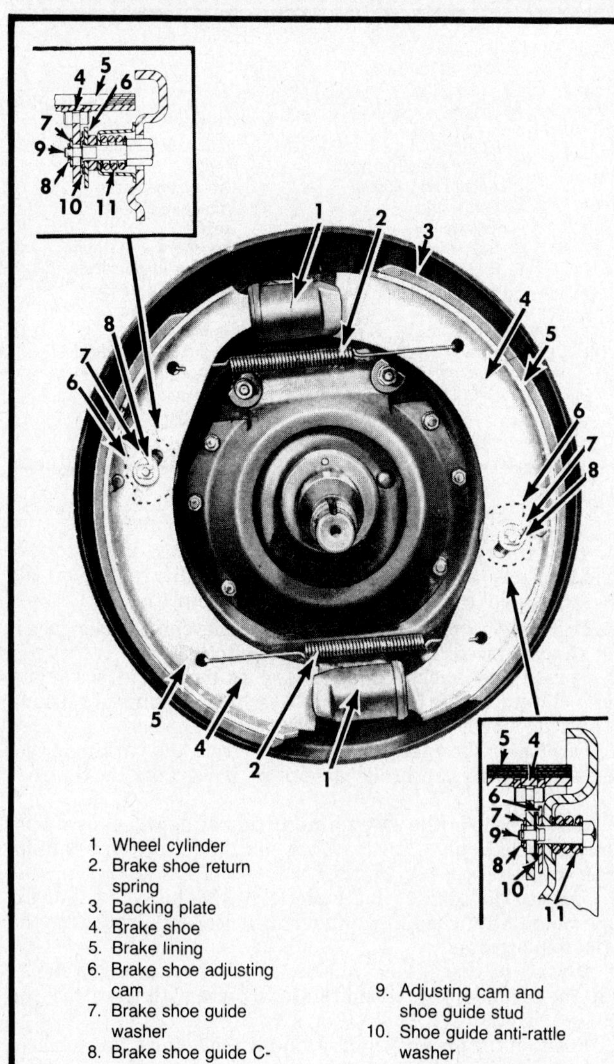

Type F brake assembly

springs. To install each spring, place spring end with short hook in toe of shoe, then using brake spring pliers, stretch spring and secure long hook end in heel of opposite shoe.

5. Install hub and brake drum assembly.
6. Adjust brake.
7. After checking pedal operation, road test vehicle.

Wagner Type FA

BRAKE SHOES

Removal

1. Block brake pedal in up position. Raise vehicle off ground and support.
2. Remove the brake drums. Disconnect the shoe retaining springs and hold down clips and lift off shoes.
3. Unhook the wedge actuating coil spring from the wedge.
4. Unhook the lever actuating spring from the shoe web, work the spring coil off the lever pivot pin and slide the spring "U" hook off the contact plug-lever pin.
5. Pull the adjuster lever from the opposite side of the shoe web, the contact plug through the shoe table and lift off the wedge washer, wedge and the wedge guide.
6. Clean all parts with the exception of the brake shoe linings in a suitable solvent. Inspect all components for wear or damage. Replace all parts that are in questionable condition.

Installation

1. Install the automatic adjuster, contact plug flush with the lining surface.
2. Position the wedge guide on the back side of the shoe with serrations facing away from the shoe table.
3. Position the wedge on the shoe with the serrations against matching serrations on the wedge guide with the slot aligned on the lever pivot pin hole.
4. Working from the drum side of the shoe, insert the contact plug, with the guide shank through the hole in the shoe table and over wedge guide and wedge.
5. Insert the adjuster lever pins through the shoe web from the opposite side, guiding actuating (center) pin into the mating hole of the contact plug shank.
6. Install the wedge washer over the shoulder of the pivot pin. Slide the U-hook of adjuster spring on the pin over the contact plug shank.
7. Attach the end of the wedge actuating spring to the U-hook of the adjusting spring. Position the coil of the adjuster torsion spring over the pivot pin and pull spring hook over the edge of shoe web.
8. Connect the wedge actuating spring on the raised hook of wedge fork.
9. Fully retract the wedge against the lever pivot pin, pressing upon contact plug to permit this movement. If the plug protrudes more than 0.005 in. above lining, clamp shoe in vise so that jaws press against adjuster lever. With a file, press down on the plug until it is even with the brake lining. Exercise caution when filing so as not to create a flat spot on the brake lining. If the fully extended plug is more than 0.005 in. below the surface of the lining, replace with a new contact plug.
10. Locate the shoe on hold-downs. Install the retracting springs, long ends of springs are at the ends of shoes.

Initial Adjustment

1. Fully release the manual cams.
2. Center each shoe by sliding up or down on its anchor slot until the leading and trailing edges of the lining are equal distant from the inner curl of the support plate.
3. Install the wheel and drum.
4. Rotate the manual adjuster cam in the direction of forward drum rotation, while rotating the drum in the same direction, until the shoe slightly drags on the brake drum. Back off adjuster until drag is just relieved. Use only sufficient adjustment torque to obtain drag that will just allow turning the wheel by hand (approximately 120–130 inch lbs.) as excessive torque may damage the adjuster mechanism.
5. Adjust other manual adjuster in the same manner, forward to tighten, and reverse to relieve drag.
6. Lower vehicle and road test. Automatic adjusters should operate from this point and additional manual adjustment should not be necessary.

Wagner Type FR–3

Each brake is equipped with two double-end wheel cylinders which apply hydraulic pressure to both the toe and the heel of two identical, self-centering shoes. The shoes anchor at either toe or heel, depending upon the direction of rotation. Each adjusting screw is threaded into or out of its support by means of an adjusting wheel. Adjusting wheels are accessible through adjusting slots in the backing plate.

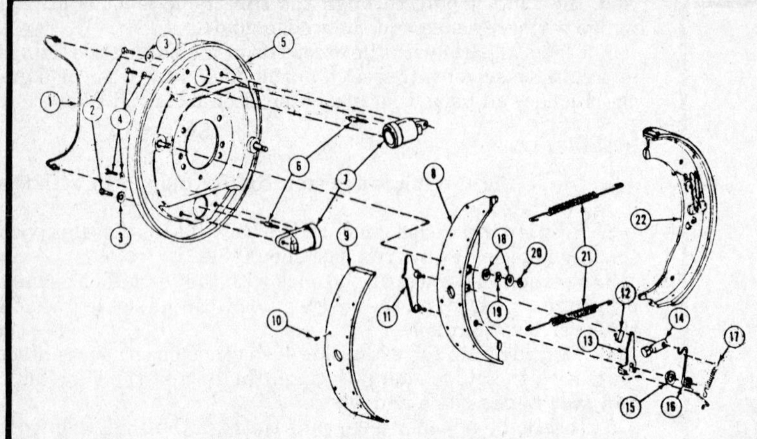

1. Connector tube
2. Cylinder anchor bolt
3. Anchor bolt washer
4. Screw and lockwasher
5. Support plate
6. Bleeder screw
7. Wheel cylinder
8. Brake shoe
9. Brake lining
10. Rivet
11. Automatic adjuster lever
12. Adjuster wedge guide
13. Automatic adjuster wedge
14. Drum contact plug
15. Wedge retainter washer
16. Adjuster wedge spring
17. Adjuster torsion spring
18. Shoe guide washer
19. Shoe guide wave washer
20. Shoe guide C-washer
21. Shoe retracting spring
22. Complete shoe assembly

Exploded view of Wagner type FA brake assembly

BRAKE SHOES

Removal

1. Remove hub and brake drum assembly.
2. Install wheel cylinder clamps to hold pistons in cylinders.
3. Remove brake shoe return springs.
4. Remove lock wires, nuts, and washers from brake shoe guide bolts, then remove brake shoe assemblies.
5. Remove screws attaching adjusting wheel lock springs to anchor supports. Thread each adjusting screw from the shoe side of its anchor support by turning adjusting wheels, then lift adjusting wheels out of slots in anchor supports.

Installation

1. Install adjusting screws and wheels in anchor supports dry; use no lubricant. Insert each adjusting wheel in slot in anchor support, insert threaded end of adjusting screw in anchor support, then turn adjusting wheel to thread adjusting screw into anchor support. Insert anchor pins into holes in anchor supports, with slots in pins facing slots in supports.
2. Install brake shoes with cutaway end of shoe web next to adjusting screw and with ends of shoes engaging slots in wheel cylinder push rods and anchor pins. Install flat washer and nut on each brake shoe guide bolt. Tighten nuts finger-tight, then back off nuts only far enough to allow movement of shoes without binding.
3. Install brake shoe return springs, hooking one end of each spring in brake shoe web, then hook other end over anchor pins.
4. Remove wheel cylinder clamps.
5. Install hub and brake drum assembly.
6. Adjust brakes.
7. After checking pedal operation, road test vehicle.

Bendix Duo Servo Type

BRAKE SHOES

Removal and Installation

1. With the vehicle raised and supported safely, loosen the parking brake equlizer nut, if working on the rear wheel brakes.
2. Remove the drums andthe brake shoe return springs, while noting the position of the secondary spring overlapping the primary spring.
3. Remove the brake shoe return retainers, springs and nails.
4. Slide the eye of the automatic adjuster cable off the top anchor and then unhook the cable from the adjusting lever. Remove the cable, cable guide and the anchor plate.
5. Disconnect the lever spring from the lever and disengage it from the shoe web. Remove the spring and lever.
6. Spread the anchor ends of the primary and secondary shoes and remove the parking brake strut and spring, if working on the rear wheels.
7. Disengage the parking brake cable from the parking brake lever and remove the brake assembly, if working on the rear wheels.
8. Remove the brake assembly and adjusting wheel assembly from the backing plate. Install a wheel cylinder piston retaining spring over the wheel cylinder.
9. Inspect the backing plate platforms for nick, burrs or extreme wear. After cleaning, apply a thin coat of lubricant to the suypport platforms.
10. If working on the rear wheels, attach the parking brake lever to the secondary shoe and retain in place with the attaching clip.
11. Position the primary and secondary shoes on a flat surface.
12. Lubricate the threads of the adjusting screw and install it between the primary and secondary shoes with the star wheel next to the secondary shoe. The star wheels are marked "R"(right side) and "L" (left side) and indicate their location on the vehicle.
13. Overlap anchor ends of the primary and secondary brake shoes and install the adjusting spring and lever.
14. Hold the brake shoes in their relative position on the backing plate and if working with the rear brake shoes, engage the parking brake cable into the parking brake lever.
15. Retain the brake shoes with the retainer nails, springs and retainer, while installing the rear wheels parking brake strut and spring in position between the two shoes, if working on the rear wheels.
16. Complete the installation of the shoes to the backing plate and install the anchor pin plate.
17. Install the eye of the adjusting cable over the anchor pin and install the return spring between the primary shoe and the anchor spring.
18. Install the cable guide in the secondary shoe. Then install the secondary return spring, being sure the the secondary spring overlaps the primary spring.
19. Place the adjusting cable in the groove of the cable guide and engage the hook of the cable into the adjusting lever.
20. Be sure the adjuster operates satisfactorily and adjust the brake shoes to match the drum diameter.
21. Install the brake drum and retaining clips, make final brake shoe adjustments and prepare for road test.

Two-Piston Single Cylinder Hydraulically Actuated Type

Both shoes pivot on anchor pins at the bottom of the support plate. The shoes are actuated by one wheel cylinder which is of the double piston type. Specifications for heel and toe clearance of the shoes should be strictly followed to obtain efficient brake operation.

BRAKE SHOES

Removal And Installation

1. Back off the adjusting cam and remove the wheel and drum assembly.
2. Remove the brake shoe return spring
3. Install wheel cylinder piston clamp to prevent the pistons from being forced from the cylinder.
4. Remove the C-washer and retainer, guide spring retainer and guide spring from the anchor bolts to remove the brake shoes.
5. To install the brake shoes, reverse the removal procedure.

ADJUSTMENTS

Since tapered brake lining is thicker at the center than at the ends, the adjustment procedures outlined must be performed in order to assure maximum braking efficiency.

Minor Adjustment

1. Raise the vehicle and support safely so that the wheels of the brakes to be adjusted can be rotated freely.
2. While rotating the wheel forward and backward. adjust the shoe out to the drum with the adjusting cam until a light drag is obtained.
3. Back off the adjustment until the wheel is free to turn.
4. Repeat this operation on the other shoe. Continue to adjust the other brake shoes in a like manner.

Major Adjustment

1. Be sure the fluid level in the master cylinder is $^3/_8$–$^1/_2$in. from the top of the reservoir.
2. Loosen the locknuts and turn the brake shoe anchor bolts to the fully released position.
3. Adjust the anchor bolt and cam, the minor anchor bolt and the minor adjustment cam at the top of the brake shoe to give equal clearance at the toe and heel of the brake shoes. Make sure that sufficient center contact is maintained to produce a slight drag.
4. Lock the anchor adjusting nut. After adjusting the clearance on one shoe, repeat the procedure on the other shoe, then apply the brakes a couple of times to make sure the adjustment is to specifications.

NOTE: Whenever cams are adjusted, check the brakes

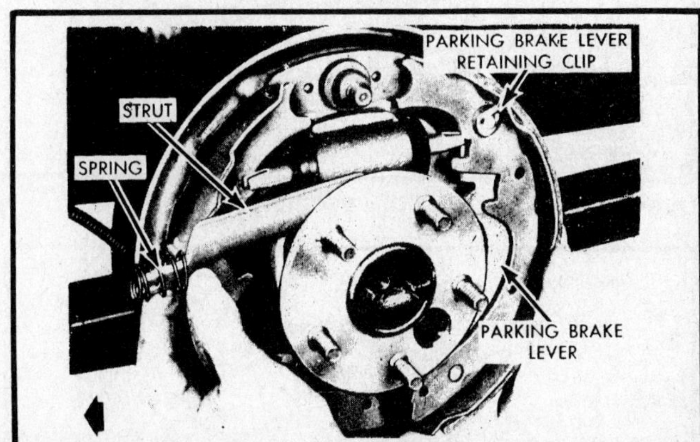

Removing or installing parking brake strut and spring—rear

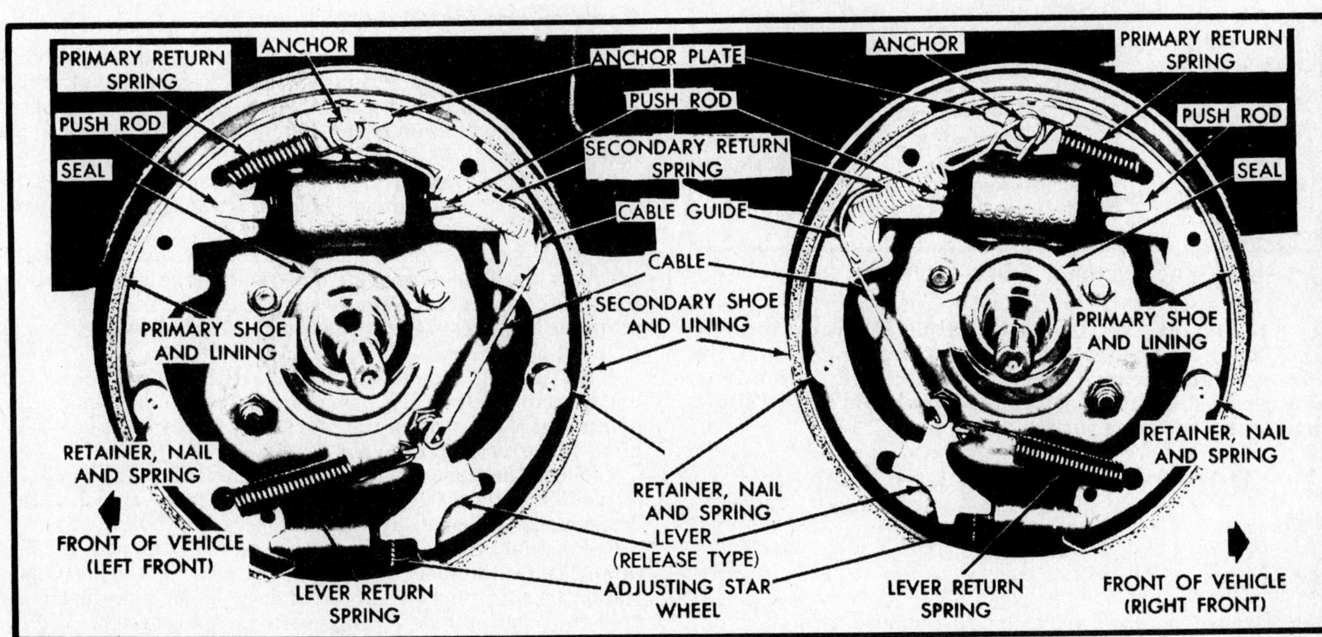

Chrysler front brake assembly

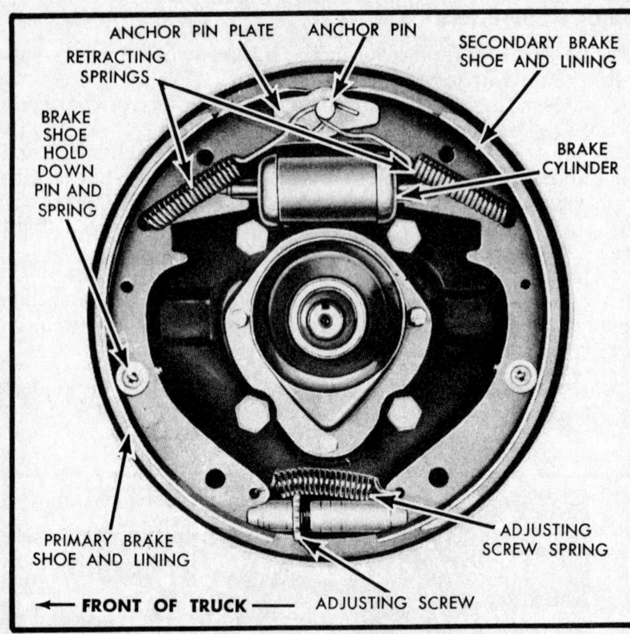

Duo-servo single anchor assembly

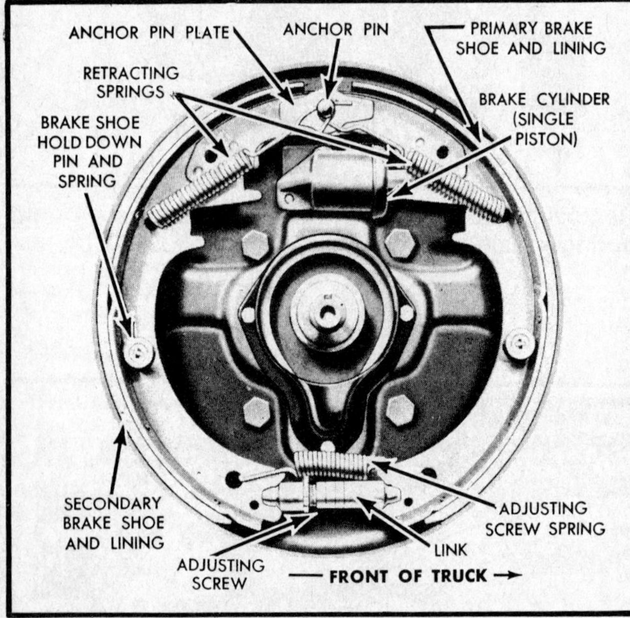

Uni-servo single anchor brake assembly

by applying pressure on the brake pedal several times so as to make sure wheel drag has not increased, since the spring loaded cams may cause shoe adjustment to change by shifting position. Wheels should have a slight drag at room temperature.

Bendix Single Anchor Brakes

BRAKE SHOES

Removal

1. Remove the wheel and drum. Do not push down the brake pedal after the brake drum has been removed. On a truck equipped with a vacuum or air booster, be sure the engine is stopped and there is no vacuum or air pressure in the system before disconnecting the hydraulic lines.
2. Clamp the brake cylinder boots against the ends of the cylinder, and remove the brake shoe retracting springs from both shoes.
3. Remove the anchor pin plate.
4. Remove the hold-down spring cups and springs from the shoes, and remove the shoes and the adjusting screw parts from the carrier plate. Do not let oil or grease touch the brake linings. If the shoes on a rear brake assembly are being removed, remove the parking brake lever, link, and spring with the shoes. Unhook the parking brake cable from the lever as the shoes are being removed.
5. If the shoes are from a rear brake assembly, remove the parking brake lever from the secondary shoe.

Installation

1. Coat all points of contact between the brake shoes and the other brake assembly parts with Lubriplate® or a similar lubricant. Lubricate the adjusting screw threads.
2. Place the adjusting screw, socket, and nut on the brake shoes so that the star wheel on the screw is opposite the adjusting hole in the carrier plate. Then install the adjusting screw spring.
3. Position the brake shoes and the adjusting screw parts on the carrier plate, and install the hold-down spring pins, springs, and cups. When assemblying a rear brake, connect the parking brake lever to the secondary shoe, and install the link and spring with the shoes. Be sure to hook the parking brake cable to the lever.
4. Install the anchor pin plate on the pin.
5. Install the brake shoe retracting springs on both shoes. The primary shoe spring must be installed first.
6. Remove the clamp from the brake cylinder boots.
7. Install the wheel and drum.
8. Bleed the system and adjust the brakes. Check the brake pedal operation after bleeding the system.

Bendix Double Anchor Brakes

BRAKE SHOES

Removal and Installation

1. Remove the wheel and drum. Do not push down the brake pedal after the brake drum has been removed. On trucks equipped with vacuum boosters, be sure the engine is stopped and there is no vacuum in the system before disconnecting the hydraulic lines.
2. Clamp the brake cylinder boots against the ends of the cylinder, and remove the brake shoe retracting springs from both shoes.
3. At each shoe, remove the 2 brake shoe retainers and washers from the hold-down pins and remove the spring and pin from the carrier plate. Remove the anchor pin retainers and remove the shoes from the anchor pins. Do not allow grease or oil to touch the linings.
4. Clean all brake assembly parts. If the adjusting cams do not operate freely apply a small quantity of lubricating oil to points where the shaft of the cam enters the carrier plate. Wipe dirt and corrosion off the plate.
5. Clean the ledges on the carrier plate with sandpaper. Coat all points of contact between the brake shoes and the other brake assembly parts with high temperature grease.
6. Position the brake shoes on the carrier plate with the heel (lower) end of the shoes over the anchor pins and the toe (upper) end of the shoes engaged in the brake cylinder link. Install the hold-down spring pins, spring, washers and retainers.
7. Install the anchor pin retainers and then install the brake shoe return spring.

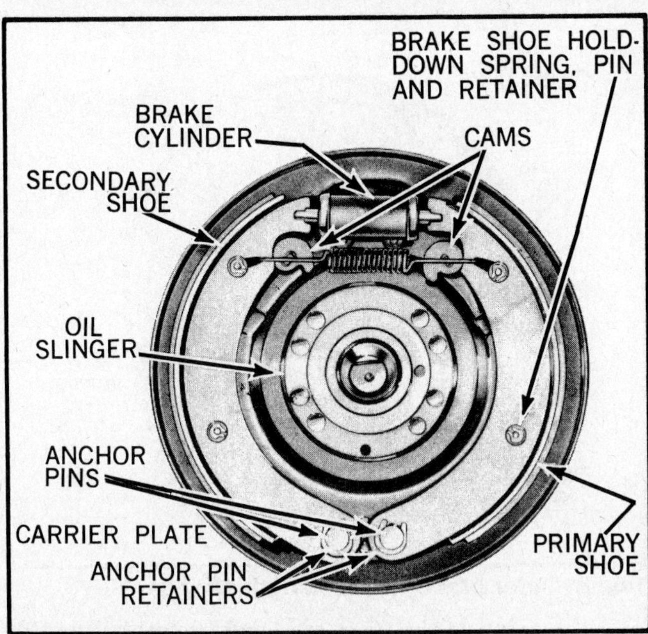

Double anchor brake assembly

8. Turn the brake shoe adjusting cams to obtain maximum clearance for brake drum installation.
9. Install the wheel and drum assembly.
10. Bleed the brake system and adjust the brakes.
11. Check brake pedal operation and road test.

Bendix Two Cylinder Brakes

BRAKE SHOE

Removal

1. Remove the wheel, and then remove the drum or the hub and drum assembly. Mark the hub and drum to aid assembly in the same position. On trucks equipped with vacuum or air boosters, be sure the engine is stopped and there is no vacuum or air pressure in the system before disconnecting the hydraulic lines.
2. Clamp the brake cylinder boots against the ends of the cylinder and remove the four brake shoe retracting springs.
3. Remove the brake shoe guide bolt cotter pin, nut, washer, and bolt from both shoes, and remove the shoes from the carrier plate.
4. Remove the clamp-type adjusting wheel lock from the anchor pin support, and unthread the adjusting screw and wheel assembly from the anchor pin support.

Installation

1. Clean the carrier plate ledges with sandpaper. Coat all points of contact between the brake shoes and other brake assembly parts with high temperature grease.
2. Thread the adjusting screw and wheel assembly into the anchor pin support and install the clamp-type adjusting wheel lock. Thread the adjusting wheel into the support so that the brake shoe will rest against the adjusting wheel end.
3. Place the brake shoe over the two brake shoe anchor pins, insert the ends in the brake cylinder links, and install the shoe guide bolt, washer, and nut. Finger tighten the nut, then back off one full turn, and install the cotter pin.
4. Install the four retracting springs.
5. Remove the cylinder clamps, install the drum or the hub and drum assembly, then install the wheel assembly. Align the marks on the hub and drum during installation.
6. Bleed and adjust the brakes.
7. Check pedal operation and road test.

BENDIX BRAKE SHOES

ADJUSTMENT

The brake drums should be at normal room temperature, when the brake shoes are adjusted. If the shoes are adjusted when the shoes are hot and expanded, the shoes may drag as the drums cool and contract.

A minor brake adjustment re-establishes the brake lining-to-drum clearance and compensates for normal lining wear.

A major brake adjustment includes the adjustment of the brake shoe anchor pins as well as the brake shoes. Adjustment of the anchor pin permits the centering of the brake shoes in the drum.

Adjustment procedures for each type of brake assembly are given under the applicable heading.

Minor Adjustment

The brake shoe adjustment procedures for the uniservo single anchor brake assembly are the same as those for the duo-servo single anchor type.

A major brake adjustment should be performed when dragging brakes are not corrected by a minor adjustment, when brake shoes are relined or replaced, or when brake drums are machined.

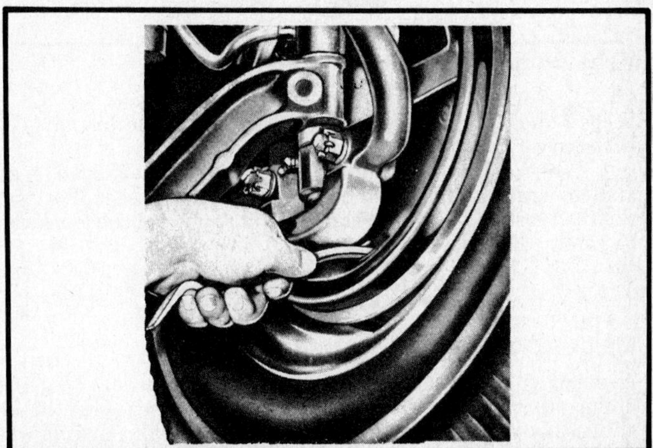

Duo-servo brake adjustment

Duo-Servo Single Anchor Brake

The duo-servo single-anchor brake is adjusted by turning an adjusting screw located between the lower ends of the shoes.

1. Raise the truck until the wheels clear the floor.
2. Remove the cover from the adjusting hole at the bottom of the brake carrier plate, and turn the adjusting screw inside the hole to expand the brake shoes until they drag against the brake drum.
3. When the shoes are against the drum, back off the adjusting screw 10 or 12 notches so that the drum rotates freely without drag.
4. Install the adjusting hole cover on the brake carrier plate.
5. Check and adjust the other three brake assemblies. When adjusting the rear brake shoes, check the parking brake cables for proper adjustment. Make sure that there is clearance between the ends of the parking brake link and the shoes.
6. Apply the brakes. If the pedal travels more than halfway down between the released position and the floor, too much clearance exists between the brake shoes and the drums. Repeat

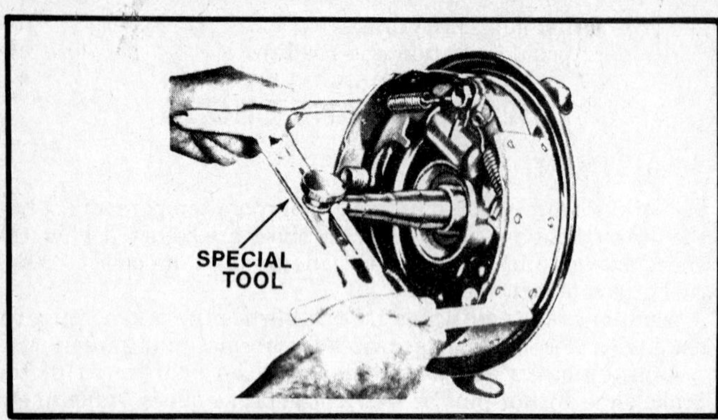

Measuring brake shoes

Measuring brake drum

Steps 2 and 3 above. Internal inspection and/or bleeding may be necessary.

7. When all brake shoes have been properly adjusted, road test the truck and check the operation of the brakes. Perform the road test only when the brakes will apply and the truck can be safely stopped.

SINGLE ANCHOR PIN

Major Adjustment

A major brake adjustment should be made when dragging brakes are not corrected by a minor adjustment, when brake shoes are relined or replaced, or when brake drums are machined.

1. Raise the truck until the wheel clears the floor.
2. Rotate the drum until the feeler slot is opposite the lower end of the secondary (rear) brake shoe.
3. Insert a 0.010 in. feeler gauge through the slot in the drum. Move the feeler up along the secondary shoe unit it is wedged between the secondary shoe and the drum.
4. Turn the adjusting screw (star wheel) to expand the brake shoes until a heavy drag is felt against the drum. Back off the adjusting screw just enough to establish a clearance of 0.010 in. between the shoe and the drum at a point 1 $\frac{1}{2}$ in. from each end of the secondary shoe. This adjustment will provide correct operating clearance for both the primary and secondary shoes. If the 0.010 in. clearance cannot be obtained at both ends of the secondary shoe, the anchor pin must be adjusted.
5. To adjust the anchor pin setting, loosen the anchor pin nut just enough to permit moving the pin up or down by tapping the nut with a soft hammer. Do not back the nut off too far or the shoes will move out of position when the nut is tightened. Tap the anchor pin in a direction that will allow the shoes to center in the drum and provide an operating clearance of 0.010 in.. Torque the anchor pin nut to 80–100 ft. lbs. Recheck the secondary shoe clearance at both the heel and toe ends of the shoe.
6. When all brake shoes and anchor pins have been properly adjusted, road test the truck and check the operation of the brakes. Perform the road test only when the brakes will apply and the truck can be safely stopped.

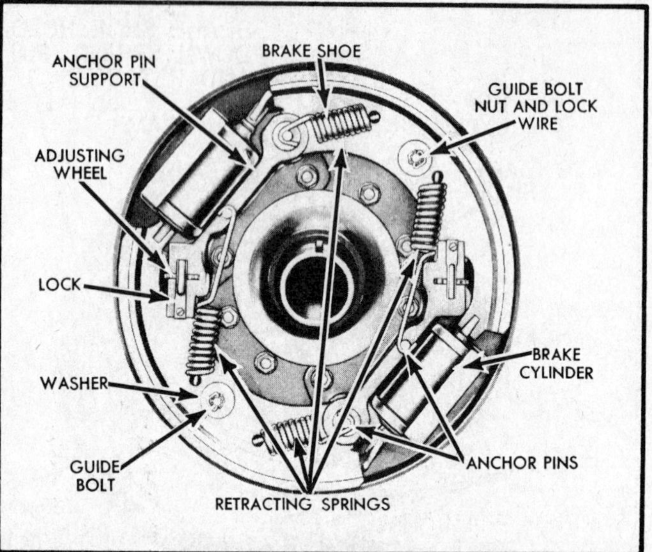

Two cylinder brake—equal length springs

Double Anchor Pin

Major Adjustment

1. Raise the truck until the wheels clear the floor.
2. Rotate the drum until the feeler slot is opposite the lower (heel) end of the secondary (rear) brake shoe.
3. Insert a 0.007 in. feeler gauge through the slot in the drum. Move the feeler up along the secondary shoe until it is wedged between the shoe and the drum.
4. Loosen the secondary shoe anchor pin nut. Turn the secondary shoe anchor pin until the brake shoe-to-drum clearance at a point 1 $\frac{1}{2}$ in. from the heel end of the shoe is 0.007 in. Remove the feeler gauge.
5. Rotate the drum until the feeler slot is opposite the upper (toe) end of the secondary brake shoe.
6. Insert a 0.010 in. feeler gauge through the slot in the drum. Move the feeler gauge down along the secondary shoe until it is wedged between the shoe and the drum. Turn the adjusting cam, to expand the brake shoe, until a heavy drag is felt against the drum.
7. Turn the anchor pin until the brake shoe-to-drum clearance at a point 1 $\frac{1}{2}$ in. from the toe end of the shoe is 0.010 in.. Remove the feeler gauge.
8. Torque the anchor pin nut to 80–100 ft. lbs. Recheck the heel and toe clearances.
9. Using the preceding secondary brake shoe adjustment procedure as a guide, adjust the primary brake shoe-to-drum clearance.
10. Road test the truck and check the operation of the brakes.

NOTE: Perform the road test only when the brakes will apply and the truck can be safely stopped.

Kelsey-Hayes

FRONT BRAKE SHOES

Removal

1. Raise the vehicle until the wheel clears the floor. Remove the wheel, drum and hub assembly.

2. Clamp the wheel cylinder boots against the ends of the cylinder.
3. Remove the brake shoe retracting springs from both shoes.
4. Remove the adjusting lever link, anchor plate and the adjusting lever spring.
5. Remove the hold down spring cups, springs and the adjusting lever.
6. Remove the brake shoes and adjuster screw assembly from the backing plate.

Installation

1. Clean all brake dust from the brake assembly parts with a clean dry rag.
2. Coat all points of contact between the shoes and other brake parts with high temperature grease.

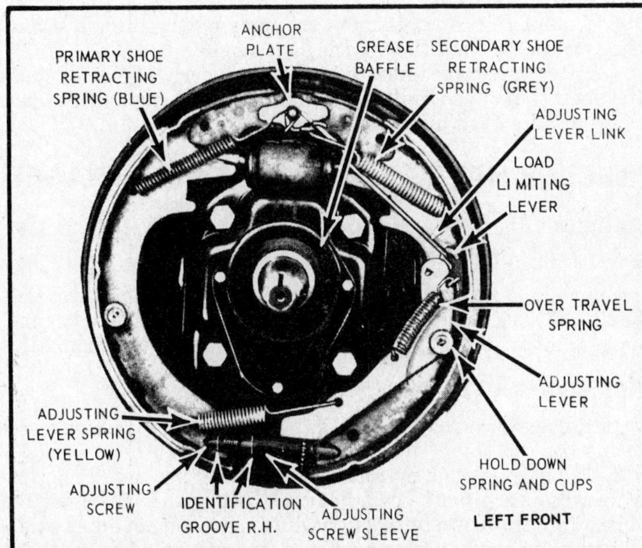

Kelsey-Hayes front brake assembly

3. Coat the adjuster screw with high temperature grease before assembly. Thread the adjuster screw into the adjuster screw sleeve.
4. Position the brake shoes on the backing plate and install the adjusting lever, hold down pins, springs and cups.
5. Position the adjuster screw assembly on the brake shoes so that the star wheel is opposite the adjusting slot in the backing plate. Install the adjusting lever spring.
6. Install the anchor plate and adjusting lever link.
7. Install the secondary brake shoe retracting spring.
8. Install the primary brake shoe retracting spring.
9. Remove the clamp from the wheel cylinder boots.
10. Install the wheel, drum and hub assembly.
11. Adjust the brakes. Subsequent adjustment will be automatic.

REAR BRAKE SHOES

Removal

1. Raise the truck until the wheel clears the floor.
2. Remove the wheel, hub and drum assembly.
3. Clamp the brake cylinder boots against the ends of the cylinder with brake piston clamps.
4. The two different types of brake shoe retracting springs and remove the springs.
5. Remove the brake shoe hold down post cotter key, nut, and shoe hold down washer.
6. Loosen and remove the eccentric adjuster bolt, lock washer, eccentric and adjusting link.
7. Remove the shoe and lining assembly from the backing plate.
8. Remove the anchor block spring and slide the adjuster assembly from the shoe web.
9. Remove the adjuster star wheel and screw from the adjuster block. Unthread the star wheel from the adjuster screw.

Installation

1. Wipe all brake dust from the brake assembly parts with a clean dry rag. Coat all points of contact between brake shoes and other parts with high temperature grease.

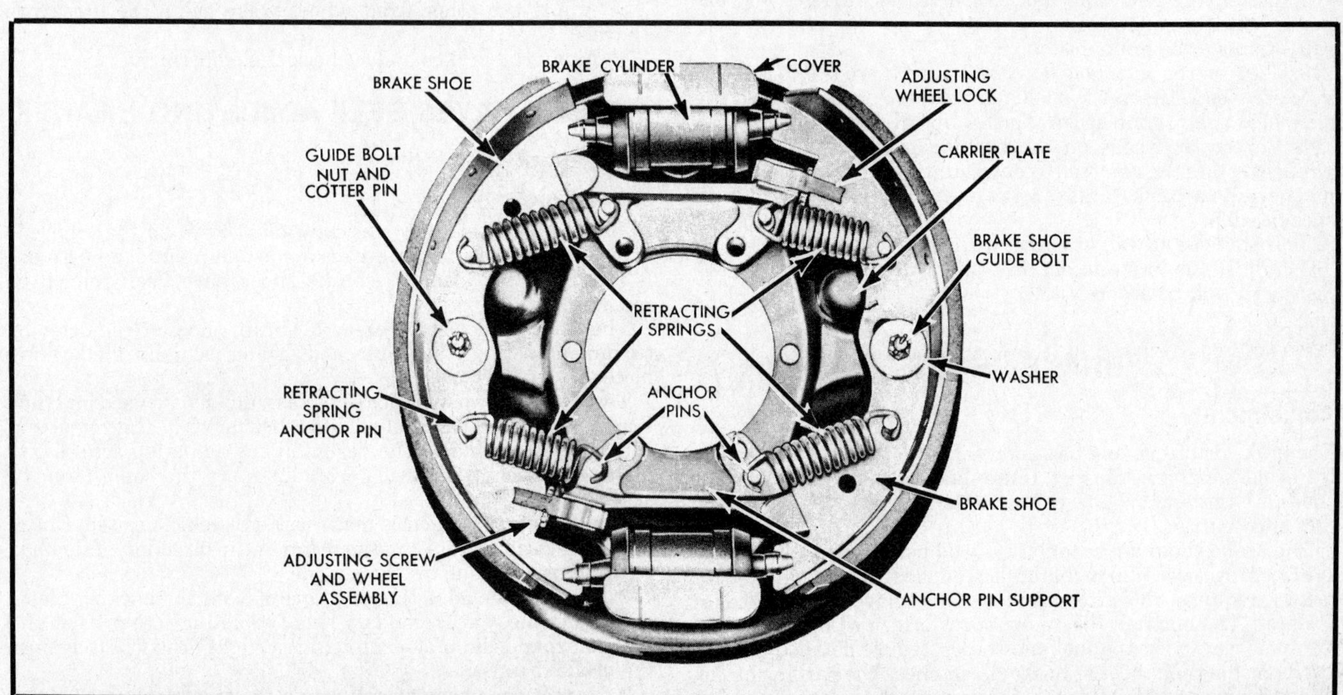

Two cylinder brake—unequal length springs

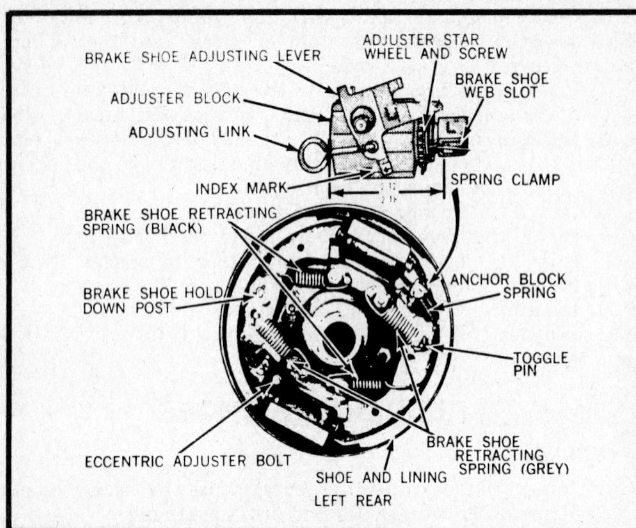

Kelsey-Hayes rear brake assembly

2. Coat the adjuster screw and the inside of the adjuster block with high temperature grease.
3. Thread the adjuster screw onto the star wheel and insert the adjuster screw assembly into the adjuster block. Maintain a 2.12–2.18 in. dimension from the end of the adjuster block to the adjuster screw web slot.
4. Install the adjuster assembly onto the shoe web and attach the anchor block spring.
5. Place the brake shoe over the retracting spring toggle pin and insert the ends of the shoe in the wheel cylinder links.
6. Install the shoe hold down washer and nut. Do not install the cotter pin.
7. Install the four brake shoe retracting springs. Make sure the retracting springs are installed. On 15 × 5 in. brakes the inner hook ends face the wheel cylinders. On 15 × 4 in. brakes the inner hook ends face the center of the axle.
8. Install the adjusting link, eccentric, lockwasher and adjuster bolt. Do not tighten.
9. Remove the brake piston clamps.
10. Tighten the shoe hold down nut until there is 0.015–0.025 in. clearance between the shoe and hold down washer with the shoe held against the backing plate. Install the cotter pin.
11. Center the shoes on the backing plate. Using a $\frac{1}{2}$ in. wrench, rotate the adjuster eccentric until the adjusting lever is at the index mark. Tighten the eccentric adjuster bolt to specification.
12. Install the wheel, hub and drum assembly.
13. Adjust the brake to obtain a slight drag. Subsequent adjustments will be automatic.

BRAKE SHOES

Adjustment

The brake drums should be at normal room temperature, when the brake shoes are adjusted. If the shoes are adjusted when the shoes are hot and expanded, the shoes may drag as the drums cool and contract.

The brake shoes are automatically adjusted when the vehicle is driven in reverse and the brakes applied. A manual adjustment is required only after the brake shoes have been relined or replaced. The manual adjustment is performed while the drums are removed, using the tool and the procedure detailed below.

When adjusting the rear brake shoes, check the parking brake cables for proper adjustment. Make sure that the equalizer operates freely.

ADJUSTMENT OF BRAKE SHOES

1. Use special drum diameter to lining gauge and adjust the lining to the inside diameter of the drum braking surface.
2. Reverse the gauge and adjust the brake shoes to touch the gauge. The gauge contact points on the shoes must be parallel to the vehicle with the center line through the center of the axle. Hold the automatic adjusting lever out of engagement while rotating the adjusting screw, to prevent burring the screw slots. Make sure the adjusting screw rotates freely.
3. Apply a small quantity of high temperature grease to the points where the shoes contact the carrier plate, being careful not to get the lubricant on the linings.
4. Install the drums. Install the retaining nuts and tighten securely.
5. Install the wheels on the drums and tighten the mounting nuts to specification.
6. Complete the adjustment by applying the brakes several times while backing the vehicle.
7. After the brake shoes have been properly adjusted, check the operation of the brakes by making several stops while operating in a forward direction.

KELSEY-HAYES SELF ADJUSTING BRAKES

Adjustment

TWO CYLINDER FRONT BRAKES

Two cylinder front brakes are adjusted by means of exposed, hex-head, self-locking cam adjusters. The brakes are to be manually adjusted initially. Subsequent adjustment is automatic.

Adjustment of Brakes

1. Raise the vehicle and check the front brakes for drag by rotating the wheels.
2. Adjust one shoe by rotating the wheel backward and forward while turning the cam hex-head with a wrench. Bring the shoe out to the drum until a light drag is felt. Do not apply excessive force on the hex head cam, as automatic adjuster parts can be damaged. Back off the adjustment until the wheel turns freely. Adjust the other cam on the same wheel in the same manner.
3. Adjust the other front wheel brake using the procedure above.
4. Apply the brakes and recheck the adjustment.

KELSEY-HAYES SELF ADJUSTING BRAKES

Adjustment

Rear Brakes

The brake shoes are automatically adjusted when the vehicle is driven in reverse and the brakes applied. A manual adjustment is required only after the brake shoes have been relined or replaced.

The two-cylinder brake assembly brake shoes are adjusted by turning adjusting wheels reached through slots in the backing plate.

Two types of two-cylinder brake assemblies are used on truck rear wheels. The assemblies differ primarily in the retracting spring hookup, and in the design of the adjusting screws and locks. However, the service procedures are the same for both assemblies.

The brake adjustment is made with the vehicle raised. Check the brake drag by rotating the drum in the direction of forward rotation as the adjustment is made.

1. Remove the adjusting slot covers from the backing plate.
2. Turn the rear (secondary shoe) adjusting screw inside the hole to expand the brake shoe until a slight drag is felt against the brake drum.
3. Repeat the above procedure on the front (primary) brake shoe.

4. Replace the adjusting hole covers.
5. Complete the adjustment by applying the brakes several times while backing the vehicle.
6. After the brake shoes have been properly adjusted, check the operation of the brakes by making several stops while operating in a forward direction.

Rear Brake Assembly Used With Hydro-Max Power Booster

1984 AND LATER

The rear drum brakes are a completely new simplified design incorporating many air brake type features. Shoe and lining removal requires only removal of the two shoe retractor springs. The automatic adjusting mechanisms are part of the wheel cylinder pistons and are submerged in the brake fluid protected from any road contaminants. Automatic adjustment will take place in either forward or reverse direction. The lining blocks, four per wheel, are tapered from $^3/_4$ in. thick in the center to $^5/_8$ in. thick at the ends. There are two lining inspection holes in the backing plate with removable rubber plugs. The lining blocks have a wear limit groove in the edge of the material visible through the inspection holes.The shoes can be backed off manually through two 'adj' access holes in the backing plate for drum removal.

MANUAL ADJUSTMENT

Manual adjustment should not be considered as an alternative to the auto-adjuster. It has two functions:

1. To initially set shoe to drum clearance with automatic adjusting brakes, it is important to set the shoe to drum clearance prior to driving the vehicle. To adjust, using the backing plate as a fulcrum, turn the manual override wheel in a counter-clockwise direction as viewed when looking down the piston.
2. To de-adjust the brake shoes (where there is a lipped drum condition), remove the plugs from the adjustment holes marked 'ADJ' in the backing plate. Insert a brake adjustment tool or a flat-bladed screwdriver until it engages a slot in the manual override wheel. Use the backing plate as a fulcrum to turn the manual override wheel in a clockwise direction (as viewed when looking down the piston) until the lining clears the drum. Repeat with the other shoe and remove the drum.

BRAKE SHOE AND LINING

Removal

NOTE: Always replace brake shoes and linings in axle sets. When replacing shoes, always replace the return springs to insure proper operation of the auto-adjuster.

1. Raise the vehicle and install safety stands. Remove the wheel and tire assembly.
2. Remove the adjuster plugs from the slots in the backing plate marked 'ADJ'. Remove the adjuster sight hole plugs.
3. Insert a brake adjustment tool or a flat-bladed screwdriver into the adjustment slot until the blade engages the slots in the adjustment wheel. Turn the wheel in a clockwise direction (when viewed looking down the piston) until the shoe and lining clears the drum. Remove the drum.
4. In order for de-adjustment to take place, there must be a load applied to the wheel cylinder pistons. For this reason, fully de-adjust both wheel cylinders before removing the shoes.

NOTE: To avoid locking the auto-adjust mechanism in the fully de-adjusted position, wind out each wheel cylinder piston one complete turn after fully de-adjusting the pistons.

5. Remove the springs, with a removal tool.
6. Insert the removal tool in the loop on the return spring. Rest the fulcrum of the tool against the wheel cylinder body. Unhook the spring from the shoe web. Support the lower shoe and repeat procedure for other spring. Remove the shoes. Remove and discard the springs.

NOTE: Make sure the fulcrum of the tool does not rest on the adjusting wheel or the dust boot.

CAUTION

Do not use an air gun to remove dust from the backing plate. Remove dust with Brake Service Vacuum. Dust may also be removed with a damp rag.

7. Inspect the wheel cylinder/adjuster for leaks by removing the tappet head assembly. Lift the dust boot from the piston. If fluid escapes, rebuild or replace the wheel cylinder/adjuster.
8. Inspect the wheel cylinder/parking brake expander by removing the dust boot and inspecting for leaks. If leaks are present, rebuild or replace the wheel cylinder/expander.
9. If leakage is not evident, install the dust boot and tappet head assembly on the wheel cylinder. Temporarily place an elastic band around the cylinders to keep the pistons in place. Use a wire brush to remove any corrosion from the backing plate, taking care not to damage the wheel cylinder and boots.

Installation

1. Remove the elastic band from the wheel cylinders.
2. Lightly smear the abutment ends of the new shoes and the tips of the steady posts with high temperature grease. Keep the grease away from all hydraulic components and the shoe linings. The replacement brake shoes must be installed correctly to the brake, i.e. the linings are symmetrical on platform, although there is a taper on the shoe, the only way to correct installation is via the web profile.
3. Use the correct color of new shoe return springs. The RED colored springs with one coil is used on wheel cylinder/parking brake expander side of the backing plate on the right and left side. The GREEN colored shoe return spring with two coils is used on the wheel cylinder/adjuster side of the LEFT brake assembly. The YELLOW colored spring with two coils is used on the wheel cylinder/adjuster on the RIGHT brake assembly.

NOTE: After a spring is removed, it must be discarded and replaced with a new spring to insure proper operation of the auto-adjuster.

4. Install the springs on the shoes into position. Insert the end of the spring opposite the loop in the shoe. Use the spring removal-installation tool by placing it in the loop of the spring. Rest the fulcrum of the tool on the wheel cylinder body. Use the tool as a lever to lift up the spring and insert it into the hole in the shoe.

CAUTION

Make sure the fulcrum of the tool does not rest on the manual override wheel or dust boot of the wheel cylinder.

5. Install the drum or spider/drum assembly.
6. Manually adjust the wheel cylinders through the backing plate adjusting holes until the shoe to drum clearance is less than 1.8 mm (0.070 in.). Apply the brake pedal to centralize the shoes and release the brake pedal.
7. Check the shoe to drum clearance by using a feeler gauge placed through the lining inspection holes in the backing plate.

If the reading is not 0.51–0.76mm (0.020–0.030 in.), manually adjust the wheel cylinder through the manual override wheel until the specified dimensions are obtained.

8. Bleed the brakes.
9. Install the wheel and tire. Install the lug nuts and tighten.
10. Insert the plugs in the inspection, adjuster slot and adjustment slots in the backing plate.
11. Check the brake fluid level in the master cylinder.

NOTE: The service brake system uses Ford Heavy Duty Brake Fluid, C6AZ-19542-A or -B (ESA-M6C25-A) or equivalent and is filled at the Hydro-Max master cylinder. The parking brake system uses Ford Automatic Transmission Fluid, ESP-M2C138-CJ, DEXRON® II or equivalent and is filled at the brake pump reservoir. DO NOT MIX FLUIDS.

12. Road test vehicle and check brake operation.

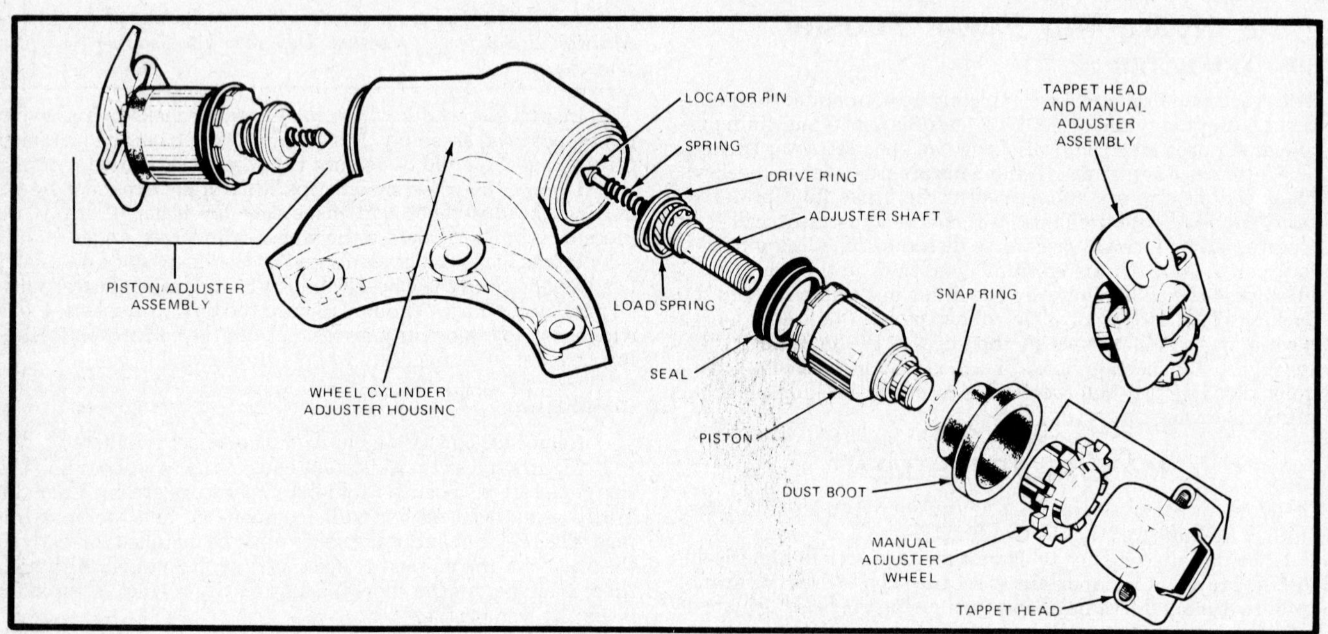

Exploded view wheel cylinder/adjuster

DISC BRAKE SERVICE

DISC BRAKES—TROUBLE DIAGNOSIS

Cause	Correction
1. Master cylinder fluid level low.	1. Fill to proper level with approved fluid. (Fluid level drops as disc brake linings wear.)
2. Poor quality brake fluid (low boiling point) in system.	2. Drain hydraulic system and fill with approved.
3. Air in hydraulic system.	3. Bleed hydraulic system and refill with approved fluid.
4. Hoses soft or weak (expanding under pressure).	4. Replace defective hoses. Combination valve and all cups and seals in complete brakes.
1. Power brake malfunctioning.	1. Check and repair power unit.
2. Linings soiled with brake fluid, oil or grease.	2. Replace shoes and linings.
3. Lines, hoses or connections dented, kinked, collapsed, clogged or disconnected.	3. Repair or replace defective parts.
4. Master cylinder cups swollen.	4. Drain hydraulic system, flush system with brake fluid and replace combination valve and all cups and seals in complete brake system.
5. Master cylinder bore corroded or rough.	5. Repair or replace master cylinder.

DISC BRAKES—TROUBLE DIAGNOSIS

Cause	Correction
6. Caliper pistons frozen or seized.	6. Disassemble caliper and free pistons (replace if necessary).
7. Caliper cylinder bores corroded or rough.	7. Disassemble caliper and remove corrosion or roughness, or replace caliper.
8. Pedal push rod and linkage binding.	8. Free and lubricate.
9. Metering valve not working.	9. Replace combination valve.
GRABBING OR PULLING (Severe Reaction To Pedal Pressure and Out of Line Stops)	
1. Linings soiled with brake fluid, oil or grease.	1. Replace shoes and linings.
2. Caliper loose.	2. Tighten caliper mounting bolts to specified torque.
3. Lines, hoses or connection dented, kinked, collapsed or clogged.	3. Repair or replace defective parts.
4. Master cylinder bore corroded or rough.	4. Repair or replace master cylinder.
5. Caliper pistons frozen or seized.	5. Disassemble caliper and free pistons (replace if necessary).
6. Caliper cylinder seals soft or swollen.	6. Drain hydraulic system, flush system with brake fluid and replace all cups and seals in complete brake system.
7. Caliper cylinder bores corroded or rough.	7. Disassemble caliper and remove corrosion or roughness, or replace caliper.
8. Pedal linkage binding (and suddenly releasing).	8. Free and lubricate linkage.
9. Metering valve not functioning properly.	9. Replace combination valve.
FADING PEDAL (Pedal Falling Away Under Steady Pressure)	
1. Poor quality brake fluid (low boiling point) in system.	1. Drain hydraulic system and fill with approved fluid.
2. Hydraulic connections loose; lines or hoses ruptured (causing leakage).	2. Tighten or replace defective parts.
3. Master cylinder cup worn or damaged. (primary, secondary or both).	3. Repair master cylinder.
4. Master cylinder bore corroded, worn or scored.	4. Repair or replace master cylinder.
5. Caliper cylinder seals worn or damaged.	5. Replace seals.
6. Caliper cylinder bores corroded, worn or scored.	6. Disassemble caliper and remove corrosion or scoring, or replace caliper.
7. Bleed screw open.	7. Close bleed screw and bleed hydraulic system.
NOISE AND CHATTER (May Be Accompanied By Brake Roughness and Pedal Pumping)	
1. Disc has excessive lateral runout.	1. Replace or machine disc.
2. Disc has excessive thickness variations (out of parallel).	2. Replace or machine disc.
3. Disc has casting imperfections.	3. Replace disc.
4. Car creeping or moving slowly with brakes applied (may produce groan or crunching noise).	4. Increase or decrease pedal effort slightly.
5. Squeal, during application.	5. A small amount of high-pitched squeal is inherent in disc brake design and must be considered normal. Some relief may be obtained with service package backing.
DRAGGING BRAKES (Slow or Incomplete Release of Brakes)	
1. Lines, hoses or connections dented, kinked, collapsed or clogged.	1. Repair or replace defective parts.
2. Master cylinder compensating port restricted by swollen primary cup.	2. Drain hydraulic system, flush system with brake fluid and replace combination valve and all cups and seals in complete brake system.
3. Residual pressure check valve in lines to front wheels.	3. Remove check valve.
4. Caliper pistons frozen or seized.	4. Disassemble caliper and free pistons (replace if necessary).
5. Caliper cylinder seals swollen.	5. Drain hydraulic system, flush system with clean brake fluid and replace combination valve and all cups and seals in complete brake system.
6. Caliper cylinder bores corroded or rough.	6. Disassemble caliper and remove corrosion or roughness, or replace caliper.
7. Hydraulic push rod on power brake out of adjustment or binding (causing primary cup to restrict master cylinder compensating port).	7. Adjust or free and lubricate.

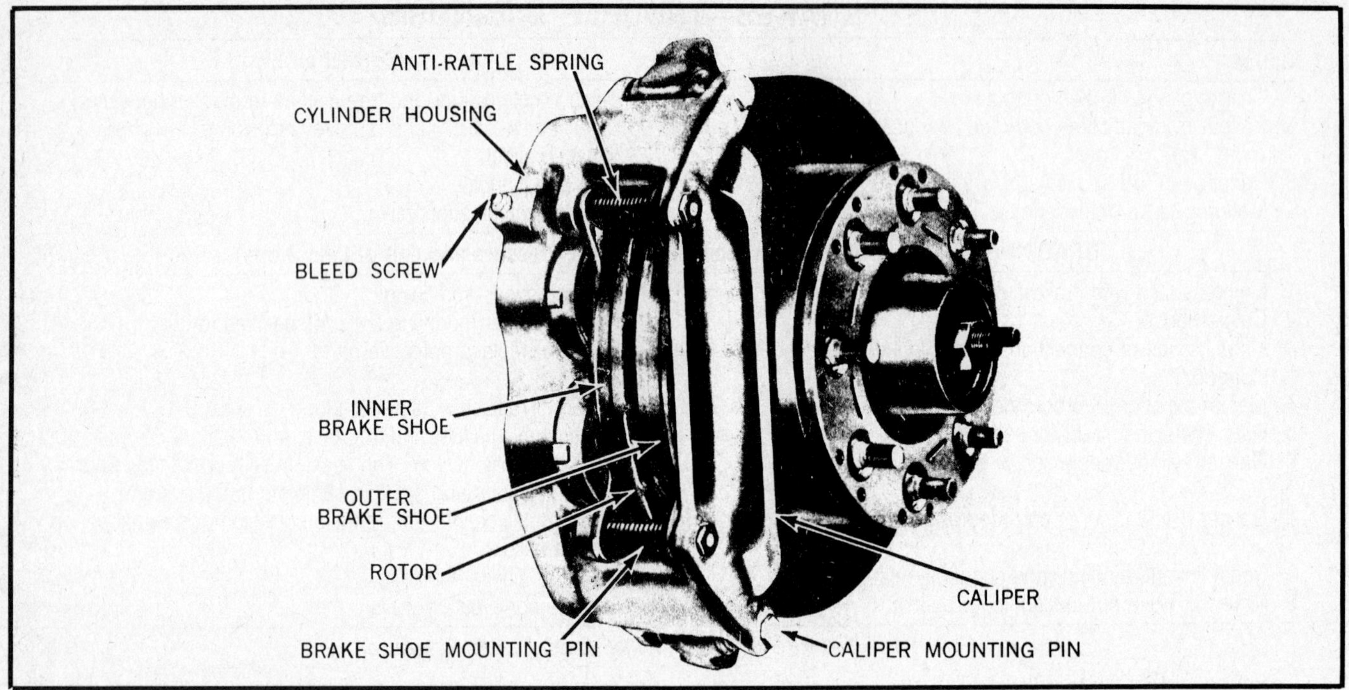

Floating disc brake caliper

Floating Caliper Disc Brakes

This disc brake is a floating caliper design with one or two pistons on one side of the rotor. It is a two piece unit consisting of the caliper and cylinder housing. The caliper is mounted to the anchor plate on two mounting pins which travel in bushings in the anchor plate. The bushings and pins are protected by toot type seals.

Two brake shoe and lining assemblies are used in each caliper, one on each side of the rotor. The shoes are identical and are attached to the caliper with two mounting pins.

The cylinder housing contains the two pistons. The pistons are fitted with an insulator on the front and a seal on the back lip. A friction ring is attached to the back of the piston with a shouldered cap screw. The pistons and cylinder bores are protected by boot seals which are fitted to a groove in the piston and attached to the cylinder housing with retainers. The cylinder assembly is attached to the caliper with two cap screws and washers.

The anchor plate is bolted directly to the spindle. It positions the caliper assembly over the rotor forward of the spindle.

DISC BRAKE SHOE ADJUSTMENT

The front disc brake assembly is designed so that it is inherently self-adjusting and requires no manual adjustment.

Automatic adjustment for lining wear is achieved by the piston and friction ring sliding outward in the cylinder bore. The piston assumes a new position in the cylinder and maintains the correct adjustment.

FRONT DISC BRAKE SHOE AND LINING

NOTE: Refer to following section for caliper and pad service for the Ford Ranger and Bronco II.

Replace shoe and lining assemblies when lining is worn to a minimum of $^1/_{16}$" in thickness (combined thickness of shoe and lining $^1/_4$ in. minimum).

Removal

1. Remove the shoe and lining mounting pins, anti-rattle springs and old shoe and lining assemblies.

Installation

1. Remove the master cylinder cover.
2. Loosen the piston housing-to-caliper mounting bolts sufficiently to permit the installation of new shoe and lining assemblies. Do not move pistons.
3. Install new shoe and lining assemblies. Install the brake shoe mounting pins and anti-rattle springs. Be sure that the spring tangs are located in the holes provided in the shoe plates.
4. Torque the brake shoe mounting pins to 17–23 ft. lbs.
5. Reset the pistons to the correct location in the cylinders by placing shims or feeler gauges of 0.023–0.035 in. thickness between the shoe plate of the outboard shoe and lining assembly and the caliper; then, retighten the piston housing-to-caliper mounting bolts. Keep the cylinder housing square with the caliper.
6. Loosen the piston housing-to-caliper mounting bolts and remove the shims.
7. Torque the piston housing-to-caliper mounting bolts to 155–185 ft. lbs.
8. Check the master cylinder reservoirs.
9. Install the master cylinder cover.

DISC BRAKE CALIPER

Removal

1. Remove the wheel and tire assembly.
2. Remove the pins and nuts retaining the caliper assembly to the anchor plate.
3. Disconnect the brake hose from the caliper and remove the caliper.

Installation

1. Connect the brake hose to the caliper.

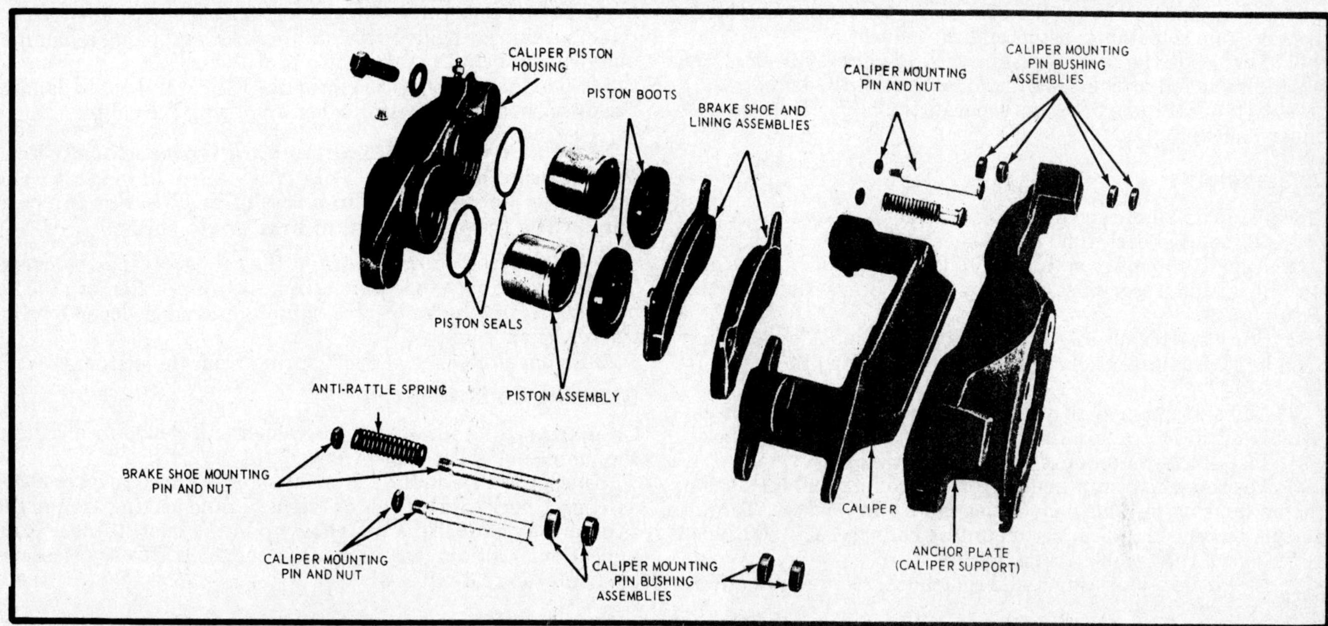

Front disc brake—exploded view

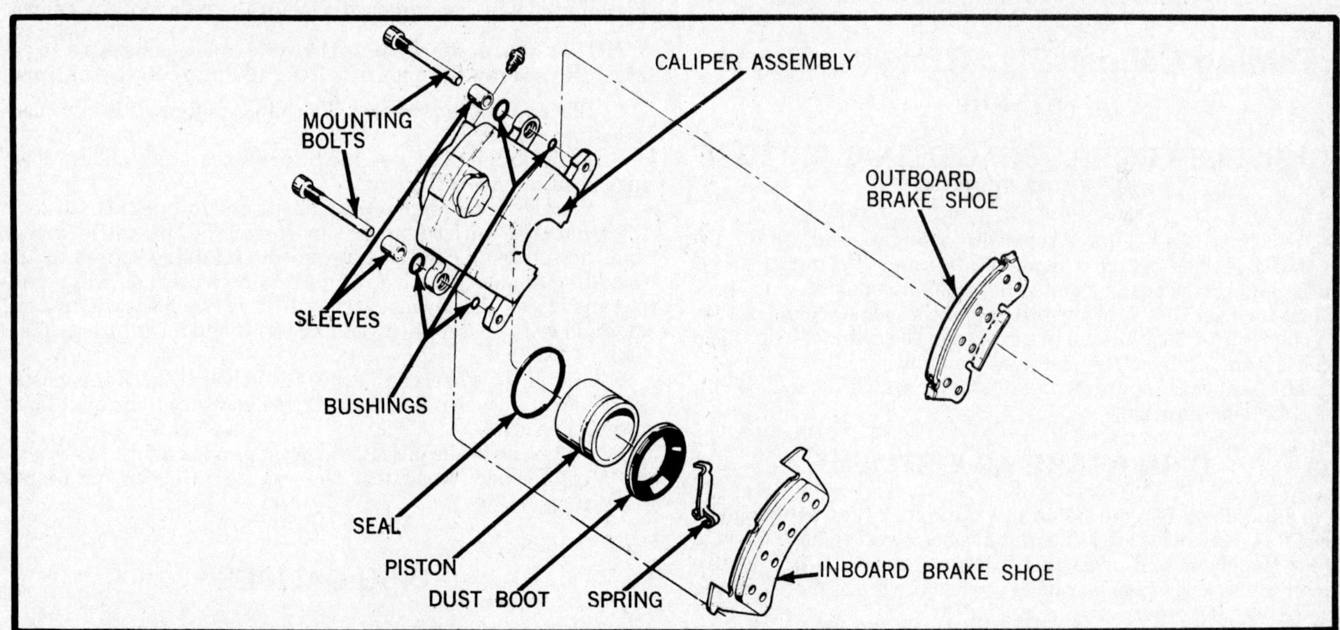

Bolt mounted caliper—exploded view

2. Position the caliper assembly to the anchor plate and install the retaining pins and nuts. Torque the nuts to specifications.
3. Install drum and wheel and bleed brake system.

NOTE: If the caliper assembly is leaking, the piston assemblies must be removed from the piston housing and replaced. If the cylinder bores are scored, corroded or excessive wear is evident, the piston housing must be replaced. Do not hone the cylinder bores. Piston assemblies are not available for oversize bores. The piston housing must be removed from the caliper for replacement.

Disassembly

1. Remove the two pins and nuts retaining the caliper to the support. Disconnect the flexible brake hose and plug the end to prevent brake fluid leakage.
2. Remove the boot retainers and remove the dust boots from the pistons and cylinder housing.
3. Position the caliper assembly in a vise.
4. Place a block of wood between the caliper and the cylinders, and apply low pressure air to the brake hose inlet. One piston will be forced out.
5. Reverse the piston and install it by hand pressure back into the cylinder bore far enough to form a seal. Block the reversed

piston from moving out of the bore and place the wooden block between the remaining piston and the caliper.

6. Force out the second piston with low pressure air. Care should be taken as the piston is forced out of the bore.

7. Remove the two bolts and separate the caliper from the cylinder housing.

Assembly

The piston assembly and dust boots are not to be reused. A new set is to be used each time the caliper is assembled.

1. Apply a film of clean brake fluid in the cylinder bores and on the piston assemblies. Do not apply brake fluid on the insulators.
2. Start the piston assemblies into the cylinder bores using firm hand pressure. Exercise care to avoid cocking the piston in the bore.
3. Lightly tapping with a rawhide mallet, seat each piston assembly until the friction ring bottoms out in the cylinder bore.
4. Install the piston dust boots and retainers.
5. Position the piston housing on the caliper and install the piston housing-to-caliper mounting bolts and washers. Torque the piston housing-to-caliper mounting bolts to 155–185 ft. lbs.
6. Install the flexible brake hose.
7. Bleed the brake system and centralize the pressure differential valve.

NOTE: Do not move the vehicle after working on the disc brakes until a firm brake pedal is obtained.

Sliding Caliper Disc Brakes—Single Piston

CHRYSLER CORP. AND GENERAL MOTORS CORP. TYPES

This caliper is a one piece type with a single piston on the inboard side. The piston is made of steel and is plated to resist wear and corrosion. The piston has a square cut seal which provides for a seal between the piston and the caliper cylinder wall. A rubber dust boot located in a groove in the cylinder helps keep contamination from the piston and cylinder wall.

The caliper is mounted on an adapter which is mounted on the steering knuckle.

DISC BRAKE ADJUSTMENT

No adjustment is required on this unit other than applying the pedal several times after the unit has been worked on. This is to seat the shoes and after this is done the hydraulic pressure maintains the proper clearance between the brake shoes and the rotor.

BRAKE DISC PADS

Replace the disc pads when the linings are worn within $\frac{1}{16}$ in. of the shoe or the rivets.

Removal

1. Remove the master cylinder cover and if the cylinder is more than $\frac{1}{3}$ full remove the fluid necessary to make the cylinder only $\frac{1}{3}$ full. This is done to prevent any overflow from the cylinder when the piston is pushed into the bore of the caliper.
2. Raise vehicle on hoist and remove the front wheels.
3. Compress the piston back into the bore by using a large C-clamp and compressing the unit until the piston bottoms in the bore.
4. Remove the two retaining bolts that hold the caliper into the support. If the caliper has retaining clips remove the retaining clips and anti-rattle springs. If the caliper has key type retainers, remove the key retaining screws, and using a hammer and drift, punch drive the key out of the caliper.
5. Slide the caliper off the rotor disc. Be careful not to damage the dust boot on the piston when removing the caliper.

NOTE: Do not let the caliper hang with the brake hose supporting the weight. This can cause damage to the hose which could result in a loss of brakes. Set the caliper on the front suspension arm or tie rod.

6. Remove the outer shoe from the caliper. It may be necessary to tap the shoe to loosen it from the caliper. Remove the inner shoe from the caliper or spindle assembly depending on where the shoe stays.
7. Remove the shoe support spring from the piston.

Cleaning and Inspection

Clean the sliding surfaces of the caliper and clean any dirt from the mounting bolts, clips or keys.

Inspect the boot on the piston for signs of cracks, cuts or other damage. Check to see if there is signs of fluid leaking around the seal on the piston. This will show up in the boot. If there is an indication of a fluid leak, the entire caliper has to be disassembled and the seal replaced.

Installation

1. Make sure that the piston is fully bottomed in the cylinder bore and install the outboard shoe in the recess of the caliper.

NOTE: On shoes with anti-rattle springs be sure to install the spring before installing the shoe in the caliper.

2. Place the outer shoe on the caliper and press it into place with finger pressure.
3. Position the caliper on the rotor and carefully slide it down into position over the rotor.
4. Install the caliper mounting bolts and torque them to 35 ft. lbs. On models with retaining clips install the anti-rattle springs and the retaining clips and torque the retaining screws to 200 inch lbs. On models with key type retainers press down the caliper and install the key in its slot and drive it in place with a hammer and drift. Install the retaining screw and torque to 12–18 ft. lbs.
5. Install the wheels and lower the vehicle. Check the master cylinder fluid level and add any fluid necessary to bring it up to the proper level.
6. Pump the brake pedal several times until a firm brake pedal is established. Road test the vehicle to check for proper operation.

DISC CALIPER

Removal

1. Remove the cover on the master cylinder and check if the fluid level is $\frac{1}{3}$ full. If it is more than $\frac{1}{3}$ full remove the necessary amount to bring the level down. This step is necessary to avoid overflow from the master cylinder when the piston is compressed into the cylinder bore.
2. Raise the vehicle and remove the wheel.
3. Compress the piston into the caliper bore and remove the brake hose from the caliper. Tape the end of the hose to prevent dirt from entering the line.
4. Remove the caliper retaining bolts, clips or wedges and remove the caliper from the vehicle.

Disassembly

1. Clean the outside of the caliper with clean brake fluid and drain any fluid from the caliper.
2. Remove the piston from the caliper by connecting the hy-

draulic line to the caliper and gently stroking the brake pedal. This will push the piston from the caliper bore.

3. With care remove the boot from the caliper piston bore.
4. Remove the piston seal from the caliper bore using a piece of wood or plastic.

NOTE: DO NOT use a metal tool to remove the seal. This can damage the bore or burr the edges of the seal groove.

5. Remove the bleeder valve.

Cleaning and Inspection

1. Clean all the parts with clean brake fluid and blow out all the passages in the caliper.

NOTE: When ever the caliper is disassembled, discard the boot and piston seal. These parts must not be reused.

2. Inspect the outside of the piston for signs of wear, corrosion, scores or any other defects. If any defects are detected replace the piston.
3. Check the caliper bore for the same defects as the piston. However, the bore can be cleaned up to a point with crocus cloth. If there are any marks that will not clean up with the cloth the caliper must be replaced.

Assembly and Installation

1. Lube the caliper bore and the piston with clean brake fluid and position the seal for the piston in the cylinder bore groove.
2. Install the dust boot into the groove in the piston with the fold faces toward the open end of the piston.
3. Install the piston in the bore being careful not to unseat the piston seal in the bore.
4. With the piston bottomed in the cylinder position the boot in the groove in the caliper. Make sure that the retaining ring in the seal is pressed down evenly around the cylinder.
5. Install the bleeder screw in the caliper and install the caliper back on the vehicle.
6. Connect the brake hoses and bleed the calipers of air. When bleeding is done pump the pedal several times to develop a firm brake pedal.

Sliding Caliper Disc Brakes (Double Piston)

BRAKE SHOE AND CALIPER

Removal

1. Drain about $^2/_3$ of the total brake fluid from the reservoir.
2. Jack up the vehicle and remove the front wheels.
3. Remove the four screws and remove the caliper hold-down assembly.
4. Lift the caliper off the hub and rotor. If the caliper is to be removed, disconnect the hydraulic line; if not, lay the caliper on the suspension or support with a length of wire.
5. Remove the inner and outer shoe and lining.

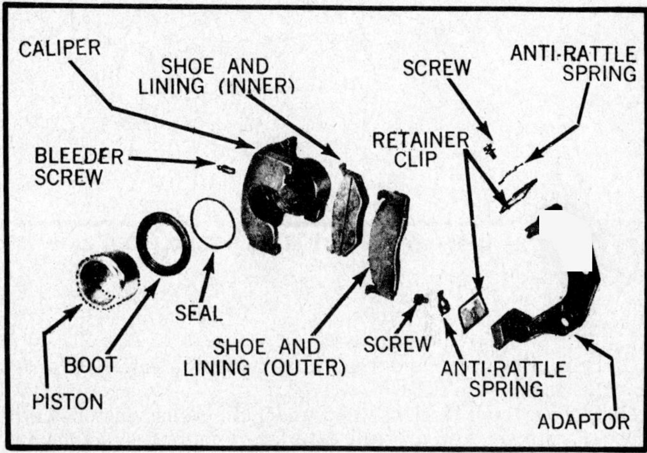

Caliper assembly retaining clip

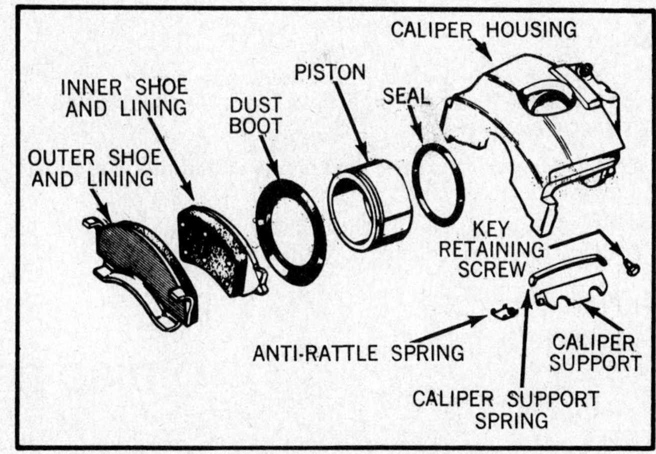

Disc brake caliper retainer—key type

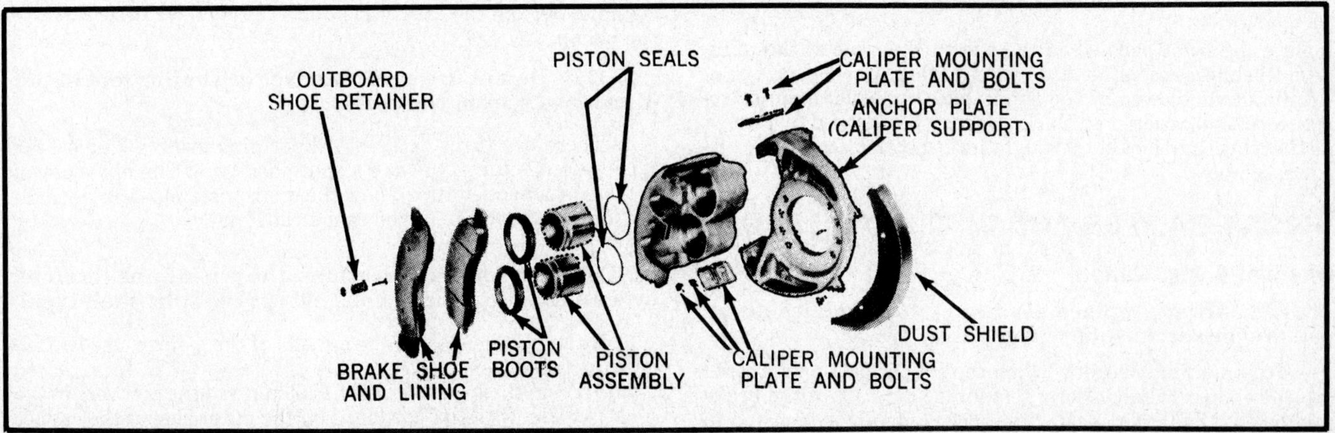

Sliding caliper disc brakes—bouble piston

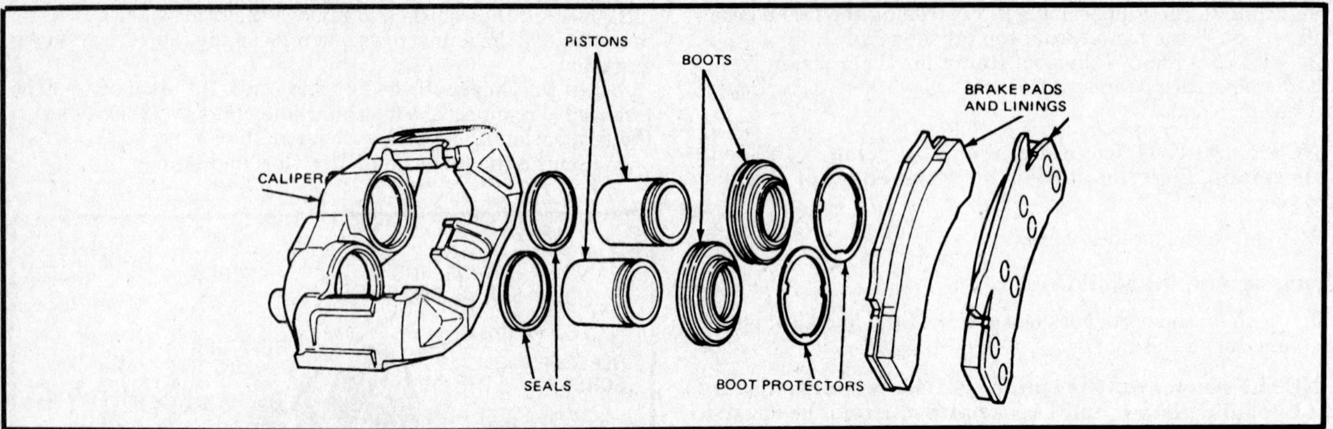

Rail slider caliper—6000 and 7000 pound front axle

Disassembly

1. Drain the brake fluid from the caliper and clean the exterior with clean brake fluid.
2. Place a small block of wood under the caliper pistons and place a protective pad over the exterior. Remove the pistons by directing compressed air into the caliper fluid outlet.
3. Remove and discard piston boots.
4. Remove the piston seals from the groove in the caliper bore.

Assembly

1. Clean all parts in clean brake fluid and blow dry.
2. Dip the new piston seal in clean brake fluid and install it into the cylinder groove.

NOTE: Be sure that the seal is not rolled or twisted in the groove.

3. Install the dust boot in the cylinder groove.
4. Coat the outside diameter of the piston with clean brake fluid. Use something plastic or wood and gradually work the dust boot around the piston.
5. Press the piston straight into the caliper bore until it bottoms. Position the boot in the piston groove.

Installation

1. Install a new shoe and lining assembly into the anchor plate.
2. Push the pistons to the bottom of the piston bore. Place a small block of wood over both pistons and boots. Push the pistons to the bottom of the bores with a C-clamp.
3. Install the outer shoe and lining onto the caliper and install the shoe hold-down spring and pin.
4. Install the caliper assembly over the hub, rotor and inner shoe, and position into the inner grooves in the anchor plate.
5. Install the caliper hold-down parts and tighten to 40 ft. lbs.
6. Add extra heavy duty brake fluid to bring the level to $\frac{1}{4}$ in. from the top of the reservoir.
7. Bleed the system and add fluid as necessary.

DISC BRAKES

Ford Ranger and Bronco II

INSPECTION

Replace the front pads when the pad thickness is at the minimum thickness recommended by Ford Motor Co. ($\frac{1}{32}$ in.), or at the minimum allowed by the applicable state or local motor vehicle inspection code. Pad thickness may be checked by removing the wheel and looking through the inspection port in the caliper assembly.

FRONT CALIPER AND DISC BRAKE PADS

Removal & Installation

NOTE: Always replace all disc pad assemblies on an axle. Never service one wheel only.

1. To avoid fluid overflow when the caliper piston is pressed into the caliper cylinder bores, siphon or dip part of the brake fluid out of the larger master cylinder reservoir (connected to the front disc brakes). Discard the removed fluid.
2. Raise the vehicle and install jack stands. Remove a front wheel and tire assembly.
3. Place an eight in. C-clamp on the caliper and tighten the clamp to bottom the caliper piston in the cylinder bore. Remove the clamp.

NOTE: Do not use a screwdriver or similar tool to pry piston away from the rotor.

4. There are three types of caliper pins used: a single tang type, a double tang type and a split-shell type. The pin removal process is dependent upon how the pin is installed (bolt head direction). Remove the upper caliper pin first.

NOTE: On some applications, the pin may be retained by a nut and torx-head bolt (except the split-shell type).

5. If the bolt head is on the outside of the caliper, use the following procedure:
   a. From the inner side of the caliper, tap the bolt within the caliper pin until the bolt head on the outer side of the caliper shows a separation between the bolt head and the caliper pin.

b. Using a hacksaw or bolt cutter, remove the bolt head from the bolt.

c. Depress the tab on the bolt head end of the upper caliper pin with a screwdriver, while tapping on the pin with a hammer. Continue tapping until the tab is depressed by the v-slot.

d. Place one end of a punch ($\frac{1}{2}$ in. or smaller) against the end of the caliper pin and drive the caliper pin out of the caliper toward the inside of the vehicle. Do not use a screwdriver or other edged tool to help drive out the caliper pin as the v-grooves may be damaged.

CAUTION

Never reuse caliper pins. Always install new pins whenever a caliper is removed.

6. If the nut end of the bolt is on the outside of the caliper, use the following procedure:

a. Remove the nut from the bolt.

b. Depress the lead tang on the end of the upper caliper pin with a screwdriver while tapping on the pin with a hammer. Continue tapping until the lead tang is depressed by the v-slot.

c. Place one end of a punch ($\frac{1}{2}$ in. or smaller) against the end of the caliper pin and drive the caliper pin out of the caliper toward the inside of the vehicle. Do not use a screwdriver or other edged tool to help drive out the caliper pin as the v-grooves may be damaged.

7. Repeat the procedure in Step 4 for the lower caliper pin.
8. Remove the caliper from the rotor. If the caliper is to be removed for service, remove the brake hose from the caliper.
9. Remove the outer pad. Remove the anti-rattle clips and remove the inner pad.
10. To install, place a new anti-rattle clip on the lower end of the inner pad. Be sure the tabs on the clip are positioned properly and the clip is fully seated.
11. Position the inner pad and anti-rattle clip in the pad abutment with the anti-rattle clip tab against the pad abutment and the loop-type spring away from the rotor. Compress the anti-rattle clip and slide the upper end of the pad in position.
12. Install the outer pad, making sure the torque buttons on the pad spring clip are seated solidly in the matching holes in the caliper.
13. Install the caliper on the spindle, making sure the mounting surfaces are free of dirt and lubricate the caliper grooves with Disc Brake Caliper Grease. Install new caliper pins, making sure the pins are installed with the tang in position.
14. The pin must be installed with the lead tang in first, the bolt head facing outward (if equipped) and the pin properly positioned. Position the lead tang in the v-slot mounting surface and drive in the caliper until the drive tang is flush with the caliper assembly. Install the nut (if equipped) and tighten to 32–47 inch lbs.

CAUTION

Never reuse caliper pins. Always install new pins whenever a caliper is removed.

15. If removed, install the brake hose to the caliper.
16. Bleed the brakes as described earlier in this chapter.
17. Install the wheel and tire assembly. Torque the lug nuts to 85–115 ft. lbs.
18. Remove the jack stands and lower the vehicle. Check the brake fluid level and fill as necessary. Check the brakes for proper operation.

Parking Brakes

INTERNAL SHOE TYPE

Adjustment

NINE INCH DIAMETER DRUM

1. Release the parking brake lever in the cab.

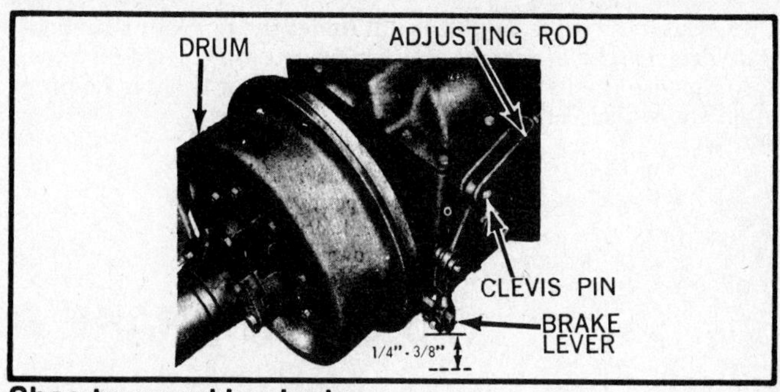

Shoe type parking brake

2. From under the truck, remove the cotter pin from the parking brake linkage adjusting clevis pin. Remove the clevis pin.
3. Lengthen the parking brake adjusting link by turning the clevis. Continue to lengthen the adjusting link until the shoes seat against the drum when the clevis pin is installed.
4. Remove the clevis pin and shorten the linkage adjustment until there is 0.010 in. clearance between the shoes and the drum. The measurement should be taken at all points around the drum with the clevis pin installed.
5. Install a new cotter pin in the clevis retaining pin and check the brake operation.

Twelve Inch Diameter Drum

There is no internal adjustment on this brake. Adjustment is made on the linkage. Remove the clevis pin, loosen the nuts on the adjusting rod, and turn the clevis on the rod until a $\frac{1}{4}$–$\frac{3}{8}$ in. free play is obtained at the brake lever. Tighten the nuts, and connect the clevis to the bellcrank with the clevis pin.

EXTERNAL BAND TYPE

Adjustment

1. On cable-controlled parking brakes, move the parking brake lever to the fully released position. On a vehicle with a rod-type linkage, set the lever at the first notch.
2. Check the position of the cam to make sure the flat portion is resting on the brake band bracket. If the cam is not flat with the bracket, remove the clevis pin from the upper part of the cam, and adjust the clevis rod to allow the flat portion of the cam to rest on the brake band bracket. Install the clevis pin and cotter pin.
3. Remove the lock wire from the anchor adjusting screw, and turn the adjusting screw clockwise until a clearance of 0.010 in. is established between the brake lining and the brake drum at the anchor bracket. Install the lock wire in the anchor adjusting screw.
4. Loosen the lock nut on the adjusting screw for the lower half of the brake band, and adjust the screw to establish a 0.010 in. clearance between the lining and the brake drum at the lower half of the brake band. Tighten the lock nut.
5. Turn the upper band adjusting rod nut until a 0.010 in. clearance is established between the upper half of the band and the drum.
6. Apply and release brake several times to insure full release.

PARKING BRAKE INCLUDED WITH REAR BRAKES

Before attempting parking brake adjustment, make sure that the rear brakes are fully adjusted.

1. Raise and support the rear axle. Release the parking brake.
2. Apply the pedal or handle one to four clicks.

3. Adjust the cable equalizer nut under the truck until a moderate drag can be felt when the rear wheels are turned forward.

4. Release the parking brake and check that there is no drag when the wheels are turned forward.

NOTE: If the parking brake cable is replaced, prestretch it by applying the parking brake hard about three times before attempting adjustment.

POWER BRAKE BOOSTER SERVICE

POWER BOOSTER TROUBLE DIAGNOSIS

Condition	Possible Cause	Correction
Vacuum leak (booster in released position)	1. End plate, center plate or control valve body gaskets leak.	1. Recondition booster unit.
	2. Distortion of end plate.	2. Replace end plate.
	3. Misalignment of control valve poppet.	3. Disassemble, clean and correctly reassemble.
	4. Loose vacuum cylinder bolts.	4. Coat vacuum cylinder bolts lightly with a suitable sealing compound and tighten to specified torque.
	5. Loose control valve body screws.	5. Tighten control valve body screws to specified torque.
	6. Large control valve poppet spring not centered in spring retainer.	6. Disassemble unit and correctly reassemble.
Vacuum leak (booster in applied position)	1. Leak at control valve poppet and seat.	1. Clean and inspect poppet and seat for damage and repair as necessary.
	2. Dry or faulty piston leather packing.	2. Clean and lubricate piston leather or replace.
	3. Faulty control valve disphragm assembly.	3. Replace faulty parts.
External hydraulic leaks	1. Gasket (O-ring) leaking at hydraulic end plate joint.	1. Disassemble clean and replace (O-ring) gasket and reassemble.
	2. Fluid leaking at copper gasket under hydraulic cylinder end cap.	2. Remove end cap and inspect copper gasket and seat install new copper gasket.
Internal hydraulic leak at low pressures	1. Control valve hydraulic piston cup failure.	1. Recondition control valve unit.
	2. Faulty push rod seal.	2. Replace push rod seal.
Internal leaks at high pressure	1. Fluid passing copper gasket under hydraulic fitting in control valve.	1. Clean and inspect gasket and fitting, replace if faulty.
	2. Inspect cups and seals of master cylinder for cuts and scores.	2. Hone master cylinder and replace cups and seals.
	3. Inspect cups of the control valve hydraulic piston.	3. Replace faulty cups.
Hydraulic pressure buildup (without added input)	1. Check hydraulic piston check valve and slot for foreign material under valve.	1. Clean or replace valve and seats as condition indicates.
Failure to release	1. Weak vacuum cylinder piston return spring.	1. Replace vacuum cylinder piston return spring.
	2. Dry vacuum piston leather packing.	2. Lubricate vacuum piston leather packing.
	3. Swollen rubber cups due to inferior or contaminated brake fluid.	3. Flush hydraulic system and recondition or replace all cylinders.

POWER BOOSTER TROUBLE DIAGNOSIS

Condition	Possible Cause	Correction
	4. Damaged or dented vacuum cylinder shell. 5. Dirty or sticky control valve piston.	4. Replace vacuum cylinder shell. 5. Recondition control valve assembly.
Failure of booster to operate within specified pressures	1. Rusty, dirty or distorted vacuum cylinder shell. 2. Dry or worn vacuum cylinder leather packing. 3. Swollen rubber cups due to inferior brake fluid. 4. Worn or scored hydraulic cups. 5. Dirt, rust or foreign matter in any component of the system.	1. Clean or replace vacuum cylinder shell. 2. Recondition and lubricate the vacuum booster. 3. Recondition the master cylinder. Replace brake fluid. 4. Recondition the master cylinder. 5. Recondition and lubricate the brake booster assembly.
Loss of fluid	1. Fluid leaking past cup in master cylinder. 2. Brake wheel cylinders leaking. 3. Loose hydraulic hose connectors. 4. Leaking stop light switch.	1. Recondition master cylinder or replace. 2. Recondition or replace wheel cylinders. 3. Inspect and tighten all hydraulic connections. 4. Replace stop light switch.
Presence of brake fluid on hy-power vacuum cylinder	1. Piston cup or push rod seal leaking.	1. Recondition master cylinder.
Pedal kicks back against foot when brakes are applied	1. Vacuum leakage. 2. Dirt under control valve or damaged seat. 3. Weak or broken spring.	1. Inspect and correct vacuum leak. 2. Clean and recondition booster assembly. 3. Replace spring.
Brakes are slow to release ①	1. Incorrect pedal linkage adjustment. 2. Compensating port of master cylinder plugged. 3. Brake shoes sticking. 4. Weak brake shoe return spring. 5. Booster control valve piston sticking. 6. Booster air filter clogged. 7. Control valve diaphragm return spring missing. 8. Defective check valve in slave cylinder piston. 9. Dirt under atmospheric valve disc.	1. Adjust and lubricate pedal linkage. 2. Clean master cylinder with compressed air. 3. Free up and lubricate brake shoes. 4. Replace brake shoe return spring. 5. Clean booster control valve piston and lubricate. 6. Clean air filter in mineral spirits. 7. Install new control valve return spring. 8. Recondition slave cylinder pistons. 9. Clean atmospheric valve.
Engine runs unevenly at idle with brakes released	1. Vacuum leakage. 2. Dirt under control valve disc or damaged seat. 3. Defective spring.	1. Inspect and tighten all vacuum fittings. 2. Clean control valve or replace. 3. Replace defective spring.
Engine runs evenly and pedal is hard with brakes applied	1. Control valve piston assembly not seating on vacuum disc. 2. Defective control valve plate and diaphragm. 3. Defective pressure plate and diaphragm.	1. Clean or replace control valve piston assembly. 2. Replace control valve plate and diaphragm. 3. Replace pressure plate and diaphragm.
Brake pedal is hard at different intervals	1. Defective manifold check valve. 2. Slave cylinder piston sticking due to dirt or inferior brake fluid. 3. Brake booster air cleaner clogged.	1. Clean or replace manifold check valve. 2. Clean and recondition slave cylinder. 3. Clean air cleaner in mineral spirits and blow dry with compressed air.

①Jack up truck and determine whether or not the brakes are dragging before further testing is done.

Brake System Preliminary Checks

Always check the fluid level in the brake master cylinder reservoir(s) before performing the test procedures. If the fluid level is not within ¼ in. of the top of the master cylinder reservoirs, add the specified brake fluid.

Push the brake pedal down as far as it will go. If the pedal travels more than halfway between the released position and the floor, adjust the brakes. If the vehicle is equipped with automatic brake adjusters, serveral sharp brake applications while backing up may be necessary to adjust the brakes.

Road test the vehicle and apply the brakes at a speed of about 20 mph to see if the vehicle stops evenly. If not, the brakes should be adjusted. Perform the road test only when the brakes will apply and the vehicle can be safely stopped.

DUAL BRAKE WARNING LIGHT SYSTEM TESTS

1. Turn the ignition switch to the ACC or ON position. If the light on the brake warning lamp remains on, the condition may be caused by a shorted or broken switch, grounded switch wires or the differential pressure valve is not centered. Centralize the differential pressure valve. If the warning light remains on, check the switch connector and wire for a grounded condition and repair or replace the wire assembly. If the condition of the wire is good, replace the brake warning lamp switch.
2. Turn the ignition switch to the start position. If the brake warning lamp does not light, check the light and wiring and replace or repair wiring as necessary. When both brake systems are functioning normally, the equal pressure at the pressure differential valve during brake pedal application keeps the valve centered. The brake warning light will be on only when the ignition key is in the start position.
3. If the brake warning lamp does not light when a pressure differential condition exists in the brake system, the warning lamp may be burned out, the warning lamp switch is inoperative or the switch to lamp wiring has an open circuit. Check the bulb and replace it, if required. Check the switch to lamp wires for an open circuit and repair or replace them, if required. If the warning lamp still does not light, replace the switch.

POWER BRAKE FUNCTION

Testing

With the engine stopped, eliminate all vacuum from the system by pumping the brake pedal several times. Then push the pedal down as far as it will go, and note the effort required to hold it in this position. If the pedal gradually moves downward under this pressure, the hydraulic system is leaking and should be checked by a hydraulic pressure test.

With the brake pedal still pushed down, start the engine. If the vacuum system is operating properly, the pedal will move downward. If the pedal position does not change, the vacuum system is not operating properly and should be checked by a vacuum test.

VACUUM BOOSTER CHECK VALVE

Testing

Disconnect the line from the bottom of the vacuum check valve, and connect a vacuum gauge to the valve. Start the engine, run it at idle speed, and check the reading on the vacuum gauge.

The gauge should register 17–19 in. Hg. with standard transmission and 14–15 in. Hg. in Drive range if equipped with an automatic transmission. Stop the engine and note the rate of vacuum drop. If the vacuum drops more than one in. Hg. in 15 seconds, the check valve is leaking. If the vacuum reading does not reach 18 in. Hg. or is unsteady, an engine tuneup is needed.

BENDIX PISTON TYPE VACUUM BOOSTER

Testing

Disconnect the vacuum line from the booster end plate. Install a tee fitting in the end plate, and connect a vacuum gauge (no. 1) and vacuum line to the fitting. Install a second vacuum gauge (no. 2) in place of the pipe plug in the booster control valve body.

Start the engine, and note the vacuum reading on both gauges. If both gauges do not register manifold vacuum, air is leaking into the vacuum system. If both gauges register manifold vacuum, stop the engine and note the rate of vacuum drop on both gauges. If the drop exceeds one in. Hg. in 15 seconds on either gauge, air is leaking into the vacuum system. Tighten all vacuum connections and repeat the test. If leakage still exists, the leak may be localized as follows:

1. Disconnect the vacuum line and gauge no. 1 from the booster.
2. Connect vacuum gauge no. 1 directly to the vacuum line. Start the engine and note the gauge reading. Stop the engine and check the rate of vacuum drop. If gauge no. 1 does not register manifold vacuum, or if the vacuum drop exceeds 1 in. Hg. in 15 seconds, the leak is in the vacuum line or check valve connections.
3. Reconnect vacuum gauge no. 1 and the vacuum line to the tee fitting. Start the engine, and run it at idle speed for one minute. Depress the brake pedal sufficiently to cause vacuum gauge no. 2 to read from zero to 1 in. Hg. Gauge no. 1 should register manifold vacuum of 17–19 in. Hg. with standard transmission and 14–16 in. Hg. in Drive range if equipped with an automatic transmission. If the drop of vacuum on gauge no. 2 is slow, the air cleaner, or air cleaner line, may be plugged. Inspect and if necessary, clean the air cleaner.
4. Release the brake pedal and observe the action of gauge no. 2. Upon releasing the pedal, the vacuum gauge must register increasing vacuum until manifold vacuum is reached. The rate of increase must be smooth, with no lag or slowness in the return to manifold vacuum. If the gauge readings are not as outlined, the booster is not operating properly and should be removed and overhauled.

DIAGRAGM TYPE VACUUM BOOSTER

Testing

This procedure can be used to test all diaphragm boosters which are equipped with a pipe thread outlet on the atmosphere portion of the diaphragm chamber.

Remove the pipe plug from the rear half of the booster chamber, and install a vacuum gauge. Start the engine and run it at idle speed. The gauge should register 18–21 in. Hg.

1. With the engine running, depress the brake pedal with enough pressure to show a zero reading on the vacuum gauge. Hold the pedal in the applied position for one minute. Any downward movement of the pedal during this time indicates a brake fluid leak. Any kickback (upward movement) of the pedal indicates brake fluid is leaking past the hydraulic piston check valve.
2. With the engine running, push down on the brake pedal with sufficient pressure to show a zero reading on the vacuum gauge. Hold the pedal down, and shut the engine off. Maintain pedal position for one minute. A kickback of the pedal indicates a vacuum leak in the vacuum check valve, in the vacuum line connections, or in the booster.

VACUUM-HYDRAULIC BOOSTER SYSTEMS

Bleeding

1. Eliminate vacuum in the booster by depressing the brake pedal several times while the engine is not running.

2. On trucks not equipped with reservoir tanks, disconnect the manifold tube at the booster side of the manifold check valve (engine not running).

3. Alternately loosen the brake tube at each unit until all air is expelled. Booster slave-cylinder is bled first.

NOTE: A piston stop is provided in the slave cylinder to eliminate the possibility of damaging the return spring while bleeding the system. This damage occurs only when bleeding the brakes with a vacuum present in the booster system.

Bendix Hydro-Boost

The Bendix Hydro-Boost uses the hydraulic pressure supplied by the power steering pump to provide a power assist to brake application.

Disassembly

1. Place the booster in a vise with the bracket end up. Using a hammer and chisel, cut the bracket nut that holds the linkage bracket to the booster assembly. The nut should be cut at the open slot in the booster cover threads. Care must be exercised to avoid damage to the threads. Spread the nut and remove the bracket.
2. Remove the pedal boot by pulling if off over the pedal rod eyelet.
3. Position pedal rod removing tool around the pedal rod. The tool should be resting on the booster cover. Insert a punch through the pedal rod from the lower side of the special tool. Push the punch through until it rests on the higher side of the tool. Push up on the punch to shear the pedal rod retainer; remove the pedal rod.
4. Remove the grommet from the groove near the end of the pedal rod and from the groove in the input rod.
5. Disengage the tabs of the spring retainer from the ledge inside the opening near the master cylinder mounting flange of the booster. Remove the retainer and piston return spring from the opening.
6. Pull straight out on the output push rod to remove the push rod and push rod retainer from inside the booster piston.
7. Press in on the spool plug, and insert a small punch into the hole on top of the housing. This unseats one side of the spool plug snap-ring from the groove in the bore. Remove the snap-ring.
8. Remove the spool plug from the bore with a pair of pliers. Remove the O-ring from the plug and discard. Remove the spool spring from the bore.
9. Place the booster cover in a soft-faced vise and remove the cover retaining bolts. Remove the booster assembly from the vise and separate the booster cover from the housing. Remove the large seal ring and discard.
10. Press in on the end of the spool assembly, and use a spiral snap-ring removing tool to remove the snap-ring from the forward groove in the spool. Discard the snap-ring.
11. Remove the input rod and piston assembly, and the spool assembly from the booster housing.
12. Remove the input rod seals from the input rod end, and the piston seal from the piston bore in the housing. Discard the seals.
13. Remove the plunger, seat, spacer and ball from the accumulator valve bore in the flange of the booster housing. Remove the O-ring from the seat and discard.
14. Thread a screw extractor into the opening in the check valve in the bottom of the accumulator valve bore, and remove the check valve from the bottom of the bore. Discard the check valve and O-ring.

NOTE: Using a screw extractor damages the seat in the check valve. A new check valve, O-ring and valve

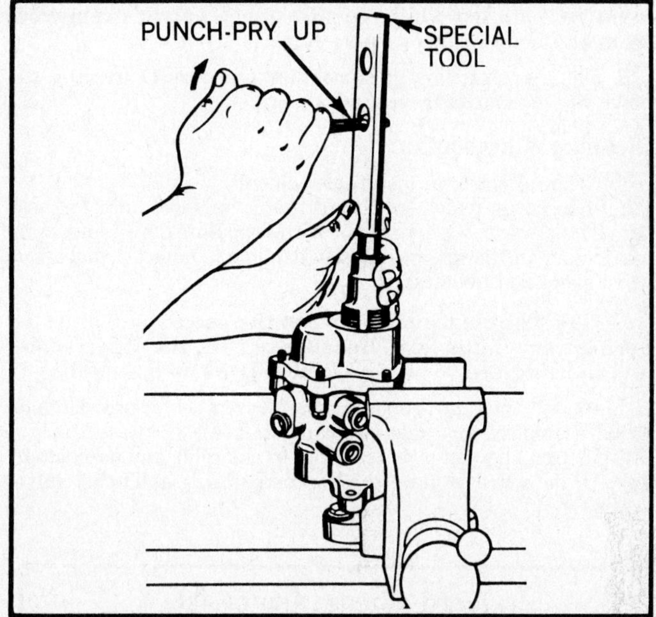

Removing the booster pedal rod—Bendix hydro boost

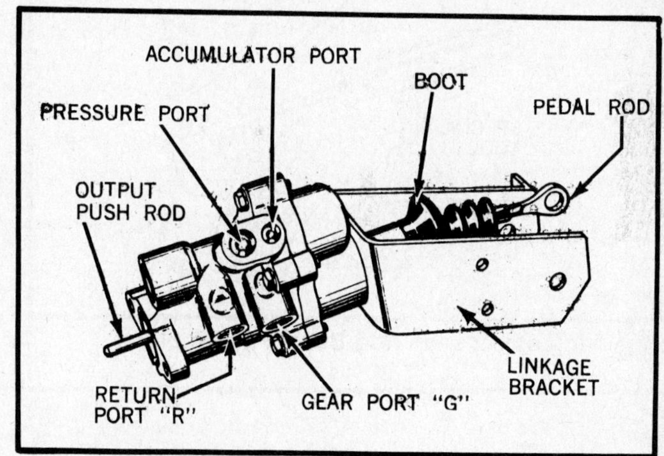

Typical Bendrix hydro boost

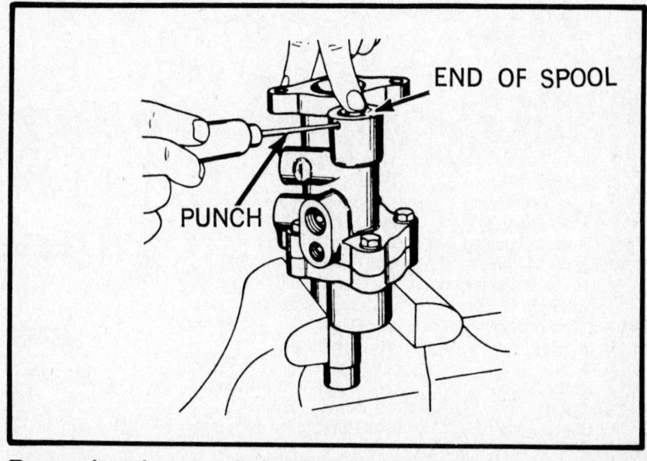

Removing the spool plug from the Bendix hydro boost

must be installed whenever the check valve is removed from the accumulator valve bore.

15. Using a $^1/_4$ or a $^5/_{16}$ in. spiral flute type screw extractor, remove the tube seats from the booster ports.

Cleaning & Inspection

1. Clean all parts in a suitable solvent.
2. Inspect the valve spool and the valve spool bore for any damage or ware. Discoloration of the spool or bore is normal, particulary in the grooves. If any damage is noted, replace the valve spool and housing.

NOTE: The clearance between the valve spool and the bore is very important. Because of this, the valve spool and housing are to be replaced only as an assembly.

3. Inspect the input rod and piston assembly for any damage or ware. Replace any defective components.
4. Inspect the piston bore in the housing for any damage or ware. If defective, replace the booster housing and spool valve assembly.

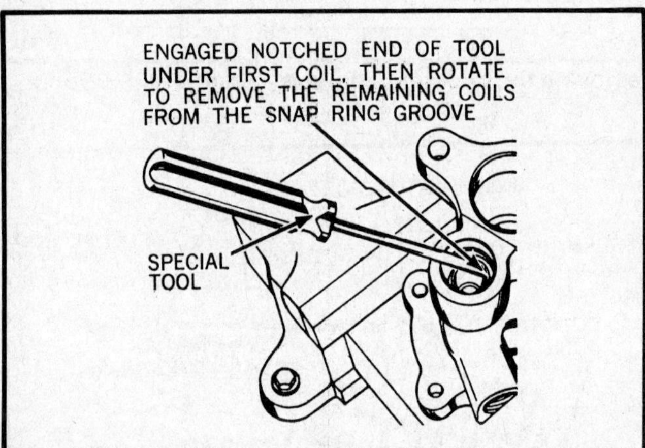

Removing spiral snap ring Bendix hydro boost

Assembly

CAUTION

Parts must be kept VERY clean. If there is any reason to doubt the cleanliness of the components, re-wash before assembly.

Lubricate all seals and metal friction points with power steering fluid before assembly. Whenever the booster is disassembled, be sure that seals, tube inserts, spiral snap-ring, check valve and ball are replaced.

1. Position a tube seat in each booster port and screw a spare tube nut in each port to press the seat down into the port. Do not tighten the tube nuts in the port as this may deface the seats. Remove the spare tube nuts and check for aluminium chips in the ports. Be sure that there is no foreign matter in the ports.
2. Coat the piston bore and piston seal with clean power steering fluid. Assemble the seal in the piston bore. The lip of the seal must be towards the rear (away from the master cylinder mounting flange). Be sure that the seal is fully seated in the housing.
3. Lubricate the input rod end, input rod seals and the seal installer tool with clean power steering fluid. Slide the seals on the tool with the lip of the cups towards the open end of the tool. Slide the tool over the input rod end end down to the second groove; then slide the forward seal off the tool and into the groove. Assemble the other seal in the first groove. Be sure, that both seals are fully seated.
4. Lubricate the piston and piston installing tool with clean power steering fluid. Insert the large end of the tool into the piston and the tool and piston into the piston bore, through the seal.
5. Position the O-ring on the accumulator check valve and coat the assembly with clean power steering fluid. Insert the check valve in the accumulator valve recess in the housing flange. Place the ball and spacer in the same recess.
6. Place the O-ring on the changing valve plunger seat and insert the plunger into the seat. Dip the assembly in clean power steering fluid and insert it into the changing valve recess.
7. Coat the spool assembly with clean power steering fluid and insert in the spool bore. Be sure that the pivot pins on the upper end of the input rod lever assembly are engaged in the groove in the sleeve. Remove piston installing tool.

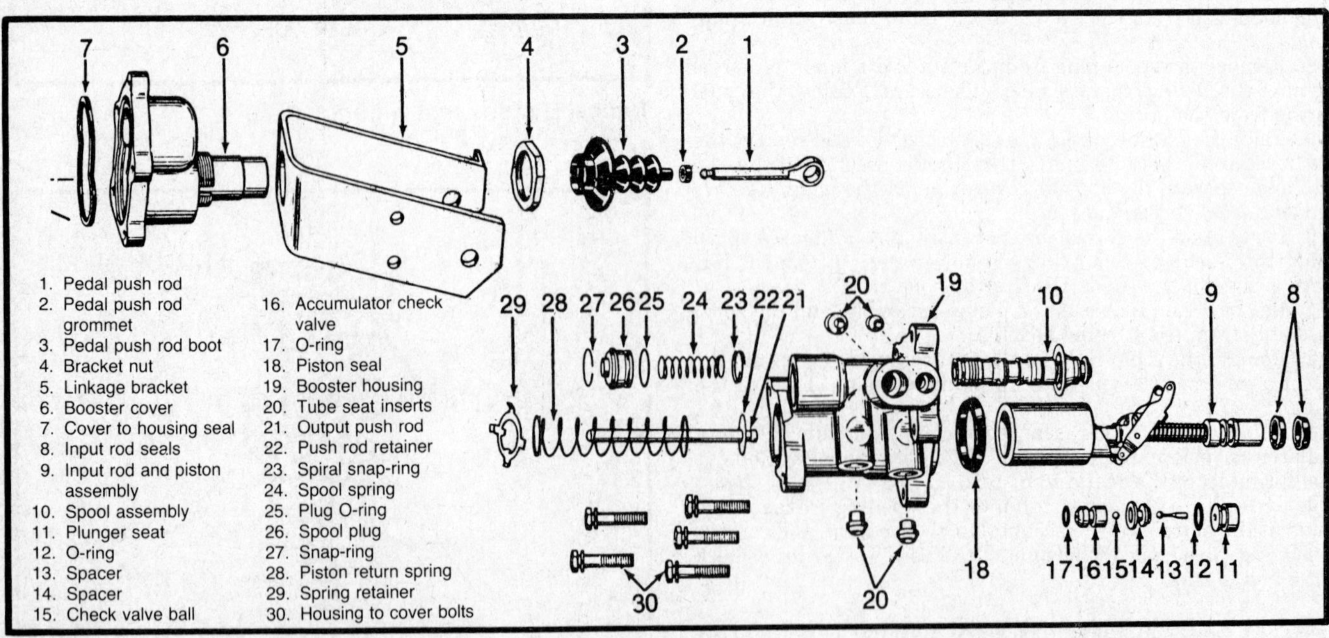

Exploded view of Bendix hydro boost

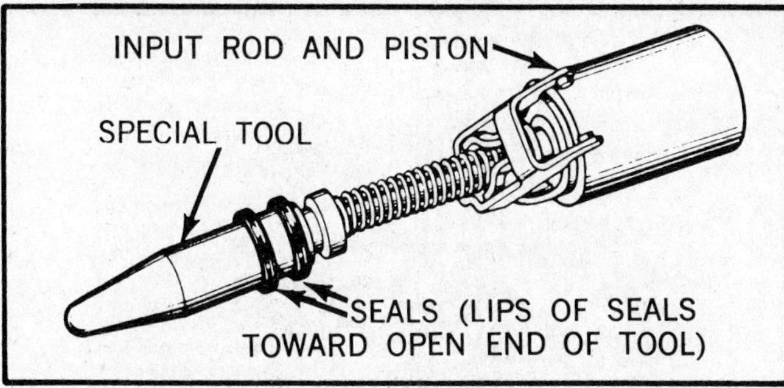

Installing input rod seals Bendix hydro boost

8. Separate the two components of the snap-ring installation tool and place the spiral snap-ring on the tool. Insert the rounded end of the installer into the spool bore. While pressing on the rear of the spool, slide the snap-ring off the tool and into the groove near the forward end of the spool by pressing in on the tool sleeve. Check to be sure that the retaining ring is fully seated.

9. Place the housing seal in the groove in the housing cover. Join the booster housing and cover and secure with five attaching bolts. Tighten the bolts to 18–26 ft. lbs.

CAUTION

It is very important that the same cover attaching bolts are used as they are designed for the booster only. If they are damaged replace with the same part numbers.

10. Place an O-ring on the spool plug. Insert the spool spring and the spool plug in the forward end of the spool bore. Press in on the plug and position the snap-ring in its groove in the spool valve bore.

11. Place the linkage bracket on the booster assembly. The tab on the inside of the large hole in the bracket should fit into the slot in the threaded portion of the booster cover.

12. Install the bracket nut with a staking groove outward on the threaded portion to the booster cover. Use special tool and tighten to 95–120 ft. lbs.

13. Insert a small punch into the staking groove of the nut, at the slot in the booster cover, and with a hammer stake the nut in place. Be sure that the threads on the nut are deformed so the nut will not loosen.

14. Position a new boot and grommet on the pedal rod. Moisten the grommet and insert the grommet end of the pedal rod into the input rod of the booster. When the grommet is fully seated, the pedal rod will rotate freely.

15. Install the boot on the booster cover.

Bendix Master Vac

Removal

1. Disconnect clevis at brake pedal to push rod.
2. Remove vacuum hoses from power cylinder.
3. Disconnect hydraulic line from master cylinder.
4. Remove the four attaching nuts and lock washers that hold the unit to the firewall. Remove the power brake unit.

Disassembly

1. Remove four master cylinder to vacuum cylinder attaching nuts and washers.
2. Separate master cylinder from vacuum cylinder, then remove the rubber seal from the outer groove at end of master cylinder.
3. Remove the push rod from the power section. (Do not disturb adjusting screw.)
4. Remove push rod boot and valve operating rod.
5. Scribe alignment marks across the rear shell and vacuum cylinder. Remove all but two of the end plate attaching screws (opposite each other). Hold down on the rear shell while removing the two remaining screws to prevent the piston return spring from expanding.
6. Scribe a mark across the face of the piston, to index the mark on the rear shell, and remove rear shell with vacuum piston and piston return spring.

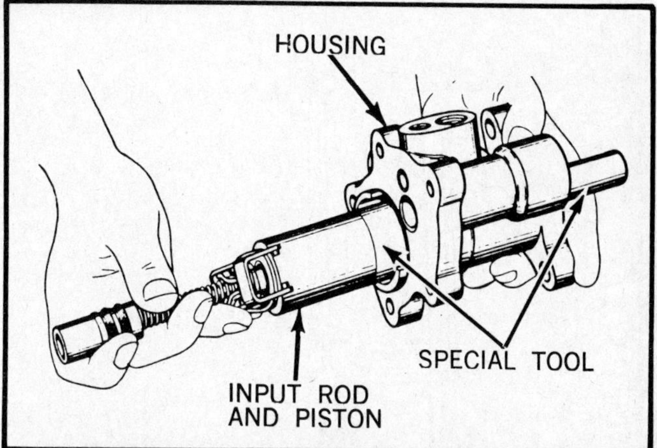

Installing input rod and piston assembly in Bendix hydro boost

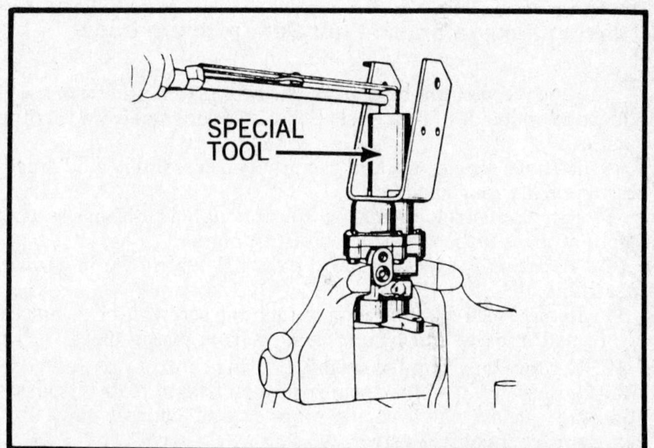

Installing linkage bracket nut Bendix hydro boost—typical

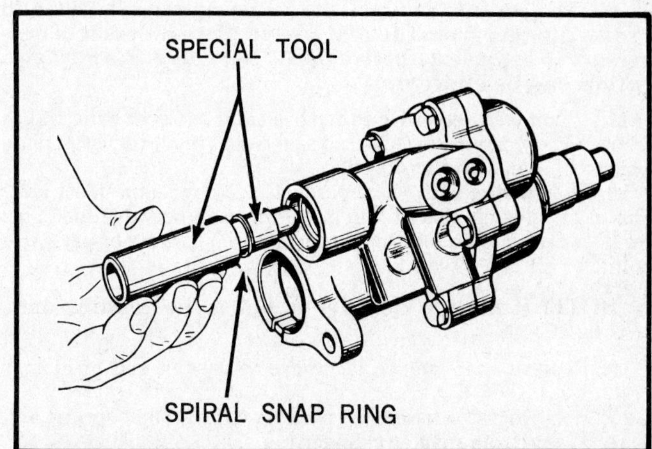

Installing spiral snap ring Bendix hydro boost

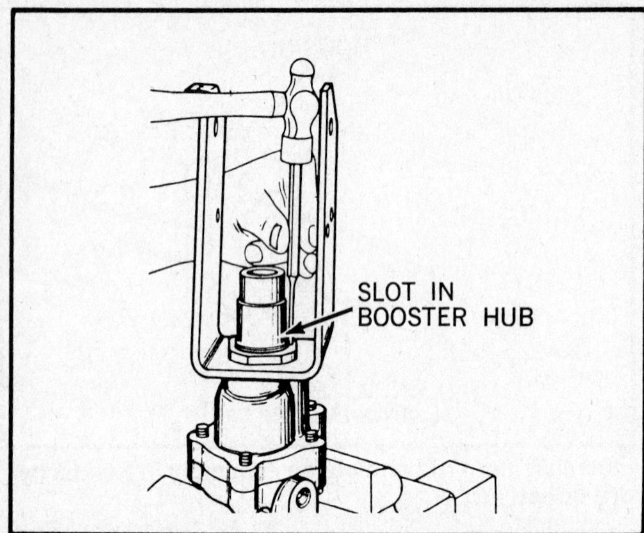

Staking linkage bracket nut Bendix hydro boost

7. Remove vacuum hose from vacuum piston and from vacuum tube on inside of rear shell. Separate rear shell from vacuum piston.

8. Remove air cleaner and vacuum tube assembly, and air filter from the rear shell.

9. Spring the felt retaining ring enough to disengage ring from grooves in bosses on rear piston plate.

10. Remove piston felt and expander ring from piston assembly.

11. Remove six piston plate attaching screws and separate front piston plate and piston packing from piston plate.

12. Remove valve return spring, floating control valve and diaphragm assembly, valve spring and diaphragm plate. Separate floating control valve spring-retainer and control valve diaphragm from control valve.

13. Remove rubber reaction disc and shim (if present) from front piston plate.

NOTE: Do not remove the valve operating rod and valve plunger from the rear piston plate unless it is necessary to replace defective parts. Normally, the next two Steps can be omitted.

14. When it is necessary to replace the valve operating rod or valve plunger, remove valve rod seal from groove in piston plate and pull seal over end of rod.

15. Hold piston with valve plunger side down and inject alcohol into valve plunger through opening around valve rod. This will wet the rubber lock in the plunger. Then drive or pry valve plunger off the valve rod.

NOTE: If master cylinder is not to be rebuilt, omit Steps 16–19.

16. Remove snap-ring from groove in base at end of master cylinder.

17. Remove piston assembly, primary cup, retainer spring, and check-valve from master cylinder.

18. Remove filler cap and gasket from master cylinder body.

19. Remove secondary cup from master cylinder piston.

Cleaning Note

After disassembly, cleaning of all metal parts in satisfactory commercial cleaner solvent is recommended. Use only alcohol or Declene on rubber parts or parts containing rubber. After cleaning and drying, metal parts should be rewashed in clean alcohol or Declene before assembly.

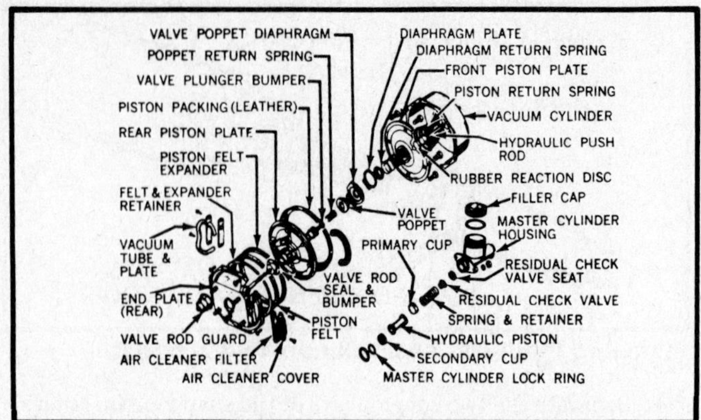

bendix master vac unit

Assembly

Steps 1–5 apply to a completely disassembled master cylinder. Otherwise, omit Steps 1–5.

1. Coat bore of master cylinder with brake fluid.

2. Dip secondary cup in brake fluid and install on master cylinder piston.

3. Dip other piston parts in brake fluid and assemble the piston. Install piston.

4. Install snap-ring into groove of cylinder.

5. Use new gasket and install filler cap.

6. Assemble valve rod seal on rod and insert valve rod through the piston. Dip valve plunger in alcohol and assemble to ball end of valve rod. Be sure ball end of rod is locked in place in plunger.

7. Assemble floating control valve diaphragm over end of floating control valve. Be sure disphragm is in recess of floating control valve. Press control valve spring retainer over end of control valve and diaphragm.

8. Clamp valve operating rod in a vise with rear piston plate up. Lay leather piston packing on rear piston plate with lip of leather over edge of piston plate.

9. Install floating control valve return spring over end of valve plunger.

10. Assemble diaphragm plate to diaphragm and assemble floating control valve with diaphragm in recess of rear piston plate.

11. Install floating control valve spring over retainer. Align and assemble front piston plate with rear piston plate. Center the floating control valve spring on front piston plate and center valve plunger stem in hole of piston.

12. Holding front and rear piston plates together, loosely install six piston plate cap screws.

13. Install shim and rubber reaction disc in recess at center of front piston plate.

NOTE: A piston assembling ring is handy in assembling the piston.

14. Place the assembling tool over piston packing, turn piston assembly upside down and assemble the expander ring against inside lip of leather packing. Saturate felt with vacuum cylinder oil or shock absorber fluid, type A. Then assemble in expander ring. Assemble retainer ring over bosses on rear piston plate. Be sure retainer is anchored in grooves of piston plate.

15. Assemble air cleaner filter over vacuum tube of air cleaner and attach air cleaner shell in position with screws.

16. Slide vacuum hose onto vacuum inlet tube of piston and align hose to lay flat against piston.

17. Wipe a coat of vacuum cylinder oil on bore of cylinder. Remove assembling ring from vacuum piston and coat leather piston packing with vacuum cylinder oil.

18. Install rear shell over end of valve operating rod and attach

vacuum hose to tube end on each side of end plate.

19. Center small diameter end of piston return spring in vacuum cylinder. Center large diameter of spring on piston. Check alignment mark on piston with marks on vacuum cylinder and rear shell, compress spring and install two attaching screws at opposite sides to hold rear shell and cylinder together. Now, install balance of screws and tighten evenly.

20. Dip small end of pushrod boot in alcohol and assemble guard over end of valve operating rod and over flange of shell.

21. Insert large end of pushrod through hole in end of vacuum cylinder and guide into hole of front piston plate.

NOTE: Before going on with assembly, check the distance from the outer end of the pushrod to the master cylinder mounting surface on the vacuum cylinder. This measurement should be 1.195–1.200 in.

22. After pushrod adjustment is correct, replace rubber seal in groove on master cylinder body.

23. Assemble master cylinder to the vacuum cylinder at four studs. Replace lock washers and nut and securely tighten.

Bendix Single Diaphragm Type Frame Mounted

Disassembly

1. Remove the booster unit and hydraulic cylinder from frame mounting bracket.

2. Scribe marks across front and rear shells and across flange of hydraulic cylinder. Disconnect the control tube nut from the control valve seat and remove the seal from the tube.

3. Remove the clamp band from the booster unit and disassemble the rear shell.

NOTE: The plug in the rear shell should be removed only if it is damaged.

4. Roll the bead of the diaphragm back from the front shell flange and compress the return spring for the diaphragm slightly. Remove the snap-ring from groove near the end of the hydraulic cylinder. Remove the hydraulic parts, push rod and diaphragm as an assembly.

5. Remove diaphragm return spring from piston end of push

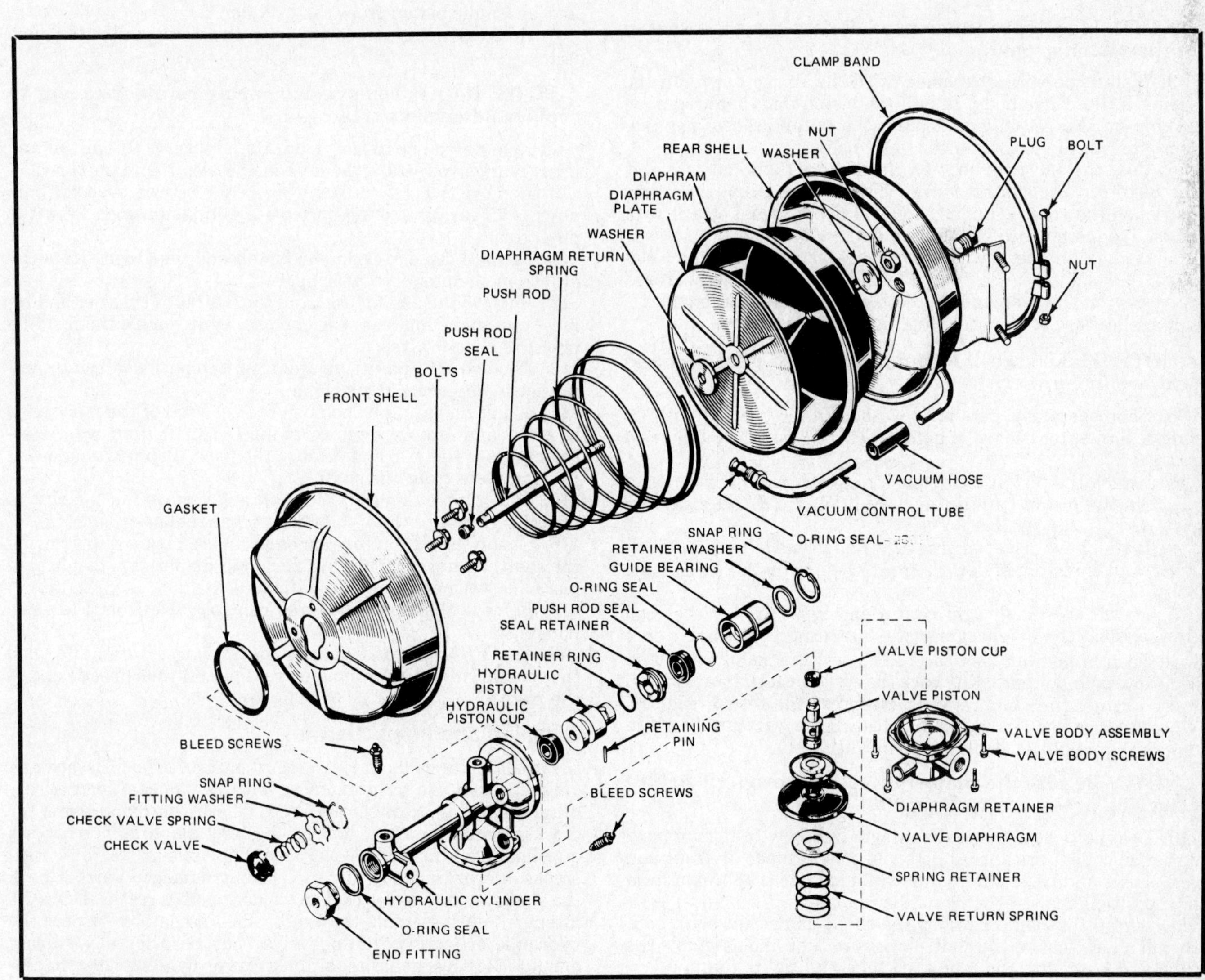

Bendix single diaphragm frame mounted booster

rod. Remove bolts securing hydraulic cylinder to front shell and remove the cylinder gasket from the shell.

NOTE: The diaphragm assembly should be removed from the push rod only if necessary to remove damaged parts.

6. Remove the retaining ring from groove in hydraulic piston and press the retaining pin from hole in push rod and piston. Remove the cup from the piston and if a new seal is to be installed in end of push rod, remove old push rod seal.

NOTE: Be careful to avoid damaging push rod. Carefully slide the seal retainer, seal, O-ring, guide bearing, retainer washer and snap-ring from push rod.

7. Scribe marks across the flanges of valve body and housing and remove the four attaching bolts. Remove the valve body and remove cups from the control valve piston.

Assembly

1. Install check valve, spring, washer and snap-ring in hydraulic cylinder end fitting. Next assemble O-ring seal and end fitting on the hydraulic cylinder.
2. Install cups, back to back, on control valve piston. Then assemble piston, diaphragm retainer and valve diaphragm.

NOTE: Make sure inner bead of diaphragm is seated in the piston groove.

3. Install the spring retainer, with the flange down, on the spring in the valve body. Install the piston and diaphragm assembly on the retainer and press the outer bead of the diaphragm into the groove in the valve body.
4. Coat the valve piston with clean brake fluid and assemble the piston in the control valve cylinder bore. Align the scribe marks on the valve cylinder body and housing and attach with bolts. Torque bolts to 40–60 inch lbs.
5. If installing new seal on push rod, place new seal on clean block of wood, with the rubber side down. Place the push rod vertically on the seal stem and strike the threaded end with a soft mallet to seat the seal stem in the push rod.

NOTE: Make sure the shoulders of the push rod and seal are in contact.

6. Slide snap-ring, retaining washer, guide bearing with O-ring seal in outer groove of guide, seal cup and seal retainer on push rod.
7. Attach the piston to the push rod with retaining ring and pin. Dip the piston cup in the clean brake fluid and install on piston.
8. Install new gasket in groove at flange end of hydraulic cylinder and install cylinder on front shell with the hold down bolts.
9. Install the diaphragm return spring, with the large coil first, against the diaphragm plate. Lubricate the cylinder bore with clean brake fluid and carefully insert the piston, cups and seals into cylinder bore. Roll back the edge of the diaphragm and press against the diaphragm to compress the return slightly. When push rod and parts are installed all the way into the cylinder bore, install the retaining snap-ring.

NOTE: Be sure the snap-ring is seated properly before releasing pressure on the spring.

10. Coat both sides of the diaphragm lightly with talcum powder or silicone lubricant. Align scribe marks made on front and rear shells and press the rear shell flange and diaphragm bead into position against the front shell flange.
11. Install the clamp band on the shells and secure with bolt. Install a new seal on the control vacuum tube and assemble the tube and hose onto the rear shell tube and tighten nut.
12. Reinstall on vehicle and check for vacuum leaks and road test to check for proper operation.

Bendix Tandem Diaphragm Type Frame Mounted

Disassembly

1. Remove all hydraulic and vacuum lines attached to booster and hydraulic cylinder. Then remove the unit from frame brackets and remove from vehicle.
2. Scribe marks across both clamp rings onto the shell surfaces, also across top of hydraulic cylinder flange onto the front shell. Scribe marks across control valve body and housing below hydraulic cylinder.
3. Disconnect the control tube and nut from control valve port and remove the three hose clamps and tee. Remove the seal ring from the control tube.
4. Remove the rear clamping ring and remove the rear shell.
5. Remove the front clamping ring and separate the front, center and rear shells and remove the diaphragm assemblies.
6. Clamp the hydraulic cylinder in a soft jawed vice being careful to avoid damaging cylinder.
7. Press on the spring retainer to compress the diaphragm return spring and remove the three bolts that hold the hydraulic cylinder to the front shell and support plate. Then carefully release the pressure on the return spring and pull the push rod and hydraulic piston from the cylinder.
8. Remove the return spring from the piston end of the push rod.

NOTE: Do not remove the spring retainer except to replace damaged parts.

9. Remove the snap-ring from the groove in the piston and press plunger pin from the hole in the piston and push rod.
10. Remove the piston, snap-ring, seal retainer, push rod cup, push rod bearing and support plate and piston stop from the push rod.
11. Remove the cup from the piston and the O-ring from the groove in the push rod bearing.
12. Remove the end fitting from the hydraulic cylinder and remove the snap-ring from the end cap. Disassemble the residual pressure check valve.
13. Remove the end fitting seal from the push rod being careful not to damage the push rod.
14. Clamp the nut, on the push rod seat end of the rear shaft, in a vise and remove by unscrewing the shaft. Remove the assembly from the vise and remove the front diaphragm and diaphragm plate from the shaft.
15. Slide center shells off the shaft and remove the O-ring seal from its groove in the hub of the center shells.
16. Clamp the nut on the rear shaft and remove by unscrewing the shaft. Remove the nut, washer, rear diaphragm, diaphragm plate and washer from the shaft.
17. Remove the valve body and control valve from the valve housing.
18. Remove the cups from the control valve piston and slide the control valve diaphragm and retainer off the opposite end of the piston.

Cleaning and Inspection

Clean all metal parts in clean metal parts cleaner. Discard any old parts that are to be replaced with new ones. Clean all hydraulic parts in clean brake fluid. Check the diaphragms for cracks, tears and kinks and replace any diaphragms that are questionable. Inspect all metal and plastic parts for nicks, cracks, scores or burrs and replace any damaged parts. Check the shells for cracked or broken welds, dents or cracks. DO NOT attempt to disassemble the center shell assembly. Inspect the hydraulic cylinder bore and valve body bore for any surface damage. Remove deposits, pitted areas or light scores with crocus cloth. Replace the part if it can not be cleaned up with crocus cloth.

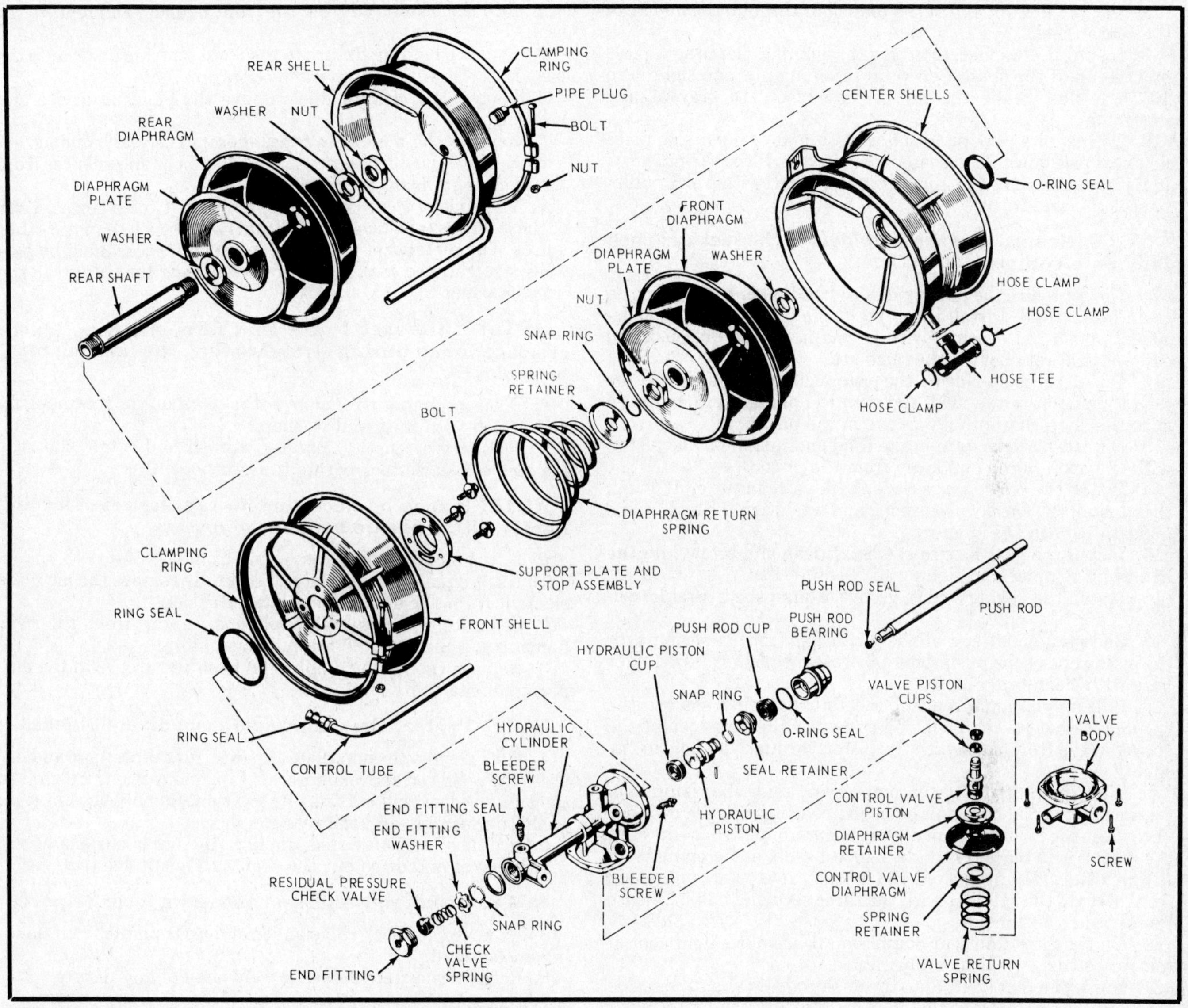

Bendix tandem diaphragm frame mounted booster

Assembly

1. Install the valve piston cups back to back in the grooves on the control valve piston.
2. Slide the valve diaphragm retainer, with the flange side first, onto the other end of the piston. Wet the inside of the valve diaphragm with alcohol and slide it over the end of the piston and seat it against the retainer. Install the spring retainer on the hub of the valve diaphragm with the flange side away from the diaphragm.
3. Install the control valve piston and diaphragm assembly on the return spring. Position the spring around the vacuum poppet guides in the valve body and press the bead of the diaphragm firmly into the groove on the flange of the valve body.
4. Dip the control valve piston and cups into clean brake fluid and install them into the control valve bore in the hydraulic cylinder. Align the scribe marks on the valve body and housing and attach with four bolts. Tighten the bolts to 40–60 inch lbs.
5. Assemble the washer, rear diaphragm plate, diaphragm and washer onto the rear shaft with the holes in the shaft towards the diaphragm.
6. Install the nut on the end of the shaft and tighten to 10–15 ft. lbs. Stake the nut in two places to prevent any movement.
7. Install the O-ring seal in its groove inside the hub of the center shells. With a silicone lubricant, coat the seal and bearing and the outer surface of the rear shaft.

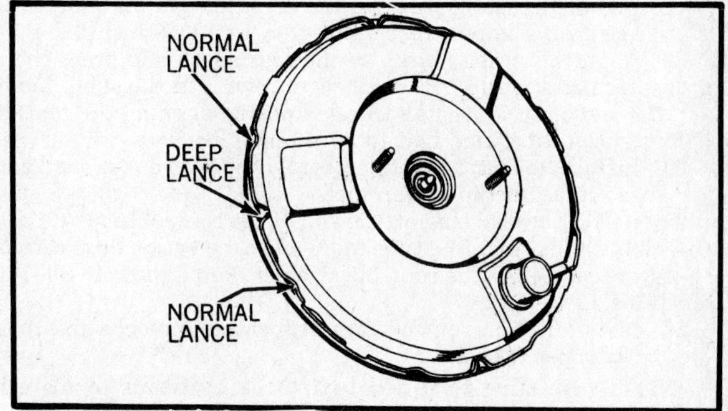

Lances in the rear housing

8. Insert the front end of the rear shaft through the middle of the center shells.
9. Install the washer, front diaphragm and diaphragm plate on the end of the shaft. Screw on retaining nut and tighten to 10–15 ft. lbs. Stake the nut in two places to prevent any movement.
10. To install a new push rod seal, in end of push rod, place new seal face down on a clean block of wood. Place the push rod uptight on the seal stem and strike end of rod with a soft mallet to seat the seal.

NOTE: Be sure that the shoulders of the seal and push rod are in contact.

11. Dip all hydraulic parts, push rod and push rod bearing in clean brake fluid. Install the support plate and piston stop assembly, push rod bearing, with O-ring in its groove, push rod cup and seal retainer on the push rod.
12. Install the snap-ring on the piston but not in its groove. Attach the piston to the push rod with the plunger pin and then slide the snap-ring into its groove in the piston.
13. Dip the piston cup in brake fluid and install on the piston with the open flared end away from the piston.
14. Install the residual pressure check valve in the end fitting, then install the check valve spring and washer in the end fitting and secure with the snap-ring.
15. Install the gasket onto the end fitting and screw into the hydraulic cylinder and tighten to 50–85 ft. lbs.
16. Install the O-ring seal in groove around the hydraulic cylinder flange.
17. Slide the small end of the diaphragm return spring over the piston end of the push rod. Lubricate the piston and cylinder bore with clean brake fluid.
18. Bottom the small end of the return spring against the spring retainer on the push rod and place the large coil of the spring in the front shell with the piston through the hole in the shell.
19. With the return slightly compressed, guide the piston, seal retainer, push rod cup, and push rod bearing into the cylinder bore. Seat the cylinder flange against the front shell, make sure the O-ring is in place. Place the support plate and stop plate on the opposite side of the shell and secure the stop assembly and front shell to the cylinder with the three securing bolts. Release the pressure on the spring.
20. On the front and rear diaphragm beads put a light coat of talcum powder or silicone lubricant.
21. Guide the rear shaft onto the push rod and align the scribe marks made on the front shell flanges. Press the shells together and seat the bead of the diaphragm all the way around in the shell flanges.
22. Install the clamp ring on the shell falnges and align the scribe marks. Tighten the clamp screw to 30–40 inch lbs.
23. Align the scribe marks on the rear shells and press them together making sure the diaphragm bead is in the shell flange all the way around. Install the clamp ring, aligning the marks, and tighten the clamp bolt to 30–40 inch lbs.
24. Install the hose tee to the control tube on the rear shell and to hose nipple on the center shell.
25. Install the seal ring on the end of the control tube and nut assembly and attach the tube to the hose tee with a hose clamp. Screw the nut onto the control valve port and tighten to 80–120 inch lbs.
26. Install unit on vehicle and test for vacuum leaks and road test for proper operation.

NOTE: Be sure to bleed hydraulic cylinder of all air before attempting to road test vehicle.

Bendix Single Diaphragm Booster

Disassembly

1. Scribe a line across the front and rear housings for reassembly.
2. Pull the piston rod from the front housing and remove the seal.
3. Attach a holding fixture to the front housing and clamp the base in a vise with the power section up.
4. Loosen the locknut and remove the pushrod device and locknut.
5. Remove the mounting bracket from the rear housing.
6. Remove the dust boot retainer, dust boot and silencer from the diaphragm plate extension.
7. The edge of the rear housing contains twelve lances. Four of these lances (one in each quadrant) are deeper than the other lances. The metal that forms the four deep lances must be partially straightened so that the lances will clear the cutouts in the front housing.

NOTE: If the metal tabs that form the deep lances crack or break during straightening, the housing must be replaced.

8. Place a spanner wrench over the studs on the rear housing and attach with nuts and washers.
9. Press down on the spanner wrench and rotate the rear housing clockwise to separate the two housings.

NOTE: It may be necessary to tap the rear housing lightly with a plastic hammer to loosen.

10. Lift the rear housing assembly from the unit.
11. Use a small screwdriver and carefully remove the air filter element from the diaphragm plate extension.
12. Separate the diaphragm plate assembly from the rear housing and disassemble the plate assembly.
13. Remove the rolling diaphragm from the groove in the diaphragm plate hub.

NOTE: Protect the diaphragm from oil, and nicks.

14. Hold the diaphragm plate in a horizontal position and depress the push rod approximately $^{1}/_{16}$ in. and rotate the piston so the air valve lock will fall from its location. Remove the air valve pushrod assembly and the reaction disc.
15. If a new seal is needed, support the outer surface of the rear housing and drive out the seal with a suitable tool.

NOTE: Do not reuse old seal once it has been removed.

16. Remove the check valve and grommet from the front housing and discard.
18. Remove the front housing from the holding fixture.

Assembly

1. Use clean brake fluid and thoroughly clean all reusable brake parts.
2. Inspect all rubber parts and replace if nicked, cut or damaged.
3. When rebuilding, make sure that no grease or mineral oil comes in contact with any of the rubber parts.
4. Install a new check valve grommet in the front housing.
5. Position and secure the holding fixture to the front housing and place in a vise.
6. Place the rear housing on a block of wood, stud side down, and position the housing seal in the center hole. Using the special installing tool seat the seal in the recess of the rear housing.
7. Assemble the diaphragm plate assembly:
   a. Apply a silicone lubricant to the outside diameter of the diaphragm plate and extension, to the bearing surfaces of the air valve and to the outer edge of the valve poppet. Insert the air valve and pushrod assembly in the extension of the diaphragm plate.
   b. Depress the pushrod slightly and install the air valve. Make sure the lock indexes and retains the air valve.
   c. Install the rolling diaphragm in the groove of the diaphragm plate.
   d. Apply silicone lubricant to the surface of the reaction

disc and position the disc in the center bore of the diaphragm plate. Use the piston rod to seat the disc in the bore.

NOTE: It is important that the disc be fully seated before removing the piston rod.

8. Apply silicone lubricant to the inside diameter of the rear housing seal and the diaphragm bead contact surface of the rear housing. Install the diaphragm plate assembly in the rear housing.
9. Position the air filter element over the pushrod and into the diaphragm plate extension. Install the air filter retainer.
10. Attach the base of the holding fixture to the front housing and clamp the base in a vise with the power section up.
11. Place a spanner wrench over the studs on the rear housing.
12. Place a diaphragm plate return spring in the front housing and position the rear housing assembly on the front housing with the small end of the spring downward. Align the scribe marks and lock in place.
13. Press down on the spanner wrench and rotate the rear housing counterclockwise to assemble the two housings.

NOTE: Bend the lances in on the rear housing. If the tangs crack or break, it will be necessary to replace that half of the housing.

14. Remove the spanner wrench from the rear shell.
15. Install the air silencer over the push rod end, then the boot retainer.
16. On vehicles with a clevis type push rod, install the locknut and clevis.
17. Install the mounting bracket to the rear shell, if so equipped.
18. Remove the cylinder from the vise and remove the holding fixture.
19. Apply silicone lubricant to the piston rod and guide the rod into the center bore of the diaphragm plate until it is fully seated.

NOTE: Keep the lubricant away from the rounded end of the rod.

20. Press the seal into the front housing until it is bottomed in the recess of the housing.

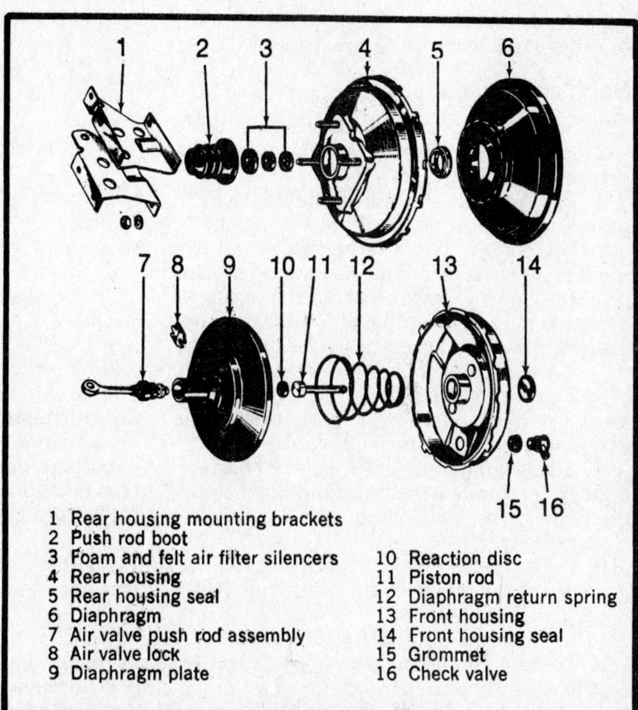

Bendix single diaphragm booster

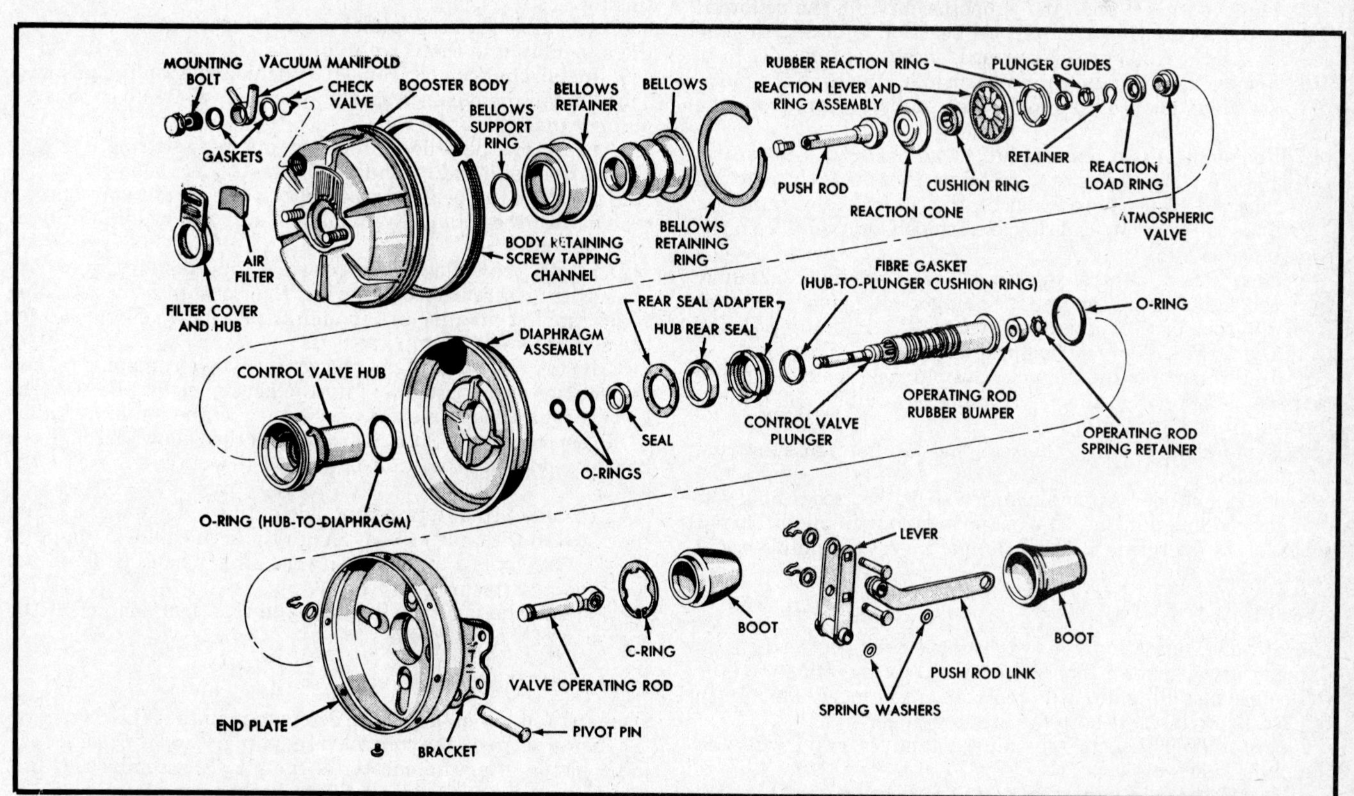

Disassembled view of booster

Midland Ross Diaphragm Type

The self-contained booster assembly is mounted on the engine side of the firewall. It is connected directly to the brake pedal. This booster is not equipped with a separate vacuum tank.

The master cylinder is attached to the forward side of the booster. The balance of the hydraulic brake system is identical to other standard service brakes.

Booster Repairs

1. Separate master cylinder from booster body.
2. Remove air filter cover and hub and the filter from the booster body.
3. Remove the vacuum manifold mounting bolt, manifold, gaskets and vacuum check valve from the booster body.
4. Disconnect the valve operating rod from the lever by removing its retaining clip, washers, and pivot pin.
5. Disconnect the lever from the booster end plate brackets by removing its retaining clip, washers, and pivot pin.
6. Remove two brackets from the end plate.
7. Remove the rubber boot from the valve operating rod.
8. To remove the bellows, control valve, and diaphragm assemblies, remove large C-ring that holds the rear seal adapter assembly to the booster end plate.
9. Scribe matching lines on the booster body and the end plate. Then remove the ten retaining screws. Tap the outside of the plate with a soft hammer and separate the plate from the booster body.
10. Push the bellows assembly into the vacuum chamber and remove the bellows, control valve, and diaphragm as an assembly from the booster body.
11. Remove the outer O-ring from the control valve hub.
12. To disassemble the bellows, pushrod, and control valve assemblies, remove the large bellows retaining ring, bellows, bellows retainer, and support ring from the diaphragm and valve assembly.
13. Remove the retainer and support ring from the bellows.
14. Remove pushrod assembly, the reaction lever and ring assembly, and the rubber reaction ring from the control valve hub.
15. Remove the reaction cone and cushion ring from the pushrod assembly. Then disassemble the reaction levers from the ring.
16. Remove the two plastic plunger guides from the control valve plunger. Then remove the retainer that holds the reaction load ring and atmospheric valve on the control valve hub.
17. Slide the reaction load ring and atmospheric valve from the control valve hub.
18. Separate the control valve hub and the plunger assembly from the diaphragm by sliding the plunger and rear seal adapter from the rear of the hub. Then remove the hub outer O-ring from the front side of the diaphragm.
19. To disassemble the control valve plunger, remove the hub rear seal adapter from the valve plunger assembly, and remove the seal from the adapter.
20. Remove the O-rings, the seal, and the fiber gaskets from the plunger.
21. If the plunger assembly needs to be replaced, hold the plunger and pull out the valve operating rod with pliers. Do not separate the operating rod and plunger unless the plunger is to be replaced.

Assembly

1. If valve operating rod was removed for replacement of plunger, install a new rubber bumper and spring retainer on the rod before installing it on the replacement plunger. Then push the rod firmly until it bottoms in the plunger.
2. Install fiber gaskets, plunger seal, and the two O-rings on the plunger assembly.
3. Install the valve hub rear seal in the adapter assembly with the sealing lip toward the rear. Then slide the adapter assembly onto the plunger with the small diameter end of the hub toward the rear.
4. To assemble the control valve, pushrod, and bellows assemblies, install the hub outer O-ring. Then install the plunger with the seal adapter and the hub on the diaphragm. To do this, hold the hub on the front side of the diaphragm and insert the plunger assembly in the hub from the rear side of the diaphragm.
5. Install atmospheric valve and then the reaction load ring onto the plunger and hub. Compress the valve spring, and install the load ring retainer into the groove of the plunger.
6. Install two plastic plunger guides into their grooves on the plunger.
7. Install rubber reaction ring into the valve hub so that the ring locating knob indexes in the notch in the hub, with the ring tips toward the front.
8. Assemble the reaction lever and ring assembly, and install the assembly into the valve hub.
9. Install the reaction cone and cushion ring on the pushrod. Then install the pushrod assembly on the valve hub so that the plunger indexes in the rod.
10. Assemble the bellows, retainer, and support ring. The ring should be positioned on the middle fold of the bellows.
11. Position the bellows assembly on the diaphragm, and secure it with the retaining ring. Make sure the retaining ring is fully seated.
12. Install the bellows, control valve, and diaphragm assemblies with a screwdriver, moving the booster body retaining screw tapping channel just enough to provide a new surface for the self-tapping attaching screws.
13. Install the diaphragm, the control valve components, and the bellows as an assembly into the booster body. (Be sure the lip of the diaphragm is evenly positioned on the retaining radius of the booster body.) Pull the front lip of the bellows through the booster body, and position it around the outer groove of the body.
14. Install O-ring in the front side of the end plate, and locate the plate on the booster body. Align the scribed lines, compress the two assemblies together with a clamp. Then install all ten self-tapping attaching screws.
15. Install the large C-ring onto the rear seal adapter at the rear side of the end plate.

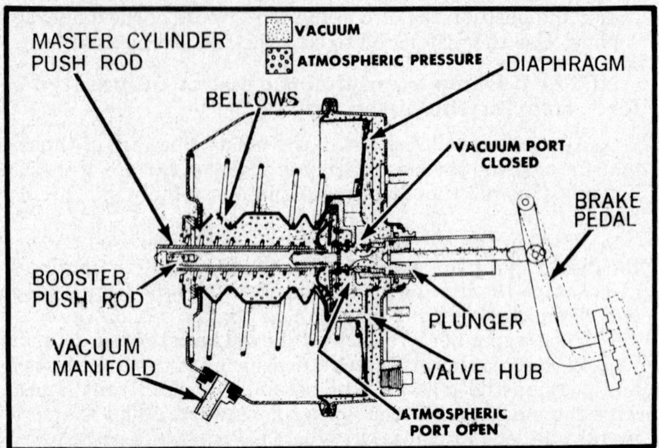

Midland diaphragm type booster—applied position

Pushrod Adjustment

The pushrod has an adjusting screw to maintain the correct relationship between the control valve plunger and the master cylinder piston after the booster is completely assembled. If this screw is not properly adjusted, the brakes may drag.

To check adjustment of the screw, make a gauge to the dimen-

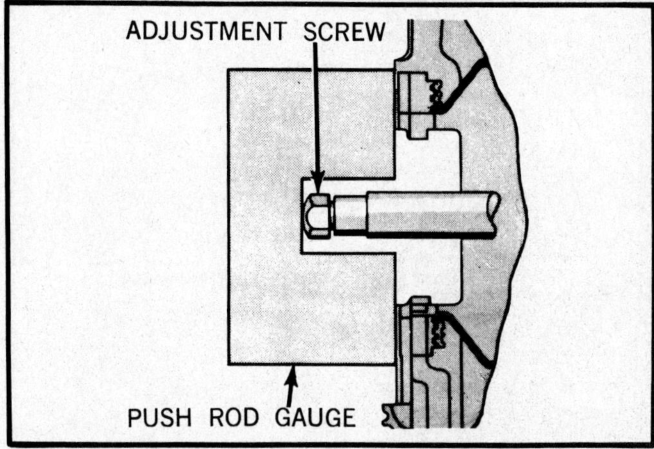

Checking pushrod screw with gauge

sions shown. Place this gauge against the master cylinder mounting surface of the booster body. The pushrod screw should be adjusted so that the end of the screw just touches the inner edge of the slot in the gauge.

Booster Installation

1. Install rubber boot on the valve operating rod.
2. Position the two mounting brackets on the end plate, and install on retaining nuts.
3. Connect the lever assembly to the lower end of the mounting brackets with its pivot pin. Then install the spring washer and retaining clip.
4. Connect the valve operating rod to the upper end of the lever with its pivot pin, washer, and retaining clip.
5. Install the vacuum check valve, the vacuum manifold, the two gaskets, and the mounting bolt. Torque the mounting bolt to 8–10 ft. lbs.

Midland Diaphragm Type Frame Mounted

The Midland frame mounted booster is a remote type, without mechanical operation, utilizing vacuum to boost the hydraulic pressure between master and wheel cylinder.

Removal

1. Remove all hydraulic lines from the booster unit hydraulic cylinder.
2. Remove all vacuum lines from the booster unit and remove the support bracket bolts.
3. Remove the unit from the vehicle and place on a clean work bench.

Disassembly

1. Remove the control tube from the control valve body and the rear body.
2. Scribe marks across the diaphragm body and across the flanges of the slave cylinder body and the control valve body.
3. Remove the body clamp carefully, and remove the rear body and diaphragm with the return spring.
4. Remove the push rod, spring retainer and collar from the return spring.
5. Scribe a line across the valve body cover and the valve body, and remove the valve body cover and gasket.
6. Remove the valve body, spring, and the piston and diaphragm assembly from the slave cylinder.
7. From the end of the slave cylinder remove the end plug, copper gasket, spring, spring seat and spring retainer.

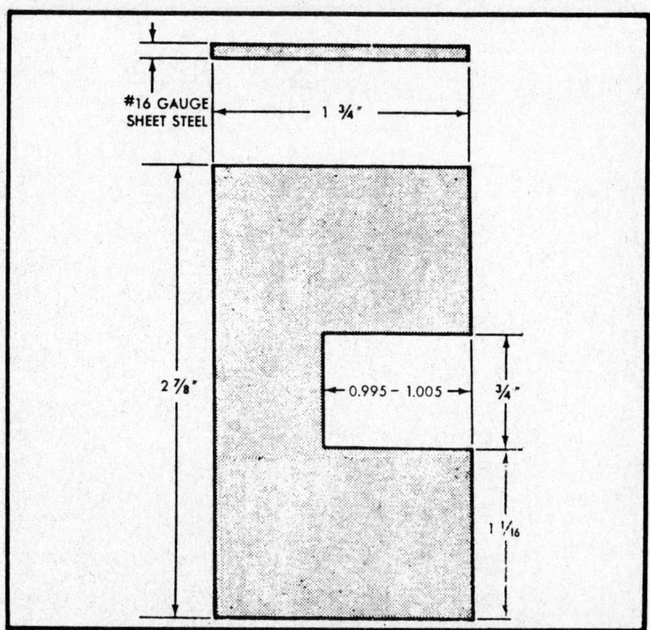

Pushrod gauge

8. Remove the piston cup and piston assembly from the cylinder.

NOTE: If the assembly does not fall free from the cylinder it may be pushed out by inserting the push rod through the bushing.

9. From the hydraulic piston remove the check valve, check valve retainer and the return spring.
10. Hold the cylinder in a soft jawed vise and remove the push rod bushing, lockwasher and front body.
11. Remove the gasket, rubber seal and transfer bushing from the slave cylinder body. From the bushing remove the two push rod bushing snap-rings, and remove the washer and two seals. From the outside of the push rod bushing remove the O-ring seal.
12. From the lower end of the control valve piston remove the seal, also remove the seal from the piston boss.
13. Remove the retaining nut from the piston boss and remove the diaphragm plate and control valve diaphragm.
14. Remove the screw, lockwasher, spacer, spring, disc., and the seal from the control valve body.

Assembly

1. Install new spring in the control valve body and assemble the spring and spacer in the valve body. Secure with the screw and locknut.
2. Secure the control valve diaphragm and plate in place with the attaching nut.
3. On the control valve piston install the piston seal.
4. In the hydraulic piston install the check valve spring, check valve and retainer, making sure that the valve floats free in the bore and does not bind.
5. On the front end of the slave cylinder body, install the transfer bushing, seal and gasket.
6. In the push rod bushing install the push rod seals, washer and snap-rings.

NOTE: Install the push rod seals with the open end of the seal towards the slave cylinder body. Install the lockwasher over the end of the rod bushing and install the bushing seal.

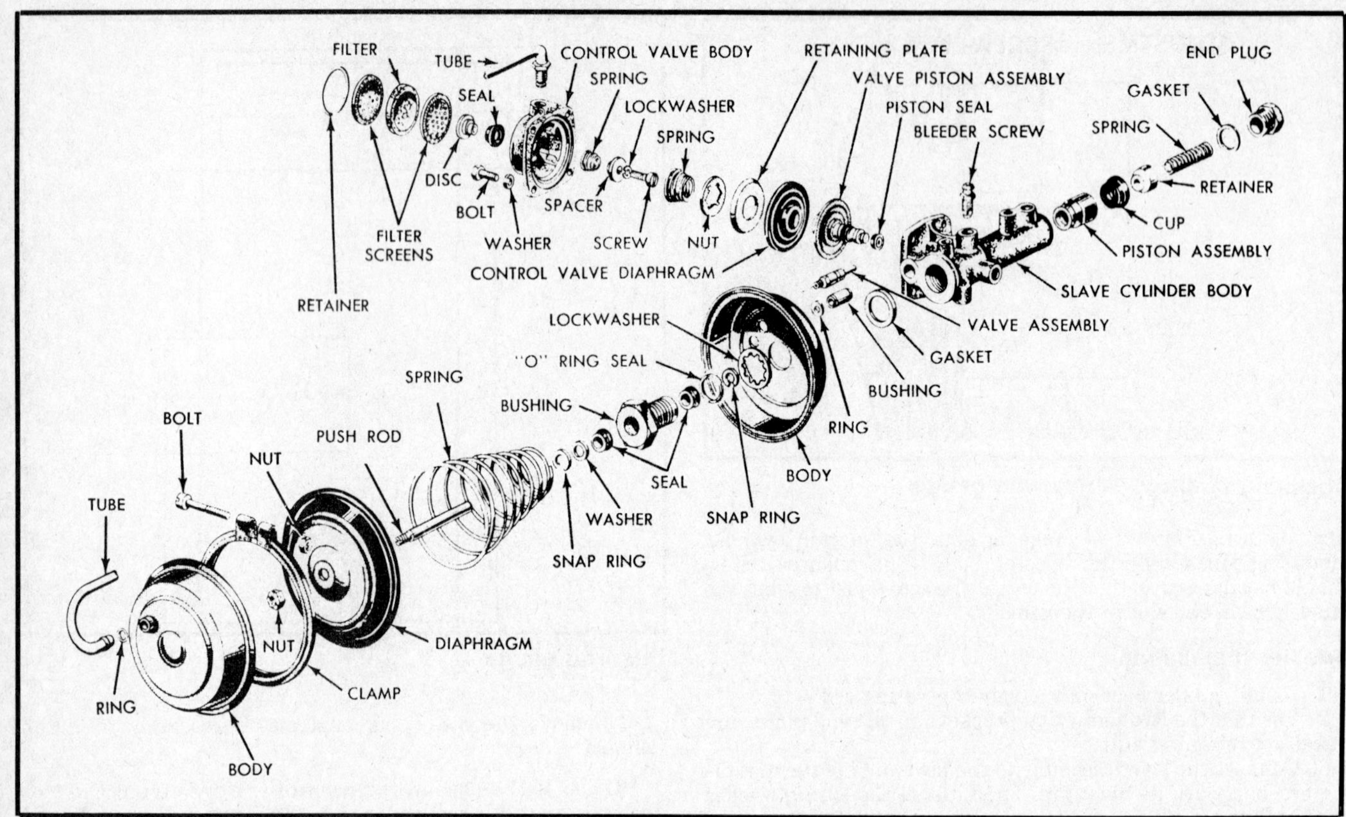

Midland vacuum booster

7. With the slave cylinder mounted in a vise, position the front body over the end of the cylinder, inserting the transfer bushing in the front body.
8. Thread push rod bushing in place and tighten securely, making sure the front body seats squarely on the slave cylinder body.
9. Coat the piston bore of the slave cylinder with brake fluid, also the hydraulic piston, seals, spring retainer and spring.
10. With the recessed end towards the push rod bushing, install the hydraulic piston in the slave cylinder bore. On top of the piston, install the piston cup, large spring retainer and spring. Install the spring seat in the spring coils.
11. Install a new copper gasket on the end plug and screw the plug into the cylinder tightening securely.
12. Dip the control valve piston and diaphragm in brake fluid and position the control valve spring on the diaphragm, making sure that the small end of the spring is over the piston boss.
13. With the control valve body positioned over the spring, and with the scribe marks aligned, secure the valve body to the slave cylinder with the four attaching bolts.
14. Install a new gasket on the valve body cover and secure the cover to the valve body with the four attaching bolts.
15. Install the collar over the threaded end of the push rod and position the retainer on the spring. Insert the rod and collar through the coils of the spring and the retainer. Install the diaphragm over the threaded end of the push rod and secure in place with the push rod nut. Coat the push rod with brake fluid.
16. Install the return spring assembly over the push rod bushing.
17. Install the rear body on the diaphragm aligning the scribe marks on the front and rear shells. Making sure the bead of the diaphragm is properly placed between the body halves, compress the return spring and install and tighten the ring clamp band.
18. Install the by-pass tube and install the unit on the vehicle.
19. Check the unit for vacuum leaks and road test the vehicle for proper operation of the unit.

NOTE: Bleed all air from the hydraulic cylinder and lines before road testing the vehicle.

Kelsey-Hayes Diaphragm Type

IDENTIFICATION

The Kelsey-Hayes power brake unit can be identified by the twistlock method of locking the housing and cover together, plus the white-colored vacuum check valve assembly.

Removal

1. With engine off, apply brakes several times to equalize internal brake pressure.
2. Disconnect hydraulic line from master cylinder.
3. Disconnect vacuum hose from power brake check valve.
4. Disconnect power brake from brake pedal (under instrument panel).
5. Disconnect power brake unit from dash panel.
6. Remove power brake and master cylinder assembly from the vehicle.

Disassembly

1. Separate master cylinder from power brake unit.
2. Remove master cylinder pushrod and air cleaner plate.
3. Mount the power unit in a vise with the master cylinder attaching studs up.
4. Scribe an index line across the housing and cover for reassembly reference.
5. Pry out the housing lock. Do not damage the lock, as it must be used at assembly.

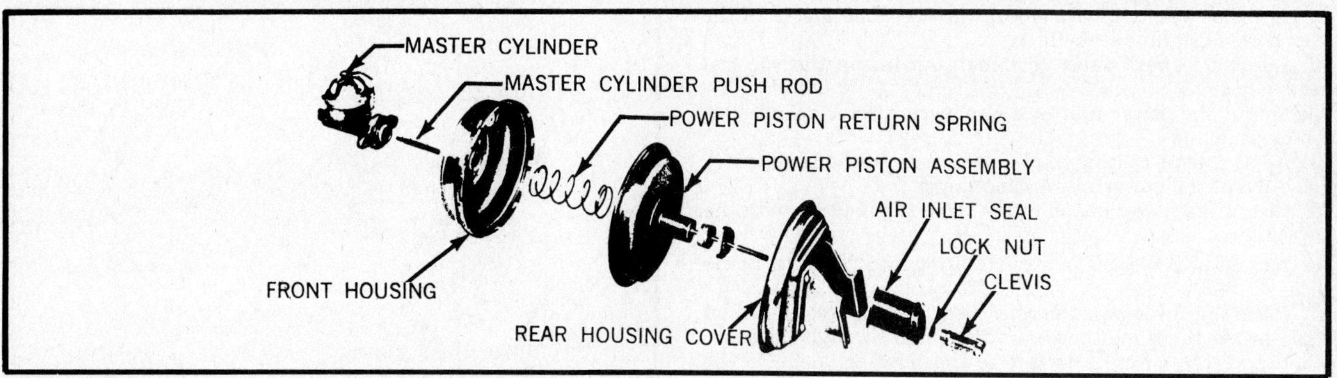

Power brake unit

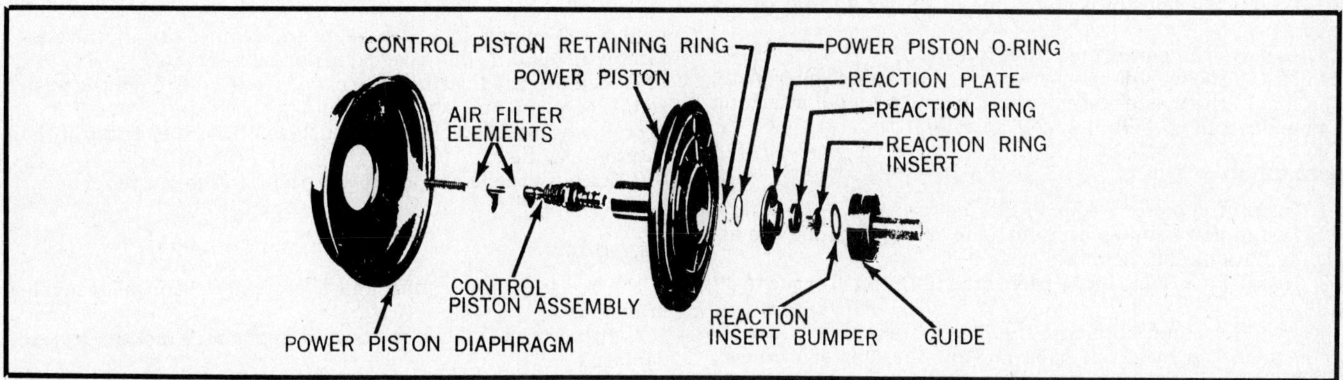

Power piston assembly

6. Remove check valve from cover by prying out of rubber grommet.
7. Place parking brake flange holding tool over the master cylinder mounting studs.
8. Rotate the tool and cover in a counterclockwise direction. Then, separate the cover from the housing. This will expose the power piston return spring and diaphragm.
9. Lift out the power piston return spring. Remove the brake unit from the vise.
10. Remove power piston by slowly lifting the piston straight up.
11. Remove air cleaner, guide seal and seal retainer from the cover.
12. Remove the block seal from the center hole of the housing, using a blunt drift. (Don't scratch the bore of the housing, it could cause a vacuum leak.)

Power Piston Disassembly

1. Remove power piston diaphragm from the power piston. Keep it clean.
2. Remove screws that attach the plastic guide to the power piston. Remove guide and place to one side.
3. Remove the power piston square seal ring, reaction ring insert, reaction ring and reaction plate.
4. Depress operating rod slightly, then remove the Truarc snap-ring.
5. Remove control piston by pulling the operating rod.
6. Remove the O-ring seal from the end of the control piston.
7. Remove the filter elements and dust felt from the control piston rod.

Cleaning and Inspection

Thoroughly wash all metal parts in a suitable solvent and dry with compressed air. The power diaphragm, plastic power piston and guide should be washed in a mild soap and water solution. Blow dust and all cleaning material out of internal passages. All rubber parts should be replaced, regardless of condition. Install new air filters at assembly. Inspect all parts for scoring, pits, dents or nicks. Small imperfections can be smoothed out with crocus cloth. Replace all badly damaged parts.

Assembly

When assembling, be sure that all rubber parts, except the diaphragm and the reaction ring are lubricated with silicone grease.

1. Install control piston O-ring onto the piston.
2. Lubricate and install the control piston into the power piston. Install the Truarc snap-ring into its groove. Wipe all lubricant off the end of the control piston.
3. Install air filter elements and felt seal over the pushrod and down past the retaining shoulder on the rod. Install the power piston square seal ring into its groove.
4. Install the reaction plate in the power piston. Align the three holes with those in the power piston.
5. Install the rubber reaction ring in the reaction plate. Do not lubricate this ring.
6. Lubricate outer diameter of the reaction insert and install in the reaction ring.
7. Install reaction insert bumper into the guide.
8. Place guide on the power piston, align the holes with the aligning points on the power piston. Install retaining screws and torque to 80–100 inch lbs.
9. Install diaphragm on power piston; be sure that the diaphragm is correctly seated in the power piston groove.
10. With the housing blocked to prevent damage, install the block seal in the housing.
11. Install a new cover seal on the retainer and lubricate thor-

oughly, inside and out, with silicone grease, then install in the cover bore. Install new air filter.

12. Lubricate check valve grommet and install the vacuum check valve.

13. Mount the power unit in a vise, with master cylinder attaching studs up.

14. Apply a light coating of silicone grease to the bead, outer edge only, of the power piston diaphragm.

15. Install the power piston assembly in the housing with the operating rod down.

16. Install the power piston return spring into the flange of the guide.

17. Place the cover over the return spring and press down on the cover. At the same time, pilot the guide through the seal.

18. Rotate the cover to lock it to the housing. Be sure the scribe lines are in correct index and that the diaphragm is not pinched during assembly.

19. Install the housing lock on one of the long tangs of the housing.

20. Remove the power unit from the vise.

21. Install the master cylinder push-rod and air cleaner plate, then install the master cylinder on the studs. Install attaching nuts and washers. Torque to 200 inch lbs.

Installation

1. Install the power brake seal to the firewall.
2. Install power brake unit onto firewall and torque the attaching nuts to 200 inch lbs.
3. Install pushrod to brake pedal attaching bolt. Torque to 30 ft. lbs.
4. Install vacuum hose onto the power brake unit.
5. Attach the hydraulic tube and fill the master cylinder. Bleed hydraulic system.
6. Adjust stop light switch if necessary.

Delco Single Diaphragm Booster

Disassembly

1. Scribe a mark on the bottom center of front and rear housings for reassembly.
2. Attach a base tool to the front housing and clamp the base in a vise with the power section up.
3. Separate the front and rear housings by securing a spanner wrench to the bracket. Press down on the wrench and rotate rear housing counterclockwise to the unlocked position. Loosen the housing carefully as it is spring loaded.
4. Remove the spanner wrench, then lift the rear housing and power piston assembly from the unit. Remove the return spring.
5. Remove the silencer by removing the retaining ring on the push rod.
6. Remove the seal, vacuum check valve and grommet from the front housing.
7. Remove the power piston assembly from the rear housing.
8. Remove the silencer from the neck of the power piston tube.
9. Remove the lock ring from the power piston.
10. Remove the reaction retainer, piston, plate, levers, bumper and spring.
11. Place a power piston wrench in a vise and position the assembly so that the three lugs on the tool fit into the three notches in the piston.
12. Press down on the support plate and rotate it counterclockwise until it separates from the power piston.
13. Remove the diaphragm from the support plate.
14. Position the power piston, tube down, in a tool fabricated from a piece of wood 2 × 4 × 8 in. long with a 1 $^3/_8$ in. hole in the center clamped in a vise.
15. Remove the snap-ring on the air valve.
16. Using the power pump and press plate insert the power piston, tube down, in a press plate and remove the air valve assembly using a $^3/_8$ in. drive extension as a remover.

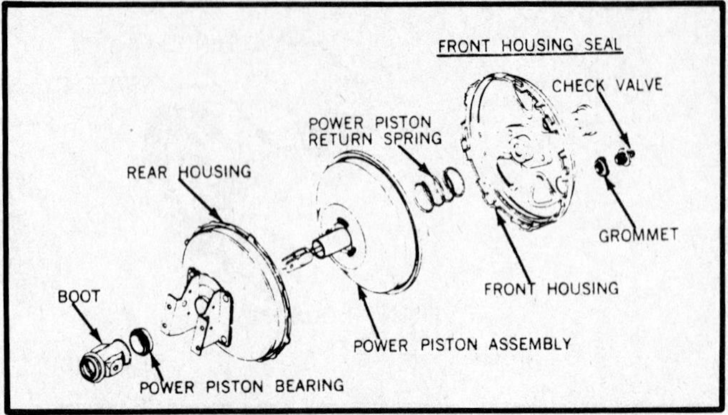

Delco single diaphragm booster

17. Remove the floating control valve assembly from the push rod. Use a new one when rebuilding.
18. Push the master cylinder push rod from the center of the reaction retainer.
19. Remove the O-ring from the groove in the master cylinder piston rod.

Assembly

1. Use clean brake fluid and thoroughly clean all resuable brake parts.
2. Inspect all rubber parts and replace if nicked, cut or damaged.
3. When rebuilding make sure that no grease or mineral oil comes in contact with any of the rubber parts.
4. Install a new vacuum check valve using a new grommet.
5. Position a new front housing seal so that the flat surface of the cup lies against the bottom depression in the housing.
6. Place a new O-ring in the groove on the master cylinder piston rod, wipe a thin film of silicone lubricant on the O-ring.
7. Insert the master cylinder piston rod through the reaction retainer so the round end protrudes from the end of the tube on the reaction retainer.
8. Place the power piston wrench in a vise and position the power piston on the wrench so that the three lugs fit into the notches.
9. Position a new O-ring on the air valve on the second groove from the push rod end.
10. Place a new floating control valve on the push rod-air valve assembly so that the flat face of the valve will seat against the valve seat on the air valve.

NOTE: The old floating control valve assembly must be replaced with a new one since the force required to remove it distorts component parts.

11. Wipe a thin film of silicone lubricant on the control valve and the O-ring on the air valve.
12. Push the air valve push rod assembly, air valve first, onto its seat in the tube of the power piston.
13. Place the control valve retainer over the push rod so that the flat side seats on the floating control valve.
14. Press the floating control valve and its retainer onto the power piston tube by use of an installer tool and pushing down by hand.
15. After the floating control valve is seated, position the push rod limiter washer over the push rod and down onto the valve.
16. Stretch the air filter element over the end of the push rod and press it into the power piston tube.
17. Assemble the power piston diaphragm to the support plate. The raised flange of the diaphragm is pressed through the hole in the center of the support plate.

NOTE: Be sure that the edge of the center hole fits into the groove in the flange of the diaphragm.

18. Pull the diaphragm away from the outside diameter of the support plate so that the support plate can be gripped with both hands.
19. With the power piston still positioned on the holding tool in a vise, coat the bead of the diaphragm that contacts the power piston with silicone lubricant.
20. Place the support plate and diaphragm assembly over the tube of the power piston with the locking tangs facing downward.

NOTE: The flange of the power piston will fit into the groove on the power piston.

21. Press down and rotate the support plate clockwise, until the lugs on the power piston come against the stops on the support plate.
22. Turn the assembly over and place tube down in a tool, fabricated from a piece of wood 2 × 4 × 8 in. long with a 1 $^3/_8$ in. hole in the center, clamped into a vise.
23. Replace the snap-ring into the groove of the air valve.
24. Place the air valve spring retainer on the snap-ring and assemble the reaction bumper into the groove in the end of the air valve.
25. Position the air valve return spring, large end down, on the spring retainer.
26. Place the three reaction levers into position with the wide ends in the slots of the power piston and the narrow ends resting on top of the air valve return springs.
27. Position the reaction plate (with the numbered side up) on top of the reaction levers. Press down on the plate until the large ends of the reaction levers pop up so the plate rests flat on the levers and is centered.
28. With the round end of the master cylinder piston rod up, and with the reaction retainer held toward the top of the piston rod, place the small end of the piston rod in the hole in the center of the reaction plate. Line up the ears on the reaction retainer with the notches in the power piston and push the reaction retainer down until the ears seat in the notches.
29. With pressure on the reaction retainer, position the large lock ring down over the master cylinder push rod.
30. There is a lug on the power piston which has a raised divider in the center. One end of the lock ring goes under the lug and on one side of the divider.
31. As you work your way around the power piston, the lockring goes over the ear of the reaction retainer and under a lug on the power piston until the other end of the lock ring is seated under the lug with the raised divider.

NOTE: Make certain both ends of the lock ring are securely under the large lug.

32. Place a new power piston bearing in the center of the rear housing so the flange on the center hole of the housing fits into the groove of the power piston bearing. The large flange on the power piston bearing will be on the stud side of the housing. Coat the inside of the bearing with silicone lubricant.
33. Place the air silencer over the holes on the tube of the power piston. Wipe the tube with silicone lubricant.
34. Attach the holding fixture to the front housing and clamp the base in a vise.
35. Place the power piston return spring over the insert in the front housing.
36. Lubricate the inside diameter of the support plate seal, the reaction retainer tube, and the beaded edge of the diaphragm with silicone lubricant.
37. Place the rear housing assembly over the front housing assembly and align the scribe marks of the two housings so they will match when in the locked position.
38. Place a spanner wrench on the rear housing and tighten the nuts and washers to the bolts.

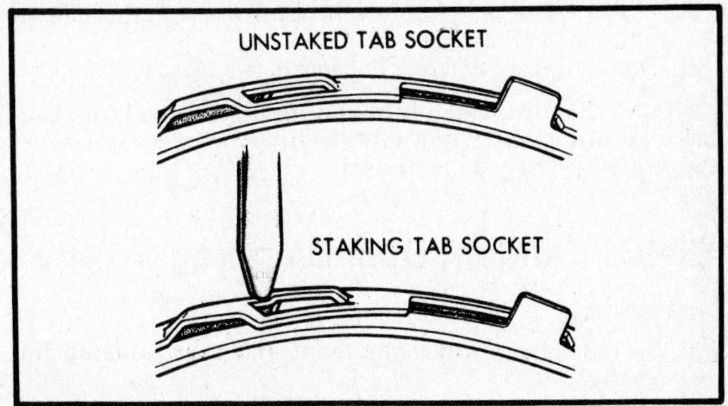

Staking housing tabs

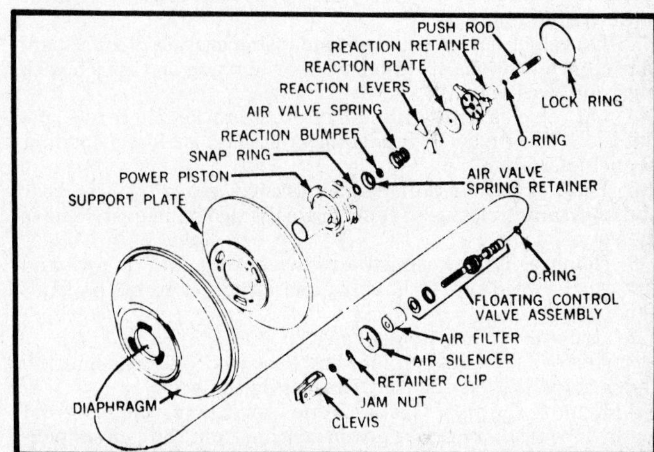

Power piston assembly

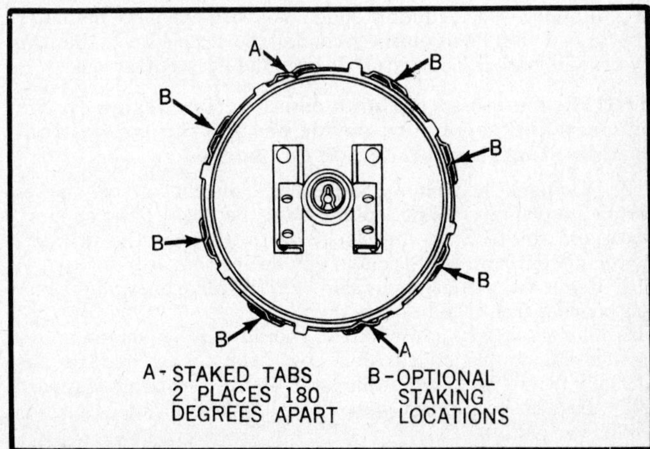

Housing locking tabs

39. Press down on the spanner wrench and twist the rear housing clockwise until fully locked.

NOTE: Do not break the studs loose in the rear housing or put pressure on the power piston tube when locking the housings.

40. Remove the spanner wrench and the holding fixture from the front housing.
41. Push the felt silencer over the pushrod and seat it against the end of the power piston tube.
42. Push the plastic boot and seat it against the rear housing.

The raised tabs on the side of the boot will locate in the holes in the center of the brackets.

43. Stake the front and rear housing in two places: 180° apart.

NOTE: The interlock tabs should not be used for staking a second time. When all tabs have been staked once, the housing must be replaced.

Delco Tandem Dual Diaphragm Type

Disassembly

1. Scribe a line across the front and rear housing for reassembly.
2. Attach the base of a special holding fixture or equivalent to the front housing with nuts and washers and draw down tight to eliminate damage to the studs. Clamp the base in a vise with the power section up.
3. On vehicles with a straight mounting bracket place a spanner wrench over the studs on the rear housing and attach with nuts and washers.
4. On vehicles with a tilted mounting bracket there is a special tool placed inside the mounting bracket with the spanner wrench placed on top.
5. Press down on the spanner wrench and rotate the rear housing counterclockwise to separate the two housings. Remove the special tools.
6. Remove the power piston return spring, and remove and discard the vacuum check valve and grommet from the front housing.
7. Remove the front housing seal.
8. Remove the boot retainer and boot from the rear housing and remove the felt silencer from inside the boot.
9. Remove the power piston group from the rear housing and remove the primary power piston bearing from the center opening of the rear housing.
10. Remove piston rod retainer and piston rod from the secondary piston.
11. Mount a special double ended tool with the large diameter end up in a vise. Position the secondary power piston so that the two radial slots in the piston fit over the ears of the tool.

NOTE: Due to an optional construction design on the primary and secondary power pistons the special tool used in Step 11 will have to be reworked.

12. Fold back the primary diaphragm from the outside diameter of the primary support plate. Grip the edge of the support plate and rotate it counterclockwise to unscrew the primary power piston from the secondary power piston.
13. Remove the housing divider from the secondary power piston bearing from the housing divider.
14. The secondary power piston should still be positioned on the special double ended tool. Fold back the secondary diaphragm from the outside diameter of the secondary support plate. Rotate the support plate clockwise to unlock the secondary power piston.
15. Remove the secondary diaphragm from the secondary support plate.
16. Remove the reaction piston and disc from the center of the secondary power piston by pushing down on the end of the piston.
17. Remove the air valve spring from the end of the valve, if not removed earlier.
18. Remove the primary diaphragm and piston using the same procedure as the secondary with the exception of turning the support plate counterclockwise to unlock it.
19. Remove the air filter from the tubular section of the primary power piston.
20. Remove the power head silencer from the neck of the power piston tube.

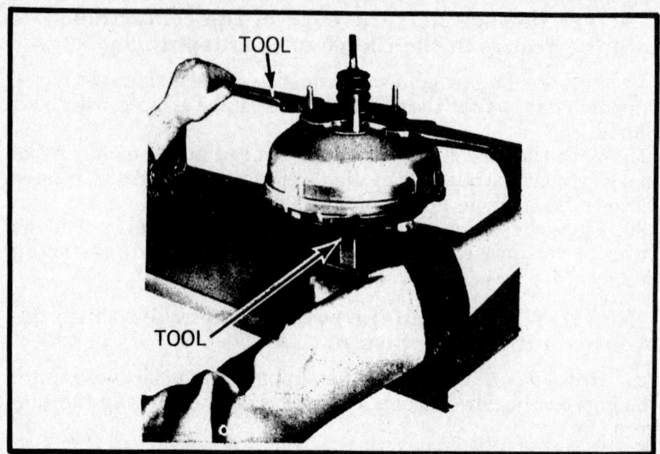

Unlocking front and rear housing

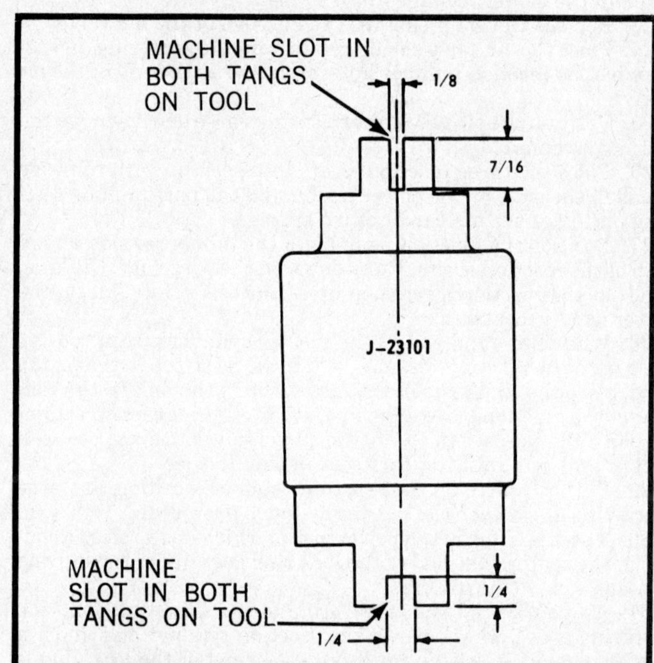

Reworking of tool for optional power piston design

21. Remove the rubber reaction bumper from the end of the air valve.
22. Using snap-ring pliers, remove the retaining ring from the air valve.
23. Remove the air valve push rod assembly.
    a. The recommended method would be to place the primary power piston in an arbor press and press the air valve push rod assembly out the bottom of the power piston tube using a rod not larger than $1/2$ in. in diameter.
    b. An alternate method would be to insert a heavy, round shanked screwdriver on both sides of the pushrod and pull the air valve push rod assembly straight out.
24. Remove the O-ring seal from the air valve.

Assembly

1. Use clean brake fluid and thoroughly clean all reusable brake parts.
2. Inspect all rubber parts and replace if nicked, cut or damaged.

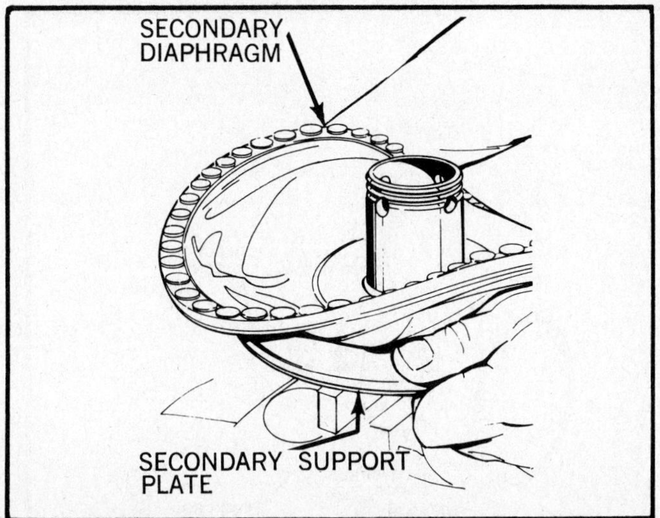

Locking or unlocking the secondary support plate and power piston

3. When rebuilding, make sure that no grease or mineral oil comes in contact with any of the rubber parts.
4. Install a new vacuum check valve and a new grommet in the front housing.
5. Place a new seal in the front housing so that the flat surface lies against the bottom of the depression in the housing.
6. Reassemble the power piston group.
7. Lubricate the inside and outside diameter of the O-ring seal with silicone lubricant and place on the air valve.
8. Wipe a thin film of silicone lubricant on the large and small outside diameter of the floating control valve. If the floating control valve needs replacement, it will be necessary to replace the complete air valve-push rod assembly.
9. Place the air valve end of the air valve push rod assembly into the tube of the primary power piston. Manually press the air valve push rod assembly so that the floating control valve bottoms on the tube section of the primary power piston.
10. Place the inside diameter of the floating control valve retainer on the outside diameter of the special installer. Place it over the pushrod so that the closed side of the retainer seats on the floating control valve. Using the installer manually press the retainer and floating control valve to seat in the tube.
11. Stretch the filter element over the pushrod and press it into the piston tube.
12. Place the retaining ring into the groove in the air valve using snap-ring pliers.
13. Position the rubber reaction bumper on the end of the air valve.
14. Determine the correct reaction piston and apply a light coat of silicone lubricant to the outside diameter of the rubber reaction disc.
15. Place the rubber reaction disc in the large cavity of the secondary power piston and push the disc down to seat on the reaction piston.
16. Unlock the secondary power piston from the primary power piston.
17. Assemble the primary diaphragm to the primary support plate opposite the locking tangs. Press the raised flange on the inside diameter of the diaphragm through the center hole of the support plate. Be sure that the edge of the support plate center hole fits into the groove of the flange.

NOTE: Lubricate the inside diameter of the diaphragm and the raised surface of the flange with a light coat of silicone lubricant.

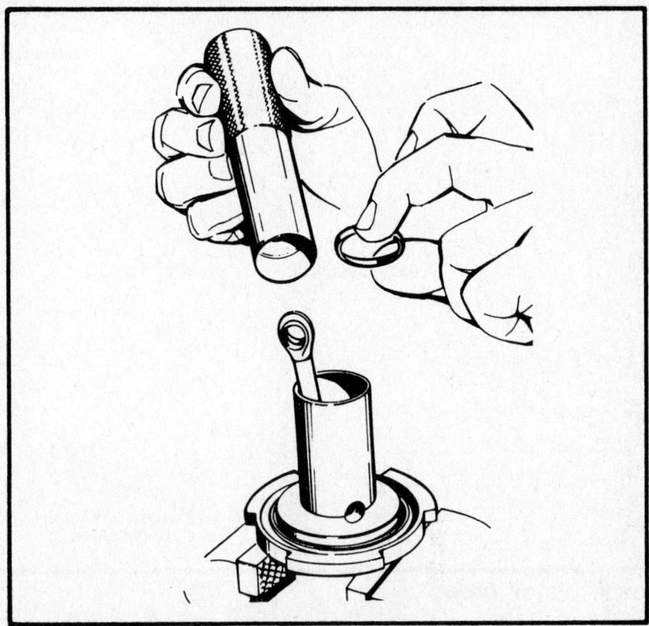

Installing the floating control valve retainer

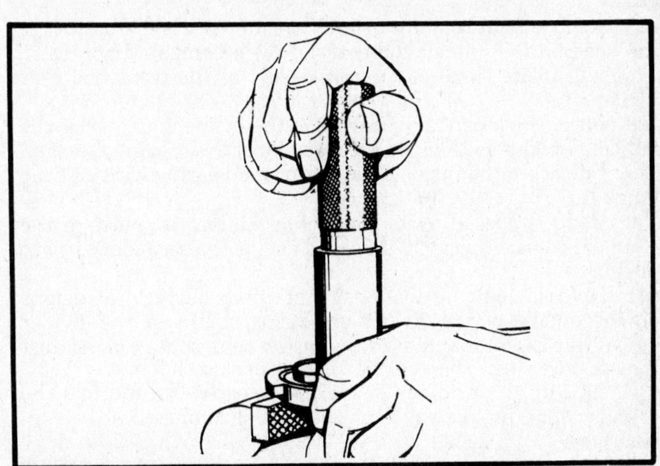

Seating the floating control valve assembly

18. Mount the special tool used in Step 11 of the disassembly procedures in a vise with the small end up. Position the primary power piston so that the two radial slots in the piston fit over the ears (tangs) of the tool.
19. Fold the primary diaphragm away from the outside diameter of the primary support plate.
20. Place the primary support plate and diaphragm assembly over the tube of the primary piston. Make sure the locking tangs are facing down.
21. Press down and rotate the support plate clockwise until the tabs on the piston contact the stops.
22. Place the power head silencer on the tube of the piston so that the holes at the base of the tube are covered.
23. Coat the outside of the tube with silicone lubricant.
24. Remove the primary piston assembly from the special tool and lay it aside.
25. Assemble the secondary diaphragm to the secondary support plate following the same steps for assembling the primary support plate except mount the special tool with the large diameter up, and press down and turn the plate counterclockwise until the piston contacts the stops.

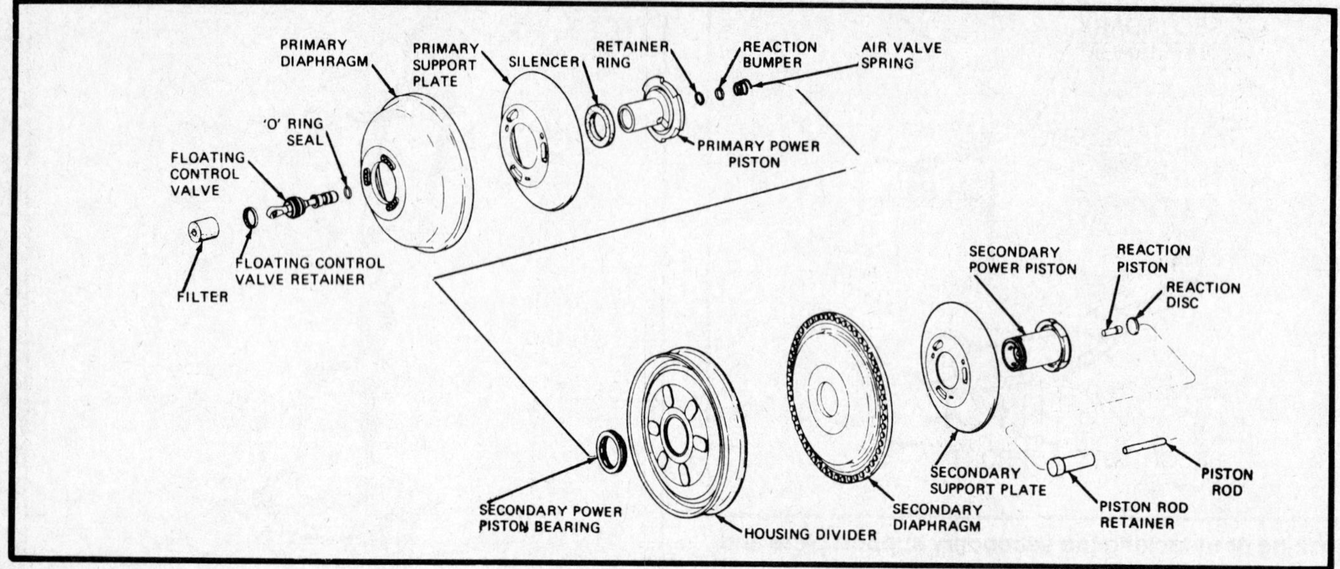

Power piston group

26. Leave the secondary power piston on the tool and in the vise.
27. Apply a light coat of talcum powder or silicone lubricant to the bead on the outside diameter of the secondary diaphragm. This will make it easier for reassembly of the front and rear housing.
28. Place the secondary bearing in the inside diameter of the housing divider so that the extended lip of the bearing faces up.
29. Lubricate the inside diameter of the bearing with silicone lubricant.
30. Using a special protector tool or equivalent, position the secondary bearing on the threaded end of the secondary power piston.
31. Hold the housing divider so that the six oblong protrusions on the middle of the divider are facing up. Press the divider down over the tool and onto the piston tube so it rests against the support ring. Remove the bearing protector tool.
32. Pick up the primary power piston assembly and fold the primary diaphragm away from the outside diameter of the support plate.
33. Place the small end of the air valve return spring on the air valve so that it contacts the air valve retaining ring.
34. Position the primary power piston. Make sure that the air valve return spring seats down over the raised center section of the secondary piston.
35. Rotate the secondary power piston clockwise into the threaded portion of the primary piston. Tighten to 5–15 ft. lbs.
36. Fold the primary diaphragm back into position.
37. Cover the outside diameter of the piston rod retainer with a light coat of silicone lubricant.
38. Insert the master cylinder piston rod retainer into the secondary power piston so that the flat end bottoms against the rubber reaction disc.
39. Place the new primary piston bearing in the rear housing center hole. The thin lip of the bearing will protrude to the outside of the housing. Coat the inside diameter of the bearing with silicone lubricant.
40. Mount the holding fixture in a vise and position the front housing so that the housing studs fit in the holes provided in the tool.
41. Place the power piston return spring over the inset in the front housing.
42. Assemble the power piston assembly to the rear housing by pressing the tube of the primary piston through the rear housing bearing until the housing divider seats in the rear housing and the primary piston bottoms against the housing.
43. Hold the rear housing with the mounting studs up and position it so that the tangs on the edge of the front housing are locked in the slots on the edge of the rear housing. The scribe marks on the top of the housings will be in line.
44. Lower the rear housing assembly onto the front housing.

NOTE: The power piston spring must seat in the depression in the face of the secondary power piston. Check that the bead on the outside diameter of the secondary diaphragm is positioned between the edges of the housing.

45. Assemble the front and rear housings with the spanner wrench.
46. Replace the silencer and boot.

Hydro-Max Electro Hydraulic Brake Booster

OPERATION

1982–83

Beneath the booster a vane type pump is attached and is integral with a 12 volt DC electric motor. If the vehicle engine was not operating or a hose or belt was broken the pump and motor would serve as a reserve power source to provide boost pressure. The electric pump draws fluid from the low pressure side of the booster piston and delivers it to the high pressure side. The electric pump provides one-half of the primary system pressure.

ELECTRICAL CONTROL CIRCUITS

The electric pump operation is controlled by a relay which is operated by a flow switch located in the booster outlet to sense the fluid flow. A pedal switch also controls the electric pump operation whenever the brake pedal is depressed and the engine is not operating. The system is monitored by two dash mounted telltale lamps and a buzzer. The two lamps will be marked to:

1. Warn of failure of the primary system.
2. Warn of failure of the reserve system.
3. To make the driver aware that the reserve is in operation, the dash lamp will light and the buzzer will sound. The monitoring system is controlled by a solid state module, and two in line

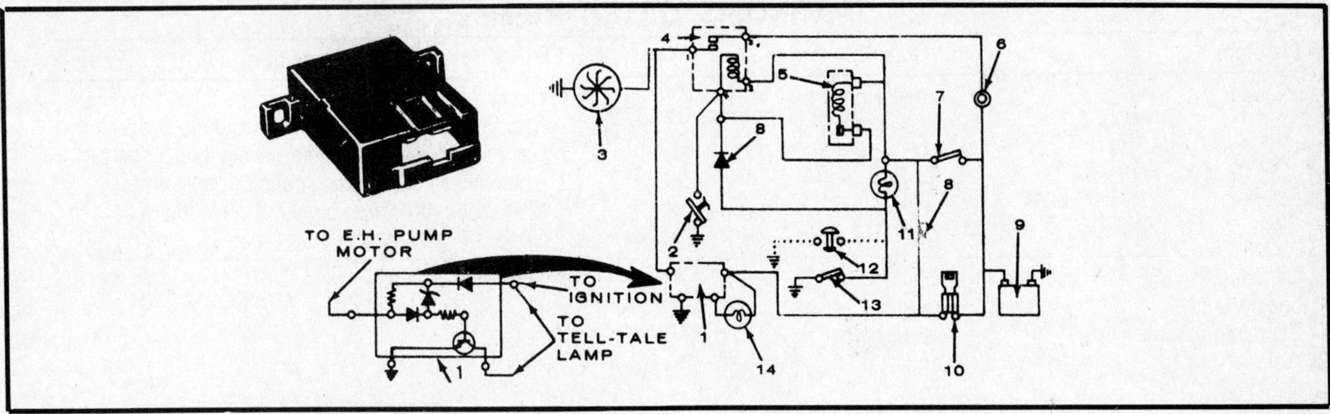

Hydraulic booster electrical diaphragm

Electro-Hydraulic Pump Diagnosis

Mode	Tell-Tale #1①	Tell-Tale #2②	Buzzer
Engine off—ignition off			
No brake apply	off	off	off
Brake apply	on	off	on
Engine off—ignition on with or without brake apply—(bulb check)	on	on	on
Engine off—ignition on start with or without brake apply	on	on	on
Engine on with or without brake apply	off	off	off
Engine on—primary boost interrupted with or without brake apply	on	on	on
Engine on—open circuit in EH pump motor with or without brake apply	off	on	off

① Brake ② Brake Elect. Hyd. Boost

DIAGNOSIS OF EH PUMP

Problem	Possible Cause	Correction
Excessive Pump Noise (gurgle, chatter, etc.)	Trapped air in pump.	Depress brake pedal lightly with the engine off for thirty seconds and release. Recheck and should the problem persist, repeat above procedure after a three minute waiting period. ①
Inoperative pump	Non-functioning motor.	1. Check electrical connection between motor lead wire and wiring harness. If loose, corroded, or disconnected, clean and secure connection. 2. Check grounding of pump housing to booster. The pump housing must be securely bolted to the booster to properly ground the motor. 3. Replace EH Pump

DIAGNOSIS OF EH PUMP

Problem	Possible Cause	Correction
	Low or no voltage at motor connection of wiring harness.	1. Check condition of battery and battery terminals.Correct an abnormally low battery condition and/or clean battery terminals if necessary. 2. Check electrical leads at battery terminal of starter or ignition bus bar—not corroded or loose.
Oil leak at booster and EH pump mating surface.	Damaged or missing O-rings at pressure and/or return port.	Replace two O-rings.
Oil leak from pump end plate	damaged or missing end plate seal.	Replace EH pump assembly.
Oil leak from EH pump motor	Damaged shaft seal.	Replace EH pump assembly.

① This noise will diminish upon continued use of the brakes under normal driving conditions.

diodes. The plug in module is not repairable and must be replaced as a unit.

WARNING MODES

The function of the system warning devices, tell-tales and alarm buzzer, under different vehicle operational modes are indicated in the Electro-Hydraulic Pump Diagnosis Chart.

ELECTRO-HYDRAULIC PUMP

Diagnosis

1. The pump and tell-tale light does not come on when the brake pedal is depressed with the engine off:
   a. Check the brake pedal switch.
   b. Check for electrical continuity through the pump flow switch.
   c. Check for voltage to the ignition side of the relay coil.
   d. Check for voltage at the battery connection to the relay coil.
   d. Check for voltage at the battery connection to the relay.
   e. Check for an open at the ignition diode.
   f. Check for voltage at the pump terminal at the relay.
2. The engine is off and the pump is operating but the light is not on when the brake pedal is depressed.
   a. Check the voltage at the warning light bulb.
   b. Replace the bulb.
3. The engine and the pump are off, but when the brake pedal is depressed, the light is on.
   a. Check the voltage at the pump motor.
   b. Replace pump.
4. The accessories, radio, heater, wipers etc. operate when the brake pedal is depressed and the engine off.
   a. Check the ignition diode for a short.
5. The pump and warning light stay on after the engine is started.
   a. Check for air in the boost systems.
   b. Check to see if the flow switch is shorted or in the stuck position.
   c. Check to see if the relay is in the closed position.

Hydro-Max

1984 AND LATER

The main features of the new style Hydro-Max system are as follows;

1. All front brakes are dual piston, disc brakes of the Dayton/Walther design.
2. The parking brake is actuated by a spring/ramp assembly, located on the rear wheel backing plate and controlled by hydraulic pressure from the Hydro-Max pump, through a parking brake control in the cab of the vehicle.
3. The hydraulic brake system is a vertically split system, with the front disc brakes as one system and the rear brakes as the other system, except on tandem equipped vehicles.
4. The tandem vehicle brakes are split with the front disc and one of the wheel cylinders of the forward axle as one system and the second wheel cylinder of the forward axle and the total rear axle as the second system.
5. The hydraulic brake pump and reservoir is completely separate from the power steering system and uses Dexron®II A/T fluid for operation of the in-wheel parking brake system. Brake fluid is used in the two brake systems.
6. Seals are located between the master cylinder and the booster, along with spacing, making it impossible for the two fluids to mix. A vent is provided between the two units to for normal fluid "weepage".

Dual Power Brake System (G.M.)

The Dual Power Brake System (DPB) is a system which utilizes two power boosting units in series to provide the power assist necessary to stop the vehicle. This is accomplished by combining a vacuum operated booster with a hydraulically operated booster in tandem arrangement with a standard dual master cylinder. Assist power generated by the vacuum booster is transmitted forward to the hydraulic booster, where the apply power is, again, assisted or augmented by the hydraulic booster. Doubly assisted power available at the hydraulic booster is transmitted to the master cylinder, thereby developing hydraulic pressure up to a maximum of approximately 600 psi. Refer to the Chevrolet or G.M.C. sections of this manual for removal and installation instructions, as they pertain to components of the dual power booster.

CAUTION

The Dual Power Brake System is comprised of two separate hydraulic systems, and should be treated as such. One system operates with hydraulic brake fluid, and the other system operates with power steering fluid. These two very different types of hydraulic fluid are not compatible, and should not be allowed to come into contact with one another, nor should they be allowed to come into contact with components of the system for which they are not intended. DO NOT mix these fluids together. DO NOT reuse the old fluid. If care is not exercised to isolate these two fluids during the overhaul procedure, then inevitable deterioration will result, causing leakage at the seals and eventual system malfunction.

VACUUM BOOSTER

Disassembly

1. Scribe a mark on the front and rear housings to ensure proper alignment and ease of assembly.
2. Remove the vacuum check valve and grommet.
3. Remove the elbow and grommet.
4. Very carefully, remove the clamp which secures the front and rear housing together.

CAUTION

Exercise caution when separating the front and rear housings, as the booster is spring loaded.

5. Separate the front and rear housings.
6. Remove the clevis.
7. Remove the boot and filter.
8. Remove the power piston from the rear housing.
9. Remove the power piston bearing from the center opening of the rear housing.
10. Pry the locking ring free from beneath the locking lug of the power piston, and remove the locking ring.
11. Remove the reaction retainer, the control valve, the reaction plate, the two reaction levers, the air valve spring, and the spring retainer.
12. Separate the control valve sleeve from the control valve. Remove the two double lip seals from the control valve.
13. Secure the square end of special tool J–21524, or its equivalent, in a vise. Position the diaphragm support plate and power piston over the raised lugs with the tubular end of the power piston facing upwards.
14. While gripping the steel support plate, press down on it, rotating it counterclockwise until the support plate separates from the power piston.
15. Remove the diaphragm support plate and the diaphragm.
16. Separate the diaphragm from the support plate.
17. Remove the silencer from the tubular end of the power piston.
18. Surround the lugged end of the power piston (the end of the power piston opposite the tubular end) with shop towels or a material of similar consistency, and secure the power piston in a vise with the tubular end facing downward.

NOTE: DO NOT tighten the vise directly on the tube, as the tube acts as a bearing surface. Tighten the vise only enough to hold the power piston in place. Excessive tightening may crack or distort the tube.

19. Working at the lugged end of the power piston, remove the retaining ring from the air valve.
20. Working at the tubular end of the power piston, thread the clevis onto the air valve. Insert the blade of a screwdriver through the hole in the clevis, and use it to pull the valve out of the power piston. Remove the clevis.
21. Remove the air valve O-ring, floating control valve retainer, spring, retainer, spring, spring seat, and the floating control valve.
22. Clean all parts in denatured alcohol, and dry with filtered, compressed air.
23. Check all parts for damage or excessive wear.

NOTE: The manufacturer states specifically that internal parts or surfaces are NOT to be remachined. DO NOT use abrasive to remove surface defects. Replace worn or damaged parts and rubber sealing components.

Assembly

1. Apply a thin film of lubricant on the air valve O-ring and on the surface of the air valve.
2. Install the O-ring in the second groove of the air valve.

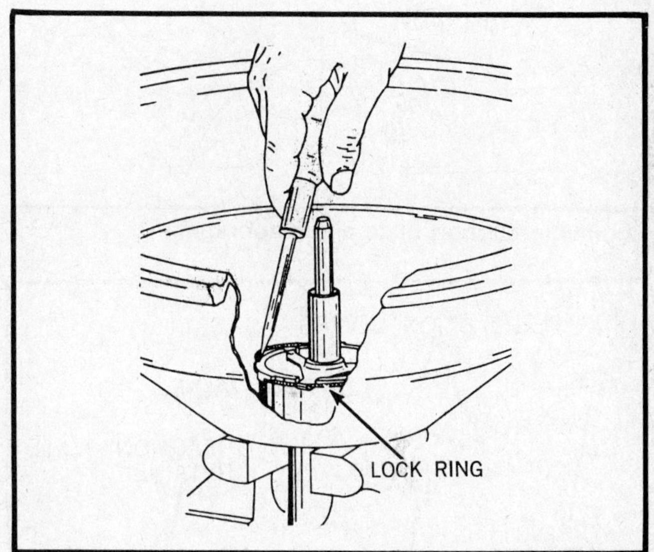

Removal of lock ring

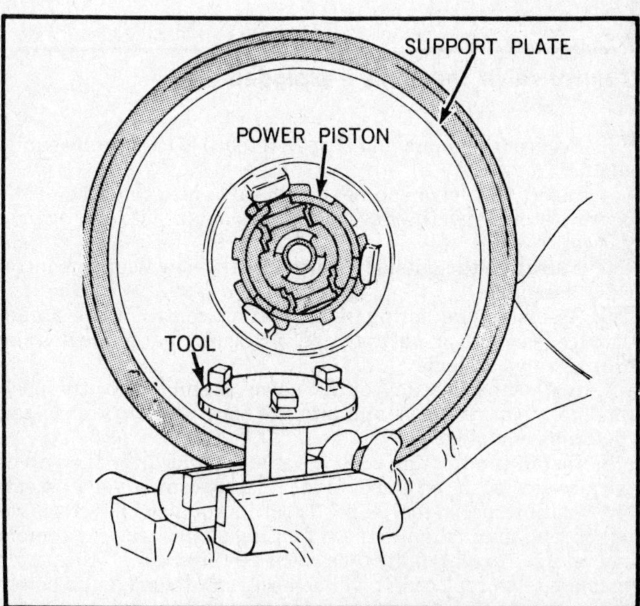

Power piston and support plate separating tool

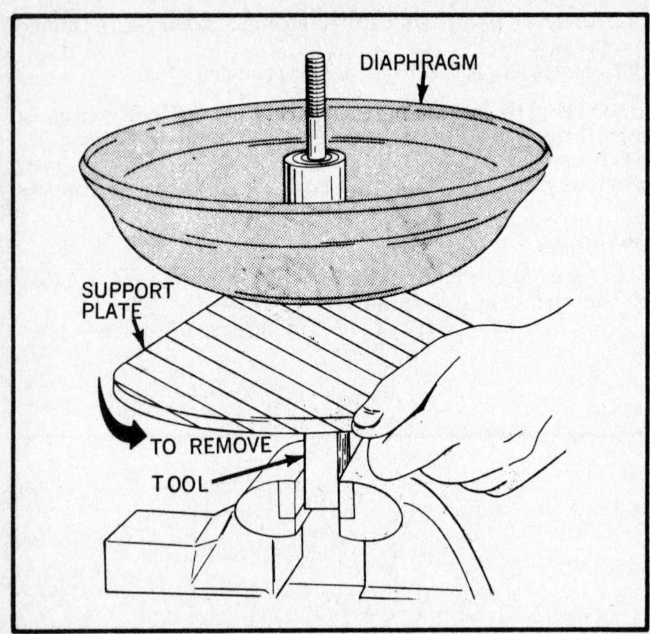

Removing support plate and diaphragm

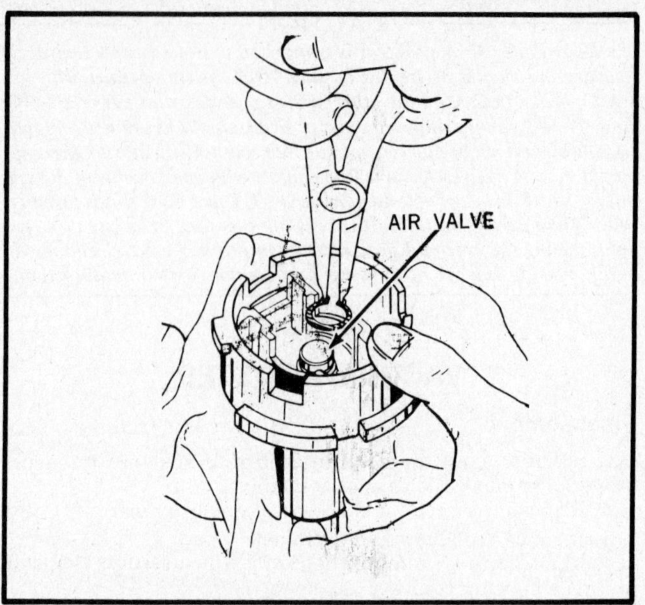

Air valve snap ring removal

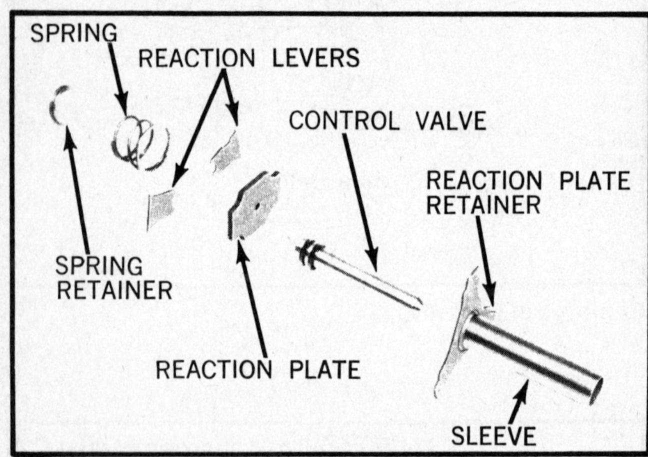

Control valve assembly—exploded view

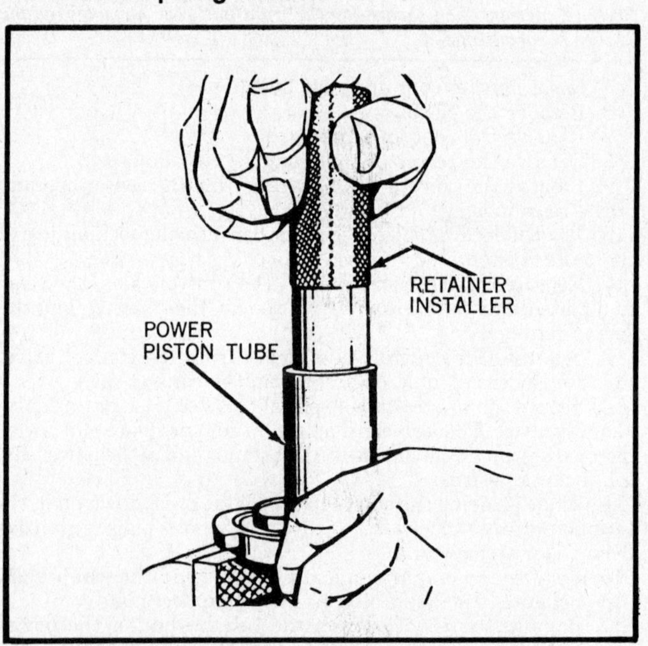

Pressing floating control assembly and retainer

3. Secure the square end of special tool J-21524, or its equivalent, in a vise.

4. Insert the valve end of the air valve into the tube of the power piston. Push the valve all the way in, until it stops against its seat.

5. Lubricate the outside diameter of the new floating control valve assembly.

6. Assemble the spring seat, floating control valve spring (small end of the spring first), and spring retainer to the floating control valve assembly.

7. Install the floating control valve assembly over the push rod end of the air valve and into the tube of the power piston (floating control valve first).

8. Install the floating control valve retainer over the end of the air valve push rod and onto the floating control valve assembly. Position special tool J-23175A or its equivalent over the retainer, and manually press the floating control valve assembly and retainer to seat in the tube of the power piston. If the power piston is to be replaced, it will be necessary to gauge the power piston-to-air valve clearance in order to select the proper control valve. To gauge, complete the following procedure;

a. Install the retaining ring into the top groove in the air valve.

b. Pull back lightly on the air valve push rod, and slowly return the air valve to its normal position.

c. Position special tool J-28673, or its equivalent, over the air valve at the lugged end of the power piston, aligning the lugs of the tool with the three cut-out lands on the large diameter of the power piston. Twist the floating pin, located in the center of the tool, a minimum of $\frac{1}{2}$ turn to relieve tension on the O-ring in the tool.

d. Insert a feeler gauge between the floating pin and the main body of the gauge tool. The clearance measured in in. or millimeters will determine which control valve will be installed during final assembly.

e. Select a control valve from the Control Valve Chart that

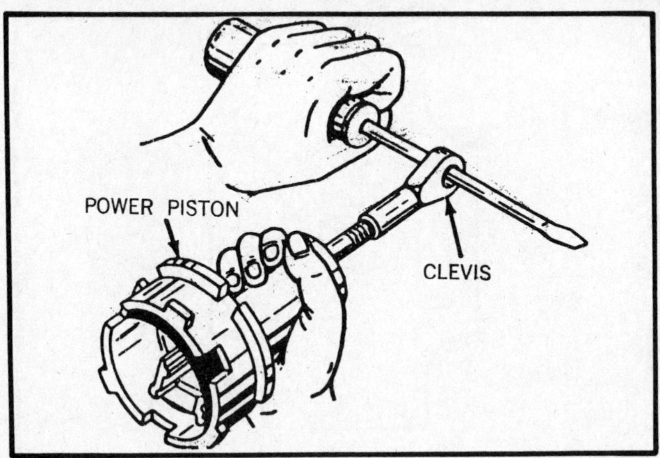

Air valve removal

comes closest to the clearance measured by the feeler gauge. Control valves are identified by grooves near the seal end of the valve. (see Control Valve Chart).

CONTROL VALVE CHART

Inches	Millimeters	Id Grooves
0.040–0.051	1.016–1.295	1
0.028–0.039	0.711–0.991	2
0.015–0.027	0.381–0.686	3

NOTE: If a new control valve is installed, it will also be necessary to regauge the piston rod of the hydraulic booster.

9. Install the silencer over the end of the push rod, and press it into the power piston tube.
10. Lubricate the inside diameter of the diaphragm with a silicone lubricant, and assemble the diaphragm to the diaphragm support plate.
11. Press the raised flange of the diaphragm through the hole in the center of the support plate.

CAUTION

Be certain that the edge of the center hole fits into the groove in the flange of the diaphragm.

12. Lubricate the section of the diaphragm that contacts the power piston with a power brake silicone lubricant.
13. Position the support plate and the diaphragm over the power piston tube. While pressing down on the support plate, turn the support plate until the locking lugs on the power piston come against the stops on the support plate.
14. Invert the piston and diaphragm assembly. Surround the lugged end of the power piston (the end of the power piston opposite the tubular end) with shop towels or a material of similar consistency, and secure the power piston in a vise with the tubular end facing downward.

CAUTION

DO NOT tighten the vise directly on the tube, as the tube acts as a bearing surface. Tighten the vise only enough to hold the power piston in place. Excessive tightening may crack or distort the tube.

15. Install the air valve spring retainer to seat on the retaining ring.

CAUTION

Check the position of the reaction plate in the power piston before placing reaction levers and spring in position. Note that the reaction plate is designed so that it will fit only one way in the power piston. DO NOT force the plate as the power piston may become damaged.

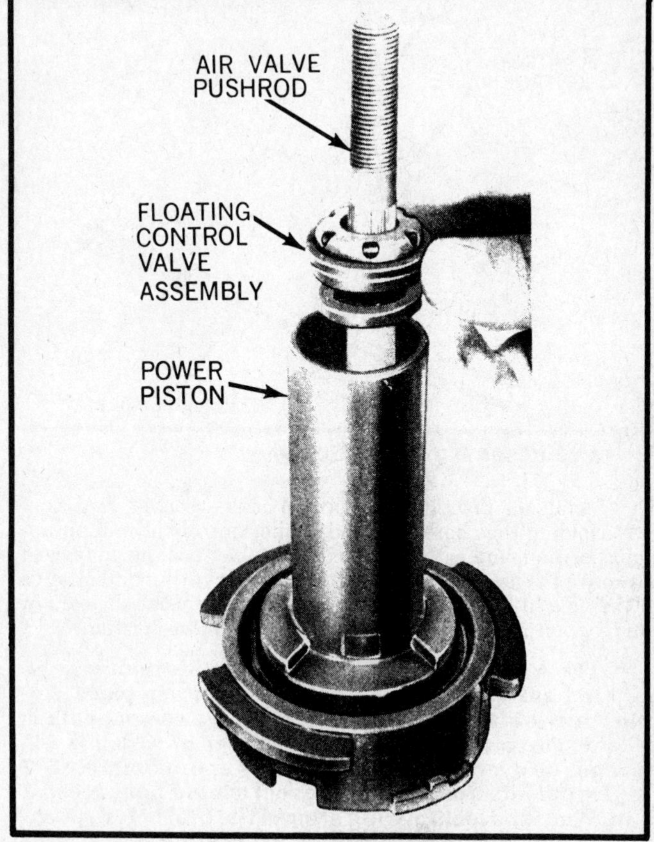

Floating control valve installation

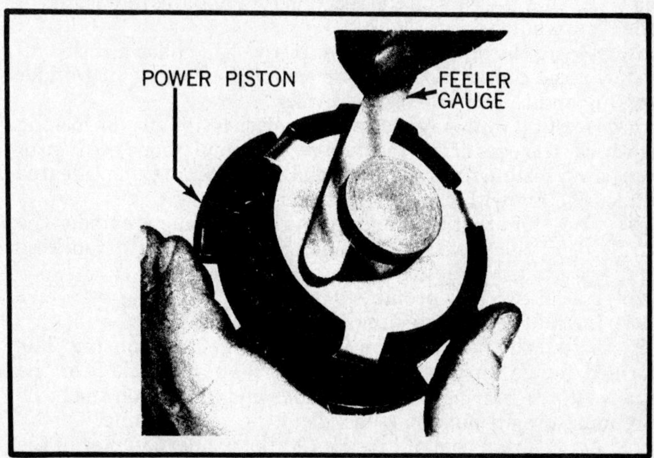

Gauging air valve clearance

16. Place the air valve return spring, small end down, on the spring retainer.
17. Place the two reaction levers into position, aligning the tabs on the wide end with the slots provided for them.
18. Install two new seals in the grooves on the control valve with the lips of the seals facing toward the chamfered end. Make sure the seals are lubricated.
19. Assemble the control valve, valve sleeve, and the reaction retainer.

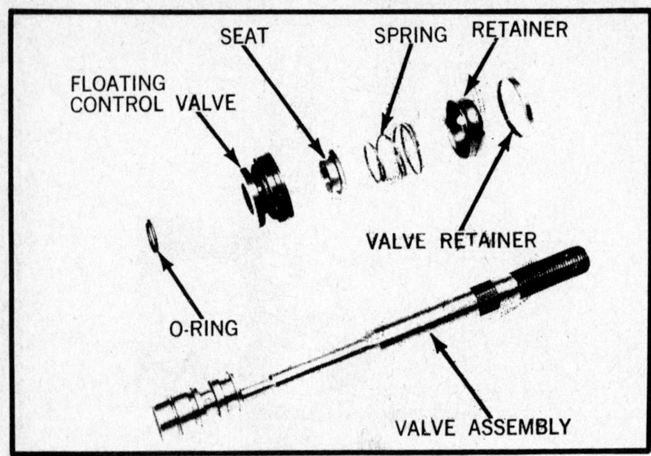

Air valve assembly—exploded view

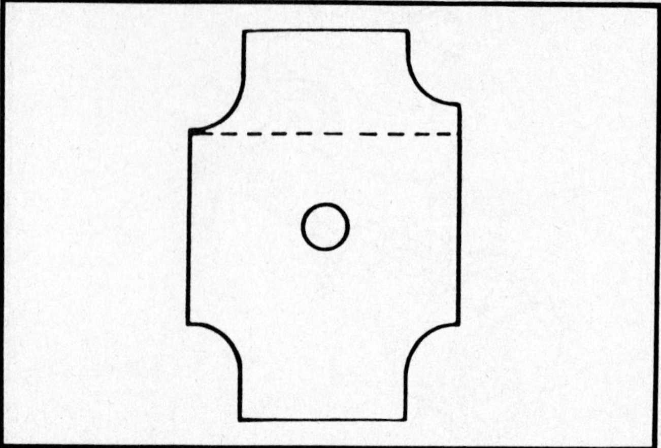

Reaction plate

20. Install the reaction plate on top of the reaction levers.

21. Holding the chamfered end of the control valve in an upright position, and with the reaction retainer positioned toward the top of the assembly, insert the small end of the control valve in the hole in the center of the reaction plate. Seat the ears of the reaction retainer in the notches of the power piston.

NOTE: A special tool J-24433 or its equivalent may be used to hold the control valve components in place. Another way of installing the control valve components is to fabricate a tool, the inside diameter of which is 1¾ in., and the overall length of which is approximately 5-7 in. The outside diameter of the tool should not exceed 1 ⅞ in. Place the locking ring around the tool before pushing components down.

22. Make sure that the reaction plate is flat on the reaction levers and that the ears on the reaction retainer are fully seated in the piston notches.

23. Locate the one lug on power piston which has a raised divider in the center. Position one end of the locking ring under the lug and to one side of the divider.

24. Working your way around the power piston, fit the locking ring over the ears of the reaction retainer and under the lugs of the power piston, until the other end of the locking ring is seated under the lug with the raised divider.

25. Be certain that both ends of the locking ring are under the large lug of the power piston, and that the ends of the locking ring are against the divider.

26. Install two new grommets in the front housing.

27. Install the new vacuum check valve and elbow.

28. Install the power piston bearing in the rear housing. The formed flange on the housing center hole must fit into the groove in the bearing. Also, the flange and thin lip on the bearing must project out the stud side of the rear housing.

29. Apply a thin coat of lubricant to the inside diameter of the power piston bearing.

30. Lay the front housing on a flat clean surface.

31. Position the power piston return spring on the front housing, and center it.

32. Apply a thin film of lubricant on the tube of the power piston. Assemble the power piston to the rear housing by pressing the tube of the piston through the rear housing bearing, until the piston bottoms against the housing.

33. Hold the rear housing and power piston assembly so that the mounting studs are facing up.

34. Position the assembly over the front housing, aligning the scribe marks made prior to disassembly.

NOTE: Vacuum may be applied to the vacuum check valve to facilitate assembly. The other vacuum tube must be plugged.

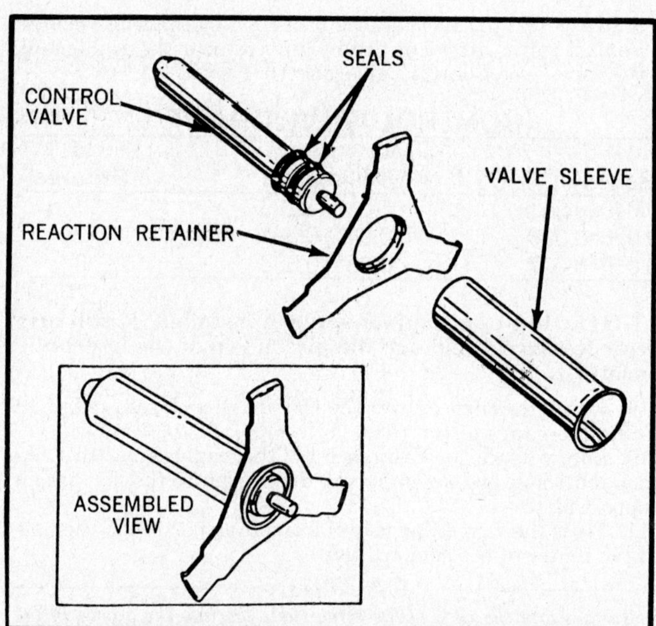

Assembled view of control valve and related components

35. Assemble the rear housing to the front housing.

CAUTION

Be certain that the return spring seats around the power piston, and that the bead on the outside diameter of the diaphragm is properly seated.

36. Install the clamp, and torque to 60 inch lbs.

37. Disconnect the vacuum source from the vacuum check valve, if used, and unplug the other tube.

38. Invert the assembly, and position it over a cylindrical device of sufficient diameter and length in order to clear the studs and accept the air valve push rod.

39. Assemble the hydraulic booster to the vacuum booster.

40. Gauge the output push rod (piston rod) of the hydraulic booster.

41. Install the filter in the boot. Install the boot assembly over the power piston tube.

Hydraulic Booster (Dual Power)

Disassembly

1. Pull the piston rod out with a twisting motion.

NOTE: It is advised that this be done over a large open container as the fluid must be drained from the booster.

2. Secure the booster in a vise by clamping across the body flange (flow switch up).
3. Remove the flow switch and the flow switch O-ring seal.
4. Insert a suitable pry tool under the lip of the cap, and pry the cap free. Be careful not to bend or distort the cap.

CAUTION

The piston return spring is under a considerable load. Exercise caution when removing the cap as spring pressure may forcibly expel the support plate, cylinder seal, and expander, resulting in personal injury.

5. Remove the O-ring from the cap.
6. Remove the support plate, cylinder seal, and seal expander.
7. Remove the return spring and the piston.
8. Remove the double lip seal from the narrow end of the booster body.
9. Remove the seal from the power piston.
10. Clean all parts, thoroughly, and check for excessive wear or damage. Replace parts as necessary.

NOTE: The manufacturer states specifically that internal parts of surfaces are NOT to be remachined. DO NOT use abrasives to remove surface defects.

Assembly

1. Secure the booster in a vise with the large bore up.
2. Lubricate the piston seal, and install it on the power piston.
3. Install the piston in the booster body bore. Press the piston to bottom in the bore. Be careful not to roll the seal.
4. Install the return spring.
5. Lubricate the inside and outside diameters of the cylinder seal.
6. Assemble the O-ring seal, support plate, cylinder seal, and

Removing booster cap

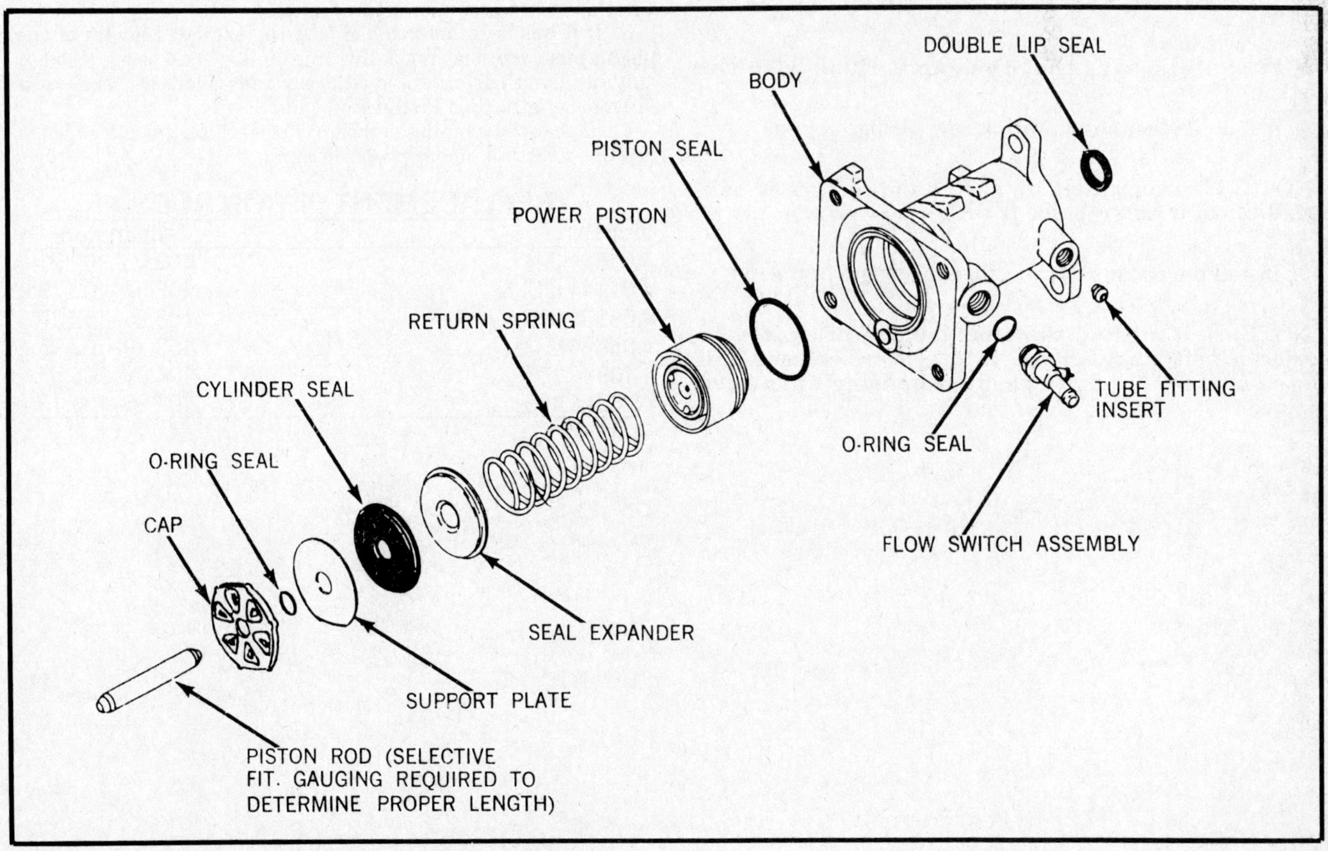

Exploded view of hydraulic booster(dual power)

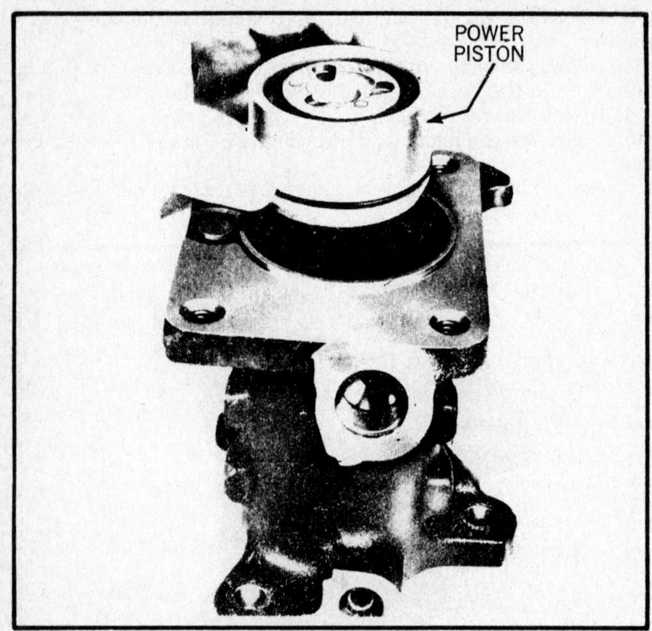

Power piston installation

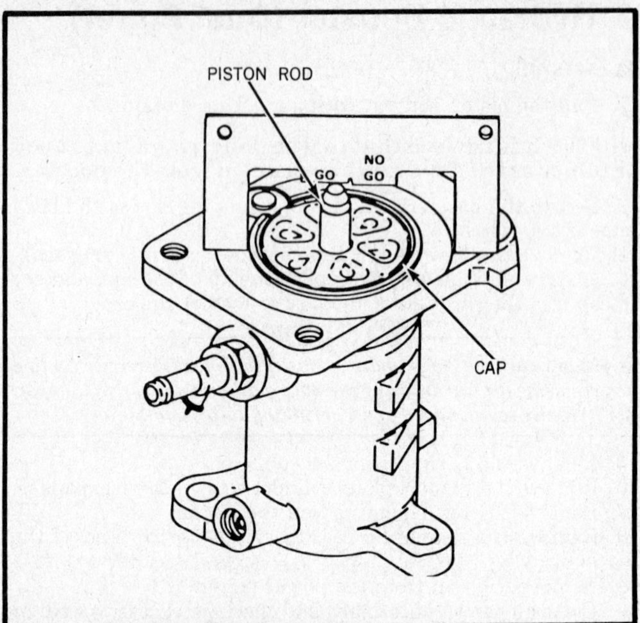

Gauging piston rod extension

seal expander against the cap in the order in which they are to be installed.

7. Position this assembly over the booster and on the return spring.

8. Push the cap down until the extensions on the cap contact the booster casting, and tap into place using a rubber or plastic mallet.

NOTE: Make sure that the cap is flush with the casting.

9. Install the flow switch with a new O-ring.

NOTE: If the original flow switch shows signs of leakage, discard it and replace it with a new switch.

10. Install the piston rod and gauge the length of the rod.

NOTE: It is advised that the gauging procedure be performed after any hard parts have been replaced, or if any components of the vacuum booster have been replaced.

Gauging the Piston Rod

1. Press down on the piston to be sure that all internal parts are bottomed in the booster.

2. Using special tool J-28675 or any suitable push rod height gauge, check the extended length of the piston rod to determine whether, or not, it falls within limits.

3. If it has been determined that the extended length of the piston push rod does not fall within limits, then select a rod of suitable length from among the six rods available, each of a differnt length. (See Piston Rod Chart).

4. Repeat the gauging procedure for each piston rod which is used in selecting one of proper length.

REPLACEMENT PISTON RODS

Inches	Millimeters
4.018–4.024	102.05–102.21
4.041–4.047	102.63–102.79
4.063–4.070	103.21–103.37
4.086–4.093	103.79–103.95
4.109–4.115	104.37–104.53
4.132–4.139	104.96–105.12

Gasoline Engine Overhaul
Domestic Trucks

INDEX

GENERAL INFORMATION

This section describes in detail, the procedures involved in rebuilding a typical gasoline engine. A rebuilt engine can be expected to give many miles of dependable service only if the proper reconditioning procedures are performed and clearances are kept within the manufacturer's recommended specifications.

The following systems of the gasoline engine should be checked to determine to what degree the rebuilding should be accomplished.

Engine Oil Pressure

The engine oil pressure developed should be compared to the manufacturer's recommended pressure, which is necessary to provide lubricating oil to the engine oil circuits. If the pressure is below specifications, the cause must be located and repaired.

The following wear points should be considered during this determination.

Oil Pump—Check Gear clearances (a new oil pump is a good investment).

Main Bearings and Journals—Check clearances, taper and roundness.

Connecting Rod Bearings and Journals—Check clearances, taper and roundness.

Camshaft and Bearings—Check clearances, taper and roundness.

Rocker Arms, Rocker Arm Shafts—Check arm and shaft wear, ball and seat wear.

Tappets—Check clearances between tappet and bore and for excessive leakdown of hydraulic tappets.

Leakage of oil pressure along external or internal oil galleries or gaskets.

Dilution of the oil by gasoline leakage through failures of the carburetor or mechanical fuel pump.

External damage to the oil pan, causing blockage or movement of the oil pick-up tube, resulting in loss of oil pick-up to the pump.

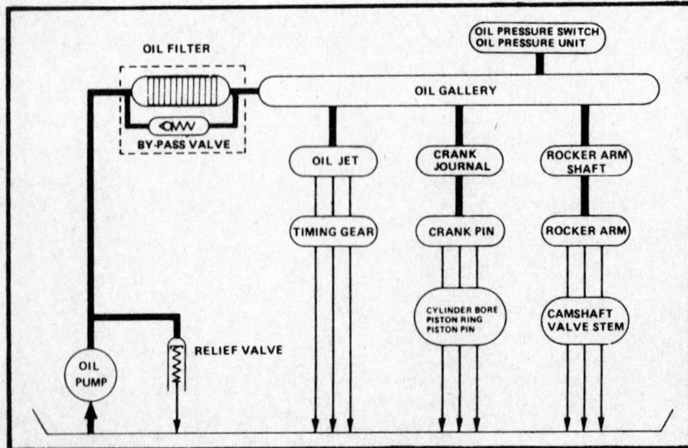

Engine oil flow diagram—typical

Compression

Compression in an engine is determined by the correct fit and sealing efficiency of the piston and rings against the cylinder walls, the quality of the seal between the valve and its seat and the seal between the cylinder head, head gasket and block. Here are some important check points.

Valve, seat and face—Machine face and seat to original specifications.

Valve guides—The reconditioned seat and face won't hold up long if the valve stem clearance isn't within specifications.

Valve seals—Oil reaching the valve seat will become a solid when it combines with the heat in the combustion chamber. This solid (carbon) will build up and eventually keep the valve from seating.

Cylinder walls—Check for taper, out-of-round and hone to proper cross hatch pattern.

Pistons—Check all dimensions. A poorly fitted piston will shorten the life of the new rings.

COMPRESSION PRESSURE COMPARISON CHART

Minimum pressure is 75% of maximum pressure

Maximum PSI	Minimum PSI	Maximum PSI	Minimum PSI	Maximum PSI	Minimum PSI
134	101	174	131	214	160
136	102	176	132	216	162
138	104	178	133	218	163
140	105	180	135	220	165
142	107	182	136	222	166
144	108	184	138	224	168
146	110	186	140	226	169
148	111	188	141	228	171
150	113	190	142	230	172
152	114	192	144	232	174
154	115	194	145	234	175
156	117	196	147	236	177
158	118	198	148	238	178
160	120	200	150	240	180
162	121	202	151	242	181
164	123	204	153	244	183
166	124	206	154	246	184
168	126	208	156	248	186
170	127	210	157	250	187
172	129	212	158		

NOTE: To Determine if the engine compression is satisfactory, most engine manufacturers require that a complete compression test be done, with the lowest cylinder pressure reading not being less than 75% of the highest reading. Look for uniformity of compression between cylinders, rather than specific compression pressures of an engine.

Cooling System

Maintaining engine temperatures within the specified range is critical to the life of a rebuilt engine. Until new parts mate properly with each other, excessive heat can cause permanent damage or substantially reduce the service life of the reconditioned engine. If the engine is operated at temperatures below normal, the oil may not properly lubricate all of the parts. Some parts that should be checked during the rebuilding process are:

Coolant passages—Should be free of rust and corrosion deposits.

Core plugs—All plugs should be replaced during the rebuilding process.

Hoses—Should be free of cracks, hard spots and oil softened spots.

Thermostat— Check for opening and closing at the specified temperature.

Radiator—Check for leaks and rust or corrosion deposits.

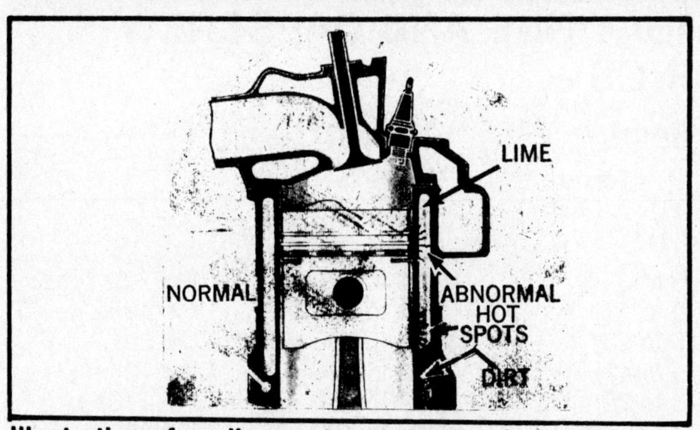

Illustration of cooling system passages being restricted, causing internal engine problems

Pressure cap – Should hold specified pressure, also check the gasket and vent valve operation.

Engine Noises

Engine noises are not only annoying, but indicate conditions inside the engine that can limit the service life of the engine or shut it down completely. Generally, noises are caused by too much clearance between parts or loss of oil supply. Engine noises can be caused by any of the following parts.

Main bearings
Connecting rod bearings
Piston and/or rings

STANDARD TORQUE SPECIFICATIONS AND CAPSCREW MARKINGS

Newton-Meter has been designated as the world standard for measuring torque and will gradually replace the foot-pound and kilogram-meter torque measuring standard. Torquing tools are still being manufactured with foot-pounds and kilogram-meter scales, along with the new Newton-Meter standard. To assist the repairman, foot-pounds, kilogram-meter and Newton-Meter are listed in the following charts and should be followed as applicable.

U.S. BOLTS

SAE Grade Number	1 or 2			5			6 or 7			8		
Capscrew Head Markings Manufacturer's marks may vary. Three-line markings on heads below indicate SAE Grade 5.												
Usage	Used Frequently			Used Frequently			Used at Times			Used at Times		
Quality of Material	Indeterminate			Minimum Commercial			Medium Commercial			Best Commercial		
Capacity Body Size	**Torque**			**Torque**			**Torque**			**Torque**		
(inches) – (thread)	Ft-Lb	kgm	Nm	Ft-Lb	kgm	Nm	Ft-Lb	kgm	Nm	Ft-Lb	kgm	Nm
1/4–20	5	0.6915	6.7791	8	1.1064	10.8465	10	1.3630	13.5582	12	1.6596	16.2698
–28	6	0.8298	8.1349	10	1.3830	13.5582				14	1.9362	18.9815
5/16–18	11	1.5213	14.9140	17	2.3511	23.0489	19	2.6277	25.7605	24	3.3192	32.5396
–24	13	1.7979	17.6256	19	2.6277	25.7605				27	3.7341	36.6071
3/8–16	18	2.4894	24.4047	31	4.2873	42.0304	34	4.7022	46.0978	44	6.0852	59.6560
–24	20	2.7660	27.1164	35	4.8405	47.4536				49	6.7767	66.4351
7/16–14	28	3.8132	37.9629	49	6.7767	66.4351	55	7.6065	74.5700	70	9.6810	94.9073
–20	30	4.1490	40.6745	55	7.6065	74.5700				78	10.7874	105.7538
1/2–13	39	5.3937	52.8769	75	10.3725	101.6863	85	11.7555	115.2445	105	14.5215	142.3609
–20	41	5.6703	55.5885	85	11.7555	115.2445				120	16.5860	162.6960
9/16–12	51	7.0533	69.1467	110	15.2130	149.1380	120	16.5960	162.6960	155	21.4365	210.1490
–18	55	7.6065	74.5700	120	16.5960	162.6960				170	23.5110	230.4860
5/8–11	83	11.4789	112.5329	150	20.7450	203.3700	167	23.0961	226.4186	210	29.0430	284.7180
–18	95	13.1385	128.8027	170	23.5110	230.4860				240	33.1920	325.3920
3/4–10	105	14.5215	142.3609	270	37.3410	366.0660	280	38.7240	379.6240	375	51.8625	508.4250
–16	115	15.9045	155.9170	295	40.7985	399.9610				420	58.0860	568.4360
7/8–9	160	22.1280	216.9280	395	54.6285	535.5410	440	60.8520	596.5520	605	83.6715	820.2590
–14	175	24.2025	237.2650	435	60.1605	589.7730				675	93.3525	915.1650
1–8	236	32.5005	318.6130	590	81.5970	799.9220	660	91.2780	894.8280	910	125.8530	1233.7780
–14	250	34.5750	338.9500	660	91.2780	849.8280				990	136.9170	1342.2420

STANDARD TORQUE SPECIFICATIONS AND CAPSCREW MARKINGS

METRIC BOLTS

Description	Torque ft-lbs. (Nm)			
Thread for general purposes (size x pitch (mm)	Head Mark 4		Head Mark 7	
6 x 1.0	2.2 to 2.9	(3.0 to 3.9)	3.6 to 5.8	(4.9 to 7.8)
8 x 1.25	5.8 to 8.7	(7.9 to 12)	9.4 to 14	(13 to 19)
10 x 1.25	12 to 17	(16 to 23)	20 to 29	(27 to 39)
12 x 1.25	21 to 32	(29 to 43)	35 to 53	(47 to 72)
14 x 1.5	35 to 52	(48 to 70)	57 to 85	(77 to 110)
16 x 1.5	51 to 77	(67 to 100)	90 to 120	(130 to 160)
18 x 1.5	74 to 110	(100 to 150)	130 to 170	(180 to 230)
20 x 1.5	110 to 140	(150 to 190)	190 to 240	(160 to 320)
22 x 1.5	150 to 190	(200 to 260)	250 to 320	(340 to 430)
24 x 1.5	190 to 240	(260 to 320)	310 to 410	(420 to 550)

CAUTION: Bolts threaded into aluminum require much less torque.

Tools

The tools required for the basic rebuilding procedure should, with minor exception, be those included in a mechanic's tool kit. Accurate torque wrench, micrometers and dial indicators should readily be available to the repairman. Special tools are available from the major tool suppliers. The services of a competent automotive machine shop must also be available.

Precautions

When assembling the engine, any parts that will be in frictional contact must be pre-lubricated, to provide protection on initial start-up.

Any product specifically formulated for this purpose may be used. Where semipermanent locked but removable installation of bolts or nuts is desired, threads should be cleaned and coated with a liquid locking compound. Studs may be permanently installed using a stud mounting compound. Bolts and nuts with no torque specification should be tightened according to size (see chart).

Aluminum has become increasingly popular for use in engines, due to its low weight and excellent heat transfer characteristics. The following precautions should be observed when handling aluminum engine parts.

Never hot-tank aluminum parts.

Remove all aluminum parts (identification tags, etc.) from engine parts before hot-tanking (otherwise they will be removed during the process).

Always coat threads lightly with engine oil or anti-seize compounds before installation, to prevent seizure.

Heli-coil

Never over-torque bolts or spark plugs in aluminum threads. Should stripping occur, threads can be restored according to the following procedure, using Heli-Coil thread inserts.

Tap drill the hole with the stripped threads to the specified size, using the Specified tap.

NOTE: Heli-Coil tap sizes refer to the size thread being replaced, rather than the actual tap size.

Tap the hole for the Heli-Coil. Place the insert on the proper installation tool (see Heli-Coil chart with kit). Apply pressure on the insert while winding it clockwise into the hole, until the top of the insert is one turn below the surface. Remove the installation tool and break the installation tang from the bottom of the insert by moving it up and down. If the Heli-Coil must be removed, tap the removal tool firmly into the hole, so that it engages the top thread and turn the tool counterclockwise to extract the insert.

Broken Bolts or Studs

Snapped bolts or studs may be removed, using a stud extractor (unthreaded) or locking pliers (threaded). Penetrating oil will often aid in breaking frozen threads. In cases where the stud or bolt is flush with, or below the surface, proceed as follows.

Drill a hole in the broken stud or bolt, approximately 1/2 its diameter. Select a screw extractor of the proper size and tap it into the stud or bolt. Turn the extractor counterclockwise to remove the stud or bolt.

Locating Metal Flaws and Cracks

Magnaflux and Zyglo are inspection techniques used to locate material flaws, such as stress cracks. Magnafluxing coats the part with fine magnetic particles and subjects the part to a magnetic field. Cracks cause breaks in the magnetic field,

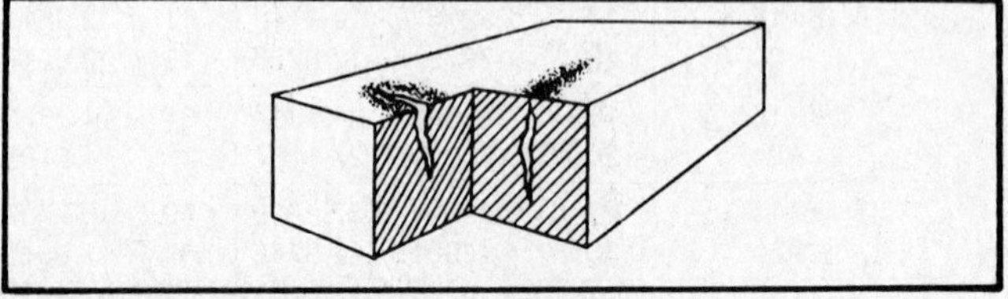

Magnaflux indication of cracks

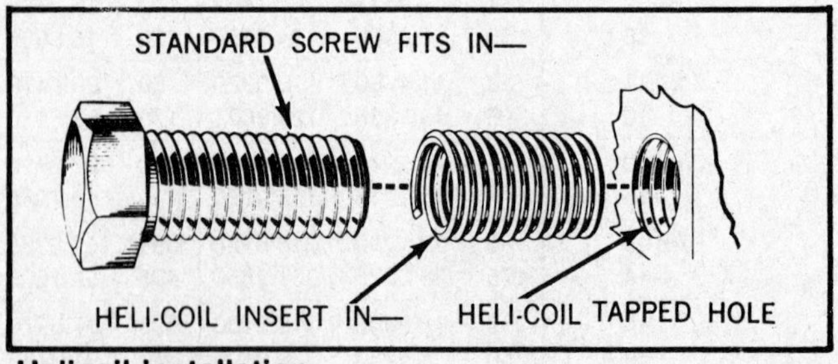

Helicoil installation

which are outlined by the particles. Since Magnaflux is a magnetic process, it is applicable only to ferrous materials. The Zyglo process coats the material with a fluorescent dye penetrant and then subjects it to blacklight inspection, under which cracks glow brightly. Parts made of any material may be tested using Zyglo. While Magnaflux and Zyglo are excellent for general inspection and locating hidden defects, specific checks of suspected cracks may be made at lower cost and more readily using spot check dye. The dye is sprayed onto the suspected area, wiped off and the area is then sprayed with a developer. Cracks then will show up brightly. Spot check dyes will only indicate surface cracks; therefore, structural cracks below the surface may escape detection. When questionable, the part should be tested using Magnaflux, Zyglo or their equivalent.

REBUILDING GASOLINE ENGINES

The section is divided into two parts. The first, Cylinder Head Reconditioning, assumes that the cylinder head is removed from the engine, all manifolds are removed and the cylinder head is on a workbench. The camshaft should be removed from overhead cam cylinder heads. The second section, Cylinder Block Reconditioning, covers the block, pistons, connecting rods and crankshaft. It is assumed that the engine is mounted on a work stand and the cylinder head and all accessories are removed.

In many cases, a choice of methods is provided. The choice of method for a procedure is at the discretion of the user.

Many makes and types of special tools are available to the rebuilder for the express purpose of making a specific rebuilding operation easier and quicker. It is the choice of the rebuilder as to the tool desired and obtained.

Cylinder Head Reconditioning

IDENTIFY THE VALVES

Invert the cylinder head and clean the carbon from the valve heads. Number the valve heads from front to rear with touch-up paint or a felt tip marking pencil. Upon removal of the valves from the cylinder head, place them in a holder, made from cardboard, wood or metal, in their respective order.

REMOVE THE ROCKER ARMS

Remove the rocker arms and shaft or balls and nuts, if not done during the cylinder head removal. Wire the sets of rockers, balls and nuts together and identify according to the corresponding valve.

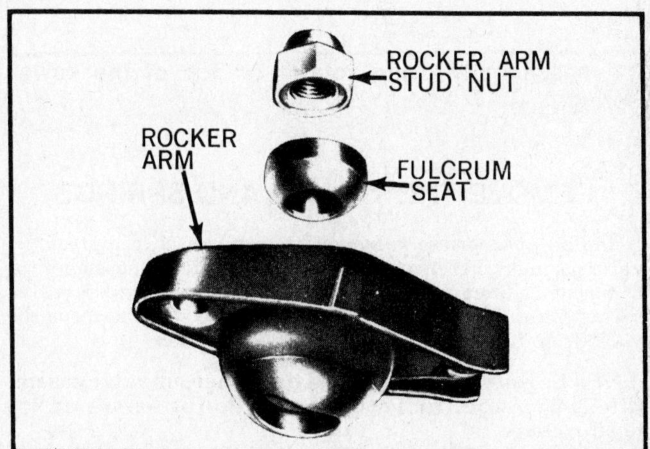

Individual rocker arm assembly

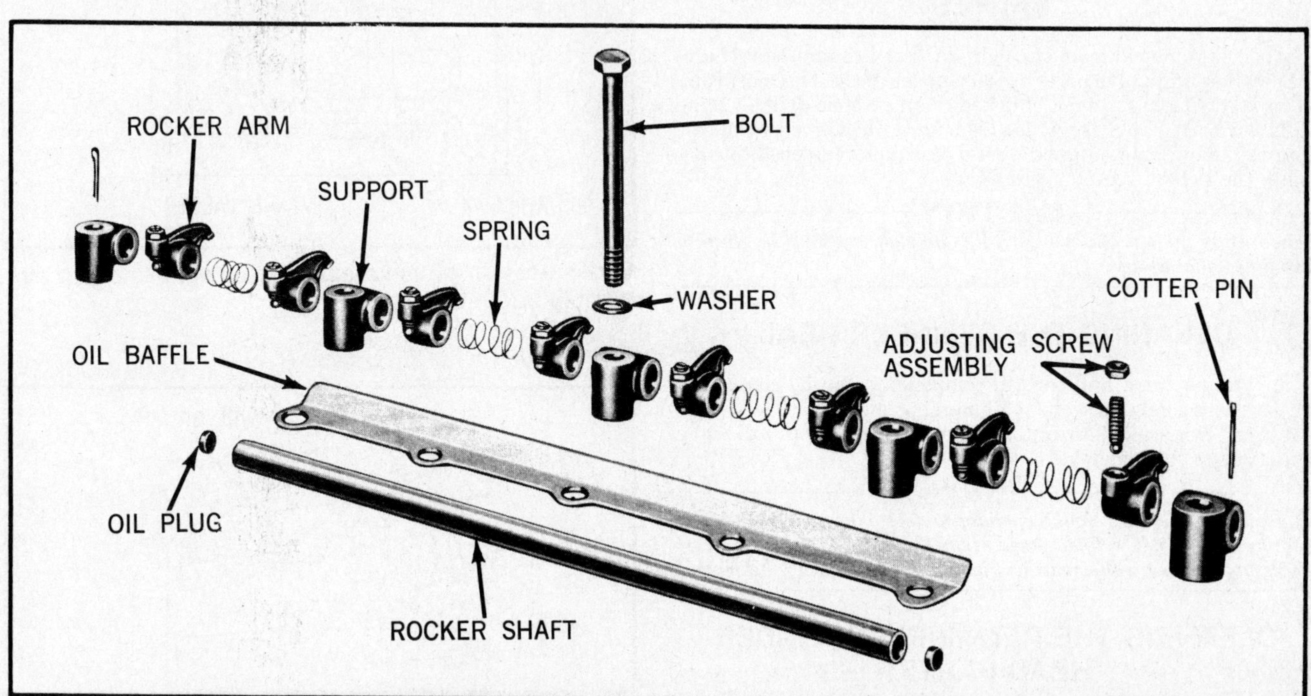

Rocker arm and shaft assembly—typical

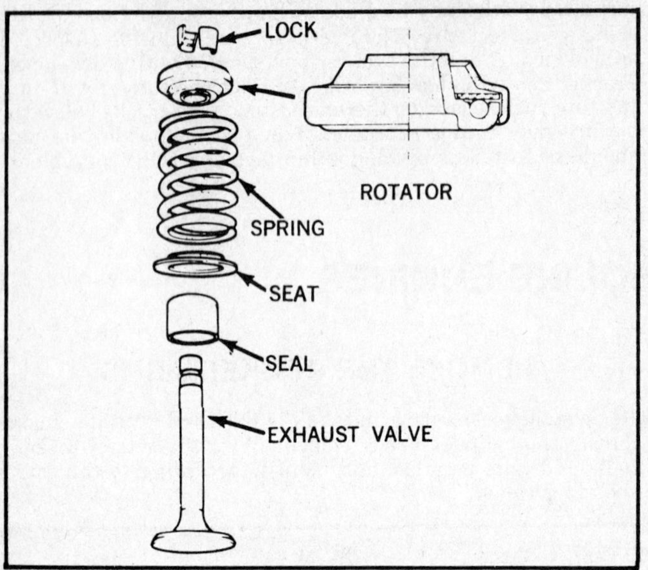

Valve assembly using rotator on top of the valve spring

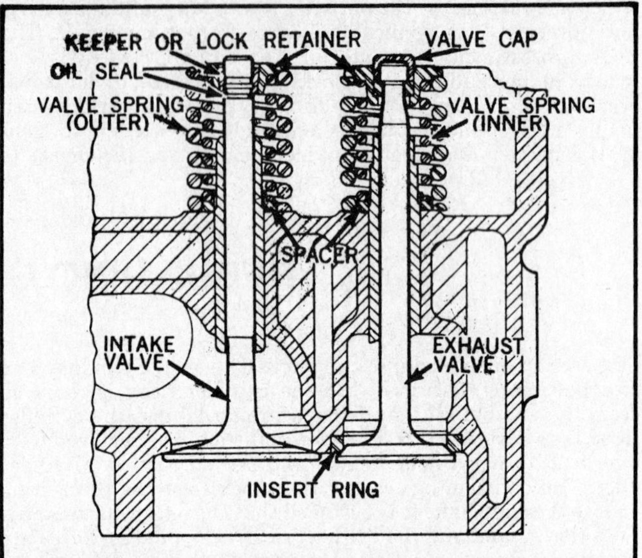

Cross section of valve assemblies with valve rotor cap on exhaust valve stem

REMOVE THE VALVES AND SPRINGS

Using an appropriate valve spring compressor, compress the valve springs and remove the keepers with needlenose pliers or a magnet. Release the compressor and remove the valve spring, retainer and oil seal from the valve stem. Remove the valve from the cylinder head and keep in order.

NOTE: Rotor units are used on numerous valve assemblies. Replace the rotor if any doubt exists on its performance.

DE-CARBON THE CYLINDER HEAD AND VALVES

Carbon is removed from the cylinder head combustion chamber, valves and valve ports by various methods. The most common is a wire brush tool, chucked to an electric drill. A hand held wire brush, a chisel made from hard wood or a special carbon removing tool supplied by a tool company is used to complete the carbon removal procedure.

CAUTION

When using a motorized wire brush, safety glasses must be worn to avoid personal injury.

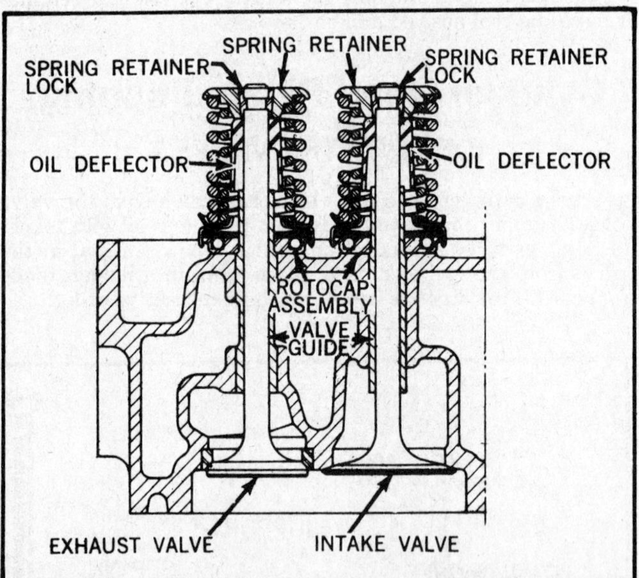

Cross section of valve assemblies with roto-cap assembly under the spring

CLEANING THE CYLINDER HEAD

The cylinder head and certain components can be cleaned of grease, corrosion and scale by immersing them in a "Hot Tank" solution. Generally, an automotive machine shop will have this type of equipment.

CAUTION

Consult with the "Hot Tank" operator to determine if overhead cam bearings of an OHC cylinder head will be damaged by the solution. If necessary to remove the bearings, replace them with new bearings.

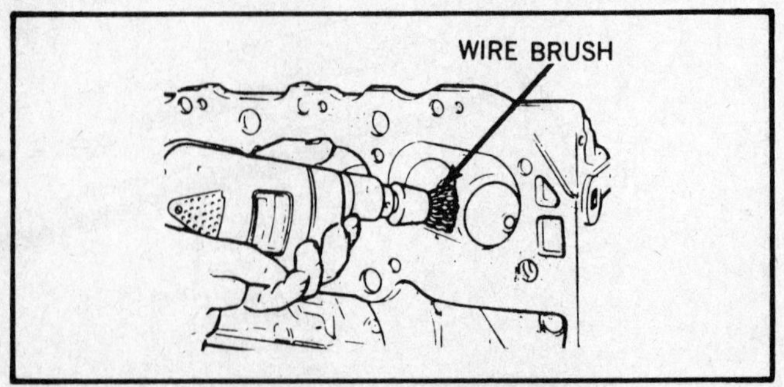

Removing carbon from the cylinder head

CLEANING THE REMAINING CYLINDER HEAD PARTS

Using solvent, clean the rocker arm assemblies, (or rocker

balls and nuts) springs, spring retainers, keepers, all bolts and nuts, push rods and rocker arm cover.

CHECK THE CYLINDER HEAD FOR WARPAGE

Place a straightedge across the gasket surface of the cylinder head. Using feeler gauges, determine the clearance at the center of the straightedge. Measure across both diagonals, along the longitudinal centerline and across the cylinder head at several points. If warpage exceeds 0.003 in. in a 6 in. span, or 0.006 in. over the total length, the cylinder head must be resurfaced.

NOTE: If warpage exceeds the manufacturer's maximum tolerance for material removal, the cylinder head must be replaced.

When milling the cylinder heads of V-type engines, the intake manifold mounting position is altered and must be corrected by milling the manifold flange a proportionate amount.

Cleaning valve guides with wire type cleaner

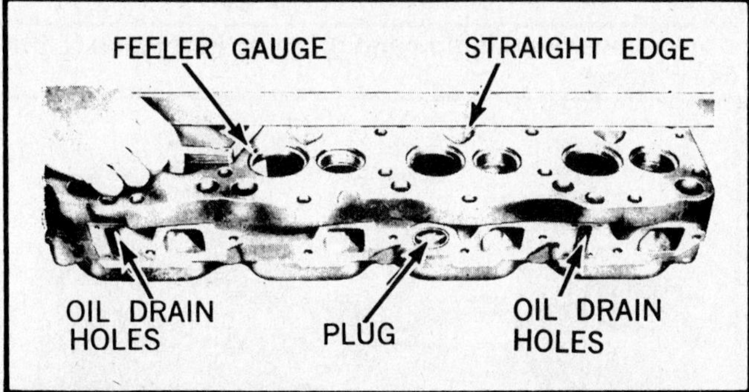

Checking cylinder head surface for flatness with feeler gauge and straight edge

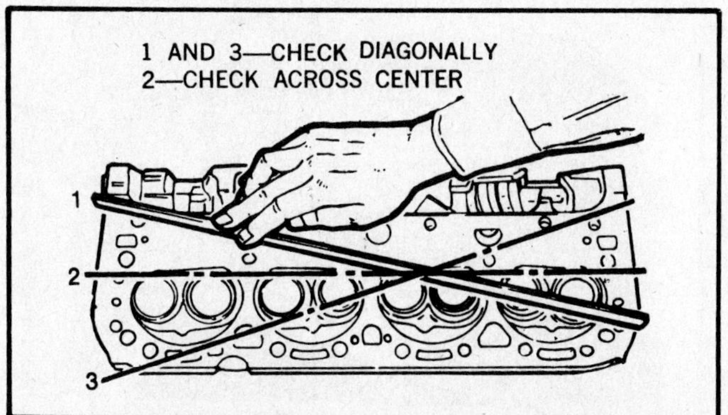

Location of straight edge to check cylinder head surface for flatness

CHECK THE VALVE STEM TO GUIDE CLEARANCE

Clean the valve stem with a solvent to remove all gum and varnish. Clean the valve guides with a solvent and/or a wire type expanding valve guide cleaner tool. Insert the proper valve into its guide and hold the valve head to the valve seat tightly. Mount a dial indicator on the spring side of the cylinder head so that the dial indicator foot is against the valve stem, protruding from the guide, at a 90° angle. Move the valve off its seat and measure the valve guide to stem clearance by moving the stem back and forth to actuate the dial indicator. Measure the

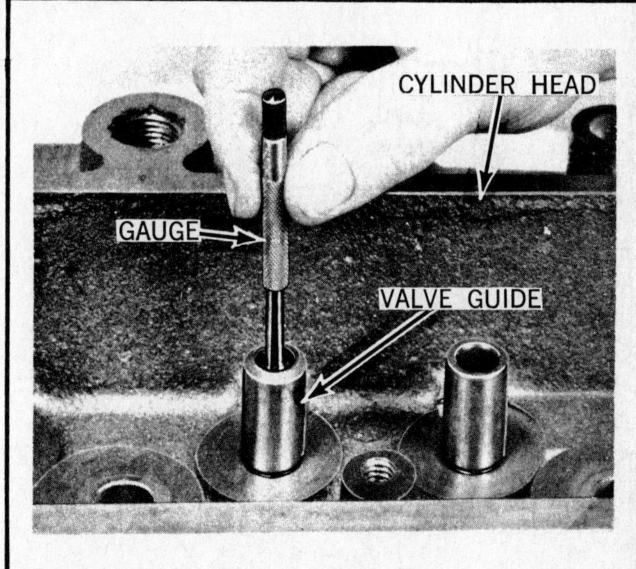

Measuring valve guide with small hole gauge

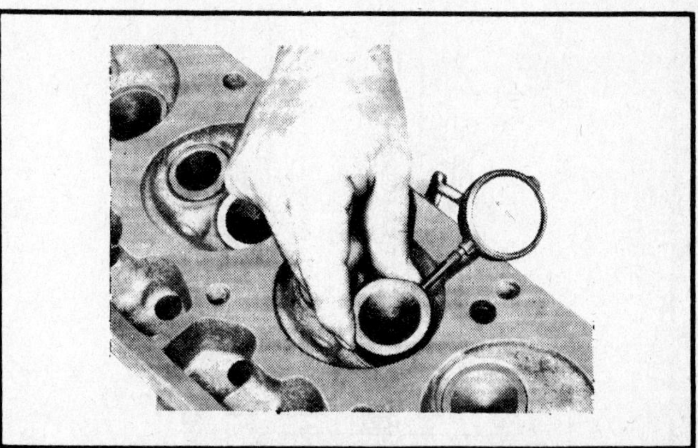

Measuring valve guide wear at valve stem

valve stems using a micrometer and compare to specifications to determine if the valve stem or valve guide is responsible for the excessive wear clearance.

An alternate method of checking the valve stem to guide clearance is to mount a dial indicator on the combustion side of the cylinder head, with the foot of the indicator to contact the side of the valve head. The valve head is moved away from its seat a predetermined distance, either by a special collar tool, placed on the valve stem between the head of the valve and the guide, or by measuring the height of the valve head above the seat with the use of a scale. The valve head is moved back and forth to actuate the dial indicator. Measure the valve stems, using a micrometer and compare to specifications.

Determination of wear from either the valve guide or valve stem can be made. Other types of measuring methods are available to the rebuilder. Go and No-Go gauge, inside caliper type small hole gauges or shim stock can be used to determine the wear of the guides.

Careful inspection will detect bellmouthing or elliptical wear of the guides, normally at the port end of the guide.

REPLACING VALVE SEAT INSERTS

Most exhaust and some intake valve seats are of the insert type and can be replaced if found to be loose, burned or cracked.

The valve seat insert can be removed by either pulling it from its counterbore with a puller, or by drilling a small hole into the seat insert on two sides and cracking it with a chisel. Care must be exercised to avoid drilling into the cylinder head. The insert counterbore in the cylinder head, should be machined prior to the insert installation, with special emphasis on having the bottom of the counterbore square to insure proper seating of the valve insert. Most inserts are supplied in standard, 0.015 in. and 0.030 in. oversizes.

After installation of the valve seat insert, grinding by a refacing machine should be made to insure the seat is angled to specification and in proper relationship to the valve guide.

REPLACING VALVE GUIDES

INTEGRAL GUIDE TYPE

These types of cylinder heads do not have removable guides but

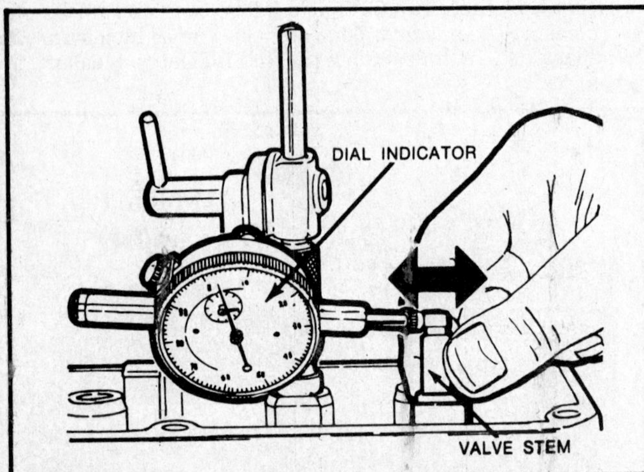

Measuring valve guide wear at valve stem

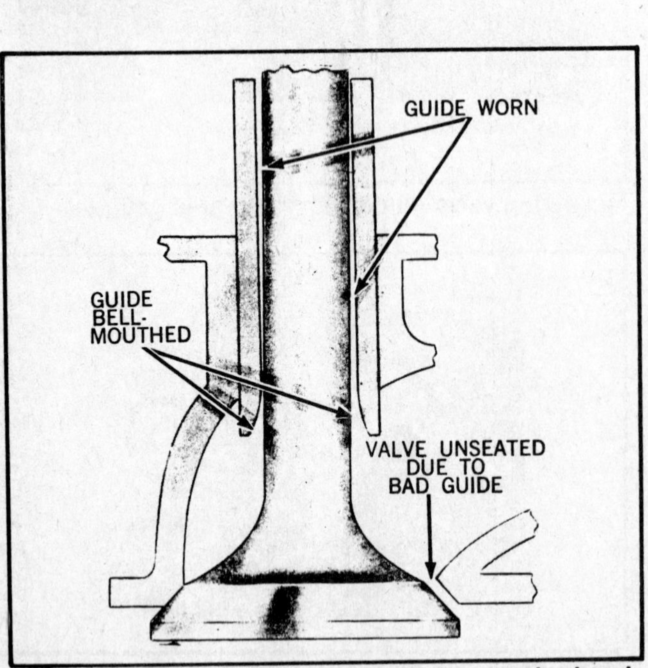

Effects of worn and bellmouthed guides on valve head seating

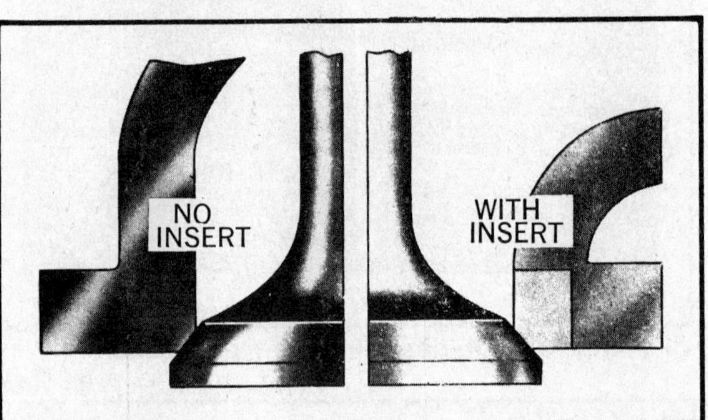

Correct seal installation and grinding in relation to the valve head

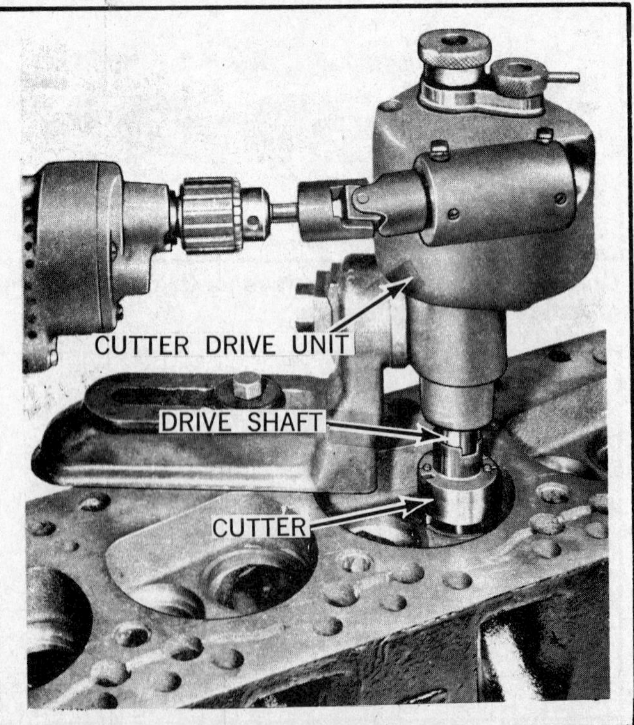

Machining cylinder head for valve seat insert installation

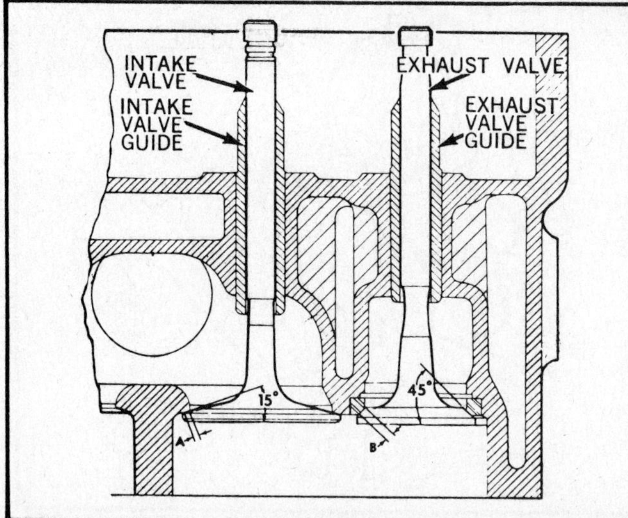

Cross section of valves showing exhaust valve seat insert and intake valve seat without insert. Method of measuring seat angle is illustrated

have the guide holes bored directly in the cylinder head material. When the clearances become excessive between the valve and guide, the guides can be reamed to an oversize dimension and oversize valves used. The "knurling" process may be used to recondition the inside of the guide surface, if the valve to guide clearance is not excessive.

A machining operation can be used to drill out the non-replaceable guide holes and have a standard type guide installed. This operation should be done by an automotive machine shop, equipped with the special boring machine.

REPLACEABLE GUIDE TYPE

Depending on the type of cylinder head, valve guides may be pressed, hammered, or shrunk in. In cases where the guides are shrunk into the head, replacement should be left to an equipped machine shop. In other cases, the guides are replaced as follows: Press or tap the valve guides out of the head using a stepped drift. Determine the height above the boss that the guide must extend and obtain a stack of washers, their I.D. similar to the guides O.D., of that height. Place the stack of washers on the guide and insert the guide into the boss.

NOTE: Valve guides are often tapered or beveled for installation.

Using the stepped installation tool, press or tap the guides into position. Ream the guides according to the size of the valve stem.

RESURFACING (GRINDING) THE VALVE FACE

Using a valve grinder, resurface the valves according to specifications.

Seat installation tool—typical

CAUTION

Valve face angle is not always identical to valve seat angle.

A minimum margin of $^{3}/_{64}$ in. should remain after grinding the valve. The valve stem tip should also be squared and resurfaced, by placing the stem in the V-block of the grinder and turning it while pressing lightly against the grinding wheel.

RESURFACING THE VALVE SEATS USING A GRINDER

Select a pilot of the correct size and a coarse stone of the correct seat angle. Lubricate the pilot if necessary and install the tool

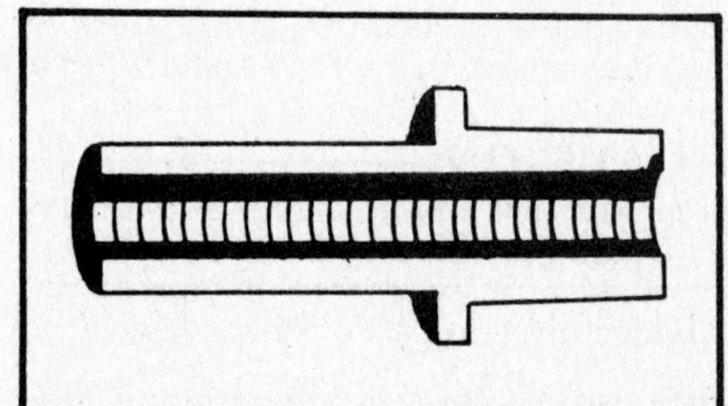

Cross section of knurled valve guide

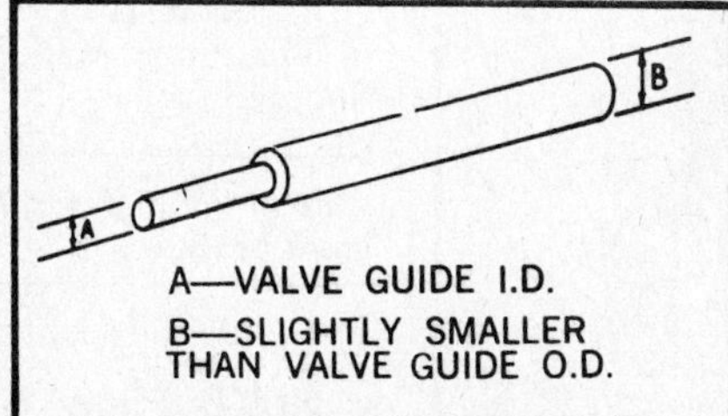

Valve guide removal tool

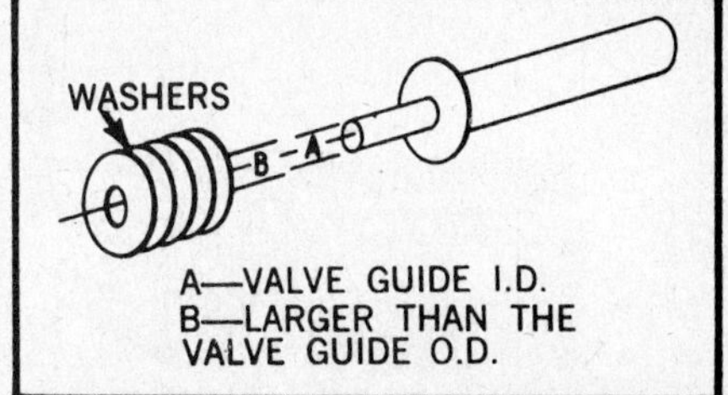

Valve guide installation tool with washer stack

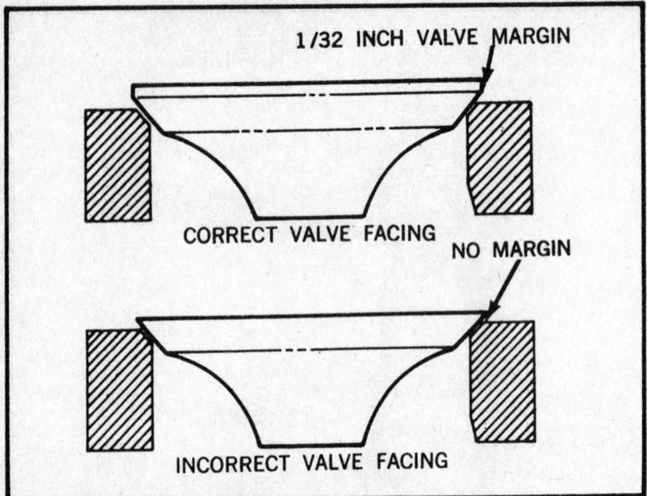

Correct and incorrect grinding of the valve face with proper margin indicated

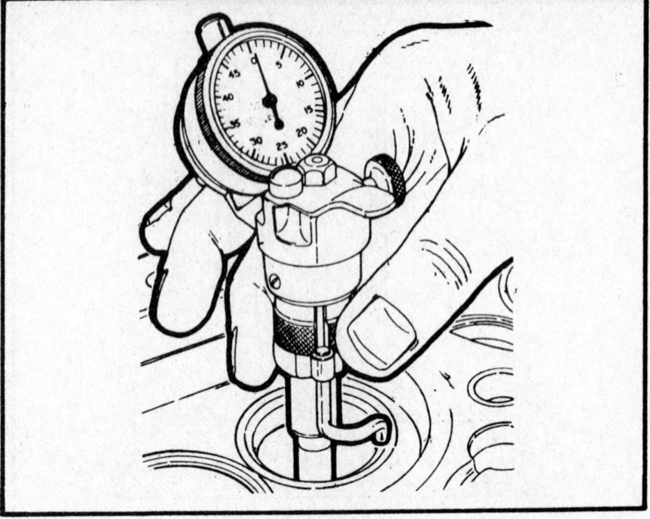

Checking valve seat run-out with a dial gauge

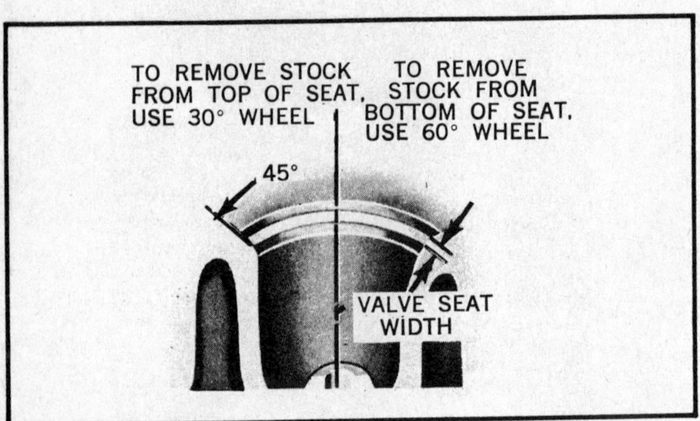

Centering and narrowing valve seat with correction stone

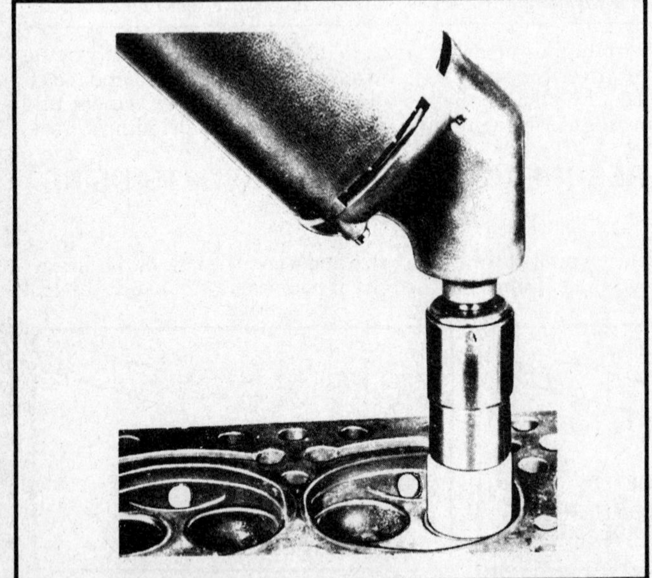

Grinding valve seats

in the valve guide. Move the stone on and off the seat at approximately two cycles per second, until all flaws are removed from the seat. Install a fine stone and finish the seat. Center and narrow the seat using correction stones. Intake seat width—$^{1}/_{16}$–$^{5}/_{64}$ in. Exhaust seat width—$^{3}/_{64}$–$^{1}/_{16}$ in.

CHECKING THE VALVE SEAT CONCENTRICITY

1. Coat the valve face with Prussian blue dye, install the valve and rotate it on the valve sat. If the entire seat becomes coated and the valve is known to be concentric, the set is concentric.
2. Install a dial gauge pilot into the guide and rest the arm on the valve seat. Zero the gauge and rotate the arm around the seat. Runout should not exceed 0.002 in.

LAPPING THE VALVES

NOTE: Valve lapping is done to ensure efficient sealing of resurfaced valves and seats. Valve lapping alone is not recommended for use as a resurface procedure.

1. Invert the cylinder head, lightly lubricate the valve stems and install the valves in the head as numbered. Coat valve seats with fine grinding compound and attach the lapping tool suction cup to a valve head.

NOTE: Moisten the suction cup.

2. Rotate the tool between the palms, changing position and lifting the tool often to prevent grooving. Lap the valve until a smooth polished seat is evident. Remove the valve and tool and rinse away all traces of grinding compound.
3. Fasten a suction cup to a piece of drill rod and mount the rod in a hand drill. Proceed as above, using the hand drill as a lapping tool.

CAUTION

Due to the higher speeds involved when using the hand drill, care must be exercised to avoid grooving the seat.

4. Lift the tool and change direction of rotation often.

NOTE: Many manufacturers do not recommend the lapping of valves to the seats after each has been reground. However, for the rebuilder to be certain a perfect

Hand lapping the valve to the seat

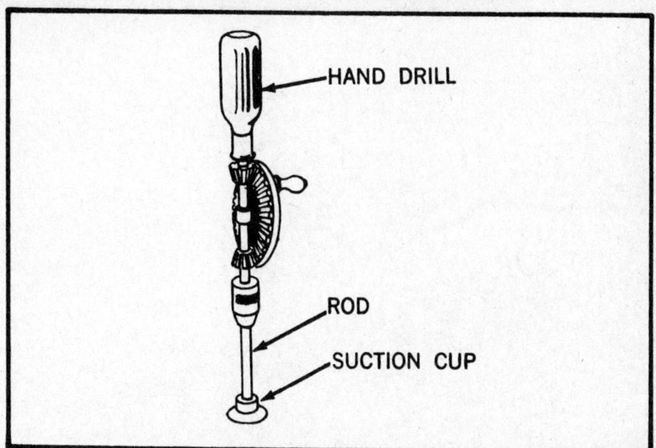

Mechanical valve lapping tool

seal exists between the valve and the seat, lapping is suggested.

CHECK THE VALVE SPRINGS

Test the spring pressure at the installed and compressed (installed height minus valve lift) height using a valve spring tester. Springs used on small displacement engines (up to 3 liters) should be ± 1 lb. of all other springs in either position. A tolerance of ± 5 lbs. is permissable on larger engines.

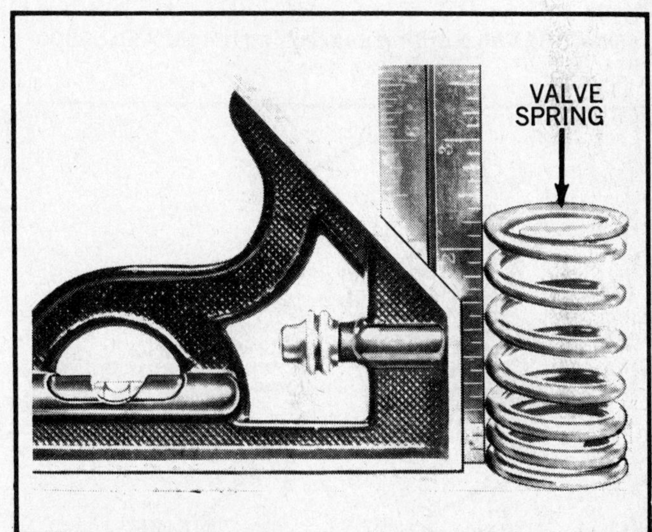

Checking valve spring for free length and squareness

INSTALL VALVE STEM SEALS

Due to the pressure differential that exists at the ends of the intake valve guides (atmospheric pressure above, manifold vacuum below), oil is drawn through the valve guides into the intake port. This has been alleviated somewhat since the addition of positive crankcase ventilation, which lowers the pressure above the guides. Several types of valve stem seals are available to reduce blow-by. Certain seals simply slip over the stem and guide boss, while others require that the boss be machined. Recently, Teflon guide seals have become popular. Consult a parts supplier or machinist concerning availability and suggested usages.

NOTE: When installing seals, ensure that a small amount of oil is able to pass the seal to lubricate the valve guides; otherwise, excessive wear may result.

INSTALL THE VALVES

Lubricate the valve stems and install the valves in the cylinder head as numbered. Lubricate and position the seals (if used, see above) and the valve springs. Install the spring retainers, compress the springs and insert the keys using needlenose pliers or a tool designed for this purpose.

NOTE: Retain the keys with wheel bearing grease during installation.

CHECK VALVE SPRING INSTALLED HEIGHT

Measure the distance between the spring pad and the lower edge of the spring retainer and compare to specifications. If the installed height is incorrect, add shim washers between the spring pad and the spring.

CAUTION

Use only washers designed for this purpose.

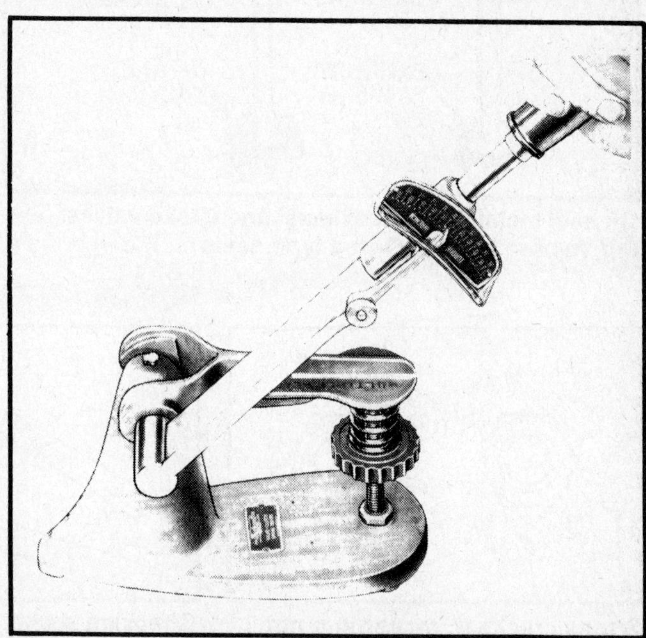

Testing valve spring compressed height

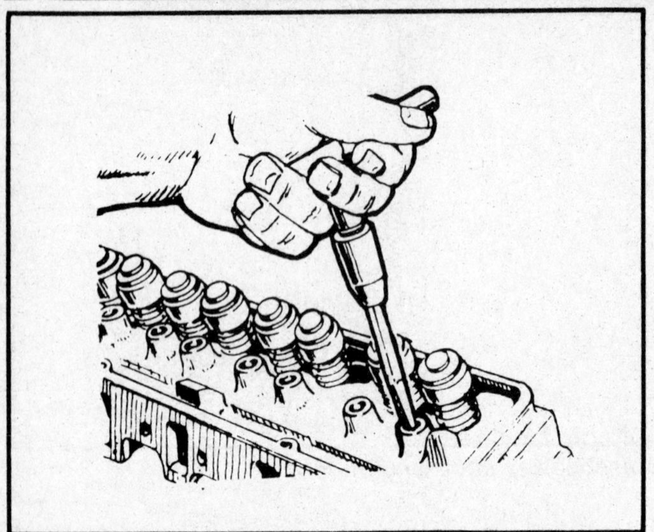

Measuring valve spring assembled height with caliper

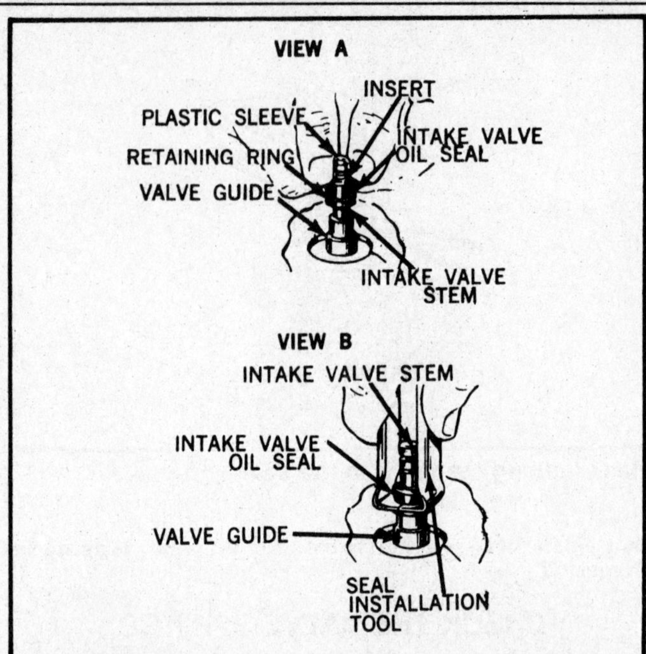

Installing intake valve oil seals, Perfect Circle type, using plastic sleeve and special installation tool

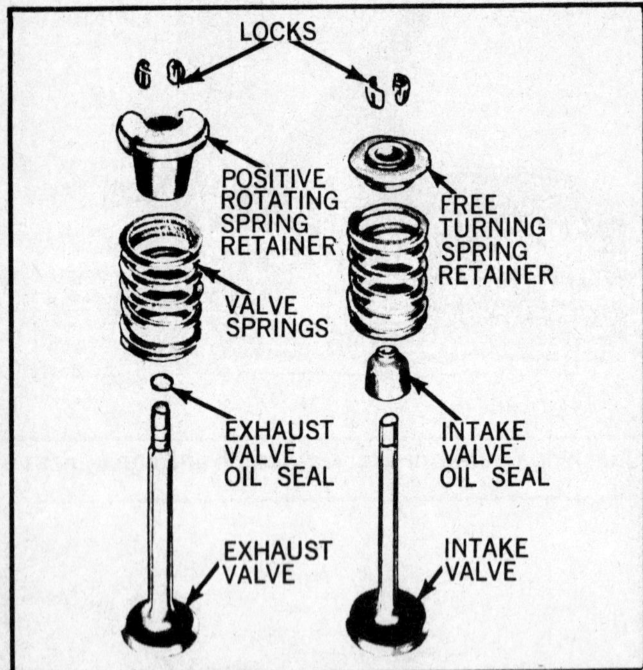

Oil seal installation on exhaust and intake valves, using "umbrella" and O-ring type seals

INSPECT THE ROCKER ARMS, BALLS, STUDS and NUTS

Visually inspect the rocker arms, balls, studs and nuts for cracks, galling, burning, scoring, or wear. If all parts are intact, liberally lubricate the rocker arms and balls and install them on the cylinder head. If wear is noted on the rocker arm at the point of valve contact, grind it smooth and square, removing as little material as possible. Replace the rocker arm if excessively worn. If a rocker stud shows signs of wear, it must be replaced. If a rocker nut shows stress cracks, replace it.

INSPECT THE ROCKER SHAFT(S) AND ROCKER ARMS

Remove rocker arms, springs and washers from rocker shaft.

NOTE: Lay out parts in the order in which they are removed.

Inspect rocker arms for pitting or wear on the valve contact point, or excessive bushing wear. Bushings need only be replaced if wear is excessive, because the rocker arm normally contacts the shaft at one point only. Grind the valve contact

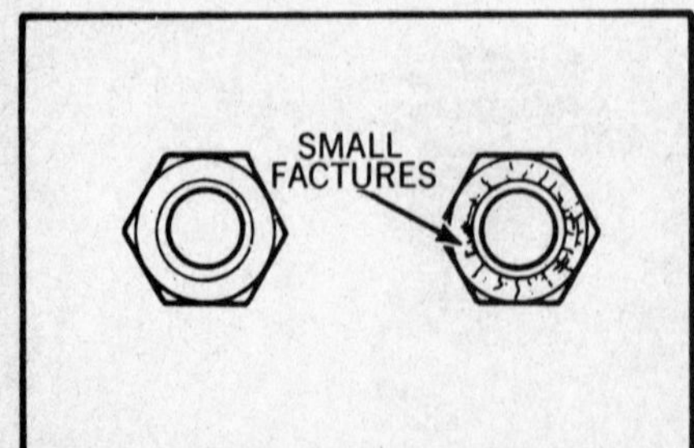

Stress cracks in rocker arm nut

Checking rocker arm shaft O.D. with mi-crometer

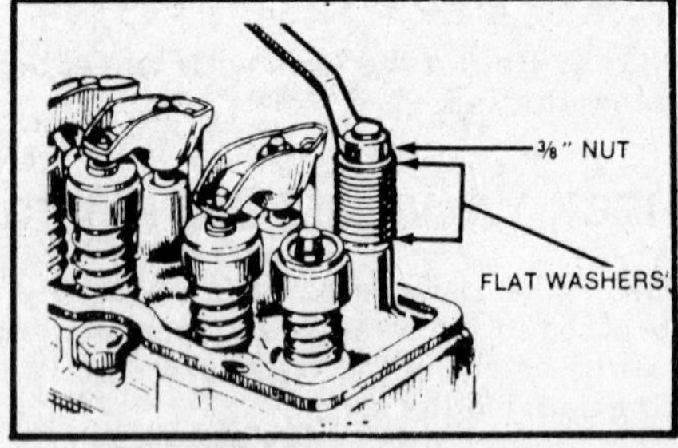

Checking rocker arms

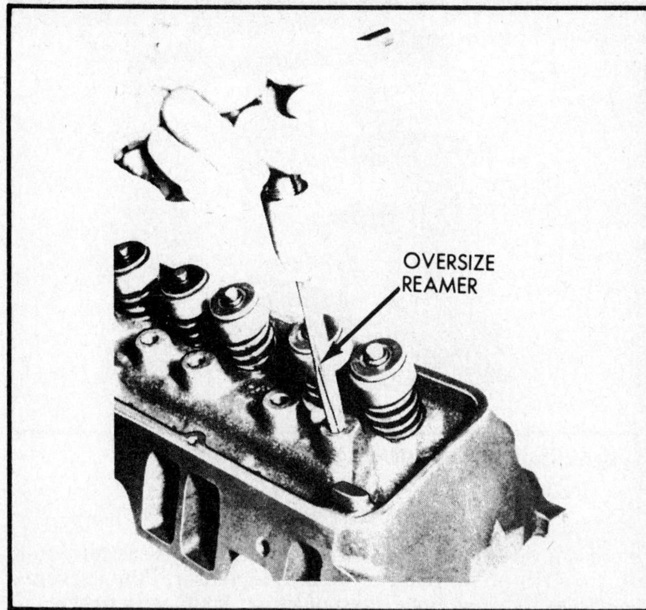

Reaming the stud bore for oversize rocker studs

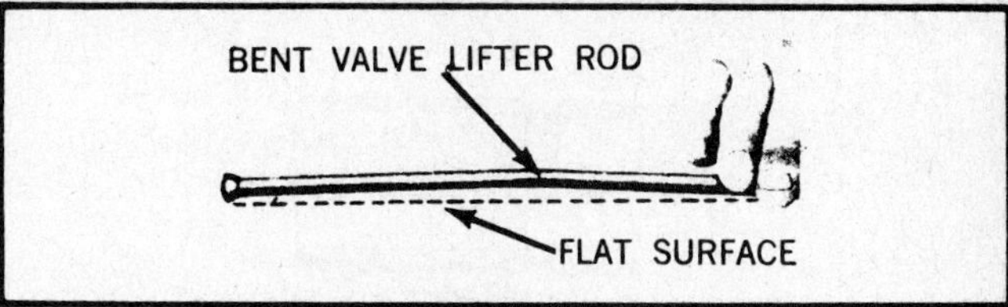

Checking for bent push rod

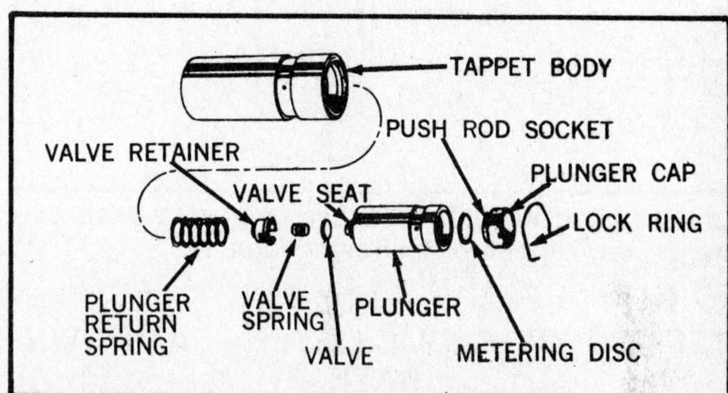

Exploded view of hydraulic lifter—typical

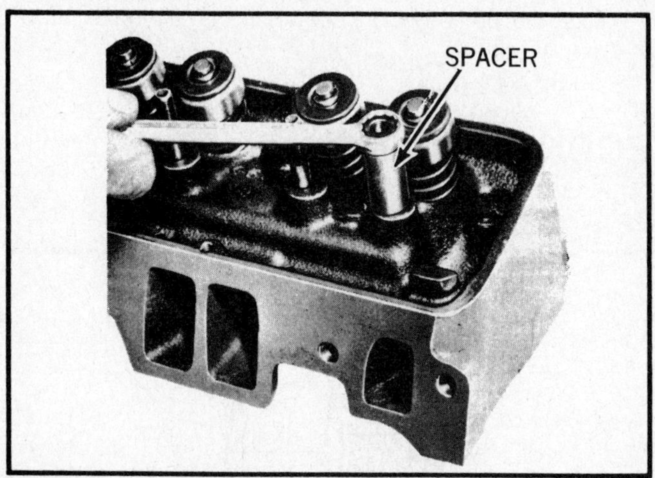

Removing a pressed in rocker stud

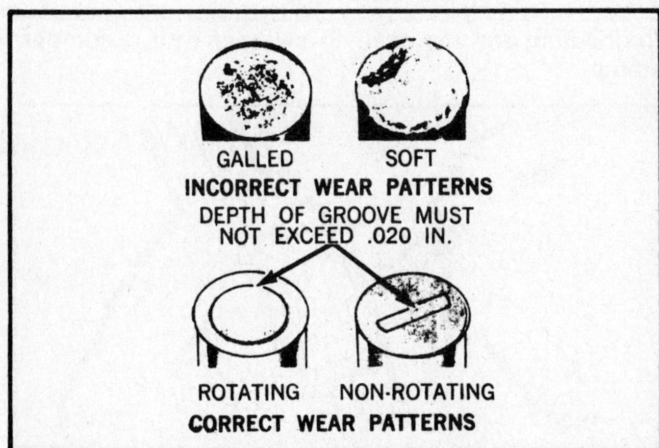

Wear patterns on base of lifter bodies

point of rocker arm smooth if necessary, removing as little material as possible. If excessive material must be removed to smooth and square the arm, it should be replaced. Clean out all oil holes and passages in rocker shaft. If shaft is grooved or worn, replace it. Lubricate and assemble the rocker shaft.

REPLACING ROCKER STUDS

In order to remove a threaded stud, lock two nuts on the stud and unscrew the stud using the lower nut. Coat the lower threads of the new stud with Loctite and install.

Two alternative methods are available for replacing pressed in studs. Remove the damaged stud using a stack of washers and a nut or use a stud puller. In the first, the boss is reamed 0.005–0.006 in. oversize and an oversize stud pressed in. Control the stud extension over the boss using washers, in the same manner as valve guides. Before installing the stud, coat it with white lead and grease. To retain the stud more positively, drill a hole through the stud and boss and install a roll pin. In the second method, the boss is tapped and a threaded stud installed. Retain the stud using a locking compound.

INSPECT THE PUSHRODS

Remove the pushrods and if hollow, clean out the oil passages using fine wire. Roll each pushrod over a piece of clean glass. If a distinct clicking sound is heard as the pushrod rolls, the rod is bent and must be replaced.

The length of all pushrods must be equal. Measure the length of the pushrods, compare to specifications and replace as necessary.

INSPECT THE VALVE LIFTERS

MECHANICAL OR HYDRAULIC

Remove lifters from their bores and remove gum and varnish, using solvent. Clean walls of lifter bores. Check lifters for concave wear as illustrated. If face is worn concave, replace lifter and carefully inspect the camshaft. Lightly lubricate lifter and insert it into its bore. If play is excessive, an oversize lifter must be installed (where possible). Consult a machinist concerning feasibility. If play is satisfactory, remove, lubricate and reinstall the lifter.

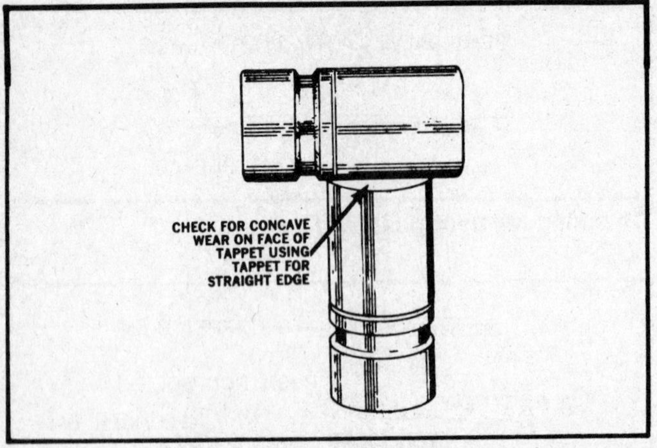
CHECK FOR CONCAVE
WEAR ON FACE OF
TAPPET USING
TAPPET FOR
STRAIGHT EDGE

Checking the tappet for concave wear on its base, using second tappet for a straight edge

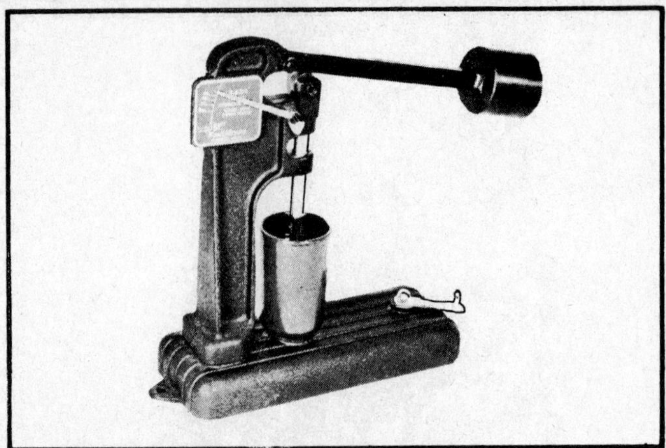

Hydraulic lifter leakdown tester—typical

TESTING HYDRAULIC LIFTER LEAK DOWN RATE

Special testers are available for the checking of the hydraulic lifter leak down rate. Special instructions accompanying the testers should be followed by the rebuilder. If the tester is not available, the following alternate method can be used.

Submerge lifter in a container of kerosene. Chuck a used pushrod or its equivalent into a drill press. Position container of kerosene so pushrod acts on the lifter plunger. Pump lifter with the drill press, until resistance increases. Pump several more times to bleed any air out of lifter. Apply very firm, constant pressure to the lifter and observe rate at which fluid bleeds out of lifter. If the fluid bleeds very quickly (less than 15 seconds), lifter is defective. If the time exceeds 60 seconds, lifter is sticking. In either case, recondition or replace lifter. If lifter is operating properly (leak down time 15–60 seconds) lubricate and reinstall.

ENGINE BLOCK RECONDITIONING

MARKING MAIN AND CONNECTING ROD CAPS

Using a punch, mark the corresponding main bearing caps and saddles according to position (i.e., one punch on the front main cap and saddle, two on the second, three on the third, etc.). Using number stamps, identify the corresponding connecting rods and caps, according to cylinder (if no numbers are present). Remove the main and connecting rod caps and place sleeves of plastic tubing over the connecting rod bolts, to protect the journals as the crankshaft is removed.

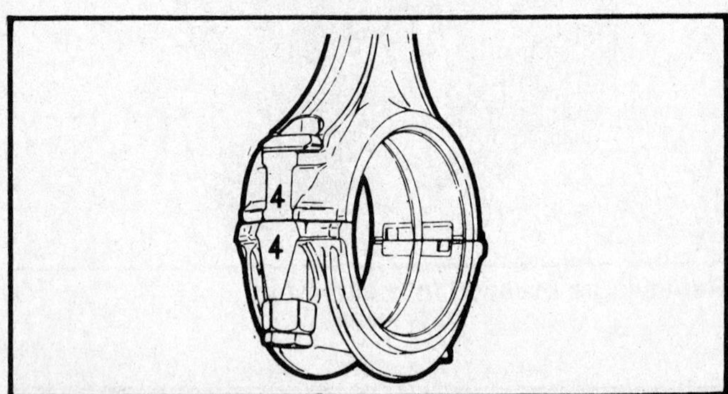
4
4

Connecting rod matched to cylinder with a number stamp

REMOVE THE RIDGE

In order to facilitate removal of the piston and connecting rod, the ridge at the top of the cylinder (unworn area; see illustration) must be removed. Place the piston at the bottom of the bore and cover it with a rag. Cut the ridge away using a ridge reamer, exercising extreme care to avoid cutting too deeply. Remove the rag and remove cuttings that remain at the piston.

CAUTION

If the ridge is not removed and new rings are installed, damage to rings will result.

REMOVING THE PISTON AND CONNECTING ROD

Invert the engine and push the pistons and connecting rods out of the cylinders. If necessary, tap the connecting rod boss with a wooden hammer handle, to force the piston out.

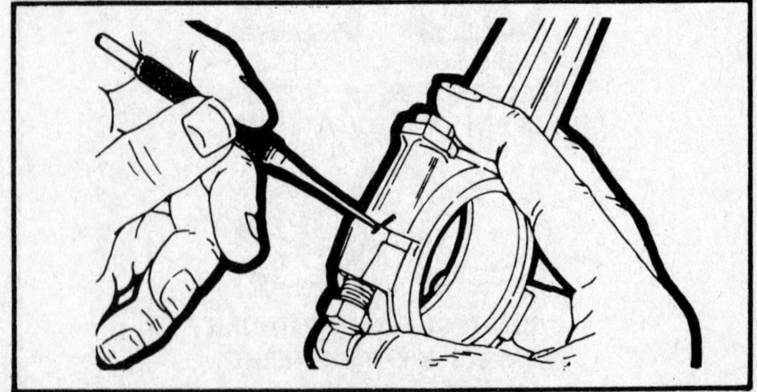

Scribe connecting rod matchmarks

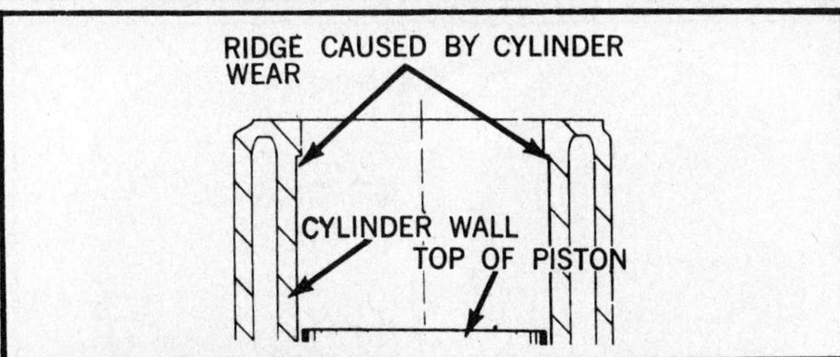

Cylinder bore ridge

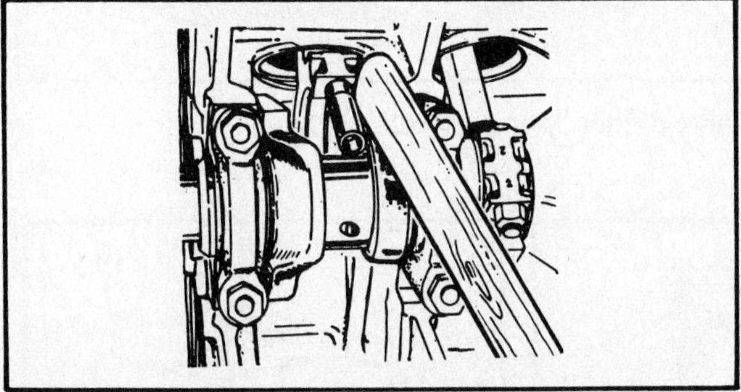

Removing the piston and connecting rod assembly

CAUTION

Do not attempt to force the piston past the uncut cylinder ridge.

REMOVE THE OIL GALLERY PLUGS

Threaded plugs should be removed using an appropriate (usually square) wrench. To remove soft, pressed in plugs, drill a hole in the plug and thread in a sheet metal screw. Pull the plug out by the screw using pliers.

REMOVING FREEZE PLUGS

Drill a hole in the center of the freeze plugs and pry them out using a drift or special puller.

CHECK THE BORE DIAMETER AND SURFACE

Visually inspect the cylinder bores for roughness, scoring, or scuffing. If evident, the cylinder bore must be bored or honed oversize to eliminate imperfections and the smallest possible oversize piston used. The new pistons should be given to the machinist with the block, so that the cylinders can be bored or honed exactly to the piston size (plus clearance). If no flaws are evident, measure the bore diameter using a telescope gauge and micrometer, or dial gauge, parallel and perpendicular to the engine centerline, at the top (below the ridge) and bottom of the bore. Subtract the bottom measurements from the top to determine taper and the parallel to the centerline measurements from the perpendicular measurements to determine eccentricity. If the measurements are not within specifications, the cylinder must be bored or honed and an oversize piston installed. If the measurements are within specifications the cylinder may be used as is, with only finish honing.

CYLINDER SLEEVE LINERS

DRY CYLINDER LINERS

Various engines are fitted with dry type cylinder liners at the

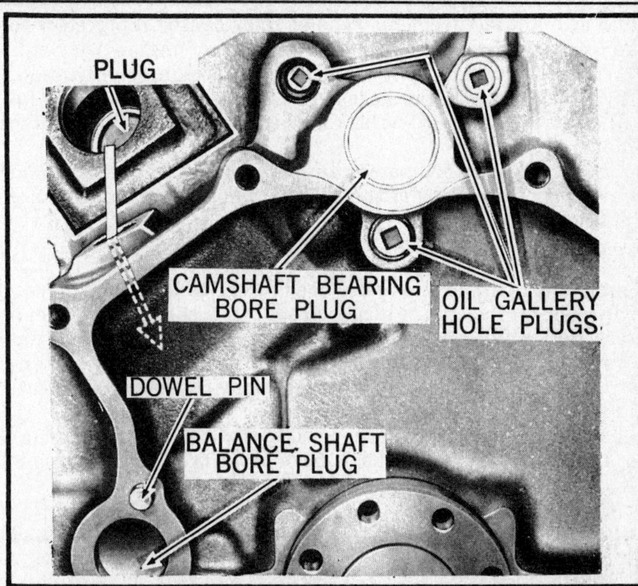

Location of oil gallery plugs, core plugs and camshaft bearing bore plug – V8 engine (some engines may be equipped with a balance shaft)

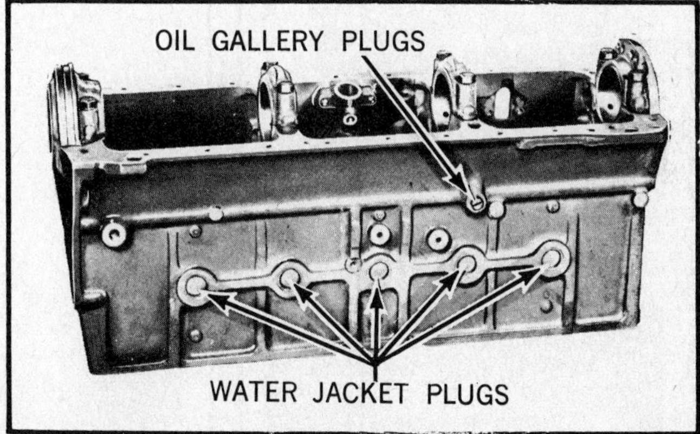

Location of oil galley and water jacket plugs – 6 cylinder engine typical

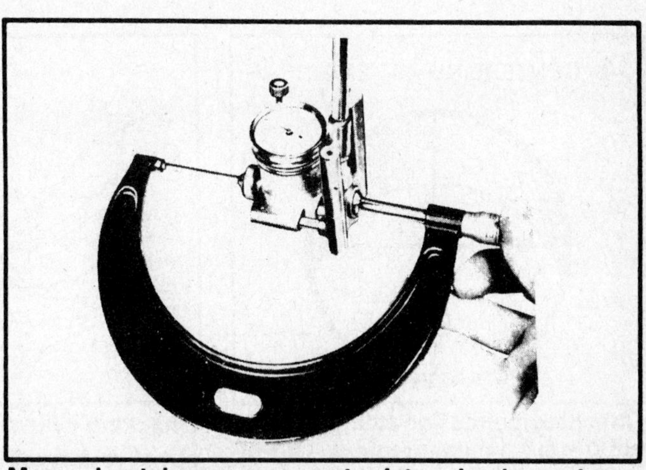

Measuring telescope gauge to determine bore size

time of manufacture. This type of liner can be replaced with the use of special pulling tools at the time of engine overhaul.

When the cylinder bore is part of the block assembly and if only one or two cylinder bores are damaged, sleeves can be installed in the damaged bores to avoid reboring all cylinders to an oversize condition.

The services of a competent automotive machine shop should be used for the boring of the cylinders and the installation of the liners.

WET CYLINDER LINERS

Removable cylinder liners are used in varied engines that can be lifted from the engine block without the use of pullers or of a press. Soft metal rings are used at the base of the liners to seal between machined surfaces on the engine block and the cylinder liner, to prevent coolant from entering the engine lubricating system.

The cylinder head gasket is used to seal the top of the cylinder liner and the cylinder head. Should the cylinder head be re-

Wet cylinder liner—typical

Cylinder reboring machine

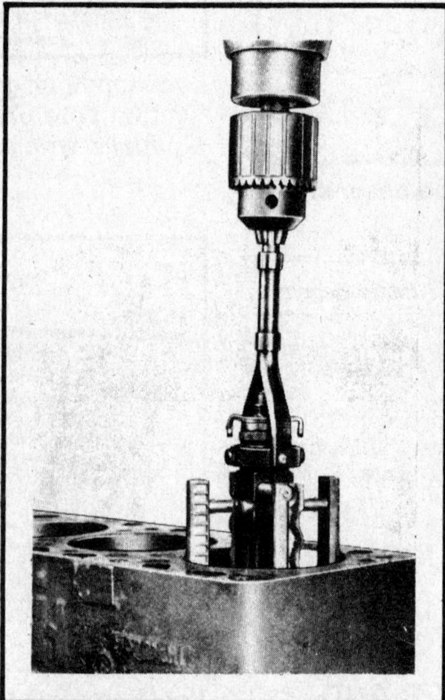

Cylinder honing tool

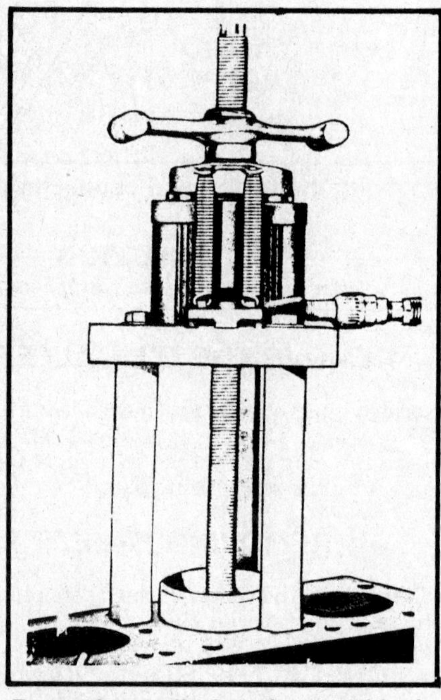

Removing cylinder sleeve with the use of hydraulic tool

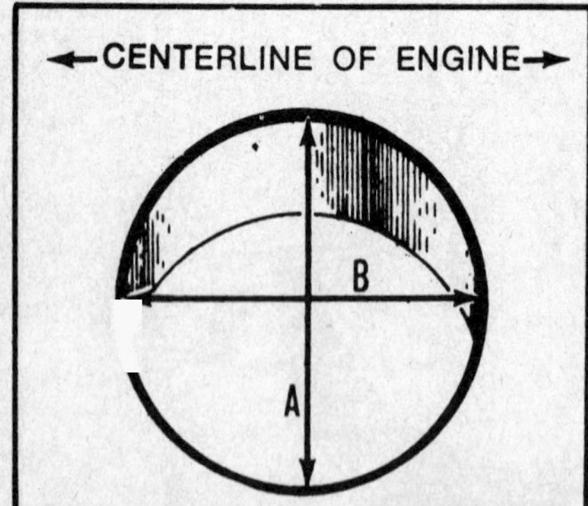

Checking points for cylinder bore out-of-round measurement. Out-of-round is difference between measurement A and B

Checking cylinder bore taper and out-of-round with a dial indicator cylinder bore gauge

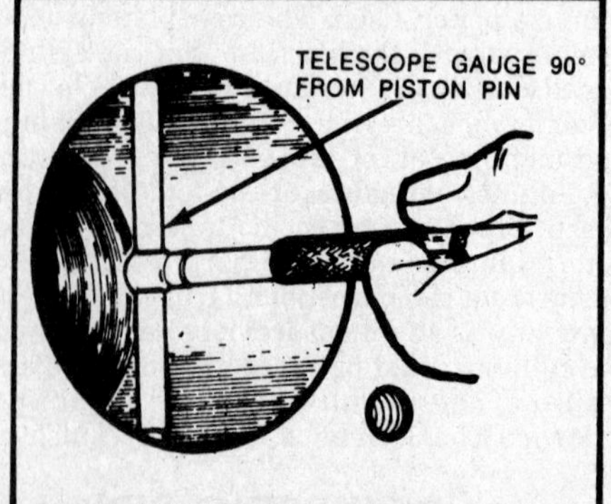

Measuring culinder bore with tele scope

moved or the engine overhauled, a projection of approximately 0.002–0.006 in. (depending upon engine manufacturer's specifications) should exist at the liner top, above the surface of the engine block. If the projection is not present, new sealing rings should be installed at the bottom of the cylinder liners to prevent coolant leakage or compression loss.

Installation of pistons, rings and liners are installed as sets to control the weight and balance of the components.

CHECK THE CYLINDER BLOCK BEARING ALIGNMENT

Remove the upper bearing inserts. Place a straightedge in the bearing saddles along the centerline of the crankshaft. If clearance exists between the straightedge and the center saddle, the block must be linebored.

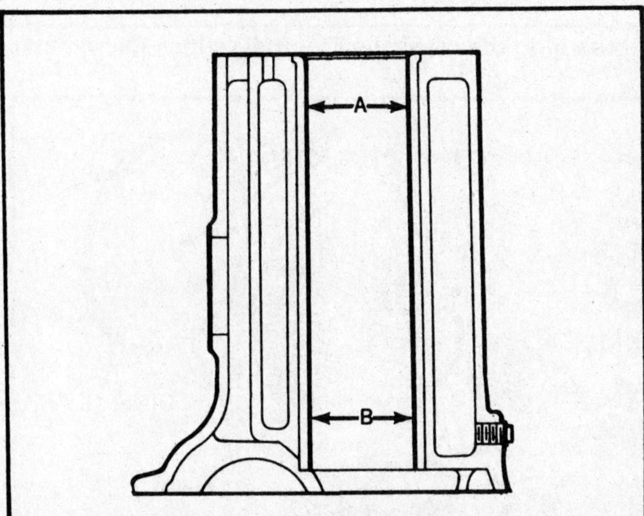

Checking points for cylinder bore taper measurement. Taper is difference between measurement A and B

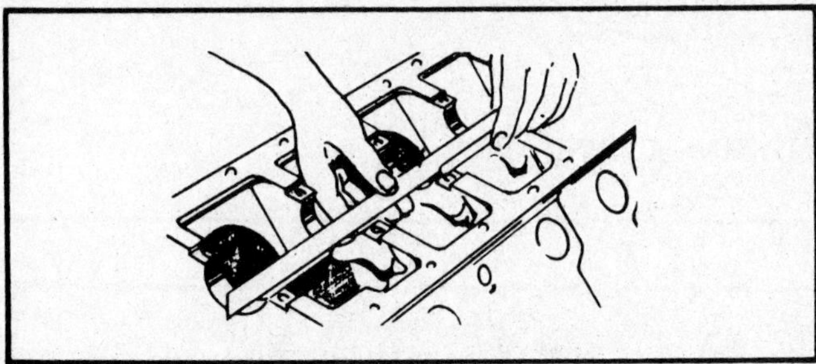

Checking main bearing saddle alignment

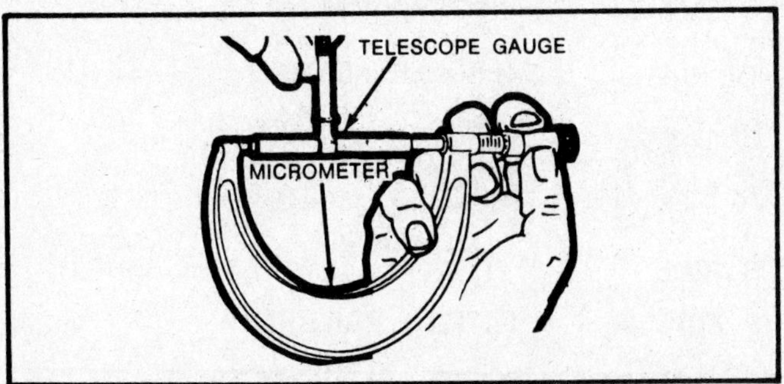

Measuring cylinder gauge to determine bore size

HOT-TANK THE BLOCK

Have the block hot-tanked to remove grease, corrosion and scale from the water jackets.

NOTE: Consult the operator to determine whether the camshaft bearings will be damaged during the hot-tank process.

SERVICE THE CRANKSHAFT

Ensure that all oil holes and passages in the crankshaft are open and free of sludge. If necessary, have the crankshaft ground to the largest possible undersize.

Have the crankshaft magnafluxed, to locate stress cracks. Consult a machinist concerning additional service procedures, such as surface hardening (e.g., Nitriding, Tuftriding) to improve wear characteristics, cross drilling and chamfering the oil holes to improve lubrication and balancing.

Measure the main bearing journals at each end twice (90° apart) using a micrometer, to determine diameter, journal taper and eccentricity. If journals are within tolerances, reinstall bearing caps at their specified torque. Using a telescope gauge and micrometer, measure bearing I.D. parallel to piston axis and at 30° on each side of piston axis. Subtract journal O.D. from bearing I.D. to determine oil clearance. If crankshaft journals appear defective, or do not meet tolerances, there is no need to measure bearings; for the crankshaft will require grinding and/or-undersize bearings will be required. If bearing appears defective, cause for failure should be determined prior to replacement.

Refer to the failure diagnosis section to help you determine the cause of the failure.

CHECK THE BLOCK FOR CRACKS

Visually inspect the block for cracks or chips. The most common locations are as follows:

1. Adjacent to freeze plugs
2. Between the cylinders and water jackets
3. Adjacent to the main bearing saddles
4. At the entrance bottom of the cylinders

Check only suspected cracks using spot check dye (see introduction). If a crack is located, consult a machinist concerning possible repairs.

Magnaflux the block to locate hidden cracks. If cracks are located, consult a machinist about feasibility of repair.

NOTE: Engine blocks that are porous or have sand holes, can be repaired with metallic plastic where coolant or oil pressure does not exist. Do not attempt to repair cracked blocks with the metallic plastic.

CHECK THE BLOCK DECK FOR WARPAGE

Using a straightedge and feeler gauges, check the block deck for warpage in the same manner that the cylinder head is checked (see Cylinder Head Reconditioning). If warpage exceeds specifications, have the deck resurfaced.

NOTE: In certain cases a specification for total material removal (Cylinder head and block deck) is provided. This specification must not be exceeded.

CHECK THE DECK HEIGHT

The deck height is the distance from the crankshaft centerline to the block deck. To measure, invert the engine and install the crankshaft, retaining it with the center main cap. Measure the distance from the crankshaft journal to the block deck, parallel to the cylinder centerline. Measure the diameter of the end (front and rear) main journals, parallel to the centerline of the cylinders, divide the diameter in half and subtract it from the previous measurement. The results of the front and rear measurements should be identical. If the difference exceeds 0.005 in., the deck height should be corrected.

NOTE: Block deck height and warpage should be corrected together.

INSTALL THE OIL GALLERY PLUGS AND FREEZE PLUGS

Coat freeze plugs with sealer and tap into position using a piece of pipe, slightly smaller than the plug, as a driver. To ensure retention, stake the edges of the plugs. Coat threaded oil

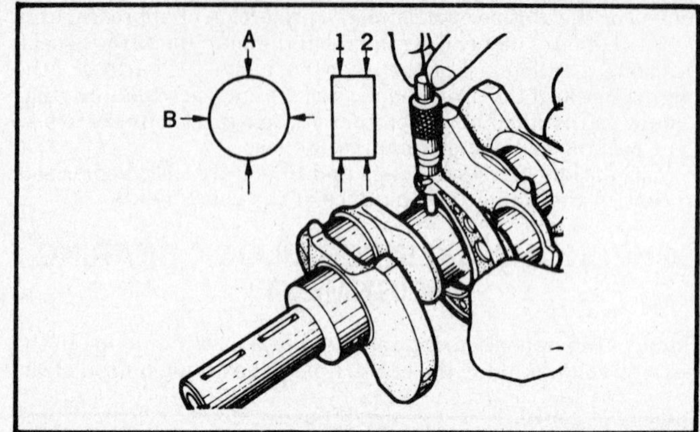

Measuring the crankshaft journals with a micrometer

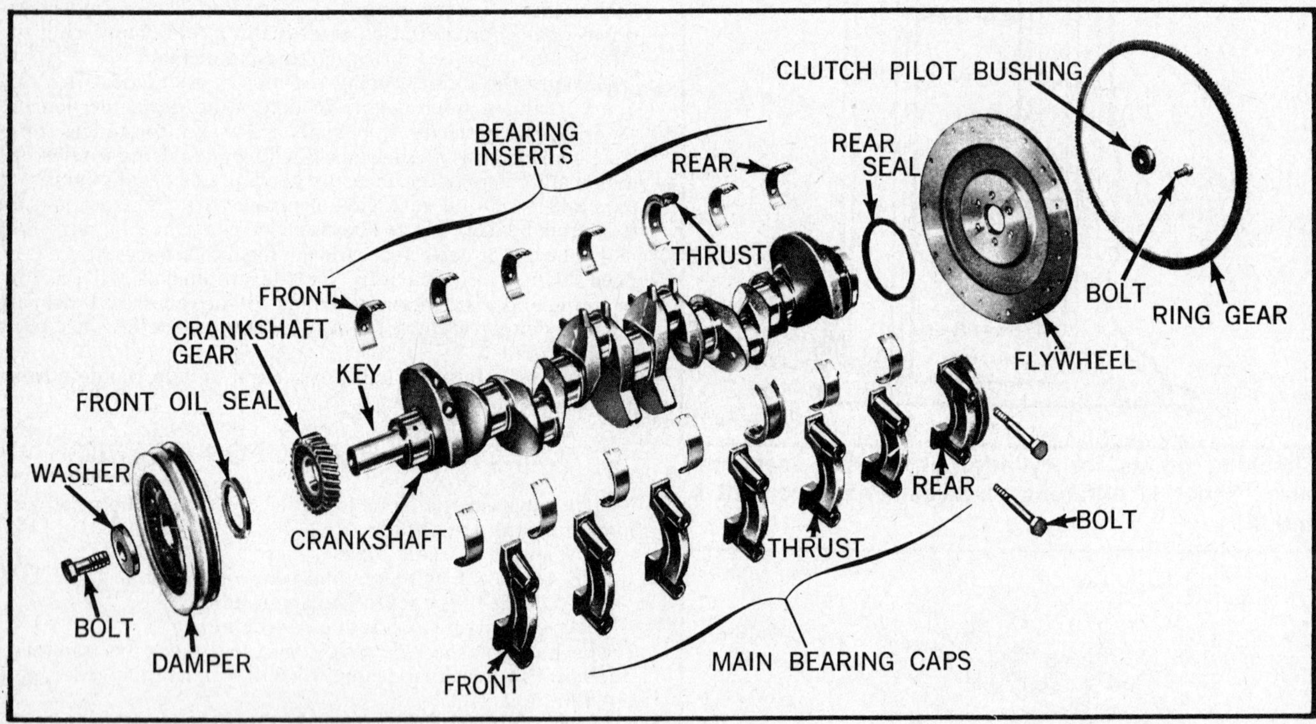

Crankshaft assembly—typical

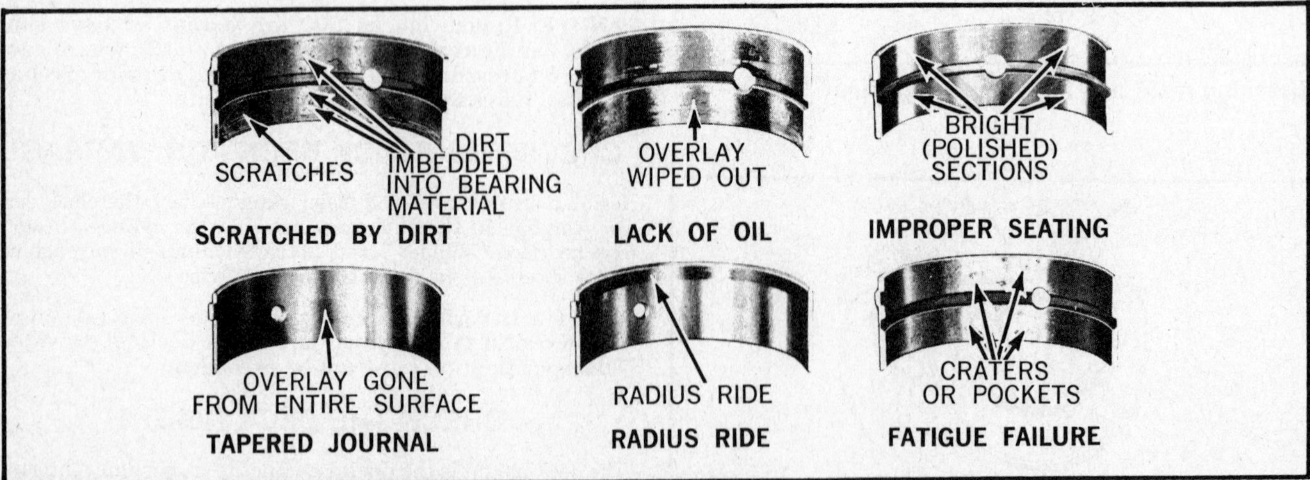

Causes of crankshaft bearing failures

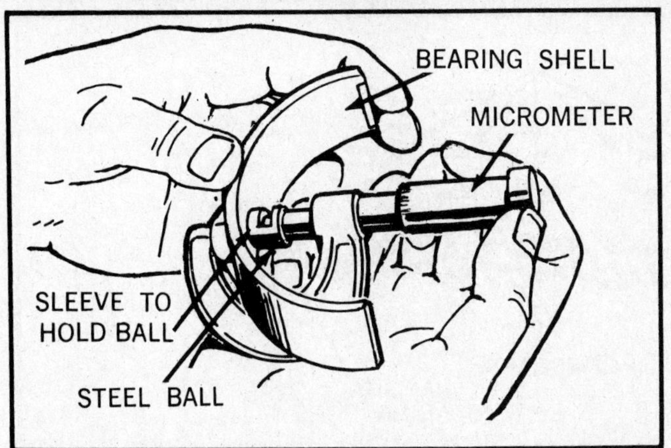

Masuring bearing insert thickness with special ball

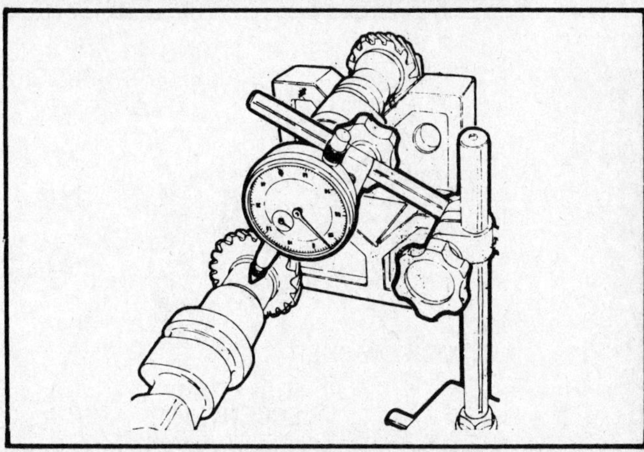

Checking the camshaft for straightness

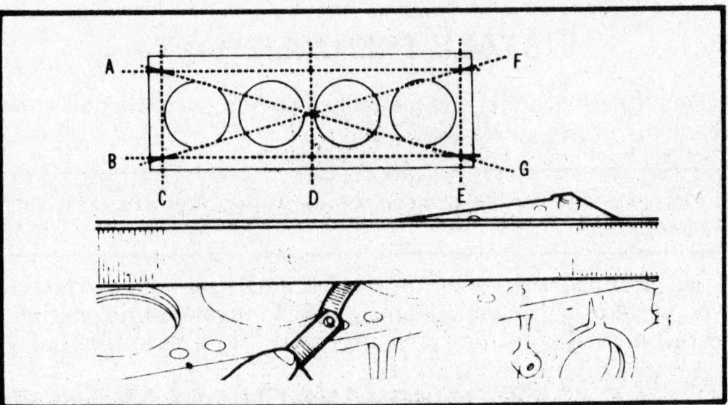

Checking the cylinder block for distortion

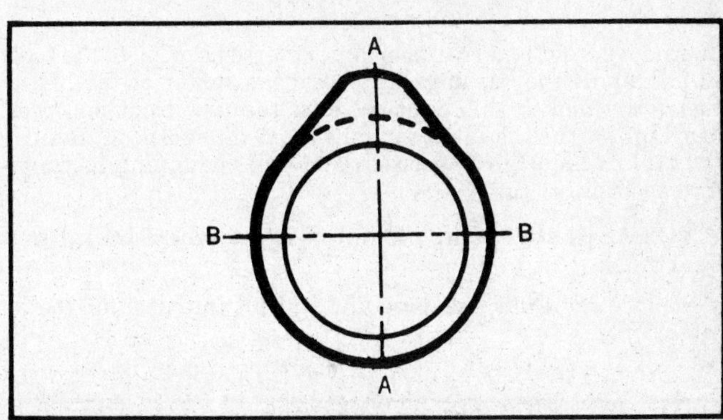

Camshaft lobe measurement—lift is difference between A and B measurement

Installation of cup type and expansion type core plugs with special tool

gallery plugs with sealer and install. Drive replacement soft plugs into block using a large drift as a driver.

Rather than reinstalling lead plugs, drill and tap the holes and install threaded plugs, where possible.

CLEAN AND INSPECT THE CAMSHAFT

Degrease the camshaft, using solvent and clean out all oil holes. Visually inspect cam lobes and bearing journals for excessive wear. If a lobe is questionable, check all lobes as indicated below. If a journal or lobe is worn, the camshaft must be reground or replaced.

NOTE: If a journal is worn, there is a good chance that the bushings are worn.

If lobes and journals appear intact, place the front and rear journals in V-blocks and rest a dial indicator on the center journal. Rotate the camshaft to check straightness. If deviation exceeds 0.001 in., replace the camshaft.

Check the camshaft lobes with a micrometer, by measuring the lobes from the nose to base and again at 90°. The lift is determined by subtracting the second measurement from the first. If all exhaust lobes and all intake lobes are not identical with specs, the camshaft must be reground or replaced.

REPLACE THE CAMSHAFT BEARINGS

If excessive wear is indicated or if the engine is being completely rebuilt, camshaft bearings should be replaced as follows: Drive the camshaft rear plug from the block. Assemble the removal puller with its shoulder on the bearing to be removed. Gradually tighten the puller nut until bearing is removed. Remove remaining bearings, leaving the front and rear for last.

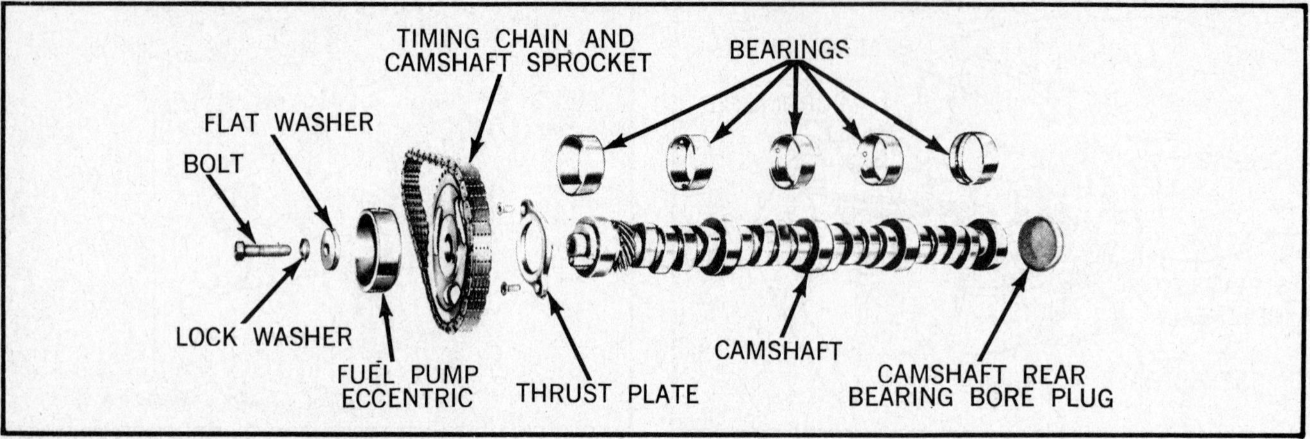

Chain driven camshaft assembly—typical

To remove front and rear bearings, reverse position of the tool, so as to pull the bearings in toward the center of the block. Leave the tool in this position, pilot the new front and rear bearings on the installer and pull them into position. Return the tool to its original position and pull remaining bearings into position.

NOTE: Ensure that oil holes align when installing bearings.

Replace camshaft rear plug and stake it into position to aid retention.

Removing and installing cam bearings with special puller tool—typical

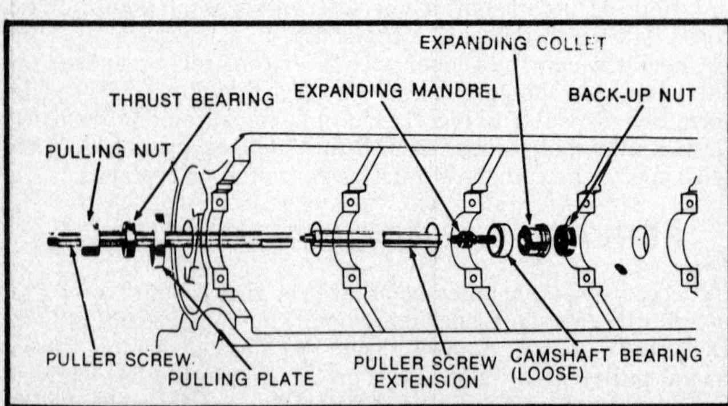

Checking camshaft alignment with Vee blocks and dial indicator

INSTALL THE CAMSHAFT

Liberally lubricate the camshaft lobes and journals and slide the camshaft into the block.

CAUTION

Exercise extreme care to avoid damaging the bearings when inserting the camshaft.

Be careful not to force the shaft towards the rear of the engine block as this can unseat the welch plugs in some engines. Install and tighten the camshaft thrust plate retaining bolts.

CHECK CAMSHAFT END-PLAY

1. Using feeler gauges, determine whether the clearance between the camshaft boss (or gear) and backing plate is within specifications. Install shims behind the thrust plate, or reposition the camshaft gear and retest end-play.
2. Mount a dial indicator stand so that the stem of the dial indicator rests on the nose of the camshaft, parallel to the camshaft axis. Push the camshaft as far in as possible and zero the gauge. Move the camshaft outward to determine the amount of camshaft end-play. If the end-play is not within tolerance, install shims behind the thrust plate or reposition the camshaft gear and retest.

INSTALLING BEARING INSERTS IN BLOCK OR CONNECTING ROD BORES

The bearing inserts must fit tightly in the connecting rod or main bearing bores. The bearing inserts are made slightly larger than the actual diameter of the bore into which they are to be used. As the bearing caps are drawn tight, the bearing inserts are compressed, assuring a positive contact between the bearing insert and the bore. This is necessary to relieve the heat and to give the bearing insert a firm support for the loads place don them during engine operation. This increased diameter of the bearing insert is referred to as bearing "crush". Because of this, the bearing caps, connecting rods and engine block must not be filed, lapped or reworked in any manner and all attaching bolts must be properly torqued.

Main and connecting rod bearing inserts are made with the width across the open end slightly larger than the main bearing or connecting rod bearing bore, so that the bearing inserts must be snapped or lightly forced into its seat. A spread of 0.025 in. is normally minimum on most engines, but will vary from engine to engine. (Some bearing kits will have instructions for the proper installation of the inserts.)

To adjust the bearing spread of the thick wall bearings, such

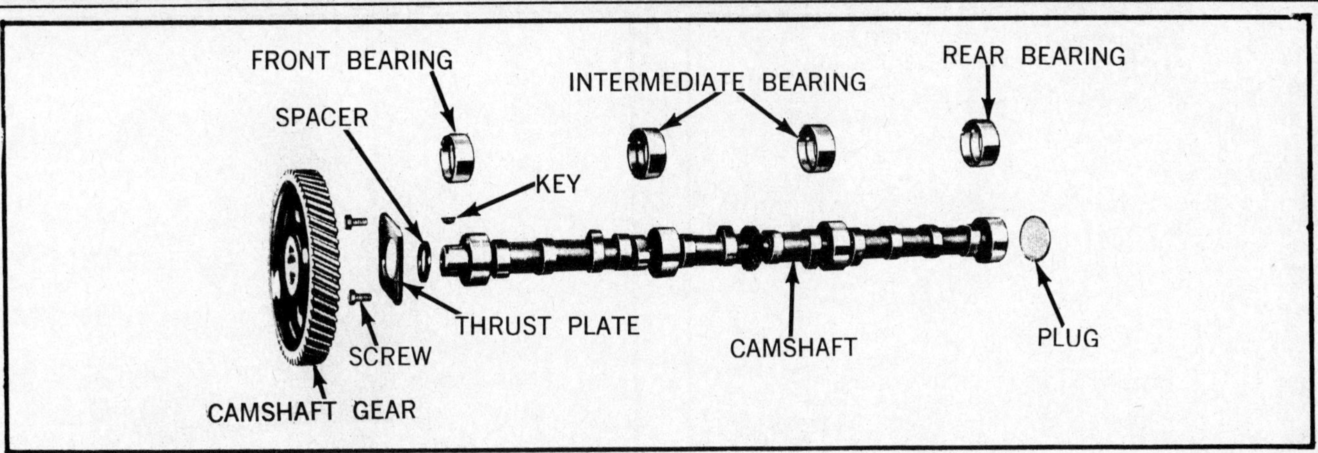

Gear driven camshaft assembly—typical

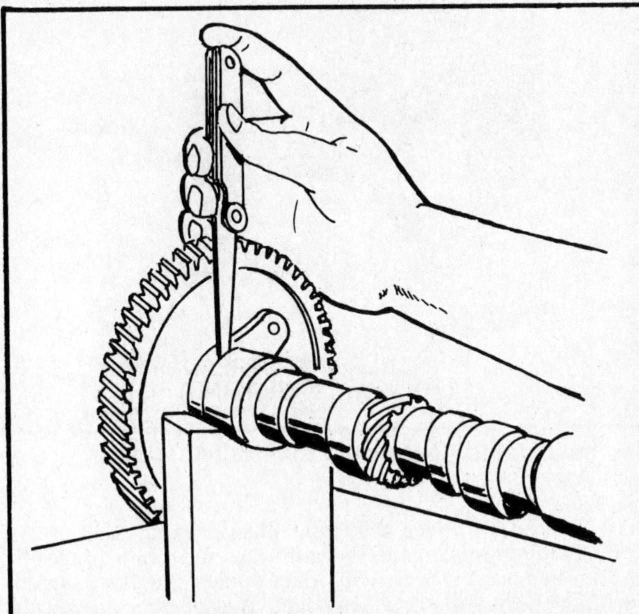

Checking clearance between timing gear and thrust plate with feeler gauge

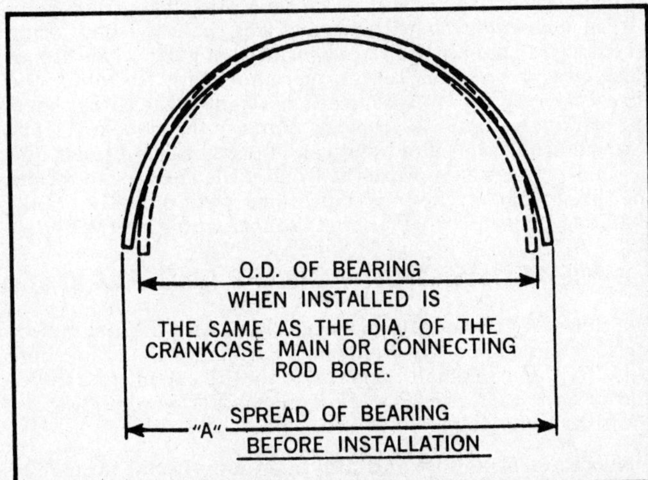

Illustration of bearing insert spread

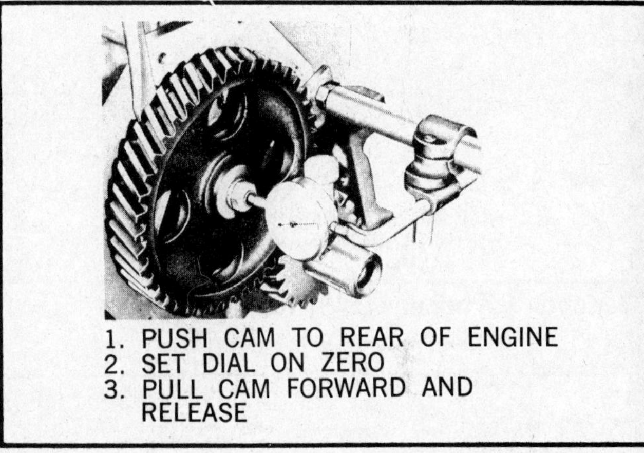

1. PUSH CAM TO REAR OF ENGINE
2. SET DIAL ON ZERO
3. PULL CAM FORWARD AND RELEASE

Checking camshaft end-play with dial indicator

as main bearing inserts, place one end of the bearing insert on a wood block and strike the other end with a soft mallet to decrease the spread. To increase the spread, place the bearing insert ends on a wood block and strike the back of the insert with a soft mallet, squarely and lightly. The bearing spread on the thin walled bearing inserts, such as connecting rod bearing inserts, can be adjusted by hand, either spreading with the thumbs and forefingers of both hands, or by squeezing the bearing insert by the palm of the hand to decrease the spread. Check the spread distance often during the adjustment procedure.

INSTALL THE REAR MAIN SEAL

Position the block with the bearing saddles facing upward. Lay the rear main seal in its groove and press it lightly into its seat. Place a piece of pipe the same diameter as the crankshaft journal into the saddle and firmly seat the seal. Hold the pipe in position and trim the ends of the seal flush if required.

INSTALL THE CRANKSHAFT

Thoroughly clean the main bearing saddles and caps. Place the upper halves of the bearing inserts on the saddles and press into position.

NOTE: Ensure that the oil holes align.

Press the corresponding bearing inserts into the main bearing caps. Lubricate the upper main bearings and lay the crank-

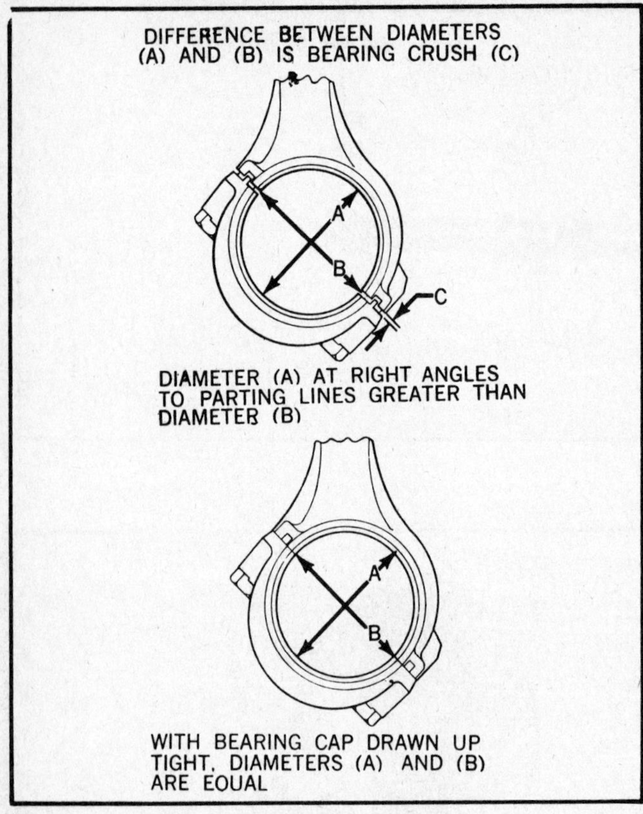

Bearing crush in connecting rod bore

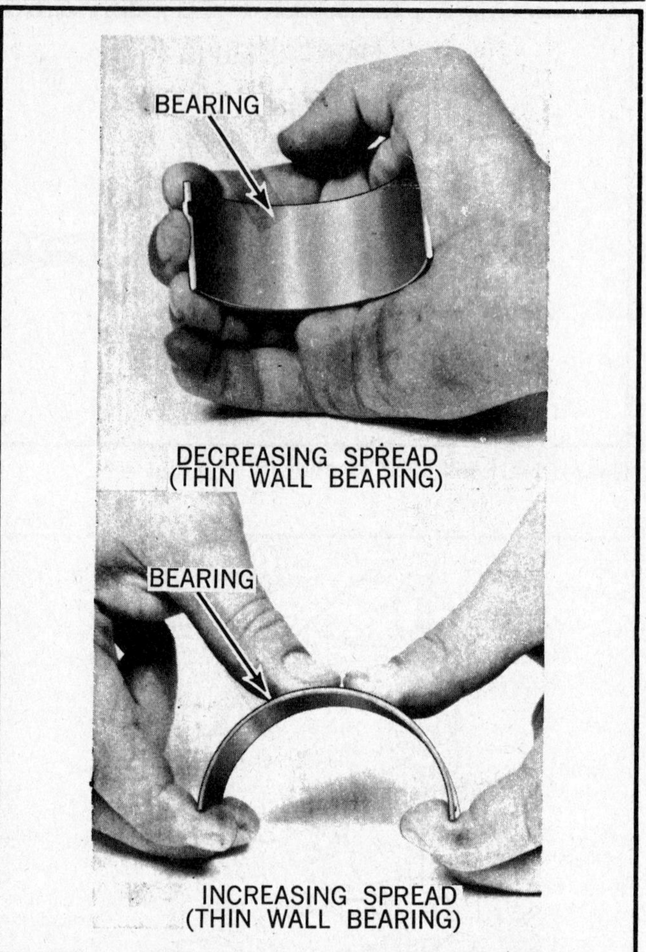

Increasing and decreasing thin-walled spread

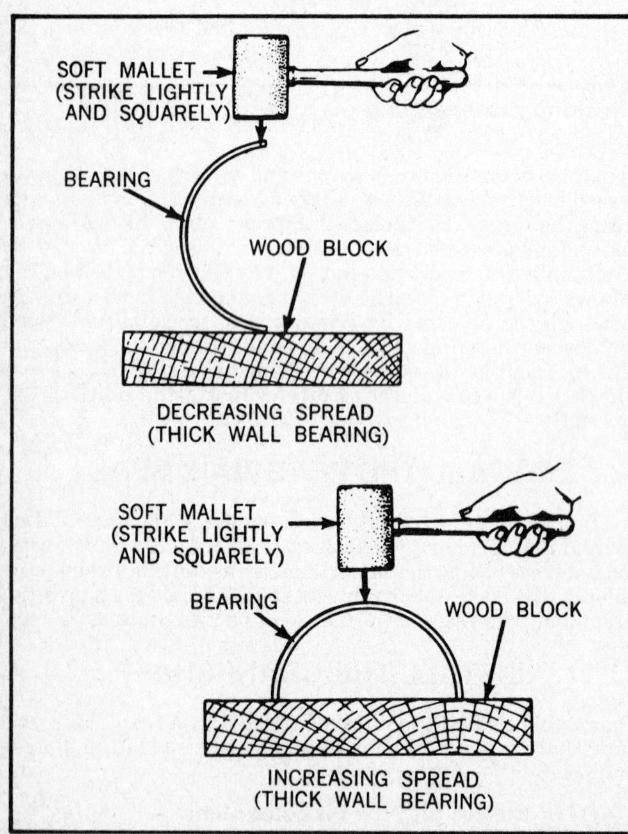

Increasing and decreasing thick-walled bearing spread

shaft in position. Place a strip of Plastigage on each of the crankshaft journals, install the main caps and torque to specifications. Remove the main caps and compare the Plastigage to the scale on the Plastigage envelope. If clearances are within tolerances, remove the Plastigage, turn the crankshaft 90°, wipe off all oil and retest. If all clearances are correct, remove all Plastigage, thoroughly lubricate the main caps and bearing journals and install the main caps.

If clearances are not within tolerance, the upper bearing inserts may be removed, without removing the crankshaft, using a bearing roll out pin. Roll in a bearing that will provide proper clearance and retest. Torque all main caps, excluding the thrust bearing cap, to specifications. Tighten the thrust bearing cap finger tight. To properly align the thrust bearing, pry the crankshaft the extent of its axial travel several times, the last movement held toward the front of the engine and torque the thrust bearing cap to specifications. Determine the crankshaft end-play and bring within tolerance with thrust washers.

MEASURE CRANKSHAFT END-PLAY

Mount a dial indicator stand on the block, with the dial indicator stem resting on the crankshaft parallel to the crankshaft axis. Pry the crankshaft rearward to the full extent of its travel and zero the indicator. Pry the crankshaft forward and record crankshaft end-play.

NOTE: Crankshaft end-play also may be measured at the thrust bearing, using feeler gauges.

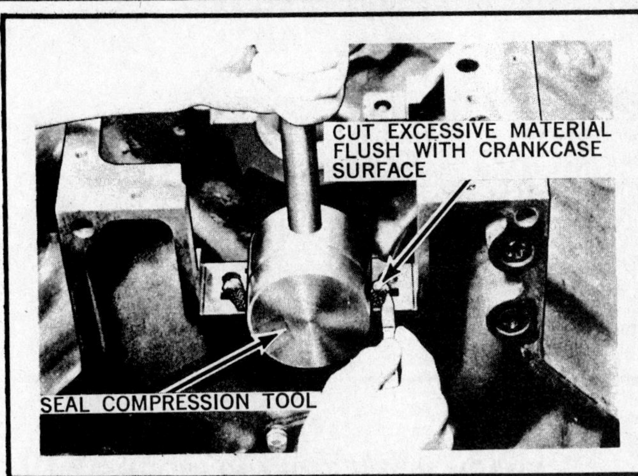

Seating the rear main bearing seal

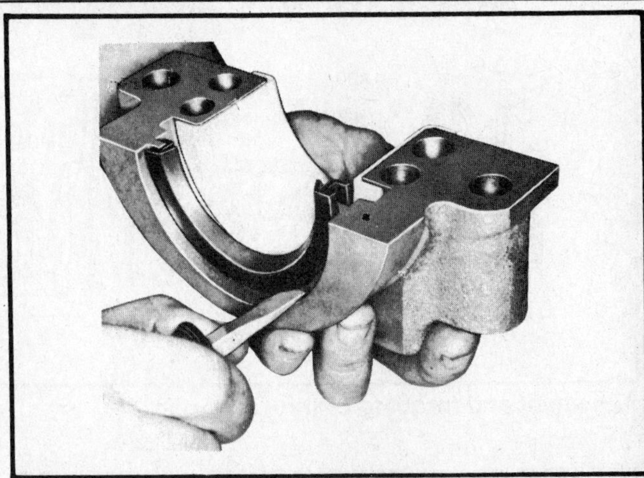

Removing the rear main bearing oil seal from the bearing cap—preformed seal type

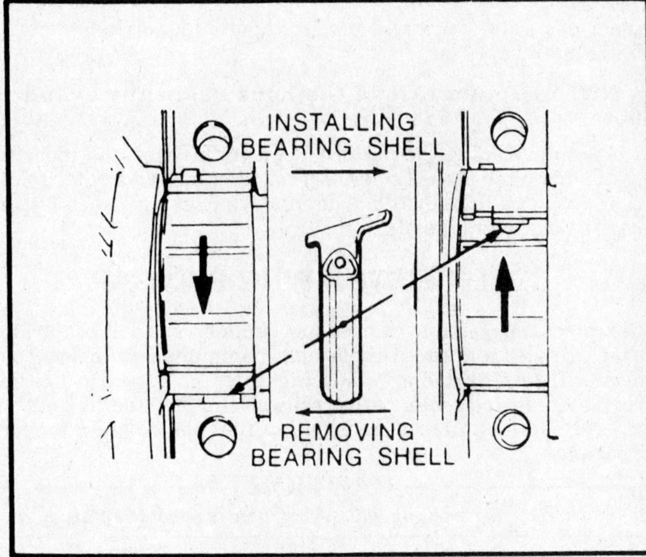

Main bearing insert identification—typical

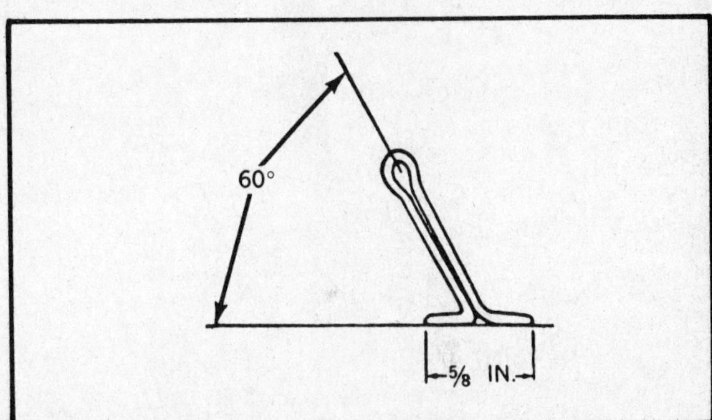

Bearing insert roll-out pin made from cotter pin

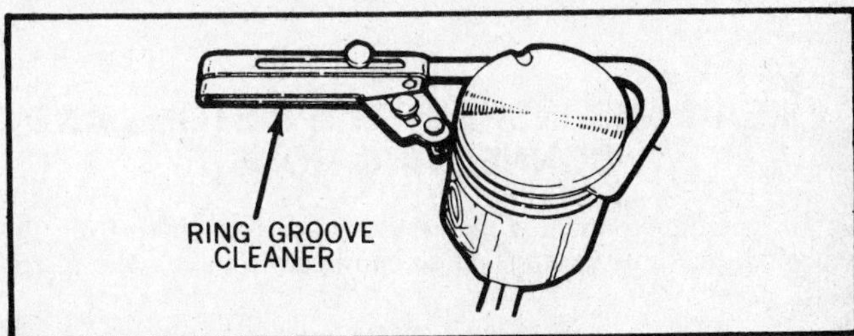

Cleaning piston ring grooves—typical

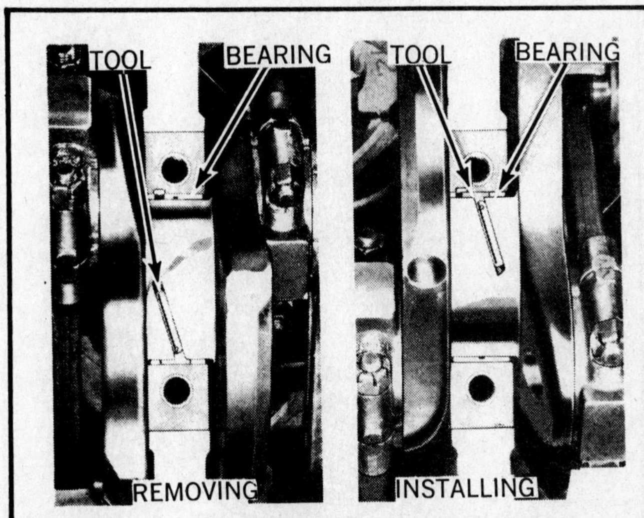

Removing and installing main bearing inserts with roll-out pins (cross section of crankshaft journal)

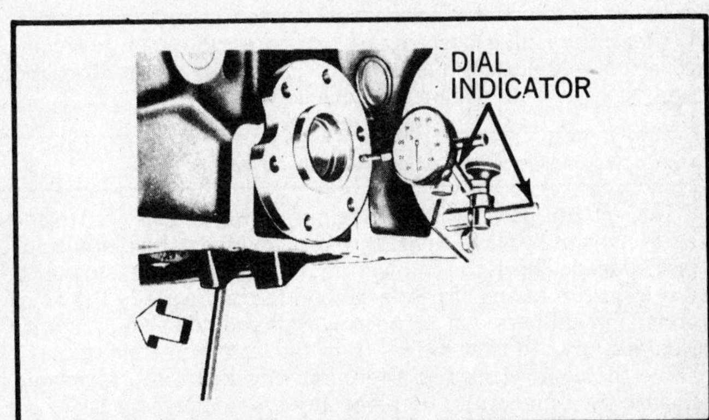

Checking crankshaft end-play—typical

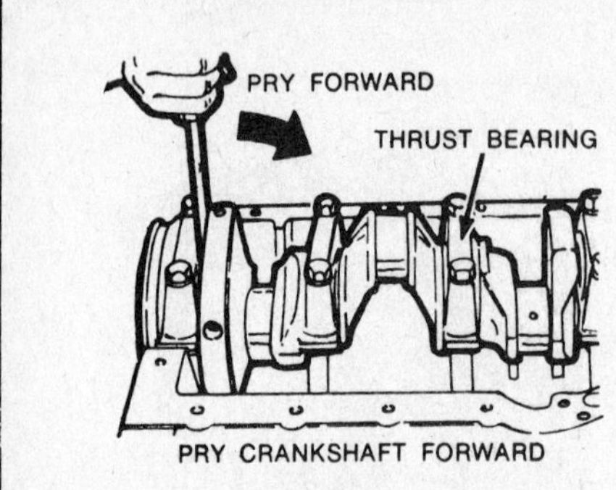

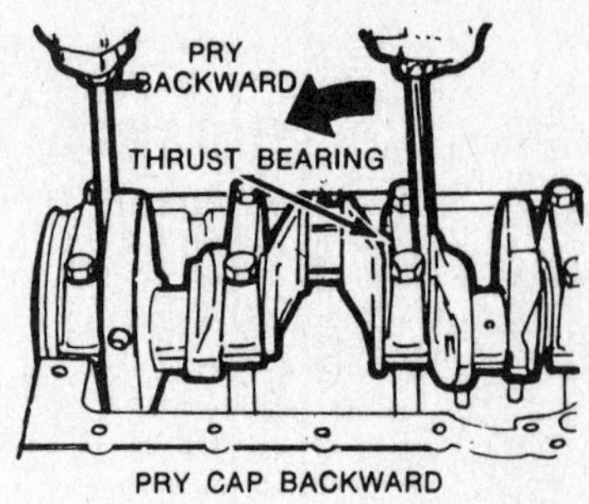

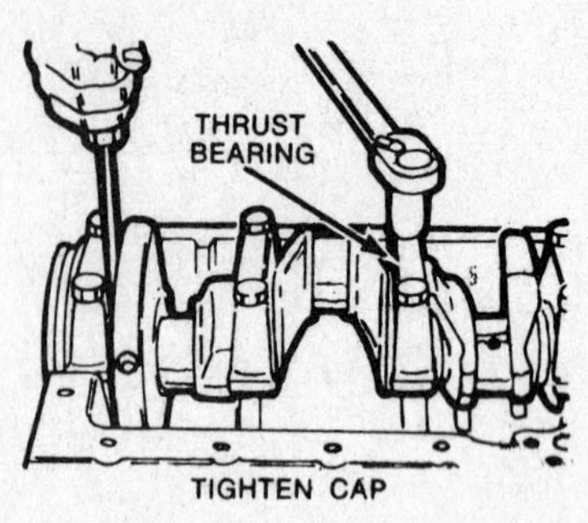

Alignment and torquing of thrust bearing

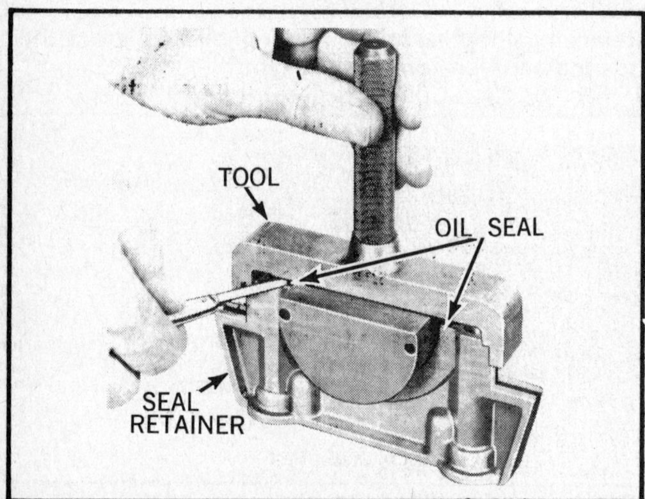

Installing the rear main bearing oil seal in bearing cap

CLEAN AND INSPECT THE PISTONS AND CONNECTING RODS

Using a ring expander, remove the rings from the piston. Remove the retaining rings (if so equipped) and remove piston pin.

CAUTION

If the piston pin must be pressed out, determine the proper method and use the proper tools; otherwise the piston will distort.

Clean the ring grooves using an appropriate tool, exercising care to avoid cutting too deeply. Thoroughly clean all carbon and varnish from the piston with solvent.

CAUTION

Do not use a wire brush or caustic solvent on pistons.

Inspect the pistons for scuffing, scoring, cracks, pitting, or excessive ring groove wear. If wear is evident, the piston must be replaced. Check the connecting rod length by measuring the rod from the inside of the large end to the inside of the small end using calipers. All connecting rods should be equal length. Replace any rod that differs from the others in the engine. Have the connecting rod alignment checked in an alignment fixture by a machinist. Replace any twisted or bent rods.

Magnaflux the connecting rods to locate stress cracks. If cracks are found, replace the connecting rod.

FINISH HONE THE CYLINDERS

Chuck a flexible drive hone into a power drill and insert it into the cylinder. Start the hone and move it up and down in the cylinder at a rate which will produce approximately a 60° cross-hatch pattern.

NOTE: Do not extend the hone below the cylinder bore.

After developing the pattern, remove the hone and recheck piston fit. Wash the cylinders with a detergent and water solution to remove abrasive dust, dry and wipe several times with a rag soaked in engine oil.

CHECK PISTON RING END-GAP

Compress the piston to be used in a cylinder, one at a time, into that cylinder and press them approximately 1 in. below the deck with an inverted piston. Using feeler gauges, measure the ring end-gap and compare to specifications. Pull the ring out of the cylinder and file the ends with a fine file to obtain proper clearance.

CAUTION

If inadequate ring end-gap exists, ring breakage could result.

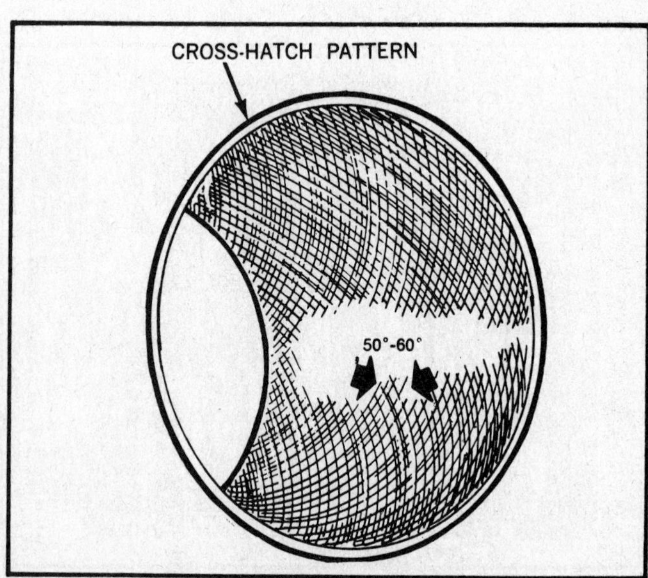

Cross hatching of cylinder bore by finish honing

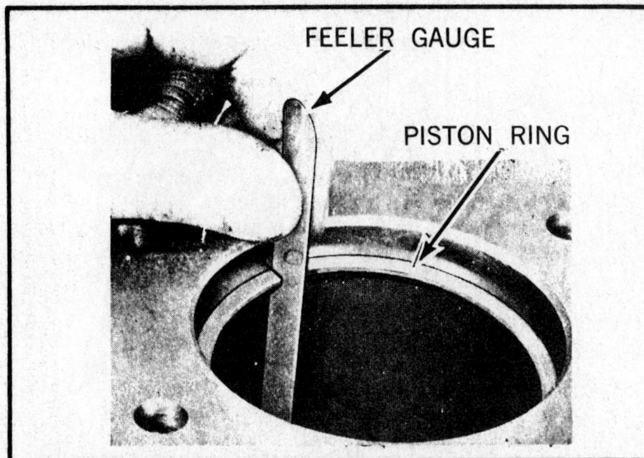

Checking ring gap in cylinder bore

FIT THE PISTONS TO THE CYLINDERS

Using a telescope gauge and micrometer, or a dial gauge, measure the cylinder bore diameter perpendicular to the piston pin, 2 ½ in. below the deck. Measure the piston perpendicular to its pin on the skirt. The difference between the two measurements is the piston clearance. If the clearance is within specifications or slightly below (after boring or honing), finish honing is all that is required. If the clearance is excessive, try to obtain a slightly larger piston to bring clearance within specifications. Where this is not possible, obtain the first oversize piston and hone (or if necessary, bore) the cylinder to size.

ASSEMBLE THE PISTONS AND CONNECTING RODS

Inspect piston pin, connecting rod, small end bushing and piston bore for galling, scoring or excessive wear. If evident, replace defective part(s). Measure the I.D. of the piston boss and connecting rod small end and the O.D. of the piston pin. If within specifications, assemble piston pin and rod.

CAUTION

CAUTION: If piston pin must be pressed in, determine the proper method and use the proper tools; otherwise the piston will distort.

Install the lock rings; ensure that they seat properly. If the parts are not within specifications, determine the service method for the type of engine. In some cases, piston and pin are serviced as an assembly when either is defective. Others specify reaming the piston and connecting rods for an oversize pin. If the connecting rod bushing is worn, it may in many cases be replaced. Reaming the piston and replacing the rod bushing are machine shop operations.

INSTALL THE PISTON RINGS

Inspect the ring grooves in the piston for excessive wear or taper. If necessary, recut the groove(s) for use with an overwidth ring or a standard ring and spacer. If the groove is worn uniformly, overwidth rings or standard rings and spacers may be installed without recutting. Roll the outside of the ring around the groove to check for burrs or deposits. If any are found, remove with a fine file. Hold the ring in the groove and measure side clearance. If necessary, correct as indicated above.

NOTE: Always install any additional spacers above the piston ring.

The ring grooves must be deep enough to allow the ring to seat below the lands. In many cases, a "go-no-go" depth gauge will be provided with the piston rings. Shallow grooves may be corrected by recutting, while deep grooves require some type of filler or expander behind the piston. Consult the piston ring supplier concerning the suggested method. Install the rings on the piston, lowest ring first, using a ring expander.

NOTE: Position the ring markings as specified by the manufacturer.

INSTALL THE PISTONS

Press the upper connecting rod bearing halves into the connecting rods and the lower halves into the connecting rod caps. Position the piston ring gaps according to specifications and lubricate the pistons. Install a ring compressor on the piston and press two long (8 in.) pieces of plastic tubing over the rod bolts. Using the plastic tubes as a guide, press the piston into the bore and onto the crankshaft with a wooden hammer handle. After seating the rod on the crankshaft journal, remove the tubes and install the cap nuts finger tight. Install the remain-

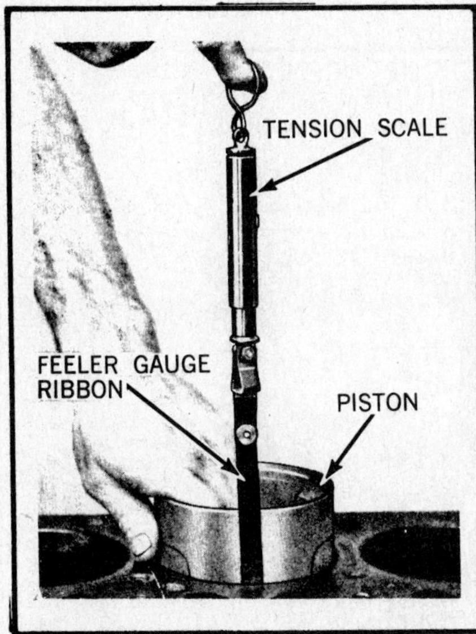

Checking piston to cylinder bore clearance

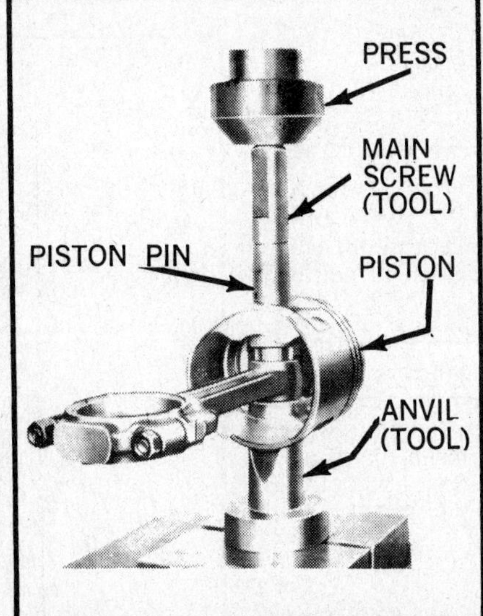

Removing or installing piston pin

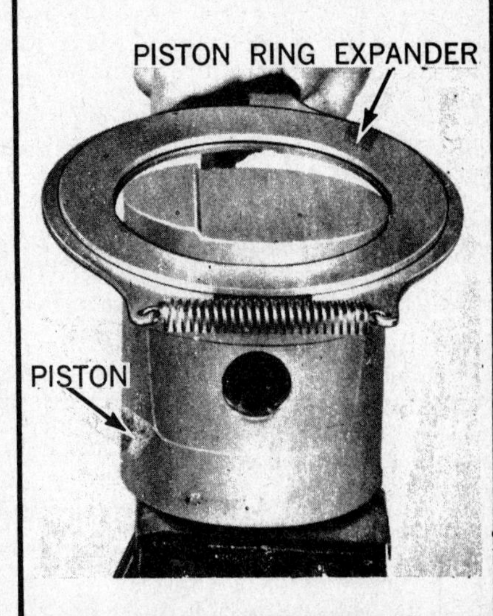

Installing rings on piston with the use of an expander tool

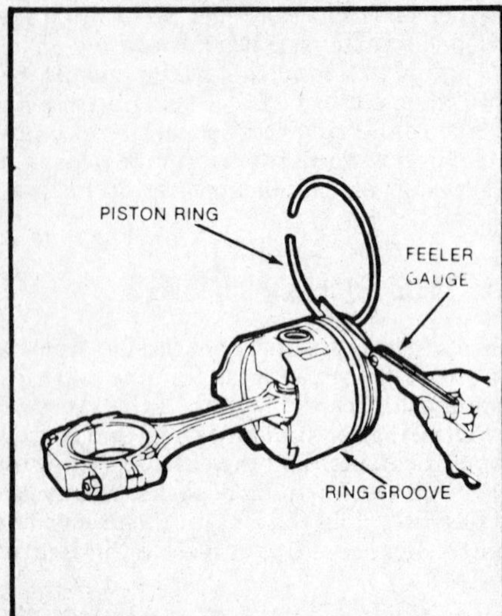

Checking ring to groove side clearance

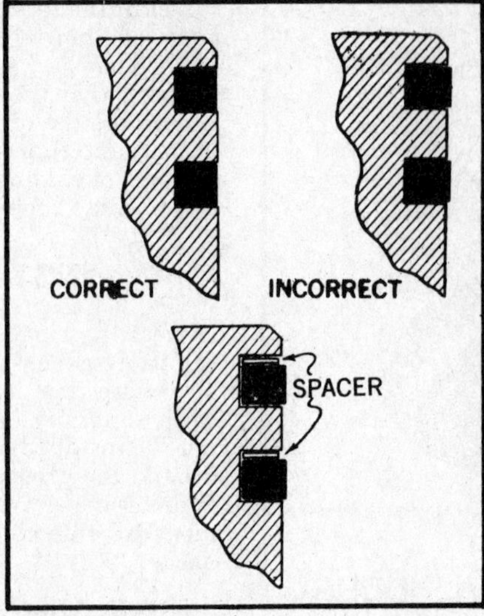

Correct ring spacer installation

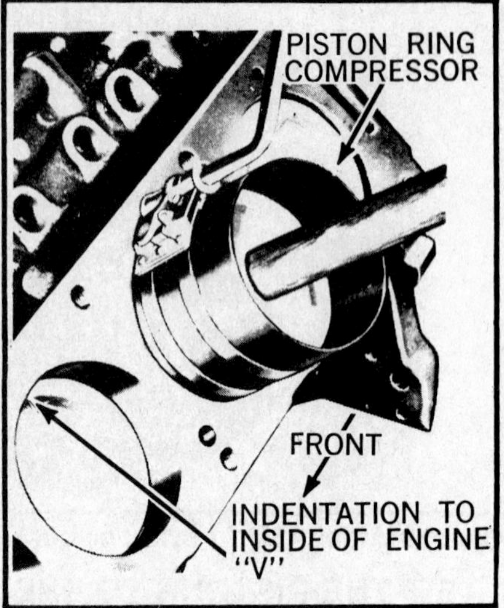

Installing piston assembly with straight sided ring compressor tool

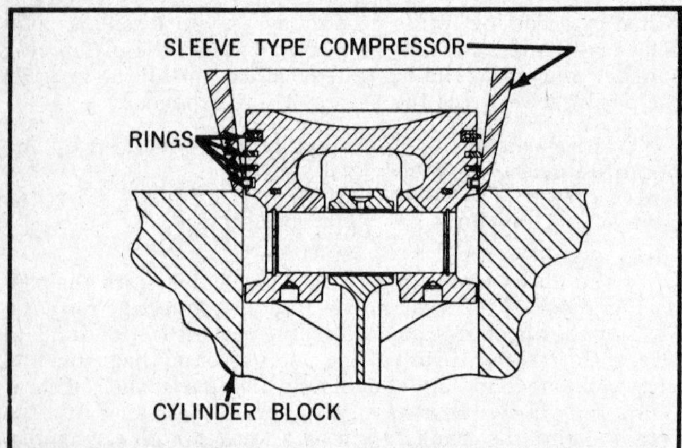

Installing piston assembly with a tapered sleeve type ring compressor tool

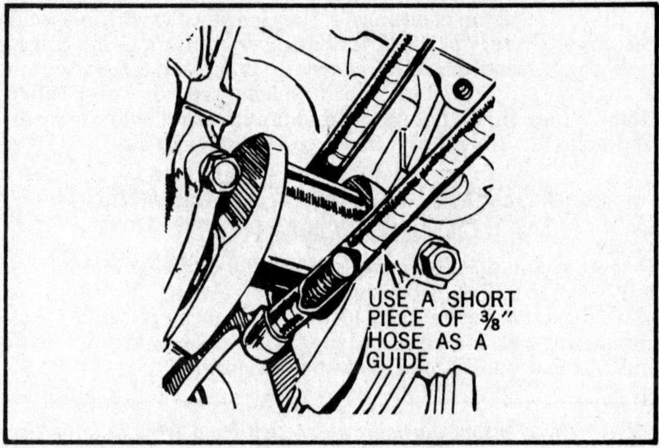

Tubing used as a guide during piston-connecting rod installation

ing pistons in the same manner. Invert the engine and check the bearing clearance at two points (90° apart) on each journal with Plastigage.

NOTE: Do not turn the crankshaft with Plastigage installed.

If clearance is within tolerances, remove all Plastigage, thoroughly lubricate the journals and torque the rod caps to specifications. If clearance is not within specifications, install different thickness bearing inserts and recheck.

CAUTION

Never shim or file the connecting rods or caps.

Always install plastic tube sleeves over the rod bolts when the caps are not installed, to protect the crankshaft journals.

CHECK CONNECTING ROD SIDE CLEARANCE

Determine the clearance between the sides of the connecting rods and the crankshaft, using feeler gauges. If clearance is below the minimum tolerance, the rod may be machined to pro-

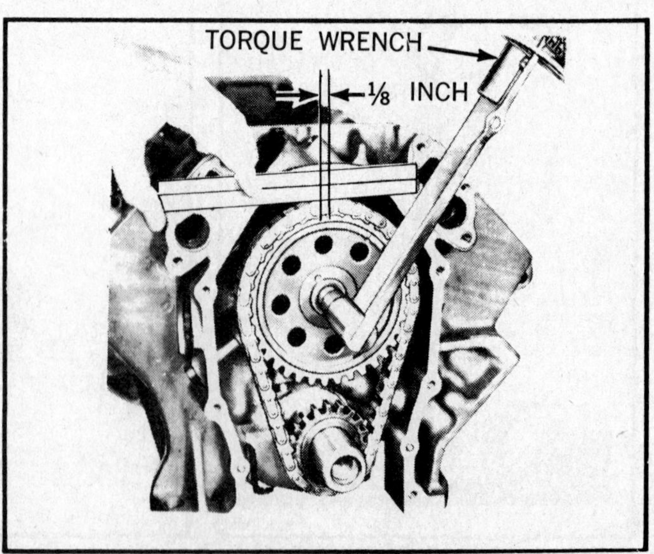

Using torque wrench to measure timing chain deflection

vide adequate clearance. If clearance is excessive, substitute an unworn rod and recheck. If clearance is still outside specifications, the crankshaft must be welded and reground, or replaced.

INSPECT THE TIMING CHAIN

Visually inspect the timing chain for broken or loose links and replace the chain if any are found. If the chain will flex sideways, it must be replaced.

NOTE: If the original timing chain is to be reused, install it in its original position.

INSPECT THE TIMING CHAIN DEFLECTION

Different methods are used by the engine manufacturers to measure the timing chain deflection and to determine the condition of the chain. Three such methods are as follows:

1. Rotate the crankshaft in a counterclockwise direction to remove the slack on the left side of the chain. Make a reference mark on the block and measure from the mark to the outside of the chain, halfway between the camshaft and crankshaft sprockets. Rotate the crankshaft in the opposite direction and remove the slack from the right side of the chain. Force the chain outward on the left side and measure from the original reference mark to the chain. The difference between the first and second measurements is the amount of chain deflection. The allowable deflection can be from $\frac{1}{4}$–$\frac{1}{2}$ in., depending upon the manufacturer.
2. The second method of chain deflection measurement is to block the crankshaft to prevent movement. Using a torque wrench and socket on the camshaft sprocket bolt and placing a scale even with the edge of a chain link, apply 30 ft. lbs. (w/cylinder head on block) or 15 ft. lbs. (w/cylinder head off block) in the direction of engine rotation and obtain a reference point on the scale to link. Apply 30 ft. lbs. (w/cylinder head on block) or 15 ft. lbs. (w/cylinder head off block) in the opposite direction and measure the chain movement on the scale. The measurement should not exceed $\frac{1}{8}$ in.
3. A third method of measuring timing chain deflection is to rotate the crankshaft clockwise until the No. 1 piston is on its firing stroke at TDC. The damper timing mark should point to TDC on the timing degree indicator. Remove the valve cover to expose the rocker arms of the companion or opposite cylinder to the No. 1 piston. Install a dial indicator on the push rod or rocker arm of the exhaust valve of this opposite or companion cylinder in a manner to register the push rod or rocker arm upward movement. Zero the dial indicator and slowly turn the crankshaft counterclockwise until the slightest movement is recorded on the dial indicator. Stop and observe the damper timing mark for the number of degrees of travel from TDC. If the reading on the timing degree indicator exceeds 6–8 degrees, replace the timing chain and sprockets.

OVERHEAD CAM TIMING CHAINS

Timing chains for the overhead cam engines are difficult to examine for looseness due to the chain tensioners used to maintain a controlled tension on the chain while in use. The chains are usually checked off the engine by measurement of a predetermined number of links with the chain stretched tight. Should the measurement of the links exceed the manufacturer's specifications, the chain should be replaced.

Another method is to wrap the chain around the sprockets and measure each chain/sprocket diameter. Should the manufacturer's specifications be exceeded, the chain and sprocket should be replaced. Where no specifications exist, the repairperson must make a professional determination to either replace the chain and sprockets or not.

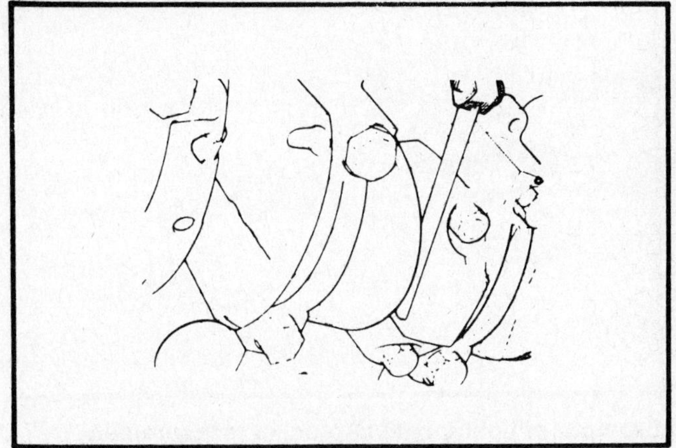

Checking connecting rod end clearance with feeler gauge blade

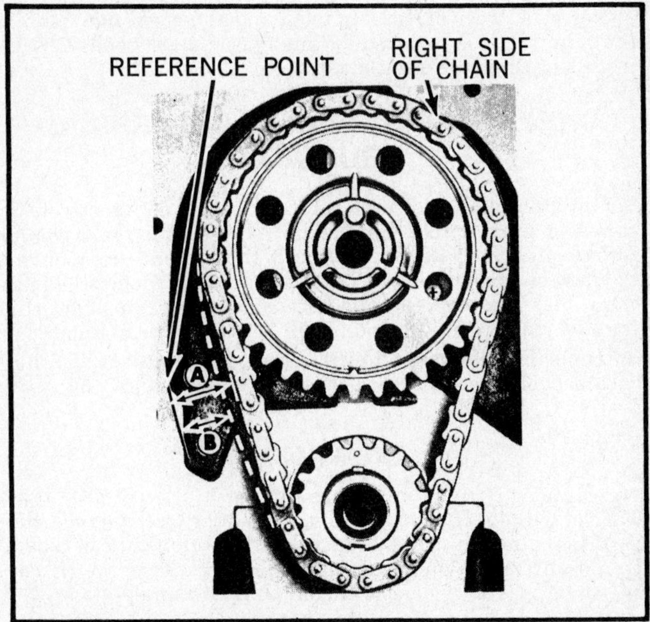

Checking timing chain deflection using point on engine blocks as reference point

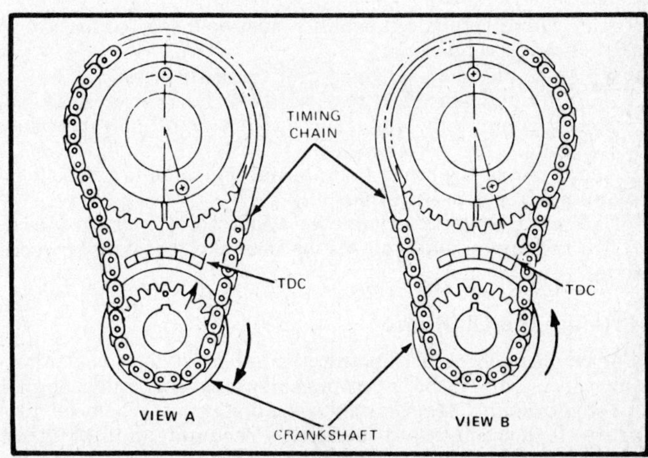

Checking timing chain deflection with timing indicator scale

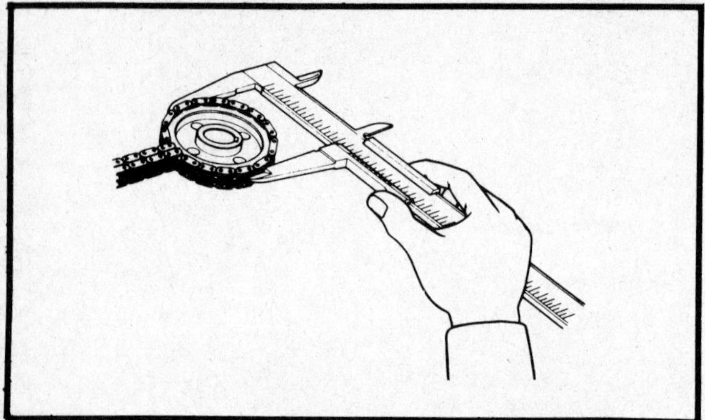

Example of timing chain/sprocket measurement

TIMING BELT INSPECTION

The timing belt should be inspected for hardness, separation of plys, cracks, worn or missing teeth and abnormal side wear. If the timing belt is removed for any reason, a new belt must be installed. Do not re-use the old belt.

CHECK TIMING GEAR BACKLASH AND RUNOUT

Mount a dial indicator with its stem resting on a tooth of the camshaft gear. Rotate the gear until all slack is removed and zero the indicator. Rotate the gear in the opposite direction until slack is removed and record gear backlash. Mount the indicator with its stem resting on the edge of the camshaft gear, parallel to the axis of the camshaft. Zero the indicator and turn the camshaft gear one full turn, recording the runout. If either backlash or runout exceed specifications, replace the worn gear(s).

OIL PUMP

Three major types of oil pumps are used, positive gear type (with or without crescent), rotor type and the trochoid type. Regardless of the type pump used, a determination must be made, by measurements and examination, in regards to the re-use, overhaul or replacement of the oil pump assembly.

NOTE: It is recommended to replace the oil pump assembly with a new unit when a major engine overhaul is done.

Inspection

The oil pump and its components must be inspected for any of the following conditions.

1. Worn, pitted or damaged gear teeth surfaces.
2. Abnormal gear side wear, scores or burrs.
3. Oil pump body and gear pockets for abnormal wear, scores, burrs, grooves or nicks.
4. Correct measurement of internal components and body to manufacturer's specifications.
5. Pressure regulator valve for wear, scores, nicks or burrs.
6. Pressure regulator spring for distortion, breakage, correct length and tension.

Priming the Oil Pump

Before the engine start-up, the oil pump must be primed. Manufacturers vary in their recommendations with either engine oil or petroleum jelly used as the priming agent. Whenever possible, follow the manufacturer's recommended priming procedure.

Completing the Rebuilding Process

Following the above procedures, complete the rebuilding process as follows:

Fill the oil pump with oil, or petroleum jelly, to prevent cavitating (sucking air) on initial engine start up. Install the oil pump and the pickup tube on the engine. Coat the oil pan gasket as necessary and install the gasket and the oil pan. Mount the flywheel and the crankshaft vibrational damper or pulley on the crankshaft.

NOTE: Always use new bolts when installing the flywheel.

Inspect the clutch shaft pilot bushing in the crankshaft. If the bushing is excessively worn, remove it with an expanding puller and a slide hammer and tap a new bushing into place.

Position the engine, cylinder head side up. Lubricate the lifters and install them into their bores. Install the cylinder head and torque it as specified in the car section. Insert the pushrods (where applicable) and install the rocker shaft(s) (if so equipped) or position the rocker arms on the pushrods. If solid lifters are utilized, adjust the valves to the "cold" specifications.

Mount the intake and exhaust manifolds, the carburetor(s), the distributor and spark plugs. Adjust the point gap and the static ignition timing. Mount all accessories and install the engine in the car. Fill the radiator with coolant and the crankcase with high quality engine oil.

BREAK-IN PROCEDURE

Before starting the engine, be sure all coolant hoses are attached and tight, the coolant level is correct, a new oil filter is installed and the crankcase filled with the proper level of oil.

The oil pump should be primed and if possible, the engine lubrication system should be charged with a pressure tank. Adjust the tappets (if required), the timing and carburetor as accurately as possible.

Start the engine and adjust the throttle to an approximate engine speed of 1000 to 2000 rpm, until the engine reaches normal operating temperature, normally within 20–30 minutes.

CAUTION

Do not leave the vehicle unattended during the warm-up period. Observe the engine operation and check for any oil or coolant leaks. Stop the engine immediately if a problem exists, to avoid engine damage.

After the engine has "run-in", lower the idle speed and stop the engine. Retorque the cylinder head bolts as required.

NOTE: Engines with aluminum heads or blocks must be allowed to cool to room temperature before any bolts are retorqued.

After rechecking the coolant and oil levels, make any further adjustments as necessary.

Follow the manufacturer's recommended driving break-in procedure or as a general rule, the following procedures may be used.

Drive the vehicle on the highway and accelerate from 30–50 mph, approximately 10–15 times, traffic flow permitting, to properly seat the piston rings to the cylinder walls. If traffic flow does not permit this procedure, accelerate the engine rapidly during shifting through the intermediate gears. The vehicle should be put in light duty service for the first 50 miles and sustained high speed should be avoided during the first 100 miles. Most important: Do not lug the engine. (Lugging exists when the engine does not respond to further opening of the throttle.)

Carburetor Service
Domestic Trucks

INDEX

CARBURETOR IDENTIFICATION

All carburetors are identified by code numbers, either stamped on the attaching flange side, the main body or on a metal tag retained by a bowl cover screw. This identification number is important in order to obtain the correct carburetor replacement or parts and to properly adjust the carburetor when matched to a specific engine.

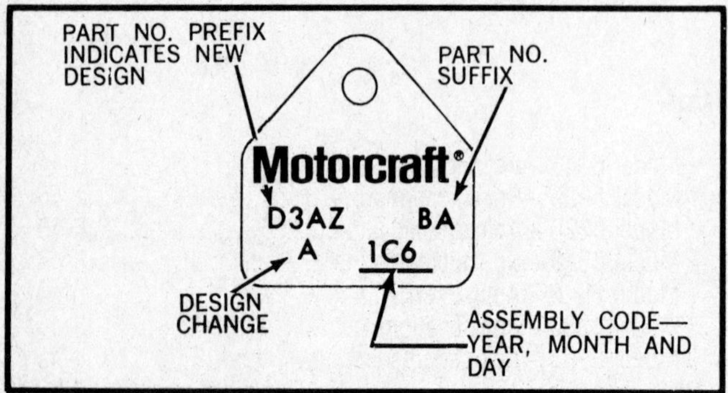

Motorcraft carburetors for Ford usage—typical

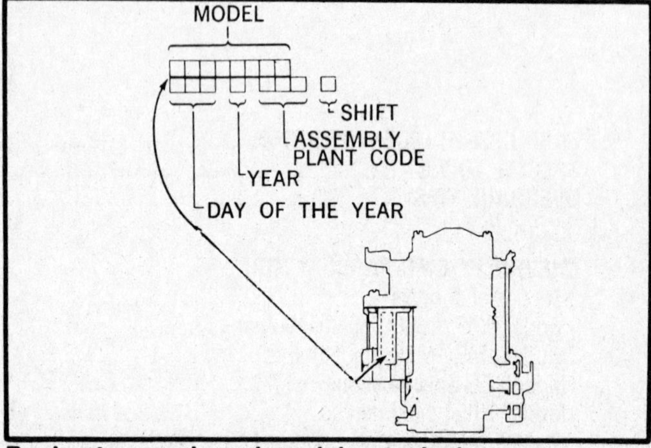

Rochester one barrel models—typical

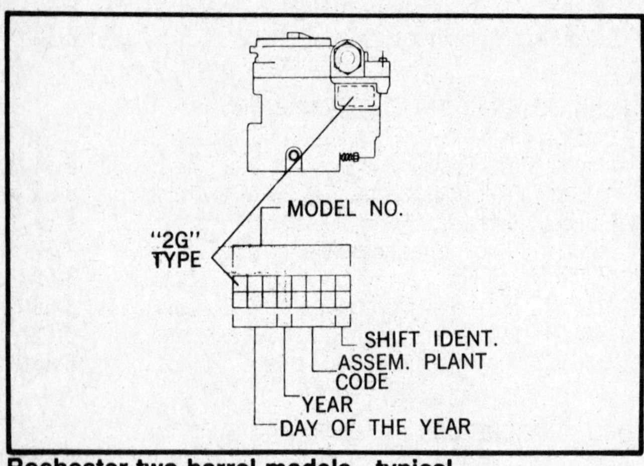

Rochester two barrel models—typical

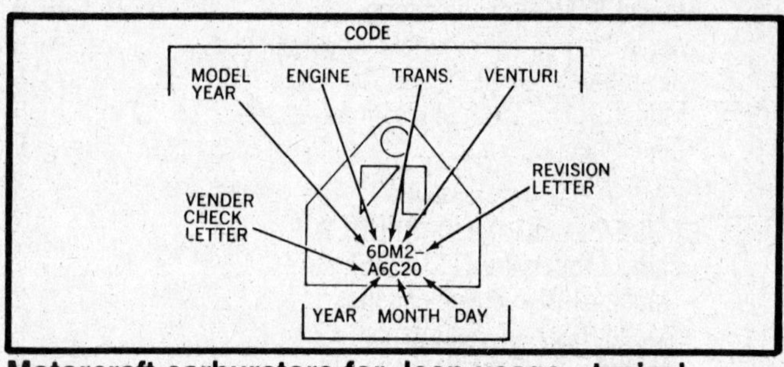

Motorcraft carburetors for Jeep usage—typical

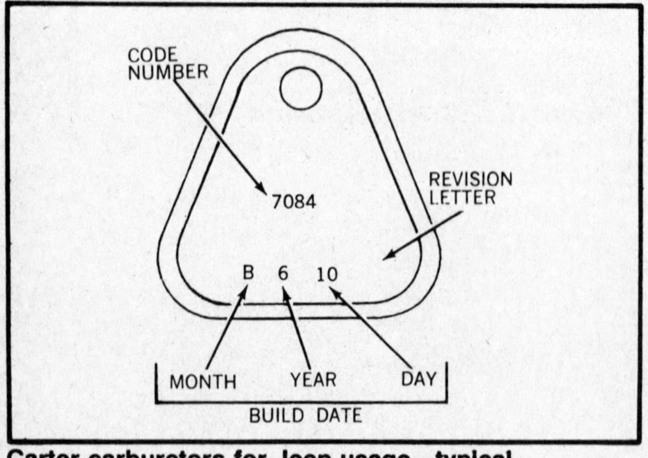

Carter carburetors for Jeep usage—typical

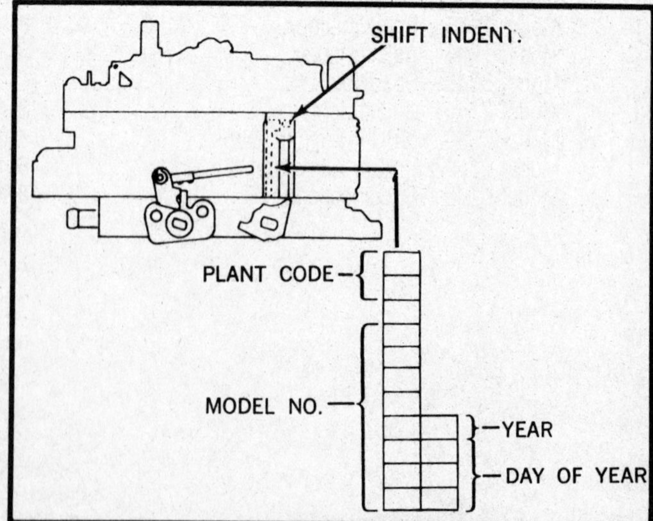

Rochester four barrel models—typical

SPECIAL TOOLS

An angle degree tool is recommended by Rochester Products Division for use to confirm adjustments to the choke valve and related linkages on late model two and four barrel carburetors in place of the plug type gauges. Decimal and degree conversion charts are provided for use with the angle degree tool. To use the angle gauge, rotate the degree scale until zero (0) is opposite the pointer. With the choke valve completely closed, place the gauge magnet squarely on top of the choke valve and rotate the bubble until it is centered. Make the necessary adjustments to have the choke valve at the specified degree angle opening as read from the degree angle tool. The carburetor may be off the engine for adjustments, but make sure the carburetor is held firmly during the use of the angle gauge.

A variety of other special adjustment tools may be necessary during the overhaul of different carburetors covered in this section. When required, the tools are illustrated and tool numbers given for reference. Most carburetor overhaul kits contain the float level gauges and specifications necessary for complete rebuilding, and if specifications differ from those given in the following charts, use the values listed in the overhaul instructions with a specific kit. Before beginning any overhaul procedures, read through each section to make sure all required special tools are on hand in order to complete the repair.

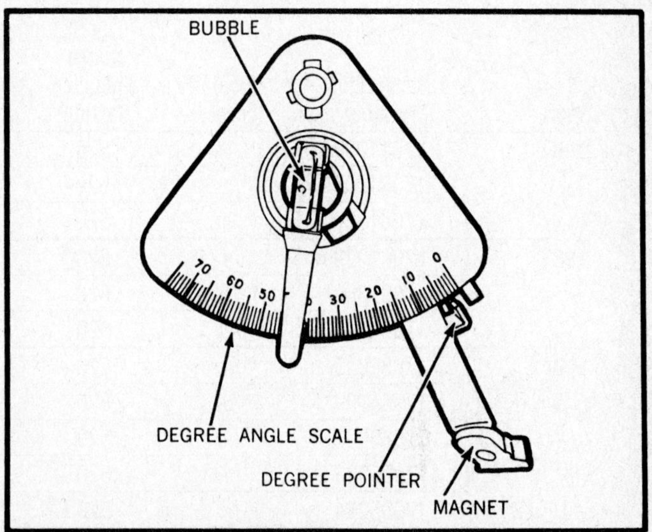

Degree angle tool-typical

Carburetor Overhaul Tips

When the carburetor is disassembled, wash all parts (except diaphragms, electric choke units, pump plunger, and any other plastic, leather, fiber, or rubber parts) in clean carburetor solvent. Do not leave parts in the solvent any longer than is necessary to sufficiently loosen the deposits. Excessive cleaning may remove the special finish from the float bowl and choke valve bodies, leaving these parts unfit for service. Rinse all parts in clean solvent and blow them dry with compressed air or allow them to air dry. Wipe clean all cork, plastic, leather, and fiber parts with a clean, lint-free cloth.

Blow out all passages and jets with compressed air and be sure that there are no restrictions or blockages. Never use wire or similar tools to clean jets, fuel passages, or air bleeds. Clean all jets and valves separately to avoid accidental interchange. Check all parts for wear or damage. If wear or damage is found, replace the defective parts. Especially check the following:

1. Check the float needle and seat for wear. If wear is found, replace the complete assembly.
2. Check the float hinge pin for wear and the float(s) for dents or distortion. Replace the float if fuel has leaked into it.
3. Check the throttle and choke shaft bores for wear or an out-of-round condition. Damage or wear to the throttle arm, shaft, or shaft bore will often require replacement of the throttle body. These parts require a close tolerance of fit. Wear may allow air leakage, which could affect starting and idling.

NOTE: Throttle shafts and bushings are not included in overhaul kits. They can be purchased separately.

4. Inspect the idle mixture adjusting needles for burrs or grooves. Any such condition requires replacement of the needle, since you will not be able to obtain a satisfactory idle.
5. Test the accelerator pump check valves. They should pass air one way but not the other. Test for proper seating by blowing and sucking on the valve. Replace the valve if necessary. If the valve is satisfactory, wash the valve again to remove breath moisture.
6. Check the bowl cover for warped surfaces with a straight edge.
7. Closely inspect the valves and seats for wear and damage, replacing as necessary.
8. After the carburetor is assembled, check the choke valve for freedom of operation.

Carburetor overhaul kits are recommended for each overhaul. These kits contain all gaskets and new parts to replace those that deteriorate most rapidly. Failure to replace all parts supplied with the kit (especially gaskets) can result in poor performance later.

After cleaning and checking all components, reassemble the carburetor, using new parts and referring to the exploded view. When reassembling, make sure that all screws and jets are tight in their seats, but do not overtighten as the tips will be distorted. Tighten all screws gradually, in rotation. Do not tighten needle valves into their seats. Uneven jetting will result. Always use new gaskets. Be sure to adjust the float level, following the instructions contained in the rebuilding kit, when reassembling.

CHEVROLET/GMC CARBURETORS

Rochester Models

Note:Refer to the individual truck section for idle speed and idle mixture adjustments, using the propane enrichment procedure on non-electronic controlled engine carburetors and with the use of a dwellmeter on the electronic controlled carburetor equipped engines.

ROCHESTER MODEL 1ME/1MEF

(All measurements in inches)

Year	Carburetor Number	Float Level	Choke Unloader Setting	Choke Setting	Fast Idle Speed (rpm)	Metering Rod Setting	Fast Idle Cam 2nd Step	Choke Vacuum Break
1982	17081009	11/32	.520	①	②	.090	.275	.400
	17081309	11/32	.520	①	②	.090	.275	.400
	17081329	11/32	.520	①	②	.090	.275	.400
1983	17081009	11/32	.520	①	②	.090	.275	.400
	17081309	11/32	.520	①	②	.090	.275	.400
	17081329	11/32	.520	①	②	.090	.275	.400
1984	17081009	11/32	.520	①	②	.090	.275	.400
	17084329	11/32	.520	①	②	.090	.275	.400
	17085009	11/32	.520	①	②	.090	.275	.400
	17085036	11/32	.520	①	②	.090	.275	.400
	17085044	11/32	.520	①	②	.090	.275	.400
	17085045	11/32	.520	①	②	.090	.275	.400
	17086096	11/32	.520	①	②	.090	.275	.400
	17086101	11/32	.520	①	②	.090	.275	.200
	17086102	11/32	.520	①	②	.090	.275	.200
1985	17081009	11/32	.520	①	②	.090	.275	.400
	17084329	11/32	.520	①	②	.090	.275	.400
	17085009	11/32	.520	①	②	.090	.275	.400
	17085036	11/32	.520	①	②	.090	.275	.400
	17085044	11/32	.520	①	②	.090	.275	.400
	17085045	11/32	.520	①	②	.090	.275	.400
	17086096	11/32	.520	①	②	.090	.275	.400
	17086101	11/32	.520	①	②	.090	.275	.200
	17086102	11/32	.520	①	②	.090	.275	.200
1986	17081009	11/32	.520	①	②	.090	.275	.400
	17084329	11/32	.520	①	②	.090	.275	.400
	17085009	11/32	.520	①	②	.090	.275	.400
	17085036	11/32	.520	①	②	.090	.275	.400
	17085044	11/32	.520	①	②	.090	.275	.400
	17085045	11/32	.520	①	②	.090	.275	.400
	17086096	11/32	.520	①	②	.090	.275	.400
	17086101	11/32	.520	①	②	.090	.275	.200
	17086102	11/32	.520	①	②	.090	.275	.200
1987-88	17081009	11/32	.520	①	②	.090	.275	.400
	17084329	11/32	.520	①	②	.090	.275	.400
	17085009	11/32	.520	①	②	.090	.275	.400
	17085036	11/32	.520	①	②	.090	.275	.400
	17085044	11/32	.520	①	②	.090	.275	.400
	17085045	11/32	.520	①	②	.090	.275	.400
	17086096	11/32	.520	①	②	.090	.275	.400
	17086101	11/32	.520	①	②	.090	.275	.200
	17086102	11/32	.520	①	②	.090	.275	.200

① Not adjustable ② See emission label under hood

MODEL 1ME/1MEF

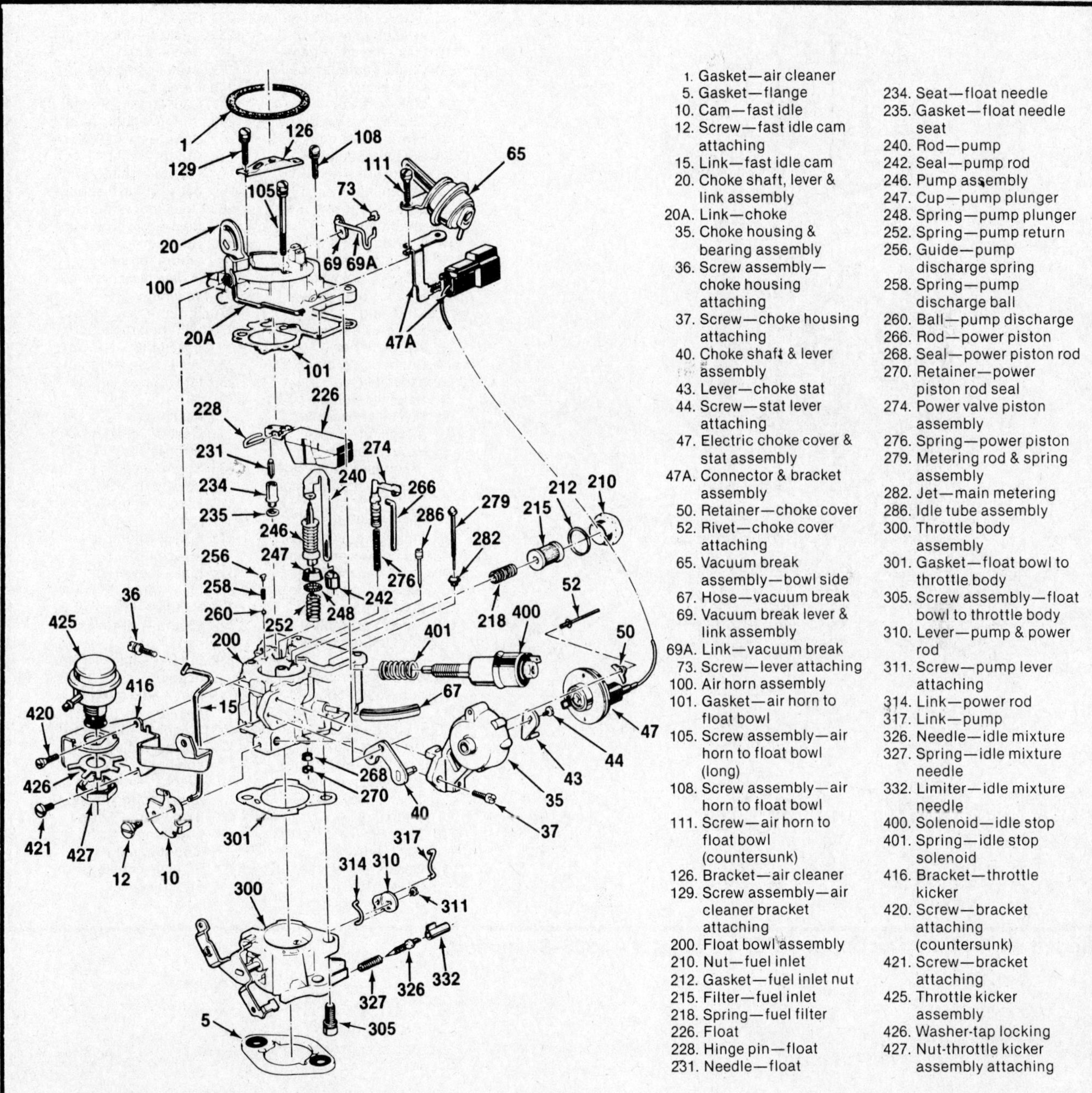
1. Gasket—air cleaner
5. Gasket—flange
10. Cam—fast idle
12. Screw—fast idle cam attaching
15. Link—fast idle cam
20. Choke shaft, lever & link assembly
20A. Link—choke
35. Choke housing & bearing assembly
36. Screw assembly—choke housing attaching
37. Screw—choke housing attaching
40. Choke shaft & lever assembly
43. Lever—choke stat
44. Screw—stat lever attaching
47. Electric choke cover & stat assembly
47A. Connector & bracket assembly
50. Retainer—choke cover
52. Rivet—choke cover attaching
65. Vacuum break assembly—bowl side
67. Hose—vacuum break
69. Vacuum break lever & link assembly
69A. Link—vacuum break
73. Screw—lever attaching
100. Air horn assembly
101. Gasket—air horn to float bowl
105. Screw assembly—air horn to float bowl (long)
108. Screw assembly—air horn to float bowl
111. Screw—air horn to float bowl (countersunk)
126. Bracket—air cleaner
129. Screw assembly—air cleaner bracket attaching
200. Float bowl assembly
210. Nut—fuel inlet
212. Gasket—fuel inlet nut
215. Filter—fuel inlet
218. Spring—fuel filter
226. Float
228. Hinge pin—float
231. Needle—float
234. Seat—float needle
235. Gasket—float needle seat
240. Rod—pump
242. Seal—pump rod
246. Pump assembly
247. Cup—pump plunger
248. Spring—pump plunger
252. Spring—pump return
256. Guide—pump discharge spring
258. Spring—pump discharge ball
260. Ball—pump discharge
266. Rod—power piston
268. Seal—power piston rod
270. Retainer—power piston rod seal
274. Power valve piston assembly
276. Spring—power piston
279. Metering rod & spring assembly
282. Jet—main metering
286. Idle tube assembly
300. Throttle body assembly
301. Gasket—float bowl to throttle body
305. Screw assembly—float bowl to throttle body
310. Lever—pump & power rod
311. Screw—pump lever attaching
314. Link—power rod
317. Link—pump
326. Needle—idle mixture
327. Spring—idle mixture needle
332. Limiter—idle mixture needle
400. Solenoid—idle stop
401. Spring—idle stop solenoid
416. Bracket—throttle kicker
420. Screw—bracket attaching (countersunk)
421. Screw—bracket attaching
425. Throttle kicker assembly
426. Washer-tap locking
427. Nut-throttle kicker assembly attaching

Exploded view of Rochester 1ME carburetor—1984 models

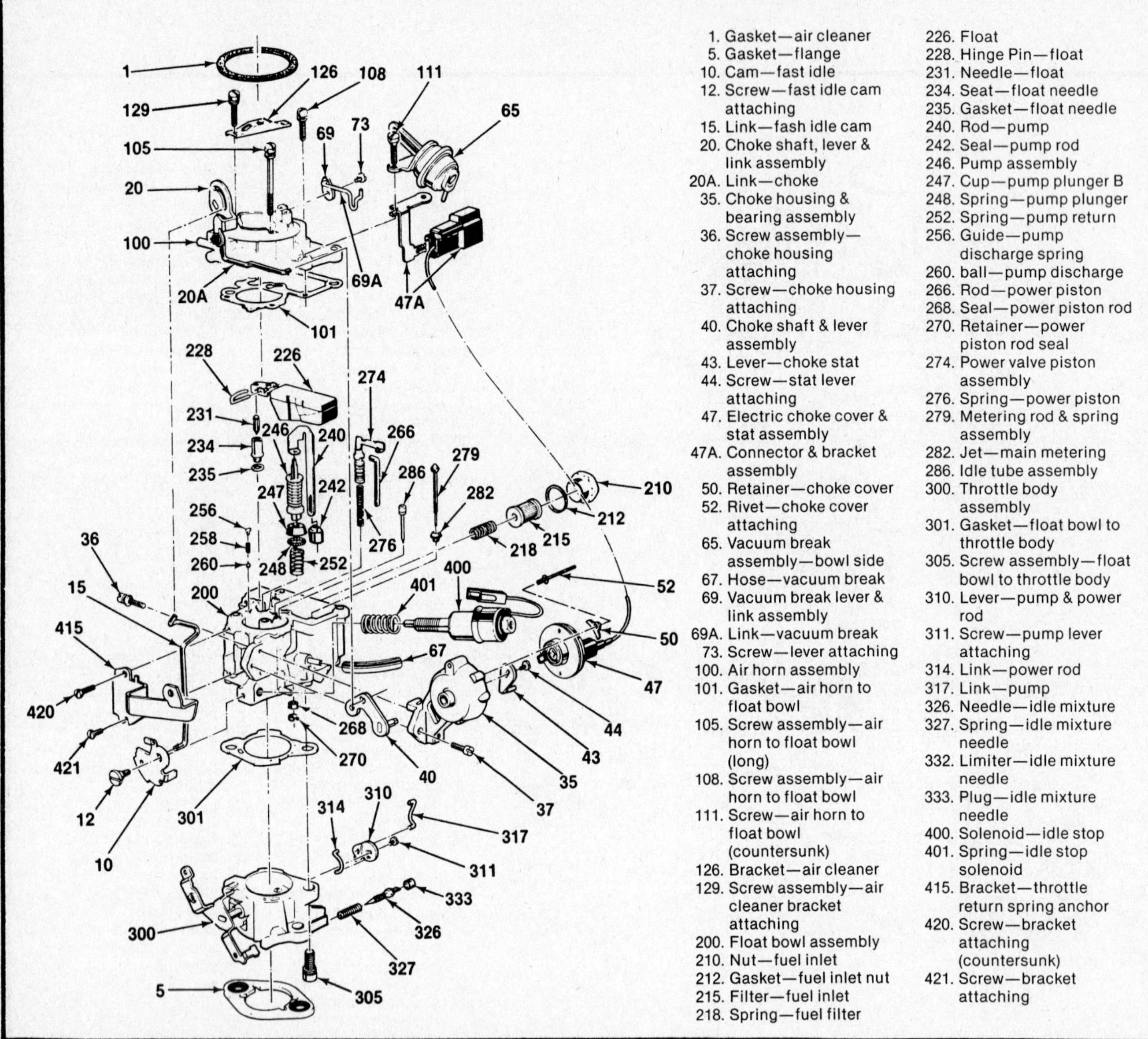

Exploded view of the Rochester 1MEF carburetor—1986–87 models

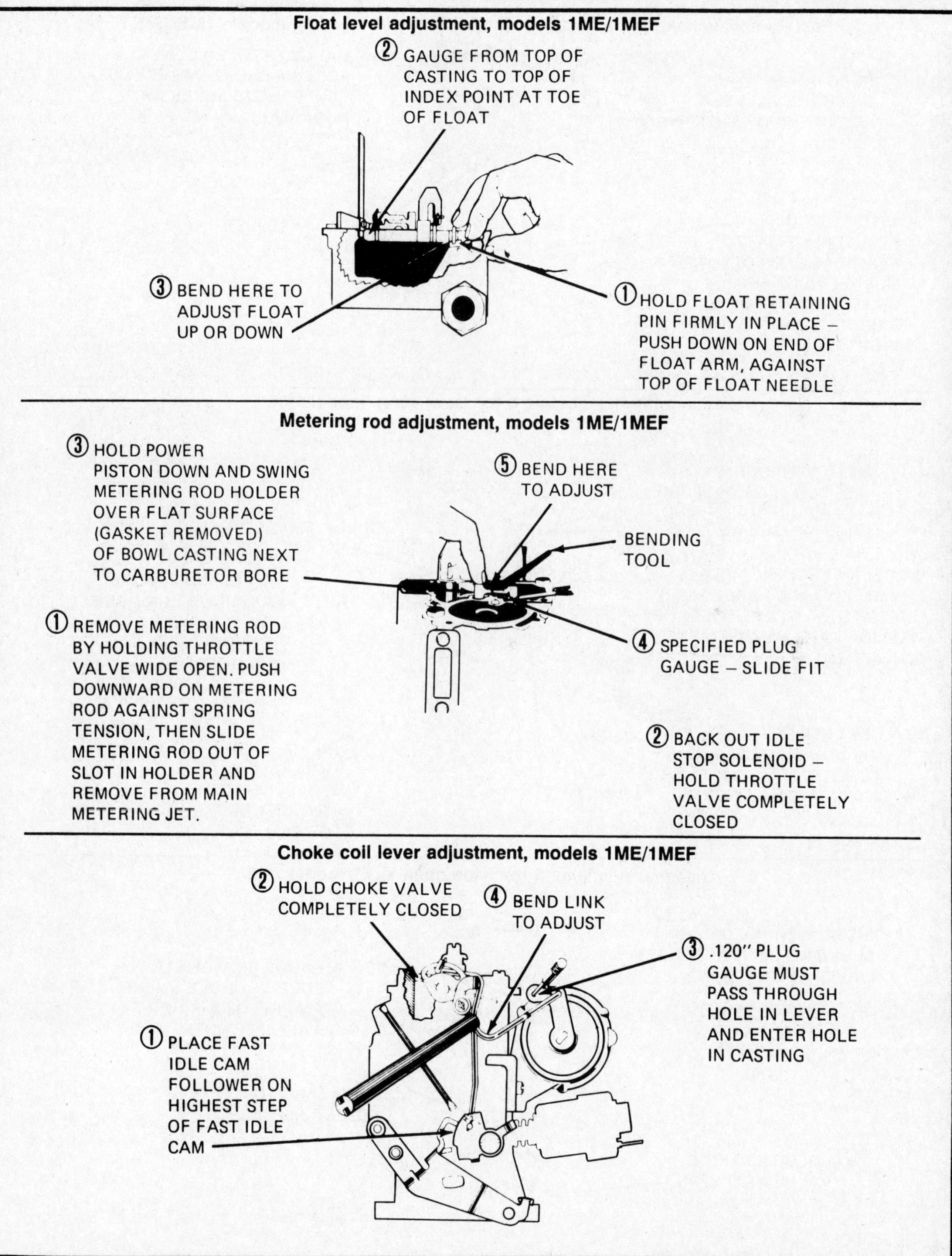
Float level adjustment, models 1ME/1MEF
② GAUGE FROM TOP OF CASTING TO TOP OF INDEX POINT AT TOE OF FLOAT
③ BEND HERE TO ADJUST FLOAT UP OR DOWN
① HOLD FLOAT RETAINING PIN FIRMLY IN PLACE – PUSH DOWN ON END OF FLOAT ARM, AGAINST TOP OF FLOAT NEEDLE
Metering rod adjustment, models 1ME/1MEF
③ HOLD POWER PISTON DOWN AND SWING METERING ROD HOLDER OVER FLAT SURFACE (GASKET REMOVED) OF BOWL CASTING NEXT TO CARBURETOR BORE
⑤ BEND HERE TO ADJUST
BENDING TOOL
① REMOVE METERING ROD BY HOLDING THROTTLE VALVE WIDE OPEN. PUSH DOWNWARD ON METERING ROD AGAINST SPRING TENSION, THEN SLIDE METERING ROD OUT OF SLOT IN HOLDER AND REMOVE FROM MAIN METERING JET.
④ SPECIFIED PLUG GAUGE – SLIDE FIT
② BACK OUT IDLE STOP SOLENOID – HOLD THROTTLE VALVE COMPLETELY CLOSED
Choke coil lever adjustment, models 1ME/1MEF
② HOLD CHOKE VALVE COMPLETELY CLOSED
④ BEND LINK TO ADJUST
③ .120" PLUG GAUGE MUST PASS THROUGH HOLE IN LEVER AND ENTER HOLE IN CASTING
① PLACE FAST IDLE CAM FOLLOWER ON HIGHEST STEP OF FAST IDLE CAM

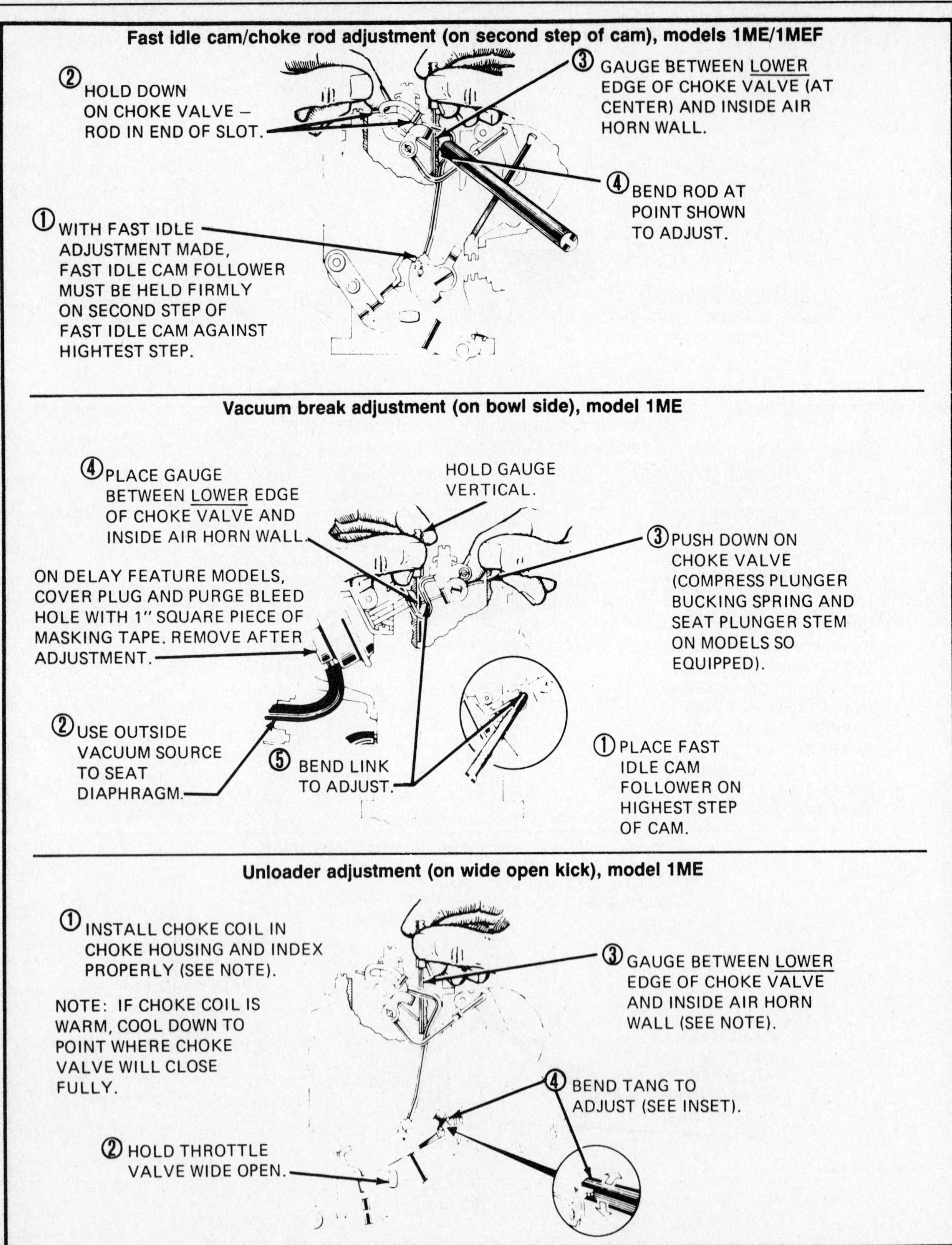
Fast idle cam/choke rod adjustment (on second step of cam), models 1ME/1MEF
② HOLD DOWN ON CHOKE VALVE – ROD IN END OF SLOT.
③ GAUGE BETWEEN LOWER EDGE OF CHOKE VALVE (AT CENTER) AND INSIDE AIR HORN WALL.
④ BEND ROD AT POINT SHOWN TO ADJUST.
① WITH FAST IDLE ADJUSTMENT MADE, FAST IDLE CAM FOLLOWER MUST BE HELD FIRMLY ON SECOND STEP OF FAST IDLE CAM AGAINST HIGHTEST STEP.
Vacuum break adjustment (on bowl side), model 1ME
④ PLACE GAUGE BETWEEN LOWER EDGE OF CHOKE VALVE AND INSIDE AIR HORN WALL.
HOLD GAUGE VERTICAL.
③ PUSH DOWN ON CHOKE VALVE (COMPRESS PLUNGER BUCKING SPRING AND SEAT PLUNGER STEM ON MODELS SO EQUIPPED).
ON DELAY FEATURE MODELS, COVER PLUG AND PURGE BLEED HOLE WITH 1" SQUARE PIECE OF MASKING TAPE. REMOVE AFTER ADJUSTMENT.
② USE OUTSIDE VACUUM SOURCE TO SEAT DIAPHRAGM.
⑤ BEND LINK TO ADJUST.
① PLACE FAST IDLE CAM FOLLOWER ON HIGHEST STEP OF CAM.
Unloader adjustment (on wide open kick), model 1ME
① INSTALL CHOKE COIL IN CHOKE HOUSING AND INDEX PROPERLY (SEE NOTE).
NOTE: IF CHOKE COIL IS WARM, COOL DOWN TO POINT WHERE CHOKE VALVE WILL CLOSE FULLY.
③ GAUGE BETWEEN LOWER EDGE OF CHOKE VALVE AND INSIDE AIR HORN WALL (SEE NOTE).
④ BEND TANG TO ADJUST (SEE INSET).
② HOLD THROTTLE VALVE WIDE OPEN.

ROCHESTER MODEL 2SE
Chevrolet/GMC

(All measurements in inches or degrees)

Year	Carburetor Number	Float Level	Choke Coil Lever	Choke Rod ①	Primary Vacuum Break	Secondary Vacuum Break	Air Valve Rod	Choke Unloader
1982	17082334	3/16	.085	15°	26°	38°	1°	42°
	17082335	3/16	.085	15°	26°	38°	1°	42°
	17082336	3/16	.085	15°	26°	38°	1°	42°
	17082337	3/16	.085	15°	26°	38°	1°	42°
	17082338	3/16	.085	15°	26°	38°	1°	42°
	17082339	3/16	.085	15°	26°	38°	1°	42°
	17082341	3/16	.085	15°	30°	37°	1°	42°
	17082342	3/16	.085	15°	30°	37°	1°	42°
	17082344	3/16	.085	15°	30°	37°	1°	42°
	17082345	3/16	.085	15°	30°	37°	1°	42°
	17082431	3/16	.085	15°	24°	38°	1°	42°
	17082433	3/16	.085	15°	24°	38°	1°	42°
	17082480	3/16	.085	15°	26°	38°	1°	42°
	17082481	3/16	.085	15°	26°	38°	1°	42°
	17082482	3/16	.085	15°	23°	38°	1°	42°
	17082483	3/16	.085	15°	26°	38°	1°	42°
	17082484	3/16	.085	15°	26°	38°	1°	42°
	17082485	3/16	.085	15°	26°	38°	1°	42°
	17082486	3/16	.085	15°	28°	38°	1°	42°
	17082487	3/16	.085	15°	28°	38°	1°	42°
	17082488	3/16	.085	15°	28°	38°	1°	42°
	17082489	3/16	.085	15°	28°	38°	1°	42°
	17082348	7/16	.085	22°	26°	32°	1°	40°
	17082349	7/16	.085	22°	28°	32°	1°	40°
	17082350	7/16	.085	22°	26°	32°	1°	40°
	17082351	7/16	.085	22°	28°	32°	1°	40°
	17082353	7/16	.085	22°	28°	35°	1°	30°
	17082355	7/16	.085	22°	28°	35°	1°	30°
1983	17083410	3/16	.085	15°	23°	38°	1°	42°
	17083411	3/16	.085	15°	26°	38°	1°	42°
	17083412	3/16	.085	15°	23°	38°	1°	42°
	17083413	3/16	.085	15°	26°	38°	1°	42°
	17083414	3/16	.085	15°	23°	38°	1°	42°
	17083415	3/16	.085	15°	26°	38°	1°	42°
	17083416	3/16	.085	15°	23°	38°	1°	42°
	17083417	3/16	.085	15°	26°	38°	1°	42°
	17083419	3/16	.085	15°	28°	38°	1°	42°

ROCHESTER MODEL 2SE
Chevrolet/GMC

(All measurements in inches or degrees)

Year	Carburetor Number	Float Level	Choke Coil Lever	Choke Rod ①	Primary Vacuum Break	Secondary Vacuum Break	Air Valve Rod	Choke Unloader
1983	17083421	3/16	.085	15°	26°	38°	1°	42°
	17083423	3/16	.085	15°	28°	38°	1°	42°
	17083425	3/16	.085	15°	26°	38°	1°	42°
	17083427	3/16	.085	15°	26°	38°	1°	42°
	17083429	3/16	.085	15°	28°	38°	1°	42°
	17083560	3/16	.085	15°	28°	38°	1°	42°
	17083562	3/16	.085	15°	28°	38°	1°	42°
	17083565	3/16	.085	15°	28°	38°	1°	42°
	17083569	3/16	.085	15°	28°	38°	1°	42°
	17083348	7/16	.085	22°	30°	32°	1°	40°
	17083349	7/16	.085	22°	30°	32°	1°	40°
	17083350	7/16	.085	22°	30°	32°	1°	40°
	17083351	7/16	.085	22°	30°	32°	1°	40°
	17083352	7/16	.085	22°	30°	35°	1°	40°
	17083353	7/16	.085	22°	30°	35°	1°	40°
	17083354	7/16	.085	22°	30°	35°	1°	40°
	17083355	7/16	.085	22°	30°	35°	1°	40°
	17083360	7/16	.085	22°	30°	32°	1°	40°
	17083361	7/16	.085	22°	28°	32°	1°	40°
	17083362	7/16	.085	22°	30°	32°	1°	40°
	17083363	7/16	.085	22°	28°	32°	1°	40°
	17083364	7/16	.085	22°	30°	35°	1°	40°
	17083365	7/16	.085	22°	30°	35°	1°	40°
	17083366	7/16	.085	22°	30°	35°	1°	40°
	17083367	7/16	.085	22°	30°	35°	1°	40°
	17083390	13/32	.085	28°	30°	35°	1°	38°
	17083391	13/32	.085	28°	30°	35°	1°	38°
	17083392	13/32	.085	28°	30°	35°	1°	38°
	17083393	13/32	.085	28°	30°	35°	1°	38°
	17083394	13/32	.085	28°	30°	35°	1°	38°
	17083395	13/32	.085	28°	30°	35°	1°	38°
	17083396	13/32	.085	28°	30°	35°	1°	38°
	17083397	13/32	.085	28°	30°	35°	1°	38°
1984	17084348	11/32	.085	22°	30°	32°	1°	40°
	17084349	11/32	.085	22°	30°	32°	1°	40°
	17084350	11/32	.085	22°	30°	32°	1°	40°
	17084351	11/32	.085	22°	30°	32°	1°	40°

ROCHESTER MODEL 2SE
Chevrolet/GMC

(All measurements in inches or degrees)

Year	Carburetor Number	Float Level	Choke Coil Lever	Choke Rod ①	Primary Vacuum Break	Secondary Vacuum Break	Air Valve Rod	Choke Unloader
1984	17084352	11/32	.085	22°	30°	35°	1°	40°
	17084353	11/32	.085	22°	30°	35°	1°	40°
	17084354	11/32	.085	22°	30°	35°	1°	40°
	17084355	11/32	.085	22°	30°	35°	1°	40°
	17084360	5/32	.085	22°	30°	32°	1°	40°
	17084362	5/32	.085	22°	30°	32°	1°	40°
	17084364	5/32	.085	22°	30°	35°	1°	40°
	17084366	5/32	.085	22°	30°	35°	1°	40°
	17084390	7/16	.085	28°	30°	38°	1°	38°
	17084391	7/16	.085	28°	30°	38°	1°	38°
	17084392	7/16	.085	28°	30°	38°	1°	38°
	17084393	7/16	.085	28°	30°	38°	1°	38°
	17084394	7/16	.085	28°	30°	40°	1°	38°
	17084395	7/16	.085	28°	30°	40°	1°	38°
	17084396	7/16	.085	28°	30°	40°	1°	38°
	17084397	7/16	.085	28°	30°	40°	1°	38°
	17084410	11/32	.085	15°	23°	38°	1°	42°
	17084412	11/32	.085	15°	23°	38°	1°	42°
	17084425	11/32	.085	15°	26°	36°	1°	40°
	17084427	11/32	.085	15°	26°	36°	1°	40°
	17084560	11/32	.085	15°	24°	34°	1°	38°
	17084562	11/32	.085	15°	24°	34°	1°	38°
	17084569	11/32	.085	15°	24°	34°	1°	38°
1985	17085348	5/32	.085	22°	32°	36°	1°	40°
	17085350	5/32	.085	22°	32°	36°	1°	40°
	17085351	11/32	.085	22°	32°	36°	1°	40°
	17085352	5/32	.085	22°	30°	34°	1°	40°
	17085354	5/32	.085	22°	30°	34°	1°	40°
	17085355	11/32	.085	22°	30°	34°	1°	40°
	17085360	5/32	.085	22°	32°	36°	1°	40°
	17085362	5/32	.085	22°	32°	36°	1°	40°
	17085363	11/32	.085	22°	32°	36°	1°	40°
	17085364	5/32	.085	22°	30°	34°	1°	40°
	17085366	5/32	.085	22°	30°	34°	1°	40°
	17085367	11/32	.085	22°	30°	34°	1°	40°
	17085372	5/32	.085	22°	32°	36°	1°	40°
	17085374	5/32	.085	22°	32°	36°	1°	40°

NOTE: Specified angle for use with angle degree tool.
① Adjust with fast idle cam on 2nd step.

ROCHESTER MODEL E2SE
Chevrolet/GMC

(All measurements in inches or degrees)

Year	Carburetor Number	Float Level	Choke Coil Lever	Choke Rod ①	Primary Vacuum Break	Secondary Vacuum Break	Air Valve Rod	Choke Unloader
1983	17083356	13/32	.085	22°	25°	35°	1°	30°
	17083357	13/32	.085	22°	25°	35°	1°	30°
	17083358	13/32	.085	22°	25°	35°	1°	30°
	17083359	13/32	.085	22°	25°	35°	1°	30°
	17083368	1/8	.085	22°	25°	35°	1°	30°
	17083370	1/8	.085	22°	25°	35°	1°	30°
	17083450	1/8	.085	28°	27°	35°	1°	45°
	17083451	1/4	.085	28°	27°	35°	1°	45°
	17083452	1/8	.085	28°	27°	35°	1°	45°
	17083453	1/4	.085	28°	27°	35°	1°	45°
	17083454	1/8	.085	28°	27°	35°	1°	45°
	17083455	1/4	.085	28°	27°	35°	1°	45°
	17083456	1/8	.085	28°	27°	35°	1°	45°
	17083630	1/4	.085	28°	27°	35°	1°	45°
	17083631	1/4	.085	28°	27°	35°	1°	45°
	17083632	1/4	.085	28°	27°	35°	1°	45°
	17083633	1/4	.085	28°	27°	35°	1°	45°
	17083634	1/4	.085	28°	27°	35°	1°	45°
	17083635	1/4	.085	28°	27°	35°	1°	45°
	17083636	1/4	.085	28°	27°	35°	1°	45°
	17083650	1/8	.085	28°	27°	35°	1°	45°
	17083430	11/32	.085	15°	26°	38°	1°	42°
	17083431	11/32	.085	15°	26°	38°	1°	42°
	17083434	11/32	.085	15°	26°	38°	1°	42°
	17083435	11/32	.085	15°	26°	38°	1°	42°
1984	17072683	9/32	.085	28°	25°	35°	1°	45°
	17074812	9/32	.085	28°	25°	35°	1°	45°
	17084356	9/32	.085	22°	25°	30°	1°	30°
	17084357	9/32	.085	22°	25°	30°	1°	30°
	17084358	9/32	.085	22°	25°	30°	1°	30°
	17084359	9/32	.085	22°	25°	30°	1°	30°
	17084368	1/8	.085	22°	25°	30°	1°	30°
	17084370	1/8	.085	22°	25°	30°	1°	30°
	17084430	11/32	.085	15°	26°	38°	1°	42°
	17084431	11/32	.085	15°	26°	38°	1°	42°
	17084434	11/32	.085	15°	26°	38°	1°	42°
	17084435	11/32	.085	15°	26°	38°	1°	42°
	17084452	5/32	.085	28°	25°	35°	1°	45°
	17084453	5/32	.085	28°	25°	35°	1°	45°
	17084455	5/32	.085	28°	25°	35°	1°	45°
	17084456	5/32	.085	28°	25°	35°	1°	45°
	17084458	5/32	.085	28°	25°	35°	1°	45°

ROCHESTER MODEL E2SE
Chevrolet/GMC

(All measurements in inches or degrees)

Year	Carburetor Number	Float Level	Choke Coil Lever	Choke Rod ①	Primary Vacuum Break	Secondary Vacuum Break	Air Valve Rod	Choke Unloader
1984	17084532	5/32	.085	28°	25°	35°	1°	45°
	17084534	5/32	.085	28°	25°	35°	1°	45°
	17084535	5/32	.085	28°	25°	35°	1°	45°
	17084537	5/32	.085	28°	25°	35°	1°	45°
	17084538	5/32	.085	28°	25°	35°	1°	45°
	17084540	5/32	.085	28°	25°	35°	1°	45°
	17084542	1/8	.085	28°	25°	35°	1°	45°
	17084632	9/32	.085	28°	25°	35°	1°	45°
	17084633	9/32	.085	28°	25°	35°	1°	45°
	17084635	9/32	.085	28°	25°	35°	1°	45°
	17084636	9/32	.085	28°	25°	35°	1°	45°
1985	17085356	4/32	.085	22°	25°	30°	1°	30°
	17085357	9/32	.085	22°	25°	30°	1°	30°
	17085358	4/32	.085	22°	25°	30°	1°	30°
	17085359	9/32	.085	22°	25°	30°	1°	30°
	17085368	4/32	.085	22°	25°	30°	1°	30°
	17085369	9/32	.085	22°	25°	30°	1°	30°
	17085370	4/32	.085	22°	25°	30°	1°	30°
	17085371	9/32	.085	22°	25°	30°	1°	30°
	17085452	5/32	.085	28°	25°	35°	1°	45°
	17085453	5/32	.085	28°	25°	35°	1°	45°
	17085458	5/32	.085	28°	25°	35°	1°	45°

Note: Specified angle for use with angle degree tool

① All models: Lean mixture screw–2½ turns
Idle mixture screw–4 turns

MODEL 2SE/E2SE

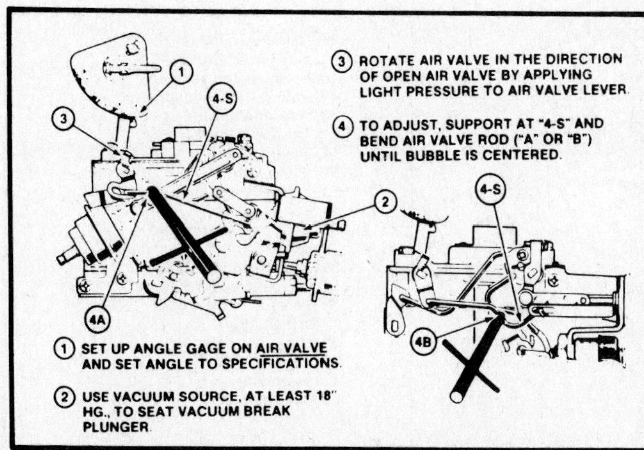

1
3
4-S
2
4A
4-S
4B
③ ROTATE AIR VALVE IN THE DIRECTION OF OPEN AIR VALVE BY APPLYING LIGHT PRESSURE TO AIR VALVE LEVER.
④ TO ADJUST, SUPPORT AT "4-S" AND BEND AIR VALVE ROD ("A" OR "B") UNTIL BUBBLE IS CENTERED.
① SET UP ANGLE GAGE ON AIR VALVE AND SET ANGLE TO SPECIFICATIONS.
② USE VACUUM SOURCE, AT LEAST 18" HG., TO SEAT VACUUM BREAK PLUNGER.

Air valve rod adjustment–2SE, E2SE carburetors

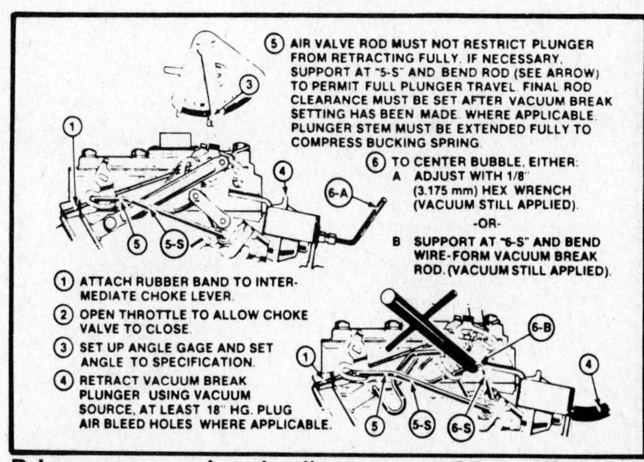

⑤ AIR VALVE ROD MUST NOT RESTRICT PLUNGER FROM RETRACTING FULLY. IF NECESSARY, SUPPORT AT "5-S" AND BEND ROD (SEE ARROW) TO PERMIT FULL PLUNGER TRAVEL. FINAL ROD CLEARANCE MUST BE SET AFTER VACUUM BREAK SETTING HAS BEEN MADE. WHERE APPLICABLE, PLUNGER STEM MUST BE EXTENDED FULLY TO COMPRESS BUCKING SPRING.
⑥ TO CENTER BUBBLE, EITHER:
A ADJUST WITH 1/8" (3.175 mm) HEX WRENCH (VACUUM STILL APPLIED).
-OR-
B SUPPORT AT "6-S" AND BEND WIRE-FORM VACUUM BREAK ROD. (VACUUM STILL APPLIED).
① ATTACH RUBBER BAND TO INTERMEDIATE CHOKE LEVER.
② OPEN THROTTLE TO ALLOW CHOKE VALVE TO CLOSE.
③ SET UP ANGLE GAGE AND SET ANGLE TO SPECIFICATION.
④ RETRACT VACUUM BREAK PLUNGER USING VACUUM SOURCE, AT LEAST 18" HG. PLUG AIR BLEED HOLES WHERE APPLICABLE.
3
1
4
6-A
5
5-S
6-B
1
4
5
5-S
6-S

Primary vacuum break adjustment–2SE, E2SE carburetors

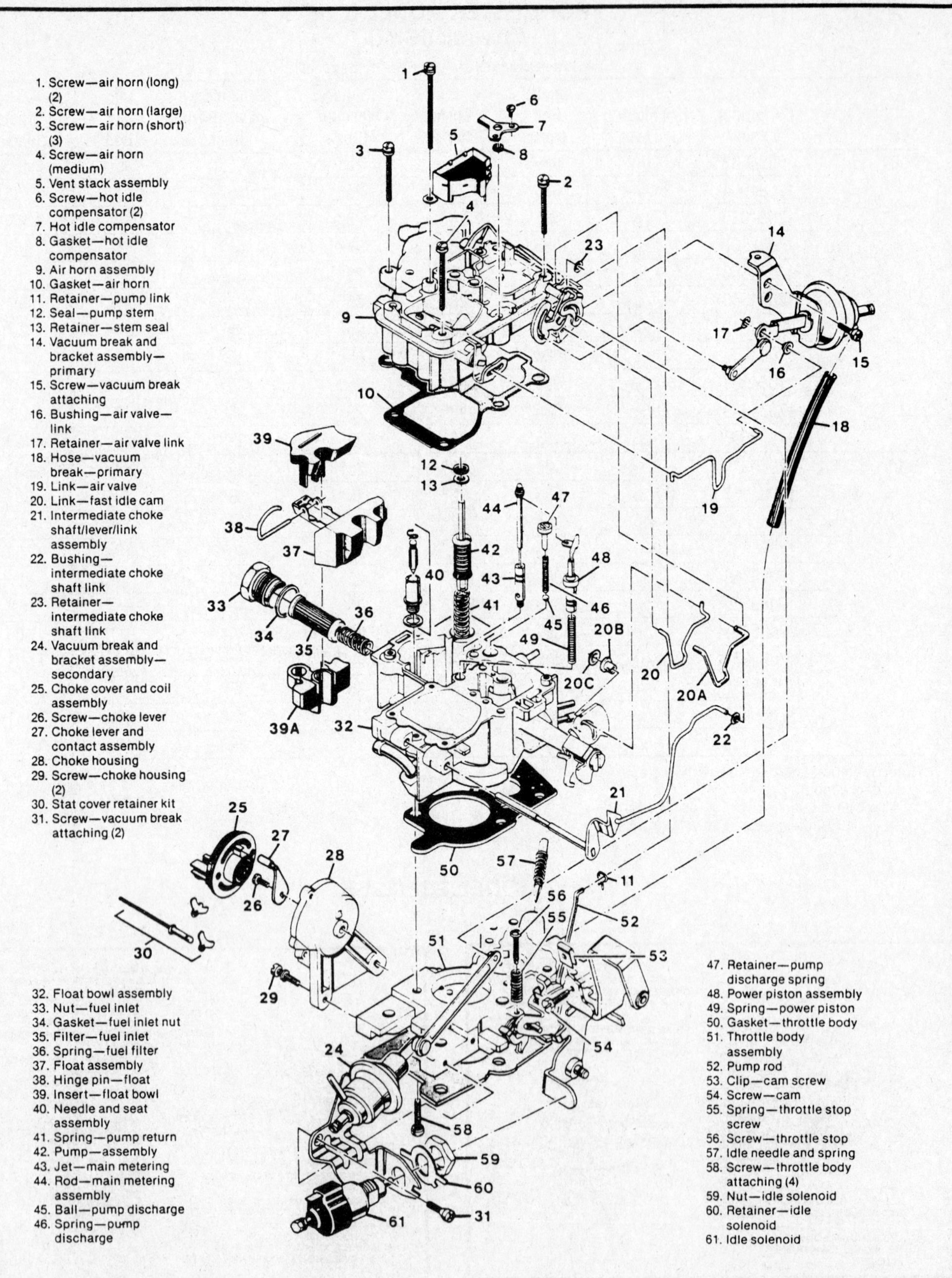
1. Screw—air horn (long) (2)
2. Screw—air horn (large)
3. Screw—air horn (short) (3)
4. Screw—air horn (medium)
5. Vent stack assembly
6. Screw—hot idle compensator (2)
7. Hot idle compensator
8. Gasket—hot idle compensator
9. Air horn assembly
10. Gasket—air horn
11. Retainer—pump link
12. Seal—pump stem
13. Retainer—stem seal
14. Vacuum break and bracket assembly—primary
15. Screw—vacuum break attaching
16. Bushing—air valve—link
17. Retainer—air valve link
18. Hose—vacuum break—primary
19. Link—air valve
20. Link—fast idle cam
21. Intermediate choke shaft/lever/link assembly
22. Bushing—intermediate choke shaft link
23. Retainer—intermediate choke shaft link
24. Vacuum break and bracket assembly—secondary
25. Choke cover and coil assembly
26. Screw—choke lever
27. Choke lever and contact assembly
28. Choke housing
29. Screw—choke housing (2)
30. Stat cover retainer kit
31. Screw—vacuum break attaching (2)
32. Float bowl assembly
33. Nut—fuel inlet
34. Gasket—fuel inlet nut
35. Filter—fuel inlet
36. Spring—fuel filter
37. Float assembly
38. Hinge pin—float
39. Insert—float bowl
40. Needle and seat assembly
41. Spring—pump return
42. Pump—assembly
43. Jet—main metering
44. Rod—main metering assembly
45. Ball—pump discharge
46. Spring—pump discharge
47. Retainer—pump discharge spring
48. Power piston assembly
49. Spring—power piston
50. Gasket—throttle body
51. Throttle body assembly
52. Pump rod
53. Clip—cam screw
54. Screw—cam
55. Spring—throttle stop screw
56. Screw—throttle stop
57. Idle needle and spring
58. Screw—throttle body attaching (4)
59. Nut—idle solenoid
60. Retainer—idle solenoid
61. Idle solenoid

Exploded view of Rochester 2SE carburetor

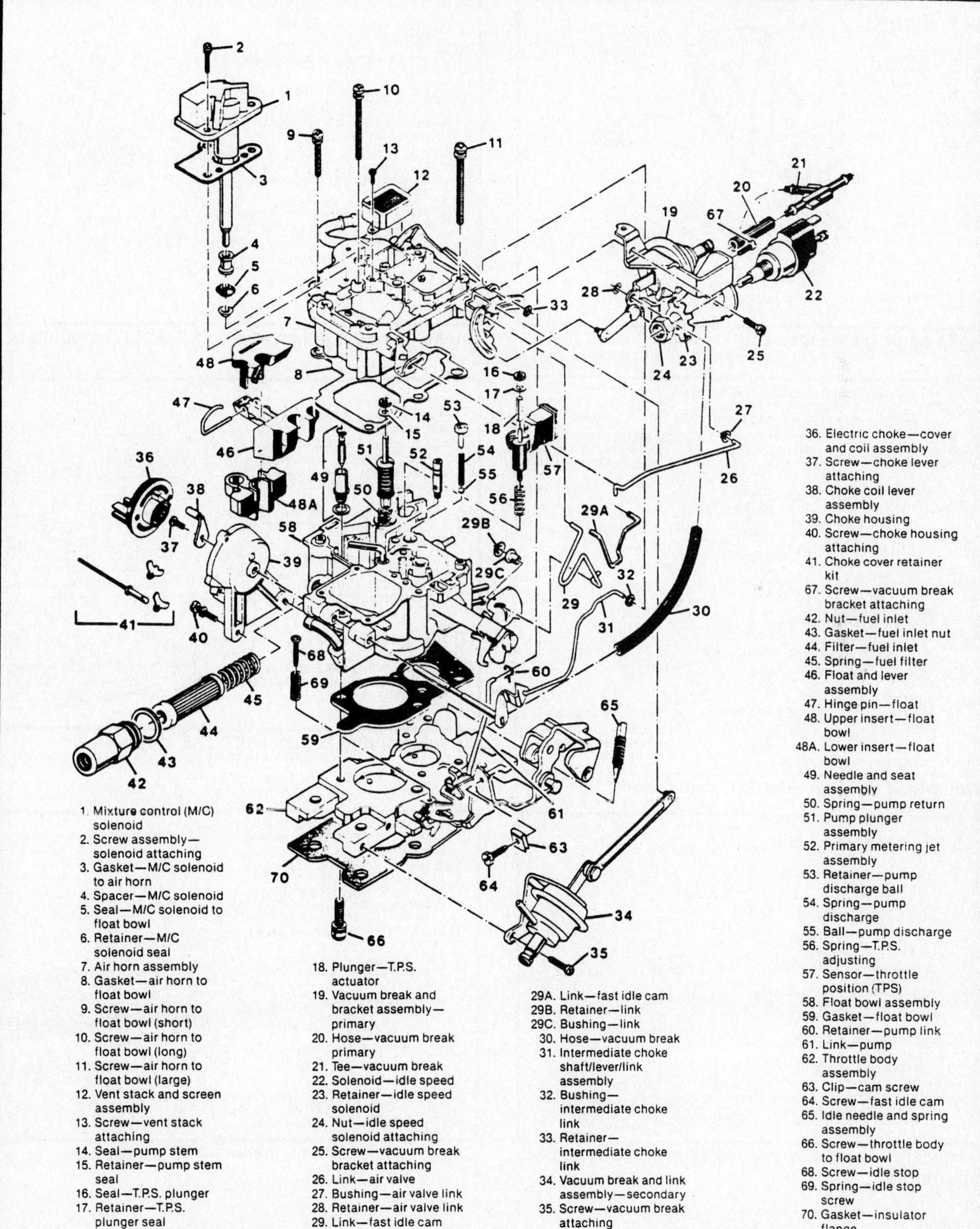
1. Mixture control (M/C) solenoid
2. Screw assembly—solenoid attaching
3. Gasket—M/C solenoid to air horn
4. Spacer—M/C solenoid
5. Seal—M/C solenoid to float bowl
6. Retainer—M/C solenoid seal
7. Air horn assembly
8. Gasket—air horn to float bowl
9. Screw—air horn to float bowl (short)
10. Screw—air horn to float bowl (long)
11. Screw—air horn to float bowl (large)
12. Vent stack and screen assembly
13. Screw—vent stack attaching
14. Seal—pump stem
15. Retainer—pump stem seal
16. Seal—T.P.S. plunger
17. Retainer—T.P.S. plunger seal
18. Plunger—T.P.S. actuator
19. Vacuum break and bracket assembly—primary
20. Hose—vacuum break primary
21. Tee—vacuum break
22. Solenoid—idle speed
23. Retainer—idle speed solenoid
24. Nut—idle speed solenoid attaching
25. Screw—vacuum break bracket attaching
26. Link—air valve
27. Bushing—air valve link
28. Retainer—air valve link
29. Link—fast idle cam
29A. Link—fast idle cam
29B. Retainer—link
29C. Bushing—link
30. Hose—vacuum break
31. Intermediate choke shaft/lever/link assembly
32. Bushing—intermediate choke link
33. Retainer—intermediate choke link
34. Vacuum break and link assembly—secondary
35. Screw—vacuum break attaching
36. Electric choke—cover and coil assembly
37. Screw—choke lever attaching
38. Choke coil lever assembly
39. Choke housing
40. Screw—choke housing attaching
41. Choke cover retainer kit
67. Screw—vacuum break bracket attaching
42. Nut—fuel inlet
43. Gasket—fuel inlet nut
44. Filter—fuel inlet
45. Spring—fuel filter
46. Float and lever assembly
47. Hinge pin—float
48. Upper insert—float bowl
48A. Lower insert—float bowl
49. Needle and seat assembly
50. Spring—pump return
51. Pump plunger assembly
52. Primary metering jet assembly
53. Retainer—pump discharge ball
54. Spring—pump discharge
55. Ball—pump discharge
56. Spring—T.P.S. adjusting
57. Sensor—throttle position (TPS)
58. Float bowl assembly
59. Gasket—float bowl
60. Retainer—pump link
61. Link—pump
62. Throttle body assembly
63. Clip—cam screw
64. Screw—fast idle cam
65. Idle needle and spring assembly
66. Screw—throttle body to float bowl
68. Screw—idle stop
69. Spring—idle stop screw
70. Gasket—insulator flange

Exploded view of Rochester E2SE carburetor

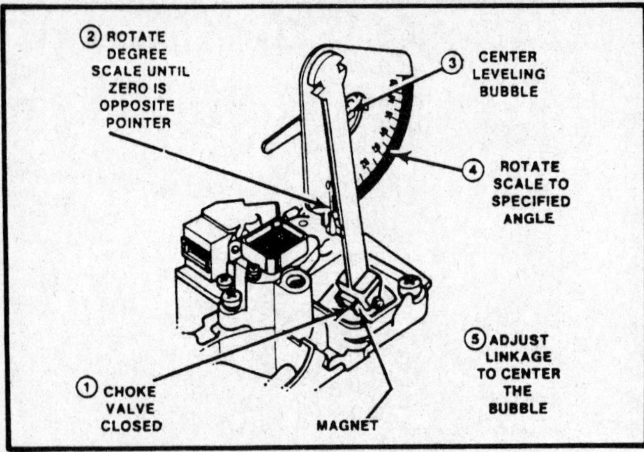

③ CENTER LEVELING BUBBLE

⑤ ADJUST LINKAGE TO CENTER THE BUBBLE

Choke angle gauge installed—typical

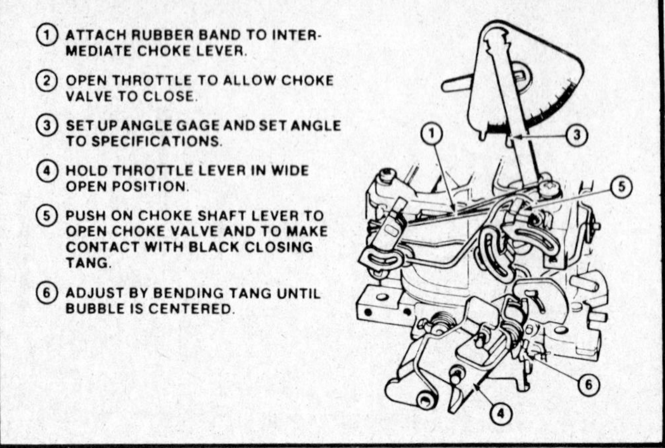

① ATTACH RUBBER BAND TO INTERMEDIATE CHOKE LEVER.
② OPEN THROTTLE TO ALLOW CHOKE VALVE TO CLOSE.
③ SET UP ANGLE GAGE AND SET ANGLE TO SPECIFICATIONS.
④ HOLD THROTTLE LEVER IN WIDE OPEN POSITION.
⑤ PUSH ON CHOKE SHAFT LEVER TO OPEN CHOKE VALVE AND TO MAKE CONTACT WITH BLACK CLOSING TANG.
⑥ ADJUST BY BENDING TANG UNTIL BUBBLE IS CENTERED.

Choke unloader adjustment—2SE, E2SE carburetors

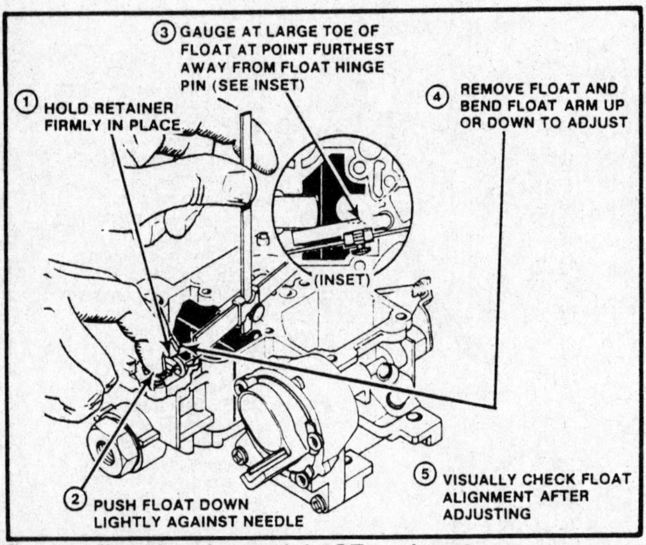

③ GAUGE AT LARGE TOE OF FLOAT AT POINT FURTHEST AWAY FROM FLOAT HINGE PIN (SEE INSET)
① HOLD RETAINER FIRMLY IN PLACE
④ REMOVE FLOAT AND BEND FLOAT ARM UP OR DOWN TO ADJUST

② PUSH FLOAT DOWN LIGHTLY AGAINST NEEDLE
⑤ VISUALLY CHECK FLOAT ALIGNMENT AFTER ADJUSTING

Setting float level—model 2SE carburetor

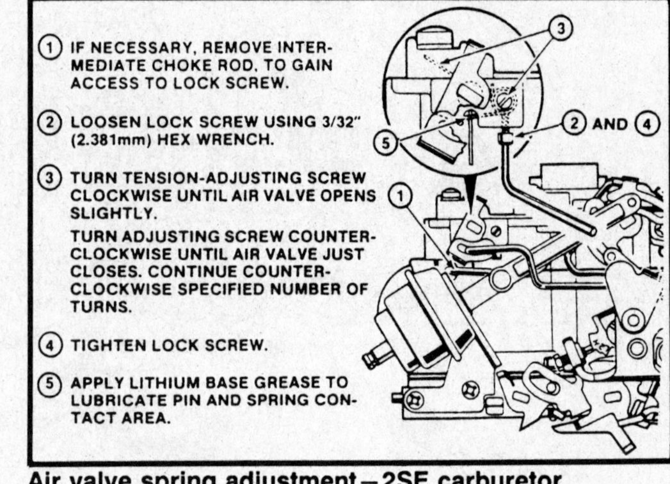

① IF NECESSARY, REMOVE INTERMEDIATE CHOKE ROD, TO GAIN ACCESS TO LOCK SCREW.
② LOOSEN LOCK SCREW USING 3/32" (2.381mm) HEX WRENCH.
③ TURN TENSION-ADJUSTING SCREW CLOCKWISE UNTIL AIR VALVE OPENS SLIGHTLY.
TURN ADJUSTING SCREW COUNTERCLOCKWISE UNTIL AIR VALVE JUST CLOSES. CONTINUE COUNTERCLOCKWISE SPECIFIED NUMBER OF TURNS.
④ TIGHTEN LOCK SCREW.
⑤ APPLY LITHIUM BASE GREASE TO LUBRICATE PIN AND SPRING CONTACT AREA.
② AND ④

Air valve spring adjustment—2SE carburetor

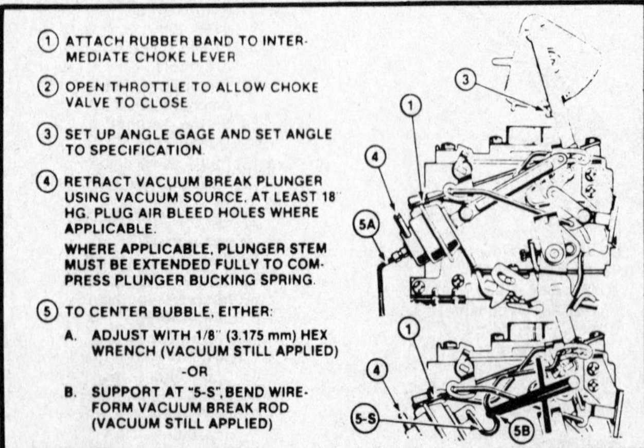

① ATTACH RUBBER BAND TO INTERMEDIATE CHOKE LEVER
② OPEN THROTTLE TO ALLOW CHOKE VALVE TO CLOSE
③ SET UP ANGLE GAGE AND SET ANGLE TO SPECIFICATION.
④ RETRACT VACUUM BREAK PLUNGER USING VACUUM SOURCE, AT LEAST 18" HG. PLUG AIR BLEED HOLES WHERE APPLICABLE.
WHERE APPLICABLE, PLUNGER STEM MUST BE EXTENDED FULLY TO COMPRESS PLUNGER BUCKING SPRING.
⑤ TO CENTER BUBBLE, EITHER:
A. ADJUST WITH 1/8" (3.175 mm) HEX WRENCH (VACUUM STILL APPLIED)
-OR
B. SUPPORT AT "5-S", BEND WIRE-FORM VACUUM BREAK ROD (VACUUM STILL APPLIED)
5A
5-S
5B

Secondary vacuum break adjustment—2SE, E2SE carburetors

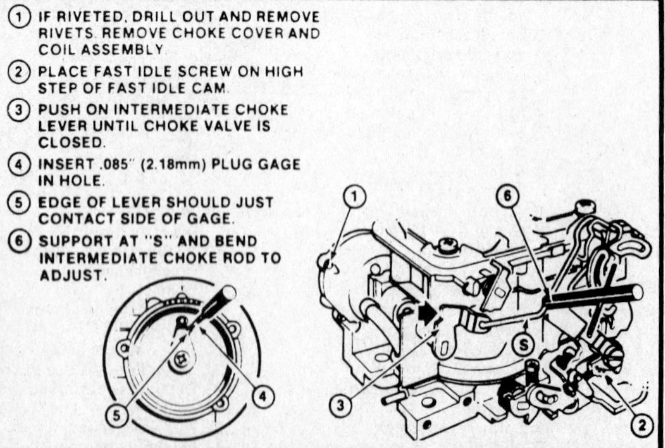

① IF RIVETED, DRILL OUT AND REMOVE RIVETS. REMOVE CHOKE COVER AND COIL ASSEMBLY.
② PLACE FAST IDLE SCREW ON HIGH STEP OF FAST IDLE CAM.
③ PUSH ON INTERMEDIATE CHOKE LEVER UNTIL CHOKE VALVE IS CLOSED.
④ INSERT .085" (2.18mm) PLUG GAGE IN HOLE.
⑤ EDGE OF LEVER SHOULD JUST CONTACT SIDE OF GAGE.
⑥ SUPPORT AT "S" AND BEND INTERMEDIATE CHOKE ROD TO ADJUST.

Choke coil lever adjustment—2SE carburetor

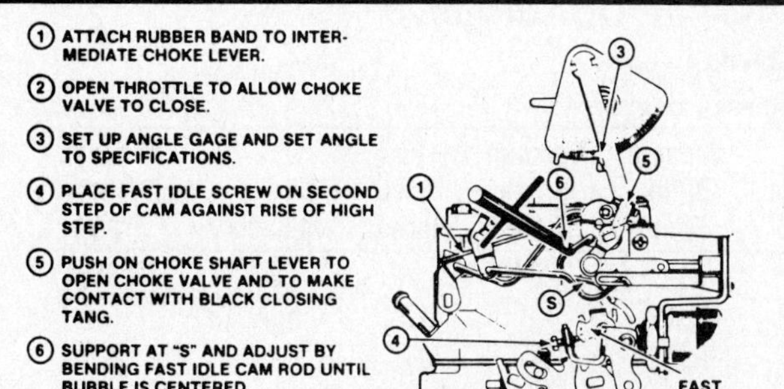
① ATTACH RUBBER BAND TO INTERMEDIATE CHOKE LEVER.
② OPEN THROTTLE TO ALLOW CHOKE VALVE TO CLOSE.
③ SET UP ANGLE GAGE AND SET ANGLE TO SPECIFICATIONS.
④ PLACE FAST IDLE SCREW ON SECOND STEP OF CAM AGAINST RISE OF HIGH STEP.
⑤ PUSH ON CHOKE SHAFT LEVER TO OPEN CHOKE VALVE AND TO MAKE CONTACT WITH BLACK CLOSING TANG.
⑥ SUPPORT AT "S" AND ADJUST BY BENDING FAST IDLE CAM ROD UNTIL BUBBLE IS CENTERED.
FAST IDLE CAM

Choke rod and fast idle cam adjustment – 2SE, E2SE carburetors

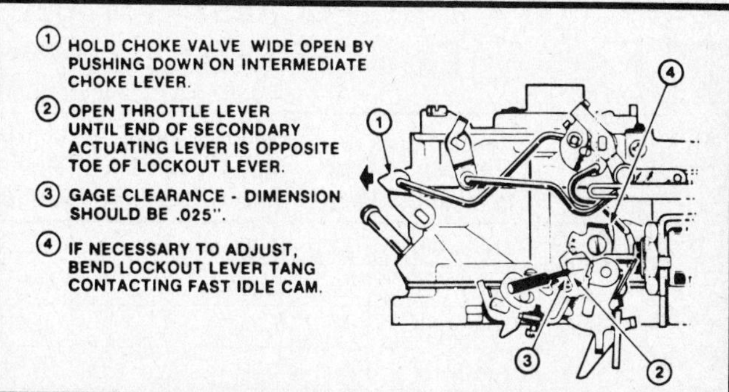
① HOLD CHOKE VALVE WIDE OPEN BY PUSHING DOWN ON INTERMEDIATE CHOKE LEVER.
② OPEN THROTTLE LEVER UNTIL END OF SECONDARY ACTUATING LEVER IS OPPOSITE TOE OF LOCKOUT LEVER.
③ GAGE CLEARANCE - DIMENSION SHOULD BE .025".
④ IF NECESSARY TO ADJUST, BEND LOCKOUT LEVER TANG CONTACTING FAST IDLE CAM.

Secondary lockout adjustment – 2SE, E2SE carburetors

ROCHESTER MODEL M4MC/M4ME QUADRAJET
Chevrolet/GMC

(All measurements in inches or degrees)

Year	Carburetor Number	Float Level	Pump Rod Hole	Pump Rod Setting	Choke Rod ① Setting	Air Valve Rod	Vacuum Break Front	Vacuum Break Rear	Air Valve Turns	Choke Unloader	Propane Enrichment (rpm)
1982	17080212	3/8	inner	9/32	46°	.025	24°	30°	3/4	40°	②
	17080213	3/8	inner	9/32	37°	.025	23°	30°	1	40°	②
	17080215	3/8	inner	9/32	37°	.025	23°	30°	1	40°	②
	17080298	3/8	inner	9/32	37°	.025	23°	30°	1	40°	②
	17080507	3/8	inner	9/32	37°	.025	23°	30°	1	40°	②
	17080512	3/8	inner	9/32	46°	.025	24°	30°	3/4	40°	②
	17080513	3/8	inner	9/32	37°	.025	23°	30°	3/4	40°	②
	17082213	3/8	inner	9/32	37°	.025	23°	30°	1	40°	②
	17082220	13/32	inner	9/32	46°	.025	24°	34°	7/8	39°	②
	17082221	13/32	inner	9/32	46°	.025	24°	34°	7/8	39°	150
	17082222	13/32	inner	9/32	46°	.025	24°	34°	7/8	39°	50
	17082223	13/32	inner	9/32	46°	.025	24°	34°	7/8	39°	100
	17082224	13/32	inner	9/32	46°	.025	24°	34°	7/8	39°	50
	17082225	13/32	inner	9/32	46°	.025	24°	34°	7/8	39°	150
	17082226	13/32	inner	9/32	46°	.025	24°	34°	7/8	39°	50
	17082227	13/32	inner	9/32	46°	.025	24°	34°	7/8	39°	50
	17082230	13/32	inner	9/32	46°	.025	26°	36°	7/8	39°	②
	17082231	13/32	inner	9/32	46°	.025	26°	36°	7/8	39°	②
	17082234	13/32	inner	9/32	46°	.025	26°	36°	7/8	39°	②
	17082235	13/32	inner	9/32	46°	.025	26°	36°	7/8	39°	②
	17082290	13/32	inner	9/32	46°	.025	24°	34°	7/8	39°	②
	17082291	13/32	inner	9/32	46°	.025	24°	34°	7/8	39°	②
	17082292	13/32	inner	9/32	46°	.025	24°	34°	7/8	39°	②
	17082293	13/32	inner	9/32	46°	.025	24°	34°	7/8	39°	100
	17082506	13/32	inner	9/32	46°	.025	23°	36°	7/8	39°	50
	17082508	3/8	inner	9/32	46°	.025	23°	36°	7/8	39°	50
	17082513	13/32	inner	9/32	46°	.025	23°	30°	3/4	40°	②
	17082524	13/32	outer	5/16	46°	.025	25°	36°	7/8	39°	20
	17082526	13/32	outer	5/16	46°	.025	25°	36°	7/8	39°	20

ROCHESTER MODEL M4MC/M4ME QUADRAJET
Chevrolet/GMC

(All measurements in inches or degrees)

Year	Carburetor Number	Float Level	Pump Rod Hole	Pump Rod Setting	Choke Rod ① Setting	Air Valve Rod	Vacuum Break Front	Vacuum Break Rear	Air Valve Turns	Choke Unloader	Propane Enrichment (rpm)
1983	17080201	15/32	inner	9/32	46°	.025	—	23°	7/8	42°	②
	17080205	15/32	inner	9/32	46°	.025	—	23°	7/8	42°	②
	17080206	15/32	inner	9/32	46°	.025	—	23°	7/8	42°	②
	17080213	3/8	inner	9/32	37°	.025	23°	30°	1	40°	②
	17080290	15/32	inner	9/32	46°	.025	—	26°	7/8	42°	②
	17080291	15/32	inner	9/32	46°	.025	—	26°	7/8	42°	②
	17080292	15/32	inner	9/32	46°	.025	—	26°	7/8	42°	②
	17080298	3/8	inner	9/32	37°	.025	23°	30°	1	40°	②
	17080507	3/8	inner	9/32	37°	.025	23°	30°	1	40°	②
	17080513	3/8	inner	9/32	37°	.025	23°	30°	1	40°	②
	17082213	9/32	inner	9/32	37°	.025	23°	30°	1	40°	②
	17083234	13/32	inner	9/32	46°	.025	—	26°	7/8	39°	20
	17083235	13/32	inner	9/32	46°	.025	—	26°	7/8	39°	100
	17083290	13/32	inner	9/32	46°	.025	—	24°	7/8	39°	40
	17083291	13/32	inner	9/32	46°	.025	—	24°	7/8	39°	100
	17083292	13/32	inner	9/32	46°	.025	—	24°	7/8	39°	40
	17083293	13/32	inner	9/32	46°	.025	—	24°	7/8	39°	100
	17083298	3/8	inner	9/32	37°	.025	23°	30°	1	40°	②
	17083507	3/8	inner	9/32	37°	.025	23°	30°	1	40°	②
	17080212	3/8	inner	9/32	46°	.025	24°	30°	3/4	40°	②
	17080512	3/8	inner	9/32	46°	.025	24°	30°	3/4	40°	②
	17083220	13/32	inner	9/32	46°	.025	—	24°	7/8	39°	150
	17083221	13/32	inner	9/32	46°	.025	—	24°	7/8	39°	150
	17083222	13/32	inner	9/32	46°	.025	—	24°	7/8	39°	50
	17083223	13/32	inner	9/32	46°	.025	—	24°	7/8	39°	150
	17083224	13/32	inner	9/32	46°	.025	—	24°	7/8	39°	50
	17083225	13/32	inner	9/32	46°	.025	—	24°	7/8	39°	150
	17083226	13/32	inner	9/32	46°	.025	—	24°	7/8	39°	50
	17083227	13/32	inner	9/32	46°	.025	—	24°	7/8	39°	50
	17083230	13/32	inner	9/32	46°	.025	—	26°	7/8	39°	20
	17083231	13/32	inner	9/32	46°	.025	—	26°	7/8	39°	100
1984	17084200	13/32	inner	9/32	46°	.025	—	26°	7/8	39°	②
	17084206	13/32	inner	9/32	46°	.025	—	26°	7/8	39°	20
	17084211	13/32	inner	9/32	46°	.025	—	26°	7/8	39°	②
	17084220	13/32	inner	9/32	46°	.025	—	26°	7/8	39°	80
	17084221	13/32	inner	9/32	46°	.025	—	26°	7/8	39°	80
	17084226	13/32	inner	9/32	46°	.025	—	24°	7/8	39°	30
	17084227	13/32	inner	9/32	46°	.025	—	24°	7/8	39°	30
	17084228	13/32	inner	9/32	46°	.025	—	26°	7/8	39°	80
	17084229	13/32	inner	9/32	46°	.025	—	26°	7/8	39°	80
	17084230	13/32	inner	9/32	46°	.025	—	26°	7/8	39°	20
	17084231	13/32	inner	9/32	46°	.025	—	26°	7/8	39°	40

ROCHESTER MODEL M4MC/M4ME/M4MEF QUADRAJET
Chevrolet/GMC

(All measurements in inches or degrees)

Year	Carburetor Number	Float Level	Pump Rod Hole	Pump Rod Setting	Choke Rod ① Setting	Air Valve Rod	Vacuum Break Front	Vacuum Break Rear	Air Valve Turns	Choke Unloader	Propane Enrichment (rpm)
1984	17084234	13/32	inner	9/32	46°	.025	—	26°	7/8	39°	20
	17084235	13/32	inner	9/32	46°	.025	—	26°	7/8	39°	80
	17084290	13/32	inner	9/32	46°	.025	—	24°	7/8	39°	30
	17084291	13/32	inner	9/32	46°	.025	—	26°	7/8	39°	100
	17084292	13/32	inner	9/32	46°	.025	—	24°	7/8	39°	30
	17084293	13/32	inner	9/32	46°	.025	—	26°	7/8	39°	100
	17084294	13/32	inner	9/32	46°	.025	—	26°	7/8	39°	30
	17084298	13/32	inner	9/32	46°	.025	—	26°	7/8	39°	30
1985	17084500	12/32	inner	9/32	37°	.025	23°	30°	1	40°	②
	17084501	12/32	inner	9/32	37°	.025	23°	30°	1	40°	②
	17084502	12/32	inner	9/32	46°	.025	24°	30°	7/8	40°	②
	17085000	12/32	inner	9/32	46°	.025	24°	30°	7/8	40°	②
	17085001	12/32	inner	9/32	46°	.025	23°	30°	1	40°	②
	17085003	13/32	inner	9/32	46°	.025	23°	—	7/8	35°	②
	17085004	13/32	inner	9/32	46°	.025	23°	—	7/8	35°	②
	17085205	13/32	inner	9/32	20°	.025	26°	38°	7/8	39°	②
	17085206	13/32	inner	9/32	46°	.025	—	26°	7/8	39°	20
	17085208	13/32	inner	9/32	20°	.025	26°	38°	7/8	39°	10
	17085209	13/32	outer	3/8	20°	.025	26°	36°	7/8	39°	50
	17085210	13/32	inner	9/32	20°	.025	26°	38°	7/8	39°	10
	17085211	13/32	outer	3/8	20°	.025	26°	36°	7/8	39°	50
	17085212	13/32	inner	9/32	46°	.025	23°	—	7/8	35°	②
	17085213	13/32	inner	9/32	46°	.025	23°	—	7/8	35°	②
	17085215	13/32	inner	9/32	46°	.025	—	26°	7/8	32°	②
	17085216	13/32	inner	9/32	20°	.025	26°	38°	7/8	39°	②
	17085217	13/32	inner	9/32	20°	.025	26°	36°	1/2	39°	②
	17085219	13/32	inner	9/32	20°	.025	26°	36°	1/2	39°	②
	17085220	13/32	outer	3/8	20°	.025	—	26°	7/8	32°	75
	17085221	13/32	outer	3/8	20°	.025	—	26°	7/8	32°	75
	17085222	13/32	inner	9/32	20°	.025	26°	36°	1/2	39°	20
	17085223	13/32	outer	3/8	20°	.025	26°	36°	1/2	39°	50
	17085224	13/32	inner	9/32	20°	.025	26°	36°	1/2	39°	20
	17085225	13/32	outer	3/8	20°	.025	26°	36°	1/2	39°	50
	17085226	13/32	inner	9/32	20°	.025	—	24°	7/8	32°	20
	17085227	13/32	inner	9/32	20°	.025	—	24°	7/8	32°	20
	17085228	13/32	inner	9/32	46°	.025	—	24°	7/8	39°	30
	17085229	13/32	inner	9/32	46°	.025	—	24°	7/8	39°	30
	17085230	13/32	inner	9/32	20°	.025	—	26°	7/8	32°	20
	17085231	13/32	inner	9/32	20°	.025	—	26°	7/8	32°	40
	17085235	13/32	inner	9/32	46°	.025	—	26°	7/8	39°	80
	17085238	13/32	outer	3/8	20°	.025	—	26°	7/8	32°	75
	17085239	13/32	outer	3/8	20°	.025	—	26°	7/8	32°	75

ROCHESTER MODEL M4MC/M4ME/M4MEF QUADRAJET Chevrolet/GMC

(All measurements in inches or degrees)

Year	Carburetor Number	Float Level	Pump Rod Hole	Pump Rod Setting	Choke Rod ① Setting	Air Valve Rod	Vacuum Break Front	Vacuum Break Rear	Air Valve Turns	Choke Unloader	Propane Enrichment (rpm)
1985	17085283	13/32	inner	9/32	20°	.025	—	24°	7/8	32°	20
	17085284	13/32	inner	9/32	20°	.025	—	26°	7/8	32°	20
	17085285	13/32	inner	9/32	20°	.025	—	24°	7/8	32°	20
	17085290	13/32	inner	9/32	46°	.025	—	24°	7/8	39°	30
	17085291	13/32	outer	3/8	46°	.025	—	26°	7/8	39°	100
	17085292	13/32	inner	9/32	46°	.025	—	24°	7/8	39°	30
	17085293	13/32	outer	3/8	46°	.025	—	26°	7/8	39°	100
	17085294	13/32	inner	9/32	46°	.025	—	26°	7/8	39°	②
	17085298	13/32	inner	9/32	46°	.025	—	26°	7/8	39°	②
1986	17084500	12/32	inner	9/32	37°	.025	23°	30°	1	40°	②
	17084501	12/32	inner	9/32	37°	.025	23°	30°	1	40°	②
	17084502	12/32	inner	9/32	46°	.025	24°	30°	7/8	40°	②
	17085000	12/32	inner	9/32	46°	.025	24°	30°	7/8	40°	②
	17085001	12/32	inner	9/32	46°	.025	23°	30°	1	40°	②
	17085003	13/32	inner	9/32	46°	.025	23°	—	7/8	35°	②
	17085004	13/32	inner	9/32	46°	.025	23°	—	7/8	35°	②
	17085205	13/32	inner	9/32	20°	.025	26°	38°	7/8	39°	②
	17085206	13/32	inner	9/32	46°	.025	—	26°	7/8	39°	20
	17085208	13/32	inner	9/32	20°	.025	26°	38°	7/8	39°	10
	17085209	13/32	outer	3/8	20°	.025	26°	36°	7/8	39°	50
	17085210	13/32	inner	9/32	20°	.025	26°	38°	7/8	39°	10
	17085211	13/32	outer	3/8	20°	.025	26°	36°	7/8	39°	50
	17085212	13/32	inner	9/32	46°	.025	23°	—	7/8	35°	②
	17085213	13/32	inner	9/32	46°	.025	23°	—	7/8	35°	②
	17085215	13/32	inner	9/32	46°	.025	—	26°	7/8	32°	②
	17085216	13/32	inner	9/32	20°	.025	26°	38°	7/8	39°	②
	17085217	13/32	inner	9/32	20°	.025	26°	36°	1/2	39°	②
	17085219	13/32	inner	9/32	20°	.025	26°	36°	1/2	39°	②
	17085220	13/32	outer	3/8	20°	.025	—	26°	7/8	32°	75
	17085221	13/32	outer	3/8	20°	.025	—	26°	7/8	32°	75
	17085222	13/32	inner	9/32	20°	.025	26°	36°	1/2	39°	20
	17085223	13/32	outer	3/8	20°	.025	26°	36°	1/2	39°	50
	17085224	13/32	inner	9/32	20°	.025	26°	36°	1/2	39°	20
	17085225	13/32	outer	3/8	20°	.025	26°	36°	1/2	39°	50
	17085226	13/32	inner	9/32	20°	.025	—	24°	7/8	32°	20
	17085227	13/32	inner	9/32	20°	.025	—	24°	7/8	32°	20
	17085228	13/32	inner	9/32	46°	.025	—	24°	7/8	39°	30
	17085229	13/32	inner	9/32	46°	.025	—	24°	7/8	39°	30
	17085230	13/32	inner	9/32	20°	.025	—	26°	7/8	32°	20
	17085231	13/32	inner	9/32	20°	.025	—	26°	7/8	32°	40
	17085235	13/32	inner	9/32	46°	.025	—	26°	7/8	39°	80
	17085238	13/32	outer	3/8	20°	.025	—	26°	7/8	32°	75

ROCHESTER MODEL M4MC/M4ME/M4MEF QUADRAJET
Chevrolet/GMC

(All measurements in inches or degrees)

Year	Carburetor Number	Float Level	Pump Rod Hole	Pump Rod Setting	Choke Rod ① Setting	Air Valve Rod	Vacuum Break Front	Vacuum Break Rear	Air Valve Turns	Choke Unloader	Propane Enrichment (rpm)
1986	17085239	13/32	outer	3/8	20°	.025	—	26°	7/8	32°	75
	17085283	13/32	inner	9/32	20°	.025	—	24°	7/8	32°	20
	17085284	13/32	inner	9/32	20°	.025	—	26°	7/8	32°	20
	17085285	13/32	inner	9/32	20°	.025	—	24°	7/8	32°	20
	17085290	13/32	inner	9/32	46°	.025	—	24°	7/8	39°	30
	17085291	13/32	outer	3/8	46°	.025	—	26°	7/8	39°	100
	17085292	13/32	inner	9/32	46°	.025	—	24°	7/8	39°	30
	17085293	13/32	outer	3/8	46°	.025	—	26°	7/8	39°	100
	17085294	13/32	inner	9/32	46°	.025	—	26°	7/8	39°	②
	17085298	13/32	inner	9/32	46°	.025	—	26°	7/8	39°	②
1987-88	17084500	12/32	inner	9/32	37°	.025	23°	30°	1	40°	②
	17084501	12/32	inner	9/32	37°	.025	23°	30°	1	40°	②
	17084502	12/32	inner	9/32	46°	.025	24°	30°	7/8	40°	②
	17085000	12/32	inner	9/32	46°	.025	24°	30°	7/8	40°	②
	17085001	12/32	inner	9/32	46°	.025	23°	30°	1	40°	②
	17085003	13/32	inner	9/32	46°	.025	23°	—	7/8	35°	②
	17085004	13/32	inner	9/32	46°	.025	23°	—	7/8	35°	②
	17085205	13/32	inner	9/32	20°	.025	26°	38°	7/8	39°	②
	17085206	13/32	inner	9/32	46°	.025	—	26°	7/8	39°	20
	17085208	13/32	inner	9/32	20°	.025	26°	38°	7/8	39°	10
	17085209	13/32	outer	3/8	20°	.025	26°	36°	7/8	39°	50
	17085210	13/32	inner	9/32	20°	.025	26°	38°	7/8	39°	10
	17085211	13/32	outer	3/8	20°	.025	26°	36°	7/8	39°	50
	17085212	13/32	inner	9/32	46°	.025	23°	—	7/8	35°	②
	17085213	13/32	inner	9/32	46°	.025	23°	—	7/8	35°	②
	17085215	13/32	inner	9/32	46°	.025	—	26°	7/8	32°	②
	17085216	13/32	inner	9/32	20°	.025	26°	38°	7/8	39°	②
	17085217	13/32	inner	9/32	20°	.025	26°	36°	1/2	39°	②
	17085219	13/32	inner	9/32	20°	.025	26°	36°	1/2	39°	②
	17085220	13/32	outer	3/8	20°	.025	—	26°	7/8	32°	75
	17085221	13/32	outer	3/8	20°	.025	—	26°	7/8	32°	75
	17085222	13/32	inner	9/32	20°	.025	26°	36°	1/2	39°	20
	17085223	13/32	outer	3/8	20°	.025	26°	36°	1/2	39°	50
	17085224	13/32	inner	9/32	20°	.025	26°	36°	1/2	39°	20
	17085225	13/32	outer	3/8	20°	.025	26°	36°	1/2	39°	50
	17085226	13/32	inner	9/32	20°	.025	—	24°	7/8	32°	20
	17085227	13/32	inner	9/32	20°	.025	—	24°	7/8	32°	20
	17085228	13/32	inner	9/32	46°	.025	—	24°	7/8	39°	30
	17085229	13/32	inner	9/32	46°	.025	—	24°	7/8	39°	30
	17085230	13/32	inner	9/32	20°	.025	—	26°	7/8	32°	20
	17085231	13/32	inner	9/32	20°	.025	—	26°	7/8	32°	40
	17085235	13/32	inner	9/32	46°	.025	—	26°	7/8	39°	80

ROCHESTER MODEL M4MC/M4ME/M4MEF QUADRAJET Chevrolet/GMC

(All measurements in inches or degrees)

Year	Carburetor Number	Float Level	Pump Rod Hole	Pump Rod Setting	Choke Rod ① Setting	Air Valve Rod	Vacuum Break Front	Vacuum Break Rear	Air Valve Turns	Choke Unloader	Propane Enrichment (rpm)
1987-88	17085238	13/32	outer	3/8	20°	.025	—	26°	7/8	32°	75
	17085239	13/32	outer	3/8	20°	.025	—	26°	7/8	32°	75
	17085283	13/32	inner	9/32	20°	.025	—	24°	7/8	32°	20
	17085284	13/32	inner	9/32	20°	.025	—	26°	7/8	32°	20
	17085285	13/32	inner	9/32	20°	.025	—	24°	7/8	32°	20
	17085290	13/32	inner	9/32	46°	.025	—	24°	7/8	39°	30
	17085291	13/32	outer	3/8	46°	.025	—	26°	7/8	39°	100
	17085292	13/32	inner	9/32	46°	.025	—	24°	7/8	39°	30
	17085293	13/32	outer	3/8	46°	.025	—	26°	7/8	39°	100
	17085294	13/32	inner	9/32	46°	.025	—	26°	7/8	39°	②
	17085298	13/32	inner	9/32	46°	.025	—	26°	7/8	39°	②

NOTE: Specified angle for use with angle degree tool. Choke coil lever setting is .120 in. for all carburetors.

① Second step of fast idle cam

② See Underhood Specifications sticker

1. Air Horn Assy.
2. Gasket—Air Horn
3. Lever—Pump Actuating
4. Roll Pin—Pump Lever Hinge
5. Screw—Air Horn Long (2)
6. Screw—Air Horn Short ( )
7. Screw — Air Horn Countersunk (2)
8. Metering Rod—Secondary (2)
9. Holder and Screw—Secondary Metering Rod
10. Baffle—Secondary Air
11. Seal—Pump Plunger
12. Retainer—Pump Seal
13. Vac. Break Control & Bracket—Front
14. Screw—Control Attaching (2)
15. Hose—Vacuum
16. Rod—Air Valve
16A. Rod—Air Valve (Truck)
17. Lever—Choke Rod (Upper)
18. Screw—Choke Lever
19. Rod—Choke
20. Lever—Choke Rod (Lower)
21. Seal—Intermediate Choke Shaft
22. Lever—Secondary Lockout
23. Link—Rear Vacuum Break
24. Int. Choke Shaft & Lever
25. Cam—Fast Idle
26. Seal—Choke Housing to Bowl (Hot Air Choke)
27. Kit—Choke Housing
28. Screw—Choke Housing to Bowl
29. Seal—Intermediate Choke Shaft (Hot Air Choke)
30. Lever—Choke Coil
31. Screw—Choke Coil Lever
32. Gasket—Stat Cover (Hot Air Choke)
33. Stat Cover & Coil Assy. (Hot Air Choke)
34. Stat Cover & Coil Assy. (Electric Choke)
35. Kit — Stat Cover Attaching
36. Rear Vacuum Break Assembly
37. Screw—Vacuum Break Attaching (2)
40. Ball—Pump Discharge
41. Retainer—Pump Discharge Ball
42. Baffle—Pump Well
43. Needle & Seat Assembly
44. Float Assembly
45. Hinge Pin — Float Assembly
46. Power Piston Assembly
47. Spring—Power Piston
48. Rod—Primary Metering (2)
49. Spring—Metering Rod Retainer
50. Insert—Float Bowl
51. Insert—Bowl Cavity
52. Spring—Pump Return
53. Pump Assembly
54. Rod—Pump
55. Baffle—Secondary Bores
56. Idle Compensator Assembly
57. Seal—Idle Compensator
58. Cover—Idle Compensator
59. Screw—Idle Compensator Cover (2)
60. Filter Nut—Fuel Inlet
61. Gasket—Filter Nut
62. Filter—Fuel Inlet
63. Spring—Fuel Filter
64. Screw—Idle Stop
65. Spring — Idle Stop Screw
66. Idle Speed Solenoid & Bracket Assembly
67. Idle Load Compensator & Bracket Assembly
68. Bracket—Throttle Return Spring
69. Actuator—Throttle Lever (Truck Only)
70. Bracket—Throttle Lever Actuator (Truck Only)
71. Washer—Actuator Nut (Truck Only)
72. Nut—Actuator Attaching (Truck Only)
73. Screw—Bracket Attaching (2)
74. Throttle Body Assembly
75. Gasket—Throttle Body
76. Screw—Throttle Body (3)
77. Idle Mixture Needle & Spring Assy. (2)
78. Screw — Fast Idle Adjusting
79. Spring — Fast Idle Screw
80. Tee—Vacuum Hose
81. Gasket—Flange

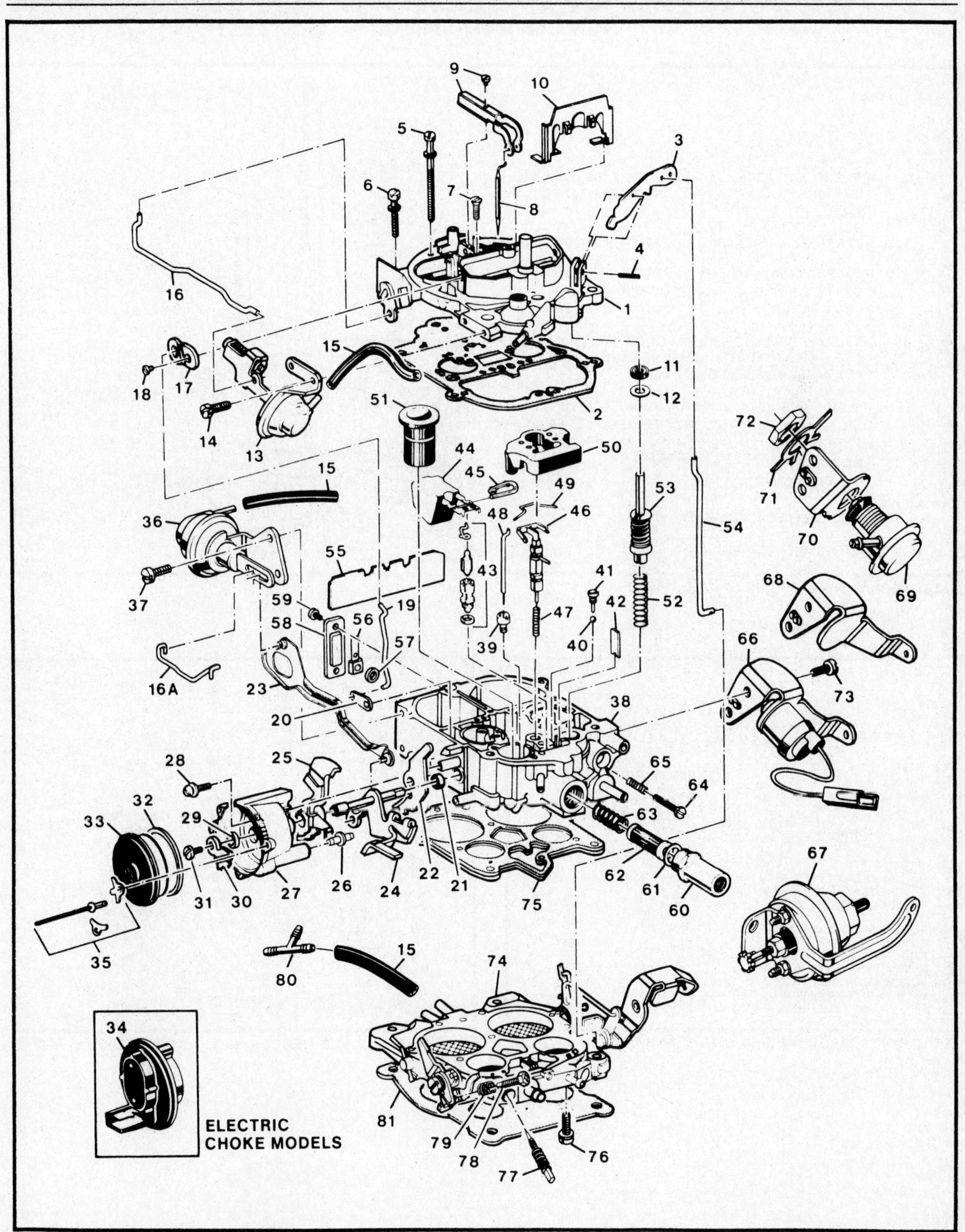

M4MC/M4ME carburetor exploded view

MODELS M4MC/M4ME

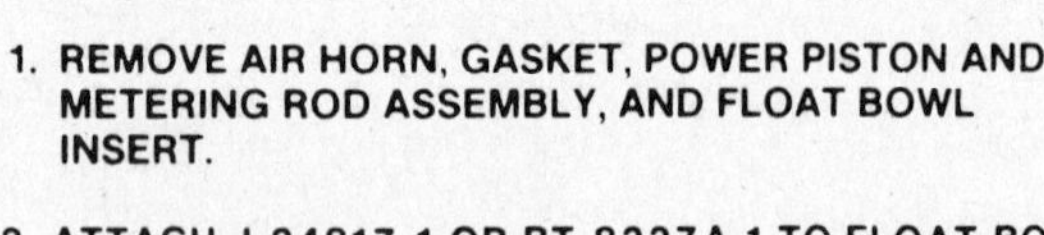

1. REMOVE AIR HORN, GASKET, POWER PISTON AND METERING ROD ASSEMBLY, AND FLOAT BOWL INSERT.
2. ATTACH J-34817-1 OR BT-8227A-1 TO FLOAT BOWL.
3. PLACE J-34817-3 OR BT-8227A IN BASE WITH CONTACT PIN RESTING ON OUTER EDGE OF FLOAT LEVER.
4. MEASURE DISTANCE FROM TOP OF CASTING TO TOP OF FLOAT, AT POINT 3/16" FROM LARGE END OF FLOAT. USE J-9789-90 OR BT-8037.
5. IF MORE THAN ±2/32" FROM SPECIFICATION, USE J-34817-25 OR BT-8427 TO BEND LEVER UP OR DOWN. REMOVE BENDING TOOL AND MEASURE, REPEATING UNTIL WITHIN SPECIFICATION.
6. CHECK FLOAT ALIGNMENT.
7. REASSEMBLE CARBURETOR.

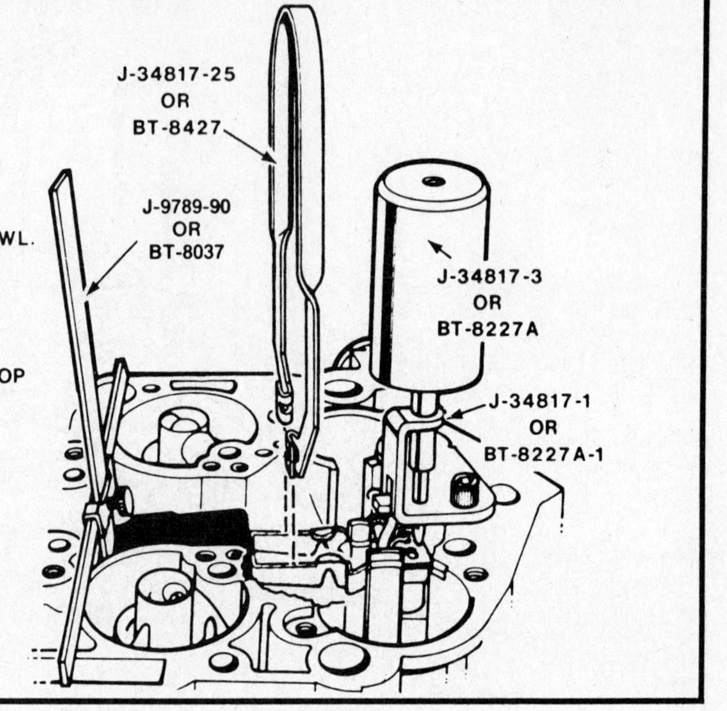
J-34817-25
OR
BT-8427
J-9789-90
OR
BT-8037
J-34817-3
OR
BT-8227A
J-34817-1
OR
BT-8227A-1

Float adjustment, models M4MC/M4ME

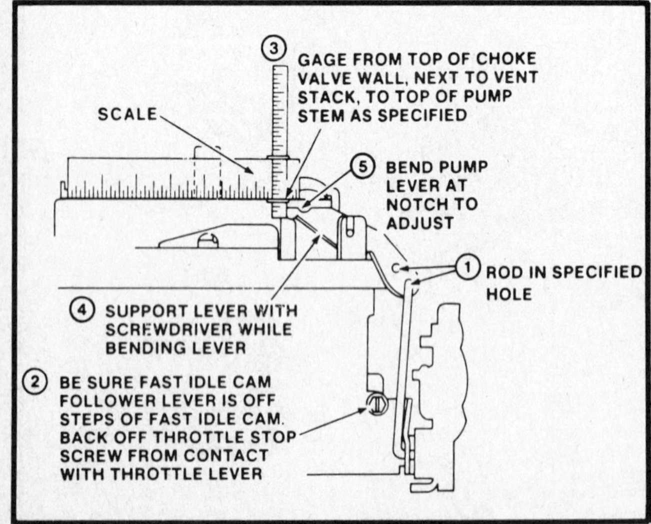
③ GAGE FROM TOP OF CHOKE VALVE WALL, NEXT TO VENT STACK, TO TOP OF PUMP STEM AS SPECIFIED
SCALE
⑤ BEND PUMP LEVER AT NOTCH TO ADJUST
① ROD IN SPECIFIED HOLE
④ SUPPORT LEVER WITH SCREWDRIVER WHILE BENDING LEVER
② BE SURE FAST IDLE CAM FOLLOWER LEVER IS OFF STEPS OF FAST IDLE CAM. BACK OFF THROTTLE STOP SCREW FROM CONTACT WITH THROTTLE LEVER

Pump adjustment, models M4MC/M4ME

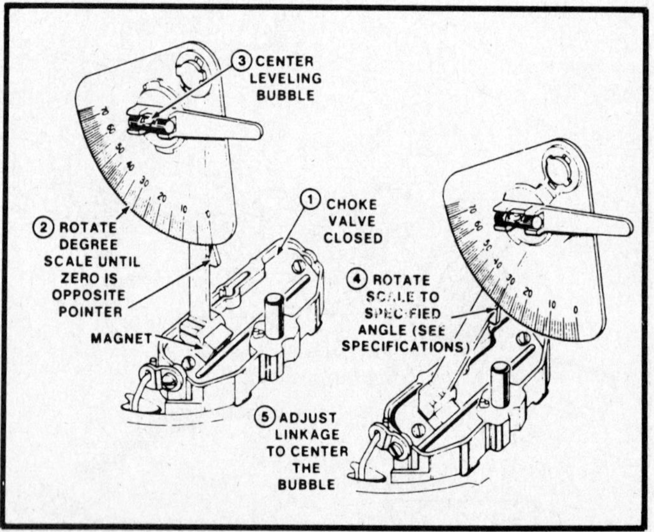
③ CENTER LEVELING BUBBLE
② ROTATE DEGREE SCALE UNTIL ZERO IS OPPOSITE POINTER
① CHOKE VALVE CLOSED
MAGNET
④ ROTATE SCALE TO SPECIFIED ANGLE (SEE SPECIFICATIONS)
⑤ ADJUST LINKAGE TO CENTER THE BUBBLE

Choke valve angle gauge usage, models M4MC/M4ME

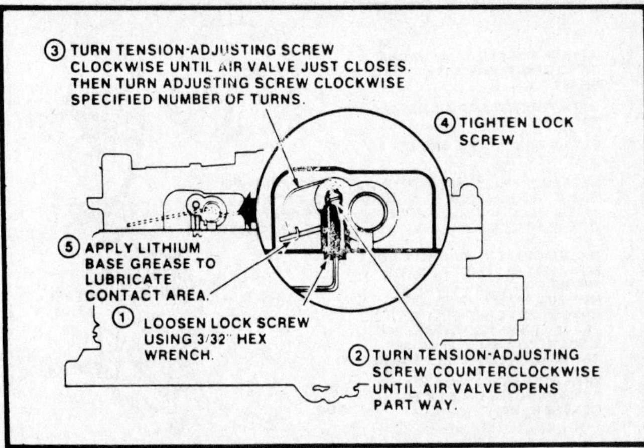

Air valve spring adjustment, models M4MC/M4ME

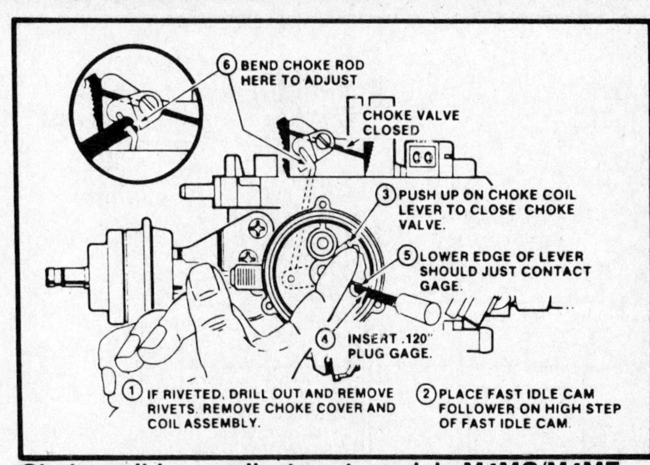

Choke coil lever adjustment, models M4MC/M4ME

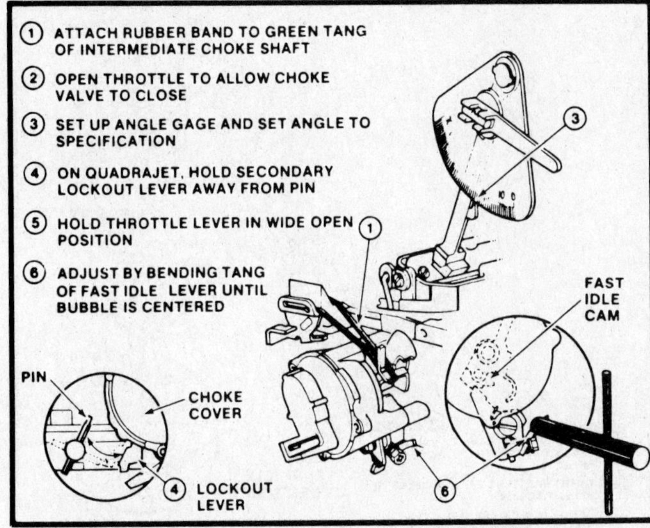

Unloader adjustment, models M4MC/M4ME

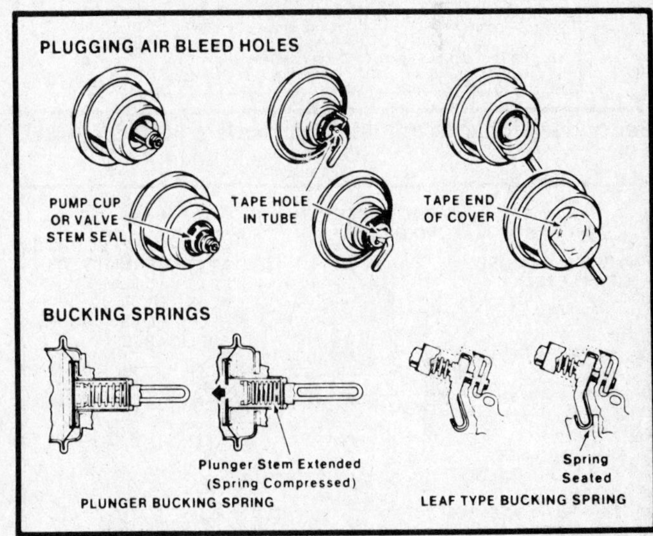

Vacuum break inspection, models M4MC/M4ME

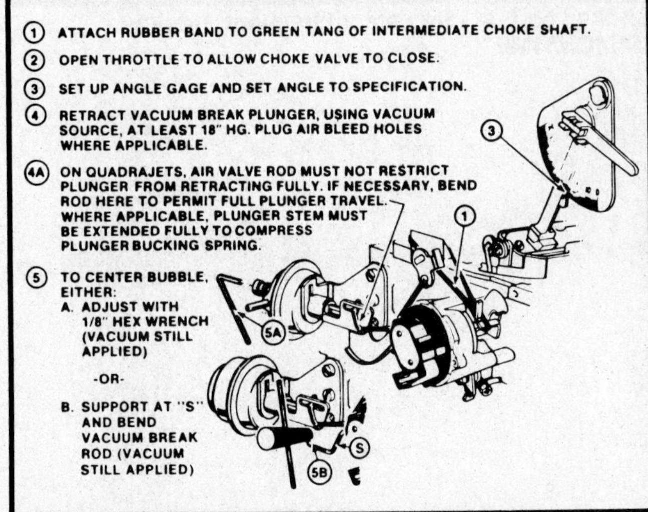

1 ATTACH RUBBER BAND TO GREEN TANG OF INTERMEDIATE CHOKE SHAFT.
2 OPEN THROTTLE TO ALLOW CHOKE VALVE TO CLOSE.
3 SET UP ANGLE GAGE AND SET ANGLE TO SPECIFICATION.
4 RETRACT VACUUM BREAK PLUNGER, USING VACUUM SOURCE, AT LEAST 18" HG. PLUG AIR BLEED HOLES WHERE APPLICABLE.
4A ON QUADRAJETS, AIR VALVE ROD MUST NOT RESTRICT PLUNGER FROM RETRACTING FULLY. IF NECESSARY, BEND ROD HERE TO PERMIT FULL PLUNGER TRAVEL. WHERE APPLICABLE, PLUNGER STEM MUST BE EXTENDED FULLY TO COMPRESS PLUNGER BUCKING SPRING.
5 TO CENTER BUBBLE, EITHER:
A. ADJUST WITH 1/8" HEX WRENCH (VACUUM STILL APPLIED)
-OR-
B. SUPPORT AT "S" AND BEND VACUUM BREAK ROD (VACUUM STILL APPLIED)
5A
5B
S

Rear (secondary) vacuum break adjustment, models M4MC/M4ME

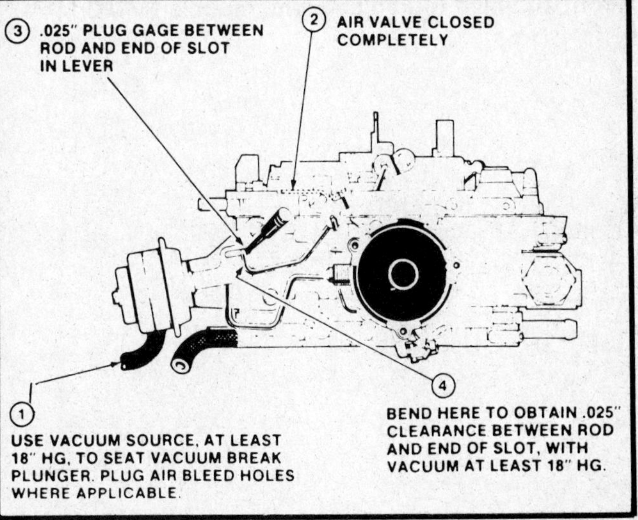

Rear air valve rod adjustment, models M4MC/M4ME

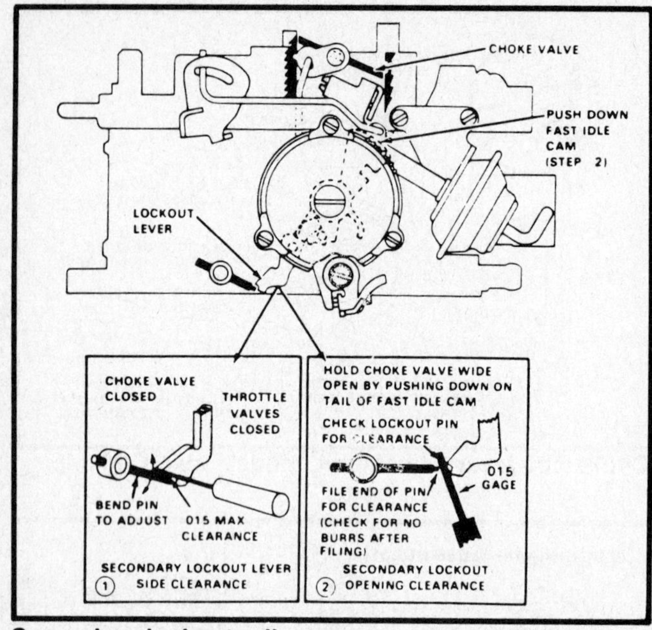
CHOKE VALVE
PUSH DOWN FAST IDLE CAM (STEP 2)
LOCKOUT LEVER
CHOKE VALVE CLOSED
THROTTLE VALVES CLOSED
BEND PIN TO ADJUST
.015 MAX CLEARANCE
SECONDARY LOCKOUT LEVER
1 SIDE CLEARANCE
HOLD CHOKE VALVE WIDE OPEN BY PUSHING DOWN ON TAIL OF FAST IDLE CAM
CHECK LOCKOUT PIN FOR CLEARANCE
.015 GAGE
FILE END OF PIN FOR CLEARANCE (CHECK FOR NO BURRS AFTER FILING)
SECONDARY LOCKOUT
2 OPENING CLEARANCE

Secondary lockout adjustment, models M4MC/M4ME

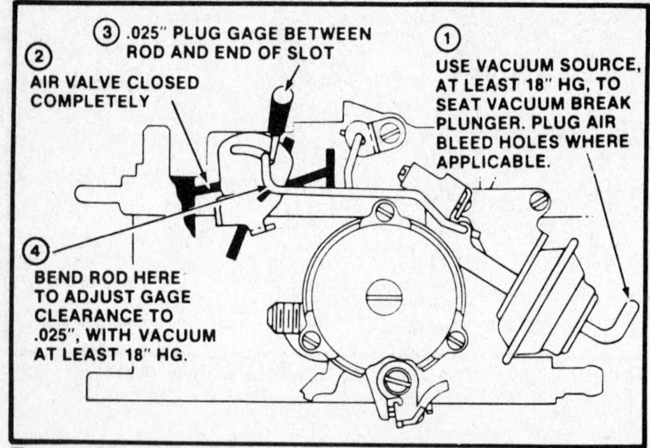
3 .025" PLUG GAGE BETWEEN ROD AND END OF SLOT
2 AIR VALVE CLOSED COMPLETELY
1 USE VACUUM SOURCE, AT LEAST 18" HG, TO SEAT VACUUM BREAK PLUNGER. PLUG AIR BLEED HOLES WHERE APPLICABLE.
4 BEND ROD HERE TO ADJUST GAGE CLEARANCE TO .025", WITH VACUUM AT LEAST 18" HG.

Front air valve rod adjustment, models M4MC/M4ME

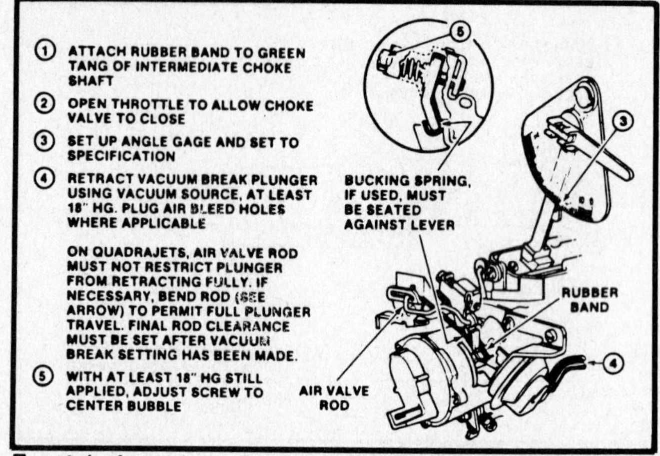
1 ATTACH RUBBER BAND TO GREEN TANG OF INTERMEDIATE CHOKE SHAFT
2 OPEN THROTTLE TO ALLOW CHOKE VALVE TO CLOSE
3 SET UP ANGLE GAGE AND SET TO SPECIFICATION
4 RETRACT VACUUM BREAK PLUNGER USING VACUUM SOURCE, AT LEAST 18" HG. PLUG AIR BLEED HOLES WHERE APPLICABLE
ON QUADRAJETS, AIR VALVE ROD MUST NOT RESTRICT PLUNGER FROM RETRACTING FULLY. IF NECESSARY, BEND ROD (SEE ARROW) TO PERMIT FULL PLUNGER TRAVEL. FINAL ROD CLEARANCE MUST BE SET AFTER VACUUM BREAK SETTING HAS BEEN MADE.
5 WITH AT LEAST 18" HG STILL APPLIED, ADJUST SCREW TO CENTER BUBBLE
BUCKING SPRING, IF USED, MUST BE SEATED AGAINST LEVER
RUBBER BAND
AIR VALVE ROD

Front (primary) vacuum break adjustment, models M4MC/M4ME

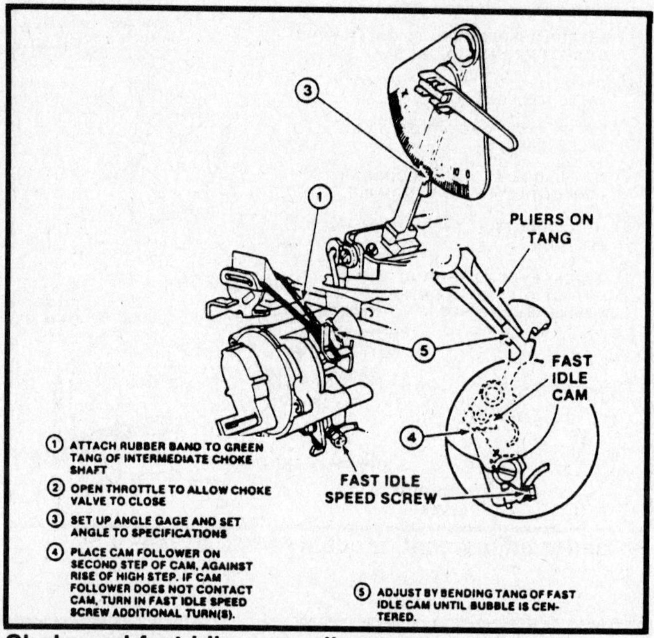
PLIERS ON TANG
FAST IDLE CAM
FAST IDLE SPEED SCREW
1 ATTACH RUBBER BAND TO GREEN TANG OF INTERMEDIATE CHOKE SHAFT
2 OPEN THROTTLE TO ALLOW CHOKE VALVE TO CLOSE
3 SET UP ANGLE GAGE AND SET ANGLE TO SPECIFICATIONS
4 PLACE CAM FOLLOWER ON SECOND STEP OF CAM, AGAINST RISE OF HIGH STEP. IF CAM FOLLOWER DOES NOT CONTACT CAM, TURN IN FAST IDLE SPEED SCREW ADDITIONAL TURN(S).
5 ADJUST BY BENDING TANG OF FAST IDLE CAM UNTIL BUBBLE IS CENTERED.

Choke rod fast idle cam adjustment, models M4MC/M4ME

MODEL E4ME

NOTE: Refer to Models M4MC/M4ME Carburetors for adjustment procedures.

ROCHESTER MODEL E4ME
Chevrolet/GMC

(All measurements in inches or degrees)

Year	Carburetor Number	Float Level	Rich Mixture Screw	Idle Mixture Needle Turns	Air Valve Spring Turns	Choke Rod	Front Vacuum Break	Rear Vacuum Break	Air Valve Rod	Choke Unloader	Idle Air Bleed Valve
1983	17083202	11/32	—	3 3/8	7/8	20°	—	27°	—	38°	①
	17083203	11/32	—	3 3/8	7/8	38°	—	27°	—	38°	①
	17083204	11/32	—	3 3/8	7/8	20°	—	27°	—	38°	①
	17083207	11/32	—	3 3/8	7/8	38°	—	27°	—	38°	①
	17083216	11/32	—	3 3/8	7/8	20°	—	27°	—	38°	①
	17083218	11/32	—	3 3/8	7/8	20°	—	27°	—	38°	①
	17083236	11/32	—	②	7/8	20°	—	27°	—	38°	1.756
	17083506	7/16	—	②	7/8	20°	27°	36°	—	36°	1.756
	17083508	7/16	—	②	7/8	20°	27°	36°	—	36°	1.756
	17083524	7/16	—	②	7/8	20°	25°	36°	—	36°	1.756
	17083526	7/16	—	②	7/8	20°	25°	36°	—	36°	1.756
1984	17084201	11/32	4/32	3 3/8	7/8	20°	27°	—	.025	38°	①
	17084205	11/32	4/32	3 3/8	7/8	38°	27°	—	.025	38°	①
	17084208	11/32	4/32	3 3/8	7/8	20°	27°	—	.025	38°	①
	17084209	11/32	4/32	3 3/8	7/8	38°	27°	—	.025	38°	①
	17084210	11/32	4/32	3 3/8	7/8	20°	27°	—	.025	38°	①
	17084507	7/16	4/32	②	1	20°	27°	36°	.025	36°	①
	17084509	7/16	4/32	②	1	20°	27°	36°	.025	36°	①
	17084525	7/16	4/32	②	1	20°	25°	36°	.025	36°	①
	17084527	7/16	4/32	②	1	20°	25°	36°	.025	36°	①
1985	17085202	11/32	4/32	3 3/8	7/8	20°	27°	—	.025	38°	①
	17085203	11/32	4/32	3 3/8	7/8	20°	27°	—	.025	38°	①
	17085204	11/32	4/32	3 3/8	7/8	20°	27°	—	.025	38°	①
	17085207	11/32	4/32	3 3/8	7/8	38°	27°	—	.025	38°	①
	17085218	11/32	4/32	3 3/8	7/8	20°	27°	—	.025	38°	①
1986	17085502	7/16	—	②	7/8	20°	26°	36°	.025	39°	①
	17085503	7/16	—	②	7/8	20°	26°	36°	.025	39°	①
	17085506	7/16	—	②	1	20°	27°	36°	.025	36°	①
	17085508	7/16	—	②	1	20°	27°	36°	.025	36°	①
	17085524	7/16	—	②	1	20°	25°	36°	.025	36°	①
	17085526	7/16	—	②	1	20°	25°	36°	.025	36°	①

Note: Specified angle for use with angle degree tool
Lean mixture screw-1.304 gauge
Choke stat lever-.120 gauge

① Preset with 1.756 gauge, final adjustment on vehicle
② Preset 3 turns, final adjustment on vehicle

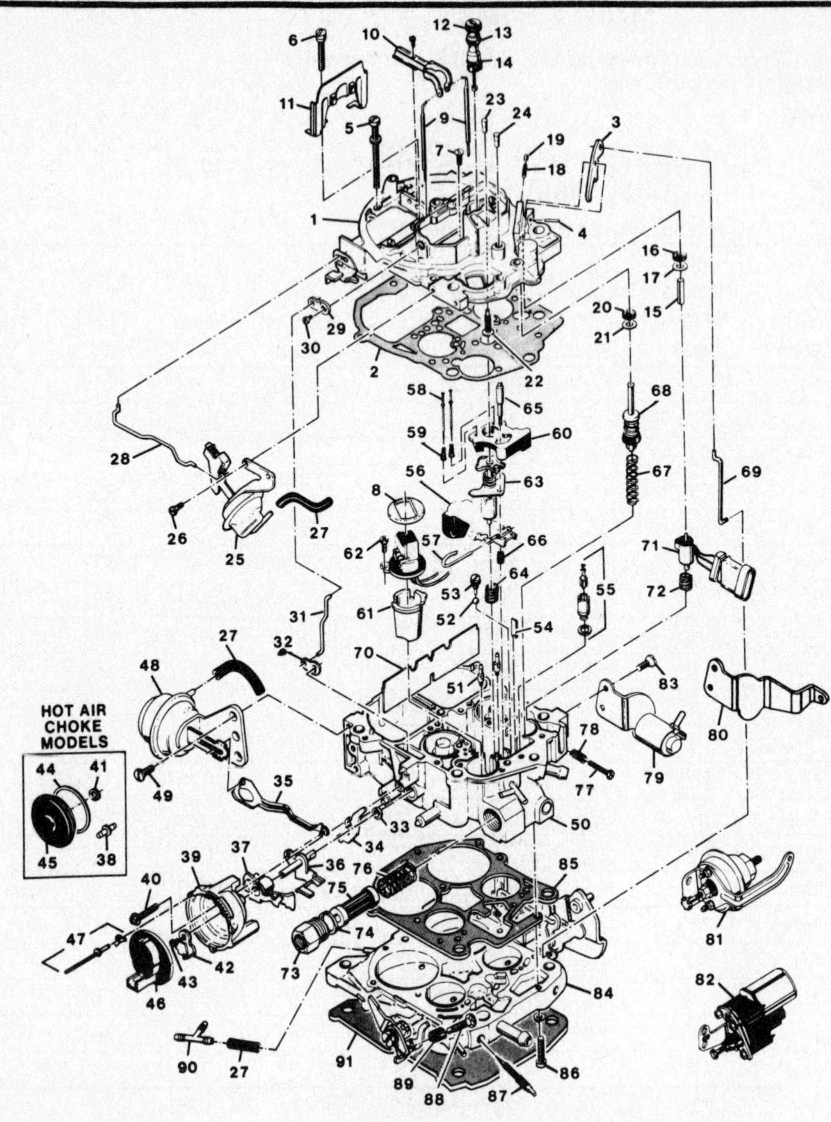

1. Air horn assembly
2. Gasket—air horn
3. Lever—pump actuating
4. Roll pin—pump lever hinge
5. Screw—air horn, long (2)
6. Screw—air horn, short
7. Screw—air horn, countersunk (2)
8. Gasket—solenoid connector to air horn
9. Metering rod—secondary (2)
10. Holder & screw—secondary metering rod
11. Baffle—secondary air
12. Valve—idle air bleed
13. "O" ring (thick)—idle air bleed valve
14. "O" ring (thin)—idle air bleed valve
15. Plunger—TPS actuator
16. Seal—TPS plunger
17. Retainer—TPS seal
18. Screw—TPS adjusting
19. Plug—TPS screw
20. Seal—pump plunger
21. Retainer—pump seal
22. Screw—solenoid plunger stop (rich mixture stop)
23. Plug—plunger stop screw (rich mixture stop)
24. Plug—solenoid adjusting screw (lean mixture)
25. Vacuum break & bracket—front
26. Screw—vacuum break attaching (2)
27. Hose—vacuum
28. Rod—air valve
29. Lever—choke rod
30. Screw—choke lever
31. Rod—choke
32. Lever—choke rod (lower)
33. Seal—intermediate choke shaft
34. Lever—secondary lockout
35. Link—rear vacuum break
36. Intermediate choke shaft & lever
37. Cam—fast idle
38. Seal—choke housing to bowl (hot air choke)
39. Choke housing
40. Screw—choke housing to bowl
41. Seal—intermediate choke shaft (hot air choke)
42. Lever—choke coil
43. Screw—choke coil lever
44. Gasket—Stat cover (hot air choke)
45. Stat cover & coil assembly (hot air choke)
46. Stat cover & coil assembly (electric choke)
47. Kit—stat cover attaching
48. Vacuum break assembly—rear
49. Screw—vacuum break attaching (2)
50. Float Bowl Assembly
51. Jet—primary metering (2)
52. Ball—pump discharge
53. Retainer—pump discharge ball
54. Baffle—pump well
55. Needle & seat assembly
56. Float assembly
57. Hinge pin—float assembly
58. Rod—primary metering (2)
59. Spring—primary metering rod (2)
60. Insert—float bowl
61. Insert—bowl cavity
62. Screw—connector attaching
63. Mixture control (M/C) solenoid & plunger assembly
64. Spring—solenoid tension
65. Screw—solenoid adjusting (lean mixture)
66. Spring—solenoid adjusting screw
67. Spring—pump return
68. Pump assembly
69. Link—pump
70. Baffle—secondary bores
71. Throttle position sensor (TPS)
72. Spring—TPS Tension
73. Filter nut—fuel inlet
74. Gasket—filter nut
75. Filter—fuel inlet
76. Spring—fuel filter
77. Screw—idle stop
78. Spring—idle stop screw
79. Idle speed solenoid & bracket assembly
80. Bracket—throttle return spring
81. Idle load compensator & bracket assembly
82. Idle speed control & bracket assembly
83. Screw—bracket attaching
84. Throttle body assembly
85. Gasket—throttle body
86. Screw—throttle body
87. Idle needle & spring assembly (2)
88. Screw—fast idle adjusting
89. Spring fast idle screw
90. Tee—vacuum hose
91. Gasket—flange

Exploded view of Rochester E4ME carburetor

GENERAL ROCHESTER CARBURETOR SPECIFICATIONS

ANGLE DEGREE TO DECIMAL CONVERSION
Rochester Model M4MC Carburetor

Angle Degrees	Decimal Equiv. Top of Valve	Angle Degrees	Decimal Equiv. Top of Valve
5	.023	33	.203
6	.028	34	.211
7	.033	35	.220
8	.038	36	.227
9	.043	37	.234
10	.049	38	.243
11	.054	39	.251
12	.060	40	.260
13	.066	41	.269
14	.071	42	.277
15	.077	43	.287
16	.083	44	.295
17	.090	45	.304
18	.096	46	.314
19	.103	47	.322
20	.110	48	.332
21	.117	49	.341
22	.123	50	.350
23	.129	51	.360
24	.136	52	.370
25	.142	53	.379
26	.149	54	.388
27	.157	55	.400
28	.164	56	.408
29	.171	57	.418
30	.179	58	.428
31	.187	59	.439
32	.195	60	.449

ANGLE DEGREE TO DECIMAL CONVERSION
Rochester Model M4MV Carburetor

Angle Degrees	Decimal Equiv. Top of Valve	Angle Degrees	Decimal Equiv. Top of Valve
5	.019	33	.158
6	.022	34	.164
7	.026	35	.171
8	.030	36	.178
9	.034	37	.184
10	.038	38	.190
11	.042	39	.197
12	.047	40	.204
13	.051	41	.211
14	.056	42	.217

ANGLE DEGREE TO DECIMAL CONVERSION
Rochester Model M4MV Carburetor

Angle Degrees	Decimal Equiv. Top of Valve	Angle Degrees	Decimal Equiv. Top of Valve
15	.060	43	.225
16	.065	44	.231
17	.070	45	.239
18	.075	46	.246
19	.080	47	.253
20	.085	48	.260
21	.090	49	.268
22	.095	50	.275
23	.101	51	.283
24	.106	52	.291
25	.112	53	.299
26	.117	54	.306
27	.123	55	.314
28	.128	56	.322
29	.134	57	.329
30	.140	58	.337
31	.146	59	.345
32	.152	60	.353

TPS ADJUSTMENT SPECIFICATIONS
Chevrolet/GMC Models

Year	Engine Code	TPS Voltage
1983	H	.51
	G	.51
	F	.40
	L	.40
1984	B	.255
	X	.31
	Z	.255
	G	.48
	H	.48
	G	.48
	F	.41
	L	.41
1985	G	.48
	H	.48
	G	.48
	F	.41
	L	.41
	N	.25
1986	F	.41
	L	.41
	N	.25

Note: Measure voltage with throttle at curb idle position, ignition ON, engine and A/C OFF. All values ± 0.1 volt.

STROMBERG MODEL DCH340
Chevrolet S-10

(All measurements in inches)

Float Needle Valve Stroke	Primary Throttle Valve Adjustment	Secondary Throttle Opening Point	Kick Lever Adjustment
.059	.050–.059 ①	.24–.30	②

① Applies to manual trans. automatic trans. .059–.069

② Zero clearance between kick lever screw and return plate—throttle fully closed.

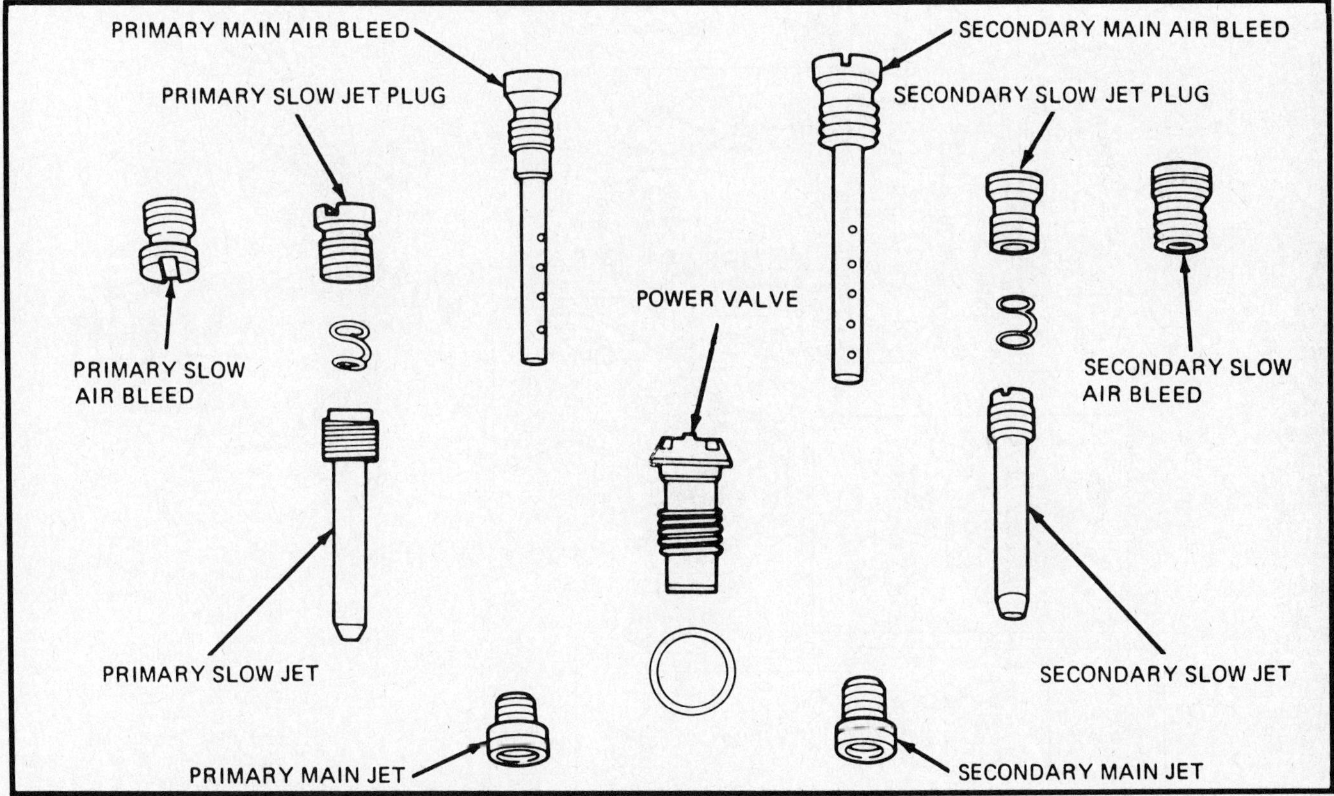

Carburetor jet identification, model DCH340

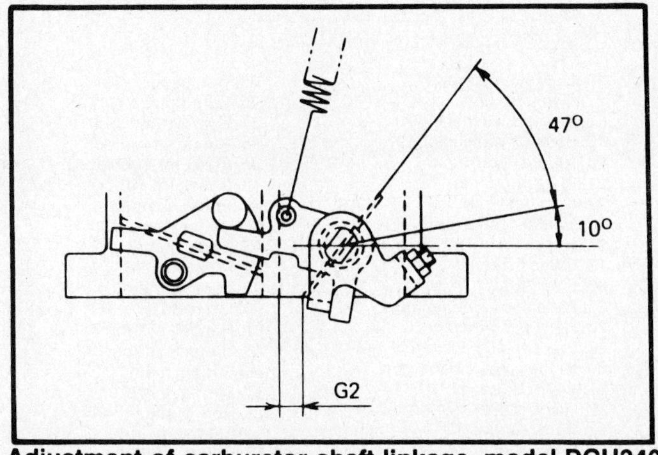

Adjustment of carburetor shaft linkage, model DCH340

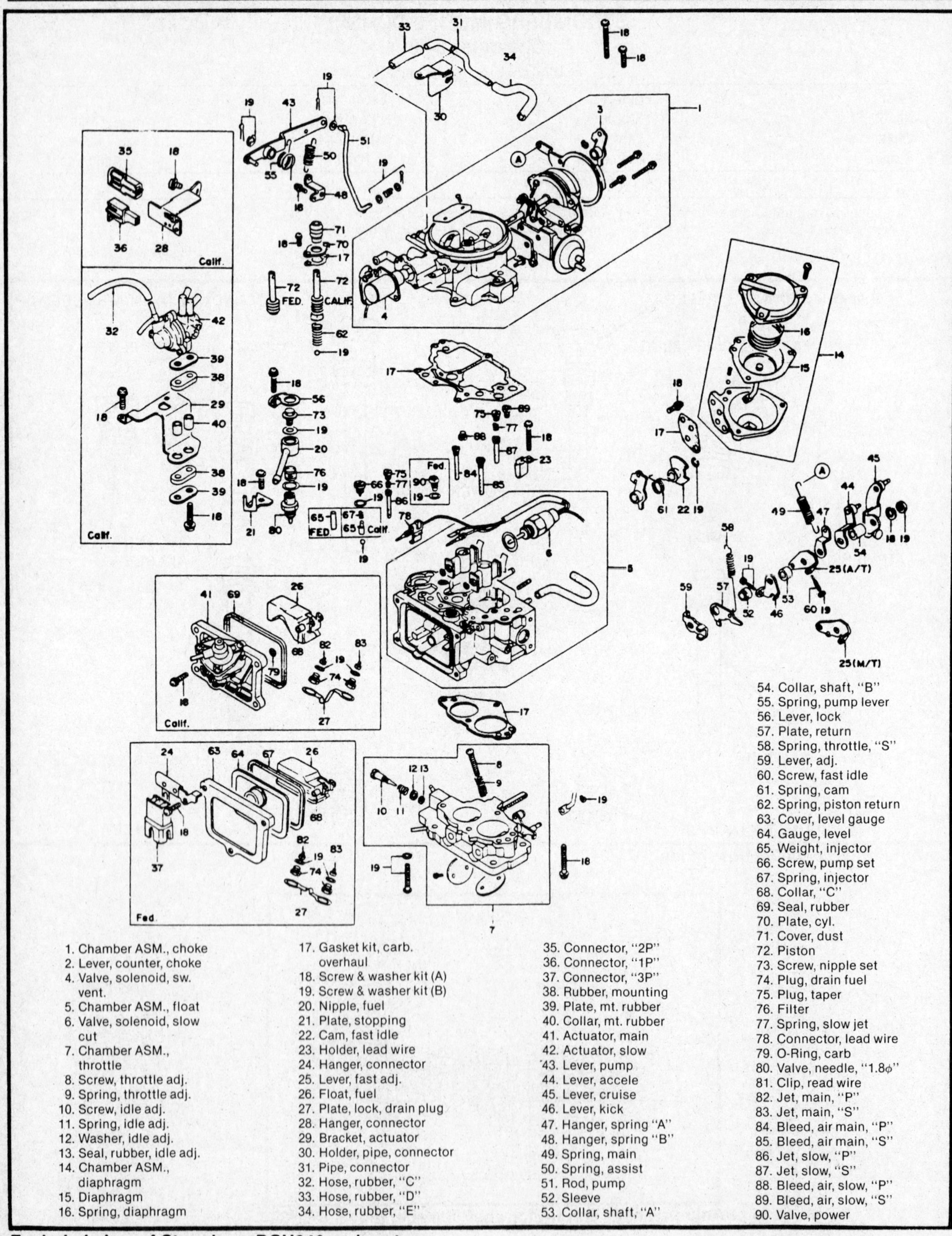

1. Chamber ASM., choke
2. Lever, counter, choke
4. Valve, solenoid, sw. vent.
5. Chamber ASM., float
6. Valve, solenoid, slow cut
7. Chamber ASM., throttle
8. Screw, throttle adj.
9. Spring, throttle adj.
10. Screw, idle adj.
11. Spring, idle adj.
12. Washer, idle adj.
13. Seal, rubber, idle adj.
14. Chamber ASM., diaphragm
15. Diaphragm
16. Spring, diaphragm
17. Gasket kit, carb. overhaul
18. Screw & washer kit (A)
19. Screw & washer kit (B)
20. Nipple, fuel
21. Plate, stopping
22. Cam, fast idle
23. Holder, lead wire
24. Hanger, connector
25. Lever, fast adj.
26. Float, fuel
27. Plate, lock, drain plug
28. Hanger, connector
29. Bracket, actuator
30. Holder, pipe, connector
31. Pipe, connector
32. Hose, rubber, "C"
33. Hose, rubber, "D"
34. Hose, rubber, "E"
35. Connector, "2P"
36. Connector, "1P"
37. Connector, "3P"
38. Rubber, mounting
39. Plate, mt. rubber
40. Collar, mt. rubber
41. Actuator, main
42. Actuator, slow
43. Lever, pump
44. Lever, accele
45. Lever, cruise
46. Lever, kick
47. Hanger, spring "A"
48. Hanger, spring "B"
49. Spring, main
50. Spring, assist
51. Rod, pump
52. Sleeve
53. Collar, shaft, "A"
54. Collar, shaft, "B"
55. Spring, pump lever
56. Lever, lock
57. Plate, return
58. Spring, throttle, "S"
59. Lever, adj.
60. Screw, fast idle
61. Spring, cam
62. Spring, piston return
63. Cover, level gauge
64. Gauge, level
65. Weight, injector
66. Screw, pump set
67. Spring, injector
68. Collar, "C"
69. Seal, rubber
70. Plate, cyl.
71. Cover, dust
72. Piston
73. Screw, nipple set
74. Plug, drain fuel
75. Plug, taper
76. Filter
77. Spring, slow jet
78. Connector, lead wire
79. O-Ring, carb
80. Valve, needle, "1.8ϕ"
81. Clip, read wire
82. Jet, main, "P"
83. Jet, main, "S"
84. Bleed, air main, "P"
85. Bleed, air main, "S"
86. Jet, slow, "P"
87. Jet, slow, "S"
88. Bleed, air, slow, "P"
89. Bleed, air, slow, "S"
90. Valve, power

Exploded view of Stromberg DCH340 carburetor

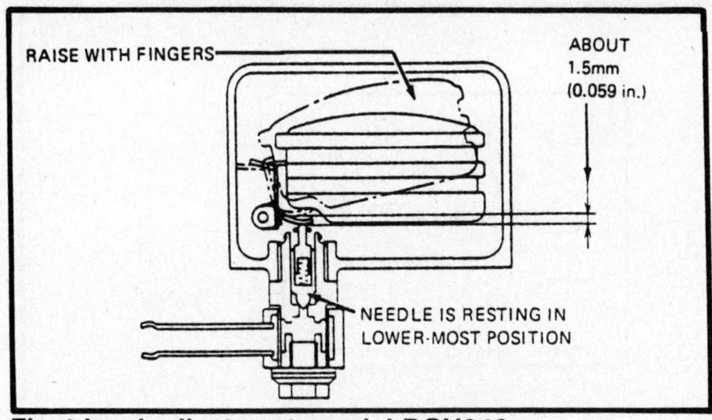

Float level adjustment, model DCH340

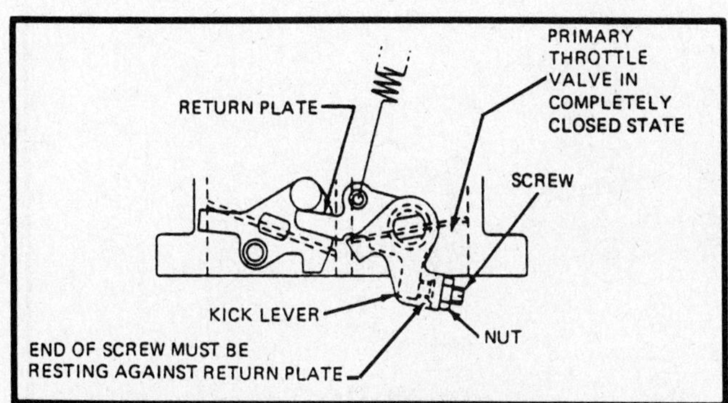

Adjustment of kick lever, model DCH340

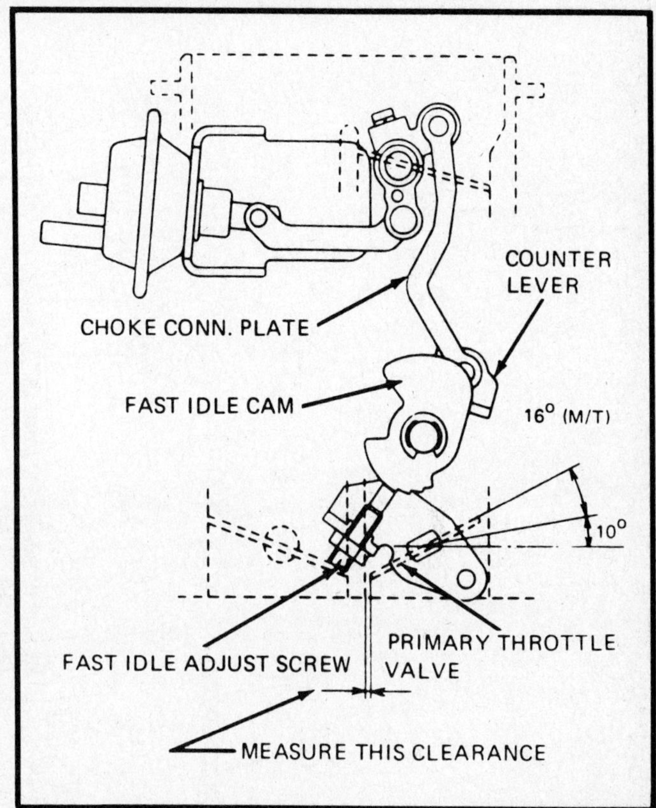

Adjustment of primary throttle valve, model DCH340

DODGE/PLYMOUTH CARBURETORS

CARTER MODEL BBD
Dodge/Plymouth

(All measurements in inches)

Year	Carburetor Number	Float Level	Choke Unloader	Fast Idle Cam Setting	Choke Valve Initial Opening v/Vacuum Kick	Fast Idle Speed (rpm)	Accelerator Pump Setting	Step-up Piston Gap
1982	8146S	.250	.310	.070	.070	1500	.500	.035
	8147S	.250	.310	.110	.150	1500	.500	.035
	8348S	.250	.310	.070	.130	1600	.500	.035
	8352S	.250	.310	.070	.130	1600	.500	.035
1983	8146S	.250	.310	.070	.070	1500	.470	.035
	8147S	.250	.310	.110	.150	1500	.470	.035
	8371S	.250	.280	.070	.130	1600	.470	.035
	8374S	.250	.280	.070	.130	1400	.470	.035
	8359S	.250	.280	.070	.130	1400	.470	.035
	8358S	.250	.280	.070	.130	1400	.470	.035
1984	8387S	.250	.310	.110	.150	1700	.470	.035
	8386S	.250	.310	.070	.070	1500	.470	.035
	8374S	.250	.280	.070	.130	1400	.470	.035
	8359S	.250	.280	.070	.130	1400	.470	.035
	8358S	.250	.280	.070	.130	1400	.470	.035

Note: Choke is fixed on all models

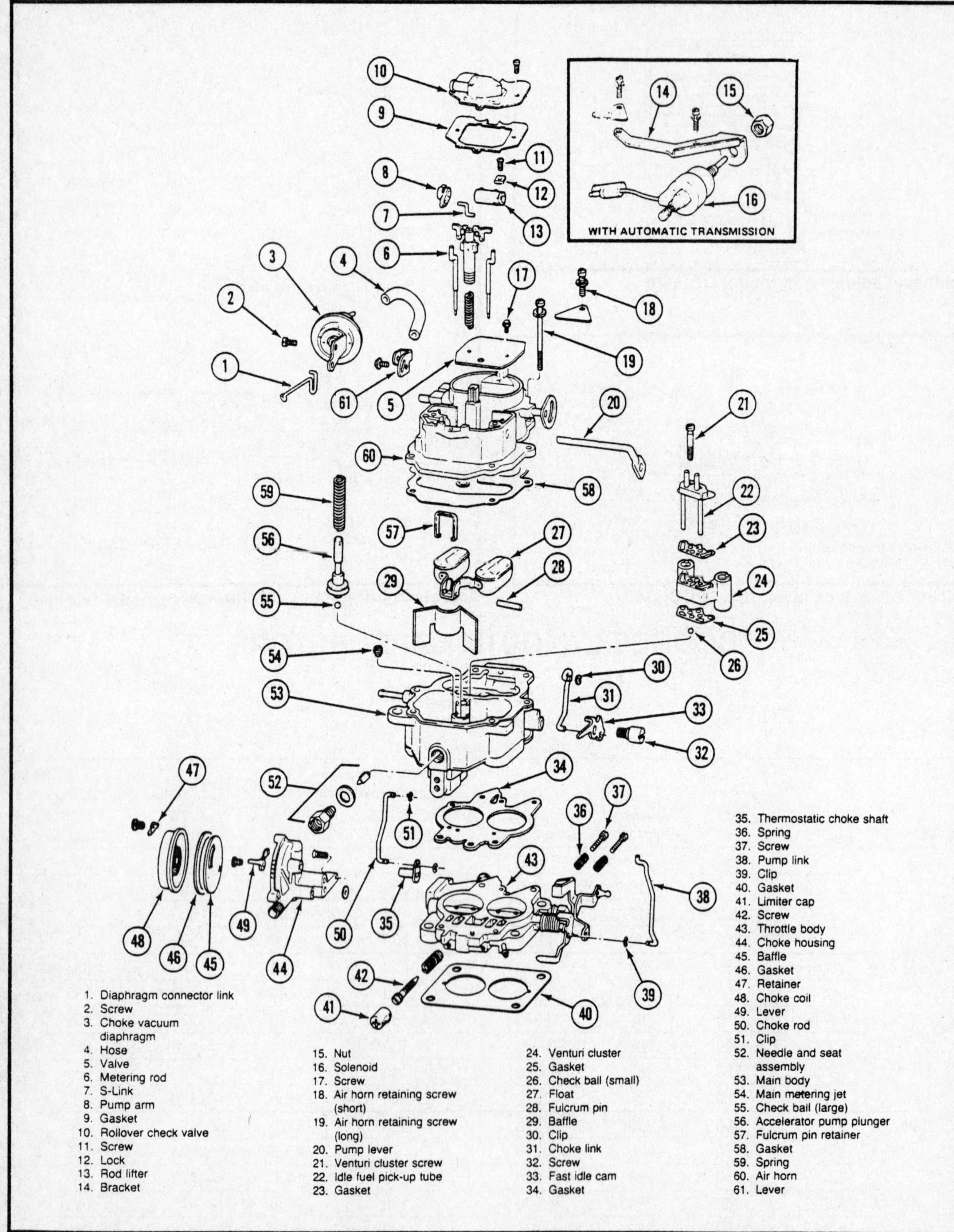
WITH AUTOMATIC TRANSMISSION
1. Diaphragm connector link
2. Screw
3. Choke vacuum diaphragm
4. Hose
5. Valve
6. Metering rod
7. S-Link
8. Pump arm
9. Gasket
10. Rollover check valve
11. Screw
12. Lock
13. Rod lifter
14. Bracket
15. Nut
16. Solenoid
17. Screw
18. Air horn retaining screw (short)
19. Air horn retaining screw (long)
20. Pump lever
21. Venturi cluster screw
22. Idle fuel pick-up tube
23. Gasket
24. Venturi cluster
25. Gasket
26. Check ball (small)
27. Float
28. Fulcrum pin
29. Baffle
30. Clip
31. Choke link
32. Screw
33. Fast idle cam
34. Gasket
35. Thermostatic choke shaft
36. Spring
37. Screw
38. Pump link
39. Clip
40. Gasket
41. Limiter cap
42. Screw
43. Throttle body
44. Choke housing
45. Baffle
46. Gasket
47. Retainer
48. Choke coil
49. Lever
50. Choke rod
51. Clip
52. Needle and seat assembly
53. Main body
54. Main metering jet
55. Check ball (large)
56. Accelerator pump plunger
57. Fulcrum pin retainer
58. Gasket
59. Spring
60. Air horn
61. Lever

Carter BBD two barrel carburetor—typical

Carter Models

MODEL BBD

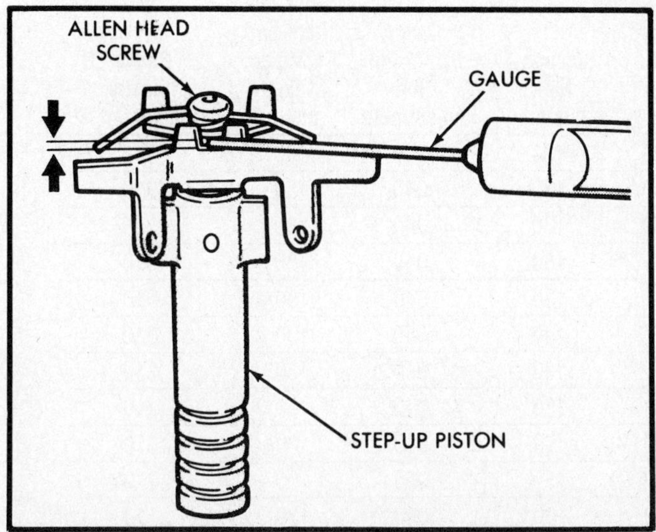

Step-up piston clearance adjustment—BBD carburetor

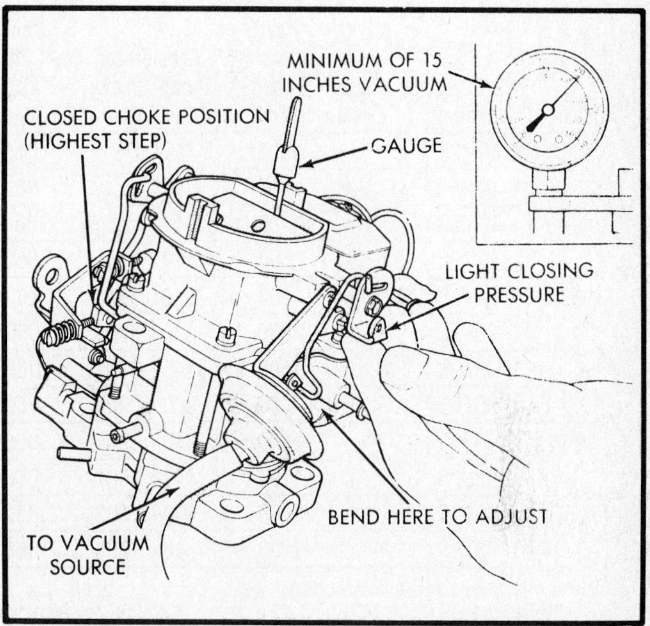

Adjustment of initial opening (vacuum kick)—BBD carburetor

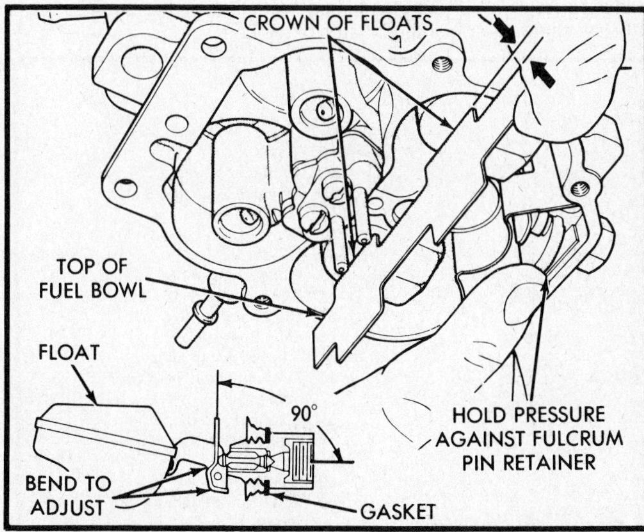

Adjusting float level with bowl inverted—BBD carburetor

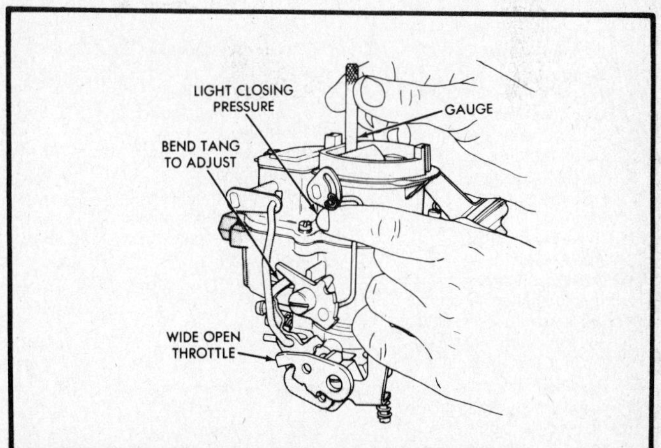

Adjusting choke unloader—BBD carburetor

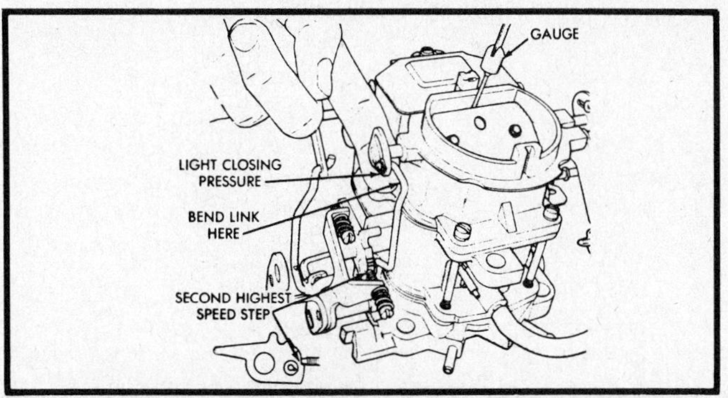

Fast idle cam position adjustment—BBD carburetor

CARTER MODEL TQ
Dodge/Plymouth

(All measurements in inches)

Year	Carburetor Number	Float Level	Fast Idle Speed (rpm)	Accelerator Pump Stroke Adjustment ①	Secondary Throttle Lock-Out Adjustment	Vacuum Kick Adjustment	Choke Diaphragm Rod Adjustment	Fast Idle Cam and Linkage Adjust-ment ③	Choke Unloader Adjustment ②
1982	9342S	29/32	1600	.340	.060–.090	.130	.040	.100 ②	.310
	9375S	29/32	1800	.340	.060–.090	.130	.040	.130 ②	.310
	9376S	29/32	1700	.340	.060–.090	.130	.040	.130 ②	.310
	9379S	29/32	1500	.340	.060–.090	.130	.040	.130 ②	.310
1983	9342S	29/32	1600	.340 (.390)	.060	.130	.040	.100 ②	.310
	9375S	29/32	1800	.340 (.390)	.060	.130	.040	.130 ②	.310
	9379S	29/32	1500	.340 (.390)	.060	.130	.040	.130 ②	.310
	9376S	29/32	1700	.340 (.390)	.060	.180	.040	.100 ②	.310
1984	9386S	29/32	1600	.340 (.190)	.060–.090	.170	.040	.100	.310
	9387S	29/32	1500	.340 (.190)	.060–.090	.150	.040	.100	.310
	9379S	29/32	1500	.340 (.190)	.060–.090	.130	.040	.130	.310
	9376S	29/32	1700	.340 (.190)	.060–.090	.180	.040	.100	.310

Note: Choke is fixed on all models

① Stage I (Stage II). Not Stage II adjustment on 1982 models

② Measure at the lowest edge of the choke valve on the throttle lever side

③ Set the linkage with idle on the second highest step of the cam

1. Fuel inlet nut and gasket
2. Idle compensator screw
3. Idle compensator
4. Idle compensator gasket
5. "E" retainer
6. Primary diaphragm choke pull-off rod washer
7. Primary diaphragm choke pull-off rod
8. Auxiliary diaphragm choke pull-off rod (if equipped)
9. Choke lever screw
10. Choke lever
11. Choke connector rod
12. Countershaft lever screw
13. Countershaft, lever, outer
14. Countershaft lever spring
15. Countershaft lever, inner
16. Fast idle cam rod
17. Throttle connector rod
18. Cover plate screw
19. Metering rod cover plate (opposite pump)
20. Metering rod cover plate (pump side)
21. Step-up piston cover plate
22. Step-up piston and hanger assembly
23. Metering rod
24. Step-up piston spring
25. Bowl cover screw
26. IH part number location
27. Bowl cover assembly
28. Float pin
29. Float assembly
30. Needle, seat, and gasket
31. Pump passage tube
32. Bowl cover gasket
33. Secondary metering jet
34. Primary metering jet
35. Quad rings
36. Pin spring retainer
37. Bowl vent valve lever, upper
38. Bowl vent valve lever spring
39. Bowl vent valve arm
40. Bowl vent valve grommet
41. Rivet plug
42. Pump housing screw
43. Pump housing
44. Pump housing gasket
45. Discharge check needle
46. Pump arm screw
47. Pump arm

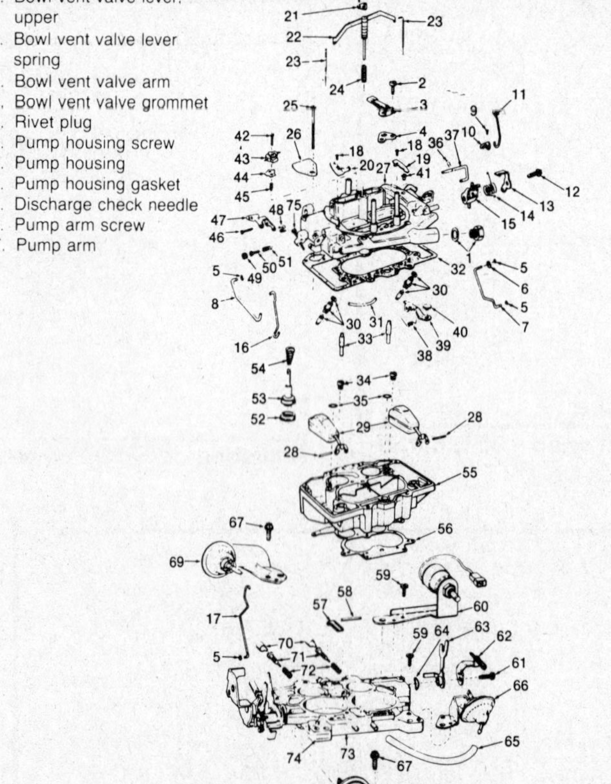

48. Pump "S" link
49. Air valve lock plug
50. Air valve adjustment plug
51. Air valve spring
52. Pump intake check assembly
53. Plunger assembly
54. Plunger spring
55. Main body
56. Main body gasket
57. Step-up piston lifter
58. Step-up piston lifter lever pin
59. Solenoid and diaphragm choke pull-off bracket screw
60. Solenoid
61. Solenoid operating lever screw
62. Curb idle speed screw and lever
63. Bowl vent lever, lower
64. Throttle shaft washer
65. Hose
66. Primary diaphragm choke pull-off bracket
67. Auxiliary choke pull-off and dashpot
68. Auxiliary choke pull-off and bracket (if equipped)
69. Dashpot and bracket
70. Limiter cap
71. Idle mixture screw
72. Idle mixture screw spring
73. Throttle body assembly
74. Carter part number location
75. Low idle speed screw

Exploded view of a typical late-model Thermo-Quad®

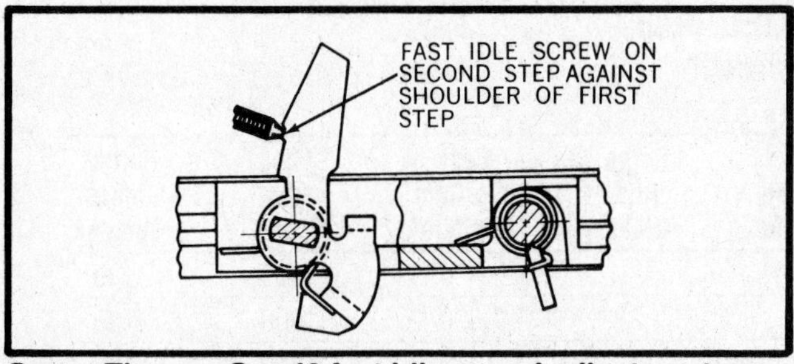

Carter Thermo-Quad® fast idle speed adjustment cam position

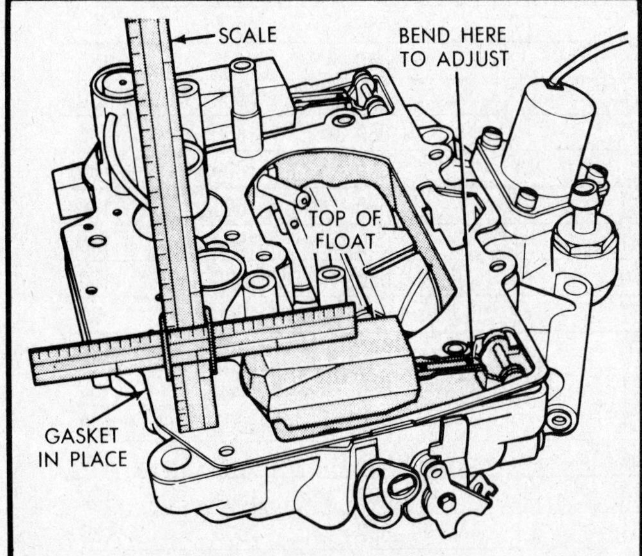

Carter TQ float height measurement

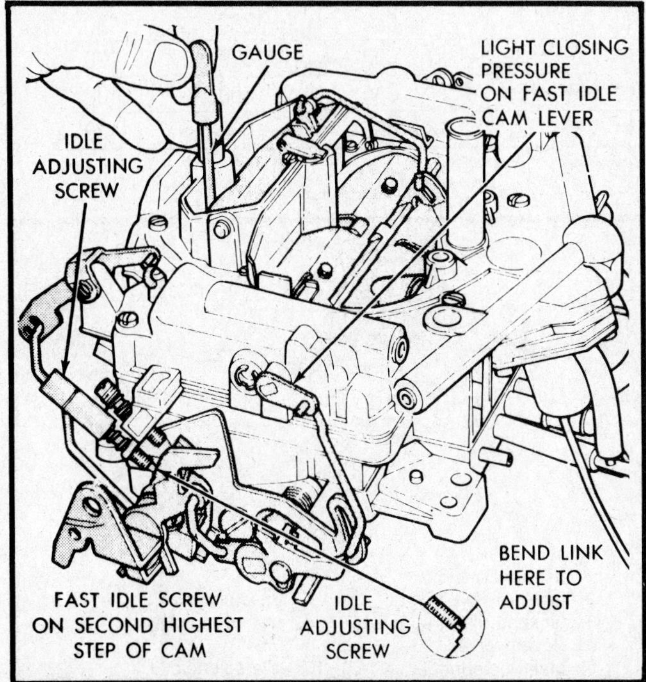

Adjustment of fast idle cam setting—Thermo-Quad® carburetor

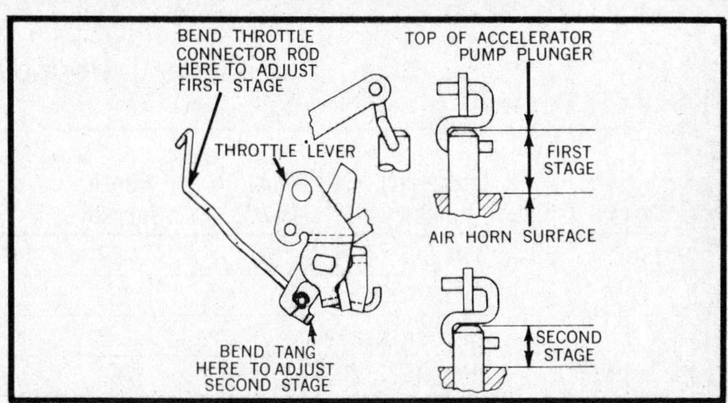

Adjustment of the primary and secondary accelerator pump—Thermo-Quad® carburetor

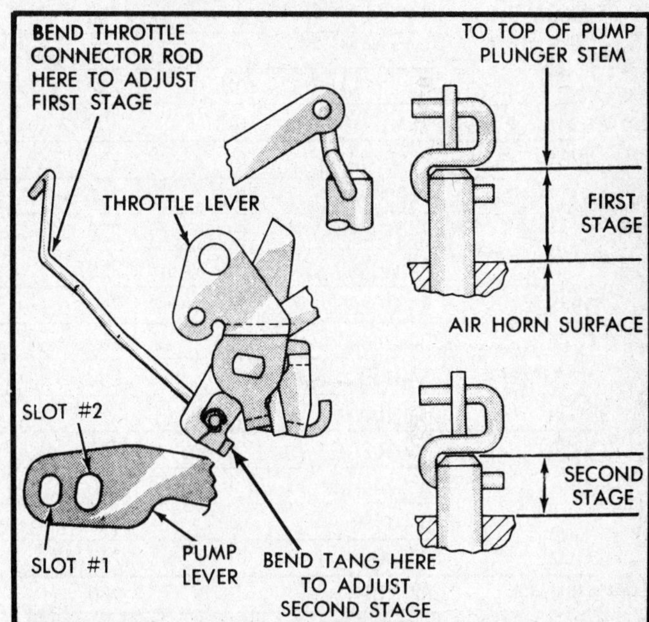

Accelerator pump stroke adjustment—Thermo-Quad® carburetor

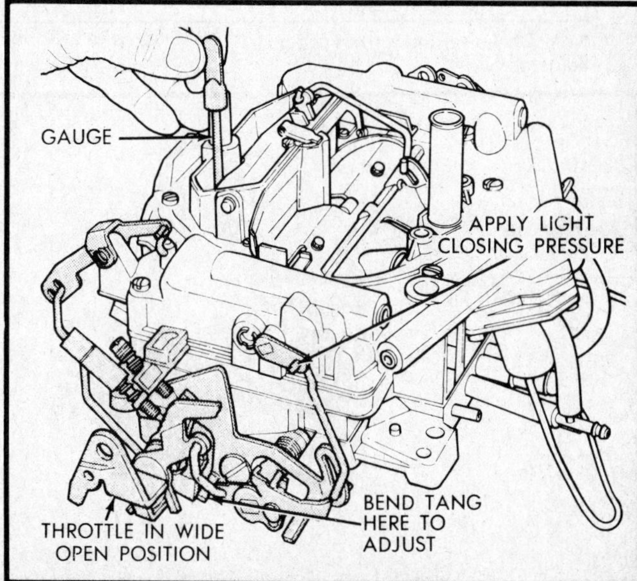

Carter TQ choke unloader adjustment

HOLLEY MODEL 1945
Dodge/Plymouth

(All measurements in inches)

Year	Carburetor Number	Dry Float Level	Choke Unloader	Pump Stroke	Pump Rod Hole	Fast Idle Cam Position	Fast Idle Speed	Initial Choke Opening
1982	R9132A	①	.250	—	2	.090	1600	.130
	R9134A	①	.250	—	2	.090	1600	.130
	R9153A	①	.250	—	2	.080	1800	.130
	R9399A	①	.250	—	2	.080	1800	.130
	R9762A	①	.250	—	2	.090	1600	.130
	R9765A	①	.250	—	2	.080	1800	.130
1983	R40055A	①	.250	—	2	.080	1600	.130
	R40056A	①	.250	—	2	.080	1600	.130
	R9399-1A	①	.250	—	2	.080	1800	.130
	R9134-1A	①	.250	—	2	.090	1800	.130
1984	R40088A	①	.250	1.61	2	.080	1600	.130
	R40089A	①	.250	1.61	2	.080	1600	.130
	R40102A	①	.250	1.70	1	.080	1800	.130
	R40103A	①	.250	1.61	2	.090	1600	.130
1985	R40102A	①	.250	1.70	1	.080	1800	.130
	R40244A	①	.250	1.61	2	.090	1600	.130
	R40159	①	.250	1.61	2	.080	1600	.130
	R40160	①	.250	1.61	2	.090	1600	.130
1986	R40102A	①	.250	1.70	1	.080	1800	.130
	R40244A	①	.250	1.61	2	.090	1600	.130
	R40159	①	.250	1.61	2	.080	1600	.130
	R40160	①	.250	1.61	2	.090	1600	.130
1987-88	R40102A	①	.250	1.70	1	.080	1800	.130
	R40244A	①	.250	1.61	2	.090	1600	.130
	R40159	①	.250	1.61	2	.080	1600	.130
	R40160	①	.250	1.61	2	.090	1600	.130

Note: Choke setting is fixed and non-adjustable.

① Flush with top of bowl over gasket, carb inverted

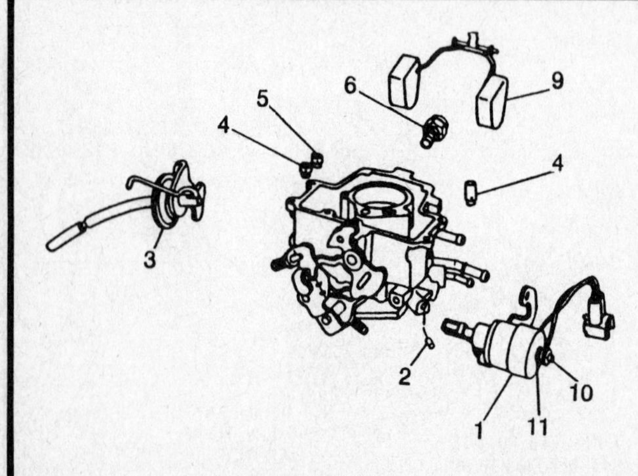

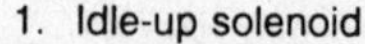

1. Idle-up solenoid
2. Idle needle plug
3. Linkage diaphragm
4. Power valve
5. Main metering jet
6. Needle and seat
7. Piston pump cup
8. Air horn gasket
9. Float
10. Idle solenoid adjusting screw

Exploded view of the Holley 1945 carburetor

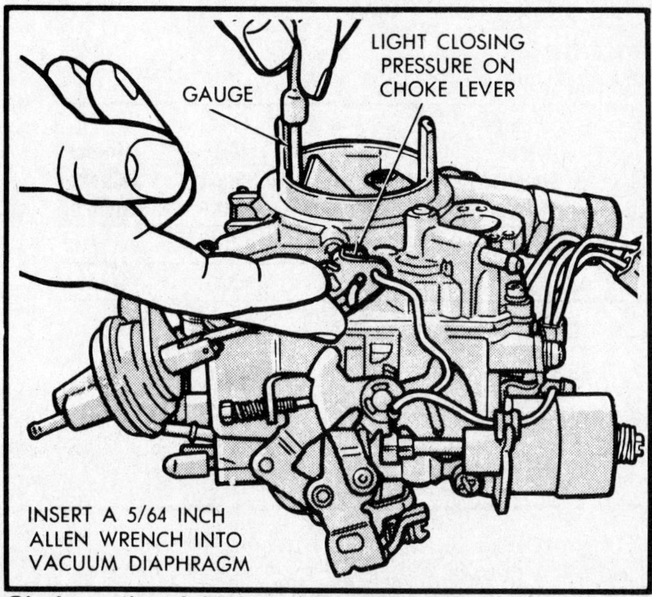

Choke valve initial setting (vacuum kick)—model 1945 carburetor

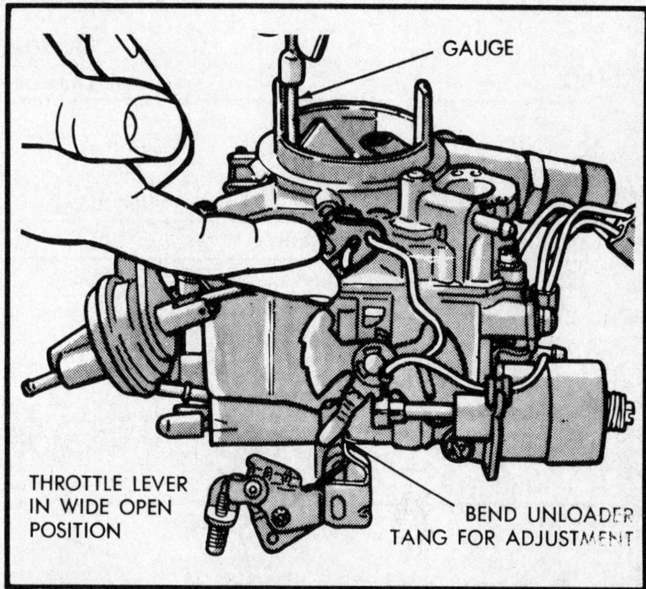

Choke valve unloader adjustment—model 1945 carburetor

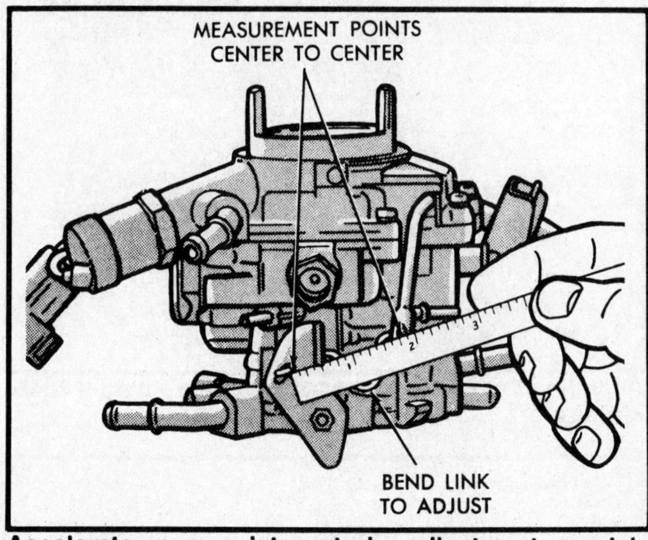

Accelerator pump piston stroke adjustment—model 1945 carburetor

Fast idle cam-to-choke valve adjustment—model 1945 carburetor

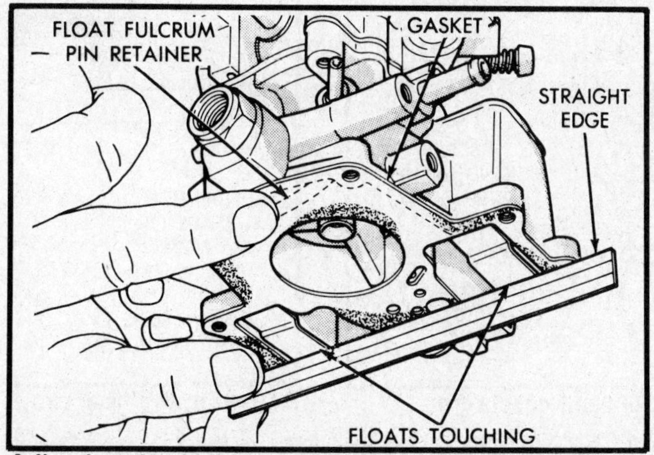

Adjusting the fuel level with the fuel bowl inverted—model 1945 carburetor

HOLLEY MODEL 2245
Dodge/Plymouth

(All measurements in inches)

Year	Carburetor Number	Float Level (Dry)	Choke Unloader	Choke Setting	Pump Rod Location (Hole)	Fast Idle Cam Position	Fast Idle Speed (rpm)	Initial Choke Opening
1982	R9816A	3/16	.170	Fixed	3	.110	1700	.150
1983	R9816A	5/32–7/32	.170	Fixed	2	.110	1700	.150

① Fixed setting
② Float drop—bottom of float to be parallel with air horn bottom

MODEL 2245

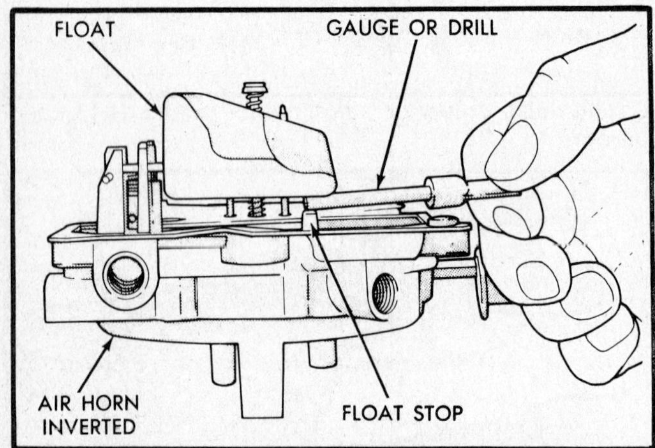

Adjusting the float level—model 2245 carburetors

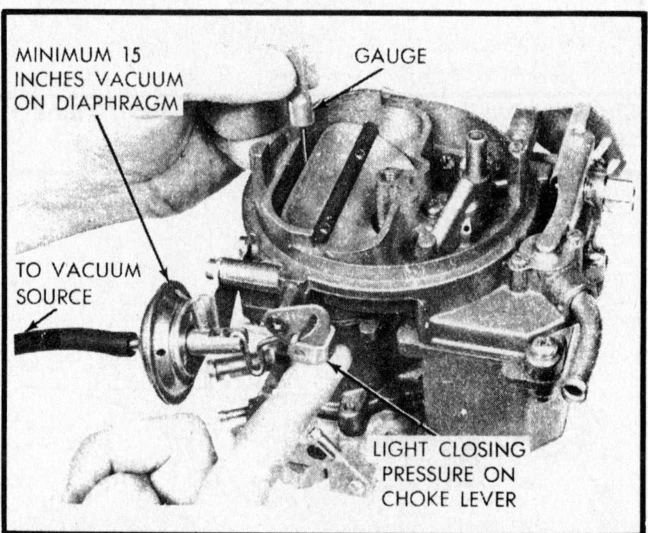

Adjusting the initial choke valve setting—model 2245 carburetors

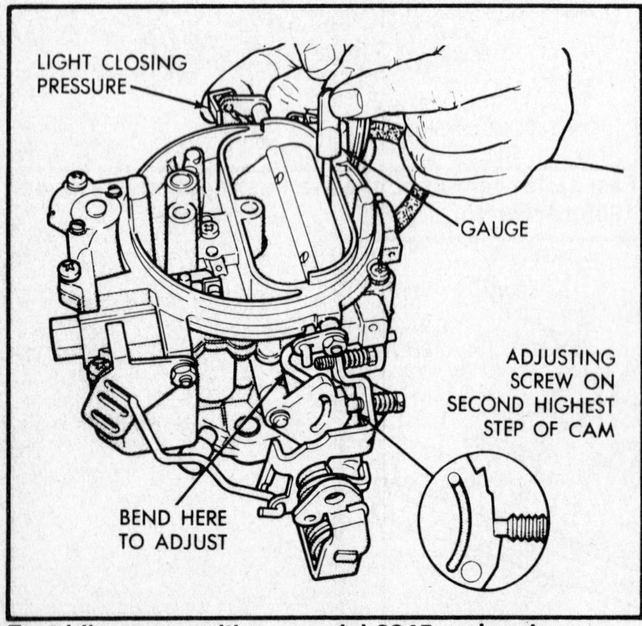

Fast idle cam position—model 2245 carburetor

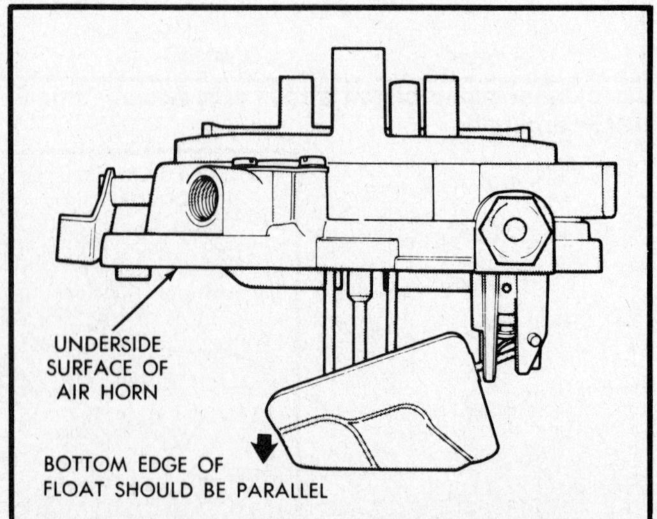

Adjusting the float drop—model 2245 carburetors

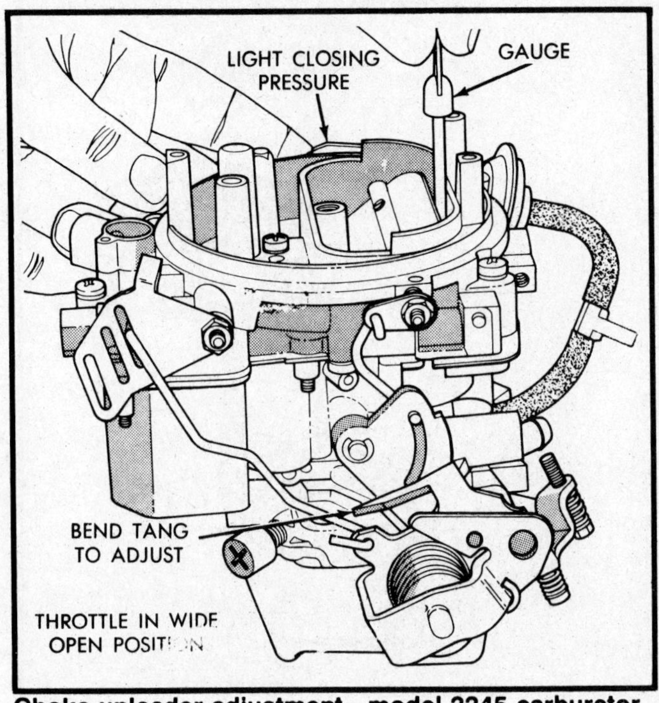

Choke unloader adjustment–model 2245 carburetor

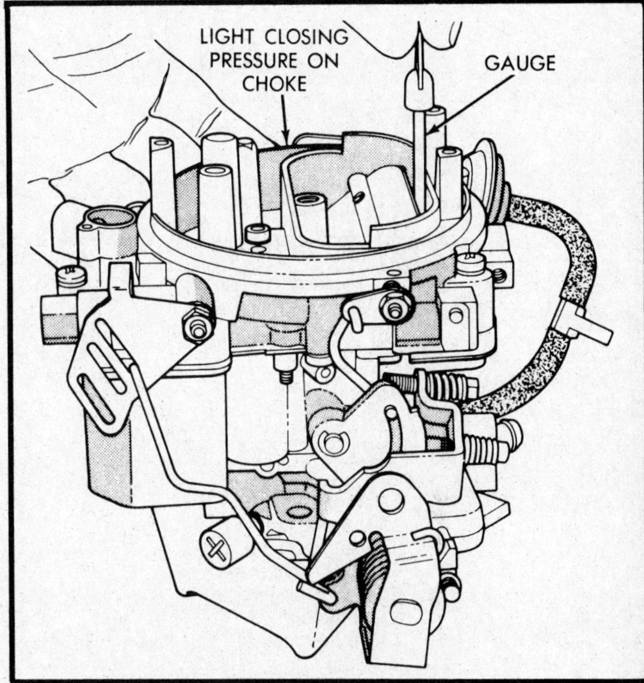

Vacuum kick adjustment–2245 carburetors

MODELS 2280, 2280G

HOLLEY MODEL 2280, 2280G
Dodge/Plymouth

(All measurements in inches)

Year	Carburetor Number	Float Level ①	Choke Vacuum Kick	Fast Idle Cam	Fast Idle (rpm)	Choke Unloader	Bowl Vent Valve
1982	R9491A	7/32–10/32	.140	.052	1500	.200	—
	R9493A	7/32–10/32	.140	.052	1500	.200	—
	R9572A	7/32–10/32	.140	.052	1500	.200	—
1983	R9499A	9/32	.140	.052	1500	.200	—
	R9951A	9/32	.140	.052	1500	.200	—
1984	R9951A	9/32	.140	.070	1500	.250	—
	R40093A	9/32	.140	.052	1500	.200	—
1985	R40164	9/32	.140	.070	1600	.150	.035
	R40167	9/32	.140	.070	1600	.150	.035
	R40172A	9/32	.140	.070	1450	.200	.035
1986–87	R40172-1A	9/32	.140	.052	②	.250	.035
	R40216A	9/32	.140	.070	②	.250	.035
	R40214A	9/32	.140	.070	②	.250	.035

① Measured from surface of fuel bowl to the toe of each float
② Refer to underhood specification sticker

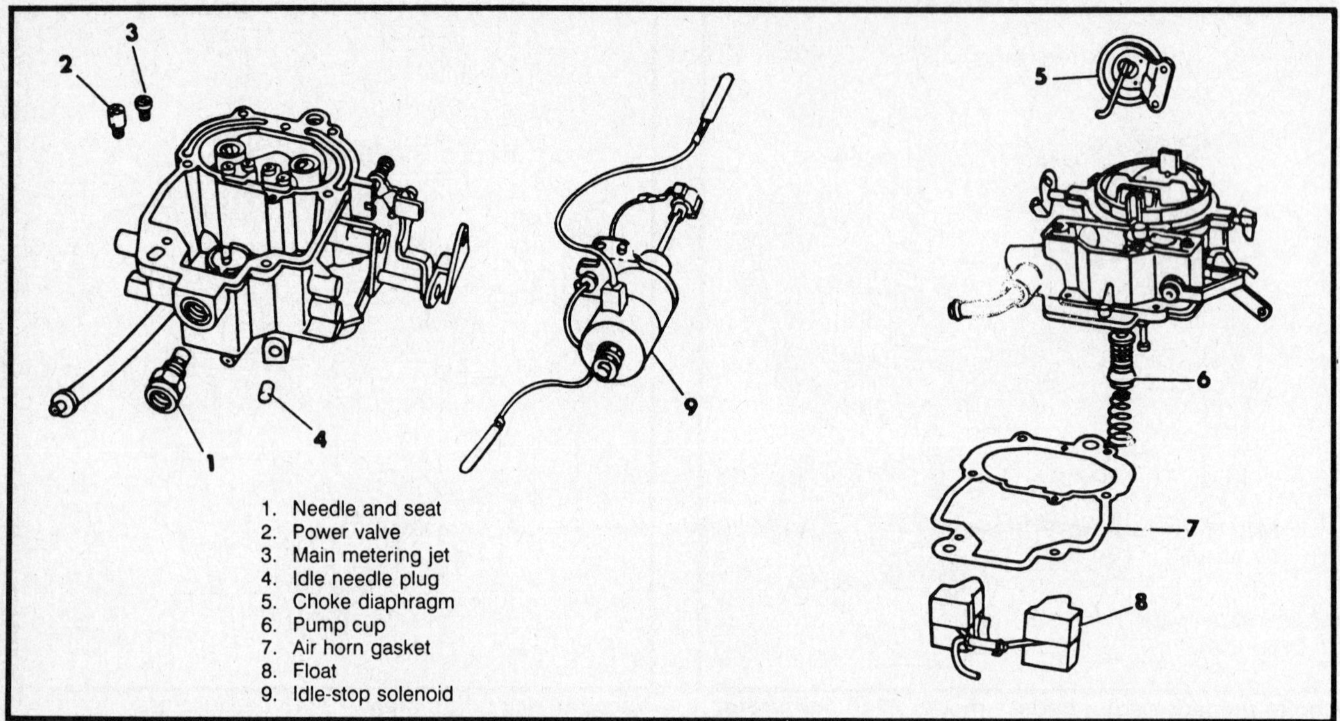

Exploded view of the Holley 2280 carburetor

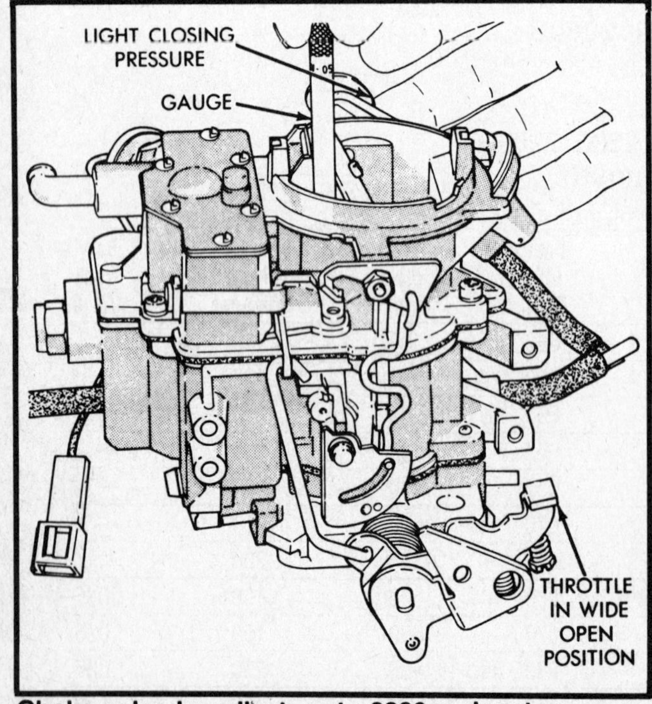

Choke unloader adjustment—2280 carburetor

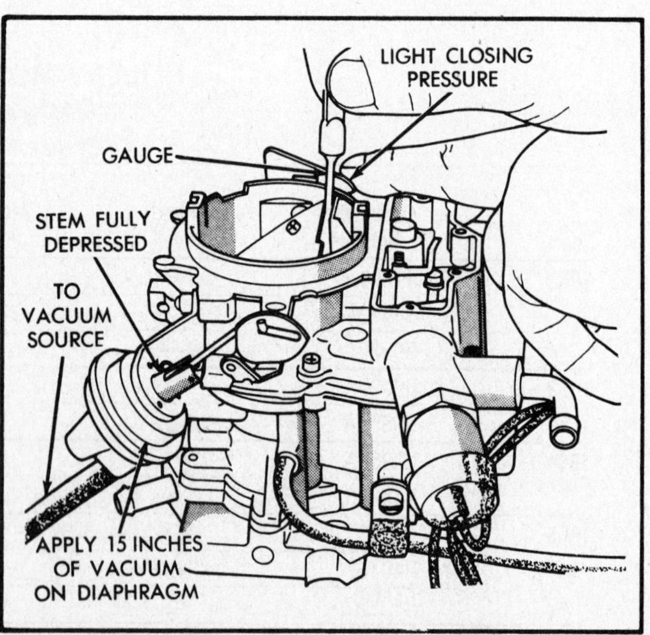

Vacuum kick adjustment—2280 carburetor

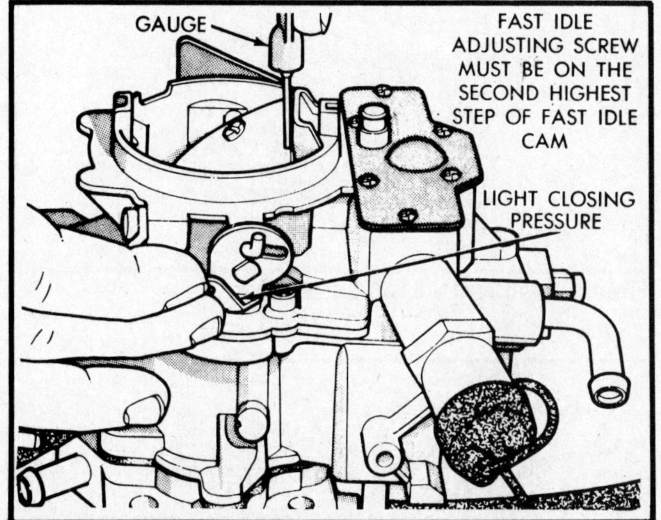

Fast idle adjustment – 2280 carburetor

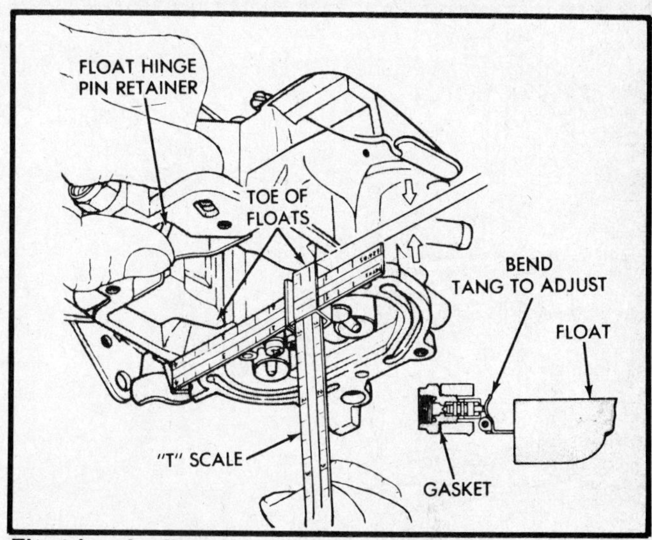

Float level adjustment – 2280 carburetor

MODEL 6145

HOLLEY MODEL 6145
Dodge/Plymouth

(All measurements in inches)

Year	Carburetor Number	Float Setting	Choke Vacuum Kick	Choke Unloader Adjustment	Fast Idle Cam Position	Fast Idle (rpm)	Pump Piston Stroke
1983	R40029A	①	.150	.250	.090	1600	1.70
	R40030A	①	.150	.250	.090	1600	1.61
1984	R40098A	①	.150	.250	.070	1600	1.61
	R40099A	①	.150	.250	.070	1600	1.61
1985	R40161	①	.150	.250	.060	1600	1.75
	R40162	①	.150	.250	.070	1600	1.75
1986	R40161	①	.150	.250	.060	②	1.75
	R40162	①	.150	.250	.070	②	1.75
1987-88	R40161	①	.150	.250	.060	②	1.75
	R40162	①	.150	.250	.070	②	1.75

① With bowl inverted, float lungs just touch a straightedge run along gasket surface.
② 1986-88: Refer to underhood specification sticker

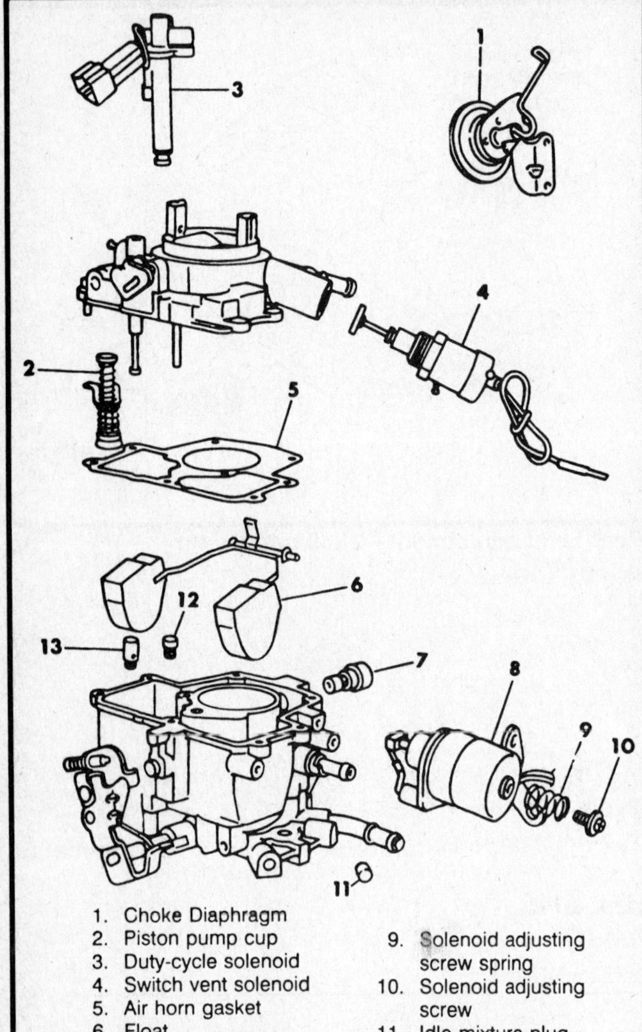

Exploded view of the Holley 6145 carburetor

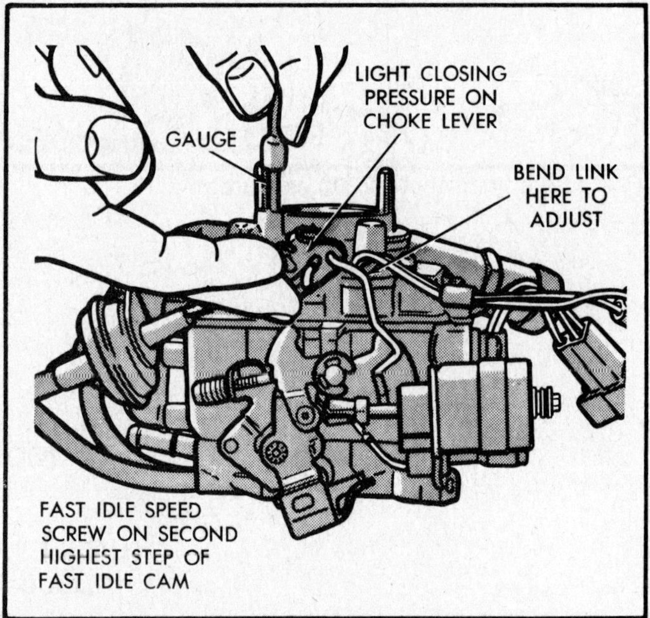

Float adjustment—6145 carburetor

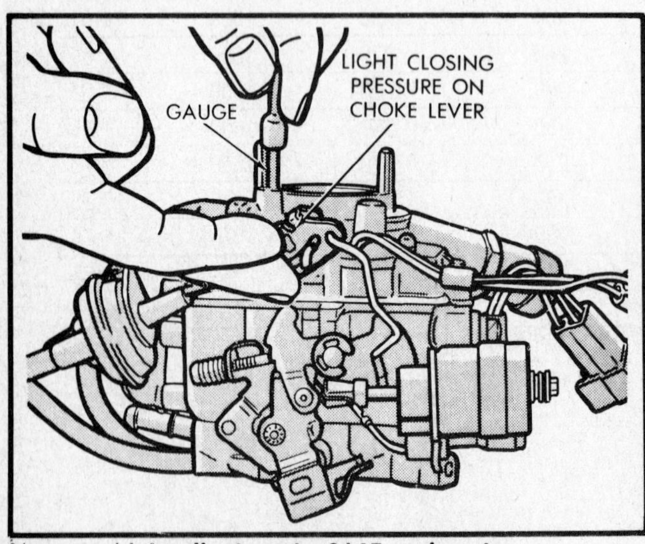

Fast idle cam adjustment—6145 carburetor

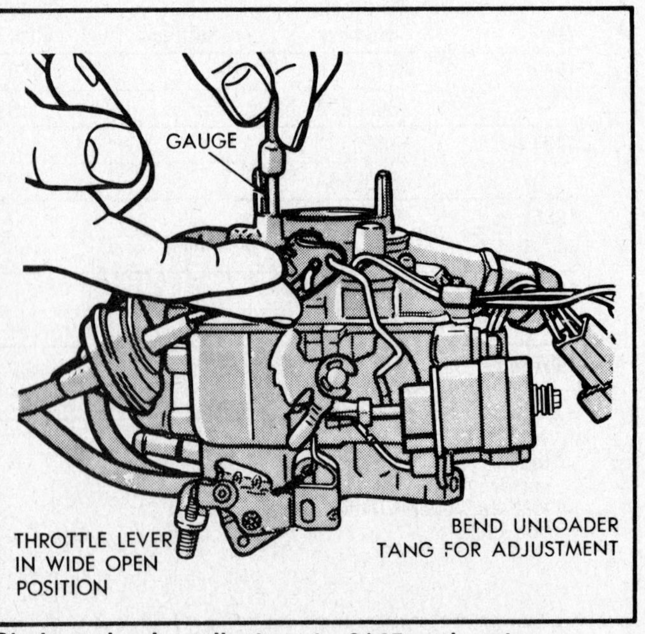

Vacuum kick adjustment—6145 carburetor

Choke unloader adjustment—6145 carburetor

HOLLEY MODEL 5220
Dodge/Plymouth

(All measurements in inches)

Year	Carburetor Number	Float Level	Choke Vacuum Kick	Accelerator Pump Hole	Fast Idle Speed	Propane Idle Speed
1984	R40069-2A	.480	.070	#3	1500	800
	R40075-2A	.480	.070	#3	1700	975
	R40128-2A	.480	.070	#3	1500	875
	R40129-2A	.480	.070	#3	1700	975
1985	R40143A	.480	.095	#3	1700	875
	R40145A	.480	.095	#3	1850	975
	R40146A	.480	.095	#3	1850	975
	R40136A	.480	.075	#3	1700	875
1986	R40229A	.480	.130	—	①	①
	R40230A	.480	.130	—	①	①
	R40231A	.480	.130	—	①	①
	R40232A	.480	.130	—	①	①
1987-88	R40234A	.480	.095	—	①	①
	R40240A	.480	.095	—	①	①
	R40303A	.480	.095	—	①	①

① Refer to underhood specification sticker

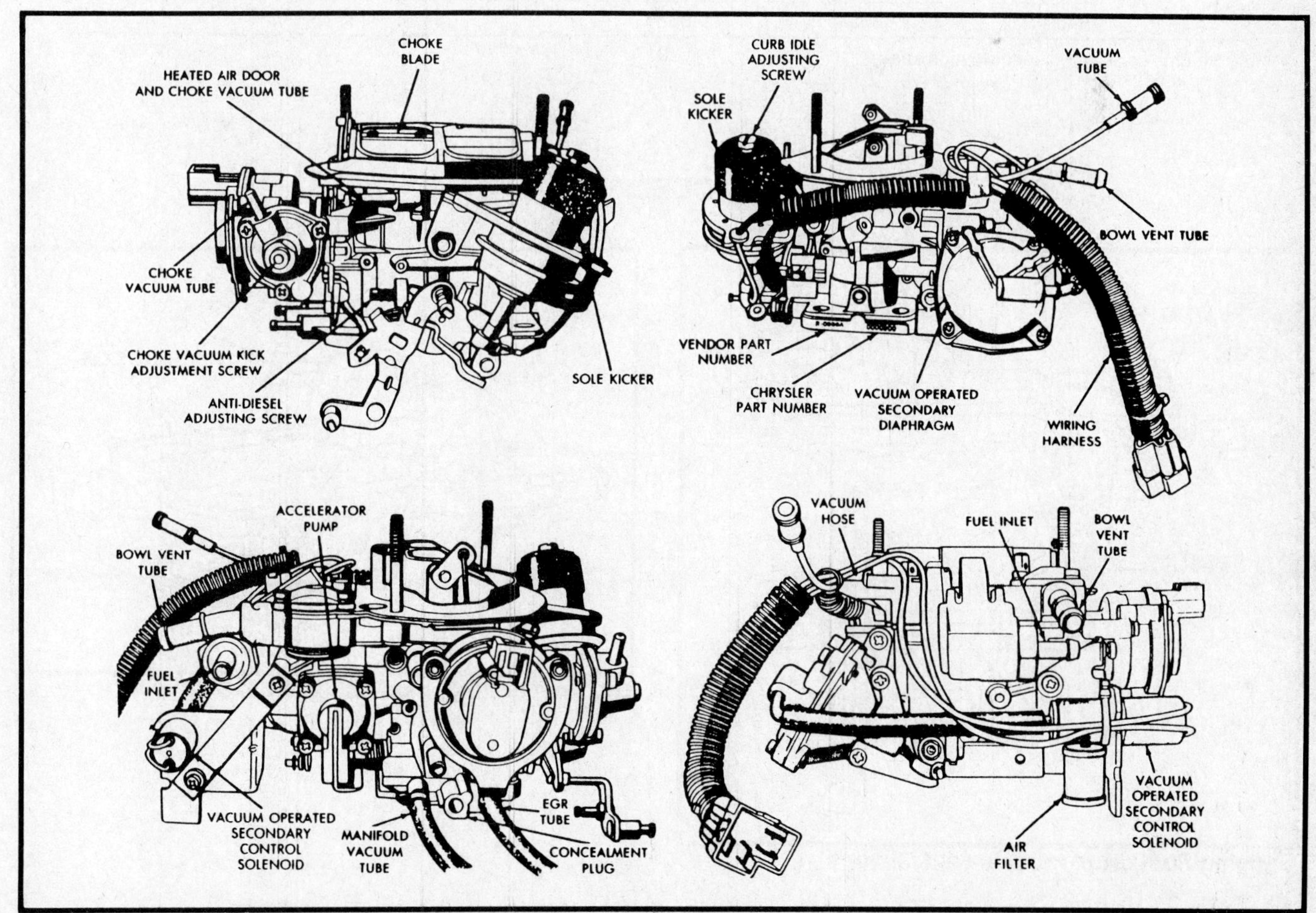

Side views of model 5220 carburetors

HOLLEY MODEL 6520
Dodge/Plymouth

(All measurements in inches)

Year	Carburetor Number	Float Level	Choke Vacuum Kick	Accelerator Pump Hole	Fast Idle Speed	Propane Idle Speed
1984	R40063-2A	.480	.080	#3	1500	975
	R40070-2A	.480	.080	#3	1500	875
	R40072-2A	.480	.080	#3	1500	875
1985	R40137A	.480	.075	#3	1850	975
	R40140A	.480	.075	#3	1700	875
	R40141A	.480	.075	#3	1850	975
1986	R40233A	.480	.160	—	①	①
	R40234A	.480	.160	—	①	①
	R40240A	.480	.160	—	①	①
1987	R40299A	.480	.075	—	①	①
	R40300A	.480	.075	—	①	①
	R40301A	.480	.075	—	①	①
	R40302A	.480	.075	—	①	①
	R40308A	.500	.082	—	①	①
	R40309A	.500	.082	—	①	①
1988	R403081	.500	.082	—	①	①
	R403091	.500	.082	—	①	①

① Refer to underhood specification sticker

MODEL 6520

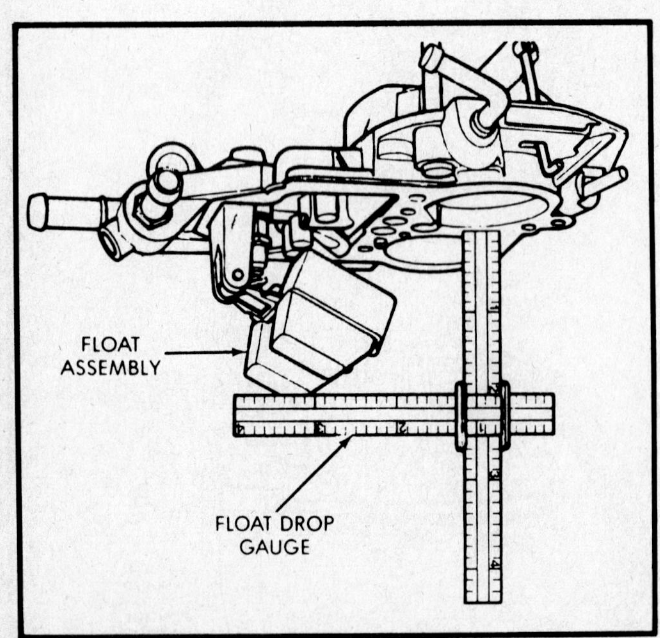

Gauging float drop, models 5220/6520

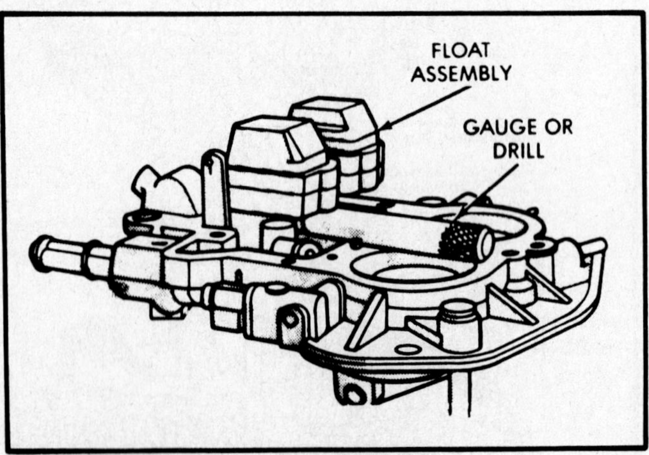

Dry float setting, models 5220/6520

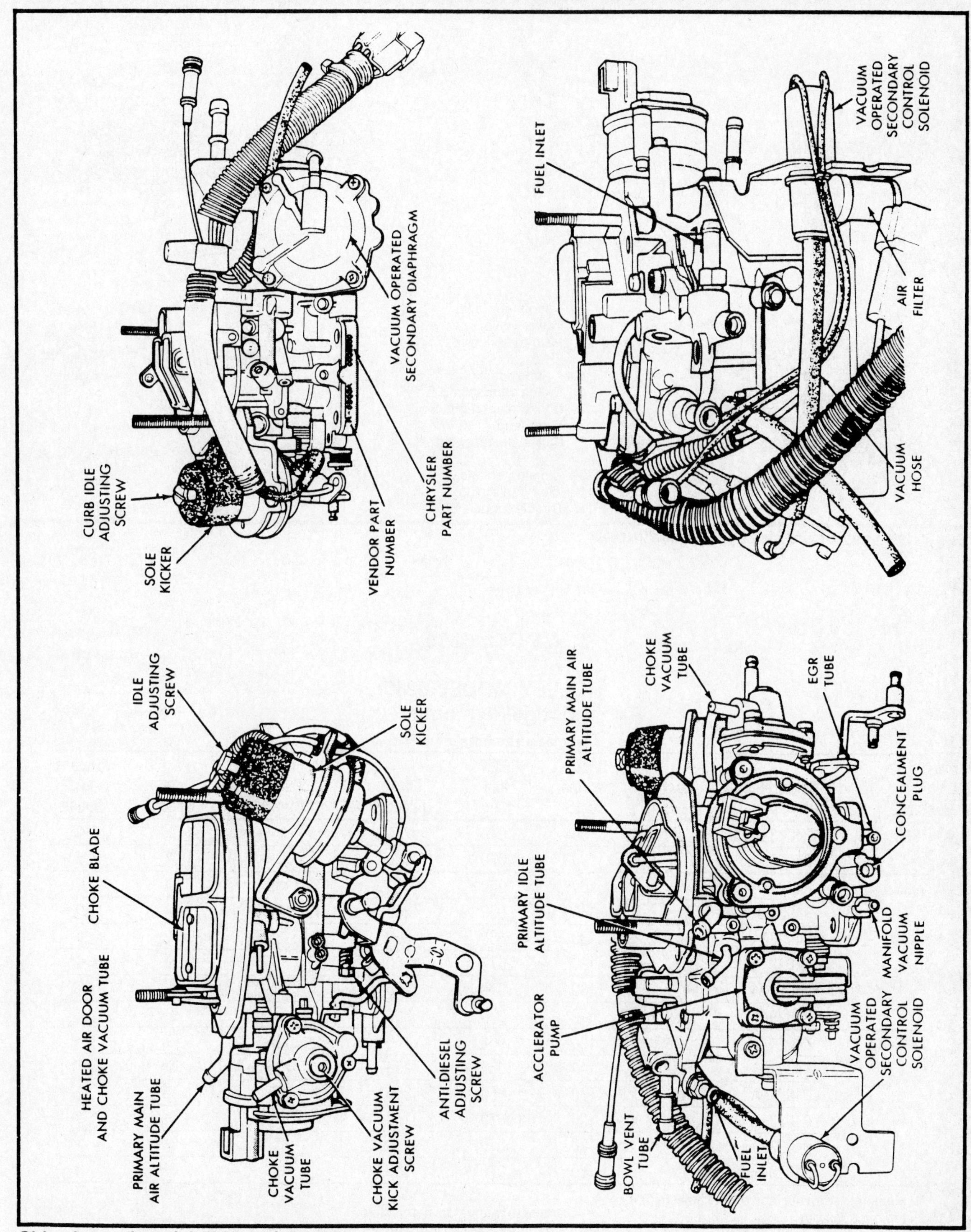

Side views of model 6520 carburetors

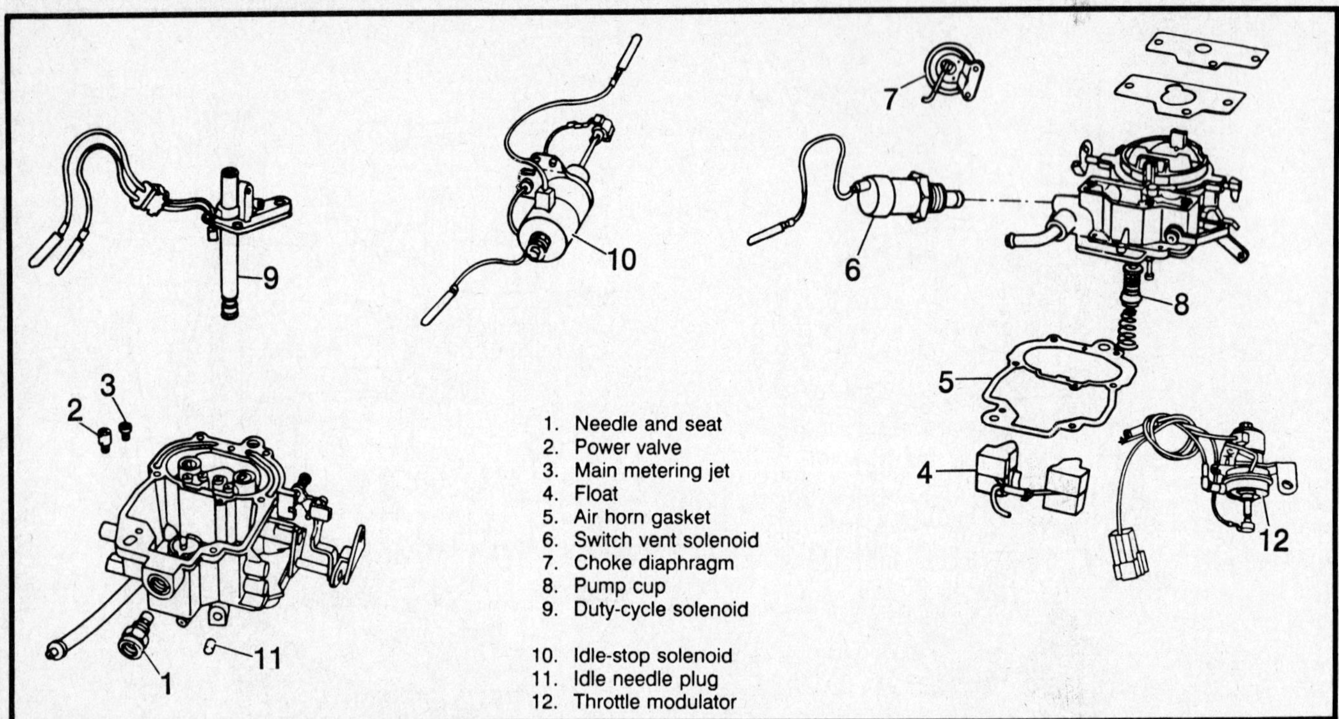

Exploded view of the Holley 6520 carburetor

MODEL 6280

HOLLEY MODEL 6280
Dodge/Plymouth

(All measurements in inches)

Year	Carburetor Number	Float Level	Choke Vacuum Kick	Fast Idle Cam	Choke Unloader	Accelerator Pump Stroke	Fast Idle Speed	Propane Idle Speed
1985	R40132	①	.150	.070	.250	②	1400	710
	R40133	①	.130	.070	.150	②	1625 ③	775 ④
1986	R40217A	9/32	.160	.060	.350	.135	⑤	⑤
	R40218A	9/32	.140	.060	.250	.135	⑤	⑤
	R40220A	9/32	.130	.060	.350	.135	⑤	⑤
	R40221A	9/32	.130	.070	.150	②	⑤	⑤
	R40222A	9/32	.130	.070	.150	②	⑤	⑤
	R40294A	9/32	.160	.070	.350	—	⑤	⑤
1987-88	R40217A	9/32	.160	.060	.350	.135	⑤	⑤
	R40218A	9/32	.140	.060	.250	.135	⑤	⑤
	R40220A	9/32	.130	.060	.350	.135	⑤	⑤
	R40221A	9/32	.130	.070	.150	②	⑤	⑤
	R40222A	9/32	.130	.070	.150	②	⑤	⑤
	R40294A	9/32	.160	.070	.350	—	⑤	⑤

① Measured from surface of fuel bowl to top of each float
② Flush with top of bowl vent
③ 1450 rpm with manual transmission
④ 740 rpm with manual transmission
⑤ Refer to underhood specification sticker

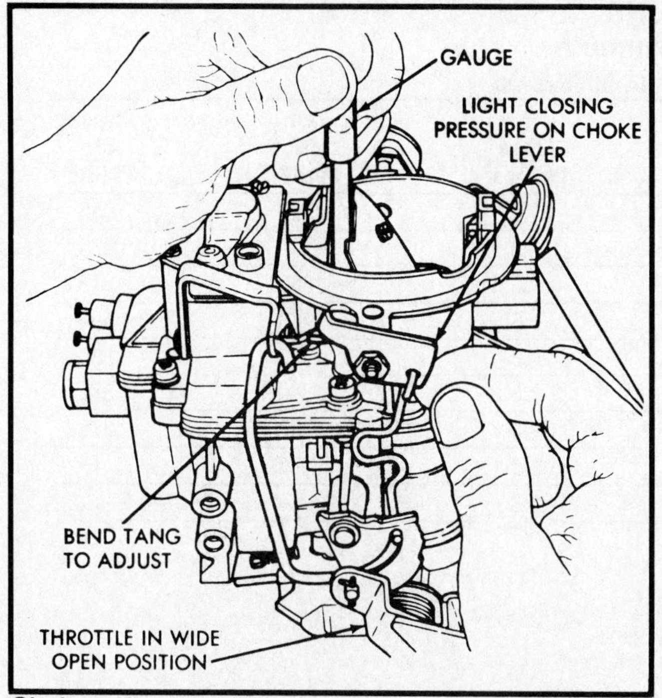

Choke unloader adjustment with wide open kick, model 6280

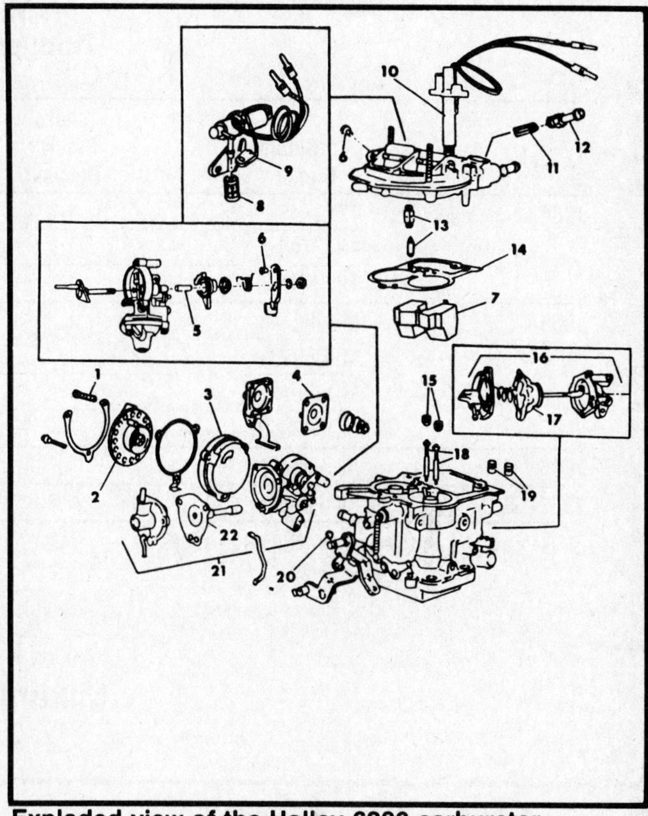

Exploded view of the Holley 6280 carburetor

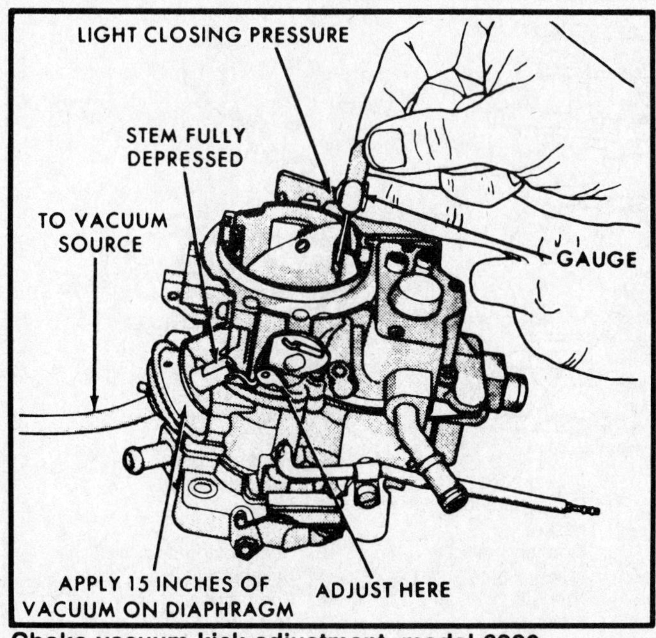

Choke vacuum kick adjustment, model 6280

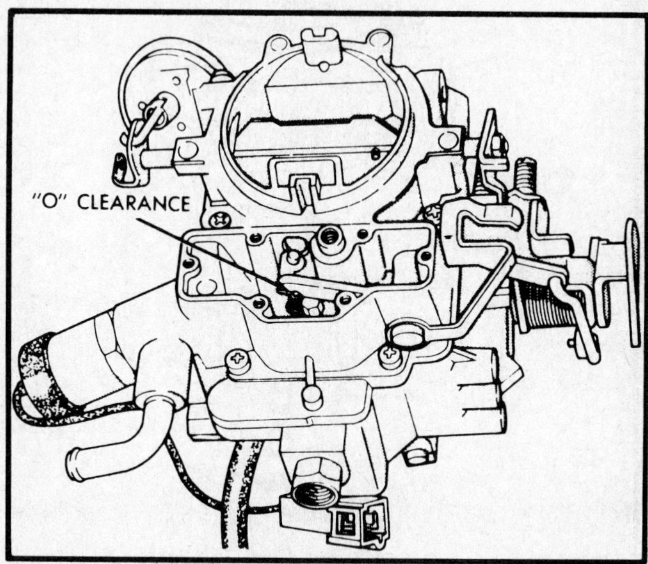

Accelerator pump stroke measurement, model 6280

MIKUNI
Dodge/Plymouth

(All measurements in millimeters)

Year	Carburetor Number	Choke Breaker Opening	Choke Unloader	Fast Idle Speed	Propane Idle Speed
1984	4243743	1.7	1.3	1300	850
	4243744	1.7	1.3	950	875
	4243745	1.7	1.3	1300	875
1985	MD082749	1.7	1.3	950	850
	MD083781	1.7	1.3	950	880
	MD088138	1.7	1.3	1300	875
	MD089840	1.7	1.3	1300	875
1986	All numbers	1.7	1.3	①	①
1987–88	All numbers	1.7	1.3	①	①

① Refer to the underhood specification sticker

Mikuni Models

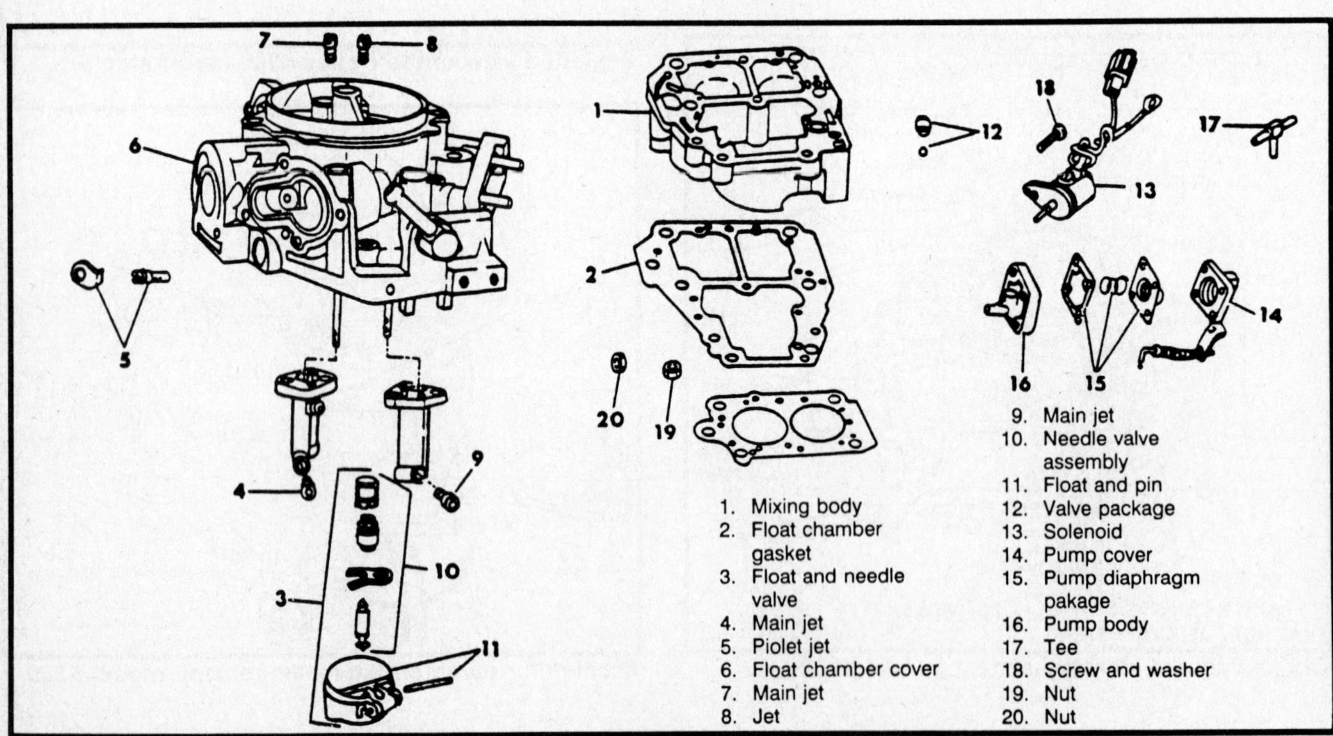

Side views, Mikuni carburetors for Federal and Canadian use

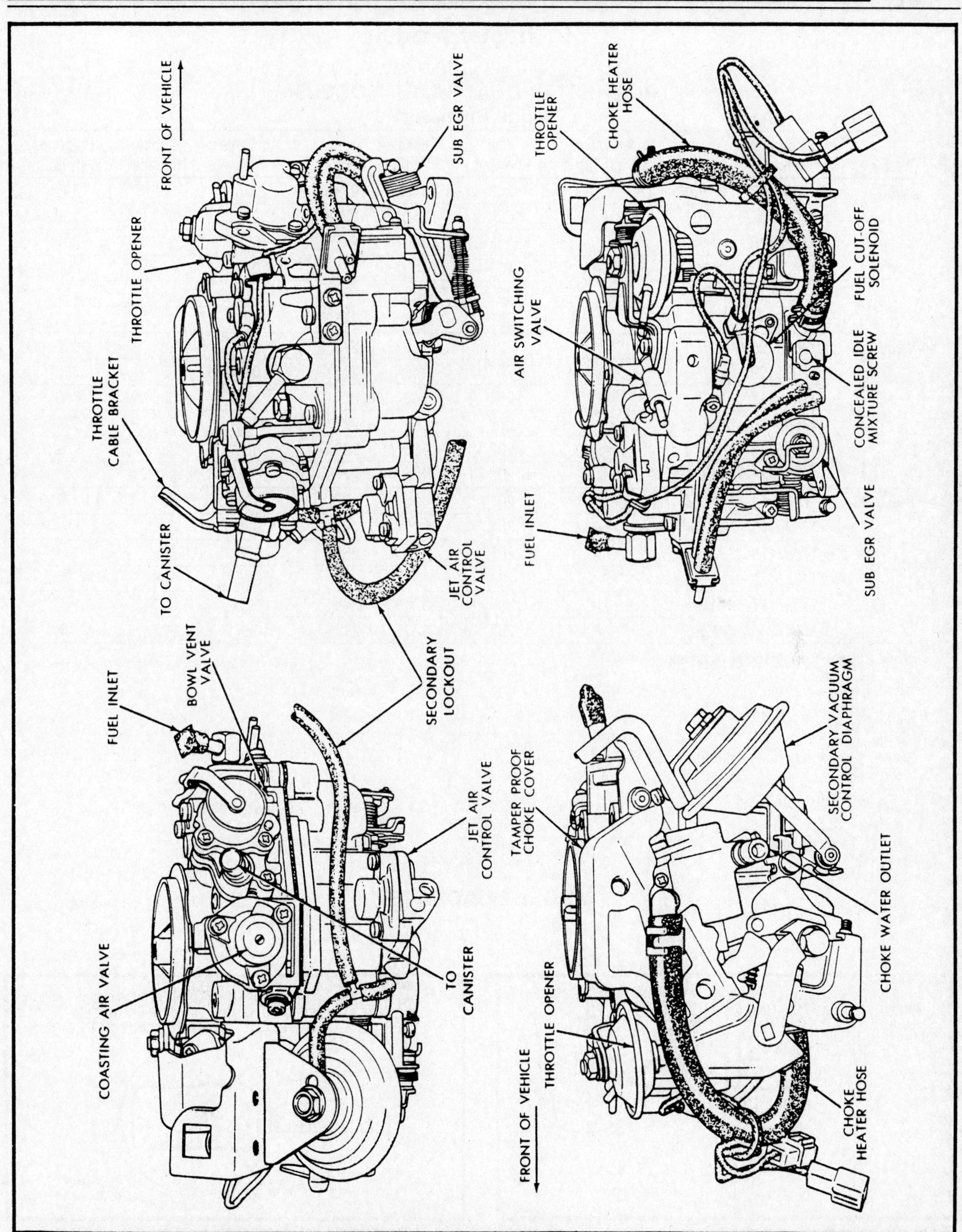

Side views, Mikuni carburetors for California and High Altitude use

Rochester Models

ROCHESTER QUADRAJET MODELS
Dodge/Plymouth

Year	Carburetor Number	Float Level	Air Valve Spring Turns	Fast Idle Cam	Choke Rod	Vacuum Kick	Air Valve Rod	Choke Unloader	Propane rpm
1985	17850408	13/32	1/2	20°	.143	27° ①	.025	38° ②	800
	17085409	13/32	5/8	20°	.143	27° ①	.025	38° ②	750
	17085415	13/32	1/2	20°	.143	27° ①	.025	38° ②	800
	17085416	13/32	3/4	20°	.143	27° ①	.025	38° ②	800
	17085417	13/32	3/4	20°	.125	27° ③	.025	38° ④	⑤
	17085431	13/32	1/2	20°	.125	27° ③	.025	38° ④	⑤
1986	17085408	13/32	1/2	20°	.143	27° ①	.025	38° ②	800
	17085409	13/32	5/8	20°	.143	27° ①	.025	38° ②	750
	17085415	13/32	1/2	20°	.143	27° ①	.025	38° ②	800
	17085416	13/32	3/4	20°	.143	27° ①	.025	38° ②	800
	17085417	13/32	3/4	20°	.125	27° ③	.025	38° ④	⑤
	17085431	13/32	1/2	20°	.125	27° ③	.025	38° ④	⑤
1987-88	17085431	13/32	1/2	20°	.125	23°	.025	32°	⑤
	17086425	15/32	1/2	20°	.125	23°	.025	38°	⑤
	17087175	13/32	3/4	20°	.125	26°	.025	30°	⑤
	17087176	13/32	3/4	20°	.125	26°	.025	30°	⑤
	17087177	13/32	1	20°	.125	27°	.025	33°	⑤
	17087245	15/32	5/8	20°	.125	23°	.025	32°	⑤

Note: Specified angle for use with angle gauge tool
① Plug gauge—.214 in.
② Plug gauge—.345 in.
③ Plug gauge—.170 in.
④ Plug gauge—.260 in.
⑤ Refer to underhood specification sticker

MODEL QUADRAJET

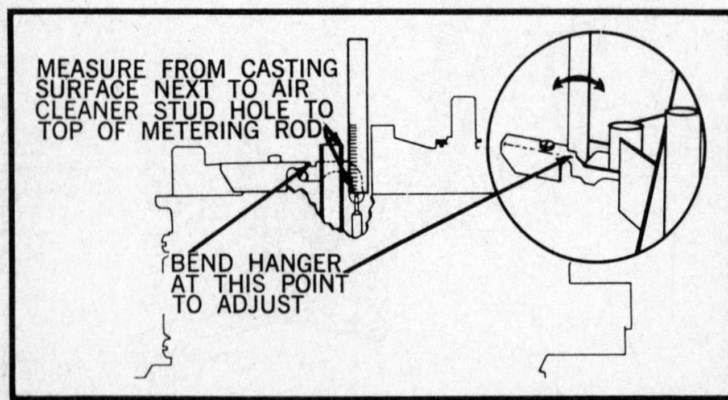

Secondary metering adjustment—typical Quadrajet® carburetor

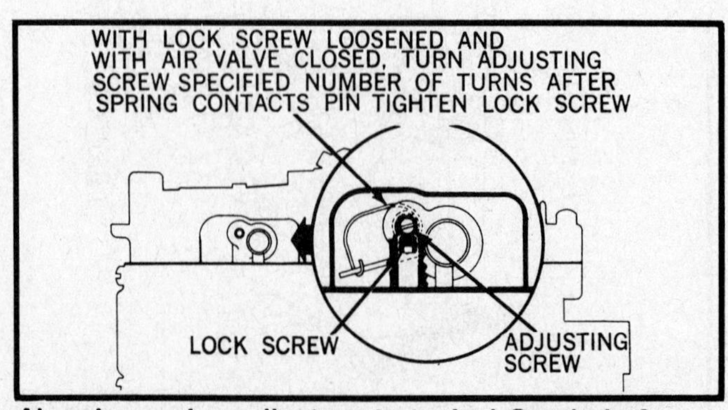

Air valve spring adjustment—typical Quadrajet® carburetor

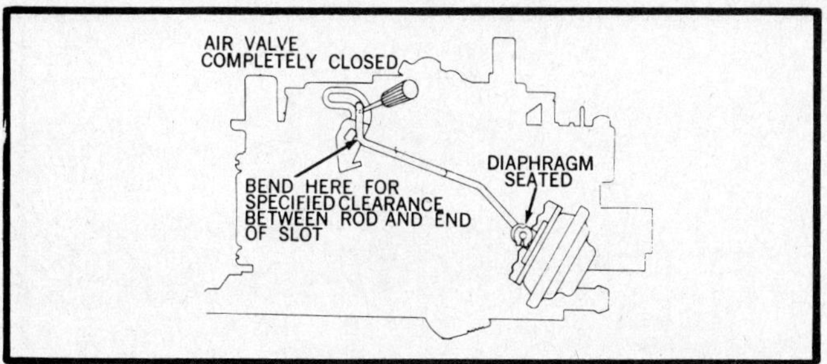

Air valve dashpot adjustment—typical Quadrajet® carburetor

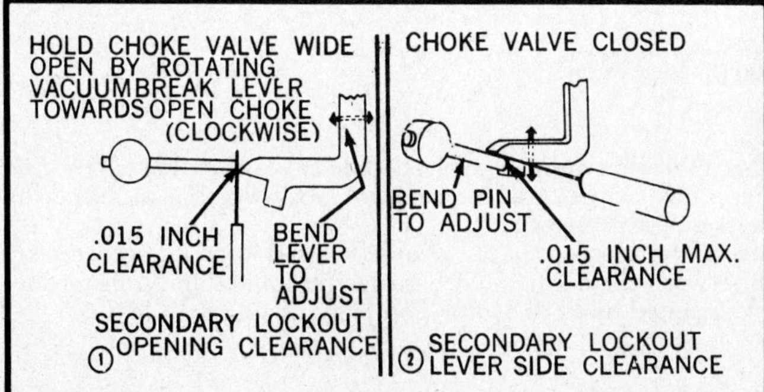

Secondary lockout adjustment—typical Quadrajet® carburetor

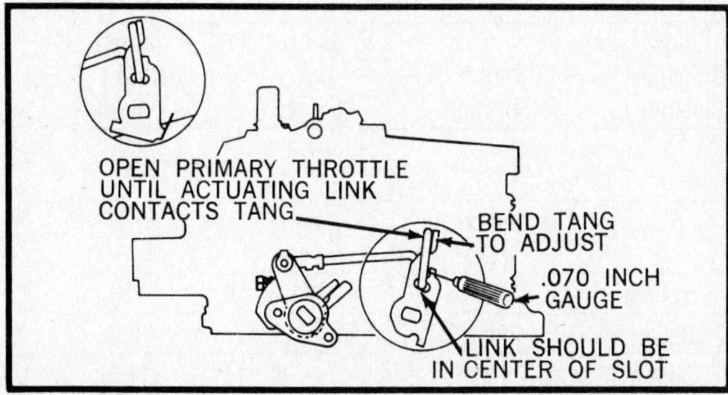

Secondary opening adjustment—typical Quadrajet® Carburetor

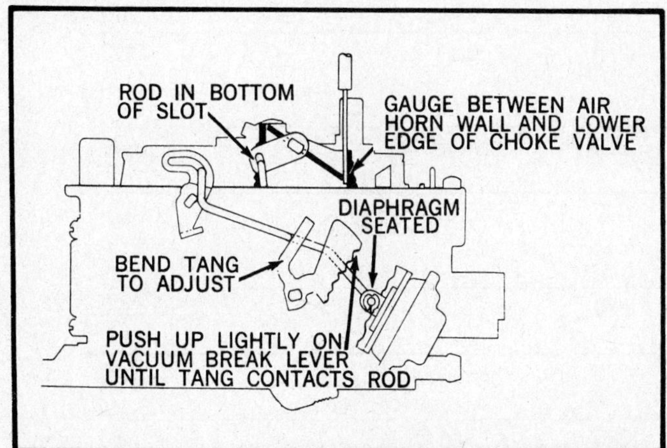

Vacuum break adjustment—typical Quadrajet® carburetor

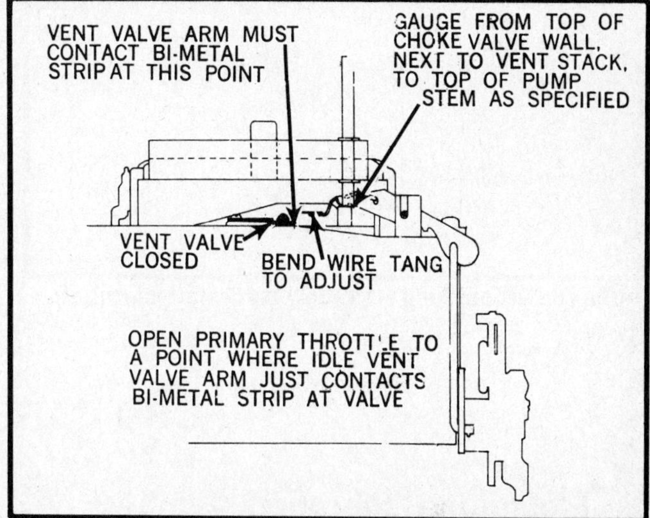

Idle vent adjustment—typical Quadrajet® carburetor

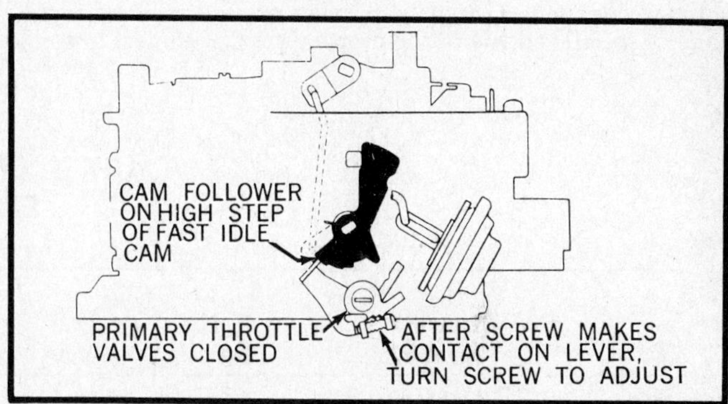

Fast idle adjustment—typical Quadrajet® carburetor

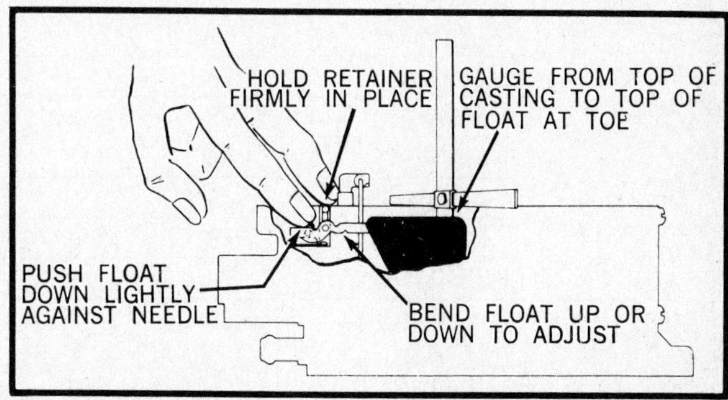

Float level adjustment—typical Quadrajet® carburetor

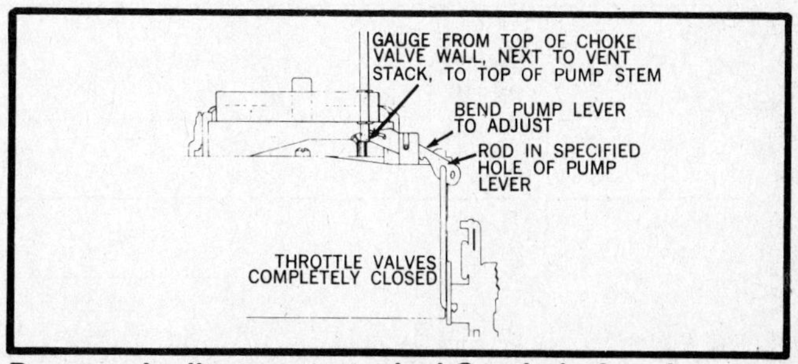

Pump rod adjustment—typical Quadrajet® carburetor

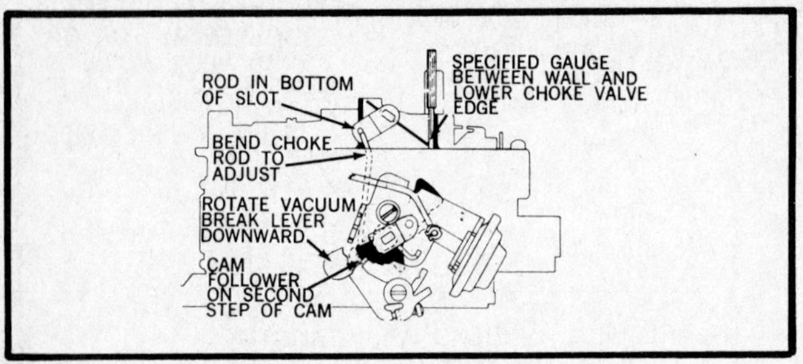

Choke rod adjustment—typical Quadrajet® carburetor

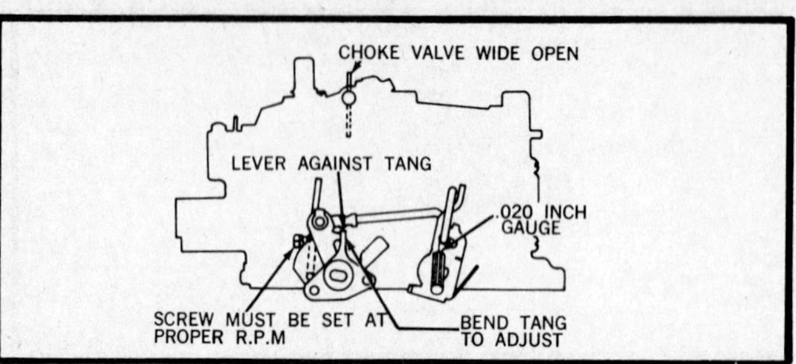

Secondary closing adjustment—typical Quadrajet® carburetor

FORD CARBURETORS

Emission Calibration Numbers

Emission calibration numbers are used by Ford Motor Company to provide the technician with the necessary specifications to adjust a specific engine to the proper emission control levels.

The calibration numbers are listed on the lower right of the Vehicle Emission Control Information label, which is attached to the engine valve cover.

The information on the decal must be used when differences exist between the decal and other specification tables, unless otherwise noted by Ford Motor Company.

CARTER MODEL YFA
Ford

(All measurements in inches)

Year	Carburetor Number	Float Level	Float Drop	Choke Unloader Setting	Choke Setting	Dash Pot Plunger	Initial Choke Opening
1982	E2TE-AMA E2UE-EA	.78	—	.28	Index	—	.230
	E2TE BZA, BVA	.78	—	.28	Index	—	.270
	CEA, JA	.78	—	.320	2 Rich	—	.330
	YA, AAA	.78	—	.280	Index	—	.300
	MA, ANA	.78	—	.280	2 Rich	—	.300
	KA	.78	—	.330	2 Rich	—	.320
	AAA	.78	—	.280	Index	—	.300
	EZUE-DA	.78	—	.330	2 Rich	—	.320
1983	E37E-9510 LB, NB, RB, TB	.65	—	.270	Gray ①	—	.320
	E37E-9510 BB	.65	—	.270	Yellow ①	—	.320
1984	E37E-9510 LB, NB, RB, TB	.65	—	.270	Gray ①	—	.320
	E37E-9510 BB	.65	—	.270	Yellow ①	—	.320
1985	E5TE-9510 DA	.65	—	.270	Gray ①	—	.320
	VA, UA, TA, BA, RA, SA, JA	.78	—	.330	Red ①	—	.360

CARTER MODEL YFA
Ford

(All measurements in inches)

Year	Carburetor Number	Float Level	Float Drop	Choke Unloader Setting	Choke Setting	Dash Pot Plunger	Initial Choke Opening
1985	FA	.78	—	.330	Red ①	—	.340
	HA	.78	—	.330	Red ①	—	.320
	DA, MA, CA ②	.78	—	.330	Red ①	—	.360
	D5TE-9510 AGB	3/8	—	.280	—	—	.230
	E0TE-9510 AMB, FB	.69	—	.280	Index	—	.290
1986	E57E-9510 DA, DB	.650	—	.270	Gray ①	—	.320
	E5TE-9510 AA, TA, UA, VA, RA, SA, JA, BA, MA, CA, GA	.780	—	.330	Red ①	—	.360
	E5TE-9510 FA	.780	—	.330	Red ①	—	.340
	E5TE-9510 HA	.780	—	.330	Red ①	—	.320
	D5TE-9510 AGB	.375	—	.280	—	—	.230

① Choke cap index plate color
② Feedback carburetor

Carter Models

MODEL YFA

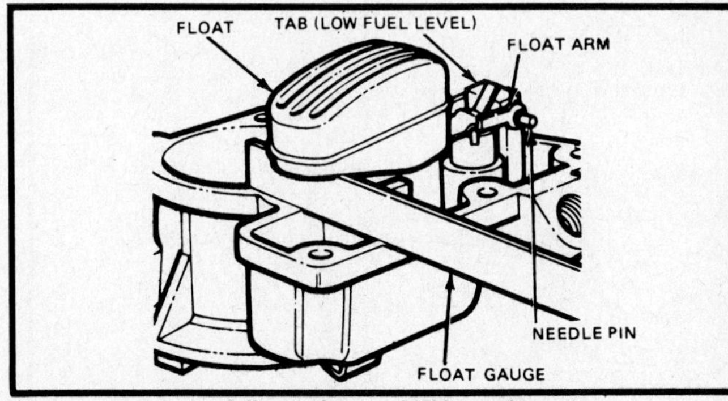

Measurement of float drop—YFA carburetor

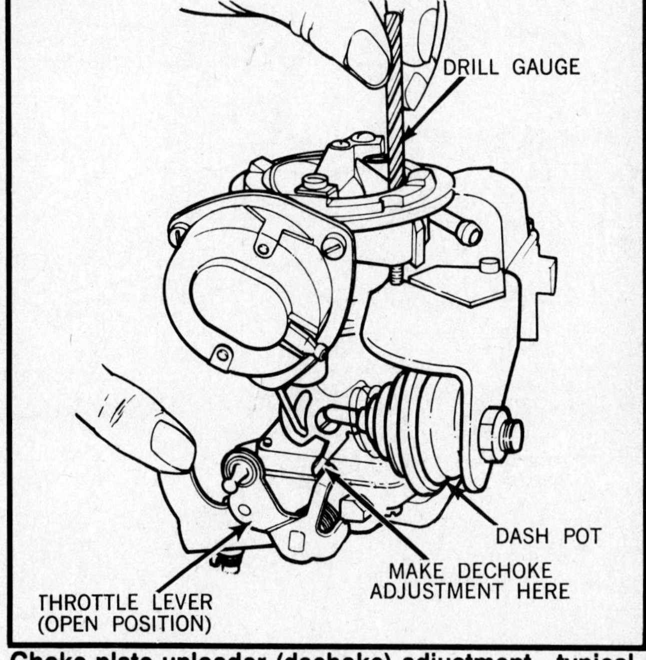

Choke plate unloader (dechoke) adjustment—typical YFA carburetor

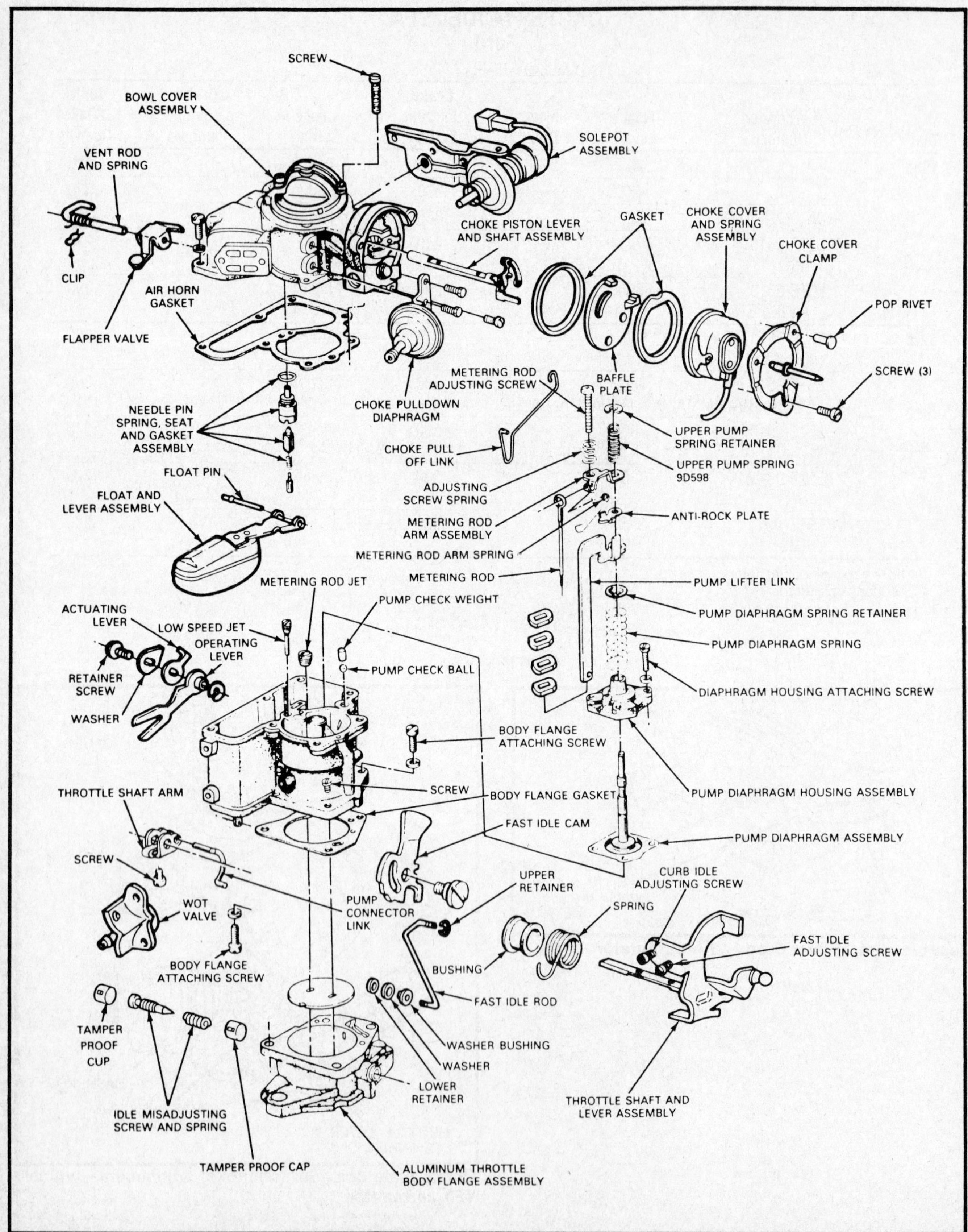

Exploded view of YFA carburetor—non-feedback type

Holley Models

MODEL 4180C

HOLLEY MODEL 4180C
Ford

(All measurements in inches)

Year	Carburetor Number	Fuel Level (Wet)	Choke Pulldown Setting	Choke Unloader Setting	Choke Setting	Pump Lever Location	Enrichment Valve Indent.
1982	E1UE-RA	①	.200–.220	.295–.335	2 Rich	#1	②
1983	E3TE- 9510-PC 9510-PC	①	.210–.230	.300–.330	3 Rich	#1	11
	E3TE- 9510-SB 9510-TB	①	.210–.230	.300–.330	3 Rich	#1	8
1984	E4TE-9510-ARA	①	.185	.300	Index	#1	13
	E3TE-9510-PD	①	.220	.295–.335	3 Rich	#1	8
	TC	①	.210–.230	.300–.330	3 Rich	#1	8
	RD	①	.200	.315	3 Rich	#1	8A
	SC	①	.210–.230	.315	3 Rich	#1	8A
1985	E4TE-9510-ARA	①	.185	.300	Index	#1	13
	E3TE-9510 PD	①	.220	.295–.335	3 Rich	#1	8
	TC	①	.210–.230	.300–.330	3 Rich	#1	8
	RD	①	.200	.315	3 Rich	#1	8A
	SC	①	.210–.230	.315	3 Rich	#1	8A
1986	E5TE-9510 ZB	①	.157	.425	Orange ③	#1	—
1987–'88	E5TE-9510 ZB	①	.144–.170	.425	Orange ③	#1	—
	E6HE-9510 AC	①	.144–.170	.425	Orange ③	#1	—
	E6HE-9510 GA,GB	①	.138–.162	.300	Natural ③	#1	—

① At bottom of sight plug
② Power valve timing 9.5–7.0/3.0–.5
③ Choke cap color index plate

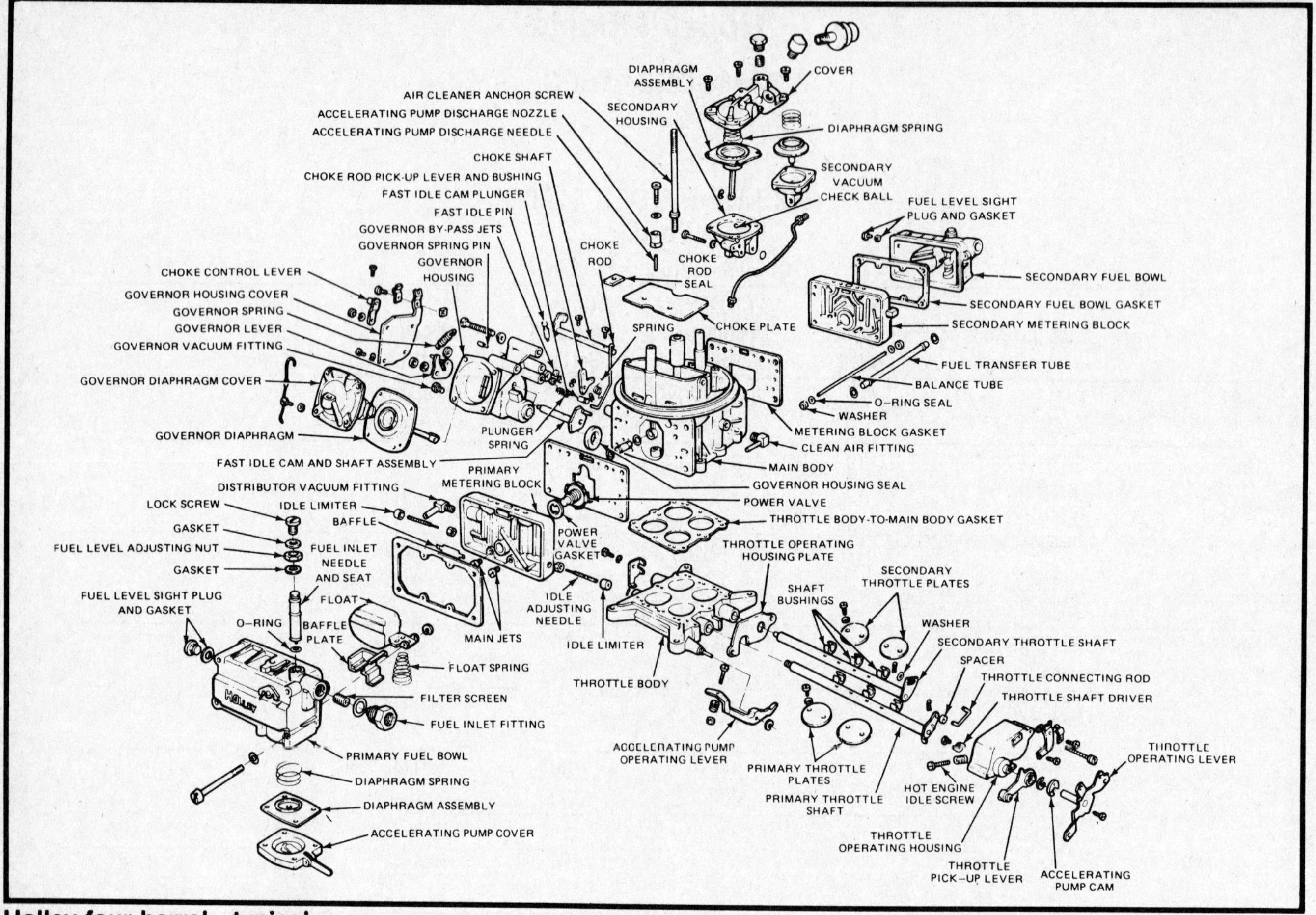

DIAPHRAGM ASSEMBLY
COVER
AIR CLEANER ANCHOR SCREW
SECONDARY HOUSING
ACCELERATING PUMP DISCHARGE NOZZLE
ACCELERATING PUMP DISCHARGE NEEDLE
DIAPHRAGM SPRING
CHOKE SHAFT
SECONDARY VACUUM CHECK BALL
CHOKE ROD PICK-UP LEVER AND BUSHING
FAST IDLE CAM PLUNGER
FUEL LEVEL SIGHT PLUG AND GASKET
FAST IDLE PIN
GOVERNOR BY-PASS JETS
GOVERNOR SPRING PIN
CHOKE ROD
GOVERNOR HOUSING
CHOKE ROD SEAL
CHOKE CONTROL LEVER
SECONDARY FUEL BOWL
GOVERNOR HOUSING COVER
SECONDARY FUEL BOWL GASKET
GOVERNOR SPRING
GOVERNOR LEVER
SPRING
CHOKE PLATE
SECONDARY METERING BLOCK
GOVERNOR VACUUM FITTING
FUEL TRANSFER TUBE
GOVERNOR DIAPHRAGM COVER
BALANCE TUBE
O-RING SEAL
WASHER
PLUNGER SPRING
METERING BLOCK GASKET
GOVERNOR DIAPHRAGM
CLEAN AIR FITTING
FAST IDLE CAM AND SHAFT ASSEMBLY
PRIMARY METERING BLOCK
MAIN BODY
DISTRIBUTOR VACUUM FITTING
GOVERNOR HOUSING SEAL
LOCK SCREW
IDLE LIMITER
POWER VALVE
BAFFLE
THROTTLE BODY-TO-MAIN BODY GASKET
GASKET
POWER VALVE GASKET
FUEL LEVEL ADJUSTING NUT
FUEL INLET NEEDLE AND SEAT
THROTTLE OPERATING HOUSING PLATE
GASKET
SECONDARY THROTTLE PLATES
FUEL LEVEL SIGHT PLUG AND GASKET
FLOAT
IDLE ADJUSTING NEEDLE
SHAFT BUSHINGS
O-RING
BAFFLE PLATE
WASHER
MAIN JETS
IDLE LIMITER
SECONDARY THROTTLE SHAFT
SPACER
FLOAT SPRING
THROTTLE BODY
THROTTLE CONNECTING ROD
FILTER SCREEN
THROTTLE SHAFT DRIVER
FUEL INLET FITTING
ACCELERATING PUMP OPERATING LEVER
THROTTLE OPERATING LEVER
PRIMARY FUEL BOWL
PRIMARY THROTTLE PLATES
HOT ENGINE IDLE SCREW
DIAPHRAGM SPRING
PRIMARY THROTTLE SHAFT
DIAPHRAGM ASSEMBLY
ACCELERATING PUMP COVER
THROTTLE OPERATING HOUSING
THROTTLE PICK-UP LEVER
ACCELERATING PUMP CAM

Holley four barrel—typical

HOT ENGINE IDLE SPEED
POWER VALVE VACUUM PICK-UP
SECONDARY FUEL BOWL
SECONDARY STAGE THROTTLE PLATES
PCV HOSE TUBE
IDLE NEEDLES
SECONDARY THROTTLE STOP SCREW
CHOKE HOUSING VACUUM PICKUP
AUTOMATIC CHOKE
FAST IDLE SPEED

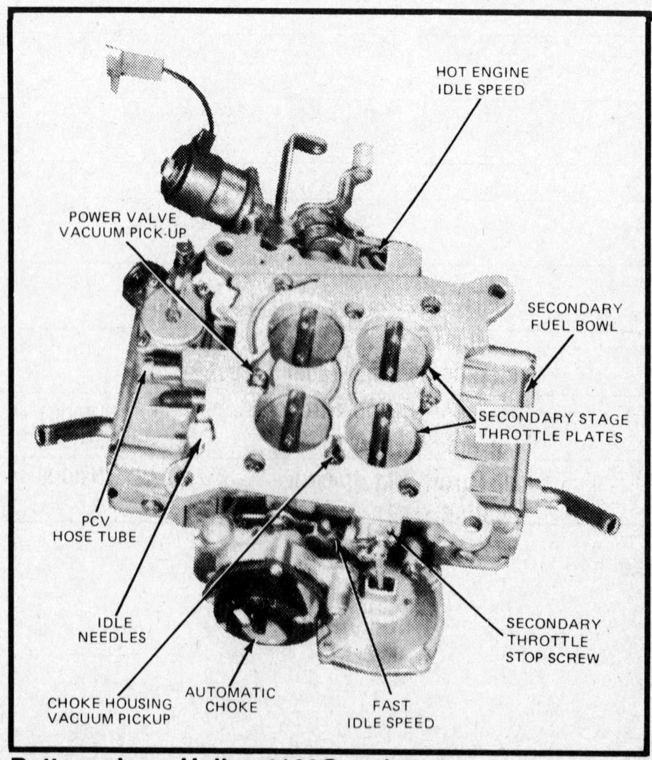

Bottom view—Holley 4180C carburetor

Motorcraft Models

MODEL 2150

MOTORCRAFT MODEL 2150
Ford

(All measurements in inches)

Year	Carburetor Number	Float Level (Dry)	Choke Unloader Setting	Choke Setting	Accelerator Pump Rod Location	Fuel Level (Wet)	Choke Pulldown Setting (Min)
1982	E2TE- BNA, CGA	7/16	.200	V notch	2	.810	.125
	BMA, CFA	7/16	.250	V notch	2	.810	.125
	DAA, CYA	7/16	.250	V notch	2	.810	.115–.135
	BEA	7/16	.200	V notch	2	.810	.130
	BLA	7/16	.200	V notch	2	.810	.125
	AYA, BEA, CJA, BFA	7/16	.200	V notch	2	.810	.130
	E2UE-JA	31/64	.200	V notch	2	.875	.130
	E2TE-BAA, BBA	7/16	.200	V notch	2	.810	.130
	CKA	7/16	.200	V notch	2	.810	.120
	E2UE-FA E1UE-JA	31/64	.200	V notch	3	.875	.120
	E2UE-KA	31/64	.200	V notch	2	.875	.120
	E2TE-BPA, BRA	31/64	.200	V notch	2	.875	.120
	E2UE-ANA AAA AKA E2UE-RA	31/64	.250	V notch	3	.875	.170–.190
	E2UE-SA	31/64	.250	V notch	3	.875	.182
	E2UE-HA ABA E1UE-KA	31/64	.250	V notch	3	.875	.170–.190
	E2TE-BHA BGA	31/64	.250	V notch	4	.875	.180
	E2TE-DCA E2TE-DBA	31/64	.250	V notch	3	.875	.170–.190
	E2TE-BKA BJA	31/64	.250	V notch	4	.875	.175
	E2TE-DDA DEA	31/64	.250	V notch	3	.875	.170–.190
1983	E3TE-9510 BCA BFA BBA BGA	—	.25	V notch	3	.810	.115–135
	AUA	7/16	.20	V notch	3	.810	.142
	BHA	7/16	.20	V notch	3	.810	.152
	AYA	7/16	.25	V notch	4	.810	.137
	AVA	7/16	.25	V notch	3	.810	.149

MOTORCRAFT MODEL 2150
Ford

(All measurements in inches)

Year	Carburetor Number	Float Level (Dry)	Choke Unloader Setting	Choke Setting	Accelerator Pump Rod Location	Fuel Level (Wet)	Choke Pulldown Setting (Min)
1983	BJA	7/16	.20	V notch	4	.810	.157
	BLA	7/16	.20	V notch	3	.810	.157
	BEA	7/16	.20	V notch	3	.810	.149
	BMA	7/16	.20	V notch	4	.810	.150
	E3UE-9510 CA, FA	31/64	.20	V notch	3	.875	.120
	BA, KA	31/64	.20	V notch	2	.875	.120
	E3TE-9510 BAA, BPA	31/64	.25	V notch	3	.875	.130
	E2UE-9510 DA EA ANA AKA	31/64	.25	V notch	3	.875	.180
	E37E-9510 LB	.650	.27	—	—	—	.320
	E37E-9510 ABA AAA ADA	7/16	.250	V notch	4	.810	.126–.146
1984	E37E-9510 AEA	7/16	.200	V notch	4	.810	.136
	E4TE-9510						
	AUA	31/64	.200	V notch	4	.875	.150
	AFA	31/64	.200	V notch	3	.875	.144
	ADA	7/16	.200	V notch	4	.810	.152
	ACA	7/16	.200	V notch	4	.810	.155
	ATA	31/64	.200	V notch	3	.875	.130
1985	E57E-9510 BA, CA	1/16	.250	3-Rich	4	.810 ④	.136
	E5TE-9510			V-notch	4	.875	.150
	YA	9/32	.220				
	ACA	9/32	.200	3 Rich	4	.875	.150
	AAA	1/4	.200	V Notch	4	.810	.155
	PA	1/4	.200	3 Rich	4	.810	.152
	E3UE-9510 EA, DA	31/64	.250	V notch	3	.875	.180
1986	E69E-9510 CA, DA	1/16	.250	V notch	4	.810	.126–.146
	AA, BA	1/16	.250	V notch	4	.810	.126–.146

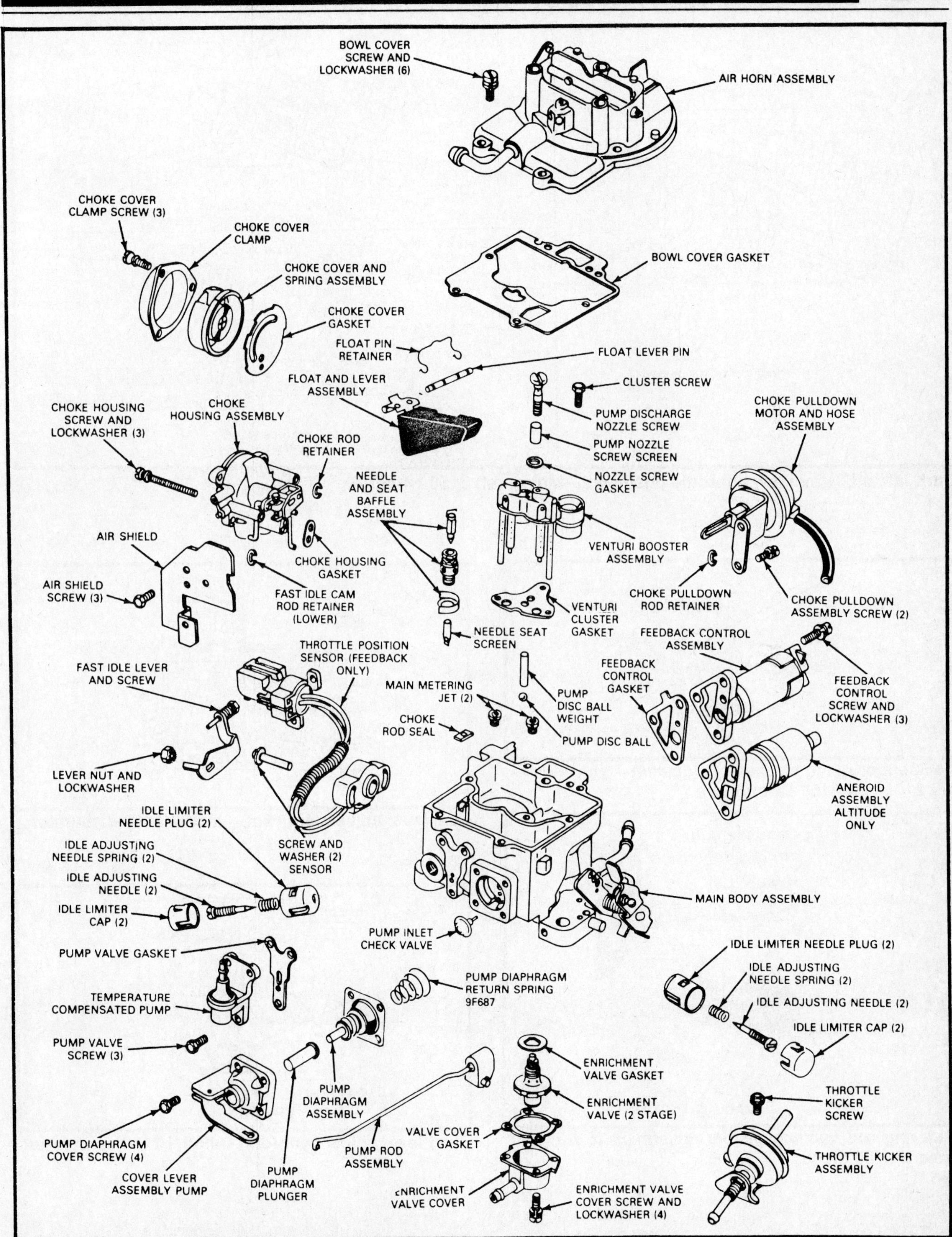

Exploded view of 2150A feedback carburetor

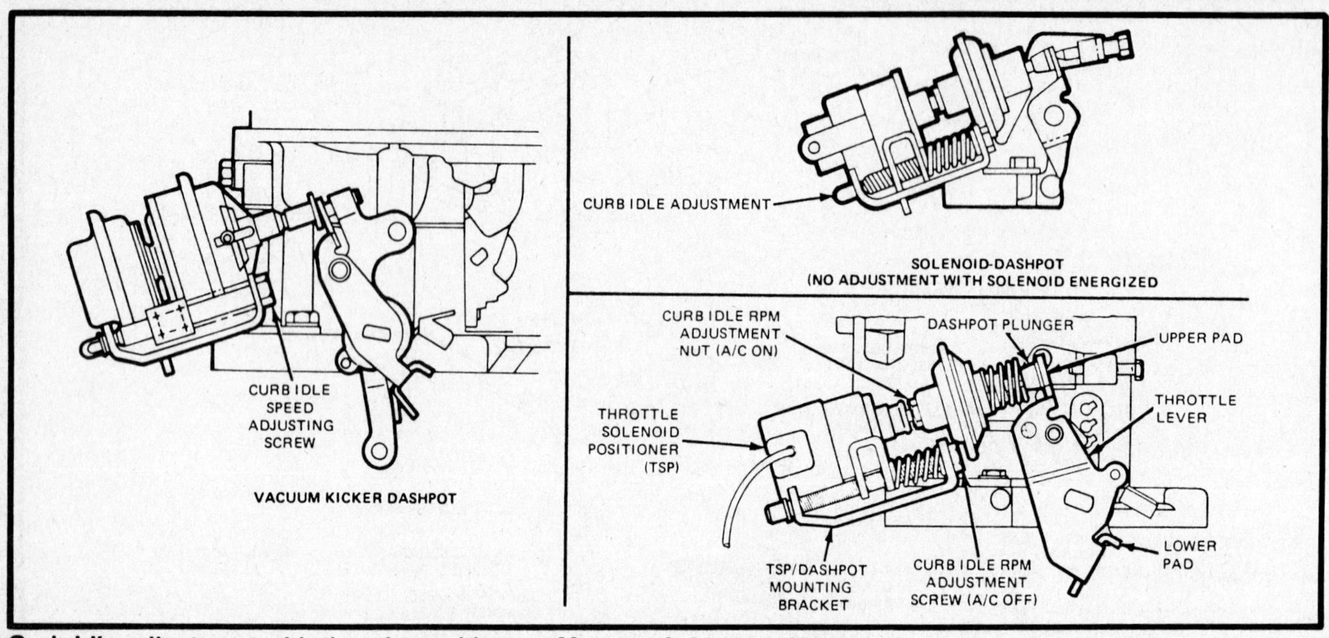

Curb idle adjustment with throttle positioner—Motorcraft 2150 carburetor

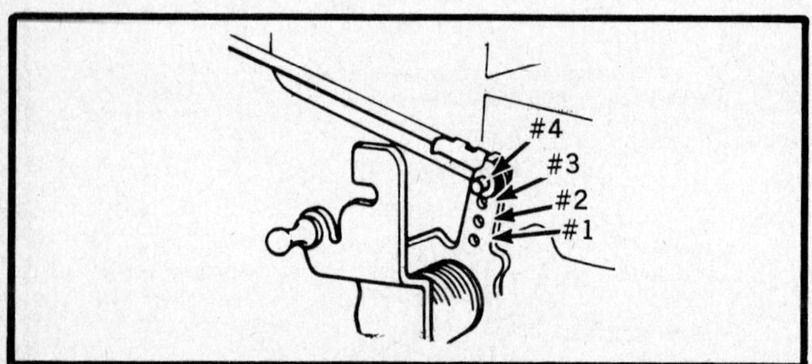

Accelerator pump stroke hole location—typical models 2100 and 2150 carburetors

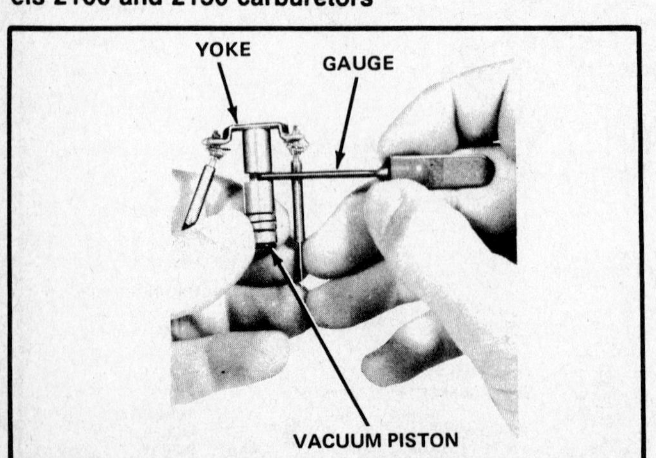

Metering rod vacuum piston adjustment to a clearance of .120 inches

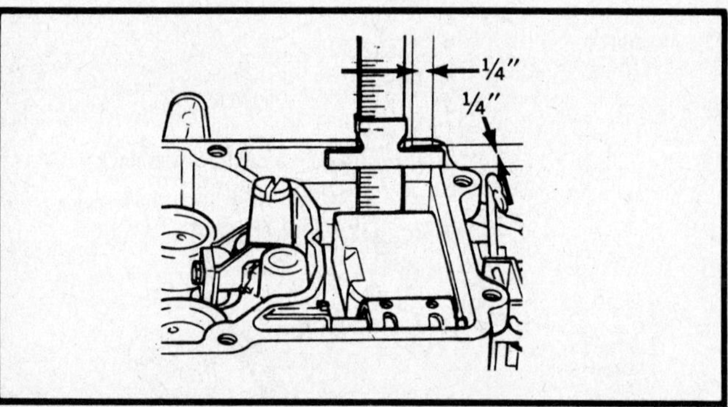

Fuel level adjustment (wet)—model 2150 carburetor

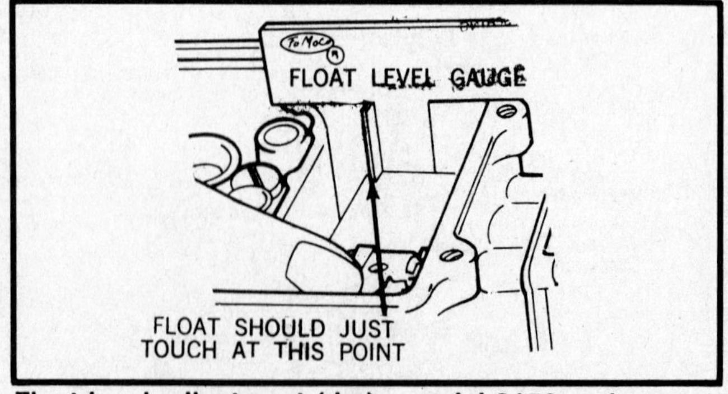

Float level adjustment (dry)—model 2150 carburetor

MOTORCRAFT MODEL 7200
Ford

(All measurements in inches)

Year	Carburetor Number	Float Setting	Float Drop	Control Vacuum Regulator	Pulldown Timing	Pump Lever Lash
1982	E1TE-2A, AHA E2TE-CDA, CCA	1.070–1.010	1.490–1.430	.245–.255	2–5 sec.	.010 ①
1983	E3TE-9510-BVA, BYA	1.070–1.010	1.490–1.430	.245–.255	2–5 sec.	.010 ①
1984	E3TE-9510-BVA, BYA	1.070–1.010	1.490–1.430	.245–.255	2–5 sec.	.010 ①
1985	E3TE-9510-BVA, BYA	1.070–1.010	1.490–1.430	.245–.255	2–5 sec.	.010 ①

① Plus one turn counter-clockwise.

MODEL 7200

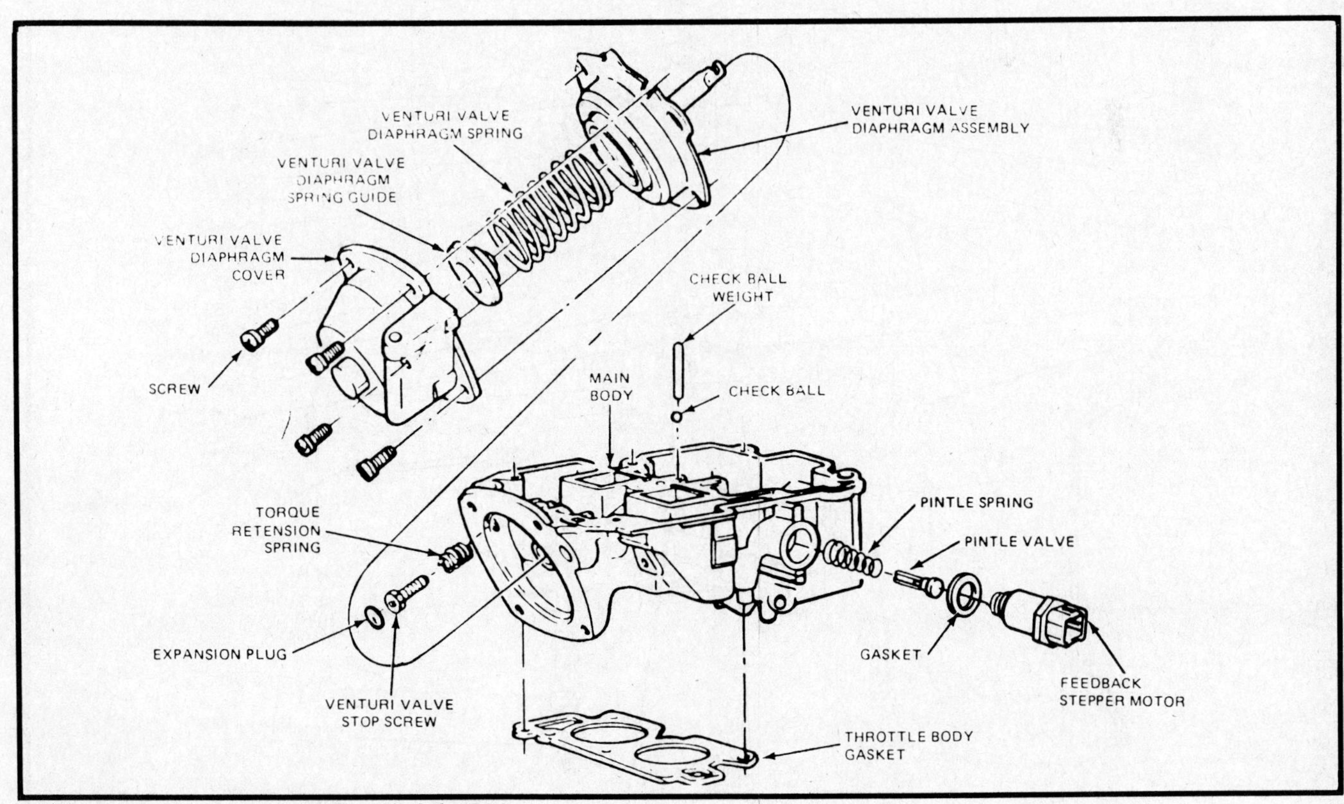

Exploded view of main body, model 7200

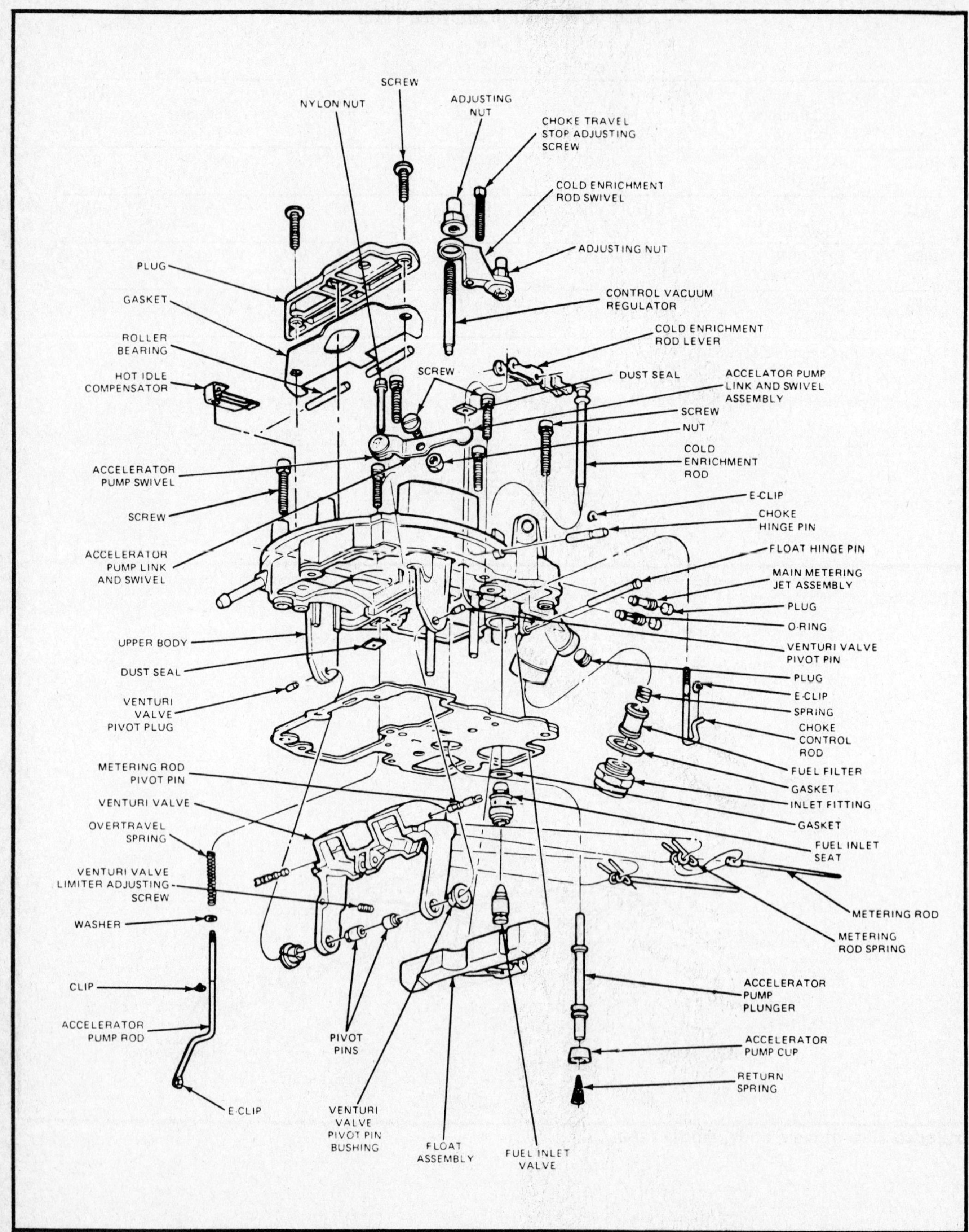

Exploded view of Upper body, model 7200

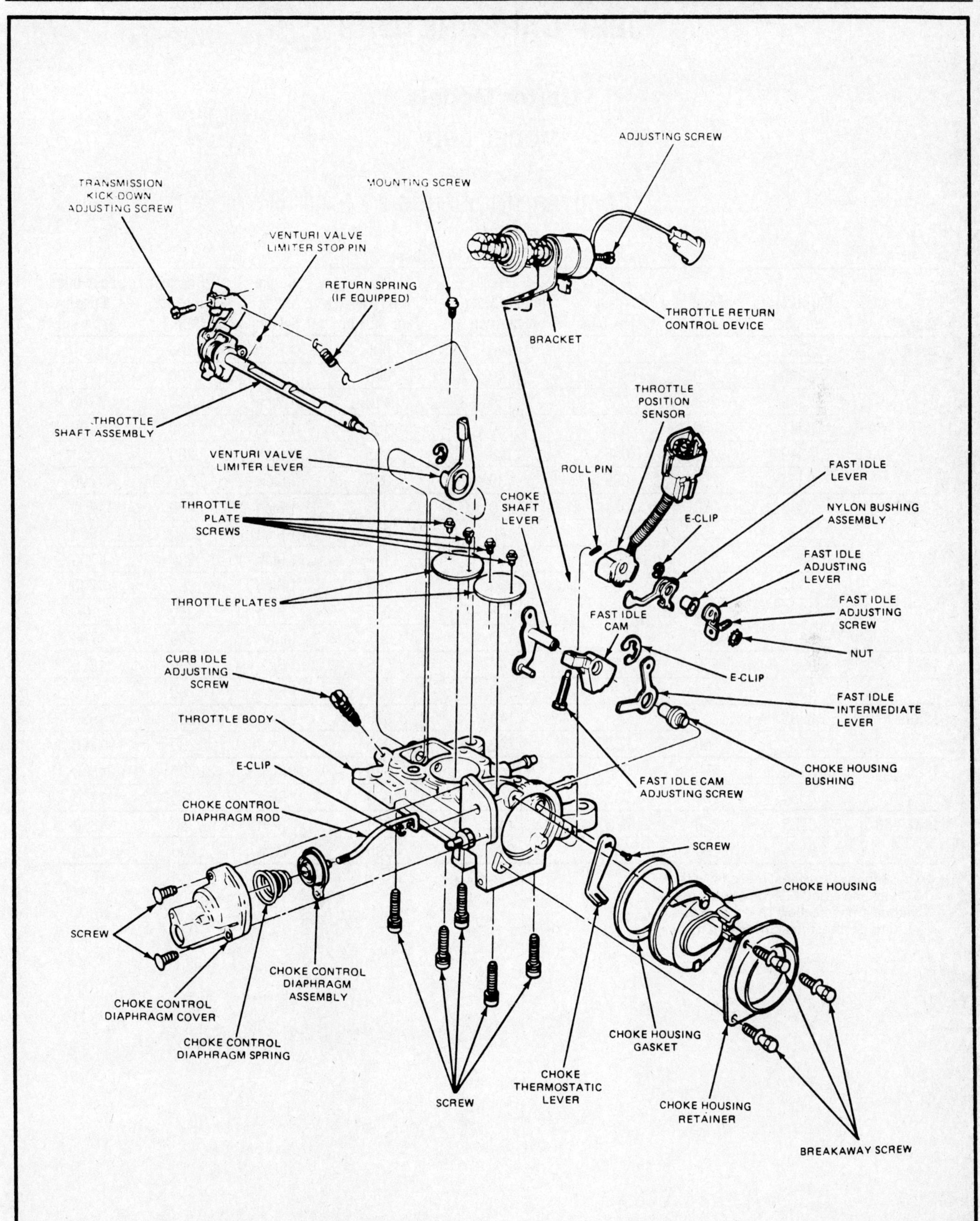

Exploded view of throttle body, model 7200

JEEP CARBURETORS

Carter Models

MODEL BBD

**CARTER MODEL BBD-2
Jeep**

(All measurements in inches)

Year	Carburetor Number	Float Level	Step-up Piston Gap	Initial Choke Clearance	Fast Idle Cam Setting	Choke Cover Setting	Choke Unloader (Min.)	Fast Idle Speed (rpm) ①
1982	8338	.250	.035	.140	.095	1 Rich	.280	1850
	8339	.250	.035	.140	.095	1 Rich	.280	1700
	8340	.250	.035	.150	.110	1 Rich	.280	1700
	8341	.250	.035	.150	.150	1 Rich	.280	1700
	8349	.250	.035	.128	.095	2 Rich	.280	②
	8351	.250	.035	.130	.095	Index	.280	1700
1983	8338	.250	.035	.140	.095	1 Rich	.280	1850
	8339	.250	.035	.140	.095	1 Rich	.280	1700
	8340	.250	.035	.150	.110	1 Rich	.280	1700
	8341	.250	.035	.150	.150	1 Rich	.280	1700
	8349	.250	.035	.128	.095	2 Rich	.280	②
	8351	.250	.035	.130	.095	Index	.280	1700
1984	8383	.250	.035	.140	.095	1 Rich	.280	1850
	8384	.250	.035	.140	.095	1 Rich	.280	1700
1985	8383	.250	.035	.140	.095	1 Rich	.280	1850
	8384	.250	.035	.140	.095	1 Rich	.280	1700
1986	8383	.250	.035	.140	.095	1 Rich	.280	1850
	8384	.250	.035	.140	.095	1 Rich	.280	1700
1987-'88	8383	.250	.035	.140	.095	1 Rich	.280	1850
	8384	.250	.035	.140	.095	1 Rich	.280	1700

① On second step of fast idle cam with TCS solenoid and EGR disconnected.
② Manual transmission 1700 rpm and automatic transmission 1850 rpm

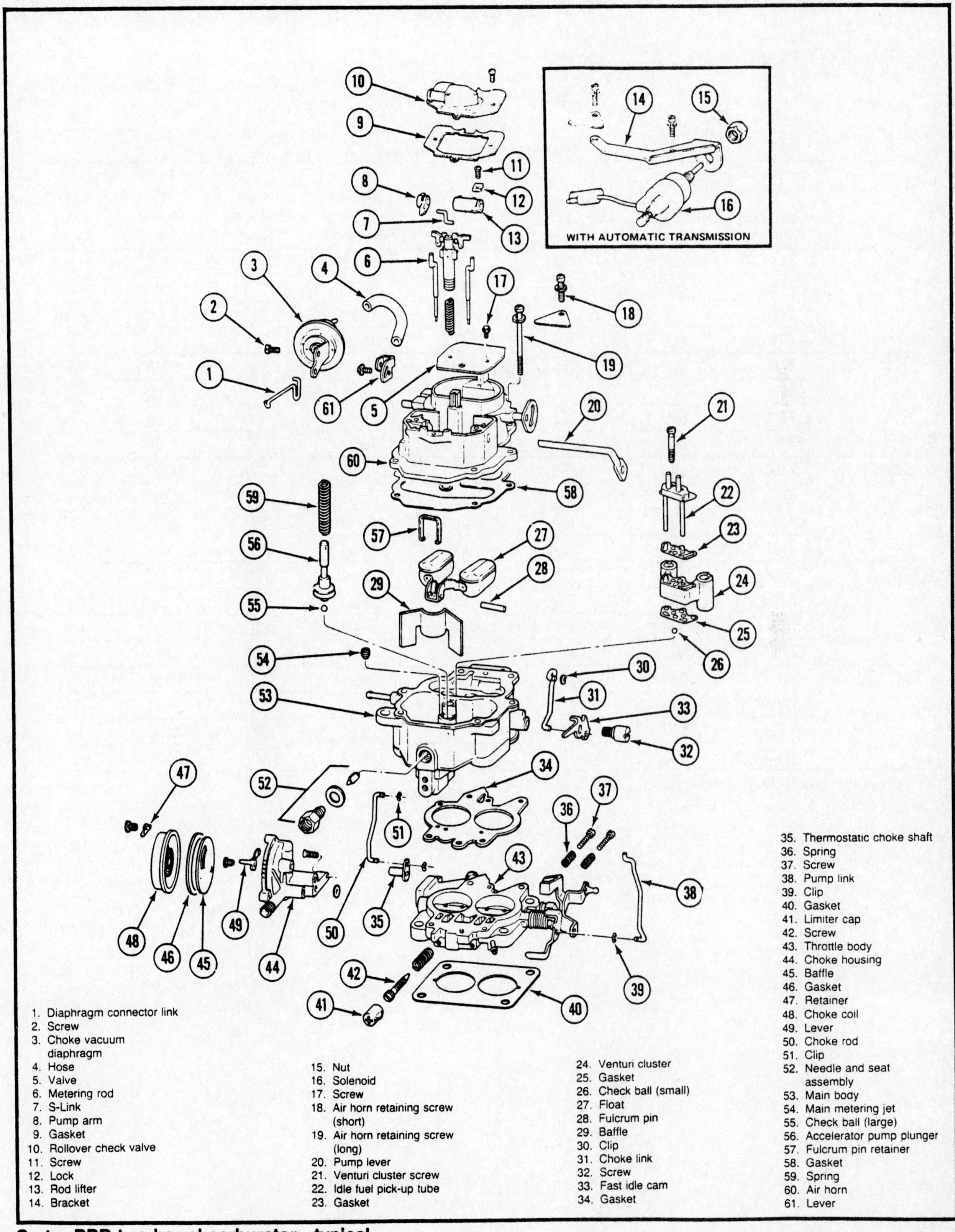

Carter BBD two barrel carburetor—typical

MODEL YFA

CARTER MODEL YFA
Jeep

(All measurements in inches)

Year	Carburetor Number	Float Level	Fast Idle Cam Setting Index	Initial Choke Clearance	Choke Cover Setting	Choke Unloader (Min.)	Fast Idle Speed (rpm) ①	Bowl Vent Opens
1983	7452	.600	.175	.280	Fixed	.280	2300	2 Step
	7453	.600	.175	.280	Fixed	.280	2000	2 Step
	7454	.600	.175	.280	Fixed	.280	2300	2 Step
	7455	.600	.175	.280	Fixed	.280	2000	2 Step
1984	7700	.600	.175	.240	Fixed	.280	2000	—
	7701	.600	.175	.240	Fixed	.280	2300	—
	7702	.600	.175	.240	Fixed	.280	2000	—
	7703	.600	.175	.240	Fixed	.280	2300	—
1985	7704	.600	.175	.280	Fixed	.280	2000	—
	7705	.600	.175	.280	Fixed	.280	2300	—
	7706	.600	.175	.280	Fixed	.280	2000	—
	7707	.600	.175	.280	Fixed	.280	2300	—
1986	7704	.600	.175	.280	Fixed	.280	2000	—
	7705	.600	.175	.280	Fixed	.280	2300	—
	7706	.600	.175	.240	Fixed	.280	2000	—
	7707	.600	.175	.280	Fixed	.280	2300	—
1987–'88	7704	.600	.175	.280	Fixed	.280	2000	—
	7705	.600	.175	.280	Fixed	.280	2300	—
	7706	.600	.175	.280	Fixed	.280	2000	—
	7707	.600	.175	.280	Fixed	.280	2300	—

① Engine hot, EGR valve disconnected

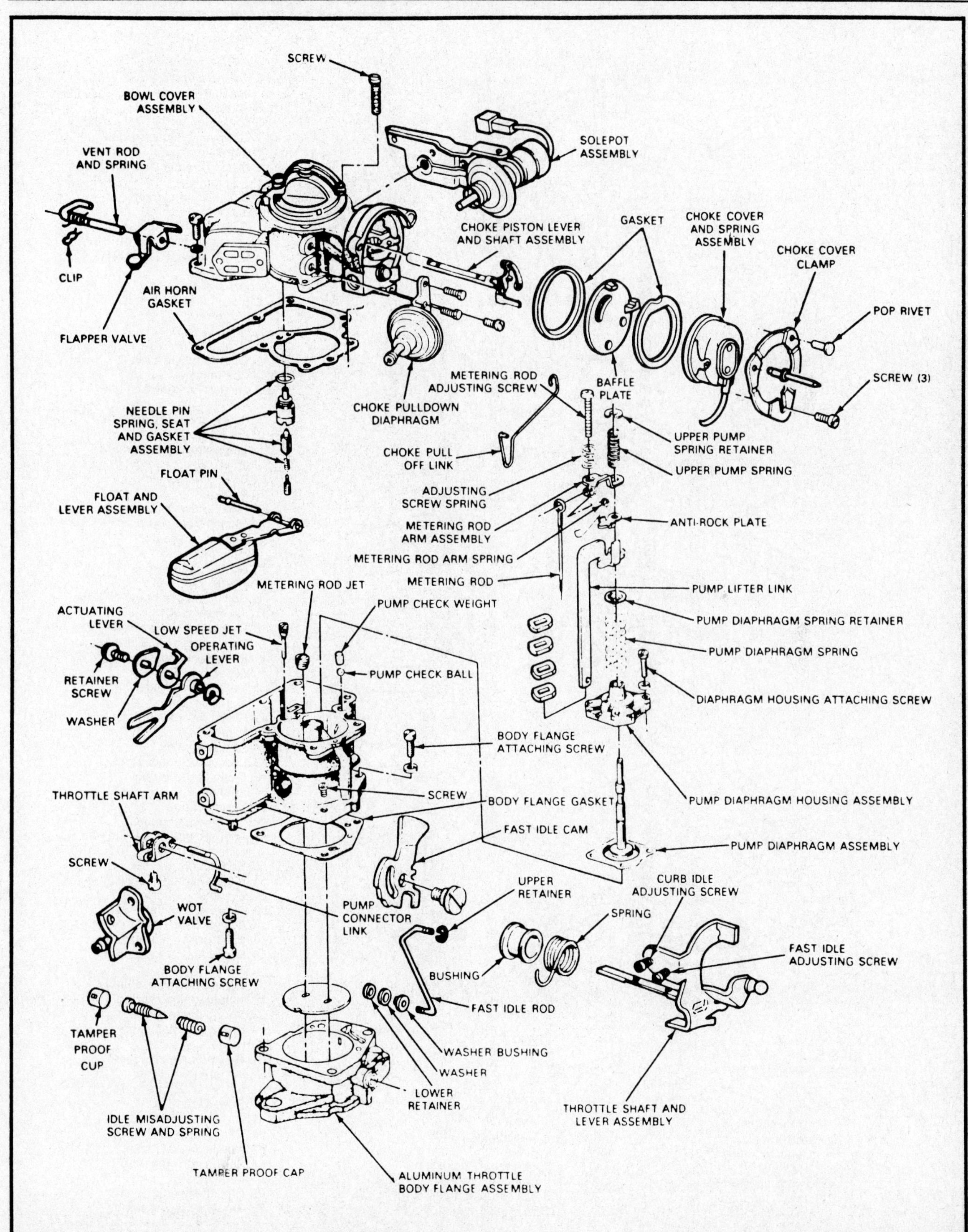

Exploded view of YFA carburetor—non-feedback type

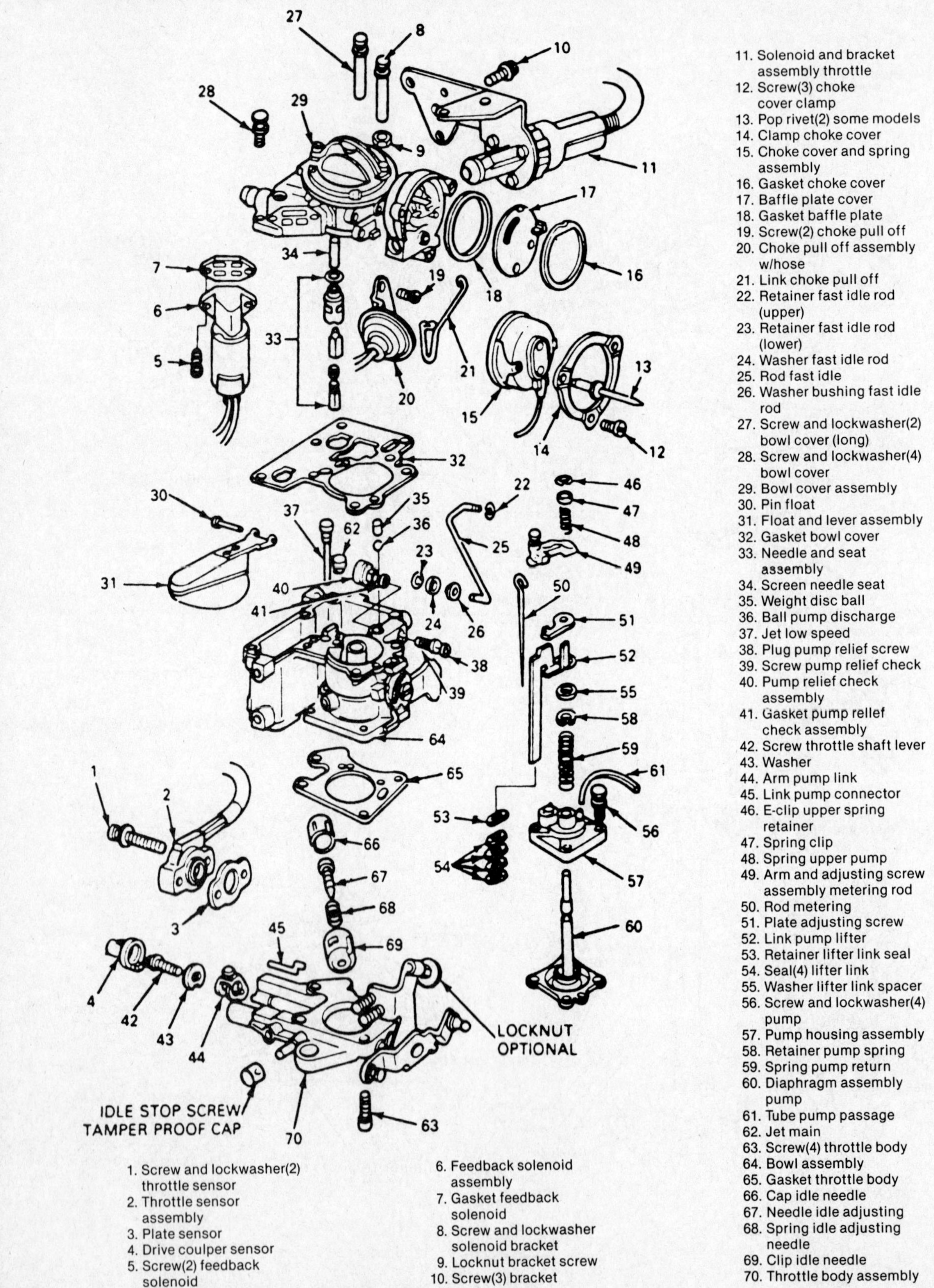

1. Screw and lockwasher(2) throttle sensor
2. Throttle sensor assembly
3. Plate sensor
4. Drive coulper sensor
5. Screw(2) feedback solenoid
6. Feedback solenoid assembly
7. Gasket feedback solenoid
8. Screw and lockwasher solenoid bracket
9. Locknut bracket screw
10. Screw(3) bracket
11. Solenoid and bracket assembly throttle
12. Screw(3) choke cover clamp
13. Pop rivet(2) some models
14. Clamp choke cover
15. Choke cover and spring assembly
16. Gasket choke cover
17. Baffle plate cover
18. Gasket baffle plate
19. Screw(2) choke pull off
20. Choke pull off assembly w/hose
21. Link choke pull off
22. Retainer fast idle rod (upper)
23. Retainer fast idle rod (lower)
24. Washer fast idle rod
25. Rod fast idle
26. Washer bushing fast idle rod
27. Screw and lockwasher(2) bowl cover (long)
28. Screw and lockwasher(4) bowl cover
29. Bowl cover assembly
30. Pin float
31. Float and lever assembly
32. Gasket bowl cover
33. Needle and seat assembly
34. Screen needle seat
35. Weight disc ball
36. Ball pump discharge
37. Jet low speed
38. Plug pump relief screw
39. Screw pump relief check
40. Pump relief check assembly
41. Gasket pump relief check assembly
42. Screw throttle shaft lever
43. Washer
44. Arm pump link
45. Link pump connector
46. E-clip upper spring retainer
47. Spring clip
48. Spring upper pump
49. Arm and adjusting screw assembly metering rod
50. Rod metering
51. Plate adjusting screw
52. Link pump lifter
53. Retainer lifter link seal
54. Seal(4) lifter link
55. Washer lifter link spacer
56. Screw and lockwasher(4) pump
57. Pump housing assembly
58. Retainer pump spring
59. Spring pump return
60. Diaphragm assembly pump
61. Tube pump passage
62. Jet main
63. Screw(4) throttle body
64. Bowl assembly
65. Gasket throttle body
66. Cap idle needle
67. Needle idle adjusting
68. Spring idle adjusting needle
69. Clip idle needle
70. Throttle body assembly

Exploded view of YFA carburetor—feedback type

MODEL 2150

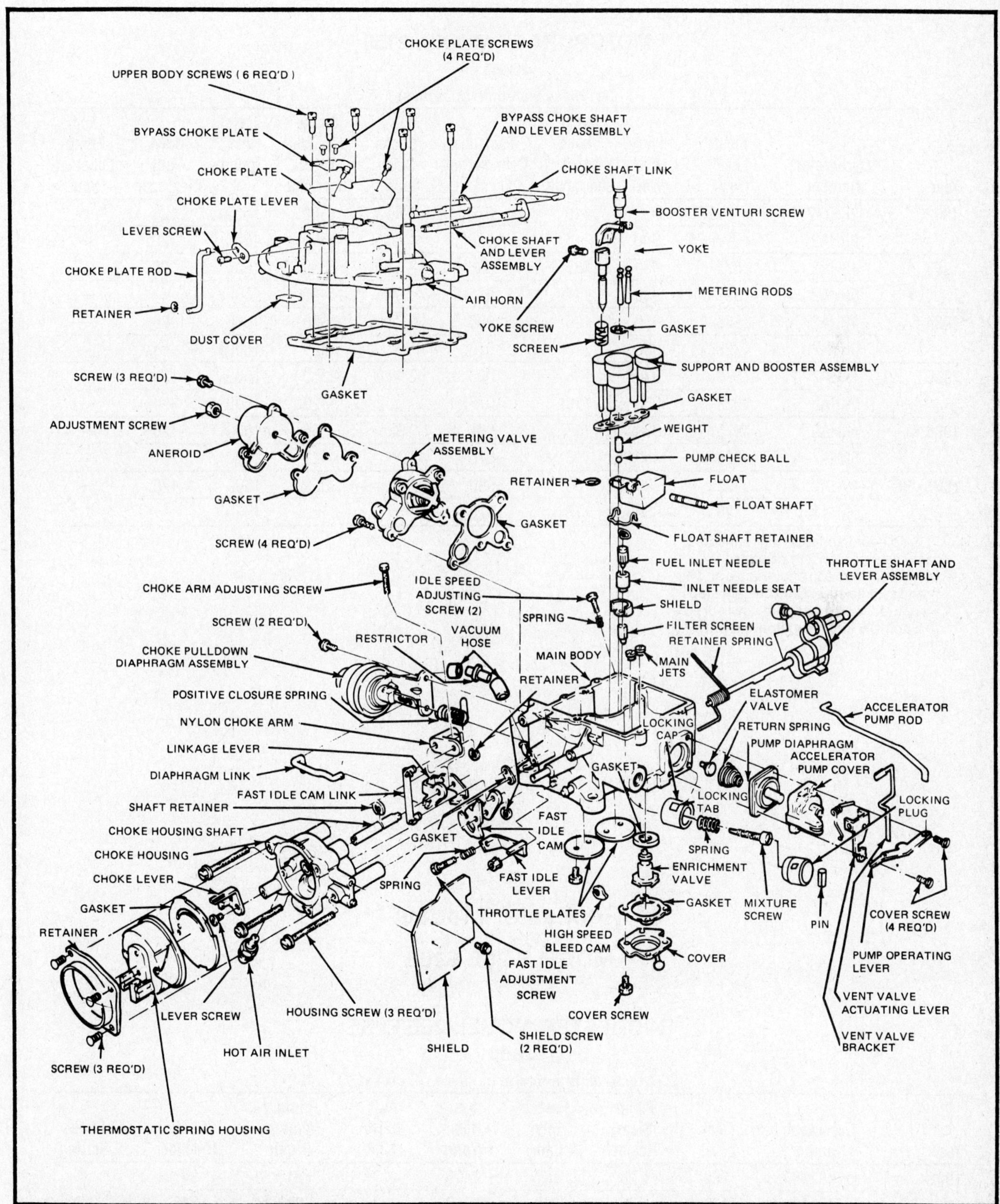
CHOKE PLATE SCREWS (4 REQ'D)
UPPER BODY SCREWS (6 REQ'D)
BYPASS CHOKE PLATE
BYPASS CHOKE SHAFT AND LEVER ASSEMBLY
CHOKE PLATE
CHOKE SHAFT LINK
CHOKE PLATE LEVER
BOOSTER VENTURI SCREW
LEVER SCREW
CHOKE SHAFT AND LEVER ASSEMBLY
YOKE
CHOKE PLATE ROD
METERING RODS
AIR HORN
RETAINER
YOKE SCREW
GASKET
DUST COVER
SCREEN
SUPPORT AND BOOSTER ASSEMBLY
SCREW (3 REQ'D)
GASKET
GASKET
WEIGHT
ADJUSTMENT SCREW
METERING VALVE ASSEMBLY
ANEROID
PUMP CHECK BALL
RETAINER
FLOAT
GASKET
FLOAT SHAFT
GASKET
SCREW (4 REQ'D)
FLOAT SHAFT RETAINER
FUEL INLET NEEDLE
THROTTLE SHAFT AND LEVER ASSEMBLY
IDLE SPEED ADJUSTING SCREW (2)
CHOKE ARM ADJUSTING SCREW
INLET NEEDLE SEAT
SHIELD
SPRING
FILTER SCREEN
SCREW (2 REQ'D)
VACUUM HOSE
RETAINER SPRING
RESTRICTOR
CHOKE PULLDOWN DIAPHRAGM ASSEMBLY
MAIN BODY
MAIN JETS
RETAINER
POSITIVE CLOSURE SPRING
ELASTOMER VALVE
ACCELERATOR PUMP ROD
NYLON CHOKE ARM
LOCKING CAP
RETURN SPRING
LINKAGE LEVER
PUMP DIAPHRAGM
ACCELERATOR PUMP COVER
GASKET
DIAPHRAGM LINK
FAST IDLE CAM LINK
LOCKING TAB
LOCKING PLUG
SHAFT RETAINER
FAST IDLE CAM
CHOKE HOUSING SHAFT
GASKET
SPRING
CHOKE HOUSING
ENRICHMENT VALVE
CHOKE LEVER
FAST IDLE LEVER
SPRING
GASKET
MIXTURE SCREW
GASKET
THROTTLE PLATES
PIN
COVER SCREW (4 REQ'D)
RETAINER
HIGH SPEED BLEED CAM
COVER
PUMP OPERATING LEVER
FAST IDLE ADJUSTMENT SCREW
VENT VALVE ACTUATING LEVER
LEVER SCREW
HOUSING SCREW (3 REQ'D)
COVER SCREW
SHIELD SCREW (2 REQ'D)
VENT VALVE BRACKET
HOT AIR INLET
SHIELD
SCREW (3 REQ'D)
THERMOSTATIC SPRING HOUSING

Typical late model 2150 carburetor

Motorcraft Models

MOTORCRAFT MODEL 2150 Jeep

(All measurements in inches)

Year	Carburetor Number	Float Level (Dry)	Fuel Level (Wet)	Initial Choke Valve Clearance	Fast Idle Cam Setting ②	Choke Cover Setting	Choke Unloader Valve Clearance	Fast Idle Speed ①	Bowl Vent Clearance	Rod Pump Location Hole
1982	2RHM2	19/64–23/64 ③	.930	.116	.076	1 Rich	.350	1500	.120	—
	2RHA2	19/64–23/64 ③	.930	.116	.076	1 Rich	.350	1600	.120	—
1983	4RHA2	.575	.930	.136	.086	2 Rich	.350	1600	.120	—
	5RHA2	.328	.930	.118	.076	Y	.420	1600	—	—
1984	4RHA2	.575	.930	.136	.086	2 Rich	.350	1600	.120	—
	5RHA2	.328	.930	.118	.076	Y	.420	1600	—	—
1985	4RHA2	.575	.930	.136	.086	2 Rich	.350	1600	.120	—
	5RHA2	.328	.930	.118	.076	Y	.420	1600	—	—
1986	4RHA2	.575	.930	.136	.086	2 Rich	.350	1600	.120	—
	5RHA2	.328	.930	.118	.076	Y	.420	1600	—	—
1987–'88	4RHA2	.575	.930	.136	.086	2 Rich	.350	1600	.120	—
	5RHA2	.328	.930	.118	.076	Y	.420	1600	—	—

① TCS solenoid and EGR disconnected, fast idle screw on 2nd cam step
② Measured between choke valve and air horn fast idle screw on 2nd cam step
③ Measured from machined bowl surface to a point 1/8 inch from float tip with the needle seated

Rochester Models

MODELS 2SE/E2SE

ROCHESTER MODEL 2SE/E2SE Jeep

(All measurements in inches or degrees)

Year	Carburetor Number	Float Level	Pump Stem Height	Fast ② Idle Cam	Fast Idle (rpm)	Air ① Valve Link	Primary Vacuum Break	Choke Unloader	Choke Setting
1982	17082380	.169	1.28	18°	2400	2°	21°	34°	③
	17082381	.169	1.28	18°	2400	2°	21°	34°	③
	17082389	.169	1.28	18°	2400	2°	19°	34°	③

ROCHESTER MODEL 2SE/E2SE
Jeep

(All measurements in inches or degrees)

Year	Carburetor Number	Float Level	Air Valve Windup	Choke Coil Lever	Fast Idle Cam 2nd Step	Primary Vacuum Break	Secondary Vacuum Break	Air Valve Rod	Choke Unloader
1983	17084580	5/32	1	.085	22°	26°	32°	1°	40°
	17084581	5/32	1	.085	22°	26°	32°	1°	40°
	17084582	5/32	1	.085	22°	26°	32°	1°	40°
	17084583	5/32	1	.085	22°	26°	32°	1°	40°
	17084384	1/8	1	.085	22°	25°	30°	1°	40°
1984	17084580	5/32	1	.085	22°	26°	32°	1°	40°
	17084581	5/32	1	.085	22°	26°	32°	1°	40°
	17084582	5/32	1	.085	22°	26°	32°	1°	40°
	17084583	5/32	1	.085	22°	26°	32°	1°	40°
	17084584	1/8	1	.085	22°	25°	30°	1°	40°
1985	17084580	5/32	1	.085	22°	26°	32°	1°	40°
	17084581	5/32	1	.085	22°	26°	32°	1°	40°
	17084582	5/32	1	.085	22°	26°	32°	1°	40°
	17084583	5/32	1	.085	22°	26°	32°	1°	40°
	17084584	1/8	1	.085	22°	25°	30°	1°	40°
1986	17085380	5/32	1	.085	22°	26°	32°	1°	40°
	17085381	5/32	1	.085	22°	26°	32°	1°	40°
	17085382	5/32	1	.085	22°	26°	32°	1°	40°
	17085383	5/32	1	.085	22°	26°	32°	1°	40°
	17085384	1/8	1	.085	22°	25°	30°	1°	40°
1987-88	17084580	5/32	1	.085	22°	26°	32°	1°	40°
	17084581	5/32	1	.085	22°	26°	32°	1°	40°
	17084582	5/32	1	.085	22°	26°	32°	1°	40°
	17084583	5/32	1	.085	22°	26°	32°	1°	40°
	17084384	1/8	1	.085	22°	25°	30°	1°	40°

NOTE: Specified angle for use with angle degree tool

① Maximum degree setting

② 2nd step on cam

③ Tamper resistant—riveted cover

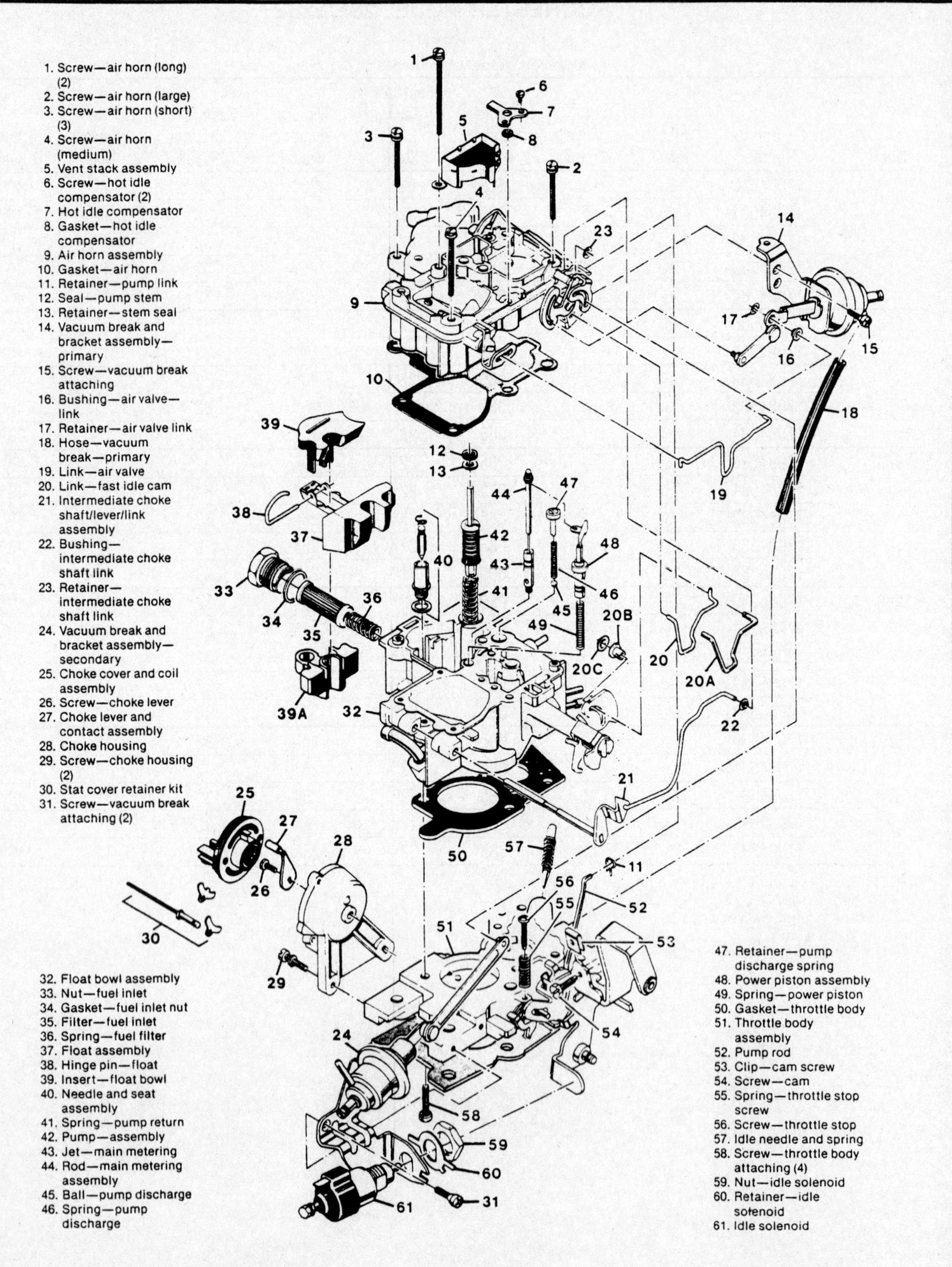

Exploded view of Rochester 2SE carburetor

Steering Gears
Domestic Trucks

INDEX

MANUAL STEERING

POWER STEERING

STEERING TROUBLE DIAGNOSIS
Manual Steering

Condition	Possible Cause	Correction
Excessive Play or Looseness in the Steering	1. Steering gear shaft adjusted too loose or shaft and/or bushing badly worn.	1. Replace worn parts and adjust according to instructions.
	2. Excessive steering gear worm end play due to bearing adjustment.	2. Adjust according to instructions.
	3. Steering linkage loose or worn.	3. Replace worn parts.
	4. Front wheel bearings improperly adjusted.	4. Adjust wheel bearings.
	5. Steering arm loose on steering gear shaft.	5. Inspect for damage to the gear shaft and steering arm, replace parts as necessary.
	6. Steering gear housing attaching bolts loose.	6. Tighten the attaching bolts to specifications.
	7. Steering arms loose at steering knuckles.	7. Tighten according to specifications.
	8. Working pins or bushings.	8. Replace king pins and bushings.
	9. Loose spring shackles.	9. Adjust or replace parts as necessary.
Hard Steering	1. Low or uneven tire pressure.	1. Inflate the tires to recommended pressures.
	2. Insufficient lubricant in the steering gear housing or in steering linkage.	2. Lubricate as necessary.
	3. Steering gear shaft adjusted too tight.	3. Adjust according to instructions.
	4. Improper caster or toe-in.	4. Align the wheels.
	5. Steering column misaligned.	5. See "Steering Gear Alignment."
Wheel Tramp (Excessive Vertical Motion of Wheels)	1. Incorrect tire pressure.	1. Inflate the tires to recommended pressures.
	2. Improper balance of wheels, tires and brake drums.	2. Balance as necessary.
	3. Loose tie rod ends or steering connections.	3. Inspect and repair as necessary.
	4. Worn or inoperative shock absorbers.	4. Replace the shock absorbers.
	5. Excessive run-out of brake drums, wheels or tires.	5. Repair or replace as required.
Shimmy	1. Badly worn and/or unevenly worn tires.	1. Rotate tires or replace if necessary.
	2. Wheels and tires out of balance.	2. Balance wheel and tire assemblies.
	3. Worn or loose steering linkage parts.	3. Replace parts are required.
	4. Worn king pins and bushings.	4. Replace king pins and bushings.
	5. Loose steering gear adjustments.	5. Adjust steering gear as necessary.
	6. Loose wheel bearings.	6. Adjust wheel bearings.
	7. Improper caster setting.	7. Adjust caster to specifications.
	8. Weak or broken springs.	8. Replace as required.
	9. Incorrect tire pressure or tire sizes not uniform.	9. Check tire sizes and inflate tires to recommended pressure
	10. Faulty shock absorbers.	10. Replace as necessary.
Pull to One Side (Tendency of the Vehicle to Veer in one Direction Only)	1. Incorrect tire pressure or tires not uniform.	1. Check tire sizes and inflate the tires to recommended pressures.
	2. Wheel bearings improperly adjusted.	2. Adjust wheel bearings.
	3. Dragging brakes.	3. Inspect for weak, or broken brake shoe spring, binding pedal.
	4. Improper caster, camber or toe-in.	4. Adjust to specifications.
	5. Grease, dirt, oil or brake fluid on brake linings.	5. Inspect, replace and adjust as necessary.
	6. Broken or sagging rear springs.	6. Replace the rear springs.
	7. Bent front axle, linkage or steering knuckle.	7. Replace the parts as necessary.
	8. Worn or tight king pin bushings.	8. Lubricate or replace as necessary.
Wander or Weave	1. Improper caster, camber or toe-in.	1. Adjust to specifications.
	2. Worn king pin and bushings.	2. Replace parts as required.
	3. Worn or improperly adjusted front wheel bearings.	3. Adjust or replace parts as necessary.
	4. Loose spring shackles.	4. Adjust or replace parts as necessary.
	5. Incorrect tire pressure or tire sizes not uniform.	5. Check tire sizes and inflate tires to recommended pressure.
	6. Loose steering gear mounting bolts.	6. Tight to specifications.

STEERING TROUBLE DIAGNOSIS
Manual Steering

Condition	Possible Cause	Correction
Wander or Weave	7. Tight king pin bushings. 8. Tight king pin thrust bearings.	7. Lubricate or ream to proper fit. 8. Adjust to .001 to .005 inch cleareance.

MANUAL STEERING GEAR

Steering Gear Alignment

Before any steering gear adjustments are made, it is recommended that the front end of the truck be raised and a thorough inspection be made for stiffness or lost motion in the steering gear, steering linkage and front suspension. Worn or damaged parts should be replaced, since a satisfactory adjustment of the steering gear cannot be obtained if bent or badly worn parts exist.

It is also very important that the steering gear be properly aligned in the truck. Misalignment of the gear places a stress on the steering worm shaft, therefore a proper adjustment is impossible. To align the steering gear, loosen the steering gear-to-frame mounting bolts to permit the gear to align itself. Check the steering gear to frame mounting seat. If there is a gap at any of the mounting bolts, proper alignment may be obtained by placing shims where excessive gap appears. Tighten the steering gear-to-frame bolts. Alignment of the gear in the truck is very important and should be done carefully so that a satisfactory, trouble-free gear adjustment may be obtained.

Gemmer Worm and Double Roller Tooth Type

WITH SCREW ADJUSTED MESH

The steering gear is of the worm and roller type with a 24 to 1 gear ratio. The cross shaft is straddle mounted with a bearing surface at the top and bottom points of the shaft mounting areas. The three tooth cross shaft roller is mounted in ball bearings. The proper lubricant used in the gear box is 90W Extreme Pressure Lubricant.

The external adjustments given below will properly adjust the steering gear.

WORM BEARING

Adjustment

1. Turn the steering wheel about one full turn from straight ahead and secure it so it doesn't move.

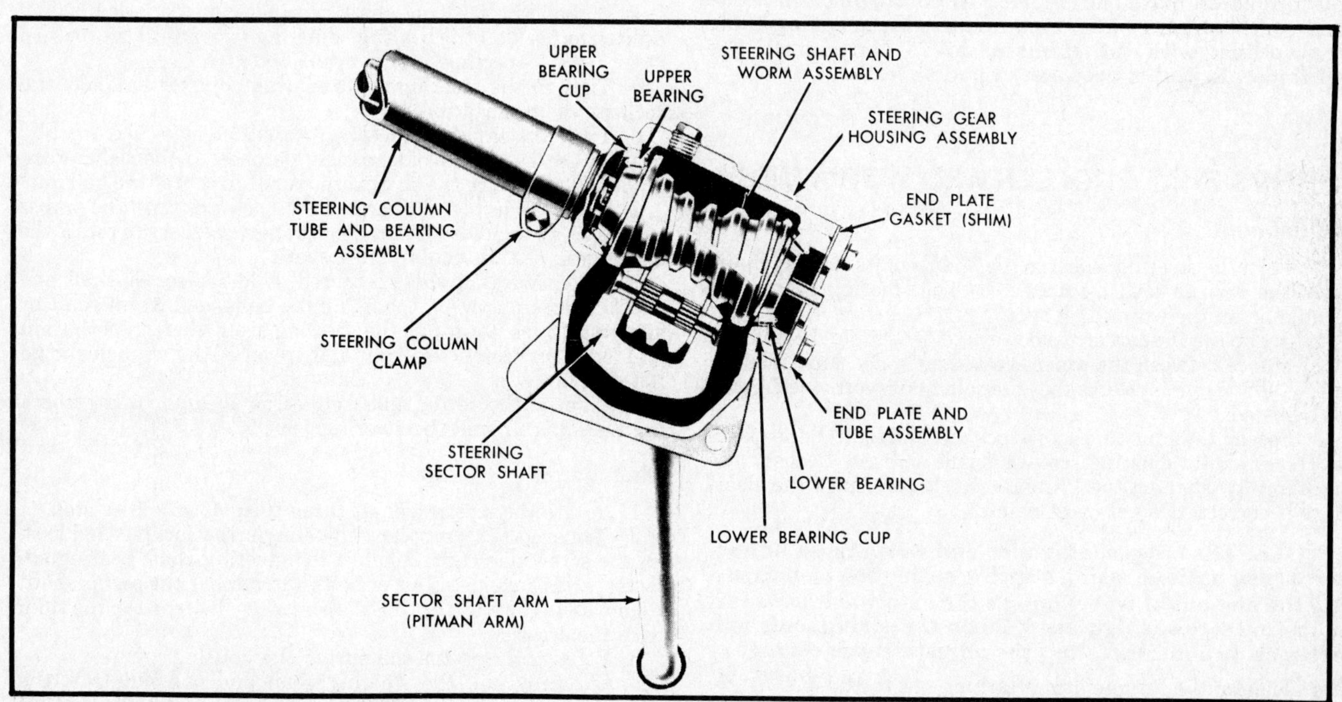

Worm and roller type steering gear

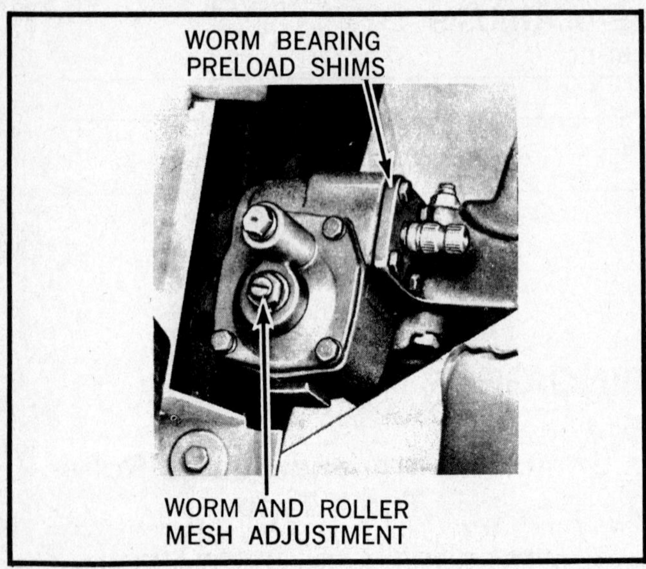

Steering gear adjustments

2. Determine if there is any worm gear end-play by shaking the front wheel sideways and noting if there is any end movement that may be felt between the steering wheel hub and the steering jacket tube. (Be sure any movement noted is not looseness in the steering jacket tube.)

3. If end play is present, adjust the worm bearings by loosening the four cover cap screws about ½ in. Separate the top shim, using a knife blade, and remove it. Do not damage the remaining shims or gaskets.

4. Replace the cover and recheck the end-play again. If necessary, repeat Steps 2 and 3 until the end-play movement is as small as possible without tightening the steering gear too much.

NOTE: Adjustment may be done with the Pitman arm disconnected. With the steering wheel turned about one full turn from straight ahead and using a spring scale tool, adjust with the shims as given above until the spring scale pull is between ¼ and ⅝ ft. lbs.

CROSS SHAFT ROLLER AND WORM MESH

Adjustment

1. Turn the steering wheel to the middle of its turning limits with the Pitman arm disconnected. The steering gear roller should be on the worm high spot.

2. Shake the Pitman arm sideways to determine the amount of clearance between the worm cross shaft roller. Movement of more than $^1/_{32}$ in. indicates that the roller and worm mesh must be adjusted.

3. Loosen the adjusting screw lock nut and tighten the external cross shaft adjusting screw a small amount. Recheck the clearance by shaking the Pitman arm. Repeat until the clearance is correct. (Do not overtighten.)

NOTE: The cross shaft roller and worm mesh adjustment may be done, using a spring scale tool, by measuring the amount of wheel pull as the external cross shaft adjusting screw is tightened. When the spring scale pull between ⅞ and 1⅛ ft. lbs., the adjustment is correct.

4. Tighten the Pitman arm attaching nut to 100–125 ft. lbs. The steering wheel nut (if loosened) should be tightened to 15–20 ft. lbs. torque.

Disassembly

1. Remove steering gear oil seal, using a suitable puller.
2. Remove cross shaft, using an arbor to prevent bearings from dropping out.
3. Remove cover, shims and cover gasket.
4. Remove worm gear, thrust bearings and bearing cups.

Assembly

1. Clean and inspect all parts, replace as necessary.

NOTE: If either thrust bearing is excessively worn, replace them both.

2. Reassemble steering gear, using new oil seal.
3. Perform worm bearing and cross shaft roller and worm mesh adjustments.
4. Lubricate to specifications.

Ford Steering Gear-Recirculating Ball Type

STEERING WORM AND SECTOR GEAR

Adjustment

The ball nut assembly and the sector gear must be adjusted properly to maintain a minimum amount of steering shaft end play and a minimum amount of backlash between the sector gear and the ball nut. There are only two adjustments that may be done on this steering gear and they should be done as given below:

1. Remove the steering gear from the vehicle.
2. Loosen the locknut on the sector shaft adjustment screw and turn the adjusting screw counterclockwise about three turns.
3. Measure the worm bearing preload by attaching an inch lbs. torque wrench to the input shaft. Note the reading required to rotate input shaft about 1½ turns either side of center. If the torque reading is not about 4–5 inch lbs., adjust the gear as given in the next step.
4. Loosen the steering shaft bearing adjuster lock nut and tighten or back off the bearing adjusting screw until the preload is within the specified limits.
5. Tighten the steering shaft bearing adjuster lock nut and recheck the preload torque.
6. Turn the input shaft slowly to either stop. Turn gently against the stop to avoid possible damage to the ball return guides. Then rotate the shaft three turns to center the ball nut.
7. Turn the sector adjusting screw clockwise until the proper torque (9–10 inch lbs.) is obtained that is necessary to rotate the worm gear past its center (high spot).
8. With the input shaft centered, hold the sector shaft and check the lash between the ball nuts, balls, and worm shaft by applying 15 lbs. torque to the steering input shaft in both right and left turn directions. The total travel of the wrench should not exceed 1¼ in..
9. Tighten the sector adjusting screw locknut, and recheck the backlash. Install the steering gear.

Disassembly

1. Rotate the steering shaft three turns from either stop.
2. Remove the sector shaft adjusting screw locknut and loosen the screw one turn. Remove the steering shaft bearing adjuster, and the housing cover bolts and remove the sector shaft. Remove the shaft by turning the screw clockwise. Keep the shim with the screw.
3. Remove the sector shaft from the housing.
4. Carefully pull the steering shaft and ball nut from the housing, and remove the steering shaft lower bearing. Do not run the ball nut to either end of the worm gear to prevent dam-

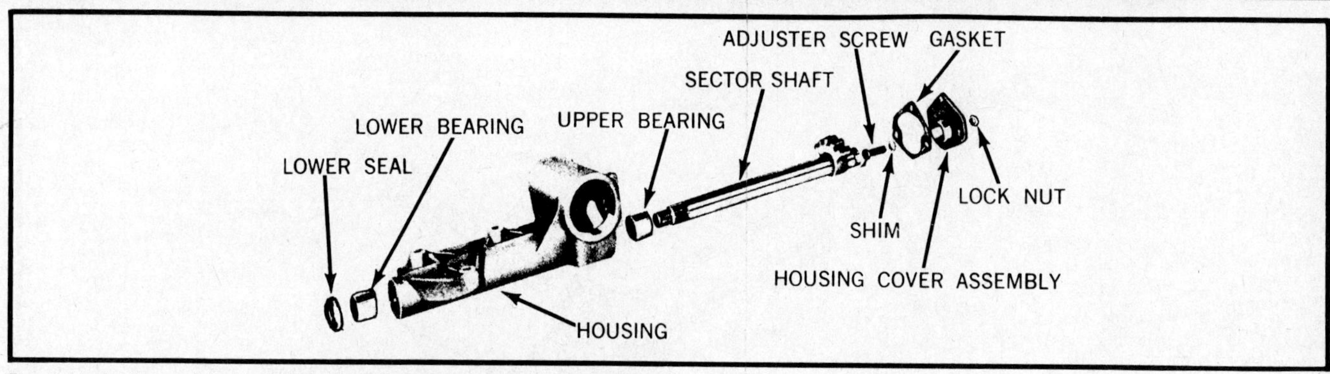

Sector shaft and housing—Ford recirculating ball model

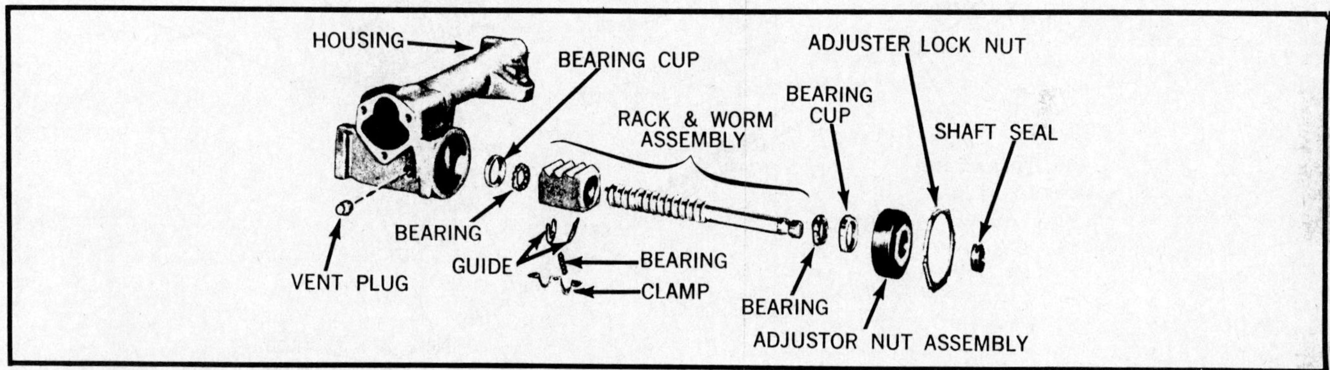

Steering shaft related parts—Ford recirculating ball model

aging the ball return guides. Disassemble the ball nut only if there are signs of binding or tightness.

5. To disassemble the ball nut, remove the ball return guide clamp and the ball return guides from the ball nut. Keep ball nut clamp side up until ready to remove the ball bearings.

6. Turn the ball nut over and rotate the worm shaft from side to side until all 50 balls have dropped out into a clean pan. With all balls removed, the nut will slide off the wormshaft.

7. Remove the upper bearing cup from the bearing adjuster and the lower cup from the housing. It may be necessary to tap the housing or the adjuster on a wooden block to jar the bearing cups loose.

Inspection

1. Carefully clean and inspect all parts. If the inspection shows bearing damage, the sector shaft bearing and the oil seal should be pressed out.

2. If the sector shaft bearing and oil seals were removed, press new bearings and oil seals into the housing. Do not clean, wash, or soak seals in cleaning solvent.

3. Apply the recommended steering gear lubricant to the housing and seals, filling the pocket between the sector shaft bearings.

Assembly

1. Install the bearing cup in the lower end of the housing and a bearing cup in the adjuster nut. Install a new seal in the bearing adjuster if the old seal was removed.

2. Apply gear lube to the outside of the worm shaft and the inside of the ball nut. Lay the steering shaft down, and position the ball nut on the shaft with the guide holes upward and the shallow end of the teeth to the left of the steering wheel position. Align the grooves in worm and ball nut by sighting through the guide holes.

3. Insert the ball guides into the holes in the ball nut, lightly tapping them, if necessary, to seat them.

4. Insert 25 balls into the hole in the top of each ball guide. If necessary, rotate the shaft slightly to distribute the balls evenly in the circuit.

5. Install the ball guide clamp, tightening the screws to the proper torque. Check that the worm shaft rotates freely.

6. Coat the threads of the steering shaft bearing adjuster, the housing cover bolts, and the sector adjusting screw with a suitable oil-resistant sealing compound. Do not apply sealer to female threads and do not get sealer on the steering shaft bearings.

7. Coat the worm bearings, sector shaft bearings, and gear teeth with steering gear lubricant.

8. Clamp the housing in a vise, with the sector shaft axis horizontal, and place the steering shaft lower bearing in its cup. Place the steering shaft and ball nut assemblies in the housing.

9. Position the steering shaft upper bearing on top of the worm gear and install the steering shaft bearing adjuster, adjuster nut, and the bearing cup. Leave the nut loose.

10. Adjust the worm bearing preload according to the instructions given earlier.

11. Position the sector adjusting screw and adjuster shim, and check for a clearance of not more than 0.002 in. between the screw head and the end of the sector shaft. If the clearance exceeds 0.002 in., add enough shims to reduce the clearance to under 0.002 in. clearance.

12. Start the sector shaft adjusting screw into the housing cover. Install a new gasket on the cover.

13. Rotate the steering shaft until the ball nut teeth mesh with the sector gear teeth, tilting the housing so the ball will tip toward the housing cover opening.

14. Lubricate the sector shaft journal and install the sector shaft and cover. With the cover moved to one side, fill the gear with lubricant (about 0.97 lb.). Push the cover and the sector shaft into place, and install the two top housing bolts. Do not tighten the bolts until checking to see that there is some lash between the ball nut and the sector gear teeth. Hold or push the

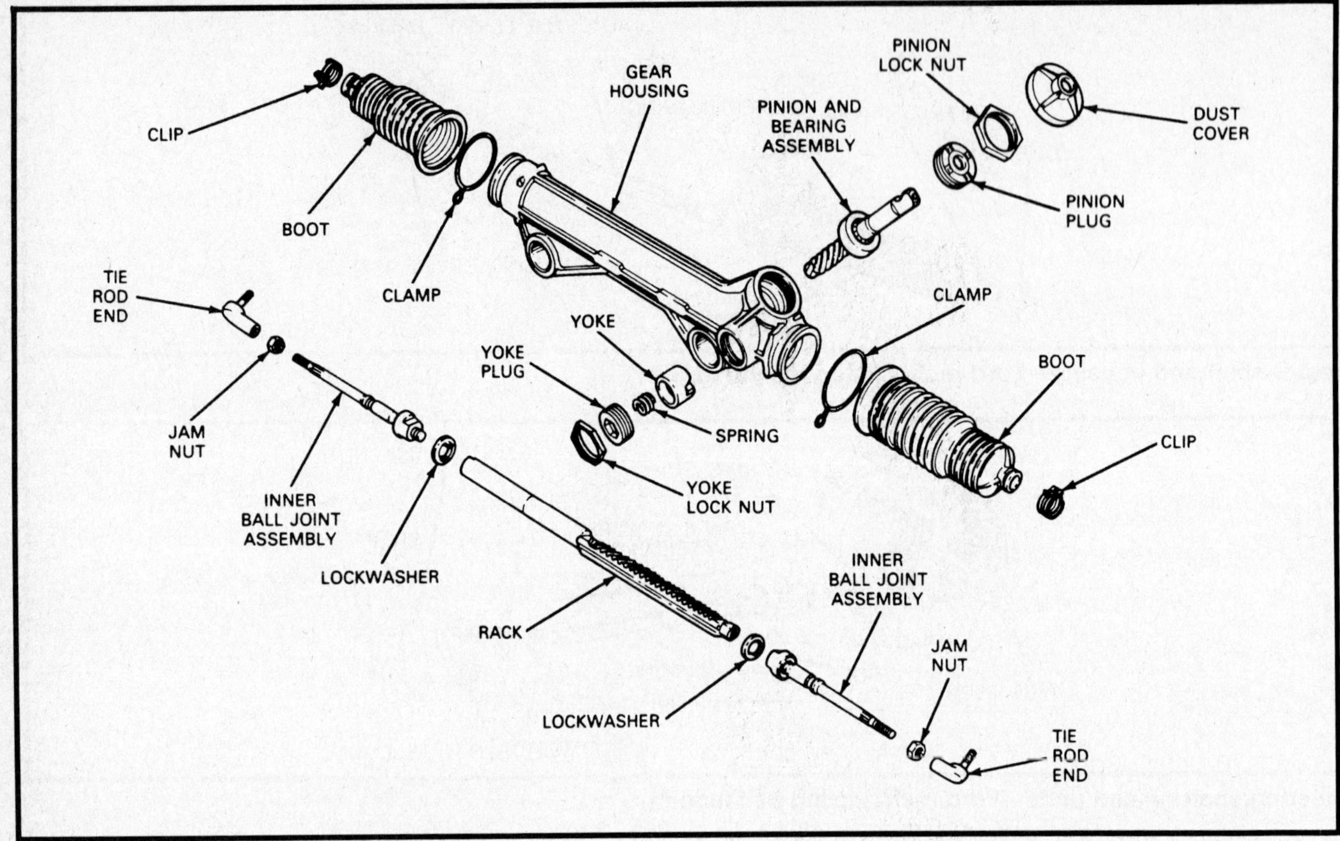

Ford manual rack and pinion assembly

cover away from the ball nut and tighten the bolts to the proper torque (30–40 ft. lbs.).

15. Loosely install the sector shaft adjusting screw lock nut and adjust the sector shaft mesh load as given earlier. Tighten the adjusting screw lock nut.

Ford Rack and Pinion

NOTE: The following manual rack and pinion assembly is used on the Ford Aerostar.

Disassembly

1. Clean the exterior of the steering gear and place in a soft jawed vise.
2. Place the gear in the on center position as follows:
   a. Rotate the pinion shaft from lock-to-lock (entire gear travel). Record the number of pinion shaft rotations.
   b. Divide the number of pinion shaft rotations by two. This provides the required number of turns to place the gear in the on-center position.
   c. From one lock position, rotate the pinion the number of turns determined in Step b to place the gear in the on-center position. The white marks on the pinion shaft and lower bearing should be in aligment.
3. Using tool, T85T–3504–AH, hold the yoke plug in place and remove the yoke locking nut with tool, T74P–3504–U.
4. Remove the yoke plug with tool, T85T–3504–BH.
5. Remove the spring from the yoke and remove the yoke from the housing.

NOTE: It may be necessary to use snap ring pliers to remove the yoke.

6. Remove the dust cover from the pinion shaft.
7. Using tool, T85T–3504–AH, hold the pinion plug lock plug in place and remove the pinion plug locknut with tool, T74P–3504–U.
8. Remove the pinion plug with tool, T85T–3504–AH.
9. Remove the pinion and bearing assembly from the housing.

Assembly

1. Coat the pinion teeth and the upper bearing with steering grease.
2. Install the pinion and bearing assembly into the housing. Make sure the pinion is seated in the lower bearing.
3. Carefully slide the pinion plug and seal assembly over the pinion shaft. Hand start the plug and seal into the housing. Using tool, T85T–3504–AH, tighten the plug to 21.30–35.40 in. oz. to set the pinion bearing preload.
4. Apply a thread lock and sealer to the pinion plug threads.
5. Hand start the pinion plug locknut onto the pinion plug. Hold the pinion plug in place using tool, T85T–3504–AH, then tighten the locknut using tool, T74P–3504–U to 50–65 ft. lbs.
6. Pack the dust cover with steering gear grease and install it over the pinion shaft on the housing.
7. Inspect the yoke to make sure that the plastic insert is firmly seated flush with the shallow rim provided on the metal portion of the yoke assembly.

NOTE: There should be no visible gap between the plastic insert and the metal.

8. Coat the plastic yoke insert and the rack bar surface that slides against the yoke with steering gear grease.
9. Install the yoke in the housing bore against the Y-section of the rack.

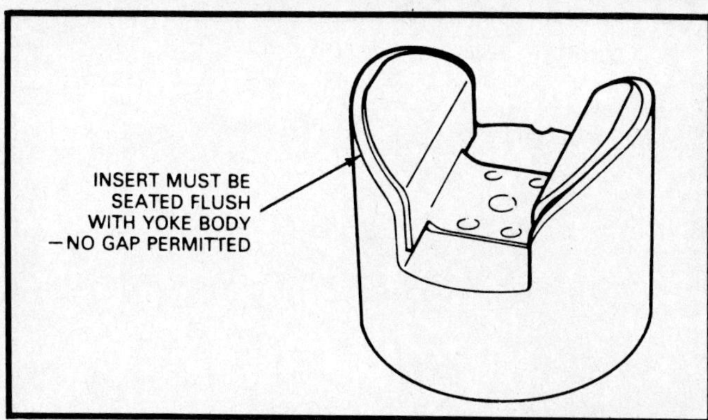

Make sure the plastic insert is seated with the shallow rim of the yoke assembly

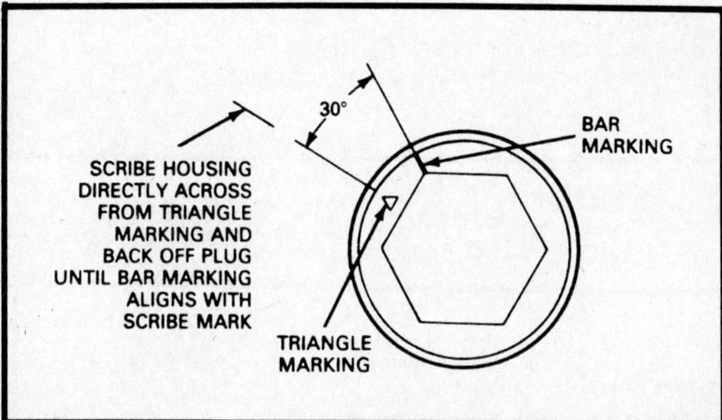

Adjusting the clearance between the yoke plug and yoke

10. Coat both ends of the spring with steering gear grease. Install the spring in the recess in the back of the yoke.
11. If necessary, install a new service yoke plug onto the spring. Hand tighten the plug, then using tool T85T–3504–AH, tighten to 65 inch lbs.
12. Mark the housing directly across from the triangle marking on the yoke plug. Back off the yoke plug about 30°, until the bar (-) marking on the yoke plug aligns with the scribed mark on the housing. This adjusts the clearance between the yoke plug and the yoke.
13. Apply a thread lock and sealer to the yoke plug threads.
14. Hand start the locknut on the yoke plug. Hold the plug in place using tool, T85T–3504–AH, then tighten the locknut using tool, T74P–3504–BH to 43–58 ft. lbs.
15. Verify that the bar (-) marking on the yoke plug aligns with the scribed mark on the housing.

Saginaw Recirculating Ball Type

The steering gear is of the recirculating ball nut type. the ball nut, mounted on the worm gear, is driven by means of steel balls which circulate in helical grooves in both the worm and nut. Ball return guides attached to the nut serve to recirculate the two sets of balls in the grooves. As the steering wheel is turned to the right, the ball nut moves upward. When the wheel is turned to the left, the ball nut moves downward.

The sector teeth on the pinion shaft and the ball nut are designed so that they fit the tightest when the steering wheel is straight ahead. This mesh action is adjusted by an adjusting screw which moves the pinion shaft endwise until the teeth mesh properly. The worm bearing adjuster provides proper preloading of the upper and lower bearings.

Before doing the adjustment procedures given below, ensure that the steering problem is not caused by faulty suspension components, bad front end alignment, etc. Then, proceed with the following adjustments.

STEERING WORM AND SECTOR

Adjustment

1. Tighten the worm bearing adjuster plug until all end play has been removed, then loosen ¼ turn.
2. Use an ¹¹⁄₁₆ in. 12 point socket to carefully turn the wormshaft all the way into the right corner then turn back about ½ turn.
3. Tighten the adjuster plug until the proper thrust bearing preload is obtained (5–8 inch lbs.). Tighten the adjuster plug locknut to 85 ft. lbs.
4. Turn the wormshaft from one stop to the other counting the number of turns. Then turn the shaft back exactly half the number of turns to the center position.
5. Turn the lash (sector shaft) adjuster screw clockwise to remove all lash between the ball nut and sector teeth. Tighten the locknut to 25 ft. lbs.
6. Using an ¹¹⁄₁₆ in. 12 point socket and an inch lb. torque wrench, observe the highest reading while the gear is turned through the center position. It should be 16 inch lbs. or less.
7. If necessary repeat Steps 5 and 6.

STEERING GEAR

Disassembly

1. Place the steering gear in a vise, clamping onto one of the mounting tabs. The wormshaft should be in a horizontal position.
2. Rotate the wormshaft from stop to stop and count the total number of turns. Turn back exactly halfway, placing the gear on center.
3. Remove the three self locking bolts which attach the sector cover to the housing.
4. Using a plastic hammer, tap lightly on the end of the sector shaft and lift the sector cover and sector shaft assembly from the gear housing.

NOTE: It may be necessary to turn the wormshaft by hand until the sector will pass through the opening in the housing.

5. Remove the locknut from the adjuster plug and remove the adjuster plug assembly.
6. Pull the wormshaft and ball nut assembly from the housing.

NOTE: Damage may be done to the ends of the ball guides if the ball nut is allowed to rotate to the end of the worm.

7. Remove the worm shaft upper bearing from inside the gear housing.
8. Pry the wormshaft lower bearing retainer from the adjuster plug housing and remove the bearing.
9. Remove the locknut from the lash adjuster screw in the sector cover. Turn the lash adjuster screw clockwise and remove it from the sector cover. Slide the adjuster screw and shim out of the slot in the end of the sector shaft.
10. Pry out and discard both the sector shaft and wormshaft seals.

Inspection

1. Wash all parts in cleaning solvent and blow dry with an air hose.
2. Use a magnifying glass and inspect the bearings and bearing caps for signs of indentation, or chipping. Replace any parts that show signs of damage.

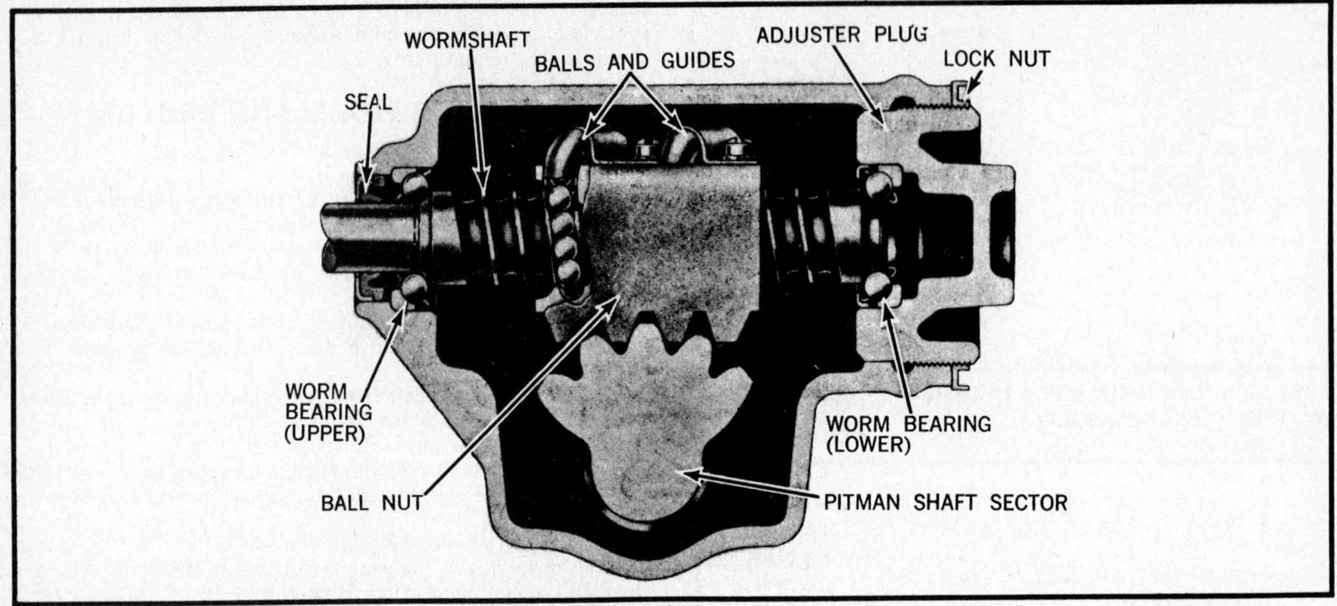

Cross section of Saginaw recirculating ball model

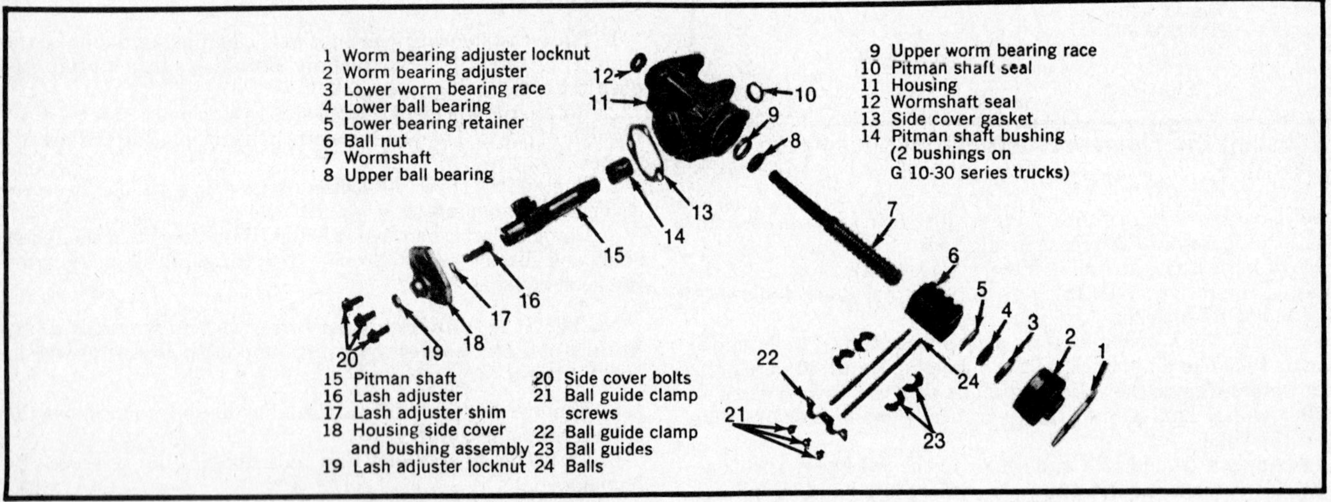

Exploded view of Saginaw recirculating ball model

Removing the bearing retainer from the worm bearing adjuster – Saginaw recirculating ball model

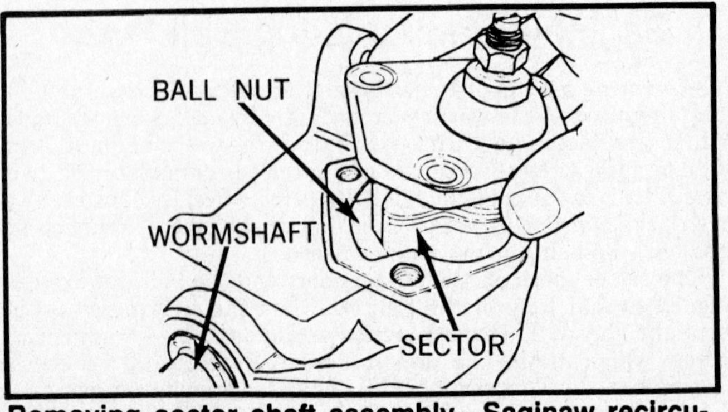

Removing sector shaft assembly—Saginaw recirculating ball model

3. Check the fit of the sector shaft in the bushings in the sector cover and housing. If these bushings are worn, a new sector cover and bushing assembly or housing bushing should be installed.

4. Check steering gear wormshaft assembly for being bent or damaged.

Shaft Seal Replacement

1. Remove the old seal from the pump body.
2. Install the new seal by pressing the outer diameter of the seal with a suitable size socket.

NOTE: Make sure the socket is large enough to avoid damaging the external lip of the seal.

Sector Shaft Bushing Replacement

1. Place the steering gear housing in an arbor press.
2. Press the sector shaft bushing from the housing.

NOTE: Service bushings are bored to size and require no further reaming.

Sector Cover Bushing Replacement

1. The sector cover bushing is not serviced separately. The entire sector cover assembly including the bushing must be replaced as a unit.

Ball Nut Service

If there is any indication of binding or tightness when the ball nut is rotated on the worm the unit should be disassembled, cleaned and inspected as follows:

1. Remove the screws and clamp retaining the ball guides in the ball nut. Pull the guides out of the ball nut.
2. Turn the ball nut upside down and rotate the wormshaft back and forth until all the balls have dropped out of the ball nut. The ball nut can now be pulled endwise off the worm.
3. Wash all parts in solvent and dry them with air. Use a magnifying glass and inspect the worm and nut grooves and the surface of all balls for signs of indentation. Check all ball guides for damage at the ends. Replace any damaged parts.
4. Slip the ball nut over the worm with the ball guide holes up and the shallow end of the ball nut teeth to the left from the steering wheel position. Sight through the ball guide to align the grooves in the worm.
5. Place two ball guide halves together and insert them in the upper circuit in the ball nut. Place the two remaining guides together and insert them in the lower circuit.
6. Count out 25 balls and place them in a suitable container. This is the proper number of balls for one circuit.
7. Load the 25 balls into one of the guide holes while turning the wormshaft gradually away from that hole.
8. Fill the remaining ball circuit in the same manner.

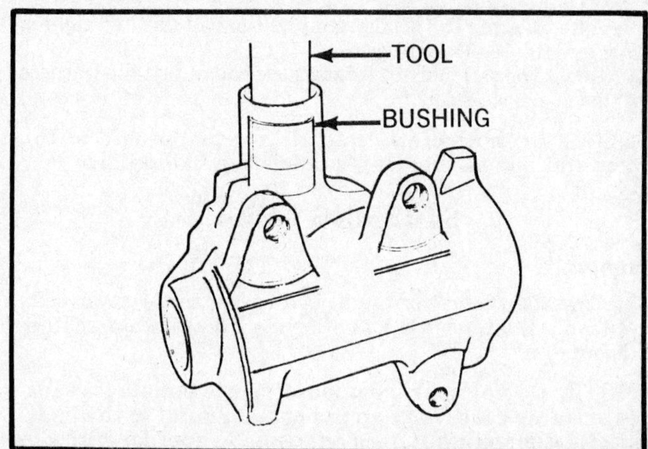

Removing sector shaft bushing—Saginaw recirculating ball model

Removing worm shaft lower bvearing cup from the adjuster plug—Saginaw recirculating ball model

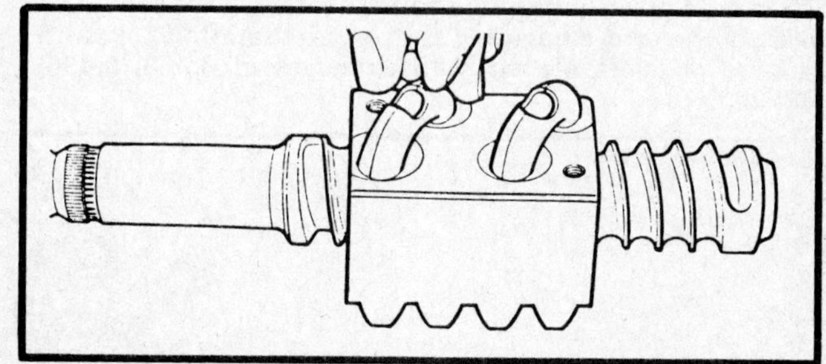
Checking lash adjuster end clearance—Saginaw recirculating ball model

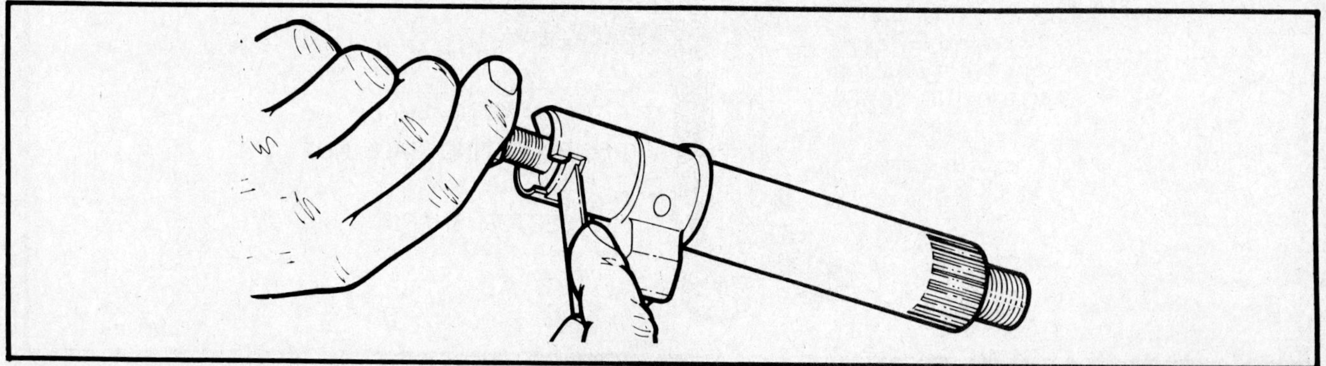
Filling the ball circuits—Saginaw recirculating ball model

9. Assemble the ball guide clamp to the ball nut and tighten the screws to 18–24 inch lbs.

10. Check the assembly by rotating the ball nut on the worm to see that it moves freely.

NOTE: Do not rotate the ball nut to the end of the worm threads as this may damage the ball guides.

STEERING GEAR

Assembly

1. Coat the threads of the adjuster plug, sector cover bolts and lash adjuster with a non-drying oil resistant sealing compound.

NOTE: Do not apply compound to the female threads. Use extreme care when applying compound to the bearing adjuster so that it does not come in contact with the wormshaft bearing.

2. Place the steering gear housing in a vise with the wormshaft bore horizontal and the sector cover opening up.
3. Make sure that all seals, bushings and bearing cups are installed in the gear housing and that the ball nut is installed on the wormshaft.
4. Slip the wormshaft upper bearing assembly over the wormshaft and insert the wormshaft and ball nut assembly into the housing, feeding the end of the shaft through the upper ball bearing cup and seal.
5. Place the wormshaft lower bearing assembly in the adjuster plug bearing cup and press the stamped retainer into place with a suitable size socket.
6. Install the adjuster plug and locknut into the lower end of the housing while carefully guiding the end of the wormshaft into the bearing until nearly all end play has been removed from the wormshaft.
7. Position the lash adjuster including the shim in the slotted end of the sector shaft.

NOTE: End clearance should not be greater than 0.002. If the end clearance is greater than 0.002 a shim package is available with thicknesses of 0.063, 0.065, 0.067, 0.069.

8. Lubricate the steering gear with 11 oz. of steering gear grease. Rotate the wormshaft until the ball nut is at the other end of its travel and then pack as much new lubricant into the housing as possible without losing out the sector shaft opening. Rotate the wormshaft until the ball nut is at the other end of its travel and pack as much lubricant into the opposite end as possible.
9. Rotate the wormshaft until the ball nut is in the center of travel. This is to make sure that the sector shaft and ball nut will engage properly with the center tooth of the sector entering the center tooth space in the ball nut.
10. Insert the sector shaft assembly including lash adjuster screw and shim into the housing so that the center tooth of the sector enters the center tooth space in the ball nut.
11. Pack the remaining portion of the lubricant into the housing and also place some in the sector cover bushing hole.
12. Place the sector cover gasket on the housing.
13. Install the sector cover onto the sector shaft by reaching through the sector cover with a screwdriver and turning the lash adjuster screw counterclockwise until the screw bottoms, then back the screw off one-half turn. Loosely install a new lock nut onto the adjuster screw.
14. Install and tighten the sector cover bolt to 30 ft. lbs.

Chrysler Recirculating Ball Type

The steering gear is of the recirculating ball nut type. The ball nut, mounted on the worm gear, is driven by means of steel balls which circulate in helical grooves in both the worm and nut. Ball return guides attached to the nut serve to recirculate the two sets of balls in the grooves. As the steering wheel is turned to the right, the ball nut moves upward. When the wheel is turned to the left, the ball nut moves downward.

The sector teeth on the pinion shaft and the ball nut are designed so that they fit the tightest when the steering wheel is straight ahead. This mesh action is adjusted by an adjusting screw which moves the pinion shaft endwise until the teeth mesh properly. The worm bearing adjuster provides proper preloading of the upper and lower bearings.

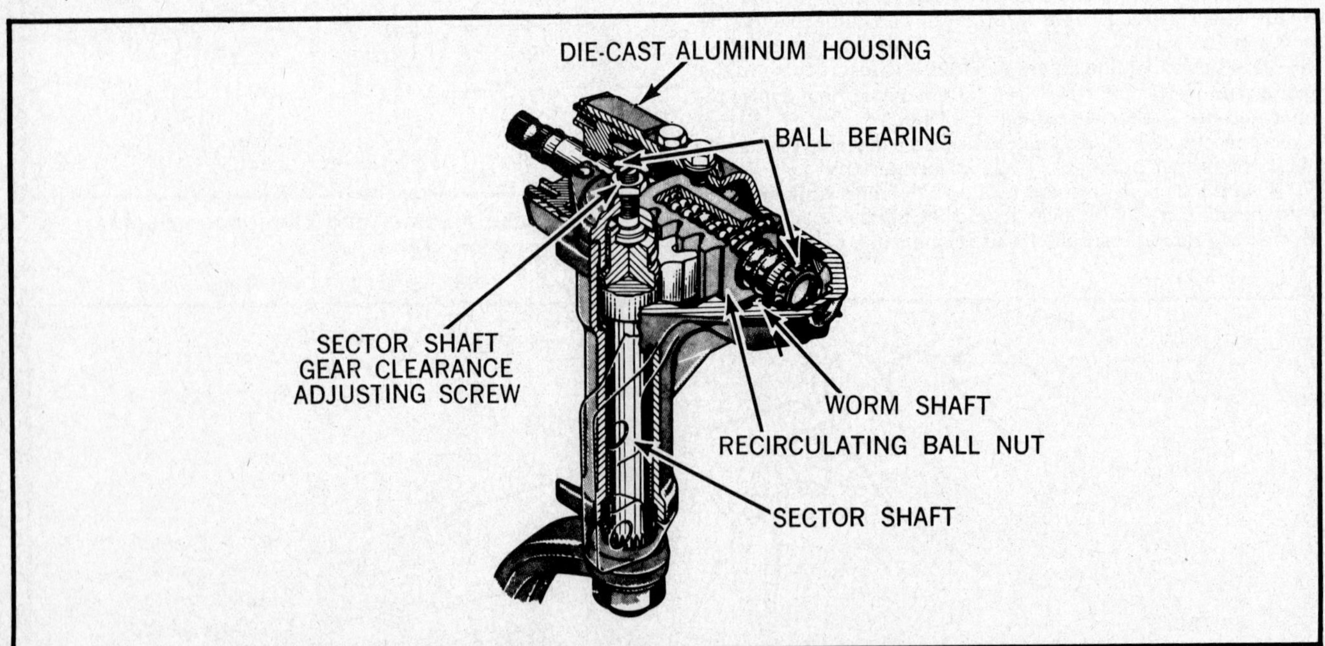

Chrysler recirculating ball type steering gear

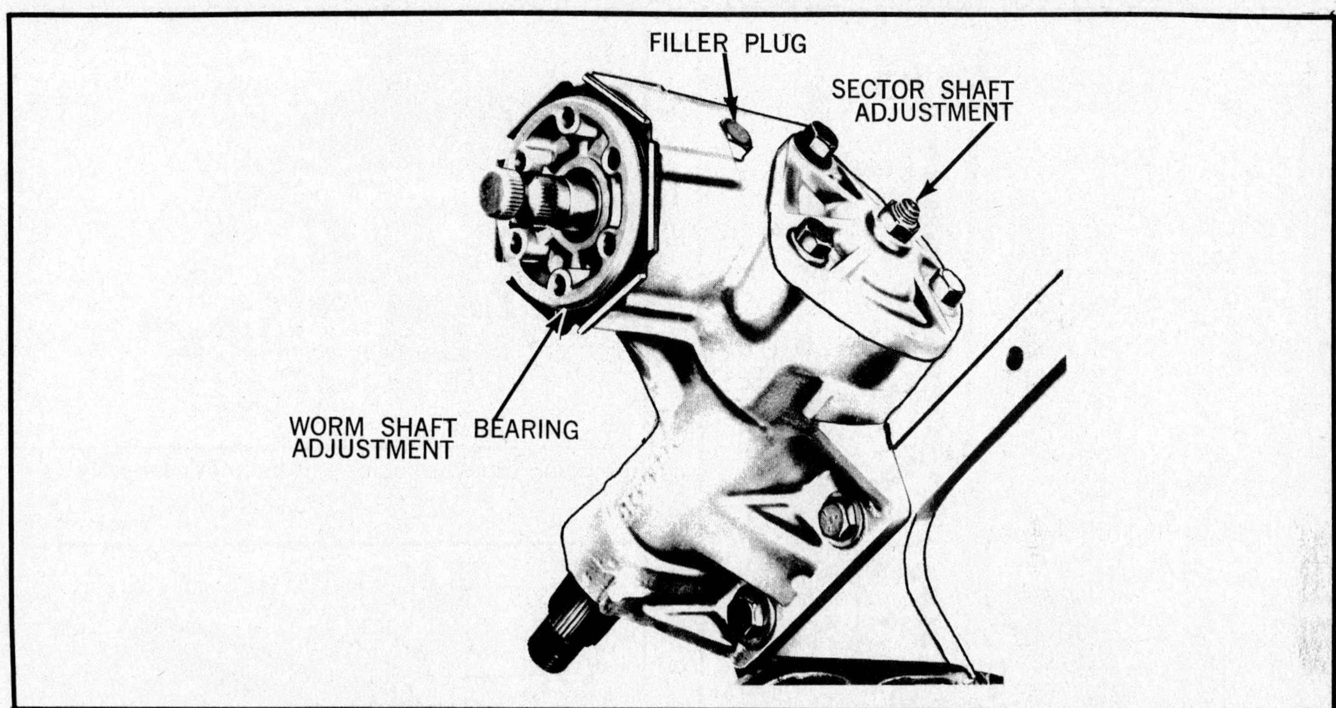

Steering gear adjustment locations

WORM BEARING PRE-LOAD

Adjustment

1. Remove the steering gear arm and lockwasher from the sector shaft, using a suitable gear puller.
2. Remove the horn button or horn ring.
3. Loosen the sector-shaft adjusting screw locknut, and back out the adjusting screw about two turns.
4. Turn the steering wheel two complete turns from the straight ahead position, and place an in. lb. torque wrench on the steering shaft nut.
5. Rotate the steering shaft at least one turn toward the straight ahead position while measuring the torque on the torque wrench. The torque should be between 1⅛ and 4½ inch lbs. to move the steering wheel. If torque is not within these limits, loosen the worm shaft bearing adjuster locknut and turn the adjuster clockwise to increase the preload or counterclockwise to decrease the preload. When the preload is correct, hold the adjuster screw steady and tighten the locknut. Recheck preload.

BALL NUT RACK AND SECTOR MESH

Adjustment

NOTE: This adjustment can be accurately made only after proper preloading of worm bearing.

1. Turn steering wheel gently from one stop to the other, counting the number of turns. Turn the steering wheel back exactly half way, to the center position.
2. Turn the sector–shaft adjusting screw clockwise to remove all lash between ball nut rack and the sector gear teeth, then tighten adjusting screw locknut to 35 ft. lbs.
3. Turn the steering wheel about ¼ turn away from the center or high spot position. With the torque wrench on the steering wheel nut measure the torque required to turn the steering wheel through the high spot at the center position. The reading should be between 8 and 11 inch lbs. This is the total of the worm shaft bearing preload and the ball nut rack and sector gear mesh load. Readjust the sector-shaft adjustment screw if necessary to obtain a correct torque reading.
4. After completing the adjustments, place the front wheels in a straight ahead position, and with the steering wheel and steering gear centered, install the steering arm on sector-shaft. Tighten the steering arm retaining nut to 180 ft. lbs.

STEERING GEAR

Disassembly and Assembly

1. Attach the steering gear assembly to a holding fixture and put the holding fixture in a bench vise. Thoroughly clean the outside surface before disassembly.
2. Loosen the sector-shaft adjusting screw locknut, and back out the adjusting screw about two turns to relieve the mesh load between the ball nut rack and the sector gear teeth.
3. Position the steering gear worm shaft in a straight ahead position.
4. Remove the attaching bolts from the sector-shaft cover and slowly remove the sector-shaft while sliding an arbor tool into the housing. Remove the locknut from the adjusting screw and remove the screw from the cover by turning it clockwise. Slide the adjustment screw and its shim out of the slot in the end of the sector-shaft.
5. Loosen the worm shaft bearing adjuster locknut with a brass drift (punch) and remove the locknut. Hold the worm shaft steady while unscrewing the adjuster. Slide the worm adjuster off the shaft.

CAUTION

Handle the adjuster carefully to avoid damaging the aluminum threads. Also, do not run the ball nut down to either end of the worm shaft to avoid damaging the ball guides.

6. Carefully remove the worm and ball nut assembly. This assembly is serviced as a complete assembly only and is not to be disassembled or the ball return guides removed or disturbed.
7. Remove the sector-shaft needle bearing by placing the gear housing in an arbor press; insert a tool in the lower end of the

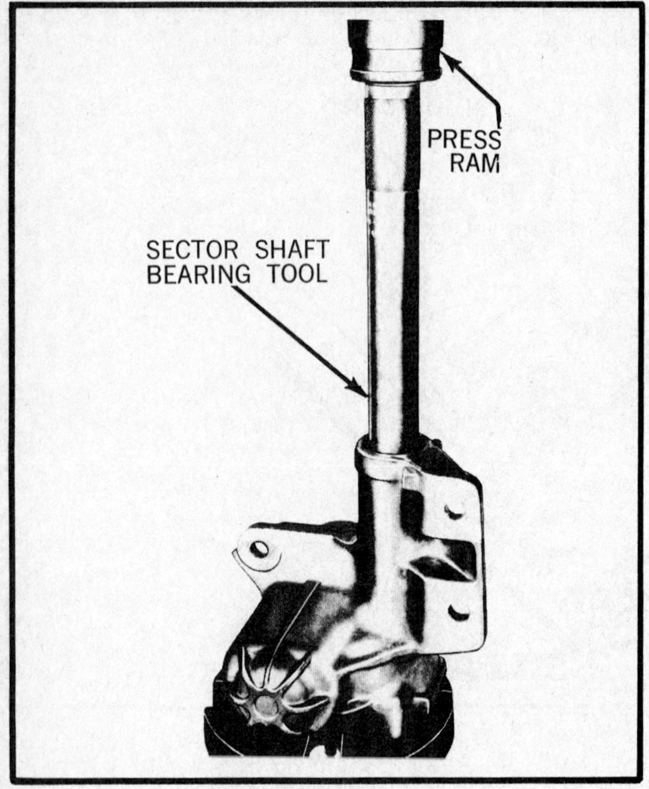

Removing the sector shaft inner and outer bearings

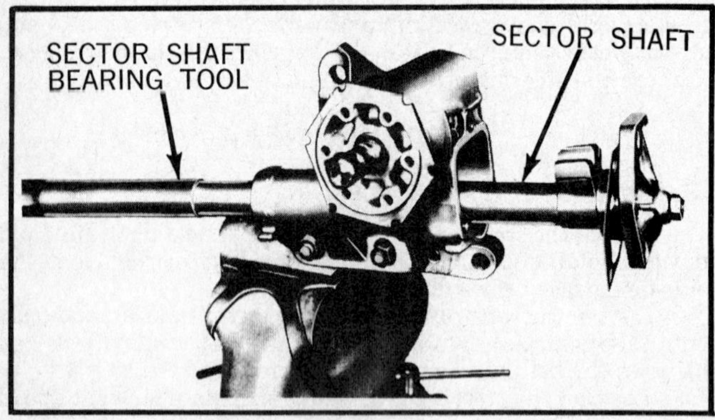

Removing the sector shaft

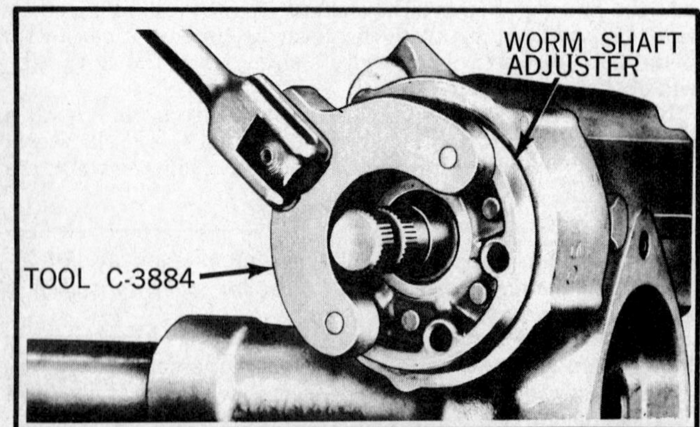

Removing the wormshaft adjuster

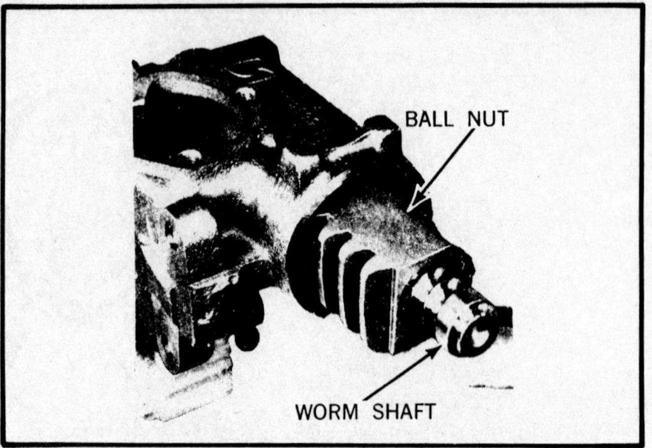

Removing the wormshaft and ball nut assembly

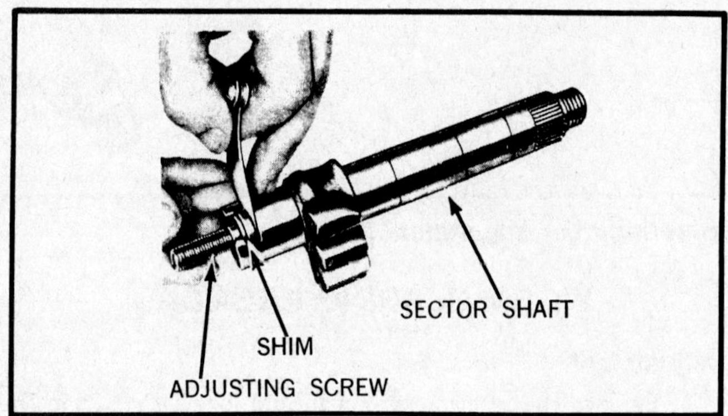

Measuring the sector shaft adjusting screw and clearance

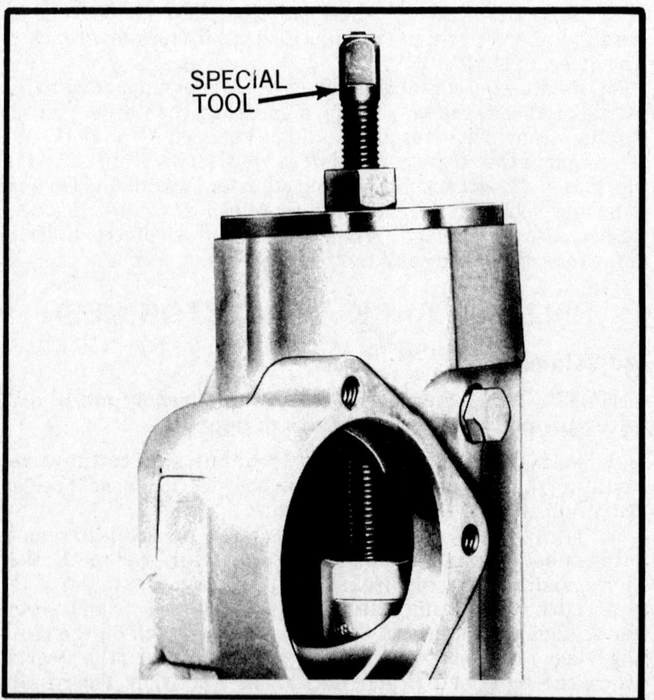

Removing the lower bearing cup

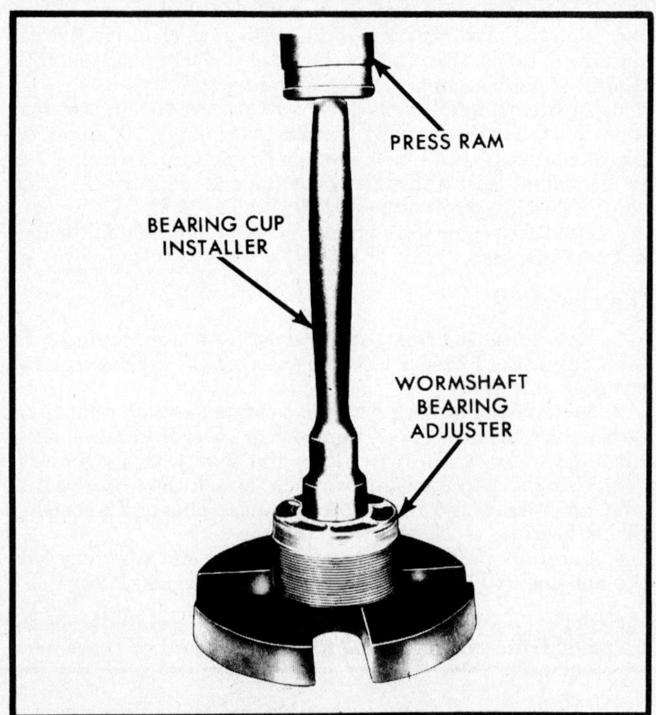

Installing the wormshaft upper bearing cup

housing and press both bearings through the housing.

The sector-shaft cover assembly, including a needle bearing or bushing, is serviced as an assembly.

8. Remove the worm shaft oil seal from the worm shaft bearing adjuster by inserting a blunt punch behind the seal and tapping alternately on each side of the seal until it is driven out of the adjuster.

9. Remove the worm shaft in the same manner as that given in Step 8. *Be careful not to cock the bearing cup and distort the adjuster counter bore.*

10. Remove the lower cup if necessary. Pull the bearing cup out.

11. Wash all parts in clean solvent and dry thoroughly. Inspect all parts for wear, scoring, pitting, etc. Test operation of the worm shaft and ball nut assembly. If ball nut does not travel smoothly and freely on the worm shaft or if there is binding, replace the assembly.

NOTE: Extreme care must be taken when handling the aluminum worm bearing adjuster to avoid thread damage. Also, be careful not to damage the threads in the gear housing. Always lubricate the worm bearing adjuster before screwing it into the housing.

12. Inspect the sector-shaft for wear and check the fit of the shaft in the housing bearings. Inspect the fit of the shaft pilot bearing in the housing. Be sure the worm shaft is not bent or damaged.

13. Install the sector-shaft lower needle bearing. Press the bearing into the housing about $^7/_{16}$ in. below the end of the bore to leave space for the new oil seal.

14. Install the upper needle bearing in the same manner and press it into the inside end of the housing bore flush with the inside end of the bore surface.

15. Install the worm shaft bearing cups (upper and lower) by placing them and their spacers in the adjuster nut and press them into place.

16. Install the worm shaft oil seal by placing the seal in the worm shaft adjuster with the metal seal retainer up. Drive the seal into place with a suitable sleeve until it is just below the end of the bore in the adjuster.

NOTE: Apply a coating of steering gear lubricant to all moving parts during assembly. Also, put lubricant on and around oil seal lips.

17. Clamp the holding fixture and housing in a bench vise with the bearing adjuster opening upward. Place a thrust bearing in the lower cup in the housing.

18. Hold the ball nut from turning and insert the worm shaft and ball nut assembly into the housing with the end of the worm shaft resting in the thrust bearing. Place the upper thrust bearing on the worm shaft. Thoroughly lubricate the threads on the adjuster and the threads in the housing.

19. Place a protective sleeve of tape over the splines on the worm shaft to avoid damaging the seal. Slide the adjuster assembly over the shaft.

20. Thread the adjuster into the housing and tighten the adjuster to 50 ft. lbs. while rotating the worm shaft to seat the bearings.

21. Loosen the adjuster so no bearing preload exists. Tighten the adjuster for a worm shaft bearing preload of 1⅛ to 4½ inch lbs. Tighten the bearing adjuster locknut and recheck the preload.

22. Before installing the sector-shaft, pack the worm shaft cavities in the housing above and below the ball nut with steering gear lubricant. A good grade of multi-purpose lubricant may be used if steering gear lubricant is not available. *Do not use gear oil.* Pack enough lubricant into the worm cavities to cover the worm.

23. Slide the sector-shaft adjusting screw and shim into the slot in the end of the shaft. Check the end clearance for no more than 0.004 in. clearance. If the clearance is not within the limit, remove old shim and install a new shim, available in three different thicknesses, to get the proper clearance.

24. Start the sector-shaft and adjuster screw into the bearing in the housing cover. Using a screwdriver through the hole in the cover, turn the screw counterclockwise to pull the shaft into the cover. Install the adjusting screw locknut, but do not tighten at this time.

25. Rotate the worm shaft to center the ball nut.

26. Place a new gasket on the housing cover and install the sector-shaft and cover aasembly into the steering gear housing. Be sure to coat the sector-shaft and sector teeth with steering gear lubricant before installing the sector-shaft in the housing. Allow some lash between the sector-shaft sector teeth and the ball nut rack. Install and tighten the cover bolts to 25 ft. lbs.

27. Place the sector-shaft seal on the cross-shaft with the lip of the seal facing the housing. Press the seal in place.

28. Turn the worm shaft about ¼ turn away from the center of the high spot position. Using a torque wrench and a ¾ in. socket on the worm shaft spline, check the torque needed to rotate the shaft through the high spot. The reading should be between 8 and 11 inch lbs. Readjust the sector-shaft adjusting screw until the proper reading is obtained. Tighten the locknut to 35 ft. lbs. and recheck sector-shaft torque.

SECTOR-SHAFT OIL SEAL

Replacement

1. Remove the steering gear arm retaining nut and lockwasher.
2. Remove seal with a seal puller or other appropriate tool.
3. Place a new oil seal onto the splines of the sector-shaft with the lip of the seal facing the housing.
4. Remove the tool, and install the steering gear arm, lockwasher, and retaining nut. Tighten the nut to 180 ft. lbs. torque.

Chrysler Corp. Manual Rack and Pinion

NOTE: The manual rack and pinion assembly used on the Rampage, Scamp, Caravan, Voyager and Dakota

cannot be adjusted or serviced. Should a malfunction occur, the complete rack and pinion assembly must be replaced.

Koyo

NOTE: The Koyo steering gear is used on 1984–88 E-150 thru E-350 vans and F-150 thru F-350 pickups.

Preload and Meshload Adjustment

GEAR REMOVED FROM VEHICLE

1. Tighten the sector cover bolts to 40 ft. lbs.
2. Loosen the preload adjuster locknut and tighten the worm bearing adjuster nut until all end play has been removed. Lubricate the wormshaft seal with a drop of Type F automatic transmission fluid.
3. Using a $^{11}/_{16}$ in., 12 point socket and an inch lbs. torque wrench, turn the wormshaft all the way to the right. Measure the left turn torque required to rotate the wormshaft at a constant speed for approximately 1½ turns. This torque reading is preload.
4. Tighten or loosen the adjuster nut as required until the correct preload of 7–9 inch lbs. is obtained. Tighten the adjuster locknut to 187 ft. lbs.
5. Rotate the wormshaft from stop to stop, counting the total number of turns, then turn back halfway, placing the gear at the center. (Approximately 7 turns stop to stop.)
6. Again, using the tools in Step 3, observe the highest reading while the wormshaft is turned approximately 90° either way across center. If the highest reading (meshload) is within 12–14 in lbs. and at least 4 inch lbs. over the preload, turn the sector shaft adjusting screw as required.
7. Hold the sector shaft adjusting screw and tighten the locknut to 25 ft. lbs.

Disassembly

1. Rotate the steering shaft from stop to stop, counting the total number of turns. Then turn exactly half-way back, placing the gear on center.
2. Remove the sector adjusting cover bolts, then remove the sector shaft with the cover. Remove the cover from the shaft by turning the screw clockwise. Keep the shim with the screw.
3. Using a special locknut wrench, loosen the worm bearing adjuster locknut and remove the adjuster plug and wormshaft thrust bearing.
4. Carefully pull the wormshaft and ball nut assembly from the housing and remove the upper thrust bearing.

NOTE: To avoid damage to the return guides, keep the ball nut from running down to either end of the worm.

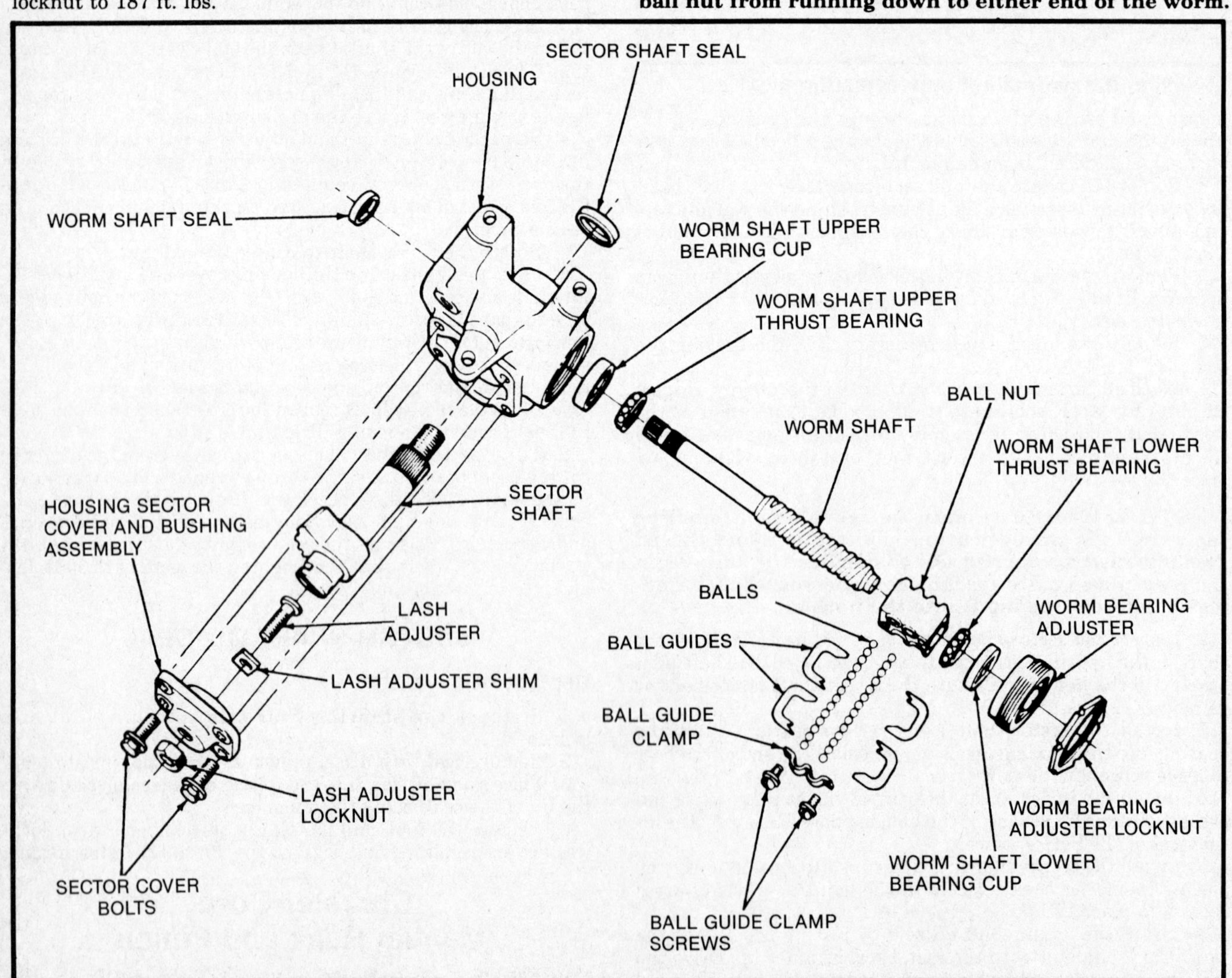

Koyo steering gear—exploded view

5. Pry out the sector shaft and wormshaft seals and discard them.

NOTE: Individual parts for this manual steering gear are not availabe for service. Do not disassemble. If the worm cannot rotate freely in the ball nut, replace the entire assembly.

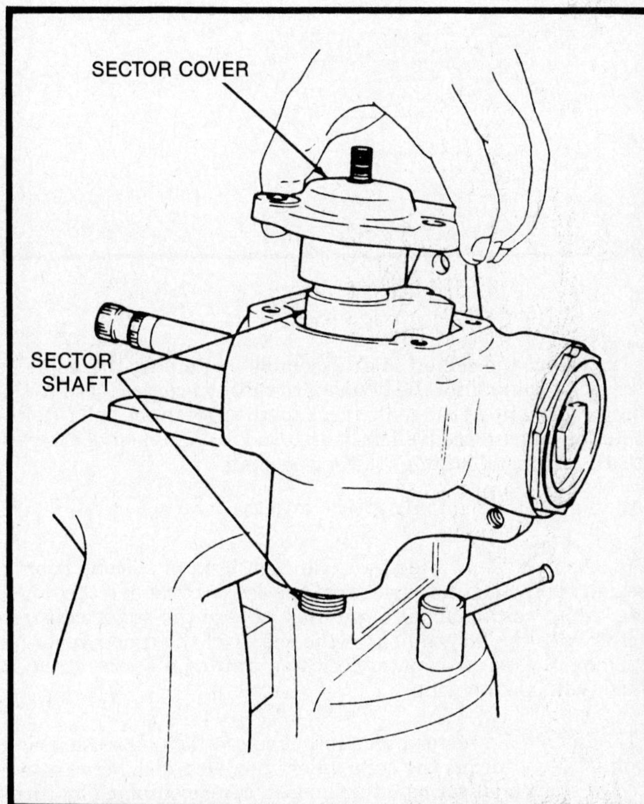

Sector shaft removal

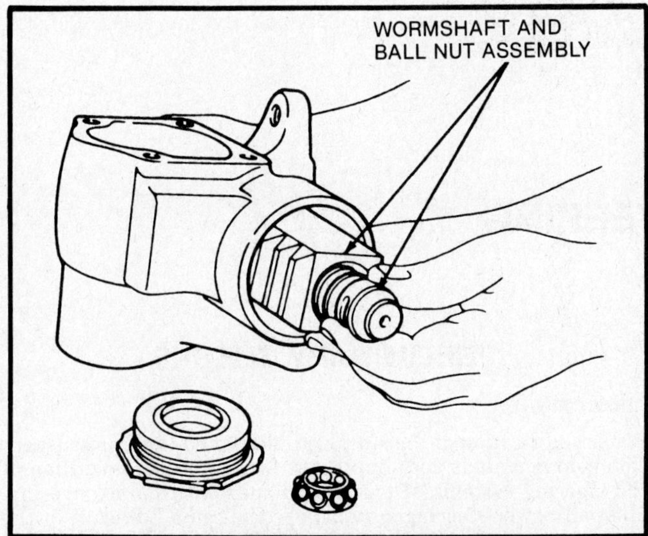

Removal of wormshaft and ball nut assembly

6. The adjuster/plug bearing cup can be removed using a puller tool and slide hammer.
7. The housing bearing cup can be removed from the housing using a hammer and a suitable size bearing driver or socket.
8. The sector cover bushing is not serviceable. If found to be defective the entire sector cover including the bushing must be replaced.
9. The sector shaft needle bearing is serviced only as part of the housing unit and is not serviced separately. If one or more needles fall out, they may be cleaned and put back using steering gear lube to hold them in place.

Inspection

1. Wash all parts in a cleaning solvent and dry thoroughly with air.
2. Inspect all bearings and bushings for wear.
3. Inspect the ball nut gear for chipping.
4. Inspect the ball nut and wormshaft for tightness and binding.
5. Inspect the housing for cracks.
6. Inspect the sector gear teeth for chipping.
7. Check the clearance between the sector adjusting screw head and the bottom of the sector shaft T-slot. If the clearance is more than 0.004 in. install a new shim as required to reduce the clearance to 0.004 in. or less. A steering gear lash adjuster kit is available containing five different size shims. While holding the sector adjusting screw, turn the sector shaft back and forth. The sector shaft must turn freely. If the sector shaft does not turn freely, increase the T-slot clearance using an appropriate shim from the lash adjuster kit. Make sure the resulting clearance is not more than 0.004 in.

Assembly

1. If the wormshaft bearing cup was removed from the housing, install a new cup Using Tool T82T–3504–AH, or equivalent.
2. If the adjuster plug bearing cup was removed, install a new cup using Tool T82T–3504–AH or equivalent.
3. Install the sector shaft seal in the housing using Tool T82T–3504–AH, or equivalent. Press the seal until it bottoms out.
4. Tap the womshaft seal in the housing, using a suitable size socket and a hammer. Assemble the seal flush with the housing surface.
5. Clamp the steering gear housing in a vise with the wormshaft bore horizontal and the sector cover opening up.
6. Apply steering gear grease to the wormshaft bearings, sector shaft needle bearing in the housing and the sector cover bushing.
7. Slip one of the wormshaft bearings over the wormshaft splined end. Insert the wormshaft and ball nut assembly into the housing. Feed the splined end of the wormshaft through the bearing cup and seal. Place the remaining wormshaft thrust bearing in the adjuster plug bearing cup.
8. Install the adjuster plug and locknut into the housing opening being careful to guide the wormshaft end into the bearing until nearly all end play has been removed from the wormshaft.
9. Position the sector adjusting screw and shim into the sector shaft slot. Check the clearance between the screw head and the sector shaft T-slot. Refer to Step 7 under Inspection above.
10. Lubricate the steering gear with 14.8 ounces by weight of steering gear grease. Rotate the wormshaft until the ball nut is near the end of its travel. Pack as much grease into the housing as possible without loosing it out at the sector shaft opening. Rotate the wormshaft to move the ball nut near the other end of its travel and pack more grease into the housing.
11. Rotate the wormshaft until the ball nut is in the center of its travel.

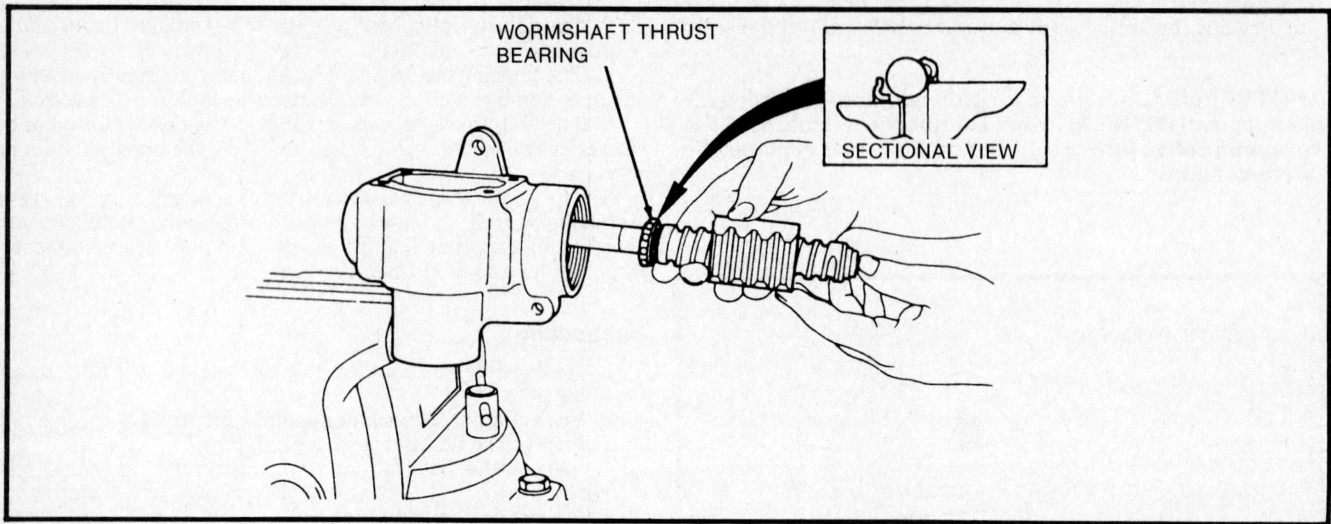

Installation of wormshaft and ball nut assembly in gear housing

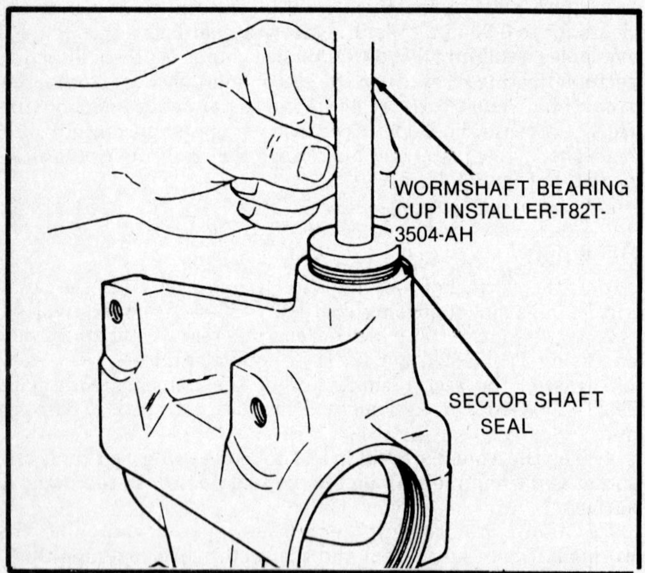

Sector shaft seal installation

12. Insert the sector shaft assembly containing the adjuster screw and shim into the housing so that the center tooth of the sector gear enters the center rack tooth space in the ball rut. Rotate the ball nut teeth slightly up to aid in alignment of the gear teeth and installation of the sector shaft.

13. Pack the remaining grease into the housing.

14. Apply a ⅛ in. wide by ⅛ in. high bead of silicone rubber sealant to the mating surfaces of the sector cover and the housing. After waiting about 5 minutes, engage the sector adjuster screw with the tapped hole in the center of the center cover by turning the screw counterclockwise until the sector cover is flush with the housing.

15. Install the sector cover to housing attaching washer and bolts. Do not torque the bolts unless there is a lash between the sector shaft and wormshaft. The lash can be obtained by turning the screw counterclockwise.

16. Tighten the sector cover attaching bolts to 40 ft. lbs.

17. Adjust the steering gear preload and meshload. Refer to adjustments above.

POWER STEERING

GENERAL INFORMATION

The procedures for maintaining, adjusting, and repairing the power steering systems and components discussed in this chapter are to be done only after determining that the steering linkages and front suspension systems are correctly aligned and in good condition. All worn or damaged parts should be replaced before attempting to service the power steering system. After correcting any condition that could affect the power steering, do the preliminary tests of the steering system components.

PRELIMINARY CHECKS

Lubrication

Proper lubrication of the steering linkage and the front suspension components is very important for the proper operation of the steering systems of trucks equipped with power steering. Most all power steering systems use the same lubricant in the steering gear box as in the power steering pump reservoir, and the fluid level is maintained at the pump reservoir.

STEERING TROUBLE DIAGNOSIS
Power Steering

Condition	Possible Cause	Correction
Hard Steering	1. Low or uneven tire pressure.	1. Inflate the tires to recommended pressures.
	2. Insufficient lubricant in the steering gear housing or in steering linkage.	2. Lubricate as necessary.
	3. Steering gear shaft adjusted too tight.	3. Adjust according to instructions.
	4. Improper caster or toe-in.	4. Align the wheels.
	5. Steering column misaligned.	5. See "Steering Gear Alignment."
	6. Loose, worn or broken pump belt.	6. Adjust or replace belt.
	7. Air in system.	7. Bleed air from system.
	8. Low fluid level in the pump reservoir.	8. Fill to correct level.
	9. Pump output pressure low.	9. See "Pressure Test."
	10. Leakage at power cylinder piston rings. (Linkage type).	10. Replace piston rings and repair as required.
	11. Binding or bent cylinder linkage. (Linkage type).	11. Replace or repair as required.
	12. Valve spool and/or sleeve sticking. (Linkage type).	12. Free-up or replace as required.
Intermittent or No Power Assist	1. Belt slipping and/or low fluid level.	1. Adjust or replace belt. Add fluid as necessary.
	2. Piston or rod binding in power cylinder. (Linkage type).	2. Repair or replace piston and rod.
	3. Sliding sleeve stuck in control valve. (Linkage type).	3. Free-up or replace sleeve.
	4. Improper pump operation.	4. Refer to "Power Steering Pump."
Poor or No Recovery from Turns	1. Improper caster setting.	1. Adjust to specifications.
	2. Steering gear adjustments too tight.	2. Adjust according to instructions.
	3. Improper spool nut adjustment. (Linkage type).	3. Adjust according to instructions.
	4. Valve spool installed backwards. (Linkage type).	4. Install valve spool correctly.
	5. Low tire pressure.	5. Inflate tires to recommended pressure.
	6. Tight steering linkage.	6. Lubricate as necessary.
	7. King pins frozen.	7. Lubricate as necessary.
Lack of Effort (Both Turns)	1. Improper sector shaft adjustment.	1. Adjust Sector Shaft.
	2. Pressure plates on wrong side of reactions rings.	2. Gear Recondition.
Lack of Effort (Left Turn Only)	1. Left turn reaction seal "O" ring worn, damaged or missing.	1. Gear Recondition.
	2. Left turn reaction oil passageway not drilled in housing or cylinder head.	2. Replace parts as required.
	3. Left turn reaction ring sticking in cylinder head.	3. Replace parts as required.
Lack of Effort (Right Turn Only)	1. Right turn U-shaped reaction seal worn, damaged, or missing.	1. Gear Recondition.
	2. Right turn reaction oil passageway not drilled in housing head, or ferrule pin.	2. Replace parts as required.
	3. Right turn reaction ring sticking in housing head.	3. Replace parts as required.
Lack of Assist (Left Turn Only)	1. Left turn reaction seal "O" ring worn, damaged, or missing.	1. Gear Recondition.
Lack of Assist (Right Turn Only)	1. Right turn U-shaped reaction seal worn, damaged, or missing.	1. Gear Recondition.
	2. Worm sealing ring (teflon) worm sleeve seal, ferrule pin "O" ring damaged or worn.	2. Gear Recondition.
	3. Excessive internal leakage thru piston end plug and/or side plugs.	3. Replace worm-piston assembly.

STEERING TROUBLE DIAGNOSIS
Power Steering

Condition	Possible Cause	Correction
Lack of Assist (Both Turns)	1. Low oil level in pump reservoir (usually accompanied by pump noise). 2. Loose pump belt. 3. Pump output low. 4. Engine idle too low. 5. Excessive internal leakage thru piston end plug and/or side plugs.	1. Fill to proper level. 2. Adjust belts. 3. Pressure test pump. 4. Adjust engine idle. 5. Replace worm-piston assembly.

With power cylinder-assist power steering, the steering gear is of the standard mechanical type and the lubricating oil is self contained within the gear box and the level is maintained by the removal of a filler plug on the gear box housing. The control valve assembly is mounted on the gear box and is lubricated by power steering oil from the power steering pump reservoir, where the level is maintained.

Air Bleeding

Air bubbles in the power steering system must be removed from the fluid. Be sure the reservoir is filled to the proper level and the fluid is warmed up to operating temperature. Then, turn the steering wheel through its full travel three or four times until all the air bubbles are removed. Do not hold the steering wheel against its stops. Recheck the fluid level.

Fluid Level

1. Run the engine until the fluid is at the normal operating temperature. Then, turn the steering wheel through its full travel three or four times, and shut off the engine.
2. Check the fluid level in the steering reservoir. If the fluid level is low, add enough fluid to raise the level to the Full mark on the dipstick or filler tube.

Pump Belt

Inspect the pump belt for cracks, glazing, or worn places. Using a belt tension gauge, check the belt tension for the proper range of adjustment. The amount of tension varies with the make of truck and the condition of the belt. New belts (those belts used less than 15 minutes) require a higher figure. The belt deflection method of adjustment may be used only if a belt tension gauge is not available. The belt should be adjusted for a deflection of ¼ to ⅜ inch.

Fluid Leaks

Check all possible leakage points (hoses, power steering pump, or steering gear) for loss of fluid. Turn engine on and rotate the steering wheel from stop to stop several times. Tighten all loose fittings and replace any defective lines or valve seats.

Turning Effort

Check the turning effort required to turn the steering wheel after aligning the front wheels and inflating the tires to the proper pressure.

1. With the vehicle on dry pavement and the front wheel straight ahead, set the parking brake and turn the engine on.
2. After a short warm-up period for the engine, turn the steering wheel back and forth several times to warm the steering fluid.
3. Attach a spring scale to the steering wheel rim and measure the pull required to turn the steering wheel one complete revolution in each direction. The effort needed to turn the steering wheel should not exceed the limits specified.

NOTE: This test may be done with the steering wheel removed and a torque wrench applied on the steering wheel nut.

POWER STEERING PUMP TEST

Since the power steering pump provides all the power assist in a power steering system, the pump must operate properly at all times for the system to work. After performing all the checks given above, the power steering pump may be tested for proper flow by the following procedures:

Two Gauges and Flow Meter

1. Disconnect the pressure and return lines at the power steering pump and connect the test pressure and return lines. The test lines are connected to a pressure gauge and two manual valves.
2. Open the two manual valves, connect a tachometer to the engine, and start the engine. Run the engine at idle speed until the reservoir fluid temperature reaches about 165–175 °F. This temperature must be maintained during the test. Manual valve B may be partially opened to create a back pressure of no more than 350 psi to aid the temperature rise. Reservoir fluid must be at the proper level.
3. After the engine and the reservoir fluid are sufficiently warmed up, close the manual valve B. Note the pressure gauge reading. It must be a minimum of 620 psi.

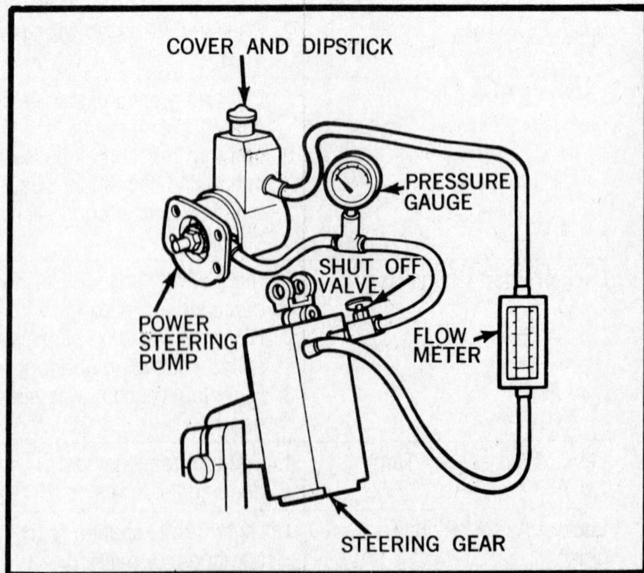

Testing power steering hydraulic system for internal leakage using a pressure gauge, shut off valve and flow meter—typical

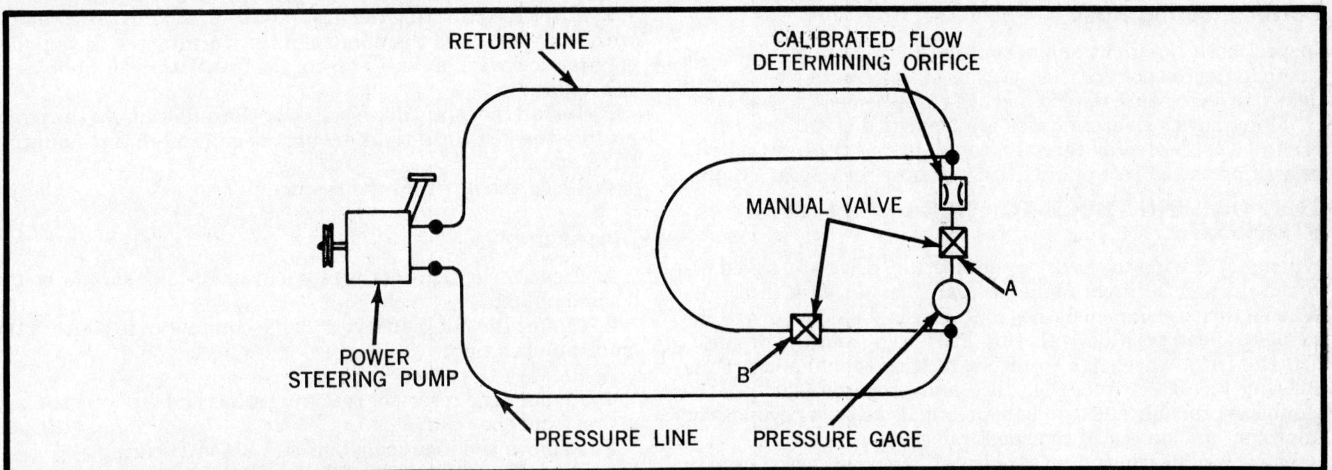

Power steering pump test circuit diagram

4. If the pressure reading is below the minimum acceptable pressure, the pump is defective and must be repaired. If the pressure reading is at or above the minimum value, the pump is normal. Open manual valve B and proceed to the pump fluid pressure test.

Power Steering Pump Fluid Pressure

1. Keep the lines and pressure gauge connected as in the Pump Flow Test.
2. With manual valve A and B opened fully, run the engine at the proper idle speed. Then, close manual valve A and manual valve B, in that order.

CAUTION

Do not keep both valves closed for more than 5 seconds since the fluid temperature will increase abnormally and cause unnecessary wear to the pump.

3. With both manual valves closed, the pressure reading should be as given in the specifications. If the pressure is below the minimum reading, the pump is defective and must be repaired. If the pressure reading is at or above the minimum reading, the pump is normal and the power steering gear or power assist control valve must be checked.

CHECKING THE OIL FLOW AND PRESSURE RELIEF VALVE IN THE PUMP ASSEMBLY

When the wheels are turned hard right, or hard left, against the stops, the oil flow and pressure relief valves come into action. If these valves are working and are not stuck there should be a slight buzzing noise.

CAUTION

Do not hold the wheels in the extreme position for over three or four seconds because, if the pressure relief valve is not working, the pressure could get high enough to damage the system.

TESTING THE PRESSURE RELIEF VALVE (SINGLE GAUGE)

1. Install the test presure gauge (O–2000 psi) between the power steering pump and the control valve.
2. With the fluid at a temperature of 170 to 190°F, the engine running above idle and the shut-off valve open, observe the pressure reading while moving the wheels to the end of their right and left travel.
3. If the gauge registers the correct relief valve pressure, the hydraulic system should be satisfactory. If pressure cannot be built up on either side of the gear, internal pump or gear problems exist.

NOTE: A shuttle valve equipped power cylinder may register a sharp drop-off in pressure at the end of the wheel travel and is considered normal.

4. To check the pump, close the shut-off valve and observe the pressure gauge. The pressure reading should be at relief valve pressure.

NOTE: Do not keep the shut-off valve closed longer than 15 seconds as damage to the pump could occur.

5. Repeat the closing of the shut-off valve twice more and record the highest pressure reading each time.
6. If the pressure readings are within 50 lbs. of each other and with-in the pump relief valve specifications, the pump operation is normal.

Example: Pump specifications 900 to 1500 psi.
Readings: 1st–1310 psi, 2nd–1290 psi, 3rd–1320

7. If the readings are high but do not repeat within 50 lbs. of each other, the flow control valve can be sticking. If 100 lbs. difference is noted below the low listed specification, replace the flow valve and recheck the system.

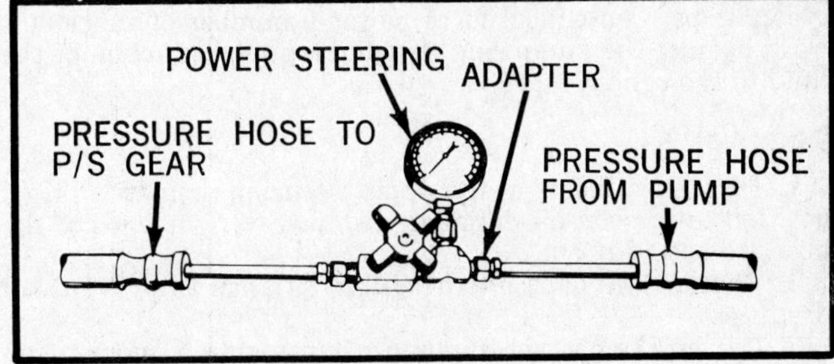

Power steering single gauge test unit

RELIEF VALVE PRESSURE

Relief valve pressures normally range between 800 to 2000 psi, depending upon the requirements of the power steering system and the axle application used on the vehicle. The lighter the truck, the less pressure is needed to operate the steering system, while the opposite is true of the heavier vehicles.

The minimum pressures with the wheels straight ahead and at engine idle should be in the 80 to 120 psi range.

Power Steering Hose

Inspect both the input and output hoses of the power steering pump for worn spots, cracks, or signs of leakage. Replace hose if defective, being sure to reconnect the replacement hose properly. Many power steering hoses are identified as to where they are to be connected by special means, such as fittings that will only fit on the correct pump fitting, or hoses of special lengths.

TEST DRIVING TRUCK TO CHECK THE POWER STEERING

When test driving to check power steering, drive at a speed between 15 and 20 mph. Make several turns in each direction. When a turn is completed, the front wheels should return to the straight ahead position with very little help from the driver.

If the front wheels fail to return as they should and yet the steering linkage is free, well oiled and properly adjusted, the trouble is probably due to misalignment of the power cylinder or improper adjustment of the spool valve.

The power steering pump supplies all the power assist used in power steering systems of all designs. There are various designs of pumps used by the truck manufacturers but all pumps supply power to operate the steering systems with the least effort. All power steering pumps have a reservoir tank built onto the oil pump. These pumps are driven by belt turned by pulleys on the engine, normally on the front of the crankshaft.

During operation of the engine at idle speed, there is provision for the power steering pump to supply more fluid pressure. During driving speeds or when the truck is moving straight ahead, less pressure is needed and the excess is relieved through a pressure relief and flow control valve. The pressure relief part of the valve is inside the flow control and is basically the same for all pumps. The flow control valve regulates, or controls, the constant flow of fluid from the pump as it varies with the demands of the steering gear. The pressure relief valve limits the hydraulic pressure built up when the steering gear is turned against its stops.

During pump disassembly, make sure all work is done on a clean surface. Clean the outside of the pump thoroughly and do not allow dirt of any kind to get inside. Do not immerse the shaft oil seal in solvent.

If replacing the rotor shaft seal, be extremely careful not to scratch sealing surfaces with tools.

Vane Type Power Steering Pump

The vane type power steering pump is used in Saginaw steering systems. The operation is basically the same as that of the roller type pumps. Centrifugal force moves a number of vanes outward against the pump ring, causing a pumping action of the fluid to the control valve.

Removal

1. Disconnect hoses at the pump, securing them in a raised position to prevent oil drainage. Cap or cover the ends of the hoses to keep dirt out.
2. Install two caps on the pump fittings to prevent oil drainage.
3. Loosen the bracket-to-pump mounting nuts, move pump toward engine slightly, and remove the pump drive belt.
4. Remove the bracket-to-pump bolts and remove the pump from the truck.
5. While holding the drive pulley steady, loosen and remove the pulley attaching nut. Slide the pulley off the shaft.

NOTE: Do not hammer the pulley off the shaft.

Installation

1. To install the pump on the truck, reverse the removal procedure. Always use a new pulley nut, tightening it to 35–45 ft. lbs. torque.
2. After reconnecting the hoses to the pump, fill the reservoir with fluid and bleed the pump of air by turning the drive pulley counterclockwise (as viewed from the front) until air bubbles do not appear.
3. Install the pump drive belt over the pulley, move the pump against the belt until tight enough, then tighten the mounting bolts and nuts.
4. Bleed the air from the system.

Disassembly

1. Clean the outside of the pump in a non-toxic solvent before disassembling.
2. Mount the pump in a vise, being careful not to squeeze the front hub too tight.
3. Remove the union and seal.
4. Remove the reservoir retaining studs and separate the reservoir from the housing.
5. Remove the mounting bolt and union O-rings.
6. Remove the filter and filter cage; discard the element.
7. Remove the end plate retaining ring by compressing the retaining ring and then prying it out with a removal tool. The retaining ring may be compressed by inserting a small punch in the ⅛ in. diameter hole in the housing and pushing in until the ring clears the groove.
8. Remove the end plate. The end plate is spring-loaded and should rise above the housing level. If it is stuck inside the housing, a slight rocking or gentle tapping should free the plate.
9. Remove the shaft woodruff key and tap the end of the shaft gently to free the pressure plate, pump ring, rotor assembly, and thrust plate. Remove these parts as one unit.
10. Remove the end plate O-ring. Separate the pressure plate, pump ring, rotor assembly, and thrust plate.

Inspection

Clean all metal parts in a non-toxic solvent and inspect them as given below:

1. Check the flow control valve for free movement in the housing bore. If the valve is sticking, see if there is dirt or a rough spot in the bore.
2. Check the cap screw in the end of the flow control valve for looseness. Tighten if necessary being careful not to damage the machined surfaces.
3. Inspect the pressure plate and the pump plate surfaces for flatness and check that there are no cracks or scores in the parts. Do not mistake the normal wear marks for scoring.
4. Check the vanes in the rotor assembly for free movement and that they were installed with the radiused edge toward the pump ring.
5. If the flow control valve plunger is defective, install a new part. The valve is factory calibrated and supplied as a unit.
6. Check the drive shaft for wornsplines, breaks, bushing material pick-up, etc.
7. Replace all rubber seals and O-rings removed from the pump.
8. Check the reservoir, studs, casting, etc. for burrs and other defects that would impair operation.

Assembly

1. Install a new shaft seal in the housing and insert the shaft at the hub end of housing, splined end entering mounting face side.
2. Install the thrust plate on the dowel pins with the ported side facing the rear of the pump housing.
3. Install the rotor on the pump shaft over the splined end. Be sure the rotor moves freely on the splines. Countersunk side must be toward the shaft.
4. Install the shaft retaining ring. Install the pump ring on the dowel pins with the rotation arrow toward the rear of the pump housing. Rotation is clockwise as seen from the pulley.

STEERING TROUBLE DIAGNOSIS
Power Steering Pump

Condition	Possible Cause	Correction
Intermittent Assist	1. Flow control valve sticking. 2. Slipping belt. 3. Low fluid level. 4. Low pump efficiency.	1. Pressure test pump and service as necessary. 2. Adjust belt. 3. Inspect and correct fluid level. 4. Pressure test pump and service as necessary.
No Assist	1. Pump seizure. 2. Broken slipper spring(s). 3. Flow control bore plug ring not in place. 4. Flow control valve sticking.	1. Replace pump. 2. Recondition pump or replace as necessary. 3. Replace snap ring. Inspect groove for depth. 4. Pressure test pump and service as necessary.
No Assist When Parking Only	1. Wrong pressure relief valve. 2. Broken "O" ring on flow control bore plug. 3. Loose pressure relief valve. 4. Low pump efficiency	1. Install proper relief valve. 2. Replace "O" ring. 3. Tighten valve. DO NOT ADJUST. 4. Pressure test pump and service as necessary.
Noisy Pump	1. Low fluid level. 2. Belt noise. 3. Foreign material blocking pump housing oil inlet hole.	1. Inspect and correct fluid level. 2. Inspect for pulley alignment, paint or grease on pulley and correct. Adjust belt. 3. Remove reservoir, visually check inlet oil hole and service as necessary.
Pump Vibration	1. Pump hose interference with sheet metal or brake lines. 2. Belt loose. 3. Pulley loose or out of round. 4. Crankshaft pulley loose or damaged. 5. Bracket pivot bolts loose.	1. Reroute hoses. 2. Adjust belt. 3. Replace pulley. 4. Replace crankshaft pulley. 5. If unable to tighten, replace bracket.
Pump Leaks	1. Cap or filler neck leaks. 2. Reservoir solder joints leak. 3. Reservoir "O" ring leaking. 4. Shaft seal leaking. 5. Loose rear bracket bolts. 6. Loose or faulty high pressure ferrule. 7. Rear bolt holes stripped or casting cracked.	1. Correct fluid level. 2. Resolder or replace reservoir as necessary. 3. Inspect sealing area of reservoir. Replace "O" ring or reservoir as necessary. 4. Replace seal. 5. Tighten bolts. 6. Tighten fitting to 24 foot-pounds or replace as necessary. 7. Repair, if possible, or replace pump.
Objectionable "Hiss"	1. Noisy valve	1. Do not replace valve unless "hiss" is extremely objectionable. A replacement valve will also exhibit sight noise and is not always a cure for the objection.
Rattle or Chuckle Noise in Steering Gear	1. Gear loose on frame. 2. Steering linkages looseness. 3. Pressure hose touching other parts of truck. 4. Loose Pitman shaft over center adjustment. **NOTE:** A slight rattle may occur on turns because of increased clearance off the "high point". This is normal and clearance must not be reduced below specified limits to eliminate this slight rattle. 5. Loose Pitman arm.	1. Check gear mounting bolts. Torque bolts to specifications. 2. Check linkage pivot points for wear. Replace if necessary. 3. Adjust hose position. Do not bend tubing by hand. 4. Adjust 5. Torque Pitman arm pinch bolt.

STEERING TROUBLE DIAGNOSIS
Power Steering Noise

Condition	Possible Cause	Correction
Squawk Noise in Steering Gear When Turning or Recovering From a Turn	1. Dampener O-ring on valve spool cut. 2. Loose or worn valve.	1. Replace dampener O-Ring. 2. Replace valve.
Chirp Noise in Steering Gear	1. Gear relief valve.	1. Replace relief valve.
Chirp Noise in Steering Pump	1. Loose belt.	1. Adjust belt tension.
Belt Squeal (Particularly Noticeable at Full Wheel Travel and Standstill Parking)	1. Loose belt.	1. Adjust belt tension.
Growl Noise in Steering Pump	1. Excessive back pressure in hoses or steering gear caused by restriction.	1. Locate restriction and correct. Replace part if necessary.
Growl Noise in Steering Pump (Particularly Noticeable at Standstill Parking)	1. Scored pressure plates, thrust plate or rotor. 2. Extreme wear of cam ring.	1. Replace parts and flush system. 2. Replace parts.
Groan Noise in Steering Pump	1. Low oil level. 2. Air in the oil. Poor pressure hose connection.	1. Fill reservoir to proper level. 2. Torque connector. Bleed system.
Rattle or Knock Noise in Steering Pump	1. Loose pump pulley nut.	1. Torque nut.
Rattle Noise in Steering Pump	1. Vanes not installed properly. 2. Vanes sticking in rotor slots.	1. Install properly. 2. Repair or replace.
Swish Noise in Steering Pump	1. Defective flow control valve.	1. Replace part.
Whine Noise in Steering Pump	1. Pump Shaft bearing scored.	1. Replace housing and shaft. Flush and bleed system.

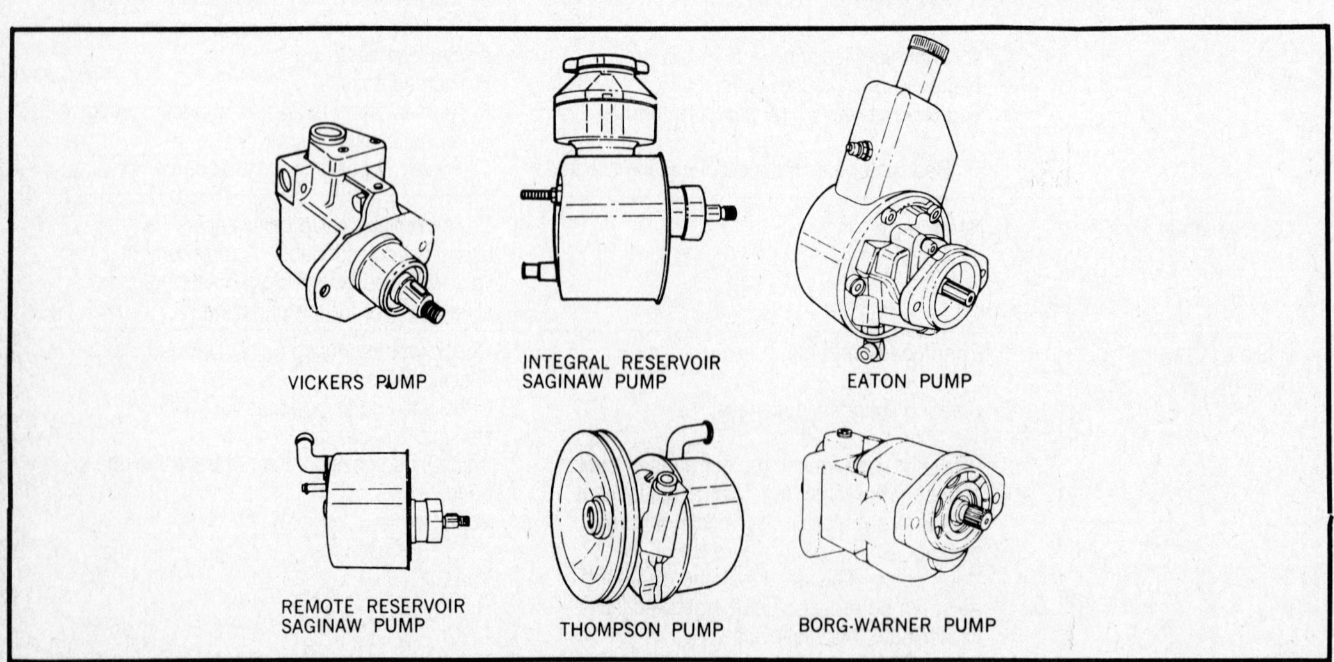

Identification of power steering pumps used on General Motors trucks—typical

5. Install the vanes in the rotor slots with the radius edge towards the outside.
6. Lubricate the outside diameter and chamfer of the pressure plate with petroleum jelly so as not to damage the O-ring and install the plate on the dowel pins with the ported face toward the pump ring. Seat the pressure plate by placing a large socket on top of the plate and pushing down with the hand.
7. Install the pressure plate spring in the center groove of the plate.
8. Install the end plate O-ring. Lubricate the outside diameter and chamfer of the end plate with petroleum jelly so as not to damage the O-ring and install the end plate in the housing, using an arbor press. Install the end plate retaining ring while pump is in the arbor press. Be sure the ring is in the groove and the ring gap is positioned properly.

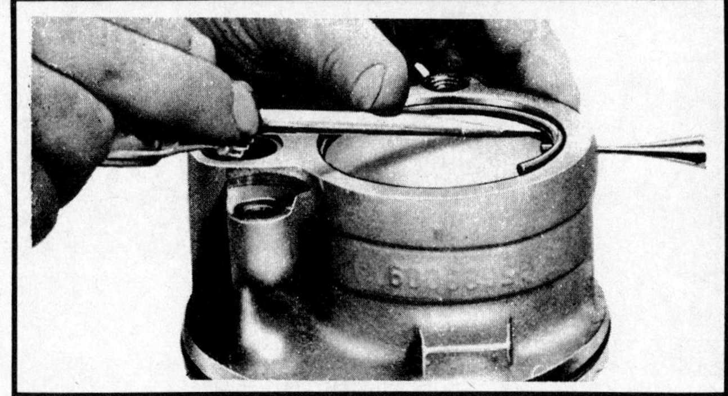

Removing end plate ring

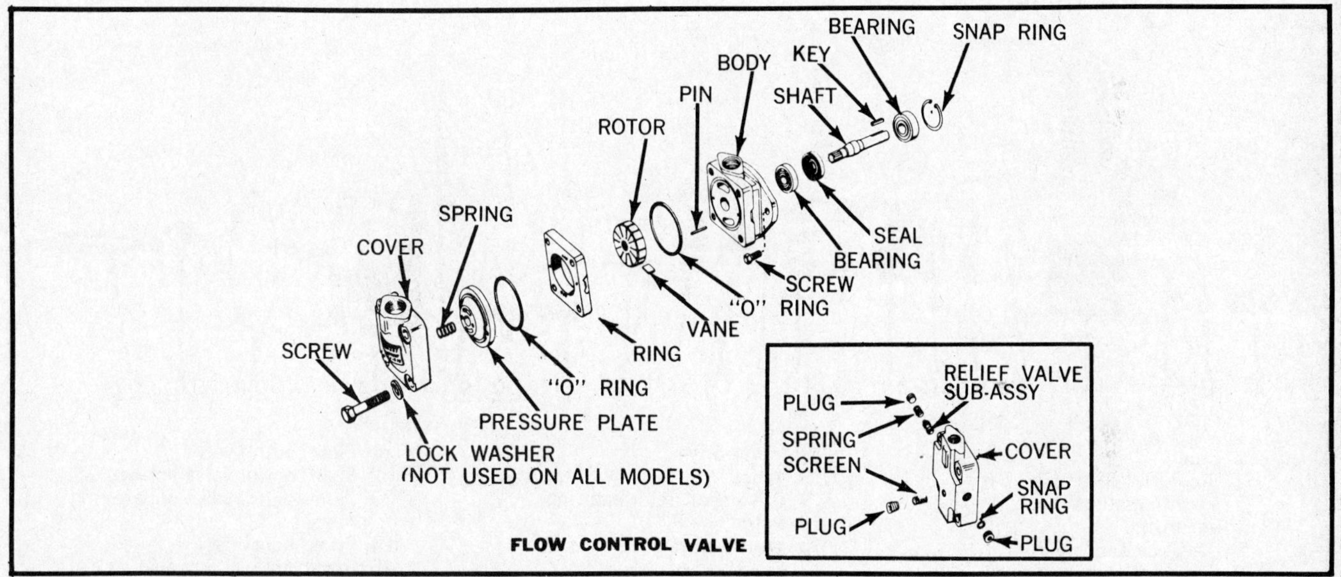

Exploded view of vane type pump—Vickers

9. Install the flow control spring and plunger, hex head screw end in bore first. Install the filter cage, new filter stud seals and union seal.
10. Place the reservoir in the normal position and press down until the reservoir seats on the housing. Check the position of the stud seals and the union seal.
11. Install the studs, union, and drive shaft woodruff key. Support the shaft on the opposite side of the key when tapping the key into place.

Roller Type Power Steering Pump

The roller type power steering pump is designed similar to other constant flow centrifugal force pumps. A star-shaped rotor forces 12 steel rollers against the inside surface of a cam ring. As the rollers follow the eccentric pattern of the cam ring, oil is drawn into the inlet ports and exhausted through the discharge ports while the rollers are moved into v shaped cavities of the rotor, forcing oil into the high pressure circuit. A flow control valve permits a regulated amount of fluid to return to the intake side of the pump when excess output is produced during high speed operation. This reduces the power needs to drive the pump and minimizes temperature build-up.

The flow control valve used in one make of pump is a two-stage valve. Fluid under high pressure passes through two holes into a metering circuit located in a sealed passage. At low speed, about 2.7 gpm. passes to the gear. As speed increases and the valve moves, excess fluid is bypassed to the inlet and the valve blocks flow through one hole. This drops the flow to about 1.6 gpm. at high speeds.

When steering conditions produce excessive pressure needs (such as turning the wheels against the stops), the pressure built up in the steering gear exerts force on the spring end of the flow control valve.

This end of the valve contains the pressure relief valve. High pressure lifts the relief valve ball from its seat, allowing fluid to flow through a trigger orifice located in the front land of the flow control valve. This reduces pressure on the spring end of the valve which then opens and allows the fluid to return to the intake side of the pump. This action limits the maximum pressure output of the pump to a safe level. Normally, the pressure needs of the pump are below the maximum limits, causing the pressure relief ball and the flow control valve to remain closed.

Removal

1. Loosen the pump mounting and locking bolts and remove the belt.
2. Disconnect both hoses at the pump. Cap and tie the hoses out of the way. Cap the hose fittings on the pump.
3. Remove the mounting and locking bolts, the pump and brackets from the truck.

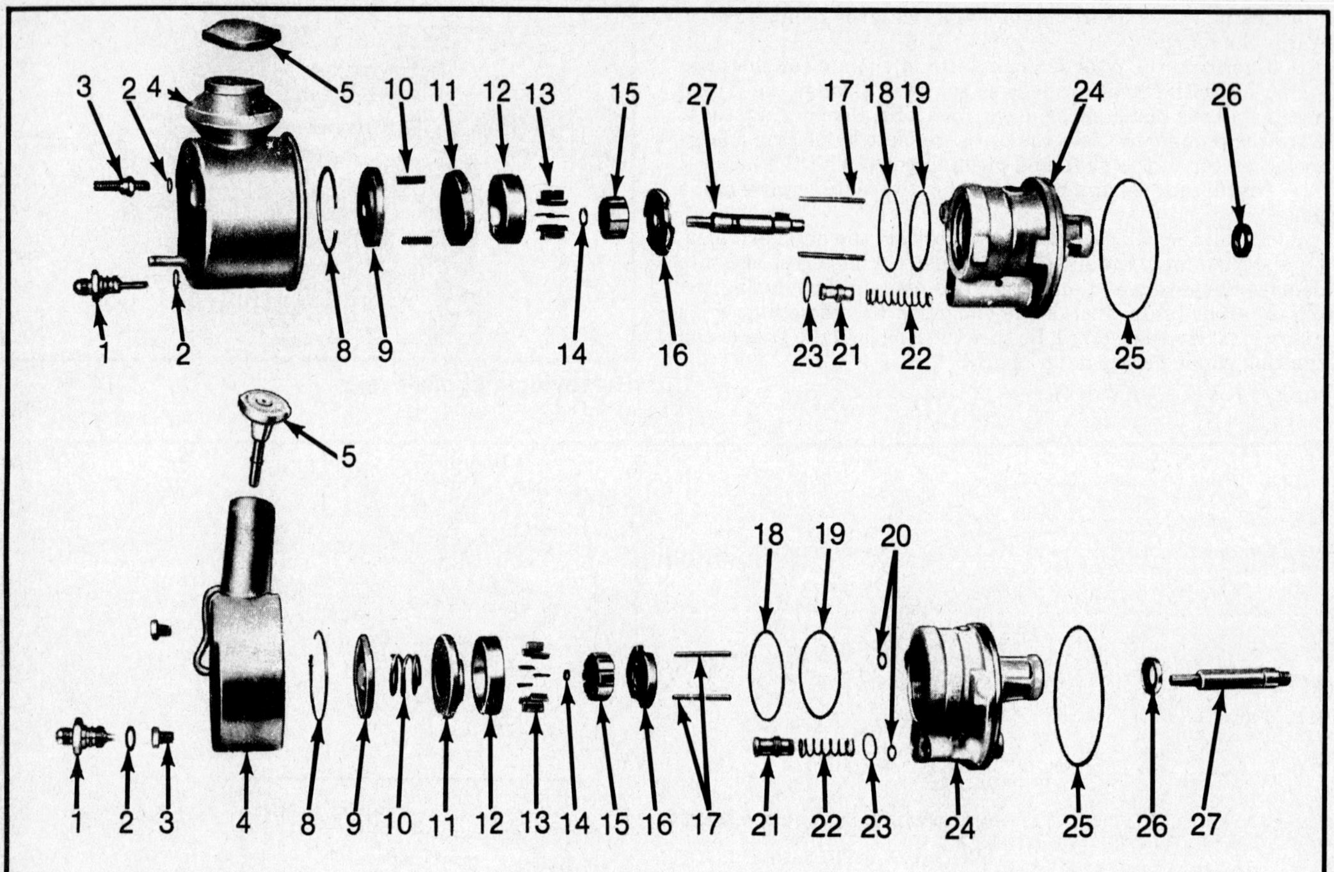

1 Union
2 Union "O" ring seal
3 Mounting studs
4 Reservoir
5 Dip stick and cover
8 End plate retaining ring
9 End plate
10 Spring
11 Pressure plate
12 Pump ring
13 Vanes
14 Drive shaft retaining ring
15 Rotor
16 Thrust plate
17 Dowel pins
18 End plate "O" ring
19 Pressure plate "O" ring
20 Mounting stud square ring
21 Flow control valve
22 Flow control valve spring
23 Flow control valve square ring seal
24 Pump housing
25 Reservoir "O" ring seal
26 Shaft seal
27 Shaft

Vane type power steering pumps

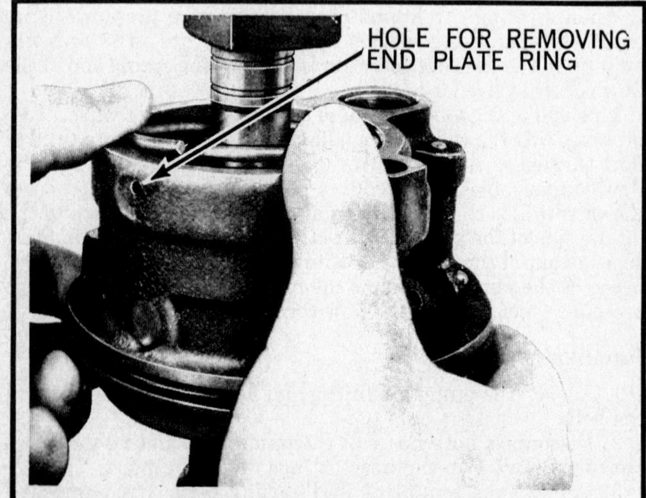

Installing end plate retaining ring

Installing flow control valve

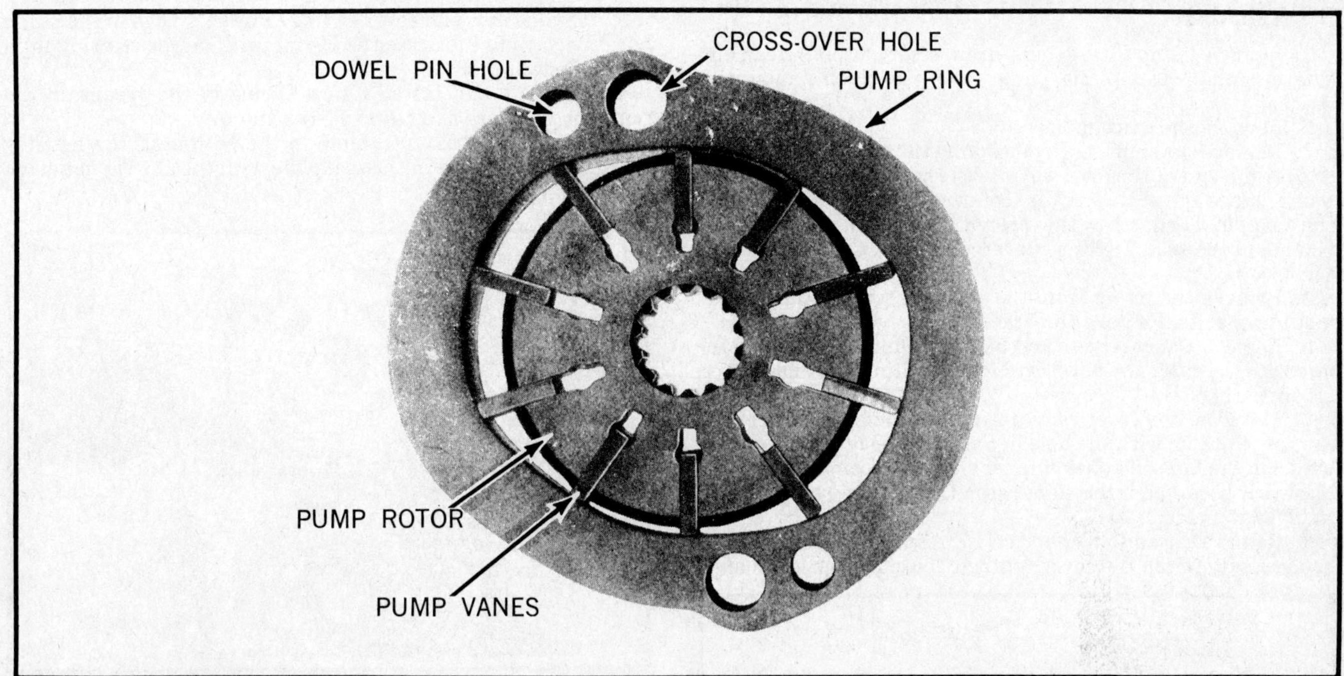

Correct vane assembly

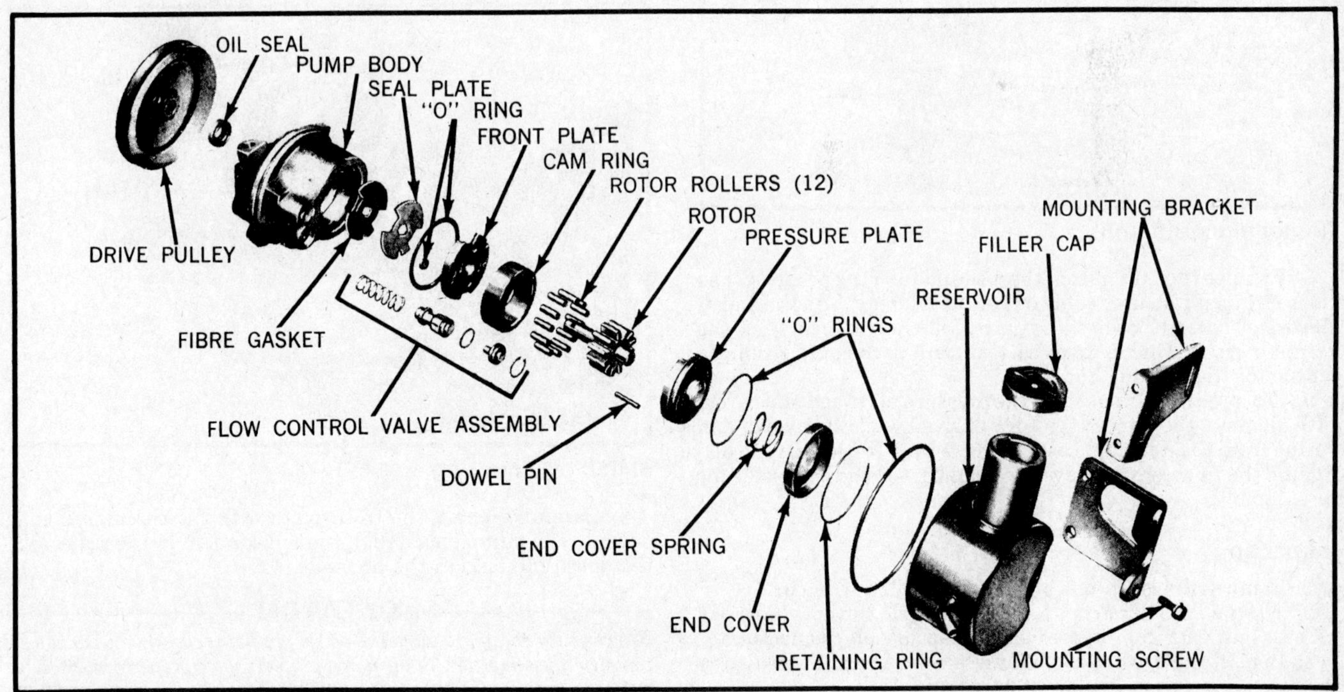

Roller type power steering pump

Installation

1. Position the pump and brackets on the engine and install the mounting and locking bolts.
2. Install the drive belt and adjust for the proper tension.
3. Connect the pressure and return hoses, using a new pressure hose O-ring.
4. Fill the pump reservoir to the top of the filler neck with power steering fluid.
5. Start the engine and turn the steering wheel several times from stop to stop to bleed the pump of air. Check the level and add fluid if necessary.

NOTE: When checking the level, see that the level is as follows: engine cold-bottom of filler tube; engine hot-half way up filler tube.

Disassembly

1. Remove pump from engine, drain reservoir, and clean outside of pump. Clamp the pump in a vise at the mounting bracket.
2. Remove the drive pulley.
3. Remove the shaft seal by installing the seal remover adapter over the end of the drive shaft with the large end toward the pump. Place the seal remover tool over the shaft and through the adapter. Then, screw the tapered thread well into the metal portion of the seal. Tighten the large drive nut and remove the seal.
4. Remove the pump from the vise and remove the bracket mounting bolts. Remove the bracket.
5. Remove the reservoir and place the pump in a soft-faced vise with the shaft down. Discard the mounting bolt and the reservoir O-rings.
6. Move the end cover retaining ring around until one end of the ring lines up with the hole in the pump body. Insert a small punch in the hole and push it in far enough to bend the ring so a screwdriver can be inserted between the ring and the housing. Remove the ring.
7. Remove the end cover and spring from the housing. It may be necessary to tap the cover gently to loosen it in the housing.

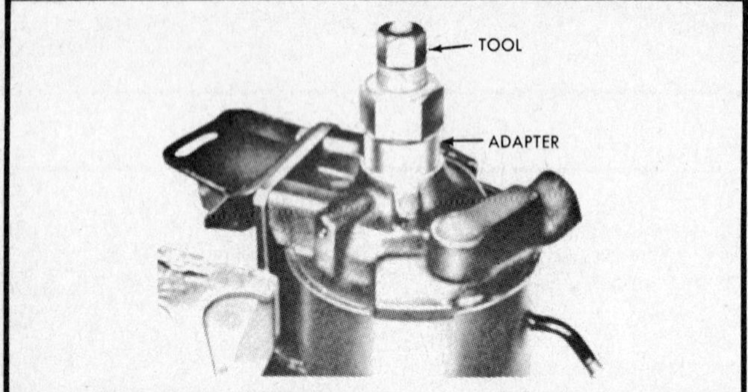

Removing shaft seal

8. Remove the pump from the vise and turn the pump over so the rotating pump may come out of the housing. Tap the end of the drive shaft to loosen these parts. Lift the pump body off the rotating group. Check that the seal plate is removed from the bottom of the housing bore.
9. Discard the O-rings from the pressure plate and end cover.
10. Remove the snap-ring, bore plug, flow control valve and spring from the housing. Discard the O-ring. If necessary to dismantle the flow control valve for cleaning, see the procedure for disassembly.

Inspection

1. Remove the clean out plug with an Allen wrench.
2. Wash all metal parts in clean, non-toxic solvent. Blow out all passages with compressed air and air dry all cleaned parts.
3. Inspect the drive shaft for excessive wear and the seal area for nicks or scoring. Replace if necessary.
4. Inspect the end plates, rollers, rotor and cam ring for nicks, burrs, or scratches. If any of the components are damaged enough to cause poor operation of the pump, all the interior parts may have to be replaced to prevent later failures.
5. Inspect the pump body drive shaft bushing for excessive wear. Replace the pump body and bushing as one assembly.

Assembly

1. Install the pipe clean out plug, tightening it to 80 inch lbs. torque.
2. Place the pump body on a clean flat surface and install a new shaft seal into the bore.
3. Install a new end cover O-ring into the groove in the pump bore. Be sure to lubricate the O-ring with power steering fluid before installing it.
4. Lubricate and install a new O-ring in the groove on the pump body where the reservoir fits snugly.
5. Install the brass seal plate to the bottom of the housing bore. Align the notch in the seal plate with the dowel pin hole in the housing.

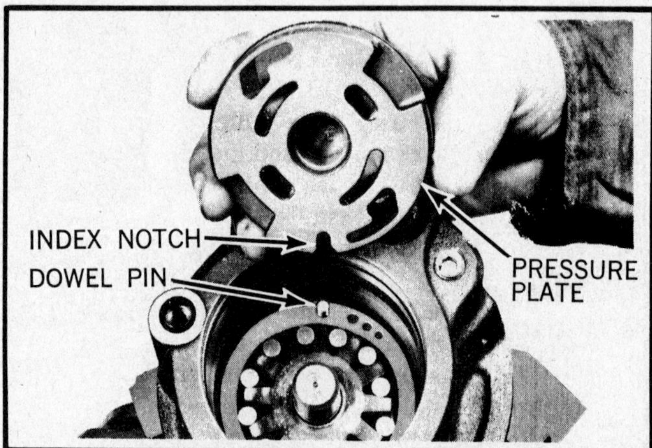

Installing pressure plate

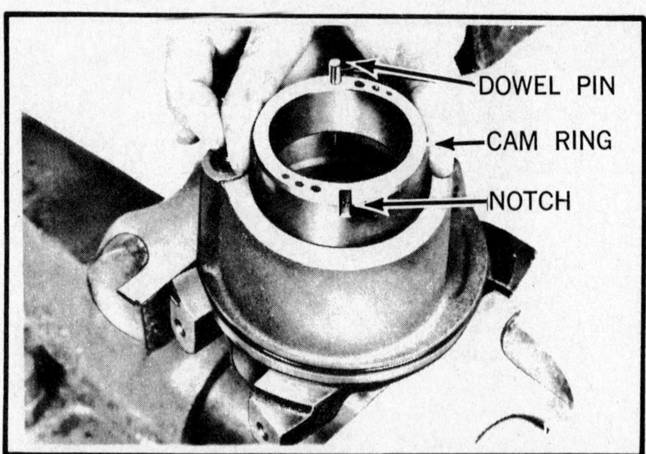

Installing cam ring

6. Carefully install the front plate with the chamfered edge down in the pump bore. Align the index notch in the plate with the dowel pin hole in the housing.

CAUTION

Be extremely careful to align the dowel pin hole properly. Pump can be completely assembled with the dowel pin not seated properly in the hole.

7. Place the dowel pin in the cam ring and position the cam ring inside the pump bore. Notch in the cam ring must be facing up (away from the pulley end of pump housing). If the cam ring has two notches, one machined and one cast, install the cam ring with the machined notch up. Check the amount of dowel pin extending above the cam ring surface. If more than $^3/_{16}$ in. is showing, the dowel pin is not seated in the index hole in the housing.
8. Install the rotor and shaft in the cam ring and carefully install the 12 steel rollers in the cavities of the rotor. Lubricate the rotor, rollers, and the inside surface of the cam ring with power steering fluid. Rotate the shaft by hand to be sure all the rollers

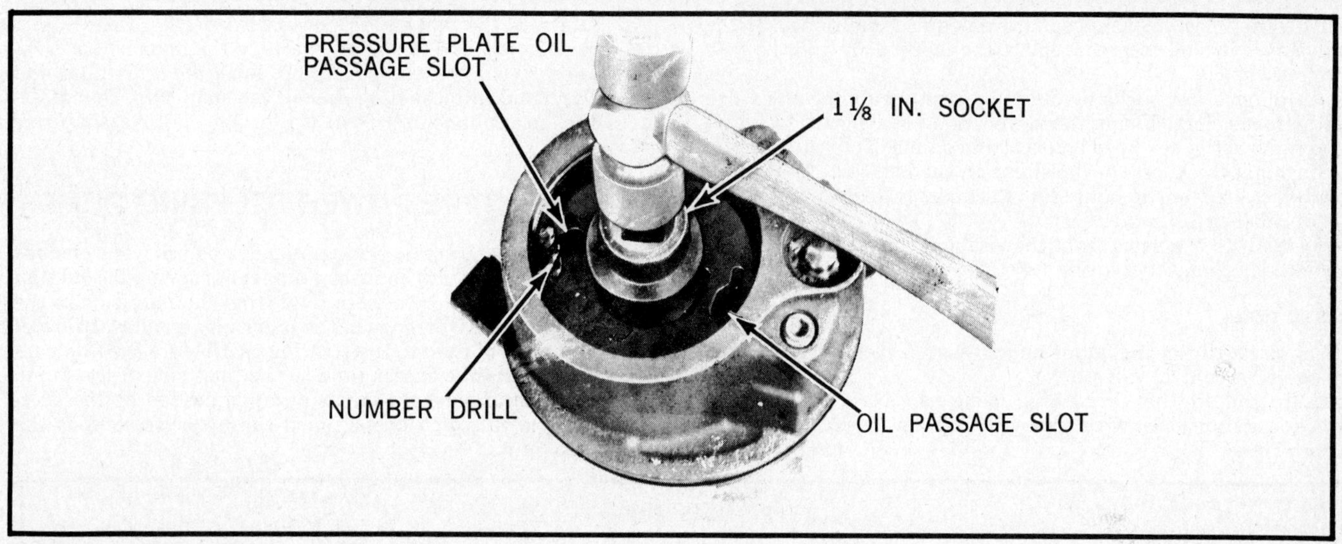

Seating pressure plate

are seated parallel with the shaft and are not sticking or binding.

9. Position the pressure plate by carefully aligning the index notch on the plate with the dowel pin and inserting a clean drill (number 13 to 16) in the cam ring oil hole next to the dowel pin notch until it bottoms on the housing floor.

10. Lubricate and install a new O-ring on the pressure plate. Position the pressure plate in the pump bore so that the dowel pin is in the index notch on the plate and the drill extends through the oil passage in the pressure plate. Seat the pressure plate on the cam ring using a clean 1⅛ in. socket and a soft-faced hammer to tap it gently. Remove the drill and inspect the plate at both oil passage slots to be sure that the plate is squarely seated on the cam ring.

11. Place the large coil spring over the raised portion of the installed pressure plate.

12. Place the end cover, lip edge facing up, over the spring. Press the end cover down below the retaining ring groove. Install the retaining ring in the groove. Be sure the end cover chamfer is squarely seated against the snap-ring.

13. Replace the reservoir mounting bolt seal.

14. Lubricate the flow control valve assembly with power steering fluid and insert the valve spring and valve in the bore. Install a new O-ring on the bore plug, lubricate with fluid, and carefully install in the bore. Install the snap-ring with the sharp edge up. Do not depress the bore plug more than $^{1}/_{16}$ in. below the snap-ring groove.

15. Place the reservoir on the pump body and visually align the mounting bolt hole. Tap the reservoir down on the pump with a plastic-faced hammer.

16. Remove the pump from the vise and install the mounting brackets with the mounting bolts on the pump. Tighten the bolts to 18 ft. lbs. torque.

17. Install the drive pulley by using the installer tool as follows: place the pulley on the end of the shaft and thread the installer tool into the ⅜ in. threaded hole in the end of the shaft. Put the installer shaft in a vise and tighten the drive nut against the thrust bearing, pressing the pulley on the shaft until it is flush. Do not try to press the pulley on the shaft without the special installer tool since the pump interior will be damaged by any other installation procedure. A small amount of drive shaft end play will be seen when the pulley is installed. This end play is necessary and will be minimized by a thin coat of oil between the rotor and the end plates when the pump is operating.

18. Install the pump assembly on the engine, install the drive belt and hoses (use new O-ring on pressure hose), and check for leaks.

FLOW CONTROL VALVE

Disassembly

1. After removing the pump from the engine and the reservoir from the pump, remove the snap-ring and plug from the flow bore. Discard the O-ring.

2. Depress the control valve against the spring pressure and allow the valve to spring out of the bore. If the valve is stuck in the bore or it did not come out of the bore far enough, it may be necessary to tap the housing lightly to remove it.

3. If the valve has dirt or foreign particles on it or in its bore, the rest of the pump needs cleaning. The hoses should be

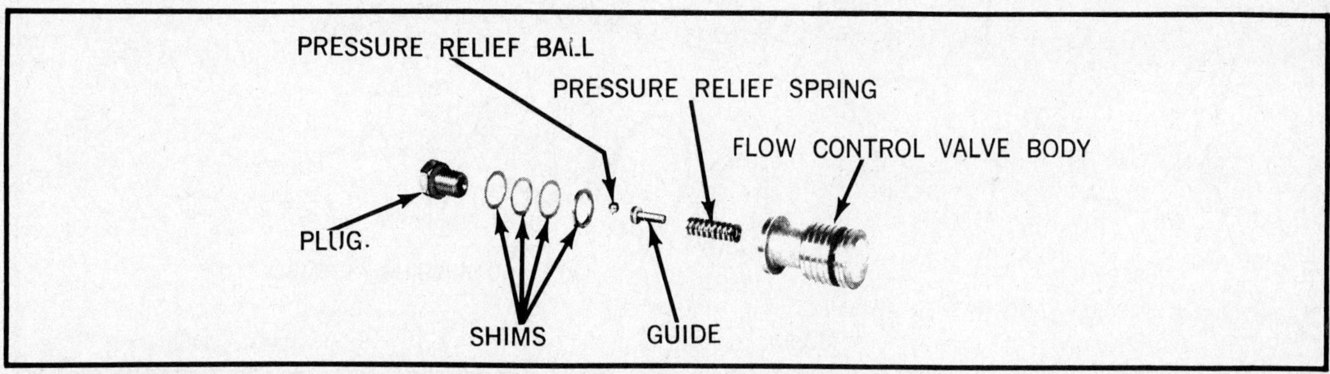

Flow control valve

flushed and the steering gear valve body reconditioned. If the valve bore is badly scored, replace the pump body and the flow control valve.

4. Remove any nicks or burrs by gently rubbing the valve with crocus cloth. Clamp the valve land in a vise with soft-jaws and remove the hex head ball seat and shims. Note the number and gauge (thickness) of the shims on the ball seat. They must be re-installed for the same shim thickness to keep the same value of relief pressure.

5. Remove the valve from the vise and remove the pressure relief ball, guide, and spring.

Assembly

1. Insert the spring, guide and pressure relief ball in the end of the flow control valve.

2. Install the hex head plug using the exact number and thickness shims that were removed. Tighten the plug to 80 inch lbs. torque.

3. Lubricate the valve with power steering fluid and insert the flow control valve spring and valve in the housing bore. Install a new O-ring on the bore plug, lubricate with fluid and carefully install into the bore. Install the snap-ring. Do not depress the bore plug more than $^{1}/_{16}$ in. beyond the snap-ring groove.

SLIPPER TYPE POWER STEERING PUMP

The slipper type power steering pump is a belt-driven constant displacement assembly that uses a number of spring-loaded slippers in the pump rotor to force fluid from the inlet side to the flow control valve. Openings in the metering pin allow a flow of about two gpm. of fluid to the steering gear before the flow control valve directs the excess fluid to the inlet side of the pump again. Maximum pressure in the pump is limited by the pressure relief valve which opens when the pressure exceeds the maximum limits.

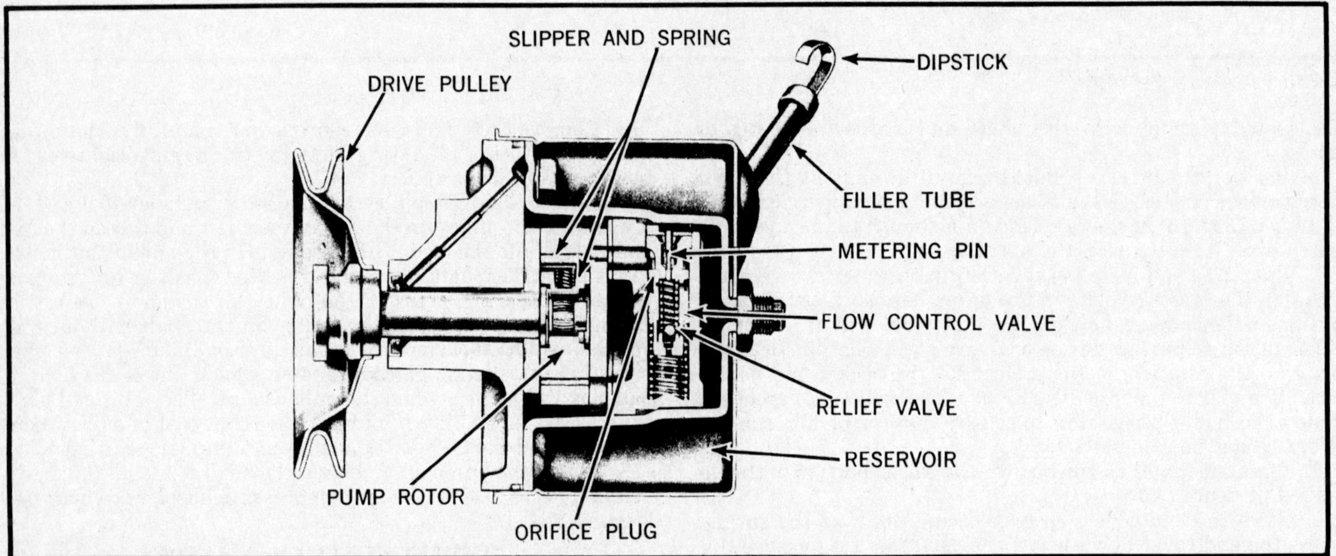

Sectional view of Ford Thompson power steering pump

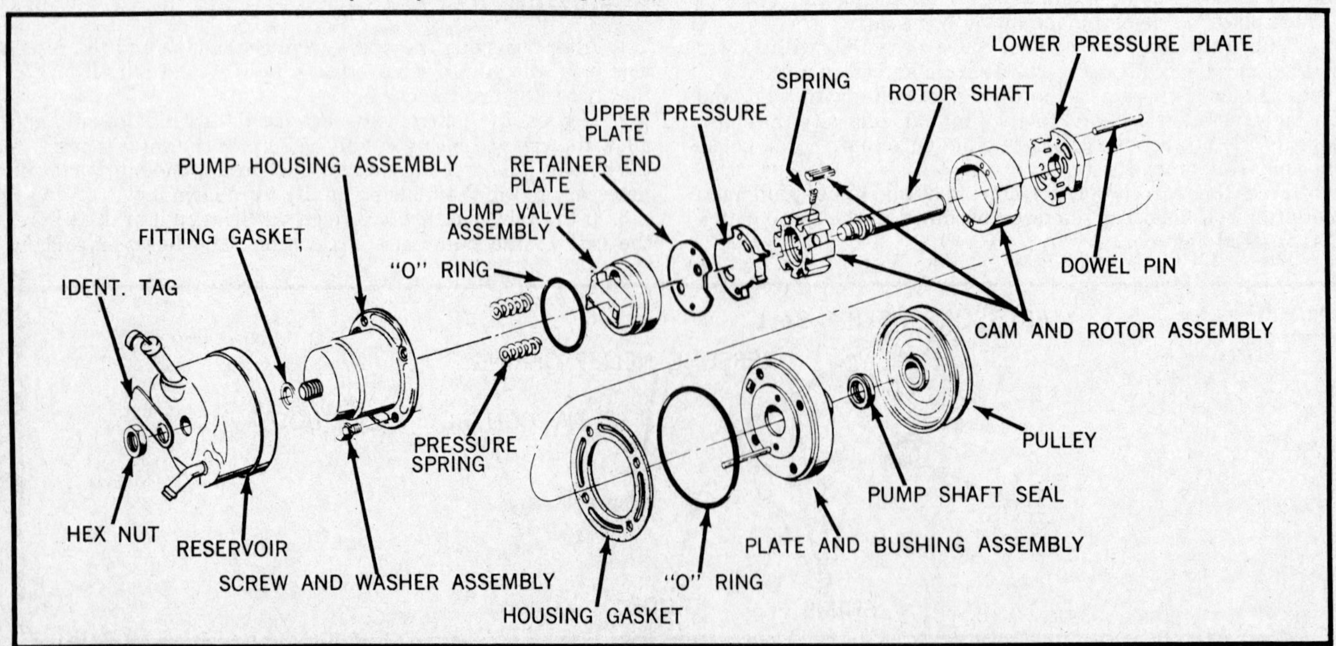

Exploded view of Ford Thompson power steering pump

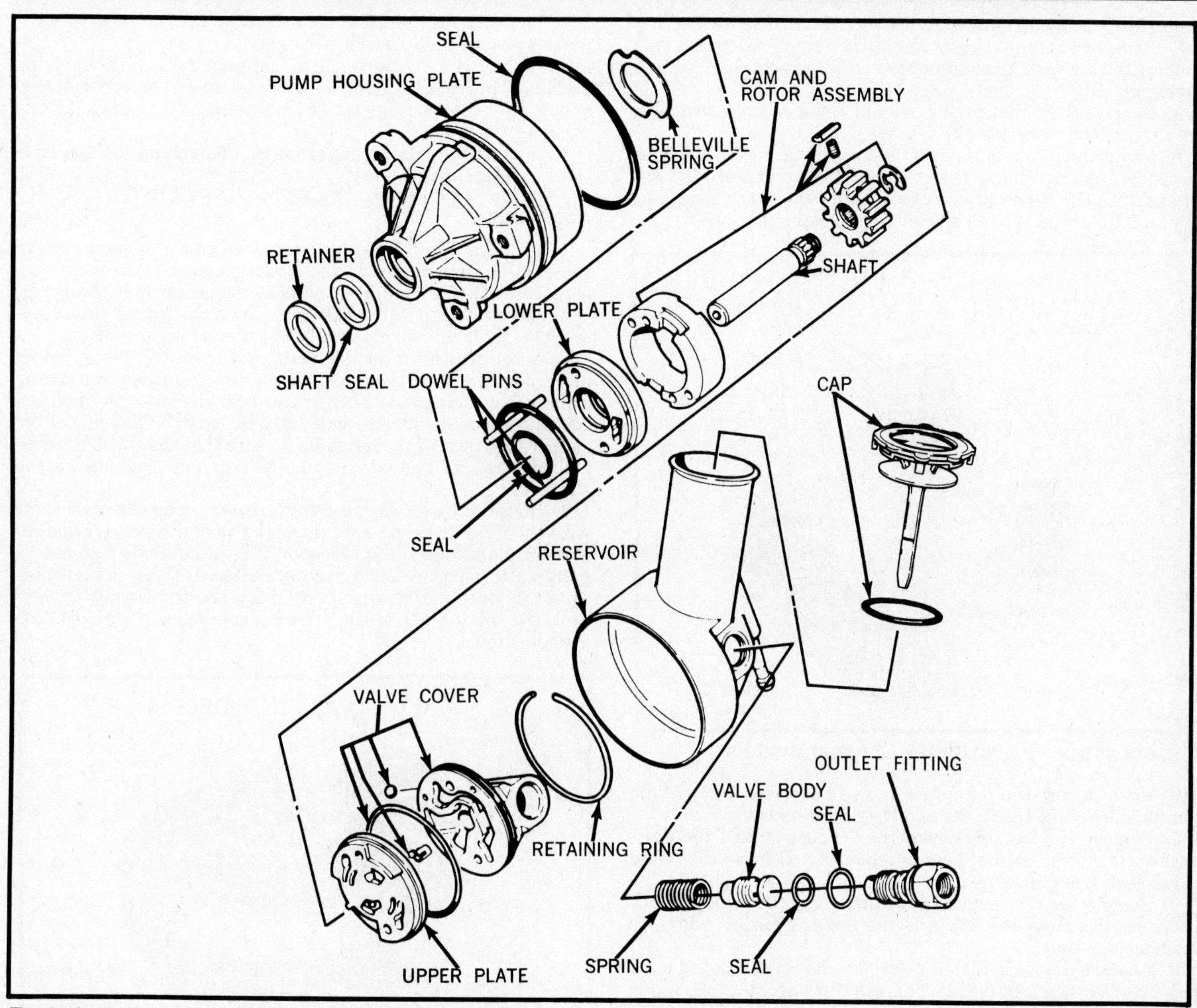

Exploded view of model C-11 slipper type pump

The slipper type power steering pump discussed in this section is used on Ford trucks and is called the Ford-Thompson power steering pump.

Removal

1. Drain the fluid from the pump reservoir by disconnecting the fluid return hose at the pump. Then, disconnect the pressure hose from the pump.
2. Remove the mounting bolts from the front of the pump. On eight cylinder engines, there is a nut on the rear of the pump that must be removed. After removing all the mounting bolts and nuts from the pump, move the unit inward to loosen the belt tension and remove the belt from the pulley. Then remove the pump from the engine.

Installation

1. Position the pump on the mounting bracket and loosely install the mounting bolts and nuts. Put the drive belt over the pulley and move the pump outward against the belt until the proper belt tension is obtained. Measure the belt tension with a gauge for the proper adjustment. Only in cases where a belt tension gauge is not available should the belt deflection method be used. If the belt deflection method is used, be sure to check the belt with a tension gauge at the earliest time since the deflection method is not accurate.
2. Tighten the mounting bolts and nuts to the specified torque limits.
3. Tighten the pressure hose fitting hex nut to the proper torque. Then connect the pressure hose to the pump and tighten the hose nut to the proper torque.
4. Connect the fluid return hose to the pump and tighten the clamp.
5. Fill the pump reservoir with power steering fluid and bleed the air bubbles from the system.
6. Check for leaks and recheck the fluid level. If necessary, add fluid to raise the level properly.

Disassembly

1. Drain as much fluid from the pump as possible after removing the pump from the truck.
2. Install a $^3/_8$ × 16 in. capscrew in the end of the pump shaft to avoid damaging the shaft end with the pulley remover tool. Install the pulley remover tool on the pulley hub and place the pump and remover tool in a vise. Hold the pump steady and turn the tool nut counterclockwise to draw the pulley off the shaft. The pulley must be removed without in and out pressure on the

pump shaft to avoid damaging the internal thrust washers.

3. Remove the pump reservoir by installing the pump in a holding fixture with an adapter plate in a vise with the reservoir facing up.

4. Remove the outlet fitting hex nut and any other attaching parts from the reservoir case.

5. Invert the pump so the reservoir is now facing down. Using a wooden block, remove the reservoir by tapping around the flange until the reservoir is loose. Remove the reservoir O-ring seal and the outlet fitting gasket from the pump.

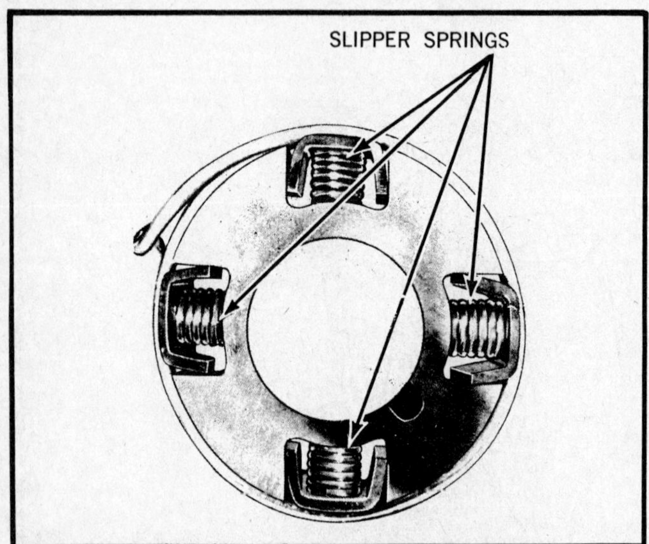

Correct slipper installation—Chrysler models

6. Again invert the pump assembly in the vise, remove the pump housing holding bolts and the pump housing.

7. Remove the housing cover, the O-ring seal and the pressure springs from inside the pump housing. Remove the pump cover gasket and discard it.

8. Remove the retainer end plate and upper pressure plate. In some pumps, the end plate and the upper pressure plate are made as one unit.

9. Remove the loose fitting dowel pin. Be careful not to bend the fixed dowel pin which remains in the housing plate assembly.

10. Remove the rotor assembly being careful not to let the slippers and springs fall out of the rotor. It may not be necessary to disassemble the rotor assembly unless the lower pressure plate, housing plate, rotor shaft and/or seal is to be replaced. However, the rotor assembly may be disassembled by removing the slippers and springs from the cam ring.

11. Remove any rust, dirt, burrs, or scoring from the pulley end of the rotor shaft before removing the shaft from the housing plate. The shaft must come out without restrictions to avoid scoring or damaging the bushing. Remove the pump rotor shaft.

12. Remove the lower pressure plate.

13. Remove the rotor shaft seal after first wrapping a piece of 0.005 in. shim stock around the shaft and pushing it into the inside of the seal until it touches the bushing. With a sharp tool, pierce the seal body and pry the seal out. Do not damage the bushing, housing, or the shaft. Install a new seal using a soft-faced hammer.

14. If the pump has a flow control valve, disassemble according to instructions given in the section on the roller type power steering pump.

Inspection

1. Wash all metal parts in clean, non-toxic solvent. Blow out all oil passages with compressed air and air dry all cleaned parts.

2. Inspect the drive shaft for excessive wear and seal area for nicks or scoring. Replace if necessary.

3. Inspect the pressure plates, slippers, rotor, and cam ring for nicks, burrs, or scratches. If any of the parts are damaged enough to cause poor operation or binding of the pump, replace the defective part.

4. Inspect the pump body drive shaft bushing for excessive wear. Replace if necessary.

Assembly

1. With the pump assembly positioned on the adapter plate in the holding fixture, install the lower pressure plate on the anchor pin with the chamfered slots at the center hole facing up.

2. Lubricate the rotor shaft with power steering fluid and insert the shaft into the lower pressure and housing plates.

3. Assemble the rotor, slippers, and springs by wrapping a piece of wire around the rotor, installing the springs, and sliding a slipper in each groove of the rotor over the springs. Then, insert the assembly into the cam ring. Be sure the flat side of the slippers are toward the left side. Be sure that the springs are installed straight and are not cocked to one side under the slippers.

4. Install the cam ring and rotor assembly on the drive shaft with the fixed dowel passing through the first hole to the left of the cam notch when the arrow on the cam outside diameter is pointing toward the lower pressure plate. If the cam and rotor assembly does not seat properly, turn the rotor shaft slightly until the spline teeth mesh, allowing the cam and rotor to drop into position.

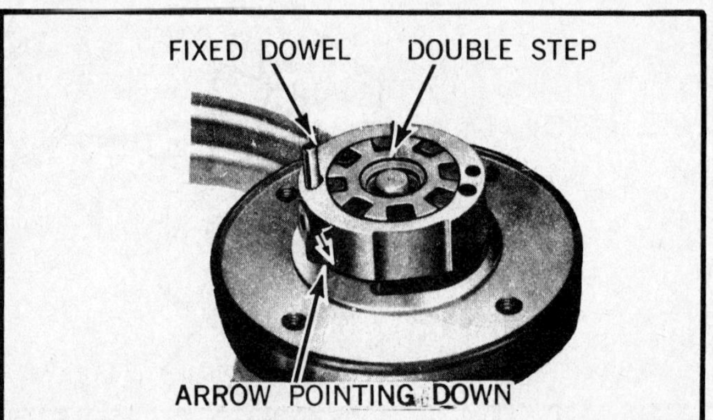

Cam and rotor installation

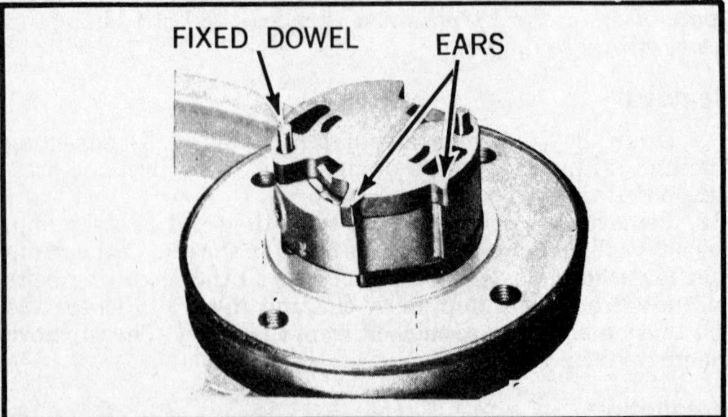

Upper pressure plate installation

5. Insert the loose fitting dowel through the cam insert and lower pressure plate into the hole in the housing plate assembly. When both dowels are installed properly, they will be the same height.

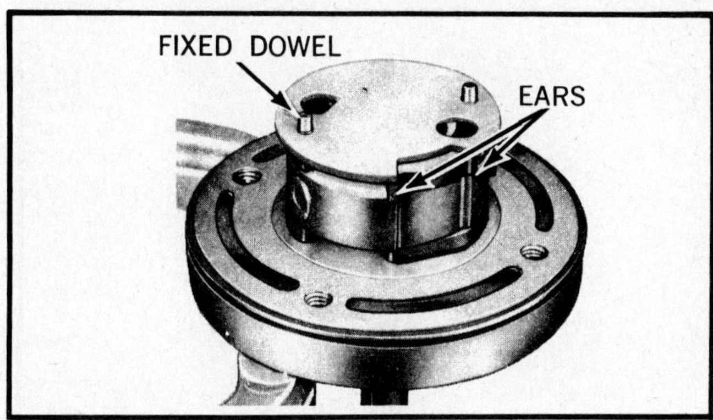

Retainer end plate installation

6. Install the upper pressure plate so the tapered notch is facing down against the cam insert. The fixed dowel should pass through the round dowel hole and the loose dowel through the long hole. The slot between the ears on the outside of the pressure plate should match the notch on the cam insert.

7. Install the retainer end plate so the slot on the end plate matches the notches on the upper pressure plate and the cam insert.

8. Install the pump valve assembly O-ring seal on the pump valve assembly. Do not twist the seal.

9. Place the pump valve assembly on top of the retainer end plate with the large exhaust slot on the pump valve in line with the outside notches of the cam, upper pressure plate, and retainer end plate. All parts must be fully seated. If correctly installed, the relief valve stem will be in line with the lube return hole in the pump housing plate.

10. Put small amounts of vaseline on the pump housing plate to hold the cover gasket in place. Install the cover gasket in place.

11. Insert the pressure plate springs into the pockets in the pump valve assembly.

12. Plug the intake hole in the housing.

13. Lubricate the inside of the housing and the housing cover seal with power steering fluid. Install two studs for use as positioning guides, one in the bolt hole nearest the drain hole and the other in the bolt hole on the opposite side of the housing plate.

14. Align the small lube hole in the housing rim and the lube hole in the housing plate. Install the housing, using a steady, even, downward pressure. Do not jar the pressure spring out of position. Remove the guide studs and loosely install the housing retaining bolts finger tight.

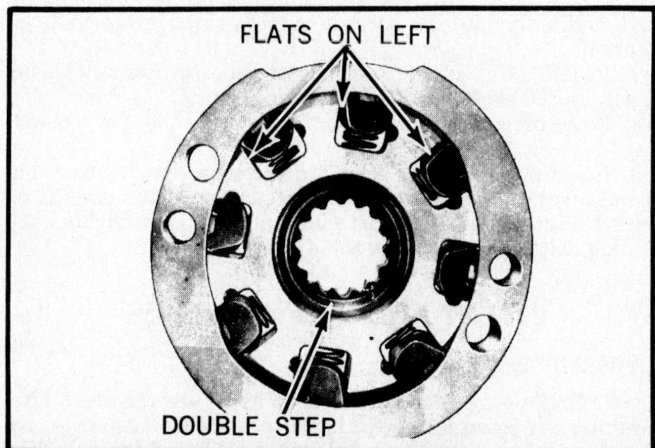

Correct slipper installation—Ford model

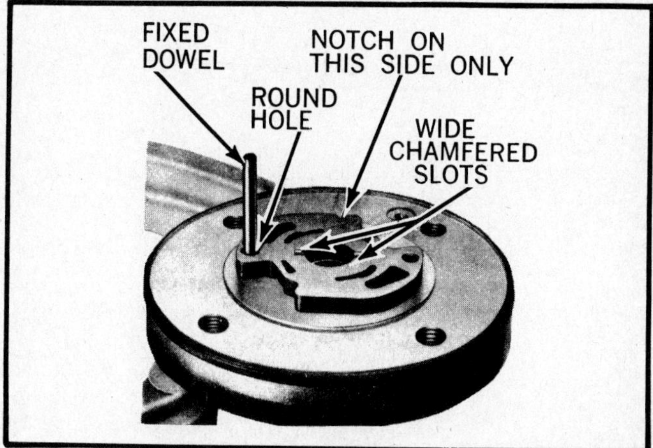

Lower pressure plate installed

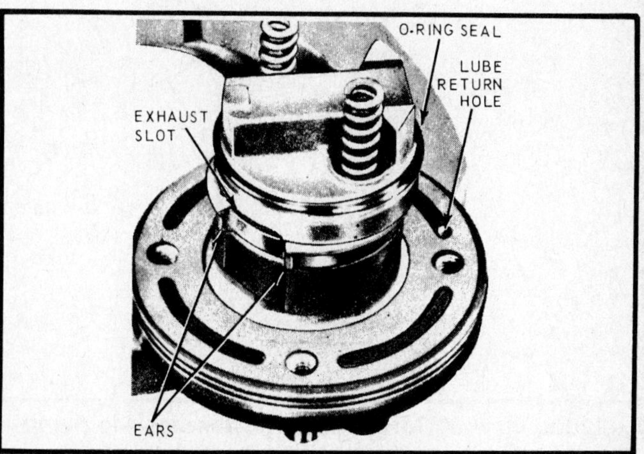

Valve and pressure spring installation

15. Tighten the retaining bolts evenly to 28–32 ft. lbs. until the housing flange contacts the gasket.

16. Install a 3/8–16 hex head screw into the end of the rotor shaft and put a torque wrench on it. Check the amount of torque needed to rotate the rotor shaft. If the torque is more than 15 inch lbs., loosen the retaining bolts slightly and rotate the rotor shaft. Then, retighten the retaining bolts evenly. Do not use the pump if the shaft torque exceeds 15 inch lbs.

17. Release the pin in the bench holding fixture and shake the pump assembly back and forth. If there is a rattle, the pressure springs have fallen out of their seats and must be reinstalled.

18. Install the reservoir O-ring seal on the housing plate without twisting it. Lubricate the seal and install the reservoir, aligning the notch in the reservoir flange with the notch in the outside edge of the pump housing plate and bushing assembly. Using only a soft-faced hammer, tap at the rear outer corners of the reservoir. Inspect the assembly to be sure the reservoir is fully seated on the housing plate.

19. Install the identification tag (if one was removed) on the outlet valve fitting. Install the outlet valve fitting nut and tighten to 48–45 ft. lbs. torque.

20. Turn the pump assembly over and install the pulley using the tool used to remove the pulley. Turn the tool nut clockwise to draw the pulley on the shaft until it is flush with the shaft end. Do not exert inward and outward pressures on the shaft to avoid damaging the internal thrust areas. Remove the tool.

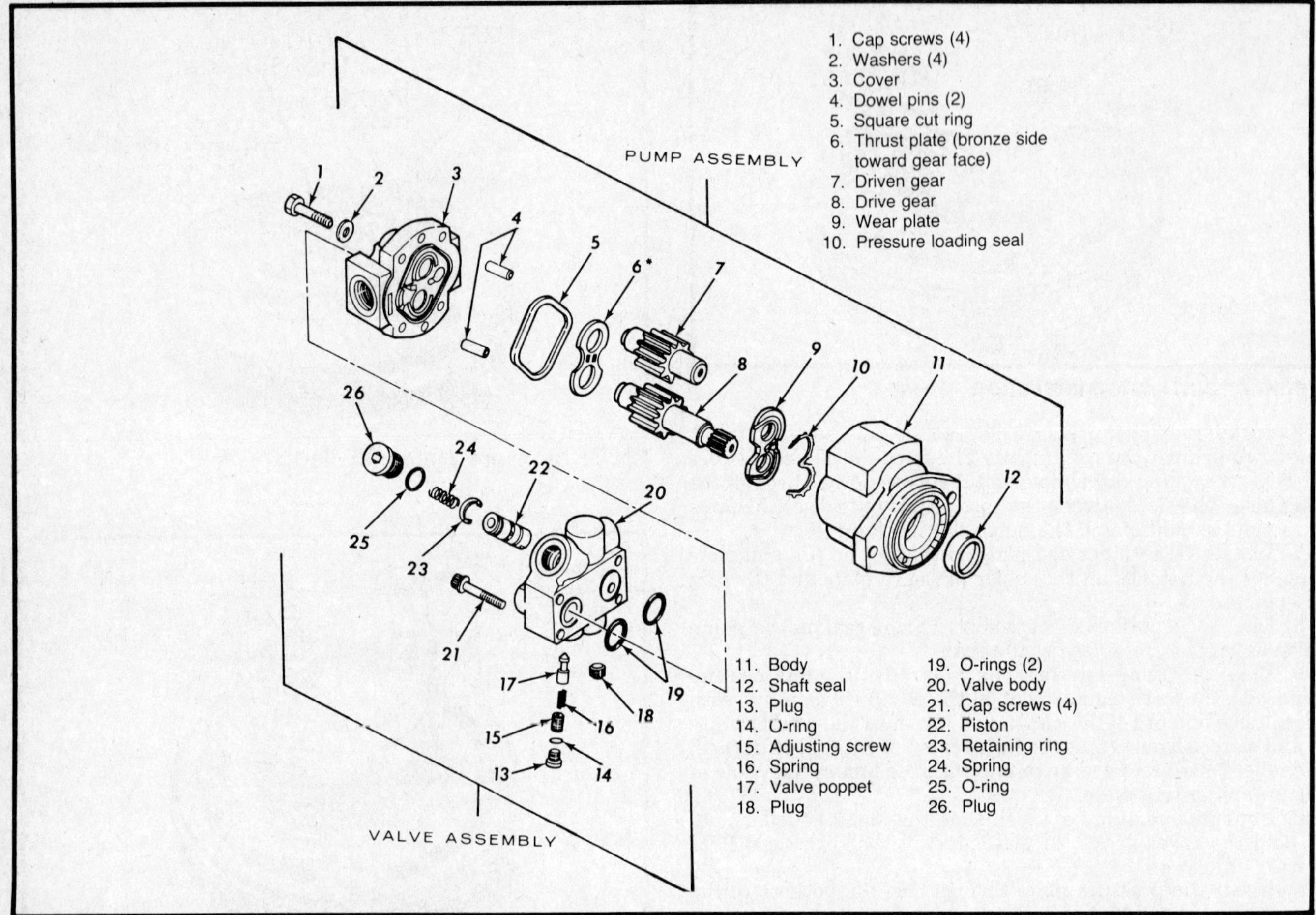

Exploded view of Borg Warner power steering pump

BORG WARNER POWER STEERING PUMP

The Borg Warner pump is a gear-type power steering pump and is used on on series of diesel engines. The pump is mounted directly to the engine and is gear driven. A bolt-on oil flow control valve is attached to the pump assembly.

VICKERS POWER STEERING PUMP

Disassembly

1. Clamp pump in vise with cover end up and remove cover screws. Lift off cover and remove O-ring.
2. If pump is equipped with flow control valve, remove plug spring and valve subassembly.
3. Remove pressure plate and spring.
4. Mark position of ring and remove it along with locating pin.
5. Separate vanes from rotor and slide rotor from shaft.
6. Turn pump body over and remove shaft key and outer bearing snap ring. Tap on splined end of shaft with a soft hammer to force it out of housing.
7. If bearing is to be removed, support the inner race and press shaft out of bearing.
8. Pull shaft seal out of body.
9. Press inner bearing out of body.

Assembly

1. Coat all parts with hydraulic fluid before assembly.
2. If flow control valve is used, assemble components into cover. If cover has a blind bore, install spring first, then valve. Install snap ring and plug. Install screen and retaining plug.
3. Press shaft into outer bearing while supporting inner race. Press inner bearing into body using a driver on the outer race.
4. Install seal. Seals should be assembled with holes facing the shaft end of the pump. Lube lip with petroleum jelly.
5. Slide driveshaft in place until outer bearing is sealed. Install bearing retaining snap ring in body.
6. Install new O-ring in body. Insert ring locating pins in body and assemble ring so that arrow points in direction of rotation.
7. Install rotor on shaft and insert vanes in rotor slots. Be sure radiused edge of vanes is toward the ring.
8. Place pressure plate over locating pins and flat against ring.
9. Insert pressure plate spring in pressure plate recess, then install cover using new O-ring. Be sure outlet port in cover is in correct position with respect to inlet port in body. Tighten attaching bolts to specified torque. Check binding.

VTM 27 AND VTM 42 SERIES

Disassembly

NOTE: Two versions of the VTM 27 are in use. The noncurrent production pump uses needle bearings on the shaft; the current models use ball bearings and dispense with the thrust spacers.

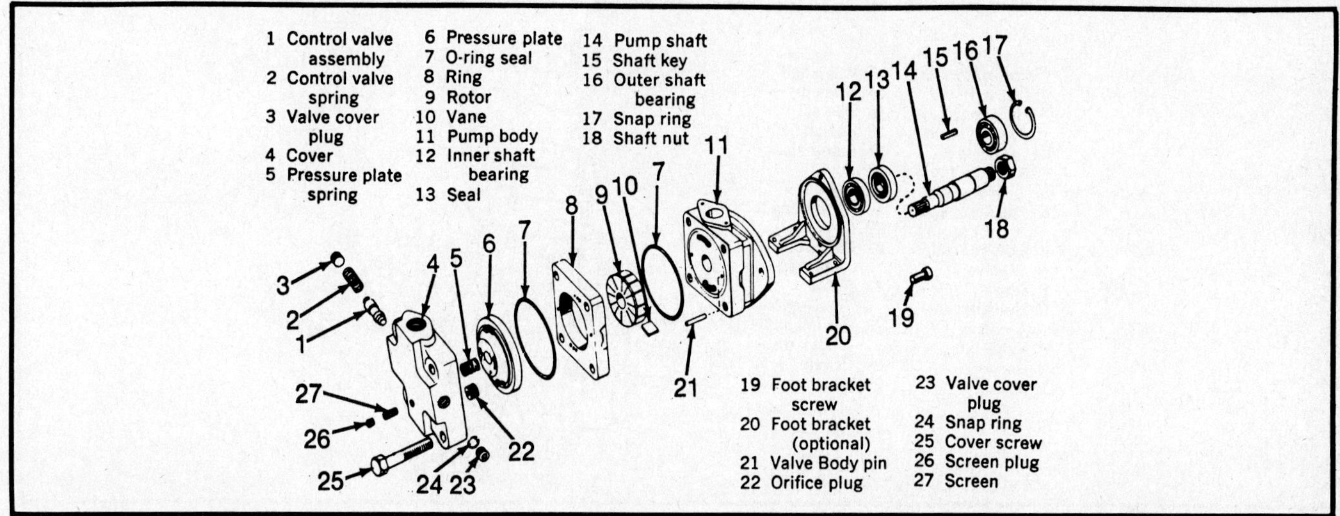

Vickers V2000 series pump

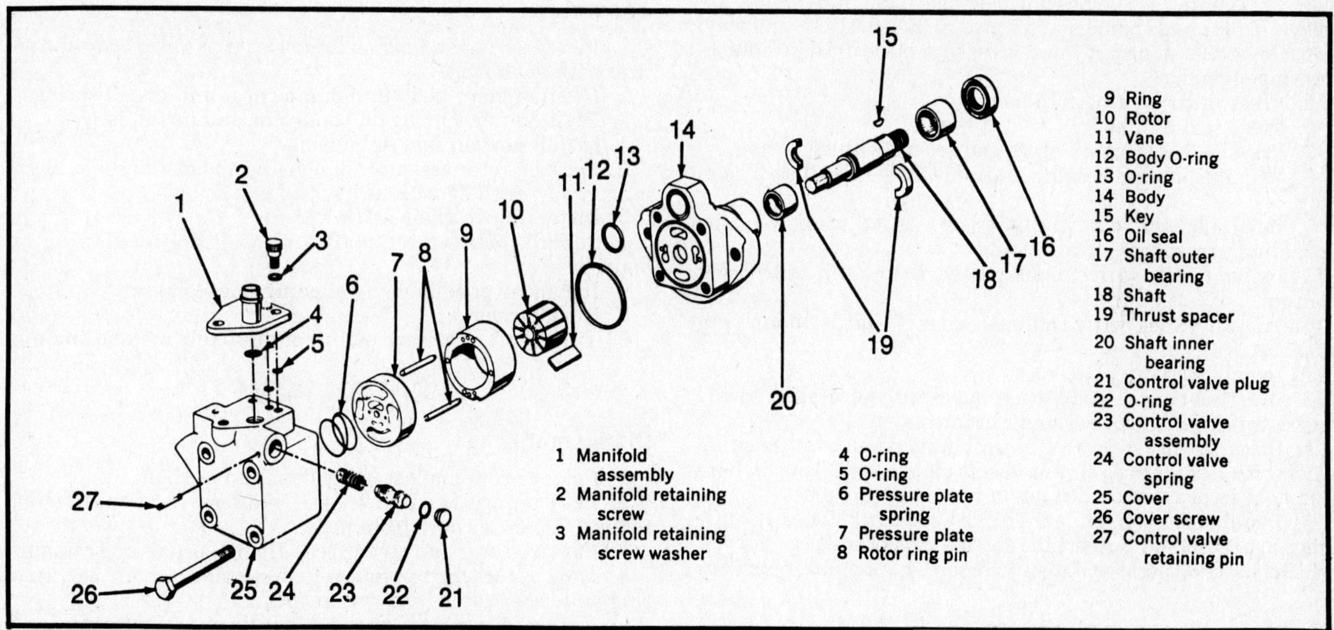

Vikers VTM27 series pump—non current models

1. If the pump has an attached reservoir, remove it before working by removing wing nut, washer, cover and gasket. Lift washer, filter retainer, spring and filter element from stud. Remove reservoir stud and nut, two reservoir retaining screws, baffle and reinforcing plate. Separate reservoir from pump. Discard O-rings.
2. If pump has manifold instead of reservoir, remove it along with attaching cap screws, copper washer and O-rings.
3. Clamp pump mounting flange in a vise with soft jaws. Remove cover attaching bolts and separate cover from body.
4. Remove pressure plate spring and pressure plate.
5. Remove ring, locating pins and rotor and vane assembly. Remove and discard O-rings found between body and cover.
6. Mount cover in a vise and drive relief valve retaining pin out. Do not allow relief valve plug and subassembly to fall from bore. Remove plug, valve and spring from bore.
7. Non-current VTM 27: support shaft outer end of pump body on a two inch pipe coupling and using an arbor press, remove the shaft assembly, shaft thrust spacers, outer needle bearing and shaft seal.
8. Current VTM 27 and all VTM 42: remove large snap ring retaining ball bearing in body. Press shaft and bearing assembly from body. Remove snap ring that retains bearing on shaft and remove bearing if not serviceable.
9. Inner bearing, if used, and seal in current production pumps, can be driven from body using a pin punch.

Assembly

NOTE: Lubricate all parts in hydraulic fluid before assembly. For non-current production VTM 27 pump, use Steps 1 thru 4 and Steps 9 thru 15. For current production VTM 27 and 42 pumps use Steps 5–15.

1. Install inner bearing by pressing into body with an arbor press.
2. Assemble thrust spacers on shaft and install shaft in pump body.

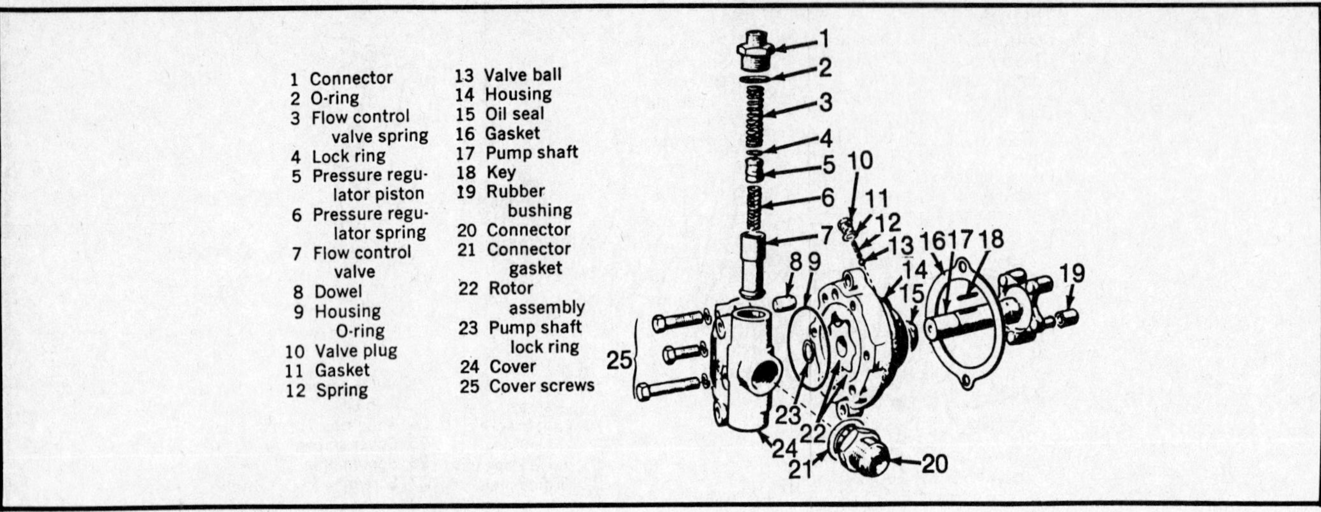

Exploded view of Scania pump

3. Press outer needle bearing over shaft and into pump body to $\frac{1}{64}$ in. past seal shoulder. This gives 0.010–0.015 in. end play.
4. Position seal on body and press into place until it contacts locating shoulder.
5. Press inner bearing into body.
6. Press seal into body.
7. Press ball bearing on shaft and secure with snap ring.
8. Install shaft and bearing assembly into body. Install snap ring.
9. Install locating pins in pump body. Install ring over pins according to direction of rotation.
10. Install rotor with chamfered edge towards inner ring contour.
11. Install vanes with radiused edge towards inner ring contour.
12. Install pressure plate.
13. Insert O-ring in body, then install pressure plate spring and cover. Tighten cover screws to torque.
14. Place spring and valve assembly in relief bore. Position valve with hex towards spring. Insert plug, with O-ring, in bore and hold in place while driving in new retaining pin.
15. Install reservoir or manifold as required. Place new O-rings over reservoir outlet tube and use copper washer on screw which enters oil passage if manifold is used. Assemble reservoir.

SCANIA PUMP

Disassembly

1. Remove cover retaining cap screws.
2. Tap cover with soft mallet to separate from housing.
3. Remove housing O-ring from groove in pump housing.
4. Remove lock ring from shaft and lift rotor assembly out of housing.
5. Remove key from shaft and tap shaft out of housing.
6. Remove oil seal.
7. Remove connector from valve body.

CAUTION

Take care when removing connector as it compresses the flow control spring and could cause injury if not restrained when unscrewed.

8. Remove flow control spring.
9. Turn cover assembly over and tap lightly to remove valve assembly.
10. Use suitable pliers and remove snap ring.
11. Remove piston and spring from valve body.

Assembly

1. Install spring and piston in flow control valve body and secure with snap ring.
2. Position valve body into pump cover and install spring.
3. Position new O-ring on connector and install in cover.
4. Install new oil seal in housing.
5. Position rotor assembly in housing and install shaft, aligning keyway in shaft with key slot in rotor.
6. Install key in shaft and rotor.
7. Install lockring on shaft and position new O-ring on housing.
8. Install cover-to-housing aligning dowelpins.
9. Install cover.
10. Turn shaft to be sure pump rotates freely with no binding.

EATON PUMP

Disassembly

1. Remove coupling assembly from pump shaft.
2. Place pumps in soft jawed vise and remove cover attaching screws. Separate cover from body.
3. Remove cover and O-ring seal. Do not lose O-ring retainer.
4. Mark rotors for reference. Remove pump shaft, key, snap ring and inner rotor from pump body.
5. Remove outer rotor by turning body over and tapping on a soft surface.
6. Slide rotor and key off pump shaft.
7. Remove oil seal from body.
8. Disassemble flow control relief valve by:
   a. Remove connector, O-ring and flow control valve spring.
   b. Tap cover on soft surface to dislodge valve assembly.
   c. Remove relief valve by pushing valve into flow control valve and removing snap ring. Remove valve and spring.

Assembly

NOTE: Lubricate all parts before assembly.

1. Install new oil seal in pump body. Press seal in place using a driver on outer edge of seal.
2. Install inner rotor and key on shaft and insert shaft and rotor assembly into body, coupling end front.
3. Place outer rotor in body. Be sure rotors are aligned according to marks made during disassembly.
4. Locate O-rings in body and insert thrust washer in cover. Place cover in position on body and tighten to torque.

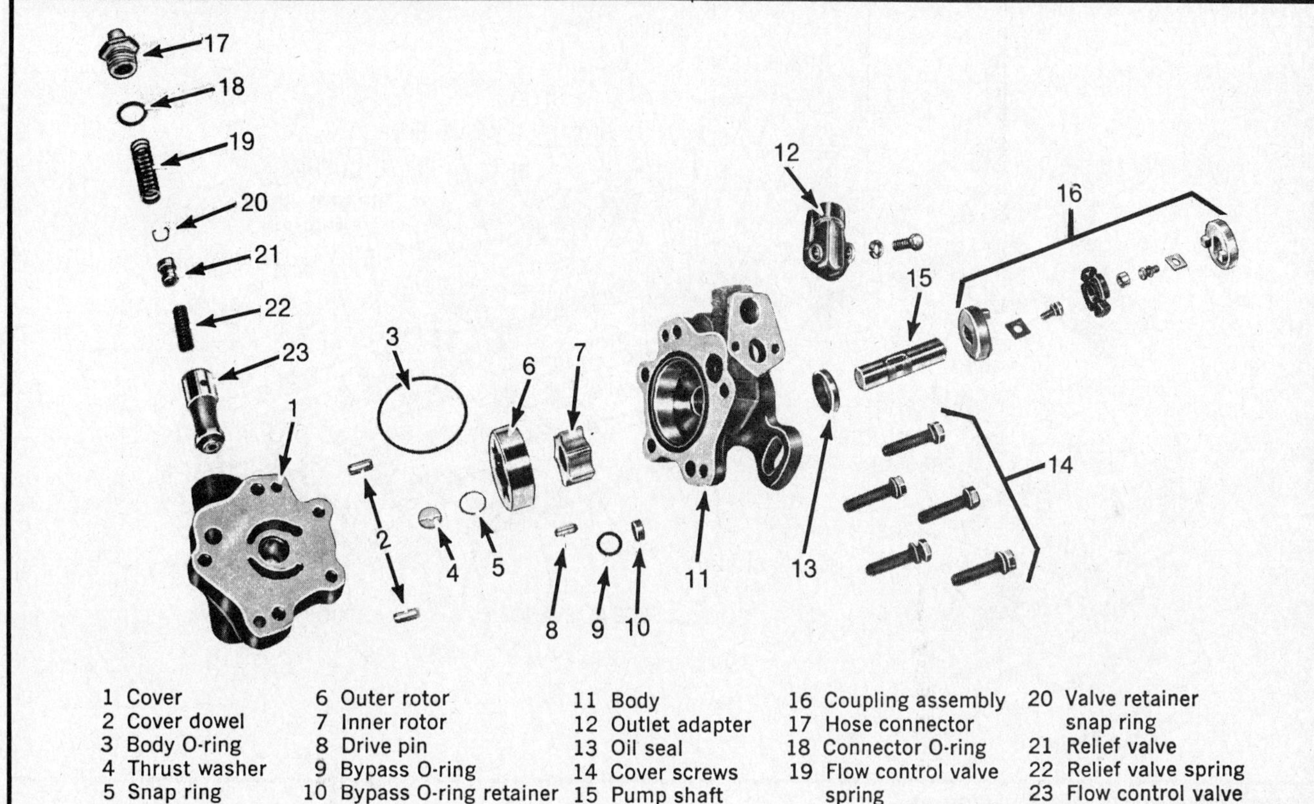

Exploded view of Eaton pump

5. Reassemble flow control relief valve by:
   a. Insert spring and relief valve into flow control valve, small end first.
   b. Push relief valve into flow control valve far enough to allow installation of snap ring.
   c. Install valve assembly into pump body, narrow land first, insert spring and install connector using new O-ring.

Bendix Linkage-Type Power Steering System

The Bendix linkage-type power steering is a hydraulically controlled system composed of an integral pump and fluid reservoir, a control valve, a power cylinder, connecting fluid lines, and the steering linkage. The hydraulic pump, which is driven by a belt turned by the engine, draws fluid from the reservoir and provides pressure through hoses to the control valve and the power cylinder. There is a pressure relief valve to limit the pressures within the steering system to a safe level. After the fluid has passed from the pump to the control valve and the power cylinder, it returns to the reservoir.

CONTROL VALVE CENTERING SPRING

Adjustment

1. Raise the truck and remove the spring cap attaching screws and remove the spring cap.

CAUTION

Be very careful not to position the hoist adapters of two post hoists under the suspension and/or steering components. Place the hoist adapters under the front suspension lower arms.

2. Tighten the adjusting nut snug (about 90–100 inch lbs.); then, loosen the nut ¼ turn (90 degrees). Do not turn the adjusting nut too tight.
3. Place the spring cap on the valve housing. Lubricate and install the attaching screws and washers. Tighten the screws to 72–100 inch lbs. torque.
4. Lower the truck and start the engine. Check the steering effort using a spring scale attached to the steering wheel rim for a pull of no more than 12 lbs.

POWER STEERING CONTROL VALVE

Removal

1. Raise the truck and support safely. If a two post hoist is used, be sure to place the hoist adapters under the front suspension steering arms. Do not allow the hoist adapters to contact the steering linkage.
2. Disconnect the four fluid line fittings at the control valve and drain the fluid from the lines. Turn the front wheels back and forth to force all the fluid from the system.
3. Loosen the clamping nut and bolt at the right end of the sleeve.
4. Remove the roll pin from the steering arm-to-idler arm rod through the slot in the sleeve.
5. Remove the control valve ball stud nut.
6. Remove the ball stud from the sector shaft arm.
7. After turning the front wheels fully to the left, unthread the control valve from the center link steering arm-to-idler arm rod.

Installation

1. Thread the valve on the center link until about four threads are still visible.

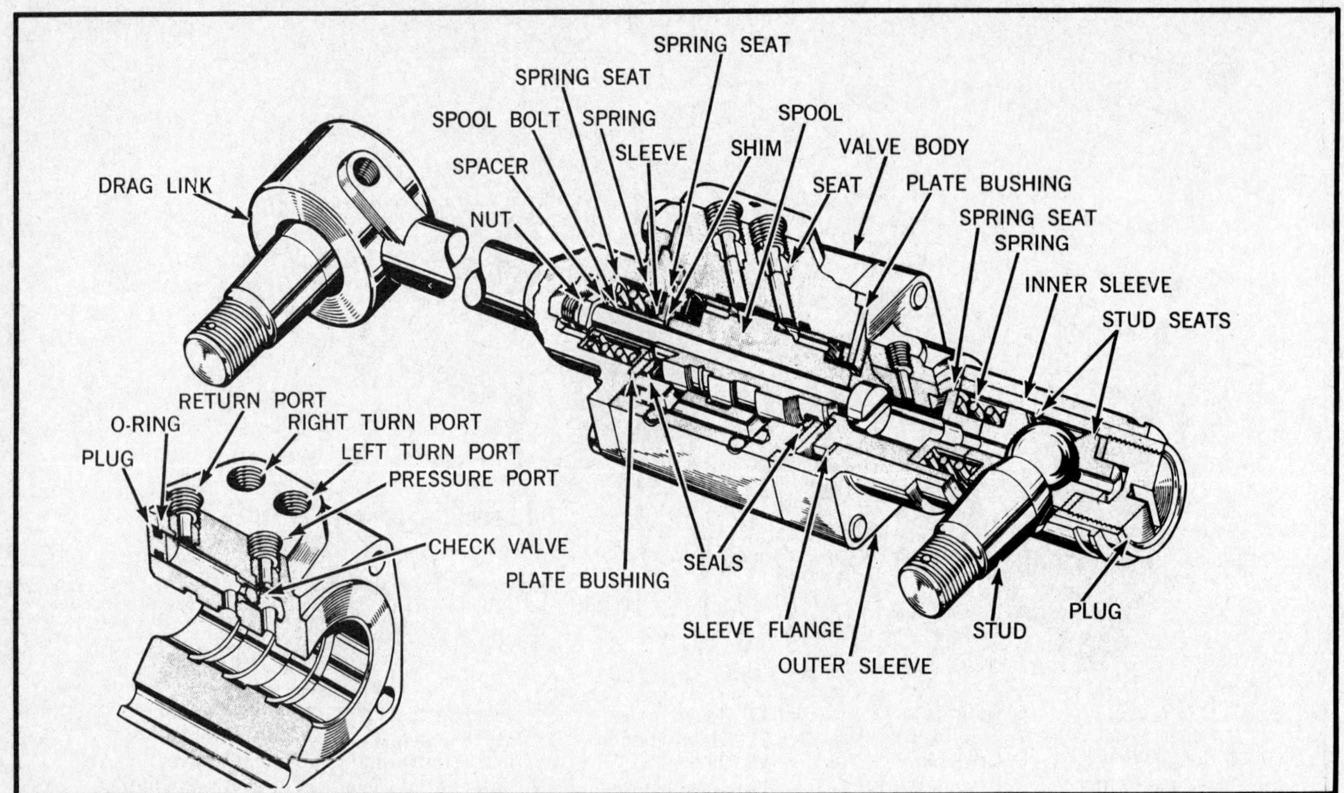

Control valve cross section—typical

2. Position the ball stud in the sector shaft arm.
3. Measure the distance between the grease plug in the sleeve and the stud at the inner end of the left spindle connecting rod. If the distance is not correct, disconnect the ball stud from the sector shaft arm and turn the valve on the center link until the correct distance is obtained.
4. When the distance is correct and the ball stud is positioned in the sector shaft arm, align the hole in the steering arm-to-idler arm rod with the slot near the end of the valve sleeve. Install the roll pin in the rod hole to lock the valve in place on the rod.
5. Tighten the valve sleeve clamp bolt to the proper torque.
6. Install the ball stud nut and tighten to the proper torque. Install a new cotter pin.
7. Connect all fluid lines to the control valve and tighten all fittings securely. Do not over-tighten.
8. Fill the fluid reservoir with power steering fluid to the full mark on the dipstick.
9. Start the engine and run it for a few minutes to warm the fluid in the power steering system. Turn the steering wheel back and forth to the stops and check the system for leaks.
10. Increase the engine idle speed to about 1000 rpm. Turn the steering wheel back and forth several times, then stop the engine. Check the control valve and hose connections for leaks.
11. Recheck the fluid level and add fluid if necessary.
12. Start the engine again, and check the position of the steering wheel when the front wheels are straight ahead. Do not make any adjustments until toe-in is checked.
13. With engine running, check front wheel toe-in.
14. Check steering wheel turning effort which should be equal in both directions.

POWER STEERING POWER CYLINDER

Removal and Installation

1. Disconnect the two fluid lines from the power cylinder and drain the fluid.
2. Remove the pal nut, attaching nut, washer and the insulator from the end of the power cylinder rod. Remove the cotter pin and castellated nut holding the power cylinder stud to the center link.
3. Disconnect the power cylinder stud from the center link.
4. Remove the insulator sleeve and washer from the end of the power cylinder.
5. Inspect the tube fittings and seats in the power cylinder for nicks, burrs, or other damage. Replace the seats or tubes if damaged.
6. Install the washer, sleeve and the insulator on the end of the power cylinder rod.
7. While extending the rod as far as possible, insert the rod in the bracket on the frame and then, compress the rod so the stud may be inserted in the center link. Secure the stud with the castellated nut and a new cotter pin.
8. Install the insulator, washer, nut, and a pal nut on the power cylinder rod.
9. Connect the two fluid lines to their proper ports on the power cylinder.
10. Fill the reservoir with power steering fluid to the full mark on the dipstick. Start the engine and run for a few minutes to warm the fluid. Turn the steering wheel back and forth to the stops to fill the system. Stop the engine.
11. Recheck the fluid level and add fluid if necessary. Check for fluid leaks.
12. Start the engine again, turn the steering wheel back and forth, and check for leaks while the engine is running.

CONTROL VALVE

Disassembly

1. Clean the outside of the control valve of dirt and fluid.
2. Remove the centering spring cap from the valve housing. The control valve should be put in a soft-faced bench vise during

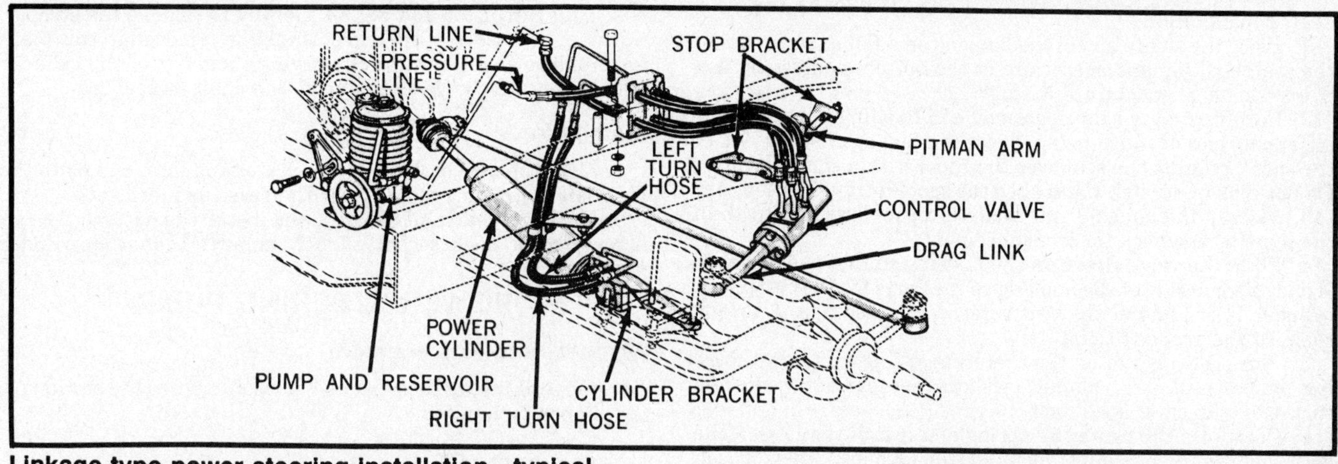

Linkage type power steering installation—typical

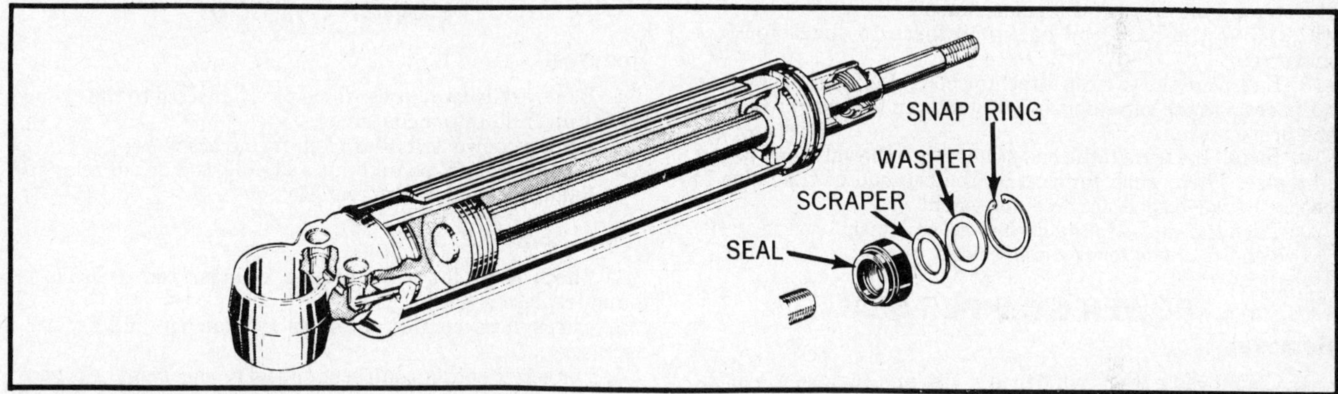

Power cylinder—typical

disassembly. Clamp the control valve around the sleeve flange only to avoid damaging the valve housing, spool, or sleeve.

3. Remove the nut from the end of the valve spool bolt. Remove the washers, spacer, centering spring, adapter, and the bushing from the bolt and valve housing.

4. Remove the two bolts holding the valve housing and the sleeve together. Separate the valve housing and the sleeve.

5. Remove the plug from the sleeve. Push the valve spool out of the centering spring end of the valve housing, and remove the seal from the spool.

6. Remove the spacer, bushing and valve housing.

7. Drive the pin out of the travel regulator stop with a punch and hammer. Pull the head of the valve spool bolt tightly against the travel regulator stop before driving the pin out of the stop.

8. Turn the travel regulator stop counterclockwise in the valve sleeve to remove the stop from the sleeve.

9. Remove the valve spool bolt, spacer, and rubber washer from the travel regulator stop.

10. Remove the rubber boot and clamp from the valve sleeve. Slide the bumper, spring, and ball stud seat out of the valve sleeve and remove the ball stud socket from the sleeve.

11. Remove the return port hose seat and the return port relief valve.

12. Remove the spring plug and O-ring. Then remove the reaction limiting valve.

13. Replace all worn or damaged hose seats by using an Easy-Out screw extractor or a bolt of proper size as a puller. Tap the existing hole in the hose seat, using a starting tap of the correct size. Remove all metal chips from the hose seat after tapping. Place a nut and washer on a bolt of the same size as the tapped hole. The washer must be large enough to cover the hose seat port. Insert the bolt in the tapped hole and remove the hose seat by turning the nut clockwise and drawing the bolt out. Install a new hose seal in the port, and thread a bolt of the correct size in the port. Tighten the bolt enough to bottom the seal in the port.

Assembly

1. Coat all parts of the control valve assembly with power steering fluid. Seals should be coated with lubricant before installation.

2. Install the reaction limiting valve, spring and plug. Install the return port relief valve and the hose seat.

3. Insert one of the ball stud seats (flat end first) into the ball stud socket, and insert the threaded end of the ball stud into the socket.

4. Place the socket in the control valve sleeve so that the threaded end of the ball stud can be pulled out through the slot.

5. Place the other ball stud seat, spring, and bumper in the socket. Install and securely tighten the travel regulator stop.

6. Loosen the stop just enough to align the nearest hole in the stop with the slot in the ball stud socket and install the stop pin in the ball stud socket, travel regulator stop, and valve spool bolt.

7. Install the rubber boot, clamp, and the plug on the control valve sleeve. Be sure the lubrication fitting is turned on tightly and does not bind on the ball stud socket.

8. Insert the valve spool in the valve housing, rotating it while installing it.

9. Move the spool toward the centering spring end of the housing, and place the small seal bushing and spacer in the sleeve end of the housing.

10. Press the valve spool against the inner lip of the seal and, at the same time, guide the lip of the seal over the spool with a small screwdriver. Do not nick or scratch the seal or the spool

during installation.

11. Place the sleeve end of the housing on a flat surface so that the seal, bushing and spacer are at the bottom end; then push down the valve spool until it stops.

12. Carefully install the spool seal and bushing in the centering spring end of the housing. Press the seal against the end of the spool, guiding the seal over the spool with a small flat tool. Do not nick or scratch the seal or the spool during installation.

13. Pick up the housing, and slide the spool back and forth in the housing to check for free movement.

14. Place the valve sleeve on the housing so that the ball stud is on the same side of the housing as the ports for the two power cylinder lines. Install the two bolts in the sleeve, and torque them to the proper torque.

15. Place the adapter on the centering spring end of the housing, and install the bushing, washers, spacers and centering spring on the valve spool bolt.

16. Compress the centering spring and install the nut on the bolt. Tighten the nut snug (about 90–100 inch lbs.); then, loosen it not more than 1/4 turn. Do not over-tighten to avoid breaking the stop pin at the travel regulator stop.

17. Move the ball stud back and forth to check for free movement.

18. Lubricate the two cap attaching bolts. Install the centering spring cap on the valve housing, and tighten the two cap bolts to the proper torque.

19. Install the nut on the ball stud so that the valve can be put in a vise. Then, push forward on the cap end of the valve to check the valve spool for free movement.

20. Turn the valve around in the vise, and push forward on the sleeve end to check for free movement.

POWER CYLINDER SEAL

Removal

1. Clamp the power cylinder in a vise and remove the snap-ring from the end of the cylinder. Do not distort or crack the cylinder in the vise.

2. Pull the piston rod out all the way to remove the scraper, bushing, and seals. If the seals cannot be removed in this manner, remove them by carefully prying them out of the cylinder with a sharp pick. Do not damage the shaft or seal seat.

Installation

1. Coat the new seals with power steering fluid and place the parts on the piston rod. Coat with grease or lubricant.

2. Push the rod in all the way, and install the parts in the cylinder with a deep socket slightly smaller than the cylinder opening.

POWER STEERING PUMP

Removal and Replacement

To remove or install the power steering pump, see the section on the slipper type pump.

Saginaw Linkage-Type Power Cylinder

Removal

1. Remove the two hoses which are connected to the cylinder and drain fluid into a container.
2. Remove power cylinder from frame bracket.
3. Remove cotter pin and nut and pull stud out of relay rod.
4. Remove cylinder from vehicle.

Inspection

1. Check seals for leaks around cylinder rod. If leaks are found, replace seals.
2. Check hose connection seats for damage and replace if necessary.
3. For service other than seat or seal replacement, it is necessary to replace the power cylinder.
4. The ball stud may be replaced by removing snap-ring.

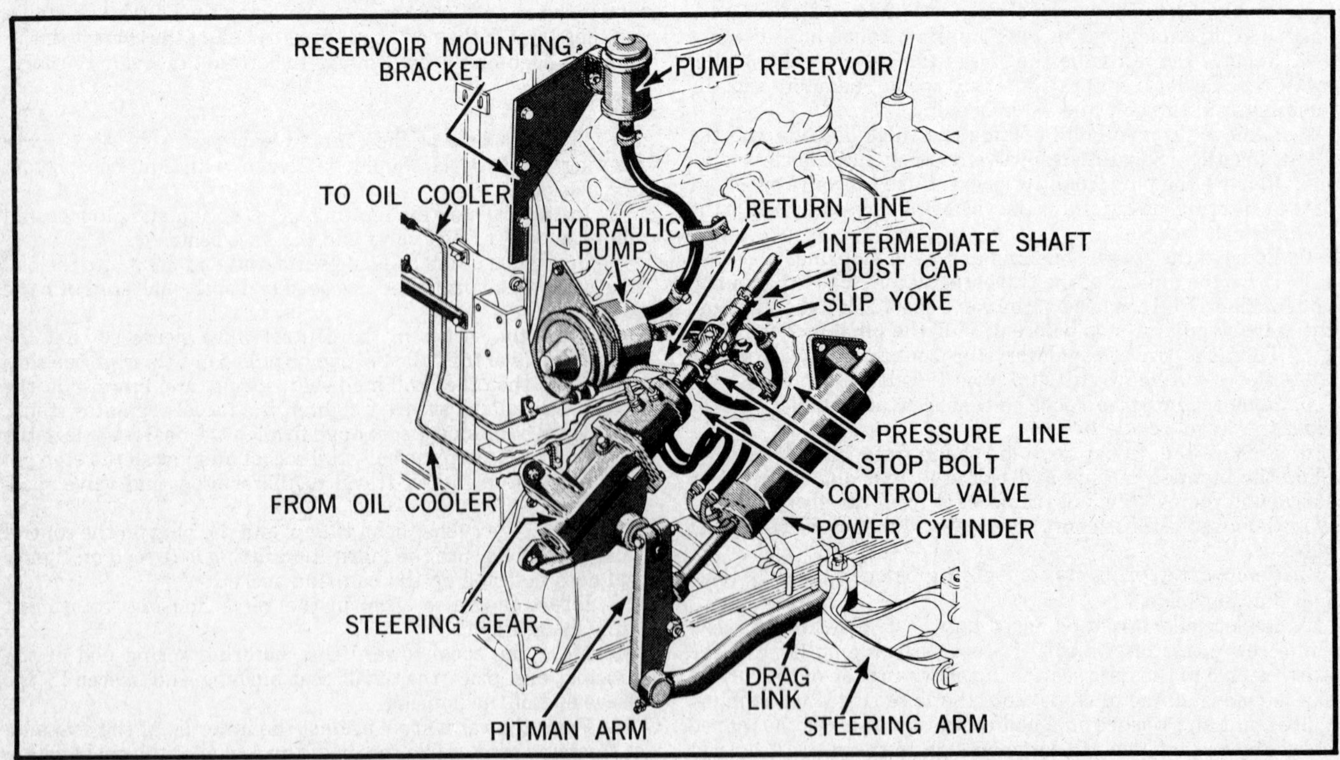

General Motors power steering system—tilt cab

Disassembly and Assembly

1. To remove piston rod seal, remove snap-ring and pull out on rod. Remove back-up washer, piston rod scraper and piston rod seal from rod.
2. To remove the ball stud, depress the end plug and remove the snap-ring. Push on the end of the ball stud and the end plug, spring, spring seat, ball stud and seal may be removed. If the ball seat is to be replaced, it must be pressed out.
3. Reverse disassembly procedure. Be sure snap-ring is properly seated.

Installation

1. Install power cylinder on vehicle in reverse of removal procedure.
2. Reconnect the hydraulic lines, fill system and bleed out air as described in the installation and balancing section of control valve servicing.

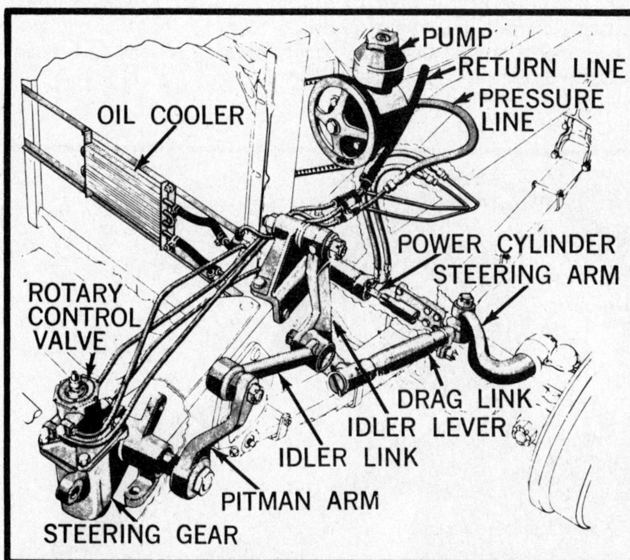

General Motors power steering system—conventional cab—typical

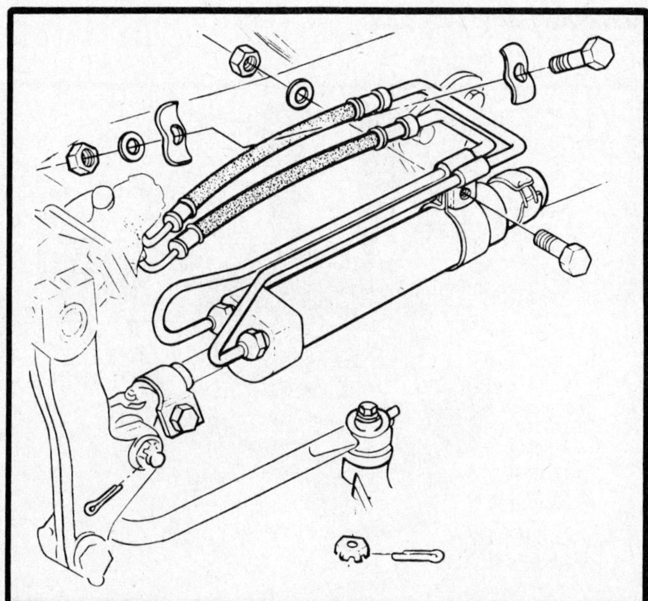

General Motors side mounted power cylinder

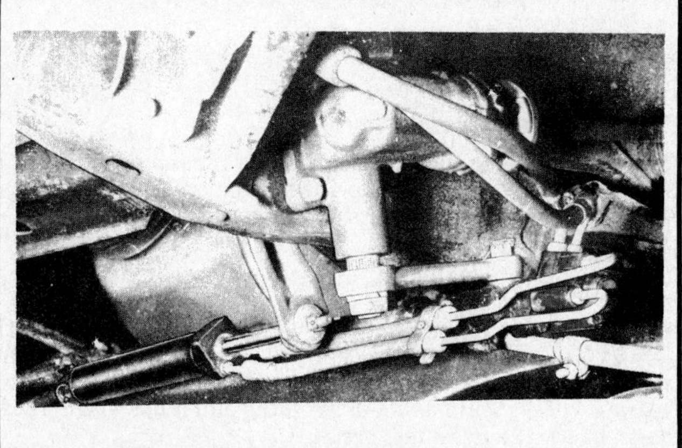

Typical light duty power cylinder

POWER STEERING HOSES

Carefully inspect the hoses. When installing, be sure to place in such a position as to avoid all chafing or other abuse when making sharp turns.

Saginaw Rotary-Type Power Steering

The rotary-type power steering gear is designed with all components in one housing.

The power cylinder is an integral part of the gear housing. A double-acting type piston allows oil pressure to be applied to either side of the piston. The one-piece piston and power rack is meshed to the sector shaft.

The hydraulic control valve is composed of a sleeve and valve spool. The spool is held in the neutral position by the torsion bar and spool actuator. Twisting of the torsion bar moves the valve spool, allowing oil pressure to be directed to either side of the power piston, depending upon the directional rotation of the steering wheel, to give power assist.

On many trucks of the General Motors Corporation, a modified version of the rotary valve power steering system provides variable ratio steering to assist the driver to steer the truck easier and safer. The steering gear ratio will vary from a high ratio of about 16:1 while steering straight ahead to a lower gear ratio of about 12.1:1 while making a full turn to either side.

ROLLER PUMP

Removal

Remove the reservoir cover and use a suction gun to empty the reservoir. Disconnect the hoses from the pump and tie them in a raised position to prevent oil drainage. Loosen the pump adjusting screw and remove the pump belt, then take out the retaining bolts and remove the pump and reservoir.

Installation

Position the pump assembly and install the retaining bolts. Be sure there is clearance between the pump bracket and the engine front support bracket. Install the hoses and place the pump belt on the pulley. Adjust the belt to ½ in. deflection, then tighten the adjusting screw.

Connect the hoses to the pump assembly. Fill the reservoir to within ½ in. of the top with Dexron® II automatic transmission fluid.

Start the engine and rotate the steering wheel several times to the right and left to expel air from the system, then recheck the oil level and install the reservoir cover.

POWER STEERING UNIT

This unit uses Dexron®II automatic transmission fluid. The fluid capacity is 4½ pints.

Bleeding the System

Fill the pump reservoir to within ½ in. of the top. Start and run the engine to attain normal operating temperatures. Now, turn the steering wheel through its entire travel three or four times to expel air from the system, then recheck the fluid level.

Checking Steering Effort

Run the engine to attain normal operating temperatures. With the wheels on a dry floor, hook a pull scale to the spoke of the steering wheel at the outer edge. The effort required to turn the steering wheel should be 3½–5 lbs. If the pull is not within these limits, check the hydraulic pressure.

Pressure Test

To check the hydraulic pressure, disconnect the pressure hose from the gear. Now connect the pressure gauge between the pressure hose from the pump and the steering gear housing. Run the engine to attain normal operating temperatures, then turn the wheel to a full right and a full left turn to the wheel stops.

Hold the wheel in this position only long enough to obtain an accurate reading.

The pressure gauge reading should be within the limits specified. If the pressure reading is less than the minimum needed for proper operation, close the valve at the gauge and see if the reading increases. If the pressure is still low, the pump is defective and needs repair. If the pressure reading is at or near the minimum reading, the pump is normal and needs only an adjustment of the power steering gear or power assist control valve.

WORM BEARING PRELOAD AND SECTOR MESH

Adjustment

Disconnect the pitman arm from the sector shaft, then back off on the sector shaft adjusting screw on the sector shaft cover.

Center the steering on the high point, then attach a pull scale to the spoke of the steering wheel at the outer edge. The pull required to keep the wheel moving for one complete turn should be ½–⅔ lbs.

If the pull is not within these limits, loosen the thrust bearing locknut and tighten or back off on the valve sleeve adjuster locknut to bring the preload within limits. Tighten the thrust bearing locknut and recheck the preload.

Slowly rotate the steering wheel several times, then center the steering on the high point. Now, turn the sector shaft adjusting screw until a steering wheel pull of 1–1½ lbs. is required to move the worm through the center point. Tighten the sector shaft adjusting screw locknut and recheck the sector mesh adjustment.

Install the pitman arm and draw the arm in position with the nut.

Service Operations

ADJUSTER PLUG AND ROTARY VALVE

Removal

1. Thoroughly clean exterior of gear assembly. Drain by holding valve ports down and rotating worm back and forth through entire travel.
2. Place gear in vise.
3. Loosen adjuster plug locknut with punch. Remove adjuster plug with spanner.
4. Remove rotary valve assembly by grasping stub shaft and pulling it out.

ADJUSTER PLUG

Disassembly and Assembly

1. Remove upper thrust bearing retainer with screwdriver. Be careful not to damage bearing bore. Discard retainer. Remove spacer, upper bearing and races.
2. Remove and discard adjuster plug O-ring.
3. Remove stub shaft seal retaining ring (Truarc pliers will help) and remove and discard dust seal.
4. Remove stub shaft seal by prying out and discard.
5. Examine needle bearing and, if required, remove same by pressing from thrust bearing end.
6. Inspect thrust bearing spacer, bearing rollers and races.
7. Reassemble in reverse of above.

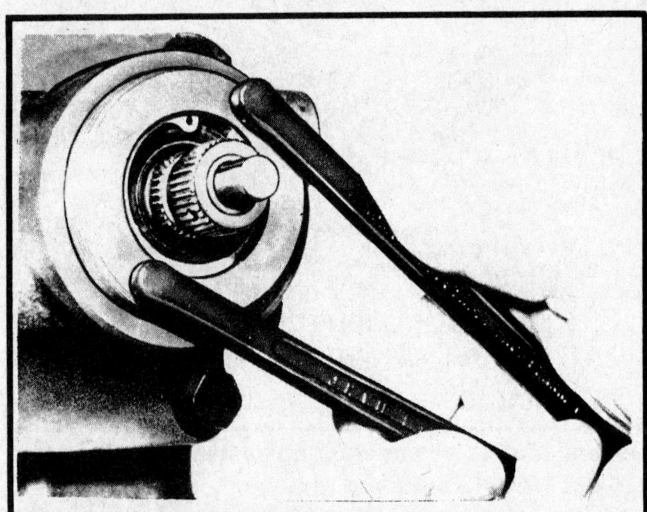

Removing adjuster plug

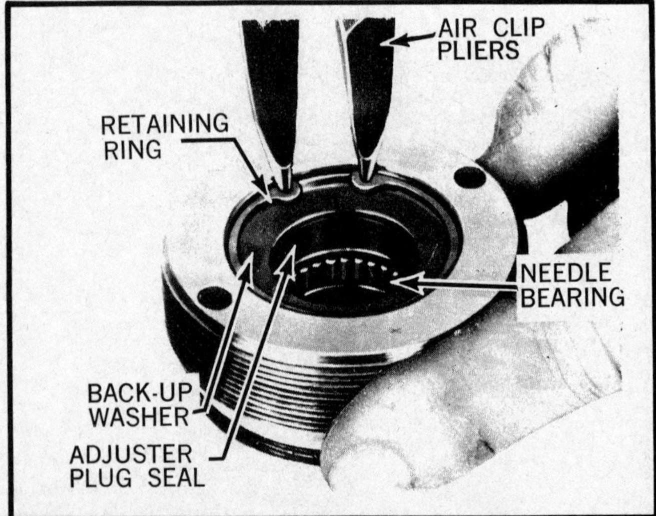

Removing adjsuter plug seal retainer ring

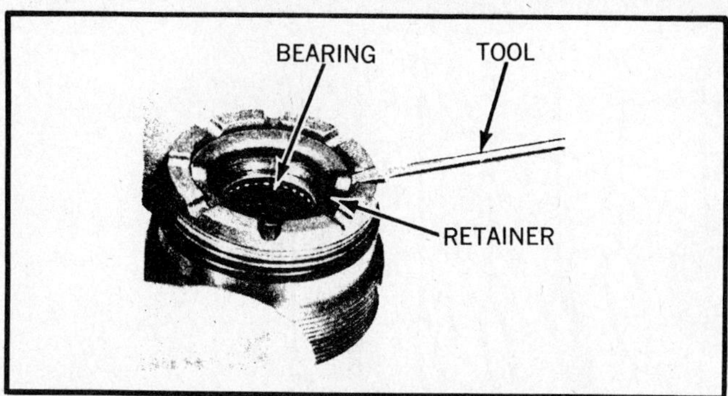

Exploded view of adjuster plug asembly

ROTARY VALVE

Disassembly

Repairs are seldom needed. Do not disassemble unless absolutely necessary. If the O-ring seal on valve spool dampener needs replacement, perform this portion of operation only.

1. Remove cap-to-worm O-ring seal and discard.
2. Remove valve spool spring by prying on small coil with a small tool to work spring onto bearing surface of stub shaft. Slide spring off shaft. Be careful not to damage shaft surface.
3. Remove valve spool by holding the valve assembly in one hand with the stub shaft pointing down. Insert the end of pencil or wood rod through opening in valve body cap and push spool until it is out far enough to be removed. In this procedure, rotate to prevent jamming. If spool becomes jammed it may be necessary to remove stub shaft, torsion bar and cap assembly.

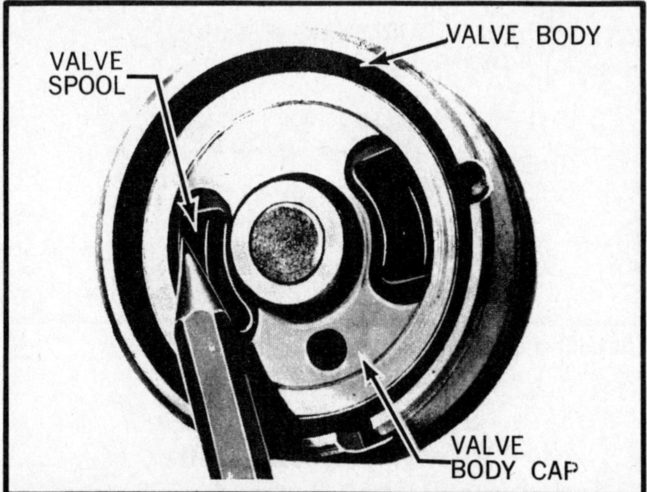

Separating valve spool from valve body

Assembly

NOTE: All parts must be free and clear of dirt, chips, etc., before assembly and must be protected after.

1. Lubricate three new back-up O-ring seals with automatic transmission oil and reassemble in the ring grooves of valve body. Assemble three new valve body rings in the grooves over the O-ring seals by carefully slipping over the valve body.

NOTE: If the valve body rings seem loose or twisted in the grooves, the heat of the oil during operation will cause them to straighten.

2. Lubricate a new dampener O-ring with automatic transmission fluid and install in valve spool groove.
3. Assemble stub shaft torsion bar and cap assembly in the valve body, aligning the groove in the valve cap with the pin in the valve body. Tap lightly with soft remainder of assembly. Valve body pin must be in the cap groove. Hold parts together during the remainder of assembly.
4. Lubricate spool. With notch in spool toward valve body, slide the spool over the stub shaft. Align the notch on the spool with the spool drive pin on stub shaft and carefully engage spool in valve body bore. Push spool evenly and with slight rotating motion until it reaches the drive pin. Rotate slowly, with some pressure, until notch engages pin. Be sure dampener O-ring seal is evenly distributed in the spool groove.

CAUTION

Use extreme care because spool to valve body clearance is very small. Damage is easily caused.

5. With seal protector over stub shaft, slide valve spool spring over shaft, with small diameter of spring going over shaft last. Work spring onto shaft until small coil is located in stub shaft groove.
6. Lubricate a new cap to O-ring seal and install in valve body.

ADJUSTER PLUG AND ROTARY VALVE

Installation

1. Align narrow pin slot on valve body with valve body drive pin on the worm. Insert the valve assembly into gear housing by pressing against valve body with finger tips. Do not press on stub shaft or torsion bar. The return hole in the gear housing should be fully visible when properly assembled.

CAUTION

Do not press on stub shaft as this may cause shaft and cap to pull out of valve body, allowing the spool dampener O-ring seal to slip into valve body oil grooves.

2. With seal protector over end of stub shaft, install adjuster plug assembly into gear housing snugly with spanner, then back plug off approximately one-eighth turn. Install plug locknut but do not tighten. Adjust preload as described in the adjustment section.
3. After adjustment, tighten locknut.

PITMAN SHAFT

Removal and Installation

1. Completely drain the gear assembly and thoroughly clean the outside.
2. Place gear in vise.
3. Rotate stub shaft until pitman shaft gear is in center position. Remove side cover retaining bolts.
4. Tap end of pitman shaft with soft hammer and slide shaft out of housing.
5. Remove and discard side cover O-ring seal.
6. The seals, washers, retainers and bearings may now be removed and examined.
7. Examine all parts for wear or damage and replace as required.
8. Install in reverse of above. Make proper adjustment as described in adjustment section.

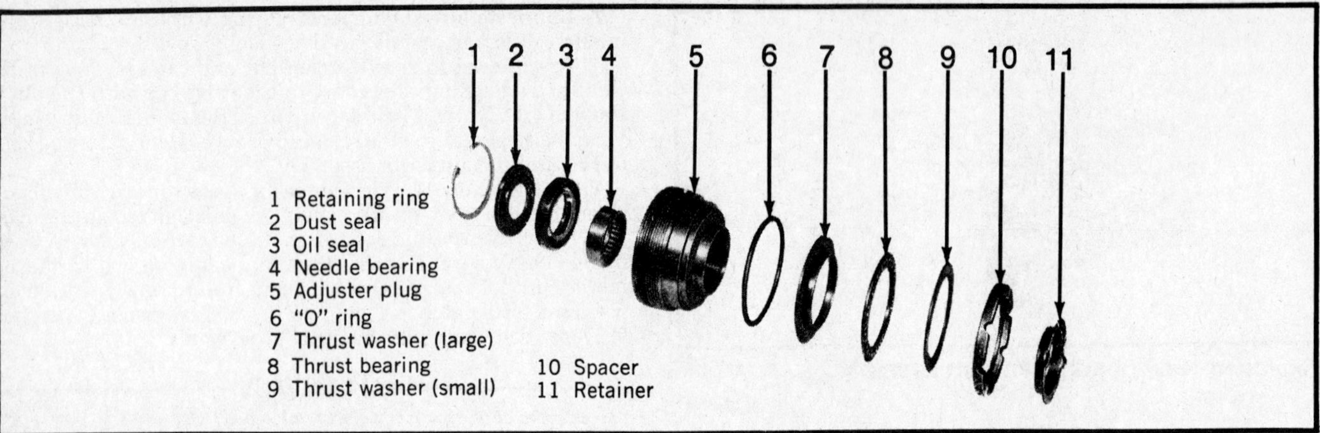

Removing thrust bearing retainer

RACK-PISTON NUT AND WORM ASSEMBLY

Removal

1. Completely drain the gear assembly and thoroughly clean the outside.
2. Remove pitman shaft assembly as previously described.
3. Rotate housing end plug retaining ring so that one end of ring is over hole in gear housing. Spring one end of ring so pin punch can be inserted to lift it out.
4. Rotate stub shaft to full left turn position to force end plug out of housing.
5. Remove and discard housing end plug O-ring seal.
6. Remove rack-piston nut end plug with ½ square drive.
7. Insert special tool in end of worm. Turn stub shaft so that rack-piston nut will go into tool and then remove rack-piston nut from gear housing.
8. Remove adjuster plug and rotary valve assemblies as previously described.
9. Remove worm and lower thrust bearing and races.
10. Remove cap O-ring seal and discard.

RACK-PISTON NUT AND WORM

Disassembly and Assembly

1. Remove and discard piston ring and back-up O-ring on rack piston nut.
2. Remove ball guide clamp and return guide.
3. Place nut on clean cloth and remove ball retaining tool. Make sure all balls are removed.
4. Inspect all parts for wear, nicks, scoring or burrs. If worm or rack-pinion nut need replacing, both must be replaced as a matched pair.
5. In reassembling reverse the above.

NOTE: When assembling, alternate black and white balls, and install guide and clamp. Packing with grease helps in holding during assembly. When new balls are used, various sizes are available and a selection must be made to secure proper torque when making the high point adjustment.

RACK-PISTON NUT AND WORM ASSEMBLY

Installation

1. Install in reverse of removal procedure.
2. In all cases use new O-ring seals.
3. Make adjustments as previously described.

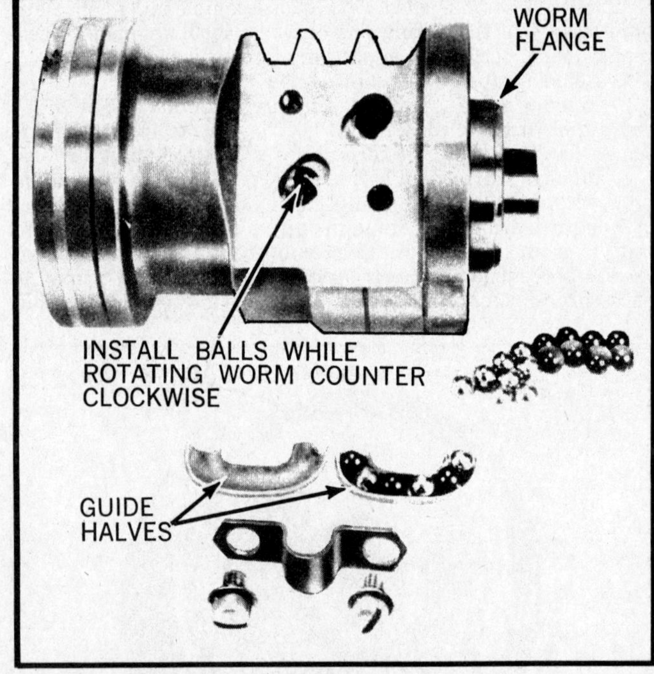

Installing balls in rack piston

Saginaw Model 605 Power Steering Gear

This is a recirculating ball type power steering gear used on light duty Chevrolet and GMC trucks between 1982–83.

Disassembly

1. Remove the pitman arm.
2. Remove the retaining ring.
3. Start the engine and turn the wheels fully to the right to force the seals and washers out. Turn off the engine.
4. The stub shaft seals may be removed by removing the retaining ring and dust seal then wraping a piece of 0.005 to 0.008 in. shim stock around the shaft and inserting it between the shaft and sealing lip until it bottoms. Pry out the seal.
5. Remove the pitman shaft and side cover by removing the preload adjuster nut (left hand thread). Rotate the shaft to the center gear, then tap on the threaded end of the pitman shaft with a plastic hammer and remove it.

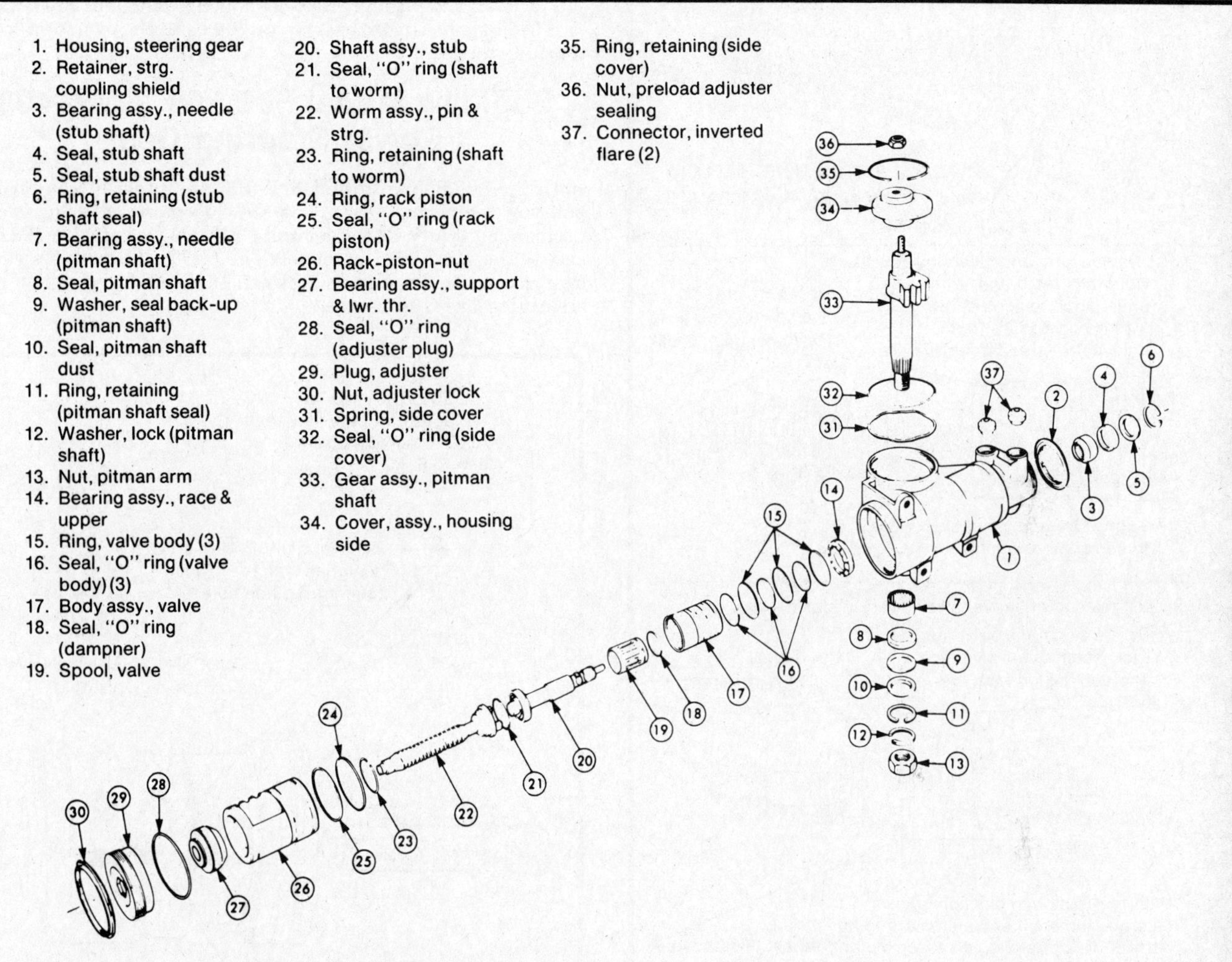

Exploded view of the Model 605 power steering gear

6. The lower bearing and adjuster may be removed by loosening the locknut with a punch against the edge of one slot, then remove the adjuster plug with a 17 mm hexagon driver.
7. Remove the rack piston and valve assembly.
8. Unscrew the valve and worm from the rack and remove the teflon ring and O-ring seal from the rack piston.
9. Remove the retaining ring and remove the valve assembly from the worm assembly.
10. Disassemble the valve by tapping the shaft lightly on a block of wood.
11. Rotate and remove the spool.
12. Disengage the pin on the shaft at the hole in the spool and remove the stub shaft.
13. If necessary, use tool J–8524–2, and remove the stub shaft seals and bearings.
14. If necessary, remove the pitman shaft seals and bearing by first removing the snap ring then prying out the seals and washer with a suitable tool.

Assembly

1. If the pitman shaft seals and bearing were removed install as follows:
   a. Install the bottom oil seal in the counterbore, then install the washer.
   b. Coat the seal lip and washer face with anhydrous calicum grease.
   c. Install the dust seal and retaining ring.

NOTE: When using installer No. J–8810, install with the lettered edge of the bearing against the tool and flush with the bottom of the counterbore.

2. If the stub shaft seals and bearings were removed install as follows:
   a. Install the new stub shaft needle bearing and bottom tool on the housing counterbore.
   b. Install the upper thrust bearing centered on the valve body.

NOTE: The service thrust bearing does not snap on the needle bearing.

   c. Install the stub shaft seal and liberally coat the top of the seal with anhydrous calicum grease.
   d. Install the dust seal just deep enough to clear the retaining ring groove, then install the retaining ring.
3. Assemble the valve as follows:
   a. For ease of assembly soak the teflon rings in warm water.
   b. Engage the stub shaft. The notch must fully engage the pin and the cap must seat against the shoulder.

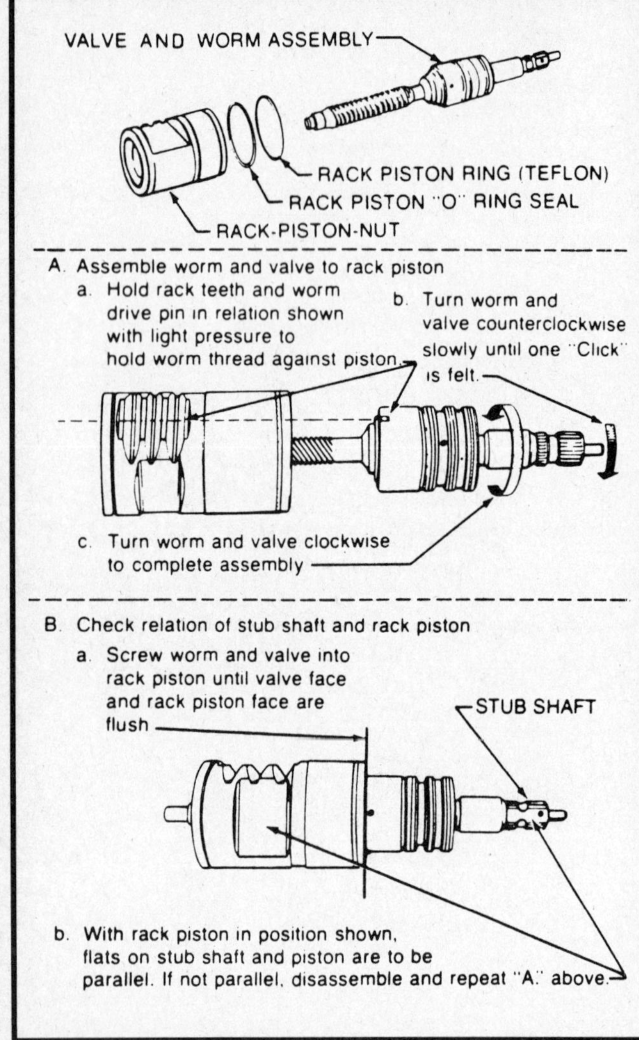

Assembling the worm valve to the worm assembly-Model 605 power steering gear

c. Lubricate the spool and body with with power steering fluid and rotate while installing

4. Assemble the worm valve to the valve assembly. Install the retaining ring with the curved in end on the same side as the access hole.

5. Assemble the worm and valve to the rack piston as follows:
   a. For ease of assembly soak the teflon ring in warm water.
   b. Install the O-ring and then the teflon ring on the rack-piston-nut.
   c. Assemble the worm and valve to the rack piston.

6. Install the rack piston and valve assembly to the housing with the teeth positioned toward the side cover opening.

7. Install the lower bearing and adjuster. Adjust the thrust bearing preload before tightening the locknut.

8. Install the pitman shaft and side cover. Use a new retaining ring and make sure that the open end of the retaining ring is approximately ½ in. from the access hole. The side cover must be depressed to install the ring. Tighten the preload adjustment nut to 20 ft. lbs.

9. To install the stub shaft seals first install protector J-29810 on the stub shaft. Install the seal, then coat the top of the seal with anhydrous calicum grease. Install the dust seal just deep enough to clear the retaining ring groove, then install the retaining ring.

10. Install the pitman shaft seals using tool J-6133-01.

11. Adjust the thrust bearing preload and the over-center sector adjustment.

Saginaw Model 800/808, GMT-400 Power Steering Gear

Both the 800/808 and the GMT-400 are integral recirculating ball power steering gears. The 800/808 power steering gear is used on light duty Chevrolet and GMC trucks between 1982-88 except the 1987-88 CK model. The GMT-400 power steering gear is used on CK models between 1987-88. Overhaul on both steering gears is the same.

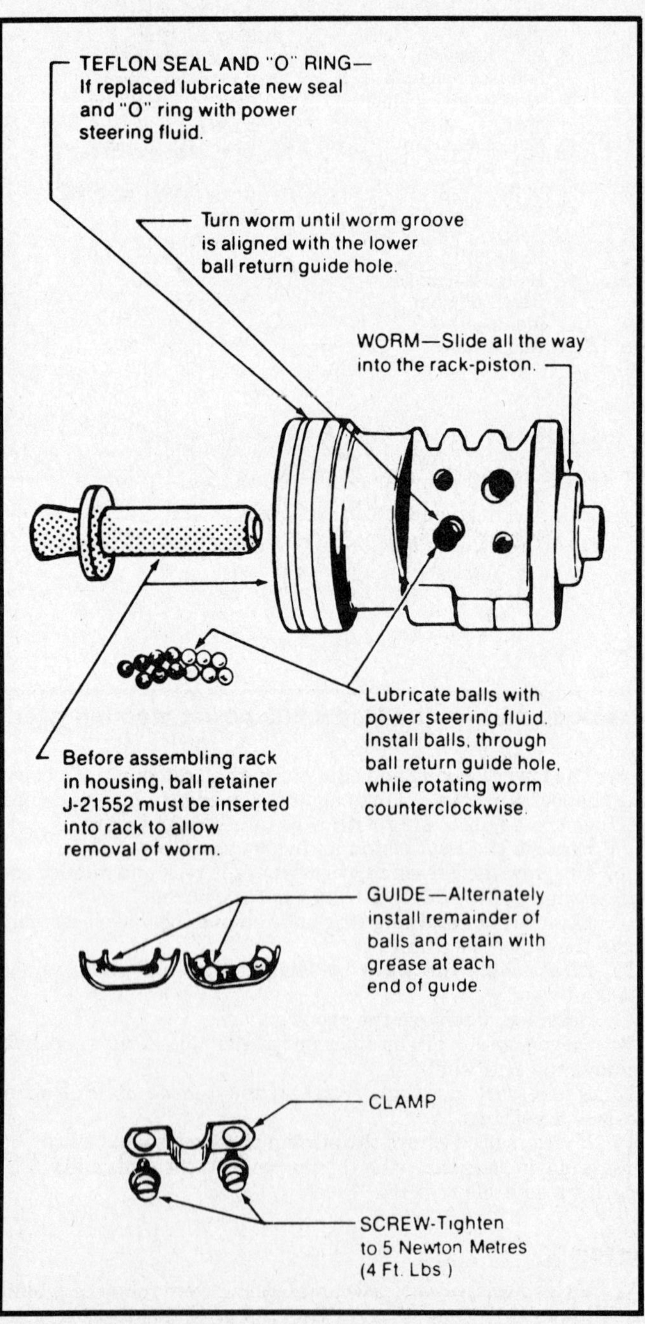

Assembling the rack piston-Model 800/808 and 400 power steering gear

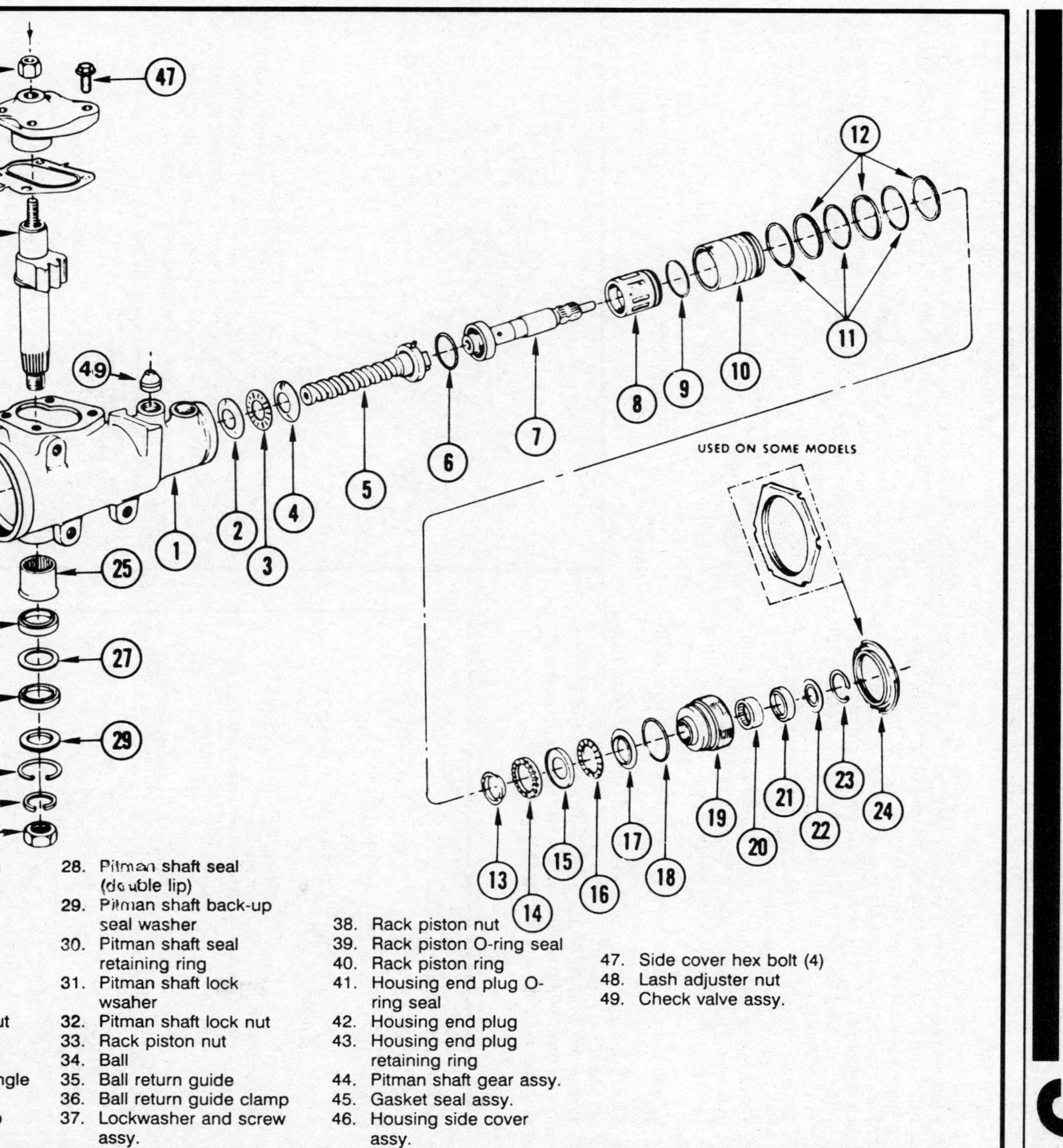

1. Steering gear housing
2. Worm thrust bearing race
3. Worm thrust bearing
4. Thrust bearing worm race
5. Steering worm
6. Stub shaft O-ring seal
7. Stub shaft
8. Valve spool
9. Spool O-ring seal
10. Valve body
11. Valve body O-ring (3)
12. Valve body O-ring seal
13. Bearing adjuster retainer
14. Thrust bearing spacer
15. Upper thrust bearing race (small)
16. Upper thrust bearing
17. Upper thrust bearing race (large)
18. Adjuster O-ring seal
19. Adjuster plug
20. Needle bearing
21. Stub shaft seal
22. Stub shaft dust seal
23. Retaining ring
24. Adjuster plug lock nut
25. Pitman shaft needle bearing
26. Pitman shaft seal (single lip)
27. Pitman shaft back-up seal washer
28. Pitman shaft seal (double lip)
29. Pitman shaft back-up seal washer
30. Pitman shaft seal retaining ring
31. Pitman shaft lock wsaher
32. Pitman shaft lock nut
33. Rack piston nut
34. Ball
35. Ball return guide
36. Ball return guide clamp
37. Lockwasher and screw assy.
38. Rack piston nut
39. Rack piston O-ring seal
40. Rack piston ring
41. Housing end plug O-ring seal
42. Housing end plug
43. Housing end plug retaining ring
44. Pitman shaft gear assy.
45. Gasket seal assy.
46. Housing side cover assy.
47. Side cover hex bolt (4)
48. Lash adjuster nut
49. Check valve assy.

Exploded view of the 800/808 and 400 power steering gear

Disassembly

1. Remove the pitman arm.
2. Remove the retaining ring.
3. Start the engine and turn the wheels fully to the right to force the seals and washers out. Turn off the engine.
4. Remove the pitman shaft and side cover by removing the preload adjuster nut. Rotate the shaft to the center gear, then tap on the threaded end of the pitman shaft with a plastic hammer and remove it.
5. Remove the housing end plug by using a punch in the access hole and removing the retaining ring.
6. Remove the rack piston plug and remove the rack piston.
7. Remove the adjuster plug assembly as follows:
   a. Use a punch against the edge of the slots and loosen the lock nut.
   b. Remove the adjuster plug using a spanner wrench J–7624.
8. Pry the bearing retainer at the raised edge and disassemble the adjuster plug assembly.
9. Grasp the stub shaft and remove the valve and worm assembly as a unit. When separating the valve from the worm note how the pin in the worm fits the slot in the valve.
10. Disassemble the valve by tapping the shaft lightly on a block of wood.
11. Rotate and remove the spool.
12. Disengage the pin on the shaft at the hole in the spool and remove the stub shaft.
13. Disassemble the rack piston.
14. If necessary, remove the pitman shaft seals and bearing by first removing the snap ring then prying out the seals and washer with a suitable tool.
15. If necessary, remove the check valve by prying out of the housing with a suitable tool. Be careful not to damage the threads on the housing.

Assembly

1. To replace the check valve, use a piece of ⅜ in. tubing, 4 inches long and carefully drive the check valve into the housing.
2. Install the pitman shaft bearing with tools J-22407 and J-8092, coat the seal lip and washer face with anhydrous calicum

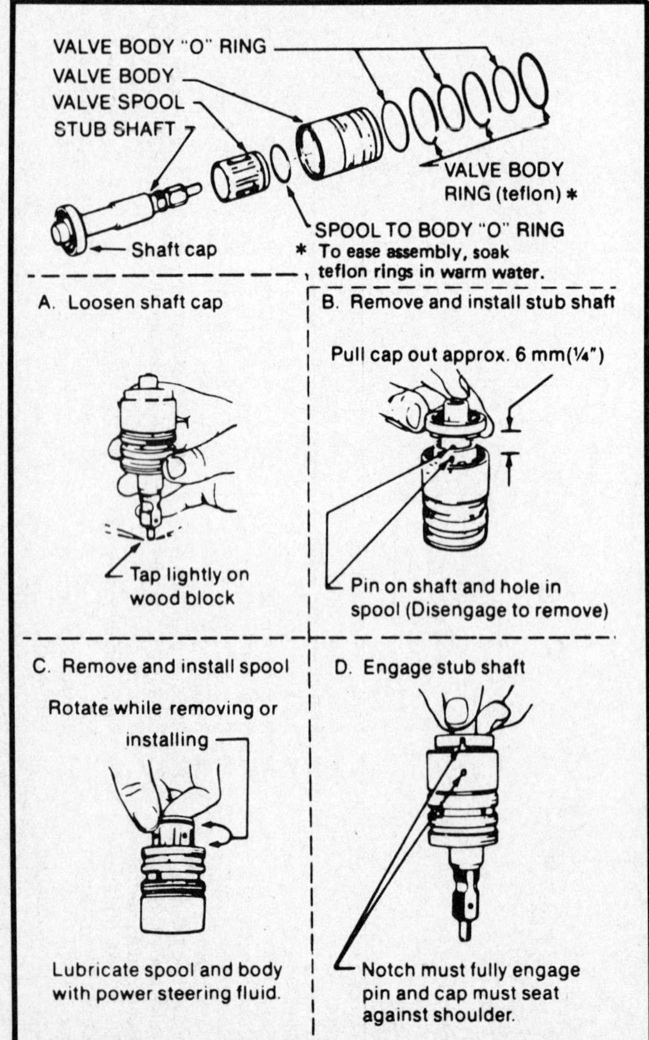

Assembling the worm valve to the worm assembly-Model 800/808 and 400 power steering gear

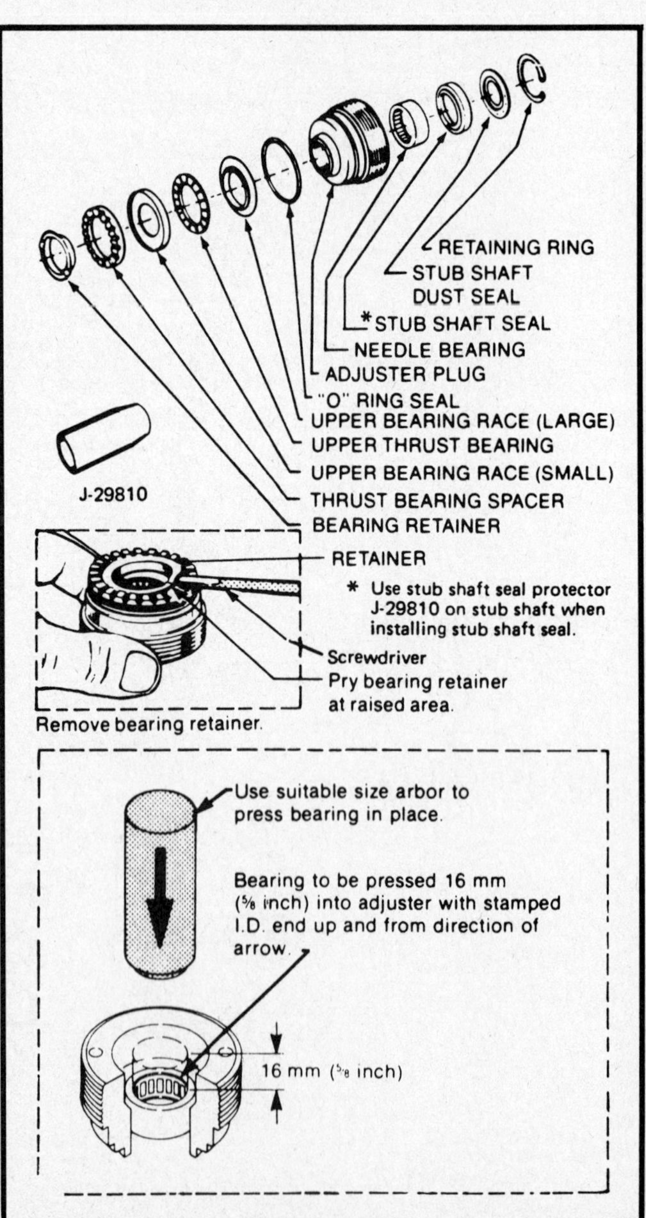

Assembling the adjuster plug assembly-Model 800/808 and 400 power steering gear

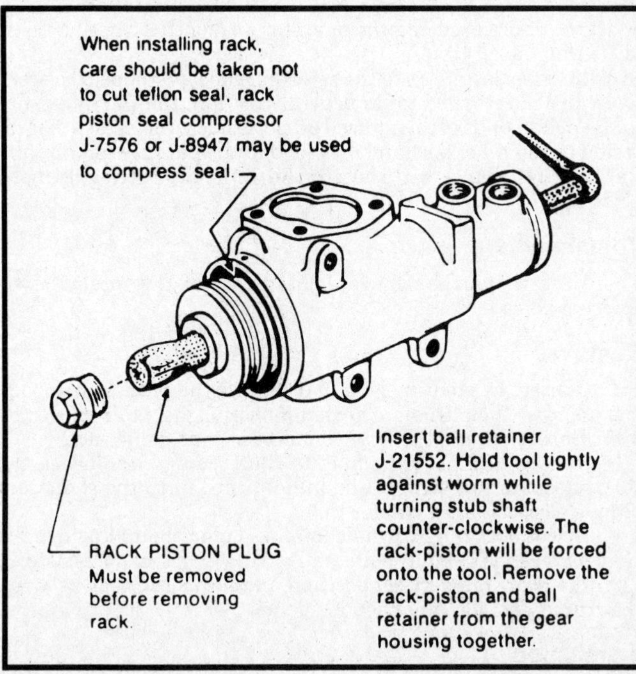

When installing rack, care should be taken not to cut teflon seal, rack piston seal compressor J-7576 or J-8947 may be used to compress seal.

Installation of the rack piston-Model 800/808 and 400 power steering gear

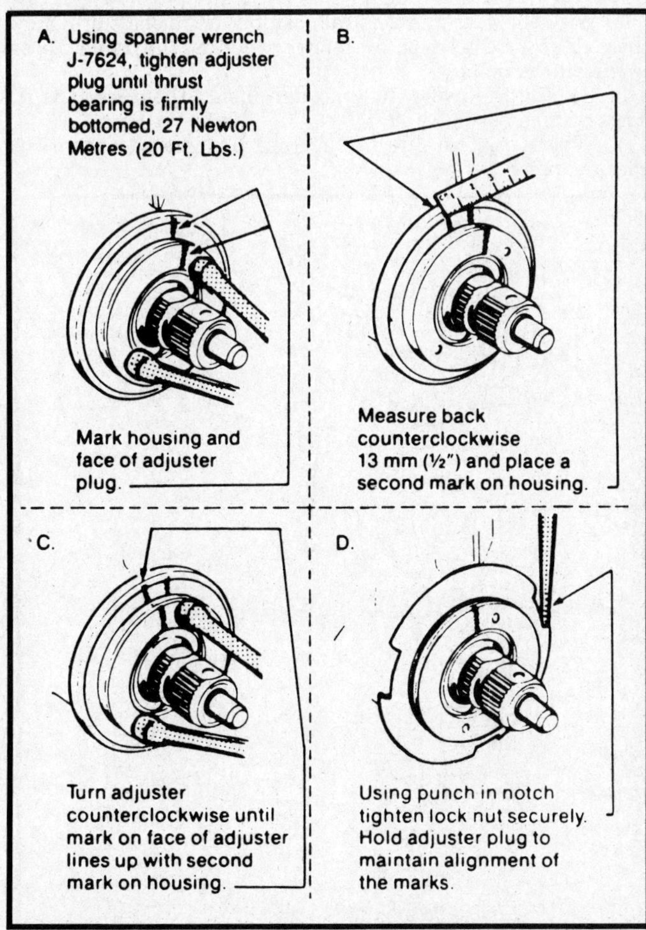

A. Using spanner wrench J-7624, tighten adjuster plug until thrust bearing is firmly bottomed, 27 Newton Metres (20 Ft. Lbs.)
Mark housing and face of adjuster plug.
B.
Measure back counterclockwise 13 mm (½") and place a second mark on housing.
C.
Turn adjuster counterclockwise until mark on face of adjuster lines up with second mark on housing.
D.
Using punch in notch tighten lock nut securely. Hold adjuster plug to maintain alignment of the marks.

Thrust bearing preload-Model 800/808 and 400 power steering gear

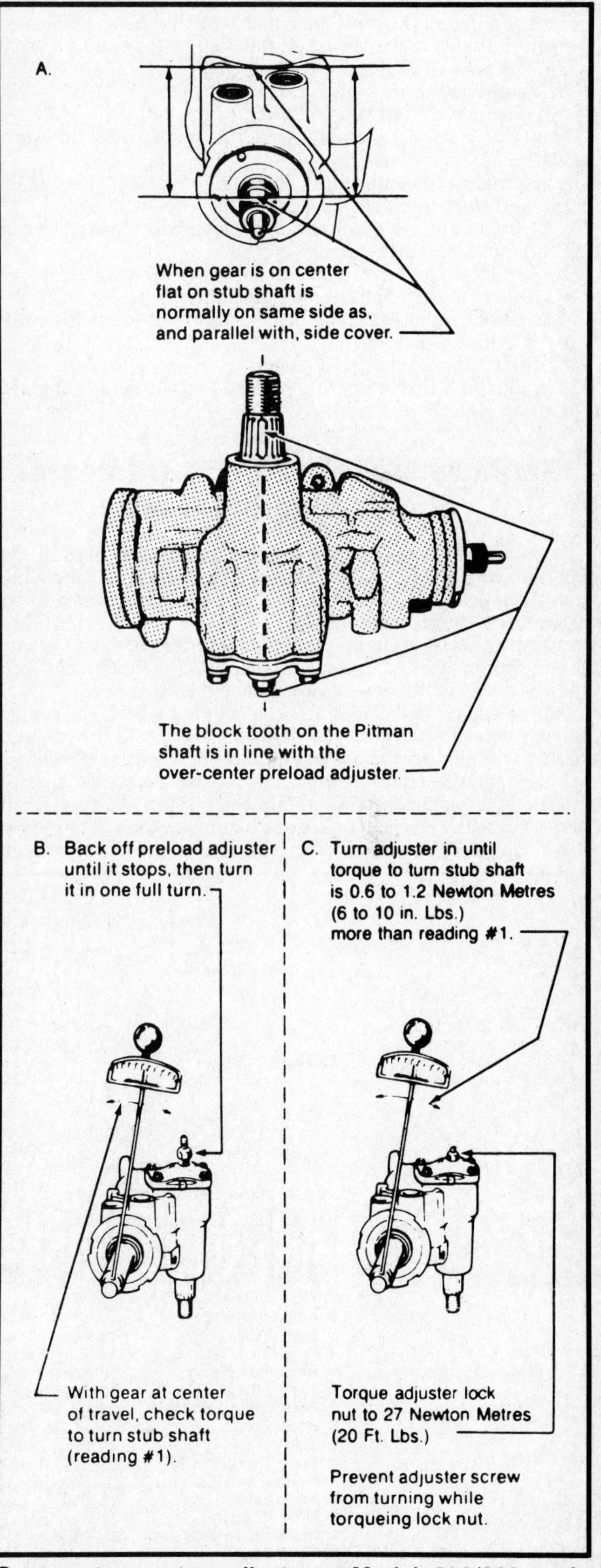

A.
When gear is on center flat on stub shaft is normally on same side as, and parallel with, side cover.
The block tooth on the Pitman shaft is in line with the over-center preload adjuster.
B. Back off preload adjuster until it stops, then turn it in one full turn.
With gear at center of travel, check torque to turn stub shaft (reading #1).
C. Turn adjuster in until torque to turn stub shaft is 0.6 to 1.2 Newton Metres (6 to 10 in. Lbs.) more than reading #1.
Torque adjuster lock nut to 27 Newton Metres (20 Ft. Lbs.)
Prevent adjuster screw from turning while torqueing lock nut.

Over-center sector adjustment-Model 800/808 and 400 power steering gear

grease and install the seals with tool J–6219. The single lip seal goes first, then a back up washer, followed by the double lip seal, a back up washer and the retaining ring.

3. Assemble the rack piston.
4. Assemble the valve as follows:
   a. For ease of assembly soak the teflon rings in warm water.
   b. Engage the stub shaft. The notch must fully engage the pin and the cap must seat against the shoulder.
   c. Lubricate the spool and body with with power steering fluid and rotate while installing
5. Assemble the worm valve to the valve assembly.
6. Assemble the adjuster plug assembly.
7. Install the adjuster plug being careful not to cut the seals.
8. Install the rack piston.
9. Install the pitman shaft seals.
10. Adjust the thrust bearing preload and the over-center sector adjustment.

Saginaw Model 170, 170-D Integral Power Steering Gear

The model 170, 170-D power steering gear unit is used in conjunction with the heavier pitman and steering arms, and eliminates the need for power cylinder assist units attached to the axle and to the steering linkage.

The unit uses a remote mounted, belt driven, vane type hydraulic pump for fluid pressure and directs the fluid to and from the gear unit by the use of pressure and return hoses.

As the vehicle operator turns the steering wheel, the control valve is moved within the gear housing, and closes the pressure relief port and directs fluid pressure to the opposite ends of the primary and secondary pistons. The pressure assists the movement of the pistons as they rotate the pitman shaft, which in turn, moves the steering linkage to turn the wheels. The greater the turning effort, the more pressure is applied to the piston ends, therefore assuring the operator a smooth hydraulic assist in turning at all times.

As the steering effort to the steering wheel is stopped, the control valve is returned to its neutral position, the fluid pressure to the piston ends are equalized on both sides, the pressure is directed to the relief port and returned to the pump reservoir, and the steering gear is returned to the neutral or straight ahead position.

Adjustments

There are no on-the-vehicle adjustments of the integral type steering gear.

Removal

1. Center the steering gear and remove the pitman arm bolt.
2. Spread the pitman arm clamp boss slightly to remove the arm. Do not spread the arm clamp boss over 0.004 inch.
3. Remove the pot joint to stub shaft clamp bolt, loosen the steering column assembly and pull upward until the shaft coupling clears the stub shaft.
4. Disconnect the hydraulic lines and plug them. Remove the steering gear attaching bolts and with the aid of an assistant, turn the gear in a vertical position and lower the gear between the frame and the inner fender panel.

Installation

1. Install adapter plate to the gear assembly, if removed. (Install the lower forward bolt through the adapter plate before attaching it to the gear housing.)
2. With the gear in a vertical position, (stub shaft up), move the gear upward between the fender panel and the frame. Loosely install the bolts.
3. Unplug the hydraulic lines and install them into the fittings of the gear housing.
4. Tighten the gear to frame bolts and torque to specifications.

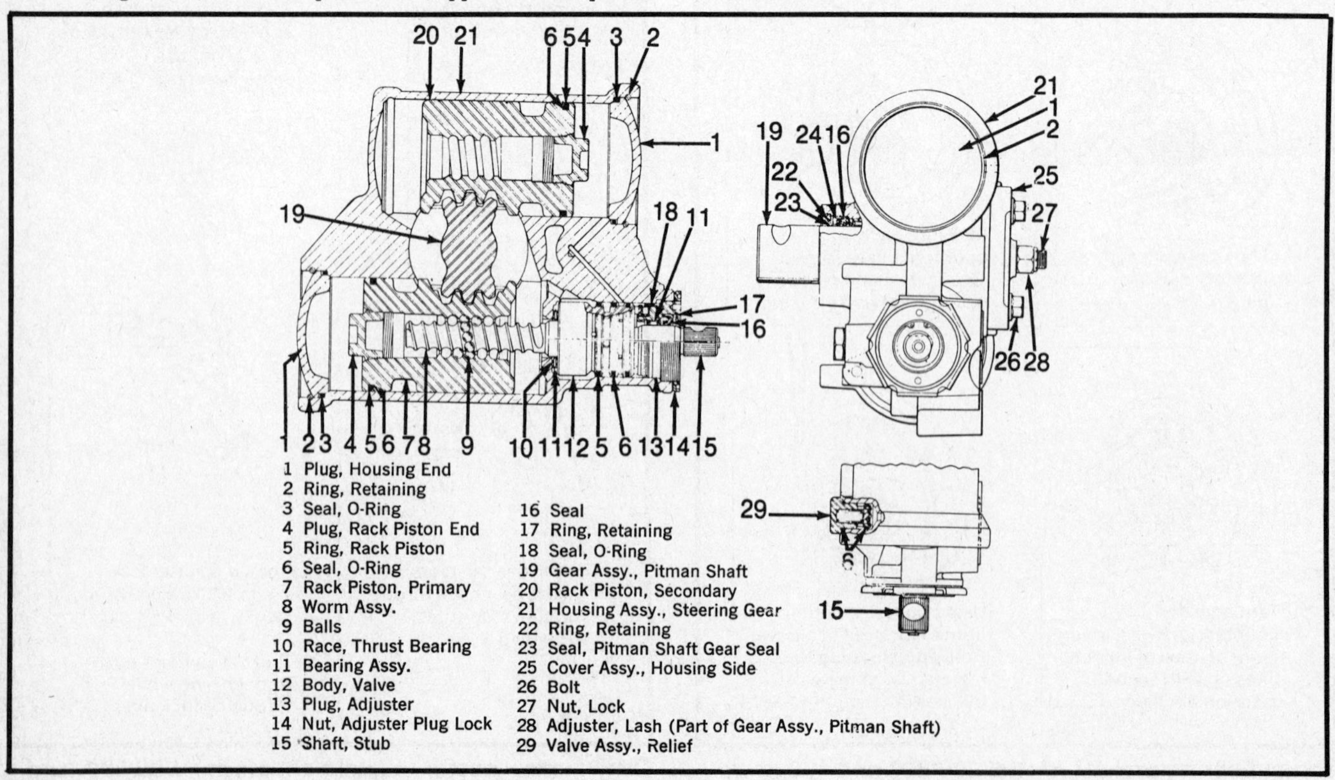

Integral power steering gear and control unit—models 170-170D

5. With the aid of one or more assistants, center and push the steering shaft over the stub shaft until the coupling lines up with the cross groove in the stub shaft.

6. Install the clamp bolt in the cross groove clamp and tighten. Tighten the steering column assembly.

7. Install the pitman arm, install the bolt and torque to specifications.

8. Fill the reservoir and bleed the system as outlined previously.

GEAR UNIT

Disassembly

1. Place the steering gear box in a holding fixture or a vise. With a small pin punch, dislodge the end cover retaining rings from their grooves in the primary and secondary piston housings and pry them out.

2. Turn the stub shaft counterclockwise to force the cover from the primary cylinder. Remove the cover and O- ring seal.

3. Remove the rack piston end plug, the sector preload adjuster nut, and the four side cover bolts.

4. Using a 1/4 in. Allen wrench, turn the preload adjusting nut clockwise until the side cover separates from the sector shaft and remove the cover.

5. Turn the stub shaft counterclockwise until the sector shaft teeth are out of engagement with the teeth of the rack piston.

NOTE: The secondary piston end cover is stuck, turn the stub shaft counterclockwise until the rack piston bottoms in the housing, then engage the sector end tooth in the center tooth spacing on the primary rack piston. Turn the stub shaft counterclockwise until the secondary rack piston forces the end cover from the housing.

6. Remove the secondary rack piston from the bore in the gear housing. Do not remove the end plug unless it is to be replaced.

7. Rotate the stub shaft clockwise until the teeth of the sector and the rack piston clear each other and the rack piston can move freely.

8. Insert a ball retainer tool or its equivalent into the bore of the rack piston. Turn the stub shaft counterclockwise while

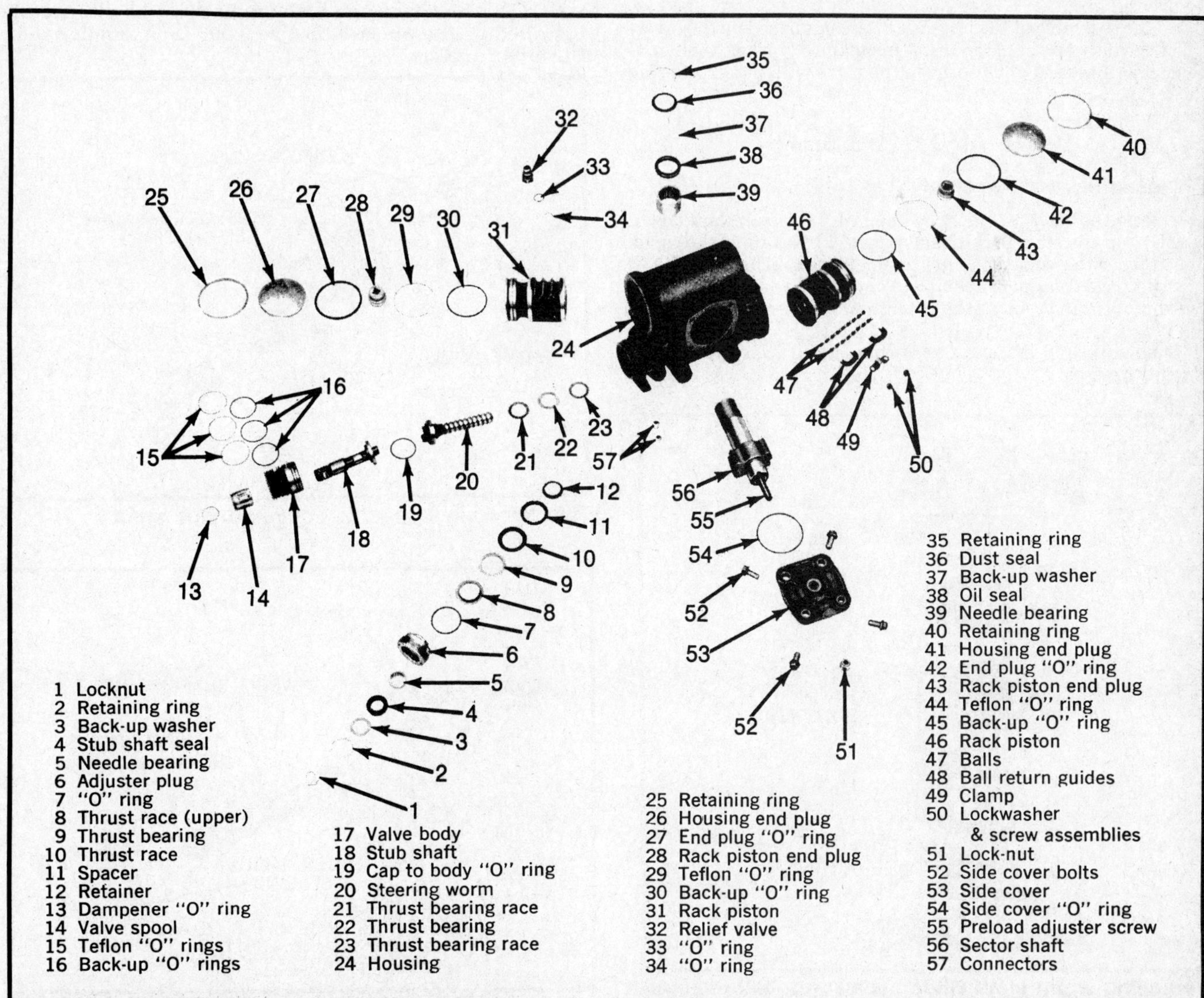

Exploded view of models 170-170D steering gear

holding the tool firmly against the worm, forcing the rack piston over the tool and retaining the recirculating balls in place. Remove the rack piston from the housing.

9. Rotate the sector shaft teeth to clear the housing and remove the shaft from the gear housing.

10. Remove the adjuster plug lock nut and with the aid of a spanner wrench, remove the adjuster plug from the stub shaft end of the gear housing.

11. Remove the valve and worm as an assembly with the thrust bearings and races and separate the worm from the valve assembly.

ADJUSTER PLUG

Disassembly and Assembly

1. Reinstall the adjuster plug into the gear housing and snug it finger tight. Remove the snap retaining ring and the back-up washer.
2. Remove the seal from the plug by prying the seal outward, being careful not to damage the bore.
3. Pry the thrust bearing retainer from the bore. Remove the spacer, washer, bearing and second washer.
4. The needle bearing assembly can be removed from the plug by driving it out.
5. The assembly of the plug can be accomplished by the reversal of the disassembly procedure. Install new O-rings, seals, and bearings as needed and lubricate the parts with power steering fluid.

VALVE AND STUB SHAFT

Disassembly and Assembly

1. Hold the valve assembly by hand with the stub shaft down. Lightly tap the stub shaft against a wood block until the cap is raised from the valve body approximately 1/4 inch.
2. Remove the shaft assembly from the spool by disengaging the shaft pin, and remove the spool from the valve body by rotating it.
3. Remove and discard the O-rings and replace the teflon rings if needed.

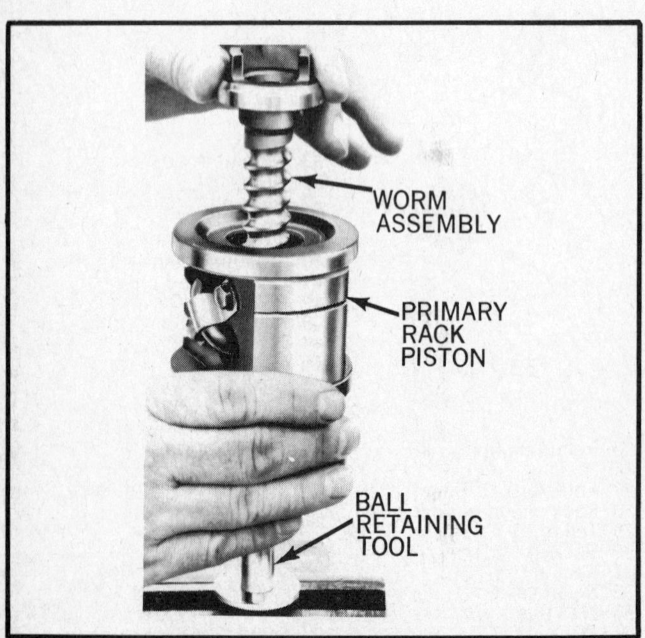

Removing worm shaft while installing a ball retainer tool

4. The assembly is in the reverse of disassembly. All parts should be lubricated with power steering fluid.

NOTE: The valve body pin must mate with the cap notch before the valve body is assembled into the gear assembly and a new O-ring placed in the shaft end of the valve body assembly.

PRIMARY RACK PISTON

Disassembly

1. Remove the two screws from the ball return clamp. Remove the guide, retaining tool and the recirculating balls.
2. Remove the teflon ring and O-ring from the rack piston.

Assembly

1. Install the teflon and O-rings.
2. Slide the worm into the rack piston and rotate the worm to align the grooves with the ball return guide hole nearest the piston ring.
3. While turning the worm shaft, feed 28 balls into the rack piston.

NOTE: The silver and black balls must be alternately installed as the black balls are 0.005 inch smaller than the silver balls.

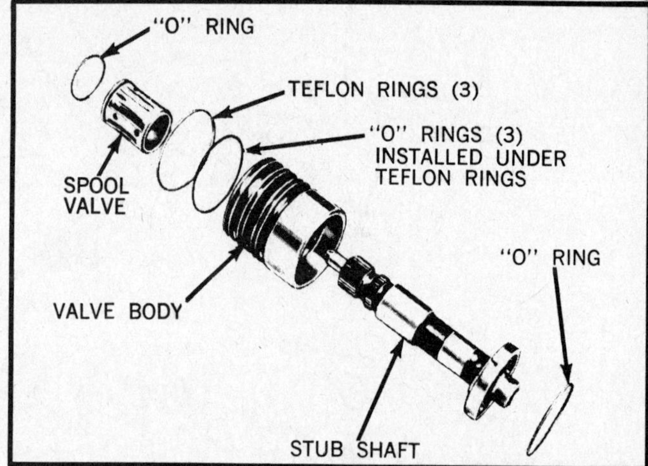

Exploded view of valve body and stub shaft

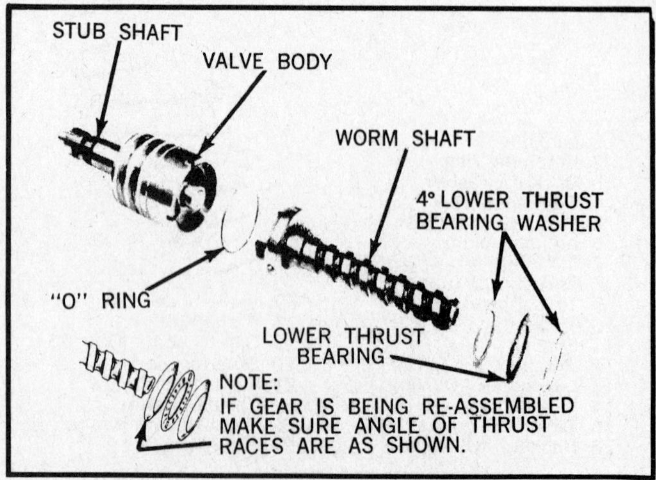

Exploded veiw of worm shaft and valve body

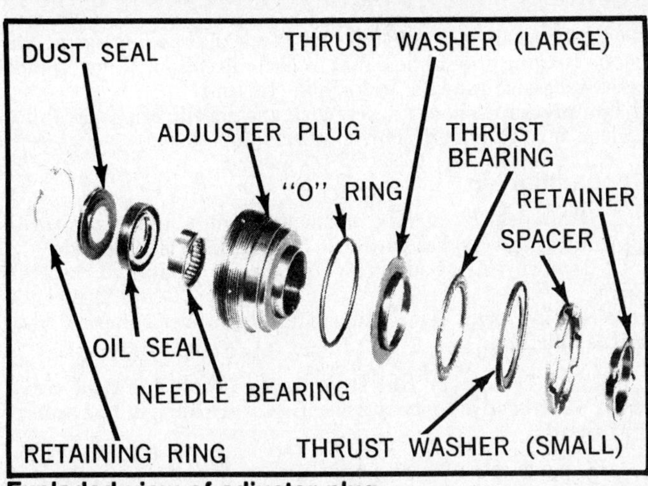

Exploded view of adjuster plug

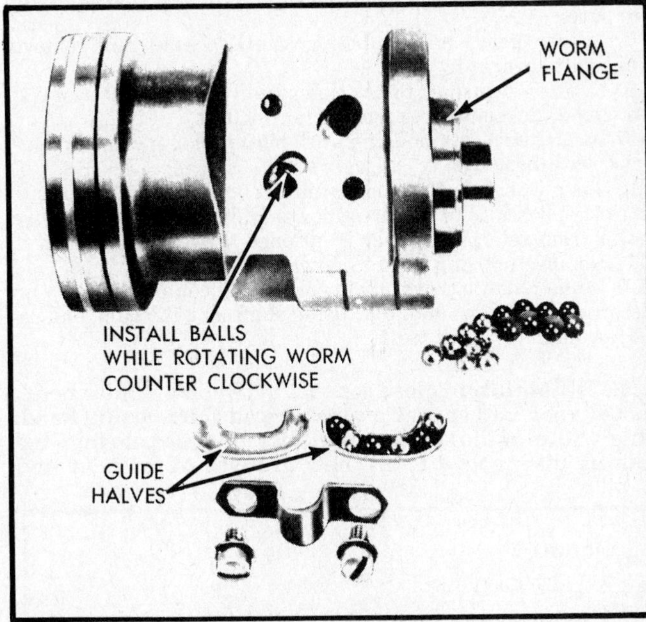

Exploded view of primary rack piston

4. Place the remaining 6 balls alternately into the ball return guide, holding the balls in place with grease. Install the guide into the holes of the rack piston, retaining with the guide clamps and screws.

5. Install the ball retaining tool in place of the worm shaft, being careful not to allow any balls to drop.

NOTE: When installing the teflon rings, looseness will be noticed. The teflon rings will heat-shrink when the gear is operated. Therefore, care must be exercised when assembling the internal parts into the housing, to insure that all parts are lubricated with power steering fluid and not forced during the reassembly. The seals and O-rings may be damaged if this is allowed to happen.

SECONDARY RACK PISTON

No disassembly is necessary on this unit unless the teflon and O-rings are to be replaced.

GEAR UNIT

Assembly and Adjustment

1. Install the thrust washer, bearing and second thrust washer over the end of the worm and lubricate with power steering fluid.

NOTE: The tapered surfaces of the washers should be parallel to each other and the cupped side towards the stub shaft.

2. Install the O-ring in the valve body so that it is seated against the lower shaft cap and lubricate the valve body, rings and seals with power steering fluid.
3. Align the narrow notch in the valve body with the pin in the worm and install the unit into the gear housing, by exerting pressure on the valve body and not the stub shaft.
4. The return hole in the gear housing should be fully uncovered when the valve body is fully seated. Screw in the adjuster plug assembly and seat it against the valve body.
5. Adjust the thrust bearing preload by torquing the adjuster plug to 20 ft. lbs. to seat the thrust bearings.
6. Mark the steering housing in line with one of the tool hole locations on the adjuster plug. Measure counterclockwise $^{3}/_{16}$ to ¼ inch and remark the housing.
7. Loosen the adjuster until the tool hole is in line with the second mark on the steering housing and install the lock nut and tighten while maintaining the alignment of the adjuster tool hole with the mark on the housing.
8. With the aid of a torque wrench, turn the stub shaft evenly and observe the torque reading. The reading should be from 4 to 10 inch pounds.
9. Continue the adjustment as necessary to obtain the specified torque reading.
10. With the ball retaining tool in position, lubricate and install the primary rack piston into the gear housing until the retaining tool bottoms against the center of the worm.
11. Turn the stub shaft clockwise to thread the rack piston onto the worm. Keep the retaining tool tight against the worm while turning the stub shaft.
12. Remove the ball retainer tool when the rack piston is completely threaded onto the worm. Center the rack teeth in the sector shaft opening.
13. Install the secondary rack piston in the gear housing and line up the center tooth space with the teeth of the primary rack piston.
14. Slide the sector shaft into the gear housing with the tapered teeth engaging the primary rack piston.
15. Install a new O-ring on the side cover and push the cover into the housing until contact is made with the preload adjuster screw. With the aid of a ¼ inch Allen wrench inserted through the cover, turn the adjusting screw counterclockwise until the cover bottoms on the housing.
16. Install the side cover bolts and torque to 45 ft. lbs. Install the rack piston plug and torque to 75 ft. lbs.
17. Install the primary and secondary end covers, O-rings, and install the retainer rings.
18. With the steering gear on center, tighten the sector adjusting screw. Install and tighten the lock nut and check the overcenter torque while rotating the stub shaft through an arc of 180 degrees, with a torque wrench. Adjust the sector shaft accordingly until the correct torque is obtained.
    a. New gears 4 to 8 inch lbs., but not over 18 inch lbs. combined torque.
    b. Used gears 4 to 5 inch lbs., but not over 14 inch lbs. combined torque.
    c. Combined torque includes the thrust bearing adjustment reading, over-center and internal friction.

Chrysler Full-Time Power Steering (Constant Control Type)

The Chrysler Corporation Constant Control Type Power Steering Gear System consists of a hydraulic pressure pump, a power steering gear and connecting hoses.

The power steering gear housing contains a gear shaft and sector gear, a power piston with gear teeth milled into the side of the piston which is in constant mesh with the gear shaft sector teeth, a worm shaft which connects the steering wheel to the power piston through a coupling. The worm shaft is geared to the piston through recirculating ball contact.

A pivot lever is fitted into the spool valve at the upper end and into a drilled hole in the center thrust bearing race at the lower end. The center thrust bearing race is held firmly against the shoulder of the worm shaft by two thrust bearings, bearing races and an adjusting nut. The pivot lever pivots in the spacer which is held in place by the pressure plate.

When the steering wheel is turned to the left the worm shaft moves out of the power piston a few thousandths of an inch, the center thrust bearing race moves the same distance since it is clamped to the worm shaft. The race thus tips the pivot lever and moves the spool valve down, allowing oil under pressure to flow into the left-turn power chamber and force the power piston down. As the power piston moves, it rotates the cross-shaft sector gear and, through the steering linkage, turns the front wheels.

On a right turn the worm shaft moves into the power piston, the center thrust bearing race thus tips the pivot lever and moves the spool valve up, allowing oil under pressure to flow into the right power chamber and force the power piston up.

Pressure Test

Connect the pressure test hoses with the pressure gauge installed between the pump and steering gear.

Now, fill the reservoir to the level mark, then start the engine and bleed the system. Allow the engine to idle until the fluid in the reservoir is between 150° F. and 170° F. Now turn the steering wheel to the extreme right and check the pressure reading, then turn to the extreme left and check the reading again. The gauge reading should be equal in each direction. If not, it indicates excessive internal leakage in the unit.

The pressure should agree with the specifications in Pump section for satisfactory power steering operation.

Reconditioning

1. Drain gear by turning worm shaft from limit to limit with oil connections held downward. Thoroughly clean outside.
2. Remove valve body attaching screws, body and three O-rings.
3. Remove pivot lever and spring. Pry under spherical head with a small bar.

NOTE: Take care not to collapse slotted end of valve lever as this will destroy bearing tolerances of the spherical head.

4. Remove steering gear arm from sector shaft.
5. Remove snap-ring and seal back-up washer.
6. Remove seal, using proper tool to prevent damage to relative parts.
7. Loosen gear shaft adjusting screw locknut and remove gear shaft cover nut.
8. Rotate wormshaft to position sector teeth at center of piston travel. Loosen power train retaining nut.
9. Insert tools into housing until both tool and shaft are engaged with bearings.
10. Turn worm shaft either to full left or full right (depending on car application) to compress power train parts. Then remove power train retaining nut as mentioned above.
11. Remove housing head tang washer.
12. While holding power train completely compressed, pry on piston teeth with a small bar, using shaft as a fulcrum, and remove complete power train.

NOTE: Maintain close contact between cylinder head, center race and spacer assembly and the housing head. This will eliminate the possibility of reactor rings becoming disengaged from their grooves in cylinder and

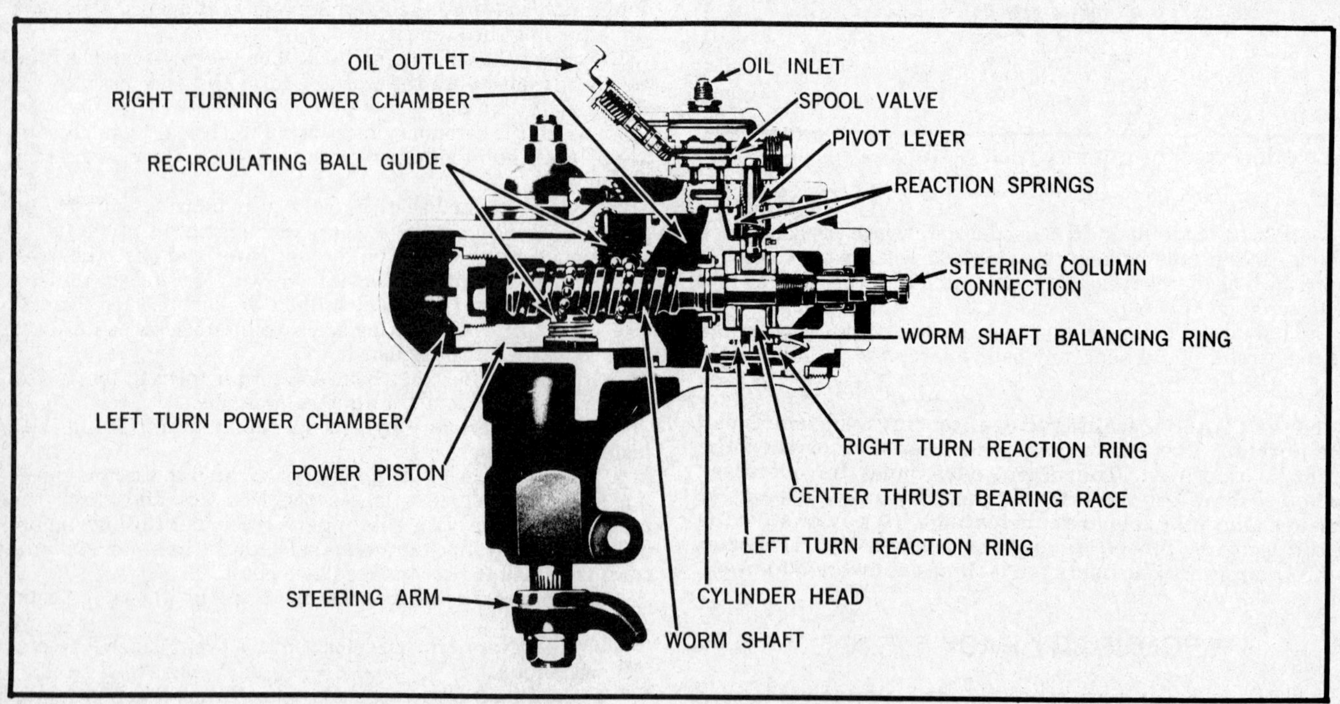

Cross section of Chrysler power steering gear

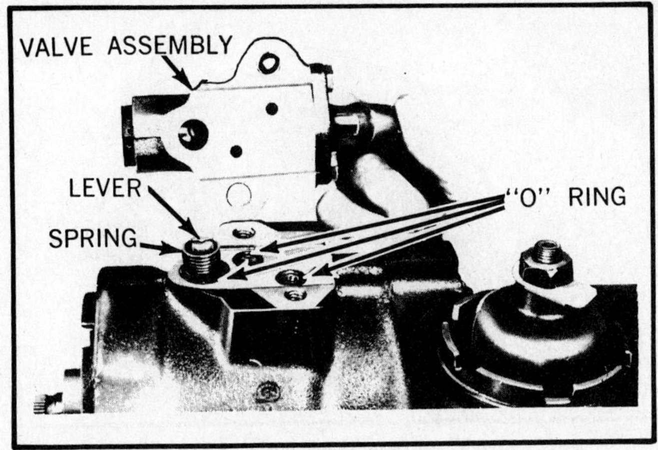

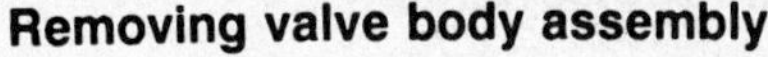
Removing valve body assembly

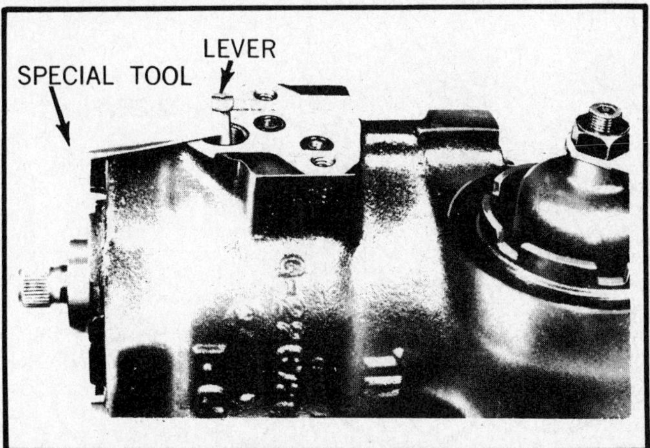

Ball nut and valve housing

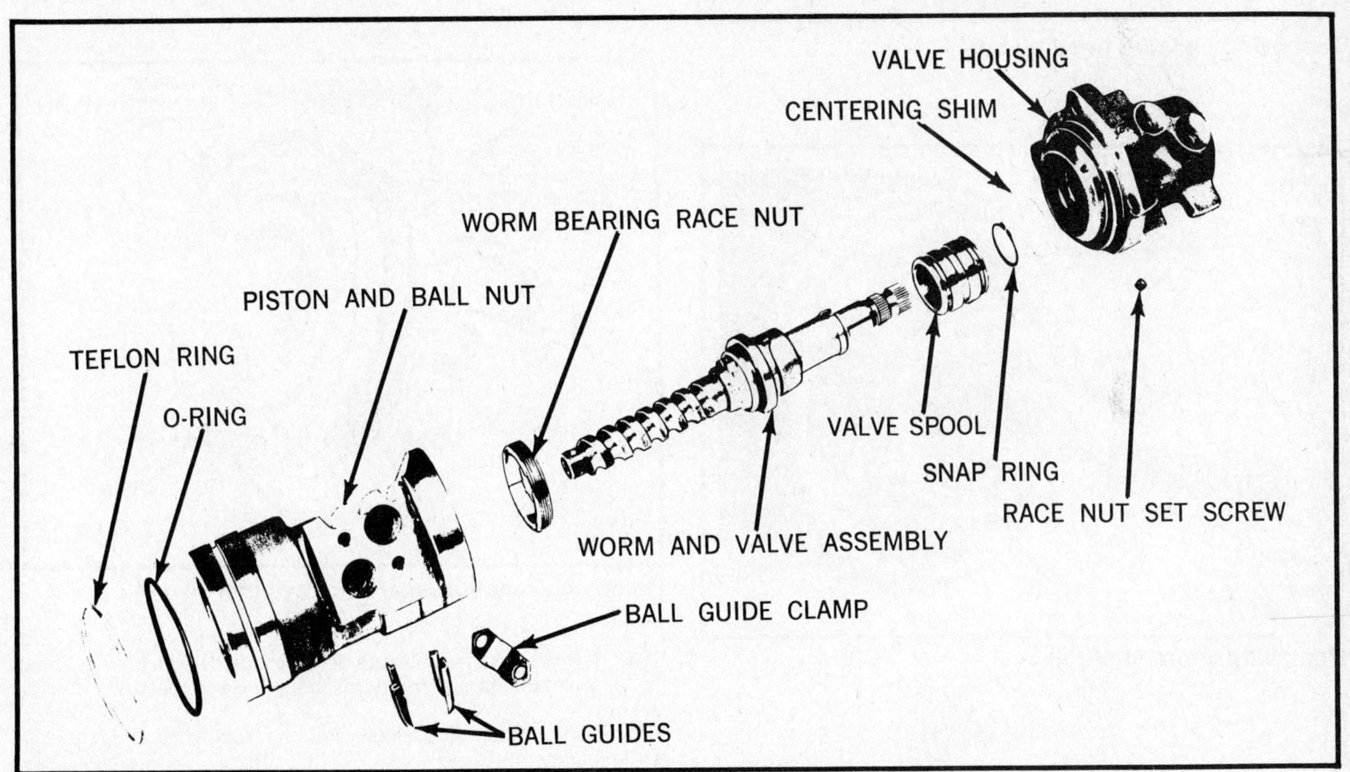

Removing pilot lever

housing head. It will prohibit center spacer from separating from center race and cocking in the housing. This could make it impossible to remove the power train without damaging involved parts.

13. Place power train in soft-jawed vise in vertical position. The worm bearing rollers will fall out. Use of arbor tool will hold roller when the housing is removed.
14. Raising housing head until wormshaft oil shaft just clears the top of wormshaft and position arbor tool on top of shaft and into seal. With arbor in position, pull up on housing head until arbor is positioned in bearing. Remove when the housing is removed.
15. Remove large O-ring from housing head groove.
16. Remove reaction seal from groove in face of head with air pressure directed into ferrule chamber.
17. Remove reactor spring, reactor ring, worm balancing ring and spacer.
18. While holding wormshaft from turning, turn nut with enough force to release staked portions from knurled section and remove nut.

NOTE: Pay strict attention to cleanliness.

19. Remove upper thrust bearing race (thin) and upper thrust bearing.
20. Remove center bearing race.
21. Remove lower thrust bearing and lower thrust bearing race (thick).
22. Remove lower reaction ring and reaction spring.
23. Remove cylinder head assembly.
24. Remove O-rings from outer grooves in head.

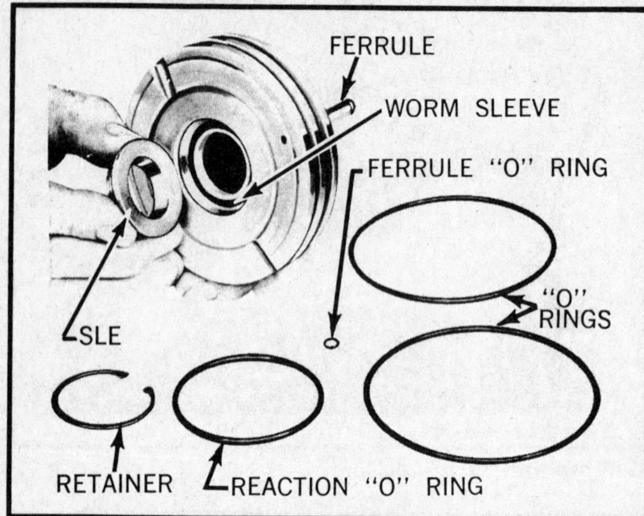

Removing cylinder head oil seal

Retaining bearing rollers with arbor tool

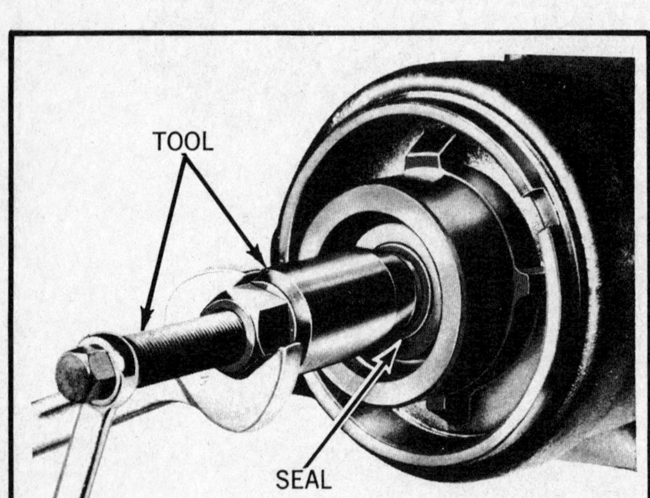

Removing worm shaft oil seal

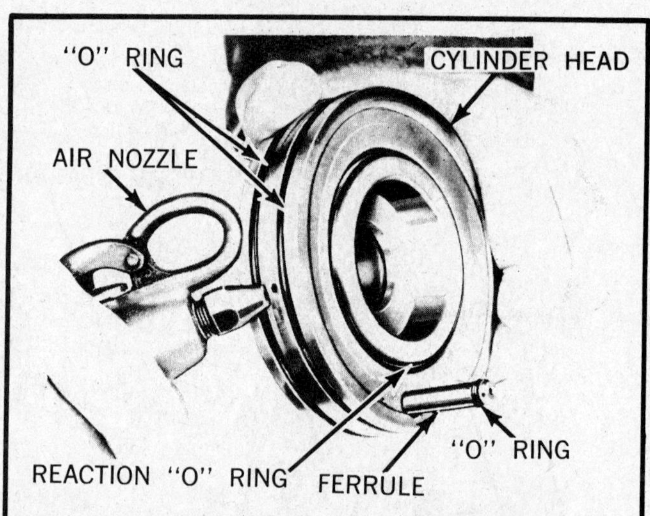

Removing reaction seal from cylinder head

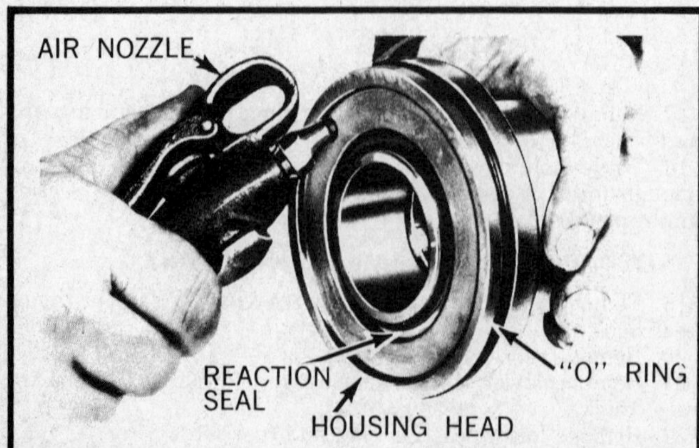

Removing reaction seal from worm shaft support

25. Remove reaction O-ring from groove in face of cylinder head. Use air pressure in oil hole located between O-ring grooves.
26. Remove snap-ring, sleeve and rectangular oil seal from cylinder head counterbore.
27. Test wormshaft operation. Not more than 2 inch lbs. should be required to turn it through its entire travel, and with a 15 ft. lb. side load.

NOTE: The worm and piston is serviced as a complete assembly and should not be disassembled.

28. Shaft side play should not exceed 0.008 in. under light pull applied 2 $^{5}/_{16}$ in. from piston flange.
29. Assemble in reverse of above, noting proper adjustments and preload requirements following.
30. When cover nut is installed, tighten to 20 ft. lbs. torque.
31. Valve mounting screws should be tightened to 200 inch lbs. torque.
32. With hoses connected, system bled, and engine idling roughly, center valve unit until not self-steering. Tap on head of valve body attaching screws to move valve body up, and tap on end plug to move valve body down.
33. With steering gear on center, tighten gear shaft adjusting screw until lash just disappears.

34. Continue to tighten ⅜ to ½ turn and tighten locknut to 50 ft. lbs.

TRW Power Rack and Pinion Assembly

NOTE: This system is used on the Rampage, Scamp, Caravan, Voyager and Dakota.

OUTER TIE ROD

Removal

1. Loosen the rod jam nut.
2. Remove the tie rod from the steering knuckle.
3. Remove the outer tie rod by unscrewing it from the inner tie rod. Count the number of turns to unscrew.

Installation

1. Screw the outer tie rod onto the inner tie rod the same number of turns necessary to remove.
2. Expand the outer boot clamp and leave loose on the tie rod.
3. Do not tighten the jam nut until the toe adjustment is made. Do not twist the boot.
4. Torque the jam nut to 50 ft. lbs. and install the outer boot clamp.
5. Be sure the boot is not twisted when done.

BOOT SEAL

Removal

1. With the outer tie rod off, remove the jam nut from the inner tie rod.
2. Expand the outer boot clamp and cut the inner boot clamp and discard.
3. Mark the location of the breather tube on the rubber boot. Remove the boot.

Installation

1. Install the boot and inner boot clamp. Align the boot mark and breather tube.
2. Install thee boot seal over the housing lip with the hole in the boot aligned with the breather tube.
3. Install the inner boot clamp. Lubricate the tie rod boot groove with a silicone type lubricant before installing the outer clamp.

INNER TIE ROD

Removal

1. Remove the roll pin from the inner tie rod to the rack.
2. Put a wrench on the tie rod pivot housing flats and turn the housing counterclockwise until the inner tie rod assembly separates from the rack.

Installation

1. Install the inner tie rod onto the rack and bottom the threads.
2. Torque the housing while holding the rack with a wrench. Torque to 60 ft. lbs. for the TRW gear.

RACK BEARING

Removal

1. Loosen the lock nut for the adjuster plug.
2. Remove the adjuster plug from the housing. Remove the spring and rack bearing.

Installation

1. Lubricate the metal parts and install the rack bearing, the spring, the adjuster plug and the lock nut.
2. Turn the adjuster plug in until it bottoms and then back off 40–60°.
3. Tighten the lock nut while holding the adjuster plug in place. The torque must be 50 ft. lbs.

STUB SHAFT SEALS

Removal

1. Remove the retaining ring and the dust cover.
2. Using a special holder or its equivalent, remove the lock nut from the pinion.

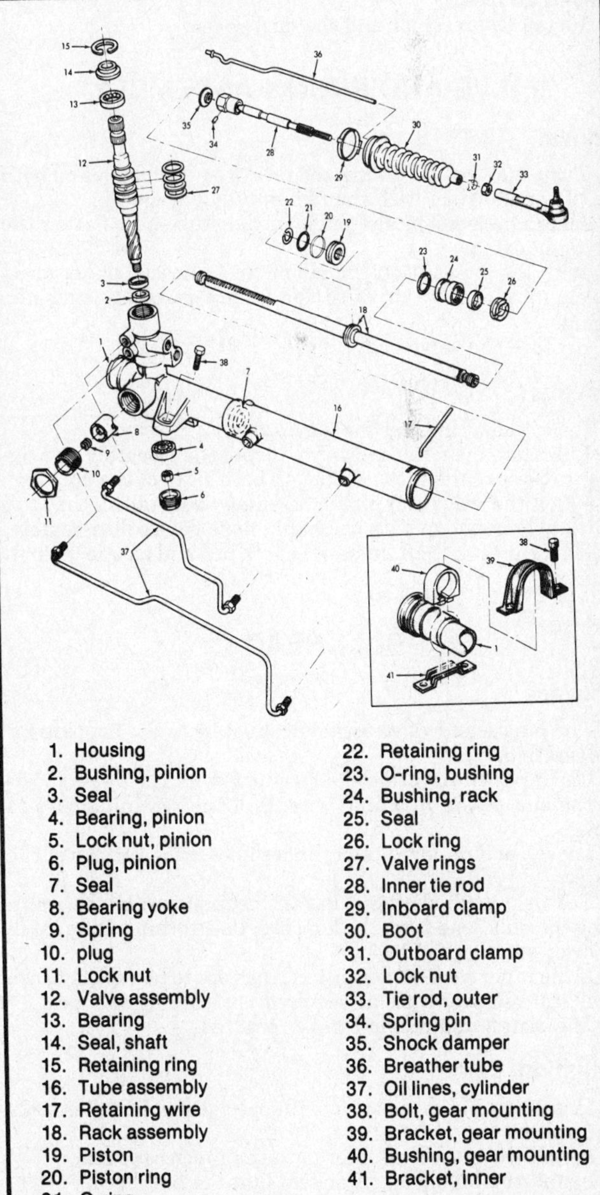

1. Housing
2. Bushing, pinion
3. Seal
4. Bearing, pinion
5. Lock nut, pinion
6. Plug, pinion
7. Seal
8. Bearing yoke
9. Spring
10. plug
11. Lock nut
12. Valve assembly
13. Bearing
14. Seal, shaft
15. Retaining ring
16. Tube assembly
17. Retaining wire
18. Rack assembly
19. Piston
20. Piston ring
21. O-ring
22. Retaining ring
23. O-ring, bushing
24. Bushing, rack
25. Seal
26. Lock ring
27. Valve rings
28. Inner tie rod
29. Inboard clamp
30. Boot
31. Outboard clamp
32. Lock nut
33. Tie rod, outer
34. Spring pin
35. Shock damper
36. Breather tube
37. Oil lines, cylinder
38. Bolt, gear mounting
39. Bracket, gear mounting
40. Bushing, gear mounting
41. Bracket, inner

Exploded view of the TRW power steering gear

CAUTION

If the stub shaft is not held, damage to the pinion teeth will occur.

3. Using the special puller or its equivalent, pull the valve and pinion assembly until flush with the ball bearing assembly. The complete assembly does not have to be removed.
4. Remove the stub shaft dust seal, stub shaft seal, needle bearing and stub shaft bearing annulus.

NOTE: The bearing and annuls are pressed together and disassembly is required only if bearing replacement is necessary.

Installation

1. Lubricate the seals and install in the reverse order of removal, using seal protectors on the pinion shaft. Seal installers are available to assist in seating the seal properly.
2. While holding the stub shaft, firmly seat the lock nut and torque to 26 ft. lbs.
3. Install the retainer and the dust cover.

VALVE AND PINION ASSEMBLY

Removal

1. Turn the stub shaft until the rack is equal distance on both sides of the housing, with the pinion fully engaged.
2. Mark the location and angle of the stub shaft flat on the steering housing.
3. With the lock nut off the pinion, use a special puller or its equivalent, and pull the valve and pinion assembly from the housing.
4. Remove the valve body rings.

Installation

1. Install new rings on the valve body.
2. Lubricate the rings and valve. Install the assembly into the housing. Be sure the rack is equal on both sides of the housing.
3. When the valve and pinion assembly is installed, the stub shaft flat should align with the mark made before disassembly.
4. Hold the stub shaft, install the lock nut and torque to 26 ft. lbs.

BULKHEAD

Removal

1. The pinion and valve assembly must be in the housing for this operation.
2. Use a punch to rotate the retaining wire clockwise to expose the end of the retaining wire. Pull the retaining wire to remove.
3. Loosen and remove both cylinder lines. Plug fittings at the cylinder.
4. Turn the stub shaft so that the rack moves to the right, forcing the bulkhead from the housing. Use a drain pan to catch the power steering fluid.
5. If the inner rack seal or piston rings are to be replaced, use special seal remover tools as required.
6. The piston and pinion can be removed.

Installation

1. Install the inner rack seal with special seal installer tools or equivalent.
2. Install the plastic retainer onto the inner rack seal.
3. Install the bulkhead outer seal into the bulkhead.
4. Install the bulkhead onto the rack.
5. Install the retaining wire by rotating the bulkhead assembly counterclockwise.

PINION BALL BEARING, UPPER PINION BUSHING AND SEAL

Removal and Installation

1. The pinion and piston must be out of the housing.
2. The bearing is removed by the use of a drift and hammer. To install, a bearing installer is available.
3. To remove the seal and bushing, a drift and hammer is used. To install, the use of special installing tools are necessary.

Ford Integral Power Steering Gear

The Ford integral power steering unit is a torsion-bar type.

The torsion bar power steering unit includes a worm and one-piece rack piston, which is meshed to the gear teeth on the steering sector shaft. The unit also includes a hydraulic valve, valve actuator, input shaft and torsion bar assembly which are mounted on the end of the worm shaft and operated by the twisting action of the torsion bar.

The torsion-bar type of power steering gear is designed with the one piece rack-piston, worm and sector shaft in one housing and the valve spool in an attaching housing. This makes possible internal fluid passages between the valve and cylinder, thus eliminating all external lines and hoses, except the pressure and return hoses between the pump and gear assembly.

The power cylinder is an integral part of the gear housing. The piston is double acting, in that fluid pressure may be applied to either side of the piston.

A selective metal shim, located in the valve housing of the gear is for the purpose of tailoring steering gear efforts. If efforts are not within specifications they can be changed by increasing or decreasing shim thickness as follows:

1. Efforts heavy to the left-increase shim thickness.
2. Efforts light to the left-decrease shim thickness.

Adjustments

The only adjustment which can be performed is the total over center position load, to eliminate excessive lash between the sector and rack teeth.

1. Disconnect the Pitman arm from the sector shaft.
2. Disconnect the fluid return line at the reservoir, at the same time cap the reservoir return line pipe.
3. Place the end of the return line in a clean container and cycle the steering wheel in both directions as required, to discharge the fluid from the gear.
4. Turn the steering wheel to 45 degrees from the left stop.
5. Using an in. lb. torque wrench on the steering wheel nut, determine the torque required to rotate the shaft slowly through an approximately ⅛ turn from the 45 degree position.
6. Turn the steering gear back to center, then determine the torque required to rotate the shaft back and forth across the center position. Loosen the adjuster nut, and turn the adjuster screw until the reading is 11–12 inch lbs. greater than the torque 45 degrees from the stop. Tighten the lock nut while holding the screw in place.
7. Recheck the readings and replace the Pitman arm and the steering wheel hub cover.
8. Correct the fluid return line to the reservoir and fill the reservoir with specified lubricant to the proper level.

VALVE CENTERING SHIM

Removal and Installation

1. Hold the steering gear over a drain pan in an inverted position and cycle the input shaft several times to drain the remaining fluid from the gear.
2. Mount the gear in a soft-jawed vise.
3. Turn the input shaft to either stop then, turn it back approximately 1¾ turns to center the gear.

4. Remove the two sector shaft cover attaching screws, the brake line bracket and the identification tag.
5. Tap the lower end of the sector shaft with a soft-faced hammer to loosen it, then lift the cover and shaft from the housing as an assembly. Discard the O-ring.
6. Remove the four valve housing attaching bolts. Lift the valve housing from the steering gear housing while holding the piston to prevent it from rotating off the worm shaft.
7. Remove the valve housing and the lube passage O-rings and discard them.
8. Place the valve housing, worm and piston assembly in the bench mounted holding fixture with the piston on the top.
9. Rotate the piston upward (back off) 3½ turns.
10. Insert tool T66P–3553–C or equivalent (with the arm facing away from the piston) into a bolt hole in the valve housing. Rotate the arm into position under the piston.
11. Loosen the Allen head race nut set screw from the valve housing.
12. Using tool T66P–3553–B or equivalent, loosen the worm bearing race nut.
13. Lift the piston-worm assembly from the valve housing. During removal hold the piston to prevent it from spinning off at the shaft.
14. Change the power steering valve centering shim.
15. Install the piston-worm assembly into the valve housing. Hold the piston worm to prevent it from spinning off of the shaft.
16. Install the worm bearing race nut and torque to 2–8 inch lbs. using tool T66P–3553–B or equivalent.
17. Install the race nut set screw (Allen head) through the valve housing.
18. Rotate the piston upward (back off) ½ turn and remove tool T66P–3553–C or equivalent.
19. Remove the valve housing, worm, and piston assembly from the holding fixture.
20. Position a new lube passage O-ring in the counterbore of the gear housing.
21. Apply vaseline to the teflon seal on the piston.
22. Place a new O-ring on the valve housing.
23. Slide the piston and valve into the gear housing being careful not to damage the teflon seal.
24. Align the lube passage in the valve housing with the one in the gear housing, and install but do not tighten the attaching bolts.
25. Rotate the ball nut so that the teeth are in the same place as the sector teeth. Tighten the four valve housing attaching bolts to 35–45 ft. lbs.
26. Position the sector shaft cover O-ring in the steering gear housing. Turn the input shaft as required to center the piston.
27. Apply vaseline to the sector shaft journal; then, position the sector shaft and cover assembly in the gear housing. Install the brake line bracket, steering gear identification tag and the two sector shaft cover attaching studs.
28. Position an in. lb. torque wrench on the gear input shaft and adjust the meshload to approximately 4 inch lbs. Then, torque the sector shaft cover attaching studs to 55–70 ft. lbs.
29. After the cover attaching bolts have been tightened to specification, adjust the mesh load to 17 inch lbs. with an in. lb. torque wrench.

STEERING GEAR

Disassembly

1. Hold the steering gear over a drain pan in an inverted position and cycle the input shaft several times to drain the remaining fluid from the gear.
2. Mount the gear in a soft-jawed vise.
3. Remove the lock nut from the adjusting screw.
4. Turn the input shaft to either stop then, turn it back approximately 1¾ turns to center the gear.

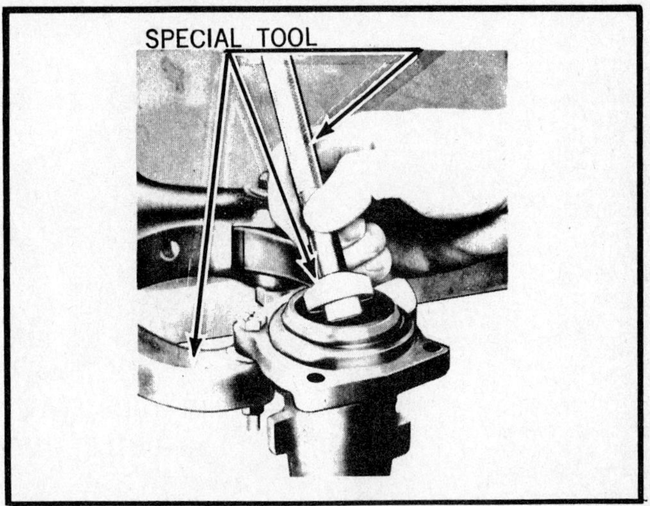

Removing bearing and oil seal

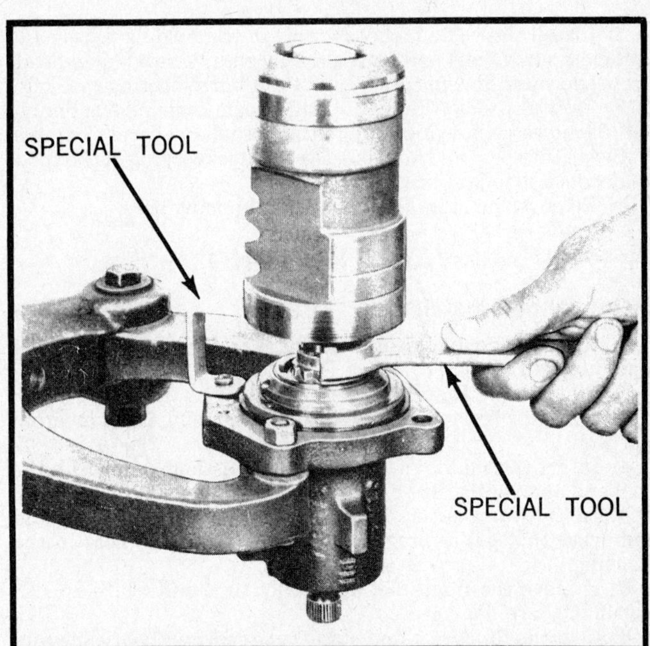

Removing worm bearing race nut

5. Remove the two sector shaft cover attaching studs, the brake line bracket and the identification tag.
6. Tap the lower end of the sector shaft with a soft-hammer to loosen it, then lift the cover and shaft from the housing as an assembly. Discard the O-ring.
7. Turn the sector shaft cover counterclockwise off the adjuster screw.
8. Remove the four valve housing attaching bolts. Lift the valve housing from the steering gear housing while holding the piston to prevent it from rotating off the worm shaft. Remove the valve housing and the lube passage O-rings and discard them.
9. Stand the valve body and piston on end with the piston end down. Rotate the input shaft counterclockwise out of the piston allowing the ball bearings to drop into the piston.
10. Place a cloth over the open end of the piston and turn it upside down to remove the balls.
11. Remove the two screws that attach the ball guide clamp to the ball nut and remove the clamp and the guides.

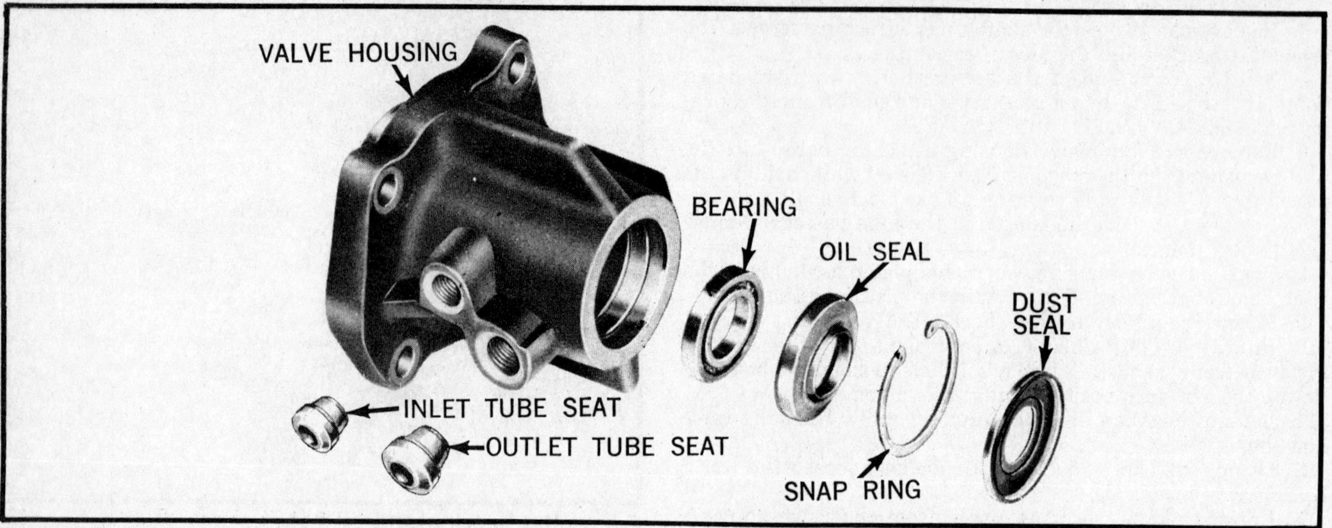

Valve housing disassembled

12. Install the valve body assembly in the holding fixture (do not clamp in a vise) and loosen the race nut screw (Allen head) from the valve housing and remove the worm bearing race nut.
13. Carefully slide the input shaft, worm and valve assembly out of the valve housing. Due to the close diametrical clearance between the spool and housing, the slightest cocking of the spool may cause it to jam in the housing.
14. Remove the shim from the valve housing bore.

VALVE HOUSING

Removal and Installation

1. Remove the dust seal from the rear of the valve housing and discard the seal.
2. Remove the snap-ring from the valve housing.
3. Turn the fixture to place the valve housing in an inverted position.
4. Insert special tool in the valve body assembly opposite the seal end and gently tap the bearing and seal out of the housing. Discard the seal. Caution must be exercised when inserting and removing the tool to prevent damage to the valve bore in the housing.
5. Remove the fluid inlet and outlet tube seats with an EZ-out if they are damaged.
6. Coat the fluid inlet and outlet tube seats with vaseline and position them in the housing. Install and tighten the tube nuts to press the seats to the proper location.
7. Coat the bearing and seal surface of the housing with a film of vaseline.
8. Seat the bearing in the valve housing. Make sure that the bearing is free to rotate.
9. Dip the new oil seal in gear lubricant; then, place it in the housing with the metal side of the seal facing outward. Drive the seal into the housing until the outer edge of seal does not quite clear the snap-ring groove.
10. Place the snap-ring in the housing; then, drive on the ring until the snap-ring seats in its groove to properly locate the seal.
11. Place the dust seal in the housing with the dished side (rubber side) facing out. Drive the dust seal into place. The seal must be located behind the undercut in the input shaft when it is installed.

WORM AND VALVE

Removal and Installation

1. Remove the snap-ring from the end of the actuator.
2. Slide the control valve spool off the actuator.
3. Install the valve spool evenly and slowly with a slight oscillating motion into the flanged end of valve housing with the valve identification groove between the valve spool lands outward, checking for freedom of valve movement within the housing working area. The valve spool should enter the housing bore freely and fall by its own weight.
4. If the valve spool is not free, check for burrs at the outward edges of the working lands in the housing and remove with a hard stone.
5. Check the valve for burrs and if burrs are found, stone the valve in a radial direction only. Check for freedom of the valve again.
6. Remove the valve spool from the housing.
7. Slide the spool onto the actuator making sure that the groove in the spool annulus is toward the worm.
8. Install the snap-ring to retain the spool. The beveled ID of the snap-ring must be assembled toward the spool.
9. Check the clearance between the spool and the snap-ring. The clearance should be between 0.0005–0.035 inch. If the clearance is not within these limits, select a snap-ring that will allow a clearance of 0.002 inch.

PISTON AND BALL NUT

Removal and Installation

1. Remove the teflon ring and the O-ring from the piston and ball nut.
2. Dip a new O-ring in gear lubricant and install it on the piston and ball nut.
3. Install a new teflon ring on the piston and ball nut being careful not to stretch it any more than necessary.

STEERING GEAR HOUSING

Removal and Installation

1. Remove the snap-ring and the spacer washer from the lower end of the steering gear housing.
2. Remove the lower seal from the housing. Lift the spacer washer from the housing.
3. Remove the upper seal in the same manner as the lower seal. Some housings require only one seal and one spacer.
4. Dip both sector shaft seals in gear lubricant.
5. Apply lubricant to the sector shaft seal bore of the housing and position the sector shaft inner seal into the housing with the lip facing inward. Press the seal into place. Place a spacer

washer (0.090 in.) on top of the seal and apply more lubricant to the housing bore.

6. Place the outer seal in the housing with the lip facing inward and press it into place. Then, place a 0.090 in. spacer washer on top of the seal.

7. Position the snap-ring in the housing. Press the snap-ring into the housing to properly locate the seals and engage the snap-ring in the groove.

STEERING GEAR ASSEMBLY

Disassembly

NOTE: Do not clean, wash, or soak seals in cleaning solvent.

1. Mount the valve housing in the holding fixture with the flanged end up.
2. Place the required thickness valve spool centering shim in the housing.
3. Carefully install the worm and valve in the housing.
4. Install the race nut in the housing and torque it to 42 ft. lbs.
5. Install the race nut set screw (Allen head) through the valve housing and torque to 20–25 inch lbs.
6. Place the piston on the bench with the ball guide holes facing up. Insert the worm shaft into the piston so that the first groove is in alignment with the hole nearest to the center of the piston.
7. Place the ball guide in the piston. Place the 27 to 29 balls, depending on the piston design, in the ball guide turning the worm in a clockwise direction as viewed from the input end of the shaft. If all of the balls have not been fed into the guide upon reaching the right stop, rotate the input shaft in one direction and then in the other while installing the balls. After the balls have been installed, do not rotate the input shaft or the piston more than 3½ turns off the right stop to prevent the balls from falling out of the circuit.
8. Secure the guides in the ball nut with the clamp.
9. Position a new lub passage O-ring in the counterbore of the gear housing.
10. Apply petroleum jelly to the teflon seal on the piston.
11. Place a new O-ring on the valve housing.
12. Slide the piston and valve into the gear housing being careful not to damage the teflon seal.
13. Align the lube passage in the valve housing with the one in the gear housing and install but do not tighten the attaching bolts.
14. Rotate the ball nut so that the teeth are in the same plane as the sector teeth. Tighten the four valve housing attaching bolts to 35–45 ft. lbs.
15. Position the sector shaft cover O-ring in the steering gear housing. Turn the input shaft as required to center the piston.

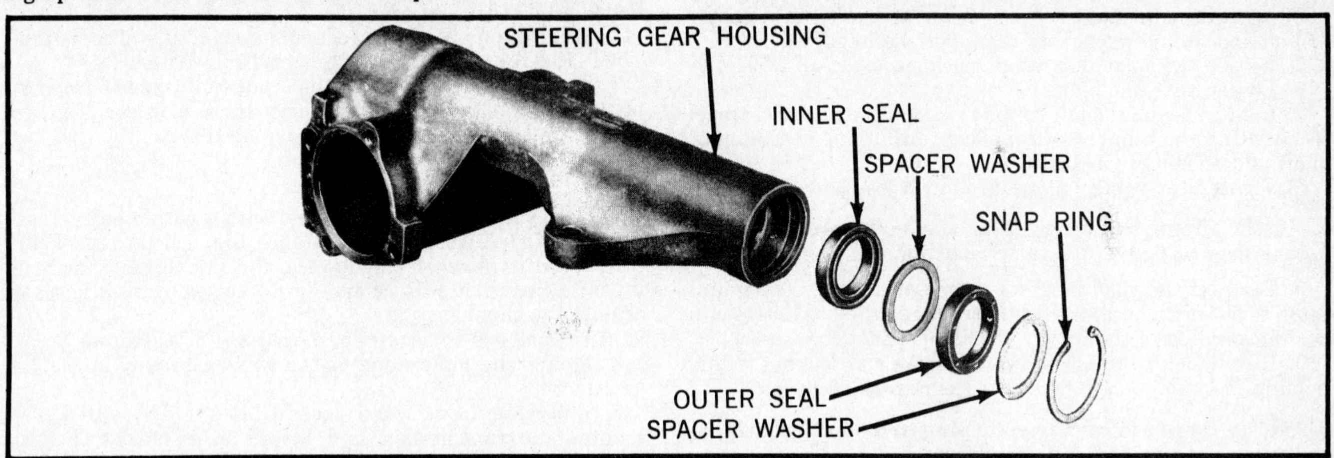

Steering gear housing and sector shaft seal assembly

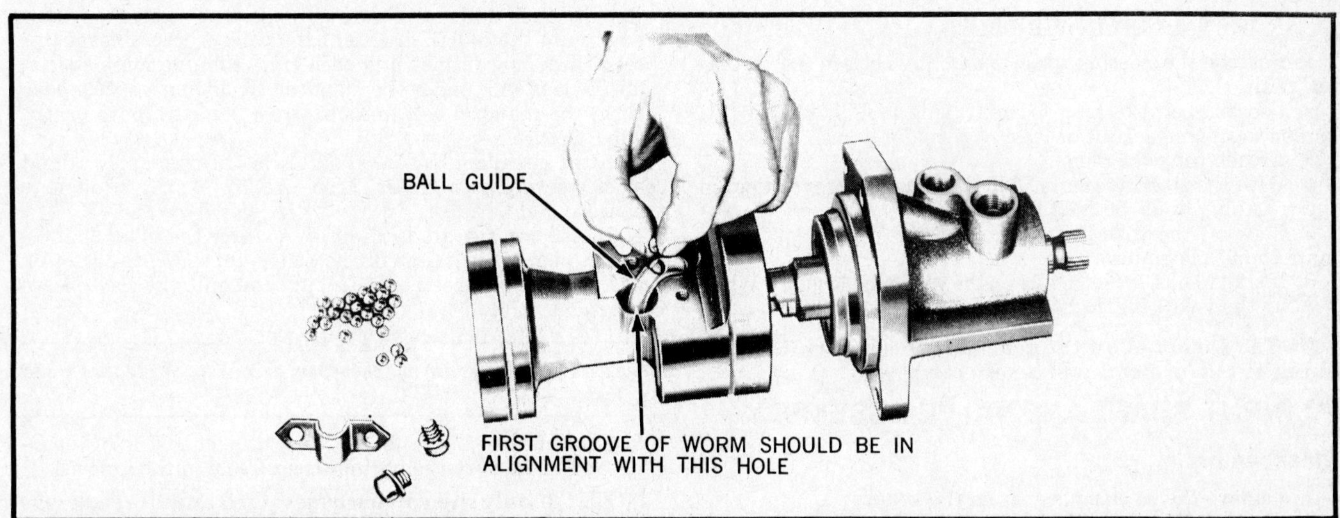

Loading balls into the ball guides

16. Apply vaseline to the sector shaft journal then position the sector shaft and cover assembly in the gear housing. Install the brake line bracket, the steering identification tag and two sector shaft cover attaching bolts. Torque the bolts to 55–70 ft. lbs.
17. Attach an inch lb. torque wrench to the input shaft. Adjust the mesh load to 17 inch lbs.

Ford Integral Power Rack and Pinion Gear

NOTE: The following power rack and pinion assembly is used on the Ford Aerostar.

RACK YOKE PLUG PRELOAD

Adjustment

GEAR REMOVED FROM VEHICLE

1. Attach the gear to a vise.
2. Do not remove the external pressure lines unless thay need replacement.
3. Drain the power steering fluid by rotating the input shaft lock-to-lock twice using the Pinion Shaft Torque Adapter, T74P–3504–R. Cover the ports with a shop towel while draining.
4. Insert an inch lb. torque wrench with a maximum capacity of 30–60 ft.lbs. into tool T74P–3504–R, then position the adapter tool and torque wrench on the input shaft splines.
5. Loosen the yoke plug locknut using tool, T78P–3504–H.
6. Loosen the yoke plug.
7. Rotate the input shaft so the rack is in the center of travel by counting the number of complete revolutions of the input shaft and dividing by two.
8. Tighten the yoke plug to 45–50 inch lbs.

NOTE: Clean the threads of the yoke plug prior to tightening to prevent a false reading.

9. Back off the yoke plug approximately ⅛ turn (44° minimum to 54° maximum) until the torque required to initate and sustain rotation of the input shaft is 7–18 inch lbs.
10. Install tool, T78P–3504–H on the yoke plug locknut. While holding the yoke plug, tighten the locknut 44–66 ft. lbs.

NOTE: Do not allow the yoke plug to move while tightening or the preload will be affected.

11. Recheck the input shaft torque after tightening the locknut.

GEAR INSTALLED IN VEHICLE

1. Position the steering wheel and front wheels in the 'on center' position.
2. Loosen the yoke plug locknut using tool, T78P–3504–H and back off the locknut at least ¼ turn.
3. Loosen the yoke plug.
4. With the steering gear still in the center of travel, tighten the yoke plug to 45–50 inch lbs.
5. Back off the yoke plug approximately ⅛ turn (44° minimum to 54° maximum).
6. Install tool, T78P–3504–H on the yoke plug locknut. While holding the yoke plug, tighten the locknut 44–66 ft. lbs.

NOTE: Do not allow the yoke plug to move while tightening or the preload will be affected.

INPUT SHAFT AND VALVE ASSEMBLY

Disassembly

1. Remove the steering gear from the vehicle.
2. Position the assembly in a suitable holding fixture and clean the exterior.
3. Do not remove the external pressure lines (right and left turn lines) unless they are leaking or damaged. If the lines are removed new teflon seals must be installed.
4. Using tool T78P–3504–H, loosen the yoke plug locknut and the yoke plug to relieve pressure on the rack.
5. Remove the pinion bearing plug.
6. Install a pinion shaft torque adapter, T74P–3504–R on the input shaft. Hold the input shaft and remove the pinion bearing locknut.

CAUTION

Do not allow the rack to reach full travel when loosening or tightening the locknut.

7. Using a suitable tool, pry the input shaft dust seal from the housing.
8. Remove the snap ring, located beneath the dust seal, from the valve housing.
9. Install a valve body puller, T78P–3504–B on the input shaft. Tighyen the nut on the tool to remove the input shaft and valve assembly.
10. To remove the lower pinion shaft seal, insert tool T78P–3504–E2 and spacer collet, D82P–3504–E1 until it bottoms. Hold the large nut and tighten the small nut on the tool until the expander fully tightens.
11. Install slide hammer, T50T–100–A in the rear of the tool T78P–3504–E2 and pull the lower pinion shaft seal from the housing.
12. If the pinion bearing needs replacement use slide hammer T50T–100–A and puller attachment T58L–101–A.
13. The four O-ring seals on the input shaft may be removed, however it is not necessary to replace these seals each time the valve is removed unless they are damaged.

Assembly

1. Coat the lower pinion oil seal with steering gear grease, ESW–M1C87–A or equivalent. Place the seal on tool T78P–3504–F, with the seal facing towards the tool. Support the housing on a clean flat surface and drive the seal until it is seated against the shoulder.
2. If the valve O-rings were removed install as follows:
   a. Mount the pinion end of the valve assembly in a soft jawed vise.
   b. Lubricate the Mandral Tool, T75L–3517–A1 with Type F automatic transmission fluid. Install the mandral tool over the valve assembly. Slide one valve sleeve O–ring over the tool.
   c. Slide Ring Pusher, T75L–3517–A2 over the mandral. Rapidly push down on the ring pusher and force the O-ring down into the fourth groove of the valve sleeve. Repeat this step three more times and each time add one more spacer, T75L–3517–A3, under the mandral. By adding a spacer each time, the mandral will line up with the next groove on the valve sleeve.
3. After installing the four valve seal O-rings, apply a light coat of steering gear grease, ESW–M1C87–A or equivalent to the sleeve and O-rings.
4. Install one spacer, T75L-3517–A3, over the input shaft to act as a pilot. Slowly install the sizing tube, T75L–3517–A4, over the sleeve valve end of the input shaft onto the vlave sleeve O-rings.

CAUTION

Make sure the O-rings are not being bent over as the sizing tube is slid over them.

5. Remove the sizing tube and check the condition of the O-rings and make sure the O-rings turn freely in the grooves.

NOTE: If only the valve was serviced and the rack was not moved while the valve was out, Step 6 may be omitted.

6. If the rack was removed and marked with paint, position the rack so that the paint mark is centered in the valve bore. If the rack was not removed, position the rack in the housing so the right end of the rack protrudes 14mm ($^{9}/_{16}$ in.) from the socket to the housing.

7. Insert the Valve Body Insertion Tool, T78P–3504–C in the top of the valve housing. Line up the 'D'-flat on the input shaft 180° from the yoke plug hole center and insert the valve assembly into the bore. The 'D'-flat must point straight to the rear when the gear is installed in the vehicle with the gear in the 'on center' (straight ahead) position. If necessary rotate the input shaft slightly from side to side to mesh the pinion to the rack teeth. Push the valve assembly in by hand until seated properly.

8. Insert the Pinion Shaft Torque Adapter, T74P–3504–R on the input shaft. Check if the pinion is centered by rotating the input shaft and counting the number of turns from center to each stop. If the number of turns is unequal, pull the valve assembly out far enough to free the pinion teeth. Rotate the input shaft 60° (one tooth) in the direction that requires the least turns. Reinsert the valve assembly and check if the pinion is centered. Repeat if necessary.

9. Install the nut on the pinion end of the valve assembly. Hold the input shaft with the Pinion Shaft Torque Adapter, T74P–3504–R and tighten the nut to 30–40 ft. lbs. The rack must be away from the stops during this operation.

10. Position the input shaft bearing over the shaft in the bore. drive the bearing into the bore with tool, T78P–3504–D until firmly seated.

11. Coat the input shaft seal with a thin coat of steering gear grease, ESW–M1C87–A or equivalent.

12. Install the input shaft seal with the lip towards the gear housing.

13. Install the input shaft seal over the seal protector tool, so the seal lip faces the valve.

14. Drive the seal into the bore with the seal installer, TP78–3504–D until seated.

15. Install the snap ring into the valve bore.

16. Coat the input shaft in the dust seal area with Polyethylene grease.

17. Install the input shaft seal tool, T85T–3504–CH1 over the input shaft.

18. Install the input shaft dust seal and drive into position using seal installer, T85T–3504–CH2. Remove the tool from the seal and the input shaft. This allows trapped air to be released.

19. Install the bearing cap and tighten to 50 ft. lbs.

20. Adjust the rack yoke preload.

GEAR HOUSING, RACK YOKE PLUG, RACK ASSEMBLY, RACK BUSHING AND OIL SEALS

Disassembly

1. Remove the tie rod socket assemblies from both ends of the rack. Remove the input shaft and valve assembly from the gear housing.

2. Remove the yoke plug locknut using tool, T78P–3504–H.

3. Remove the yoke plug from the housing using a suitable socket.

4. Remove the yoke spring and yoke from the gear housing. The yoke may be removed by gripping on the guide post with a pair of pliers.

5. From the right end of the gear (opposite the pinion), push the rack into the housing far enough to gain access to the snap ring.

6. Remove the snap ring from the right end of the gear housing.

7. Using a hammer and a brass drift, slowley drive the rtack out of the right side of the housing along with the bushing. Remove the rack from the housing.

8. To remove the high pressure rack oil seal, insert tool, T78P–3504–J into the housing until it bottoms.

9. Activate the expander with a wrench until the expander fully tightens against the oil seal.

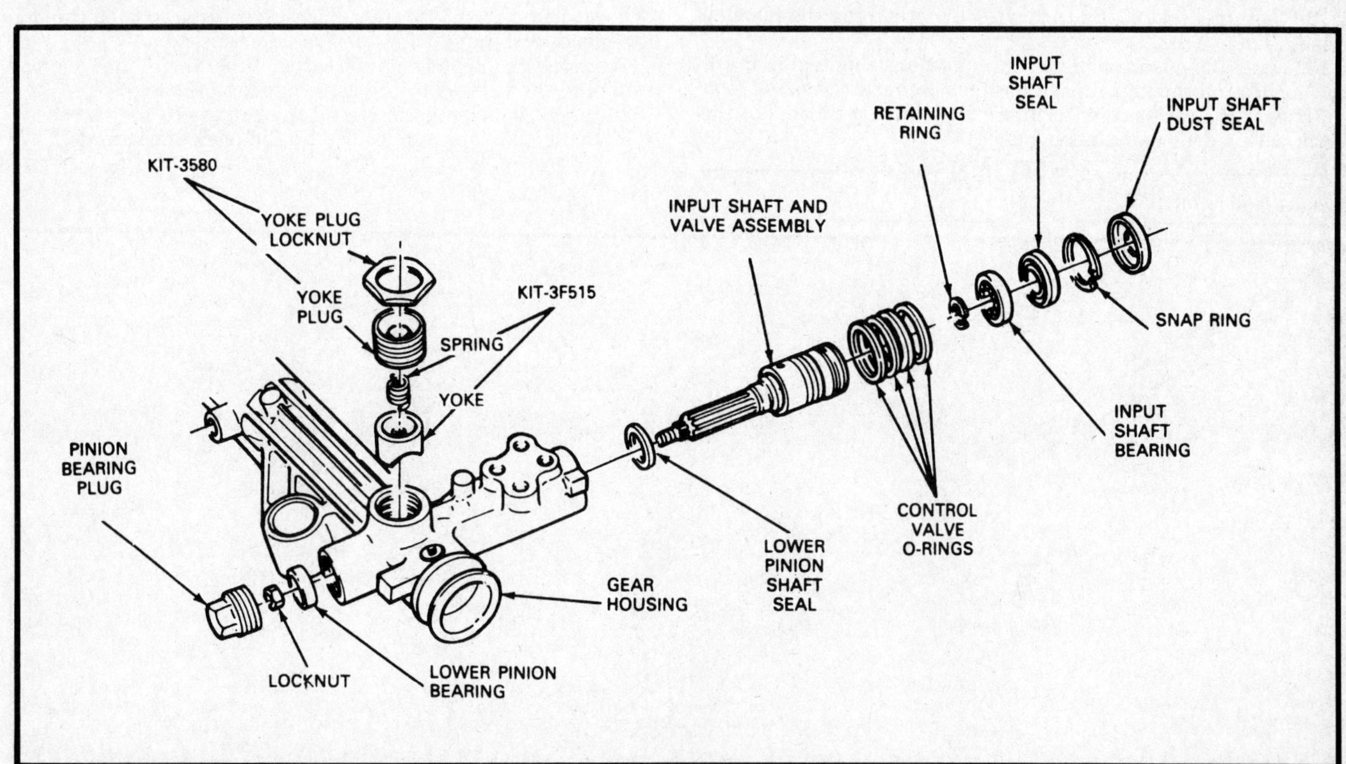

Input shaft and valve assembly-Ford Integral rack and pistion assembly

10. Install Slide Hammer, T50T-100-A into the end of the Rack Oil Seal Remover, T78P-3504-J and pull the seal from the housing. Discard the seal.

NOTE: On the first attempt, the plastic insert may pull out of the seal, leaving the seal in the housing. Repeat the procedure until the seal is removed.

11. Remove the plastic O-ring and the rubber O-ring from the rack piston with a suitable tool.
12. To remove the rack bushing seal, grip the seal in a vise and squeeze the seal to distort it. Repeat this procedure if the bushing slips out of the vise. With the seal distorted, it can easily removed using a suitable prying tool.

Assembly

1. Mark the center tooth (the eleventh tooth) on the rack so the mark will be visible in the valve bore.
2. Slide the Teflon Ring Replacer, T74P-3504-G on the rack until it seats on the piston. Install the rubber O-ring in the rack piston groove.
3. slide the plastic (Teflon) O-ring over the tool into the piston groove over the rubber O-ring.
4. Remove the plastic insert from the rack seal. Save the insert for reinstallation.
5. Install the Rack Seal Protector Tool, T85L-3504-B over the rack teeth.
6. Lubricate the rack and the protector tool with type F transmission fluid.
7. Install the seal so that the lip faces the piston. Push the seal all the way against the piston. Remove the rack seal protector.
8. Install the plastic insert in the rack seal.
9. Pack the rack teeth with steering gear grease and apply a light coat to the yoke contact area in back of the rack teeth.
10. Lubricate the piston seal and and rack seal outside diameter with type F transmission fluid.
11. Install the Teflon Ring Sizing Tool, T78P-3504-M into the end of the gear housing.
12. Carefully install the rack without scratching the housing piston bore.
13. Carefully push the piston through the sizing tool. Continue pushing on the rack until it bottoms. Remove the sizing tool.
14. Seat the rack seal with the rack by driving the end of the rack with a drift and plastic mallet.

CAUTION

Do not remove the rack.

15. Install the left tie rod and ball socket on the rack and hand tighten.
16. Thread the Rack Sleeve Protector, T74P-3504-J over the threads on the right side of the rack. Coat the protective sleeve with type F transmission fluid.

CAUTION

The rack must not move too far from the center since excessive travel can cause the rack teeth to cut the left (inner) oil seal.

17. Apply steering grease to the outer rack oil seal, then install the high pressure oil seal in the rack bushing using tool T74P-3504-F.
18. Lubricate the short protective sleeve on the rack end and the seal outside diameter on the rack bushing with steering grease.
19. Start the bushing on the rack with the seal facing forward. Pass the bushing and the seal over the protective sleeve and into the housing bore. Using The Teflon Ring Sizing Tool, T78P-3504-M, apply hand pressure to the rack bushing until the bushing seats in the gear housing. If hand pressure will not seat the bushing, use a 1⅛ in., 12 point socket or larger and a plastic mallet and tap the bushing in place.
20. Install the snap ring in the right end of the gear housing./
21. Install the right tie rod assembly. Tighten both tie rod sockets simultaneously to 55-65 ft. lbs. by holding one and turning the other.
22. Tap new coiled pins in the sockets until fulley seated.
23. Fill the yoke plug hole with 2 ounces of steering gear grease, ESW-MIC87-A or equivalent.
24. Install the yoke plug in the gear housing.
25. Install the yoke in the gear housing.
26. Install the yoke spring in the yoke.
27. Start the yoke plug and locknut in the gear housing.
28. Install the input shaft and valve assembly as outlined earlier.
29. Adjust the rack plug preload.
30. Apply lubricant to the undercut in the tie rods where the bellows clamp to the tie rods. This is required to keep the bellows from twisting during toe—in adjustment.
31. Install the bellows and breather tube. Install new clamps retaining the bellows to the gear housing.
32. Install the clamps retaining the bellows to the tie rods.
33. Install the jam nuts to the tie rod ends on the rods.

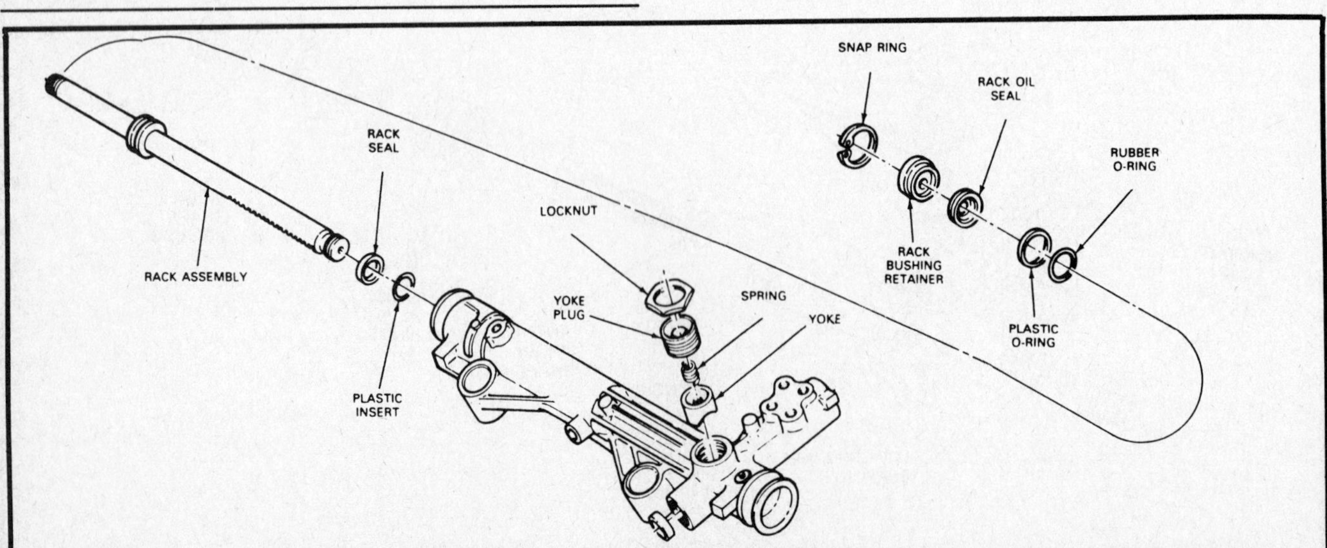

Gear housing, rack yoke plug, rack assembly, rack bushing and oil seals

Suspensions
Domestic Trucks

10

FRONT SUSPENSION TROUBLE DIAGNOSIS

UNEVEN TIRE WEAR

1. Tire pressure's low
2. Excessive camber
3. Tires out of balance
4. Tires overloaded
5. Out of round tires and rims
6. Caster incorrect
7. Toe-in incorrect
8. High speed driving into turns
9. Unequal tire size
10. Improper tracking
11. Bent or worn steering and suspension components

STEERING WHEEL SPOKE POSITION NOT PROPERLY CENTERED

1. Steering gear set off "high-spot"
2. Improper toe-in
3. Relationship between lengths of tie-rods not equal
4. Bent steering components
5. Steering wheel improperly placed on steering shaft

HARD STEERING

1. Tire pressure low
2. Wheel spindle bent
3. Steering assembly binding or maladjusted
4. Tie rod ends tight
5. Caster excessive
6. Kingpins or ball joints too tight
7. Lack of lubrication to steering and suspension units.

SHIMMY

1. Tire pressure incorrect
2. Tires of unequal size
3. Loose wheel bearings
4. Loose steering arms or steering gear adjustment
5. Steering gear loose on frame
6. Loose or broken steering linkage rods or internal adjustment parts
7. Spring shackles loose
8. Ball joints or kingpins and bushings worn
9. Front end alignment out of specifications
10. Wheels and tires out of balance
11. Wheels and tires out of round or loose on hub
12. Shock absorbers worn out.
13. U-bolts loose on axle to spring.
14. Worn or out-of-round brake drum or rotor (shimmy felt upon brake application)

WANDER OR WEAVE

1. Tire pressure incorrect
2. Tires of unequal size
3. Bent spindle
4. Wheel bearings loose or worn
5. Kingpins worn or bent
6. Kingpins tight in steering knuckle or bushings
7. Steering gear assembly too tight or too loose
8. Too little caster
9. Too much or too little chamber
10. Too much or too little toe-in
11. Front axle bent or shifted
12. Springs broken
13. Frame diamond shaped
14. Rear axle housing shifted or bent
15. Steering linkage tight or binding
16. Lack of lubrication to front suspension or steering linkage
17. Defective power steering assembly

FRONT END RIDES HARD

1. Improper tire pressure
2. Springs broken or too stiff
3. Shock absorbers too stiff or malfunctioning
4. Front end alignment incorrect
5. Loose suspension components

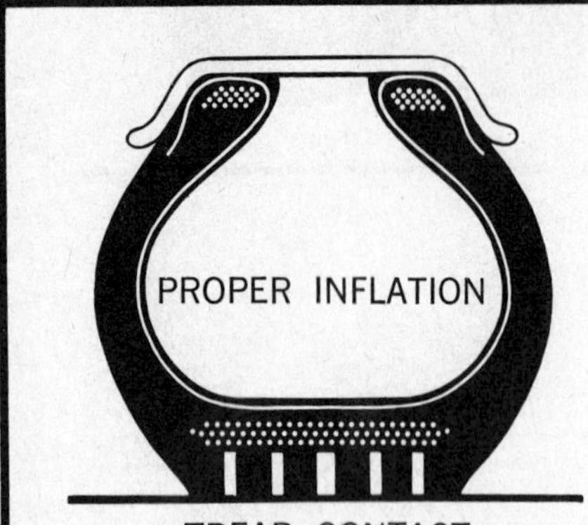

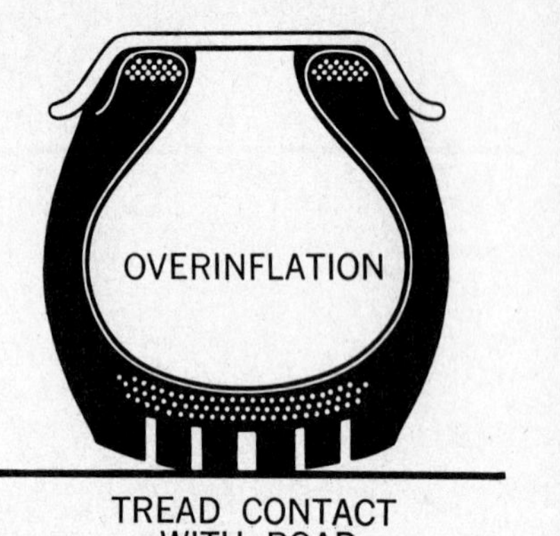

Comparison of normal, under and over tire inflation and effect on the tire tread

VEHICLE STEERS TO ONE SIDE AT ALL TIMES

1. Incorrect caster setting
2. Incorrect camber setting
3. Incorrect kingpin inclination or wheel support angle
4. Unequal tire pressure or tire size
5. One side brake drag
6. Unequal shock absorber control
7. Bent or damaged steering and suspension components
8. Uneven or weak spring condition, front or rear
9. Broken center or shackle bolts
10. Frame bent causing improper tracking

NOISY FRONT END

1. Lack of, or improper lubrication
2. Loose steering linkage
3. Loose suspension parts
4. Loose brake parts
5. Worn universal (FWD)
6. Worn differential (FWD)
7. Loose sheet metal

LUBRICATION LEAKING INTO DRUM OR ON ROTOR

1. Excessive differential lubricant (FWD)
2. Clogged axle housing vent (FWD)
3. Damage or worn universal driveshaft oil seal (FWD)
4. Loose steering knuckle flange bearings (FWD)
5. Defective outer seal
6. Rough spindle to oil seal surface
7. Wheel bearings overpacked or use of wrong lubricant
8. Clogged oil slinger drain
9. Cracked steering knuckle outer flange

EXCESSIVE TIRE WEAR

1. Incorrect wheel alignment
2. Failure to rotate tires
3. Improper tire inflation
4. Overload or improperly loaded vehicle
5. High tire temperature operation
6. Excessive speed, quick starts and quick stops
7. Bent suspension, frame or wheel parts
8. Tires out of balance
9. Uneven brake application
10. Excessive hard turning of tandem and spread axle wheels

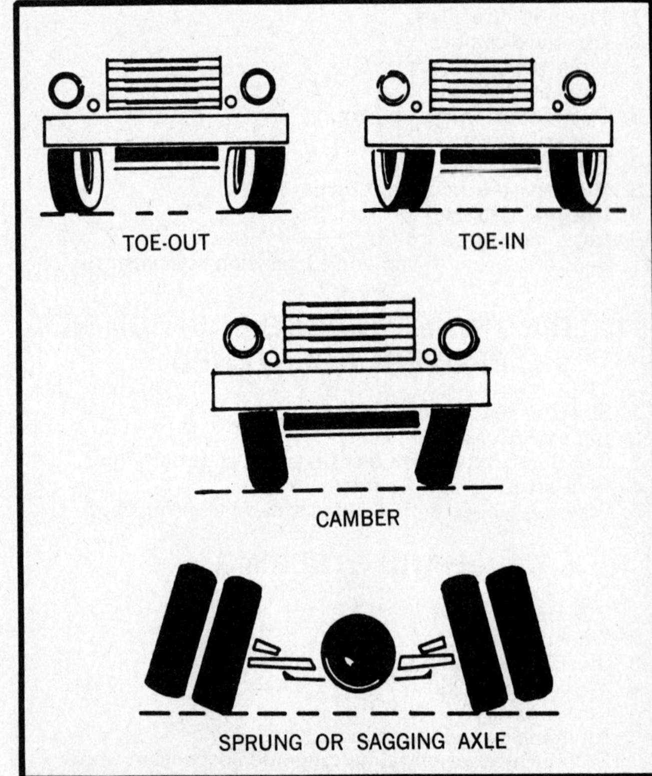

Exaggerated views of alignment problems

Wheel Alignment

For a truck to have safe steering control with a minimum of tire wear, certain established rules must be followed. These rules fix the values of planes, angles and radii relative to each other and to truck and tire dimensions. Some factors are built in, with no provision for adjustment; others are adjustable within limits. The entire system depends upon all value factors, separately and combined. It is therefore difficult to change some of the established settings without influencing others.

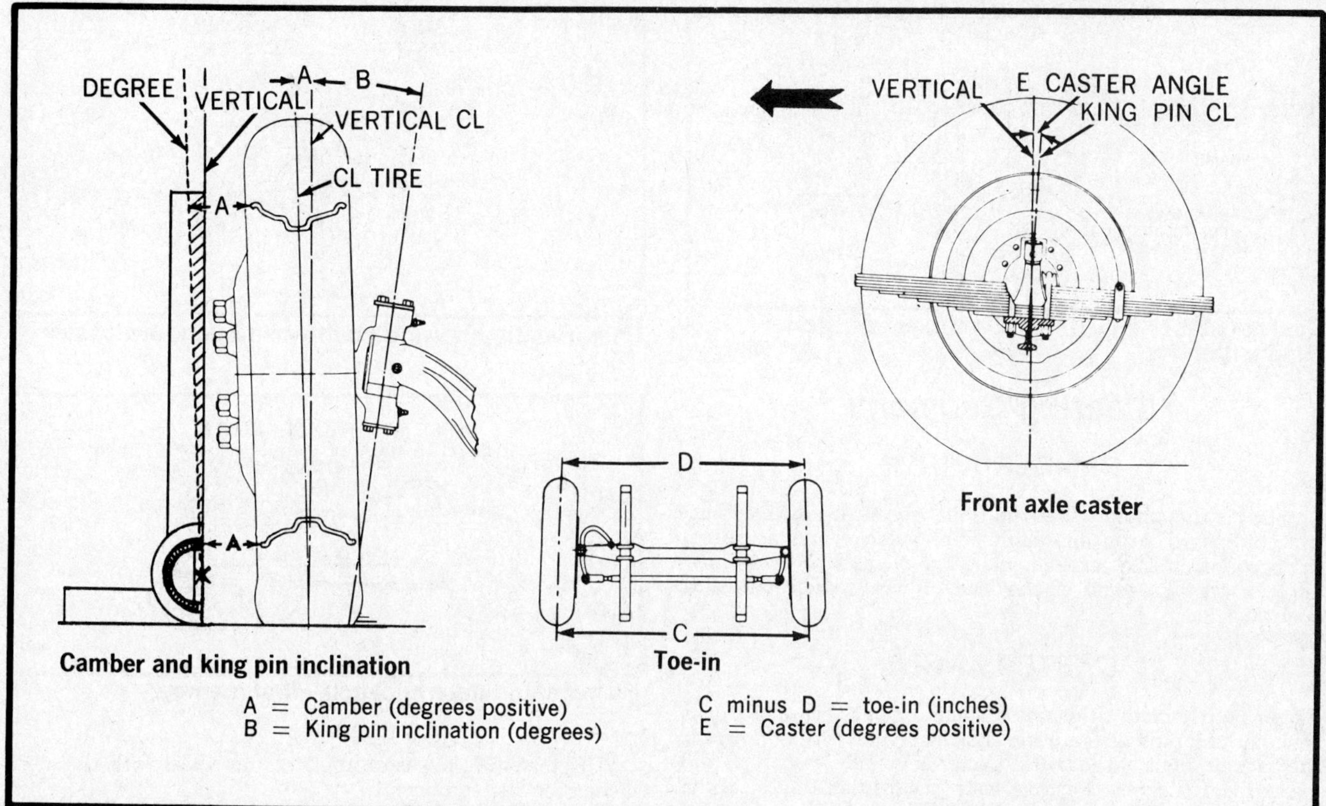

Steering geometry

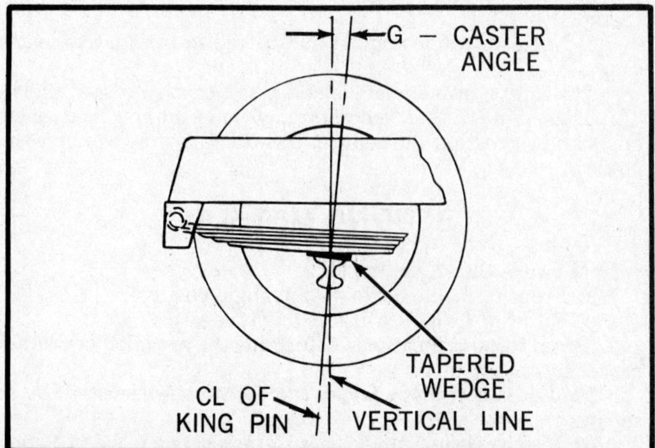

Use of tapered wedge between the axle and spring to adjust caster angle

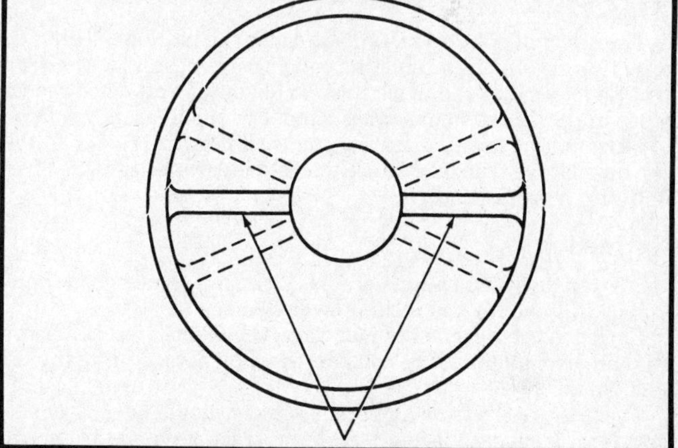
Steering wheel position

This system is called steering geometry or wheel alignment and requires a complete check of all the factors involved. Definitions of these factors and the effect each one has on the truck are given in the following paragraphs. For adjustment data relative to each separate truck and year, refer to the individual truck sections.

STEERING WHEEL POSITION

Always check steering wheel alignment in conjunction with and at the same time as toe-in. In fact, the steering wheel spoke position, with the truck on a straight section of highway, may be the first indication of front end misalignment.

If the truck has been wrecked, or indicates any evidence of steering gear or linkage disturbance, the Pitman arm should be disconnected from the sector shaft. The steering wheel (or gear) should be turned from extreme right to extreme left to determine the halfway point in its turning scope. This will be the spot on the gear that is in action during straight ahead driving and in which position the steering gear should be adjusted. With the steering wheel in the straight-ahead position and the steering gear adjusted to zero lash status, reconnect the Pitman arm.

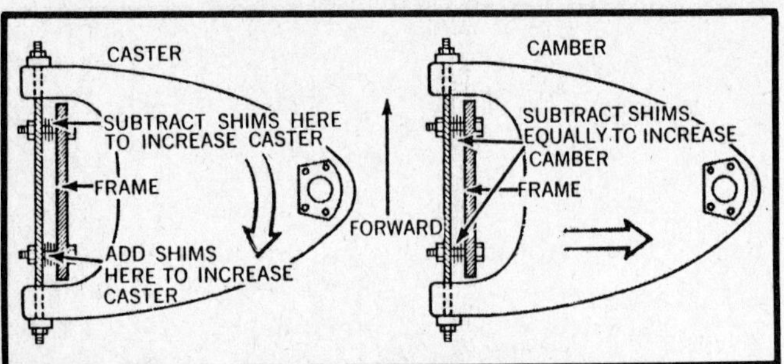

Caster-camber adjustment on upper arm front suspension

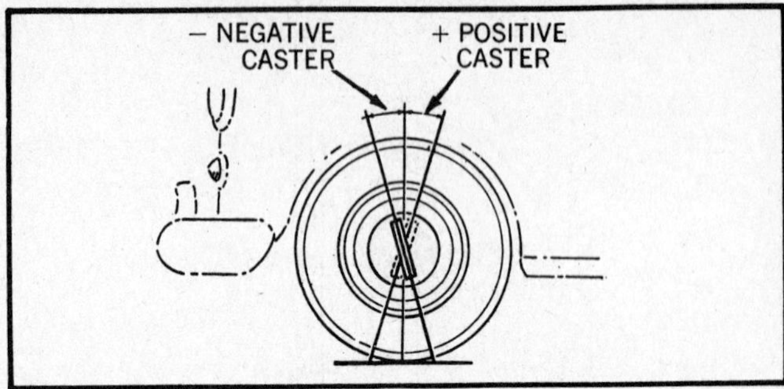

Caster angle showing positive and negative caster

Steering Geometry

CAMBER ANGLE

Camber is the amount that the front wheels are inclined outward or inward at the top. Chamber is spoken of, and measured, in degrees from the perpendicular. The purpose of the camber angle is to take some of the load off the spindle outboard bearing.

CASTER ANGLE

Caster is the amount that the kingpin (or in the case of trucks without king-pins, the knuckle support pivots) is tilted towards the back or front of the truck. Caster is usually spoken of, and measured, in degrees. Positive caster means that the top of the kingpin is tilted toward the back of the truck. Positive caster is indicated by the sign "+".

Negative caster is exactly the opposite; the top of the kingpin is tilted toward the front of the truck. This is generally indicated by the sign "-". Negative caster is sometimes referred to as reverse caster.

The effect of positive caster is to cause the truck to steer in the direction in which it tends to go. Positive caster in the front wheels may cause the truck to steer down off a crowned road or steer in the direction of a cross wind. For this reason, a number of our modern trucks are arranged with negative caster so that the opposite is true; the truck tends to steer up a crowned road and into a cross wind.

Correction

Caster angle specifications are based on the vehicle load limits, which will usually result in a level frame.

Since load requirements may vary, the frame does not always remain level and must be considered when determining the correct caster angle.

To measure the from angle, the vehicle should be on a smooth and level surface. Place a bubble protractor on the frame rail and measure the degree of frame tilt and in what direction, either front or rear.

Two methods of determining caster angles are used. The first method is to determine the caster angle from the wheel with alignment equipment, and the second method is to obtain the desired caster angle from the specification charts. The frame angle is then added to or subtracted fro the caster angles as necessary. The two methods are outlined. Examples and diagrams are provided for use by the repairman to assist in determining the proper caste angle to use.

FIRST METHOD

1. Determine the frame angle.
   a. Frame high at rear–frame angle is negative.
   b. Frame low at rear–frame angle is positive.

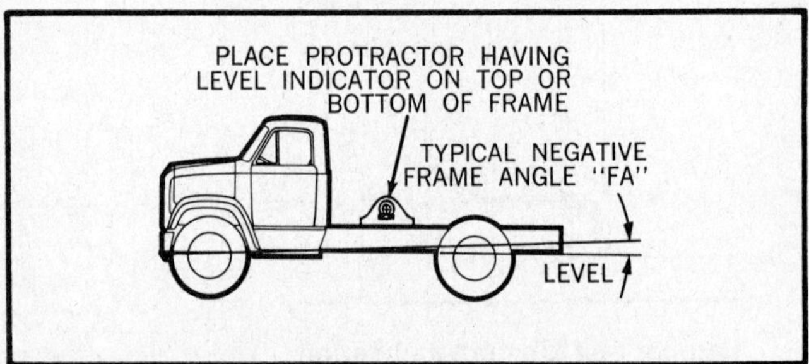

Frame angle determination—first method

2. Determine the caster angle at the wheel with the alignment checking equipment.
3. Add or subtract frame angle from or to the determined caster angle.
   a. Negative frame angle is added to positive caster angle.
   b. Positive frame angle is subtracted from positive caster angle.
   c. Negative frame angle is subtracted from negative caster angle.
   d. Positive frame angle is added to negative caster angle.
4. Determine the correct caster angle and the specified caster angle and correct on the vehicle. Use the following examples as guides.

SECOND METHOD

1. Measure the frame angle.
   a. Front of frame down–frame angle positive.
   b. Front of frame up–frame angle negative
2. From the specifications, determine the specified or desired caster setting.
3. Add or subtract the frame angle from the specified caster setting.
   a. Positive frame angle is subtracted from the specified setting.
   b. Negative frame angle is added to the specified caster setting.
4. Using wheel alignment equipment, obtain the measured caster angle from the wheel and determine the corrected specified setting, using the following examples as guides.

ANGLE OF KINGPIN INCLINATION

In addition to the caster angle, the kingpins (or knuckle support pivots) are also inclined toward each other at the top. This angle is known as kingpin inclination and is usually spoken of, and measured, in degrees.

The effect of kingpin inclination is to cause the wheels to steer in a straight line, regardless of outside forces such as crowned

EXAMPLE NO. 1 (FRAME LOWER AT REAR—POSITIVE)

Measured wheel caster angle	+2°
Frame angle	3°
Actual caster angle (Frame at zero degrees)	−1°
Specifications (desired)	+2°
Necessary degrees to change	+3°

REFER TO EXAMPLE 1

WHEEL CL
CA +2°
FRONT
POSITIVE FA
FRAME 0°
FA 3°

ACTUAL CASTER ANGLE = −1° @ 0° FA

WHEEL CL
CA-2°
FRONT
NEGATIVE
FRAME 0°
FA 2°

ACTUAL CASTER ANGLE = −4° @ 0° FA

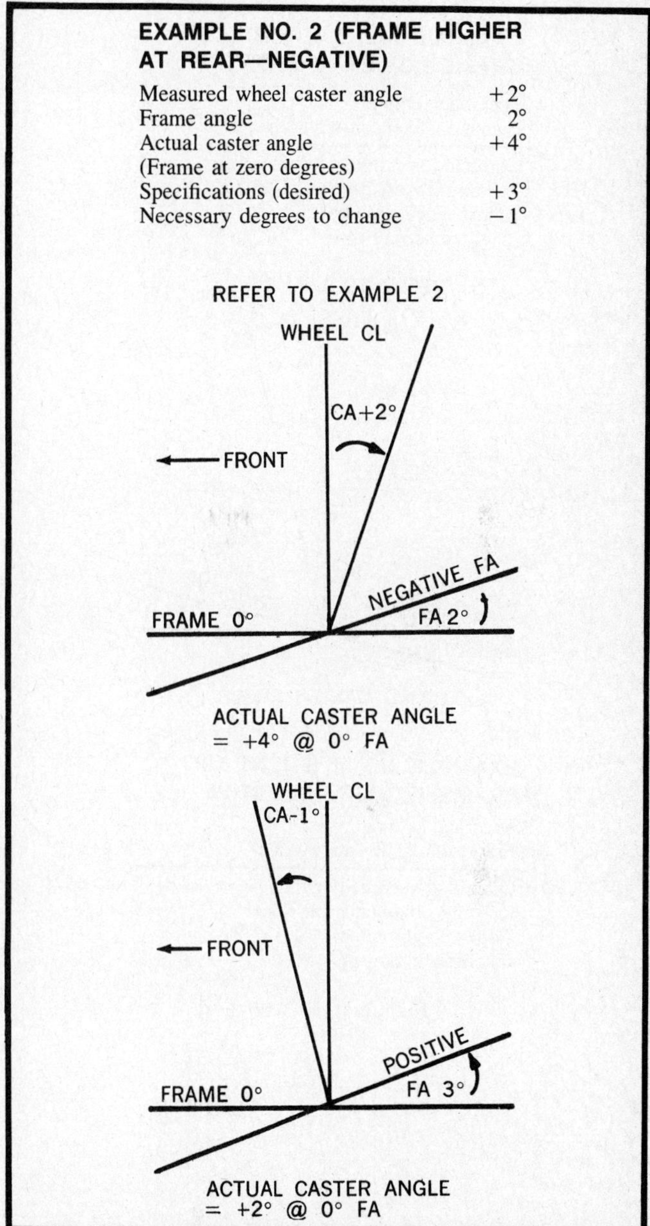

EXAMPLE NO. 2 (FRAME HIGHER AT REAR—NEGATIVE)

Measured wheel caster angle	+2°
Frame angle	2°
Actual caster angle (Frame at zero degrees)	+4°
Specifications (desired)	+3°
Necessary degrees to change	−1°

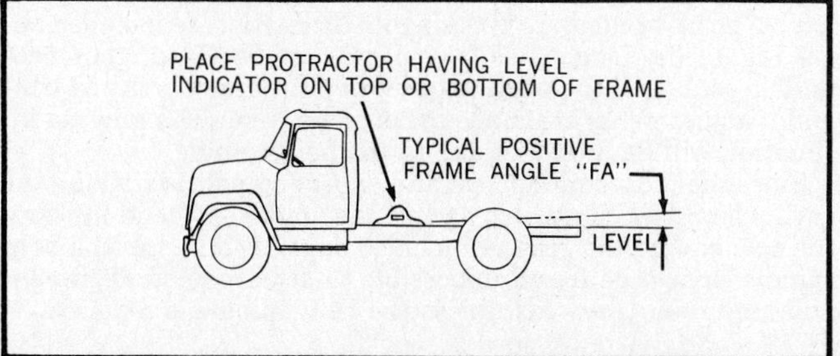

Frame angle determination—second method

roads, cross winds, etc., which may tend to make it steer at a tangent. As the spindle is moved from extreme right to extreme left it apparently rises and falls. Notice that it reaches its highest position when the wheels are in the straight-ahead position. In actual operation, the spindle cannot rise and fall because because the wheel is in constant contact with the ground.

Therefore, the truck itself will rise at the extreme right turn and come to its lowest point at the straight-ahead position, and again rise for an extreme left turn. The weight of the truck will tend to cause the wheels to come to the straight-ahead position, which is the lowest position of the truck itself.

INCLUDED ANGLE

Included angle is the name given to that angle which includes kingpin inclination and camber. It is the relationship between the centerline of the wheel and the centerline of the kingpin (or the knuckle support pivots). This angle is build into the knuckle

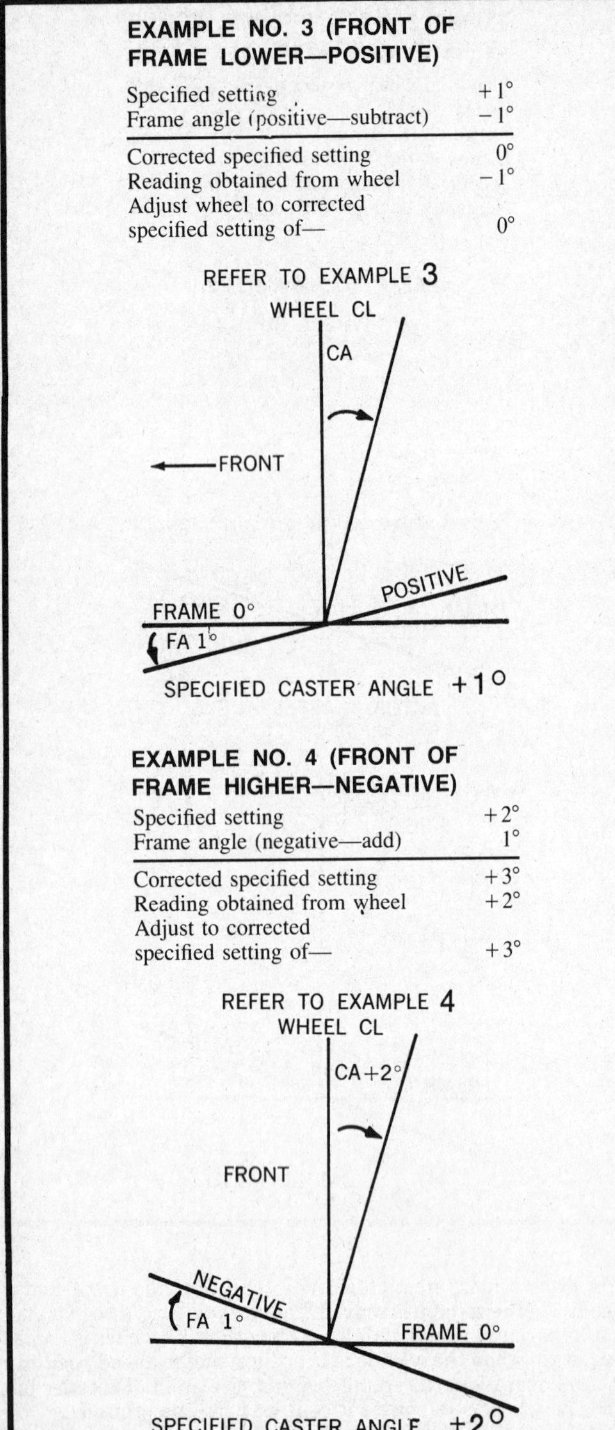

EXAMPLE NO. 3 (FRONT OF FRAME LOWER—POSITIVE)

Specified setting	+1°
Frame angle (positive—subtract)	−1°
Corrected specified setting	0°
Reading obtained from wheel	−1°
Adjust wheel to corrected specified setting of—	0°

EXAMPLE NO. 4 (FRONT OF FRAME HIGHER—NEGATIVE)

Specified setting	+2°
Frame angle (negative—add)	1°
Corrected specified setting	+3°
Reading obtained from wheel	+2°
Adjust to corrected specified setting of—	+3°

(spindle) forging and will remain constant throughout the life of the truck, unless the spindle itself is damaged.

When checking a truck on the front end stand, always measure kingpin inclination as well as camber unless some provision is made on the stand for checking condition of the spindle. Where no such provision is made, add the kingpin inclination inclination to the camber for each side of the truck. These totals

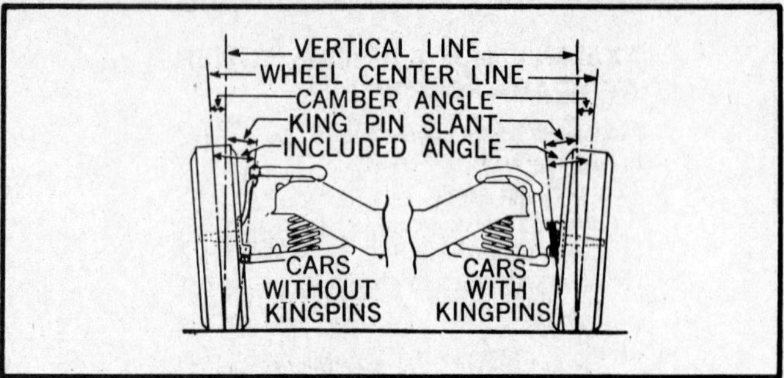

Camber, king pin slant and included angle

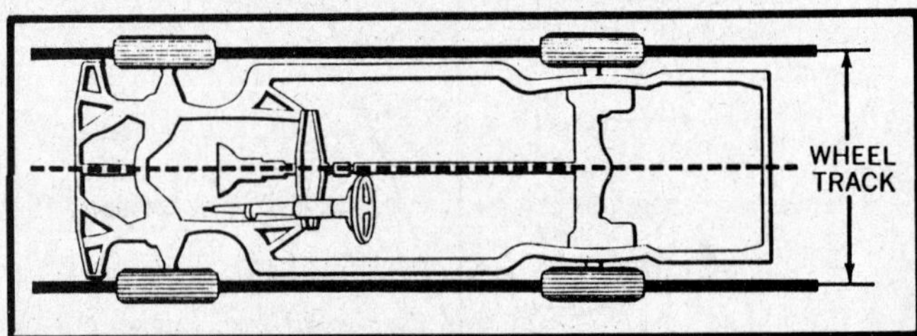

Typical parallel wheel track

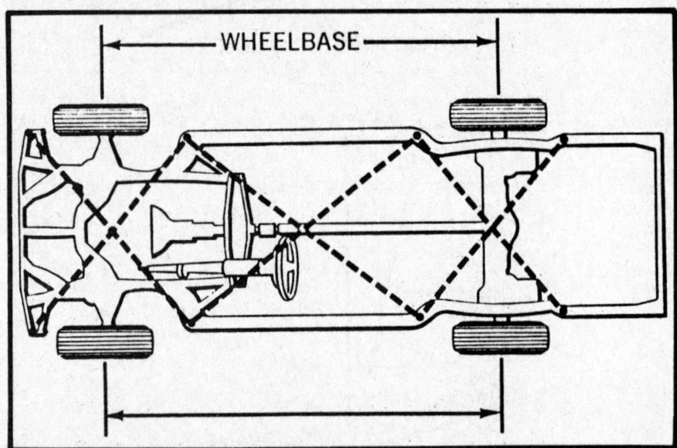

Measuring corresponding points of frame

should be exactly the same, regardless of how far from the norm the readings may be.

For example, the left side of the truck checks 5 $^1/_2$° kingpin inclination and 1° positive camber–total 6 $^1/_2$°. Since both sides check exactly the same for the included angle, it is unlikely that both spindles, in this instance, are bent. Adjusting to correct for camber will automatically set correct kingpin inclination.

A bent spindle would show up like this: left side of the truck has 3/4° positive camber, 5¼° kingpin inclination–6° included angle. Right side of truck has 1¼° positive camber, 6° kingpin inclination–total 7¼° included angle. One of these spindles is bent and if adjustments are made to correct camber, the kingpin inclination will be incorrect due to the bent spindle.

Since the most common cause of a bent spindle is striking the curb when parking, which causes the spindle to bend upward, the side having the greater included angle usually has the bent spindle. It will be found impossible to achieve good alignment and minimum tire wear unless the bent spindle is replaced.

TOE-IN

Toe-in is the amount that the front wheels are closer together at

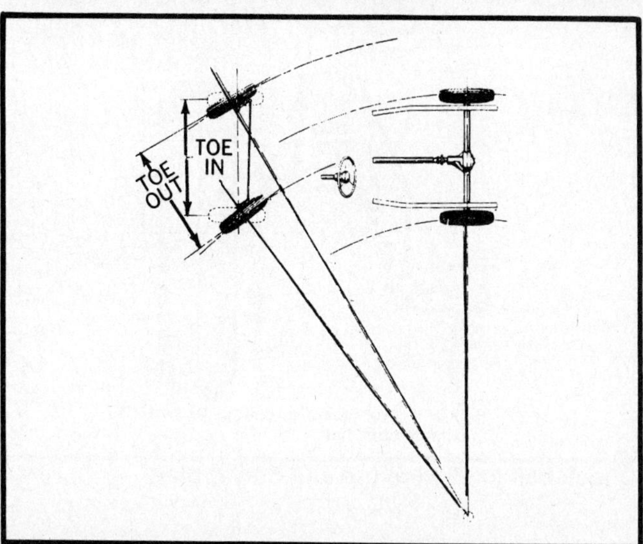

Steering geometry on turns

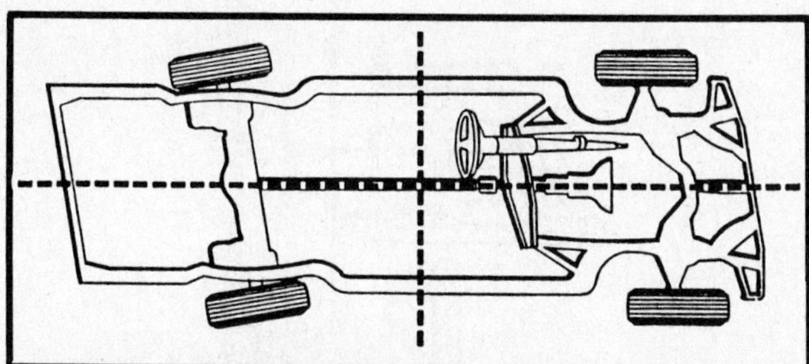
Bent frame, diamond shaped

the front than they are at the back. This dimension is usually spoken of, and measured, in inches or fractions of inches.

Generally speaking, the wheels are toed-in because they are cambered. When a truck operates with 0° camber it will be found to operate with zero toe-in. As the required camber increases, so does the toe-in. The reason for this is that the cambered wheel tends to steer in the direction in which it is cambered. Therefore it is necessary to overcome this tendency of the wheel by compensating very slightly in the direction opposite to that in which it tends to roll. Caster and camber both have an effect on toe-in. Therefore toe-in is the last thing on the front end which should be corrected.

TOE-OUT STEERING RADIUS

When a truck is steered into a turn, the outside wheel of the vehicle scribes a much larger circle than the inside wheel. Therefore, the outside wheel must be steered to a somewhat less angle than the inside wheel. This difference in the angle is often called toe-out.

The change in angle from toe-in in the straight-ahead position to toe-out in the turn is caused by the relative position of the steering arms to the kingpin and to each other.

If a line were drawn from the center of the kingpin through the center of the steering arm-tie rod attaching hole at each wheel, these lines would be found to cross almost exactly in the center of the rear axle.

If the front end angles, including toe-in, are set correctly, and the toe-out is found to be incorrect, one or both of the steering arms are bent.

TRACKING

While tracking is more a function of the rear axle and frame, it is difficult to align the front suspension when the truck does not track straight. Tracking means that the centerline of the rear axle follows exactly the path of the centerline of the front axle when the truck is moving in a straight line.

On trucks that have equal tread, front and rear, the rear tires will follow in exactly the thread of the front tires, when moving in a straight line. However, there are many trucks whose rear tread is wider than the front tread. On such trucks, the rear axle tread will straddle the front axle tread an equal amount on both sides, when moving in a straight line.

Perhaps the easiest way to check a truck for tracking is to stand directly in back of it and watch it more in a straight line down the street. If the observer will stand as near to the center of the truck as possible, he can readily observe, even with the difference in perspective between the front and rear wheels, whether or not they are tracking properly. If the truck is found to track incorrectly, the difficulty will be found in either the frame or in the rear axle alignment.

Another more accurate method to check tracking is to park the truck on a level floor and drop a plumb-line from the extreme outer edge of the front suspension lower A-frame. Use the same drop point on each side of the truck. Make a chalk lie where the plumb-line strikes the floor. Do the same with the rear axle, selecting a point on the rear axle housing for the plumb-line.

Measure diagonally from the left rear mark to the right front mark and from the right rear mark to the left front mark. These two diagonal measurements should be exactly the same. A 1/4 in. variation is acceptable.

If the diagonal measurements taken are different, measure from the right rear mark to the right front mark and from the left rear to the left front. These two measurements should also be the same within 1/4 in..

If the diagonal measurements are different, but the longitudinal measurements are the same, the frame is swayed (diamond shaped).

However, in the event that the diagonal measurements are unequal and the longitudinal measurements are also unequal, and the truck is tracking incorrectly, the rear axle is misaligned.

If the diagonal and longitudinal measurements are both unequal, but the truck appears to track correctly on the street, a kneeback is indicated.

NOTE: A kneeback means that one complete side of the front suspension is bent back. This is often caused by crimping the front wheels against the curb when parking the vehicle, then starting up without straightening the wheels out.

Suspension And Ball Joint System

When checking the suspension and ball joints, it is advisable to follow the manufacturer's recommendations. For all practical purposes, however, the following general procedures are applicable.

SUSPENSION SYSTEM

Inspection

This check is made with the ball joints fully loaded, so that suspension elements other than the ball joints may be checked.
When the front spring or torsion bar is supported by lower control arm, the jackstand should be located under the front crossmember or frame.
When the front spring is supported by the upper control arm, the jackstand should be located under the lower control arm.

Vertical or horizontal movement at the road wheel should not exceed the following:

1. Up to and including 16 in. – ¼ in. movement.
2. 16 to 18 in. – ⅓ in. movement.
3. More than 18 in. – ½ in. movement.

Ball Joint

Inspection

When checking the ball joints for any wear, they must be free of any load.

When the front spring or torsion bar is supported by the lower control arm, the jackstand should be positioned under the lower control arm.

When the front spring is supported by the upper control arm, the jackstand should be located under the front crossmember or frame.

Replace the upper ball joint if any noticeable play is present in the joint when the spring is supported by the upper control arm; If the sideplay (horizontal motion) of the wheel, when rocked, exceed specifications; or if the up and down (vertical motion) exceed specifications.

WHEEL BEARING AND SEAL

Replacement

NOTE: Refer to individual truck section for oil filled hub service.

1. Place jack under lower suspension arm. Remove hub cover and grease cap. Remove spindle nut, keyed washer and outer bearing. Slide off hub and drum.

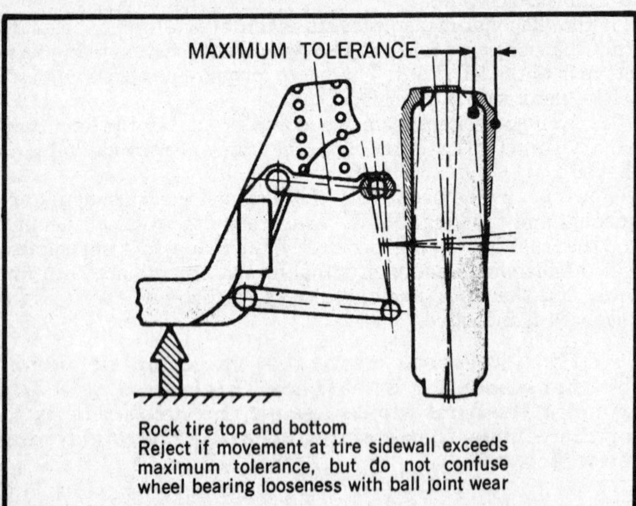
MAXIMUM TOLERANCE
Rock tire top and bottom
Reject if movement at tire sidewall exceeds maximum tolerance, but do not confuse wheel bearing looseness with ball joint wear

Check ball joint radial (side play)

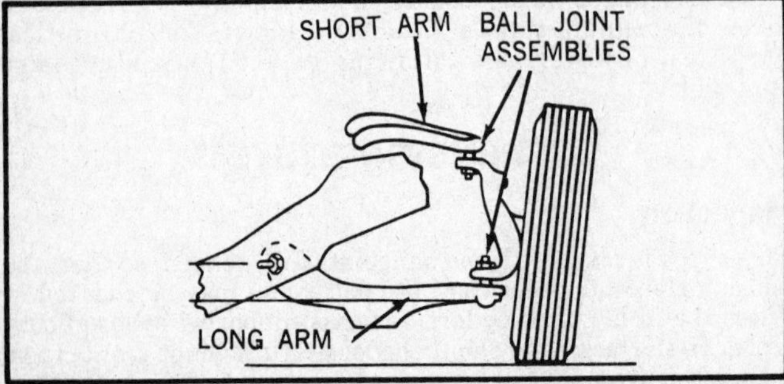
SHORT ARM
BALL JOINT ASSEMBLIES
LONG ARM

Use of control arms and ball joints for independent suspension

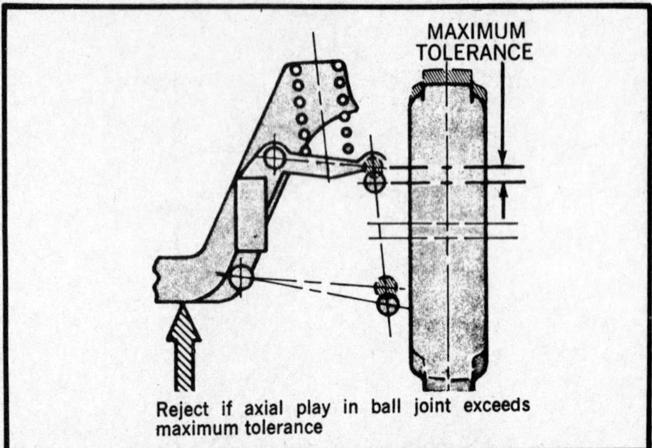
MAXIMUM TOLERANCE
Reject if axial play in ball joint exceeds maximum tolerance

Check ball joint axial (up and down) play

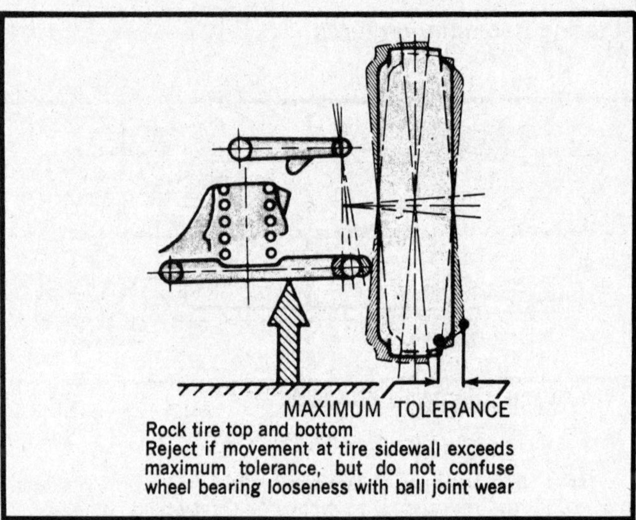
MAXIMUM TOLERANCE
Rock tire top and bottom
Reject if movement at tire sidewall exceeds maximum tolerance, but do not confuse wheel bearing looseness with ball joint wear

Maximum tolerance

NOTE: In some cases, drum removal may require loosening of brake adjustment.

2. At this point, brakes and drums should be inspected for their condition.
3. With hub and drum on bench, remove seal and inner bearing. Thoroughly clean all parts. Drive out inner and outer races of roller type. Use care not to mar the bearing surfaces.
4. Pack bearings with approved lubricant. When replacing cups, use a bearing race driver if possible. If a punch is used, make sure it is blunt and then drive parts in every carefully to avoid cocking the bearings.
5. Install new grease seal in hub. Assemble hub and drum on spindle and replace the outer bearing, key washer and nut.
6. A common method of adjustment is to tighten to zero clearance and then back off to first cotter pin castellation. Some manufacturers recommend tightening to approximately 10 to 12 ft. lbs., then backing off nut ⅙ turn. If cotter pin hole does not line up, loosen slightly.
7. Readjust brake if necessary and install grease cap and hub cover. Remove jack.

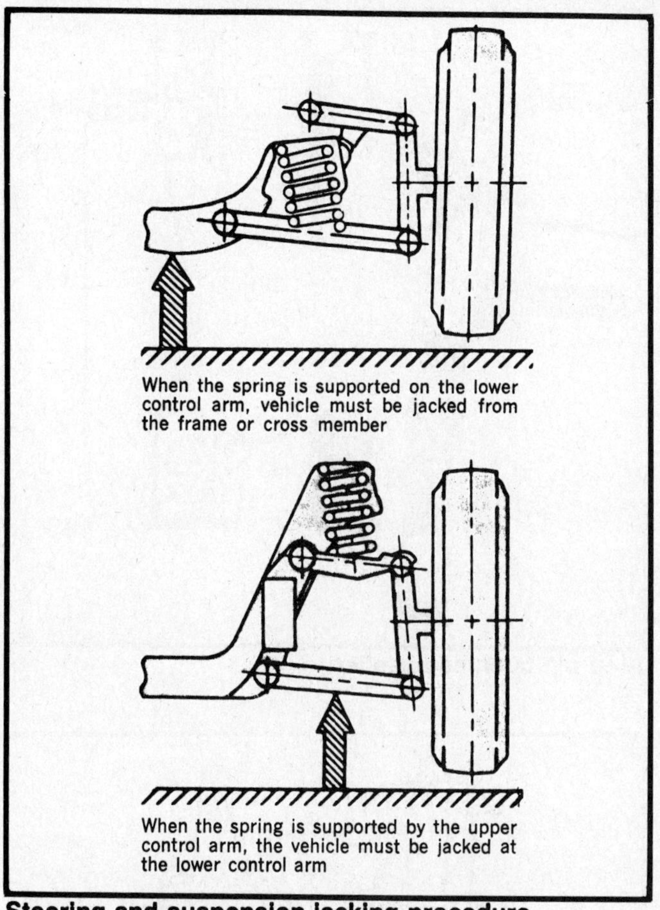
When the spring is supported on the lower control arm, vehicle must be jacked from the frame or cross member
When the spring is supported by the upper control arm, the vehicle must be jacked at the lower control arm

Steering and suspension jacking procedure

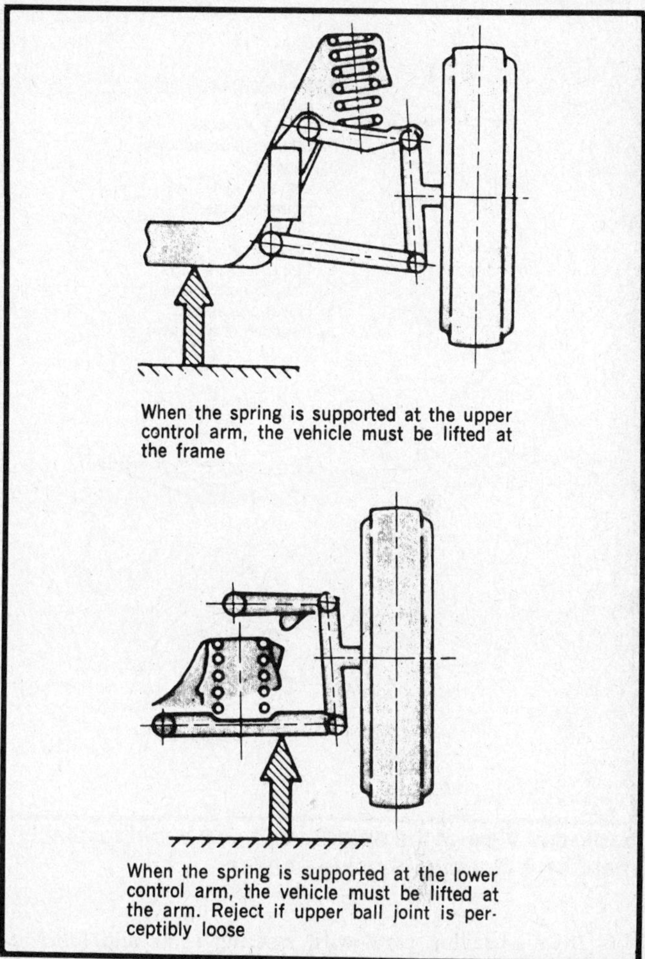
When the spring is supported at the upper control arm, the vehicle must be lifted at the frame
When the spring is supported at the lower control arm, the vehicle must be lifted at the arm. Reject if upper ball joint is perceptibly loose

The bearing and seal replacement procedure is the same as for the drum brakes

NOTE: When disc brakes are used on the front wheels, the calipers must be removed before the rotors can be taken from the spindle. Hang the calipers by wire from the frame rail so the weight of the caliper is not on the brake hose. The bearing and seal replacement procedure is the same as for the drum brakes.

KINGPIN AND BUSHING

Kingpins and bushings can be placed in two general classes:

1. With bushings in knuckle.
2. With bushings in spindle.

Replacement

1. Jack up the truck and remove the hub as described in the wheel bearing section. Remove the backing plate to knuckle bolts and lift assembly, with brakes, from the knuckle. Suspend it with a piece of wire to prevent damage to brake hose.
2. Drive out lock pin or bolt. with a sharp punch, remove top welch plug. Drive pin and lower welch plug down through knuckle and support.

NOTE: Remove top and bottom threaded plugs with wrench.

3. Drive bushings from the spindle and replace them. Be sure, when driving new bushing, that grease holes line up with those in knuckle.
4. Align and ream bushings to a snug running fit for the new kingpin.

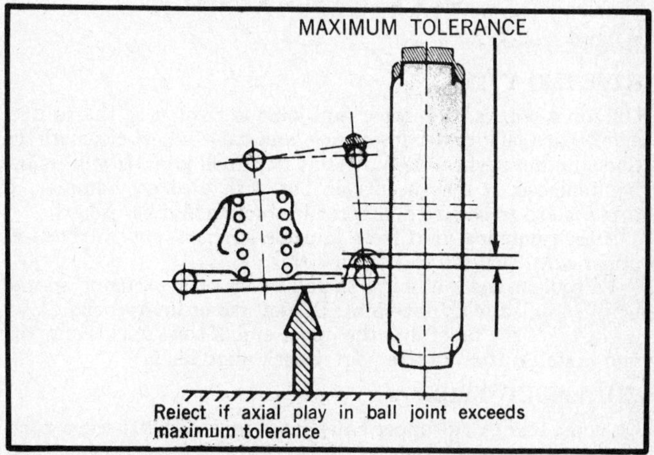
MAXIMUM TOLERANCE
Reiect if axial play in ball joint exceeds maximum tolerance

Check ball joint axial (up and down) play

5. Insert the kingpin through the top of the spindle, support, thrust bearing (with shims to control vertical play) and into the spindle bottom. Keep the kingpin in proper rotation so that the lockpin can be inserted. Install lockpin or bolt. Install upper and lower welch plugs.

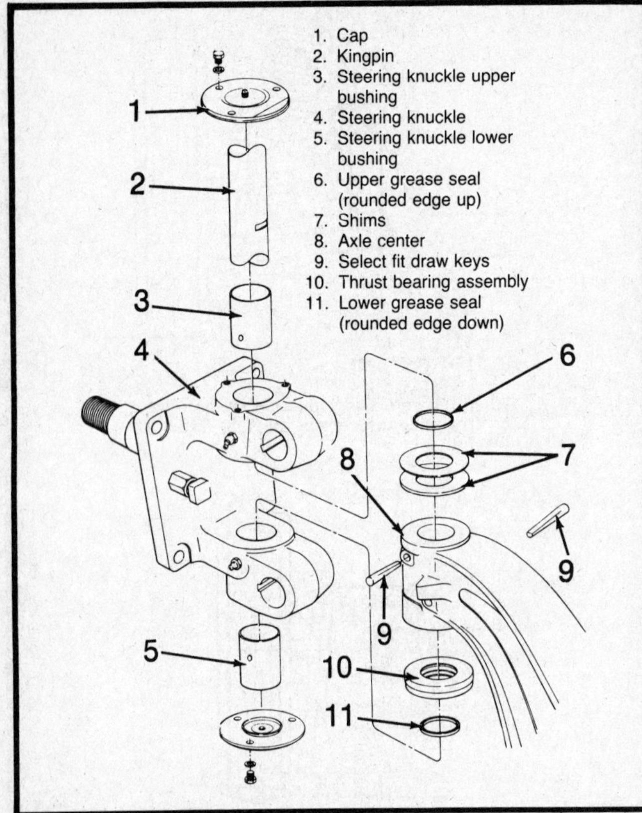

Exploded view of the spindle bolt and bushing attachment of a steering knuckle–typical

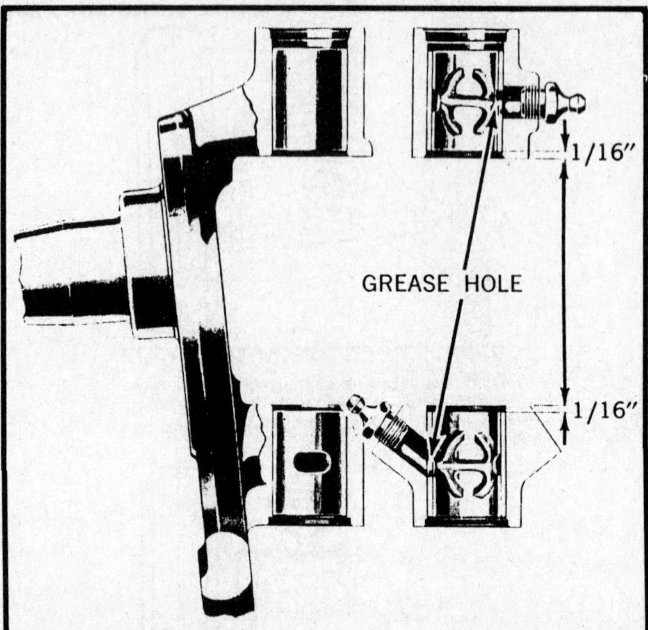

King pin bushins installed

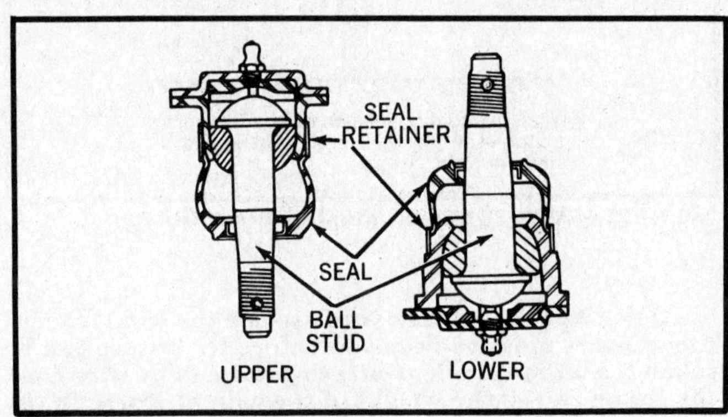

Typical ball joint assemblies

6. Install backing plate with steering arms and lubricate properly.
7. Install hubs, drums and wheels, then remove jack.

UPPER BALL JOINT

Replacement

RIVETED TYPE

On some trucks, the upper ball joint is riveted to the control arm. Place jack under lower arm and raise wheel clear off the floor. Remove wheel. Remove nut from ball joint. If joint is being replaced, it may be driven out with a heavy hammer. If threads are to be saved, a spreader tool should be used.

After removing joint from knuckle support, cut off rivets at upper arm. Drilling rivets eases this job.

To replace the ball joint: install in upper arm, using special bolts supplied with new joint. Do not use ordinary bolts.

Next, set the taper into the upper end of the knuckle support and install nut and cotter pin. Check alignment.

THREADED TYPE

On some trucks, the upper ball joint is threaded into the control arm.

Place jack under lower control arm and relieve load on torsion bar. Raise wheel clear of floor. Remove wheel. Remove nut from ball joint. If ball joint is being replaced, it may be driven out with a heavy hammer. If threads are to be saved, use a spreader tool.

After removing from knuckle support, the ball joint can be unscrewed from the support arm. Special tools are recommended for this operation.

When replacing the ball joint, be sure to engage the threads into the control arm squarely. Torque to 125 ft. lbs. If this torque cannot be obtained, check for bad threads in arm or on joint. Install new balloon seal.

Place joint in knuckle and install nut. Reload torsion bar (if so equipped) and reset height.

LOWER BALL JOINT

Removal and Installation

PRESSED TYPE

These ball joints are pressed into support arms. To replace pressed-in units, it is necessary to remove the front spring and support arm.

After removing wheel and drum, loosen nut slightly at ball joint taper and hammer lightly around area to loosen. If new ball joints are being installed, it is not necessary to protect the threads.

Place support arm in an arbor press with a suitable tool and press ball joint from the arm.

Install ball joint by reversing the pressing procedure.

NOTE: Special tools of the C-clamp type are available and an be used n some trucks to avoid removal of front spring and support arm.

INTEGRAL TYPE

On some trucks, the lower ball joint is integral with the steering arm and is not serviced separately. To service this unit, remove the upper arm bumper. Raise truck so that the front suspension is under no load. If jacks are used, a support must be placed between the jack and K-member.

1. Remove the wheel and drum assembly. Remove the two lower bolts holding the steering arm to the backing plate.
2. Disconnect tie-rod end from the steering arm. Do not damage seal.
3. Remove the ball joint stud from the lower control arm. A spreading tool will aid in this operation.
4. Install new seal on ball joint. Bolt the steering arm to the backing plate. Insert the ball joint into control arm and torque nut.
5. Connect the tie-rod end. Install drum and wheel.

TIRE REPLACEMENT

Specialized tools and equipment have been designed for use in the replacement of a tire on multipiece rims. The manufacturers instructions should be followed in the use of the machines in the amounting and dismounting of tires to avoid personal injury.

For the safety of the repairman, the word "D.I.P." should be remembered when working with tires and wheels.

1. D–DEFLATE–The tire before working on it.
2. I–INSPECT–The rim, rings, lug holes and tires for damage and proper sealing.
3. P–PROTECT–Yourself by placing the tire and wheel assembly in a cage before inflating.

Tire safety. Remember the word D.I.P.

STRUT SUSPENSION

Design

In a conventional front suspension, the wheel is attached to a spindle, which is in turn connected to upper and lower control arms through upper and lower ball joints. A coil spring between the control arms (sometimes on top of the upper arm) supports the weight of the vehicle and a shock absorber controls rebound and dampens oscillations. In a MacPherson strut type suspension, the strut performs a shock dampening function like a shock absorber, but unlike a conventional shock absorber the strut is a structural part of the vehicle's suspension.

The strut assembly usually contains a spring seat to retain the coil spring that supports the vehicle's weight. The shock absorber is built into the body of the strut housing. The strut is normally attached at the bottom to the lower control arm and at the top to the car body. The upper mount usually features a bearing that permits the coil spring to rotate as the wheels turn for smoother steering. The entire design eliminates the need for the upper control arm, upper ball joint and many of the conventional suspension bushings. The lower ball joint is no longer a load carrying unit, because it is isolated from the weight of the vehicle.

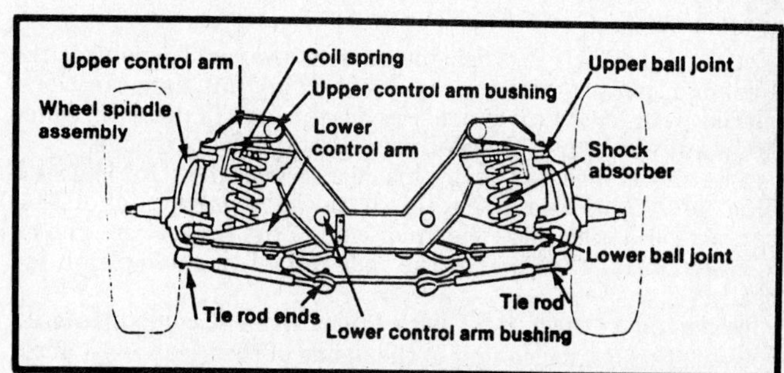

Conventional upper and lower arm suspension

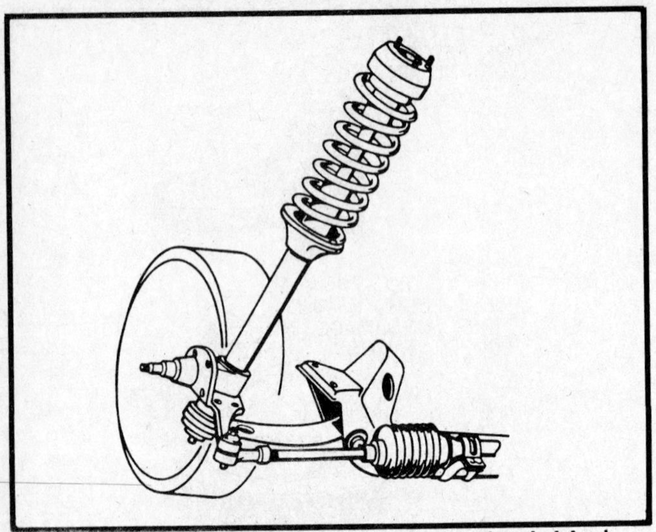

Strut with concentric coil spring (rear wheel drive)

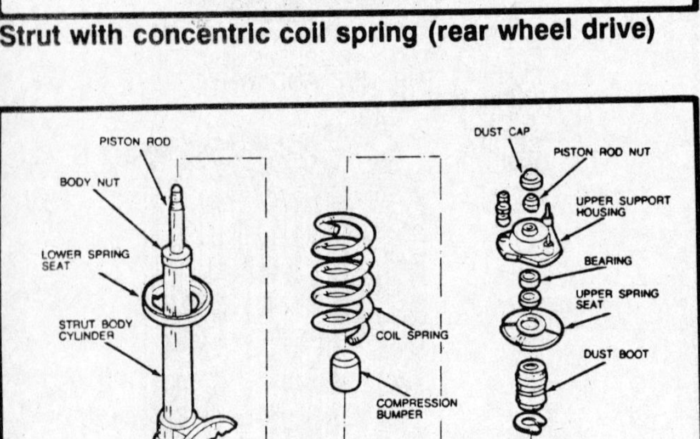

Exploded view of a typical strut

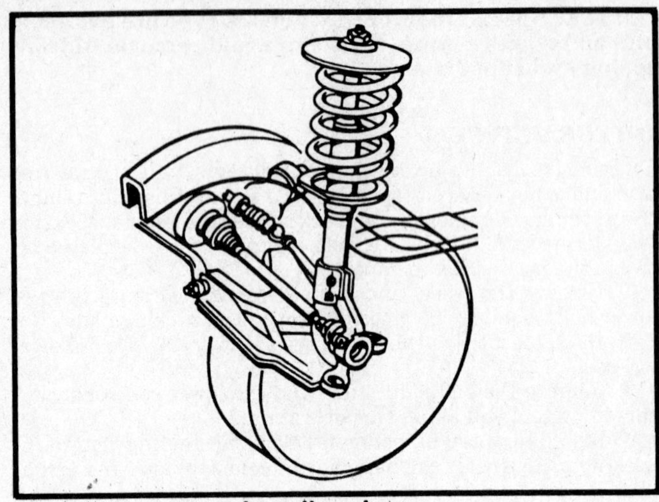

Strut with concentric coil spring

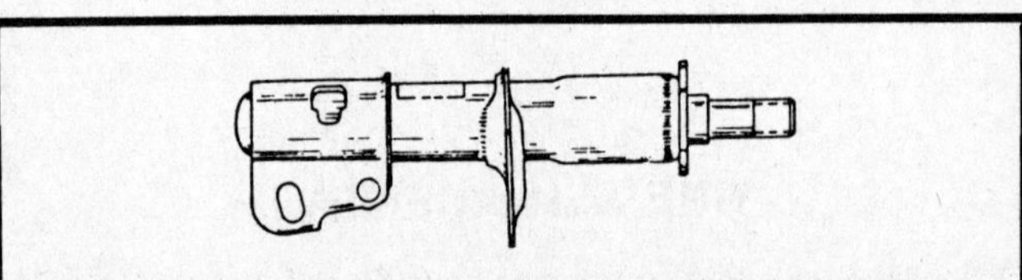

A sealed strut has no body nut and is servicable by replacement

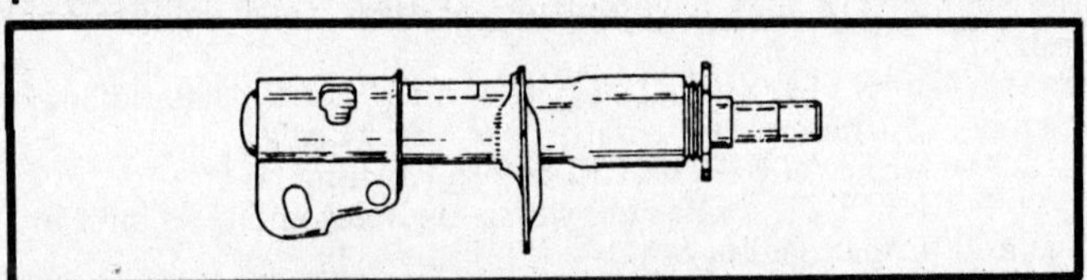

Serviceable struts have removable body nut to allow replacement of the strut cartridge

Serviceability

Struts fall into 2 broad categories; serviceable and sealed units. A sealed strut is designed so that the top closure of the strut assembly is permanently sealed. There is no access to the shock absorber cartridge inside the strut housing and no means of replacing the cartridge. It is necessary to replace the entire strut unit.

A serviceable strut is designed so that the cartridge inside the housing, that provides the shock absorbing function, can be replaced with a new cartridge. Serviceable struts use a threaded body nut in place of a sealed cap to retain the cartridge.

The shock absorber device inside a serviceable strut is generally "wet." This means that the shock absorber contains oil that contacts and lubricates the inner wall of the strut body. The oil is sealed inside the strut by the body nut, O-ring and piston rod seal.

Servicing a "wet" strut with the equivalent components involves a thorough cleaning of the inside of the strut body, absolute cleanliness and great care in reassembly.

Cartridge inserts were developed to simplify servicing "wet" struts. The insert is a factory sealed replacement for the strut shock absorber. The replacement cartridge is simply substituted for the original shock absorber cartridge and retained with the body nut, avoiding the near laboratory-like conditions required to service a "wet" strut with "wet" service components.

Sealed, OEM units can also be serviced by replacement with an aftermarket unit, that will permit future servicing by cartridge replacement.

Wheel Alignment

It is not always necessary to re-align the wheels after struts are serviced. If care is taken matchmarking affected components and in reassembling, alignment may be unaffected. However, if wheels were not in proper alignment prior to service, or if the entire strut assembly was replaced, a wheel alignment check should be made. Generally, only camber is adjustable, and then only within a narrow range.

Do not attempt to bend components to correct wheel alignment.

Since the majority of OEM struts are serviced by replacement, most manufacturers recommend wheel alignment following strut replacement.

Transfer Case
Domestic Trucks

11

INDEX

TRANSFER CASE APPLICATION CHART

Model	Chev./GMC	Dodge/Plymouth	Ford	Jeep
Borg Warner 13–45	—	—	X	—
Borg Warner 13–50	—	—	X	—
Borg Warner 13–56	—	—	X	—
Borg Warner 13–59	—	—	X	—
Dana 300				X
Jeep Selec-Trac 229	—	—	—	X
New Process 205	X	X	X	
New Process 207	X	X	—	X
New Process 208	X	X	X	X
New Process 219	—	—	—	X
New Process 228	—	—	—	X
New Process 231	—	X	—	—
New Process 241	X	—	—	—

TRANSFER CASE

Trouble Analysis

SLIPS OUT OF GEAR (HIGH-LOW)

1. Shifting poppet spring weak.
2. Bearing broken or worn.
3. Shifting fork bent.
4. Improper control rod adjustment.

SLIPS OUT OF FRONT WHEEL DRIVE

1. Shifting poppet spring weak or broken.
2. Bearing worn or broken.
3. Excessive shaft end-play.
4. Shifting fork bent.

HARD SHIFTING

1. Lack of lubricant.
2. Shift lever binding on shaft.
3. Shifting poppet ball scored.
4. Shifting fork bent.
5. Low tire pressure.

BACKLASH

1. Companion yoke loose.
2. Transfer case loose on mounts.
3. Internal parts excessively worn.

NOISY

1. Low lubricant level.
2. Bearings improperly adjusted or excessively worn.
3. Gears worn or damaged.
4. Improper alignment of driveshafts or U-joints.

OIL LEAKAGE

1. Excessive amount of lubricant in case.
2. Vent clogged.
3. Gaskets or seals leaking.
4. Bearings loose or damaged.
5. Driveshaft yoke mating surfaces scored.

OVERHEATING

1. Excessive or insufficient amount of lubricant.
2. Bearing adjustment too tight.

CLEANING & INSPECTION

Cleaning

During overhaul, all components of the transfer case (except bearing assemblies) should be thoroughly cleaned with solvent and dried with air pressure prior to inspection and reassembly.

1. Clean the bearing assemblies as follows.

NOTE: Proper cleaning of bearings is of utmost importance. Bearings should always be cleaned separately from other parts.

a. Soak all bearing assemblies in clean solvent or fuel oil. Bearings should never be cleaned in a hot solution tank.

b. Slush bearings in solvent until all old lubricant is loosened. Hold races so that bearings will not rotate; then clean bearings with a soft bristled brush until all dirt has been removed. Remove loose particles of dirt by tapping bearing flat against a block of wood.

c. Rinse bearings in clean solvent; then blow bearings dry with air pressure.

CAUTION

Do not spin bearings while drying.

d. After drying, rotate each bearing slowly while examining balls or rollers for roughness, damage, or excessive wear. Replace all bearings that are not in first class condition.

NOTE: After cleaning and inspecting bearings, lubricate generously with recommended lubricant, then wrap each bearing in clean paper until ready for reassembly.

2. Remove all portions of old gaskets from parts, using a stiff brush or scraper.

Inspection

1. Inspect all parts for discoloration or warpage.
2. Examine all gears and splines for chipped, worn, broken or nicked teeth. Small nicks or burrs may be removed with a fine abrasive stone.

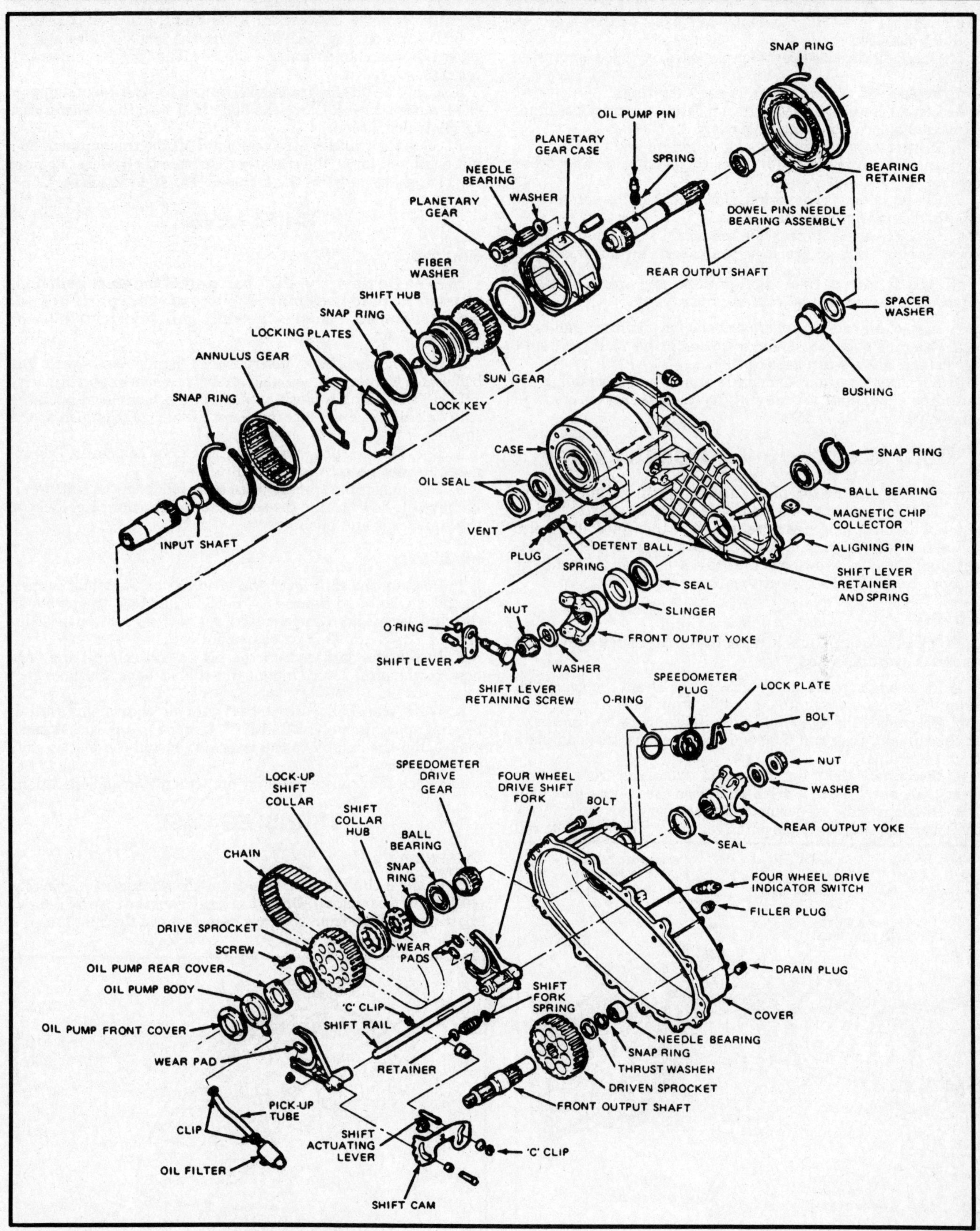

Exploded view of the 1345 transfer case

3. Inspect the breather assembly to make sure that it is open and not damaged.
4. Check all threaded parts for damaged, stripped, or crossed threads.
5. Replace all gaskets, oil seals and snap-rings.
6. Inspect housings, retainers and covers for cracks or other damage. Replace the damaged parts.
7. Inspect keys and keyways for condition and fit.
8. Inspect shift forks for wear, distortion or any other damage.
9. Check detent ball springs for free length, compressed length, distortion or collapsed coils.
10. Check bearing fit on their respective shafts and in their bores or cups. Inspect bearings, shafts and cups for wear.

NOTE: If either bearings or cups are worn or damaged, it is advisable to replace both parts.

11. Inspect all bearing rollers or balls for pitting or galling.
12. Examine detent balls for corrosion or brinneling. If shift bar detents show wear, replace them.
13. Replace all worn or damaged parts. When assembling the transfer case, coat all moving parts with recommended lubricant.

Borg Warner 13–45 Transfer Case

This transfer case is a two piece all aluminum part time transfer case. The unit lubrication is done by a positive displacement oil pump. This oil pump, channels the oil flow through drilled holes in the rear output shaft. The oil pump turns with the rear output shaft and allows towing of the vehicle for extended distances without having to disconnect the drive shaft.

Removal

NOTE: Do not proceed with this procedure when the exhaust system is hot.

1. Raise and support the vehicle safely. Drain the gear fluid from the transfer case into a suitable drain pan.
2. Disconnect the four wheel drive indicator switch connector at the transfer case and if so equipped, remove the skid plate from the frame.
3. Disconnect the front driveshaft from the front output yoke. Disconnect the rear drive shaft from the rear output yoke.
4. Disconnect the speedometer driven gear from the transfer case bearing retainer. Remove the retaining clips and shift rod from the transfer case control lever and transfer shift lever.
5. Disconnect the vent hose from the transfer case and remove the heat shield from the engine mount bracket and transfer case.
6. Using a suitable transmission jack or equivalent, support the transfer case. Remove the bolts that hold the transfer case to the transmission.
7. Slide the transfer case rear ward off the transmission output shaft and lower the transfer case from the vehicle. Remove the old gasket between the transfer case and the adapter.

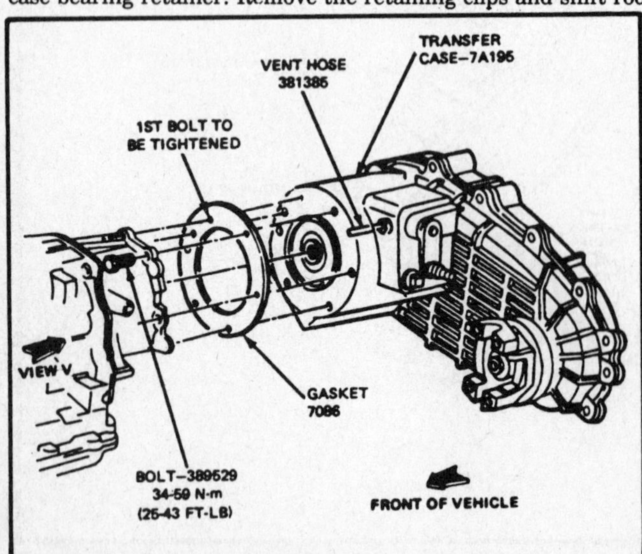

Proper shift cam engagement

SHIFT LEVER

Removal

NOTE: Remove the shift ball only if the shift ball, boot or lever have to be replaced. If any of these parts are not being replaced, remove the shift ball, boot and lever as an assembly.

1. Remove the plastic insert from the shift ball. Warm the ball with a heat gun or equivalent until it reaches approximately 140°–180°F. Using a block of wood and a hammer, knock the shift ball off the lever. Be careful not to damage the finish on the shift lever.
2. Remove the rubber boot with the floor pan cover. Disconnect the vent hose from the shift lever.
3. Disconnect the transfer case shift rod from the shift lever. Remove the bolt holding the shift lever to transfer case. Remove the shift lever and bushings.

Installation

1. Position the shift lever and bushings on the transfer case. Install the bolt and tighten to 70–90 ft. lbs. Coat the pivots on the shift lever and transfer case lever with a multi-purpose lubricant C1AZ–19590–B or equivalent.
2. Install the shift rod on the pivots and connect the vent hose to the shift lever. Install the rubber boot and floor pan cover.
3. Warm the ball with a heat gun or equivalent until it reaches approximately 140°–180°F. Using a $^{7}/_{16}$ in. socket and a mallet, tap the ball on to the lever and install the plastic shift pattern insert.
4. Check the transfer case for proper shifting and operation.

TRANSFER CASE

Disassembly

1. Remove the transfer case from the vehicle as previously outlined in this section. Drain the fluid from the case by removing the filler plug from the case half. Remove the speedometer cover.

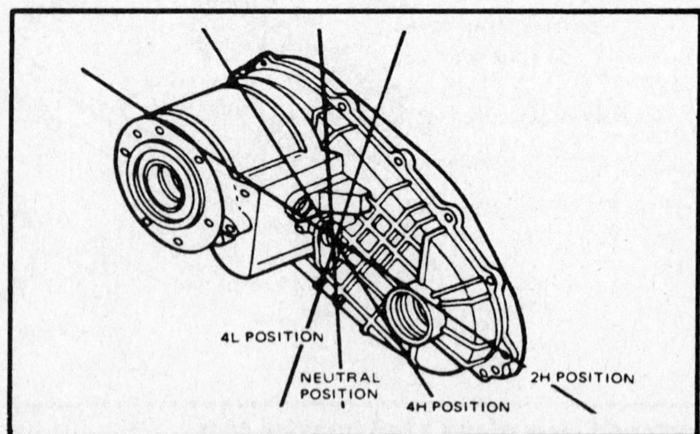

Proper shift lever installation

2. Remove both output shaft yoke nuts and washers. Remove the front and rear output yokes. Remove the four-wheel drive indicator switch.

3. Separate the cover from the case by removing the attaching bolts. Pry the case and cover apart by inserting a suitable tool. Remove the magnetic chip collector from the boss in the bottom of the case half.

4. Slide the shift collar hub off the rear output shaft and compress the shift fork spring. Remove the upper and lower spring retainers from the shaft.

5. As an assembly lift out from the case the four wheel lock-up shift collar. Be careful not to lose the nylon wear pads on the lock-up fork. Note the location of the holes on the nylon wear pad and lock-up fork. Lift the output shaft from the case.

6. Remove the snap ring from the front output shaft and remove the thrust washer. Grip the chain and both sprockets and lift straight up to to remove the drive sprockets, driven sprocket and chain from the output shafts. Remove the thrust washer from the rear output shaft.

7. Lift the front output shaft out from the case. Remove the four oil pump attaching bolts and remove the oil pump rear cover, pick-up tube filter and pump body, two pump pins, pump spring and oil pump front cover from the rear output shaft. Disconnect the oil pump pick-up tube from the pump body.

8. Remove the snap ring that holds the bearing retainer inside the gas. Lift the rear output shaft while tapping on the bearing retainer with a plastic or soft mallet. Lift the rear output shaft and bearing retainer from the case.

NOTE: Two dowel pins will fall into the case when the retainer is removed, be sure not to lose them.

9. Remove the rear output shaft from the bearing retainer and if necessary, press the needle bearing assembly out from the bearing retainer. Remove the C-clip that holds the shift cam to the shift actuating lever inside the case.

10. Remove the shift lever retaining screw and remove the shift lever from the case. When removing the lever, the shift cam will disengage from the shift lever and may release the detent ball and spring from the case.

11. As an assembly, remove the planetary gear set, shift rail, shift cam, output shaft and shift forks from the case. Be careful not to lose the two nylon wear pads on the shift fork.

12. Remove the spacer washer from the bottom of the case and remove the bushing. Using a drift pin or equivalent, drive out the plug from the detent spring bore.

Assembly

NOTE: Before starting the assembly procedure, lubricate all the internal parts, with DEXRON®II transmission fluid or equivalent.

1. Assemble the planetary gear set, shift rail, shift cam, input shaft and shift fork together as a unit. Be sure that the boss on the shift cam is installed toward the case. Install the spacer washer on the input shaft.

2. Place the rear output shaft in the planetary gear set, being sure that the shift cam engages the shift fork actuating pin. Lay the case on its side and insert the rear output shaft with planetary gear set into the case. Be sure that the spacer washer remains on the input shaft.

3. Install the shift rail into the hole in the case. Install the outer roller bushing into the guide in the case. Remove the rear output shaft and position the shift fork in neutral.

4. Place the shift control lever shaft through the cam and install the clip ring. Be sure that the shift control lever is pointed downward and is parallel to the front face of the case in the neutral position.

5. Check the shift fork and planetary gear engagement. The unit should move freely with out any binding. Press a new needle bearing into the needle bearing retainer using output bearing replacer tool # T80T-7127-C or equivalent.

6. Insert the output shaft through the bearing retainer from the bottom side outward. Insert the rear output shaft pilot into the input shaft rear bushing. Align the dowel holes and lower the bearing into position.

7. Install the dowel pins. Install the snap ring that retains the bearing retainer in the case. Insert the detent ball and spring in the detent bore in the case half.

8. Coat the seal plug with RTV sealant or equivalent. Drive the plug into the case until the lip of the plug is $^{1}/_{32}$ in. below the surface of the case. Peen the case over the plug in two places.

9. Install the oil pump front cover over the output shaft with the flanged side down. The word "TOP" must be facing the top of the transfer case as the position the case is installed in the vehicle.

10. Install the oil pump spring and two pump pins with the flat side outward in the hole in the output shaft. Push both pins in to install the oil pump body, pick-up tube and filter. The rear markings on the pump must be facing upward. Be sure to prime the pump with DEXRON®II transmission fluid or equivalent.

11. Place the oil pump rear cover on the output shaft with the flanged side outward. The word "TOP REAR" is positioned toward the the top of the transfer case in the position the transfer case is installed in the vehicle. Apply Loctite® or equivalent to the oil pump bolts and install the pump cover. Torque the bolts to 3–4 ft. lbs. and be sure to rotate the pump while tightening.

NOTE: When the oil pump is correctly installed, it will rotate freely on the output shaft.

12. Install the thrust washer on the rear output shaft next to the oil pump. Install the chain on the drive sprocket and driven sprocket. Lower the chain and sprockets into position in the case. The driven sprocket is installed over the front output shaft and the drive the sprocket is placed on the rear output shaft.

13. Assemble the washer and snap ring behind the driven sprocket. Engage the four wheel drive fork on the shift collar.

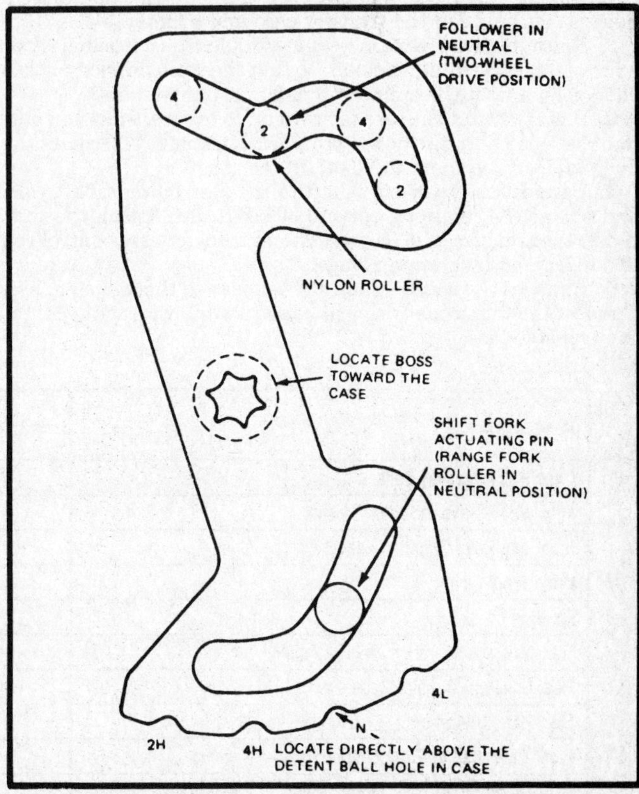

Torque sequence for the transfer case to transmission mounting bolts

14. Slide the shift fork over the shift shaft and the shift collar over the rear output shaft. Be sure that the nylon pads are installed on the shift fork tips and the necked down part of the shift collar lock-up fork are assembled correctly. Note that the location of the holes in the nylon wear pad and the lock-up fork are assembled correctly.

15. Push the four wheel drive shift spring downward and install the upper spring retainer. Push the spring upward and install the lower retainer. Install the shift collar hub on the rear output shaft.

16. Apply a bead of RTV sealant or equivalent on the case mounting surface. Lower the cover over the rear output shaft and align the shift rail to its blind hole in the cover. Be sure the front output shaft is fully seated in its support bearing. Install the attaching bolts and torque the bolts to 40–45 ft. lbs. Allow one hour curing time for the gasket material prior to the operating vehicle.

17. Install the four wheel drive indicator switch and torque the bolts down at 8–12 ft. lbs. Press an oil slinger on the front yoke.

18. Install the front and rear output shaft yokes. Install the anti-spill oil seal. Coat the faces of the yoke nuts and output shaft threads with a suitable thread sealer. Torque the yoke nuts to 100–130 ft. lbs. Install the speedometer assembly.

19. Refill the transfer case with 6.5 pints of DEXRON® II transmission fluid or equivalent. Torque the level plug and the drain plugs to 6–14 ft. lbs. Torque the fill plug to 15–22 ft. lbs.

20. Install the transfer case as outlined in this section.

21. Start the engine and check the transfer case for correct operation. Stop the engine and check the fluid level, add as necessary.

22. Fluid should drip from the level hole. If the fluid flows out level hole in a stream, the pump may not be operating properly.

Installation

1. Install the heat shield onto the transfer case and place a new gasket between the transfer case and adapter.

2. Raise the transfer case with a suitable transmission jack or equivalent, raise it high enough so that the transmission output shaft aligns with the splined transfer case input shaft.

3. Slide the transfer case forward on to the transmission output shaft and onto the dowel pin. Install transfer case retaining bolts and torque them to 26–43 ft. lbs.

4. Connect the rear driveshaft to the rear output shaft yoke and torque the retaining bolts to 20–28 ft. lbs. Attach the shift rod to the transfer case shift lever and transfer case control rod and attach with retaining rings.

5. Connect the speedometer driven gear to the transfer case. Connect the four wheel drive indicator switch wire connector at the transfer case.

6. Connect the front driveshaft to the front output yoke and torque the yoke nut to 8–15 ft. lbs. Attach the heat shield to the engine mounting bracket and mounting lug on the transfer case.

7. Install the skid plate to the frame. Install the transfer case drain plug and torque the plug to 6–14 ft. lbs.

8. Fill the transfer case with 6.5 pints of DEXRON®II transmission fluid or equivalent. Torque the fill plug to 15–22 ft. lbs. Start the engine and check the transfer case for correct operation. Stop the engine and check the fluid level, add as necessary.

Borg Warner 13–50 Transfer Case

The Borg Warner 13–50 is a three-piece aluminum part time transfer case. It transfers power from the transmission to the rear axle and when actuated, also to the front drive axle. The unit is lubricated by a positive displacement oil pump that channels oil flow through drilled holes in the rear output shaft. The pump turns with the rear output shaft and allows towing of the vehicle at maximum legal road speeds for extended distances without disconnecting the front and/or rear driveshaft.

Removal

1. Raise the vehicle on a hoist.
2. If so equipped, remove the skid plate from frame.
3. Place a drain pan under transfer case, remove the drain plug and drain fluid from the transfer case.
4. Disconnect the four-wheel drive indicator switch wire connector at the transfer case.
5. Disconnect the front driveshaft from the axle input yoke.
6. Loosen the clamp retaining the front driveshaft boot to the transfer case, and pull the driveshaft and front boot assembly out of the transfer case front output shaft.
7. Disconnect the rear driveshaft from the transfer case output shaft yoke.
8. Disconnect the speedometer driven gear from the transfer case rear cover.
9. Disconnect the vent hose from the control lever.
10. Loosen or remove the large bolt and the small bolt retaining the shifter to the extension housing. Pull on the control lever until the bushing slides off the transfer case shift lever pin. If necessary, unscrew the shift lever from the control lever.
11. Remove the heat shield from the transfer case.

CAUTION

The catalytic converter is located beside the heat shield. Be careful when working around the converter because of the extremely high temperatures generated by the converter.

12. Support the transfer case with a transmission jack.

Description	Torque Limits	
	N·m	Ft-Lbs
Case Half Attaching Bolts	48-54	35-40
Four Wheel Drive Indicator Switch	11-16	8-12
Front and Rear Output Yokes to Transfer Case	163-203	120-150
Drain Plug	13-24	14-22
Fill Plug	21-33	15-25
Transfer Case to Transmission Adapter	34-58	25-43
Heat Shield to Transfer Case	54-61	40-45
Skid Plate to Frame	20-27	15-20
Front Driveshaft to Front Output Yoke	163-203	120-150
Rear Driveshaft to Rear Output Yoke	163-203	120-150

13-45 transfer case torque specifications

13. Remove the five bolts retaining the transfer case to the transmission and the extension housing.

14. Slide the transfer case rearward off the transmission output shaft and lower the transfer case from the vehicle. Remove the gasket from between the transfer case and extension housing.

SHIFT LEVER

Removal

NOTE: Remove the shift ball only if the shift ball, boot or lever is to be replaced. If the ball, boot or lever is not being replaced, remove the ball, boot and lever as an assembly.

1. Remove the plastic insert from the shift ball. Warm the ball with a heat gun to 60°–87°C (140°–180°F) and knock the ball off the lever with a block of wood and a hammer. Be careful not to damage the finish on the shift lever.
2. Remove the rubber boot and floor pan cover.
3. Disconnect the vent hose from the control lever.
4. Unscrew the shift lever from the control lever.
5. Remove the bolts retaining the shifter to the extension housing. Remove the control lever and bushings.

TRANSFER CASE

Disassembly

1. Remove the transfer case from the vehicle.
2. Remove the transfer case drain plug with a $^{3}/_{8}$ in. drive ratchet and drain the fluid.
3. Remove the four-wheel drive indicator switch and the breather vent.
4. Remove the rear output shaft yoke by removing the 30mm nut, steel washer and rubber seal from the output shaft.
5. Remove the nine 15mm bolts which retain the front case to the rear cover. Insert a $^{1}/_{2}$ in. drive breaker bar between the three pry bosses and separate the front case from the rear cover. Remove all traces of RTV gasket sealant from the mating surfaces of the front case and rear cover.

CAUTION

When removing RTV sealant, take care not to damage the mating surface of the aluminum case.

6. If the speedometer drive gear or ball bearing assembly is to be replaced, first, drive out the output shaft oil seal from either the inside of the rear cover with a brass drift and hammer or from the outside by bending and pulling on the curved-up lip of

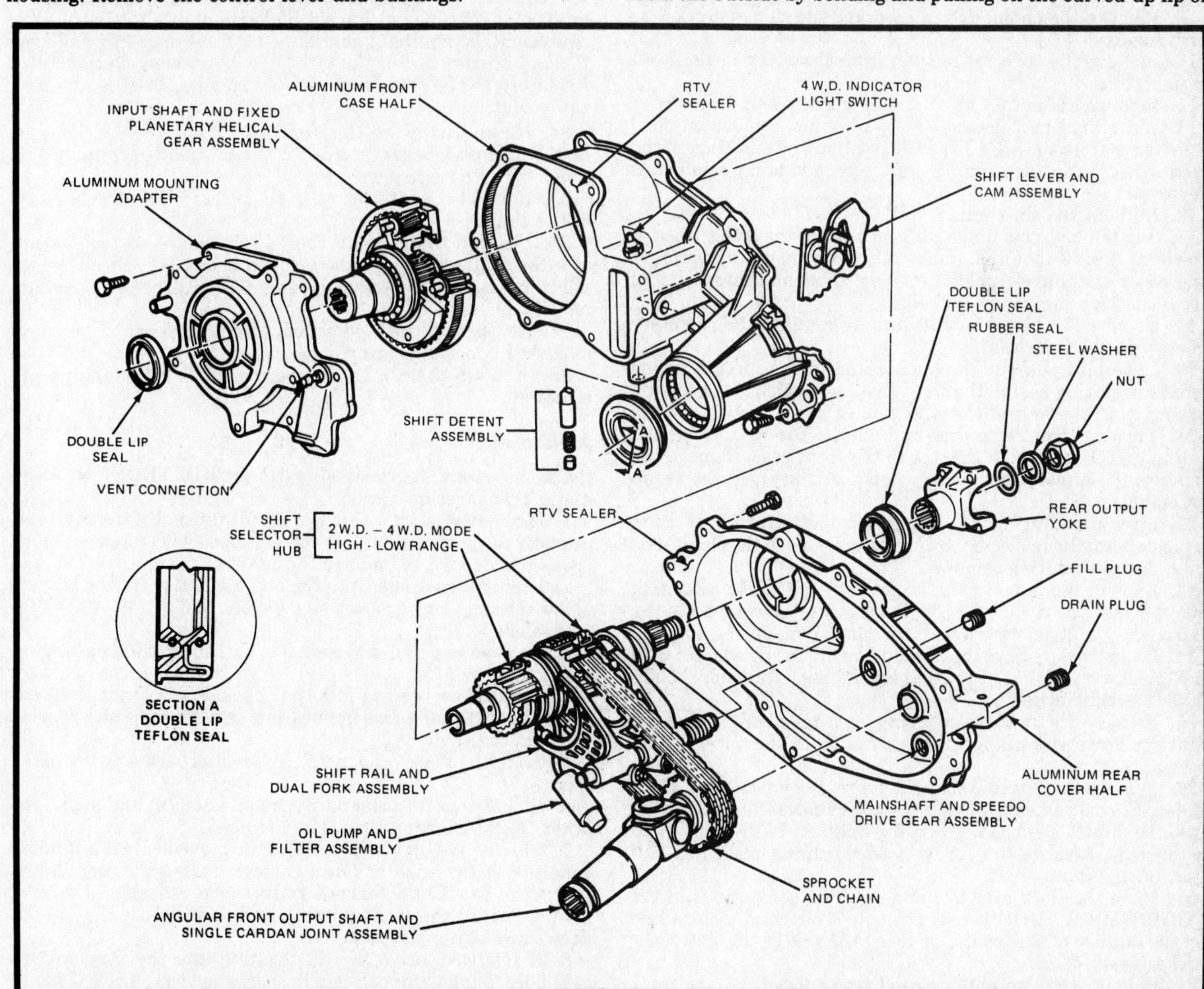

Borg-Warner 13-50 transfer case

the oil seal. Remove and discard the oil seal. Remove the speedometer drive gear assembly (gear, clip and spacer). Note that the round end of the speedometer gear clip faces the inside of the rear cover.

7. Remove the internal snap-ring that retains the rear output shaft ball bearing in the bore. From the outside of the case, drive out the ball bearing with Output Shaft Bearing Replacer, T83T–7025–B and Drive Handle, T80T–4000–W or equivalent.

8. If required, remove the front output shaft caged needle bearing from the rear cover with Puller Collet, D80L–100–S and Impact Slide Hammer, T50T–100–A or equivalent.

9. Remove the 2W–4W shift fork spring from the boss in the rear cover.

10. Remove the shift collar hub from the output shaft. Remove the 2W–4W lock-up assembly and the 2W–4W shift fork together as an assembly. Remove the 2W–4W fork from the 2W–4W lock-up assembly. If required, remove the external clip and remove the roller bushing assembly (bushing, shaft and external clip) from the 2W–4W shift fork.

11. If required to disassemble the 2W–4W lock-up assembly, remove the internal snap-ring and pull the lock-up hub and spring from the lock-up collar.

12. Remove the external snap-ring and thrust washer that retains the drive sprocket to the front output shaft.

13. Remove the chain, driven sprocket and drive sprocket as an assembly.

14. Remove the collector magnet from the notch in the front case bottom.

15. Remove the output shaft and oil pump as an assembly.

16. If required to disassemble the oil pump, remove the four 8mm bolts from the body. Note the position and markings of the front cover, body, pins, spring, rear cover, and pump retainer as removed.

17. Pull out the shift rail.

18. Slip the high-low range shift fork out of the inside track of the shift cam. If required, remove the external clip and remove the roller bushing assembly (bushing, shaft and external clip) from the high-low range shift fork.

19. Remove the high-low shift hub from out of the planetary gearset in the front case.

20. Push and pull out the anchor end of the torsion spring from the locking post in the front case half. Remove the torsion spring and roller out of the shift cam (if so equipped).

21. Turn the front case over and remove the six 15mm bolts retaining the mounting adapter to the front case. Remove the mounting adapter, input shaft and planetary gearset as an assembly.

22. If required, remove the ring gear from the front case using a press. Note the relationship of the serrations to the chamfered pilot diameter during removal.

23. Expand the tangs of the large snap-ring in the mounting adapter and pry under the planetary gearset and separate the input shaft and planetary gearset from the mounting adapter.

24. If required, remove the oil from the mounting adapter with Seal Remover, Tool 1175–AC and Impact Slide Hammer, T50T–100–A or equivalent.

25. Remove the internal snap-ring from the planetary carrier and separate the planetary gearset from the input shaft assembly.

26. Remove the external snap-ring from the input shaft. Place the input shaft assembly in a press and remove the ball bearing from the input shaft using Bearing Splitter, D79L–4621–A or equivalent. Remove the thrust washer, thrust plate and sun gear off the input shaft.

27. Move the shift lever by hand until the shift cam is in the FOUR WHEEL HIGH detent position (4WH) and mark a line on the outside of the front case using the side of the shift lever and a grease pencil.

28. Remove the two phillips head set screws from the front case and from the shift cam.

29. Turn the front case over and remove the external clip. Pry the shift lever out of the front case and shift cam.

CAUTION

Do not pound on the external clip during removal.

NOTE: Removal of four-wheel drive indicator switch will ease removal of the shift lever and shift cam assembly.

30. Remove the O-ring from the second groove in the shift lever shaft.

31. Remove the detent plunger and compression spring from the inside of the front case.

32. Remove the internal snap-ring and remove the ball bearing retainer from the front case by tapping on the face of the front output shaft and U-joint assembly with a plastic hammer. Remove the internal snap-ring and drive the ball bearing out of the bearing retainer using Output Shaft Bearing Replacer, T83T–7025–B and Driver Handle, T80T–4000–W or equivalent.

NOTE: The clip is required to prevent the bearing retainer from rotating. Do not discard the clip.

33. Remove the front output shaft and U-joint assembly from the front case. If required, remove the oil seal with Seal Remover, Tool–1175–AC and Impact Slide Hammer, T50T–100–A or equivalent. If required, remove the internal snap-ring and drive the ball bearing out of the front case bore using Output Shaft Replacer, T83T–7025–B and Driver Handle, T80T–4000–W or equivalent.

34. If required, place the front output shaft and U-joint assembly in a vise, being careful not to damage the assembly. Use copper or wood vise jaws.

35. Remove the internal snap-rings that retain the bearings in the shaft.

36. Position the U-Joint Tool, T74P–4635–C or equivalent, over the shaft ears and press the bearing out. If the bearing cannot be pressed all the way out, remove it with vise grip or channel lock pliers.

37. Re-position the U-joint tool on the spider in order to remove the opposite bearing.

38. Repeat the above procedure until all bearings are removed.

Assembly

Before assembly, lubricate all parts with DEXRON® II, Automatic Transmission Fluid.

1. If removed, start a new bearing into an end of the shaft ear. Support the output shaft in a vise equipped with copper or wood jaws, in order not to damage the shaft.

2. Position the spider into the bearing and press the bearing below the snap-ring groove using U-joint Tool, T74P–4635–C or equivalent.

3. Remove the tool and install a new internal snap-ring on the groove.

4. Start a new bearing into the opposite side of the shaft ear and using the tool, press the bearing until the opposite bearing contacts the snap-ring.

5. Remove the tool and install a new internal snap-ring in the groove.

6. Re-position the front output shaft assembly and install the other two bearings in the same manner.

7. Check the U-joint for freedom of movement. If a binding condition occurs due to misalignment during the installation procedure, tap the ears of both shafts sharply to relieve the bind. Do not install the front output shaft assembly if the U-joint shows any sign of binding.

8. If removed, drive the ball bearing into the front output case bore using Output Shaft Bearing Replacer, T83T–7025–B and Drive Handle, T80T–4000–W or equivalent. Drive the ball bearing in straight, making sure that it is not cocked in the bore.

Install the internal snap-ring that retains the ball bearing to the front case.

9. If removed, install the front output oil seal in the front case bore using Output Shaft Seal Installer, T83T–7065–B and Driver Handle, T80T–4000–W or equivalent.

10. If removed, install the ring gear in the front case. Align the serrations on the outside diameter of the ring gear to the serations previously cut in the front case bore. Using a press, start the piloted chamfered end of the ring gear first and press in until it is fully seated. Make sure the ring gear is not cocked in the bore.

11. If removed, install the ball bearing in the bearing retainer bore. Drive the bearing into the retainer using Output Shaft Bearing Replacer, T83T–7025–B and Driver Handle, T80T–4000–W or equivalent. Make sure the ball bearing is not cocked in the bore. Install the internal snap-ring that retains the ball bearing to the retainer.

12. Install the front output shaft and U-joint assembly through the front case seal. Position the ball bearing and retainer assembly over the front output shaft and install in the front case bore. Make sure the clip on the bearing retainer aligns with the slot in the front case. Tap the bearing retainer into place with a plastic hammer. Install the internal snap-ring that retains the ball bearing and retainer assembly to the front case.

13. Install the compression spring and the detent plunger into the bore from the inside of the front case.

14. Install a new O-ring in the second groove of the shift lever shaft. Coat the shaft and O-ring with Multi-Purpose Long-Life Lubricant.

NOTE: Use a rubber band to fill the first groove so as not to cut the O-ring. Discard the rubber band.

15. Position the shift cam inside the front case with the 4WH detent position over the detent plunger. Holding the shift cam by hand, push the shift lever shaft into the front case to engage the shift cam aligning the side of the shift lever with the mark previously scribed on the front case. Install the external clip on the end of the shift lever shaft.

16. Install the two phillips head set screws in the front case and in the shift cam. Tighten the screws to 6.8–9.5 Nm (5–7 ft. lbs.). Make sure the set screw in the front case is in the first groove of the shift lever shaft and not bottomed against the shaft itself. The shift lever should be able to move freely to all detent positions.

17. Slide the sun gear, thrust plate, thrust washer, and press the ball bearing over the input shaft. Install the external snap-ring to the input shaft.

NOTE: The sun gear recessed face and ball bearing snap-ring groove should be toward the rear of the transfer case. The stepped face of the thrust washer should face towards the ball bearing.

18. Install the planetary gear set to the sun gear and input shaft assembly. Install the internal snap-ring to the planetary carrier.

19. Drive the oil seal into the bore of the mounting adapter with Input Shaft Seal Installer, T83–T–7065–A and Driver Handle, T80T–4000–W or equivalent.

20. Place the tanged snap-ring in the mounting adapter groove. Position the input shaft and planetary gearset in the mounting adapter and push inward until the planetary assembly and input shaft assembly are seated in the adapter. When properly seated, the tanged snap-rig will snap into place. Check installation by holding the mounting adapter by hand and tapping the face of the input shaft against a wooden block to ensure that the snap-ring is engaged.

21. Remove all traces of RTV gasket sealant from the mating surfaces of the front case and mounting adapter. Install a bead of RTV gasket sealant on the surface of the front case.

22. Position the mounting adapter on the front case. Install six bolts and tighten to 31–41 Nm (25–30 ft. lbs.).

23. Position the roller on the 90° bent tang of the torsion spring. The larger diameter end of the spring must be installed first.

24. Install the roller into the torsion spring roller track of the shift cam while locating the center spring in the pivot groove in the front case. Push the anchor end of the torsion spring behind the locking post adjacent to the ring gear face.

25. Position the high-low shift hub into the planetary gearset. Slip the high-low shift fork bushing into the high-low roller track of the shift cam and the groove of the high-low shift hub.

NOTE: Make sure the nylon wear pads are installed on the shift fork. Make sure the dot on the pad is installed in the fork hole.

26. Install the shift rail through the high-low fork and make sure the shift rail is seated in the bore in the front case.

27. Install the oil pump front cover over the output shaft with the flanged side down. The word "TOP" must be facing the top of the transfer case as the position the case id installed in the vehicle.

28. Install the oil pump spring and two pump pins with the flat side outward in the hole in the output shaft. Push both pins in to install the oil pump body, pick-up tube and filter. The rear markings on the pump must be facing upward. Be sure to prime the pump with DEXRON® II transmission fluid or equivalent.

29. Place the oil pump rear cover on the output shaft with the flanged side outward. The word "TOP REAR" is positioned toward the the top of the transfer case in the position the transfer case is installed in the vehicle. Apply Loctite® or equivalent to the oil pump bolts and install the pump cover. Torque the bolts to 3–4 ft. lbs. and be sure to rotate the pump while tightening.

NOTE: When the oil pump is correctly installed, it will rotate freely on the output shaft.

30. Install the thrust washer on the rear output shaft next to the oil pump. Install the chain on the drive sprocket and driven sprocket. Lower the chain and sprockets into position in the case. The driven sprocket is installed over the front output shaft and the drive the sprocket is placed on the rear output shaft.

31. If disassembled, assemble the 2W–4W shift fork to the 2W–4W lock up assembly. Install the spring in the lock up collar. Place the lock up hub over the spring and engage the lock up hub in the notches in the lock up collar. Retain the lock up hub to the lock up collar with an internal snap ring.

32. Install the 2W–4W shift fork to the 2W–4W lock up assembly. If removed, make sure the nylon wear pads are installed on the fork. The dot on the pad must be installed in the hole in the fork. Install the 2W–4W lock up collar and hub assembly over the the output shaft and onto the shift rail. If removed, install the shaft, bushing and external clip to the 2W–4W lock up fork.

33. Install the shift collar hub to the output shaft.

34. If removed, drive the gaged needle bearing into the rear cover bore with the needle bearing replacer tool T83T–7127–A and driver handled T80T–4000–W or equivalent.

35. If removed, install the ball bearing in the rear cover bore. Drive the bearing into the rear cover bore with output shaft bearing replacer tool # T83T–7025–B and driver handled T80–4000–W or equivalent. Make sure the ball bearing is not cocked in the bore. Install the internal snap ring that retains the ball bearing to the rear cover.

36. Install the speedometer drive gear assembly into the rear cover bore with round end of the speedometer gear clip facing towards the inside of the rear cover. Drive the oil seal into the rear cover bore with output shaft seal installer tool # T83T–7065–B and driver handle # T80T–4000–W or equivalent.

37. Install the 2W–4W shift fork spring on the inside boss of the rear cover.

38. Prior to final assembly of the rear cover to front case half, the transfer case shift lever assembly should be shifted into

"4H" detent position to assure positioning of the shift rail to the rear cover.

39. Coat the mating surface of the front case with a bead of Loctite® sealant or equivalent.

40. Position the rear cover on the front case, making sure that the 2W–4W shift fork spring engages the shift rail and does not fall off the rear cover boss. Install the nine bolts, starting with the bolts on the rear cover and torque the bolts to 23–30 ft. lbs.

NOTE: If the rear cover assembly does not seat properly, move the rear cover up and down slightly to permit the end of the shift rail to enter the shift rail hole in the rear cover boss.

41. Install the front and rear output shaft yokes. Install the anti-spill oil seal. Coat the faces of the yoke nuts and output shaft threads with a suitable thread sealer. Torque the yoke nuts to 120–150 ft. lbs.

42. Install the four wheel drive indicator switch and torque the bolts down at 23–35 ft. lbs.

43. Refill the transfer case with 3.0 pints of DEXRON®II transmission fluid or equivalent. Torque the level plug and the drain plugs to 14–22 ft. lbs. Torque the fill plug to 14–22 ft. lbs.

44. Install the transfer case as outlined in this section.

45. Start the engine and check the transfer case for correct operation. Stop the engine and check the fluid level, add as necessary.

46. Fluid should drip from the level hole. If the fluid flows out level hole in a stream, the pump may not be operating properly.

TRANSFER CASE

Installation

1. Install the heat shield onto the transfer case and place a new gasket between the transfer case and adapter.

2. Raise the transfer case with a suitable transmission jack or equivalent, raise it high enough so that the transmission output shaft aligns with the splined transfer case input shaft.

3. Slide the transfer case forward on to the transmission output shaft and onto the dowel pin. Install transfer case retaining bolts and torque them to 26–43 ft. lbs.

4. Connect the rear driveshaft to the rear output shaft yoke and torque the retaining bolts to 20–28 ft. lbs. Attach the shift rod to the transfer case shift lever and transfer case control rod and attach with retaining rings.

5. Connect the speedometer driven gear to the transfer case. Connect the four wheel drive indicator switch wire connector at the transfer case.

6. Connect the front driveshaft to the front output yoke and torque the yoke nut to 8–15 ft. lbs. Attach the heat shield to the engine mounting bracket and mounting lug on the transfer case.

7. Install the skid plate to the frame. Install the transfer case drain plug and torque the plug to 6–14 ft. lbs.

8. Fill the transfer case with 6.5 pints of DEXRON®II transmission fluid or equivalent. Torque the fill plug to 15–22 ft. lbs. Start the engine and check the transfer case for correct operation. Stop the engine and check the fluid level, add as necessary.

TORQUE SPECIFICATIONS
Borg-Warner 13-50 Transfer Case

Description	Torque N•m	Torque Ft. Lb.
Breather Vent	8-19	6-14
Case to Cover Bolts	31-41	23-30
Drain and Fill Plug	19-30	14-22
Four-Wheel Drive Indicator Switch	34-47	25-35
Front and Rear Driveshaft Bolts	16-20	12-15
Shift Control Bolts—Large	95-122	70-90
Shift Control Bolts—Small	42-57	31-42
Shift Shaft and Shift Cam Set Screw	6.8-9.5	5-7
Skid Plate to Frame Bolt	30-41	22-30
Transfer Case to Transmission Adapter	34-47	25-35
Upper Shift Control Lever and Heat Shield Bolts	37-50	27-37
Yoke Nut	163-203	120-150
	N•m	**In. Lb.**
Oil Pump Bolts	4.0-4.5	36-40
Speedometer Screw	2.3-2.8	20-25

NOTE: The output shaft must turn freely within the oil pump. If binding occurs, loosen the four bolts and re-tighten again.

Borg Warner 13–56 Transfer Case

This transfer case is a three piece all magnesium, (except for the manual shift unit equipped for a power take off which will have an aluminum case), part time transfer case. The unit lubrication is done by a positive displacement oil pump. This oil pump, channels the oil flow through drilled holes in the rear output shaft. The oil pump turns with the rear output shaft and allows towing of the vehicle for extended distances without having to disconnect the drive shaft.

Removal

NOTE: Do not proceed with this procedure when the exhaust system is hot.

1. Raise and support the vehicle safely. Drain the gear fluid from the transfer case into a suitable drain pan.

2. Disconnect the four wheel drive indicator switch connector at the transfer case and if so equipped, remove the skid plate from the frame.

3. Disconnect the front driveshaft from the front output yoke. Disconnect the rear drive shaft from the rear output yoke.

4. Disconnect the speedometer cable from the transfer case bearing retainer.

5. Disconnect the vent hose from the transfer case and remove the heat shield from the engine mount bracket and transfer case.

6. Using a suitable transmission jack, support the transfer case. Remove the bolts that hold the transfer case to the transmission.

7. Slide the transfer case rear ward off the transmission output shaft and lower the transfer case from the vehicle. Remove the old gasket between the transfer case and the adapter.

SHIFT LEVER

Removal

NOTE: Remove the shift ball only if the shift ball, boot or lever have to be replaced. If any of these parts are not being replaced, remove the shift ball, boot and lever as an assembly.

1. Remove the plastic insert from the shift ball. Warm the ball with a heat gun or equivalent until it reaches approximately 140°to 180°F. Using a block of wood and a hammer, knock the shift ball off the lever. Be careful not to damage the finish on the shift lever.

2. Remove the rubber boot with the floor pan cover. Disconnect the vent hose from the shift lever.

3. Disconnect the transfer case shift rod from the shift lever.

Remove the bolts holding the shift lever to transfer case. Remove the shift lever and bushings.

Installation

1. Before installing the shifter assembly, move the transfer case lever to the "4L" position.
2. Install the shifter assembly with the bolts finger tight, and move the cam plate rearward until the bottom chamfered corner of the neutral lug just contact the foreward right edge of the shift lever, (Point "C" in the illustration).
3. Hold the cam plate in the position mentioned above and tighten the bolts to 71–90 ft. lbs.
4. Move the transfer case in-cab shift lever to all positions to check for positive engagement. There should be clearance between the shift lever and the cam plate in the "2H" front, and "4H" rear (clearance should not exceed 2.0mm), and the "4L" shift positions.
5. Attach the shift lever to the control lever and tighten to 23–32 ft. lbs.
6. Install the vent assembly so the white marking on the housing is in the position in the notch in the shifter. Install the rubber boot and the floor pan cover
7. Warm the ball with a heat gun or equivalent until it reaches approximately 140°to 180°F. Using a $^{7}/_{16}$ in. socket and a mallet, tap the ball on to the lever and install the plastic shift pattern insert.
8. Check the transfer case for proper shifting and operation.

TRANSFER CASE

Disassembly

1. Remove the transfer case from the vehicle as previously outlined in this section. Drain the fluid from the case by removing the filler plug from the case half. Remove the speedometer cover.
2. Remove both output shaft yoke nuts and washers. Remove the front and rear output yokes. Remove the four-wheel drive indicator switch.
3. Remove the front and rear output shaft yoke seals using special Tool T74P–77248–A and T50L–100–A or equivalent.
4. Remove the input shaft seals using the tools mentioned above.
5. Remove the four No.50 torx head bolts securing the rear bearing retainer to the cover. Pry the rear bearing retainer from the cover using a ½ in. drive breaker bar between the pry bosses and separate and remove the bearing retainer from the cover. Remove all traces of RTV gasket sealant from the mating surfaces of the cover and the bearing retainer.

NOTE: When removing the RTV sealer, be careful not to damage the mating surfaces of the magnesium cases.

6. Lift the rear output shaft and using a small prybar, remove the speedometer gear retaining clip.
7. Slide the speedometer gear foreward and remove the ball with a small magnet. The speedometer gear can now be removed off of the rear output shaft.
8. Remove the snap ring on the output shaft retaining the upper rear ball bearing using a suitable tool.
9. Remove the 12 No. 50 torx bolts that retain the front case to the rear cover. Insert a ½ in. drive breaker bar between the pry bosses and separate. Lift the front case from the rear cover. Remove all traces of RTV gasket sealant from the mating surfaces of the cover and the bearing retainer.

NOTE: When removing the RTV sealer, be careful not to damage the mating surfaces of the magnesium cases.

10. Remove the front output shaft inner needle bearing from the rear cover with special tool T50T–100–A, slide hammer, and D80L–100–T, collet from D80L–100–A, Blind Hole Puller Set.
11. Drive out the rear output shaft bearing from the inside of the case using the appropriate tools.
12. Remove the snap ring on the output shaft securing the clutch hub. Slide the 4WD hub off of the output shaft.
13. Remove the spring from the shift rail and lift the mode shift fork complete with the shifting collar from the upper sproket spline.
14. Dissassemble the 2WD/4WD lockup assembly by removing the internal snap ring and pull the lockup hub and spring from the collar.
15. Remove the snap ring retaining the lower sprocket to the lower output shaft. Grasp the upper and lower sprocket complete with the chain and lift them at the same time from the upper and lower output shafts.
16. Remove the snap ring retaining the lower sprocket complete with the chain and lift them at the same time from the upper and lower output shafts.
17. Remove the shift rail by sliding it straight out from the shift fork.
18. Remove the high and low shift fork by first rotating it until the rollar is free from the cam then sliding out of the engagement from the shift hub.
19. Remove the chip collecting magnet from its slot in the case.

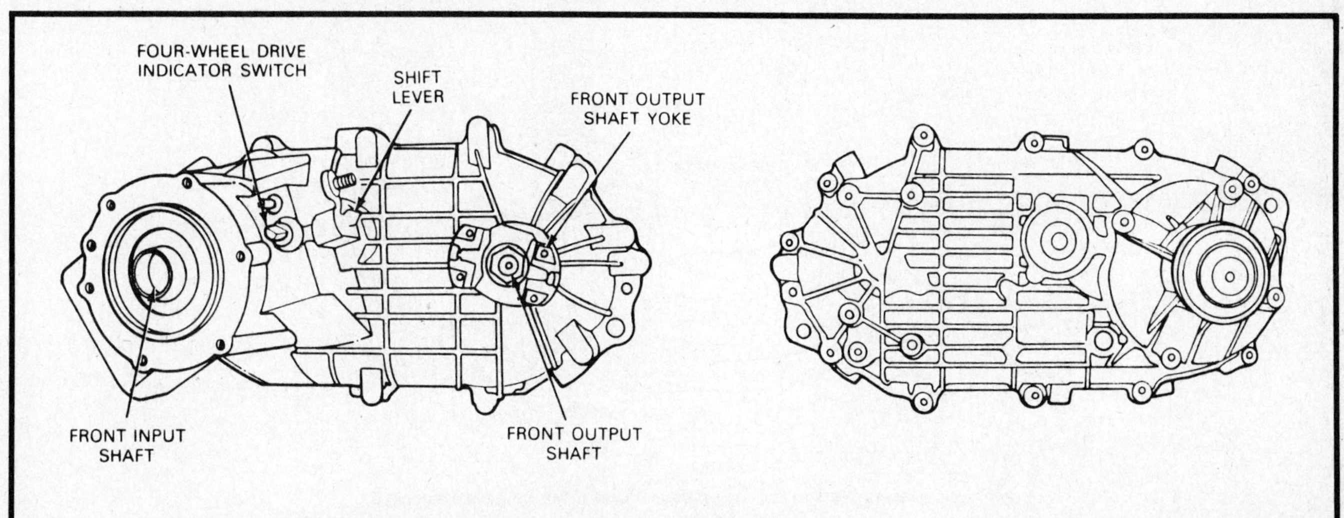

Borg Warner 13-56 transfer case—Manual shift shown, electric shift similar

20. Lift out the pump screen and remove the output shaft assembly with the pump assembled on it. If the pump is to be disassembled, remove the four bolts from the pump body. Note the position of the pump front body, pins, spring, rear cover and pump retainer as removed.

21. Remove the high low shift hub.

22. Remove the front output shaft from the case.

23. Turn the front case over and remove the front oil seal from the case using tool T74P–77248–A and T50T–100–A.

24. Reaching through the front opening with a pair of snap ring pliers, expand the snap ring on the input shaft allowing it to drop out of the bearing. The carrier assembly, including the input shaft is serviced as an assembly only. If the bearing or bushing is to be replaced, drive out both of them through the input spline using suitable tools.

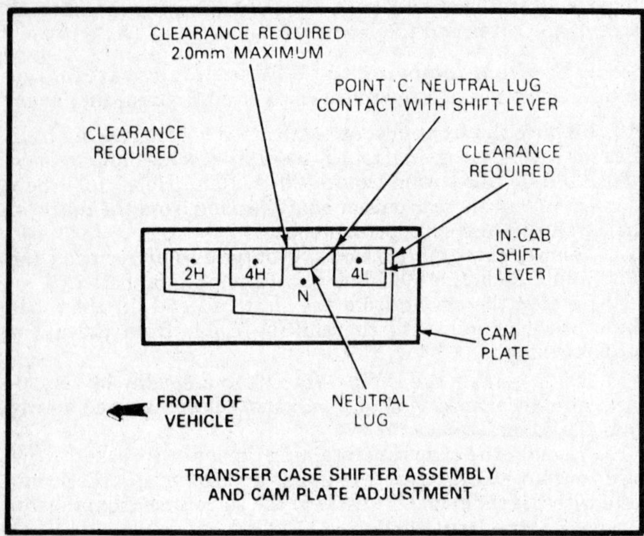

Transfer case shifter assy and cam plate adjustment

25. Remove the ring gear by prying out the internal snap ring and lift out the gear.

26. Remove the PTO drive gear from the input shaft carrier assembly, if equipped using appropriate tools.

27. Remove the internal snap ring securing the input shaft bearing to the case and drive it out from the outside of the case using Tool T73T–1202–A ans T80T–4000–W.

28. Remove the internal snap ring securing the front output shaft bearing in the magnesium housing and drive the bearing out from the front of the case using Tool T73T–1202–B and T80T–4000–W.

29. Remove the shift cam by removing the retaining clip and sliding the shift shaft out of the case.

30. Remove the shift shaft seal by carefully prying it out of the case, being careful not to damage the case.

31. Remove the shift cam, assist spring, and the assist spring bushing from the case.

Assembly

NOTE: Before starting the assembly procedure, lubricate all the internal parts, with DEXRON®II transmission fluid or equivalent.

1. Install the input shaft and the front output shaft bearings in the case using the appropriate tools. Install the internal snap rings retaining the bearings in the case.

2. Drive the front output shaft seal into the case unit until it is fully seated against the case using Tool T86T–7034–CH.

3. Install the front output shaft through the lower bearing. The front output shaft is held in place in the case by the front output yoke and oil seal slinger assembly. Install the front yoke assembly onto the front output shaft then the rubber seal, flat washer and 30mm locknut. Torque the yoke locknut to 130–180 ft. lbs.

4. Press the power take-off drive gear onto the input shaft assembly if it was removed.

5. Press the needle bearing and bronze bushing into the input shaft with the appropriate tools.

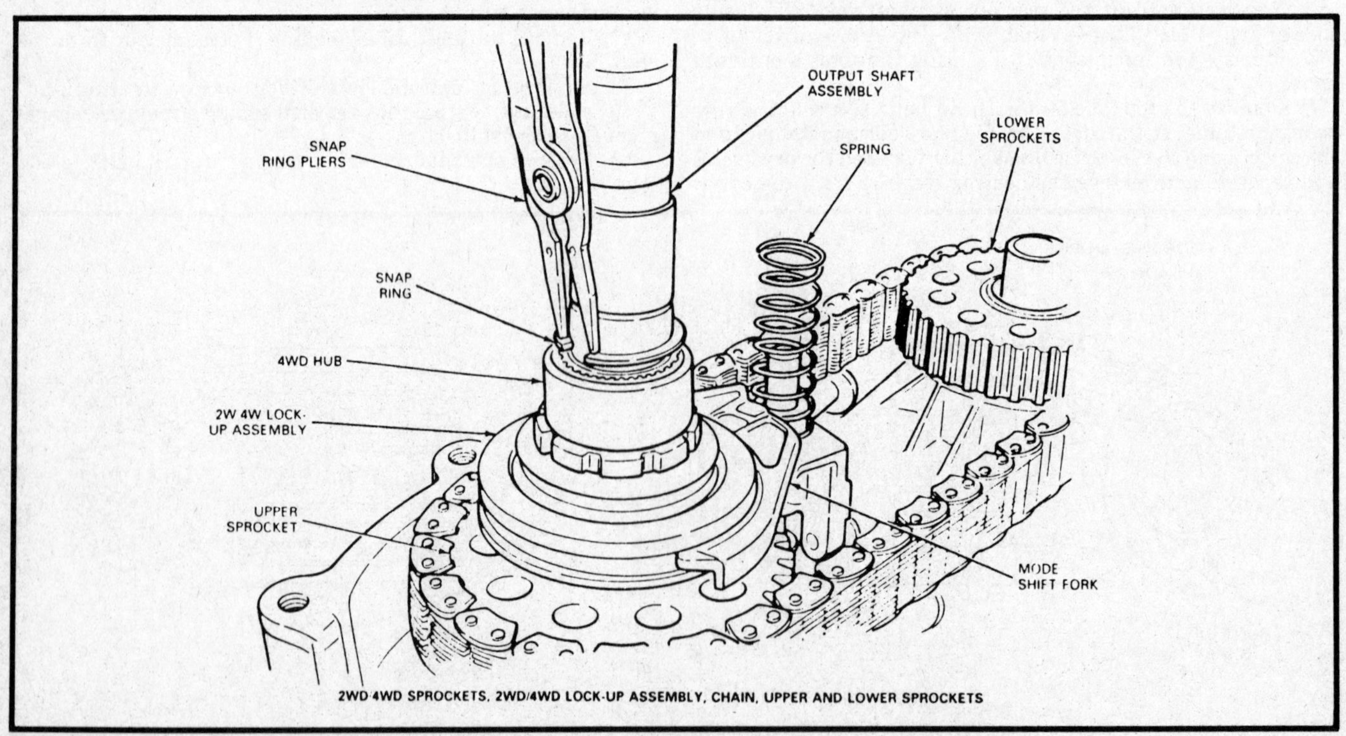

2WD, 4WD sprokets, 2WD, 4WD lock-up assembly, chain, upper and lower sprockets

6. Install the ring gear into the slots in the case and retain it with the large internal snap ring making sure that it is fully seated.

7. Install the input shaft and carrier assembly in the case through the input shaft bearing being careful not to damage the gear teeth when aligning them with the ring gear teeth.

8. While supporting the carrier assembly in position, install a new spring on the front side of the input bearing making sure that it is fully seated in the snap ring groove of the input shaft.

9. Install the upper input shaft oil seal into the case using an appropriate tool until it is fully seated against the case.

10. Install a new shifter shaft seal into the case using an appropriate tool.

11. Assemble the shift cam assembly into the case by sliding the shift shaft and lever assembly through the case and seal into engagement with the shift cam. Secure the shift cam with the retaining clip.

12. Install the shift cam assist spring in position in the bushing of the shift cam and in the recess in the case.

13. Assemble the pump and output shaft as follows: Place the oil pump cover with the word "TOP" facing the front of the front case. Install the two pins (with the flats facing upwards) with the spring between the pins and place the assembly in the oil pump bore in the output shaft. Place the oil pump body and the pick up tube over the shaft and make sure that the pins are riding against the inside of the pump body. Place the oil pump rear cover with the words "TOP REAR" facing the rear of the case. The word "TOP" on the front cover and the rear cover should be on the same side. Install the pump retainer with the tabs facing the front of the transfer case. Install the four retaining bolts and rotate the output shaft while tightening the bolts to prevent the pump from binding. Tighten the bolts to 36–40 inch lbs. Lubricate the assembly with automatic transmission fluid.

NOTE: The output shaft must turn freely within the oil pump. If binding occurs, loosen the four bolts and retighten again.

14. Install the high low shift hub. Install the high low shift fork by engaging it with the shift hub flange and rotating it until the roller is engaged with the lower groove of the cam.

15. Install the shift rail through the high low fork bore and into the rail bore in the case.

16. Install the output shaft and oil pump assembly in the input shaft. Make certain that the external splines of the output shaft engage the internal splines of the high low shift hub. Make sure that the oil pump retainer and oil filter leg are in the groove and notch of the front case. Install the collector magnet in the notch in the front case.

17. Assemble the upper and lower sprockets with the chain and place them as an assembly over the upper and lower output shafts. Install the washer and snap ring which retain the lower sprocket to the front output shaft.

18. Assemble the 2WD/4WD lockup assembly by installing the tapered compression spring in the lockup collar with the small end installed first. Place the lockup hub over the spring and compress the spring while installing the internal snap ring which holds the lockup assembly together.

19. Install the lockup assembly and its shift fork over the external splines of the upper sprocket and the shift rail with the long boss of the shift rail facing foreward.

20. Assemble the 4WD return spring over the shift rail and against the shift fork.

21. Place the 4WD hub over the external splines of the output shaft and secure with the appropriate snap ring. Make sure that the snap ring is fully seated in the snap ring groove.

22. Press the lower output needle bearing in its bore in the rear cover using an appropriate tool.

23. Press the rear output shaft bearing into position in the cover. Install the bearing snap ring retainer in the cover.

24. Install the rear output shaft oil seal in the bearing retainer using the appropriate tool making sure it is fully seated.

25. Coat the mating surface of the front case with a bead of RTV.

26. Place the cover on the case making sure that the lower output shaft, shift shaft and the shift rail are aligned. Install and torque the 12 No. 50-torx head case to cover bolts to 22–36 ft. lbs.

27. Install the bearing retainer snap ring on the output shaft making sure that the snap ring is fully seated in the groove on the shaft.

28. Place the speedometer drive gear over the shaft with the slot aligned with the hole for the drive ball. The gear should go completely against the snap ring which retains the output shaft. Place the ball in the hole and pull the speedometer gear over the ball. Snap the retaining clip between the snap ring and the speedometer gear.

29. Apply a bead of RTV to the face of the rear bearing retainer or to the rear slip yoke extension housing.

30. Place the rear bearing retainer or the rear slip yoke extension housing in its position and secure with the 4 torx head bolts.

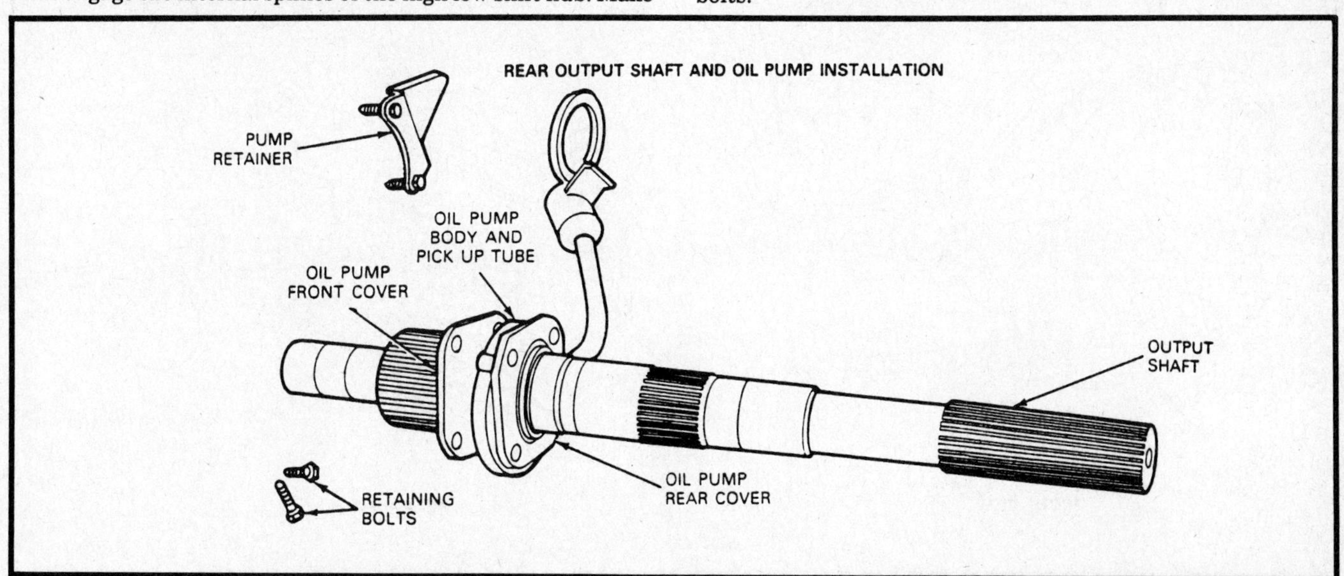

Rear output shaft and oil pump installation

31. On the transfer case with the slip yoke bearing retainer housing remove the extension oil seal using Tool T74P–77248–A and T50T–100–A. Remove the extension housing bushing using Tool T85–7034–AH. Install a new bushing using Tool T85T–7034–BH and T80T–4000–W. Install a new seal using Tool T61L–7657–B.

32. Install the rear output shaft yoke and slinger assembly onto the rear splines of the output shaft. Install the rubber seal, flat steel washer and 30mm locknut on the output shaft and torque to 150–180 ft. lbs.

33. Install the drain plug and tighten to 14–22 ft. lbs.

34. Install the 4WD indicator light switch and aluminum washer into the case.

35. Place a ⅜ in. drive ratchet in the fill plug and remove the plug. Fill the transfer case with 64 oz. of Dexron®II transmission fluid.

36. Install the fill plug and tighten to 14–22 ft. lbs.

37. Install the transfer case as described below.

38. Start the engine, check the transfer case for proper operation. Stop the engine and check the fluid level. The fluid should drip out of the "LEVEL" hole. If the fluid flows out of the "LEVEL" hole, the oil pump may not be funtioning properly.

TRANSFER CASE

Installation

1. Install the heat shield onto the transfer case and place a new gasket between the transfer case and adapter.

2. Raise the transfer case with a suitable transmission jack or equivalent, raise it high enough so that the transmission output shaft aligns with the splined transfer case input shaft.

3. Slide the transfer case forward on to the transmission output shaft and onto the dowel pin. Install transfer case retaining bolts and torque them to 26–43 ft. lbs. Remove the Transmission jack from the transfer case.

4. Connect the rear driveshaft to the rear output shaft yoke and torque the retaining bolts to 20–25 ft. lbs. for the Bronco, and 8–15 ft. lbs. for the "F" series trucks. Attach the shift rod to the transfer case shift lever and transfer case control rod and attach with retaining rings.

5. Connect the speedometer driven gear to the transfer case. Connect the four wheel drive indicator switch wire connector at the transfer case.

6. Connect the front driveshaft to the front output yoke and torque the yoke nut to 8–15 ft. lbs. Attach the heat shield to the engine mounting bracket and mounting lug on the transfer case.

7. Install the skid plate to the frame. Install the transfer case drain plug and torque the plug to 6–14 ft. lbs.

8. Fill the transfer case with 6.5 pints of DEXRON®II transmission fluid or equivalent. Torque the fill plug to 15–25 ft. lbs. Start the engine and check the transfer case for correct operation. Stop the engine and check the fluid level, add as necessary.

Borg Warner 13–59 Transfer Case

The Borg Warner 13–59 is a in-line three-piece aluminum transfer case. It transfers power from the transmission to the rear axle and is used on the Bronco II 4 × 2 models. The unit contain no lubricant and none should be added. The front and rear bearings are pre-lubricated and sealed. The internal roller bearings are lubricated during assembly and since the front and rear shafts are locked together, no rotating wear is developed.

Removal

CAUTION

The catalytic converter is located beside the heat shield. Be careful when working around the converter because of the extremely high temperatures generated by the converter.

1. Raise the vehicle and support safely.

2. Disconnect the rear driveshaft from the transfer case output shaft flange.

3. Disconnect the speedometer driven gear from the transfer case rear cover.

4. Support the transfer case with a transmission jack.

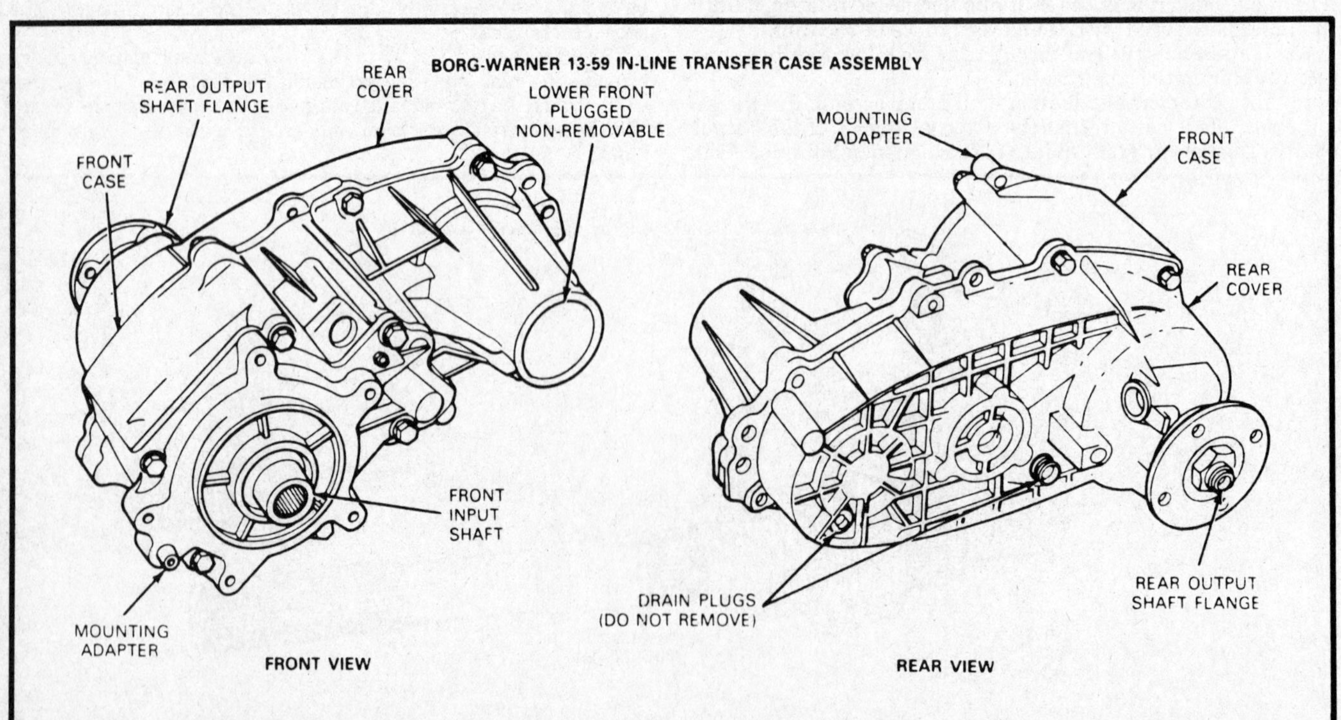

Borg Warner 13-59 transfer case

5. Remove the five bolts retaining the transfer case to the transmission and the extension housing.
6. Slide the transfer case rearward off the transmission output shaft and lower the transfer case from the vehicle. Remove the gasket from between the transfer case and extension housing.

Disassembly

1. Remove the transfer case from the vehicle.
2. Remove the rear output shaft yoke by removing the 30mm nut, steel washer and rubber seal from the output shaft. Remove the flange from the output shaft.
3. Remove the rear output shaft oil seal from the rear cover using Tool T74P-77248-A and T50T-100-A or equivalent.
4. Remove the nine 15mm bolts which retain the front case to the rear cover. Insert a ½ in. drive breaker bar between the three pry bosses and separate the front case from the rear cover.
5. Remove the speedometer drive gear assembly (gear, clip and spacer). Note that the round end of the speedometer gear clip faces the inside of the rear cover.
6. Remove the rear spacer collar from the rear output shaft.
7. Remove the rear output shaft and snap ring assembly by lifting it out of the locking coupling and front input shaft in the front case.
8. Remove the locking coupling from the external splined end of the input shaft assembly.

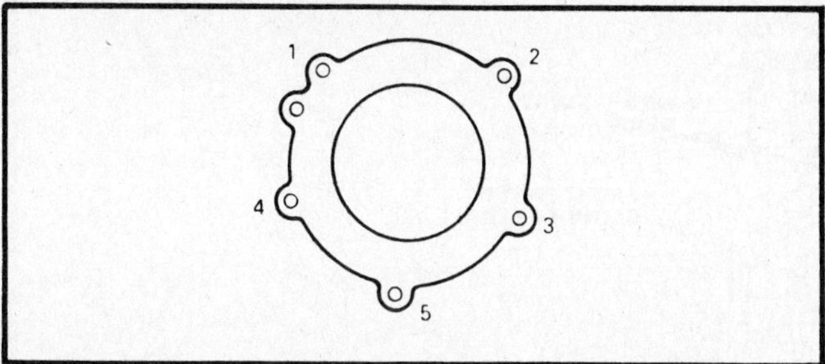

Transmission adapter to Transfer case torque sequence

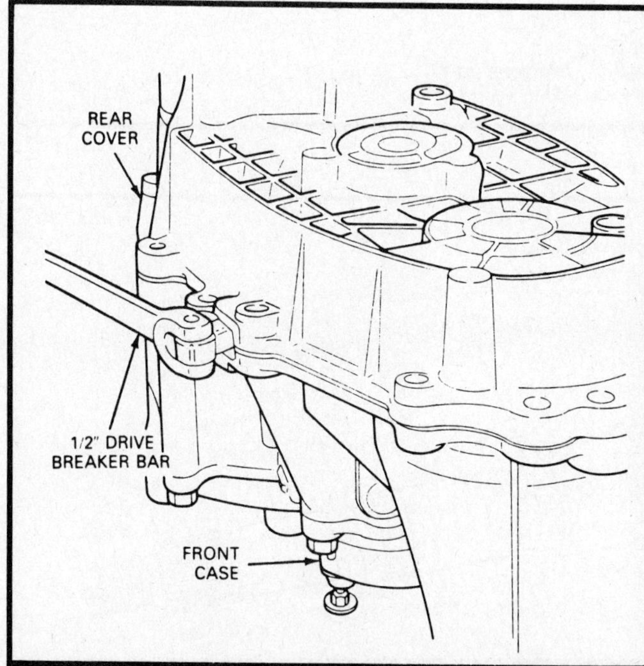

Separating the rear cover from the front case

9. Remove the internal snap-ring that retains the rear output shaft ball bearing in the bore. From the outside of the case, drive out the ball bearing with Output Shaft Bearing Replacer, T83T-7025-B and Drive Handle, T80T-4000-W or equivalent.
10. Turn the front case over and remove the six 15mm bolts retaining the mounting adapter to the front case. Remove the mounting adapter, input shaft bearing, thrust plate and sleeve as an assembly.
11. Place the mounting adapter in a suitable holding fixture and remove the output shaft pilot and needle bearing and bushing from the rear bore of the input shaft.
12. Expand the tangs of the large snap ring in the mounting adapter and pry the snap ring apart and remove the input shaft assembly from the mounting adapter.
13. Remove the external snap ring from the input shaft. Place the input shaft assembly in a press and remove the ball bearing from the input shaft using bearing splitter D79L-4621-A. Remove the thrust plate and sleeve off the input shaft.
14. Remove the OK seal from the mounting adapter with Seal Remover, Tool T77248-A and Impact Slide Hammer, T50T-100-A or eqivalent.

Assembly

Before assembly, lubricate all parts with DEXRON® II, Automatic Transmission Fluid.

1. If removed, install the front output oil seal in the front case bore using Output Shaft Seal Installer, T83T-7065-B and Driver Handle, T80T-4000-W or equivalent.
2. Slide the spacer sleeve, thrust plate, and press the ball bearing onto the input shaft assembly. Install the external snap ring to the input shaft to retain the ball bearing.

NOTE: The snap ring groove of the ball bearing should be facing toward the rear of the transfer case. The stepped face of the thrust plate should face toward the front of the case, against the bearing. The spacer sleeve is installed between the thrust plate and the external splines of the input shaft assembly.

3. Place the tanged snap-ring in the mounting adapter groove. Position the input shaft in the mounting adapter and push inward until the input shaft assembly is seated in the adapter. When properly seated, the tanged snap-rig will snap

TORQUE SPECIFICATIONS
Borg-Warner 13-59 Transfer Case

Description	Torque N•m	Torque Ft. Lb.
Case to Cover Bolts	31–41	23–30
Rear Driveshaft Bolts	83–118	61–87
Skid Plate to Frame Bolt	30–41	22–30
Transfer Case to Transmission Adapter	34–47	25–35
Yoke Nut	203–244	150–180
Speedometer Screw	2.3–2.8	20–25

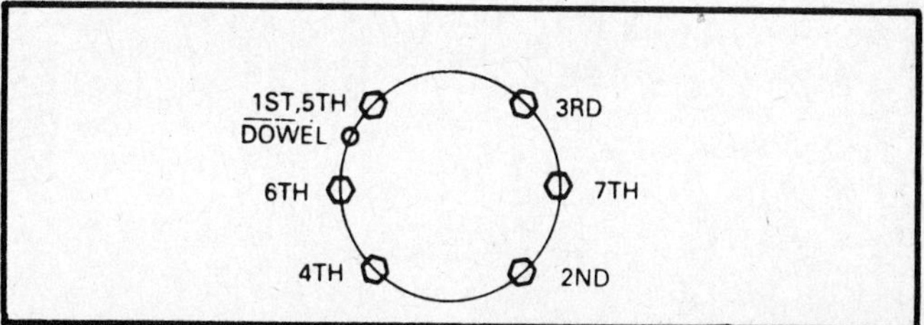

Transmission adapter to Transfer case torque sequence

into place. Check installation by holding the mounting adapter by hand and tapping the face of the input shaft against a wooden block to ensure that the snap-ring is engaged.

4. Position the mounting adapter on the front case. Install six bolts and tighten to 31–41 Nm (25–30 ft. lbs.).

5. Install the locking coupling onto the external splines of the input shaft assembly.

6. Install the output shaft, and snap ring assembly into the locking coupling and the input shaft. Make sure the external splines of the output shaft engauge the internal splines of the locking coupling and the input shaft.

7. Install the spacer hub onto the output shaft assembly with the square teeth side facing toward the front of the transfer case.

8. If removed, install the ball bearing in the rear cover bore. Drive the bearing into the rear cover bore with output shaft bearing replacer tool # T83T–7025–B and driver handled T80–4000–W or equivalent. Make sure the ball bearing is not cocked

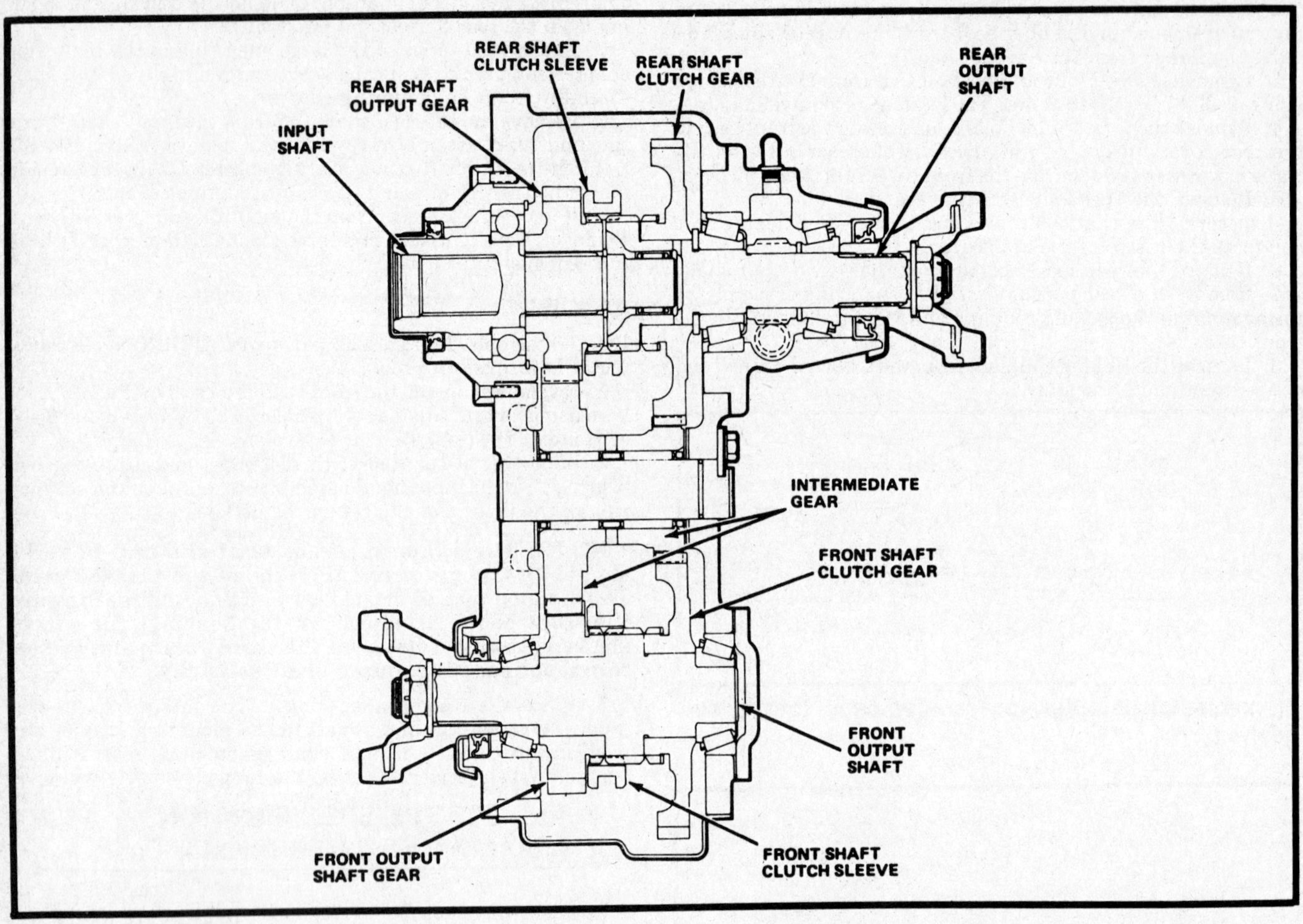

Dana 300 power flow

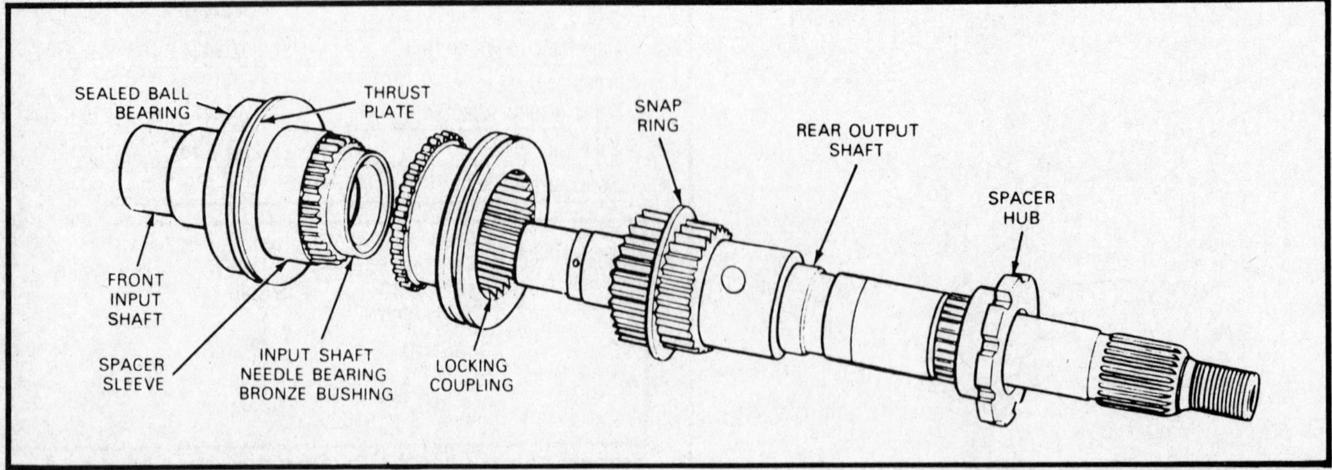

Input shaft assembly—Borg Warner 13-59

in the bore. Install the internal snap ring that retains the ball bearing to the rear cover.

9. Install the speedometer drive gear assembly into the rear cover bore with round end of the speedometer gear clip facing towards the inside of the rear cover. Pack the speedometer gear cavity in the rear cover with long life lubricant. Drive the oil seal into the rear cover bore with output shaft seal installer tool # T83T-7065-B and driver handle # T80T-4000-W or equivalent.

10. Position the rear cover on the front case. Install the nine bolts, starting with the bolts on the rear cover and torque the bolts to 23–30 ft. lbs.

11. Install the rear output shaft flange. Coat the faces of the yoke nuts and output shaft threads with a suitable thread sealer. Torque the yoke nuts to 150–180 ft. lbs.

12. Install the transfer case as outlined in this section.

TRANSFER CASE

Installation

1. Place a new gasket between the transfer case and adapter.
2. Raise the transfer case with a suitable transmission jack or equivalent, raise it high enough so that the transmission output shaft aligns with the splined transfer case input shaft.

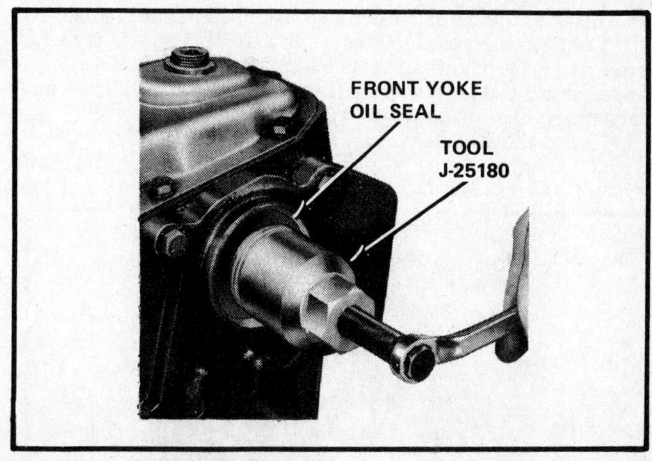

Yoke oil seal removal

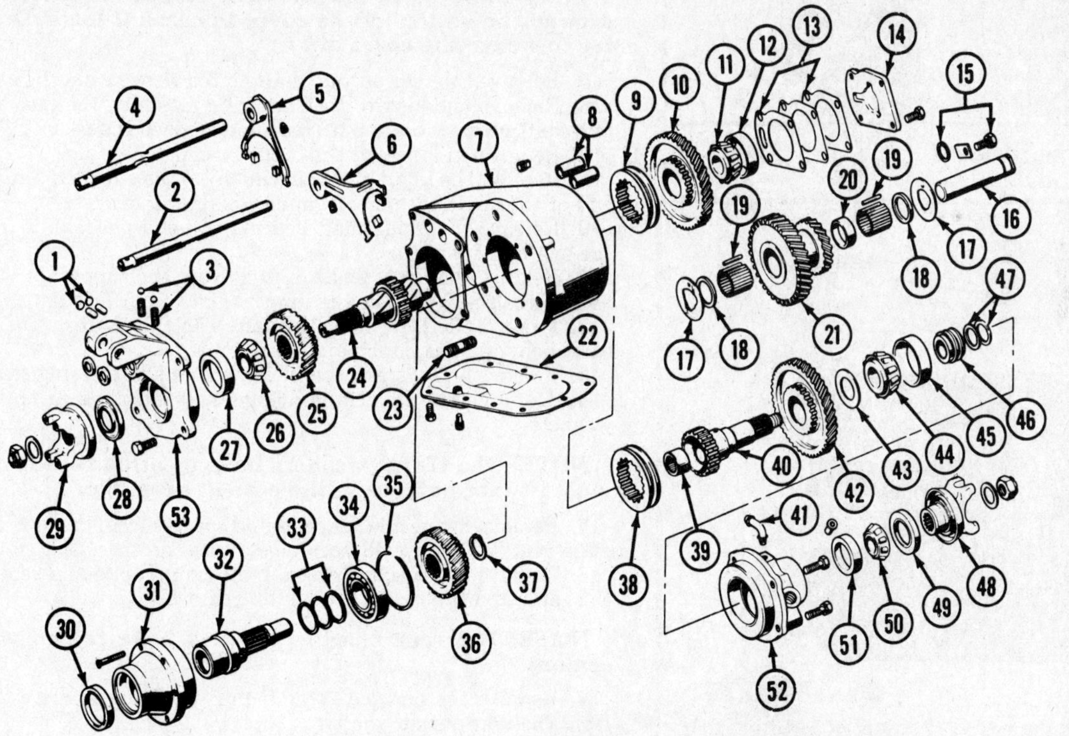

1. Interlock plugs and interlocks
2. Shift rod—rear output shaft fork
3. Poppet balls and springs
4. Shift rod—front output shaft fork
5. Front output shaft shift fork
6. Rear output shaft shift fork
7. Transfer case
8. Thimble covers
9. Clutch sleeve—front output shaft
10. Clutch gear—front output shaft
11. Bearing—front output shaft rear
12. Race—front output shaft bearing
13. End-play shims—front output shaft
14. Cover plate
15. Lock plate, bolt and washer
16. Intermediate gear shaft
17. Thrust washer
18. Bearing spacer (thin)
19. Intermediate gear shaft needle bearings
20. Bearing spacer (thick)
21. Intermediate gear
22. Bottom cover
23. Stud (case-to-trans.)
24. Front output shaft
25. Front output shaft gear
26. Front output shaft bearing (front)
27. Front output shaft bearing race
28. Oil seal
29. Front yoke
30. Seal
31. Support—input shaft
32. Input shaft
33. Shims
34. Input shaft bearing
35. Input shaft bearing snap-ring
36. Rear output shaft gear
37. Snap-ring
38. Clutch sleeve—rear output shaft
39. Input shaft rear bearing (needle) (or pilot bearing)
40. Rear output shaft
41. Vent
42. Clutch gear—rear output shaft
43. Thrustwasher
44. Bearing—rear output shaft front
45. Race—rear output shaft bearing
46. Speedometer drive gear
47. End-play shims
48. Rear yoke
49. Rear output shaft oil seal
50. Bearing—rear output shaft rear
51. Bearing race
52. Rear bearing cap
53. Front bearing cap

Exploded view of the Dana 300

3. Slide the transfer case forward on to the transmission output shaft and onto the dowel pin. Install transfer case retaining bolts and torque them to 26–43 ft. lbs.
4. Remove the transmission jack from the transfer case.
5. Connect the speedometer cable assembly to the transfer case rear cover. Tighten the screw to 20–25 inch lbs.
6. Connect the rear driveshaft to the output shaft flange and torque the yoke nut to 61–87 15 ft. lbs.
7. Lower the vehicle.

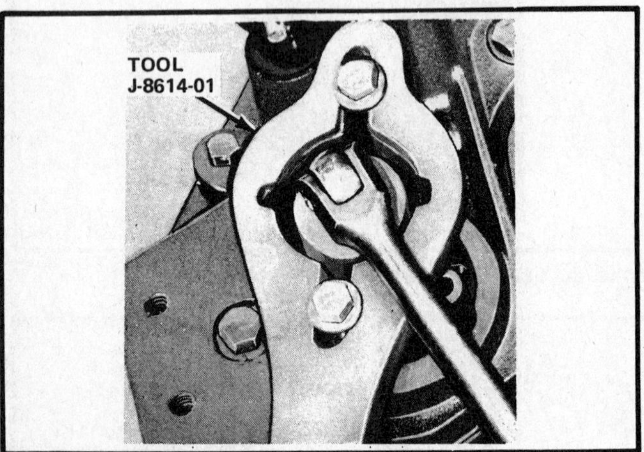

Output shaft yoke nut removal

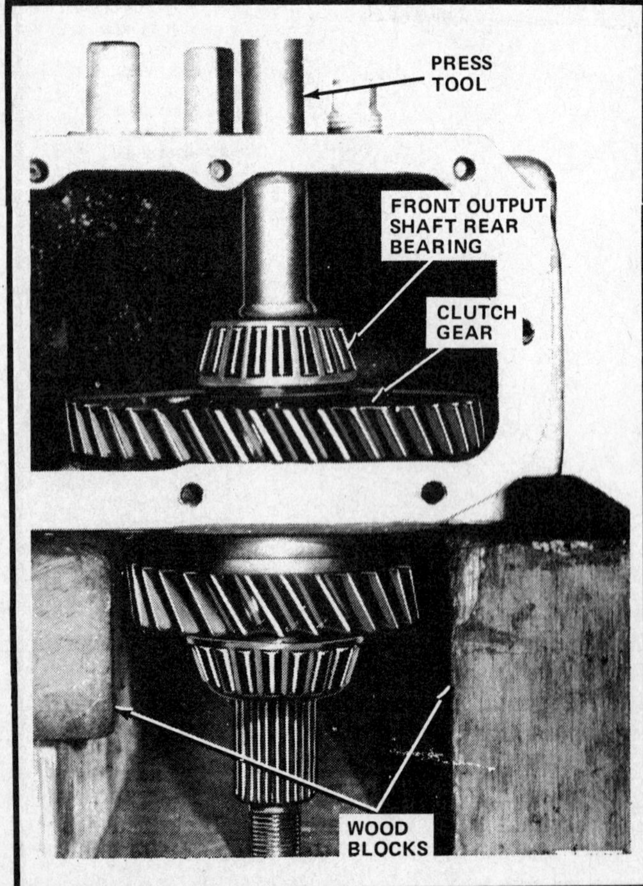

Front output shaft

Dana 300 Transfer Case

The 300 is used in Jeep® CJ models only. It has a cast iron case, four gear positions and employs an external floor mounted gearshift linkage for range control. It is a part time, 2 speed unit with undifferentiated high and low ranges. It is used with both manual and automatic transmission. Low range reduction is 2.6:1.

Disassembly

1. Drain the unit and remove the shift lever assembly.
2. Remove the bottom cover.

NOTE: The bottom cover has been coated with a sealant. Use a putty knife to break the seal and work the knife around the bottom of the cover to break it loose. Don't try to wedge the cover off.

3. With a puller, remove the front and rear yokes.
4. Unbolt and remove the input shaft support from the case. The rear output shaft gear and input shaft will come with it as an assembly.

NOTE:The support has been coated with sealant. Use a putty knife to break the seal and work the knife around the bottom of the cover to break it loose. Don't try to wedge the cover off.

5. Remove the rear output shaft clutch sleeve from the case.
6. Remove and discard the snap ring retaining the rear output shaft gear on the input shaft and remove the gear.
7. Remove and discard the input bearing snapring.
8. Remove the input shaft bearing from the support. Tap the end of the shaft with a soft mallet to aid removal.
9. Remove the input shaft bearing and end-play shims from the shaft with an arbor press.
10. Remove the input shaft oil seal from the support.
11. Unbolt and remove the intermediate shaft lockplate.
12. Remove the intermediate shaft. Tap the shaft out of the case using a brass punch and plastic mallet.
13. Remove and discard the intermediate shaft O-ring seal.
14. Remove the intermediate gear assembly and thrust washers.

NOTE: The thrust washers have locating tabs which must fit into notches in the case at assembly.

15. Remove the needle bearings and spacers from the intermediate gear. There are 48 needle bearings and three spacers.
16. Remove the rear bearing cap attaching bolts and remove the cap. A plastic mallet will aid in removal.

NOTE: The rear bearing cap has been coated with sealant.

17. Remove the end play shims and speedometer drive gear from the rear output shaft.
18. Remove and discard the rear output shaft oil seal. Remove the bearings and races from the rear cap.
19. Unbolt and remove the front and rear output shaft shift forks from the shift rods.
20. Remove the shift rods. Insert a punch through the clevis pin holes in the rods and rotate the rods while pulling them out of the case.

NOTE: The shift rods are free of the case, take care to avoid losing the shift rod poppet balls and springs.

21. Remove the shift forks from the case.
22. Remove the bolts attaching the front cap to the case and remove the cap.

NOTE: The front cap has been coated with sealant.

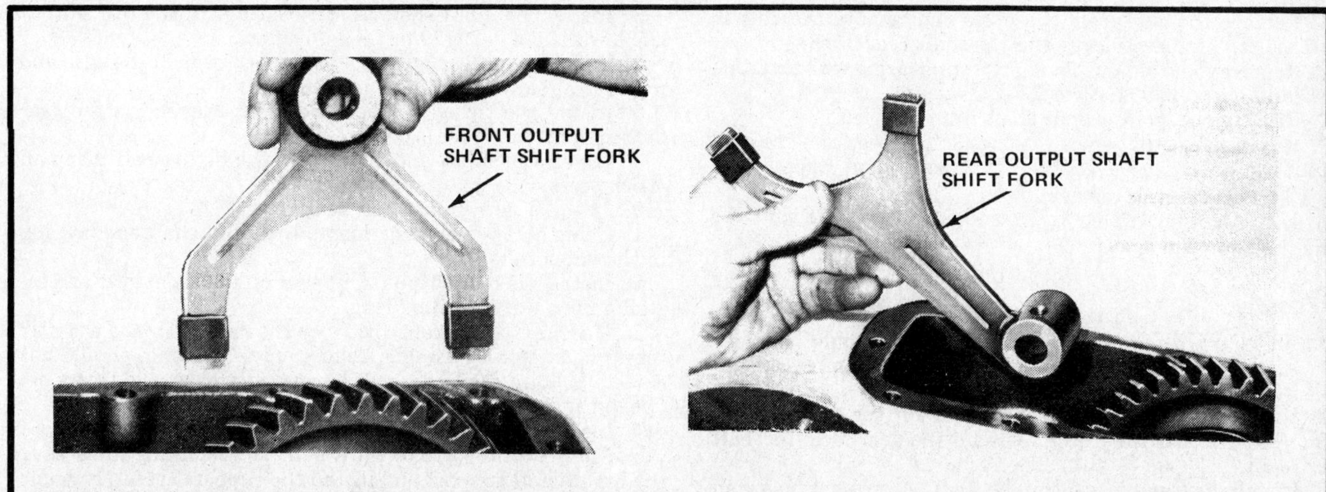

Shift fork installation

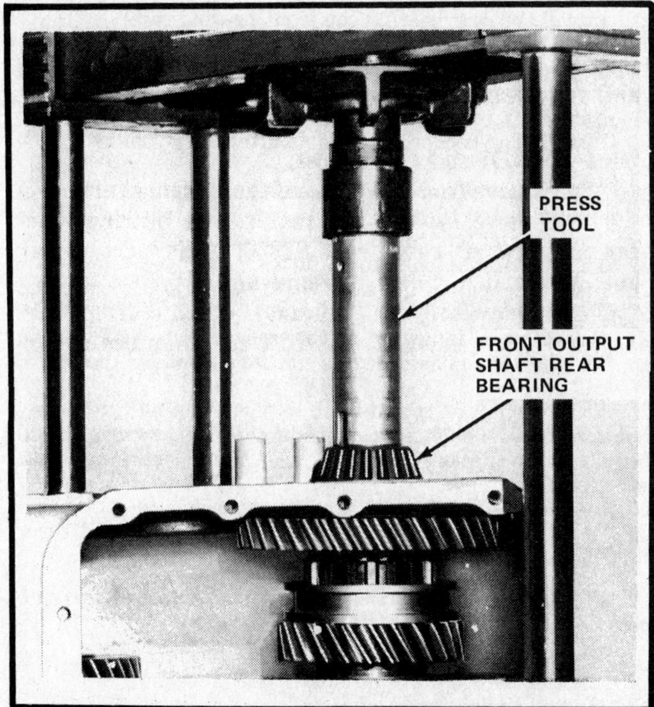

Front output shaft rear bearing installation

23. Remove the front output shaft and shift rod oil seals from the front cap.
24. Remove the bearing race from the front cap.
25. Remove the cover plate bolts and remove the plate and end play shims from the case. Keep the shims together for assembly.
26. Move the front output shaft toward the front of the case.
27. Remove the front output shaft rear bearing race.
28. Remove the rear output shaft front bearing. Position the case on wood blocks. Seat the clutch gear on the case interior surface and tap the shaft out of the bearing with a soft mallet.

NOTE: If the bearing is difficult to remove, an arbor press may have to be used.

29. Remove the rear output shaft front bearing, thrust washer, clutch gear and output shaft from the case.

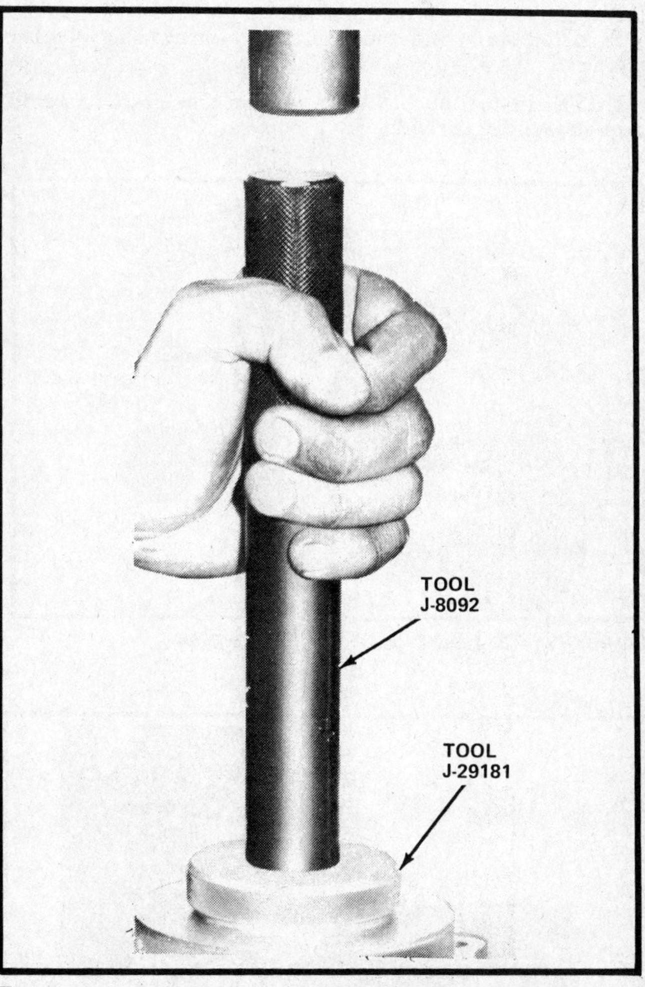

Front output shaft fornt bearing race installtion

30. Remove the front output shaft rear bearing with an arbor press.

CAUTION

Be sure to support the case with wood blocks positioned on either side of the case bore.

31. Remove the case from the press and remove the output shaft, clutch gear and sleeve and the shaft rear bearing.
32. Remove the front output shaft front bearing with an arbor press and tool J–22912–01 or its equivalent.
33. Remove the front output shaft from the gear.
34. Remove the input shaft rear needle bearing from the rear output shaft using tool J–29369–1 or its equivalent. Support the shaft in a vise during removal.
35. Using a $^3/_8$ in. drive, $^7/_{16}$ in. socket, remove the shift rod thimbles from the case.

Assembly

Coat all parts with SAE 85W–90 oil before assembly.

1. Apply Loctite® 220 or its equivalent to the thimbles and install them in the case.
2. Install the front output shaft gear on the front output shaft. Be sure that the clutch teeth on the gear face the shaft gear teeth.
3. Install the front bearing on the front output shaft using an arbor press. Be sure that the bearing is seated against the gear.
4. Install the front output shaft in the case and install the clutch sleeve and gear on the shaft.
5. Install the front output shaft rear bearing using an arbor press.

NOTE: Install an old yoke nut on the shaft to avoid damage to the threads.

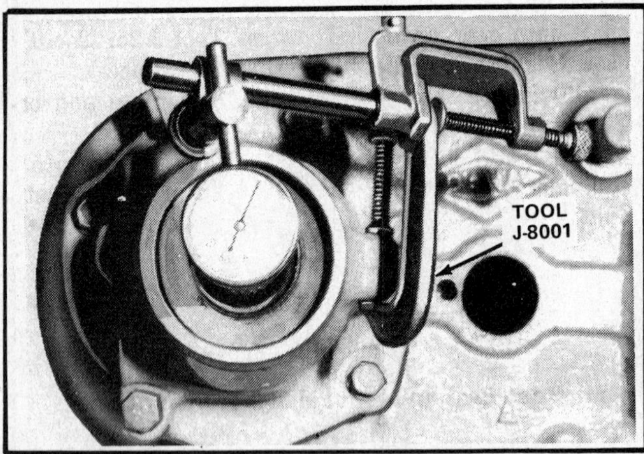

Checking the rear output shaft end-play

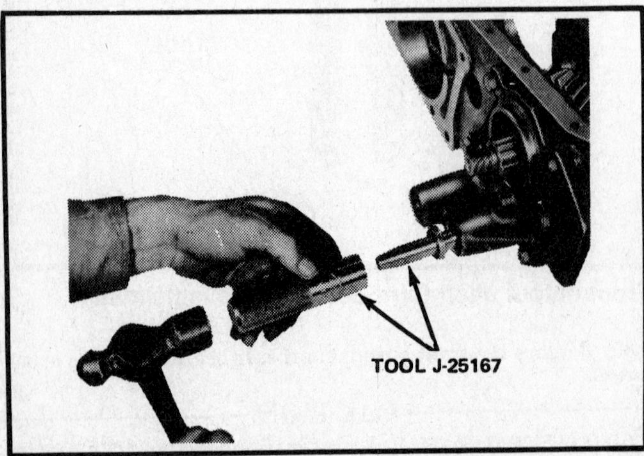

Shift rod oil seal installation

6. Install the input shaft needle bearings in the rear output shaft with tool J–29179 or its equivalent.
7. Position the rear output shaft clutch gear in the case and insert the rear output shaft into the gear.
8. Install the thrust washer and front bearing on the rear output shaft using an arbor press.
9. Install the shims and bearing on the input shaft using an arbor press.
10. Install a new input shaft seal.
11. Using a new snap-ring, install the input shaft and bearing in the support.
12. Install the rear output shaft gear on the input gear and install a new gear retaining ring.
13. Measure the clearance between the input gear and the gear retaining snap-ring using a feeler gauge. Clearance should not exceed 0.003 in. If clearance is beyond tolerance, add shims between the input shaft and bearing.
14. Install the clutch sleeve on the rear output shaft.
15. Apply Loctite® 515 or equivalent to the mating surfaces of the input shaft support and install the support assembly, shaft and gear in the case. Use two support bolts to align the support on the case and tap the support into position with a soft mallet. Torque the support bolts to 10 ft. lbs.
16. Install the rear bearing cap front bearing race.
17. Install the rear bearing cap rear bearing race.
18. Position the rear output shaft rear bearing in the rear bearing cap.
19. Install the rear output shaft yoke oil seal.
20. Install the speedometer gear and end-play shims on the rear output shaft.
21. Apply Loctite® 515 or equivalent to the mating surfaces of the cap and install the rear bearing cap. Use two cap bolts to align the cap and tap it into place with a soft mallet.
22. Tighten the cap bolts to 35 ft. lbs.
23. Install the rear output shaft yoke. Torque a new locknut to 120 ft. lbs.
24. Clamp a dial indicator on the rear output shaft bearing cap. Position the indicator stylus so that it contacts the end of the shaft.
25. Pry the shaft back and forth to check end-play. End-play should be 0.001–0.005 in. If play is not correct, remove or add shims between the speedometer drive gear and the output shaft rear bearing.
26. Install the front output shaft rear bearing race.
27. Install the front output shaft end play shims and cover plate. Tighten the cover plate bolts to 35 ft. lbs.

NOTE: Apply Loctite® 220 to the bolts before installation.

28. Install the front output shaft front bearing race.
29. Install the front output shaft yoke oil seal.
30. Install the shift rod oil seals.
31. Install the front bearing cap, using Loctite® 515 on the mating surfaces. Use two bolts to align the cap and tap it into position with a soft mallet.
32. Install and tighten the bearings cap bolts to 35 ft. lbs.
33. Seat the rear bearing cup against the cover plate by tapping the end of the front output shaft with a plastic mallet. Mount a dial indicator on the front bearing cap and position the stylus against the end of the output shaft. Pry the shaft back and forth to check end-play. End-play should be 0.001–0.005 in. If the play is not correct, add or remove shims between the cover plate and case. If shims are added seat the rear bearing cup again before checking.
34. Install the front output shaft yoke. Tighten the new locknut to 120 ft. lbs.
35. Install the front and rear output shaft shift forks.
36. Install the front output shaft shift rod poppet ball and spring in the front bearing cap.
37. Compress the poppet ball and spring and install the front output shaft shift rod part way in the case.

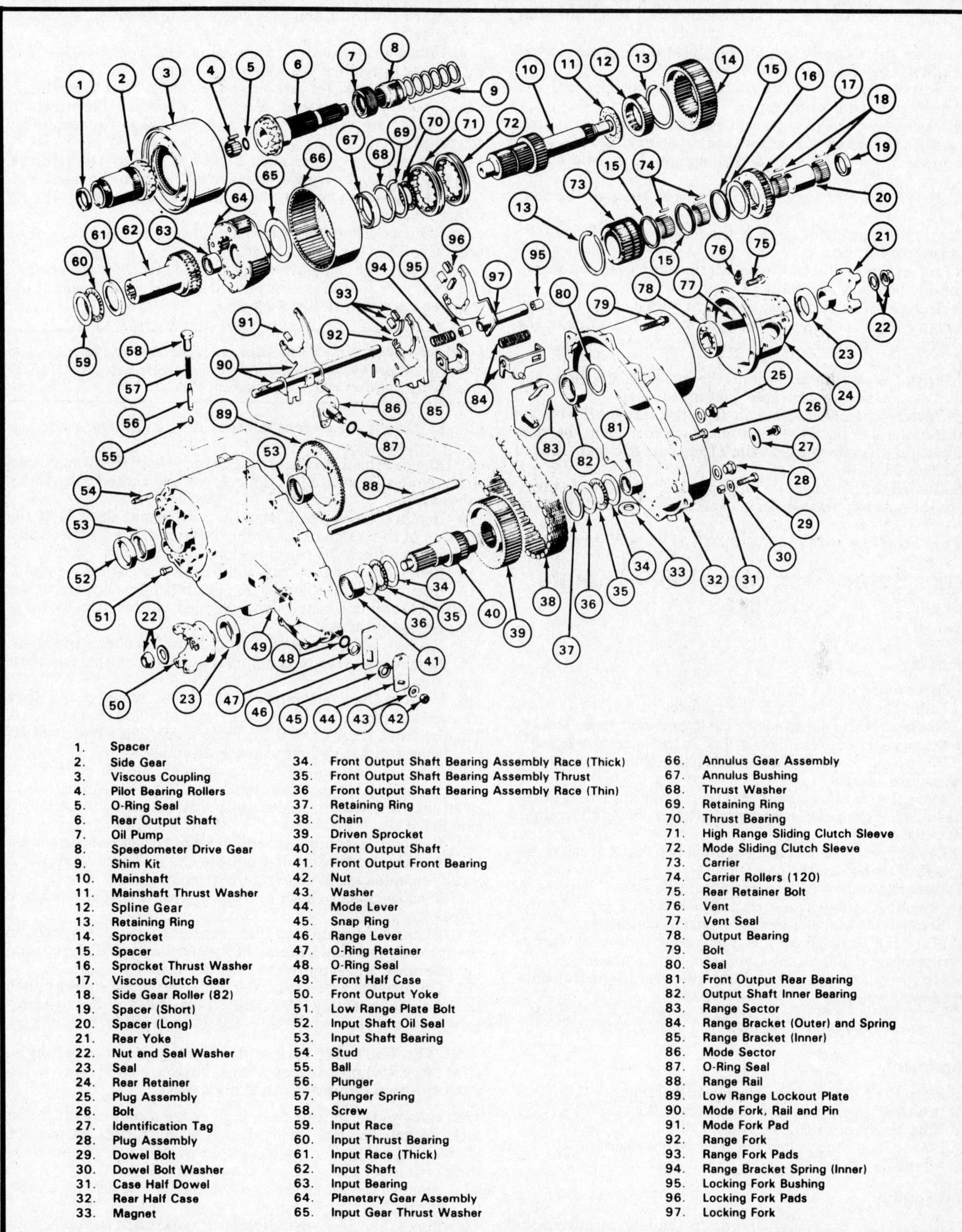

1. Spacer
2. Side Gear
3. Viscous Coupling
4. Pilot Bearing Rollers
5. O-Ring Seal
6. Rear Output Shaft
7. Oil Pump
8. Speedometer Drive Gear
9. Shim Kit
10. Mainshaft
11. Mainshaft Thrust Washer
12. Spline Gear
13. Retaining Ring
14. Sprocket
15. Spacer
16. Sprocket Thrust Washer
17. Viscous Clutch Gear
18. Side Gear Roller (82)
19. Spacer (Short)
20. Spacer (Long)
21. Rear Yoke
22. Nut and Seal Washer
23. Seal
24. Rear Retainer
25. Plug Assembly
26. Bolt
27. Identification Tag
28. Plug Assembly
29. Dowel Bolt
30. Dowel Bolt Washer
31. Case Half Dowel
32. Rear Half Case
33. Magnet
34. Front Output Shaft Bearing Assembly Race (Thick)
35. Front Output Shaft Bearing Assembly Thrust
36. Front Output Shaft Bearing Assembly Race (Thin)
37. Retaining Ring
38. Chain
39. Driven Sprocket
40. Front Output Shaft
41. Front Output Front Bearing
42. Nut
43. Washer
44. Mode Lever
45. Snap Ring
46. Range Lever
47. O-Ring Retainer
48. O-Ring Seal
49. Front Half Case
50. Front Output Yoke
51. Low Range Plate Bolt
52. Input Shaft Oil Seal
53. Input Shaft Bearing
54. Stud
55. Ball
56. Plunger
57. Plunger Spring
58. Screw
59. Input Race
60. Input Thrust Bearing
61. Input Race (Thick)
62. Input Shaft
63. Input Bearing
64. Planetary Gear Assembly
65. Input Gear Thrust Washer
66. Annulus Gear Assembly
67. Annulus Bushing
68. Thrust Washer
69. Retaining Ring
70. Thrust Bearing
71. High Range Sliding Clutch Sleeve
72. Mode Sliding Clutch Sleeve
73. Carrier
74. Carrier Rollers (120)
75. Rear Retainer Bolt
76. Vent
77. Vent Seal
78. Output Bearing
79. Bolt
80. Seal
81. Front Output Rear Bearing
82. Output Shaft Inner Bearing
83. Range Sector
84. Range Bracket (Outer) and Spring
85. Range Bracket (Inner)
86. Mode Sector
87. O-Ring Seal
88. Range Rail
89. Low Range Lockout Plate
90. Mode Fork, Rail and Pin
91. Mode Fork Pad
92. Range Fork
93. Range Fork Pads
94. Range Bracket Spring (Inner)
95. Locking Fork Bushing
96. Locking Fork Pads
97. Locking Fork

Jeep Select Trac 229

38. Insert the front output shaft shift rod through the shift fork.

39. Align the setscrew hole in the shift fork and rod. Install and tighten the setscrew to 14 ft. lbs.

40. Install the rear output shaft shift rod poppet ball and spring in the front bearing cap.

41. Compress the ball and spring and install the rear output shaft shift rail part way. The front output shaft shift rod should be in neutral and the interlocks seated in the front bearing cap bore.

42. Insert the rear output shaft shift rod through the shift fork.

43. Align the setscrew holes in the fork and rod. Torque the setscrew to 14 ft. lbs.

44. Insert tool J–25142 in the intermediate gear and install the needle bearings and spacer.

45. Install the intermediate gear thrust washers in the case. Make sure that the tangs are aligned with the grooves in the case. The thrust washers may be held in place with petroleum jelly.

46. Install a new O-ring seal on the intermediate shaft.

47. Position the intermediate gear in the case.

48. Install the intermediate shaft in the case bore. Tap the shaft into the gear until the shaft forces the tool out of the case.

49. Install the intermediate shaft lock plate and bolt. Torque the bolt to 23 ft. lbs.

50. Install the bottom cover, applying Loctite® 515 or equivalent to the mating surfaces. Install and torque the bolts to 15 ft. lbs.

51. Fill the case with 4 pints of SAE 85W–90W gear oil.

Jeep Selec–Trac Model 229 Transfer Case

Removal

1. Raise and support the vehicle.
2. Drain the lubricant from the transfer case.
3. Disconnect the speedometer cable and vent hose. Disconnect the transfer case shift lever link at the operating lever.
4. Place a support stand under the transmission and remove the rear crossmember.
5. Mark the transfer case front and rear output shafts at the transfer case yokes and propeller shafts for installation alignment reference.
6. Disconnect the front and rear propeller shafts at the transfer case yokes. Secure the shafts.
7. Disconnect the shift motor vacuum hoses.
8. Disconnect the transfer case shift linkage.
9. Remove the transfer case-to-transmission bolts.
10. Move the transfer case assembly rearward until clear of the transmission output shaft and remove the assembly.
11. Remove all gasket material from the rear of the transmission adapter housing.

RANGE CONTROL LINKAGE

Adjustment

1. Place the range control lever in high range.
2. Insert a $\frac{1}{8}$ in. spacer between gate and lever.
3. Hold the lever in this position.
4. Place range control lever in high range position.
5. Adjust as needed.

Disassembly

1. Remove the drain plug and drain the lubricant from the transfer case.
2. Remove the front and rear yoke nuts and seal washers. Discard the washers.
3. Mark the front and rear yokes for installation alignment reference.
4. Remove the front and rear yokes. Use Tool J–8614–01 or equivalent to remove the yokes if necessary.
5. Place the transfer case on wooden blocks. Cut V-notches in the blocks for clearance for the front case mounting studs.
6. Mark the rear retainer and rear case for assembly reference.
7. Remove the rear retainer bolts and remove the retainer. Use two prybars to pry the retainer off the transfer case. Position the prybars in slots in the retainer and case to pry the retainer loose.
8. Remove the differential shim(s) and speedometer drive gear from the rear output shaft.
9. Remove the bolts attaching the rear transfer case half to the front case half. Note that the bolts used at each end of the transfer case require flat washers.

CAUTION

Insert two prybars in the slots at each end of the rear transfer case half to loosen it. Do not attempt to wedge the transfer case halves apart or the case mating surfaces will be damaged.

10. Remove the rear transfer case half from the front case half using two prybars.
11. Remove the thrust bearing and races from the front output shaft. Note the position of the bearing and races for assembly reference.
12. Remove the oil pump from the rear output shaft. Note the position of the pump for assembly reference. The recessed side of the pump faces the case interior.
13. Remove the rear output shaft from the viscous coupling.
14. Remove the 15 main shaft pilot bearing rollers from the shaft or coupling (if the rollers dropped off during removal of the rear output shaft).
15. Remove the main shaft O-ring from the end of the shaft.
16. Remove the viscous coupling from the main shaft and side gear.
17. Remove the front output shaft, driven sprocket and drive chain assembly. Lift the front shaft, sprocket and chain upward. Tilt the front shaft toward the main shaft. Slide the chain off the drive sprocket and remove the assembly.
18. Remove the main shaft, side gear, clutch gear, drive sprocket and spline gear as an assembly. Place the assembly on a clean shop towel and set aside until the front case disassembly is completed.
19. Remove the front output shaft front thrust bearing assembly from the front case, or from the shaft (if the bearing and races remained on the shaft during removal).
20. Remove the drive chain from the front output shaft and sprocket.
21. Remove the snap-ring that retains the driven sprocket on the front output shaft. Mark the sprocket and shaft for assembly reference and remove the sprocket from the shaft.
22. Remove the mode fork, shift rail, and mode sliding clutch sleeve as an assembly. Mark the sleeve and fork for assembly reference and remove the sleeve from the fork.

NOTE: The mode fork and rail are pinned together so that they will operate as a unit. Remove the pin to separate the two components if necessary.

23. Remove the locking fork, high range sliding clutch sleeve, fork brackets and fork springs as an assembly. Note the position of the components for assembly reference and disassemble the components for cleaning and inspection.
24. Remove the range sector detent screw and remove the detent spring, plunger and ball.
25. Move the range operating lever downward to the last detent position.
26. Disengage the low range fork lug from the range sector slot.

27. Remove the retaining snap-ring from the annulus gear and remove the thrust washer.
28. Remove the annulus gear, range fork and rail as an assembly. Separate the components for cleaning and inspection.
29. Remove the planetary thrust washer from the planetary assembly hub.
30. Remove the planetary assembly. Grasp the planetary hub and lift the assembly upward to remove it.
31. Remove the main shaft thrust bearing from the input shaft.
32. Remove the input shaft and remove the input shaft thrust bearing and race.
33. Remove the range sector and operating lever attaching nut and lockwasher. Remove the lever.
34. Remove the range sector and shaft from the front case.
35. Remove the range sector O-ring and retainer.

TORQUE SPECIFICATIONS
Model 229

Component	Service Set-To Torque
Detent Retainer Bolt	31 N•m (23 ft-lbs)
Drain and Fill Plugs	24 N•m (18 ft-lbs)
Front/Rear Yoke Nuts	163 N•m (120 ft-lbs)
Operating Lever Locknut	24 N•m (18 ft-lbs)
Rear Case-to-Front Case Bolts (All)	31 N•m (23 ft-lbs)
Rear Retainer Bolts	31 N•m (23 ft-lbs)
Transfer Case-to-Transmission Adapter Nuts	35 N•m (26 ft-lbs)
Universal Joint Strap Bolt-to-Transfer Case	19 N•m (170 in-lbs)

MAIN SHAFT

Disassembly

1. Grasp the drive sprocket and lift the sprocket clutch gear and side gear upward and off the main shaft.
2. Remove the main shaft needle bearings and two bearing spacers from the main shaft; a total of 82 bearings are used; note the spacer position for assembly reference.
3. Remove the spline gear and thrust washer from the main shaft.
4. Remove the side gear, clutch gear, and clutch gear thrust washer from the sprocket carrier and sprocket.
5. Remove the clutch gear and thrust washer from the side gear.
6. Remove one sprocket carrier snap-ring and remove the drive sprocket from the carrier; mark for assembly reference.

CAUTION

The sprocket carrier and main shaft needle bearings are different in size. Take care to avoid intermixing them.

7. Remove the three bearing spacers and all sprocket carrier needle bearings from the carrier; a total of 120 needle bearings are used.
8. Remove the rear output bearing and rear yoke seal from the rear retainer; the bearing is shielded on one side; note the bearing position for assembly reference.
9. Remove the input gear and front yoke seals from the front case; use a small prybar to pry the seals out of the case.

Cleaning & Inspection

1. Wash all components thoroughly in clean solvent. Ensure that all lubricant, metallic particles, dirt, and foreign material are removed from the surfaces of every component.
2. Apply compressed air to each oil supply port and channel in each transfer case half to remove any obstructions or cleaning solvent residue.
3. Inspect all gear teeth for excessive wear or damage. Inspect all gear splines for burrs, nicks, wear or damage.
4. Remove minor nicks or scratches using an oilstone. Replace any component exhibiting excessive wear or damage.
5. Inspect all snap-rings and thrust washers for excessive wear, distortion and damage. Replace any component exhibiting these conditions.
6. Inspect the transfer case halves and rear retainer for cracks, porosity, damaged mating surfaces, stripped bolt threads and distortion. Replace any component exhibiting these conditions.
7. Inspect the viscous coupling and differential pinions. If the pinions or carrier are damaged or worn excessively, replace the coupling as an assembly only. If the coupling is cracked, leaking, or damaged, replace the coupling as an assembly only.
8. Inspect the condition of all needle, roller, ball and thrust bearings in the front and rear transfer case halves. Also inspect to determine the condition of the bearing bores in both transfer case halves and in the input gear, rear output shaft, side gear, and rear retainer.
9. Replace any component that is excessively worn or damaged. If any shaft, case half or input gear bearing requires replacement, refer to Bushing/Bearing Replacement.

NOTE: The front output shaft thrust bearing race surfaces are heat treated during manufacture. Heat treatment causes a brown or blue discoloration of these surfaces. Do not replace a front output shaft because of this type of discoloration.

BEARING & BUSHING

CAUTION

All of the bearings used in the transfer case must be correctly positioned to avoid blocking the bearing oil supply holes. After replacing any bearing, check the bearing position and ensure that the supply hole is not obstructed by the bearing.

REAR OUTPUT SHAFT BEARING

Removal and Installation

1. Remove the bearing using Remover Tool J–26941 and Slide Hammer J–2619–01 or equivalent. Remove the rear output lip seal using a small awl.
2. Install a replacement lip seal.
3. Install a replacement bearing using Driver Handle J–8092 and Installer Tool J–29166 or equivalent.
4. Remove the tools and inspect the oil supply hole. The bearing must not obstruct the supply hole.

FRONT OUTPUT SHAFT FRONT BEARING

Removal and Installation

1. Remove the bearing using Tools J–8092 and J–29168 or equivalent.
2. Remove the tools and inspect the oil supply hole. The bearing must not obstruct the supply hole.

FRONT OUTPUT SHAFT REAR BEARING

Removal and Installation

1. Remove the bearing using Remover Tool J–26941 and Slide Hammer J–2619–01 or equivalent.

2. Install a replacement bearing using Driver Handle J–8092 and Installer Tool J–29163 or equivalent.

3. Remove the installer tools and inspect the bearing position to ensure the oil supply hole is not obstructed. Also ensure that the bearing is seated flush with the edge of the bore in the case to allow clearance for the thrust bearing assembly.

INPUT GEAR FRONT & REAR BEARINGS

Removal and Installation

1. Remove both bearings simultaneously using Driver Handle J–8092 and Remover Tool J–29170 or equivalent.

2. Install the new bearings one at a time. Install the rear bearing first; then install the front bearing. Use Driver Handle J–8092 and Installer Tool J–29169 or equivalent.

3. Remove the installer tools and inspect the bearing position to ensure the oil supply holes are not obstructed. Also ensure that the bearings are flush with the transfer case bore surfaces.

4. Install a replacement oil seal using seal Installer Tool J–29162 or equivalent.

MAIN SHAFT PILOT BUSHING

Removal and Installation

1. Remove the bushing using Slide Hammer J–2619–01 and Remover Tool J–29369–1 or equivalent.

2. Install a replacement bearing using Driver Handle J–8092 and Installer Tool J–29174 or equivalent.

3. Inspect bushing position to ensure that the oil supply hole is not obstructed.

ANNULUS GEAR BUSHING

Removal and Installation

1. Remove the bushing using Driver Handle J–8092 and Remover/Installer Tool J–29185 or equivalent.

2. Install a replacement bushing using Tools J–8092 and J–29185–2 or equivalent.

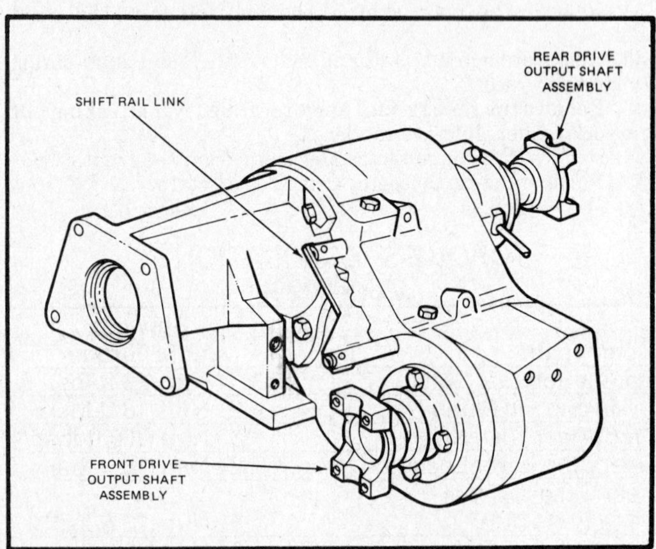

Front view of a model 205 transfer case

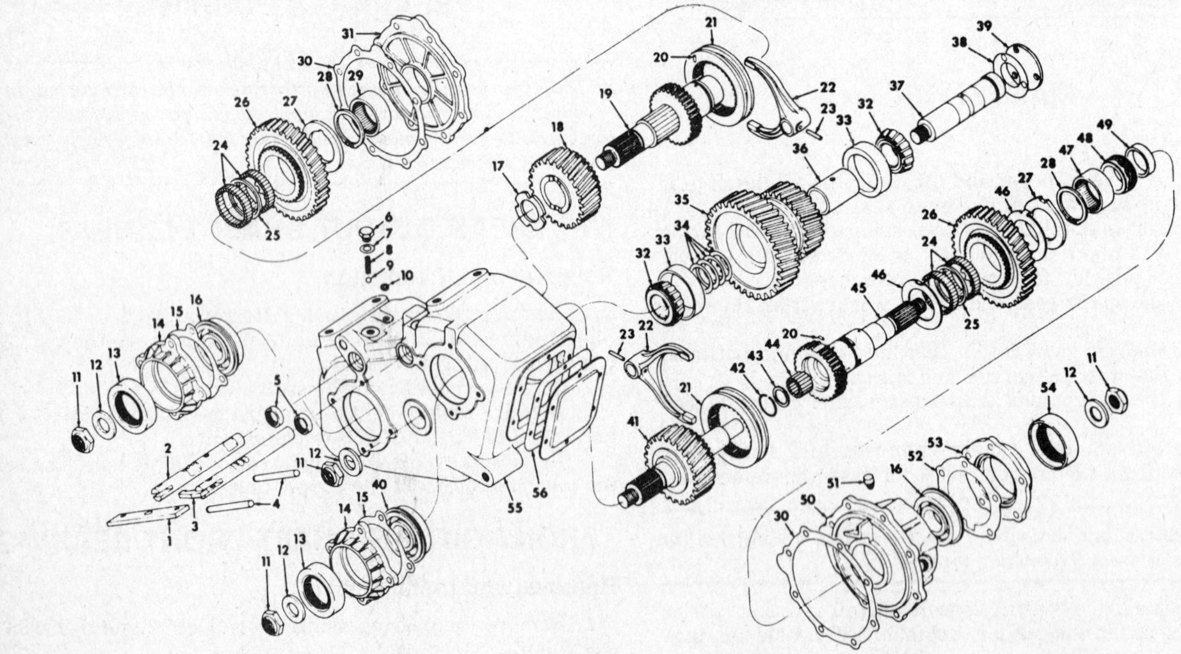

1. Shift lever link
2. Bar
3. Bar
4. Plunger
5. Seal
6. Screw
7. Gasket
8. Spring
9. Ball
10. Plug
11. Nut
12. Washer
13. Seal
14. Retainer
15. Gasket
16. Bearing
17. Washer
18. Gear
19. Shaft
20. Pin
21. Clutch
22. Fork
23. Pin
24. Bearing
25. Spacer
26. Gear
27. Washer
28. Ring
29. Bearing
30. Gasket
31. Retainer
32. Cone
33. Cup
34. Shim set
35. Gear
36. Spacer
37. Shaft
38. Gasket
39. Cover
40. Bearing
41. Shaft
42. Ring
43. Washer
44. Bearing
45. Gear
46. Washer
47. Bearing
48. Gear
49. Spacer
50. Retainer
51. Breather
52. Gasket
53. Retainer
54. Seal
55. Case
56. Gasket

Exploded view of a new process 205 transfer case

3. Remove any chips generated by the bushing removal and/or installation.

REAR OUTPUT BEARING AND REAR YOKE SEAL

Removal and Installation

1. Remove the bearing using a brass drift and hammer.
2. Remove the seal from the retainer using a brass drift and hammer.

CAUTION

The rear output bearing is shielded on one side. Ensure that the shielded side faces the transfer case interior after installation.

3. Install a replacement bearing using Driver Handle J–8092 and Installer Tool J–7818 or equivalent.
4. Install a replacement seal in the retainer using Tool J–29162 or equivalent.

New Process Model 205 Transfer Case

The New Process Model 205 transfer case is a two-speed gearbox mounted between the main transmission and the rear axle. The gearbox transmits power from the transmission and engine to the front and rear driving axles.

Disassembly

TRANSFER CASE

1. Clean the exterior of the case.
2. Remove the nuts from the universal joint flanges.
3. Remove the front output shaft rear bearing retainer, front bearing retainer and drive flange.
4. Tap the front output shaft assembly from the case with a soft hammer. Remove the sliding clutch, front output high gear, washer and bearing from the case.
5. Remove the rear output shaft housing attaching bolts and remove the housing, output shaft, bearing retainer and speedometer gear.
6. Slide the rear output shaft from the housing.

NOTE: Be careful not to lose the 15 needle bearings that will be loose when the rear output shaft is removed.

7. Drive the two $\frac{1}{4}$ in. shift rail pin access hole plugs into the transfer case with a punch and hammer.
8. Remove the two shift rail detent nuts and springs from the case. Use a magnet to remove the two detent balls.
9. Position both shift rails in neutral and remove the shift fork retaining roll pins with a long punch.
10. Remove the clevis pin from one shift rail and rail link.
11. Remove the range shift rail first, then the 4WD shift rail.
12. Remove the shift forks and and sliding clutch from the case. Remove the input shaft bearing retainer, bearing and shaft.
13. Remove the cup plugs and rail pins, if they were driven out, from the case.
14. Remove the locknut from the idler gear shaft.
15. Remove the idler gear shaft rear cover.
16. Remove the idler gear shaft, using a soft hammer and a drift.
17. Roll the idler gear assembly to the front output shaft hole and remove the assembly from the case.

REAR OUTPUT SHAFT AND YOKE

1. Loosen rear output shaft yoke nut.
2. Remove shaft housing bolts, then remove the housing and retainer assembly.
3. Remove retaining nut and yoke from the shaft, then remove the shaft assembly.
4. Remove and discard snap-ring.
5. Remove thrust washer and pin.
6. Remove tanged bronze washer. Remove gear needle bearings, spacer and second row of needle bearings.
7. Remove tanged bronze thrust washer.
8. Remove pilot rollers, retainer ring and washer.
9. Remove oil seal retainer, ball bearing, speedometer gear and spacer. Discard gaskets.
10. Press out bearing.
11. Remove oil seal from the retainer.

FRONT OUTPUT SHAFT

1. Remove lock nut, washer and yoke.
2. Remove attaching bolts and front bearing retainer.
3. Remove rear bearing retainer attaching bolts.
4. Tap output shaft with a soft-faced hammer and remove shaft, gear assembly and rear bearing retainer.
5. Remove sliding clutch, gear, washer and bearing from output high gear.
6. Remove sliding clutch from the high output gear; then remove gear, washer and bearing.
7. Remove gear retaining snap-ring from the shaft, using large snap-ring picks. Discard ring.
8. Remove thrust washer and pin.
9. Remove gear, needle bearings and spacer.
10. Replace rear bearing, if necessary.

CAUTION

Always replace the bearing and retainer as an assembly. Do not try to press a new bearing into an old retainer.

SHIFT RAILS AND FORKS

1. Remove the two poppet nuts, springs, and using a magnet, the poppet balls.
2. Remove cup plugs on top of case, using a $\frac{1}{4}$ in. punch.
3. Position both shift rails in neutral, then remove fork pins with a long handled screw extractor.
4. Remove clevis pins and shift rail link.
5. Lower shift rails; upper rail first and then lower.
6. Remove shift forks and sliding clutch.
7. Remove the front output high gear, washer and bearing. Remove the shift rail cup plugs.

INPUT SHAFT

1. Remove snap-ring in front of bearing. Tap shaft out rear of case and bearing out front of case, using a soft-faced hammer or mallet.
2. Tilt case up on power take-off and remove the two interlock pins from inside.

IDLER GEAR

1. Remove idler gear shaft nut.
2. Remove rear cover.
3. Tap out idler gear shaft, using a soft-faced hammer and a drift approximately the same diameter as the shaft.
4. Remove idler gear through the front output shaft hole.
5. Remove two bearing cups from the idler gear.

Assembly

TRANSFER CASE

1. Assemble the idler shaft gears, bearings, spacer and shims, and bearings on a dummy shaft tool and install the assembly into the case through the front output shaft bore, large end first.
2. Install the idler shaft from the large bore side, using a soft hammer to drive it through the bearings, spacer, gears, and shims.

3. Install a washer and new locknut on the end of the idler shaft. Check to make sure the idler gear rotates freely. Tighten the locknut to specification.
4. Install the idler shaft cover with a new gasket so the flat side faces the rear bearing retainer of the front output shaft. Install and tighten the two retaining screws to the proper torque.
5. Install the interlock pins into the interlock bore through the front of the output shaft opening.
6. Start the 4WD shift rail into the front of the case, solid end of the rail first, with the detent notches facing up.
7. Position the shift fork onto the shift rail with the long end facing inward. Push the rail through the fork and into the Neutral position.
8. Position the input shaft and bearing in the case.
9. Start the range shift rail into the case from the front, with the detent notches facing up.
10. Position the sliding clutch to the shift fork. Place the sliding clutch on the input shaft and align the fork with the shift rail. Push the rail through the fork into the Neutral position.
11. Install the roll pins that lock the shift forks to the shift rails with a long punch.
12. Position the front wheel drive high gear and its thrust washer in the case. Position the sliding clutch in the shift fork. Shift the rail and fork into the front wheel drive (4WD-Hi) position, while at the same time, meshing the clutch with the mating teeth on the front wheel drive high gear.
13. Align the thrust washer, high gear and sliding clutch with the bearing bore in the case and insert the front output shaft and low gear into the high gear assembly.
14. Install a new seal in the front bearing retainer of the front output shaft, and install the bearing and retainer and new gasket in the case. Tighten the bearing retainer cap screws to the proper torque.
15. Lubricate the roller bearing in the front output shaft rear bearing retainer, which is the aluminum cover, and install it over the front output shaft and to the case. Install and tighten the retaining screws to the proper torque.
16. Move the range shift rail to the High position and install the rear output shaft and retainer assembly to the housing and input shaft. Use one or two new gaskets, as required, to adjust the clearance on the input shaft pilot. Install the rear output shaft housing retaining bolts and tighten them to specification.
17. Using a punch and sealing compound, install the shift rail pin access plugs.
18. Install the fill and drain plugs and the cross-link clevis pin.

IDLER GEAR

1. Press the two bearing cups in the idler gear.
2. Assemble the two bearing cones, spacer, shims and idler gear on a dummy shaft, with bore facing up. Check end-play.
3. Install idler gear assembly (with dummy shaft) into the case, large end first, through the front output shaft bore.
4. Install idler shaft from large bore side, driving it through with a soft-faced hammer or mallet.
5. Install washer and new locknut. Check for free rotation and measure end-play. Torque locknut to specifications.
6. Install idler shaft cover and new gasket. Torque cover bolts to specifications.

NOTE: Flat side of cover must be positioned towards front output shaft rear cover.

SHIFT RAILS AND FORKS

1. Press the two rail seals into the case.

NOTE: Install seals with metal lip outward.

2. Install interlock pins from inside case.
3. Insert slotted end of front output drive shift rail (with poppet notches up) into back of case.
4. While pushing rail through to neutral position, install shift fork (long end inward).
5. Install input shaft and bearing into case.
6. Install end of range rail (with poppet notches up) into front of case.
7. Install sliding clutch on fork, then place over input shaft in case.
8. Push range rail, while engaging sliding clutch and fork, through to neutral position.
9. Drive new lockpins into forks through holes at top of case.

NOTE: Tilt case on power take-off opening to install range rail lockpin.

FRONT OUTPUT SHAFT AND GEAR

1. Install two rows of needle bearings in the front low output gear and retain with grease.

NOTE: Each row consists of 32 needle bearings and the two rows are separated by a spacer.

2. Position front output shaft in a soft-jaw vise, with spline end down. Place front low gear over shaft with clutch gear facing down; then install thrust washer pin, thrust washer and new snap-ring.

NOTE: Position snap-ring gap opposite the thrust washer pin.

3. Place front drive high gear and washer in case. Install sliding clutch in the shift fork, then put fork and rail into 4-High position, meshing front drive high gear and clutch teeth.
4. Align washer, high gear and sliding clutch and bearing bore. Insert front output shaft and low gear assembly through the high gear assembly.
5. Install front output bearing and retainer with a new seal in the case.
6. Clean and grease rollers in front output rear bearing retainer. Install on case with one gasket and bolts coated with sealant. Torque bolts to specifications.
7. Install front output yoke, washer and locknut. Torque locknut to specifications.

REAR OUTPUT SHAFT

1. Install two rows of needle bearings into the output low gear, retaining them with grease.

NOTE: Each row consists of 32 needle bearings and the two rows are separated by a spacer.

2. Install thrust washer (with tang down in clutch gear groove) onto the rear output shaft.
3. Install output low gear onto shaft with clutch teeth facing downward.
4. Install thrust washer over gear with tab pointing up and away. Install washer pin.
5. Install large thrust washer over shaft and pin. Turn washer until tab fits into slot located approximately 90° away from pin.
6. Install snap-ring and measure shaft end-play.
7. Grease pilot bore and install needle bearings.

NOTE: There are 15 pilot needle bearings.

8. Install thrust washer and new snap-ring in pilot bore.
9. Press new bearing into retainer housing.
10. Install housing on output shaft assembly.
11. Install spacer and speedometer gear. Install rear bearing.
12. Install rear bearing retainer seal.
13. Install bearing retainer assembly on housing, using one or two gaskets to achieve specified clearance. Torque attaching bolts to specifications.
14. Install yoke, washer and locknut on output shaft.
15. Position range rail in high, then install output shaft and retainer assembly on case. Torque housing bolts to specifications.

CASE

1. Install power take-off cover and gasket. Torque attaching bolts to specifications.
2. Install cup plugs at rail pin holes.

NOTE: After installing, seal the cup plugs.

3. Install drain and filler plugs. Torque to specifications.
4. Install shift rail cross link, clevis pins and lock pins.

New Process Model 207 Transfer Case

The 207 transfer case is an aluminum case, chain drive, four position unit providing four-wheel drive high and low ranges, a two-wheel high range, and a neutral position. It is a part-time four-wheel drive unit. Torque input in four-wheel high and low ranges is undifferentiated. The range positions on the 207 transfer case are selected by a floor mounted gearshift lever.

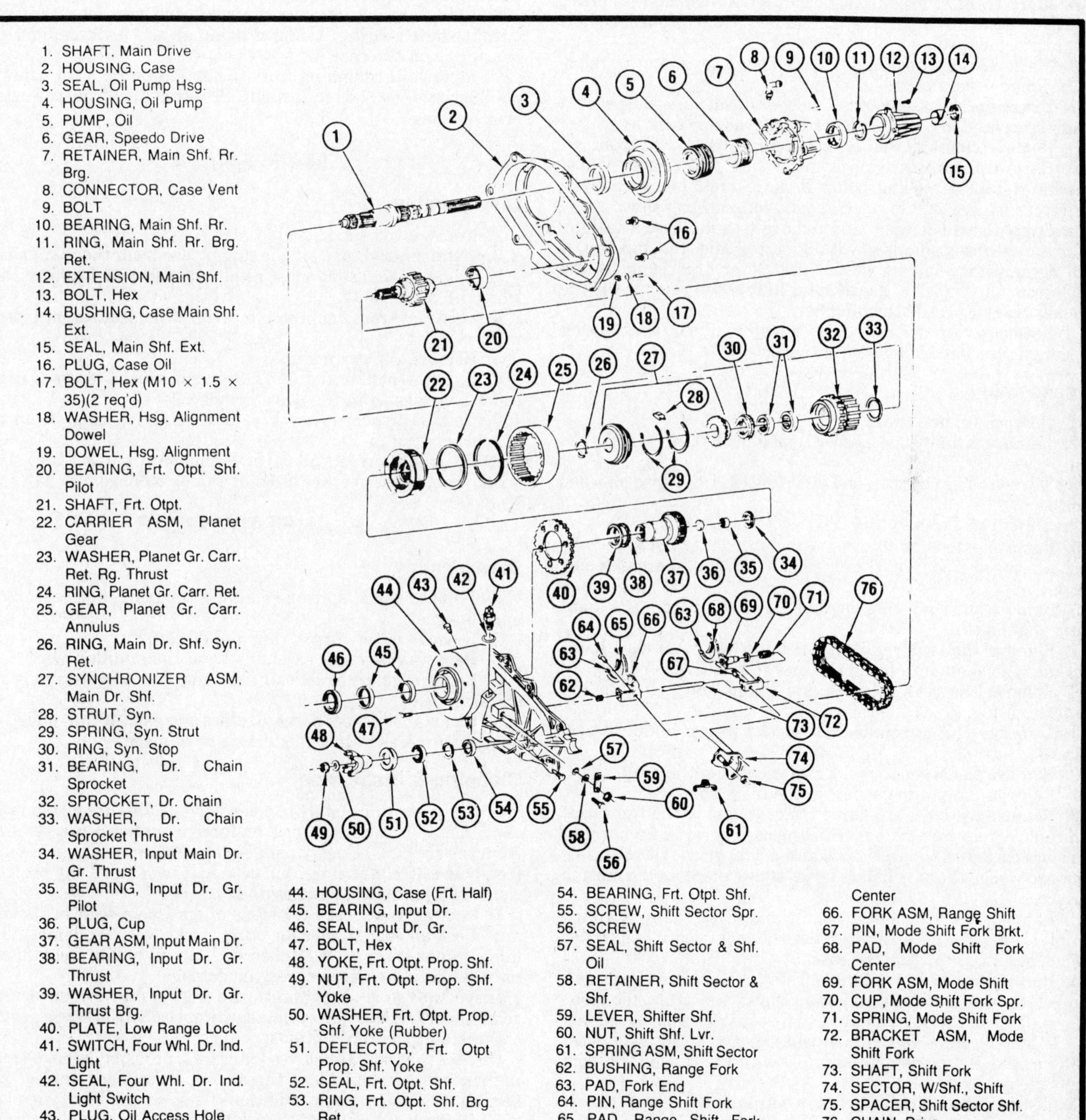

Exploded view of a new process 207 transfer case

The 207 case is a two-piece aluminum case containing front and rear output shafts, two drive sprockets, a shift mechanism and a planetary gear assembly. The drive sprockets are connected and operated by the drive chain. The planetary assembly which consists of a three pinion carrier and an annulus gear provide the four-wheel drive low range when engaged.

Removal

1. Shift transfer case into 4 Hi.
2. Disconnect negative cable at battery.
3. Raise vehicle and remove skid plate.
4. Drain lubricant from transfer case.
5. Mark transfer case front output shaft yoke and propeller shaft for assembly reference. Disconnect front propeller shaft from transfer case.
6. Mark rear axle yoke and propeller shaft for assembly reference. Remove rear propeller shaft.
7. Disconnect speedometer cable and vacuum harness at transfer case. Remove shift lever from transfer case.
8. Remove catalytic converter hanger bolts at converter.
9. Raise transmission and transfer case and remove transmission mount attaching bolts. Remove mount and catalytic converter hanger and lower transmission and transfer case.
10. Support transfer case and remove transfer case attaching bolts. On vehicles equipped with an automatic transmission, it will be necessary to remove the shift lever bracket mounting bolts from the transfer case adapter in order to remove the upper left transfer case attaching bolt.
11. Separate transfer case from adapter (auto) or extension housing (man.) and remove from vehicle.

Disassembly

1. Remove fill and drain plugs.
2. Remove front yoke. Discard yoke seal washer and yoke nut.
3. Turn transfer case on end and position front case on wood blocks.
4. Shift transfer case to 4 Lo.
5. Remove extension housing attaching bolts. Using a hammer, tap the shoulder on the extension housing to break sealer loose.
6. Remove the snap-ring for the rear bearing from the main shaft and discard.
7. Remove the rear retainer attaching bolts. Using a hammer, tap the shoulder on the retainer to break sealer loose.
8. Remove the rear retainer and pump housing from the transfer case.
9. Remove the pump seal from the pump housing and discard.
10. Remove the speedometer drive gear from the main shaft.
11. Remove the pump gear from the main shaft.
12. Remove the bolts attaching the rear case to the front case and remove rear case. To separate the case, insert a prybar into the slots casted in the case ends and pry upward. DO NOT attempt to wedge the case halves apart at any point on the mating surfaces.
13. Remove the front output shaft and drive chain as an assembly. It may be necessary to raise the main shaft slightly for the output shaft to clear the case.
14. Pull up on the mode fork rail until rail clears range fork and rotate mode fork and rail and remove from transfer case.
15. Pull up on the main shaft until it separates from the planetary assembly. Remove the main shaft from the transfer case.
16. Remove the planetary assembly with the range fork from the transfer case.
17. Remove the planetary thrust washer, input gear thrust bearing and front thrust washer from the transfer case.
18. Remove the shift sector detent spring and retaining bolt.
19. Remove the shift sector, shaft and spacer from the transfer case.
20. Remove the locking plate retaining bolts and lock plate from the transfer case.
21. Remove the input gear pilot bearing using J-29369-1 or equivalent with a slide hammer.
22. Remove the front output shaft seal, input shaft seal and the rear extension seal using a brass drift.
23. Using J-33841 with J-8092 or equivalent, press the 2 caged roller bearings for the front input shaft gear from the transfer case.
24. Using J-29369-2 with J-33367 or a slide hammer, remove the rear bearing for the front output shaft.
25. Using a hammer and drift, remove the rear main shaft bearing from the rear retainer.
26. Using an awl, remove the snap-ring retaining the front output shaft bearing. Using a hammer and drift, remove the bearing from the case.
27. Remove the bushing from the extension housing using J-33839 with J-8092 or equivalent. Press bushing from the extension housing.

MAIN SHAFT

Disassembly

1. Remove the speedometer gear.
2. Using an awl, pry off the pump gear from the main shaft.
3. Remove the snap-ring retaining the synchronizer hub from the main shaft.
4. Using a brass hammer, tap the synchronizer hub from main shaft.
5. Remove the drive sprocket.
6. Using J-33826 and J-8092 or equivalent, press 2 caged roller bearings from the drive sprocket.
7. Remove synchronizer keys and retaining rings from the synchronizer hub.
8. Clean and inspect all parts. Replace any parts if they show evidence of excessive wear, distortion or damage.

PLANETARY GEAR

Disassembly

1. Remove the snap-ring retaining the planetary gear in the annulus gear.
2. Remove outer thrust ring and discard.
3. Remove planetary assembly from the annulus gear.
4. Remove inner thrust ring from the planetary assembly and discard.
5. Clean and inspect parts. Replace any parts if they show evidence of excessive wear, distortion or damage.

Cleaning & Inspection

Wash all parts thoroughly in clean solvent. Be sure all old lubricant, metallic particles, dirt, or foreign material are removed from the surfaces of every part. Apply compressed air to each oil feed port and channel in each case half to remove any obstructions or cleaning solvent residue.

Inspect all gear teeth for signs of excessive wear or damage and check all gear splines for burrs, nicks, wear or damage. Remove minor nicks or scratches with an oil stone. Replace any part exhibiting excessive wear or damage.

Inspect all snap-rings and thrust washers for evidence of excessive wear, distortion or damage. Replace any of these parts if they exhibit these conditions.

Inspect the two case halves for cracks, porosity damaged mating surfaces, stripped bolt threads, or distortion. Replace any part that exhibits these conditions. Inspect the low range lock plate in the front case. If the lock plate teeth or the plate hub is cracked, broken, chipped, or excessively worn, replace the lock plate and the lock plate attaching bolts.

Inspect the condition of all needle, roller and thrust bearings in the front and rear case halves and the input gear. Also, check the condition of the bearing bores in both cases and in the input gear, rear output shaft and rear retainer. Replace any part that exhibits signs of excessive wear or damage.

PLANETARY GEAR

Assembly

1. Install the inner thrust ring on planetary assembly.
2. Install the planetary assembly into the annulus gear.
3. Install the outer thrust ring and then the snap-ring.

MAIN SHAFT

Assembly

1. Using J–33828 and J–8092 or equivalent, install the front drive sprocket bearing. Press bearing until tool bottoms out. Bearing should be flush with front surface. Reverse tool on J–8092 or equivalent and press rear bearing into sprocket until tool bottoms out. The rear bearing should be recessed after installation.
2. Install thrust washer on the main shaft.
3. Install drive sprocket on the main shaft.
4. Install blocker ring and synchronizer hub on the main shaft. Seat hub on main shaft and install a new snap-ring to retain.
5. Install pump gear on the main shaft. Tap the gear with a hammer to seat on main shaft.
6. Install speedometer gear on the main shaft.

TRANSFER CASE

Assembly

All of the bearings used in the transfer case must be correctly positioned to avoid covering the bearing oil feed holes. After installation of bearings, check the bearing position to be sure the feed hole is not obstructed or blocked by a bearing.

1. Install the lock plate in the transfer case. Coat case and lock plate surfaces around bolt holes with Loctite®515 or equivalent.
2. Position the lock plate to the case and align bolt holes in lock plat with case. Install attaching bolts and torque to specification.
3. Install the roller bearings for the input shaft into the transfer case using J–33830 and J–8092 or equivalent. Press bearings until tool bottoms in bore.
4. Install the front output shaft rear bearing, using J–33832 and J–8092 or equivalent. Press bearing until tool bottoms in case.
5. Install the front output shaft front bearing using J–33833 and J–8092 or equivalent. Press bearing until tool bottoms in bore.
6. Install the snap-ring that retains the front output shaft bearing in case.
7. Install the front output shaft seal using J–33834 or equivalent.
8. Install the input shaft seal using J–33831 or equivalent.
9. Install spacer on shift sector shaft and install sector in transfer case. Install shift lever and retaining nut. Torque to specification.
10. Install shift sector detent spring and retaining bolt.
11. Install the pilot bearing into the input gear using J–33829 and J–8092 or equivalent. Press bearing until tool bottoms out.
12. Install the input gear front thrust bearing and input gear in transfer case.
13. Install the planetary gear thrust washer on the input gear. Position range fork on planetary assembly and install planetary assembly into the transfer case.

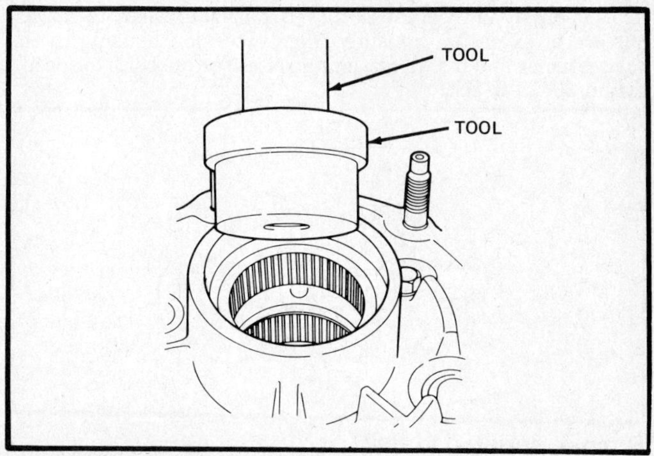

Input gear beareing removal

14. Install the main shaft into the transfer case. Make sure the thrust washer is aligned with the input gear and planetary assembly before installing main shaft.
15. Install mode fork on synchronizer sleeve and rotate until mode fork is aligned with range fork. Slide mode fork rail down through range fork until rail is seated in bore of transfer case.
16. Position drive chain on front output shaft and install chain on drive sprocket. Install front output shaft in the transfer case. It may be necessary to slightly raise the main shaft to seat the output shaft in the case.
17. Install the magnet into pocket of transfer case.

TORQUE SPECIFICATIONS
Model 207

Description	N•m	Ft. Lb.
Bolt Locking Plate to Transfer Case	27–40	20–30
Nut-Front Output Yoke	122–176	90–130
Switch Vacuum	20–34	15–25
Nut-Shift Lever	20–27	15–20
Bolt-Transfer Case	27–34	20–25
Bolt-Rear Retainer	20–27	15–20
Bolt-Extension Housing	27–34	20–25
Bolt-Drain-Fill	40–54	30–40
Bolt-Adapter to Transfer Case	26–40	19–29
Bolt-Shift Bracket	65–85	47–62
Bolt-Shift Lever Pivot	120–140	88–103
Bolt-Shift Lever Adjusting	34–48	25–35

18. Apply $\frac{1}{8}$ in. bead of Loctite®515 or equivalent to the mating surface of the front case. Install rear case on the front case aligning dowel pins. Install bolts and torque to 20–25 ft. lbs. Install the two bolts with washers into the dowel pin holes.
19. Install the output bearing into the rear retainer using J–33833 and J–8092 or equivalent. Press bearing until seated in bore.
20. Install pump seal in pump housing using J–33835 or equivalent. Apply petroleum jelly to pump housing tabs and install housing in rear retainer.
21. Apply $\frac{1}{8}$ in. bead of Loctite®515 or equivalent to mating surface of rear retainer. Align retainer to case and install retaining bolts. Torque bolts to specification 15–20 ft. lbs.
22. Using a new snap-ring, install snap-ring on main shaft. Pull up on main shaft and seat snap-ring in its groove.
23. Install bushing in extension housing using J–33826 and J–8092 or equivalent. Press bushing until tool bottoms in bore.
24. Install a new seal in the extension housing using J–33843 or equivalent.

25. Apply ⅛ in. bead of Loctite®515 or equivalent to mating surface of extension housing. Align extension housing to the rear retainer and install attaching bolts. Torque bolts to specification 20–25 ft. lbs.

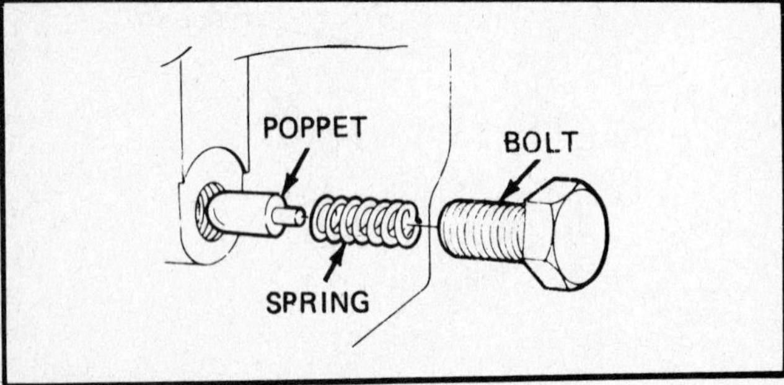

Poppet, spring and bolt

26. Install front yoke on output shaft. Install a new yoke seal washer with a new nut and torque to specification.

27. Install drain plug and torque to specification. Install fill plug.

New Process 208 Transfer Case

The NP208 is a part-time unit with a two piece aluminum housing. On the front case half, the front output shaft, front input shaft, four wheel drive indicator switch and shift lever assembly are located. On the rear case half, the rear output shaft, bearing retainer and drain and fill plugs are located.

Disassembly

1. Drain the fluid from the case.
2. Remove the attaching nuts from the front and rear output yokes. Remove the yokes and sealing washers.

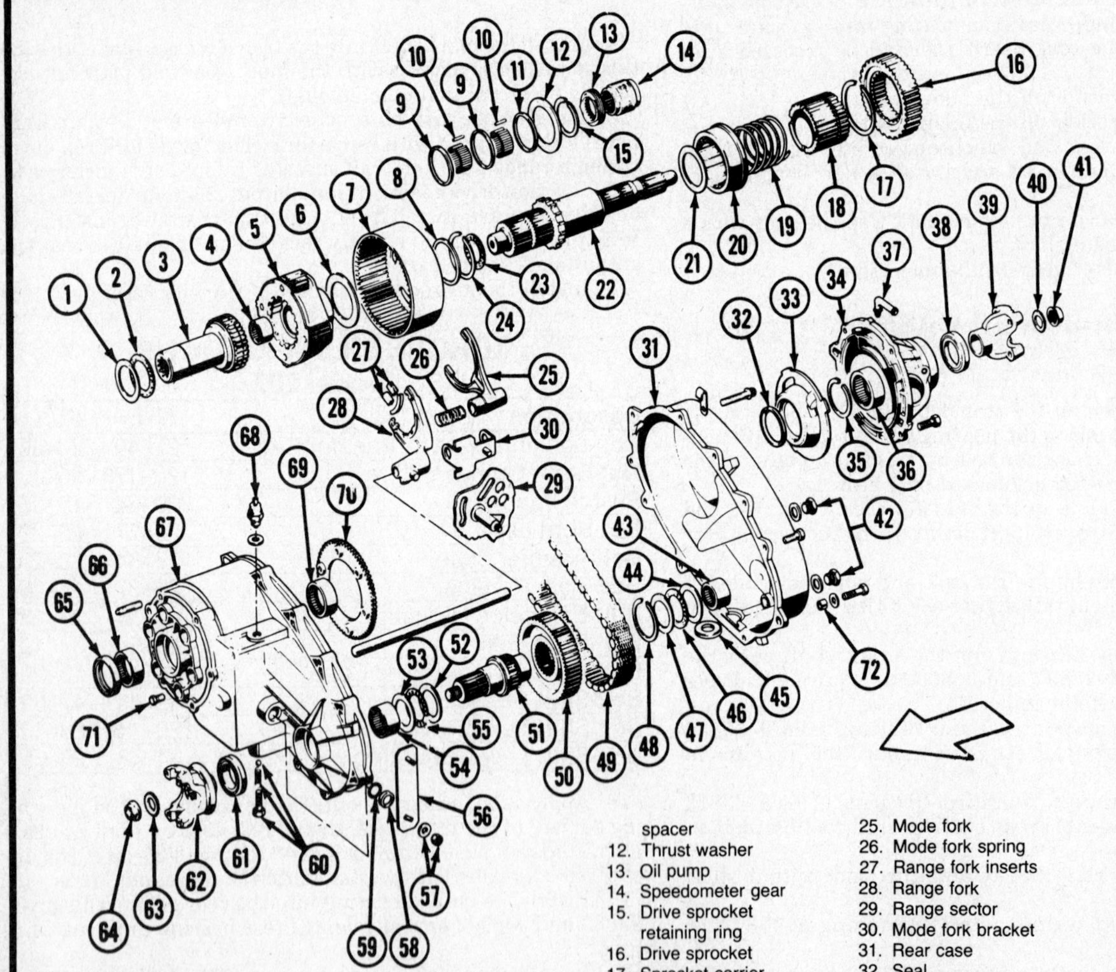

1. Input gear thrust washer
2. Input gear thrust bearing
3. Input gear
4. Mainshaft pilot bearing
5. Planetary assembly
6. Planetary thrust washer
7. Annulus gear
8. Annulus gear thrust washer
9. Needle bearing spacers
10. Mainshaft needle bearings (120)
11. Needle bearing spacer
12. Thrust washer
13. Oil pump
14. Speedometer gear
15. Drive sprocket retaining ring
16. Drive sprocket
17. Sprocket carrier stop ring
18. Sprocket carrier
19. Clutch spring
20. Sliding clutch
21. Thrust washer
22. Mainshaft
23. Mainshaft thrust bearing
24. Annulus gear retaining ring
25. Mode fork
26. Mode fork spring
27. Range fork inserts
28. Range fork
29. Range sector
30. Mode fork bracket
31. Rear case
32. Seal
33. Pump housing
34. Rear retainer
35. Rear output bearing
36. Bearing snap-ring
37. Vent tube
38. Rear seal
39. Rear yoke
40. Yoke seal washer
41. Yoke nut
42. Drain and fill plugs
43. Front output shaft rear bearing
44. Front output shaft rear thrust bearing race (thick)
45. Case magnet
46. Front output shaft rear thrust bearing
47. Front output shaft rear thrust bearing race (thin)
48. Driven sprocket retaining ring
49. Drive chain
50. Driven sprocket
51. Front output shaft
52. Front output shaft front thrust bearing race (thin)
53. Front output shaft front thrust bearing race (thick)
54. Front output shaft front bearing
55. Front output shaft front thrust bearing
56. Operating lever
57. Washer and locknut
58. Range sector shaft seal retainer
59. Range sector shaft seal
60. Detent ball, spring and retainer bolt
61. Front seal
62. Front yoke
63. Yoke seal washer
64. Yoke nut
65. Input gear oil seal
66. Input gear front bearing
67. Front case
68. Lock mode indicator switch and washer
69. Input gear rear bearing
70. Lockplate
71. Lockplate bolts
72. Case alignment dowels

Exploded view of the new process 208 transfer case

3. Remove the four bolts and separate the rear bearing retainer from the rear case half.

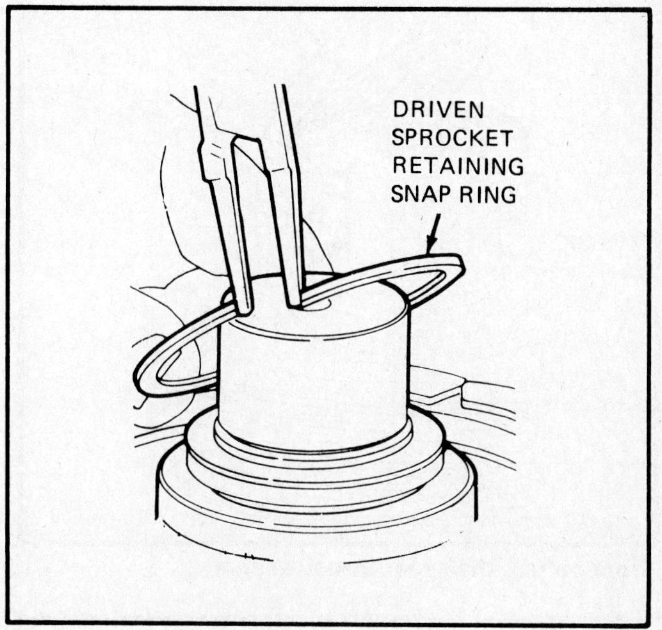

Driven sprocket retaining snap-ring

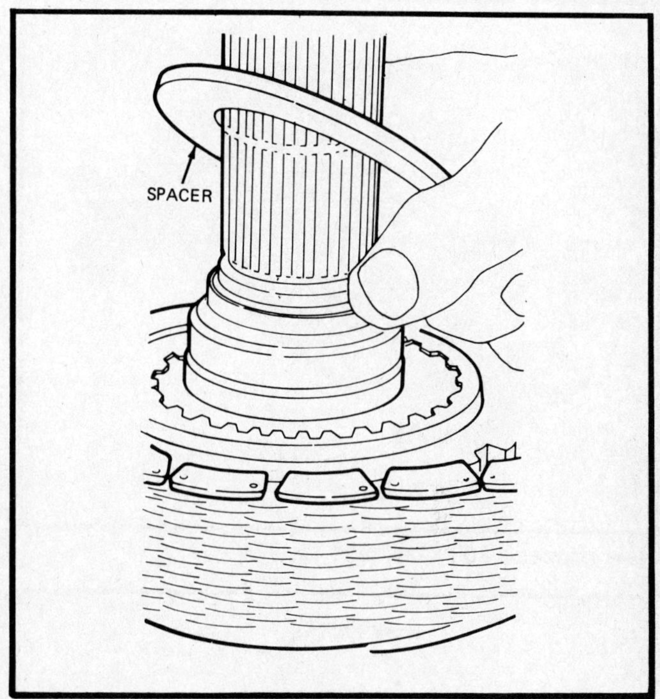

Drive sprocket thrust washer

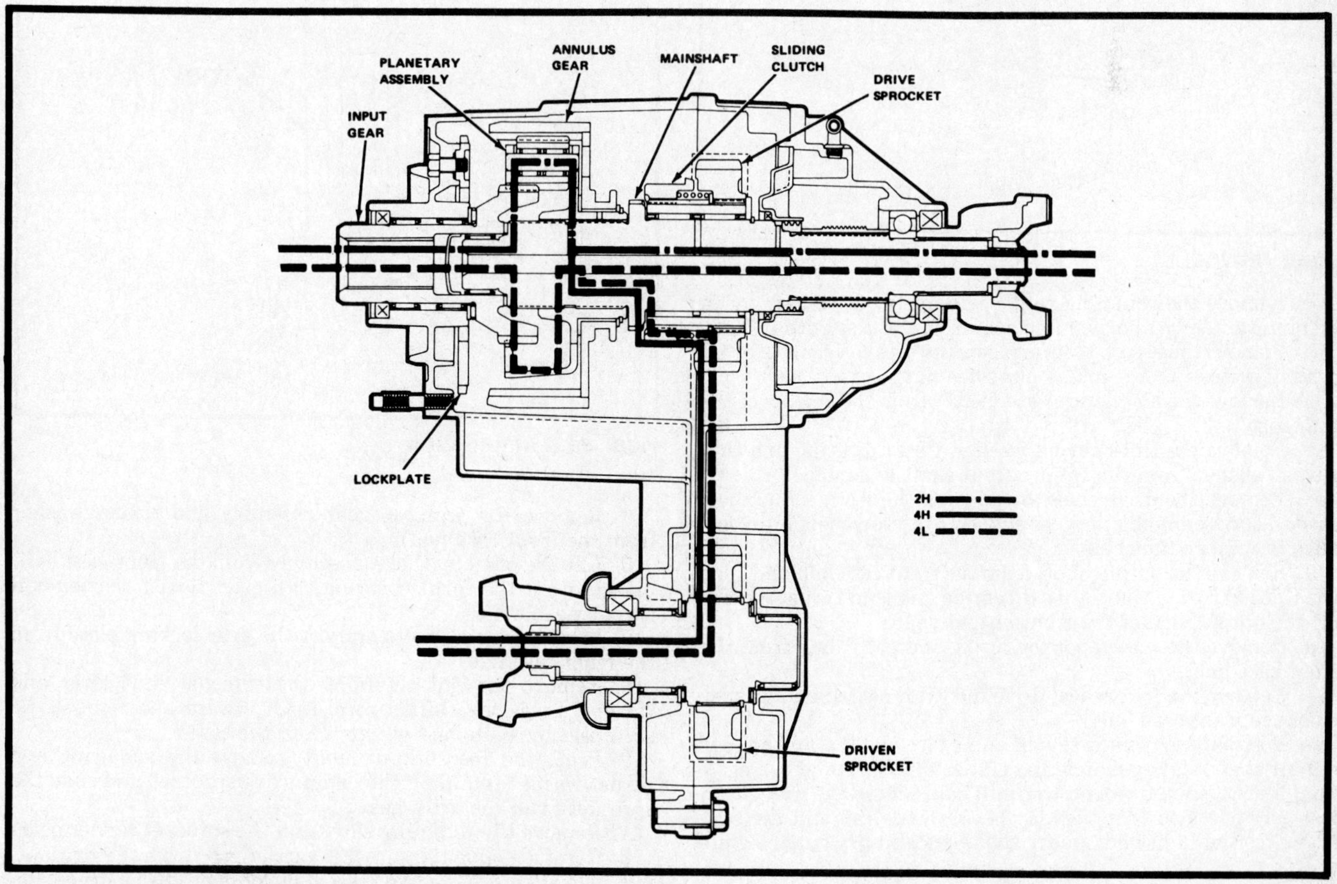

Power flow new process 208 transfer case

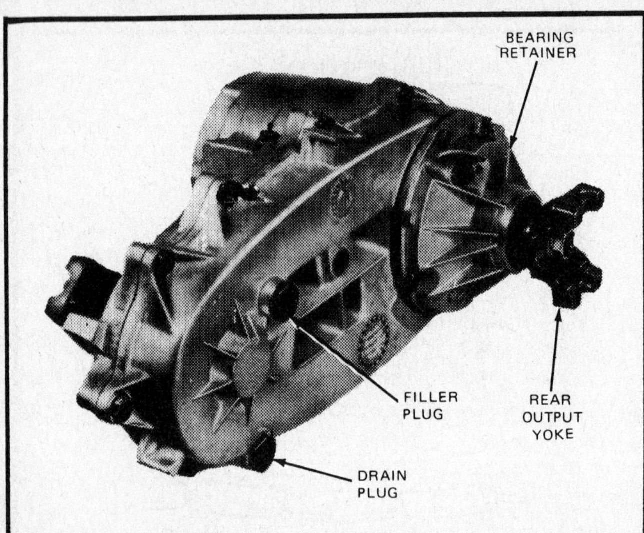

New process 208 rear case view

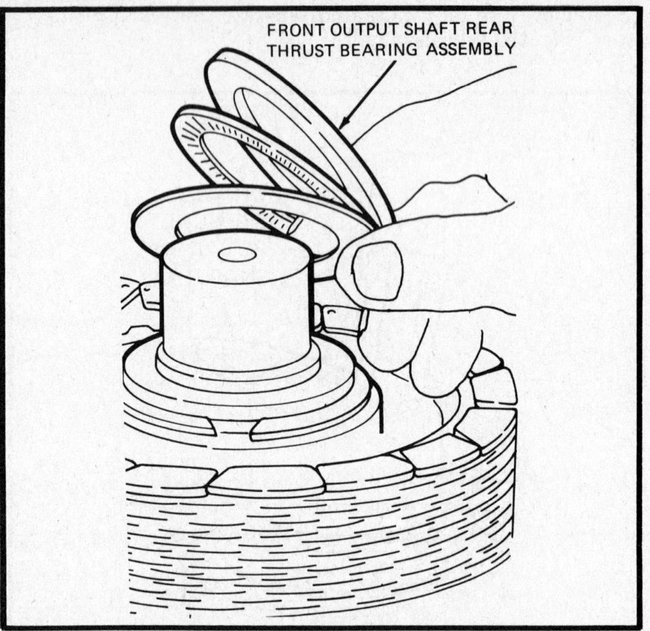

Front output shaft rear thrust washer

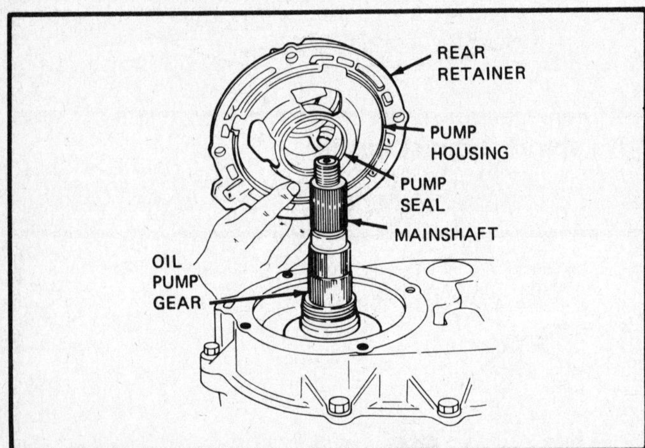

Rear retainer

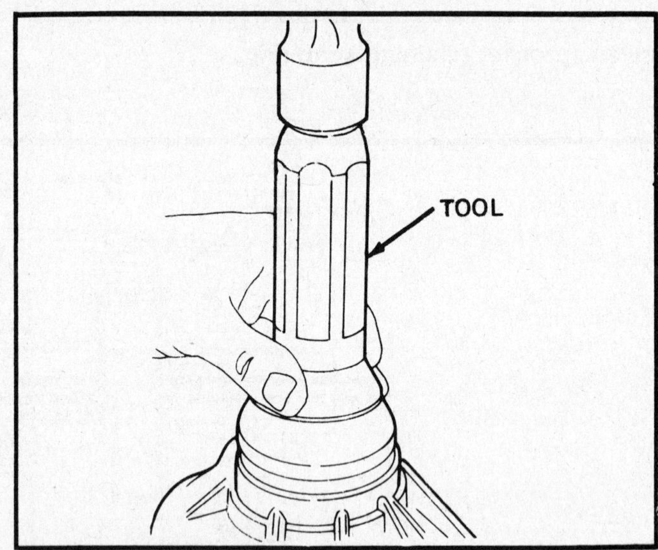

Rear seal installation

4. Remove the retaining ring, speedometer drive gear nylon oil pump housing, and oil pump gear from the rear output shaft.
5. Remove the eleven bolts and separate the case halves by inserting a screw driver in the pry slots on the case.
6. Remove the magnetic chip collector from the bottom of the rear case half.
7. Remove the thick thrust washer, thrust bearing and thin thrust washer from the front output shaft assembly.
8. Remove the drive chain by pushing the front input shaft inward and by angling the gear slightly to obtain adequate clearance to remove the chain.
9. Remove the output shaft from the front case half and slide the thick thrust washer, thrust bearing and thin thrust washer off the output side of the front output shaft.
10. Remove the screw, poppet spring and check ball from the front case half.
11. Remove the four wheel drive indicator switch and washer from the front case half.
12. Position the front case half on its face and lift out the rear output shaft, sliding clutch and clutch shift fork and spring.
13. Place a shop towel on the shift rail. Clamp the rail with a vise grip pliers so that they lay between the rail and the case edge. Position a pry bar under the pliers and pry out the shift rail.
14. Remove the snap ring and thrust washer from the planetary gear set assembly in the front case half.
15. Remove the annulus gear assembly and thrust washer from the front case half.
16. Lift the planetary gear assembly from the front case half.
17. Lift out the thrust bearing, sun gear, thrust bearing and thrust washer.
18. Remove the six bolts and lift the gear locking plate from the front case half.
19. Remove the nut retaining the external shift lever and washer. Press the shift control shaft inward and remove the shift selector plate and washer from the case.
20. From the rear output shaft, remove the snap-ring and thrust washer retaining the chain drive sprocket and slide the sprocket from the drive gear.
21. Remove the retaining ring from the sprocket carrier gear.
22. Carefully slide the sprocket carrier gear from the rear output shaft. Remove the two rows of 60 loose needle bearings. Remove the three separator rings from the output shaft.

Assembly

1. Slide the thrust washer against the gear on the rear output shaft.
2. Place the three space rings in position on the rear output shaft. Liberally coat the shaft with petroleum jelly and install the two rows (60 each) of needle bearings in position on the rear output shaft.
3. Carefully slide the sprocket gear carrier over the needle bearings. Be careful not to dislodge any of the needles.
4. Install the retaining ring on the sprocket gear.
5. Slide the chain drive sprocket onto the sprocket carrier gear.
6. Install the thrust washer and snap ring on the rear output shaft.
7. Install the shift selector plate and washer through the front of the case.
8. Place the shift lever assembly on the shift control shaft and torque the nut to 14–20 ft. lbs.
9. Place the locking plate in the front case half and torque the bolts to 25–35 ft. lbs.
10. Place the thrust bearing and washer over the input shaft of the sun gear. Insert the input shaft through the front case half from the inside and insert the thrust bearing.
11. Install the planetary gear assembly so the fixed plate and planetary gears engage the sun gear.
12. Slide the annulus gear and clutch assembly with the shift fork assembly engaged, over the hub of the planetary gear assembly. The shift fork pin must engage the slot in the shift selector plate. Install the thrust washer and snap ring.
13. Position the shift rail through the shift fork hub in the front case. Tap lightly with a soft hammer to seat the rail in the hole.
14. Position the sliding clutch shift fork on the shift rail and place the sliding clutch and clutch shift spring into the front case half. Slide the rear output shaft into the case.
15. On the output side of the front output shaft, assemble the thin thrust washer, thrust bearing, and thick thrust washer and partially insert the front output shaft into the case.
16. Place the drive chain on the rear output shaft drive gear. Insert the rear output shaft into the front case half and engage the drive chain on the front output shaft drive gear. Push the front output shaft into position in the case.
17. Assemble the thin thrust washer, thrust bearing and thick thrust washer on the inside of the front output shaft drive gear.
18. Position the magnetic chip collector into position in the front case half.
19. Place a bead of RTV sealant completely around the face of the front case half and assemble the case halves being careful that the shift rail and forward output shafts are properly retained.
20. Alternately tighten the bolts to 20–25 ft. lbs.
21. Slide the oil pump gear over the input shaft and slide the spacer collar into position.
22. Engage the speedometer drive gear onto the rear output shaft and slide the retaining ring into position.
23. Use petroleum jelly to hold the nylon oil pump housing in position at the rear bearing retainer. Apply a bead of RTV sealant around the mounting surface of the retainer and carefully position the retainer assembly over the output shaft and onto the rear case half. The retainer must be installed so that the vent hole is vertical when the case is installed.
24. Torque the retainer bolts alternately to 20–25 ft. lbs.
25. Place a new thrust washer under each yoke and install the yokes on their respective shafts. Place the oil slinger under the front yoke. Torque the nuts to 90–130 ft. lbs.
26. Install the poppet ball, spring and screw in the front case half. Torque the screw to 20–25 ft. lbs.
27. Install the 4WD indicator switch and washer and tighten to 15–20 ft. lbs.
28. Fill the unit with 6 pints of Ford CJ fluid or DEXRON®II.

New Process 219 Transfer Case (Quadra-Trac®)

Introduced in Jeep® vehicles as the Quadra-Trac®, this is a full-time unit. The 4WD mode is fully differentiated in 4H only. The 4L and Lock ranges are undifferentiated. The 4H differentiation is accomplished by a torque biasing viscous coupling and an open differential connected to the coupling. Two drive sprockets and an interconnecting drive chain are used to distribute input torque.

Disassembly

1. Drain the lubricant from the case.
2. Remove the front and rear output shaft yokes and discard the yoke seal washers and yoke nuts.
3. Mark the rear retainer and rear case for an alignment reference.
4. Unbolt and remove the rear retainer. If necessary, use a soft mallet to loosen the retainer. Under no circumstances should the retainer be pried off.

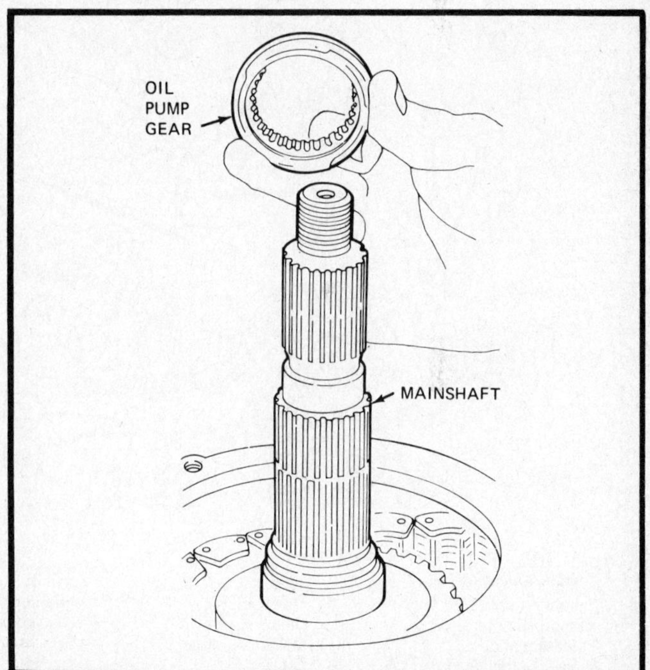

Oil pump

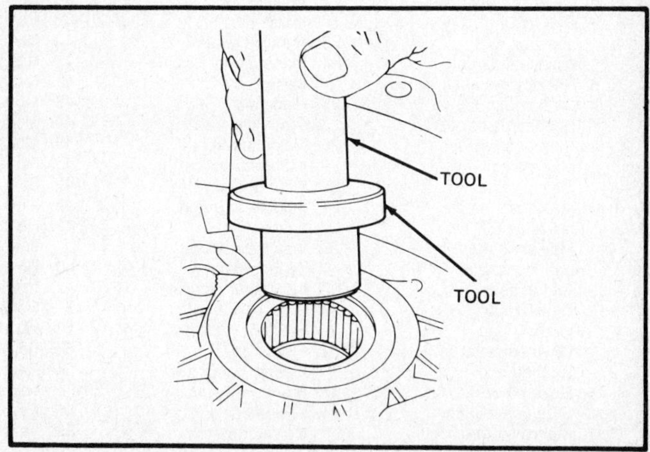

Front output shaft rear bearing installation

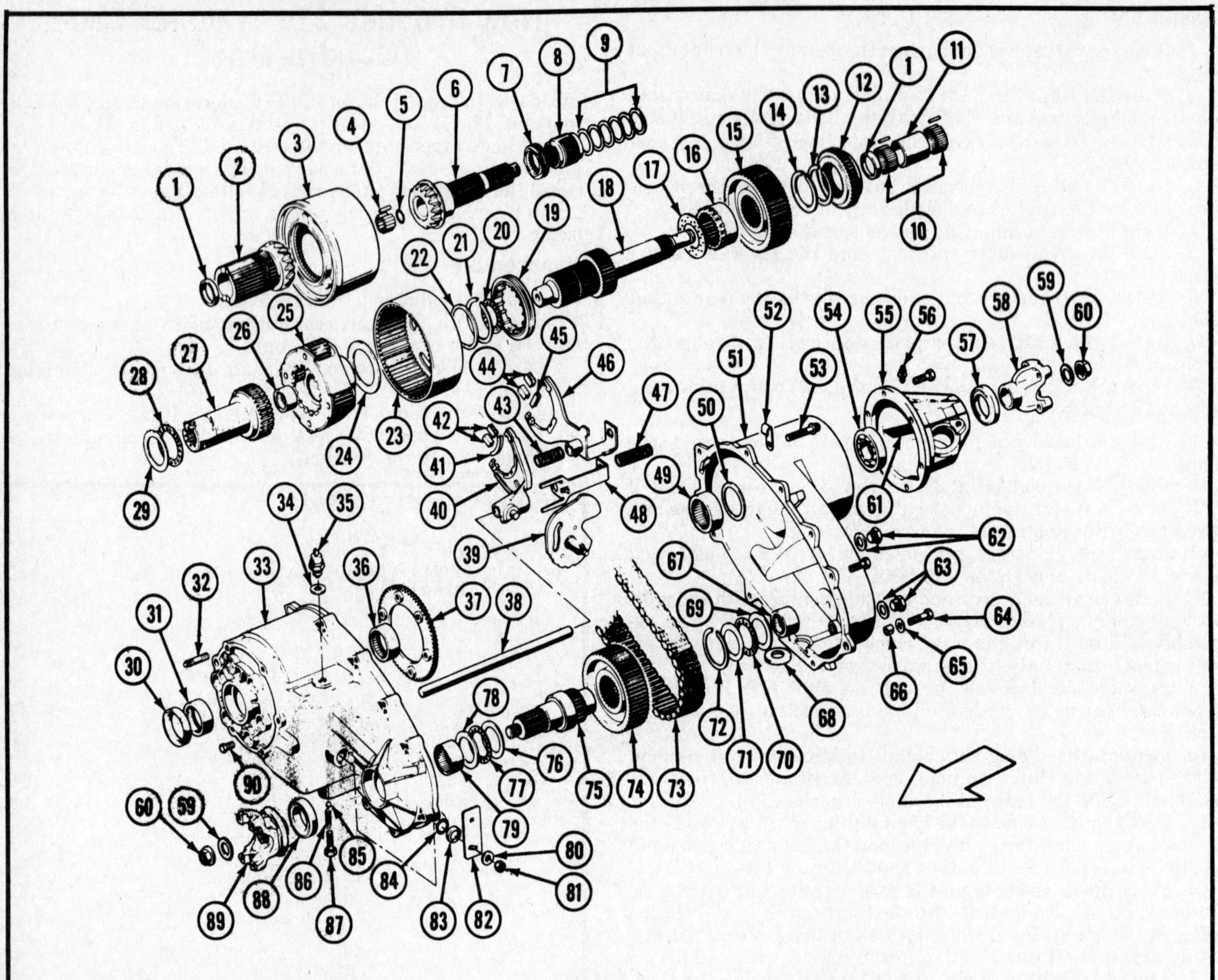

1. Mainshaft rear bearing spacer—short (2)
2. Side gear
3. Viscous coupling and differential assembly
4. Mainshaft rear pilot roller bearings (15)
5. Mainshaft O-ring
6. Rear output shaft
7. Oil pump
8. Speedometer gear
9. Differential end play shims (selective)
10. Mainshaft needle bearings (82)
11. Mainshaft rear bearing spacer
12. Clutch gear
13. Clutch gear locating ring
14. Drive sprocket locating ring
15. Drive sprocket
16. Side gear clutch
17. Mainshaft thrust washer
18. Mainshaft
19. Clutch sleeve
20. Mainshaft thrust bearing
21. Annulus gear retaining ring
22. Annulus gear thrust washer
23. Annulus gear
24. Planetary thrust washer
25. Planetary assembly
26. Mainshaft front pilot bearing
27. Input gear
28. Input gear thrust bearing
29. Input gear thrust bearing race
30. Input gear oil seal
31. Input gear front bearing
32. Front case mounting stud (6)
33. Front case
34. Lock mode indicator switch gasket
35. Lock mode indicator switch
36. Input gear rear bearing
37. Low range lockplate
38. Shift rail
39. Range sector
40. Range fork
41. Range fork insert
42. Range fork pads
43. Mode fork spring
44. Mode fork pads
45. Mode fork insert
46. Mode fork
47. Shift rail spring
48. Mode fork bracket
49. Rear output shaft bearing
50. Rear output shaft bearing seal
51. Rear case
52. Wiring clip
53. Spline bolt
54. Rear output bearing
55. Rear retainer
56. Vent
57. Output shaft oil seal
58. Rear yoke
59. Yoke seal washer
60. Yoke locknut
61. Vent chamber seal
62. Fill plug and gasket
63. Drain plug and gasket
64. Rear case bolt
65. Washer (2)
66. Case alignment dowel
67. Front output shaft rear bearing
68. Magnet
69. Front output shaft rear thrust bearing race (thick)
70. Front output shaft rear thrust bearing
71. Front output shaft rear thrust bearing race (thin)
72. Driven sprocket retaining snap-ring
73. Drive chain
74. Driven sprocket
75. Front output shaft
76. Front output shaft front thrust bearing race (thin)
77. Front output shaft front thrust bearing
78. Front output shaft front thrust bearing race (thick)
79. Front output shaft front bearing
80. Washer
81. Locknut
82. Operating lever
83. Range sector shaft seal retainer
84. Range sector shaft seal
85. Detent ball
86. Detent spring
87. Detent retaining bolt
88. Front output shaft seal
89. Front yoke
90. Lockplate bolts

Exploded view of the new process 219 transfer case

5. Remove the differential shims and speedometer drive gear from the rear output shaft. Mark the shims for reference.

6. Remove the rear output bearing snap-ring and remove the bearing from the retainer using a soft mallet.

NOTE: The rear output bearing has one side shielded. Note this for reassembly.

7. Remove the rear output shaft seal from the retainer using a small prybar or punch.

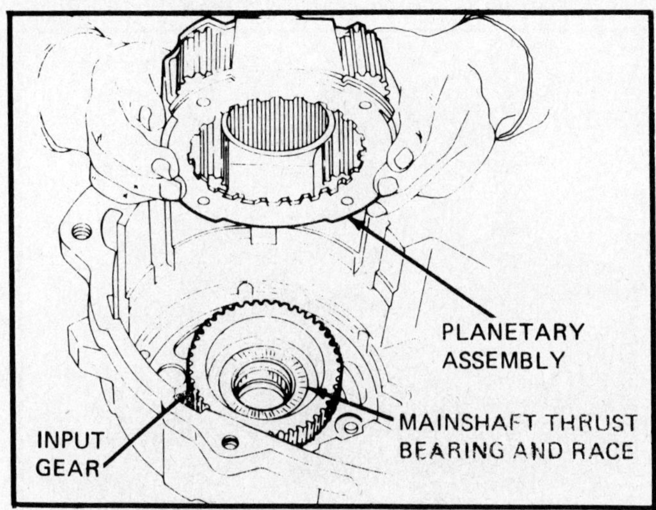

Input gear, mainshaft thrust bearing and planetary installaiton

8. Position the front case assembly on wood blocks. The blocks should have V cuts made in them for more positive support of the case.

9. Remove the case halve bolts. The case halves may be pried apart using a small prybar in the notches provided at the case ends.

NOTE: The two case end bolts have flat washers and alignment dowels. Note their location for assembly.

10. Remove the rear output shaft and viscous coupling as an assembly. Tap the shaft with a plastic mallet if necessary.

11. Remove the O-ring seal and pilot roller bearings from the main shaft.

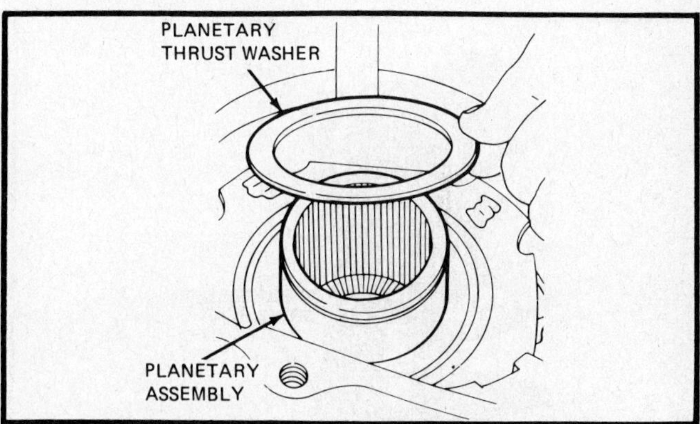

Planetary thrust washer and planetary assembly

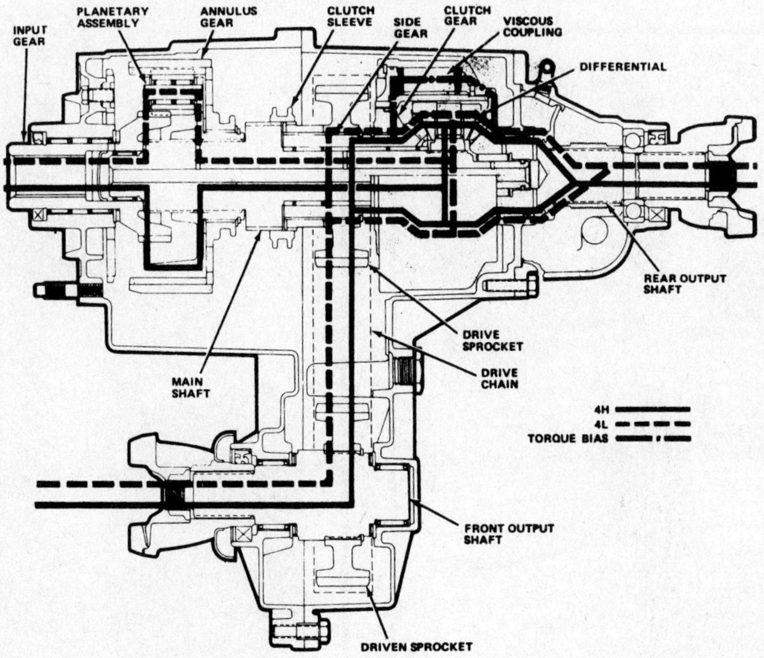

Power flow new process 219 transfer case

12. Remove the rear output shaft from the viscous coupling.
13. Remove the shift rail spring from the rail.
14. Remove the plastic oil pump from the shaft bore in the rear case. Note the pump position for assembly reference. The end with the recess must face the shaft bore when installed.
15. Remove the rear output shaft bearing seal from the case. A small prybar may be used to pry it out.
16. Remove the front output shaft thrust bearing assembly. Remove the thick washer, bearing and thin washer.
17. Remove the driven sprocket retaining snap-ring.
18. Remove the drive sprocket, drive chain, driven sprocket, side gear clutch and clutch gear as an assembly. Place the assembly on a workbench and mark the components for assembly.

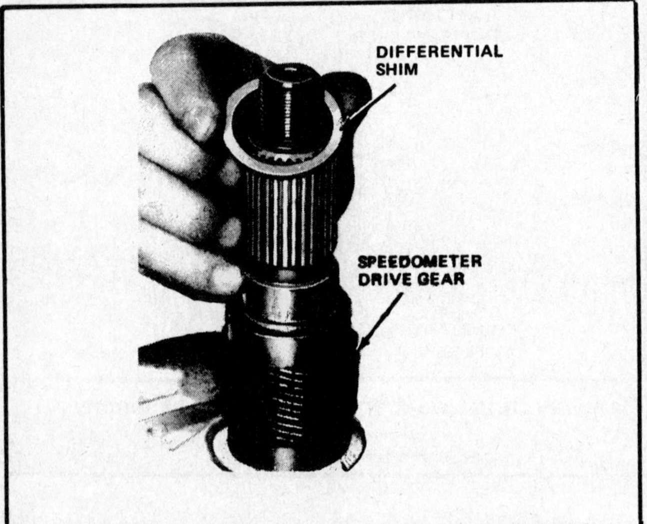

Differential shim, speedometer gear and oil pump

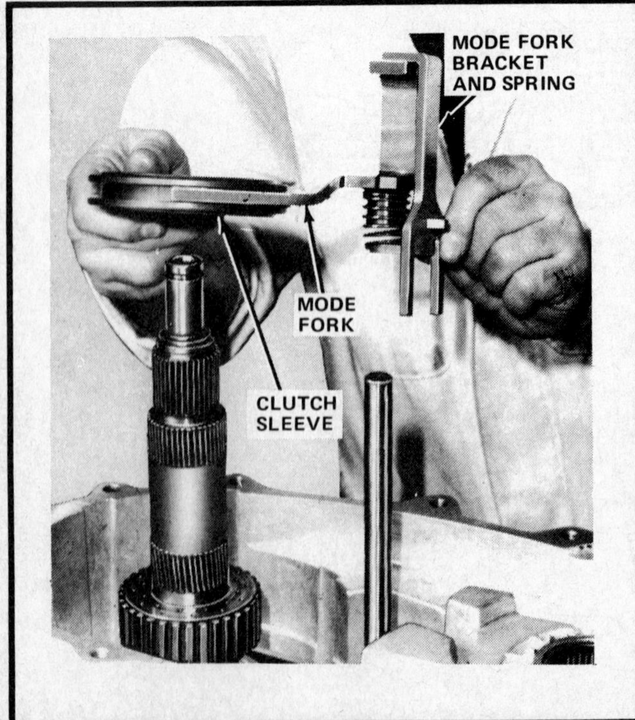

Clutch sleeve and mode fork removal and installation

19. Remove the needle bearings and spacers from the main shaft and side gear bore. A total of 82 bearings and three spacers is used.
20. Remove the side gear/clutch gear assembly from the drive sprocket. Remove two snap-rings and remove the clutch gear from the side gear.
21. Remove the side gear clutch, main shaft thrust washer and remaining main shaft needle bearing spacer.
22. Remove the front output shaft and shaft thrust bearing assembly. Note the installation sequence of the bearing assembly.

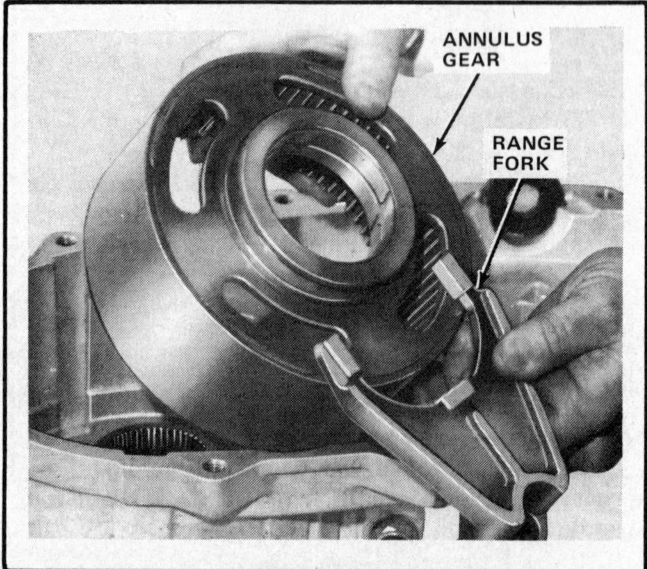

Annulus gear and range fork removal and installation

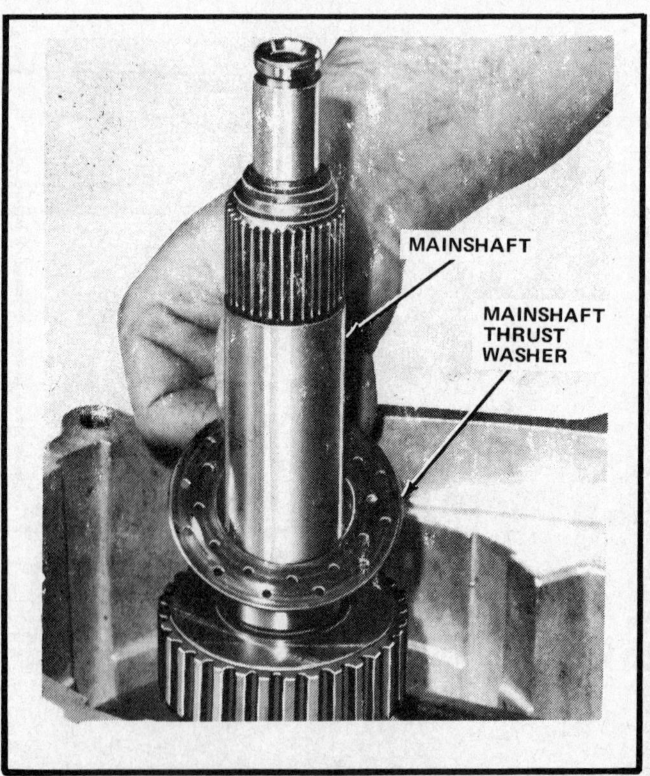

Mainshaft and thrust washer

23. Remove the front output shaft seal from the front case using a small prybar or punch.
24. Remove the shift rail spring from the shift rail.
25. Remove the clutch sleeve, mode fork and spring as an assembly.
26. Remove the main shaft thrust washer and main shaft. Grasp the shaft and pull it straight up and out.
27. Move the range operating lever downward to the last detent position.
28. Disengage the range fork lug from the range sector slot.
29. Remove the annulus gear retaining snap-ring and thrust washer.
30. Remove the annulus gear and range fork.
31. Remove the planetary thrust washer from the hub.
32. Remove the planetary assembly.
33. Remove the main shaft thrust bearing from the input gear.

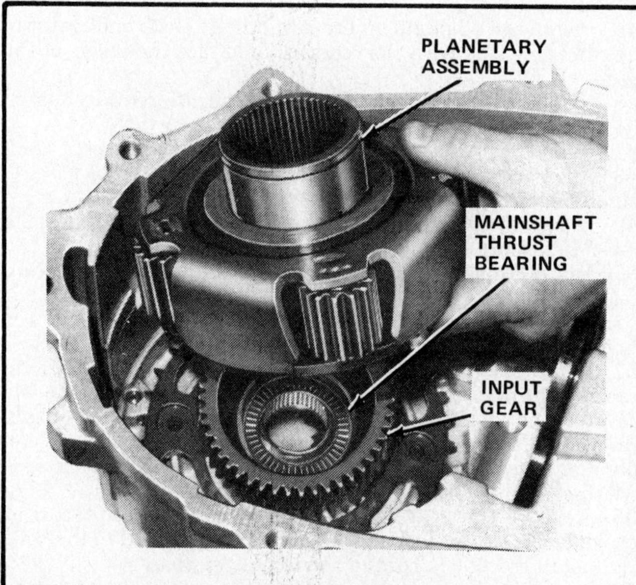

Planetary assembly removal and installation

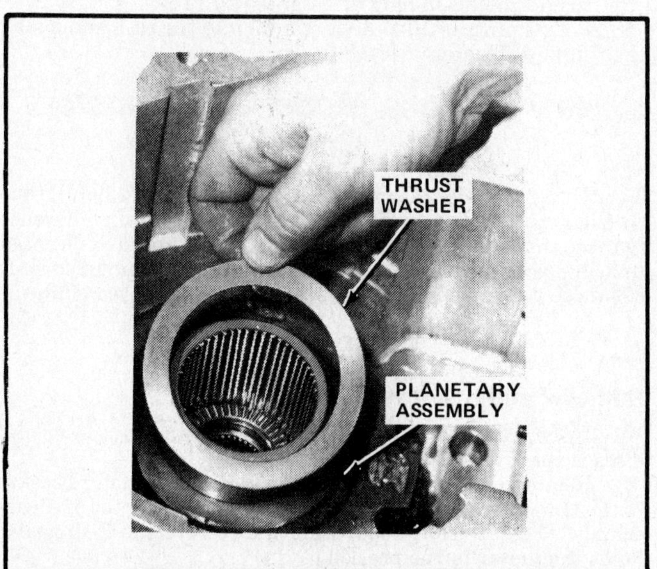

Planetary thrust washer removal and installation

34. Remove the input gear and remove the input gear thrust bearing and race.
35. Remove the range selector detent ball and spring retaining bolt and remove the detent ball and spring.
36. Remove the range selector and operating lever attaching nut and lockwasher, and remove the lever.
37. Remove the range selector.
38. Remove the range selector O-ring and retainer.
39. Remove the input gear oil seal from the front case with a small prybar.

Assembly

Lubricate all parts before assembly with 10W–30 motor oil. Petroleum jelly will be indicated for some assemblies. Do not use chassis lube or other heavy lubricants.

1. Install new input gear and rear output shaft bearing oil seals. Seat the seals flush with the edge of the seal bore or with the seal groove in the case. Coat the seal lips with petroleum jelly after installation.
2. Install the input gear thrust bearing race in the case counterbore.
3. Install the input gear thrust bearing on the input gear and install the gear and bearing in the case.
4. Install the main shaft thrust bearing in the bearing recess in the input gear.
5. Install the planetary assembly on the input gear. Make sure that the planetary pinion teeth mesh fully with the input gear.
6. Install the planetary thrust washer on the planetary hub.
7. Install a new sector shaft O-ring and retainer in the shaft bore in the case.
8. Install the range selector in the front case. Install the operating lever on the sector shaft and install the lever attaching washer and locknut on the shaft. Tighten the locknut to 17 ft. lbs.
9. Install the detent spring, ball and retaining bolt in the front case detent bore. Tighten the bolt to 22 ft. lbs.
10. Move the range selector to the last detent position.

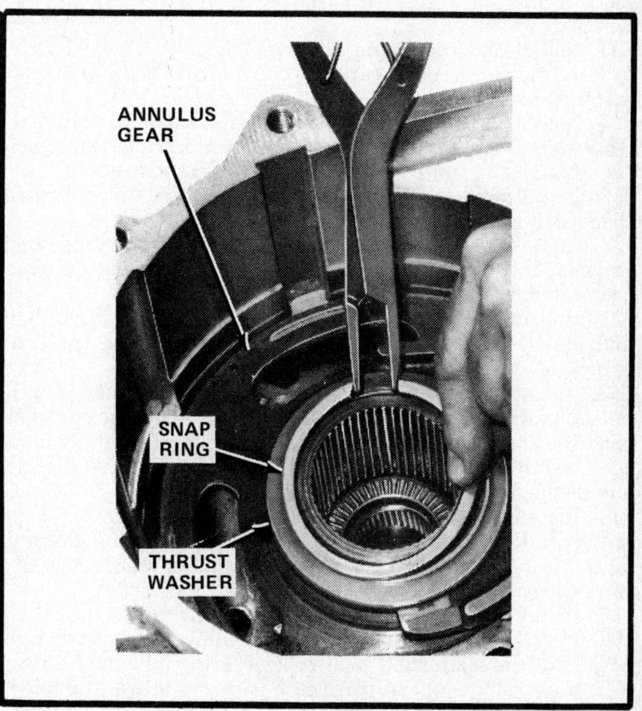

Annulus gear snap-ring and thrust washer

11. Assemble the annulus gear and range fork. Install the assembled fork and gear over the planetary assembly. Be sure that the annulus gear is fully meshed with the planetary pinions.
12. Insert the range fork lug in the range detent slot.
13. Install the annulus thrust washer and retaining ring on the annulus gear hub.
14. Align the main shaft thrust washer in theinput gear, if necessary.
15. Install the main shaft. Be sure the shaft is fully seated in the input gear.
16. Install the main shaft thrust washer on the main shaft.
17. Install the short main shaft needle bearing spacer on the shaft.
18. Apply a liberal coating of petroleum jelly to the main shaft needle bearing surface and install 41 of the 82 needle bearings on the shaft. Be sure the bearings seat on the short spacer.
19. Install the long needle bearing spacer on the shaft. Lower the spacer onto the previously installed needle bearings carefully to avoid displacing them.
20. Align the shift rail bore in the case with the bore in the range fork and install the shift rail.

NOTE: Remove all traces of oil from the case shift rail bore before installing the rail. Oil in the case bore may prevent the rail from seating completely and prevent rear case installation.

21. Assemble the mode fork, mode fork spring and mode fork bracket.
22. Install the clutch sleeve in the mode fork. Be sure the sleeve is positioned so that the ID numbers on the sleeve face upward when the sleeve is installed.
23. Align the clutch sleeve and mode fork assembly with the shift rail and install the assembly on the shift rail and main shaft. Be sure that the clutch sleeve is meshed with the main shaft gear.
24. Lubricate the remaining 41 needle bearings and place them on the main shaft.
25. Install the side gear clutch on the main shaft with the teeth facing downward. Be sure the gear teeth mesh with the clutch sleeve.
26. Install the remaining short main shaft needle bearing spacer. Install the spacer carefully to avoid displacing previously installed bearings.
27. Install the front output shaft front thrust bearing in the front case. Correct sequence is thick race, bearing, thin race.
28. Install the front output shaft in the front case.
29. Install the clutch gear on the side gear. The tapered side of the clutch gear teeth must face the side gear teeth.
30. Install the clutch gear and drive sprocket locating snaprings on the side gear. Install the snap-rings so that they face each other.
31. Position the drive and driven sprockets in the drive chain and install the assembled side and clutch gears in the drive sprocket.
32. Install the assembled drive chain, sprockets and side gear on the main shaft and front output shaft. Align the sprockets with the shaft, keeping the assembly level and carefully lower the assembly onto both shafts simultaneously. Do not displace any of the needle bearings.
33. Install the driven sprocket retaining snap-ring.
34. Install the front output shaft rear thrust bearing assembly on the front output shaft. Correct installation sequence is thin race, thrust bearing, thick race.
35. Install the shift rail spring on the shift rail.
36. Install a new O-ring on the main shaft pilot bearing hub.
37. Coat the main shaft pilot roller bearing hub and bearings with a liberal amount of petroleum jelly and install the rollers on the shaft.
38. Install the rear output shaft in the viscous coupling. Be sure it is fully seated.
39. Install the assembled viscous coupling and rear output shaft on the main shaft. Align the main shaft pilot hub with the pilot bearing bore in the rear output shaft and carefully lower the assembly onto the main shaft. Take care to avoid displacing the roller bearings.
40. Align the clutch gear teeth with the viscous coupling teeth and seat the coupling fully onto the clutch gear.

NOTE: When correctly installed, the clutch gear teeth will not be visible or extend out of the coupling.

41. Install the magnet in the front case, if removed.
42. Clean the mating surfaces of the case halves thoroughly.
43. Apply Loctite®515 or equivalent to the mating surfaces and all attaching bolts.
44. Join the case halves, aligning the dowels and install the bolts. Torque the bolts to 22 ft. lbs.

NOTE: The two end bolts require flat washers.

45. Install the oil pump on the rear output shaft and seat it in the case. The side with the recess should face the inside of the case.
46. Install the speedometer drive gear and differential shift, on the output shaft.
47. Install the vent chamber seal in the rear retainer.
48. Align and install the rear retainer on the case. Make the retainer finger tight only.
49. Install the yoke on the rear output shaft. Make the yoke finger tight only.
50. Mount a dial indicator on the rear retainer. Position the indicator stylus so that it contacts the top of the yoke nut.
51. Install the yoke on the front output shaft and rotate the shaft ten complete revolutions.
52. Rotate the front output shaft again and note the play indicated on the dial. End play should be 0.002–0.010 in. If the end play must be adjusted, remove the rear retainer and add or subtract shims as required.
53. Remove both output shaft yokes and discard the nuts.
54. Install the front and rear yoke seals.
55. Remove the rear retainer bolts, apply Loctite®515 or equivalent to the mating surface of the retainer and to the bolts and install the bolts. Torque them to 22 ft. lbs.
56. Install new yoke seal washers on the output shafts, install yokes on the shafts and install new yoke nuts. Tighten the nuts to 110 ft. lbs.
57. Install the drain plug and tighten to 18 ft. lbs.
58. Pour 4 pints of 10W–30 motor oil into the case and install the fill plug. Tighten it to 18 ft. lbs.

New Process Model 228 Transfer Case

The NP228 transfer case is very similar to the NP229 full time transfer case used on previous Jeep models. The main difference in these two transfer cases, is that the NP228 uses a differential unit in place of the viscous coupling. It also uses modified shift collars to preclude engine run away during a delayed shift.

SHIFT MOTOR

Removal and Installation

1. Disconnect the shift motor link from the range lever and discard the lever grommet.
2. Remove the nut and bolt that hold the shift motor bracket to the transfer case and remove the bracket and motor as an assembly. Slide the shift boot inside and remove the E-ring that holds the motor in the bracket.
3. Remove the motor from the transfer case.
4. Replace old gaskets with new gaskets where ever necessary and installation is the reverse order of the removal procedure.

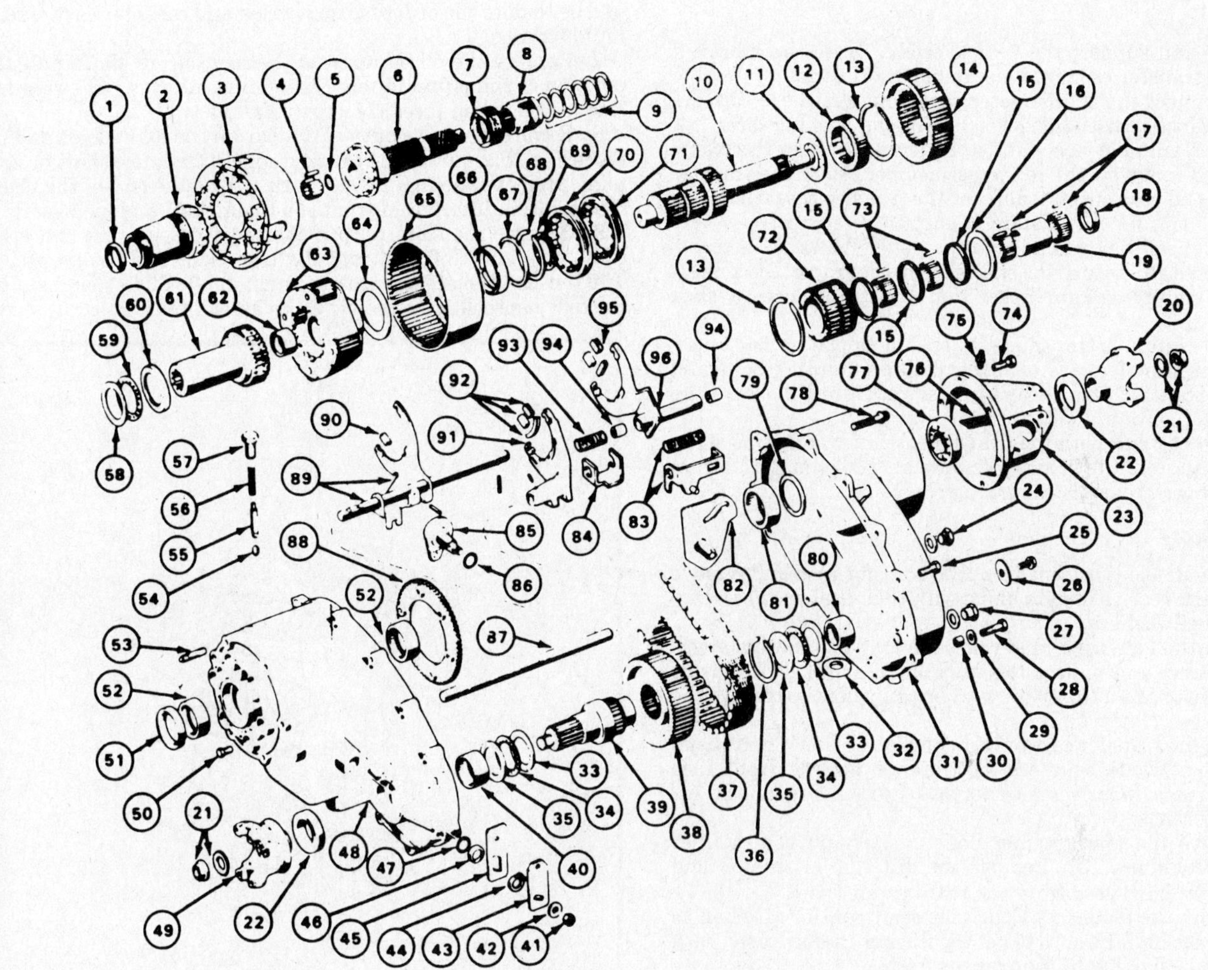

1. Spacer
2. Side gear
3. Differential
4. Pilot bearing rollers (15)
5. O-ring seal
6. Rear output shaft
7. Oil pump
8. Speedometer drive gear
9. Shim kit
10. Mainshaft
11. Mainshaft thrust washer
12. Spline gear
13. Retaining ring
14. Sprocket
15. Spacer
16. Sprocket thrust washer
17. Side gear roller (82)
18. Spacer (short)
19. Spacer (long)
20. Rear yoke
21. Nut and seal washer
22. Seal
23. Rear retainer
24. Plug assembly
25. Bolt
26. Identification tag
27. Plug assembly
28. Dowel bolt
29. Dowl bolt washer
30. Case half dowell
31. Rear half case
32. Magnet
33. Front output shaft bearing assembly race (thick)
34. Front output shaft bearing assembly thrust
35. Front output shaft bearing assembly race (thin)
36. Retaining ring
37. Chain
38. Driven sprocket
39. Front output shaft
40. Front output front bearing
41. Nut
42. Washer
43. Mode lever
44. Snap ring
45. Range lever
46. O-ring retainer
47. O-ring seal
48. Front half case
49. Front output yoke
50. Low range plate bolt
51. Input shaft oil seal
52. Input shaft bearing
53. Stud
54. Ball
55. Plunger
56. Plunger spring
57. Screw
58. Input race
59. Input thrust bearing
60. Input race (thick)
61. Input shaft
62. Input bearing
63. Planetary gear assembly
64. Input gear thrust washer
65. Annulus gear assembly
66. Annulus bushing
67. Thrust washer
68. Retaining ring
69. Thrust bearing
70. High range sliding clutch sleeve
71. Mode sliding clutch sleeve
72. Carrier
73. Carrier rollers (120)
74. Rear retainer bolt
75. Vent
76. Vent seal
77. Output bearing
78. Bolt
79. Seal
80. Front output rear bearing
81. Output shaft inner bearing
82. Range sector
83. Range bracket (outer) and spring
84. Range bracket (inner)
85. Mode sector
86. O-ring seal
87. Range rail
88. Low range lockout plate
89. Mode fork, rail and pin
90. Mode fork pad
91. Range fork
92. Range fork pads
93. Range bracket spring (inner)
94. Locking fork bushing
95. Locking fork pads
96. Locking fork

Exploded view of the 228 transfer case

TRANSFER CASE

Removal

1. Raise and support the vehicle safely. Drain the lubricant out of the transfer case into a suitable drain pan.
2. Disconnect the speedometer cable and vent hose. Disconnect the transfer case shift lever link at the opening lever.
3. Place a suitable jack stand or equivalent, under the transmission and removew the rear crossmember. Mark the transfer case front and rear output shafts at the transfer case yokes and propeller shafts for installation alignment reference.
4. Disconnect the front and rear propeller shafts at the transfer case yokes and secure the shafts along the frame. Disconnect the shift motor vacuum hoses and the transfer case shift linkage.
5. Place a suitable transmission jack under the transfer case. Remove the transfer case to transmission mounting bolts and move the transfer case assembly rearward until it clears the transmission output shaft.
6. Lower the jack with the transfer case on it and remove the transfer case from the vehicle. Remove all gasket material from the rear of the transmission adapter housing.

Disassembly

1. Drain all the lubricant from the transfer case and remove the front and rear yoke nuts along with their seal washers. Discard the seal washers.
2. Mark the front and rear yokes for easy installation alignment reference and remove the front and rear yokes. It may be necessary to use tool No. J-8614-01 or equivalent to remove the yokes.
3. Place the transfer case on wooden blocks. Cut V-notches in the blocks of wood so there is clearance for the front case mounting studs. Mark the retainer and the rear case for easy assembly reference.
4. Remove the rear retainer bolts and pry off the retainer with a suitable pry bar. Remove the differential shim(s) and speedometer drive gear from the rear output shaft.
5. Remove the bolts that attach the rear transfer case half to the front case half. Be sure to get the washer that are used with the bolts on each end of the transfer case.

NOTE: Insert two small pry bars into the slots at each end of the rear of the transfer case half to loosen it. Do not attempt to wedge the transfer case halves apart or the case mating surface will be damages.

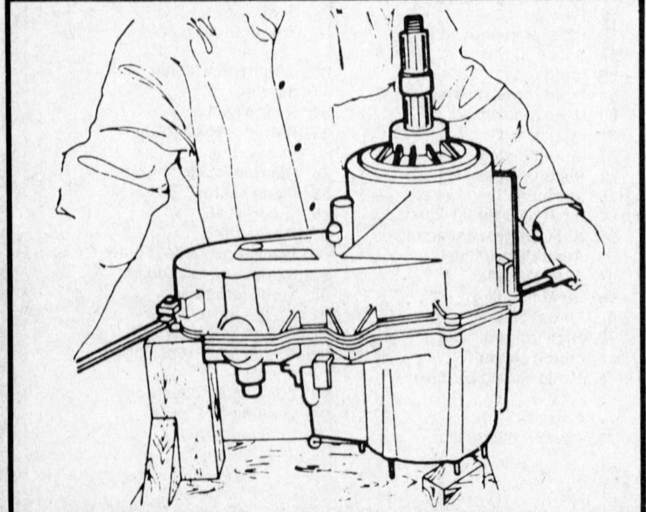

Separating the transfer case halves

6. Remove the rear transfer case half from the front case. Remove the thrust bearing and races from the front output shaft and be to note the order of the bearing and races for easy assembly reference.
7. Remove the oil pump from the rear output shaft, note the position of the pump for easy assembly reference. The recessed side of the pump faces the case interior.
8. Remove the rear output shaft from the main shaft and remove the 15 main needle bearing rollers from the shaft or coupling. Remove the main shaft O-ring from the end of the shaft. Remove the differential from the main shaft and side gear.
9. Remove the front output shaft, driven sprocket and drive chain assembly. Lift the front shaft, sprocket and chain upward. Tilt the front shaft toward the main shaft. Slide the chain off the drive sprocket and remove the assembly.

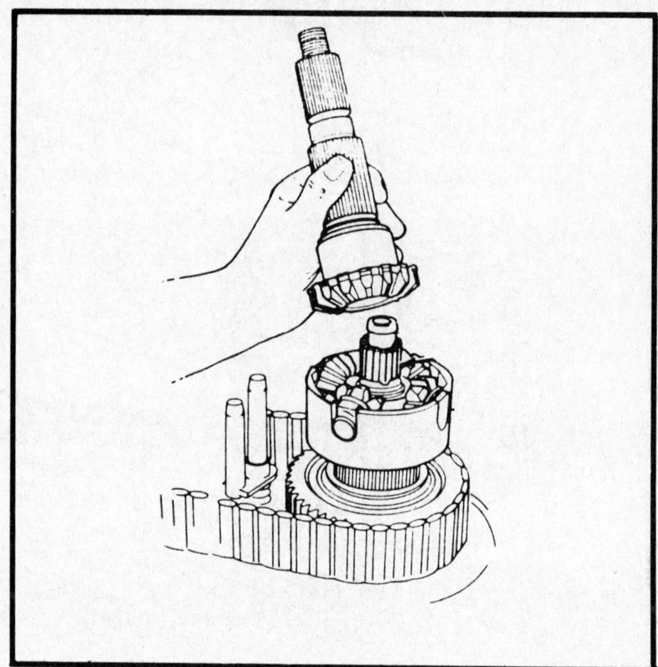

Removing the rear output shaft

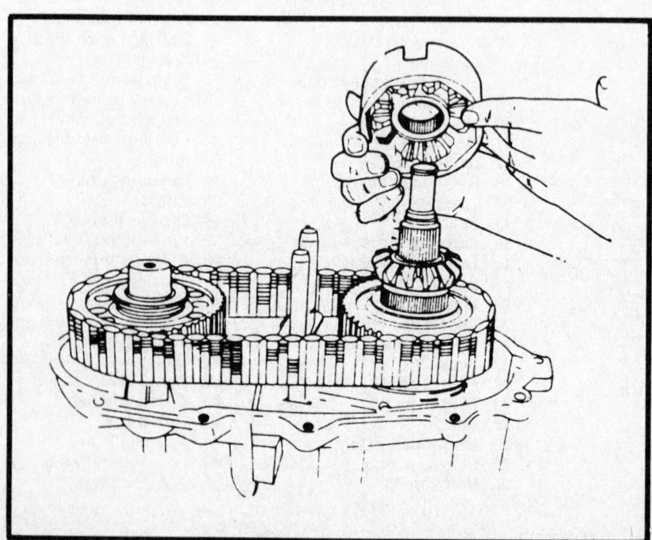

Removing the differential

10. Remove the front output shaft and front thrust bearing assembly from the front case. Remove the drive chain from the output shaft and sprocket.

11. Remove the snap ring that retains the riven sprocket on the front output shaft. Mark the sprocket and shaft for assembly reference and remove the sprocket from the shaft.

12. Remove the main shaft, side gear, drive sprocket and spline gear as an assembly. Place the assembly on a clean shop towel and set it aside until the front case disassembly is completed.

13. Remove the mode fork, shift rail and mode sliding clutch sleeve as an assembly. Mark the sleeve and fork for easy assembly reference and remove the sleeve from the fork.

NOTE: The mode fork and rail are pinned together so that they will operate as a unit. Remove the pin to separate the two components if necessary.

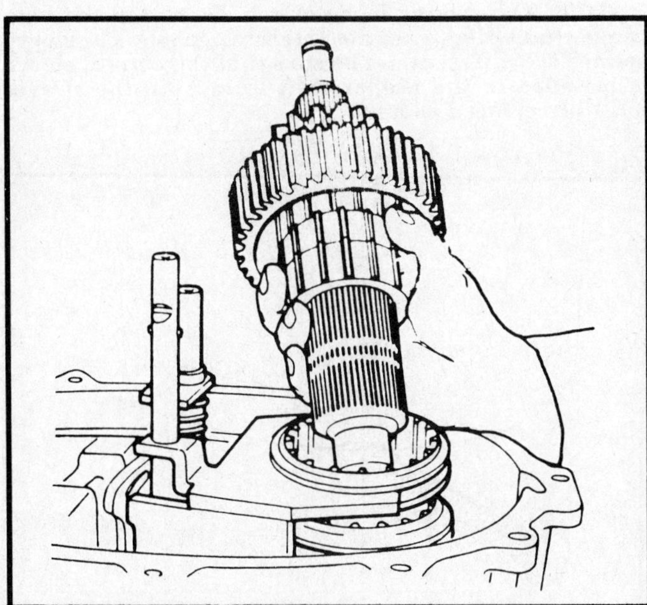

Removing the mainshaft

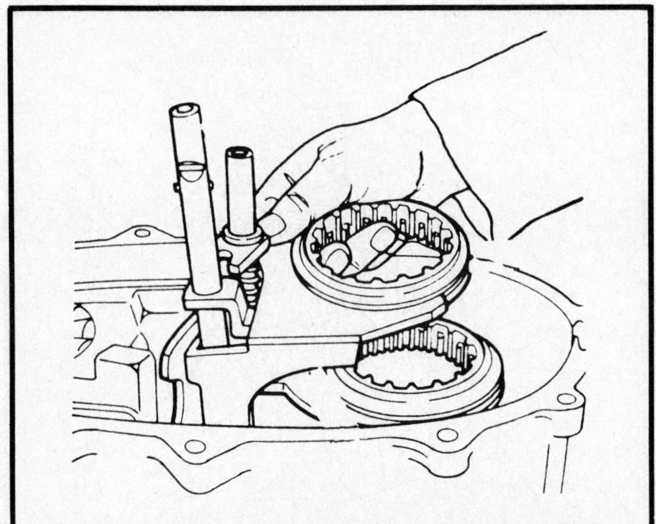

Removing the mode fork and shift rail assembly

14. Remove the locking fork, high range sliding clutch sleeve, fork brackets and fork spring as an assembly. Be sure to take note of the position of these components for an easy assembly reference.

15. Remove the range sector detent screw and remove the detent spring, plunger and ball. Move the range operating lever downward to the last detent position and disengage the low range fork lug from the range sector slot.

16. Remove the retaining snap ring from the annulus gear and remove the thrust washer. Remove the annulus gear, range fork and rail as an assembly and separate the components for cleaning and inspection.

17. Remove the planetary thrust washer from the planetary assembly hub. Remove the planetary assembly, by grasping the planetary hub and lifting the assembly upward.

18. Remove the main shaft thrust bearing from the input shaft. Remove the input shaft, input shaft thrust bearing and race.

19. Remove the range sector and operating lever attaching nut and lockwasher. Remove the lever.

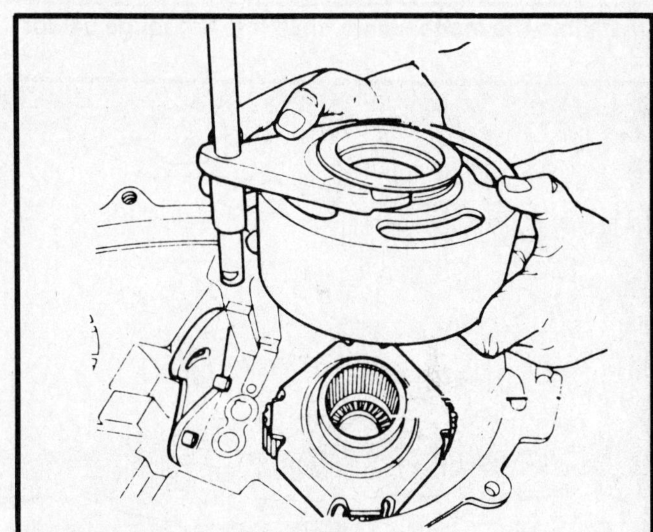

Removing the annulus gear

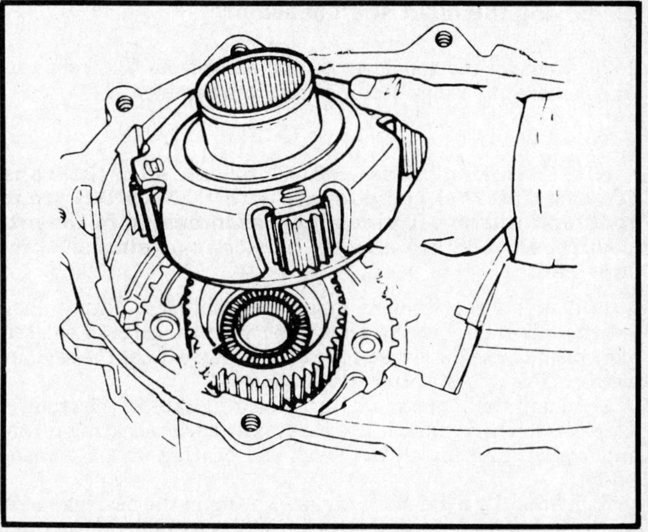

Removing the planetary assembly

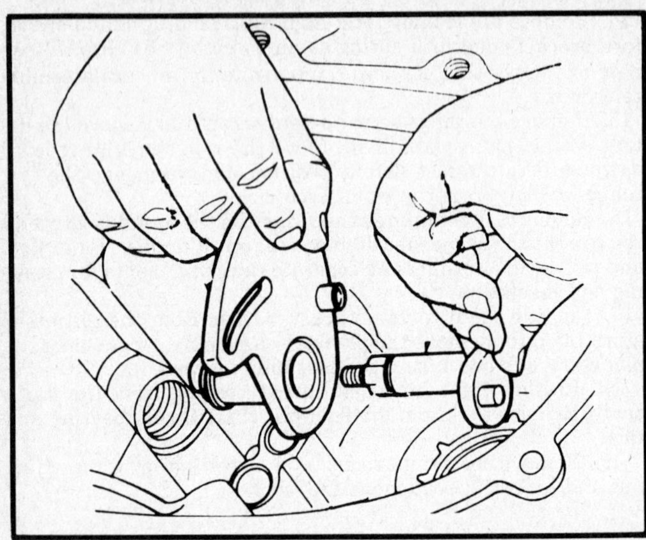
Installing the mode sector shaft into the range sector

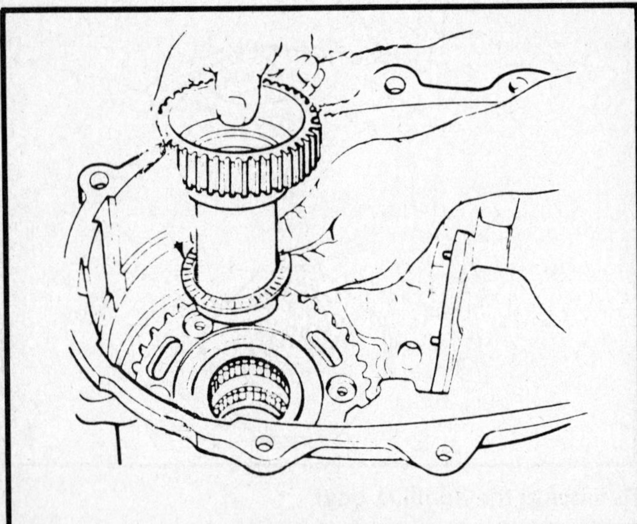
Removing the input shaft assembly

20. Remove the range sector and shaft from the front case and remove the range sector O-ring and retainer.

Assembly

NOTE: During the assembly, lubricate all of the transfer case internal components with DEXRON®II transmission fluid or petroleum jelly as indicated in the procedure. Do not use chassis lubricant or similar thick lubricants.

1. Install a replacement input shaft and rear output shaft bearing oil seals. Set the seals flush with the edge of the seal bore or in the seal groove in the transfer case. Coat the seal lips with petroleum jelly after installation.
2. Install the input shaft thrust bearing race in the transfer case counterbore. Install the input gear thrust bearing on the input shaft and install the shaft and bearing in the transfer case.
3. Install the main shaft thrust bearing in the bearing recess in the input shaft. Install the planetary assembly on the input shaft. Ensure that the planetary pinion teeth mesh fully with the input shaft.
4. Install the planetary thrust washer on the planetary hub. Install a replacement sector shaft O-ring and install the retainer in the shaft bore in the transfer case.
5. Install the O-ring on the mode sector shaft and insert the mode sector through the range sector. Install the range sector in the front of transfer case half. Install the operating lever and the snap ring on the range sector shaft.
6. Install the lever, attaching washer and lock nut on the mode sector shaft. Torque the lock nut to 17 ft. lbs. Assemble the annulus gear, range fork and rail. Install the assembled fork on and over the planetary assembly.
7. Be sure that the annulus gear is fully meshed with the planetary pinions. Engage the range sector lug into the range sector.
8. Install the annulus thrust washer and the annulus retaining ring onto the annulus gear hub. Install the detent ball, plunger, spring and retaining screw in the front transfer case half detent bore. Torque the retaining screw to 22 ft. lbs.

NOTE: The locking mode clutch sleeve and the high range clutch sleeve are not interchangeable. The sleeve splines are different. So be sure that the correct sleeve is installed in the proper shift fork. Also, the sleeves must be replaced as a set.

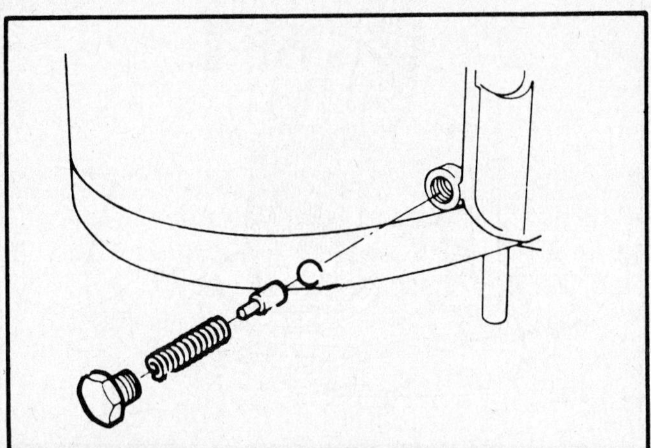
Installing the detent ball assembly

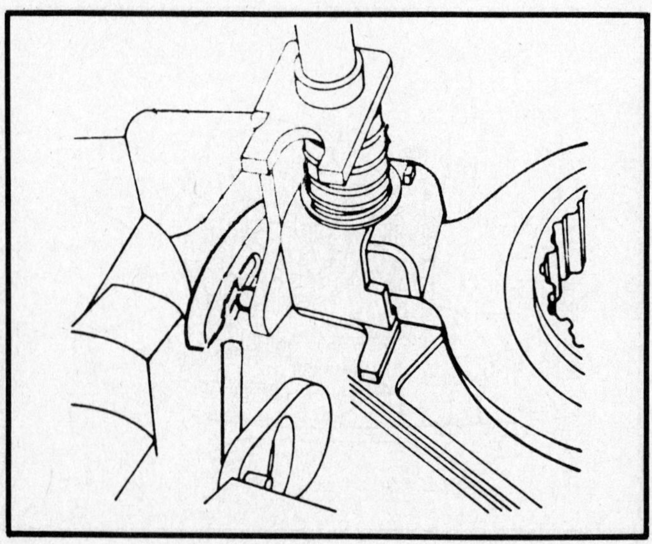
Installing the locking fork

9. Assemble and install the locking fork, fork bracket, fork springs and high range clutch sleeves. Be sure that the lug on the fork is seated in the range sector detent slot.

10. Install the range fork lug in the range sector detent notch. Move the range sector to the high range position. Assemble and install the range fork, shift rail and mode clutch sleeve.

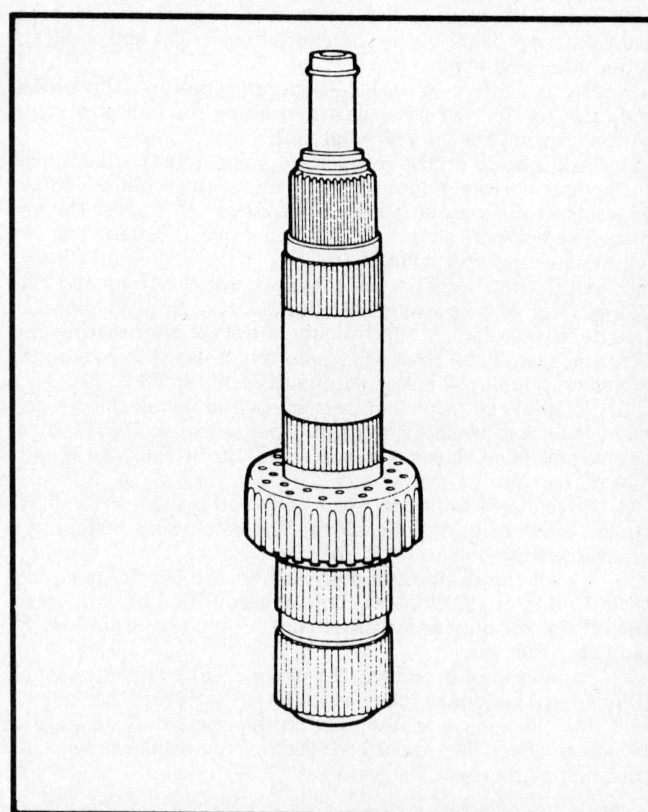

Installing the needle bearing and bearing spacers on the mainshaft

NOTE: Steps 11–16 are to be used if the main shaft was disassembled, when the transfer case was disassembled.

11. Install the thrust washer and a replacement O-ring on the main shaft. Install the needle bearings and bearing spacers on the main shaft. Coat the shaft bearing surface and all needle bearings with petroleum jelly.

12. Install the first 41 needle bearings and install the long bearing spacer, the remaining 41 needle bearings and the remaining short spacer. Be careful to avoid displacing the bearing when the spacers are installed. Apply additional petroleum jelly to hold the bearing in place if necessary.

13. Install the spline gear on the main shaft, be careful not to displace the bearing while installing the gear. Install the sprocket carrier in the drive sprocket and install the sprocket carrier snap rings. Make sure that the carrier and sprockets are aligned according to the reference marks made during disassembly.

NOTE: The sprocket carrier teeth are tapered on one side and the drive sprocket has a deep recess on one side. Be sure that these components are assembles so that the carrier tapered teeth and sprocket recess are on the same side.

14. Install the sprocket carrier bearings and spacers. Coat the carrier bore and all the 120 carrier needle bearings with petroleum jelly. Install the center spacer.

15. Install the 60 needle bearings in each end of the carrier and install the remaining two spacers, one at each side of the carrier. Apply additional petroleum jelly to hold the bearings in place if necessary.

16. Install the assembled sprocket carrier and drive sprocket on the main shaft. Do not displace the main shaft bearing during installation. Be sure that the recessed side of the drive sprocket is facing downward.

17. Install the trust washer in the main shaft, position the washer on the sprocket carrier. Install the side gear on the main shaft and be sure that the side gear is fully seated in the sprocket carrier. Be careful not to displace any of the carrier or main shaft needle bearings.

18. Install the main shaft and gear assembly in the case, making sure that the main shaft is fully seated in the input gear. Install the driven sprocket on the front output shaft and install the sprocket retaining snap ring. Be sure that the sprocket is installed according to the reference marks made during disassembly.

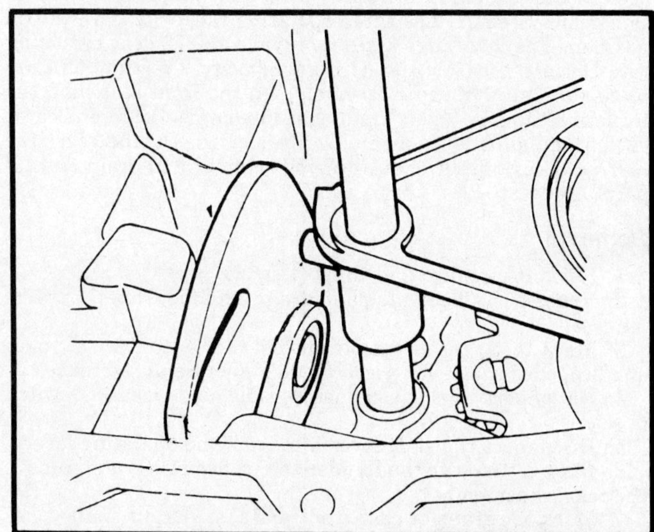

Engage the range sector lug into the range sector

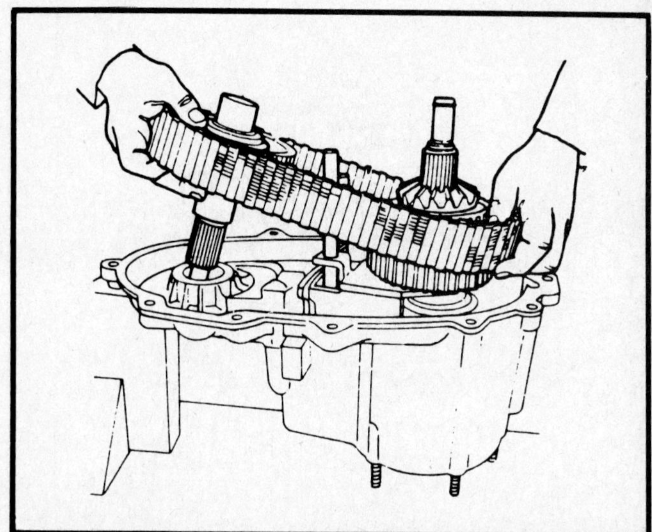

Installing the drive chain, front output shaft and driven socket

19. Install the front output shaft front thrust bearing assembly in the transfer case front half. Install the thick race in the transfer case and then install the bearing and the thin race.

20. Install the drive chain, front output shaft and driven sprocket. Install the chain on the driven sprocket. Raise and tilt the driven sprocket and chain and install the opposite end of the chain on the drive sprocket.

21. Align the front output shaft with the shaft bore in the transfer case front half and install the shaft in the transfer case. Be sure that the front shaft thrust bearing assembly is seated in the transfer case.

22. Install the front output shaft rear thrust bearing assembly on the front output shaft. Install the tin race first, then install the bearing and the thick race. Install the differential on the side gear, making sure that the differential is fully seated.

23. Coat the main shaft pilot bearing surface and all 15 needle bearings with petroleum jelly and install thew bearing on the shaft. Apply additional petroleum jelly to hold the bearings in place if necessary.

24. Install the rear output shaft on the main shaft and into the differential, making sure that the shaft is completely seated. If necessary tap the shaft with a plastic mallet or equivalent to seat the shaft. Do not displace the pilot bearing during shaft installation.

25. Install the oil pump and the rear output shaft. Install the oil pump with the recessed side facing down. Install a replacement rear output shaft bearing seal in the rear transfer case half.

26. Apply a bead of Loctite®515 sealant or equivalent, to the mating surface of the rear transfer case half. Install the magnet in the case and attach the rear transfer case half to the front transfer case half. Be sure that the alignment dowels at the front case half ends are aligned with the bolt holes in the rear case half and mate the rear case half with the front case half.

NOTE: If the rear transfer case half will not mate completely with the front case. Inspect the following; oil in the range fork rail bore, the front output shaft rear thrust bearing assembly is not aligned with the rear case half, the main shaft is not completely seated or the rear case half is not aligned with the oil pump.

27. Install the rear case half to the front case half bolts. Torque the bolts to 23 ft. lbs. Be sure that the flat washers are used on the bolts at the case end where the alignment dowels are located. Install the speedometer drive gear on the rear output shaft.

Checking the end play on the rear output shaft

28. Measure the thickness of the shim pack and record. Install a 0.030 in. shim on the rear output shaft. Align the rear retainer on the rear transfer case half and install the retainer. Install the retainer bolts and tighten them securley, do not torque to specifications.

29. Install the front and rear output shaft yokes and the original yoke nuts. Tighten the yoke nuts finger tight and check the differential end play.

30. Set the shift lever in the 4-high range position. Place a dial indicator on the rear retainer and position the indicator stylus so that it contacts the rear yoke nut.

31. Pull upward on the rear output yoke, note the dial indicator pointer position and record it. Remove the retainer and add or subtract differential shims as necessary to correct the end play. The end play should be between 0.002–0.010 in. The recommended end play is 0.006 in.

32. After adjusting the end play, remove the front and rear yokes. Discard the original yoke nuts. Apply a bead of Loctite®515 sealant or equivalent, to the retainer mating surface and install the retainer. Apply the sealer to the retaining bolts and install the bolts. Torque the bolts to 23 ft. lbs.

33. Position the front and rear yokes and install the replacement yoke seal washers and nuts. Using tool # J-8614-01 or equivalent hold the yokes in place and torque the yoke nuts to 120 ft. lbs.

34. Install the detent ball, spring and bolt if these were not installed previously. Apply sealer to the bolt before installing it and torque the bolt to 23 ft. lbs.

35. Install the drain plug and washer. Fill the transfer case with 7 pints of DEXRON®II transmission fluid or equivalent. Install the fill plug and washer and torque the drain and fill plugs to 18 ft. lbs.

36. Install the plug and washer in the front transfer case half (if removed) and torque the plug to 18 ft. lbs. Install the transfer case into the vehicle as described in this section. Road test the vehicle to check for proper operation of the transfer case, stop the engine and check for leaks.

New Process Model 231 Transfer Case

The NP231 is a part-time unit with a built-in low range reduction gear system. It has three operating ranges plus a Neutral position. The low-range system provides a 2.72 gear reduction ratio for increased low-speed torque capacity. The unit has a two piece aluminum housing assembly. On the front case half, the front output shaft, front input shaft, four wheel drive indicator switch and shift lever assembly are located. On the rear case half, the rear output shaft, bearing retainer and drain and fill plugs are located.

Removal

1. Raise the vehicle and support safely.
2. Remove the drain plug and drain the fluid from the transfer case.
3. Mark the transfer case front and rear output shaft yokes and propeller shafts for assembly alignment and reference.
4. Disconnect the speedometer cable and vacuum switch hoses.
5. Disconnect the shift lever link from the operating lever.
6. Place a support stand under the transmission and remove the rear crossmember.
7. Mark the transfer case front and rear output shaft yokes and drive shafts for assembly alignment reference.
8. Disconnect the front and rear drive shafts at the transfer case yokes. Secure the shafts to the frame rails with wire.

Component	Service Set-To Torque	Service Recheck Torque
Detent Retainer Bolt	31 N·m (23 ft-lbs)	27-34 N·m (20-25 ft-lbs)
Drain and Fill Plugs	24 N·m (18 ft-lbs)	20-34 N·m (15-25 ft-lbs)
Front/Rear Yoke Nuts	163 N·m (120 ft-lbs)	122-176 N·m (90-130 ft-lbs)
Operating Lever Locknut	24 N·m (18 ft-lbs)	20-27 N·m (15-20 ft-lbs)
Rear Case-to-Front Case Bolts (All)	31 N·m (23 ft-lbs)	27-34 N·m (20-25 ft-lbs)
Rear Retainer Bolts	31 N·m (23 ft-lbs)	27-34 N·m (20-25 ft-lbs)
Transfer Case-to-Transmission Adapter Nuts	35 N·m (26 ft-lbs)	27-41 N·m (20-30 ft-lbs)
Universal Joint Strap Bolt-to-Transfer Case Yoke	19 N·m (170 in-lbs)	16-23 N·m (140-200 in-lbs)

228 transfer case torque specifications

NOTE: Do not allow the shafts to hang.

9. Remove the bolts attaching the exhaust pipe support bracket to the transfer case, if necessary.
10. Remove the transfer case-to-transmission nuts.
11. Move the transfer case assembly rearward until free of the transmission output shaft and remove the assembly.
12. Remove all the gasket material from the rear of the transmission adapter housing.

Disassembly

1. Remove the transfer case from the vehicle as descibed above.
2. Remove the attaching nuts from the front and rear output yokes. Remove the yokes and sealing washers.
3. Remove the bolts and tap the extension housing off of the rear retainer.
4. Remove the snap ring from the rear bearing, then, remove the four bolts and separate the rear bearing retainer from the rear case half.
5. Remove the retaining bolts and separate the case halves by inserting a small pry bar in the pry slots on the case.
6. Remove the oil pump, pickup tube and pickup screen from the rear case.
7. Remove the mode spring from the shift rail.
8. Remove the drive chain by pushing the front input shaft inward and by angling the gear slightly to obtain adequate clearance to remove the chain.
9. Remove the mainshaft assembly from the front case half.
10. Remove the snap ring and thrust washer from the planetary gear set assembly in the front case half.
11. Remove the annulus gear assembly and thrust washer from the front case half.
12. Lift the planetary gear assembly from the front case half.
13. Using an arbor press ram, press the input gear out of the front case assembly.
14. Remove the detent spring bolt from the front case and remove the detent spring.
15. Remove the shift selector, then the low-range lock plate from the front case assembly.

Assembly

Assembly of the transfer case is the reverse of the above disassembly procedures. Lubricate all components with Dexron®II ATF. Seal the case halves and the extension housing with a 1/8 in. bead of RTV on assembly. Fill the unit with DEXRON®II transmission fluid.

TORQUE SPECIFICATIONS
New Process 231 Transfer Case

Description	Torque Ft. Lbs.	N•m
Bolt, Low Range Lock Plate	25	34
Vacuum Switch	20	27
Nut, Range Lever	18	24
Bolt, Front Case-to-Rear Case	22	30
Bolt, Rear Retainer	18	24
Bolt, Extension Housing	22	30
Plug, Drain/Fill	35	47
Bolt, Adapter-to-Transfer Case	24	33
Nut, Transfer Case-to-Adapter	26	35
U-Joint Clamp Strap Bolts	14	19

Installation

1. Apply Permatex® No.3 sealer, or equivalent to both sides of the transfer case-to-transmission gasket and position the gasket on the transmission.
2. Align and install the transfer case assembly on the transmission. Be sure the transfer case input gear splines are aligned with the transmission output shaft. Align the splines by rotating the transfer case rear output shaft yoke as necessary.

NOTE: Do not install any transfer case attaching nuts until the transfer case is completely seated against the transmission.

3. Align and install the transfer case attaching nuts. Tighten the nuts to 35 ft. lbs.
4. Install the rear crossmember and remove the transmission support stand.

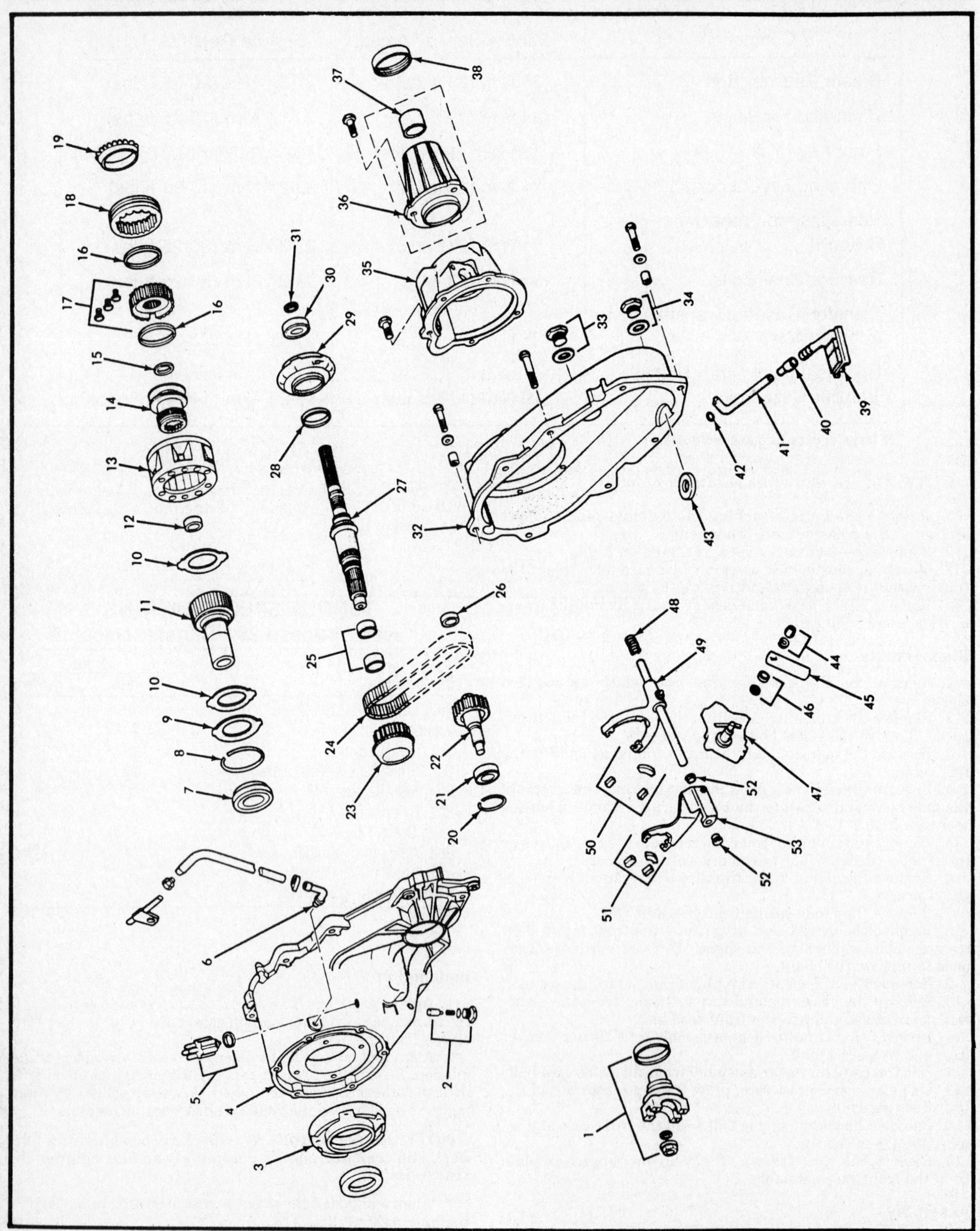

Exploded view of the NP231 Transfer case

LEGEND FOR NP231 TRANSFER CASE

1. Front yoke nut, seal washer, yoke, and oil seal
2. Shift detent plug, spring, and pin
3. Front retainer and seal
4. Front case
5. Vacuum switch and seal
6. Vent assembly
7. Input gear bearing and snap ring
8. Low range gear snap ring
9. Input gear retainer
10. Low range gear thrust washers
11. Input gear
12. Input gear pilot bearing
13. Low range gear
14. Range fork shift hub
15. Synchronizer hub snap ring
16. Synchronizer hub springs
17. Synchronizer hub and inserts
18. Synchronizer sleeve
19. Synchronizer stop ring
20. Snap ring
21. Output shaft front bearing
22. Output shaft (front)
23. Drive sprocket
24. Drive chain
25. Drive sprocket bearings
26. Output shaft rear bearing
27. Mainshaft
28. Oil seal
29. Oil pump assembly
30. Rear bearing
31. Snap ring
32. Rear case
33. Fill plug and gasket
34. Drain plug and gasket
35. Rear retainer
36. Extension housing
37. Bushing
38. Oil seal
39. Oil pickup screen
40. Tube connector
41. Oil pickup tube
42. Pickup tube O-ring
43. Magnet
44. Range lever nut and washer
45. Range lever
46. O-ring and seal
47. Sector
48. Mode spring
49. Mode fork
50. Mode fork inserts
51. Range fork inserts
52. Range fork bushings
53. Range fork

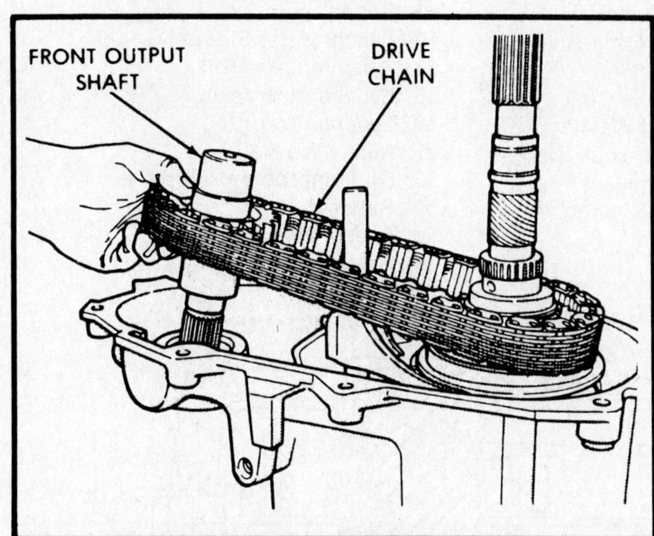

Drive chain removal and installation

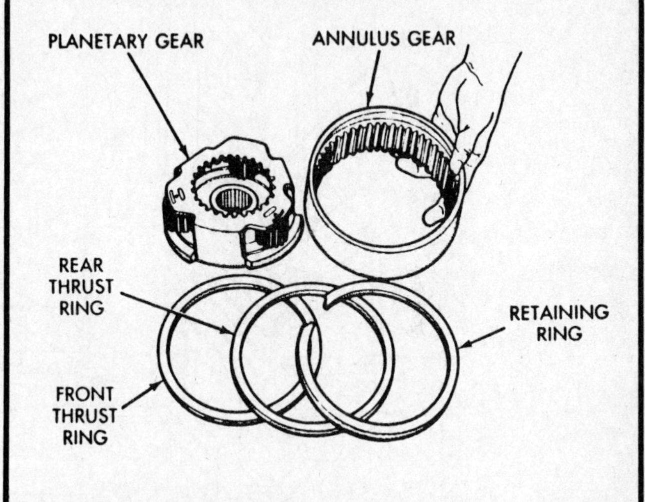

Planetary assembly components

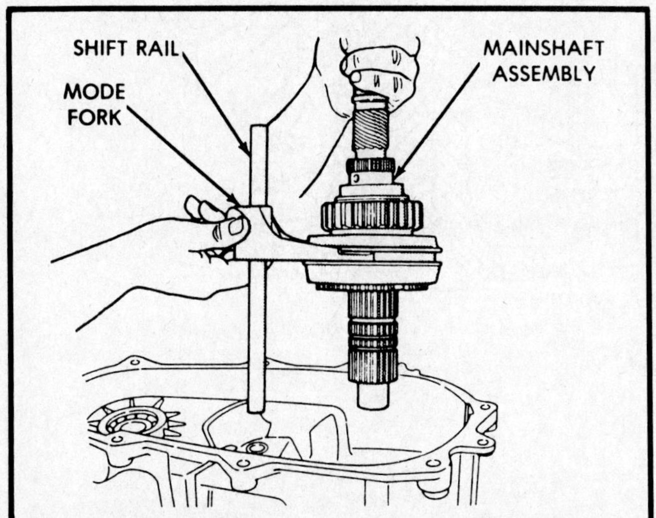

Mainshaft assembly removal

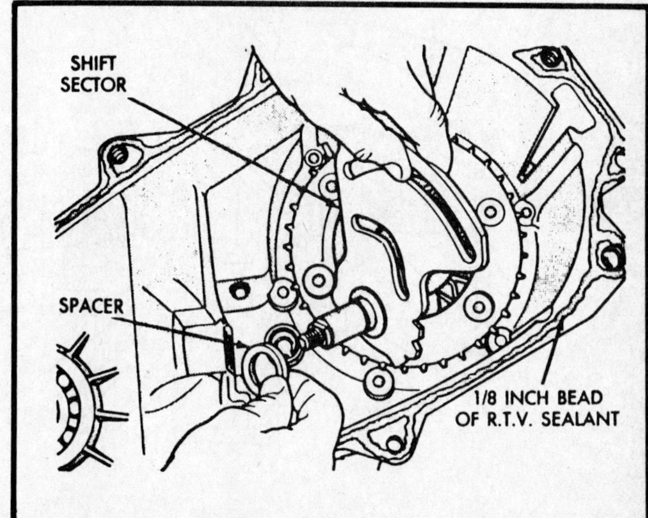

Shift selector removal

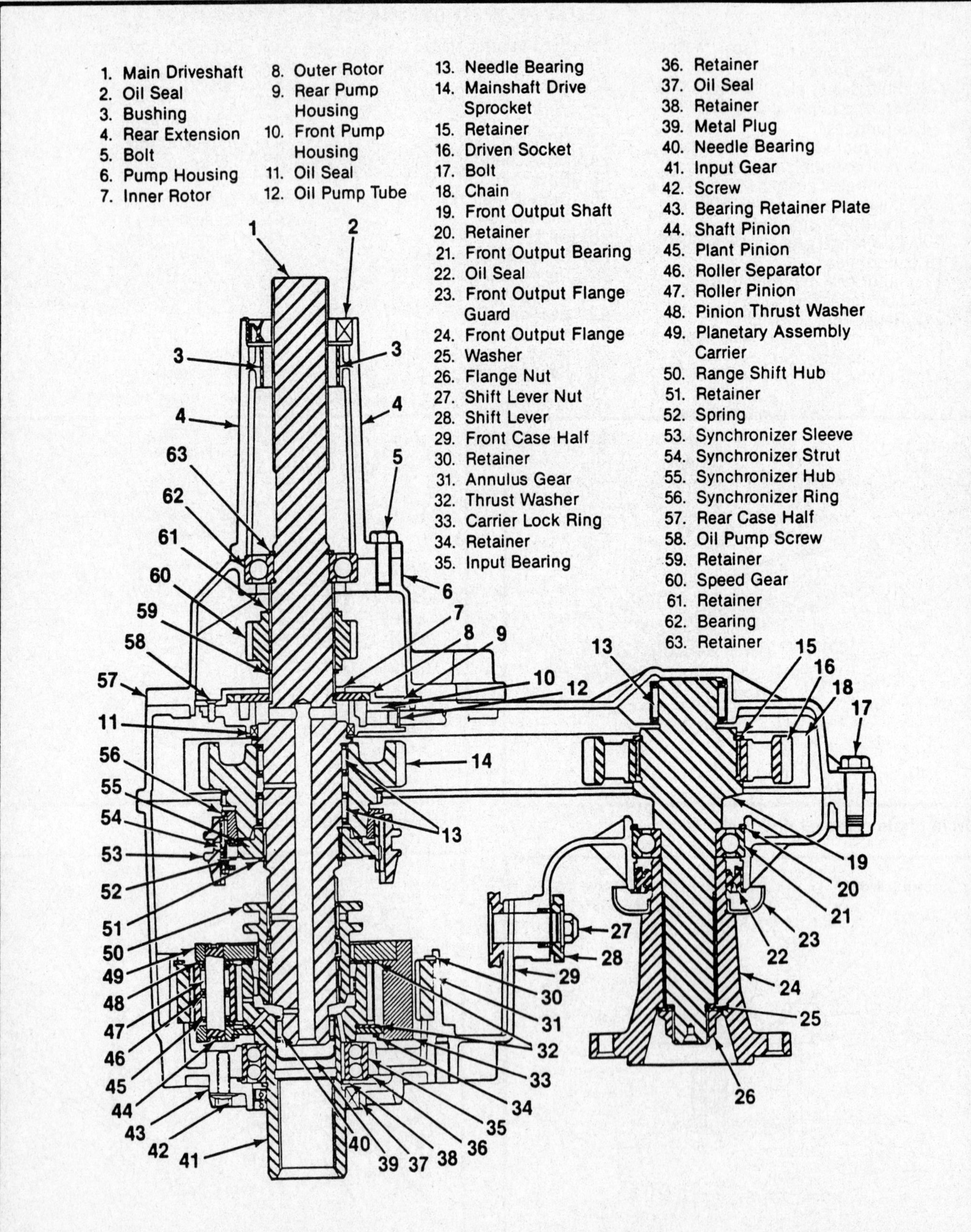
1. Main Driveshaft
2. Oil Seal
3. Bushing
4. Rear Extension
5. Bolt
6. Pump Housing
7. Inner Rotor
8. Outer Rotor
9. Rear Pump Housing
10. Front Pump Housing
11. Oil Seal
12. Oil Pump Tube
13. Needle Bearing
14. Mainshaft Drive Sprocket
15. Retainer
16. Driven Socket
17. Bolt
18. Chain
19. Front Output Shaft
20. Retainer
21. Front Output Bearing
22. Oil Seal
23. Front Output Flange Guard
24. Front Output Flange
25. Washer
26. Flange Nut
27. Shift Lever Nut
28. Shift Lever
29. Front Case Half
30. Retainer
31. Annulus Gear
32. Thrust Washer
33. Carrier Lock Ring
34. Retainer
35. Input Bearing
36. Retainer
37. Oil Seal
38. Retainer
39. Metal Plug
40. Needle Bearing
41. Input Gear
42. Screw
43. Bearing Retainer Plate
44. Shaft Pinion
45. Plant Pinion
46. Roller Separator
47. Roller Pinion
48. Pinion Thrust Washer
49. Planetary Assembly Carrier
50. Range Shift Hub
51. Retainer
52. Spring
53. Synchronizer Sleeve
54. Synchronizer Strut
55. Synchronizer Hub
56. Synchronizer Ring
57. Rear Case Half
58. Oil Pump Screw
59. Retainer
60. Speed Gear
61. Retainer
62. Bearing
63. Retainer

NP241 Transfer case—phantom view

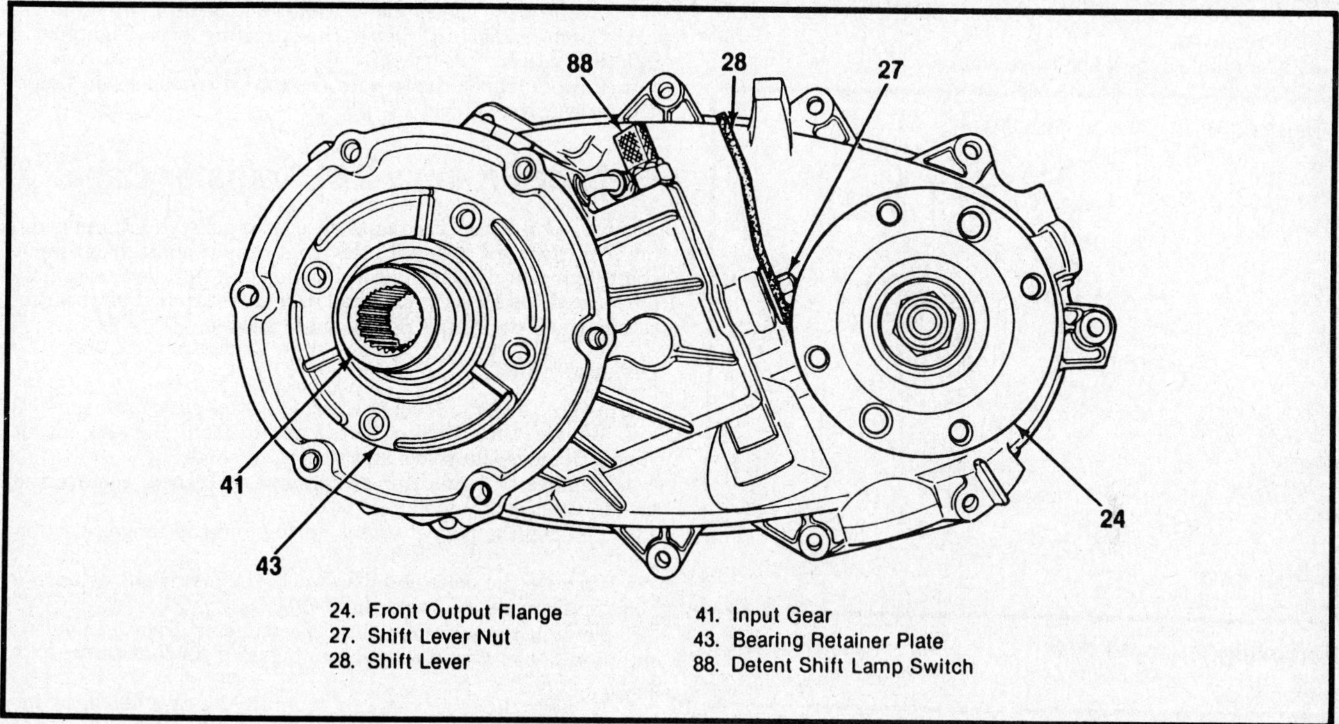

NP241 Transfer case—front view

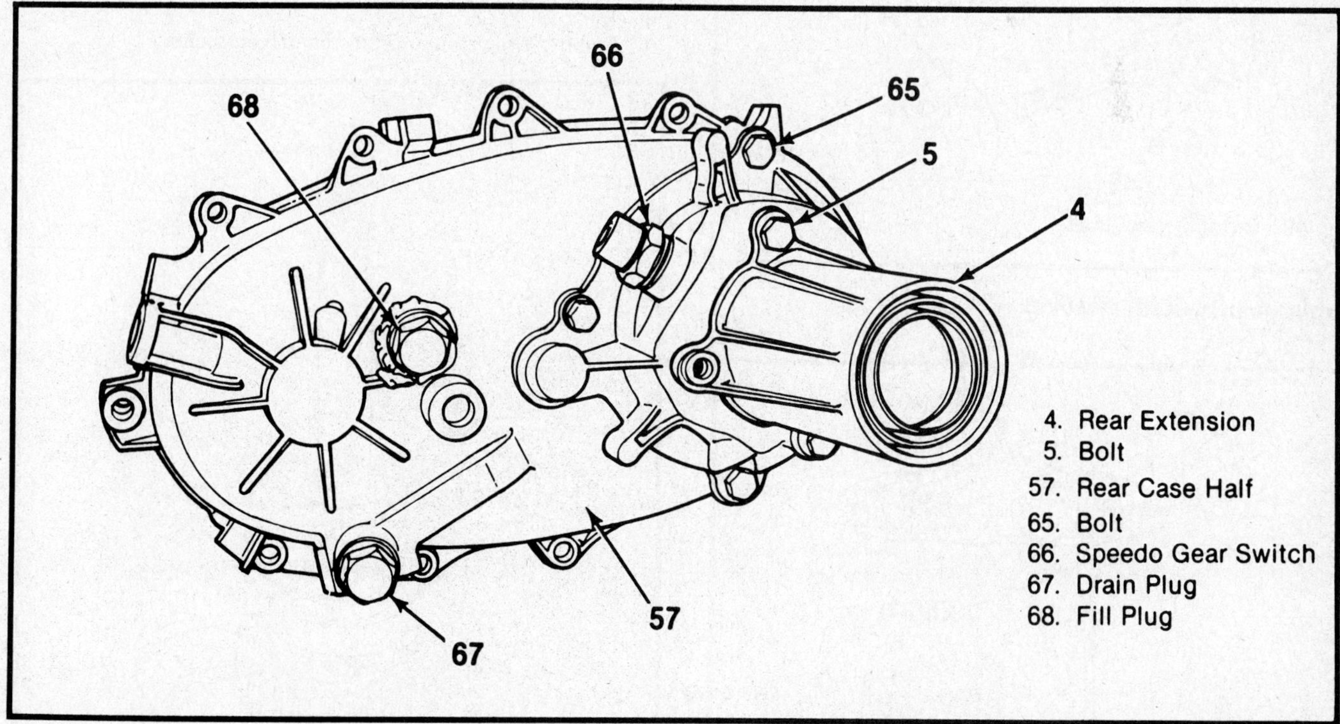

NP241 Transfer case—rear view

5. Attach the exhaust pipe support bracket to the transfer case, if removed.
6. Align and connect the drive shafts.

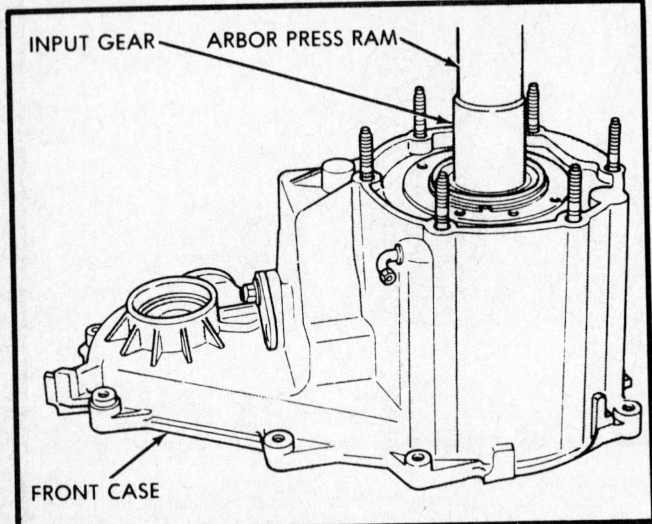

Removing the input gear

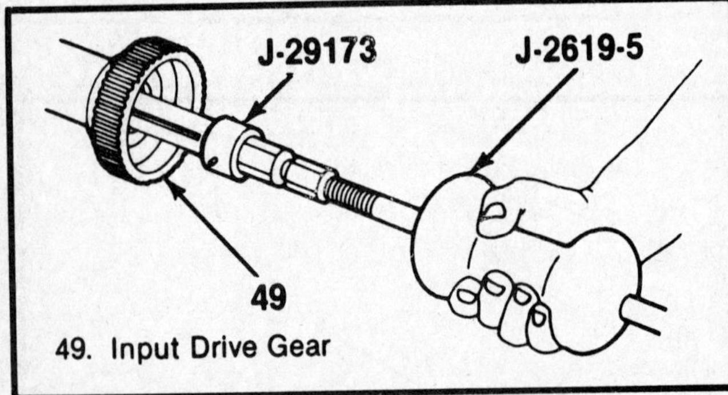

Input gear bearing removal

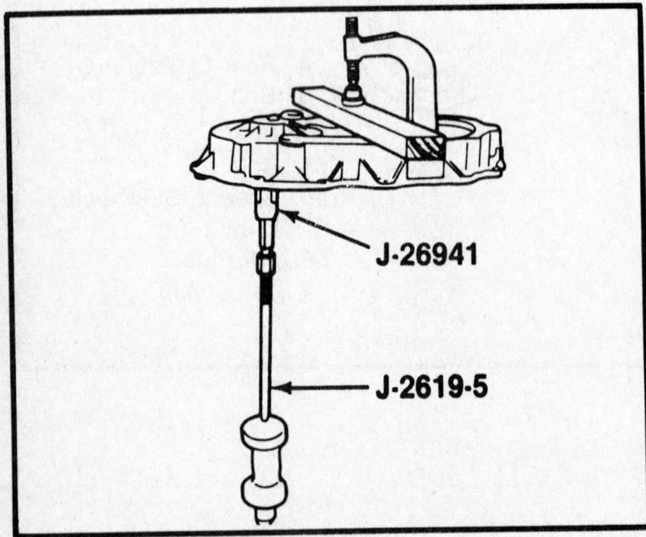

Output shaft bearing removal

7. Connect the speedometer cable and vacuum switch hoses.
8. Connect the shift lever to the operating lever. Tighten the locknut to 18 ft. lbs.
9. Fill the transfer case with Dexron®II transmission fluid.
10. Lower the vehicle.

New Process 241 Transfer Case

The NP241 is a part-time unit with a two piece aluminum housing. On the front case half, the front output shaft, front input shaft, four wheel drive indicator switch and shift lever assembly are located. On the rear case half, the rear output shaft, bearing retainer and drain and fill plugs are located.

Disassembly

1. Drain the fluid from the case if not already drained.
2. Remove the attaching nuts from the front and rear output yokes. Remove the yokes and sealing washers.
3. Remove the indicator switch and seal, then, remove the speedometer switch and seal.
4. Remove the poppet screw, spring and the range selection plunger.
5. Remove the bolts and disconnect the mainshaft extension housing from the rear case half.
6. Remove the retaining ring, speedometer drive gear nylon, oil pump housing, and the oil pump gear from the rear output shaft.
7. Remove the case bolts and separate the case halves by inserting a small pry bar in the pry slots on the case.
8. Remove the fork shift spring.
9. Remove the oil pump pick-up tube and the magnetic chip collector.
10. Remove the retainer from the driven socket.

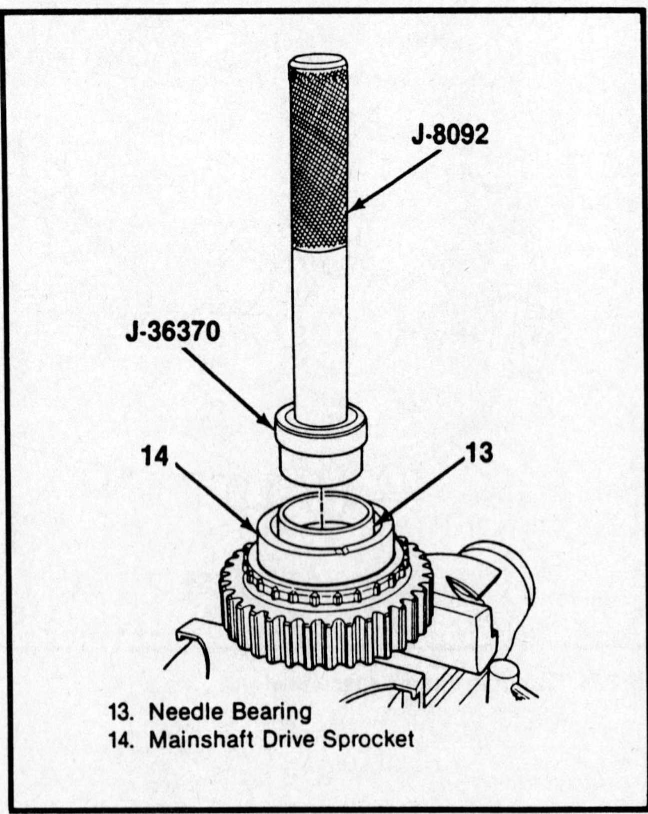

11. Remove the mainshaft, chain and driven sprocket as a unit from the front case half.
12. Remove the synchronizer assembly retainer, then remove the syncro. assembly, sleeve, thrust washer, hub and ring.
13. Remove the range fork, range selector, mode fork and range shift hub. Remove the shift lever nut, washer, and shift lever.
14. Remove the input shaft bearing retainer plate and seal.
15. Remove the input shaft bearing retainer, bearing, and the planetary assembly. Remove the bearing from the input gear with special tool J-22912-1.
16.Remove the retainer, lock ring and thrust washer from the annulus gear assembly.
17. Remove the needle bearing from the input gear as follows:
   a. Insert needle bearing tool J-29369-1 and adapter with J-2619-5 slide hammer.
   b. Using the tools mentioned above, hammer the bearing from the input gear.
18. Remove the drive sprocket from the main drive shaft.
19. Remove the needle bearings from the drive sprocket as follows:
   a. Insert needle bearing tool J-29369-2 and adapter with J-2619-5 slide hammer.
   b. Using the tools mentioned above, hammer the bearing from the drive sprocket.
20. Remove the retainer and bearing from the front output shaft. Use bearing remover tool J-33832 and driver J-8092 to drive the bearing from the case.
21. Remove the seal from the mainshaft extension housing and the seal from the front input bearing retainer.
22. Remove the needle bearing from the rear case half as follows:
   a. Insert needle bearing tool J-29369-2 and adapter with J-2619-5 slide hammer.
   b. Using the tools mentioned above, hammer the bearing from the case.

Assembly

1. Use tools J-36370 and J-8092 to drive the needle bearings onto the main shaft drive sprocket.
2. With special tools J-36372 and J-8092, drive the needle bearing into the rear case half.
3. With tools J-36373 and J-8092, drive the needle bearing into the input gear.
4. Install the bearing into the front case half, using J-36371 and J-36373 to insert the bearing. Install the bearing.
5. Use J-36371 and install the bearing into the oil pump housing.
6. Install the bearing to the input gear, then, install the thrust washer, carrier lock ring and the retainer. Install the bearing to the input gear with tool J-36372.
7. Install the input gear, bearing and planetary assembly into the annulus ring. Use a hammer and a brass drift to seat the bearing.
8. Install the retainer to the input shaft bearing.
9. Install the retainer to the input gear.
10. Install the input shaft bearing retainer, seal and bolts. Tighten the bolts to 14 ft. lbs.
11. Install the range shift hub, mode fork, range selector and range fork. Install the shift lever, washer and nut and tighten to 20 ft. lbs.
12. Install the drive sprocket and needle bearings to the main drive shaft.
13. Assembly the synchronizer assembly; ring, hub, thrust washer and sleeve, then install the retainer.
14. Install the mainshaft, chain and driven sprocket as a unit into the front case half.
15. Install the retainer to the driven sprocket. Install the shift fork spring.
16. Install the oil pump pick-up, filler and magnetic washer to the rear case half.
17. Apply a bead of Loctite® 515 sealer or equivalent to the

TORQUE SPECIFICATIONS
New Process 241 Transfer Case

Description	Torque N•m	Torque Ft. Lbs.
Input Shaft Retainer Bolts	19	14
Shift Selector Lever Nut	27	20
Shift Selector Light Switch	24	17
Case Half Bolts	31	23
Pump Housing Bolts	41	30
Mainshaft Extension Housing Bolts	31	23
Speedometer Pick-up Switch	31	23
Front Propeller Shaft Flange Bolts	149	110

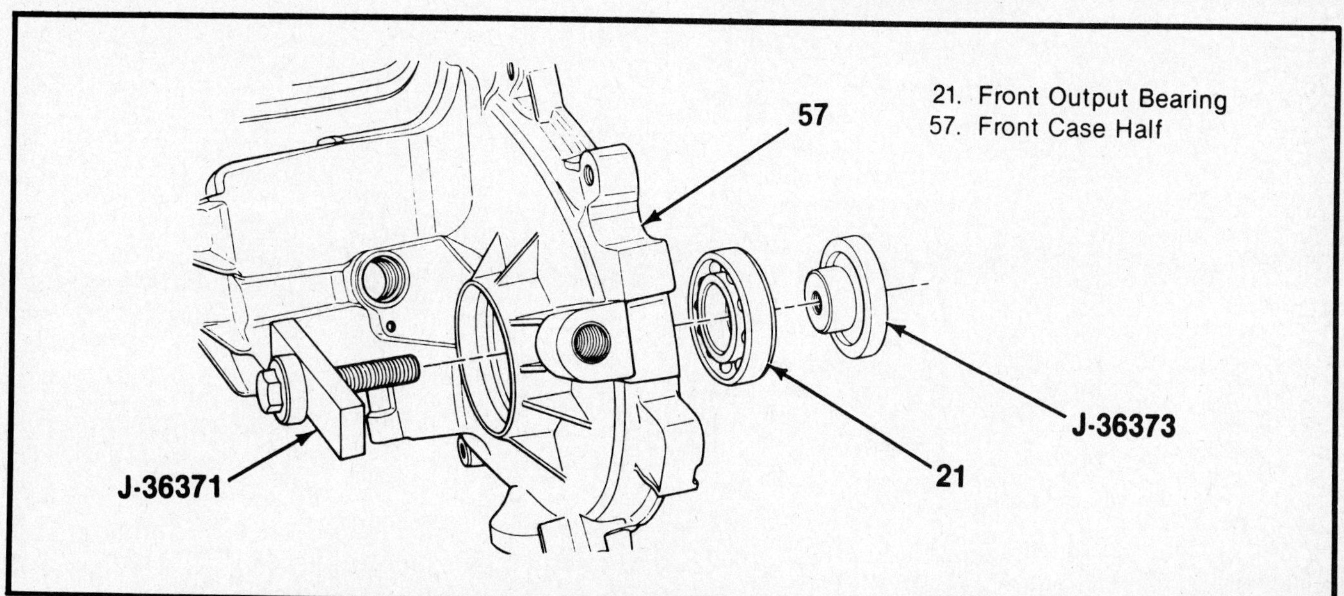

Installing the needle bearings on the main drive sprocket

case matinng surfaces, then connect the rear and front case halves. Install the bolts and tighten to 23 ft. lbs.

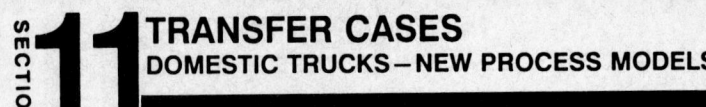

18. Install the speedometer gear retainer, speedometer gear, then the 2nd retainer.

19. Apply a bead of Loctite® 515 sealer or equivalent to the mating surfaces of the pump housing, then connect the housing. Install the bolts and tighten to 30 ft. lbs.

20. Install the bearing retainer to the mainshaft.

21. Apply a bead of Loctite® 515 sealer or equivalent to the mating surfaces of the extension housing, then connect the housing. Install the bolts and tighten to 23 ft. lbs.

22. Install the range selector plunger, spring and poppet screw.

23. Install the speedometer pick-up switch and seal. Tighten the switch to 23 ft. lbs.

24. Install the indicator lamp switch and seal. Tighten the switch to 17 ft. lbs.

25. Install the front output flange, washer and nut. Tighten the nut to 110 ft. lbs.

26. Install the transaxle into the vehicle.

27. Fill the unit with 4.6 pints of DEXRON®II transmission fluid.

Drive Axles
Domestic Trucks

12

INDEX

Types of Drive Axles

FULL FLOATING AXLES

Support of the vehicle and the payload weight is by the axle housing. The wheels are driven by splined shafts which "float" within the axle housing.

SEMI-FLOATING AXLE

This axle design provides for the support of the payload and vehicle weight to be carried by the axle shaft through the wheel bearings to the axle housing.

SINGLE REDUCTION AXLE

Final drive ratio is obtained by the use of a single ring gear and pinion set. This type is used for most light and medium duty applications.

LOCK-UP TYPE DIFFERENTIALS

Unlike the standard differential, the locking differential equally divides the torque load between the driving wheels. The vehicle equipped with the locking differential can be operated on any surface (sand, snow, etc.) with a minimum of slippage through one wheel and provides the greatest power to the wheel getting traction. The vehicle with the standard differential provides power to the wheel that's easiest to turn; that is, the one experiencing the poorest traction while the other wheel may be gripping well.

When negotiating a turn, the locking differential allows the outer wheel to turn faster than the inner. When traveling in a straight direction, and the vehicle loses traction over a rough or slippery road, the clutches will lock up and neither wheel will spin. A specified lubricant must be used for locking differentials.

The overhaul procedures are basically the same as for the conventional rear axle assemblies. The noted differences are within the differential carrier case where the lock-up mechanism is located. In some instances where wear is noted within the lock-up mechanism, the lock-up assembly should be replaced as a unit.

AXLE SERVICE AND INSPECTION

Cleaning Bearings

Proper bearing cleaning is important. Bearings should always be cleaned separately from other rear axle parts.

1. Soak all bearings in clean kerosene or diesel fuel oil.

CAUTION

Ordinary gasoline should not be used. Bearings should not be cleaned in hot solution tank.

2. Slush bearings in cleaning solution until all oil lubricant is loosened. Brush bearings with soft bristled brush until ALL dirt has been removed. Remove loose particles of dirt by striking flat against a wood block.
3. Rinse bearings in clean fluid. While holding races to prevent rotation, blow dry with compressed air.

CAUTION

Do not spin bearings while drying.

4. After bearings have been inspected, lubricate thoroughly with regular axle lubricant; then wrap each bearing in clean cloth until ready to use.

Cleaning Parts

Immerse all parts in suitable cleaning fluid and clean thoroughly. Use a stiff bristle brush as required to remove foreign deposits. Clean all lubricant passages or channels in pinion cage, carrier, caps and retainers. Make certain that interior of housing is thoroughly cleaned. Clean vent plugs and breathers.

Small parts such as cap screws, bolts, studs, nuts etc., should be cleaned thoroughly.

Inspection

Magna Flux all steel parts, except ball and roller bearings, to detect presence of wear and cracks.

Bearings

Rotate each bearing and check to see if the rollers are worn, chipped, rough or in any other way damaged. Check the cage to see if it is in any way damaged. If either the bearing rollers or the cage are damaged the bearing must be replaced.

Gears

Examine drive gear and drive pinion, differential pinions and differential side gears carefully, for damaged teeth, worn spots in surface hardening, distortion and where drive gear is attached to differential case with rivets, inspect rivets for looseness, replace loose rivets. Check radial clearances between differential side gears and differential case. Check fit of differential pinions on spider.

Differential Case

Inspect case for cracks, distortion or damage, if in good condition, thoroughly clean case and cover; then assemble case with bolts and mount in lathe centers of "V" block stand. If lathe is not available, install differential side bearings and mount case in differential carrier. Install dial indicator and check differential case run out.

Differential case with drive gear installed is checked in the same manner, except that dial indicator reading must be taken at gear instead of at case flange.

Whenever run-out exceeds limits, it may be corrected as later described under "Repair" in this section. However, the support case used in the 2-speed axle cannot be repaired and should be replaced with new case.

Axle Shafts

Examine splined end of axle shaft for twisted or cracked splines, twisted shaft, and worn dowel holes in flange. Install new shafts if necessary.

Checking the drive gear run-out

Install axle shaft assembly in lathe centers and check shaft run-out with dial indicator so that indicator shaft end contacts inner surface of flange near outer edge of flange and check flange run-out.

Shims

Carefully inspect shims for uniform thickness. Where various thickness of shims are used in a pack, it is recommended that the thickest shims be used between the thin shims.

Thrust Washers

Replace all thrust washers.

Spider

Carefully inspect spider arms for wear or defects.

Differential Pinion Bushings

Examine bushings (when used) for excessive wear, looseness, or damage. Check fit or gears on spider for excessive clearance.

Axle Housing Sleeves

Sleeves showing damaged threads, wear, or other damage should be replaced if hydraulic press is available, otherwise replace housing.

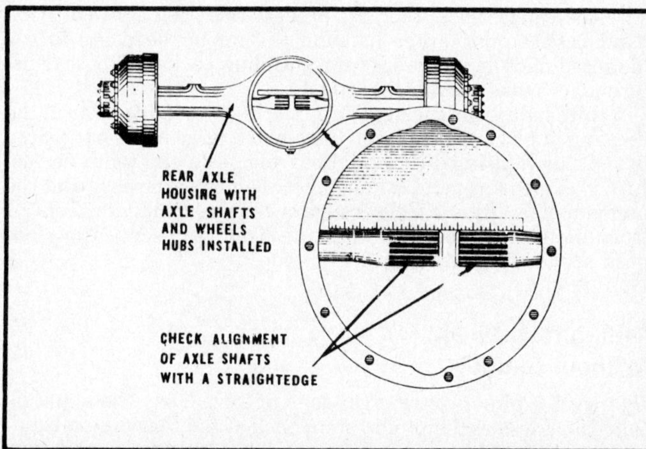

Method of checking the axle housing alignment with full floating axles

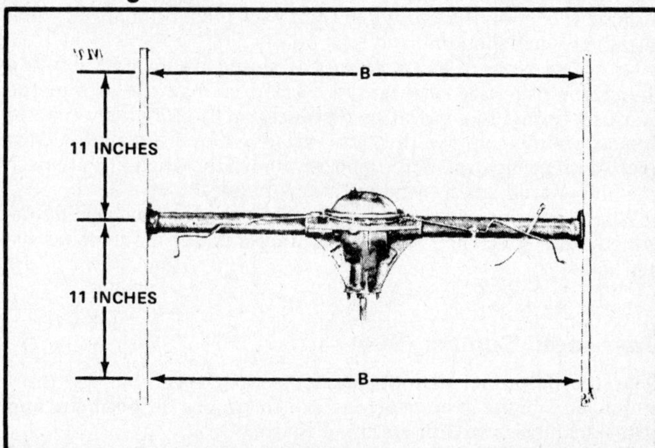

Checking the housing alignment with straight edge bars

HOUSING CHECK

Before Removal

A check for bent axle housing can be made with unit in vehicle; however, conventional alignment instruments can be used if available.

1. Raise rear axle with a jack until wheels clear floor. Block up axle under each spring seat.
2. Check wheel bearing adjustment and adjust if necessary, then check wheels for looseness and tighten wheel nuts if necessary.
3. Place a chalk mark on outer side wall of tires at bottom. Measure across tires at chalk marks with a toe-in gauge.
4. Turn wheels half-way around so that chalk marks are positioned at top of wheel. Measure across tires again. If measurement at top is $^1/_3$ in. or more, smaller than measurement at bottom of wheels, axle housing has sagged and is bent. If measurement at top exceeds bottom dimension by $^1/_3$ in. or more, axle housing is bent at ends.
5. Turn chalk marks on both wheels so that marks are level with axle and at rear of vehicle. Take measurement with toe-in gauge at chalk marks; then turn both chalk marks to front and level with axle and take another measurement. If measurement at front exceeds rear dimension by $^1/_3$ in. or more, axle is bent to the rear. If the measurement condition is the reverse, the axle is bent forward.

After Removal

Place two straightedges across the housing flanges and measure the distance between the ends of the straightedges at a point 11 inches from the tube center. Relocate the straightedge 180 degrees and remeasure. If the straightedges are parallel in both measurements within $^3/_{32}$ in., the housing is serviceable.

GENERAL REPAIR

Oil Seal Contact Surfaces

Surface of parts, contacted by oil seals must be free of corrosion, pits and grooves. When abrasive cleaning fails to clean up the seal contact surface and restore smooth finish, a new part must be installed.

OIL SEAL

Removal

Oil seals can be removed with a drift pin. When removing a seal, be careful that it does not become cocked and result in damage to the retainer. Clean surface of retainer carefully, so that seal will seat properly in retainer.

Installation

Coat outer surface of seal retainer with a light coat of sealer, to prevent lubricant leaks. Carefully start seal in retainer. Cutting, scratching, or curling of lip of seal seriously impairs its efficiency and usually results in premature replacement. Lip of seal should be coated with a high temperature grease containing zinc oxide to help prevent scoring and damage to parts during installation.

Seals must always be installed so that seal lip is toward the lubricant.

PINION BEARING ADJUSTMENTS (PRE-LOAD)

Pinion bearing must be adjusted for pre-load before assembly is installed in carrier.

Do not install oil seal until after adjustment is made. Installation of seal would produce false rotating torque.

Cage Type

1. With pinion bearings, and adjusting spacers (or shims) installed in cage, check bearing contact by rotating cage.
2. Using a press, apply pressure (approx. 20,000 lbs.) to outer bearing.
3. Wrap soft wire around cage and pull on horizontal line with spring scale. Rotating (not starting) torque should be within limits recommended by manufacturer.

NOTE: Method of determining inch-pounds torque with scale is to determine radius of cage. Multiply radius in inches by pounds pull required to rotate cage to determine inch-pounds torque. Example: An 8 in. diameter divided by 2 equals 4 in. radius. Multiply 4 in. (radius) by 5 pounds (pull) equals 20 in. pounds torque.

4. If press is not available, check preload torque by installing propeller shaft yoke, washer, and nut and torque to specifications; then check as previously explained. Remove yoke after correct adjustment is obtained.

BEVEL GEAR SHAFT BEARING ADJUSTMENT

Bevel gear shaft bearings must be adjusted for pre-load before pinion and cage assembly and differential assembly are installed in carrier.

1. Wrap several turns of soft wire around gear teeth on cross shaft, then pull on a horizontal line with spring scale. Rotating (not starting) torque should be used.

NOTE: Method of determining inch-pounds torque with scale is to determine radius. Multiply radius in inches by pounds pull required to rotate shaft to determine inch-pounds torque. Example: An 8 in. diameter divided by 2 equals 4 in. radius times 5 pounds (pull) equals 20 inch lbs. torque.

2. Remove or add shims from under cage or cap opposite bevel gear to obtain specified bearing pre-load.
3. When making bevel gear and pinion tooth contact or backlash adjustments it is sometimes necessary to remove or add shims from one side.

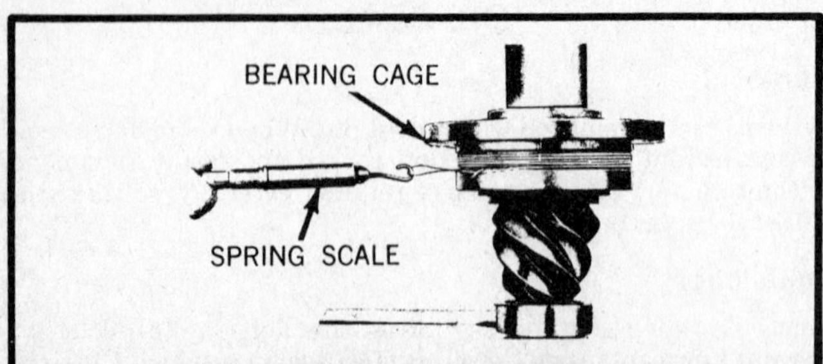

Checking the pinion bearing pre-load

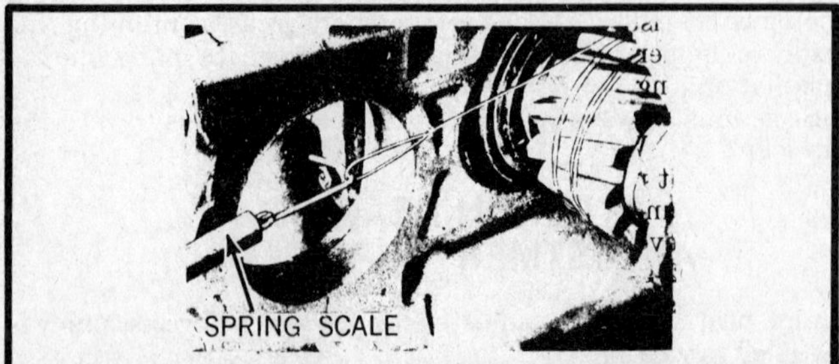

Checking the pre-load on bevel gear cross shaft

NOTE: Always remove or add an equal thickness to the opposite side so to maintain correct pre-load.

GEAR TOOTH CONTACT AND BACKLASH

Pinion Depth Measurement Methods

Methods of adjusting pinions to obtain the proper depths will vary with the axle type and the manufacturers recommendations. Pinion depth settings and gear teeth contact may be determined by the use of pinion setting gauges or by the use of marking dye on the gear teeth.

When using the gauge method, backlash is established after the pinion has been properly set. With the dye method, backlash is obtained first, then the proper pinion tooth contact is established.

The pinion gauge method can be a direct reading micrometer, mounted on or through an arbor bar, set in adapter discs and located in the side carrier bearing cup locations on the differential housing and held in place by the bearing cup caps. The arbor bar coincides and represents the center line of the axle shafts. A reading is taken by the mounted micrometer, from the arbor bar to the head of the pinion to determine the need to add to or remove shims from the shim pack total, to adjust the pinion to the proper nominal assembly dimension or standard pinion depth.

Another method using the arbor bar and discs, is the use of a gauge block with a spring loaded plunger and a thumb screw to lock the plunger upon expansion. A micrometer is used to measure the gauge block after the plunger has been allowed to expand between the arbor bar and the pinion head. As in the mounted micrometer procedure, the shim pack thickness is determined by the reading obtained.

A third method is the use of a gauge block tool, installed in the housing in place of the pinion gear, and a large arbor bar placed in the axle housing differential bearing seats and tightened securely. A measurement is taken between the arbor bar and the pinion tool by either a feeler gauge or the use of individual shims from the shim pack. This measurement represents the shim pack needed for a zero marked pinion.

Setting New Pinion (Without Gauge)

Whenever a pinion setting gauge is not available, the approximate thickness of the pinion shim pack at the rear pinion bearing cup, change the sign of the marking (individual variation distance) on the *new* pinion (plus to minus or minus to plus), then add the variation of the old pinion (sign unchanged) which will determine the amount the original shim pack must be changed when installing a new pinion.

On those types of axles where the shims are located between the pinion cage and differential carrier, change the sign of the marking (individual variation distance) on the *old* pinion (plus to minus or minus to plus), then add variation of the new pinion (sign unchanged) which will determine how much the original shim pack must be altered when installing a new pinion.

When the approximate thickness of shim pack has been determined, final check of gear tooth contact must be made using dye method.

Gear Tooth Contact (Dye)

Gear tooth contact cannot be successfully accomplished until pinion and bevel gear bearings are in proper adjustment and gear backlash is within specified limits.

Check for proper tooth contact by painting a few teeth of bevel gear with marking dye. Turn pinion in direction of normal rotation, then check tooth impression on bevel gear.

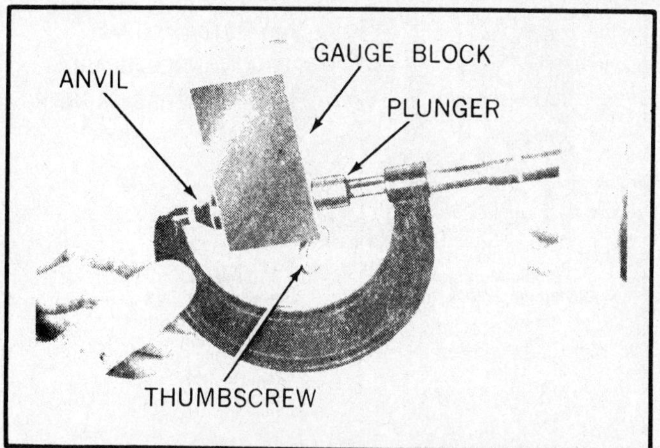

Method of measurement of the gauge block

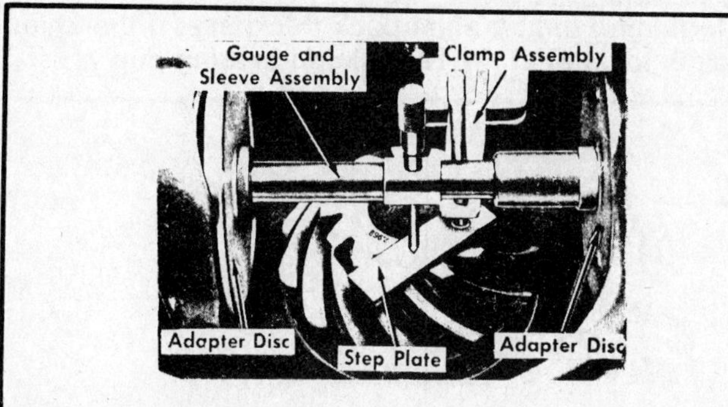

Installment of the pinion gauge

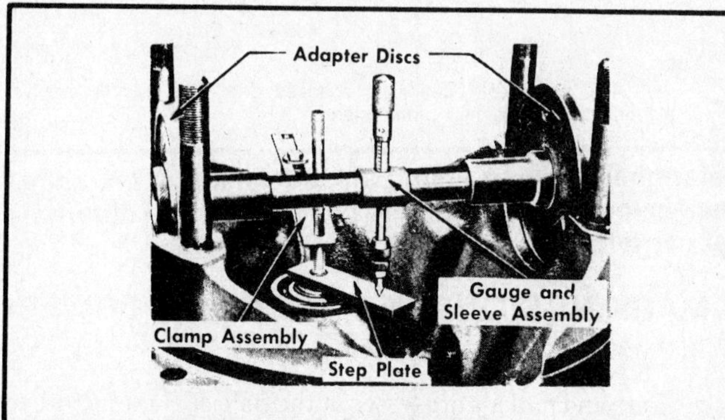

Position of pinion setting gauge

Checking the gear backlash-bevel gear

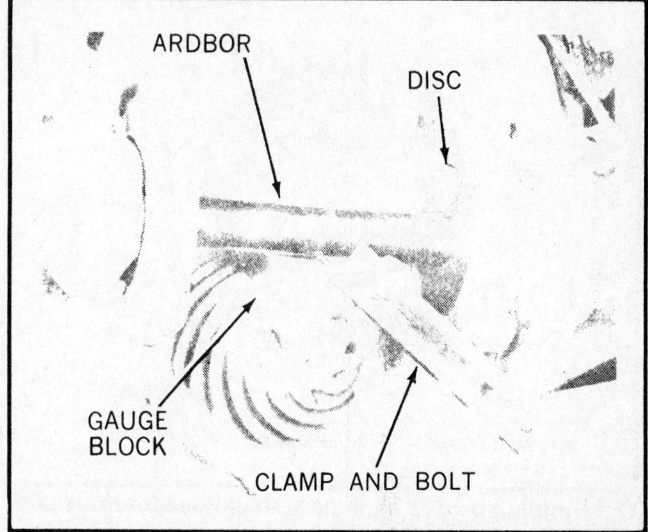

Placement of arbor and gauge block for pinion depth

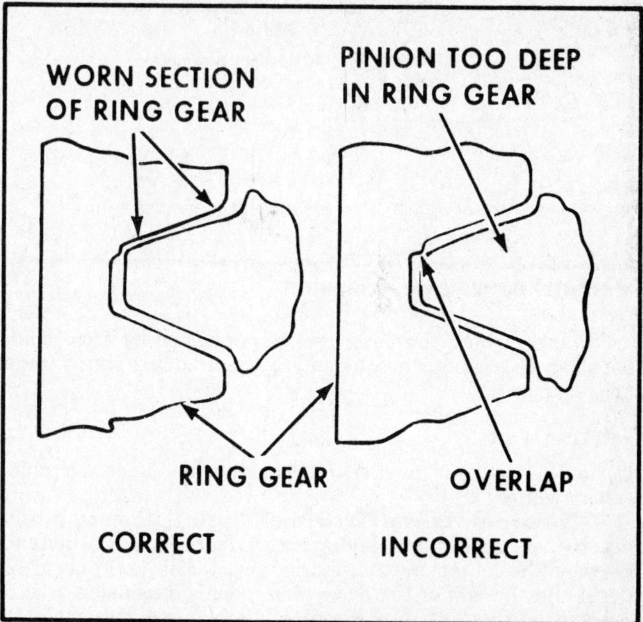

Avoid overlap of worn section of gear teeth during backlash adjustments when using original gears

Gear Backlash

Gears that have been in extended service, form running contacts due to wear of teeth; therefore the original shim pack (between pinion cage and carrier) should be maintained when checking backlash. If backlash exceeds maximum tolerance, reduce backlash only in the amount that will avoid overlap of worn tooth section. Smoothness and roughness can be noted by rotating bevel gear.

If a slight overlap is present at worn tooth section, rotation will be rough.

If new gears are installed, check backlash with dial indicator.

Backlash is increased by moving bevel gear away from pinion, and may be decreased by moving bevel gear toward pinion.

When the drive gear is attached to the differential, backlash is accomplished is differential bearing adjusting rings. It should be remembered that when one ring is tightened, the opposite ring must be loosened an equal amount to maintain previously established bearing adjustment.

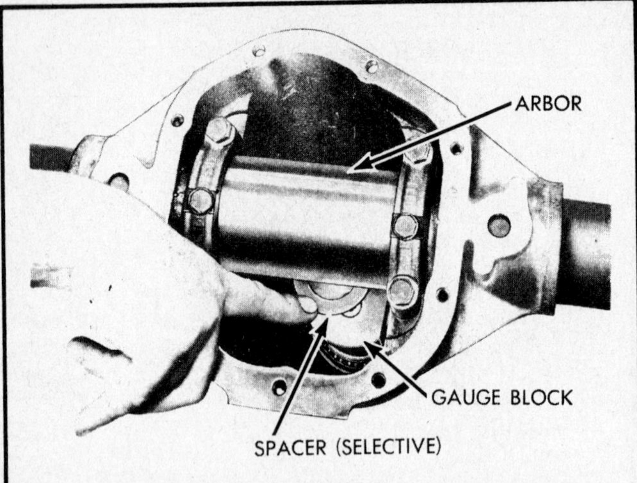

Determining proper shim pack thickness for drive pinion depth of mesh

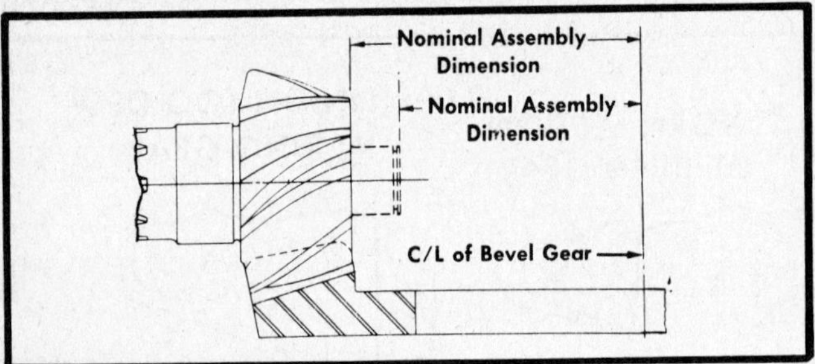

Nominal assembly dimension

On axles where the bevel gear is supported by cross shaft, backlash is accomplished by adding or removing shims under bearing cages.

Terms Used

Certain dimensions must be determined when using the pinion setting gauge:

1. **Nominal Assembly Dimension:** (standard pinion depth) This dimension (varying with axle model) is the distance between the center line of the drive gear (or differential carrier bore) and the end of the drive pinion. This dimension may be marked on the pinion or listed on the Nominal Assembly Dimension and Adapter Disc chart.
2. **Individual Variation Distance:** (pinion depth variance) This dimension is a plus or minus variation of the **Nominal Assembly Dimension** on each individual pinion which may be caused by manufacturing variations.
3. **Corrected Nominal Dimension:** (desired pinion depth) This dimension is the **Nominal Assembl[illegible]sion** plus or minus the **Individual Variation Distance.**
4. **Corrected Micrometer Distance is the Corrected Nominal Dimension** less the thickness of the gauge set step plate (0.400 in.) mounted on end of pinion.
5. **Initial Micrometer Reading** is the dimension taken by micrometer to the gauge step plate.
6. **Shim Pack Correction** is determined by the difference between the **Corrected Micrometer Distance** and the **Initial Micrometer Reading,** and represents the amount of shim pack to be added or removed as later explained.
7. **Measured Pinion Depth.** This measurement is the distance between the axle center line and the top of the pinion gear. If a step plate or other type gauge tool is used, this measurement is included in the total.

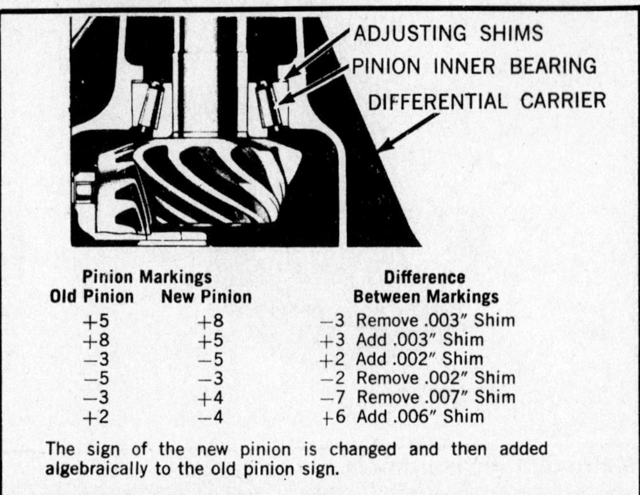

Pinion Markings Old Pinion	New Pinion	Difference Between Markings
+5	+8	−3 Remove .003″ Shim
+8	+5	+3 Add .003″ Shim
−3	−5	+2 Add .002″ Shim
−5	−3	−2 Remove .002″ Shim
−3	+4	−7 Remove .007″ Shim
+2	−4	+6 Add .006″ Shim

The sign of the new pinion is changed and then added algebraically to the old pinion sign.

Determining pinion shim pack thickness, if the shim pack is located at the rear pinion bearing cup

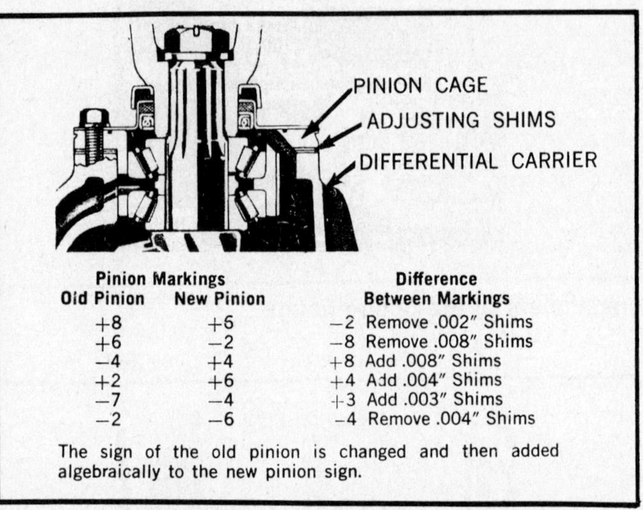

Pinion Markings Old Pinion	New Pinion	Difference Between Markings
+8	+6	−2 Remove .002″ Shims
+6	−2	−8 Remove .008″ Shims
−4	+4	+8 Add .008″ Shims
+2	+6	+4 Add .004″ Shims
−7	−4	+3 Add .003″ Shims
−2	−6	−4 Remove .004″ Shims

The sign of the old pinion is changed and then added algebraically to the new pinion sign.

Determining pinion shim pack thickness, if the shim pack is located between the pinion cage and differential carrier

MARKINGS ON THE PINION AND DRIVE GEARS

Drive gears and pinions are tested at the time of manufacture to detect machining variances and to obtain desirable tooth contact and quietness. When the correct setting is achieved, the gears are considered matched and a set of numbers, along with other identifying marks are etched on the gear set.

A + (plus) or − (minus) sign is used, followed by a digit to represent the factory setting where the tooth contact and quietness were the best. This is called the *Pinion Depth Variance* or *Individual Variation Distance.*

If the pinion is marked +5 for example, this means the distance from the pinion gear rear face to the axle shaft center line is .005 in. more than the standard setting, and if the pinion gear is marked −5, this means that the distance is .005 in. less than the standard setting. To move the pinion to the standard setting, compensating for the variation, shims must be either added to subtracted from the total shim pack, located under the rear pinion bearing cup, between the pinion cage and the differential carrier, or under the rear pinion bearing, depending upon the differential model being serviced.

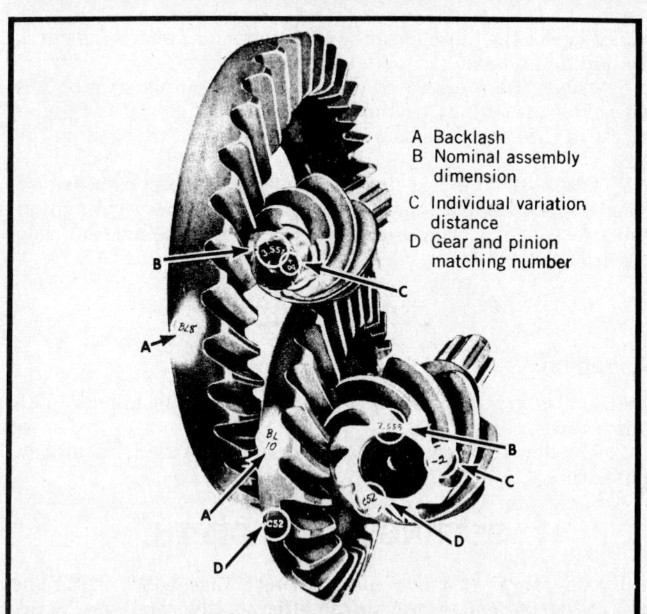

Typical gear set marking coded

The procedures to follow in the adjustment of the pinion and drive gears are outlined in the respective differential model disassembly and assembly chapters.

As a rule of thumb on the addition or removal of shims for the pinion depth adjustment, draw a diagram as shown and determine which way the pinion must be moved to obtain the desired pinion depth.

STANDARD TORQUE SPECIFICATIONS AND CAPSCREW MARKINGS

Because of the varied bolt sizes used in the many models of differentials, the torque specifications are not always available to the technician for a specific bolt. By determining the grade of bolt, size, and thread, the proper torque limit can be found in the following chart.

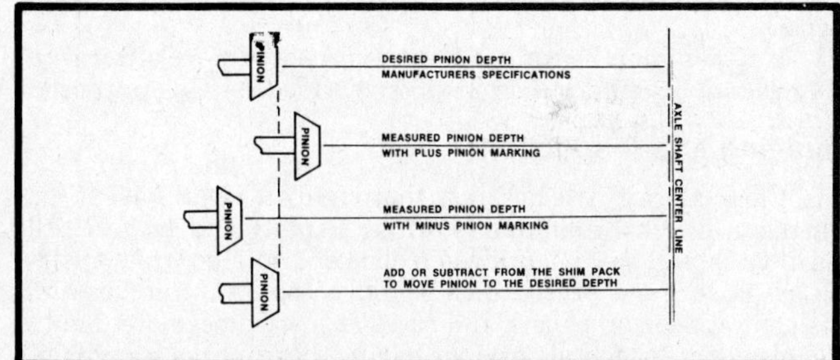

Movement of pinion to obtain desired pinion depth

Chevrolet and GMC Rear Axle Assemblies

The single speed rear axles used on the Chevrolet and GMC light and medium trucks are categorized by the ring gear diameter and are identified as follows:
7 $^1/_2$, 8 $^1/_2$, 8 $^7/_8$ in. (GMC) semi-floating axles, 9 $^3/_4$, 10 $^1/_2$ in. (Dana) full floating axles, 10 $^1/_2$ in. (GMC) full floating axles, 12 $^1/_4$ in. (Corporation) full floating axles.

Two speed axles are used by both Chevrolet and GMC trucks that are manufactured by General Motors Corporation or by Eaton Corporation. The Eaton Corporation models can be identified by their use of a spiral bevel pinion gear arrangement, while the remaining axles are of the hypoid gear arrangement.

General Motors Corporation 7 $^1/_2$ Inch Ring Gear Axle Assembly

REAR AXLE CASE

Removal

1. Before removing the rear axle case from the housing, ring gear to drive pinion backlash should be checked. This will indicate gear or bearing wear or an error in backlash or preload setting which will help in determining cause of axle noise.
2. Remove rear axle bearing cap bolts. Bearing caps should be marked "R" and "L" to make sure they will be reassembled in their original location.
3. Remove rear axle case. Excercise caution in prying on carrier so that gasket sealing surface is not damaged. Place right and left bearing outer races and shims in sets with marked bearing caps so that they can be reinstalled in their original positions.

Disassembly

1. If rear axle side bearings are to be replaced, they must be removed using a puller.
2. Remove rear axle pinions, side gears and thrust washers from case. Mark side gear and case after removing bolts. (L.H. Threads), drive it off using a brass drift and hammer. Do not pry between ring gear and case.

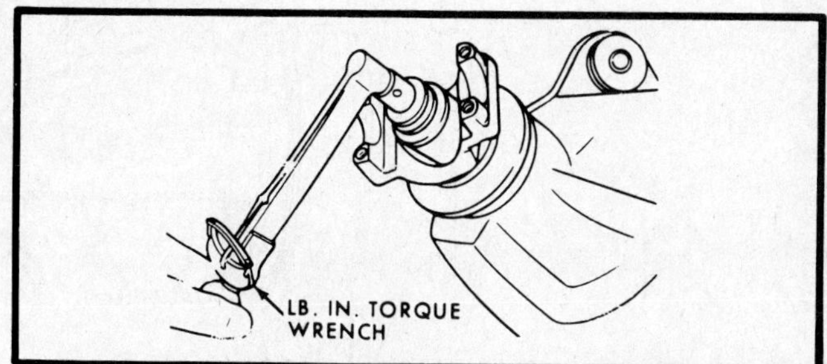

Checking the pinion pre-load

DRIVE PINION, BEARING AND RACES

Removal

1. Check drive pinion bearing pre-load. If there is no preload reading, check for looseness of pinion assembly by shaking. Looseness could be caused by defective bearings or worn pinion flange. If rear axle was operated for an extended period with very loose bearings, the ring gear and drive pinion will also require replacement.

2. Remove pinion flange nut and washer.
3. Remove pinion flange.
4. Install drive Pinion Remover J–22536 or its equal and drive out pinion. Apply heavy hand pressure on pinion remover toward rear axle housing to keep front bearing seated to avoid damage to outer race.

BEARING REPLACEMENT

Disassembly

The rear pinion bearing must be removed when it becomes necessary to change the pinion depth adjustment.

1. With drive pinion removed from carrier, press bearing from the pinion gear.
2. Drive pinion oil seal from carrier and remove front pinion bearing. If this bearing is to be replaced, remove outer race from carrier.
3. If rear pinion bearing is to be replaced, remove outer race from carrier using a punch in slots provided for this purpose.

Cleaning and Inspection

1. Clean all rear axle bearings thoroughly in clean solvent (do not use a brush). Examine bearings visually and by feel. All bearings should feel smooth when oiled and rotated while applying as much hand pressure as possible. Minute scratches and pits that appear on rollers and races at low mileage are due to the initial pre-load, and bearings having these marks should not be rejected.
2. Examine sealing surface of pinion flange for nicks, burrs, or rough tool makrs which would cause damage to the seal and result in an oil leak. Replace if damaged.
3. Examine carrier bore and remove any burrs that might cause leaks around the O.D. of the pinion seal.
4. Examine the ring gear and drive pinion teeth for excessive wear and scoring. If any of these conditions exist, replacement of the gear set will be required.
5. Inspect the pinion gear shaft for unusual wear; also check the pinion and side gears and thrust washers.
6. Check the press fit of the side bearing inner race on the rear axle case hub by prying against the shoulder at the puller recess in the case. Side bearings must be a tight press fit on the hub.
7. Diagnosis of a rear axle failure such as: chipped bearings, loose (lapped-in) bearings, chipped gears, etc., is a warning that some foreign material is present; therefore, the axle housing must be cleaned.

DRIVE PINION

Assembly

1. If a new rear pinion bearing is to be installed, install new outer races.
2. If a new front pinion bearing is to be installed, install new outer race.

SETTING PINION DEPTH

Pinion depth is set with Pinion Setting Gauge J–21777–01. The pinion setting gauge provides in effect, a "Normal" or "zero" pinion as a gauging reference. Instructions are included in gauge set.

1. Make certain all of the gauge parts are clean.
2. Lubricate front and rear pinion bearings liberally with rear axle lubricant.
3. While holding bearings in position, install depth setting gauge assembly.
4. Hold stud stationary with a wrench positioned over the flats on the ends of stud and tighten nut to 2.2 Nm (20 inch lbs.) torque. Rotate gauge plate assembly several complete revolutions to seat the bearings. Then tighten nut until a torque between 1.6 and 2.2 Nm (15 and 25 inch lbs.) is obtained to keep the gauge plate in rotation.

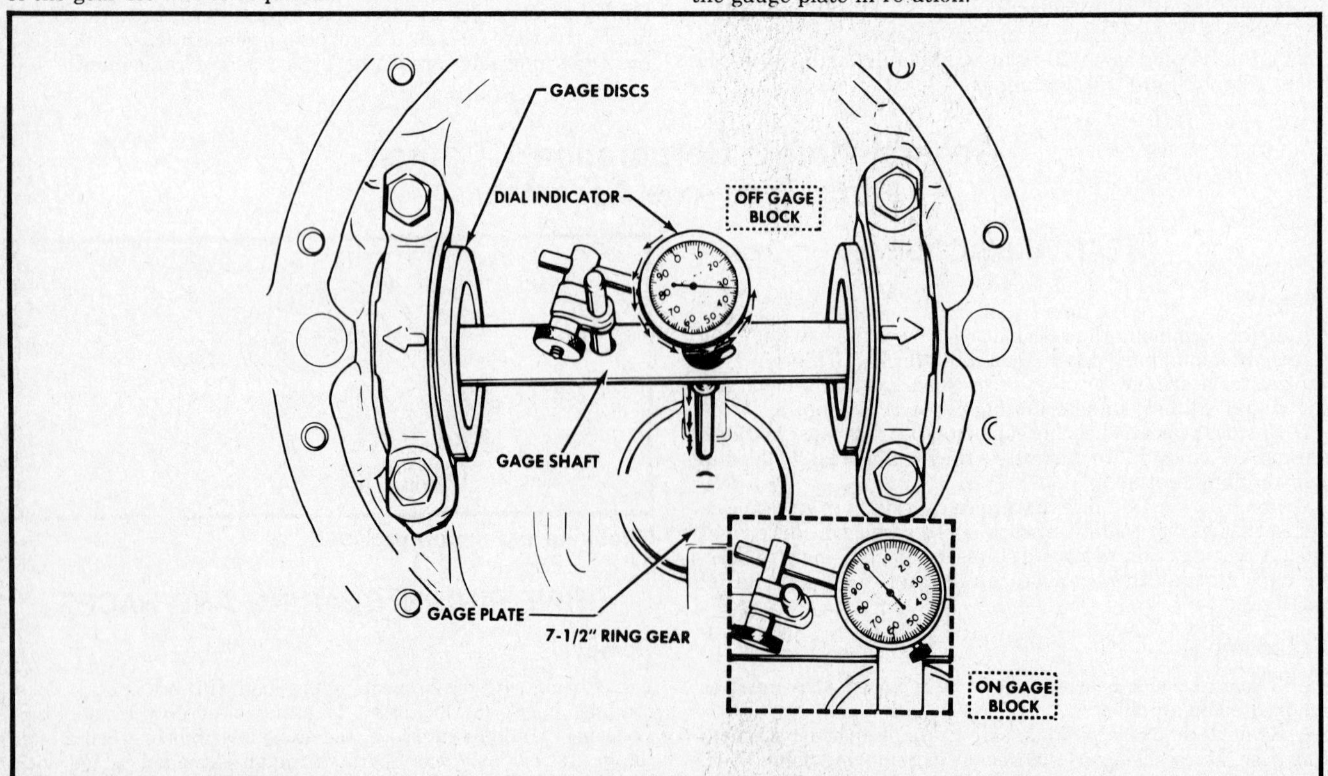

Checking the pinion depth

5. Rotate the gauge plate until the gauging areas are parallel with the discs.

6. Make certain rear axle side bearing support bores are clean and free of burrs.

7. Install the correct discs on the gauge shaft.

8. Position the gauge shaft assembly in the carrier so that the dial indicator rod is centered on the gauging area of the gauge block, and the discs seated fully in the side bearing bores. Install side bearing caps and torque bolts to 75 Nm (55 ft. lbs.). Use dial indicator J–8001 or an equivalent indicator reading from 0.0–2.5mm (0.00–100.0 inch).

9. Set dial indictor at ZERO. Then position on mounting post of the gauge shft with the contact button touching the indicator pad. Push dial indicator downward until the needle rotates approximately $^{3}/_{4}$ turn clockwise. Tighten the dial indicator in this position and recheck.

10. Rotate gauge shaft slowly back and forth until the dial indicator reads the greatest deflection. At the point of greatest deflection, set the dial idicator to ZERO. Repeat rocking action of gauge shaft to verify the ZERO setting.

11. After the ZERO setting is obtained, rotate gauge shaft until the dial indicator rod does not touch the gauge block.

12. Record dial reading at pointer position. Example: If pointer moved counterclockwise 1.70mm (0.067 in.) to a dial reading of 0.84mm (0.033 in.) except as follows: Dial indicator reading should be within the range of 0.50–1.27mm (0.020–0.050 in.).

13. Loosen Stud J–21777–43 and remove gauge plate, washer and both bearings from carrier.

14. Position correct shim on drive pinion and install the drive pinion rear bearings.

REAR AXLE CASE

Assembly

Before assembling the rear axle case, lubricate all parts with rear axle lubricant.

1. Place side gear thrust washer over side gear hubs and install side gears in case. If same parts are reused, install in original sides.

2. Position one pinion (without washer) between side gears and rotate gears until pinion is directly opposite from loading opening in case. Place other pinion between side gears so that pinion shaft holes are in line; then rotate gears to make sure holes in pinions will line up with holes in case.

3. If holes line up, rotate pinions back toward loading opening just enough to permit sliding in pinion thrust washers.

4. After making certain that mating surfces of case and ring gear are clean and free of burrs, thread two bolts into opposite sides of ring gear; then install ring gear on case. Install NEW ring gear attaching bolts just snug. NEVER REUSE OLD BOLTS. Torque bolts alternately in progressive stages to 120 Nm (90 ft. lbs.).

5. If case side bearings were removed, re-install bearings.

SIDE BEARING PRE-LOAD ADJUSTMENT

The side bearing pre-load adjustment is to be made before installing the pinion. If the pinion is installed, remove ring gear. Case side bearing pre-load is adjusted by changine the thickness of both the right and left shims by an equal amount. By changing the thickness of both shims equally, the original backlash will be maintained. Production shims are cast iron and vary in thickness from 5.33–6.91mm (0.210–0.272 in.) in increments of 0.05mm (0.002 in.). Standard service spacers are 4.32mm (0.170 in.) thick and steel service shims are available from 1.02–2.08mm (0.040–0.082 in.) in increments of 0.05mm (0.002 in.).

Do not attempt to reinstall the production shims as they may break when tapped into place. If service shims were previously installed, they can be reused, but (whether using new or old bearings) adhere to the following procedure in all cases.

1. Before installation of the case assembly, make sure that side bearing surfaces in the carrier are clean and free of burrs. If the same bearings are being reused, they must have the originl outer races in place.

2. Determine the approximate thickness of shims needed by measuring each production shim or each service spacer and shim pack.

3. In addition to the service spacer, a service shim will be needed. To select a starting point in service shim thickness, use the following chart:

4. Place case with bearing outer races in position in carrier. Slip the service spacer between each bearing race and carrier housing with chamfered edge against housing.

Install the left bearing cap loose so that the case may be moved while checking adjustments. Another bearing cap bolt can be added in the lower right bearing cap hole. This will prevent case from dropping while making shim adjustments.

Select one or two shims totaling the amount shown in the right-hand column and position between the right bearing race and the service spacer. Be sure left bearing race and spacer are against left side of housing.

4.32mm (.170") SERVICE SPACER

Total Thickness of Both Prod. Shims Removed	Total Thickness of Service Shims to be Used as a Starting Point
10.57mm .420"	1.52mm .060"
10.92mm .430"	1.78mm .070"
11.18mm .440"	2.03mm .080"
11.43mm .450"	2.29mm .090"
11.68mm .460"	2.54mm .100"
11.94mm .470"	2.79mm .110"
12.19mm .480"	3.05mm .120"
12.45mm .490"	3.30mm .130"
12.70mm .500"	3.56mm .140"
12.95mm .510"	3.81mm .150"
13.21mm .520"	4.06mm .160"
13.46mm .530"	4.32mm .170"
13.97mm .550"	4.83mm .190"

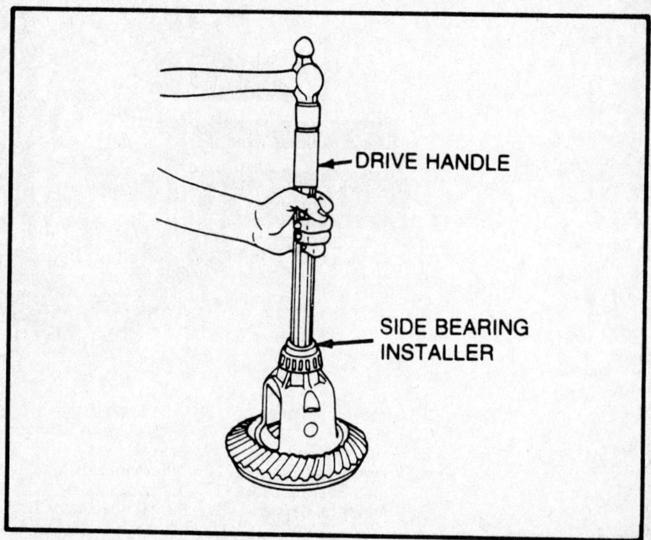

Installing case side bearings

5. Insert progressively larger feeler gauge sizes 0.25mm, 0.30mm, 0.36mm, etc. (0.010 in, 0.012 in., 0.014 in., etc.) between the right shim and service spacer until there is noticeable increased drag. Push the feeler gauge downward until the end of the gauge makes contact with the carrier bore so as to obtain a correct reading. The point just before additional drag begins is correct feeler gauge thickness. Rotate case while using feeler gauge to asure an even reading.
The original light drag is caused by weight of the case against the carrier while additional drag is caused by side bearing preload. By starting with a thin feeler gauge, a sense of "feel" is obtained so that the beginning of pre-load can be recognized to obtain Zero clearance. It will be necessary to work case in and out and to the left in order to insert the feeler gauge.

6. Remove left bearing cap and shim from carrier. The total shim pack needed (with no pre-load on side bearings) is the feeler gauge reading found in Step 5 plugs thickness of shims installed in Step 4.

7. Select two shims of approximately equal size whose total thickness is equal to the value obtained in Step 5. These shims will be installed between each side bearing race and service spacer when the case is installed in the carrier. The object of Step 7 is to obtain the equivalent of a slip fit" of the case in the carrier. For convenience in setting backlash, the "preload will not be added until the final step.

8. If the pinion is in position, install the ring gear, then proceed to REAR AXLE BACKLASH ADJUSTMENT.

DRIVE PINION, BEARING AND RACES

Installtion

1. Install NEW collapsible spacer on pinion and position assembly in carrier. Lubricate pinion bearings with Rear Axle Lubricant before installing pinion.

2. Hold forward on pinion into case assembly.

3. Install front bearing on pinion and drive bering on pinion shaft until sealed in race.

4. Position pinion oil seal in carrier. Install seal.

5. Coat lips of pinion oil seal an seal surface of pinion flange with Lubricant No. 1050169 or equivalent. Install pinion flange on pinionby tapping with a soft hammer until a few pinion threads project through flange.

6. Install pinion washer and nut. Hold pinion flange. While intermittently rotating pinion to seat pinion bearings, tighten pinion flange nut until end play begins to be taken up. When no further end play is detectable and when holder will no longer pivot freely as pinion is rotated, pre-load specifications are being approached. No further tightening should be attempted until the pre-load has been checked.

7. Check pre-load by using an in. pound torque wrench. After pre-load has been checked, final tightening should be done very carefuly. For example, if when checking, pre-load was found to be 0.6 Nm (5 inch lbs.), any additional tightening of the pinion nut can add many additional in. pounds of torque. Therefore, the pinion nut should be further tightened only a little at a time and the pre-load specifications will compress the collapsible spacer too far and require the installation of a new collpsible spacer.
While observing the preceding note, carefully set pre-load at 2.7–3.6 Nm (24 to 32 inch lbs.) on new bearings or 1.0–1.4 Nm (8–12 inch lbs.) on used bearings.

8. Rotate pinion several times to assure that bearings have been seated. Check pre-load again. If pre-load has been reduced by rotating pinion, reset pre-load to specifications.

REAR AXLE BACKLASH ADJUSTMENT

1. Install rear axle case into carrier, using shims as determined by the side bearing pre-load adjustment.

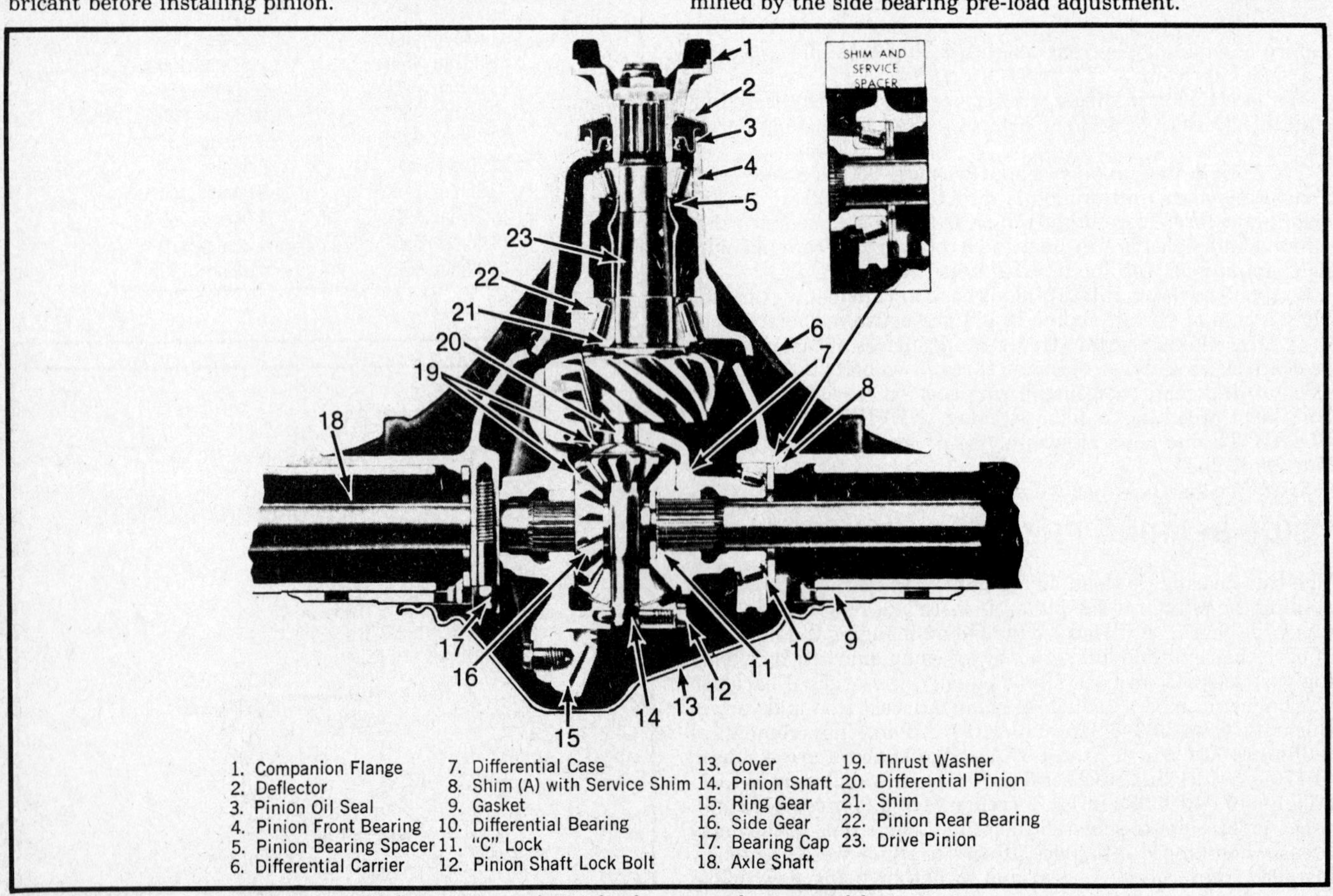

Cross section of the General Motors 8½ and 8⅞ inch rear axle assembly

2. Rotate rear axle case several times to seat bearings, then mount dial indicator. Use a small button on the indicator stem so that contct can be made near heel end of tooth. Set dial indicator so that stem is in line as nearly as possible with gear rotation and perpendicular to tooth angle for accurate backlash reading.

3. Check backlash at three or four points around ring gear. Lash must not vary over 0.05mm (0.00 in.) around ring gear. Pinion must be held stationary when checking backlash. If variation is over 0.05mm (0.002 in.) check for burrs, uneven bolting conditions or destorted case flange and make corrections as necessary.

4. Backlash at the point of minimum lash should be between 0.13 and 0.23mm (0.005 and 0.009 in.) for all new gears.

5. If backlash is not within specifications, correct by increasing thickness of one shim and decreasing thickness of other shim the same amount. This will maintain correct rear axle side bearing pre-load. For each 0.03mm (0.001 in.) change in backlash desired, transfer 0.05mm (0.002 in.) in shim thickness. To decrease backlash 0.03mm (0.001 in.), decrease thickness of right shim 0.05mm (0.002 in.) and increase thickness of left shim 0.5mm (0.002 in.). To increase backlash 0.05mm (0.002 in.), increase thickness of right shim 0.10mm (0.004 in.) and decrease thickness of left shim 0.10mm (0.004 in.).

6. When backlash is correctly adjusted, remove both bearing caps and both shim packs. Keep packs in their respective position, right or left side.
Select a shim 0.10mm (0.004 in.) thicker than one removed from left side, then insert left side shim pack between the spacer and the left bearing race. Loosely install bearing cap.

7. Select a shim 0.10mm (0.004 in.) thicker than the one removed from right side and insert between the spacer and the right bearing race. It will be necessary to drive the right shim into position.

8. Torque to 75 Nm (55 ft. lbs.).

9. Recheck backlash and correct if necessary.

10. Install axles.

11. Install new cover gasket. Install over and torque cover bolts to 27 Nm (20 ft. lbs.).

12. Fill rear axle to proper level.

General Motors Corporation 8 ½ and 8 ⅞ Inch Ring Gear Axle Assembly

This axle assembly is the semi-floating type with Hypoid type drive pinion and ring gears. The drive pinion gear is supported by two bearings. The differential case contains two pinion gears. The carrier assembly is not removable since it is part of the axle assembly but the design allows for the differential assembly to be serviced while the axle is still in the vehicle. The ring gear is bolted to a one piece differential case that is supported by two preloaded roller bearings.

DIFFERENTIAL CASE

Removal

1. Remove the inspection cover from the axle housing and drain the gear lubricant into a pan.

2. Remove the screw or pin that holds the pinion shaft in place and remove the shaft.

3. Push the axle shaft(s) in a little and remove the "C" locks from the ends of the shafts. Remove the axle shafts from the housing.

4. Before going any further, the backlash should be measured and recorded. This will allow the old gears to be reassembled at the same amount of lash to avoid changing the gear tooth pattern. It also helps to indicate if there is gear or bearing wear, and if there is any error in the original backlash setting.

5. Roll the differential pinions and thrust washers out of the case and also remove the side gears and thrust washers. Make sure to mark the pinions and side gears so they can be reassembled in their original position.

6. Mark the bearing caps and housing and loosen the retaining bolts. Tap the caps lightly to loosen them. When the caps are loose, take the bolts all the way out and then reinstall the bolts just a few turns. This will keep the case from falling out of the housing when it is pried loose.

7. With a pry bar, very carefully pry the case assembly loose. Be careful not to damage the gasket surface on the housing when prying. The case assembly may suddenly come free if the bearings were preloaded, so pry very slowly.

8. When the case assembly is loose, remove the bolts for the bearing caps and remove the caps. Place the caps so they may be reinstalled in the same position. Place any shims that are removed with the cap they were removed from.

DRIVE PINION

Removal

1. With the differential removed, check the pinion preload. Do this by checking the amount of torque needed to turn the pinion gear. For a new bearing, it should be 20–25 inch lbs., and for a used bearing it should be 10–15 inch lbs. If there is no preload reading check the pinion for looseness. If there is any looseness the bearing should be replaced.

2. With a holder assembly installed on the flange, use a socket of the proper size and remove the flange nut and washer.

3. Remove the flange by using a puller assembly and drawing the flange off the pinion splines.

4. Thread the pinion nut a few turns onto the pinion shaft. Using a brass drift and hammer, lightly tap the end of the pinion shaft to remove the pinion from the carrier. Be careful not to allow the pinion to fall out of the carrier after it breaks loose.

5. With the pinion removed from the carrier, discard the old seal pinion nut and collapsible spacer and install new ones when reassembling.

Cleaning and Inspection

1. Clean all parts in solvent and blow dry.

2. Check all of the parts for any signs of wear, chips, cracks or distortion. Replace any parts that are defective.

3. Check the fit of the differential side gears in the case and the fit of the side gear and axle shaft splines.

DIFFERENTIAL BEARING

Replacement

1. With a bearing puller attached to the bearing, pull the bearing from the case.

2. Place the new bearing on the case hub with the thick side of the inner race toward the case. Using a bearing driver, drive the bearing onto the case until it seats against the shoulder on the case.

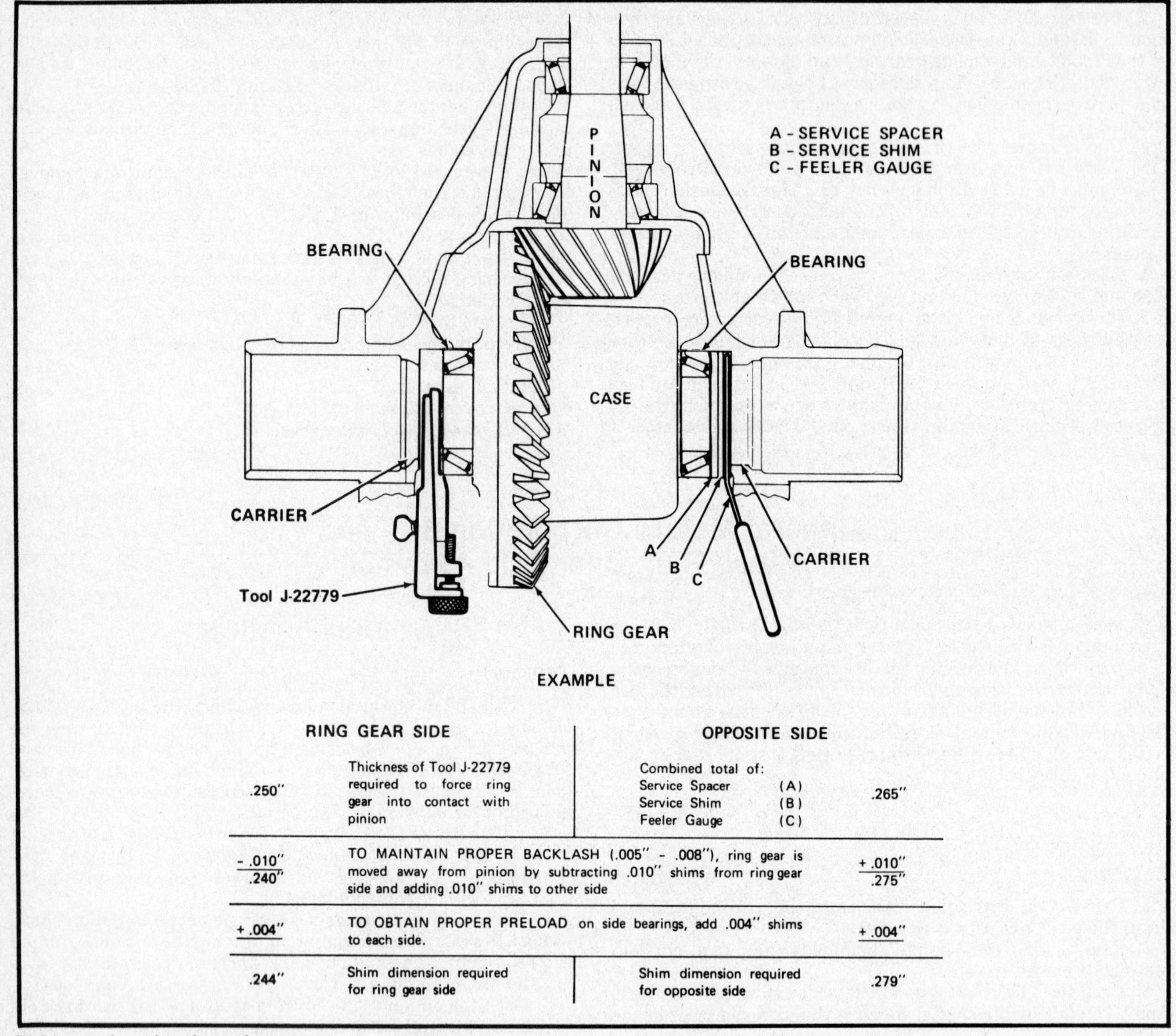

RING GEAR SIDE		OPPOSITE SIDE	
.250"	Thickness of Tool J-22779 required to force ring gear into contact with pinion	Combined total of: Service Spacer (A) Service Shim (B) Feeler Gauge (C)	.265"
-.010" / .240"	TO MAINTAIN PROPER BACKLASH (.005" - .008"), ring gear is moved away from pinion by subtracting .010" shims from ring gear side and adding .010" shims to other side		+.010" / .275"
+.004"	TO OBTAIN PROPER PRELOAD on side bearings, add .004" shims to each side.		+.004"
.244"	Shim dimension required for ring gear side	Shim dimension required for opposite side	.279"

Shim pack selection chart

DRIVE PINION BEARING

Replacement and Adjustment

1. Depending on the bearing that is being replaced, remove the front or rear bearing cup from the carrier assembly.
2. With the pinion gear mounted in a press, press the rear bearing from the pinion shaft. Be sure to record the thickness of the shims that are removed from between the bearing and the gear.
3. Using a bearing driver of the proper size, install a new bearing cup for each one that was removed. Make sure the cups are seated fully against the shoulder in the housing.
4. The pinion depth must now be checked to determine the nominal setting. This allows for machining variations in the housing and enables you to select the proper shim so that the pinion depth can be set for the best bear tooth contact.
5. Clean the housing and carrier assemblies to insure accurate measurement of the pinion depth.
6. Lubricate the front and rear pinion bearings with gear lubricant and install them in their races in the carrier assembly.
7. Using a pinion setting gauge, select the proper clover leaf plate, and install it on the preload stud.
8. Insert the stud through the rear bearing, with the proper size pilot on the stud, and through the front bearing using the proper pilot. Install the hex nut and tighten it until it is just snug.
9. Holding the preload stud with a wrench, tighten the hex nut until 20 inch lbs. of torque are required to rotate the bearings.
10. Install the side bearing discs on the ends of the arbor assembly, using the step of the disc that fits the bore of the carrier.
11. Install the arbor and plunger assembly into the carrier. Make sure the side bearing discs fit properly.
12. Install the bearing caps in the carrier assembly finger tight to make sure the discs do not move.
13. Mount a dial indicator on the mounting post of the arbor. Have the contact button resting on the top surface of the plunger.
14. Preload the dial indicator by turning it one-half revolution and tightening it in this position.

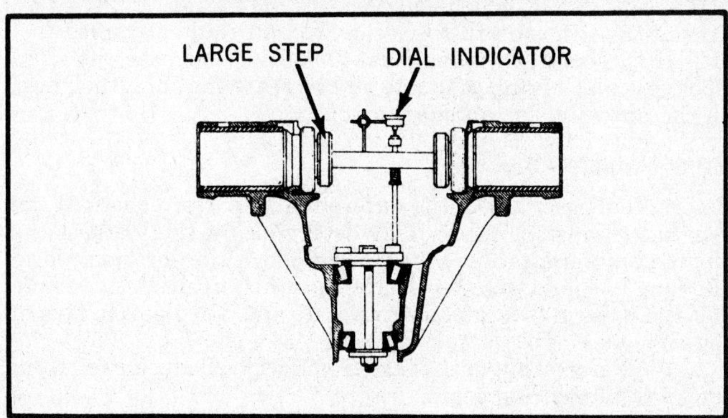

Gauge tools installed in carrier

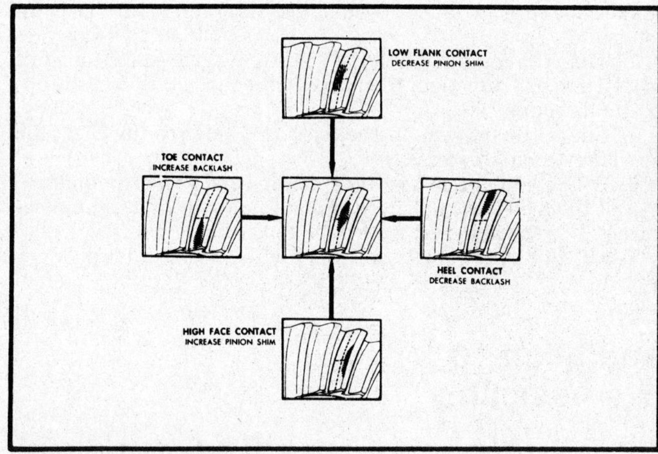

Gear tooth contact check

15. Use the button on the gauge plate that corresponds to the ring gear size and turn the plate so the plunger rests on top of it.
16. Rock the plunger rod back and forth across the top of the button until the dial indicator reads the greatest amount of variation. Set the dial indicator to zero at the point of most variation. Repeat the rocking of the plunger several times to check the setting.
17. Turn the plunger until it is removed from the gauging plate button. The dial indicator will now read the pinion shim thickness required to set the nominal pinion depth. Make a note of the reading.
18. Check for the pinion code number on the rear face of the pinion gear being used. This number will indicate the necessary change to the pinion shim thickness. If the pinion is marked with a plus (+) and a number, add that much to the reading you got from the dial indicator. If the pinion has no mark, use the reading from the dial indicator as the correct shim thickness. If the pinion is marked with a minus (−) and a number, subtract that much from the reading on the dial indicator.
19. Remove the depth gauging tools from the carrier assembly and install the proper size shim on the pinion gear.
20. Lubricate the bearing with gear lubricant and using a press, press the bearing into place on the pinion shaft.

PINION GEAR

Installation and Adjustment

1. Lubricate the front bearing with gear lubricant and install it in the front cup.
2. Install the pinion seal in the bore. Using a seal driver and the proper size gauge plate, drive the seal in until the gauge plate is flush with the shoulder of the carrier.
3. Coat the seal lips with gear lubricant and install a new bearing spacer on the pinion gear.
4. Install the pinion gear in the carrier assembly and using a large washer and nut, draw the pinion gear in through the front bearing far enough to get companion flange in place.
5. With the companion flange installed on the pinion shaft, use a holder assembly and tighten the pinion nut until all of the end play is removed from the drive pinion.
6. When there is no more end play the preload should be checked. The preload of the bearing is the amount of torque required to turn the pinion gear. The preload should be 20–25 iinch lbs. on new bearings and 10–15 inch lbs. on reused bearings. Tighten the pinion nut until these figures are reached. Do Not over tighten the pinion. This will collapse the spacer too much and make it necessary to replace it.
7. Turn the pinion gear several times to make sure the bearings are seated and recheck the preload.

RING GEAR

Replacement

1. Remove all of the bolts that hold the ring gear to the differential case and with a soft hammer, tap the ring gear off the case.

NOTE: Do not try to pry the ring gear off the case. This will damage the machined surfaces.

2. Clean all dirt from the case assembly and lubricate the case with gear lube. Align the ring gear bolt holes with the holes in the carrier and lightly press the ring gear onto the case assembly. Install all of the bolts and tighten them all evenly, using a criss-cross pattern to avoid cocking the ring gear.
3. When the ring gear is firmly seated against the case, tighten the bolts to 60 ft. lbs.

DIFFERENTIAL CASE ASSEMBLY

Installation and Adjustment

1. Install the thrust washers and side gears into the case assembly. If the original parts are being used, be sure to place them in their original position.
2. Place the pinions in the case so they are 180 degrees apart as they engage the side gears.
3. Turn the pinion gears so the hole in the case lines up with the holes in the gears. When the holes are aligned, install the pinion shaft and lock screw. Do not tighten the lock screw too tightly at this time.
4. Check the bearings, bearing cups, cup seat and carrier caps to make sure they are in good condition.
5. Lubricate the bearings with gear lube. Install the cups on the proper bearings and install the differential assembly in the carrier. Support the carrier assembly to keep it from falling.
6. Install a support strap on the left side bearing and tighten the bearing bolts to an even, snug fit.
7. With the ring gear tight against the pinion gear, insert a gauging tool between the left side bearing cup and the carrier housing.
8. While lightly shaking the tool back and forth, turn the adjusting wheel until a slight drag is felt. Tighten the lock nut.
9. Between the right side bearing and carrier, install a service spacer, 0.170 in. thick, a service shim and a feeler gauge. The feeler gauge must be thick enough so a light drag is felt when it is moved between the carrier and the shim.
10. Add the total of the service spacer, service shim and the feeler gauge. Remove the gauging tool from the left side of the carrier and using a micrometer, measure the thickness in at least three places. Average the readings and record the result.
11. Refer to the chart to determine the proper thickness of the shim packs.

12. Install the left side shim first, then install the right side shim between the bearing cup and spacer. Position the shim so the chamfered side is outward or next to the spacer. If there is not enough chamfer around the outside of the shim, file or grind the chamfer a little to allow for easy installation.

13. If there is difficulty in installing the shim, partially remove the case from the carrier and slide both the shim and case back into place.

14. Install the bearing caps and torque them to 60 ft. lbs. Tighten the pinion shaft lock screw.

NOTE: The differential side bearings are now preloaded. If any adjustments are made in later procedures, make sure not to change the preload. Do Not change the total thickness of the shim packs.

15. Mount a dial indicator on the carrier assembly with the indicator button perpendicular to the tooth angle and in line with the gear rotation.

16. Measure the amount of backlash between the ring and pinion gears. The backlash should be between 0.005–0.008 in. Take readings at four different spots on the gear. There should not be variations greater than 0.002 in.

17. If there are variations greater than 0.002 in. between the readings, check the runout between the case and ring gear. The gear runout should not be greater than 0.003 in. If the runout does exceed 0.003 in. check the case and ring gear for the deformation or dirt between the case and gear.

18. If the gear backlash exceeds 0.008 in., increase the thickness of the shims on the ring gear side and decrease the thickness of the shims on the opposite side, an equal amount.

19. If the backlash is less than 0.005 in., decrease the shim thickness on the ring gear side and increase the shim thickness on the opposite side an equal amount.

Gear Pattern Check

Before final assembly of the differential, a pattern check of the gear teeth must be made. This determines if the teeth of the ring and pinion gears are meshing properly, for low noise level and long life of the gear teeth. The most important thing to note is if the pattern is located centrally up and down on the face of the ring gear.

1. Wipe any oil out of the carrier and wipe all dirt and oil from the teeth of the ring gear.
2. Coat the teeth of the ring gear with a gear marking compound.
3. With the bearing caps torqued to 55 ft. lbs., expand the brake shoes until it takes 20–30 ft. lbs. of torque to turn the pinion gear.
4. Turn the companion flange so the ring gear makes one full rotation in one direction, then turn it one full rotation in the opposite direction.
5. Check the pattern on the teeth and refer to the chart for any adjustments necessary.
6. With the gear tooth pattern checked and properly adjusted, install the axle housing cover gasket and cover and tighten securely. Fill the axle with gear lube to the correct level.
7. Road test the vehicle to check for any noise and proper operation of the rear.

General Motors Corporation 10 1/2 Inch Ring Gear Axle Assembly

This axle is a full floating type that uses special hypoid type drive and pinion gears. The pinion gear is supported by three bearings, two in front of the pinion gear and one behind. The differential assembly has either two or four pinions depending on the application of the axle. This axle assembly must be removed from the vehicle to remove and service the differential.

DIFFERENTIAL

Removal

1. With the axle assembly removed from the vehicle, place the axle assembly in a vise or holding fixture.
2. Remove the bolts that retain the cover assembly and remove the cover, allowing the gear lubricant to drain into a pan.
3. Remove the axle shafts from the axle assembly.

NOTE: Before going any further, check the pinion backlash and record the measurement so that if the same gears are reused they may be installed at the same backlash to avoid changing the gear tooth pattern.

4. From the bearing caps, remove the adjusting nut lock retainers.
5. Mark the bearing caps so they may be reinstalled in the same position and remove the bearing caps.
6. Loosen the side bearing adjusting nut and remove the differential carrier from the axle housing.

PINION ASSEMBLY

Removal

1. Remove the differential assembly from the axle.
2. Check the pinion bearing for the proper preload. The force required to turn the pinion should be 25–35 inch lbs. for used bearings. If there is no reading, shake the companion flange to check for any looseness in the bearing. If there is any looseness present the bearing should be replaced.
3. Remove the retaining bolts for the pinion bearing from the axle housing.
4. Remove the bearing retainer and pinion assembly from the axle housing. It may be necessary to tap the pilot end of the pinion shaft to help remove the pinion assembly from the carrier.
5. Record the thickness of the shims that are removed from between the carrier assembly and the bearing retainer assembly.

DRIVE PINION

Disassembly

1. With the pinion assembly clamped in a vise, install a holder assembly on the flange.
2. Using the proper size socket, remove the pinion nut and washer from the pinion. When reassembling the pinion use a new nut and washer assembly.
3. With the holder assembly still in place, use a puller to remove the flange from the pinion.
4. With the bearing retainer supported in a press, press the pinion out of the retainer assembly. Be careful not to allow the pinion gear to fall onto the floor because this can damage the gear.
5. Separate the pinion flange, oil seal, front bearing and the bearing retainer. If the oil seal needs to be replaced it may have to be driven from the retainer.
6. Using a drift, drive the front and rear bearing cups from the bearing retainer.
7. Support the pinion assembly in a press, with the bearing supported. Press the bearing from the pinion gear.
8. Using a drift, drive the straddle bearing from the carrier assembly.

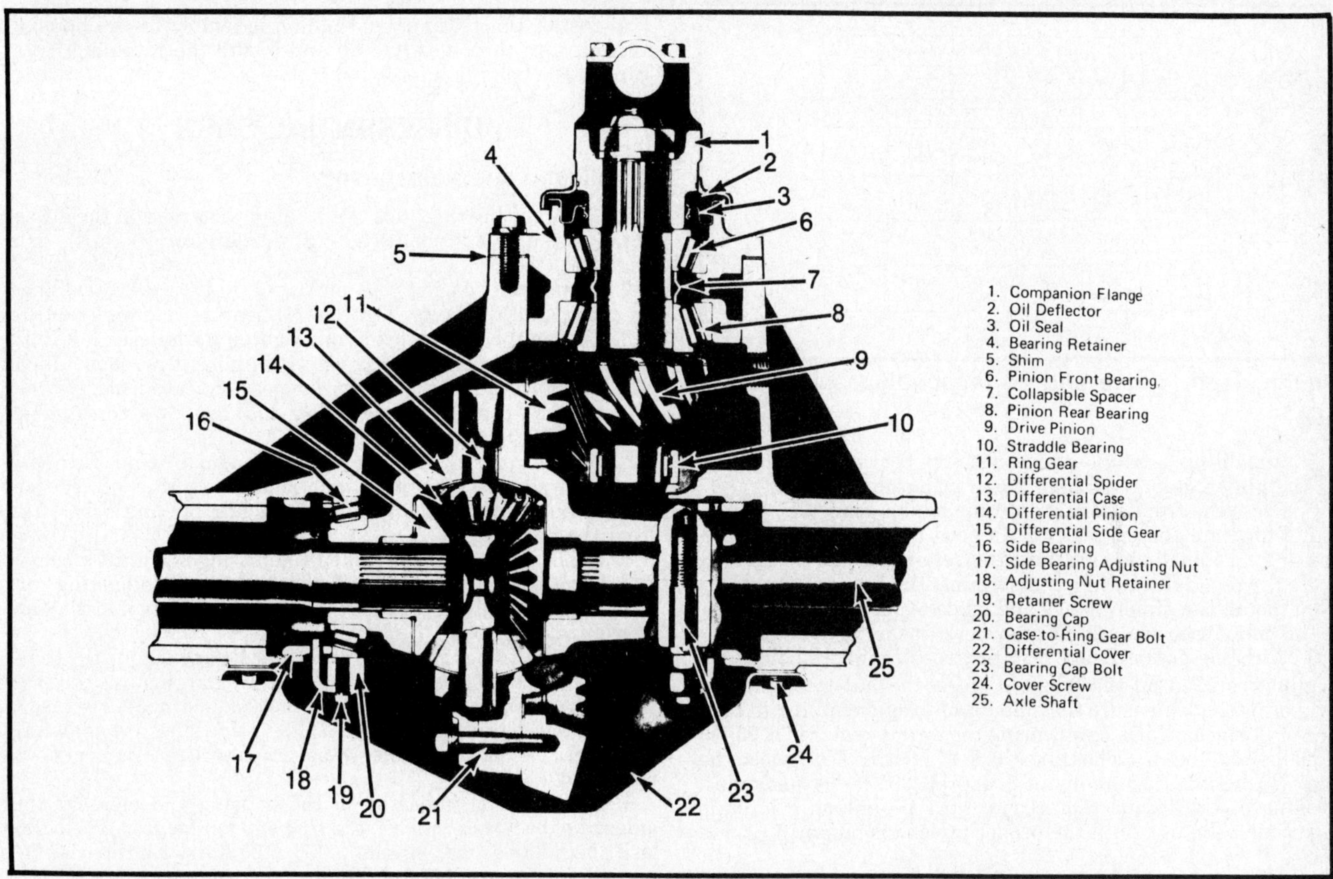

Cross section of General Motors 10½ inch rear assembly

Cleaning and Inspection

1. Clean off all the parts in solvent and blow dry.
2. Check the pinion gear for signs of wear, chips, cracks or any other imperfections. Check the splines for signs of wear or distortion.
3. Check the bearings for signs of wear or pitting on the rollers and races and check the bearing cage for dents and bends. Check the bearing retainer for any cracks, pits, grooves or corrosion.
4. Check the pinion flange splines for any signs of wear or distortion.
5. Replace parts that show any of the signs mentioned above.

DIFFERENTIAL CASE

Disassembly

1. Scribe a line across the two halves of the differential case so they may be reassembled in the same position, and with the ring gear removed, separate the two halves. To remove the ring gear, remove the ring gear bolts and washers, and using a soft hammer tap the ring gear from the case.
2. Remove the internal parts from the inside of the case and set them aside in order that they may be reassembled in the same position.

Cleaning and Inspection

1. Check the differential gears, pinions, thrust washers and spider for any signs of unusual wear, chips, cracks or pitting.
2. Check all mating surfaces for signs of wear.
3. Replace parts that show any of the signs mentioned above.

DIFFERENTIAL CASE

Assembly

1. Using a good quality gear lubricant coat all of the parts.
2. Assemble the differential pinions and thrust washers onto the spider and install the assembly into the differential case.
3. Line up the scribe marks on the two halves of the differential case and install the ring gear. Install the ring gear washers and bolts and torque the bolts to approx. 10 ft. lbs.

SIDE BEARING

Replacement

1. Install a bearing puller on the bearing and remove the bearing assembly from the differential case.
2. Check the bearings for any signs of wear on distortion.
3. Install the new bearing by setting it in place on the differential case and, using a bearing driver, drive the bearing onto the case assembly until it seats against the shoulder on the case.

DRIVE PINION

Assembly and Adjustment

1. Coat all of the parts with a good quality gear lubricant.
2. With the pinion gear in a press, press the rear bearings onto the pinion assembly.
3. In the bearing retainer, install the front and rear bearing cups using a driver of the proper size.
4. In the axle housing, install the straddle bearing assembly using the proper size driver.

		CODE NUMBER ON ORIGINAL PINION				
		+2	+1	0	-1	-2
CODE NUMBER ON SERVICE PINION	+2	–	ADD .001	ADD .002	ADD .003	ADD .004
	+1	SUBT. .001	–	ADD .001	ADD .002	ADD .003
	0	SUBT. .002	SUBT. .001	–	ADD .001	ADD .002
	-1	SUBT. .003	SUBT. .002	SUBT. .001	–	ADD .001
	-2	SUBT. .004	SUBT. .003	SUBT. .002	SUBT. .001	–

Pinion depth codes and corresponding shim thickness

5. Install the bearing retainer with the bearing cups in place on the pinion gear and install a new collapsible spacer.
6. Press the front bearing onto the pinion gear.
7. Lubricate the oil seal with a good quality high pressure grease and install the seal into the retainer bore. Be sure to press the seal down until it rests against the internal shoulder.
8. Install the pinion flange and oil deflector onto the splines of the pinion gear and install a new lock washer and pinion nut.
9. With the pinion flange clamped in a vise and a holder assembly installed on the flange, tighten the nut to obtain the proper preload. Measure the amount of torque required to turn the pinion gear. For a new bearing the torque required is 25–35 inch lbs. and for an old bearing it is 5–15 inch lbs. To preload the bearing, tighten the pinion nut to approx. 350 ft. lbs. and take a reading of the torque required to turn the pinion. Continue tightening the nut until the proper preload is obtained.

CAUTION

Do not tighten the nut too tightly because it will collapse the spacer too much. This will make replacement necessary.

DRIVE PINION ASSEMBLY

Installation

1. If installing a new pinion gear, check the top of the new gear for the depth code number.
2. Compare the new number with the old number on top of the old pinion and check the pinion depth chart for preliminary setting of the pinion depth.
3. Check the thickness of the original shims removed from the pinion and either add or subtract from the shims according to the chart.
4. Place the shim on the carrier assembly and line the holes up with those in the axle housing. Make sure the surfaces are clean of all dirt and grease.
5. Install the retainer and pinion assembly in the housing making sure the holes line up and install the retaining bolts. Torque the bolts to approx. 45 ft. lbs.

DIFFERENTIAL CASE

Installation and Adjustments

1. Place the bearing cups over the side bearings on the differential assembly and place the unit into the carrier in the axle housing.
2. Install the bearing caps making sure the marks are lined up and install the bolts. Tighten the bearing retaining bolts.
3. Loosen the right side nut and tighten the left side nut until the ring gear comes in contact with the pinion gear. Do not force the gears together. This brings the gears to zero lash.
4. Back off the left side adjusting nut about two slots and install the lock fingers into the nut.
5. In this order tighten the right side adjusting nut firmly to force the case assembly into tight contact with the left side adjusting nut and then loosen the right side nut until it is free from the bearing.
6. Again retighten the right side adjusting nut until it comes in contact with the bearing. Tighten the right adjusting nut about two slots if it is an old bearing or three slots if it is a new bearing.
7. Install the lock retainers into the slots and torque the bearing cap bolts to 100 ft. lbs. This procedure now insures that the bearings are preloaded properly. If more adjustments are made, make sure the preload stays the same. To do this, one adjusting nut must be loosened the same amount the other nuts is tightened.
8. Install a dial indicator on the housing and measure the amount of backlash between the ring and pinion gear. The backlash should measure between 0.003–0.012 in. with the best figure being between 0.005–0.008 in.
9. If the backlash is more than 0.012 in., loosen the right side adjusting nut one slot and tighten the left side one slot. If the backlash is less than 0.003 in., loosen the left side nut one slot and tighten the right side one slot. These adjustments should bring the backlash measurement into an acceptable range.

Pattern Check

1. Clean all the oil off the ring gear and using a gear marking compound, coat all of the teeth of the ring gear.
2. Make sure the bearing caps are torqued to 110 ft. lbs. and apply load to the gears while rotating the pinion. Rotate the ring gear one full turn in both directions.

NOTE: Load must be applied to the assembly while rotating or the pattern will not show completely.

3. Check the pattern on the ring gear and following the chart, adjust the assembly to get the contact pattern located centrally on the face of the ring gear teeth.

Dana Corporation

9 3/4 AND 10 1/2 Inch RING GEAR AXLE ASSEMBLIES

The Dana Corporation's 9 3/4 and 10 1/2 in. ring gear axle assemblies are basically the same, but with certain exceptions. The differential side bearing shims are located between the side bearing cup assembly and the differential case on the 9 3/4 in. ring gear axle assembly, while on the 10 1/2 in. ring gear axle assembly, the side bearing shims are located between the side bearing cup and the axle housing. Both axles use inner and outer shims on the pinion gear. The inner shims are used to control the pinion depth in the housing, while the outer shims are used to preload the pinion bearings. The 9 3/4 in. ring gear axle uses a solid differential carrier with a removable side and pinion gear shaft. The 10 1/2 in. ring gear axle uses a split differential carrier with the side and pinion gears mounted on a cross shaft.

DIFFERENTIAL CASE

Removal

9 3/4 AND 10 1/2 INCH RING GEAR ASSEMBLIES

1. The axle assembly can be overhauled either in or out of the vehicle, depending on the repairman's discretion. Either way,

the free-floating axles and wheel assemblies must be removed.

2. Drain the lubricant and remove the rear cover and gasket.

3. Matchmark the bearing caps and the housing for reassembly in the same position. Remove the bearing caps and bolts.

4. Using a spreader tool mounted to the carrier housing, spread the housing a maximum of 0.015 in.

CAUTION

Do not exceed this measurement. The housing could be permanently damaged. The use of a dial indicator is recommended to prevent overstretching the housing.

5. Using a pry bar, remove the differential case from the housing. Separate the shims and record the dimensions and location on the 10 1/2 in. ring gear axle. Remove the spreader tool from the housing.

Disassembly

10 1/2 in.

1. Remove the differential side bearings from the case, using the necessary puller tools.

2. Remove the ring gear bolts and tap the ring gear from the case with a soft-faced hammer.

3. Scribe the case halves for reassembly and remove the retaining bolts.

4. Tap the top half of the case to separate it from the bottom half. Remove the internal gears, washers and cross.

Inspection

9 3/4 AND 10 1/2 INCH

1. Clean the gears, bearings and component parts with solvent and inspect for scoring, chipping or excessive wear.

2. Replace the necessary parts as required.

Assembly

10 1/2 INCH

1. Install new thrust washers to the side gears and lubricate the contact surfaces.

2. Assemble the side gears, pinion bears, washers and cross shaft into the flanged half of the case.

3. Install the top half of the case to the bottom half, making sure the scribe marks are lined up.

4. Install the retaining bolts finger tight. Then tighten the bolts alternately to the proper torque specifications.

5. If a new ring gear is to be installed or the old one used, install it to the differential case and align the bolt holes. Tighten the bolts aternately to the proper torque specifications.

6. Install the side carrier bearings by using the proper installation tools.

7. Cover the assembled unit and set aside until ready for the installation into the housing.

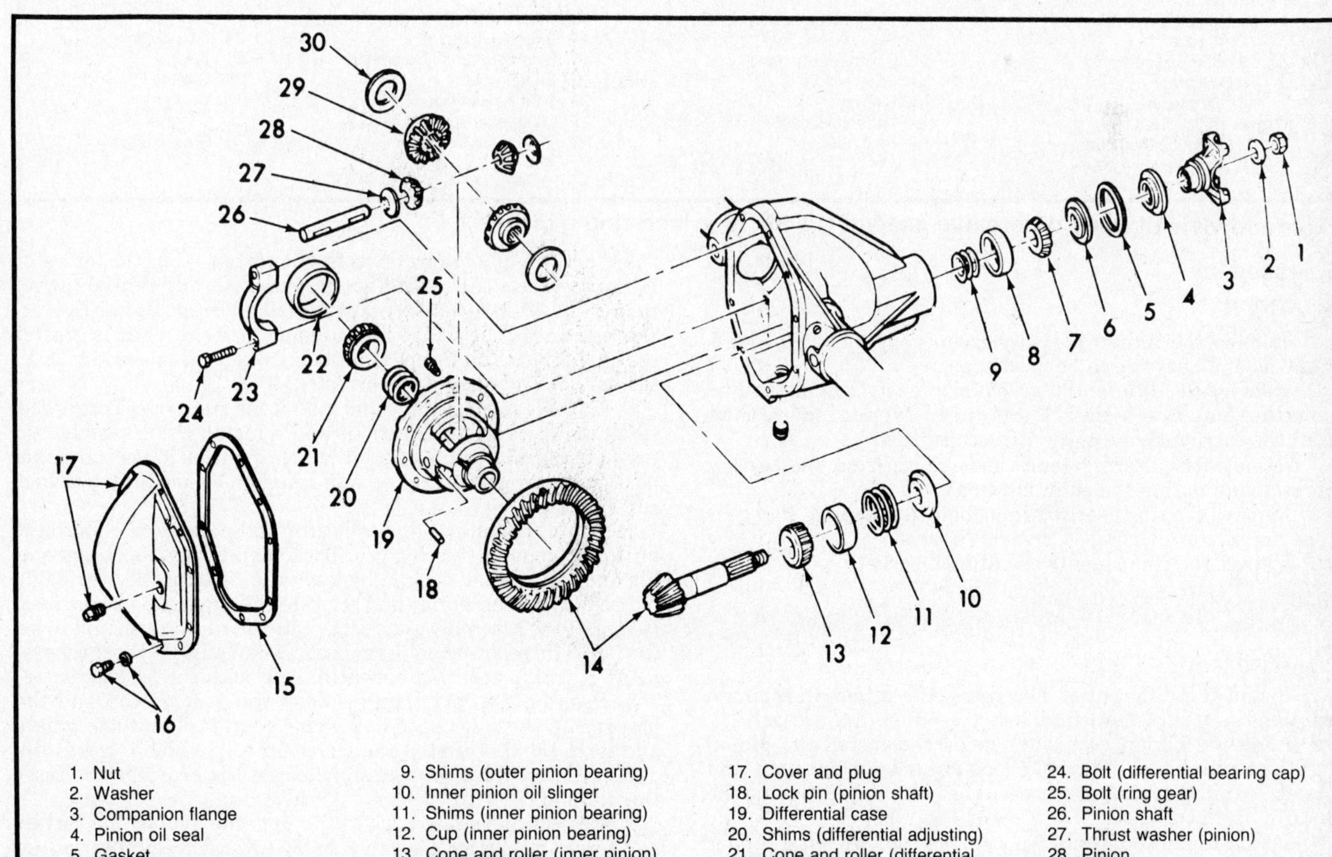

Exploded view of the Dana differential assembly with 9¾ inch ring gear

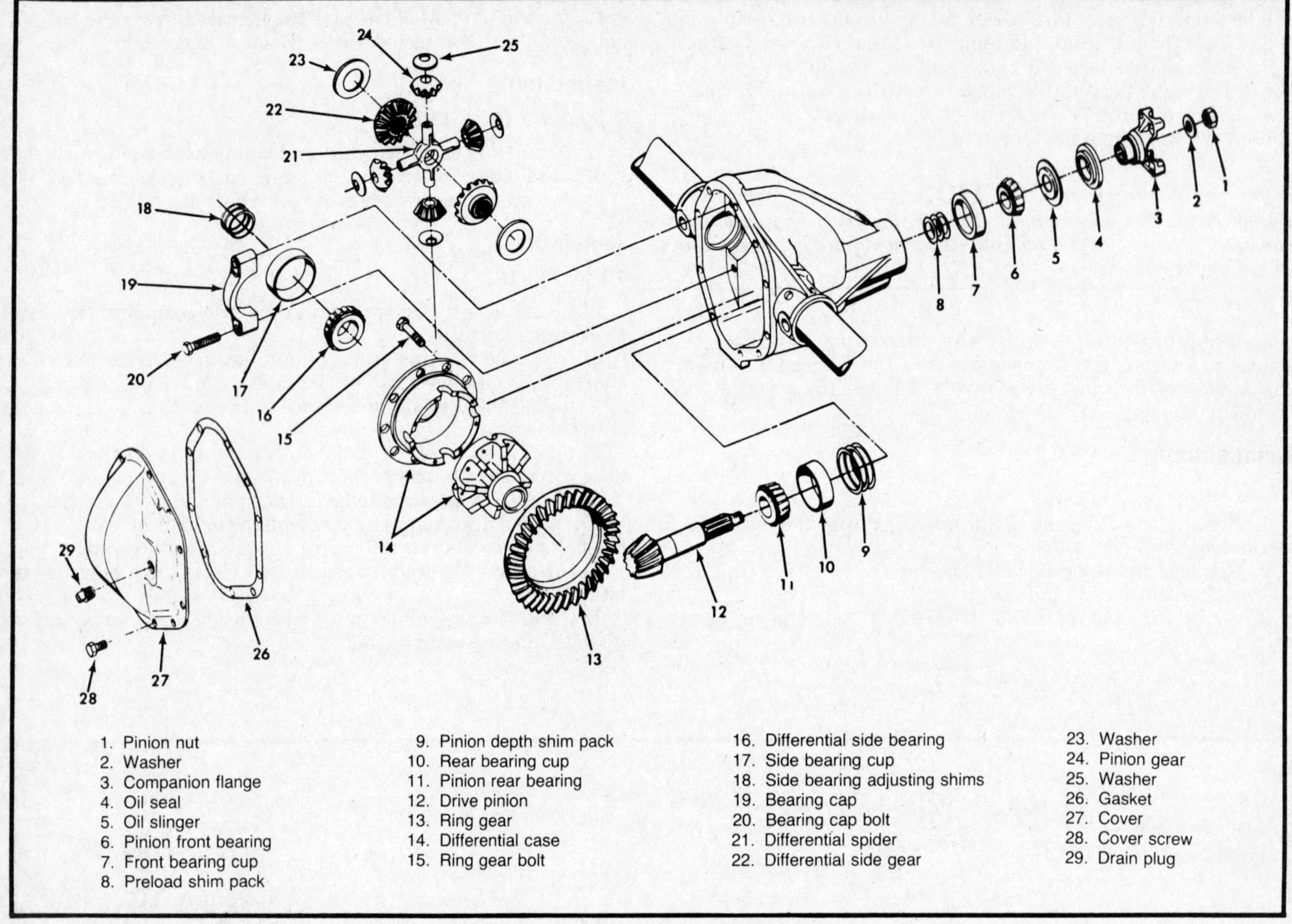

Exploded view of Dana differential assembly with 10¾ inch ring gear

Disassembly

9 3/4 INCH

1. Remove the differential side bearing cups and tag to identify the side, if they are to be used again.
2. Remove the differential gear pinion shaft lock pin and remove the shaft. Rotate the side and pinion gears to remove them from the carrier. Remove the thrust bearings.
3. Remove the bearing cones and rollers from the carrier, marking and noting the shim locations.
4. Remove the ring gear retaining bolts and tap the ring gear from the carrier housing.
5. Inspect the components as outlined earlier.

Assembly

9 3/4 INCH

1. Install the differential side gears, the differential pinion gears and new thrust washers into the differential carrier.
2. Align the pinion gear shaft holes and install the pinion shaft into the carrier. Align the lock pin hole in the shaft and carrier. Install the lock pin and peen the hole to avoid having the pin drop from the carrier.
3. Install the differential case side bearings with the proper installation tools. Do not install the shims at this time.
4. Place the carrier assembly into the axle housing with the bearing cups on the bearing cones. Install the bearing caps in their original position and tighten the bearing cap bolts enough to keep the bearing caps in place.
5. Install a dial indicator on the housing so that the indicator button contacts the carrier flange. Press the differential carrier to prevent side play and center the dial indicator. Rotate the carrier and check the flange for run-out. If the run-out is greater than 0.002 in., the defect is probably due to the bearings or to the carrier and should be corrected.
6. Remove the assembly and install the ring gear. Torque the retaining bolts to specifications and reinstall the assembly into the housing and again install the bearing caps in their original position and tighten the cap bolts enough to keep the bearings caps in place.
7. Again, install the dial indicator and position the indicator button to contact the ring gear back surface. Rotate the assembly and the run-out should be less than 0.002 in. If over 0.002 in., remove the assembly and relocate the ring gear 180 degrees. Reinstall the assembly and recheck. If the run-out remains over the 0.002 in. tolerance, the ring gear is defective. If the measurement is within tolerances, continue on with the assembly.
8. Position two pry bars between the bearing cap and the housing on the side opposite the ring gear. Pull on the pry bars and force the differential carrier as far as possible towards the dial indicator. Rock the assembly to seat the bearings and reset the dial indicator to "0".
9. Reposition the prybars to the opposite side of the carrier and force the carrier assembly as far towards the center of the housing. Read the dial indicator scale. This will be the total amount of shims required for setting the backlash during the reassembly, less the bearing preload. Record the measurement.
10. Remove the differential carrier from the housing and set aside.

SIDE BEARING SHIM SELECTION FOR THE 10 $^1/_2$ INCH

1. With the pinion gear not in the axle housing, place the bearing cups over the side bearings and install the differential carrier into the axle housing.
2. Place the shim that was originally installed on the ring gear side back into its original position.
3. Install the bearing caps in their proper positions and tighten the bolts enough to keep the bearings in place.
4. Mount a dial indicator on the axle housing with the indicator button contacting the back of the ring gear.
5. Position two prybars between the bearing shim and the housing on the ring gear side of the differential carrier. Force the differential carrier away from the dial indicator and set the indicator to "0".
6. Reposition the prybars to the opposite side of the differential carrier and force the carrier back towards the dial indicator. Repeat several times until the same reading is obtained each time.
7. To the dial indicator reading, add the thickness of the shim and record the results to be used later in the assembly.

DRIVE PINION

Removal

9 $^3/_4$ AND 10 $^1/_2$ INCH

1. Remove the pinion nut and flange from the pinion gear, using the proper removing tools.
2. Remove the pinion gear assembly from the housing. It may be necessary to tap the pinion from the housing with a soft faced hammer. Catch the pinion so as not to allow it to drop on the floor.
3. With a long drift, remove the inner bearing cup, pinion seal, slinger, gasket, outer pinion bearing and the shim pack. Tag the shim pack for reassembly.
4. Remove the rear pinion bearing cup and shim pack from the housing. Tag the shims for reassembly.
5. Remove the rear pinion bearing from the pinion gear with an arbor press and special plates.

Inspection of the Components

1. Clean all components in a solvent and inspect the bearings, cups and rollers for scoring, chipping or excessive wear. Inspect the flanges and splines for excessive wear. Inspect all gear surfaces for excessive wear or chipping.
2. Replace the necessary bearing assemblies, gears and thrustwashers as required.

PINION SHIM SELECTION

Ring gears and pinions are supplied in matched sets only. The matched numbers are etched on both gears for verification. On the rear face of the pinion, a + (plus) or a − (minus) number will be etched, indicating the best running position for each particular gear set. This dimension is controlled by the shimming behind the inner bearing cup. Whenever baffles or oil slingers are used, they become part of the adjusting shim pack. An example: If a pinion is etched +3, this pinion would require 0.003 in. less shims than a pinion etched 0. This means by removing shims, the mounting distance of the pinion is increased by 0.003 in., which is just what a + (plus) etching indicates. If a pinion is etched −3, it would be necessary to add 0.003 in. more shims than would be required if the pinion was etched 0. By adding the 0.003 in. shims, the mounting distance of the pinion is decreased 0.003 in., which is just what the − (minus) etching indicates. Pinion adjusting shims are available in thicknesses of 0.003, 0.005 and 0.010 in. An example: If a new gear set is used and the old pinion reads +2 and the new pinion reads −2, add 0.004 in. shims to the original shim pack.

Assembly

9 $^3/_4$ AND 10 $^1/_2$ INCH

1. Select the correct pinion depth shims and install in the rear pinion bearing cup bore.
2. Install the rear bearing cup in the axle housing with the proper tool.
3. Add or subtract an equal amount of shim thickness to or from the preload or outer shim pack, as was added or subtracted from the inner shim pack.
4. Install the front pinion bearing cup into its bore in the axle housing.

Old Pinion Marking	New Pinion Marking								
	- 4	- 3	- 2	- 1	0	+ 1	+ 2	+ 3	+ 4
+ 4	+ 0.008	+ 0.007	+ 0.006	+ 0.005	+ 0.004	+ 0.003	+ 0.002	+ 0.001	0
+ 3	+ 0.007	+ 0.006	+ 0.005	+ 0.004	+ 0.003	+ 0.002	+ 0.001	0	- 0.001
+ 2	+ 0.006	+ 0.005	+ 0.004	+ 0.003	+ 0.002	+ 0.001	0	- 0.001	- 0.002
+ 1	+ 0.005	+ 0.004	+ 0.003	+ 0.002	+ 0.001	0	- 0.001	- 0.002	- 0.003
0	+ 0.004	+ 0.003	+ 0.002	+ 0.001	0	- 0.001	- 0.002	- 0.003	- 0.004
- 1	+ 0.003	+ 0.002	+ 0.001	0	- 0.001	- 0.002	- 0.003	- 0.004	- 0.005
- 2	+ 0.002	+ 0.001	0	- 0.001	- 0.002	- 0.003	- 0.004	- 0.005	- 0.006
- 3	+ 0.001	0	- 0.001	- 0.002	- 0.003	- 0.004	- 0.005	- 0.006	- 0.007
- 4	0	- 0.001	- 0.002	- 0.003	- 0.004	- 0.005	- 0.006	- 0.007	- 0.008

Correction of shims from old pinion to new pinion—Dana 9¾ and 10½ inch ring gear

5. Press the rear pinion bearing onto the pinion gear shaft and install the pinion gear with bearing into the axle housing.

6. Install the preload shims and the front pinion bearing. Do not install the oil seal at this time.

7. Install the flange with the holding bar tool attached, the washer and the nut on the pinion shaft end. Torque the nut to 250 ft. lbs. for the 10 $^1/_2$ in. and 255 ft. lbs. for the 9 $^3/_4$ in.

8. Remove the holding bar from the flange and with an in. pound torque wrench, measure the rotating torque of the pinion gear. The rotating torque should be 10–20 inch lbs. with the original bearings and 20–40 inch lbs. with new bearings. Disregard the torque reading necessary to start the shaft to turn.

9. If the preload torque is not in specifications, adjust the shim pack as required.

a. To increase preload, decrease the thickness of the preload shim pack.

b. To decrease preload, increase the thickness of the preload shim pack.

10. When the proper preload is obtained, remove the nut, washer and flange from the pinion shaft.

11. Install a new pinion seal into the housing and reinstall the flange, washer and nut. Using the holder tool, torque the nut to 250 ft. lbs. for the 10 $^1/_2$ in. and 255 ft. lbs. for the 9 $^3/_4$ in.

Assembly of Differential Carrier Into Axle Housing

9 $^3/_4$ INCH

1. As outlined in the Differential Carrier Assembly procedure, the amount of shims required for setting the backlash less bearing preload had been selected and the measurement recorded.

2. With the pinion gear installed and properly set, position the differential carrier assembly into the axle housing and install the bearing caps in their proper positions. Tighten the cap bolts just enough to hold the bearing cups in place.

3. Install a dial indicator on the axle housing with the indicator button contacting the back of the ring gear.

4. Position two prybars between the bearing cup and the axle housing on the ring gear side of the case and pry the ring gear into mesh with the pinion gear teeth, as far as possible. Rock the ring gear to allow the teeth to mesh and the bearings to seat. With the pressure still applied by the prybars, set the dial indicator to "0".

5. Reposition the prybars on the opposite side of ring gear and pry the gear as far as it will go. Take the dial indicator reading. Repeat this procedure until the same reading is obtained each time. This reading represents the necessary amount of shims between the differential carrier and the bearing on the ring gear side.

6. Remove the bearing from the differential carrier on the ring gear side and install the proper amount of shims. Reinstall the bearing.

7. Remove the differential carrier bearing from the opposite side of the ring gear. To determine the amount of shims needed, use the following method.

a. Subtract the size of the shim pack just installed on the ring gear side of the carrier from the reading obtained and recorded when measurement was taken without the pinion gear in place during the Differential Carrier Assembly procedure. To this figure, add an additional 0.015 in. to compensate for preload and backlash. An example: If the first reading was 0.085 in. and the shims installed on the ring gear side of the carrier were 0.055 in., the correct amount of shims whould be 0.085 − 0.055 + 0.015 = 0.045 in.

8. Install the required shims as determined under step 7 and install the differential side bearing. The installation of the shims should give the proper preload to the bearings and the proper backlash to the ring and pinion gears.

10 $^1/_2$ INCH

1. Install the differential carrier, with the side bearings and cups installed, in place in the axle housing.

2. Select the smallest of the original shims as a gauging shim and place it between the bearing cup and the housing on the ring gear side.

3. Install the bearing caps and tighten the bolts enough to hold the cups in place.

4. Mount a dial indicator on the ring gear side of the axle housing and position the indicator button on the rear side of the ring gear.

5. Position two prybars between the bearing cup and the housing on the side opposite the ring gear. With the prybars, force the differential carrier towards the dial indicator and set the indicator dial to "0".

6. Reposition the prybars on the ring gear side of the carrier and force the ring gear into mesh with the pinion gear while observing the dial indicator reading. Repeat this operation until the same reading is obtained each time.

7. Add this indicator reading to the gauging shim thickness to determine the correct shim dimension for installation on the ring gear side of the differential carrier.

8. An example: If the gauging shim was 0.115 in. and the indicator reading was 0.017 in., the correct shim would be 0.115 + 0.017 = 0.172 in.

9. Remove the gauging shim and install the correct shim into position between the bearing cup and the axle housing on the ring gear side of the housing.

10. To determine the correct dimension for the remaining shim, refer to the Side Bearing Shim Selection for the 10 $^1/_2$ in. and obtain the recorded shim size. From that figure, subtract the size of the shim installed in step 9 and then add 0.006 in. for the bearing preload and backlash.

11. An example: If the reading of the shim just installed on the ring gear side of the carrier was 0.172 in. and the reading obtained during the checking of clearance without the pinion installed was 0.329, the correct shim dimension would be as follows: 0.329 − 0.172 = 0.157 + 0.006 = 0.163 in.

Installation of Differential Carrier Into Axle Housing

9 $^3/_4$ INCH

1. Spread the axle housing with the spreader tool no more than 0.015 in. Install the differential bearing outer cups in their correct locations and install the cups in their respective locations.

2. Install the bolts and tighten finger-tight. Rotate the differential carrier and ring gear and tap with a soft-faced hammer to insure proper seating of the assembly in the axle housing.

3. Remove the spreader tool and torque the cap bolts to specifications.

4. Install a dial indicator and check the ring gear backlash at four equally spaced points of the ring gear circle. The backlash must be within a range of 0.004–0.009 in. and must not vary more than 0.002 in. between the points checked.

5. If the backlash is not within specifications, the shim packs must be corrected to bring the backlash within limits.

6. Check the tooth contact pattern and verify.

7. Complete the assembly, fill to proper level with lubricant and operate to verify proper assembly.

10 $^1/_2$ INCH

1. Spread the axle housing with a spreader tool, no more than 0.015 in. The carrier assembly is in place in the housing.

2. Assemble the shim, as determined previously, into place between the bearing cup and the housing. Remove the spreader tool.

3. Install the bearing caps in their marked positions and torque the bolts to specifications.

4. Install a dial indicator and check the ring gear backlash at four equally spaced points around the ring gear.

5. The backlash must be within 0.004–0.009 in. and must not vary more than 0.002 in. between the positions checked.

6. Whenever the backlash is not within the allowable limits, it must be corrected. Changing of the shim packs is required.

a. Low backlash is corrected by decreasing the shim on the ring gear side and increasing the opposite side shim an equal amount.

b. High backlash is corrected by increasing the shim on the ring gear side and decreasing the opposite side shim an equal amount.

7. Check the tooth contact pattern and correct as required.

8. Complete the assembly, fill to the correct level and operate to verify correct repairs.

Dana–Spicer—Single Reduction Models 30, 44, 44–1, 60–1–2, 70

DIFFERENTIAL

Removal

1. Drain lubricant.
2. Remove cover and gasket.

NOTE: Attached to a cover bolt is a metal tag which shows the number of teeth on pinion and ring (drive) gear.

3. Remove bearing cap screws. Note the matching marks on cap and carrier and make sure caps are reassembled to correct markings.
4. Using a spreader tool, spread carrier a maximum of 0.020 in. and measure amount of spread with a dial indicator.

CAUTION

Carrier may be permanently damaged if spread more than 0.020 in. Do not attempt differential removal without using a spreader.

5. Carefully lift differential assembly out of carrier.
6. Remove the spreader assembly after removing the differential assembly from the housing.

DRIVE PINION

Disassembly

1. Pull flange (yoke) from shaft splines of drive pinion.
2. Using a press or soft hammer, drive pinion and inner bearing cone assembly out of carrier.
3. Remove and tag shim pack from splined end of pinion.

NOTE: If either ring (drive) gear or pinion are to be replaced, write down markings (+), (–), or (0) located at face end of pinion for reassembly reference.

4. Remove oil seal assembly from carrier bore. This frees oil seal gasket, oil slinger, and bearing cone.
5. If replacement of the pinion tapered bearings is necessary, the bearing cups should be removed from carrier as follows:
   a. Use remover with a driver or slide hammer to remove inner bearing cup from carrier. This frees shim pack. Remove and tag shims for reassembly.
   b. Remove outer bearing cup.
6. Use remover set to separate bearing cone from drive pinion.
7. Separate oil slinger from pinion. This oil slinger is only found on some axle models.

DIFFERENTIAL

Disassembly

1. Remove and label the two bearing cups.
2. Use a suitable type puller to remove the bearing cones. Remove and label adjusting shims.
3. Drive out pinion shaft lock pin.

NOTE: On the Spicer Model 70 rear axle, punch-mark the differential case halves (for reassembly reference) and separate. Remove the differential spider, pinion gears, side gears and thrust washers.

4. Separate ring gear from case.
5. Remove pinion shaft, two pinions, two side gears, and four thrust washers from case.

Assembly

1. Place side gears with new thrust washers in position inside case.
2. Place pinions and thrust washers in position in case.
3. Install the differential pinion shaft in position in case between two pinions. Align shaft lock pin hole with lock pin hole in case and install pinion shaft lock pin. Peen hole to prevent pin from falling out.

NOTE: On the Spicer Model 70 rear axle, install the differential spider along with its pinion gears, side gears and thrust washers into the differential case halves. Bolt the two halves together making sure the punch-marks line up.

4. Place ring (drive) gear in proper position against flange of case and bolt ring gear to case. Alternately tighten these bolts until all bolts are tightened to proper torque.

NOTE: Do not install differential cones or shim packs until pinion depth and bearing preload have been checked out. Differential bearing adjustment is a part of axle assembly procedure.

DIFFERENTIAL BEARING

Adjustment

1. Press fit bearing cones tightly against shoulders on case. Do not install shims at this time.
2. Install bearing cups.
3. Install spreader tool and dial indicator, and spread carrier as described in Differential Removal.
4. Place differential assembly into carrier.
5. Install bearing caps using their respective cap screws. Make sure caps are assembled to their correct markings. Hand tighten bearing cap screws.
6. Install dial indicator at carrier with indicator button contacting back of ring (drive) gear. Rotate ring gear and check run-out.
7. If run-out exceeds 0.002 in., remove the differential assembly and remove the ring gear from the case.
8. Reinstall differential assembly without ring gear and check run-out of differential case flange. If run-out still exceeds 0.002 in., the defect is probably due to bearings or case, and should be corrected before proceeding.
9. Remove differential from carrier. Do not install shims behind the bearings until final installation.

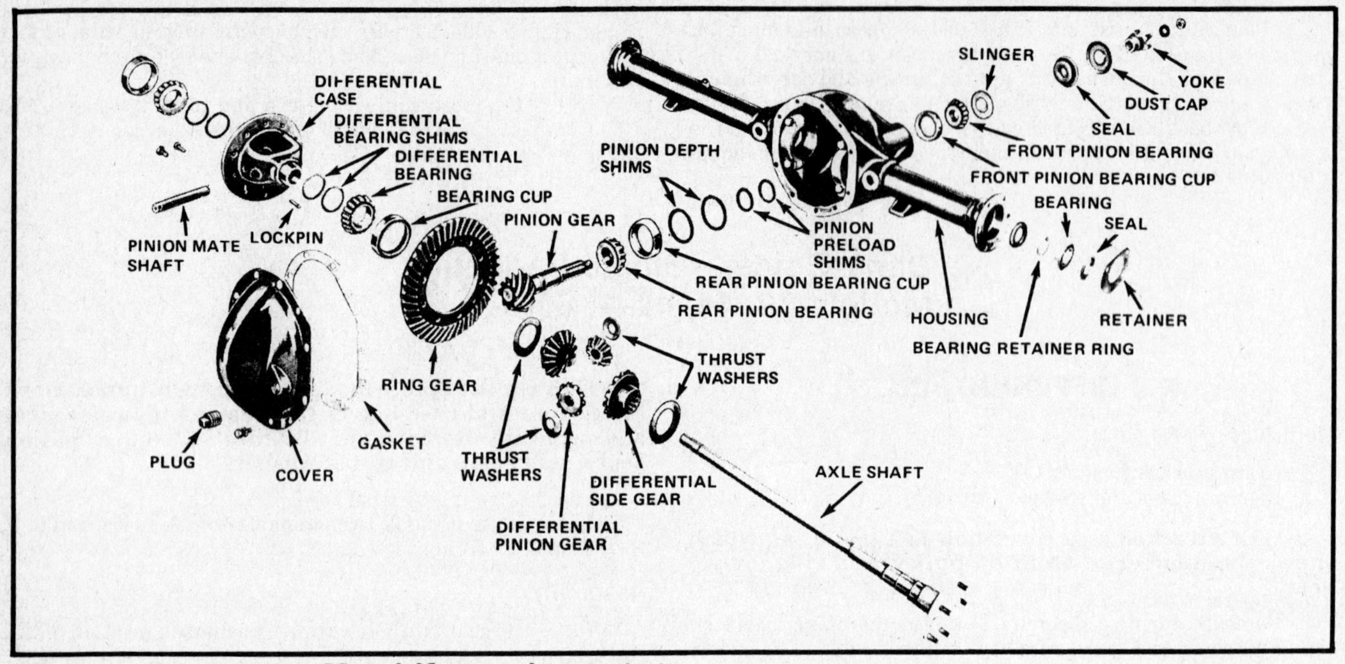

Exploded view of models 30 and 40 rear axles—typical

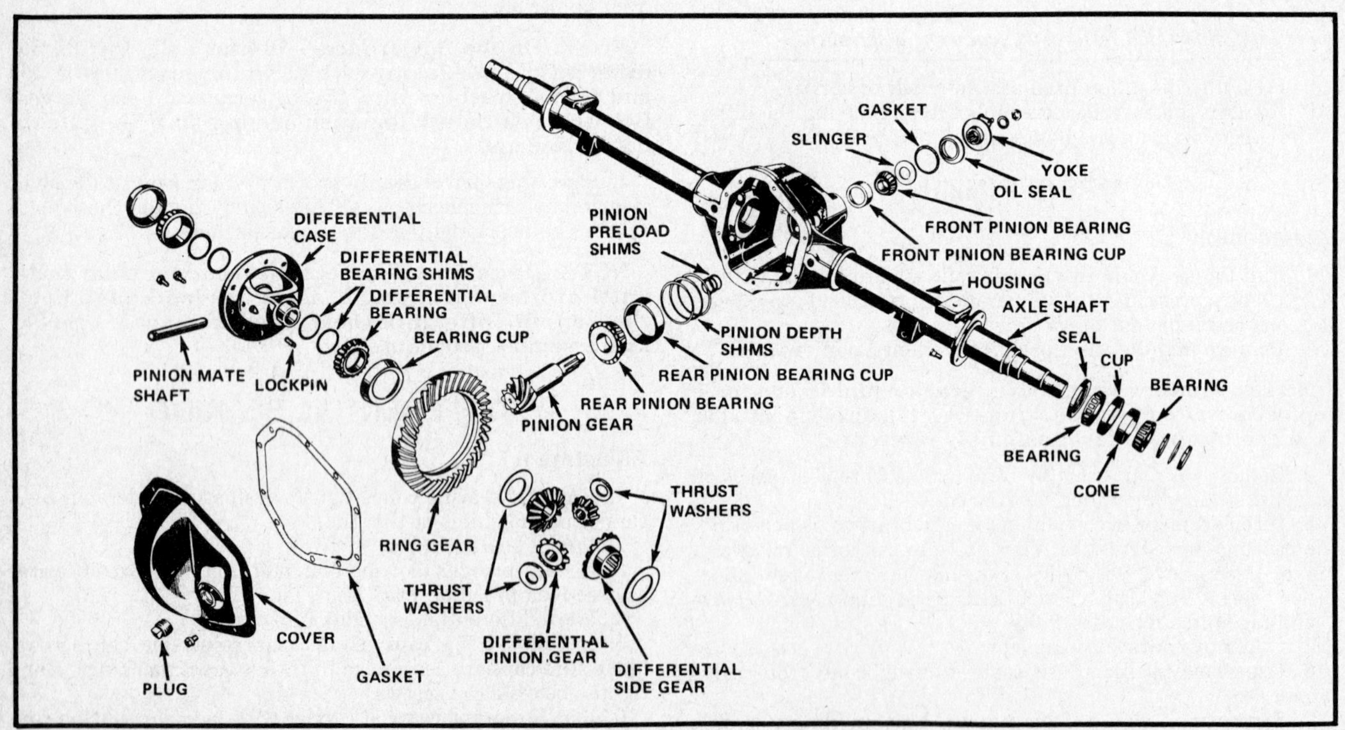

Exploded view of models 60 rear axle—typical

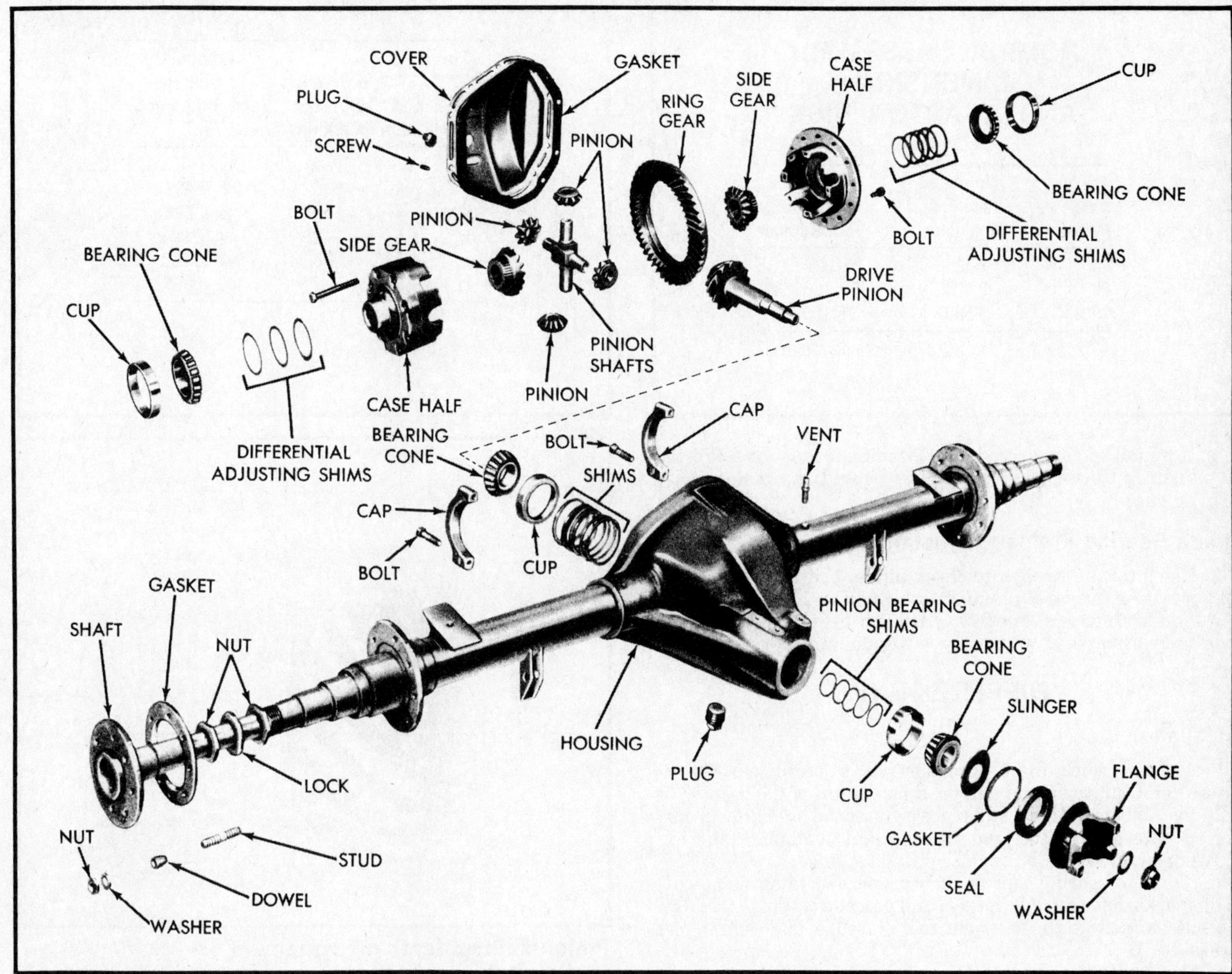

Exploded view of Dana Model 70 rear axle assembly

DRIVE PINION

Installation

1. If either drive pinion or ring (drive) gear must be replaced, they must be installed as a set. (These parts are matched and lapped at time of manufacture to obtain the correct gear tooth contact.)

2. Whenever it is necessary to install a new drive pinion, the plus (+) or minus (–) marking on face of rear end of pinion must be considered. Select a new pinion and ring gear set with markings as near as possible to those on old pinion. If marking on both old and new pinion is the same, do not change thickness of shim pack.

3. The approximate difference between markings on old and new drive pinion is the adjustment that will have to be made in the shim packs.

4. In the first listing below note that the new pinion is a plus eight (+8) while the old pinion is a plus five (+5). Making a difference of plus three (+3). This means that the thickness of each shim pack must be decreased by 0.003 in.

5. Once proper adjustment in shim packs has been made, place oil slinger, if so equipped, over pinion shaft. Install pinion inner bearing cone over shaft, and use bearing installer and an arbor press to press bearing onto pinion shaft. Bearing must be seated tightly against shoulder or oil slinger.

6. Use pinion front bearing cup installer to install outer bearing cup into carrier bore.

7. Install the selected inner shim pack in carrier. Then use pinion rear bearing cup installer to install inner bearing cup.

8. Insert pinion, oil slinger (when used) and inner bearing cone assembly into carrier and place the selected shim pack into position on outer end of pinion shaft.

9. Place outer bearing cone over pinion shaft, then use installer to seat bearing tight against shim pack.

10. Install pinion flange (yoke), washer and nut. Hold flange while tightening the nut to proper torque.

Note: Install oil slinger and oil seal only after pinion depth and pinion bearing preload have been checked out.

Checking Pinion Depth Adjustment

1. A pinion depth gauge and correct adapter, which gives a micrometer reading, should be used to determine pinion depth. The actual pinion depth setting can be determined by adding gauge reading to thickness of step plate and comparing result with the nominal dimension of 2.625 in. (models 44/60) or 3.125 in. (model 60), or 3.500 in. (model 70).

2. If the pinion setting is within minus (–) 0.001 in. to plus (+) 0.003 in. of this nominal dimension, the pinion position can be considered satisfactory.

NOMINAL ASSEMBLY DIMENSION AND ADAPTOR DISC CHART

Axle Model	Nominal Assembly Dimension	Adapter Disc Tool Number
44	2.625″	SE-1065-9-SS
60	3.125″	SE-1065-9-Y
70①	3.500″	SE-1065-9-Y

① Model 70—Use a 0.375 shim under dial pointer

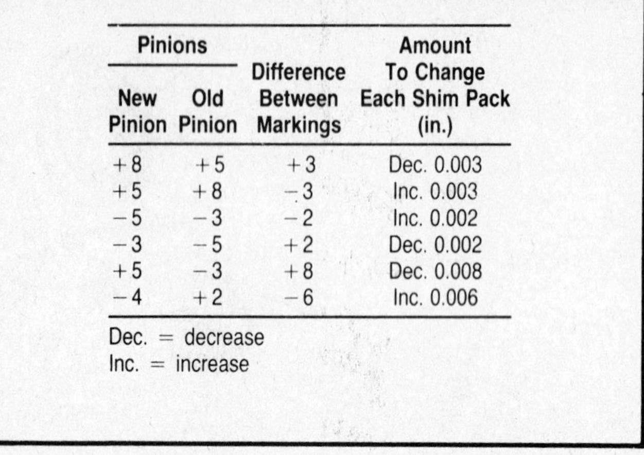

Pinions		Difference	Amount
New Pinion	Old Pinion	Between Markings	To Change Each Shim Pack (in.)
+8	+5	+3	Dec. 0.003
+5	+8	−3	Inc. 0.003
−5	−3	−2	Inc. 0.002
−3	−5	+2	Dec. 0.002
+5	−3	+8	Dec. 0.008
−4	+2	−6	Inc. 0.006

Dec. = decrease
Inc. = increase

3. If pinion setting exceeds these limits, it must be corrected by adjusting thickness of shim pack behind the pinion inner bearing cup.

Pinion Bearing Preload Adjustment

1. Use a torque wrench to check pinion bearing preload.
2. Rotating torque of pinion should be from 15 to 30 inch lbs.
3. Add or remove shims from pack just behind outer bearing cone to bring preload within these torque limits.

DIFFERENTIAL

Installation

1. Use dial indicator and spreader tool as described in Differential Removal, to spread carrier a maximum of 0.020 in.
2. Install bearing cups and place differential assembly in carrier. Rotate differential and, with a soft hammer, tap ring (drive) gear to assure a proper bearing seating.
3. Reinstall bearing caps in their proper locations as indicated by marks made during the removal procedure. Finger tighten cap screws. Relieve the spreader tool pressure, and tighten cap screws to 70–90 ft. lbs.
4. Move differential assembly tightly against drive pinion.
5. Install dial indicator securely to carrier, then set button at zero and against back of drive gear.
6. Move the differential toward the dial indicator and note the reading. For accuracy, repeat this operation several times.
7. Remove the differential assembly from carrier. Install a shim pack behind differential bearing cone at drive gear side, equal to the dimension indicated by dial indicator.
8. Subtract the indicator reading from the reading previously obtained in paragraph Differential Bearing Adjustment.
9. To the above result should be added 0.015–0.020 in. in shims to provide bearing preload.
10. Install the above shim pack behind differential bearing cone at side opposite to drive gear.
11. Spread differential carrier, using spreader tool.

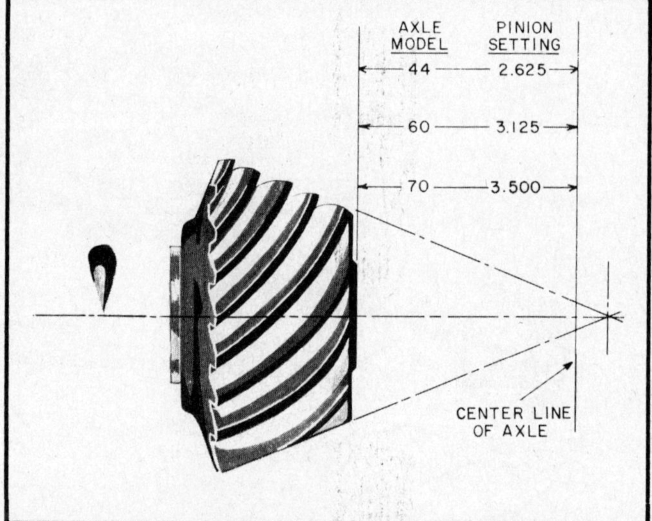

Pinion setting depth measurement

12. Install differential bearing cups then locate differential assembly in carrier.
13. Rotate differential assembly, tapping gear to seat bearings.
14. Install differential bearing caps in their correct location as indicated by marks made upon disassembly. Finger tighten cap screws.
15. Remove differential carrier spreader tool. Tighten differential bearing cap screws to proper torque.
16. Install dial indicator and check drive gear to drive pinion backlash at four equally spaced points around the drive gear. Backlash must be held to 0.003–0.006 in. and must not vary more than 0.002 in. between positions checked.
17. Whenever backlash is not within limits, differential bearing shim pack should be corrected.

AMC/JEEP

All the Jeep, Grand Wagoneer, Comanche and J–10 models are using a Jeep semi-floating type rear axle with flanges axle shafts. Both standard (7 $^{9}/_{16}$ in.) and heavy duty (8 $^{7}/_{8}$ in.) are being used. The J-20 models are using the Dana–Model 60 full-floating rear axle. The standard and heavy duty Jeep rear axle housings are made up of a modular cast iron center section and two steel tubes which are pressed into the center section. The rear drum brake support plates are attached to the mounting flanges at the axle tube outboard ends.

The differential assembly consists of a cast iron case containing two differential side gears, two differential pinion gears and a pinion shaft on which the pinion gears are mounted. The differential side and pinion gears are in constant mesh.

The axle ratio and the ring and pinion gear tooth combina-

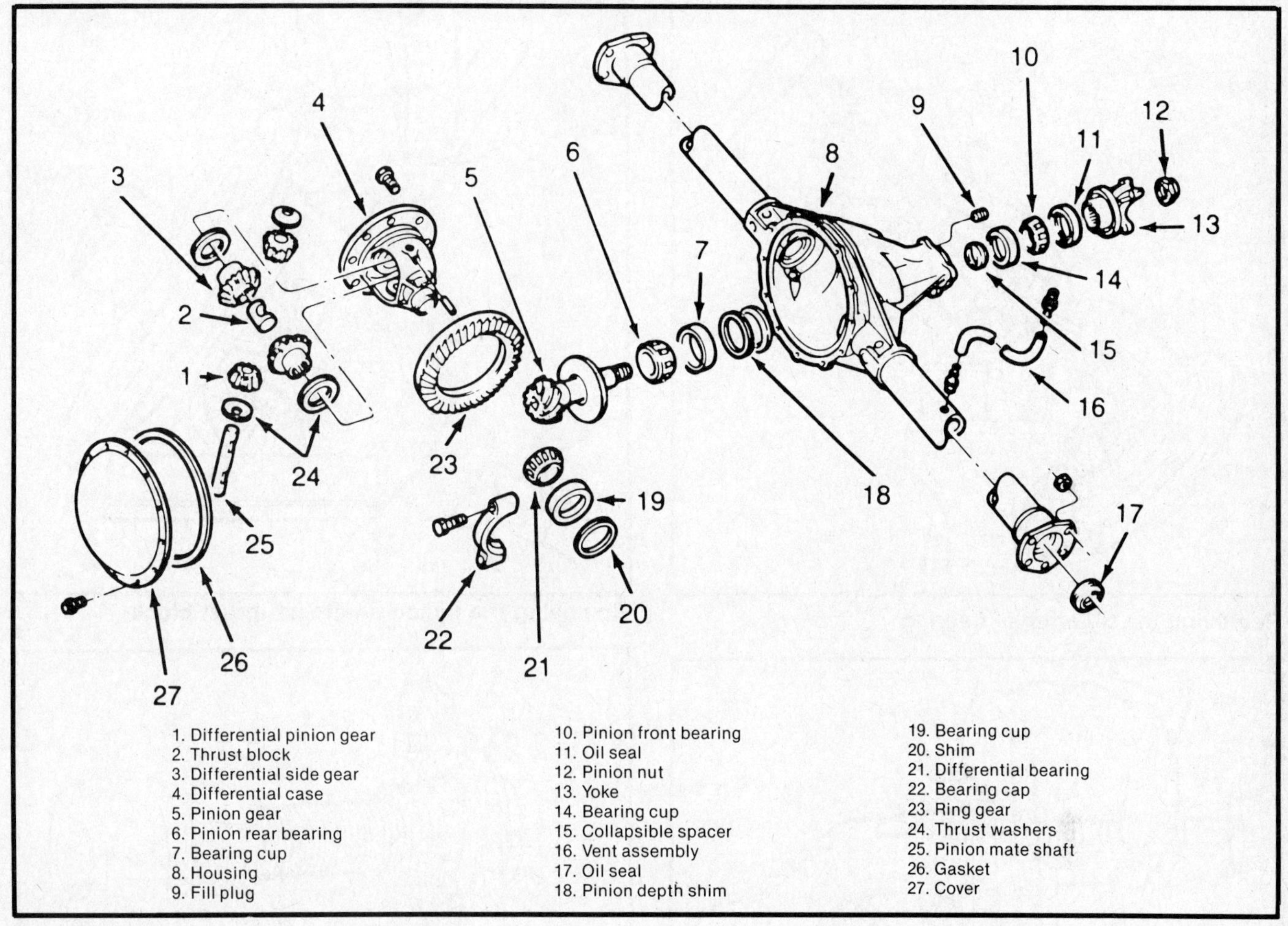

Exploded view of the 8⅞ heavy duty axle

tions are stamped on a tag attached to the differential housing cover. On the Jeep rear axles, the axle code letters are stamped on the right side axle housing tube boss.

NOTE: The Trac-Lok limited slip differentials are available as an option. The Trac-Lok is used only in rear axles and there are two Trac-Lok units used.

7 $^9/_{16}$ AND 8 $^7/_8$ INCH RING GEAR

Removal

NOTE: It is not necessary to remove the rear axle assembly in order to overhaul the differential.

1. Raise and support the vehicle safely. Remove the axle housing cover and drain the lubricant into a suitable drain pan.
2. Remove the wheels, brakedrums, axle shafts and seals. Keep the left and right-side axle parts separated.
3. Mark the bearing caps with a center punch for assembly reference. Loosen the bearing cap bolts until only several threads are engaged, then pull the bearing caps away from the bearings. This will prevent the differential from falling out and sustaining damage when pried from the axle housing.
4. Pry the differential loose in the axle housing. Remove the bearing caps and remove the differential. Tie the differential bearing shims to their respective bearing caps and cups to prevent misplacement.

Differential Disassembly

1. Use Puller J–29721 and adapters or equivalent to remove the differential bearings. When using this tool, be sure the differential case is secure. When the bearing is removed the differential case can drop if not supported.
2. Remove the ring gear-to-differential case bolts.

NOTE: Do not chisel or wedge the gear from the case.

3. Remove the ring gear from the case. Use a brass drift and hammer to tap the ring gear from the case. Do not nick the ring gear face of the differential case or drop the gear.
4. Remove the pinion mate shaft lockpin using a suitable drift. Remove the pinion mate shaft and remove the thrust block.
5. Rotate the pinion gears on the side gears until the pinion gears are aligned with the case opening. Remove the pinion gears and thrust washers and remove the side gears and thrust washers.
6. Remove the pinion nut using Tool J–8614–01 or equivalent. Remove the axle yoke using Tool J–8614–01, –02, –03 or equivalent.
7. Install the axle housing cover to prevent the pinion gear from falling out when the gear is driven out of the bearings and housing. Loosely attach the cover using two bolts.
8. Remove the pinion seal using tool J–9233 or equivalent. Tap the end of the pinion gear with a soft face mallet to drive the pinion gear out of the front bearing. Remove the front bearing and collapsible spacer. Discard the spacer.

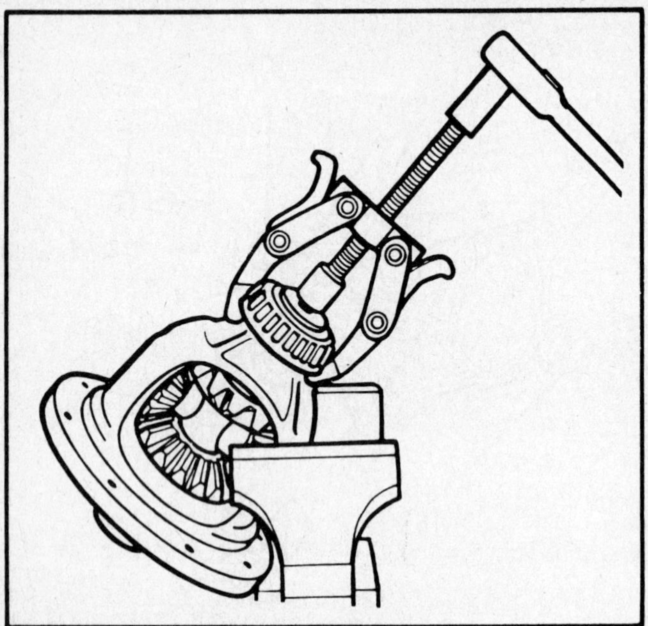
Removing the differential bearing

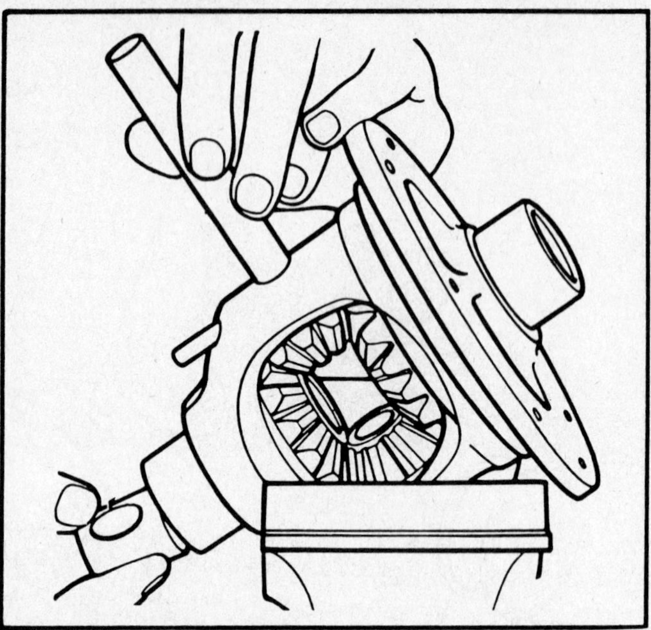
Removing the pinion shaft and thrust block

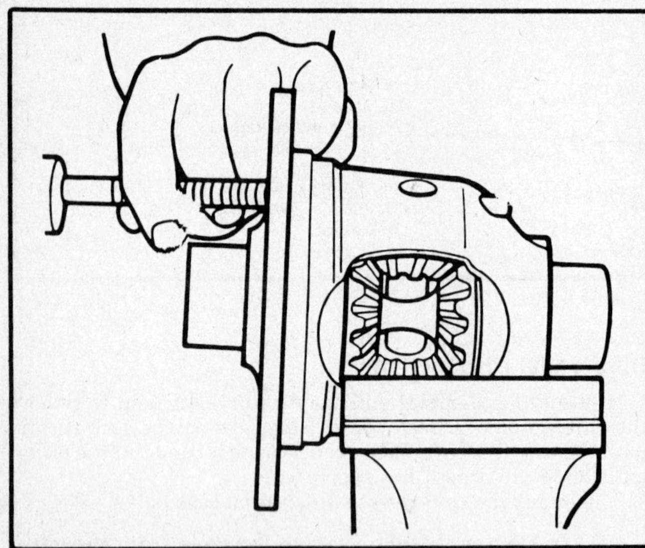
Removing the pinion shaft lock pin

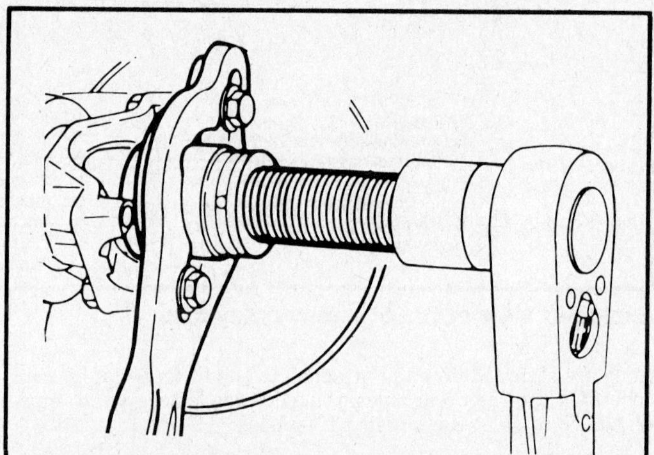
Removing the axle yoke

NOTE: The collapsible spacer is used to control pinion bearing preload. Discard this spacer after removal, it is not reusable.

9. Remove the axle housing cover and remove the pinion gear and rear bearing from the housing. Remove the rear bearing cup using Tools J–8092 and J–21786 or equivalent

NOTE: The pinion gear depth adjustment shims are located under the rear bearing cup. Tag these shims for assembly reference.

10. Remove the front bearing cup using Tools J–8092 and J–21787 or equivalent.

NOTE: Keep the bearing cup remover tool seated squarely on the cup to prevent damaging the cup bores during removal.

Differential Axle Housing Alignment

1. Place two straightedges across the tube flanges and measure the distance between the flange ends. If the straightedges are parallel within $^3/_{32}$ in. at a distance of 11 inches from the tube centerline, the axle housing is serviceable.
2. Perform this inspection with the straightedges placed in horizontal and vertical positions.

Pinion Gear Installation and Depth Adjustment

Ring and pinion gear sets are factory tested to detect machining variances. Tests are started at a standard setting which is then varied to obtain the most desirable tooth contact pattern and quiet operation. When this setting is determined, the ring and pinion gear are etched with identifying numbers.
The ring gear receives one number. The pinion gear receives two numbers which are separated by a plus (+) or a minus (–) sign.

The second number on the pinion gear indicates pinion position, in relation to the centerline of the axle shafts, where tooth contact was best and gear operation was most quiet. This number represents pinion depth variance and indicates the amount

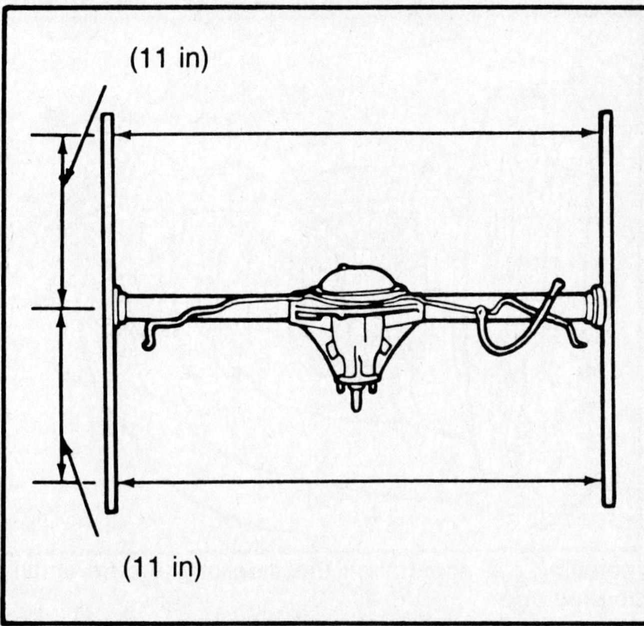

Checking the axle housing alignment

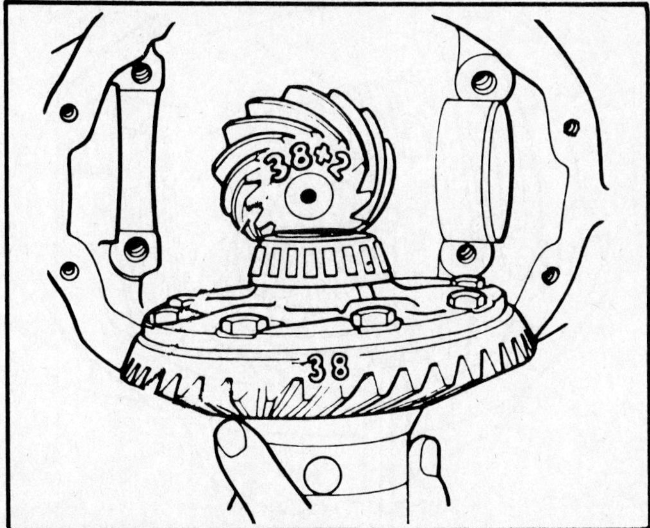

Pinion and ring gear identifying numbers

in thousands of an inch that the gear set varied from the standard setting.

The number on the ring gear and first number on the pinion gear identify the gears as a matched set. Do not attempt to use a ring and pinion set having different numbers. The standard setting for AMC/Jeep axles is 2.547 in. If the pinion is marked +2, the gear set varied from standard by + 0.002 in. and will require 0.002 in. less shims than a gear set marked zero (0).

When a gear set is marked plus (+), the distance from the pinion end face to the axle shaft centerline must be more than the standard setting. If the pinion gear is marked -3, the gear set varied from standard by 0.003 in. more shims than a set marked zero (0). When a set is marked minus (–), the distance from the pinion end face to the axle shaft centerline must be less than the standard setting.

NOTE: On some factory installed gear sets, an additional 0.010 or 0.020 in. may have been machined off the pinion gear bottom face. This does not affect the gear operation but does affect the pinion gear marking and depth measurement.

Pinion gears machined in this fashion have different identifying numbers. For example, if the pinion is marked +23, the number 2 indicates that 0.020 in. was removed from the pinion bottom face and the number 3 indicates that variance from the standard setting is + 0.003 in. If the pinion is marked +16, the number 1 indicates that 0.010 in. was removed from the pinion bottom face and the number 6 indicates that variance from the standard setting is + 0.006 in.

Gear sets with additional amounts machined off the pinion bottom face are factory installed items exclusively. All service replacement gear sets will be machined to standard settings only. In addition, replacement gear sets marked + or - 0.009 in. or more, or sets with mismatched identifying numbers must be returned to the parts distributor center. Do not attempt to install these gear sets.

The chart provided in this section will help to determine the approximate "starter shim" thickness needed for the initial pinion depth measurement. However, the chart will not provide the exact shim thickness required for final adjustment and must not be used as a substitute for an actual pinion depth measurement. The chart should be used as follows.

1. Measure the thickness of the original pinion depth shim. Note the pinion depth variance numbers marked on the old and new pinion gears.

2. Now use the chart to determine the starter shim thickness. An example of this is as follows:

If the old pinion is marked -3 and the new pinion is marked +2, the chart procedure would be as follows. Go to the old pinion col-

Old Pinion Marking	New Pinion Marking								
	−4	−3	−2	−1	0	+1	+2	+3	+4
+4	+0.008	+0.007	+0.0006	+0.005	+0.004	+0.003	+0.002	+0.001	0
+3	+0.007	+0.006	+0.005	+0.004	+0.003	+0.002	+0.001	0	−0.001
+2	+0.006	+0.005	+0.004	+0.003	+0.002	+0.001	0	−0.001	−0.002
+1	+0.005	+0.004	+0.003	+0.002	+0.001	0	−0.001	−0.002	−0.003
0	+0.004	+0.003	+0.002	+0.001	0	−0.001	−0.002	−0.003	−0.004
−1	+0.003	+0.002	+0.001	0	−0.001	−0.002	−0.003	−0.004	−0.005
−2	+0.002	+0.001	0	−0.001	−0.002	−0.003	−0.004	−0.005	−0.006
−3	+0.001	0	−0.001	−0.002	−0.003	−0.004	−0.005	−0.006	−0.007
−4	0	−0.001	−0.002	−0.003	−0.004	−0.005	−0.006	−0.007	−0.008

Pinion Variance chart for AMC/Jeep $7^{9}/_{16}$ & $8^{7}/_{8}$ inch ring gear

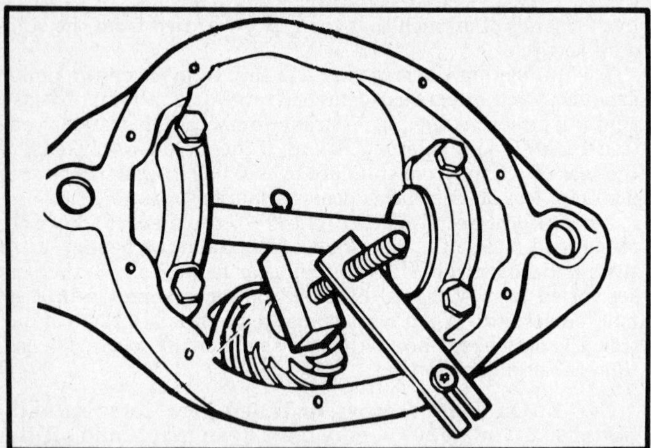
Installing the gauge arbor tool, discs and the gauge block tool

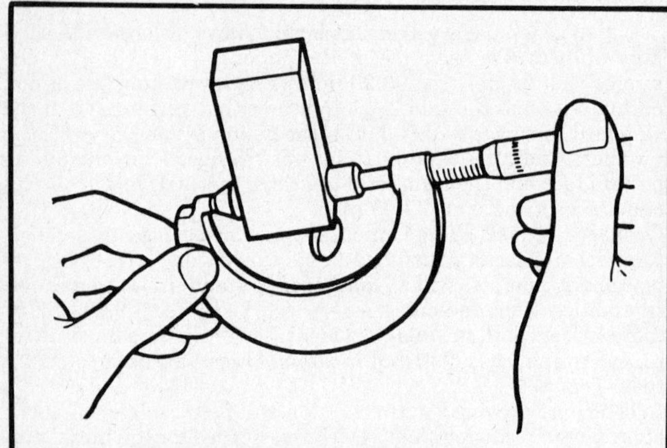
Measuring the anvil with a micrometer

umn and locate the -3, then go across the chart until the +2 figure is reached in the new pinion column. The box where the two columns intersect will indicate the amount of starter shim thickness required.

Pinion Depth Measurement Adjustment

1. Measure the thickness of the original pinion depth shim. Note the pinion depth variance numbers marked on the old and new pinion gears.
2. Determine the starter shim thickness. With the use of the chart, determine the amount to be added to or subtracted from the original shim thickness for starter shim thickness.

NOTE: The starter shim thickness must not be used as a final shim setting. An actual pinion depth measurement must be performed and the final shim thickness adjusted as necessary.

3. Install the ring bearing on the pinion gear with the large diameter of the bearing cage facing the gear end of the pinion. Press the bearing against the rear face of the gear.
4. Clean the pinion bearing bores in the axle housing thoroughly. This is important in obtaining the correct pinion gear depth adjustment. Install the starter pinion depth shim in the housing rear bearing cup bore. Be sure the shim is centered in the bearing cup bore.

NOTE: If the shim is chamfered, be sure the chamfered side faces the bottom of the bearing cup bore.

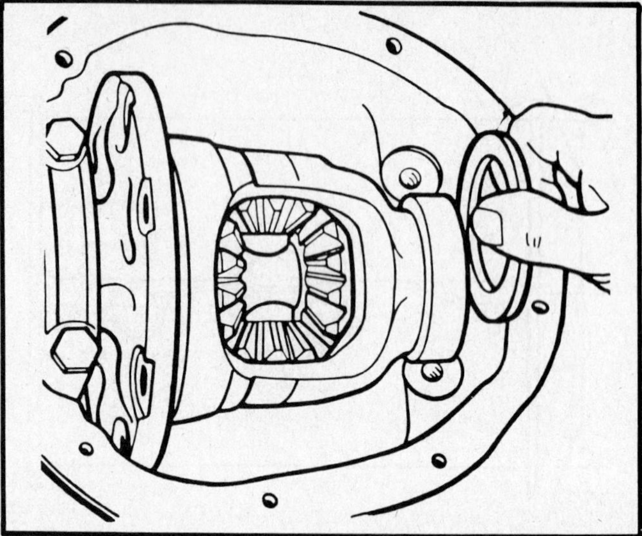
Installing the shim(s) on the side of the differential bearing cup

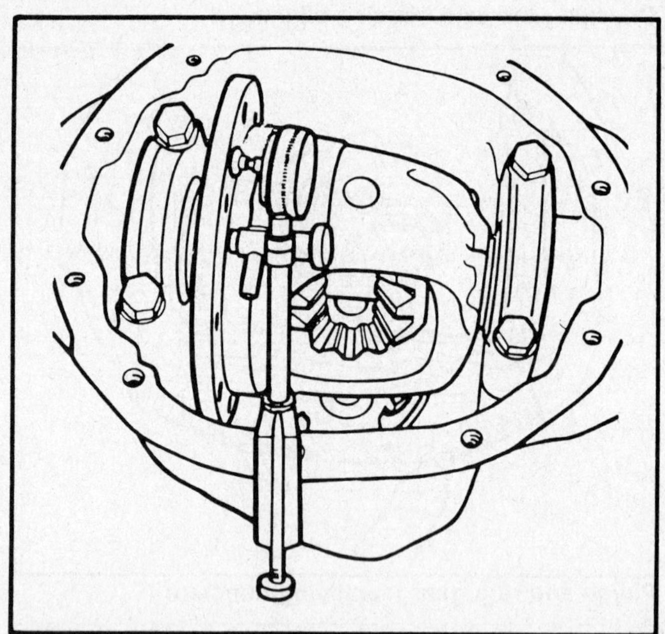
Installation of the dial indicator

5. Install the ring bearing cup using Tools J–8092 and J–8608 or equivalent. Install the front bearing cup using Tools J–8092 and J–8611–01 or equivalent. Install the pinion gear in the rear bearing cup.
6. Install the front bearing, rear universal joint yoke and original pinion nut on the pinion gear. Tighten the pinion nut only enough to remove the bearing end play.

NOTE: Do not install a replacement pinion nut and collapsible spacer at this time as the pinion gear will be removed after depth measurement.

7. Note the pinion depth variance marked on the pinion gear. If the number is preceded by a plus (+) sign, add that amount (in thousandths) to the standard setting for the axle model being overhauled. If the number is preceded by a minus (–) sign, subtract that amount (in thousandths) from the standard set-

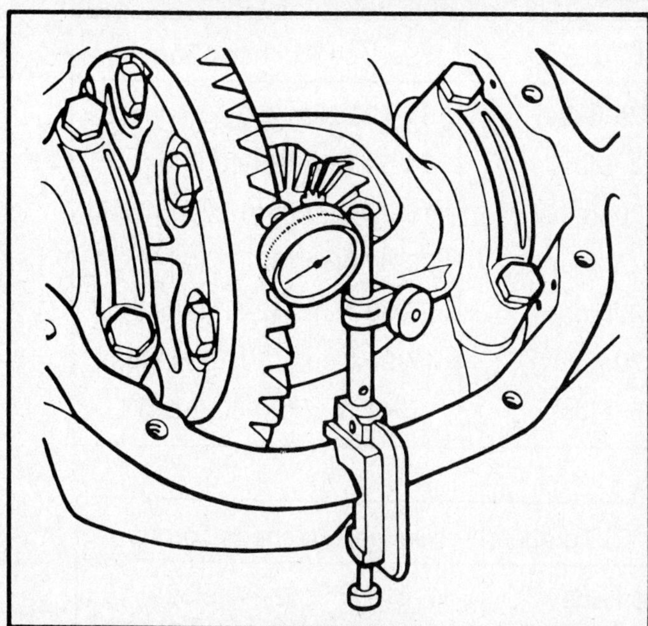

Measuring the ring gear backlash

ting. The result of this addition or subtraction is the desired pinion depth. Record this figure for future reference.

8. Assemble Arbor tool J-5223-4 and Discs J-5223-23 or equivalent, install the assembled tools in the differential bearing cup bores. Be sure discs are completely seated in bearing cup bores.

9. Install the bearing caps over the discs and install the bearing cap bolts. Tighten the bearing cap bolts securely, but not with the specified torque.

10. Position Gauge Block J-5223-20 or equivalent, on the end face of the pinion gear with the anvil end of the gauge block seated on the gear and the gauge plunger underneath Arbor Tool J-5223-4 or equivalent.

11. Assemble and mount Clamp J-5223-24 and bolt J-5223-29 or equivalent, on the axle housing. Use the axle housing cover bolt to attach the clamp to the housing.

12. Extend the clamp bolt until it presses against the gauge block with enough force to prevent the gauge block from moving. Loosen the gauge block thumbscrew to release the gauge block plunger. When the plunger contacts the arbor tool, tighten the thumbscrew to lock the plunger in position. Do not disturb the plunger position.

13. Remove the clamp and bolt assembly from the axle housing. Remove the gauge block and measure the distance from the end of the anvil to the end of the plunger using a 2–3 in. micrometer. This dimension represents the measured pinion depth. Record this dimension for assembly reference.

14. Remove the bearing caps and remove the arbor tool and discs from the axle housing. Remove the pinion gear, rear bearing cup and pinion depth shim from the axle housing.

15. Measure the thickness or the depth shim. Add this dimension to the measured pinion depth. From this total, subtract the desired pinion depth. The result represents the correct shim thickness required.

NOTE: The desired pinion depth is the standard setting plus or minus the pinion depth variance.

Pinion Gear Bearing Preload Adjustment

1. Install the correct thickness pinion depth shim(s) in the axle housing bearing cup bore. Install the rear bearing cup and pinion gear.

NOTE: The collapsible spacer controls the pinion bearing preload. Do not reuse the old spacer. Use a replacement spacer only.

2. Install the replacement collapsible spacer and front bearing on the pinion gear. Install the pinion oil seal using Tool J-22661 or equivalent.

3. Install the pinion yoke and replacement pinion nut. Tighten the pinion nut finger-tight only. Tighten the pinion nut only enough to remove end play and seat the pinion bearings. Use Tool J-22575 or equivalent to tighten the nut and use Tool J-86141-01 or equivalent to hold the yoke while tightening the nut.

4. Rotate the pinion while tightening the nut to seat the bearings evenly. Remove the tools.

NOTE: Do not exceed the specified preload torque and do not loosen the nut to reduce the preload torque if the specified torque is exceeded.

5. Measure the torque required to turn the pinion gear using an inch-pound torque wrench and Tool J-22575 or equivalent. The correct pinion bearing preload torque is 17–25 inch lbs. torque. Continue tightening the pinion nut until the required preload torque is obtained.

6. If the pinion bearing preload torque is exceeded, remove the pinion gear, replace the collapsible spacer and pinion nut and adjust the preload again.

DIFFERENTIAL ASSEMBLY

NOTE: The following items should be done before begining the reassembly of the differential.

Clean each part thoroughly in solvent. Towel dry bearings or allow them to air dry, do not use compressed air to dry bearings as damage might result. Dry all other parts with compressed air or shop towels. If the parts are not to be assembled immediately, cover them to prevent dust or dirt contamination.

Inspect the housing for cracks and sand holes. Replace the housing if it is cracked or porous. Check for burrs and deep scratches or nicks on the gasket and oil seal surfaces. An oil stone or fine tooth file may be used to remove nicks or burrs. The bearing cup bores should be carefully inspected for nicks or burrs that may have been created during bearing cup removal. Inspect and clean the axle tubes. Inspect the vent to be sure that it is not obstructed.

Check housing for bent or loose tubes or other physical damage.

Whenever one rear wheel is stationary and the opposite wheel is spinning, the differential pinion shaft is subject to high torque loads. Inspect the shaft for scoring and wear. The shaft should be a press fit of 0.000–0.010 in. in the case. Replace the shaft if worn or scored.

Inspect the side gears for worn, cracked or chipped teeth. The gears should fit snugly on the axle shaft splines. Also inspect the fit of the gears in the differential case bore. With the gears installed, side clearance must not exceed 0.007 in. Excessive side clearance must be corrected to avoid driveline backlash resulting in a "clunk" noise when the transmission is initially engaged in Drive or Reverse (with automatic transmission).

1. Install the differential bearings on the case using Tools J-21784 and J-8092 or equivalent.

2. Install the thrust washers on the differential side gears and install the gears in the differential case. Install the differential pinion gears in the case. Install the thrust washers behind the pinion gears and align the pinion gear bores.

3. Rotate the differential side and pinion gears until the pinion mate shaft bores in the pinion gears are aligned with the shaft bores in the case.

Install the thrust block in the case. Insert the block through the side gear bore. Align the bore in the block with the pinion mate shaft bores in the pinion gears and case.

Component	Service Set-To Torque	Service Recheck Torque
Wheel Lug Nuts	102 N·m (75 ft-lbs)	81-122 N·m (60-90 ft-lbs)
Brake Support Plate Nuts	43 N·m (32 ft-lbs)	34-54 N·m (25-40 ft-lbs)
U-Joint Strap Bolts	19 N·m (170 in-lbs)	15-23 N·m (140-200 in-lbs)
Differential Bearing Cap Bolts	77 N·m (57 ft-lbs)	70-91 N·m (52-67 ft-lbs)
Ring Gear-to-Case Bolts	70 N·m (52 ft-lbs)	57-88 N·m (42-65 ft-lbs)
Rear Axle Cover Screws	19 N·m (170 in-lbs)	17-21 N·m (150-190 in-lbs)
Rear Axle Filler Plug	34 N·m (25 ft-lbs)	27-41 N·m (20-30 ft-lbs)

8⁷⁄₈ inch (heavy duty) ring gear torque specifications

Component	Service Set-To Torque	Service Recheck Torque
Axle Housing Cover Bolts	19 N·m (14 ft-lbs)	17-21 N·m (12-17 ft-lbs)
Brake Tube-to-Rear Wheel Cylinder	11 N·m (97 in-lbs)	10-12 N·m (90-105 in-lbs)
Differential Bearing Cap Bolts	115 N·m (85 ft-lbs)	102-129 N·m (75-95 ft-lbs)
Ring Gear-to-Case Bolt	142 N·m (105 ft-lbs)	135-149 N·m (95-115 ft-lbs)
Rear Brake Support Plate Bolts	43 N·m (32 ft-lbs)	34-54 N·m (25-40 ft-lbs)
Universal Joint Strap Bolts	19 N·m (170 in-lbs)	16-22 N·m (140-200 in-lbs)

4. Install the pinion mate shaft. Align the lockpin bore in the shaft with the bore in the case and install the shaft lockpin.

DIFFERENTIAL BEARING ADJUSTMENT

1. Place the bearing cup over each differential bearing and install the differential case assembly in the axle housing.
2. Install the shim on each side between the bearing cup and the housing. Use 0.080 in. shims as the starting point.
3. Install the bearing caps and tighten the bolts finger-tight. Mount the Dial Indicator J–8001 or equivalent on the housing. Using an appropriate pry tool, pry between the shims and housing. Pry the assembly to one side and zero the indicator, then pry the assembly to the opposite side and read the indicator.

NOTE: Do not zero or read the indicator while prying.

4. The amount read on the indicator is the shim thickness that should be added to arrive at the zero preload and zero end play. Repeat the procedure to ensure accuracy and adjust if necessary. Shims are available in thicknesses from 0.080 – 0.110 in. in 0.002 in. increments.
5. When sideplay is eliminated, a slight bearing drag will be noticed. Install the bearing caps and tighten the bearing cap bolts with 85 ft. lbs. torque. Attach the dial indicator to the axle housing and check the ring gear mounting face of the differential case for runout. Runout should not exceed 0.002 in.
6. Remove the case from the housing. Retain the shims used to adjust the sideplay.

RING GEAR INSTALLATION

1. Position the ring gear on the differential case. Install the two ring gear bolts in the opposite holes and tighten the bolts to pull the gear into position.
2. Install the remaining ring gear attaching bolts. Tighten the bolts with 105 ft. lbs. torque.
3. Position the shims previously selected to remove the differential bearing sideplay on the bearing cups and install the differential assembly in the axle housing. Install the bearing cap bolts and tighten the bolts with 85 ft. lbs. torque.
4. Attach the dial indicator to the housing. Position the indicator so the indicator stylus contacts the drive side of a ring gear tooth and at a right angle to the tooth. Move the ring gear back and forth and note the movement registered on the dial indicator. The ring gear backlash should be 0.005–0.009 in., with 0.008 in. desired.
5. Adjust the backlash as follows: to increase the backlash, install the thinner shim on the ring gear side and the thicker shim on the opposite side. To decrease the backlash, reverse the procedure; however, do not change the total thickness of the shims.

NOTE: The following is an example on how to decrease backlash. The sideplay was removed using 0.090 in. shims on each side totaling 0.180 in. Backlash is checked and found to be 0.011 in. To correct the backlash, add 0.004 in. the the shim on the ring gear side and subtract 0.004 in. from the shim on the opposite side. This will result in 0.094 in. shim on the ring gear side and 0.086 in. shim on the other side. The backlash will be approximately 0.007 – 0.008 in. The total shim thickness remains 0.180 in.

DIFFERENTIAL INSTALLATION AND BEARING PRELOAD ADJUSTMENT

NOTE: The differential bearings must be preloaded to compensate for heat and loads during operation. The

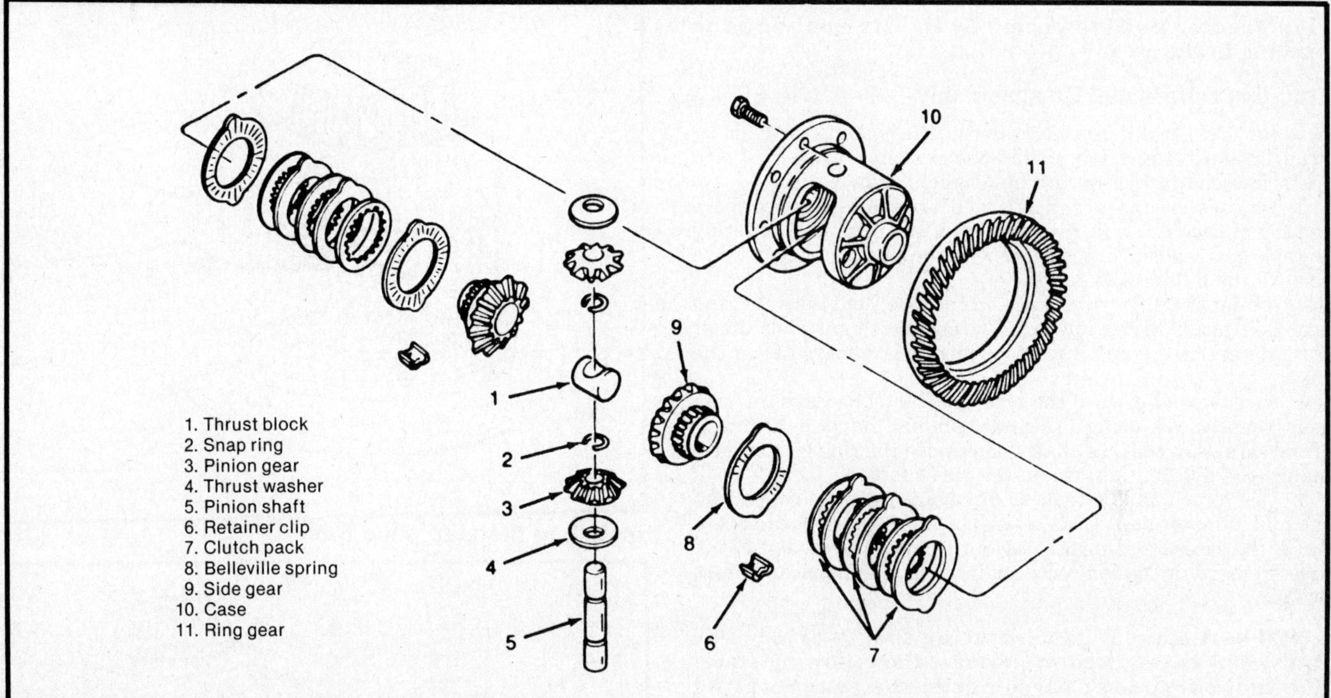

Exploded view of the Trac-Lok differential

differential bearings are preloaded by increasing the shim pack thickness at each side of the differential by 0.004 in. for a total of 0.008 in.

1. Remove the differential assembly from the housing. Be sure to keep the differential bearing shim packs together for the proper assembly. Do not distort the shims in the axle housing bearing bores.
2. Install the differential bearing cups on the differential bearings. The cups should cover the differential bearing rollers completely. Position the differential assembly in the housing so the bearings just start into the housing bearing bores.

NOTE: Slightly tipping the bearing cups will ease starting them into the bores. Also keep the differential assembly square in the housing during installation and push it in as far as possible.

3. Tap the outer edge of the bearing cups until the differential is seated in the housing.
4. Install the differential bearing caps. Position the caps accordingly to the alignment punch marks made at disassembly. Tighten the bearing cap bolts with 85 ft. lbs. torque. Preloading the differential bearings may change the backlash setting. Check and correct the backlash if necessary.
5. Install the propeller shaft, aligning the index marks made at disassembly. Install the axle shafts, bearings, seals and brake support plates. Fill the rear axle with the specified axle lubricant.
6. Check and adjust the axle shaft end play if necessary. Adjust the end play at the left side of the axle shaft only. Install the hubs, drums and wheels.

Lower the vehicle and road test the vehicle to check the rear axle assembly for proper operation.

TRAC-LOK DIFFERENTIAL

Operational Test

If a noisy or rough operation such as a chatter occurs when turning corners, the most probalbe cause of this chatter or noise is incorrect or contaminated lubricant. Before removing the Trac-Lok unit for repair, drain flush and refill the axle with the specified lubricant. A complete lubricant drain and refill with the specified fluid will usually correct the chatter problem. A quick operational test of the Trac-Lok differential can be done easily by performing the following steps.

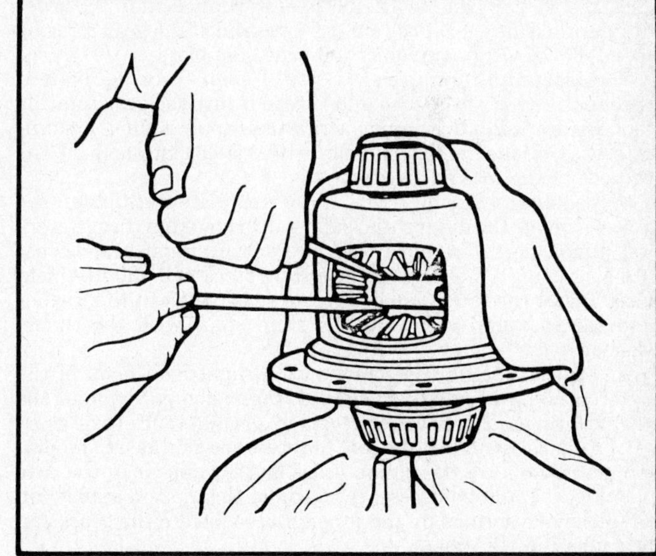

Removing the snap ring from the pinion mate shaft

1. Position one wheel on solid dry pavement and the opposite wheel on ice, mud grease or a similar low traction surface.
2. Gradually increase the engine rpm to obtain the maximum traction prior to a breakaway. The ability to move the vehicle effectively will demonstrate the proper performance.

NOTE: If the test is performed on extremely slick surfaces such as ice or grease coated surfaces, some question may exist as to proper performance. In these extreme cases, a properly performing Trac-Lok will pro-

vide greater pulling power by lightly applying the parking brake.

Trac-Lok Differential Dissassembly

1. Remove the differential from the axle housing as previously outlined in this section. Install one axle shaft in the vise with the spline end facing upward and tighten thew vise.
2. Do not allow more than 2 $^3/_4$ in. of the shaft to extend above the top of the vise. This prevents the shaft from fully entering the side gear, causing interfernce with the step plate tool used to remove the differential gears.
3. Mount the differential case on the axle shaft with the ring gear bolt heads facing upward. Place some shop towels under the ring gear to protect the gear when it is removed from the case.
4. Remove and discard the ring gear bolts. Remove the ring gear from the case using a rawhide hammer. Remove the differential case from the axle shaft and remove the ring gear and remount the differential case on the axle shaft.
5. Use some suitable tools to disengage the snap rings from the pinion mate shaft. Place a shop towel on the opposite opening of the case to prevent the snap rings from flying out of the case. Remove the pinion mate shaft using a hammer and brass drift.

NOTE: A special gear rotating tool J-23781-3 or equivalent is required to perform the following steps. The tool consists of three parts; the gear rotating tool,forcing screw and step plate.

6. Install step plate tool J-23781-7 or equivalent in the lower differential side gear. Position the pawl end of the gear rotating tool J-23781-7 or equivalent onto the step plate.
7. Insert the forcing screw tool J-8646-2 or equivalent through the top of the case and thread it into the gear rotating tool. Before using the forcing screw tool, apply a small amount of grease to the centering hole in the step plate and oil the threads of the forcing screw.
8. Center the forcing screw in the step plate and tighten the screw to move the differential side gears away from the differential pinion gears. Remove the differential pinion gear thrust washers using a feeler gauge or a shim stock of 0.030 in. thickness. Insert the feeler gauge or shim stock between the washer and the case and withdraw the shim stock with the thrust washer.
9. Tighten the forcing screw until a slight movement of the differential pinion gear is observed. Insert the pawl end of the gear rotating tool between the teeth of one differential side gear.
10. Pull the handle of the tool to rotate the side gears and pinion gears. Remove the pinion gears as they appear in the case opening. It could be necessary to adjust the tension applied on the Belleville springs by the forcing screw before the gears can be rotated in the case.
11. Retain the upper side gear and clutch pack in the case by holding your hand on the bottom of the rotating tool while removing the forcing screw. Remove the rotating tool, upper side gear and clutch pack.
12. Remove the differential case from the axle shaft. Invert the case with the flange or ring gear side up and remove the step plate tool, lower the side gear and clutch pack from the case. Remove the retainer clips from both the clutch packs to allow separation of the plates and discs.

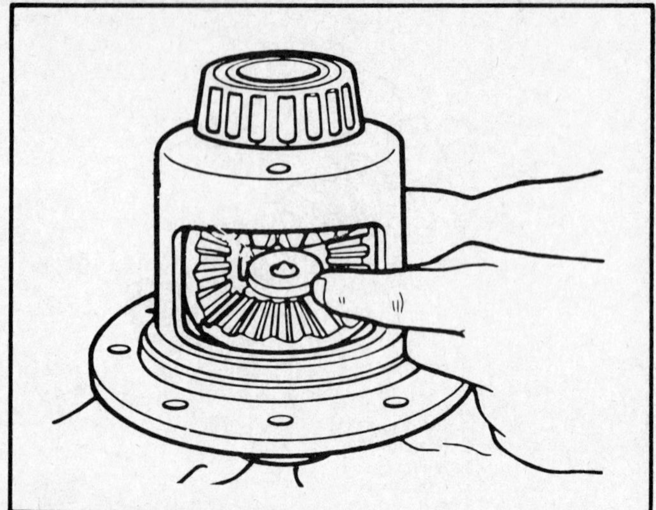
Installing the step plate tool

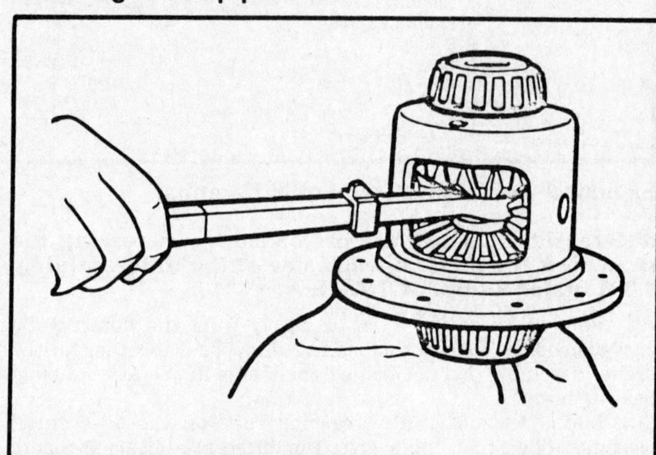
Installing the gear rotating tool

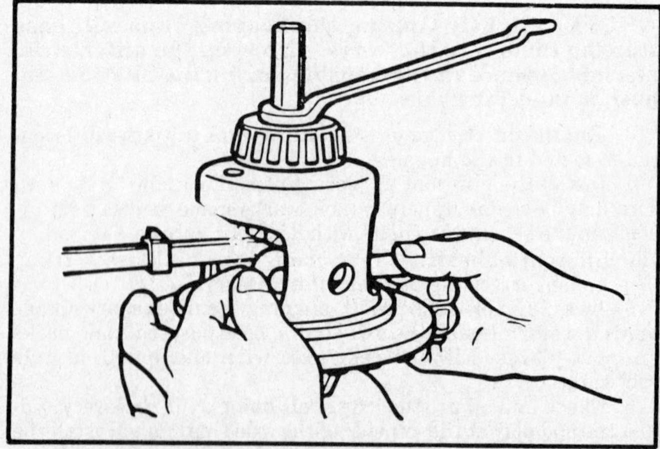
Removing the pinion gear thrust washers

Trac-Lok Differential Assembly

If any one member of either clutch pack shows evidence of excessive wear or scoring, the complete clutch pack must be replaced on both sides.
Clean each part thoroughly in solvent. Towel dry bearings or allow them to air dry, do not use compressed air to dry bearings as damage might result. Dry all other parts with compressed air or shop towels. If the parts are not to be assembled immediately, cover them to prevent dust or dirt contamination.

Inspect the housing for cracks and sand holes. Replace the housing if it is cracked or porous. Check for burrs and deep scratches or nicks on the gasket and oil seal surfaces. An oil stone or fine tooth file may be used to remove nicks or burrs. The bearing cup bores should be carefully inspected for nicks or

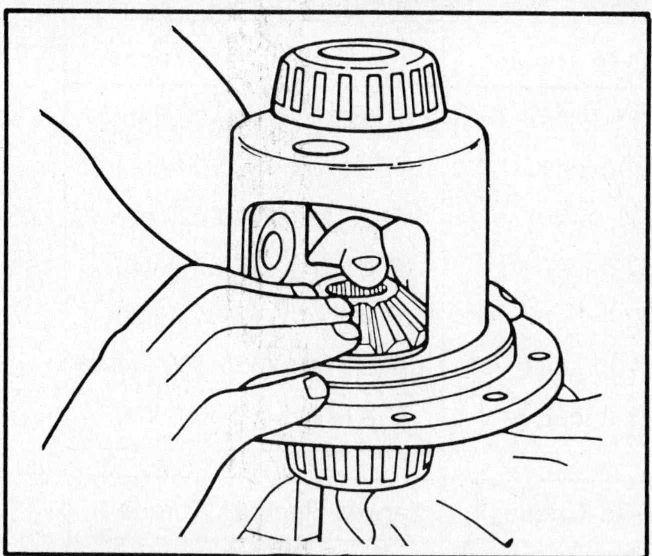
Installing the clutch packs

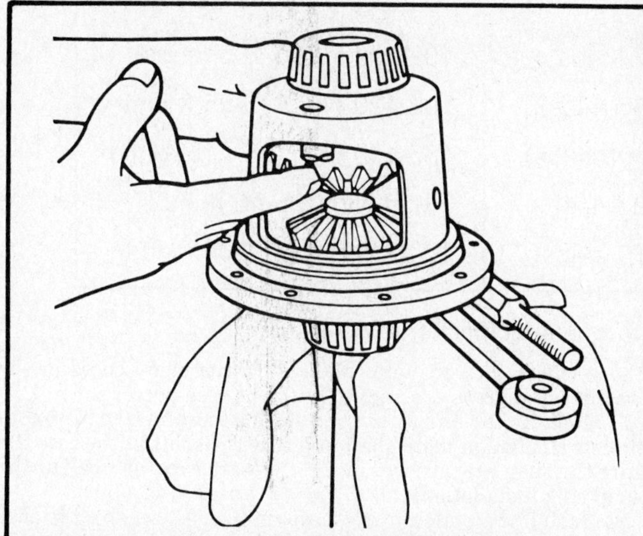
Keeping the side gear rotating tool in position

burrs that may have been created during bearing cup removal. Inspect and clean the axle tubes. Inspect the vent to be sure that it is not obstructed.

Check housing for bent or loose tubes or other physical damage.

Inspect the side gears for worn, cracked or chipped teeth. The gears should fit snugly on the axle shaft splines. Also inspect the fit of the gears in the differential case bore.

1. Lubricate all the differential components with the specified gear lubricant. Assemble the clutch packs. Install the plates and discs in the same position as when removed regardless of whether they are replacement or original parts.
2. Install the clutch retainer clips on the ears of the clutch plates. Be sure the clutch packs are completely assembled and seated on the ears of the plates. Install the clutch packs on the differential side gears and install the assembly in the case.
3. Make sure the clutch pack stays assembled on the side gear splines and that the retainer clips are completely seated in the case pockets. To prevent the pack from falling out of the case, it will be necessary to hold it in place by hand while mounting the case on the axle shaft.

NOTE: When installing the differential case on the axle shaft, make sure that the splines of the side gears are aligned with those of the axle shaft. Make sure the clutch pack is still properly assembled in the case after installing the case on the axle shaft.

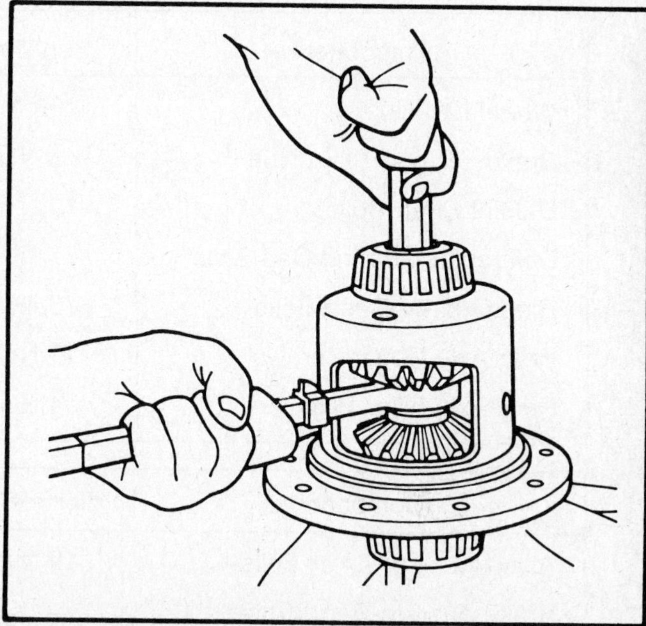
Installing the forcing screw into the rotating tool

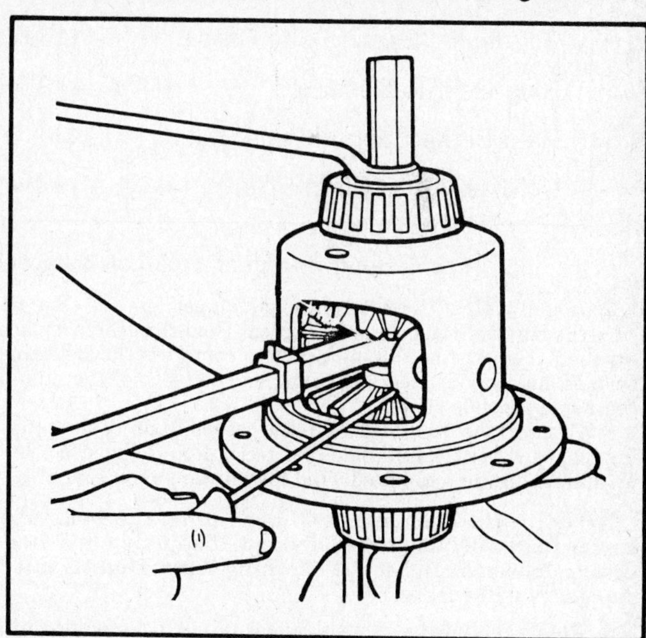
Installing the thrust washers

4. Mount the case assembly on the axle shaft. Install the step plate tool in the side gear and apply a small amount of grease in the centering hole of the step plate.
5. Install the remaining clutch pack and side gear. Make sure the clutch pack stays assembled on the side gear splines and that the retainer clips are completely seated in the pockets of the case.
6. Position the gear rotating tool in the upper side of the gear. Keep the side gear and rotating tool in position by holding them with your hand. Insert the forcing screw through the top of the case and thread it into the rotating tool.

Component	Service Set-To Torque	Service Recheck Torque
Wheel Lug Nuts	102 N·m (75 ft-lbs)	81-122 N·m (60-90 ft-lbs)
Brake Support Plate Nuts	43 N·m (32 ft-lbs)	34-54 N·m (25-40 ft-lbs)
U-Joint Strap Bolts	19 N·m (170 in-lbs)	15-23 N·m (140-200 in-lbs)
Differential Bearing Cap Bolts	77 N·m (57 ft-lbs)	64-91 N·m (47-67 ft-lbs)
Ring Gear-to-Case Bolts	70 N·m (52 ft-lbs)	57-88 N·m (42-65 ft-lbs)
Rear Axle Cover Screws	19 N·m (170 in-lbs)	17-21 N·m (150-190 in-lbs)
Rear Axle Filler Plug	34 N·m (25 ft-lbs)	27-41 N·m (20-30 ft-lbs)

Component	Service Set-To Torque	Service Recheck Torque
Axle Housing Cover Bolts	19 N·m (170 in-lbs)	17-21 N·m (150-190 in-lbs)
Brake Tube-to-Rear Wheel Cylinder	11 N·m (97 in-lbs)	10-12 N·m (90-105 in-lbs)
Differential Bearing Cap Bolts	115 N·m (85 ft-lbs)	102-129 N·m (75-95 ft-lbs)
Ring Gear-to-Case Bolt	142 N·m (105 ft-lbs)	135-149 N·m (95-115 ft-lbs)
Rear Brake Support Plate Bolts	43 N·m (32 ft-lbs)	34-54 N·m (25-40 ft-lbs)
Universal Joint Strap Bolts	19 N·m (170 in-lbs)	16-22 N·m (140-200 in-lbs)

8⅞ inch (heavy duty) ring gear Trak-Lok differential torque specifications

7. Install both of the differential pinion gears in the case. Be sure the bores of the gears are aligned. Hold the gears in place by hand. Tighten the forcing screw to compress the Belleville springs and provide clearance between the teeth of the pinion gears and the side gears.
8. Position the pinion gears in the case and insert the rotating tool pawl between the side gear teeth. Rotate the side gears by pulling on the tool handle and install the pinion gears.

NOTE: If the side gears will not rotate, the Belleville spring load will have to be adjusted. If adjustment is necessary, loosen or tighten the forcing screw slightly until the gears will rotate.

9. Rotate the side gears, using the rotating tool handle, until the shaft bores in both the pinion gears are aligned with the case bore. Lubricate both sides of the pinion gear thrust washers.
10. Tighten or loosen the forcing screw to permit the thrust washer installation. Install the thrust washers and using a suitable tool, guide the washers into position. Make sure the shaft bores in the washers and gears are aligned with the case bores.
11. Remove the forcing screw, rotating tool and step plate. Lubricate the pinion mate shaft and seat the shaft in the case. Be sure the snap ring grooves in the shaft are exposed to allow the snap ring installation.
12. Install the pinion mate shaft snap rings, remove the case from the axle shaft and install the ring gear on the case. Be sure to use replacement ring bolts only. Do not reuse the original bolts.
13. Align the ring gear and case bolt holes and install the ring gear bolts finger tight only. Remove the case on the axle shaft and tighten the bolts down evenly to the proper torque specifications.
14. Install the Trac–Lok differential assembly in the axle housing. and follow the procedures previously outline for the other Jeep axles to complete the differential and axle assembly servicing.

Dodge/Plymouth

8 3/8 AND 9 1/4 INCH Integral Carrier Axle

See the Dodge/Plymouth truck section for external identification and axle shaft service. Some of the Dodge /Plymouth models are using a Spicer 60 and a heavy duty Spicer 60 series rear drive axle. The removal, installation, disassembly and assembly procedures are basically the same as the procedures for the coventional drive axles already covered in this section.

DIFFERENTIAL

Removal

1. Raise the rear of the vehicle and support safely.
2. Remove the wheels, drums and the housing cover screws.

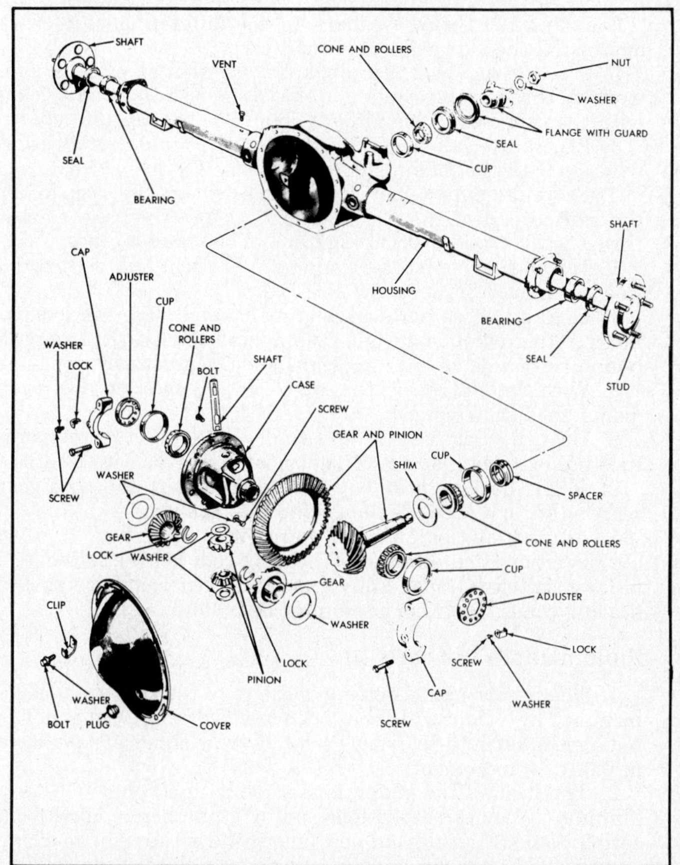

Exploded view of Chrylser Corp. 9¼ inch rear axle assembly

Exploded view of Chrylser Corp. 8³⁄₈ inch rear axle assembly

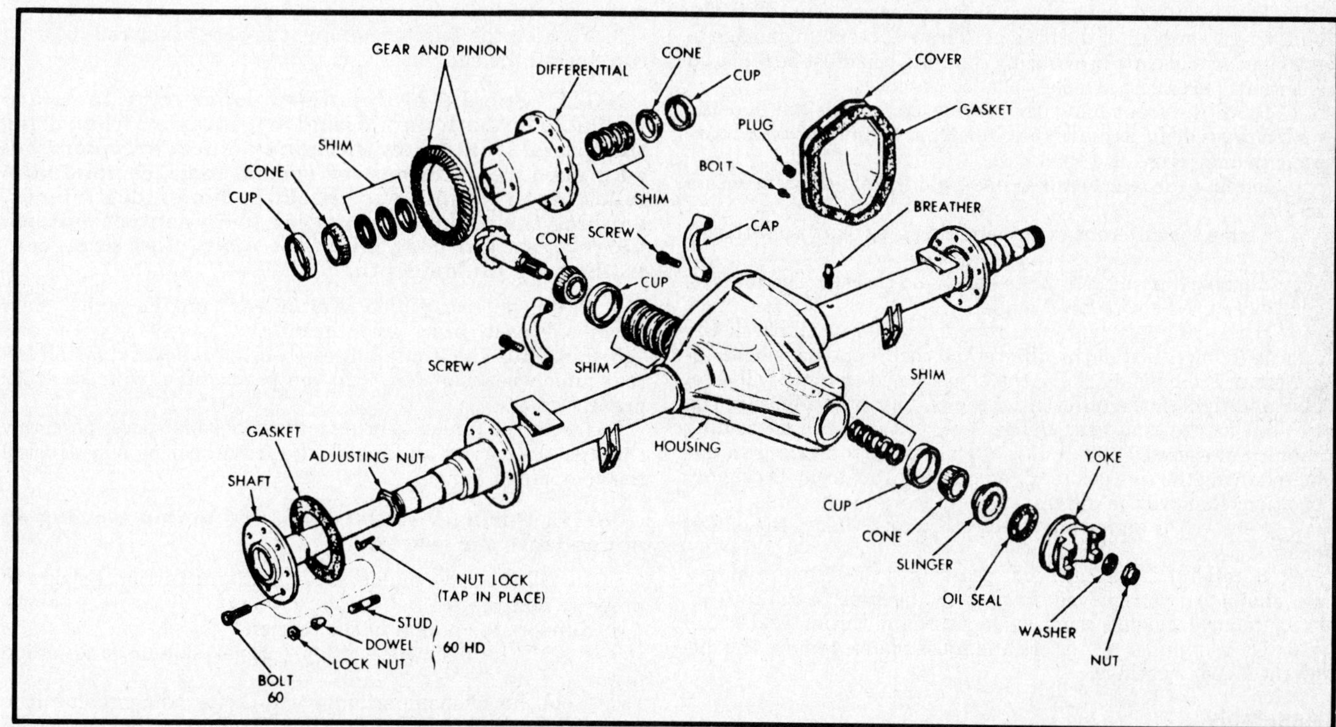

Exploded view of the Spicer 60 and Spicer 60 heavy duty rear axle assembly

Drain the lubricant from the axle housing by removing the cover.

3. Turn the differential carrier case to make the differential pinion shaft lock screw accessible and remove it from the case. Slide the pinion shaft from the case.

4. Push both axle shafts towards the center of the axle assembly and remove the C-washer clips from the recessed grooves of the axle shafts. Withdraw the axle shafts carefully to avoid damaging the axle shaft bearings in the axle tubes.

5. Clean the inside of the differential case with solvent and blow dry with compressed air.

6. Check for differential side-play by inserting a pry-bar between the left side of the axle housing and the differential case flange. Using a prying motion, determine whether side-play exists. There should be no side-play.

7. Paint the ring gear teeth and make a gear tooth contact pattern. Determine if proper depth of mesh can be obtained.

8. If side-play was found in step six, proceed to step nine. If no side-play was found in step six, check the drive gear run-out. Mount a dial indicator and index the indicator stem at right angles in the rear face of the ring gear. Rotate the ring gear and mark the ring gear and case at the point of greatest run-out. Total indicator reading should not exceed 0.005 in. If it does, the possibility exists that the case must be replaced.

9. Measure and record the pinion bearing preload. Use an in. lb. torque wrench to measure the preload.

10. Remove the pinion nut, washer and pinion flange.

11. Remove and discard the pinion oil seal.

12. Match-mark the axle housing and the differential bearing caps.

13. Remove the threaded adjusters and the differential bearing caps. There is a special wrench to do this through the axle tube.

14. Remove the differential case from the housing. The differential bearing cups and threaded adjuster must be kept together so they can be installed in their original position.

Disassembly

1. To remove the drive pinion or front bearing cone, drive the pinion rearward out of the bearing. This will result in damage to the bearing and cup. The bearing cone and cup must be replaced with new parts. Discard the collapsible spacer.

2. Drive the front and rear bearing cups from the housing with a brass drift. Remove the shim from behind the rear bearing cup and record the thickness.

3. Remove the rear bearing cone from the pinion stem with a puller.

4. Clamp the differential case and ring gear in a vise with soft jaws.

5. Remove the ring gear bolts (left-hand thread). Tap the ring gear loose with a soft-faced mallet.

6. If the ring gear run-out exceeded 0.005 in., recheck the case as follows. Install the differential case, cups, caps, and adjusters in the housing. Turn the adjusters to eliminate all side-play and tighten the differential cap bolts snugly. Measure the run-out at the ring gear flange face. Total indicator reading should not exceed 0.003 in. It is often possible to reduce run-out by removing the ring gear and remounting 180° from its original position. Remove the differential case from the housing.

7. Remove the pinion shaft lock-screw and remove the pinion shaft.

8. Rotate the differential side gears until the differential pinion shafts can be removed through the opening in the case.

9. Remove the differential side gears and thrust washers.

10. Using a puller or a press and press plates, remove the differential side bearings.

Assembly

1. Lubricate all parts, before assembly, with rear axle lubricant.

2. Install the thrust washers on the differential side gears and install the side gears into the case.

3. Place thrust washers on both differential pinions and, working through the opening in the case, mesh the pinion gears with the side gears. The pinions should be exactly 180° apart.

4. Rotate the side gears 90° to align the pinions and thrust washers with the pinion shaft holes.

5. From the pinion shaft lockpin hole side of the case, insert the slotted end of the pinion shaft through the case, conical thrust washer and just through one of the pinion gears.

6. Install a thrust block through the side gear hub, so that the slot is centered between the side gears.

7. Hold all these parts in alignment, and align the lockpin holes in the pinion shaft and case. Install the lockpin from the pinion shaft side of the ring gear flange, temporarily.

8. With a stone, relieve the edge of the chamfer on the inside diameter of the ring gear.

9. Heat the ring gear (fluid bath or heat lamp) to a temperature not exceeding 300°F. Do not heat ring gear with a torch.

10. Align the ring gear with the case. Insert the ring gear screws through the case flange and into the ring gear.

11. Alternately tighten each cap screw to 70 ft. lbs.

12. Position each differential bearing cone on the hub of the differential case (taper away from ring gear) and install the bearing cones. An arbor press may be helpful.

Pinion Depth of Mesh

1. The proper pinion setting (relative to the ring gear) is determined by a shim which has been selected before the pinion is to be installed in the carrier. Pinion bearing shims are available in 0.001 in. increments.

2. The head of the pinion is marked with a "plus" (+) or a "minus" (–) mark that is followed by a number ranging from zero to four. If the old and new pinions have the same marking and the old bearing is being installed, use a shim of the original thickness. If the old pinion is marked zero (0), however, and the new pinion is marked plus two (+2), try a shim that is 0.002 in. thinner. If the new pinion is marked axle housing cup bore and install minus two (–2), try a shim that is 0.002 in. thicker.

3. Position the selected shim in the bore of the rear bearing cup. Install the cup.

NOTE: Special pinion depth measuring tools are available for both the 8 $^3/_8$ and 9 $^3/_8$ in. axles. When using the special tools, follow the manufacturer's recommended procedures. Without the special tools, complete the following procedure and check the pinion depth by examining the pinion to ring gear tooth contact pattern. Correct as required by adding or subtracting shims controlling the pinion depth.

4. Place the rear pinion bearing cone on the pinion stem (small side away from pinion head).

5. Lubricate the front and rear bearing cones and install the rear pinion bearing cone onto the pinion stem with an arbor press.

6. Insert the pinion bearing and collapsible spacer assembly through the carrier and install the front bearing cone. Install the companion flange.

NOTE: During installation of the pinion bearing do not collapse the spacer.

7. Install the drive pinion oil seal into the carrier. Be sure to properly seat the seal.

8. Support the pinion in the carrier.

9. Install the Belleville washer (convex side up) and pinion nut.

10. Hold the companion flange and tighten the pinion nut to remove all end-play, while rotating the pinion to ensure proper bearing seating. Remove the tools and rotate the pinion several revolutions.

Type	Semi-Floating Hypoid	
Ring Gear Diameter	8.375" (212.7mm)	
Number of Teeth		
Drive Gear	47	45
Pinion	16	14
Ratio to 1	2.94	3.21
Number of Teeth		
Drive Gear	39	39
Pinion	11	10
Ratio to 1	3.55	3.90
PINION BEARINGS		
Type	Taper Roller	
Number Used	Two	
Adjustment	Collapsible Spacer	
Pinion Bearing Preload New Bearings	20-35 in. lbs. (2.25-3.95 N·m)	
Used Rear And New Front	10-25 in. lbs. (1.12-2.82 N·m)	
DIFFERENTIAL	Conventional	
Bearings (Type)	Taper Roller	
Number Used	Two	
Preload Adjustment	Threaded Adjustment	
RING GEAR AND PINION	Hypoid	
Serviced In	Matched Sets	
Pinion Depth Of Mesh Adjustment	Select Shims	
Pinion and Ring Gear Backlash	.005-.008" (.13-.20mm) At Point Of Minimum Backlash	
Runout-Differential Case and Ring Gear Backface	.006" (.15mm) Maximum	
WHEEL BEARINGS		
Type	Straight Roller	
Adjustment	None	
End Play	Built-In	
Lubrication	Rear Axle Lubricant	
LUBRICATION		
Capacity	4.4 PTS. (3-1/2 Imperial) (2 Liters)	

Type . . . Multi-Purpose Lubricant, as defined by MIL-L-2105B (API GL-5) should be used in all rear axle with conventional differentials, such a lubricant is available under Part. No. 4318058 MOPAR Hypoid Gear Lubricant or an equivalent. In Sure-Grip differentials 4 ounces (.1183 liters) of MOPAR Hypoid Gear Oil Additive Friction Modifier, Part No. 4318060 or equivalent must be included with every refill.

8⅜ inch rear axle specifications

TYPE	Semi-Floating Hypoid	
Ring Gear Diameter	9.250" (234.9mm)	
Number of Teeth		
Drive Gear	39	
Pinion	10	
Ratio to 1	3.90	
Number of Teeth		
Drive Gear	45	39
Pinion	14	11
Ratio to 1	3.21	3.55
PINION BEARINGS		
Type	Taper Roller	
Number Used	Two	
Adjustment	Collapsible Spacer	
Pinion Bearing Preload New Bearings	20-35 in. lbs. (2.25-3.95 N·m)	
Used Rear And New Front	10-25 in. lbs. (1.12-2.82 N·m)	
DIFFERENTIAL	Conventional	
Bearings (Type)	Taper Roller	
Number Used	Two	
Preload Adjustment	Threaded Adjustment	
RING GEAR AND PINION	Hypoid	
Serviced In	Matched Sets	
Pinion Depth Of Mesh Adjustment	Selected Shims	
Pinion and Ring Gear Backlash	.005-.008" (.13-.20mm) At Point Of Minimum Backlash	
Runout-Differential Case and Ring Gear Backface	.005" (.127mm) Max.	
WHEEL BEARINGS		
Type	Straight Roller	
Adjustment	None	
End Play	Built-In	
Lubrication	Rear Axle Lubricant	
LUBRICATION		
Capacity	4.5 PTS. (3-3/4 Imperial) (2.1 Liters)	

Type . . . Multi-Purpose Lubricant, as defined by MIL-L-2105B (API GL-5) should be used on all rear axles; such a lubricant is available under Part No. 4318058 MOPAR Hypoid Gear Lubricant or an equivalent. In Sure-Grip Differentials 4 ounces (.1183 liters) of MOPAR Hypoid Gear Oil Additive Friction Modifier, Part No. 4318060 or equivalent must be included with every refill.

9¼ inch rear axle specifications

8-3/8 Inch (212.72mm) Axle	Pounds Foot	N·m
Differential Bearing Cap Bolts	70	95
Ring Gear to Differential Case Bolts (Left Hand Thread)	70	95
Drive Pinion Flange Nut	210 (Min.)	285 (Min.)
Carrier Cover Bolts		
Brake Support Plate Retainer Nuts	30-35	41-47
Propeller Shaft Bolts (Rear)		
Spring Clip (U Bolt) Nuts	45	61

9-1/4 Inch (234.95mm) Axle (HD)	Pounds Foot	N·m
Brake Support Plate Retainer Nuts	75	102
Carrier Cover Bolts		
Differential Bearing Cap Bolts	100	136
Drive Pinion Flange Nut	210 (Min.)	285 (Min.)
Propeller Shaft Bolts (Rear)		
Ring Gear to Differential Case Bolts (Left Hand Thread)	70	95

Spicer 60 and 60HD	Pounds Foot	N·m
Differential Bearing Cap Bolts	70-90	95-122
Differential Case Half Retaining Bolts	35-45	41-47
Ring Gear to Differential Case Bolts (Left Hand Thread)	100-120	136-163
Drive Pinion Flange Nut	250-270	339-366
Carrier Cover Bolts	30-40	41-54
Axle Shaft Retainer Bolts (60), Nuts (60HD)	50-90 (SP60), 55-90 (SP60HD)	68-122 74-122
Propeller Shaft Bolts (Rear)		
Spring Clip (U Bolt) Nuts	125-150-210	169-203-285

Rear axle torque specifications

TYPE	Full-Floating Hypoid	
Ring Gear Diameter	9.750" (247.64mm)	
Number of Teeth		
Drive Gear	46	
Pinion	13	
Ratio to 1	3.54	
Number of Teeth		
Drive Gear	41	41
Pinion	11	10
Ratio to 1	3.73	4.10
PINION BEARINGS		
Type	Taper Roller	
Number Used	2	
Adjustment	Select Shims	
Pinion Bearing Drag Torque (Seal Removed)	10-20 in. lbs. (1.12-2.25 N·m)	
DIFFERENTIAL	Trak-Lok and Standard	
Bearings (Type)	Taper Roller	
Number Used	2	
Preload Adjustment	Select Shims	
RING GEAR AND PINION	Hypoid	
Serviced In	Matched Sets	
Pinion Depth Of Mesh Adjustment	Select Shims	
Pinion and Ring Gear Backlash	.004-.009" (.101-.228mm) at point Of minimum backlash	
Runout-Differential Case and Ring Gear Backface	.006" (.15mm) Maximum	
LUBRICATION		
Capacity	6 Pints (5 Imperial) (2.8 Liters)	
Type	Multi-Purpose Gear Lubricant, as defined by MIL-L-2105B (API GL-5) should be used on all rear axles; such a lubricant is available under Part No. 4318058 MOPAR Hypoid Gear Lubricant or an equivalent. In Trak-Lok Differentials 4 ounces (.1183 liters) of MOPAR Hypoid Gear Oil Additive Friction Modifier, Part No. 4318060 or equivalent must be included with every refill.	

Spicer 60 and 60 heavy duty rear axle specifications

11. Torque the pinion nut to 210 ft. lbs. With an inch lbs. torque wrench, measure the pinion bearing preload, which would be 20–35 inch lbs. for new bearings or 10 inch lbs. over the original figure if the old pinion bearing is used.

NOTE: The correct preload reading can only be obtained with the carrier nose upright. The final assembly is incorrect if the final pinion nut torque is below 210 ft. lbs. or if the pinion bearing preload is not within specifications. Under no circumstances should the pinion nut be backed off to reduce the pinion bearing preload; if this is done, a new collapsible spacer will have to be installed and the unit adjusted again until proper preload is obtained.

DIFFERENTIAL BEARING PRELOAD AND RING GEAR-TO-PINION BACKLASH

The threaded adjuster uses a hex drive hole, and requires special tool C–4164 to adjust the side bearing preload through the axle tube. An adjuster lock with two pointed teeth which engage in the exposed adjuster thread when the lock is tightened is provided. The shims will range from 0.020–0.038 in. and will be equipped with internal centering tabs. The shims, marked with a number which represents its thickness in thousandths of an in., can be installed with either side against the pinion head.

1. Index the gears so that the same gear teeth are in contact throughout the adjustment.

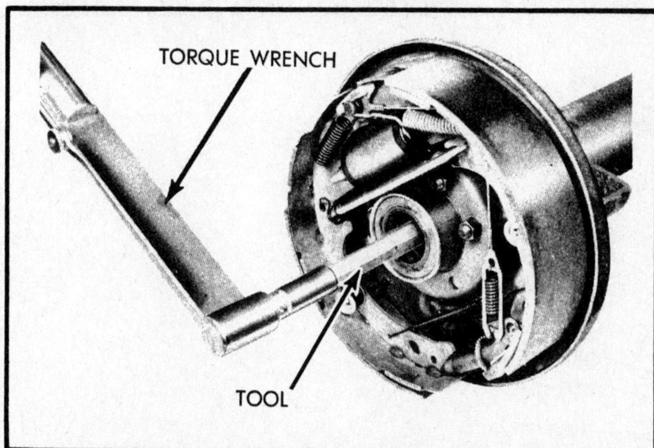

Use of long bar tool with hex end to adjust diffferential bearing pre-load and gear backlash

2. The differential bearing cups will not always move with the adjusters. It is important to seat the bearings by rotating them 5–10 times in each direction, each time the adjusters are moved.

3. With the pinion bearings installed and the preload set, install the differential with adjusters, caps and bearings. Lubricate the bearings and adjuster threads. Check to be sure that there are no crossed threads. Tighten the top cap screws on the right and left to 10 ft. lbs. Tighten the bottom cap screws fingertight until the head is just seated on the bearing cap.

4. Using the tool, check to be sure that the adjuster rotates freely. Turn both adjusters in until bearing play is eliminated with some drive gear backlash (0.010 in.). Seat the bearing rollers.

5. Install and register a dial indicator against the drive side of a gear tooth. Check the backlash at four positions to find the point of minimum backlash. Rotate the gear to the position of least backlash and mark the tooth so that all readings will be taken at the same point.

6. Loosen the right adjuster and turn the right adjuster until the backlash is 0.003–0.004 in. with each adjuster tightened to 10 ft. lbs. Seat the bearings rollers.

7. Tighten the differential bearing cap screws to 100 ft. lbs.

8. Tighten the right adjuster to 70 ft. lbs. and seat the rollers, until the torque remains constant at 70 ft. lbs. Measure the backlash. If the backlash is not 0.006–0.008 in. increase the torque on the right adjusters and seat the rollers until the correct backlash is obtained. Tighten the left adjuster to 70 ft. lbs. and seat the bearings until the torque remains constant.

9. If the assembly is properly done, the initial reading on the left adjuster will be approximately 70 ft. lbs. If it is substantially less, the entire procedure should be repeated.

10. After adjustments are complete, install the adjuster locks. Be sure the teeth are engaged in the adjuster threads. Torque the lockscrews to 90 inch lbs.

Final Assembly

1. Install the axle shafts, C-clips, reinstall the pinion shaft and lock screw and tighten securely.

2. Install the cover on the differential housing, using a new gasket.

3. Refill the rear axle housing with lubricant.

Ford—Semi-Floating Single Speed Axle, Removable Carrier Type

This is a conventional type axle used on light duty Ford trucks. The axle design uses a removable carrier with the assembly bolted to the axle housing. The axle uses hypoid type gears and has the pinion gear mounted below the center line on the ring gear. The pinion gear is supported by two bearings in front of the gear and one behind. It is important to refer to the tag showing the axle and model number which is secured to the housing to obtain proper replacement parts.

CARRIER ASSEMBLY

Removal

1. With the vehicle raised on a lift, remove the axle shafts from the housing.

2. Remove the drive shaft from the carrier assembly.

3. With a drain pan under the axle, remove the retaining bolts from the carrier and drain the gear lube.

4. Remove the carrier assembly from the axle.

Installation

1. Clean the surfaces of the carrier and the axle housing. Install a new gasket.

2. Position the carrier assembly on the studs in the housing and install the retaining nuts. Torque the nuts to 30–40 ft. lbs.

3. Install the drive shaft and torque the bolts to 13–17 ft. lbs.

4. Install the axles in the housing and secure.

5. Fill the axle housing to the proper level with gear lube and road test for proper operation.

DIFFERENTIAL CASE

Removal and Disassembly

1. Remove the carrier assembly from the axle housing and mount the carrier in a holding fixture.

2. Mark the bearing caps and adjusting nuts so they may be installed in their original positions when assembling.

3. Remove the adjusting nut locks, bearing caps and adjusting nuts.

4. Lift the differential assembly out of the carrier. Using a bearing puller, remove the side bearings from the differential case.

5. Mark the side of the case, the ring gear and the cover so they can be installed in their original positions.

6. Remove the bolts that retain the ring gear to the case and using a soft hammer, tap the ring gear from the case.

7. Using a drift, drive the lock pin from the pinion shaft and separate the halves of the differential case.

8. Drive the pinion shaft out of the case using a brass drift and remove the thrust washers and gears.

DRIVE PINION AND BEARING RETAINER

Removal and Disassembly

1. With a holding fixture installed on the flange, remove the pinion nut and washer. Leave the holding fixture on the flange and using a puller, remove the flange from the pinion shaft.

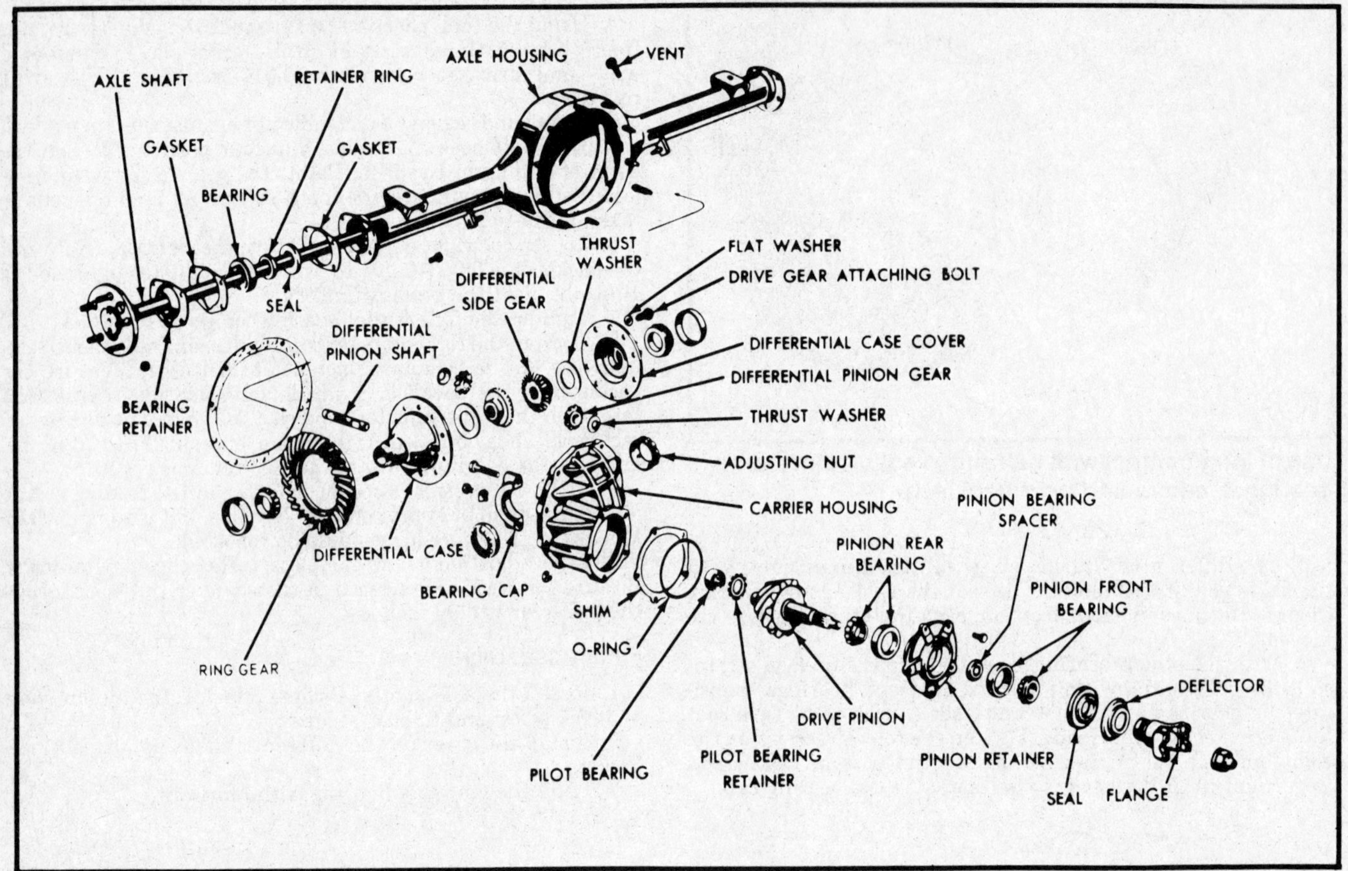

Removeable carrier axle—disassembled

2. Using a seal puller, remove the pinion seal from the retainer assembly.
3. Remove the bolts from the retainer assembly and lift the retainer from the carrier. Measure the thickness of the shim that was between the retainer and the carrier assembly. Record the result.
4. Install a piece of hose on the pinion pilot bearing surface in front of the pinion gear. Mount the retainer assembly in a press and press the pinion gear out of the retainer.
5. Mount the pinion shaft in a press and press the rear bearing from the pinion shaft.

PINION BEARING CUP

Replacement

1. With the retainer assembly mounted in a press, using the proper tool, press the front and rear bearing cups from the assembly.
2. Check the inside surfaces of the retainer for any nicks, dirt or distortion.
3. Install the new cups by pressing them into place with the proper tool. When the cups are installed, make sure they are seated in the retainer by trying to fit a 0.0015 in. feeler gauge, between the cup and the bottom of the bore.

PILOT BEARING

Replacement

1. Using a bearing driver, drive the bearing and retainer out of the carrier assembly.
2. Using the same tool, drive the new bearing into place until the driver bottoms against the case.
3. Drive a new retainer into place with the concave side up.

DRIVE PINION AND BEARING RETAINER

Assembly and Installation

1. Mount the pinion gear in a press and press the rear bearing into place.
2. Install the bearing spacer, bearing retainer and front bearing on the pinion shaft and press them into place. Be careful not to crush the bearing spacer.
3. Install a new O-ring in the groove in the retainer assembly. Do not twist the O-ring when fitting it into place.
4. Lubricate both pinion bearings.
5. Check the thickness of the original shim that was recorded earlier. Located on the head of the pinion gear is the shim adjustment number. Compare the number on the old pinion with the one on the new pinion. Refer to the table which indicates the amount of change to the original shim thickness for proper operation.
6. Install the new shim on the housing and install the pinion and retainer assembly, being careful not to damage the O-ring.
7. Install the bearing retainer bolts and torque them to 30–40 ft. lbs.
8. Using a seal driver, install a new pinion seal in the retainer assembly.
9. Position a holding tool on the flange and install the flange on the pinion shaft. With the holding tool still in place, install the washer and nut on the pinion shaft and torque the nut to 175 ft. lbs. Check the pinion bearing preload. The preload should be 8–14 inch lbs. for used bearings and 22–32 inch lbs. for new bearings. *Do not* overtighten the nut. *Do not* back off the nut to obtain the proper preload. If the 175 ft. lbs. initial torque was

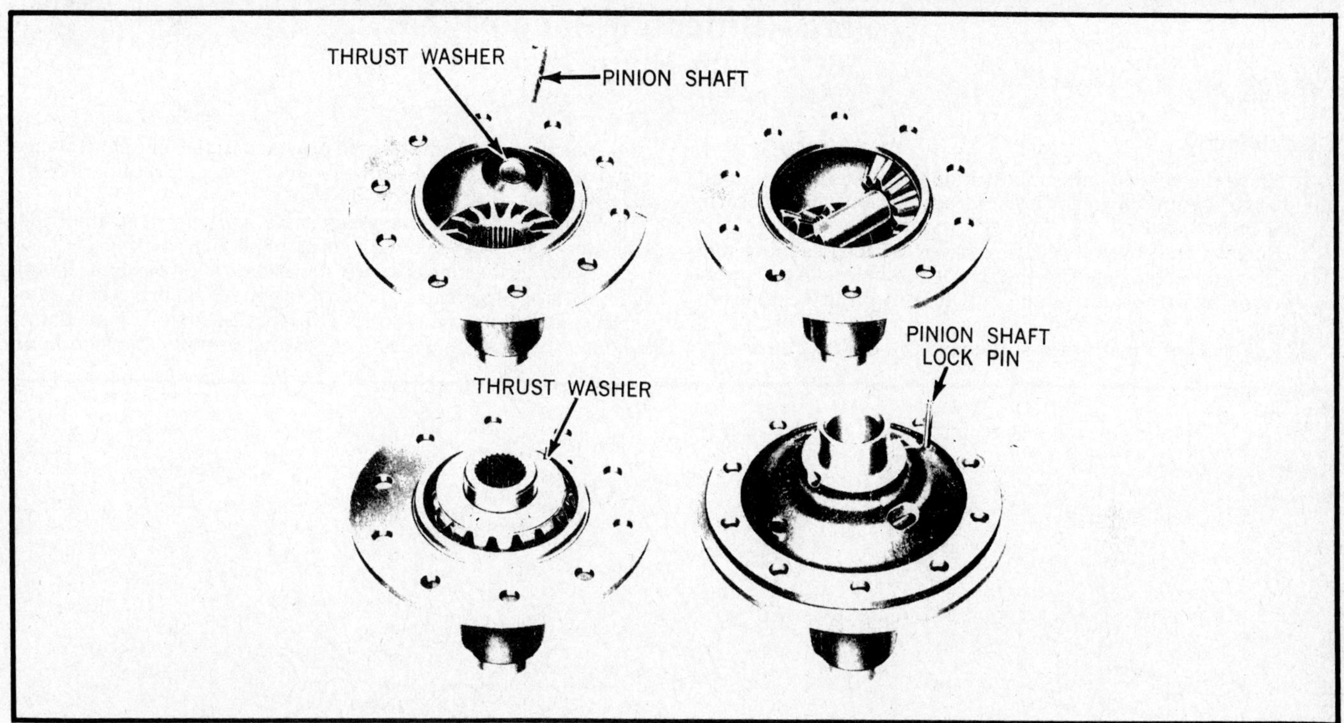

Differential case assembly

too much, the collapsible spacer must be replaced. Tighten the pinion only enough to obtain the right preload torque.

DIFFERENTIAL CASE

Assembly and Installation

1. Lubricate all of the differential parts with gear lube before assembling.
2. Install a side gear and thrust washer in the case bore. Using a soft hammer, drive the pinion shaft into the case far enough to hold a pinion thrust washer and gear. Place the second pinion thrust washer and gear in position and carefully tap the pinion shaft into place. Be sure to line up the holes for the lock pin in the pinion shaft.
3. With the second side gear and thrust washer in place, install the cover on the differential case. Drive the pinion lock pin into place. Insert an axle shaft spline into the side gear and check for free rotation of the gears.
4. Install two, two in. long $^{7}/_{16}$ (N.F.) bolts through the differential case and thread them a little way into the ring gear. These will act as a guide when installing the ring gear on the case. Tap the ring gear into place.
5. Remove the guide pins and install the ring gear bolts. Tighten the bolts evenly to 65–85 ft. lbs.
6. If the differential bearings were removed, install the assembly in a press and press the new bearings into place.
7. Coat the bearing bores in the carrier with gear lube and install the bearing cups on the bearings. Place the differential assembly in the carrier.
8. Slide the differential case in the carrier bore until there is a slight amount of backlash between the gears.
9. Install the adjusting nuts in the carrier so that they just contact the bearing cups. The nuts should be engaged about the same number of threads on each side.
10. Position the bearing caps in the carrier. Be careful to line up the marks. Install the cap bolts and torque them to 70–80 ft. lbs. Make sure the adjusting nuts turn freely as the bolts are being tightened.
11. Adjust the backlash and bearing preload as follows:
    a. Loosen the bearing cap bolts then retighten them to 35 ft. lbs.
    b. Loosen the adjusting nut on the pinion side so that it is away from the bearing cup. Tighten the nut on the opposite side so that the ring gear is forced into the pinion with no backlash.
    c. Recheck the nut on the pinion side to make sure it is still loose. Now tighten this nut until it contacts the bearing cup. After it contacts the cup, turn it two more notches.
    d. Rotate the ring gear several times in each direction. This helps to seat the bearings in the cups.
    e. Again loosen the nut on the pinion side. If there is any backlash between the gears, tighten the nut on the ring gear side until the backlash is removed.
    f. Install a dial indicator on the carrier assembly. Tighten the nut on the pinion side until it just contacts the cup. With the dial indicator set at zero, tighten the pinion side nut until the case is spread 0.008–0.012 in. with new bearings and 0.005–0.008 in. with old bearings. As this preload is applied the ring gear is forced away from the pinion and usually results in the correct backlash.
    g. Mount the dial indicator on the ring gear and check the gear for backlash. Make sure the bearing caps are torqued to 75–85 ft. lbs.
    h. The backlash should be between 0.008–0.012 in. If the backlash is not correct, loosen one nut and tighten the other an equal amount to move the ring gear in or out to correct the measurement. When making final adjustments, always move the adjusting nuts in a tightening direction. To do this, if a nut had to be loosened one notch, loosen it two notches and tighten it one. This makes certain the nut is in contact with the cup and will not shift when the vehicle is in operation.
    i. Coat the ring gear teeth with a marking compound and check the tooth pattern. If the pattern is not correct make the necessary changes to bring it into adjustment.
12. Install the carrier assembly in the vehicle and road test for proper operation.

Ford—Bronco II/Ranger
6 3/4 Inch Ring Gear

Disassembly

1. Raise the vehicle and support it on the underbody, so that the rear axle drops down as far as the springs and shock absorbers permit.

2. Remove the cover from the carrier casting rear face and drain the lubricant. Perform the inspection before disassembly of carrier as directed under the Cleaning and Inspection Section.

3. Remove both rear wheels. Remove the brake drums.

4. Working through the hole provided in the axle shaft flange, remove the nuts that attach the wheel bearing retainers to the axle housing. Pull the axle shafts.

5. Remove the brake backing plate and wire it to the frame rail. Remove both seals with the tool shown.

6. Make scribe marks on the driveshaft end yoke and the axle U-joint flange to ensure proper position of the driveshaft at assembly. Disconnect the driveshaft from the axle U-joint flange. Remove the driveshaft from the transmission extension hous-

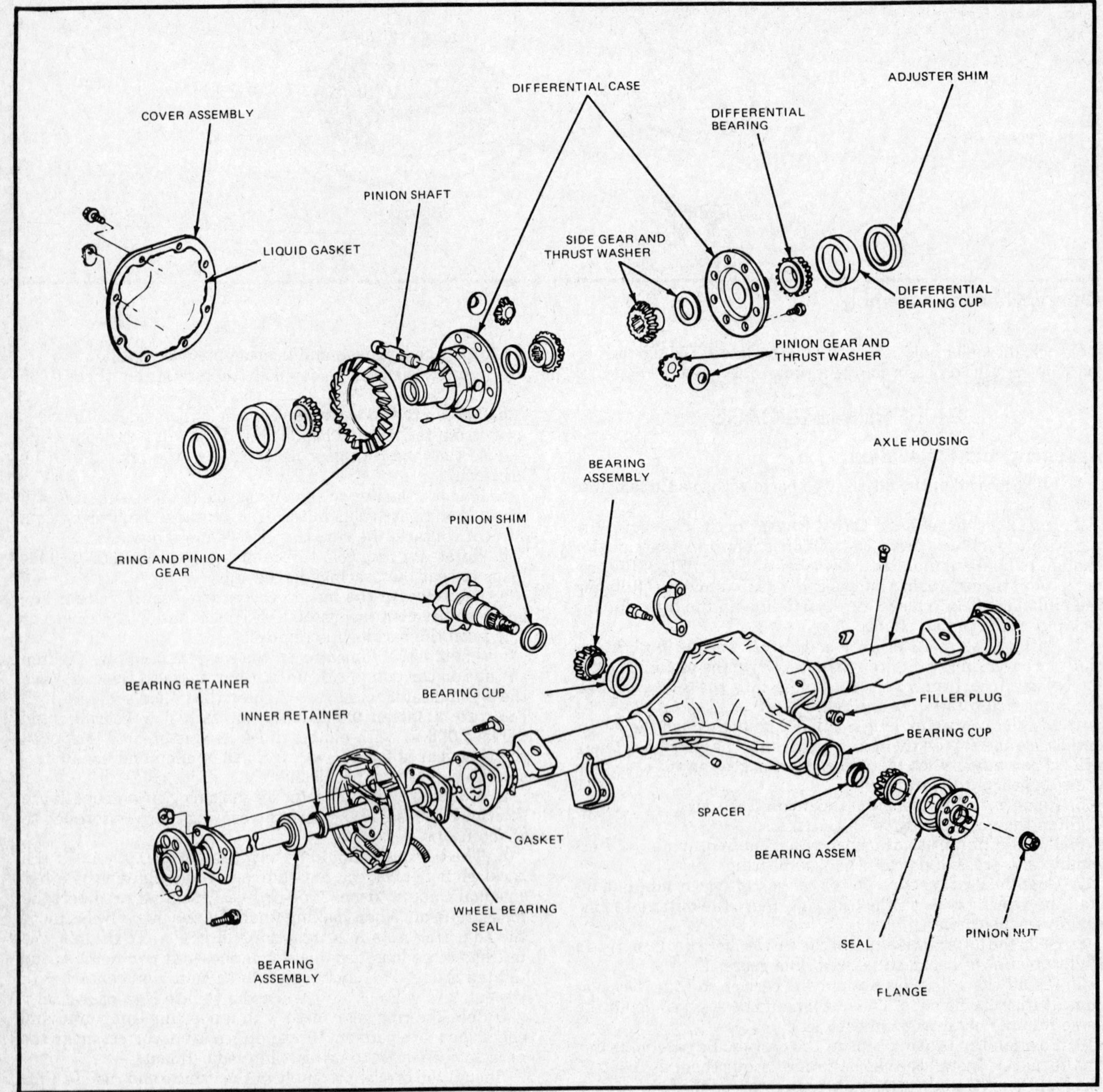

Exploded view 6¾ inch axle assembly

ing. Install an oil seal replacer tool in the transmission extension housing to prevent transmission leakage.

7. Check and record the ring gear runout and the ring gear backlash.

8. Mark one differential bearing cap and the case to help ensure proper position of the parts during assembly.

9. Loosen the differential bearing cap bolts and bearing caps. Pry the differential case, bearing cups and shims out until they are loose in the bearing caps. Remove the bearing caps and the differential assembly from the carrier.

NOTE: The direction of arrows on bearing caps must be noted. When reassembled, the arrows must be pointing outward.

10. Mark the companion flange in relation to the pinion shaft. Hold the rear axle companion flange with the proper tool and remove the pinion nut. If a new gear set is being installed, the companion flange need not be marked.

11. Remove the companion flange.

12. With a soft-faced hammer, drive the pinion out of the front bearing cone and remove it through the rear of the carrier casting.

13. Remove the pinion seal and front bearing cone from the front of the carrier casting.

DRIVE PINION

Disassembly

1. Remove the drive pinion, front bearing cone, spacer, and seal.

2. Remove the pinion rear bearing cone. Measure the shim found under the bearing cone with a micrometer. Record the thickness of the shim.

NOTE: Before assembling the rear bearing cone to the piston, it will be necessary to adjust Pinion.

DRIVE PINION DEPTH ADJUSTMENT

Individual differences in machining the carrier casting and the gear set and variation in bearing widths require a shim between the pinion rear bearing and pinion head, in order to locate the pinion head, in order to locate the pinion for correct tooth contact with the ring gear. When replacing a ring and pinion gear, the correct shim thickness for the new gear set to be installed is determined by the following procedure using Tool T79P–4020–A or equivalent.

1. Place the rear pinion bearing (new or used if in good condition) over the aligning disc and insert it into the pinion bearing cup of the carrier. Place the front bearing into the front bearing cup and assemble the tool handle into the screw and tighten to 27 Nm (20 ft. lbs.).

NOTE: The gauge block must be offset to obtain an accurate reading.

2. Center the gauge tube into the differential bearing bore. Install the bearing caps and torque the bolts to specification. (Caps to be installed with the arrows pointing outboard).

3. Make sure that the gauge handle adapter screw, aligning adapter, gauge disc and gauge block assembly are securely mounted between front and rear bearing. Recheck tool handle torque prior to gauging to ensure that bearings are properly seated. This can affect final shim selection when improperly assembled. Clean bearing cups and differential pedestal surfaces thoroughly. Apply only light oil film on bearing assemblies prior to gauging.

4. Gauge block should then be rotated several half turns to ensure rollers are properly seated in bearing cups. Rotational torque on the gauge assembly should be 20 inch lbs. with new bearings. Final position should be approximately 45° across gauge tube to ensure that gauge block is in line with gauge tube high point. This area should be utilized for pinion shim selection. Selection of pinion shim with gauge block not lined up with tube high point will cause improper shim selection and may result in axle noise.

5. Utilize pinion shims as the gauge for shim selection, this will minimize errors in attempting to stack feeler gauge stock together or simple addition errors in calculating correct shim thickness.

NOTE: Shims must be flat. Do not use dirty, bent, nicked or mutilated shims as a gauge.

6. It is important to utilize a light drag on the shim for the correct selection. Do not attempt to force the shim between the gauge block and gauge tube. This will minimize selection of a shim thicker than required, which results in a deep tooth contact in final assembly for integral axles. If the pinion has a plus (+) marking, subtract this amount from the feeler gauge measurement.

7. If the pinion has a minus (–) marking, add this amount to the feeler gauge measurement.

DRIVE PINION REAR BEARING

NOTE: The same rear pinion bearing used in this procedure must be used in final assembly of the axle.

1. Place the selected shim(s) on the pinion shaft and press the pinion bearing until firmly seated on the shaft.

PINION BEARING CUPS

Disassembly and Assembly

Do not remove the pinion bearing cups from the carrier casting unless the cups are to be replaced; drive them out of the carrier casting with a drift. Install the new cups with tool T71P–4616–A or equivalent. Make sure the cups are properly seated in their bores. If a 0.0015 in. feeler gauge can be inserted between a cup and the bottom of its bore at any point around the cup, the cup is not properly seated. Whenever the cups are replaced, the cone and roller assemblies should also be replaced.

DIFFERENTIAL CASE

Disassembly

1. If the differential bearings are to be removed, use tool T77F–4220–B or equivalent. Mark the differential case, cover and ring gear for assembly in the original position.

2. Remove the bolts that attach the ring gear to the differential case and discard them. Press the ring gear from the case or tap it off with a soft-faced hammer.

3. Remove the left side of the differential case.

4. With a drift, drive out the differential pinion shaft lock pin.

5. Drive out the pinion shaft with a brass drift. Remove the gears and thrust washers. Clean and inspect all the parts. Repair or replace all parts as indicated by the inspection.

Assembly

1. Install the differential side gears and thrust washers in their bores.

2. Install the pinion shaft aligning the pinion gears and thrust washers.

3. Install the left case on the right and tap them together.

4. Install the pinion shaft lockpin.

5. Install the differential bearing.

AXLE

Assembly

The drive pinion should be set to the correct depth before final assembly setting is proper. Drive pinion preload requires that a new spacer be used when the pinion is removed. Drive pinion bearing preload is set with the drive pinion assembly installed and the pinion nut tightened to specification. Correct preload is indicted when the rotational torque is 0.9–1.6 Nm (8–14 inch lbs.) with original bearing or 1.8–3.2 Nm (16–29 inch lbs.) for new bearings.

Differential Bearing Preload and Ring Gear Backlash is adjusted with the drive pinion and differential case installed. Adjustment is performed by the installation of shims between the differential bearing cup and axle housing.

DRIVE PINION AND DRIVE PINION BEARING PRELOAD ADJUSTMENT

1. Install the pinion front bearing.
2. Install the pinion seal.
3. Insert the companion flange into the seal and hold it firmly against the pinion front bearing cone. From the rear of the carrier casting, insert the pinion shaft with a new spacer into the flange.
4. Start a new pinion nut. Hold the flange and tighten the pinion shaft nut. As the nut is tightened, the pinion shaft is pulled into the front bearing cone and into the flange.
5. the pinion shaft is pulled into the front bearing cone, pinion shaft end play is reduced. While there is still end play in the pinion shaft, the flange and bearing cone will be felt to bottom on the collapsible spacer.

From this point, a much greater torque must be applied to turn the pinion nut, since the spacer must be collapsed. Very slowly, tighten the nut, but check the pinion shaft end play often, to see that the pinion bearing preload does not exceed the limits.

6. If the pinion nut is tightened to the point that the pinion bearing preload exceeds the limits, the pinion shaft must be removed and a new collapsible spacer installed. Do not decrease the preload by loosening the pinion nut. This will remove the compression between the pinion front and rear bearing cones and the collapsible spacer and may permit the front bearing cone to turn on the pinion shaft.
7. As soon as there is a preload on the bearings, turn the pinion shaft in both directions several times to set the bearing rollers.
8. Adjust the bearing preload to specification. Measure the preload with a torque wrench.

DIFFERENTIAL ASSEMBLY

For shim selection after a complete replacement of the rear axle housing, the differential assembly or differential side bearing, use the following instructions. For a ring and pinion replacement only or a backlash adjustment, follow Steps 9 through 13 and Step 15, using the side bearing shims that were originally in the axle.

1. With pinion depth set and pinion installed, place differential case and gear assembly with bearings and cups in carrier.
2. Install a 6.73mm (0.265 in.) shim on left side.
3. Install left bearing cap and tighten bolts finger tight.
4. Install progressively larger shims on the right side until the largest shim selected can be assembled with a slight drag feel.

NOTE: Apply pressure towards left side to ensure bearing cup is seated.

5. Install right side bearing cap and tighten bearing cup bolts to 95–115 Nm (70–85 ft. lbs.).
6. Rotate assembly to ensure free rotation.
7. Check ring gear and pinion backlash. If the backlash is 0.20–0.38mm (0.008–0.015 in.) with 0.30–0.38 (0.012–0.015 in.) preferred, proceed to Step 14. If backlash is not within specifications, go to Step 10, unless zero backlash is measured, then go to Step 8.
8. If a zero backlash condition occurs, add 0.020 in. to the right side and subtract 0.020 in. from the left side to allow backlash indication.
9. Recheck backlash.
10. If backlash is not to specification, correct backlash by increasing thickness of one shim and decreasing thickness on the other shim the same amount. Refer to chart for approximate shim change.
11. Install shim and bearing caps. Tighten cap bolts to 95–110 Nm (70–85 ft. lbs.).
12. Rotate assembly several times.
13. Recheck backlash. If backlash is within specification, go to Step 14. If backlash is not within specification, repeat Step 10. Backlash specification is 0.20–0.38mm (0.008–0.015 in.). Preferred range is 0.30–0.38mm (0.012–0.015 in.).
14. Increase both left and right shim sizes by 0.006 and install for correct differential bearing preload. Make sure shims are fully seated and assembly turns freely.
15. Utilize white marking compound to obtain a tooth mesh contact pattern in your assembly.

NOTE: Reincorporation of pattern inspection is intended to allow technicians the ability to detect gross

BACKLASH CHANGE REQUIRED (INCH)	THICKNESS CHANGE REQUIRED (INCH)	BACKLASH CHANGE REQUIRED (INCH)	THICKNESS CHANGL REQUIRED (INCH)
.001	.002	.009	.012
.002	.002	.010	.014
.003	.004	.011	.014
.004	.006	.012	.016
.005	.006	.013	.018
.006	.008	.014	.018
.007	.010	.015	.020
.008	.010		

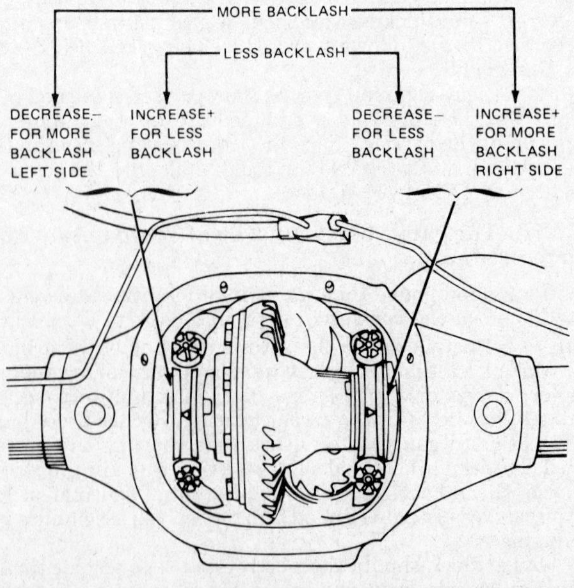

MORE BACKLASH
LESS BACKLASH
DECREASE– FOR MORE BACKLASH LEFT SIDE
INCREASE+ FOR LESS BACKLASH
DECREASE– FOR LESS BACKLASH
INCREASE+ FOR MORE BACKLASH RIGHT SIDE

Shim changes for ring gear and pinion backlash

errors in set up prior to complete reassembly. Pattern contact should be within the primary area of the ring gear tooth surface, avoiding any "narrow" or "hard" contact with outer perimeter of tooth (top to root, toe to heel). Pattern inspection should be on the drive (pull) side. Correct assembly of drive pattern will result in satisfactory coast performance. If gross pattern error is detected, with preferred backlash 0.30–0.38mm (0.012–0.05 in.), recheck pinion shim selection.

16. Install bearing caps and tighten cap bolts to 95–115 Nm (70–85 ft. lbs.).
17. Inspect the machined surfaces of the axle shaft and the axle housing for rough spots, or other irregularities which would affect the sealing action of the oil seal. Check the axle shaft splines for burrs, wear or damage. Carefully remove any burrs or rough spots. Replace worn or damaged parts. Install a new gasket on the housing flange and install the brake backing plate.
18. Carefully slide the axle shaft into the housing so that the rough forging of the shaft will not damage the oil seal. Start the axle splines into the side gar, and push the shaft in until the bearing bottoms in the housing. Install the bearing retainer plate on the mounting bolts t the axle housing, and install the attaching nuts. Tighten the nuts to 27-54 Nm (20–40 ft. lbs.).
19. Remove the oil seal replacer from the transmission extension housing. Align the scribe marks on the flange and driveshaft and connect the driveshaft at the drive pinion flange. Apply Loctite (EOAZ–19554–B) or equivalent to the threads of the attaching bolts and tighten to 95–128 Nm (70–95 ft. lbs.).
20. Install the brake drum and attaching shakeproof retainers. Install the wheel and tire on the brake drum. Install the wheel covers.
21. Clean the gasket mating surface of the rear axle housing and cover. Apply a new continuous bead of silicone rubber sealant (D6AX–19562–B or equivalent) to the carrier casting face.

NOTE: Make sure machined surfaces on both cover and carrier are clean before installing the new silicone sealant. Inside of axle must be covered when cleaning the machined surface to prevent axle contamination.

22. Install cover and tighten cover bolts to 34–47 Nm (25–35 ft. lbs.), except the ratio tag bolt, which is tightened to 20–34 Nm (15–25 ft. lbs.).

NOTE: Cover assembly must be installed within 15 minutes of application of the silicone or new sealant must be applied.

23. Add EOAZ–19580–A (ESP–M2C154–A) lubricant or equivalent through the filler hole until the lubricant level reaches the bottom of the filler hole with the axle in the running position. Install filler plug and tighten to 21–40 Nm (15–30 ft. lbs.).
24. Lower vehicle and road test.

Ford—Bronco II/Ranger

7 1/2 INCH RING GEAR AXLE ASSEMBLY

Disassembly

NOTE: The Aerostar is equipped with a 7 1/2 in. ring gear and the service procedures are the same as outlined below, except for a few minor changes. There are now two new special tools used in the rear axle service procedures. Tool T85L–4067–AH is a driver which is designed to install shims as needed to adjust the ring gear and pinion backlash. The backlash specification is 0.001 to 0.015 in., but 0.012 to 0.015 in. is preferred. Tool T85L–1225–AH is is used to remove the wheel bearing seal from the axle. Both of these tools or their equivalent are needed to complete the rear axle overhaul on the Aerostar. All service operations on the differential case assembly and the drive pinion can be performed with the axle housing installed in the vehicle.

1. Raise the vehicle and place jackstands under the rear frame crossmember. Lower the hoist so that the axle drops down far enough for working ease.
2. Remove the cover from the carrier casting rear face an drain the lubricant. Inspect the case assembly and drive pinion before removal.
3. Remove the rear wheels and brake drums.
4. Remove the axle shafts.
5. Make scribe marks on the driveshaft and yoke and the rear axle companion flange to ensure proper alignment at assembly. Disconnect the driveshaft from the rear axle companion flange. Remove the driveshaft assembly from the vehicle. Insert an oil seal replacement tool in the transmission extension housing to prevent leakage.
6. Check and record the ring gear runout. Check and record the ring gear backlash.
7. Mark on differential bearing cap to help position the caps properly during assembly.
8. Loosen the differential bearing cap bolts and bearing caps.

NOTE: The direction of arrows on bearing caps must be noted. When reassembled, the arrows must be pointing in the same direction as before removal.

9. Pry the differential case, bearing cups and shims out until they are loose in the bearing caps. Remove the bearing caps and remove the differential assembly out of the carrier. On conventional differentials, if the ring is removed, discard the bolts. Install new bolts, coated with Loctite or equivalent. Tighten to 95–115 Nm (70–85 ft. lbs.).
10. Mark the companion flange in relation to the pinion shaft. Hold the rear axle companion flange with the proper tool and remove the pinion nut. If a new gear set is being installed, the companion flange need not be marked.
11. Remove the companion flange. With a soft-faced hammer, drive the pinion out of the front bearing cone and remove it through the rear of the carrier casting.
12. Remove the drive pinion oil seal with Tool 1125–AC and T50T–100–A or their equivalent. Remove the front pinion bearing cone and roller and slinger from the carrier casting.

DRIVE PINION

Disassembly

1. Remove the drive pinion, front bearing cone, spacer, and seal.
2. To remove the pinion rear bearing cone, use tool T71P–4621–B or equivalent. Measure the shim found under the bearing cone with a micrometer. Record the thickness of the shim.

NOTE: Before assembling the rear bearing cone to the pinion, it will be necessary to adjust pinion depth.

DRIVE PINION DEPTH ADJUSTMENT

Individual differences in machining the carrier casting and the gear set and variation in bearing widths require a shim between the pinion rear bearing and pinion head, in order to locate the

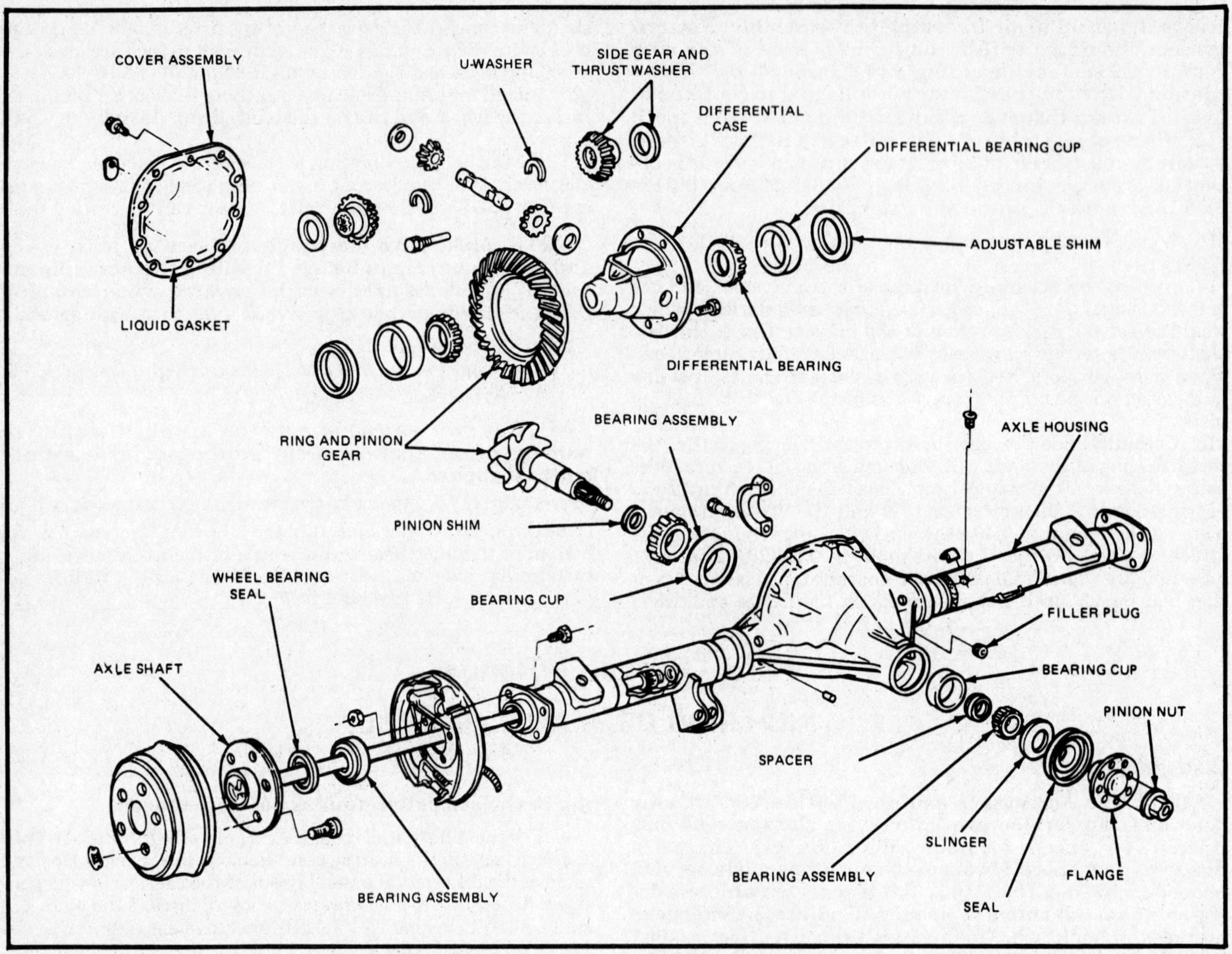

Exploded view 7½ inch axle assembly

pinion for correct tooth contact with the ring gear. When replacing a ring and pinion gear, the correct shim thickness for the new gear set to be installed, is determined by the following procedure using tool T79P–4020–A or equivalent.

PINION DEPTH TOOL SET

1. Place the rear pinion bearing (new or used if in good condition) over the aligning disc and insert it into the pinion bearing cup of the carrier. Place the front bearing into the front bearing cup and assemble the tool handle into the screw and tighten to 27 Nm (20 ft. lbs.).

NOTE: The gauge block must be offset to obtain an accurate reading.

2. Center the gauge tube into the differential bearing bore. Install the bearing caps and torque the bolts to specification. (Caps to be installed with the arrows point outboard.).

3. Make sure that the gauge handle adapter screw, aligning adapter, gauge disc and gauge block assembly are securely mounted between front and rear bearing. Recheck tool handle torque prior to gauging to ensure that bearings are properly seated. This can affect final shim selection when improperly assembled. Clean bearing cups and differential pedestal surfaces thoroughly. Apply only light oil film on bearing assemblies prior to gauging.

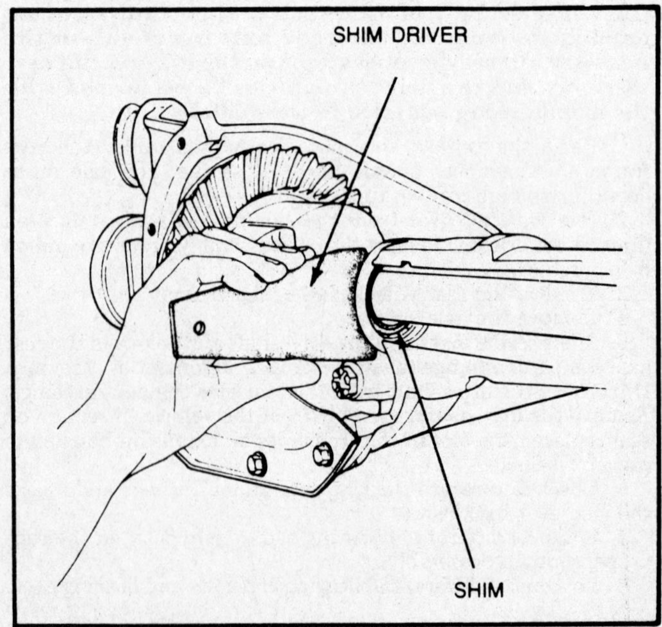

Typical Aerostar shim driver

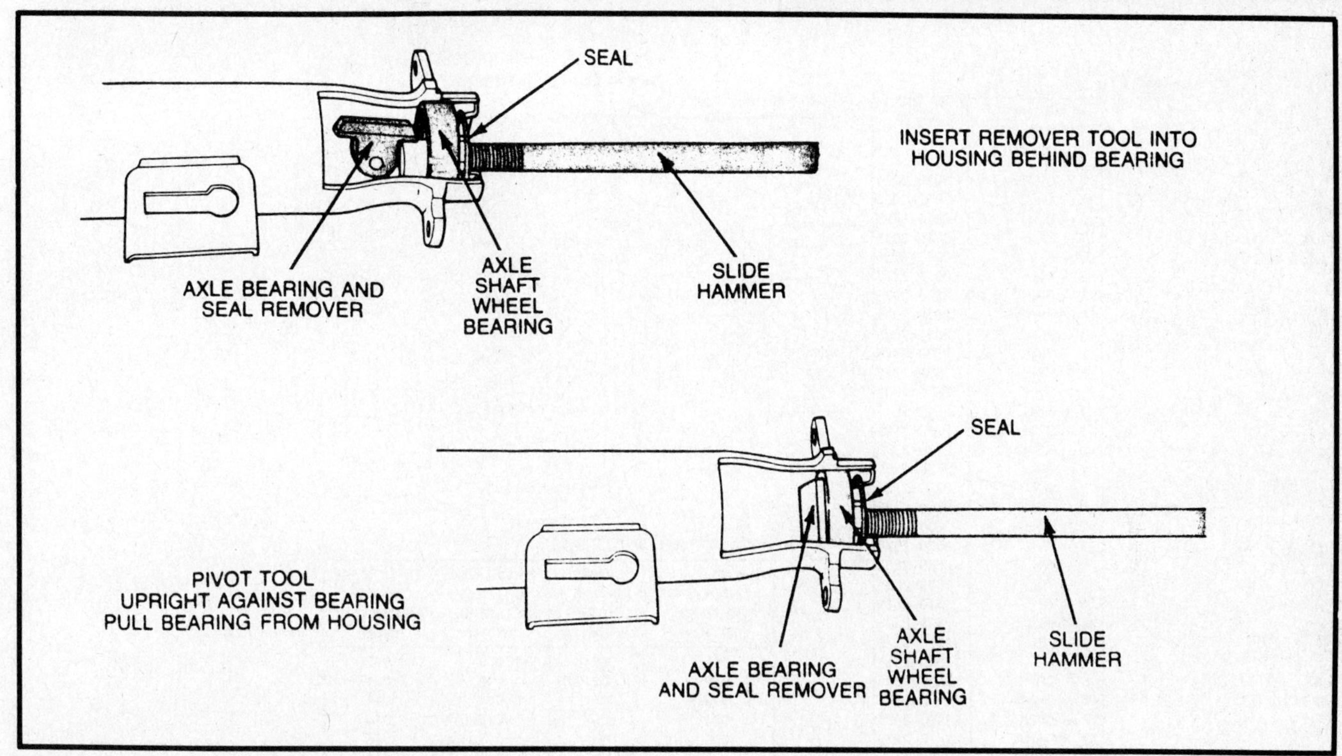

Exploded view of the axle shaft wheel bearing removal

4. Gauge block should then be rotated several half turns to ensure rollers are properly seated in bearing cups. Rotational torque on the gauge assembly should be 20 inch lbs. with new bearings. Final position should be approximately 45° across gauge tube to ensure that gauge block is in line with gauge tube high point. This area should be utilized for pinion shim selection. Selection of pinion shim with gauge block not lined up with tube high point will cause improper shim selection and may result in axle noise.

5. Utilize pinion shims as the gauge for shim selection. This will minimize errors in attempting to stack feeler gauge stock together or simple addition errors in calculating correct shim thickness.

NOTE: Shims must be flat. Do not use dirty, bent, nicked or mutilated shims as a gauge.

6. It is important to utilize a light drag on the shim for the correct selection. Do not attempt to force the shim between the gauge block and gauge tube. This will minimize selection of a shim thicker than required which results in a deep tooth contact in final assembly for integral axles.

7. If the pinion has a plug (+) marking, subtract his amount from the feeler gauge measurement. If the pinion has a minimum (–) marking, add this amount to the feeler gauge measurement.

ASSEMBLY OF DRIVE PINION REAR BEARING CONE

NOTE: The same rear pinion bearing used in this procedure must be used in final assembly of the axle.

1. Place the selected shim(s) on the pinion shaft an depress the pinion bearing until firmly seated on the shaft.

DRIVE PINION BEARING CUPS

Disassembly and Assembly

Do not remove the pinion bearing cups from the carrier casting unless the cups are worn or damaged. If the pinion bearing cups are to be replaced, drive them out of the carrier casting with a drift. Install the new cups. Make sure the cups are properly seated in their bores. If a 0.0015 in. feeler gauge can be inserted between a cup and the bottom of its bore at any point around the cup, the cup is not properly seated. Whenever the cups are replaced, the cone and roller assemblies should also be replaced.

Assembly

The drive pinion must be set to the correct depth before final assembly. Drive pinion preload requires that a new spacer be used when the pinion is removed. Drive pinion bearing preload is set with the drive pinion assembly installed and the pinion nut tightened to specification. Correct preload is indicted when the rotational torque is 0.9–1.6 Nm (8–14 inch lbs.) with the original bearings or 1.8–3.2 Nm (16–29 inch lbs.) for used bearings. Differential Bearing Preload and Ring Gear Backlash is adjusted with the drive pinion and differential case installed. Adjustment is performed by the installation of shims between the differential bearing cup and axle housing.

DRIVE PINION AND DRIVE PINION BEARING PRELOAD ADJUSTMENT

1. Install the pinion front bearing and slinger.
2. Apply grease, C1AZ–19590–B or equivalent between the lips of the pinion seal and install the pinion seal.
3. Insert the companion flange into the seal and hold it firmly against the pinion front bearing cone. From the rear of the carrier casting, insert the pinion shaft, with a new spacer, into the flange.

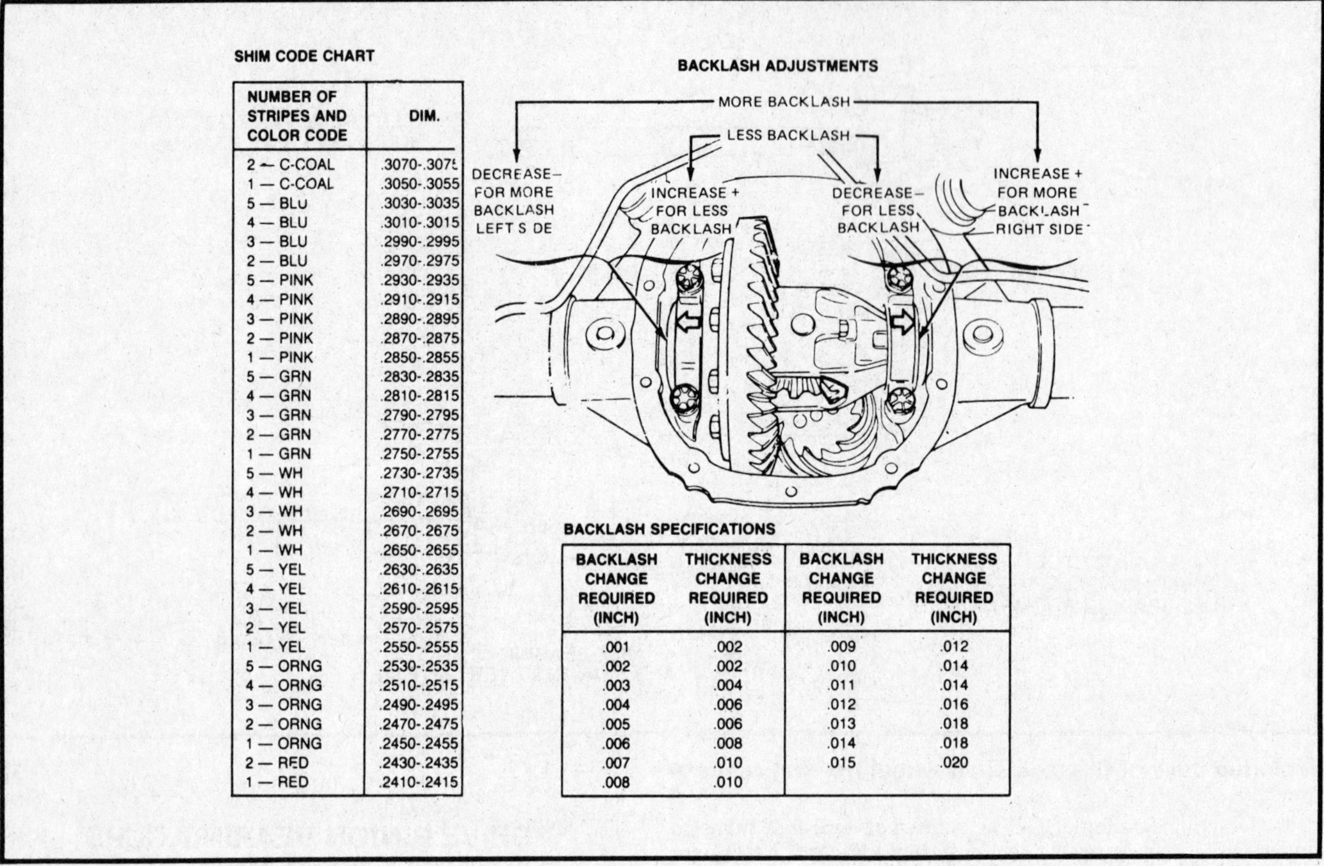

SHIM CODE CHART

NUMBER OF STRIPES AND COLOR CODE	DIM.
2 — C-COAL	.3070-.3075
1 — C-COAL	.3050-.3055
5 — BLU	.3030-.3035
4 — BLU	.3010-.3015
3 — BLU	.2990-.2995
2 — BLU	.2970-.2975
5 — PINK	.2930-.2935
4 — PINK	.2910-.2915
3 — PINK	.2890-.2895
2 — PINK	.2870-.2875
1 — PINK	.2850-.2855
5 — GRN	.2830-.2835
4 — GRN	.2810-.2815
3 — GRN	.2790-.2795
2 — GRN	.2770-.2775
1 — GRN	.2750-.2755
5 — WH	.2730-.2735
4 — WH	.2710-.2715
3 — WH	.2690-.2695
2 — WH	.2670-.2675
1 — WH	.2650-.2655
5 — YEL	.2630-.2635
4 — YEL	.2610-.2615
3 — YEL	.2590-.2595
2 — YEL	.2570-.2575
1 — YEL	.2550-.2555
5 — ORNG	.2530-.2535
4 — ORNG	.2510-.2515
3 — ORNG	.2490-.2495
2 — ORNG	.2470-.2475
1 — ORNG	.2450-.2455
2 — RED	.2430-.2435
1 — RED	.2410-.2415

BACKLASH SPECIFICATIONS

BACKLASH CHANGE REQUIRED (INCH)	THICKNESS CHANGE REQUIRED (INCH)	BACKLASH CHANGE REQUIRED (INCH)	THICKNESS CHANGE REQUIRED (INCH)
.001	.002	.009	.012
.002	.002	.010	.014
.003	.004	.011	.014
.004	.006	.012	.016
.005	.006	.013	.018
.006	.008	.014	.018
.007	.010	.015	.020
.008	.010		

Shim changes for ring gear and pinion backlash

4. Start new pinion nut. Hold the flange with special tool T78P–4851–A or equivalent and tighten the pinion nut. As the nut is tightened, the pinion shaft is pulled into the front bearing cone and into the flange.
5. As the pinion shaft is pulled into the front bearing cone, pinion shaft end play is reduced. While there is still end play in the pinion shaft, the flange and bearing cone will be felt to bottom on the collapsible spacer.
6. From this point, a much greater torque must be applied to turn the pinion nut, since the spacer must be collapsed. Very slowly, tighten the nut, but check the pinion shaft end play often to see that the pinion bearing preload does not exceed the limits.
7. If the pinion nut is tightened to the point that pinion bearing preload exceeds the limits, the pinion shaft must be removed and a new collapsible spacer installed.

NOTE: Do not decrease the preload by loosening the pinion nut. This will remove the compression between the pinion front and rear bearing cones and the collapsible spacer, and may permit the front bearing cone to turn on the pinion shaft.

8. As soon as there is a preload on the bearings, turn the pinion shaft in both directions several times to set the bearing rollers.
9. Adjust the bearing preload to specification. Measure the preload.

Differential Assembly

For shim selection after a complete replacement of the rear axle housing, the differential assembly or differential side bearings use the following instructions. For a ring and pinion replacement only or a backlash adjustment, follow Steps 9 through 13 and Step 15, using the side bearing shims that were originally in the axle.

1. With pinion depth set and pinion installed, place differential case gear assembly with bearings and cups in carrier.
2. Install a 6.73mm (0.265 in.) shim on left side.
3. Install left bearing cap and tighten bolts finger tight.
4. Install progressively larger shims on the right side until the largest shim selected can be assembled with a slight drag feel.

NOTE: Apply pressure towards the left side to ensure bearing cup is seated.

5. Install right side bearing cap and tighten bearing cup bolts to 95–15 Nm (70–85 ft. lbs.).
6. Rotate assembly to ensure free rotation.
7. Check ring gear and pinion backlash. If the backlash is 0.20–0.38mm (0.008–0.015 in.) with 0.304–0.381mm (0.012–0.015 in.) preferred, proceed to Step 14. If backlash is not within specifications, go to Step 10, unless zero backlash is measured, then go to Step 8.
8. If a zero backlash conditions occurs, add 0.020 in. to the right side and subtract 0.020 in. from the left side to allow backlash indication.
9. Recheck backlash.
10. If backlash is not to specification, correct backlash by increasing thickness of one shim and decreasing thickness on the other shim the same amount. Refer to chart for approximate shim change.
11. Install shim and bearing caps. Tighten cap bolts to 95–115 Nm (70–85 ft. lbs.).
12. Rotate assembly several times.

13. Recheck backlash. If backlash is within specification, go to Step 14. If backlash is not within specification, repeat Step 10. Backlash specification is 0.20–0.38mm (0.008–0.015 in.). Preferred range is 0.304–0.381mm (0.012–0.015 in.).
14. Increase both left and right shim sizes by 0.006 in. and install for correct differential bearing preload. Make sure shims are fully seated and assembly turns freely.
15. Utilize white marking compound to obtain a tooth mesh contact pattern in the assembly.

NOTE: pattern inspection is intended to allow technicians the ability to detect gross errors in set up prior to complete reassembly. Pattern contact should be within the primary area of the ring gear tooth surface avoiding any "narrow" or "hard" contact with outer perimeter of tooth (top to root, toe to heel). Pattern inspection should be on the drive (pull) side. Correct assembly of drive pattern will result in satisfactory coast performance. If gross pattern error is detected, the preferred backlash of 0.30–0.38mm (0.012–0.015 in.), recheck pinion shim selection.

16. Install bearing caps and tighten cap bolts to 95–115 Nm (70–85 ft. lbs.).
17. Install the axle shafts.
18. Remove the oil seal replacer from the transmission extension housing. Install the driveshaft in the extension housing. align the scribe marks on the flange and driveshaft and connect the driveshaft at the drive pinion flange. Apply Loctite (EOAZ–19554–B) or equivalent to the threads of the attaching bolts. Tighten attaching bolts to 90–128 Nm (70–95 ft. lbs.).
19. Install the brake drum and attaching shakeproof retainers. Install the wheel and tire on the brake drum. Install the wheel covers.
20. Clean the gasket mating surface of the rear axle housing and cover.
Apply a new continuous bead of silicone rubber sealant (D6AZ–19562–B or equivalent) to the carrier casting face.

CAUTION

MAKE SURE MACHINED SURFACES ON BOTH COVER AND CARRIER ARE CLEAN BEFORE INSTALLING THE NEW SILICONE SEALANT. INSIDE OF AXLE MUST BE COVERED WHEN CLEANING THE MACHINED SURFACE TO PREVENT AXLE CONTAMINATION.

21. Install cover and tighten cover bolts to 34–47 Nm (25–35 ft. lbs.), except the ratio tag bolt, which is tightened to 20–34 Nm (15–25 ft. lbs.).

NOTE: Cover assembly must be installed within 15 minutes of application of the silicone or new sealant must be reapplied.

22. Add EOAZ–19580–A (ESP–MC2154–A) or equivalent through the filler hole until the lubricant level is 9.5mm ($^3/_8$ in.) below the filler hole with the axle in the running position.
23. Lower vehicle and road test.

Ford—Bronco, E-150 and F-150

9.0 INCH RING GEAR REAR AXLE

Carrier Removal

1. Raise and support the rear of the vehicle safely, and remove the two rear wheel and tire assemblies.
2. Remove the two brake drums and the axle flange studs. Working through the access hole provided in each axle shaft flange, remove the nuts that secure the rear wheel bearing retainer plate. Pull each axle shaft assembly out of the axle housing, using axle shaft puller adapter tool T66l–4234–A or equivalent. Wire the backing plate to the frame rail . Remove and discard the old gasket if so equipped.
3. Make scribe marks on the drive shaft yoke end and the axle companion flange to insure proper position at assembly. Disconnect the drive shaft at the rear axle U-joint. Hold the cups on the spider with tape. Mark the cups so that they will be in their original position relative to the flange when they are assembled.
4. Remove the drive shaft from the transmission extension housing. Install an oil seal replacer tool or equivalent in the housing to prevent transmission fluid leakage.
5. Clean the area around the carrier with a wire brush and wipe it clean to prevent any dirt from entering the housing. Place a suitable drain pan under the carrier, remove the carrier attaching nuts and washers and drain the axle. Remove the carrier assembly from the axle housing.

Carrier Disassembly

1. Place the carrier assembly into a suitable holding fixture, check and record the ring gear runout and the ring gear backlash.
2. Mark one of the differential bearing cap and the mating bearing support with punch marks to help position the parts during reassembly of the carrier. Remove the adjusting nut locks, bearing caps, (remove the bearing caps with a soft mallet) and adjusting nuts. Lift the differential case assembly out of the carrier.
3. Remove the differential side bearings with special tools T57L–4220–A or T66P–4220–A or their equivalent. Mark the differential case, differential cover and ring gear for assembly in the original position.

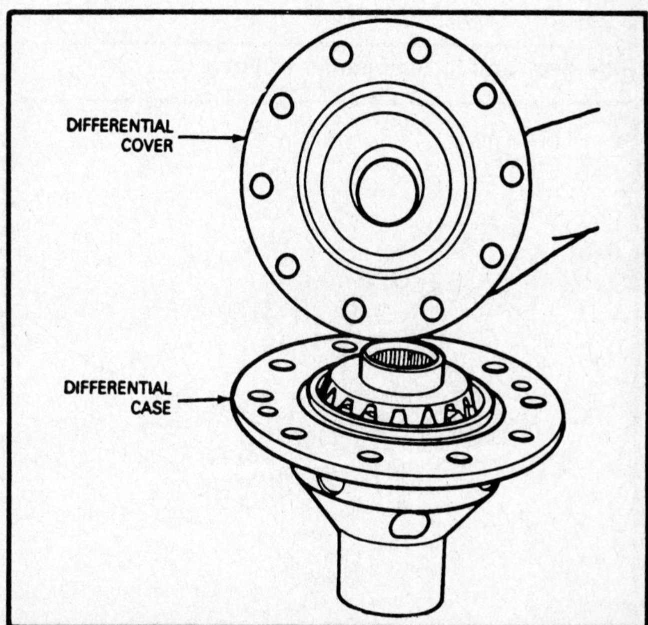

Removing the differential cover

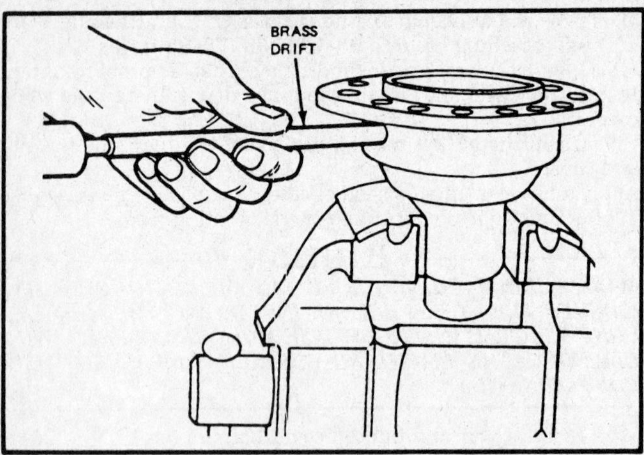

Removing the long differential pinion shaft

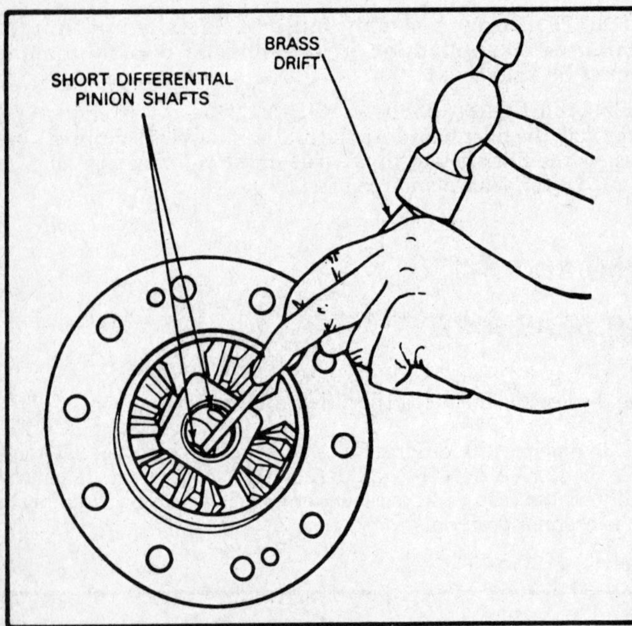

Side gear and thrust washer removal

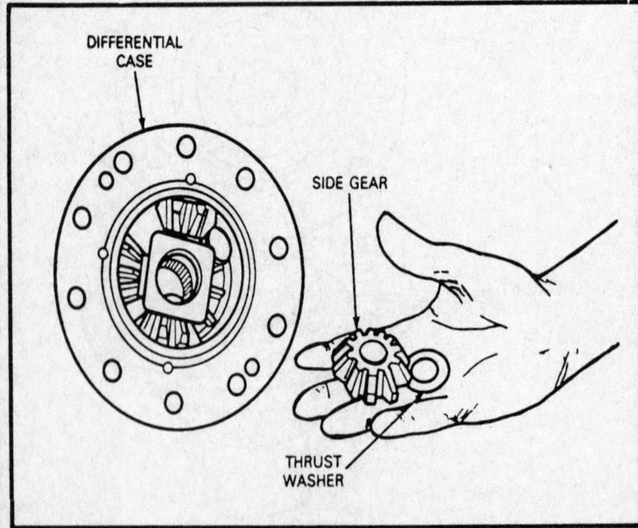

Removing the short differential pinion shaft

4. Separate the differential cover from the differential case. Remove the side gear thrust washer and the side gear. Using a drift, drive out the three diferential pinion shaft lock pins. Drive out the long differential pinion shaft with a brass drift.

5. With a brass drift carefully positioned inside the case, drive out the two short differential pinion shafts. Remove the positioning block, differential pinions and the thrust washers from the differential case.

6. Remove the side gear and side gear thrust washer from the case.

7. Position the carrier assembly in a manner that will permit the removal of the drive pinion shaft nut. Remove the campanion flange from the drive pinion shaft and remove the pinion seal.

8. Remove the pinion and retainer assembly from the carrier housing. If a new pinion bearing and or gear set is installed, a new shim will have to installed. Be very careful not to damage the mounting surfaces of the retainer and the carrier.

9. Place a protective sleeve on the pinion pilot bearing surface. Press the pinion shaft out of the pinion retainer. Press the pinion shaft out of the pinion rear bearing cone, using tool # T71P–4621–B or equivalent.

10. Remove and install a new pinion shaft pilot bearing. Remove the old pinion shaft pilot bearing by pressing it off and install the new one by pressing it on. Install a new pinion shaft pilot bearing retainer, concave side up, on the same press.

NOTE: Do not remove the drive pinion bearing cups from the retainer unless the cups are worn or damaged or if the cone and roller assemblies are damaged.

11. If the cups are worn or damaged, remove them with the use of bearing cup puller T77F–1102–A or T78P–1225–B or equivalent. Install the new bearing cups by pressing them into the retainer with pinion bearing cup replacer T71P–4616–A or eqivalent.

12. After the new cups have been installed, make sure that they are seated in the retainer by trying to insert a 0.0015 in. feeler gauge between the cup and the bottom of the bore. Whenever the cups are replaced, the cone and roller assemblies should also be replaced.

Drive Pinion and Ring Gear Set Assembly

NOTE: When replacing a ring gear and a drive pinion or pinion bearings, select the proper pinion shim thickness by using the following procedure and tool T79P–4020–A or equivalent.

1. Select the proper rear pinion bearing aligning adapter and gauge disc to correspond to the axle size (nine in. ring gear). Slide these adapters over the screw or threaded shaft and install the gauge block on the threaded shaft and tighten it securely.

2. Place this assembly, along with the rear drive pinion bearing, into the pinion bearing retainer assembly. Install the front pinion bearing (new or used, if in good condition) and screw the handle onto the threaded shaft, with the tapered end into the front pinion bearing.

3. The flat end of the handle has a $^3/_8$ in. square hole broached in it. This is designed so that an inch pound torque wrench may be used to obtain the proper pinion bearing preload.

4. Install the pinion bearing retainer assembly into the carrier (without a pinion shim) and tighten the attaching bolts to 30–45 ft. lbs. Rotate the gauge block so that it rests against the pilot boss.

5. Place the differential gauge tube into the differential bearing bore and tighten the bearing caps to the specified torque. Using a feeler gauge, gauge the space between the differential bearing gauge block and gauge tube. Insert a feeler blade direct-

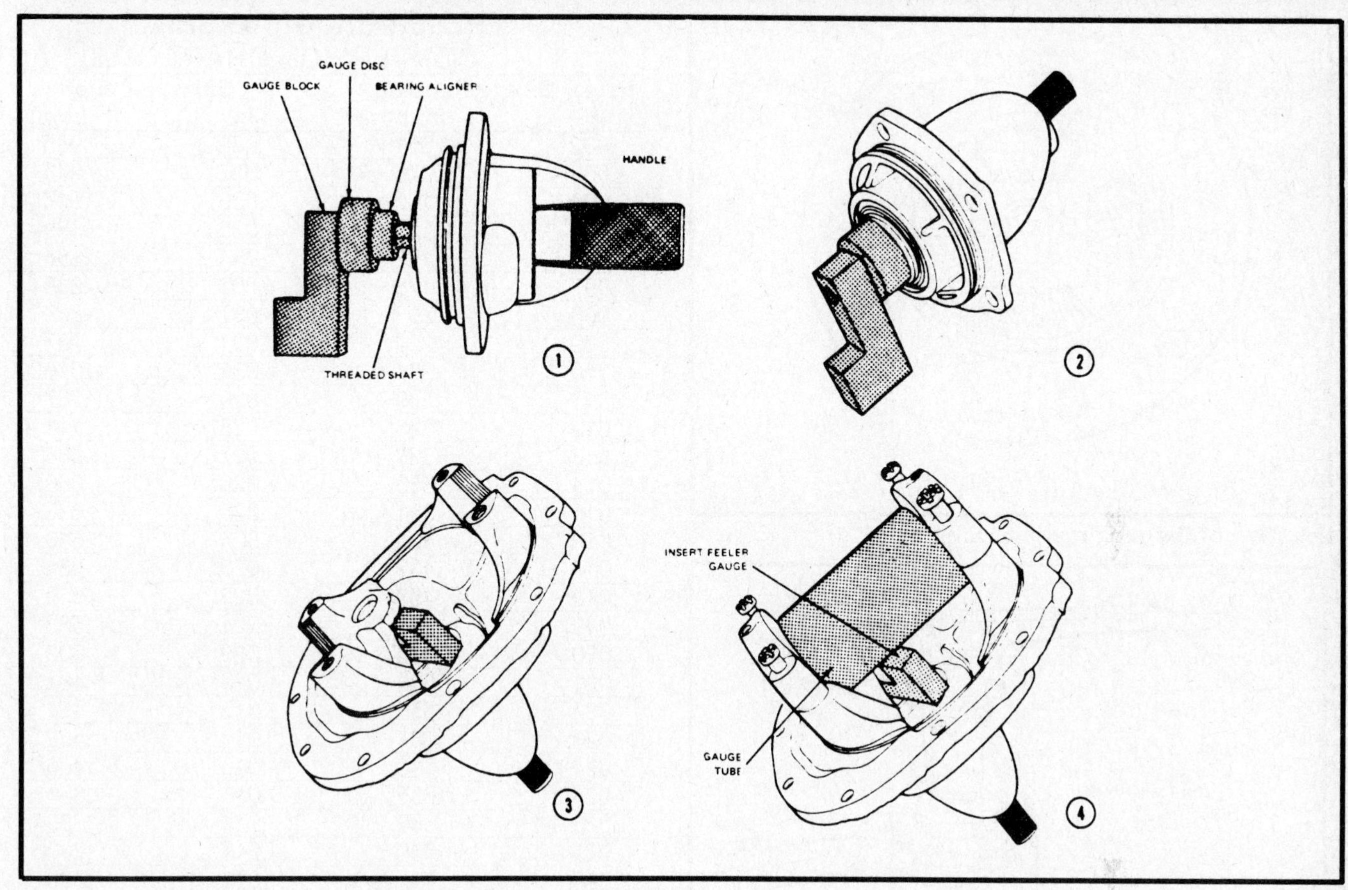

Proper use of the pinion depth gauge tool

ly along the gauge block top to insure a correct reading. The fit should be a slight drag-type feeling.

6. After a correct feeler gauge is obtained, use the conversion chart provided to find the correct shim thickness needed according to the feeler gauge reading.

7. After determining the correct shim thickness as just outlined in this procedure, assemble the pinion bearing retainer as follows.

NOTE: A new ring gear and drive pinion should always be installed in an axle as a matched set, never separately. Be sure the same matching number appears on the ring gear and on the head of the drive pinion.

8. Install the pinion retainer attaching bolts and torque them to 30–45 ft. lbs. . Install the oil slinger, if so equipped.

9. Install a new pinion oil seal in the bearing retainer,install the companion flange. Start a new pinion nut on the drive pinion shaft and apply a small amount of thread lubricant to the flange side of the nut.

10. Hold the flange with tool T57T–4851–B and tighten the pinion nut. Do not use impact tools. Check the pinion bearing preload, the correct preload will be obtained when the torque required to rotate the pinion in the retainer is as specified in the specifications.

11. If the torque required to rotate the pinion is less than specified, tighten the pinion shaft nut a little at a time until the proper preload is established.

NOTE: Do not over-tighten the pinion nut. If excessive preload is obtained as a result of over tightening, replace the collapsible bearing spacer. Do not back off the pinion shaft nut to establish pinion bearing preload.

Differential Case Assembly

NOTE: Lubricate all the differential components liberally with Hypoid Gear Lubricant, EOAZ–19580–A or equivalent during assembly.

1. Place a side gear thrust washer and side gear in the differential case bore. With a soft faced hammer, drive a short differential pinion shaft into the case far enough to retain a pinion thrust washer and pinion gear.

2. Carefully line up the pinion shaft lock pin holes with the holes provided in the case. Drive a short differential pinion shaft only far enough into the case to retain the pinion thrust washer pinion gear.

3. Install the remaining two pinion thrust washers along with the pinion gears into the case. Install the positioning block into the case. Use a soft face hammer, to drive the short differential pinion shafts into the case until the shafts are flush with the side of the case.

4. Insert the long differential pinion shaft and drive it into the case. Be sure the pinion shaft lock holes line up with the holes in the case. Place a second side gear and thrust washer into position. Install the three pinion shaft lock pins. Press the differential cover on the case.

Differential Carrier Assembly

1. Clean the tapped holes in the ring gear with a suitable solvent. Insert two $^{7}/_{16}$ (N.F.) bolts two inches long through the differential case flange and turn them three or four turns into the ring gear as a quide in aligning the ring gear bolt holes. Press or tap the ring gear into position.

2. If the new bolts are coated with a green or yellow coating of approxitmately $^{1}/_{2}$ in. or over the threaded area, use as is. If it is

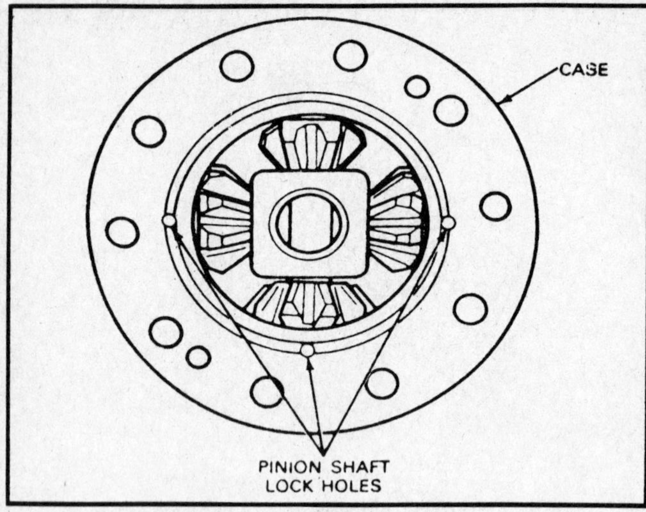

Location of the pinion shaft lock holes

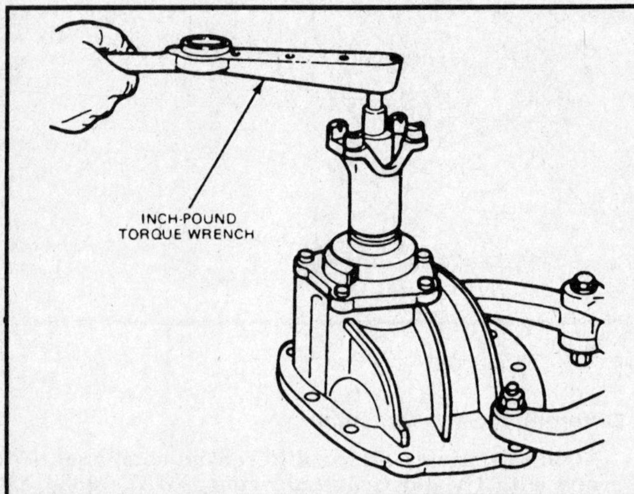

Checking the pre-load on the pinion bearing

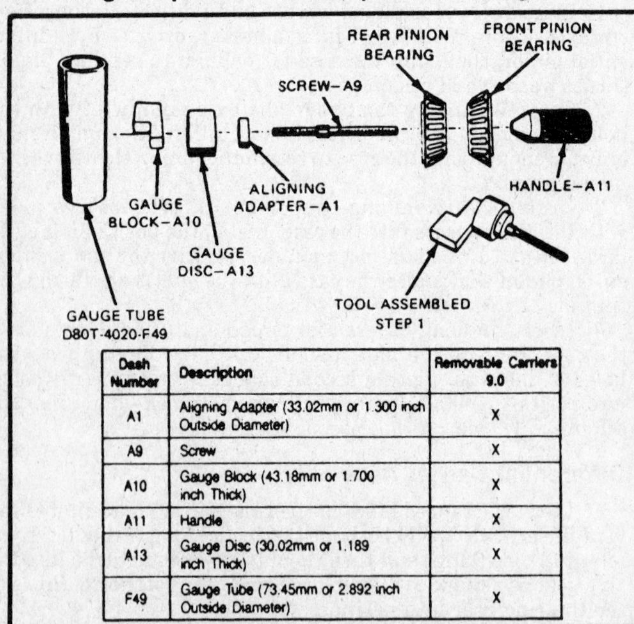

Dash Number	Description	Removable Carriers 9.0
A1	Aligning Adapter (33.02mm or 1.300 inch Outside Diameter)	X
A9	Screw	X
A10	Gauge Block (43.18mm or 1.700 inch Thick)	X
A11	Handle	X
A13	Gauge Disc (30.02mm or 1.189 inch Thick)	X
F49	Gauge Tube (73.45mm or 2.892 inch Outside Diameter)	X

Typical rear axle pinion depth gauge tool

FEELER GAUGE TO SHIM CONVERSION CHART

Feeler Gauge Reading in.	(mm)	Shim Required in.	(mm)
.002	.051	.038	.965
.003	.076	.037	.940
.004	.102	.036	.914
.005	.127	.035	.889
.006	.152	.034	.864
.007	.178	.033	.838
.008	.203	.032	.813
.009	.229	.031	.787
.010	.254	.030	.0762
.011	.279	.029	.737
.012	.305	.028	.711
.013	.330	.027	.686
.014	.356	.026	.660
.015	.381	.025	.635
.016	.406	.024	.610
.017	.432	.023	.584
.018	.457	.022	.559
.019	.483	.021	.533
.020	.508	.020	.508
.021	.533	.019	.483
.022	.559	.018	.451
.023	.584	.017	.432
.024	.610	.016	.406
.025	.635	.015	.381
.026	.660	.014	.356
.027	.686	.013	.330
.028	.711	.012	.305
.029	.737	.011	.279
.030	.762	.010	.254
.031	.787	.009	.229
.032	.813	.008	.208
.033	.838	.007	.178
.034	.864	.006	.152
.035	.889	.005	.127

not coated, apply a suitable thread sealer and torque the bolts to 70–85 ft. lbs. Do not re-use the old bolts.

3. If the differential bearings have been removed, press them in using tool T57L–4221–A2 or equivalent. Wipe a thin coating of axle lubricant on the differential bearing bores so that the differential bearing cups will move easily.

4. Place the cups on the bearings and set the differential case assembly in the carrier. Assemble the differential case and ring gear assembly in the carrier so that the marked tooth on the drive pinion indexes between the marked teeth on the ring gear. Be sure to match the marked gears as indicated. When assembled out of time, the result is noise and improper mating.

5. Slide the assembly along the bores until a slight backlash is felt between the gear teeth. Set the adjusting nuts in the bores using differential bearing nut wrench T70P–4067–A so that they just contact the bearing cups.

6. The nuts should be engaged about the same number of threads (turns) on each side. Carefully position the differential bearing caps on the carrier. Match the marks made when the caps were removed. Before tightening the bearing cap bolts, be sure that the adjuster nuts are properly threaded in the cap and carrier and turn freely.

7. Install the bearing cap bolts and alternately torque them to 70–85 ft. lbs. If the adjusting nuts do not turn freely as the cap bolts are tightened, remove the differential bearing caps and

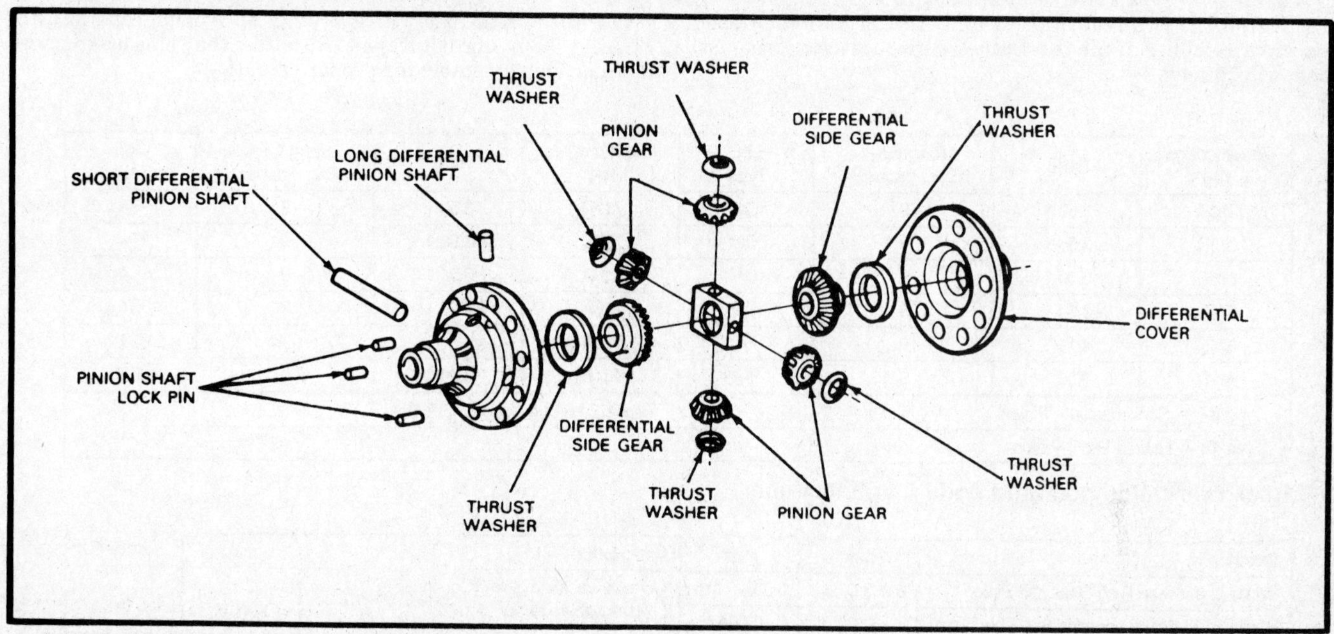

Exploded view of the differential case

again inspect for damaged threads or incorrectly positioned caps.

8. Tightening the bolts to the specified torque is done to be sure that the cups and adjusting nuts are seated. Loosen the cap bolts and tighten them to only 25 ft. lbs. before making adjustments.

9. Adjust the backlash between the ring gear and pinion and the differential bearing preload as described in the following section.

Backlash and Differential Bearing Preload Adjustment

1. Remove the adjusting nut locks, loosen the differential bearing cap bolts, then torque the bolts to 15–20 ft. lbs. before making adjustments.

2. The left adjusting nut is on the ring gear side of the carrier. The right nut is on the pinion side. Loosen the right nut until it is away from the cup. Tighten the let nut until the ring gear is just forced into the pinion with 0.000 backlash, then rotate the pinion several revolutions to be sure there is no binding. Recheck the right nut at this time to make sure that it is still loose.

3. Install a suitable dial indicator. Tighten the right nut until it first contacts the bearing cups. Set the dial indicator to zero and apply pressure to the bearing by tightening the right nut until the indicator reading shows 0.008–0.012 in. case spread.

4. Turn the pinion gear several times in each direction to seat the bearings in the cups and be sure no bind is evident (this step is important). Tighten the bearing cap bolts to 70–85 ft. lbs.

5. Measure the backlash on several teeth around the ring gear. If the backlash is out of specification, loosen one adjusting nut and tighten the opposite nut an equal amount, to move the ring gear away from or toward the pinion.

6. Tightening the left nut moves the ring gear into the pinion to decrease the backlash and tightening the right nut moves the ring gear away.

NOTE: When moving the adjusting nuts, the final movement should always be made in a tightening direction. An example of this is, if the left nut had to be loosened one notch, loosen the nut two turns and tighten it one. This insures that the nut is contacting the bearing cup and that the cup can not shift after being put in service. After all such adjustments, check to be sure that the case spread remains as specified for the new or original bearings used.

7. Use a white marking compound to obtain a tooth mesh contact pattern in the assembly. Pattern contact should be within the primary area of the ring gear tooth surface avoiding any narrow or hard contact with the outer perimeter of tooth (top to root, toe to heel).

8. The pattern inspection should be on the drive (pull) side. The correct assembly of the drive pattern will result in a satisfactory coast performance. If gross pattern error is detected with preferred backlash of 0.012–0.015 in. recheck the pinion shim selection.

Carrier Installation

NOTE: Any synthetic type wheel bearing seals must not be cleaned, soaked or washed in cleaning solvent. Clean the axle housing and shafts with kerosene and swabs. Do not allow any quantity of solvent to touch the wheel bearings. Clean the mating surfaces of the axle housing and carrier.

1. Position the differential carrier on the studs in the axle housing using a new gasket between the carrier and the housing. Apply a bead of Silicone rubber sealant or equivalent to the gasket. Install the carrier to housing attaching nuts and washers. Torque them to 25–40 ft. lbs.

2. Remove the oil seal replacer tool from the transmission extension housing. Position the the drive shaft so that the front U-joint slip yoke splines to the transmission output shaft.

3. Connect the drive shaft to the axle U-joint flange, aligning the scribe marks made on the drive shaft end yoke and the axle U-joint flange during the removal procedure. Install the U-bolts and nuts, tighten the nuts on the U-bolts evenly.

4. Install the two axle shaft assemblies in the axle housing. Be careful not to damage the oil seals. Slowly slide the axle shaft into the housing (Timken bearing axle shafts do not require a gasket). Start the axle splines into the differential side gear and push the shaft until the bearing bottoms in the housing.

5. Install the bearing retainer plates on the attaching bolts on the axle housing flange. Install the nuts on the bolts and alternately torque them to 20–40 ft. lbs.

6. Install the two rear brake drums. Install the rear wheel and tire assemblies. If the rear brakes were backed off, readjust them accordingly.

7. Fill the rear axle with 5.5 pints of hypoid gear lubricant EOAZ–19580–A or equivalent. Road test the vehicle and check the rear axle assembly for proper operation.

Identification Tag	Ratio	Ring Gear Dia. (Inches)	Diff. Type	Identification Tag	Ratio	Ring Gear Dia. (Inches)	Diff. Type
320C	3.50:1	9	C4	717P	3.50:1	9	T4
318D	3.50:1	9	C2	705B	3.00:1	9	T4
316D	3.00:1	9	C4	715A	3.50:1	9	T4
319D	3.50:1	9	T2	716P	3.50:1	9	C4
321C	4.11:1	9	T4	714A	3.50:1	9	C4
317D	3.00:1	9	T4	704B	3.00:1	9	C4
Type C4 — Conventional 4-Pinion				Type C2 — Conventional 2-Pinion			
Type T4 — Limited-Slip 4-Pinion							

Rear axle ratios gear and code identifications

Description	mm	Inch	Description	mm	Inch
Backlash Between Ring Gear and Pinion	0.203-0.381	0.008-0.015	Nominal Locating Shim (Continued) Removable Carrier	0.381	0.015
Maximum Backlash Variation Between Teeth	0.102	0.004			
Maximum Runout of Backface of Ring Gear	0.102	0.004	Shims Available (Steps of 0.001) Removable Carrier	0.254-0.736	0.010-0.029
Differential Side Gear Thrust Washer Thickness	0.762-0.812	0.030-0.032	Differential Bearing Preload Used	0.127-0.177	0.005-0.007
Differential Pinion Gear Thrust Washer Thickness	0.762-0.838	0.030-0.033	New	0.203-0.304	0.008-0.012

Rear axle adjustment

Description	ft-lbs	in-lbs	N·m
Pinion Retainer to Carrier Bolts	30-45		41-60
Ring Gear Attaching Bolts	70-85		95-115
Bearing Cap Bolts	70-85		95-115
Carrier to Housing Nuts	25-40		34-54
Adjusting Nut Lock Bolts	12-25		17-33
Axle Shaft Bearing Retainer Nut	20-40		28-54
Pinion Bearing Preload — Original Bearing		8-14	1.0-1.5
Pinion Bearing Preload — New Bearing		16-29	1.8-3.3

Rear axle torque specifications

Manual Transmissions 13

INDEX

Sequence of Diagnosis

In order to determine the problems that may exist in a transmission, a systematic diagnosis procedure should be followed to locate and repair the malfunction.

1. Consult with the owner or operator to identify the problem.
2. Road test, whenever possible with the owner or operator, to verify the problem is within the transmission and not caused by a related component.
3. Verify that all controls are operating properly and in good condition.
4. With the unit removed from the vehicle, inspect it prior to the disassembly.
5. During the disassembly, inspect the varied parts to locate the source of the problem.
6. Replace companion gears to defective or worn gears. Do not reinstall a part that does not have a long service life remaining.
7. Make any modifications or changes as recommended by the manufacturer.

Transmission Diagnosis and Troubleshooting

Noises with Transmission in Neutral (Always Leave Main Box in Neutral, Auxiliary in Gear When Idling)

1. Misalignment of transmission.
2. Worn flywheel pilot bearing.
3. Worn or scored countershaft bearings.
4. Worn or rough reverse idler gear.
5. Sprung or worn countershaft.
6. Excessive backlash in gears.
7. Worn mainshaft pilot bearing.
8. Scuffed gear tooth contact surface.
9. Insufficient lubrication.
10. Use of incorrect grade of lubricant.

Noises with Transmission in Gear

1. Worn or rough mainshaft rear bearing.
2. Rough, chipped or tapered sliding gear teeth.
3. Noisy speedometer gears.
4. Excessive end play of mainshaft gears.
5. Refer to conditions listed above under noises with transmission in neutral.

Growling, Humming and Grinding

1. Pitted, chipped or cracked gears.
2. Damaged gears or chips in lubricant from failed power-take-off.
3. Excessive gear wear from high mileage or overloading.

Hissing, Thumping and Bumping

1. Bad bearings on way to failure.
2. Broken bearings and retainers.

Metallic Rattles

1. Engine torsional vibration.
2. Clutch disc assembly worn or without torsional vibration dampers.
3. Engine idle speed too low.
4. Rough engine idle.
5. Excessive backlash in power take off mounting.

Squealing, Gear Whine and Gear Seizure

1. One of the free running gears seizing on thrust face or fluted diameter momentarily, then letting go.
2. Whine of excessive backlash in mating gears or improper shimming of power take off unit.

Walking or Jumping out of Gear

CAUSES OUTSIDE TRANSMISSION

1. Improperly positioned forward remote control which limits full travel forward and backward from the remote neutral position.
2. Improper adjustment or length shift rods or linkage that limits travel of forward remote from neutral position.
3. Loose bell cranks, sloppy ball and socket joints.
4. Shift rods, cables, etc., too spongy, flexible, or not secured properly at both ends.
5. Worn or loose engine mounts if forward unit is mounted to frame.
6. Forward remote mount too flimsy, loose on frame, etc.
7. Set screws loose at remote control joints.
8. Air shift system partially inoperative.
9. Transmission and engine out of alignment either vertically or horizontally.

CAUSES INSIDE TRANSMISSION

1. Shift tower or cover loose or interlock balls or pins worn or springs broken.
2. Shift fork pads not square with shift rod bore.
3. Shift rod poppet springs broken.
4. Shift rod poppet notches worn.
5. Shift rod bent or sprung out of line.
6. Shift fork pads or groove in sliding gear or collar worn excessively.
7. Shift fork pads not square with rod bore.
8. Worn taper on gear teeth, spacers or bearings.
9. Backing rings or retaining rings not installed properly on rear unit.

Hard Shifting

PRELIMINARY INVESTIGATION

1. Not enough clutch pedal free play.
2. Worn or inoperative clutch hydraulic cylinder.
3. Worn or loose clutch shaft, levers.
4. Worn or loose throwout bearing or carrier.
5. Low air pressure to main auxiliary unit shift cylinder.
6. Air leaks in cylinders, control lines or cab control valve.
7. Improper remote control function.
8. No lubricant in remote control units.
9. No lubricant in (or grease fittings on) U-joints or swivels of remote controls.

UNSYNCHRONIZED (CONSTANT MESH) TRANSMISSIONS

1. Lack of lubricant or wrong lubricant used causing buildup of sticky varnish and sludge deposits on splines of shaft and gears.
2. Sliding clutch gears tight on splines of shaft.
3. Clutch teeth burred over, chipped or badly mutilated due to improper shifting.
4. Driver not familiar with proper shifting procedure for this transmission. Also includes proper shifting if used with two speed axle, auxiliary, etc.
5. Clutch or drive gear pilot bearing seized, rough, or dragging.
6. Clutch brake engaging too soon when clutch pedal is depressed.

SYNCHRONIZED TRANSMISSION

1. Badly worn or bent shift rods.
2. Loose or flimsy remote controls, spongy or flexible rods and/or cables preventing full application of force to hold and synchronize gears.

3. Further, driver may not be able to feel the synchronizer action which usually results in a snap type shift.
4. Synchronizer bronze or aluminum rings worn or steel chips imbedded in rings prevent proper synchronization.
5. Damaged synchronizer such as broken poppet springs, poppets jammed, loose or broken blocker pins.
6. Free running gears, seized or galled on either the thrust face or diameters.

Sticking in Gear

1. Clutch not releasing.
2. Inoperative slave power units.
3. Sliding clutch gears tight on splines.
4. Chips wedged between or under splines of shaft and gear.
5. Improper adjustment, excessive wear or lost motion in shifter linkage.
6. Clutch brake set too high on clutch pedal locking gears behind hopping guard.

Crash Shifting or Raking Gears

SYNCHRONIZED TRANSMISSIONS

1. Raking of gears during manual shift may be caused by a defective synchronizer or improper shifting technique for synchronized transmission.
2. Occurs with cold, heavy oil, but synchronizer begins to work properly when transmission oil reaches normal operating temperature.
3. Heavy oil prevents the synchronizer cone from breaking through oil film and doing job properly.
4. Glazing of synchronizer cones due to use of E.P. addition in multi-purpose axle lubricant.
5. Synchronizer cones worn smooth causing loss of clutching action, which causes failure to control engine speed drop off during upshift, failure to bring engine speed nearly up to governor speed when driver shifting and attempted shifting without using clutch.
6. Blocker pin detents worn resulting in loss of blocker action.
7. Blocker pins loose, broken or turned over.

Oil Leaks

1. Oil level too high.
2. Wrong lubricant in unit.
3. Non-shielded bearing used at front or rear bearing cap (where applicable.)
4. Seals (if used) defective or omitted from bearing cap, wrong type seal used, etc.
5. Screwback threads in bearing caps off location, worn out, or filled with varnish, sludge, dirt, etc.
6. Transmission breather omitted, plugged internally, etc.
7. Capscrews loose, omitted or missing from remote control, shifter housing, bearing caps, P.T.O. or covers, etc.
8. Welch "seal" plugs loose or missing entirely from machine openings in case.
9. Oil drain back openings in bearing caps or case plugged with varnish, dirt, covered with gasket material, etc.
10. Broken gaskets, gaskets shifted or squeezed out of position, pieces still under bearing caps, clutch housing, P.T.O. and covers, etc.
11. Cracks or holes in castings.
12. Drain plug loose.
13. Also possibility that oil leakage could be from engine.
14. Internal O-ring worn in air cylinders, leaking air into transmission, pressurizing transmission.

Vibration

ORIGINATING IN TRANSMISSION

1. Sprung mainshafts and countershaft.
2. Gears that have seized to shaft and broken loose.
3. Bearings that are extremely worn allowing rotating shafts to oscillate from intended centers.

ORIGINATING ELSEWHERE BUT APPARENTLY IN TRANSMISSION

1. Drive lines out of static or dynamic balance.
2. Out of phase, wrong drive line working angles.
3. Worn crosses and bearings in U-joints.
4. Loose mounting or worn center bearings.
5. Worn and pitted teeth on ring gear and pinion of driving axle(s).
6. Wheels out of balance.
7. Warped parking brake drum or disc.

Bearing Failure

1. Dirt, always abrasive enters through seals, breathers, dirty containers.
2. Lapping action of fine steel particles from balls and raceways.
3. Entry of chips from hammers, chisels, punches during disassembly and assembly.
4. Bearing jammed with chip(s) may turn on shaft or in housing.
5. Brinnelling, ball depressions, spalling.
6. Excessive looseness under load scrubs shaft and bearing bore.
7. Failure due to heat. Failure of lubricant circulation. Lubricant deterioration or low level.
8. Radically tight bearing caused by expansion of inner race when mounted on shaft or compression of outer race when pressed into housing. Off-square mounting producing heat at retainers.

Air Shift System Diagnosis and Troubleshooting

Failure to Shift

LOW AIR PRESSURE IN SHIFT SYSTEM

1. Low air pressure in brake system air tank.
2. Air pressure regulator out of adjustment.
3. Air pressure regulator defective.
4. Leaks in controls, valves or air lines.
5. Frozen lines or valves during cold weather.

INTERNAL SHIFT CYLINDER(S) WEAK OR INOPERATIVE

1. Worn O-ring on piston shift bar, or piston rod, bad gaskets.
2. Cover insert valve inoperative.
3. Main air valve inoperative.

EXTERNAL SHIFT CYLINDERS WEAK OR INOPERATIVE

1. Worn O-rings on piston rod, or defective gaskets.
2. Cylinder link clevis, or cylinder anchor pivot excessively worn or poor link adjustment.

COVER INSERT VALVE INOPERATIVE

1. Leaking at retainer nut or external O-ring.
2. Piston jammed or by-passing air.

MAIN AIR VALVE INOPERATIVE

1. No air from drivers shift valve.
2. Excessive O-ring or piston wear with air by-passing or leaking in one or both range positions.
3. Actuating piston held by jammed actuating pin in shift bar housing remaining in protruded position.
4. Plunger rusted causing excess moisture.

DRIVER SHIFT VALVE(S) INOPERATIVE

1. No air to drivers shift valve(s).

2. Valve(s) worn or defective.

MECHANICAL RESISTANCE OR BLOCK TO INTERNAL RANGE OR AUXILIARY GEAR SECTION

1. Worn shift bar(s) jammed or broken poppets or interlock pins, or springs.
2. Internal shift fork, clutch gear, or synchro wear or failure.

Slow Shifting

LOW AIR PRESSURE IN SHIFT SYSTEM

1. Low air pressure in brake system air tank.
2. Air pressure regulator out of adjustment.
3. Air pressure regulator defective.
4. Leaks in controls, valves or air lines.
5. Frozen lines or valves during cold weather.

INTERNAL SHIFT CYLINDERS WEAK SLOW RESPONSE

1. Worn O-ring on piston, shift bar, or piston rod/bad gasket.
2. Cover insert valve slow.
3. Main air valve slow.

COVER INSERT VALVE SLOW RESPONSE

1. Leaking at retainer nut or external O-ring.
2. Piston dragging or by-passing air.

MAIN AIR VALVE SLOW RESPONSE

1. Low air from drivers shift valve.
2. Excessive O-ring or piston wear with air by-passing or leaking in one or both range positions.
3. Rust, moisture from air tank.

EXTERNAL SHIFT CYLINDER(S) SLOW RESPONSE

1. Cylinder shaft locknut under clevis worked loose allowing shaft to back out of adjustment. Cylinder shaft will not return to neutral position.
2. Air leaks around cylinder shaft or piston.
3. Air cylinder cap anchor pin hole worn excessively, allowing cylinder to be loose during shifts to gear positions.
4. Air cylinder shaft slightly bent causing piston to bind in cylinder.
5. Fittings on cylinders, regulator leaking, or fittings from main air supply ahead of rear unit shifting system, leaking before it reaches rear unit air system.
6. Pin.ed air line at regulator or cylinders.
7. Lockwire on regulator fatigued or broken apart, allowing regulator setting screw to back off, producing low air pressure to shifting system.
8. Regulator (non-adjustable) defective.
9. Filter contamination blow off butterfly nut not tight or seated properly.
10. Cab control valve dry of O-ring lubrication or excessive dirt in unit that will adhere to rotor.
11. Worn O-rings in cab control valve under rotor.
12. Cab control valve loose on shift lever.

Crash Shifting or Raking of Gears

HIGH AIR PRESSURE

1. Improperly set pressure regulator (adjustable type).
2. Defective regulator.
3. Regulator or valve freeze-up in cold weather.
4. Poor driver technique.
5. Failure to control engine speed drop off during upshift.
6. Failure to bring engine up to near governed speed when downshifting.

Transfer Case Diagnosis and Troubleshooting

Slips Out of Gear (High-Low)

1. Shifting poppet spring weak.
2. Bearing broken or worn.
3. Shifting fork bent.
4. Improper control rod adjustment.

Slips Out of Front Wheel Drive

1. Shifting poppet spring weak or broken.
2. Bearing worn or broken.
3. Excessive shaft end-play.
4. Shifting fork bent.

Hard Shifting

1. Lack of lubricant.
2. Shift lever binding on shaft.
3. Shifting poppet ball scored.
4. Shifting fork bent.
5. Low tire pressure.

Backlash

1. Companion yoke loose.
2. Transfer case loose on mounts.
3. Internal parts excessively worn.

Noisy

1. Low lubricant level.
2. Bearings improperly adjusted or excessively worn.
3. Gears worn or damaged.
4. Improper alignment of driveshafts or U-joints.

Oil Leakage

1. Excessive amount of lubricant in case.
2. Vent clogged.
3. Gaskets or seals leaking.
4. Bearings loose or damaged.
5. Driveshaft yoke mating surfaces scored.

Overheating

1. Excessive or insufficient amount of lubricant.
2. Bearing adjustment too tight.

CLEANING OF TRANSMISSION COMPONENTS

Cleanliness of parts, tools and work area is of the utmost importance. All transmission components (except bearing assemblies) should be cleaned in cleaning solvent and dried with compressed air before any inspection or work is begun. Great care should be taken when cleaning bearings. Bearings should always be cleaned separately from other parts in clean cleaning solvent and not gasoline. They must never be cleaned in a hot solution tank. It is advisable that they be soaked in cleaning fluid and then tapped against a block of wood in order to free any solidified lubricant that may be trapped inside. Rinse bearings thoroughly in clean solvent and then dry them with moisture-free compressed air being careful not to spin the bearings with the air stream. Rotate each bearing slowly and inspect rollers or balls for any signs of excessive wear, roughness, or damage. Those bearings not in excellent condition must be replaced. If they pass this inspection, they should be dipped in clean oil and wrapped in clean lintless cloth to protect them until installation.

INSPECTION OF TRANSMISSION COMPONENTS

All parts must be completely and carefully inspected and replaced for any signs of wear, stress, discoloration or warpage due to excessive heat. Whenever available, the magna flux process should be used on all parts except roller and ball bearings, to detect small cracks unseen by the eye. Inspect the breather assembly to see that it is not clogged or damaged and check all threaded parts for stripped or cross threads. Oil passages must be cleared of obstructions by the use of air pressure or brass rods and all gaskets, oil seals, lock wires, cotter pins and snap rings are to be replaced. Small nicks or burrs in gears or splines can be removed with a fine abrasive stone. It is important that any housings or covers having cracks or other damage should be replaced and not welded. Synchronizers, not in excellent condition, must be replaced. The bronze synchronizer cone should be checked for wear or for any steel chips that may have become imbedded in it. Springs must be inspected for free length, compressed length, distortion, or collapsed coils.

NOTE: The splines on many clutch gears, mainshafts, etc., are equipped with a machined relief called a "hopping guard". With the clutch gear engaged, the mating gear is free to slip into this notch, preventing the two gears from separating or "walking out of gear" under various load conditions. This is not a worn or chipped gear. Do not grind or discard the gear.

Check all shafts for spline wear or damage. If the mainshaft 1st and reverse sliding gear or clutch hub have worn into the sides of the splines, the shaft should be replaced. Shift forks, shift rods, interlock balls and pins must be replaced if scored, worn, distorted or damaged.

MANUAL TRANSMISSION SERVICE

AMC (Jeep)

Model AX4 is a 4-speed manual transmission while AX5 is a 5-speed manual transmission. Both transmissions have synchromesh engagement in all forward gears controlled by a floor shift mechanism integrated into the transmission top cover.

NOTE: The following components and materials must be replaced whenever the transmission is overhauled. Lip-type oil seals, lock nuts, all roll pins and all snaprings.

Disassembly

1. Remove the clutch housing.
2. Remove the straight screw plug, spring and ball using a Torx bit to remove the screw plug and a magnet to remove spring and ball.
3. Remove five adapter housing bolts and one nut.
4. Remove the shift lever housing set bolt and lock plate.
5. Remove the plug at the rear of the shift fork shaft.
6. Remove the large magnet to pull the shaft out.
7. Remove the select lever from the top while rotating.
8. Remove the five adapter housing bolts two studs and one nut.
9. Using a plastic hammer, tap and remove the extension housing. Leave the gasket attached to the intermediate plate.

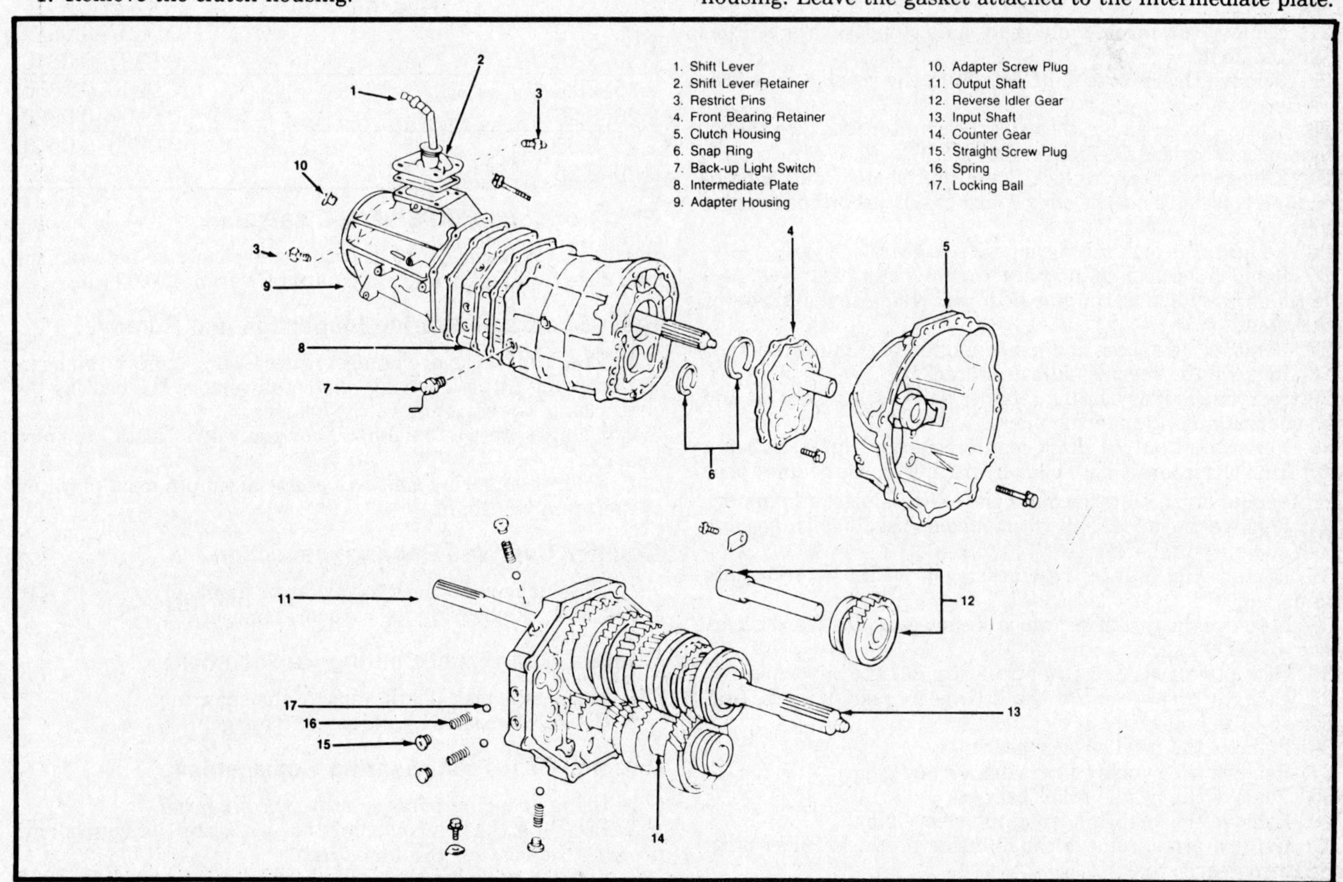

Jeep 4-5 speed

10. Remove the front bearing retainer and outer snaprings from the two front bearings.
11. Separate the intermediate plate from the transmission case using a small plastic hammer and remove the case.
12. Mount the intermediate plate in a vise. Be careful not to damage the plate.

NOTE: Before placing the intermediate plate in a vise, insert bolts, washers and nuts in the open holes at the bottom of plate. Tighten vise against these bolts to prevent damage to the plate.

13. Remove the straight screw plug, locking balls and springs using a Torx bit and magnet.
14. Remove the five slotted spring pins using a hammer and punch and then remove the two E-rings from the shift rails The locking ball from the reverse shift head and locking ball and pin from the intermediate housing will fall from the holes so be sure to catch them with a magnet.
15. Pull out the shift fork shaft No. 4 from the intermediate plate and catch the locking ball.
16. Remove shift fork shaft No. 4 and the 5th gear fork.
17. Pull out shift fork shaft No. 5 from the intermediate plate, and remove it with the reverse shift head. The interlock pins will fall from their hole. If they do not come out, remove them with a magnet.
18. Remove the shift fork shaft No. 3 from the intermediate plate and catch the interlock pins. The interlock pin will fall from the hole so be sure to catch it. If it does not come out, remove it with a magnet.
19. Remove shift fork shaft No. 1 from the intermediate plate being careful not to drop the interlock pin.
20. Remove shift fork shaft No. 2, shift fork No. 2 and shift fork No. 1.
21. Remove the reverse idle gear shaft stopper, reverse idler gear and shaft.
22. Remove the reverse shift arm from the reverse shift arm bracket.
23. Using a feeler gauge, measure the counter fifth gear thrust clearance. Standard Clearance: 0.004–0.012 in.
24. Engage two gears to lock the output shaft. Using a hammer and chisel, loosen the staked part of the nut on the counter shaft.
25. Remove the lock not disengage the gears.
26. Remove the gear spline piece No. 5, synchronizer ring, needle roller bearing and counter fifth gear using tool J-22888 or equivalent.
27. Remove the spacer and use a magnet to remove the ball.
28. Remove the reverse shift arm bracket.
29. remove the rear bearing retainer bolts with a Torx bit and the snapring using snapring pliers.
30. Remove the output shaft, counter gear and input shaft as a unit from the intermediate plate by pulling on the counter gear and tapping on the intermediate plate with a plastic hammer.
31. Remove the input shaft with fourteen needle roller bearing from the output shaft.
32. Remove the counter rear bearing from the intermediate plate.
33. Measure the thrust clearance of each gear. Standard Clearance: 0.004–0.010 in.
34. Using two awls and a hammer, tap out the snapring.
35. Using a press, remove the fifth gear, rear bearing, first gear and the inner race.
36. Remove the needle roller bearing.
37. Remove the synchronizer ring, second gear.
39. Remove the needle roller bearing.
40. Remove the snapring from hub sleeve No. 2.
41. Using a press, remove the hub sleeve, synchronizer ring, and third gear.
42. Remove the needle roller bearing.

Component Inspection

Output Shaft and Inner Race

1. Check the output shaft and inner race for wear or damage.
2. Using calipers, measure the output shaft flange thickness. Minimum Thickness. Minimum Thickness: 0.189 in.
3. Using calipers, measure the inner face flange thickness. Minimum Thickness: 0.157 in.
4. Using a micrometer, measure the outer diameter of the output shaft journal surface. 2nd Gear Minimum: 1.495 in., 3rd Gear Minimum: 1.377 in.
5. Using a micrometer, measure the outer diameter of the inner race. Minimum Diameter: 1.535 in.
6. Using a dial indicator, measure the shaft runout. Maximum Runout: 0.002 in.

First Gear Oil Clearance

1. Using a dial indicator, measure the oil clearance between the gear and inner race with the needle roller bearing installed. Standard Clearance: 0.0004–0.0013 in.
2. Using a dial indicator, measure the oil clearance between the gear and shaft with the needle roller bearing installed. Standard Clearance: 2nd and 3rd Gears: 0.0004–0.0013 in., Counter 5th Gear: 0.0004–0.0013 in.

Synchronizer Ring Inspection

1. Check for wear or damage. Turn the ring and push it in to check the braking action.
2. Measure the clearance between the synchronizer ring back and the gear spline end. Standard Clearance: 0.040–0.078 in., Minimum Clearance 0.031 in.

Thickness mm (in.)	
2.05–2.10	(0.0807–0.0827)
2.10–2.15	(0.0827–0.0846)
2.15–2.20	(0.0846–0.0866)
2.20–2.25	(0.0866–0.0886)
2.25–2.35	(0.0886–0.0906)
2.30–2.35	(0.0906–0.0925)

Shift Fork and Hub Sleeve Clearance

1. Using a feeler gauge, measure the clearance between the hub sleeve and shift fork. Maximum Clearance: 0.039 in.

Input Shaft and Bearing Inspection and Removal

1. Check for wear or damage. If necessary, remove the bearing snapring using snapring pliers and remove the bearing.
2. Using a press, remove the bearing.
3. Using a press a tool J-34603 or equivalent, install the new bearing.
4. Select a snapring that will allow minimum axial play and install it on the shaft.

Counter Gear and Bearing Inspection

1. Check the gear teeth for werar or damage.
2. Check the bearing for wear or damage.

Counter Gear Front Bearing Replacement

1. Using snapring pliers, remove the snapring.
2. Check the bearing for wear or damage.

Counter Gear Front Bearing Replacement

1. Using snapring pliers, remove the snapring.
2. Press out the bearing using tool J-22912-01 or equivalent, press in the bearing and inner race.
3. Select a snapring that will allow minimum axial play and install it on the shaft.

Thickness mm (in.)	
1.75–1.80	(0.0689–0.0709)
1.80–1.85	(0.0709–0.0728)
1.85–1.90	(0.0728–0.0748)
1.90–1.95	(0.0748–0.0768)
1.95–2.00	(0.0768–0.0787)
2.00–2.05	(0.0788–0.0807)
2.05–2.10	(0.0807–0.0827)

Front Bearing Retainer Inspection

1. Check retainer for damage.
2. Check the oil seal lip for wear or damage.

Oil Seal Replacement

1. Using a awl, pry the old seal out of the housing.
2. Press in the new oil seal using tool J-34602 or equivalent.
3. The oil seal depth is 0.441–0.480 in. from the housing to transmission surface to the top edge of the seal.

Reverse Restrict Pin replacement

1. Check for wear or damage.
2. Using a Torx bit, remove the screw plug.
3. Using a hammer and pin punch, drive out the slotted spring pin.
4. Pull off the lever housing and slide out the shaft.
5. Install the lever housing.
6. Using a hammer and pin punch, drive out the slotted spring pin.
7. Using a Torx bit, install and torque the screw plug to 27 ft. lbs. torque.

Adapter Housing and Oil Seal Inspection and Replacement

1. Check the adapter housing for wear or damage.
2. Replace the oil seal with tool J-29184 or equivalent.

OUTPUT SHAFT

Assemble

1. Install the clutch hub No. 1 and No. 2 into hub sleeves along with the shifting keys. Install the key springs so their gaps are not in line.
2. Install the shifting springs under the shifting keys.
3. Apply gear oil on the output shaft and 3rd gear needle roller bearing.
4. Place the 3rd gear synchronizer ring on the gear and align the ring slots with the shifting keys.
5. Install the needle roller bearing in the 3rd gear and hub sleeve No. 2.
6. Select a new snapring (2) that will allow minimum axial play and install it on the shaft.
7. Using a feeler gauge, measure the 3rd gear thrust clearance. Standard Clearance: 0.004–0.010 in.
8. Apply gear oil on the output shaft and 2nd gear needle bearing.
9. Place the 2nd gear synchronizer ring on the 2nd gear and align the ring slots with the shifting keys.
10. Install the needle roller bearing in the 2nd gear.
11. Using a press install the 2nd gear and hub sleeve No.1.
12. Install the first gear locking ball in the output shaft.
13. Apply gear oil to the needle roller bearing.
14. Assemble the first gear, synchronizer ring, needle roller bearing and bearing inner race.

Thickness mm (in.)	
1.75–1.80	(0.0689–0.0709)
1.80–1.85	(0.0709–0.0728)
1.85–1.90	(0.0728–0.0748)
1.90–1.95	(0.0748–0.0768)
1.95–2.00	(0.0768–0.0787)
2.00–2.05	(0.0788–0.0807)
2.05–2.10	(0.0807–0.0827)

15. Install the assembly on the output shaft, with the synchronizer ring slots aligned with the shifting keys.
16. Turn the inner race to align it with the locking ball.
17. Install the output shaft rear bearing using tool J-34603 or equivalent and a press.
18. Install the bearing on the output shaft with the outer race snapring groove toward the rear. Hold the 1st gear inner race to prevent it from falling.
19. Measure the 1st and 2nd gear thrust clearance with a feeler gauge. Standard Clearance: 0.004–0.010 in.
20. Install 5th gear on the output shaft using tool J-35603 or equivalent and a press.
21. Select a snapring that will allow minimum axial play.
22. Using the proper tools tap the snap into position.
23. Apply multi-purpose grease to the fourteen needle bearings and install them in the input shaft.
24. Install the output shaft into the intermediate plate by pulling on the output shaft and tapping on the intermediate plate.
25. Install the input shaft to the output shaft with the synchronizer ring slots aligned with the shifting keys.
26. Install the counter gear into the intermediate plate while holding the counter gear and install the counter rear bearing with a suitable driver.

Thickness mm (in.)	
2.67–2.72	(0.1051–0.1071)
2.73–2.78	(0.1075–0.1094)
2.79–2.84	(0.1098–0.1118)
2.85–2.90	(0.1122–0.1142)
2.91–2.96	(0.1146–0.1165)
2.97–3.02	(0.1169–0.1189)
3.03–3.08	(0.1193–0.1213)
3.09–3.14	(0.1217–0.1236)
3.15–3.20	(0.1240–0.1260)
3.21–3.26	(0.1264–0.1283)
3.27–3.32	(0.1287–0.1307)

27. Install the bearing snapring using snapring pliers. Be sure the snapring is flush with the intermediate plate surface.
28. Using a Torx bit, install and tighten the screws to 13 ft. lbs. torque.
29. Install the reverse shift arm bracket and tighten the bolts to 13 ft. lbs. torque.
30. Install the ball and spacer.
31. Install the shifting keys and hub sleeve No. 3 onto the counter 5th gear. Install the key springs positioned so the end gaps are not in line.
32. Install shifting key springs under the shifting keys.
33. Apply gear oil to the needle roller bearing and install the counter 5th gear with hub sleeve No. 3 and needle roller bearings.
34. Install the synchronizer ring on gear spline piece.
35. Using tool J-28406 or equivalent drive in gear spline piece No.5 with the synchronizer ring slots aligned with the shifting keys. When installing gear spline piece No. 5, support the counter gear in front with a 3–5 lb. hammer or equivalent.

36. Engage two gears to lock the output shaft.
37. Install and tighten the lock nut to 90 ft. lbs. torque on the counter shaft.
38. Stake the lock nut.
39. Disengage the gears.
40. Measure the counter fifth gear thrust clearance using a feeler gauge. Standard Clearance: 0.004–0.012 in.
41. Install the reverse shift arm to the pivot of the reverse shift arm bracket.
42. Install the reverse idler gear on the shaft.
43. Align the reverse shift arm shoe to the reverse idler gear groove and insert the reverse idler gear shift to the intermediate plate.
44. Install the reverse idler gear shaft stopper and tighten the bolt to 13 ft. lbs. torque.
45. Place shift forks No. 1 and No. 2 into groove of hub sleeves No. 1 and No. 2 and install fork shaft No. 2 to the shift fork No. 1 and No. 2 through the intermediate plate.
46. Apply multi-purpose grease to the interlock pins.
47. Using a magnet and a suitable tool, install the interlock pin onto the intermediate plate.
48. Install the interlock pin into the shaft hole.
49. Install fork shaft No. 1 to shift fork No. 1 through the intermediate plate.
50. Using a magnet and a suitable tool, install the interlock pin into the intermediate plate.
51. Install the interlock pin into the shaft hole.
52. Install fork shaft No. 3 to the reverse shift arm through the intermediate plate.
53. Install the reverse shift head into fork shaft No. 5.
54. Insert fork shaft No. 5 to the intermediate plate and put in the reverse shift head to the shift fork No. 3.
55. Using a magnet and a suitable tool, install the locking ball into the reverse shift head hole.
56. Shift hub sleeve No. 3 to the 5th speed position.
57. Place shift fork No. 3 into the groove of hub sleeve No. 3 and install fork shaft No.4 to shift fork No. 3 and reverse shift arm.
58. Using a magnet and a suitable tool, install the locking ball into the intermediate plate and insert fork shaft No. 4 to the intermediate plate.
59. Check the interlock by positioning the shift fork shaft No.1 to the 1st speed position.
60. Fork shafts No. 2, No. 3, No. 4 and No. 5 should not move.
61. Using a pin punch and a hammer, drive in new slotted springs pins in each shift fork, reverse shift arm and reverse shift head.
62. Install two fork shaft E-rings.
63. Apply liquid sealer to the screw plugs.
64. Install the locking balls, springs and screw plugs with a Torx bit and tighten to 14 ft. lbs. torque. Install the short spring into the tower of the intermediate plate.
65. Remove the intermediate plate from the vise.
66. Remove the bolts, nuts, washers and gasket.

Transmission Case Installation

1. Align each bearing outer race, each fork shaft end and reverse idler gear with the holes in the case and install the case on the intermediate plate. If necessary, tap on the case with a plastic hammer.
2. Instll two new bearing snaprings.
3. Install front bearing retainer with a new gasket.
4. Apply liquid sealer to the bolts.
5. Install and tighten the bolts to 12 ft. lbs. torque.
6. Instll the new gasket to the intermediate plate.
7. Install the adapter housing.
8. Install and tighten the adapter bolts to 27 ft. lbs. torque.
9. Install the shift lever housing.
10. Insert the shift lever into the adapter and shift lever housing.
11. Install and tighten shift lever housing bolt with a lock plate to 28 ft. lbs. torque. Lock the lock plate.
12. Install and tighten the adapter screw plug to 13 ft. lbs. torque.
13. Apply liquid sealer to the plug.
14. Install the locking ball, spring and screw plug and tighten the plug to 14 ft. lbs. torque.
15. Check to see that the input shaft and output shafts rotate smoothly.
16. Check to see that shifting can be done smoothly to all positions.
17. Install the black restrict pin on the reverse gear/5th gear side.
18. Install the remaining pin and tighten the pins 20 ft. lbs. torque.
19. Install the shift lever retainer with a new gasket and tighten the bolts to 13 ft. lbs. torque.
20. Install the back-up light switch and tighten to 27 ft. lbs. torque.
21. Install the clutch housing and tighten the bolts to 27 ft. lbs. torque.

Chevrolet/GM S Series

77mm 4-SPEED TRANSMISSION

Disassembly

1. Remove drain plug and drain lubricant from transmission.
2. Thoroughly clean the exterior of the transmission assembly.
3. Using a hammer and punch, remove the roll pin that retains
the offset lever to shift rail.
4. Remove extension housing attaching bolts. Separate the extension housing from the transmission case and remove housing and offset lever as an assembly.
5. Remove detent ball and spring from offset lever and remove roll pin from extension housing or offset lever.
6. Remove transmission shift cover attaching bolts. Pry the shift cover loose using the proper tool and remove cover from transmission case.
7. Remove clip that retains reverse lever to reverse lever pivot bolt.
8. Remove reverse lever pivot bolt and remove reverse lever and fork as an assembly.
9. Using a hammer and punch, mark position of front bearing cap to transmission case. Remove front bearing cap bolts and remove bearing cap.
10. Remove small retaining and large locating snaprings from front drive gear bearing.
11. Install bearing puller J-22912-01 on front bearing and puller J-8433-1 with two bolts on end of drive gear and remove and discard bearing. A new bearing must be used when assembling the transmission.
12. Remove retaining and locating snaprings from rear bear-

ing and mainshaft. Install puller J-22912-01 on bearing and puller J-8433-1 with two bolts (J-33171) on end of mainshaft and remove and discard used bearing. A new bearing must be used when assembling transmission.

13. Remove drive gear from mainshaft and transmission case as shown.

14. remove mainshaft from transmission case by tipping mainshaft down at the rear and lifting shaft out through shift cover opening.

15. Using a hammer and punch, remove rollpin retaining reverse idler gear shift in transmission case. Remove idler gear and shaft from case.

16. Remove countershaft from rear of case using loading tool J-26624. Remove countershaft gear and loading tool as an assembly from case along with thrust washers.

Mainshaft Disassembly

1. Scribe alignment mark on third/fourth synchronizer hub and sleeve for reassembly. remove retaining snapring and remove third/fourth synchronizer assembly from mainshaft.
2. Slide third gear off mainshaft.
3. Remove second gear retaining snapring. Remove tabbed thrust washer, second gear and blocker ring from mainshaft.
4. Remove first gear thrust washer and roll pin from mainshaft. Use pliers to remove roll pin.
5. Remove first gear and blocker ring from mainshaft.
6. Scribe alignment mark on first/second synchronizer hub and sleeve for reassembly.
7. Remove synchronizer springs and keys from first/second sleeve and remove sleeve from shaft.

77mm four speed transmission

NOTE: Do not attempt to remove the first/second hub from the mainshaft. The hub and mainshaft are assembled and machined as a unit.

8. Remove loading Tool J-26624, roller bearings, spacers and thrust washers from the countershaft gear.

Drive Gear Disassembly

1. Remove roller bearings from cavity of drive gear.
2. Wash parts in a cleaning solvent.
3. Inspect gear teeth for wear.
4. Inspect drive shaft pilot for wear.

Cover Disassembly

1. Place selector arm plates and shift rail in neutral position (centered).
2. Rotate shift rail until selector arm disengages from selector arm plates and roll pin is accessible.
3. Remove selector arm roll pin using a pin punch and hammer.
4. Remove shift rail, shift forks, selector arm plates, selector arm, interlock plate and roll pin.
5. Remove shift cover to extension housing O-ring seal using a suitable tool.
6. Remove nylon inserts and selector arm plates from shift forks. Note position of inserts and plates for assembly reference.

Assembly

1. Install nylon inserts and selector arm plates in shift forks.
2. If removed, install shift rail plug. Coat edges of plug with sealer before installing.
3. Coat shift rail and rail bores with light weight grease and insert shift rail in cover. install rail until flush with inside edge of cover.
4. Place first/second shift fork in cover with fork offset facing rear of cover and push shift rail through fork. The first/second shift fork is the larger of the two forks.
5. Position selector arm and C-shaped interlock plate in cover and insert shift rail through arm. Widest part of interlock plate must face away from cover and selector arm roll pin hole must face downward and toward rear of cover.
6. Position third/fourth shift fork in cover with fork offset facing rear of cover. Third/fourth shift fork selector arm plate must be under first/second shift for selector arm plate.
7. Push shift rail through third/fourth shift fork and into front bore in cover.
8. Rotate shift rail until selector arm plate at forward end of rail faces away from, but is parallel to cover.
9. Align roll pin holes in selector arm and shift rail and install roll pin. Roll pin must be flush with surface of selector arm to prevent pin from contacting selector arm plates during shifts.
10. Install a new shift cover to extension housing O-ring seal. Coat O-ring seal with transmission lubricant.

Drive Gear Assembly

1. Coat roller bearings and drive gear bearing bore with light weight grease. Install roller bearings into bore of drive gear.

Mainshaft Assembly

1. Coat mainshaft and gear bores with transmission lubricant.
2. Install first/second synchronizer sleeve on mainshaft, aligning marks previously made.
3. Install synchronizer keys and springs into the first/second synchronizer sleeve. Engage tang end of springs into the same synchronizer key but position open ends of springs so they face away from one another.
4. Place blocking ring on first gear and install gear and ring on mainshaft. Be sure synchronizer keys engage notches in first gear blocking ring.
5. Install first gear roll pin in mainshaft.
6. Place blocking ring on second gear and install gear and ring on mainshaft. Be sure synchronizer keys engage notches in second gear blocking ring. Install second gear thrust washer and snap ring on mainshaft. Be sure thrust washer tab is engaged in mainshaft notch.
7. Measure second gear end play using feeler gauge. Insert gauge between gear and thrust washer. End play should be 0.004–0.014 in. If end play is over 0.014 in., replace thrust washer and snap ring and inspect synchronizer hub for excessive wear.
8. Place blocking ring on third gear and install gear and ring on mainshft.
9. Install third/fourth synchronizer sleeve on hub, aligning marks previously made.
10. Install synchronizer keys and springs in third/fourth synchronizer sleeve. Engage tang end of each spring in same key but position open ends of springs so they face away from one another.
11. Install third/fourth synchronizer assembly on the mainshaft with machined groove in hub facing forward. Install snapring on mainshaft. Be sure synchronizer keys are engaged in notches in third gear blocker ring.
12. Install Tool J-26624 into countershaft gear. Using a light weight grease, lubricate roller bearings and install into bores at front and rear of countershaft gear. Install roller bearing retainers on Tool J-26624.

Transmission Assembly

1. Coat countershaft gear thrust washers with grease and position washer in case.
2. Position countershaft gear in case and install countershaft from rear of case. Be sure that thrust washers stay in place during installation of countershaft and gear.
3. Position reverse idler gear in case with shift lever groove facing rear of case and install reverse idler shaft from rear of case. Install roll pin in shaft and center pin in shaft.
4. Install mainshaft assembly into the case. Do not disturb position of synchronizer assemblies during installation.
5. Install fourth gear blocking ring in third/fourth synchronizer sleeve. Be sure synchronizer keys ingaged in notches in blocker ring.
6. Install drive gear into case and engage with mainshaft.
7. Position mainshaft first gear against the rear of the case. Using a new bearing, start front bearing onto drive gear. Align bearing with bearing bore in case and drive bearing onto drive gear and into case using Tool J-25234.
8. Install front bearing retaining and locating snaprings.
9. Apply a $\frac{1}{8}$ in. diameter bead of RTV sealant, #732 or equivalent, on case mating surface of front bearing cap. Install bearing cap aligning marks previously made. Apply non-hardening sealer on attaching bolts and install bolts. Torque bolts to specification.
10. Install first gear thrust washer with oil grove facing first gear on mainshaft, aligning slot in washer with first gear roll pin.
11. Using a new bearing, position rear bearing on mainshaft. Align bearing with bearing bore in case and drive bearing into case using Tool J-25234.
12. Install locating and retaining snaprings on rear bearing.
13. Install speedometer gear and retaining clip on mainshaft.
14. Apply non-hardening sealer to threads of reverse lever pivot bolt and start bolt into case. Engage reverse lever fork in the reverse idler gear and reverse lever on pivot bolt. Tighten bolt to specifications and install retaining clip.
15. Rotate drivegear and mainshaft gear. If blocker rings tend to stick on gears, release the rings by gently prying them off the cones.
16. Apply a $\frac{1}{8}$ in. diameter bead or RTV Sealant, #732 or equivalent, on the cover mating surface of transmission. Place reverse lever in neutral and position cover on case.

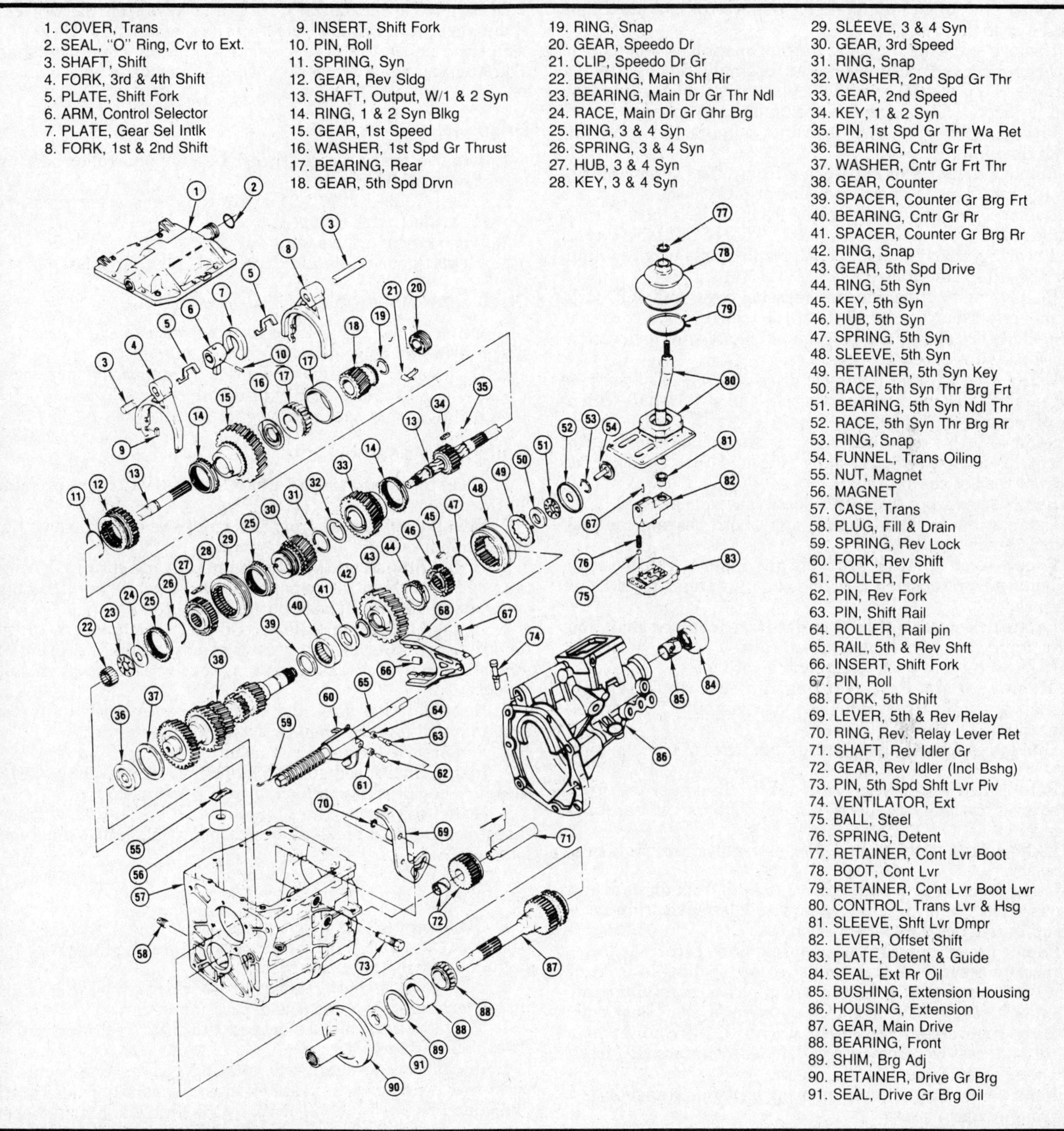

77mm five speed transmission

17. Install 2 dowel type bolts first to align cover on case. Install remaining cover bolts and torque to specifications. The offset lever to shift rail roll pin hole must be in the vertical position after cover installation.

18. Apply a ⅛ in. diameter bead of RTV Sealant, #732 or equivalent, on the extension housing to transmission case mating surface.

19. Place extension housing over mainshaft to a position where shift rail is in shift cover opening.

20. Install detent spring in offset lever. Place ball in neutral guide plate detent position. Apply pressure on the offset lever, slide offset lever onto shift rail and seat extension housing to transmission case.

21. Install extension housing retaining bolts. Torque bolts to specifications.

22. Align hole in offset lever and shift rail and install roll pin.

23. Fill transmission to its proper level with recommended lubricant.

Five Speed Transmission

Disassembly

1. Remove drain bolt on transmission case and drain lubricant.

2. Thoroughly clean the exterior of the transmission assembly.

3. Using pin punch and hammer, remove roll pin attaching offset lever to shift rail.
4. Remove extension housing to transmission case bolts and remove housing and offset lever as an assembly. Do not attempt to remove the offset lever while the extension housing is still bolted in place. The lever has a positioning lug engaged in the housing detent plate which prevents moving the lever far enough for removal.
5. Remove detent ball and spring from offset lever and remove roll pin from extension housing or offset lever.
6. Remove plastic funnel, thrust bearing race and thrust bearing from rear of counter shaft. The countershaft rear thrust bearing, bearing washer and plastic funnel may be found inside the extension housing.
7. Remove bolts attaching transmission cover and shift fork assembly and remove cover. Two of the transmission cover attaching bolts are alignment-type dowel bolts. Note the location of these bolts for assembly reference.
8. Using a punch and hammer, drive the roll pin from the fifth gearshift fork while supporting the end of the shaft with a block of wood.
9. Remove fifth synchronizer gear snapring, shift fork, fifth gear synchronizer sleeve, blocking ring and fifth speed drive gear from rear of counter shaft.
10. Remove snapring from fifth speed driven gear.
11. Using a hammer and punch, mark both bearing cap and case for assembly reference.
12. Remove front bearing cap bolts and remove front bearing cap. Remove front bearing race and end play shims from front bearing cap.
13. Rotate drive gear until flat surface faces counter shaft and remove drive gear from transmission case.
14. Remove reverse lever C-clip and pivot bolt.
15. Remove mainshaft rear bearing race and then tilt mainshaft assembly upward and remove assembly from transmission case.
16. Unhook overcenter link spring from front of transmission case.
17. Rotate fifth gear/reverse shift rail to disengage rail from reverse lever assembly. Remove shift rail from rear of transmission case.
18. Remove reverse lever and fork assembly from transmission case.
19. Using hammer and punch, drive roll pin from forward end of reverse idler shaft and remove reverse idler shaft, rubber O-ring and gear from the transmission case.
20. Remove rear countershaft snapring and spacer.
21. Insert a brass drift through drive gear opening in front of transmission case and, using an arbor plress, carefully press countershaft rearward to remove rear counter shaft bearing.
22. Move countershaft assembly rearward, tilt countershaft upward and remove from case. Remove countershaft front thrust washer and rear bearing spacer.
23. Remove countershaft front bearing from transmission case using an arbor press.

Mainshaft Disassembly

1. Remove thrust bearing washer from front end of mainshaft.
2. Scribe reference mark on third/fourth synchronizer hub and sleeve for reassembly.
3. Remove third/fourth synchronizer blocking ring, sleeve, hub and third gear as an assembly from mainshaft.
4. Remove snapring, tabbed thrust washer and second gear from mainshaft.
5. Remove fifth gear with Tool-J-22912-01 or its equal and arbor press. Slide rear bearing of mainshaft.
6. Remove first gear thrust washer, roll pin, first gear and synchronizer ring form mainshaft.
7. Scribe reference mark on first/second synchronizer hub and sleeve for reassembly.
8. Remove synchronizer spring and keys from first/reverse sliding gear and remove gear from mainshaft hub. Do not attempt to remove the first second reverse hub from mainshaft. The hub and shaft are assembled and machined as a matched set.

Drive Gear Disassembly

1. Remove bearing race, thrust bearing and roller bearings from cavity of drive gear.
2. Using Tool- J-22912-01 or its equal and arbor press, remove bearing from drive gear.
3. Wash parts in a cleaning solvent.
4. Inspect gear teeth and drive shaft pilot for wear.

Drive Gear Assembly

1. Using Tool J-22912-01 or its equal with an arbor press, install bearing on drive gear.
2. Coat roller bearings and drive gear bearing bore with grease. Install roller bearings into bore of drive gear.
3. Install thrust bearing and race in drive gear.

Mainshaft Assembly

1. Coat mainshaft and gear bores with transmission lubricant.
2. Install first/second synchronizer sleeve on mainshaft hub aligning marks made at disasssembly.
3. Install first/second synchronizer keys and springs. Engage tang end of each spring in same synchronizer key but position open end of springs opposite of each other.
4. Install blocker ring and second gear on mainshaft. Install tabbed thrust washer and second gear retaining snapring on mainshaft. Be sure washer tab is properly seated in mainshaft notch.
5. Install blocker ring and first gear on mainshaft. Install first gear roll pin and then first gear thrust washer.
6. Slide rear bearing on mainshaft.
7. Install fifth speed gear on mainshaft using Tool J-22912-01 and arbor press. Install snapring on mainshaft.
8. Install third gear, third/fourth synchronizer assembly and thrust bearing on mainshaft. Synchronizer hub offset must face forward.

Assembly

1. Coat countershaft front bearing bore with Loctite®601, or equivalent and install front countershaft bearing flush with facing of case using an arbor press.
2. Coat countershaft tabbed thrust washer with grease and install washer so tab engages depression in case.
3. Tip transmission case on end and install countershaft in front bearing bore.
4. Install countershaft rear bearing spacer. Coat countershaft rear bearing with grease and install bearing using Tool J-29895 and sleeve J-33032, or its equivalent. The bearing when correctly installed will extend beyond the case surface 0.125 in..
5. Position reverse idler gear in case with shift lever groove facing rear of case and install reverse idler shaft from rear of case. Install roll pin in idler shaft.
6. Install assembled mainshaft in transmission case. Install rear mainshaft bearing race in case.
7. Install drive gear in case and engage in third/fourth synchronizer sleeve and blocker ring.
8. Install front bearing race in front bearing cap. Do not install shims in front bearing cap at this time.
9. Temporarily install front bearing cap.
10. Install fifth speed/reverse lever, pivot bolt and retaining clip. Coat pivot bolt threads with non-hardening sealer. Be sure to engage reverse lever fork in reverse idler gear.
11. Install countershaft rear bearing spacer and retaining snap ring.

12. Install fifth speed gear on countershaft.
13. Insert fifth speed/reverse rail in rear of case and install into reverse fifth speed lever. Rotate rail during installation to simplify engagement with lever. Connect spring to front of case.
14. Position fifth gear shift fork on fifth gear synchronizer assembly and install synchronizer on countershaft and shift fork on shift rail. Make sure roll pin hole in shift fork and shift rail are aligned.
15. Support fifth gear shift rail and fork on a block of wood and install roll pin.
16. Install thrust race against fifth speed synchronizer hub and install snap ring. Install thrust bearing against race on countershaft. Coat both bearing and race with petroleum jelly.
17. Install lipped thrust race over needle-type thrust bearing and install plastic funnel into hole in end of counter shaft gear.
18. Temporarily install extension housing and attaching bolts. Turn transmission case on end and mount a dial indicator on extension housing with indicator on the end of mainshaft.
19. Rotate mainshaft and zero dial indicator. Pull upward on mainshaft until end play is removed and record reading. Mainshaft bearings require a preload of 0.001–0.005 in. to set preload, select a shim pack measuring 0.001–0.005 in. greater than the dial indicator reading recorded.
20. Remove front bearing cap and front bearing race Install necessary shims to obtain prelaod and reinstall bearing race.
21. Apply a $\frac{1}{8}$ in. bead of RTV sealant, #732 or equivalent, on case mating surface of front bearing cap. Install bearing cap aligning marks made during disassembly and torque bolts to specification.
22. Remove extension housing.
23. Move shift forks on transmission cover and synchronizer sleeves inside transmission to the neutral position.
24. Apply a $\frac{1}{8}$ in. bead of RTV sealant, #732 or equivalent, or cover mating surface of transmission.
25. Lower cover onto case while aligning shift forks and synchronizer sleeves. Center cover and install the two dowel bolts. Install remaining bolts and torque to specification. The offset lever to shift rail roll pin hole must be in the vertical position after cover installation.
26. Apply a $\frac{1}{8}$ in. bead of RTV Sealant, #732 or equivalent, on extension housing to transmission case mating surface.
27. Install extension housing over mainshaft and shift rail to a position where shift rail just enters shift cover opening.
28. Install detent spring into offset lever and place steel ball in neutral guide plate detent. Position offset lever on steel ball and apply pressure on offset lever and at the time seat extension housing against transmission case.
29. Install extension housing bolts and torque to specification.
30. Align and install roll pin in offset lever and shift rail.
31. Fill transmission to its proper level with lubricant.

Clark 280V Series Transmissions

FIVE SPEED TRANSMISSIONS

The Clark 280V series transmissions are available in two direct drive and an overdrive ratio. The 285V has normal steps between the gears while the 282V has a "short fourth", meaning a small step between direct and fourth, which can be used to split the step with a two speed axle. The OD model is designated 280VO and has the OD gear as an integral part of the gear train. The direct drive and overdrive types of gear trains differ in gear ratios and in the power flow. However, the basic construction of the transmissions are the same.

Disassembly

1. Remove the remote control or shift tower from the control cover. Remove the control cover capscrews and lock washers. Remove the control cover assembly from the transmission. Remove the back-up light switch.
2. Remove the universal joint assembly and the drive shaft from the parking brake drum.
3. Remove the parking brake drum. Disconnect the parking brake actuating lever from the linkage.
4. Remove the transmission spline flange. Remove the bolts holding the carrier plate to the transmission housing. Slide the plate with the brake shoes and retaining springs off the transmission.
5. Lock the transmission in two gears and remove the brake drum retaining nut. Remove the brake drum.
6. Remove the output shaft rear bearing retainer and the speedometer drive gear.
7. Remove the countershaft rear bearing retainer. Remove the bearing snapring.
8. Remove the input shaft bearing retainer and pull the input shaft out of the case. Be careful not to drop the output shaft pilot bearing rollers into the transmission case.
9. Move the output shaft rearward until the rear bearing is exposed. Remove the rear bearing with a suitable bearing puller.
10. Lift the output shaft out of the transmission case.
11. Remove the reverse idler shaft using the special tool. Lift the reverse idler gear, bearing and thrust washer out of the case.
12. Move the countershaft rearward until the rear bearing is exposed. Remove the bearing and the oil slinger with a suitable puller.
13. Lift the countershaft out of the case.
14. If the countershaft front bearing or the pilot bearing is to be replaced, remove the clutch housing from the transmission.
15. Press the pilot bearing out of the transmission case. Do not hammer or drive the bearing out of the bearing bore.

OUTPUT SHAFT

Disassembly

1. Remove the first reverse gear from the output shaft.
2. Clamp the output shaft, front end facing up, in a soft jawed vise. Remove the fourth/fifth speed synchronizer assembly from the shaft. Remove the snap ring retaining the fourth gear and remove the shift hub sleeve and the fourth gear.
3. Remove the third gear snapring and lift the locating washer and the gear off the shaft.
4. Lift the second/third speed synchronizer off the shaft.
5. Remove the snapring retaining the second/third speed gear shift hub sleeve and lift the sleeve off the shaft.
6. Remove the second gear snapring and remove the locating washer and the gear.

Assembly

1. Install the output shaft, forward end up, in a soft jawed vise.
2. Install the second gear lower snapring and the locating washer on the output shaft. Install the second gear on the output shaft with the clutching teeth facing upward. Install the upper snapring.

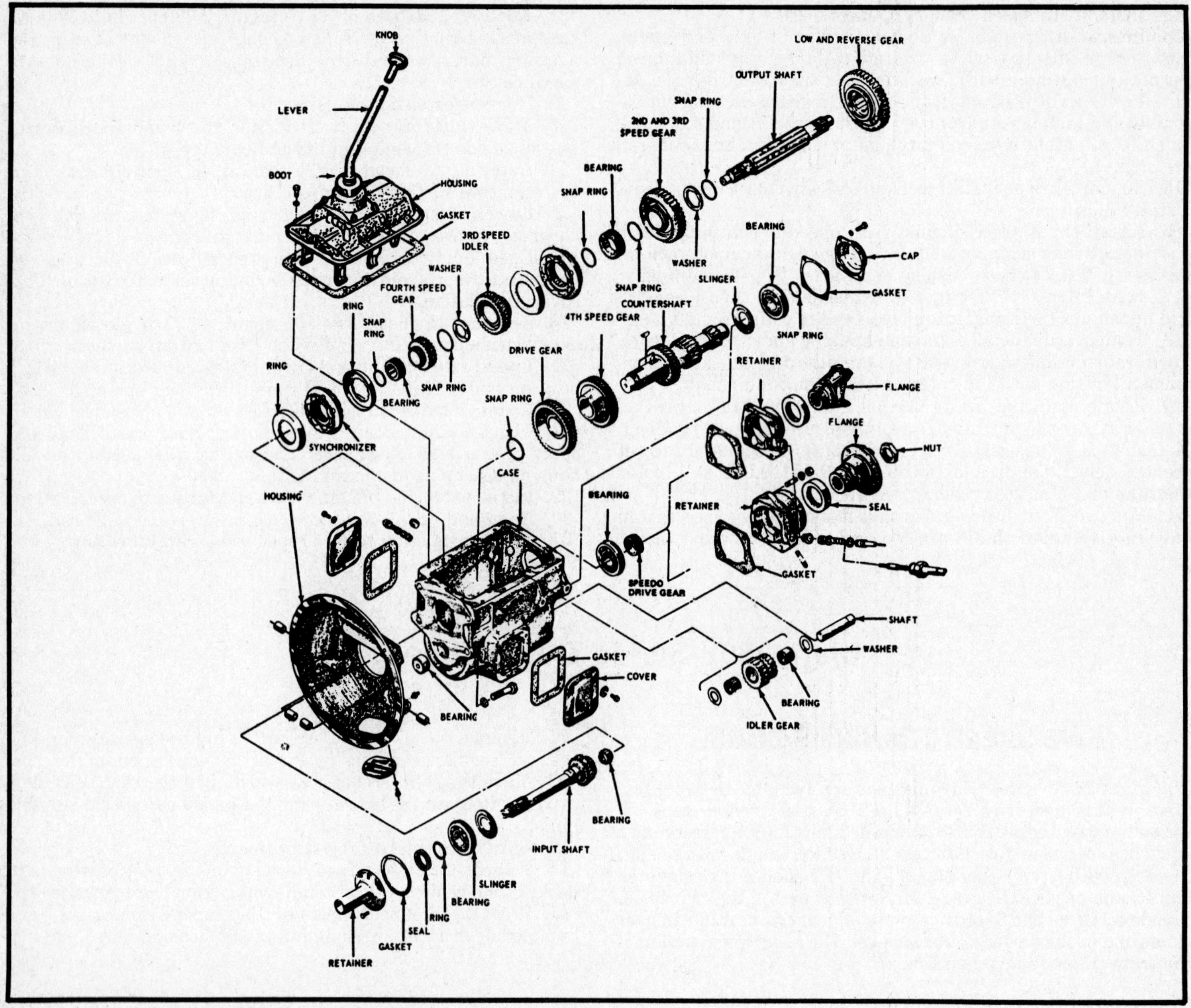

Exploded view Clark 280V transmission

3. Install the second/third shift hub sleeve and snapring. While pressing downward on the second gear to compress the lower helical snapring, check the gap between the second gear and the upper snapring. This gap must be minimum of 0.006 in.
4. Install the second/third speed synchronizer assembly on the shaft.
5. Install the third gear on the shaft with clutching teeth facing downward. Install the third gear locating washer and snapring.
6. Install the fourth gear with the clutching teeth facing upward.
7. Install the bottom cone of the fourth/fifth synchronizer over the clutching teeth of the fourth gear.
8. Install the fourth/fifth shift sleeve hub. Be sure the chamfered side is facing down. Install the snapring.
9. Install the fourth/fifth synchronizer on the shift hub sleeve.
10. Reverse the output shaft and install the first/reverse gear with the shift fork facing downward. A minimum of 0.006 in. end play must be maintained on all mainshaft gears. Synchronizer end play on both synchronizers must be maintained at 0.060 in. minimum and 0.160 in. maximum.

INPUT SHAFT

Disassembly

1. Remove the bearing retaining snapring from the input shaft. Remove the bearing, using the special tool.

Assembly

1. Install the oil slinger and press the bearing on the input shaft. Be sure the snapring groove is facing the forward end of the shaft.

NOTE: To prevent damage to the bearing, apply pressure on the inner race of the bearing only.

2. Install the bearing snapring.

COUNTERSHAFT

Disassembly

1. Remove the snapring at the forward end of the countershaft.

2. Place the countershaft assembly in a hydraulic press and press the drive gear off the shaft.

3. Remove the key from the shaft and press the fourth gear off the shaft. Remove the remaining key.

Assembly

1. Install the fourth speed gear key in the slot on the shaft. Position the fourth gear on the shaft with the long hub facing toward the front.

2. Install the countershaft main drive gear key in the keyway in the shaft. Install the countershaft drive gear on the shaft with the long hub facing toward the rear. Install the snapring on the countershaft.

GEAR SHIFT HOUSING

Disassembly

NOTE: It is not necessary to disassemble the gear shift housing assembly to determine if the parts are worn. Note the condition of the shifter fork shafts and forks by visual inspection. If the forks are excessively worn or if they bind when shifted, disassemble the gear shift housing assembly to make repairs. Check the interlocking system.

1. With the control cover in neutral, pry the fourth/fifth shift fork to the fourth speed position (toward the rear of the cover). Remove the front rail support capscrews and remove the front rail support.

2. Remove the interlock tapered pin supports. Note the position of the interlock tapered pins for reassembly.

3. Remove the rear rail support capscrews and remove the rear rail support.

4. Remove the first/reverse shift fork and rail assembly. Remove the fourth, fifth, second and third shift fork and rail assembly. Use caution so as not to lose the interlock cross pin, interlock tapered pins, or the mesh lock poppet balls.

5. Remove the first/reverse shift rail. Remove the four mesh lock poppet balls. Remove the four poppet springs.

6. Remove the first/reverse rocker arm. Remove the reverse latch plunger spring retaining plug and the reverse latch plunger spring and plunger.

7. If the fork bushings are worn, secure the fork in a soft jawed vise and remove the worn bushings with a drift. Install

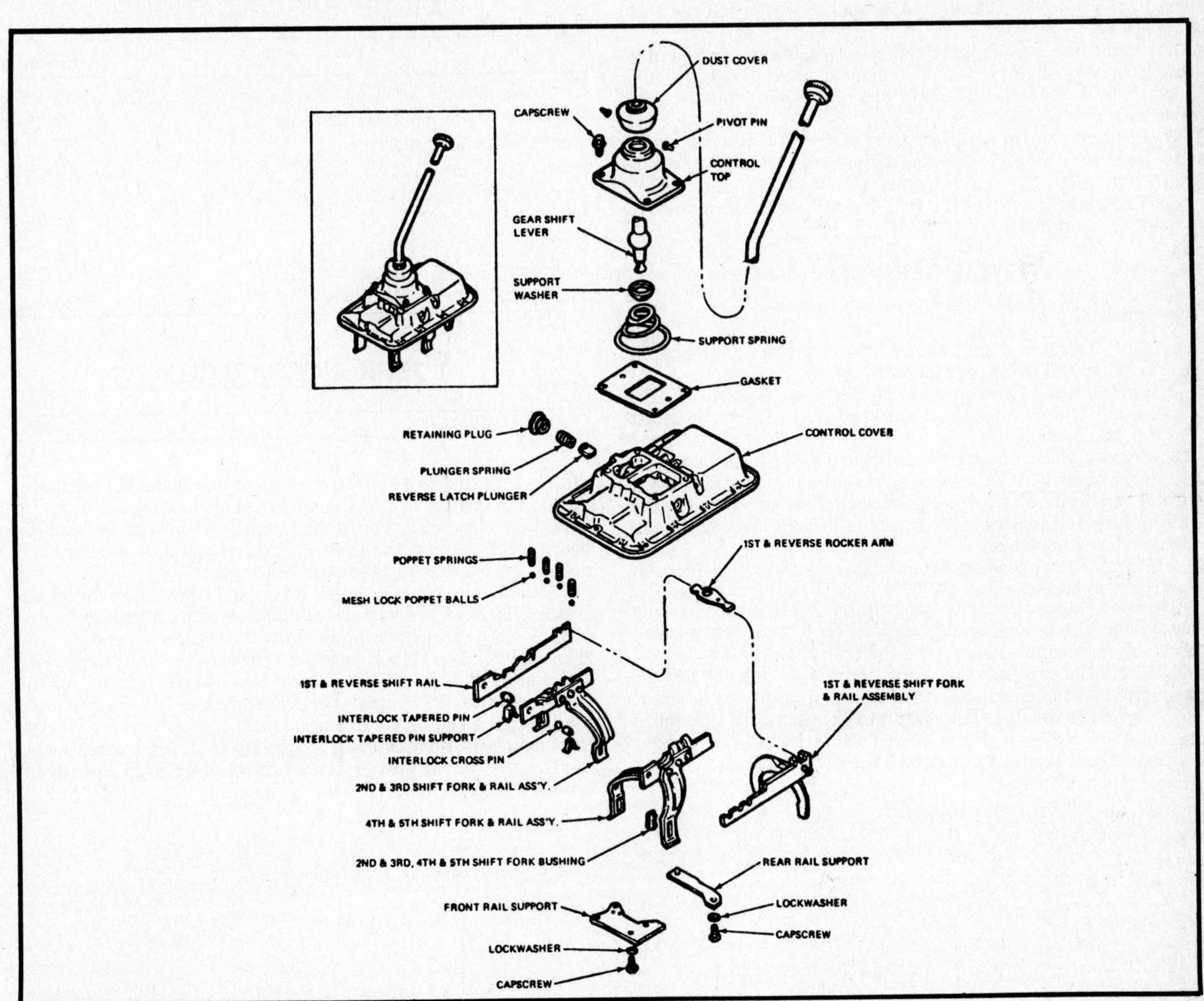

Exploded view Clark 280V gear shift housing

new bushings in the fork. Turn the fork over on the anvil of the vise and secure the bushings in the fork, using a prick punch and upsetting the bushing metal on the outside of the fork.

Assembly

1. Position the first/reverse rocker arm on the pivot pin. Install the reverse latch plunger, spring and retaining plug. Tighten the plug securely.
2. Install the four poppet springs and the four mesh lock poppet balls. Note the first/reverse shift fork rail poppet ball in the pocket.
3. Align one tapered interlock cross pin with the hole in the first/reverse shift rail. Position the rail on the poppet ball, in neutral position with the interlock pin aligned with the first interlock tapered pin. Install the second interlock tapered pin.
4. Align the pin with the interlock cross pin hole.
5. Position the fourth/fifth shift fork and rail assembly on the poppet ball in neutral position. Slightly raise the rear of the rail and align the second interlock tapered pin with the cross hole in the rail. Note the positions of the tapered interlock pins and the shift rails.
6. Install the first/reverse shift fork and rail assembly on the poppet ball in a neutral position. Align the first/reverse rocker arm in the notch at the rear of the rail. Position the rear rail support.
7. Install the rail support capscrews and washers. Tighten the capscrews slightly. Install the interlock tapered pin supports. Tap the fourth/fifth shift fork to the rear (fourth speed position).
8. Position the front rail support and install the capscrews and washers. Tighten the front and rear support capscrews 20–25 ft. lbs.
9. Tap the fourth/fifth shift fork and rail assemble forward to a neutral position.

TRANSMISSION

Assembly

1. Coat the countershaft needle bearings with grease and install them in the front countershaft bore.
2. Tip the rear of the countershaft down and lower it into the case. Push the countershaft forward and insert the shaft through the bearing.
3. Position the countershaft rear bearing oil slinger and bearing on the shaft. Drive the bearing in to the bearing bore in the case. The countershaft drive gear should be supported while driving the shaft to prevent damage to the front bearing. Install the rear bearing retainer.
4. Coat the reverse idler thrust washers with grease and position them in the case.
5. Insert the two roller bearings in the reverse idler bearing bore. Place the gear assembly in position in the transmission case, with the small gear toward the rear of the case.
6. Insert the reverse idler shaft through the hole in the case through the reverse idler gear and into the forward support boss. Drive the reverse idler shaft into the case until the slot in the shaft is lined up with the lock bolt hole. Install the retainer in the slot and secure the retainer with the lock bolt. Tighten the bolt to specifications.
7. Tilt the rear of the output shaft assembly downward and insert the end of the shaft through the output shaft bore in the case. Lower the front end of the output shaft until it is in line with the pilot bearing opening. Move the assembly forward into position.
8. Insert the pilot bearing in the input shaft bore.
9. Position the input shaft and bearing assembly in the forward end of the transmission case. Tap the front end of the shaft with a soft faced hammer until the snapring is seated against the case. Be sure the clutching teeth of the input shaft gear mesh with the fifth speed synchronizer without binding.
10. Position a new gasket on the input shaft bearing retainer. Be sure that the oil return holes in the retainer and gasket are aligned with the holes in the transmission case.
11. Install the lock washers and bolts on the input shaft bearing retainer and tighten the bolts to specifications.
12. Position the output shaft rear bearing on the shaft and drive the bearing into the bore until the snapring is seated against the case.
13. Position the countershaft rear bearing cap and gasket on the case and install the lock washers and bolts. Tighten the bolts to specification.

TORQUE SPECIFICATIONS

	ft. lbs.
Companion flange nut	350–420
Countershaft rear bearing cap	20–25
Input shaft bearing retainer	20–25
Output shaft bearing retainer	20–25
Reverse idler shaft lock bolt	20–25
Shift control to case	20–25
Shift cover to case	20–25
Shift tower to shift cover	20–25
Transmission to clutch housing	60–80

LUBRICANT CAPACITY

	Pints
Clark 280V series	8

14. Install the speedometer drive gear on the output shaft and position a new oil seal in the output shaft bearing retainer. Be sure the seal is correctly installed. Position a new gasket and the bearing retainer on the case and install the lock washers and bolts. Tighten the bolts to specification.
15. Install the parking brake drum and companion flange assembly. Tighten the yoke retaining nut to specification.
16. With the transmission in neutral, position the control cover over the gears, aligning the shift forks in the shift cover with the gear shift hubs. If the control cover is in neutral and the transmission is in neutral, the transmission drive gear should turn without the brake drum or output shaft turning. Install the capscrews and washers. Tighten 20–25 ft. lbs. Install the remote control or shift tower in the control cover. Tighten the capscrews 20–25 ft. lbs.

Clark 390V and 280 VHD Series

FIVE SPEED TRANSMISSIONS

The Clark 390V and 280VHD series transmissions are five speed units and have split pin synchronizers in all gears except low and reverse. The shift forks have replaceable bronze inserts and numerous needle bearings. Two tapered roller bearings and one large straight roller bearing is used to support the power shafts. Certain differences exist between the transmissions, but are both basically the same.

Disassembly

1. Remove the remote control or shift tower from the control cover. Remove the control cover capscrews and lockwashers. Remove the control cover assembly from the transmission. Remove the back-up light switch.
2. Remove the universal joint assembly and the drive shaft from the parking brake drum.
3. Remove the parking brake drum. Disconnect the parking brake actuating lever from the linkage.
4. Remove the transmission spline flange. Remove the bolts holding the carrier plate to the transmission housing. Slide the plate with the brake shoes and retaining springs off the transmission.
5. Lock the transmission in two gears and remove the brake drum retaining nut. Remove the brake drum from the output shaft.
6. Remove the output shaft rear bearing retainer and the speedometer drive gear.
7. Remove the countershaft rear bearing retainer, then remove the bearing snapring.
8. Remove the input shaft bearing retainer and pull the input shaft out of the case. Be careful not to drop the output shaft pilot bearing rollers into the transmission case.

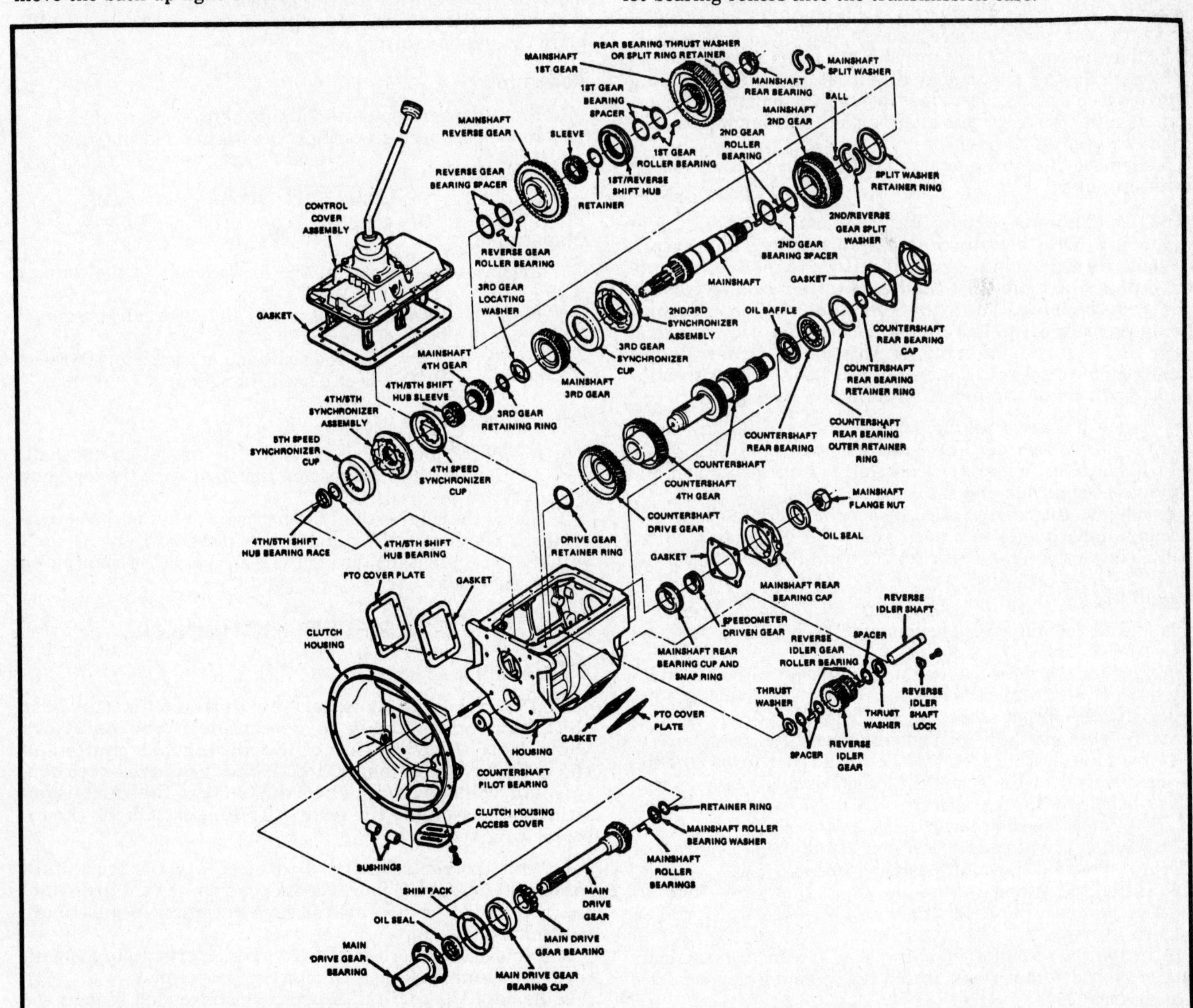

Exploded view Clark 390V transmission

9. Force the output shaft rearward until the rear bearing is exposed. Working with a bearing puller, remove the rear bearing from the bore.
10. Lift the output shaft out of the case.
11. Remove the reverse idler shaft using special tool. Lift the reverse idler gear, bearing and thrust washer out of the transmission case.
12. Move the countershaft rearward until the rear bearing is exposed. Remove the bearing and oil slinger with a suitable gear puller.
13. Lift the countershaft from the case.
14. If the countershaft front bearing or pilot bearing is to be replaced, remove the clutch housing from the transmission.
15. Press the pilot bearing out of the case. Do not hammer or drive the bearing out as damage or distortion to the bearing bore will result.

OUTPUT SHAFT

Disassembly

1. Clamp the output shaft, front end facing upward, in a soft jawed vise. Remove the fifth gear synchroninizer and the fourth and fifth gear synchronizer assembly.
2. Remove the shift hub thrust bearing and race.
3. Remove the fourth and fifth shift hub sleeve and the fourth speed synchronizer ring. Remove the fourth gear.
4. Remove the third gear snapring and locating washer. Lift the third gear off the shaft.
5. Remove the third gear synchronizer ring and the synchronizer assembly.

NOTE: There is a variation in the mainshaft first gear retention. One version has a split washer and a split washer retainer ring. Working with a three legged puller, pull against the split washer retainer ring to remove the rear bearing. The other version of the mainshaft first gear retention is a thrust washer between the first gear and the rear bearing. In this version there is not enough room to get a puller behind the thrust washer and it will be necessary to pull on the first gear.

6. Remove the rear bearing and the first gear. Be sure not to lose the needle bearings under the first gear.
7. Remove the first and reverse shift hub sleeve retainer and remove the shift hub and sleeve.
8. Remove the reverse gear. Be sure not to lose the needle bearings under the reverse gear.
9. Remove the second gear retainer and the second gear.

Assembly

1. Install the output shaft, forward end up, in a soft jawed vise.
2. Position the third gear on the output shaft with the clutching teeth down. Install the locating washer and snapring.
3. Turn the output shaft over and install the third gear synchronizer ring and the second and third synchronizer assembly.
4. With the clutching teeth of the second gear down, coat the inside diameter of the gear with a high quality heavy grease. This will hold the needle rollers in place during assembly. Install the first row of needle rollers.
5. Position the bearing spacer and install the second row of bearings. Position the outer bearing spacer.
6. Install the second gear on the output shaft, using caution so as not to catch the needle rollers on the edge of a spline or snap-ring groove.
7. Install the second gear split washer locating ball and split washer on the output shaft. Install the retaining ring over the split washer.
8. Coat the inside of the reverse gear with grease and install the bearing spacers and the bearings.
9. Install the reverse gear on the output shaft, position the shift hub sleeve and the shift hub and install the shift hub sleeve snapring.
10. Install the spacers and bearings in the first gear and install the gear on the output shaft.
11. Install the first gear retaining washer. Install the output shaft bearing. Be sure that the bearing is tight against the washer.
12. Turn the output shaft over and install the fourth gear with the clutching teeth facing upward.
13. Position the fourth gear synchronizer ring on the clutching teeth of the fourth gear. Install the fourth and fifth shift hub sleeve on the output shaft.
14. Install the fourth and fifth synchronizer and the fifth speed synchronizer ring on the output shaft.
15. Install the thrust bearing and race.

INPUT SHAFT

Disassembly

1. Remove the bearing snapring from the input shaft. Remove the bearing with the special tool.
2. Remove the needle bearing retainer and the washer. Remove the needle bearings.

Assembly

1. Press the bearing on the input shaft.
2. Install the needle bearings, the washer and snapring.

COUNTER SHAFT

Disassembly

1. Remove the snapring at the forward end of the counter shaft.
2. Place the countershaft assembly in a hydraulic press and press the drive gear off the shaft.
3. Remove the key from the shaft and press the fourth/speed gear off the shaft. Remove the remaining key.

Assembly

1. Install the fourth/speed gear key in the slot on the shaft. Position the fourth/speed gear on the shaft with the long hub facing toward the front.
2. Install the countershaft main drive gear key in the keyway on the shaft. Install the countershaft drive gear on the shaft with the long hub facing toward the rear. Install the snapring on the countershaft.

GEAR SHIFT HOUSING

Disassembly

NOTE: It is not necessary to disassemble the gear shift housing assembly to determine if the parts are worn. Note the condition of the shifter fork shafts and the forks by visual inspection. If the forks are excessively worn, or if they bind when shifted into the various positions, disassemble the gear shift housing. Check the interlocking system.

1. With the control cover in neutral, pry the fourth/fifth speed shift fork to the fourth speed position (toward the rear of the cover). Remove the front rail support capscrews and remove the front rail support.
2. Remove the interlock tapered pin supports. Note the position on the interlock tapered pins for reassembly.
3. Remove the rear rail support capscrews and remove the rear rail support.
4. Remove the first/reverse shift fork and rail assembly, re-

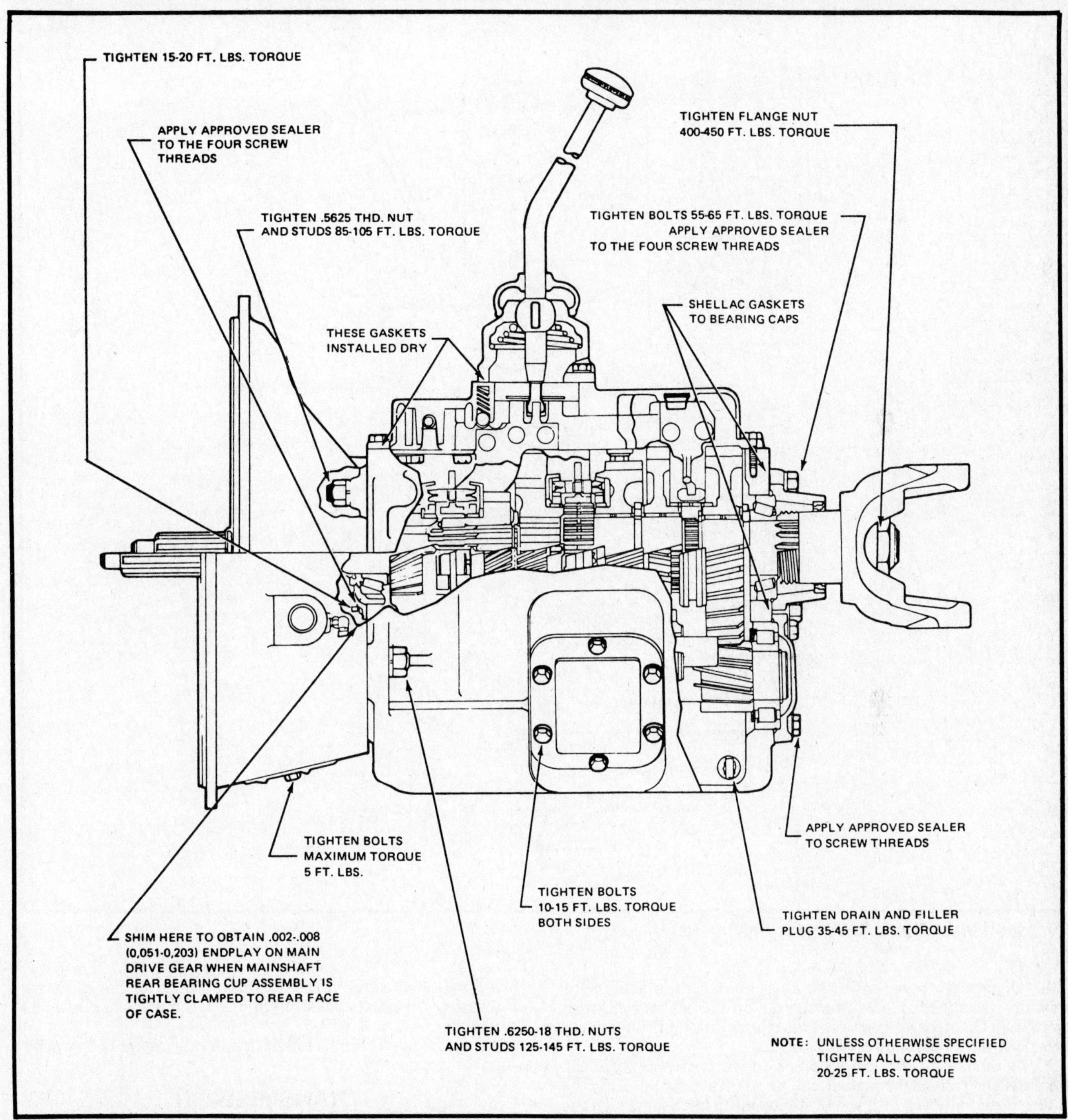
TIGHTEN 15-20 FT. LBS. TORQUE
APPLY APPROVED SEALER TO THE FOUR SCREW THREADS
TIGHTEN FLANGE NUT 400-450 FT. LBS. TORQUE
TIGHTEN .5625 THD. NUT AND STUDS 85-105 FT. LBS. TORQUE
TIGHTEN BOLTS 55-65 FT. LBS. TORQUE APPLY APPROVED SEALER TO THE FOUR SCREW THREADS
SHELLAC GASKETS TO BEARING CAPS
THESE GASKETS INSTALLED DRY
APPLY APPROVED SEALER TO SCREW THREADS
TIGHTEN BOLTS MAXIMUM TORQUE 5 FT. LBS.
TIGHTEN BOLTS 10-15 FT. LBS. TORQUE BOTH SIDES
TIGHTEN DRAIN AND FILLER PLUG 35-45 FT. LBS. TORQUE
SHIM HERE TO OBTAIN .002-.008 (0,051-0,203) ENDPLAY ON MAIN DRIVE GEAR WHEN MAINSHAFT REAR BEARING CUP ASSEMBLY IS TIGHTLY CLAMPED TO REAR FACE OF CASE.
TIGHTEN .6250-18 THD. NUTS AND STUDS 125-145 FT. LBS. TORQUE
NOTE: UNLESS OTHERWISE SPECIFIED TIGHTEN ALL CAPSCREWS 20-25 FT. LBS. TORQUE

Torque specifications—Clark 390V transmission

move the fourth, fifth, second and third shift fork and rail assembly. Use caution so that the interlock cross pin, interlock tapered pins, or the mesh lock poppet balls are not lost.

5. Remove the first/reverse shift rail. Remove the four mesh lock poppet balls and then remove the four poppet springs.

6. Remove the first/reverse rocker arm. Remove the reverse latch plunger spring retaining plug and the reverse latch plunger spring and plunger.

7. If the fork bushings are worn, secure the fork in a soft jawed vise and remove the worn bushings with a suitable drift. Install the new bushings in the fork. Turn the fork over on the anvil of the vise and secure the bushing in the fork, using a pick punch and upsetting the bushing metal on the outside of the fork.

Assembly

1. Position the first/reverse rocker arm on the pivot pin. Install the reverse latch plunger, spring and the retaining plug. Tighten the plug securely.

2. Install the four poppet springs and the four mesh lock poppet balls.

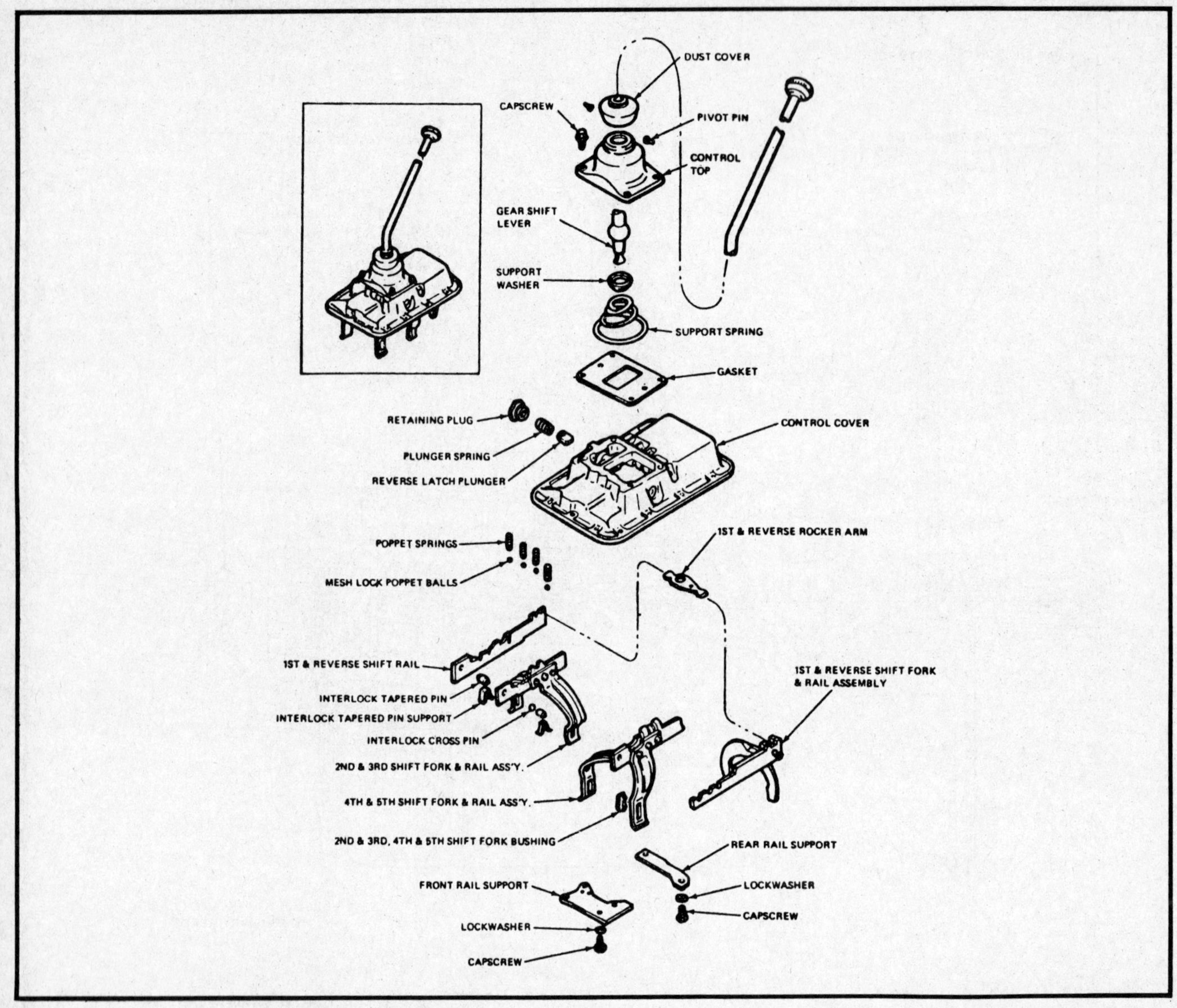

Exploded view Clark 390V gear shift housing

3. Align one tapered interlock cross pin with the hole in the first/reverse shift rail. Position the rail on the poppet ball, with the rail in the neutral position. Note the position of the tapered interlock pin in relation to the rail.

4. Install the interlock cross pin in the second/third shift rail. Position the rail on the poppet ball, in neutral position with the interlock pin aligned with the first interlock pin aligned with the first tapered pin. Install the second interlock tapered pin. Align the pin with the interlock cross pin hole.

5. Position the fourth/fifth shift fork rail assembly on the poppet ball in the neutral position. Slightly raise the rear of the rail and align the second interlock tapered pin with the cross hole in the rail. Note the positions of the tapered interlock pins in the shift rails.

6. Install the first/reverse shift fork and rail assembly on the poppet ball in a neutral position. Align the first/reverse rocker arm in the rear of the rail.

7. Install the rail support capscrews and washers. Tighten the capscrews slightly. Install the interlock tapered pin supports. Tap the fourth/fifth shift fork to the rear (fourth speed position).

8. Position the front rail support and install the capscrews and washers. Tighten the front and rear support capscrews 20–25 ft. lbs.

9. Tap the fourth/fifth shift fork and rail assembly forward to a neutral position.

TRANSMISSION

Assembly

1. Coat the front counter shaft needle bearings with grease and install them in the front countershaft bore.

2. Tap the rear of the countershaft down and lower into the case. Push the countershaft forward and insert the shaft into the front bearing.

3. Position the countershaft rear bearing oil slinger and bearing on the shaft. Drive the bearing into the bore. The countershaft drive gear should be supported while driving the shaft to prevent damage to the front bearing. Install the rear bearing retainer.

4. Coat the reverse idler thrust washer with grease and position them in the transmission case.

5. Insert the bearings in the reverse idler bore. Place the gear assembly in position in the case, with the small gear toward the rear of the case.

6. Insert the reverse idler shaft through the hole in the case through the reverse idler gear and into the forward support boss. Drive the reverse idler shaft into the case until the slot in the shaft is lined up with the lock bolt hole. Install the retainer in the slot and secure the retainer with the lock bolt. Tighten the bolt to specification.

7. Tilt the rear of the output shaft assembly downward and insert the end of the shaft through the output shaft in the bore in the case. Lower the front end of the output shaft until it is in line with the pilot bearing opening. Move the assembly forward into position.

8. Insert the pilot bearing in the input shaft bore.

9. Position the input shaft and bearings in the forward end of the transmission case. Tap the front end of the shaft with a soft faced hammer until the snapring is seated against the case. Be sure the clutching teeth of the input shaft gear mesh with the fifth speed synchronizer without binding.

10. Position a new gasket on the input shaft bearing retainer. Be sure that the oil return holes in the retainer and gasket are aligned with the holes in the transmission case.

11. Install the lock washers and bolts on the input shaft bearing retainer and tighten the bolts to specification.

12. Position the output shaft rear bearing on the shaft and drive the bearing into the bore until the snapring is seated against the case.

13. Position the countershaft rear bearing cap and gasket on the case and install the lock washers and bolts. Tighten to specification.

14. Install the speedometer drive gear on the output shaft and position a new oil seal in the output shaft bearing retainer. Be sure the seal is correctly installed. Position a new gasket and the bearing retainer on the case and install the lock washers and bolts. Tighten to specification.

15. Install the parking brake drum and companion flange assembly. Tighten the yoke retaining nut to specification.

16. With the transmission in neutral, position the control cover over the gears, aligning the shift forks in the shift cover with the gear shift hubs. If the control cover is in Neutral and the transmission is in Neutral, the transmission drive gear should turn without the brake drum or output shaft turning. Install the capscrews and washers and tighten 20–25 ft. lbs. Install the remote control or shift tower in the control cover. Tighten the capscrews 20–25 ft. lbs.

Chrysler Corporation

A-230 THREE SPEED TRANSMISSION

The A-230 is a three speed transmission equipped with two synchronizer units to assist in the engagement of all forward gears. Lubricant capacity is 5 pints.

Disassembly

SHIFT HOUSING AND MECHANISM

1. Shift to second gear.

2. Remove side cover. If shaft O-ring seals need replacement, pull shift forks out of shafts. Remove nuts and operating levers from shafts. Deburr and remove the shafts.

DRIVE PINION RETAINER AND EXTENSION HOUSING

1. Remove pinion bearing retainer from front of transmission case. Pry off retainer oil seal for clearance. With a brass drift, tap drive pinion as far forward as possible. Rotate cut away part of second gear next to countershaft gear. Shift second–third synchronizer sleeve forward. Remove speedometer pinion adapter retainer. Work adapter and pinion out of extension housing.

2. Unbolt extension housing. Break housing loose with plastic hammer and carefully remove.

IDLER GEAR AND MAINSHAFT

1. Insert dummy shaft in case to push reverse idler shaft and key out of case.

2. Remove dummy shaft and idler rollers.

3. Remove both tanged idler gear thrust washers.

4. Remove mainshaft assembly through rear of case.

COUNTERSHAFT GEAR AND DRIVE PINION

1. Using a mallet and dummy shaft, tap the countershaft rearward enough to remove key. Drive countershaft out of case, being careful not to drop the washers.

2. Lower countershaft gear to bottom of case.

3. Remove snapring from pinion bearing outer race (outside front of case).

4. Drive pinion shaft into case with plastic hammer. Remove assembly through rear of case.

5. If bearing is to be replaced, remove snapring and press off bearing.

6. Lift counter shaft gear and dummy shaft out through rear of case.

MAINSHAFT

1. Remove snapring from front end of mainshaft along with second gear stop ring and second gear.

2. Spread snapring in mainshaft bearing retainer. Slide retainer back off the bearing race.

3. Remove snapring at rear of mainshaft. Support front side of reverse gear. Press bearing off mainshaft.

4. Remove from press. Remove mainshaft bearing and reverse gear from shaft.

5. Remove snapring and first/reverse synchronizer assembly from shaft. Remove stop ring and first gear rearward.

Cleaning and Inspection

See Cleaning and Inspection instructions at the beginning of the Transmission section.

Assembly

COUNTERSHAFT GEAR

1. Slide dummy shaft into countershaft gear.

2. Slide one roller thrust washer over dummy shaft and into gear, followed by 22 greased rollers.

3. Repeat Step 2, adding one roller thrust washer on end.

4. Repeat Steps 2–3 at other end of countershaft gear. There is a total of 88 rollers and 6 thrust washers.

5. Place greased front thrust washer on dummy shaft against gear with tangs forward.

6. Grease rear thrust washer and stick it in place in the case, with tangs rearward. Place countershaft gear assembly in bottom of transmission case until drive pinion is installed.

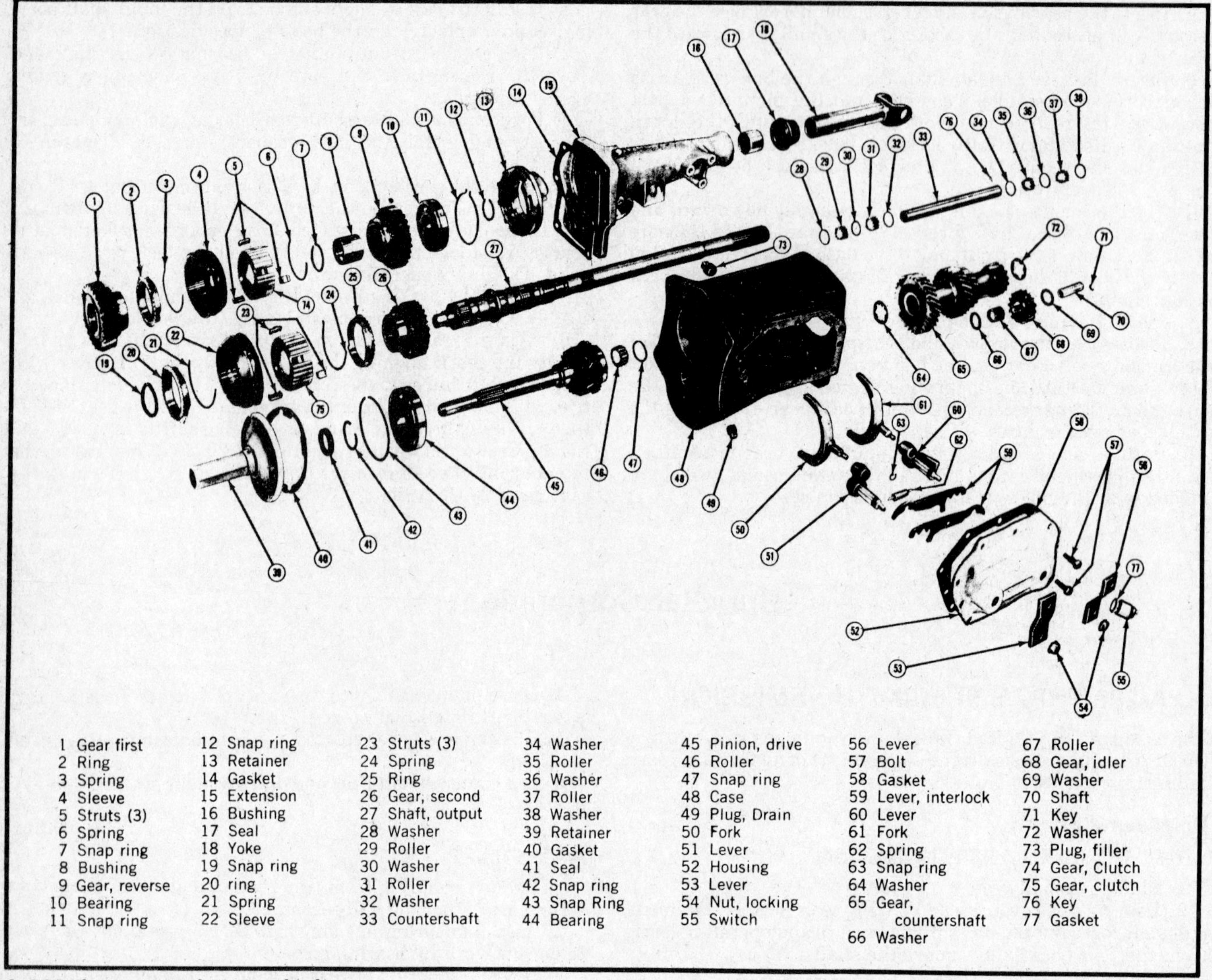

A-230 three speed transmission

PINION GEAR

1. Press new bearing on pinion shaft with snapring groove forward. Install new snapring.
2. Install 15 rollers and retaining ring in drive pinion gear.
3. Install drive pinion and bearing assembly into case.
4. Position countershaft gear assembly by positioning it and thrust washers so countershaft can be tapped into position. Be careful to keep the countershaft against the dummy shaft to keep parts from falling between them. Install key in countershaft.
5. Tap drive pinion forward for clearance.

MAINSHAFT

1. Place a stop ring flat on the bench. Place a clutch gear and a sleeve on top. Drop the struts in their slots and insert a strut spring with the tang inside on strut. Turn the assembly over and install second strut spring, tang in a different strut.
2. Slide first gear and stop ring over rear of mainshaft and against thrust flange between assembly over rear of mainshaft, first and second gears on shaft.
3. Slide first/reverse synchronizer indexing hub slots to first gear stop ring lugs.
4. Install first/reverse synchronizer clutch gear snapring on mainshaft.
5. Slide reverse gear and mainshaft bearing on shaft, supporting inner race of bearing. Be sure snapring groove on outer race is forward.
6. Install bearing retaining snapring on mainshaft. Slide snapring over the bearing and seat it in groove.
7. Place second gear over front of mainshaft with thrust surface against flange.
8. Install stop ring and second/third synchronizer assembly against second gear. Install second/third synchronizer clutch gear snapring on shaft.
9. Move second/third synchronizer sleeve forward as far as possible. Install front stop ring inside sleeve with lugs indexed to struts.
10. Rotate cut out on second gear toward countershaft gear for clearance.
11. Insert mainshaft assembly into case. Tilt assembly to clear cluster gears and insert pilot rollers in drive pinion gear. If assembly is correct, the bearing retainer will bottom to the case without force. If not, check for a misplaced strut, pinion roller, or stop ring.

REVERSE IDLER GEAR

1. Place dummy shaft into idler gear. Insert 22 greased rollers.

2. Position reverse idler thrust washers in case with grease.
3. Position idler gear and dummy shaft in case. Install idler shaft and key.

EXTENSION HOUSING

1. Remove extension housing yoke seal. Drive bushing out from inside housing.
2. Align oil hole in bushing with oil slot in housing. Drive bushing into place. Drive new seal into housing.
3. Install extension housing and gasket to hold mainshaft and bearing retainer in place.

DRIVE PINION BEARING RETAINER

1. Install outer snapring on drive pinion bearing. Tap assembly back until snap-ring contacts case.
2. Using seal installer tool or equivalent, install a new seal in retainer bore.
3. Position main drive pinion bearing retainer and gasket on front of case. Coat threads with sealing compound, install bolts, torque to 30 ft. lbs.

GEARSHAFT MECHANISM AND HOUSING

1. If removed, place two interlock levers in pivot pin with spring hangers offset toward each other, so that spring installs in a straight line. Place E-clip on pivot pin.
2. Grease and install new O-ring seals on both shift shafts. Grease housing bores and insert shafts.
3. Install spring on interlock lever hangers.
4. Rotate each shift shaft fork bore to straight up position. Install shift forks through bores and under both interlock levers.
5. Position second/third synchronizer sleeve to rear, in second gear position. Position first–reverse synchronizer sleeve to middle of travel, in neutral position. Place shift forks in the same positions.
6. Install gasket and gearshift mechanism. The bolt with the extra long shoulder must be installed at the center rear of the case. Torque bolts to 15 ft. lbs.
7. Install speedometer drive pinion gear and adapter. Range number on adapter, which represents the number of teeth on the gear, should be in 6 o'clock position.

TORQUE SPECIFICATIONS

Manual A-203 3-Speed	ft. lbs.
Back up light switch	15
Extension housing bolts	50
Drive pinion bearing retainer bolts	30
Gearshift operating lever nuts	18
Transmission to clutch housing bolts	50
Transmission cover retaining bolts	12
Transmission drain plug	25

Chrysler Corporation

A-250 THREE SPEED TRANSMISSION

The A-250 is a three speed transmission equipped with a synchronizer between second and third gears. Lubricant capacity is 4 ½ pints.

Disassembly

1. Remove case cover and gasket.
2. Measure the synchronizer "float" with a pair of feeler gauges. Measurement is made between the synchronizer outer ring pin and the opposite synchronizer outer ring. This measurement must be made on two pins 180 degrees apart with equal gap on both ends for "float" determination. The measurement should be between 0.060–0.117 in. A snug fit should be maintained between feeler gauge and pins.
3. Remove the bolt and retainer holding the speedometer pinion adapter in the extension housing. Carefully work the adapter and pinion out of the extension housing.
4. Remove extension housing bolts and extension housing.
5. Remove the bolts that attach the drive pinion bearing retainer to case, then slide the retainer off the pinion. Pry the seal out of retainer using a suitable tool. Be cautious not to nick or scratch the bore.
6. Rotate the drive pinion so that the blank clutch tooth area is opposite the countershaft for removal clearance.
7. Slide drive pinion assembly slightly out of case. Move the synchronizer front inner stop ring from the short splines on the pinion shaft. Slowly remove drive pinion assembly.
8. Remove snapring that holds bearing on pinion shaft. Remove pinion bearing washer. Using an arbor press, press pinion shaft out of bearing. Remove oil slinger.
9. Remove snapring and bearing rollers from the end of the drive pinion.

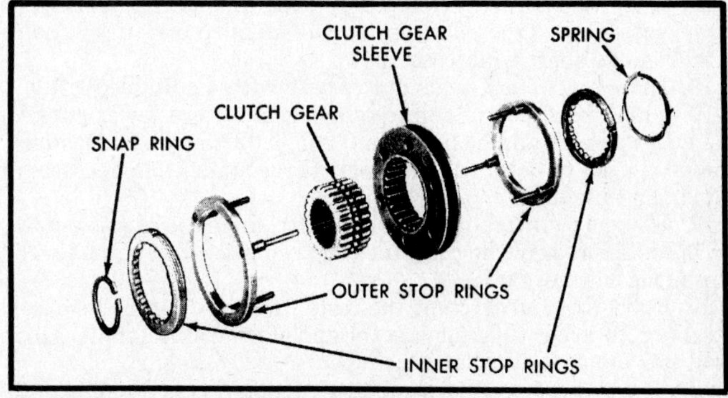

Exploded view A-250 synchronizer

10. Remove clutch gear retaining snapring from the mainshaft.
11. Remove the mainshaft bearing securing snapring from case.
12. Slide mainshaft and bearing rearward out of case while holding the gears as they drop free.
13. Remove the snapring from mainshaft and press the bearing off of mainshaft.
14. Remove the synchronizer components, second gear, first/reverse gear and shift forks from case.

NOTE: Steps 15–18 need only be performed if gear shift lever seals are leaking.

15. Remove the shift levers from the shift shafts.
16. Drive out the tapered retaining pin from the first/reverse shift shaft. Remove the shift shaft from inside the case.

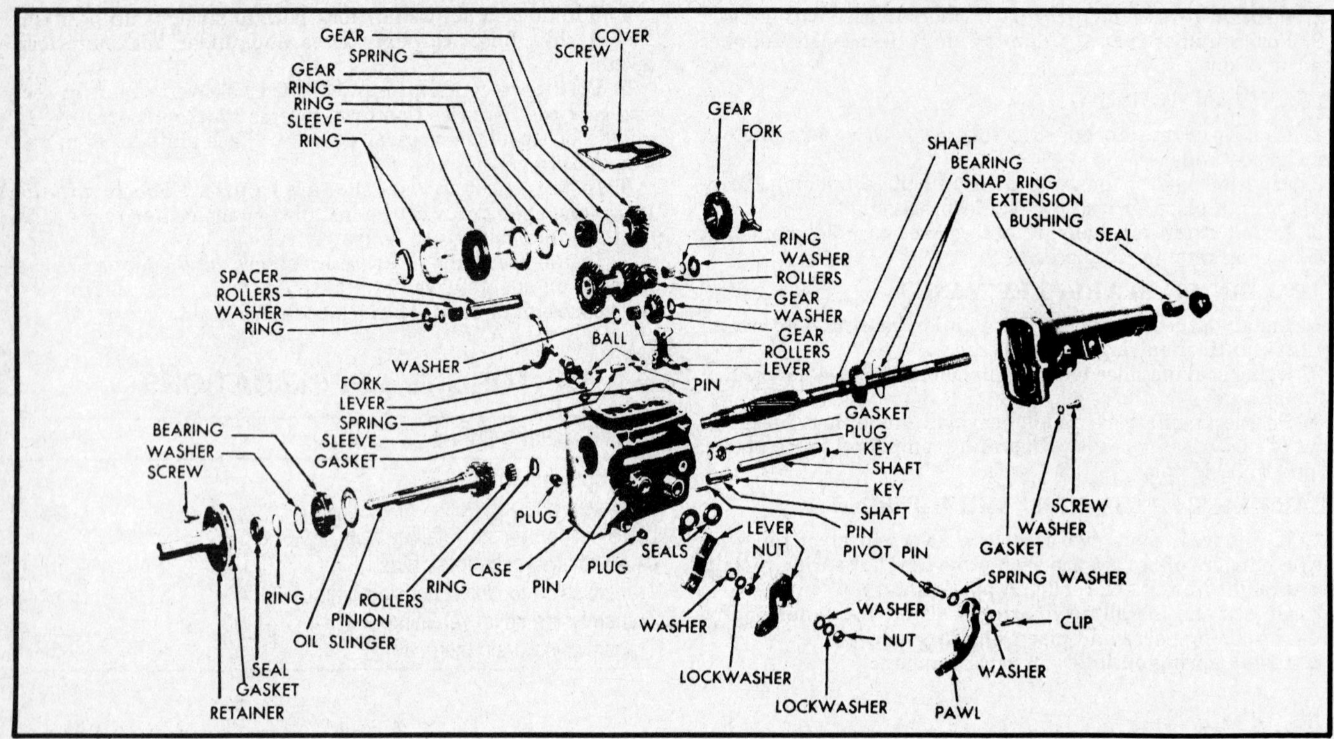

Exploded view A-250 transmission

NOTE: As the detent balls are spring loaded, when the shafts are removed the balls will drop to the bottom of the transmission case.

17. Remove the interlock sleeve, spring and both detent balls from case. Drive tapered retaining pin out of second–third shaft and remove shaft from case.
18. Drive shift shaft seals out of case with a suitable drift.
19. Check end play of countershaft gear with a feeler gauge. The end play should be between 0.005–0.022 in. This measurement is used to determine if a new thrust washer is necessary during reassembly.
20. Using a countershaft bearing arbor, drive the countershaft towards the rear of the case until the small key can be removed from the countershaft.
21. Drive the countershaft the rest of the way out of the case, keeping the arbor tight against the end of the countershaft. This will prevent loss of roller bearings.
22. Remove the countershaft gear, front thrust washer and rear thrust washer from the case.
23. Remove the bearing rollers, spacer ring and center spacer from the countershaft gear.
24. Drive the reverse idler gear shaft out of the transmission case using a suitable drift. Remove the Woodruff key from the end of the reverse idler shaft.
25. Remove the reverse idler gear and thrust washers out of the case. Remove the bearing rollers from the gear.

Cleaning and Inspection

See Cleaning and Inspection instructions at the beginning of the Transmission section.

Assembly

1. Slide the countershaft gear bearing roller spacer over arbor tool. Coat the bore of gear with lubricant and slide tool and spacer into gear bore.
2. Lubricate the bearing rollers with heavy grease and install two rows of 22 rollers each in both ends of gear in area around arbor. Cover with heavy grease and install bearing spacer rings in each end of gear and between roller rows.
3. If countershaft gear end play was found to be excessive during disassembly, install new thrust washers. Cover with heavy grease and install thrust washer and thrust needle bearing and cap at each end of countershaft gear and over arbor. Install gear and arbor in the case and make sure that tabs on rear thrust washer slide into grooves in the case.
4. Drive the arbor forward out of the countershaft gear and through the bore in the front of the case using the countershaft and a soft faced hammer. When the countershaft is almost in place, make certain the keyway in the countershaft is aligned with the key slot in the rear of the case. Insert the shaft key and continue to drive the countershaft into the case until the key is bottomed in the slot.
5. Position special arbor tool in the reverse idler gear and install the 22 roller bearings using a heavy grease.
6. Place the front and rear thrust washers at each end of the reverse idler gear. Position the assembly in the transmission case with the chamfered end of the gear teeth towards the front. Make sure that the thrust washer tabs engage the slots in case.
7. Insert reverse idler shaft into the bore at rear of case with keyway to the rear, pushing the arbor towards the front of the case.
8. When the keyway is aligned with the slot in the case, insert the key in the keyway. Drive the shaft forward until the key is seated in the recess.

NOTE: Steps 9–14 need only be performed if the shift levers have been disassembled.

9. Place new shift shaft seals in the case and drive it into position with suitable drift.
10. Carefully slide the first/reverse shift shaft into the case and lock into place with a tapered retaining pin. Position the lever so that the center detent is aligned with the interlock bore.

11. Install the interlock sleeve into the bore followed by a detent ball, spring and pin.
12. Install remaining detent ball and hold in place with detent ball holding tool.
13. Depress the detent ball and carefully install the second/third shift shaft. Align center detent with detent ball and secure lever with tapered retaining pin.
14. Install shift levers and tighten retaining nuts to 18 ft. lbs.
15. Press the bearing on the mainshaft and select and install snapring that gives minimum end play.
16. Move shift lever to reverse position and then place the first/reverse gear and shift fork in the case. Both shift forks are offset toward the rear of the transmission case.
17. Assemble the synchronizer parts with shift fork and second gear.
18. Place the second gear assembly in the transmission case and insert the shift fork into its lever.
19. Install the mainshaft carefully through the gear assembly until it bottoms in rear of case.
20. Install synchronizer clutch gear snapring on mainshaft.
21. Select and install mainshaft bearing snapring in case.
22. If "float" measurement was found to be outside specifications, install or remove shims to place "float" within range.
23. Install oil slinger on drive pinion shaft and slide against the gear.
24. Slide the bearing over the pinion shaft with snapring groove away from gear, then seat bearing on shaft using an arbor press.
25. Install keyed washer between bearing and retaining snapring groove.
26. Secure bearing and washer with selected thickness snapring. If large snapring around bearing was removed, install it at this time.
27. Place drive pinion shaft in a vise with soft faced jaws and install the 14 roller bearings in the shaft cavity. Coat the roller bearings with a heavy grease and install retaining ring in groove.
28. Rotate the drive pinion so that the blank clutch tooth area is next to the countershaft. Guide the drive pinion through the front of case and engage the inner stop ring with the clutch teeth. Then seat pinion bearing. The pinion shaft is fully seated when the snapring is in full contact with the case.
29. Install a new seal in the pinion bearing retainer.
30. Position retainer assembly and new gasket on the case. Use sealing compound on bolts and tighten to 30 ft. lbs.
31. Slide the extension housing and a new gasket over mainshaft. Guide shaft through bushing and oil seal. Use sealing compound on the bolt used in the hole tapped through the transmission case. Install remaining bolts and tighten all to 50 ft. lbs.
32. Install the transmission cover and gasket and tighten cover bolts to 12 ft. lbs.
33. Rotate the speedometer pinion gear and adapter assembly so that the number on the adapter corresponding to the number of teeth on the gear is in the 6 o'clock position as the assembly is installed.
34. Fill the transmission with the proper lubricant and install the drain plug and tighten to 25 ft. lbs. Install the back-up light switch and tighten to 15 ft. lbs.
35. Rotate the drive pinion shaft and check operation of transmission by running the transmission through all gear ranges.

Chrysler Corporation

A-390 THREE SPEED TRANSMISSION

The A-390 is a three speed synchromesh transmission. Lubricant capacity is 4 ½ pints.

Disassembly

1. Remove the bolts that attach the cover to the case. Remove the cover and gasket.
2. Remove the long spring that retains the detent plug in the case. Remove the detent plug with a small magnet.
3. Remove the bolt and retainer securing the speedometer pinion adapter to the transmission case. Carefully work the adapter and pinion out of the extension housing.
4. Remove the bolts that attach the extension housing to the transmission case. Slide the extension housing off the output shaft.
5. Remove the bolts that attach the input shaft bearing retainer to the case. Slide the retainer off the shaft. Using a suitable tool, pry the seal out of the retainer. Be careful not to nick or scratch the bore in which the seal is pressed or the surface on which the seal is bottomed.
6. Remove the lubricant fill plug from the right side of the case. Working through the fill plug opening, drive the roll pin out of the countershaft with a ¼ in. punch.
7. Working with the countershaft bearing arbor and a soft faced hammer, tap the countershaft toward the front of the case with the arbor tool to remove the expansion plug from the countershaft bore at the front of the case. The countershaft is a loose fit in the case and will slide easily.
8. Insert the arbor tool through the front of the case and push the countershaft out of the rear of the case so the roll pin hole in the countershaft does not travel through the roller bearings. The countershaft gear will drop to the bottom of the case. Remove the countershaft from the rear of the case.
9. Place both shift levers in neutral (center) position.
10. Remove the input shaft assembly and stop ring from the front of the case.
11. Remove the set screw that secures the first/reverse shift fork to the shift rail. Slide the first/reverse shift rail out through the rear of the case.
12. Move the second/third shift fork rearward for access to the set screw. Remove the set screw from the fork. Using a suitable tool, rotate the shift rail one quarter turn.
13. Lift the interlock plug from the case with a magnet.
14. Tap on the inner end of the second/third shift rail to remove the expansion plug from the front of the case. Remove the shift rail through the front of the case.
15. Remove the second/third shift rail detent plug and spring from the detent bore with a magnet.
16. Tap the output shaft assembly rearward until the output shaft bearing clears the case. Remove both shift forks. Remove the snapring that retains the output shaft bearing to the output shaft.
17. Assemble the output shaft bearing removal tool over the output shaft and bearing. Remove the output shaft bearing.
18. Remove the output shaft assembly through top of the case.
19. Using a suitable drift, drive the reverse idler gear shaft toward the rear and out of the transmission case.
20. Lift the reverse idler gear and thrust washer out of the case.
21. Remove the countershaft gear, arbor assembly and thrust washers from the bottom of the case.
22. Remove the countershaft roll pin from the bottom of the case.

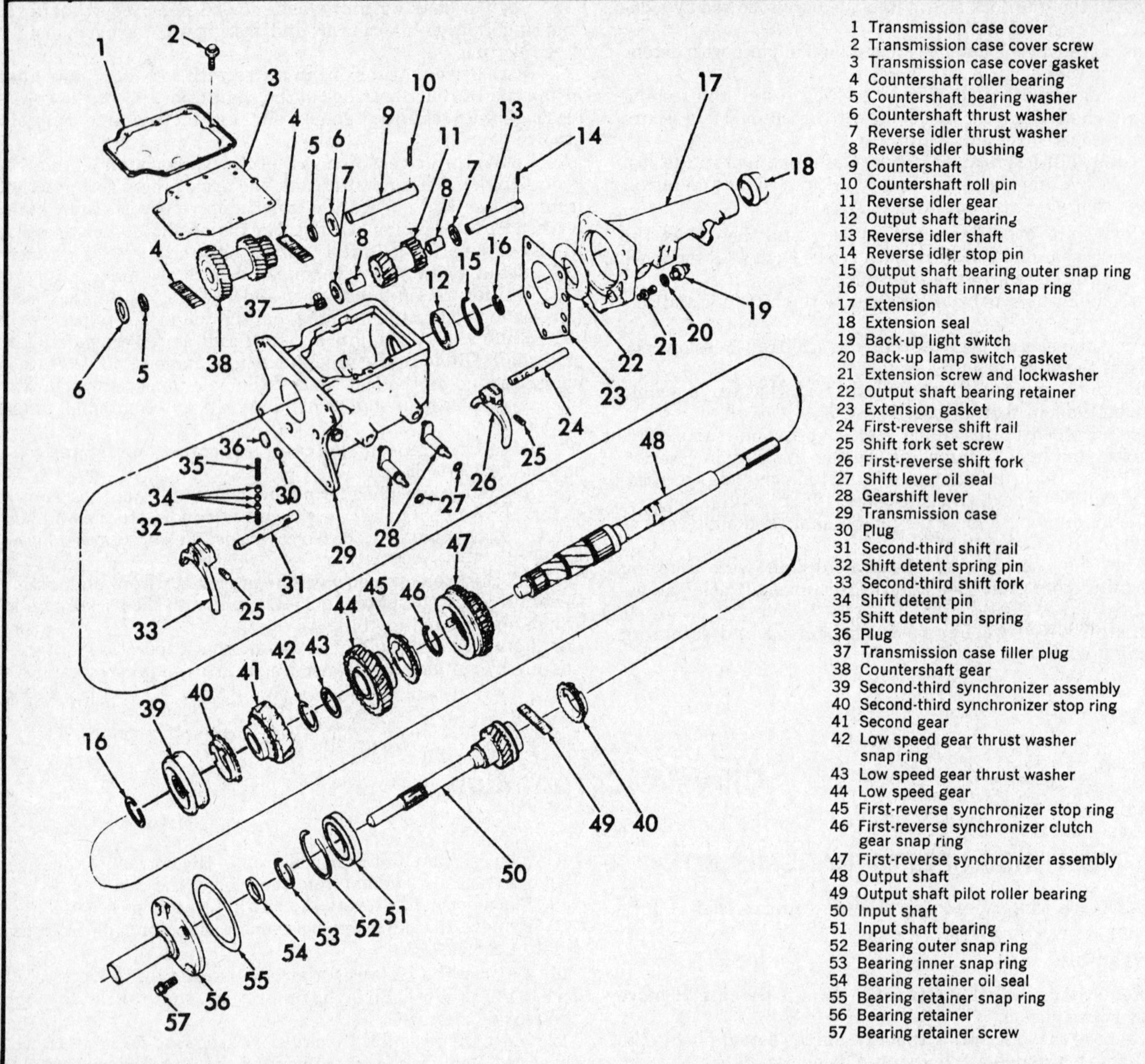

Exploded view A-390 transmission

23. Remove the snapring that retains the second/third synchronizer clutch gear and sleeve assembly on the output shaft. Slide the second/third synchronizer assembly off the end of the output shaft.

NOTE: Do not separate the second/third synchronizer clutch gear, sleeve, struts, or spring unless inspection reveals that a replacement is necessary.

24. Slide the second gear and stop ring off the output shaft.
25. Remove the snapring and thrust washer retaining the first gear. Slide the first gear and stop ring off the output shaft.
26. Remove the snapring that retains the first/reverse synchronizer hub on the output shaft. The first/reverse synchronizer hub is a press fit on the output shaft. To avoid damage to the synchronizer, remove the synchronizer hub using an arbor press. Do not attempt to remove or install the hub by hammering or prying.

Overhaul

SHIFT LEVERS AND SEALS

1. Remove the operating levers from their respective shafts. Remove any burrs from the shafts to avoid damage to the case.
2. Push the shift levers out of the transmission case. Remove and discard the O-ring seal from each shaft.
3. Lubricate the new seals with transmission oil and install them on the shafts.
4. Install the shift levers in the case.
5. Install the operating levers and tighten the retaining nuts to 18 ft. lbs.

INPUT SHAFT BEARING AND ROLLERS

1. Remove the snapring securing the bearing on the input shaft. Carefully press the input shaft out of the bearing with an arbor press.

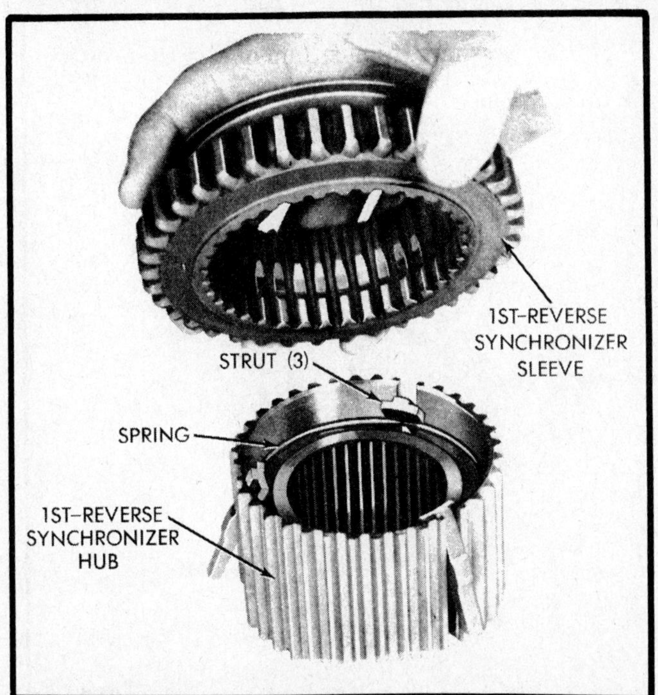

Assembling the first/reverse synchronizer—A-390 transmission

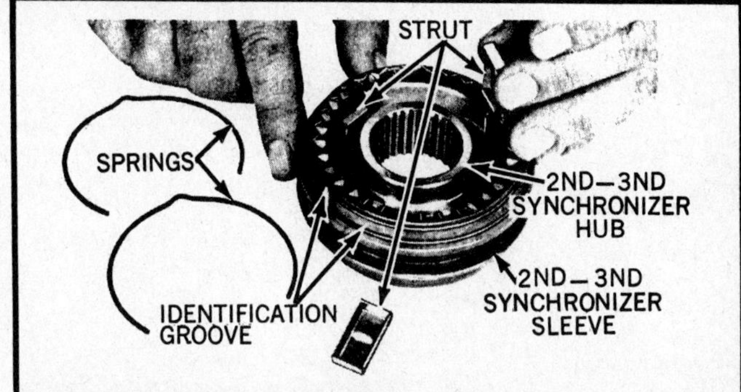

Assembling the second/third synchronizer—A-390 transmission

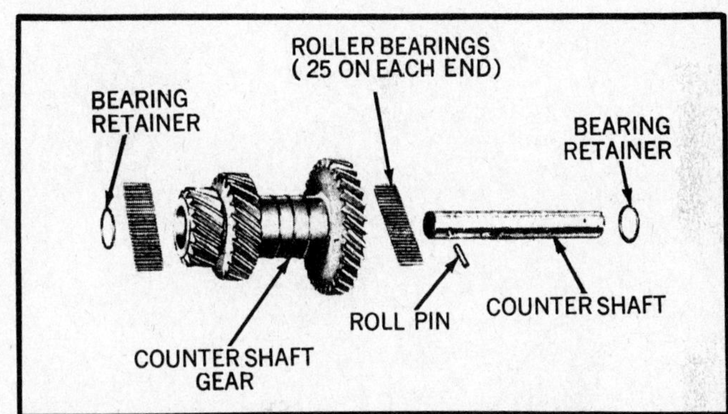

Exploded view A-390 countershaft and gear

2. Remove the fifteen bearing rollers from the cavity in the end of the input shaft.

3. Install the 15 bearing rollers in the cavity of the input shaft. Coat the rollers with a thin film of grease to retain them during installation.

4. Slide the input shaft bearing over the input shaft, snapring groove away from the gear end. Seat the bearing assembly on the input shaft with an arbor press.

5. Secure the bearing with the snapring. Be sure the snapring is properly seated. If a large snapring around the bearing was removed, be sure to install it at this time.

SYNCHRONIZERS

NOTE: If either synchronizer is to be disassembled, mark all parts so that they will be reassembled in the same position. Do not mix parts from the two synchronizers.

1. Push the synchronizer hub off each synchronizer sleeve.

2. Separate the struts and springs from the hubs.

3. Install the spring on the front side of the first/reverse synchronizer hub, making sure that all three strut slots are fully covered. Hang the three struts on the spring and in the slots with the wide end of the strut inside the hub.

4. With the alignment marks on the hub and sleeve aligned, push the sleeve down on the hub until the struts are in the neutral detent. Place the stop ring on top of the synchronizer assembly.

5. With the alignment marks on the second/third synchronizer sleeve and hub aligned, slide the sleeve on the hub. Drop in the three struts in the strut slots. Install the spring with the hump in the center, into the hollow of the strut. Turn the assembly over and install the other spring so that the hump in the center of the spring is inserted in the same strut. Place the stop ring on each end of the synchronizer assembly.

COUNTERSHAFT GEAR AND BEARING

1. Remove the countershaft bearing arbor, the roller bearings and the two bearing retainers from the countershaft gear.

2. Coat the bore in each end of the countershaft gear with grease.

3. Insert the countershaft arbor and install twenty five roller bearings and the retainer washer in each end of the countershaft gear.

4. Position the countershaft gear and arbor assembly in the transmission case. Align the gear bore and the thrust washers with the bores in the case and install the countershaft.

5. Using a feeler gauge, check the countershaft gear end play. The end play should be within 0.004–0.018 in. If the clearance is not within limits, replace the thrust washers.

6. After establishing the correct end play, install the arbor tool in the countershaft gear and lower the gear and tool out of the bottom of the transmission case.

Assembly

1. Coat the countershaft gear thrust surfaces in the case with a thin film of grease and position the two thrust washers in place. Place the countershaft gear and arbor assembly in the proper position in the bottom of the transmission case. The countershaft gear will remain in the bottom of the case until the output and input shafts are installed.

2. Coat the reverse idler gear thrust surfaces in the case with a thin film of grease and position the two thrust washers in place. Install the reverse idler gear in the case and align the gear bore with the thrust washers in the case bore. Install the reverse idler shaft.

3. Measure the reverse idler gear end play with a feeler gauge. End play should be 0.004–0.018 in. If the clearance is not within limits, replace the thrust washers. If the end play is correct, leave the reverse idler gear in place.

4. Lubricate the output shaft splines and the machined surfaces with transmission oil.

5. Slide the first/reverse synchronizer onto the output shaft

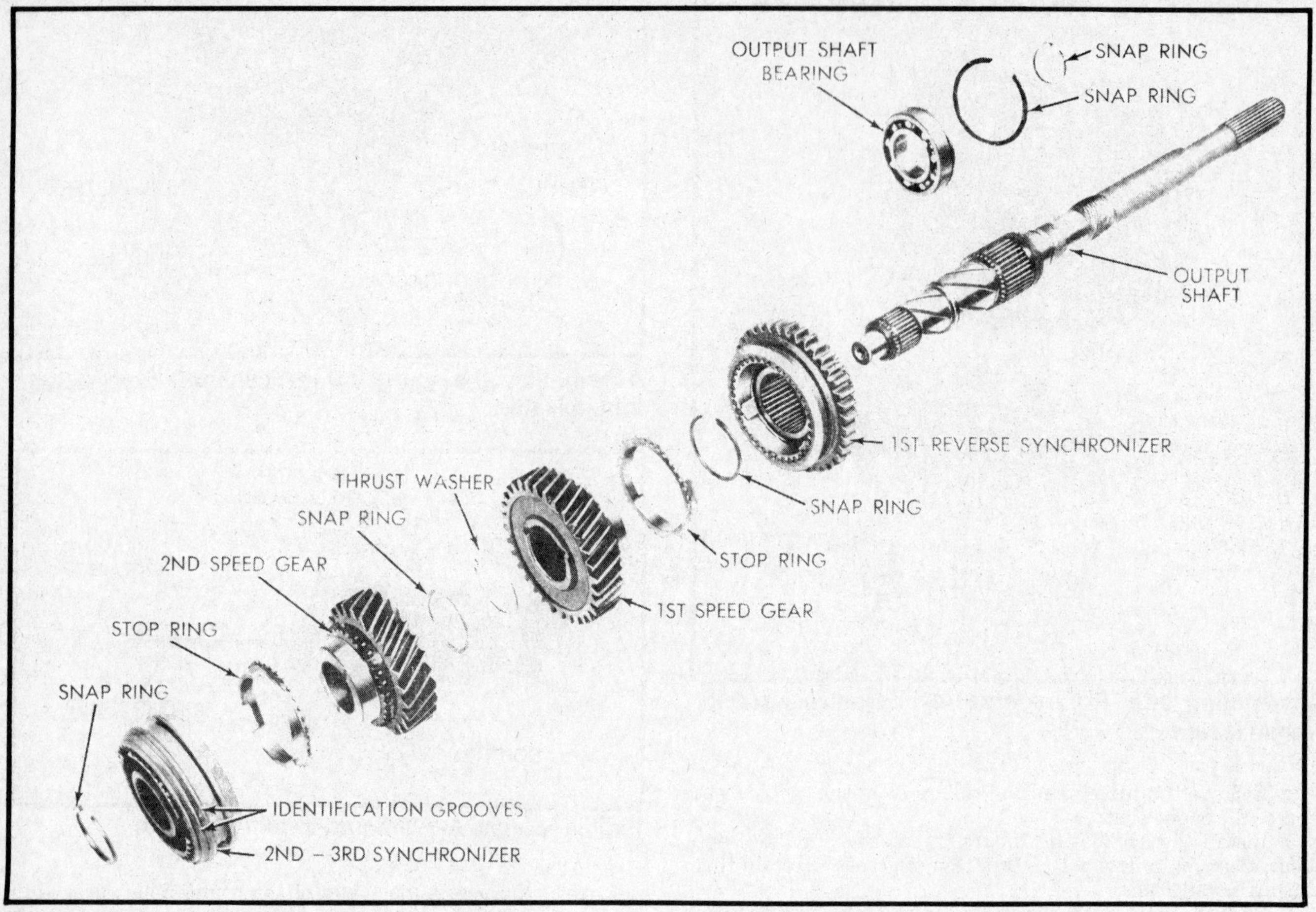

Exploded view A-390 output shaft assembly

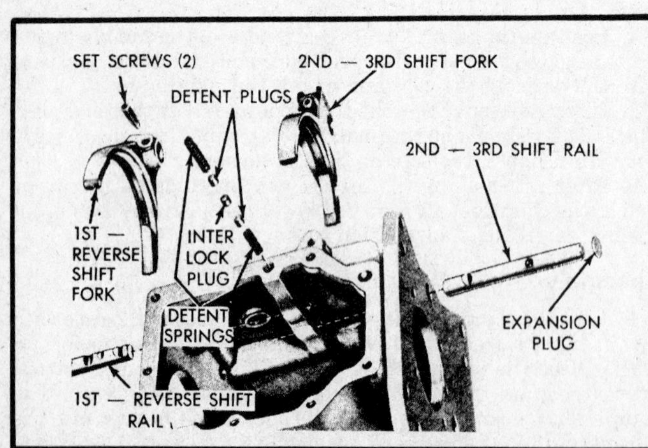

Exploded view A-390 shift rails and forks

with the fork groove toward the front. The first/reverse synchronizer hub is a press fit on the output shaft. To eliminate the possibility of damage to the hub, install the hub using an arbor press. Do not attempt to install the hub by hammering or driving. Secure the hub on the output shaft with the snapring.

6. Slide the first gear and stop ring onto the output shaft, aligning the slots in the stop ring with the struts. Install the thrust washer and snapring.

7. Slide the second gear and stop ring on the output shaft.

8. Install the second/third synchronizer assembly on the output shaft. Rotate the second gear to index the struts with the slots in the stop ring. Secure the synchronizer with a snapring.

9. Position the output shaft assembly in the transmission case. Place the transmission in a vertical position with the front of the case flat on the work bench. Place a 1 ¼ in. block of wood under the end of the output shaft. The block of wood will hold the output shaft assembly up during installation of the output shaft bearing.

10. Install the large snapring on the output shaft bearing. Place the bearing on the output shaft with the large snapring up. Drive the bearing on the shaft until it is seated on the shaft. Secure the bearing on the output shaft with the snapring. Return the transmission to a horizontal position.

11. Insert both shift forks in the case and in their proper sleeves. Push the output shaft assembly into position and tap it forward until the output shaft bearing is seated in the transmission case.

12. Install the shortest detent spring followed by a detent plug into the case. Place the second/third synchronizer assembly in the second gear position.

13. Align the second/third shift fork and install the second/third shift rail. The second/third shift rail is the shortest of the two shift rails. It will be necessary to depress the detent plug to enter the shift rail in the bore. Move the rail inward until the detent plug engages the forward notch (second gear position).

14. Secure the fork to the rail with the set screw. Move the synchronizer to the neutral position.

15. Install a new expansion plug in the transmission case.

16. Install the interlock plug in the transmission case with a magnet. If the second/third shift rail is in the neutral position,

the top of the interlock plug will be slightly lower than the surface of the first/reverse shift rail bore.

TORQUE SPECIFICATIONS

	ft. lbs.
Cover to case screws	22
Back-up light switch	15
Extension housing to case bolts 50	
Extension housing to cross member bolts	50
Gearshift lever nuts	18
Input shaft bearing retainer bolts	30
Shift fork to shift rail set screw	10
Transmission to clutch housing bolts	50
Transmission drain plug	25
Transmission filler plug	15

17. Align the first/reverse fork and install the first/reverse shift rail. Move the rail inward until the center notch (neutral) is aligned with the detent bore. Secure the fork to the rail with the set screw.
18. Using a suitable tool, install a new oil seal in the input shaft bearing retainer bore.
19. Coat the bore of the input shaft gear with a thin film of grease. A thick, heavy grease will plug the lubricant holes and prevent lubrication of the roller bearings. Install the fifteen roller bearings in the bore.
20. Place the stop ring, slots aligned with the struts, into the second/third synchronizer. Tap the input shaft assembly into place in the case while holding the output shaft to prevent the roller bearings from dropping.
21. Roll the transmission over so that it rests on both the top edge and the shift levers. The countershaft gear will drop into place. Using a suitable tool, align the countershaft gear and thrust washers with the bore in the transmission case.
22. Working from the rear of the case, slide the countershaft into position being careful to keep the countershaft in contact with the arbor to avoid dropping parts out of position. Be sure that the roll pin hole in the countershaft aligns with the roll pin hole in the case.
23. Install the roll pin. Install a new expansion plug in the countershaft bore at the front of the case. Install the plug flush or below the face of the case to prevent interference with the clutch housing.
24. Slide the extension housing, with a new gasket, over the output shaft and against the case. Coat the attaching bolt threads with a sealing compound. Install and tighten the attaching bolts to 50 ft. lbs.
25. Install the input shaft bearing retainer and a new gasket. Make sure that the oil return slot is at the bottom. Coat the threads with a sealing compound, install the attaching bolts and tighten to 30 ft. lbs.
26. Install the remaining detent plug into the case followed by the detent spring.
27. Install the filler plug and the back-up light switch. Pour lubricant over the entire gear train while rotating the input shaft and the output shaft.
28. Place the cover and a new gasket on the transmission. Coat the attaching screw threads with a sealing compound. Install and tighten the attaching screws to 22 ft. lbs.

Chrysler Corporation

FOUR SPEED OVERDRIVE TRANSMISSION

The four speed overdrive transmission is a four speed unit with all forward gears synchronized. Third gear is direct, while the fourth gear is the overdrive ratio. Lubricant capacity is 7 pints.

Disassembly

GEARSHIFT HOUSING AND MECHANISM

1. If available, mount transmission in a repair stand.
2. Disconnect gearshift control rods from the shift control levers and the transmission operating levers.
3. Remove the two gearshift control housing mounting bolts.
4. Remove gearshift control housing from the transmission extension housing or mounting bracket (if so equipped).
5. Remove the gearshift control housing mounting bracket bolts, then remove the bracket (if so equipped).
6. Remove back-up light switch (if so equipped).
7. Remove output companion flange nut and washer, if used, then pull the flange from the mainshaft (output shaft).
8. Remove gearshift housing to transmission case attaching bolts.
9. With all levers in the neutral detent position, pull housing out and away from the case. If first and second, or third and fourth shift forks remain in engagement with the synchronizer sleeves, move the sleeves and remove forks from the case.
10. Remove nuts, lock washers and flat washers that hold first/second and third/fourth speed shift operating levers to the shafts.
11. Disengage shift levers from the flats on the shafts and remove levers. Remove the E-ring on the overdrive four speed.

EXTENSION HOUSING, MAINSHAFT AND MAIN DRIVE PINION

1. Remove the bolt and retainer holding the speedometer pinion adapter in the extension housing, then remove the pinion adapter.
2. Remove the bolts attaching the extension housing to the transmission case.
3. Rotate the extension housing on the output shaft to expose the rear of the countershaft. Install one bolt to hold the extension in place.
4. Drill a hole in the countershaft extension plug at the front of the case.
5. Reaching through this hole, push the countershaft to the rear to expose the Woodruff key, when exposed, remove it. Push the countershaft forward against the expansion plug and using a brass drift, tap the countershaft forward until the expansion plug is removed.
6. Using a countershaft arbor, push the countershaft out the rear of the case, but don't let the countershaft washers fall out of position. Lower the cluster gear to the bottom of the transmission case.
7. Remove the bolt and rotate the extension back to the normal position.
8. Remove the drive pinion attaching bolts and slide the retainer and gasket from the pinion shaft, then pry the pinion or seal from the retainer. When installing the new seal, don't nick or scratch the seal bore in the retainer or the surface on which the seal bottoms.
9. Using a brass drift, tap the pinion and bearing assembly forward and remove through the front of the case.
10. Slide the third and overdrive synchronizer sleeve slightly

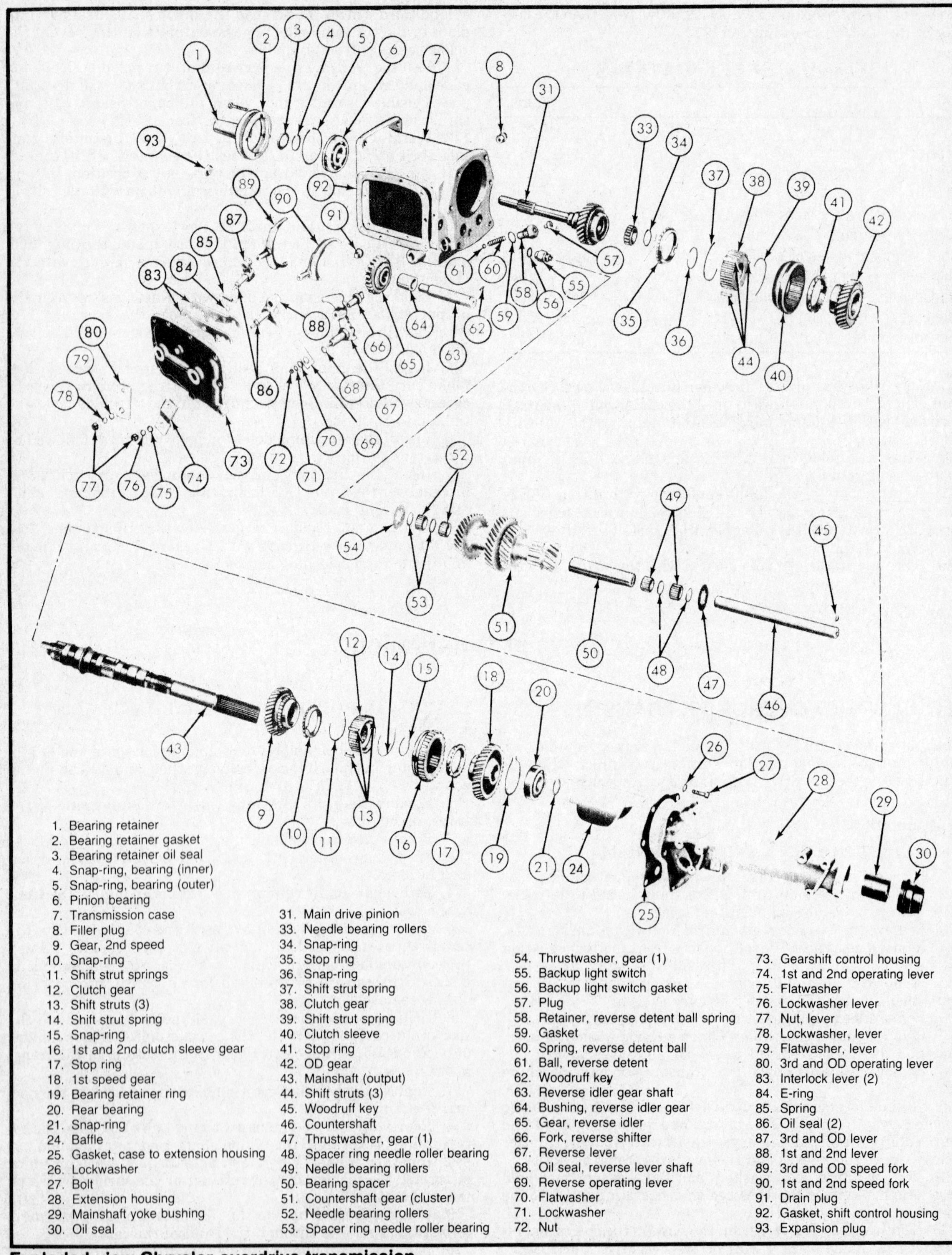
1. Bearing retainer
2. Bearing retainer gasket
3. Bearing retainer oil seal
4. Snap-ring, bearing (inner)
5. Snap-ring, bearing (outer)
6. Pinion bearing
7. Transmission case
8. Filler plug
9. Gear, 2nd speed
10. Snap-ring
11. Shift strut springs
12. Clutch gear
13. Shift struts (3)
14. Shift strut spring
15. Snap-ring
16. 1st and 2nd clutch sleeve gear
17. Stop ring
18. 1st speed gear
19. Bearing retainer ring
20. Rear bearing
21. Snap-ring
24. Baffle
25. Gasket, case to extension housing
26. Lockwasher
27. Bolt
28. Extension housing
29. Mainshaft yoke bushing
30. Oil seal
31. Main drive pinion
33. Needle bearing rollers
34. Snap-ring
35. Stop ring
36. Snap-ring
37. Shift strut spring
38. Clutch gear
39. Shift strut spring
40. Clutch sleeve
41. Stop ring
42. OD gear
43. Mainshaft (output)
44. Shift struts (3)
45. Woodruff key
46. Countershaft
47. Thrustwasher, gear (1)
48. Spacer ring needle roller bearing
49. Needle bearing rollers
50. Bearing spacer
51. Countershaft gear (cluster)
52. Needle bearing rollers
53. Spacer ring needle roller bearing
54. Thrustwasher, gear (1)
55. Backup light switch
56. Backup light switch gasket
57. Plug
58. Retainer, reverse detent ball spring
59. Gasket
60. Spring, reverse detent ball
61. Ball, reverse detent
62. Woodruff key
63. Reverse idler gear shaft
64. Bushing, reverse idler gear
65. Gear, reverse idler
66. Fork, reverse shifter
67. Reverse lever
68. Oil seal, reverse lever shaft
69. Reverse operating lever
70. Flatwasher
71. Lockwasher
72. Nut
73. Gearshift control housing
74. 1st and 2nd operating lever
75. Flatwasher
76. Lockwasher lever
77. Nut, lever
78. Lockwasher, lever
79. Flatwasher, lever
80. 3rd and OD operating lever
83. Interlock lever (2)
84. E-ring
85. Spring
86. Oil seal (2)
87. 3rd and OD lever
88. 1st and 2nd lever
89. 3rd and OD speed fork
90. 1st and 2nd speed fork
91. Drain plug
92. Gasket, shift control housing
93. Expansion plug

Exploded view Chrysler overdrive transmission

forward, slide the reverse idler gear to the center of its shaft, and tap the extension housing rearward. Slide the housing and mainshaft assembly out and away from the case.

11. Remove the snapring holding the third and overdrive synchronizer clutch gear and sleeve assembly to the mainshaft, then remove the synchronizer assembly.

12. Slide the overdrive gear and stop ring off the mainshaft. Using pair of long nose pliers, compress the snap ring holding the mainshaft bearing in the extension housing. With it compressed, pull the mainshaft assembly and bearing out of the extension housing.

13. Remove the snapring holding the mainshaft on the shaft. The bearing is removed by inserting steel plates on the front side of the first speed gear, then pressing the mainshaft through the bearing being careful not to damage the gear teeth.

14. Remove the bearing, retainer ring, first speed gear and stop ring from the shaft.

15. Remove the snapring. Remove the first and second clutch gear and sleeve assembly from the mainshaft.

16. Remove the drive pinion bearing inner snapring, then using an arbor press, remove the bearing. Remove the snapring and bearing rollers from the cavity in the drive pinion.

17. Remove the countershaft gear from the bottom of the case, then remove the arbor, needle bearings, thrust washers and spacers from the center of the countershaft gear.

18. Remove the reverse gearshift lever detent spring retainer, gasket, plug and detent ball spring from the rear of the case.

19. The reverse idler gear shaft is a tight fit in the case and will have to be pressed out.

20. If there is oil leakage visible around the reverse gearshift lever shaft, push the lever shaft in and remove it from the case. Remove the detent ball from the bottom of the transmission case and remove the shift fork from the shaft and detent plate.

Assembly

REVERSE SHAFT

Follow the first four steps only if the reverse shaft is removed in the disassembly procedure.

1. Install a new oil seal O-ring on the lever shaft and coat the shaft with grease; insert it into its bore and install the reverse fork in the lever.

2. Install the reverse detent spring and gasket; insert the ball and spring and install the plug and gasket.

3. Place the reverse idler gear shaft in position in the end of the case and drive it in far enough to position the reverse idler gear on the protruding end of the shaft with the fork slot toward the rear. While doing this, engage the slot with the reverse shift fork.

4. With the reverse idler gear correctly positioned, drive the reverse gear shaft into the case far enough to install the Woodruff key. Drive the shaft in flush with the end of the transmission case. Install the back-up light switch and gasket.

COUNTERSHAFT GEAR AND DRIVE PINION

1. Coat the inside bore of the countershaft gear with a thin film of grease and install the roller bearing spacer with an arbor into the gear, center the spacer and arbor.

2. Install the roller bearings and a spacer ring on each end.

3. Replace worn thrust washers, coat the new ones with grease and install them over the arbor with the tang side toward the case boss.

4. Install the countershaft assembly into the case and allow the gear assembly to sit on the bottom of the case so that the thrust washers won't come out of position.

5. Press the drive pinion bearing on the pinion shaft. Make sure the outer snap ring groove is toward the front end and the bearing is seated against the shoulder on the gear.

6. Install a new snapring on the shaft to hold the bearing in place. Be sure the snapring is seated and that there is minimum end play. There are several snapring thicknesses available for adjustment.

7. Place the pinion shaft in a soft jawed vise and install the roller bearings in the cavity of the shaft. Coat them with grease and install the bearing retaining snapring.

8. Install a new oil seal in the bore.

EXTENSION HOUSING BUSHING

1. Remove the yoke seal from the extension housing.

2. Drive out the old bushing and drive in a new one, aligning the oil hole in the bushing with the slot in the housing.

3. Place a new seal in the opening of the extension housing and then drive it into place.

MAINSHAFT

1. Place a stop ring flat on a bench followed by the clutch gear and sleeve, drop the struts in their slots and snap in a strut spring placing the tang inside one strut. Install the second strut spring tang in a different strut after turning the assembly over.

2. Slide the second speed gear over the mainshaft with the synchronizer cone toward the rear and down against the shoulder on the shaft.

3. Slide the first and second gear synchronizer assembly including stop rings with lugs indexed in the hub slots, over the mainshaft down against the second gear cone and hold it there with a new snapring. Slide the next snapring over the shaft and index the lugs into the clutch hub slots.

4. Slide the first speed gear with the synchronizer cone toward the clutch sleeve just installed over the mainshaft and into position against the clutch sleeve gear.

5. Install the mainshaft bearing retaining ring followed by the mainshaft rear bearing, press the bearing down into position and install a new snap ring to secure it. There are several snapring thicknesses available for minimum end play.

6. Install the partially assembled mainshaft into the extension housing far enough to engage the bearing retaining ring in the slot in the extension housing. Compress the ring with pliers so that the mainshaft ball bearing can move in and bottom against its thrust shoulder in the extension housing. Release the ring and make sure that it is seated.

7. Slide the overdrive gear over the mainshaft with the synchronizer cone toward the front followed by the gears snapring.

8. Install the third overdrive gear synchronizer clutch gear assembly on the mainshaft against the overdrive gear. Make sure to index the rear stop ring with the clutch gear struts.

9. Install the snapring and position the front stop ring over the clutch gear again lining up the ring lugs with the struts. Coat a new extension gasket with grease and place it in position.

10. Slide the reverse idler gear to the center of its shaft and move the third–overdrive synchronizer as far forward as possible without losing the struts.

TORQUE SPECIFICATIONS

	ft. lbs.
Back up light switch	15
Drive pinion bearing, retainer bolts	30
Extension housing to case bolts	50
Gearshift to mounting plate	24
Gearshift mounting plate to extension	12
Shift lever nuts	18
Transmission to clutch housing bolts	50
Transmission drain plug	25

11. Insert the mainshaft assembly in the case tilting it as necessary. Place the third overdrive sleeve in the neutral detent.

12. Rotate the extension on the mainshaft to expose the rear of the countershaft and install one bolt to hold it in position.

13. Install the drive pinion and bearing assembly through the

front of the case and position it in the front bore. Install the outer snapring in the bearing groove and tap lightly into place. If it doesn't bottom easily, check to see if a strut, pinion roller or stop ring is out of position.

14. Turn the transmission upside down while holding the countershaft gear to prevent damage. Then lower the countershaft gear assembly into position making sure that the teeth mesh with the drive pinion gear.

15. Start the countershaft into the bore at the rear of the case and push until it is in about halfway, then install the Woodruff key and push it in until it is flush with the rear of the case.

16. Rotate the extension back to normal position and install the bolts. Turn the transmission upright and install the drive pinion bearing retainer and gasket. Coat the threads with sealing compound and tighten the attaching bolts to 30 ft. lbs.

17. Install a new expansion plug in its bore.

GEARSHIFT HOUSING AND MECHANISM

1. Install the interlock levers on the pivot pin and secure with the E-ring. Install the spring with a pair of pliers.
2. Grease and install new O-ring seals on both shift shafts. Grease the housing bores and push the shafts through.
3. Install the operating levers and tighten the retaining nuts to 18 ft. lbs. Make sure the third overdrive lever points down.
4. Rotate each shift shaft fork bore straight up and install the third overdrive shift fork in its bore and under both interlock levers.
5. Position both synchronizer sleeves in neutral and place the first and second gear shift fork in the groove of the first and second gear synchronizer sleeve. Slide the reverse idler gear to neutral. Turn the transmission on its right side and place the gearshift housing gasket in place holding it there with grease. Install the reverse detent ball and spring into the case bore.
6. As the shift housing is lowered in place, guide the third overdrive shift fork into its synchronizer groove then lead the shaft of the first and second shift lever.
7. Raise the interlock lever with a suitable tool to allow the first and second shift fork to slip under the levers. The shift housing will now seat against the case.
8. Install the bolts lightly and shift through all the gears to check for proper operation.
9. The reverse shift lever and the first and second gear shift lever have cam surfaces which mate in reverse position to lock the first and second lever, the fork and synchronizer in the neutral position.
10. To check for proper operation, put the transmission in reverse and, while turning the input shaft, move the first and second lever in each direction. If it locks up or becomes harder to turn, select a new shift lever size with more or less clearance. If there is too little cam clearance, it will be difficult or impossible to shift into reverse.
11. Grease the reverse shaft, install the operating lever and nut and install the speedometer drive pinion gear and adapter, making sure the range number is in the straight down position.

Chrysler A-412 Manual Transaxle

Gear reduction, ratio selection and differential functions are combined in a single unit. The transaxle assembly is housed in a two piece magnesium case. One piece is the transmission housing and the other piece is the clutch and differential assembly housing.

Disassembly

1. Remove the clutch push rod.
2. Remove the dirve flange dust plug. snapring, cone washer drive flange and drive flange oil seal.
3. Remove the selector shaft cover, push out the selector shaft and remove the selector shaft oil seal.
4. Remove the mainshaft bearing retaining nut rubber plugs, and remove the clutch release bearing end cover. While removing, hold the clutch release lever in upward position to avoid loading end cover and damaging case threads.
5. Remove the release bearing and the sleeve.
6. Remove the circlips from the torque shaft and remove the clutch torque shaft, return spring and release lever.
7. Remove the mainshaft bearing retainer nuts. The three studs and clips will drop into the case.
8. Remove the case attaching bolts, the reverse idler shaft set screw and the backup light switch. Remove the transmission case and mark the shims for installation reference.
9. Remove the reverse shift fork supports and remove the reverse shift fork.
10. Remove the mainshaft assembly and pinion shaft fourth speed gear.
11. Disassemble the mainshaft by removing the bearing and fourth speed gear, the third/fourth synchronizer and third speed gear and needle hearing.

NOTE: Synchronizers are serviced as an assembly.

12. Remove the shift rail "E" clips and remove the shift forks assembly.
13. Remove the clutch push rod seal and bushing assembly.
14. On the pinion shaft, remove the snapring, third speed gear, and needle bearing.
15. Remove the reverse gear idler shaft.

16 Complete pinion shaft disassembly by removing the first/second gears synchronizer, the second speed gear sleeve, the first gear stop ring and the first speed gear. The inner sleeve for second speed gear and the first speed gear are removed together.

NOTE: Before installing the puller to remove the synchronizer, remove the plastic thrust bottom and install Tool L-4443-4 or equivalent in the pinion shaft. The pinion shaft bearing retainer is notched in two places for puller jaws.

17. Remove the pinion shaft retainer and first gear thrust washer and remove the pinion shaft.

Differential Repair

1. Remove the axle shaft circlips.
2. Remove differential bearing cone and cup. Bearing cones and cups are matched sets and must be replaced as assemblies.
3. Remove the side gears.
4. Remove the pinion shaft snapring and drive out the pinion shaft. Pinion shaft gears and plastic thrust washer can now be removed from differential case. When installing pinion shaft be sure to align plastic thrust washer with case to avoid damaged to thrust washer holes.
5. Drill out the ring gear rivets. The new ring gear is installed with bolts and nuts.

Differential Bearing Preload Adjusting

NOTE: Differential Bearing Preload adjustment is necessary after replacement of the transmission case, clutch housing, differential case or differential bearings.

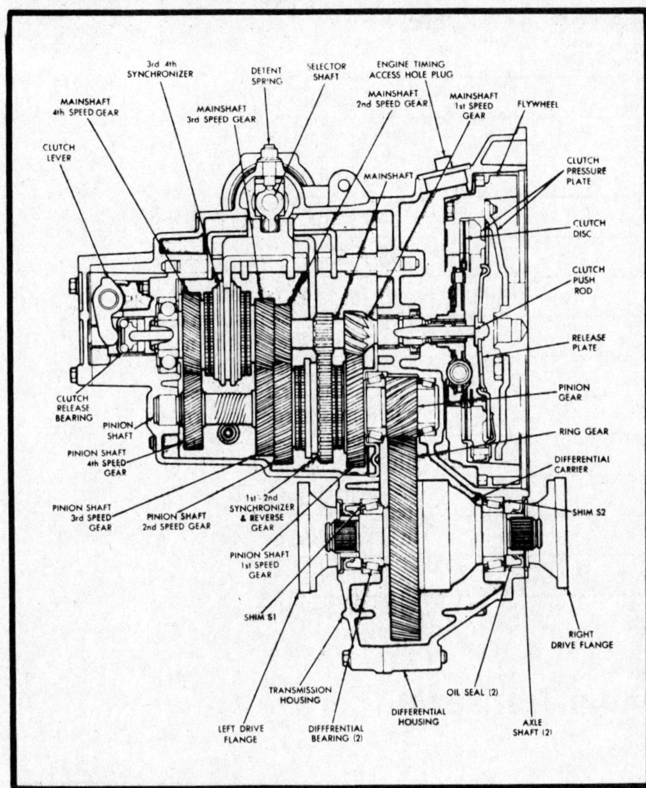

Chrysler A-412 transaxle

1. Install cup of bearing (opposite ring gear) with shim S2 in clutch/differential housing. Shim S2 is always 0.039 in. thick.
2. Install outer race on ring gear side without shim S1 in transmission housing.
3. Install differential in its housing.
4. Place transmission housing in position with gasket and tighten five bolts to 14 ft. lbs.
5. Install a dial indicator and move the differential up and down for measurement reading.

NOTE: Do not turn differential when measuring because bearings will settle and give incorrect reading.

6. Correct bearing preload is obtained by adding a constant figure 0.015 in. to measured reading. For example, measured reading plus preload is 0.035 in. the constant figure is 0.015 in. add them together and the result is 0.050 in. which is the shim thickness.
7. Remove the transmission case and drive out the outer bearing cup.
8. insert selected shim S1; the thickest shim first. Shims are available in sizes ranging from 0.006–0.031 in.
9. Drive in bearing cup and install transmission housing with gasket and tighten. Before installing transmission housing, remove one axle shaft to check turning torques

Checking Turning Torque

1. Lubricate bearings with transmission oil and check for the following turning torque, new bearings 10.4–21.7 inch lbs. used bearings minimum 2.7 in. lbs.

Pinion Shaft Bearing Preload Adjustment

1. If clutch housing, ring and pinion gears or differential bearing are changed, it is necessary to adjust prelaod on pinion shaft bearing.
2. Place a 0.65 mm shim in bearing housing and press in the small bearing cup.
3. Install pinion shaft and tighten cover nuts to 14 ft. lbs.
4. Mount a dial gauge and move pinion shaft up and down for measurement reading. Do not turn pinion shaft when measuring because bearings will settle and give incorrect measurement.
5. Specified bearing prelaod is obtained by adding a constant figure 0.20 mm to measured reading and shim thickness 0.65 mm. For example, installed shim is 0.025 in. the measured reading is 0.012 in. the preload is 0.008, which is a constant figure, and the shims are available from 0.025–0.055 in.
6. Remove ball bearing retainer, pinion shaft and small bearing cup and 0.65 mm shim. Install correct shim.

Transaxle Assembly

1. Install the pinion shaft.
2. Install first gear thrust washer flat side up and install pinion shaft retainer.
3. Install first gear and stop ring and first/second gears synchronizer. The lowest thrust collar on the hub must go toward second gear. Install the sleeve with reverse teeth nearest fifth gear. Slots in synchronizer ring must be aligned with struts in first/second gears synchronizer assembly to avoid damage to stop ring on assembly.
4. Install second gear bearing race.
5. Install and correctly align reverse idler gear shaft.
6. Install needle bearing and second speed gear.
7. Install third speed gear. Select and install a retaining snapring which will provide 0.000–0.004 in. end play.
8. Install the mainshaft and third/fourth gears synchronizer assembly.
9. Install fourth speed gear mainshaft needle bearing and mainshaft fourth speed gear.
10. Install fourth speed gear and snapring on pinion shaft.
11. Use Tool L-4442 to correctly adjust mainshaft position to specifications.
12. Adjust mainshaft end play only if transmission case, clutch housing or mainshaft has been changed.
13. Install shift forks and "E" clips.
14. Install reverse shift fork and support brackets.
15. Use guide pins to install transmission case on clutch housing. Be sure pinion shaft is aligned with pinion shaft needle bearing in transmission case.
16. Install mainshaft bearing snapring.
17. Install reverse idler shaft bolt and install selector shaft assembly.
18. Install mainshaft bearing retainer and washer.
19. Install clutch torque shaft, return spring, release lever and circlips.
20. Install release bearing and sleeve.
21. Install the clutch release bearing end cover and mainshaft bearing retainer nut rubber plug.
22. Install selector shaft cover.
23. Install back-up light switch.
24. Install the detent plunger. Adjust the plunger as follows. Loosen lock nut. Tighten adjusting sleeve until gap can be seen between lock ring and adjusting sleeve. Loosen adjusting sleeve ¼ turn. Hold adjusting sleeve in this position and tighten lock nut.
25. install the clutch push rod and the selector shaft boot seal.

A-412 MANUAL TRANSAXLE TORQUE SPECIFICATIONS

Clutch Housing Case Bolt	250 in/lbs
Clutch Housing Case Stud	250 in/lbs
Release Bearing End Cover Screw	105 in/lbs
Back-up Light Switch	144 in/lbs
Electronic Timing Probe Retainer	80 in/lbs
Gearshift Selector Shaft Cover	35 ft/lbs
Gearshift Detent Body Lock Nut	175 in/lbs
Drain Plug	175 in/lbs
Fill Plug	175 in/lbs
Pinion Shaft Bearing Retainer Bolt	29 ft/lbs
Mainshaft Ball Bearing Retaining Nut	155 in/lbs
Reverse Idler Shaft Set Screw	175 in/lbs
Reverse Idler Fork Bracket—Clutch Housing Screw	105 in/lbs

Chrysler A-460 Manual Transaxle

Intermediate Shaft Assembly

The 1–2 and 3–4 shift forks and synchronizer stop rings are interchangeable. However, if parts are to be reused, reassemble them in their original position. When assembling the intermediate shaft, make sure all gears turn freely and have a minimum of 0.003 in. end play.

INPUT SHAFT

Shim thickness calculation need only be done if any of the following parts are replaced. Refer to Bearing Adjustment Procedure to determine the proper shim thickness for correct bearing preload and proper bearing turning torque.

1. Transaxle case.
2. Input shaft seal retainer.
3. Bearing retainer plate.
4. Rear end cover.
5. Input Shaft.
6. Input shaft bearings.

DIFFERENTIAL

Shim thickness calculation need only be done if any of the following parts are replaced. Refer to Bearing Adjustment Procedure to determine the proper shim thickness for correct bearing preload and proper bearing turning torque.

1. Transaxle case.
2. Differential bearing retainer.
3. Extension housing.
4. Differential case.
5. Differential bearings.

BEARING ADJUSTMENT PROCEDURE

1. Take extreme care when removing and installing bearing cups and cones. Use only an arbor press for instllation, as a hammer may not properly align the bearing cup or cone. Burrs or nicks on the bearing seat will give a false end play reading while gauging for proper shims. Improperly seated bearings cups and cones are subject to low mileage failure.

2. Bearing cups and cones should be replaced if they show signs of pitting or heat distress. If distress is seen on either the cup or bearing rollers, both cup and cone must be replaced.

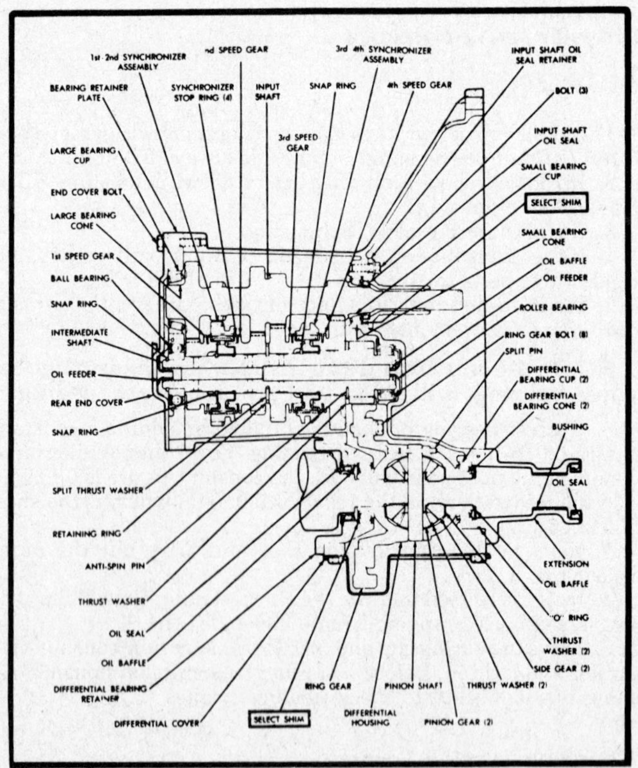

A-460 manual transaxle

3. Bearing end play and drag torque specifications must be maintained to avoid premature bearing failures.

4. Used (original) bearing may lose up to 50% of the original drag torque after break in.

NOTE: All bearing adjustments must be made with no other component interference or gear mesh.

5. Replace bearings as a pair. for example, if one differential bearing is defective, replace both differential bearings. If one input shaft bearing is defective, replace both input shaft bearings.

6. Bearing cones must be reused if removed.

7. Turning torque readings should be obtained while smoothly rotating in either direction (breakaway reading is not indicative of the true turning torque).

Ford 3.03 Three Speed Transmission

The Ford 3.03 is a fully synchronized three speed transmission. All gears except reverse are in constant mesh. Forward speed gear changes are accomplished with synchronizer sleeves.

Disassembly

1. Drain the lubricant by removing the lower extension housing bolt.
2. Remove the case cover and gasket.
3. Remove the long spring that holds the detent plug in the case and remove the detent plug with a small magnet.
4. Remove the extension housing and gasket.
5. Remove the front bearing retainer and gasket.
6. Remove the filler plug on the right side of the transmission case. Working through the plug opening, drive the roll pin out of the case and countershaft with a ¼ in. punch.
7. Hold the countershaft gear with a hook. Install dummy shaft and push the countershaft out of the rear of the case. As the countershaft comes out, lower the gear cluster to the bottom of the case. Remove the countershaft.
8. Remove the snapring that holds the speedometer drive gear on the output shaft. Slip the gear off the shaft and remove the gear lock ball.
9. Remove the snapring that holds the output shaft bearing. Using a special bearing puller, remove the output shaft bearing.
10. Place both shift levers in the neutral (center) position.
11. Remove the set screw that holds the first/reverse shift fork to the shift rail. Slip the first/reverse shift rail out through the rear of the case.
12. Move the first/reverse synchronizer forward as far as possible. Rotate the first/reverse shift fork upwards and lift it out of the case.
13. Place the second/third shift fork in the second position. Remove the set screw. Rotate the shift rail 90 degrees.
14. Lift the interlock plug out of the case with a magnet.
15. Remove the expansion plug from the second/third shift rail by lightly tapping the end of the rail. Remove the second/third shift rail.
16. Remove the second/third shift rail detent plug and spring from detent bore.
17. Remove the input gear and shaft from the case.
18. Rotate the second/third shift fork upwards and remove from case.
19. Using caution, lift the output shaft assembly out through top of case.
20. Lift the reverse idler gear and thrust washers out of case. Remove the countershaft gear, thrust washer and dummy shaft from case.
21. Remove the snapring from the front of the output shaft. Slip the synchronizer and second gear off shaft.
22. Remove the second snapring from output shaft and remove the thrust washer, first gear and blocking ring.
23. Remove the third snapring from the output shaft. The first/reverse synchronizer hub is a press fit on the output shaft. Remove the synchronizer hub with an arbor press. Do not attempt to remove or install the synchronizer hub by prying or hammering.

Disassembly and Assembly of Sub-Assemblies

SHIFT LEVERS AND SEALS

1. Remove shift levers from the shafts. Slip the levers out of case. Discard shaft sealing O-rings.

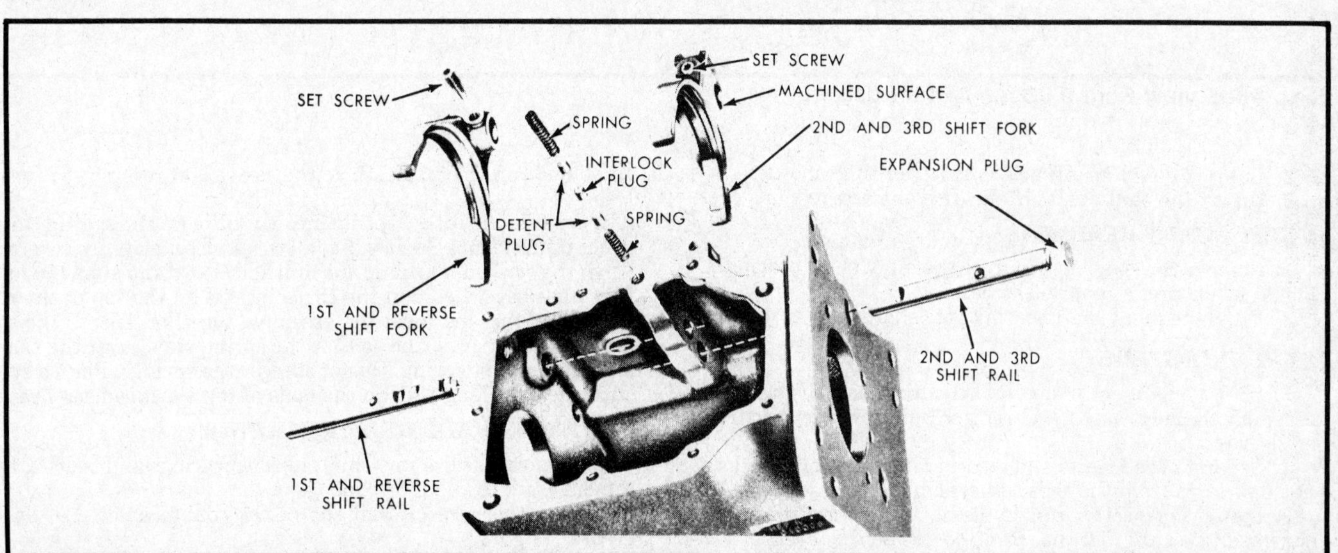

Exploded view Ford 3.03 shift rails and forks

Rotating second/third shift rail—Ford 3.03 transmission

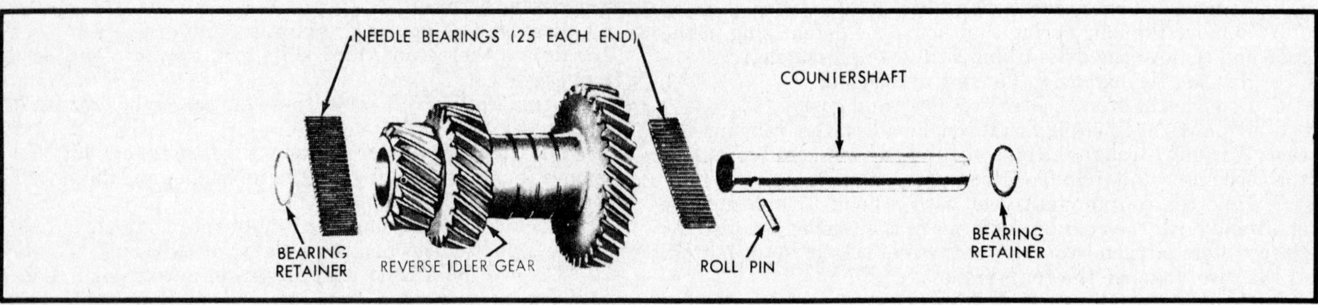

Exploded view Ford 3.03 countergear

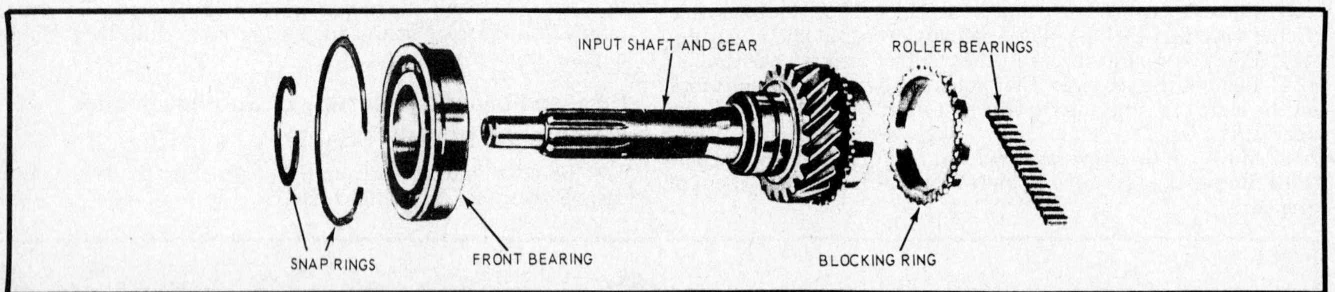

Exploded view Ford 3.03 input shaft gear

2. Lubricate and install new O-rings on shift shafts.
3. Install the shift shafts in the case and secure shift levers.

INPUT SHAFT BEARINGS

1. Remove the snapring securing the input shaft bearing. Using an arbor press, remove the bearing.
2. Press the input shaft bearing onto shaft using correct tool.

SYNCHRONIZERS

1. Scribe alignment marks on synchronizer hubs before disassembly. Remove each synchronizer hub from the synchronizer sleeves.
2. Separate the inserts and insert springs from the hubs. Do not mix parts from the separate synchronizer assemblies.
3. Install the insert spring in the hub of the first/reverse synchronizer. Be sure that the spring covers all the insert grooves. Start the hub on the sleeve making certain that the scribed marks are properly aligned. Place the three inserts in the hub, small ends on the inside. Slide the sleeve and reverse gear onto hub.
4. Install one insert spring into a groove on the second/third synchronizer hub. Be sure that all three insert slots are covered. Align the scribed marks on the hub and sleeve and start the hub into the sleeve. Position the three inserts on the top of the retaining spring and push the assembly together. Install the remaining retainer spring so that the spring ends cover the same slots as the first spring. Do not stagger the springs. Place a synchronizer blocking ring on the ends of the synchronizer sleeve.

COUNTERSHAFT GEAR BEARINGS

1. Remove the dummy shaft, needle bearings and bearing retainers from the countershaft gear.
2. Coat the bore in each end of the countershaft gear with grease.
3. Hold the dummy shaft in the gear and install the needle bearings in the case.

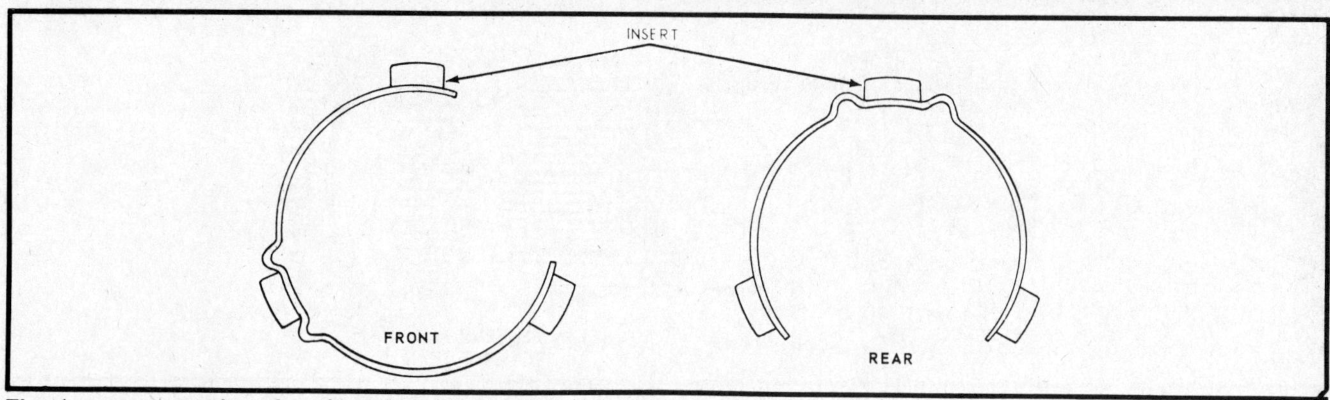

First/reverse synchronizer insert spring installation Ford 3.03

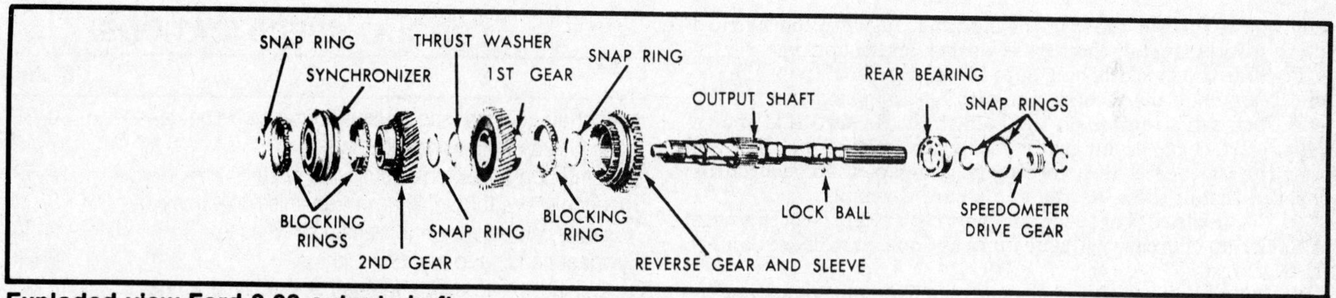

Exploded view Ford 3.03 output shaft

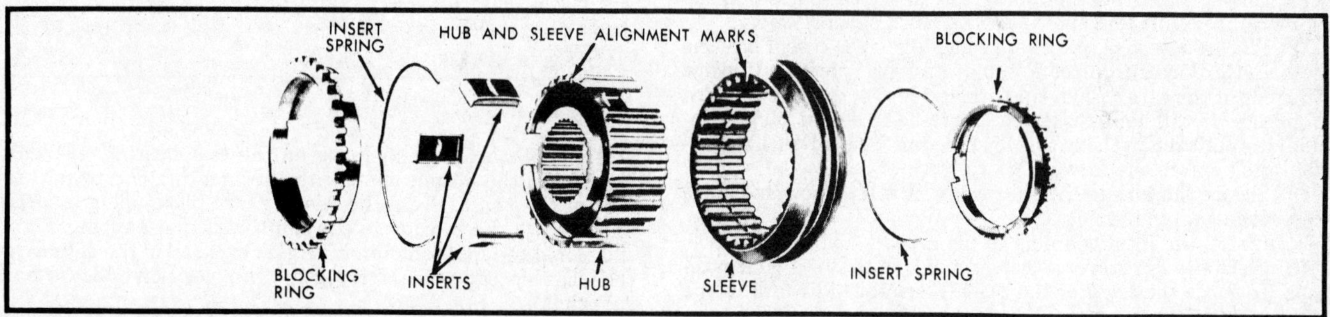

Exploded view Ford 3.03 second/third synchronizer

4. Place the countershaft gear, dummy shaft and needle bearings in the case.

5. Place the case in a vertical position. Align the gear bore and the thrust washers with the bores in the case and install the countershaft.

6. Place the case in a horizontal position. Check the countershaft gear end play with a feeler gauge. Clearance should be between 0.004–0.018 in. If clearance does not come within specifications, replace the thrust washers.

7. Install the dummy shaft in the countershaft gear and leave the gear at the bottom of the transmission case.

Assembly

1. Cover the reverse idler gear thrust surfaces in the case with a thin film of lubricant and install the two thrust washers in the case.

2. Install the reverse idler gear and shaft in the case. Align the case bore and thrust washers with gear bore and install the reverse idler shaft.

3. Measure the reverse idler gear end play with a feeler gauge, clearance should be between 0.004–0.018 in. If end play is not within specifications, replace the thrust washers. If clearance is correct, leave the reverse idler gear in case.

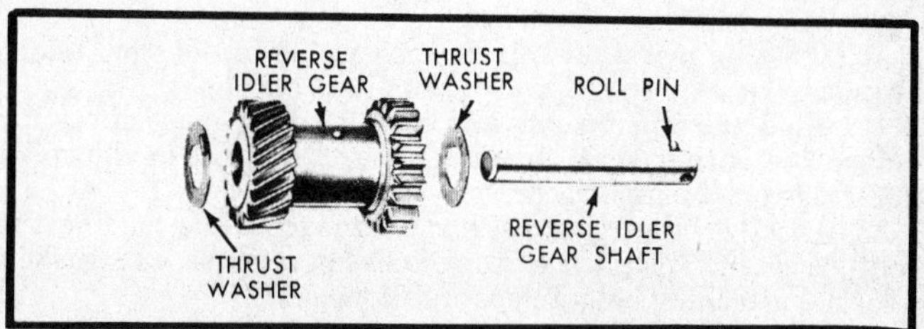

Exploded view Ford 3.03 reverse idler shaft

4. Lubricate the output shaft splines and machined surfaces with transmission oil.

5. The first/reverse synchronizer hub is a press fit on the output shaft. Hub must be installed in an arbor press. Install the synchronizer hub with the teeth-end of the gear facing towards the rear of the shaft. Do not attempt to install the first/reverse synchronizer with a hammer.

6. Place the blocking ring on the tapered surface of the first gear.

7. Slide the first gear on the output shaft with the blocking ring toward the rear of the shaft. Rotate the gear as necessary to

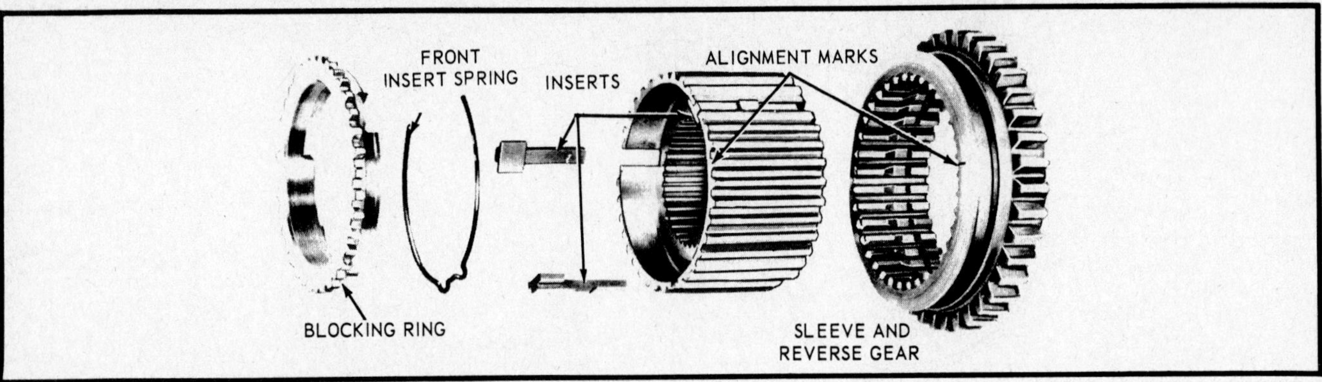

Exploded view Ford 3.03 first/reverse synchronizer

engage the three notches in the blocking ring with the synchronizer inserts. Install the thrust washer and snapring.

8. Slide the blocking ring onto the tapered surface of the second gear. Slide the second gear with blocking ring and the second/third synchronizer on the mainshaft. Be sure that the tapered surface of second gear is facing the front of the shaft and that the notches in the blocking ring engage the synchronizer inserts. Install the snapring and secure assembly.

9. Cover the core of the input shaft with a thin coat of grease. A thick film of grease will plug lubricant holes and cause damage to bearings.

10. Install the input shaft through the front of the case and insert snapring in the bearing groove.

11. Install the output shaft assembly in the case. Position the second/third shift fork on the second/third synchronizer.

12. Place a detent plug spring and a plug in the case. Place the second–third synchronizer in the second gear position (toward the rear of the case). Align the fork and install the second/third shift rail. It will be necessary to depress the detent plug to install the shift rail in the bore. Move the rail forward until the detent plug enters the forward notch (second gear).

13. Secure the fork to the shift rail with a set screw and place the synchronizer in neutral.

14. Install the interlock plug in the case.

15. Place the first/reverse synchronizer in the first gear position (towards the front of the case). Place the shift fork in the groove of the synchronizer. Rotate the fork into position and install the shift rail. Move the shift rail inward until the center notch (neutral) is aligned with the detent bore. Secure shift fork with set screw.

16. Install a new shift rail expansion plug in the front of the case.

17. Hold the input shaft and blocking ring in position and move the output shaft forward to seat the pilot in the roller bearings on the input gear.

18. Tap the input gear bearing into place while holding the output shaft. Install the front bearing retainer and gasket. Torque attaching bolts to specifications.

Lubricant Refill Capacity

	U.S. Pints	Imp. Pints
Ford Type 3.03	3.5	3.0

TORQUE SPECIFICATIONS

	ft. lbs.
Input shaft gear bearing retainer to transmission case	30–36
Transmission to flywheel housing	37–42
Transmission cover to transmission case	14–19
Speedometer cable retainer to transmission extension	3–4.5
Transmission extension to transmission case	42–50
Flywheel housing to engine	40–50
Gear shift lever to cam and shaft assembly lock nuts	18–23
U-Joint flange to output shaft	60–80
Filler plug	10–20
Shifter fork set screws	10–18
T.R.S. switch to case	15–20

19. Install the large snapring on the rear bearing. Place the bearing on the output shaft with the snapring end toward the rear of the shaft. Press the bearing into place using a special tool. Secure the bearing to the shaft with the snapring.

20. Hold the speedometer drive gear lock ball in the detent and slide the speedometer drive gear into position. Secure with snapring.

21. Place the transmission in the vertical position. Using a suitable tool insert it through the drain hole in the bottom of the case, align the bore of the countershaft gear and the thrust washer with the bore in the case.

22. Working from the rear of the case, push the dummy shaft out of the countershaft gear with the countershaft. Align the roll pin hole in the countershaft with the matching hole in the case. Drive the shaft into place and install the roll pin.

23. Position the new extension housing gasket on the case with sealer. Install the extension housing and torque to specification.

24. Place the transmission in gear and pour gear oil over entire gear train while rotating the input shaft.

25. Install the remaining detent plug and long spring in case.

26. Position cover gasket on case with sealer and install cover. Torque cover bolts to specifications.

27. Check operation of transmission in all gear positions.

Ford Four Speed Transmission (Diesel Engines)

Disassembly

1. If not already drained, remove the drain plug and drain the transmission fluid into a suitable container. Remove the fork and release bearing from the clutch housing.
2. Install transmission in Holding Fixture T57L-500-B. Remove six bolts attaching the front cover to the transmission case and remove the front cover shim and gasket.
3. Remove front cover oil seal.
4. Remove the input shaft snapring.
5. Remove outer snapring on input shaft bearing. Install Bearing Collet tool T75L-7025-E or its equal on main input shaft front bearing, Remover Tube T75L-7025-B and Forcing Screw T75L-7025-J or their equal. slide Bearing Collet Sleeve T75L-7025-G or its equal over remover tube and bearing collet, and turn forcing screw to remove input shaft bearing.
6. Remove the eight bolts attaching the extension housing to the transmission case., Slide the extension housing off the mainshaft, with the control lever end laid down and to the left as far as it will go.
7. Remove the bolt attaching the control lever end to the control rod and remove the control lever end and rod from the extension housing.
8. Remove the speedometer driven gear assembly from the extension housing.
9. Remove the back-up lamp switch and neutral sensing switch.
10. Remove the snapring that secures the speedometer drive gear on the mainshaft. Slide the speedometer drive gear off the mainshaft and remove the lock ball.
11. Install Bearing Pusher Tool T83T-7111-A or its equal over countershaft front bearing. Turn forcing screw to force countershaft, together with the countershaft front bearing, from the transmission housing.
12. Slide Bearing Holder and Gear Shaft Assembly from the transmission housing.
13. Remove three spring cap bolts, three springs and shift locking balls. The reverse spring is shortest. The lower ball is spring loaded and will pop out.
14. Remove the reverse shift rod and shift fork assembly and reverse gear from the bearing housing.
15. Remove roll pins fixing shift forks to the rods. Push each of the shift rods rearward through the fork and bearing housing and remove the shift rods and forks.

NOTE: Mark 3rd–4th and 1st–2nd shift forks before removal to simplify installation.

16. Remove the lower reverse shift rod locking ball and spring, and the interlock pins from the bearing housing.
17. Straighten the tab of the lockwasher. Lock transmission synchronizers into any two gears and remove the mainshaft lock nut using Adapter Tool T83T-7025-A and Tool Shaft T77J-7025-C or its equal.
18. Remove the snapring from the rear end of the countershaft and slide off the counter reverse gear.
19. Remove the five bearing cover bolts and cover and the reverse idler gear shaft from the bearing housing.
20. With a soft hammer, tap the rear end of the mainshaft and countershaft in turn, being careful not to damage the shafts, and remove these shafts from the bearing housing.
21. Carefully separate the input shaft and caged needle roller bearing from the mainshaft.
22. Remove rear countershaft bearing from the bearing housing using Remover Tube Tool T77J-7025-B or its equal.
23. Remove rear mainshaft bearing from the bearing housing using Bearing Remover Tool T77F-4222-A and Remover Tube Tool T77J-7025-B or its equal.
24. Remove the thrust washer, first gear, sleeve and synchronizer ring from the rear of the mainshaft.
25. Using snapring pliers, remove the snapring from the front of the mainshaft.
26. Using a press and Remover Tool T71P-4621-B or its equal, remove the third and fourth clutch hub, sleeve, synchronizer ring and third gear from the front of the mainshaft.
27. Using a press and Remover Tool T71P-4621-B or its equal, remove the first and second clutch hub and sleeve assembly synchronizer ring and second gear from the rear of the mainshaft in the same manner as described in the above step.
28. Press front bearing from countershaft using Remover Tool D79L-4621-A or T71P-4621-B or its equal and a suitable stock piece.
29. Perform cleaning and inspection procedures described in a separate section of this manual.

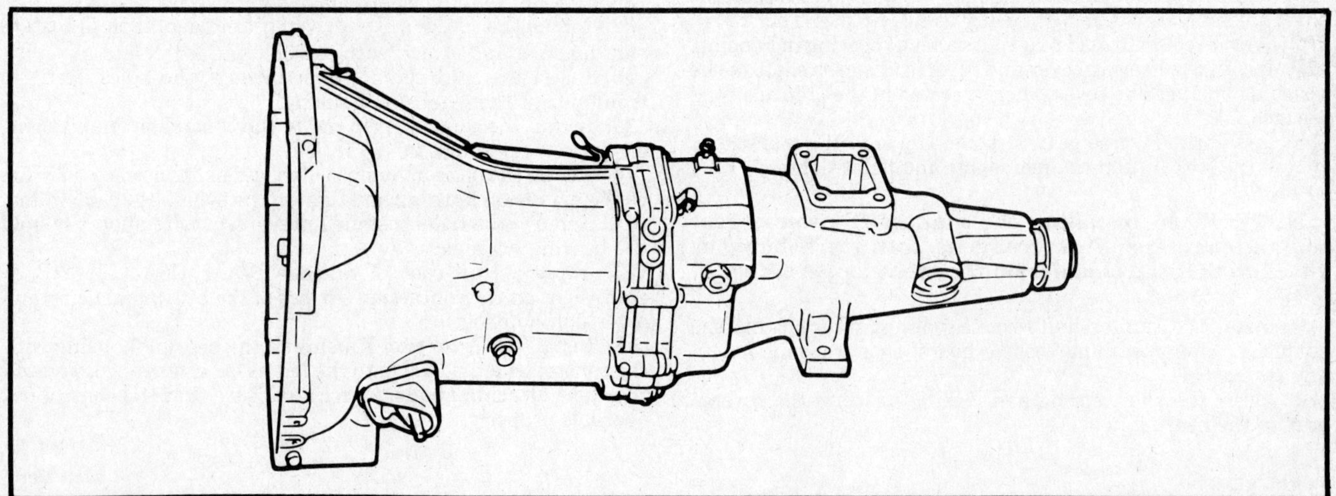

Four speed manual (diesel engine)

Assembly

1. Assemble the third and fourth clutch by installing the clutch hub and synchronizer into the sleeve, placing the three keys into the clutch hub slots and installing the springs onto the hub.

NOTE: When installing the key springs, the open end tab of the springs should be inserted into the hub holes. This will keep the springs tension on each key uniform

2. Assemble the first and second clutch hub and sleeve in the same manner as described in Step 1 above.
3. Install the third gear and synchronizer ring onto the front section of the mainshaft.
4. Install the third and fourth clutch hub assembly onto the mainshaft by using a press. Hold assembly together and slowly press into place.
5. Fit the snapring on the mainshaft.
6. Install the second gear, synchronizer ring onto the rear section of the mainshaft.
7. Install the first and second clutch hub assembly onto the mainhshaft by using a press.
8. Install the synchronizer ring, first gear with sleeve and thrust washer onto the mainshaft.
9. Install the input shaft and the needle roller bearing to the mainshaft.
10. Check the countershaft rear bearing clearance. Measure the depth of the countershaft bearing bore in the bearing housing using a depth micrometer (D80P-4201-A or Equivalent). Then, measure the countershaft bearing height. The difference between the two measurements, indicates the required thickness of the adjusting shim. The clearance should be less than 0.0039 in. The adjusting shims are available in the following thickness, 0.0039 in. and 0.0118 in.
11. Check the mainshaft bearing clearance in the same manner as for the countershaft rear bearing clearance. The clearance should be less than 0.0039 in. The adjusting shims are available in the following thickness, 0.0039 in and 0.0118 in.
12. Position proper shim on countershaft rear bearing and press into bearing housing using Installer Tool T77J-7025-B.
13. Position proper shim on mainshaft bearing and press into bearing housing using Insttaller Tool T77J-7025-K or its equal.
14. Position front bearing on countershaft and press into place using Bearing Repalcer Tool T71P-7025-A or its equal.
15. Mesh counter shaft and mainshaft assembly and positon the two on the bearnig housing. Make certain that thrust washer is installed on mainshaft assembly at the rear of the first gear.
16. While holding mainshaft assembly in place, press countershaft assembly into bearing housing using Replacer Tool T71P-7025-A or its equal to hold rear countershaft bearing in housing.
17. Install the bearing cover and reverse idle gear shaft to the bearing housing. The cover must be seated in the groove on the idle gear shaft.
18. Install the reverse gear with the key onto the mainshaft. Install the lock nut on the mainshaft and hand tighten.

NOTE: When installing the mainshaft reverse gear and the countershaft reverse gear, both gears should be fitted so that the chamfer on the teeth faces rearward.

19. Install the countershaft reverse gear and secure it with the snapring. After installing reverse gears, lock transmission in any two gears.
20. Insert the short spring and locking ball into the reverse bore of the bearing housing.
21. While holding down the ball with a punch or other suitable tool, install the reverse shift rod and shift lever assembly with the reverse idle gear at the same time.
22. Using the dummy shift rails (Tool Number T72J-7280 or its equal), install each shift fork rod and interlock pins.
23. Install the first and second shift fork and third and fourth shift fork to their respective clutch sleeves.
24. Align the roll pin holes of each shift fork and rod. Install the new roll pins.

NOTE: When assembling the shift fork and control end, a new roll pin should be installed with a pin slit positioned in the direction of the shift rod axis.

25. Install the shift locking balls and springs into their respective positions and install the spring cap bolt. The short spring and ball are installed in the reverse bore.
26. Apply a thin coat of Silicone Sealer D6AZ-19562-B, or equivalent, on both contacting surfaces of the bearing housing.
27. Install the bearing housing assembly to the transmission case.
28. Temporarily attach the bearing housing to the transmission with two top and two bottom bolts and tighten the extension housing mounting bolts to position the countershaft front bearing in the bore.

NOTE: If necessary, remove plugs from bell housing shift rod bores to align shift rods. After installation of bearing housing assembly is complete, reinstall plugs using a silicone sealer (D6AZ-19562-B or equivalent).

29. Tighten the mainshaft locknut 116–174 ft. lbs. using Adapter T83T-7025-A and Tool Shaft T77J-7025-C or equivalent.
30. Bend a tab on the lockwasher using Staking Tool T77J-7025-F or equivalent.
31. Install the speedometer drive gear with the lock ball onto the mainshaft and secure it with a snapring.
32. With the outer snapring in place on the main driveshaft front bearing, place bearing, shim 38917-2S and Adapter Tool T75L-7025-N or equivalent over the input shaft.
33. Thread the Replacer Shaft T75L-7025-K or equal onto the Adapter Tool. Install the Replacer Tube T75L-7025-B or equal over the Replacer shaft and install the nut and washer on the forcing screw.
34. Slowly tighten the nut until the adapter is secure on the input shaft. Make certain that all tools are aligned.
35. Tighten the nut on the forcing screw until the bearing outer snapring is seating against the housing. Remove the installation tools.
36. Install the input shaft snapring.
37. Install the speedometer driven gear assembly to the extension housing and attach with the bolt and lock plate.
38. Insert the shift control lever through the holes from the front side of the extension housing.
39. Install the control lever end to the control lever and tighten the attaching bolt 20–25 ft. lbs.
40. Install the back-up lamp switch and neutral sensing switch to the extension housing and tighten the switches 20–25 ft. lbs.
41. Remove the bolts installed previously to temporarily hold the bearing housing.
42. Apply a thin coat of Silicone Sealer D6AZ-19562-B or equivalent on the contacting surface of the bearing housing and extension housing.
43. Install the extension housing to the bearing housing with the control lever laid down to the left as far as it will go. Tighten the eight attaching bolts. Check to ensure that the control rod operates properly.

Ford Four Speed Transmission (Gasoline Engines)

Disassembly

1. Remove the nuts attaching the bell housing to the transmission case. Remove the bell housing and gasket.
2. Remove the drain plug and drain lubricant from the transmission. Clean the metal filings from the magnet of the drain plug (if necessary). Install the drain plug.
3. Place transmission in neutral.
4. Remove the four bolts attaching the gearshift lever retainer to the extension housing. Remove the gearshift lever retainer and gasket.
5. Remove the six bolts attaching the extension housing to the transmission case.
6. Raise the control lever to the left and slide toward the rear of the transmission. Slide the extension housing off the mainshaft, being careful not to damaged the oil seal.
7. If required, remove the bolt attaching the gearshift control lower end to the gearshift control lever and remove the control lever end and control lever.
8. If required, remove the back-up lamp switch from the extension housing.
9. Remove the anti spill seal from the output shaft and discard (a seal is not necessary for assembly).
10. Remove the snapring that secures the speedometer drive gear to the mainshaft. Slide the drive gear off the mainshaft, and remove the lock ball.
11. Evenly loosen the fourteen bolts securing the transmission case cover to the transmission case and remove the cover and gasket.
12. Remove the three spring cap bolts the detent springs and the detent balls with a magnet from the transmission case.
13. Remove the four bolts attaching the blind covers to the transmission case and remove the blind covers and gaskets.
14. Slide the reverse shift fork shaft assembly and reverse idler gear out of the transmission case.
15. Shift the transmission into fourth gear. This will provide adequate space to drive out the roll pin. With a small drift, drive the roll pin from third and fourth fork assembly. Slide the third and fourth shift fork shaft out of the rear of the transmission case.
16. Remove the roll pin from the first and second shift fork. Slide the first and second shift fork shaft assembly out the rear of the transmission case. Remove both interlock pins.
17. Reinstall the reverse idler gear to lock the gears. Install the Synchronizer Ring Holder and countershaft Spacer (T77J-7025-E) or its equal between the fourth speed synchronizer ring and synchromesh gear on the mainshaft. Shift the transmission gear into second gear to lock the mainshaft and prevent the assembly from rotating.
18. Straighten the bent portion of the lockwasher with a chisel.
19. Remove the locknut and washer using Locknut Wrench Adapter T82T-7003-CH and Locknut Wrench, T77J-7025-C or their equal. Slide the reverse/idler gear off the mainshaft.
20. Remove the key from the mainshaft.
21. Remove the reverse idler gear.
22. Remove the snapring from the rear end of the countershaft. Slide the countershaft reverse gear off the countershaft.
23. Remove the four bearing retainer attaching bolts.
24. Remove the baring retainer together with the reverse idler gear shaft.
25. To remove the countershaft rear bearing, install Puller, T77J-7025-H; Puller Rings, T77J-7025-J; Remover Tube, T77J-7025-B; and Forcing Screw, T75L-7025-J or their equal.

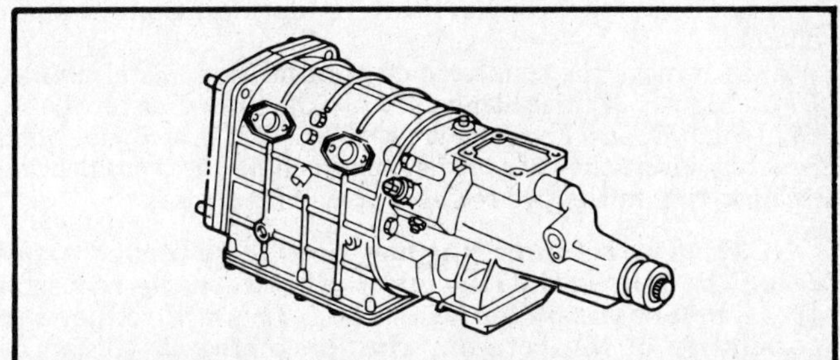

Four speed manual (gasoline engine)

Squarely insert the jaws of the puller behind the front bearing retainer ring in the two recessed areas of the case.

NOTE: The retainer ring may need to be turned to position the split in the retainer ring midway between the recessed area, before the puller is installed. This will reduce the possibility of the retainer ring becoming distorted as the bearing is removed.

26. Turn the forcing screw clockwise to remove the bearing.
27. To remove the mainshaft rear bearing, install Puller T77J-7025-H; Puller Rings, T77J-7025-J; Remover and Replacer Tube (Long Tube), T75L-7025-C and Forcing Screw, T75L-7025-J or their equal. Squarely insert the jaws of the puller behind the rear mainshaft bearing retainer ring in the two recessed areas of the case.

NOTE: The retainer ring may need to be turned to position the split in the ring midway between the recessed areas before the puller is installed. This will reduce the possibility of the retainer ring becoming distorted as the bearing is removed.

28. Turn the forcing screw clockwise to remove the bearing.
29. Remove the shim and spacer from behind the mainshaft rear bearing.
30. Remove the front cover by removing the four studs attaching the cover to case. Remove the studs by installing two nuts on the stud and drawing the stud out of the case. Remove the four bolts and remove the cover. Save the shim found on the inside of the cover.
31. Remove the snapring from the input shaft.
32. Remove the mainshaft drive gear bearing by installing Puller, T77J-7025-H; Puller Rings, T77J-7025-J; Remover and Replacer Tube (Short Tube), T75L-7025-B; and Forcing Screw, T75L-7025-J or their equal. Squarely insert the jaws of the puller behind the mainshaft drive gear bearing retainer ring in the two recessed areas of the case.

NOTE: The retainer ring may need to be turned to position the split in the ring midway between the recessed areas before the puller is installed. This will reduce the possibility of the retainer ring becoming distorted as the bearing is removed.

33. Turn the forcing screw clockwise to remove the bearing.
34. Rotate both shift forks so that the main gear train will fall to the bottom of the case. Remove the shift forks. Rotate the input shaft so that one of the two flats on the input shaft face upward.
35. Insert Synchronizer Ring Holder and Countershaft Spacer, T77J-7025-E or its equal between the first gear on the countershaft and the rear of the case.

36. Remove the snapring from the front of the countershaft.
37. Install Forcing Screw, T75L-7025-J; Press Frame, T77J-7025-N; and Press Frame Adapter, T82T-7003-BH or their equal against the countershaft assembly.
38. Turn the forcing screw clockwise to press the countershaft rearward. Press the countershaft ($^3/_{16}$ in. movement) until it contacts the Synchronizer Ring Holder and Countershaft Spacer.
39. To remove the countershaft front bearing, install Puller, T77J-7025-H; Puller Rings, T77J-7025-J; Remover Tube, T77J-7025-B; and Forcing Screw, T75L-7025-J or their equal. Squarely insert the jaws of the puller behind the front bearing retainer ring in the two recessed areas of the case.

NOTE: The retainer ring may need to be turned to position the split in the ring midway between the recessed areas, before the puller is installed. This will reduce the possibility of the retainer ring becoming distorted as the bearing is removed.

40. Turn the forcing screw clockwise to remove the bearing.
41. Remove the shim from behind the countershaft front bearing.
42. Remove the input shaft from the transmission case. Remove the synchronizer ring and caged bearing from the main driveshaft.
43. Remove the countershaft from the transmission case.
44. Remove the inner race of the countershaft center bearing from the countershaft in a press frame using Axle Bearing Seal Plate, T75L-1165-B and Pinion Bearing Cone Remover, D79L-4621-A or their equal.
45. Remove the mainshaft and gear assembly from the transmission case.
46. Remove the snapring from the front of the mainshaft.
47. Slide the third/fourth clutch hub and sleeve assembly, the third synchronizer ring and third gear off of the front of the mainshaft. Do not mix the synchronizer rings.
48. Slide the thrust washer, first gear and gear sleeve off the rear mainshaft. Press the bushing from the first gear using a press and suitable presssing stock.
49. Remove the first and second clutch hub and sleeve assembly from the mainshaft.
50. Clean and inspect transmission case, gears, bearings and shafts

Assembly

Before beginning the assembly procedure, three measurements must be performed: Mainshaft Thrust Play, Countershaft Thurst Play and Mainshaft Bearing clearance.

Mainshaft Thrust Play

Check the mainshaft thrust play by measuring the depth of the mainshaft bearing bore in the transmission rear cage by using a depth micrometer (D80P-4201-A) or its equal. Then measure the mainshaft rear bearing height. The difference between the two measurements indicates the required thickness of the adjusting shim. The standard thrust play is 0–0.0039 in. Adjusting shims are available in 0.0039 in. and 0.0118 in.

Countershaft Thrust Play

Check the countershaft thrust play by measuring the depthmicrometer (D80P-4201-A) or its equal. Then measure the countershaft front bearing height. The difference between the two measurements indicates the required thickness of the adjusting shims. The standard thrust play is 0–0.0039 in. Adjusting shims are available in 0.0039 in. and 0.0118 in. sizes.

Mainshaft Bearing Clearance

Check the main driveshaft bearing clearance by measuring the depth of the bearing bore in the clutch adapter plate with a depth micrometer, D80P-4201-A or its equal. Make sure the micrometer is on the second step of the plate. Measure the bearing height. The difference between the two measurements indicates the required adjusting shim thickness. The standard clearance is 0–0.0039 in. If an adjusting shim is required, select one to bring the clearance to within specifications.

1. Assemble the first and second synchromesh mechanism by installing the clutch hub to the sleeve, placing the three synchronizer keys into the clutch hub key slots and installing the key springs to the clutch hub.

NOTE: When installing the Key springs, the open end tab of the springs should be inserted into the hub holes with the springs turned in the same direction. This will keep the spring tension on each key uniform.

2. Assemble the third and fourth synchromesh mechanisms in the same manner as first and second synchromesh mechanism.
3. Place the synchronizer ring on the third gear to the front of the mainshaft with the synchronizer ring toward the front.
4. Slide the third and fourth clutch hub and sleeve assembly to the front of the mainshaft, making sure that the three synchronizer keys in the synchromesh mechanism engage the notches in the synchronizer ring. Note the proper direction of the third and fourth clutch hub and sleeve assembly.
5. Install the snapring to the front of the mainshaft.
6. Place the synchronizer ring on the second gear and slide the second gear to the mainshaft with the synchronizer ring toward the rear of the shaft.
7. Slide the first and second clutch hub and sleeve assembly to the mainshaft with the oil grooves of the clutch hub toward the front of the mainshaft. Make sure that the three synchronizer keys in the synchromesh mechanism engage the notches in the second synchronizer ring.
8. Insert the first gear sleeve in the mainshaft.
9. Press the bushing in the first gear using a press and suitable press stock.
10. Placc the synchronizer ring on the first gear and slide the first gear onto the mainshaft with the synchronizer ring facing the front of the shaft. Rotate the first gear as necessary to engage the three notches in the synchronizer ring with the synchronizer keys.
11. Install the original thrust washer on the mainshaft.
12. Position the mainshaft and gears assembly in the case.
13. Position the caged bearing in the front end of the mainshaft.
14. Place the synchronizer ring on the input shaft (fourth gear) and install the input shaft to the front end of the mainshaft, making sure that the three synchronizer keys in the third and fourth synchromesh mechanism engage the notches in the synchronizer ring.
15. Position the first and second shift fork and third-and fourth shift fork in the groove of the clutch hub and sleeve assembly.
16. Press the inner race of the countershaft rear bearing onto the countershaft using Center Bearing Replacer, T77J-7025-K or its equal.
17. Position the countershaft gear in the case, making sure that the countershaft gear engages each gear of the mainshaft assembly.
18. Install the correct shim in the mainshaft rear bearing bore as determined in the Mainshaft Thrust Play Measurement.
19. Position the main drive gear bearing and the mainshaft rear bearing into the proper bearing bores. Be sure the synchronizer and shifter forks have not been moved out of position.
20. Install the Dummy Bearing Replacer, T75L-7025-Q; Mainshaft Front Bearing Replacer, T82T-7003-DH; Replacer Tube, T77J-7025-M; Press Frame Adapter, T82T-7003-BH; and Press Frame, T77J-7025-N or their equal on the case. Position the Synchronizer Ring Holder and Countershaft Spacer, T77J-

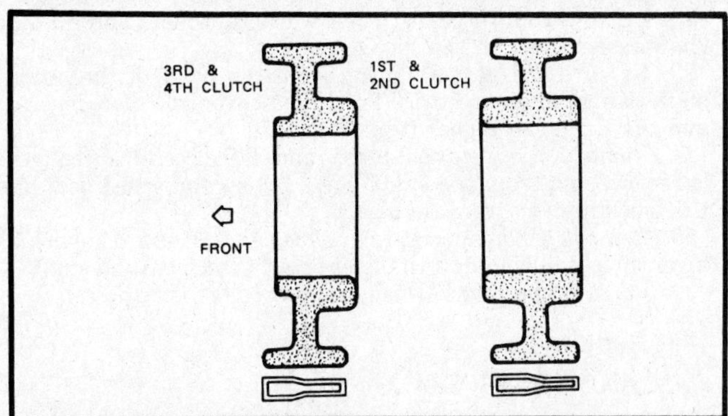

Clutch hub assembly direction

7025-E or their equal between the mainshaft drive gear and synchronizer ring. Turn the forcing screw on the press frame until both bearings are properly seated.

21. Install the main drive gear bearing snapring.

22. Place the correct shim in the countershaft front bearing bore as determined by the Countershaft Thrust Play Mesurement.

23. Position the countershaft front and rear bearings in the bores and install the tools. Turn the forcing screw until the bearing is properly seated. Use the rear bearing as a pilot.

24. Install the snapring to secure the countershaft front bearing.

25. Install the bearing retainer together with the reverse idler gear shaft to the transmission case and tighten the four attaching bolts.

26. Slide the counter reverse gear onto the countershaft with the chamfer to the rear. Install the snapring to secure the counter reverse gear.

27. Install the key on the mainshaft.

28. Slide the reverse gear and lockwasher(tab facing outward) onto the mainshaft (chamfer on teeth should be to rear). Install a new locknut and hand tighten.

29. Shift into second gear and reverse gear to lock rotation of the mainshaft. Tighten the locknut 145–203 ft. lbs. using the Locknut Wrench (T77J-7025-C) and Locknut Adapter, T82T-7003-CH or their equal.

30. Place the fourth and third clutch sleeve in third gear using Synchronizer Ring Holder and Countershaft Spacer, T77J-7025-E or its equal.

31. Check the clearance between the synchronizer key and the exposed edge of the synchronizer ring with a feeler gauge. If the measurement is greater than 0.079 in., the synchronizer key can pop out of position. To correct this, change the thrust washer (selective fit) between the mainshaft rear bearing and the first gear. Available thrust washer sizes are 0.098, 0.118 and 0.138.

32. Check the clearance again with a feeler gauge. If the clearance is within specifications, bend the tab of the lockwasher.

33. Slide the first and second shift fork shaft assembly into the case (from rear of case). Install the roll pin. Secure the first and second shift fork to the fork shaft by staking the roll pin. Be sure to use a new roll pin.

34. Insert the interlock pin into the transmission using the lockout pin replacer tool.

35. Slide the third and fourth shift fork shaft assembly into the case (from rear of case). Secure the third and fourth shift fork to the fork shaft by staking the roll pin. Place transmission in neutral. Be sure to use a new roll pin.

36. Insert the interlock pin into the transmission.

37. Slide the reverse fork shaft assembly and reverse idler gear into the transmission case from the rear of the case with the gear chamfer forward. Secure the reverse shift fork to the fork shaft by staking the roll pin. Be sure to use a new roll pin.

38. Position the three detent balls and three springs into the case place copper washer on the top two bolts and install the three spring cap bolts.

39. Install the two blind covers and gaskets. Tighten the attaching bolts.

40. Install the lock all, speedometer drive gear and snapring onto the mainshaft.

41. Apply a thin coat of sealing agent, Gasket Maker, E2AZ-19562-A (ESEM4G234-A2) or equivalent to the contacting surfaces of the transmission case and extension housing.

42. Position the extension housing with the gearshift control lever end laid down to the left as far as it will go. tighten the four attaching bolts. The lower two bolts must be coated with Loctite or equivalent.

43. If removed, insert the speedometer driven gear assembly to the extension housing and secure it with the bolt.

44. Check to ensure the gearshift control lever operates properly.

45. Install the transmission case cover gasket and cover with drain plug to rear. Install and tighten the fourteen attaching bolts.

46. Position the gasket and gearshift lever retainer to the extension housing and tighten the four attaching bolts.

47. Install the correct size shim on the second step of the clutch adapter plate as determined by the Mainshaft Bearing Clearance Measurement.

48. Coat the clutch adapter plate with sealer, Gasket Maker, E2AZ-19562-A (ESEM4G234-A2) or equivalent. Install the clutch adapter plate to the transmission case and tighten the four bolts and four studs.

49. Remove the filler plug and install 3.0 pints of Ford Manual Transmission Lube, D8DZ-19C547-A (ESPM2C83-C) or equivalent. Reinstall filler plug and tighten 18–29 ft. lbs.

Ford Four Speed Overdrive Transmission

The Ford four speed overdrive transmission is fully synchronized in all forward gears. The four speed shift control is serviced as a unit and should not be disassembled. The lubricant capacity is 4.5 pints.

Disassembly

1. Remove retaining clips and flat washers from the shift rods at the levers.

2. Remove shift linkage control bracket attaching screws and remove shift linkage and control brackets.

3. Remove cover attaching screws. Then lift cover and gasket from the case. Remove the long spring that holds the detent plug in the case. Remove the plug with a magnet.

4. Remove extension housing attaching screws. Then, remove extension housing and gasket.

5. Remove input shaft bearing retainer attaching screws. Then, slide retainer from the input shaft.

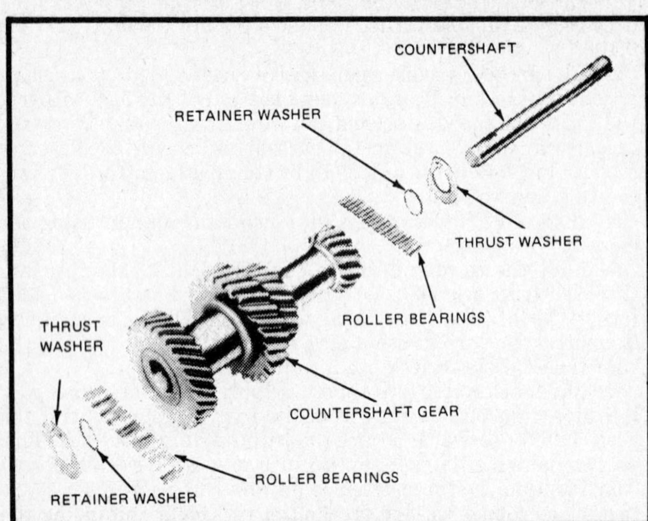

Exploded view of countershaft gear

6. Working a dummy shaft in from the front of the case, drive the countershaft out the rear of the case. Let the countergear assembly lie in the bottom of the case. Remove the set screw from the first/second shift fork. Slide the first/second shift rail out of the rear of the case. Use a magnet to remove the interlock detent from between the first/second and third/fourth shift rails.
7. Locate first/second speed gear shift lever in neutral. Locate third/fourth speed gear shift lever in third speed position. On overdrive transmissions, locate third/fourth speed gear shift lever in the fourth speed position.
8. Remove the lockbolt that holds the third–fourth speed shift rail detent spring and plug in the left side of the case. Remove spring and plug with a magnet.
9. Remove the detent mechanism set screw from top of case. Then, remove the detent spring and plug with a small magnet.
10. Remove attaching screw from the third/fourth speed shift fork. Tap lightly on the inner end of the shift rail to remove the expansion plug from front of case. Then, withdraw the third/fourth speed shift rail from the front. Do not lose the interlock pin from rail.
11. Remove attaching screw from the first and second speed shift fork. Slide the first/second shift rail from the rear of case.
12. Remove the interlock and detent plugs from the top of the case with a magnet.
13. Remove the snapring or disengage retainer that holds the speedometer drive gear to the output shaft, then remove speedometer gear drive ball.
14. Remove the snapring used to hold the output shaft bearing to the shaft. Pull out the output shaft bearing.
15. Remove the input shaft bearing snaprings. Use a press to remove the input shaft bearing. Remove the input shaft and blocking ring from the front of the case.
16. Move output shaft to the right side of the case. Then, maneuver the forks to permit lifting them from the case.
17. Support the thrust washer and first speed gear to prevent sliding from the shaft, then lift output shaft from the case.
18. Remove reverse gear shift fork attaching screw. Rotate the reverse shift rail 90°, then, slide the shift rail out the rear of the case. Lift out the reverse shift fork.
19. Remove the reverse detent plug and spring from the case with a magnet.
20. Using a dummy shaft, remove the reverse idler shaft from the case.
21. Lift reverse idler gear and thrust washers from the case. Be careful not to drop the bearing rollers or the dummy shaft from the gear.
22. Lift the countergear, thrust washers, rollers and dummy shaft assembly from the case.
23. Remove the next snapring from the front of the output shaft. Then, slide the third/fourth synchronizer blocking ring and the third speed gear from the shaft.
24. Remove the next snapring and the second speed gear thrust washer from the shaft. Slide the second speed gear and the blocking ring from the shaft.
25. Remove the snapring, then slide the first/second synchronizer, blocking ring and the first speed gear from the shaft.
26. Remove the thrust washer from rear of the shaft.

Unit Repairs

CAM AND SHAFT SEALS

1. Remove attaching nut and washers from each shift lever, then remove the three levers.
2. Remove the three cams and shafts from inside the case.
3. Replace the old O-rings with new ones that have been well lubricated.
4. Slide each cam and shaft into its respective bore in the transmission.
5. Install the levers and secure them with their respective washers and nuts.

SYNCHRONIZERS

1. Push the synchronizer hub from each synchronizer sleeve.
2. Separate the inserts and springs from the hubs. Do not mix parts of the first–second with parts of third–fourth synchronizers.
3. To assemble, position the hub in the sleeve. Be sure the alignment marks are properly indexed.
4. Place the three inserts into place on the hub. Install the insert springs so that the irregular surface (hump) is seated in one of the inserts. Do not stagger the springs.

COUNTERSHAFT GEAR

1. Dismantle the countershaft gear assembly.
2. Assemble the gear by coating each end of the countershaft gear bore with grease.
3. Install dummy shaft in the gear. Then install 21 bearing rollers and a retainer washer in each end of the gear.

REVERSE IDLER GEAR

1. Dismantle reverse idler gear.
2. Assemble reverse idler gear by coating the bore in each end of reverse idler gear with grease.
3. Hold the dummy shaft in the gear and install the 22 bearing rollers and the retainer washer into each end of the gear.
4. Install the reverse idler sliding gear on the splines of the reverse idler gear. Be sure the shift fork groove is toward the front.

INPUT SHAFT SEAL

1. Remove the seal from the input shaft bearing retainer.
2. Coat the sealing surface of a new seal with lubricant, then press the new seal into the input shaft bearing retainer.

Assembly

1. Grease the countershaft gear thrust surfaces in the case. Then, position a thrust washer at each end of the case.
2. Position the countershaft gear, dummy shaft and roller bearings in the case.
3. Align the gear bore and thrust washers with the bores in the case. Install the countershaft.
4. With the case in a horizontal position, countershaft gear endplay should be from 0.004–0.018 in. Use thrust washers to obtain play within these limits.
5. After establishing correct endplay, place the dummy shaft in the countershaft gear and allow the gear assembly to remain on the bottom of the case.

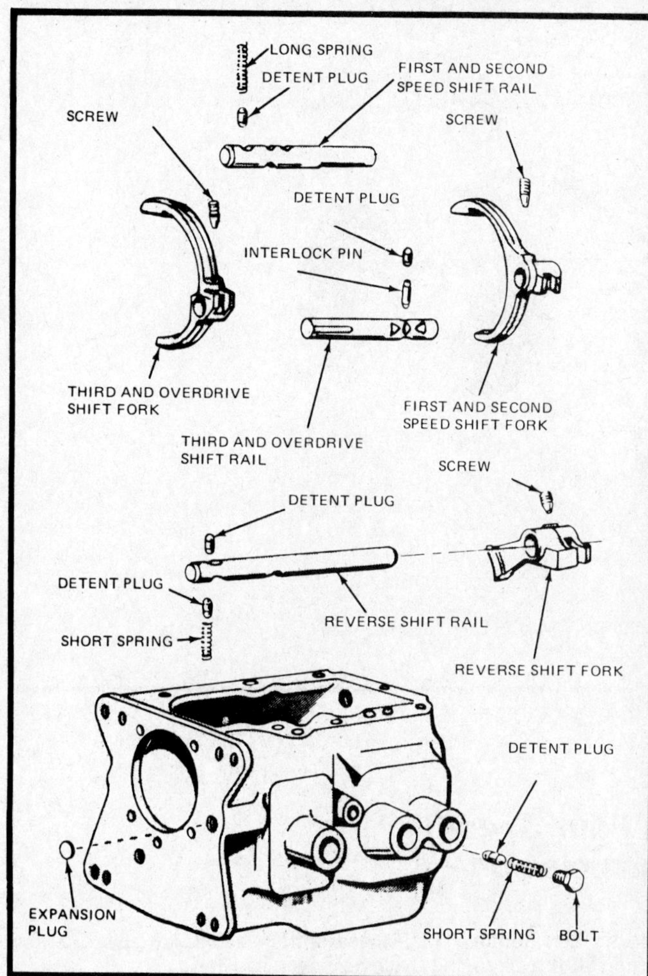

Exploded view of shift mechanism Ford four speed overdrive

6. Grease the reverse idler gear thrust surfaces in the case, and position the two thrust washers.
7. Position the reverse idler gear, sliding gear, dummy, etc., in place. Make sure that the shift fork groove in the sliding gear is toward the front.
8. Align the gear bore and thrust washers with the case bores and install the reverse idler shaft.
9. Reverse idler gear endplay should be 0.004–0.018 in. Use selective thrust washers to obtain play within these limits.
10. Position reverse gear shift rail detent spring and detent plug in the case. Hold the reverse shift fork in place on the reverse idler sliding gear and install the shift rail from the rear of the case. Lock the fork to the rail with the Allen head set screws.
11. Install the first/second synchronizer onto the output shaft. The first and reverse synchronizer hub are a press fit and should be installed with gear teeth facing the rear of the shaft.

On overdrive transmissions, first and reverse synchronizer hub is a slip fit.

12. Place the blocking ring on second gear. Slide second speed gear onto the front of the shaft with the synchronizer coned surface toward the rear.
13. Install the second speed gear thrust washer and snapring.
14. Slide the fourth gear onto the shaft with the synchronizer coned surface front.
15. Place a blocking ring on the fourth gear.
16. Slide the third/fourth speed gear synchronizer onto the shaft. Be sure that the inserts in the synchronizer engage the notches in the blocking ring. Install the snapring onto the front of the output shaft.
17. Put the blocking ring on the first gear.
18. Slide the first gear onto the rear of the output shaft. Be sure that the inserts engage the notches in the blocking ring and that the shift fork groove is toward the rear.
19. Install heavy thrust washer onto the rear of the output shaft.
20. Lower the output shaft assembly into the case.
21. Position the first/second speed shift fork and the third/fourth speed shift fork in place on their respective gears. Rotate them into place.
22. Place a spring and detent plug in the detent bore. Place the reverse shift rail into neutral position.
23. Coat the third/fourth speed shift rail interlock pin (tapered ends) with grease, then position it in the shift rail.
24. Align the third/fourth speed shift fork with the shift rail bores and slide the shift rail into place. Be sure that the three detents are facing the outside of the case. Place the front synchronizer into fourth speed position and install the set screw into the third/fourth speed shift fork. Move the synchronizer to neutral position. Install the third/fourth speed shift rail detent plug, spring and bolt into the left side of the transmission case. Place the detent plug (tapered ends) in the detent bore.
25. Align first/second speed shift fork with the case bores and slide the shift rail into place. Lock the fork with the set screw.
26. Coat the input gear bore with a small amount of grease. Then install the 15 bearing rollers.
27. Put the blocking ring in the third/fourth synchronizer. Place the input shaft gear in the case. Be sure that the output shaft pilot enters the roller bearing of the input shaft gear.
28. With a new gasket on the input bearing retainer, dip attaching bolts in sealer, install bolts and torque 30–36 ft. lbs.
29. Press on the output shaft bearing, then install the snapring to hold the bearing.
30. Position the speedometer gear drive ball in the output shaft and slide the speedometer drive gear into place. Secure gear with snapring.
31. Align the countershaft gear bore and thrust washers with the bore in the case. Install the countershaft.
32. With a new gasket in place, install and secure the extension housing. Dip the extension housing screws in sealer, then torque screws 42–50 ft. lbs.
33. Install the filler plug and the drain plug.
34. Pour E.P. gear oil over the entire gear train while rotating the input shaft.
35. Place each shift fork in all positions to make sure they function properly. Install the remaining detent plug in the case, followed by the spring.
36. With a new cover gasket in place, install the cover. Dip attaching screws in sealer, then torque screws 14–19 ft. lbs.
37. Coat the third/fourth speed shift rail plug bore with sealer. Install a new plug.
38. Secure each shift rod to its respective lever with a spring washer, flat washer and retaining pin.
39. Position the shift linkage control bracket to the extension housing. Install and torque the attaching screws 12–15 ft. lbs.

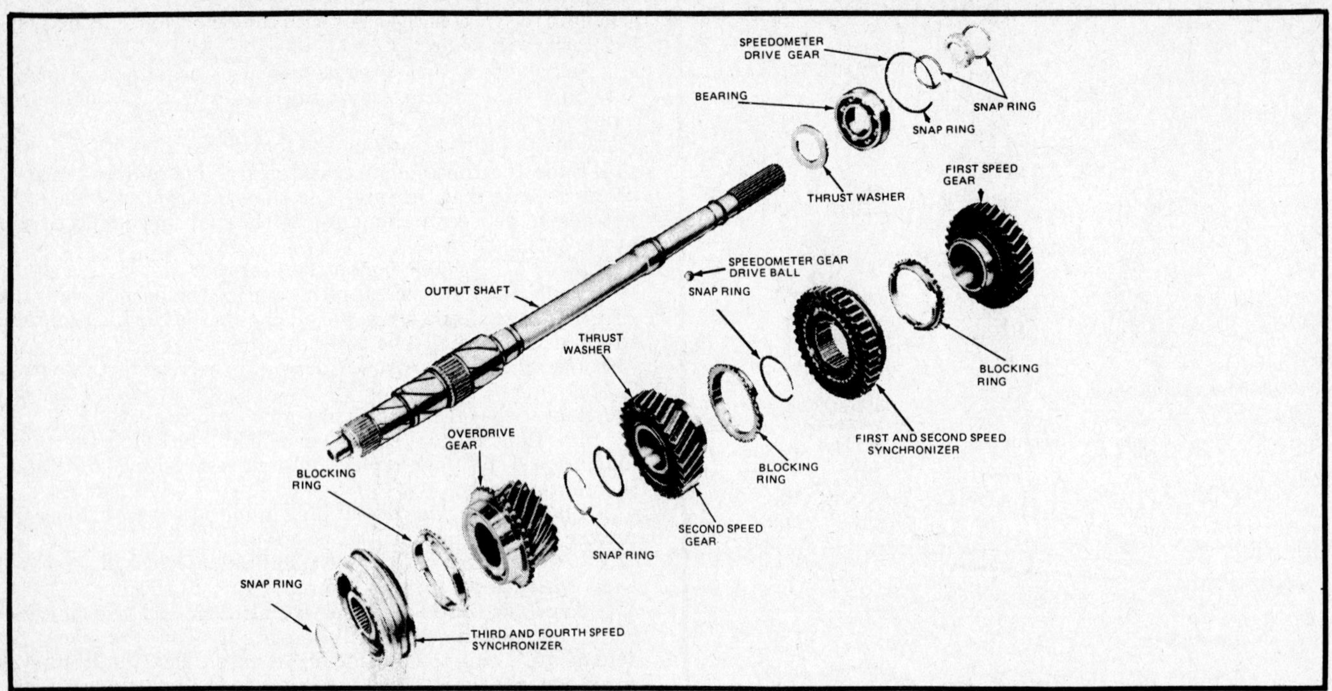

Exploded view of four speed overdrive transmission

Ford Single Rail Four Speed, Overdrive Transmission

The Single Rail Overdrive (SROD) transmission is a four speed unit that has all forward speeds synchronized. A single control rod (rail) connects the shift lever to the transmission shift lever rails. The lubricant capacity is 4.5 pints.

Disassembly

1. Remove the lower extension housing bolt to drain the transmission.
2. Remove the cover screws. Remove the cover and discard the gasket.
3. Remove the screw, detent spring and plug from the case; a magnetized rod will aid in removal.
4. Drive the roll pin from the shifter shaft.
5. Remove the backup lamp switch, snapring and the dust cover from the rear of the extension housing.
6. Remove the shifter shaft from the turret assembly.
7. Remove the extension housing bolts and housing; discard the gasket.
8. Remove the speedometer gear snapring. Slide the gear from the shaft and remove the drive ball.
9. Remove the output shaft bearing snapring. Remove the bearing.
10. Use a dummy shaft to push the countershaft out of the rear of the case. Lower the countershaft gear to the bottom of the case.
11. Remove the input shaft bearing retainer attaching bolts and slide the retainer and gasket from the input shaft and discard the gasket.
12. Remove the input shaft bearing snapring and remove the bearing.
13. Remove the input shaft and blocking ring (including roller bearings) from the case.
14. Remove the overdrive shift pawl, gear selector and interlock plate. Remove the 1–2 gearshift selector arm plate. Remove the roll pin from the 3rd/overdrive shift fork.
15. Drive the 3rd/overdrive shift rail and expansion plug from the rear of the case. Remove the mainshaft.
16. Remove the 1st and 2nd gear shift fork; remove the 3rd/overdrive shift fork.
17. Remove the countershaft gear and thrust washers from the case.
18. Remove the snapring from the front of the output shaft. Slide the 3rd gear and overdrive synchronizer, blocking ring, and gear from the shaft.
19. Remove the next snapring and washer and remove second gear. Remove next snapring and remove the 1st and 2nd synchronizer. Slide the 1st gear and blocking ring from the rear of the shaft.
20. Remove the roll pin from the reverse fork, slide the reverse shifter rail through the rear of the case and remove the reverse gearshift fork and spacer.
21. Drive the reverse gear shaft out the rear of the case.
22. Remove the reverse idler gear, thrust washers and roller bearings.
23. Remove the retaining clip, reverse gearshift relay lever and reverse gear selector fork pivot pin. Remove the overdrive shift control link assembly. Remove the shift shaft seal from the rear of the case. Remove the expansion plug from the front of the case.

Assembly

Assembly is the reverse. Tighten the extension housing bolts in a criss cross pattern 42–50 ft. lbs. The bearing rollers, extension housing bushing, shifter shaft and gear shift damper bushing are to be lubricated with grease before assembly (Ford #ESW-M1C109-A or the equivalent). The gear shift shaft sleeve and

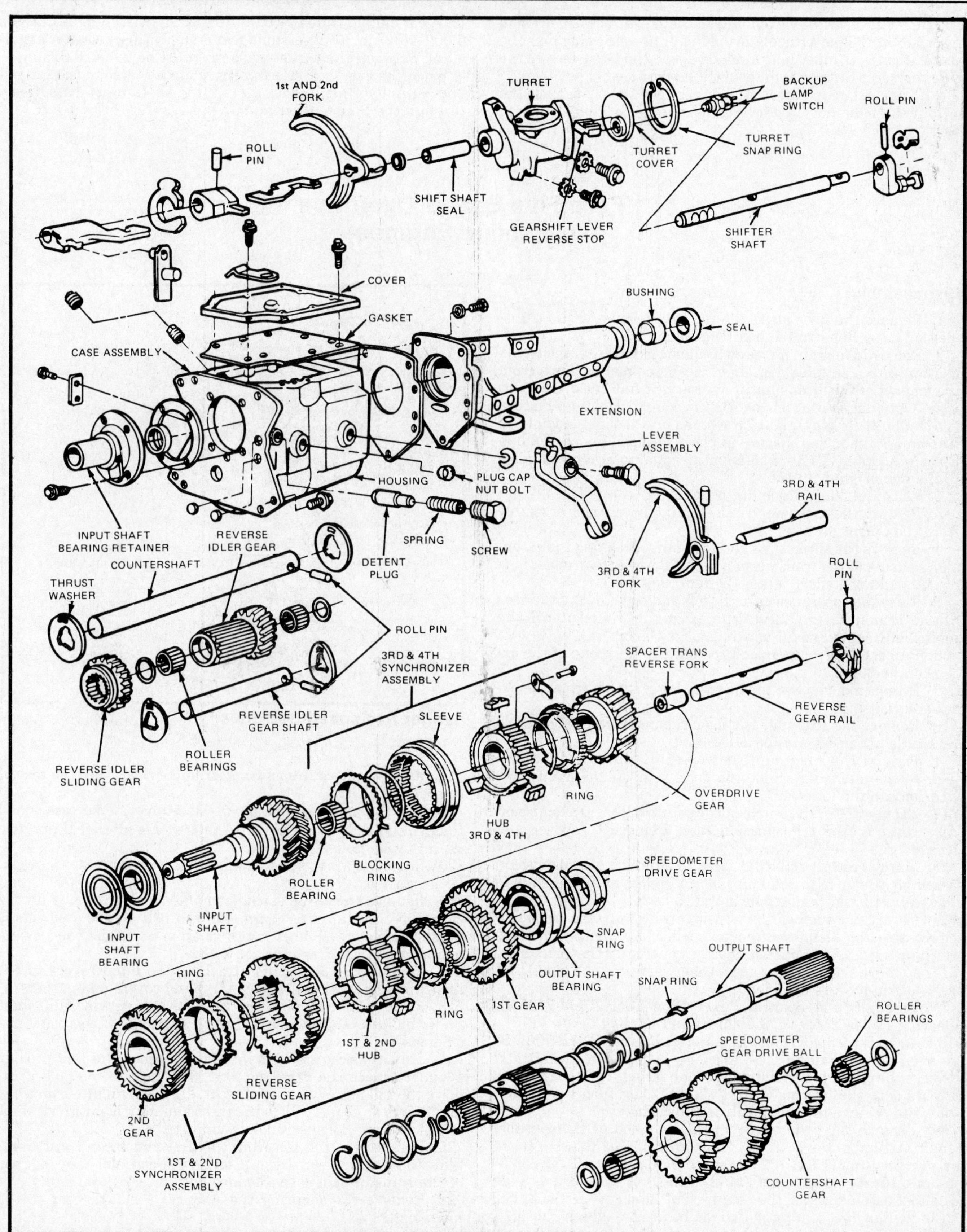
1st AND 2nd FORK
TURRET
BACKUP LAMP SWITCH
ROLL PIN
ROLL PIN
TURRET COVER
TURRET SNAP RING
SHIFT SHAFT SEAL
GEARSHIFT LEVER REVERSE STOP
SHIFTER SHAFT
COVER
BUSHING
GASKET
SEAL
CASE ASSEMBLY
EXTENSION
LEVER ASSEMBLY
HOUSING
PLUG CAP NUT BOLT
3RD & 4TH RAIL
INPUT SHAFT BEARING RETAINER
REVERSE IDLER GEAR
SPRING
SCREW
COUNTERSHAFT
DETENT PLUG
3RD & 4TH FORK
ROLL PIN
THRUST WASHER
ROLL PIN
3RD & 4TH SYNCHRONIZER ASSEMBLY
SPACER TRANS REVERSE FORK
REVERSE IDLER GEAR SHAFT
SLEEVE
REVERSE GEAR RAIL
ROLLER BEARINGS
REVERSE IDLER SLIDING GEAR
RING
OVERDRIVE GEAR
HUB 3RD & 4TH
BLOCKING RING
ROLLER BEARING
SPEEDOMETER DRIVE GEAR
INPUT SHAFT
INPUT SHAFT BEARING
SNAP RING
OUTPUT SHAFT
RING
OUTPUT SHAFT BEARING
SNAP RING
1ST GEAR
RING
ROLLER BEARINGS
1ST & 2ND HUB
SPEEDOMETER GEAR DRIVE BALL
REVERSE SLIDING GEAR
2ND GEAR
1ST & 2ND SYNCHRONIZER ASSEMBLY
COUNTERSHAFT GEAR

Disassembly if single rail four speed overdrive transmission

the turret cover assembly should be coated with sealer prior to installation. The intermediate and high rail welch plug must be seated firmly; it must not protrude above the front face of the case, nor seat below 0.6 in. below the front face.

With the 1st gear thrust washer clamped tightly against the output shaft shoulder, 1st gear endplay must be 0.005–0.024 in. 2nd gear endplay must be 0.003–0.021 in. O.D. endplay must be 0.009–0.023 in. Countershaft gear endplay, checked after installation between the thrust washers, must be 0.004–0.018 in.

When the gearshift selector arm plate is seated in the 1st and 2nd shift fork plate slot, the shifter shaft must pass freely through the bore without binding.

Ford Five Speed Overdrive (Gasoline Engines)

Disassembly

1. Remove the nuts attaching the bell housing to the transmission case. Remove the bell housing gasket.
2. Remove the drain plug and drain lubricant from the transmission into a suitable container. clean the metal filings from the magnet of the drain plug, if necesary. Install the drain plug.
3. (Optional) Position the Bench Mount Holding Fixture (T57L-500-B) or its equal to the studs on the right side of the transmission housing. Secure in place with the Bench Holding Fixture Adapter (T77J-7025-D) or its equal to prevent damage to the metric stud threads.
4. Place the transmission in neutral.
5. Remove the speedometer sleeve and driven gear assembly from the extension housing.
6. Remove the three bolts and four nuts attaching the extension housing to the transmission case. There are two longer outer bolts and one short center (bottom) bolt used.
7. Raise the control lever to the left and slide toward the rear of the transmission. Slide the extension housing off the mainshaft, being careful not to damage the oil seal.
8. Pull the control lever and rod out the front end of the extension housing.
9. If required, remove the back-up lamp switch from the extension housing.
10. Remove the anti-spill seal from the mainshaft and discard (A seal is not necessary for assembly.).
11. Remove the snapring that secures the speedometer drive gear to the mainshaft. Slide the drive gear off the mainshaft, and remove the lock ball.
12. Evenly loosen the fourteen bolts securing the transmission case cover to the transmission case. Remove the cover and gasket.
13. Mark the shift rails and forks to aid during transmission assembly. Remove the roll pins attaching the shift rod ends to the shift rod and remove the shift rod ends.
14. Gently pry the bearing housing away from the transmission case using the proper tool and being careful not to damage the housing or case. Slide the bearing housing off the mainshaft.
15. Remove the snapring and washer retaining the mainshaft rear bearing to the mainshaft.
16. Assembly the Bearing Puller Ring Tool (T77J-7025-J), Bearing Puller Tool (T77J-7025-H) and Forcing Screw (T75L-7025-J) on the Remover and Replacer Tube Tool (T75L-7025-B) or their equal. Slide the tool assembly over the mainshaft and engage the puller jaws behind the rear bearing. Tighten the jaws evenly onto the bearing with a wrench, then turn the forcing screw to remove the mainshaft rear bearing.
17. Remove the snapring from the rear end of the countershaft. Assemble the Bearing Puller Tool (T77J-7025-H), Bearing Puller Ring (T77J-7025-J) and Forcing Screw (T75L-7025-J) onto the Remover Tube (T77J-7025-B) or their equal. Slide the tool assembly over the countershaft and engage the puller jaws behind the countershaft rear bearing. Tighten the jaws evenly onto the bearing with a wrench, then turn the forcing screw to remove the bearing.

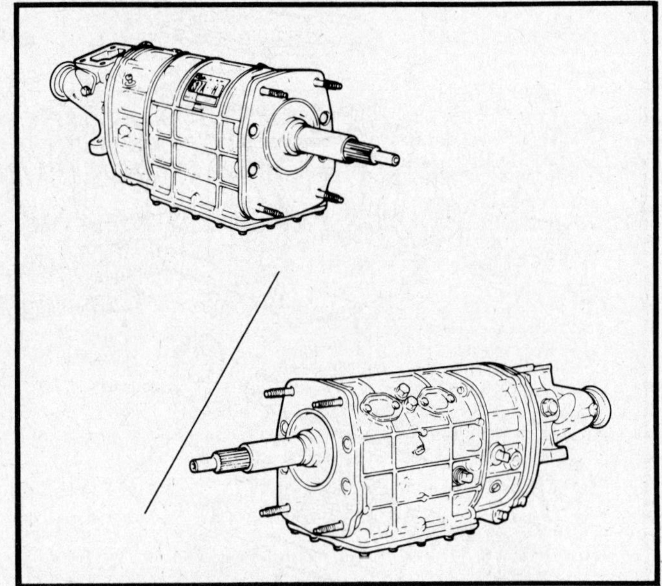

Ranger five speed overdrive

18. Remove the counter fifth gear and spacer from the rear of the countershaft.
19. Tap the housing with a plastic hammer, if necessary and remove center housing. Remove the reverse idler gear and two spacers with housing.
20. Remove the cap screw from center housing and remove idler gear shaft.
21. Remove the three spring cap bolts. The two bolts on the case upper portion are 17mm and the bolt on the case side is 14mm. Remove the detent springs and the detent balls with a magnet from the transmission case.
22. Remove the four bolts attaching the blind covers to the transmission case and remove the blind covers and gaskets.
23. Remove the roll pin from the fifth and reverse shift fork. Slide the fifth and reverse shift fork shaft out of the transmission case.
24. Shift the transmission into fourth gear. This will provide adequate space the drive out the roll pin. With a small drift, drive the roll pin. With a small drift, drive the rollpin from third and fourth shift fork. Slide the third and fourth shift fork shaft out of the rear of the transmission case.
25. Remove the roll pin from the first and second shift fork. Slide the first and second shift fork shaft assembly out the rear of the transmission case. Remove both interlock pins.
26. Remove the snapring that secures the fifth gear to the mainshaft.
27. Remove the thrust washer and lock ball, fifth gear and synchronizer ring from the rear of the mainshaft.

28. Install the Synchronizer Ring Holder and Countershaft Spacer (T77J-7025-E) or its equal between the fourth-speed synchronizer ring and synchromesh gear on the mainshaft. Shift the transmission into second gear to lock the mainshaft and prevent the assembly from rotating.

29. Straighten the staked portion of the mainshaft bearing locknut with the Staking Tool (T77J-7025-C) or its equal. Using the Locknut Wrench ((T77J-7025-C) or its equal. remove the mainshaft bearing locknut.

30. Slide the reverse gear and clutch hub assembly off the mainshaft.

31. Remove the counter reverse gear from the countershaft.

32. If installed, remove the transmission from the holding fixture and set on a workbench.

33. Remove the bolts attaching the mainshaft center bearing cover to the transmission and remove the bearing cover.

34. To remove the countershaft center bearing, install Puller T77J-7025-H, Puller Rings T77J-7025-J, Remover Tube T77J-7025-B and Forcing Screw T75L-7025-J or their equal. Squarely insert the jaws of the puller behind the center bearing retainer ring in the recessed areas of the case.

NOTE: The retainer ring may need to be turned to position the split in the retainer ring midway between the recessed areas before the puller is installed. this will reduce the possibility of the retainer ring becoming distorted as the bearing is removed.

35. Turn the forcing screw to remove the bearing.

36. To remove the mainshaft center bearing, install Puller T77J-7025-H, Puller Rings T77J-7025-J, Long Remover Tube T75L-7025-C and Forcing Screw T75L-7025-J or their equal. Squarely insert the jaws of the puller behind the jaws of the puller behind the rear mainshaft bearing retainer ring in the tow recessed areas of the case.

37. Turn the forcing screw clockwise to remove the bearing.

38. Remove the shim an spacer from behind the mainshaft rear bearing along with the bearng.

39. Remove the front cover by first removing the four studs attaching the cover to case. Remove the studs by installing two nuts (10mm x 1.5) on the stud and drawing the stud out of the case. Remove the four 14mm bolts and remove the cover. Save the shim found on the inside of the cover.

40. Remove the snapring from the input shaft.

41. Remove the input shaft bearing by installing Puller T77J-7025-H, Puller Rings T77J-7025-J, Remover Tube T75L-7025-B and Forcing Screw T75L-7025-J or their equal. Squarely insert the jaws of the puller behind the input shaft bearing retainer ring in the two recessed areas of the case.

NOTE: The retainer ring may need to turned to position the slit in the ring midway between the recessed areas before the puller is installed.

42. Turn the forcing screw clockwise to remove the bearing.

43. Rotate both shift forks so that the main gear train will fall to the bottom of the case. Remove the shift forks. Rotate the input shaft so that one of the two flats on the input shaft faces upward.

44. Remove the snapring from the front of the countershaft.

45. Remove Synchronizer Ring Holder T77J-7025-E or its equal from the front of the case and insert between the first gear on the counter shaft and the rear of the case.

46. Install Forcing Screw T75L-7025-J, Press Frame T77j-7025-N and Press Frame Adapter T82T-7003-BH or their equal against the countershaft assembly.

47. Turn the forcing screw clockwise to press the countershaft rearward. Press the countershaft ($^3/_{16}$ in. movement) until it contacts the Synchronizer Ring Holder and Countershaft Spacer.

48. To remove the countershaft front bearing, first remove the press frame. The, install Puller T77J-7025-H, Puller Rings T77J-7025-J, Remover Tube T777J-7025-B and Forcing Screw T75L-7025-J or their equal. Squarely insert the jaws of the puller behind the front bearing retainer ring in the two recessed areas of the case.

NOTE: The retainer ring may need to be turned to position the split in the ring midway between the recessed areas before the puller is installed.

49. Turn the forcing screw clockwise to remove the bearing.

50. Remove the shim form behind the countershaft front bearing.

51. Remove the countershaft from the transmission case.

52. Remove the input shaft from the transmission case. Remove the synchronizer ring and caged bearing from the mainshaft.

53. Remove the mainshaft and gear assembly from the transmission case.

54. Remove the inner race of the countershaft center bearing from the countershaft in a press frame using Axle Bearing Seal Plate T75L-1165-B and Pinion Bearing Cone Remover D79L-4621-A or their equal.

55. Remove first gear and first and second synchronizer ring. Remove snapring retainer from mainshaft. Do not mix synchronizer rings.

56. Install Bearing Remover Tool T71P-4621-B or its equal between second and third gear.

57. Press the mainshaft out of third gear and third and fourth clutch hub sleeve.

58. Press the first and second clutch hub and sleeve assembly, and first gear sleeve from the mainshaft.

59. Clean and inspect the case, gears, bearings and shafts.

Assembly

NOTE: As each part is assembled, Coat the part with manual transmission oil D8DZ-19C547-A (ESP-M2C83-C) or equivalent. Before beginning the assembly procedure, three measurements must be performed: Mainshaft Thrust Play, Countershaft Thrust Play and Mainshaft Bearing Clearance.

Mainshaft Thrust Play

Check the mainshaft thrust play by measuring the depth of the mainshaft bearing bore in the transmission rear case by using a depth micrometer (D80P-4201-A). Then the measure the mainshaft rear bearing height. The difference between the two mesurements indicates the required thickness of the adjusting shim. The standard thrust play is 0–0.0039 in. Adjusting shims are available in 0.0039 in. and 0.0118 in. sizes.

Countershaft Thrust Play

Check the countershaft thrust play by measuring the depth of the countershaft front bearing bore in the transmission case by using a depth micrometer (D80P-4201-A). Then measure the countershaft front bearing height. The difference between the two measurements indicates the required thickness of the adjusting shims. The standard thrust play is 0–0.0039 in. Adjusting shims are available in 0.0039 in. and 0.0118 in.sizes.

Mainshaft Bearing Clearance

Check the mainshaft bearing clearance by measuring the depth of the bearing bore in the clutch adapter plate with a depth micrometer, D80P-4201-A. Make sure the micrometer is on the second step of the plate. Measure the bearing height. The difference between the two measurements indicates the required adjusting shim thickness. The standard clearance is 0–0.0039 in. If an adjusting shim is required, select one to bring the clearance to within specifications.

1. Assemble the first and second synchromesh mechanism and the third and fourth synchromesh mechanism by installing

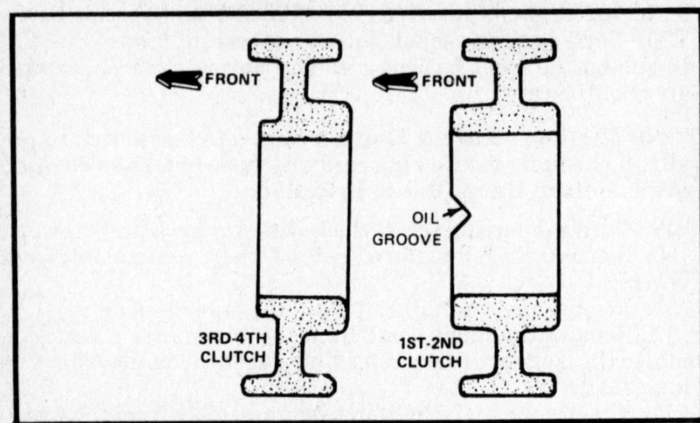

Clutch hub assembly direction

the clutch hub to the sleeve. Place the three synchronizer keys into the clutch hub key slots and install the key springs to the clutch hub.

NOTE: When installing the key springs, the open end tab of the springs should be inserted into hub holes with springs turned in the same direction. This will keep the spring tension on each key uniform.

2. Place the synchronizer ring on the second gear and position the second gear to the mainshaft with the synchronizer ring toward the rear of the shift.
3. Slide the first and second clutch hub and sleeve assembly to the mainshaft with the oil grooves of the clutch hub toward the front of the mainshaft. Make sure that the three synchronizer keys in the synchromesh mechanism engage the notches in the second synchronizer ring.
4. Press into position using press and suitable replacer tool.
5. Insert the first gear sleeve on the mainshft.
6. Place the synchronizer ring on the third gear along with the caged roller bearing and slide the third gear to the front of the mainshaft with the synchronizer ring toward the front.
7. Press the third and fourth clutch hub and sleeve assembly to the front of the mainshaft. Make sure that the three synchronizer keys in the synchromesh mechanism engage the notches in the synchronizer ring. Note the proper direction of the third and fourth clutch hub and sleeve assembly.
8. Install the snapring to the front of the mainshaft.
9. Slide the needle bearing for the first gear to the mainshaft.
10. Place the synchronizer ring on the first gear. Slide the first gear on to the mainshaft with the synchronizer ring facing the front of the shaft. Rotate the first gear, as necessary, to engage the three notches in the synchronizer ring with the synchronizer keys.
11. Install the original thrust washer to the mainshaft.
12. Position the mainshaft and gear assembly in the case.
13. Position the first and second shift fork and third and fourth shift fork in the groove of the clutch hub and sleeve assembly.
14. Position the caged bearing in the front end of the mainshaft.
15. Place the synchronizer ring on the input shaft (fourth gear) and install the input shaft to the front end of the mainshaft. Make sure that the three synchronizer keys in the third and fourth synchromesh mechanism engage the notches in the synchronizer ring.
16. Press the inner race of the countershaft rear bearing onto the countershaft using Center Bearing Replacer T77J-7025-K or its equal.
17. Position the countershaft gear in the case, Making sure that the countershaft gear engages each gear of the mainshaft assembly.
18. Install the correct shim on the mainshaft center bearing as determined in the Mainshaft Thrust Play Mesurement.
19. Position the input shaft bearing and the mainshaft center bearing to the proper bearing bores. Be sure the synchronizer and shifter forks have not been moved out of position.
20. Install the Synchronizer Ring Holder ToolT77J-7025-E or its equal between the fourth synchronizer ring and the synchromesh gear on the mainshaft.
21. Install the Dummy Bearing Replacer T82T-7003-DH, Replacer Tube T77J-7025-M and Press Frame T77J-7025-N or their equal on the case. Turn the forcing screw on the press frame until both bearings are properly seated.
22. Install the input shaft bearing snapring. Be sure that the synchronizer and shift forks are properly positioned during seating of bearings. After bearings are seated, make certain that both synchronizers operate freely.
23. Place the correct shim in the countershaft front bearing bore.
24. Position the countershaft front and center bearings in the bores and install the tools. Turn the forcing screw until the bearing is properly seated. Use the center bearing as a pilot.
25. Install the snapring to secure the countershaft front bearing.
26. Remove the synchronizer ring holder.
27. Install the bearing cover to the transmission case and tighten the four attaching bolts. Tighten 41–59 ft. lbs.
28. Install the reverse idler gear and shaft with a spacer on each side of shaft.
29. Slide the counter reverse gear (chamfer side forward) and spacer onto the countershaft.
30. Slide the thrust washer, reverse gear, caged roller bearings and clutch hub assembly onto the mainshaft. Install a new locknut (hand tight).
31. Shift into second gear and reverse gear to lock the rotation of the mainshaft. Tighten the locknut 115–175 ft. lbs. using the Locknut Wrench T77J-7025-C or its equal.
32. Stake the locknut into the mainshaft keyway using the staking tool.
33. Place the fourth and third clutch sleeve in third gear using Synchronizer Ring Holder and Countershaft Spacer T77J-7025-E.
34. If new synchronizers have been installed, Check the clearance between the synchronizer key and the exposed edge of the synchronizer ring with a feeler gauge. If the measurement is greater than 0.079 in., the synchronizer key can pop out of position. To correct this, change the thrust washer (selective fit) between the mainshaft center bearing and the first gear Available thrust washer sizes are 0.089, 0.118 and 0.138.
35. If new synchronizers were installed, check the clearance again with a feeler gauge, If the clearance is within specifications, bend the tab of the lockwasher.
36. Position the fifth synchronizer ring on the fifth gear. Slide the fifth gear onto the mainshaft with the synchronizer ring toward the front of the shft. Rotate the fifth gear, as necessary, to engage the three notches in the synchronizer ring with the synchronizer keys in the reverse and clutch hub assembly.
37. Install the lock ball and thrust washer on the rear of the fifth gear.
38. Install the snapring on the rear of the thrust washer. Check the clearance between the thrust washer and the snapring. If the clearance is not within 0.0039–0.0118 in., select the proper size thrust washer to bring the clearance within specifications.
39. Slide the first and second shift fork shaft assembly into the case (front rear of case). Secure the first and second shift fork shaft assembly into the case). Secure the first and second shift fork to the fork shaft with the roll pin. Be sure to use a new roll pin.
40. Insert the interlock pin into the transmission using the lockout pin replacer tool.
41. Shift transmission into fourth gear. Slide the third and

fourth shift fork shaft into the case, from rear of case. Secure the third and fourth shift fork to the fork shaft with the roll pin. Insert interlock pin. Be sure to use a new roll pin.

42. Shift synchronizer hub into fifth gear. Position reverse and fifth fork on the clutch hub and slide the reverse and fifth fork shaft into the case (from rear of case). Secure the reverse and fifth shift fork to the fork shaft with the roll pin. Be sure to use a new roll pin.

43. Install the two blind covers and gasket. Tighten the attaching bolts 23–34 ft. lbs.

44. Position the three detent balls and three springs into the case and install the spring cap bolts.

45. Apply a thin coat of Gasket Maker E2AZ-19562-A (ESE-M4G234-A2) or equivalent to the contacting surfaces of the center housing and transmission case.

46. Position the center housing on the case. Align the reverse idler gear shaft boss with the center housing attaching bolt boss. Install and tighten the idler shaft capscrew and tighten 41–59 ft. lbs.

47. Slide the counter fifth gear to the countershft.

48. Position the countershaft rear bearing on the countershaft. Press into positon using the Adjustable Press Frame T77J-7025-N and Forcing Screw T75L-7025-J or their equal.

49. Install the thrust washer and snapring to the rear of the countershaft rear bearing. Check the clearance between the thrust washer and the snapring using a feeler gauge.

50. If the clearance is not within 0.0000–0.0059 in., select the proper size thrust washer to bring the clearance within specifications, 0.0748, 0.0787, 0.0827, or 0.0866.

51. If installed, remove filler plugs. Position the mainshaft rear bearing on the mainshaft. Press into place using the adjustable Press Frame T77J-7025-N, Dummy Bearing T75L-7025-QI and Forcing Screw T75L-7025 or their equal.

52. Install the thrust washer and snapring to the rear of the mainshaft rear bearing. Check the clearance between the thrust washer and the snapring. The Clearance should be 0.0000–0.0039 in. If the clearance is not within specifications, replace the thrust washer to bring the clearance within specifications, 0.0787, 0.0846, or 0.0906.

53. Apply a thin coat of Gasket Maker E2AZ-19562-A (ESE-M4G234-A2) or equivalent to the contacting surfaces of the bearing housing and center housing.

54. Position the bearing housing on the center housing.

55. Install each shift fork shaft end onto the proper shift fork shaft. (Note the scribe marks made during disassembly) and secure with roll pins.

56. Install the lock ball. Speedometer drive gear and snapring onto the mainshaft.

57. If removed, install control lever and rod in extension housing.

58. Apply a thin coat of Gasket Maker E2AZ-19562-A (ESE-M4G234-A2) or equivalent to the contacting surfaces of the bearing housing and extension housing.

59. Position the extension housing in the bearing housing with the gearshift control lever end laid down to the left as far as it will go. Tighten the attaching bolts and nuts 60–80 ft. lbs. There are two longer outer bolts and one shorter center (bottom) bolt used.

60. If removed, insert the speedometer driven gear assembly to the extension housing and secure it with the bolt.

61. Check the ensure the gearshift control lever operates properly.

62. Install the transmission case cover gasket and cover with drain plug to the rear. Install and tighten the fourteen attaching bolts 23–34 ft. lbs.

63. Install the correct size shim on the second step of the front cover as determined by the mainshaft bearing clearance measurement.

64. Coat the front cover with Gasket Maker E2AZ-19562-A (ESE-M4G234-A2) or equivalent. Install the front cover to the transmission case and tighten the four bolts and four studs.

65. Install 3.0 pints of Ford Manual Transmission Lube D8DZ-19C547-A (ESP-M2C83-C) or equivalent. Reinstall the filler plugs and tighten 18–29 ft. lbs.

Ford Five Speed Overdrive (Diesel Engines)

Disassembly

1. If not already drained, remove the drain plug and drain the transmission fluid into a suitable container. Remove the fork and release bearing from the transmission case.

2. Install the transmission in Bench Mounted Holding Fix-

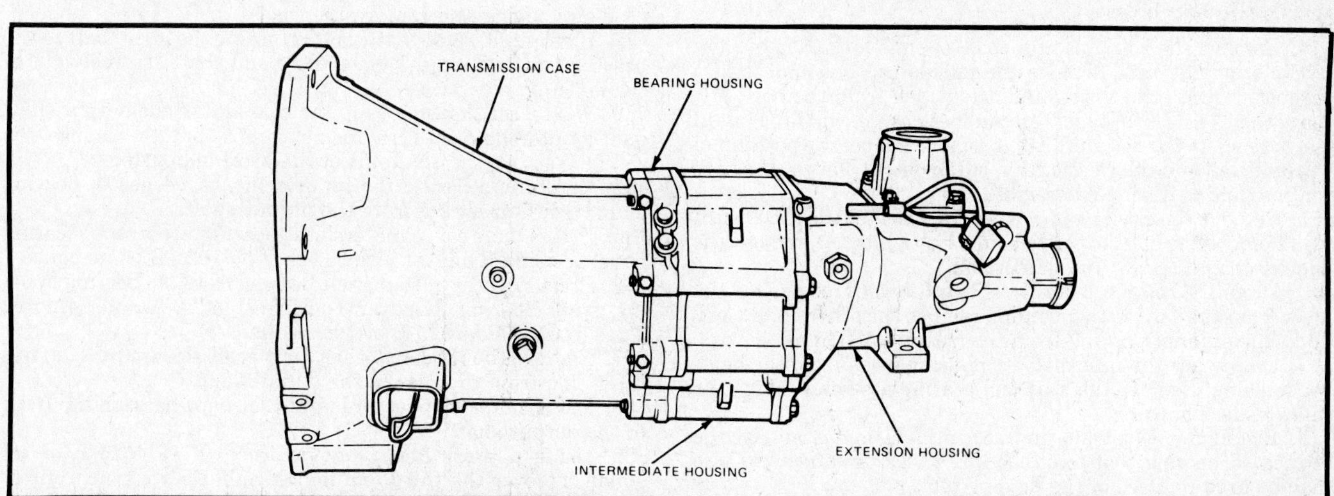

Five speed manual overdrive (diesel engine)

ture, T57L-500-B or its equal. Remove the six bolts attaching the front cover to the transmission case and remove the front cover, shim (located in cover) and gasket.

3. Remove the front cover oil seal using Inner Seal Removal Tool, T75P-3504-G and Impact Slide Hammer, T50T-100-A or their equal.

4. Remove the input shaft snapring.

5. If installed, remove the gearshift lever. Remove the four bolts and remove the retainer and gasket from the extension housing.

6. Remove the outer retaining ring on the input shaft bearing. Install Bearing Collet Tool, T75L-7025-E on the input shaft bearing and Remover Tube, T75L-7025-B and Forcing Screw T75L-7025-J or their equal. Slide Bearing Collet Sleeve, T75L-7025-G or its equal over the Remover Tube and Bearing Collet, and turn the forcing screw to remove the input shaft bearing.

7. Remove the bolt that attaches the control lever end to the control rod an remove the control lever end and rod from the extension housing.

8. Remove the eight bolts attaching the extension housing to the intermediate housing and transmission housing. Slide the extension housing off the output shaft with the control lever end laid down and to the left as far as to will go.

9. Remove the speedometer driven gear assembly from the extension housing.

10. Remove the back-up lamp switch and the neutral safety switch.

11. Remove the grommet from the end of the output shaft. Remove the snapring that secures the speedometer drive gear on the output shaft. Slide the speedometer drive gear off the output shaft and remove the lock ball.

12. Install Bearing Pusher Tool, T83T-7111-A or its equal over the countershaft front bearing. Turn the forcing screw to force the countershaft (together with the countershaft front bearing) from the transmission case. Remove the pusher tool assembly. The countershaft front bearing may remain in the transmission case. Remove the Bearing with a suitable driver.

13. Remove and discard the roll pin from the 1–2 shift fork. Remove the circlip from the rail. Remove the upper cap bolt and with a magnet, remove the spring and detent ball from the bore. Remove the 1–2 shift fork.

NOTE: Note the position of the 1–2 shift fork in relation to the 3–4 shift fork for positioning during reassembly. The shift forks and rails are not interchangeable. Check the position of the shift rail and the relationship of the detent slots to the bore for positioning during reassembly. The three detent slots in the shift rails face towards the cap bolts.

14. Remove the roll pin from the 3–4 shift fork. Remove the circlip from the rail. Remove the middle cap bolt and with a magnet, remove the spring and detent ball from the bore. Remove the 3–4 shift fork and rail. An inerlock pin will drop out of the bore when the 3–4 shift rail is removed. Note the position of the shift rail and the relationship of the detent slots to the bore for positioning during reassembly.

15. Remove the circlip and washer from the 5R (Reverse) shift rail. Remove the bottom cap bolt and with a magnet, remove the shorter length spring and detent ball.

16. Drive the roll pin from the 5R shift lever and remove the lever from the rail. With a magnet remove the other detent ball and shorter length spring from the bottom (5R) bore.

17. Gently pry the intermediate housing away from the bearing housing. Remove the gear and bearing assembly out of the intermediate housing.

18. Install the gear train and bearing housing assembly in a fabricated holding tool positioned in a vise. A soft jawed vise may be used in place of the holding tool.

19. Remove the bottom cap bolt and with a magnet, remove the shorter length spring and detent ball from the bore. Drive the roll pin out of the 5R shift fork and discard. Remove the 5R shift rail. An interlock pin will drop out of the bore when the 5R shift rail is removed.

NOTE: Note the position of the 5R shift fork in relation to the bearing housing for positioning during reassembly. Check the position of the shift rail and the relationship of the detent slots to the bore for positioning during reassembly. The three detent slots in the shift rail face towards the cap bolt.

20. Remove the retaining ring from the output shaft ball bearing. Remove the thrust washer.

21. To remove the output shaft rear bearing, place Shaft Protectors, D80L-625-2 and D80L-625-3 or their equal on the end of the output shaft. It may be necessary to hold the shaft protectors in place with putty. Install Puller, T77J-7025-H, Collet (2), T77J-7025-J or their equal against the bearing so the jaws of the puller are against the rear of the bearing. Place Tube (Long), T75L-7025-C or its equal over the output shaft. Install Forcing Screw, T75L-7025-J or its equal into the tube and turn the forcing screw clockwise to remove the bearing. Discard the bearing and install a new one during reassembly.

22. Remove the snapring from the countershaft rear bearing. Install Puller. T77J-7025-H, Collet (2), T77J-7025-J, Tube (Short, T77J-7025-B) and Forcing Screw, T75L-7025-J or their equal. Turn the forcing screw clockwise and remove the bearing. Discard the bearing and install a new one during reassembly.

23. Remove the retaining ring, thrust washer and lock ball from the output shaft.

24. Remove the fifth gear and sleeve from the countershaft. The collar of the fifth gear faces towards the bearing housing.

25. Remove the reverse gear from the countershaft. The collar of the counter/reverse gear faces towards the bearing housing.

26. Remove the fifth gear form the output shaft and remove the 5R sychronizer ring.

27. Straighten the peen on the locknut with Staking Tool, T77J-7025-F or its equal. Lock the transmission gears in reverse and any forward gear. Install Lock Nut Wrench T77J-7025-C or its equal on the locknut and remove the locknut and discard.

28. Remove the 5R synchronizer assembly from the output shaft.

29. Pry the reverse gear caged needle bearing. Sleeve and thurst washer from the output shaft.

30. Remove the snapring and remove the reverse idler gear from the idler shaft. Remove the keyed thrust washer from the shaft.

31. Remove the five bolts that attach the bearing cover to the bearing housing and remove the cover.

32. If required, remove the bolt retaining the idler shaft to the bearing housing and drive the plate and shaft assembly out of the housing.

33. With a soft hammer. tap the rear end of the output shaft and countershaft in turn, being careful not to damage the shafts. Remove the shafts form the bearing housing.

34. Carefully separate the input shaft, caged needle bearing and synchronizer ring from the output shaft.

35. Press the rear countershaft bearing from the bearing housing using Remover Tube Tool, T77J7025-B or its equal.

36. Press the rear output shaft bearing from the bearing housing using Bearing Remover Tool, T77F-4222-A and Remover Tube Tool, T77J-7025-B or their equal.

37. Remove the thrust washer, first gear, sleeve and synchronizer ring from the rear of the output shaft.

38. Using snapring pliers, remove the snapring from the front of the output shaft.

39. Using a press and Remover Tool, T71P-4621-B or its equal, remover the third and fourth hub, sleeve, synchronizer ring and third gear from the front of the output shaft.

40. Using a press and Remover Tool,T71P-4621-B or its equal,

remove the first and second hub and sleeve assembly synchronizer ring and second gear from the rear of the output shaft in the same manner as described in the previous step.

41. Press the front bearing from the countershaft using Remover Tool D79L-4621-A or T71P-4621-B and suitable press stock.

42. Inspect all parts.

Assembly

1. Assemble the 3–4 synchronizer assembly by installing the keys in the hub and sliding the sleeve over the hub and keys. Install the springs onto the hub.

NOTE: When installing the springs, the open end tab of the springs should be inserted into the hub holes. This will keep the spring tension on each key uniform.

2. Assemble the 1–2 synchronizer assembly in the same manner as described in Step 1. Assemble the 5R synchronizer assembly as also described in Step 1 and install the retaining ring in the 5R assembly.

3. Install the third gear and synchronizer ring onto the front section of the output shaft.

4. Install the 3–4 synchronizer assembly onto the output shaft by using a press. Hold the assembly together and slowly press in place. Make sure the three recesses in the synchronizer ring are aligned with the three keys in the synchronizer hub. Note the proper direction of the hub. The recesses in each synchronizer sleeve must face each other.

5. Fit the snapring on the output shaft.

6. Instll the second gear, synchronizer ring onto the rear section of the output shaft.

7. Install the 1–2 synchronizer assembly onto the output shaft by using a press. Hold the assembly together and slowly press in place. Make sure the three keys recesses in the synchronizer ring are aligned with the three keys in the synchronizer hub. Note the proper direction of the hub. The recesses in the synchronizer sleeve must face each other.

8. Install the synchronizer ring, first gear with sleeve and thrust washer onto the output shaft.

9. Install the input shaft and the needle roller bearing to the output shaft.

10. Check the countershaft rear bearing clearance. Measure the depth of the countershaft bearing bore in the bearing housing with a depth micrometer (D80P-4201-A or equivalent). Install the retaining ring on the bearing and with a depth micrometer measure the distance betwen the inside edge of the ring and the end of the bearing. The difference between the two measurements indicates the required thickness of the adjusting shim. The clearance should be less than 0.0039 in. The adjusting shims are available in 0.0039 in. and 0.0118 in. sizes.

11. Check the output shaft bearing clearance. Measure the depth of the bearing bore with a depth micrometer. Measure the width of the bearing with a micrometer. The difference between the two measurements indicates the required thickness of the adjusting shim. The clearance should be less than 0.0039 in. Adjusting shims are available in 0.0039 in. and 0.0118 in. sizes.

12. Position the proper shim on the countershaft rear bearing and press into the bearing housing using Installer Tool, T77J-7025-B or its equal.

13. Position the proper shim on the output shaft bearing and press the bearing into the bearing housing using Installer Tool, T77J-7025-K or its equal.

14. Position the front bearing on the countershaft and press the bearing into place using Bearing Replacer Tool, T71P-7025-A or its equal.

15. Mesh the countershaft and the output shaft assembly and position the two in the bearing housing. Make sure that the thrust washer is installed on the mainshaft assembly at the rear of the first gear. Make sure that the recesses in the synchronizer ring are aligned with the three keys in the synchronizer hub.

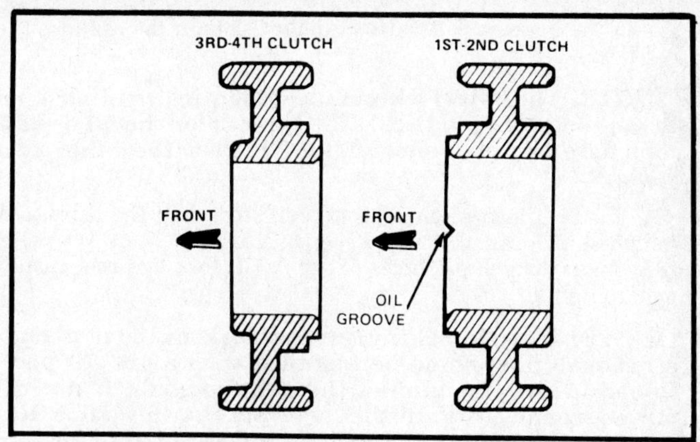

Synchronizer hub installation

16. While holding the mainshaft assembly in place, press the countershaft assembly into the bearing housing using Replacer Tool T71P-7025-A or its equal to hold the rear countershaft bearing in the housing.

17. Position the bearing cover on the bearing housing. Install the five bolts and tighten.

18. If removed, drive the reverse idler shaft into the bearing housing. Install the bolt and tighten.

19. Install the thrust washer, sleeve, caged needle bearing and reverse gear on the output shaft.

20. Install the reverse gear on the countershaft. The offset on the gear must face the bearing housing.

21. Place the keyed thrust washer so the tab is in the groove in the bearing housing. Install the reverse idler gear so the squared portion of the gear faces the bearing housing. Make sure the reverse idler gear and reverse gear are in mesh. Install the spacer and snapring on the idler shaft.

22. Install the 5R synchronizer assembly on the output shaft.

23. Lock the transmission in Reverse and any forward gear. Install a new locknuton the output shaft and tighten 94 to 152 ft. lbs. using Locknut Wrench, T77J-7025-C or its equal.

24. Bend the tab on the locknut with Staking Tool, T77J-7025-F or its equal.

25. Install the 5R synchronizer ring and gear on the output shaft. Make sure the three recesses in the synchronizer ring are aligned with the three keys in the synchronizer hub.

26. Install the sleeve and the counter fifth gear on the countershaft.

27. Install the lock ball in the output shaft and position the thrust washer so the slot in the washer is over the lock ball. Install the retaining ring.

28. Position the output shaft assembly in a press and press the output shaft bearing on the shaft using Dummy Bearing Replacer, T75L-7025-Q or its equal and an appropriate length of press stock. Install the thrust washer and retaining ring.

29. Position the countershaft in a press and press the countershaft rear bearing on the shaft using Dummy Bearing Replacer, T75L-7025-Q or its equal and an appropriate length of press stock. Install the thrust washer and retaining ring.

30. Position all synchronizers in the neutral position. Install the shorter length spring and detent ball in the bottom (5R) bore. Compress the ball and spring with Dummy Shift Rail Tools, T72J-7280 or its equal and install the dummy shift rail in the bore. Install the 5R shift rail in the bottom bore and make sure the three detent slots in the rail face the cap bolt and the interlock slot in the 5R rail baces towards the 1–2 bore. Install the interlock pin through the top bore so it is positioned in the channel between the 5R rail bore and 3–4 rail bore. Install the 3–4 rail in the housing and make sure the three detent slots in the rail face the middle bore. Insert the interlock pin in the channel the 3–4 rail and the 1–2 rail bore. Install the 1–2 shift

rail in the housing so the three detent slots in the rail face the top bore.

NOTE: The interlock pins are identical and all four detent balls are identical. The springs for the 5R or bottom bore are of a shorter length than the other two springs.

31. Install the first and second shift fork and the third and fourth shift forks to their respective sleeves.
32. Align the roll pin holes of each shift fork and rod. Install new roll pins.

NOTE: When installing the shift fork and control end, a new roll pin should be installed with a pin slit positioned in the direction of the shift rod axis. If not removed, remove the shift levers from the shift rails. Remember from which rail each lever was removed for correct installation upon assembly.

33. Install the detent balls and springs into their respective bores and install the three cap bolts. The shorter length spring is installed in the bottom (reverse) bore.
34. Install the circlips on the 1–2 and 3–4 shift rails. Install the circlip and washer on the 5R shift rail.
35. Apply a thin coating of Silicone Sealer D6AZ-19562-B or equivalent to the mating surfaces of the transmission case and the bearing housing. Install the transmission case on the bearing housing.
36. Apply a thin coating of Silicone Sealer, D6AZ-19562-B or equivalent to the mating surfaces of the bearing housing and intermediate housing. Install the intermediate housing to the bearing housing.
37. Position the shift lever gates on the appropriate shift rails. Install new roll pins.
38. Place the lock ball in the output shaft and position the speedometer drive gear over the ball. Install the snapring. Install the grommet on the end of the output shaft.
39. Apply a thin coating of Silicone Sealer, D6AZ-19562-B or equivalent to the extension housing and the intermediate housing. Slide the extension housing over the output shaft (the control lever must be moved to the far left) and onto the extension housing. Install the bolts and tighten.

NOTE: If necessary, remove the plugs from the transmission case shift rod bores to align the shift rods. After the installation of the bearing housing assembly, reinstall the plugs using Silicone Sealer, D6AZ-19562-B or equivalent.

40. With the outer snapring in place on the input shaft front bearing, place the bearing, shim and Adapter Tool, T75L-7025-N or its equal over the input shaft.
41. Thread the Replacer Shaft, T75L-7025-K or its equal onto the Adapter Tool. Install the Replacer Tube, T75L-7025-B or its equal over the Replacer Shaft and install the nut and washer on the forcing screw.
42. Slowly tighten the nut until the adapter is securely on the input shaft. Make sure the tools are aligned.
43. Tighten the nut on the forcing screw until the bearing outer snapring is seated. Remove the installation tools.

NOTE: The input shaft bearing retaining ring must be flush with the transmission case. If not flush, it will be necessary to tap on the end of the input shaft with a soft hammer until the bearing is seated.

44. Install the input shaft snapring.
45. Measure the distance between the end of the installed input bearing in the transmission case with a depth micrometer. Measure the distance between the bearing cover gasket and the bottom of the bearing bore in the cover. The difference between the two measurements is the clearance between the outer bearing race and the front cover. The clearance should be less than 0.0039 in.. Clearance can be adjusted by installing an adjusting shim. Shims are available in sizes of 0.006 in. and 0.012 in..
46. Install a new oil seal in the front cover using Installer Tool, T71P-7025-A. Install the shim in the recess in the front cover.
47. Apply gear lubricant to the lip of the oil seal inside the front cover and install the front cover to the transmission case. Install the six bolts and tighten.
48. Install the control lever end to the control lever and tighten the attaching bolt 20–25 ft. lbs.
49. Install the back-up lamp switch and the neutral safety switch to the extension housing and tighten the switches 20–25 ft. lbs.
50. Install the gearshift lever retainer and gasket to the extension housing. Install the four bolts and tighten 20–27 ft. lbs. If required, install the gearshift lever.
51. Install the release bearing and fork.

Muncie Model SM330 Three Speed (83MM)

The G.M. Corporation Model SM 330 (83MM) (Muncie) is a three speed transmission using helical constant mesh gears. The engagement of all gears except reverse is assisted by synchronizers.

TRANSMISSION UNIT

Disassembly

1. Remove side cover and shift forks.
2. Unbolt extension and rotate to line up groove in extension flange with reverse idler shaft. Drive reverse idler shaft and key out of case with a brass drift.
3. Move second/third synchronizer sleeve forward. Remove extension housing and mainshaft assembly.
4. Remove reverse idler gear from case.
5. Remove third speed blocker ring from clutch gear.
6. Expand snapring which holds mainshaft rear bearing. Tap gently on end of mainshaft to remove extension.

GENERAL DATA

Type	3-Speed
Synchromesh gears	1st, 2nd, and 3rd
Model	SM330 (83MM)
Gear ratios	
1st speed	3.03:1
2nd speed	1.75:1
3rd speed	1.00:1
Reverse	3.02:1

7. Remove clutch gear bearing retainer and gasket.
8. Remove snapring. Remove clutch gear from inside case by gently tapping on end of clutch gear.
9. Remove oil slinger and 16 mainshaft pilot bearings from clutch gear cavity.
10. Slip clutch gear bearing out front of case. Aid removal with a screwdriver between case and bearing outer snapring.
11. Drive countershaft and key out to rear.
12. Remove countergear and two tanged thrust washers.

MAINSHAFT

Disassembly

1. Remove speedometer drive gear. Some speedometer drive gears, made of metal, must be pulled off.
2. Remove rear bearing snapring.
3. Support reverse gear. Press on rear of mainshaft to remove reverse gear, thrust washer and rear bearing. Be careful not to cock the bearing on the shaft.
4. Remove first and reverse sliding clutch hub snapring.
5. Support first gear. Press on rear of mainshaft to remove clutch assembly, blocker ring and first gear.
6. Remove second and third speed sliding clutch hub snapring.
7. Support second gear. Press on front of mainshaft to remove clutch assembly, second speed blocker ring and second gear from shaft.

CLEANING AND INSPECTION

For more detailed information, see the "Cleaning and Inspection" instructions at front of transmission section.
1. Wash all parts in solvent.
2. Air dry.

CLUTCH KEYS AND SPRINGS

Replacement

Keys and springs may be replaced if worn or broken, but the hubs and sleeves must be kept together as originally assembled.
1. Mark hub and sleeve for reassembly.
2. Push hub from sleeve. Remove keys and springs.
3. Place three keys and two springs, one on each side of hub, so all three keys are engaged by both springs. The tanged end of the springs should not be installed into the same key.
4. Slide the sleeve onto the hub, aligning the marks.

EXTENSION OIL SEAL AND BUSHING

Replacement

1. Remove seal.
2. Using bushing remover and installer, or other suitable tool, drive bushing into extension housing.
3. Drive new bushing in from rear. Lubricate inside of bushing and seal. Install new oil seal with extension seal installer or suitable tool.

CLUTCH BEARING RETAINER OIL SEAL

Replacement

1. Pry old seal out.
2. Install new seal using seal installer or suitable tool. Seat seal in bore.

MAINSHAFT

Assembly

1. Lift front of mainshaft.
2. Install second gear with clutching teeth up; the rear face of the gear butts against the mainshaft flange.
3. Install a blocking ring with clutching teeth downward. All three blocking rings are the same.
4. Install second and third synchronizer assembly with fork slot down. Press it onto mainshaft splines. Both synchronizer assemblies are identical but are assembled differently. The second/third speed hub and sleeve is assembled with the sleeve fork slot toward the thrust face of the hub; the first-reverse hub and sleeve, with the fork slot opposite the thrust face. Be sure that the blocker ring notches align with the synchronizer assembly keys.

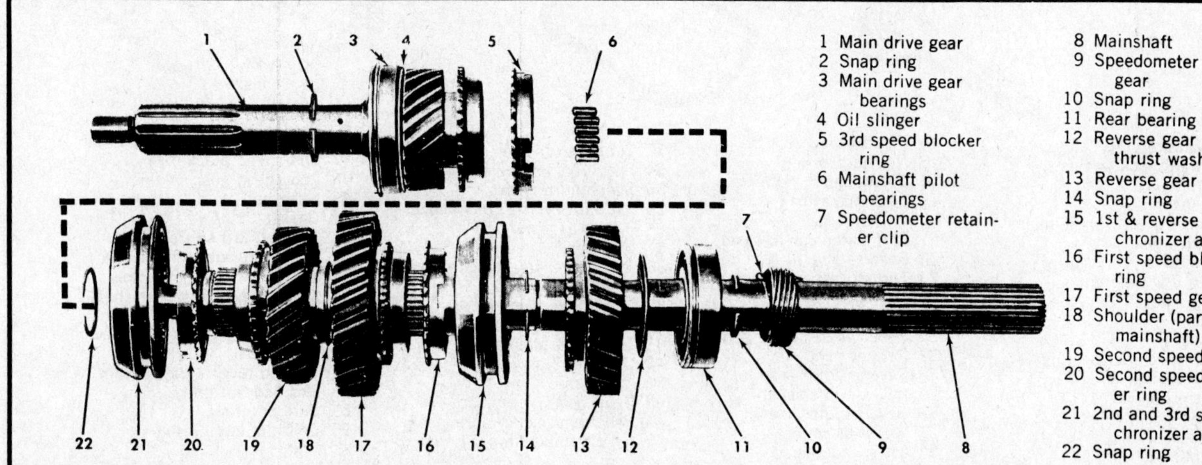

Main drive gear and mainshaft assembly

5. Install synchronizer snapring. Both synchronizer snaprings are the same.
6. Turn rear of shaft up.
7. Install first gear with clutching teeth upward; the front face of the gear butts against the flange on the mainshaft.
8. Install a blocker ring with clutching teeth down.
9. Install first and reverse synchronizer assembly with fork slot down. Press it onto mainshaft splines. Be sure blocker ring notches align with synchronizer assembly keys and synchronizer sleeves face front of mainshaft.
10. Install snapring.
11. Install reverse gear with clutching teeth down.
12. Install steel reverse gear thrust washer with flats aligned.
13. Press rear ball bearing onto shaft with snapring slot down.
14. Install snapring.
15. Install speedometer drive gear and retaining clip.

TRANSMISSION UNIT

Assembly

1. Place a row of 29 roller bearings, a bearing washer, a second row of 29 bearings and a second bearing washer at each end of the countergear. Hold in place with grease.
2. Place countergear assembly through rear case opening with a tanged thrust washer, tang away from gear, at each end. Install countershaft and key from rear of case. Be sure that thrust washer tangs are aligned with notches in case.
3. Place reverse idler gear in case. Do not install reverse idler shaft yet. The reverse idler gear bushing may not be replaced separately, it must be replaced as a unit.
4. Expand snapring in extension. Assemble extension over mainshaft and onto rear bearing. Seat snapring.
5. Load 16 mainshaft pilot bearings into clutch gear cavity.

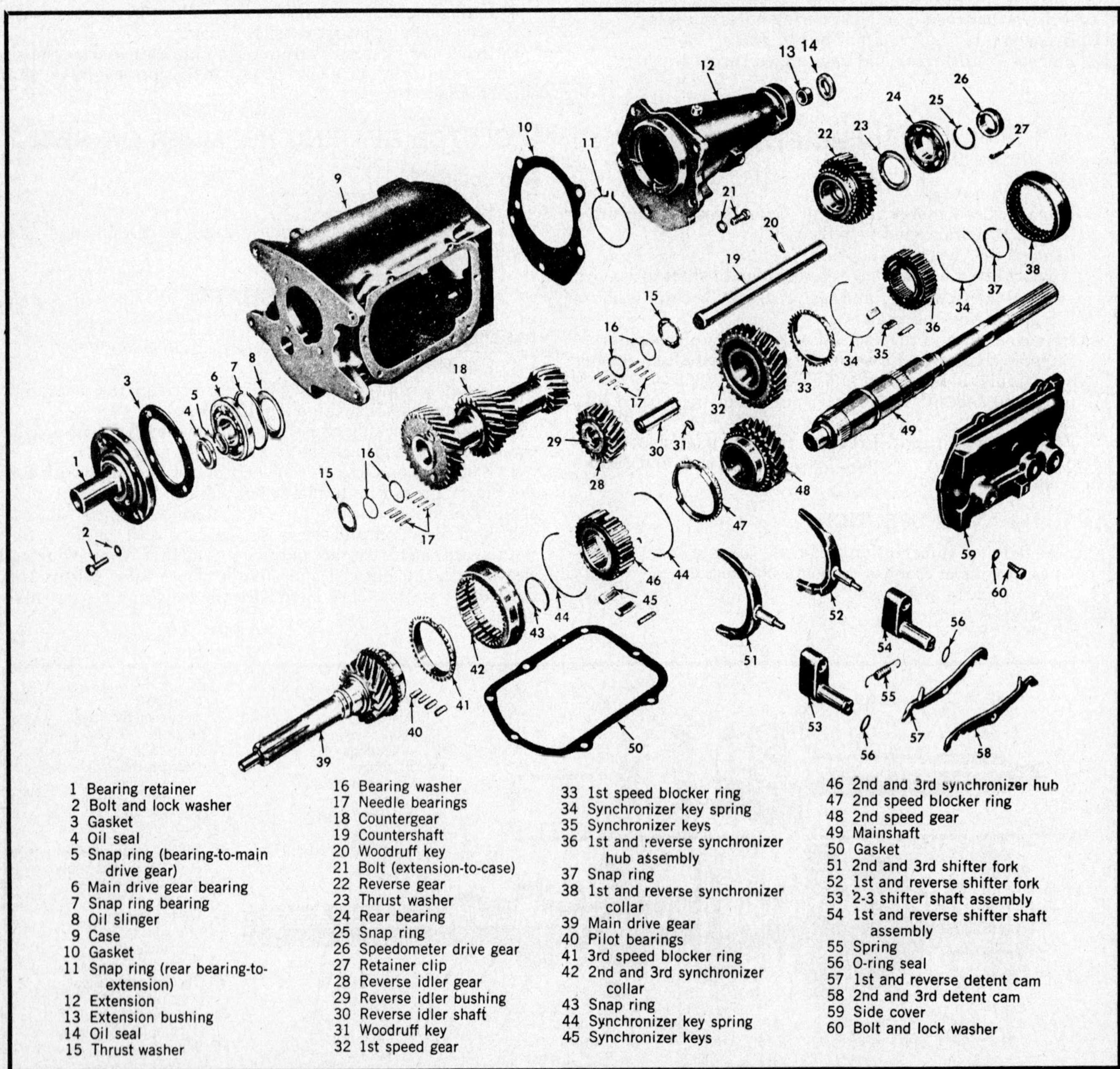

SM330 transmission components

Assemble third speed blocker ring onto clutch gear clutching surface with teeth toward gear.

6. Place clutch gear assembly, without front bearing, over front of mainshaft. Make sure that blocker ring notches align with keys in second/third synchronizer assembly.

7. Stick gasket onto extension housing with grease. Assemble clutch gear, mainshaft and extension to case together. Make sure that clutch gear teeth engage teeth of countergear anti-lash plate.

8. Rotate extension housing. Install reverse idler shaft and key.

9. Torque extension bolts to 45 ft. lbs.

10. Install oil slinger with inner lip facing forward. Install front bearing outer snapring and slide bearing into case bore.

11. Install snapring to clutch gear stem. Install bearing retainer and gasket and torque to 20 ft. lbs. Retainer oil return hole must be at 6 o'clock.

12. Shift both synchronizer sleeves to neutral positions. Install side cover, inserting shifter forks in synchronizer sleeve grooves.

13. Torque side cover bolts to 20 ft. lbs.

TORQUE SPECIFICATIONS Muncie-83MM

	ft. lbs.
Extension to case attaching	45
Drain plug	30
Filler plug	15
Side cover attaching bolts	22
Main drive gear retainer bolts	22
Transmission case to clutch housing bolts	45

Muncie Model SM465 Four Speed (117mm)

Muncie model CH-465-SM-465 transmission is a four speed transmission using helical gears. The action of all gears except reverse is aided by synchronizers.

TRANSMISSION UNIT

Disassembly

1. Remove transmission cover assembly. Move reverse shifter fork so that reverse idler gear is partially engaged before attempting to remove cover. Forks must be positioned so rear edge of the slot in the reverse fork is in line with the front edge of the slot in the forward forks as viewed through tower opening.

2. Lock transmission into two gears. Remove the universal joint flange nut, universal joint front flange and brake drum assembly.

NOTE: On 4-wheel drive models, use a special tool to remove mainshaft rear lock nut.

3. Remove parking brake and brake flange plate assembly on those vehicles having a driveshaft parking brake.
4. Remove rear bearing retainer and gasket.
5. Slide speedometer drive gear off mainshaft.
6. Remove clutch gear bearing retainers and gasket.
7. Remove countergear front bearing cap and gasket.
8. Using a prybar, pry off countershaft front bearing.
9. Remove countergear rear bearing snaprings from shaft and bearing. Using special tool, remove countergear rear bearings.
10. Remove clutch gear bearing outer race to case retaining ring.
11. Remove clutch gear and bearing by tapping gently on bottom side of clutch gear shaft and prying directly opposite against the case and bearing snapring groove at the same time. Remove fourth gear synchronizer ring. Index cut out section of clutch gear in down position with countergear to obtain clearance for removing clutch gear.
12. Remove rear mainshaft bearing snapring and, using special tools, remove bearing from case. Slide 1st speed gear thrust washer off mainshaft.
13. Lift mainshaft assembly from case. Remove synchronizer cone from shaft.
14. Slide reverse idler gear rearward and move countergear rearward, then lift to remove from case.
15. To remove reverse idler gear, drive reverse idler gear shaft out of case from front to rear using a drift. Remove reverse idler gear from case.

SUBASSEMBLIES TRANSMISSION COVER

Disassembly

1. Remove shifter fork retaining pins and drive out expansion plugs. The third and fourth shifter fork must be removed before the reverse shifter head pin can be removed.
2. With shifter shafts in neutral position, remove shafts. Care should be taken when removing the detent balls and springs since removal of the shifter shafts will cause these parts to be forcibly ejected.
3. Remove retaining pin and drive out reverse shifter shaft.

Assembly

1. In reassembling the cover, care should be taken to install the shifter shafts in order, reverse, 3rd/4th and 1st/2nd.
2. Place fork detent ball springs and balls in cover.
3. Start shifter shafts into cover and, while depressing the detent balls, push the shafts over the balls. Push reverse shaft through the yoke.
4. With the 3rd–4th shaft in neutral, line up the retaining holes in the fork and shaft. Detent balls should line up with detents in shaft.
5. After 1st and 2nd fork is installed, place two innerlock balls between the low speed shifter shaft and the high speed shifter shaft in the crossbore of the front support boss. Grease the interlock pin and insert it in the 3rd/4th shifter shaft hole. Continue pushing this shaft through cover bore and fork until retainer hole in fork lines up with hole in shaft.
6. Place two interlock balls in crossbore in front support boss between reverse and 3rd and 4th shifter shaft. Then push remaining shaft through fork and cover bore, keeping both balls in position between shafts until retaining holes line up in fork and shaft. Install retaining pin.
7. Install 1st/2nd fork and reverse fork retaining pins. Install new shifter shaft hole expansion plugs.

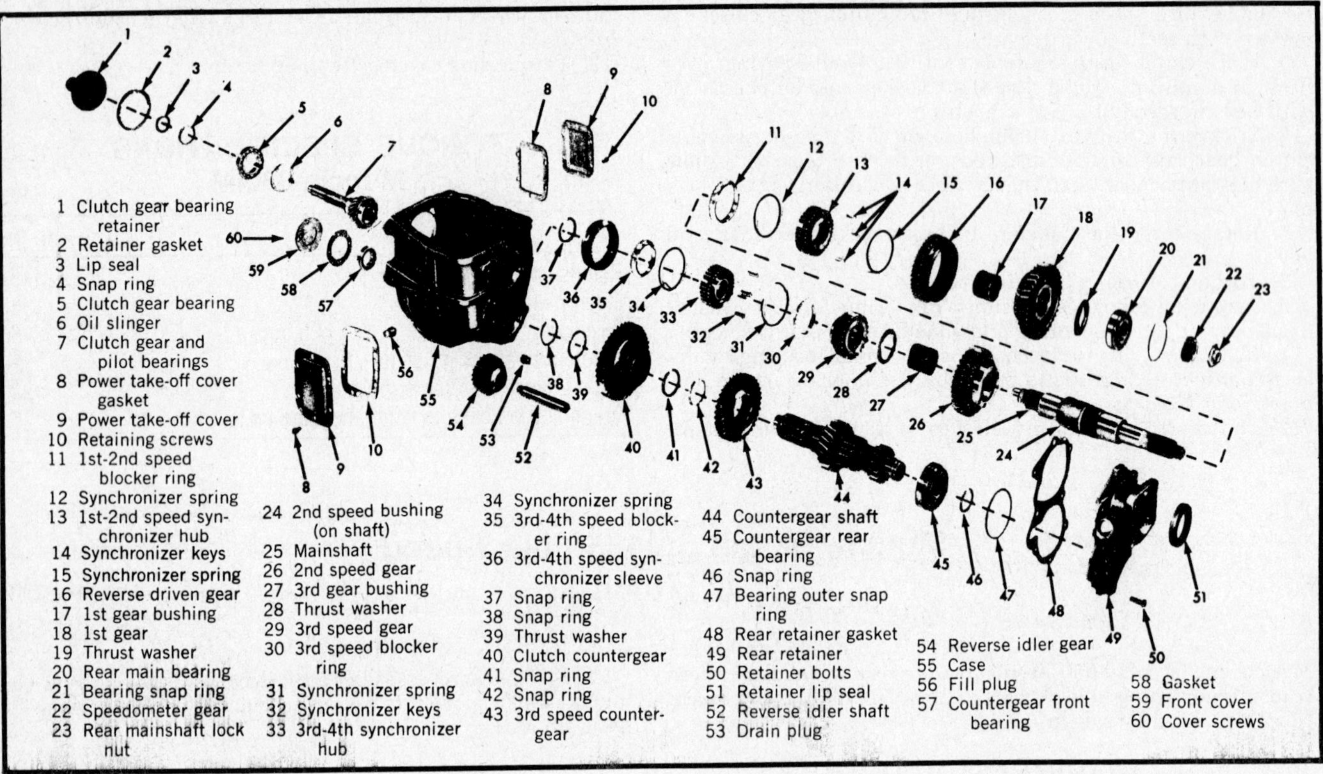

Transmission components

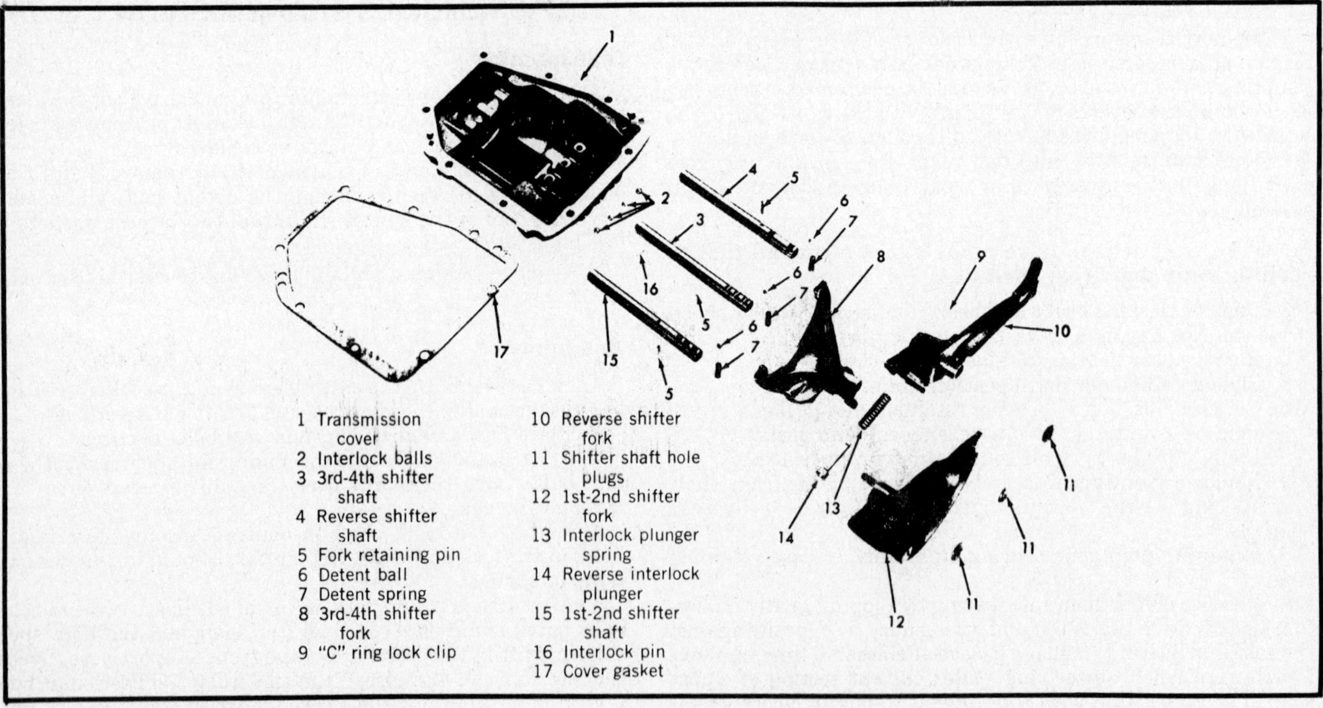

Shift cover assembly components

CLUTCH GEAR AND SHAFT

Disassembly

1. Remove mainshaft pilot bearing rollers from clutch gear if not already removed and remove roller retainer. Do not remove snapring on inside of clutch gear.
2. Remove snapring securing bearing on steam of clutch gear.
3. To remove bearing, position a special tool to the bearing and, with an arbor press, press gear and shaft out of bearing.

Assembly

1. Press bearing and new oil slinger onto clutch gear shaft using a special tool. Slinger should be located flush with bearing shoulder on clutch gear. Be careful not to distort oil slinger.
2. Install bearing snapring on clutch gear shaft.
3. Install bearing retainer ring in groove on O.D. of bearing. The bearing must turn freely on the shaft.
4. Install snapring on I.D. of mainshaft pilot bearing bore in clutch gear.
5. Lightly grease bearing surface in shaft recess, install transmission mainshaft pilot roller bearings and install roller bearing retainer. This roller bearing retainer holds bearings in position and, in final transmission assembly, is pushed forward into recess by mainshaft pilot.

BEARING RETAINER OIL SEAL

Replacement

1. Remove retainer and oil seal assembly and gasket.
2. Pry out oil seal.
3. Install new seal with lip of seal toward flange of tool.
4. Support front surface of retainer in press and drive seal into retainer.
5. Install retainer and gasket on case.

MAINSHAFT

Disassembly

1. Remove first speed gear.
2. Remove reverse driven gear.
3. Press behind second speed gear to remove 3rd/4th synchronizer assembly, 3rd speed gear and 2nd speed gear along with 3rd speed gear bushing and thrust washer.
4. Remove 2nd speed synchronizer ring and keys.
5. Using a press, remove 1st speed gear bushing and 2nd speed synchronizer hub.
6. Without damaging the mainshaft, chisel out the 2nd speed gear bushing.

Inspection

Wash all parts in cleaning solvent and inspect them for excessive wear or scoring.

NOTE: Third and fourth speed clutch sleeve should slide freely on clutch hub but clutch hub should fit snugly on shaft splines. Third speed gear must be running fit on mainshaft bushing and mainshaft bushing should be press fit on shaft. First and reverse sliding gear must be sliding fit on synchronizer hub and must not have excessive radial or circumferential play. If sliding gear is not free on hub, inspect for burrs which may have rolled up on front end of half tooth internal splines and remove by honing as necessary.

Assembly

1. Lubricate with E.P. oil and press onto mainshaft. 1st, 2nd and 3rd speed gear bushings are sintered iron, exercise care when installing.
2. Press 1st and 2nd speed synchronizer hub onto mainshaft with annulus toward rear of shaft.
3. Install 1st and 2nd synchronizer keys and springs.
4. Press 1st speed gear bushing onto mainshaft until it bottoms against hub. Lubricate all bushings with E.P. oil before installation of gears.
5. Install synchronizer blocker ring and 2nd speed gear onto mainshaft and against synchronize hub. Align synchronizer key slots with keys in synchronizer hub.
6. Install 3rd speed gear thrust washer onto mainshaft inserting washer tang in slotted shaft. Then press 3rd speed gear bushing onto mainshaft against thrust washer.
7. Install 3rd speed gear and synchronizer blocker ring against 3rd speed gear thrust washer.
8. Align synchronizer key ring slots with synchronizer assembly keys and drive 3rd and 4th synchronizer assembly onto mainshaft. Secure assembly with snapring.
9. Install reverse driven gear with fork groove toward rear.
10. Install 1st speed gear against 1st and 2nd synchronizer hub. Install 1st speed gear thrust washer.

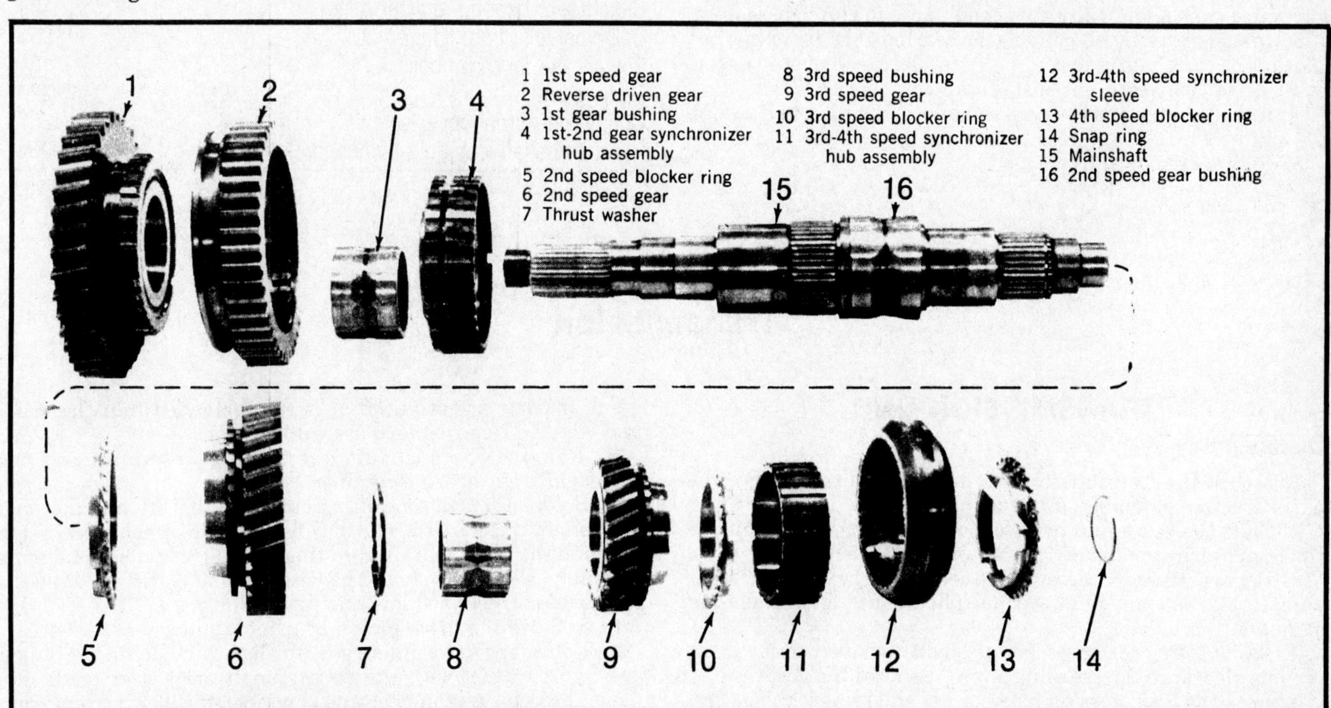

Mainshaft assembly

COUNTERSHAFT

Disassembly

1. Remove front countergear retaining ring and thrust washer. Do not re-use this snapring or any others.
2. Press countershaft out of clutch countergear assembly.
3. Remove clutch countergear and 3rd speed countergear retaining rings.
4. Press shift from 3rd speed countergear.

Assembly

1. Press the 3rd speed countergear onto the shaft. Install gear with marked surface toward front of shaft.
2. Using snapring pliers, install new 3rd speed countergear retaining ring.
3. Install new clutch countergear rear retaining ring. Do not over stress snapring. Ring should fit tightly in groove with no side play.
4. Press countergear onto shaft against snapring.
5. Install clutch countergear thrust washer and front retaining ring.

TRANSMISSION UNIT

Assembly

1. Lower the countergear into the case.
2. Place reverse idler gear in transmission case with gear teeth toward the front. Install idler gear shaft from rear to front, being careful to have slot in end of shaft facing down and flush with case.
3. Install mainshaft assembly into case with rear of shaft protruding out rear bearing hole in case. Rotate case onto front end. Install 1st speed gear thrust washer on shaft, if not previously installed.
4. Install snapring on bearing O.D. and place rear mainshaft bearing on shaft. Drive bearing onto shaft and into case.
5. Install synchronizer cone on mainshaft and slide rearward to clutch hub. Make sure three cut out sections of 4th speed synchronizer cone align with three clutch keys in clutch assembly.
6. Install snapring on clutch gear bearing O.D. Index cut out portion of clutch gear teeth to obtain clearance over countershaft drive gear teeth and install into case.
7. Install clutch gear bearing retainer and gasket and torque 15–18 ft. lbs.
8. Rotate case onto front end.
9. Install snapring on countergear rear bearing O.D. and drive bearing into place. Install snapring on countershaft at rear bearing.
10. Tap countergear front bearing assembly into case.
11. Install countergear front bearing cap and new gasket and torque 20–30 inch lbs.
12. Slide speedometer drive gear over mainshaft to bearing.
13. Install rear bearing retainer with new gasket. Be sure snapring ends are in lube slot and cut out in bearing retainer. Install bolts and tighten 15–18 ft. lbs. Install brake backing plate assembly on those models having driveshaft brake.

NOTE: On models equipped with 4-wheel drive, install rear lock nut and washer and torque to 120 ft. lbs. and bend washer tangs to fit slots in nut.

14. Install parking brake drum and/or universal joint flange. Lightly oil seal surface.
15. Lock transmission in two gears at once. Install universal joint flange locknut and tighten 90–120 ft. lbs.
16. Move all transmission gears to neutral except the reverse idler gear which should be engaged approximately $^3/_8$ in. (leading edge of reverse idler gear taper lines up with the front edge of the 1st speed gear). Install cover assembly and gasket. Shifting forks must slide into their proper positions on clutch sleeves and reverse idler gear. Forks must be positioned as in removal.
17. Install cover attaching bolts and gearshift lever and check operation of transmission.

TORQUE SPECIFICATIONS
Muncie-117MM

	ft. lbs.
Rear bearing retainer	18
Cover bolts	25
Filler plug	35
Drain plug	35
Clutch gear bearing retainer bolts	18
Universal joint front flange nut	95
Power take off cover bolts	18
Parking brake	22
Countergear front cover screws	25
Rear mainshaft lock nut (4 wheel drive models)	95

New Process 435 Four Speed Transmission

TRANSMISSION UNIT

Disassembly

1. Mount the transmission in a holding fixture. Remove the parking brake assembly, if one is installed.
2. Shift the gears into neutral by replacing the gear shift lever temporarily, or by using a bar or a suitable tool.
3. Remove the cover screws, the second screw from the front on each side is shouldered with a split washer for installation alignment.
4. While lifting the cover, rotate slightly counterclockwise to provide clearance for the shift levers. Remove the cover.
5. Lock the transmission in two gears and remove the output flange nut, the yoke and the parking brake drum as a unit assembly. The drum and yoke are balanced and unless replacement of parts are required, it is recommended that the drum and yoke be removed as a assembly.
6. Remove the speedometer drive gear pinion and the mainshaft rear bearing retainer.
7. Before removal and disassembly of the drive pinion and mainshaft, measure the end play between the synchronizer stop ring and the third gear. Record this reading for reference during assembly. Clearance should be within 0.050–0.070 in.. If necessary, add corrective shims during assembly.
8. Remove the drive pinion bearing retainer.
9. Rotate the drive pinion gear to align the space in the pinion gear clutch teeth with the countershaft drive gear teeth. Remove the drive pinion gear and the tapered roller bearing from the transmission by pulling on the pinion shaft and rapping the face of the case lightly with a brass hammer.

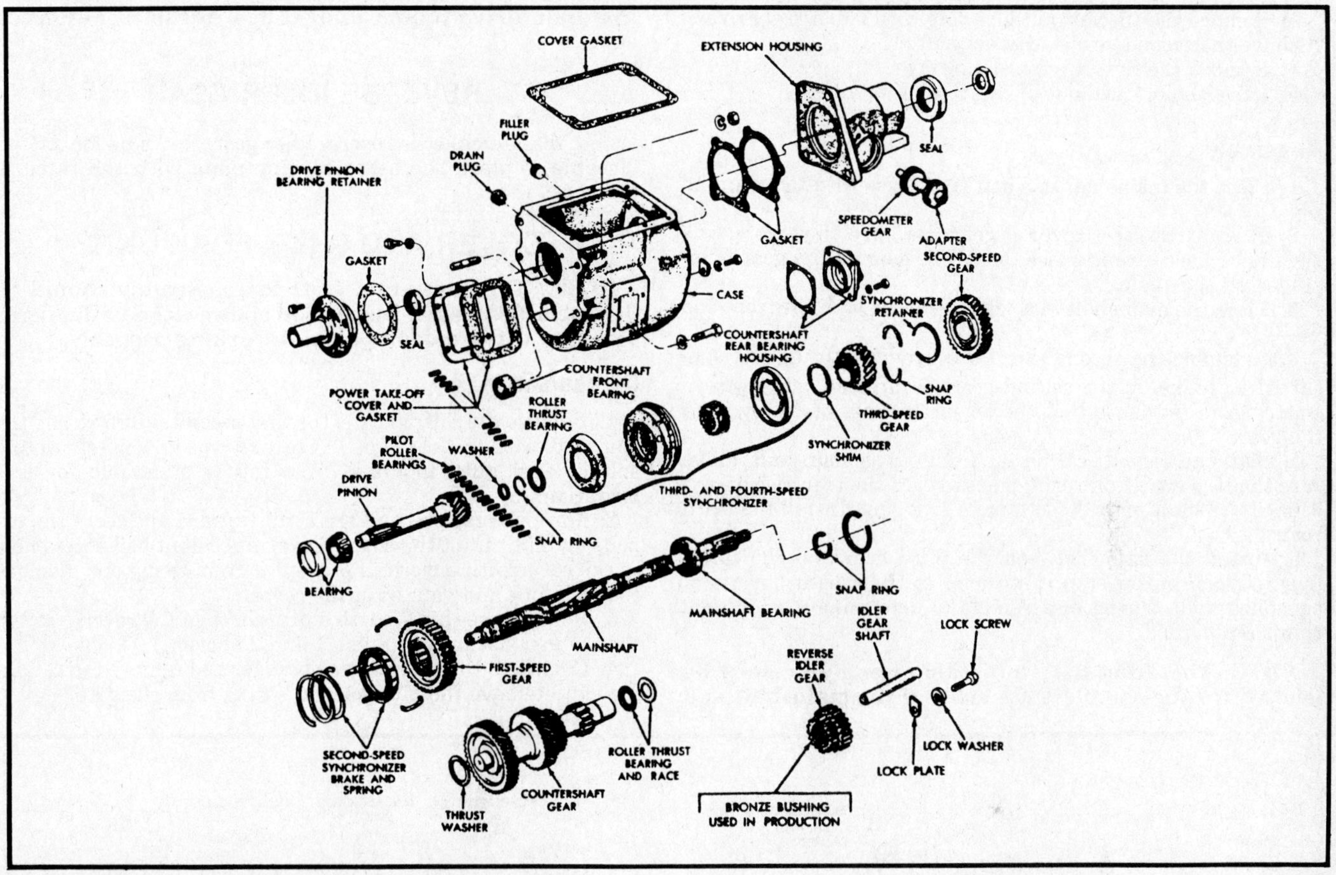

Exploded view of NP435 transmission

10. Remove the snapring, washer and the pilot roller bearings from the recess in the drive pinion gear.
11. Place a brass drift in the front center of the mainshaft and drive the shaft rearward.
12. When the mainshaft rear bearing has cleared the case, remove the rear bearing and the speedometer drive gear with a suitable gear puller.
13. Move the mainshaft assembly to the rear of the case and tilt the front of the mainshaft upward.
14. Remove the roller type thrust washer.
15. Remove the synchronizer and stop rings separately.
16. Remove the mainshaft assembly.
17. Remove the reverse idler lock screw and lock plate.
18. Using a brass drift held at an angle, drive the idler shaft to the rear while pulling.
19. Lift the reverse idler gear out of the case. If the countershaft gear does not show signs of excessive side play or end play and the teeth are not badly worn or chipped, it may not be necessary to replace the countershaft gear.
20. Remove the bearing retainer at the rear end of the countershaft. The bearing assembly will remain with the retainer.
21. Tilt the cluster gear assembly and work it out of the transmission case.
22. Remove the front bearings from the case with a suitable driver.

SUBASSEMBLIES MAINSHAFT

Disassembly

1. Remove the clutch gear snapring.
2. Remove the clutch gear, the synchronizer outer stop ring to third gear shim and the third gear.

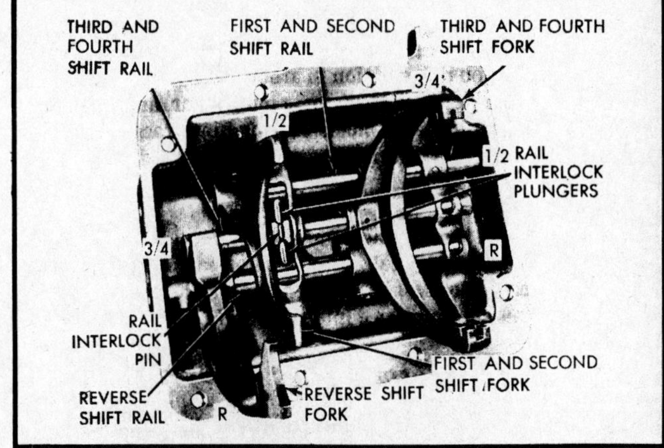

NP435 cover and shift fork assembly

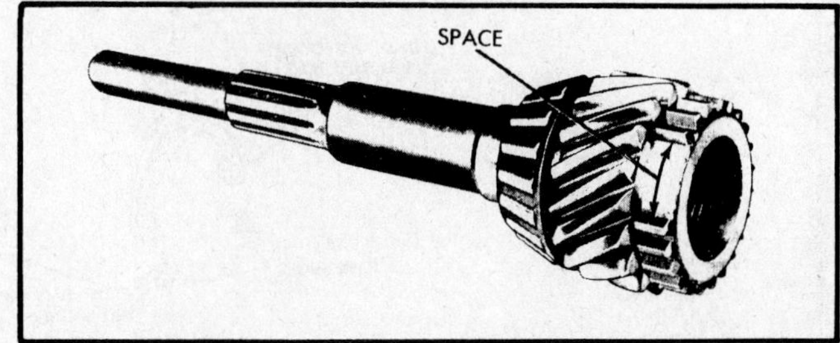

NP435 drive pinion gear showing teeth removal

3. Remove the special split lock ring with two screw drivers. Remove the second gear and synchronizer.
4. Remove the first/reverse sliding gear.
5. Drive the old seal out of the bearing retainer.

Assembly

1. Place the mainshaft in a soft jawed vise with the rear end up.
2. Install the first/reverse gear. Be sure the two spline springs, if used, are in place inside the gear as the gear is installed on the shaft.
3. Place the mainshaft in a soft jawed vise with the front end up.
4. Assemble the second speed synchronizer spring and synchronizer brake on the second gear. Secure the brake with a snapring making sure that the snapring tangs are away from the gear.
5. Slide the second gear on the front of the mainshaft. Make sure that the synchronizer brake is toward the rear. Secure the gear to the shaft with the two piece lock ring. Install the third gear.
6. Install the shim between the third gear and the third/fourth synchronizer stop ring. Refer to the measurements of end play made during disassembly to determine if additional shims are needed.

NOTE: The exact determination of end-play must be made after the complete assembly of the mainshaft and the main drive pinion is installed in the transmission case.

REVERSE IDLER GEAR

Do not disassemble the reverse idler gear. If it is no longer serviceable, replace the assembly complete with the integral bearings.

COVER AND SHIFT FORK UNIT

NOTE: The cover and shift fork assembly should be disassembled only if inspection shows worn or damaged parts, or if the assembly is not working properly.

Disassembly

1. Remove the roll pin from the first/second shift fork and the shift gate with an "easy out". A square type or a closely wound spiral "easy out" mounted in a tap is preferable for this operation.
2. Move the first/second shift rail forward and force the expansion plug out of the cover. Cover the detent ball access hole in the cover with a cloth to prevent it from flying out. Remove the rail, fork and gate from the cover.
3. Remove the third/fourth shift rail, then the reverse rail in the manner outlined in Steps 1 and 2 above.
4. Compress the reverse gear plunger and remove the retaining clip. Remove the plunger and spring from the gate.

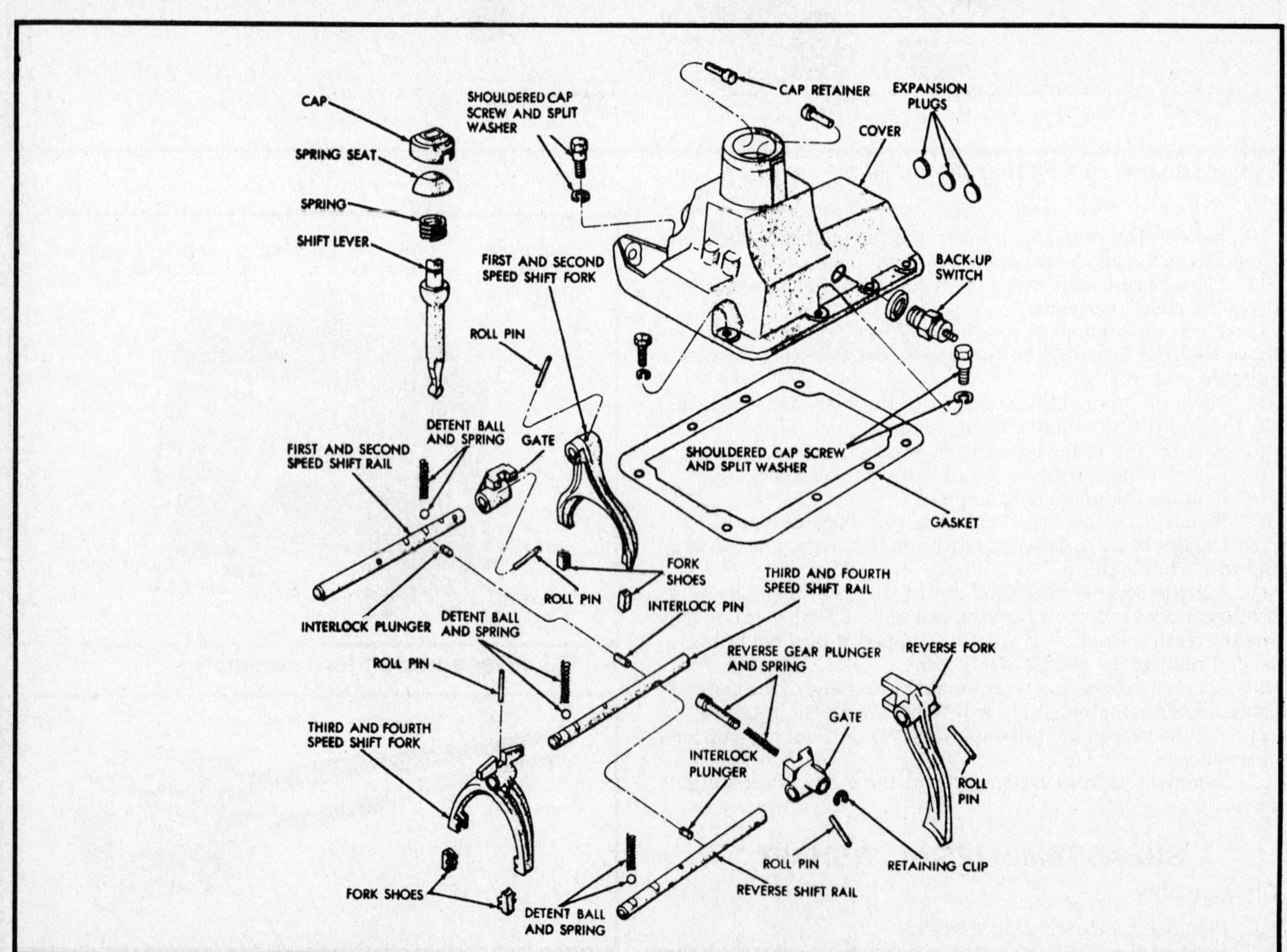

NP435 cover and shift fork assembly

Assembly

1. Install the spring on the reverse gear plunger and hold it in the reverse shift gate. Compress the spring in the shift gate and install the retaining clip.
2. Insert the reverse shift rail in the cover and place the detent ball and spring in position. Depress the ball and slide the shift rail over it.
3. Install the shift gate and fork on the reverse shift rail. Install a new roll pin in the gate and the fork.
4. Place the reverse fork in the neutral position.
5. Install the two interlock plungers in their bores.
6. Insert the interlock pin in the third/fourth shift rail. Install the shift rail in the same manner as the reverse shift rail.
7. Install the first/second shift rail in the same manner as outlined above. Make sure the interlock plunger is in place.
8. Check the interlocks by shifting the reverse shift rail into the Reverse position. It should be impossible to shift the other rails with the reverse rail in this position.
9. If the shift lever is to be installed at this point, lubricate the spherical ball seat and place the cap in place.
10. Install the back-up light switch.
11. Install new expansion plugs in the bores of the shift rail holes in the cover. Install the rail interlock hole plug.

DRIVE PINION AND BEARING RETAINER

Disassembly

1. Remove the tapered roller bearing from the pinion shaft with a suitable tool.
2. Remove the snapring, washer and the pilot rollers from the gear bore, if they have not been previously removed.
3. Pull the bearing race from the front bearing retainer with a suitable puller.
4. Remove the pinion shaft seal with a suitable tool.

Assembly

1. Position the drive pinion in an arbor press.
2. Place a wood block on the pinion gear and press it into the bearing until it contacts the bearing inner race.
3. Coat the roller bearings with a light film of grease to hold the bearings in place and insert them in the pocket of the drive pinion gear.
4. Install the washer and snapring.
5. Press a new seal into the bearing retainer. Make sure that the lip of the seal is toward the mounting surface.
6. Press the bearing race into the retainer.

TRANSMISSION UNIT

Assembly

1. Press the front countershaft roller bearings into the case until the cage is flush with the front of the transmission case. Coat the bearings with a light film of grease.
2. Place the transmission with the front of the case facing down. If uncaged bearings are used, hold the loose rollers in place in the cap with a light film of grease.
3. Lower the countershaft assembly into the case placing the thrust washer tangs in the slots in the case and inserting the front end of the shaft into the bearing.
4. Place the roller thrust bearing and race on the rear end of the countershaft. Hold the bearing in place with a light film of grease.
5. While holding the gear assembly in alignment, install the rear bearing retainer gasket, retainer and bearing assembly. Install and tighten the cap screws.
6. Position the reverse idler gear and bearing assembly in the case.
7. Align the idler shaft so that the lock plate groove in the shaft is in position to install the lock plate.
8. Install the lock plate, washer and cap screw.
9. Make sure the reverse idler gear turns freely.
10. Lower the rear end of the mainshaft assembly into the case, holding the first gear on the shaft. Maneuver the shaft through the rear bearing opening. With the mainshaft assembly moved to the rear of the case, be sure the third-fourth synchronizer and shims remain in position.
11. Install the roller type thrust bearing.
12. Place a wood block between the front of the case and the front of the mainshaft.
13. Install the rear bearing on the mainshaft by carefully driving the bearing onto the shaft and into the case, snapring flush against the case.
14. Install the drive pinion shaft and bearing assembly. Make sure that the pilot rollers remain in place.
15. Install the spacer and speedometer drive gear.
16. Install the rear bearing retainer and gasket.
17. Place the drive pinion bearing retainer over the pinion shaft, without the gasket.
18. Hold the retainer tight aginst the bearing and measure the clearance between the retainer and the case with a feeler gauge. End play in Steps 19 and 20 below allows for normal expansion of parts during operation, preventing seizure and damage to bearings, gears, synchronizers and shafts.
19. Install a gasket shim pack 0.010–0.015 in. thicker than measured clearance between the retainer and case to obtain the required 0.007–0.017 in. pinion shaft end play. Tighten the front retainer bolts and recheck the end play.
20. Check the synchronizer end play clearance 0.050–0.070 in. after all mainshaft components are in position and properly tightened. Two sets of feeler gauges are used to measure the clearance. Care should be used to keep both gauges as close as possible to both sides of the mainshaft for best results.

NOTE: In some cases, it may be necessary to disassemble the mainshaft and change the thickness of the shims to keep the end play clearance within the specified limits, 0.050–0.070 in.. Shims are available in two thicknesses.

21. Install the speedometer drive pinion.
22. Install the yoke flange, drum and drum assembly.
23. Place the transmission in two gears at once and tighten the yoke flange nut.
24. Shift the gears and/or synchronizers into all gear positions and check for free rotation.

TORQUE SPECIFICATIONS
New Process 435

	ft. lbs.
Cover screws	20–40
Drive gear retaining screw	15–25
Front countershaft retainer screw	15–25
Front countershaft bearing washer screw	12–22
Flange nut	125
Mainshaft rear retainer screw	15–25
Rear countershaft retainer screw	15–25
PTO cover screws	8–12
Filler and drain plugs	25–45
Reverse idler shaft lock screw	20–40
Brake link shoulder screw	20–40

LUBRICANT CAPACITY

New Process 435	7 pt.

25. Cover all transmissions components with a film of transmission oil to prevent damage during start up after initial lubricant fill up.

26. Move the gears to the neutral position.

27. Place a new cover gasket on the transmission case and lower the cover over the transmission.

28. Carefully engage the shift forks into their proper gears. Align the cover.

29. Install a shouldered alignment screw with split washer in the screw hole second from the front of the cover. Try out gear operation by shifting through all ranges. Make sure everything moves freely.

30. Install the remaining cover screws.

New Process 445 Four Speed Transmission

TRANSMISSION UNIT

Disassembly

1. Place the transmission in a holding fixture and drain the lubricant.

2. Shift the transmission gears into neutral. Remove the gearshift cover attaching bolts. Note that the two bolts opposite the tower are shouldered to properly position the cover. Lift the cover straight up and remove.

3. Lock the transmission in two gears at once and remove the mainshaft nut and yoke.

4. Loosen and remove the extension housing bolts. Remove the mainshaft extension housing and the speedometer drive pinion.

5. Remove the bolts from the drive pinion front bearing retainer and pull the bearing retainer and gasket off.

6. Rotate the drive pinion gear to align the pinion gear flat with the countershaft drive gear teeth. Remove the drive pinion gear and the tapered roller bearing from the transmission.

7. Remove the mainshaft thrust bearing.

8. Push the mainshaft assembly to the rear of the transmission and tilt the front of the mainshaft up.

9. Remove the mainshaft assembly from the transmission case.

10. Remove the reverse idler lock screw and lock plate.

11. Using a suitable size brass drift, carefully drive the reverse idler shaft out the REAR of the case. Do not attempt to drive the reverse idler shaft forward. This will damage the transmission case and the reverse idler shaft.

12. Remove the countershaft rear bearing retainer.

13. Slide the countershaft to the rear, then up and out of the case.

14. Drive the countershaft forward, out of the bearing and the case.

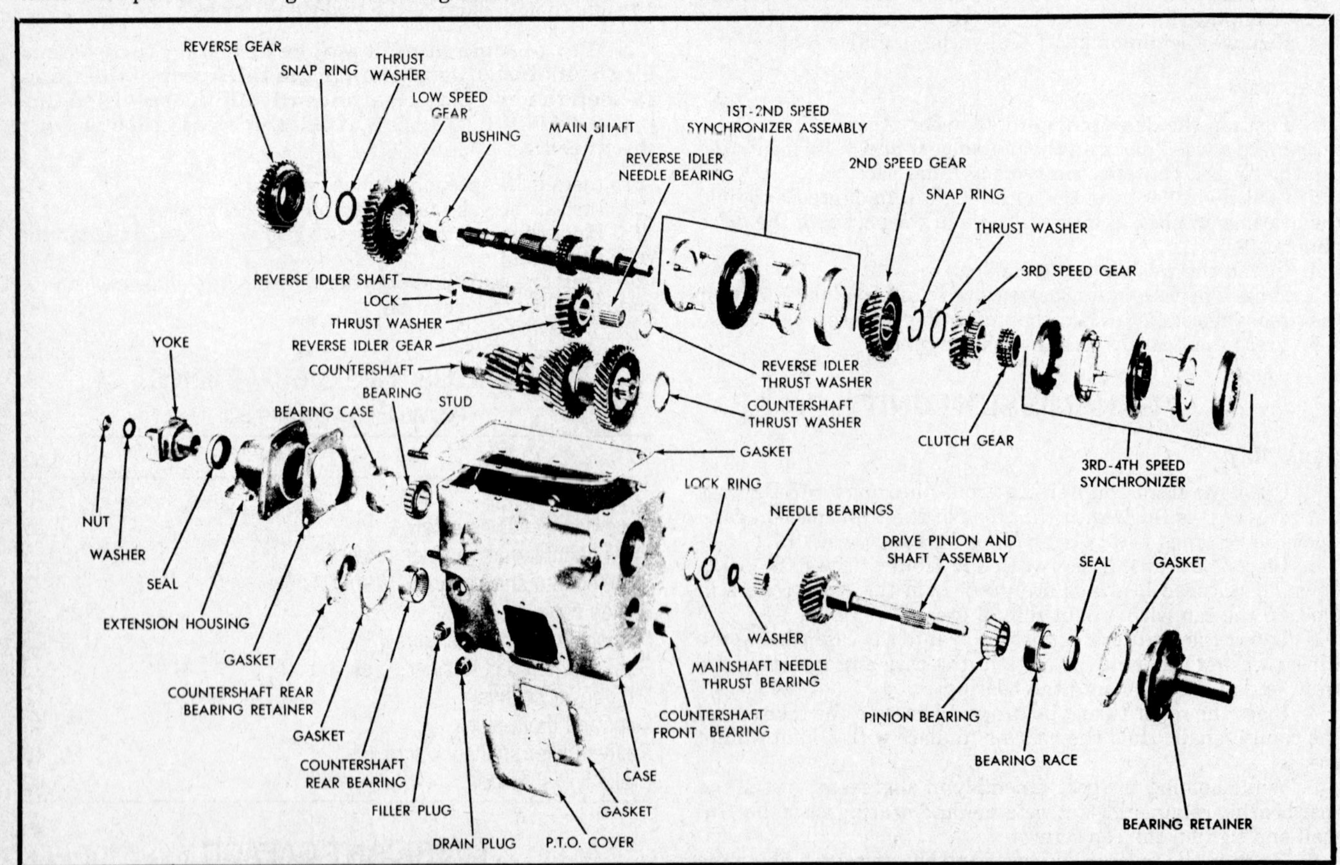

NP445 transmission—exploded view

SUBASSEMBLIES MAINSHAFT

Disassembly

1. Place the mainshaft in a soft jawed vise with the front end up.
2. Lift the third/fourth synchronizer and high speed clutch off the mainshaft.
3. Remove the third gear.
4. Remove the second gear snapring. Lift off the thrust washer.
5. Remove the second gear.
6. Remove the first/reverse synchronizer and clutch gear.
7. Install the mainshaft in the vise rear end up.
8. Remove the tapered bearing from the shaft with a suitable gear puller.
9. Remove the first gear snapring and thrust washer.
10. Remove the first gear.

Assembly

1. Lubricate all parts with transmission lubricant prior to assembly.
2. Place the mainshaft in a soft jawed vise with the rear end up.
3. Slide the first gear over the mainshaft, with the clutch gear facing down. Install the thrust washer and snapring.
4. Install the revese gear over the end of the mainshaft with the fork groove facing down.
5. Install the mainshaft rear bearing on the mainshaft with a sleeve of suitable size. Press the bearing on its inner race.
6. Install the mainshaft in the vise with the front end facing up.
7. Install the first/reverse synchronizer.
8. Install the second gear on the mainshaft.
9. Install the keyed thrust washer, ground side toward the second gear and secure with the snapring.
10. Install the third gear and one shim on the mainshaft.
11. Install the third fourth synchronizer over the mainshaft. Make sure that the slotted end of the clutch gear is positioned toward the third gear.

COVER AND SHIFT FORK UNIT

Disassembly

NOTE: The cover and shift fork assembly should be disassembled only if inspection shows worn or damaged parts, or if the assembly is not working properly.

1. Remove the roll pin from the first/second shift fork and the shift gate. Use a square-type or spirial wound "easy-out" mounted in a tap handle for these operations.
2. Move the first/second shift rail rearward and force the expansion plug out of the cover. Cover the detent ball access hole in the cover with a cloth to prevent it from flying out. Remove the rail fork and gate from the cover.
3. Remove the third/fourth shift rail, then the reverse rail in the manner outlined in steps 1 and 2 above.
4. Compress the reverse gear plunger and remove the retaining clip. Remove the plunger and spring from the gate.

Assembly

1. Apply a thin film of grease on the interlock slugs and slide them into the openings in the shift rail supports.
2. Install the reverse shift rail through the reverse shift fork plate and the reverse shift fork.
3. Secure the reverse shift plate and the shift fork with the roll pins. Install the interlock pin in the third-fourth shift rail. Hold in place with a thin film of grease.
4. Slide the third/fourth shift rail into the rail support from the rear of the cover. Slide the rail through the third-fourth shift fork and poppet ball and spring. Secure the third/fourth shift fork with the roll pin.
5. Install the interlock pin in the first/second shift rail and secure with a light coat of grease. Slide the first/second shift rail into the case, through the shift fork and shift gate. Hold the poppet ball and spring down until the shaft rail passes.
6. Secure the first-second shift rail and gate with the roll pins.

TRANSMISSION UNIT

Assembly

1. Install the countershaft front bearing in the case using a 1 $^3/_8$ in. socket as a driver. Grease the needle bearings prior to installation. Hold the bearings in place with a socket of suitable size while seating the bearing retainer. Drive the retainer in until it is flush with the case.
2. Install the tanged thrust washer on the countershaft with the tangs facing out. Install the countershaft in the transmission case.
3. Install the countershaft rear bearing retainer over the rear bearing. Use a new washer and position the retainer with the curved segment toward the bottom of the case.
4. Install the reverse idler gear into the case with the chamfered section facing the rear. Hold the thrust washer and needle bearings in position.
5. Slide the reverse idler shaft into the case, from the rear, and through the reverse idler gear. Make sure that the lock notch is down and at the rear of the case.
6. Install the reverse idler shaft lock and bolt.
7. Place the mainshaft in a soft jawed vise with the front end facing up.
8. Install the drive gear on top of the mainshaft.
9. Measure the clearance between the high speed synchronizer and the drive gear with two feeler gauges. If the clearance is greater than 0.043–0.053 in., install synchronizer shims between the third gear and the synchronizer brake drum. After the required shims have been installed, remove the drive gear from the mainshaft.
10. Install the mainshaft into the transmission case. Place the thrust washer over the pilot end of the mainshaft.
11. Position the drive gear so that the cutaway portion of the gear is facing down. Slide the drive gear into the front of the case and engage the mainshaft pilot in the pocket of the drive gear.
12. Slip the drive gear front bearing retainer over the shaft on gasket and do not secure with bolts.
13. Install the mainshaft rear bearing retainer. Tighten the screws to specifications.

LUBRICANT CAPACITY

New Process 445	7½ pts.

TORQUE SPECIFICATIONS
New Process 445

	ft. lbs.
Cover screws	20–40
Drive gear retaining screw	15–25
Front countershaft retaining screw	15–25
Front countershaft bearing washer screw	12–22
Flange nut	125
Mainshaft rear retainer screw	15–25
Rear countershaft retainer screw	15–25
PTO cover screws	8–12
Filler and drain plugs	25–45
Reverse idler shaft lock screw	20–40
Brake link shoulder screw	20–40

14. Hold the retainer against the front of the transmission case and measure the clearance between the front bearing retainer and the front of the case with a feeler gauge. Record the measurement and remove the bearing retainer.

15. Install a gasket pack on the front bearing retainer which is 0.010–0.015 in. thicker than the clearance measured in Step 14. Install the front bearing retainer and torque attaching screws to specification.

16. The end play float of the front synchronizer must be checked before installation of the transmission cover assembly. Measure the end play "float" by inserting two feeler gauges opposite one another between the third gear and the synchronizer stop ring. Accurate measurement can be made only after all mainshaft parts are in place and torqued to specification.

17. If the front synchronizer end play "float" does not fall between 0.050–0.070 in., shims should be added or removed as required, from between the third gear and the synchronizer stop ring.

18. Install the yoke retaining nut on the rear of the mainshaft. Shift the transmission into two gears at the same time and torque the yoke nut to 125 ft. lbs.

19. Shift the transmission into neutral.

20. Install the cover gasket.

21. Shift the transmission into second gear. Shift the cover into second.

22. Carefully lower the cover into position. It may be necessary to position the reverse gear to permit the fork to engage its groove.

23. Install the cover aligning screws (shouldered) and tighten with fingers only.

24. Install the remaining cover screws and tighten to specifications.

New Process 7550 and 7590 Five Speed Transmissions

TRANSMISSION UNIT

Disassembly

1. Mount the transmission in a housing fixture and remove the parking brake assembly.
2. Shift the gears into neutral.
3. Remove the shift cover screws, the second screw from the front on each side is shouldered with split washers for installation alignment.
4. Lift the cover and turn slightly either way to clear the shift forks, remove the cover.
5. Lock the transmission in two gears at once and remove the output flange nut.
6. Remove the brake drum and yoke assembly by tapping with a brass hammer.

NOTE: The drum and yoke assembly are balanced and unless replacement of parts is required, it is recommended that the drum and yoke be removed as a single unit.

7. Remove the brake band assembly bracket and support bolts and lock washers. Remove the brake band assembly as a complete unit.
8. Before removal and disassembly of the drive pinion and mainshaft, measure the end-play between the synchronizer stop ring and the fourth gear. Record this measurement for reference during assembly. The correct end-play is 0.050–0.070 in.. Note any difference from the limits so that corrective shims can be added or removed as required.
9. Remove the drive pinion bearing retainer.
10. Remove the drive pinion gear and ball bearing from the transmission by pulling on the shaft and rapping the face of the case with a brass hammer.
11. Remove the speedometer drive pinion and the mainshaft rear bearing retainer.
12. Place a brass drift in the front center of the mainshaft and drive the mainshaft to the rear.
13. Pull the rear bearing from the mainshaft with a suitable gear puller.
14. Once the mainshaft rear bearing has cleared the case, remove the rear bearing and the speedometer gear with a suitable puller.
15. Move the mainshaft assembly to the rear and tilt the front of the mainshaft up.
16. Hold the first/reverse gear and the fourth/fifth synchronizer to keep them from sliding off the shaft, remove the mainshaft from the transmission case.
17. Remove the reverse idler lock screw and lock plate.
18. Using a brass drift, held at an angle, drive the idler shaft to the rear while pulling.
19. Lift the reverse idler gear and thrust washers out of the case. Loose needle bearings are usually replaced. Never mix old and new bearings.
20. Remove the countershaft rear bearing retainer, gasket and bearing.
21. Tip the countershaft upward and remove it from the case. Remove the thrust washer from the front end of the countershaft.
22. Remove the countershaft front needle bearing from the case bore by tapping on the bearing cage from inside the case, with a suitable driver.

SUBASSEMBLIES DRIVE PINION

Disassembly

1. Remove the snapring and washer holding the pilot needle bearings in place and remove the bearings.
2. Relieve the staked area, remove the drive pinion ball bearing retainer nut and remove the ball bearing. The ball bearing retainer nut has left hand threads.
3. Remove the snapring from the drive pinion ball bearing.
4. Remove the seal from the drive pinion bearing retainer.

Assembly

1. Grease the loose pilot bearings to hold them in place and insert them into the pocket of the drive gear. Install the washer and snapring.
2. Press the large bearing on the pinion shaft. Make sure the bearing is properly seated.
3. Install the bearing retainer nut and tighten securely. Stake in place.
4. Install the snapring on the large bearing. Make sure the snapring is properly seated. The bearing retainer nut has left hand threads.

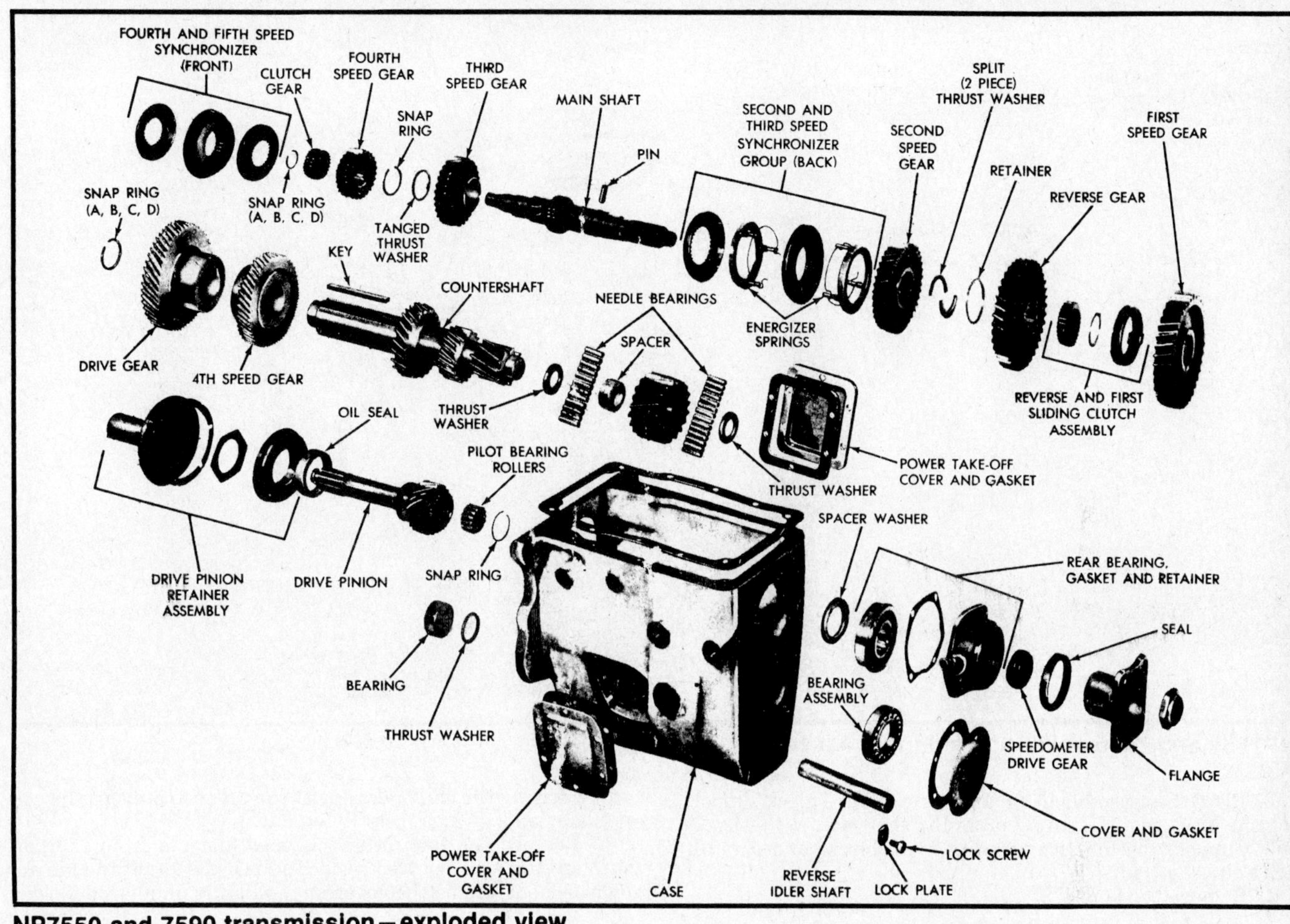

NP7550 and 7590 transmission—exploded view

MAINSHAFT

Disassembly

1. Remove the spacer washer and the first gear from the mainshaft.
2. Remove the retaining ring and the first/reverse clutch and clutch gear assembly.
3. Remove the reverse gear.
4. Remove the second gear retaining thrust washer. This two piece split washer consists of two halves held in position on the mainshaft by a pin in a hole on the mainshaft together with a retaining ring.
5. Remove the second gear.
6. Remove the second/third synchronizer assembly. The second/third clutch gear is integral with the mainshaft.
7. Remove the snapring and the fourth/fifth synchronizer assembly and clutch gear.
8. Remove the fourth gear, retain the shims for assembly.
9. Remove the retaining snapring, tanged thrust washer and the third gear.

Assembly

1. Place the mainshaft, front end up, in a soft jawed vise.
2. Place the third gear on the shaft with the clutching teeth facing down. Install the tanged thrust washer and the one piece snap ring.
3. Place the fourth gear on the shaft with the clutching teeth up.
4. Check the end-play measurements recorded during disassembly and select shims to provide 0.050–0.070 in. end-play between the fourth gear and the fourth/fifth synchronizer.
5. Place the fourth/fifth synchronizer clutch gear, with the oil slots down, on the mainshaft. Select a snapring of the greatest possible thickness to eliminate all end-play of the clutch gear.
6. Remove the mainshaft from the vise and install the second-third synchronizer group. The synchronizer sleeve is marked "Front" for proper installation.
7. Place the second speed gear on the mainshaft.
8. Place the thrust washer retaining pin in the hole in the mainshaft and position the two thrust washer halves. Install the thrust washer retaining ring with the large diameter contacting the second gear.
9. Install the reverse gear.
10. Position the reverse/first clutch gear on the shaft. Install the retaining snapring. Select a snapring with the greatest possible thickness to eliminate all end-play of the clutch gear.
11. Position the sliding clutch on the clutch gear. Install the first gear on the mainshaft.
12. Place the spacer washer on the mainshaft.

COUNTERSHAFT

It is only necessary to disassemble the countershaft if inspection shows signs of damage or malfunction.

Disassembly

1. Remove the snapring.

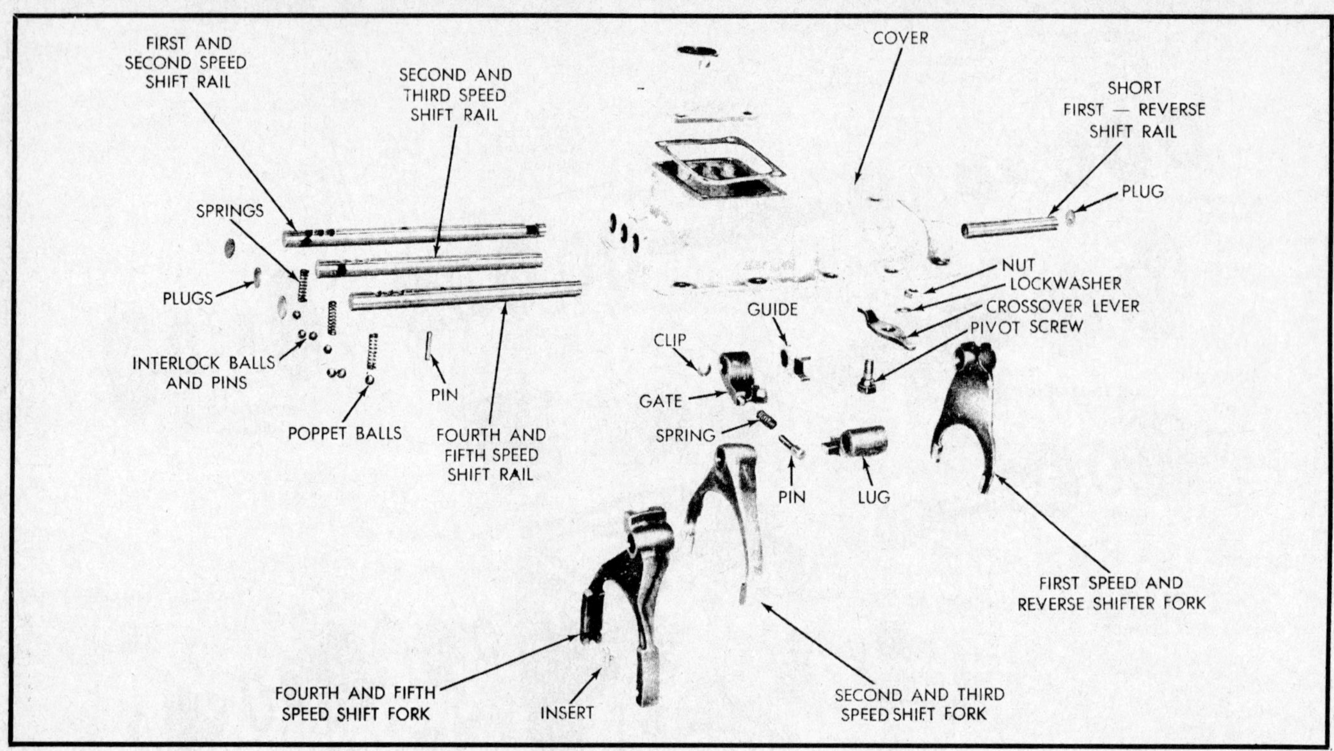

NP7550 and 7590 cover and shift fork assembly

2. Place the assembly in an arbor press with a block supporting the drive gear. Carefully press the shaft out.
3. Support the fourth gear with wood blocks and carefully drive the shaft out.
4. Remove the key.

Assembly

1. Place the key in position on the countershaft.
2. Press the gears on the countershaft until properly seated. Make sure that the key does not move out of position as the gears are being pressed on the shaft.
3. Install the snapring on the countershaft. Select a snapring with the greatest possible thickness to eliminate all possible end-play.
4. Install the washer on the countershaft drive gear.

COVER AND SHIFT FORK UNIT

The cover and shift fork assembly should be disassembled only if inspection shows worn or damaged parts, or if the assembly is not working properly.

Disassembly

1. Mount the cover assembly in a soft jawed vise. Mark each fork and rail for location during assembly.
2. Place the shift forks in neutral. Remove the spiral roll pins from the shift forks and lugs. The roll pins may be removed by working with a "easy-out" mounted in a tap handle.
3. Drive the short first/reverse shift rail toward the rear and out of the shift cover. Remove the fork.
4. Remove the first/reverse shift rail pivot bolt and nut. Remove the crossover level.
5. Drive the fourth/fifth and the second/third shift rail forward and out of the shift cover. Remove the long first/reverse shift rail in the same manner. Place a cloth over the shift rails while driving the shift rails out of the cover to prevent the poppet balls and springs from flying out.
6. Remove the four interlock balls and pin from the bore through the width of the cover. To make sure that the pin and balls are out, shake the cover or tap lightly on a wood block.

Assembly

1. Push the long first/reverse shift rail into the cover bore far enough to permit the installation of the gates, poppet ball and springs and the roll pins. Move the shift rail into neutral position.
2. Place a small quantity of grease on the four interlock balls and pin.
3. Place two balls in the interlock bore. Move both of the balls toward the shift rail to seat the ball in the neutral notch.
4. Grease the interlock pin and place it in the hole located in the second-third shift rail. Install the second/third shift rail, gate and fork as outlined in Step 1. Move the rail into neutral.
5. Install the remaining balls into the interlock bore.
6. Push the fourth/fifth shift rail into the cover bore and install the shift fork as outlined in Step 1. Move the shift rail into neutral.
7. Place the crossover lever in position in the cover in such a way that the short first/reverse shift rail, fork and roll pin can be installed. Install the short first/reverse shift rail and parts.
8. Reposition the crossover level to mate in the notches in both the long and short first/reverse shift rails.
9. Install the pivot bolt through the crossover level and the cover. Install the retaining nut and washer.
10. Install new expansion plugs in the shift cover.

TRANSMISSION UNIT

Assembly

1. Coat all parts and assemblies with transmission fluid prior to assembly. This will insure that there is no damage during initial start up.

2. Install the front bearing assembly into the countershaft bearing bore in the case.

3. Grease the thrust washer and place in position in the transmission case.

4. Install the countershaft front bearing journal into the front bearing and seat it against the thrust washer. Be sure to keep the centerline of the countershaft aligned with the rear bearing bore during installation to prevent damage to the countershaft front bearing. Install the countershaft rear bearing assembly, gasket and cover. Tighten the screws to specification.

5. Check the counter shaft end clearance, it should be 0.008–0.020 in.. Clearance can be adjusted by changing the countershaft rear bearing cover gasket.

6. With the reverse idler needle bearings held in place on each side of the spacer with grease, place the reverse idler gear and thrust washer in position in the case.

7. Drive the shaft through the case and gear using a hammer and a brass drift. Be sure that the needles stay in place and that the lock strap slot in the shaft will line up so that the lock strap, cap and cap screw can be installed.

8. Install the lock strap on the shaft and tighten the cap screw securely.

9. Carefully lower the rear end of the mainshaft into the case while holding the first gear and washer on the shaft.

10. Place a hardwood block at the front of the mainshaft and drive the mainshaft bearing onto the shaft and into the case.

11. Install the drive pinion by carefully driving on the bearing outer race, forcing it into the case while guiding the front end of the mainshaft into the pilot bearing pocket. Make sure the bearing is fully seated.

12. Replace the retainer oil seal, pressing the seal into the retainer until the seal makes contact with its seat. Do not press beyond this point.

13. Install the bearing retainer and gasket and torque the screws to specification.

14. Install the speedometer drive gear on the output shaft.

15. Install the oil seal on the mainshaft flange, pressing the seal on until it makes contact with its seat. Do not press beyond this point.

16. Place the gasket on the output shaft bearing retainer and install the retainer on the case. Tighten the screws to specifications.

17. Position the universal joint flange and brake drum on the output shaft.

18. Shift the transmission into two gears at the same time and install the flange nut. Tighten to specifications.

19. Check the fourth/fifth synchronizer end-play "float" as follows. With all transmission parts in place, with the exception of the cover, place two feeler gauges between the fourth-fifth synchronizer and the stop ring. End-play should be 0.050–0.070 in.. If end-play is not within limits, shims should be added or removed, as required, from between the fourth-fifth synchronizer and the stop ring. Reassemble and recheck the end-play.

20. Check the second/third synchronizer end-play "float" as follows. With all transmission parts in place, with the exception of the cover, place two feeler gauges between the second/third synchronizer and the outer stop ring. End-play should be 0.070–0.090 in.. If the end-play is not within limits, install new parts as required. Shims cannot be used at this point. Reassemble and recheck the end-play.

21. Place the transmission gears and the shift cover in neutral.

22. Position the cover gasket on the transmission.

23. Carefully lower the cover into position on the transmission. Make sure that all shift forks engage their grooves correctly.

24. Install the shouldered aligning screws and split washers, in the second hole from the front and tighten finger tight.

25. Install the remaining screws and tighten all screws to specification.

26. Shift the transmission through all gear ranges to be sure that the transmission is working properly.

LUBRICANT CAPACITY

New Process 7550 & 7590	18¼ pts.

TORQUE SPECIFICATIONS
New Process 7550 & 7590

	ft. lbs.
Cover screws	20–40
Drive gear retaining screw	15–25
Front countershaft retaining screw	15–25
Front countershaft bearing washer screw	12–22
Flange nut	125–175
Mainshaft rear retainer screw	20–40
Rear countershaft retainer screw	20–40
PTO cover screws	8–12
Filler and drain plugs	25–45
Reverse idler shaft lock screw	20–40
Bar brake screw	70–110
Bell housing screw	70–110
Brake link shoulder screw	25–45

New Process 540 and 542 Five Speed Transmissions

TRANSMISSION UNIT

Disassembly

1. Place the transmission on a stand or a bench.

2. Shift the transmission into the 2nd speed for the 540 and 3rd speed for the 542.

3. Remove the screws and remove the transmission cover by lifting upward and carefully rotating the housing counterclockwise. Note the location of the alignment screws. The alignment screws use split type lockwashers.

On the 542 transmission, it may be necessary to move the 1st speed gear back slightly allowing the offset curve in the shift fork to clear the rim of the gear.

4. Lock the transmission in two gears and remove the output flange nut, with the yoke and parking brake drum as an assembly. The drum and yoke are balanced and unless replaced it is recommended that the drum and yoke be removed as a unit assembly.

5. Before removal and disassembly of the drive pinion and mainshaft measure the end play between the synchronizer outer stop ring and the 4th speed gear. Record the reading for reference during reassembly and shim as necessary to obtain the ideal end play of 0.050–0.070 in..

6. Remove the drive pinion bearing retainer.

7. Remove the drive pinion assembly from the case while pulling on the shaft and tapping with a small hammer.

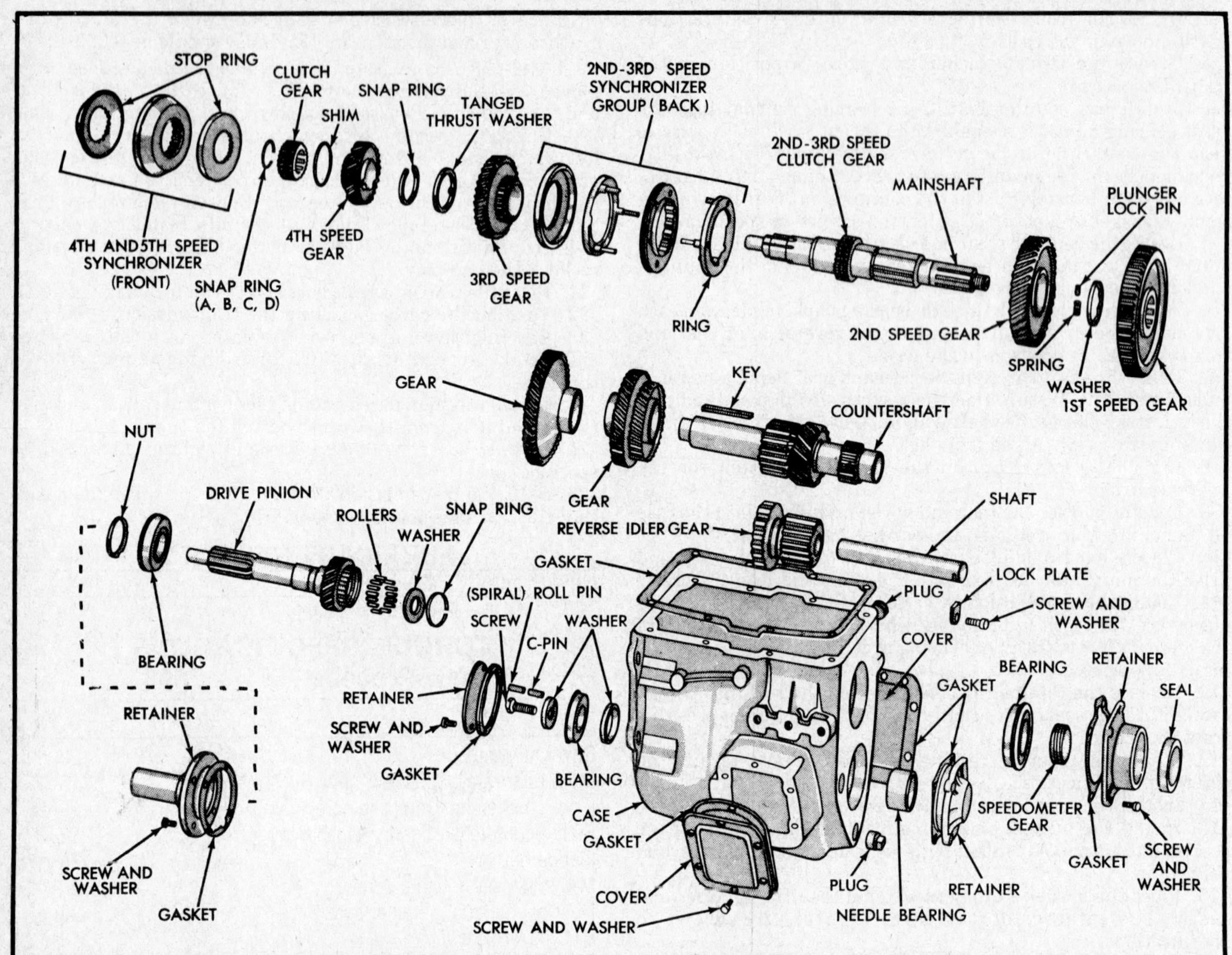

NP540 transmission—exploded view

8. Remove the mainshaft rear bearing retainer and speedometer drive gear.
9. Using a brass hammer, tap the front of the mainshaft rearward to drive the rear bearing from its bore then using a puller remove the bearing from the mainshaft.
10. Remove the mainshaft assembly from the case by lifting the front end upward and forward until the 1st speed can pass through the notch areas in the case.
11. Remove the reverse idler lock screw and lock plate.
12. With a brass drift held at an angle drive the idler shaft to the rear and pull the shaft.
13. Lift the reverse idler gear from the shaft.
14. On the 542 transmission, push the bearing retainer including the needle bearings and radial thrust bearing out the back of the case. On the 542 transmission, the countershaft must be laid in the bottom of the case to make easier the reverse idler gear removal.
15. Remove the reverse gear shaft with the integral gear, sliding gear and thrust washer.
16. Push the caged front needle bearing out of the case.
17. Remove the countershaft front bearing cover and gasket.
18. To prevent the countershaft from turning, insert a hammer handle between the gear set and the case.
19. Remove the spiral roll pin, screw, retaining washer and C-pin.
20. After removing the gear bearing retainer cap screws, drive against the front end of the countershaft with a brass drift, driving through the front bearing toward the rear, until the countershaft rear bearing and retainer cap comes out of the case. On the 542 transmission, the idler gear must be removed before the countershaft can be removed from the case.
21. Remove the bearing and cap from the countershaft and lift the countershaft from the case.
22. Remove the countershaft front bearing from the bore in the case by tapping the outer bearing race from inside the case.

SUBASSEMBLIES MAINSHAFT

Disassembly

1. Remove the 1st speed gear from the mainshaft.
2. Remove the 2nd speed gear by depressing the plunger lock, and rotating the splined thrust washer. On the 542 remove the snapring and thrust washer.
3. Remove the 2nd/3rd speed synchronizer unit.
4. Clamp the mainshaft in a soft jawed vise and remove the 4th and 5th speed synchronizer assembly, clutch gear snapring and clutch gear.
5. Remove the 4th speed gear and shim.
6. Remove the 3rd speed gear snapring and tanged washer. Remove the 3rd speed gear.

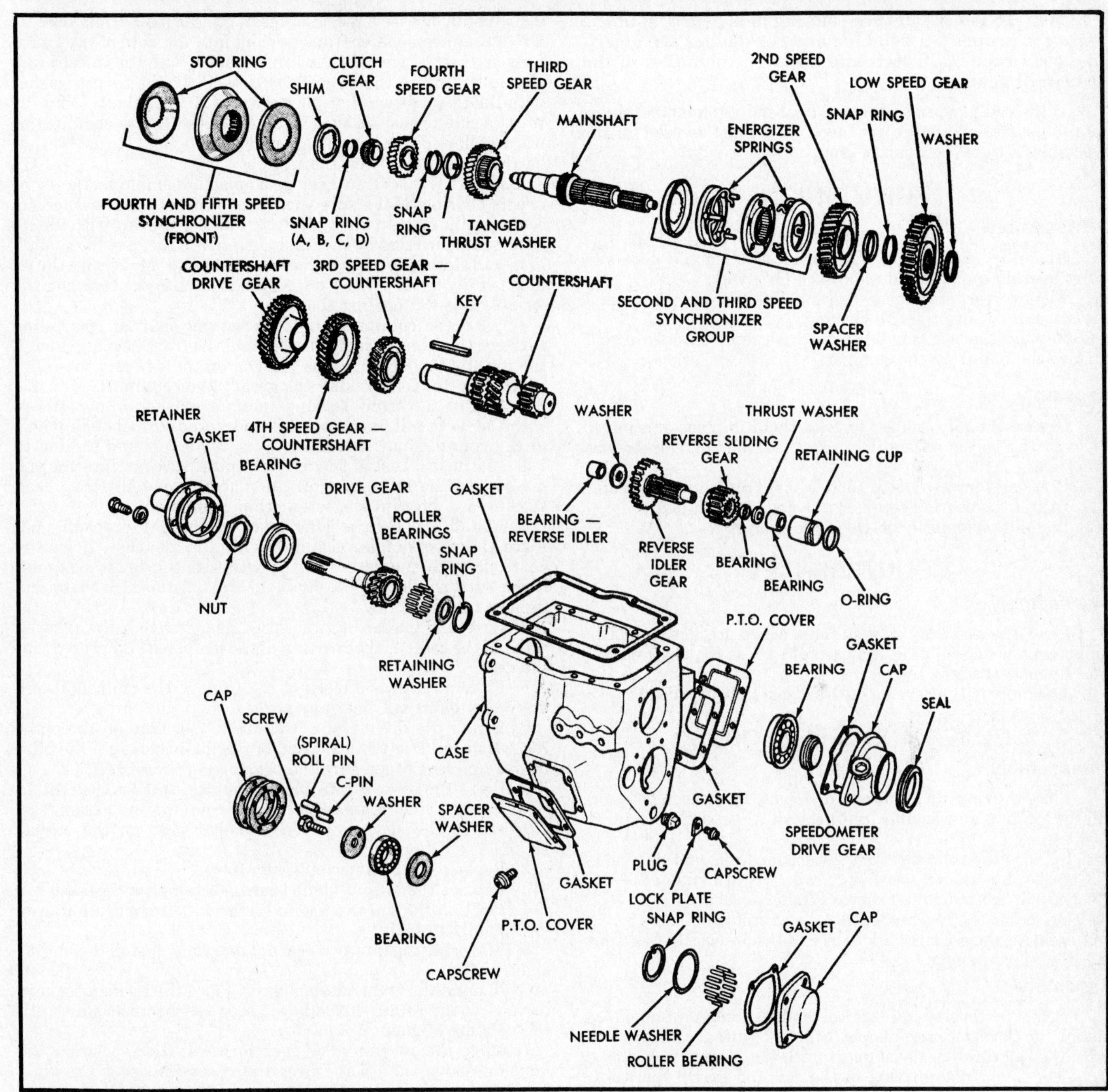

NP542 transmission—exploded view

Assembly

1. Place the mainshaft with the forward end up in a soft jawed vise.
2. Place the 3rd speed gear on the shaft with the clutching teeth facing down. Install the one piece snapring and thrust washer.
3. Place the 4th speed gear on the shaft with the clutching teeth up. Refer to the end-play dimension recorded earlier and select shims to provide 0.050–0.070 in. end play between the gear and the front synchronizer.
4. Place the 4th/5th speed synchronizer clutch gear with the oil slots down on the mainshaft. Select a snapring of the greatest possible thickness to eliminate all end play of the clutch gear.
5. Remove the mainshaft from the vise and install the 2nd/3rd speed synchronizer group. The synchronizer sleeve is marked "FRONT" for proper installation.
6. Place the 2nd speed gear on the shaft. On the 540 lock in place by installing the plunger spring, plunger and splined washer. Push in the washer and lock by rotating until the splines are aligned. On the 542 install the thrust washer and snapring. Place the 1st speed gear on the shaft with fork groove facing the front end of the shaft.
7. Checking the end play float (0.050–0.090) at the rear synchronizer (2nd/3rd speeds) is mandatory and be performed during the mainshaft. This can be done by using two equal size feeler gauges diametrically opposite each other between the 3rd speed outer stop ring and the 3rd speed gear.

NOTE: To get the proper reading make sure all of the parts are properly assembled and the gauges are inserted close to the mainshaft and up on the shoulder of the 3rd speed gear.

8. If the end-play is less that 0.070 or more than 0.090 shims cannot be used and new component parts must be used for the assembly of the synchronizer group.

DRIVE PINION

Disassembly

1. Remove the snapring and washer holding the pilot and roller bearing in place and remove the bearing.
2. Remove the drive gear bearing retainer nut (left hand thread) and remove the ball bearing.
3. Remove the snapring from the drive gear ball bearing and remove the seal from the retainer.

Assembly

1. Grease the pilot rollers to hold them in place and insert them in the pocket of the drive gear. Install the washer and snapring.
2. Press and properly seat the large bearing onto the shaft.
3. Install the bearing retainer nut and stake in place.
4. Install the snapring on the large bearing.

COUNTERSHAFT

Disassembly

1. Place the assembly in a suitable arbor press with blocks supporting 3rd speed gear and carefully press the shaft out.
2. Remove the key.
3. Assembly is the reverse of the disassembly procedure.

COVER AND SHIFT FORKS

Disassembly

1. Place the cover in a soft jawed vise and mark each fork and rail for location at assembly. Shift the shifter rails into neutral position.
2. Remove the roll pins from the shifter forks and rail ends.
3. Drive the 4th/5th speed shift rails forward and out of the cover, then, the remaining center (2nd/3rd) rail.
4. Drive out the reverse and 1st speed rails.
5. Remove the six interlock balls and two interlock pins from the shift rail support.

Assembly

1. Drive the reverse rail into the housing only far enough to install the reverse gate, poppet ball and spring. Continue to drive the rail through the support until the reverse fork can be installed, then finish driving in the rail and install the welch plug.
2. Install the 1st speed rail in a similar manner.
3. Place a small quantity of grease on the six interlock balls.
4. Shift the reverse and 1st speed rails into neutral and install the interlock balls in the shift rail support.
5. Install the 4th/5th speed shift rail and fork and the 2nd/3rd speed shift rail, fork and rail end in the same manner described in Step 1, then install the interlock pins.

TRANSMISSION UNIT

Assembly

1. Lay the countershaft in the bottom of the transmission. Make sure the spacer washer is in place in the front of the drive gear. The reverse idler gear should be installed on the 542 transmission, however on the 540 transmission, install the reverse idler gear after the countershaft installation is complete.
2. Install the reverse idler gear on the 542 transmission. Drive the reverse idler front bearing into the bore of the transmission case. The end of the front bearing with the thicker wall should be toward the rear of the case. Place the thrust washer with the tangs forward on the front of the idler shaft. Place the reverse sliding gear on the shaft with the shift fork channel forward, followed by the radial thrust bearing and thrust washer on the small end of the shaft.
3. Insert the reverse idler gear shaft assembly in the front needle bearing. Make sure the tangs on the thrust washer are seated in the slots in the case. Push the rear bearing with the retainer cup encircled by the oiled O-ring into the case far enough to install the lock plate, washer and cap screw. Make sure the oil hole is fully in view as seen looking down into the case and the lock plate is flat against the case.
4. With the countershaft front bearing journal protruding through the front bearing bore, install the front bearing. Install the countershaft rear needle bearing on the 540 and the roller bearing on the 542. Install the gasket and retainer.
5. Install the front bearing retainer washer into position, with the large roll pin through it and in the corresponding hole in the countershaft. Install a $^5/_8$ in. cap screw and tighten to 100–135 ft. lbs. Install the smaller spiral lock pin into the roll pin leaving the lock pin protruding about one half screw head thickness to prevent the screw from coming out.
6. Install the reverse idler gear on the 540 transmission. Place the reverse idler gear in position in the case. Drive the shaft through the case and the gear using a brass hammer. Make sure the lock plate lines up. Install the lock plate and tighten the cap screw.
7. Carefully guide the first speed gear through the relieved areas in the case, as the rear end of the mainshaft is lowered into the case.
8. Place a hardwood block at the front of the mainshaft and drive the mainshaft bearing onto the shaft and into the case.
9. Install the drive pinion by carefully driving on the outer race while guiding the front end of the mainshaft into the pilot bearing pocket. Make sure the bearing is fully seated.
10. Press the oil seal into the retainer until it makes contact with its seat, then install the bearing retainer and gasket.
11. Install the spacer and speedometer gear on the output shaft.
12. Replace the retainer oil seal.
13. Replace the output shaft bearing retainer and gasket.
14. Position the universal joint flange and brake drum if used on the output shaft.
15. After shifting into two gears at one time, install the output shaft nut.
16. Replace the transmission cover. Place the transmission in third gear and rotate the 2nd/3rd speed synchronizer unit until the pins are aligned.
17. Move the reverse idler gear forward, then, position the housing above the case. Lower the cover into position while guiding the reverse fork through the case and pass the synchronizer pins. Move the first speed gear slightly forward as necessary to engage the fork in the groove in the gear.
18. Install the shouldered aligning screws and split lockwashers in the second hole from the front and tighten thumb tight. Install the remaining cover screws.

GENERAL DATA

Type	3-Speed
Synchromesh gears	1st, 2nd, and 3rd
Models SM 326 and SM326 w/Overdrive	
Gar ratios	
1st speed	2.85:1
2nd speed	1.68:1
3rd speed	1.00:1
Reverse	2.95:1

Saginaw Three Speed (GM–SM326–76mm)

The G.M. Corporation Model SM326 (Saginaw) is a synchromesh three speed transmission using helical constant mesh gears. The engagement of all gears except reverse is assisted by synchronizers.

TRANSMISSION UNIT

Disassembly

1. Remove side cover assembly and shift forks.
2. Remove clutch gear bearing retainer.
3. Remove clutch gear bearing to gear stem snapring. Pull clutch gear outward until a screwdriver can be inserted between bearing and case. Remove clutch gear bearing.
4. Remove speedometer driven gear and extension bolts.
5. Remove reverse idler shaft snapring. Slide reverse idler gear forward on shaft.
6. Remove mainshaft and extension assembly.
7. Remove clutch gear and third speed blocker ring from inside case. Remove 14 roller bearings from clutch gear.

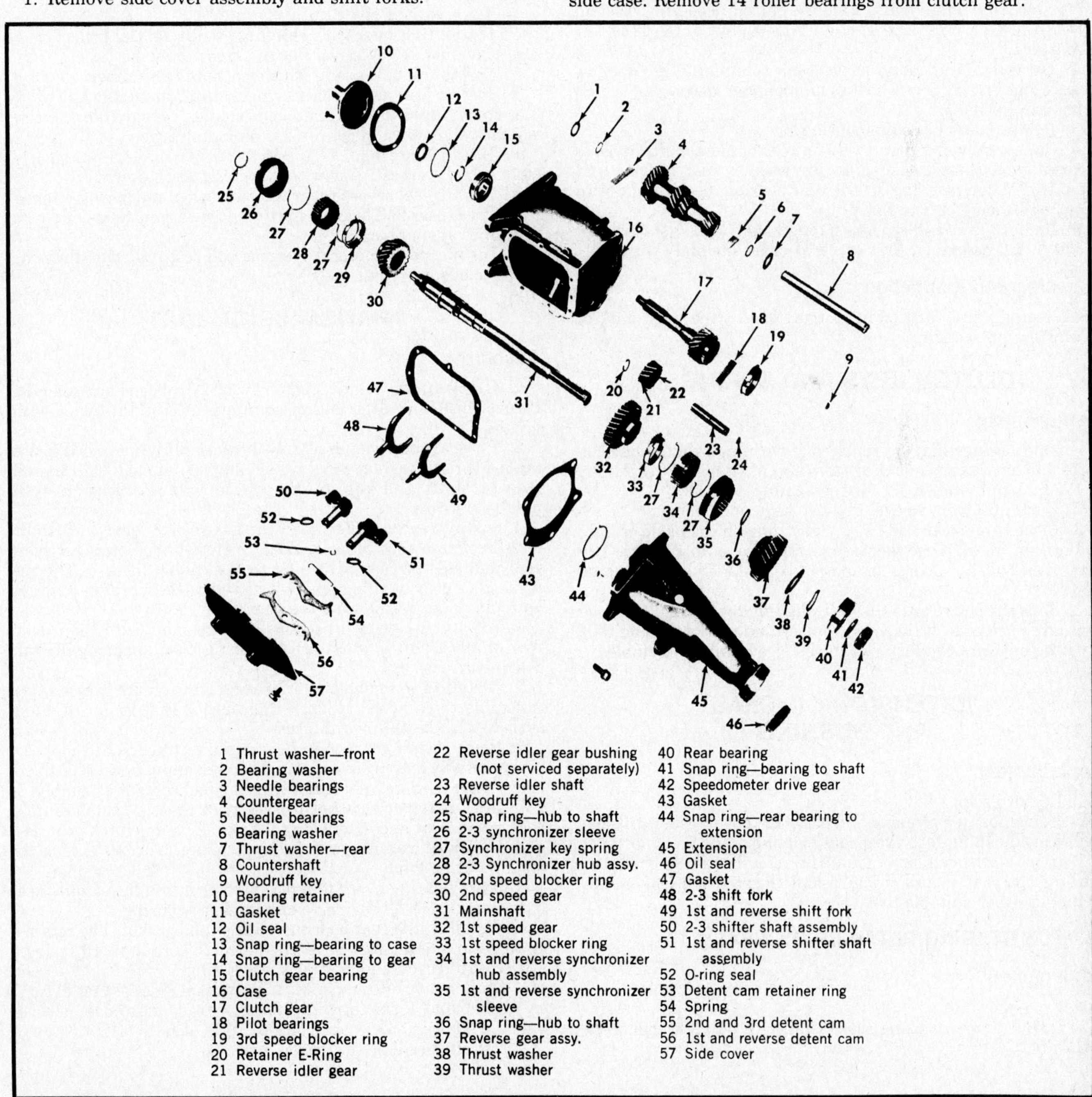

SM326 transmission components

8. Expand the snapring which retains the mainshaft rear bearing. Remove the extension.

9. Using a dummy shaft, drive the countershaft and key out the rear of the case. Remove the gear, two tanged thrust washers and dummy shaft. Remove bearing washer and 27 roller bearings from each end of countergear.

10. Use a long drift to drive the reverse idler shaft and key through the rear of the case.

11. Remove reverse idler gear and tanged steel thrust washer.

MAINSHAFT

Disassembly

1. Remove second and third speed sliding clutch hug snapring from mainshaft. Remove clutch assembly, second speed blocker ring and second speed gear from front of mainshaft.
2. Depress speedometer drive gear retaining clip. Remove gear. Some units have a metal speedometer drive gear which must be pulled off.
3. Remove rear bearing snapring.
4. Support reverse gear. Press on rear of mainshaft. Remove reverse gear, thrust washer, spring washer, rear bearing and snapring. When pressing off the rear bearing, be careful not to cock the bearing on the shaft.
5. Remove first and reverse sliding clutch hub snapring. Remove clutch assembly, first speed blocker ring and first gear.

Cleaning and Inspection

See Cleaning and Inspection instructions at the beginning of Transmission section.

CLUTCH KEYS AND SPRINGS

Replacement

Keys and springs may be replaced if worn or broken, but the hubs and sleeves are matched pairs and must be kept together.

1. Mark hub and sleeve for reassembly.
2. Push hub from sleeve. Remove keys and springs.
3. Place three keys and two springs, one on each side of hub, in position, so all three keys are engaged by both springs. The tanged end of the springs should not be installed into the same key.
4. Slide the sleeve onto the hub, aligning the marks. A groove around the outside of the synchronizer hub marks the end that must be opposite the fork slot in the sleeve when assembled.

EXTENSION OIL SEAL AND BUSHING

Replacement

1. Remove seal.
2. Using bushing remover and installer tool, or other suitable tool, drive bushing into extension housing.
3. Drive new bushing in from the rear. Lubricate inside of bushing and seal. Install new oil seal with extension seal installer tool or other suitable tool.

CLUTCH BEARING RETAINER OIL SEAL

Replacement

1. Pry old seal out.
2. Install new seal using seal installer or suitable tool. Seat seal in bore.

MAINSHAFT

Assembly

1. Turn front of mainshaft up.
2. Install second gear with clutching teeth up; the rear face of the gear butts against the flange on the mainshaft.
3. Install a blocker ring with clutching teeth down. All three blocker rings are the same.
4. Install second and third speed synchronizer assembly with fork slot down. Press it onto mainshaft splines. Both synchronizer assemblies are the same. Be sure that blocker ring notches align with synchronizer assembly keys.
5. Install synchronizer snapring. Both synchronizer snaprings are the same.
6. Turn rear of shaft up.
7. Install first gear with clutching teeth up; the front face of the gear butts against the flange on the mainshaft.
8. Install a blocker ring with clutching teeth down.
9. Install first and reverse synchronizer assembly with fork slot down. Press it onto mainshaft splines. Be sure blocker ring notches align with synchronizer assembly keys.
10. Install snapring.
11. Install reverse gear with clutching teeth down.
12. Install steel reverse gear thrust washer and spring washer.
13. Press rear ball bearing onto shaft with snapring slot down.
14. Install snapring.
15. Install speedometer drive gear and retaining clip. Press on metal speedometer drive gear.

TRANSMISSION UNIT

Assembly

1. Using dummy shaft load a row of 27 roller bearings and a thrust washer at each end of countergear. Hold in place with grease.
2. Place countergear assembly into case through rear. Place a tanged thrust washer, tang away from gear at each end. Install countershaft and key, making sure that tangs align with notches in case.
3. Install reverse idler gear thrust washer, gear and shaft with key from rear of case. Be sure thrust washer is between gear and rear of case with tang toward notch in case. The reverse idler gear bushing may not be replaced separately it must be replaced as a unit with the gear.
4. Expand snapring in extension. Assemble extension over rear of mainshaft and onto rear bearing. Seat snapring in rear bearing groove.
5. Install 14 mainshaft pilot bearings into clutch gear cavity. Assemble third speed blocker ring onto clutch gear clutching surface with teeth toward gear.
6. Place clutch gear, pilot bearings and third speed blocker ring assembly over front of mainshaft assembly. Be sure blocker rings align with keys in second-third synchronizer assembly.
7. Stick extension gasket to case with grease. Install clutch gear, mainshaft and extension together. Be sure clutch gear engages teeth of countergear anti-lash plate. Torque extension bolts to 45 ft. lbs.
8. Place bearing over stem of clutch gear and into front case bore. Install front bearing to clutch gear snapring.
9. Install clutch gear bearing retainer and gasket. The retainer oil return hole must be at the bottom. Torque to 10 ft. lbs.
10. Install reverse idler gear shaft E-ring.
11. Shift synchronizer sleeves to neutral positions. Install cover, gasket and forks, aligning forks with synchronizer sleeve grooves. Torque side cover bolts to 10 ft. lbs.
12. Install speedometer driven gear.

TORQUE SPECIFICATIONS
Saginaw-76mm

	ft. lbs.
Extension to case attaching bolts	35–55
Drain and filler plugs	10–15
Side cover attaching bolts	18–24
Clutch gear retainer bolts	18–24

Spicer 5000 Series Five Speed Transmission

The extra heavy duty five speed transmission (Spicer), is a manually shifted, synchromesh, helical gear type. Fifth forward speed is direct drive. A power take off base is located on the right and left side of the transmission case.

TRANSMISSION UNIT

Disassembly

1. Remove the gear shift housing from the transmission case. Remove the detent balls from the housing and shift the transmission into two gears.
2. Remove the brake drum and spline flange.
3. Remove the brake shoe assembly, the output shaft bearing retainer, speedometer driving gear and spacer.
4. Remove the countershaft rear bearing retainer, gasket, and countershaft nut.
5. Remove the left side power take off cover.
6. Remove the input shaft bearing retainer and gasket from the case. Using a soft drift, drive the input shaft and front bearing from the case. Remove the pilot rollers from the drive gear.
7. With a hardwood or fiber block placed against the front side of the second-speed gear, drive the input shaft assembly rearward until the output shaft bearing clears the case. Be careful not to hit the second speed gear against the countershaft reverse gear. Remove the bearing from the output shaft.
8. When removing the output shaft from the case, slide off the first speed gear.
9. Using a puller, remove the countershaft rear bearing.
10. Lift the countershaft assembly out of the case.
11. Remove the countershaft front bearing retainer, gasket and bearing from the front of the case.
12. Remove the reverse idler gear and bearings from the gear bores.
13. Remove any of the 14 output shaft pilot rollers which may have dropped into the case.

OUTPUT SHAFT

Disassembly

1. Remove the fourth and fifth speed synchronizer assembly snapring and thrust washer at the front of the fourth speed gear. Remove the gear.
2. Remove the snapring at the front of the third speed gear sleeve. The second and third speed synchronizer can then be re-

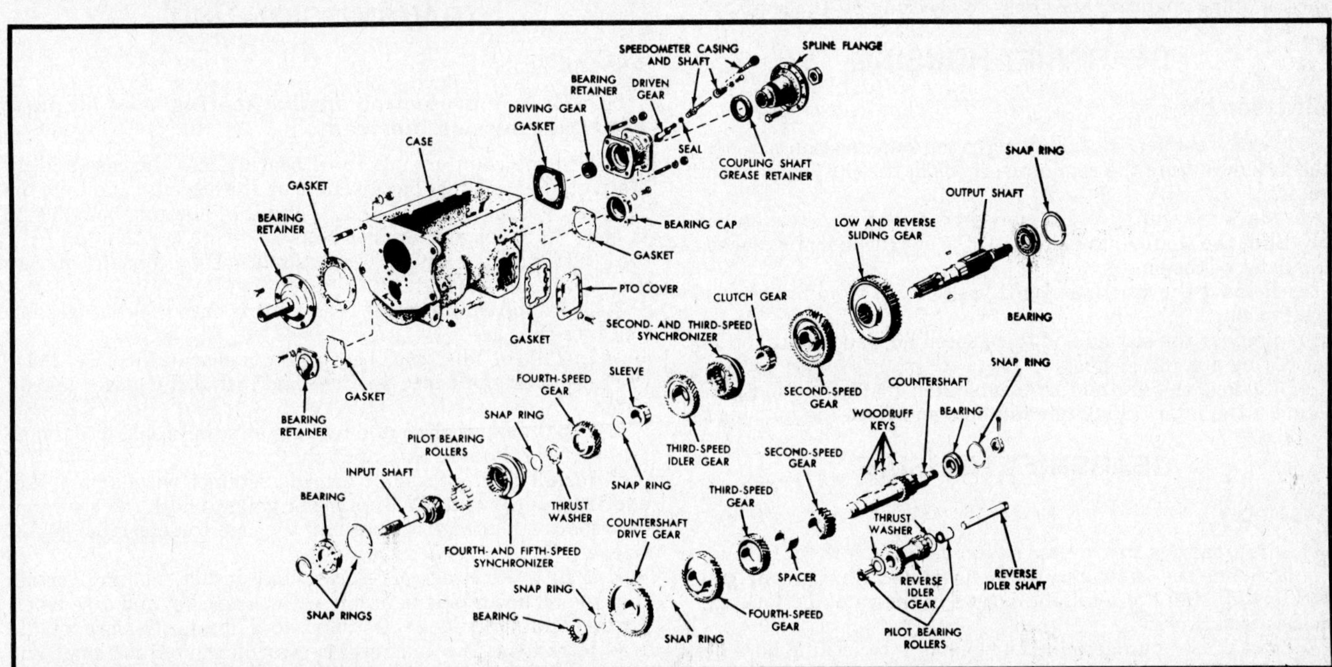

Spicer five speed transmission

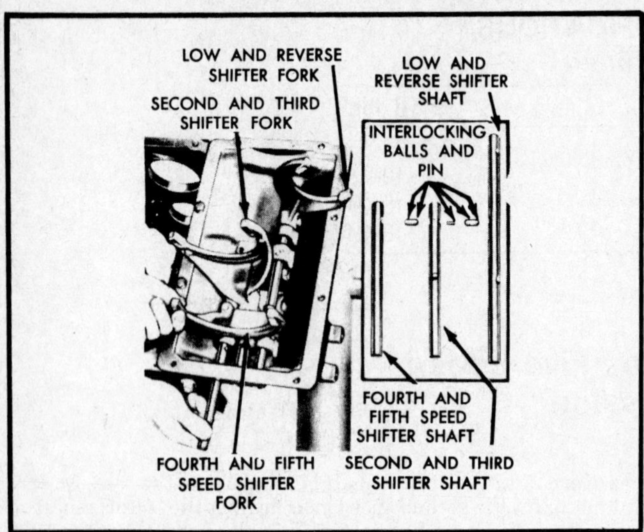

Gearshift housing

moved by bouncing the front of the output shaft on a block of wood.

3. Press the output shaft out of the second and third speed synchronizer clutch gear and second speed gear.

COUNTERSHAFT

Disassembly

When replacing the countershaft or countershaft gear, press off one gear at a time. To remove the second speed gear use special tool.

INPUT SHAFT

Disassembly

Remove the input shaft bearing only for replacement. Remove the retaining snapring and press the bearing off the shaft.

GEARSHIFT HOUSING

Disassembly

1. Attach the gear shift housing to the transmission case. Cut the lock wire from the retaining screws in the shifter forks and gates.
2. Mark the shifter forks, shafts and gates for correct assembly. Shift the shafts into neutral. Drive out the housing plugs at the front of the shafts.
3. Remove the fourth and fifth speed shaft from the front of the housing.
4. Remove the second and third speed fork and shaft and interlocking pin.
5. Remove the low and reverse shifter shaft, fork and gate. Remove the interlocking pin and plungers from the housing.

GEARSHIFT HOUSING

Assembly

1. Place the low and reverse shifter gate and fork in the housing and slide the shaft into the housing and through the gate and fork. Install the retaining screws in the gate and fork and hold with lock wire.
2. Install two plungers in the housing interlocking bore between the low and reverse and second and third shifter shaft bores. Install the interlock pin in the shaft and the second and third speed fork in the housing. Slide the shaft into the housing and through the fork. Install the retaining screw and lock wire.
3. Install the interlocking pin and plunger in the housing interlocking bore between the second and third speed and fourth and fifth speed shifter shaft guides. Install the fourth and fifth speed shaft and fork. Install the retaining screw and lock wire.
4. Check the interlocking system for correct operation and, using sealer, install the housing plugs. Remove the housing from the transmission case.

OUTPUT SHAFT

Assembly

1. Place the second speed gear onto the output shaft, with the clutch teeth facing forward.
2. Insert the two Woodruff keys in the output shaft and install the second and third speed synchronizer clutch gear.
3. Place the second and third speed synchronizer and third speed gear and sleeve on the output shaft. Press the sleeve onto the shaft until it bottoms on the synchronizer clutch gear. The third speed gear sleeve slots must line up with the Woodruff keys in the output shaft.
4. Remove the assembly from the press and install the snapring at the front of the third speed gear sleeve.
5. Install the fourth speed gear, thrust washer and snapring on the output shaft. Install the fourth and fifth speed synchronizer on the output shaft.

COUNTERSHAFT

Assembly

Install gears and spacer onto shaft and hold with the snaprings. Each gear takes a specific Woodruff key, so install them one at a time.

INPUT SHAFT

Assembly

Press the input shaft bearing onto the shaft using special tool.

TRANSMISSION UNIT

Assembly

NOTE: As a protection against scoring, coat all parts with transmission lubricant.

1. Tap the countershaft front bearing into the case and install retainer and new gasket. Line up the oil return holes in the retainer, gasket and case and torque the retaining bolts 50–55 ft. lbs. (30 ft. lbs. for smaller bolts).
2. Place the assembled countershaft in the transmission case into the front bearing.
3. Drive the countershaft rear bearing onto the countershaft and into the case.
4. Install the idler gear bearings and gear in the case. Drive the idler gear shaft into position and install the power takeoff cover.
5. Tap the input shaft and bearing into the case. Place the pilot bearing rollers in the input shaft.
6. Install the input shaft bearing retainer without a gasket and tighten the bolts. With a feeler gauge, check the clearance between the bearing retainer and the case to determine gasket size.
7. Install the bearing retainer and gasket, making certain that the oil drain-hole is in line with the gasket and case holes. Torque retainer bolts to 30 ft. lbs., 40 ft. lbs. for the larger bolt.
8. Install the low and reverse gear on the output shaft and place the assembly in the case. Drive the output shaft bearing into position.

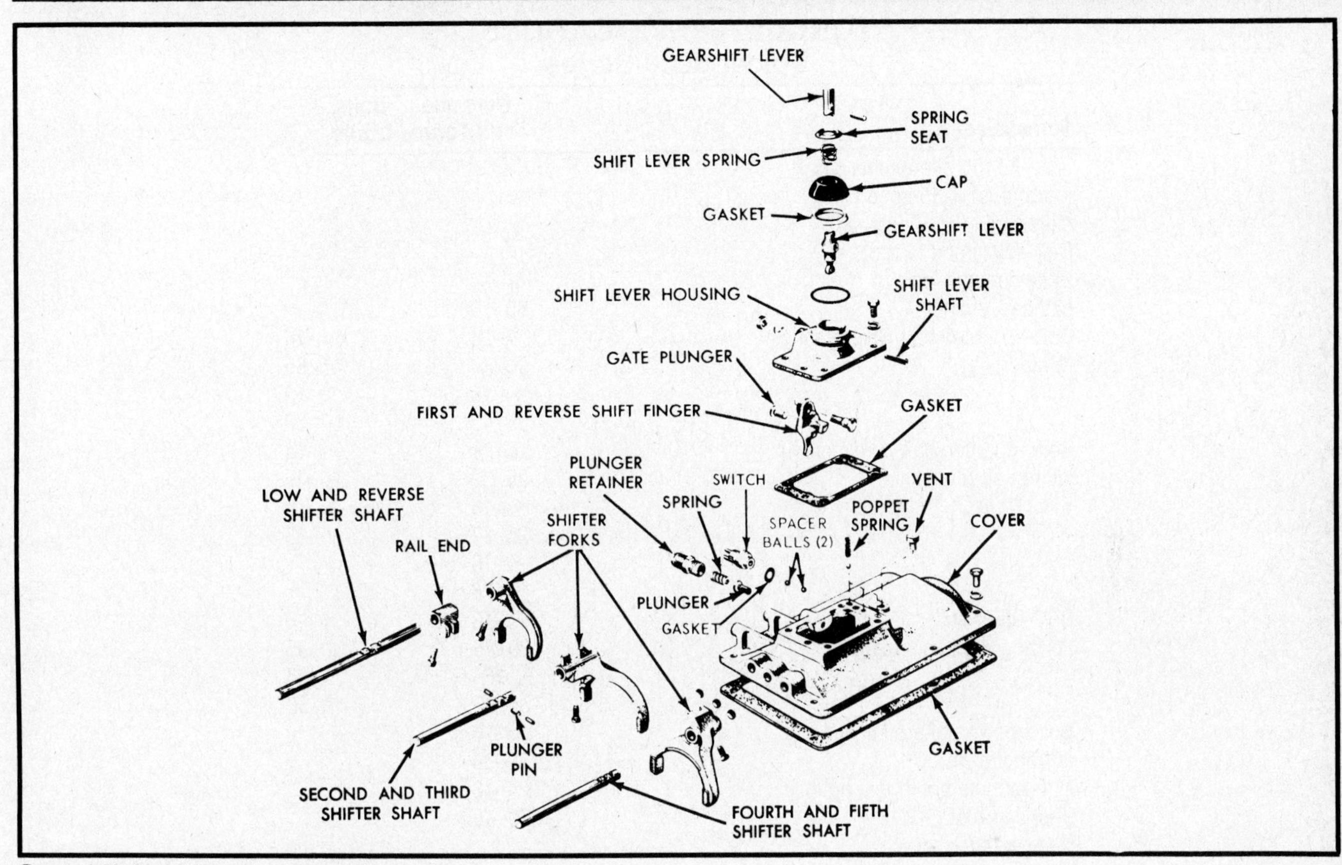

Gearshift housing components

9. Shift the transmission into two gears. Install the countershaft nut and torque at 350–450 ft. lbs. Install the countershaft rear bearing retainer and torque the $^7/_{16}$ in. bolts to 45 ft. lbs.

10. Install a new oil seal in the output shaft bearing retainer. Place the spacer and speedometer driving gear on the output shaft and install the bearing retainer. Torque the bolts to specification.

11. Install the parking brake shoe assembly.

12. Install the brake drum and the spline flange. Torque the output shaft nut to specification.

13. Shift the transmission and gear shift housing into neutral, and install the gear shift housing and, using $^7/_{16}$ in. bolts, torque to 45 ft. lbs.

TORQUE SPECIFICATIONS
Spicer 5000 Series

Nomenclature		Nuts and/or Bolts and Torque Limits	
Bolt-gear shift lever tower to gearshift housing		⅜–16 20–25	7/16–14 30–35
Bolt-clutch housing to trans. case		7/16–14 30–38 ⅝–11 96–120	9/16–12 70–90
Nut-U-joint flange to trans. output shaft	1¼–18 225–275	1.00–20 90–125	1½–18 275–350
Nut—drum parking brake to companion flange		⅜–24 35–45	7/16–20 50–70
Nut—bellcrank to trans.		9/16–18 70–90	
Bolt—lever assy. to trans.		⅜–16 20–25	

TORQUE SPECIFICATIONS
Spicer 5000 Series

Nomenclature	Nuts and/or Bolts and Torque Limits	
Nut—handbrake anchor bar		
to trans. case (5-speed		
extra-heavy duty only)		
Bolt—bellcrank to trans.		
Bolt—reverse lockout	11/16–16	
plunger retainer	80–100	
Bolt—countershaft rear bearing	5/16–18	7/16–14
retainer	25–30	45–55
	3/8–16	1/2–13
	35–40	67–70
Bolt—countershaft & reverse	5/16–18	7/16–14
idler shaft retainer	25–30	40–45
	3/8–16	1/2–13
	25–37	80–85
	3/8–16	
	18–25	
Bolt—gear shift	5/16–18	3/8–16
housing to trans. case	20–25	30–35
	3/8–16	7/16–14
	35–40	45–50
Bolt—power take off cover	3/8–16	
to trans. case	20–30	
Nut—countershaft bearing lock	1 1/4–18	
(5-speed extra h.d. &	350–450	
5-speed exclusive)		
Nut—countershaft bearing lock		
(5-speed exclusive h.d.)		
Bolt—input shaft bearing retainer to trans.	5/16–18	7/16–14
case	25–30	40–45
	3/8–16	
	25–30	
Bolt—countershaft	5/16–18	7/16–14
front bearing retainer	25–30	50–55
	3/8–16	
	25–35	

Spicer 6000 Series Five Speed Transmissions

This transmission is a 5 speed synchromesh helical gear design with direct drive in 5th speed on all models, except the 6853C, which has overdrive in 5th speed.

Engagement of all gears, except first and reverse, is aided by sleeve type synchronizers. All gears are of helical design, with the exception of first and reverse gears. Lubricant capacity is 17 pints.

TRANSMISSION MAINSHAFT

Removal

1. Remove clutch housing and clutch release mechanism as a unit.
2. Engage 2nd and 3rd synchronizer with mainshaft 2nd speed gear and engage 4th and 5th synchronizer with mainshaft 4th speed or overdrive gear to lock transmission in two gears.
3. Remove companion flange or yoke retaining nut. Use puller to remove flange or yoke.
4. Remove speedometer driven gear and adapter (if used) from mainshaft rear bearing cap.
5. Remove mainshaft and countershaft rear bearing caps and gaskets.
6. Remove cotter pin and countershaft rear bearing nut.
7. Remove speedometer drive gear or spacer from rear end of mainshaft.
8. Remove mainshaft rear bearing snapring.
9. Using bearing puller, remove mainshaft rear bearing.
10. Remove mainshaft and gear assembly from the transmis-

GENERAL DATA

Make		Spicer
Type		5-Speed Synchromesh
Models		6852S, 6852K, 6852G, and 6853C
Clutch housing		S.A.E. #2
Gear ratios—all ratios are (to 1)		
Transmission Model	6852G	6852K
1st	6.70	6.70
2nd	3.52	4.02
3rd	1.97	2.49
4th	1.17	1.57
5th	1.00	1.00
Reverse	6.72	6.72
Transmission Model	6852S	6852C
1st	5.71	5.71
2nd	3.20	3.00
3rd	1.89	1.78
4th	1.15	1.00
5th	1.00	0.85
Reverse	5.73	5.73

sion case by clearing it from main drive gear and sliding assembly up and forward out of rear bearing bore.

MAINSHAFT

Disassembly

1. Remove the 1st and reverse sliding gear from mainshaft.
2. Remove 4th and 5th synchronizer.
3. Remove snapring and thrust washer.
4. Slide mainshaft 4th speed or overdrive gear from end of mainshaft.
5. Remove mainshaft 3rd speed gear and mainshaft 4th speed or overdrive gear sleeve.

NOTE: If necessary to press off gear and sleeve, shift 2nd and 3rd synchronizer into engagement with mainshaft 2nd speed gear and support under 3rd speed gear. Be sure to remove sleeve pin from the inside of 4th speed or overdrive gear sleeve.

6. Slide 2nd and 3rd synchronizer from mainshaft.
7. Remove snapring from 2nd and 3rd speed clutch gear.
8. Support mainshaft 2nd speed gear under arbor press and press mainshaft out of 2nd and 3rd speed clutch gear and 2nd speed gear.

MAINDRIVE GEAR

Removal

1. Remove 14 mainshaft pilot bearing rollers which may have remained in cavity of main drive gear.
2. Remove main bearing cap and gasket.
3. Remove snapring from main drive gear bearing.
4. Remove main drive gear and bearing assembly from transmission case.

Disassembly

1. Remove main drive gear bearing retaining snapring.
2. Using bearing remover plates with an arbor press, remove bearing from main drive gear.

REVERSE IDLER GEAR

Removal

NOTE: When removing the reverse idler gear shaft, support the gear to prevent it from being damaged.

1. Using remover tool, remove reverse idler gear shaft, gear and bearings.

COUNTERSHAFT

Removal

1. Using puller, remove countershaft rear bearing.
2. Lift the countershaft assembly out of transmission case.
3. Press or drive countershaft front bearing from bore of transmission case.

Disassembly

1. Support countershaft drive gear with parallel bars under hub and press countershaft free of gear.
2. Remove exposed countershaft gear key and snapring. Support 4th speed or overdrive gear and press countershaft free of gear.
3. Follow the same procedure and remove 2nd and 3rd speed gear.
4. Remove the remaining countershaft gear key.

SUBASSEMBLIES

Assembly

Cleanliness is of the utmost importance. The transmission should be rebuilt in a clean working area. All parts, except those actually being worked on should be covered with clean lint-free paper. Avoid nicking, marring, or burring all surfaces.

NOTE: Coat all thrust washers, splines of shafts and bores of all gears with lubricant to provide initial lubrication thus preventing scoring or galling.

MAINSHAFT

Assembly

1. Position mainshaft in a soft jawed vise, front end up. Fit of new parts may require the use of an arbor press. If so, set up vertically and follow same procedure.
2. Position 2nd speed gear on mainshaft with clutch teeth and synchronizer cone facing up.
3. Using a suitable sleeve, press or drive 2nd and 3rd speed clutch gear on mainshaft. Install snapring in mainshaft groove. Minimum end clearance between 2nd and 3rd speed clutch gear and 2nd speed gear should be 0.004 in. Correct accordingly.
4. Slide 2nd and 3rd speed synchronizer on mainshaft until engaged with 2nd and 3rd speed clutch gear. The 2nd and 3rd speed synchronizer is often assembled backward on the mainshaft. Make sure that the long hub on synchronizer clutch gear faces the 2nd speed gear.
5. Place 3rd speed gear on mainshaft with clutch teeth and synchronizer cone facing downward.
6. Assemble sleeve pin to 4th speed or overdrive gear sleeve with head of pin inside sleeve, with flanged end of sleeve facing the 3rd speed gear, align sleeve pin with splines and press on the mainshaft.
7. Place 4th speed or overdrive gear on sleeve with clutch hub facing up and secure with thrust washer and snapring.

MAIN DRIVE GEAR

Assembly

1. Press or drive main drive gear bearing onto main drive gear shaft and install snapring.

1 Main drive gear
2 Main drive gear bearing cap
3 Mainshaft pilot bearing rollers
4 Snap ring
5 Clutch housing
6 4th and 5th shift rod
7 4th and 5th shift fork
8 4th and 5th synchronizer
9 Poppet ball
10 Poppet spring
11 Snap ring
12 Thrust washer
13 Mainshaft 4th speed or overdrive gear
14 Mainshaft 4th speed or overdrive gear sleeve
15 Mainshaft 3rd speed gear
15 Mainshaft 3rd speed gear
16 2nd and 3rd shift fork
17 Snap ring
18 Mainshaft 2nd and 3rd speed clutch gear
19 2nd and 3rd synchronizer
20 Mainshaft 2nd speed gear
21 1st and reverse shift rod
22 1st and reverse shift fork
23 Mainshaft 1st and reverse sliding gear
24 Mainshaft
25 Shifter housing
26 Mainshaft rear bearing
27 Snap ring
28 Speedometer driven gear
29 Mainshaft rear bearing cap oil seal
30 Companion flange
31 Companion flange nut
32 Mainshaft rear bearing cap
33 Speedometer drive gear
34 Countershaft rear bearing
35 Countershaft rear bearing cap
36 Countershaft rear bearing nut
37 Snap ring

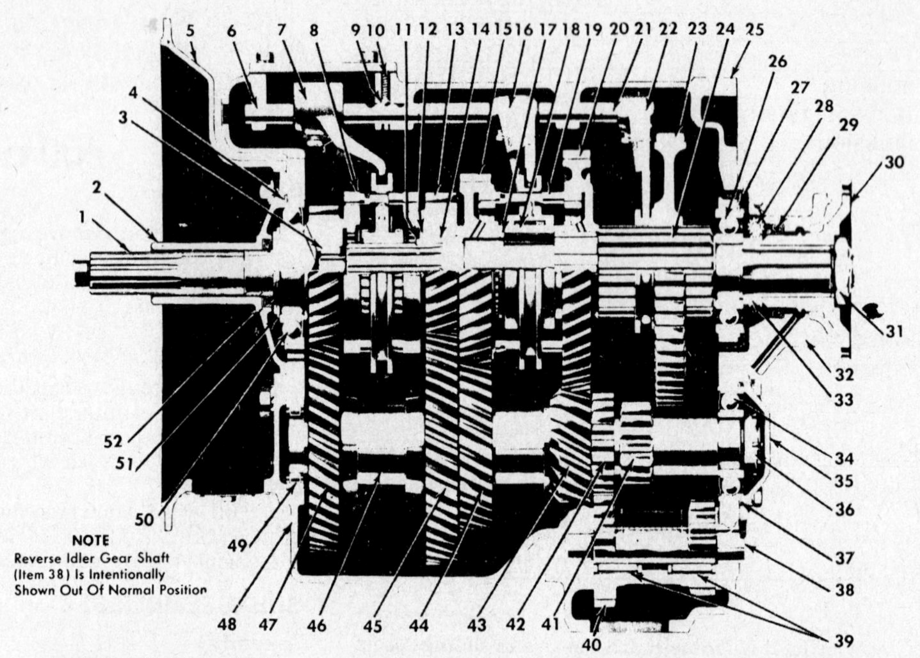

NOTE
Reverse Idler Gear Shaft (Item 38) Is Intentionally Shown Out Of Normal Position

38 Reverse idler gear shaft
39 Reverse idler gear bearings
40 Reverse idler gear
41 Countershaft 1st gear teeth
42 Countershaft reverse gear teeth
43 Countershaft 2nd speed gear
44 Countershaft 3rd speed gear
45 Countershaft 4th speed or overdrive gear
46 Countershaft
47 Countershaft drive gear
48 Transmission case
49 Countershaft front bearing
50 Main drive gear bearing
51 Snap ring
52 Main drive gear bearing cap oil seal

Spicer 6000 series five speed transmission

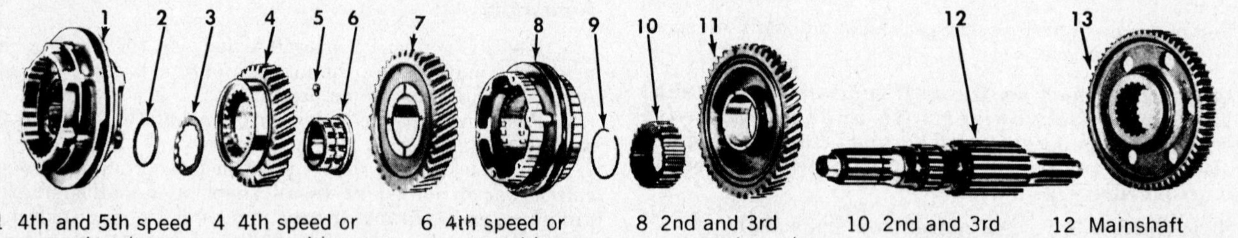

1 4th and 5th speed synchronizer
2 Snap ring
3 Thrust washer
4 4th speed or overdrive gear
5 Sleeve pin
6 4th speed or over-drive gear sleeve
7 3rd speed gear
8 2nd and 3rd speed synchronizer
9 Snap ring
10 2nd and 3rd clutch gear
11 2nd speed gear
12 Mainshaft
13 1st and reverse sliding gear

Mainshaft components

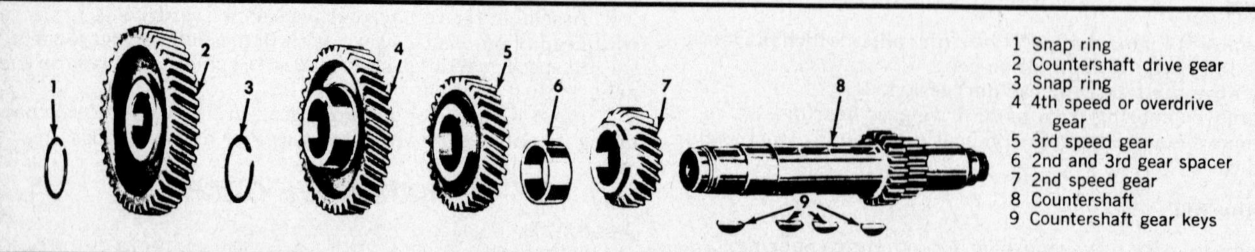

1 Snap ring
2 Countershaft drive gear
3 Snap ring
4 4th speed or overdrive gear
5 3rd speed gear
6 2nd and 3rd gear spacer
7 2nd speed gear
8 Countershaft
9 Countershaft gear keys

Countershaft components

COUNTERSHAFT

Assembly

1. Position first countershaft gear key in slot of countershaft. Press 2nd speed gear and, 2nd and 3rd gear spacer onto countershaft.
2. Install the remaining countershaft gear keys. It may be necessary to dress the keys with a file.
3. Press 3rd speed gear on the countershaft, followed by 4th speed gear, a snapring and drive gear secured by a snapring.

MAINSHAFT

Installation

1. Place mainshaft 1st and reverse sliding gear at an angle in the rear of the transmission case with shift fork collar facing toward front of case.
2. Place 4th and 5th synchronizer on mainshaft. Shift synchronizer clutch collar into engagement with mainshaft 4th speed or overdrive gear to help lock synchronizer in place during installation in case.
3. Lower rear of mainshaft into case, through 1st and reverse sliding gear and out mainshaft rear bearing bore. There must be fourteen pilot bearing rollers in the main drive gear pocket.
4. Lower front of mainshaft to mesh with countershaft gears. Slide rear of mainshaft into pocket of main drive gear.
5. Slide rear bearing onto mainshaft with snapring facing the rear.
6. Tap bearing into case bore with its snapring flush with rear of case.
7. Press speedometer drive gear or spacer onto the mainshaft against bearing. Install new oil seal in mainshaft rear bearing cap.
8. Install gasket with sealing cement and mainshaft rear bearing cap and torque cap screws 35–40 ft. lbs. Install speedometer driven gear (when used) through opening in mainshaft rear bearing cap.
9. Engage 2nd and 3rd synchronizer with mainshaft 2nd speed gear and 4th and 5th synchronizer with mainshaft 4th speed or overdrive gear to lock transmission in two gears.
10. Install companion flange or yoke on mainshaft and secure with a washer and nut at a torque of 320–350 ft. lbs.
11. Remove rear bearing cap from countershaft and torque bearing nut to 320–350 ft. lbs. and secure with cotter pin.
12. Install gasket and countershaft rear bearing (with sealing cement) and torqe cap screws to 35–40 ft. lbs. The projection on the countershaft rear bearing cap locks the reverse idler gear shaft into proper position.
13. Rotate main drive gear to check for free rotation of all gears and shafts.
14. Use pressure type oil can, filled with transmission lubricant (S.A.E. 50 engine oil of good quality) to force oil through holes and end slots of all mainshaft gears to open oil passageways. Using the pressure type oil can, spray gear teeth with transmission lubricant to provide initial lubrication and to prevent corrosion.

MAIN DRIVE GEAR

Installation

1. Install main drive gear and bearing from inside the transmission case, by tapping bearing through case bore.
2. Install snapring on outer race of bearing. Tap bearing rearward, so snapring is flush with case. Install new oil seal in main drive gear bearing cap.
3. Install gasket (with sealing cement) and main drive gear bearing cap to transmission case and torque 60–80 ft. lbs. Be sure the oil passages in the bearing cap, gasket and transmission case are all aligned.
4. Coat the pocket of main drive gear with light weight ball and roller bearing grease.
5. Place the fourteen pilot bearing rollers in main drive gear pocket.

REVERSE IDLER GEAR

Installation

1. Install reverse idler gear bearings into gear and install in transmission case, with large gear on idler gear toward front of case. Mesh idler gear with countershaft and align bore of bearings with hole in transmission case.
2. Insert reverse idler gear shaft in rear of case, noting that "flat" on shaft is squared toward countershaft so that it can be locked by rear bearing cap.
3. Set countershaft rear bearing cap in place to check lock of reverse idler shaft. Finger tighten bearing cap screws to prevent countershaft from moving during installation of mainshaft.

COUNTERSHAFT

Installation

1. Press countershaft front bearing on front of countershaft.
2. Lower countershaft assembly into case, guiding rear end of shaft out through rear of case.
3. Guide countershaft front bearing into countershaft front bearing bore.
4. Place two strips of flat steel stock, approximately $^3/_8$ in. thick, between countershaft drive gear and wall of case.
5. Seat bearing on shaft (should be tight fit) then remove the two steel strips and tap bearing into bore seating snapring against case.
6. Hand tighten countershaft rear bearing nut.

REMOTE CONTROL ASSEMBLY

Removal

NOTE: The Spicer 6000 transmission uses two different remote control assemblies: prop shaft type and rod type.

1. Remove retainer, plunger pin spring and plunger.
2. Remove remote control assembly from transmission as described below. Tilt the remote control assembly slightly to the left during removal to prevent the plunger from falling into the transmission.
3. Remove the plunger from the 1st and reverse shift finger.

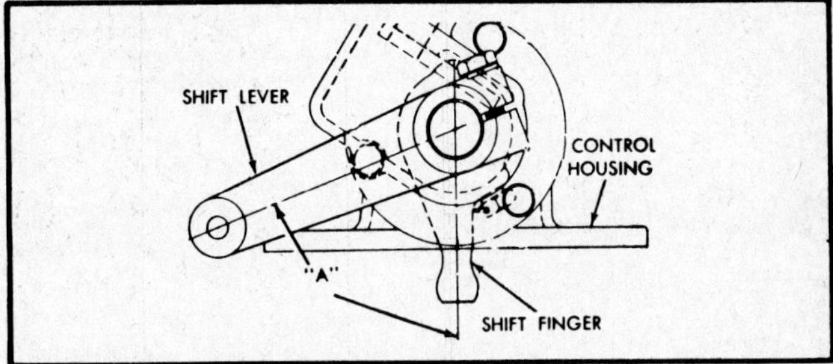

Rod type remote control adjustment

Installation

1. Coat remote control assembly position on shifter housing.
2. Position plunger in 1st and reverse shift finger; then carefully install remote control assembly as shown, keeping the assembly slightly tilted to the left to prevent the plunger from falling into transmission.

3. Install plunger pin, plunger pin spring and retainer.
4. Install remote control assembly-to-shifter housing attaching parts. Tighten cap screws firmly.

CONTROL TOWER

Installation

Install control tower as described below only when the transmission is going into storage.

1. Coat gasket with sealing cement and position on shifter housing.
2. Position plunger in 1st and reverse shift finger, then place the assembly and new gasket (with cement) on the shifter housing.
3. Install plunger, plunger spring and plunger retainer and tighten down the tower with washers and capscrews.

SHIFTER HOUSING

Removal

NOTE: The Spicer 6000 transmission uses a forward control shifter housing and a center control shifter housing.

1. Remove shifter housing to transmission case attaching parts. Carefully remove forward control shifter housing to prevent loss of the three poppet balls and springs.
2. Carefully remove shifter housing from the case.

Installation

NOTE: Make certain that shift forks and transmission clutch collars are in neutral position.

1. Carefully position shifter housing and gasket (use cement) on transmission case and make sure all three shift forks are in their corresponding shift collar and tighten down.
2. Use small pry bar and check movement of each shift rod for proper shift action. Return shift rods to neutral position. On transmissions using the forward control shifter housing, place the three poppet balls and springs in the shifter housing.

TORQUE SPECIFICATIONS
Spicer 6000 Series

Location	ft. lbs.
Shift fork set screws	45–50
Main drive gear bearing cap retaining cap screws	60–80
Mainshaft rear bearing cap retaining cap screws	35–40
Mainshaft flange or yoke retaining nut	320–350
Countershaft rear bearing retaining nut	320–350
Countershaft rear bearing cap retaining cap screws	35–40
Clutch housing retaining cap screws	90–95

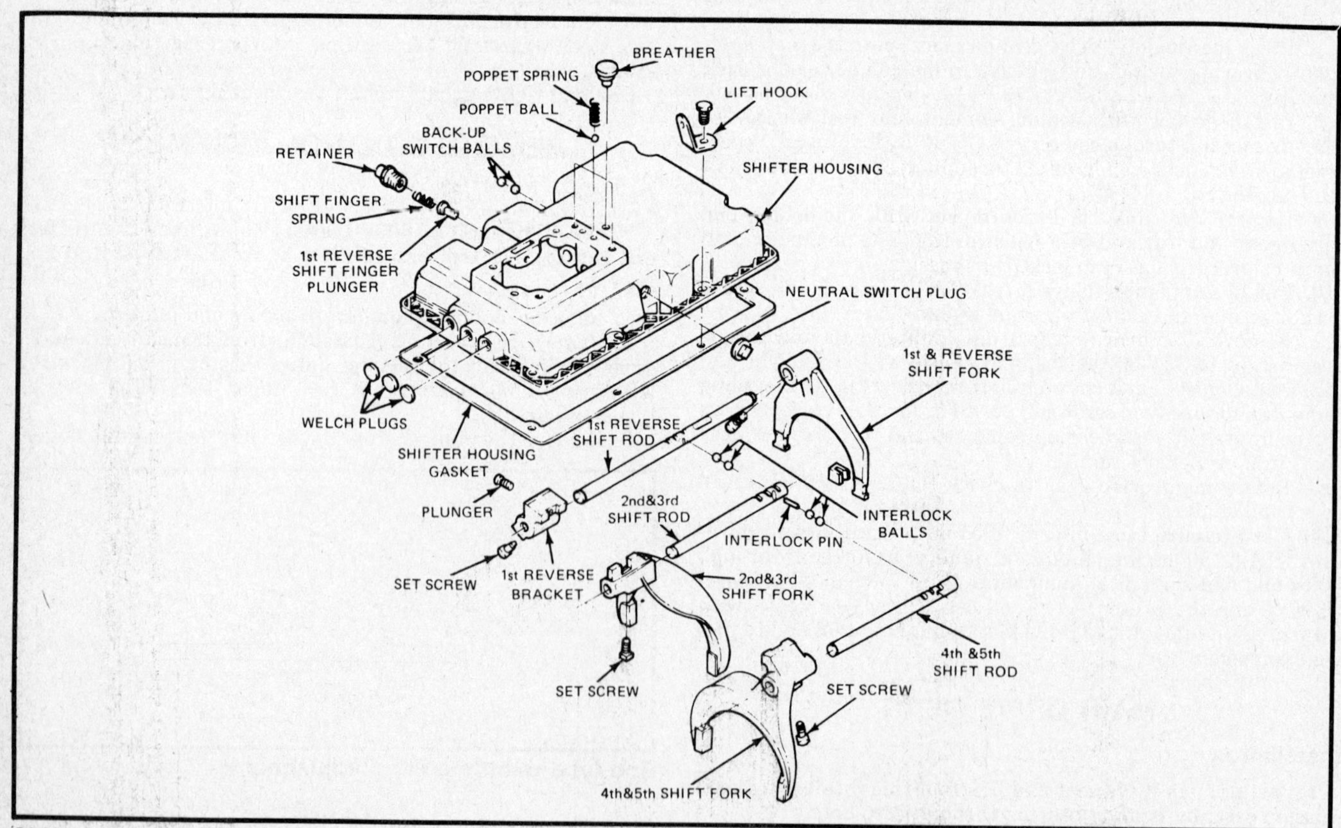

Shifter housing—exploded view

Spicer 50 and 60 Series Five Speed

MAIN TRANSMISSION

Disassembly

1. Remove the shifter housing from the transmission. Lift the housing straight up and use caution not to lose the poppet balls and springs.
2. Use a pry bar and engage the 2nd/3rd speed synchronizer with the 2nd/3rd speed gear and the 4th/5th speed synchronizer with the 4th/5th speed gear. Lock the transmission in two gears.
3. Using a suitable puller, remove the flange retaining nut from the mainshaft and remove the output flange.
4. Remove the mainshaft rear bearing capscrews and pry the bearing cap from the case. If either bearing or seal needs replacing tap out using a drift or a punch.
5. Remove the speedometer gear from the mainshaft.
6. Remove the capscrews retaining the drive gear front bearing cap and remove the bearing cap. A split ring shim is located behind the bearing cup to set the mainshaft end play.
7. Remove the drive gear from the case. If the drive gear bearing needs to be replaced, use a suitable puller on the inner race of the bearing.
8. Inspect the pocket bearing cup in the drive gear for damage. If it is damaged on the C50 transmission the drive gear must be replaced since the cup is machined into the gear. On the C60 transmission the cup is pressed in and out.
9. Carefully lift the mainshaft assembly from the transmission case by using a suitable hook or another lifting device around the 2nd/3rd speed synchronizer.
10. Remove the countershaft rear bearing cap. The countershaft may be moved to the rear by the removal of the bearing cap, allowing the bearing cup to fall out of the transmission case bore.
11. Using a puller, remove the reverse gear idler shaft while holding the reverse idler gear and bearings inside the case, then remove the idler gear, bearings, spacer and thrust washers from the case.
12. Tie a rope around the countershaft, behind the drive gear. Carefully pry the countershaft assembly rearward until the bearing cup is out of the case bore and the front bearing is clear of the front bearing cup. Carefully lift the countershaft assembly from the case.
13. Inspect the countershaft front bearing cup and if damaged remove the clutch housing and gasket. Then remove the spacer ring. From inside the case tap forward on the bearing cup using a soft drift and a hammer.

SUBASSEMBLIES MAINSHAFT

CM50—Disassembly

1. Using a suitable puller, remove the rear bearing, thrust washer and reverse gear. The caged needle bearings can be removed from the end of the shaft once the reverse gear is removed.
2. Remove the 1st/reverse sliding clutch collar from the mainshaft.
3. Using a suitable puller on the 4th/5th speed synchronizer, remove the drive gear pocket bearing and synchronizer from the mainshaft.
4. Remove the 4th speed gear snapring, located deep inside the gear bore, with a pair of snapring pliers.

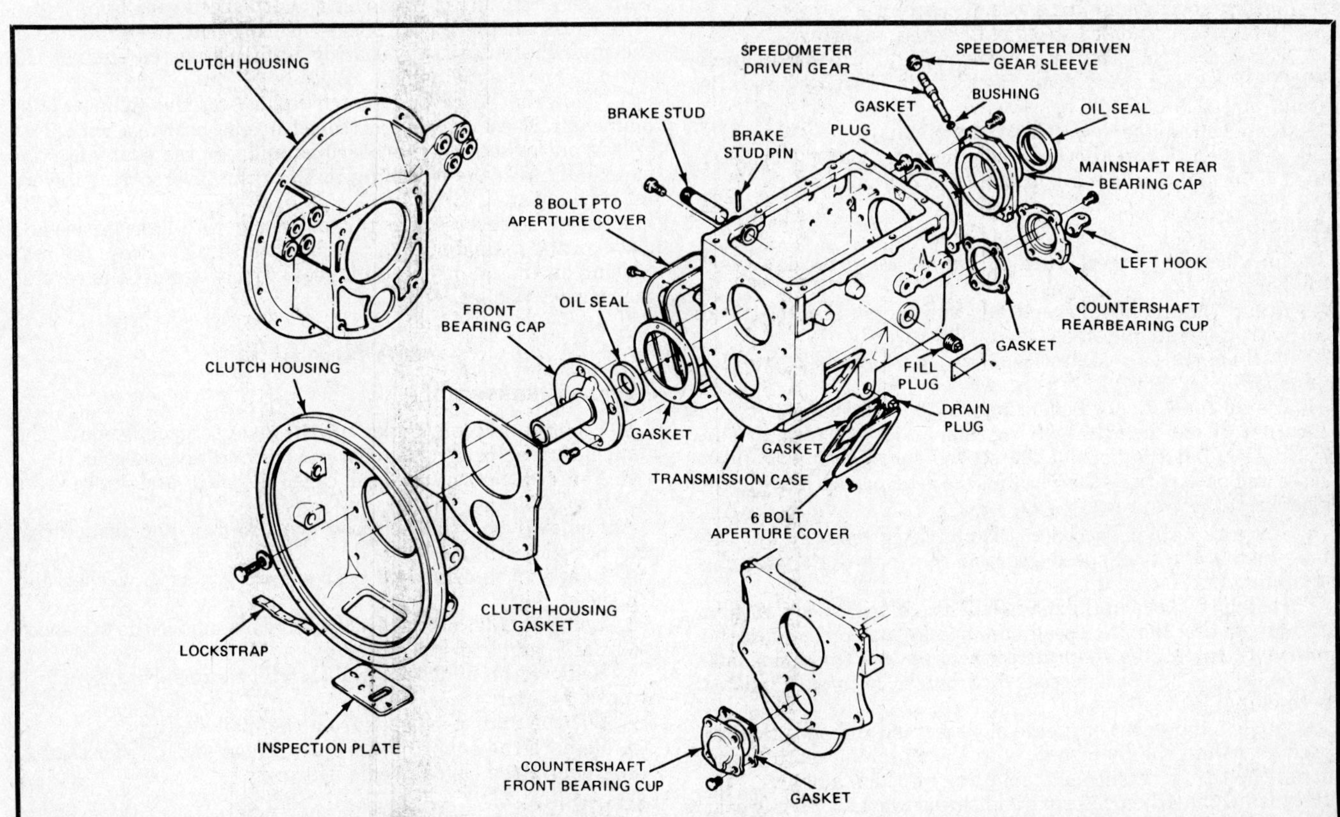

Typical transmission case

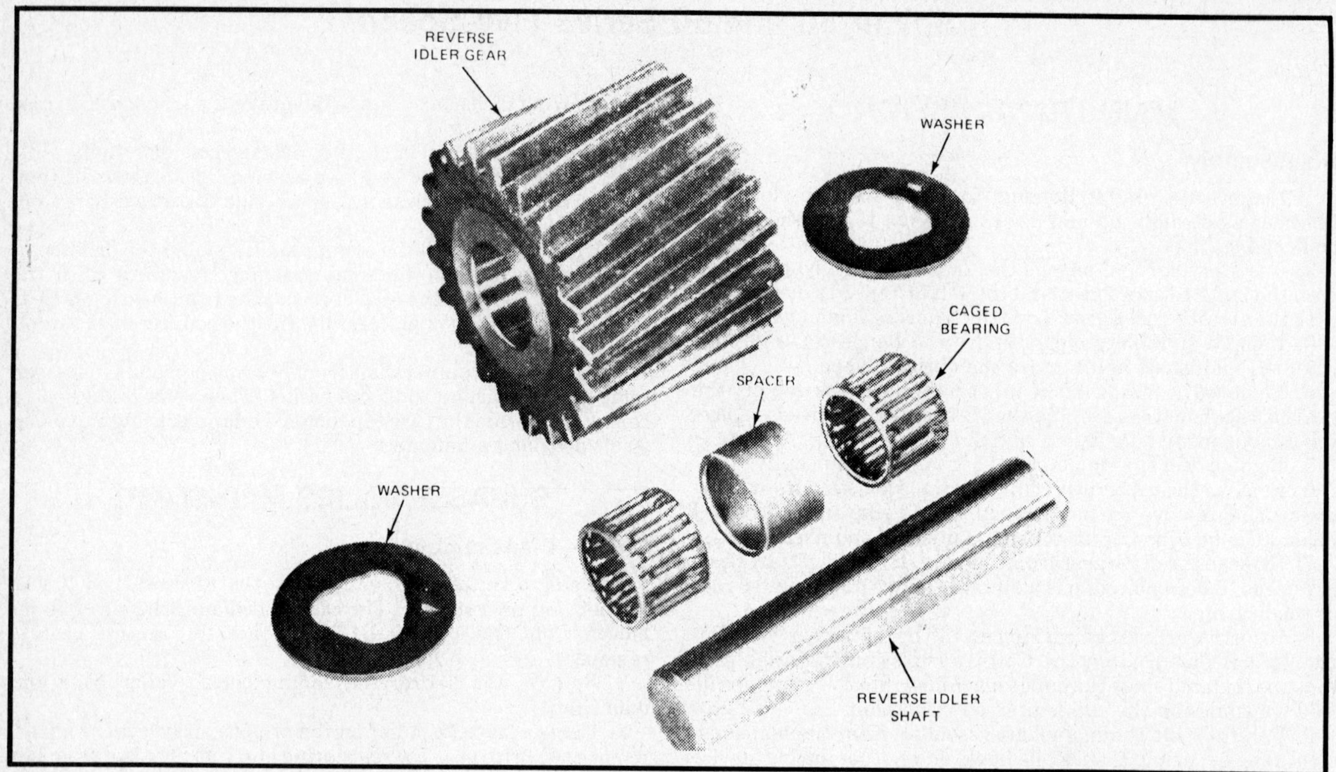

Reverse gear idler shaft assembly

5. Remove the 3rd speed gear snapring, thrust washer, 3rd speed gear and 2nd and 3rd speed synchronizer.
6. Remove the 2nd/3rd speed clutch gear snapring.
7. Using a suitable puller remove the 2nd/3rd speed clutch gear. Pull the 2nd speed gear off the main shaft by hand. Be careful not to lose needle bearings.
8. Remove the two keys from the mainshaft.
9. Remove the three loose needle bearing spacer rings, 1st speed snapring, thrust washer and 1st speed gear.

Assembly

1. Lubricate the caged bearings and install in the 1st speed gear bore.
2. Stand the mainshaft vertically and install the 1st speed gear with the clutching teeth facing downward.
3. Lubricate the thrust washer and install it on the mainshaft.
4. Install the 1st speed snapring on the mainshaft.
5. Install the needle bearing spacer to the rear of the mainshaft. Coat the bore of the second speed gear with light grease and pack with two rows of needle bearings with one spacer between the two rows.
6. Place the other spacer in the clutching teeth end of the bore. Install the 2nd speed gear on the mainshaft with the clutching teeth facing up.
7. Install the keys in the mainshaft and align the keyways in the bore of the 2nd/3rd speed clutch gear and press onto the mainshaft. Install the snapring in the groove of the mainshaft.
8. Slide the 2nd/3rd speed synchronizer onto the 2nd/3rd speed clutch gear.
9. Apply a light coat of grease as necessary and slide the 3rd speed gear onto the mainshaft with the clutching teeth down. Install the thrust washer and snapring on the mainshaft.
10. Install the 4th speed gear and thrust washer. Firmly seat the 4th speed gear snapring under the bore of the gear in the groove on the mainshaft.
11. Slide the 4th/5th speed synchronizer onto the mainshaft with the larger brass ring over the 4th speed gear hub.
12. Press the drive gear pocket bearing onto the front end of the mainshaft until the bearing is firmly seated against the shoulder on the mainshaft.
13. Slide the 1st/reverse clutch collar over the splines of the mainshaft. Coat the reverse caged needle bearings with light grease and assemble the bearings and reverse gear onto the mainshaft with the clutching teeth of the reverse gear toward 1st speed gear.
14. Coat the reverse gear thrust washer with light grease and place on the mainshaft against the reverse gear. Press the rear bearing on the mainshaft so it seats firmly against the reverse gear thrust washer.

MAINSHAFT

CM60—Disassembly

1. Using a suitable puller on the reverse gear, remove the mainshaft rear bearing, thrust washer and reverse gear.
2. Remove the reverse gear caged bearings and 1st–reverse clutch collar.
3. Remove the 4th/5th speed synchronizer and front drive gear pocket bearing.
4. Remove the 4th/speed gear snapring, thrust washer and 4th speed gear.
5. Using a puller on the 3rd speed gear, remove the 4th speed gear sleeve and 3rd speed gear.
6. Remove the 2nd/3rd speed clutch gear snapring, synchronizer and clutch gear.
7. Lift the 2nd speed gear from the mainshaft.
8. Remove the snapring, thrust washers and 1st speed gear.
9. Remove the caged needle bearings.

Assembly

1. Lubricate the caged needle bearings and install in the 1st speed gear.

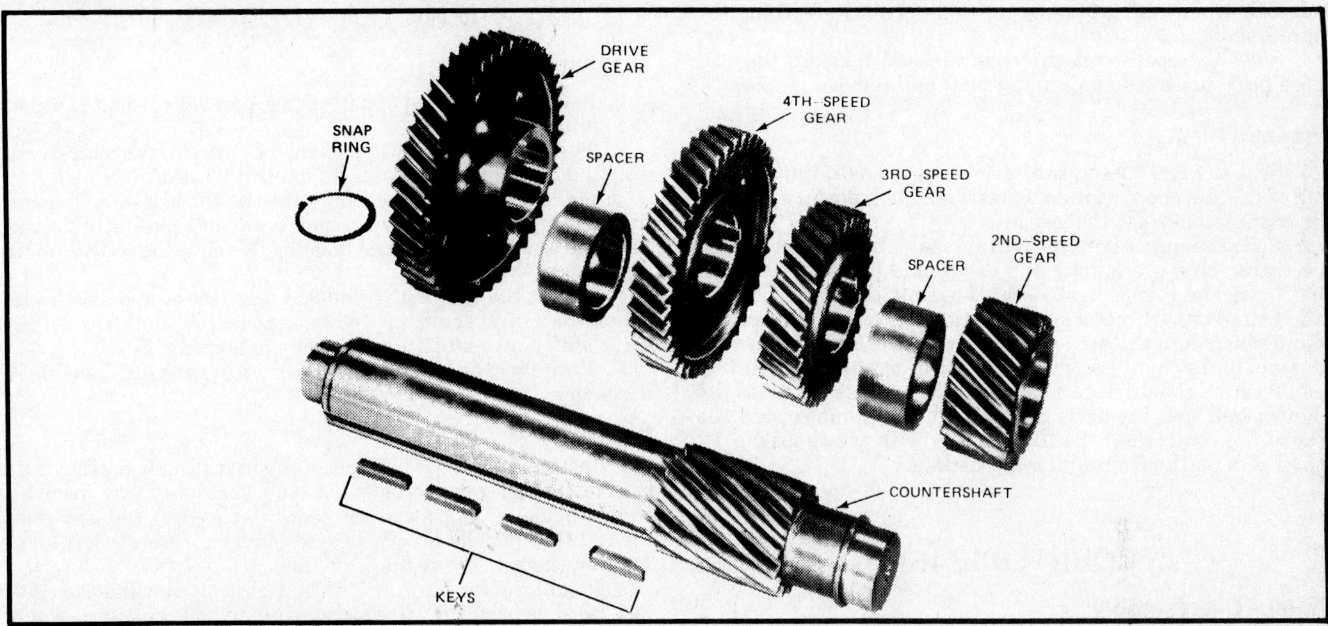

CM60 countershaft assembly

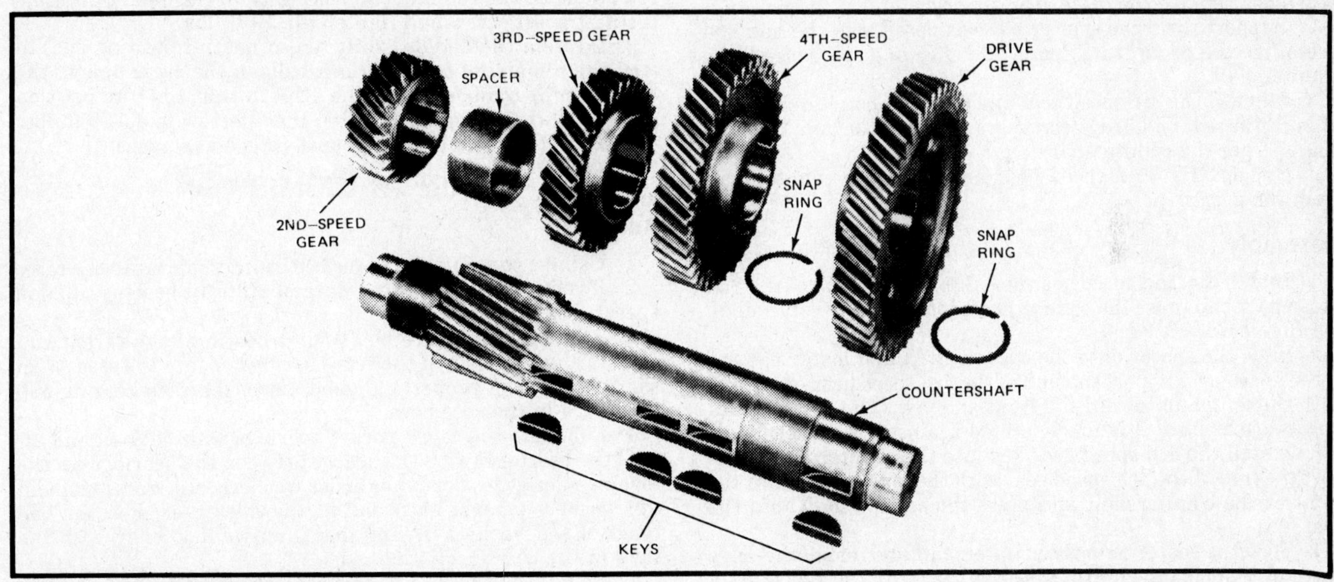

CM50 countershaft assembly

2. Install the 1st speed gear with the clutch teeth toward the front, lubricate the thrust washer and install it and the snapring.

3. Slide the 2nd speed gear on the mainshaft with the clutch teeth toward front. Install the 2nd–3rd speed clutch gear, synchronizer (with the long hub toward 2nd gear) and snapring.

4. Install the 3rd–speed gear with the clutch teeth toward the rear of the mainshaft. Align the pin in the bore or the 4th–speed gear sleeve with the spline of the mainshaft and slide the sleeve into place with the flange facing the 3rd speed gear.

5. Drive the 4th speed into position with a suitable driver.

6. Lubricate the thrust washer and assemble the 4th speed gear, thrust washer and snapring on the mainshaft.

7. Install the 4th/5th speed synchronizer on the mainshaft with the larger brass ring toward the 4th speed gear.

8. Press the drive gear pocket bearing onto the mainshaft with the inner race against the shoulder on the mainshaft.

9. Lubricate the caged bearings and install them in the bore of the reverse gear. Slide the 1st/reverse clutch collar and install the reverse gear on the mainshaft with the clutch teeth toward 1st speed gear.

10. Lubricate the thrust washer and install it on the mainshaft against the reverse gear. Press the rear bearing on the main shaft.

COUNTERSHAFT

CM50—Disassembly

1. Using a puller on the inner race remove the front and rear bearings from the countershaft. Remove the drive gear snapring.

2. Support the drive gear as close as possible to the hub and press out the countershaft.

3. Remove the 4th speed gear snapring. Support the 3rd speed gear and press the countershaft until it is free of both the

3rd and 4th speed gears. Remove the gear keys from the countershaft.

4. Slide the spacer off the counrershaft. Support the 2nd speed gear, press out the countershaft and remove the key.

Assembly

1. Seat the 2nd speed gear in the countershaft. Support the hub of the 2nd speed gear on a press (long hub down) and press the countershaft into the gear.
2. Slide the spacer onto the countershaft and position the 3rd speed gear on a press (long hub down) and press the countershaft until the gear is firmly seated against the spacer.
3. Install the 4th speed gear onto the countershaft. Press the countershaft into the 4th speed gear with the long hub toward the front of the countershaft. Secure the gear with the snapring.
4. Position the drive gear key onto the crankshaft. Press the countershaft into the drive gear with the long hub toward the rear of the coutershaft. Secure the gear with the snapring.
5. Press on the front and rear bearings.

COUNTERSHAFT

CM60—Disassembly

1. Using a puller on the inner race, remove the front and rear bearings. Remove the drive gear snapring.
2. Support the drive gear as close as possible to the hub and press free the drive gear. Remove the key and spacer from the countershaft.
3. Support the 3rd speed gear and press the countershaft free of both the 4th and 3rd speed gears. Remove the two keys and spacer from the countershaft.
4. Support the 2nd speed gear and press the countershaft from the gear.

Assembly

1. Install the 2nd speed gear key. Support the hub of the 2nd speed gear and press the countershaft into the gear while aligning the keyway.
2. Slide the spacer onto the countershaft and install the 3rd speed gear key. Support the hub of the 3rd speed gear on a press with the long hub toward the front and press the countershaft into the gear until it is firmly seated against the spacer.
3. Install the 4th speed gear key into the countershaft. Support the hub of the 4th speed gear with the long hub toward the front of the countershaft and press the countershaft into the gear.
4. Slide the spacer onto the countershaft and install the drive gear key. Support the hub of the drive gear with the long hub toward the rear of the countershaft and press the countershaft into the drive gear. Secure with the snapring.
5. Press on the front and rear bearings.

OVERHEAD CONTROL

Disassembly

1. Position the gearshift housing on edge in a vise.
2. Depress the collar against the spring and remove the lockpin.
3. Slide the compression cup up the lever and remove the rock shaft snapring.
4. Tap the rock shaft free of the dome and remove the gearshift lever and ring.
5. Remove the knob and slide the collar, spring and cup off of the lever.
6. Assembly is the reverse of the disassembly procedure.

SHIFTER HOUSING

Disassembly

1. Remove the three poppet springs and balls from the top of the shifter housing.
2. Turn the shifter upside down and position the 1st/reverse and 2nd/3rd shift forks into the neutral position.
3. Remove the set screw from the 4th/5th shift fork. Tap the 4th/5th shift rod forward with a drift pin until the end of the rod pops the welch plug from the housing. Remove the rod and shift fork.
4. Repeat Step 3 for the 2nd/3rd and 1st/reverse shift rods. When the 1st/reverse shift rod is removed, lift both the 1st/reverse shift fork and bracket out of the housing.
5. Remove the interlock balls and back-up switch if necessary.

Assembly

1. Install the lockout plunger in the first/reverse bracket. Lubricate the 1st–reverse shift rod and slide part way into the shifter housing. Align the bracket with the shift rod and slide the rod through the bracket, bosses and 1st–reverse shift fork. Tighten the set screws 40–50 ft. lbs.
2. Install the two interlock balls. Lubricate the 2nd/3rd shift rod and slide part way into the housing. Install the interlock pin and hold in place with heavy grease. Align the shift fork with the rod and slide the rod into the boss until in the detent position. Install the set screw and tighten 40–50 ft. lbs.
3. Position the 2nd/3rd shift rod in neutral position and install the remaining two interlock balls in the cross hole of the 4th/5th shift rod boss. Slide the 4th/5th shift rod into position and install the shift fork. Tighten the setscrew to 40–50 ft. lbs.
4. Install the welch plug, poppet balls and springs.

MAIN TRANSMISSION

Assembly

1. Using a rope or sling lower the countershaft into the case.
2. If removed, install the countershaft front bearing cup and spacer ring.
3. Position the countershaft front bearing in the front cup and start installation of the rear bearing cup into the case. With the rear bearing properly aligned, drive the rear bearing cup into place in the case bore.
4. Lubricate the caged pocket bearings with 30W oil and install the bearings (with the spacer between the bearings) in the reverse idler gear. Coat the thrust washers with grease to hold the washers against each end of the idler gear. Position the tangs of the washers up and facing outward to align with the slots in the boss inside the case.
5. Hold the idler gear and thrust washers inside the case with the tangs of the washer up. Insert the idler shaft part way into the bore of the case with the shoulder and threaded hole facing out. Carefully align the washer tangs with the slots in the case, and lower the idler gear until it is aligned with the shaft. Insert the shaft into the case through the idler gear with the flat on the shoulder in alignment with position of the flat on the countershaft rear bearing cap. Drive the idler shaft in with a soft mallet until the bottom of the flat is flush with the case.

NOTE: While driving the idler shaft into the case it may be necessary to hold the countershaft rear bearing cup in place using one of the retainer capscrews and a large flat washer.

6. Clean the countershaft rear bearing cap gasket surface and also the gasket surface on the transmission case. Position the countershaft rear bearing cap and gasket to the case with the flat on the side of the cap aligned with the flat on the reverse idler shaft. Tighten the capscrews 60–80 ft. lbs. and remove the rope or sling from the countershaft.

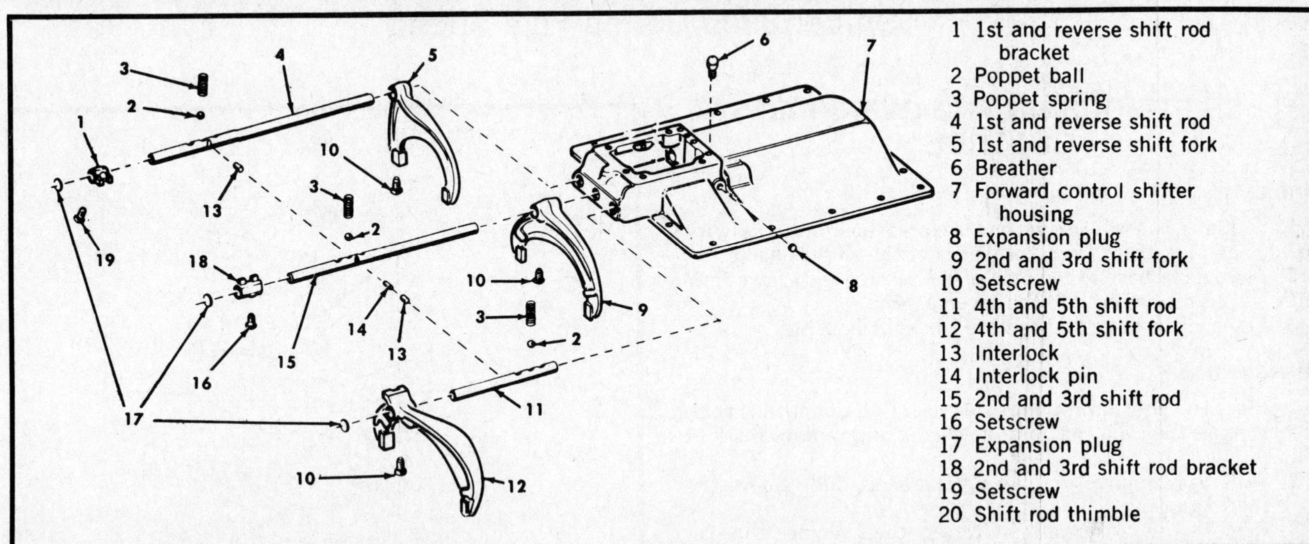

Shifter housing components

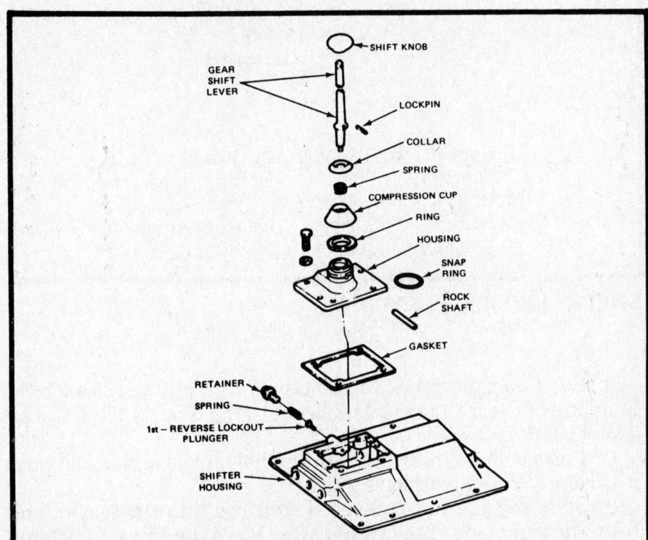

Gear shift housing—exploded view

7. Attach a suitable hook to the mainshaft assembly and carefully lower the assembly into the case. Mesh the mainshaft gears with the mating countershaft gears.

8. If previously removed press the bearing on the drive gear.

9. Lubricate the pocket bearing on the front of the mainshaft with light grease.

10. Install the drive gear through the front of the transmission case and onto the mainshaft.

11. Assemble the drive gear front bearing cap and gasket on the case. Be sure the oil return hole is properly aligned in the cap, gasket and case. Tighten the cap screws 25–32 ft. lbs. The clutch housing removal installation is only required if the countershaft front bearing cup was replaced or the clutch housing was defective.

12. Position the clutch housing gasket on the front of the case and hold in place with a light coat of grease. Be sure the gasket clears the countershaft front bearing spacer. Assemble the clutch housing on the case using the drive gear front bearing cap as a pilot. Tighten the housing capscrews 120–150 ft. lbs. Overtightening of the capscrews on the front of the case will distort the end-play of the mainshaft and countershaft.

13. If removed, install the oil seal and bearing cup in the mainshaft rear bearing cap.

14. Lubricate the mainshaft rear bearing with light grease. Assemble the rear bearing cap and gasket on the mainshaft. Apply even pressure on all sides and tighten the capscrews 68–80 ft. lbs. Make certain the oil holes in the case, gasket and cap are aligned.

15. Slide the speedometer drive gear onto the mainshaft until it is seated against the shoulder on the mainshaft.

16. Install the output flange, washer and locknut on the mainshaft. Rotate the mainshaft to seat the bearings. Lock the transmission in two gears and tighten the locknut to 500 ft. lbs. Pry on the mainshaft or output flange and check the end play. End-play should measure 0.006–0.010 in.. If end-play is not within the prescribed limits, remove the drive gear front bearing cap. Remove the bearing cup from the cap and remove the shim. Measure the thickness of the shim and replace if needed.

NOTE: The countershaft end play specifications are 0.006–0.013 in. with "set right" bearings used. End-play should not require checking.

17. Lock the transmission in gear and tighten the output flange locknut 500–550 ft. lbs. Shift the transmission into neutral.

18. Install the shifter housing gasket on top of the transmission case. With the shifter forks in neutral, align the forks with the respective synchronizers and 1st reverse clutch collar. Assemble the shifter housing on the case and tighten the cover screws 25–32 ft. lbs. Using a small pry bar check the movement of the shift rods for proper operation.

TORQUE SPECIFICATIONS
Spicer 50 and 60 Series

Location	ft. lbs.
Engine to Transmission Bolts	60–80
Countershaft Rear Bearing Cap Capscrews	60–80
Drive Gear Front Bearing Cap Capscrews	25–32
Clutch Housing Capscrews	120–150
Mainshaft Rear Bearing Cap Capscrews	60–80
Output Flange Locknut	500–550
Shifter Housing Cover Screws	25–32
Shifter Fork Setscrews	40–50

Spicer 8000 Series Five Speed

SHIFT HOUSING AND OVERHEAD CONTROL

Removal

1. Remove the overdrive and reverse lockout pins with springs and retainers from both sides of the shift housing.
2. Place a pry bar in the notch of the reverse shift finger and shift the transmission into the reverse gear.
3. Remove the bolts and remove the shift housing.

Disassembly

1. Place the shift lever dome in a vise. Pull up on the grommet, depress the collar against the spring and remove the lock pin.
2. Slide the compression cup up the shaft and remove the rock shaft snapring.
3. Remove the rock shaft and lever, then remove the ball grommet, collar, spring and cup off the lever.
4. Place the shifter housing in a vise with the forks facing out and the front of the housing to the left.
5. Remove the interlock crosshole plug.
6. Hold the reverse shift finger stud and remove the locknut and washer. Tap the stud free of the housing and remove the reverse shift finger. Remove the locknut plunger pin from the counterbore of the shift finger.
7. Cut the lockwire and remove the set screw from the reverse shift rod bracket.
8. Tap the reverse shift fork forward to move the shift rod against the welsh plug. Drive the plug free of the case and tap the fork forward until stopped by the housing. Cut the lockwire and remove the set screw from the reverse fork. Tap the shift rod free of the fork and bracket and out of the housing.
9. Remove the interlock from the cross hole between the rods.
10. Cut the lockwire and remove the set screw from the 3rd and 4th shift fork. Use a soft rod and drive the shift rod forward to remove the welch plug. Remove the rod and shift fork from the housing.
11. Cut the lockwire and remove the set screw from the 1st and 2nd shift rod bracket. Tap the 1st and 2nd shift fork forward to remove the welch plug from the front of the housing. Remove the set screw from the 1st and 2nd fork. Pull the rod free of the fork, bracket and housing.
12. Remove the short interlock from the cross hole between the shift rods.
13. Cut the lock wire and remove the set screws from the 5th speed or overdrive shift rod bracket and shift fork. Drive the shift rod out the front of the cover removing the welch plug. Pull the rod free of the fork, bracket and housing.
14. Remove the four poppet springs from the holes in the shifter housing center boss.

Assembly

1. Place the reverse relay shift finger stud in the shift finger.
2. Place the reverse lockout plunger in the reverse relay shift finger.
3. Position the reverse shift finger and tap the stud through the shift cover housing. Install the nut and washer.
4. Set the four shift rod poppet ball springs in the holes.
5. Place the overdrive lockout plunger in the overdrive shift rod bracket and slide the overdrive shift rod into the hole in the cover.
6. Place the overdrive rod bracket on the shift rod.
7. Place the poppet ball on the spring, hold it down and slide the rod past it.

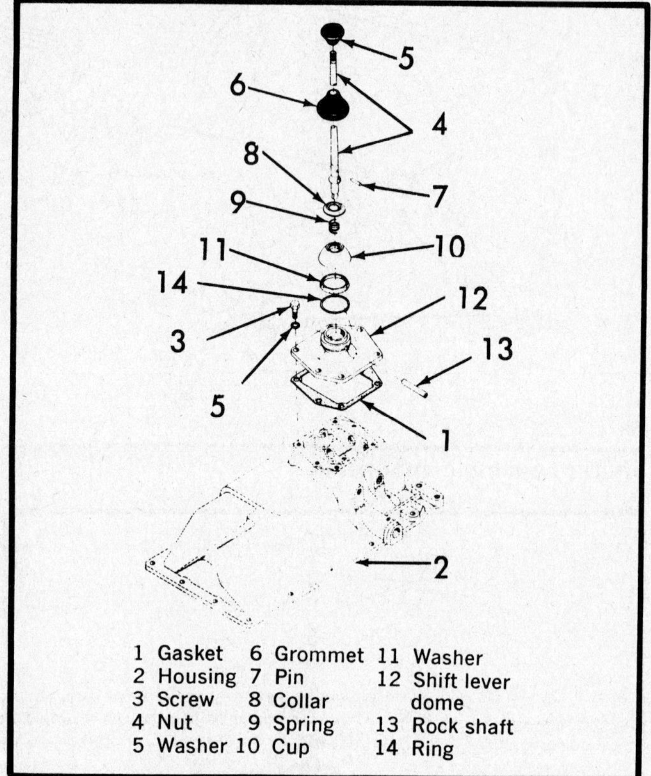

Shifter housing assembly

8. Position the upper overdrive shift fork on the rod with the long hub of the fork toward the front of the cover. Install the set screws and lock wire.
9. Place a short interlock into the hole in the cover and push it through to the overdrive shift rod.
10. Slide the 1st and 2nd speed shift rod into the second hole from the right side of the front cover. Place the 1st and 2nd shift rod bracket on the rod.
11. Install the small interlock pin on the rod. Place a poppet ball on the poppet spring. Hold the ball and spring compressed and slide the rod past the center boss. Place the 1st and 2nd speed shift fork on the rod, with the long hub toward the front. Install the set screws and lockwire.
12. Install a short interlock into the cover and push it through to the 1st and 2nd speed rod.
13. Slide the 3rd and 4th shift rod into the front of the cover. Place a small interlock pin in the rod. Place the 3rd and 4th speed shift fork on the rod, with the long hub toward the front. Set the poppet ball on the spring and depress it. Slide the rod through the case boss. Line up the holes and install the set screw and lock wire.
14. Place the long interlock in the cover hole and push it over to the 3rd and 4th speed rod.
15. Install the reverse shift rod and position the reverse bracket. Set a poppet ball on the poppet spring, hold it down and push the shift rod past it. Install the reverse shift fork. Install the set screws and wire securely.
16. Install the four expansion plugs in the shift rod holes in the front of the cover and expand them by striking with a flat ended bar and a hammer.
17. Install the interlock cross-hole plug in the side of the cover.

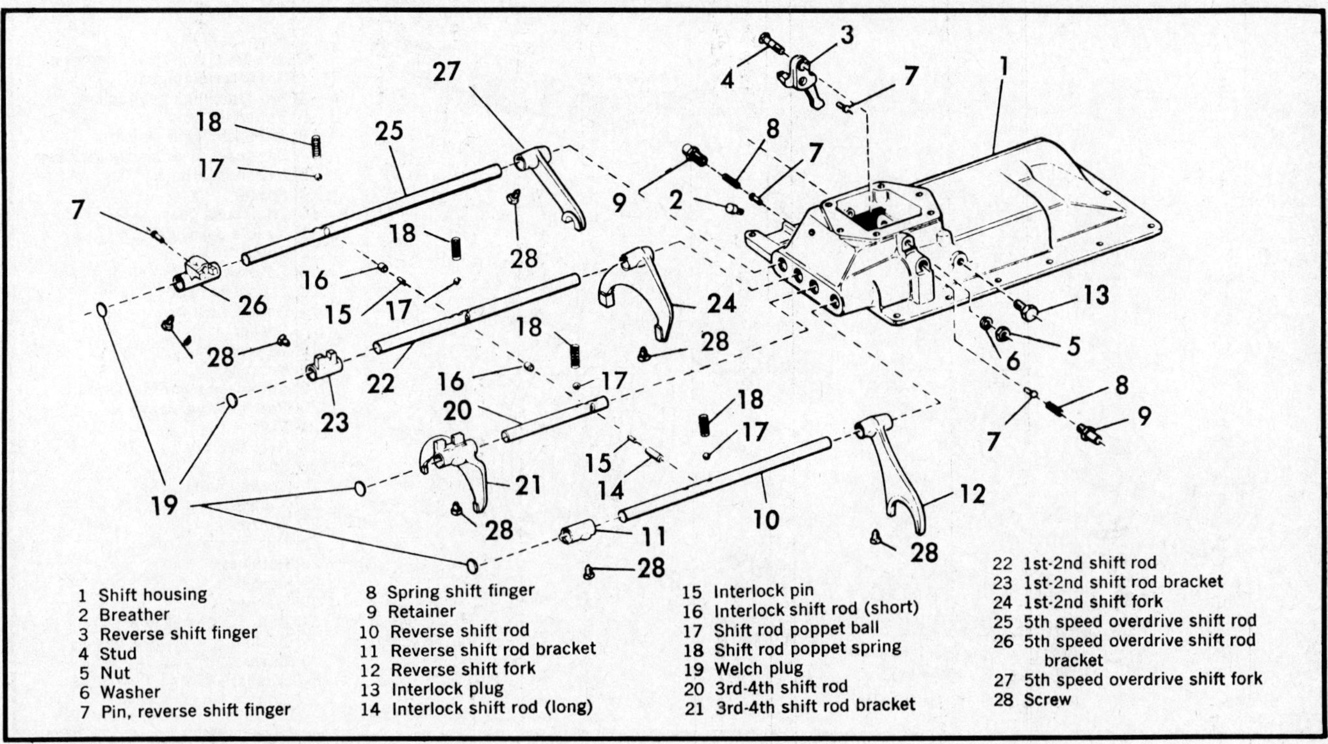

Overhead shift control assembly

TRANSMISSION UNIT

Disassembly

1. Using a bar shift the transmission into the reverse gear and remove the cover from the case.
2. Remove the clutch release cross shaft, yoke and clutch brake discs.
3. Pull the bearing retainer and the input gear assembly out of the case.
4. Remove the parking brake drum and the speedometer driven gear and bushing.
5. Lock the transmission in two gears, remove the companion flange nut and remove the companion flange with a puller.
6. Remove the mainshaft rear bearing cap.
7. Remove the speedometer gear and the bearing spacer.
8. Tap on the mainshaft 1st speed gear and move the mainshaft as far back to the rear as possible.
9. Using a puller remove the mainshaft rear bearing.
10. Remove the transmission rear cover using a puller.
11. Remove the overdrive shift fork guide rod with a bolt and a puller. Remove the fork from the case.
12. Shift the transmission into two gears. Remove the countershaft rear cotter key and nut.
13. Remove the countershaft overdrive clutch gear by pulling on the collar or by attaching a puller to the three threaded holes in the clutch gear.
14. Remove the 5th or overdrive countershaft gear and thrust washer then pry the gear off the shaft.
15. Tap the mainshaft assembly toward the rear of the case and install a splitter type puller on the mainshaft center bearing outer race. Tap the mainshaft as far forward as possible and then to the rear again until the bearing is loose on the shaft.
16. Remove the mainshaft and gears from the case with the use of a sling. The center bearing and the low speed gear needle bearings will come off during the above operations.
17. Remove the rear bearing retainer.
18. Remove the reverse idler gear. Two identical caged roller bearings support the gear and sleeve.
19. Pry the countershaft assembly toward the rear of the case until a bearing puller can be installed on the rear bearing. Remove the countershaft assembly.

SUBASSEMBLIES MAINSHAFT

Disassembly

1. Place the mainshaft, front end up, in an arbor press.
2. Remove the snapring from the groove behind the front bearing and press the bearing, 3rd and 4th speed clutch gear, mainshaft 3rd speed gear, sleeve and mainshaft 2nd speed gear from the mainshaft.
3. Remove the snapring from between the bearing cap and the drive gear. Pull the cap off toward the front of the drive gear.
4. Remove the left hand threaded nut with a spanner wrench and press the bearing off the shaft.

NOTE: Some early production units used the old style loose needle bearings in the bores of the mainshaft gears. Be careful not to lose them as the gears are removed.

Assembly

1. Press the ball bearing on the input gear with the shielded side of the bearing toward the gear.
2. Install the bearing lock nut on the gear and tighten and stake the nuts.
3. Place the bearing cap over the bearing and press into position.
4. Insert the snapring into the slot in the bearing cap.
5. Use grease and assemble the caged needle bearings onto the shaft diameter just to the front of the center splined area. Install the mainshaft 2nd speed gear over the caged needle bearing, with the clutch teeth toward the rear.

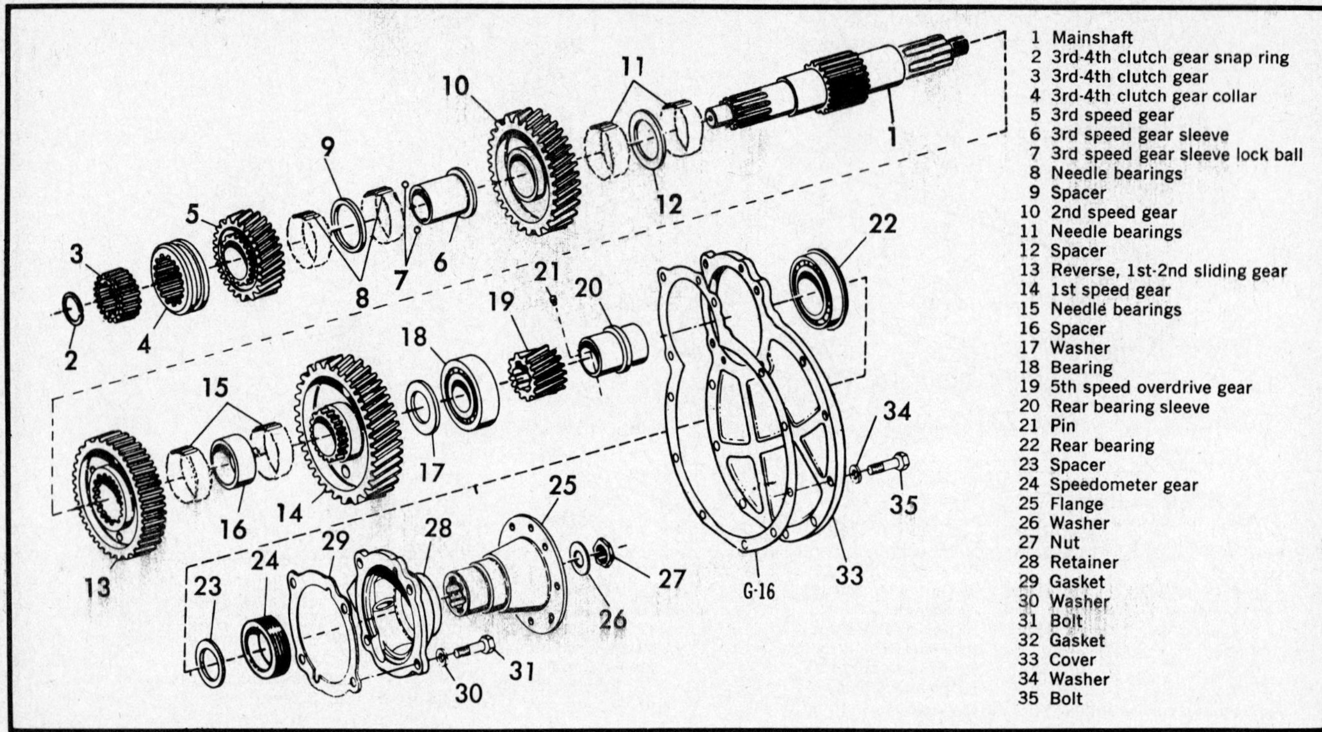
1 Mainshaft
2 3rd-4th clutch gear snap ring
3 3rd-4th clutch gear
4 3rd-4th clutch gear collar
5 3rd speed gear
6 3rd speed gear sleeve
7 3rd speed gear sleeve lock ball
8 Needle bearings
9 Spacer
10 2nd speed gear
11 Needle bearings
12 Spacer
13 Reverse, 1st-2nd sliding gear
14 1st speed gear
15 Needle bearings
16 Spacer
17 Washer
18 Bearing
19 5th speed overdrive gear
20 Rear bearing sleeve
21 Pin
22 Rear bearing
23 Spacer
24 Speedometer gear
25 Flange
26 Washer
27 Nut
28 Retainer
29 Gasket
30 Washer
31 Bolt
32 Gasket
33 Cover
34 Washer
35 Bolt
G-16

Mainshaft assembly—exploded view

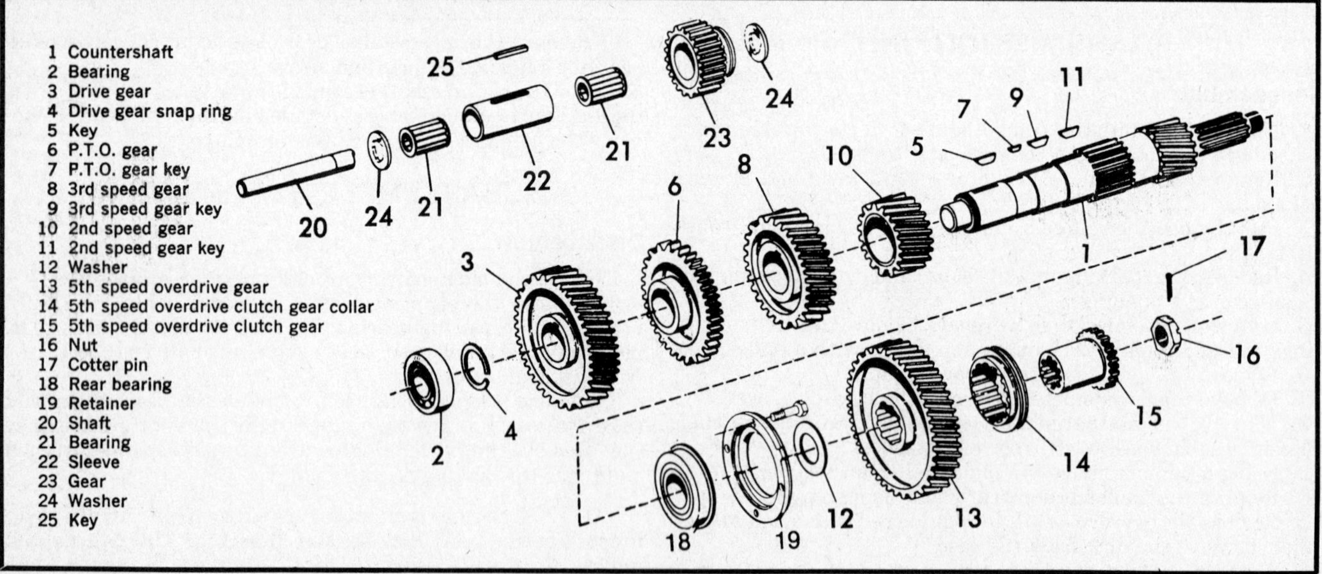
1 Countershaft
2 Bearing
3 Drive gear
4 Drive gear snap ring
5 Key
6 P.T.O. gear
7 P.T.O. gear key
8 3rd speed gear
9 3rd speed gear key
10 2nd speed gear
11 2nd speed gear key
12 Washer
13 5th speed overdrive gear
14 5th speed overdrive clutch gear collar
15 5th speed overdrive clutch gear
16 Nut
17 Cotter pin
18 Rear bearing
19 Retainer
20 Shaft
21 Bearing
22 Sleeve
23 Gear
24 Washer
25 Key

Countershaft and reverse idler gear

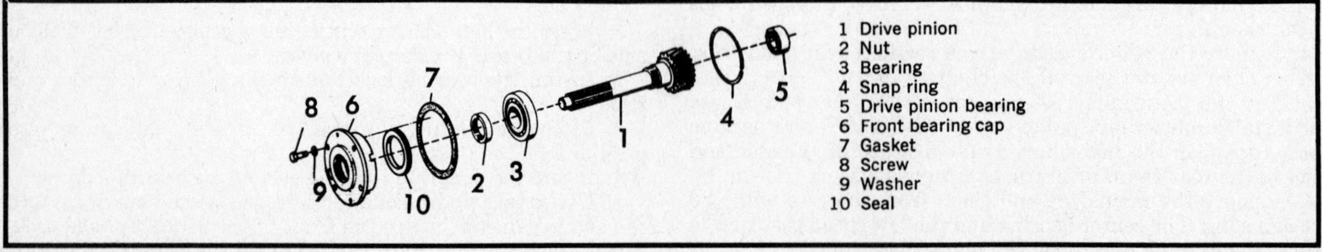
1 Drive pinion
2 Nut
3 Bearing
4 Snap ring
5 Drive pinion bearing
6 Front bearing cap
7 Gasket
8 Screw
9 Washer
10 Seal

Drive pinion assembly

6. Install the mainshaft 3rd speed gear sleeve onto the front of the shaft with the flange facing to the rear and the notches aligned with the splines and the balls.
7. Install the caged needle bearings on the mainshaft. Use grease as a retainer.
8. Slide the mainshaft 3rd speed gear over the needle bearings with the clutch teeth toward the front.
9. Press the mainshaft 3rd and 4th speed clutch gear onto the front of the mainshaft with the flat side toward the rear and the clutch hub toward the front.
10. Install the snapring in the groove on the front of the mainshaft.
11. Press the front ball bearing on with the beveled edge of the inner race toward the rear.
12. Press the 3rd and 4th speed clutch collar on the 3rd and 4th speed clutch gear, with the long portion of the hub toward the rear.
13. Slide the 1st and 2nd speed clutch gear onto the splines, with the shift fork collar toward the rear.
14. Using grease, install two rows of 71 needle bearings per row, with the wide spacer between them, on the shaft diameter to the rear of the center splined area.
15. Place the mainshaft 1st speed gear over the needle bearings with the clutch teeth toward the front.
16. Grease one side of the 1st speed gear thrust washer and place it on the mainshaft with the greased side toward the 1st speed gear.

COUNTERSHAFT

Disassembly

1. Remove the countershaft front bearing with a puller.
2. Remove the snapring from the front of the countershaft.
3. Press the drive gear off the countershaft and the remainder of the gears with a suitable press.

Assembly

1. Position the 2nd gear key and press the 2nd speed gear on the shaft with the chamfered bore toward the front.
2. Insert the 3rd speed gear key and press the 3rd speed gear on the shaft with the long hub of the gear toward the front.
3. Place the P.T.O. gear key in position then press the P.T.O. gear on the shaft with the long hub toward the front.
4. Insert the drive gear key on the shaft then press the drive gear on the shaft with the long hub facing the P.T.O. gear.
5. Install the snapring in its groove in the front of the countershaft. Press the countershaft front bearing on.

TRANSMISSION UNIT

Assembly

1. Lower the countershaft assembly into the case, rear end first and down, so the rear of the countershaft enters the rear bearing bore. Lower the front of the countershaft assembly until the front bearing will enter its bore in the case. Tap the rear bearing until the front bearing enters the bore.
2. Install the countershaft rear bearing, with the snapring toward the rear, in the bore and on the countershaft. Tap in place with a tool that contacts the inner bearing race.
3. Assemble the reverse idler gear, sleeve, key and bearings. Place them in the case with the shift fork collar toward the rear of the transmission case. Make sure the sleeve small diameter is facing toward the front.
4. Install the reverse idler shaft. The tang on the edge of the countershaft rear bearing retainer must align with the flat on the rear end of the shaft.
5. Install the countershaft rear bearing retainer, with the tang locking the idler shaft. Install the bolts and torque to specifications. Install the lockwire.
6. Using a sling lower the mainshaft assembly into the case rear end first. Start the center support bearing over the rear of the shaft and into the case center web with the bearing snapring toward the rear.
7. Install the input gear, bearing and cap, with a new gasket into the front of the case. Pilot the mainshaft front bearing into place in the bore of the input gear. Start but do not tighten the nuts.
8. Drive the mainshaft center support bearing into place.
9. Install the 5th or overdrive gear onto the rear of the mainshaft.
10. Install the 5th or overdrive gear thrust washer and gear onto the rear of the countershaft with the clutch teeth toward the rear. Install the countershaft 5th or overdrive clutch collar and gear with the large diameters of the collar and gear toward the rear. Install the clutch gear nut and torque to specification.
11. Place the pin on the inside of the mainshaft rear bearing sleeve and press the sleeve onto the rear of the mainshaft 5th or overdrive gear. The ground surface of the hub is to the rear.
12. Install the 5th or overdrive shift fork and shaft guide. The long hub of the shift fork must face toward the front. Place the shift fork guide rod into the hole in the rear of the case, through the shift fork and into the hole in the center web of the case.
13. Install the transmission rear cover, using a new gasket. Do not tighten the bolts.
14. Install the mainshaft rear bearing.
15. Install the mainshaft rear bearing thrust washer and speedometer drive gear.
16. Using a new gasket, install the rear bearing cap onto the transmission cover. Torque the cap bolts to specifications.
17. Place the speedometer driven gear and bushing in the mainshaft rear bearing cap and secure with the two bolts and nuts.
18. Torque the transmission rear cover bolts to specifications.
19. Torque the input gear bearing cap bolts to specifications.
20. Install the clutch release yoke and cross shafts in the clutch housing. Install the clutch brake discs.
21. Shift the transmission and the cover assembly into the reverse position and install the shift cover using a new gasket. Be sure the forks line up with the shift collars. Install the cover bolts and torque to specifications.

Spicer SST-6, SST-6+ 1, SST-1007, Six and Seven Speeds

TRANSMISSION REAR CASE

Disassembly

1. Remove the nut from the end of the output shaft. Remove the yoke or flange.
2. Remove the output shaft bearing cap and gasket.
3. Pull back on the output shaft to expose the snapring and remove the snapring, bearing and thrust spacer from the shaft.
4. Remove the bolts from the piston body and rear cover and remove the piston body and gasket from the case face and off piston.
5. Remove the shift piston locknut and remove the piston from the shaft.
6. Remove the rear cover and gasket by lifting straight up off the dowel pins.
7. Remove the rear bearing caps with shims from the rear cover.
8. Remove the cups from the countershaft bores of the rear cover.
9. Remove the output shaft and gear from the rear case.
10. Remove the piston shift rod with the fork and stop spacer as an assembly. The curvic clutch collar will pull away with the fork.
11. Remove the curvic clutch collar from the fork and the positive stop spacer of the piston shift rod.
12. Before removing both countershafts, turn the head end gear until the timing marks or paint marks align to each other. Remove both countershafts from the rear case.
13. If the countershaft bearing cones need replacement, use a split puller tool for removal.
14. Remove the selflocking lock nut if so equipped, or unstake the lockwasher tang from the groove of the locknut and remove the locknut. Remove the lockwasher from the end of the shaft.
15. Use a puller tool to remove the pocket bearing from the shaft.
16. Slide the gear and thrust washer from the splines of the shaft.
17. Cut the lockwire from the bolts. Remove the bolts and remove the rear case from the front transmission unit.
18. Inspect the oil seal and replace if necessary.
19. Remove the air vent and replace if necessary.
20. Press the head and timing gears from the countershaft using parallel bars under the gear hub. Press the shaft from the key bore and remove the key from the shaft.

Assembly

1. Install the rear case gasket on the back face of the front unit and install the O-rings into the countershaft bore of the front case.
2. Assemble the rear case on the gasket and secure the rear case to the front case with the bolts and lockwashers. Tighten the $^3/_8$ in. screws 25–32 ft. lbs. and the $^1/_2$ in. screws 60–80 ft. lbs. Lockwire the bolts.
3. Install the taper bearing cups into the countershaft bores and the output shaft bore seral into the center bore.
4. Install the mainshaft head end gear on the shaft splines. Assemble the thrust washer on the shaft. Install the pocket bearing on the shaft. Tap the bearing on with a tubing pressed against the inner race of the bearing.
5. Install the bearing self locking locknut if so equipped or with lockwasher and locknut. Tighten the locknut 500–600 ft. lbs. Bend the tang on the lockwasher if so equipped.
6. Press the key into the keyway of the countershaft. Support

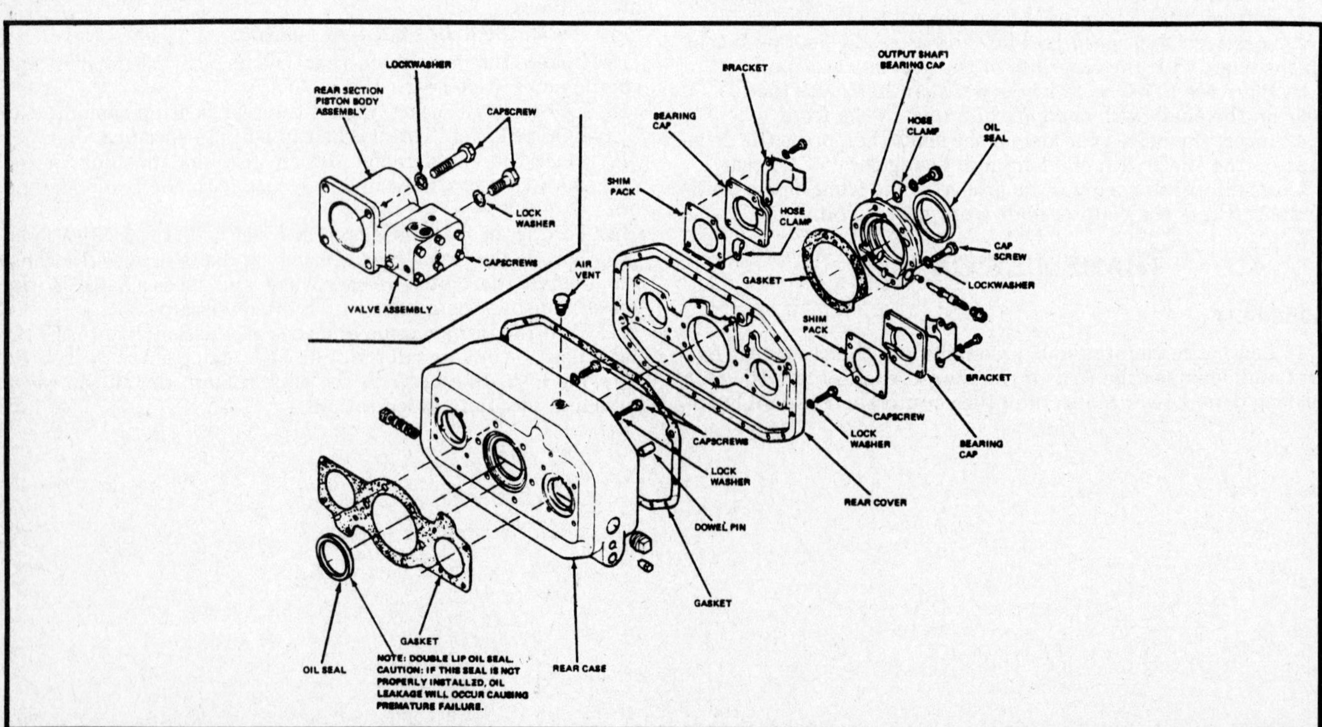

Rear case assembly

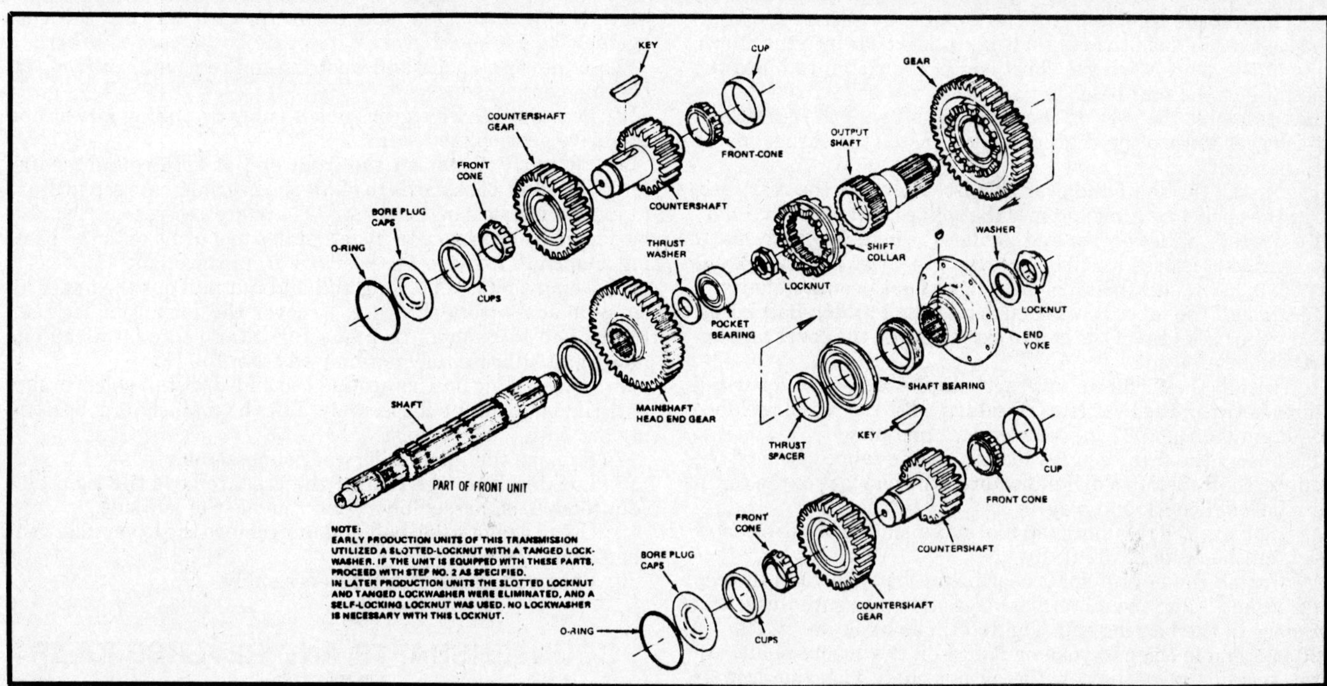

Rear case gears

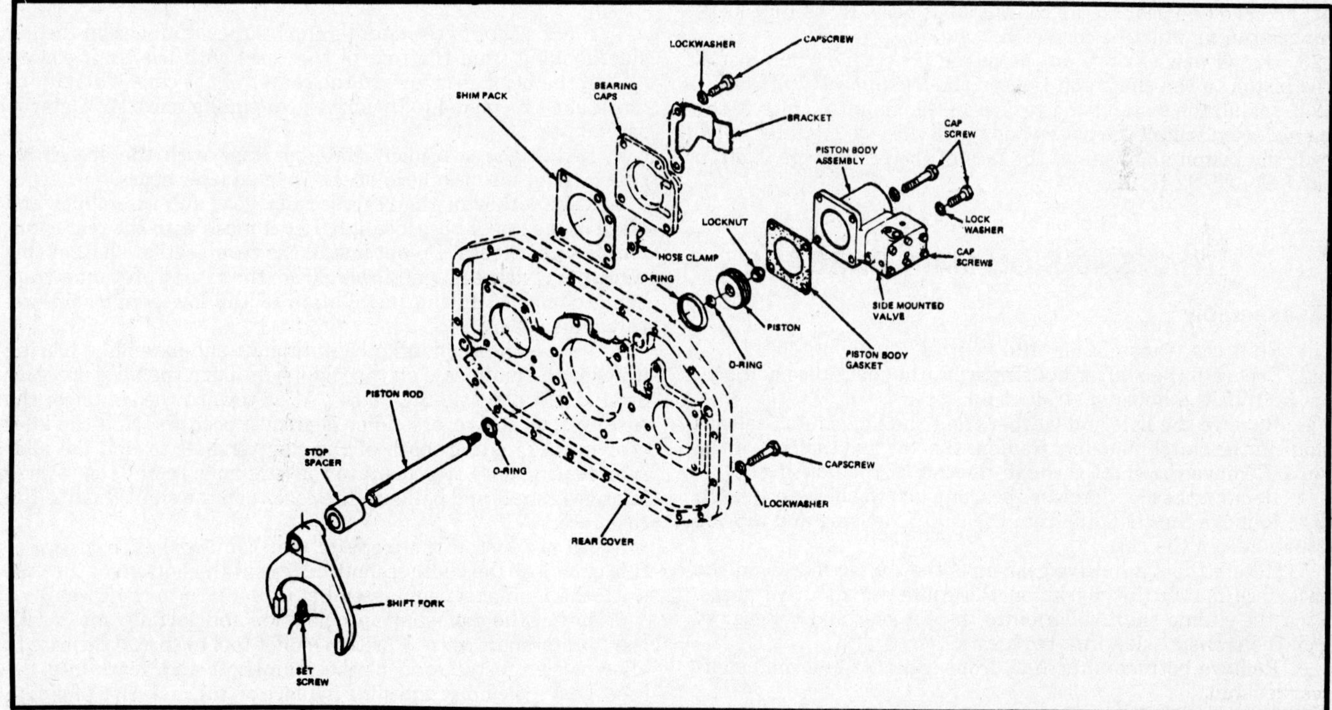

Rear cover

the head end timing gear with the long hub end up. Press the shaft into the bore of the gear. Seat the gear face firmly against the shoulder of the shaft.

7. With the cones installed on the countershaft ends, install the countershafts, large OD gear toward the inner face of the rear case. Align the timing marks of the countershaft in mesh with the head end gear timing marks.

8. Install the gasket on the rear case face.

9. If the piston rod, stop spacer and shift fork were previously disassembled, reassemble these parts for installation into the rear case.

10. Assemble the long hub end of the shift fork toward the oil groove end of the piston shaft. Install the set screw and tighten 40–50 ft. lbs. and lockwire securely. Assemble the top spacer on the piston end of the rod. Assemble the shift collar on the shift fork pads.

11. Install the complete shift fork and rod sub-assembly into the rear case. Mesh the curvic ring clutch collar into the curvic ring of the gear. Mesh the short end of the piston rod into the rod bore of the rear case.
12. Assemble the gear on the output shaft with the curvic end of the gear toward the shaft shoulder. Install the thrust spacer on the shaft.
13. Install the shaft and gear sub-assembly into the rear case, over the pocket bearing and into the splines of the clutch collar.
14. Install the rear cover and tighten the bolts 25–32 ft. lbs. If a new gasket is used it will be necessary to check the end-play of 0.004–0.007 in. on the taper bearings of both countershafts.
15. Install the taper bearing cups into the countershaft bores. Allow the back face of the cup to extend out of the cover face approximately $^{3}/_{32}$ in..
16. Install the 0.080 in. (average) shim pack with rubberized shims between the over cup OD and against the rear cover face to obtain 0.004–0.007 in. countershaft end-play.
17. Insert the 5 in. long $^{1}/_{2}$ in. bolt in the tapped hole of the countershaft. Set up a dial indicator at the end face of the countershaft and check end-play.
18. Remove the retaining cap tool and install the bearing caps. Tighten the bolts 25–32 ft. lbs.
19. Install the output shaft bearing on the shaft then the cap and gasket. Align the oil return holes and make sure the seal is in place in the bearing cap. Tighten the bolts 60–80 ft. lbs.
20. Assemble the end yoke or flange on the output shaft.
21. Install the washer on the output shaft with the locknut and tighten the locknut 550–600 ft. lbs.
22. Rotate the output shaft several times to correct the timing of the head end gear to the countershaft gear. If the unit locks up the timing must be corrected.
23. Install new O-rings on the piston if necessary and install the piston to the shaft and tighten the locknut 40–50 ft. lbs.
24. Install the piston body gasket on the mounting face of the piston body. Install the piston body with the side mounted valve over the piston and against the face of the rear cover. Tighten the bolts 25–32 ft. lbs.

TRANSMISSION MAIN CASE

Disassembly

1. Shift the transmission into neutral.
2. Separate the shifter housing from the main case and gasket and lift the housing straight up.
3. Remove the bolt and washer from the long clutch release shaft in the clutch housing. Remove the key and tap free of the yoke. Remove the shaft through the side of the housing.
4. Remove the clutch release bearing, two washers and clutch disc. Remove the six bolts from the clutch housing and tap the housing from the case.
5. Rotate the main drive gear until the timing marks on the back face match the marks on the countershaft drive gears. Lock the sliding shaft collars into the 1st gear and six gear to lock the transmission into two gears.
6. Remove both countershaft front locknuts and mainshaft rear locknut.
7. Use a puller tool and remove the end yoke or flange.
8. Remove the mainshaft rear bearing cap. Remove the speedometer driven gear, bushing and seal.
9. Engage the collar into the 5th speed gear. Use a pry bar against the front face of the collar and force the mainshaft subassembly rearward to expose the mainshaft rear bearing snapring. Install a puller on the snapring and remove the bearing.
10. Remove the thrust washer from the shaft. Remove the split rings from the shaft. Remove the snapring located in the reverse gear bore.
11. Engage the 1st–reverse shift collar under the reverse gear. Slide the reverse gear and collar forward butting the gear against the 1st speed gear. Wire or tie both gears together.
12. Remove the bolts and washers and remove the drive gear bearing cap.
13. Remove the drive gear subassembly by pulling forward on the drive gear splined stem.
14. Using a soft bar on the front end of both countershafts, force the shaft backwards to allow the bearings to creep forward to expose the bearing snapring. There are recesses in the case face to allow clearance to install puller tool arms onto the bearing snapring. Remove the bearings from the shaft.
15. Using a pilot tube, long bolt and nut pull out the upper idler gear shaft from the case. Recover the idler gear lockball. Leave the idler gear in place for later removal after the mainshaft subassembly is removed from the case.
16. Place a sling or wire around the 2nd–3rd shift collar to support the mainshaft subassembly. Lift the mainshaft subassembly out with a chain hoist.
17. Remove the upper idler gear subassembly.
18. Looking from the rear of the case, remove the right side countershaft subassembly. Then remove the left side.
19. Using a pilot tube, bolt and nut remove the lower idler gear shaft from the case.
20. Remove the idler gear sub-assembly.

COUNTERSHAFTS AND REVERSE IDLER GEARS

Assembly

1. Place either of the countershaft sub-assemblies on the left side (looking from the rear of the case) with the timing mark "A" of the head gear toward the center of the case. This timing mark must be mated to the drive gear timing mark "V" later in assembly.
2. Install the two idler shaft bearings with the spacer between them into the bore of the reverse idler gears.
3. Take either of the reverse idler gear sub-assemblies and place in the upper boss location. Lay it mesh with the rear countershaft gear teeth. Do not install the reverse idler shaft at this time. Remove the magnetic plug from the case to prevent it from being damaged during installation of the lower right side reverse idler gear.
4. Install the remaining countershaft sub-assembly, placing it inside the main case on the right side. Turn the head end gear around until the timing mark "A" is toward the center of the case. Install the reverse idler gear into position. Roll the idler gear on the mating tooth of the countershaft to find the idler gear bearing bore alignment to the case hole. Install the reverse idler gear shaft and ball into the case. Tap the shaft flush to the case face.
5. Do not install the front or rear countershaft bearings at this time. Let the countershaft lie free at the bottom of the case until the mainshaft sub-assembly is placed into the case.
6. Lower the mainshaft into position and partially mesh with the countershaft gears. Position a pilot tool to spread the case to allow easier installation of the mainshaft and gears into the case. Leave the hoist and sling in place on the mainshaft for support until all bearings and reverse idler shafts have been installed in the case.
7. Install the thrust washer on the output end of the mainshaft. Push the washer forward and against the thrust washer previously installed, then force both washers against the snapring that is on the rear of the mainshaft.
8. Cut the wire used to tie both gears together then slide the reverse idler gear backwards into approximate location on the reverse gear bore thrust washer.
9. Install the snapring into location in the groove of the bore of the gear.
10. Coat two split rings with heavy grease and install the rings

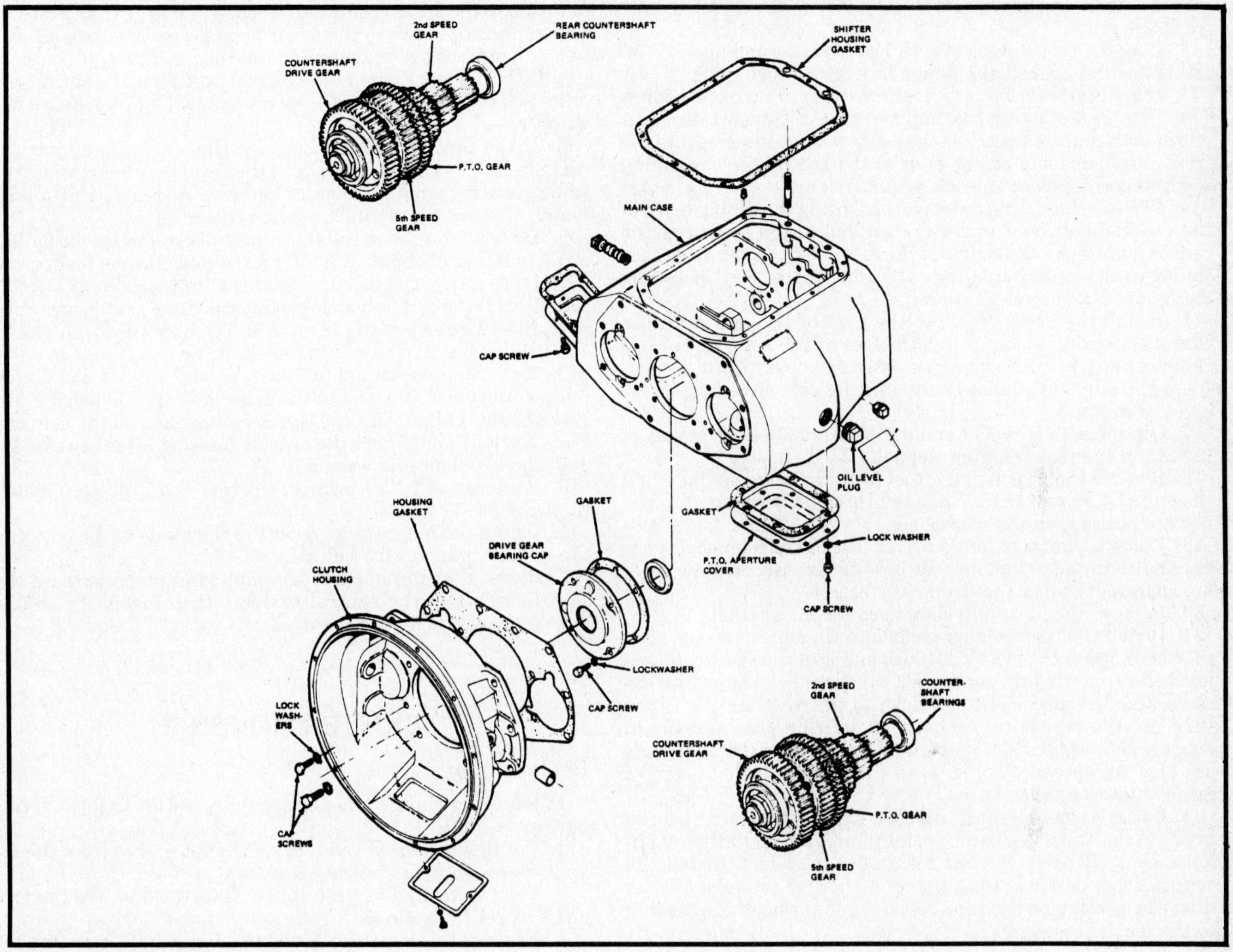

Main section—exploded view

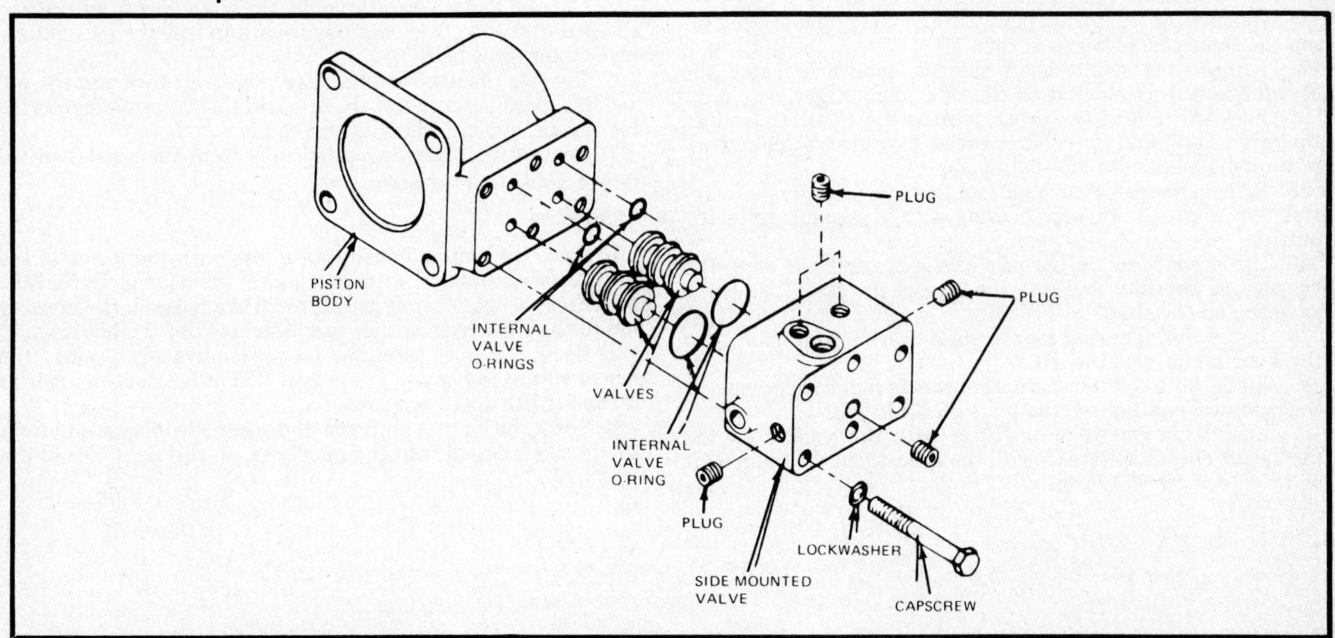

Piston body and valve assemblies

into the recess on the rear of the mainshaft, with the flanges toward the gears.

11. Coat the thrust washer with heavy grease and install it on the mainshaft against the flange face of the split rings.

12. Install the bearing pilot tool for the rear mainshaft bore.

13. Use the front bore bearing pilot tools to support the front end of both countershafts. As the pilot tools are inserted into the front case bores and on the ends of the shaft, keep the timing teeth in correct mesh to each respective gear.

14. With all the timing gears painted, bring the timing teeth of the countershaft head end gears parallel to the bottom of the case or pointing to the center of the case. Position the drive gear timing teeth (two) where they will match and mate to the timing teeth of the countershaft gears.

15. Install the drive gear into the bore of the case until the bearing snapring seats against the face of the main case.

16. Install the front drive gear bearing cap with the gasket. Align the oil return holes of the bearing cap with the oil port holes of the case.

17. Dip the bolts in sealer and use washers to attach the bearing cap to the case. Tighten the bolts 25–32 ft. lbs.

18. Remove the bearing pilot tool from the rear case bore and the end of the mainshaft. Slide the three shift collars into the neutral position on the mainshaft.

19. Using a pilot tool and a driver install the mainshaft rear bearing on the shaft and into the bore of the case. Seat the bearing snapring against the main case face.

20. Remove the hoist and sling used for installation.

21. Install the reverse idler shaft into the upper reverse idler gear bore. Place the idler shaft lock ball into the shaft ball hole just before entering the recess. With the lock ball locked into the recess, tap the idler shaft end flush to the case face.

22. Use the rear bore countershaft bearing piloting tools to support the rear ends of both countershafts. As the pilot tools are inserted into the bores, keep the timing teeth in correct mesh with each other.

23. Using a countershaft support hook tool, place the rod hooks in the web hole of each gear. Support the tool with a chain hoist hook. Remove the left front bore pilot tool. Install the countershaft bearing using the front face of the pilot tool to drive the bearing on the shaft. Seat the snapring of the bearing to the face of the case.

24. Install the countershaft front lockout on the shaft. Bring the lockout against the bearing face hand tight.

25. Remove the right front pilot tool and install the bearing using the same procedure as in Step 23.

26. Remove the countershaft support hook and install the countershaft front locknut on the shaft, hand tight.

27. Lock the unit in two gears, moving the clutch collar into the reverse gear and the collar into the drive gear. Tighten both countershaft locknuts 550–600 ft. lbs.

28. Remove the left rear pilot tool from the countershaft. Install the countershaft rear bearing with the snapring to the outside.

29. Use a pilot tool on the face of the bearing and drive the bearing on the shaft and into the bore of the case. Install the snapring on the shaft.

30. Install the right rear countershaft bearing and snapring in the same manner as the left.

31. Install both countershaft rear bearing caps with gaskets to the case face and tighten the bolts 25–32 ft. lbs.

32. Install the end yoke or flange with the washer on the mainshaft output splines. Install the locknut on the mainshaft and tighten 550–600 ft. lbs.

33. Move the clutch collar out of the reverse gear and into its neutral position. Leave the collar engaged in the drive gear.

34. Turn the drive gear stem to roll the gear train. If the teeth on the timing marks are in the correct positions, the entire gear train will roll freely, if not the gear train will lock up after a few turns.

35. If the unit locks up, disengage the shift collar from the drive gear. Turn the drive gear in the reverse rotation until the timing marks come into match or close mis-match. If a mismatch appears the shafts must be retimed.

36. Place all the clutch collars in their neutral positions for later installation of the shift housing assembly on the main case.

37. Place a new clutch housing gasket in position.

38. Install the clutch housing using the drive gear bearing cap as a guide. Use sealer on the bolts and tighten the $^5/_8$ in. screws 120–150 ft. lbs. and the $^1/_2$ in. 60–80 ft. lbs.

39. Install the washer, clutch disc, second washer and clutch release bearing on the end of the drive gear on the housing. Install the short shaft with the clutch release yoke in the housing. Slide the long shaft from the outside housing into the yoke. Install the key, bolt and washer.

40. Replace the P.T.O. aperture covers and gaskets. Tighten the bolts 25–32 ft. lbs.

41. Install the magnetic plug on the right side of the unit and the oil level plug on the left side.

42. Check the shifter cover assembly and make sure all the shift forks are in the neutral position, then install the shifter housing to the main case using a new gasket.

SHIFTER HOUSING

Disassembly

1. Place the shifter housing in a vise with the forks facing out.

2. Cut the lock wires and remove the set screws from the 1st and reverse shift rod bracket and fork.

3. Tap the 1st and reverse shift rod forward to free the fork and bracket from the shift rod.

4. Remove the interlock from the cross hole between the rods.

5. Cut the lockwire and remove the set screw from the 2nd and 3rd shift fork. Tap the rod forward to free the fork and recover the poppet ball.

6. Remove the 4th speed bracket and shift fork and the 5th and 6th speed bracket and shift fork in the same manner as the 1st and reverse and the 2nd and 3rd.

7. Remove the four poppet springs from their holes in the shifter housing front boss.

Assembly

1. Place the shifter housing in a vise with the inside of the housing facing out and with the front of the housing facing left.

2. Apply a light coat of grease to all the bores in the housing and to the shift rods as they are assembled to the housing.

3. Using a poppet assembly tool or equivalent, preload the poppet spring and ball in the poppet detent bore of the top boss or the 5th/6th speed rod location.

4. Select the longest shift rod and enter the longest end from the interlock detent into the rear boss, on the right side of the housing.

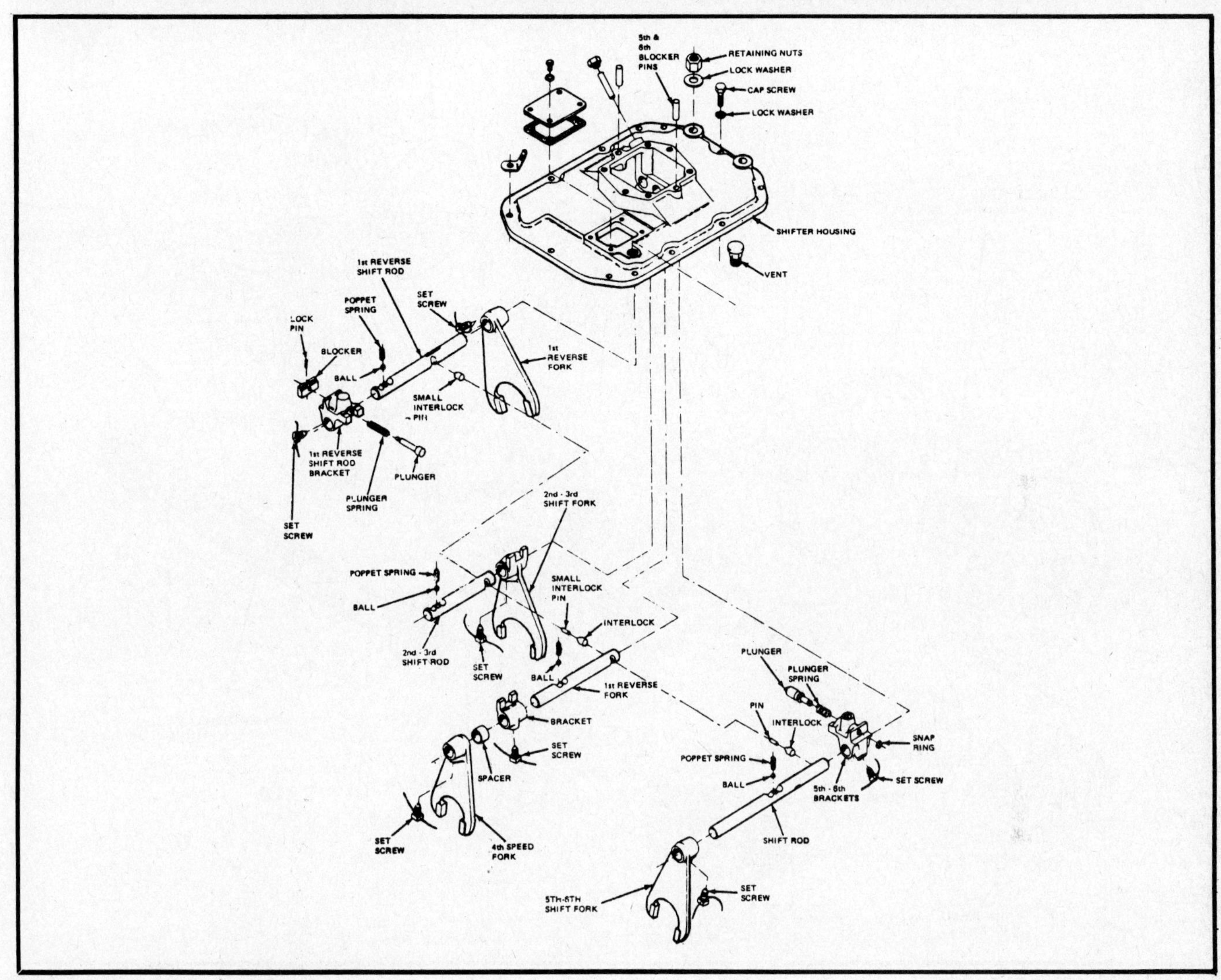

Shifter housing—exploded view

5. Assemble the shift rod bracket to the rod with the shift gate downward. Tap the shift rod sharply to remove the poppet ball loading tool in the front boss and continue the assembly until the poppet ball registers in the neutral detent of the shift rod.

6. Install the 5th and 6th shift fork to the rod with the extended hub toward the right. Install the bracket and fork in the proper positions and secure with the set screws and torque 40–50 ft. lbs.

7. With the poppet assembly tool or equivalent, preload the poppet spring and ball in the poppet detent bore of the 2nd top opening (4th speed) in the front boss.

8. Coat the small interlock pin of the 4th speed shift rod with heavy grease and insert the pin into the hole of the shift rod. Enter the rod with the interlocking pin to the right, through the rear boss.

9. Install the bracket to the rod with the shift gate down, then install the spacer on the rod. As the shift rod enters the front boss tap the rod sharply to remove the poppet loading tool. Assemble the 4th speed fork to the rod with the extended hub of the fork to the left. Place the shift fork and bracket in its proper position and install the set scew and torque 40–50 ft. lbs. Tie with lock wire.

10. Coat the interlock with heavy grease and install the interlock into the access hole of the rear boss through the 2nd and 3rd shift rod bore.

11. With the poppet assembly tool or equivalent, preload the poppet spring and ball in the poppet detent bore.

12. Coat the small interlock with heavy grease and insert the pin into the hole of the 2nd and 3rd shift rod. Enter the rod through the rear boss with the interlock pin to the right.

13. Assemble the 2nd and 3rd shift fork to the rod with the extended hub of the fork to the left. As the shift rod enters the front boss, tap it sharply to remove the poppet loading tool. Install the shift fork in its proper position. Torque the set screw 40–50 ft. lbs. and secure with lock wire.

14. Coat the interlock with heavy grease and install the interlock into the access hole of the rear boss with the interlock pin to the right.

15. With a poppet assembly tool or equivalent, preload the poppet spring and ball in the poppet detent bore.

16. Select the 1st and reverse shift rod. Start the end closest to the set screw counter sink hole through the front boss of the housing, then through the middle boss containing the preloading tool. Install the 1st and reverse bracket on the rod after tapping the shift rod sharply to remove the poppet loading tool. Make sure the bracket top boss is down and the shift gate is toward the tower opening. Slide the rod through the rear boss and install the 1st and reverse fork on the rod with the extended hub of the fork to the right. Install the shift fork and rod in the prop-

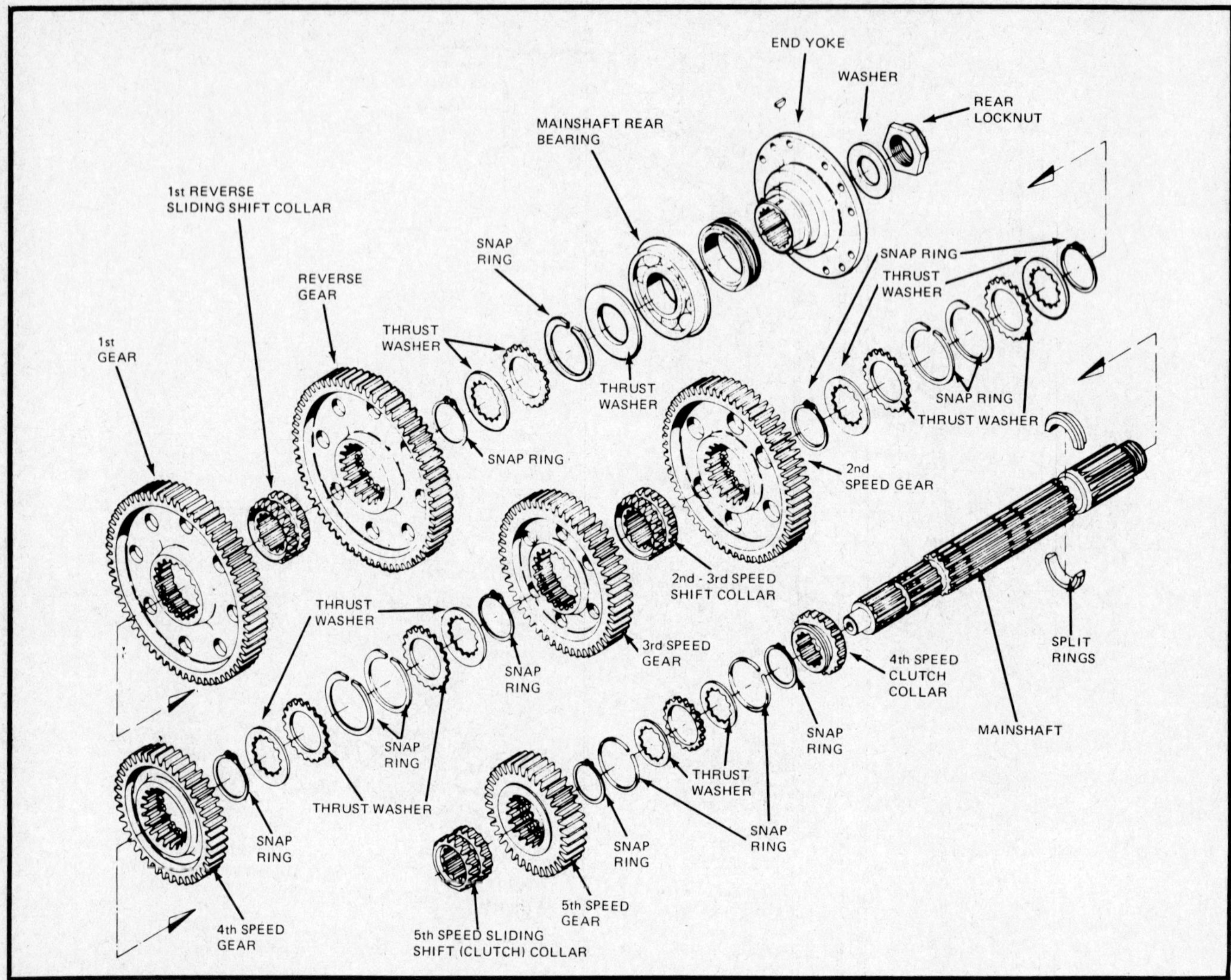

Mainshaft—exploded view

er position and torque the set screws to 40–50 ft. lbs. Secure with lock wire.

17. Shift the 1st/reverse speed fork into gear and try to shift the other three rods. If functioning correctly the other rods should be locked in neutral.

MAINSHAFT

Disassembly

1. Remove the 5th speed clutch collar. Remove the snapring from the mainshaft groove. Remove the 5th gear sub-assembly then remove the 2nd snapring from the shaft groove.
2. Remove the 4th speed clutch collar, the snapring, then the 4th speed gear sub-assembly.
3. Remove the 3rd speed gear sub-assembly then the snapring from the shaft groove.
4. Remove the 2nd–3rd speed gear shift collar. Remove the snapring under the 2nd speed gear bore. Remove the 2nd speed gear sub-assembly.
5. Cut the holding wire on the 1st and reverse gears. Remove the 1st speed gear sub-assembly, snapring and shift collar from the shaft.
6. Remove the reverse gear sub-assembly from the output end of the shaft.

Assembly

1. Position the mainshaft vertically in a vise.
2. Install the thrust washer on the mainshaft. Let the washer rest on the shoulder near the output splines.
3. Install the snapring in the bottom groove of the mainshaft.
4. Install the 1st/reverse clutch collar on the shaft, with either end of the collar down. Rest the clutch collar on the snapring.
5. Install the 2nd snapring and thrust washer on the shaft. Seat the snapring securely in the groove closest to the 1st and reverse clutch collar.
6. Install the thrust washer and snapring into the 1st speed gear and install the sub-assembly on the shaft, with the 35 degree chamfer in the bore of the gear down toward the clutch collar.
7. Install the 2nd set of washers and snapring into the 2nd speed gear and install the sub-assembly on the shaft, with the 35 degree bore chamfer up. Rest the gear against the face of the 1st speed. Install the 3rd snapring on the shaft under the bore of the 2nd speed gear.
8. Install the 2nd/3rd speed gear clutch collar, either end of the collar down, resting in the bore of the 2nd speed gear.
9. Install the 4th snapring in the groove closest to the 2nd/3rd clutch collar and install the thrust washers on the ring.

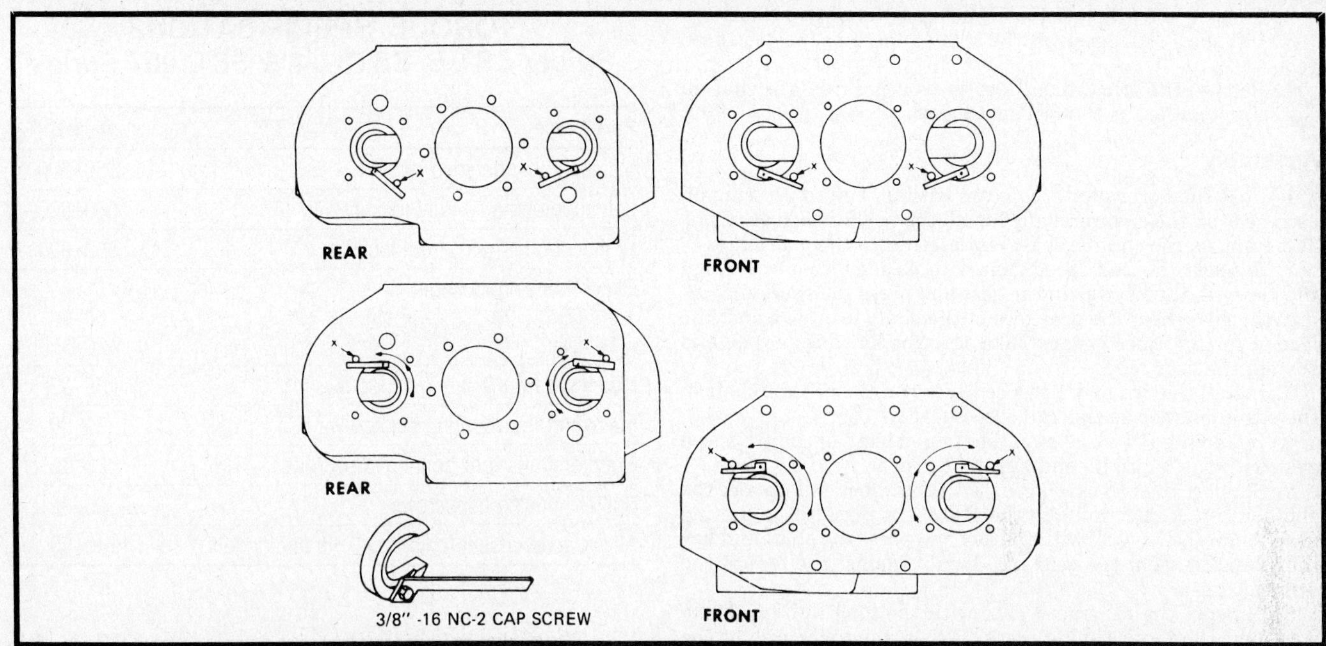

Tool for positioning mainshaft gears in case

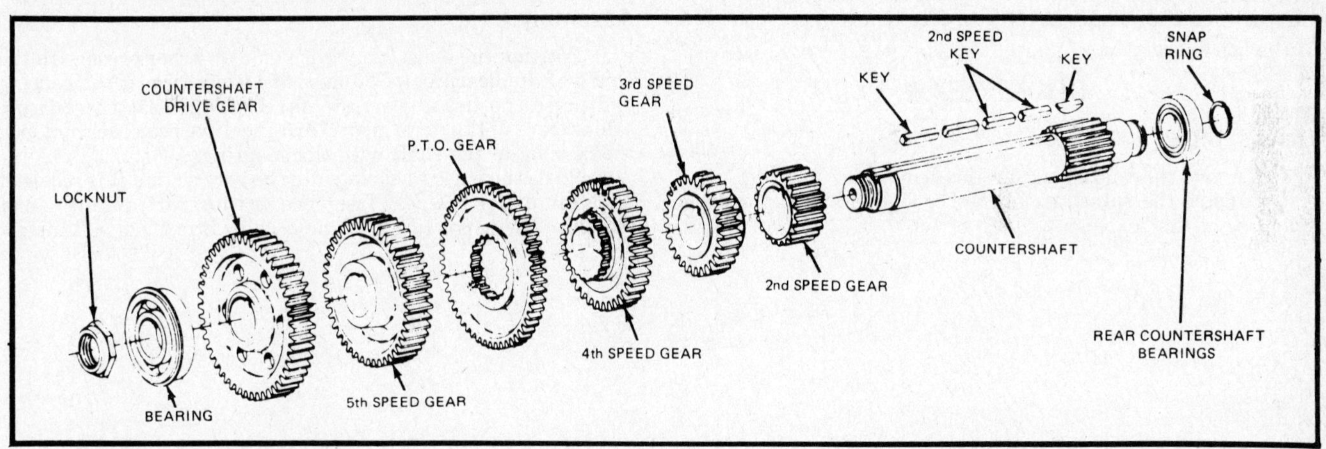

Countershaft—exploded view

10. Install the 3rd snapring into the 3rd speed gear and install the sub-assembly with the 35 degree chamfer in the bore of the gear down toward the clutch collar. Rest the gear on the washer of the shaft.
11. Install the fourth set of washers and snapring into the 4th speed gear and install the sub-assembly on the shaft with the 35 degree chamfer bore up. Rest the gear against the face of the 3rd speed gear. Install the fifth snapring in the groove of the shaft under the bore of the 4th speed gear.
12. Install the 4th speed clutch collar on the shaft, with the shift fork collar up. Rest the clutch collar in the bore of the 4th speed gear.
13. Install the first snapring in the shaft groove closest to the 4th speed clutch collar.
14. Install the snapring into the groove of the 5th speed gear. Install the washer, snapring, thrust washer and second snapring in the gear bore.
15. Install the sub-assembly on the shaft, with the 35 degree bore chamfer up. Rest the gear internal thrust washer on the shaft snapring. Install the 2nd snapring in the shaft groove under the bore of the 5th speed gear.
16. Install the 5th–6th speed clutch collar on the shaft and rest it in the bore of the 5th speed gear.
17. Remove the assembly from the vise and place on a work bench.
18. Slide the 1st/reverse shift collar into the bore of the 1st gear, also slide the thrust washer on the end of the shaft against the snapring.
19. Install the reverse gear on the rear of the shaft and slide it forward onto the clutch collar. Match the OD teeth to the 1st speed gear teeth. Wire or tie the two gears together.
20. Install the remaining parts, relating to the reverse gear and to the rear of the mainshaft, after the mainshaft sub-assembly has been placed into the main case.

COUNTERSHAFT

Disassembly

1. Support the 6th speed gear with parallel bars as close to the hub as possible. Using an arbor press, press the countershaft out of the gear.

2. Remove the 5th speed gear, using a standard puller.
3. Lift the P.T.O. gear off the splined teeth of the 4th speed gear.
4. Remove the 4th, 3rd and 2nd speed gears from the shaft in the same manner as the 6th speed gear.

Assembly

1. Coat the bores of all the gears with oil before pressing on each gear on the countershaft. Install the key for each gear, one at a time, as the countershaft is pressed into the gear bore.
2. Support the 2nd speed gear with either face down. Align the key with the keyway in the gear and press the shaft and key into the gear. Seat the gear face of the shaft firmly against the face of the 2nd speed gear. Make sure the key does not extend beyond the gear face.
3. Install the 3rd and 4th speed gears on the countershaft in the same manner as the 2nd speed gear.
4. Install the P.T.O. gear on the splined teeth of the 4th speed gear with the long hub end against the gear.
5. Support the 5th speed gear with the short end up. Set the shaft into the gear, holding the P.T.O. in place to its mating gear. Align the keyway with the key and press the shaft and key into the gear. Seat the gear face firmly against the face of the 4th speed gear.
6. Support the 6th speed gear with the long hub up. Make sure that the tooth timing mark "A" on the tooth web of the gear aligns itself to the center of the gear keyway. Set the shaft into the gear, align the keyway with the key and press the shaft and key into the gear. Seat the gear face firmly against the face of the 5th speed gear.

DRIVE GEAR

Disassembly

1. Remove the snapring from the drive gear.
2. Support the outer race of the bearing and press the drive gear free of the bearing.

TORQUE SPECIFICATIONS
Spicer SST-6, SST6+1 & SST1007 Series

Part Name	ft. lbs.
Mainshaft flange/yoke locknut	550–600
Left countershaft—front locknut	550–600
Right countershaft—front locknut	550–600
Clutch housing locknuts	
½″ Dia.	60–80
⅝″ Dia.	120–150
Mainshaft front bearing capscrews	25–32
Mainshaft rear bearing capscrews	60–80
Countershafts rear bearing capscrews	25–32
Shifter housing capscrews	25–32
All set screws shift forks, brackets and fingers	40–50

3. The pocket bearing in the drive gear is a press OD fit. If the pocket bearing must be replaced, use a small puller tool.

Assembly

1. Position the drive gear bearing on an arbor press with the shield of the bearing up. Support the inner race of the bearing and press the drive gear into the bearing. Seat the bearing against face of the drive gear. Turn the drive gear over and lock the bearing to the shaft with the snapring.
2. Press the pocket bearing into the bore so that it is recessed 0.062 in. under the gear face. The bearing part number must face out. The opposite end of the bearing is made of soft metal.

Tremec T-150 Three Speed Transmission (77mm)

The Tremec T-150 (77mm) transmission is used in varied vehicle applications, with or without transfer cases. The gear selection is controlled by either a top shift housing or by a remote control shift lever assembly. Although some of the gears and case applications are not interchangeable, the gear arrangement is basically the same.

Disassembly

1. Remove the bolts securing the transfer case to the transmission. Remove the transfer case.
2. Remove the transfer case drive gear locknut, flat washer, and drive gear. Remove the large fiber washer from the rear bearing adapter. Move the second-third clutch sleeve forward and the first/reverse sleeve to the rear before removing the locknut.
3. Remove the transmission oil plug and drive the countershaft out of the case with a suitable size drift. Do not lose the countershaft access plug when removing the countershaft. With the countershaft removed the countershaft gear will lie at the bottom of the case, leave it there until the mainshaft is removed.
4. Punch alignment marks in the front bearing cap and the transmission case for assembly reference.
5. Remove the front bearing cap and gasket.
6. Remove the large lock ring from the front bearing.
7. Remove the clutch shaft, front bearing and the second/third synchronizer assembly. A special tool is required for this operation.
8. Remove the rear bearing and adapter assembly with a brass drift and hammer. Drive the adapter out the rear of the case with light blows from the hammer.
9. Remove the mainshaft assembly. Tilt the spline end of the shaft downward and lift the front end up and out of the case.
10. Remove the countershaft tool and arbor as an assembly. Remove the countershaft thrust washers, countershaft roll pin and any pilot roller bearings that may have fallen into the case.

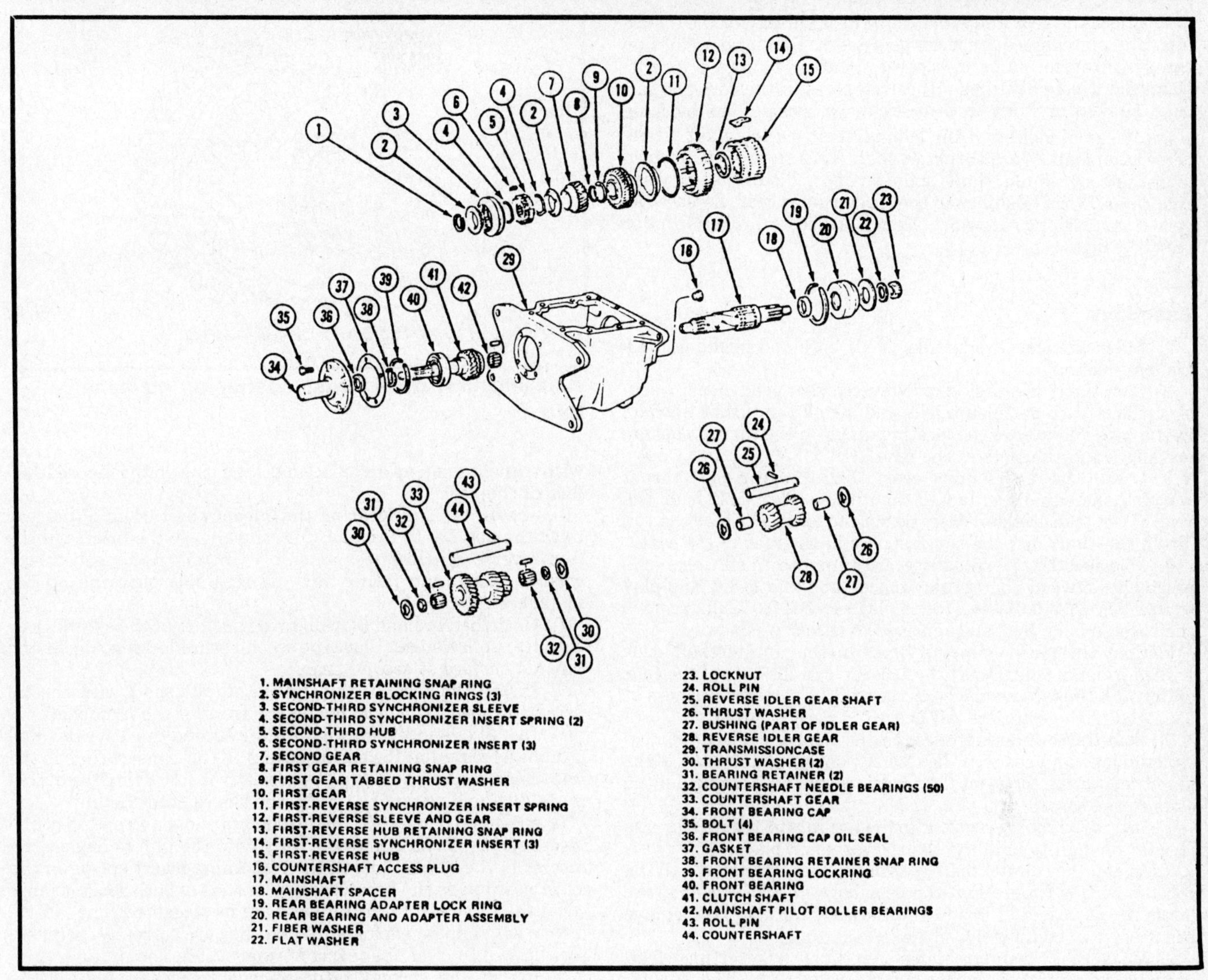

T-150 transmission—exploded view

11. Remove the reverse idler shaft. Insert a brass drift through the clutch shaft bore in the front of the case and tap the shaft until the end with the roll pin clears the counter bore in the rear of the case. Remove the shaft.

12. Remove the reverse idler gear and thrust washers from the case.

13. Remove the retaining snapring from the front of the mainshaft. Remove the second/third synchronizer assembly and second gear. Mark the hub and sleeve for reference during assembly. Observe the position of the insert springs and the inserts during removal for correct assembly.

14. Remove the insert springs from the second/third synchronizer, remove the three inserts and separate the sleeve from the synchronizer hub retaining snapring.

15. Remove the snapring and the tabbed thrust washer from the mainshaft and remove the first gear blocking ring.

16. Remove the first/reverse synchronizer hub snapring. Observe the position of the insert springs and the inserts during removal for correct assembly.

17. Remove the first/reverse sleeve, insert spring and the three insert from the hub. Remove the spacer from the rear of the mainshaft. Do not attempt to remove the press fit hub by hammering. Hammer blows will damage the hub and mainshaft.

18. Remove the front bearing retaining snapring and any remaining roller bearings from the clutch shaft.

19. Press the front bearing off the clutch shaft with an arbor press. Do not attempt to remove the bearing by hammering. Hammer blows will damage the bearing and the clutch shaft.

20. Clamp the rear bearing adapter in a soft jawed vise. Do not over tighten.

21. Remove the rear bearing retaining snapring. Remove the bearing adapter from the vise.

22. Press the rear bearing out of the adapter with an arbor press.

Cleaning and Inspection

1. Thoroughly wash all parts in clean solvent and dry with compressed air. Do not dry the bearings with compressed air, use a clean shop cloth.

2. Clean the needle and clutch shaft bearings by placing them in a shallow parts cleaning tray and covering them with solvent. Allow the bearings to air dry on a clean shop cloth.

3. Check the case for the following. Cracks in the bores, bosses, or bolt holes. Stripped threads in bolt holes. Nicks, burrs, rough surfaces in the shaft bores or on the gasket surfaces.

4. Check the gear and synchronizer assemblies for the following. Broken, chipped, or worn gear teeth. Damaged splines on the synchronizer hubs or sleeves. Bent or damaged inserts. Damaged needle bearings or bearing bores in the countershaft gear. Broken or worn teeth or excessive wear of the blocking rings. Wear of galling of the countershaft, clutch shaft, or reverse idler shaft. Worn thrust washers. Nicked, broken, or worn mainshaft or clutch shaft splines. Bent, distorted, or weak snaprings. Worn bushings in the reverse idler gear. Replace the gear if the bushings are worn. Rough, galled, or broken front or rear bearings.

Assembly

1. Lubricate the reverse idler shaft bore and bushings with transmission oil.
2. Coat the transmission case reverse idler gear thrust washer surfaces with petroleum jelly and install the thrust washers in the case. Make sure the locating tangs on the thrust washers are aligned in the slots in the case.
3. Install the reverse idler gear. Align the gear bore, thrust washers and case bore. Install the reverse idler shaft from the rear of the transmission case. Be sure to align and seat the roll pin in the shaft into the counter bore in the rear of the case.
4. Measure the reverse idler gear end-play by inserting a feeler gauge between the thrust washer and the gear. End-play should be 0.004–0.018 in.. If end play exceeds 0.018 in., remove the reverse idler gear and replace the thrust washers.
5. Coat the needle bearing bores in the countershaft gear with petroleum jelly. Insert the arbor tool in the bore of the gear and install the (25) needle bearings and the retainer washers at each end of the countershaft gear.
6. Coat the countershaft gear thrust washer surface with petroleum jelly and position the thrust washers in the case. Make sure the locating tangs on the thrust washers are aligned in the slots in the case.
7. Insert the countershaft into the bore at the rear of the case just far enough to hold the thrust washer in place.
8. Install the countershaft gear in the case. Do not install the roll pin at this time. Align the gear bore, thrust washers, the bores in the case and install the countershaft. Do not remove the arbor tool completely.
9. Measure the countershaft gear end-play by inserting a feeler gauge between the washer and the countershaft gear. End-play should be 0.004–0.018 in.. If the end-play exceeds 0.018 in., remove the gear and replace the thrust washer.
10. When the correct countershaft gear end-play has been obtained, install the countershaft arbor and remove the countershaft. Allow the countershaft gear to remain at the bottom of the case, leave the countershaft in the case enough to hold the thrust washer in place.
11. Coat the splines and machined surfaces on the mainshaft with transmission oil. Install the first/reverse synchronizer on the output shaft splines by hand. The end of the hub with the slots should face the front of the shaft. Use an arbor press to complete the hub installation. Install the retaining snapring in the groove farthest to the rear. Do not attempt to drive the hub on the shaft with a hammer.
12. Coat the splines of the first/reverse hub with transmission oil and install the first reverse sleeve and gear halfway onto the hub, with the gear end of the sleeve facing the rear of the shaft. Align the marks made during disassembly.
13. Install the insert spring in the first/reverse hub. Make sure the spring bottoms in the hub and covers all three insert slots. Position the three "T" shaped inserts in the hub with the small ends in the hub slots and the large ends inside the hub. Push the inserts fully into the hub so they seat on the insert spring, slide the first/reverse sleeve and gear over the inserts until the inserts engage in the sleeve.
14. Coat the bore and the blocking ring surface of first gear with transmission oil and place blocking ring on the tapered surface of the gear.

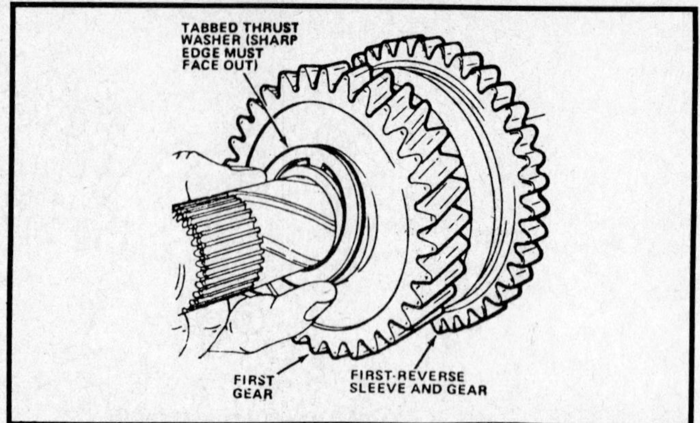

Installing first gear thrust washer on mainshaft—T-150

15. Install the first gear on the output shaft. Rotate the gear until the notches in the blocking ring engage the inserts in the first/reverse synchronizer assembly. Install the tanged thrust washer, sharp end facing out and retaining snapring on the mainshaft.
16. Coat the bore and blocking ring surface of the second gear with transmission oil. Place the second gear blocking ring on the tapered surface of second gear.
17. Install the second gear on the output shaft with the tapered surface of the gear facing the front of the mainshaft.
18. Install one insert spring into the second/third synchronizer hub. Be sure that the spring covers all three insert slots in the hub. Align the second-third sleeve with the hub using the marks made during disassembly. Start the sleeve onto the hub.
19. Place the three inserts into the hub slots and on top of the insert spring. Push the sleeve fully onto the hub to engage the inserts in the sleeve. Install the remaining insert spring in the exact position as the first spring. The ends of both springs must cover the same slot in the hub and not be staggered. The inserts have a small lip on each end. When they are correctly installed, this lip will fit over the insert spring.
20. Install the second/third synchronizer assembly on the mainshaft. Rotate the second gear until the notches in the blocking ring engage the inserts in the second/third synchronizer assembly.
21. Install the retaining snapring on the mainshaft and measure the end-play between the snapring and the second/third synchronizer hub. The end-play should be 0.040–0.014 in.. If the end-play exceeds the limit, replace the thrust washer and all the snaprings on the mainshaft assembly. Install the spacer on the rear of the mainshaft.
22. Install the mainshaft assembly in the case. Be sure that the first/reverse sleeve and gear is in the neutral (centered) position.
23. Press the rear bearing into the rear bearing adapter with an arbor press. Install the rear bearing retaining ring and the bearing adapter lockring.
24. Support the mainshaft assembly and install the rear bearing and adapter assembly in the case. Use a soft faced hammer to seat the adapter in the case.
25. Install the large fiber washer in the rear bearing adapter. Install the transfer drive gear, flat washer and locknut. Tighten the locknut to 150 ft. lbs. torque.
26. Press the front bearing onto the clutch shaft. Install the bearing retaining snapring on the clutch shaft and the lockring into its groove.
27. Coat the bore of the clutch shaft assembly with petroleum jelly and install the (15) roller bearings in the clutch shaft bore.

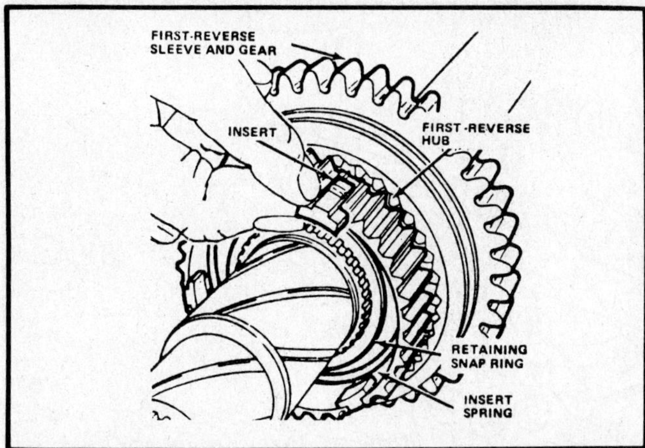

Installing the inserts in the first/reverse synchronizer hub—T-150

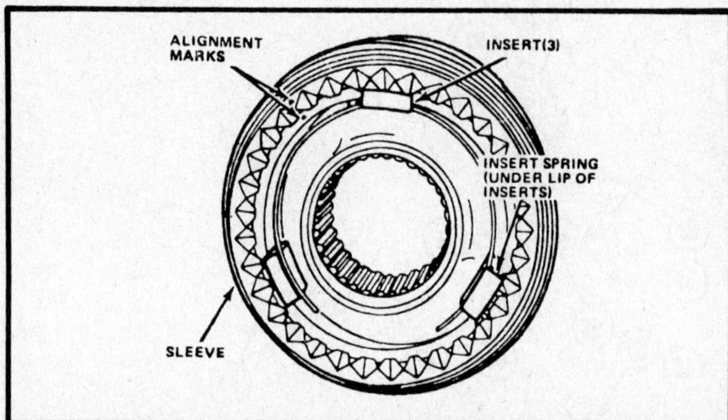

Installing second gear on mainshaft—T-150

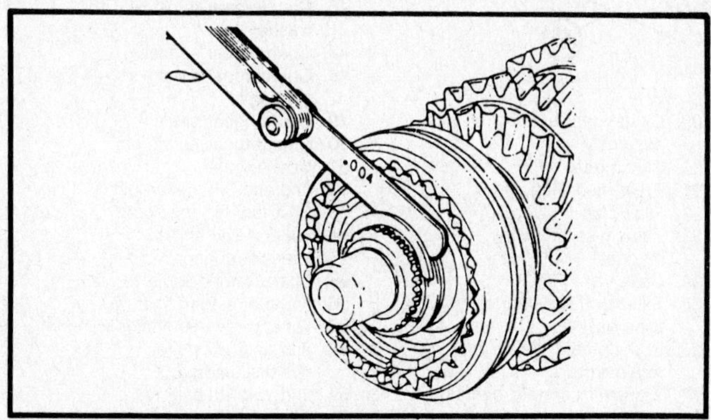

Measuring mainshaft endplay—T-150

Do not use chassis grease or a similar heavy grease in the clutch shaft bore. Heavy grease will plug the lubricant holes in the shaft and prevent proper lubrication of the roller bearings.

28. Coat the blocking ring surface of the clutch shaft with transmission oil. Position the blocking ring on the clutch shaft.

29. Support the mainshaft assembly and insert the clutch shaft through the front bearing bore in the case. Seat the mainshaft pilot in the clutch shaft roller bearings. Tap the bearings into place with a soft faced hammer.

30. Apply a thin film of sealer to the front bearing cap gasket and position the gasket on the case. Be sure the cutout in the gasket is aligned with the oil return hole in the case.

31. Remove the front bearing cap oil seal with a suitable tool. Install a new seal with a suitable driver.

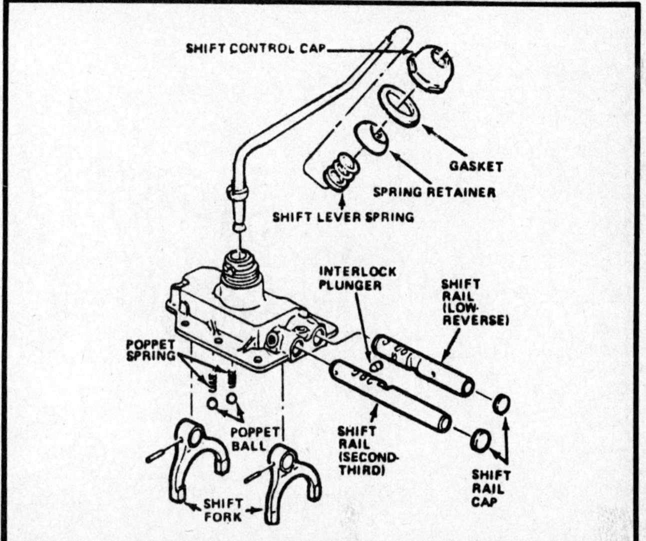

Shift control housing—T-150

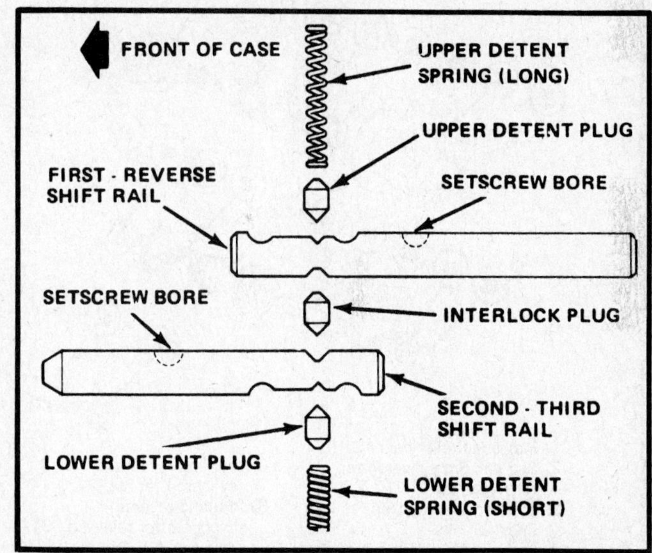

Proper positioning of detent plugs and springs in the remote shifting control shift rails

32. Install the front bearing cap and tighten the bolts to 33 ft. lbs. Be sure that the marks on the cap and the transmission case are aligned and the oil return slot in the cap lines up with the oil return hole in the case.

33. Make a wire loop about 18–20 in. long and pass the wire under the countershaft gear assembly. The wire loop should raise and support the countershaft gear assembly when it is pulled upward.

34. Raise the countershaft gear with the wire. Align the bore in the countershaft gear with the front thrust washer and the countershaft. Start the countershaft into the gear with a soft faced hammer.

35. Align the roll pin hole in the countershaft with the roll pin holes in the case and complete the installation of the countershaft. Install the countershaft access plug in the rear of the case and seat with a soft faced hammer.

36. Install the countershaft roll pin in the case. Use a magnet or needle nose pliers to insert and start the pin in the case. Use a $\frac{1}{2}$ in. punch to seat the pin. Install the transmission filler plug.

37. Shift the synchronizer sleeves through all gear ranges and

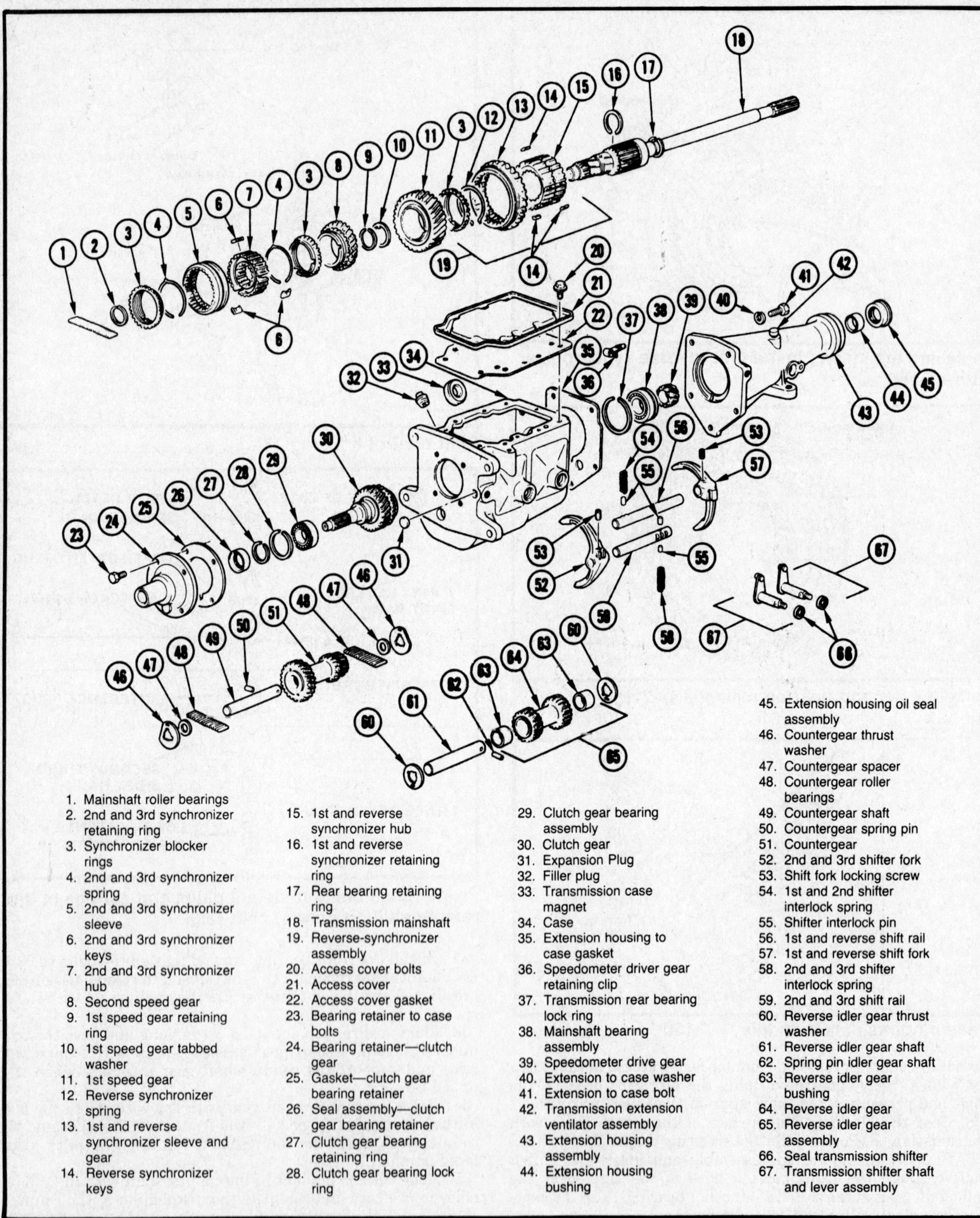
1. Mainshaft roller bearings
2. 2nd and 3rd synchronizer retaining ring
3. Synchronizer blocker rings
4. 2nd and 3rd synchronizer spring
5. 2nd and 3rd synchronizer sleeve
6. 2nd and 3rd synchronizer keys
7. 2nd and 3rd synchronizer hub
8. Second speed gear
9. 1st speed gear retaining ring
10. 1st speed gear tabbed washer
11. 1st speed gear
12. Reverse synchronizer spring
13. 1st and reverse synchronizer sleeve and gear
14. Reverse synchronizer keys
15. 1st and reverse synchronizer hub
16. 1st and reverse synchronizer retaining ring
17. Rear bearing retaining ring
18. Transmission mainshaft
19. Reverse-synchronizer assembly
20. Access cover bolts
21. Access cover
22. Access cover gasket
23. Bearing retainer to case bolts
24. Bearing retainer—clutch gear
25. Gasket—clutch gear bearing retainer
26. Seal assembly—clutch gear bearing retainer
27. Clutch gear bearing retaining ring
28. Clutch gear bearing lock ring
29. Clutch gear bearing assembly
30. Clutch gear
31. Expansion Plug
32. Filler plug
33. Transmission case magnet
34. Case
35. Extension housing to case gasket
36. Speedometer driver gear retaining clip
37. Transmission rear bearing lock ring
38. Mainshaft bearing assembly
39. Speedometer drive gear
40. Extension to case washer
41. Extension to case bolt
42. Transmission extension ventilator assembly
43. Extension housing assembly
44. Extension housing bushing
45. Extension housing oil seal assembly
46. Countergear thrust washer
47. Countergear spacer
48. Countergear roller bearings
49. Countergear shaft
50. Countergear spring pin
51. Countergear
52. 2nd and 3rd shifter fork
53. Shift fork locking screw
54. 1st and 2nd shifter interlock spring
55. Shifter interlock pin
56. 1st and reverse shift rail
57. 1st and reverse shift fork
58. 2nd and 3rd shifter interlock spring
59. 2nd and 3rd shift rail
60. Reverse idler gear thrust washer
61. Reverse idler gear shaft
62. Spring pin idler gear shaft
63. Reverse idler gear bushing
64. Reverse idler gear
65. Reverse idler gear assembly
66. Seal transmission shifter
67. Transmission shifter shaft and lever assembly

T-150 transmission—exploded view

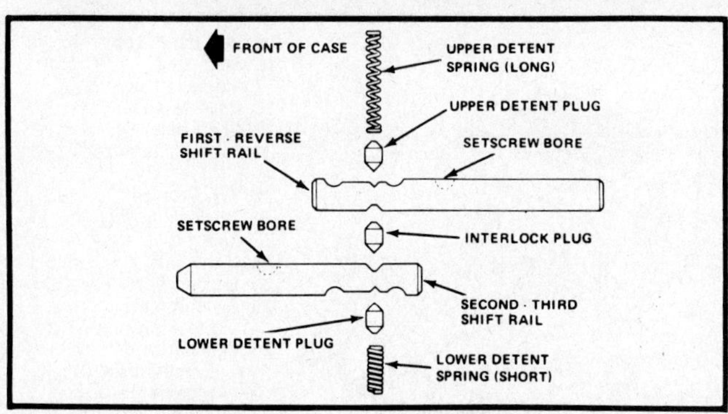

Installation sequence—interlock and detent plugs and springs

check their operation. If the clutch shaft and mainshaft appear to bind in the neutral position, check for blocking rings sticking on the first or second gear tapers.

38. Install the transfer case on the transmission. Tighten the attaching bolts to 30 ft. lbs.

SHIFT CONTROL HOUSING

Disassembly

1. Remove the back-up light switch and the transmission controlled spark switch (TCS) if so equipped.
2. Remove the shift control housing cap, gasket, spring retainer and the shift lever spring as an assembly.
3. Invert the housing and mount in a soft jawed vise.
4. Move the second/third shift rail to the rear of the housing, rotate the shift fork toward the first/reverse rail until the roll pin is accessible. Drive the roll pin out of the fork and rail with a pin punch. Remove the shift fork and the roll pin. The roll pin hole in the shift fork is offset. Mark the position of the shift fork for assembly reference.
5. Remove the second/third shift rail using a brass drift or hammer. Catch the shift rail plug as the rail drives it out of the housing. Cover the shift and poppet ball holes in the cover to prevent the poppet ball from flying out. Mark the location of the shift rail for assembly reference.
6. Rotate the first/reverse shift fork away from the notch in the housing until the roll pin is accessible. Drive the roll pin out of the fork and rail using a pin punch. Remove the shift fork and roll pin. The roll pin hole in the shift fork is offset. Mark the position of the shift fork for assembly reference.
7. Remove the first/reverse shift rail using a brass drift or hammer. Catch the shift rail plug as the rail drives it out of the housing. Cover the shift and poppet ball holes in the cover to prevent the poppet ball from flying out. Mark the location of the shift rail for assembly reference.
8. Remove the poppet balls, springs and the interlock plunger from the housing.

Assembly

1. Install the poppet springs and the detent plug in the housing.
2. Insert the first/reverse shift rail into the housing and install the shift fork on the shift rail.
3. Install the poppet ball on the top of the spring in the first/reverse rail.
4. Using a punch or wooden dowel, push the poppet ball and spring downward into the housing bore and install the first/reverse shift rail.
5. Align the roll pin holes in the first/reverse shift fork and install the roll pin. Move the shift rail to the neutral (center) detent.
6. Insert the second/third shift rail into the housing and install the poppet ball on top of the spring in the shift rail bore.
7. Using a punch or wooden dowel, push the poppet ball and spring downward into the housing bore and install the second/third shift rail.
8. Align the roll pin holes in the second/third shift rail and the shift fork and install the roll pin. Move the shift rail to the neutral (center) position.
9. Install the shift rail plugs in the housing and remove the shift control cover from the vise.
10. Install the shift lever, shift lever spring, spring retainer, gasket and the shift control housing cap as an assembly. Tighten the cap securely.
11. Install the back-up light switch and the TCS switch if so equipped.

LUBRICANT CAPACITY

SAE 80-90 gear lube	3 pts.

TORQUE SPECIFICATIONS
Tremec T-150

	ft. lbs.
Back-up light switch	15–20
Fill and drain plugs	10–20
Front bearing cap bolt	30–36
Shift control housing bolts	20–25
Transfer case drive gear locknut	150
Transfer case to transmission bolts	30
TCS switch	18

Warner T–4 and T–5 4 and 5 Speed

NOTE: For T–5 procedures, refer to the GM S–Series (5 Speed)

Disassembly

1. Drain the transmission lubricant. 2WD models are not equipped with a drain plug; the fluid must be siphoned from the transmission.
2. Use a pin punch and hammer to remove the offset lever-to-shift rail roll pin.
3. Remove the extension housing (2WD) or the adapter (4WD). Remove the housing and the offset lever as an assembly.
4. Remove the detent ball and spring from the offset lever. Remove the roll pin from the extension housing or adapter.
5. Remove the countershaft rear thrust bearing and race.
6. Remove the transmission cover and shift fork assembly. Two of the transmission cover bolts are alignment type dowel pins. Mark their location so that they may be reinstalled in their original locations.
7. Remove the reverse lever to reverse lever pivot bolt C-clip.
8. Remove the reverse lever pivot bolt. Remove the reverse lever and fork as an assembly.

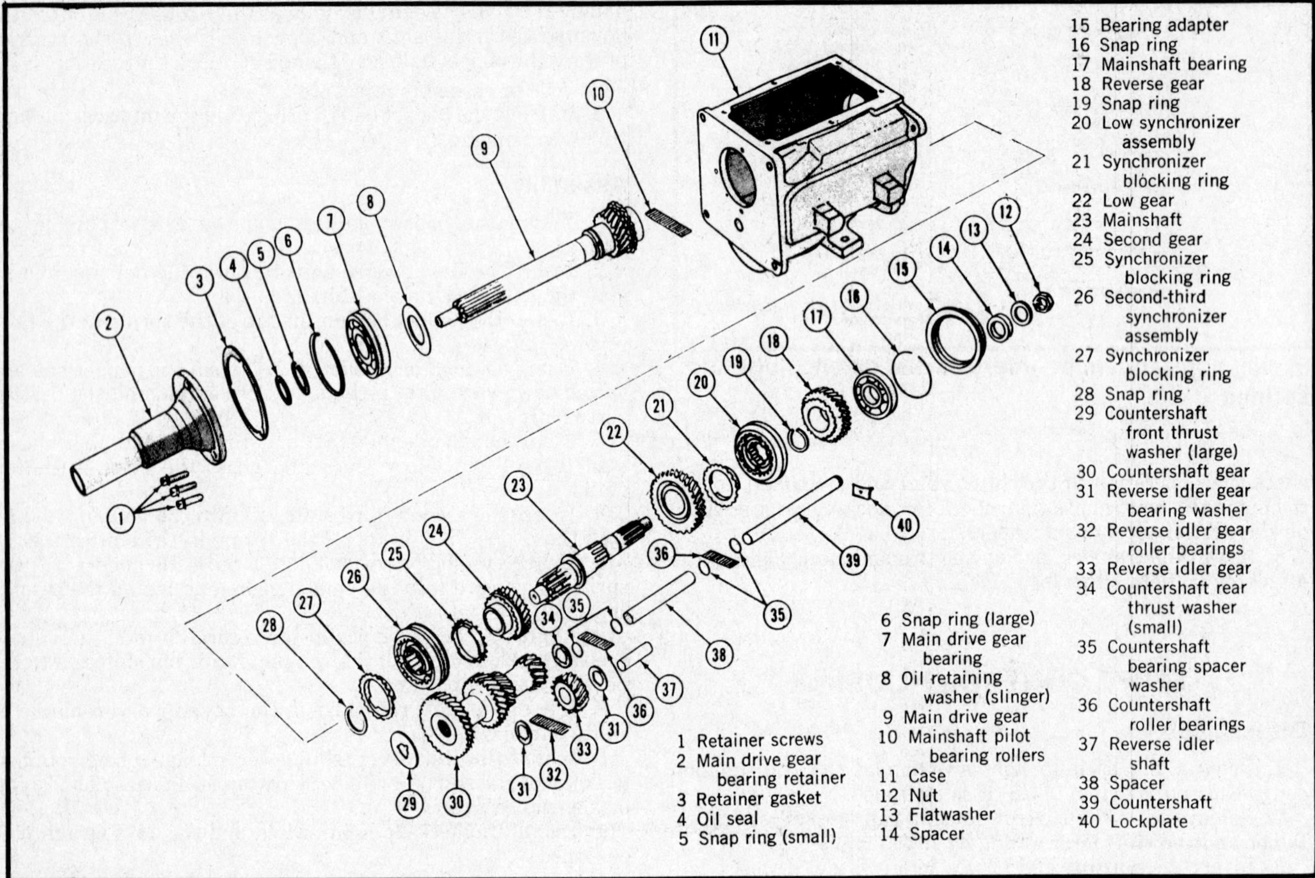

T-14A and T-15A three speed transmissions

9. Mark the position of the front bearing cap to case, then remove the bearing cap bolts and cap.

10. Remove the front bearing race and the shims from the bearing cap. Use a small pry bar and remove the front seal from the bearing cap.

11. Rotate the main drive gear shaft until the flat portion of the gear faces the countershaft, then remove the main drive gear shaft assembly.

12. Remove the thrust bearing and 15 roller bearings from the clutch shaft. Remove the output shaft bearing race. Tap the output shaft with a plastic hammer to loosen it if necessary.

13. Tilt the output shaft assembly upward and remove the assembly from the case.

14. Carefully pull off the countershaft rear bearing with the proper puller after marking the position for reinstallation.

15. Move the countershaft rearward and tilt it upward to remove it from the transmission case. Remove the countershaft bearing spacer.

16. Remove the reverse idler shaft roll pin, then remove the reverse idler shaft and gear.

17. Press off the countershaft front bearing. Use the appropriate pullers and remove the bearing from the main drive gear shaft.

18. Remove the extension housing or adapter oil seal and remove the back-up light switch from the case.

OUTPUT SHAFT DISASSEMBLY

1. Remove the thrust bearing washer from the front of the output shaft.

2. Scribe matchmarks on the hub and sleeve of the 3rd–4th synchronizer so that these parts may be reassembled properly.

3. Remove the 3rd–4th synchronizer blocking ring, sleeve and hub as an assembly.

4. Remove the insert springs and the inserts from the 3rd–4th synchronizer and separate the sleeve from the hub.

5. Remove the 3rd speed gear from the shaft.

6. Remove the 2nd speed gear to output shaft snapring, the tabbed thrust washer and the 2nd speed gear from the shaft.

7. Use an appropriate puller and remove the the output shaft bearing.

8. Remove the 1st gear thrust washer, the roll pin, the 1st speed gear and the blocking ring.

9. Scribe matchmarks on the 1st–2nd synchronizer sleeve and the output shaft.

10. Remove the insert spring and the inserts from the 1st–reverse sliding gear, then remove the gear from the output hub.

OUTPUT SHAFT ASSEMBLY

1. Coat the output shaft and the gear bores with transmission lubricant.

2. Align the matchmarks and install the 1st–2nd synchronizer sleeve on the output shaft hub.

3. Install the three inserts and two springs into the 1st–reverse synchronizer sleeve.

NOTE: The tanged end of each spring should be positioned on the same insert but the open face of each spring should be opposite each other.

4. Install the blocking ring and the 2nd speed gear onto the output shaft.

5. Install the tabbed thrust washer and 2nd gear snapring in

the output shaft; be sure that the washer is properly seated in the notch.

6. Install the blocking ring and the 1st speed gear onto the output shaft, then install the 1st gear roll pin.

7. Press the rear bearing onto the shaft.

8. Install the remaining components onto the output shaft: The 1st gear thrust washer. The 3rd speed gear. The 3rd–4th synchronizer hub inserts and the sleeve (the hub offset must face forward). The thrust bearing washer on the rear of the countershaft.

COVER AND FORKS DISASSEMBLY

1. Place the selector arm plates and the shift rail centered in the Neutral position.

2. Rotate the shift rail counterclockwise until the selector arm disengages from the selector arm plates; the selector arm roll pin should now be accessible.

3. Pull the shift rail rearward until the selector contacts the 1st–2nd shift fork.

4. Use a $^{3}/_{16}$ in. pin punch and remove the selector arm roll pin and the shift rail.

5. Remove the shift forks, the selector arm, the roll pin and the interlock plate.

6. Remove the shift rail oil seal and O-ring.

7. Remove the nylon inserts and the selector arm plates from the shift forks.

NOTE: Mark the position of the parts so that they may be properly installed.

COVER AND FORK ASSEMBLY

1. Attach the nylon inserts to the selector arm plates and through the shift forks.

2. If removed, coat the edges of the shift rail plug with sealer and install the plug.

3. Coat the shift rail and the rail bores with petroleum jelly, then slide the shift rail into the cover until the end of the rail is flush with the inside edge of the cover.

4. Position the 1st–2nd shift fork into the cover; with the offset of the shift fork facing the rear of the cover. Push the shift rail through the fork. The 1st–2nd fork is the larger of the two forks.

5. Position the selector arm and the C-shaped interlock plate into the cover, then push the shift rail through the arm. The widest part of the interlock plate must face away from the cover and the selector arm roll pin must face downward, toward the rear of the cover.

6. Position the 3rd–4th shift fork into the cover with the fork offset facing the rear of the cover. The 3rd–4th shift selector arm plate must be positioned under the 1st–2nd shift fork selector arm plate.

7. Push the shift rail through the 3rd–4th shift fork and into the front cover rail bore.

8. Rotate the shift rail until the forward selector arm plate faces away from parallel to the cover.

9. Align the roll pin holes of the selector arm and the shift rail and install the roll pin. The roll pin must be installed flush with the surface of the selector arm to prevent selector arm plate to pin interference.

10. Install the O-ring into the groove of the shift rail oil seal, then install the oil seal carefully after lubricating it.

Case Assembly

1. Apply a coat of Loctite® 601, or equivalent, to the outer cage of the front countershaft bearing, then press the bearing into the bore until it is flush with the case.

2. Apply petroleum jelly to the tabbed countershaft thrust washer and install the washer with the tab engaged in the corresponding case depression.

3. Tip the transmission case on end and install the countershaft into the front bearing bore.

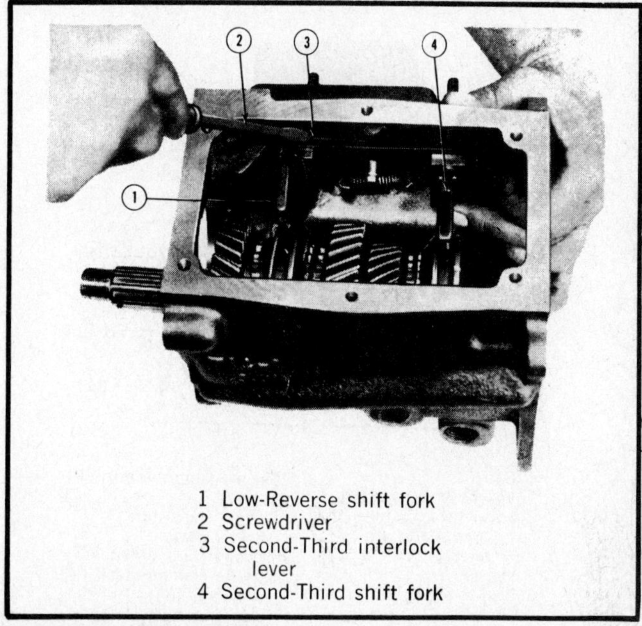

Installing shifter forks

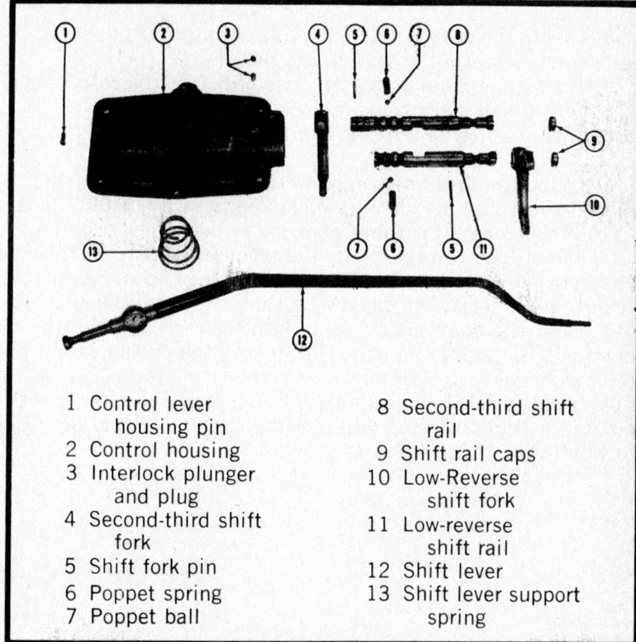

Shift control components

4. Install the rear countershaft bearing spacer and coat the rear bearing with petroleum jelly. Install the rear countershaft bearing using the appropriate tools. The rear bearing is properly installed when 0.125 in. is extended beyond the case surface.

5. Position the reverse idler into the case (the shift lever groove must face rearward) and install the reverse idler shaft into the case. Install the shaft retaining pin.

6. Install the output shaft assembly into the transmission case.

7. Install the main drive gear bearing onto the main drive shaft using the appropriate tools. Coat the roller bearings with petroleum jelly and install them in the main drive gear recess. Install the thrust bearing and race.

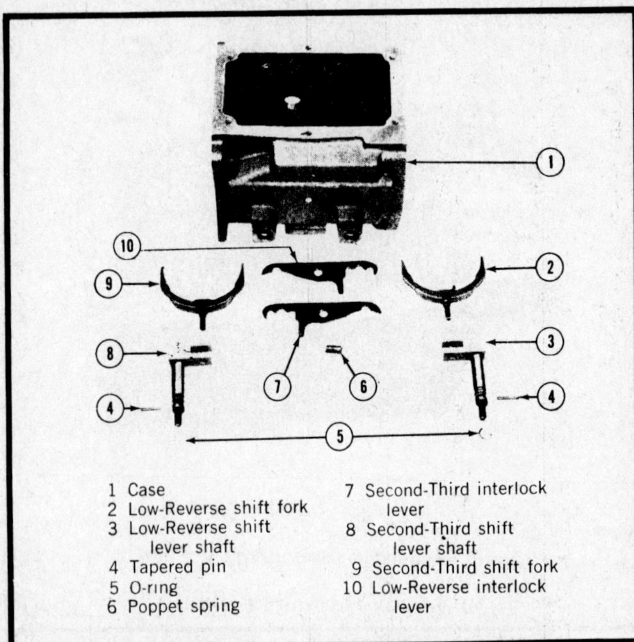

Remote control shift bar housing components

8. Install the 4th gear blocking ring onto the output shaft. Install the rear output shaft bearing race.

9. Install the main drive gear assembly into the case, engaging the 3rd–4th synchronizer blocking ring.

10. Install a new seal in the front bearing cap and in the rear extension or adapter.

11. Install the front bearing into the front bearing cap but do not (at this time) install the shims. Temporarily install the cap to the transmission without applying sealer.

12. Install the reverse lever, the pivot pin (coat the threads with non-hardening sealer) and the retaining C-clip. Be sure the reverse lever fork is engaged with the reverse idler gear.

13. Coat the countershaft rear bearing race and the thrust bearing with petroleum jelly, then install the parts into the extension housing or adapter.

14. Temporarily install the extension housing or adapter without sealer, tighten the retaining bolts slightly, but do not final torque them.

15. Turn the transmission case on end and mount a dial indicator in position to measure output shaft end play. To eliminate end play the bearings must be preloaded from 0.001–0.005 in. Check the endplay. Select a shim pack that measures 0.001–0.005 in. thicker than the measured endplay.

16. Install the shims under the front bearing cap. Apply an $1/8$ in. bead of RTV sealer to the cap. Align the reference marks and install the cap on the front of the transmission. Torque the mounting bolts to 15 ft. lbs. Recheck the output shaft end play, none should exist. Adjust if necessary.

17. Remove the extension housing or adapter. Move the shift forks and synchronizer sleeves to their neutral position. Apply an $1/8$ in. bead of RTV sealer to the cover to case mounting surface. Align the forks with their sleeves and carefully lower the cover into position. Center the cover and install the alignment dowels. Install the mounting bolts and tighten to 9 ft. lbs.

NOTE: The offset lever to shift rail roll pin must be position vertically; if not, repeat Step 17.

18. Apply a $1/8$ in. bead of RTV sealer to the extension housing or adapter and install over the output shaft.

NOTE: The shift rail must be positioned so that it just enters the shift cover opening.

19. Install the detent spring into the offset lever and place the steel ball into the Neutral guide plate detent. Apply pressure to the detent spring and offset lever, then slide the offset lever on the shift rail and seat the extension housing or adapter plate against the transmission case. Install and tighten the mounting bolts to 25 ft. lbs.

20. Install the roll pin into the offset lever and shift rail. Install the damper sleeve in the offset lever. Coat the back up lamp switch threads with sealer and install the switch, tighten to 15 ft. lbs.

TORQUE SPECIFICATIONS

Location	N.m.	ft. lbs.
Front bearing retainer to case	14–20	10–15
Cover to case	14–24	10–18
Control levers to lever shafts	20–34	15–25
Rear bearing retainer to case	31–37	23–27
Companion flange to mainshaft	122–163	90–120
Control lever housing bolt	14–20	10–15

Warner T-14A, T-15A Three Speed Transmission

The Warner T-14A, T-15A are fully synchronized three-speed transmissions having helical drive gears throughout. Lubricant capacity is 2 $1/2$ pints.

TRANSMISSION UNIT

Disassembly

1. Separate transfer case from transmission by removing five capscrews.

2. Remove gearshift housing and disassembly by removing shift rails, poppet balls, springs and shift forks.

3. Remove nut, flat washer, transfer case drive gear, adapter, and spacer.

4. Remove main drive gear bearing retainer gasket.

5. Remove main drive gear and mainshaft bearing snaprings and bearings.

6. Remove main drive gear and mainshaft assembly.

NOTE: The T-15A transmission must be shifted into second gear to allow removal of the mainshaft and gear assembly.

7. On remote shift models, remove roll pins from lever shafts and housing. From inside case, slide levers and interlock assembly out. Remove forks and lever assemblies.

8. Remove lock plate from reverse idler shaft and countershaft.

9. Drive countershaft out to rear with dummy shaft. Remove countergear and two thrust washers. Remove spacer washers, rollers and spacer from gear.

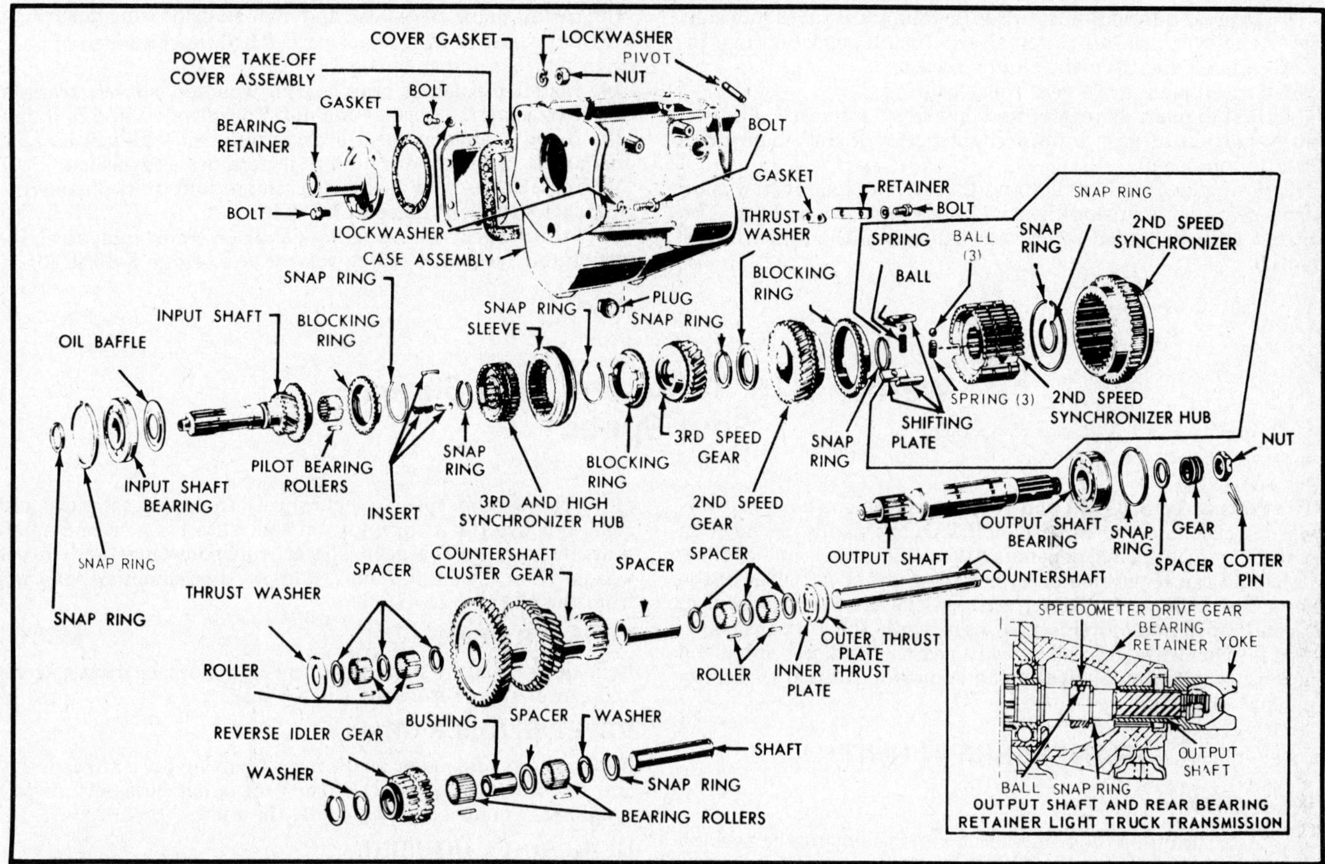

T-18 four speed transmission

10. Drive reverse idler shaft out to rear. Remove gear, washers and roller bearings.
11. Remove clutch hub snapring and second/third synchronizer assembly.
12. Remove second and reverse gears.
13. Remove clutch hub snapring and low synchronizer assembly.
14. Remove low gear.

SYNCHRONIZER

Disassembly and Assembly

1. Remove springs. low synchronizer has only one spring, second/third, two.
2. Mark sleeve and hub before separating.
3. Remove hub.
4. Remove three shifter plates from hub.
5. Inspect all parts for wear.
6. Assembly in reverse order of disassembly. On second/third unit, make sure that spring openings are 120 degrees from each other, with spring tension opposed.

NOTE: If a synchronized assembly is replaced on a floor shift unit, the shift fork operating the synchronizer being replaced must have the letter A just under the shaft hole on the side opposite the pin.

Inspection

1. Wash all parts in solvent.
2. Air dry but do not spin bearings with air pressure.
3. Check case bearing and shaft bores for cracks or burrs.
4. Check all gears and bronze blocking rings for cracks and chipped, worn, or cracked teeth. If any gears are replaced, also replace the meshing gears.
5. Check all bearings and bushings for wear or damage.
6. Check that synchronizer sleeves slide freely on clutch hubs.

TRANSMISSION UNIT

Assembly

1. Place reverse idler gear with dummy shaft, roller bearing, and thrust washers in case. Install reverse idler shaft.
2. Assemble countershaft center spacer, four bearing spacers, and bearing rollers in countershaft gear.
3. Install large countergear thrust washer in front of case. Position small thrust washer on countergear hub with lip facing groove in case. Holding countergear in position, push in countershaft from rear.
4. Install lock plate in slots of reverse idler shaft and countershaft.
5. Install the following components to the mainshaft. Low gear, bronze blocking ring, low synchronizer assembly, the largest snapring that fits in groove, second gear, the bronze blocking ring, second/third synchronizer assembly, the largest snapring that fits in groove and the reverse gear.
6. Install mainshaft assembly through top of case.
7. Install bronze blocking ring to second/third synchronizer assembly.
8. On remote shift units, install shifter shafts, with new O-rings, into case.

NOTE: T-15 interlock levers are marked as to location. T-14 levers have no marks and are interchangeable.

9. Depress interlock lever while installing shift fork into shift lever and synchronizer clutch sleeve. Install poppet spring. Install tapered pins securing shafts in case.
10. Install main drive gear roller bearings.
11. Install main drive gear and oil slinger into case with cutaway portion of gear toward countergear. Install main drive gear to mainshaft.
12. Using bearing installer and thrust yoke tool, install main drive gear and mainshaft bearings and drive into position. The thrust yoke is needed to prevent damage to the synchronizer clutch.
13. Install main drive gear and mainshaft bearing snaprings. The mainshaft bearing snapring is 0.010 in. thicker than main drive gear bearing snapring.
14. Install mainshaft rear bearing adapter, spacer, transfer case drive gear, flat washer and nut. Torque nut 130–170 ft. lbs.
15. Install main drive gear bearing retainer (with new oil seal) and gasket. Align oil drain holes in retainer and gasket.
16. Install case cover gasket. On remote shift units, install cover gasket with vent holes to left side.
17. Position gear train and floor shift assembly in neutral. Insert shifter forks into clutch sleeves and torque 8–15 ft. lbs.

Warner T-18, T-18A and T-19 Series Four Speed

The Warner T-18, T-18A and T-19 transmissions have four forward speeds and one reverse. A P.T.O. opening is provided on certain transmissions, depending upon the models and applications and can be located on either the right or left sides of the case. The T-18 and T-18A transmissions are synchronized in second, third and fourth speeds only, while the T-19 transmission is synchronized in all forward gears. The disassembly and assembly remains basically the same for the transmission models.

TRANSMISSION UNIT

Disassembly

1. After draining the transmission and removing the parking brake drum (or shoe assembly), lock the transmission in two gears and remove the U-joint flange, oil seal, speedometer driven gear and bearing assembly. Lubricant capacity is 6 ½ pints.
2. Remove the output shaft bearing retainer and the speedometer drive gear and spacer.
3. Remove the output shaft bearing snapring and remove the bearing.
4. Remove the countershaft and idler shaft retainer and the P.T.O. cover.
5. After removing the input shaft bearing retainer, remove the snaprings from the bearing and the shaft.
6. Remove the input shaft bearing and oil baffle.
7. Drive out the countershaft (from the front). Keep the dummy shaft in contact with the countershaft to avoid dropping any rollers.
8. After removing the input shaft and the synchronizer blocking ring, pull the idler shaft.
9. Remove the reverse gear shifter arm, the output shaft assembly, the idler gear and the cluster gear. When removing the cluster, do not lose any of the rollers.

SUBASSEMBLIES

Disassemby

OUTPUT SHAFT

1. Remove the third and high speed synchronizer hub snapring from the output shaft and slide the third and high speed synchronizer assembly and the third speed gear off the shaft. Remove the synchronizer sleeve and the inserts from the hub. Before removing the two snaprings from the ends of the hub, check the end play of the second speed gear (0.005–0.024 in.).
2. Remove the second speed synchronizer snapring. Slide the second speed synchronizer hub gear off the hub. Do not lose any of the balls, springs, or plates. Pull the hub off the shaft and remove the second speed synchronizer from the second speed gear. Remove the snapring from the rear of the second speed gear and remove the gear, spacer, roller bearings and thrust washer from the output shaft. Remove the remaining snapring from the shaft.

CLUSTER GEAR

Remove the dummy shaft, pilot bearing rollers, bearing spacers, and center spacer from the cluster gear.

REVERSE IDLER GEAR

Rotate the reverse idler gear on the shaft and if it turns freely and smoothly, disassembly of the unit is not necessary. If any roughness is noticed, disassemble the unit.

GEAR SHIFT HOUSING

1. Remove the housing cap and lever. Be sure all shafts are in neutral before disassembly.
2. Tap the shifter shafts out of the housing while holding one hand over the holes in the housing to prevent loss of the springs and balls. Remove the two shaft lock plungers from the housing.

SUBASSEMBLIES

Assembly

CLUSTER GEAR ASSEMBLY

Slide the long bearing spacer into the cluster gear bore and insert the dummy shaft in the spacer. Hold the cluster gear in a vertical position and install one of the bearing spacers. Position the 22 pilot bearing rollers in the cluster gear bore. Place a spacer on the rollers and install 22 more rollers and another spacer. Hold a large thrust washer against the end of cluster gear and turn the assembly over. Install the rollers and spacers in the other end of the gear.

REVERSE IDLER GEAR ASSEMBLY

1. Install a snapring in one end of the idler gear and set the gear on end, with the snapring at the bottom.
2. Position a thrust washer in the gear on top of the snapring. Install the bushing on top of the washer, insert the 37 bearing rollers and then a spacer followed by 37 more rollers. Place the remaining thrust washer on the rollers and install the other snapring.

OUTPUT SHAFT ASSEMBLY

1. Install the second speed gear thrust washer and snapring on the output shaft. Hold the shaft vertically and slide on the second speed gear. Insert the bearing rollers in the second speed gear and slide the spacer into the gear. (The T-18 model does not contain second speed gear rollers or spacer). Install the snapring

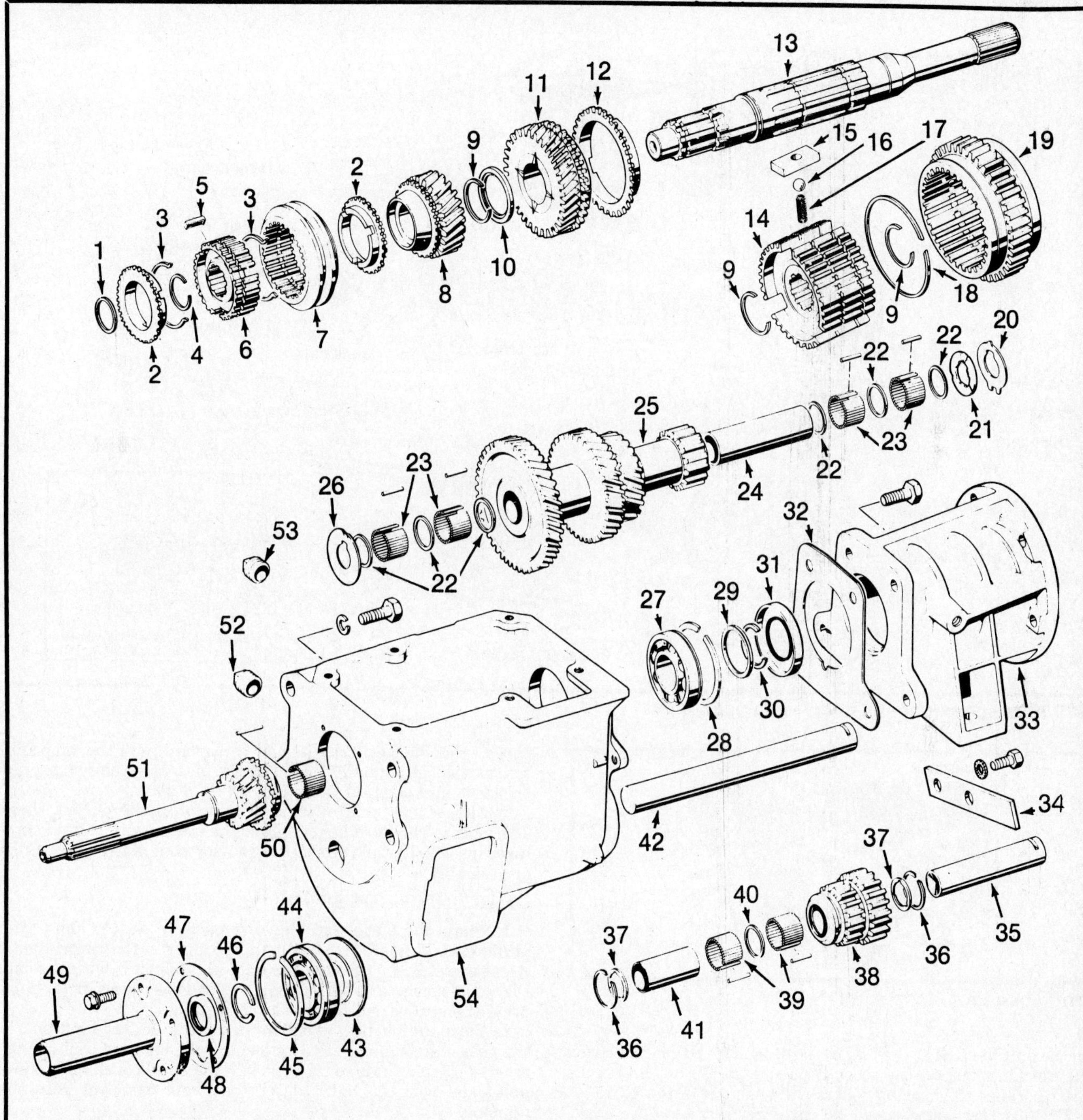

1. Mainshaft pilot bearing roller spacer
2. Third-fourth blocking ring
3. Third-fourth retaining ring
4. Third-fourth synchronizer snap-ring
5. Third-fourth shifting plate (3)
6. Third-fourth clutch hub
7. Third-fourth clutch sleeve
8. Third gear
9. Mainshaft snap-ring
10. Second gear thrust washer
11. Second gear
12. Second gear blocking ring
13. Mainshaft
14. First-second clutch hub
15. First-second shifting Plate (3)
16. Poppet ball
17. Poppet spring
18. First-second insert ring
19. First-second clutch sleeve
20. Countershaft gear thrust washer (steel) (rear)
21. Countershaft gear thrust washer (steel backed bronze) (rear)
22. Countershaft gear bearing washer
23. Countershaft gear bearing rollers (88)
24. Countershaft gear bearing spacer
25. Countershaft gear
26. Countershaft gear thrust washer (front)
27. Rear bearing
28. Rear bearing locating snap-ring
29. Rear bearing spacer ring
30. Rear bearing snap-ring
31. Adapter plate seal
32. Adapter plate to transmission gasket
33. Adapter to transmission
34. Countershaft-reverse idler shaft lockplate
35. Reverse idler gear shaft
36. Reverse idler gear snap-ring
37. Reverse idler gear thrust washer
38. Reverse idler gear
39. Reverse idler gear bearing rollers (74)
40. Reverse idler gear bearing washer
41. Reverse idler shaft sleeve
42. Countershaft
43. Front bearing retainer washer
44. Front bearing
45. Front bearing locating snap-ring
46. Front bearing lock ring
47. Front bearing cap gasket
48. Front bearing cup seal
49. Front bearing cap
50. Mainshaft pilot bearing rollers (22)
51. Clutch shaft
52. Drain plug
53. Filler plug
54. Transmission case

T-18A transmission—exploded view

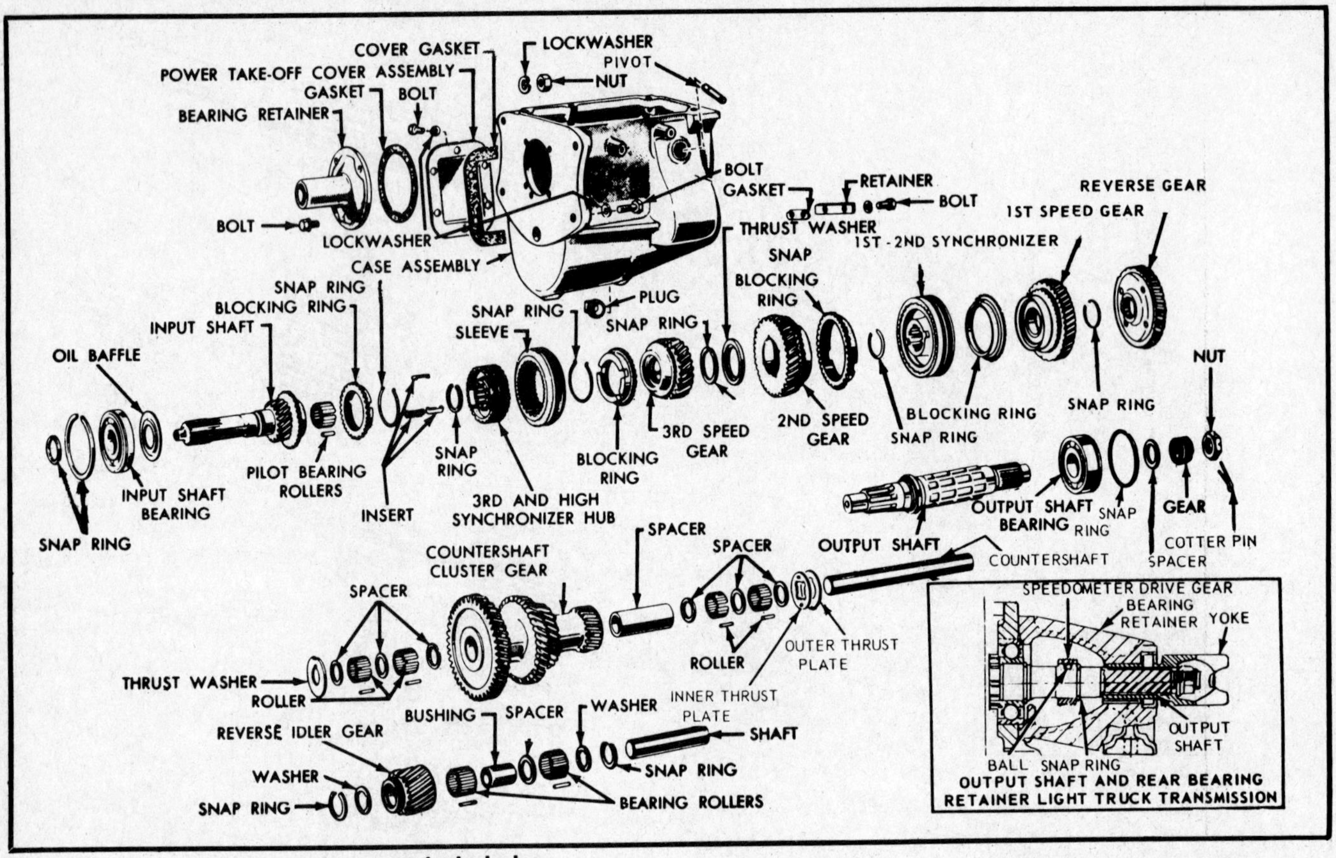

T-19 four speed transmission—exploded view

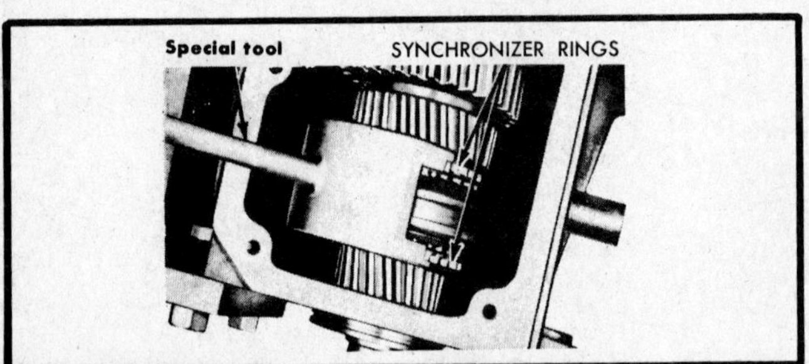

Stop yoke tool

on the output shaft at the rear of the second speed gear. Position the blocking ring on the second speed gear. Do not invert the shaft because the bearing rollers will slide out of the gear.

2. Press the second speed synchronizer hub onto the shaft, and install the snapring. Position the shaft vertically in a soft jawed vise. Position the springs and plates in the second speed synchronizer hub and place the hub gear on the hub.

3. With the T-19 model, press the first and second speed synchronizer onto the shaft and install the snapring. Install the first speed gear and snapring on the shaft and press on the reverse gear. For the T-19, ignore Steps 2 and 4.

4. Hold the gear above the hub spring and ball holes and position one ball at a time in the hub and slide the hub gear downward to hold the ball in place. Push the plate upward and insert a small block to hold the plate in position, thereby holding the ball in the hub. Follow these procedures for the remaining balls.

5. Install the third speed gear and synchronizer blocking ring on the shaft.

6. Install the snaprings at both ends of the third and high speed synchronizer hub. Stagger the openings of the snaprings so that they are not aligned. Place the inserts in the synchronizer sleeve and position the sleeve on the hub.

7. Slide the synchronizer assembly onto the output shaft. The slots in the blocking ring must be in line with the synchronizer inserts. Install the snapring at the front of the synchronizer assembly.

GEAR SHIFT HOUSING

1. Place the spring on the reverse gear shifter shaft gate plunger and install the spring and plunger in the reverse gate. Press the plunger through the gate and fasten it with the clip. Place the spring and ball in the reverse gate poppet hole. Compress the spring and install the cotter pin.

2. Place the spring and ball in the reverse shifter shaft hole in the gear shift housing. Press down on the ball and position the reverse shifter shaft so that the reverse shifter arm notch does not slide over the ball. Insert the shaft part way into the housing.

3. Slide the reverse gate onto the shaft and drive the shaft into the housing until the ball snaps into the groove of the shaft. Install the lock screw lock wire to the gate.

4. Insert the two interlocking plungers in the pockets between the shifter shaft holes. Place the spring and ball in the low and second shifter shaft hole. Press down on the ball and insert the shifter shaft part way into the housing.

5. Slide the low and second shifter shaft gate onto the shaft, and install the corresponding shifter fork on the shaft so that the offset of the fork is toward the rear of the housing. Push the shaft all the way into the housing until the ball engages the shaft groove. Install the lock screw and wire that fastens the fork to the shaft. Install the third and high shifter shaft in the same manner. Check the interlocking system. Install new expansion plugs in the shaft bores.

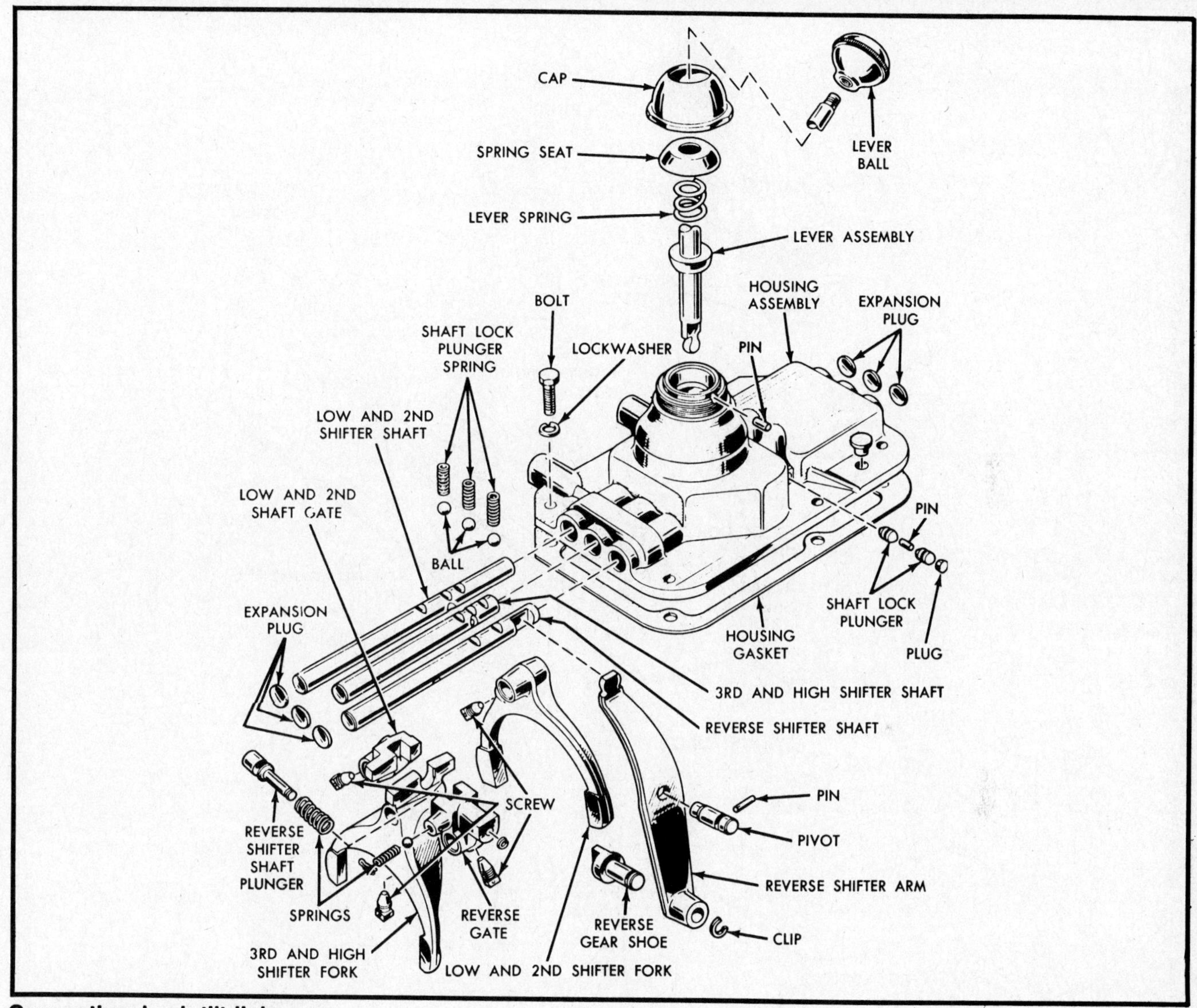

Conventional cab tilt linkage

TRANSMISSION UNIT

Assembly

1. Coat all parts, especially the bearings, with transmission lubricant to prevent scoring during initial operation.
2. Position the cluster gear assembly in the case. Do not lose any rollers.
3. Place the idler gear assembly in the case and install the idler shaft. Position the slot in the rear of the shaft so that it can engage the retainer. Install the reverse shifter arm.
4. Drive out the cluster gear dummy shaft by installing the countershaft from the rear. Position the slot in the rear of the shaft so that it can engage the retainer. Use thrust washers as required to get 0.006–0.020 in. cluster gear end play. Install the countershaft and idler shaft retainer.
5. Position the input shaft pilot rollers and the oil baffle, so that the baffle will not rub the bearing race. Install the input shaft and the blocking ring in the case.
6. Install the output shaft assembly in the case and use a special tool to prevent jamming the blocking ring when the input shaft bearing is installed.
7. Drive the input shaft bearing onto the shaft. Install the thickest select-fit snapring that will fit on the bearing. Install the input shaft snapring.
8. Install the output shaft bearing.
9. Install the input shaft bearing without a gasket and tighten the bolts only enough to bottom the retainer on the bearing snapring. Measure the clearance between the retainer and the case and select a gasket (or gaskets) that will seal in the oil and prevent end play between the retainer and the snapring. Torque the bolts to specification.
10. Position the speedometer drive gear and spacer and install a new output shaft bearing retainer seal.
11. Install the output shaft bearing retainer. Torque the bolts to specification and install safety wire.
12. Install the brake shoe (or drum) and torque the bolts to specification. Install the U-joint flange. Lock the transmission in two gears and torque the nut to specification.
13. Install the P.T.O. cover plates with new gaskets. Fill the transmission according to specifications.

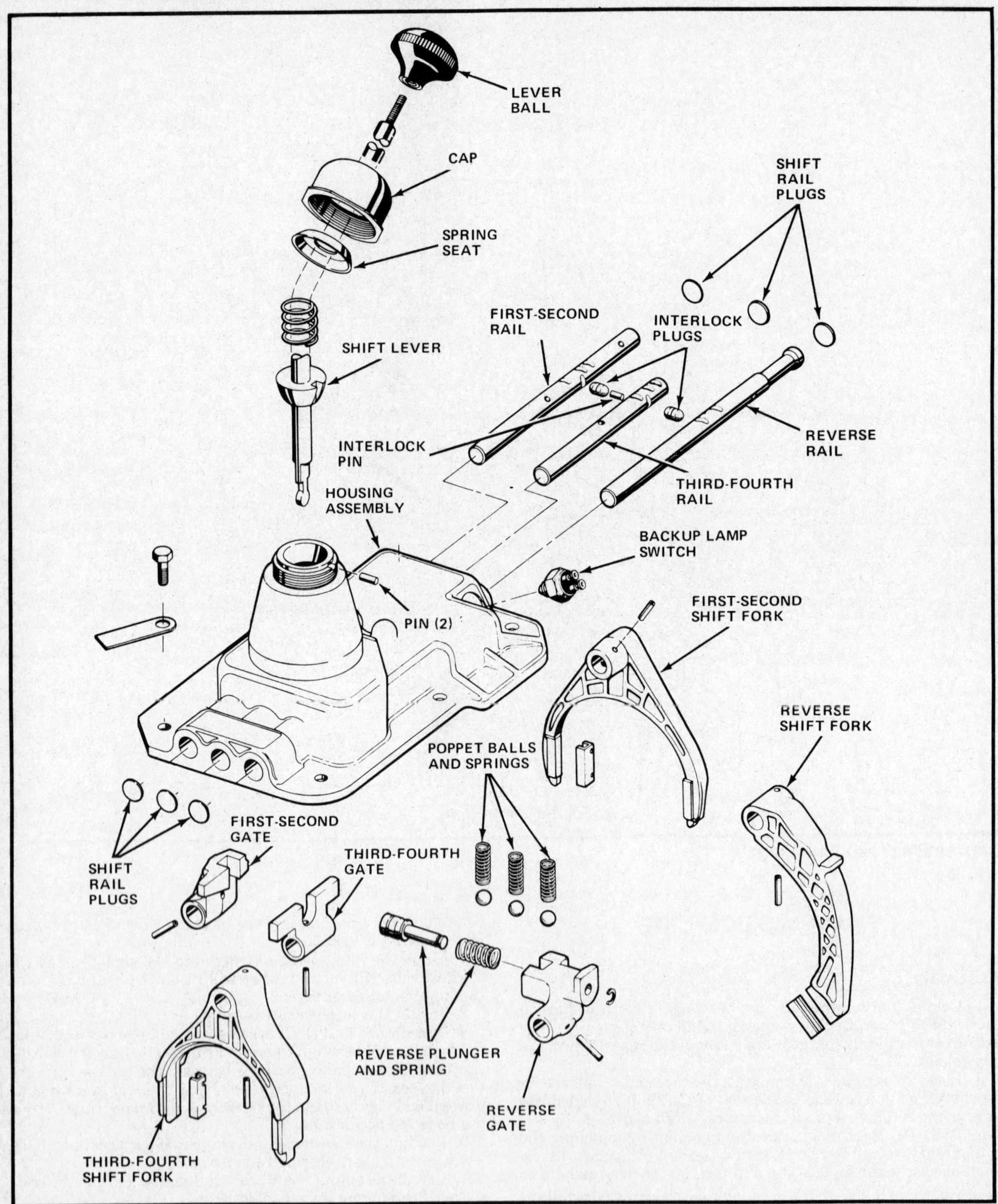

T-18a shift control housing—exploded view

TORQUE SPECIFICATIONS

Nomenclature		Nuts and/or Bolts and Torque Limits	
Bolt—gear shift lever tower to gearshift housing		3/8–16 20–25	7/16–14 30–35
Bolt—clutch housing to trans. case		7/16–14 30–38 5/8–11 96–120	9/16–12 70–90
Nut—U-joint flange to trans. output shaft	1.00–20 90–125	1½–18 275–350	1¼–18 225–275
Nut—drum parking brake to companion flange		3/8–24 35–45	7/16–20 50–70
Nut—bellcrank to trans.		9/16–18 70–90	
Bolt—lever assy. to trans.		3/8–16 20–25	
Nut—handbrake anchor bar to trans. case (5-speed extra-heavy duty only)		9/16–18 120–130	
Bolt—bellcrank to trans.		3/8–16 20–25	
Bolt—reverse lockout plunger retainer		11/16–16 80–100	
Bolt—countershaft rear bearing retainer		5/16–18 25–30 3/8–16 35–40	7/16–14 45–55 1/2–13 60–70
Bolt—countershaft & reverse idler shaft retainer		5/16–18 25–30 3/8–16 25–37 3/8–16 18–25	7/16–14 40–45 1/2–13 80–85
Bolt—gear shift housing to trans. case		5/16–18 20–25 3/8–16 35–40	3/8–16 30–35 7/16–14 45–50
Bolt—power take off cover to trans. case.		3/8–16 20–30	
Nut—countershaft bearing lock (5-speed extra h.d. & 5-speed exclusive)		1¼–18 350–450	
Nut—countershaft bearing lock (5-speed exclusive h.d.)		1½–18 350–450	
Bolt—input shaft bearing retainer to trans. case		5/16–18 25–30 3/8–16 25–30	7/16–14 40–45
Bolt—countershaft front bearing retainer		5/16–18 25–30 3/8–16 25–35	7/16–14 50–55

Warner T-15-D Three Speed Transmission

The Warner T-15-D transmission has three synchronized forward speeds and one reverse. The transmission has either a remote controlled shift lever on the steering column or a top cover shift lever assembly. This transmission can be used with or without a transfer case in the drive line with the use of different extension housing or bearing retainer designs.

MAINSHAFT

Removal

1. Drain the transmission of its lubricant and remove either the top cover or the shift lever assembly from the top of the transmission. Remove the front bearing retainer.
2. Remove the front main drive gear bearing snaprings and remove the bearing from the shaft and transmission case with the aid of a bearing puller or its equivalent.
3. Remove the main drive gear from the transmission case by having the cutaway portion of the gear teeth positioned downward towards the cluster gear. As the gear is removed from the mainshaft, do not lose the needle roller bearing from the bearing pocket.
4. Remove the rear extension housing or the bearing retainer from the rear of the transmission case.
5. Remove the mainshaft rear bearing snaprings and remove the bearing from the mainshaft and transmission case with a bearing puller or its equivalent.
6. Column shift: Position the gears in second speed, move the mainshaft to the left and remove the shift forks.
7. Remove the mainshaft by tilting the front of the assembly upward and lifting it through the top of the case.

IDLER GEAR, CLUSTER GEAR AND SHAFTS

Removal

1. Tap the reverse idler gear shaft and the countershaft rearward to allow the removal of the lockplate from the slots in both shafts.
2. Using a brass drift, drive the reverse idler gear shaft towards the rear and out of the transmission case. Avoid losing the needle roller bearings from the gear bore.
3. Using a dummy countershaft or its equivalent, drive the countershaft from the rear of the transmission case. Lift the cluster gear assembly from the transmission case. Mark the thrust washer locations.

MAINSHAFT

Disassembly

1. Remove the second/third speed synchronizer snapring from the front of the mainshaft. Remove the synchronizer from the mainshaft, after matchmarking the sleeve and hub.
2. Remove the second speed gear from the mainshaft.
3. Remove the reverse gear from the rear of the mainshaft. Remove the rear synchronizer (first/reverse) hub snapring.
4. Remove the first/reverse synchronizer unit from the rear of the mainshaft. Only one blocker ring is used with the first/reverse synchronizer assembly as the reverse speed gear is not a synchromesh unit.
5. Remove the first speed gear from the mainshaft.

Cleaning and Inspection

1. Clean the transmission case with solvent and inspect for cracks, worn bearing bores or other damages.
2. Clean and inspect all gears and bronze blocking rings for cracks, chipped or cracked teeth or excessive wear on the teeth. Should a gear require replacement, the meshing gear should be replaced also.
3. Inspect all bearings and bushings for wear or damage. The thrust washers should be renewed upon transmission assembly, if grooved or distorted.
4. Inspect the synchronizer clutch sleeves for abnormal wear and ease of operation.
5. Lubricate all internal transmission components before installation.

MAINSHAFT

Assembly

1. The assembly of the mainshaft gears is in the reverse of the removal procedure. During the assembly, the snaprings are of the selective thickness type and should be selected to obtain the following end-play measurements.
2. Second/third speed synchronizer 0.004–0.020 in. measured between the snapring and the second speed synchronizer hub.
3. First/reverse synchronizer 0.005–0.020 in. measured between the first speed gear and the collar on the mainshaft.

IDLER GEAR AND COUNTERSHAFT

Installation

1. Using the dummy countershaft or its equivalent, install the needle roller bearings, spacers and thrust washers in the cluster gear bore. Use vaseline type lubricant to hold the needle, roller bearings in place.
2. Place the cluster gear assembly into the transmission case and install the countershaft from the rear to the front of the case, through the cluster gear, forcing the dummy shaft out the front shaft bore of the case.
3. During the installation of the countershaft, be sure to maintain alignment of the spacers and thrust washers.
4. Install the needle roller bearings into the bore of the reverse idler gear and hold in place with a vaseline type lubricant.
5. Position the thrust washers on the gear and place the assembly between the transmission case web and the rear inner surface of the case.
6. Carefully drive the reverse idler gear shaft through the case bore and into the reverse idler gear assembly. Be sure to keep the thrust washers aligned to avoid damage to them.
7. With both the countershaft and the reverse idler gear shaft in Place, install the lock plate with the tabs on the top side, into the slots of each shaft. Drive the shafts forward until the lock plate is flush against the case surface.

MAINSHAFT

Installation

1. Tilt the mainshaft assembly and install the rear of the shaft assembly into the case. Lower the mainshaft assembly into the case. If the transmission is controlled by a steering column shift lever, move the mainshaft and install the shifting forks into place on the clutch sleeves and shift mechanism.
2. Using a mainshaft support or equivalent, block and support the front of the mainshaft. Install the rear mainshaft bearing with a bearing installer tool or equivalent.
3. Install the large and small snaprings on the rear bearing and mainshaft. Remove the front shaft support.

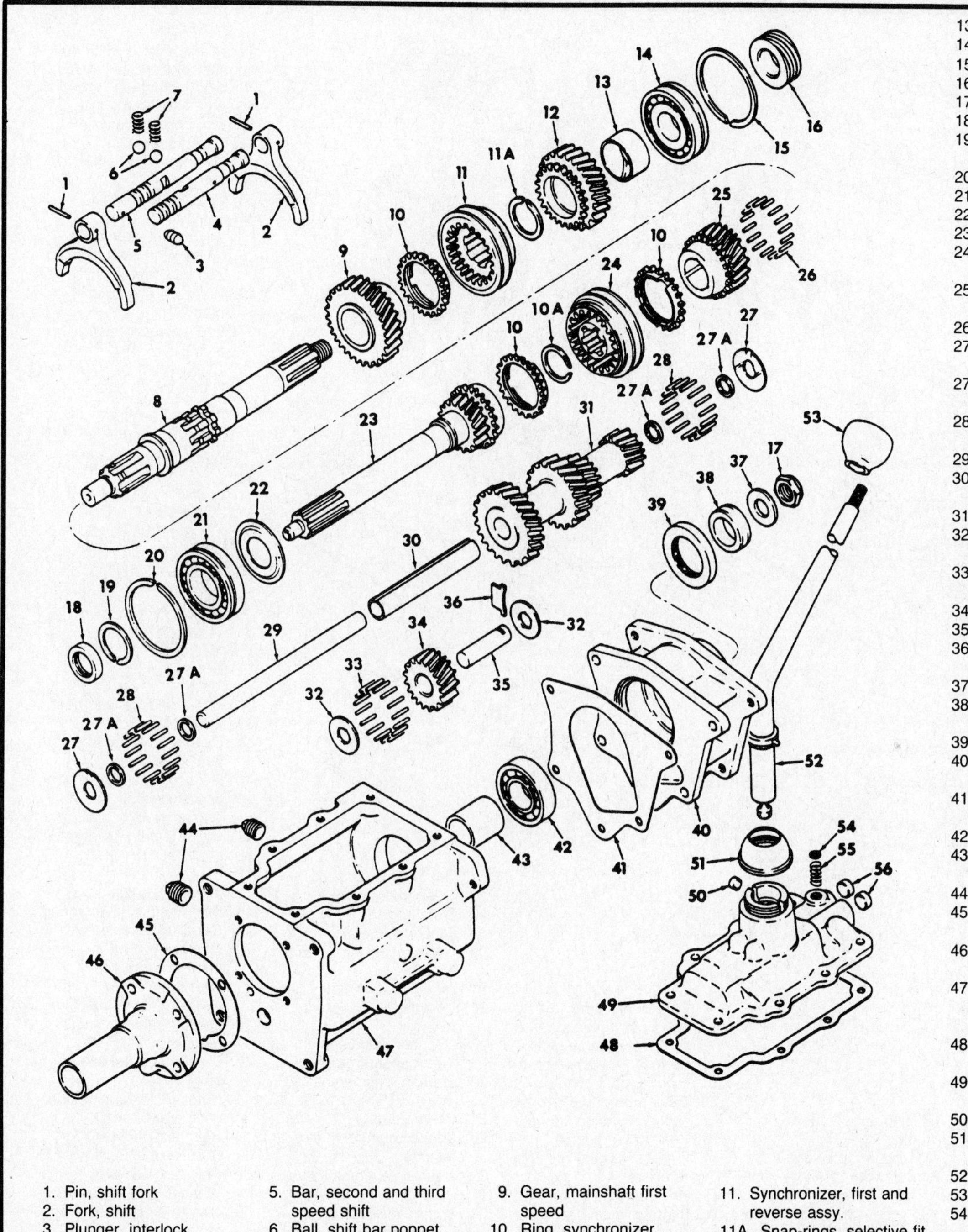

1. Pin, shift fork
2. Fork, shift
3. Plunger, interlock
4. Bar, first and reverse speed shift
5. Bar, second and third speed shift
6. Ball, shift bar poppet
7. Spring, shift bar poppet
8. Mainshaft
9. Gear, mainshaft first speed
10. Ring, synchronizer blocking
10A. Snap-ring, selective fit
11. Synchronizer, first and reverse assy.
11A. Snap-rings, selective fit
12. Gear, w/bushing, mainshaft reverse
13. Bushing, reverse gear
14. Bearing, mainshaft rear
15. Ring, snap bearing
16. Gear, speedometer drive
17. Nut, companion flange
18. Seal, drive gear oil
19. Ring, drive gear bearing snap selective fit
20. Ring, bearing snap
21. Bearing, main drive gear
22. Baffle, drive gear oil
23. Gear, main drive
24. Synchronizer, second and third, assy.
25. Gear, mainshaft second speed
26. Bearing, mainshaft roller
27. Washer, countershaft thrust
27A. Spacer, countershaft gear bearing
28. Bearing, countershaft roller
29. Countershaft
30. Spacer, countershaft gear bearing
31. Gear, countershaft cluster
32. Washer, reverse idler gear
33. Bearing, reverse idler gear roller
34. Gear, reverse idler
35. Shaft, reverse idler gear
36. Lock, reverse idler gear shaft
37. Washer, mainshaft nut
38. Spacer, mainshaft bearing
39. Seal, mainshaft oil
40. Retainer, w/bushing and seal, rear brg.
41. Gasket, rear bearing retainer
42. Bearing, mainshaft rear
43. Spacer, mainshaft bearing
44. Plug, sq-hd ¾ (filler)
45. Gasket, main drive gear brg. retainer
46. Retainer, w/bushing, main drive gear
47. Case, w/studs, transmission nut, hex washer, lock
48. Gasket, control housing to trans. case
49. Housing, control lever bolt, hex-hd washer, lock
50. Plug, taper
51. Cover, control housing dust
52. Lever, control Assy.
53. Handle, control lever
54. Washer, control lever spring
55. Spring, control lever
56. Plug, special cup

T-15A transmission with top mounted shifter lever exploded view

4. Install the main drive gear with the oil baffle, into the case. Position the cutaway portion of the gear downward towards the countershaft/cluster gear assembly, to aid in the installation of the drive gear. Use caution to avoid dropping the needle roller bearings as the mainshaft front stub enters the main drive gear bearing pocket.

5. Install the main drive gear bearing and the retaining snaprings. Be sure the oil baffle is in place.

6. Install the front bearing retainer with a new gasket.

7. Install the rear bearing retainer or extension housing, using a new gasket. Install the oil seal as required.

8. Floor Shift: Place the gears in a neutral position and the shift lever housing components in neutral. Place the shifting levers in their respective sliding sleeve grooves and bolt the cover to the transmission case. Column Shift: Install the top cover with a new gasket and bolt into place on the transmission.

9. Fill the transmission with lubricant to its proper level (3 pints) and move the gear shifting mechanism by hand to be assured of proper gear selection before installation of the transmission into the vehicle.

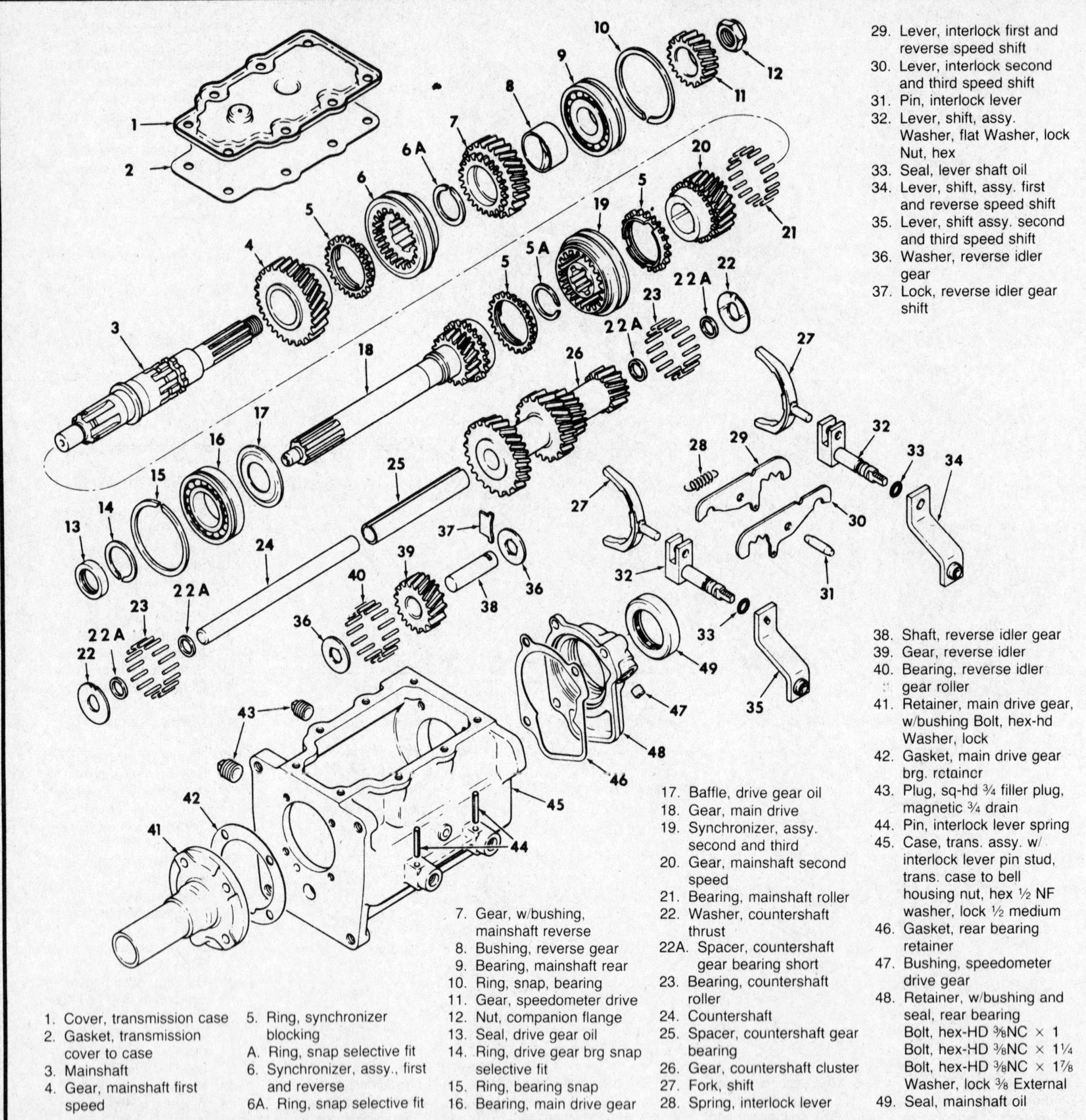
1. Cover, transmission case
2. Gasket, transmission cover to case
3. Mainshaft
4. Gear, mainshaft first speed
5. Ring, synchronizer blocking
A. Ring, snap selective fit
6. Synchronizer, assy., first and reverse
6A. Ring, snap selective fit
7. Gear, w/bushing, mainshaft reverse
8. Bushing, reverse gear
9. Bearing, mainshaft rear
10. Ring, snap, bearing
11. Gear, speedometer drive
12. Nut, companion flange
13. Seal, drive gear oil
14. Ring, drive gear brg snap selective fit
15. Ring, bearing snap
16. Bearing, main drive gear
17. Baffle, drive gear oil
18. Gear, main drive
19. Synchronizer, assy. second and third
20. Gear, mainshaft second speed
21. Bearing, mainshaft roller
22. Washer, countershaft thrust
22A. Spacer, countershaft gear bearing short
23. Bearing, countershaft roller
24. Countershaft
25. Spacer, countershaft gear bearing
26. Gear, countershaft cluster
27. Fork, shift
28. Spring, interlock lever
29. Lever, interlock first and reverse speed shift
30. Lever, interlock second and third speed shift
31. Pin, interlock lever
32. Lever, shift, assy. Washer, flat Washer, lock Nut, hex
33. Seal, lever shaft oil
34. Lever, shift, assy. first and reverse speed shift
35. Lever, shift assy. second and third speed shift
36. Washer, reverse idler gear
37. Lock, reverse idler gear shift
38. Shaft, reverse idler gear
39. Gear, reverse idler
40. Bearing, reverse idler gear roller
41. Retainer, main drive gear, w/bushing Bolt, hex-hd Washer, lock
42. Gasket, main drive gear brg. retainer
43. Plug, sq-hd 3/4 filler plug, magnetic 3/4 drain
44. Pin, interlock lever spring
45. Case, trans. assy. w/ interlock lever pin stud, trans. case to bell housing nut, hex 1/2 NF washer, lock 1/2 medium
46. Gasket, rear bearing retainer
47. Bushing, speedometer drive gear
48. Retainer, w/bushing and seal, rear bearing Bolt, hex-HD 3/8NC × 1 Bolt, hex-HD 3/8NC × 1 1/4 Bolt, hex-HD 3/8NC × 1 7/8 Washer, lock 3/8 External
49. Seal, mainshaft oil

T-15A transmission with remote shifter lever—exploded view

Warner SR-4 Four Speed Transmission

The Warner SR-4 transmission is a four speed, constant mesh unit, providing synchromesh engagement in all forward gears.

TRANSMISSION UNIT

Disassembly

1. Separate the transmission from the transfer case, if attached.
2. Drain the lubricant from the transmission by removing the lower adapter housing bolt.
3. If the shift lever housing has not been removed, place the shift lever in the neutral position, remove the retaining bolts and lift the shift lever housing from the transmission.
4. Remove the flanged nut holding the offset lever to the shift rail. Remove the offset lever.
5. Remove the adapter housing retaining bolts and the housing from the transmission case.
6. Remove the shift control housing retaining bolts and remove the cover and gasket. Mark the location of the two dowel bolts to reinstall in their original position.
7. Remove the spring clip holding the reverse lever to the reverse lever pivot bolt. Remove the reverse lever pivot bolt, allowing the removal of the reverse lever and reverse lever fork as an assembly.
8. Match mark the front bearing retainer to the transmission case and remove the bearing retainer and gasket.
9. Remove the large and small snaprings from the front and rear ball bearings on the input and output shafts.
10. With the aid of a bearing puller tool or equivalent, remove the input shaft ball bearing and remove the input shaft from the case.
11. Remove the rear (output shaft) bearing from the shaft with the aid of a bearing puller tool or equivalent.
12. Remove the output shaft assembly as a unit from the transmission case. Do not allow the synchronizer sleeves to separate from the hubs during the removal.
13. Push the reverse idler gear shaft rearward and remove the shaft and gear from the case.
14. Using a dummy countershaft, push the countershaft to the rear of the case. Remove the cluster gear assembly and dummy countershaft as a unit, from the transmission case.
15. Separate the dummy countershaft and remove the 50 needle roller bearings, spacers and thrust washers from the cluster gear. The cluster gear front thrust washer is of a plastic material, while the rear thrust washer is metal.

COUNTERSHAFT GEAR BEARING

Replacement

1. Remove the dummy shaft, bearing retainer washers and needle bearings from the countershaft gear. Clean and inspect the parts.
2. Coat the bore at each end of the countershaft gear with grease to retain the needle bearings.
3. While holding the dummy shaft in the gear, install the needle bearings and retainer washers in each end of the gear.
4. Slide first gear off the output shaft and remove the first speed blocker ring. Take care not to lose the sliding gear from the first and second speed synchronizer assembly.
5. Clean and inspect all parts.

Assembly

1. Place a blocker ring on the cone of first gear and slide the gear and ring assembly onto the output shaft. Make sure that the inserts in the synchronizer engage in the blocker ring notches.
2. Install the spring pin retaining first gear to the output shaft.
3. Install a blocker ring on the cone of second gear and slide the gear and ring assembly onto the output shaft. Make sure that the inserts in the synchronizer engage in the blocker ring notches.
4. Install the second gear thrust washer and new snapring on the shaft.
5. Install a blocker ring on the cone of third gear and slide the gear and ring assembly onto the output shaft. Install the third and fourth speed synchronizer. Make sure that the inserts in the synchronizer engage in the blocker ring notches.
6. Install a new third and fourth gear synchronizer snapring.
7. Place the first gear thrust washer (oil slinger) on the shaft and on the spring pin retaining first gear.
8. Assembly end play measurements are as follows. Second gear 0.004–0.014 in., measured between the second speed gear and the thrust washer. Third/fourth synchronizer hub 0.004–0.014 in., measured between the output shaft snapring and the third speed synchronizer hub.

COVER ASSEMBLY

Disassembly

1. Remove the detent screw, spring and plunger.
2. Pull the shifter shaft rod rearward, rotating it counterclockwise.
3. Remove the spring pin retaining the manual selector and interlock to the shifter shaft.
4. Remove the shifter shaft from the cover taking care not to damage the seal.
5. Remove the manual selector and interlock plate.
6. Remove the first and second speed shifter fork. Remove the third and fourth speed shifter fork.
7. Clean and inspect all parts. Replace the shifter shaft seal and welch plug, if damaged.

Assembly

1. Assemble the two plastic inserts to each shift fork; the two projections on the inside of the inserts fit into the blind holes in the ends of the shift forks. Insert the selector arm plates into the shift forks.
2. Install the third and fourth speed shifter fork into the cover.
3. Install the first and second speed shifter fork into the cover. Lubricate the shifter shaft bore with grease.
4. Install the manual selector arm through the interlock plate and position the two pieces into the cover, with the wide leg of the interlock plate towards the inside of the transmission case.
5. Align the shifter shaft in the cover and insert the shaft through the shifter forks and manual selector. Coat the shifter shaft with a light coating of grease. Make sure the detent grooves face the plunger side of the cover.
6. Align the pin holes in the manual selector arm and shifter shaft. Install the spring pin flush with the surface of the selector arm.
7. Install the detent plunger, spring and plug. Tighten the plug 8–12 ft. lbs.
8. Check the operation of the shift forks in each gear position.

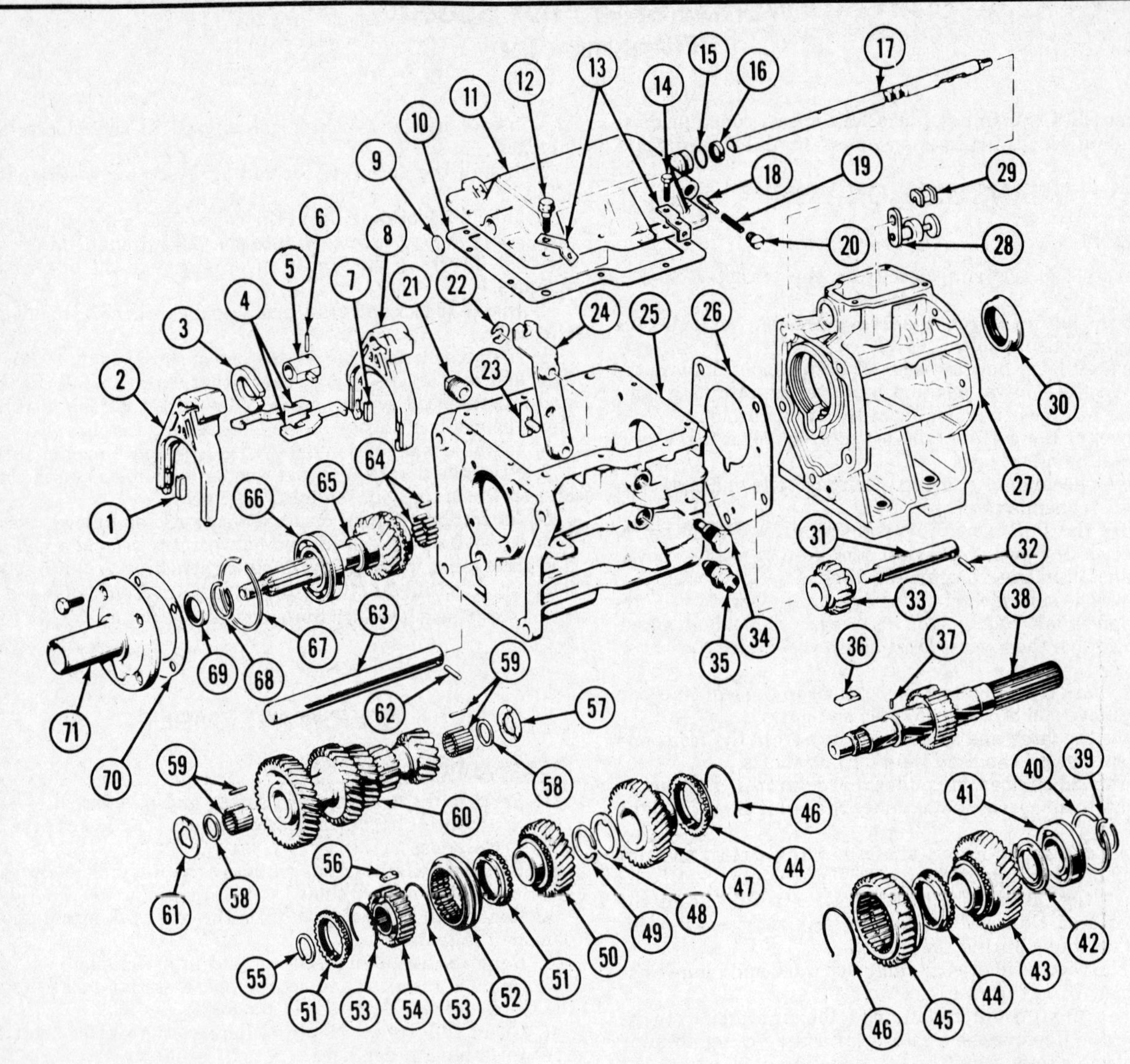

1. Third-fourth shift insert
2. Third-fourth shift fork
3. Selector interlock plate
4. Selector arm plate (2)
5. Selector arm
6. Selector arm roll pin
7. First-second shift fork insert
8. First-second shift fork
9. Shift rail plug
10. Transmission cover gasket
11. Transmission cover
12. Transmission cover dowel bolt (2)
13. Clip
14. Transmission cover bolt (8)
15. Shift rail O-ring seal
16. Shift rail oil seal
17. Shift rail
18. Detent plunger
19. Detent spring
20. Detent plug
21. Fill plug
22. Reverse lever pivot bolt C-clip
23. Reverse lever fork
24. Reverse lever
25. Transmission case
26. Gasket
27. Adapter housing
28. Offset lever
29. Offset lever insert
30. Extension housing oil seal
31. Reverse idler shaft
32. Reverse idler shaft roll pin
33. Reverse idler gear
34. Reverse lever pivot bolt
35. Backup lamp switch
36. First-second synchronizer insert (3)
37. First gear roll pin
38. Output shaft and hub assembly
39. Rear bearing retaining snap-ring
40. Rear bearing locating snap-ring
41. Rear bearing
42. First gear thrust washer
43. First gear
44. First-second synchronizer blocking ring (2)
45. First-reverse sleeve and gear
46. First-second synchronizer insert spring (2)
47. Second gear
48. Second gear thrust washer (tabbed)
49. Second gear snap-ring
50. Third gear
51. Third-fourth synchronizer blocking ring (2)
52. Third-fourth synchronizer sleeve
53. Third-fourth synchronizer insert spring (2)
54. Third-fourth synchronizer hub
55. Output shaft snap-ring
56. Third-fourth synchronizer insert (3)
57. Countershaft gear rear thrust washer (metal)
58. Countershaft needle bearing retainer (2)
59. Countershaft needle bearing (50)
60. Countershaft gear
61. Countershaft gear front thrust washer (plastic)
62. Countershaft roll pin
63. Countershaft
64. Clutch shaft roller bearings (15)
65. Clutch shaft
66. Front bearing
67. Front bearing locating snap-ring
68. Front bearing retaining snap-ring
69. Front bearing cap oil seal
70. Front bearing cap gasket
71. Front bearing cap

SR-4 four speed transmission—exploded view

OUTPUT SHAFT

Disassembly

1. Scribe alignment marks on the synchronizer and blocker rings. Remove the snapring from the front of the output shaft. Slide the third and fourth speed synchronizer assembly, blocker rings and third gear off the shaft.

2. Remove the next snapring and the second gear thrust washer from the shaft. Slide second gear and the blocker ring off the shaft, taking care not to lose the sliding gear from the first and second speed synchronizer assembly. The first and second speed synchronizer hub cannot be removed from the output shaft.

3. Remove the first gear thrust washer (oil slinger) from the rear of the output shaft. Remove the spring pin retaining first gear onto the shaft.

SYNCHRONIZER

Disassembly and Assembly

1. Scribe reference marks on the hub and sleeve of the synchronizer.

2. Push the sleeve from the hub of each synchronizer.

3. Separate the inserts and insert springs from the hubs. Do not mix the parts between the first/second speed synchronizer and the third/fourth speed synchronizer. Clean and inspect all parts.

NOTE: The first/second speed synchronizer hub is not to be removed from the shaft. They have been assembled and machined as a matched unit during manufacturing to assure concentricity.

4. To assemble, position the sleeve on the hub, aligning the previously marked reference points.

5. Position the three inserts per hub and install the insert springs, being sure that the bent end of the springs are seated in one of the inserts. The springs on each side of the hubs must face in opposite directions and the openings be 180 degrees apart.

TRANSMISSION UNIT

Assembly

1. Coat the countershaft thrust washers with a vaseline type lubricant and position the plastic type washer at the front of the case and the metal washer at the rear of the case.

2. With the 50 needle roller bearings in place in the cluster gear and the dummy countershaft in place, install the countershaft/cluster gear assembly into the case. Be sure the thrust washers are not displaced during the gear installation.

3. Align the cluster gear bore with the case bores and install the countershaft from the rear to the front of the case, pushing the dummy countershaft from the gear and case.

4. Position the reverse idler gear with the shift lever groove facing to the front and install the shaft from the rear of the case.

5. Being careful not to disturb the synchronizers, install the output shaft assembly into the transmission case. Install the fourth gear blocking ring in the third speed synchronizer sleeve, engaging the inserts on the hub with the grooves of the blocking ring.

6. Install the 15 roller bearings in the input shaft pocket and retain with a vaseline type lubricant. Install the input shaft into the case and engage the shaft in the third/fourth synchronizer, while the stub of the output shaft is installed in the pocket of the input shaft. Do not jam or drop the 15 roller bearings during the input shaft installation.

7. Install the input shaft front bearing. Block the first speed gear against the rear of the case, align the bearing with the bearing bore in the case and drive the bearing completely onto the input shaft and into the transmission case. To identify the front and rear bearings, look for a notch in the front bearing race. The rear bearing has no notch.

8. Install the front bearing retaining and locating snaprings.

9. Install the front bearing cap oil seal and install the cap (bearing retainer) with a new gasket to the transmission case. Install the retaining bolts.

10. Install the first speed thrust washer on the output shaft with the oil grooves facing the first speed gear. Install the rear bearing onto the output shaft and into the case bearing bore. Be sure the first gear thrust washer is engaged on the first gear roll pin before installing the rear bearing.

11. Install the retaining and locating snaprings on the rear bearing and output shaft.

12. Position the reverse lever in the case, on the pivot bolt and install the retaining clip. Tighten the pivot bolt. Be sure the reverse lever fork is engaged in the reverse idler gear.

13. Rotate the input shaft and output shaft gears and blocking rings to insure freeness of movement. Blocking ring to gear clutch tooth face should have a clearance of 0.030 in..

14. Place the reverse lever in the neutral position and install the cover assembly on the transmission case. Place the two dowel bolts in their original positions and install the remaining retaining bolts.

15. Install a new oil seal in the adapter housing and, using a new gasket, install the adapter housing to the transmission case.

16. Install 3 pints of lubricant into the transmission.

17. Install the offset lever and retain with the flanged nut.

18. Depending upon the installation of the transmission into a vehicle, the shift lever housing can be installed and the transmission attached to the transfer case.

TORQUE SPECIFICATIONS①

	ft. lbs.	N.m.
Backup lamp switch	10	14
Adapter housing bolt	23	31
Detent plug (in housing)	10	14
Fill plug	20	27
Front bearing cap bolt	13	18
Offset lever nut	10	14
Reverse lever pivot bolt	20	27
Shift control housing bolt	10	14
Transmission-to-clutch housing bolt	55	75
Universal joint clamp strap bolt	14	19

①All torque values given in foot-pounds and newton-meters with dry fits unless otherwise specified.

Warner T-176 Four Speed Transmission

The Warner T-176 transmission is a constant mesh unit, synchronized in all forward gears and with one reverse gear.

TRANSMISSION UNIT

Disassembly

1. Remove the transfer case from the rear of the transmission.
2. Remove the shift control housing. Mark the location of the two dowel bolts in the housing.
3. Drain the lubricant from the transmission, if not previously done. Remove the rear adapter housing.
4. With a dummy countershaft tool, remove the countershaft from the transmission, front to rear. Allow the cluster gear to lay on the bottom of the case.
5. Remove the rear bearing locating and retaining snaprings. Remove the rear bearing with a bearing remover tool or equivalent.
6. Match mark the front bearing retainer to the case for easier installation, remove the retaining bolts and the retainer.
7. Remove the locating and retaining snaprings from the front bearing. Remove the front bearing and the input shaft using a puller tool or equivalent.
8. Remove the mainshaft pilot bearing rollers from the input shaft pocket. Engage the third speed synchronizer.
9. Remove the mainshaft assembly by lifting the front of the shaft upward and out.
10. Remove the cluster gear assembly from the case. Locate and remove any thrust washers and needle roller bearings from the case.
11. Tap the reverse idler gear shaft from the case and remove the reverse idler gear and thrust washers.
12. Separate the reverse idler gear from the sliding gear. Do not lose the needle roller bearings.

MAINSHAFT

Disassembly

1. Remove the third/fourth speed synchronizer snapring from the front of the mainshaft.
2. Remove the third/fourth synchronizer from the mainshaft and slide the hub from the sleeve. Remove the inserts and springs. Inspect the blocking rings for wear and damage.
3. Remove the third speed gear and the second speed gear snapring. Remove the second speed gear and the blocking ring. Remove the tabbed thrust washer.
4. Remove the snapring from the first/second synchronizer hub. Remove the hub and the reverse gear with sleeve as an assembly. Match mark the hub and sleeve for assembly references. Remove the inserts and springs as the sleeve is removed.
5. Remove the first speed gear thrust washer from the rear of the shaft and remove the first speed gear and the blocking ring.

Inspection of Transmission Components

CASE

1. Cracks in the bores, sides, bosses or at bolt holes.
2. Stripped bolt hole threads.
3. Nicks, burrs, roughness on gasket or shaft bore surfaces.

GEARS, SHAFTS AND SYNCHRONIZER UNITS

1. Chipped, broken or worn gear teeth.
2. Damaged splines.
3. Worn or broken teeth or blocking rings.
4. Bent or broken synchronizer inserts or springs.
5. Damaged needle bearings or operating surfaces.
6. Wear or galling of the mainshaft, countershaft, clutch shaft or idler gear shaft.
7. Worn or broken thrust washers.
8. Bent, distorted, broken or weak snaprings.
9. Rough, galled, worn or broken front or rear bearing.

MAINSHAFT

Assembly

1. Assemble the first/second synchronizer hub, inserts and springs. Install the clutch sleeve. Be sure to position the spring ends 180 degrees apart.
2. Install the assembled first/second speed synchronizer hub and the reverse gear with sleeve, on the mainshaft. Secure with a new snapring.
3. Install the first speed gear and blocking ring on the rear of the mainshaft and install the first gear thrust washer.
4. Install a new tabbed thrust washer on the mainshaft with the tab seated in the mainshaft tab bore.
5. Install the second speed gear and the blocking ring on the mainshaft and secure with a new snapring.
6. Install the third speed gear and blocking ring on the mainshaft.
7. Assemble the third/fourth speed synchronizer hub, inserts and springs. Be sure the spring ends are 180 degrees apart.
8. Install the assembled third/fourth speed synchronizer on the mainshaft and secure with a new snapring.
9. The measured end play between the snapring and the third/fourth speed synchronizer should be 0.004–0.014 in..

TRANSMISSION UNIT

Assembly

1. Load the reverse idler gear with the 44 needle roller bearings and a bearing retainer on each end of the gear. Install the sliding gear on the reverse idler gear. Install lubricated thrust washers into the case.
2. Install the reverse idler assembly into the case and install the reverse idler gear shaft.
3. Be sure to engage the thrust washer locating tabs in the case locating slots.
4. Seat the reverse idler gear shaft roll pin into the counterbore in the case. The reverse idler gear end play should be 0.004–0.018 in..
5. Install the 42 needle roller bearings in the cluster gear, using the dummy countershaft as a bearing holder. Use of a vaseline type lubricant is suggested to hold the bearings in place.
6. Position the lubricated thrust washers in place on the inside of the transmission case. Position the thrust washer tabs in the tab slots of the case.
7. Insert the countershaft into the rear case bore, just far

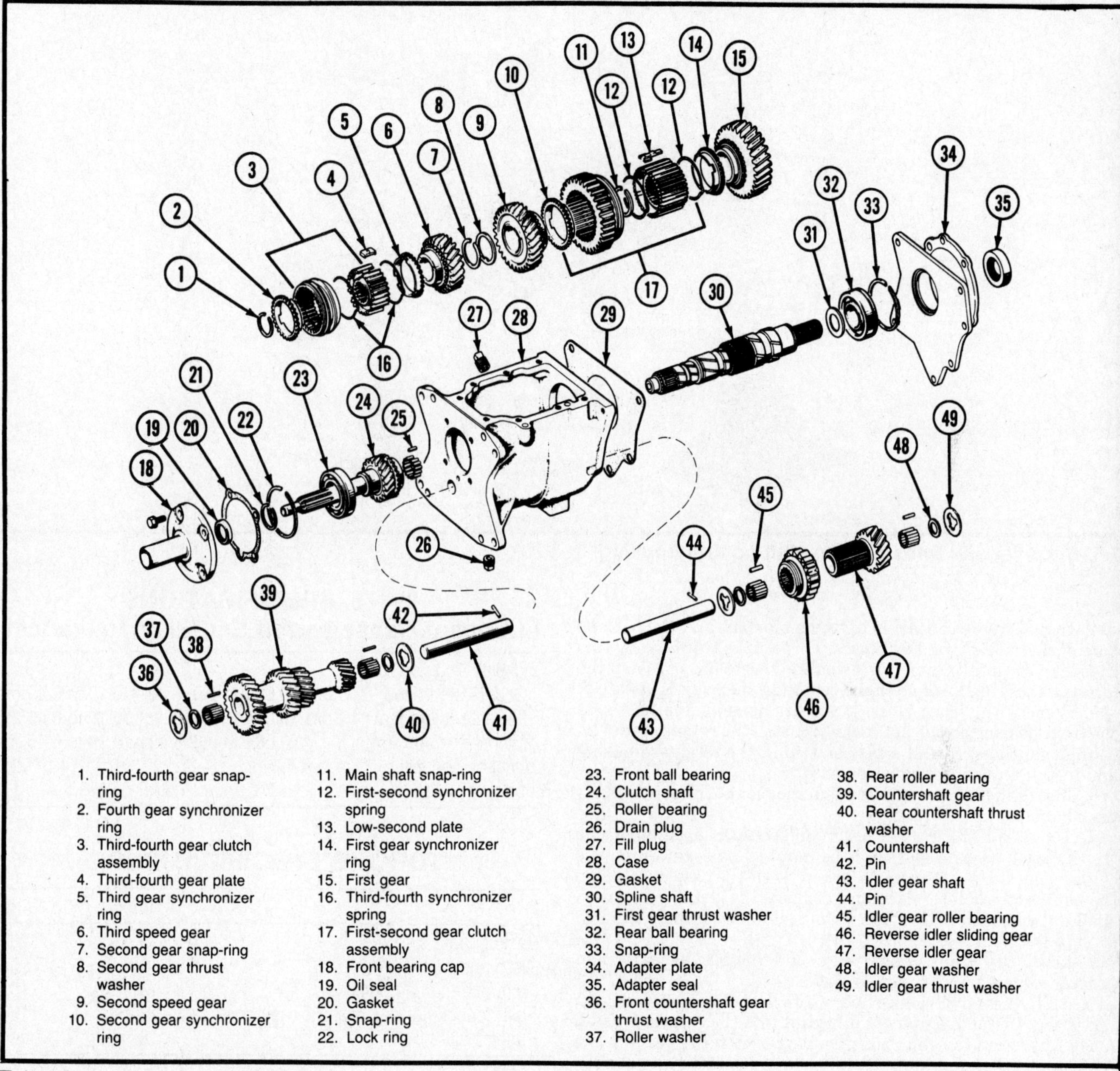

T-176 four speed transmission

enough to hold the rear thrust washer. Lower the cluster gear assembly into the case and align the gear bore with the case bore. Push the countershaft into the cluster gear, displacing the dummy countershaft out the front case bore hole. Do not completely remove the dummy countershaft.

8. Measure the cluster gear end play which should be 0.004–0.018 in.. Correct as required and reinstall the dummy countershaft into the cluster gear, pushing the countershaft from the gear.

9. Allow the cluster gear to remain at the bottom of the case until the input and mainshaft has been installed to provide the necessary assembly clearance.

10. With the synchronizers in the neutral position, install the mainshaft assembly into the case.

11. Install the front bearing part way on the input shaft and install the 15 roller bearing in the shaft pocket. Do not use a heavy grease to hold the bearings in the pocket as the grease can plug the lubrication holes. Use only a vaseline type lubricant.

12. Position the blocking ring on the third/fourth synchronizer. Support the mainshaft assembly and insert the input shaft through the front bearing bore of the case. Seat the mainshaft pilot hub into the bearing pocket of the input shaft and tap the front bearing and input shaft into the case, using a soft faced hammer.

13. When the bearing is fully seated, install the bearing retainer housing, but not the snaprings at this time.

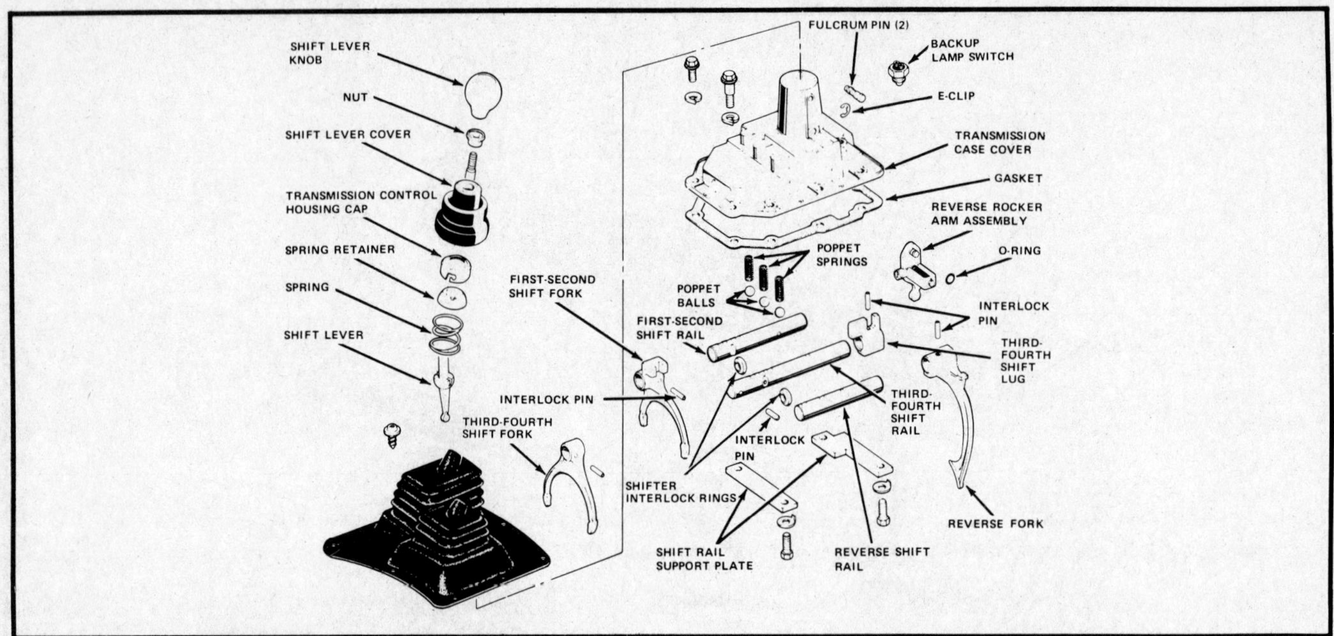

T-176 four speed transmission shift control housing

14. Install the rear bearing on the mainshaft and the bearing bore of the case. It will be necessary to seat the rear bearing further than the locating snapring would allow, so do not install the locating snapring until after the retaining snapring is installed.

15. Remove the front bearing retainer housing and fully seat the front bearing on the input shaft. Install the retaining and locating snaprings. Install a new oil seal in the retainer housing and install on the transmission case.

16. Install the locating snapring on the rear bearing, if not previously done.

17. To install the cluster gear and countershaft, turn the transmission case on end with the input shaft down. Align the cluster gear bore and thrust washers with the case bores. Tap the countershaft into place and displace the dummy countershaft out the front of the case. Do not allow the dummy shaft to drop to the floor.

18. Level the transmission case and install the extension adapter housing with a new gasket.

19. Shift the synchronizer sleeves by hand to insure correct operation. Install 3.5 pints of lubricant into the case and install a new gasket on the shift housing flange. With the gears in the neutral position and the shift lever forks in their neutral position, install the shift lever housing in place on the transmission case.

T-176 SPECIFICATIONS
Lubricant Capacity and End-Play Tolerances

End-Play Tolerances:	
Countershaft Gear to Case	0.004 to 0.018 inch (0.10 to 0.45 mm)
Reverse Idler Gear to Case	0.004 to 0.018 inch (0.10 to 0.45 mm)
Mainshaft Gear Train	0.004 to 0.018 inch (0.10 to 0.45 mm)
Lubricant Capacity	3.5 pints (1.7 liters)
Lubricant Type	SAE 85W-90, APJ GL5

TORQUE SPECIFICATIONS①

	ft. lbs.	N.m.
Backup lamp switch	15	20
Drain and fill plugs	15	20
Front bearing cap bolts	13	18
Shift housing-to-transmission case bolts	13	18
Support plate bolts	18	24

①All torque values given in foot-pounds and newton-meters with dry fits unless otherwise specified.

Mitsubishi 14

INDEX

BEFORE SERVICING, SEE THE SAFETY NOTICE AT THE FRONT OF THE BOOK

CHRYSLER/MITSUBISHI

ENGINE IDENTIFICATION CODES BY VIN NUMBER

Engine Cu. In. (liter)	Cylinders	1982	1983	1984	1985	1986	1987	1988
122 (2.0)	4	G63B	G63B	G63B	G63B	G63B	—	—
122 (2.0)	4	—	—	—	—	—	G63B	G63B
143 (2.3)	4	4D55	4D55	4D55	4D55	4D55	—	—
143 (2.4)	4	—	—	—	—	—	G64B	G64B
156 (2.6)	4	G54B	G54B	G54B	G54B	G54B	—	—
156 (2.6)	4	—	—	—	—	—	4G54	4G54

MODEL IDENTIFICATION
Chrysler/Mitsubishi Trucks and Vans

Year	Model Designation	Model Name
1982	Ram 50	Dodge Pickup
	Ram 50 Custom	Dodge Pickup
	Ram 50 Royal	Dodge Pickup
	Ram 50 Sport	Dodge Pickup
1983	Montero Utility	Mitsubishi 4 Wheel Drive
	Mighty Max	Mitsubishi Pickup
	Pickup S	Mitsubishi Pickup
	Pickup SP	Mitsubishi Pickup
	Pickup SPX	Mitsubishi Pickup
	Pickup SP 4WD TD	Mitsubishi 4 Wheel Drive Turbo Diesel Pickup
	Ram 50	Dodge Pickup
	Ram 50 Custom	Dodge Pickup
	Ram 50 Royal	Dodge Pickup
	Ram 50 Sport	Dodge Pickup
1984	Montero Utility	Mitsubishi 4 Wheel Drive
	Mighty Max	Mitsubishi Pickup
	Pickup SP	Mitsubishi Pickup
	Pickup SPX	Mitsubishi Pickup
	Ram 50 Custom	Dodge Pickup
	Ram 50 Royal	Dodge Pickup
	Ram 50 Sport	Dodge Pickup
1985	Montero Utility	Mitsubishi 4 Wheel Drive
	Mighty Max	Mitsubishi Pickup
	Pickup SP	Mitsubishi Pickup
	Pickup SPX	Mitsubishi Pickup
1985	Ram 50 Custom	Dodge Pickup
	Ram 50 Royal	Dodge Pickup
	Ram 50 Sport	Dodge Pickup
1986	Montero Utility	Mitsubishi 4 Wheel Drive
	Mighty Max	Mitsubishi Pickup
	Mighty Max Sport	Mitsubishi Pickup
	Pickup SPX	Mitsubishi Pickup
	Ram 50 Custom	Dodge Pickup
	Ram 50 Sport	Dodge Pickup
1987–88	Montero Utility	Mitsubishi 4 Wheel Drive
	Montero Utility Sport	Mitsubishi 4 Wheel Drive
	Mighty Max	Mitsubishi Pickup
	Mighty Max Sport	Mitsubishi Pickup
	Mighty Max 1 Ton Long Bed	Mitsubishi Pickup
	Mighty Max Sport Long Bed	Mitsubishi Pickup
	Mighty Max 4WD Long Bed	Mitsubishi Pickup
	Pickup SPX	Mitsubishi Pickup
	Raider①	Dodge 4 Wheel Drive
	Ram 50 Custom	Dodge Pickup
	Ram 50 Sport	Dodge Pickup
	Ram 50 Long Bed	Dodge Pickup
	Van	Mitsubishi Van

① Imported by Mitsubishi for Dodge

GENERAL ENGINE SPECIFICATIONS

Year	VIN	No. Cylinder Displacement cu. in. (liter)	Fuel System Type	Net Horsepower @ rpm	Net Torque @ rpm (ft.lbs.)	Bore × Stroke (in.)	Com- pression Ratio	Oil Pressure @ 2000 rpm
1982	G63B	4–122 (2.0)	2bbl	93 @ 5200①④	108 @ 3000①	3.31 × 3.54	8.5:1	50–64
	4D55	4–143 (2.3)	TD	84 @ 4200	136 @ 2500	3.59 × 3.54	21.0:1	56
	G54B	4–156 (2.6)	2bbl	105 @ 5000	139 @ 2500	3.59 × 3.86	8.2:1	50–64
1983	G63B	4–122 (2.0)	2bbl	93 @ 5200①④	108 @ 3000②	3.31 × 3.54	8.5:1	50–64
	4D55	4–143 (2.3)	TD	84 @ 4200	136 @ 2500	3.59 × 3.54	21.0:1	56
	G54B	4–156 (2.6)	2bbl	105 @ 5000	139 @ 2500	3.59 × 3.86	8.2:1	50–64
1984	G63B	4–122 (2.0)	2bbl	93 @ 5200①④	108 @ 3000②	3.31 × 3.54	8.5:1	50–64
	4D55	4–143 (2.3)	TD	84 @ 4200	136 @ 2500	3.59 × 3.54	21.0:1	56
	G54B	4–156 (2.6)	2bbl	105 @ 5000	139 @ 2500	3.59 × 3.86	8.2:1	50–64
1985	G63B	4–122 (2.0)	2bbl	93 @ 5200①④	108 @ 3000②	3.31 × 3.54	8.5:1	50–64
	4D55	4–143 (2.3)	TD	84 @ 4200	136 @ 2500	3.59 × 3.54	21.0:1	56
	G54B	4–156 (2.6)	2bbl	105 @ 5000	139 @ 2500	3.59 × 3.86	8.2:1	50–64
1986	G63B	4–122 (2.0)	2bbl	93 @ 5200①④	108 @ 3000②	3.31 × 3.54	8.5:1	50–64
	4D55	4–143 (2.3)	TD	84 @ 4200	136 @ 2500	3.59 × 3.54	21.0:1	56
	G54B	4–156 (2.6)	2bbl	105 @ 5000	139 @ 2500	3.59 × 3.86	8.2:1	50–64
1987–88	G63B	4–122 (2.0)	2bbl	88 @ 5000	108 @ 3500	3.31 × 3.54	8.5:1	63
	G64B	4–143 (2.4)	MPI③	110 @ 4500	138 @ 5000	3.41 × 3.94	8.5:1	63
	G54B	4–156 (2.6)	2bbl	145 @ 5000	185 @ 2500	3.57 × 3.86	7.0:1	63
	4G54	4–156 (2.6)	2bbl	145 @ 5000	185 @ 2500	3.57 × 3.86	7.0:1	63

① Canada: 96 @ 5500
② Canada: 109 @ 3500
③ Multi Point Injection
④ Canada: 150 @ 5000
⑤ 1982–86 California: 88 @ 5000
TD Turbo Diesel

GASOLINE ENGINE TUNE-UP SPECIFICATIONS

Year	VIN	No. Cylinder Displacement cu. in. (liter)	Spark Plugs Type	Spark Plugs Gap (in.)	Ignition Timing (deg.) MT	Ignition Timing (deg.) AT	Com- pression Pressure (psi)	Fuel Pump (psi)	Idle Speed (rpm) MT	Idle Speed (rpm) AT	Valve Clearance (in.) In.	Valve Clearance (in.) Ex.
1982	G63B	4–122 (2.0)	W20EP-U10	.035	5B	5B	①	4.6–6.0	800	800	.006 Hot②	.010 Hot②
	G54B	4–156 (2.6)	W20EP-U10	.035	7B	7B	①	4.6–6.0	750	750	.006 Hot②	.010 Hot②
1983	G63B	4–122 (2.0)	W20EP-U10	.035	5B	5B	①	4.6–6.0	800	800	.006 Hot②	.010 Hot②
	G54B	4–156 (2.6)	W20EP-U10	.035	7B	7B	①	4.6–6.0	750	750	.006 Hot②	.010 Hot②
1984	G63B	4–122 (2.0)	W20EP-U10	.035	5B	5B	①	4.6–6.0	800	800	.006 Hot②	.010 Hot②
	G54B	4–156 (2.6)	W20EP-U10	.035	7B	7B	①	4.6–6.0	750	750	.006 Hot②	.010 Hot②

GASOLINE ENGINE TUNE-UP SPECIFICATIONS

Year	VIN	No. Cylinder Displacement cu. in. (liter)	Spark Plugs Type	Spark Plugs Gap (in.)	Ignition Timing (deg.) MT	Ignition Timing (deg.) AT	Compression Pressure (psi)	Fuel Pump (psi)	Idle Speed (rpm) MT	Idle Speed (rpm) AT	Valve Clearance In.	Valve Clearance Ex.
1985	G63B	4–122 (2.0)	W20EP-U10	.035	5B	5B	①	4.6–6.0	800	800	Hyd.②	Hyd.②
	G54B	4–156 (2.6)	W20EP-U10	.035	7B	7B	①	4.6–6.0	750	750	Hyd.②	Hyd.②
1986	G63B	4–122 (2.0)	W20EP-U10	.035	5B	5B	①	4.6–6.0	800	800	Hyd.②	Hyd.②
	G54B	4–156 (2.6)	W20EP-U10	.035	7B	7B	①	4.6–6.0	750	750	Hyd.②	Hyd.②
1987–88	G63B	4–122 (2.0)	W20EP-U10	.035	7B	7B	①	3.0–4.5	750	750	Hyd.	Hyd.
	G64B	4–143 (2.4)	NGK	.043	5B	5B	①	37	750	750	Hyd.	Hyd.
	4G54	4–156 (2.6)	W20EP-U10	.035	7B	7B	①	3.0–4.5	750	750	Hyd.	Hyd.

① When analyzing compression results, look for uniformity among cylinders, rather than specific pressures

② Jet valve clearance: 0.010 Hot①

FIRING ORDERS

NOTE: To avoid confusion, always replace spark plug wires one at a time.

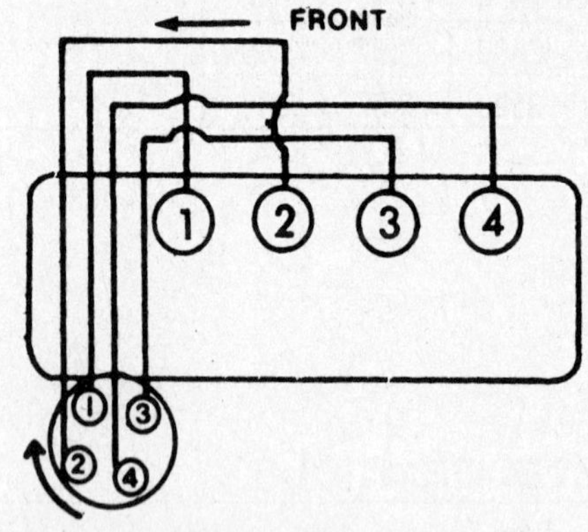

2.6L engine—firing order 1-3-4-2

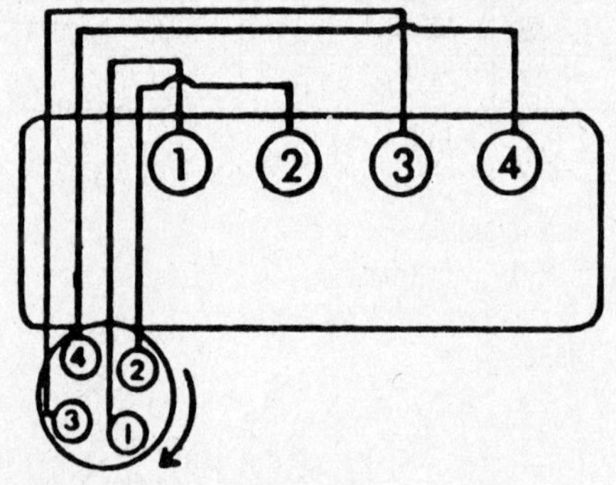

2.0L & 2.4L engines—firing order 1-3-4-2

CAPACITIES

Year	Model	No. Cylinder Displacement cu. in. (liter)	Engine Crankcase with Filter	Engine Crankcase without Filter	Transmission (pts.) 4-Spd	Transmission (pts.) 5-Spd	Transmission (pts.) Auto.	Drive Axle (pts.)	Fuel Tank (gal.)	Cooling System (qts.)
1982	Pickups	4–122 (2.0)	4.5	4.0	2.2	—	6.8	2.8①	15.8②	9.5
		4–143 (2.3)	5.9	5.3	2.2	2.5	—	2.3①	15.1②	8.5
		4–156 (2.6)	4.5	4.0	—	2.4	6.8	2.8①	15.8②	9.7
1983	Pickups	4–122 (2.0)	4.5	4.0	2.2	—	6.8	2.8①	15.8②	9.5
		4–143 (2.3)	5.9	5.3	2.2	2.5	—	2.3①	15.1②	8.5
		4–156 (2.6)	4.5	4.0	—	2.4	6.8	2.8①	15.8②	9.7
	Montero	4–156 (2.6)	4.5	4.0	—	2.4	6.8	2.3①②	15.9	8.5

CAPACITIES

Year	Model	No. Cylinder Displacement cu. in. (liter)	Engine Crankcase with Filter	Engine Crankcase without Filter	Transmission (pts.) 4-Spd	5-Spd	Auto.	Drive Axle (pts.)	Fuel Tank (gal.)	Cooling System (qts.)
1984	Pickups	4–122 (2.0)	4.5	4.0	2.2	—	6.8	2.8①	15.8②	9.5
		4–143 (2.3)	5.9	5.3	2.2	2.5	—	2.3①	15.1②	8.5
		4–156 (2.6)	4.5	4.0	—	2.4	6.8	2.8①	15.8②	9.7
	Montero	4–156 (2.6)	4.5	4.0	—	2.4	6.8	2.3①②	15.9	8.5
1985	Pickups	4–122 (2.0)	4.5	4.0	2.2	—	6.8	2.8①	15.8②	9.5
		4–143 (2.3)	5.9	5.3	2.2	2.5	—	2.3①	15.1②	8.5
		4–156 (2.6)	4.5	4.0	—	2.4	6.8	2.8①	15.8②	9.7
	Montero	4–156 (2.6)	4.5	4.0	—	2.4	6.8	2.3①②	15.9	8.5
1986	Pickups	4–122 (2.0)	4.5	4.0	2.2	—	6.8	2.8①	15.8②	9.5
		4–143 (2.3)	5.9	5.3	2.2	2.5	—	2.3①	15.1②	8.5
		4–156 (2.6)	4.5	4.0	—	2.4	6.8	2.8①	15.8②	9.7
	Montero	4–156 (2.6)	4.5	4.0	—	2.4	6.8	2.3①②	15.9	8.5
1987–88	Pickups	4–122 (2.0)	4.5	4.0	—	2.4	7.2	2.3①	15.7④	7.4
		4–156 (2.6)	4.5	4.0	—	2.4	7.2	2.3①	15.7④	8.3
	Montero/ Raider	4–156 (2.6)	5.3	4.8	—	2.8	7.6	2.3①	15.9	9.4
	Van	4–143 (2.4)	4.2	3.7	—	—	7.7	2.7	14.3	8.5⑤

① Front axle; Rear axle: 3.8 pints
② Optional fuel tank: 18.0 gallons
③ Limited slip rear axle: 3.2 pints
④ Long wheel base: 19.8 gallons
⑤ With rear heater: 9.0 quarts

CRANKSHAFT AND CONNECTING ROD SPECIFICATIONS

All measurements are given in inches.

Year	VIN	No. Cylinder Displacement cu. in. (liter)	Crankshaft Main Brg. Journal Dia.	Main Brg. Oil Clearance	Shaft End-play	Thrust on No.	Connecting Rod Journal Diameter	Oil Clearance	Side Clearance
1982	G63B	4–122 (2.0)	2.2440	0.0008–0.0020	0.002–0.007	3	1.7720	0.0008–0.0020	0.004–0.010
	4D55	4–143 (2.3)	2.5980	0.0008–0.0020	0.0008–0.0020	3	2.0866	0.0008–0.0020	0.004–0.010
	G54B	4–156 (2.6)	2.3622	0.0008–0.0020	0.002–0.007	3	2.0866	0.0008–0.0020	0.004–0.010
1983	G63B	4–122 (2.0)	2.2440	0.0008–0.0020	0.002–0.007	3	1.7720	0.0008–0.0020	0.004–0.010
	4D55	4–143 (2.3)	2.5980	0.0008–0.0020	0.0008–0.0020	3	2.0866	0.0008–0.0020	0.004–0.010
	G54B	4–156 (2.6)	2.3622	0.0008–0.0020	0.002–0.007	3	2.0866	0.0008–0.0020	0.004–0.010

CRANKSHAFT AND CONNECTING ROD SPECIFICATIONS

All measurements are given in inches.

Year	VIN	No. Cylinder Displacement cu. in. (liter)	Crankshaft				Connecting Rod		
			Main Brg. Journal Dia.	Main Brg. Oil Clearance	Shaft End-play	Thrust on No.	Journal Diameter	Oil Clearance	Side Clearance
1984	G63B	4–122 (2.0)	2.2440	0.0008–0.0020	0.002–0.007	3	1.7720	0.0008–0.0020	0.004–0.010
	4D55	4–143 (2.3)	2.5980	0.0008–0.0020	0.0008–0.007	3	2.0866	0.0008–0.0020	0.004–0.010
	G54B	4–156 (2.6)	2.3622	0.0008–0.0020	0.002–0.007	3	2.0866	0.0008–0.0020	0.004–0.010
1985	G63B	4–122 (2.0)	2.2440	0.0008–0.0020	0.002–0.007	3	1.7720	0.0008–0.0020	0.004–0.010
	4D55	4–143 (2.3)	2.5980	0.0008–0.0020	0.0008–0.0020	3	2.0866	0.0008–0.0020	0.004–0.010
	G54B	4–156 (2.6)	2.3622	0.0008–0.0020	0.002–0.007	3	2.0866	0.0008–0.0020	0.004–0.010
1986	G63B	4–122 (2.0)	2.2440	0.0008–0.0020	0.002–0.007	3	1.7720	0.0008–0.0020	0.004–0.010
	4D55	4–143 (2.3)	2.5980	0.0008–0.0020	0.0008–0.0020	3	2.0866	0.0008–0.0020	0.004–0.010
	G54B	4–156 (2.6)	2.3622	0.0008–0.0020	0.002–0.007	3	2.0866	0.0008–0.0020	0.004–0.010
1987–88	G63B	4–122 (2.0)	2.2440	0.0008–0.0020	0.002–0.007	3	1.7720	0.0008–0.0020	0.004–0.010
	G64B	4–143 (2.4)	2.2441	0.0008–0.0020	0.002–0.007	3	2.0866	0.0008–0.0020	0.004–0.010
	4G54	4–156 (2.6)	2.3622	0.0008–0.0020	0.002–0.007	3	2.0866	0.0008–0.0020	0.004–0.010

VALVE SPECIFICATIONS

Year	VIN	No. Cylinder Displacement cu. in. (liter)	Seat Angle (deg.)	Face Angle (deg.)	Spring Test Pressure (lbs.)	Spring Installed Height (in.)	Stem-to-Guide Clearance (in.)		Stem Diameter (in.)	
							Intake	Exhaust	Intake	Exhaust
1982	G63B	4–122 (2.0)	45	45	72	1.59	0.0012–0.0024	0.0020–0.0035	0.3150	0.3150
	4D55	4–143 (2.3)	45	45	61	1.59	0.0012–0.0024	0.0020–0.0035	0.3150	0.3150
	G54B	4–156 (2.6)	45	45	72	1.59	0.0012–0.0024	0.0020–0.0035	0.3150	0.3150
		Jet valve	45	45	5.5	0.846	–	–	0.1693	0.1693
1983	G63B	4–122 (2.0)	45	45	72	1.59	0.0012–0.0024	0.0020–0.0035	0.3150	0.3150
	4D55	4–143 (2.3)	45	45	61	1.59	0.0012–0.0024	0.0020–0.0035	0.3150	0.3150
	G54B	4–156 (2.6)	45	45	72	1.59	0.0012–0.0024	0.0020–0.0035	0.3150	0.3150
		Jet valve	45	45	5.5	0.846	–	–	0.1693	0.1693

VALVE SPECIFICATIONS

Year	VIN	No. Cylinder Displacement cu. in. (liter)	Seat Angle (deg.)	Face Angle (deg.)	Spring Test Pressure (lbs.)	Spring Installed Height (in.)	Stem-to-Guide Clearance (in.)		Stem Diameter (in.)	
							Intake	Exhaust	Intake	Exhaust
1984	G63B	4–122 (2.0)	45	45	72	1.59	0.0012–0.0024	0.0020–0.0035	0.3150	0.3150
	4D55	4–143 (2.3)	45	45	61	1.59	0.0012–0.0024	0.0020–0.0035	0.3150	0.3150
	G54B	4–156 (2.6)	45	45	72	1.59	0.0012–0.0024	0.0020–0.0035	0.3150	0.3150
		Jet valve	45	45	5.5	0.846	–	–	0.1693	0.1693
1985	G63B	4–122 (2.0)	45	45	72	1.59	0.0012–0.0024	0.0020–0.0035	0.3150	0.3150
	4D55	4–143 (2.3)	45	45	61	1.59	0.0012–0.0024	0.0020–0.0035	0.3150	0.3150
	G54B	4–156 (2.6)	45	45	72	1.59	0.0012–0.0024	0.0020–0.0035	0.3150	0.3150
		Jet valve	45	45	5.5	0.846	–	–	0.1693	0.1693
1986	G63B	4–122 (2.0)	45	45	72	1.59	0.0012–0.0024	0.0020–0.0035	0.3150	0.3150
	4D55	4–143 (2.3)	45	45	61	1.59	0.0012–0.0024	0.0020–0.0035	0.3150	0.3150
	G54B	4–156 (2.6)	45	45	72	1.59	0.0012–0.0024	0.0020–0.0035	0.3150	0.3150
		Jet valve	45	45	5.5	0.846	–	–	0.1693	0.1693
1987–88	G63B	4–122 (2.0)	45	45	72	1.59	0.0012–0.0024	0.0020–0.0035	0.3150	0.3150
	G64B	4–143 (2.4)	45	45	72	1.59	0.0012–0.0024	0.0020–0.0035	0.3150	0.3150
	4G54	4–156 (2.6)	45	45	72	1.59	0.0012–0.0024	0.0020–0.0035	0.3150	0.3150
		Jet valve	45	45	5.5	0.846	–	–	0.1693	0.1693

PISTON AND RING SPECIFICATIONS

All measurements are given in inches.

Year	VIN	No. Cylinder Displacement cu. in. (liter)	Piston Clearance	Ring Gap			Ring Side Clearance		
				Top Compression	Bottom Compression	Oil Control	Top Compression	Bottom Compression	Oil Control
1982	G63B	4–122 (2.0)	0.0008–0.0016	0.0020–0.0035	0.0008–0.0024	Snug	0.010–0.018	0.008–0.016	0.0078–0.028
	4D55	4–143 (2.3)	0.0016–0.0024	0.0010–0.0020	0.0010–0.0030	0.001–0.003	0.001–0.016	0.001–0.016	0.001–0.016
	G54B	4–156 (2.6)	0.0008–0.0016	0.0020–0.0035	0.0008–0.0024	Snug	0.012–0.018	0.010–0.015	0.012–0.024

PISTON AND RING SPECIFICATIONS

All measurements are given in inches.

Year	VIN	No. Cylinder Displacement cu. in. (liter)	Piston Clearance	Ring Gap Top Compression	Ring Gap Bottom Compression	Ring Gap Oil Control	Ring Side Clearance Top Compression	Ring Side Clearance Bottom Compression	Ring Side Clearance Oil Control
1983	G63B	4–122 (2.0)	0.0008–0.0016	0.0020–0.0035	0.0008–0.0024	Snug	0.010–0.018	0.008–0.016	0.0078–0.028
	4D55	4–143 (2.3)	0.0016–0.0024	0.0010–0.0020	0.0010–0.0030	0.001–0.003	0.001–0.016	0.001–0.016	0.001–0.016
	G54B	4–156 (2.6)	0.0008–0.0016	0.0020–0.0035	0.0008–0.0024	Snug	0.012–0.018	0.010–0.015	0.012–0.024
1984	G63B	4–122 (2.0)	0.0008–0.0016	0.0020–0.0035	0.0008–0.0024	Snug	0.010–0.018	0.008–0.016	0.0078–0.028
	4D55	4–143 (2.3)	0.0016–0.0024	0.0010–0.0020	0.0010–0.0030	0.001–0.003	0.001–0.016	0.001–0.016	0.001–0.016
	G54B	4–156 (2.6)	0.0008–0.0016	0.0020–0.0035	0.0008–0.0024	Snug	0.012–0.018	0.010–0.015	0.012–0.024
1985	G63B	4–122 (2.0)	0.0008–0.0016	0.0020–0.0035	0.0008–0.0024	Snug	0.010–0.018	0.008–0.016	0.0078–0.028
	4D55	4–143 (2.3)	0.0016–0.0024	0.0010–0.0020	0.0010–0.0030	0.001–0.003	0.001–0.016	0.001–0.016	0.001–0.016
	G54B	4–156 (2.6)	0.0008–0.0016	0.0020–0.0035	0.0008–0.0024	Snug	0.012–0.018	0.010–0.015	0.012–0.024
1986	G63B	4–122 (2.0)	0.0008–0.0016	0.0020–0.0035	0.0008–0.0024	Snug	0.010–0.018	0.008–0.016	0.0078–0.028
	4D55	4–143 (2.3)	0.0016–0.0024	0.0010–0.0020	0.0010–0.0030	0.001–0.003	0.001–0.016	0.001–0.016	0.001–0.016
	G54B	4–156 (2.6)	0.0008–0.0016	0.0020–0.0035	0.0008–0.0024	Snug	0.012–0.018	0.010–0.015	0.012–0.024
1987–88	G63B	4–122 (2.0)	0.0008–0.0016	0.0112–0.0177	0.0098–0.0158	0.0118–0.0315	0.0020–0.0035	0.0008–0.0024	0.0078–0.028
	G64B	4–143 (2.4)	0.0008–0.0016	0.0098–0.0157	0.0079–0.0157	0.0079–0.0276	0.0012–0.0028	0.0008–0.0024	0.0078–0.028
	4G54	4–156 (2.6)	0.0008–0.0016	0.0112–0.0177	0.0098–0.0158	0.0118–0.0315	0.0020–0.0035	0.0008–0.0024	0.0078–0.028

TORQUE SPECIFICATIONS

All readings in ft. lbs.

Year	VIN	No. Cylinder Displacement cu. in. (liter)	Cylinder Head Bolts②	Main Bearing Bolts	Rod Bearing Bolts	Crankshaft Pulley Bolts	Flywheel Bolts	Manifold Intake	Manifold Exhaust	Spark Plugs
1982	G63B	4–122 (2.0)	65–72①	37–39	33–35	80–94	94–101	11–14	11–14	NA
	4D55	4–143 (2.3)	76–83②	55–61	33–35	123–137	94–101	11–14	11–14	—
	G54B	4–156 (2.6)	65–72①	55–61	33–35	80–94	94–101	11–14	11–14	NA
1983	G63B	4–122 (2.0)	65–72①	37–39	33–35	80–94	94–101	11–14	11–14	NA
	4D55	4–143 (2.3)	76–83②	55–61	33–35	123–137	94–101	11–14	11–14	—
	G54B	4–156 (2.6)	65–72①	55–61	33–35	80–94	94–101	11–14	11–14	NA

TORQUE SPECIFICATIONS

All readings in ft. lbs.

Year	VIN	No. Cylinder Displacement cu. in. (liter)	Cylinder Head Bolts②	Main Bearing Bolts	Rod Bearing Bolts	Crankshaft Pulley Bolts	Flywheel Bolts	Manifold Intake	Manifold Exhaust	Spark Plugs
1984	G63B	4-122 (2.0)	65-72①	37-39	33-35	80-94	94-101	11-14	11-14	NA
	4D55	4-143 (2.3)	76-83①	55-61	33-35	123-137	94-101	11-14	11-14	—
	G54B	4-156 (2.6)	65-72①	55-61	33-35	80-94	94-101	11-14	11-14	NA
1985	G63B	4-122 (2.0)	65-72①	37-39	33-35	80-94	94-101	11-14	11-14	NA
	4D55	4-143 (2.3)	76-83①	55-61	33-35	123-137	94-101	11-14	11-14	—
	G54B	4-156 (2.6)	65-72①	55-61	33-35	80-94	94-101	11-14	11-14	NA
1986	G63B	4-122 (2.0)	65-72①	37-39	33-35	80-94	94-101	11-14	11-14	NA
	4D55	4-143 (2.3)	76-83②	55-61	33-35	123-137	94-101	11-14	11-14	—
	G54B	4-156 (2.6)	65-72①	55-61	33-35	80-94	94-101	11-14	11-14	NA
1987-88	G63B	4-122 (2.0)	65-72①	37-39	33-34	80-94	94-101	11-14	11-14	NA
	G64B	4-143 (2.4)	65-72①	37-39	37-38	80-94	94-101	11-14	11-14	NA
	4G54	4-156 (2.6)	65-72①	55-61	33-34	80-94	94-101	11-14	11-14	NA

① Specification is for cold engine. Hot engine: 73-79 ft. lbs.

② Specification is for cold engine. Hot engine: 84-90 ft. lbs.

③ Do not torque the front two bolts on gasoline engines, to this specification. Torque the front two bolts to 11-15 ft. lbs.

WHEEL ALIGNMENT

Year	Model	Caster Range (deg.)	Caster Preferred Setting (deg.)	Camber Range (deg.)	Camber Preferred Setting (deg.)	Toe-in (in.)	Steering Axis Inclination (deg.)
1982	2WD Pickups	$1\frac{1}{2}$-$3\frac{1}{2}$	$2\frac{1}{2}$	$\frac{1}{2}$-$1\frac{1}{2}$	1	.08-.35	NA
	4WD Pickups	1-3	2	$\frac{1}{2}$-$1\frac{1}{2}$	1	.08-.35	NA
1983	2WD Pickups	$1\frac{1}{2}$-$3\frac{1}{2}$	$2\frac{1}{2}$	$\frac{1}{2}$-$1\frac{1}{2}$	1	.08-.35	NA
	4WD Pickups	1-3	2	$\frac{1}{2}$-$1\frac{1}{2}$	1	.08-.35	NA
	Montero	2-3	$2\frac{1}{2}$	$\frac{1}{2}$-$1\frac{1}{2}$	1	.08-.35	NA
1984	2WD Pickups	$1\frac{1}{2}$-$3\frac{1}{2}$	$2\frac{1}{2}$	$\frac{1}{2}$-$1\frac{1}{2}$	1	.08-.35	NA
	4WD Pickups	1-3	2	$\frac{1}{2}$-$1\frac{1}{2}$	1	.08-.35	NA
	Montero	2-3	$2\frac{1}{2}$	$\frac{1}{2}$-$1\frac{1}{2}$	1	.08-.35	NA
1985	2WD Pickups	$1\frac{1}{2}$-$3\frac{1}{2}$	$2\frac{1}{2}$	$\frac{1}{2}$-$1\frac{1}{2}$	1	.08-.35	NA
	4WD Pickups	1-3	2	$\frac{1}{2}$-$1\frac{1}{2}$	1	.08-.35	NA
	Montero	2-3	$2\frac{1}{2}$	$\frac{1}{2}$-$1\frac{1}{2}$	1	.08-.35	NA
1986	2WD Pickups	$1\frac{1}{2}$-$3\frac{1}{2}$	$2\frac{1}{2}$	$\frac{1}{2}$-$1\frac{1}{2}$	1	.08-.35	NA
	4WD Pickups	1-3	2	$\frac{1}{2}$-$1\frac{1}{2}$	1	.08-.35	NA
	Montero	2-3	$2\frac{1}{2}$	$\frac{1}{2}$-$1\frac{1}{2}$	1	.08-.35	NA
1987-88	2WD Pickups	$1\frac{1}{2}$-$3\frac{1}{2}$	$2\frac{1}{2}$	$\frac{1}{2}$-$1\frac{1}{2}$	1	.08-.35	NA
	4WD Pickups	1-3	2	$\frac{1}{2}$-$1\frac{1}{2}$	1	.08-.35	NA
	Montero/Raider	2-3	$2\frac{1}{2}$	$\frac{1}{2}$-$1\frac{1}{2}$	1	.08-.35	NA
	Van	$2\frac{1}{2}$-$3\frac{1}{2}$	3	0-1	$\frac{1}{2}$	.00-.24	NA

ENGINE ELECTRICAL

Refer to the Overhaul Section for Starter and Alternator Overhaul.

Alternator

The charging system consists of an alternator with an IC integral voltage regulator. With the exception of belt tension, no adjustments are possible on the systems.

Removal and Installation

ALL MODELS EXCEPT VAN

NOTE: Vehicles equipped with A/C may require the removal of the A/C compressor in order to remove the alternator. If this is necessary, remove the compressor from the mounts without disconnecting the refrigerant lines and support the compressor out of the way.

1. Disconnect the negative battery cable.
2. Disconnect and tag the wires on the back of the alternator.
3. Remove the alternator brace bolt, spacer and support bolt nut. Remove the drive belt.
4. On 2.6L engines with an automatic transmission, disconnect and plug the transmission cooling lines under the alternator.
5. Support the alternator and remove the support bolt. Remove the alternator assembly noting the position of any shims.
6. To install, align the hole in the alternator leg with the hole in the front case and install the alternator support bolt and spacer from the front.

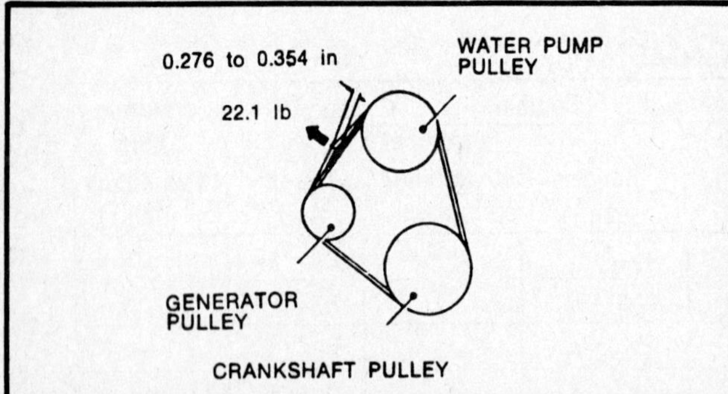

Drive belt tension adjustment

7. Tighten the alternator brace bolt hand tight.
8. Install drive belt.
9. Push the alternator toward the front of the engine and check the clearance between the alternator leg and the front case. If the clearance is less than 0.008 inch, insert spacers as required. 0.0078 inch spacers are available.
10. Connect the wires on the back of the alternator and adjust the drive belt tension.
11. Install the A/C compressor and connect the transmission cooling lines, if removed.
12. Torque the alternator support bolt nut to 15–18 ft. lbs. and the brace bolt to 9–11 ft. lbs.

VAN

1. Raise and support the vehicle safely.
2. Remove the oil filter.
3. Disconnect and tag the alternator wiring.
4. Remove the alternator adjustment bolt.

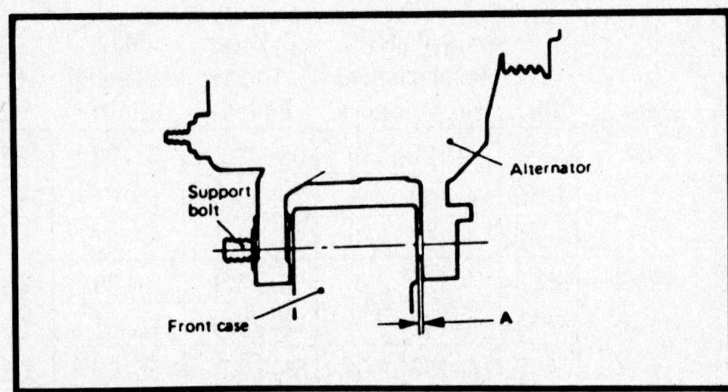

Gap "A" shows shim placement for alternator mounting

5. Remove the alternator drive belt.
6. Support the alternator and remove the brace bolt and nut.
7. Remove the alternator from the engine.
8. Installation is the reverse of the removal procedure.
9. Torque the alternator brace bolt and nut to 14–18 ft. lbs. Torque the alternator adjustment bolt to 9–11 ft. lbs. after adjusting the belt tension.

Voltage Regulator

INTEGRAL

Removal and Installation

All models are equipped with an integral circuit type voltage regulator. Removal and Installation requires alternator disassembly. Refer to the Unit Repair Section for the procedure.

Starter

Removal and Installation

ALL MODELS

NOTE: Vehicles equipped with A/C may require removal of the A/C compressor in order to remove the starter. If this is necessary, remove the compressor from the mounts without disconnecting the refrigerant lines and support the compressor out of the way.

1. Disconnect the negative battery cable. Raise and support the vehicle safely.
2. Disconnect and tag the starter motor wiring.
3. Support the starter and remove the two starter motor mounting bolts.
4. Remove the starter motor.
5. Installation is the reverse of the removal procedure. Torque the starter motor mounting bolts to 20–25 ft. lbs.

OVERHAUL

For Starter Overhaul procedures, refer to the Electrical Section in the Unit Repair Section.

Distributor

Removal and Installation

ELECTRONIC

1. Disconnect the battery ground cable.

2. Disconnect the wiring harness from the distributor control unit.
3. Tag the spark plug wires at the distributor cap and remove the wires from the cap by pulling on the boot of the wire.
4. Remove the distributor cap.
5. Matchmark the distributor mounting flange to the mounting stud on the engine for correct positioning during assembly. Matchmark the position of the rotor to the distributor housing.
6. Disconnect and tag the vacuum hose(s) from the vacuum control unit(s).
7. Remove the distributor mounting nut and remove the distributor.
8. If the engine has been turned while the distributor is out: (Go to Step 12 if the engine has not been turned). Rotate the engine until the No. 1 cylinder is at top dead center on compression stroke. To find No. 1 cylinder compression stroke, remove the distributor cap and turn the engine until the rotor assembly is pointing toward the No. 1 cylinder lead in the distributor cap. Verify top dead center on the crankshaft pulley.
9. Align the matchmark on the distributor housing with the punch mark on the distributor driven gear.
10. Install the distributor so the matchmark on the distributor mounting flange is in line with the center of the distributor mounting stud. Tighten the mounting nut and install the distributor cap, wires, hoses and spark plug wires.

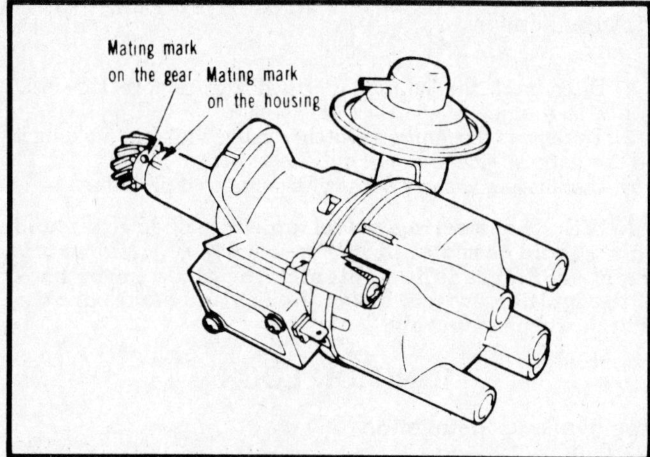

Mating mark alignment

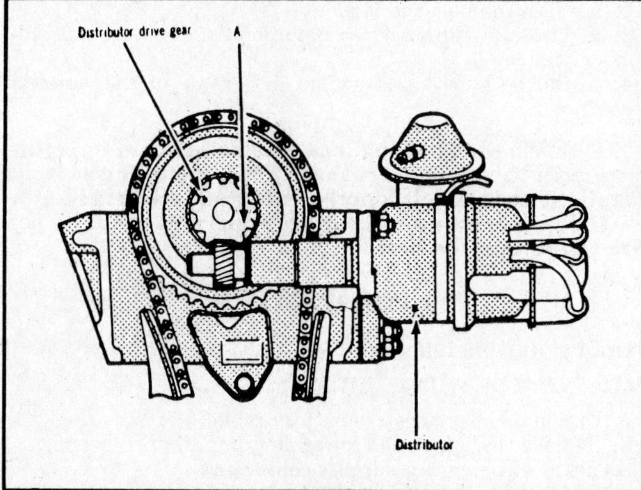

Distributor mounting

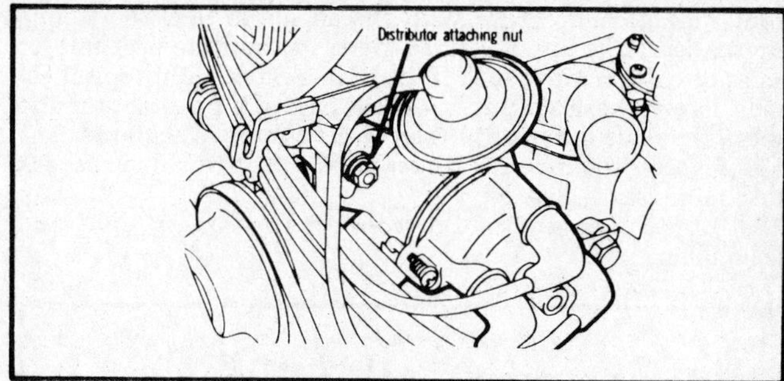

Distributor locknut location

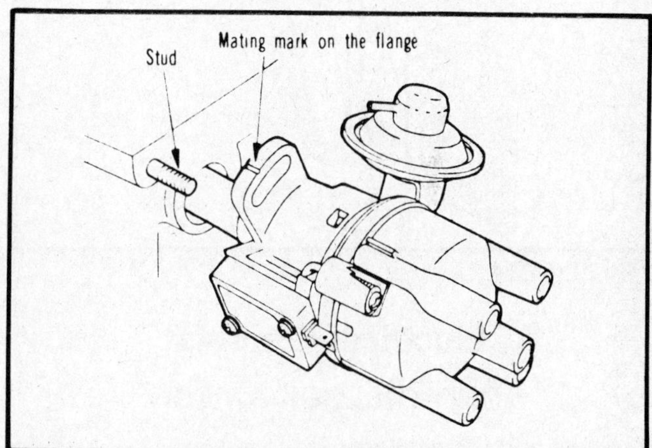

Align mark on flange with stud

11. Check and adjust the ignition timing.
12. If the engine has not been disturbed while the distributor was out; install the distributor in the engine by aligning the marks made during removal.
13. Install the mounting nut, distributor cap, wires, hoses and plug wires.
14. Reconnect the negative battery cable, start the engine and check the ignition timing.

TIMING LIGHT AND TACHOMETER CONNECTIONS

All timing lights and tachometers should be connected according to their manufacture's recommedations.

IGNITION TIMING

Adjustment

1. Run the engine until it reaches normal operating temperature. Connect a tachometer and check the engine idle speed. Adjust it as outlined if not within specifications. If the timing mark on the front pulley is difficult to see, use chalk or a dab of paint to make it more visible.
2. Connect a timing light to the engine, as outlined in the instructions supplied by the manufacturer of the light.
3. Allow the engine to run at the specified idle speed with the gear shift in Neutral (Park, if automatic) and the air conditioning compressor and lights off.

CAUTION

Be sure the parking brake is firmly set and that the wheels are chocked.

4. Point the timing light at the timing marks indicated on the

front timing chain cover. With the engine at idle, the timing should be at the specifications given in the tune-up chart or emission information label. If the timing is not within specifications, loosen the mounting nut at the base of the distributor and rotate the distributor until the correct timing is achieved.

5. Tighten the mounting nut. Start the engine and recheck the timing.

6. Stop the engine and disconnect the timing light and tachometer.

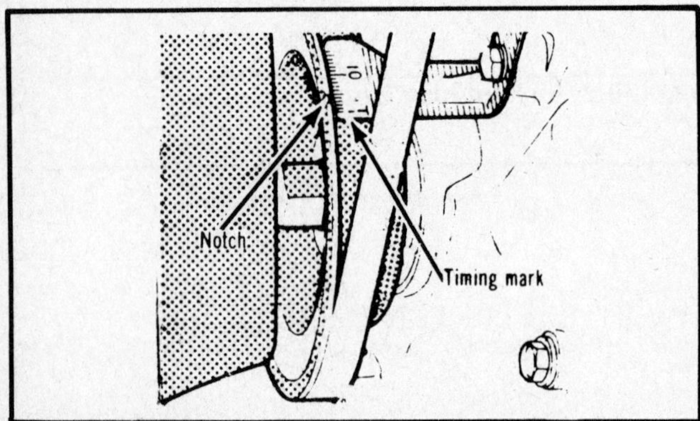

Timing marks

Electrical Controls

IGNITION LOCK/SWITCH

Removal and Installation

PICKUPS

1. Disconnect the negative battery cable. Remove the steering column cover.
2. Cut a notch in the lock bracket bolt head with a hacksaw.
3. Remove the lock bolts.

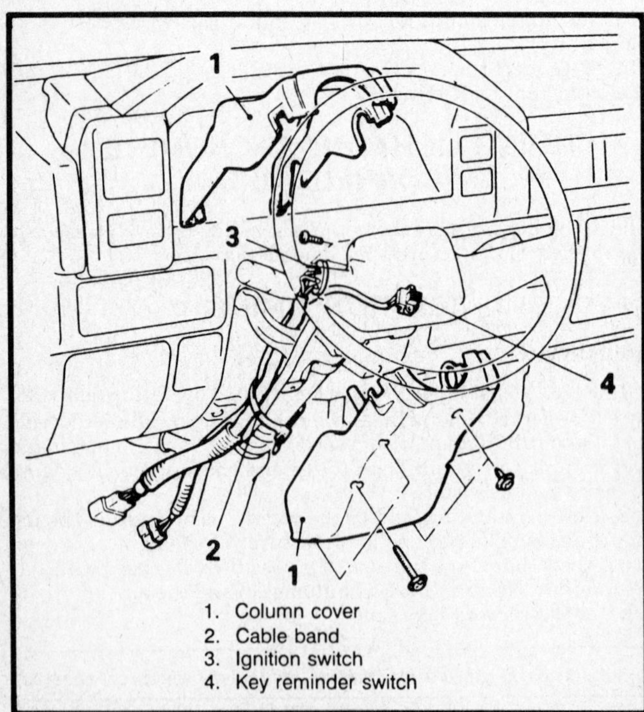

Ignition switch installation—Van

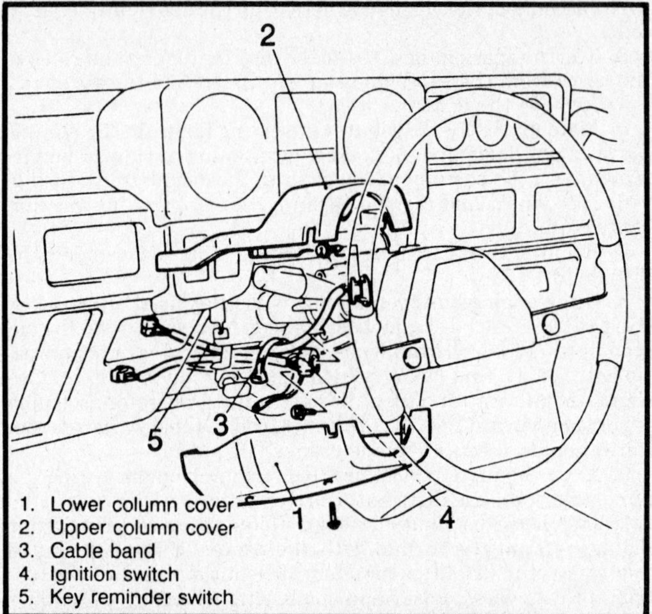

Ignition switch installation—Montero/Raider shown—pickups similar

4. Disconnect the ignition harness and remove the lock/switch as a unit.
5. To remove the ignition switch, remove the screw holding it on the harness side and pull out the switch.
6. Installation is the reverse of the removal procedure.

NOTE: The steering wheel upper lock bracket and bolts should be replaced with new parts when the unit is installed. Before fully tightening the screw in the back of the ignition switch, insert the key and make sure the switch works smoothly.

IGNITION LOCK

Removal and Installation

VAN AND MONTERO/RAIDER

1. Disconnect the negative battery cable. Cut a notch in the lock bracket bolt head with a hacksaw.
2. Remove the bolt and lock.
3. Remove the column cover and unbolt and remove the ignition switch.
4. Install both lock and switch in reverse of the removal procedure.

NOTE: When installing lock, the bolt should be tightened until the head is crushed. When installing switch, install the switch bolt loosely. Insert and work the key a few times to make sure the switch operates properly before tightening the bolt.

IGNITION SWITCH

Removal and Installation

VAN AND MONTERO/RAIDER

1. Disconnect the negative battery cable.
2. Remove the upper and lower steering column covers.
3. Remove the wiring harness cable band.
4. Disconnect the wiring harness from the ignition switch.
5. Remove the ignition switch mounting bolts and remove the switch.

6. Installation is the reverse of the removal procedure. Use care not to pinch the wiring harness when installing the column covers.

COMBINATION SWITCH

The Combination Switch incorporates the Headlight, Dimmer, W/Wiper and Turn Signal Switches into one switch.

Removal and Installation

ALL MODELS

1. Disconnect the negative battery cable.
2. Remove the horn cover from the steering wheel. Matchmark and remove the steering wheel.
3. If the vehicle is equipped with a tilt steering column, put the tilt handle in its lowest position.
4. Remove the upper and lower column covers.
5. Remove the wiring harness band clip and disconnect the harness.
6. Remove the combination switch mounting screws and remove the switch.
7. Installation is the reverse of removal with the following notes: Make sure the column switch aligns with the steering shaft center.
8. Place the wiring harness along the column tube as close as possible to the center line. Be sure to replace the adjustable wiring harness bands.
9. Install the steering wheel in the same position as when removed. Torque the steering wheel nut to 26–33 ft. lbs.

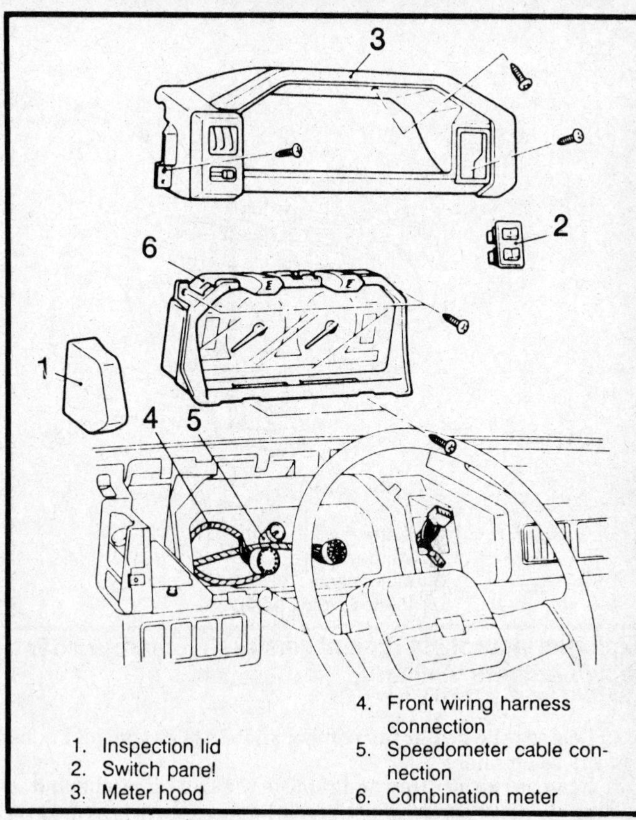

Instrument cluster mounting – Van shown – others similar

W/WIPER MOTOR

Removal and Installation

ALL MODELS

1. Remove the wiper arms. Remove the arm shaft lock nuts and push in the shafts. Disconnect the electrical wiring.
2. Remove the bolts holding the motor bracket to the body and pull the wiper assembly outward and away from the body.
3. Hold the motor shaft and the linkage at right angles to each other and disconnect them. Remove the motor.
4. The linkages can be pulled from the opening in the front deck.
5. Installation is the reverse of the removal procedure. Make sure to insert the linkage shaft bracket positioning boss positively in the hole provided in the body before tightening the wiper shaft nut.
6. Locate the wiper blades in the stopped position approximately $^1/_2$–$^3/_4$ in. above the bottom moulding or sealer of the windshield.

INSTRUMENT CLUSTER

Removal and Installation

PICKUPS

1. Disconnect the negative battery cable.

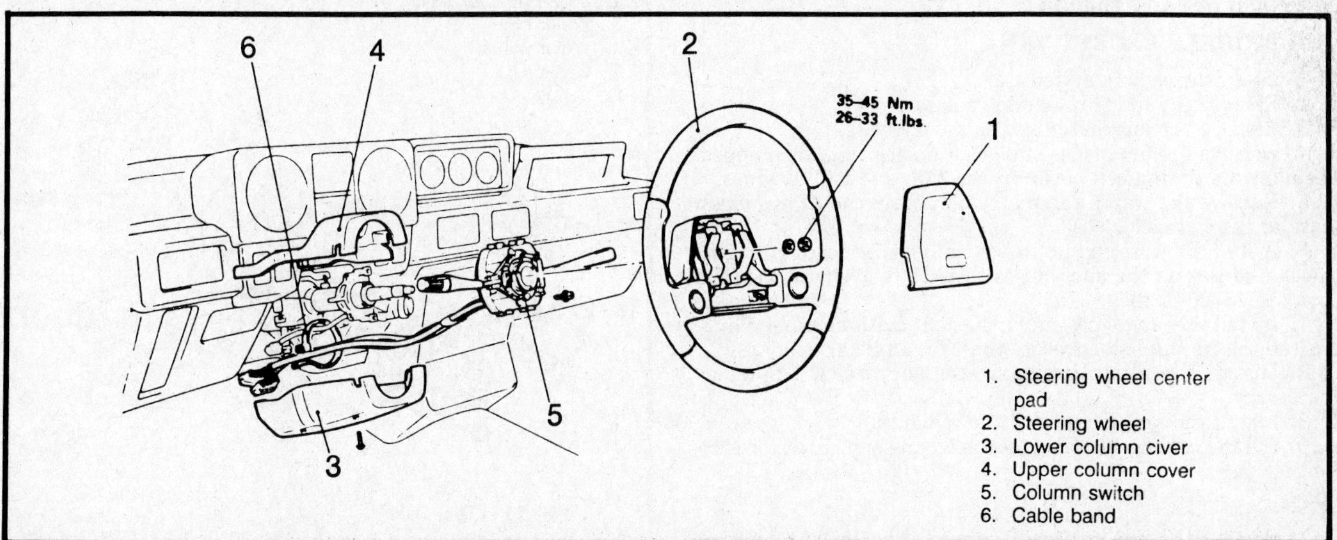

Combination switch mounting – Montero/Raider shown – others similar

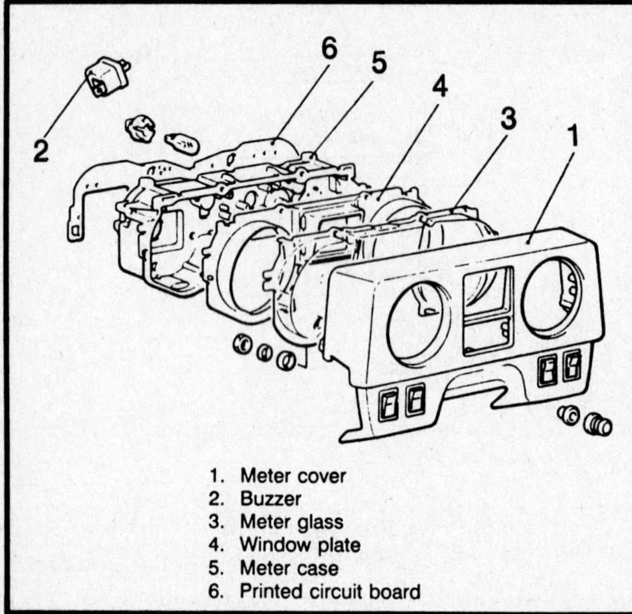

Exploded view of instrument cluster—Montero/Raider shown—others similar

2. Remove the heater fan control knob, heater control knobs and the radio knobs.
3. Remove the ash tray and remove the two screws behind it holding the instrument panel bezel. Remove the two screws at the top of the bezel and remove the bezel.
4. Remove the four screws in the corners of the meter case.
5. Disconnect the speedometer cable and connectors from the back of the meter and remove the meter assembly.
6. Installation is the reverse of the removal procedure.

MONTERO/RAIDER

1. Disconnect the negative battery cable.
2. Remove the four instrument panel bezel screws and remove the bezel.
3. Remove the four instrument cluster mounting screws and slide the instrument cluster out enough to reach behind it.
4. Disconnect the speedometer cable.
5. Disconnect and tag the instrument cluster wiring.
6. Remove the wiring harness from the clips on the rear of the instrument cluster.
7. Remove the instrument cluster.
8. Installation is the reverse of the removal procedure.

VAN

1. Disconnect the negative battery cable.
2. Remove the left side inspection cover on the instrument cluster.
3. Remove the hazard switch on the right side of the instrument panel by pressing in the clips on the side of the switch and pulling the switch outwards.
4. Remove the instrument cluster top cover panel.
5. Disconnect and tag the wiring harness on the rear of the instrument cluster.
6. Disconnect the speedometer cable from the speedometer.
7. Remove the instrument cluster mounting bolts and remove the cluster.
8. Installation is the reverse of the removal procedure.

SPEEDOMETER

Removal and Installation

ALL MODELS

1. Disconnect the negative battery cable.
2. Remove the instrument cluster.
3. Remove the speedometer from the case, noting the position of any light bulbs and wires.
4. Installation is the reverse of the removal procedure.

COOLING AND HEATING SYSTEMS

Water Pump

Removal and Installation

ALL MODELS EXCEPT VAN

1. Drain the cooling system.
2. Remove the fan shroud and radiator.
3. Remove the alternator and accessory belts.
4. Remove the fan blades and/or automatic hub, if equipped. Remove the timing belt cover on the 2.0L and 2.4L engines.
5. Remove the water pump assembly from the timing chain case or the cylinder block.
6. Install the water pump to the timing chain case or engine block and torque the short bolts to 9–11 ft. lbs. and the long bolts to 15–20 ft. lbs.
7. Install the fan blades and/or the automatic clutch fan hub. Install the timing belt cover on the 2.0L and 2.4L engines.
8. Install the alternator and accessory belts. Adjust as necessary.
9. Install the fan shroud and the radiator.
10. Fill the cooling system, run the engine and check for coolant leakage.

VAN

1. Remove the drivers seat. Remove the parking brake lever and fuel tank filler door release lever.

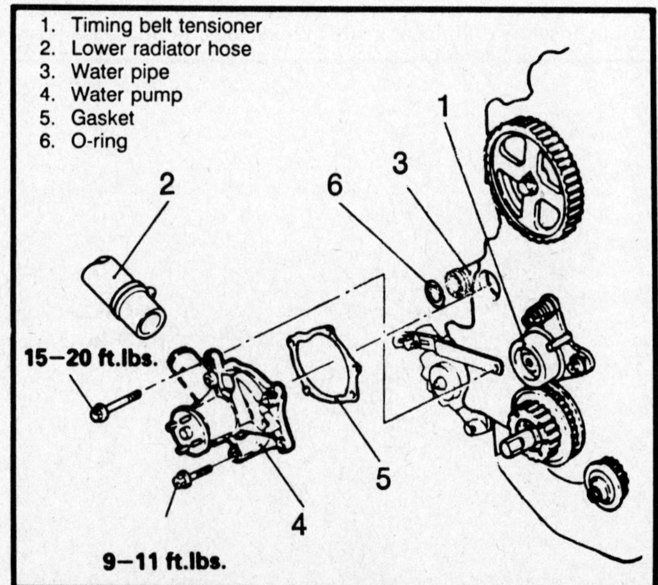

Water pump mounting—2.0L & 2.4L engines

2. Remove the battery cover. Remove the bolts retaining the seat underframe in place. Remove the seat underframe.
3. Disconnect the negative battery cable. Drain the cooling system.
4. Remove the radiator shroud. Remove the drive belts. Remove the cooling fan.
5. Remove the water pump pulley. Remove the tension pulley bracket if the vehicle is equipped with air conditioning. Disconnect the lower radiator hose.
6. Remove the crankshaft pulley. Remove the upper and lower timing belt covers. Remove the timing belts.
7. Remove the water pipe connection. Remove the water pump mounting bolts. Remove the water pump from the engine.
8. Installation is the reverse of the removal procedure.

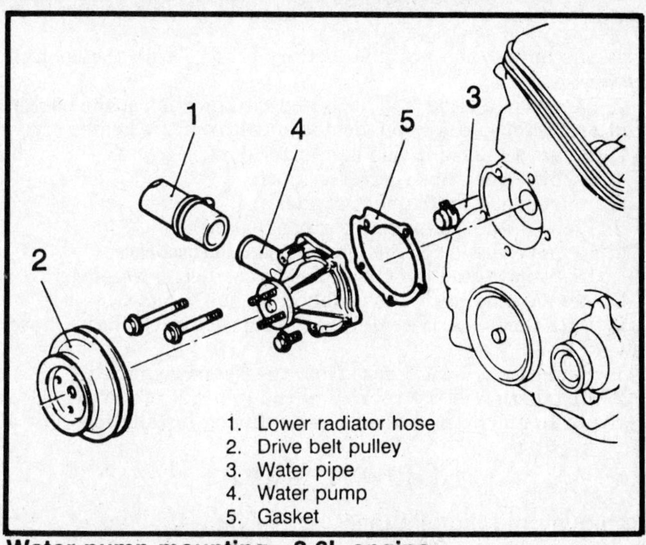

Water pump mounting—2.6L engine

Thermostat

Removal and Installation

ALL MODELS

1. Drain the coolant below the level of the thermostat.
2. Remove the two retaining bolts and lift the thermostat housing off the intake manifold with the upper radiator hose still attached.
3. Lift the thermostat out of the manifold.
4. Using a new gasket and with the mating surfaces coated with sealer, install the thermostat with the spring facing the engine.

Heater Core

Removal and Installation

PICKUPS

Removing the heater unit with air conditioning attached is similar to procedures used on units without air conditioning. It may be necessary to loosen or remove certain components of the air conditioning system to facilitate heater unit removal.

CAUTION

Use care when loosening the refrigerant hoses that lead into the air conditioning evaporator assembly. The hoses are filled with a noxious fluid which, under certain conditions, could cause severe damage to eyes or skin.

1. Drain the cooling system.
2. Place the hot water flow control lever in the off position.
3. Remove the glove box, the center ventilation grille and duct and the defroster duct.
4. Disconnect and tag all control cables at the heater side.
5. Disconnect the water hoses.
6. Disconnect the harness from the heater fan motor.
7. Remove the top mounting bolts and the center mounting nuts. Remove the heater assembly.

MONTERO/RAIDER

1. Remove the heater control lever arm and water valve cover on the heater.
2. Drain the cooling system. Remove the heater pipe and water valve.
3. Disconnect the control lever linkage.
4. Remove the control lever.
5. Remove the heater core from the side.

NOTE: To prevent foreign material from getting in between the heater core and case, be careful not to remove the heater core felt when removing the heater core.

6. To install, after the center ventilator open/close damper has been placed in the fully closed position, turn the arm fully clockwise, then connect it to the link.
7. With the defroster/changeover damper in the fully closed defroster position, turn the arm fully counterclockwise, then connect it to the link.
8. With the water valve fully closed and the air intake damper fully closed, connect the arm to the link.
9. Connect each heater hose up to the proper inlet/outlet.
10. When installing the water hoses, apply a non-drying adhesive to the engine compartment side of the grommet. Tighten the clamps so that the bolt heads are accessible.

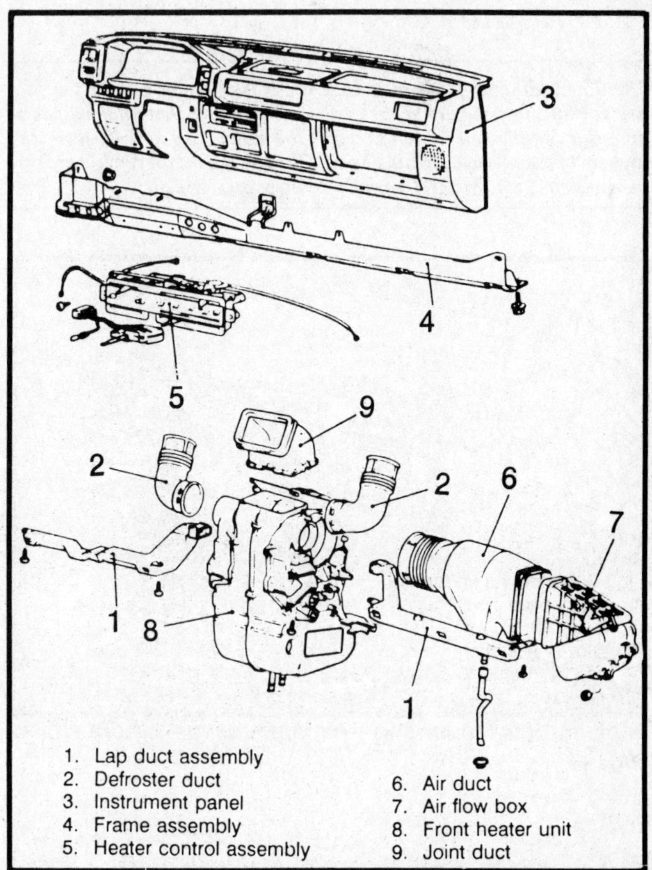

Heater assembly—Van shown—others similar

VAN

1. Disconnect the negative battery cable. Drain the cooling system.
2. Place a pan under the heater hose connection at the heater unit and remove the lower heater hoses from the heater core.
3. Remove the right side lap heater duct.
4. Remove the upper defroster duct.
5. Remove the instrument cluster.
6. Remove the complete instrument panel.
7. Remove the lower instrument panel crossbrace.
8. Disconnect and tag the cables at the heater assembly.
9. Remove the heater assembly from the vehicle.
10. With the heater assembly removed, remove the heater core cover.
11. Remove the heater core from the heater assembly.
12. Installation is the reverse of the removal procedure. Use care not to pinch any hoses or cable during installation.

Blower Motor

Removal and Installation

PICKUPS WITHOUT A/C

1. Remove the instrument cluster panel.
2. Disconnect the cable between the motor and the heater unit.
3. Remove the three bolts holding the motor in the heater unit and pull out the fan.

NOTE: It may be necessary to disconnect the fan from the motor to remove them from under the dashboard.

4. Installation is the reverse of the removal procedure.

PICKUPS WITH A/C

CAUTION

The air conditioning system utilizes the blower motor assembly of the heater unit. However, it may be necessary to remove some of the air conditioning components to gain access to the motor. Use care when loosening any of the air conditioning hoses. The hoses contain refrigerant under pressure, which could severely damage eyes or skin.

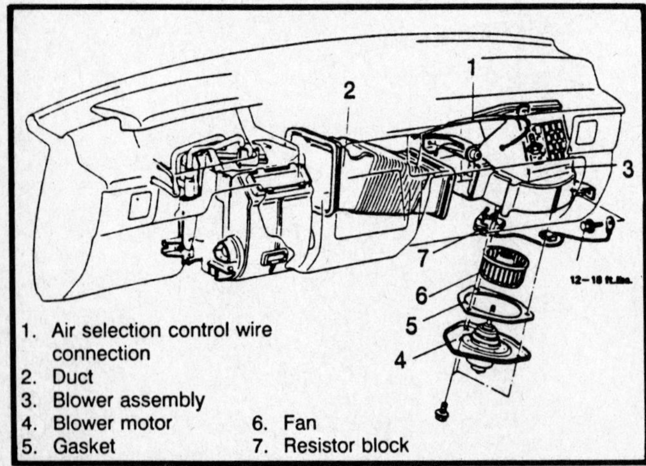

Blower motor mounting – pickup shown – others similar

MONTERO/RAIDER

1. Disconnect and tag the front wiring harness and blower motor coupling connectors.
2. Remove the lower mounting bolts of the blower assembly.
3. Remove the lap heater duct.
4. Remove the stopper of the glove box and push the glove box down.
5. Remove the "Recirc-Fresh" control wire and blower assembly mounting bolts.
6. Remove the blower assembly.
7. Installation is the reverse of the removal procedure.

VAN

1. Disconnect the negative battery cable.
2. Disconnect and tag the blower motor wiring at the heater assembly.
3. Remove the blower motor from the heater box.
4. Remove the blower motor cage and install it on the new motor.
5. Installation is the reverse of the removal procedure.

Cooling Fans

Inspection

All vehicles with A/C use a belt driven cooling fan equipped with a fan clutch. Vehicles without A/C use the same fan but it is not equipped with a clutch. Whenever the fan is removed, inspect the fan for cracked or broken fan blades. Inspect the fan clutch for signs of leaking fluid. With the cooling fan and clutch installed, check the fan clutch by rotating the fan and checking for any resistance.

Removal and Installation

ALL MODELS

1. If the vehicle is equipped with A/C, remove the upper radiator shroud.
2. Remove the four fan clutch to water pump mounting bolts and remove the fan and clutch as an assembly.
3. Remove the fan clutch to fan mounting bolts and separate the fan from the clutch.
4. Installation is the reverse of the removal procedure. Torque the fan to clutch and clutch to water pump bolts to 7–9 ft. lbs.

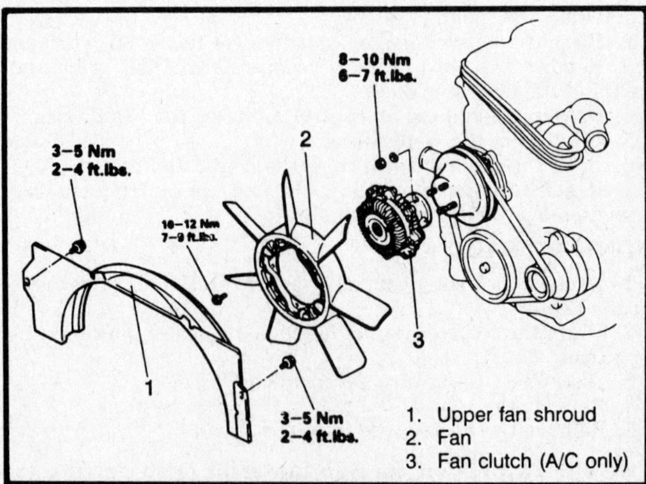

Cooling fan mounting – all models

FUEL SYSTEMS

Carburetor

FEEDBACK CARBURETORS

Removal and Installation

1. Remove the solenoid valve wiring.
2. Disconnect the air cleaner breather hose, air duct and vacuum tube.
3. Remove the air cleaner.
4. Remove the air cleaner case.
5. Disconnect the accelerator and shift cables (automatic transmission) at the carburetor.
6. Disconnect the purge valve hose.
7. Remove the vacuum compensator and fuel lines.
8. Drain the cooling system.
9. Remove the water hose between the carburetor and the cylinder head.
10. Remove the carburetor.
11. Installation is the reverse of the removal procedure. Check for water and fuel leaks when finished.

Adjustment

IDLE SPEED AND MIXTURE

1. Remove the carburetor from the engine. To gain accessto the mixture screws, drill out the casting around the mixture screw using a $^5/_{64}$ in. drill.
2. Start and run the engine at idle until it reaches normal operating temperature.
3. Check the tune-up specifications chart or the underhood decal for the correct curb idle speed.
4. Connect a tachometer and adjust the idle speed screw until the correct rpm is reached. Connect a CO meter.
5. If a CO meter is not available, adjust carburetor to the correct curb idle speed. Watch the tachometer scale, listen to the engine and slowly turn the idle mixture screw clockwise. When the engine drops in rpm, stop. Then, slowly turn the mixture screw counterclockwise until once again a drop in rpm or engine roughness is noted. A point, in between the clockwise or counterclockwise positions that gives the highest rpm or smoothest running engine, is the best setting.
6. Check and readjust the curb idle speed, if necessary.
7. If a CO meter is available, adjust the mixture until the CO meter reads 0.1–0.3 % at idle.

FUEL INJECTION

Relieve Pressure

VAN

CAUTION

Before working on any part of the fuel system, the fuel pressure must be relieved. Failure to do so may result in a sudden spray of fuel causing injury and an unsafe condition.

1. Raise and support the vehicle safely.
2. Disconnect the electric fuel pump connector, located at fuel tank.
2. Lower the vehicle. Start the engine and allow it to run until it stalls.
3. Turn the key to the OFF position.
4. Raise and support the vehicle safely. Connect the fuel pump connector.
5. Lower the vehicle. Do not turn the key to the ON position until all work on the fuel system is complete.

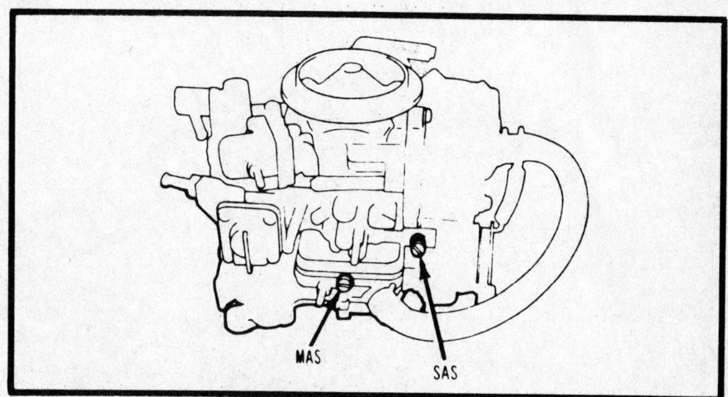

Carburetor idle adjustments

FUEL INJECTORS

Removal and Installation

1. Relieve the fuel pressure.
2. Disconnect the negative battery cable.
3. Disconnect and tag the wire connectors at the fuel injectors.
4. Disconnect and plug the fuel inlet hose at the fuel pressure regulator.
5. Disconnect the high pressure hose on the fuel rail. Save the O-rings for installation.
6. Remove the fuel injector rail mounting bolts.
7. Remove the fuel rail with the injectors.
8. Remove the injector from the fuel rail.
9. To install, lightly coat the O-ring on the injector with engine oil.
10. Install the injector in the fuel rail.
11. The remainder of the installation is the reverse of the removal procedure.
12. Torque the high pressure hose and the fuel rail mounting bolts to 7–9 ft.

IDLE SPEED

1. Run the engine until it reaches normal operating temperature. Make sure all lights and accessories are turned off.
2. Apply the parking brake and block the wheels. Place the transmission in neutral and stop the engine.
3. Attach a tachometer and timing light. Start the engine and increase the engine speed to 2000–3000 rpm several times, return the engine to idle and check the ignition timing, adjust if necessary.
4. Remove the rubber cap covering the idle speed adjuster switch, leaving the cable connector connected. The idle adjuster switch is located on the throttle linkage. Adjust the idle speed.

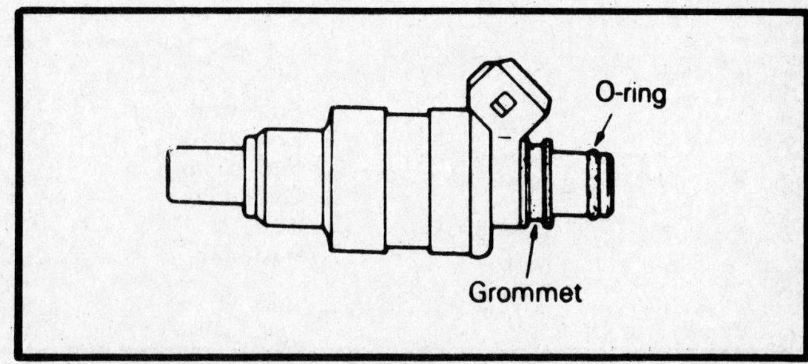

Fuel injector showing O-ring and grommet placement

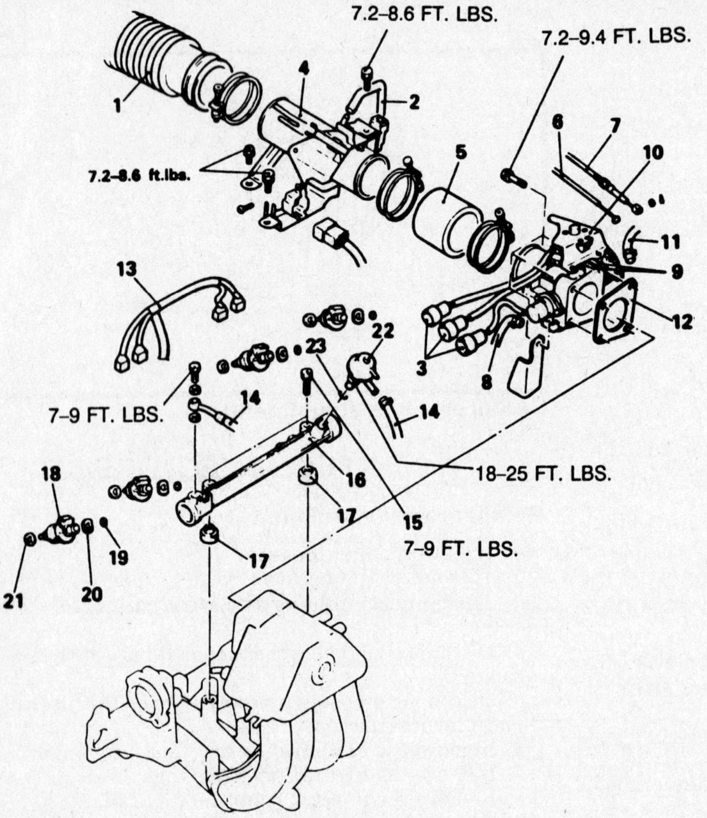

1. Air intake hose
2. Breather hose
3. Wiring harness connector
4. Air intake pipe
5. Air hose
6. Accelerator cable
7. Kick down cable
8. Water hose
9. Vacuum hose connection
10. Throttle body
11. Water hose
12. Gasket
13. Fuel injector harness connector
14. High pressure fuel hose
15. Bolt
16. Fuel delivery pipe
17. Insulator
18. Fuel injector
19. O-ring
20. Grommet
21. Insulator
22. Fuel pressure regulator
23. O-ring

2.4L engine fuel injection system—exploded view

1. Hose clamp (2)
2. Fuel hose
3. Bolt (2)
4. Fuel pump
5. Gasket (2)
6. Insulator
7. Push rod

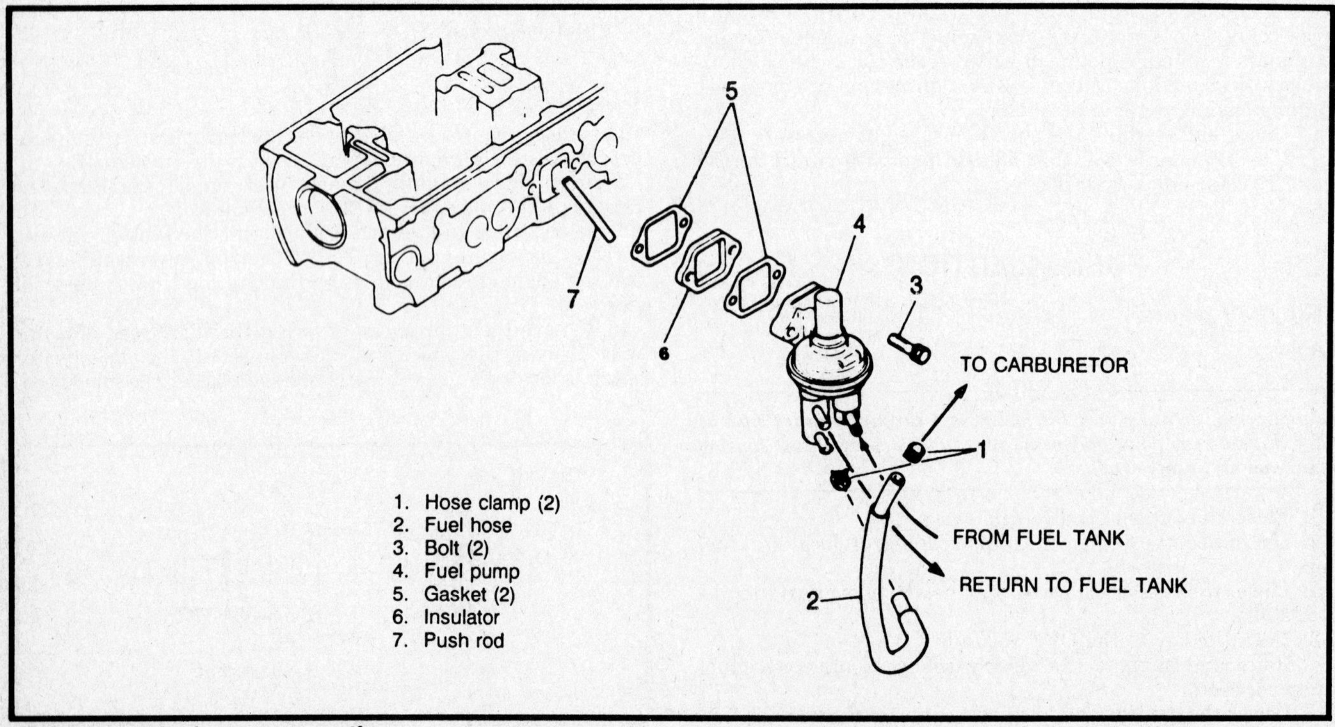

Mechanical fuel pump mounting

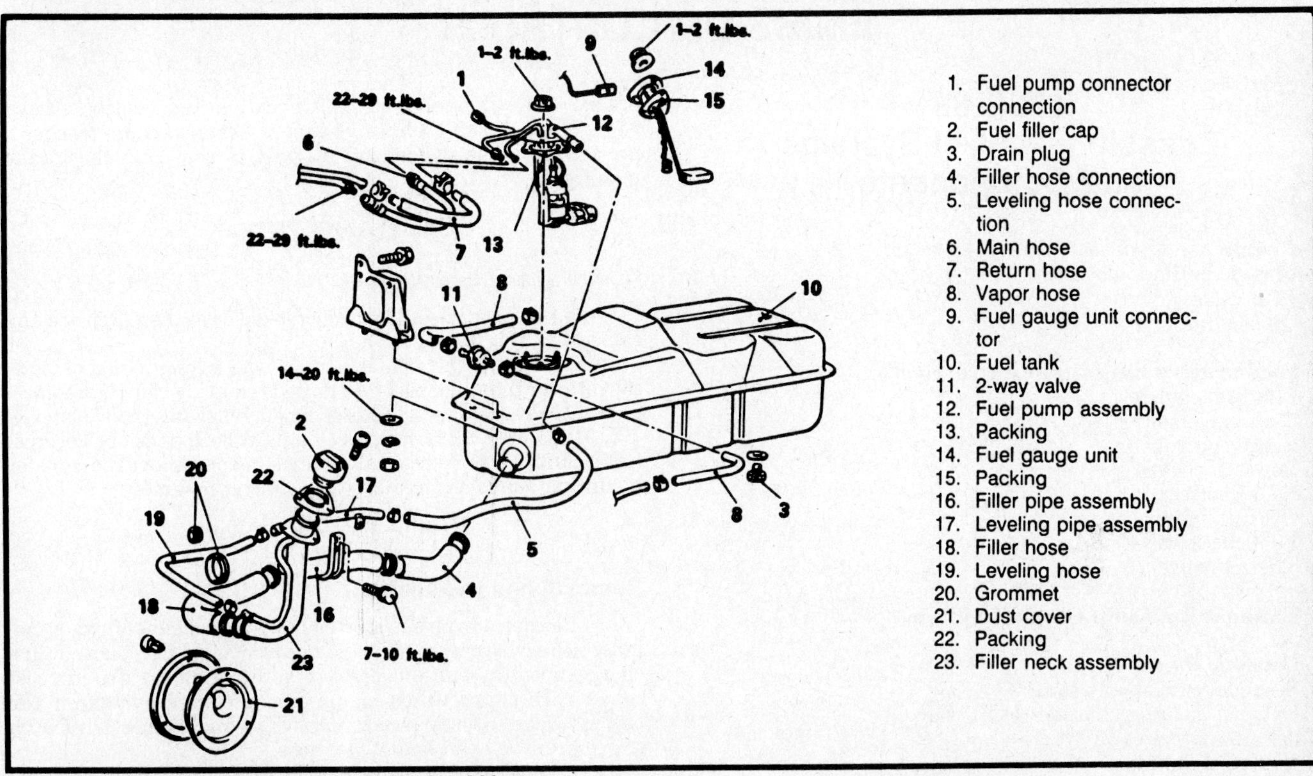

Electrical fuel pump mounted in tank of Van

5. If the idle adjustment screw must be turned more than 1 turn during adjustment, disconnect the connector from the speed adjust switch and plug it into the dummy terminal on the injector base. Adjust to correct idle speed and reconnect to the idle switch. Remove the tachometer and timing light.

Fuel Pump

With the exception of the Mitsubishi Van, all vehicles use a mechanical fuel pump.

MECHANICAL

Removal and Installation

1. Disconnect and plug the fuel lines at the fuel pump.
2. Remove the fuel pump mounting bolts and remove the fuel pump, insulator and gasket.
3. Clean and inspect the fuel pump sealing surface on the engine.
4. Using a new insulator and gasket coated with sealer, install the fuel pump on the engine.
5. Connect the fuel lines, run the engine and check for leaks.

ELECTRICAL

Removal and Installation

Removal and installation of the electric fuel pump requires that the fuel tank be removed from the vehicle.

1. Relieve the fuel pressure. Disconnect the negative battery cable. Remove the fuel tank filler cap.
2. Raise and support the vehicle safely.
3. Remove the fuel tank drain plug and drain the fuel tank into a suitable container. Install the drain plug after the tank is empty.
4. Disconnect the fuel pump connector at the fuel pump.
5. Disconnect the fuel filler hose from the fuel tank.
6. Disconnect the fuel leveling hose above the fuel filler hose.
7. Disconnect the fuel feed and return hoses at the fuel pump.
8. Disconnect the fuel guage sending unit connector.
9. Disconnect the two-way valve and fuel vapor hose at the fuel tank.
10. Support the fuel tank and remove the fuel tank retaining straps. Remove the fuel tank from the vehicle.
11. Remove the fuel pump/sending unit retaining ring and remove the fuel pump from the fuel tank.
12. Inspect the packing around the fuel pump to tank surface. Replace if necessary.
13. Installation is the reverse of the removal procedure.
14. Check for fuel leaks when finished.

EMISSION CONTROLS

1982–88 Emission Control Systems and Components

Crankcase Emission Control System
Closed ventilation system
PCV valve
Oil separator

Evaporative Emission Control System
Charcoal canister
Carbon element
Purge control valve
Bowl vent valve
Fuel filler cap relief valve
Overfill limiter (two-way valve)
Fuel check valve
Thermo valve

Exhaust Emission Control System
Jet valve
Catalytic converter
Secondary sir supply source
Exhaust gas recirculation (EGR) valve
Jet air control valve
Heated air intake
Fuel control system (ECI)
Deceleration device
Coasting air valve (CAV)
Air switching valve (ASV)
Deceleration spark advance
Idle speed control system (A/C models)
High altitude compensation system
Tamper-proof choke and mixture

Crankcase Emission Control Systems

A closed crankcase ventilation system is used to prevent blow-by gases from escaping into the atmosphere. The system has a positive (one-way) crankcase vent valve (PCV valve) at the rocker arm cover. Blow-by gases are drawn through two passages; one by a rubber vent hose from the rocker arm cover through the PCV valve into the intake manifold and the other by a rubber hose from the rocker arm cover to the air cleaner.

Removal and Installation

1. Check the PCV valve for operation, the oil separator and oil return pipe (if equipped) for clogging and leaks.
2. Check the PCV valve by removing the valve and the hose from the rocker cover while the engine is at idle speed. If the valve is not clogged, a hissing noise will be heard and strong vacuum will be felt when a finger is placed over the bottom of the valve.
3. Shut off the engine and disconnect the PCV valve from the hose. Blow through the threaded end. If air will not pass through, the valve is clogged and replacement will be required.

Evaporative Emission Control System

When the engine is not operating, fuel vapor generated inside the fuel tank is absorbed and stored in the charcoal canister. When the engine is running, the fuel vapor absorbed in the canister is drawn into the air intake hose through the purge valve. The purge valve is kept closed at idle when vacuum reaches a pre-set value the valve opens. On carbureted models, a bowl vent valve controls carburetor vapors. When vacuum reaches a pre-set level, the vapors are allowed to pass into the intake manifold.

CANISTER

Removal and Installation

1. Replace any hoses that are cracked or broken. Replace any canister that is damaged.
2. When the canister is in service over a long period of time, the interior filter will become clogged requiring canister replacement. Always replace the hoses when renewing the canister.
3. Disconnect all hoses and clamps at both ends of the canister(s) and from the purge valve. Unclamp or remove the canister mounting bands and remove the canister assembly.

THERMO VALVE

Removal and Installation

1. The thermo valve is located on the intake manifold or cylinder head where it's bottom will be immersed in coolant. It discharges into the purge control valve located near the charcoal canister. Disconnect the vacuum/pressure line coming from the thermo valve to the purge control valve and connect a vacuum gauge into the open end of the hose.
2. The engine must be overnight cold. Start the engine and run it at about 2000 rpm to get the throttle past the purge port.
3. The gauge should indicate zero vacuum pressure when the engine is started and, by the time thermostat opens and coolant begins to circulate in the radiator, there should be pressure or vacuum. Replace the thermo valve if pressure and/or vacuum exists.

PURGE CONTROL VALVE

Removal and Installation

1. Once the intake vacuum exists and the hose connections are inspected, the purge control valve can be tested. With the engine warm, disconnect the large vacuum line passing from the purge valve to the canister. Use a vacuum gauge to verify that when the engine speed is increased, there is vacuum at the end of the line.
2. If there is no vacuum, verify the test by disconnecting the large vacuum line going into the purge control valve from the intake manifold. If there is vacuum there when the engine is revved, but not on the canister side of the purge control valve and the thermo valve is working, replace the canister purge valve.

Exhaust Emission Control System

Exhaust emissions are controlled by engine modifications and addition of special control components. All engines contain jet air valves, one for each cylinder and are installed in the cylinder head. A jet air passage is provided in the carburetor, intake manifold and cylinder head. Air flows through the passages and when the jet valve opens, into combustion chambers. Air provided by the jet valve leans out the fuel mixture.

Catalytic Converters are used for the purpose of decreasing harmful emissions. Secondary air systems are used to supply air into the exhaust system for the purpose of promoting oxidation of exhaust emissions into the converter. Exhaust gas recirculation (EGR) is used to reduce oxides of nitrogen in the exhaust by recirculating a portion of the exhaust gases back into the intake manifold below the air/fuel source.

PULSE AIR FEED (SECONDARY AIR)

Removal and Installation

1. Remove the hose connected to the air cleaner and check for vacuum. If no vacuum is present, check for cracked or broken hoses.

EGR VALVE

Removal and Installation

1. Check the vacuum hose to the EGR valve for cracks or cuts, replace any if necessary.
2. Start the engine and run at idle speed (cold engine). Run the engine to 2500 rpm and check the secondary EGR valve. If the secondary EGR valve is operating the thermo valve is defective.
3. Warm the engine to about 131°F. The secondary EGR valve should operate when the engine is at 2500 rpm. If the valve is not operating, check the EGR control valve and the thermo valve.
4. Disconnect the green stripped hose from the thermo valve. Connect a hand vacuum pump to the thermo valve and apply vacuum. If no vacuum passes, the thermo valve is good.
5. Disconnect the green stripped hose from the carburetor fitting and connect the hose to the hand pump.
6. Open the sub EGR valve by hand and apply approx. 6 in. of vacuum with the hand pump.
7. If the idle speed becomes unstable, the secondary EGR valve is operating properly. If the idle speed remains unchanged, the EGR valve is not working. Replace the EGR valve.

TROUBLESHOOTING

Symptoms

NOTE: Vacuum hoses and wiring connections are problems commonly found with emission systems. However, when diagnosing a system, all components of the system should be checked. Symptoms and solutions given, only pertain to the emission system. Other problems may exist with other non-emission systems that cause the same symptom.

Engine cranks, but won't start

1. Vacuum hose disconnected or damaged.
2. Mixture control valve stuck open.
3. EGR valve stuck open.
4. Purge control system malfunction.

Rough idle or engine stalls

1. Vacuum hose disconnected or damaged.
2. High altitude compensation system faulty.
3. EGR valve stuck open.
4. Faulty purge control system.
5. Faulty bowl vent valve.
6. Mixture control valve open.
7. Faulty PCV system.

Hesitation or poor acceleration

1. Exhaust gas recirculation system faulty.
2. High altitude compensation system faulty.
3. Thermo valve faulty.
4. Intake air temperature system faulty.

Excessive oil consumption

1. PCV line clogged.

Poor fuel mileage

1. Intake air temperature system faulty.
2. Exhaust gas recirculation system faulty.
3. High altitude compensation system faulty.

Maintenance Lamp Reset

Procedure

ALL MODELS

1. Disconnect the negative battery cable.
2. Remove the instrument cluster bezel.
3. The switch to reset the lamp is located on the rear of the speedometer.
4. Reset the switch by sliding the lever to the opposite side, connect the negative battery cable and confirm the the lamp is off.
5. Install the instrument cluster bezel.

ENGINE MECHANICAL

Engine

Removal and Installation

ALL MODELS WITH GASOLINE ENGINES EXCEPT VAN

1. Working inside the engine compartment, remove the splash shield below the engine. Drain the cooling system.
2. Disconnect the battery cables, negative first and remove the battery.
3. Disconnect the ground strap. Identify and remove the wiring of the ignition coil, fuel cut-off solenoid valve, alternator, starter motor, water temperature gauge unit and oil pressure gauge unit.
4. Disconnect the air cleaner breather hose. Remove the air cleaner and disconnect the hot air duct and the vacuum hose.
5. Disconnect the accelerator control cable. For automatic transmissions, disconnect the transmission control rod.
6. Disconnect the radiator hoses.
7. Disconnect the heater hose.
8. Disconnect the exhaust pipe from the exhaust manifold. The muffler pipe bracket should be detached at the transmission.
9. Disconnect the fuel hoses and vapor hose.
10. Remove the radiator and radiator cowl. Four bolts hold the radiator in place. On vehicles with automatic transmissions, remove and plug the two oil cooling pipes in the bottom of the radiator.
11. For vehicles with four and five speed transmissions:
    a. Remove the lock screws and lift up the console box, inside the driver's compartment. On vehicles without a console box, remove the carpet.
    b. Remove the attaching screws and lift out the dust cover retainer plate.
    c. Pull up the dust cover and remove the four attaching bolts holding the shift lever to the transmission extension housing. Remove the shift lever control assembly.

NOTE: On four speed transmissions, remove the gear shift lever with the lever in 2nd speed position. On five

speed transmissions, place the lever in 1st speed position.

12. Mark the position of the hood retaining bolts in relation to the hood and remove the hood.
13. Raise and support the vehicle safely.
14. Disconnect the speedometer cable and backup light switch wiring from the transmission.
15. For vehicles with manual transmissions, disconnect the clutch cable from the transmission by removing the cotter key and sliding it off the arm. Disconnect the cable from the cable bracket. For automatic transmissions, remove shift linkage between transmission and shift lever.
16. Drain the transmission.
17. Remove the bolts holding the rear of the driveshaft to the rear axle. Remove the two nuts holding the center bearing assembly of the driveshaft to the frame and pull the driveshaft out of the rear of the transmission.
18. On two wheel drive models, support the transmission and remove the bolts holding the front motor mounts. For four wheel drive models, support the transfer case and, after removing the transfer case mounting bracket and support insulator, remove the plate from the side frame. Detach the transfer case mounting bracket from the transfer case.
19. Unbolt the rear transmission mount crossmember and remove the two bolts holding it to the transmission. Remove the crossmember.
20. Attach steel lifting cables to the engine front and rear hangers and attach the cables to a suitable hoist.
21. Have an assistant slowly lower the transmission and pull the engine/transmission out of the vehicle by tilting it upwards and pulling forward.

NOTE: If the transmission will not clear the steering relay rod, raise it until the bell housing is above the rod, then remove the engine/transmission from the vehicle.

22. Installation is the reverse of the removal procedure. Adjust all transmission and carburetor linkages as detailed in the appropriate sections. Install and adjust the hood. Refill the engine, transmission and radiator to capacity.

ALL MODELS WITH TURBO DIESEL ENGINE

1. Disconnect the negative battery cable. Matchmark and remove the hood. Drain the cooling system.
4. Remove the air cleaner duct. Remove the heater hoses.
5. Disconnect the throttle cable.
6. Disconnect and plug the fuel lines. Disconnect the water level sensor connector and remove the fuel filter.
7. Remove the power steering pump, if equipped.
8. Disconnect and tag the glow plug system cable and the gauge unit harness connectors.
9. Disconnect the engine ground cable. Disconnect and tag the alternator wiring harness.
10. Disconnect and tag the starter motor wiring harness.
11. Separate the clutch release cylinder from the transmission.
12. Disconnect and plug the engine oil cooler hoses. Remove the radiator.
13. Disconnect the brake booster vacuum hose.
14. Disconnect the oil pressure switch harness or the oil pressure gauge unit harness.
15. Raise and support the vehicle safely. Drain the engine oil.
16. Disconnect the front exhaust pipe from the exhaust manifold.
17. On 4WD models, remove the engine and transfer case skid plates and under cover. On 2WD models, remove the under cover.
18. Disconnect the speedometer cable at the transmission.
19. For 2WD models, disconnect the back-up light switch harness. On 4WD models, disconnect the backup light switch harness and 4WD indicator light switch harness.
20. Matchmark and remove the driveshafts.
21. Remove the gearshift lever assembly.
22. Support the transmission.
23. Detach the rear insulator from the transmission. Remove the No. 2 crossmember.
24. On 4WD models, support the transfer case and, after removing the transfer case mounting bracket and support insulator, remove the plate from the side frame. Detach the transfer case mounting bracket from the transfer case.
25. Remove the engine mounting nuts from the front insulators. Using a suitable engine lifting device, raise and remove the engine and transmission assembly diagonally from the engine compartment.
26. Installation is the reverse of the removal procedure. Adjust the clutch and accelerator controls, align the hood and add coolant, engine oil and transmission lubricant. Check all controls for proper function before road testing the vehicle.

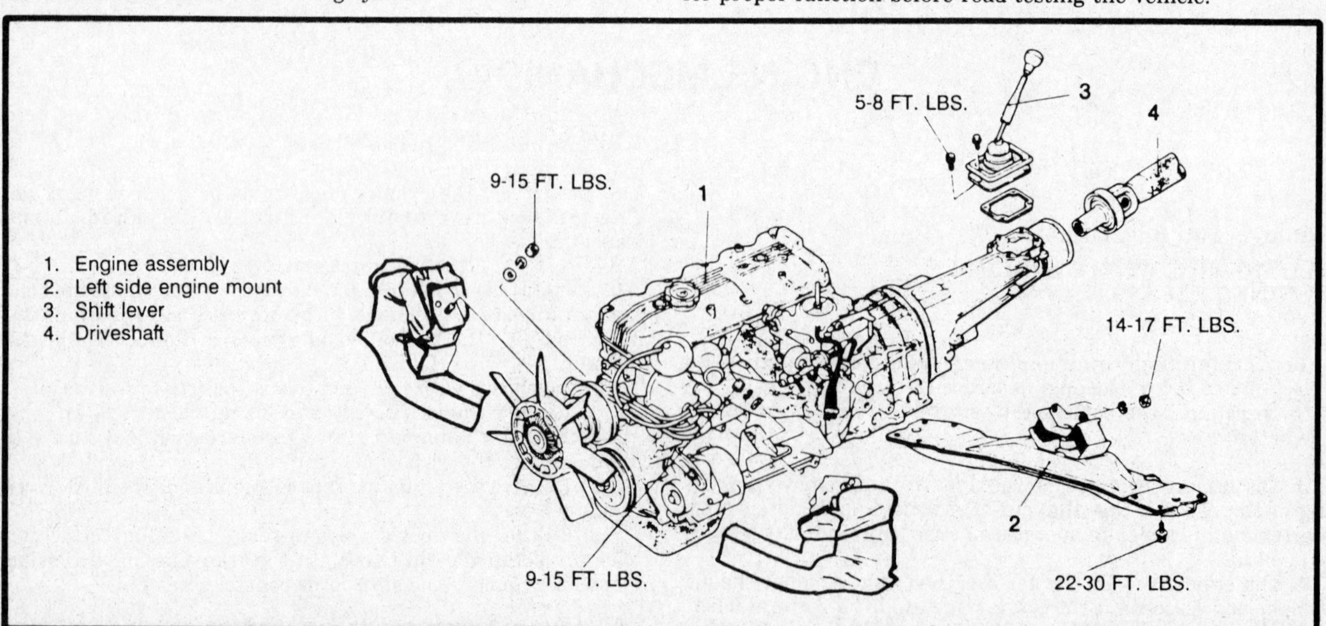

2WD Pickup engine mounting-others similar

VAN

1. Disconnect the negative battery cable. Drain the cooling system.

NOTE: In order to remove the engine, the seat underframe inside the vehicle must be removed.

2. To remove the seat and frame, remove the drivers seat. Remove the parking brake lever and fuel tank filler door release lever.
3. Remove the battery cover. Remove the bolts retaining the seat underframe in place. Remove the seat underframe.
4. Remove the radiator. Remove the radiator fan shroud. Remove the fan assembly. Remove the power steering pump assembly.
5. Remove the upper and lower radiator hoses. Disconnect and tag all electrical connections from the engine. Disconnect the oxygen sensor harness connector connections.
6. Disconnect the accelerator cable connection. Disconnect the kickdown cable connection, if equipped.
7. Disconnect and tag all vacuum hoses. Disconnect the power brake vacuum hose line. Remove the air condition compressor without disconnecting the refrigerant lines. Support the compressor out of the way.
8. Raise and support the vehicle safely. Remove the strut bars. Remove the starter asembly.
7. Disconnect the speedometer cable at the transmission assembly. Disconnect the exhaust pipe at the exhaust manifold.
8. Disconnect and tag the alternator and oil pressure switch electrical connectors. Disconnect and plug the automatic transmission lines, if equipped.
9. Disconnect and plug the fuel line hose. Disconnect the heater hoses. Disconnect the transmission control cable.
10. Matchmark and remove the driveshaft. Remove the engine mount bolts. Remove the transmission crossmember bolt.
11. Lower the vehicle. Using the proper lifting equipment, remove the assembly from the vehicle.
12. Installation is the reverse of the removal procedure.

Intake Manifold

Removal and Installation

ALL MODELS EXCEPT VAN

1. Disconnect the negative battery cable. Drain the cooling system.
2. Remove the air cleaner assembly with its hoses from the engine.
3. Disconnect the fuel line and EGR lines.
4. Disconnect the accelerator linkage. If equipped with automatic transmission, disconnect the automatic transmission shift cables at the carburetor.
5. Remove the water hose at the intake manifold and at the carburetor.
6. Disconnect the water temperature sending unit.
7. Remove the intake manifold mounting nuts and remove the intake manifold with the carburetor as an assembly.
8. Installation is the reverse of the removal procedure. Torque the manifold nuts to 11–14 ft. lb.

VAN

1. Disconnect the negative battery cable. Remove the air cleaner and duct hose assembly.

NOTE: In order to remove the intake manifold, the seat underframe must be removed from the vehicle.

2. Relieve the fuel pressure. Disconnect and plug the fuel lines, EGR lines, vacuum hoses and wire harness connectors at the intake manifold.
3. Disconnect and tag the throttle positioner solenoid and fuel cutoff solenoid wires.

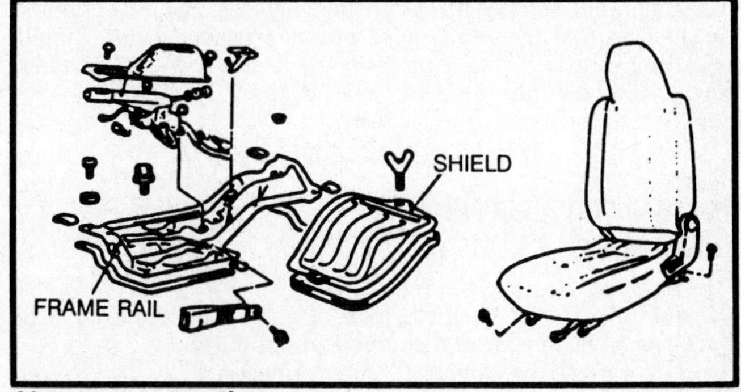

Van seat mounting

4. Disconnect the accelerator linkage and, if equipped with automatic transmission, the shift cables at the carburetor/injector.
5. Drain the cooling system.
6. Remove the water hose from the carburetor and cylinder head.
7. Remove the heater and water outlet hoses.
8. Disconnect the water temperature sending unit.
9. Starting with the outer bolts and working inwards, remove the manifold and carburetor/injector assembly mounting bolts and remove the manifold assembly.

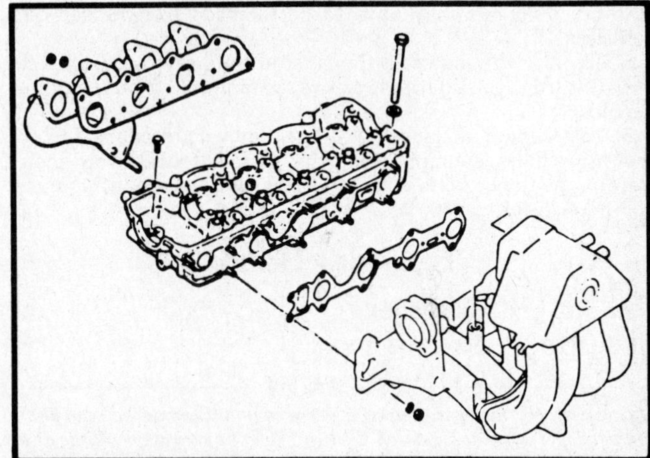

Intake and exhaust manifold mounting – 2.4L engine

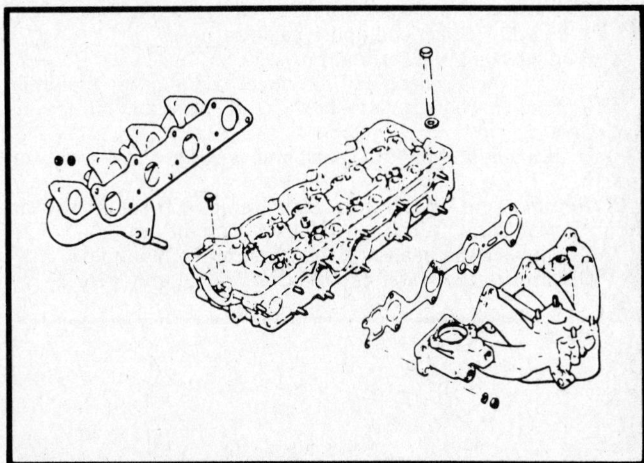

Intake and exhaust manifold mounting – 2.0L & 2.6L engines

10. Clean and inspect all mounting surfaces. Before reinstalling the manifold, coat both sides with new gasket sealer. Install mounting nuts/bolts starting from the center toward the ends. Torque the bolts and nuts to 11–14 ft. lbs.

Exhaust Manifold

Removal and Installation

ALL MODELS EXCEPT VAN

1. Remove the air cleaner.
2. Remove the heat shield from the exhaust manifold. Remove the EGR lines and reed valve, if equipped.
3. Disconnect the exhaust flange connection.
4. Remove the exhaust manifold to cylinder head mounting nuts and remove the exhaust manifold.
5. Clean and inspect the mounting surfaces of the exhaust manifold and cylinder head.
6. Installation is the reverse of the removal procedure. Torque the flange connection bolts to 11–18 ft. lbs. Torque the manifold bolts to 11–14 ft. lbs.

VAN

1. Disconnect the negative battery cable. Remove the air cleaner and duct hose assembly.
2. Remove the manifold heat stove and hose. Disconnect the EGR lines and reed valve, if equipped.
3. Disconnect the exhaust pipe bracket from the engine block.
4. Remove the exhaust pipe flange bolts from the manifold. One bolt and nut may have to be removed from under the vehicle.
5. Remove the manifold flange stud nuts starting from the ends toward the middle and remove the manifold from the cylinder head.
6. Installation is the reverse of the removal procedure. Install mounting nuts starting from the middle toward the ends. Torque the flange bolts to 11–18 ft. lbs. and the mounting nuts to 11–14 ft. lbs.

Cylinder Head

Removal and Installation

ALL MODELS EXCEPT VAN

CAUTION

Do not perform this operation on a warm engine. Remove the head bolts in the proper sequence. Loosen the head bolts in even steps a little at a time.

1. Disconnect the negative battery cable. Drain the cooling system and disconnect the upper radiator hose.
2. Remove the breather and purge hose.
3. Remove the air cleaner. Disconnect and plug the fuel line.
4. Remove the vacuum hose at the distributor and purge control valve.
5. Disconnect and tag the spark plug wires at the distributor cap.
6. Remove the distributor cap. Remove the distributor mounting nut and pull the distributor straight out.
7. Disconnect the heater hose at the intake manifold.
8. Disconnect the water temperature gauge unit wire.

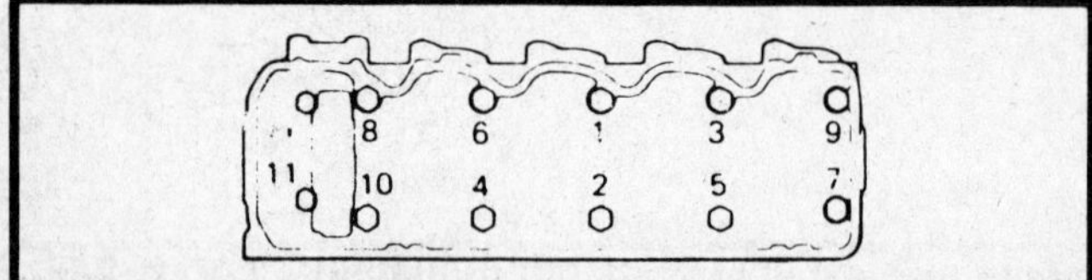

2.6L engine cylinder head bolt torque sequence

9. Place No. 1 piston in the Top Dead Center position to take pressure off the fuel pump rocker arm. Disconnect the fuel hoses and plug the line leading to the gas tank to prevent fuel leakage.
10. Remove the fuel pump mounting nuts and remove the fuel pump. Remove the insulator and gaskets.
11. Disconnect the exhaust pipe at the exhaust manifold flange.
12. Remove the rocker cover.
13. Remove the rocker cover breather and semicircular seal.
14. Loosen the camshaft sprocket bolt and turn the crankshaft until No. 1 piston is at top dead center on compression stroke (both valves closed).

NOTE: Never turn the engine over using the camshaft bolt: it puts undue strain on the chain and other components.

15. Remove the camshaft sprocket bolt and distributor drive gear. Remove the camshaft sprocket and allow it to rest in the chain on the holder below.
16. Starting with the outer bolts and working inwards, remove the cylinder head bolts. Head bolts should be loosened in two or three stages to prevent head warpage.

NOTE: The cylinder head assembly is located with two dowel pins, front and rear, on the cylinder block. When removing, be careful not to slide it, or twist the camshaft sprocket and chain.

17. Remove the cylinder head assembly and cylinder head gasket.
18. Clean all gasket surfaces of cylinder block and cylinder head.
19. Install a new cylinder head gasket. Install the cylinder head assembly.

NOTE: Do not apply sealant to the head gasket and do not reuse an old head gasket.

20. Install the TEN cylinder head bolts. The two bolts at the front extend into the timing case and are not included in the head bolt torqueing sequence. In the torqueing illustration,

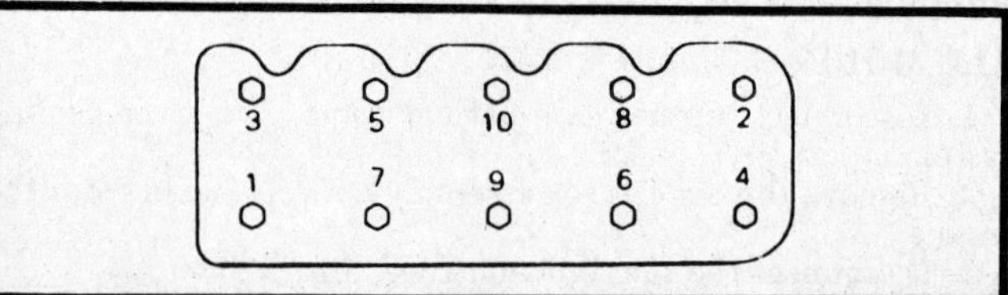

2.0L & 2.4L engines cylinder head bolt removal sequence

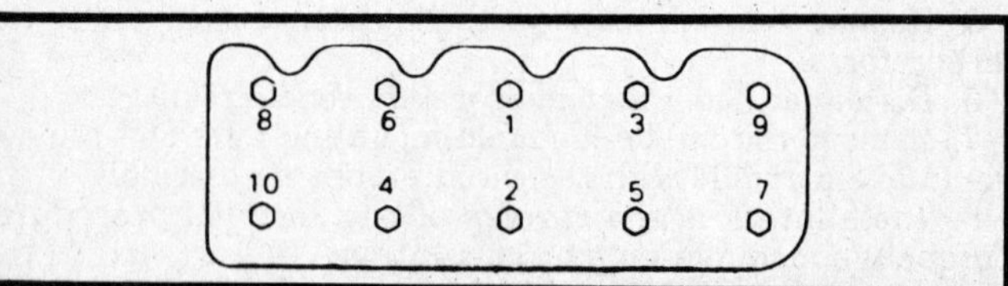

2.0L & 2.4L engines cylinder head bolt torque sequence

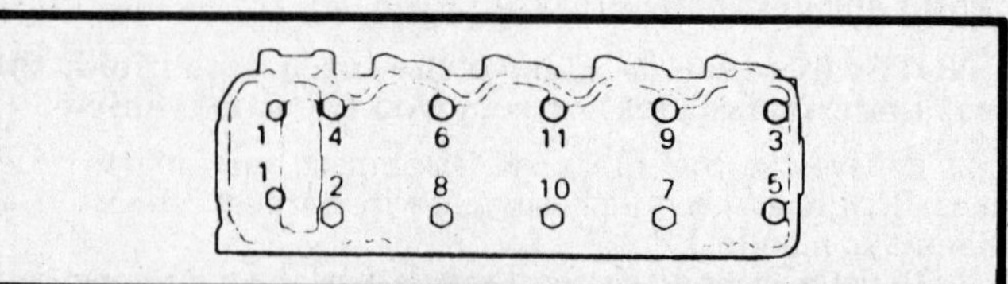

2.6L engine cylinder head bolt removal sequence

they are labeled No. 11. Starting at top center, Torque all ten cylinder head bolts to 35 ft. lbs. in the proper sequence. Repeat the torqueing procedure, this time torque the bolts to 65–72 ft. lbs. (cold engine), (72–80 ft. lbs. hot engine).

21. Torque the two front bolts (No. 11) to 11–15 ft. lbs.

22. Verify that No. 1 cylinder is at top dead center. Align the dowel pin in the end of the camshaft sprocket with the groove in the top of the front camshaft bearing cap and install the camshaft sprocket and chain while pulling up on the sprocket.

23. Install the distributor drive gear and the sprocket bolt.

24. Turn the crankshaft 90° backwards and torque the camshaft sprocket bolt to 37–43 ft. lbs. Slowly turn the engine over two times to make sure the valve timing is correct. If the engine locks at a certain point in these two revolutions, the valve timing is not correct. Repeat Steps 22–24.

CAUTION

Do not turn the engine over using the starter. If the valve timing is off, several of the valves could be bent.

25. Install the breather and semicircular seal to the cylinder head after applying sealant to surface contact points. Install the rocker cover with a new gasket.

26. Connect the exhaust pipe to the exhaust manifold flange. Torque the bolts to 11–18 ft. lbs.

27. Put No. 1 cylinder at top dead center and install the fuel pump with a new gasket and insulator. Connect all hoses.

28. Connect the water temperature gauge unit wire. Connect the heater hose to the intake manifold.

29. Install the distributor in the correct postion and spark plug cables.

30. Connect the vacuum hose to the distributor and purge control valve. Connect the upper radiator hose and fill the cooling system with coolant.

VAN

NOTE: In order to remove the cylinder head from the engine, the seat underframe must be removed from the vehicle.

1. Remove the drivers seat. Remove the parking brake lever and fuel tank filler door release lever.

2. Remove the battery cover. Remove the bolts retaining the seat underframe in place. Remove the seat underframe.

3. Turn the engine until the No. 1 piston is at TDC on the compression stroke. Disconnect the negative battery cable. Remove the air cleaner assembly.

4. Drain the engine coolant. Remove the upper radiator hose and disconnect the heater hoses.

5. Disconnect and tag the fuel lines, wiring harnesses, distributor vacuum lines, spark plug wires at spark plugs, purge valves, accelerator linkage and water temperature unit wire.

6. Remove the distributor and fuel pump from the cylinder head.

7. Remove the nuts connecting the exhaust pipe to the manifold. Lower the exhaust pipe.

8. Remove the exhaust manifold.

9. Remove the intake manifold assembly.

10. Remove the upper, outer front cover. Align the timing mark on the cylinder head with the mark on the camshaft sprocket (engine should already be on the No.1 piston TDC of the compression stroke.

11. Matchmark the timing belt with the timing mark on the camshaft sprocket, using a felt tip marker.

12. Remove the sprocket and insert a 2 in. piece of rubber or other material between the camshaft sprocket and sprocket holder on the lower front cover, to hold the sprocket and belt so that the valve timing will not be changed.

13. Remove the timing belt upper under cover and the rocker arm cover.

11. Remove the cylinder head mounting bolts and remove the cylinder head from the engine.

12. Clean the cylinder head and block mating surfaces and install a new cylinder head gasket.

13. Position the cylinder head on the engine block, engage the dowel pins front and rear and install the cylinder head bolts.

14. The bolts must be torqued to cold specification, which is 65–72 ft. lbs. in two equal stages. Using the proper sequence, torque the bolts in order to 32.5–36 ft. lbs. then, repeat the operation torquing them to the full torque.

15. Locate the camshaft in original position. Pull the camshaft sprocket and belt or chain upward and install on the camshaft.

NOTE: If the dowel pin and the dowel pin hole does not line up between the sprocket and the spacer or camshaft, move the camshaft by bumping either of the two projections provided at the rear of No. 2 cylinder exhaust cam of the camshaft, with a light hammer or other tool, until the hole and pin align. Be certain the crankshaft does not turn.

16. Install the camshaft sprocket bolt and distributor gear.

17. Install the timing belt upper front cover and spark plug wire support.

18. Apply sealant to the intake manifold gasket on both sides. Position the gasket and install the intake manifold. Torque the nuts to specifications. Be sure that no sealant enters the jet air passages.

19. Install the exhaust manifold gaskets and the manifold assembly. Torque the nuts to 11–14 ft. lbs.

20. Connect the exhaust pipe to the exhaust manifold and install the fuel pump. Install the purge valve.

21. Install the water temperature gauge wire, heater hoses and the upper radiator hose.

23. Connect the fuel lines, accelerator linkage, vacuum hoses and the spark plug wires.

24. Fill the cooling system and connect the negative battery cable. Install the distributor.

25. Temporarily adjust the valve clearance to the cold engine specifications.

26. Install the gasket on the rocker arm cover and temporarily install the cover on the engine.

27. Run the engine bring until it reaches normal operating temperature. Stop the engine and remove the rocker arm cover.

28. Adjust the valves to hot engine specifications.

29. Reinstall the rocker arm cover and tighten securely.

30. Install the air cleaner and purge valve hose.

Rocker Arms and Shaft

Removal and Installation

2.0L, 2.4L AND 2.6L ENGINES

NOTE: On 1985–88 gasoline engines with hydraulic lash adjusters, eight special holders are needed, Mitsubishi tool NO. MD998443 or equivalent, to retain the hydraulic lash adjusters when the valve train is disassembled. On the Van, it will be necessary to remove the drivers seat and the seat underframe.

1. On the Van, remove the drivers seat, parking brake lever and fuel tank filler door release lever.

2. Remove the battery cover. Remove the bolts retaining the seat underframe in place. Remove the seat underframe.

3. Disconnect the negative battery cable. Remove the rocker cover. On the Van, remove the upper timing belt cover. Loosen the camshaft sprocket bolt until it can be turned by hand. On the Van, turn the engine over until the camshaft sprocket timing mark lines up with the timing mark on the cylinder head. On other models, the timing mark on the sprocket ends up on the extreme right of the sprocket bolt as viewed from the front. In both cases, the TDC mark on the front crankshaft pulley must line up with the timing scale on the front cover.

4. Remove the camshaft sprocket bolt without allowing the

tension on the timing chain or belt to be lost. Place the sprocket in the sprocket holder of the front cover or lower timing belt cover. Make sure not to loose tension on the belt/chain. Make sure also that the crankshaft is not turned throughout the work. On the Van with hydraulic lash adjusters, put the special clips on the eight hydraulic adjusters at the outer ends of all eight rocker arms. Note that these clips go over the lash adjusters that actuate the large intake valves, not on the small adjusting screw for the smaller jet valves.

5. Loosen, but do not remove the camshaft bearing cap bolts. After all bolts have been loosened, remove them and, holding the ends so the assembly stays together, remove the rocker shaft assembly from the cylinder head. Note that on all models except the Van, the rearmost cam bearing cap is not associated with the rocker shafts and need not be removed.

6. Keep all parts in original order. Assemble the parts of the rocker assembly as follows:

a. Install left and right side rocker shafts into the front bearing cap. Notches in the ends of the shaft must be upward. Install the bolts for the front cap to retain the shafts in place. Note that the left rocker shaft is longer than the right rocker shaft.

b. Install the wave washer onto the left rocker shaft with the bulge forward. Then, coat the inner surfaces of the rockers and the upper bearing surfaces of the bearing caps with clean engine oil and assemble rockers, springs and the remaining bearing caps in the order in which removed. Note that the intake rockers are the only ones with the jet valve actuators. Note also that the rockers are labeled for cylinders 1–3 and 2–4 because the direction that the jet valve actuator faces, changes.

c. Use mounting bolts to hold the caps in place after each is assembled. When the assembly is complete, install it onto the head and start all mounting bolts into the head and tighten finger tight.

7. Torque the attaching bolts for the rocker assembly 14–15 ft. lbs. working from the center outward.

8. Without removing tension from the timing chain or belt, lift the sprocket out of the holder and position it against the front of the cam. Make sure the locating tang on the sprocket goes into the hole in the front of the cam.

9. Torque the bolt to 58–72 ft. lbs.

10. Adjust the valve lash.

11. Apply sealant to the top surface of the semicircular seals in the head and then install the valve cover. Install the upper timing belt cover on the Van.

Valve Arrangement

Front to Rear

2.0L, 2.4L AND 2.6L ENGINES

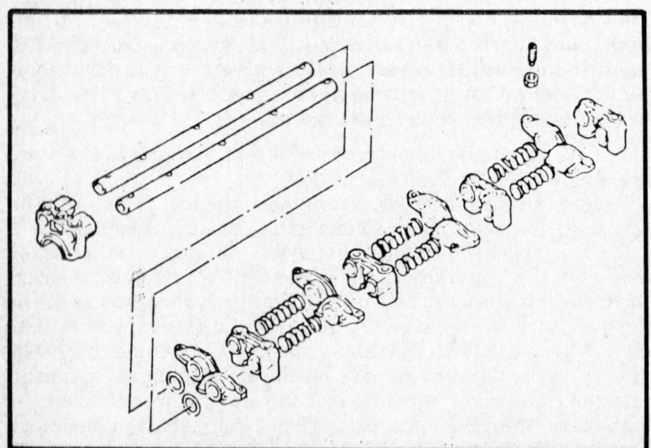

Rocker arms and shaft assembly—all engines

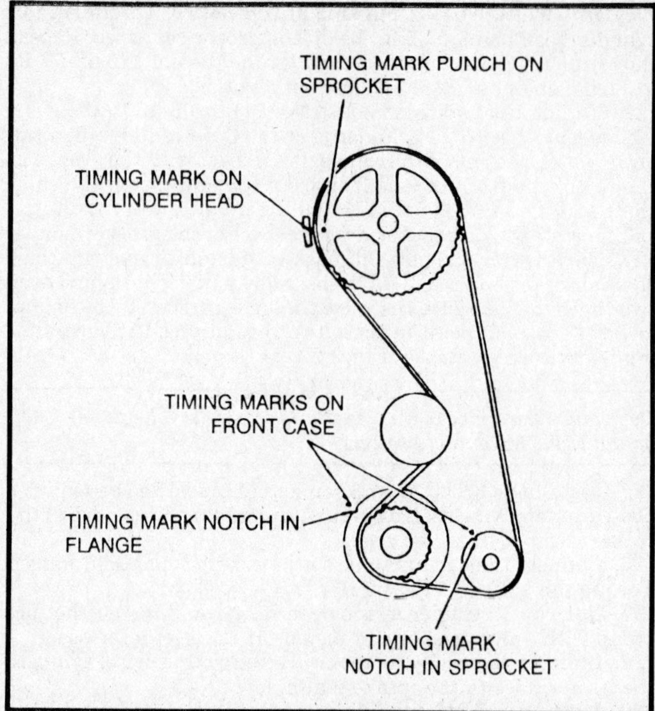

2.4L engine timing belt alignment marks

Valve Adjustment

Procedure

2.0L, 2.4L AND 2.6L ENGINES

Valve lash must be adjusted on all engines not equipped with hydraulic lash adjusters. All the engines except 1985–88 2.0L, 2.4L and 2.6L have solid valve train systems requiring valve adjustments.

All engines have a third valve called a Jet Valve located beside the intake valve of each cylinder. The Jet valve works off the intake valve rocker arm and injects a swirl of air into the combustion chamber to promote more complete burning of fuel. The Jet Valve must be adjusted on all engines, whether or not the engine has hydraulic lash adjusters. On engines equipped with hydraulic lash adjusters, only the Jet valve must be adjusted.

NOTE: When adjusting valve clearances, the jet valve must be adjusted before the intake valve.

1. Start the engine and allow it to reach normal operating temperature (170–190°F).

2. Stop the engine and remove the air cleaner. Remove rocker cover.

3. Disconnect the coil-to-distributor wire at the coil.

4. Watch the rocker arms for No. 1 cylinder and rotate the crankshaft until the exhaust valve is closing and the intake valve has just started to open. At this point, No. 4 cylinder will be at top dead center (TDC), commencing its firing stroke.

5. Loosen the lock nut on cylinder No. 4 intake valve and back off the intake valve adjusting screw 2 or more turns.

6. Loosen the lock nut on the jet valve adjusting screw.

7. Turn the jet valve adjusting screw counterclockwise and insert a 0.006 in. feeler gauge between the jet valve stem and the adjusting screw.

8. Tighten the adjusting screw until it touches the feeler gauge. Take care not to press in the valve while adjusting because the jet valve spring is very weak.

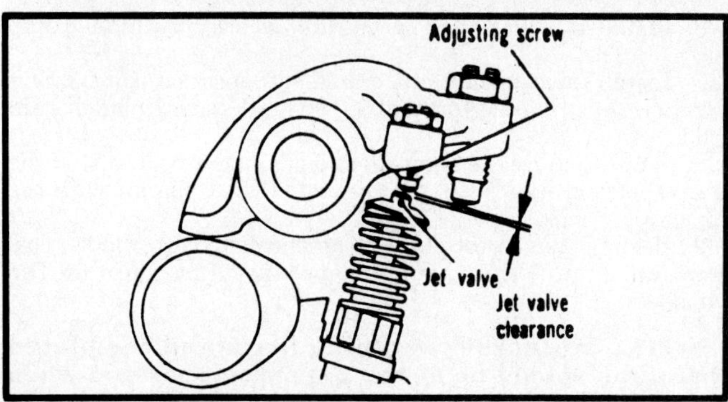

Jet valve adjustment

NOTE: If the adjusting screw is tight, special care must be taken to avoid pressing down on the jet valve when adjusting the clearance or a false reading will result.

9. Tighten the lock nut securely while holding the rocker arm adjusting screw with a screwdriver to prevent it from turning.
10. Make sure that a 0.006 in. feeler gauge can just be inserted between the jet valve and the rocker arm.
11. Adjust No. 4 cylinder's intake valve to 0.006 in. and exhaust valve to 0.010 in. Tighten the adjusting screw locknuts and recheck each clearance.
12. Perform Step 4 in conjunction with the chart to adjust the remaining three cylinders.
13. Replace the valve cover and all other components. Run the engine and check for oil leaks at the valve cover.

Valve adjustment

Exhaust Valve Closing	Adjust
No. 1 cylinder	No. 4 cylinder valves
No. 2 cylinder	No. 3 cylinder valves
No. 3 cylinder	No. 2 cylinder valves
No. 4 cylinder	No. 1 cylinder valves

Timing Chain, Cover, Silent Shafts and Tensioner

Removal and Installation

2.0L AND 2.6L ENGINES

NOTE: All pickup engines are equipped with two Silent Shafts which cancel the vertical vibrating force of the engine and the secondary vibrating forces, which include the sideways rocking of the engine due to the turning direction of the crankshaft and other rolling parts. The secondary vibrating forces can be cancelled if forces equivalent in magnitude but opposite in direction are produced. In these engines, the opposite force is produced by silent shafts located in the upper left and lower right sides in the front of the cylinder block. The shafts are driven by a duplex chain and are turned by the crankshaft. The silent shaft chain assembly is mounted in front of the timing chain assembly and must be removed to service the timing chain.

1. Disconnect the negative battery cable.
2. Drain the radiator and remove it from the vehicle.
3. Remove the cylinder head.
4. Remove the cooling fan, spacer, water pump pulley and belt.
5. Remove the alternator. Remove the water pump.
6. Raise and support the vehicle safely.
7. Remove the oil pan and screen. Remove the crankshaft pulley.
8. Remove the timing case cover.
9. Remove the chain guides, side (A), top (B), bottom (C), from the "B" chain (outer).
10. Remove the locking bolts from the "B" chain sprockets.
11. Remove the crankshaft sprocket, silent shaft sprocket and the outer chain.

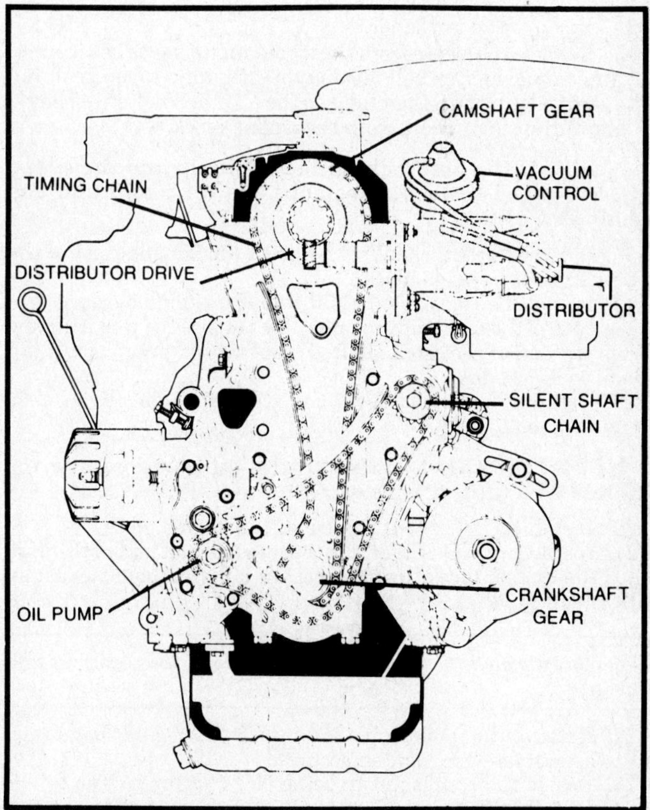

Front view of gasoline engine showing timing and silent shaft chains

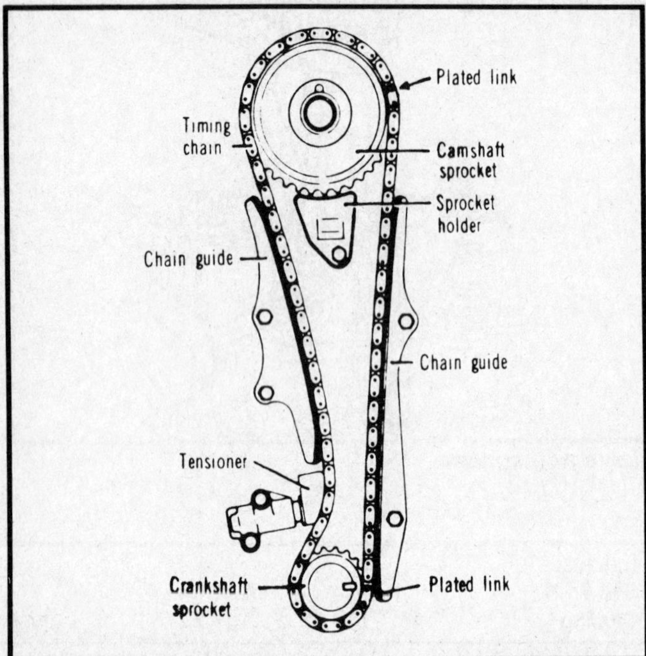

Timing chain installation: align the plated links with the punch-marks on the cam sprocket and the crankshaft sprocket

12. Remove the crankshaft and camshaft sprockets and the timing chain.
13. Remove the camshaft sprocket holder and the chain guides, both left and right.
14. Remove the tensioner.
15. Remove the sleeve from the oil pump. Remove the oil pump by first removing the bolt locking the oil pump driven gear and the right silent shaft, then remove the oil pump mounting bolts. Remove the silent shaft from the engine block.

NOTE: If the bolt locking the oil pump and the silent shaft is hard to loosen, remove the oil pump and the shaft as a unit.

16. Remove the left silent shaft thrust washer and remove the shaft from the engine block.
17. Install the right silent shaft into the engine block.
18. Install the oil pump assembly. Do not lose the woodruff key from the end of the silent shaft. Torque the oil pump mounting bolts to 6–7 ft. lbs.
19. Tighten the silent shaft and the oil pump driven gear mounting bolt.

NOTE: The silent shaft and the oil pump can be installed as a unit, if necessary.

20. Install the left silent shaft into the engine block.
21. Install a new O-ring on the thrust plate and install the unit into the engine block, using a pair of bolts without heads, as alignment guides.

CAUTION

If the thrust plate is turned to align the bolt holes, the O-ring may be damaged.

22. Remove the guide bolts and install the regular bolts into the thrust plate and tighten securely.
23. Rotate the crankshaft to bring No. 1 piston to TDC.
24. Install the cylinder head.
25. Install the sprocket holder and the right and left chain guides.
26. Install the tensioner spring and sleeve on the oil pump body.
27. Install the camshaft and crankshaft sprockets on the timing chain, aligning the sprocket punch marks to the plated chain links.
28. While holding the sprocket and chain as a unit, install the crankshaft sprocket over the crankshaft and align it with the keyway.
29. Keeping the dowel pin hole on the camshaft in a vertical position, install the camshaft sprocket and chain on the camshaft.

NOTE: The sprocket timing mark and the plated chain link should be at the 2–3 o'clock position when correctly installed. The chain must be aligned in the right and left chain guides with the tensioner pushing against the chain. The tension for the inner chain is predetermined by spring tension.

30. Install the crankshaft sprocket for the outer or "B" chain.
31. Install the two silent shaft sprockets and align the punched mating marks with the plated links of the chain.
32. Holding the two shaft sprockets and chain, install the outer chain in alignment with the mark on the crankshaft sprocket. Install the shaft sprockets on the silent shaft and the oil pump driver gear. Install the lock bolts and recheck the alignment of the punch marks and the plated links.
33. Temporarily install the chain guides, side (A), top (B) and bottom (C).
34. Tighten side (A) chain guide securely.
35. Tighten bottom (B) chain guide securely.
36. Adjust the position of the top (B) chain guide, after shaking the right and left sprockets to collect any chain slack, so that when the chain is moved toward the center, the clearance between the chain guide and the chain links will be approximately $^9/_{64}$ inch. Tighten the top (B) chain guide bolts.
37. Install the timing chain cover using a new gasket, being careful not to damage the front seal.
38. Using a new gasket, install the oil screen and oil pan. Torque the bolts to 4.5–5.5 ft. lbs.
39. Install the crankshaft pulley, alternator and accessory belts and the distributor.
40. Install the oil pressure switch, if removed. Connect the negative battery cable.
41. Install the fan blades, radiator, fill the cooling system and run the engine. Check for oil and water leaks.

Silent Shafts

Removal and Installation

2.4L ENGINE

NOTE: A special oil seal guide, MD998285 or equivalent is necessary to complete this operation.

1. Disconnect the negative battery cable. Remove the timing belt covers, timing belts and sprockets.
2. Drain the oil and remove the oil filter. Remove the oil pan and gasket. Remove the oil pump pickup and gasket.
3. Remove the oil pressure relief plunger plug and gasket. Remove the spring and plunger from the oil filter bracket. Remove the four bracket mounting bolts and remove the oil filter mount and gasket.
4. Remove the cap and gasket that cover the oil pump driven gear shaft. This is located on the right side of the front case at the front of the engine, just above the protruding silent shaft.
5. Using a long socket, remove the retaining bolt from the oil pump driven gear located behind the plug removed earlier.
6. Remove the mounting bolts for the front case and remove it from the block. Remove the front case gasket. Slide the silent shafts from the block, noting their installation angles.

7. Inspect the silent shaft bearing journals for signs of excessive wear of seizure. If there are signs of critical wear problems, the bushings should also be inspected. The bushings may be replaced by pulling them out and pressing new ones in, using special tools. This is done with the crankshaft removed, since it normally is required only at time of major engine overhaul.

8. Lubricate the silent shaft bearing journals with clean engine oil and install the shafts into the block. Insert the shafts so they are positioned as they were when removed.

9. Install a special seal guide to the crankshaft, MD998285-01 or equivalent so the smaller diameter faces outward. Coat the outer diameter of the seal with clean engine oil. Install a new front case gasket. Install the front case by carefully positioning the crankshaft seal over the seal guide and lining up all bolt holes. Install all eight mounting bolts. Tighten the bolts hand tight.

10. Install the oil filter mounting bracket gasket. Install the mounting bracket and four bolts; torque the front case bolts to 15–19 ft. lbs. and the oil filter mounting bracket bolts to 11–15 ft. lbs.

11. The remainder of the installation is the reverse of the removal procedure.

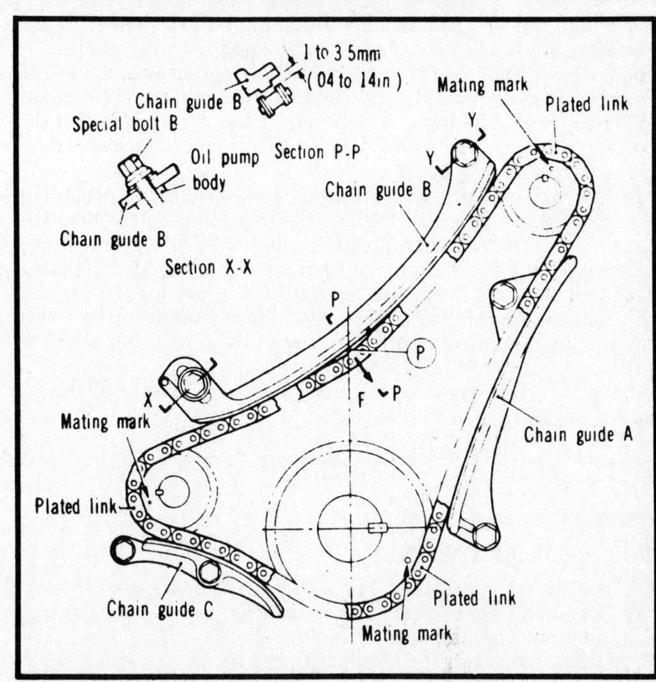

"Silent Shaft" balancing system—gasoline engine shown

Timing Belt and Sprockets

Removal and Installation

2.4L ENGINE

1. Disconnect the negative battery cable. Remove the timing belt cover. Rotate the engine until the timing marks on the camshaft sprocket and cylinder head or rear belt cover and the crankshaft sprocket and front cover are aligned.

2. Loosen the timing belt tensioner adjusting bolt and mounting bolt. Shift the tensioner as far as it will go toward the left or water pump side to remove belt tension. Retighten the adjusting bolt. If the belt is to be reused, draw an arrow on it in the direction of rotation. Remove the belt. Hold the tensioner in position while removing the tensioner adjusting bolt. Slowly release tension, remove the mounting bolt and remove the tension, spring and spacer.

3. Remove the bolt and camshaft sprocket.

4. If the inner timing belt which drives the oil pump and right silent shaft is being replaced or removed to remove the sprockets, proceed as follows; otherwise, proceed with Step 5:

a. Remove the crankshaft front sprocket bolt and front crankshaft sprocket and flange. Remove the plug from the left side of the engine block. Insert a suitable tool about .3 in. in diameter and about 2.5 in. long or longer into the hole to keep the left silent shaft in position.

b. Remove the oil pump sprocket retaining nut and remove the nut and the sprocket. Loosen the right silent shaft sprocket bolt until the sprocket can be turn it by hand.

c. Remove the inner tensioner bolts and remove the tensioner. Remove the inner timing belt. Remove the large crankshaft sprocket from the crankshaft and the right silent shaft bolt, sprocket and spacer.

5. Inspect all components. Replace any defective parts.

6. Install the larger crankshaft sprocket onto the crankshaft with the flatter or flanged side forward and the boss which is there to extend the sprocket forward from the front of the crankshaft at the rear. Align the timing mark on the sprocket with the mark on the front case. Apply a light coating of engine oil to the inner surface of the right silent shaft spacer and install the spacer. The chamfer must face inward, toward the engine. Install the right silent shaft sprocket and bolt and tighten the bolt finger tight. Align the timing mark on this sprocket also with the timing mark on the front case.

7. Install the inner belt over the sprockets so that the timing marks are in alignment and the upper side is under slight tension. Install the inner belt tensioner with the center of the pulley on the left side of the mounting bolt and the flange of the pulley facing the front of the engine. Lift the tensioner until there is tension on the inner belt's upper length. Hold the tensioner in this position and tighten the tensioner mounting bolt. Make sure the turning of the bolt does not alter the position of the tensioner, or belt tension will be excessive. Tighten the right silent shaft retaining flange bolt to 25–28 ft. lbs.

8. Check to make sure the timing marks affected by this belt are in alignment. Shift the position of the belt's teeth and adjust the tension if necessary. Depressing the belt's upper span should enable the belt to be depressed about 0.2–0.3 inches. Adjust the tension again to produce this amount of deflection if necessary.

9. Torque the right silent shaft mounting bolt to 25–28 ft. lbs. Install the flange and crankshaft sprocket onto the crankshaft. The concave (inner) side of the flange must face to the rear to fit the curved front of the inner crankshaft sprocket. The flat side of the outer crankshaft sprocket must face the flange, to the rear. Install the washer and bolt to the front of the crankshaft and torque it to 80–94 ft. lbs.

10. Install the camshaft sprocket to the camshaft and torque the bolt to 58–72 ft. lbs.

11. Install the spacer and main timing belt tensioner, installing the bolts finger tight. Install the spring between the locking tang on the right side of the tensioner and the tang on the right side of the water pump, just above the tensioner. This will force the tensioner to turn counterclockwise on the pivot bolt. Push the tensioner all the way toward the water pump and lock it by tightening the adjusting bolt.

12. Check alignment of all timing marks: the mark on the camshaft sprocket must align with the mark on the head; the mark on the crankshaft sprocket must align with that on the front case; and the mark on the oil pump sprocket must align with that on the front case.

13. Install the timing belt. The belt should be fitted over the sprockets in order: first the crankshaft, then the oil pump and then the camshaft sprocket. The (right) side of the belt which is normally straight must be straight during installation so the timing marks will remain lined up when the belt is actually tensioned. Remove the tool installed to keep the silent shaft in position and replace the plug. Making sure there is no tension on the

pivot bolt, loosen the tensioner adjusting bolt so the spring applies tension to the belt. Make sure the belt remains completely engaged with the teeth on the camshaft sprocket and that all timing marks remain aligned. Correct if necessary. Tighten the adjusting bolt. Tighten the pivot bolt. Make sure to tighten the bolts in that order, or tension will not be correct. Recheck alignment of the timing marks.

14. Turn the engine one full turn clockwise only. Loosen the tensioner pivot bolt and tighten the adjusting bolt. Allow the tensioner spring to again position the tensioner without interference from bolt friction. Tighten the adjusting bolt. Tighten the pivot bolt. Try to pry the belt outward by placing from under the belt on the seal line at the right side of the timing belt rear cover. The distance between the back of the belt and seal line will be about .55 in. if the tension is correct.

15. The remainder of the installation is the reverse of the removal procedure.

Camshaft

Removal and Installation

2.0L AND 2.6L ENGINES

1. Remove the breather hoses and purge hose.
2. Remove the air cleaner and fuel line.
3. Remove the fuel pump. Remove the distributor.
4. Disconnect and tag the spark plug wires.
5. Remove the rocker cover.
6. Remove the breather and semicircular seal.
7. After slightly loosening the camshaft sprocket bolt, turn the crankshaft until No. 1 piston is at top dead center on compression stroke (both valves closed).
8. Remove the camshaft sprocket bolt and distributor drive gear.
9. Remove the camshaft sprocket with chain and allow it to rest on the camshaft sprocket holder.
10. Remove the camshaft bearing cap tightening bolts. Do not remove the front and rear bearing cap bolts altogether, but keep them inserted in the bearing caps so that the rocker assembly can be removed as a unit.
11. Remove the rocker arms, rocker shafts and bearing caps as an assembly.
12. Remove the camshaft.
13. To install, lubricate the camshaft lobes and bearings and fit camshaft into head.
14. Install the assembled rocker arm shaft assembly. The camshaft should be positioned so that the dowel pin on the front end of the cam is in the 12 o'clock position and in line with the notch in the top of the front bearing cap.
15. Install the bearing cap bolts. Starting at the center and working out, Torque the bolts to 7 ft. lbs. Repeat the procedure and torque the bolts to 14–15 ft. lbs.
16. Install the camshaft sprocket and distributor drive gear onto the camshaft while pulling it upward. Temporarily tighten the locking bolt.

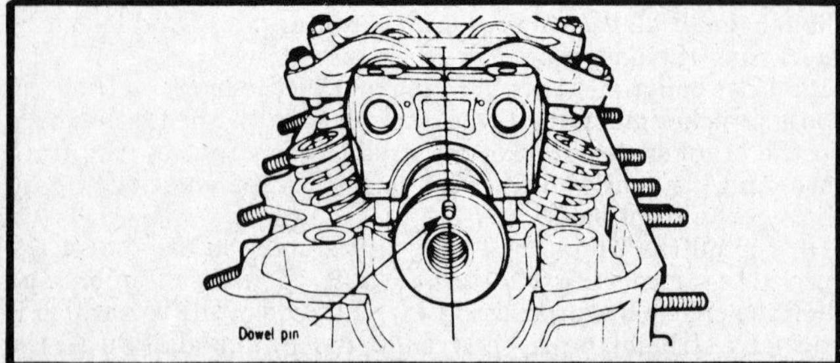

Installing the camshaft: align the dowel pin with the notch in the top of the front bearing cap

17. Turn the crankshaft backwards 90° and torque the camshaft sprocket bolt to 37–43 ft. lbs.
18. Temporarily set the valve clearance to cold engine specifications.
19. Temporarily install the breather, semicircular seal and rocker cover. Start the engine and run it at idle speed.
20. After the engine is at normal operational temperature, adjust the valves to hot engine specifications.
21. Install breather and seal. Apply sealant to the contact surfaces.
22. Install the rocker cover and torque the nuts to 4–5 ft. lbs.
23. Install the distributor, fuel pump, air cleaner, fuel line and plug wires.

2.4L ENGINE

1. Remove the drivers seat. Remove the parking brake lever and fuel tank filler door release lever.
2. Remove the battery cover. Remove the bolts retaining the seat underframe in place. Remove the seat underframe.
4. Disconnect the negative battery cable. Remove the distributor. Remove the rocker cover, disconnect the camshaft sprocket and remove the rocker arm shaft and cam bearing assembly. The camshaft may then be lifted off the top of the cylinder head.
5. Check and replace defective components as required.
6. Thoroughly lubricate the camshaft bearing journals, bearing saddles in the cylinder head and the inner surfaces of the caps with clean engine oil. Then continue the installation in the reverse order of the removal procedure.

Piston and Connecting Rods

IDENTIFICATION

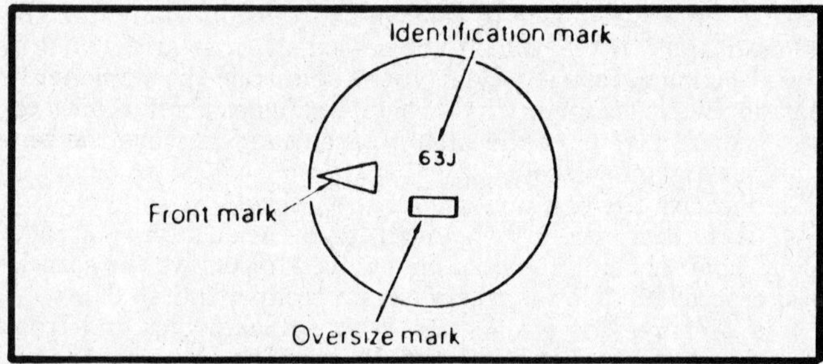

Piston positioning—all engines

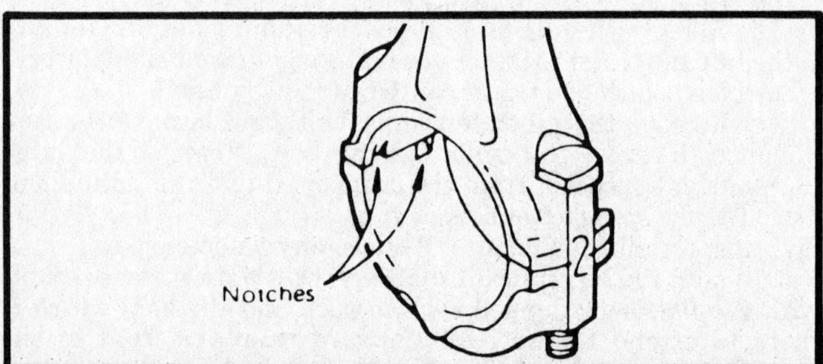

Connecting rod cap installation—all engines

Connecting Rod and Main Bearings

Removal and Installation

Refer to the Unit Repair Section for Procedures.

ENGINE LUBRICATION

Oil Pan

Removal and Installation

2.0L, 2.4L AND 2.6L ENGINE

NOTE: The engine must be raised off its mounts and safely supported for the oil pan to clear the suspension crossmember.

1. Raise and support the vehicle safely. Drain the engine oil.
2. Remove the underbody splash shield.
3. Disconnect the left and right engine mounts.
3. Raise the engine under the bell housing.
4. Remove the oil pan mounting bolts and remove the oil pan.
5. Installation is the reverse of the removal procedure. Always use a new gasket during installation.

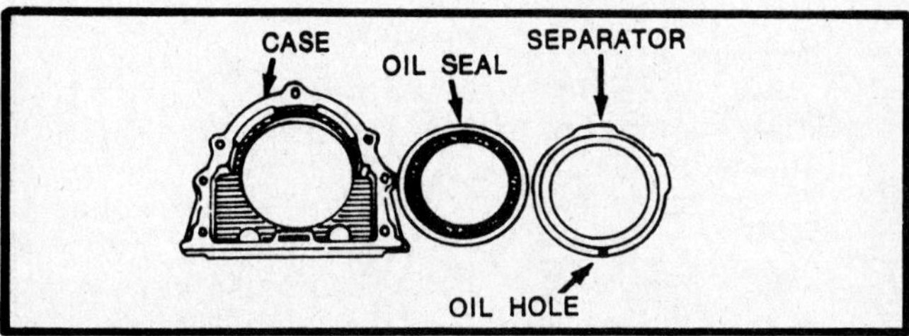

Rear main oil seal

Oil Pump

Removal and Installation

2.0L, 2.4L AND 2.6L ENGINE

Refer to Timing Chain, Cover, Silent Shaft and Tensioner Removal and Installation procedure.

Rear Main Bearing Oil Seal

Removal and Installation

2.0L, 2.4L AND 2.6L ENGINES

NOTE: The rear main bearing oil seal is located in a housing on the rear of the engine. To replace the seal, remove the transmission and work from underneath the vehicle.

1. On manual transmission models, remove the transmission, clutch and flywheel. On automatic transmission models, remove the transmission and flywheel. Remove the oil seal housing from the rear of the engine.
2. Remove the separator from the housing.
3. Pry out the old seal.
4. Lightly oil the replacement seal. The oil seal should be installed so that the seal plate fits into the inner contact surface of the seal case. Install the separator with the oil holes facing down.
5. Install the flywheel, clutch and transmission. Check the engine oil level when finished.

2WD FRONT SUSPENSION

Coil Spring

Removal and Installation

PICKUPS

1. Raise and support the vehicle safely.
2. Remove the wheel assembly.
3. Remove the shock absorber.
4. Remove stabilizer and strut bar.
5. Compress the coil spring with a spring compressor.
6. Remove the relay rod from the steering arm.
7. Separate the upper and lower ball joints.
8. Remove the coil spring.
9. Installation is the reverse of the removal procedure.

NOTE: The coil springs are color coded. The left side spring has a green band on it and the right side spring has a pink band on it. Do not mix the left and right springs.

10. Torque the ball joint castle nuts to: Upper, 43–65 ft. lbs.; Lower, 87–130 ft. lbs.

Torsion Bar

Removal and Installation

VAN

1. Raise and support the vehicle safely so that the front suspension is hanging freely.
2. Remove the torsion bar locknut. Remove the torsion bar adjusting nut. Remove the seat holding nut.
3. Before removing the anchor bolt, measure the protrusion through the assembly, this will aid in reinstallation of the assembly. Remove the anchor bolt that retains the torsion bar to the mount on the frame.
4. Remove the nuts that retain the torsion bar to the control arm.
5. Remove the torsion bar from the vehicle.

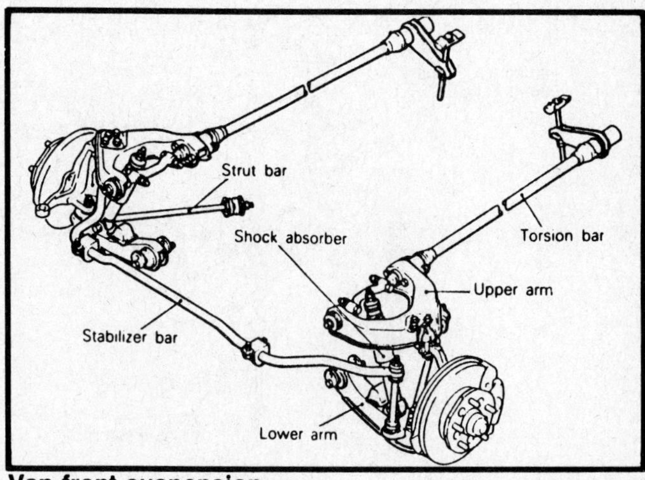

Van front suspension

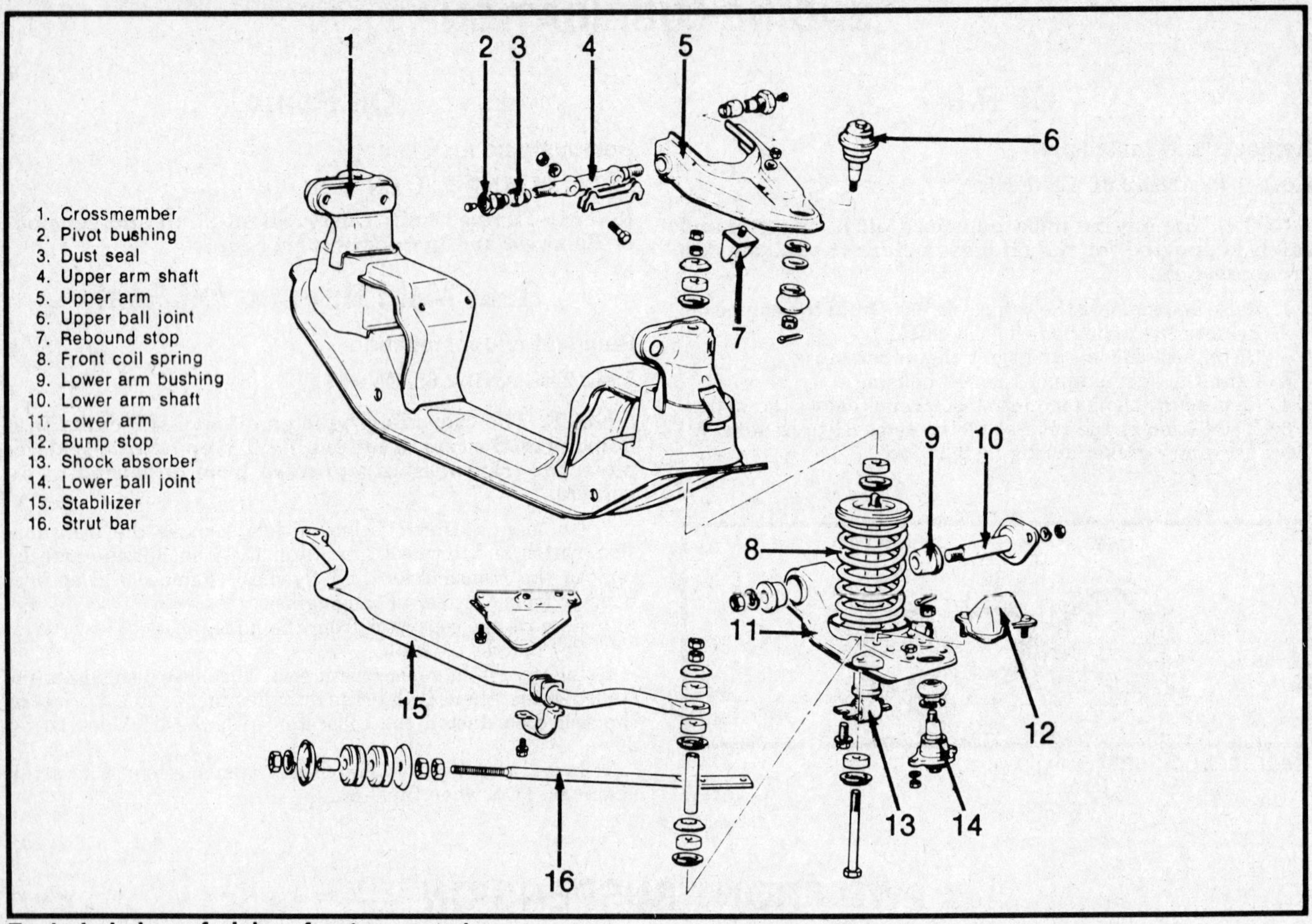

1. Crossmember
2. Pivot bushing
3. Dust seal
4. Upper arm shaft
5. Upper arm
6. Upper ball joint
7. Rebound stop
8. Front coil spring
9. Lower arm bushing
10. Lower arm shaft
11. Lower arm
12. Bump stop
13. Shock absorber
14. Lower ball joint
15. Stabilizer
16. Strut bar

Exploded view of pickup front suspension

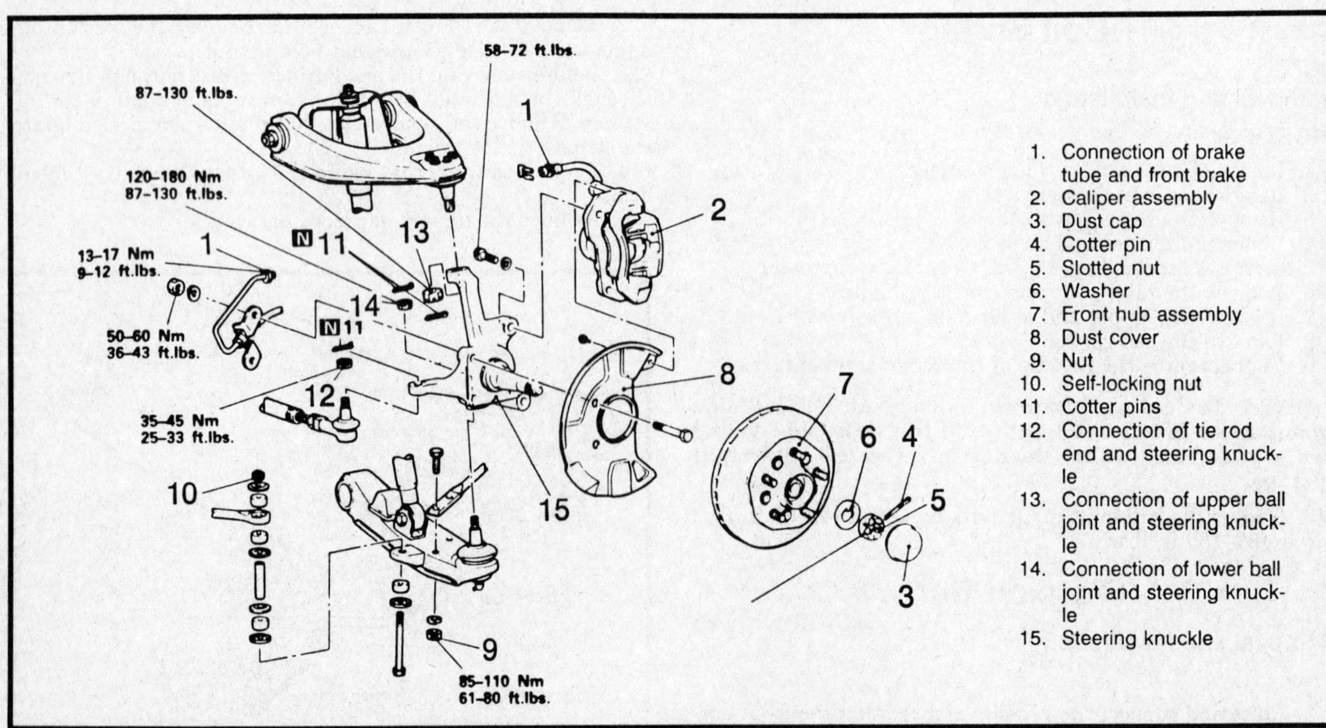

Exploded view of Van upper control arm, lower control arm and steering knuckle

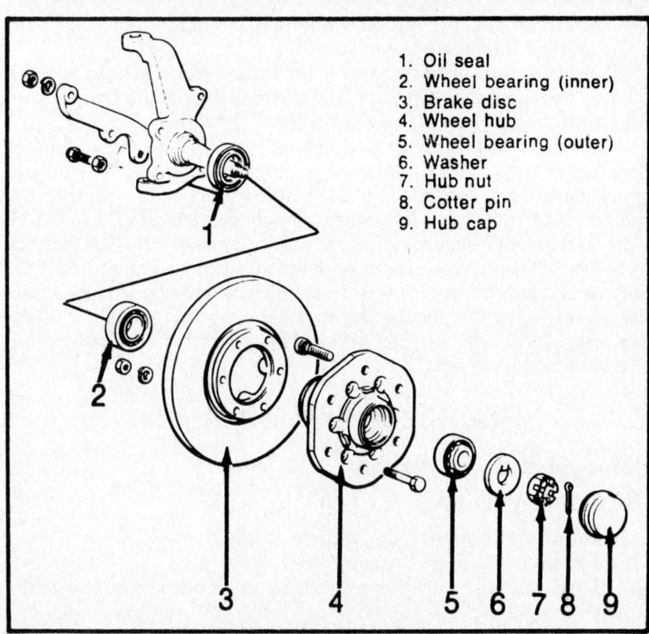

Steering knuckle and hub assembly

6. Installation is the reverse of the removal procedure. Check and adjust the alignment when finished.

Shock Absorbers

Removal and Installation

PICKUPS AND VAN

1. Raise and support the vehicle safely.
2. Remove the wheel assembly.
3. Remove the double lock nuts at the top of the shock absorber along with the rubber washer and metal caps.
4. Remove the two bolts at the bottom of the shock absorber and withdraw the shock absorber through the bottom control arm.
5. Installation is the reverse of the removal procedure. Refit all of the rubber cushion washers and metal caps in the correct order. Torque the upper shock absorber nut to 9–13 ft. lbs. and install the lock nut. Torque the two lower shock absorber bolts to 6–9 ft. lbs.

Upper Control Arm

Removal and Installation

PICKUPS AND VAN

1. Raise and support the vehicle safely.
2. Remove the wheel assembly.
3. Remove the shock absorber. Compress the coil spring with a coil spring compressor.
4. Remove the cotter pin and castle nut from the upper ball joint.
5. Using a ball joint remover, free the ball joint from the steering knuckle.
6. Remove the bolts holding the upper control arm to the crossmember and remove the control arm as an assembly.

NOTE: Save all of the adjustment shims from the upper control arm for reassembly.

7. Installation is the reverse of the removal procedure. Replace all camber adjustment shims, in the proper position, behind the upper control arm. Observe the following torques: upper control arm to crossmember bolts, 40–54 ft. lbs., ball joint to knuckle, 43–65 ft. lbs.

Lower Control Arm

Removal and Installation

PICKUPS AND VAN

1. Raise and support the vehicle safely.
2. Remove the wheel assembly.
3. Remove the shock absorber. On the pickup, compress the coil spring with a coil spring compressor. On the van, disconnect the torsion bar from the upper control arm.
4. Remove the stabilizer and strut bar.
5. Remove the cotter pin and castle nut from the lower ball joint and separate the ball joint from the steering knuckle using a ball joint remover.
6. On the pickup, remove the coil spring.
7. Remove the nut in the front of the lower control arm mounting shaft. Remove the nuts at the rear of the shaft. Remove the shaft and remove the lower arm.
8. Installation is the reverse of the removal procedure. Torque the front mounting shaft nut to 40–54 ft. lbs. Torque the rear nut to 6–9 ft. lbs. Torque the ball joint castle nut to 87–130 ft. lbs. Torque control arm shaft only after vehicle is on the ground.

Ball Joints

UPPER

Removal and Installation

PICKUPS AND VAN

1. Raise and support the vehicle safely. Remove the upper control arm.
2. Remove the ball joint seal by prying upwards evenly.
3. Remove the snap ring using snap ring pliers.
4. Using a press, remove the ball joint from the control arm.

NOTE: A minimum of 2,200 lbs. pressure will be required to remove the upper ball joint from the control arm.

5. To install the ball joint, with the joint and upper arm mating marks aligned, press the ball joint into the control arm hole. Make sure the ball joint snap ring is a tight fit and install the dust cover.
6. Install the control arm on the vehicle. Torque the ball joint to steering knuckle nut to 43–65 ft. lbs.

LOWER

Removal and Installation

PICKUPS AND VAN

1. Raise and support the vehicle safely. Remove the wheel assembly.
2. Remove the coil spring.
3. Free the lower ball joint from the steering knuckle using a ball joint remover. Remove the dust cover from the ball joint.
4. Remove the ball joint.
5. Installation is the reverse of the removal procedure. Install the ball joint with the tab side pointing to the rear of the vehicle. Torque the ball joint to lower control arm bolts to 22–30 ft. lbs.

Wheel Bearings

Removal and Installation

PICKUPS AND VAN

1. Raise and support the vehicle safely. Remove the wheel assembly. Remove the caliper.

2. Pry off the dust cap. Tap out and discard the cotter pin. Remove the locknut.
3. Being careful not to drop the outer bearing, pull off the brake disc and wheel hub.
4. Remove the grease inside the wheel hub.
5. Using a brass drift, carefully drive the outer bearing race out of the hub.
6. Remove the inner bearing seal and bearing.
7. Check the bearings for wear or damage and replace them if necessary.
8. Coat the inner surface of the hub with grease.
9. Grease the outer surface of the bearing race and drift it into place in the hub.
10. Pack the inner and outer wheel bearings with grease. If the brake disc has been removed and/or replaced, tighten the retaining bolts to specification.
11. Install the inner bearing in the hub. Being careful not to distort it, install the oil seal with its lip facing the bearing. Drive the seal on until its outer edge is even with the edge of the hub.
12. Install the hub/disc assembly on the spindle, being careful not to damage the oil seal.
13. Install the outer bearing, washer and spindle nut. Adjust the bearing.

Adjustment

1. Remove the wheel and dust cover. Remove the cotter pin and lock cap from the nut.
2. Torque the wheel bearing nut to 14.5 ft. lbs. and loosen the nut. Retorque the nut to 3.6 ft. lbs.
3. Install the lock cap and cotter pin.
3. Install the dust cover and wheel assembly.

Alignment

Procedures

PICKUPS

1. Camber is preset at the factory and cannot be adjusted.
2. Caster is adjusted by varying the length of the strut bar and the amount of shims under the upper control arms.
3. Loosen both nuts and turn the strut bar in or out. Add or subtract shims under the upper control arm to obtain the proper reading.
4. Toe adjustment is possible by adjusting both tie rod end turnbuckles the same amount.

VAN

1. Measure the toe in. Toe should be 0.024 inch. Adjust toe by turning the turnbuckles of the right and left tie rods the same amount in opposite directions.
2. Turn the left turnbuckle in the forward direction of the vehicle and the right one in the reverse direction in order to reduce toe in. Toe in can be adjusted about 0.12 inch by turning both turnbuckles half a turn each.
3. Adjust camber and caster after first checking that the vehicle tire pressure is within specification. Position the front wheel on the turning radius gauge and level the vehicle.
4. Remove the hubcap and cotter pin. Measure the camber and caster with the camber/caster/kingpin attached. The proper specification for camber is 0°31' ± 30' (difference in camber between right hand and left hand wheels is within 30').
5. The proper specification for caster is 0°08 ± 30' (difference in caster between right hand and left hand wheels is within 30').
6. If the camber is not within specification, adjust it by rotating the lower arm's shaft assembly. One marking on the control is a change of 2°18' of the camber. Turn the control away from the lower control arm.

Stabilizer and Strut Bar

Removal and Installation

PICKUPS AND VAN

1. Raise and support the vehicle safely.
2. Remove the wheel assemblies.
3. Disconnect the stabilizer and the strut bars from the lower control arms.

CAUTION

When removing the strut bar, loosen the adjusting nut at the other end of the bar before loosening the bolts at the control arm.

NOTE: Before removing the stabilizer bar, note the order and direction of the rubber cushion washers and metal caps for reassembly.

4. Remove the nut and spacers at the threaded end of the strut bar and remove the bar.
5. Remove the two stabilizer brackets and remove the stabilizer.
6. Installation is the reverse of the removal procedures. Observe the following: There is a letter L on the left side strut bar, do not confuse it with the right side bar. The rubber cushions on the front of the strut bar are different. The cushion with a protruded lip is mounted at the front and the regular cushion is mounted at the back.

When installing the strut bar, set the standard distance of 3.8 in. from the tip of the threaded end of the bar to the rear face of the rear double nut. Lower the vehicle to the ground and tighten all nuts and bolts. Check the front wheel alignment after installing the strut bar in order to obtain the correct caster and then re-adjust the distance as required.

When installing both ends of the stabilizer, tighten the first nut (adjustment nut) to obtain length 0.87–0.94 in., then torque the lock nut to 18–25 ft. lbs.

4WD FRONT SUSPENSION

Upper Control Arm

Removal and Installation

1. Raise and support the vehicle safely.
2. Loosen, but do not remove, the anchor bolt of the torsion bar.
3. Remove the shock absorber.
4. Disconnect and plug the brake hose at the caliper.
5. Loosen, but do not remove, the nut holding the upper ball joint to the steering knuckle.
6. Using a ball joint separater, disconnect the upper ball joint from the knuckle. Do not tear the rubber ball joint boot.
7. Remove the bolts connecting the upper arm shaft to the arm post of the side frame. Remove the upper control arm.

NOTE: The camber adjusting shims should be marked for later assembly.

8. Replace the upper ball joint, if necessary.
9. Reassemble the upper control arm in the reverse order of disassembly, while noting the following:
   a. When installing the upper arm assembly into the crossmember, insert the upper arm shaft mounting bolts from the outside of the crossmember and put adjusting shims between the crossmember and the upper arm shaft in the order in which they were removed.

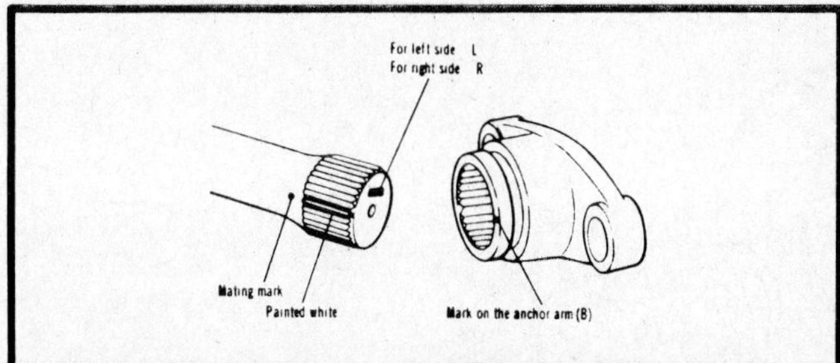

Torsion bar installation – 4WD pickups and Montero

b. Torque the upper arm shaft-to-crossmember bolts to 72–87 ft. lbs.

c. Torque the upper ball joint-to-knuckle nut to 43–65 ft. lbs.

10. Check the front wheel alignment.

Lower Control Arm

Removal and Installation

1. Raise and support the vehicle safely. Remove the front skid plate and under cover, if equipped.
2. Remove the torsion bar.
3. Remove the stabilizer bar.
4. Remove the shock absorber.
5. Remove the lower ball joint to the steering knuckle nut. Using a ball joint tool, disconnect the lower ball joint from the knuckle.
6. Remove the front mounting bolts for the lower control arm. Remove the lower control arm.
7. Replace the lower ball joint, if necessary.
8. To install, temporarily mount the lower control arm shaft to the crossmember.

NOTE: Assembly is easier if a solution of soapy water is applied to the lower arm shaft and to the rubber bushing.

9. Install the shock absorber and torsion bar.
10. Torque the lower arm shaft to 101–116 ft. lbs. with the vehicle lowered to the ground and unloaded.
11. Install the stabilizer bar.
12. The remainder of the installtion is the reverse of the removal procedure.

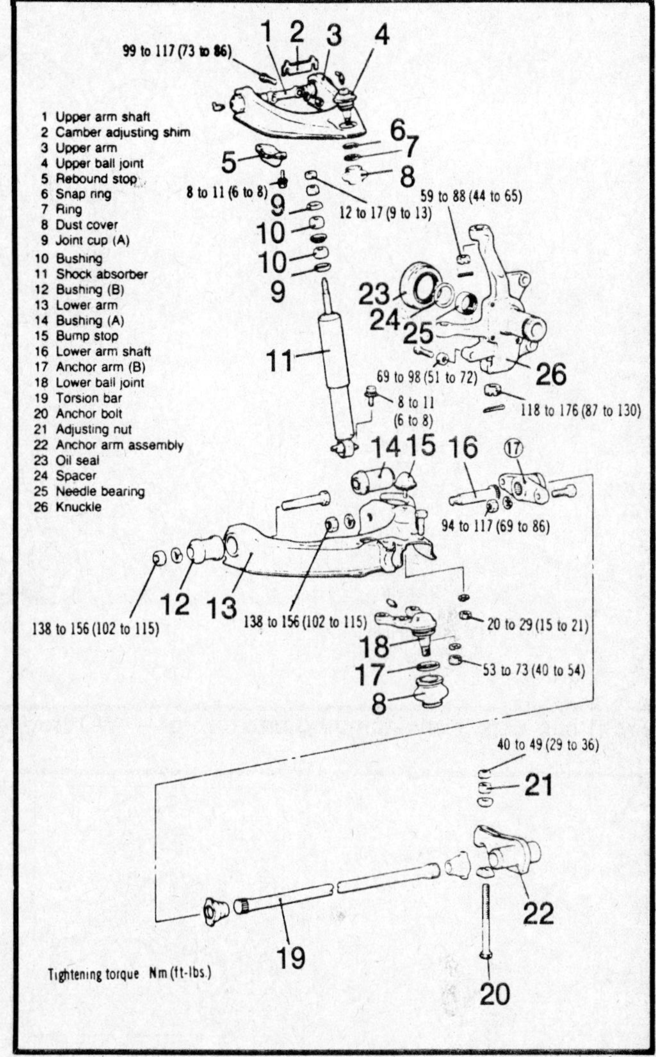

4WD pickup and Montero front suspension and knuckle assemblies

Ball Joints

UPPER

Removal and Installation

1. Raise and support the vehicle safely. Remove the wheel assembly.
2. Separate the upper ball joint from the steering knuckle.
3. Remove the rubber dust boot together with the ring.
4. Remove the snapring from the ball joint.
5. The upper ball joint must be pressed out of the arm. Depending on the type of press available, the control arm may or may not have to be removed.
6. The ball joint must be pressed into position when installing. Make sure the mating mark on the ball joint and the mark center of the control arm are aligned.

NOTE: Check to make sure there is no play between the ball joint groove and the snapring. If play exists, replace the snapring with a new one.

7. Fill the boot and upper ball joint with an SAE No. 2 EP multipurpose grease.
8. Apply a semi-drying sealant to the grooves in the upper ball joint. Secure the boot to the ball joint with the ring.
9. The remainder of the installation is the reverse of the removal procedure. Torque the ball joint-to-knuckle nut to 43–65 ft. lbs. Check the front end alignment.

LOWER

Removal and Installation

1. Raise and support the vehicle safely. Remove the wheel assembly.
2. Remove the lower shock absorber bolts at the control arm.
3. Remove the nut which retains the lower ball joint to the steering knuckle.
4. Using a ball joint tool, disconnect the lower ball joint from the knuckle.
5. Unbolt the lower ball joint from the control arm.
6. Installation is the reverse of the removal procedure. Fill the rubber ball joint boot with an SAE No. 2 multipurpose grease. Apply the grease to the ball joint. Apply a semi-drying sealant to the grooves in the lower ball joint. Secure the boot to the joint with the ring.

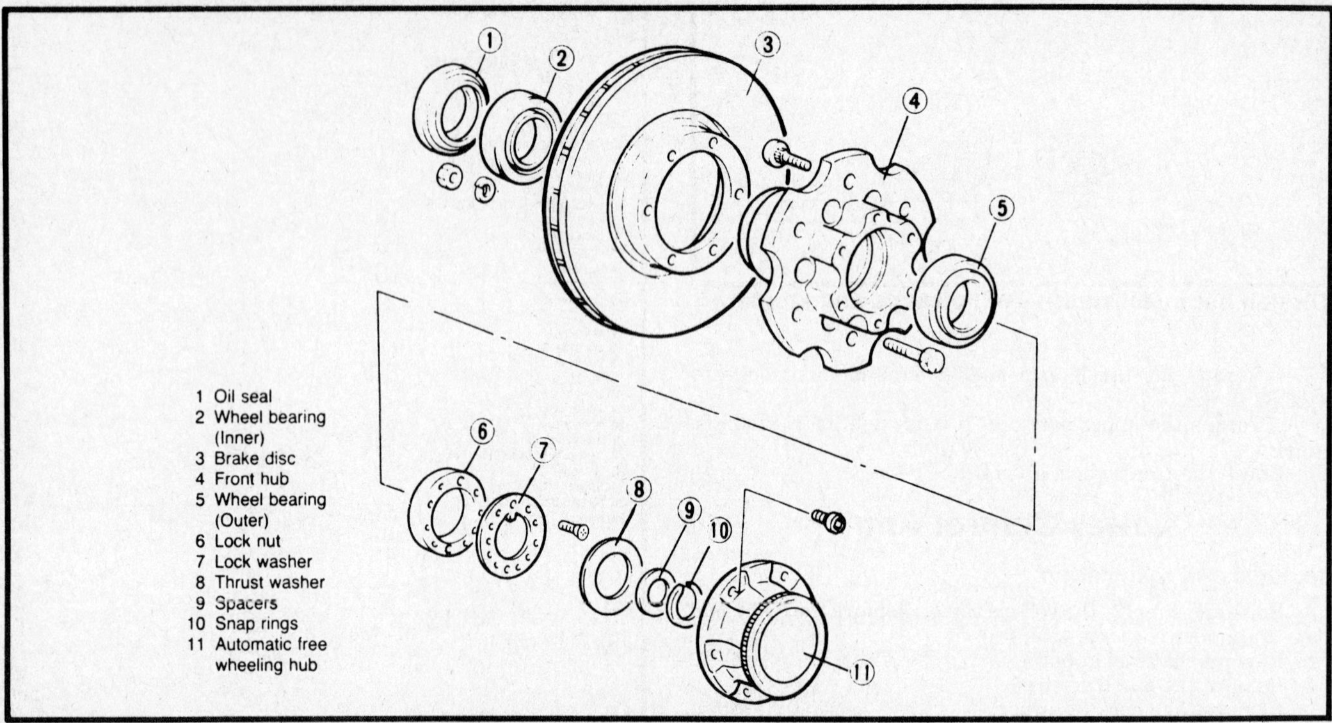

Front hub assembly including brake rotor—4WD trucks and Montero

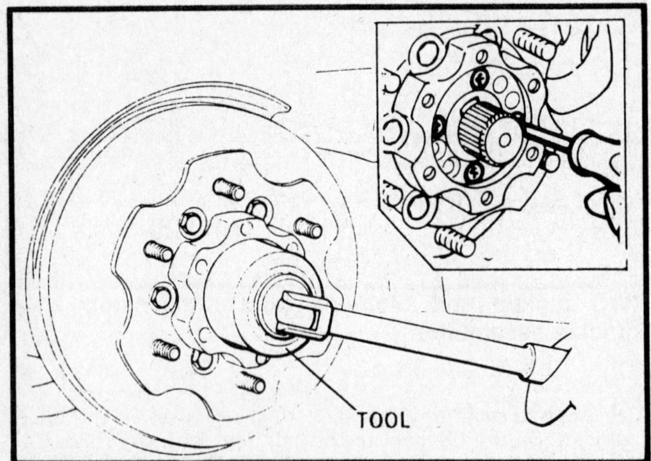

Removing front hub lock nut

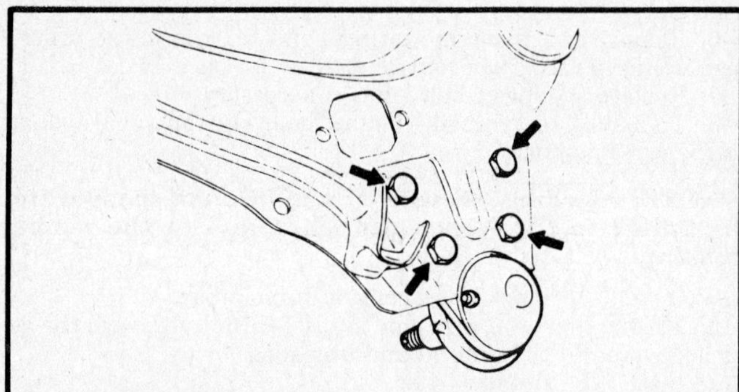

Removing lower ball joint

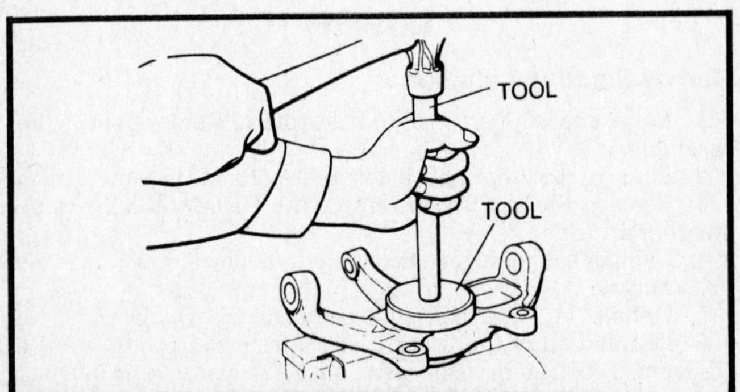

Press fitting oil seal into steering knuckle

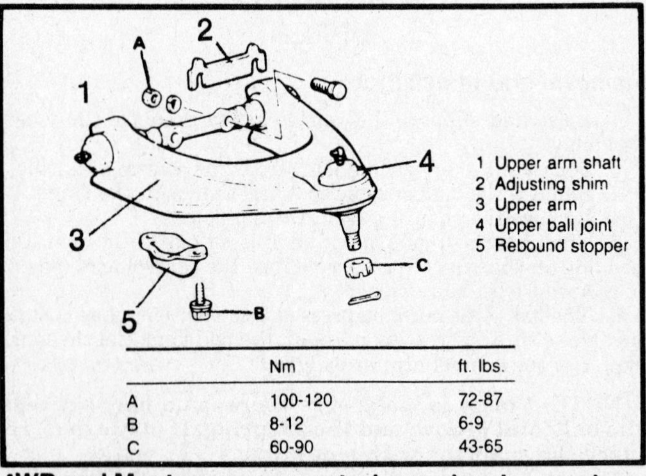

	Nm	ft. lbs.
A	100-120	72-87
B	8-12	6-9
C	60-90	43-65

4WD and Montero upper control arm showing camber adjustment shim(s)

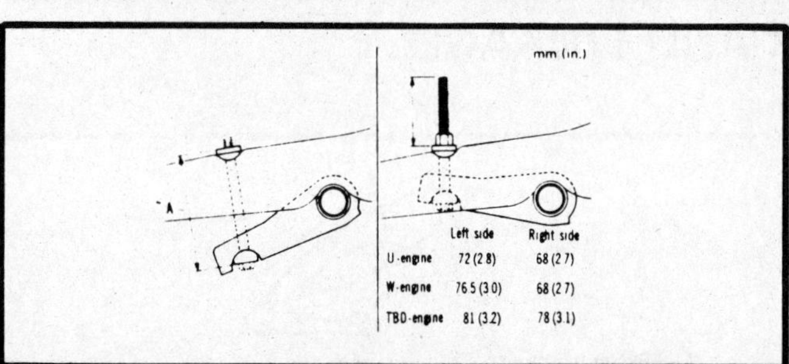

Torsion bar installation showing anchor arm and bolt adjustment

Alignment

Procedure

PICKUPS AND MONTERO/RAIDER

1. To adjust caster, tighten the upper control arm shaft. A half turn of the upper control arm shaft will cause 0.049 in. play in the upper control arm shaft resulting in a $^1/_4$ degree caster adjustment.
2. To adjust the camber, it is necessary to adjust the number and thickness of the shims under the upper control arm shaft. A total of 0.16 in. shim thickness between the upper control arm shaft and the crossmember is normally required for standard camber.
3. A 0.024 in. adjustment in thickness of shims will provide about 8 minutes adjustment of camber.
4. Toe-in can be adjusted by turning the left tie rod turnbuckle in or out. One revolution of the turnbuckle will vary about 0.3 in. of toe-in adjustment.
5. The toe-in may be increased or decreased by turning the tie rod turnbuckle toward the front or the rear of the vehicle respectively.

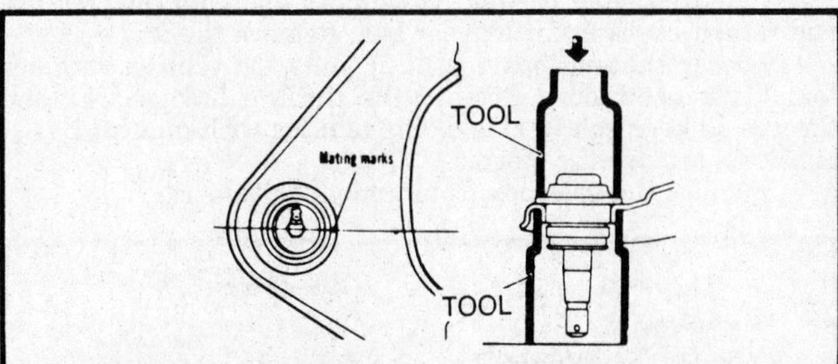

Press fitting upper ball joint—4WD and Montero

6. After completion of the toe-in adjustment, check the difference in the length of the left and the right tie rods. If the difference exceeds 0.2 in., remove the right tie rod and adjust the length until the difference is reduced to 0.2 in. or less. An "L" stamped on the outer surface of the tie rod stands for left hand thread end.

Stabilizer Bars and Shafts

Removal and Installation

1. Raise and support the vehicle safely.
2. Remove the front skid plate.
3. Unbolt the stabilizer bar from its front support bushings on the stabilizer link and from the control arm. Remove the stabilizer bar.
4. When mounting the stabilizer link to the No. 1 crossmember, tighten the nut so as to obtain a 0.63–0.71 in. dimension between the bottom of the nut and the top of the threaded bolt end. Torque the stabilizer bar-to-control arm nut so that the bottom of nut-to-top of threaded bolt end dimension is 0.63–0.71 in.

Torsion Bars

Removal and Installation

1. Raise and support the vehicle safely.
2. Remove the front wheel assembly. Remove the brake caliper without disconnecting the brake hose. Remove the front hub assembly.
3. Support the lower control arm away from where the torsion bar is to be removed.
4. Detach the torsion bar dust covers from the torsion bar anchor arm assembly and slide the covers a few inches down the torsion bar and out of the way.
5. Matchmark the torsion bar to the anchor arm.
6. Loosen the adjusting nut and remove the torsion bar from the anchor arm.

NOTE: Remove the anchor arm assembly as necessary to make torsion bar removal easier.

7. To install, apply a multi-purpose grease to the torsion bar splines, the anchor arm splines and the inside of the dust boot and the anchor boot thread.
8. Make sure that the torsion bars are replaced on their proper sides respectively, if both bars were removed. Face the end of the bar with the identification mark forward and align the mark on the anchor arm with the mating mark on the torsion bar when the bar is inserted in the anchor arm.

NOTE: When installing a new torsion bar, align the spline painted white with the mark on the anchor arm.

9. Select the relative position of the torsion bar splines and the anchor arm splines so that the dimension is as specified below, when the torsion bar and anchor arm are assembled and with the rebound stop in contact with the side frame.

Dimension A

LEFT SIDE

Montero/Raider: 5.43–5.73 in.
Pickups: 5.52–5.82 in.

RIGHT SIDE

Montero/Raider: 5.04–5.35 in.
Pickups: 5.32–5.62 in.

10. Tighten the adjusting nut so that the anchor bolt protrusion will become the dimensions shown in the illustration. Pickup dimensions vary, according to the engine in the vehicle. Montero/Raider dimensions are: 2.17 in. left side; 2.68 in. right side.
11. Install the stabilizer bar to the lower arm. Tighten the nut so that the dimension from the bottom of the nut to the top of the bolt end is about 17mm.
12. Install the front hub assembly and brake caliper. Install the front wheel. Torque the lower arm-to-side frame bracket bolt to 108 ft. lbs.
13. Measure the distance between the suspension bump stop bumper and bump stop bracket on the side frame with the vehicle unloaded. Distance should be 2.8 in. Tighten the adjusting nut on the anchor bolt if it is out of specification.

STEERING GEAR AND LINKAGE

Refer to the Unit Overhaul Section for Overhaul Procedures.

Manual Steering Gear

Removal and Installation

PICKUPS AND MONTERO/RAIDER

1. Remove the clamp bolt connecting the steering shaft with the steering gear housing mainshaft. Raise and support the vehicle safely.
2. Disconnect the tie rod and pitman arm from the relay rod using a ball joint remover or gear puller.
3. Remove the three bolts holding the gear box to the frame and remove the gear box from under the vehicle.
4. Installation is the reverse of the removal procedure. Torque the Pitman arm to relay rod nut to 94–109 ft. lbs. and the tie rod socket to relay rod to 29–33 ft. lbs.

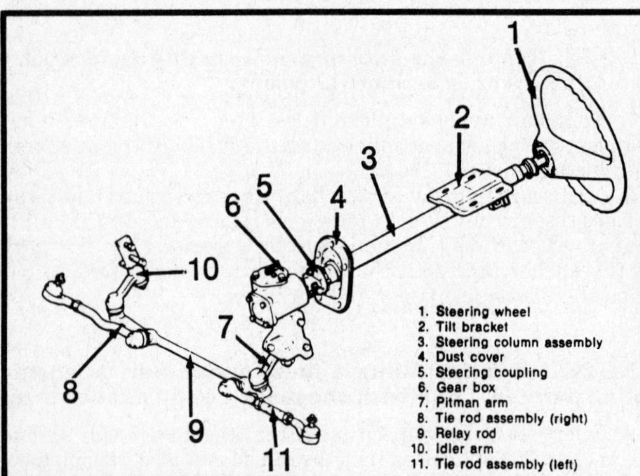

Manual steering columnm and gear assembly—Pick-up and Montero/Raider

Manual and Power Steering Gear

Removal and Installation

VAN

1. Raise and support the vehicle safely.
2. Remove the splash guard plate. If equipped with power steering, remove the power steering tube protector. Disconnect the right and left tie rod connection using the proper tools.
3. Disconnect and cap the power steering lines, if equipped with power steering. Remove the steering gear housing retaining clamps.
4. Separate the steering gear from the steering shaft.
5. Remove the steering gear from the vehicle.
6. Installation is the reverse of the removal procedure. If equipped with power steering, fill and bleed the system when finished.

Power Steering Gear

Removal and Installation

PICKUPS AND MONTERO/RAIDER

1. Disconnect the steering shaft from the gear box mainshaft. Raise and support the vehicle safely.

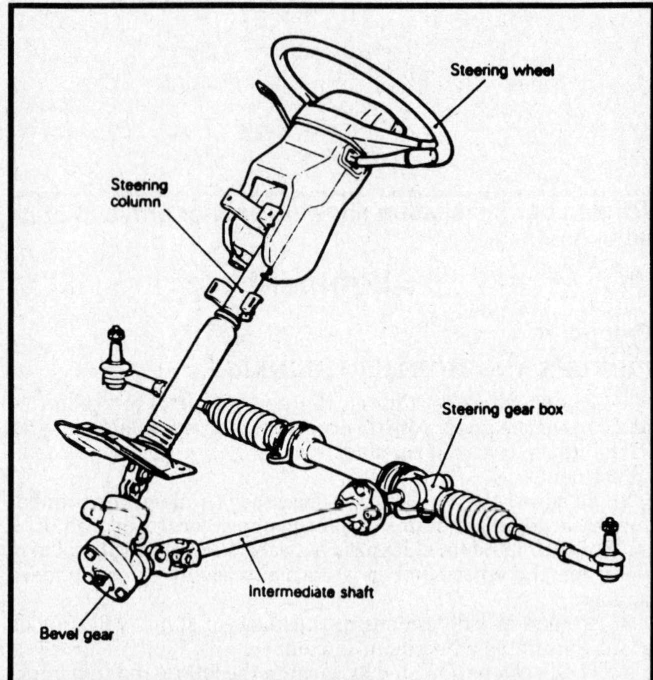

Van manual steering assembly

2. Disconnect the tie rod from the relay rod and the Pitman arm from the relay rod using a gear puller.
3. Remove the air cleaner. Disconnect and plug the pressure and return hoses from the gear box. Remove the undercover.
4. Loosen the gear box mounting bolts. On vehicles with automatic transmissions, remove the throttle linkage with the throttle linkage splash shield. On vehicles with manual transmissions, remove the starter.
5. Remove the gear box from under the vehicle.

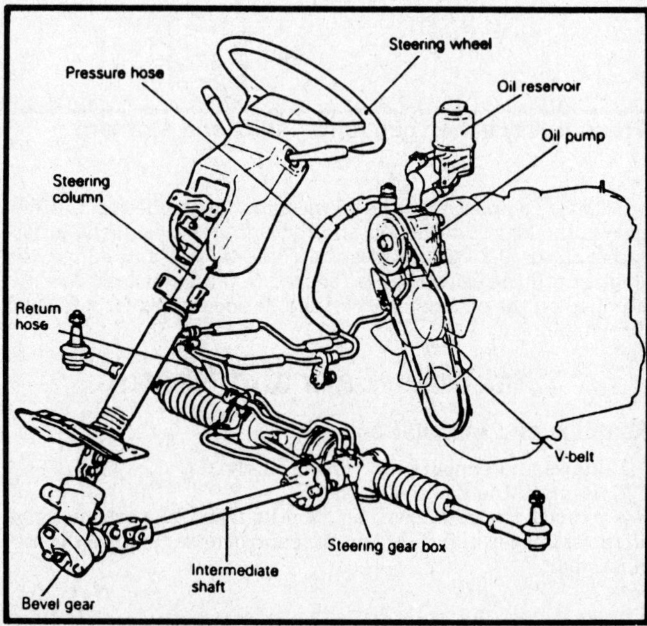

Van power steering assembly

6. Remove the Pitman arm with a gear puller.
7. Installation is the reverse of the removal procedure. Observe the following torques: gear box to frame, 40–47 ft. lbs.; tie rod socket and relay rod connection, 25–33 ft. lbs.; pressure hose connection, 22–29 ft.lbs.; return hose connection 29–36 ft. lbs.

Power Steering Pump

Removal and Installation

ALL MODELS

1. Remove the drive belt.
2. Disconnect and plug the pressure and return lines.
3. Remove the pump attaching bolts and lift the pump from the brackets.
4. Make sure the bracket bolts are tight and install the pump to the brackets.
5. If pulley had been removed, install the pulley and tighten the nut securely. Bend the lock tab over the nut.
6. Install the drive belt and adjust to a tension of 22 lbs. at a deflection of 0.28–0.39 in. at the top center of the belt. Tighten the pump bolts securely to hold the tension.
7. Connect the pressure and return lines and fill the reservoir with Dexron®II fluid.
8. Bleed the power steering system.

Steering Linkage

Removal and Installation

PICKUPS AND MONTERO/RAIDER

1. Raise and support the vehicle safely.
2. Remove the cotter pins and castle nuts holding the tie rod ends to the steering arms and relay rod. Disconnect the tie rod ends.
3. Unbolt and remove the relay rod.

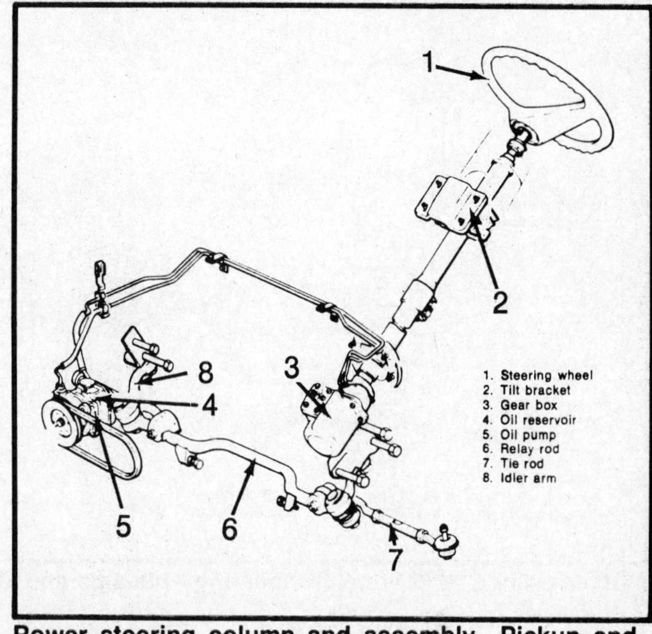

Power steering column and assembly—Pickup and Montero/Raider

4. Remove the two bolts holding the idler arm to the frame and remove the idler arm.

NOTE: The outer tie rod end has a left hand thread and the inner tie rod has a right handed thread on the driver's side.

5. Installation is the reverse of the removal procedure. Torque all tie rod end nuts and relay rod nuts to 25–33 ft. lbs.

BRAKE SYSTEM

Refer to the Unit Repair Section for Overhaul Procedures.

Master Cylinder

Removal and Installation

ALL MODELS EXCEPT VAN

1. Disconnect the brake fluid level sensor connector.
2. Disconnect and plug the brake fluid lines at the master cylinder.
3. Remove the master cylinder to booster mounting nuts.
4. Remove the master cylinder.
5. If the master cylinder is being replaced, remove the fluid reservoir from the master cylinder and install it on the new master cylinder.
6. Bleed the new master cylinder before installing.
7. Installation is the reverse of the removal procedure.
8. Bleed the brake system and check the brake fluid level when finished.

VAN

1. Disconnect the negative battery cable. Remove the instrument cluster assembly.
2. The brake fluid reservoir is separate from the master cylinder. Disconnect and plug the hoses at the master cylinder.
3. Disconnect all the brake lines at the master cylinder. Remove the nuts and lockwashers attaching the master cylinder to the booster. Remove the master cylinder from the vehicle.
4. Installation is the reverse of the removal. Torque the attaching nuts to 6–9 ft. lbs. Refill the reservoir with approved fluid and bleed the system.

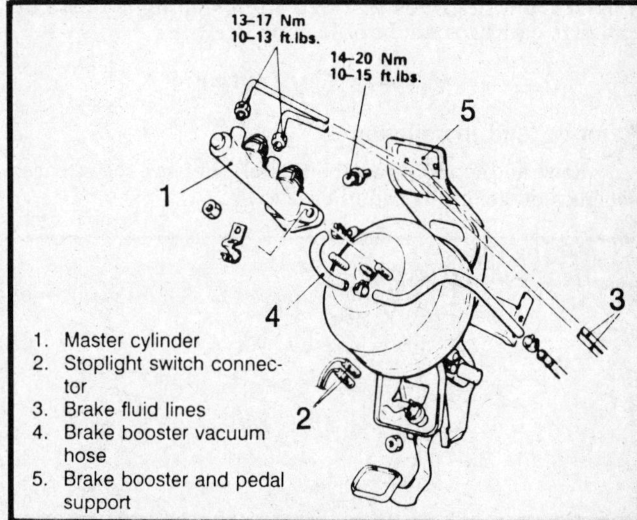

Master cylinder mounting—Van

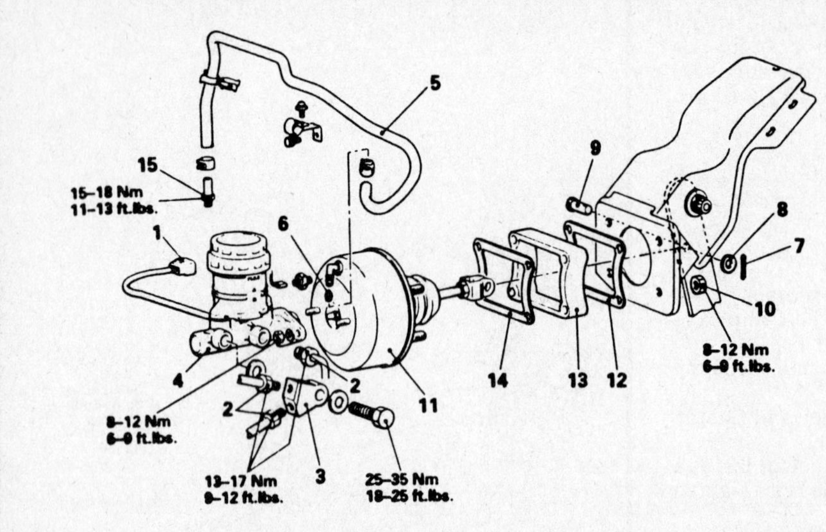

1. Brake fluid level sensor connection
2. Brake tube connection
3. Connector
4. Master cylinder
5. Vacuum hose
6. Check valve
7. Cotter pin
8. Washer
9. Clevis pin
10. Nuts
11. Brake booster
12. Sealer
13. Spacer
14. Sealer
15. Fitting

Master cylinder and booster mounting – pickups and Montero/Raider

BLEEDING

Procedure

1. Clean all dirt from around the master cylinder filler plug.
2. If a bleeder tank is used, follow the manufacturer's instructions. Remove the filler plug and fill the master cylinder to the lower edge of the filler neck.
3. Clean off the bleeder connections at all of the wheel cylinders or disc brake calipers. Attach the bleeder hose and fixture to the right rear wheel cylinder bleeder screw and place the end of the tube in a glass jar, submerged in brake fluid.
4. Open the bleeder valve $^{1}/_{2}$–$^{3}/_{4}$ of a turn. Have an assistant depress the brake pedal and allow it to return slowly. Continue this pumping action to force any air out of the system. When bubbles cease to appear at the end of the bleeder hose, close the bleeder valve and remove the hose.
5. Check the level of the brake fluid in the master cylinder and add fluid, if necessary.
6. After the bleeding operation at each caliper or wheel cylinder has been completed, fill the master cylinder reservoir and replace the filler plug.

NOTE: Never reuse brake fluid which has been removed from the lines through the bleeding process because it contains air bubbles and dirt.

Wheel Cylinder

Removal and Installation

1. Raise and support the vehicle safely. Remove the wheel assemblies brake drums and brake shoes.

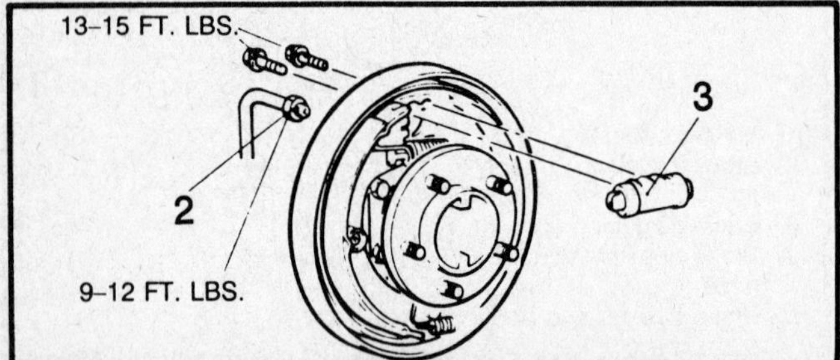

Rear wheel cylinder mounting – all models

2. Disconnect and plug the brake line from the rear of the wheel cylinder.
3. Remove the wheel cylinder from the brake backing plate.
4. Installation is the reverse of the removal procedure. Bleed the brake system when finished.

Disc Brakes

Removal and Installation

1. Raise and support the vehicle safely. Remove the wheel assemblies.
2. Remove the brake caliper pivot bolt and pivot the caliper upwards taking care not to pinch the fluid line.
3. Remove the brake pads and silencing clips.
4. Install the clips on the new brake pads.
5. Using a suitable tool, push the caliper piston into the caliper body.
6. Install the new brake pads and caliper.
7. The remainder of the installation is the reverse of the removal procedure.

Calipers

Removal and Installation

1. Raise and support the vehicle safely. Remove the wheel assembly.
2. Disconnect and plug the brake fluid line at the caliper.
3. Disconnect and plug the ruuber brake fluid line from the metal line.
4. Remove the rubber line clip.
5. Remove the brake caliper mounting bolts and remove the caliper.
6. Installation is the reverse of the removal procedure.

Rotors

Removal and Installation

1. Raise and support the vehicle safely. Remove the wheel assembly.
2. Remove the brake caliper.
3. Remove the dust cap, cotter pin, lock nut and rotor nut.
4. Remove the brake rotor.
5. Installation is the reverse of the removal procedure. Adjust the front wheel bearings when finished.

Power Brake Booster

VACUUM

Removal and Installation

ALL MODELS EXCEPT VAN

1. Remove the master cylinder.
2. Disconnect the vacuum hose from the power brake.
3. Remove the pin connecting the power brake operating rod to the pedal.
4. Loosen the nuts attaching the power brake to the fire wall and remove the power brake.
5. Installation is the reverse of the removal procedure. Apply sealer to all mounting surfaces before assembling.

VAN

1. Disconnect the negative battery cable. Remove the lap heater duct. Remove the steering column cover.
2. Remove the steering column switch connector. Remove the steering column assembly.
3. Remove the master cylinder.
4. Remove the stoplight switch connector. Remove the brake tube, vacuum hose and pipe.
5. Remove the brake pedal assembly retaining bolts. Remove the power brake booster along with the brake pedal assembly.
6. Installation is the reverse of the removal procedure.

Stoplight Switch

Removal and Installation

1. Disconnect the negative battery cable.
2. Locate the stoplight switch on the brake pedal support.
3. Disconnect the switch wiring connector.
4. Remove the switch from the brake pedal support.
5. Install the new switch on the pedal support.
6. Adjust the switch until the dimension between the switch and the pedal is 0.19–0.39 in.
7. Connect the switch connector and negative battery cable.

Parking Brake

CABLE

Removal and Installation

4 WHEEL DRIVE

1. Raise and support the vehicle safely.
2. Remove the console and rear seat. Disconnect the brake cable at the parking brake lever (brakes released). Remove the cable clamps inside the driver's compartment (two bolts). Disconnect the clamps on the rear suspension arm.
3. Remove the rear brake drums and the brake shoe assemblies. Disconnect the parking brake cable from the lever on the trailing (rear) brake shoe by removing the snapring. Remove the brake cables.
4. Installation is the reverse of the removal procedure. Make sure the grommets through which the cables pass into the passenger compartment are installed with the concave side outward. Adjust the parking brake. Adjust the switch so the indicator light comes on when the parking brake lever is pulled one notch.

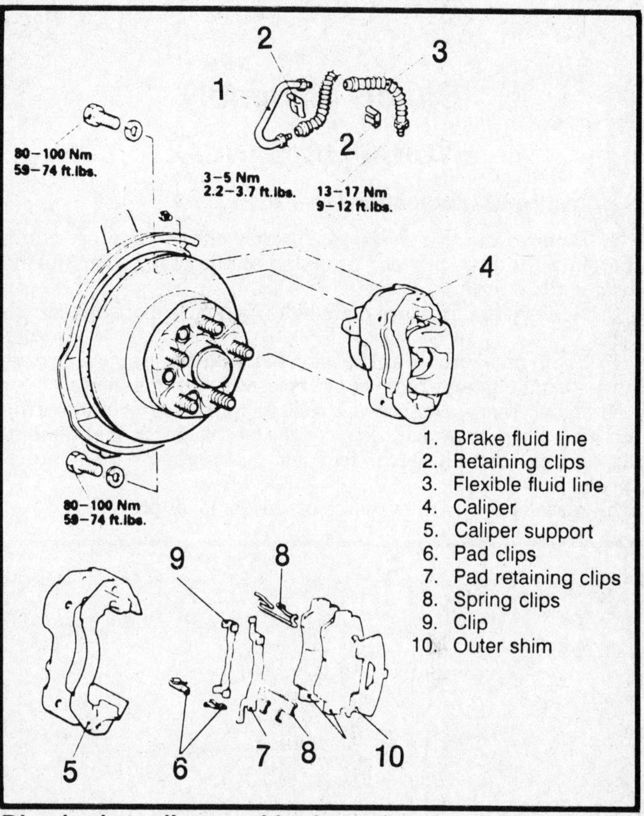

Disc brake caliper and brake pads—exploded view—2WD shown—4WD similar

2 WHEEL DRIVE EXCEPT VAN

1. Remove the console and rear seat.
2. Raise and support the vehicle safely.
3. Disconnect all clevis pin connecting and the cable ends.
4. Pull the cable through the floor.
5. Install in reverse order.
6. Adjust the cable. Apply sealer to the edge of the grommet at the floor opening. Check the parking brake indicator, the light should come on when the brake is applied one notch.

VAN

1. Disconnect the negative battery cable.
2. Remove the parking brake lever cover. Disconnect the parking brake cable from the parking brake lever. Remove the electrical switch connector. Remove the parking brake lever.
3. Remove the front cable retaining bolts from under the vehicle. Remove the front cable after removing the heat protector.
4. Remove the fuel tank.
5. Remove the left and right parking brake cables. Remove the lever assembly.
6. Installation is the reverse of the removal procedure.

CLUTCH

Clutch Assembly

HYDRAULIC/MANUAL

Removal and Installation

1. Remove the transmission. Insert a clutch aligning tool in the clutch hub to prevent dropping of the clutch disc during disassembly.
2. Remove the pressure plate bolts, pressure plate and clutch disc.
3. From inside the transmission bell housing, remove the return spring clip and remove the release bearing assembly.
4. If necessary, remove the release control lever and spring pin with a $^3/_{16}$ in. punch. Remove the control lever shaft assembly and clutch shift arm, two felt packings and two return springs.
5. Installation is the reverse of the removal procedure.

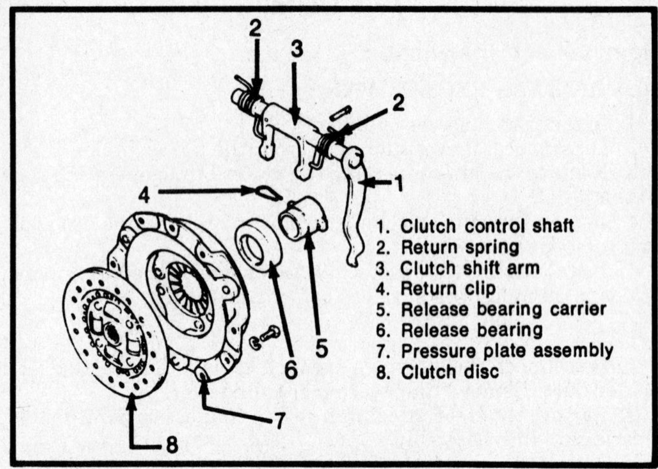

Exploded view of clutch assembly

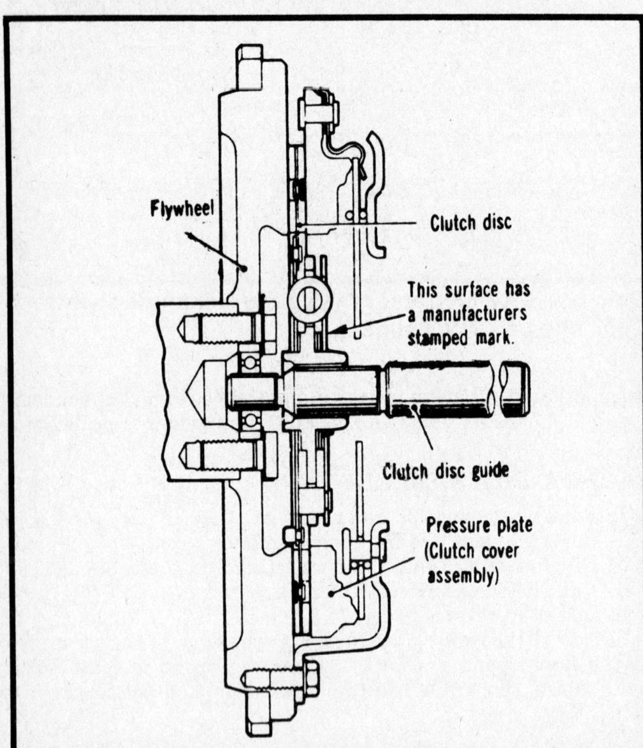

Installing the clutch disc—use clutch disc guide as shown

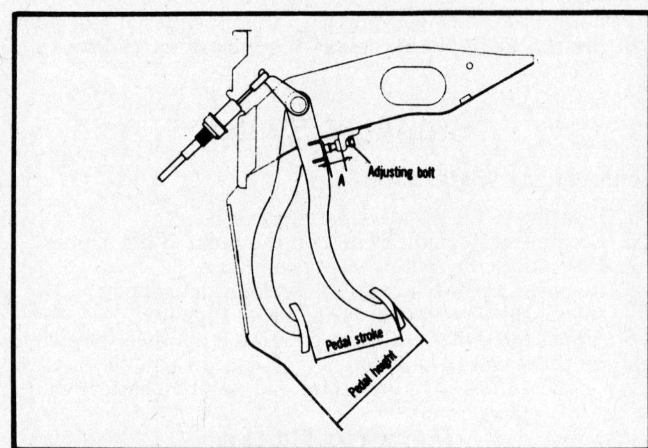

Adjusting clutch pedal height

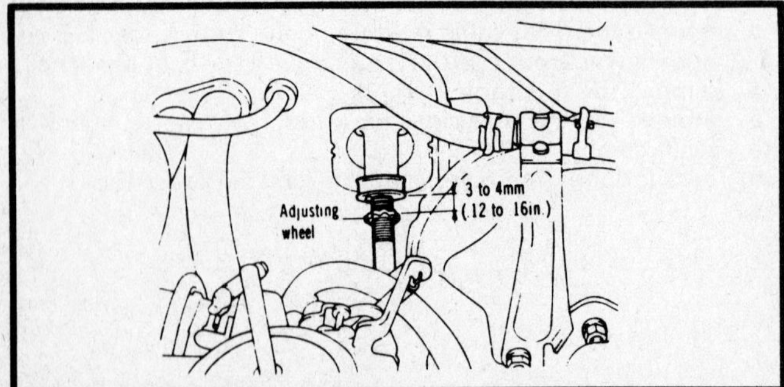

Adjusting the clutch cable

LINKAGE

Adjustment

HYDRAULIC

No adjustments are possible on the hydraulic clutch system. If the clutch is not functioning properly, bleed the clutch system before replacing any parts.

MANUAL

1. Loosen the cable adjusting wheel inside the engine compartment while pulling the cable.
2. Loosen the clutch pedal adjusting bolt locknut and loosen the adjusting bolt.
3. Remove the cable end from the clutch throwout lever.
4. Remove the cable end from the clutch pedal.
5. Installation is the reverse of the removal procedure.

NOTE: Apply engine oil to the cable before replacing. Make sure the isolating pad is fitted on the cable after installation to keep the cable from rubbing the motor mount during operation.

MASTER CYLINDER

Removal and Installation

Montero/Raider models utilize a hydraulic clutch system. Clutch pedal pressure is converted, through the master cylinder, into fluid pressure, which operates a slave cylinder at the clutch. The slave cylinder operates the clutch control lever and shift arm, which moves the clutch release bearing and operates the clutch.

1. Disconnect the clutch fluid line from the master cylinder. Slowly depress the clutch pedal to drain the fluid.
2. Remove the cotter pin connecting the master cylinder pushrod to the clutch pedal.
3. Remove the two retaining nuts and remove the master cylinder.
4. Reverse the order of removal for installation. Torque the master cylinder and clutch tube flare nut to 8–10 ft. lbs. and 10–12 ft. lbs., respectively.
5. Adjust the clutch pedal free play and bleed the hydraulic system.

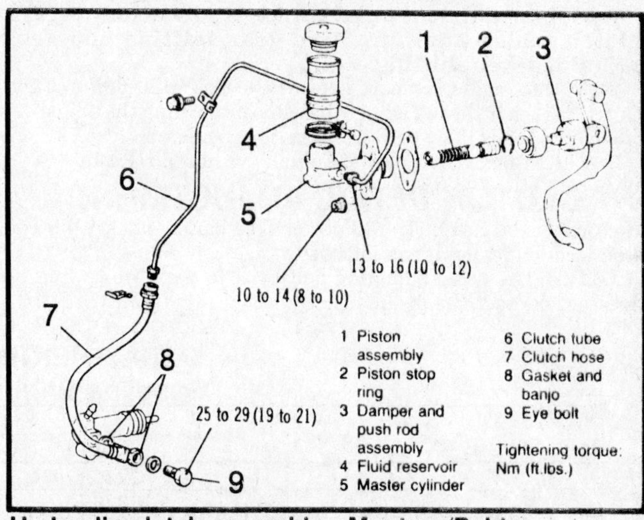

Hydraulic clutch assembly—Montero/Raider

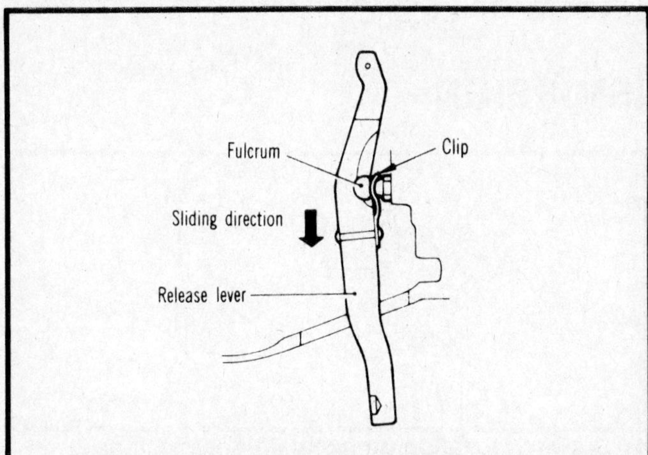

Montero/Raider clutch release lever

SLAVE CYLINDER

Removal and Installation

1. Remove the eye bolt and gaskets and disconnect the clutch hose from the clutch slave cylinder.
2. Remove the two bolts securing the clutch slave cylinder and clutch housing and remove the slave cylinder assembly.
3. Install the slave cylinder to the clutch housing and torque the two bolts to 22–30 ft. lbs.
4. Connect the clutch fluid line to the cylinder and tighten the eye bolt.
5. Bleed the clutch system.

HYDRAULIC CLUTCH BLEEDING

Whenever the clutch fluid line, clutch hose and/or clutch master cylinder have been removed, or if the clutch pedal feels spongy (indicating air in the system), bleed the system.

1. Raise and support the vehicle safely. Loosen the bleeder screw on the clutch slave cylinder.
2. Connect a length of rubber tubing to the bleeder screw, with the other end of the tube submerged in a clear glass jar filled with clean brake fluid. Make sure the clutch master cylinder is topped up with fluid. Keep it topped up throughout the procedure.
3. Have an assistant push the clutch pedal down slowly until air bubbles stop coming out of the rubber hose in the jar. All air is now expelled from the system.
4. Have the assistant hold the clutch pedal down until while retightening the bleeder screw.
5. Refill the clutch master cylinder with DOT 3 brake fluid.

CAUTION

Never reuse brake fluid which has been removed from the lines through the bleeding process because it may contain air bubbles and dirt. Never mix brake fluids. Use only approved DOT 3 fluid.

Adjustment

PEDAL HEIGHT

1. Adjust the pedal height to the standard value with the adjusting bolt and check the pedal stroke and distance "A".

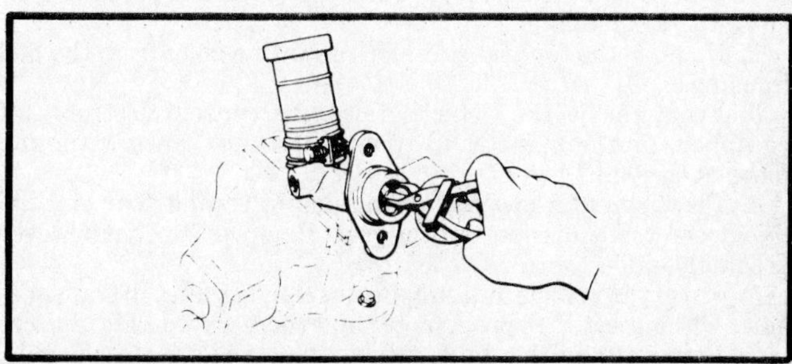
Removing master cylinder piston stop ring, hydraulic clutches

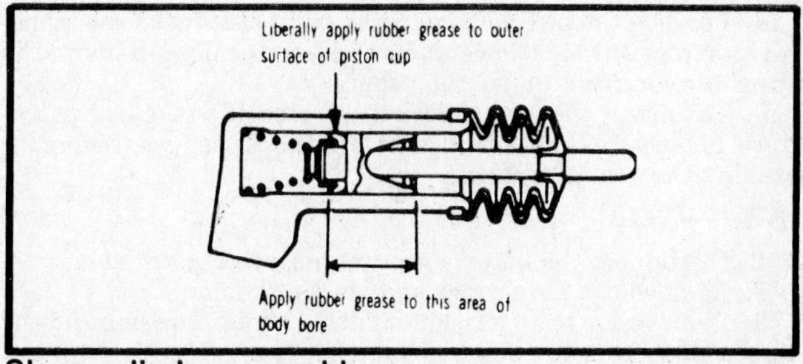

Slave cylinder assembly

NOTE: Insufficient pedal stroke results in only partial clutch release, causing hard gear shifting and gear grinding when shifting.

2. In the engine compartment at the fire wall, pull out the clutch cable a little and adjust the cable by turning the adjusting wheel until it is 0.12–0.16 in. from the insulator.
3. Clutch pedal free play should be within 0.8–1.4 in.

CLUTCH PEDAL ADJUSTMENT

If clutch pedal height from floor or free play is not within the standard value, adjust as follows:

1. Turn the pedal adjusting bolt back to a position where it does not contact the pedal arm.
2. Loosen the push rod lock nut and adjust the pedal height to the standard value by turning the push rod.
3. Turn the pedal adjusting bolt until it comes into contact with the pedal arm and then tighten the lock nut.
4. After making the adjustment, depress the clutch pedal several times and check the clutch pedal-to-floorboard clearance. The pedal on diesel pickups should be within 22mm (0.9 in.) or more when the clutch is fully disengaged. The Montero/Raider pedal should be close to this same distance. If the pedal-to-floor clearance is less then this, air may be in the hydraulic system. If so, the system should be bled. Also, the clutch plates could be worn.

PEDAL HEIGHT ADJUSTMENT
Gasoline Engined Pickup Trucks

Description	Standard valve mm (in.) 2.0L	2.6L
Distance A	22 (.9)	20 (.8)
Pedal height	166 (6.5)	176 (6.9)
Pedal stroke	140 (5.5)	150 (5.9)

MANUAL TRANSMISSION

The pickups use both a 4-speed, the KM130 and a 5-speed, the KM132. The Montero/Raider uses only a 5-speed, the KM145. All three transmissions are virtually identical, the 5-speed boxes being just a 4-speed box with an overdrive 0.856:1 fifth gear. For Transmission and Transfer Case Overhaul, refer to the Unit Repair Section.

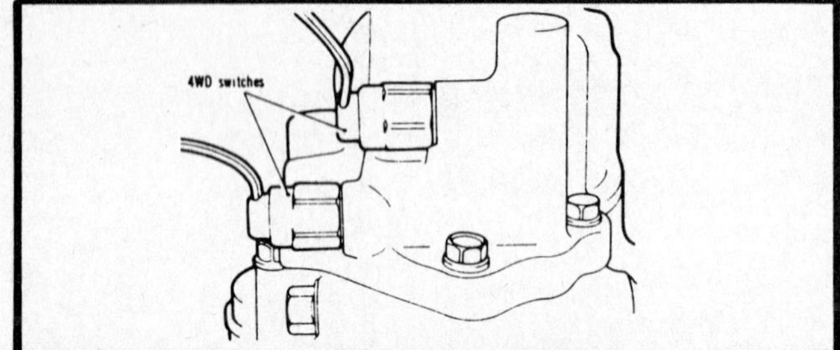

4WD switch location on manual transmissions

Manual Transmission 4 & 5 Speed

Removal and Installation

2WD PICKUP

1. Disconnect the battery ground cable, remove the air cleaner and the starter.
2. Remove the top transmission mounting bolts from the bell housing.
3. From inside the vehicle, raise the console assembly, if equipped, or the carpet and remove the dust cover retaining plate at the shift lever.
4. Place the four speed transmission in second gear and the five speed transmission in first gear. Remove the control lever assembly.
5. Raise the vehicle and support it safely. Drain the transmission. Disconnect the speedometer and the back up light switch.
6. Remove the driveshaft, exhaust pipe and the clutch cable. On diesel vehicles, remove the clutch release cylinder.
7. Support the transmission and remove the engine rear support bracket.
8. Remove the bell housing cover and bolts, move the transmission rearward and lower it carefully to the floor. Remove the transmission from under the vehicle.
9. To install the transmission, reverse the removal procedure. Make sure the transmission is in the proper gear before installing the gear shift lever.

4WD PICKUP

1. Disconnect the battery ground (negative) terminal.
2. Remove the air cleaner and starting motor.
3. Remove the transmission mounting bolts (two bolts on the upper side) from the bell housing.
4. In the cab, remove the lock screws and lift up the console box. In vehicles without a console box, remove the carpet.
5. Remove the attaching screws and lift out the dust cover retaining plate.
6. Turn up the dust cover and remove the control housing attaching bolts from the extension housing and remove the control lever assembly.
7. Raise and support the vehicle safely.
8. Drain the gearbox.
9. Remove the driveshafts. Disconnect the speedometer cable at the transmission.
10. Disconnect the back-up light switch harness and the 4WD indicator light switch harness, which is resting on the upper middle section of the transfer case.
11. Disconnect the front exhaust pipe.
12. Disconnect the clutch cable from the clutch control lever.
13. Support the rear of the engine.
14. Disconnect and remove the transfer case mounting bracket.
15. Raise the transmission from underneath. Remove the No.2 crossmember.

CAUTION

The transmission supporting area should be as wide as possible.

16. After removing the bell housing cover, remove the remaining transmission bolts from the bell housing.
17. Remove the transmission from the vehicle. Use care not to twist the front end of the main drive gear.
18. Installation is the reverse of the removal procedure.

Torque the transmission mounting bolts to 31–40 ft. lbs.; the transmission-to-rear insulator bolts to 14–18 ft. lbs.; the transfer case support insulator-to-transfer case mounting bracket bolts to 14–18 ft. lbs.; the transfer case mounting bracket bolts to 14–18 ft. lbs. Set the transmission shift lever to the "neutral" position and the transfer case shift lever to the 4H position when installing the gear shift lever assembly. Adjust the clutch and fill the KM130 transmission with 2.2 qts. of hypoid gear oil; the KM132 with 2.4 qts.; the KM144 and KM145 transmission and transfer case with 2.3 qts.

MONTERO/RAIDER

1. Disconnect the negative cable from the battery.
2. Place the transmission lever in neutral and the transfer case lever in 4H. Remove the gearshift lever assembly. Cover the opening with a shop rag to prevent any dirt from entering.
3. Raise and support the vehicle safely. Remove the transfer case skid plate.
4. Drain the transfer case and transmission gearbox.
5. Remove the front and rear driveshafts.
6. Disconnect the speedometer cable, back-up light switch harness and the 4WD indicator light harness, which rests on the top center of the transfer case.
7. Detach the clutch release cylinder from the transmission.
8. Remove the bell housing cover.
9. Detach the starter motor from the bell housing.

NOTE: On vehicles with air conditioning, remove the front driveshaft, then lower the starting motor downward from underneath the vehicle to remove it.

10. Remove the front exhaust pipe mounting bracket.
11. Detach the engine support rear insulator from the No. 2 crossmember and remove the No. 2 crossmember.
12. Support the transmission and transfer case assembly.
13. Unbolt the transfer case from the transfer case mounting bracket.
14. Remove the transmission mounting bolts from the engine.
15. Remove the transmission mounting bolts from the engine. With the assembly supported and securely positioned, pull the transfer case and transmission assembly away from the engine.
16. Tilt the front of the transmission and transfer case assembly downward. Slowly lower the assembly, being careful that the rear of the transmission does not hit the No. 3 crossmember.

VAN

NOTE: In order to remove the transmission, the seat underframe must be removed from the vehicle.

1. Disconnect the negative battery cable. Remove the air cleaner. Remove the starter.
2. Remove the drivers seat. Remove the parking brake lever and fuel tank filler door release lever.
3. Remove the battery cover. Remove the bolts retaining the seat underframe in place. Remove the seat underframe.
4. Remove the top transmission mounting bolts from the bell housing.
5. From inside the vehicle, remove the dust cover retaining plate at the shift lever.
6. Place the transmission in the neutral position. Remove the control lever assembly.
7. Raise and support the vehicle safely. Drain the transmission. Disconnect the speedometer and the backup light switch.
8. Remove the driveshaft. Disconnect the exhaust pipe. Remove the slave cylinder.
9. Support the engine and transmission and remove the engine rear support bracket.
10. Remove the bellhousing cover and bolts, move the transmission rearward and lower it carefully to the floor. Remove the transmission from under the vehicle.
11. To install the transmission, reverse the removal procedure. Make sure the transmission is in the proper gear before installing the gear shift lever.

Linkage

Adjustment

No adjustments are possible on the manual transmission shifting linkage.

AUTOMATIC TRANSMISSION

Automatic Transmission

Removal and Installation

ALL MODELS EXCEPT VAN

NOTE: The transmission and converter must be removed as an assembly. Otherwise, the converter drive plate, pump bushing, or oil seal may be damaged. The drive plate will not support a load. Therefore, none of the weight of the transmission should be allowed to rest on the plate during removal.

1. Disconnect the battery ground cable, drain the transmission and remove the cooler lines at the transmission.
2. Remove the starter and cooler line bracket.
3. Rotate the crankshaft clockwise and remove the bolts attaching the torque converter to drive plate.
4. Remove the driveshaft(s).
5. Disconnect the gearshift rod and torque shaft.
6. Disconnect the throttle rod from the lever at the left side of the transmission. Remove the linkage bellcrank from the transmission if so equipped.
7. Remove the oil filler tube and speedometer cable.
8. On 2WD models, disconnect the back-up light switch harness. On 4WD models, disconnect the back-up light switch har-

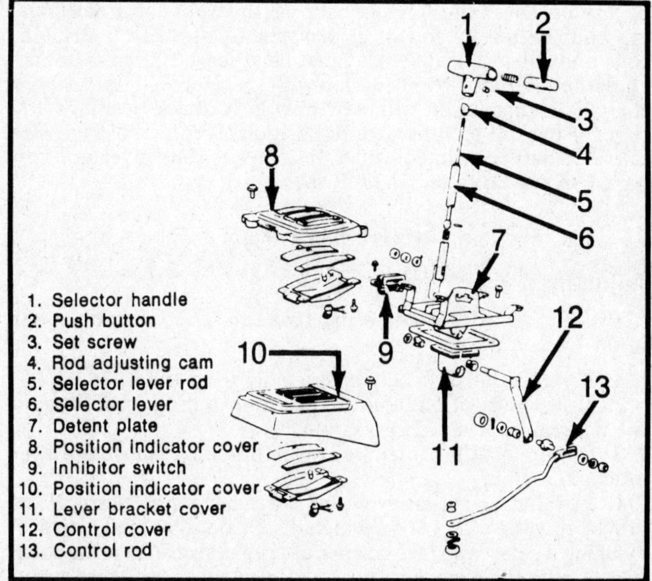

Exploded view of automatic transmission shift control

ness and 4WD indicator light switch harness which are located near the upper middle of the transfer case.

9. Support the rear of the engine.
10. Raise the transmission slightly.
11. Remove the crossmember.
12. Remove all bell housing bolts.
13. Carefully work the transmission converter assembly rearward off the engine block dowels and disengage the converter hub from the end of the crankshaft. Attach a small C-clamp to the edge of the bell housing to hold the converter in place during transmission removal.
14. Remove the transmission.
15. Installation is the reverse of the removal procedure.

VAN

1. Raise and support the vehicle safely. Loosen the oil pan mounting screws, tap the oil pan at one corner to break it loose and then allow the fluid to drain out one side. Remove the pan and remaining fluid.
2. Lower the vehicle. Disconnect the negative battery cable. Remove the attaching bolt and remove the transmission pan filler tube by pulling it upward and out of the transmission case.
3. Raise and support the vehicle safely. Remove the two top transmission attaching bolts from the converter housing.
4. Disconnect and tag the starter wiring and remove the starter.
5. Disconnect the oil cooler hoses at the metal tubes near the engine block. Unbolt and remove the tubes and mounting brackets from the block.
6. Remove the four bolts and remove the converter housing cover. Remove the torque converter bolts.
7. Disconnect the speedometer cable. Disconnect the transmission control rod and the connection lever at the cross shaft assembly.
8. Disconnect the transmission ground cable. Remove the driveshaft.
9. Support the rear of the transmission. Unbolt the transmission rear support bracket by removing two bolts on either side. Then, unbolt the bracket from the transmission.
10. Remove the remaining mounting bolts from the area of the converter housing. Separate the transmission from the engine and remove it.
11. Installation is the reverse of the removal procedure. Before beginning, check the distance between the front of the bell housing and the torque converter driveplate bolts with a straightedge and ruler. The distance must be at least 1.38 in. After installation, refill the transmission with the approved fluid. Check that the transmission will start only in N and P positions and that the backup light lights in R position. Torque the driveplate to crankshaft bolts to 94–100 ft. lbs. Torque the converter housing to engine bolts to 31–39 ft. lbs.

Shift Linkage

Adjustment

NOTE: To adjust the shift linkage, the control cover must be removed.

1. Remove the shift handle assembly from the lever.
2. Take the position indicator assembly out upward. Remove the position indicator lamp.
3. Disconnect the control rod from the arm. Remove the lever bracket assembly.
4. Installation is the reverse of the removal procedure. If the proper turning effort (13–29 inch lbs.) is not obtained, adjust it by using a selective wave washer of proper size. When the turning effort at the pivot A is checked, the pin at the forward end of the rod assembly must not slide with the detent plate. If the arm is loose, the bushing should be replaced.

Band Adjustment

LOW AND REVERSE BAND

Procedure

1. Raise and support the vehicle safely. Drain the transmission fluid and remove the pan.
2. This transmission has an allen socket adjustment screw at the servo end of lever. After removing the locknut, torque the screw to 43 inch lbs. Back the screw off 7 turns. Torque the locknut to 30 ft. lbs.
3. Reinstall the pan and fill the transmission to the proper level.

KICKDOWN

Procedure

The kickdown band adjusting screw is located on the left side of the transmission case.

1. Loosen the locknut and back off approximately 5 turns. Test the adjusting screw for free turning in the transmission case.
2. Torque the adjusting screw to 69 inch lbs.
3. Back off the adjusting screw 3 $^{1}/_{2}$ turns. Torque the locknut to 35 ft. lbs.

Throttle Linkage

Adjustment

The throttle rod adjustment is very important to proper transmission operation. This adjustment positions a valve which controls shift speed, shift quality and part throttle down shift sensitivity. If the setting is too short, early shifts and slippage between shifts may occur. If the setting is too long, shifts may be delayed and part throttle down shifts may be very sensitive.

1. Warm up the engine until it reaches normal operating temperature. With the carburetor automatic choke disengaged from the fast idle cam, adjust the engine idle speed by rotating speed adjusting screw (SAS).
2. Loosen the bolts on the linkage so that both rod "B" and "C" can slide properly.
3. Lightly push rod "A" or the transmission throttle lever and rod "C" toward the idle stopper and set the rods to the idle position. Tighten the bolt securely that connects rods "B" and "C".

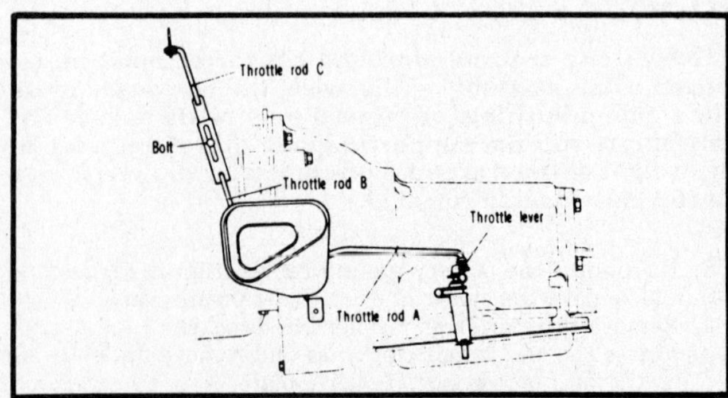

Throttle rod adjustment – automatic transmission

4. Make sure that when the carburetor throttle valve is wide open, the transmission throttle lever smoothly moves from the IDLE to the WIDE OPEN position (from 47.5°–54°) and that there is some range in the lever stroke.

5. Make sure that when the throttle linkage alone is slowly returned from the fully closed position, the transmission throttle lever completely returns to idle by the return spring force.

Neutral Start Switch

Removal and Installation

1. Raise and support the evhicle safely.
2. Remove the switch from the right side of the transmission.
3. Install the new switch and adjust the shift cable so that the engine will start only while the shift lever is in the Neutral or Park positions.
4. Check to make sure that the back-up lamps only work when the shifter is in Reverse.

Oil Pan, Fluid and Filter

Replacement

1. Raise and support the vehicle safely.
2. Loosen the pan bolts from one end to the other allowing the fluid to drain out.
3. Remove the old filter from the pan.
4. Clean the pan and install a new filter. Torque the filter bolts to 35 inch lbs.
5. Install the pan and new gasket. Torque the pan bolts to 6–9 ft. lbs.
6. Add four quarts of Dexron®II fluid, start the engine and move the lever through all positions, pausing momentarily in each. Add enough fluid to bring the level to the full mark on the dipstick.

TRANSFER CASE

Refer to the Unit Repair Section for Overhaul Procedures.

Transfer Case

Removal and Installation

4WD PICKUPS AND MONTERO/RAIDER

The transfer case is removed from the transmission while the transmission/transfer case assembly is out of the vehicle.

1. Remove the back-up light switch from the lower right of the adapter. Take out the steel ball (manual transmission models only).
2. Remove the plug from the right side of the transfer case and take out the select spring and the select plunger.
3. Remove the six bolts securing the control lever assembly and remove the control lever assembly and gasket.
4. On the four speed only, remove the plug from the top of the adaptor and take out the neutral return spring and plunger.
5. On five speed models, remove the plugs from the top of the adaptor and take out the resistance spring, steel ball, neutral springs and plungers.
6. On the four speed and automatic transmission transfer case, remove the bolts securing the transfer case adapter to the transmission.
7. On the four speed model only, with the change shifter tilted to the left, remove the control finger from the shift lug groove. Take out the transfer case assembly.
8. On the five speed model, drive out the lock pin from the change shifter using a $^{3}/_{16}$ in. punch. Remove the four bolts and two nuts securing the transfer case to the adapter and remove the transfer case assembly from the adapter. Remove the change shifter from the control shaft.
9. Reverse the above procedure for installation. Make sure to mount the neutral return plungers and the springs in the hole on top of the adapter and tighten the plug until it is flush with the adapter surface.

DRIVE LINES AND UNIVERSAL JOINTS

Drive Lines

FRONT AND REAR

Removal and Installation

2WD MODELS

1. Make mating marks on the flange yoke and the differential companion flange.
2. Remove the bolts connecting the flange yoke to the differential companion flange and remove the nuts attaching the center bearing assembly.
3. Remove the driveshaft by pulling it out. Installation is reverse of the removal procedure.

NOTE: When the sleeve yoke end of the driveshaft is pulled out from the transmission extension housing, transmission oil will flow out, if the front of the vehicle is raised higher than the rear.

CAUTION

When removing the driveshaft, be careful not to damage the oil seal lip and that no foreign substance is present in the lip area.

4WD MODELS

1. Set the free wheeling hubs to UNLOCKED and set the transfer case gear shift lever to the 2H position.
2. Make mating marks on the U-joint flange yoke and the companion flange on the differential and/or transfer case.
3. Remove the bolts connecting the flange yoke to the differential and/or transfer case companion flange.
4. Remove the driveshaft by pulling it out. Be careful not to damage the oil seal lip.

NOTE: When the driveshaft is pulled out of the transmission extension housing or the transfer case, transmission or transfer case oil may leak out depending on the angle of the vehicle.

CENTER BEARING

Removal and Installation

2WD MODELS

1. Remove driveshaft.
2. Disconnect the center universal joint.
3. Remove the nut holding the center yoke and remove the

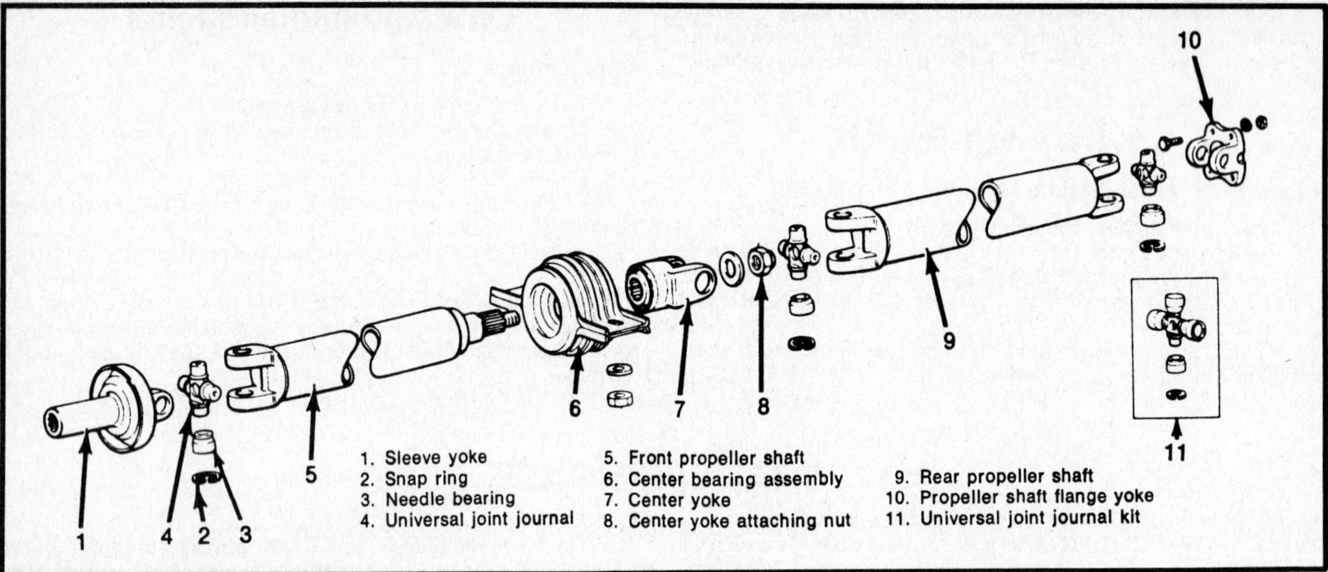

Exploded view of driveshaft

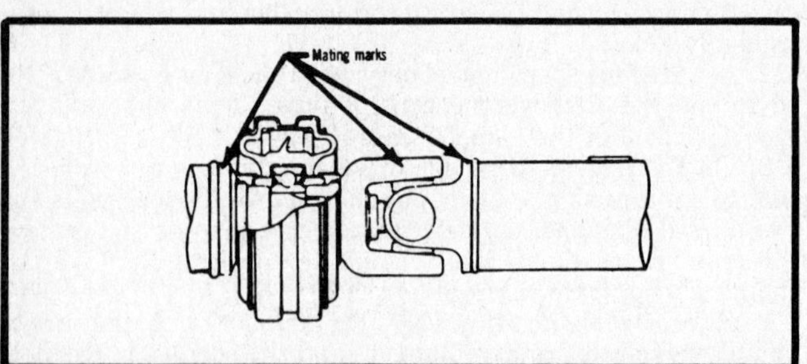

When installing center bearing align three mating marks

yoke. Remove the center bearing bracket from the bearing by prying on it.

4. Remove the center bearing using a gear puller.

NOTE: The center bracket and the mounting rubber must be replaced as a unit.

5. Fill the bearing grease cavity with multipurpose grease.
6. Partially insert the center bearing into the shaft and install the bracket to the bearing.
7. Verify that the bracket mounting rubber is properly fitted in the bearing groove.
8. Refit the center yoke, making sure to align the notch on the yoke with the notch on the front driveshaft. Replace the attaching nut and torque to 116–159 ft. lbs.
9. Replace the center universal joint, making sure to align the notch on the rear driveshaft with the notch on the yoke.
10. Install the driveshaft.

NOTE: The manufacturer suggests that a new center yoke locking nut be used when the center bearing is removed.

Universal Joints

Removal, Overhaul and Installation

1. Raise and support the vehicle safely. Matchmark and remove the driveshaft.
2. If the front yoke is to be disassembled, matchmark the driveshaft and sliding splined yoke so that driveline balance is preserved upon reassembly. Remove the snap rings that retain the bearing caps.
3. Select two press components, with one small enough to pass through the yoke holes for the bearing caps and the other large enough to receive the bearing cap.
4. Use a vise or a press and position the small and large press components on either side of the U-joint. Press in on the smaller press component so that it presses the opposite bearing cap out of the yoke and into the larger press component. If the cap does not come all the way out, grasp it with a pair of pliers and work it out.
5. Reverse the position of the press components so that the smaller press component presses on the cross. Press the other bearing cap out of the yoke.
6. Repeat the procedure on the other bearings.
7. To install, grease the bearing caps and needles thoroughly if they are not pregreased. Start a new bearing cap into one side of the yoke. Position the cross in the yoke.

NOTE: Some U-joints have a grease fitting that must be installed in the joint before assembly. When installing the fitting, make sure that once the driveshaft is installed in the vehicle, the fitting is accessible to be greased at a later date.

8. Select two press components small enough to pass through the yoke holes. Put the press components against the cross and the cap and press the bearing cap ¼ in. below the surface of the yoke. If there is a sudden increase in the force needed to press the cap into place, or if the cross starts to bind, the bearings are cocked. They must be removed and restarted in the yoke. Failure to do so will cause premature bearing failure.
9. Install a new snap-ring.
10. Start the new bearing into the opposite side. Place a press component on it and press in until the opposite bearing contacts the snap ring.
11. Install a new snap ring. It may be necessary to grind the facing surface of the snap ring slightly to permit easier installation.
12. Install the other bearings in the same manner.
13. Check the joint for free movement. If binding exists, smack the yoke ears with a brass or plastic faced hammer to seat the bearing needles. If binding still exists, dissassemble the joint and check to see if the needles are in place. Do not strike the bearings unless the shaft is supported firmly. Do not install the driveshaft until free movement exists at all joints.

FRONT DRIVE AXLE–FOUR WHEEL DRIVE

Refer to the Unit Repair Section for Overhaul Procedures.

Axle Housing

Removal and Installation

1. Raise and support the vehicle safely. Remove the under cover.
2. Matchmark and remove the driveshaft.
3. Remove the inner axle circlips. Remove the axle assemblies.
4. Support the front axle housing.
5. Remove the axle housing mounting brackets and nuts.
5. Save all rubber bushings from the mounting brackets for installation.
6. Remove the axle housing from the vehicle.
7. Installation is the reverse of the removal procedure.
8. Torque the mounting bracket to housing nuts and bolts to 58–72 ft. lbs. and the mounting bracket to frame nuts and bolts to 22–30 ft. lbs.

Locking Hubs

Removal and Installation

MANUAL LOCKING HUBS

1. Set the control handle to the FREE position. Unbolt the six cover bolts and remove the hub cover.
2. Using snapring pliers, remove the snapring from the driveshaft.
3. Remove the hub assembly from the front wheel.
4. To install, apply a semi-drying sealant to the front hub mounting surface of the hub body assembly, then torque the bolts to 36–43 ft. lbs.
5. Measure axleshaft end play using a dial indicator. If endplay exceeds 0.008–0.020 in., install a spacer on the axleshaft end so that the measurement will be within specifications.
6. Install the snapring. Install the hub cover.

AUTOMATIC LOCKING HUBS

1. Remove the hub cover. If the cover cannot be loosened by hand, protect the cover with a shop towel to avoid damaging it and use an oil filter strap wrench to loosen it.
2. Remove the O-ring from the hub cover.
3. Using snapring pliers, remove the snapring and spacer.
4. Remove the hub.
5. To install, apply a semi-drying sealer to the hub surface.

NOTE: Make sure there is no excess sealer on the outside of the hub.

6. Align the key of brake "B" with the slot in the knuckle spindle. Loosely install the automatic hub assembly.

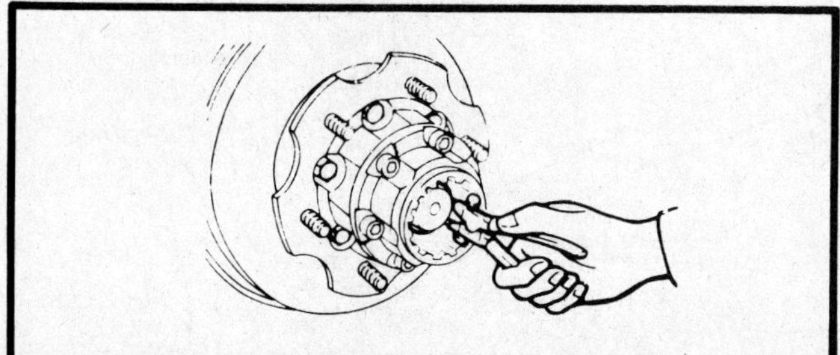

Removing snap-ring from front hub–4WD models

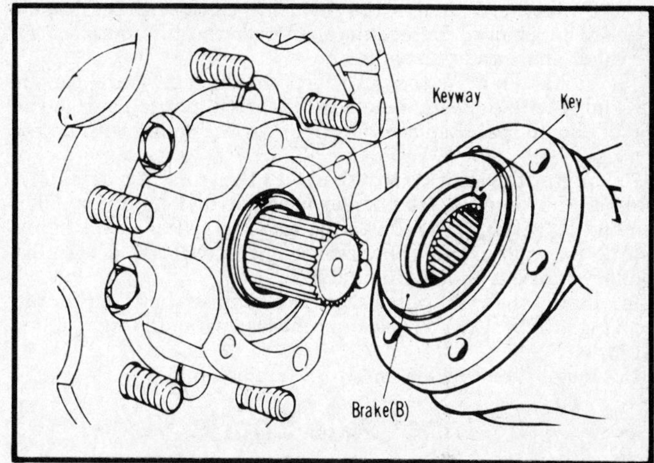

Free-wheeling hub installation. Notice keyway

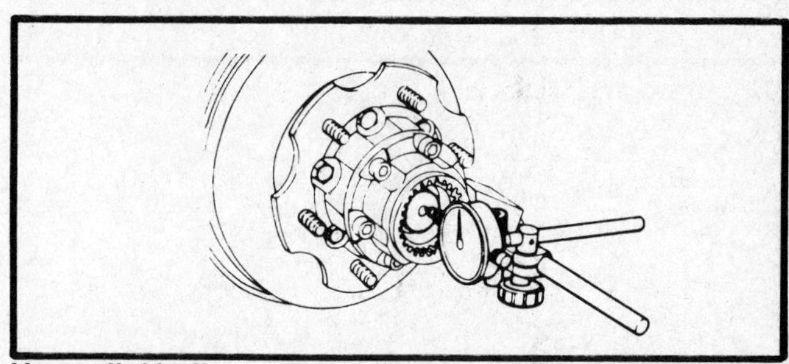

Use a dial indicator to measure axial drive shaft play–4WD models

7. Make sure that the hub and the free wheeling hub assembly are in close contact when the assembly is forced lightly against the hub. If not, turn the hub until close contact is obtained.
8. Torque the free wheeling hub mounting bolts to 37–43 ft. lbs.
9. Apply a suitable grease to the O-ring before mounting it into the cover.
10. Install the cover securely.

Outer Axle Shafts

Removal and Installation

1. Raise and support the vehicle safely. Remove the wheel assembly.
2. Remove the front brake caliper assembly. Do not disconnect the brake hose. Support the caliper out of the way.
3. Remove the free wheeling hub cover assembly and remove the snapring from the axleshaft.
4. Remove the knuckle and the front hub together as a unit.
5. Remove the outer shaft as follows: for the left side on all 4WD pickups and Montero/Raiders, pull the shaft out of the differential carrier assembly. When pulling the left shaft from the differential carrier assembly, be careful that the shaft splines do not damage the oil seal.
6. On 4WD pickups, raise the right lower suspension arm. Remove the right shock absorber.

NOTE: Do not lower the control arm while disconnecting the shock absorber or after it is disconnected. The control arm should not be removed until the upper part of the shock absorber has been reconnected to the arm post of the side frame.

7. On 4WD pickups, detach the right shaft from the inner shaft assembly and remove the shaft.
8. On Montero/Raiders, the right side shock absorber doesn't have to be removed. Detach the shaft from the differential carrier inner shaft and remove it.
9. To install; drive the left shaft into the differential carrier assembly with a plastic hammer. Be careful not to damage the lip of the oil seal. Replace the circlip on the spline with a new one.
10. Mount the knuckle together with the front hub assembly. Adjust the outer shaft endplay using a dial indicator. Play should be within 0.008–0.020 in. Install a spacer (available in 0.012 in. increments from Dodge and Mitsibishi dealers) if endplay exceeds the above limits.
11. Install the right outer shaft to the inner shaft and torque to 37–43 ft. lbs. On 4WD pickup vehicles, install the right shock absorber.
12. Install the knuckle and front hub assembly.

Inner Axle Shafts

Removal and Installation

1. Raise and support the vehicle safely.

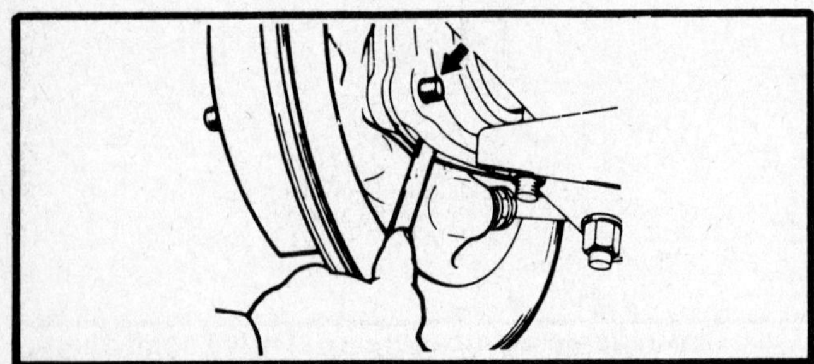

Measuring clearance between bearing case and axle housing face

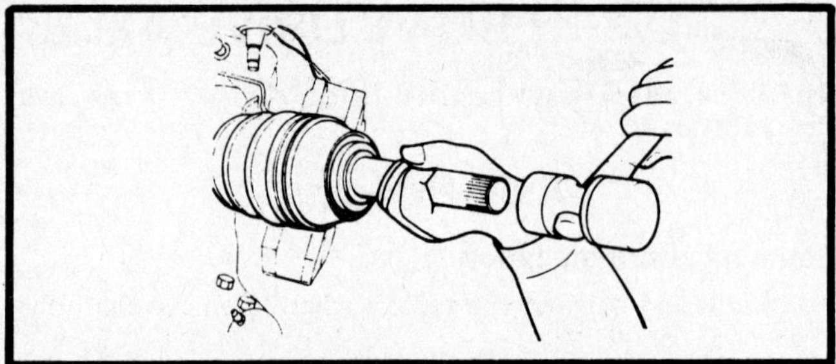

Use a plastic mallet to drive in left drive shaft

2. Remove the mounting nut from the top of the shock absorber and detach the shock absorber from the crossmember. The shock absorber must be removed when working on either side.

NOTE: When removing the shock absorber, do not lower the vehicle. The vehicler must be lowered only when the shock absorber is properly mounted.

3. Remove the outer axle shaft.
4. Attach a special axle shaft puller, Mitsubishi part MB990906 or equivalent, to the inner shaft flange. Pull the inner axle shaft from the front differential carrier.

NOTE: When pulling the inner shaft from the carrier, be careful that the spline part of the inner shaft does not damage the oil seal.

5. If necessary, remove the housing tube.
6. Check for unusual wear or discoloration on the inner shaft.
7. Install the housing tube onto the front differential carrier and differential mounting bracket.
8. Drive the inner shaft into the front differential with the same special tool used to remove the shaft.

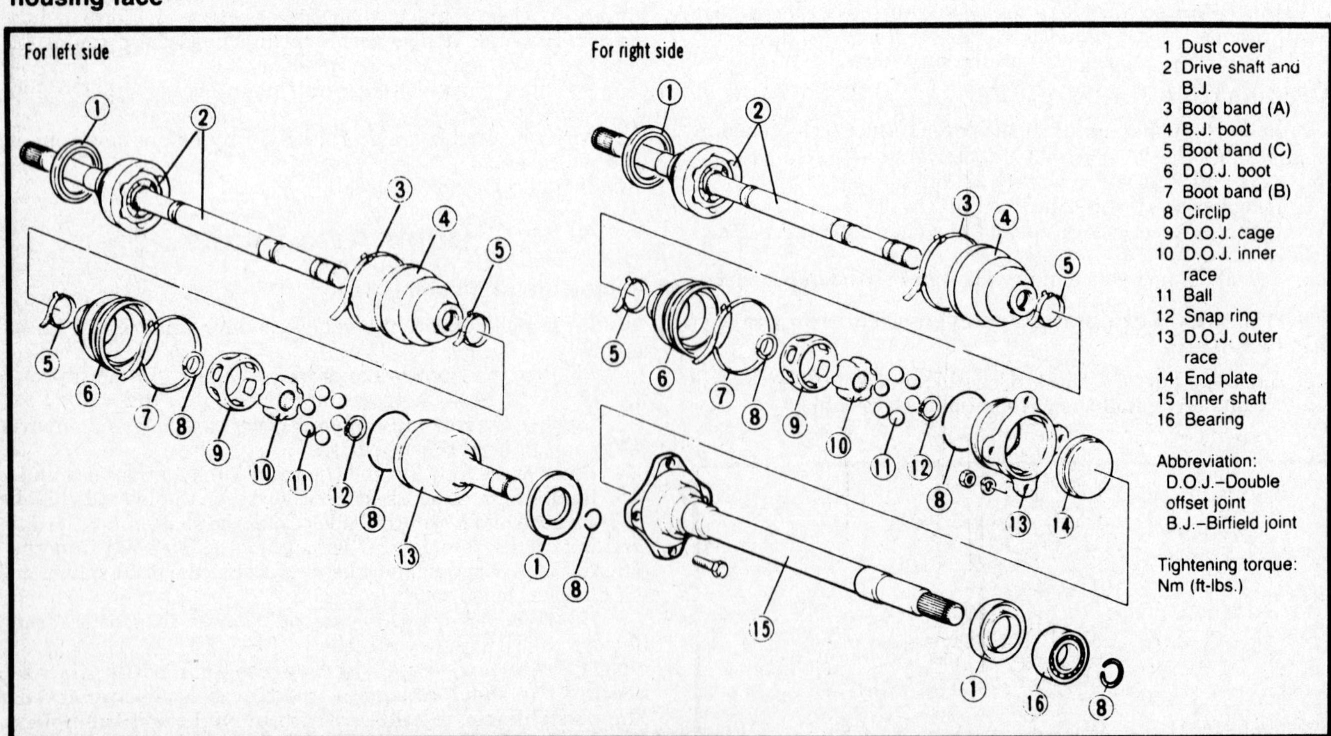

Axle shaft and CV-joint assemblies—4WD models and Montero

NOTE: Replace the circlip on the spline part of the inner shaft with a new one. Use care not to damage the lip of the oil seal.

9. Install the right outer shaft.

Axle Shaft Seal

Removal and Installation

1. Remove the inner axleshaft.
2. Pry out the seal, using care not to damage the sealing surface.
3. Coat the lip of the new seal with engine oil and, with the lip facing inward, drive the seal into the same depth as the old seal.
4. Install the inner axleshaft. Check the lubricant level when finished.

Oil Seal and Needle Bearing

Removal and Installation

1. Raise and support the vehicle safely. Remove the steering knuckle.
2. Remove the oil seal and spacer. Remove the needle bearing by tapping the needles uniformly.

NOTE: Never reuse the needle bearing. It must be replaced.

3. To install, apply an SAE No. 2 EP grease to the roller surface of the new needle bearing. Press in the needle bearing using a bearing installation tool until it is flush with the knuckle end face. Be careful not to drive the bearing in too far.
4. Apply the SAE No. 2 EP grease to the knuckle contacting surface of the spacer. Install the spacer onto the knuckle with chamfered side toward the center of the vehicle.
5. Press the new oil seal with the bearing tools until it is flush with the knuckle end face. Apply the grease to the inside and lip of the oil seal.
6. Install the steering knuckle.

Front Axle Hub and Bearings

Removal and Installation

1. Raise and support the vehicle safely. Remove the front wheel assembly. Remove the front brake caliper without disconnecting the brake hose. Support the caliper out of the way.
2. Remove the free wheeling hub.
3. Remove the lock washer. Remove the lock nut with special tool MB990954 or equivalent.
4. Remove the front hub assembly from the knuckle, together with the inner and outer bearings.
5. Remove the outer bearing race from the brake rotor. Remove the oil seal and the inner bearing race.
6. If necessary, make matchmarks on the brake rotor and front hub and separate.
7. Carefully wipe all old grease from inside the front hub.
8. Using a brass drift, carefully tap out the inner and outer bearing races. Tap around each race uniformly.
9. Apply an SAE No. 2 EP grease to the outside surface of the new inner and outer bearings.

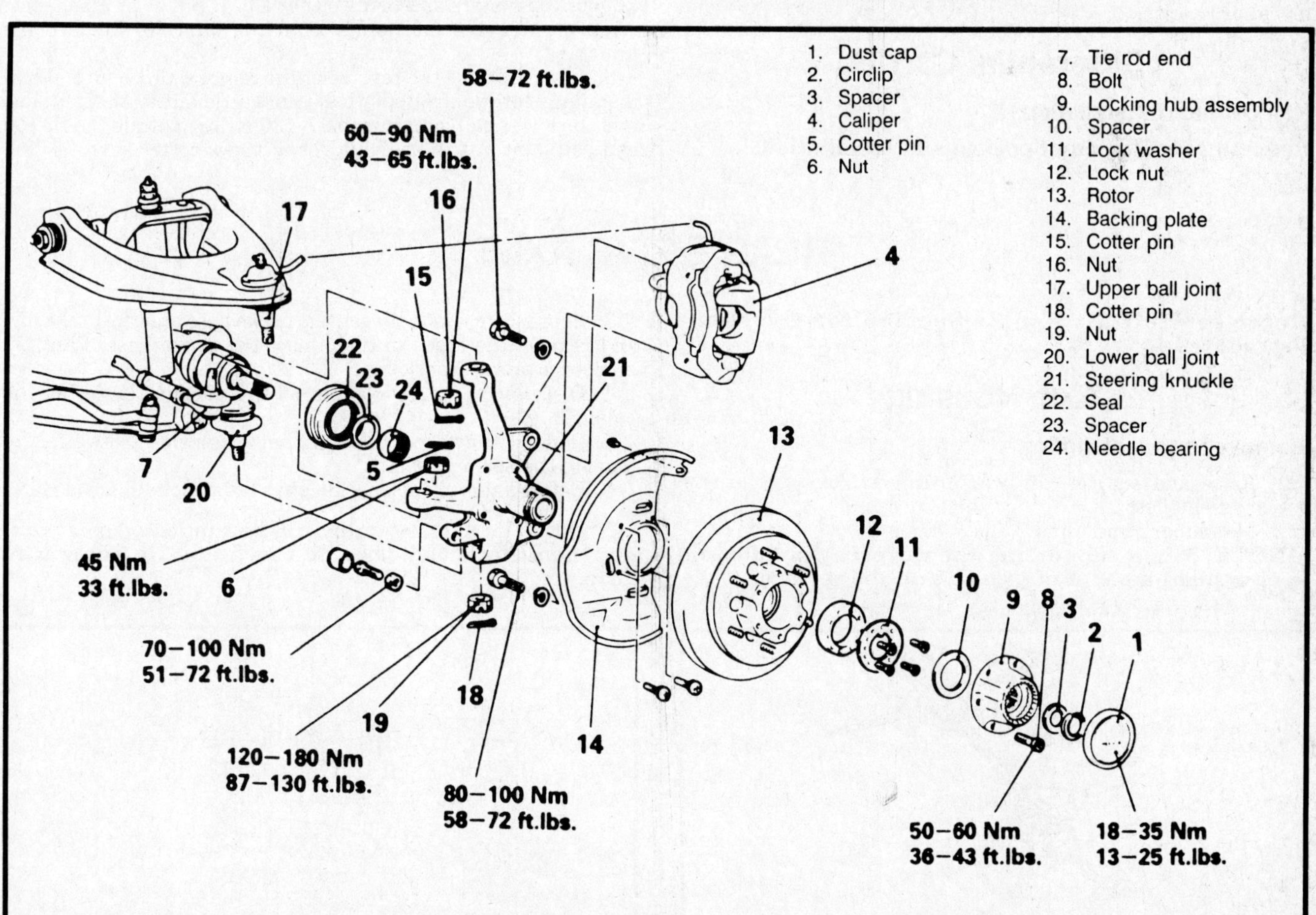

4WD steering knuckle, hub and bearing—exploded view

NOTE: The bearing inner and outer race must always be replaced as an assembly.

10. Bearing installation tool, Mitsubishi part No. MB990938 and MB990933 or equivalent are necessary to replace the inner and outer races.
11. Apply an SAE No. 2 EP multipurpose grease to the outer bearing outer race, oil seal lip and inside surface of the front hub.
12. Apply the grease to the inner bearing inner race and fit the inner race into the front hub.
13. Press the new oil seal into the front hub with the special tools until it is flush with the front hub end face.
14. Fit the knuckle into the front hub assembly. Using a special tool, part No. MB990954 or equivalent, which fits standard torque wrenches, torque the lock nut to 95–145 ft. lbs. Loosen the lock nut to 0 ft. lbs. then, torque to 18 ft. lbs. Loosen the nut 30°.
15. Install the lock washer. If the lock washer and lock nut holes do not align, align the holes by loosening the nut by not more than 20°.
16. Before installing the free wheeling hub assembly, measure the turning force of the front hub using a spring scale. If the measured value does not meet specifications (1–4 lbs.) retorque the lock nut to the specified torque given earlier.
17. Apply a semi-drying sealant to the free wheeling hub surface of the front hub and then torque the front hub to the specified torque, 36–43 ft. lbs.
18. Measure front driveshaft end play and correct , if necessary.
19. The remainder of the installation is the reverse of the removal procedure.

Differential Carrier

Removal and Installation

Refer to Axle Housing Removal and Installation.

Axle Shaft Bearings

Removal and Installation

Refer to Front Wheel Hub and Bearing Removal and Installation.

Steering Knuckle

WITH KING PINS

Removal and Installation

1. Raise and support the vehicle safely. Remove the wheel assembly.
2. Remove the front hub assembly, including the brake rotor.
3. Disconnect the tie rod from the steering knuckle.
4. Remove the upper and lower ball joints.
5. Remove the steering knuckle from the outer shaft.
6. Replace the oil seal or needle bearing, if necessary.
7. Installation is the reverse of the removal procedure.

WITH BALL JOINTS

1. Raise and support the vehicle safely.
2. Remove the wheel assembly.
3. Remove the brake caliper and front hub assembly.
4. Disconnect the stabilizer and strut bar from the lower arm.
5. Remove the shock absorber and compress the coil spring.
6. Remove the relay rod from the steering arm using a ball joint remover.
7. Remove the cotter pins and castle nuts from the steering knuckle ball joints and using either a gear puller or a ball joint remover, free the ball joints from the knuckle. Remove the knuckle.
8. Installation is the reverse of the removal procedure. When installing, torque the upper ball joint castle nut to 43–65 ft. lbs. and the lower ball joint nut to 87–130 ft. lbs. Torque the tie rod end ball joint nut to 25–33 ft. lbs. Fit new cotter keys.

REAR DRIVE AXLE

Refer to the Unit Repair Section for Overhaul Procedures.

Axle Housing

Removal and Installation

1. Raise and support the vehicle safely. Remove the rear wheel assemblies.
2. Matchmark and remove the driveshaft.

NOTE: When supporting the differential housing, keep a slight amount of pressure on the springs.

3. Loosen the joint between the brake hose and the brake line and remove the stops to disconnect the brake hose. Plug the lines to prevent fluid loss.
4. Disconnect the rear cable of the parking brake at the balancer.
5. Remove the shock absorbers and the spring seats after removing the spring U-bolts.
6. Remove the spring shackle pin nuts and the shackle plate.

NOTE: The axle assembly will be supported solely under the differential case. Be careful not to allow it to drop.

Removing the rear drive axle seal

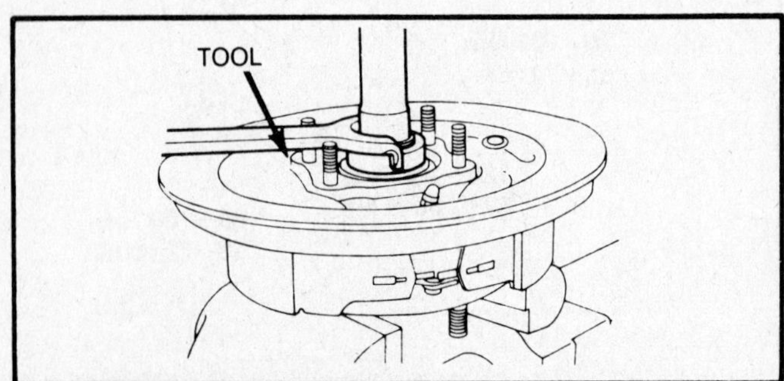

Removing axle shaft locknut

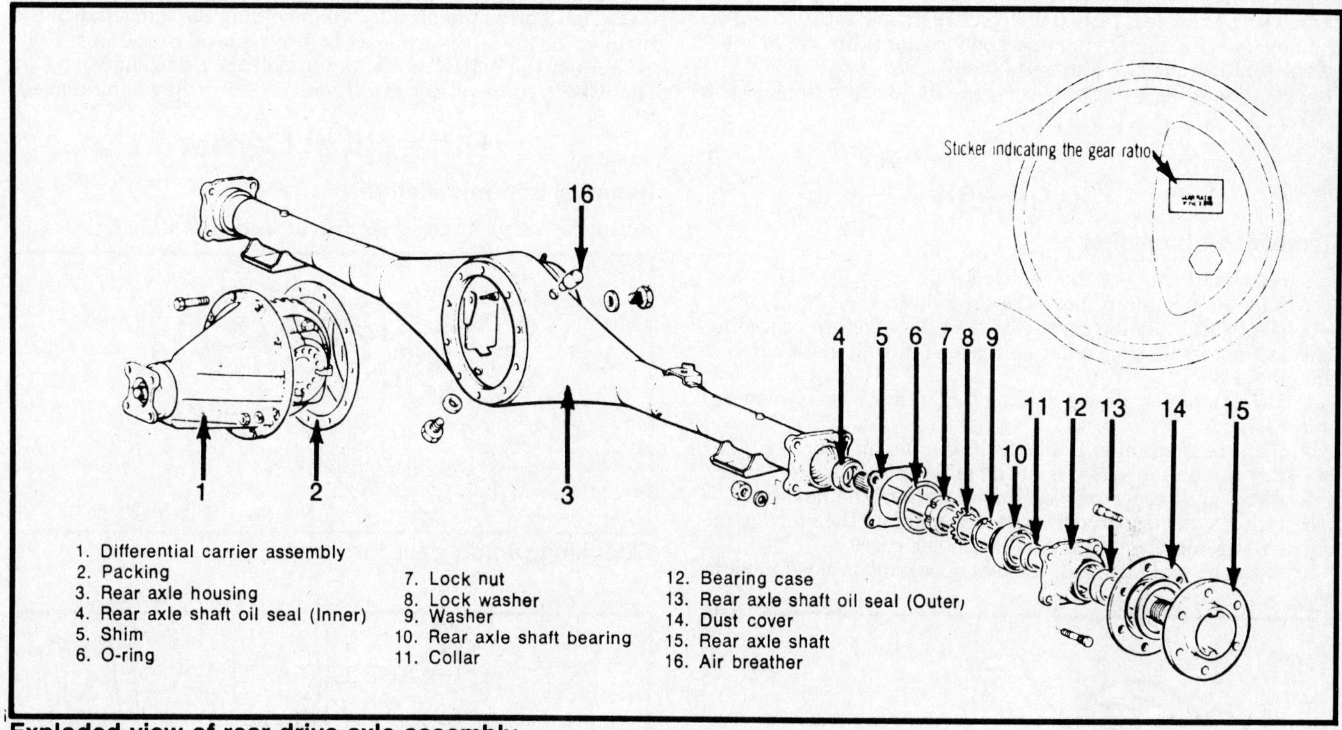

Exploded view of rear drive axle assembly

7. With an assistant holding the axle assembly, slowly lower it to the ground.
8. Installation is the reverse of the removal procedure. Bleed the brakes after assembly.

Axle Shaft, Bearing and Seal

Removal and Installation

ALL MODELS

1. Raise and support the vehicle safely.
2. Remove the rear wheel assemblies and brake drums.
3. Disconnect and plug the brake line from the wheel cylinder and plug it to prevent fluid loss.
4. Remove the four nuts behind the brake backing plate holding the bearing case to the axle housing assembly.
5. Remove the backing plate, bearing case and the axle shaft as an assembly.

NOTE: It may be necessary to use a slide hammer to remove the assembly.

6. Remove the O-ring and the bearing preload shims. Save the preload shims for reassembly.
7. Remove the oil seal with a hooked slide hammer.
8. To remove the axle shaft bearing, remove the notched locknut with a brass drift.
9. Remove the lock washer and plain washer.
10. Screw the lock nut back on to the axle shaft about three turns.
11. It will be necessary to fabricate a metal plate that fits over the axle shaft and butts the lock nut. Drill four holes in the plate that align with the four bearing case studs and fit the plate. Refit two nuts and washers to the bearing case studs diagonally across from each other and tighten them evenly to free the bearing case and the bearing.
12. Use a hammer and drift to remove the bearing outer race from the bearing case.
13. Remove the outer oil seal from the bearing case.

NOTE: Always use new O-rings and check the condition of all oil seals and dust covers.

14. Apply grease to the outer surface on the bearing outer race and to the lip of the outer oil seal and drive them into the bearing case from each side.
15. Slide the bearing case and bearing over the rear axle shaft. Apply grease on the bearing rollers and fit the inner race by pressing it into place.

CAUTION

Be careful not to damage or deform the dust cover.

16. Pack the bearing with grease.
17. Install the washer, the crowned lock washer and the lock nut in the order just given and torque the lock nut to 130–159 ft. lbs. if possible.
18. Bend the tab on the lock washer into the groove on the lock nut. If the tab and the groove do not line up, slightly tighten the lock nut until they do.
19. Drive the new inner oil seal into place after greasing it and refit the assembly. Be sure to fit the O-ring and shim and apply silicone rubber sealant to the bearing case face.

NOTE: Be sure to bleed the brakes before road testing!

20. To adjust preload: Begin with the left side rear axle assembly and insert a 0.04 in. shim between the bearing case and the axle shaft housing. Torque the four nuts to 36–43 ft. lbs.

NOTE: Be sure to fit the O-ring and apply sealant.

21. Install the right side axle assembly into the right side housing without its shim and O-ring. Torque the four nuts to 0.4 ft. lbs.
22. Using a flat blade feeler gauge, measure the gap between the bearing case and the axle housing face. It should range between 0.002–0.008 in. Record the measurement.
23. Remove the axle shaft and select a shim that is the same thickness as the gap between the faces just measured, plus a

shim with a thickness from 0.002–0.0079 in. and install them on the housing. Fit the O-ring and apply sealant. Fit the axle assembly and torque the four nuts to 36–43 ft. lbs.

24. Assemble the remaining components. Be sure to bleed the brakes.

Pinion Seal

Removal and Installation

1. Raise and support the vehicle safely.
2. Matchmark and remove the driveshaft.
3. Check the turning torque of the pinion before proceding. This is the torque that must be reached during installation of the pinion nut.
4. Using a pinion flange holding tool, remove the pinion nut and washer.
5. Remove the pinion flange from the pinion gear.
6. Pry the pinion seal out of the differential carrier.
7. Clean and inspect the sealing surface of the housing.
8. Using a seal driver, drive the new seal into the housing until the flange on the seal is flush with the carrier.
9. With the seal installed, the pinion bearing preload must be set.
10. Tighten the pinion nut, while holding the flange, until the turning torque is the same as before removal of the nut.
11. Align the matchmarks and install the drive shaft.
12. Check the level of the differential lubricant when finished.

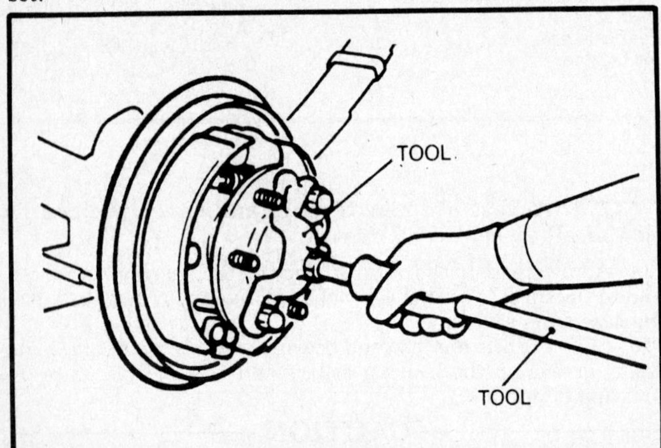

Removing the axleshaft using a puller

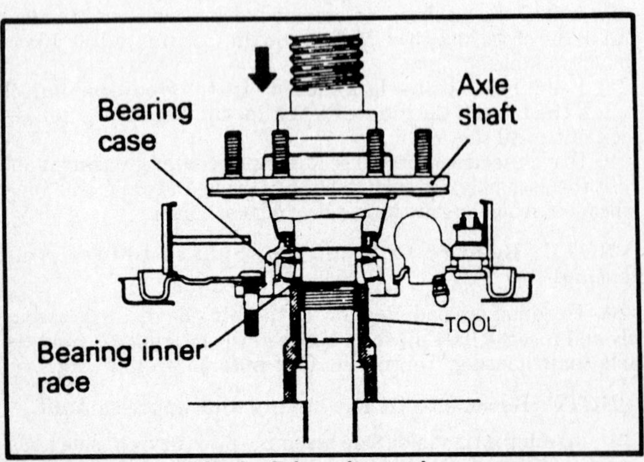

Removing the axleshaft bearing using a press

Differential Carrier

Removal and Installation

Refer to Axle Housing Removal and Installation.

Checking pinion gear turning torque

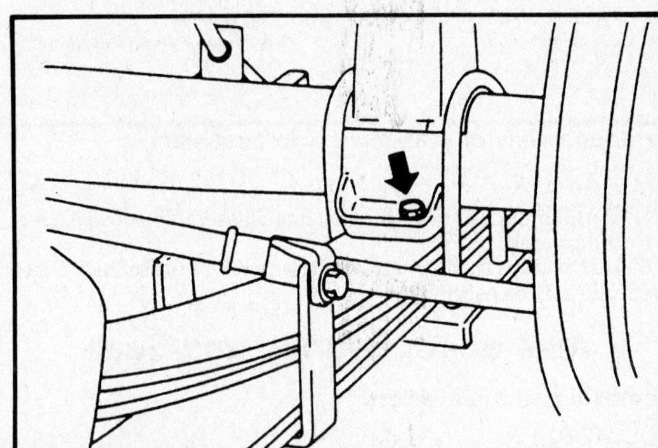
Rear spring plate bolt location

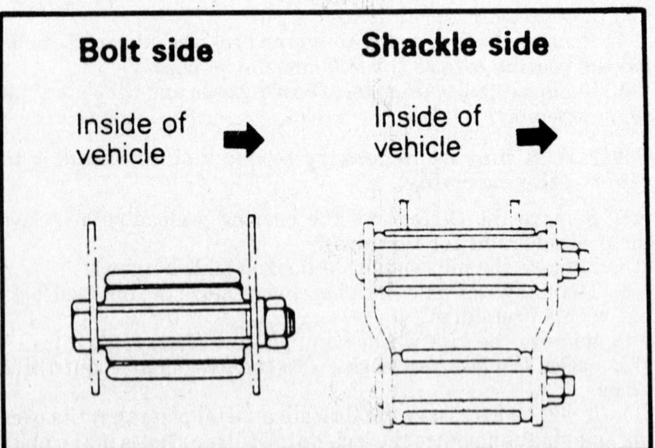

Rear leaf spring shackle position

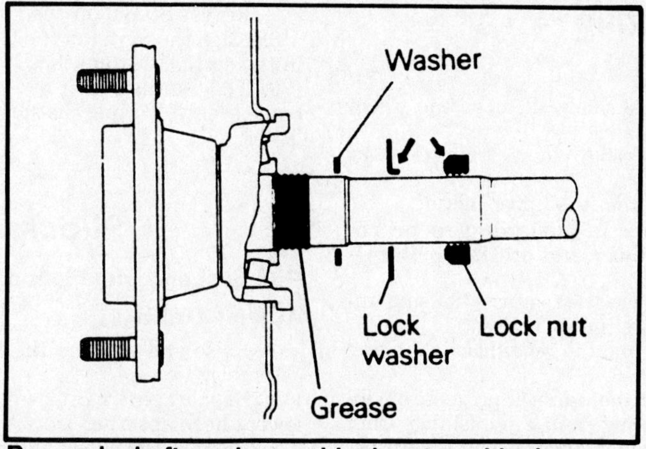

Rear axleshaft washer and lock nut positioning

AXLE SHAFT ASSEMBLY PRELOAD SHIMS

Part No.	Thickness of shim mm	in.
MB092491	0.05 ± 0.005	.0020 ± .0002
MB092492	0.10 ± 0.010	.0040 ± .0004
MB092493	0.20 ± 0.015	.0079 ± .0006
MB092494	0.30 ± 0.020	.0118 ± .0008
MB092495	0.50 ± 0.025	.0197 ± .0010
MB092496	1.00 ± 0.040	.0394 ± .0016
MB092497	1.50 ± 0.050	.0591 ± .0020
MB092498	2.00 ± 0.055	.0787 ± .0022

REAR SUSPENSION

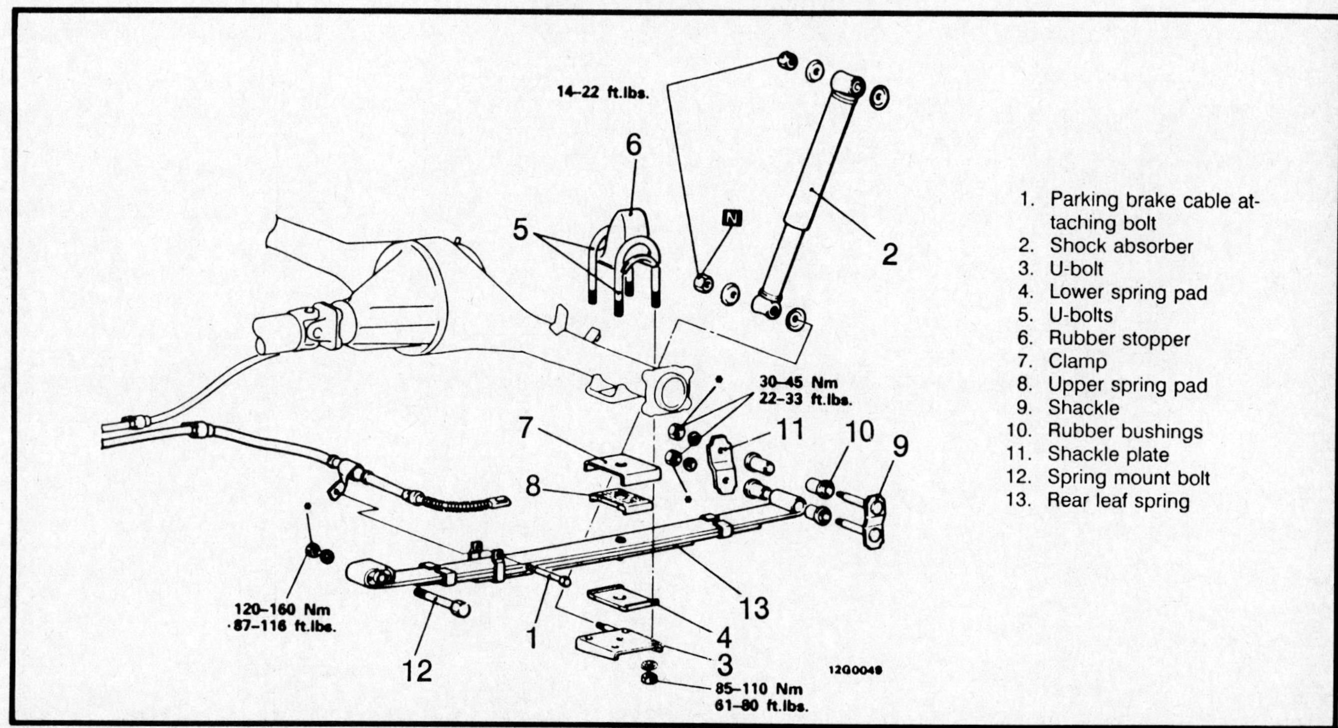

Rear suspension—exploded view—Van shown—others similar

Leaf Spring

Removal and Installation

1. Raise and support the vehicle safely. Remove the wheel assembly.
2. Remove the parking brake cable clamp from the leaf spring.
3. Remove the shock absorber from the upper mount.

NOTE: If the shock absorber is not going to be replaced or serviced, leave the lower end on the spring U-bolt seat.

4. Loosen the U-bolt nuts and raise the rear axle housing until it clears the spring seat. Remove the spring seat.
5. Remove the front spring pin and the rear shackle pin and remove the spring.
6. Installation is the reverse of the removal procedure. Observe the following: Install the spring front eye bushings from both sides of the eye with the bushing flanges facing out. Insert the spring pin assembly from the wheel side and secure it to the hanger bracket with its bolt. Temporarily tighten the spring pin nut.
7. Repeat Step 6 on the rear spring mount.
8. Align the center of the U-bolt seat with the center bolt hole in the spring. Torque the U-bolts to 47–54 ft. lbs.
9. Tighten the U-bolt nuts until all of the U-bolt threads protrude evenly. Torque the spring pins and shackle pins to 22–33 ft. lbs.

Shock Absorbers

Removal and Installation

ALL MODELS

1. Raise and support the vehicle safely. Remove the wheel assembly.
2. Support the rear axle housing and remove the upper and lower shock absorber mounting bolts.
3. Remove the shock absorber from the vehicle.
4. Installation is the reverse of the removal procedure.
5. Torque the shock absorber mounting bolts to 13–18 ft. lbs. for Pickups and Montero and to 14–22 ft. lbs. for the Van.

Isuzu 15

INDEX

BEFORE SERVICING, SEE THE SAFETY NOTICE AT THE FRONT OF THE BOOK

MODEL IDENTIFICATION
Isuzu Pickups and Trooper II

Model Name	Model Designation	Model Name	Model Designation
P'up	Pickup	P'up LS Spacecab	Pickup
P'up Long Bed	Pickup	P'up LS Spacecab Turbo Diesel	Pickup
P'up DLX	Pickup	P'up DLX Long Bed 4WD TD	4WD Pickup
P'up Long Bed DLX	Pickup	P'up DLX Spacecab	Pickup
P'up Long Bed DLX 4WD	Pickup	Trooper II Utility	4WD
P'up DLX 4WD	4WD Pickup	Trooper II Utility	4WD
P'up MPG Diesel	Pickup	Trooper II Utility 2 Dr DLX	4WD
P'up Spacecab	Pickup	Trooper II Utility 4 Dr DLX	4WD
P'up DLX Spacecab	Pickup		

ENGINE IDENTIFICATION CODES BY VIN NUMBER
Isuzu Pickup and Trooper II

Engine Cu. In. (liter)	Cylinders	1982	1983	1984	1985	1986	1987	1988
4–119 (2.0)	4	G200Z	G200Z	G200Z	G200Z	G200Z	G200	G200
4–137 (2.2)	4	—	—	—	—	4DZ1	4DZ1	4DZ1
4–137 (2.2)①	4	C223	C223	C223	C223	C223	C223	C223
4–137 (2.2)②	4	—	—	—	—	C223TD	C223TD	C223TD

① Diesel Engine ② Turbo Diesel Engine

GENERAL ENGINE SPECIFICATIONS

Year	VIN	No. Cylinder Displacement cu. in. (liter)	Fuel System Type	Net Horsepower @ rpm	Net Torque @ rpm (ft.lbs.)	Bore × Stroke (in.)	Com-pression Ratio	Oil Pressure @ 1400 rpm
1982	G200Z	4–119 (2.0)	2bbl	82 @ 4600	101 @ 3000	3.42 × 3.23	8.4:1	56
	C223	4–136 (2.2)	Diesel	58 @ 4300	93 @ 2200	3.46 × 3.62	21.1:1	55
	C223T	4–136 (2.2)	TD	80 @ 4000	128 @ 2200	3.46 × 3.62	21.1:1	55
1983	G200Z	4–119 (2.0)	2bbl	82 @ 4600	101 @ 3000	3.42 × 3.23	8.4:1	56
	C223	4–136 (2.2)	Diesel	58 @ 4300	93 @ 2200	3.46 × 3.62	21.1:1	55
	C223T	4–136 (2.2)	TD	80 @ 4000	128 @ 2200	3.46 × 3.62	21.1:1	55
1984	G200Z	4–119 (2.0)	2bbl	82 @ 4600	101 @ 3000	3.42 × 3.23	8.4:1	56
	C223	4–136 (2.2)	Diesel	58 @ 4300	93 @ 2200	3.46 × 3.62	21.1:1	55
	C223T	4–136 (2.2)	TD	80 @ 4000	128 @ 2200	3.46 × 3.62	21.1:1	55
1985	G200Z	4–119 (2.0)	2bbl	82 @ 4600	101 @ 3000	3.42 × 3.23	8.4:1	56
	C223	4–136 (2.2)	Diesel	58 @ 4300	93 @ 2200	3.46 × 3.62	21.1:1	55
	C223T	4–136 (2.2)	TD	80 @ 4000	128 @ 2200	3.46 × 3.62	21.1:1	55
1986	G200	4–119 (2.0)	2bbl	82 @ 4600	101 @ 3000	3.42 × 3.23	8.4:1	56
	4ZD1	4–137 (2.2)	2bbl	96 @ 4600	123 @ 3000	3.52 × 3.54	8.3:1	57
	C223	4–136 (2.2)	Diesel	58 @ 4300	93 @ 2200	3.46 × 3.62	21.1:1	55
	C223T	4–136 (2.2)	TD	80 @ 4000	128 @ 2200	3.46 × 3.62	21.1:1	55
1987–88	G200	4–119 (2.0)	2bbl	82 @ 4600	101 @ 3000	3.42 × 3.23	8.4:1	56
	4ZD1	4–137 (2.2)	2bbl	96 @ 4600	123 @ 3000	3.52 × 3.54	8.3:1	57
	C223	4–136 (2.2)	Diesel	58 @ 4300	93 @ 2200	3.46 × 3.62	21.1:1	55
	C223T	4–136 (2.2)	TD	80 @ 4000	128 @ 2200	3.46 × 3.62	21.1:1	55

TD Turbo Diesel Engine

GASOLINE ENGINE TUNE-UP SPECIFICATIONS

Year	VIN	No. Cylinder Displacement cu. in. (liter)	Spark Plugs Type	Spark Plugs Gap (in.)	Ignition Timing (deg.) MT	Ignition Timing (deg.) AT	Compression Pressure (psi)	Fuel Pump (psi)	Idle Speed (rpm) MT	Idle Speed (rpm) AT	Valve Clearance (in.) In.	Valve Clearance (in.) Ex.
1982	G200Z	4–119 (2.0)	BPR–6ES11	0.040	6B	6B	NA	3.0	800	900	0.006	0.010
1983	G200Z	4–119 (2.0)	BPR–6ES11	0.040	6B	6B	NA	3.0	800	900	0.006	0.010
1984	G200Z	4–119 (2.0)	BPR–6ES11	0.040	6B	6B	NA	3.0	800	900	0.006	0.010
1985	G200Z	4–119 (2.0)	BPR–6ES11	0.040	6B	6B	NA	3.0	800	900	0.006	0.010
1986	G200	4–119 (2.0)	BPR–6ES11	0.040	6B	6B	NA	3.0	800	900	0.006	0.010
	4ZD1	4–137 (2.2)	BPR–6ES11	0.040	6B	6B	NA	3.0	800	900	0.006	0.010
1987–88	G200	4–119 (2.0)	BPR–6ES11	0.040	6B	6B	NA	3.0	800	900	0.006	0.010
	4ZD1	4–137 (2.2)	BPR–6ES11	0.040	6B	6B	NA	3.0	800	900	0.006	0.010

FIRING ORDER

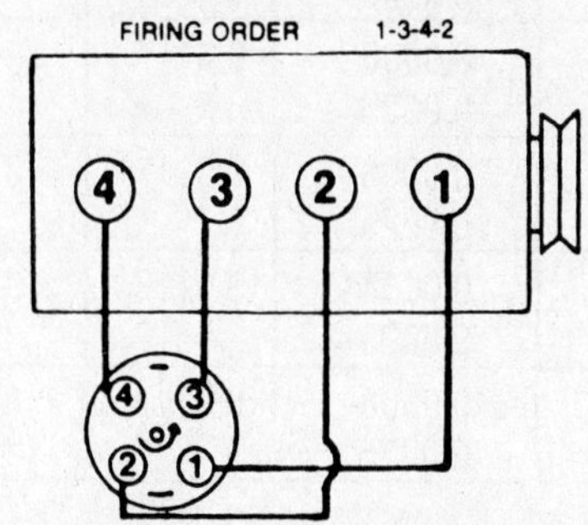

Gasoline engine firing order

CAPACITIES

Year	Model	No. Cylinder Displacement cu. in. (liter)	Engine Crankcase with Filter	Engine Crankcase without Filter	Transmission (pts.) 4-Spd	Transmission (pts.) 5-Spd	Transmission (pts.) Auto.	Drive Axle (pts.)	Fuel Tank (gal.)	Cooling System (qts.)
1982	All	4–119 (2.0)	4.1	3.8	2.7	2.7	12.8	3.2①	13.2②	8.5
1983	All	4–119 (2.0)	4.1	3.8	2.7	2.7	12.8	3.2①	13.2②	8.5
1984	All	4–119 (2.0)	4.1	3.8	2.7	2.7	12.8	3.2①	13.2②	8.5
1985	Pickups	4–119 (2.0)	4.1	3.8	2.7	2.7	12.8	3.2①	13.2②	8.5
	Pickups	4–136 (2.2)	4.1	3.8	2.7	2.7	12.8	3.2①	13.2②	8.5
	Trooper II	4–119 (2.0)	4.1	3.8	2.7	2.7	NA	3.2①	13.2	8.5
1986	Pickups	4–119 (2.0)	4.1	3.8	2.7	2.7	12.8	3.2①	13.2②	8.5
	Pickups	4–136 (2.2)	4.1	3.8	2.7	2.7	12.8	3.2①	13.2②	8.5
	Trooper II	4–136 (2.2)	4.1	3.8	2.7	2.7	NA	3.2①	13.2	8.5
1987–88	Pickups	4–119 (2.0)	4.1	3.8	2.7	2.7	12.8	3.2①	13.2②	8.5
	Pickups	4–136 (2.2)	4.1	3.8	2.7	2.7	12.8	3.2①	13.2②	8.5
	Trooper II	4–136 (2.2)	4.1	3.8	2.7	2.7	NA	3.2①	13.2	8.5

① Front Drive Axle: 2.1 pints
② Optional Fuel Tank: 19.1 gallons

CRANKSHAFT AND CONNECTING ROD SPECIFICATIONS

All measurements are given in inches.

Year	VIN	No. Cylinder Displacement cu. in. (liter)	Crankshaft Main Brg. Journal Dia.	Crankshaft Main Brg. Oil Clearance	Crankshaft Shaft End-play	Crankshaft Thrust on No.	Connecting Rod Journal Diameter	Connecting Rod Oil Clearance	Connecting Rod Side Clearance
1982	G200Z	4–119 (2.0)	2.2050	0.0008–0.0025	0.0117	3	1.9290	0.0007–0.0030	0.0137
1983	G200Z	4–119 (2.0)	2.2050	0.0008–0.0025	0.0117	3	1.9290	0.0007–0.0030	0.0137
1984	G200Z	4–119 (2.0)	2.2050	0.0008–0.0025	0.0117	3	1.9290	0.0007–0.0030	0.0137
1985	G200Z	4–119 (2.0)	2.2050	0.0008–0.0025	0.0117	3	1.9290	0.0007–0.0030	0.0137
	4ZD1	4–137 (2.2)	2.2050	0.0008–0.0025	0.0117	3	1.9290	0.0007–0.0030	0.0137
1986	G200	4–119 (2.0)	2.2050	0.0008–0.0025	0.0117	3	1.9290	0.0007–0.0030	0.0137
	4ZD1	4–137 (2.2)	2.2050	0.0008–0.0025	0.0117	3	1.9290	0.0007–0.0030	0.0137
1987–88	G200	4–119 (2.0)	2.2050	0.0008–0.0025	0.0117	3	1.9290	0.0007–0.0030	0.0137
	4ZD1	4–137 (2.2)	2.2050	0.0008–0.0025	0.0117	3	1.9290	0.0007–0.0030	0.0137

TORQUE SPECIFICATIONS

All readings in ft. lbs.

Year	VIN	No. Cylinder Displacement cu. in. (liter)	Cylinder Head Bolts	Main Bearing Bolts	Rod Bearing Bolts	Crankshaft Pulley Bolts	Flywheel Bolts	Manifold Intake	Manifold Exhaust	Spark Plugs
1982	G200Z	4–119 (2.0)	72	72	43	87	69	13	15	22
1983	G200Z	4–119 (2.0)	72	72	43	87	69	13	15	22
1984	G200Z	4–119 (2.0)	72	72	43	87	69	13	15	22
1985	G200Z	4–119 (2.0)	72	72	43	87	69	13	15	22
1986	G200	4–119 (2.0)	72	72	43	87	69	13	15	22
	4ZD1	4–137 (2.2)	72	72	43	87	69	13	15	22
1987–88	G200	4–119 (2.0)	72	72	43	87	69	13	15	22
	4ZD1	4–137 (2.2)	72	72	43	87	69	13	15	22

PISTON AND RING SPECIFICATIONS

All measurments are given in inches.

Year	VIN	No. Cylinder Displacement cu. in. (liter)	Piston Clearance	Ring Gap Top Compression	Ring Gap Bottom Compression	Ring Gap Oil Control	Ring Side Clearance Top Compression	Ring Side Clearance Bottom Compression	Ring Side Clearance Oil Control
1982	G200Z	4–119 (2.0)	0.0018–0.0026	0.014–0.020	0.014–0.020	0.008–0.035	0.0059	0.0059	0.0059
1983	G200Z	4–119 (2.0)	0.0018–0.0026	0.014–0.020	0.014–0.020	0.008–0.035	0.0059	0.0059	0.0059
1984	G200Z	4–119 (2.0)	0.0018–0.0026	0.014–0.020	0.014–0.020	0.008–0.035	0.0059	0.0059	0.0059
1985	G200Z	4–119 (2.0)	0.0018–0.0026	0.014–0.020	0.014–0.020	0.008–0.035	0.0059	0.0059	0.0059
1986	G200	4–119 (2.0)	0.0018–0.0026	0.014–0.020	0.014–0.020	0.008–0.035	0.0059	0.0059	0.0059
	4ZD1	4–137 (2.2)	0.0018–0.0026	0.014–0.020	0.014–0.020	0.008–0.035	0.0059	0.0059	0.0059
1987–88	G200	4–119 (2.0)	0.0018–0.0026	0.014–0.020	0.014–0.020	0.008–0.035	0.0059	0.0059	0.0059
	4ZD1	4–137 (2.2)	0.0018–0.0026	0.014–0.020	0.014–0.020	0.008–0.035	0.0059	0.0059	0.0059

VALVE SPECIFICATIONS

Year	VIN	No. Cylinder Displacement cu. in. (liter)	Seat Angle (deg.)	Face Angle (deg.)	Spring Test Pressure (lbs.)	Spring Installed Height (in.)	Stem-to-Guide Clearance (in.) Intake	Stem-to-Guide Clearance (in.) Exhaust	Stem Diameter (in.) Intake	Stem Diameter (in.) Exhaust
1982	G200Z	4–119 (2.0)	45	45	184	1.614	0.0009–0.0022	0.0015–0.0031	0.3102	0.3091
1983	G200Z	4–119 (2.0)	45	45	184	1.614	0.0009–0.0022	0.0015–0.0031	0.3102	0.3091
1984	G200Z	4–119 (2.0)	45	45	184	1.614	0.0009–0.0022	0.0015–0.0031	0.3102	0.3091
1985	G200Z	4–119 (2.0)	45	45	184	1.614	0.0009–0.0022	0.0015–0.0031	0.3102	0.3091
1986	G200	4–119 (2.0)	45	45	184	1.614	0.0009–0.0022	0.0015–0.0031	0.3102	0.3091
	4DZ1	4–137 (2.2)	45	45	184	1.614	0.0009–0.0022	0.0015–0.0031	0.3102	0.3091
1987–88	G200	4–119 (2.0)	45	45	184	1.614	0.0009–0.0022	0.0015–0.0031	0.3102	0.3091
	4ZD1	4–137 (2.2)	45	45	184	1.614	0.0009–0.0022	0.0015–0.0031	0.3102	0.3091

WHEEL ALIGNMENT

Year	Model	Caster Range (deg.)	Caster Preferred Setting (deg.)	Camber Range (deg.)	Camber Preferred Setting (deg.)	Toe-in (in.)	Steering Axis Inclination (deg.)
1982	2WD Pickups	0–1P	1/2P	0–1P	1/2P	0.08	NA
	4WD Pickups	1/6N–5/6P	2/3P	1/6P–1 1/6P	1/2P	0.08	NA
1983	2WD Pickups	0–1P	1/2P	0–1P	1/2P	0.08	NA
	4WD Pickups	1/6N–5/6P	2/3P	1/6P–1 1/6P	1/2P	0.08	NA
1984	2WD Pickups	0–1P	1/2P	0–1P	1/2P	0.08	NA
	4WD Pickups	1/6N–5/6P	2/3P	1/6P–1 1/6P	1/2P	0.08	NA
1985	2WD Pickups	0–1P	1/2P	0–1P	1/2P	0.08	NA
	4WD Pickups	1/6N–5/6P	2/3P	1/6P–1 1/6P	1/2P	0.08	NA
	Trooper II	1 1/2P–3 1/2P	2 1/2P	0–1P	1/2P	0.08	NA
1986	2WD Pickups	0–1P	1/2P	0–1P	1/2P	0.08	NA
	4WD Pickups	1/6N–5/6P	2/3P	1/6P–1 1/6P	1/2P	0.08	NA
	Trooper II	1 1/2P–3 1/2P	2 1/2P	0–1P	1/2P	0.08	NA
1987–88	2WD Pickups	0–1P	1/2P	0–1P	1/2P	0.08	NA
	4WD Pickups	1/6N–5/6P	2/3P	1/6P–1 1/6P	1/2P	0.08	NA
	Trooper II	1 1/2P–3 1/2P	2 1/2P	0–1P	1/2P	0.08	NA

ENGINE ELECTRICAL

Refer to the Electrical Section for Alternator and Starter Overhaul.

Alternator

Removal and Installation

ALL MODELS

1. Disconnect the negative battery cable. Remove the air pump.
2. Disconnect and tag the alternator wiring.
3. Remove the alternator pivot bolt on the lower part of the alternator. Remove the alternator belt from the pulley.
4. Remove the alternator mounting bolt and remove the alternator from the engine.
5. Installation is the reverse of the removal procedure. Adjust the belt tension when finished.

Voltage Regulator

EXTERNAL

Removal and Installation

ALL MODELS

1. Disconnect the negative battery cable.
2. Disconnect and tag the electrical leads at the regulator.
3. Remove the two regulator mounting screws and remove the regulator.
4. Installation is the reverse of the removal procedure.

Adjustment

1. Remove the regulator from the vehicle and remove the regulator cover.
2. If the points are pitted, clean them carefully with fine emery paper.
3. Check and adjust the core gap first and then the point gap.
4. Adjust the core gap by loosening the screws attaching the contact set to the yoke. Move the contact set up or down as required. The standard core gap is 0.024–0.039 in. Tighten the attaching screw.

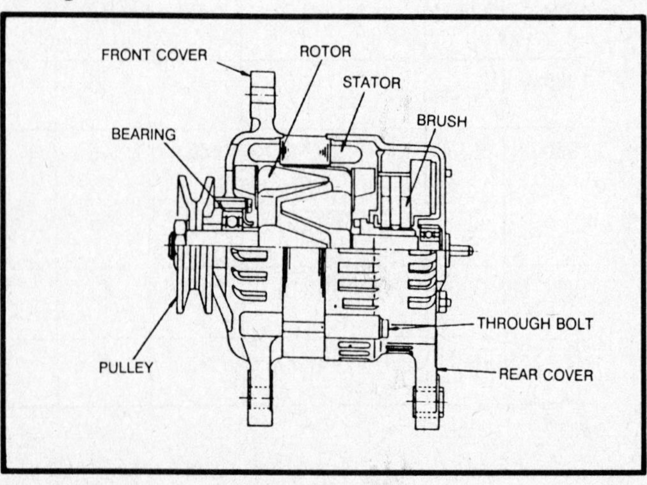

Alternator mounting and cut-away view

5. Adjust the point gap by loosening the screw attaching the upper contact. Move the upper contact up or down as required. The standard point gap is 0.012–0.016 in.

6. Adjust the regulated voltage by turning the adjusting screw. Turn the adjusting screw in to increase voltage and out to reduce voltage. When the correct adjustment is obtained, secure the adjusting screw by tightening the locknut. The regulated voltage is 13.8–14.8 volts.

7. Install the regulator cover, reconnect the electrical leads and install the regulator.

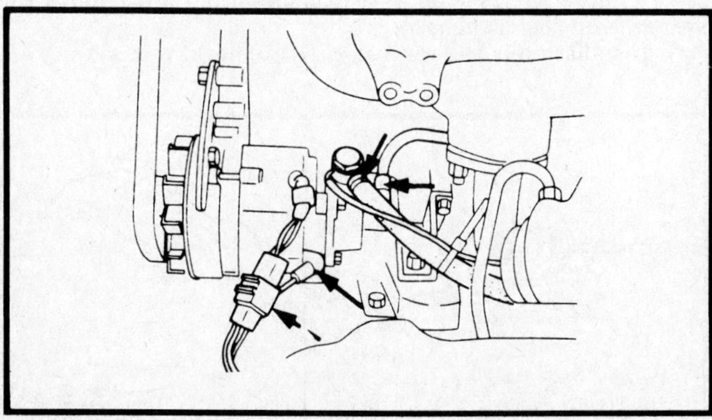

Vacuum hose and alternator wiring disconnection points

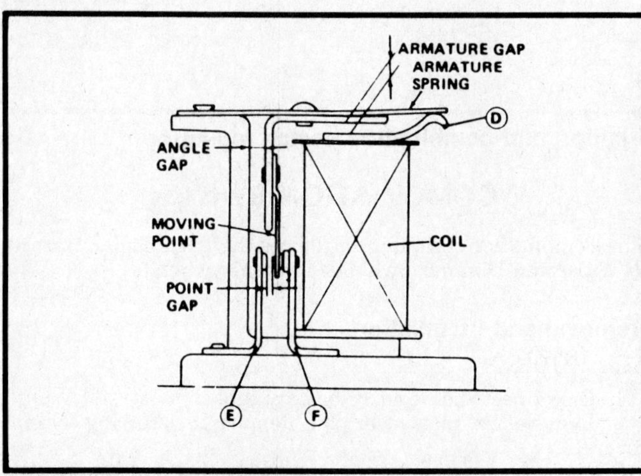

Voltage regulator adjustment

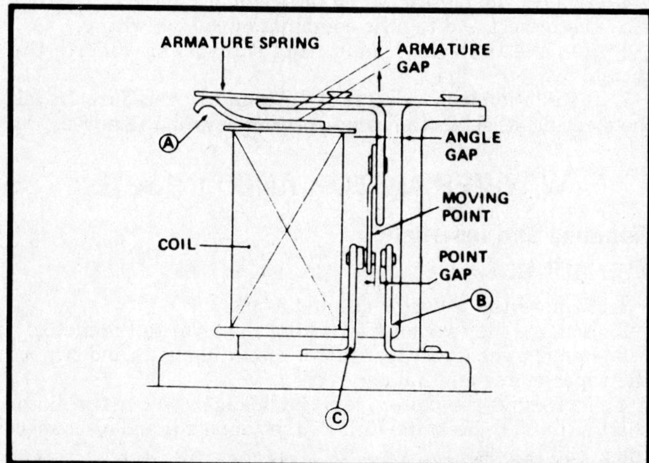

Voltage relay adjustment

6. Installation is the reverse of the removal procedure. Check and adjust the ignition timing when finished.

NOTE: If the engine was disturbed while the distributor was removed, remove the No. 1 spark plug and rotate the crankshaft in the normal direction of rotation until compression is felt at the spark plug hole. Continue rotating the engine in the same direction while observing the timing marks at the indicator line up when No. 1 cylinder is at TDC. Install the distributor with the rotor lined up with the No. 1 lug on the distributor cap.

Starter

OVERHAUL

Refer to the Unit Repair Section.

Removal and Installation

ALL MODELS

1. Disconnect the negative battery cable. Disconnect and remove the EGR pipe, if equipped.
2. Disconnect and tag the starter wiring at the starter.
3. Remove the bolts attaching the starter to the engine and remove the starter from the vehicle.
4. Installation is the reverse of the removal procedure.

Distributor

Removal and Installation

ELECTRONIC

1. Disconnect the negative battery cable.
2. Disconnect and tag the spark plug wires at the distributor cap.
3. Remove the distributor cap from the distributor. Disconnect and tag the distributor wiring.
4. Remove the distributor mounting nut.
5. Note the position of the rotor in relation to the distributor housing and lift the distributor from the engine.

TIMING LIGHT AND TACHOMETER CONNECTIONS

All timing lights and tachometers should be connected according to the manufacturers instructions.

IGNITION TIMING

Procedure

The timing marks are located near the front crankshaft pulley and consist of a pointer with graduations attached to the engine block and a mark on the crankshaft pulley.

1. Check and correct the air gap in the distributor.
2. Locate and clean the timing marks on the crankshaft pulley and the front of the engine.
3. Attach a tachometer and timing light to the engine.
4. Disconnect and plug the vacuum line to the distributor.
5. Make sure that all wires from the timing light and tachometer are clear of the fan and belts. Start the engine.
6. Adjust the idle to the correct rpm.
7. Aim the timing light at the timing marks. Rotate the distributor until the timing marks are aligned.
8. Tighten the distributor mounting bolt and check the timing again.
9. Turn the engine off and remove the timing light and tachometer. Connect the distributor vacuum line.

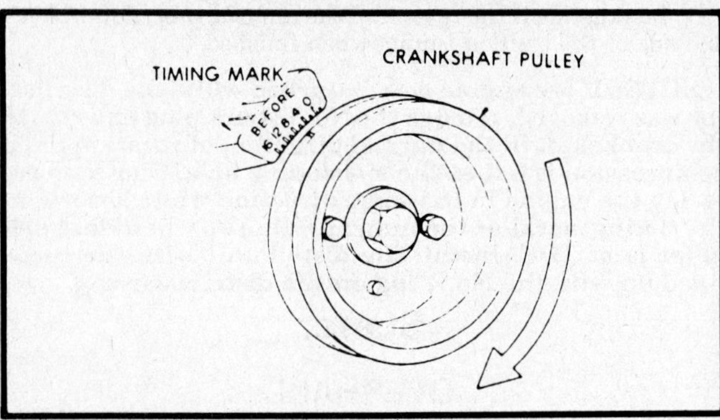

Ignition timing marks

Air Gap Setting

An electronic ignition is used with all models. The air gap setting in the distributor should be checked and adjusted before the ignition timing is adjusted.

Procedure

1. Remove the distributor cap, O-ring and rotor.
2. Use a feeler gauge to measure the air gap at the pick up coil projection. The gap should be 0.008–0.016 in. Adjust if necessary.
3. Loosen the screws and move the signal generator until the gap is correct. Tighten the screws and recheck the gap.

NOTE: The electrical parts in this system are not repairable. If found to be defective, they must be replaced.

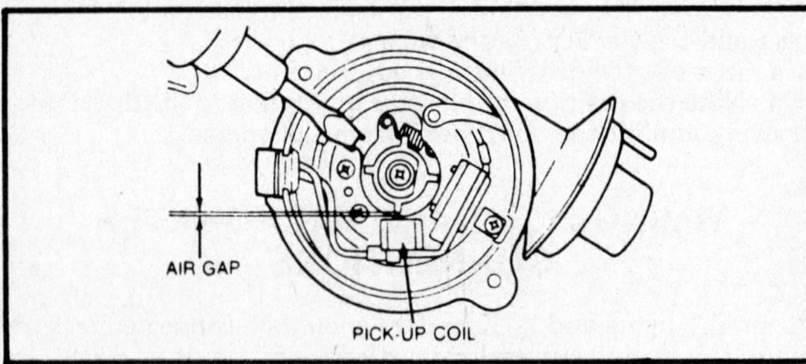

Adjusting the air gap

Electrical Controls

IGNITION LOCK/SWITCH

Removal and Installation

ALL MODELS

1. Disconnect the negative battery cable.
2. Remove the multi-connector from the rear of the ignition switch.
3. Remove the steering wheel, horn ring and steering column covers.
4. Disconnect and tag the combination switch wiring and remove the combination switch from the steering column.
5. Remove the ignition switch mounting bolts. Remove the switch from the steering column.
6. Installation is the reverse of the removal procedure.
7. Place the transmission in park when installing the switch and make sure that the lock bolt in the switch fits into the steering shaft slot.

HEADLIGHT SWITCH

Removal and Installation

ALL MODELS

1. Disconnect the negative battery cable.
2. Unscrew the headlight switch knob.
3. Disconnect and tag the headlight switch wiring under the dashboard.
4. Remove the headlight switch lock ring and remove the switch from the dashboard.
5. Installation is the reverse of the removal procedure.

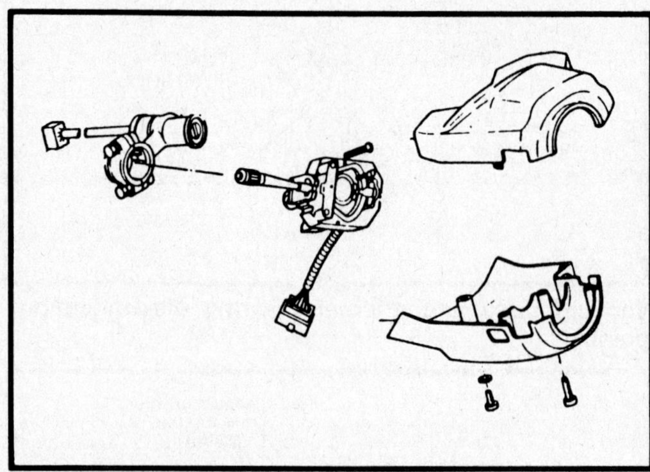

Ignition and combination switch mounting

COMBINATION SWITCH

The Combination Switch incorporates the Turn Signal, Hazard, W/Wiper and Dimmer Switches into one switch.

Removal and Installation

ALL MODELS

1. Disconnect the negative battery cable.
2. Remove the horn cover pad. Remove the steering column covers.
3. Note the position of the steering wheel and remove the wheel.
4. Remove the plastic switch protector ring.
5. Disconnect and tag the combination switch wiring.
6. Remove the switch mounting screws and remove the switch.
7. Installation is the reverse of the removal procedure. Install the steering wheel in the same position as when removed.

W/WIPER MOTOR AND LINKAGE

Removal and Installation

ALL MODELS

1. Remove the wiper blades and arms.
2. Remove the two bolts attaching the pivot to the motor.
3. Remove the four wiper motor mounting bolts and remove the wiper motor and linkage.
4. To remove the motor from the linkage, remove the motor shaft nut and three bolts. Pull off the connector and disconnect the ground cable.
5. Installation is the reverse of the removal procedure. Make

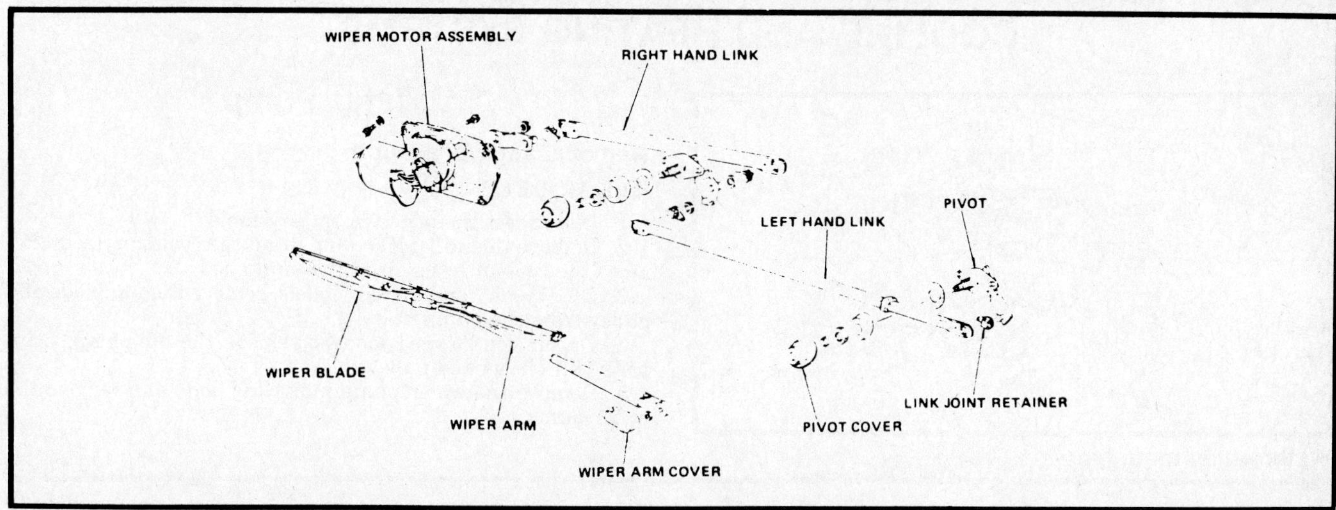

Windshield wiper motor and linkage

sure to install the wiper motor linkage so that it is not twisted or touching any adjacent parts.

INSTRUMENT CLUSTER

Removal and Installation

ALL MODELS

1. Disconnect the negative battery cable.
2. Remove the screws and/or nuts securing the instrument cluster and pull the assembly part way out.

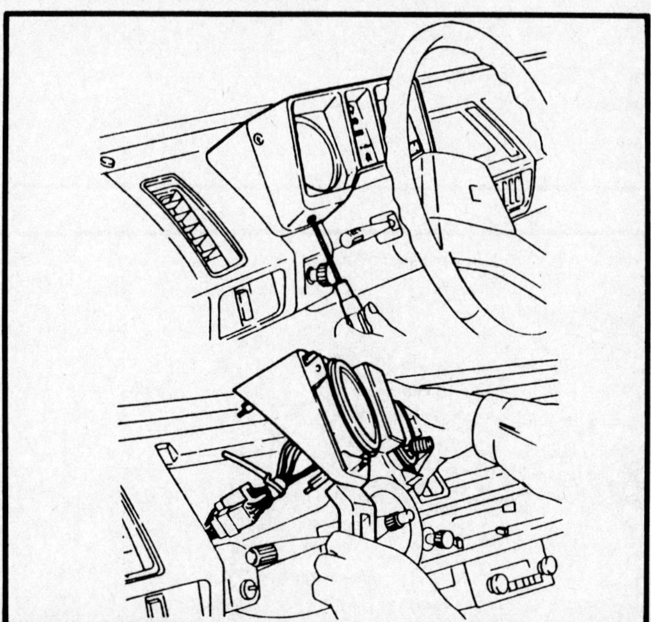

Instrument cluster removal – Trooper II shown – Pick-up similar

3. Disconnect the instrument cluster wiring harness and speedometer cable. Remove the instrument panel.
4. Installallation is the reverse of the removal procedure.

SPEEDOMETER

Removal and Installation

ALL MODELS

1. Disconnect the negative battery cable.
2. Remove the instrument cluster.
3. Remove the speedometer from the cluster, noting the position of any light bulbs and wires.
4. Installation is the reverse of the removal procedure.

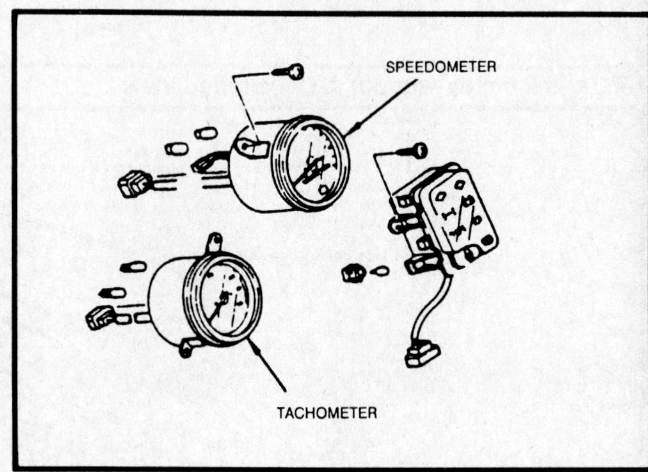

Speedometer mounting

COOLING AND HEATING SYSTEMS

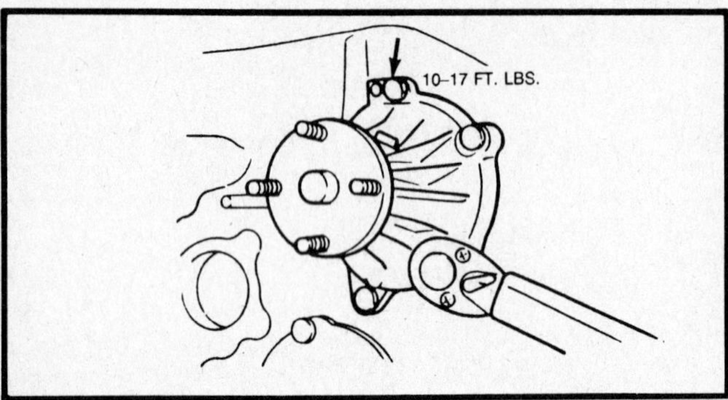

Water pump mounting

Water Pump

Removal and Installation

ALL MODELS

1. Disconnect the negative battery cable.
2. Remove the undercover and drain the cooling system. Remove the coolant hoses from the pump body.
3. On non-air conditioned models, remove the fan blade and pulley from the pump hub.
4. On air conditioned models, remove the air pump, drive belts, fan blades and pulleys.
5. Remove the water pump mounting bolts and remove the water pump.

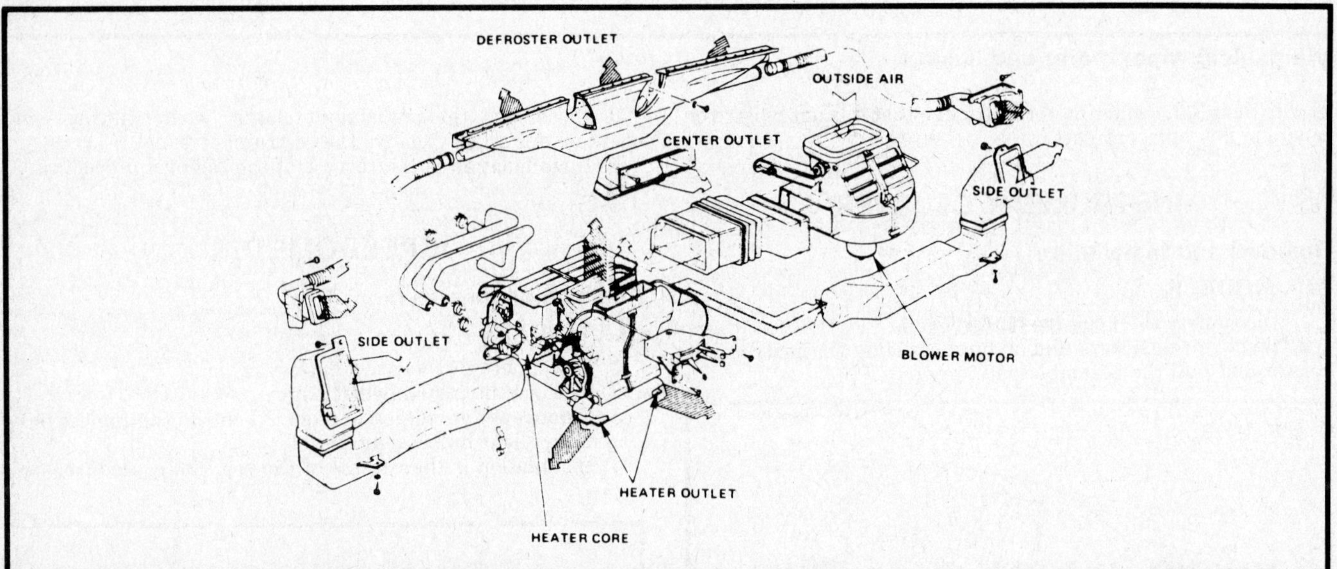

Heater assembly-without A/C-exploded view

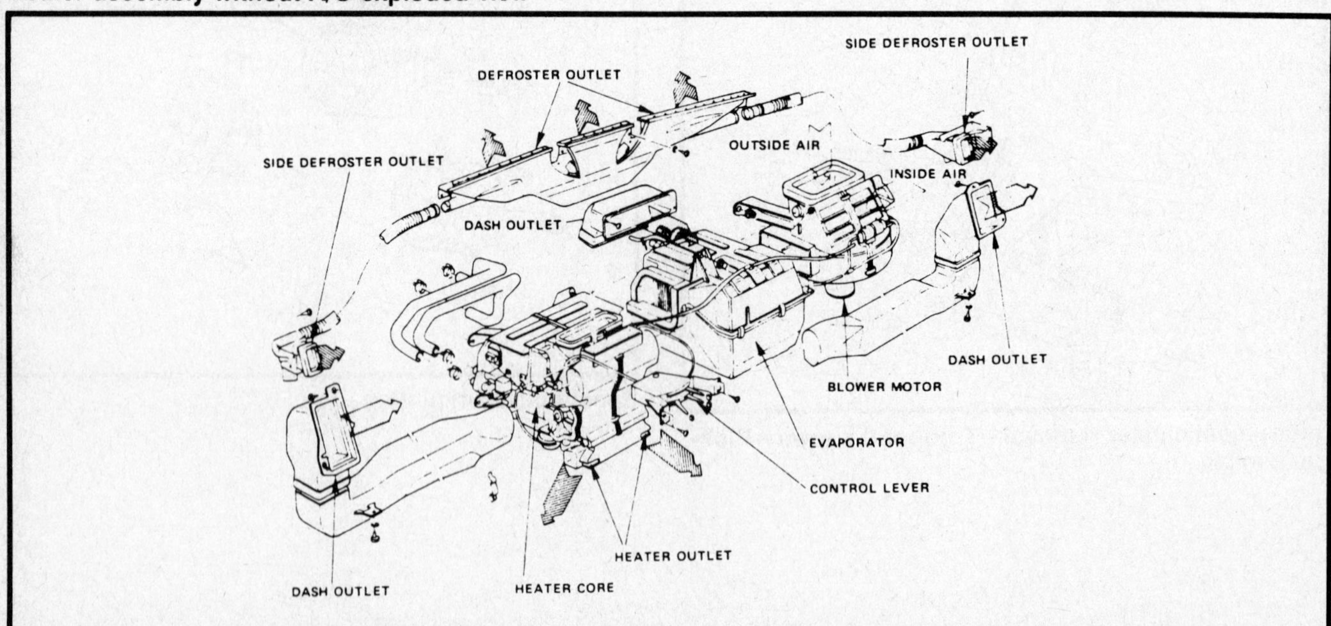

Heater assembly-with A/C-exploded view

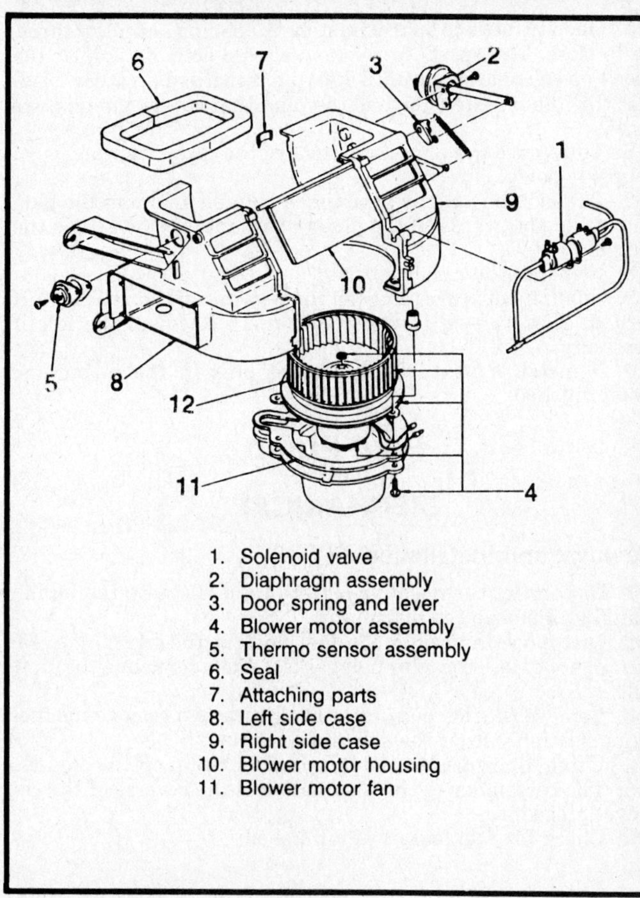

Exploded view of heater unit

6. Clean and inspect the mounting sufaces of the water pump and engine.
7. Installation is the reverse of the removal procedure.
8. Use a new gasket during installation and torque the mounting bolts to 10–17 ft. lbs.

Thermostat

Removal and Installation

ALL MODELS

1. Drain the cooling system.
2. Remove the air cleaner assembly. Disconnect the upper radiator hose.
3. Disconnect the water outlet from the intake manifold.
4. Remove the thermostat.
5. Using a new gasket, install the thermostat, with the spring facing the engine and the thermostat housing.
6. Connect the radiator hose and fill the cooling system.
7. Run the engine until it reaches normal operating temperature and check the thermostat operation.

Heater Core

Removal and Installation

ALL MODELS

1. Disconnect the negative battery cable.
2. Place a drain pan under the heater hoses at the heater core. Remove the heater hoses from the core tubes, securing the heater hoses in a raised position to prevent further loss of coolant. Plug the heater core tubes to prevent spillage of coolant in the passenger compartment when removing.
3. Remove the five parcel shelf attaching screws and remove the shelf.
4. Loosen the air diverter and defroster door bowden cable clamps at the heater case and disconnect and tag the cables at the doors.
5. Disconnect the blower resistor leads.
6. Remove the control assembly-to-instrument panel screws, swing the control to the left and lay it on the floor. Be careful not to kink the water valve bowden cable.
7. Remove the four heater-to-firewall screws. Pull the heater rearward until the core tubes clear the dash opening, then remove the heater by moving it to the right and down.
8. Remove the core tube clamp screw and remove the clamp.
9. Remove the seven screws and separate the heater case halves.
10. Remove the core from the case.
11. Install and assemble the heater core and heater case in the reverse order of the removal procedure, using new seals around the heater core.

Blower Motor

Removal and Installation

ALL MODELS

1. Disconnect the negative battery cable.
2. Disconnect and tag the blower motor electrical leads.
3. Remove the blower-to-heater core screws and remove the blower motor assembly.
4. Installation is the reverse of the removal procedure.

Cooling Fan

Removal and Installation

Refer to Water Pump Removal and Installation for the procedure.

FUEL SYSTEM

Carburetor

FEEDBACK

Removal and Installation

ALL MODELS

1. Remove the air cleaner wing nut and disconnect the rubber hoses from the clips on the air cleaner cover and the vacuum hose from the vacuum motor.
2. Remove the bracket bolts at the air cleaner and remove the air cleaner cover and filter element.
3. Disconnect the hot air hose (to the hot air duct), the air hose to the air pump at the air cleaner and the vacuum hose at the joint nipple side of the intake manifold.
4. Loosen the bolt clamping the air cleaner to the carburetor. Separate the air cleaner body from the carburetor, but do not remove it completely.
5. Disconnect the PCV hose (to the camshaft cover), the rubber hoses to the check and relief valve. Remove the air cleaner body.

6. Disconnect the vacuum hoses from the EGR valve.
7. Disconnect the choke control wire.
8. Disconnect the lead from the throttle solenoid.
9. Disconnect the throttle linkage return spring.
10. Disconnect the accelerator linkage wire.
11. Disconnect the fuel line at the carburetor.
12. Remove the four retaining nuts and lockwashers securing the carburetor to the manifold and remove the carburetor.
13. Installation is the reverse of the removal. Check for fuel leaks when finished.

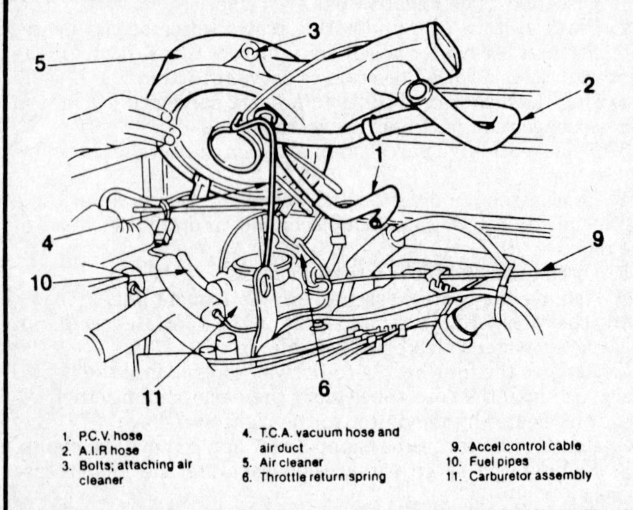

Removing the carburetor

Idle Speed and Mixture

Adjustment

1. Make the idle speed adjustment with the engine at normal operating temperature. Be sure the choke is fully opened, air conditioning off and the air cleaner installed.
2. Disconnect and plug the distributor vacuum, the canister purge and EGR vacuum lines. Shut off the vacuum to the idle compensator by bending the rubber hose.
3. Adjust to required idle speed with throttle adjusting screw.
4. If equipped with air conditioning, turn A/C to max cold and high blower.

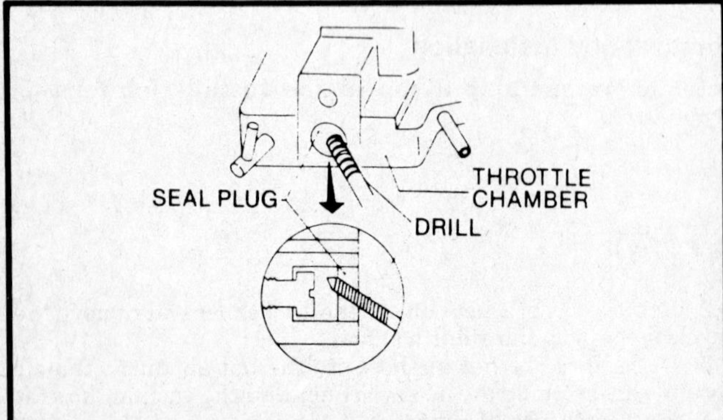

Removing the idle mixture plug

5. Open throttle to approximately ⅓ opening and allow throttle to close. The speed-up solenoid should activate. Adjust the speed-up solenoid screw until 900 rpm is reached. In order to adjust the idle mixture, remove the plug that covers the mixture screw.
6. To remove the plug, first remove the carburetor and turn it upside down.
7. Remove the plug by inserting a suitable tool into the plug and pulling outwards. If the plug pushes into the hole, drill the plug out.
8. Reinstall the carburetor.
9. Turn the mixture screw all the way in and then back it out 2 turns (Federal) or 1 turn (California). Readjust the idle if necessary.
10. Reinstall a mixture adjustment plug in the carburetor when finished.

Fuel Pump

MECHANICAL

Removal and Installation

1. Disconnect the negative battery cable. Remove the intake manifold. Remove the distributor.
2. Disconnect and plug the fuel lines at the fuel pump. Be careful not to lose the joint bolt gaskets when removing the joint bolt.
3. Remove the fuel pump mounting nuts and remove the fuel pump assembly from the side of the engine.
4. Using a new gasket, install the fuel pump on the engine.
5. The remainder of the installation is the reverse of the removal procedure.
6. Check for fuel leaks when finished.

ELECTRIC

The electric fuel pump is installed on the inner face of the third crossmember at the left hand side. The fuel pump is a totally enclosed type and cannot be disassembled.

Removal and Installation

1. Disconnect the negative battery cable.
2. Disconnect the wiring connection to the fuel pump.
3. Disconnect and plug the hoses at the fuel pump.
4. Remove the two bolts and one nut mounting the fuel pump and remove the fuel pump assembly.
5. Installation is the reverse of the removal procedure.
6. Check for fuel leaks when finished.

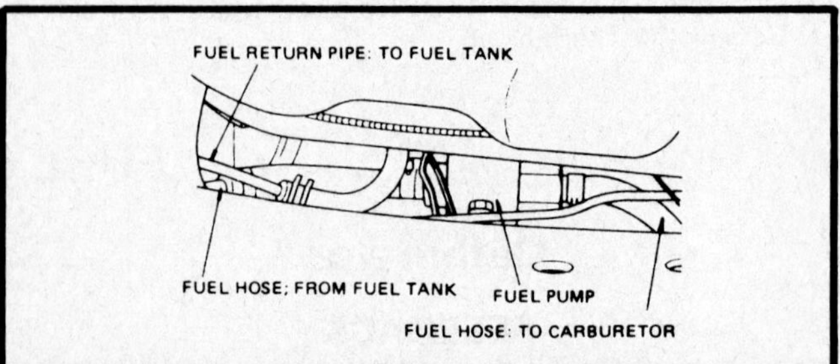

Electric fuel pump mounted on frame rail

EMISSION CONTROLS

1982–88 Emission Controls and Separate Components

Crankcase Emission Control Systems
Positive Crankcase Ventilation (PCV) Valve
Oil Separater

Evaporative Emission Control Systems
Thermostatically Controlled Air Cleaner
Over Temperature Control Valve
Coasting Enrichment Valve
Charcoal Canister
Fuel Check Valve
Vent Switching Valve-California models only
Thermo Switch

Exhaust Emission Control Systems
Injection Reactor (Air Pump)-California models only
Exhaust Gas Recirculation (EGR) Valve
Coolant Temperature Sensor-California models only
Catalytic Converter
Oxygen Sensor
Electronic Control Module (ECM)

Crankcase Emission Control Systems

A closed crankcase ventilation system is used to prevent blow-by gases from escaping into the atmosphere. The system has a positive (one-way) crankcase vent valve (PCV valve) at the rocker arm cover. Blow-by gases are drawn through two passages; one by a rubber vent hose from the rocker arm cover through the PCV valve into the intake manifold and the other by a rubber hose from the rocker arm cover to the air cleaner.

Removal and Installation

ALL MODELS

1. Check the PCV valve for operation, the oil separator and oil return pipe (if equipped) for clogging and leaks.
2. Check the PCV valve by removing the valve and the hose from the rocker cover while the engine is at idle speed. If the valve is not clogged, a hissing noise will be heard and strong vacuum will be felt when a finger is placed over the bottom of the valve.
3. Shut off the engine and disconnect the PCV valve from the hose. Blow through the threaded end. If air will not pass through, the valve is clogged and replacement will be required.

Evaporative Emission Control System

When the engine is not operating, fuel vapor generated inside the fuel tank is absorbed and stored in the charcoal canister. When the engine is running, the fuel vapor absorbed in the canister is drawn into the air intake hose through the purge valve. The purge valve is kept closed at idle. When vacuum reaches a pre-set value, the valve opens. On carbureted models, a bowl vent valve controls carburetor vapors. When vacuum reaches a pre-set level, the vapors are allowed to pass into the intake manifold.

CANISTER

Removal and Installation

ALL MODELS

1. Replace any hoses that are cracked or broken. Replace any canister that is damaged.
2. When the canister is in service over a long period of time, the interior filter will become clogged requiring canister replacement. Always replace the hoses when renewing the canister.
3. Disconnect all hoses and clamps at both ends of the canister(s) and from the purge valve. Unclamp or remove the canister mounting bands and remove the canister assembly.

THERMO VALVE

Removal and Installation

ALL MODELS

1. The thermo valve is located on the intake manifold or cylinder head where it's bottom will be immersed in coolant. It discharges into the purge control valve located near the charcoal canister. Disconnect the vacuum/pressure line coming from the thermo valve to the purge control valve and connect a vacuum gauge into the open end of the hose.
2. The engine must be overnight cold. Start the engine and run it at about 2000 rpm to get the throttle past the purge port.
3. The gauge should indicate zero vacuum pressure when the engine is started and, by the time thermostat opens and coolant begins to circulate in the radiator, there should be pressure or vacuum. Replace the thermo valve if pressure and/or vacuum exists.

Exhaust Emission Control System

Catalytic Converters are used for the purpose of decreasing harmful emissions. Secondary air systems are used to supply air into the exhaust system for the purpose of promoting oxidation of exhaust emissions into the converter. Exhaust gas recirculation (EGR) is used to reduce oxides of nitrogen in the exhaust by recirculating a portion of the exhaust gases back into the intake manifold below the air/fuel source.

PULSE AIR FEED (SECONDARY AIR)

Removal and Installation

ALL MODELS

1. Remove the hose connected to the air cleaner and check for vacuum. If no vacuum is present, check for cracked or broken hoses.

EGR VALVE

Removal and Installation

ALL MODELS

1. Check the vacuum hose to the EGR valve for cracks or cuts, replace any if necessary.
2. Start the engine and run at idle speed (cold engine). Run the engine to 2500 rpm and check the secondary EGR valve. If the secondary EGR valve is operating, the thermo valve is defective.
3. Warm the engine to about 131°F. The secondary EGR valve should operate when the engine is at 2500 rpm. If the valve is not operating, check the EGR control valve and the thermo valve.
4. Disconnect the hose from the thermo valve. Connect a hand vacuum pump to the thermo valve and apply vacuum. If no vacuum passes, the thermo valve is good.
5. Disconnect the green stripped hose from the carburetor fitting and connect the hose to the hand pump.
6. Open the sub EGR valve by hand and apply approximately 6 in. of vacuum with the hand pump.

7. If the idle speed becomes unstable, the secondary EGR valve is operating properly. If the idle speed remains unchanged, the EGR valve is not working. Replace the EGR valve.

Trouble Codes

Diagnosis Procedure

When the Electronic Control Module (ECM) finds a problem in the system, it will record a trouble code in its memory and the "Check Engine" light will come on. If the problem is intermittent, the code will be recorded, but the light will go out. Trouble codes can be identified by a series of light flashes with the "Check Engine" light. With the engine running at idle, disconnect and ground the ECM test lead under the left side of the dashboard, next to the hood release lever. The light flashes will begin in a pattern that will identify which system is at fault. For example; two flashes followed by a pause, then four more flashes, identifies that trouble code No. 24 is recorded in the ECM memory. If more than one trouble code is recorded, the system will flash the first code three times, then the second code three times, before returning to the first code. After completion of any repairs, reconnect the ECM power wire.

Identifying Trouble Codes

Trouble Code 12 – No ignition reference signal to the ECM. The code will not be stored in the ECM memory.

Trouble Code 13 – Oxygen sensor circuit is open or grounded. The engine must run for up to one minute, at partial throttle and under driving conditions, before the code will be recorded.

Trouble Code 14 – Coolant temperature circuit is shorted. The engine must run for up to two minutes before the code will be recorded.

Trouble Code 15 – Coolant temperature switch circuit is open. The engine must run at least five minutes before the code will be recorded.

Trouble Code 21 – Idle or wide open throttle switch circuit is shorted. The engine must run for at least two minutes before the code will be recorded.

Trouble Code 22 – Fuel cut solenoid circuit is open or grounded. The engine must run over 2000 rpm and under deceleration conditions before the code will be recorded.

Trouble Code 23 – Mixture control solenoid circuit is open or grounded.

Trouble Code 25 – Air switching solenoid circuit is open or grouunded.

Trouble Code 31 – No ignition reference signal to the ECM for at least ten seconds. This code will be stored in the memory.

Trouble Code 44 – Lean oxygen sensor indication. The engine must run for up to two minutes at partial throttle for the code to be recorded.

Trouble Code 45 – Rich fuel system indication. The engine must run for up to two minutes at partial throttle for the code to be recorded. The code will not set if the engine speed goes over 2500 rpm.

Trouble Code 51 – Shorted fuel cut solenoid circuit and/or faulty ECM.

Trouble Code 52 – Faulty ECM.

Trouble Code 53 – Shorted air switching solenoid and/or faulty ECM.

Trouble Code 54 – Shorted vacuum control solenoid and/or faulty ECM.

Trouble Code 55 – Faulty converter in ECM.

Clearing Trouble Codes

Procedure

Once the problem in the system is corrected, the trouble codes must be cleared from the ECM memory. The "Check Engine" light can be reset by disconnecting the negative battery cable for at least ten seconds and then reconnecting the cable.

ENGINE MECHANICAL

Refer to the Unit Overhaul Section for General Overhaul Procerdures.

Engine

Removal and Installation

2WD AND 4WD WITH GASOLINE ENGINE

NOTE: On pickup models with 2WD, the engine and transmission may be removed as an assembly. 4WD models require the engine and transmission to be removed separately.

1. Disconnect the battery cables, negative cable first. Drain the cooling system. Matchmark and remove the hood.

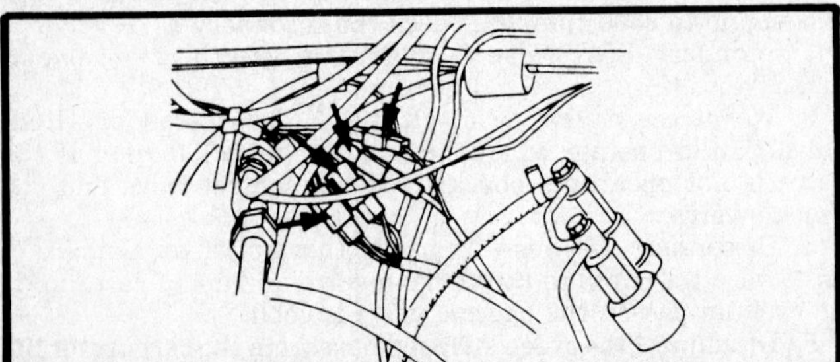

Disconnect points for the air compressor switch, sensing resistor, and thermoswitch connectors

2. Disconnect and tag the vacuum hoses to the air cleaner and remove the air cleaner.
3. Disconnect the upper and lower radiator hoses. Disconnect the heater hoses.
4. Disconnect and tag the vacuum hoses and electrical leads to the engine.
5. Remove the radiator and fan blade assembly.
6. Raise and support the vehicle safely. Disconnect the exhaust pipe from the exhaust manifold.
7. Remove the clutch return spring and the clutch cable, if equipped with a manual transmission.
8. Disconnect and tag the starter motor wiring and remove the starter motor. On 2WD, matchmark and remove the driveshaft. Remove transmission mount bolts. Remove gearshift lever assembly.
9. On 4WD; remove the flywheel cover pan.
10. On 4WD; remove the bell housing bolts and support the transmission.
11. Lift the engine slightly and remove the engine mount nuts.
12. Make certain that all lines, hoses, cables and wires have been disconnected from the engine and frame.
13. Lift the engine from the vehicle with the front of the engine raised slightly to clear the transmission input shaft.
14. Installation is the reverse of the removal procedure.
15. With the engine mounted properly, fill the cooling system with the proper coolant and fill the crankcase with engine oil. Check and adjust the clutch pedal free play.
16. Adjust the belt tension. Start the engine, check for leaks and adjust the idle speed and ignition timing.

2WD WITH DIESEL ENGINE

1. Matchmark and remove the hood.
2. Disconnect the battery cables, negative first and remove the battery from the vehicle.
3. Drain the cooling system.
4. Remove the air cleaner assembly as follows: Remove the intake silencer. Remove the bolts mounting the air cleaner and loosen the clamp bolt. Lift the air cleaner slightly and disconnect the breather hose. Remove the air cleaner assembly.
5. Disconnect the upper radiator hose at the engine.
6. Loosen the compressor drive belts by moving the power steering pump or idler.
7. Remove the cooling fan and fan shroud.
8. Disconnect the lower radiator hose at the engine.
9. Remove the radiator grille.
10. Remove the radiator attaching bolts and remove the radiator.
11. Disconnect the accelerator control cable from the injection pump.
12. If equipped with A/C, disconnect the A/C compressor control cable.
13. Disconnect and plug the fuel hoses from the injection pump.
14. Disconnect the ground cable from the engine.
15. Raise and support the vehicle safely. Disconnect and tag the transmission wiring.
16. Disconnect the vacuum hose from the fast idle actuator.
17. Disconnect the fuel cut solenoid wiring.
18. Disconnect the A/C compressor wiring, sensing resistor and thermoswitch connectors.
19. Disconnect the heater hoses extending from the heater unit from the dash panel side.
20. Disconnect the hose for power brake booster from the vacuum pump.
21. Disconnect vacuum hose from the vacuum pump.
22. Disconnect the alternator wiring.
23. Disconnect the exhaust pipe from the exhaust manifold at the flange.
24. Remove the exhaust pipe mounting bracket from the engine.
25. Disconnect and tag the starter motor wiring.
26. Slide the gearshift lever boot upwards on the lever. Remove the two gearshift lever attaching bolts and the remove lever.
27. Disconnect speedometer and ground cables at the transmission.
28. Matchmark and remove the driveshaft.
29. Remove the clutch fork return spring from the clutch fork.
30. Disconnect clutch cable from the hooked portion of clutch fork and pull it out forward through the stiffener bracket.
31. Remove two bracket to transmission rear mount bolts and nuts.
32. Raise the engine and transmission and remove the crossmember to frame bracket bolts.
33. Remove the rear mounting nuts from the transmission rear extension.
34. Disconnect electrical connectors at CRS switch and backup lamp switch.
35. Raise the engine and remove the engine mounting bolts and nuts.
36. Remove the engine towards the front of the vehicle making sure that the front part of the engine is lifted slightly above the level.
37. Installation is the reverse of the removal procedure.
38. With the engine mounted properly in the vehicle, fill the cooling system. Fill the crankcase with engine oil. Check and adjust the clutch pedal free play.
38. Adjust the fan belt tension. Start the engine, run at idle and check for leakage. Adjust the ignition timing and engine idle speed.

4WD WITH DIESEL ENGINE

1. Matchmark and remove the hood.
2. Disconnect the battery cables, negative first and remove the battery from the vehicle.
3. Drain the cooling system and disconnect the upper and lower radiator hoses from the engine and radiator.
4. Remove the intake silencer. Remove the air cleaner mounting bolts and loosen the clamp bolt. Lift the air cleaner slightly and disconnect the breather hose. Remove the air cleaner assembly.
5. Loosen the compressor drive belts by moving the power steering pump or idler.
6. Remove the cooling fan and fan shroud.
7. Remove the radiator grille.
8. Remove the radiator attaching bolts and remove the radiator.
9. Disconnect the accelerator control cable from the injection pump side.
10. If equipped with A/C, disconnect the air conditioner compressor control cable.
11. Disconnect and plug the fuel hose from the injection pump.
12. Disconnect the ground cable from the cylinder body.
13. Disconnect the transmission wiring.
14. Disconnect the vacuum hose from the fast idle actuator.
15. Disconnect the fuel cut solenoid wiring.
16. Disconnect the A/C compressor switch wiring, sensing resistor and the thermoswitch connectors.
17. Disconnect the heater hoses extending from the heater unit from the dash panel side.
18. Disconnect the hose for the power brake booster from the vacuum pump.
19. Disconnect the vacuum hose from the vacuum pump.
20. Disconnect and tag the alternator wiring.
22. Disconnect the exhaust pipe from the exhaust manifold at the flange.
23. Remove the exhaust pipe mounting bracket from the engine back plate.
24. Disconnect and tag the starter motor wiring. Remove the starter motor.
25. Slide the transmission/transfer case gearshift lever boots upwards on each lever. Remove the gearshift lever attaching bolts.
26. Remove return spring from transfer gear shift lever then remove levers.
27. Remove the transmission/transfer case assembly.
28. Raise the engine slightly and remove the engine mounting bolts and nuts.
29. To remove the engine, check to make certain all the parts have been removed or disconnected frame the engine that are fastened to the frame side. Remove the engine toward front of the vehicle with the front part of the engine lifted slightly above the level.
30. Installation is the reverse of the removal procedure.
31. With the engine mounted in the vehicle, fill the cooling system. Fill the crankcase with engine oil. Check and adjust the clutch pedal free play.
32. Adjust the fan belt tension. Start the engine, run at idle and check for leakage.
33. Adjust the ignition timing and idle speed.

Intake Manifold

Refer to the Unit Repair Section for Diesel Engine Service Procedures.

Removal and Installation

1982–88 GASOLINE ENGINES

1. Disconnect the negative battery cable and remove the air cleaner assembly.

2. Remove the EGR pipe clamp bolt at the rear of the cylinder head.
3. Raise and support the vehicle safely. Remove the EGR pipe from the intake and exhaust manifolds.
4. Remove the EGR valve and bracket assembly from the intake manifold.
5. Lower the vehicle and drain the cooling system.
6. Remove the upper coolant hoses from the manifold.
7. Disconnect the accelerator linkage, vacuum lines, electrical wiring and fuel line from the intake manifold.
8. Remove the intake manifold mounting nuts and remove the manifold from the cylinder head.

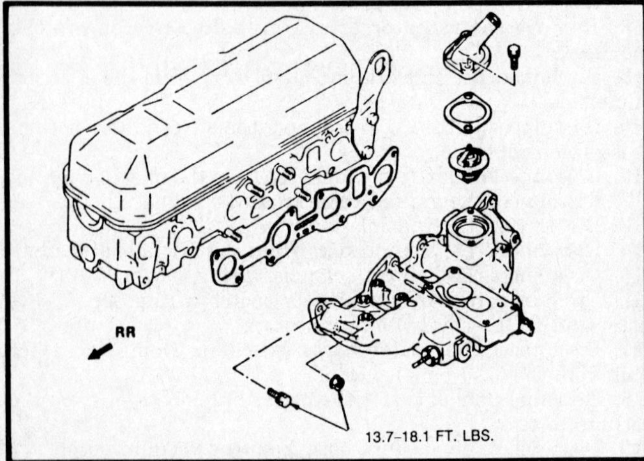

Intake manifold mounting

9. Remove the lower heater hose while holding the manifold away from the engine. Remove the manifold from the vehicle.
10. Installation is the reverse of the removal procedure.

Exhaust Manifold

Removal and Installation

1982–88 GASOLINE ENGINES

1. Disconnect the negative battery cable and remove the air cleaner assembly.
2. Remove the EGR pipe clamp bolt at the rear of the cylinder head.

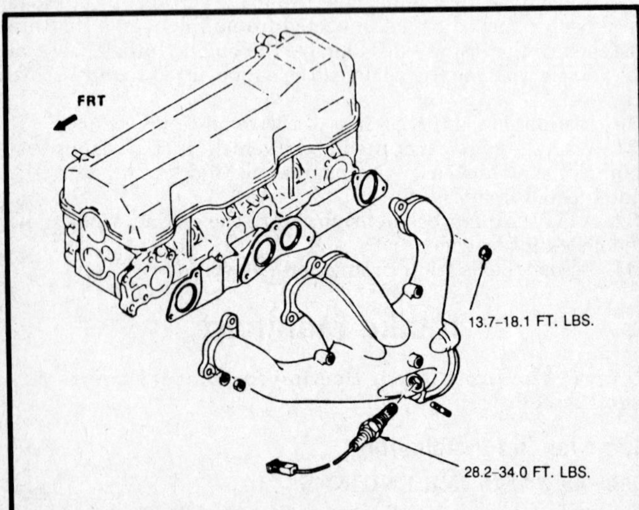

Exhaust manifold mounting

3. Raise and support the vehicle safely. Remove the EGR pipe from the intake and exhaust manifolds.
4. Disconnect the exhaust pipe from the exhaust manifold.
5. Remove the manifold shield and heat stove.
6. Remove the manifold retaining nuts and remove the manifold from the engine.
7. Installation is the reverse of the removal procedure.

Cylinder Head

Removal and Installation

1982–88 GASOLINE ENGINES

1. Disconnect the negative battery cable. Remove the rocker cover.
2. Remove the EGR pipe clamp bolt at the rear of the cylinder head.
3. Raise and support the vehicle safely. Disconnect the exhaust pipe at the exhaust manifold.
4. Lower the vehicle and drain the cooling system.
5. Disconnect the heater hoses at the intake manifold and at the rear of the cylinder head. Remove the A/C compressor and/or power steering pump with hoses attached and support them out of the way.
6. Disconnect the accelerator linkage and fuel line at the carburetor. Disconnect and tag the electrical connections, spark plug wires and vacuum lines at the cylinder head.
7. Rotate the engine until the No.4 cylinder is in the firing position. Remove the distributor cap and mark the rotor to housing relationship. Remove distributor and the fuel pump.
8. Lock the timing chain adjuster by depressing and turning the automatic adjuster side pin 90° clockwise.
9. Remove the timing sprocket to camshaft bolt and remove the sprocket from the camshaft.

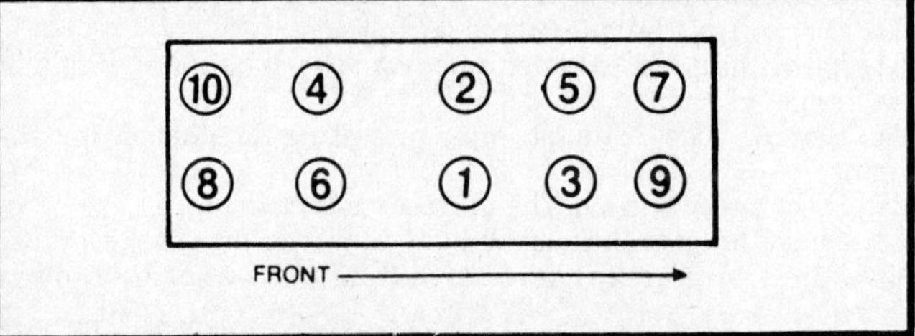

Gasoline engine head bolt torque sequence

NOTE: Keep the sprocket on the chain damper and chain.

10. Disconnect the AIR hose and the check valve at the exhaust manifold.
11. Remove the cylinder head to timing cover bolts.
12. Starting with the outer bolts and working inward, remove the cylinder head bolts.
13. Remove the cylinder head, intake and exhaust manifold as a unit.
14. To install, use a new gasket and install the cylinder head on the engine.
15. Torque the bolts to 57 ft. lbs. in the first step and to 65–79 ft. lbs. in the final step.
16. The remainder of the installation is the reverse of the removal. Check for fuel and water leaks when finished.

Rocker Arms and Shaft

Removal and Installation

1982–88 GASOLINE ENGINES

1. Disconnect the negative battery cable. Remove the rocker cover.

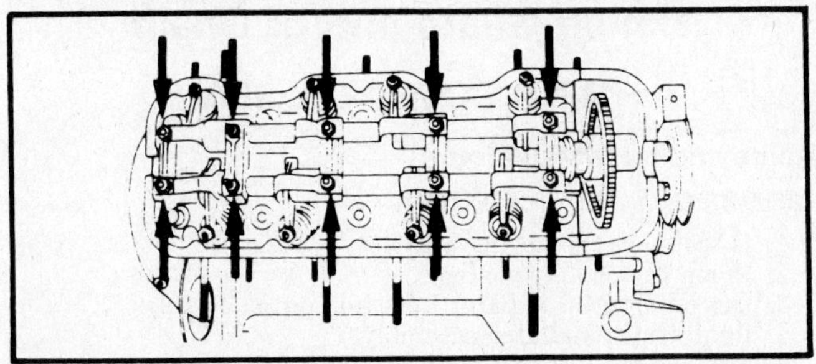

Rocker arm shaft bracket nut locations--gasoline engine

2. Loosen the rocker arm shaft bracket nuts a little at a time, in sequence, starting with the outer nuts.
3. Remove the nuts from the rocker arm shaft brackets. Remove shaft assembly.
4. To disassemble the rockers and shafts; remove the spring from the rocker arm shaft and remove the rocker brackets and arms. Keep parts in order for reassembly.
5. Before installing apply a generous amount of clean engine oil to the rocker arm shaft, rocker arms and valve stems.
6. Install the longer shaft on the exhaust valve side and the shorter shaft on the intake side so that the aligning marks on the shafts are turned on the front side of the engine.
7. Assemble the rocker arm shaft brackets and rocker arms to the shafts so that the cylinder number that is on the upper face of the brackets is pointed toward the front of the engine.
8. Align the mark on the No. 1 rocker arm shaft bracket with the mark on the intake and exhaust valve side rocker arm shaft.
9. Make certain the amount of projection of the rocker arm shaft beyond the face of the No. 1 rocker arm shaft bracket, is longer on the exhaust side shaft than on the intake shaft when the rocker arm shaft stud holes are aligned with the rocker arm shaft bracket stud holes.
10. Place the rocker arm shaft springs in position between the shaft bracket and rocker arm.
11. Check that the punch mark on the rocker arm shaft is turned upward, then install the rocker arm shaft bracket assembly onto the cylinder head studs. Align the mark on the camshaft with the mark on the No. 1 rocker arm shaft bracket.
12. Torque the rocker arm shaft brackets stud nuts to 16 ft. lbs.

NOTE: Hold the rocker arm springs while torquing the nuts to prevent damage to the spring. Start with the center nut and work outward.

13. Adjust the valves and install the camshaft cover, with a new gasket and sealer. Check the ignition timing.

Valve Adjustment

Procedure

NOTE: The valves are adjusted with the engine COLD. It is best to allow an engine to sit overnight before beginning a valve adjustment. While all valve adjustments must be made as accurately as possible, it is better to have the valve adjustment slightly loose rather than slightly tight. A burned valve may result from overly tight valve adjustments.

1. Make sure that both the cylinder head and camshaft retaining bolts are tightened to the proper torque.
2. Remove the camshaft carrier sidecover and discard the gasket.

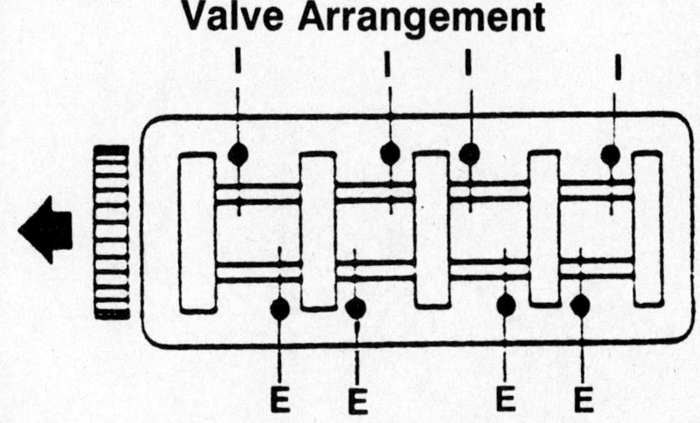

Valve \ Cylinder	1	2	3	4
Intake	○	○	●	●
Exhaust	○	●	○	●

Note: ○ When piston in No. 1 cylinder is at TDC on compression stroke.
● When piston in No. 4 cylinder is at TDC on compression stroke.

Valve adjusting sequence

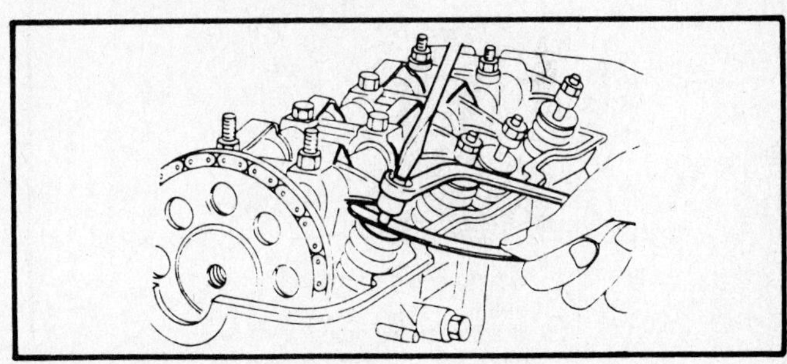

Valve clearance adjustment

3. Turn the crankshaft by the front pulley attaching bolt until the No. 1 piston is at TDC of the compression stroke. To make sure that the piston is on the correct stroke, remove the spark plug and place a finger over the hole. Feel for air being forced out of the spark plug hole. Both valves on No. 1 cylinder will be closed. Stop turning the crankshaft when the TDC timing mark on the crankshaft pulley is directly aligned with the timing mark pointer.
4. With the No. 1 piston at TDC of the compression stroke, check the clearance between the rocker arm and valve stem with the proper thickness feeler gauge on Nos. 1 and 2, intake valves and Nos. 1 and 3 exhaust valves.
5. Adjust the clearance by loosening the locknut and turning the adjusting screw. Retightening the locknut when the proper thickness feeler gauge passes between the camshaft or valve stem and has a slight drag when the clearance is corrected.
6. Turn the crankshaft one full turn (360°) to position the No. 4 piston at TDC of its compression stroke. Adjust the remaining valves: Nos. 2 and 4 exhaust and Nos. 3 and 4 intake in the same manner.
7. Install the camshaft carrier sidecover with a new gasket and sealer.

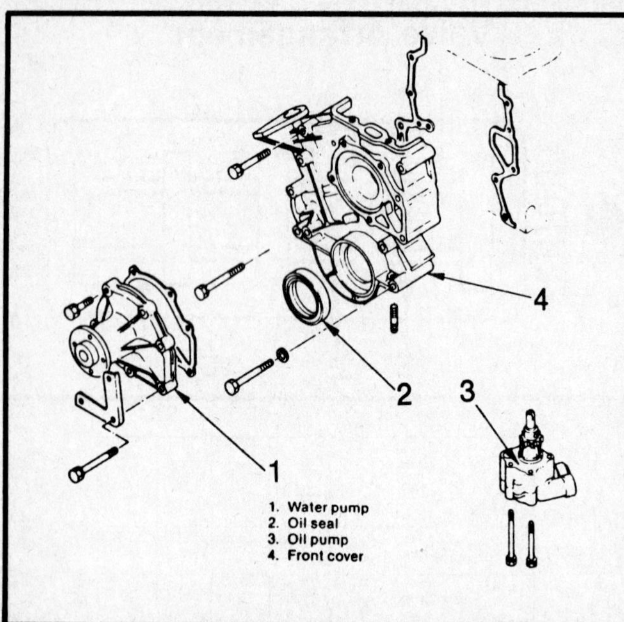

1982–85 Front timing chain cover and water pump

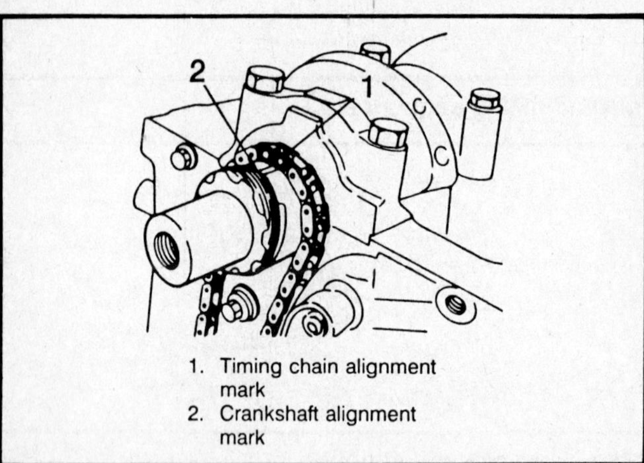

1982–85 Crankshaft gear and timing chain alignment marks

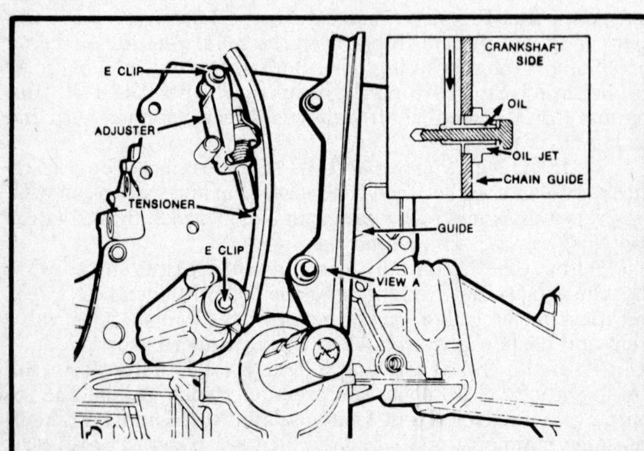

Timing chain adjuster

Timing Gears and/or Chain

TIMING COVER OIL SEAL

Removal and Installation

1982–85 GASOLINE ENGINE

1. Disconnect the negative battery cable.
2. Drain the cooling system.
3. Disconnect the radiator inlet and outlet hoses.
4. Remove the radiator assembly.
5. Remove the alternator and compressor drive belts.
6. Remove the cooling fan.
7. Remove the crankshaft pulley center bolt and remove the pulley and balancer assembly.
8. Using care not to damage the crankshaft and cover sealing surfaces, carefully pry out the timing cover seal.
9. Using suitable tool, carefully tap the new seal into place on the cover with the lip of the seal facing the engine.
10. Use a new gasket and sealer between the timing cover and engine block.
11. The remainder of the installation is the reverse of the removal procedure.

TIMING BELT COVER

Removal and Installation

1986–88 GASOLINE ENGINE

1. Disconnect the negative battery cable. Remove all accessory drive belts.
2. Remove the crankshaft pulley bolt.
3. Remove the upper timing belt cover.
4. Remove the lower timing belt cover.
5. Installation is the reverse of the removal procedure.

TIMING CHAIN, SPROCKETS AND TENSIONER

Removal and Installation

1982–85 GASOLINE ENGINE

1. Rotate the engine until No. 1 piston is at TDC on the compression stroke. Remove the front cover assembly. Depress or lock the shoe of the automatic chain adjuster in the retracted position.
2. Remove the timing chain from the crankshaft sprocket.
3. Remove the sprocket and the pinion gear from the crankshaft using a puller.
4. Remove the bolt or E-clip and remove the automatic chain adjuster.

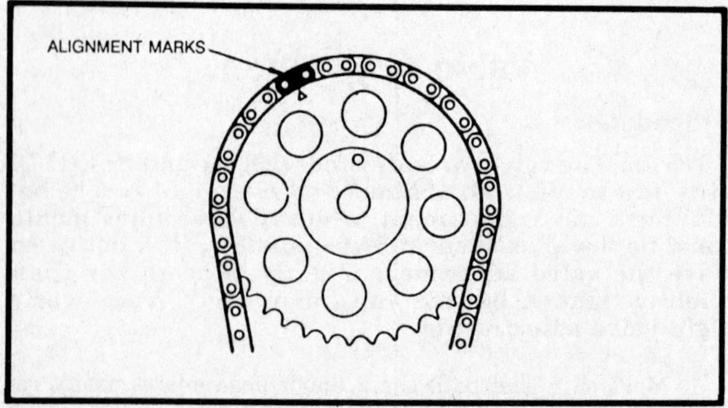

1982–85 Camshaft gear and timing chain alignment marks

5. Inspect the adjuster pin, arm, wedge and rack teeth. Replace assembly if worn. Remove the chain tensioner.
6. Check the timing chain for wear. Stretch the chain with a pull of approximately 22 lbs., the standard length is 15.00 in.; replace the chain if it is greater than 15.16 in.
7. Check the tensioner pins for wear or damage and replace if necessary.
8. Replace the chain tensioner and adjuster using the E-clips or bolt.
9. Install the timing sprocket and pinion gear with the groove side toward the front cover. Align the key grooves with the key on the crankshaft, then drive into position.
10. Confirm No. 1 piston at TDC. If not, turn the crankshaft so that the key is turned toward the cylinder head side (No. 1 and No. 4 pistons at top dead center).
11. Install the timing chain by aligning the mark plate on the chain with the mark on the crankshaft timing sprocket. The side of the chain with the mark plate is on the front side and the side of the chain with the most links between the mark plates is on the chain guide side.
12. Install the camshaft timing sprocket so that the mark side of the sprocket faces forward and so that the triangular mark aligns with the chain mark plate.

NOTE: Keep the timing chain engaged with the camshaft timing sprocket until the sprocket is installed on the camshaft.

13. Install the front cover assembly, using a new gasket and sealer.

TIMING BELT AND SPROCKETS

Removal and Installation

1986–88 GASOLINE ENGINE

1. Disconnect the negative battery cable.
2. Remove the upper and lower timing belt covers.
3. Remove the timing belt tensioner and pulley.
4. Remove the timing belt. If the belt is being reinstalled, mark the direction of rotation of the belt to insure proper installation.

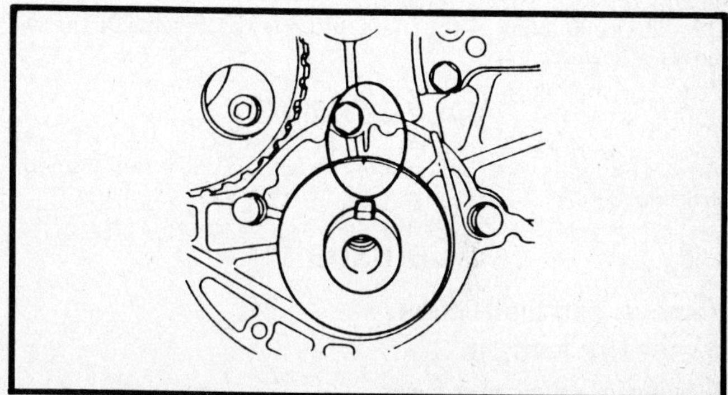

1986–88 Crankshaft alignment marks for timing belt installation

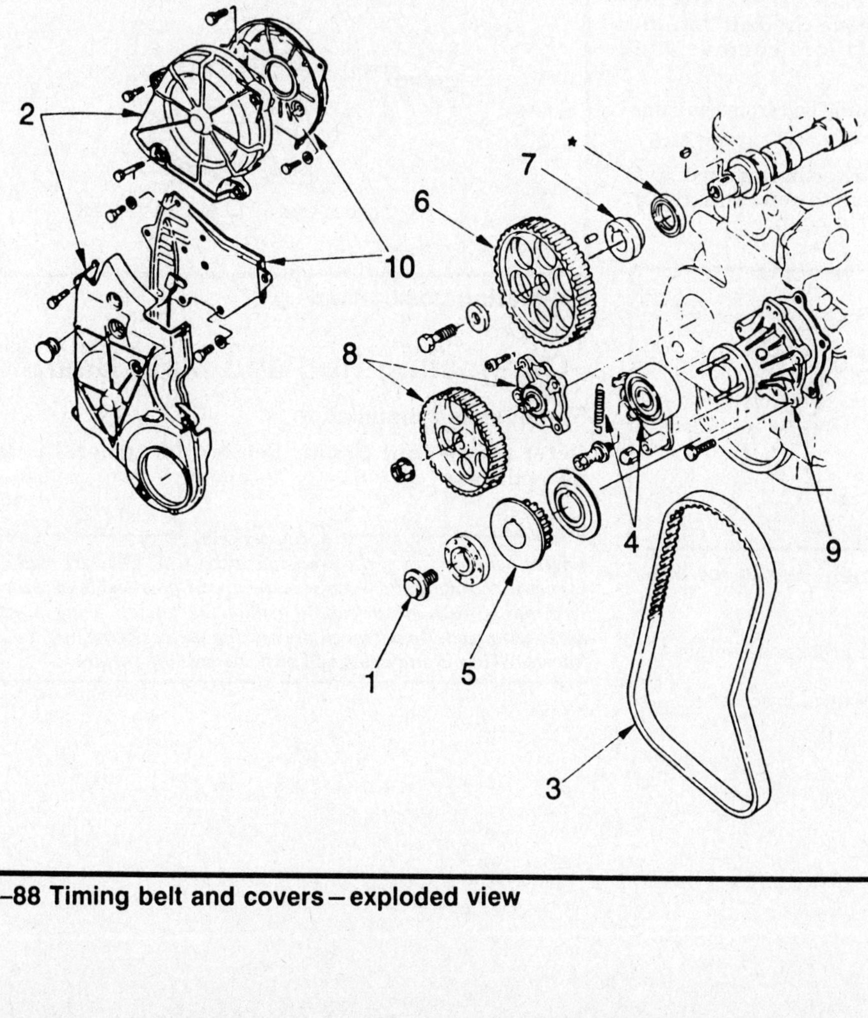

1. Crankshaft pulley bolt
2. Timing belt cover
3. Timing belt
4. Tensioner pulley and spring
5. Crankshaft timing sprocket
6. Camshaft timing sprocket
7. Camshaft boss
8. Oil pump and pulley
9. Water pump
10. Rear timing belt covers

1986–88 Timing belt and covers—exploded view

5. Remove the camshaft sprocket bolt and remove the sprocket.
6. Remove the crankshaft sprocket and washer.
7. Rotate the crankshaft until the timing marks on the washer line up with the mark on the oil seal cover.
8. Rotate the camshaft until the timing mark on the sprocket lines up with the mark on the rear timing belt cover.
9. Install the timing belt with the marks in this position. After the belt is installed, check the marks again to insure proper alignment.
10. Install the tensioner and spring. Correct tension is predetermined by the spring tension.
11. The remainder of the installation is the reverse of the removal procedure.

VALVE TIMING

Valve timing is not adjustable. Refer to Valve Adjustment Procedure

Camshaft

Removal and Installation

GASOLINE ENGINE

1. Remove the rocker cover.
2. Rotate the engine until the No. 4 cylinder is at TDC (top dead center) on the compression stroke. Remove the distributor cap and mark the rotor to housing position.
3. On 1982–85 engines, lock the timing chain adjuster by depressing and turning the automatic adjuster slide pin 90° in a clockwise position.

NOTE: Make sure that the chain is in a free state, after locking the chain adjuster. Remove the bolt retaining the sprocket to the camshaft and remove the sprocket.

4. On 1986–88 engines, remove the timing belt from the camshaft sprocket and remove the sprocket.

NOTE: On 1982–85 engines, keep the timing sprocket on the chain damper and tensioner without removing the chain from the sprocket.

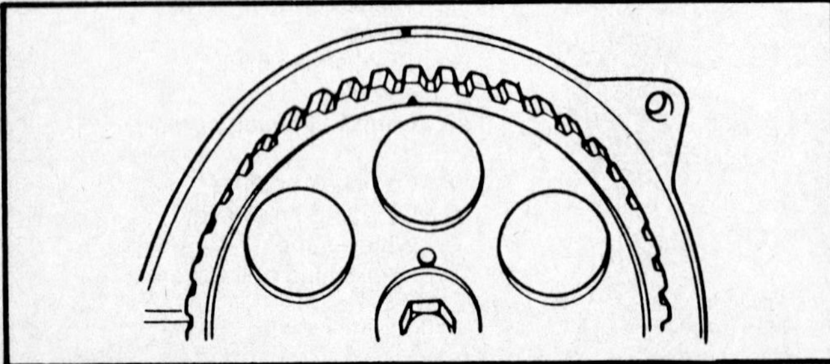

1986–88 Camshaft sprocket alignment marks for timing belt installation

5. Remove the rocker arms, shaft and bracket assembly.
6. Remove the camshaft assembly.
7. Installation is the reverse of the removal procedure.
8. Adjust the valve lash when finished. Check the timing mark alignment before starting the engine.

Piston and Connecting Rod

IDENTIFICATION

NOTE: Whenever pistons and connecting rods are removed or replaced, they must be marked to identify the cylinder and direction of assembly. The pistons are marked with the word "Front" and/or a notch in the piston head. When installed in the engine the "Front" and notch markings must face the front of the engine. The connecting rods are numbered corresponding to the cylinders in which they are installed in. Install the connecting rods in their correct cylinders with the marking to the right of the notch in the piston, looking from the rear of the engine.

Removal and Installation

Refer to the Unit Overhaul Section for general overhaul procedures.

NOTE: Remove the ridge at the top of the cylinder wall before removing. Replace the connecting rod caps on the connecting rod immediately after removal and inspect for cylinder number markings.

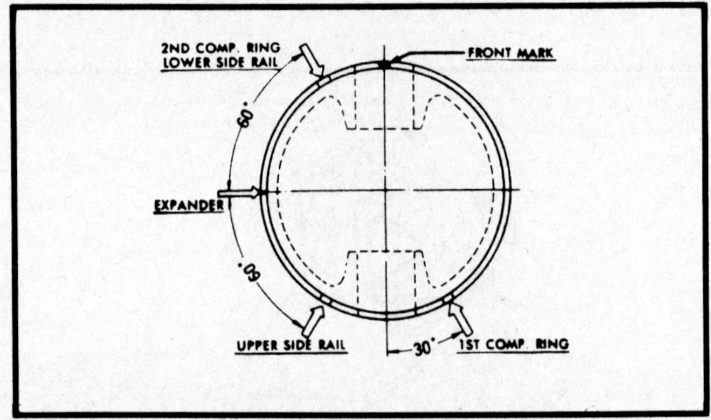

Piston ring positioning

Connecting Rod and Main Bearings

Removal and Installation

Refer to the Unit Repair Section for general overhaul procedures.

CAUTION

Engine bearings are of the precision insert type. They are available for service in standard and various undersizes. Upper and lower bearing inserts may be different. Be careful to align the holes. Bearing inserts must not be shimmed. Do not touch the bearing surface of the insert with bare fingers. Skin oil and acids will etch the bearing surface.

ENGINE LUBRICATION

Oil Pan

Removal and Installation

NOTE: On 4WD gasoline engine models, the engine must be removed before removing the oil pan.

1. Disconnect the negative battery cable.
2. Raise and support the vehicle safely.
3. Drain the engine oil.
4. Remove the front splash shield.
5. On 1982–85 models, remove the front crossmember.
6. Disconnect the relay rod at the idler arm and lower the relay rod.
7. Remove the left side bellhousing bracket.
8. Disconnect the vacuum line at the oil pan.
9. Remove the oil pan bolts and remove the oil pan.
10. Installation is the reverse of the removal procedure. Tighten the retaining bolts to 43 inch lbs. On models with a separate crankcase, tighten the bolts 15 ft. lbs. (180 inch lbs.). Always use a new gasket and sealer.

Oil Pump

Removal and Installation

1982–85 GASOLINE ENGINE

1. Raise and support the vehicle safely.
2. Drain the engine oil and remove the oil pan.
3. Disconnect the oil feed pipe.
4. Remove the two bolts securing the oil pump to the cylinder block and remove the oil pump.
5. Installation is the reverse of the removal procedure.

1986–88 GASOLINE ENGINE

1. Remove the upper and lower timing belt covers.

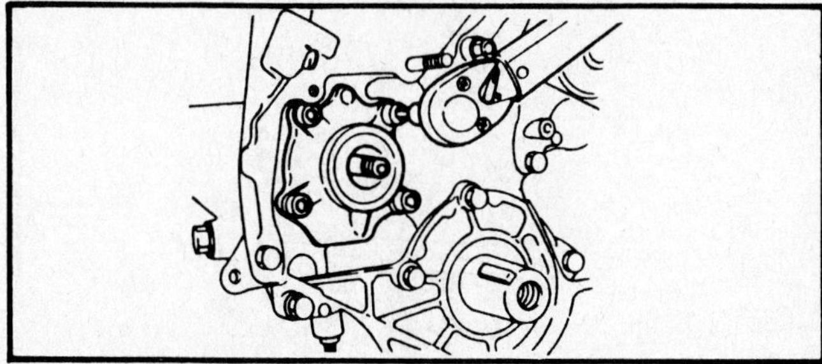

Oil pump mounting – 1986–88

2. Remove the timing belt from the crankshaft and oil pump sprockets.
3. Remove the oil pump mounting bolts and remove the oil pump.
4. Install the oil pump and torque the bolts to 10–17 ft. lbs.
5. Line up the timing marks on the camshaft and crankshaft sprockets and install the timing belt.
6. Install the timing belt covers and drive belts.

Rear Main Bearing Oil Seal

LIP TYPE SEAL

Removal and Installation

GASOLINE ENGINE

1. Disconnect the negative battery cable.
2. Drain the engine oil and remove the oil pan.
3. On automatic transmission models, remove the transmission. On manual transmission models, remove the transmission and clutch assembly.
4. Remove the starter without disconnecting the wires and secure it out of the way.
5. Remove the flywheel.
6. Remove the rear main seal retainer.
7. Carefully remove the oil seal, using a suitable tool. Work the tool around the diameter of the seal until the seal begins to lift out. Use care not to damage the seat and area around the seal.
8. Fill the space between the seal lips with grease and lubricate the seal lips with clean engine oil. Install the new oil seal.
9. Installation is the reverse of the removal procedure.
10. Install the oil pan with a new gasket and sealer.

Use sealer at the points indicated when installing the pan gasket

2WD FRONT SUSPENSION

Spring

TORSION BAR

Removal and Installation

1. Raise and support the vehicle safely.
2. Remove the adjusting bolt from the height control arm.
3. Mark the location and remove the height control arm from the torsion bar and the third crossmember.
4. Mark the location and withdraw the torsion bar from the lower control arm.
5. To install, apply a generous amount of grease to the serrated ends of the torsion bar.
6. Hold the rubber bumpers in contact with the lower control arm. Raise the vehicle up under the lower control arm to accomplish this.
7. Insert the front end of the torsion bar into the control arm.
8. Install the height control arm in position so that it's end is reaching the adjusting bolt. Be sure to lubricate the part of the height control arm that fits into the chassis with grease.
9. Install a new cotter pin in the control arm.
10. Turn the adjusting bolt to the location marked before removal.
11. Lower the vehicle and check the vehicle height.

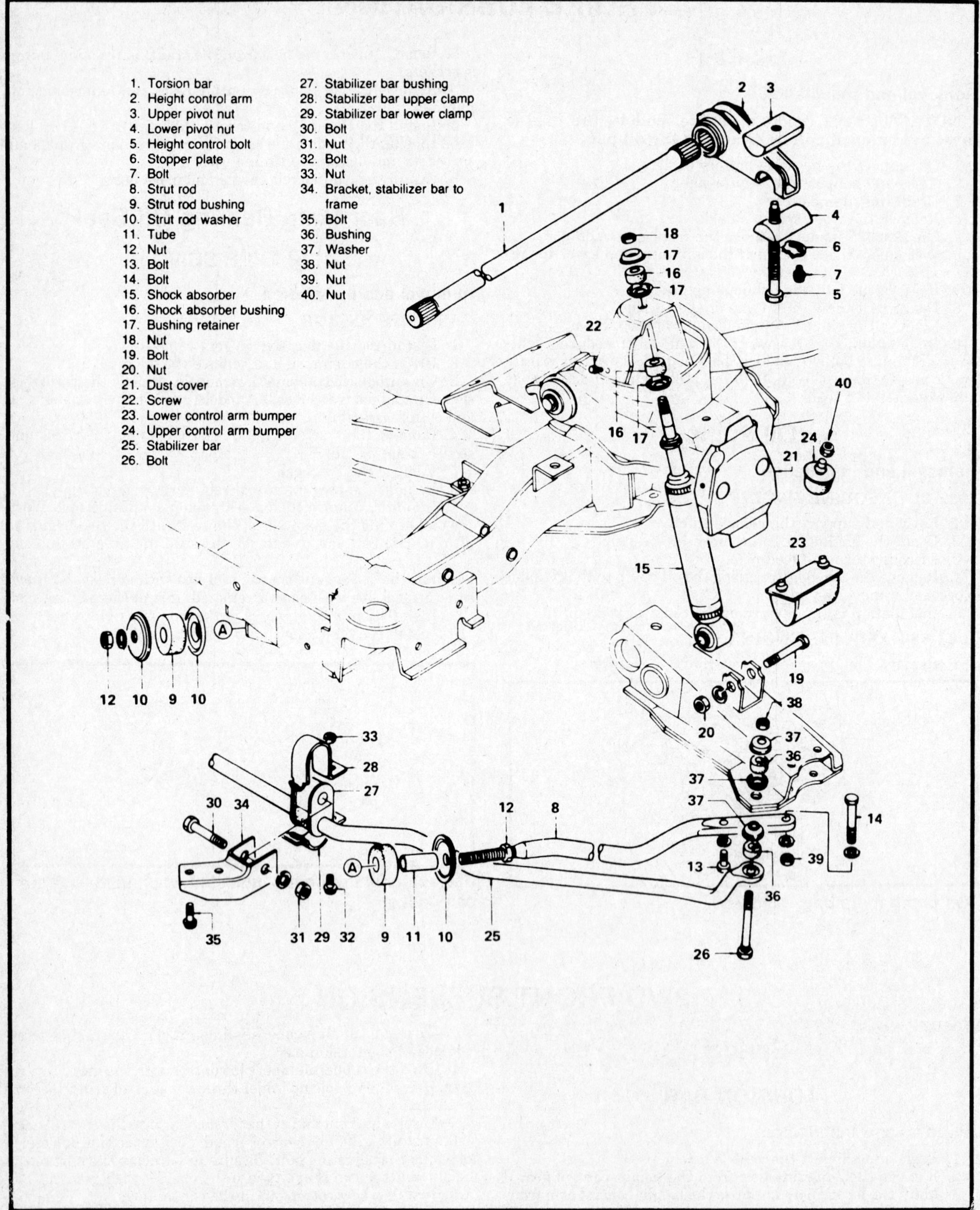
1. Torsion bar
2. Height control arm
3. Upper pivot nut
4. Lower pivot nut
5. Height control bolt
6. Stopper plate
7. Bolt
8. Strut rod
9. Strut rod bushing
10. Strut rod washer
11. Tube
12. Nut
13. Bolt
14. Bolt
15. Shock absorber
16. Shock absorber bushing
17. Bushing retainer
18. Nut
19. Bolt
20. Nut
21. Dust cover
22. Screw
23. Lower control arm bumper
24. Upper control arm bumper
25. Stabilizer bar
26. Bolt
27. Stabilizer bar bushing
28. Stabilizer bar upper clamp
29. Stabilizer bar lower clamp
30. Bolt
31. Nut
32. Bolt
33. Nut
34. Bracket, stabilizer bar to frame
35. Bolt
36. Bushing
37. Washer
38. Nut
39. Nut
40. Nut
A

2-wheel drive torsion, strut and stabilizer bars

Shock Absorbers

Removal and Installation

1. Raise and support the vehicle safely.
2. Hold the upper stem of the shock absorber from turning and remove the upper stem retaining nut, retainer and rubber grommet.
3. Remove the bolt retaining the lower shock absorber pivot to the lower control arm and remove the shock absorber from the vehicle.
4. Install the shock absorber by first installing the lower retainer and rubber grommet over the upper stem and then, installing the shock fully extended up through the upper control arm so that the upper stem passes through the mounting hole in the frame bracket.
5. Install the upper rubber grommet, retainer and attaching nut over the shock absorber upper stem.
6. Hold the upper stem of the shock absorber from turning and tighten the retaining nut.
7. Install the retainers attaching the shock absorber lower pivot to the lower control arm and tighten them.
8. Lower the vehicle.

Upper Control Arm and Ball Joint

Removal and Installation

NOTE: The upper control arm and ball joint are replaced as an assembly.

1. Raise and support the vehicle on the lower control arms safely.
2. Remove the wheel assembly.
3. Remove the cotter pin nut fastening the upper control arm and upper ball joint assembly and disconnect the upper control arm from the steering knuckle.

NOTE: Do not allow the steering knuckle to hang by the flexible brake line. Wire the steering knuckle up to the frame temporarily.

4. Remove the two bolts from the upper pivot shaft and remove the upper control arm from the bracket. Be sure to note the position and number of shims used for adjusting the camber and caster angles when removing the upper control arm. The shims must be replaced in their original position.
5. To remove the pivot shaft and bushings from the upper control arm assembly, remove the bushing nuts from the pivot shaft by loosening them alternately, then remove the pivot shaft.
6. To install the upper control arm and ball joint assembly, first install the pivot shaft boots to the pivot shaft.
7. Fill the internal part of the bushings with grease and screw the bushings into the pivot shaft. Be sure to screw the right-side and the left-side bushings alternately into the pivot shafts carefully avoiding getting grease on the outer face of the bushings. Tighten the nuts to 250 ft. lbs.

NOTE: Be sure that the control arm and bushings are centered properly and that the control arm rotates with resistance but not binding on the pivot shaft when tightened to the proper torque.

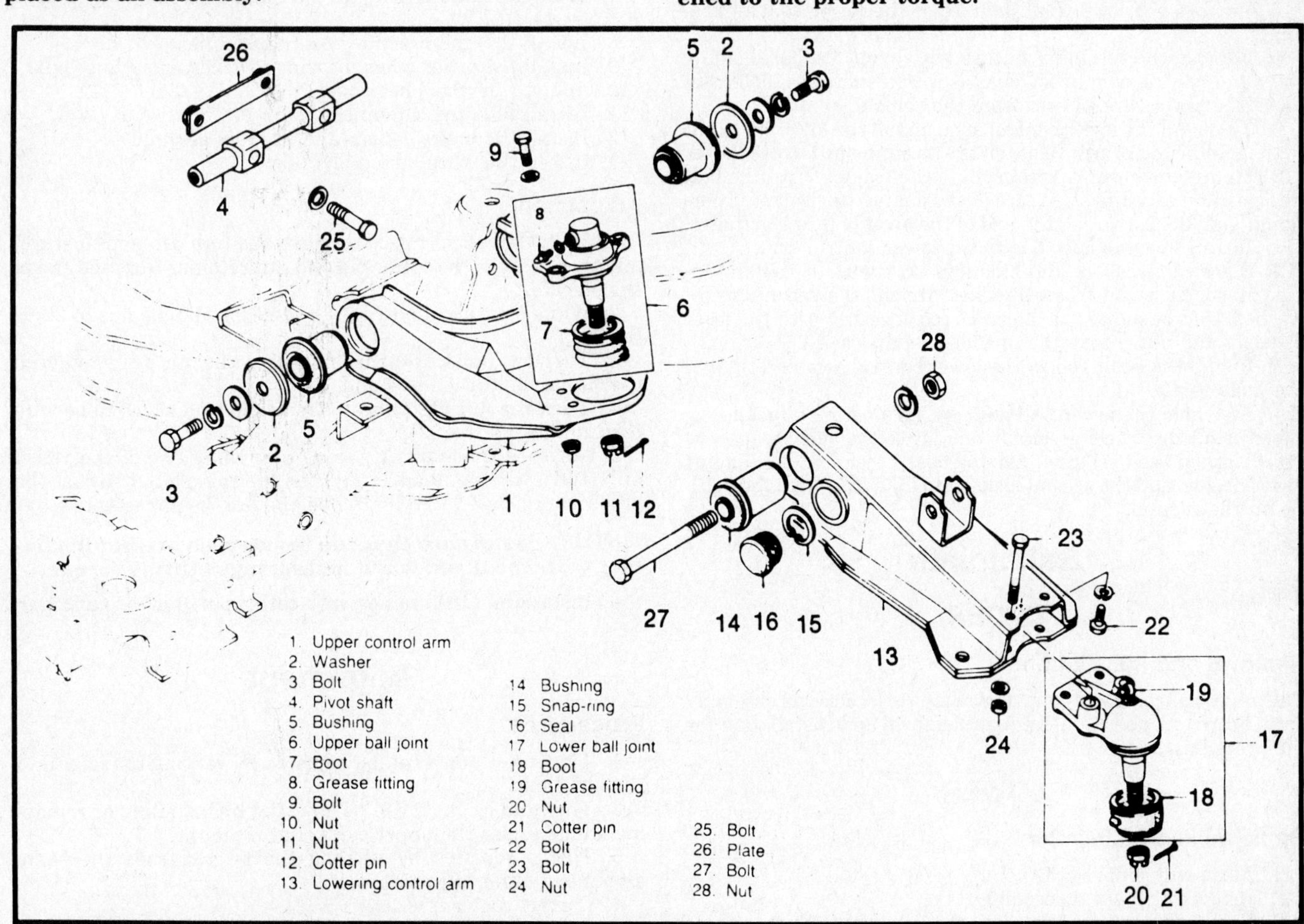

2-wheel drive front suspension

8. Install the grease fittings and lubricate the parts with grease through the grease fittings.
9. Install the ball joint stud through the steering knuckle. Install the castellated nut and tighten it to 75 ft. lbs. and just enough additional torque to install the cotter pin. Use a new cotter pin.
10. Mount the upper control arm to the chassis frame and install the shims in their original positions between the pivot shaft and bracket. Tighten the pivot shaft attaching nuts to 55 ft. lbs.

NOTE: Tighten the thinner shim pack's nut first for improved shaft-to-frame clamping force and torque retention.

11. Install the dust cover.
12. Install the wheel assembly and lower the vehicle.

Lower Control Arm

Removal and Installation

1. Raise and support the vehicle safely.
2. Remove the wheel assembly.
3. Remove the strut bar by removing the frame side bracket and the double nuts, washer and the rubber bushing from the front side of the strut bar. Remove the two bolts fastening the strut bar to the lower control arm and remove the bar.
4. Disconnect the stabilizer bar from the lower control arm.
5. Remove the torsion bar.
6. Disconnect the shock absorber from the lower control arm.
7. Remove the lower ball joint from the lower control arm joint.
8. Remove the retaining nut and drive out the bolt holding the lower control arm to the chassis with a soft metal drift. Remove the lower control arm from the vehicle.
9. To install the lower control arm, install the lower ball joint to the lower control arm. Tighten the retaining nuts to 45 ft. lbs.
10. Mount the lower control arm to the frame. Drive the bolt into position carefully. Use care not to damage the serrated portions. Tighten the nut on the end of the pivot bolt to 135 ft. lbs.
11. Install the stabilizer bar to the lower control arm.
12. Place the washers and bushings on the strut rod and install it through the frame bracket. Install the second set of washers and bushings on the strut rod together with the lockwashers and nut. Leave the nut loose temporarily.
13. Install the strut rod to the lower control arm and tighten the bolts to 45 ft. lbs.
14. Assemble the lower ball joint to the steering knuckle.
15. Install the wheel assembly and lower the vehicle.
16. Tighten the first strut bar-to-chassis frame attaching nut to 175 ft. lbs. and the second locknut to 55 ft. lbs. with the vehicle on the ground.

Ball Joints

UPPER

Removal and Installation

The upper ball joint and control arm are replaced as an assembly only. Refer to Upper Control Arm Removal and Installation for the procedure.

LOWER

Removal and Installation

1. Raise and support the vehicle safely.
2. Remove the wheel assembly.
3. Remove the cotter pin and castellated nut which retains the ball joint to the steering knuckle.
4. Remove the two bolts retaining the lower ball joint and strut rod.
5. Remove the remaining two bolts.
6. Remove the ball joint.
7. Install the lower ball joint by mounting the joint to the lower control arm and tightening the four bolts to 45 ft. lbs.
8. Install the ball joint stud into the steering knuckle and install the castellated nut and torque it to 75 ft. lbs. and just enough additional torque to align the cotter pin hole with one of the castellations on the nut. Install a new cotter pin.
9. Lubricate the lower ball joint through the grease fitting.
10. Install the wheel assembly and lower the vehicle.

Wheel Bearings

Removal and Installation

1. Raise and support the vehicle safely. Remove the wheel assembly. Remove the hub assembly.
2. Remove the outer roller bearing assembly from the hub. Pry out the inner bearing lip seal and remove the inner bearing assembly.
3. Wash all parts in a cleaning solvent and dry with compressed air.
4. Check the bearings for pitting or scoring. Also check for smooth rotation and lack of noise.
5. Thoroughly lubricate the bearings with new wheel bearing lubricant.
6. Apply a light coat of lubricant to the spindle and inside surface of the hub.
7. Place the inner bearing in the race of the hub and install a new grease seal.
8. Install the hub assembly on the spindle.
9. Install the outer wheel bearing, washer and adjust nut.
10. Adjust the wheel bearings.
11. Install the dust cap on the hub.
12. Install the brake caliper and support assembly.
13. Install the wheel assembly.

Adjustment

1. With the wheel raised, remove the hub cap and dust cap and then remove the cotter pin and nut retainer from the end of the spindle.
2. While rotating the wheel, tighten the spindle nut to 22 ft. lbs.
3. Turn the hub 2–3 turns and loosen the nut just enough so that it can be turned by hand.
4. Turn the nut all the way hand tight and check to be sure the hub has no free play.
5. Measure the starting torque by pulling one of the wheel hub studs with a pull scale. Tighten the spindle nut so that the pull scale reads 1.1–2.6 lbs. when the hub begins to rotate.

NOTE: Make sure that the brake pads are not in contact with the drum when measuring rotating torque.

6. Install the nut retainer, new cotter pin, dust cap and hub cap.

Alignment

Procedures

1. The caster angle can be adjusted by varying the length of the strut bar.
2. The camber angle can be adjusted by installing or removing shims under the upper control arm mount.
3. Toe is adjusted by turning the tie rod ends the same amount in either direction.
4. Correct caster is +½°, ± ½°.
5. Correct camber is +½°, ± ½°.
6. Correct toe is +2′, ± 2′.

4WD FRONT SUSPENSION

Torsion Bar

Removal and Installation

1. Raise and support the vehicle safely.
2. Remove the adjusting bolt from the height control arm.
3. Mark the location and remove the height control arm from the torsion bar and the third crossmember.
4. Mark the location and withdraw the torsion bar from the lower control arm.
5. To install, apply a generous amount of grease to the serrated ends of the torsion bar.
6. Hold the rubber bumpers in contact with the lower control arm. Raise the vehicle up under the lower control arm to accomplish this.
7. Insert the front end of the torsion bar into the control arm.
8. Install the height control arm in position so that it's end is reaching the adjusting bolt. Be sure to lubricate the part of the height control arm that fits into the chassis with grease.
9. Install a new cotter pin in the control arm.
10. Turn the adjusting bolt to the location marked before removal.
11. Lower the vehicle and check the vehicle height.

Shock Absorbers

Removal and Installation

1. Raise and support the vehicle safely.
2. Hold the upper stem of the shock absorber from turning and remove the upper stem retaining nut, retainer and rubber grommet.
3. Remove the bolt retaining the lower shock absorber pivot to the lower control arm and remove the shock absorber from the vehicle.
4. Install the shock absorber by first installing the lower retainer and rubber grommet over the upper stem and then, installing the shock fully extended up through the upper control arm so that the upper stem passes through the mounting hole in the frame bracket.
5. Install the upper rubber grommet, retainer and attaching nut over the shock absorber upper stem.
6. Hold the upper stem of the shock absorber from turning and tighten the retaining nut.
7. Install the retainers attaching the shock absorber lower pivot to the lower control arm and tighten them.
8. Lower the vehicle.

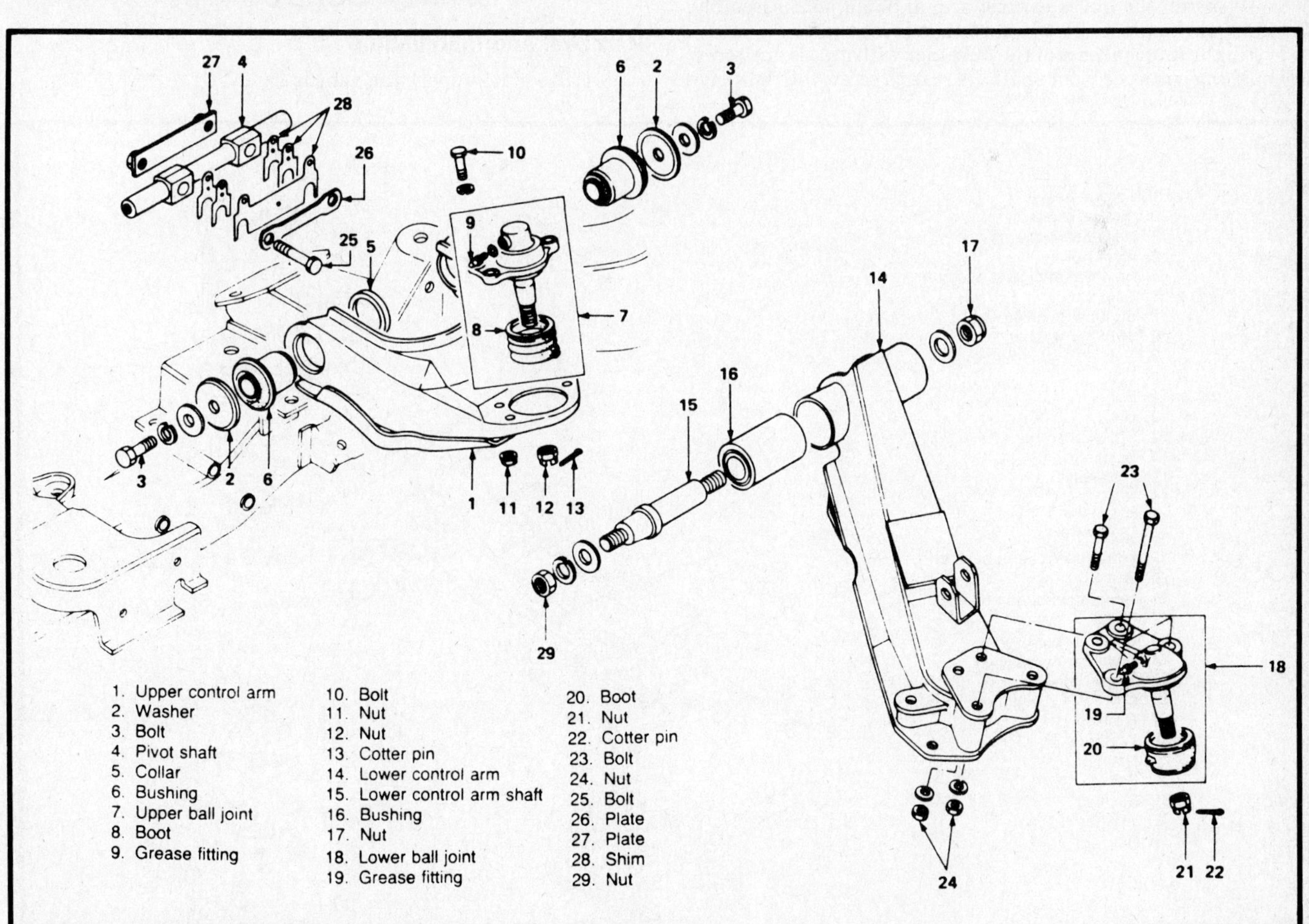

4-wheel drive front suspension

Upper Control Arm and Ball Joint

Removal and Installation

NOTE: The upper control arm and ball joint are replaced as an assembly.

1. Raise and support the vehicle on the lower control arms safely.
2. Remove the wheel assembly.
3. Remove the cotter pin nut fastening the upper control arm and upper ball joint assembly and disconnect the upper control arm from the steering knuckle.

NOTE: Do not allow the steering knuckle to hang by the flexible brake line. Wire the steering knuckle up to the frame temporarily.

4. Remove the two bolts from the upper pivot shaft and remove the upper control arm from the bracket. Be sure to note the position and number of shims used for adjusting the camber and caster angles when removing the upper control arm. The shims must be replaced in their original position.
5. To remove the pivot shaft and bushings from the upper control arm assembly, remove the bushing nuts from the pivot shaft by loosening them alternately, then remove the pivot shaft.
6. To install the upper control arm and ball joint assembly, first install the pivot shaft boots to the pivot shaft.
7. Fill the internal part of the bushings with grease and screw the bushings into the pivot shaft. Be sure to screw the right-side and the left-side bushings alternately into the pivot shafts carefully avoiding getting grease on the outer face of the bushings. Tighten the nuts to 250 ft. lbs.

NOTE: Be sure that the control arm and bushings are centered properly and that the control arm rotates with resistance but not binding on the pivot shaft when tightened to the proper torque.

8. Install the grease fittings and lubricate the parts with grease through the grease fittings.
9. Install the ball joint stud through the steering knuckle. Install the castellated nut and tighten it to 75 ft. lbs. and just enough additional torque to install the cotter pin. Use a new cotter pin.
10. Mount the upper control arm to the chassis frame and install the shims in their original positions between the pivot shaft and bracket. Tighten the pivot shaft attaching nuts to 55 ft. lbs.

NOTE: Tighten the thinner shim pack's nut first for improved shaft-to-frame clamping force and torque retention.

11. Install the dust cover.
12. Install the wheel assembly and lower the vehicle.

Lower Control Arm

Removal and Installation

1. Raise and support the vehicle safely.

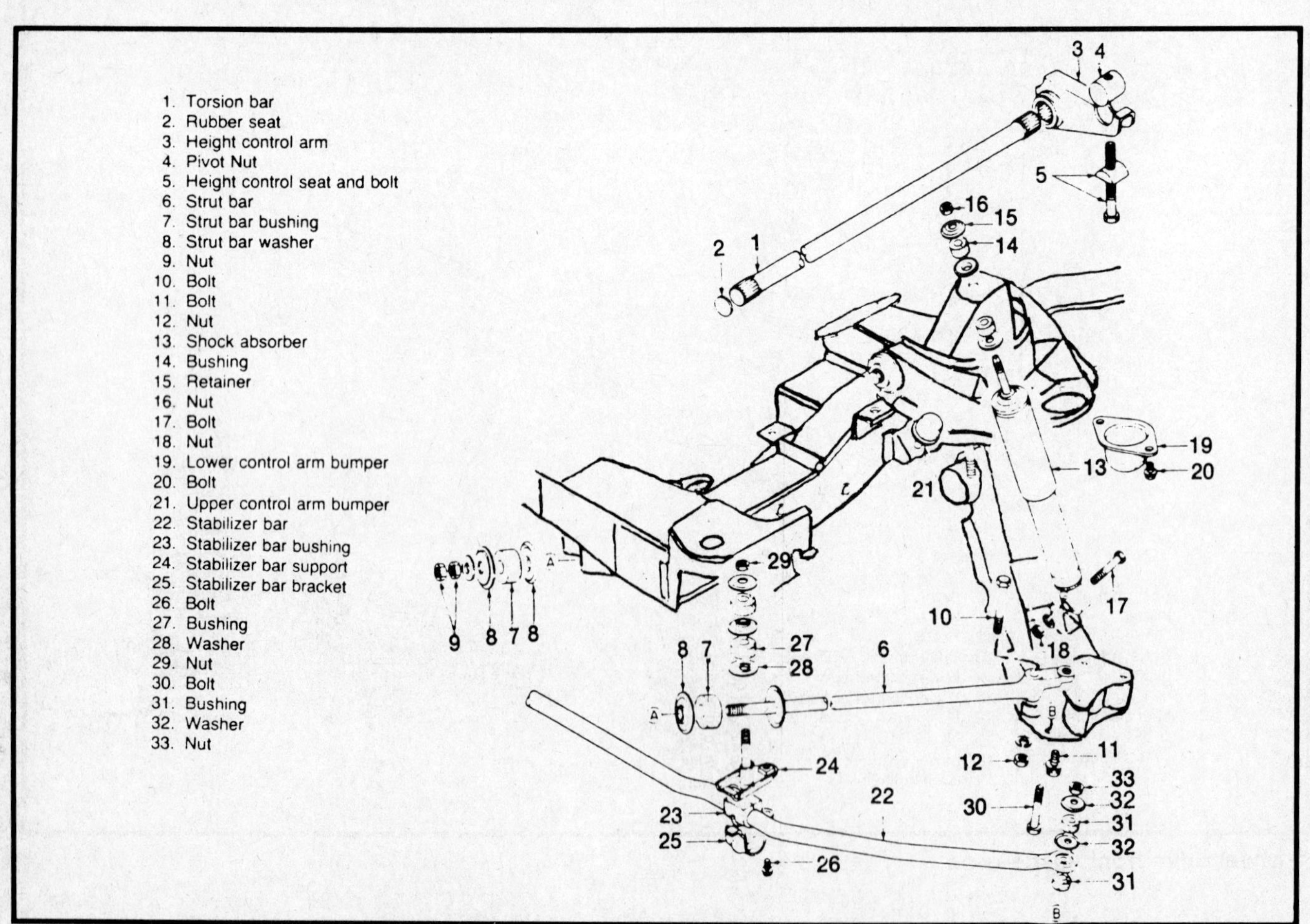

4-wheel drive torsion, strut and stabilizer bars

2. Remove the wheel assembly.

3. Remove the strut bar by removing the frame side bracket and the double nuts, washer and the rubber bushing from the front side of the strut bar. Remove the two bolts fastening the strut bar to the lower control arm and remove the bar.

4. Disconnect the stabilizer bar from the lower control arm.

5. Remove the torsion bar.

6. Disconnect the shock absorber from the lower control arm.

7. Remove the lower ball joint from the lower control arm joint.

8. Remove the retaining nut and drive out the bolt holding the lower control arm to the chassis with a soft metal drift. Remove the lower control arm from the vehicle.

9. To install the lower control arm, install the lower ball joint to the lower control arm. Tighten the retaining nuts to 45 ft. lbs.

10. Mount the lower control arm to the frame. Drive the bolt into position carefully. Use care not to damage the serrated portions. Tighten the nut on the end of the pivot bolt to 135 ft. lbs.

11. Install the stabilizer bar to the lower control arm.

12. Place the washers and bushings on the strut rod and install it through the frame bracket. Install the second set of washers and bushings on the strut rod together with the lockwashers and nut. Leave the nut loose temporarily.

13. Install the strut rod to the lower control arm and tighten the bolts to 45 ft. lbs.

14. Assemble the lower ball joint to the steering knuckle.

15. Install the wheel assembly and lower the vehicle.

16. Tighten the first strut bar-to-chassis frame attaching nut to 175 ft. lbs. and the second locknut to 55 ft. lbs. with the vehicle on the ground.

Ball Joints

UPPER

Removal and Installation

The upper ball joint and control arm are replaced as an assembly only. Refer to Upper Control Arm Removal and Installation for the procedure.

LOWER

Removal and Installation

1. Raise and support the vehicle safely.
2. Remove the wheel assembly.
3. Remove the cotter pin and castellated nut which retains the ball joint to the steering knuckle.
4. Remove the two bolts retaining the lower ball joint and strut rod.
5. Remove the remaining two bolts.
6. Remove the ball joint.
7. Install the lower ball joint by mounting the joint to the lower control arm and tightening the four bolts to 45 ft. lbs.
8. Install the ball joint stud into the steering knuckle and install the castellated nut and torque it to 75 ft. lbs. and just enough additional torque to align the cotter pin hole with one of the castellations on the nut. Install a new cotter pin.
9. Lubricate the lower ball joint through the grease fitting.
10. Install the wheel assembly and lower the vehicle.

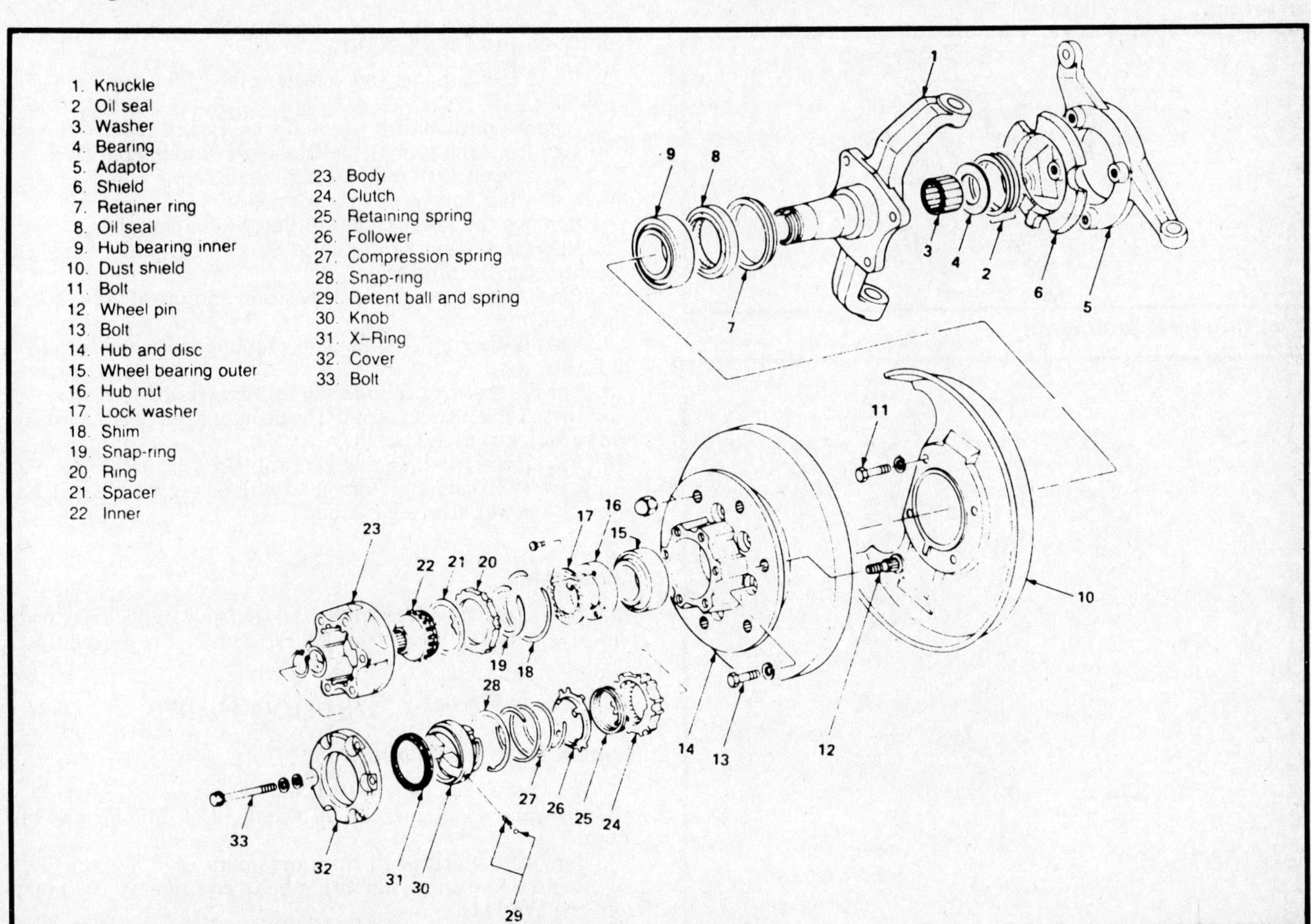

4WD Front hub, steering knuckle and bearings-exploded view

Front Wheel Bearings

Removal and Installation

1. Raise and support the front end. Place the hub in 2H.
2. Remove the free wheeling hub cover assembly.
3. Remove the snap-ring and shims from the spindle.
4. Remove the free wheeling hub body and lock washer.
5. Remove the outer roller bearing assembly from the hub with a finger.
6. Using a brass or wood drift, drive out the inner bearing assembly along with the oil seal. Replace the seal.
7. Wash all parts in a non-flammable solvent.
8. Check all parts for cracks or wear. Thoroughly lubricate all bearing parts with a high-temperature (molybdenum-disulfide) wheel bearing grease. Remove any excess. Apply about 2 ounces of the grease to the hub.
9. Lightly coat the spindle with the same grease.
10. Place the inner bearing into the hub race and install a new seal and retaining ring.
11. Carefully install the hub on the spindle and install the outer bearing.
12. Install the spindle nut.
13. While rotating the hub, tighten the hub so that the wheel can just be turned by hand.
14. Turn the hub 2–3 turns and back off the nut just enough so that it can be loosened by hand.
15. Finger-tighten the nut so that all play is taken up at the bearing.
16. Attach a pull scale to one of the lugs and check the amount of pull needed to start the wheel turning. Initial pull should be 2.6–4.0 lbs. When performing this test, make sure the brake pads are not touching the rotor. If the rotating torque is not correct, tighten the spindle nut until it is.
17. Install the snap-ring and shims, gasket and cover. Torque the cover bolts to 14 ft. lbs.

Alignment

Procedure

1. The caster angle can be adjusted by varying the length of the strut bar.
2. The camber angle can be adjusted by installing or removing shims under the upper control arm mount.
3. Toe is adjusted by turning the tie rod ends the same amount in either direction.
4. Correct caster is +20′, ± ½°.
5. Correct camber is +½° 5′, ± ½°.
6. Correct toe is +0°, ± 0.20°.

STEERING GEAR AND LINKAGE

Refer to the Unit Overhaul Section for Steering Gear Overhaul.

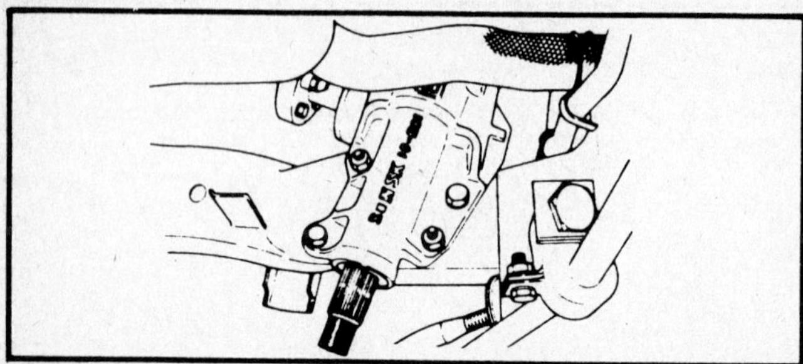

Steering gear mounting

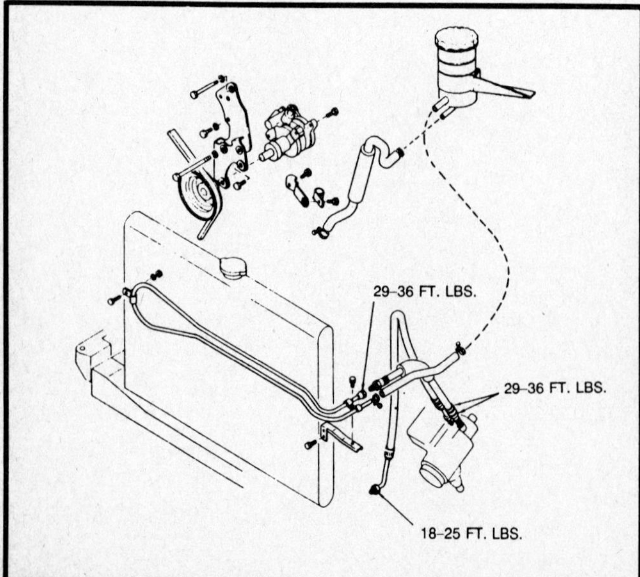

Power steering system

Manual and Power Steering Gear

Removal and Installation

1. Raise and support the vehicle safely. Remove the engine stone shield.
2. Remove pitman arm nut and washer and remove the pitman arm from the pitman shaft using a suitable puller.
3. If equipped with power steering, disconnect and plug the power steering lines at the steering gear.
4. Remove the lower clamp to flexible coupling bolts.
5. Remove the steering gear to frame bolts and remove the steering gear from vehicle.
6. Place the steering gear in position and install and tighten the mounting bolts.
7. Install steering gear flexible coupling bolts and torque to 22 ft. lbs.
8. Torque steering column mounting bolts to 13 ft. lbs.
9. Install the pitman arm to the pitman shaft. Install washer and torque nut to 160 ft. lbs.
10. Install the lower engine stone shield.
11. Lower the vehicle. If equipped with power steering, fill and bleed the power steering system.

Adjustment

Adjustments are possible on the steering gear only during overhaul. Refer to the Unit Overhaul Section for the procedure.

Power Steering Pump

Removal and Installation

1. Disconnect the negative battery cable.
2. Disconnect and plug the inlet and outlet fluid lines at the pump.
3. Remove the drive belt from the pump.
4. Remove the pump mounting bolts and remove the pump from the brackets.
5. Installation is the reverse of the removal procedure.
6. Fill and bleed the system when finished.

Bleeding System

1. Fill the power steering reservoir to the proper level when cold.
2. Run the engine until it reaches normal operating temperature.
3. Turn the engine off and check the fluid level. Fill the reservoir to the proper level when hot.
4. Run the engine and turn the steering wheel to lock in both directions.
5. Return the steering wheel to center, turn the engine off and allow the fluid to sit for 5 minutes before adding any more.
6. Repeat Steps 4 and 5 again. Fill the system to the proper level when finished.

Tie Rod Ends

Removal and Installation

1. Raise and support the vehicle safely.
2. Matchmark the tie rod ends and sleeves for installation.
3. Remove the cotter pin and nut from the tie rod end and loosen the clamping bolts on the sleeve.
4. Using a puller, remove the tie rod from the steering knuckle.
5. Unscrew the tie rod while counting the number of turns required to remove it.
6. Check the tie rod end for damage and replace it if necessary.
7. Install the tie rod end in the sleeve the same number of turns as when removing it.
8. Install the tie rod end in the steering knuckle. Install the nut and new cotter pin.
9. Check the toe in when finished.

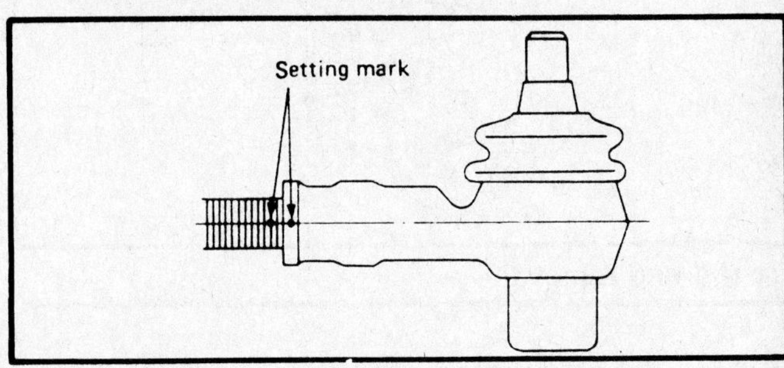

Match-mark the tie rod ends before removal

Intermediate Rod and Tie Rods

Removal and Installation

1. Raise and support the vehicle safely.
2. Remove cotter pin from the ball studs connecting tie rods to intermediate rod and steering damper. Remove the castellated nuts and disconnect the parts using tool J21687–02 or equivalent.
3. Remove the nut and lockwasher on ball stud connecting the intermediate rod to idler arm. Disconnect the parts using tool J21687–02 or equivalent.

1. Coupling
2. Flange, upper coupling
3. Flange, lower coupling
4. Cross-strap
5. Cross-strap
6. Thrust washer
7. Spring
8. Through-bolt
9. Lock nut
10. Pinch bolt, lock washer
11. Steering unit assembly
12. Bolt
13. Nut
14. Shaft nut and washer
15. Bolt
16. Capsule
17. Bezel, starter switch
18. Bolt
19. Nut
20. Bracket, RH
21. Bracket, LH
22. Bolt
23. Bracket
24. Gasket
25. Grommet
26. Steering shaft assembly
27. Wheel assembly
28. Emblem
29. Button
30. Screw
31. Contact plate
32. Screw
33. Contact ring
34. Screw
35. Screw
36. Cowling screws and washer
37. Column cowling

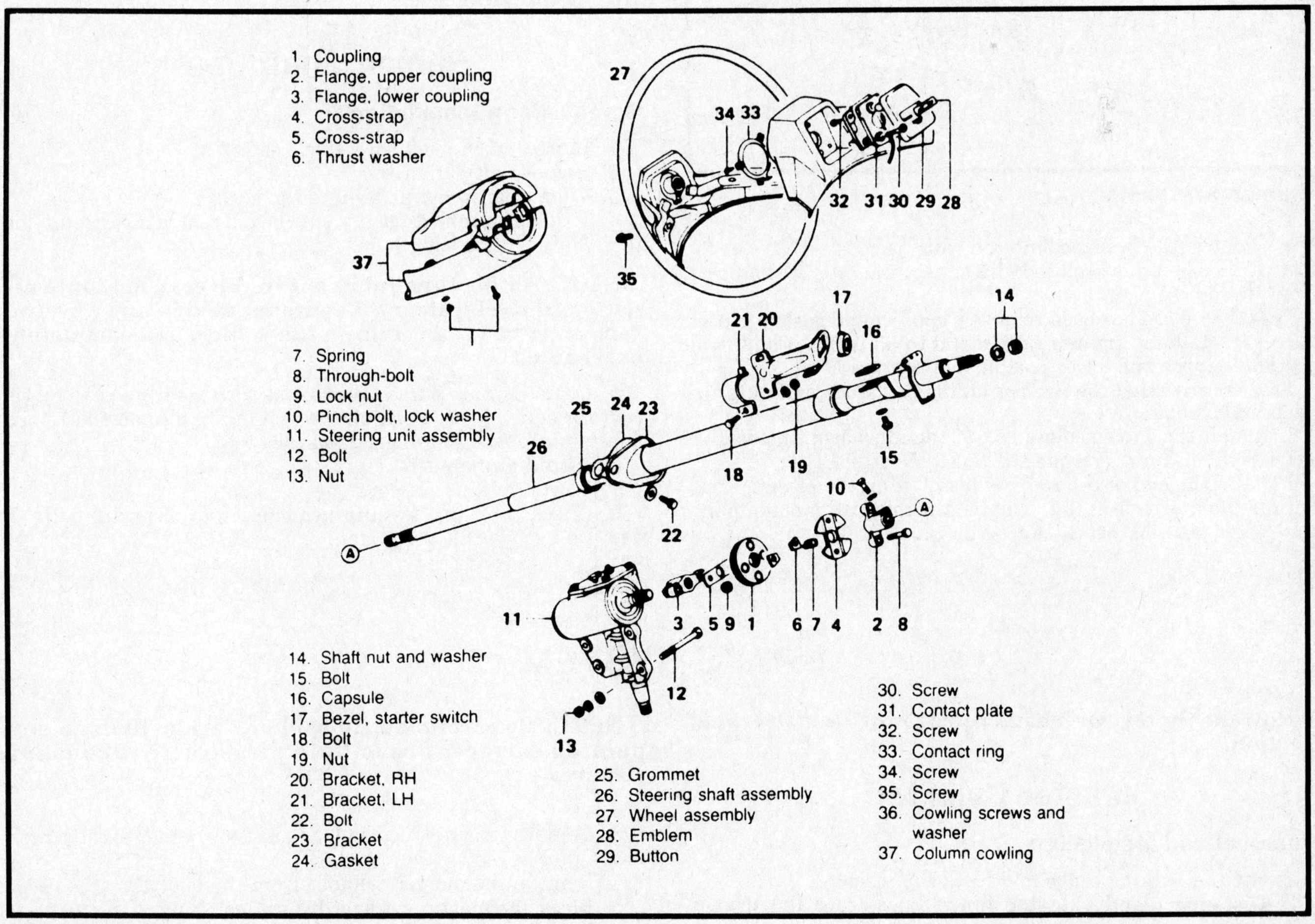

Steering column

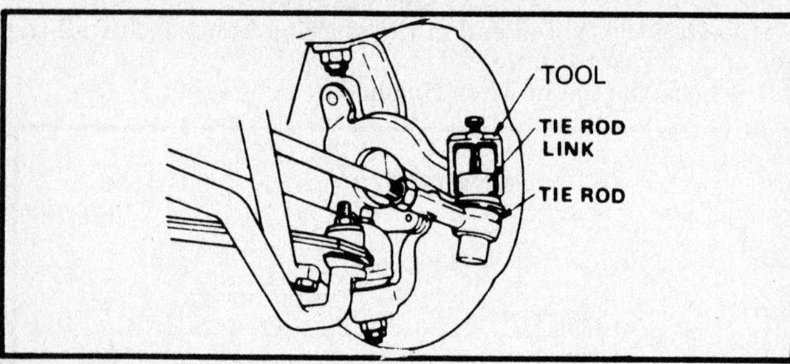

Tie rod end removal

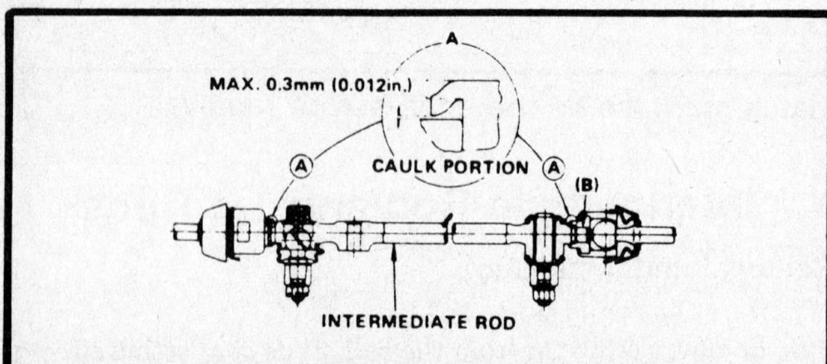

Installing tie rod to intermediate rod

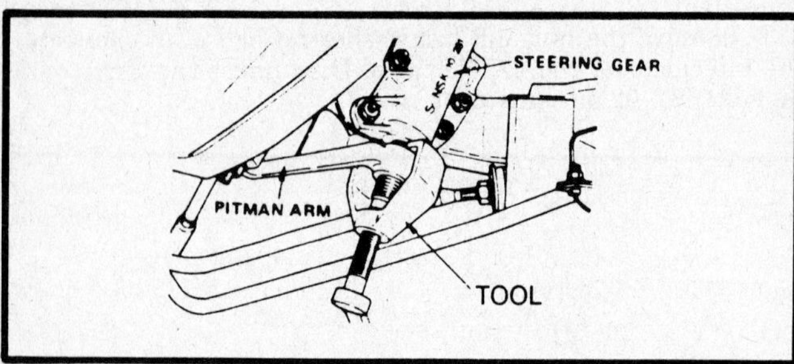

Pitman arm removal

4. Remove the intermediate rod with tie rods.
5. If the tie rod is replaced, disconnect the intermediate rod from tie rod.
6. If the tie rod has been removed, apply liquid gasket to portion B. Install and tighten tie rod end to 65 ft. lbs. Caulk two portions (upper and lower portions) of portion A.
7. Make sure that the threads on the ball studs and nuts are clean and smooth.
8. Install the intermediate rod to the idler arm, install the lockwasher and nut. Torque the nut to 50 ft. lbs.
9. Raise the end of the rod and install it on the pitman arm. Torque the nut to 44 ft. lbs. Tighten the nut just enough to insert cotter pin and install new cotter pin.
10. Install intermediate rod to steering damper end. Torque nut to 87 ft. lbs., then advance nut just enough to insert cotter pin and install new cotter pin.
11. Install the tie rods to adapter, torque nut to 44 ft. lbs., then advance nut just enough to insert cotter pin and install new cotter pin and lubricate tie rod ball studs.

Idler Arm and Pitman Shaft

Removal and Installation

1. Raise and support the vehicle safely.
2. Remove lockwasher and nut that retains the intermediate rod to the idle arm.
3. The ball studs may be removed using tool J21687–02 or equivalent.
4. Remove the four bolts, nuts and washers retaining the bracket to the frame and remove the idler arm pivot shaft and bracket with idler arm.
5. If the idler arm is being replaced, remove the idler arm to idler arm pivot shaft nut and lockwashers. Remove the idler arm from the pivot shaft.
6. Install bracket and shaft assembly to frame and torque the bolts to 29 ft. lbs.
7. Install the idler arm to the shaft and torque the nut to 87 ft. lbs.
8. Install the ball studs and intermediate rod to the idler arm. Torque the castellated nuts to 50 ft. lbs. Line up the cotter pin holes by adding additional torque if necessary. Install new cotter pins.
9. Lubricate idler arm pivot shaft.
10. Lower the vehicle.

Pitman Shaft Seal

Removal and Installation

1. Raise and support the vehicle safely.
2. Remove pitman arm.
3. Wipe clean the area around the seal.
4. Using a suitable tool, pry out the old seal being careful not to damage the housing bore.

NOTE: Inspect the lubricant in the gear for contamination. If the lubricant is contaminated in any way, the gear must be removed from the vehicle and completely overhauled.

5. Coat the new pitman shaft seal with steering gear lubricant (or equivalent). Position the seal in the pitman shaft bore and tap into position using a suitable tool.
6. Install pitman arm.
7. Lower vehicle to floor.
8. Check lubricant level in gear box; total capacity 0.2L (7 oz.). Do not overfill the system.

BRAKE SYSTEM

For Brake System Overhaul, refer to the Unit Overhaul Section.

Master Cylinder

Removal and Installation

1. Set the parking brake and block the wheels.
2. Disconnect and plug the brake lines from the master cylinder.

NOTE: Be careful not to spill any brake fluid on any painted surface. Brake fluid acts exactly like paint remover.

3. Remove the nuts securing the master cylinder to the power brake unit.
4. Remove the master cylinder from the booster.
5. Bleed the master cylinder before installing.
6. Install the master cylinder on the booster.

7. Connect the fluid lines, fill the master cylinder with the proper brake fluid and bleed the brake system.

BLEEDING

Procedure

1. To bleed the brakes, first carefully clean all dirt from around the master cylinder filler cap.
2. If a bleeder tank is used, follow the manufacturer's instructions.
3. Remove the filler cap and fill the master cylinder to the lower edge of the filler neck.
4. Clean off the bleeder connections at all of the wheel cylinders or disc brake calipers. Attach the bleeder hose and fixture to the right rear wheel cylinder bleeder screw and place the end of the tube in a glass jar, submerged in brake fluid.
5. Open the bleeder valve $1/2$–$3/4$ of a turn. Have an assistant depress the brake pedal and allow it to return slowly. Continue this pumping action to force any air out of the system.
6. When bubbles cease to appear at the end of the bleeder hose, close the bleeder valve and remove the hose. Check the level of the brake fluid in the master cylinder and add fluid, if necessary.
7. After the bleeding operation at each caliper or wheel cylinder has been completed, fill the master cylinder reservoir and replace the filler plug.

CAUTION

Never reuse brake fluid which has been removed from the lines through the bleeding process because it contains air bubbles and dirt.

Wheel Cylinder

Removal and Installation

1. Raise and support the vehicle safely. Remove the wheel assembly, brake drums and shoes.
2. Disconnect and plug the brake line at the wheel cylinder.
3. Remove the wheel cylinder attaching bolts from the backing plate.
4. Cap the openings of the brake line and the wheel cylinder.
5. Installation is the reverse of the removal procedure. Bleed the brake system when finished.

Disc Brakes

Removal and Installation

1. Raise and support the vehicle safely. Remove the wheel assembly.
2. Remove the brake caliper mounting bolts and remove the caliper without disconnecting the brake fluid line. Support the caliper so it does not hang on the brake line.
3. Remove the brake pads and retaining clips from the caliper.
4. Using a suitable tool, push the brake caliper piston into the caliper until it bottoms out.
5. Install the new brake pads and clips in the caliper and install the caliper in the mounting bracket.
6. Install the wheel assembly. Check the brake fluid level.
7. Pump the brake pedal until pressure is felt before moving the vehicle.

Calipers

Removal and Installation

1. Raise and support the vehicle safely. Remove the wheel assembly.
2. Disconnect and plug the brake fluid line at the caliper.
3. Remove the brake caliper mounting bolts and remove the caliper from the mount.
4. Remove the brake pads and clips from the caliper. Inspect the brake pads for wear. Replace if necessary.
5. Fill the brake caliper with brake fluid and connect the fluid line to the caliper. Install the brake pads and clips in the new caliper.
6. Install the caliper on the mounting bracket.
7. Install the wheel assembly. Lower the vehicle and bleed the brake system.

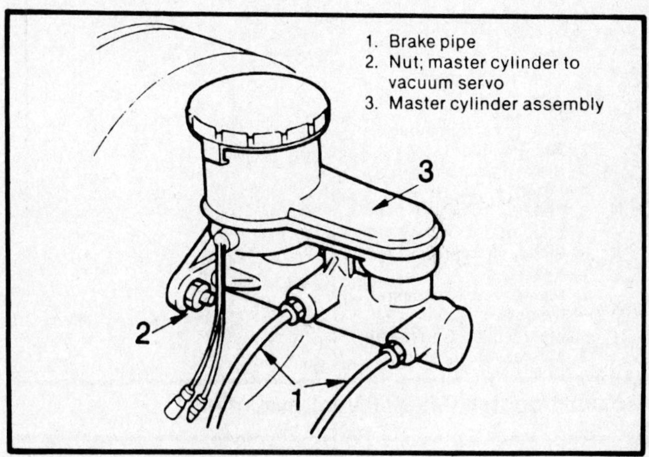

Master cylinder removal points

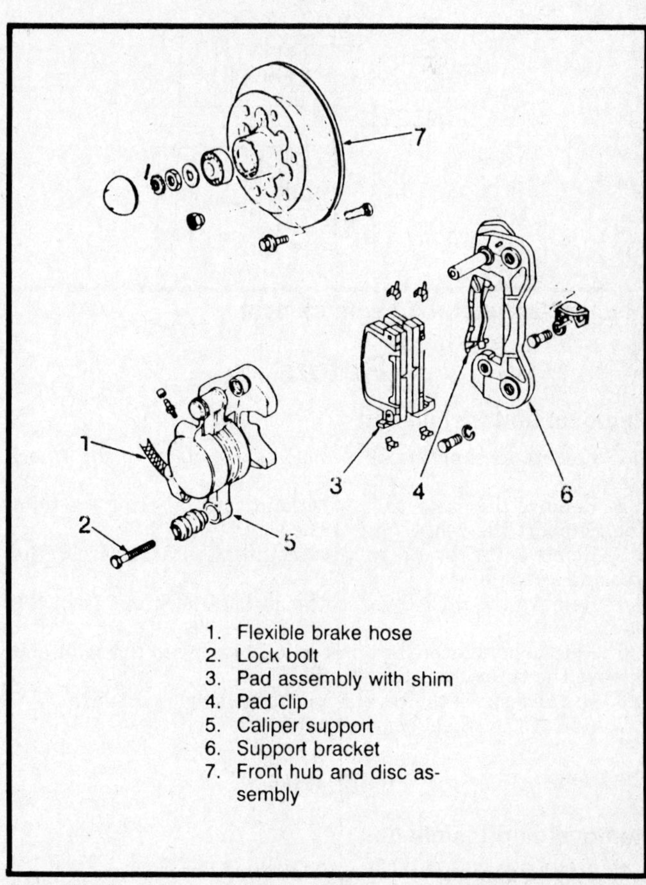

Front hub, rotor and disc brakes—exploded view

Power Brake Booster

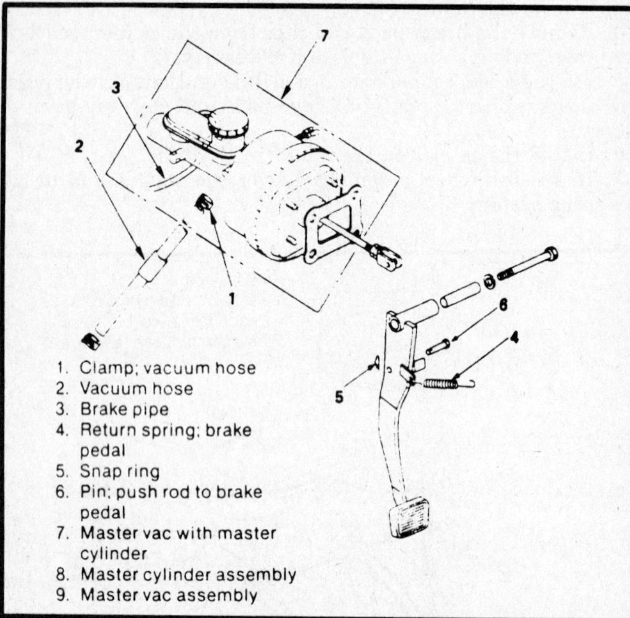

Power booster (Master Vac) mounting

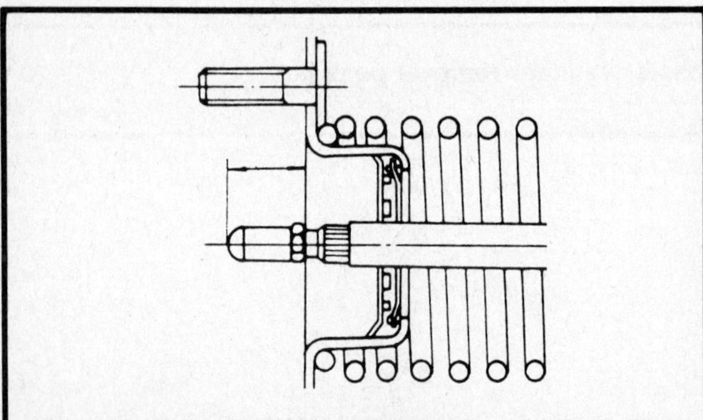

Master Vac pushrod measurement

Rotors

Removal and Installation

1. Raise and support the vehicle safely. Remove the wheel assembly.
2. Remove the brake caliper without disconnecting the fluid linc. Support the caliper out of the way.
3. Remove the brake caliper mounting bracket from the steering knuckle.
4. Remove the dust cover, cotter pin and lock nut from the rotor.
5. Place a hand over the outer wheel bearing in the rotor and remove the rotor from the spindle.
6. Installation is the reverse of the removal procedure.
7. Adjust the wheel bearings when finished.

VACUUM

Removal and Installation

1. Set the parking brake and block the wheels.
2. Disconnect the vacuum hose to the vacuum booster.
3. Disconnect and plug the brake fluid lines at the master cylinder. Place rags under the master cylinder to catch any leaking fluid.

NOTE: Be careful not to spill any brake fluid on any painted surface. Brake fluid acts exactly like paint remover.

4. Inside the vehicle, remove the snap ring from the clevis pin and separate the clevis pin from the brake pedal.
5. Remove the vacuum booster mounting nuts at the firewall and lift out the power unit and master cylinder/reservoir as an assembly.
6. Installation is the reverse of the removal procedure. Check the distance from the flange face of the vacuum booster to the end of the push-rod before installation of the master cylinder.
7. The distance should be 0.709–0.717 in. If the measurement deviates from the specified range, make an adjustment with the lock nut at the end of the push-rod.
8. Bleed the brake system when finished.

Brake Pedal Adjustment

Procedure

1. Check the distance from the flange face of the vacuum booster to the end of the push-rod.
2. The distance should be 0.709–0.717 in. If the measurement deviates from the specified range, make an adjustment with the lock nut at the end of the booster pushrod.

Stoplight Switch

Removal and Installation

1. Disconnect the negative battery cable.
2. Locate the stoplight switch on the brake pedal support.
3. Disconnect the stoplight switch wiring and remove the lock nut.
4. Install the switch on the support and adsjust the switch so that there is 0.020–0.040 in. clearance between the switch and the brake pedal.
5. Connect the wiring to the switch and the negative battery cable.
6. Check the operation of the switch.

Parking Brake

CABLE

Removal and Installation

1. Raise and support the vehicle safely.
2. Loosen the cable adjusting nut and remove the lever return spring. Remove the adjusting nut.
3. Remove the cotter pin from the retaining pin on the second lever assembly and remove the front cable.
4. Remove the two cotter pins from the retaining pins on the intermediate cable and remove the cable.
5. Remove the retaining clips from the rear fixing brackets and lower the rear brake cables.
6. Remove the rear wheel assemblies and brake drums. Remove the rear brake shoes and disconnect the rear brake cables from the lever in the rear brake shoes.
7. Installation is the reverse of the removal procedure. Adjust the cables when finished.

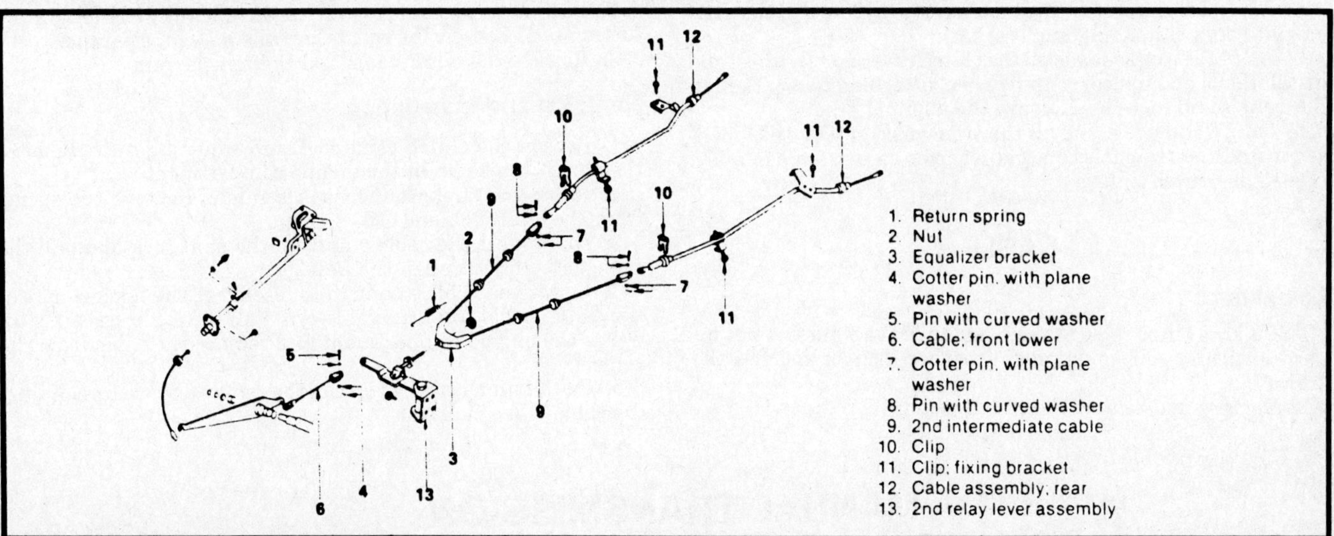

Parking brake cable assembly

Adjustment

NOTE: Adjustment of the parking brake is necessary every time the rear brake cables are disconnected or after overhauling the rear brake assembly.

1. Fully release the parking brake lever and check the cable for free movement.
2. Firmly grab the second relay lever rod. Rotate the adjusting nut until all the slack is removed from the cable. Tighten the adjusting nut.
3. Apply the parking brake to the fully set position three or four times.
4. If the parking brake is properly adjusted, the traveling range should be between 12–14 notches. If the travel is incorrect, readjust to specifications.

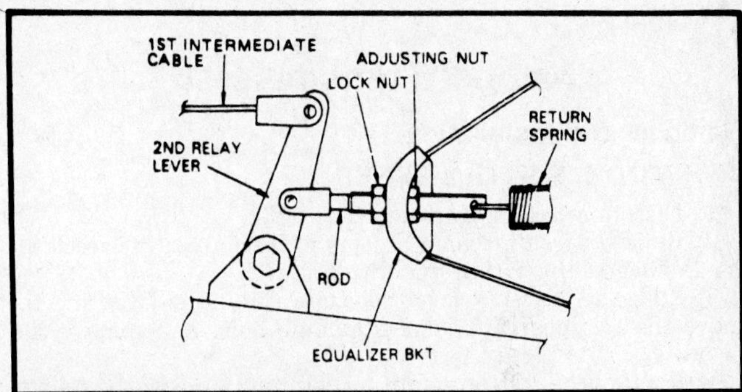

Parking brake adjustment

CLUTCH

Clutch Assembly

Removal and Installation

1. Raise and support the vehicle safely.
2. On 2WD models, remove the transmission. On 4WD models, remove the transmission and transfer case as an assembly.
3. Matchmark the clutch assembly to the flywheel so that the clutch assembly can be reassembled in the same position.

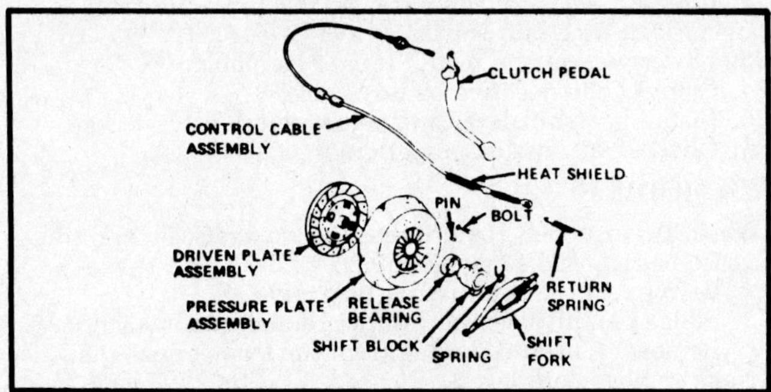

Clutch components

4. Loosen the six clutch cover-to-flywheel attaching bolts, one turn at a time in an alternating sequence, until the spring tension is relieved to avoid distorting or bending the clutch cover.
5. Support the clutch pressure plate and cover assembly with a clutch aligning tool and remove the bolts and clutch assembly.
6. Apply a thin coat of grease to the pressure plate wire ring, diaphragm spring, clutch cover grooves and the drive bosses on the pressure plate.
7. Apply a thin coat of lubricant to the splines in the driven plate.

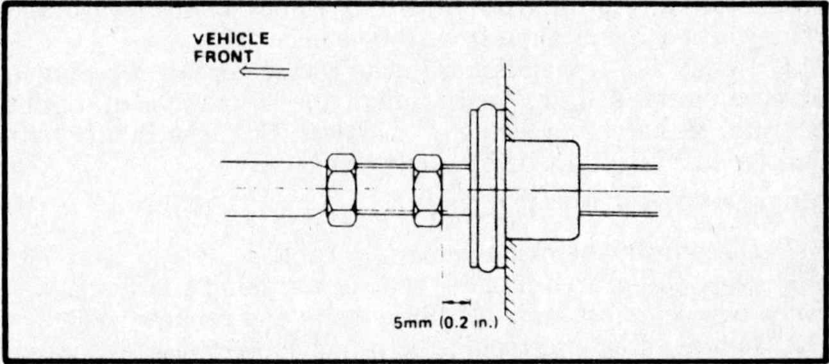

Clutch cable adjustment

8. Assemble the clutch cover and pressure plate and the driven plate on a clutch alignment arbor.
9. Align the marks made on the clutch cover and flywheel and install the six clutch cover-to-flywheel attaching bolts. Tighten the bolts to 50 inch lbs. Remove the aligning arbor.
10. On 2WD models, install the transmission. On 4WD models, install the transmission and transfer case as an assembly. Adjust the clutch linkage.

CABLE

Adjustment

1. Pull the outer cable forward and turn the adjusting nut inward until the rubber lip on the washer damper touches the firewall.
2. Depress and release the clutch pedal three times.
3. Pull the outer cable forward again and fully tighten the adjusting nut. Loosen the nut to provide a $\frac{1}{5}$ in. clearance.
4. Release the outer cable and tighten the nut.

Removal and Installation

1. Loosen the clutch cable lock and adjusting nuts. Remove the clutch cable clip in the engine compartment.
2. Raise and support the vehicle safely. Remove the spring from the shift fork end.
3. Disconnect the cable end from the shift fork and pull the cable assembly through the bracket.
4. Lower the vehicle enough to disengage the hooked part of the clutch pedal from the cable eye. Pull the cable assembly towards the engine compartment and remove the cable from the vehicle.
5. Installation is the reverse of the removal procedure. Adjust the cable when finished.

MANUAL TRANSMISSION

Refer to the Unit Overhaul Section for Overhaul Procedures.

Manual Transmission

Removal and Installation

2WD MODELS WITH 4 SPEED

1. Disconnect the negative battery cable.
2. Remove the air cleaner assembly. Disconnect the accelerator linkage at the carburetor throttle lever.
3. Slide the gearshift lever boot upward on the lever and remove the two gearshift lever attaching bolts and remove the lever.
4. Remove the starter mounting bolts and support the starter out of the way.
5. Raise and support the vehicle safely. Disconnect the exhaust pipe at the flange and disconnect the exhaust pipe hanger at the transmission.
6. Disconnect the speedometer cable at the transmission. Drain the transmission. Matchmark and remove the driveshaft.
7. Disconnect the clutch cable from the bell housing and clutch fork.
8. Remove the bolts attaching the stiffeners. Remove the skid plate.
9. Remove the three frame bracket-to-transmission rear mounting bolts.
10. Raise the engine and transmission and remove the four crossmember-to-frame bracket bolts.
11. Lower the engine and transmission and support the rear of the engine.
12. Disconnect the electrical connectors at the TCS or CRS switch and tho back-up light switch.
13. Remove the transmission-to-engine attaching bolts and slide the transmission straight back until the input shaft is clear of the clutch. Tip the front of the transmission downward and remove the transmission from the vehicle.
14. Install the transmission in the reverse order of removal, using a clutch aligning tool to align the clutch disc and pilot bearing, if the clutch was also removed. Coat the input shaft lightly with lubricant before installation.

2WD MODELS WITH 5 SPEED

1. Disconnect the negative battery cable.
2. Slide the gearshift lever boot upwards on the lever. Remove two gearshift lever attaching bolts and remove lever.
3. Remove starter attaching bolts and support starter assembly out of the way.
4. Raise and support the vehicle safely and disconnect exhaust pipe hanger at transmission.
5. Drain the transmission. Disconnect the speedometer cable and ground cable. Matchmark and remove the driveshaft.
6. Remove return spring from clutch fork and remove the clutch cable.
7. Remove the two lower bolts mounting the flywheel stone guard.
8. Remove two frame bracket to transmission rear mount bolts and nuts.
9. Raise engine and transmission and remove four crossmember to frame bracket bolts.
10. Remove the two rear mounting nuts from the transmission rear extension.
11. Lower engine and transmission assembly and support rear of engine.
12. Disconnect electrical connector at back-up lamp switch.
13. Remove transmission to engine mouinting bolts.
14. Pull transmission straight back and disengage it from clutch. Tip front of transmission downward and remove the transmission.
15. To install, position transmission in vehicle and slide forward guiding imput shaft into pilot bearing.
16. Install transmission to engine mounting bolts.
17. Raise and lower engine and transmission and install crossmember frame bracket and rear mount.
18. Install the two lower bolts mounting the flywheel stone guard.
19. Align the matchmarks on the driveshaft and install the driveshaft.
20. Connect speedometer cable, ground cable and exhaust pipe hanger.
21. Connect clutch cable and adjust shift fork.
22. Connect oloctrical connector at back-up lamp switch. Fill transmission with lubricant.
23. Lower vehicle and install starter assembly.
24. Connect the negative battery cable.
25. Install gearshift lever and adjust clutch cable.
26. Check transmission operation.

4WD MODELS

4 Wheel Drive models require that the transmission and transfer case be removed as an assembly.

1. Disconnect the negative battery cable.
2. Slide the shift lever boots upward and unbolt each lever.
3. Remove the return spring from the transfer case shift lever and remove both levers.
4. Raise and support the vehicle safely. Disconnect and tag

the starter wiring. Remove the starter mounting bolts and remove the starter.

5. Disconnect the exhaust pipe from the manifold and disconnect the pipe support from the transmission.

6. Drain the transmission. Matchmark and remove the driveshaft.

7. Disconnect the speedometer cable and ground strap at the transmission.

8. Matchmark and remove the front and rear driveshaft from the transfer case.

9. Disconnect the clutch return spring.

10. Disconnect the clutch cable at the clutch fork.

11. Remove the flywheel stoneguard.

12. Remove the transmission rear crossmember bolts.

13. Raise the engine and transmission and remove the rear crossmember-to-frame bolts.

14. Remove the rear mounting bolts from the transfer case.

15. Remove the side case from the transmission.

16. Remove the stud bolt from the transfer case.

17. Lower the engine and transmission and support the rear of the engine.

18. Disconnect the CRS switch and backup light switch.

19. Remove the shifter cover and gasket from the transfer case.

20. Remove the transmission-to-engine bolts. When removing the transmission, turn the side case fitting face downward and pull the case straight back until it is free from the clutch. Lower the front of the transmission and remove it.

21. Installation is the reverse of the removal procedure.

Linkage

Adjustment

No adjustments are possible on the transmission or transfer case linkage.

AUTOMATIC TRANSMISSION

Refer to the Unit Repair Section for Overhaul Procedures.

Automatic Transmission

The automatic transmission is used only with the 2WD pickups.

Removal and Installation

1. Disconnect the negative battery cable. Remove the throttle valve cable from the carburetor.

2. Remove the transmission dipstick assembly.

3. Raise and support the vehicle safely. Remove the pan from the converter housing. Drain the transmission fluid.

4. Remove the starter assembly.

5. Matchmark and remove the driveshaft. Plug the rear of the transmission to prevent fluid leakage.

6. Disconnect the shift lever control rod from the transmission shift lever.

7. Remove the exhaust pipe bracket. Remove the speedometer cable from the transmission.

8. Remove the oil cooler lines and position them along the vehicle frame to prevent damage.

9. Remove the torque converter bolts and nuts at the flywheel.

10. Remove the frame bracket to the transmission rear mount bolts.

11. Raise the engine and transmission assembly and remove the frame bracket from the crossmember. Remove the rear mount from the transmission.

12. Remove the bellhousing bolts and remove the transmission and converter assembly.

CAUTION

Do not allow the torque converter to drop from the transmission during removal.

13. Installation is the reverse of the removal procedure. Fill the transmission with the proper fluid and check the transmission operation.

Shift Linkage

Adjustment

1. Loosen the control rod lock nuts so that the trunnion will slide on the control rod.

2. Turn the shaft of the transmission counterclockwise, viewed from the left side of the transmission, as far as it will go.

3. Loosen the three shaft stops to the neutral position.

4. Holding the shaft in this position, move the shift lever to the neutral position and push the shift control lower lever rearward to remove play. Tighten the lock nuts.

5. Check for proper operation of the transmission in all ranges.

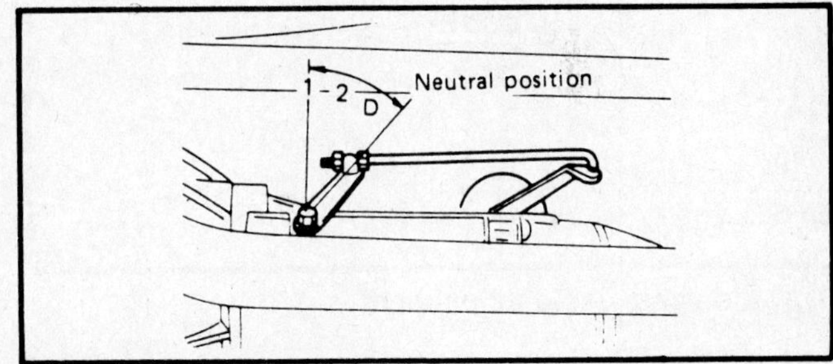

Shift linkage adjustment

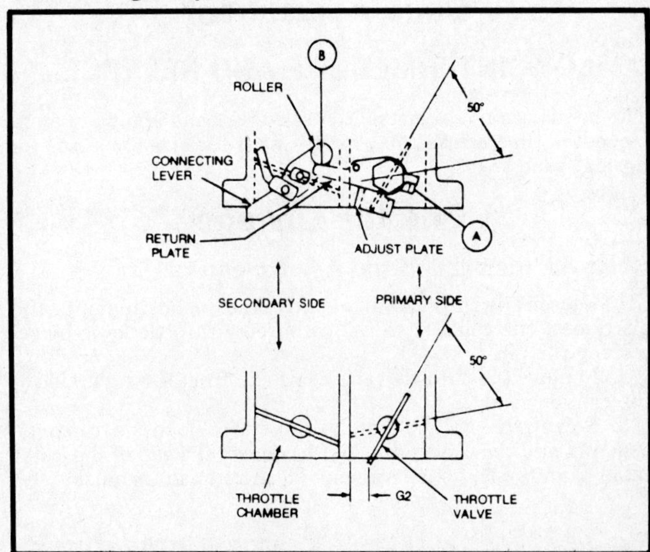

Throttle linkage adjustment

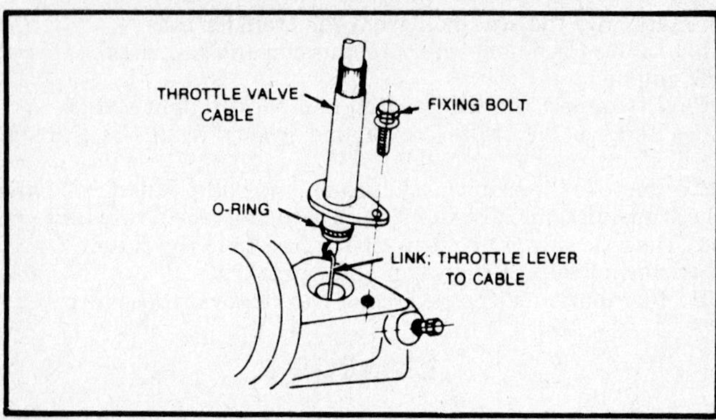

Throttle valve cable removal

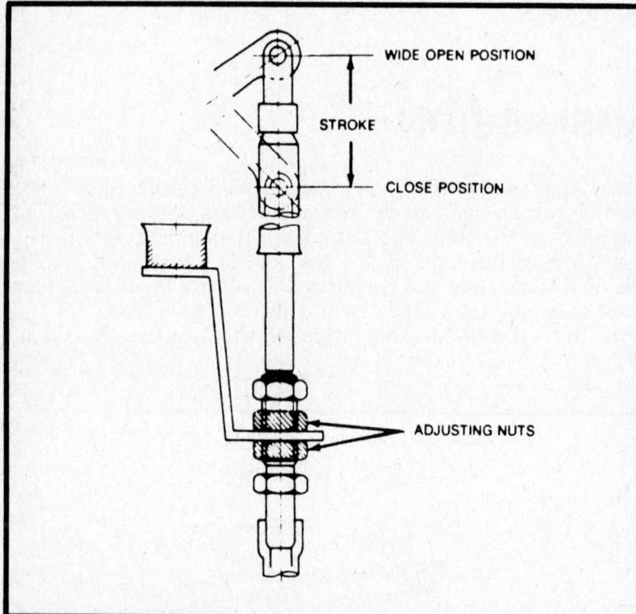

Throttle valve cable adjustment

Band Adjustment

LOW, INTERMEDIATE AND REVERSE

The bands are not adjustable. A selective band apply pin is installed at time of assembly or overhaul that compensates for normal band wear.

Throttle Linkage

Removal, Installation and Adjustment

1. Loosen the throttle valve control cable adjusting nuts and disconnect the cable from the carburetor throttle lever by removing the pin.
2. Remove the throttle valve cable clip from the right side of the cylinder body.
3. Remove the bolt holding the throttle cable to the transmission and pull the cable upward. Disconnect the end of the inner cable from the throttle lever link on the transmission side.
4. Remove the cable assembly from the vehicle.
5. Installation is the reverse of the removal procedure.
6. To adjust the linkage, loosen the throttle valve control cable adjusting nuts.
7. Open the carburetor throttle lever to the wide open position and adjust the inner cable by turning the adjustment nut on the outer cable by hand so that the inner cable has a free play of approximately 0.040 in.
8. Tighten the lock nut securely.
9. Make sure that the stroke of the inner cable from the wide open position to the closed position is within the range of 1.370–1.410 in.

Neutral Start Switch

Removal, Installation and Adjustment

1. Disconnect the switch wiring. Loosen the screws mounting the switch and remove the switch.
2. Install the switch and move the switch body so that the center of the moveable part of the switch aligns with the neutral position indicator line on the steel case, when the shift lever is in the neutral position.
3. Tighten the mounting screws and connect the wiring.
4. Make sure that the engine does not start in gear.

Inhibitor switch adjustment

Oil Pan, Fluid and Filter

Replacement

1. Raise and support the vehicle safely. Support the transmission and remove the oil pan retaining bolts from the front and sides of the fluid pan.
2. Loosen the rear fluid pan bolts approximately four (4) turns.
3. Carefully the front of the pan to allow the fluid to drain.
4. Remove and clean the pan.
5. Remove the two retaining screen-to-valve body bolts, screen and gasket. Clean the screen thoroughly.
6. Install screen and new gasket in place on valve body. Tighten retaining bolts to 6–10 ft. lbs.
7. Install the pan with a new gasket and torque the pan retaining bolts to 10–13 ft. lbs.
8. Lower the vehicle and install six pints of Dexron® II in the transmission. Start the engine and move the selector lever through each gear position.
9. Recheck the fluid level and fill to the following levels. Fluid at room temperature: Level should be $\frac{1}{8}$–$\frac{3}{8}$ in. below the add mark on the dip stick. Fluid at normal operating temperature should be at the full mark on the dip stick.

NOTE: Normal operating temperature is reached after approximately 15 miles of highway type driving or equivalent.

TRANSFER CASE

Refer to the Unit Overhaul Section for Overhaul Procedures.

Removal and Installation

NOTE: The transfer case housing is integrated into the transmission housing. Although the two cases can be separated, the transfer case should be removed with the transmission. Refer to 4 Wheel Drive Transmission Removal and Installation. The transfer case linkage is not adjustable.

DRIVE LINES AND UNIVERSAL JOINTS

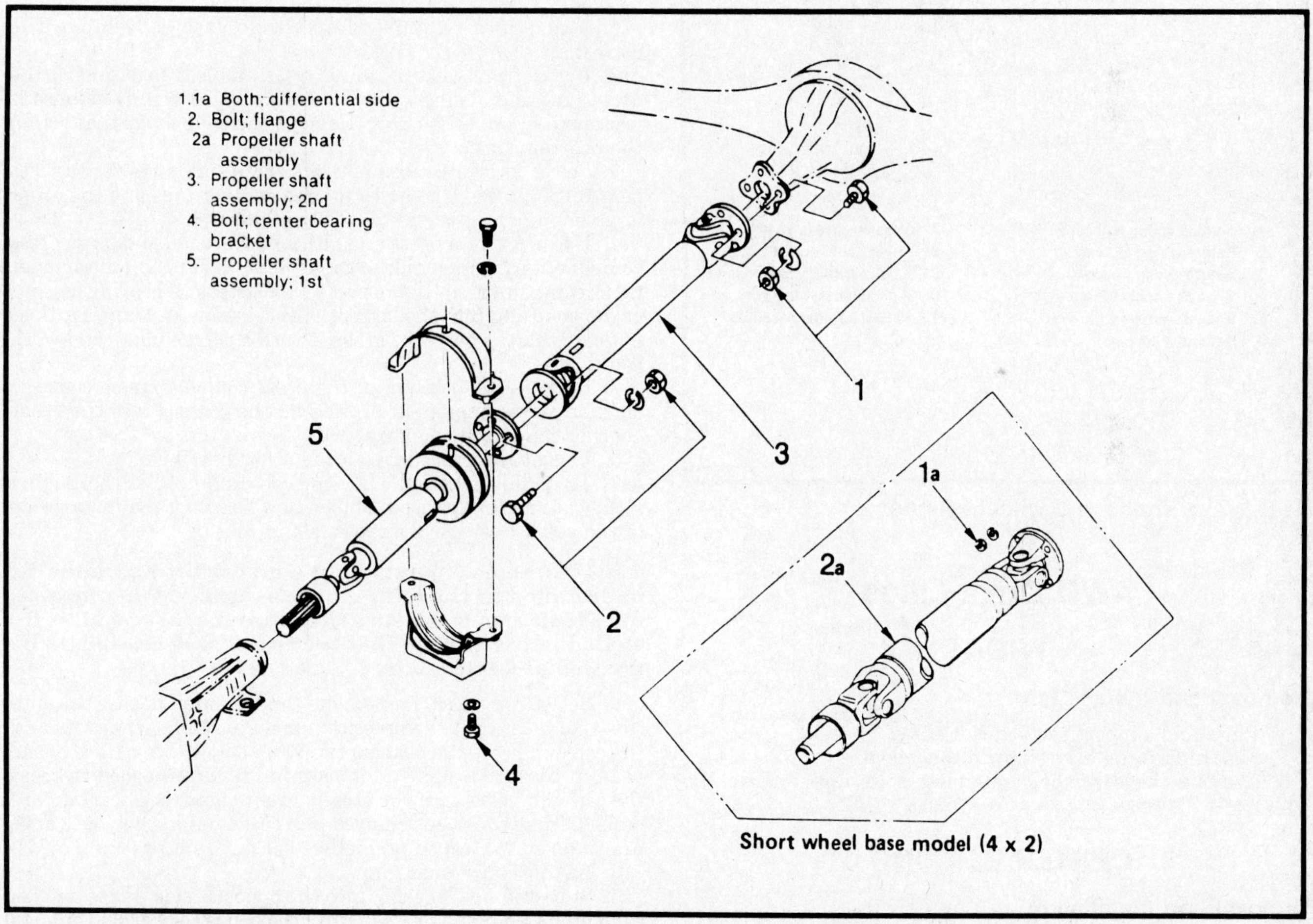

1. 1a Both; differential side
2. Bolt; flange
2a Propeller shaft assembly
3. Propeller shaft assembly; 2nd
4. Bolt; center bearing bracket
5. Propeller shaft assembly; 1st
1
1a
2
2a
3
4
5
Short wheel base model (4 x 2)

Rear driveshaft assembly

2WD Drive Line

REAR

Removal and Installation

1. Raise and support the vehicle safely.
2. Matchmark the driveshaft to the yokes.
3. Remove the driveshaft retaining bolts and remove the driveshaft.
4. Installation is the reverse of the removal procedure.

Setting mark
Front differential side
Transfer side
Front propeller shaft
Splined yoke

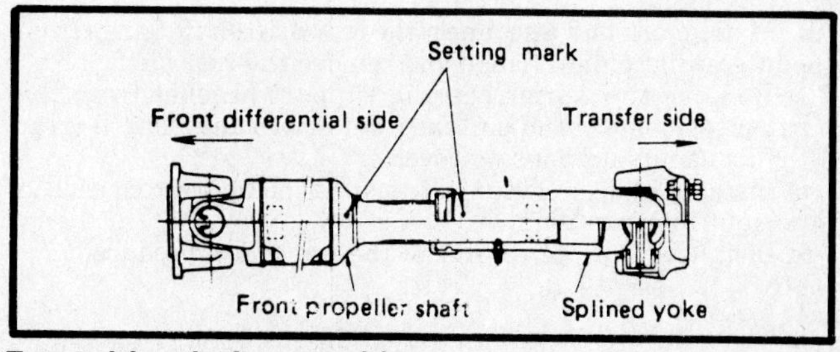

Front driveshaft assembly

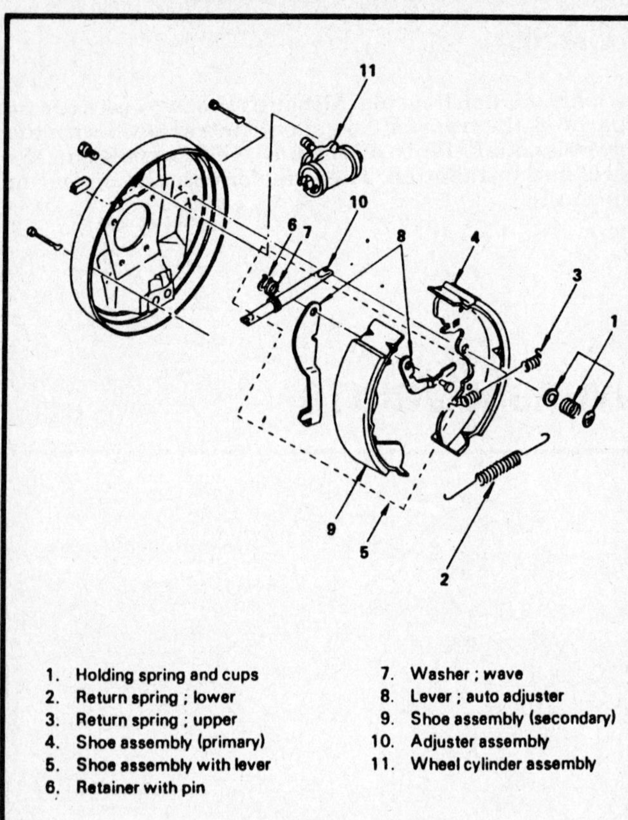

Rear brake shoes and wheel cylinder

4WD Drive Lines

FRONT

Removal and Installation

1. Raise and support the vehicle safely.
2. Matchmark the driveshaft to the yokes.
3. Remove the driveshaft retaining bolts and remove the driveshaft.

CENTER BEARING

Removal and Installation

1. Raise and support the vehicle safely.
2. Matchmark and disconnect the flanged yokes between the two driveshafts.
2. Matchmark and disconnect the rear driveshaft flange from the differential pinion flange and remove the rear shaft.
3. Remove the center bearing support bracket from the fourth crossmember and pull the front driveshaft from the rear of the transmission housing cover.
4. Install a plug or cover the transmission housing cover end to prevent lubricant loss.
5. Installation is the reverse of the removal procedure.

REAR

Removal and Installation

1. Raise and support the vehicle safely. Matchmark the driveshaft at the yokes.
2. Matchmark and disconnect the flanged yokes between the rear driveshaft and differential.
3. Remove the center bearing support bracket from the fourth crossmember and pull the front driveshaft from the rear of the transmission housing cover.
4. Install a plug or cover the transmission housing cover end to prevent lubricant loss.
5. Installation is the reverse of the removal procedure.

Universal Joints

Removal, Overhaul and Installation

1. Raise and support the vehicle safely. Remove the driveshaft.
2. If the front yoke is to be disassembled, matchmark the driveshaft and sliding splined yoke so that driveline balance is preserved upon reassembly. Remove the snap rings that retain the bearing caps.
3. Select two press components, with one small enough to pass through the yoke holes for the bearing caps and the other large enough to receive the bearing cap.
4. Use a vise or a press and position the small and large press components on either side of the U-joint. Press in on the smaller press component so that it presses the opposite bearing cap out of the yoke and into the larger press component. If the cap does not come all the way out, grasp it with a pair of pliers and work it out.
5. Reverse the position of the press components so that the smaller press component presses on the cross. Press the other bearing cap out of the yoke.
6. Repeat the procedure on the other bearings.
7. To install, grease the bearing caps and needles thoroughly if they are not pregreased. Start a new bearing cap into one side of the yoke. Position the cross in the yoke.

NOTE: Some U-joints have a grease fitting that must be installed in the joint before assembly. When installing the fitting, make sure that once the driveshaft is installed in the vehicle that the fitting is accessible to be greased at a later date.

8. Select two press components small enough to pass through the yoke holes. Put the press components against the cross and the cap and press the bearing cap ¼ in. below the surface of the yoke. If there is a sudden increase in the force needed to press the cap into place, or if the cross starts to bind, the bearings are cocked. They must be removed and restarted in the yoke. Failure to do so will cause premature bearing failure.
9. Install a new snap-ring.
10. Start the new bearing into the opposite side. Place a press component on it and press in until the opposite bearing contacts the snap ring.
11. Install a new snap ring. It may be necessary to grind the facing surface of the snap ring slightly to permit easier installation.
12. Install the other bearings in the same manner.
13. Check the joint for free movement. If binding exists, smack the yoke ears with a brass or plastic faced hammer to seat the bearing needles. If binding still exists, dissassemble the joint and check to see if the needles are in place. Do not strike the bearings unless the shaft is supported firmly. Do not install the driveshaft until free movement exists at all joints.

FRONT DRIVE AXLE FOUR WHEEL DRIVE

Refer to the Unit Overhaul Section for Overhaul Procedures.

Axle Housing

Removal and Installation

1. Raise and support the vehicle safely.
2. Disconnect the front driveshaft at the differential.
3. Remove the wheels and skid plate.
4. Loosen the torsion bar completely with the height control adjusting bolts.
5. Remove the strut bars.
6. Disconnect the stabilizer bars at the lower control arms.
7. Remove the caliper assemblies and wire them to the frame. It is not necessary to disconnect the brake lines.
8. Remove the ball joints from the tie rods.
9. Disconnect the upper control arms at the frame. Make sure to note the number and positions of the shims.
10. Remove the steering link ends from the lower control arms.
11. Disconnect the shock absorbers from the lower control arms.
12. Disconnect the lower control arms from the frame.
13. Remove the locking hub.
14. Remove the rotors and upper links.
15. Remove the pitman arm and idler arm along with the steering linkage assembly.
16. Support the differential housing and lower it clear of the vehicle. Take care to avoid damaging the Birfield joints.
17. Installation is the reverse of the removal procedure. Bleed the brake system and check the level of the axle lubricant when finished.

Locking Hubs

Removal and Installation

Manual locking hubs are the only type used on these vehicles.

MANUAL

1. Place the transfer case in the 2H position. Raise and support the vehicle safely.
2. Set the hubs in the free position.
3. Remove the hub cover bolts and remove the hub cover.
4. While pushing the follower toward the knob, turn the clutch assembly clockwise and then remove the clutch assembly from the knob.
5. Remove the snap-ring and remove the knob from the cover. Do not loose the detent ball.
6. Remove the ball and spring from the knob.
7. Remove the X-ring from the knob by pressing it off.

NOTE: Do not use a sharp instrument to remove this ring because it may scratch the ring.

8. Remove the compression spring, retaining spring and the follower from the clutch assembly.
9. Remove the retaining spring from the clutch assembly by turning it counterclockwise.
10. Remove the snap-ring and then remove the inner assembly from the body.
11. Separate the ring, inner and spacer by removing the snap-ring.
12. Installation is the reverse of the removal procedure. Apply grease to the X-ring, the inner cover and the outside circumference of the knob.

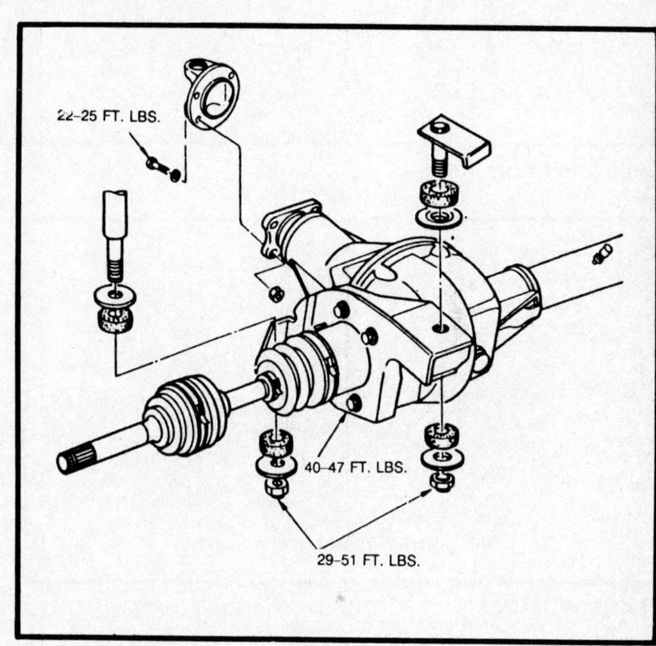

Front drive axle mounting

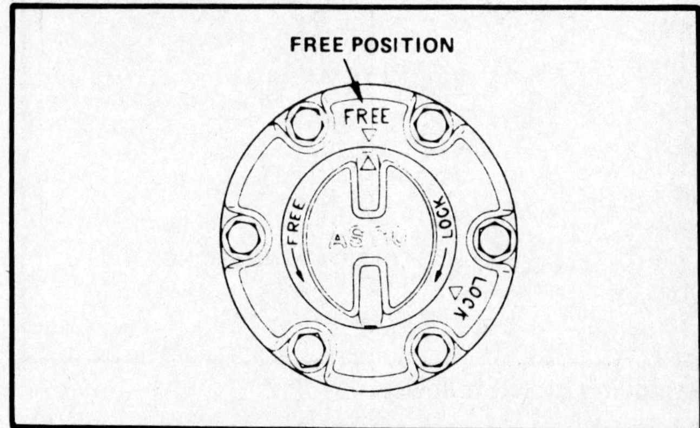

Locking hub set in FREE position

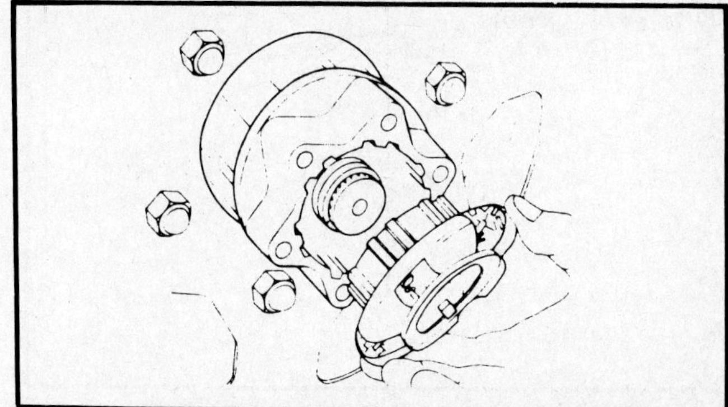

Locking hub cover teeth alignment for installation

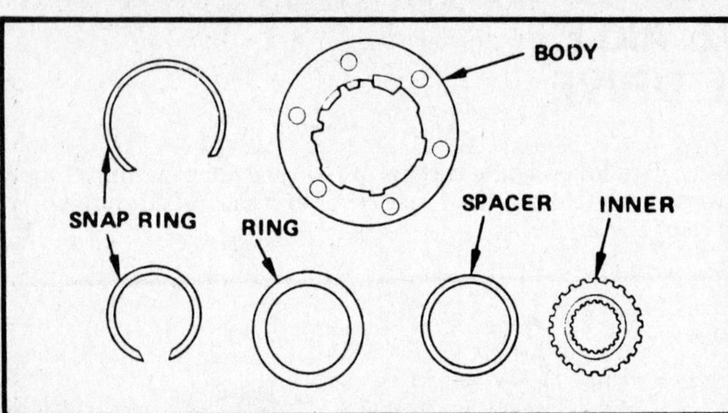

Hub body components

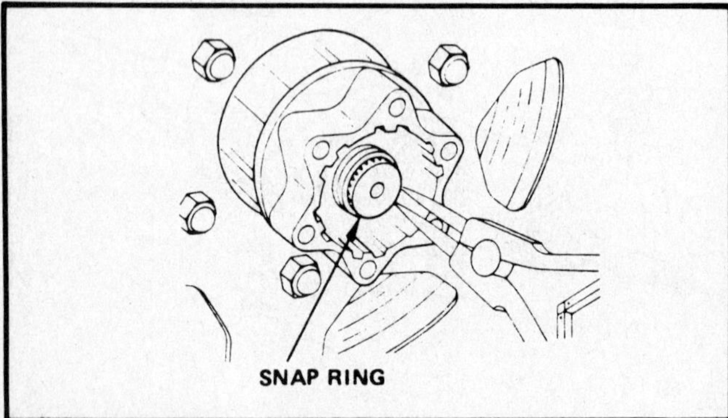

Hub snap-ring

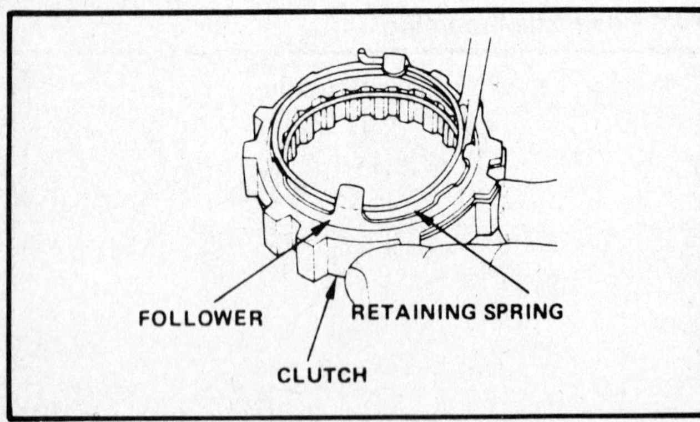

Removing clutch follower

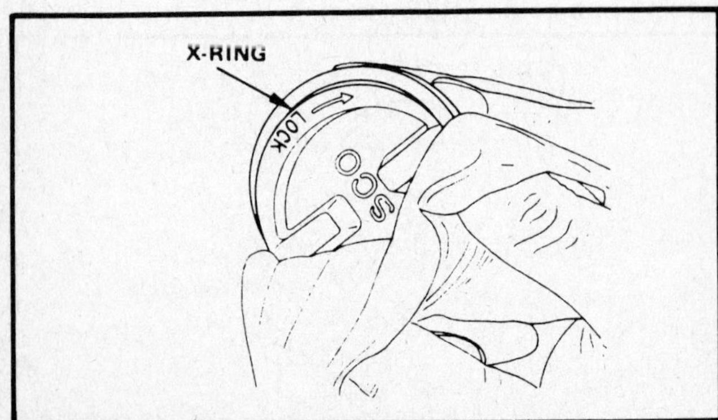

Removing X-ring

Axle Shaft

Removal and Installation

1. Raise and support the vehicle safely.
2. Disconnect the front driveshaft at the differential.
3. Remove the wheels and skid plate.
4. Loosen the torsion bar completely with the height control adjusting bolts.
5. Remove the strut bars.
6. Disconnect the stabilizer bars at the lower control arms.
7. Remove the caliper assemblies and wire them to the frame. It is not necessary to disconnect the brake lines.
8. Remove the ball joints from the tie rods.
9. Disconnect the upper control arms at the frame. Make sure to note the number and positions of the shims.
10. Remove the steering link ends from the lower control arms.
11. Disconnect the shock absorbers from the lower control arms.
12. Disconnect the lower control arms from the frame.
13. Remove the locking hub.
14. Remove the rotors and upper links.
15. Remove the pitman arm and idler arm along with the steering linkage assembly.
16. Support the differential housing and lower it clear of the vehicle. Take care to avoid damaging the Birfield joints.
17. Drain the differential case and remove the four bolts attaching the axle mounting bracket to the case.
18. Pull the shaft assemblies from the case on both sides.
19. Installation is the reverse of the removal procedure.
20. Check the level of the axle lubricant and bleed the brake system when finished.

Axle Shaft Seal

Removal and Installation

1. Raise and support the vehicle safely. Remove the wheel assembly.
2. Remove the axle from the housing.
3. Remove the seal from the housing.
4. Clean and inspect the sealing surfaces of the housing and axle.
5. Using a suitable tool, drive the seal into the housing with the lip of the seal facing the housing.
6. Lightly coat the lip of the seal with oil and install the axle in the housing.
7. The remainder of the installation is the reverse of the removal procedure.
8. Check the level of the axle lubricant when finished.

Differential Carrier

Removal and Installation

1. Raise and support the vehicle safely.
2. Drain the differential oil.
3. Matchmark and remove the front driveshaft.
4. Remove the axle shafts from the differential.
5. Remove the differentail carrier mounting bolts and remove the carrier.
6. Installation is the reverse of the removal procedure. Use a new gasket when installing.
7. Fill the differential to the correct level when finished.

Axle Shaft Bearings

Removal and Installation

1. Raise and support the vehicle safely.
2. Remove the axle shaft from the housing.

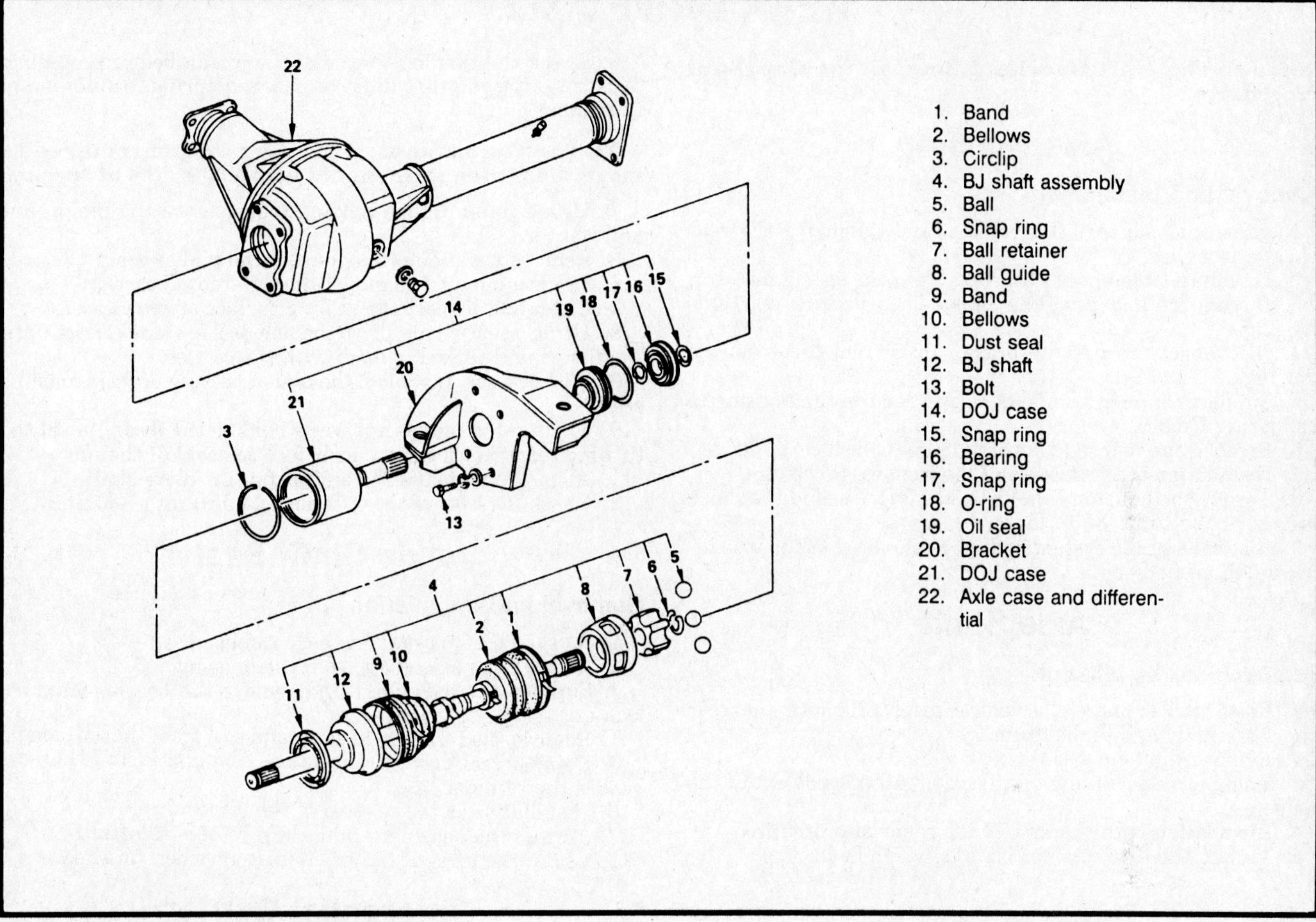

Front drive axle—exploded view

3. Support the axle shaft and remove the bearing retainer lock nut and washer.
4. Remove the retainer, bearing and seal from the axle shaft.
5. Installation is the reverse of the removal.
6. Always replace the seal and lock washer when removing the axle shaft from the housing.
7. Torque the bearing retainer nut to 188–195 ft. lbs.

Wheel Bearings

Removal, Installation and Adjustment

1. Place the transfer case in 2H. Raise and support the vehicle safely.
2. Remove the free wheeling hub cover assembly.
3. Remove the snap-ring and shims from the spindle.
4. Remove the free wheeling hub body and lock washer.
5. Remove the outer roller bearing assembly from the hub with a finger.
6. Using a brass or wood drift, drive out the inner bearing assembly along with the oil seal. Replace the seal.
7. Wash all parts in a non-flammable solvent.
8. Check all parts for cracks or wear. Thoroughly lubricate all bearing parts with a high-temperature wheel bearing grease. Remove any excess. Apply about 2 ounces of the grease to the hub.
9. Lightly coat the spindle with the same grease.
10. Place the inner bearing into the hub race and install a new seal and retaining ring.
11. Carefully install the hub on the spindle and install the outer bearing.
12. Install the spindle nut.
13. While rotating the hub, tighten the hub so that the wheel can just be turned by hand.
14. Turn the hub 2–3 turns and back off the nut just enough so that it can be loosened with the fingers.
15. Finger-tighten the nut so that all play is taken up at the bearing.
16. Attach a pull scale to one of the lugs and check the amount of pull needed to start the wheel turning. Initial pull should be 2.6–4.0 lbs. When performing this test, make sure the brake pads are not touching the rotor. If the rotating torque is not correct, tighten the spindle nut until it is.
17. Install the snap-ring and shims, gasket and cover. Torque the cover bolts to 14 ft. lbs.

Steering Knuckle

WITH BALL JOINTS

Removal and Installation

1. Raise and support the vehicle safely. Remove the wheel assembly.
2. Remove the brake caliper, rotor and dust shield.
3. Support the lower control arm and separate the steering knuckle from the lower ball joint.
4. Separate the steering knuckle from the upper ball joint.
5. Remove the steering knuckle from the vehicle.
6. Installation is the reverse of the removal procedure.
7. Torque the ball joint nuts to 75 ft. lbs.

REAR DRIVE AXLE

Refer to the Unit Overhaul Section for Overhaul Procedures.

Axle Housing

Removal and Installation

1. Raise and support the vehicle safely. Remove the rear wheel assemblies.
2. Disconnect the shock absorbers from the spring plates.
3. Disconnect and plug the brake lines on the rear axle housing.
4. Disconnect the parking brake cables from the rear axle housing.
5. Support the rear axle housing and remove the housing to leaf spring U-bolts.
6. Remove the rear axle housing from the vehicle.
7. Installation is the reverse of the removal procedure.
8. Torque the housing U-bolts to 36–43 ft. lbs. and the shock absorber bolts to 27–30 ft. lbs.
9. Bleed the brake system and check the level of the axle lubricant when finished.

Axle Shaft

Removal and Installation

1. Raise and support the vehicle safely. Remove the rear wheel assembly and brake drum.
2. Remove the four axle retainer bolts.
3. Using a slide hammer on the axle, pull the axle out of the housing.
4. Installation is the reverse of the removal procedure.
5. Torque the axle retainer bolts to 51–58 ft. lbs.

Pinion Seal

Removal and Installation

1. Raise and support the vehicle safely.
2. Matchmark and remove the driveshaft.
3. Check the turning torque of the pinion before proceding. This is the torque that must be reached during installation of the pinion nut.

NOTE: The amount of turning torque required to move the pinion gear should be 20–30 ft. lbs of torque.

4. Using pinion flange holding tool, remove the pinion nut and washer.
5. Remove the pinion flange from the pinion gear.
6. Pry the pinion seal out of the differential carrier.
7. Clean and inspect the sealing surface of the carrier.
8. Using a seal driver, drive the new seal into the carrier until the flange on the seal is flush with the carrier.
9. With the seal installed, the pinion bearing preload must be set.
10. Tighten the pinion nut while holding the flange, until the turning torque is the same as before removal of the nut.
11. Align the matchmarks and install the drive shaft.
12. Check the level of the differential lubricant when finished.

Axle Shaft Seal

Removal and Installation

1. Raise and support the vehicle safely.
2. Remove the axle shaft from the housing.
3. Support the axle shaft and remove the bearing retainer lock nut.
4. Remove the retainer, bearing and seal from the axle shaft.
5. Using a seal driver, remove the seal and install the new seal in the retainer.
6. Installation is the reverse of the removal.
7. Torque the bearing retainer nut to 188–195 ft. lbs.
8. Check the level of the axle lubricant when finished.

Differential Carrier

Removal and Installation

1. Raise and support the vehicle safely.
2. Drain the differential oil.
3. Matchmark and remove the rear driveshaft.

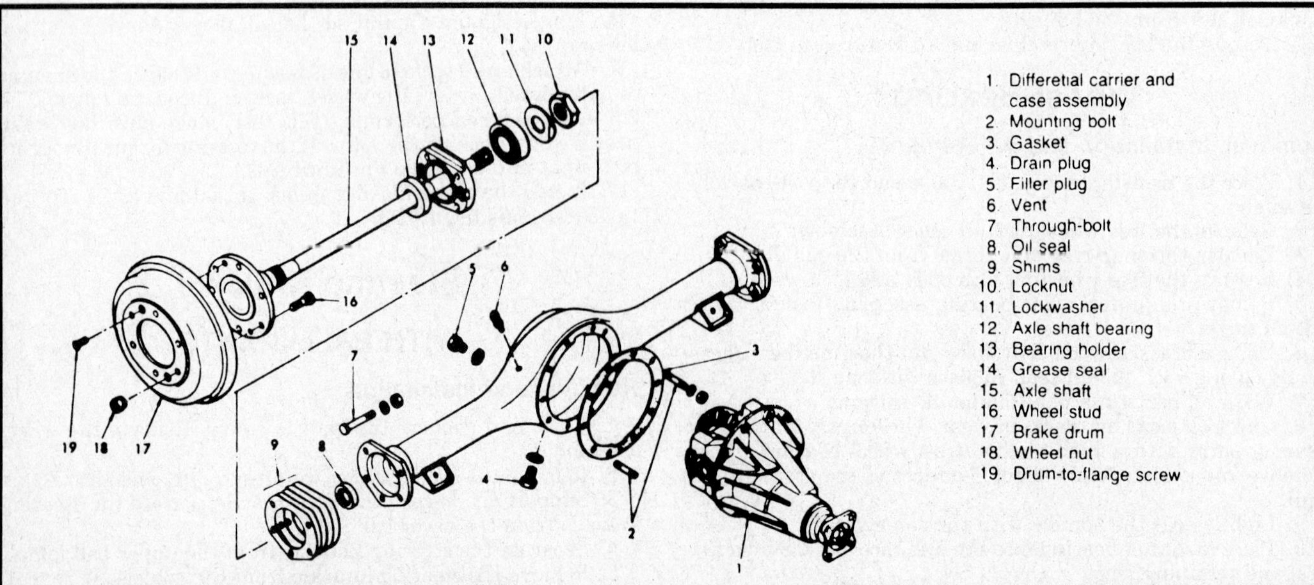

Rear axleshaft and housing-exploded view

4. Remove the axle shafts from the differential.
5. Remove the differentail carrier mounting bolts and remove the carrier.
6. Installation is the reverse of the removal procedure. Use a new gasket when installing.
7. Fill the differentail to the correct level when finished.

Axle Shaft Bearings

Removal and Installation

Refer to Axle Shaft Seal Removal and Installation for the procedure.

REAR SUSPENSION

Leaf Spring

Removal and Installation

ALL MODELS

1. Raise and support the vehicle safely so that the leaf springs are hanging freely.
2. Remove the rear shock absorbers.
3. Remove the parking brake cable clips.
4. Remove the nuts from the U-bolts holding the springs to the axle housing.
5. Support the rear axle housing to remove the weight of the axle housing from the springs.
6. Remove the front and rear shackle pin nuts.
7. Drive out the rear shackle pin by using a hammer and drift. Lower the rear end of the leaf spring assembly to the floor.
8. Drive out the front shackle pin and remove the leaf spring assembly rearward.
9. Remove the shackle pin from the rear spring bracket and remove the shackle.
10. Check the leaf springs for cracks, wear and broken leaves. Replace any leaves found to be cracked, broken, fatigued or seriously worn.
11. Check the shackles for bending and the pins for wear.
12. Check the U-bolts for distortion or other damage.
13. Mount the shackle to the bracket.
14. Align the front end of the leaf spring assembly with the front bracket and install the shackle pin.
15. Align the rear end of the leaf spring assembly with the shackle and install the shackle pin.
16. Loosely install the shackle pin nuts and install the U-bolts. Tighten the U-bolt nuts to 40 ft. lbs.
17. Install the shock absorbers.
18. Clip the parking brake cable to the bracket.
19. Remove the axle housing support and lower the vehicle so that the weight is on the leaf springs.
20. Tighten the shackle pin nuts to 130 ft. lbs.

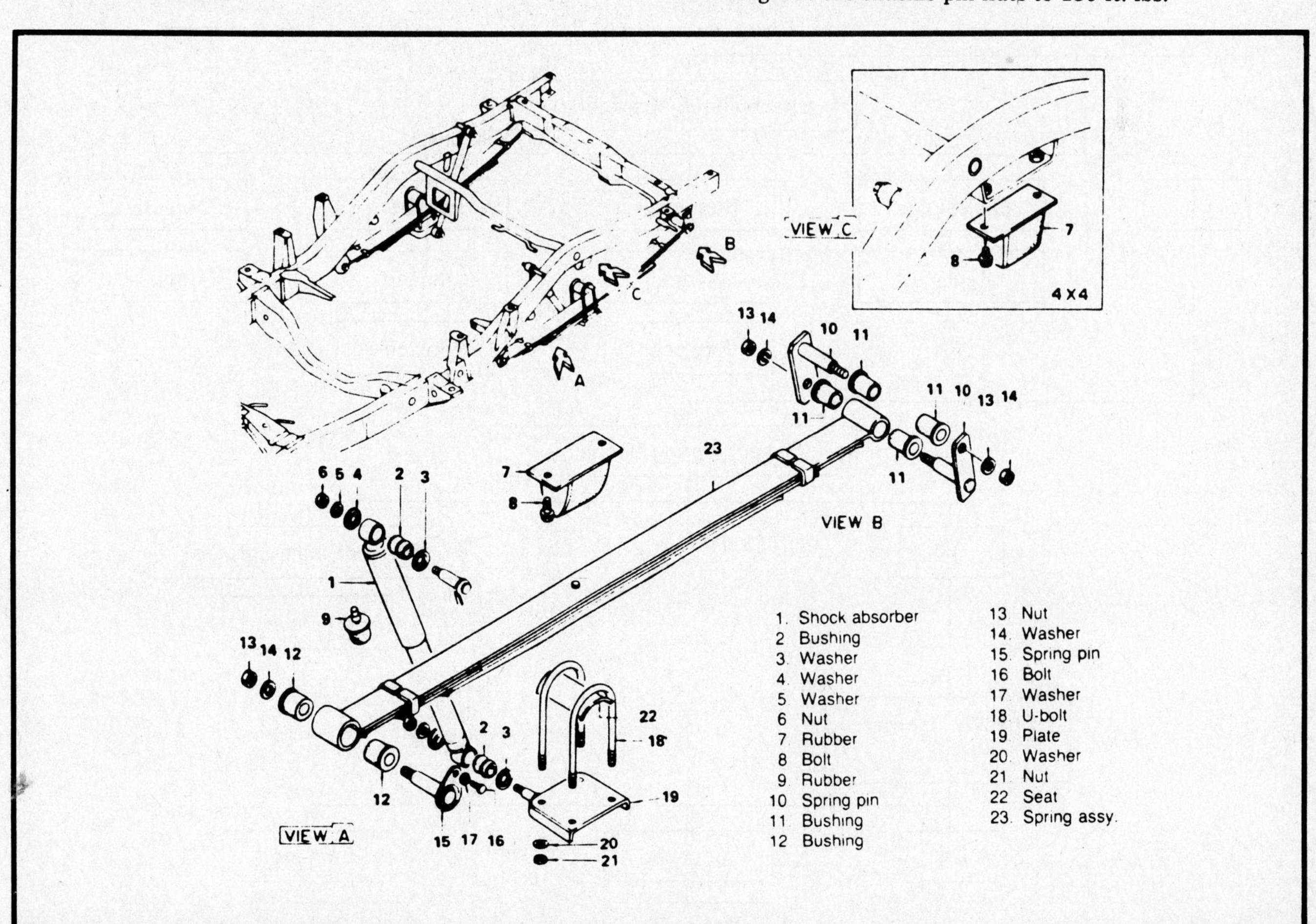

Rear suspension-exploded view

REAR SUSPENSION

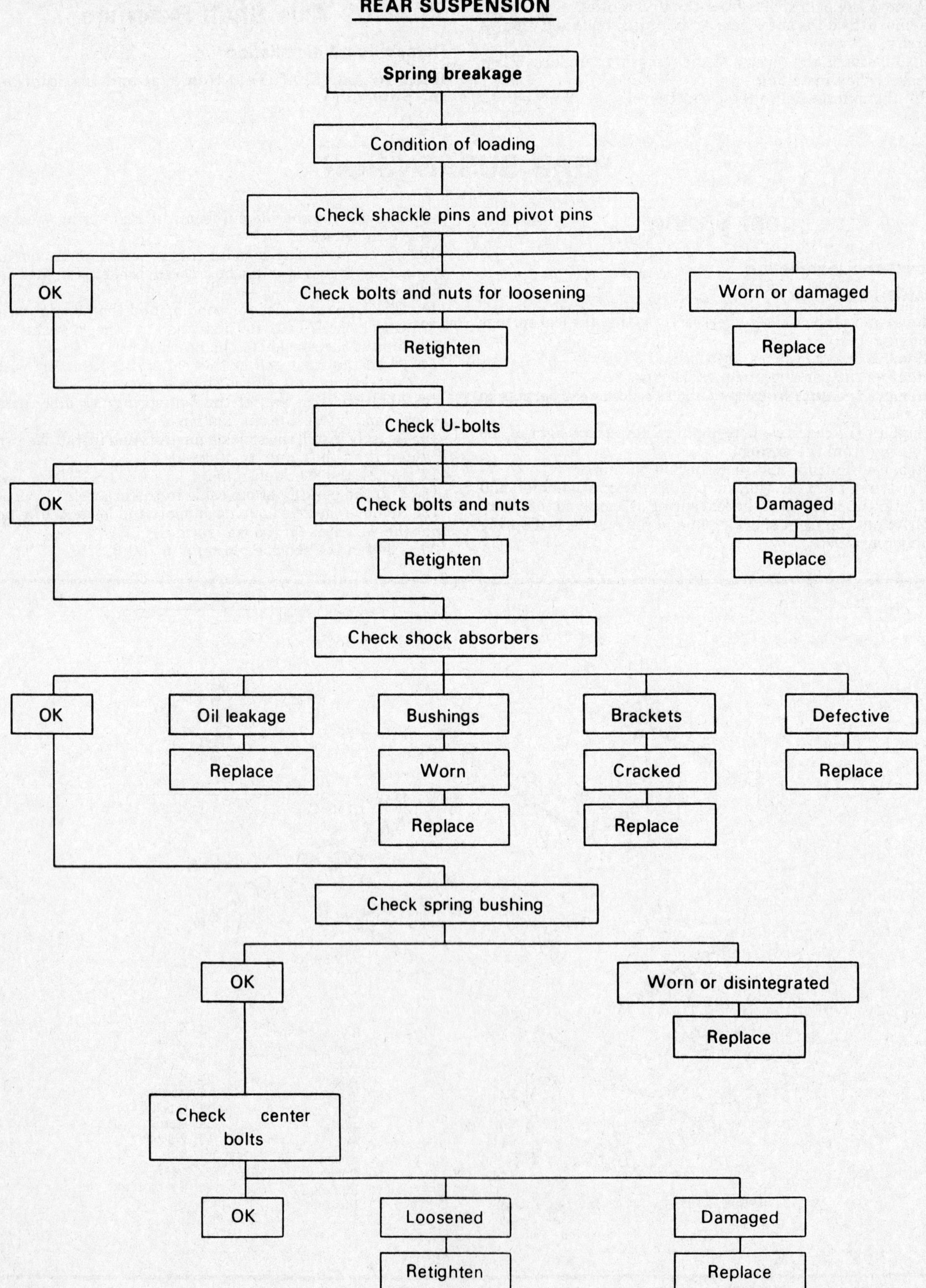

Mazda 16

INDEX

BEFORE SERVICING, SEE THE SAFETY NOTICE AT THE FRONT OF THE BOOK

MAZDA

ENGINE IDENTIFICATION CODES BY VIN NUMBER

Engine Cu. In. (liter)	Cylinders	1982	1983	1984	1985	1986	1987	1988
120 (2.0)	4	MA	MA	MA	①	—	—	—
122 (2.0)	4	—	—	—	①	FE	—	—
133 (2.2)	4	—	—	—	①	—	F2	F2
134 (2.2)	4	S2	S2	S2	①	—	—	—
156 (2.6)	4	—	—	—	①	—	G54B	G54B

① Mazda did not manufacture 1985 truck until mid-year 1985. The trucks sold in 1985 were identical in every respect to the 1984 trucks.

MODEL IDENTIFICATION

Mazda Pickup Trucks

Model Name	Model Designation
B2000 Sundowwner	Pickup
B2000 Sundownwer Long Bed	Pickup
B2000 Sundowner DLX	Pickup
B2000 Sundowner Sport	Pickup
B2000 Sundowner Sport Long Bed	Pickup
B2000 Cab Plus	Pickup
B2000 LX	Pickup
B2000 LX Plus	Pickup
B2000 LX Long Bed	Pickup
B2000 LX Long Bed Plus	Pickup
B2000 LX Cab Plus	Pickup
B2000 LX Long Bed Cab Plus	Pickup
B2200 Diesel	Pickup
B2200 Diesel DLX	Pickup
B2200 Long Bed Diesel	Pickup
B2200 Long Bed Diesel DLX	Pickup
B2200 Diesel	Pickup
B2600	Pickup

GENERAL ENGINE SPECIFICATIONS

Year	VIN	No. Cylinder Displacement cu. in. (liter)	Fuel System Type	Net Horsepower @ rpm	Net Torque @ rpm (ft.lbs.)	Bore × Stroke (in.)	Com-pression Ratio	Oil Pressure @ 2000 rpm
1982	MA	4–122 (2.0)	2bbl	77 @ 4300	109 @ 2400	3.15 × 3.86	8.6:1	50–64
	S2	4–134 (2.2)	Diesel	58 @ 4000	88 @ 2500	3.50 × 3.50	21.1:1	55–60
1983	MA	4–122 (2.0)	2bbl	77 @ 4300	109 @ 2400	3.15 × 3.86	8.6:1	50–64
	S2	4–134 (2.2)	Diesel	58 @ 4000	88 @ 2500	3.50 × 3.50	21.1:1	55–60
1984	MA	4–122 (2.0)	2bbl	77 @ 4300	109 @ 2400	3.15 × 3.86	8.6:1	50–64
	S2	4–134 (2.2)	Diesel	58 @ 4000	88 @ 2500	3.50 × 3.50	21.1:1	55–60
1985	MA	4–122 (2.0)	2bbl	77 @ 4300	109 @ 2400	3.15 × 3.86	8.6:1	50–64
	S2	4–134 (2.2)	Diesel	58 @ 4000	88 @ 2500	3.50 × 3.50	21.1:1	55–60
1986	FE	4–122 (2.0)	2bbl	80 @ 4500	110 @ 2500	3.39 × 3.39	8.6:1	55–60
1987–88	F2	4–134 (2.2)	2bbl	NA	NA	3.39 × 3.70	8.6:1	55–60
	G54B	4–156 (2.6)	2bbl	105 @ 5000	139 @ 2500	3.59 × 3.86	8.2:1	54–64

GASOLINE ENGINE TUNE-UP SPECIFICATIONS

Year	VIN	No. Cylinder Displacement cu. in. (liter)	Spark Plugs Type	Spark Plugs Gap (in.)	Ignition Timing (deg.) MT	Ignition Timing (deg.) AT	Compression Pressure (psi)	Fuel Pump (psi)	Idle Speed (rpm) MT	Idle Speed (rpm) AT	Valve Clearance (in.) In.	Valve Clearance (in.) Ex.
1982	MA	4–120 (2.0)	BPR–6ES	.031	8B	8B	171	2.8–3.6	650	650	.012	.012
1983	MA	4–120 (2.0)	BPR–6ES	.031	8B	8B	171	2.8–3.6	650	650	.012	.012
1984	MA	4–120 (2.0)	BPR–6ES	.031	8B	8B	171	2.8–3.6	650	650	.012	.012
1985	MA	4–120 (2.0)	BPR–6ES	.031	8B	8B	171	2.8–3.6	650	650	.012	.012
1986	FE	4–122 (2.0)	BPR–5ES	.031	6B	—	164	3.9–4.4	850	—	.012	.012
1987–88	F2	4–134 (2.2)	BPR–5ES	.031	6B	6B	173	2.8–3.6	850	850	Hyd.	Hyd.
	G54B	4–156 (2.6)	BPR–6ES	.031	7B	7B	171	19–25	850	850	Hyd.①	Hyd.①

① Jet Valve Clearance: .010 HOT

FIRING ORDERS

NOTE: To avoid confusion, always replace spark plug wires one at a time.

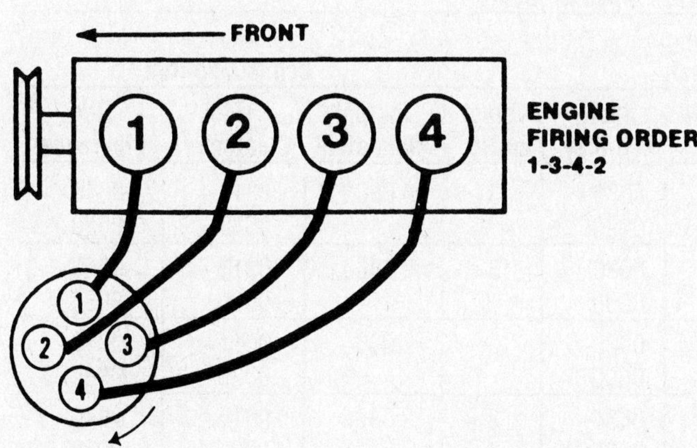

1986–88 2.0L and 2.2L engines – firing order

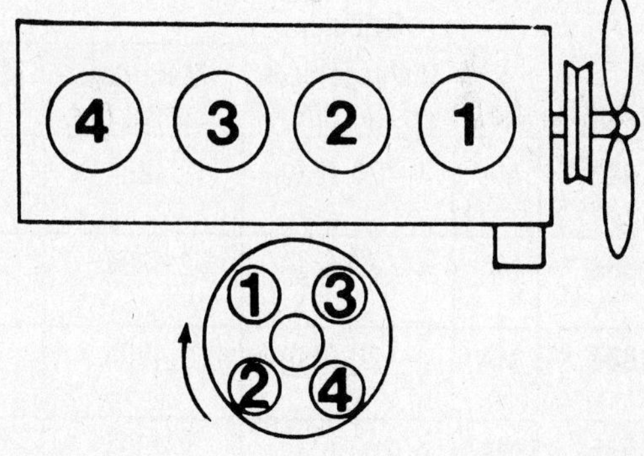

1982–85 2.0L engine – firing order 1-3-4-2

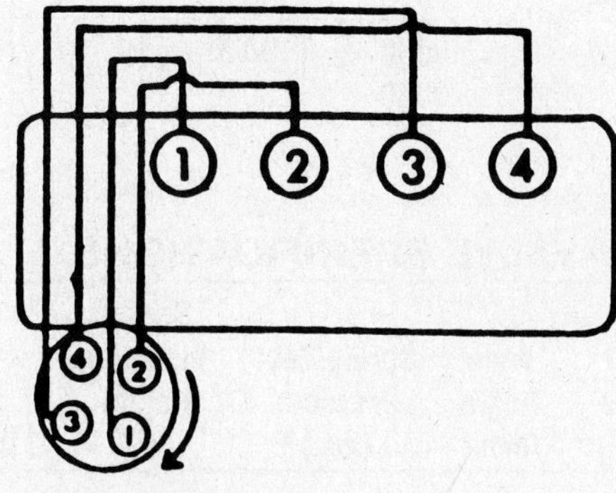

2.6L engine firing order: 1–3–4–2

CAPACITIES

Year	Model	No. Cylinder Displacement cu. in. (liter)	Engine Crankcase with Filter	Engine Crankcase without Filter	Transmission (pts.) 4-Spd	5-Spd	Auto.	Drive Axle (pts.)	Fuel Tank (gal.)	Cooling System (qts.)
1982	Pickups	4–120 (2.0)	4.5	5.0	3.2	3.6	13.2	2.8	①	7.5
		4–133 (2.2)	5.0	5.3	—	3.6	—	2.8	①	11.1
1983	Pickups	4–120 (2.0)	4.5	5.0	3.2	3.6	13.2	2.8	①	7.5
		4–133 (2.2)	5.0	5.3	—	3.6	—	2.8	①	11.1
1984	Pickups	4–120 (2.0)	4.5	5.0	3.2	3.6	13.2	2.8	①	7.5
		4–133 (2.2)	5.0	5.3	—	3.6	—	2.8	①	11.1
1985	Pickups	4–120 (2.0)	4.5	5.0	3.2	3.6	13.2	2.8	①	7.5
		4–133 (2.2)	5.0	5.3	—	3.6	—	2.8	①	11.1
1986	Pickups	4–122 (2.0)	4.0	4.5	3.0	2.6	—	2.8	②	7.9
1987–88	Pickups	4–134 (2.2)	4.0	4.5	—	2.6	—	2.8	②	7.9
		4–156 (2.6)	4.0③	4.5④	—	2.6	8.4	2.8	②	7.9

① Long Bed: 15.0; Short Bed: 17.5
② Long Bed: 15.6; Short Bed: 14.6
③ 4 Wheel Drive: 4.8
④ 4 Wheel Drive: 5.0

CRANKSHAFT AND CONNECTING ROD SPECIFICATIONS

All measurements are given in inches.

Year	VIN	No. Cylinder Displacement cu. in. (liter)	Crankshaft Main Brg. Journal Dia.	Main Brg. Oil Clearance	Shaft End-play	Thrust on No.	Connecting Rod Journal Diameter	Oil Clearance	Side Clearance
1982	MA	4–120 (2.0)	2.4804	.0012–.0020	.0030–.0090	3	2.0866	.0011–.0030	.0040–.0080
1983	MA	4–120 (2.0)	2.4804	.0012–.0020	.0030–.0090	3	2.0866	.0011–.0030	.0040–.0080
1984	MA	4–120 (2.0)	2.4804	.0012–.0020	.0030–.0090	3	2.0866	.0011–.0030	.0040–.0080
1985	MA	4–120 (2.0)	2.4804	.0012–.0020	.0030–.0090	3	2.0866	.0011–.0030	.0040–.0080
1986	FE	4–122 (2.0)	2.3597–2.3604	.0012–.0019	.0030–.0070	3	2.0050–2.0060	.0010–.0026	.0040–.0100
1987–88	F2	4–134 (2.2)	2.3597–2.3604	.0012–.0019	.0030–.0070	3	2.0050–2.0060	.0010–.0026	.0040–.0100
	G54B	4–156 (2.6)	2.3622	.0008–.0020	.0020–.0070	3	2.0866	.0008–.0020	.004–.010

VALVE SPECIFICATIONS

Year	VIN	No. Cylinder Displacement cu. in. (liter)	Seat Angle (deg.)	Face Angle (deg.)	Spring Test Pressure (lbs.)	Spring Installed Height (in.)	Stem-to-Guide Clearance (in.) Intake	Exhaust	Stem Diameter (in.) Intake	Exhaust
1982	MA	4–120 (2.0)	45	45	①	②	.0007–.0021	.0007–.0021	.3164	.3163

VALVE SPECIFICATIONS

Year	VIN	No. Cylinder Displacement cu. in. (liter)	Seat Angle (deg.)	Face Angle (deg.)	Spring Test Pressure (lbs.)	Spring Installed Height (in.)	Stem-to-Guide Clearance (in.) Intake	Stem-to-Guide Clearance (in.) Exhaust	Stem Diameter (in.) Intake	Stem Diameter (in.) Exhaust
1983	MA	4–120 (2.0)	45	45	①	②	.0007–.0021	.0007–.0021	.3164	.3163
1984	MA	4–120 (2.0)	45	45	①	②	.0007–.0021	.0007–.0021	.3164	.3163
1985	MA	4–120 (2.0)	45	45	①	②	.0007–.0021	.0007–.0021	.3164	.3163
1986	FE	4–122 (2.0)	45	45	③	④	.0010–.0024	.0010–.0024	.3177–.3185	.3159–.3165
1987–88	F2	4–134 (2.2)	45	45	③	④	.0010–.0024	.0010–.0024	.3177–.3185	.3159–.3165
	G54B	4–156 (2.6)	45	45	72	1.59	.0012–.0024	.0020–.0035	.3150	.3150

① Inner: 20.9 @ 1.26
Outer: 31.4 @ 1.34

② Inner: 1.306
Outer: 1.385

③ Outer: 96.3 @ 2.007
Inner: 95.8 @ 1.722

④ Outer: 2.007
Inner: 1.722

PISTON AND RING SPECIFICATIONS

All measurments are given in inches.

Year	VIN	No. Cylinder Displacement cu. in. (liter)	Piston Clearance	Ring Gap Top Compression	Ring Gap Bottom Compression	Ring Gap Oil Control	Ring Side Clearance Top Compression	Ring Side Clearance Bottom Compression	Ring Side Clearance Oil Control
1982	MA	4–120 (2.0)	.0019–.0025	.0080–.0160	.0080–.0160	.0120–.0350	.0012–.0028	.0012–.0025	Snug
1983	MA	4–120 (2.0)	.0019–.0025	.0080–.0160	.0080–.0160	.0120–.0350	.0012–.0028	.0012–.0025	Snug
1984	MA	4–120 (2.0)	.0019–.0025	.0080–.0160	.0080–.0160	.0120–.0350	.0012–.0028	.0012–.0025	Snug
1985	MA	4–120 (2.0)	.0019–.0025	.0080–.0160	.0080–.0160	.0120–.0350	.0012–.0028	.0012–.0025	Snug
1986	FE	4–122 (2.0)	.0014–.0030	.0080–.0120	.0060–.0120	.0120–.0350	.0012–.0028	.0012–.0028	Snug
1987–88	F2	4–134 (2.2)	.0014–.0030	.0080–.0120	.0060–.0120	.0120–.0350	.0012–.0028	.0012–.0028	Snug
	G54B	4–156 (2.6)	.0008–.0016	.0112–.0177	.0098–.0158	.0118–.0315	.0020–.0035	.0008–.0024	.0078–.0280

TORQUE SPECIFICATIONS

All readings in ft. lbs.

Year	VIN	No. Cylinder Displacement cu. in. (liter)	Cylinder Head Bolts	Main Bearing Bolts	Rod Bearing Bolts	Crankshaft Pulley Bolts	Flywheel Bolts	Manifold Intake	Manifold Exhaust	Spark Plugs
1982	MA	4–120 (2.0)	①	61–65	30–33	101–108	112–118	14–19	14–19	16–21
1983	MA	4–120 (2.0)	①	61–65	30–33	101–108	112–118	14–19	14–19	16–21
1984	MA	4–120 (2.0)	①	61–65	30–33	101–108	112–118	14–19	14–19	16–21

TORQUE SPECIFICATIONS

All readings in ft. lbs.

Year	VIN	No. Cylinder Displacement cu. in. (liter)	Cylinder Head Bolts	Main Bearing Bolts	Rod Bearing Bolts	Crankshaft Pulley Bolts	Flywheel Bolts	Manifold		Spark Plugs
								Intake	Exhaust	
1985	MA	4-120 (2.0)	①	61–65	30–33	101–108	112–118	14–19	14–19	16–21
1986	FE	4-122 (2.0)	59–64	61–65	37–41	9–12 ③	71–76	14–19	14–19	16–21
1987–88	F2	4-134 (2.2)	59–64	61–65	37–41	9–12 ③	71–76	14–19	14–19	16–21
	G54B	4-156 (2.6)	65–72②	55–61	33–34	80–94	94–101	11–14	11–14	NA

① Torque cold to 65–69 ft. lbs.; then retorque hot to 69–72 ft. lbs.

② Specification is for Cold engine; Hot engine: 84–90 ft. lbs.

③ Balancer bolt—80-94 ft. lbs.

WHEEL ALIGNMENT

Year	Model	Caster		Camber		Toe-in (in.)	Steering Axis Inclination (deg.)
		Range (deg.)	Preferred Setting (deg.)	Range (deg.)	Preferred Setting (deg.)		
1982	2WD Pickups	½P–1½P	1P	⅓P–1⅓P	¾P	0–¼P	NA
1983	2WD Pickups	½P–1½P	1P	⅓P–1⅓P	¾P	0–¼P	NA
1984	2WD Pickups	½P–1½P	1P	⅓P–1⅓P	¾P	0–¼P	NA
1985	2WD Pickups	½P–1½P	1P	⅓P–1⅓P	¾P	0–¼P	NA
1986	2WD Pickups	0–1⅔P①	1⅚P	⅓P–1⅓P	¾P	0–¼P	NA
1987–88	2WD Pickups	0–1⅔P①	1⅚P	⅓P–1⅓P	¾P	0–¼P	NA
	4WD Pickups	0–1⅔P②	1⅚P	½P–1½P	1P	0–¼P	NA

① Specification is for Manual Steering; Power Steering: 1⅓–2⅓P

② Specification is for Manual Steering; Power Steering: 2¾P

ENGINE ELECTRICAL

Refer to the Unit Overhaul Section for Alternator and Starter Overhaul.

Alternator

Removal and Installation

ALL MODELS

1. Disconnect the negative battery cable.
2. Disconnect and tag the alternator wiring.
3. Remove the alternator adjusting bolt.
4. Remove the drive belt.
5. On diesel engine models, disconnect the vacuum and oil hoses from the alternator. Plug the oil hose.
6. Support the alternator, remove the pivot bolt, and remove the alternator.
7. Before installing the alternator, tighten the alternator mount to engine bolts.

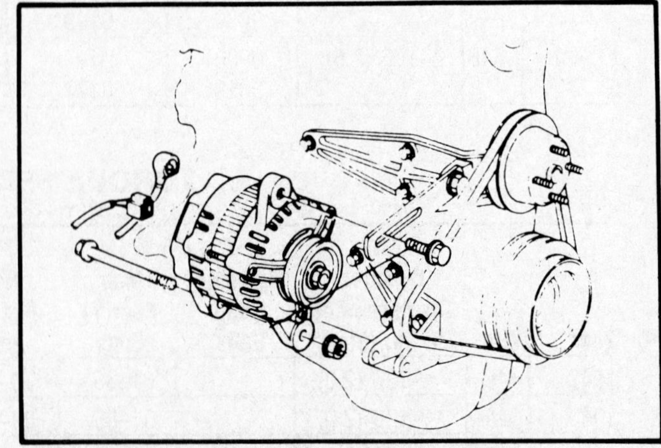

Alternator mounting 2.0L and 2.2L engines

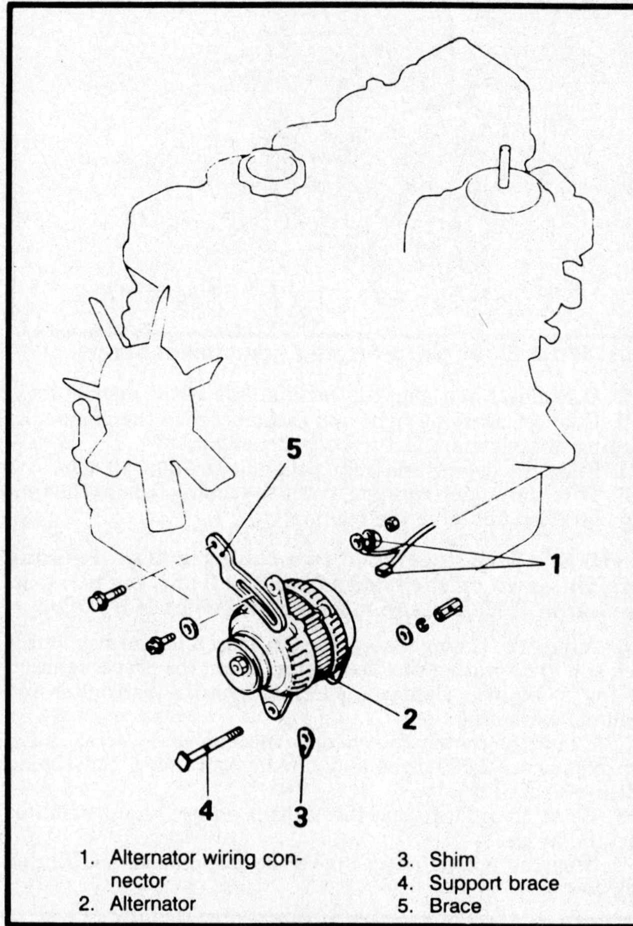

1. Alternator wiring connector
2. Alternator
3. Shim
4. Support brace
5. Brace

Alternator mounting 2.6L engine

7. Installation is the reverse of the removal procedure.
8. Reconnect the alternator wiring and negative battery cable. Adjust the belt tension when finished.

Voltage Regulator

Removal and Installation

NOTE: All models are equipped with an integral voltage regulator. Removal and installation requires alternator disassembly. Refer to the Unit Overhaul Section for the procedure.

Starter

OVERHAUL

Refer to the Unit Overhaul Section.

Removal and Installation

ALL MODELS

1. Disconnect the negative battery cable.
2. Remove the air cleaner and air intake tube.
3. Disconnect the positive battery cable from the starter solenoid.
4. Remove the ignition switch wire from the solenoid terminal.
5. Raise and support the vehicle safely.

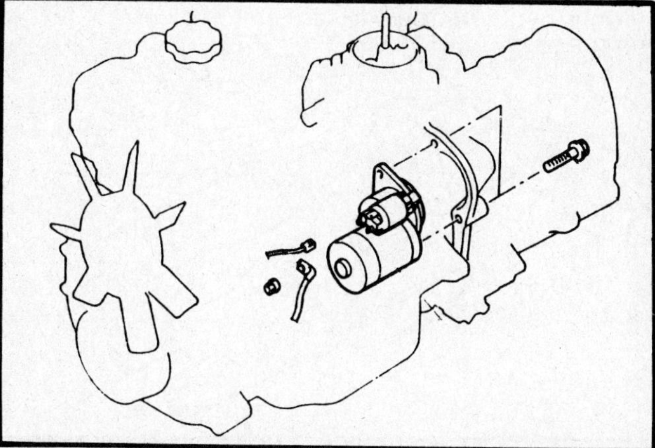

Typical starter motor mounting

6. Support the starter and remove the two starter mounting bolts and nuts.
7. Tilt the drive end of the starter downwards and remove the starter.
8. Installation is the reverse of the removal procedure.
9. Torque the starter mounting bolts to 23–34 ft. lbs.

Distributor

Removal and Installation

ALL MODELS

1. Remove the distributor cap without removing the spark plug wires from the cap.
2. Disconnect the vacuum hose from the distributor.
3. Remove the rubber plug from the timing belt cover. Scribe matchmarks on the distributor body and the engine to indicate their positions.
4. Scribe another mark on the distributor body indicating the position of the rotor. On 2.0L engines, scribe a mark on the cam pulley and on the indicator inside the timing belt cover to mark the position of the pulley relative to the indicator.
5. Disconnect and tag the primary wires from the distributor.
6. Remove the distributor lock nut and washers.
7. Remove the distributor from the engine.
8. To install, align the matchmarks made during the removal.
9. Install the distributor with the rotor pointing in the same direction as when removed.

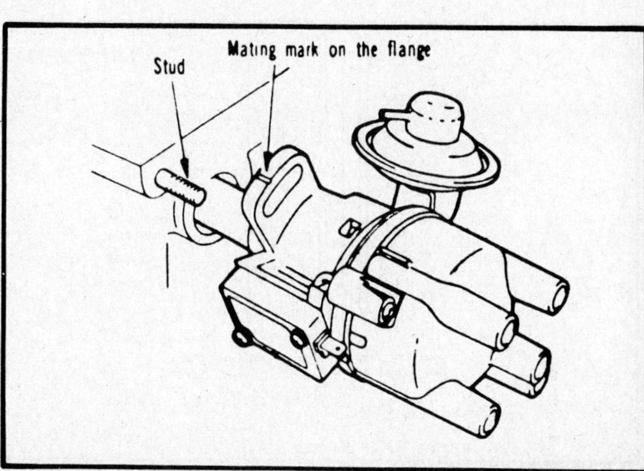

Aligning distributor and cylinder head matchmarks

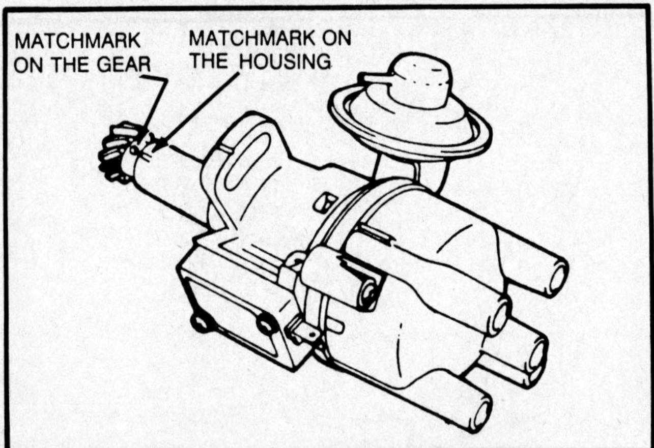

Aligning matchmarks on distributor gear and housing

10. Align the distributor body to engine matchmarks. Install the lock nut and washer.
11. Connect the wires and vacuum hose to the distributor. Install the distributor cap.
12. Start the engine and adjust the ignition timing.
13. With the timing correct, tighten the lock nut and recheck the timing.

NOTE: If the engine was disturbed while the distributor was removed, rotate the crankshaft until No.1 cylinder is at TDC. This can be determined by removing the No.1 spark plug, placing a finger over the spark plug hole while turning the engine and feeling for compression. Continue rotating the engine, until the TDC mark on the crankshaft pulley is aligned with the timing pointer. Install the distributor into the engine with the rotor pointing to the No.1 lug on the distributor cap. Install the distributor lock nut, start the engine and correct the ignition timing.

TIMING LIGHT AND TACHOMETER CONNECTIONS

All timing lights and tachometers should be connected according to their manufacture's instructions.

IGNITION TIMING

Procedure

1. Before starting the engine, clean and mark the timing marks.

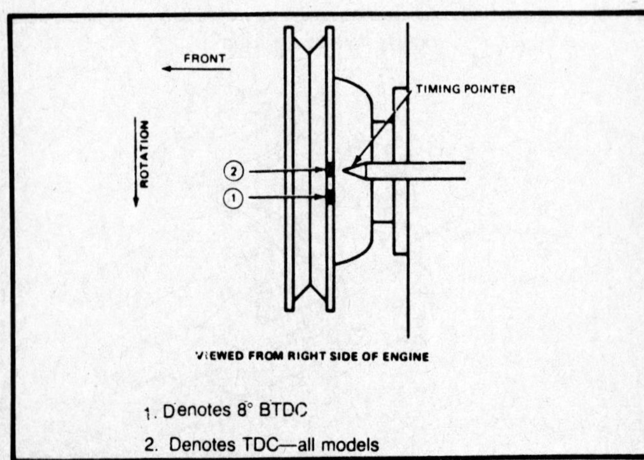

1982–85 2.0L engine timing marks

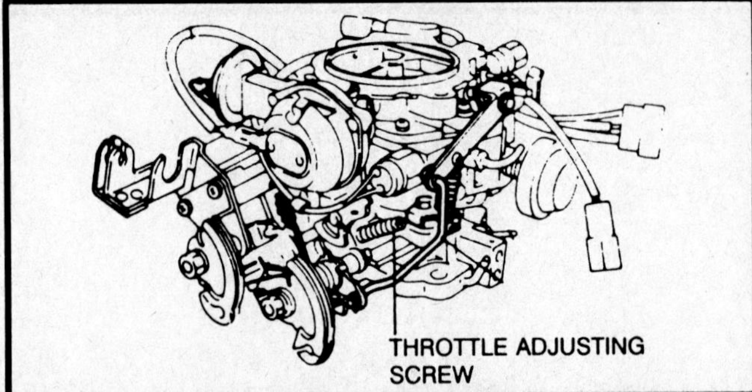

2.0L and 2.2L engines throttle adjustment screw

2. Disconnect and plug the vacuum line at the distributor.
3. Connect a timing light and tachometer to the engine according to their manufacturer's instructions.
4. Start the engine and adjust the idle to 700–750 rpm.
5. With the engine running, point the timing light at the timing marks and observe the reading.

NOTE: All engines have two timing marks. Looking straight down on the marks from the front, the mark on the left is TDC and the mark on the right is BTDC.

6. Adjust the timing if necessary, by loosening the distributor lock bolt and rotating the distributor. When the proper ignition timing is obtained, tighten the lock bolt on the distributor and recheck the timing.
7. Check the centrifugal advance mechanism by accelerating the engine to 2,000 rpm and making sure that the timing advances.
8. Reset the idle to specifications. Connect the distributor vacuum hose.
9. Stop the engine and remove the tachometer and timing light.

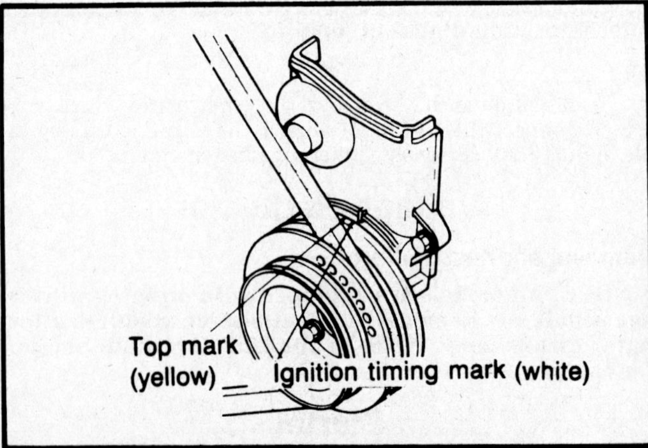

1986–88 2.0L and 2.2L engines timing marks

Electrical Controls

IGNITION LOCK

Removal and Installation

ALL MODELS

1. Disconnect the negative battery cable.
2. Matchmark and remove the steering wheel.
3. Remove the steering column cover.
4. Disconnect and tag the multiple connectors at the base of the combination switch.

5. Remove the switch retaining snap ring. Pull the turn signal indicator cancelling cam off the shaft.
6. Remove the switch retaining bolt and remove the switch from the steering column.

NOTE: Make a groove on the head of the bolts attaching the steering lock body to the column shaft using a suitable tool.

7. Remove the ignition lock attaching bolts. Remove the ignition lock.
8. Tighten the ignition lock bolts until the heads of the bolts break off.
9. The remainder of the installation is the reverse of the removal procedure.

IGNITION SWITCH

Removal and Installation

1982–85

1. Disconnect the negative battery cable.
2. Matchmark and remove the steering wheel.
3. Remove the steering column shroud.
4. Disconnect and tag the multiple connectors at the base of the combination switch.
5. Remove the switch retaining snap ring. Pull the turn signal indicator cancelling cam off the shaft.
6. Remove the switch retaining bolt and remove the complete switch from the column.
7. Installation is the reverse of the removal procedure.

1986–88

1. Disconnect the negative battery cable.
2. Remove the steering column covers.
3. Disconnect the wiring harness connector at the switch.
4. Remove the switch mounting screws and remove the switch.
5. Installation is the reverse of the removal procedure.

COMBINATION SWITCH

NOTE: The Combination Switch incorporates the Dimmer, Turn Signal, Headlight and W/Wiper switches into one switch.

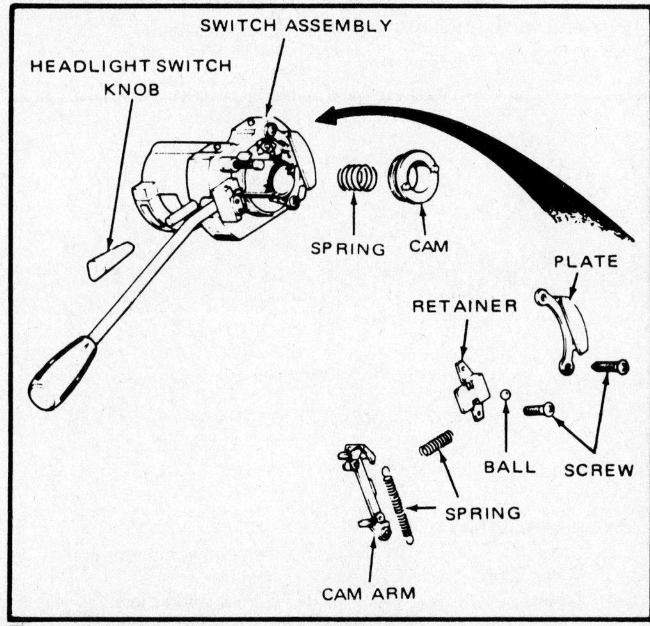

Turn signal switch—exploded view

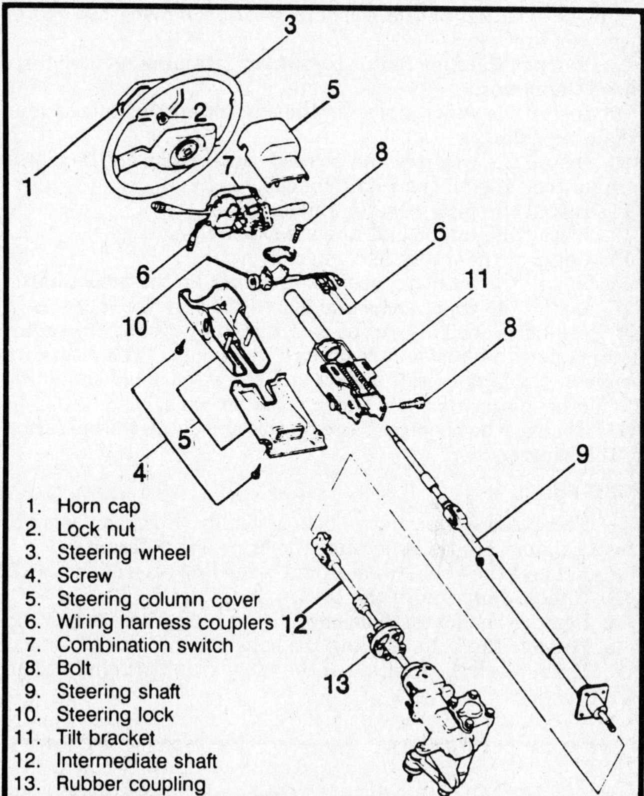

Steering column—exploded view

Removal and Installation

ALL MODELS

1. Disconnect the negative battery cable.
2. Matchmark and remove the steering wheel.
3. Remove the "Lights-Hazard" Indicator and steering column shroud.
4. Disconnect and tag the electrical connectors at the base of the steering column.
5. Pull the headlight switch knob off the shaft.
6. Remove the snap ring which retains the switch on the steering shaft. Pull the turn signal canceling cam off the shaft.
7. Remove the switch mounting bolt at the bottom of the switch. Remove the switch from the steering column.
8. Installation is the reverse of removal. Check the operation of the switch before installing the steering wheel.

W/WIPER MOTOR AND LINKAGE

Removal and Installation

1982–85

1. Disconnect the negative battery cable.
2. Remove the wiper arms and blades.
3. Remove the rubber cap, nut, tapered spacer and rubber grommet from each pivot shaft.
4. Remove the two motor and bracket retaining bolts and washers.
5. Disconnect the wiper motor leads at the multiple connector.
6. Remove the wiper motor and bracket assembly. Note the position of the ground washer and the rubber washer at the bracket mounting holes. Remove the plastic water shield.
7. To disconnect the motor from the bracket, remove the retaining clip that holds the linkage to the motor output arm.

Note the position of the washers before removing the motor from the bracket.

8. Remove the four motor to bracket retaining bolts and remove the motor.
9. Install the wiper motor on the bracket and install the four retaining bolts.
10. Install the washers and position the linkage on the motor output arm. Install the retaining clip.
11. Install the plastic water shield.
12. Install the motor and bracket assembly.
13. Connect the multiple connector.
14. Install the washers, spacers and nuts on the pivot shafts.
15. Install the wiper arms and blades. Be sure the motor is in the Park position. This can be determined by cycling the motor several times. Adjust the position of the wipers. The clearance between the tips of the blades and the windshield moulding should be 20mm with the wiper motor in park.
16. Connect the negative battery cable and check the operation of the wipers.

1986–88

1. Remove the wiper arm/blade assembly. Keep the arms in there original positions because the arms are different.
2. Remove the rubber seal from the leading edge of the cowl.
3. Unbolt and remove the cowl.
4. Remove the access hole covers.
5. Remove the bolts holding the wiper shaft drives.
6. Matchmark the position of the wiper crank arm in relation to the face of the wiper motor. Disconnect the wiper linkage from the wiper motor crank arm.
7. Remove the wiper linkage.
8. Unbolt and remove the wiper motor. Disconnect the wiring harness.
9. Installation is the reverse of the removal procedure. Make sure that the parked height of the wiper arms, measured from the blade tips to the windshield moulding, is 20mm. Torque the arm retaining nuts to 8–10 ft. lbs.

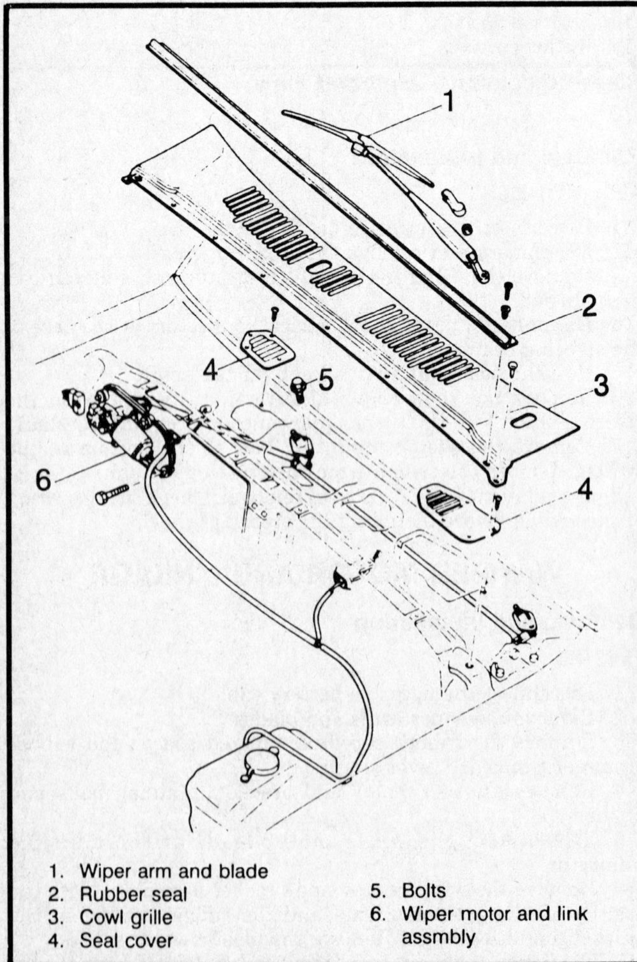

W/Wiper motor and linkage

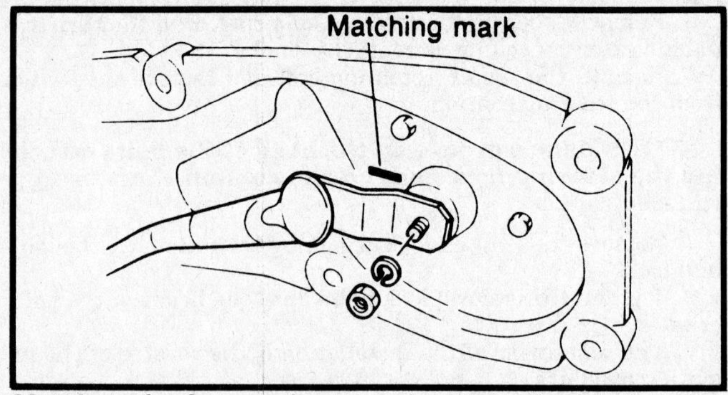

Matchmarks for crankarm and motor alignment

INSTRUMENT CLUSTER

Removal and Installation

1982–85

1. Disconnect the negative battery cable.
2. Remove the instrument cluster trim panel.
3. Remove the screws holding the cluster to the instrument panel.
4. Pull the cluster rearward enough to gain access to the cluster assembly.
5. Reach behind the cluster and disconnect the speedometer cable.
6. Pull the multiple connector from the printed circuit.
7. Note the position of and disconnect the two ammeter leads.
8. Remove the screw attaching the ground wire to the rear of the cluster. On vehicles equipped with a coasting richer valve, remove the two connectors at the speedometer sensor switch.
9. Remove the instrument cluster.

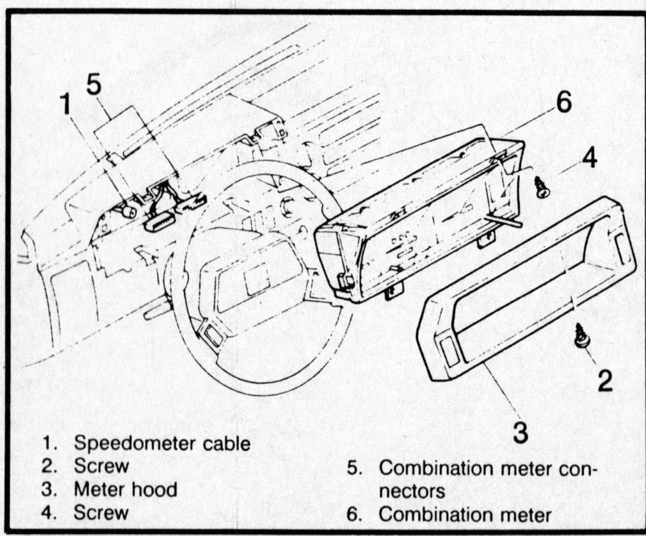

Instrument cluster mounting

10. To install, position the cluster assembly near the opening and connect the ground lead.
11. Connect the two ammeter leads to the ammeter.
12. Install the multiple connector at the rear of the cluster. On vehicles equipped with a coasting richer valve, connect the two wires to the speedometer speed sensor.
13. Connect the speedometer cable to the speedometer head.
14. Install the four attaching screws.
15. Replace the trim panel.
16. Connect the negative battery cable.
17. Run the engine and check the operation of all gauges.

1986–88

1. Disconnect the negative battery cable.
2. Reach behind the cluster and disconnect the speedometer cable.
3. Remove the screws attaching the cluster hood and carefully lift the hood off.
4. Remove the screw attaching the cluster pod to the dash panel and pull the pod outwards gradually. Reach behind the pod and disconnect the wiring connectors.
5. Remove the trip meter knob and, on clusters w/tachometer, the clock adjust knob.
6. Remove the screws retaining the lens cover and lift off the cover.
7. Remove the screws retaining the cluster bezel and lift off the bezel.
8. Lift out the warning light plate.
9. On clusters without a tachometer, in order remove:
   a. fuel gauge.
   b. speedometer.
   c. temperature gauge.
   d. printed circuit board.
10. On cluster with tachometers, in order remove:
    a. speedometer.
    b. digital clock.
    c. tachometer.
    d. fuel gauge.
    e. temperature gauge.
    f. printed circuit board.
11. Installation is the reverse of the removal procedure.

SPEEDOMETER

Removal and Installation

ALL MODELS

NOTE: The speedometer can be replaced by, removing the instrument cluster and disassembling the cluster in order to gain access to the speedometer. Note the position of any bulbs and wiring connection during the removal procedure.

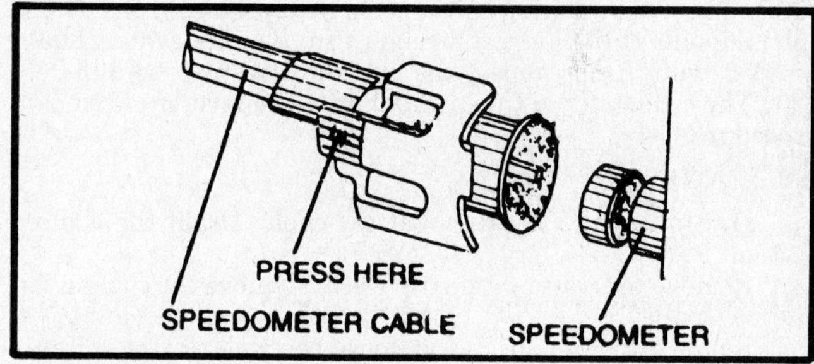

Speedometer cable connector

COOLING AND HEATING SYSTEMS

Water Pump

Removal and Installation

2.0 & 2.2L GASOLINE ENGINES

1. Disconnect the negative battery cable. Drain the cooling system.
2. Remove the distributor. Remove the fan shroud, fan blades, pulley, hub and bracket.

NOTE: Always store the fan clutch in an upright position after removal to avoid fluid loss.

3. Remove the alternator. Disconnect the air injection pipes.
4. Remove the drive belts.
5. Remove the crankshaft pulley and baffle plate.
6. Remove the upper and lower timing belt covers.
7. Rotate the crankshaft so that the "A" mark on the camshaft pulley is at the top, aligned with the notch in the front housing.
8. Loosen the tensioner lock bolt and remove the tensioner spring.
9. Mark the direction of rotation of the timing belt for installation. Remove the belt.
10. Remove the water inlet pipe and gasket from the water pump.
11. Remove the water pump mounting bolts and remove the water pump.
12. To install, use a new O-ring coated with clean coolant and a new gasket coated with sealer. Torque the water pump mounting bolts to 14–19 ft. lbs.
13. Install the coolant inlet pipe, using a new gasket coated with sealer.

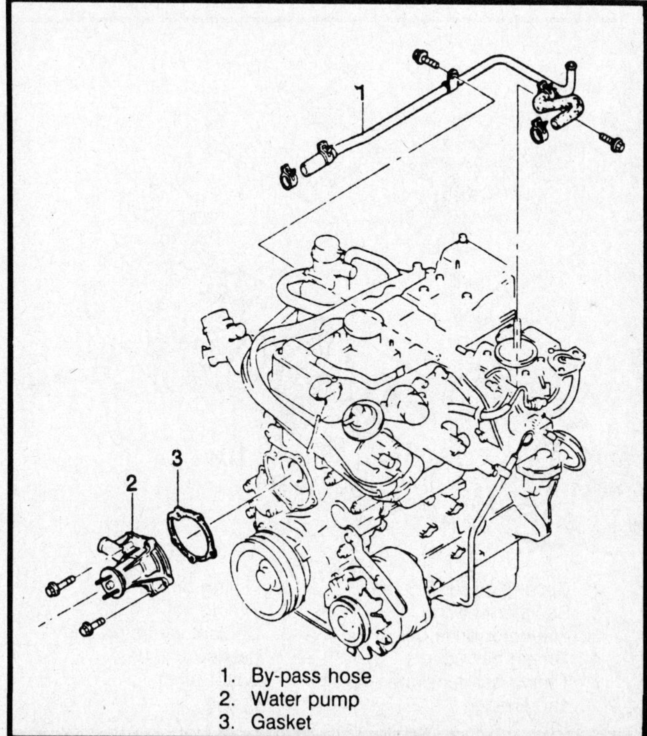

1986–88 2.0L and 2.2L engine water pump installation

14. Replace the timing belt if it has been contaminated by oil or grease, or shows any sign of damage, wear, cracks or peeling.

15. To ease installation of the belt, remove all the spark plugs.

16. Make sure that the timing mark on the camshaft is aligned and that the timing mark on the crankshaft sprocket is aligned with the triangular shaped mark on the front housing.

17. Install the tensioner and spring. Position the tensioner all the way to the intake manifold side and temporarily secure it there with the lock bolt.

18. Install the belt onto the sprockets from the right side. If the original belt is being reused, follow the directional mark previously made.

19. Loosen the lock bolt so that the tensioner applies tension to the belt.

20. Turn the crankshaft two full revolutions in the direction of normal rotation. This will apply equal tension to all points of the timing belt.

26. Make sure that the timing marks are still aligned. If not, repeat the timing belt installation procedure.

27. Tighten the timing belt tensioner lock bolt to 30–35 ft. lbs.

28. Measure the timing belt tension by pressing on the belt at the midpoint of the longest straight run. Belt deflection should be 11–13mm. If not, repeat the belt adjustment procedure.

29. The remainder of the installation is the reverse of removal procedure.

2.6L ENGINE

1. Disconnect the negative battery cable. Drain the cooling system.

2. Remove the water pump drive belt. Remove the cooling fan and belt pulley.

3. Remove the fan shroud. Remove the water by-pass hose.

4. Disconnect the lower radiator hose at the water pump.

5. Remove the water pump mounting bolts and remove the water pump.

6. Clean and inspect the water pump sealing surface of the engine.

7. Using a new gasket, install the water pump on the engine and torque the bolts to 14–19 ft. lbs.

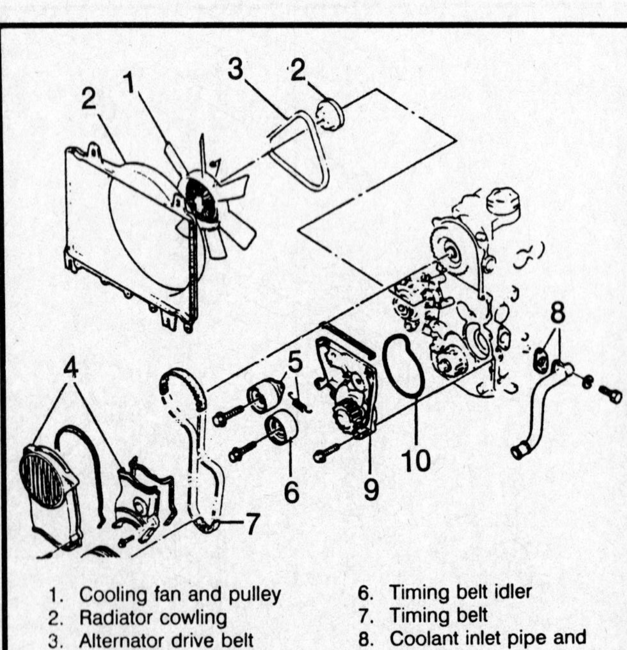

1. Cooling fan and pulley
2. Radiator cowling
3. Alternator drive belt
4. Timing belt covers
5. Timing belt tensioner and spring
6. Timing belt idler
7. Timing belt
8. Coolant inlet pipe and gasket
9. Water pump
10. O-ring

1987–88 2.6L engine water pump installation

8. Connect the lower radiator hose and water by-pass hose.

9. Install the drive belt pulley, colling fan and drive belt.

10. Adjust the drive belt tension. Install the fan shroud.

11. Fill the cooling system, run the engine and check for leaks.

Thermostat

Removal and Installation

ALL MODELS

1. Drain the cooling system down below the thermostat housing. Disconnect the coolant temperature sending unit wire.

2. Remove the coolant outlet elbow. If equipped, position the vacuum control valve out of the way. The vacuum control valve is not used on California trucks.

3. Disconnect the coolant by-pass hose from the thermostat housing.

4. Remove the thermostat and housing from the engine.

5. Note the position of the jiggle pin and remove the thermostat from the housing.

6. Clean and inspect the sealing surfaces of the housing and engine.

7. Position the thermostat in the housing with the jiggle pin up. Coat the new gasket with sealer and install it on the thermostat housing.

8. Install the thermostat housing using a new gasket with sealer. Torque the bolts to 20 ft. lbs.

9. Install the coolant outlet elbow and vacuum control valve, if equipped.

10. Connect the by-pass and radiator hoses.

11. Connect the temperature sending unit wire.

12. Fill the cooling system with the proper coolant. Run the engine, check the coolant level and check for leaks.

Heater Core/Blower Motor

Removal and Installation

ALL MODELS

1. Disconnect the negative battery cable.

2. Drain the cooling system.

3. Remove the water valve shield at the left side of the heater.

4. Disconnect the two hoses from the left side of the heater.

5. At the heater-defoster door, at the water valve and at the outside recirculation door, disengage the control cable housing from the mounting clip on the heater. Disconnect each of the three cable wires from the crank arms.

6. Disconnect the fan motor electrical lead.

7. Working inside the engine compartment, remove the two retaining nuts and the single bolt and washer which hold the heater to the firewall. A retaining bolt inside the passenger compartment must also be removed.

8. Disconnect the two defroster ducts from the heater and remove the heater.

Installation of heater control cable and clip

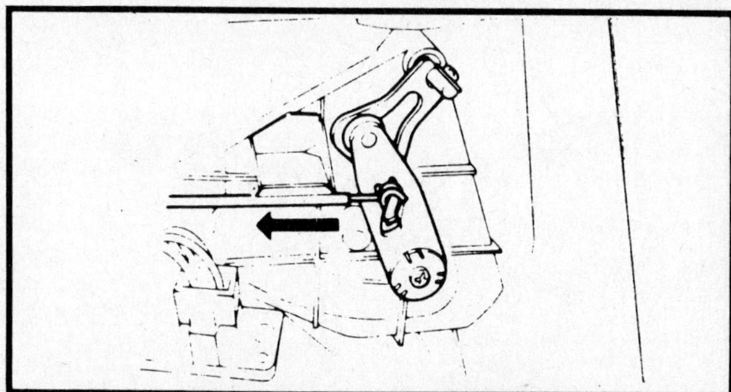
Installation of temperature control cable

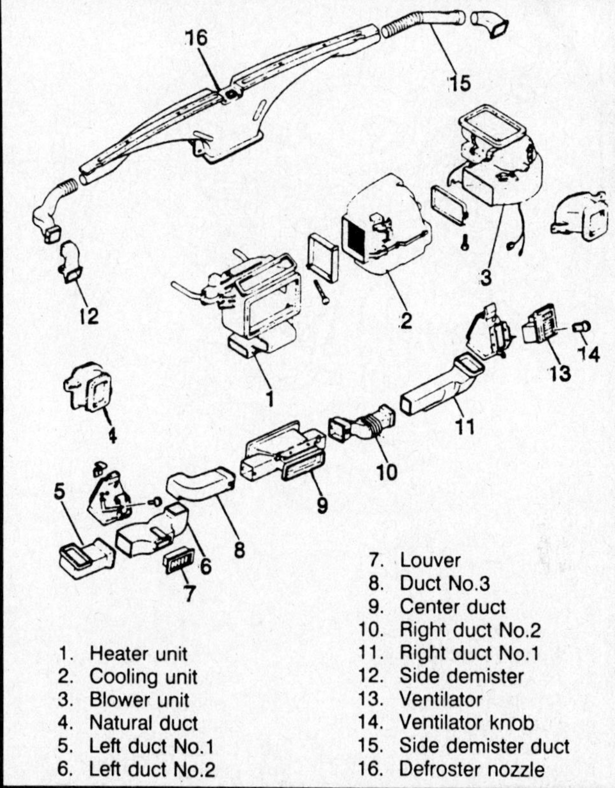

1. Heater unit
2. Cooling unit
3. Blower unit
4. Natural duct
5. Left duct No.1
6. Left duct No.2
7. Louver
8. Duct No.3
9. Center duct
10. Right duct No.2
11. Right duct No.1
12. Side demister
13. Ventilator
14. Ventilator knob
15. Side demister duct
16. Defroster nozzle

Heater assembly—exploded view

9. With the heater assembly removed, remove the five screws and separate the halves of the heater assembly. To replace the heater core, loosen the hose clamps and slide the heater core from the case. Replace the heater core, if necessary.
10. To replace the blower motor, loosen the fan retaining nut. Lightly tap on the nut to loosen the fan. Remove the fan and nut from the motor shaft.
11. Remove the three motor-to-case retaining screws and disconnect the bullet connector to the resistor and ground screw.
12. Rotate the motor and remove it from the case.
13. Install the motor in the case, rotating it slightly.
14. Install the retaining screws and connect the bullet connector and ground wire.
15. Install the fan on the shaft and install the nut.
16. Assemble the halves together and install the five retaining screws.
17. Install the heater on the dash so that the heater duct indexes with the air intake duct and the two mounting studs enter their respective holes.
18. From the engine side of the firewall, install the nuts on the mounting studs. While an assistant holds the heater in position, install the mounting bolt.
19. Connect the defroster ducts.
20. Connect the heat-defrost door control cable to the door crank arm. Set the control lever (upper) in the HEAT position and turn the crank arm toward the mounting clip as far as it will go. Engage the cable housing in the clip and install the screw in the clip.
21. Connect the water valve control cable wire to the crank arm on the water valve lever. Locate the cable housing in the mounting clip. Set the control lever in the HOT position and pull the valve plunger and lever to the full outward position. This will move the lever crank arm toward the cable mounting clip as far as it will go. Tighten the clip and screw.
22. Insert the outside-recirculation door control cable into the hole in the door crank arm. Bend the wire over and tighten the screw. Set the center control lever in the REC position and turn the door crank arm toward the mounting clip as far as it will go. Engage the cable housing in the clip and install the screw in the clip.
23. Connect the fan motor electrical lead.
24. Connect the two hoses to the heater core tubes, at the left side of the heater and tighten the clamp.
25. Install the water valve shield and tighten the three screws on the left side of the heater.
26. Refill the cooling system and connect the negative battery cable.
27. Run the engine and check for leaks. Check the operation of the heater.

FUEL SYSTEM

Carburetor

Removal and Installation

1. Disconnect the negative battery cable. Remove the air cleaner and air inlet duct.
2. Disconnect the accelerator shaft from the throttle lever.
3. Disconnect and plug the fuel supply and return lines.
4. Disconnect the leads from the throttle solenoid and deceleration valve at the quick-disconnects.
5. Disconnect the carburetor to distributor vacuum line.
6. Disconnect the throttle return spring.
7. Disconnect the choke cable and if equipped, the cruise control cable.
8. Remove the carburetor attaching nuts from the intake manifold studs and remove the carburetor.
9. Install a new carburetor gasket on the manifold.
10. Install the carburetor and tighten the carburetor attaching nuts.
11. Connect the throttle return spring.
12. Connect the accelerator shaft to the throttle shaft.
13. Connect the electrical leads to the throttle solenoid and deceleration valve.
14. Connect the distributor vacuum line.
15. Connect the fuel supply and return lines.
16. Connect and adjust the choke cable and if equipped, the cruise control cable.
17. Install the air cleaner and air inlet duct. Connect the negative battery cable.
18. Run the engine and check for fuel leaks.

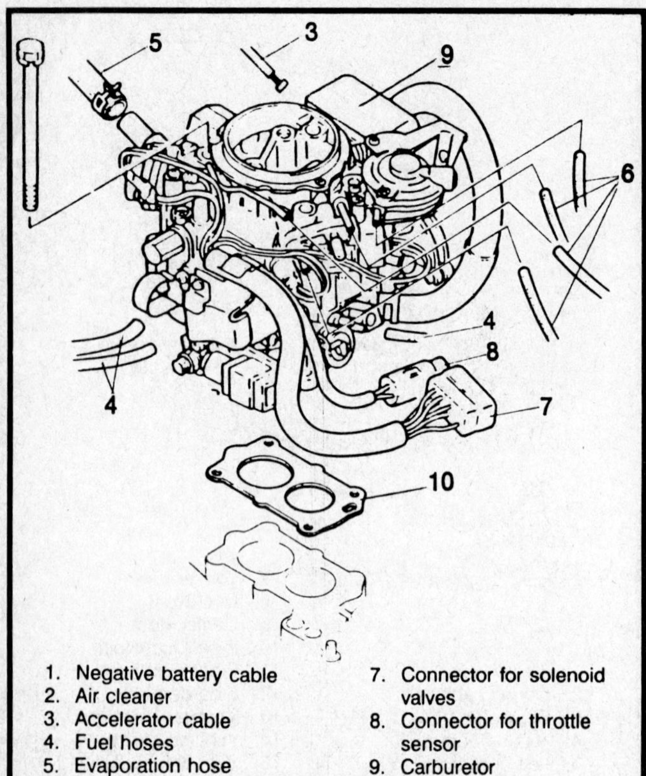

1. Negative battery cable
2. Air cleaner
3. Accelerator cable
4. Fuel hoses
5. Evaporation hose
6. Vacuum hoses
7. Connector for solenoid valves
8. Connector for throttle sensor
9. Carburetor
10. Gasket

Carburetor mounting—all engines

Fuel Pump

MECHANICAL

Removal and Installation

1982–86

1. Disconnect and plug the inlet, outlet and return hoses at the fuel pump.
2. Remove the fuel pump mounting bolts and remove the fuel pump, insulator and gaskets.
3. Clean and inspect the mounting surfaces of the fuel pump and engine
4. Using a new gasket with sealer, install the fuel pump on the engine and tighten the bolts to 11–14 ft. lbs.
5. Connect the fuel lines, run the engine and check for leaks.

ELECTRIC

Removal and Installation

1987–88

NOTE: On 1987–88 models, the electric fuel pump is mounted inside the fuel tank. Removing the fuel pump, requires that the fuel tank be drained and removed from the vehicle. When draining the fuel tank, check the fuel level with the gauge before draining the tank. Estimate how much fuel is in the tank and have enough containers to drain the fuel into.

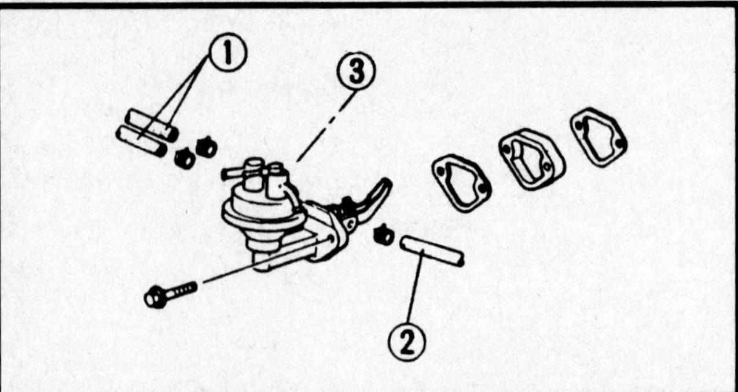

1986–88 2.0L and 2.2L engines fuel pump and components

1. Disconnect the negative battery cable. Raise and support the vehicle safely.
2. Disconnect the fuel pump and sending unit wires at the connector, next to the tank.
3. Remove the fuel tank drain plug and drain the fuel tank into approved containers. With the fuel tank drained, support the tank.
4. Remove the fuel tank mounting straps and lower the tank enough to disconnect the fuel hoses. Disconnect the fuel filler hose at the fuel tank.

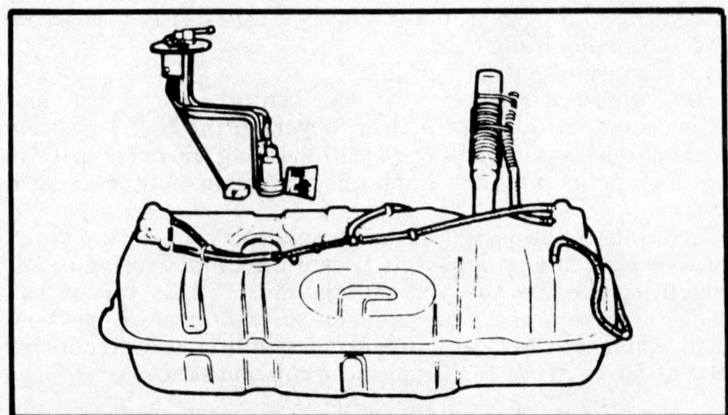

Installation of electric fuel pump in fuel tank

5. Disconnect and tag the fuel hoses at the fuel pump.
6. Remove the fuel tank from the vehicle.
7. Installation is the reverse of the removal procedure. Check the fuel pump operation when finished.

EMISSION CONTROLS

Emission Control Systems

1982–85 2.0L ENGINE

Crankcase Emission Control Systems
Closed Ventilation System
Positive Crankcase Ventilation (PCV) Valve
Oil Separater

Evaporative Emission Control Systems
Charcoal Canister
Water Thermo Valve
Air Cleaner
Fuel Vapor Valve
Purge Control Valve
Evaporative Shutter Valve

Exhaust Emission Control Systems
Fuel Cut Valve
Fuel Check Valve
Intake Air Temperature System
Air Injection Control System (California Only)
Vacuum Delay Valve
Exhaust Gas Recirculation (EGR) Valve
Vacuum Amplifier
EGR Solenoid Valve
Engine Speed Switch (California Only)
Catalytic Converter
Deceleration Control System
Air By-pass Valve (California Only)
Throttle Position Sensor (All Except Canada)

Emission Control Systems

1986–88 2.0L, 2.2L AND 2.6L ENGINES

Crankcase Emission Control Systems
Closed Ventilation System
Positive Crankcase Ventilation (PCV) Valve
Oil Separater

Evaporative Emission Control Systems
Charcoal Canister
High Altitude Compensator
Coasting Richer Soleniod Valve
Electronic Control Unit
Dash Pot
Duty Solenoid Valve
Idle Compensator
EGR Position Sensor
Idle Switch
Water Thermo Valve
Air Cleaner
Fuel Vapor Valve
Purge Control Valve
Evaporative Shutter Valve

Exhaust Emission Control Systems
Fuel Cut Valve
Fuel Check Valve
Jet Valve (1987–88 2.6L Only)
Intake Air Temperature System
Vacuum Delay Valve
Exhaust Gas Recirculation (EGR) Valve
EGR Solenoid Valve
Engine Speed Switch (California Only)

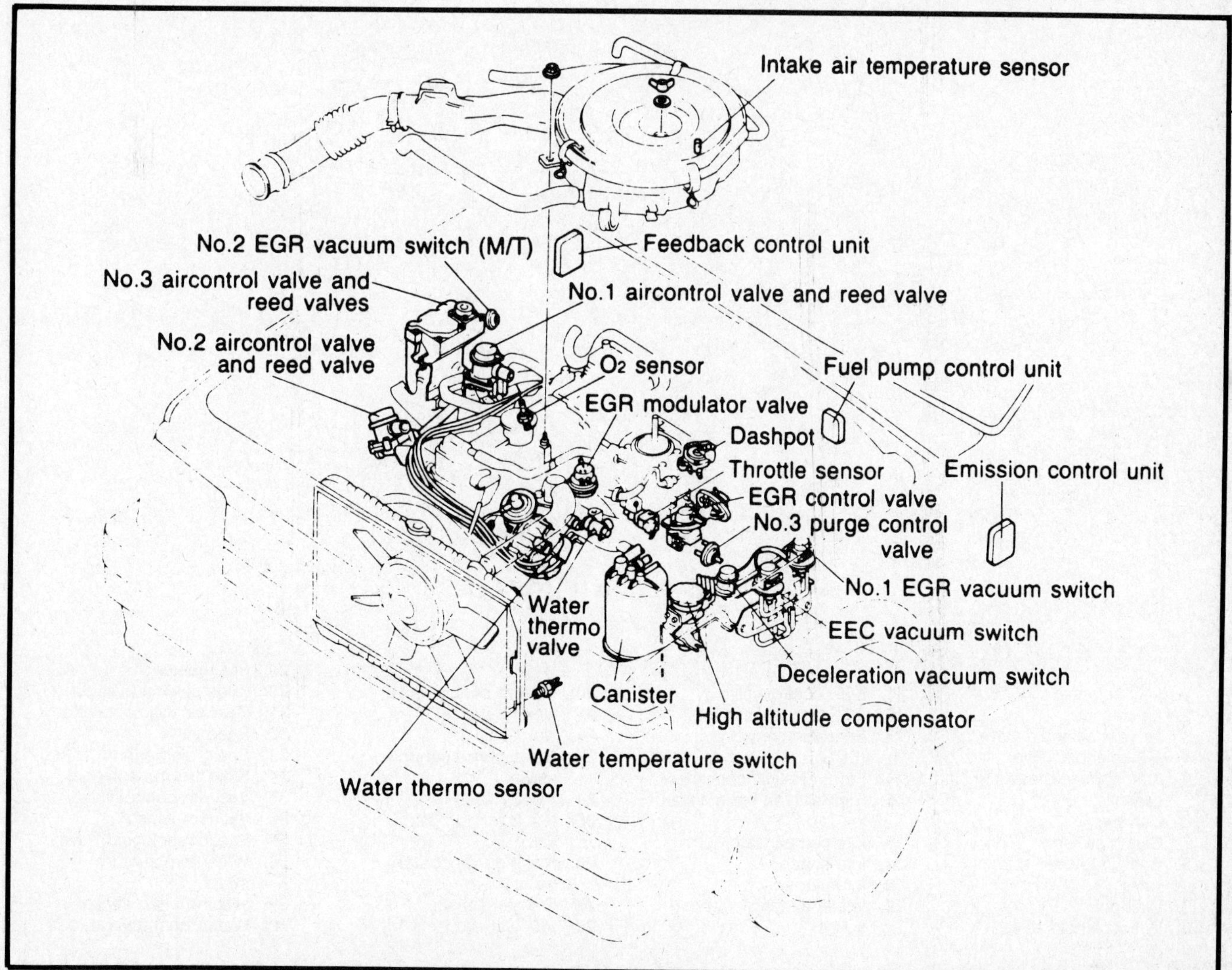

1987–88 2.6L engine emission control system component location

Front and Rear Catalytic Converters
Servo Diaphragm
Deceleration Control System
Throttle Position Sensor (All Except Canada)

Crankcase Emission Control Systems

A closed crankcase ventilation system is used to prevent blow-by gases from escaping into the atmosphere. The system has a positive (one-way) crankcase vent valve (PCV valve) at the rocker arm cover. Blow-by gases are drawn through two passages; one by a rubber vent hose from the rocker arm cover through the PCV valve into the intake manifold and the other by a rubber hose from the rocker arm cover to the air cleaner.

PCV VALVE

Removal and Installation

1. Check the PCV valve for operation, the oil separator and oil return pipe (if equipped) for clogging and leaks.
2. Check the PCV valve by removing the valve and the hose

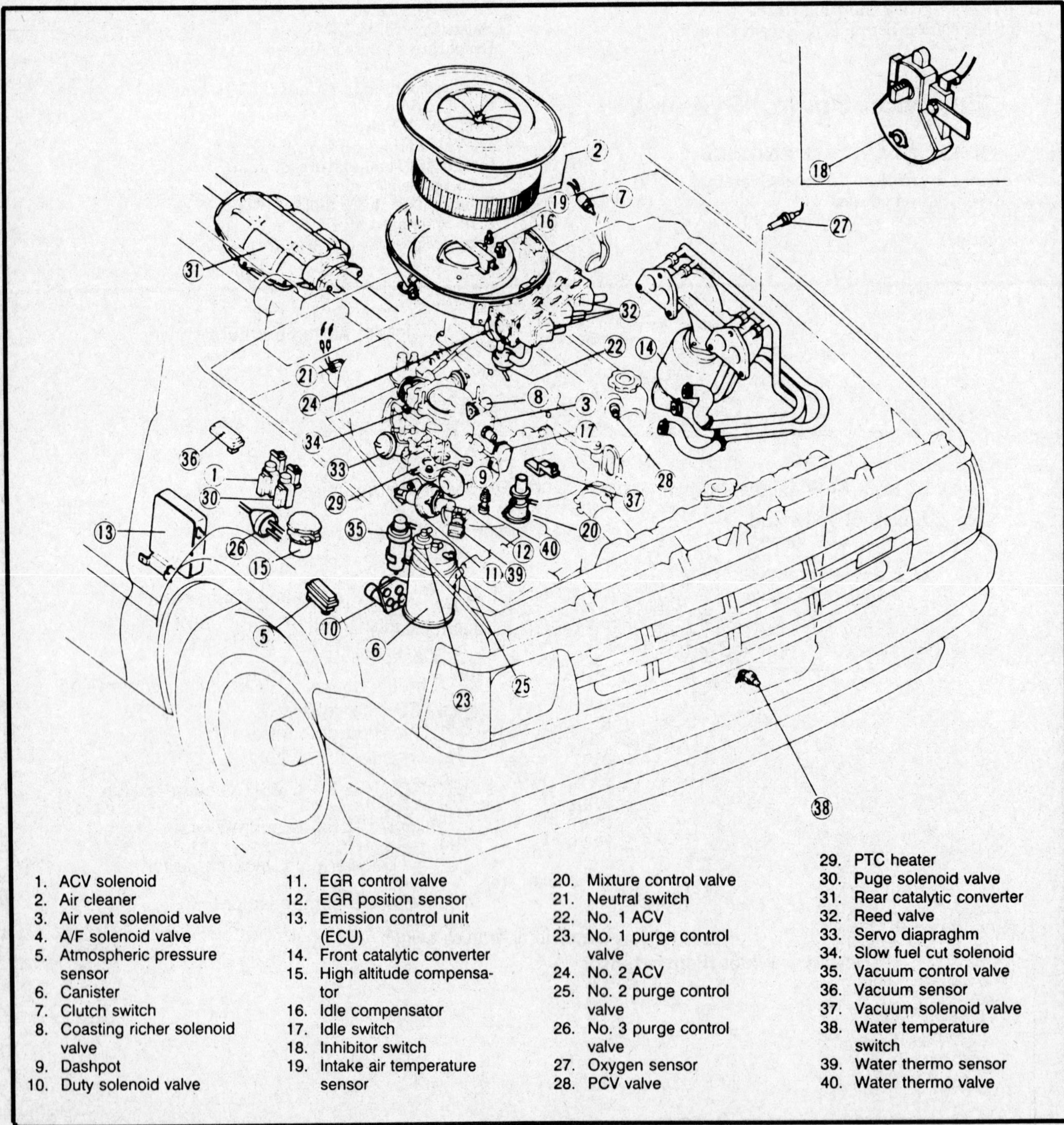

1986–88 2.0L and 2.2L engines emission control system component location

from the rocker cover while the engine is at idle speed. If the valve is not clogged, a hissing noise will be heard and strong vacuum will be felt when a finger is placed over the bottom of the valve.

3. Shut off the engine and disconnect the PCV valve from the hose. Blow through the threaded end. If air will not pass through, the valve is clogged and replacement will be required.

Evaporative Emission Control Systems

When the engine is not operating, fuel vapor generated inside the fuel tank is absorbed and stored in the charcoal canister. When the engine is running, the fuel vapor absorbed in the canister is drawn into the air intake hose through the purge valve. The purge valve is kept closed at idle when vacuum reaches a pre-set value the valve opens. On carbureted models, a bowl vent valve controls carburetor vapors. When vacuum reaches a pre-set level, the vapors are allowed to pass into the intake manifold.

CANISTER

Checking, Removal and Installation

1. Replace any hoses that are cracked or broken. Replace any canister that is damaged.
2. When the canister is in service over a long period of time, the interior filter will become clogged requiring canister replacement. Always replace the hoses when renewing the canister.
3. Disconnect all hoses and clamps at both ends of the canister and from the purge valve. Unclamp or remove the canister mounting bands and remove the canister assembly.

THERMO VALVE

Checking, Removal and Installation

1. The thermo valve is located on the intake manifold or cylinder head where it's bottom will be immersed in coolant. It discharges into the purge control valve located near the charcoal canister. Disconnect the vacuum/pressure line coming from the thermo valve to the purge control valve and connect a vacuum gauge into the open end of the hose.
2. The engine must be overnight cold. Start the engine and run it at about 2000 rpm to get the throttle past the purge port.
3. The gauge should indicate zero vacuum pressure when the engine is started and, by the time thermostat opens and coolant begins to circulate in the radiator, there should be pressure or vacuum. Replace the thermo valve if pressure and/or vacuum exists.

PURGE CONTROL VALVE

Checking, Removal and Installation

1. Once the intake vacuum exists and the hose connections are inspected, the purge control valve can be tested. With the engine warm, disconnect the large vacuum line passing from the purge valve to the canister. Use a vacuum gauge to verify that when the engine speed is increased, there is vacuum at the end of the line.
2. If there is no vacuum, verify the test by disconnecting the large vacuum line going into the purge control valve from the intake manifold. If there is vacuum there when the engine speed is increased, but not on the canister side of the purge control valve and the thermo valve is working, replace the canister purge valve.

Exhaust Emission Control Systems

JET AIR VALVE

1987–88 2.6L engines contain a jet air valve in the cylinder head. A jet air passage is provided in the carburetor, intake manifold and cylinder head. Air flows through the passages and when the jet valve opens, into combustion chambers. Air provided by the jet valve leans out the fuel mixture.

Removal and Installation

1. Remove the cylinder head from the engine.
2. Remove the jet valve from the cylinder head using socket wrench 49 U012 007 or equivalent.

CAUTION

When removing the jet valve from the cylinder head, make certain that the wrench is not tilted with respect to the centerline of the valve. Failure to do so, may result in damage to the valve, cylinder head and/or valve guide.

3. With the valve removed, remove the valve spring and retainer from the valve, using spring compressor 49 P005 100 or equivalent.
4. Check that the valve moves easily in and out of the guide.
5. Check the face of the valve and valve guide for damage or sticking.
6. If found to be defective, replace the valve and guide as an assembly.
7. Check the valve spring for damage. Replace if necessary.
8. To install, apply oil to the valve guide and install the valve in the guide.
9. Compress the valve spring and install the retainer.
10. Install a new O-ring on the valve body. Coat the O-ring with engine oil.
11. Install the valve in the cylinder head and torque the valve to 13–15 ft. lbs. using socket wrench 49 U102 007 or equivalent.
12. Install the cylinder head on the engine.

CATALYTIC CONVERTER

Two Catalytic Converters are used for the purpose of decreasing harmful exhaust emissions. The converters are installed in the exhaust system, one at the exhaust manifold and one rearward before the muffler.

Inspection, Removal and Installation

1. Check the catalytic converter for deterioration, damage or restrictions.
2. Check the insulator cover for damage, corrosion and fit.
3. The front catalytic converter is replaced by disconnecting the exhaust system at the converter and disconnecting the converter from the exhaust manifold.
4. Always use new gaskets when installing the converter.
5. The rear converter is replaced in the same order as a muffler.

CAUTION

When replacing the rear converter, use caution not to install the converter with the insulation cover touching the floor of the vehicle. The extreme heat of a converter could ignite the paint or under coating and cause a fire.

SECONDARY AIR SYSTEM

Secondary air systems are used to supply air into the exhaust system for the purpose of promoting oxidation of exhaust emissions into the converter and to control the O_2 signal for the emission control system.

Inspection

1. Remove the top of the air cleaner and air filter. Run the engine until it reaches normal operating temperature.
2. Increase the engine speed to 1500 rpm and check that air is being pulled in through the reed valves in the air cleaner.
3. Increase the engine speed to 3000 rpm and check that no exhaust gases are coming out of the air inlet port.
4. If either is incorrect, replace the reed valve.
5. Disconnect and plug the vacuum line at the No. 2 air control valve.
6. Increase the engine speed to 1500 rpm and make sure that air is being pulled in at the valve. If not, replace the valve.
7. With the No. 2 air control valve vacuum line still plugged, apply 3.54 in. Hg of vacuum to the No. 2 air control valve. Increase the engine speed to 1500 rpm.
8. Check that air is being pulled in at the No. 1 air control valve. If not, replace the No. 2 valve.
9. Stop the engine and disconnect the water temperature sensor connector.
10. Start and run the engine at idle. Check that there is no vacuum at the No. 2 air control valve.
11. Increase the engine speed to 1500 rpm and check that there is vacuum at the vacuum hose.
12. If either is incorrect, replace the ACV solenoid.
13. Turn off the engine and reconnect the vacuum hoses and water temperature switch connector.

Removal and Installation

If after inspection a component is found defective, removal and installation is accomplished by disconnecting the vacuum lines to the defective component and installing the new component on the lines.

EGR SYSTEM

Exhaust gas recirculation (EGR) is used to reduce oxides of nitrogen in the exhaust by recirculating a portion of the exhaust gases back into the intake manifold below the air/fuel source. These gases are then reburned to promote less emissions.

Inspection, Removal and Installation

1. Check the vacuum hose to the EGR valve for cracks or cuts, replace any if necessary.
2. Start the engine and run at idle speed. Run the engine to 2500 rpm and check the secondary EGR valve. If the secondary EGR valve is operating, the thermo valve is defective.
3. Warm the engine to about 131°F. The secondary EGR valve should operate when the engine is at 2500 rpm. If the valve is not operating, check the EGR control valve and the thermo valve.
4. Disconnect the green stripped hose from the thermo valve. Connect a hand vacuum pump to the thermo valve and apply vacuum. If no vacuum passes, the thermo valve is good.
5. Disconnect the green stripped hose from the carburetor fitting and connect the hose to the hand pump.
6. Open the sub EGR valve by hand and apply approx. 6 in. of vacuum to the valve.
7. If the idle speed becomes unstable, the secondary EGR valve is operating properly. If the idle speed remains unchanged, the EGR valve is not working. Replace the EGR valve.
8. When replacing the valve, always use a new gasket.

Trouble Codes

Diagnosis Procedure

1986–88

When the Electronic Control Unit (ECU) finds a problem in the system, it will record a trouble code in it's memory. Trouble codes can be identified by a series of light flashes and a buzzer while using a Self Diagnosis Checker, Part No. 49 H018 9A1, or an equivalent.

Inspection Procedure

1. Connect the Self Diagnosis Checker to the check connector located at the firewall where the wiring harness protrudes.
2. Ground the check connector with a jumper wire.
3. Turn the ignition switch to the ON position.
4. Check that the number 88 flashes on the checker.
5. If 88 does not flash, check the connections.
6. If 88 flashes and the buzzer sounds continuously for more than 20 seconds, replace the ECU and start the procedure again.
7. Note the code number displayed and repair as necessary.

Reset Maintenance Lamp

Procedure

1. Disconnect the negative battery cable for at least five seconds and then reconnect it.
2. Turn the ignition switch on for at least six seconds.
3. Run the engine for at least four minutes at 2000 rpm.
4. Check to make sure that there are no codes displayed.

TROUBLECODES

Code	Location of Malfunction
01	IG Impulse Circuit
09	Water Thermo Sensor or Circuit
13	Vacuum Sensor or Circuit
14	Atmospheric Pressure Sensor
15	O_2 Sensor or Circuit
16	EGR Control System
17	Feedback System
18	A/F Solenoid Circuit or Valve
22	Slow Fuel Cut Solenoid or Valve
23	Coasting Richer Solenoid or Circuit
26	Purge Solenoid Valve or Circuit
28	Duty Solenoid Vacuum Valve
29	Duty Solenoid Vent Valve
30	ACV Solenoid Valve or Circuit
35	Idle-Up Solenoid Valve
45	Vacuum Solenoid Valve or Circuit

Trouble code identification chart

Terminal	Connection to	Voltage with ignition ON	Voltage various conditions
1A (output)	No 1 EGR solenoid valve	0 – 0 6V at normal operating temp	0 – 0 6V at idle
1B (ground)		0V	0V at idle
1C (input)	No 1 EGR vacuum switch	0 – 0 6V	0 – 0 6V at idle Approx 12V at 3 000 rpm
1D (input)	Ignition coil	Approx 0 9V	Approx 5V at idle
1E (output)	No 2 EGR solenoid valve	0 – 0 6V at operating temperature	0 – 0 6 V at idle Approx 12V at 2 500 rpm
1F (input)	Battery	Approx 12V	Approx 12V at idle
1H (output)	EEC solenoid valve	Approx 12V	Approx. 12V at idle
1J (input)	Water temp switch	0V (12 – 13V below 17°C (63°F))	0V at idle
1K (input)	No 2 EGR vacuum switch (M/T only)	0 – 0 6V	0 – 0 6V at idle
1L (output)	No. 3 AIS solenoid valve	0 – 0 6V	0V at idle
2A	Battery	12V	12 – 15V at idle
2B (power supply)	Air vent solenoid valve	Approx. 12V	12 – 15V at idle
2C (input)	Ignition coil (—) terminal	Approx 0 9V	Approx 5V at idle
2D (power supply)	Air vent solenoid valve	Approx 12V	12 – 15V at idle
2E (ground) 2F	Engine ground	0V	0V at idle
2H (input)	Deceleration vacuum switch	Approx. 12V	0 – 1V at idle
2I (input)	Water thermo sensor	Approx 2 2V (normal operating temp)	Approx 2 2V (25°C (77°F)) at idle
2J (input)	Intake air temperature sensor	Approx. 2 2V (normal operating temp)	Approx. 2 2V (25°C (77°F)) at idle
2K (input)	Throttle sensor TVO terminal	0 – 0 6V (4 – 4 5V accelerator pedal depressed)	0 – 0 6V
2L (input)	Throttle sensor Vref terminal	Approx. 5V	Approx. 5V at idle
2M (input)	O_2 sensor	0V	0 – 1V at idle
2N (input)	Water thermo sensor Intake air temp. sensor Throttle sensor	0V	0V at idle
3A (output)	A/C cut relay	0 – 0 6V	0 – 0 6V at idle
3B (output)	Enrichment solenoid valve	Approx 12V	12 – 15V at idles Approx 5V at quick acceleration (A/T)
3C (output)	Distributor vacuum solenoid valve	0V	0V at idle 13 – 15V at 2,000 rpm
3D (output)	No 1 AIS solenoid valve	0 – 0 6V (normal operating temp)	11 – 13V at idle, after warm up 0 – 0 6V at quick deceleration, from 2,000 rpm
3F (output)	Idle-up solenoid valve	0 – 0 6 V	13 – 15V 2,000 rpm with A/C switch ON
3G (output)	Jet mixture solenoid valve	Approx. 12V	2 – 10V at idle
3H (output)	Slow fuel cut solenoid valve	0 – 0 6V	0 – 0 6V at idle 12 – 15V at quick deceleration

Connector

2M	2K	2I		2E	2C	2A
2N	2L	2J	2H	2F	2D	2B

3G		3C	3A
3H	3F	3D	3B

Feedback control unit

1K	1I		1E	1C	1A
1L	1J	1H	1F	1D	1B

Emission control unit

Checking the emission and feedback systems with a voltmeter

ENGINE MECHANICAL

Refer to the Unit Overhaul Section for General Engine Overhaul Procedures.

Engine

Removal and Installation

GASOLINE ENGINES

1. Matchmark and remove the hood.
2. Drain the cooling system.
3. Disconnect the battery cables, negative first and remove the battery.
4. Remove the air cleaner and the engine oil dipstick.
5. Remove the radiator shroud and the engine fan. Place the fan in an upright position to avoid fluid loss from the fan clutch. Remove the radiator.
6. Disconnect and tag all wires, hoses, cables, pipes and linkage from the engine.
7. Remove the 3-way and duty solenoid valves without disconnecting the vacuum hoses. Remove the charcoal canister.
8. Disconnect the exhaust pipe at the exhaust manifold and remove the exhaust manifold.
9. Without disconnecting the refrigerant lines, disconnect the A/C compressor from the mounts and support it out of the way.
10. Disconnect the power steering pump from the engine and support it out of the way without disconnecting any hoses.
11. Raise and support the vehicle safely. Remove the engine splash shield and drain the engine oil.
12. Disconnect and tag the starter wiring and remove the starter.
13. Support the transmission and remove the transmission to engine mounting bolts.
14. Remove the engine support plates and mounting nuts. Lower the vehicle.
15. Remove the engine from the vehicle by pushing the engine forward to clear the transmission.

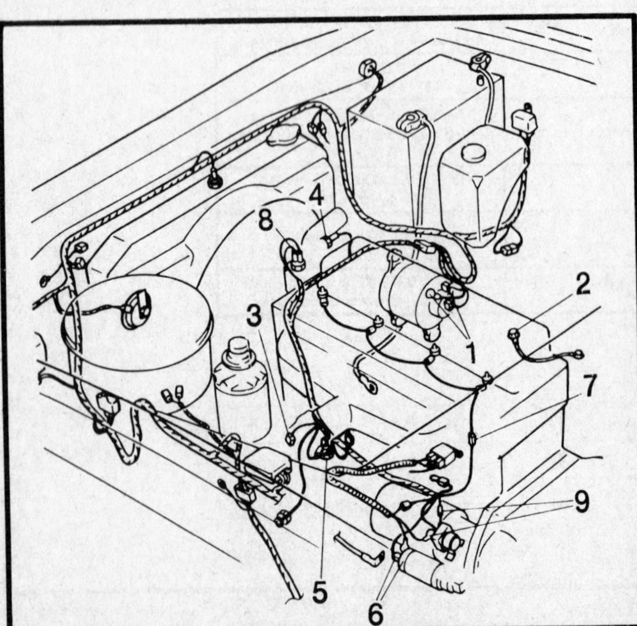

Electrical disconnections for engine removal

16. Installation is the reverse of the removal procedure. Torque the engine mounting nuts to 26–47 ft. lbs. and the exhaust manifold-to-engine nuts to 16–21 ft. lbs.

DIESEL ENGINE

1. Matchmark and remove the hood. Drain the cooling system.
2. Disconnect the battery cables, negative first and remove the battery.
3. Remove the air cleaner and engine oil dipstick.
4. Remove the radiator shroud and engine fan. Place the fan in an upright position to avoid fluid loss from the fan clutch.
5. Disconnect and tag all wires, hoses, cables, pipes and linkage from the engine.
6. Remove the clutch release cylinder from the transmission.
7. Remove the engine oil cooler and radiator.
8. Disconnect the exhaust pipe at the manifold and remove the exhaust manifold.
9. Without disconnecting any refrigerant lines, disconnect the A/C compressor from the mounts and position it out of the way.
10. Disconnect the power steering pump and position it out of the way without disconnecting the hoses.
11. Raise and support the vehicle safely. Remove the engine splash shield and drain the engine oil.
12. Support the engine to take up the weight of the engine off of the mounts.
13. Support the transmission and remove the transmission to engine mounting bolts.
14. Remove the engine support plates and mounting nuts. Lower the vehicle.
15. Remove the engine by pushing the engine forward to clear the transmission and lift it out of the vehicle.
16. Installation is the reverse of the removal procedure.

Intake Manifold

Removal and Installation

GASOLINE ENGINES

1. Drain the cooling system.
2. Remove the air cleaner.
3. Disconnect the accelerator linkage from the carburetor.
4. Disconnect the choke cable and fuel line. Plug the fuel line.
5. Disconnect the PCV valve hose.
6. Disconnect the heater return hose and by-pass hose.
7. Remove the intake manifold to cylinder head mounting nuts.
8. Remove the manifold and carburetor as an assembly.
9. Clean and inspect the gasket mating surfaces.
10. Install a new gasket and the manifold on the studs. Torque the mounting nuts to 14–19 ft. lbs., working from the center outward.
11. Connect the PCV valve hose to the manifold.
12. Connect the by-pass and heater return hoses.
13. Connect the accelerator linkage.
14. Connect the fuel line and choke cable.
15. Install the air cleaner.
16. Fill the cooling system. Run the engine and check for leaks.

Exhaust Manifold

Removal and Installation

GASOLINE ENGINES

1. Raise and support the vehicle safely.
2. Disconnect the exhaust pipe from the exhaust manifold. Remove the exhaust manifold heat shield.

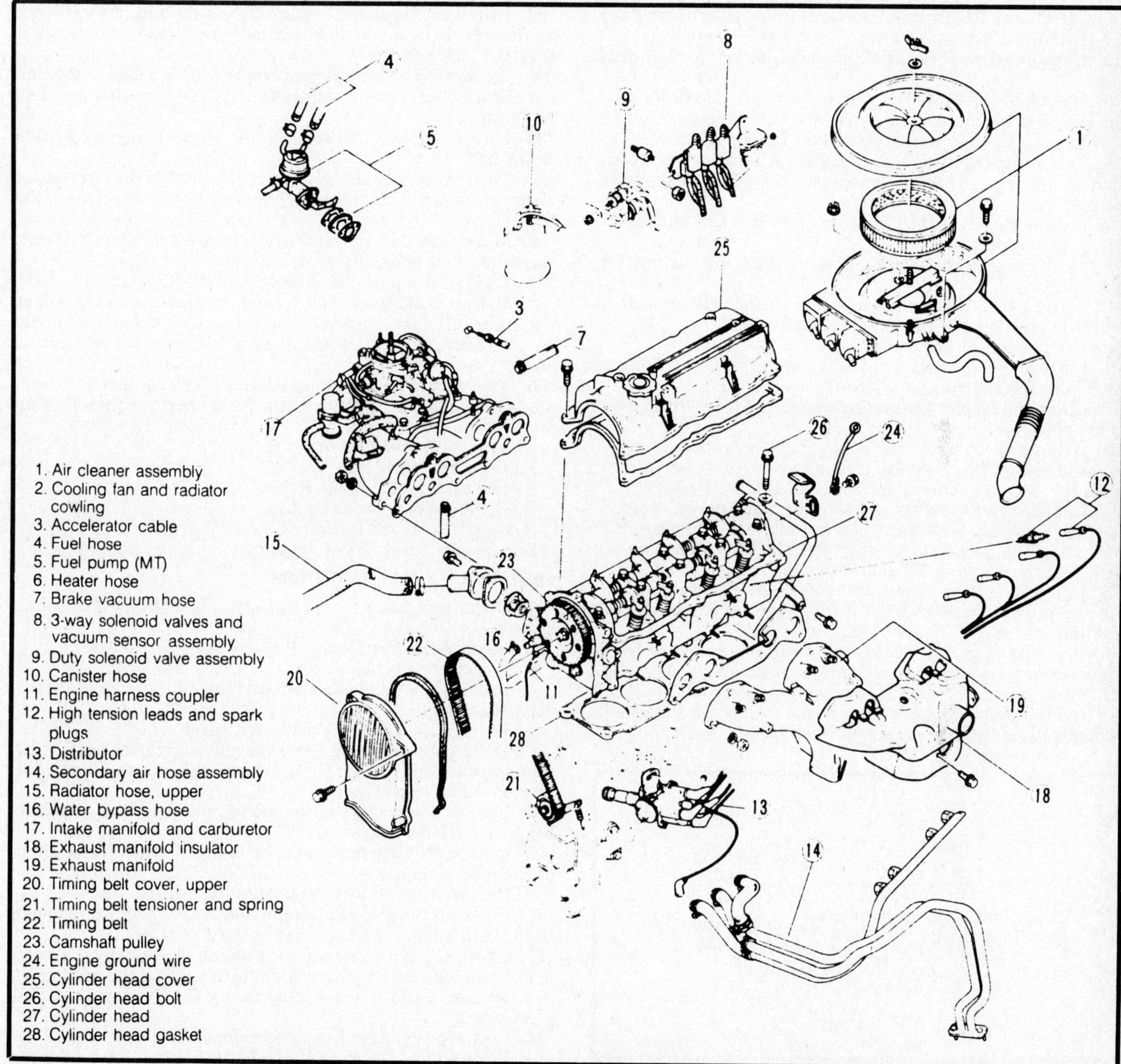

1986–88 2.0L and 2.2L engine assembly upper half – exploded view

3. Remove the exhaust manifold mounting nuts and remove the manifold.
4. To install, apply a light film of grease to the exhaust manifold mating surfaces before installation.
5. Install the manifold on the studs and install the mounting nuts. Torque the attaching nuts to 16–21 ft. lbs.
6. Install a new exhaust pipe gasket. Connect the exhaust pipe to the exhaust manifold and torque the nuts to 16–21 ft. lbs.

Cylinder Head

Removal and Installation

1982–86 2.0L GASOLINE ENGINE

NOTE: The engine must be cold whenever removing or installing the cylinder head.

1. Matchmark and remove the hood. Drain the cooling system.
2. Remove the air cleaner.
3. Disconnect, and tag, all wires, hoses, cables, pipes and linkage from the cylinder head.
4. Remove the 3-way and duty solenoid valves without disconnecting the vacuum tubes.
5. Remove the charcoal canister.
6. Remove the distributor cap. Matchmark the rotor position to the distributor body and the distributor body to cylinder head position. Remove the distributor. Remove the spark plugs.
7. Remove the intake manifold and carburetor as an assembly.
8. Remove the exhaust manifold.
9. Disconnect and tag the alternator wiring and remove the alternator.

10. Disconnect the air injection pipes from the cylinder head.
11. Remove the drive belt, fan pulley, hub and bracket.
12. If equipped, remove the air conditioning compressor drive belt.
13. If equipped, remove the power steering pump drive belt.
14. Remove the crankshaft pulley and baffle plate.
15. Remove the upper, then the lower timing belt covers.
16. Rotate the crankshaft so that the "A" mark on the camshaft pulley is at the top, aligned with the notch in the front housing.
17. Loosen the timing belt tensioner lock bolt and remove the tensioner spring.
18. Mark the forward rotation of the belt for installation. Remove the belt.
19. Insert a tool through the hole in the camshaft sprocket to hold it in position and remove the sprocket bolt.
20. Remove the rocker cover.
21. Remove the cylinder head bolts and remove the cylinder head from the engine.
22. Clean and inspect the mating surfaces of the cylinder head and engine.
23. Using a new gasket, install the cylinder head and tighten the head bolts to 60–64 ft. lbs. If new head bolts are being used, make sure to use the new, surface treated plain washers.
24. Install the camshaft pulley with the dowel pin on the camshaft engaging the pulley slot just below the "A" mark on the pulley. Tighten the bolt to 40–48 ft. lbs. The timing mark on the front housing and the "A" mark must be aligned.
25. Lubricate the distributor O-ring with clean engine oil, align all the matchmarks made during removal and install the distributor.
26. Replace the timing belt if it has been contaminated by oil or grease, or shows any sign of damage, wear, cracks or peeling.
27. Make sure that the timing mark on the camshaft is aligned and that the timing mark (notch) on the crankshaft sprocket is aligned with the triangular shaped mark on the front housing.

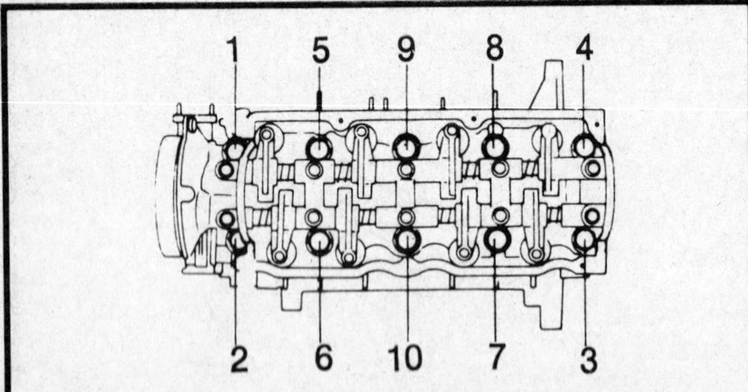

1986–88 2.0L and 2.2L engines cylinder head bolt removal sequence

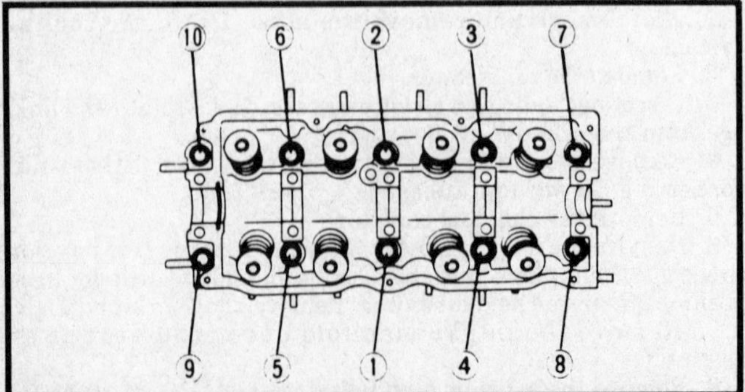

1986–88 2.0L and 2.2L engines cylinder head bolt torque sequence

28. Install the tensioner and spring, positioning the tensioner all the way to the intake manifold side and temporarily secure it with the lock bolt.
29. Install the belt onto the sprockets from left side. If the timing belt is being reused, install the belt in the direction as when removed.
30. Loosen the lock bolt so that the tensioner applies tension to the belt.
31. Turn the crankshaft two full revolutions in the direction of normal rotation. This will apply equal tension to all points of the belt.
32. Make sure that the timing marks are still aligned. If not, repeat the belt installation procedure.
33. Tighten the tensioner lock bolt to 30–35 ft. lbs.
34. Measure the timing belt tension by pressing on the belt at the midpoint of the longest straight run. Belt deflection should be 11–13mm. If not, repeat the belt adjustment procedure, above.
35. The remainder of the installtion is the reverse of the removal procedure. Observe the following torques during installation:

Timing belt covers: 80 inch lbs.
Fan bracket: 40 ft. lbs.
Exhaust manifold: 16–21 ft. lbs.
Intake manifold: 14–19 ft. lbs.
Spark plugs: 11–17 ft. lbs.
Rocker arm cover: 24–36 inch lbs.

1987–88 2.0 & 2.2L ENGINES

1. Disconnect the negatve battery cable. Drain the cooling system.
2. Remove the air cleaner. Remove the spark plugs.
3. Remove the rocker cover.
4. Remove the intake and exhaust manifolds from the cylinder head.
5. Remove the camshaft drive belt cover.
6. Loosen the drive belt tensioner and slip the belt off of the cam sprocket and tensioner. It is not necessary to remove the tensioner from the head.
7. Remove the coolant outlet elbow, with the hose attached, from the cylinder head.
8. Loosen the cylinder head bolts evenly, in the reverse order of the torque sequence.
9. Remove the cylinder head from the engine.
10. Clean all the gasket material and sealer from the cylinder head, engine block, rocker cover and water outlet..
11. Check the cylinder head for flatness. It should not exceed 0.003 in. in any 6 in. span, or 0.006 in. overall. If the head must be machined, do not remove more than 0.010 in. from the original surface.
12. Clean the cylinder head and engine bolt holes.
13. Place a new gasket on the cylinder block.
14. Position the camshaft with the pin in position.

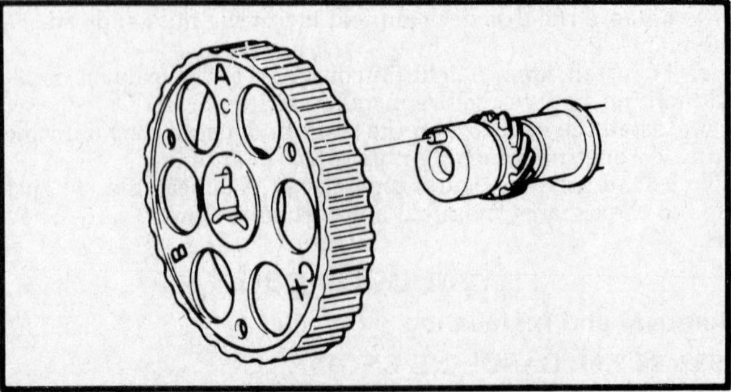

1986–88 2.0L and 2.2L engines camshaft pin alignment with timing mark

15. Lower the head carefully onto the block and gasket.
16. Lightly oil the threads of the cylinder head bolts before installation. Torque the bolts to specification in at least three passes, increasing the amount of torque used each time.
17. Slip the camshaft drive belt back over the cam sprocket and tensioner, then adjust the camshaft timing.
18. Install the camshaft drive belt cover. Make sure the two spacers are installed correctly. Tighten the bolts to 6–13 ft. lb.
19. Install the water outlet elbow and a new gasket onto the cylinder head. Tighten the bolts to 12–15 ft. lb.
20. Install the intake and exhaust manifolds.
21. Install the rocker cover, using a new gasket. Install the air cleaner. Install the spark plugs and wires.
22. Fill the cooling system. Adjust the valve lash, if necessary. Run the engine and check for leaks.

1987–88 2.6L GASOLINE ENGINE

NOTE: Do not perform this operation on a warm engine. Remove the head bolts in the proper sequence. Loosen the head bolts in even steps a little at a time.

1. Disconnect the negative battery cable. Drain the cooling system and disconnect the upper radiator hose.
2. Remove the breather and purge hose.
3. Remove the air cleaner. Disconnect and plug the fuel line.
4. Remove the vacuum hose at the distributor and purge control valve.
5. Disconnect and tag the spark plug wires at the distributor cap.
6. Remove the distributor cap. Remove the distributor mounting nut and pull the distributor straight out.
7. Disconnect the heater hose at the intake manifold.
8. Disconnect the water temperature gauge unit wire.
9. Place No. 1 piston in the Top Dead Center position to take pressure off the fuel pump rocker arm. Disconnect the fuel hoses and plug the line leading to the gas tank to prevent fuel leakage.
10. Remove the fuel pump mounting nuts and remove the fuel pump. Remove the insulator and gaskets.
11. Disconnect the exhaust pipe at the exhaust manifold flange.
12. Remove the rocker cover.
13. Remove the rocker cover breather and semicircular seal.
14. Loosen the camshaft sprocket bolt and turn the crankshaft until No. 1 piston is at top dead center on compression stroke (both valves closed).

NOTE: Never turn the engine over using the camshaft bolt: it puts undue strain on the chain and other components.

15. Remove the camshaft sprocket bolt and distributor drive gear. Remove the camshaft sprocket and allow it to rest in the chain on the holder below.
16. Starting with the outer bolts and working inwards, remove the cylinder head bolts. Head bolts should be loosened in two or three stages to prevent head warpage.

NOTE: The cylinder head assembly is located with two dowel pins, front and rear, on the cylinder block. When removing, be careful not to slide it, or twist the camshaft sprocket and chain.

17. Remove the cylinder head assembly and cylinder head gasket.
18. Clean all gasket surfaces of cylinder block and cylinder head.
19. Install a new cylinder head gasket. Install the cylinder head assembly.

NOTE: Do not apply sealant to the head gasket and do not reuse an old head gasket.

20. Install the TEN cylinder head bolts. The two bolts at the front extend into the timing case and are not included in the head bolt torqueing sequence. In the illustration, they are labeled No. 11. Starting at top center, Torque all ten cylinder head bolts to 35 ft. lbs. in the proper sequence. Repeat the procedure, this time torque the bolts to 65–72 ft. lbs. (cold engine), (72–80 ft. lbs. hot engine).
21. Torque the two front bolts (No. 11) to 11–15 ft. lbs.
22. Verify that No. 1 cylinder is at top dead center. Align the dowel pin in the end of the camshaft sprocket with the groove in the top of the front camshaft bearing cap and install the camshaft sprocket and chain while pulling up on the sprocket.
23. Install the distributor drive gear and the sprocket bolt.
24. Turn the crankshaft 90° backwards and torque the camshaft sprocket bolt to 37–43 ft. lbs. Slowly turn the engine over two times to make sure the valve timing is correct. If the engine locks at a certain point in these two revolutions, the valve timing is not correct. Repeat Steps 22–24.

CAUTION

Do not turn the engine over using the starter. If the valve timing is off, several of the valves could be bent.

25. Install the breather and semicircular seal to the cylinder head after applying sealant to surface contact points. Install the rocker cover with a new gasket.
26. Connect the exhaust pipe to the exhaust manifold flange. Torque the bolts to 11–18 ft. lbs.
27. Put No. 1 cylinder at top dead center and install the fuel pump with a new gasket and insulator. Connect all hoses.
28. Connect the water temperature gauge unit wire. Connect the heater hose to the intake manifold.
29. Install the distributor, with the rotor pointing to the No. 1

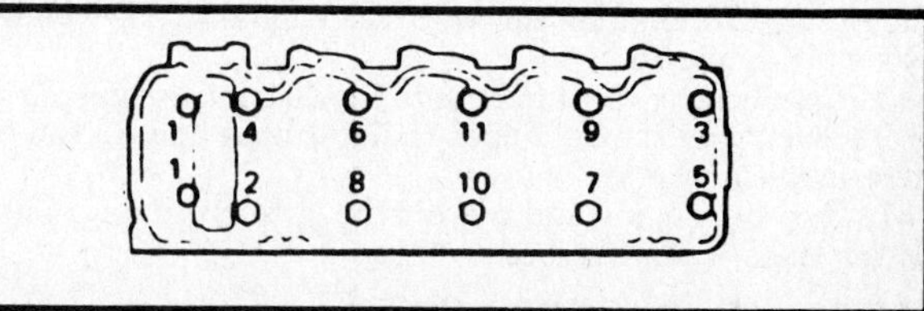

1987–88 2.6L engine cylinder head bolt removal sequence

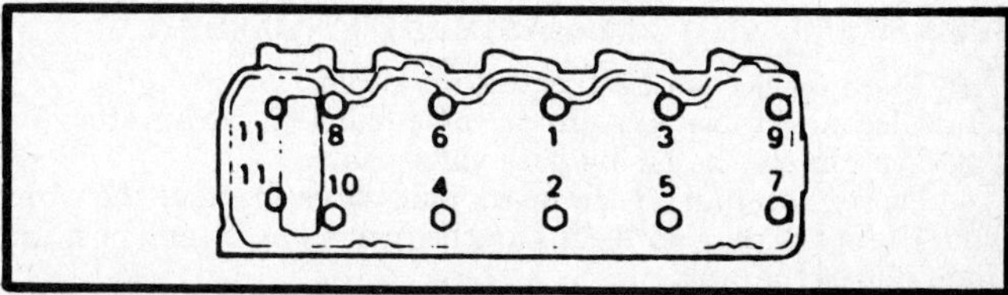

1987–88 2.6L engine cylinder head bolt torque sequence

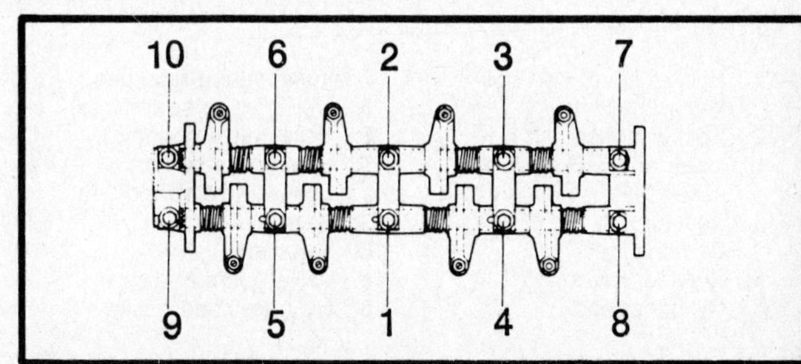

1986–88 2.0L and 2.2L engines rocker arm shaft bolt torque sequence

lug on the distributor cap, with the engine at TDC and in the No. 1 firing position.

30. Connect the vacuum hose to the distributor and purge control valve. Connect the upper radiator hose and fill the cooling system with coolant.

31. Run the engine and correct the ignition timing. Check for water leaks when finished.

Rocker Arms and Shaft

Removal and Installation

1982–88 2.0L AND 2.2L GASOLINE ENGINES

1. Disconnect the negative battery cable.
2. Disconnect the accelerator cable from the carburetor.
3. Disconnect the air by-pass valve cable.
4. Disconnect and tag the spark plug wires. Remove the wires from the spark plug wire clips on the rocker covers and position them out of the way.
5. Remove the rocker cover and discard the gasket.
6. Remove the rocker arm shaft attaching bolts evenly and remove the rocker arm shafts.

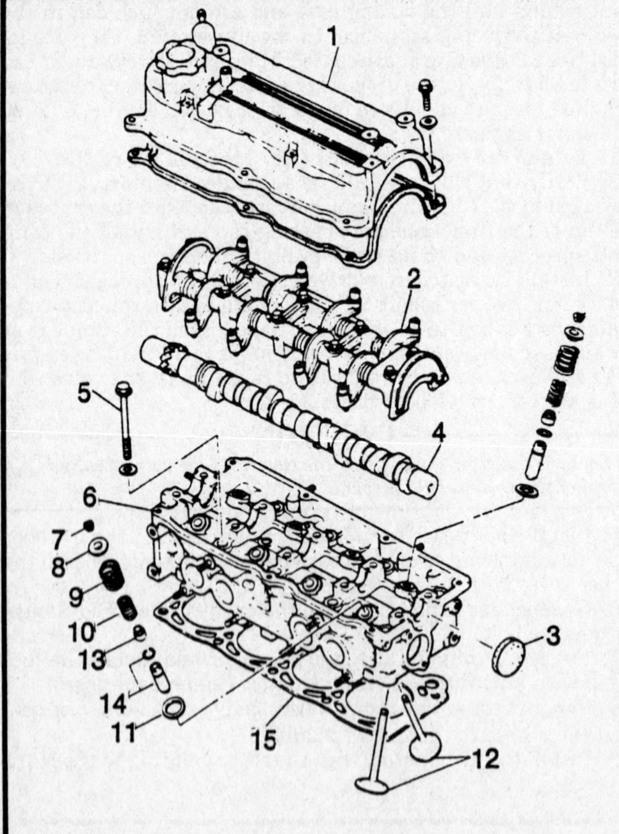

1. Rocker cover and gasket
2. Rocker arms, lash adjuster and rocker shaft assembly
3. Seal cap
4. Camshaft
5. Cylinder head bolt
6. Cylinder head
7. Valve spring retainers
8. Upper valve spring seat
9. Outer valve spring
10. Inner valve spring
11. Lower valve spring seat
12. Valve
13. Valve sael
14. Valve guide and clip
15. Cylinder head gasket

1986–88 2.0L and 2.2L engine cylinder head – exploded view

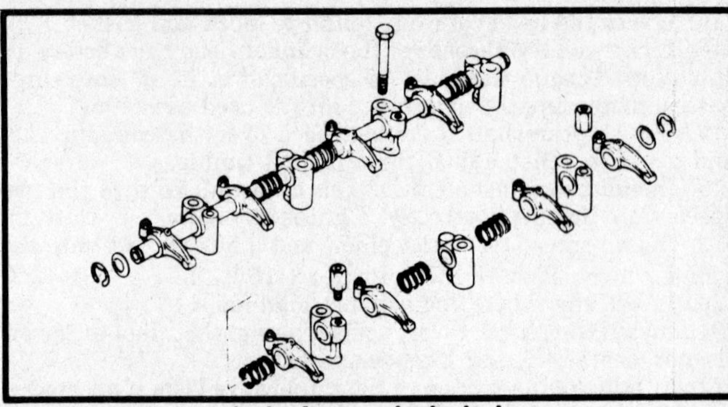

Rocker arms and shaft – exploded view

7. Install the rocker arm assemblies on the cylinder head. Torque the bolts to 13–20 ft. lbs.
8. Check and adjust the valve adjustment.
9. Clean the mating surfaces of the cylinder head and rocker cover.
10. Install the rocker cover with a new gasket. Torque the bolts to 24–36 inch lbs.
11. Install the spark plug wires on the spark plugs. Place the wires in the clips on the rocker cover. Connect the choke and air by-pass valve cable.
12. Start the engine and check for leaks.
13. Allow the engine to reach operating temperature, torque the cylinder head bolts to 60–64 ft. lbs. and adjust the valves lash with the engine hot.

1987–88 2.6L GASOLINE ENGINE

NOTE: On 1987–88 gasoline engines with hydraulic lash adjusters, eight special holders are needed, tool NO. MD998443 or equivalent, to retain the hydraulic lash adjusters when the valve train is disassembled.

1. Disconnect the negative battery cable. Remove the rocker cover. Loosen the camshaft sprocket bolt until it can be turned by hand. The timing mark on the sprocket ends up on the extreme right of the sprocket bolt as viewed from the front. The TDC mark on the front crankshaft pulley must line up with the timing scale on the front cover.
2. Remove the camshaft sprocket bolt without allowing the tension on the timing chain or belt to be lost. Place the sprocket in the sprocket holder of the front cover or lower timing belt cover. Make sure not to loose tension on the belt/chain. Make sure also that the crankshaft is not turned throughout the work. If equipped with hydraulic lash adjusters, put the special clips on the eight hydraulic adjusters at the outer ends of all eight rocker arms. Note that these clips go over the lash adjusters that actuate the large intake valves, not on the small adjusting screw for the smaller jet valves.
3. Loosen, but do not remove the camshaft bearing cap bolts. After all bolts have been loosened, remove them and, holding the ends so the assembly stays together, remove the rocker shaft assembly from the cylinder head. The rearmost cam bearing cap is not associated with the rocker shafts and need not be removed.
4. Keep all parts in original order. Assemble the parts of the rocker assembly as follows:
   a. Install left and right side rocker shafts into the front bearing cap. Notches in the ends of the shaft must be upward. Install the bolts for the front cap to retain the shafts in place. Note that the left rocker shaft is longer than the right rocker shaft.
   b. Install the wave washer onto the left rocker shaft with the bulge forward. Then, coat the inner surfaces of the rockers and the upper bearing surfaces of the bearing caps with clean engine oil and assemble rockers, springs and the re-

maining bearing caps in the order in which removed. Note that the intake rockers are the only ones with the jet valve actuators. Note also that the rockers are labeled for cylinders 1–3 and 2–4 because the direction that the jet valve actuator faces, changes.

c. Use mounting bolts to hold the caps in place after each is assembled. When the assembly is complete, install it onto the head and start all mounting bolts into the head and tighten finger tight.

5. Torque the attaching bolts for the rocker assembly 14–15 ft. lbs. working from the center outward.

6. Without removing tension from the timing chain or belt, lift the sprocket out of the holder and position it against the front of the cam. Make sure the locating tang on the sprocket goes into the hole in the front of the cam.

7. Torque the bolt to 58–72 ft. lbs.

8. Adjust the valve lash.

9. Apply sealant to the top surface of the semicircular seals in the head and then install the valve cover.

Valve Adjustment

Procedure

1982–86 2.0L GASOLINE ENGINES

1. Run the engine until normal operating temperature is reached.

2. Turn off the engine and remove the rocker cover.

3. Torque the cylinder head bolts to 60–64 ft. lbs.

4. Rotate the crankshaft so that the No.1 cylinder is at TDC. This can be determined, by removing the spark plug from the No.1 cylinder and placeing a finger over the spark plug hole while rotating the engine. When compression is felt, the No. 1 cylinder is on the compression stroke. Rotate the engine with a wrench on the crankshaft pulley and stop it at TDC of the compression stroke on the No. 1 cylinder, as confirmed by the alignment of the TDC mark in the crankshaft pulley and the timing pointer.

5. Check the valve clearances with by inserting a feeler gauge between the end of the valve stem and the rocker arm. The clearance can be checked for Nos. 1 and 2 intake valves and Nos. 1 and 3 exhaust valves.

6. If the valve clearance is incorrect, loosen the adjusting screw locknut and adjust the clearance by turning the adjusting screw with the feeler blade inserted. Hold the adjusting screw in the correct position and tighten the locknut. Recheck the clearence.

7. Rotate the crankshaft, in the normal direction of rotation, until No. 4 piston is at TDC compression. Adjust Nos. 3 and 4 intake valves and Nos. 2 and 4 exhaust valves.

8. Install the rocker arm cover and torque the nuts to 18 inch lbs.

1987–88 2.6L GASOLINE ENGINES

NOTE: 1987–88 2.6L engines, are equipped with hydraulic valve lash adjusters. The engines have a third valve called a Jet Valve located beside the intake valve of each cylinder. The Jet valve works off the intake valve rocker arm and injects a swirl of air into the combustion chamber to promote more complete burning of fuel. The Jet Valve must be adjusted on all engines, whether or not the engine has hydraulic lash adjusters. On engines equipped with hydraulic lash adjusters, only the Jet valve must be adjusted. When adjusting valve clearances, the jet valve must be adjusted before the intake valve.

1. Start the engine and allow it to reach normal operating temperature (170–190°F).

2. Stop the engine and remove the air cleaner. Remove the rocker cover.

1982–85 2.0L engine valve adjustment

3. Disconnect the coil-to-distributor wire at the coil.

4. Watch the rocker arms for No. 1 cylinder and rotate the crankshaft until the exhaust valve is closing and the intake valve has just started to open. At this point, No. 4 cylinder will be at top dead center (TDC), commencing its firing stroke.

5. Loosen the lock nut on cylinder No. 4 intake valve and back off the intake valve adjusting screw 2 or more turns.

6. Loosen the lock nut on the jet valve adjusting screw.

7. Turn the jet valve adjusting screw counterclockwise and insert a 0.006 in. feeler gauge between the jet valve stem and the adjusting screw.

8. Tighten the adjusting screw until it touches the feeler gauge. Take care not to press in the valve while adjusting because the jet valve spring is very weak.

NOTE: If the adjusting screw is tight, special care must be taken to avoid pressing down on the jet valve when adjusting the clearance or a false reading will result.

Adjusting valve clearance – 2.0L engine shown – others similar

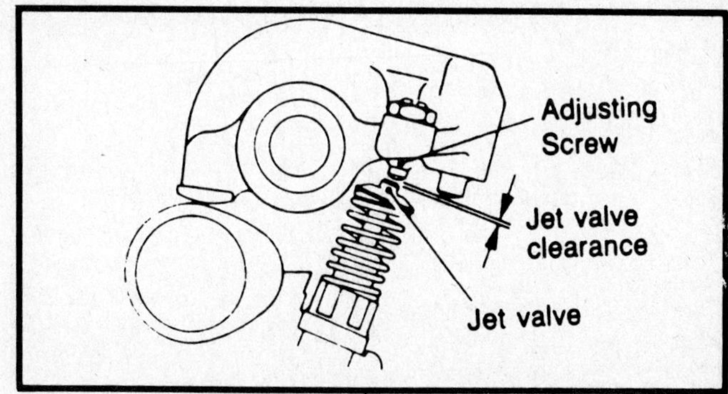

Adjusting Jet Valve clearance – 2.6L engine

9. Tighten the lock nut securely while holding the rocker arm adjusting screw with a screwdriver to prevent it from turning.
10. Make sure that a 0.006 in. feeler gauge can just be inserted between the jet valve and the rocker arm.
11. Adjust No. 4 cylinder's intake valve to 0.006 in. and exhaust valve to 0.010 in. Tighten the adjusting screw locknuts and recheck each clearance.
12. Perform Step 4 in conjunction with the chart to adjust the remaining three cylinders.
13. Install the rocker cover and all other components. Run the engine and check for oil leaks at the valve cover.

Timing Chain and/or Gears

TIMING CHAIN AND GEARS

Removal and Installation

1982–85 2.0L GASOLINE ENGINES

NOTE: Chain adjuster guide 49 3953 260, or its equivalent, is necessary for this procedure.

1. Remove the cylinder head and front cover. It is not necessary to remove intake and exhaust manifolds from the cylinder head.
2. Remove the oil pan, oil pump and pump drive chain.
3. Install the chain adjuster guide.

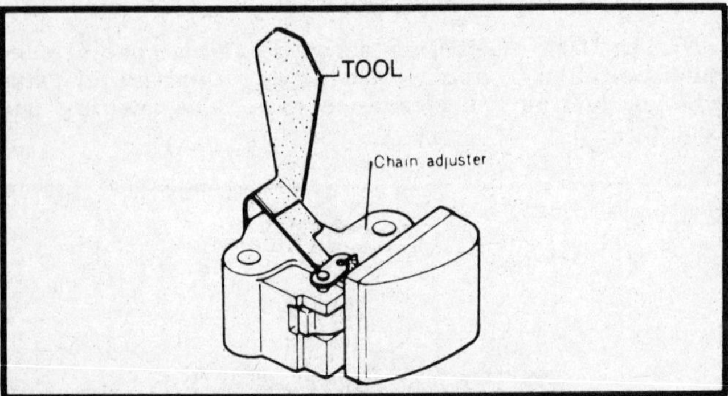

1982–85 2.0L engine timing chain adjuster guide

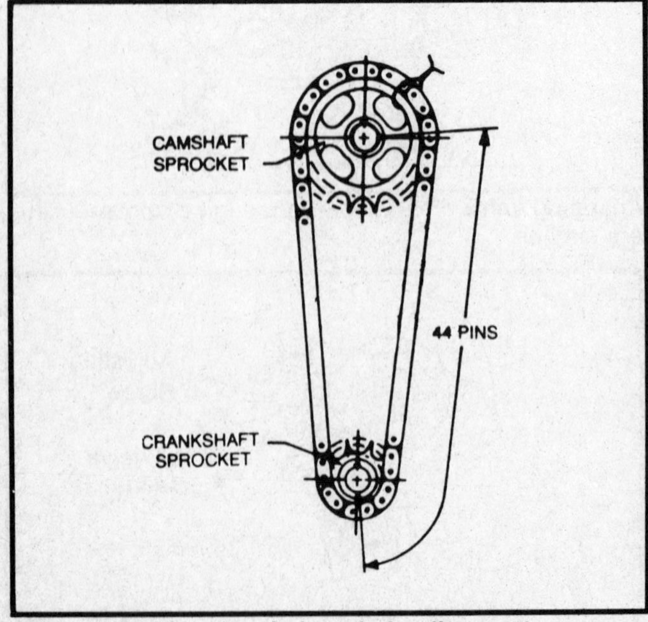

1982–85 2.0L engine timing chain alignment

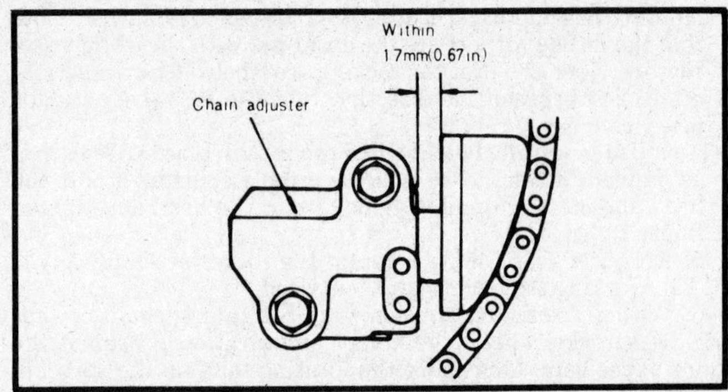

1982–85 2.0L engine timing chain adjuster positioning

4. Loosen the chain guide strip adjusting screws. Slightly rotate the timing chain in the direction of normal engine rotation. Press the top of the chain guide strip with a prybar and tighten the guide strip adjusting screws. Check the protrusion of the chain adjuster head. If protrusion exceeds 17mm, replace the chain.
5. Remove the timing chain tensioner.
6. Remove the timing chain from the gears. Remove the gears with a puller if necessary.
7. When installing the chain, make sure that the gears and chained are aligned. The alignment marks on the gears must appear on the left and fall between the nickel plated links.
8. Check the slack in the oil pump drive chain after installation. Press on the chain, midway between the gears. If slack exceeds 4.0mm, install adjusting shims between the block and oil pump body. Shims are available in thicknesses of 0.15mm. Tighten the oil pump sprocket bolt to 25 ft. lbs.
9. Follow Step 4 and adjust the timing chain. Remove the guide tool.

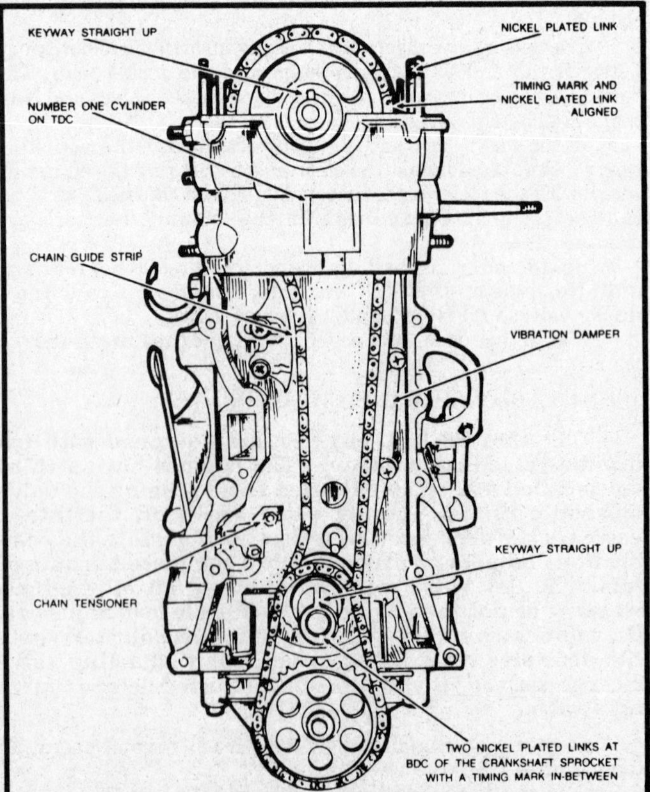

1982–85 2.0L engine timing chain details

10. Install the oil pan, using a new gasket and sealer.
11. The remainder of the installation is the reverse of the removal procedure.

1987–88 2.6L ENGINE

NOTE: All 2.6L engines are equipped with two Silent Shafts which cancel the vertical vibrating force of the engine and the secondary vibrating forces, which include the sideways rocking of the engine due to the turning direction of the crankshaft and other rolling parts. The secondary vibrating forces can be cancelled if forces equivalent in magnitude but opposite in direction are produced. In these engines, the opposite force is produced by silent shafts located in the upper left and lower right sides in the front of the cylinder block. The shafts are driven by a duplex chain and are turned by the crankshaft. The silent shaft chain assembly is mounted in front of the timing chain assembly and must be removed to service the timing chain.

1. Disconnect the negative battery cable.
2. Drain the radiator and remove it from the vehicle.
3. Remove the cylinder head.
4. Remove the cooling fan, spacer, water pump pulley and belt.
5. Remove the alternator. Remove the water pump.
6. Raise and support the vehicle safely.
7. Remove the oil pan and screen. Remove the crankshaft pulley.
8. Remove the timing case cover.
9. Remove the chain guides, side (A), top (B), bottom (C), from the "B" chain (outer).
10. Remove the locking bolts from the "B" chain sprockets.
11. Remove the crankshaft sprocket, silent shaft sprocket and the outer chain.
12. Remove the crankshaft and camshaft sprockets and the timing chain.
13. Remove the camshaft sprocket holder and the chain guides, both left and right.
14. Remove the tensioner.
15. Remove the sleeve from the oil pump. Remove the oil pump by first removing the bolt locking the oil pump driven gear and the right silent shaft, then remove the oil pump mounting bolts. Remove the silent shaft from the engine block.

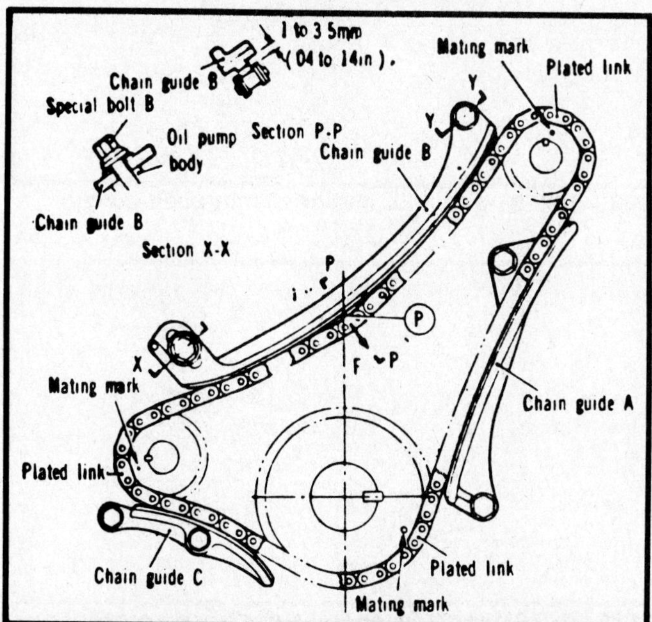

2.6L engine silence shaft chain alignment marks

NOTE: If the bolt locking the oil pump and the silent shaft is hard to loosen, remove the oil pump and the shaft as a unit.

16. Remove the left silent shaft thrust washer and remove the shaft from the engine block.
17. Install the right silent shaft into the engine block.
18. Install the oil pump assembly. Do not lose the woodruff key from the end of the silent shaft. Torque the oil pump mounting bolts to 6–7 ft. lbs.
19. Tighten the silent shaft and the oil pump driven gear mounting bolt.

NOTE: The silent shaft and the oil pump can be installed as a unit, if necessary.

20. Install the left silent shaft into the engine block.
21. Install a new O-ring on the thrust plate and install the unit into the engine block, using a pair of bolts without heads, as alignment guides.

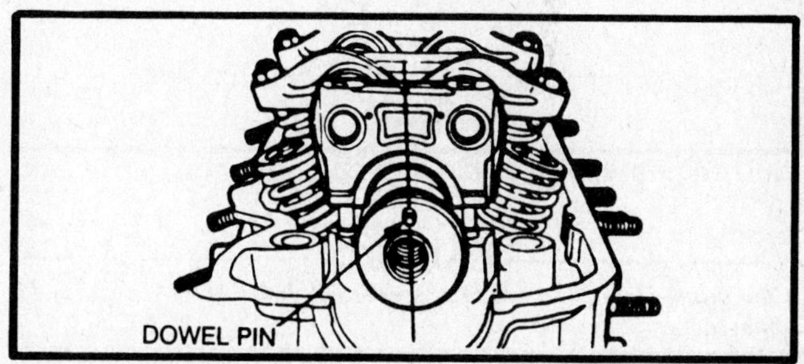

2.6L engine camshaft dowel pin alignment for timing chain installation

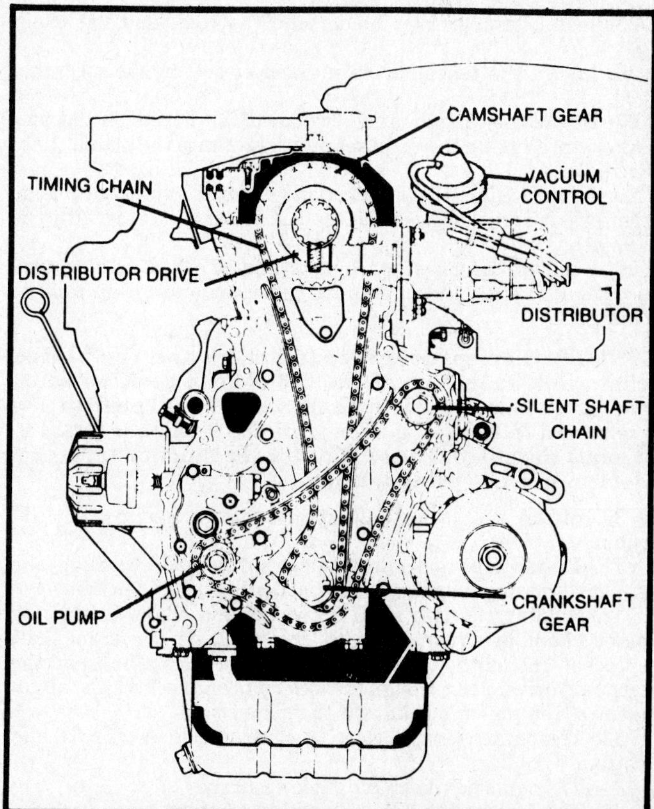

2.6L engine timing and silence shaft chains

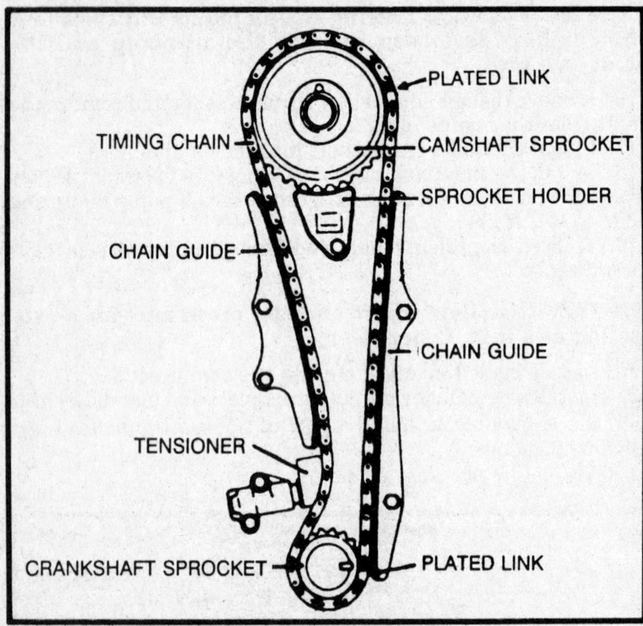

2.6L engine timing chain and components

CAUTION

If the thrust plate is turned to align the bolt holes, the O-ring may be damaged.

22. Remove the guide bolts and install the regular bolts into the thrust plate and tighten securely.
23. Rotate the crankshaft to bring No. 1 piston to TDC.
24. Install the cylinder head.
25. Install the sprocket holder and the right and left chain guides.
26. Install the tensioner spring and sleeve on the oil pump body.
27. Install the camshaft and crankshaft sprockets on the timing chain, aligning the sprocket punch marks to the plated chain links.
28. While holding the sprocket and chain as a unit, install the crankshaft sprocket over the crankshaft and align it with the keyway.
29. Keeping the dowel pin hole on the camshaft in a vertical position, install the camshaft sprocket and chain on the camshaft.

NOTE: The sprocket timing mark and the plated chain link should be at the 2–3 o'clock position when correctly installed. The chain must be aligned in the right and left chain guides with the tensioner pushing against the chain. The tension for the inner chain is predetermined by spring tension.

30. Install the crankshaft sprocket for the outer or "B" chain.
31. Install the two silent shaft sprockets and align the punched mating marks with the plated links of the chain.
32. Holding the two shaft sprockets and chain, install the outer chain in alignment with the mark on the crankshaft sprocket. Install the shaft sprockets on the silent shaft and the oil pump driver gear. Install the lock bolts and recheck the alignment of the punch marks and the plated links.
33. Temporarily install the chain guides, side (A), top (B) and bottom (C).
34. Tighten side (A) chain guide securely.
35. Tighten bottom (B) chain guide securely.
36. Adjust the position of the top (B) chain guide, after shaking the right and left sprockets to collect any chain slack, so that when the chain is moved toward the center, the clearance between the chain guide and the chain links will be approximately $^9/_{64}$ inch. Tighten the top (B) chain guide bolts.
37. Install the timing chain cover using a new gasket, being careful not to damage the front seal.
38. Using a new gasket, install the oil screen and oil pan. Torque the bolts to 4.5–5.5 ft. lbs.
39. Install the crankshaft pulley, alternator and accessory belts and the distributor.
40. Install the oil pressure switch, if removed. Connect the negative battery cable.
41. Install the fan blades, radiator, fill the cooling system and run the engine. Check for oil and water leaks.

Timing Belt and/or Sprockets

TIMING BELT, TENSIONER, COVER AND CAMSHAFT OIL SEAL

Removal and Installation

1986–88 2.0 & 2.2L GASOLINE ENGINES

1. Disconnect the negative battery cable.
2. Drain the cooling system.
3. Remove the distributor cap, with the wires attached and remove the distributor.
4. Remove the fan shroud and fan.
5. Disconnect and tag the alternator wiring and remove the alternator.
6. Disconnect the air injection pipes from the engine.
7. Remove the fan pulley, hub and bracket.
8. If equipped, remove the air conditioning compressor drive belt.
9. If equipped, remove the power steering pump drive belt.
10. Remove the crankshaft pulley and baffle plate.

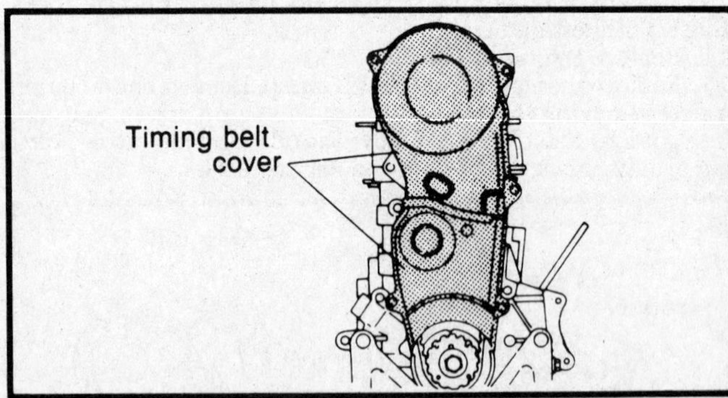

1986–88 2.0L and 2.2L engines timing belt covers

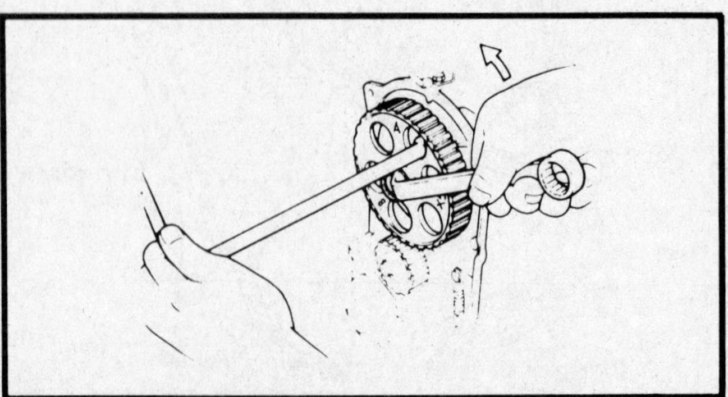

1986–88 2.0L and 2.2L engines camshaft sprocket removal

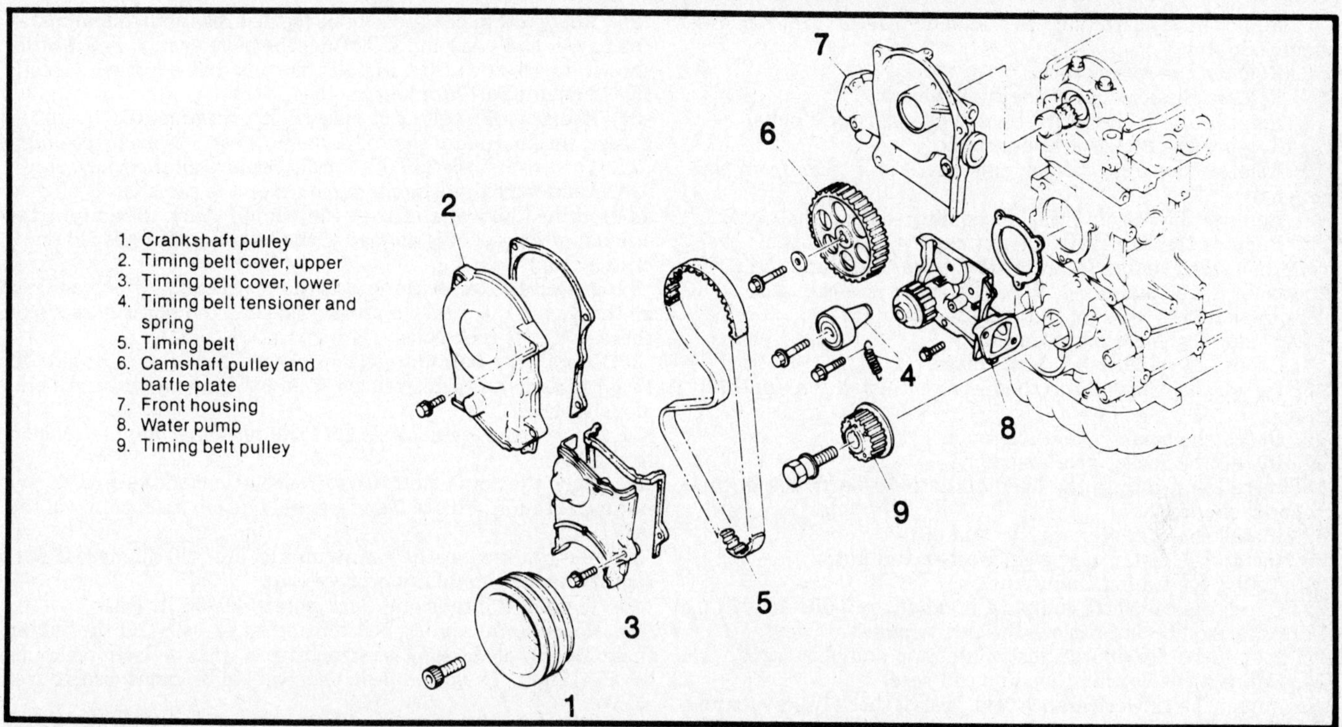

1986–88 2.0L and 2.2L engines timing belt, cover and sprockets—exploded view

11. Remove the upper and lower timing belt covers.
12. Turn the crankshaft so that the "A" mark on the camshaft pulley is at the top, aligned with the notch in the front housing.
13. Loosen the timing belt tensioner lock bolt and remove the tensioner spring.
14. Mark the forward rotation of the belt for installation. Remove the belt.
15. Unbolt and remove the front housing.
16. Carefully, drive the camshaft seal from the housing.
17. Coat the outside of a new seal with clean engine oil and press it into place in the front housing.
18. Coat the seal lip with clean engine oil. Install the front housing, using a new gasket. Torque the bolts to 14–19 ft. lbs.
19. Replace the timing belt if it has been contaminated by oil or grease, or shows any sign of damage, wear, cracks or peeling.
20. To ease installation of the belt, remove all the spark plugs.
21. Make sure that the timing mark on the camshaft is aligned and that the timing mark (notch) on the crankshaft sprocket is aligned with the triangular shaped mark on the front housing.
22. Install the tensioner and spring, positioning the tensioner all the way to the intake manifold side and temporarily secure it there with the lock bolt.
23. Install the belt onto the sprockets from the right side. If the original belt is being reused, follow the directional mark previously made.
24. Loosen the lock bolt so that the tensioner applies tension to the belt.
25. Turn the crankshaft two full revolutions in the direction of normal rotation. This will apply equal tension to all points of the belt.
26. Make sure that the timing marks are still aligned. If not, repeat the belt installation procedure.
27. Tighten the tensioner lock bolt to 30–35 ft. lbs.
28. Measure the timing belt tension by pressing on the belt at the midpoint of the longest straight run. Belt deflection should be 11–13mm. If not, repeat the belt adjustment procedure, above.

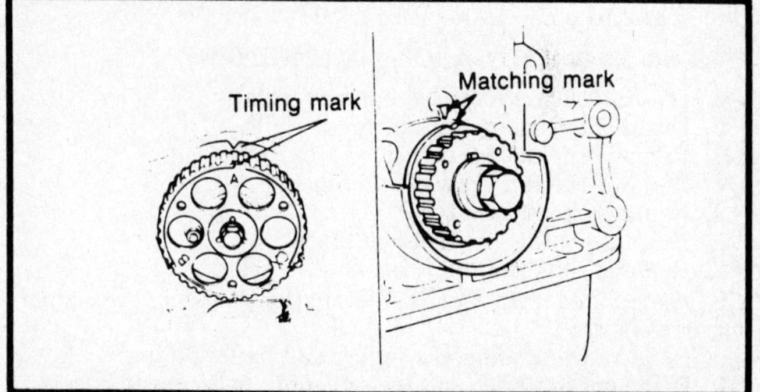

1986–88 2.0L and 2.2L engines timing belt sprocket alignment

29. Installation of all other parts is the reverse of removal. Torque the belt cover bolts to 80 inch lbs.; the fan bracket bolts to 40 ft. lbs. When installing the drive belts on the various accessories, check the belt deflection.

Camshaft

Removal and Installation

1982–85 2.0L GASOLINE ENGINE

1. Matchmark and remove the hood.
2. Remove the water pump.
3. Disconnect the coil wire and vacuum line from the distributor.
4. Rotate the crankshaft to place the No.1 cylinder on TDC of the compression stroke. This can be determined by removing the spark plug and feeling compression with a finger. When compression is felt, rotate the crankshaft until the pointer aligns with the TDC mark on the pulley.

5. Remove the spark plug wires and distributor cap. Remove the distributor.
6. Remove the rocker cover.
7. Release the tension on the timing chain.
8. Remove the rocker arm shaft to cylinder head bolts.
9. Remove the rocker arm assembly.
10. Remove the nut, washer and distributor gear from the camshaft.
11. Remove the nut and washer holding the camshaft gear.
12. Remove the camshaft. Do not remove the camshaft gear from the timing chain. Be sure that the gear teeth and chain relationship is not disturbed. Wire the chain and cam gear to a place so that they will not fall into the front cover.
13. Clean all the gasket surfaces.
14. Clean the cylinder head bolt holes.
15. Install the camshaft on the head and install the camshaft gear.
16. Check the timing chain alignment.
17. Install the rocker arm assembly.
18. Install and torque the head bolts to 60–64 ft. lbs in the proper sequence.
19. Install the cam gear washer and nut.
20. Install the distributor gear, washer and nut.
21. Adjust the timing chain tension.
22. Check the camshaft end-play. It should be 0.001–0.007 in. If it exceeds 0.008 in., replace the thrust plate.
23. Install the distributor, distributor cap and plug wires.
24. Connect the vacuum line and coil wire.
25. Adjust the valve clearance cold. Install the valve cover and fill the cooling system.
26. Run the engine and check for leaks. When normal operating temperature is reached, adjust the valve clearance.
27. Adjust the carburetor and ignition timing.
28. Install the air cleaner and hood.

1986–88 2.0 & 2.2L GASOLINE ENGINES

1. Disconnect the negative battery cable.
2. Drain the cooling system.
3. Remove the distributor.
4. Remove the fan shroud and fan.
5. Remove the alternator.
6. Disconnect the air injection pipes.
7. Remove the fan pulley, hub and bracket.
8. If equipped, remove the A/C compressor and power steering drive belts.
9. Remove the crankshaft pulley and baffle plate.
10. Remove the upper and lower timing belt covers.
12. Turn the crankshaft so that the "A" mark on the camshaft pulley is at the top, aligned with the notch in the front housing.
13. Loosen the tensioner lock bolt and remove the tensioner spring.
14. Mark the forward rotation of the belt for installation. Remove the belt.
15. Insert a bar through the hole in the camshaft sprocket to hold it in position and remove the sprocket bolt.
16. Disconnect the accelerator cable, if necessary.
17. If equipped, disconnect the air by-pass valve cable.
18. Disconnect the spark plug wires. Remove the wires from the spark plug wire clips on the rocker covers and position them out of the way.
19. Remove the rocker cover and discard the gasket.
20. Remove the rocker arm shaft attaching bolts evenly in the correct order and remove the rocker arm shafts.
21. Remove the camshaft rear seal cap.
22. Lift out the camshaft.
23. Inspect the camshaft for wear, heat scoring or obvious damage. Replace it if necessary. Check the lobes and journals for wear.
24. Coat the camshaft with clean engine oil and install it in position, making sure that the lug on the nose of the shaft is at the 12:00 o'clock position.
25. Apply a thin coat of sealant to the areas shown and install the rocker shaft assembly. Torque the bolts evenly, in the order shown, to 15–20 ft. lbs. Install the camshaft sprocket. Torque the camshaft sprocket bolt to 40–45 ft. lbs.
26. Replace the belt if it has been contaminated by oil or grease, or shows any sign of damage, wear, cracks or peeling.
27. To ease installation of the belt, remove all the spark plugs.
28. Make sure that the timing mark on the camshaft is aligned as described above, and that the timing mark (notch) on the crankshaft sprocket is aligned with the triangular shaped mark on the front housing.
29. Install the tensioner and spring, positioning the tensioner all the way to the intake manifold side and temporarily secure it there with the lock bolt.
30. Install the belt onto the sprockets from the right side. If the original belt is being reused, follow the directional mark previously made.
31. Loosen the lock bolt so that the tensioner applies tension to the belt.
32. Turn the crankshaft two full revolutions in the direction of normal rotation. This will apply equal tension to all points of the belt.
33. Make sure that the timing marks are still aligned. If not, repeat the belt installation procedure.
34. Tighten the tensioner lock bolt to 30–35 ft. lbs.
35. Measure the timing belt tension by pressing on the belt at the midpoint of the longest straight run. Belt deflection should be 11–13mm. If not, repeat the belt adjustment procedure, above.
36. Check the valve adjustment and reset, if necessary.
37. Clean the mating surfaces of the cylinder head and rocker cover.
39. Install the rocker cover with a new gasket. Torque the bolts to 24–36 inch lbs.
40. Install the spark plug wire on the plugs. Place the wires in the clips on the rocker cover. Connect the choke and air by-pass valve cable.
41. Installation of all other parts is the reverse of removal. Torque the belt cover bolts to 80 inch lbs.; the fan bracket bolts to 40 ft. lbs.
41. The remainder of the installation is the reverse of the removal procedure.

1987–88 2.6L GASOLINE ENGINE

1. Disconnect the negative battery cable.
2. Drain the radiator and remove it from the vehicle.
3. Remove the cylinder head.
4. Remove the cooling fan, spacer, water pump pulley and belt.
5. Remove the alternator. Remove the water pump.
6. Raise and support the vehicle safely.
7. Remove the oil pan and screen. Remove the crankshaft pulley.
8. Remove the timing case cover.
9. Remove the chain guides, side (A), top (B), bottom (C), from the "B" chain (outer).
10. Remove the locking bolts from the "B" chain sprockets.
11. Remove the crankshaft sprocket, silent shaft sprocket and the outer chain.
12. Remove the crankshaft and camshaft sprockets and the timing chain.
13. Remove the camshaft sprocket holder and the chain guides, both left and right.
14. Remove the tensioner.
15. Remove the sleeve from the oil pump. Remove the oil pump by first removing the bolt locking the oil pump driven gear and the right silent shaft, then remove the oil pump mounting bolts. Remove the silent shaft from the engine block.

NOTE: If the bolt locking the oil pump and the silent shaft is hard to loosen, remove the oil pump and the shaft as a unit.

16. Remove the left silent shaft thrust washer and remove the shaft from the engine block.
17. Install the right silent shaft into the engine block.
18. Install the oil pump assembly. Do not lose the woodruff key from the end of the silent shaft. Torque the oil pump mounting bolts to 6–7 ft. lbs.
19. Tighten the silent shaft and the oil pump driven gear mounting bolt.

NOTE: The silent shaft and the oil pump can be installed as a unit, if necessary.

20. Install the left silent shaft into the engine block.
21. Install a new O-ring on the thrust plate and install the unit into the engine block, using a pair of bolts without heads, as alignment guides.

CAUTION

If the thrust plate is turned to align the bolt holes, the O-ring may be damaged.

22. Remove the guide bolts and install the regular bolts into the thrust plate and tighten securely.
23. Rotate the crankshaft to bring No. 1 piston to TDC.
24. Install the cylinder head.
25. Install the sprocket holder and the right and left chain guides.
26. Install the tensioner spring and sleeve on the oil pump body.
27. Install the camshaft and crankshaft sprockets on the timing chain, aligning the sprocket punch marks to the plated chain links.
28. While holding the sprocket and chain as a unit, install the crankshaft sprocket over the crankshaft and align it with the keyway.
29. Keeping the dowel pin hole on the camshaft in a vertical position, install the camshaft sprocket and chain on the camshaft.

NOTE: The sprocket timing mark and the plated chain link should be at the 2-3 o'clock position when correctly installed. The chain must be aligned in the right and left chain guides with the tensioner pushing against the chain. The tension for the inner chain is predetermined by spring tension.

30. Install the crankshaft sprocket for the outer or "B" chain.
31. Install the two silent shaft sprockets and align the punched mating marks with the plated links of the chain.
32. Holding the two shaft sprockets and chain, install the outer chain in alignment with the mark on the crankshaft sprocket. Install the shaft sprockets on the silent shaft and the oil pump driver gear. Install the lock bolts and recheck the alignment of the punch marks and the plated links.
33. Temporarily install the chain guides, side (A), top (B) and bottom (C).
34. Tighten side (A) chain guide securely.
35. Tighten bottom (B) chain guide securely.
36. Adjust the position of the top (B) chain guide, after shaking the right and left sprockets to collect any chain slack, so that when the chain is moved toward the center, the clearance between the chain guide and the chain links will be approximately $^{9}/_{64}$ inch. Tighten the top (B) chain guide bolts.
37. Install the timing chain cover using a new gasket, being careful not to damage the front seal.
38. Using a new gasket, install the oil screen and oil pan. Torque the bolts to 4.5–5.5 ft. lbs.
39. Install the crankshaft pulley, alternator and accessory belts and the distributor.
40. Install the oil pressure switch, if removed. Connect the negative battery cable.
41. Install the fan blades, radiator, fill the cooling system and run the engine. Check for oil and water leaks.

Pistons and Connecting Rods

IDENTIFICATION

NOTE: Whenever pistons and connecting rods are removed or replaced, they must be marked to identify which cylinder and direction to be installed.

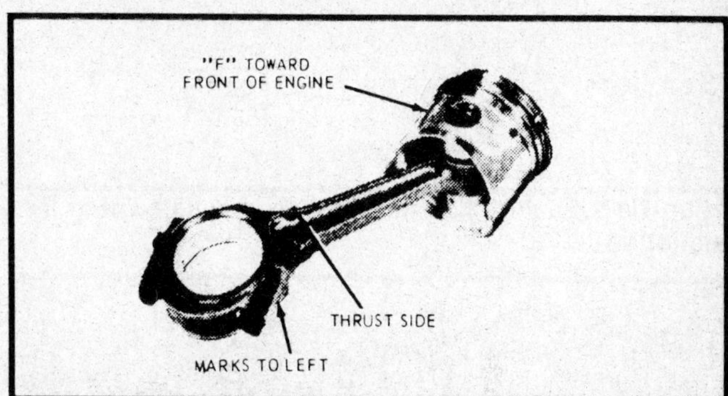

1982–85 2.0L engine piston and connecting rod relationship

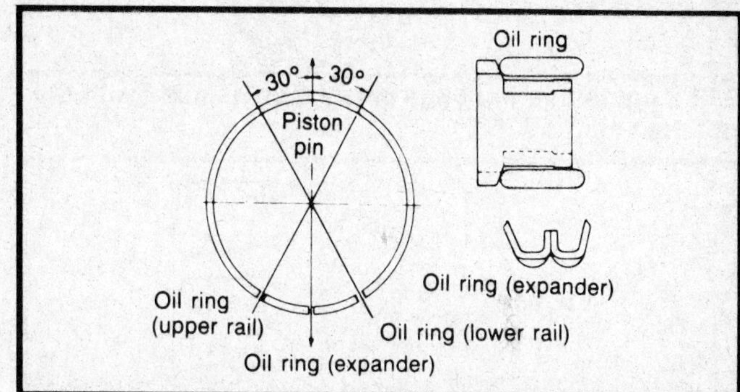

1986–88 2.0L and 2.2L engines oil ring installation position

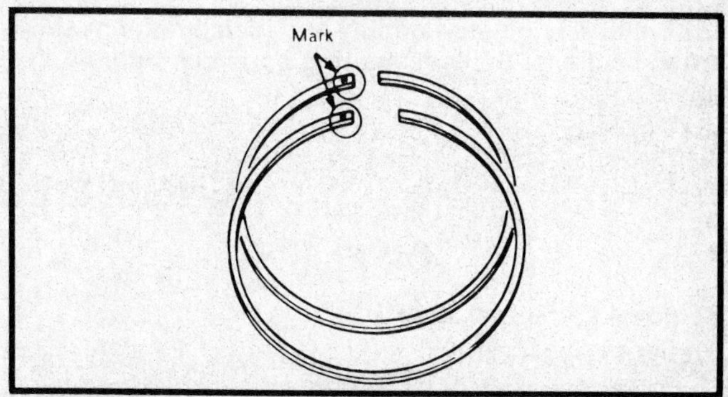

1982–88 All engines – install rings with the stamped marks facing top

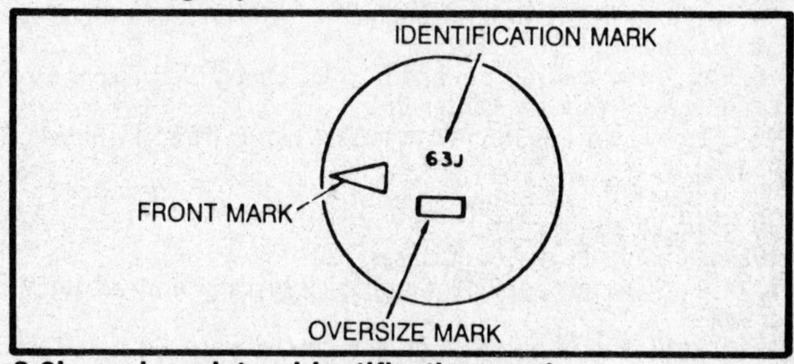

2.6L engine piston identification marks

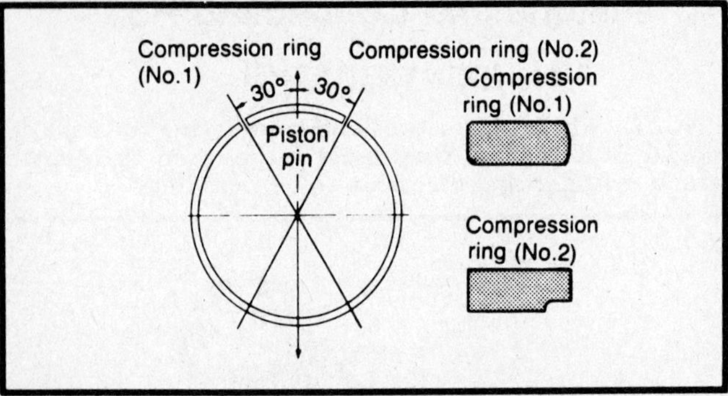

1986–88 2.0L and 2.2L engines compression ring installation

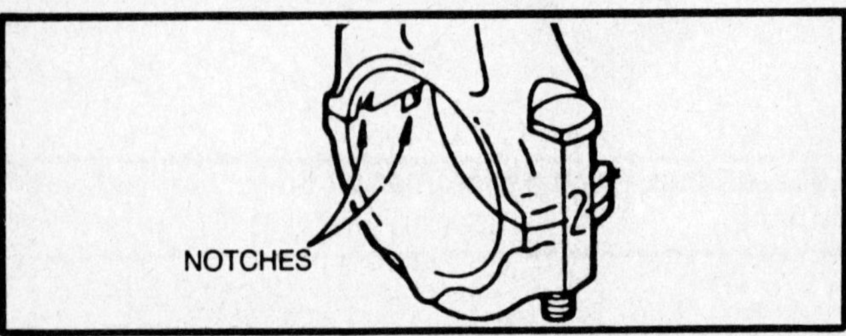

2.6L engine bearing caps must be reinstalled with the notches aligned

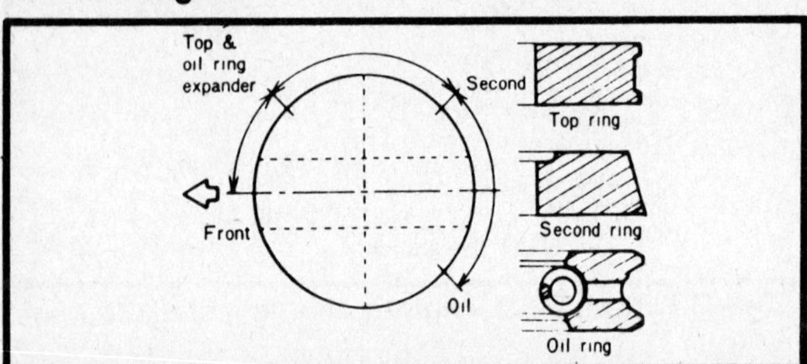

1982–88 All engines – identify and install rings by the cross-sections. Stagger the ring gaps accordingly

Removal and Installation

NOTE: Remove the ridge at the top of the cylinder wall before removing. Replace the connecting rod caps on the connecting rod immediately after removal and inspect for cylinder number markings.

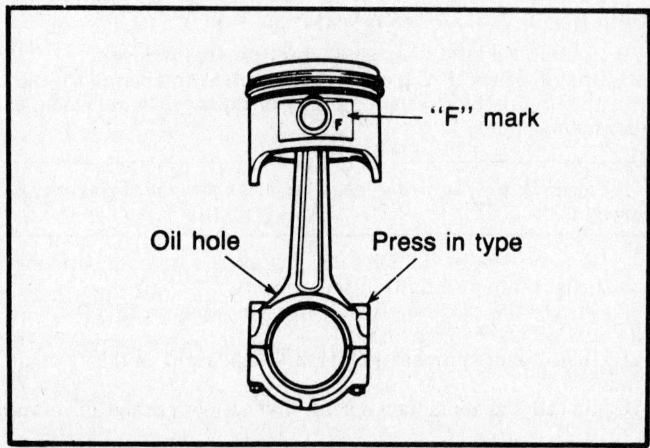

1986–88 2.0L and 2.2L engines piston and connecting rod matchmarks

Connecting Rod and Main Bearings

Removal and Installation

Refer to the Unit Overhaul Section for General Procedures.

Engine bearings are of the precision insert type. They are available for service in standard and various undersizes. Upper and lower bearing inserts may be different. Be careful to align holes. Do not obstruct any oil passages. Bearing inserts must not be shimmed. Do not touch the bearing surface of the insert with bare fingers. Skin oil and acids will etch the bearing surface.

ENGINE LUBRICATION

Oil Pan

Removal and Installation

GASOLINE ENGINES

1. Disconnect the negative battery cable.
2. Raise and support the vehicle safely. Drain the engine oil.
3. On 4WD models, remove the skid plate.
4. Support the front of the engine near the crankshaft pulley.
5. Remove the crossmember.
6. Remove the cotter pin and nut. Using a puller, disconnect the idler arm from the center link.
7. Remove the engine mount gusset plates from the sides of the engine.
8. Remove the bell housing front cover.
9. Remove the oil pan.
10. Clean all the gasket surfaces.
11. Clean the oil pan, oil pump pickup tube and oil pump screen.
12. Install a new oil pan gasket coated with oil resistant sealer.Tighten the pan bolts to 5–9 ft. lbs.
13. The remainder of the installation is the reverse of the removal procedure. Torque the idler arm nut to 25–30 ft. lbs. and the bell housing cover to 15–20 ft. lbs.

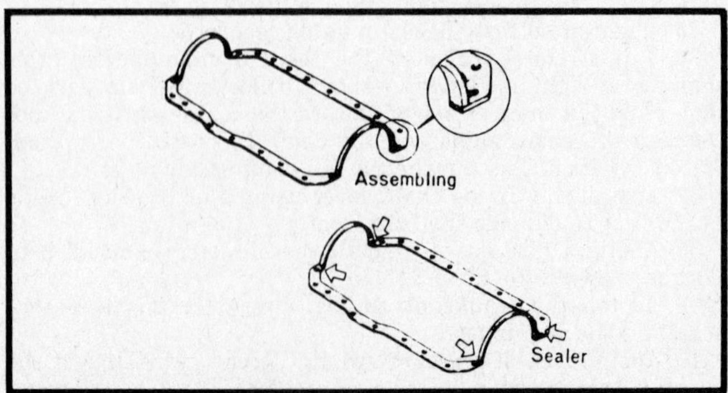

1982–85 2.0L engine apply sealer to the sections shown

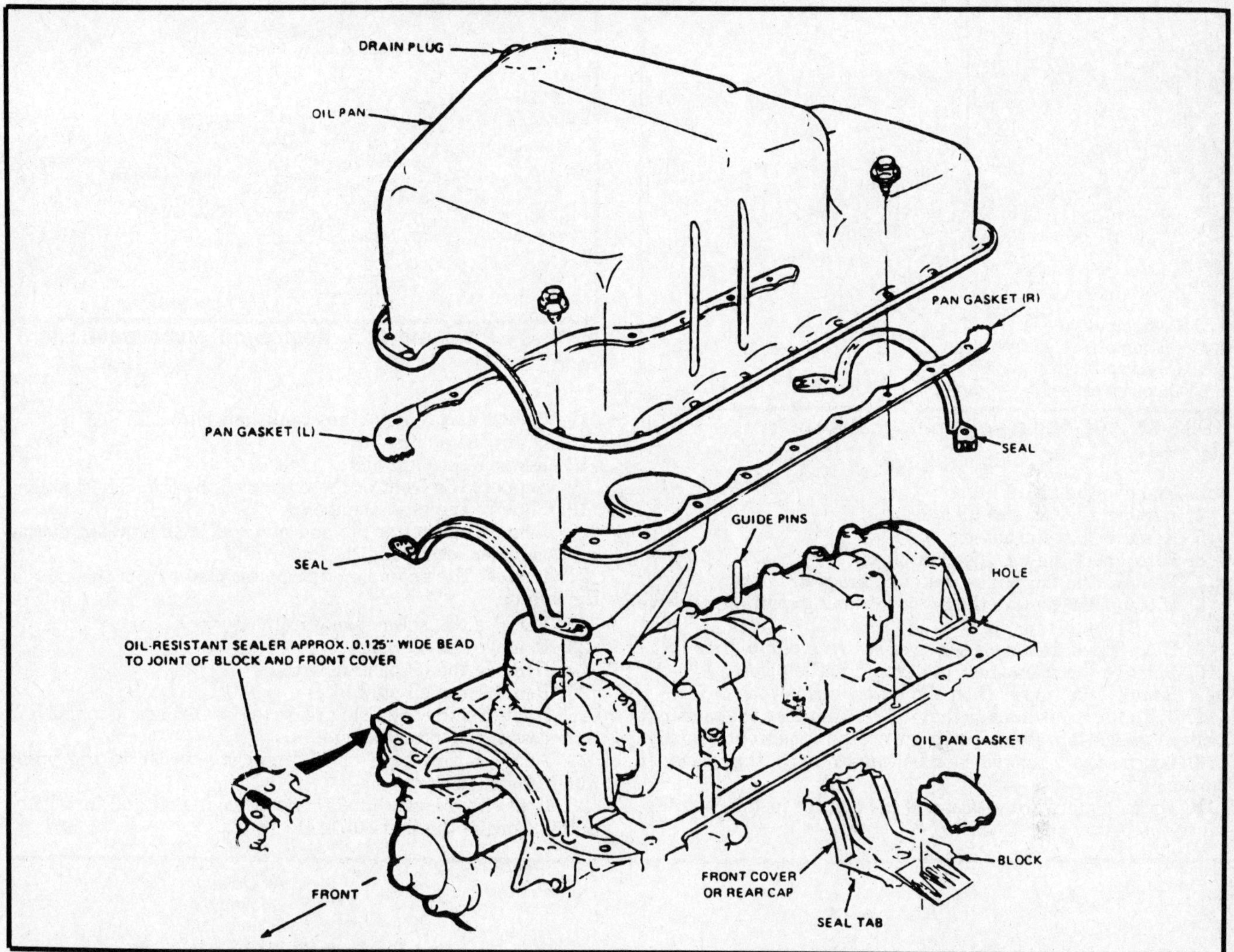

1982–85 2.0L engine oil pan installation

Oil Pump

Removal and Installation

1982–85 2.0L GASOLINE ENGINES

1. Remove the oil pan.
2. Remove the oil pump drive gear attaching nut.
3. Remove the oil pump mounting bolts. Loosen the gear on the pump.

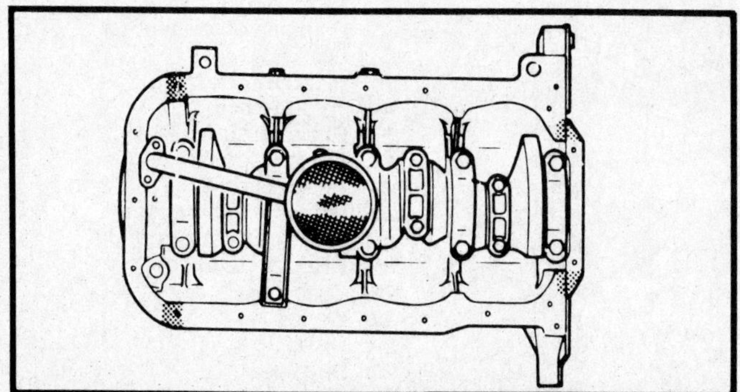

1986–88 2.0L and 2.2L engines sealer application for engines with a gasket

4. Remove the oil pump and gear.
5. Install the oil pump gear in the chain.
6. Prime the oil pump and install it on the cylinder block. Install the bolts and tighten them to 13–24 ft. lbs.
7. Install the washer, gear and nut on the shaft of the oil pump. Bend the locktab on the washer.
8. Install the oil pan. Fill the engine with oil. Start the engine and check for oil pressure. Check for leaks.

1986–88 2.0 & 2.2L GASOLINE ENGINES

1. Disconnect the negative battery cable.
2. Drain the cooling system.

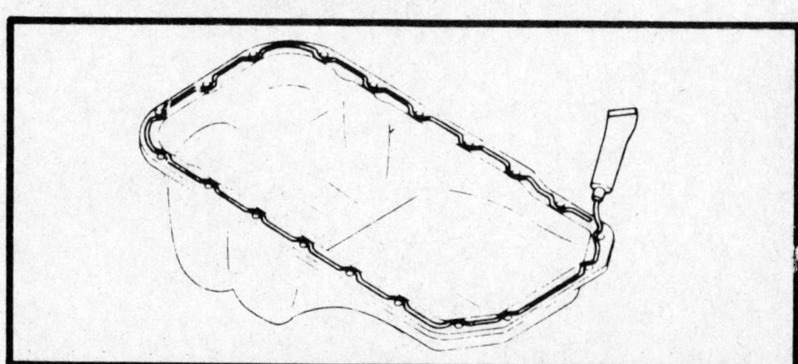

1986–88 2.0L and 2.2L engines sealer application for engines without a gasket

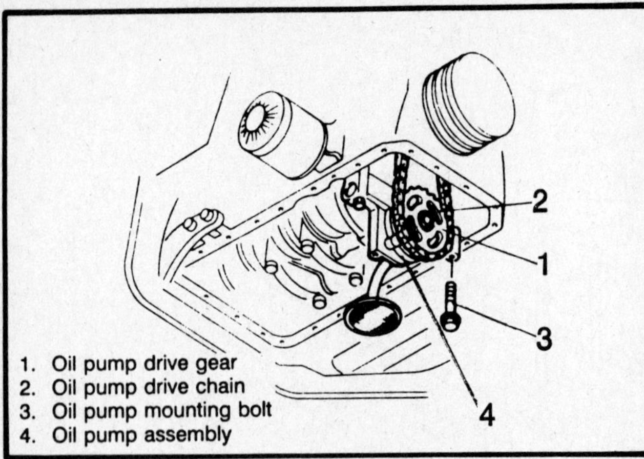

1982–85 2.0L engine oil pump installation

3. Remove the distributor.
4. Remove the fan shroud and fan.
5. Remove the alternator.
6. Disconnect the air injection pipes.
7. Remove the fan pulley, hub and bracket.
8. If equipped, remove the air conditioning compressor drive belt.
9. If equipped, remove the power steering pump drive belt.
10. Remove the crankshaft pulley and baffle plate.
11. Remove the upper, then the lower, belt covers.
12. Turn the crankshaft so that the "A" mark on the camshaft pulley is at the top, aligned with the notch in the front housing.
13. Loosen the tensioner lock bolt and remove the tensioner spring.
14. Mark the forward rotation of the belt for installation. Remove the belt.

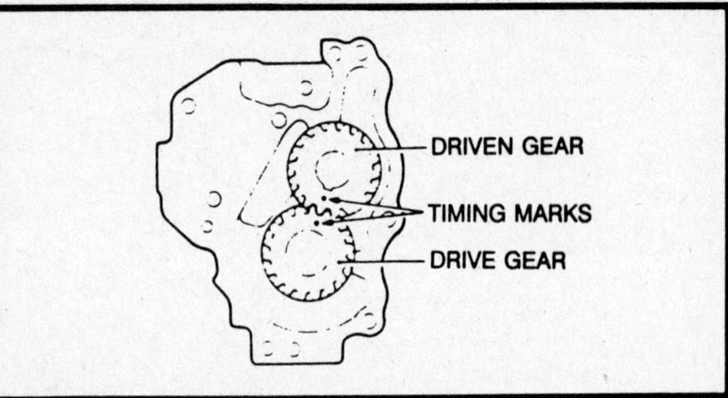

1986–88 2.0L and 2.2L engine oil pump gear alignment

15. Unbolt and remove the crankshaft sprocket.
16. Drain the engine oil.
17. Remove the skid plate.
18. Support the front of the engine at the crankshaft pulley.
19. Remove the crossmember.
20. Remove the cotter pin and nut and, with a puller, disconnect the idler arm from the center link.
21. Remove the engine mount gusset plates from the sides of the engine.
22. Remove the bell housing front cover.
23. Remove the oil pan.
24. Remove the oil pick-up tube.
25. Remove the oil pump.
26. Apply a thin coating of grease to the O-ring and install it in its recess in the pump body.
27. Apply a thin bead of RTV silicone sealer to the pump mounting surface.
28. Coat the oil seal lip with clean engine oil and install the pump. Torque the bolts to 14–19 ft. lbs.

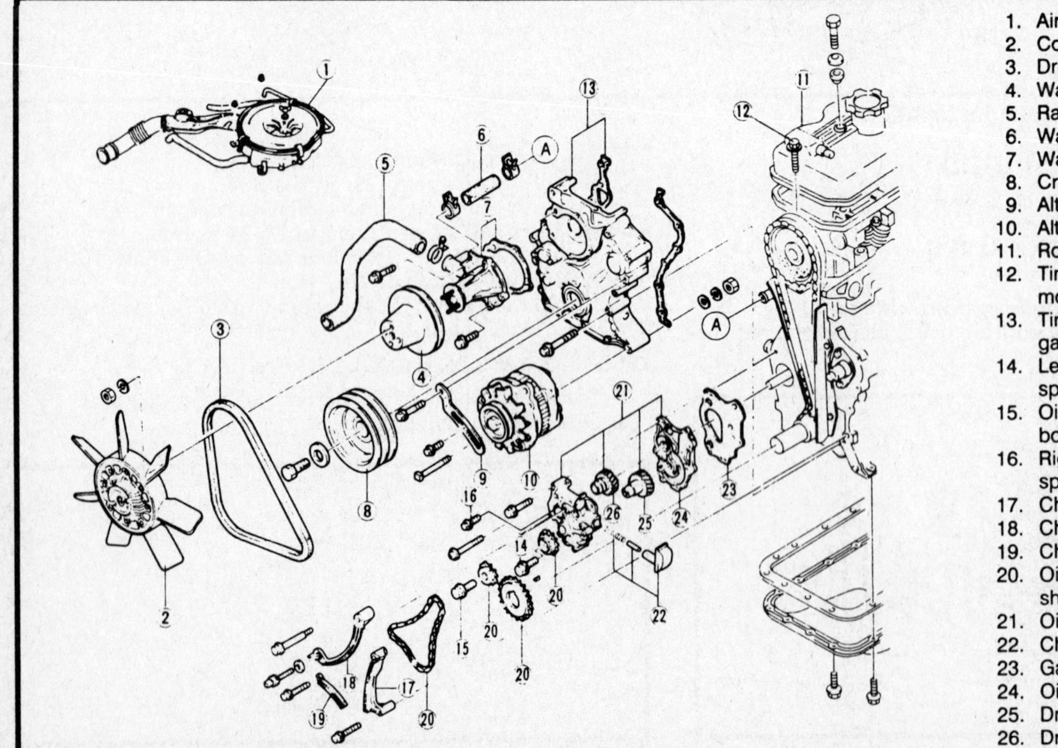

1987–88 2.6L engine oil pump installation

29. Clean all the gasket surfaces. Straighten the portion of the pan rim that may be bent.
30. Clean the oil pan, oil pump pickup tube and oil pump screen.
31. Using a new gasket, install the oil pan on the engine. Tighten the oil pan bolts to 5–9 ft. lbs.
32. Install all other parts in reverse order of removal. Torque the idler arm nut to 25–30 ft. lbs. and the bell housing cover to 15–20 ft. lbs.
33. Replace timing the belt if it has been contaminated by oil or grease, or shows any sign of damage, wear, cracks or peeling.
34. To ease installation of the belt, remove all the spark plugs.
35. Make sure that the timing mark on the camshaft is aligned and that the timing mark (notch) on the crankshaft sprocket is aligned with the triangular shaped mark on the front housing.
36. Install the tensioner and spring, positioning the tensioner all the way to the intake manifold side and temporarily secure it there with the lock bolt.
37. Install the belt onto the sprockets from the right side. If the original belt is being reused, follow the directional mark previously made.
38. Loosen the lock bolt so that the tensioner applies tension to the belt.
39. Turn the crankshaft two full revolutions in the direction of normal rotation. This will apply equal tension to all points of the belt.
40. Make sure that the timing marks are still aligned. If not, repeat the belt installation procedure.
41. Tighten the tensioner lock bolt to 30–35 ft. lbs.
42. Measure the timing belt tension by pressing on the belt at the midpoint of the longest straight run. Belt deflection should be 11–13mm. If not, repeat the belt adjustment procedure.
43. The remainder of the installation is the reverse of the removal procedure. Torque the timing belt cover bolts to 80 inch lbs. and the fan bracket bolts to 40 ft. lbs. When installing the drive belts on the various accessories, check the belt deflection.

1987–88 2.6L GASOLINE ENGINES

1. Disconnect the negative battery cable.
2. Drain the radiator and remove it from the vehicle.
3. Remove the cylinder head.
4. Remove the cooling fan, spacer, water pump pulley and belt.
5. Remove the alternator. Remove the water pump.
6. Raise and support the vehicle safely.
7. Remove the oil pan and screen. Remove the crankshaft pulley.
8. Remove the timing case cover.
9. Remove the chain guides, side (A), top (B), bottom (C), from the "B" chain (outer).
10. Remove the locking bolts from the "B" chain sprockets.
11. Remove the crankshaft sprocket, silent shaft sprocket and the outer chain.
12. Remove the crankshaft and camshaft sprockets and the timing chain.
13. Remove the camshaft sprocket holder and the chain guides, both left and right.
14. Remove the tensioner.
15. Remove the sleeve from the oil pump. Remove the oil pump by first removing the bolt locking the oil pump driven gear and the right silent shaft, then remove the oil pump mounting bolts.
16. Install the oil pump assembly. Do not lose the woodruff key from the end of the silent shaft. Torque the oil pump mounting bolts to 6–7 ft. lbs.
17. Tighten the silent shaft and the oil pump driven gear mounting bolt.

NOTE: The silent shaft and the oil pump can be installed as a unit, if necessary.

18. Install the left silent shaft into the engine block.
19. Install a new O-ring on the thrust plate and install the unit into the engine block, using a pair of bolts without heads, as alignment guides.

CAUTION

If the thrust plate is turned to align the bolt holes, the O-ring may be damaged.

20. Remove the guide bolts and install the regular bolts into the thrust plate and tighten securely.
21. Rotate the crankshaft to bring No. 1 piston to TDC.
22. Install the cylinder head.
23. Install the sprocket holder and the right and left chain guides.
24. Install the tensioner spring and sleeve on the oil pump body.
25. Install the camshaft and crankshaft sprockets on the timing chain, aligning the sprocket punch marks to the plated chain links.
26. While holding the sprocket and chain as a unit, install the crankshaft sprocket over the crankshaft and align it with the keyway.
27. Keeping the dowel pin hole on the camshaft in a vertical position, install the camshaft sprocket and chain on the camshaft.

NOTE: The sprocket timing mark and the plated chain link should be at the 2–3 o'clock position when correctly installed. The chain must be aligned in the right and left chain guides with the tensioner pushing against the chain. The tension for the inner chain is predetermined by spring tension.

28. Install the crankshaft sprocket for the outer or "B" chain.
29. Install the two silent shaft sprockets and align the punched mating marks with the plated links of the chain.
30. Holding the two shaft sprockets and chain, install the outer chain in alignment with the mark on the crankshaft sprocket. Install the shaft sprockets on the silent shaft and the oil pump driver gear. Install the lock bolts and recheck the alignment of the punch marks and the plated links.
31. Temporarily install the chain guides, side (A), top (B) and bottom (C).
32. Tighten side (A) chain guide securely.
33. Tighten bottom (B) chain guide securely.
34. Adjust the position of the top (B) chain guide, after shaking the right and left sprockets to collect any chain slack, so that when the chain is moved toward the center, the clearance between the chain guide and the chain links will be approximately $^{9}/_{64}$ inch. Tighten the top (B) chain guide bolts.
35. Install the timing chain cover using a new gasket, being careful not to damage the front seal.
36. Using a new gasket, install the oil screen and oil pan. Torque the bolts to 4.5–5.5 ft. lbs.
37. Install the crankshaft pulley, alternator and accessory belts and the distributor.
38. Install the oil pressure switch, if removed. Connect the negative battery cable.
39. Install the fan blades and radiator. Fill the cooling system and run the engine. Check for oil and water leaks.
40. Adjust the ignition timing.

Oil Pump Chain

CHECKING TENSION AND ADJUSTMENT

Procedure

1982–85 2.0L GASOLINE ENGINES

Oil pump chain tension can be checked with a straightedge and a ruler. Lay the straightedge against the oil pump and crankshaft gears, alongside the chain. Depress the chain and measure the slack with a ruler. If slack exceeds 0.157 inches, the chain tension will have to be adjusted. Chain slack is reduced by the addition of shims between the oil pump and the cylinder block. The shims should be of equal thickness on each side of the pump.

Rear Main Bearing Oil Seal

LIP TYPE SEAL

Removal and Installation

1982–85 2.0L GASOLINE ENGINES

1. Raise and support the vehicle safely. Remove the transmission.
2. On vehicles with a manual transmission, remove the clutch disc, pressure plate and flywheel. On vehicles with an automatic transmission, remove the drive plate.
3. Using an awl, punch two holes in the crankshaft rear oil seal. They should be punched on opposite sides of the crankshaft, just above the bearing cap-to-cylinder block split line.
4. Install a sheet metal screw in each hole. Pry against both screws at the same time to remove the oil seal. Do not scratch the oil seal surface on the crankshaft.
5. Clean the oil recess in the cylinder block and bearing cap. Clean the oil seal surface on the crankshaft.
6. Coat the oil seal surfaces with oil. Coat the oil surface and the seal surface on the crankshaft with Lubriplate®. Install the oil seal and be sure that it is not twisted. Be sure that the seal surface was not damaged.
7. Install the flywheel. Coat the threads of the flywheel or drive plate attaching bolts with oil resistant sealer. Torque the bolts to specifications in sequence across from each other. Flywheel: 115–120 ft. lbs.; Drive plate: 60–69 ft. lbs.
8. On manual transmission models, install the clutch, pressure plate and transmission.
9. On automatic transmission models, install the transmission.

1986–88 2.0 & 2.2L GASOLINE ENGINE

1. Remove the transmission.
2. On manual transmission models, remove the clutch assembly.
3. Remove the flywheel or drive plate.
4. Remove the end plate.
5. The seal is located in the rear cover. Remove the rear cover. Discard the gasket.
6. Place the cover on a hard, flat surface. Drive the old seal from the rear cover.
7. Apply clean engine oil to the outer rim of the new seal and the seal bore in the rear cover. Press the new seal into place.
8. Coat the seal lip with clean engine oil. Install the rear cover and new gasket. Torque the bolts to 72–102 inch lbs., (6–8.5 ft. lbs.).
9. Using a suitable tool, cut away the part of the gasket that projects below the rear cover.
10. Install the end plate. Torque the bolts to 14–22 ft. lbs.
11. On manual transmission models, install the flywheel, clutch and transmission. On automatic transmission models, install the drive plate and transmission.
12. The remainder of the installation is the reverse of the removal procedure.

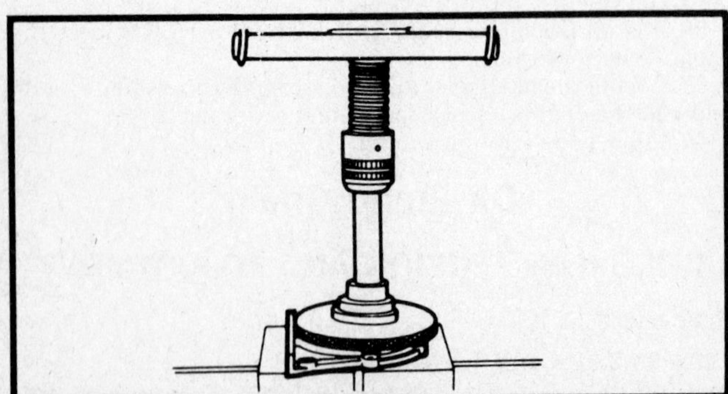

1986–88 2.0L and 2.2L engines rear main seal installation

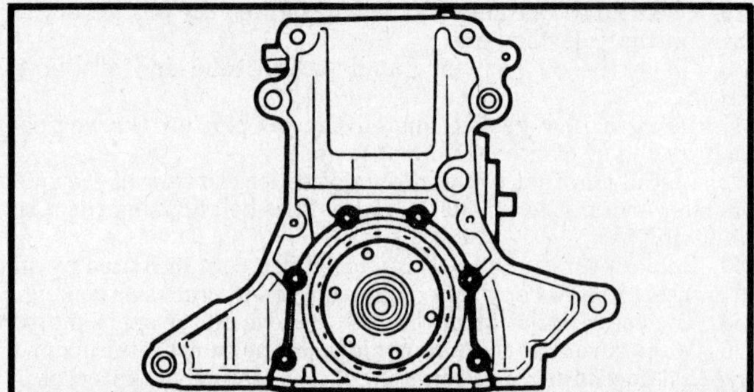

1986–88 2.0L and 2.2L engines rear main seal housing installation

1987–88 2.6L GASOLINE ENGINE

NOTE: The rear main bearing oil seal is located in a housing on the rear of the engine. To replace the seal, remove the transmission and work from underneath the vehicle.

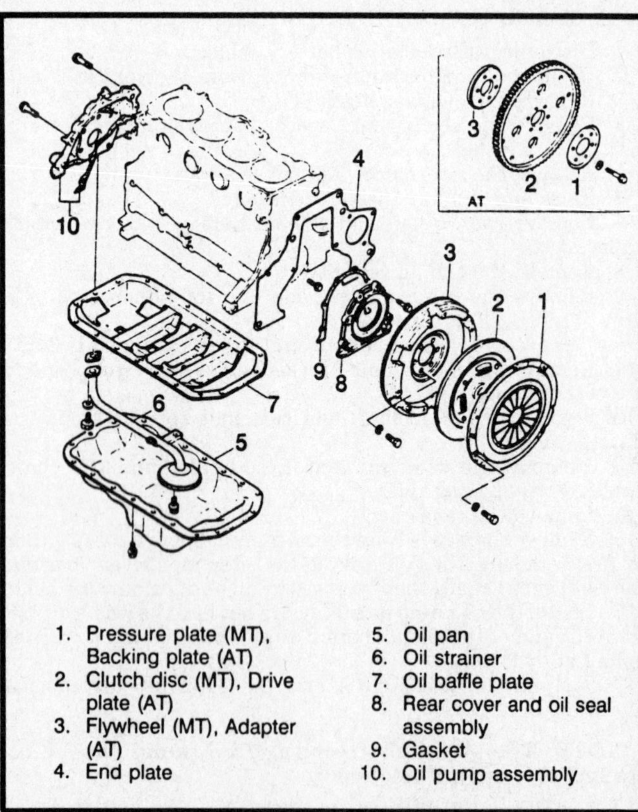

1. Pressure plate (MT), Backing plate (AT)
2. Clutch disc (MT), Drive plate (AT)
3. Flywheel (MT), Adapter (AT)
4. End plate
5. Oil pan
6. Oil strainer
7. Oil baffle plate
8. Rear cover and oil seal assembly
9. Gasket
10. Oil pump assembly

2.6L engine rear main bearing oil seal installation

1. On manual transmission models, remove the transmission, clutch and flywheel. On automatic transmission models, remove the transmission and flywheel. Remove the oil seal housing from the rear of the engine.
2. Remove the separator from the housing.
3. Pry out the old seal.
4. Lightly oil the replacement seal. The oil seal should be installed so that the seal plate fits into the inner contact surface of the seal case. Install the separator with the oil holes facing down.
5. Install the flywheel, clutch and transmission. Check the engine oil level when finished.

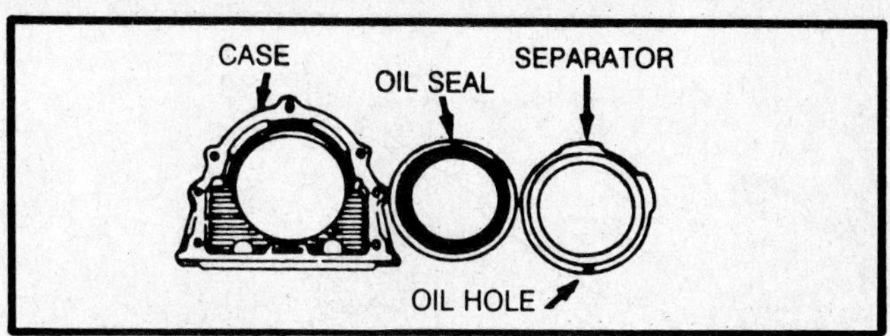

1986–88 2.0L, 2.2L and 2.6L engines rear main bearing oil seal

2WD FRONT SUSPENSION

Coil Spring

Removal and Installation

1982–85 MODELS

1. Raise and support vehicle safely so that the front suspension is hanging freely.
2. Remove the wheel assembly.
3. Remove the shock absorber. Install a coil spring compressor.
4. Remove the stabilizer bar.
5. Support the lower control arm.
6. Disconnect the upper and lower ball joints from the knuckle by removing the cotter pins and nuts and separating the ball joints with a ball joint separator tool.

CAUTION

Before separating the upper and/or lower ball joints from the control arms, make sure that the coil spring compressor is securely installed. Failure to do so, could cause the spring to jump out of the compressor, causing possible injury.

7. Remove the upper control arm.
8. Lower the lower control arm until the spring can be removed. With the spring removed, release the spring compressor to remove spring tension.
9. Installation is the reverse of the removal procedure.

Torsion Bar and Lower Control Arm

Removal and Installation

1986–88 MODELS

1. Raise and support the vehicle safely, with the front suspension hanging freely.
2. Remove the wheel assembly.
3. Remove the cotter pin and nut from the lower ball joint.
4. Remove the lower shock absorber mounting bolt.
5. Matchmark the anchor arm bolt and anchor swivel. Remove the bolt and swivel.

NOTE: The matchmarks made determine and are critical to, the vehicles ride height. Failure to do so, will result in having to set the vehicles ride hieght when finished.

6. Matchmark the torsion bar and anchor arm. Matchmark the torsion bar and torque plate.
7. Remove the anchor arm and torsion bar from the torque plate. Separate the anchor arm from the torsion bar.
8. Remove the torque plate.
9. Remove the lower control arm to frame bolt. Separate the lower arm from the frame bracket with bushing puller/installer 49 0727 575 or its equivalent.
10. Disconnect and remove the tension rod from the lower control arm.

NOTE: Do not change the position of the double nut at the rear of the tension rod bushing. It will affect the vehicles caster alignment.

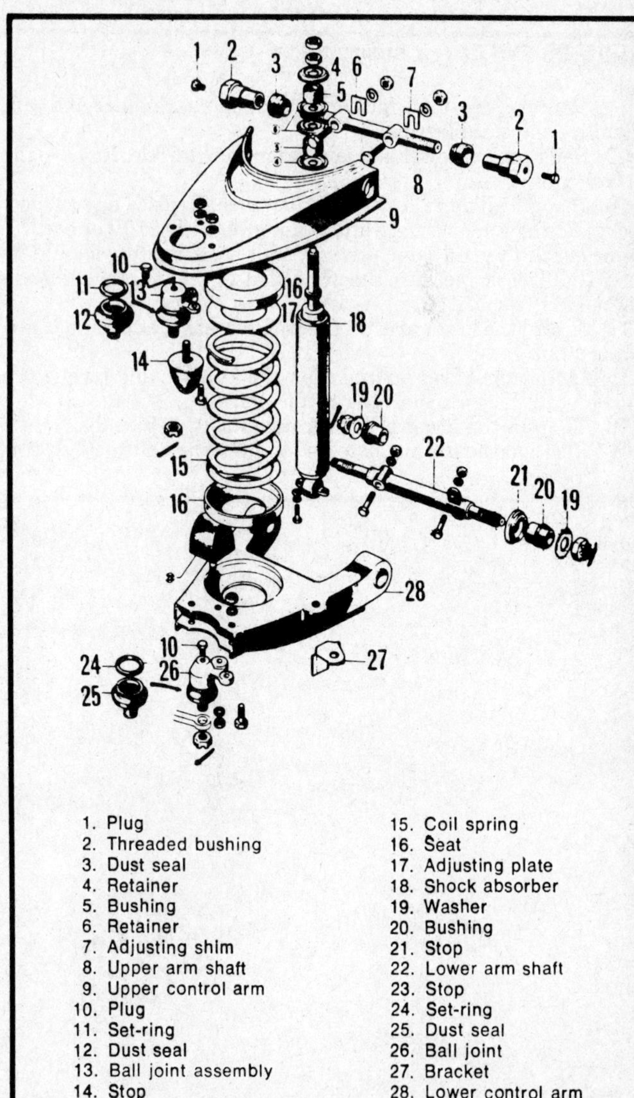

1982–85 Front suspension – exploded view

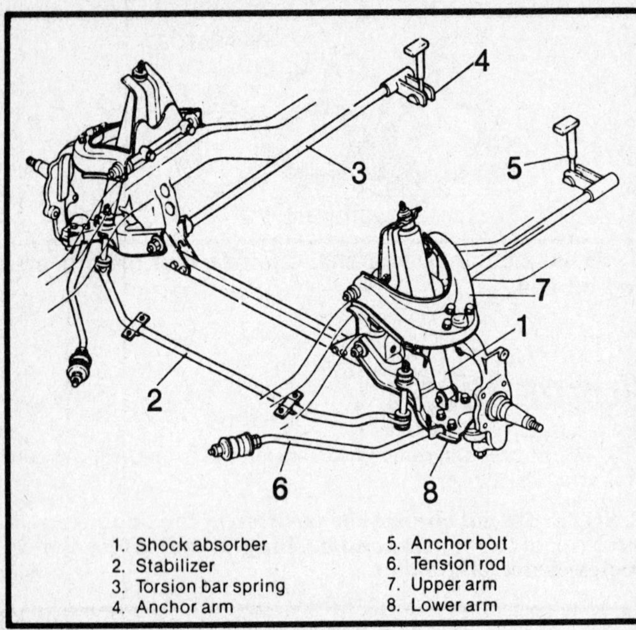

1986–88 2WD front suspension

11. Remove the stabilizer bar bolt, bushing, retainer and nut. Remove the stabilizer bar.

12. Separate the lower ball joint from the knuckle. Remove the lower control arm.

13. Inspect all parts for wear or damage. Replace any suspect parts. Using a spring scale and adapter 49 0180 510B or equivalent, check the ball joint preload. Pull scale reading should be 39.6 lbs. or less. Measure the preload after first shaking the ball joint stud to make sure it is free.

14. Install the lower arm on the frame bracket and hand tighten the nut.

15. Install the lower ball joint on the knuckle and torque the nut to 115 ft. lbs. Install the cotter pin.

16. Tighten the lower arm to frame nut to 115 ft. lbs.

17. Position the torque plate and tighten the bolt to 68 ft. lbs.

18. Coat the splines on the torsion bar with grease. Check the ends of the torsion bar. The bars are marked L for left and R for right. Align the matchmarks and install the torsion bar in the torque plate.

19. Coat the splines on the torsion bar with grease. Align the matchmarks and install the anchor arm on the torsion bar.

20. Install the anchor bolt and swivel and tighten the bolt until the matchmarks are mated.

21. Install the tension rod. Torque the bushing end nut to 90 ft. lbs.; the lower arm end bolts to 85 ft. lbs.

22. Install the stabilizer bar. Torque the bolt to 19 ft. lbs.

23. Install the shock absorber bolt. Torque the bolt to 55–59 ft. lbs.

24. Install the wheel assembly and lower the vehicle to the ground.

25. Retorque the lower arm to frame bracket nut.

26. Check the front and rear tire pressures. Set the pressures to what are specified on the vehicle rating plate, except for P-metric radials. Set them at the maximum pressure shown on the side wall.

27. Measure the distance from the center of the wheel hub to the lip of the fender. This is the ride height. Proper ride height is obtained when the difference between the left and the right side is less than 10mm. Adjust the ride height by turning the anchor bolt.

NOTE: If the torsion bar anchor bolt was not matchmarked, the matchmarks were lost, or new, unmarked torsion bar is being installed, follow this procedure to obtain the correct ride height.

28. Install the anchor arm on the torsion bar so that there is 125mm between the lowest point on the arm and the crossmember directly above it.

29. Tighten the anchor bolt until the anchor arm contacts the swivel. Then, tighten the bolt an additional 45mm travel.

Shock Absorbers

Removal and Installation

1. Raise and support the vehicle safely.

2. Remove the upper end nut, bushings and washers from the shock absorber stem.

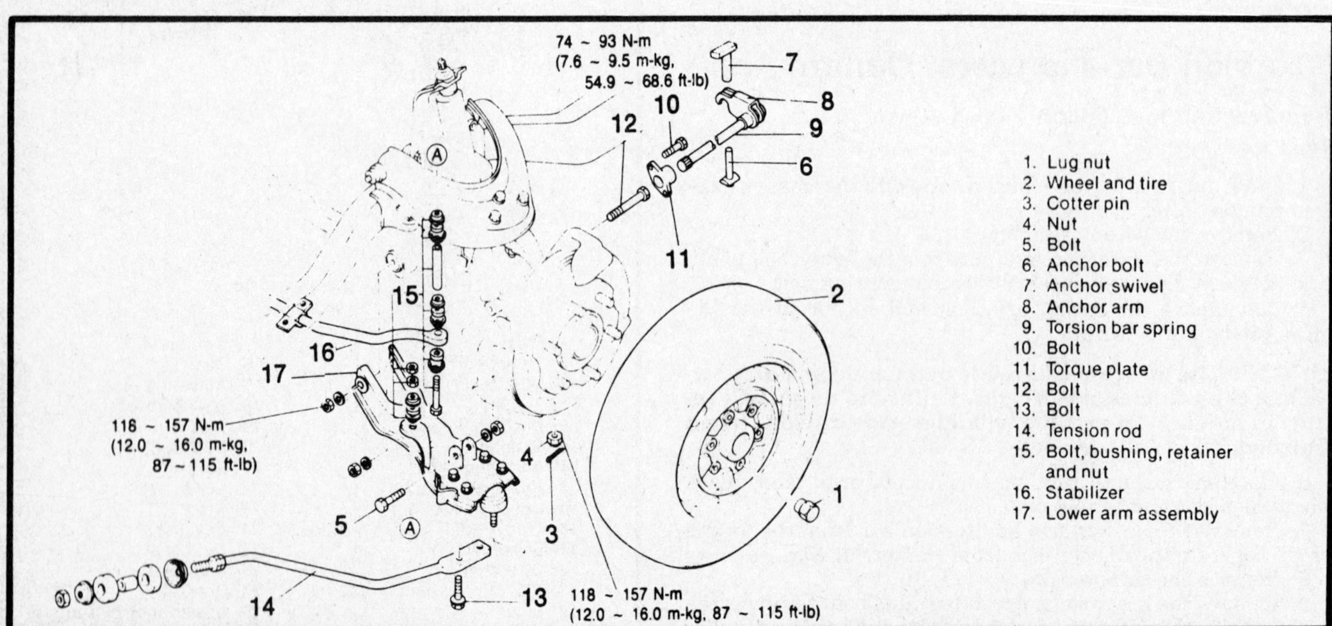

1986–88 2WD torsion bar removal

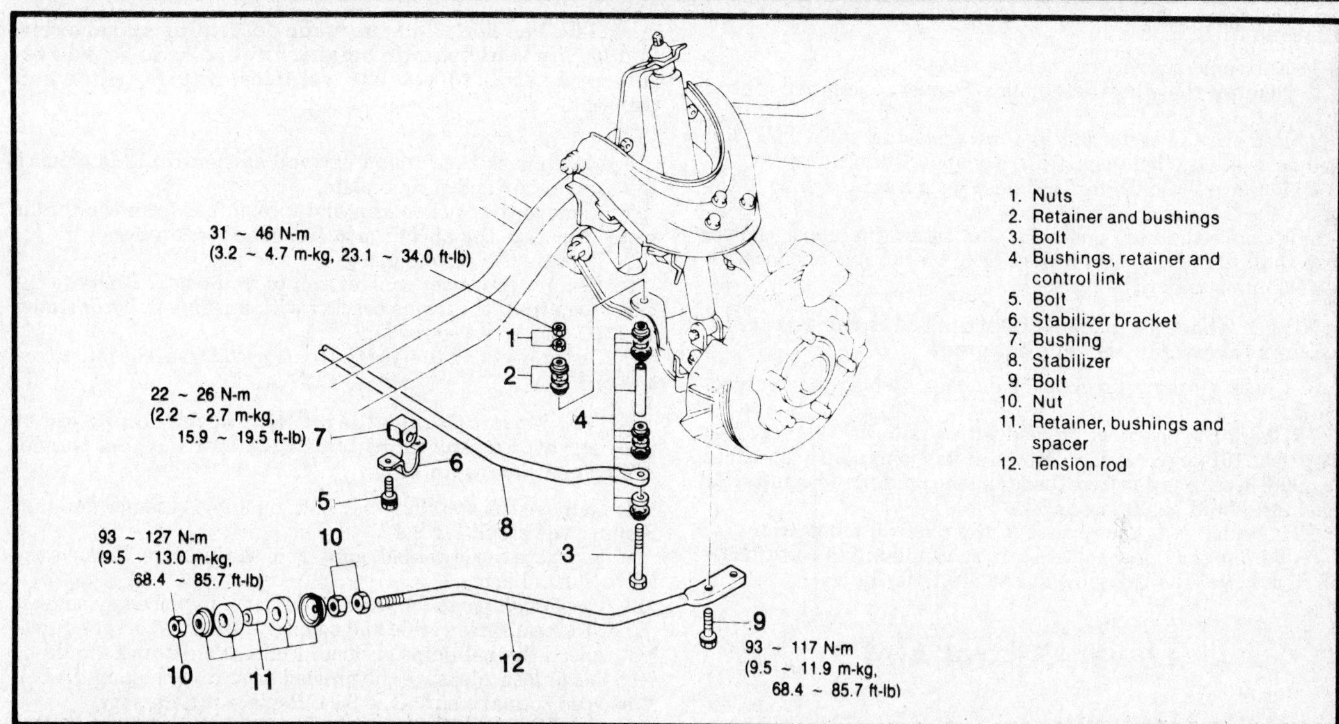

1986–88 2WD tension and stabilizer bar removal

3. Remove the lower shock absorber attaching bolts.
4. Remove the shock absorber from beneath the lower control arm.
5. Installation is the reverse of the removal procedure.
6. Tighten the lower bolts to 25 ft. lbs. on 1982–84 models and 55–59 ft. lbs. on 1985–88 models.
7. Tighten the upper nut until 1/4 inch of thread is visible above the locknut on 1982–84 models.
8. On the 1985–88 models, tighten the upper nut to 17–25 ft. lbs. At this point, 7mm of thread should be visible above the nut.

Upper Control Arm

Removal and Installation

1982–85 MODELS

1. Raise and support the vehicle safely.
2. Raise the lower control arm until the upper control arm is off the bumper stop.
3. Remove the wheel assembly.
4. Install a spring compressor on the coil spring.

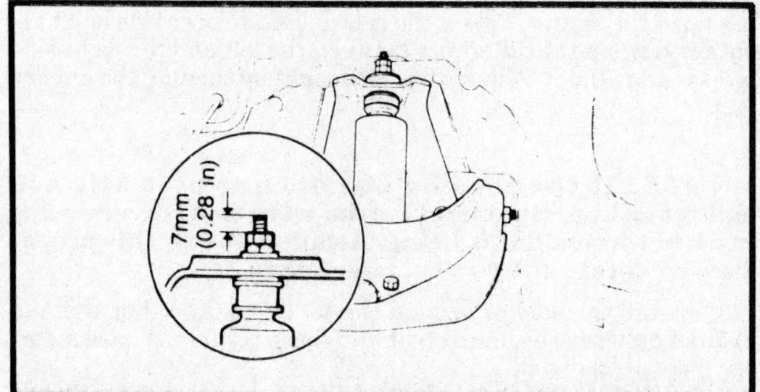

1986–88 Upper shock absorber nut installation

CAUTION

Before separating the upper and/or lower ball joints from the control arms, make sure that the coil spring compressor is securely installed. Failure to do so, could cause the spring to jump out of the compressor, causing possible injury.

5. Remove the cotter pin and nut retaining the upper ball joint.
6. Disconnect the upper ball joint from the spindle. Unbolt and replace the ball joint, if necessary.
7. Inside the engine compartment, remove the two upper control arm retaining bolts and remove the control arm from the truck. Note the number and position of any shims.
8. Installation is the reverse of the removal procedure.
9. Place the shims in their original locations. Torque the two arm retaining bolts to 65–75 ft. lbs., the ball joint to control arm bolts to 15–20 ft. lbs. and the ball joint to spindle nut to 40–55 ft. lbs.

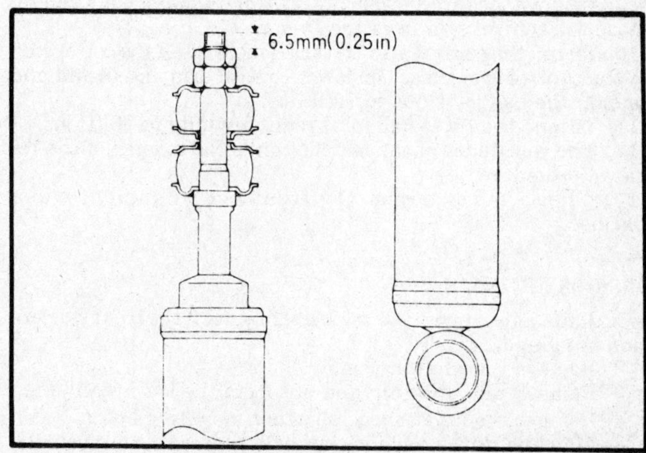

1982–85 Upper shock absorber nut installation

1986–88 MODELS

1. Raise and support the vehicle safely.
2. Remove the wheel assemblies. Support the lower control arm.
3. Remove the cotter pin and nut from the upper ball joint and separate the ball joint from the upper control arm.
4. Remove the bushings and dust seals from the ends of the upper control arm shaft.
5. Remove the nuts and bolts that retain the upper control arm shaft to the support bracket. Note the number and location of the shims under the nuts.

NOTE: These shims must be installed in their exact locations for proper wheel alignment.

6. Check all parts for wear or damage. Replace any suspect parts.
7. Check the ball joint preload with a pull scale and adapter 49 0180 510B or equivalent. Move the ball joint stud a few times to make sure that it is free, then take the reading. The pull scale reading should be 40 lbs. or less.
8. Installation is the reverse of the removal procedure.
9. Torque the upper control arm shaft mounting bolts to 60–68 ft. lbs. and the ball joint nut to 30–37 ft. lbs.

Lower Control Arm

Removal and Installation

1982–85 MODELS

1. Raise and support the vehicle safely.
2. Remove the wheel assemblies.
3. Remove the lower shock absorber mounting bolts and compress the shock absorber upwards, out of the way.
4. Disconnect the front stabilizer bar from the control arms.
5. Raise the lower control arm to compress the spring. Install a spring compressor.

CAUTION

Before separating the upper and/or lower ball joints from the control arms, make sure that the coil spring compressor is securely installed. Failure to do so, could cause the spring to jump out of the compressor, causing possible injury.

6. Disconnect the ball joint from the lower control arm.
7. Pull the spindle and ball joint away from the control arm. Unbolt and replace the ball joint, if necessary.
8. Carefully lower the control arm and remove the coil spring. Release the pressure on the spring after removal.
9. Remove the three lower control arm retaining bolts and remove the control arm from the frame.
10. Install the control arm on the frame. Install the coil spring in the control arm, raise the lower control arm and install and tighten the ball joint nut to 70 ft. lbs.
11. Torque the three ball joint retaining nuts to 70 ft. lbs.
12. The remainder of the installation is the reverse of the removal procedure.
13. Check and/or adjust the front end alignment when finished.

1986–88 MODELS

1. Raise and support the vehicle safely, with the front suspension hanging freely.
2. Remove the wheel assembly.
3. Remove the cotter pin and nut from the lower ball joint.
4. Remove the lower shock absorber mounting bolt.
5. Matchmark the anchor arm bolt and anchor swivel. Remove the bolt and swivel.

NOTE: The matchmarks made determine and are critical to, the vehicles ride height. Failure to do so, will result in having to set the vehicles ride hieght when finished.

6. Matchmark the torsion bar and anchor arm. Matchmark the torsion bar and torque plate.
7. Remove the anchor arm and torsion bar from the torque plate. Separate the anchor arm from the torsion bar.
8. Remove the torque plate.
9. Remove the lower control arm to frame bolt. Separate the lower arm from the frame bracket with bushing puller/installer 49 0727 575 or its equivalent.
10. Disconnect and remove the tension rod from the lower control arm.

NOTE: Do not change the position of the double nut at the rear of the tension rod bushing. It will affect the vehicles caster alignment.

11. Remove the stabilizer bar bolt, bushing, retainer and nut. Remove the stabilizer bar.
12. Separate the lower ball joint from the knuckle. Remove the lower control arm.
13. Inspect all parts for wear or damage. Replace any suspect parts. Using a spring scale and adapter 49 0180 510B or equivalent, check the ball joint preload. Pull scale reading should be 39.6 lbs. or less. Measure the preload after first shaking the ball joint stud to make sure it is free. Replace if necessary.
14. Install the lower arm on the frame bracket and hand tighten the nut.
15. Install the lower ball joint on the knuckle and torque the nut to 115 ft. lbs. Install the cotter pin.
16. Tighten the lower arm to frame nut to 115 ft. lbs.
17. Position the torque plate and tighten the bolt to 68 ft. lbs.
18. Coat the splines on the torsion bar with grease. Check the ends of the torsion bar. The bars are marked L for left and R for right. Align the matchmarks and install the torsion bar in the torque plate.
19. Coat the splines on the torsion bar with grease. Align the matchmarks and install the anchor arm on the torsion bar.
20. Install the anchor bolt and swivel and tighten the bolt until the matchmarks are mated.
21. Install the tension rod. Torque the bushing end nut to 90 ft. lbs.; the lower arm end bolts to 85 ft. lbs.
22. Install the stabilizer bar. Torque the bolt to 19 ft. lbs.
23. Install the shock absorber bolt. Torque the bolt to 55–59 ft. lbs.
24. Install the wheel assembly and lower the vehicle to the ground.
25. Retorque the lower arm to frame bracket nut.
26. Check the front and rear tire pressures. Set the pressures to what are specified on the vehicle rating plate, except for P-metric radials. Set them at the maximum pressure shown on the side wall.
27. Measure the distance from the center of the wheel hub to the lip of the fender. This is the ride height. Proper ride height is obtained when the difference between the left and the right side is less than 10mm. Adjust the ride height by turning the anchor bolt.

NOTE: If the torsion bar anchor bolt was not matchmarked, the matchmarks were lost, or new, unmarked torsion bar is being installed, follow this procedure to obtain the correct ride height.

28. Install the anchor arm on the torsion bar so that there is 125mm between the lowest point on the arm and the crossmember directly above it.
29. Tighten the anchor bolt until the anchor arm contacts the swivel. Then, tighten the bolt an additional 45mm travel.

Ball Joints

UPPER BALL JOINT

Inspection

2WD MODELS

1. Inspect the dust seals. If cracked or brittle, replace them.
2. Check end play of both the upper and lower ball joints. If either exceeds 0.0039 in., it is defective and must be replaced.

Removal and Installation

ALL 2WD MODELS

1. Raise and support the vehicle safely.
2. Remove the wheel assemblies. Support the lower control arm. On 1982–85 models, install a coil spring compressor on the spring.
3. Remove the cotter pin and nut from the upper ball joint and separate the ball joint from the upper control arm. On 1982–85 models, remove the coil spring and release the tension on the compressor.
4. Remove the bushings and dust seals from the ends of the upper control arm shaft.
5. Remove the nuts and bolts that retain the upper control arm shaft to the support bracket. Note the number and location of the shims under the nuts.

NOTE: These shims must be installed in their exact locations for proper wheel alignment.

6. Check all parts for wear or damage. Replace any suspect parts.
7. Check the ball joint preload with a pull scale and adapter 49 0180 510B or equivalent. Move the ball joint stud a few times to make sure that it is free, then take the reading. The pull scale reading should be 40 lbs. or less. Replace if necessary, using a press.
8. Installation is the reverse of the removal procedure.
9. Torque the upper control arm shaft mounting bolts to 60–68 ft. lbs. and the ball joint nut to 30–37 ft. lbs.

LOWER BALL JOINT

Inspection

2WD MODELS

1. Inspect the dust seals. If cracked or brittle, replace them.
2. Check end play of both the upper and lower ball joints. If either exceeds 0.0039 in., it is defective.

Removal and Installation

1982–85 2WD MODELS

1. Raise and support the vehicle safely.
2. Remove the wheel assemblies.
3. Remove the lower shock absorber mounting bolts and compress the shock absorber upwards, out of the way.
4. Disconnect the front stabilizer bar from the control arms.
5. Raise the lower control arm to compress the spring. Install a spring compressor.

CAUTION

Before separating the upper and/or lower ball joints from the control arms, make sure that the coil spring compressor is securely installed. Failure to do so, could cause the spring to jump out of the compressor, causing possible injury.

6. Disconnect the ball joint from the lower control arm.
7. Pull the spindle and ball joint away from the control arm. Unbolt and replace the ball joint, if necessary.
8. Carefully lower the control arm and remove the coil spring. Release the pressure on the spring after removal.
9. Remove the three lower control arm retaining bolts and remove the control arm from the frame. Using a press, remove and install the ball joint.
10. Install the control arm on the frame. Install the coil spring in the control arm, raise the lower control arm and install and tighten the ball joint nut to 70 ft. lbs.
11. Torque the three ball joint retaining nuts to 70 ft. lbs.
12. The remainder of the installation is the reverse of the removal procedure.
13. Check and/or adjust the front end alignment when finished.

1986–88 MODELS

1. Raise and support the vehicle safely, with the front suspension hanging freely.
2. Remove the wheel assembly.
3. Remove the cotter pin and nut from the lower ball joint.
4. Remove the lower shock absorber mounting bolt.
5. Matchmark the anchor arm bolt and anchor swivel. Remove the bolt and swivel.

NOTE: The matchmarks made determine and are critical to, the vehicles ride height. Failure to do so, will result in having to set the vehicles ride hieght when finished.

6. Matchmark the torsion bar and anchor arm. Matchmark the torsion bar and torque plate.
7. Remove the anchor arm and torsion bar from the torque plate. Separate the anchor arm from the torsion bar.
8. Remove the torque plate.
9. Remove the lower control arm to frame bolt. Separate the lower arm from the frame bracket with bushing puller/installer 49 0727 575 or its equivalent.
10. Disconnect and remove the tension rod from the lower control arm.

NOTE: Do not change the position of the double nut at the rear of the tension rod bushing. It will affect the vehicles caster alignment.

11. Remove the stabilizer bar bolt, bushing, retainer and nut. Remove the stabilizer bar.
12. Separate the lower ball joint from the knuckle. Remove the lower control arm.
13. Inspect all parts for wear or damage. Replace any suspect parts. Using a spring scale and adapter 49 0180 510B or equivalent, check the ball joint preload. Pull scale reading should be 39.6 lbs. or less. Measure the preload after first shaking the ball joint stud to make sure it is free. Replace if necessary, using a press.
14. Install the lower arm on the frame bracket and hand tighten the nut.
15. Install the lower ball joint on the knuckle and torque the nut to 115 ft. lbs. Install the cotter pin.
16. Tighten the lower arm to frame nut to 115 ft. lbs.
17. Position the torque plate and tighten the bolt to 68 ft. lbs.
18. Coat the splines on the torsion bar with grease. Check the ends of the torsion bar. The bars are marked L for left and R for right. Align the matchmarks and install the torsion bar in the torque plate.
19. Coat the splines on the torsion bar with grease. Align the matchmarks and install the anchor arm on the torsion bar.
20. Install the anchor bolt and swivel and tighten the bolt until the matchmarks are mated.
21. Install the tension rod. Torque the bushing end nut to 90 ft. lbs.; the lower arm end bolts to 85 ft. lbs.
22. Install the stabilizer bar. Torque the bolt to 19 ft. lbs.
23. Install the shock absorber bolt. Torque the bolt to 55–59 ft. lbs.

24. Install the wheel assembly and lower the vehicle to the ground.
25. Retorque the lower arm to frame bracket nut.
26. Check the front and rear tire pressures. Set the pressures to what are specified on the vehicle rating plate, except for P-metric radials. Set them at the maximum pressure shown on the side wall.
27. Measure the distance from the center of the wheel hub to the lip of the fender. This is the ride height. Proper ride height is obtained when the difference between the left and the right side is less than 10mm. Adjust the ride height by turning the anchor bolt.

NOTE: If the torsion bar anchor bolt was not matchmarked, the matchmarks were lost, or new, unmarked torsion bar is being installed, follow this procedure to obtain the correct ride height.

28. Install the anchor arm on the torsion bar so that there is 125mm between the lowest point on the arm and the crossmember directly above it.
29. Tighten the anchor bolt until the anchor arm contacts the swivel. Then, tighten the bolt an additional 45mm travel.

Wheel Bearings

Removal and Installation

2WD MODELS

1. Raise and support the vehicle safely.
2. Remove the wheel assembly.
3. Remove the grease cap, cotter pin, hub nut and flat washer.
4. Without disconnecting the brake line from the caliper, remove the caliper and support it out of the way. Place a hand over the outer wheel bearing and remove the hub from the spindle.
5. Remove the spacer, inner seal and inner bearing. Discard the seal.
6. Thoroughly clean the inside of the hub with solvent. Allow to dry completely before proceeding.
7. Inspect the bearings for wear, damage, heat discoloration or other signs of fatigue. If they are at all suspect, replace them.

NOTE: When replacing wheel bearings, replace the bearings and races as a set. Never mixmatch bearings and races.

8. To replace the races, carefully press them out of the hub.
9. Coat the outside of the new races with clean wheel bearing grease and drive them into place until they are seated in the hub. Make certain that they are completely seated.
10. Pack the inside of the hub with clean wheel bearing grease.
11. Pack each bearing with clean grease, making sure that it is thoroughly packed.
12. Install the inner bearing and seal. Drive the seal into place carefully until it is seated to the same depth as when removed.
13. Install the spacer and the hub on the spindle.
14. Install the outer bearing, flat washer and hub nut.
15. Adjust the wheel bearing.
16. Install the nut cap, cotter pin and grease cap. Install the wheel assembly.

Adjustment

1. Raise and support the vehicle safely.

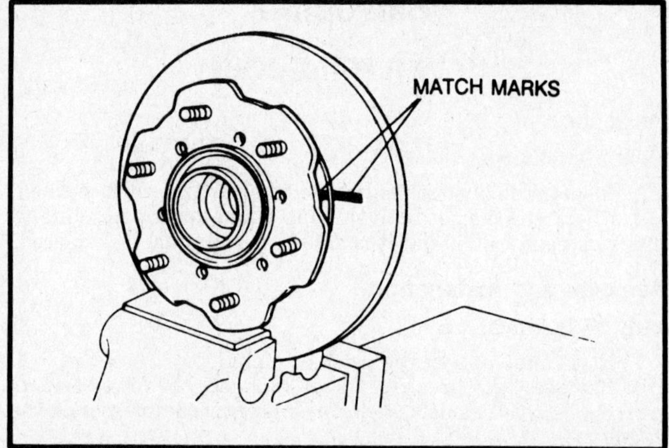

Matchmark the rotor to the hub before disassembly

2. Remove the wheel assembly. Without disconnecting the brake line, remove the disc brake caliper. Support the caliper out of the way.
3. Attach a spring scale to a wheel stud on the hub.
4. Pull the scale horizontally and check the force needed to start the hub turning. The force should be 1.3–2.4 lbs. If the reading is not correct, adjust the bearing.
5. To adjust, remove the grease cap and cotter pin.
6. Tighten or loosen the hub nut until the correct pull rating is obtained.
7. Align the cotter pin holes and insert a new cotter pin. Install the grease cap and wheel assembly.

Alignment

Procedures

1982–88 2WD MODELS

1. Check the air pressure in the tires. Correct if necessary.
2. Raise and support the vehicle safely.
3. Check the front suspension for any loose or broken components.
4. Lower the vehicle and procede with the alignment.
5. On 1982–85 models, caster should be 1° 0′. On 1986–88 models, caster should be 0° 50′, ± 45′, for manual steering models and 1° 50′ ± 45′, for power steering models.
6. On all models, caster is adjusted by increasing or decreasing the amount of shims under the upper control arm mounting shaft.
7. Camber, on all 1982–88 models, should be 0° 45′ ± 25′.
8. Camber is adjusted by the turning of the upper control arm shaft until the proper specification is obtained.

NOTE: Turning the upper control arm shaft will result in a change in the caster reading. While turning the shaft, observe both readings for caster and camber until both are within specification.

9. Toe is adjusted by turning the outer tie rod ends the same amount in either direction.
10. On 1982–85 models, toe in should be 0–0.240 in. On 1986–88 models, toe in should be 0.120 in. ± 0.120 in.

4WD FRONT SUSPENSION

Torsion Bar

Removal and Installation

1987-88 4WD MODELS

1. Raise and support the vehicle safely. Remove the wheel assembly.
2. Support the torsion bar. Matchmark the torsion bar anchor bolt to the torsion bar and remove the torsion bar anchor bolt.
3. Matchmark the torsion bar to the anchor plate and remove the anchor plate from the body. Remove the torsion bar to torque plate bolts. Remove the torsion bar from the plate.
4. Support the lower control arm and remove the lower ball joint cotter pin and nut. Disconnect the shock absorber from the lower control arm.
5. Separate the lower ball joint from the steering knuckle.
6. Remove the front torsion bar to lower control arm bolt. Remove the torsion bar.
7. Installation is the reverse of the removal procedure. Alignment the matchmarks made during the removal.
8. Torque the ball joint nut to 87–115 ft. lbs. and the torsion bar anchor plate to 55–69 ft. lbs. Torque the shock absorber bolt to 40–59 ft. lbs.
9. Check and adjust the vehicle ride height if necessary, when finished.

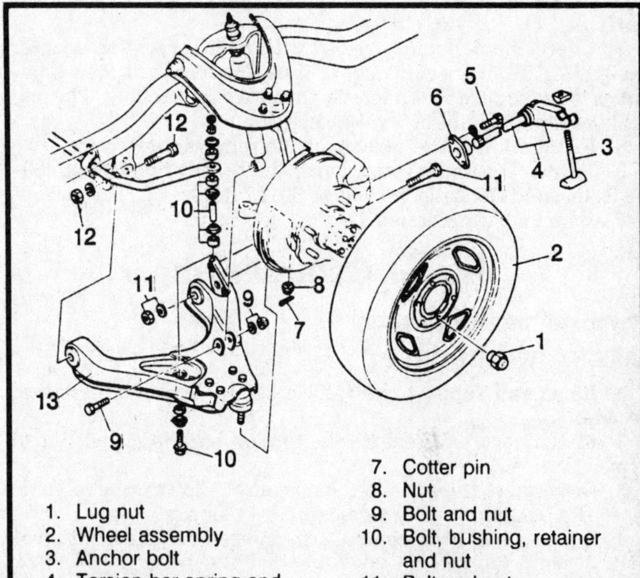

4WD front suspension – exploded view

Shock Absorbers

Removal and Installation

1987-88 4WD MODELS

1. Raise and support the vehicle safely. Remove the wheel assembly.
2. Remove the upper shock absorber mounting nut, washers and bushings.
3. Compress the shock absorber to a level under the upper control arm.
4. Remove the lower shock absorber mounting bolt and nut.
5. Remove the shock absorber from the vehicle.
6. Installation is the reverse of the removal procedure.
7. Torque the lower shock aborber bolt and nut to 40–59 ft. lbs.
8. Torque the upper shock absorber nut to 17–25 ft. lbs. or, until there is a of 7mm of thread protruding from the shock absorber threads.

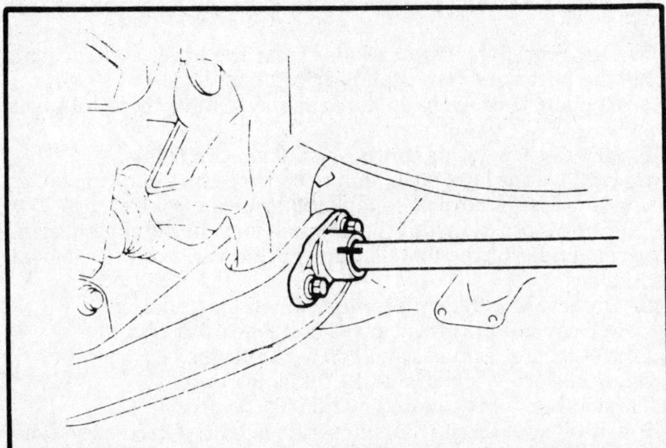
Install matchmarks on the front torsion bar mount before removal

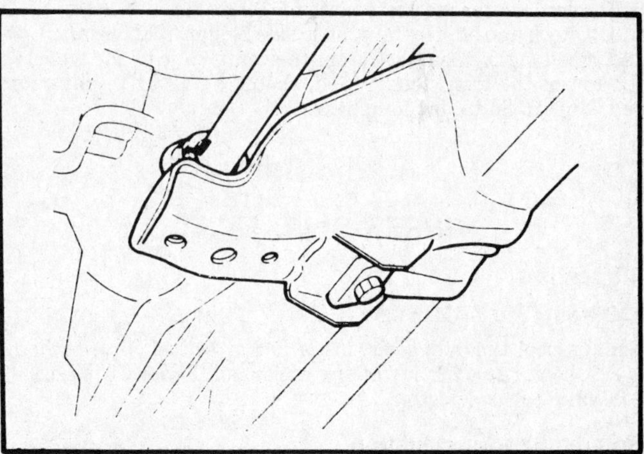
Install matchmarks on the rear torsion bar mount before removal

Upper Control Arm

Removal and Installation

1987-88 4WD MODELS

1. Raise and support the vehicle safely.
2. Remove the wheel assemblies. Support the lower control arm.
3. Remove the cotter pin and nut from the upper ball joint and separate the ball joint from the upper control arm.
4. Remove the bushings and dust seals from the ends of the upper control arm shaft.
5. Remove the nuts and bolts that retain the upper control arm shaft to the support bracket. Note the number and location of the shims under the nuts.

NOTE: These shims must be installed in their exact locations for proper wheel alignment.

6. Check all parts for wear or damage. Replace any suspect parts.
7. Check the ball joint preload with a pull scale and adapter 49 0180 510B or its equivalent. Move the ball joint stud a few times to make sure that it is free, then take the reading. The pull scale reading should be 40 lbs. or less.
8. Installation is the reverse of the removal procedure.
9. Torque the upper control arm shaft mounting bolts to 60–68 ft. lbs. and the ball joint nut to 30–37 ft. lbs. Check the front end alignment if necessary.

Lower Control Arm

Removal and Installation

1987–88 4WD MODELS

1. Raise and support the vehicle safely. Remove the wheel assembly.
2. Matchmark and remove the torsion bar from the control arm.
3. Disconnect the stabilizer bar from the lower control arm. Note the position of the stabilizer bar bushings.
4. Support the lower control arm and remove the front pivot bolt.
5. Remove the lower control arm from the frame.
6. Installation is the reverse of the removal procedure.
7. Observe the follwing torques during installation:
Lower control arm front pivot bolt 87–115 ft. lbs.
Lower control arm rear bolt 115–145 ft. lbs.
Shock absorber lower bolt 40–59 ft. lbs.
Torsion bar torque plate bolts 55–69 ft. lbs.
8. Check and adjust the vehicle ride height, if necessary. Correct ride height, measured from the center line of the wheel to the top of the front fender well, should be 17.01 in. for short beds and 16.85 in. for long beds.

Ball Joints

UPPER BALL JOINT

Inspection

1987–88 4WD MODELS

1. Inspect the dust seals. If cracked or brittle, replace them.
2. Check the end play of the upper ball joints. If it exceeds 0.0039 in., it is defective.

Removal and Installation

1. Raise and support the vehicle safely.
2. Remove the wheel assembly. Support the lower control arm.
3. Remove the cotter pin and nut from the upper ball joint and separate the ball joint from the upper control arm.
4. Remove the bushings and dust seals from the ends of the upper control arm shaft.
5. Remove the nuts and bolts that retain the upper control arm shaft to the support bracket. Note the number and location of the shims under the nuts.

NOTE: These shims must be installed in their exact locations for proper wheel alignment.

6. Check all parts for wear or damage. Replace any suspect parts.
7. Check the ball joint preload with a pull scale and adapter 49 0180 510B or its equivalent. Move the ball joint stud a few times to make sure that it is free, then take the reading. The pull scale reading should be 40 lbs. or less.

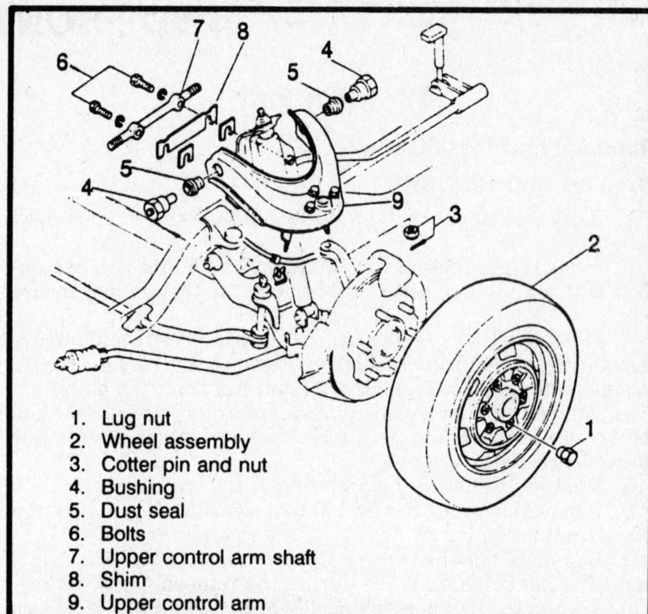

Upper control arm mounting

8. Remove the ball joint mounting bolts. Using a press, remove the upper ball joint from the control arm.
9. Installation is the reverse of the removal procedure.
10. Torque the upper control arm shaft mounting bolts to 60–68 ft. lbs. and the ball joint nut to 30–37 ft. lbs. Check the front end alignment if necessary.

LOWER BALL JOINT

Inspection

1987–88 4WD MODELS

1. Inspect the dust seals. If cracked or brittle, replace them.
2. Check the end play of the lower ball joints. If it exceeds 0.0039 in., it is defective.

Removal and Installation

1. Raise and support the vehicle safely. Remove the wheel assembly.
2. Matchmark and remove the torsion bar from the control arm.
3. Disconnect the stabilizer bar from the lower control arm. Note the position of the stabilizer bar bushings.
4. Support the lower control arm and remove the front pivot bolt.
5. Remove the lower control arm from the frame.
6. Remove the lower ball joint to control arm mounting bolts. Using a press, remove the ball joint from the control arm.
7. Using a press, install the new ball joint in the control arm. The remainder of the installation is the reverse of the removal procedure.
8. Observe the follwing torques during installation:
Lower control arm front pivot bolt 87–115 ft. lbs.
Lower control arm rear bolt 115–145 ft. lbs.
Shock absorber lower bolt 40–59 ft. lbs.
Torsion bar torque plate bolts 55–69 ft. lbs.
9. Check and adjust the vehicle ride height, if necessary. Correct ride height, measured from the center line of the wheel to the top of the front fender well, should be 17.01 in. for short beds and 16.85 in. for long beds.

Front Wheel Bearings

Removal, Installation and Adjustment

1987–88 4WD MODELS

1. Raise and support the vehicle safely. Remove the wheel assembly.
2. Remove the locking hub assembly. Remove the disc brake caliper and mount from the spindle, without disconnecting the brake line.
3. Remove the circlip and spacer from in front of the wheel bearing.
4. Remove the bearing set plate and set screw.
5. Using tool 49 S231 635 or its equivalent, remove the bearing lock nut counter clockwise.
6. Remove the hub from the axleshaft.
7. Check the hub for cracks or damage. Check the inner and outer bearings and races for wear.
8. Matchmark the rotor to the hub and, remove the rotor from the hub.
9. Drive out the inner grease seal and bearing race.
10. Drive out the outer bearing race.
11. Clean and inspect the inside of the hub.
12. Drive in the inner and outer bearing races into the hub. Make sure that they are fully seated in the hub.
13. Thoroughly pack the new wheel bearings in high temperature wheel bearing grease.
14. Install the inner wheel bearing in the hub. Drive the inner grease seal in the hub until it is flush with the surface.
15. Align the matchmarks on the rotor and the hub.
16. Install the hub on the spindle and place the outer wheel bearing in the hub.
17. Install the wheel bearing lock nut and adjust the turning torque of the hub.
18. Attach a spring scale to the wheel stud on the hub. The frictional force required to turn the hub should be 1.3–2.6 lbs.
19. Tighten the wheel bearing lock nut until the reading is correct.
20. The remainder of the installation is the reverse of the removal procedure.

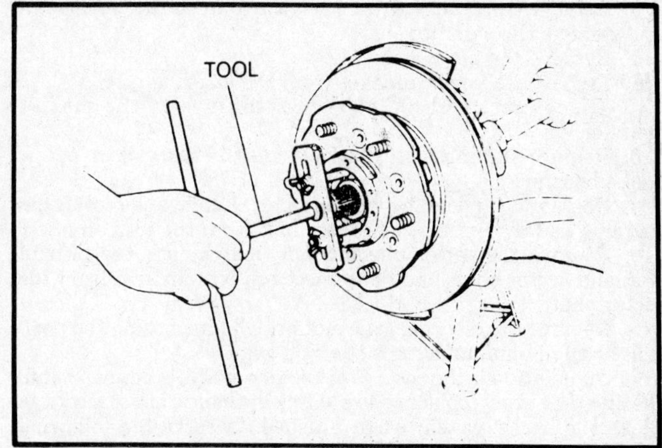

Removing the wheel bearing lock nut

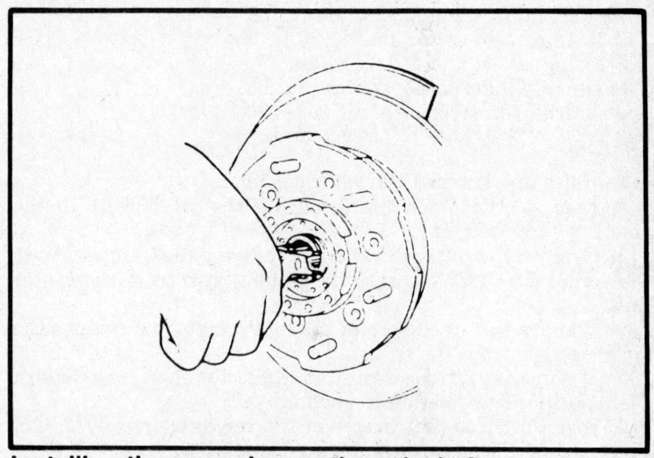
Installing the snap ring on the axleshaft

Alignment

Procedures

1987–88 4WD MODELS

1. Check and correct the air pressure in the tires.
2. Raise and support the vehicle safely. Remove the wheel assemblies.
3. Using a spring scale, check and adjust the frictional force required to turn the hub. The force should be 1.3–2.6 lbs.
4. Install the wheel assemblies. Check the suspension for loose, broken or bent components.
5. Lower the vehicle.
6. Toe is adjusted by loosening the tie rod end lock nuts and turning both tie rods the same amount until the correct reading is obtained. Toe should be 0.12 in. ± 0.12 in.
7. Caster and camber are adjusted at the same time. Remove the locking hub.
8. Attach alignment gauge 49 1205 605 or equivalent, to the hub.
9. Adjustments are made by increasing or decreasing the amount of shims under the upper control arm shaft.
10. Observe both the camber and caster readings while changing the shims.
11. With manual steering, the caster should be 0° 50′ ± 45′. With power steering, the caster should be 2° 45′.
12. The camber should be 1° ± 25′. The difference between the right and left side readings must not be more than 30′ for camber and 45′ for the caster.

STEERING GEAR AND LINKAGE

For steering gear overhaul, refer to the Unit Overhaul Section.

Manual Steering Gear

Removal and Installation

1982–85

1. Disconnect the negative battery cable. Remove the steering wheel.
2. Remove the steering column covers.
3. Remove the stop ring, cancelling cam and spring from the end of the column.
4. Disconnect and tag the combination switch wiring.
5. Remove the combination switch from the column.
6. Remove the steering column support bracket.
7. Loosen the nut securing the bottom of the steering column jacket and pull the jacket off of the shaft.
8. Remove the dust cover from the firewall at the bottom of the shaft.

9. Remove the bolt securing the yoke joint to the wormshaft and remove the steering shaft.
10. Remove the air cleaner.
11. Remove the lower bracket from the steering gear.
12. Disconnect and plug the brakes lines at the master cylinder.
13. Remove the master cylinder from the firewall or power brake booster.
14. Raise and support the vehicle safely. Remove the cotter pin and nut and disconnect the center link from the pitman arm.
15. Remove the cotter pin and nut, matchmark the pitman arm and sector shaft and disconnect the pitman arm from the sector shaft.
16. Remove the steering gear mounting bolts, noting the position of any shims under the steering gear.
17. Installation is the reverse of the removal procedure. Install the steering gear, replacing any shims in their original location. Bleed the brake system when finished. Observe the following torques during installation:
  Steering gear-to-frame: 40 ft. lbs.
  Center link-to-pitman arm: 30 ft. lbs.
  Pitman arm-to-sector shaft: 130 ft. lbs.
  Steering wheel nut: 22–29 ft. lbs.
  Master Cylinder-to-booster: 15 ft. lbs.
  Wormshaft-to-steering shaft yoke: 20 ft. lbs.

1986–88

1. Raise and support the vehicle safely.
2. Remove the pinch bolt securing the wormshaft to the steering shaft coupling.
3. Remove the cotter pin and nut securing the pitman arm to the center link and separate the pitman arm from the center link.
4. Remove the steering gear mounting bolts and remove the steering gear from the frame.
5. If removing pitman arm from the sector shaft, matchmark their positions in relation to each other.
6. Installation is the reverse of the removal procedure. Observe the following torques during installation:
  Steering gear-to-frame: 40 ft. lbs.
  Wormshaft-to-steering shaft yoke: 28 ft. lbs.
  Pitman arm-to-sector shaft: 139 ft. lbs.
  Pitman arm-to-center link: 30 ft. lbs.

1982–85 Steering linkage—exploded view

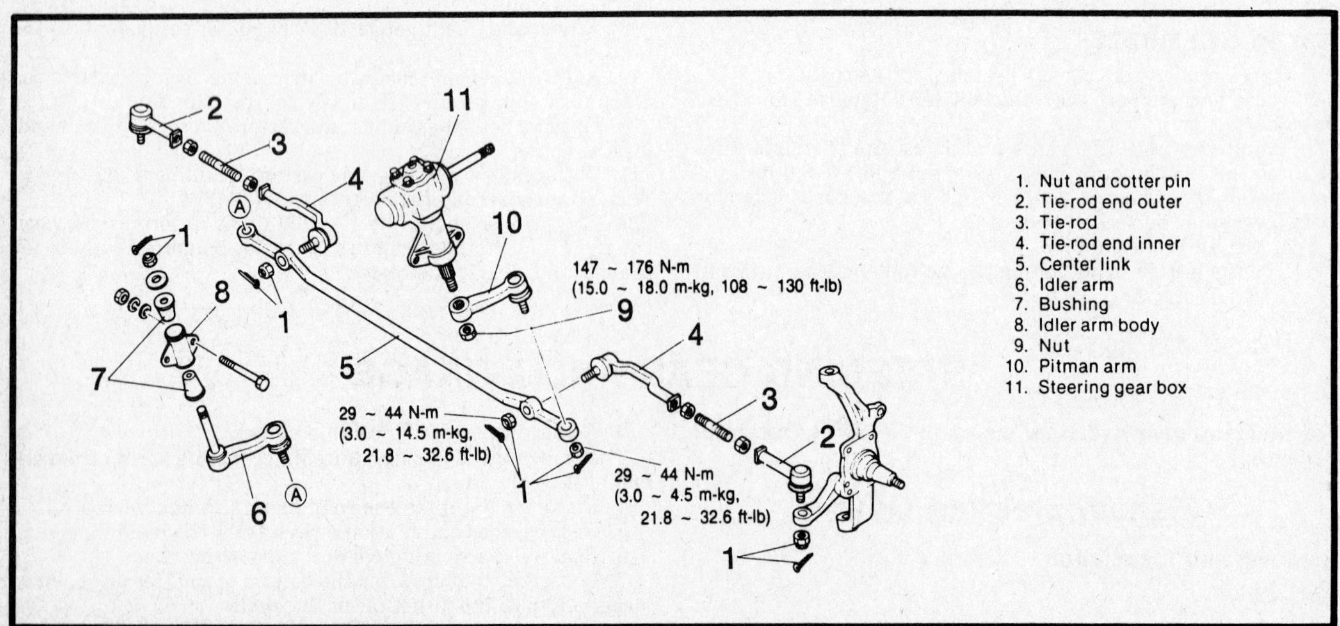

1986–88 Steering gear and linkage—exploded view

Adjustment

NOTE: The only adjustments possible on the steering gear is when the gear is being overhauled. Refer to the Unit Overhaul Section for procedures.

Power Steering Gear

Removal and Installation

NOTE: Removal and Installation of the power steering gear is the same as the manual steering gear, with the exception of disconnecting and plugging the fluid lines. After installation, bleed the power steering system.

Power Steering Pump

Removal and Installation

1. Disconnect the negative battery cable.
2. Remove the power steering pump pulley nut.
3. Loosen the drive belt tensioner pulley and remove the belt.
4. Remove the pulley from the pump.
5. Disconnect and plug the fluid lines at the pump.
6. Remove the power steering pump bracket bolts and remove the pump from the engine.
7. Installation is the reverse of the removal procedure. Adjust the drive belt tension. Fill and bleed the power steering system when finished.

Bleeding System

1. Check and fill the power steering fluid level.
2. Start and run the engine at idle. Turn the steering wheel lock-to-lock, several times. Turn the engine off, check and fill the fluid.

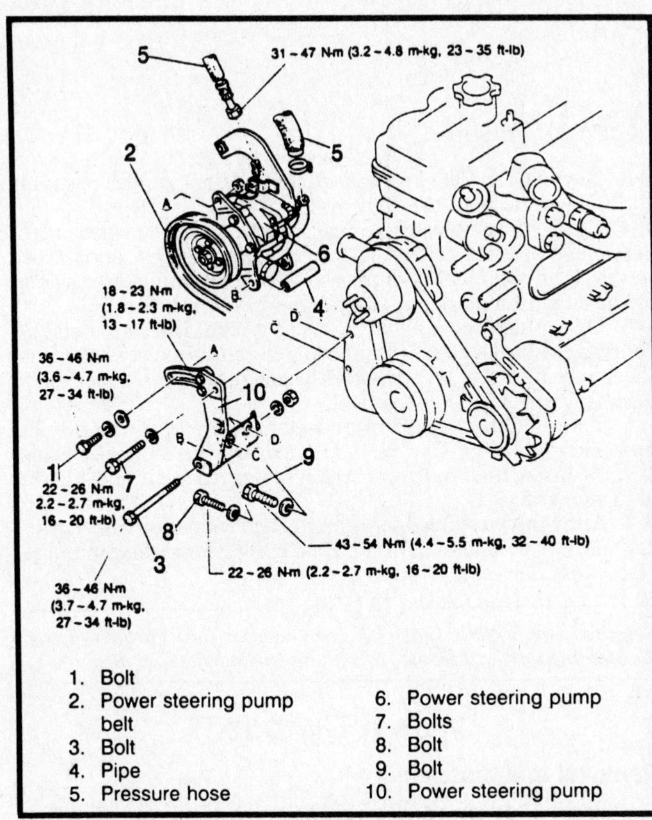

Power steering pump mounting

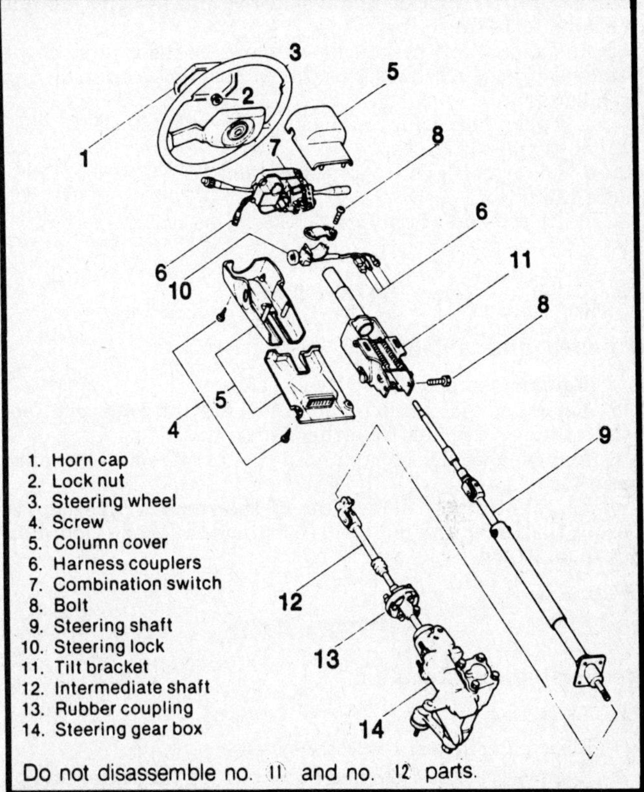

1986–88 Steering column and gear—exploded view

3. Start and run the engine at idle and turn the wheel lock-to-lock several times again.
4. Place the wheels in the straight ahead position and shut off the engine.
5. Allow the fluid to settle in the system for a few minutes and check the fluid level again.
6. Check for the presence of foaming in the fluid. Repeat the procedure until the fluid is clear and remains at the same level, with the engine off.

Steering Knuckle

Removal and Installation

ALL MODELS

1. Raise and support the vehicle safely.
2. Remove the wheel assemblies.
3. Without disconnecting the brake line, remove the brake calipers and rotors. Support the caliper out of the way.
4. Remove the hub and bearing.
5. Remove the tie rod to knuckle nut and remove the tie rod end from the knuckle.
6. On 1982–84 models, remove the shock absorber.
7. On 1985–88 models, install a spring compressor on the coil spring.
8. Support the lower control arm.
9. Remove the cotter pin and nut from the lower ball joint and disconnect the lower ball joint from the knuckle.
10. Remove the cotter pin and nut from the upper ball joint and disconnect the upper ball joint from the knuckle.
11. Pull the knuckle and spindle assembly from the control arms.
12. Remove the steering knuckle.
13. Clean and inspect all parts for wear or damage. Replace parts as necessary.

14. Secure the knuckle and install the knuckle arm. Torque the bolts to 70–74 ft. lbs.

15. Installation of the knuckle assembly is the reverse of the removal procedure. Observe the following torques during installation:

a. Upper ball joint-to-knuckle, 1982–85: 50–55 ft. lbs.; 1986–88: 35–38 ft. lbs.

b. Lower ball joint-to-knuckle, 1982–85: 70 ft. lbs.;1986–88: 116 ft. lbs.

c. Tie rod end-to-knuckle: 22–29 ft. lbs.

Idler Arm

Removal and Installation

1. Raise and support the vehicle safely.
2. Remove the idler arm to center link nut and cotter pin. Disconnect the center link from the idler arm.
3. Remove the idler arm mounting bolts and remove the idler arm.
4. Installation is the reverse of the removal procedure. Torque the center link nut to 40 ft. lbs. and the frame mounting nut to 58 ft. lbs.

Pitman Arm

Removal and Installation

ALL MODELS

1. Raise and support the vehicle safely.
2. Remove the cotter pin and nut attaching the center link to the pitman arm.
3. Disconnect the center link from the pitman arm.
4. Matchmark the pitman arm to the sector shaft.
5. Remove the pitman arm to sector shaft nut and remove the pitman arm. It may be necessary to use a puller.
6. Installation is the reverse of the removal procedure. Align the matchmarks on the pitman arm and sector shaft.
7. Tighten the pitman arm to sector shaft nut to 130 ft. lbs. and the pitman arm to center link nut to 32 ft. lbs.

Center Link

Removal and Installation

ALL MODELS

1. Raise and support the vehicle safely.
2. Disconnect the center link at the tie rods, pitman arm and idler arm.
3. Installation is the reverse of the removal procedure. Tighten all of the nuts to 30 ft. lbs. and install new cotter pins.

Tie Rods

Removal and Installation

1. Raise and supporet the vehicle safely. Loosen the tie rod jam nuts.
2. Remove and discard the cotter pin from the ball socket end and remove the nut.
3. Disconnect the ball socket stud from the center link. Remove the stud from the kingpin steering arm.
4. Unscrew the tie rod end from the threaded sleeve, counting the number of threads until it is off. The threads may be left or right hand threads. Tighten the jam nuts to 58 ft. lbs.
5. To install, lightly coat the threads with grease and turn the new end in as many turns as were required to remove it. This will give the approximate correct toe-in.
6. Install the ball socket studs into center link and kingpin steering arm. Tighten the nuts to 30 ft. lbs. Install a new cotter pin. If the cotter pin hole does not line up, tighten the nut to install the cotter pin. Never loosen the nut.
7. Tighten the tie rod clamps or jam nuts. Check and adjust the toe in.

BRAKE SYSTEM

For brake system overhaul, refer to the Unit Overhaul Section.

Master Cylinder

Removal and Installation

ALL MODELS

1. Disconnect and plug the brakes lines at the master cylinder.
2. On 1986–88 models, disconnect the fluid level sensor coupling.
3. Remove the master cylinder mounting bolts and remove the master cylinder from the firewall or power booster. 1982–85 models have a remotely mounted reservoir, so the lines will have to be unclipped and plugged.
4. Installation is the reverse of the removal procedure. Torque the mounting nuts to 15 ft. lbs.
5. Bleed the brake system when finished.

BLEEDING

Procedure

1. To bleed the brakes, clean all dirt from around the master cylinder reservoir filler cap.
2. If a bleeder tank is used, follow the manufacturer's instructions.
3. Remove the filler cap and fill the master cylinder reservoir to the lower edge of the filler neck.
4. Clean off the bleeder connections at all of the wheel cylinders and disc brake calipers. Attach the bleeder hose and fixture to the right rear wheel cylinder bleeder screw and place the end of the tube in a glass jar, submerged in clean brake fluid.
5. Open the bleeder valve $^1/_2$–$^3/_4$ of a turn. Have an assistant depress the brake pedal and allow it to return slowly. Continue this pumping action, stopping with each up and down motion, to force any air out of the system.
6. When bubbles cease to appear at the end of the bleeder hose, close the bleeder valve and remove the hose. Check the level of the brake fluid in the master cylinder reservoir and add fluid, if necessary.
7. After the bleeding operation at each caliper or wheel cylinder has been completed, fill the master cylinder reservoir and replace the filler cap.

CAUTION

Never reuse brake fluid which has been removed from the lines through the bleeding process because, it contains air bubbles and dirt.

Wheel Cylinder

Removal and Installation

1. Raise and support the vehicle safely. Remove the wheel assembly.

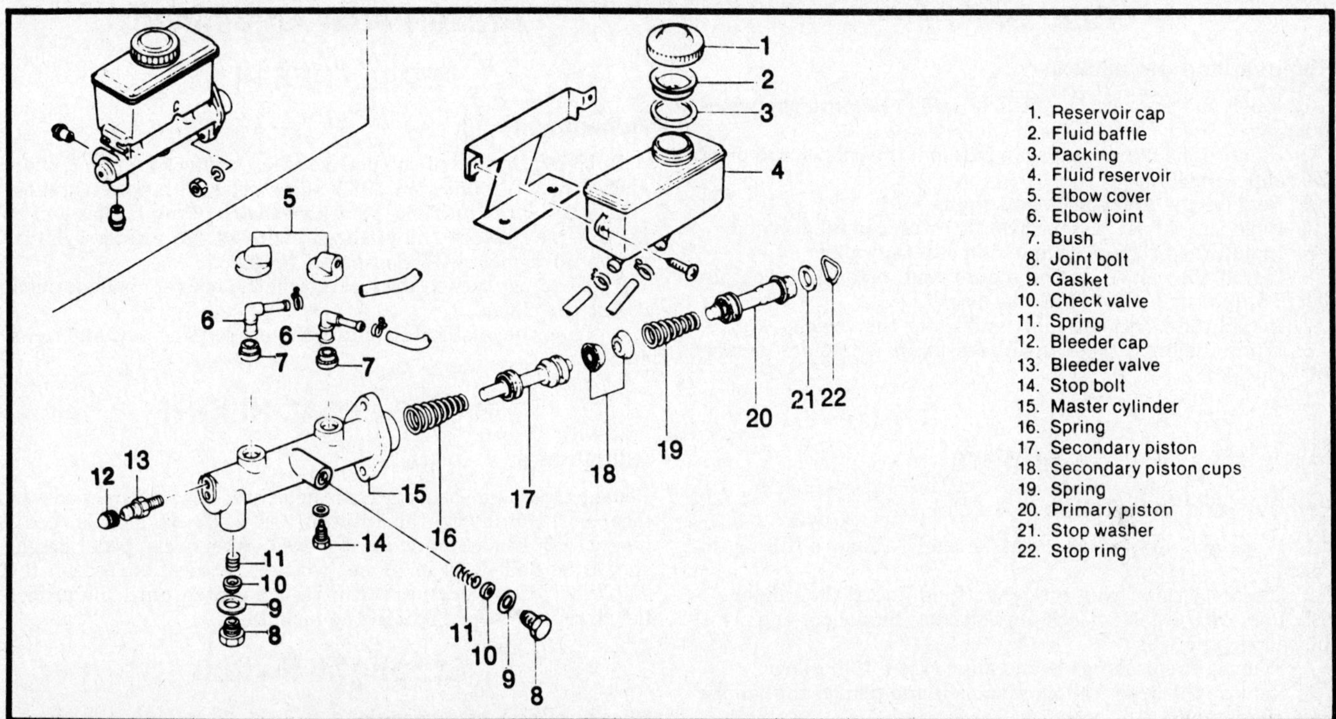

1982–85 Brake master cylinder—exploded view

2. Remove the brake drum. Inspect the brake components for signs of damage from leaking brake fluid. Replace if necessary.
3. Disconnect and plug the brake line at the wheel cylinder.
4. Remove the two wheel cylinder mounting bolts and remove the wheel cylinder from the backing plate by spreading the brake shoes apart. If necessary, remove the brake shoes from the vehicle.
5. Spread the brake shoes apart and install the new wheel cylinder on the backing plate.
6. Torque the mounting bolts to 7–9 ft. lbs.
7. Install the brake line in the wheel cylinder and torque the flare nut to 10–13 ft. lbs.

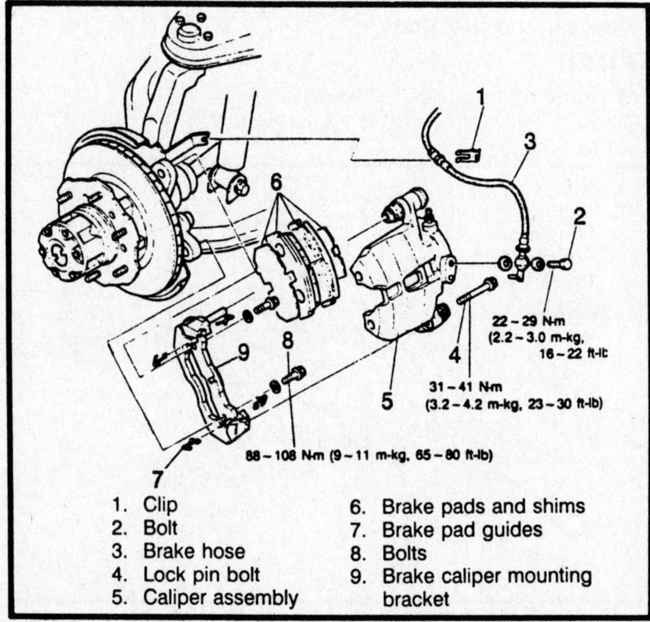

4WD front disc brake assembly—2WD similar

8. Install the brake drum and wheel assembly. Bleed the wheel cylinder.
9. Check the system operation before moving the vehicle.

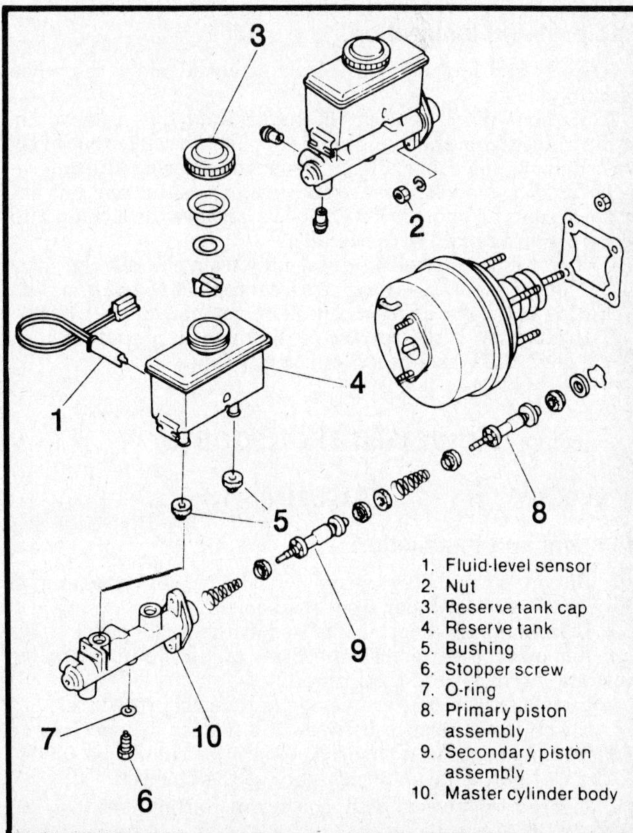

1986–88 Brake master cylinder and power booster

Disc Brakes

Removal and Installation

1. Raise and support the vehicle safely. Remove the wheel assembly.
2. Remove the bottom lock pin bolt fom the caliper and pivot the caliper upwards.
3. Remove the brake pads and shims.
4. Push the caliper piston inwards until it is fully seated.
5. Install the brake pads and shims in the caliper.
6. Install the caliper to the mount and install the lock pin bolt. Torque the bolt to 23–30 ft. lbs.
7. Install the wheel assembly and lower the vehicle.
8. Pump the brake pedal until pressure is felt before moving the vehicle.

Calipers

Removal and Installation

1. Raise and support the vehicle safely. Remove the wheel assembly.
2. Disconnect and plug the brake fluid line at the caliper.
3. Remove the bottom lock pin bolt from the caliper and pivot the caliper upwards.
4. Remove the brake pads and shims from the caliper.
5. Remove the upper caliper pivot bolt and remove the caliper from the mount.
6. Installation is the reverse of the removal procedure. Bleed the brake caliper when finished.

Rotors

Removal and Installation

1. Raise and support the vehicle safely. Remove the wheel assembly.
2. Without disconnecting the brake fluid line, remove the brake caliper from the mount and support the caliper out of the way. Remove the caliper mount from the steering knuckle.
3. On 2WD models, remove the dust cap, cotter pin, nut and washer from the hub. On 4WD models, remove the locking hub, spacer, bearing plate and lock nut.
4. Remove the brake rotor assembly from the vehicle.
5. If only the rotor is being replaced, remove the hub to rotor mounting bolts and install the hub on the new brake rotor.
6. Installation is the reverse of the removal procedure.
7. Adjust the wheel bearings when finished.

Power Brake Booster

VACUUM

Removal and Installation

1. Disconnect and plug the master cylinder fluid lines and remove the master cylinder from the booster.
2. Disconnect the booster pushrod at the brake pedal.
3. Remove the power brake booster mounting nuts and remove the booster from the firewall.
4. Installation is the reverse of the removal procedure.
5. Check the clearance between the master cylinder piston and the power booster pushrod. Clearance should be 0.004–0.020 in. If not, adjust the clearance at the pushrod.
6. Tighten the power brake booster mounting nuts to 17 ft. lbs.
7. Bleed the brake system when finished.

Brake Pedal Adjustment

PEDAL FREE-PLAY

Adjustment

1. Using the top of the pedal pad as a reference point, there should be 7.0–9.0mm on 1982–85 vehicles with power brakes.
2. 4.0–7.0mm on 1986–88 vehicles with power brakes and $^1/_8$ in. free-play before the pushrod contacts the master cylinder piston on models with non-power brakes.
3. To adjust, loosen the locknut on the master cylinder pushrod at the clevis.
4. Turn the pushrod to obtain the proper free-play and tighten the nut.

BRAKE PEDAL HEIGHT

Adjustment

Pedal height is measured from the center of the pedal pad surface, horizontally to the firewall. On 1982–84 models, pedal height should be 8.1 inches. On 1986–88 models, pedal height should be 8.23–8.43 in. If not within specification, loosen the stoplight switch locknut and turn the switch until the proper height is obtained. Tighten the locknut.

Stoplight Switch

Removal and Installation

1. Disconnect the negative battery cable.
2. Disconnect the stoplight switch wiring connector.
3. Remove the stoplight switch from the brake pedal.
4. Install the new switch on the pedal and connect the wire.
5. Adjust the switch so that there is 8.1 in. of pedal travel on 1982–84 models and 8.23–8.43 in. of clearence on 1986–88 models.
6. Connect the negative battery cable and check the switch operation.

Parking Brake

CABLE

Removal and Installation

FRONT

1. Raise and support the vehicle safely.
2. Remove the front cable adjusting nut.

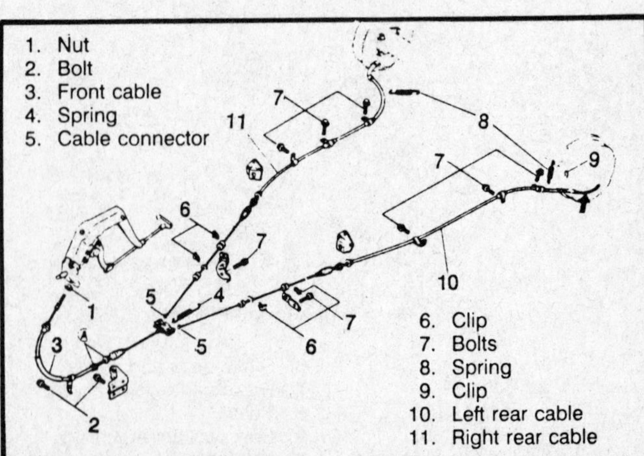

2WD parking brake cables

3. Separate the front cable from the equalizer and remove the jam nut.
4. Remove the return spring and boot from the cable housing.
5. Pull the lower cable housing forward and out of the slotted frame bracket. Slip the cable shaft sideways through the slot until the cable and housing are free of the bracket.
6. Disengage the upper cable connector from the brake lever by removing the clevis pin and retainer.
7. Remove the upper cable housing retaining clip and pull the upper cable and housing from the slotted bracket on the firewall.
8. Push the upper cable, cable housing and dust shield grommet through the firewall opening and into the engine compartment.
9. Remove the cable and housing.
10. Installation is the reverse of the removal procedure. Adjust the parking brake cable when finished.

REAR

1. Raise and support the vehicle safely.
2. Remove the pin and disconnect the equalizer from the clevis.
3. Disconnect the right side cable from the left cable.
4. Remove the rear wheels, brake drums and brake shoes.
5. Disengage the cables from the brake shoe levers.
6. Remove the cable housing retainer from the backing plate.
7. Pull the return spring to release the retainer plate from the end of the housing.
8. Loosen the cable housing to frame bracket locknut and remove the forward end of the cable housing from the frame bracket.
9. Remove the cable housing retaining clip bolts.
10. Disengage the cable housing to frame tension springs and pull the cable out of the backing plate.
11. Installation is the reverse of the removal procedure.
12. Adjust the cable when finished.

Adjustment

1. Adjust the rear brake shoes before attempting to adjust the parking brake.

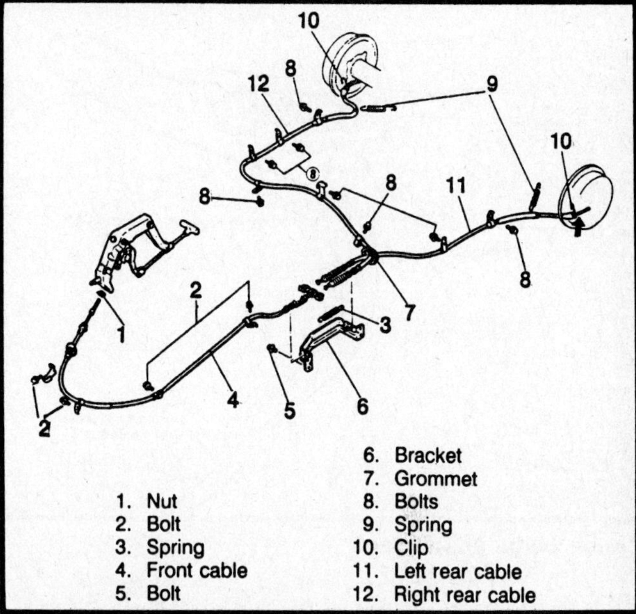

4WD parking brake cables

2. Use the adjusting nut to adjust the length of the front cable so that the rear brakes are locked when the parking brake lever is pulled out 5–10 notches on 1982–85 models, and 11–13 notches on 1986–88 models.
3. After adjustment, apply the parking brake several times. Release the parking brake and make sure that the rear wheels rotate without dragging. If they drag, repeat the adjustment.

NOTE: If the parking brake cable is replaced, prestretch it by applying the parking brake hard three or four times before attempting adjustment.

CLUTCH

Clutch Assembly

HYDRAULIC

Removal and Installation

1. Remove the transmission. If the clutch is being reused, matchmark the pressure plate to the flywheel to insure proper balance during installation.
2. Loosen the four mounting and two pilot bolts holding the clutch cover to the flywheel. Loosen the bolts evenly a turn or two at a time.
3. Support the clutch assembly and remove the mounting bolts. Remove the clutch disc.
4. Using a clutch alignment tool, install the pressure plate and disc on the flywheel.
5. Install the four standard bolts and the two pilot bolts.
6. Tighten the bolts evenly a few turns at a time.
7. Torque the bolts to 13–20 ft. lbs.
8. Remove the alignment tool.
9. Apply a light film of lubricant to the release bearing, release lever contact area on the release bearing hub and input shaft bearing retainer.
10. Install the transmission.
11. Check the operation of the clutch and if necessary, adjust the pedal free-play and the release lever.

MASTER CYLINDER

Removal and Installation

1. Disconnect and plug the fluid outlet line at the fitting on the master cylinder.

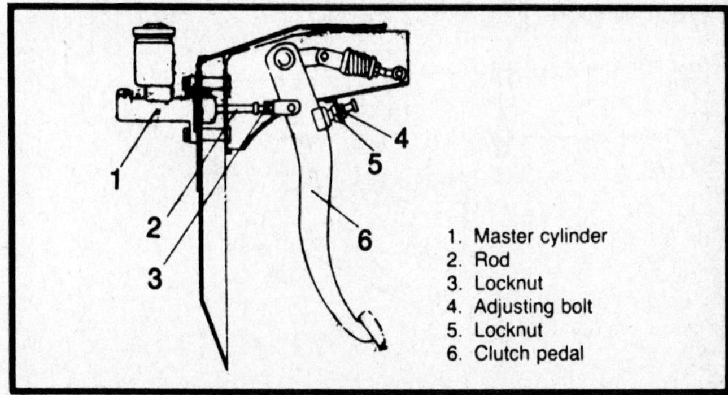

Clutch pedal height adjustment

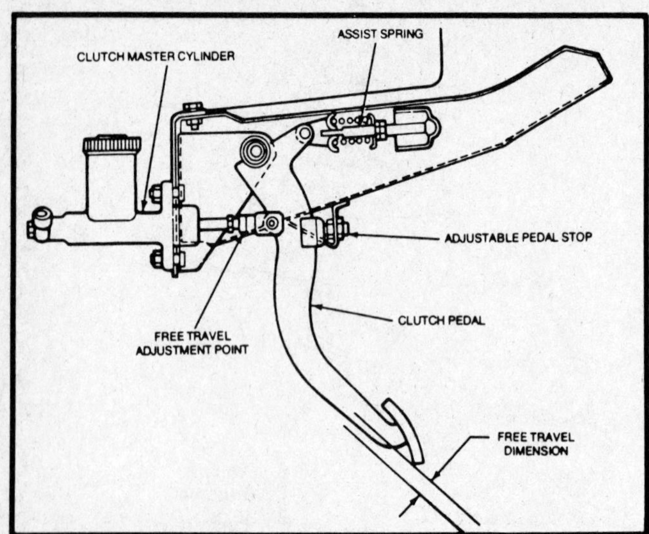

Clutch pedal adjustment

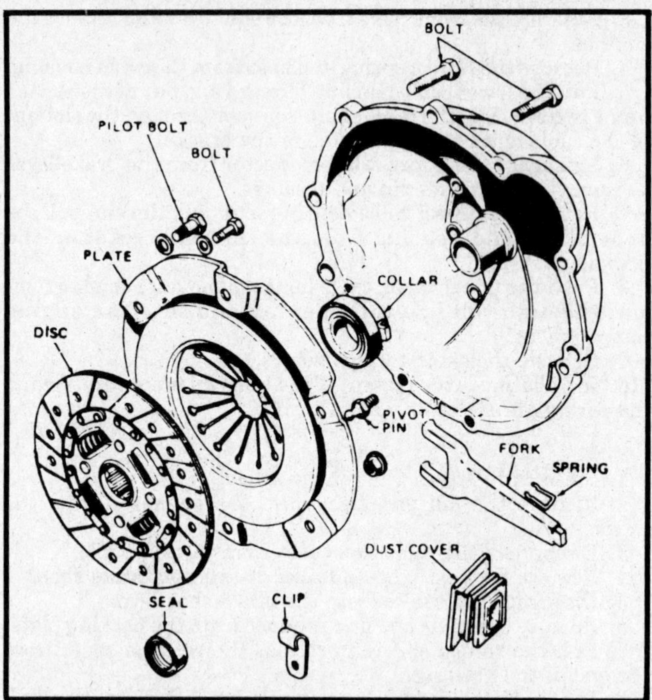

Clutch components – exploded view

2. Remove the nuts and bolts mounting the master cylinder to the firewall.
3. Remove the master cylinder from the firewall.
4. Start the pedal pushrod into the master cylinder and position the master cylinder on the firewall.
5. Install the mounting nuts and bolts. Torque the nuts to 12–17 ft. lbs.
6. Connect the fluid outlet line to the master cylinder fitting.
7. Bleed the hydraulic clutch system.
8. Check the clutch pedal free-play and adjust if necessary.

SLAVE CYLINDER

Removal and Installation

1982–85 MODELS

1. Disconnect and plug the fluid line at the slave cylinder.
2. Disconnect the release lever from the slave cylinder pushrod.
3. Remove the nuts attaching the slave cylinder to the clutch housing.
4. Installation is the reverse of removal. Torque the mounting nuts to 12–17 ft. lbs. Fill and bleed the clutch system when finished.

1986–88 MODELS

1. Raise and support the vehicle safely.
2. Disconnect the fluid line from the slave cylinder.
3. Pull off the hose retaining clip and remove the hose from the bracket. Cap the pipe to prevent fluid loss.
4. Remove the slave cylinder.
5. Installation is the reverse of removal.

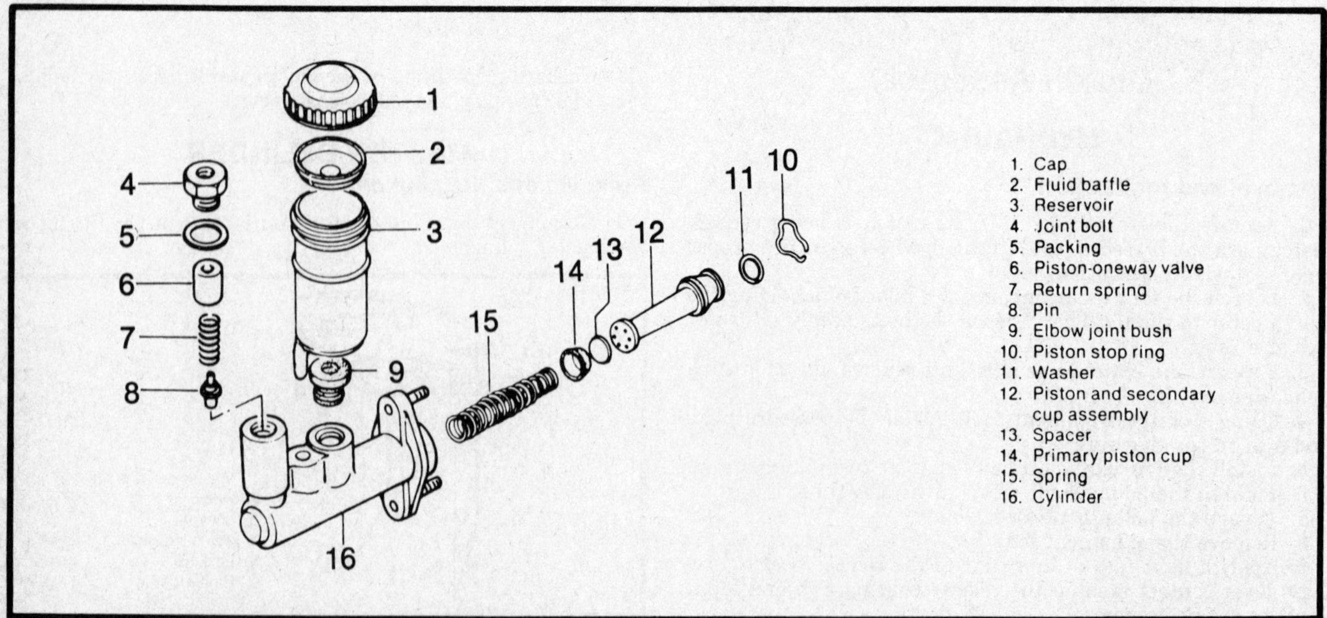

1982–85 Clutch master cylinder – exploded view

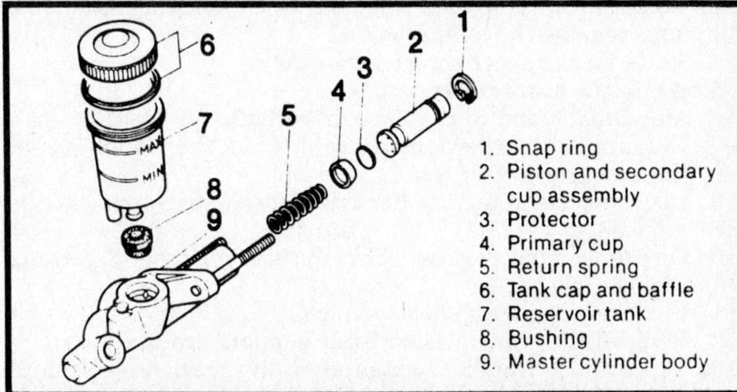

1986–88 Clutch master cylinder–exploded view

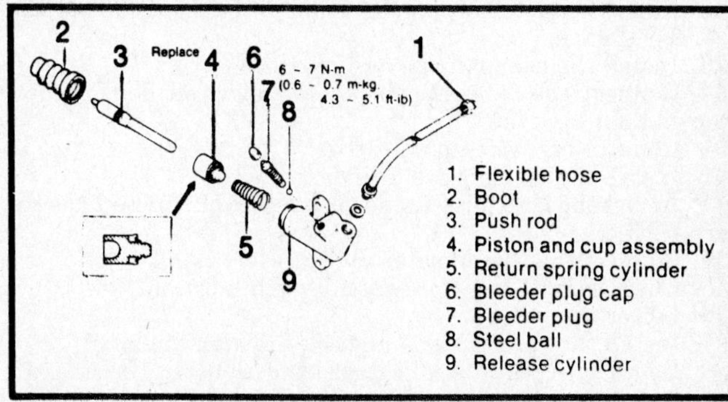

1986–88 Clutch slave cylinder–exploded view

6. Torque the slave cylinder mounting bolt to 12–17 ft. lbs.
7. Bleed the clutch system when finished.

BLEEDING SYSTEM

Procedure

The clutch hydraulic system must be bled whenever the line has been disconnected or air has entered the system.

1. To bleed the system, remove the rubber cap from the bleeder valve and attach a rubber hose to the valve.
2. Submerge the other end of the hose in a large jar of clean brake fluid.
3. Open the bleeder valve. Depress the clutch pedal and allow it to return slowly.
4. Continue slowly pumping clutch pedal and watch the jar of brake fluid.
5. When the fluid is clear of air bubbles, close the bleeder valve and remove the tube.
6. Check and fill the reservoir during and after the procedure.

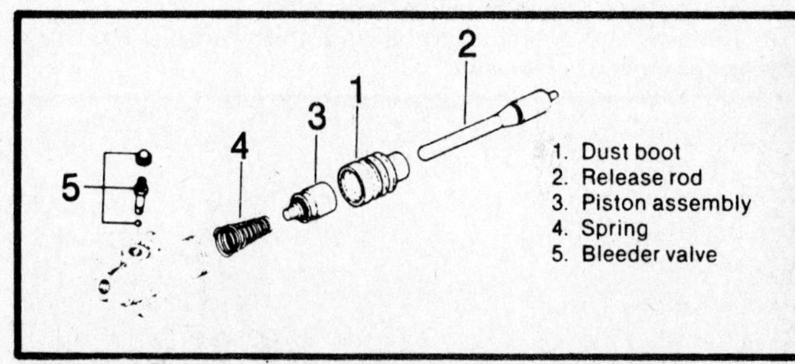

1982–85 Clutch slave cylinder–exploded view

NOTE: If the fluid in the reservoir runs out during the procedure, the entire procedure must be repeated. After the bleeding operation is finished, install the cap on the bleeder valve and fill the master cylinder to the proper level. Always use fresh DOT 3 brake fluid. Do not use the fluid that was in the jar for bleeding, since it may contains air and/or dirt.

MANUAL TRANSMISSION

Refer to the Unit Overhaul Section for Overhaul Procedures.

Manual Transmission

Removal and Installation

1982–85

1. Disconnect the negative battery cable. Place the gearshift in Neutral.
2. Lift up the boot covering the shift lever and detach the gearshift tower from the extension housing. Remove the shift lever, tower and gasket as an assembly.
3. Cover the opening in the case.
4. Raise and support the vehicle safely.
5. Matchmark and remove the driveshaft at the rear axle.
6. Remove the driveshaft center bearing support and pull the driveshaft rearward to disconnect the driveshaft from the transmission. Install a plug in the extension housing to prevent lubricant from leaking out.
7. Remove the exhaust pipe brackets from the transmission case.
8. Disconnect the exhaust pipe hanger from the clutch housing.
9. Disconnect the exhaust pipe at the manifold and muffler. Remove the exhaust pipe resonator assembly or catalytic converter.
10. Disconnect the clutch release lever return spring. Remove the clutch release cylinder and secure it out of the way.
11. Remove the speedometer cable from the extension housing.
12. Disconnect the starter motor and backup light wires.
13. Support the engine. Support the transmission separately.
14. Remove the starter motor.
15. Disconnect the transmission from the engine rear plate.
16. Disconnect the mount from the crossmember.
17. Remove the crossmember.
18. Slide the transmission rearward until the input shaft spline clears the clutch disc.
19. Remove the transmission from the vehicle.
20. Clean the mating surfaces of the transmission and engine.
21. Raise the transmission into place and start the input shaft into the clutch disc. Align the splines and move the transmission forward until the clutch housing seats on the locating dowels of the engine rear plate.
22. Torque the transmission to engine bolts to 60–65 ft. lbs. Connect the clutch housing to the rear plate.
23. Install the starter motor.
24. Raise the engine and install the rear crossmember.
25. Install the rear transmission mount on the crossmember. Bolt the transmission to the rear mount.
26. Remove the engine and transmission supports.
27. Install the driveshaft in the transmission extension housing. Install the center bearing.

28. Align the matchmarks and connect the driveshaft to the rear axle flange.
29. Install the exhaust pipe and resonator.
30. Connect the exhaust pipe to the flywheel housing and transmission brackets.
31. Connect the back-up light wire.
32. Install the clutch slave cylinder.
33. Adjust the clutch release lever free travel. Connect the return spring.
34. Connect the speedometer cable.
35. Check and fill the transmission with lubricant.
36. Lower the vehicle.
37. Install the shift tower and gasket. Install the boot.
38. Check the operation of the transmission.

1986–88 2WD MODELS

1. Disconnect the negative battery cable.
2. Remove the gearshift knob and shift console attaching screws. Remove the console.
3. Remove the shift lever to extension housing attaching bolts and remove the shift lever.
4. Raise and support the vehicle safely.
5. Drain the transmission oil.
6. Matchmark and remove the driveshaft.
7. Disconnect the speedometer cable from the transmission.
8. Remove the starter motor.
9. Disconnect and tag the back-up light switch wiring at the transmission.
10. Disconnect the parking brake return spring and parking brake cables.
11. Remove the clutch slave cylinder.
12. Remove the transmission front support bracket.
13. Disconnect the exhaust pipe at the transmission and manifold.
14. Support the transmission and engine separately.
15. Remove the transmission crossmember.
16. Lower the transmission to gain access to the top bolts and remove the transmission to engine bolts.

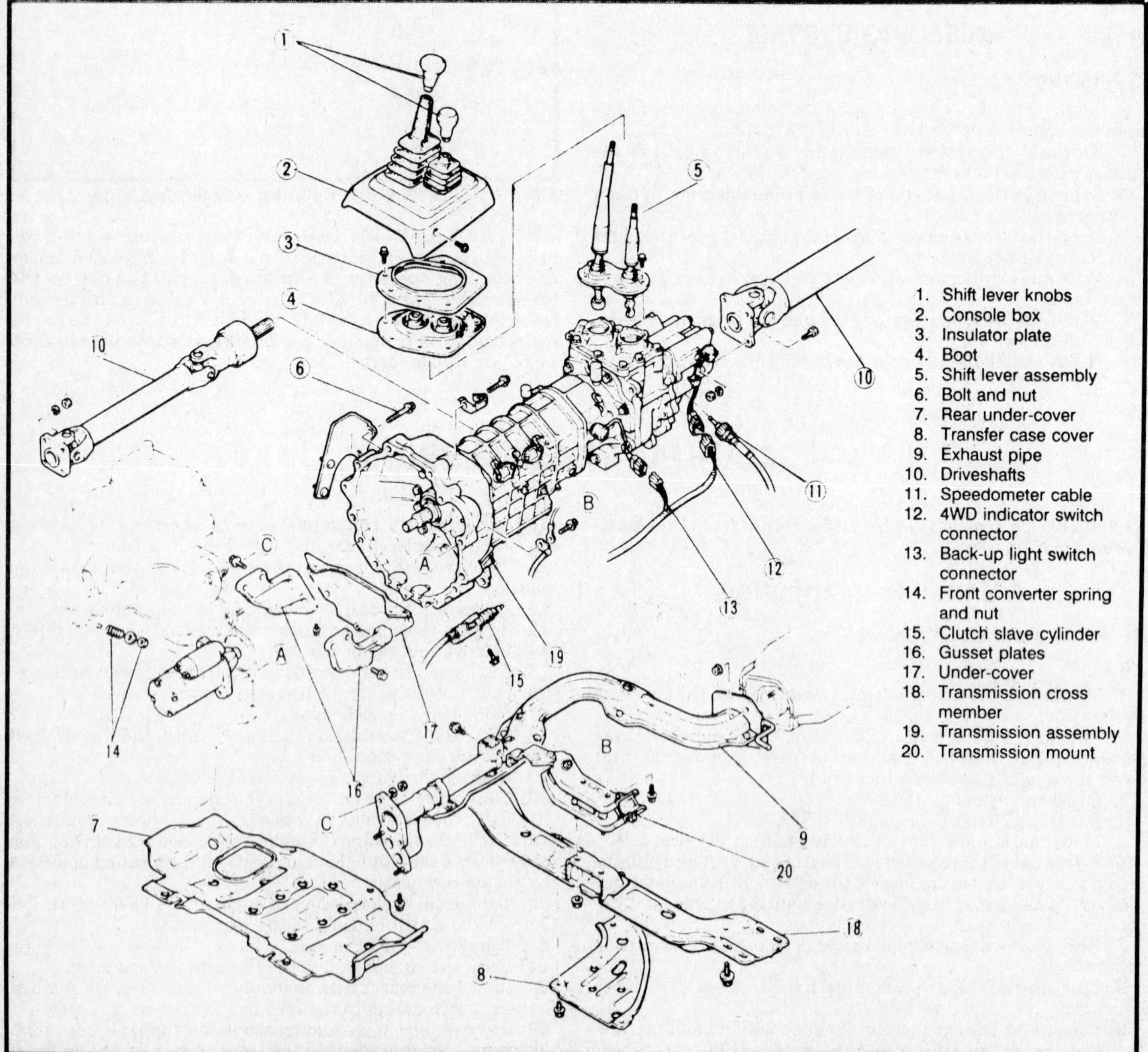

Manual transmission mounting—4WD shown—2WD similar

17. Pull the transmission straight back, away from the engine and remove transmission from the vehicle.
18. Installation is the reverse of the removal procedure.
20. Torque the transmission to engine bolts to 60–65 ft. lbs. and the gearshift lever bolts to 6–8 ft. lbs.
21. Check and fill the transmission to the proper level when finished.

1988 4WD MODELS

NOTE: Although the transmission and transfer case are separate units, they share a similar mounting and sealing surface. It is recommended that they be removed as a unit and separated once removed from the vehicle.

1. Disconnect the negative battery cable.
2. Remove the knobs from the transfer case and transmission shifters.
3. Remove the console box, if equipped.
4. Remove the insulator plate and shifter boot.
5. Remove the shift levers.
6. Raise and support the vehicle safely.
7. Remove the transmission and transfer case under covers.
8. Disconnect and remove the exhaust pipe from the manifold and catalytic converter.
9. Matchmark and remove the front and rear driveshafts.
10. Disconnect the speedometer cable, 4WD switch and back-up light switch wires from the transmission/transfer case.
11. Remove the slave cylinder without disconnecting the fluid line. Support the slave cylinder out of the way.
12. Remove the transmission/transfer case gusset plates. Support the transmission.
13. Raise the transmission/transfer case and remove the crossmember.
14. Remove the transmission and transfer case as an assembly.
15. Installation is the reverse of the removal procedure.
16. Align the matchmarks on the driveshafts during installation.
17. Check and fill the transmission and transfer case after installation.

Shift Linkage

Adjustment

No adjustments are possible on the shift linkage.

AUTOMATIC TRANSMISSION

Refer to the Unit Overhaul Section for Overhaul Procedures.

Automatic Transmission

Removal and Installation

1. Disconnect the negative battery cable.
2. Raise and support the vehicle safely.
3. Drain the transmission fluid. After the fluid has drained, install a few bolts to hold the pan in place, temporarily.
4. Remove the exhaust pipe bracket bolt from the right side of the converter housing.
5. Remove the exhaust pipe flange bolts from the rear of the resonator or catalytic converter and disconnect the pipe.
6. Matchmark and remove the driveshaft from the rear axle flange.
7. Remove the driveshaft center bearing support. Lower the driveshaft and remove it from the transmission.
8. Disconnect the speedometer cable.
9. Disconnect the shift rod from the manual lever.
10. Remove the vacuum hose from the diaphragm. Disconnect the electrical connectors from the downshift solenoid and inhibitor switch and remove their wires from the clip.
11. Disconnect and plug the cooler lines from the radiator at the transmission.
12. Remove the access cover from the lower front of the converter housing.
13. Matchmark the drive plate (flywheel) and torque converter for reassembly. Remove the four bolts holding the torque converter to the drive plate.
14. Remove the bolts connecting the crossmember to the transmission.
15. Support the transmission. Remove the crossmember to frame bolts and remove the crossmember.
16. Make sure that the transmission is securely supported.
17. Lower the transmission enough to remove the starter.
18. Remove the converter housing to engine bolts.
19. Remove the fluid filler tube.
20. Make sure that the converter is engaged in the transmission during removal.
21. Lower the transmission and converter as an assembly. Be careful not to let the converter fall out.
22. To install, make sure that the converter is properly installed in the transmission.
23. Raise the transmission into place. Install the converter housing to engine bolts and torque the bolts in two stages to 23–34 ft. lbs.
24. Lower the transmission slightly and install the starter.
25. Install the fluid filler tube with a new O-ring.
26. Raise the transmission slightly and install the crossmember to the frame. Tighten the bolts to 23–34 ft. lbs.
27. Lower the transmission and install the transmission to crossmember bolts. Tighten to 23–34 ft. lbs.
28. Align the matchmarks made earlier on the torque converter and drive plate. Install the four attaching bolts and torque to 25–36 ft. lbs. in three stages.
29. Install the access cover. Remove the support.
30. Connect the cooler lines.
31. Install the electrical connectors to the switch and solenoid and replace the wires in the clip. Install the diaphragm vacuum hose.
32. Connect the shift rod to the lever.
33. Connect the speedometer cable.
34. Insert the driveshaft into the transmission. Install the center bearing support. Bolt the driveshaft to the rear of the axle flange.
35. Connect the exhaust pipe to the catalytic converter, using a new gasket. Reinstall the exhaust pipe clamp onto the converter housing and torque the bolt to 10–15 ft. lbs.

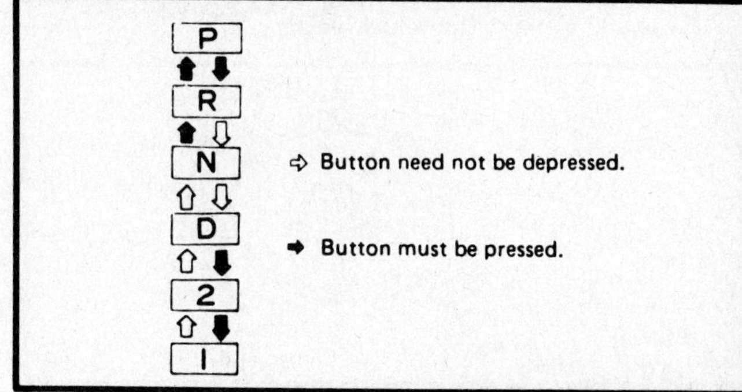

Automatic transmission shift interlock check

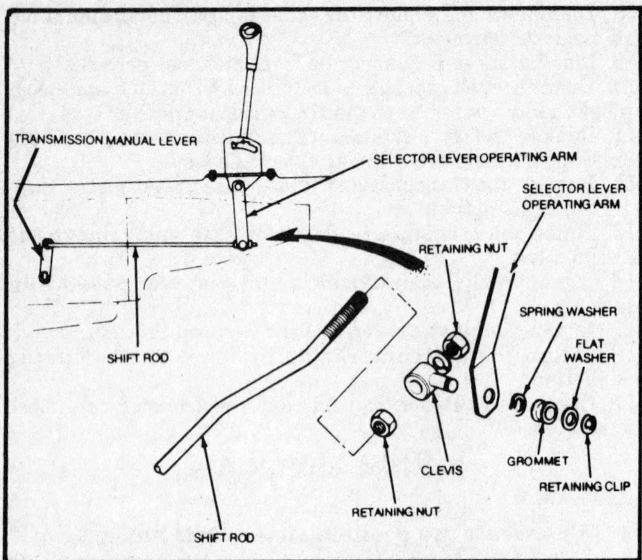

Automatic transmission shift linkage adjustment

36. Install a new pan gasket and the fluid pan.
37. Lower the vehicle. Connect the negative battery cable. Fill the transmission through the dipstick tube with the specified fluid, being careful not to overfill. Run the engine and check for leaks.

Shift Linkage

Adjustment

1. Put the gearshift lever in Neutral.
2. Raise and support the vehicle.
3. Disconnect the clevis from the lower end of the selector lever operating arm.
4. Move the transmission manual lever to Neutral, the 3rd detent position from the rear of the transmission.
5. Loosen the two clevis retaining nuts and adjust the clevis so that it freely enters the hole of the lever. Tighten the retaining nuts to secure the adjustment.
6. Connect the clevis to the lever and attach it with the spring washer, flat washer and retaining clip.
7. Lower the vehicle and check the operation of the transmission in all gears.

Band Adjustment

INTERMEDIATE

Procedure

1. Raise and support the vehicle safely.

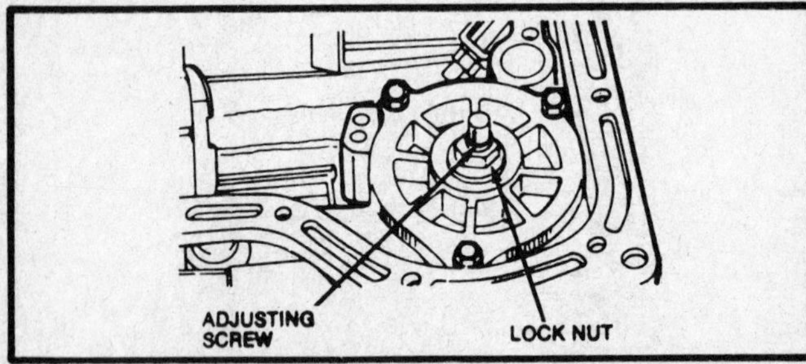

Intermediate band adjustment

2. Drain the transmission fluid.
3. When the fluid has drained, remove and thoroughly clean the pan.
4. Discard the pan gasket.
5. Loosen the brake band adjusting screw locknut and tighten the adjusting screw to 9–11 ft. lbs.
6. Back the adjusting screw off exactly two turns.
7. Hold the adjusting screw and torque the locknut to 22–29 ft. lbs.
8. Install a new pan gasket and install the pan on the transmission.
9. Lower the vehicle and fill the transmission to the proper level.

Kickdown Switch

Adjustment

1. Turn the ignition switch to the ON position.
2. Loosen the kickdown switch attaching nut (the switch is located just above the accelerator pedal) and adjust the switch to engage when the accelerator pedal is depressed about $^7/_8$ of the way. The downshift solenoid will click when the switch engages.
3. Tighten the attaching nut and check the switch for proper operation.

Neutral Interlock

Adjustment

1. Back off the locknut below the handle.
2. Position the shifter in either Neutral or Drive.
3. Turn in the handle until no play is felt at the interlock button.
4. Turn the handle one additional turn if necessary, to position the button on the driver's side.
5. Depress the button and shift to Park. If the lever cannot be moved to Park position, turn in the handle an additional turn, repeating the shift move and additional turn, until Park can be engaged smoothly.

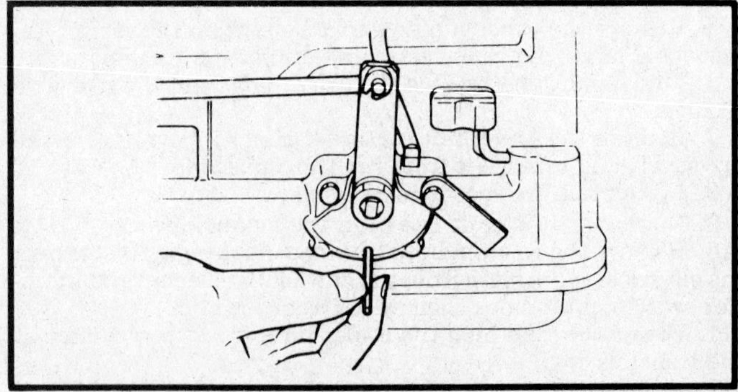

Neutral safety switch adjustment

6. From this point, shift through the various positions, confirming that the shifter works properly.
7. If the lever can be shifted to Reverse from either Park or Neutral, turn out on the handle.
8. When the adjustment is completed, check that the button protrudes 6.0mm from the handle in the Neutral or Park position. Recheck the shift pattern.
9. Tighten the locknut to 15 ft. lbs.

Neutral Safety Switch

Adjustment

1. Check and adjust the transmission linkage.

2. Place the transmission in Neutral (3rd detent from the rear of the transmission).
3. Remove the transmission manual lever retaining nut and lever.
4. Loosen the inhibitor switch attaching bolts. Remove the screw from the alignment pin hole at the bottom of the switch.
5. Rotate the switch and insert an alignment pin, 0.059 in. diameter into the alignment pin hole and internal rotor.
6. Tighten the two switch attaching bolts and remove the alignment pin.
7. Reinstall the alignment pin hole screw in the switch body.
8. Install the manual lever.
9. Check the operation of the switch. The engine should only start with the transmission selector lever in Neutral or Park.

Oil Pan, Filter and Fluid

Replacement

1. Raise and support the vehicle safely.
2. Drain the transmission.
3. Remove the fluid pan and discard the gasket.
4. Replace the transmission filter.
5. Install a new pan gasket and install the pan on the transmission.
6. Lower the vehicle and fill the transmission with Dexron® II fluid. Check the transmission operation.

TRANSFER CASE

Refer to the Unit Overhaul Section for Overhaul Procedures.

Removal and Installation

NOTE: Although the transmission and transfer case are separate units, they share similar mounting and sealing surfaces. It is recommended that they be removed as a unit and separated once removed from the vehicle. No adjustments are possible on transfer case linkage. Refer to Manual Transmission Removal and Installation for the procedure.

DRIVE LINES AND UNIVERSAL JOINTS

Drive Lines

2WD REAR

Removal and Installation

1. Raise and support the vehicle safely. Matchmark the driveshaft with the rear flange. Remove the bolts attaching the driveshaft to the rear flange and remove the driveshaft.
2. On 2-piece units, remove the center support bearing bracket from the underbody.
3. Pull the driveshaft rearward and out of the transmission.
4. Installation is the reverse of removal. Align the matchmarks made during removal. Torque the rear flange bolts to 39–47 ft. lbs. and the center bearing bracket nuts to 27–38 ft. lbs.

4WD FRONT

Removal and Installation

1. Raise and support the vehicle safely.
2. Matchmark the driveshaft to the front differential flange.
3. Remove the driveshaft from the differential and top of the transfer case.
4. Installation is the reverse of the removal procedure.
5. Torque the mounting bolts to 39–47 ft. lbs.

CENTER BEARING

Removal and Installation

1. Raise and support the vehicle safely.
2. Matchmark and remove the rear driveshaft.
3. Unbolt and remove the center bearing from the front portion of the rear driveshaft.
4. Install the center bearing on the driveshaft.
5. Install the bearing and driveshaft in the vehicle.
6. Torque the bearing mounting bolts to 27–36 ft. lbs and the flange bolts to 36–43 ft. lbs.

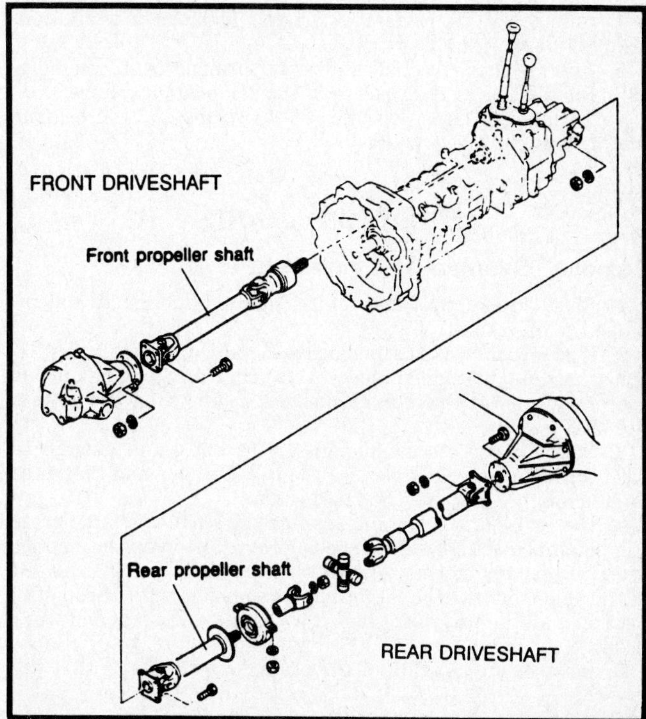

4WD driveshaft assemblies – Longbed shown – Shortbed similar

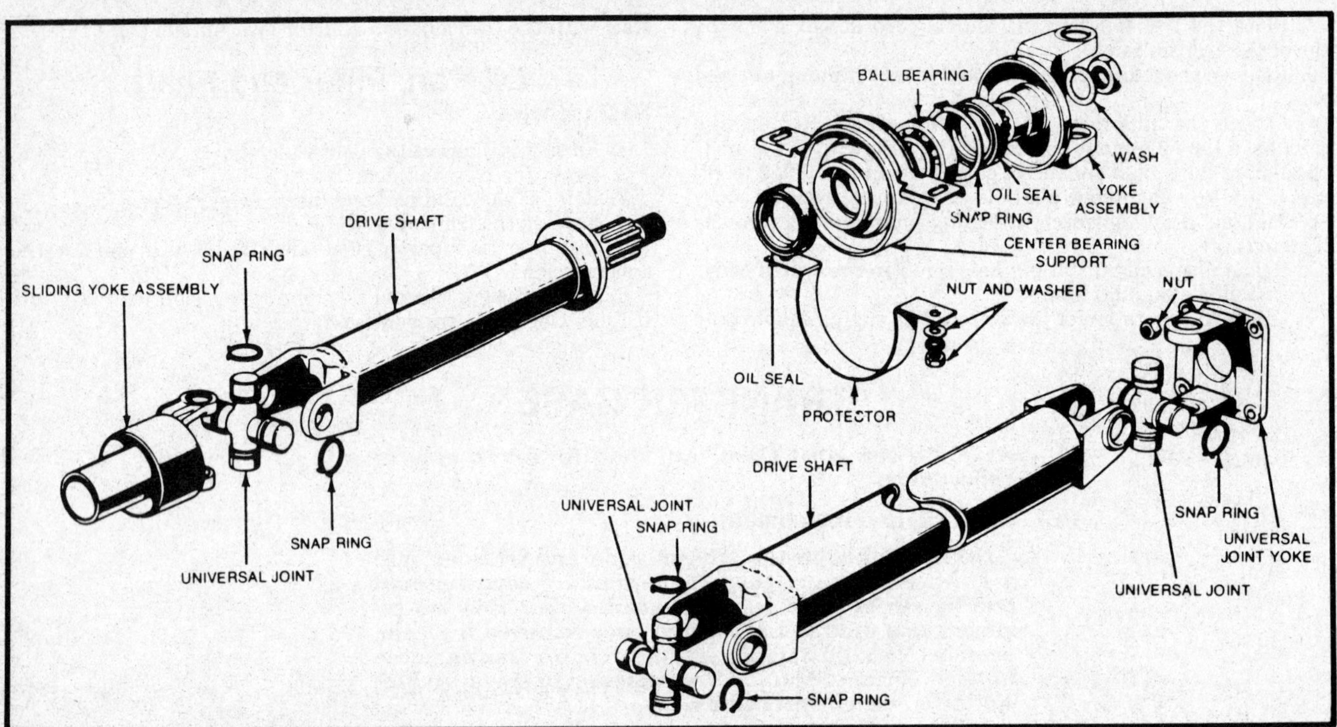

Two-piece driveshaft details

4WD REAR

Removal and Installation

1. Raise and support the vehicle safely.
2. Matchmark the front and rear flange to the driveshaft.
3. Support the driveshaft.
4. Remove the front and rear driveshaft flange bolts and center bearing mount.
5. Remove the driveshaft and center bearing as an assembly.
6. Installation is the reverse of the removal procedure.
7. Torque the flange bolts to 36–43 ft. lbs and the bearing mount bolts to 27–36 ft. lbs.

Universal Joints

Removal, Overhaul and Installation

1. Raise and support the vehicle safely. Matchmark and remove the driveshaft.
2. If the front yoke is to be disassembled, matchmark the driveshaft and sliding splined yoke so that driveline balance is preserved upon reassembly. Remove the snap rings that retain the bearing caps.
3. Select two press components, with one small enough to pass through the yoke holes for the bearing caps and the other large enough to receive the bearing cap.
4. Use a vise or a press and position the small and large press components on either side of the U-joint. Press in on the smaller press component so that it presses the opposite bearing cap out of the yoke and into the larger press component. If the cap does not come all the way out, grasp it with a pair of pliers and work it out.
5. Reverse the position of the press components so that the smaller press component presses on the cross. Press the other bearing cap out of the yoke.
6. Repeat the procedure on the other bearings.
7. To install, grease the bearing caps and needles thoroughly if they are not pregreased. Start a new bearing cap into one side of the yoke. Position the cross in the yoke.

NOTE: Some U-joints have a grease fitting that must be installed in the joint before assembly. When installing the fitting, make sure that once the driveshaft is installed in the vehicle that the fitting is accessible to be greased at a later date.

8. Select two press components small enough to pass through the yoke holes. Put the press components against the cross and the cap and press the bearing cap ¼ in. below the surface of the yoke. If there is a sudden increase in the force needed to press the cap into place, or if the cross starts to bind, the bearings are cocked. They must be removed and restarted in the yoke. Failure to do so will cause premature bearing failure.
9. Install a new snap-ring.
10. Start the new bearing into the opposite side. Place a press component on it and press in until the opposite bearing contacts the snap ring.
11. Install a new snap ring. It may be necessary to grind the facing surface of the snap ring slightly to permit easier installation.
12. Install the other bearings in the same manner.
13. Check the joint for free movement. If binding exists, strike the yoke ears with a brass or plastic faced hammer to seat the bearing needles.
14. If binding still exists, dissassemble the joint and check to see if the needles are in place. Do not strike the bearings unless the shaft is supported firmly. Do not install the driveshaft until free movement exists at all joints.

FRONT DRIVE AXLE FOUR WHEEL DRIVE

Refer to the Unit Overhaul Section for Overhaul Procedures.

Axle Housing

Removal and Installation

1. Raise and safely support the vehicle. Remove the wheel assemblies.
2. Remove the engine under cover. Drain the differential oil.
3. Matchmark and remove the front driveshaft.
4. Matchmark and disconnect the right side axleshaft from the differential.
5. Support the axle housing.
6. Remove the sub-frame mounting bolts and allow the sub-frame to hang down.
7. Remove the axle housing mounting bolts and remove the axle housing from the vehicle.
8. Installation is the reverse of the removal procedure.
9. Observe the following torques during installation:
Sub-frame bolts 59–75 ft. lbs.
Axle housing mounting bolts 41–59 ft. lbs.
Driveshaft bolts 36–43 ft. lbs.

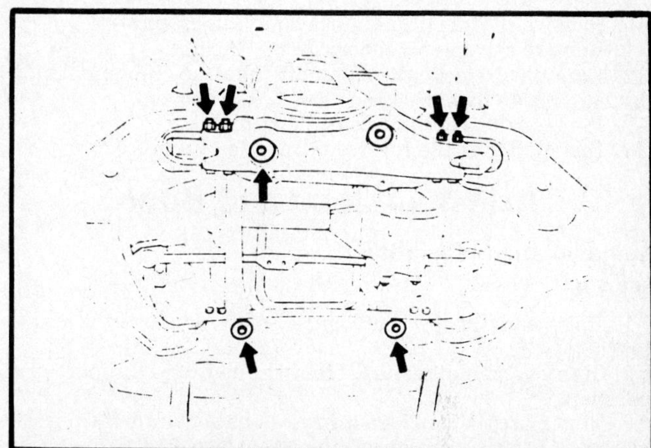
Front crossmember mounting bolt locations

Locking Hubs

Removal, Inspection and Installation

MANUAL

1. Raise and support the vehicle safely. Remove the wheel assembly.
2. Set the locking hub in the FREE position.

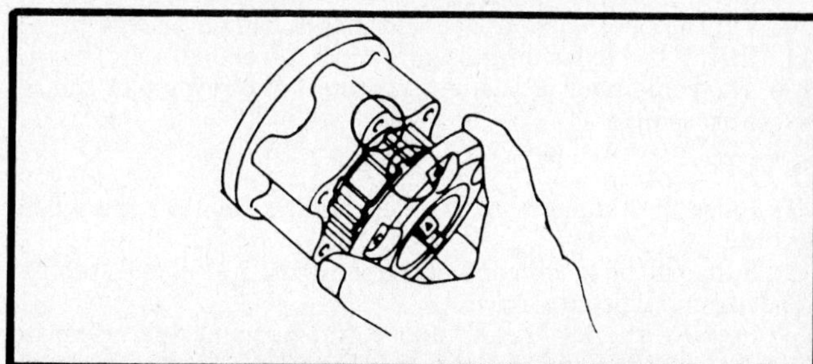
Aligning the teeth to install the locking hub

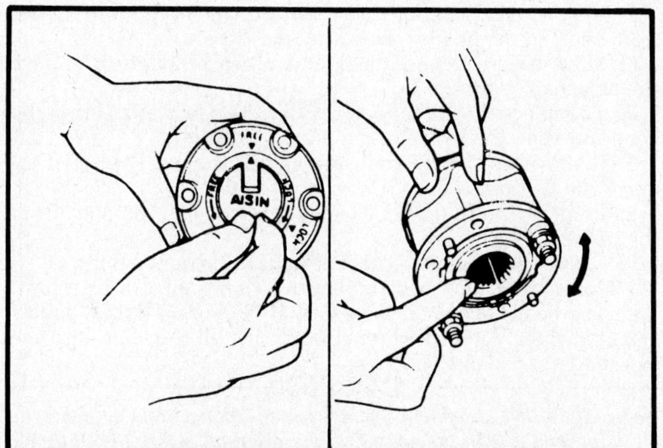

Check the hub operation before reinstalling

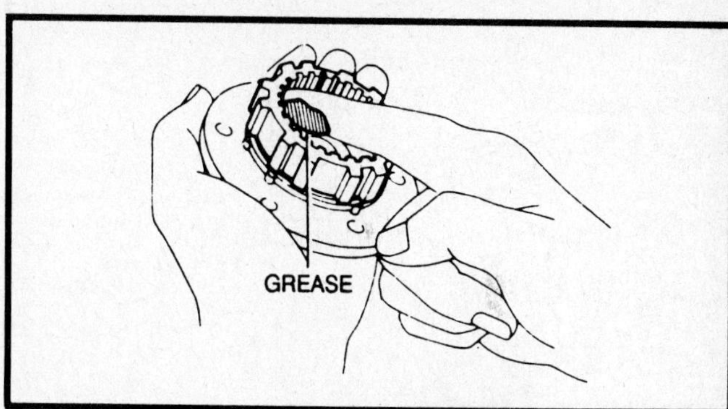

Grease the inner hub before installation

3. Remove the locking hub mounting bolts and remove the locking hub.
4. With the hub removed, install two bolts and nuts opposite each other to hold the hub together.
5. Check for smooth operation of the control handle in both the FREE and LOCK positions.
6. Check for smooth rotation of the inner hub with the control lever in the FREE position.
7. Check for no rotation of the inner hub with the control lever in the LOCK position.
8. To install, place the control lever in the FREE position.
9. Lightly grease the inner splines of the hub.
10. Install the hub on the vehicle and torque the bolts to 22–25 ft. lbs.
11. Install the wheel assembly and check the operation of the hub.

Axleshaft

Removal and Installation

1. Raise and support the vehicle safely. Remove the wheel assembly.
2. Remove the locking hub assembly.
3. Remove the brake caliper and the mount without disconnecting the fluid line. Support the caliper out of the way.
4. Disconnect the stabilizer bar and shock absorber from the lower control arm.
5. Disconnect the tie rod end from the steering knuckle.

6. Remove the circlip and spacer from the hub end of the axleshaft.
7. Support the lower control arm.
8. Remove the upper and lower ball joint cotter pins and nuts.
9. Separate the ball joints from the control arms.
10. Remove the steering knuckle and hub assembly.
11. Remove the engine under cover.
12. Carefully, remove the axleshaft from the differential end. Use care not to damage the oil seal or dust cover.
13. Remove the axleshaft from the vehicle.
14. Installation is the reverse of the removal procedure.

Axleshaft Joint and Boot

Removal and Installation

INNER

1. Raise and support the vehicle safely. Remove the wheel assembly.
2. Remove the axleshaft from the vehicle. Support the axleshaft.
3. To replace the inner boot, remove the boot clamps from the boot and slide the boot inward on the axleshaft.

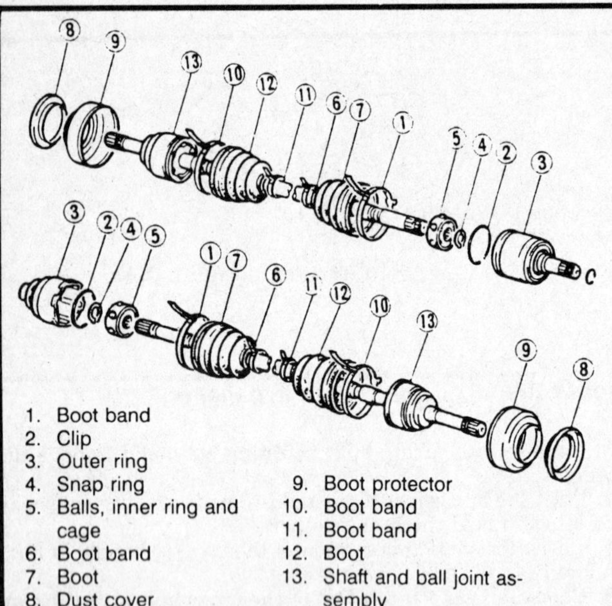

Front axleshafts—exploded view

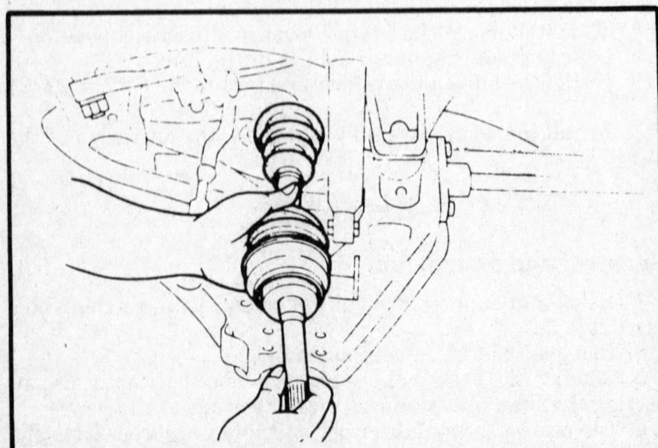

Removing the axleshaft

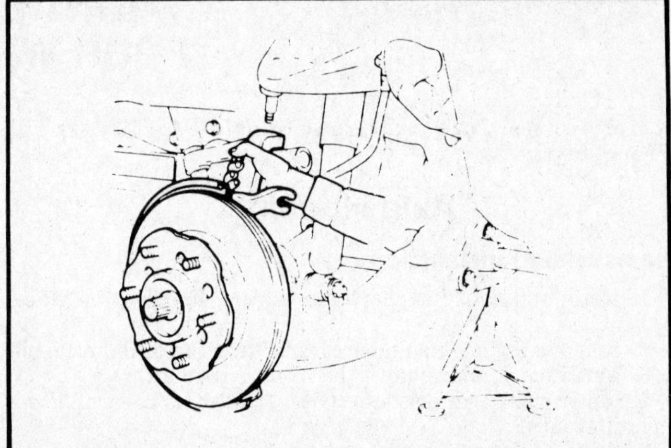

Support the lower control arm and disconnect the upper ball joint

4. Remove the circlip from the end of the axleshaft and remove the CV joint.
5. Remove the inner boot clamp and remove the boot from the axleshaft.
6. Clean the splines of the axleshaft and the CV joint.
7. Install the new boot and inner clamp on the axleshaft. Slide the boot inward on the axleshaft to install the CV joint.
8. Fill the CV joint with grease and install the joint onto the axleshaft.

CAUTION

Never hit the threads of the CV joint when installing. Make sure that the CV joint circlip is in the groove on the axleshaft before installing the boot.

9. Slide the boot into position over the CV joint and install the inner clamp.
10. Fill the boot with grease and install the outer clamp.
11. Install the axleshaft assembly in the vehicle.
12. The remainder of the installation is the reverse of the removal procedure.

OUTER

1. Raise and support the vehicle safely. Remove the wheel assembly.
2. Support the lower control arm and disconnect the stabilizer bar from the control arm.
3. Remove the lower ball joint cotter pin and nut. Separate the lower ball joint from the control arm.
4. Remove the brake caliper from the caliper mount without disconnecting the brake line. Support the caliper out of the way.
5. Remove the locking hub. Remove the circlip and spacer from the end of the axle shaft.
6. Move the steering knuckle out of way enough to remove the axleshaft from the hub.
7. To replace the inner boot, remove the boot clamps from the boot and slide the boot inward on the axleshaft.
8. Remove the circlip from the end of the axleshaft and remove the CV joint.
9. Remove the inner boot clamp and remove the boot from the axleshaft.
10. Clean the splines of the axleshaft and the CV joint.
11. Install the new boot and inner clamp on the axleshaft. Slide the boot inward on the axleshaft to install the CV joint.
12. Fill the CV joint with grease and install the joint onto the axleshaft.

CAUTION

Never hit the threads of the CV joint when installing. Make sure that the CV joint circlip is in the groove on the axleshaft before installing the boot.

13. Slide the boot into position over the CV joint and install the inner clamp.
14. Fill the boot with grease and install the outer clamp.
15. Install the axleshaft assembly in the vehicle.
16. The remainder of the installation is the reverse of the removal procedure.

Differential Carrier

Removal and Installation

1. Raise and support the vehicle safely. Remove the wheel assemblies.
2. Remove the engine undercover. Drain the differential oil.
3. Matchmark and remove the front driveshaft.
4. Remove both axleshafts from the differential.
5. Remove the differential to housing mounting nuts and remove the differential.
6. Clean and inspect the sealing surfaces of the differential and housing.
7. Install the differential in the housing and torque the nuts to 17–20 ft. lbs.
8. The remainder of the installation is the reverse of the removal procedure.
9. Fill the differential to the proper level with SAE 80W–90 oil when finished.

Output Shaft

Removal and Installation

1. Raise and support the vehicle safely. Remove the left wheel assembly.
2. Remove the left axleshaft.
3. Remove the engine undercover.
4. Remove the output shaft retainer bolts and remove the output shaft.
5. Remove the O-ring from the retainer.
6. Using a new O-ring, install the output shaft in the housing and torque the retainer bolts to 27–40 ft. lbs.
7. The remainder of the installation is the reverse of the removal procedure.

Output Shaft Oil Seal and Bearing

Removal and Installation

1. Raise and support the vehicle safely. Remove the left wheel assembly.
2. Remove the left side axleshaft. Remove the output shaft.
3. Remove the O-ring from the retainer. Remove the circlip from the retainer side of the output shaft.

NOTE: The next procedures require the use of a press. Certain adapters must also be used, to remove and install the bearing and seal.

4. Press out the output shaft, bearing and seal assembly from the retainer.
5. Remove the oil seal.
6. Press the bearing off of the output shaft.
7. Clean and inspect the output shaft.
8. Press the oil seal in the retainer using tool 49 M005 796 or equivalent.
9. Coat the lip of the oil seal with engine oil.
10. Press the output shaft into the bearing.

CAUTION

When pressing the output shaft into the bearing, only support the inner race of the bearing. If an extreme amount of binding occurs, STOP. The output shaft must be pressed into the bearing straight.

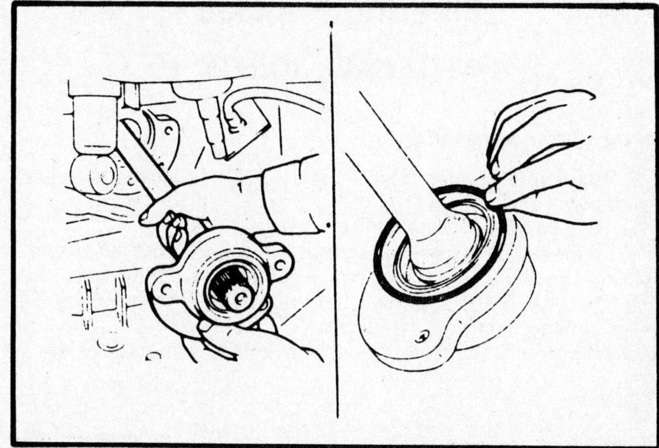

Removing the output shaft and replacing the O-ring

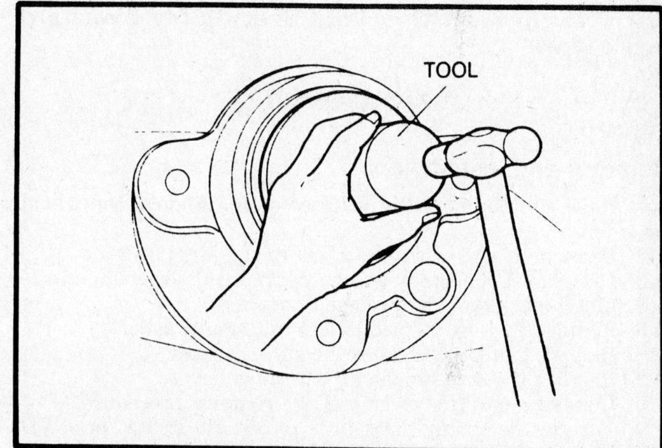

Replacing the output shaft seal

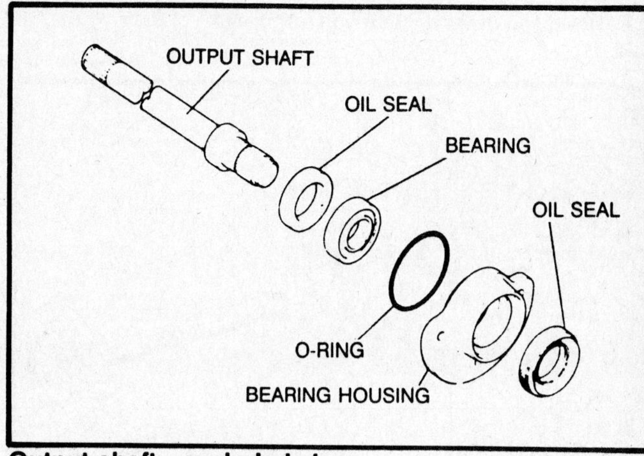

Output shaft—exploded view

11. Press the output shaft and bearing into the retainer.
12. Install the oil seal in the retainer.
13. Install a new circlip on the output shaft at the retainer.
14. Install a new O-ring on the retainer.
15. Install the output shaft into the differential.
16. Install the left side axleshaft.
17. The remainder of the installation is the reverse of the removal procedure.

Steering Knuckle

WITH BALL JOINTS

Removal and Installation

1. Raise and support the vehicle safely. Remove the wheel assembly.
2. Remove the locking hub assembly.
3. Remove the brake caliper and the mount without disconnecting the fluid line. Support the caliper out of the way.
4. Disconnect the stabilizer bar and shock absorber from the lower control arm.
5. Disconnect the tie rod end from the steering knuckle.
6. Remove the circlip and spacer from the hub end of the axleshaft.
7. Support the lower control arm. Using a puller, remove the hub and rotor assembly from the steering knuckle.
8. Remove the upper and lower ball joint cotter pins and nuts.
9. Separate the ball joints from the control arms.
10. Remove the dust shield. Remove the steering knuckle.
11. Installation is the reverse of the removal procedure. Adjust the wheel bearing when finished.
12. Observe the following torques during installation:
    Upper ball joint nut 22–38 ft. lbs.
    Lower ball joint nut 87–115 ft. lbs.
    Tie rod nut 23–43 ft. lbs.
    Brake caliper mount bolts 65–80 ft. lbs.
    Locking hub bolts 22–25 ft. lbs.

REAR DRIVE AXLE

Refer to the Unit Overhaul Section for Overhaul Procedures.

Axle Housing

Removal and Installation

1. Raise and support the vehicle safely. Remove the wheel assemblies.
2. Disconnect the brake fluid line at the junction.
3. Disconnect the shock absorbers from the lower mounts.
4. Matchmark and remove the driveshaft.
5. Remove the lower spring plate nuts and washers.
6. Remove the U-bolts from the spring plates.
7. Remove the axle housing from the vehicle.
8. Installation is the reverse of the removal procedure.
9. Torque the spring plate nuts to 88–100 ft. lbs. on 4WD models and to 47–58 ft. lbs. on 2WD models.
10. Torque the lower shock absorber bolts to 47–58 ft. lbs. for all models.
11. Bleed the brake system when finished.

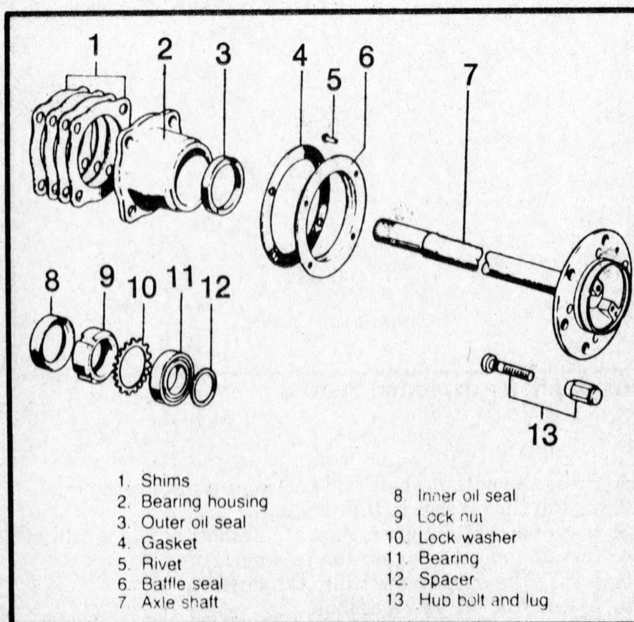

1982–85 Rear axleshaft – exploded view

Axleshaft Bearing and Seal

Removal and Installation

1982–85

1. Raise and support the vehicle safely.
2. Remove the wheel assemblies and brake drums.
3. Remove the brake shoes.
4. Remove the parking brake cable retainer.
5. Disconnect and plug the brake lines at the wheel cylinders.
6. Remove the bolts securing the backing plate and bearing housing.
7. Slide the axle shaft out of the axle housing.
8. Using a puller, remove the oil seal from the axle housing.
9. Straighten the tabs on the lockwasher and remove the nut and lockwasher from the axle shaft.
10. Using a press, remove the bearing and race from the shaft. Discard the spacer.
11. Remove the outer seal from the bearing housing and discard it.
12. Discard the gasket.
13. Using new seals and a new gasket, install all parts in reverse order of the removal procedure. Temporarily install the bearing/backing plate bolts, torquing them to 16 ft. lbs. Do not install the brake shoes.
14. Using a dial indicator, check the axleshaft end play. If only one shaft has been removed, end play should be 0.002–0.006 in. If both shaft have been removed, check the end play immediately after the first shaft has been replaced.
15. End play should be 0.026–0.033 in. Install the second shaft and check that end play. Second shaft end play should be 0.002–0.006 in.
16. If the end play at any step is not within specifications, shims are available.
17. After the end play is adjusted, torque the bearing retainer/backing plate bolts to 40–50 ft. lbs. and assemble all remaining parts.

1986–88

1. Raise and support the vehicle safely.
2. Remove the wheel assembly and brake drum.
3. Remove the brake shoes.
4. Remove the parking brake cable retainer.
5. Disconnect and plug the brake lines at the wheel cylinders.
6. Remove the bolts securing the backing plate and bearing housing.
7. Slide the axleshaft from the axle housing. Be careful to avoid damaging the oil seal with the axleshaft.
8. If the seal in the axle housing is damaged in any way, it must be replaced. The seal can be removed using a slide hammer and adapter.

9. Remove two of the backing plate bolts, diagonally from each other.
10. Using a grinding wheel, grind down the bearing retaining collar in one spot, until about 5mm remains above the axleshaft. Using a suitable tool, break the collar. Be careful to avoid damaging the shaft.
11. Using a press or puller, remove the hub and bearing assembly from the shaft. Remove the spacer from the shaft.
12. Remove the bearing and seal from the hub.
13. Using a suitable tool, remove the race from the hub.
14. Check all parts for wear or damage.

NOTE: If either race is being replaced, both must be replaced.

15. Remove the race in the axle housing with a slide hammer and adapter.
15. The outer race must be installed using an arbor press. The inner race can be driven into place in the axle housing.
16. Pack the hub with wheel bearing grease.
17. Tap a new oil seal into the axle housing until it is flush with the end of the housing. Coat the seal lip with wheel bearing grease.
18. Install a new spacer on the shaft with the larger flat surface up.
19. Install a new seal in the hub.
20. Thoroughly pack the bearing with clean wheel bearing grease.
21. Place the bearing in the hub and, using a press, press the hub and bearing assembly onto the shaft.
22. Press the new collar onto the shaft. The press pressure for the collar is critical. Press pressures should be 9,240–13,420 lbs. (4,200–6,100 kg).
23. Install one shaft in the housing being very careful to avoid damaging the inner seal.
24. If only on shaft was being serviced, the other must now be removed to check bearing play on the serviced axle. If both shafts were removed, leave the other one out temporarily.
25. Tighten the backing plate bolts on the one installed axle to 80 ft. lbs.
26. Mount a dial indicator on the backing plate, with the pointer resting on the axle shaft flange. Check the axleshaft end play. Standard bearing play should be 0.026–0.037 in. (0.65–0.95mm).

SHIM SELECTION CHART

Part Number	Thickness mm (in.)
S083 26 165	0.10 (0.004)
S083 26 166	0.15 (0.006)
S083 26 167	0.50 (0.020)
S083 23 168	0.75 (0.030)

27. If play is not within specifications, shims are available.
28. Install the other shaft and torque the backing plate bolts. Check the play as on the first shaft. Play should be 0.002–0.010 in. If not, correct it with shims.
29. Install the brake drums and wheels. Bleed the brake system.

Pinion Seal

Removal and Installation

1. Raise and support the vehicle safely.
2. Matchmark and remove the driveshaft.
3. Check the turning torque of the pinion before proceding. This is the torque that must be reached during installation of the pinion nut.

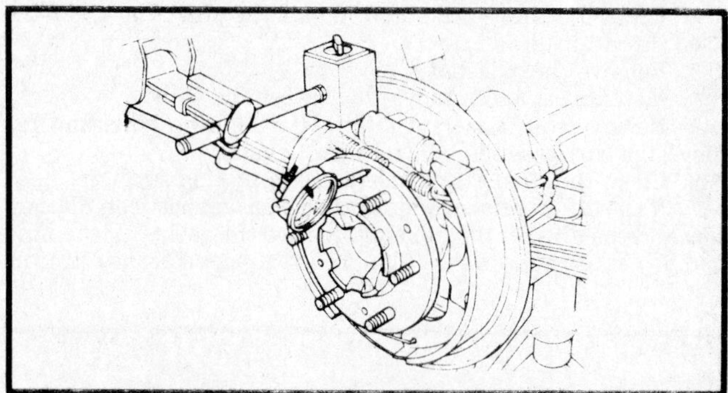

1982–85 Checking rear axleshaft endplay

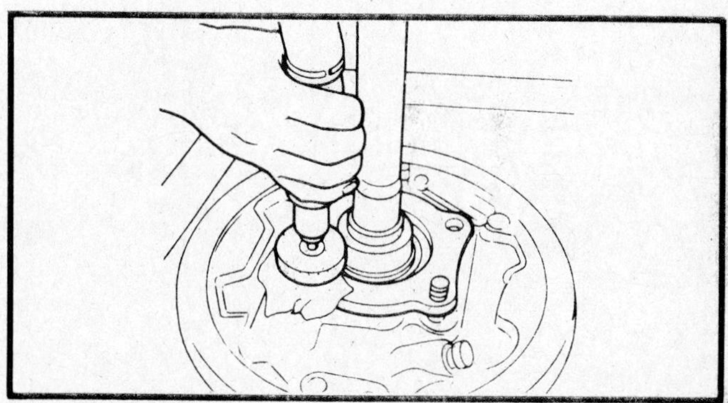

Grinding the bearing retainer collar on the 1986 trucks

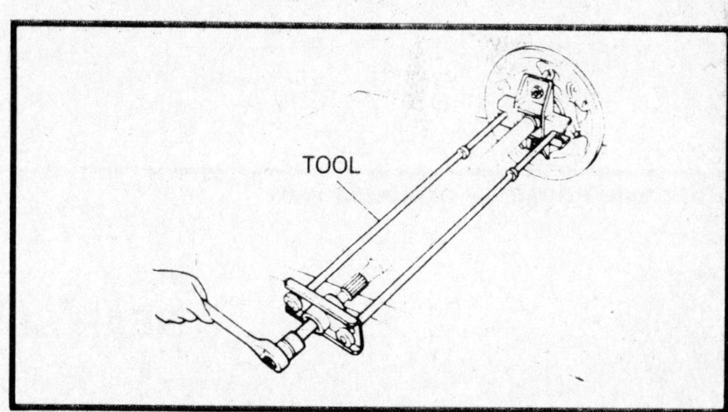

Using a puller to remove bearing housing on the rear axleshaft – 1982–85

4. Using pinion flange holding tool, remove the pinion nut and washer.
5. Remove the pinion flange from the pinion gear.
6. Pry the pinion seal out of the differential carrier.
7. Clean and inspect the sealing surface of the carrier and flange.
8. Using a seal driver, drive the new seal into the carrier until the flange on the seal is flush with the carrier.
9. With the seal installed, the pinion bearing preload must be set.
10. Tighten the pinion nut while holding the flange, until the turning torque is the same as before removal of the nut.
11. Align the matchmarks and install the driveshaft.
12. Check the level of the differential lubricant when finished.

Differential Carrier

Removal and Installation

1. Raise and support the vehicle safely.

2. Drain the differential fluid. Install the plug after all of the fluid has drained.
3. Remove the axleshafts.
4. Matchmark and remove the driveshaft.
5. Remove the carrier to differential housing bolts and remove the carrier assembly from the housing.
6. Clean the carrier and axle housing mating surfaces.
7. If the differential originally used a gasket between the carrier and the differential housing, replace the gasket. If the unit had no gasket, apply a thin film of oil-resistant silicone sealer to the mating surfaces of both the carrier and the housing and allow the sealer to set according to the manufacturer's instructions.
8. Place the carrier assembly into the housing and install the carrier to housing bolts. Torque the bolts to 12–17 ft. lbs.
9. Install the axleshafts. Align the matchmarks and install the driveshaft.
10. Install the brake drums and wheel assemblies.
11. Fill the differential with the proper amount of SAE 80W–90 fluid.

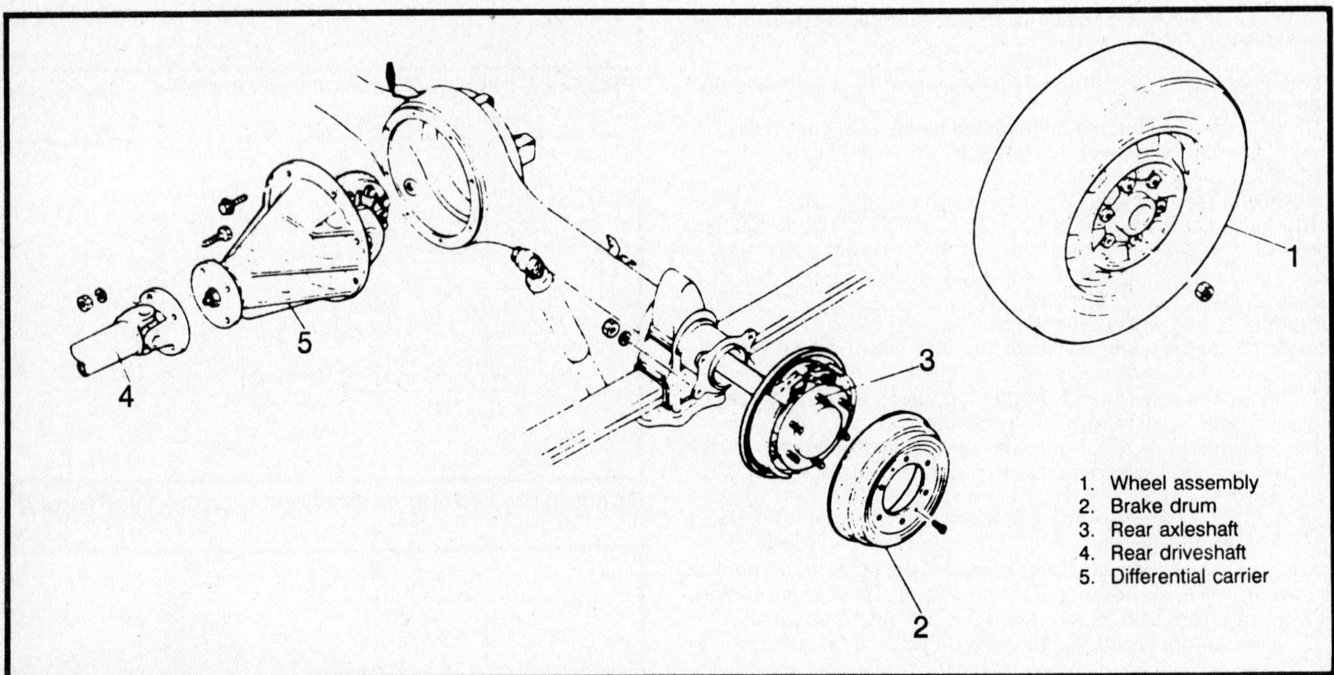

Rear axle housing – exploded view

REAR SUSPENSION

Leaf Spring

Removal and Installation

1. Raise and support the vehicle so that the leaf spring is hanging freely.
2. Support the rear axle to remove the weight from the spring.
3. Disconnect the lower shock absorber mount.
4. Remove the spring U-bolts and plate.
5. Remove the spring rear pivot bolt.
6. Remove the front shackle nuts and shackle.
7. Remove the spring from the vehicle.
8. Installation is the reverse of the removal procedure. Torque the spring rear shackle-to-frame nut to 47–58 ft. lbs.; the rear shackle-to-spring nut to 72 ft. lbs.; the U-bolt nuts to 47–58 ft. lbs. (88–100 ft. lbs. 4WD) and the front spring pin nut to 18 ft. lbs.

Shock Absorbers

Removal and Installation

1982–85

1. Raise and support the vehicle safely.
2. Unbolt the shock absorber at the top and bottom and remove it.
3. Installation is the reverse of removal. Tighten the nuts so that $^{1}/_{4}$ in. of thread is visible past the nut at each end.

1986–88

1. Raise and support the vehicle safely.
2. Remove the wheel assemblies.
3. Unbolt and remove the shock absorber at each end.
4. Installation is the reverse of removal. Torque the bolts to 57 ft. lb.

Nissan 17

INDEX

BEFORE SERVICING, SEE THE SAFETY NOTICE AT THE FRONT OF THE BOOK

MODEL IDENTIFICATION

Year	Model Designation	Model Name
1982	Z22	720 Pickup
	SD22	720 Pickup Diesel
1983	Z22	720 Pickup
	SD22	720 Pickup Diesel
1984	Z20	720 Pickup
	Z24	720 Pickup
	SD25	720 Pickup Diesel
1985	Z20	720 Pickup
	Z24	720 Pickup
	SD25	720 Pickup Diesel
1986	Z24i	720 Pickup
	VG30i	720 Pickup
	SD25	720 Pickup Diesel
1987-88	Z24i	720 Pickup, Pathfinder and Van
	VG30i	720 Pickup & Pathfinder
	SD25	720 Pickup Diesel

ENGINE IDENTIFICATION CODES BY VIN NUMBER

Engine Cu. In. (liter)	Cylinders	1982	1983	1984	1985	1986	1987	1988
133 (2.2)	4	M	M	—	—	—	—	—
132 (2.2)	4	S	S	—	—	—	—	—
119 (2.0)	4	—	—	F	F	—	—	—
146 (2.4)	4	—	—	N	N	N	N	N
152 (2.5)	4	—	—	J	J	J	J	J
181 (3.0)	6	—	—	—	—	H	H	H
146 (2.4)	4	—	—	—	—	—	S	S

GENERAL ENGINE SPECIFICATIONS

Year	VIN	No Cylinder Displacement cu. in. (liter)	Fuel System Type	Net Horsepower @ rpm	Net Torque @ rpm (ft.lbs.)	Bore × Stroke (in.)	Compression Ratio	Oil Pressure @ idle
1982	M	4-133(2.2)	2-bbl	98 @ 4000	117 @ 1800	3.43 × 3.62	8.5:1	60
	S	4-132 (2.2)	Diesel	61 @ 4000	102 @ 1800	3.27 × 3.94	21.6:1	60
1983	M	4-133 (2.2)	2-bbl	98 @ 4000	117 @ 1800	3.43 × 3.62	8.5:1	60
	S	4-132 (2.2)	Diesel	61 @ 4000	102 @ 1800	3.27 × 3.94	21.6:1	60
1984	F	4-119 (2.0)	2-bbl	97 @ 5600	102 @ 3200	3.35 × 3.39	9.4:1	60
	N	4-146 (2.4)	2-bbl	103 @ 4800	134 @ 2800	3.50 × 3.78	8.3:1	60
	J	4-152 (2.5)	Diesel	70 @ 4000	115 @ 2000	3.50 × 3.94	21.4:1	60

GENERAL ENGINE SPECIFICATIONS

Year	VIN	No Cylinder Displacement cu. in. (liter)	Fuel System Type	Net Horsepower @ rpm	Net Torque @ rpm (ft.lbs.)	Bore × Stroke (in.)	Com-pression Ratio	Oil Pressure @ idle
1985	F	4-119 (2.0)	2-bbl	97 @ 5600	102 @ 3200	3.35 × 3.39	9.4:1	60
	N	4-146 (2.4)	2-bbl	103 @ 4800	134 @ 2800	3.50 × 3.78	8.3:1	60
	J	4-152 (2.5)	Diesel	70 @ 4000	115 @ 2000	3.50 × 3.94	21.4:1 ①	60
1986	H	6-181 (3.0)	EFI	152 @ 5200	162 @ 3600	3.43 × 3.27	9.0:1	50
	N	4-146 (2.4)	EFI	103 @ 4800	134 @ 2800	3.50 × 3.78	8.3:1	60
	J	4-152 (2.5)	Diesel	70 @ 4000	115 @ 2000	3.50 × 3.94	21.4:1 ①	60
1987-88	H	6-181 (3.0)	EFI	152 @ 5200	162 @ 3600	3.43 × 3.27	9.0:1	50
	N	4-146 (2.4)	EFI	103 @ 4800	134 @ 2800	3.50 × 3.78	8.3:1	60
	J	4-152 (2.5)	Diesel	70 @ 4000	115 @ 2000	3.50 × 3.94	21.4:1	60
	S	4-146 (2.4)	EFI	103 @ 4800	134 @ 2800	3.50 × 3.78	8.3:1	60

EFI: Electronic Fuel Injection
① Calif.—21.9:1

GASOLINE ENGINE TUNE-UP SPECIFICATIONS

Year	VIN	No. Cylinder Displacement cu. in. (liter)	Spark Plugs Type	Spark Plugs Gap (in.)	Ignition Timing (deg.) MT	Ignition Timing (deg.) AT	Com-pression Pressure (psi)	Fuel Pump (psi)	Idle Speed (rpm) MT ④	Idle Speed (rpm) AT ④⑤	Valve Clearance ⑥ (in.) In.	Valve Clearance ⑥ (in.) Ex.
1982	M	4-133 (2.2)	②	0.035	3	3	8.5:1	3.4	650 ③	650	0.012	0.012
1983	M	4-133 (2.2)	②	0.033	3	3	8.5:1	3.4	650 ③	650	0.012	0.012
1984	F	4-119 (2.0)	②	0.033	5	5	9.4:1	3.0	600	650	0.012	0.012
	N	4-146 (2.4)	②	0.033	3	3	8.3:1	3.0	700	650	0.012	0.012
1985	F	4-119 (2.0)	②	0.033	5	5	9.4:1	3.0	700	—	0.012	0.012
	N	4-146 (2.4)	②	0.033	3	3	8.3:1	3.0	700 ③	650	0.012	0.012
1986	H	6-181 (3.0)	BCPR5ES-11	0.041	12	12	9.0:1	36	800	700	Hyd.	Hyd.
	N	4-146 (2.4)	BPR5ES ①	0.033	5	5	8.3:1	36	900	650	0.012	0.012
1987	H	6-181 (3.0)	BCPR5ES-11	0.041	12	12	9.0:1	36	800	700	Hyd.	Hyd.
	N	4-146 (2.4)	BPR5ES ①	0.033	5	5	8.3:1	36	900	650	0.012	0.012
	S	4-146 (2.4)	BPR5ES ①	0.033	10	10	8.3:1	36	800	750	0.012	0.012
1988	See Underhood Specifications											

① Intake & exhaust sides
② Intake side: BPR6ES
Exhaust side: BPR5ES
③ 4WD: 800 rpm
④ Before Top Dead Center (BTDC)
⑤ Transmission in Drive (D)
⑥ Engine (Hot)

FIRING ORDER

NOTE: Always remove spark plug wires one at a time.

L20B firing order: 1-3-4-2
SD22, SD25 firing order: 1-3-4-2

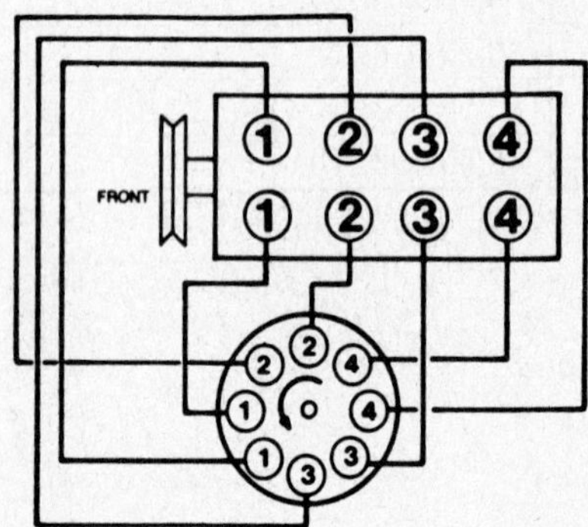

Z20, Z22, Z24 firing order: 1-3-4-2

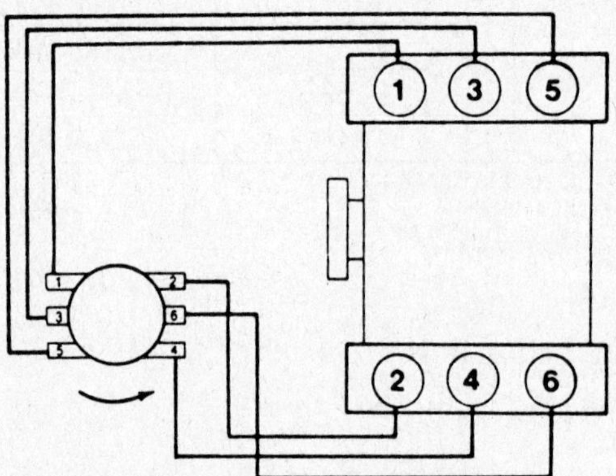

VG30i firing order: 1-2-3-4-5-6
Distributor rotation: Counterclockwise

CRANKSHAFT AND CONNECTING ROD SPECIFICATIONS

All measurements are given in inches.

Year	VIN	No. Cylinder Displacement cu. in. (liter)	Crankshaft				Connecting Rod		
			Main Brg. Journal Dia.	Main Brg. Oil Clearance	Shaft end-play	Thrust on No.	Journal Diameter	Oil Clearance	Side Clearance
1982	M	4-133 (2.2)	2.1631–2.1636	0.0008–0.0024	0.0020–0.0071	3	1.9670–1.9765	0.0010–0.0022	0.008–0.012
	S	4-132 (2.2)	2.7916–2.7921	0.0014–0.0037	0.0024–0.0055	3	2.0832–2.0837	0.0014–0.0034	0.0040–0.0080
1983	M	4-133 (2.2)	2.1631–2.1636	0.0008–0.0024	0.0020–0.0071	3	1.9670–1.9675	0.0010–0.0022	0.008–0.012
	S	4-132 (2.2)	2.7916–2.7921	0.0014–0.0037	0.0024–0.0055	3	2.0832–2.0837	0.0014–0.0034	0.0040–0.0080
1984	F	4-119 (2.0)	2.1631–2.1636	0.0008–0.0024	0.0020–0.0071	3	1.9670–1.9675	0.0005–0.0021	0.008–0.012
	N	4-146 (2.4)	2.1631–2.1636	0.0008–0.0024	0.0020–0.0071	3	1.9670–1.9675	0.0005–0.0021	0.008–0.0012
	J	4-152 (2.5)	2.7916–2.7921	0.0014–0.0034	0.0024–0.0055	3	2.0832–2.0837	0.0014–0.0032	0.004–0.008

CRANKSHAFT AND CONNECTING ROD SPECIFICATIONS

All measurements are given in inches.

Year	VIN	No. Cylinder Displacement cu. in. (liter)	Crankshaft Main Brg. Journal Dia.	Crankshaft Main Brg. Oil Clearance	Crankshaft Shaft end-play	Crankshaft Thrust on No.	Connecting Rod Journal Diameter	Connecting Rod Oil Clearance	Connecting Rod Side Clearance
1985	F	4-119 (2.0)	2.1631–2.1636	0.0008–0.0024	0.0020–0.0071	3	1.9670–1.9675	0.0005–0.0021	0.008–0.012
	N	4-146 (2.4)	2.1631–2.1636	0.0008–0.0024	0.0020–0.0071	3	1.9670–1.9675	0.0005–0.0021	0.008–0.012
	J	4-152 (2.5)	2.7916–2.7921	0.0014–0.0034	0.0024–0.0055	3	2.0832–2.0837	0.0014–0.0032	0.004–0.008
1986	H	6-181 (3.0)	2.4790–2.4793	0.0011–0.0022	0.0020–0.0067	4	1.9670–1.9675	0.0004–0.0020	0.0020–0.0067
	N	4-146 (2.4)	2.3599–2.3604	①	0.0020–0.0071	3	1.9670–1.9675	0.0005–0.0021	0.008–0.012
	J	4-152 (2.5)	2.7916–2.7921	0.0014–0.0034	0.0024–0.0055	3	2.0832–2.0837	0.0014–0.0032	0.004–0.008
1987-88	H	6-181 (3.0)	2.4790–2.4793	0.0011–0.0022	0.0020–0.0067	4	1.9670–1.9675	0.0004–0.0020	0.008–0.014
	N	4-146 (2.4)	2.3599–2.3604	①	0.0020–0.0071	3	1.9670–1.9675	0.0005–0.0021	0.008–0.012
	J	4-152 (2.5)	2.7916–2.7921	0.0014–0.0034	0.0024–0.0055	3	2.0832–2.0837	0.0014–0.0032	0.004–0.008
	S	4-146 (2.4)	2.3599–2.3604	①	0.0020–0.0071	3	1.9670–1.9675	0.0005–0.0021	0.008–0.012

① No. 1 & 5: 0.008–0.0024
No. 2, 3 & 4: 0.0008–0.0030

VALVE SPECIFICATIONS

Year	VIN	No. Cylinder Displacement cu. in. (liter)	Seat Angle (deg.)	Face Angle (deg.)	Spring Test Pressure (lbs.)	Spring Installed Height (in.)	Stem-to-Guide Clearance (in.) Intake	Stem-to-Guide Clearance (in.) Exhaust	Stem Diameter (in.) Intake	Stem Diameter (in.) Exhaust
1982	M	4-133 (2.2)	45.5	44.5	115 ①	1.18 ②	0.0008–0.0021	0.0016–0.0029	0.3136–0.3142	0.3128–0.3134
1983	M	4-133 (2.2)	45.5	44.5	115 ①	1.18 ②	0.0008–0.0021	0.0016–0.0029	0.8136–0.3142	0.3128–0.3134
1984	F	4-119 (2.0)	45.5	44.5	115 ①	1.18 ②	0.0008–0.0021	0.0016–0.0029	0.3136–0.3142	0.3128–0.3134
	N	4-146 (2.4)	45.5	44.5	115 ①	1.18 ②	0.0008–0.0021	0.0016–0.0029	0.3136–0.3142	0.3128–0.3134
1985	F	4-119 (2.0)	45.5	44.5	115 ①	1.18 ②	0.0008–0.0021	0.0016–0.0029	0.3136–0.3142	0.3128–0.3134
	N	4-146 (2.4)	45.5	44.5	115 ①	1.18 ②	0.0008–0.0021	0.0016–0.0029	0.3136–0.3142	0.3128–0.3134
1986	H	6-181 (3.0)	45.5	44.5	118 ①	1.18 ②	0.0008–0.0021	0.0012–0.0018	0.2742–0.2748	0.3136–0.3138
	N	4-146 (2.4)	45.5	44.5	51 ③	1.58 ④	0.0008–0.0021	0.0012–0.0029	0.3136–0.3142	0.3128–0.3134

VALVE SPECIFICATIONS

Year	VIN	No. Cylinder Displacement cu. in. (liter)	Seat Angle (deg.)	Face Angle (deg.)	Spring Test Pressure (lbs.)	Spring Installed Height (in.)	Stem-to-Guide Clearance (in.)		Stem Diameter (in.)	
							Intake	Exhaust	Intake	Exhaust
1987-88	H	6-181 (3.0)	45.5	44.5	118 ①	1.18 ②	0.0008–0.0021	0.0012–0.0018	0.2742–0.2748	0.3136–0.3138
	N	4-146 (2.4)	45.5	44.5	51 ③	1.58 ④	0.0008–0.0021	0.0016–0.0029	0.3136–0.3142	0.3128–0.3134
	S	4-146 (2.4)	45.5	44.5	51 ③	1.50 ④	0.0008–0.0021	0.0016–0.0029	0.3136–0.3142	0.3128–0.3134

① Inner: 57
② Inner: 0.98
③ Inner: 24
④ Inner: 1.39

PISTON AND RING SPECIFICATIONS

All measurements are given in inches.

Year	VIN	No. Cylinder Displacement cu. in. (liter)	Piston Clearance	Ring Gap			Ring Side Clearance		
				Top Compression	Bottom Compression	Oil Control	Top Compression	Bottom Compression	Oil Control
1982	M	4-133 (2.2)	0.0010–0.0018	0.0098–0.0157	0.0059–0.0118	0.0118–0.0354	0.0016–0.0029	0.0012–0.0025	—
1983	M	4-133 (2.2)	0.0010–0.0018	0.0098–0.0157	0.0059–0.0118	0.0118–0.0354	0.0016–0.0029	0.0012–0.0025	—
1984	F	4-119 (2.0)	0.0010–0.0018	0.0098–0.0157	0.0059–0.0118	0.0118–0.0354	0.0016–0.0029	0.0012–0.0025	—
	N	4-146 (2.4)	0.0010–0.0018	0.0098–0.0157	0.0059–0.0118	0.0118–0.0354	0.0016–0.0029	0.0012–0.0025	—
1985	F	4-119 (2.0)	0.0010–0.0018	0.0098–0.0157	0.0059–0.0118	0.0118–0.0354	0.0016–0.0029	0.0012–0.0025	—
	N	4-146 (2.4)	0.0010–0.0018	0.0098–0.0157	0.0059–0.0118	0.0118–0.0354	0.0016–0.0029	0.0012–0.0025	—
1986	H	G-181 (3.0)	0.0010–0.0018	0.0083–0.0134	0.0071–0.0173	0.0079–0.0299	0.0016–0.0029	0.0012–0.0025	0.0006–0.0073
	N	4-146 (2.4)	0.0010–0.0018	0.0110–0.0150	0.0098–0.0138	0.0079–0.0236	0.0016–0.0029	0.0012–0.0025	—
1987-88	H	6-181 (3.0)	0.0010–0.0018	0.0083–0.0134	0.0071–0.0173	0.0079–0.0299	0.0016–0.0029	0.0012–0.0025	0.0006–0.0073
	N	4-146 (2.4)	0.0010–0.0018	0.0110–0.0150	0.0098–0.0138	0.0079–0.0236	0.0016–0.0029	0.0012–0.0025	—
	S	4-146 (2.4)	0.0010–0.0018	0.0110–0.0150	0.0098–0.0138	0.0079–0.0236	0.0016–0.0029	0.0012–0.0025	—

TORQUE SPECIFICATIONS

All readings in ft. lbs.

Year	VIN	No. Cylinder Displacement cu. in. (liter)	Cylinder Head Bolts	Main Bearing Bolts	Rod Bearing Bolts	Crankshaft Pulley Bolts	Flywheel Bolts	Manifold Intake	Manifold Exhaust	Spark Plugs
1982	M	4-133 (2.2)	51-58	33-40	33-40	87-116	101-116	12-15	12-16	14-22
1983	M	4-133 (2.2)	51-58	33-40	33-40	87-116	101-116	12-15	12-16	14-22
1984	F	4-119 (2.0)	①	33-40	33-40	87-116	101-116	12-15	12-15	14-22
	N	4-146 (2.4)	①	33-40	33-40	87-116	101-116	12-15	12-15	14-22
1985	F	4-119 (2.0)	①	33-40	33-40	87-116	101-116	12-15	12-15	14-22
	N	4-146 (2.4)	①	33-40	33-40	87-116	101-116	12-15	12-15	14-22
1986	H	6-181 (3.0)	40-47	67-74	33-40	90-98	72-80	②	13-16	14-22
	N	4-146 (2.4)	54-61	33-40	33-40	87-116	101-116	12-15	12-15	14-22
1987-88	H	6-181 (3.0)	40-47	67-74	33-40	90-98	72-80	②	13-16	14-22
	N	4-146 (2.4)	54-61	33-40	33-40	87-116	101-116	12-15	12-15	14-22
	S	4-156 (2.4)	54-61	33-40	33-40	105-112	101-116	12-15	12-15	14-22

① Step 1: 22 ft. lbs.
Step 2: 58 ft. lbs.
Step 3: Loosen all bolts
Step 4: 22 ft. lbs.
Step 5: 54-61 ft. lbs.
② Bolt: 12-14 ft. lbs.
Nut: 17-20 ft. lbs.

CAPACITIES

Year	Model	No. Cylinder Displacement cu. in. (liter)	Engine Crankcase (qts) with Filter	Engine Crankcase (qts) without Filter	Transmission (pts.) 4-Spd	Transmission (pts.) 5-Spd	Transmission (pts.) Auto.	Drive Axle (pts.)	Fuel Tank (gal.)	Cooling System (qts.)
1982	Pickup	4-133 (2.2)	4.6 ①	4.1 ②	3.6	4.2	11.7	2.6 ③	13.25 ④	10.75
1983	Pickup	4-133 (2.2)	4.6 ①	4.1 ②	3.6	4.2	11.7	2.6 ③	13.25 ④	10.75
1984	Pickup	4-119 (2.0)	4.3 ①	3.9 ⑤	—	4.2	11.7	2.6 ⑥	13.25 ④⑦	10.75
		4-146 (2.4)	4.3 ①	3.9 ⑤	—	4.2	11.7	2.6	13.25 ④⑦	10.75
1985	Pickup	4-119 (2.0)	3.9 ⑨	3.4 ⑩	N.A.	4.5	11.7	2.6 ⑪	13.25 ④⑦⑧	10.75
		4-146 (2.4)	3.8 ⑨	3.4 ⑩	N.A.	4.5	11.7	2.6 ⑪	13.25 ④⑦⑧	10.75
1986	Pickup	6-181 (3.0)	4.3 ⑨	3.8 ⑫	N.A.	5.12 ⑭	14.8	5.6	15.8	10.5
		4-146 (2.4)	4.0 ①	3.5 ⑤	N.A.	4.25 ⑬	14.8	3.12 ⑫	15.8	8.6
1987-88	Pickup	6-181 (3.0)	4.25 ⑮	3.8 ⑫	N.A.	4.25 ⑬	15.6	5.6 ⑫	15.8	10.5
		4-146 (2.4)	4.0 ①	3.5 ⑤	N.A.	4.25 ⑬	14.8	3.12 ⑯	15.8	8.6
	Van	4-146 (2.4)	4.4	3.8	N.A.	4.25	14.8	2.8	17.12	9.25 ⑰

NA—Not available
① 4WD: 4.5
② 4WD: 3.8
③ 4WD—front axle: 2.1
④ Long bed: 16:8
⑤ 4WD: 4.0
⑥ Dual rear wheels: 2.7
⑦ 4WD long bed: 19.8
⑧ 4WD: 15.88
⑨ 4WD: 4.25
⑩ 4WD: 3.75
⑪ Front Differential (R180): 2.1 pts.
⑫ 4WD: 3.12
⑬ 4WD: 8.5 pts.
⑭ 4WD: 7.6 pts.
⑮ 4WD: 3.6 qts.
⑯ 4WD: 2.8 pts.
⑰ With front/rear heater: 3.8 qts.

WHEEL ALIGNMENT

Year	Model	Caster Range (deg.)	Caster Preferred Setting (deg.)	Camber Range (deg.)	Camber Preferred Setting (deg.)	Toe-in (in.)	Steering Axis Inclination (deg.)
1982	2WD Pickup	$\frac{5}{6}$P–$1\frac{5}{6}$P	$1\frac{1}{3}$P	0–1P	$\frac{1}{2}$P	0.20–0.28	N.A.
	4WD Pickup	$1\frac{1}{6}$P–$2\frac{1}{6}$P	$1\frac{2}{3}$P	0–1P	$\frac{1}{2}$P	0.20–0.28	N.A.
1983	2WD Pickup	$\frac{5}{6}$P–$1\frac{5}{6}$P	$1\frac{1}{3}$P	0–1P	$\frac{1}{2}$P	0.20–0.28	N.A.
	4WD Pickup	$1\frac{1}{6}$P–$2\frac{1}{6}$P	$1\frac{2}{3}$P	0–1P	$\frac{1}{2}$P	0.20–0.28	N.A.
1984	2WD Pickup	$1\frac{1}{6}$P–$2\frac{1}{6}$P	$1\frac{1}{3}$P	0–1P	$\frac{1}{2}$P	①	N.A.
	4WD Pickup	$\frac{11}{12}$P–$1\frac{11}{12}$P	$1\frac{5}{12}$P	$\frac{1}{6}$P–$1\frac{1}{6}$P	$\frac{2}{3}$P	0.08–0.16 ②	N.A.
1985	2WD Pickup	$\frac{5}{6}$P–$1\frac{5}{6}$P	$1\frac{1}{3}$P	0–1P	$\frac{1}{2}$P	①	N.A.
	4WD Pickup	$\frac{11}{12}$P–$1\frac{11}{12}$P	$1\frac{5}{12}$P	$\frac{1}{6}$P–$1\frac{1}{6}$P	$\frac{2}{3}$P	0.04–0.12 ②	N.A.
1986	2WD Pickup	$\frac{12}{15}$N–$\frac{13}{15}$P	$\frac{11}{30}$P	$\frac{1}{12}$N–$\frac{11}{12}$P	$\frac{5}{12}$P	③	$8\frac{7}{12}$–$9\frac{7}{12}$
	4WD Pickup	$\frac{12}{15}$P–$1\frac{12}{15}$P	$1\frac{3}{10}$P	$\frac{1}{6}$P–$1\frac{1}{6}$P	$\frac{2}{3}$P	0.12–0.20	$7\frac{3}{5}$–$8\frac{3}{5}$
1987-88	2WD Pickup	$\frac{2}{15}$N–$\frac{13}{15}$P	$\frac{11}{30}$P	$\frac{1}{12}$N–$\frac{11}{12}$P	$\frac{5}{12}$P	0.08–0.16 ②	$8\frac{7}{12}$–$9\frac{7}{12}$
	4WD Pickup	$\frac{12}{15}$P–$1\frac{12}{15}$P	$1\frac{3}{10}$P	$\frac{1}{6}$P–$1\frac{1}{6}$P	$\frac{2}{3}$P	0.12–0.20	$7\frac{3}{5}$–$8\frac{3}{5}$
	4WD Pathfinder	$\frac{12}{15}$P–$1\frac{12}{15}$P	$1\frac{3}{10}$P	$\frac{1}{6}$P–$1\frac{1}{6}$P	$\frac{2}{3}$P	0.04–0.12	$7\frac{3}{5}$–$8\frac{3}{5}$
	Van	1P–2P	$1\frac{1}{2}$P	$\frac{1}{4}$N–$\frac{3}{4}$P	$\frac{1}{4}$P	(−)0.04–0.04	N.A.

N.A.—Not available
① Radial tire: 0.08–0.16 in.
Bias tire: 0.20–0.28 in.
② Radial tires
③ Radial tires: 0.08–0.16 in.
Bias tires: 0.16–0.24 in.

ENGINE ELECTRICAL

Alternator

Precautions

To prevent damage to the alternator and regulator, the following precautionary measures must be taken when working with the electrical system.

1. Never reverse battery connections. Always check the battery polarity visually. This is to be done before any connections are made to be sure that all of the connections correspond to the battery ground polarity of the vehicle.
2. Booster batteries for starting must be connected properly.
3. Disconnect the battery cables before using a fast charger.
4. Never use a fast charger as a booster for starting the vehicle.
5. Never disconnect the voltage regulator while the engine is running.
6. Do not ground the alternator output terminal.
7. Do not operate the alternator on an open circuit with the field energized.
8. Do not attempt to polarize an alternator.
9. Disconnect the battery cables before using an electric arc welder on the vehicle.

Belt Tension Adjustments

Belt tension should be checked with a gauge made for the purpose. If a tension gauge is not available, tension can be checked with moderate thumb pressure applied to the belt at its longest span midway between pulleys. If the belt has a free span less than 12 in., it should deflect approximately $\frac{1}{8}$–$\frac{1}{4}$ in. If the span is longer than 12 in., deflection can range between $\frac{1}{8}$–$\frac{3}{8}$ in. To adjust or replace belts:

1. Loosen the driven accessory's pivot and mounting bolts.
2. Move the alternator toward or away from the engine until the tension is correct.

NOTE: Use a wooden hammer handle or broomstick, as a lever but do not use anything metallic, such as a pry bar.

3. Tighten the bolts and recheck the tension. If new belts have been installed, run the engine for a few minutes, then, recheck and readjust as necessary. It is better to have belts too loose than too tight, because overtight belts will lead to bearing failure, particularly in the water pump and alternator. However, loose belts place an extremely high impact load on the driven component due to the whipping action of the belt.

Removal and Installation

1. Disconnect the negative battery terminal from the battery.
2. Disconnect the two lead wires and connector from the alternator.
3. Loosen the drive belt adjusting bolt, push the alternator toward the engine and remove the drive belt.
4. Remove the alternator-to-bracket bolts and the alternator from the vehicle.
5. To install, reverse the removal procedures. Adjust the drive belt tension. Torque the alternator-to-lower bracket bolt to 27–37 ft. lbs. (gas) or 20–27 ft. lbs. (diesel), the alternator-to-adjusting bracket bolt to 14–22 ft. lbs. (Z22), 6–8 ft. lbs. (Z20 & Z24i), 10–12 ft. lbs. (VG30i) or 8–10 ft. lbs. (diesel).

Voltage Regulator

Removal and Installation

The transistorized regulator is soldered to the brush assembly inside the alternator. It is non-adjustable and must be replaced together with the brush assembly if faulty.

1. Remove the alternator from the vehicle.
2. Using a scribing awl, make alignment marks on the alternator halves. Remove the through bolts and separate the front cover from the stator housing.
3. Using a soldering iron, separate the diode plate-to-brush connection from the brush terminal.
4. Remove the diode plate-to-rear cover bolt.
5. Remove the battery terminal-to-alternator housing bolt.
6. Lift the stator slightly, together with the diode plate, to gain access to the diode plate screw, then, remove the screw.

NOTE: The regulator and brush assembly are riveted to the diode assembly. The rivets must be removed, then, reinstalled and stake new ones.

7. Separate the stator and diode, then, remove the brush/regulator assembly.
8. To install, reverse reverse the removal procedures.

NOTE: To avoid damage to the transistors and diodes, apply soldering heat sparingly, carrying out the operation as quickly as possible. Before assembling the alternator halves, bend a piece of wire in an "L" and slip it through the rear cover next to the brushes. Use the wire to hold the brushes in a retracted position until the case halves are assembled. Remove the wire carefully, to prevent damage to the slip rings.

Starter

Overhaul

For overhaul procedures, please refer to "Electrical" in the Unit Repair Section.

Removal and Installation

1. Disconnect the negative battery terminal from the battery.
2. Disconnect the wiring from the starter, taking note of the positions for correct reinstallation.
3. Remove the starter-to-engine bolts and the starter from the vehicle.
4. To install, reverse the removal procedures. Torque the starter-to-transmission bolts to 29–36 ft. lbs.

Distributor

Removal and Installation

1. Disconnect the two distributor cap retaining clips and remove the distributor cap with the plug wires attached.
2. Using a piece of chalk, make alignment marks on the distributor-to-engine and rotor-to-distributor locations; the alignment marks are used for reinstallation.
3. On the 1982-85 models, disconnect the vacuum advance hose from the distributor and the wiring connector from the coil. On the 1986-88 models, disconnect the distributor electrical harness connector.
4. Remove the distributor-to-engine bolt and lift the distributor assembly from the engine.
5. If the engine was undisturbed, install the distributor, align the match-marks and reverse the removal procedures. Check and/or adjust the timing.
6. If the crankshaft was turned, the engine disturbed in any manner (while the distributor was removed) or alignment marks were not drawn, perform the following procedures:

a. Remove the No. 1 cylinder spark plug.

b. Turn the crankshaft until the No. 1 piston is positioned on the Top Dead Center (TDC) of the compression stroke.

NOTE: To determine the TDC of the compression stroke, place your thumb over the spark plug hole and feel the air being forced from the cylinder. Stop turning the crankshaft when the timing marks that are used to time the engine are aligned.

c. Oil the distributor housing-to-cylinder block surface.

d. Install the distributor so the rotor is points toward the No. 1 spark plug terminal tower of the distributor cap (when installed).

e. When the distributor shaft has reached the bottom of the hole, move the rotor back and forth slightly until the driving lug on the end of the shaft enters the slots cut in the end of the oil pump shaft and the distributor assembly slides down into place.

7. To complete the installation, reverse the removal procedures. Check and/or adjust the ignition timing.

TIMING LIGHT AND TACHOMETER CONNECTIONS

Since the vehicle uses an electronic ignition, use a timing light with an inductive pickup. This pickup simply clamps onto the No. 1 plug wire, eliminating the adapter. It is not susceptible to cross-firing or false triggering, which may occur with a conventional light, due to the greater voltages produced by electronic ignition.

IGNITION TIMING

NOTE: Ignition timing is the measurement, in degrees of crankshaft rotation, of the point at which the spark plugs fire in each of the cylinders. It is measured in degrees before or after Top Dead Center (TDC) of the compression stroke.

Because it takes a fraction of a second for the spark plug to ignite the mixture in the cylinder, the spark plug must fire a little before the piston reaches TDC. Otherwise, the mixture will not be completely ignited as the piston passes TDC and the full power of the explosion will not be used by the engine.

The timing measurement is given in degrees of crankshaft rotation before the piston reaches TDC (BTDC). If the setting for the ignition timing is 5° BTDC, the spark plug must fire 5° before each piston reaches TDC. This only holds true, however, when the engine is at idle speed.

As the engine speed increases, the pistons go faster. The spark plugs have to ignite the fuel even sooner if it is to be completely ignited when the piston reaches TDC. To do this, the distributor has a means to advance the spark timing as the engine speed increases. On the 1982-85 models, this is accomplished by centrifugal weights within the distributor and a vacuum diaphragm, mounted on the side of the distributor. On the 1986-88 models, the ignition timing is controlled by the ECM.

If the ignition is set too far advanced (BTDC), the ignition and expansion of the fuel in the cylinder will occur too soon and tend to force the piston down while it is still traveling up. This causes engine ping. If the ignition spark is set too far retarded, after TDC (ATDC), the piston will have already passed TDC and started on its way down when the fuel is ignited. This will cause the piston to be forced down for only a portion of its travel. This will result in poor engine performance and lack of power.

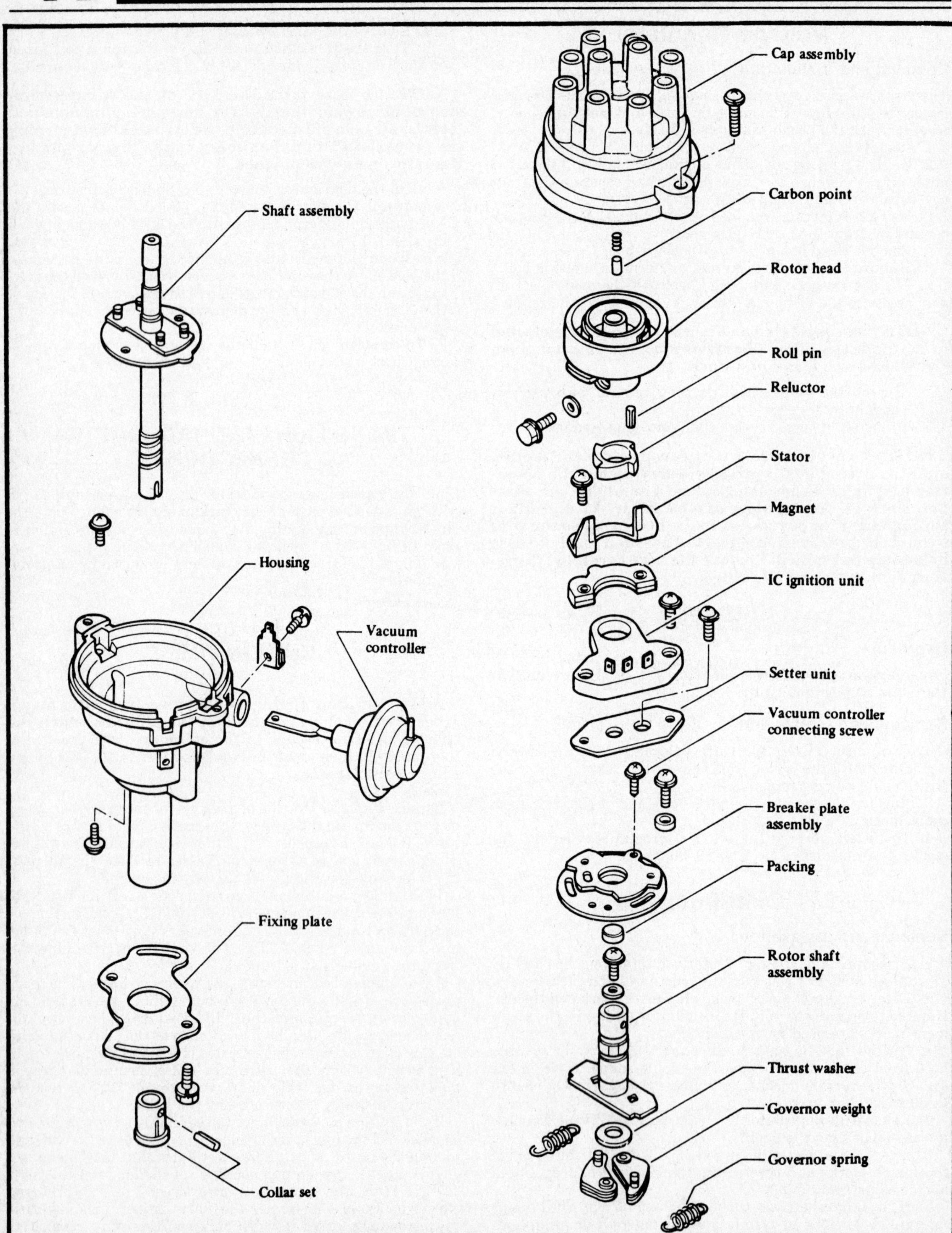

Exploded view of the distributor—Z-series engine (1982-85)

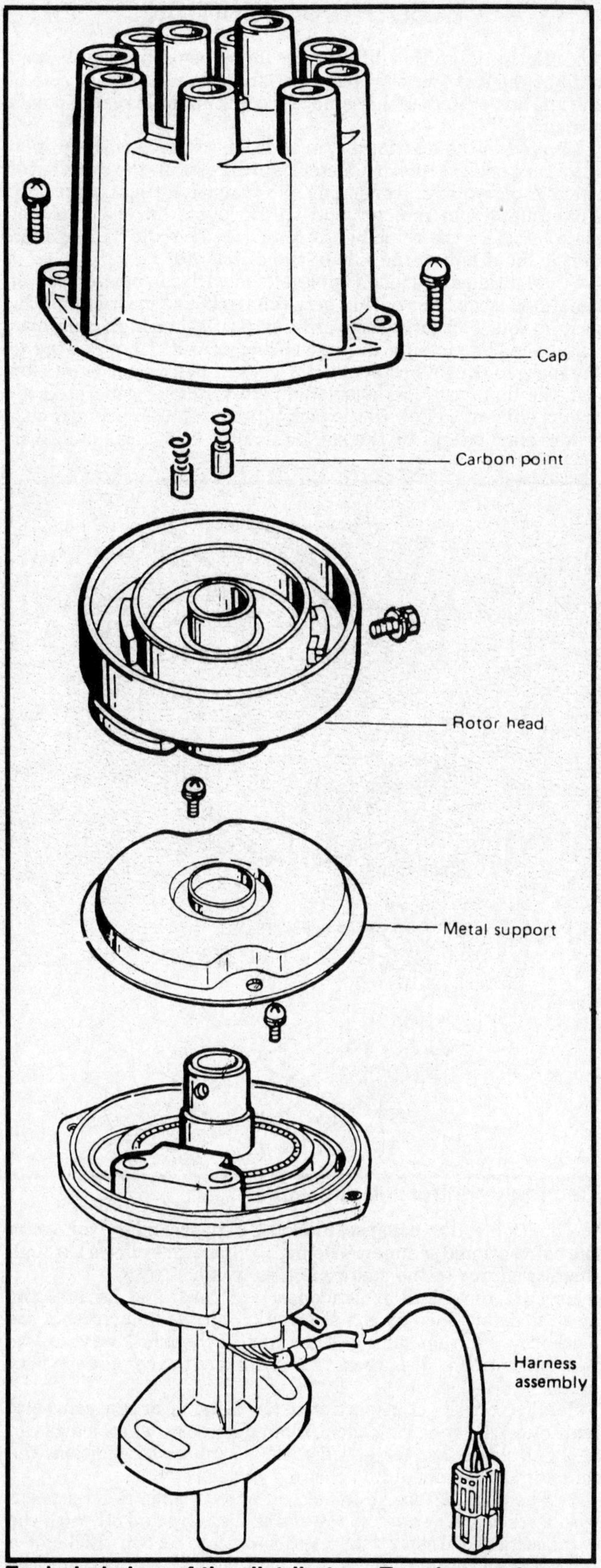

Exploded view of the distributor – Z-series engine (1986-88)

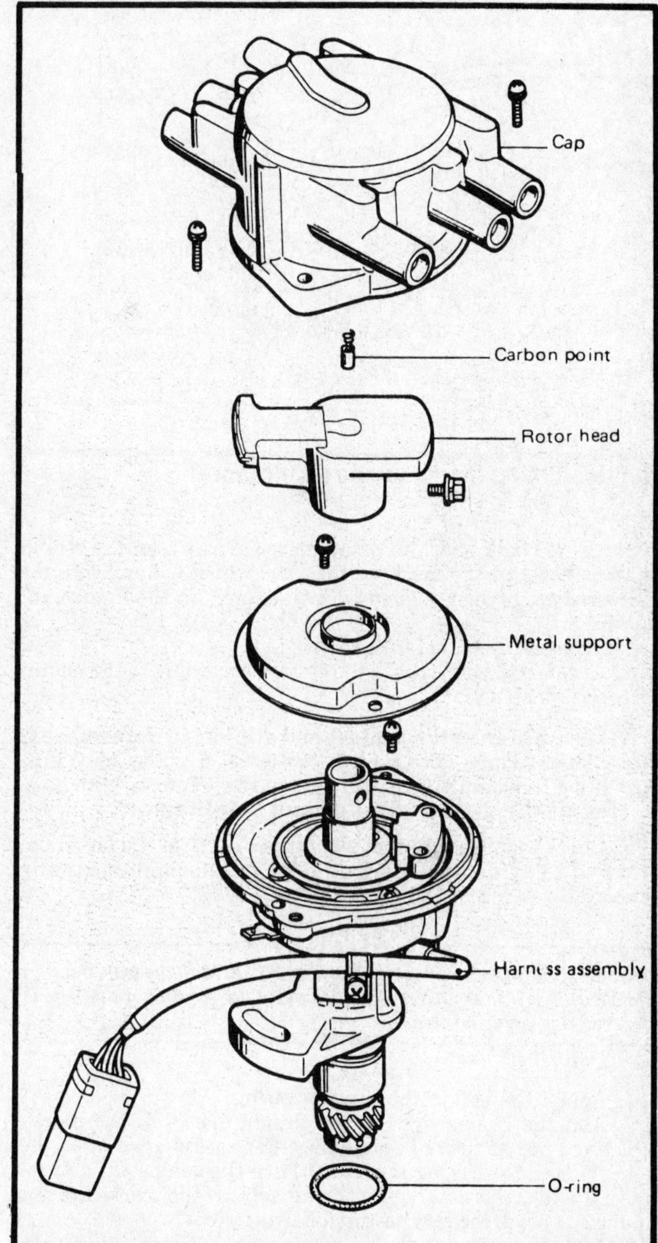

Exploded view of the distributor – V6 engine (1986-88)

Timing marks consist of a notch on the rim of the crankshaft pulley and a scale of degrees attached to the front of the engine. The notch corresponds to the position of the piston in the No. 1 cylinder. A stroboscopic (dynamic) timing light is used, which is connected to the No. 1 cylinder spark plug wire. Every time the spark plug fires, the timing light flashes. By aiming the timing light at the timing marks, the exact position of the piston within the cylinder can be read, since the stroboscopic flash makes the mark on the pulley appear to be standing still. Proper timing is indicated when the notch is aligned with the correct number on the scale.

Procedure

GASOLINE ENGINES

1. Locate the timing marks on the crankshaft pulley and the front of the engine.
2. Clean the timing marks, so you can see them.

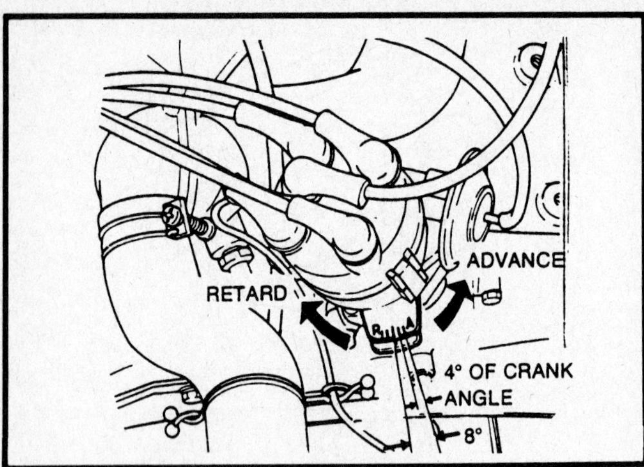

Ignition timing marks on the distributor

3. Using chalk or white paint, color the mark on the crankshaft pulley and the mark on the scale which will indicate the correct timing when aligned with the notch on the crankshaft pulley.
4. Attach a tachometer to the engine.
5. Attach a timing light to the engine, according to the manufacturer's instructions.

NOTE: Refer to the underhood sticker to determine if the vacuum hose is to be left connected to the distributor. If no instructions differ, leave the vacuum line connected to the distributor vacuum diaphragm.

6. Check to make sure that all of the wires clear the fan, then, start the engine and allow it to reach normal operating temperatures.

CAUTION

Block the front wheels and set the parking brake. Shift the transmission into Neutral (M/T) or Drive (A/T). Do not stand in front of the vehicle when making adjustments!

7. Adjust the idle to the correct setting.
8. Aim the timing light at the timing marks. If the marks which you put on the pulley and the engine are aligned when the light flashes, the timing is correct. Turn the engine Off and remove the tachometer and the timing light. If the marks are not in alignment, proceed with the following steps.
9. Turn the engine Off.
10. Loosen the distributor lockbolt just enough so that the distributor can be turned with a little effort.
11. Start the engine. Keep the wires of the timing light clear of the fan.
12. With the timing light aimed at the pulley and the marks on the engine, turn the distributor in the direction of rotor rotation to retard the spark or in the opposite direction to advance the spark. Align the marks on the pulley and the engine with the flashes of the timing light.
13. Tighten the distributor lockbolt and recheck the timing.

DIESEL ENGINES

The ignition timing is controlled by the position of the fuel injection pump. Locate the injection pump and inspect the alignment of the timing marks (one on the engine and the injection pump). If necessary, loosen the injection pump-to-engine bolts, then, turn the pump to align the timing marks. Torque the injection pump-to-engine bolts to 14–18 ft. lbs.

ELECTRONIC IGNITION

The electronic ignition differs from its conventional counterpart only in the distributor component area. The secondary side of the ignition system is the same as a conventional breaker points system.

Located in the distributor, in addition to the normal ignition rotor, is a spoked rotor (reluctor) which rests on the distributor shaft. A pick-up coil, consisting of a magnet, a ring type pickup surrounding the reluctor and wiring, rests on the "breaker plate" next to the reluctor. An integrated circuit (IC) ignition unit is mounted on the side of the distributor.

When a reluctor spoke is not aligned with the pick-up coil, it generates large lines of flux between itself, the magnet and the pick-up coil. This large flux variation results in a high generated voltage in the pick-up coil, preventing current from flowing to the pick-up coil. When a reluctor spoke align with the pick-up coil, the flux variation is low and zero voltage is generated, allowing current to flow to the pick-up coil. Ignition primary current is then cut off by the electronic unit, allowing the field in

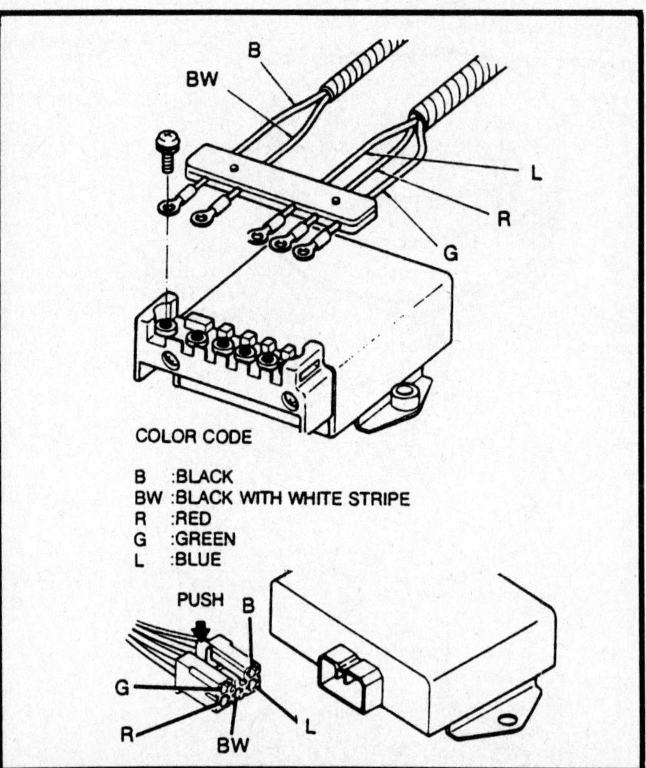

Electronic control unit connection

the ignition coil to collapse, inducing high secondary voltage in the conventional manner. The high voltage then flows through the distributor to the spark plug, as usual.

Because no points or condenser are used, and because the dwell is determined by the electronic unit, no adjustments are necessary. Ignition timing is checked in the usual way; unless the distributor is disturbed, it is not likely to ever change very much.

Service consists of inspection of the distributor cap, rotor and ignition wires, replacing them when necessary. These parts can be expected to last for at least 40,000 miles. In addition, the reluctor air gap should be checked periodically.

1. The distributor cap is held on by two clips. Release them with a screwdriver and lift the cap straight up and off, with the wires attached. Inspect the cap for cracks, carbon tracks or a worn center contact. Replace it, if necessary, transferring the

wires one at a time from the old cap to the new.

2. Pull the ignition rotor (not the spoked reluctor) straight up to remove. Replace it if its contacts are worn, burned or pitted. Do not file the contacts. To replace, press it firmly onto the shaft. It only goes on one way, so be sure it is fully seated.

3. Before replacing the ignition rotor, check the reluctor air gap. Use a non-magnetic feeler gauge. Rotate the engine until a reluctor spoke is aligned with the pick-up coil (either bump the engine around with the starter or turn it with a wrench on the crankshaft pulley bolt). The gap should measure 0.012–0.020 in. Adjustment, if necessary, is made by loosening the pick-up coil mounting screws and shifting its position to center the pick-up coil (ring) around the reluctor. Tighten the screws and recheck the gap.

4. Inspect the wires for cracks or brittleness. Replace them one at a time to prevent cross-wiring, carefully pressing the replacement wires into place. The cores of electronic wires are more susceptible to breakage than those of standard wires, so treat them gently.

Electrical Controls

IGNITION SWITCH

Removal and Installation

1. Disconnect the negative battery terminal from the battery.
2. From the upper steering column, remove the shell cover screws and the covers.
3. Disconnect the electrical connector from the rear of the ignition switch.
4. Using a drill, remove the self-shear type screws from the ignition switch.

NOTE: Remove the four screws (1982-85) or the two screws (1986-88).

5. Remove the ignition switch.
6. To install, reverse the removal procedures. Torque the shear-type screws until the heads shear.

HEADLIGHT SWITCH

Removal and Installation

1982-85

1. Refer to the "Combination Switch, Removal and Installation" procedures in this section, then, remove the steering wheel and the shell covers.
2. Disconnect the headlight/turn signal electrical connector.
3. Remove the headlight/turn signal-to-combination switch screws and the headlight/turn signal switch from the combination switch.
4. To install, reverse the removal procedures.

1986-88

1. Disconnect the negative battery terminal from the battery.
2. Remove the shell covers-to-steering column screws and the covers from the steering column.
3. Disconnect the headlight/turn signal switch electrical connector.
4. Remove the headlight/turn signal switch-to-combination switch screws and the headlight/turn signal switch from the steering column.
5. To install, reverse the removal procedures.

COMBINATION SWITCH

The combination switch consists of the headlight, turn signal and dimmer switches.

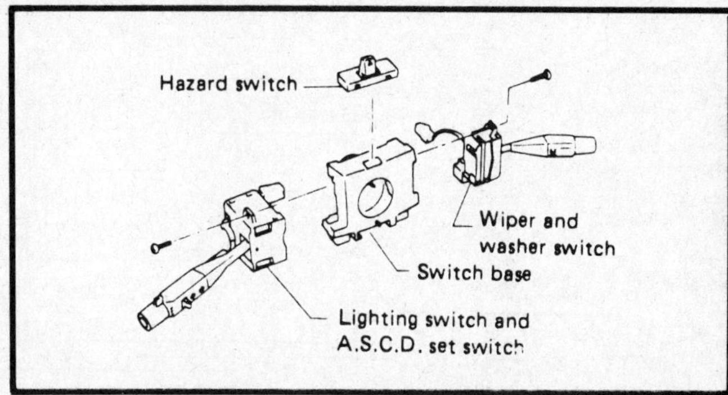

Exploded view of the combination switch – 1986-88

NOTE: On the 1986-88 models, the switches can be removed from the combination switch base without removing the base.

Removal and Installation

1. Disconnect the negative battery terminal from the battery.
2. Remove the horn pad and the steering wheel nut. Using the Puller tool No. ST27180001 or equivalent, press the steering wheel from the steering column.
3. Disconnect the wiring harness from the clip which retains it to the lower instrument panel.
4. Disconnect the electrical connectors from the combination switch.
5. Remove the steering column shell cover screws and the covers (upper and lower).
6. Loosen the combination switch-to-steering column screw and remove the switch assembly.
7. To install, align the hole in the steering column with the protrusion on the switch body and reverse the removal procedures.

WINDSHIELD/WIPER SWITCH

Removal and Installation

1982-85

1. Refer to the "Combination Switch, Removal and Installation" procedures in this section, then, remove the steering wheel and the shell covers.
2. Disconnect the windshield/wiper switch electrical connector.
3. Remove the windshield/wiper-to-combination switch screws and the windshield/wiper switch from the combination switch.
4. To install, reverse the removal procedures.

1986-88

1. Disconnect the negative battery terminal from the battery.
2. Remove the shell covers-to-steering column screws and the covers from the steering column.
3. Disconnect the windshield/wiper switch electrical connector.
4. Remove the windshield/wiper switch-to-combination switch screws and the windshield/wiper switch from the steering column.
5. To install, reverse the removal procedures.

WINDSHIELD/WIPER MOTOR

Removal and Installation

FRONT

1. Remove the wiper blades and arms as an assembly from the pivots. The arms are retained to the pivots by nuts; remove

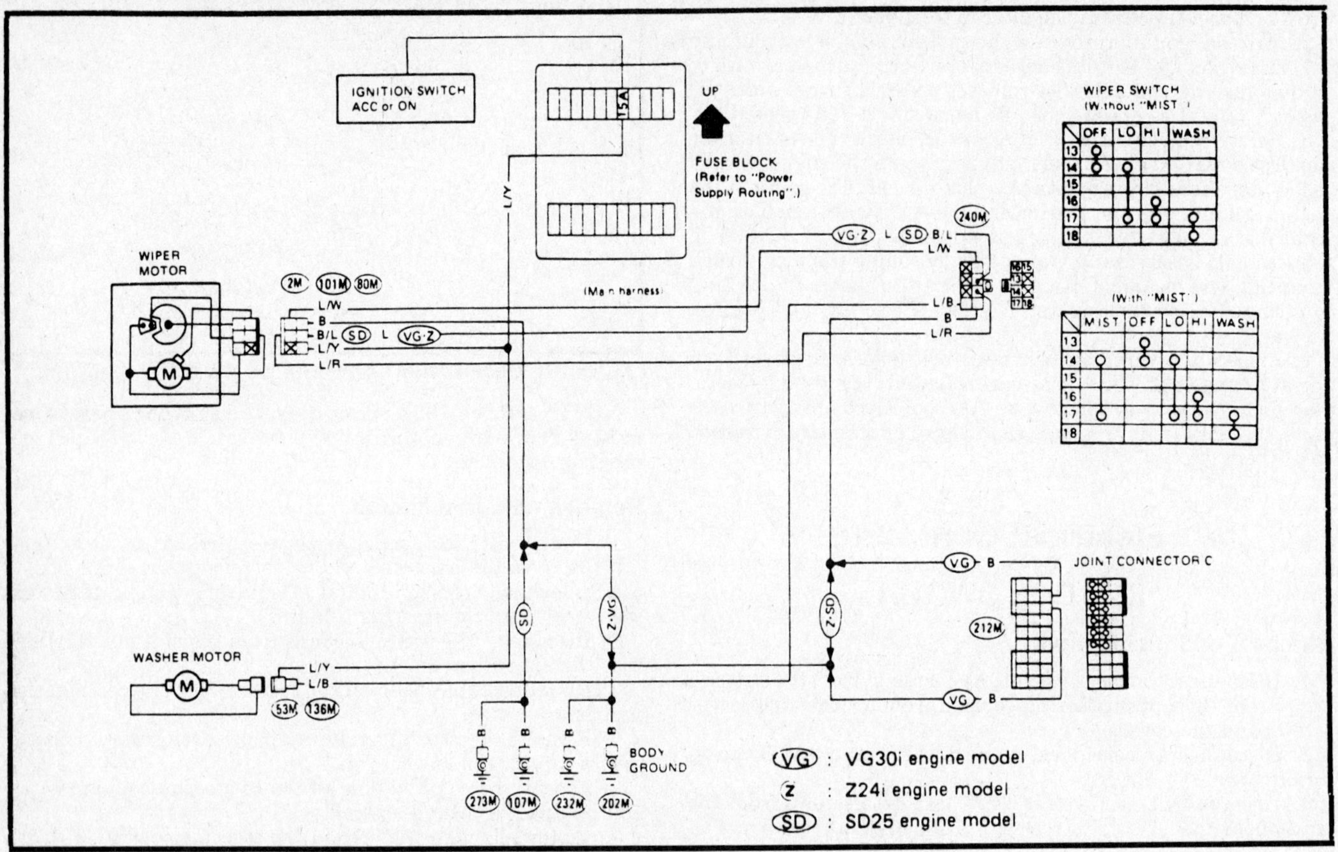

Wiring schematic of the front wiper/washer system—without intermittent wiper

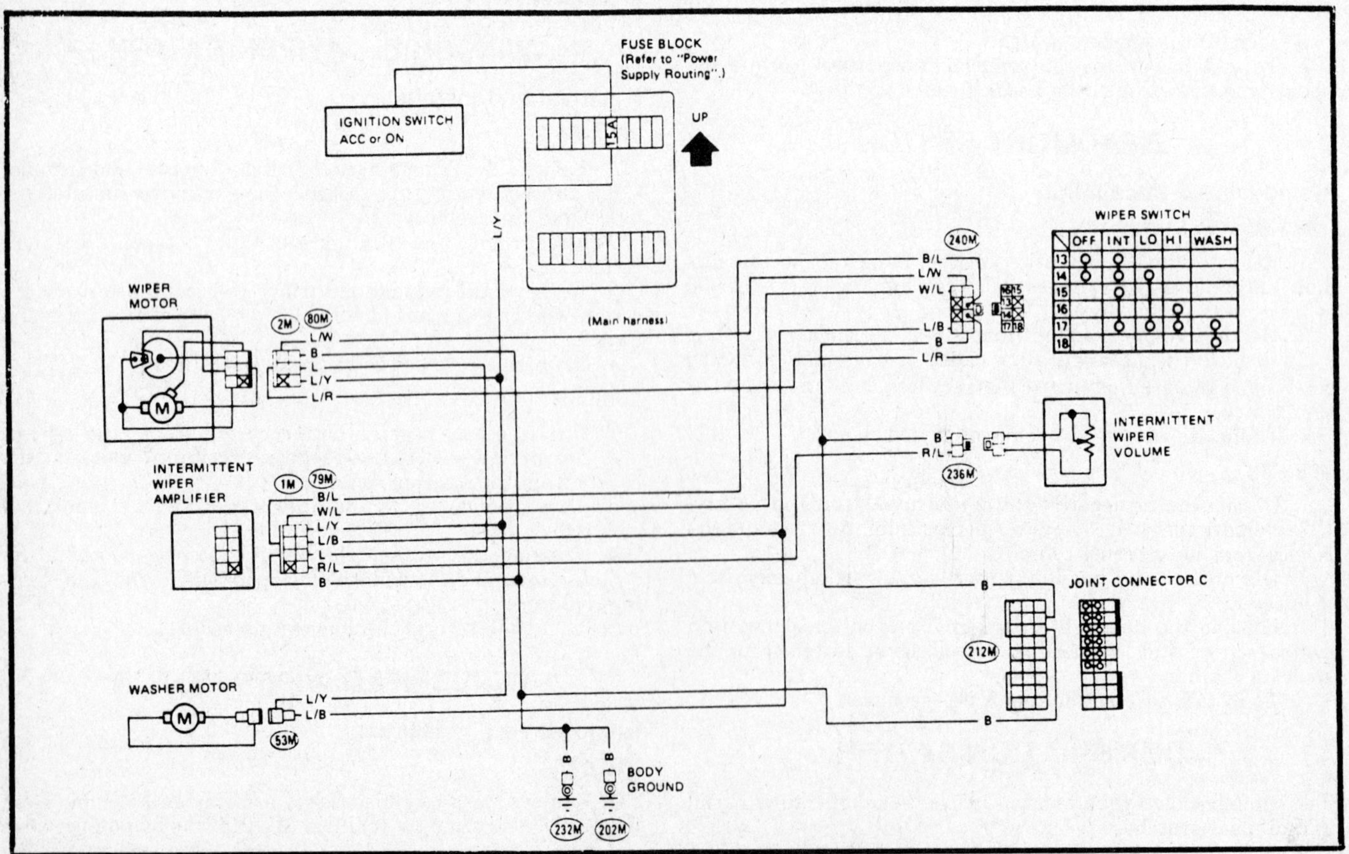

Wiring schematic of the front wiper/washer system—with intermittent wiper

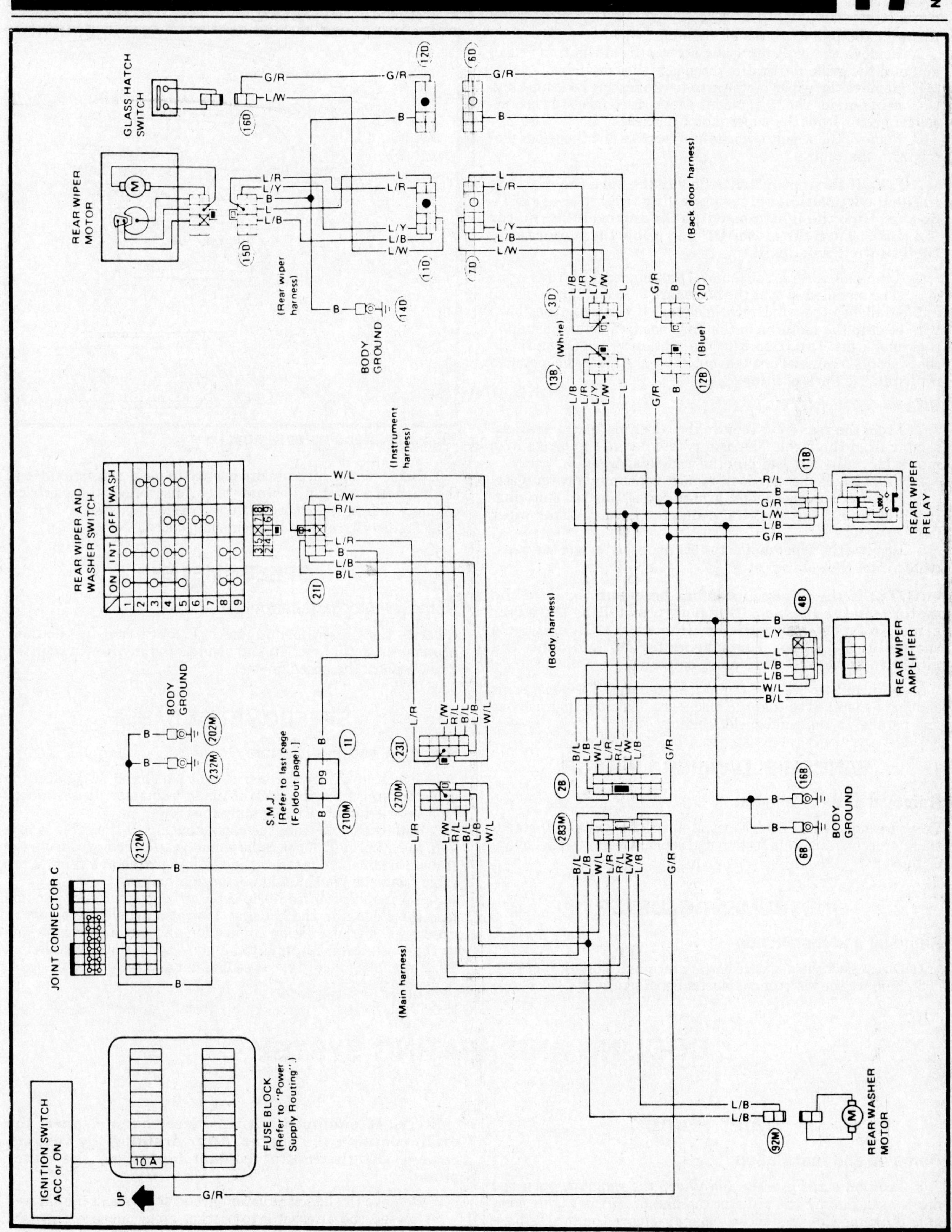

Wiring schematic of the rear wiper/washer system

the nuts and pull the arms straight off.

2. Remove the cowl top grille screws (from the front edge) and pull the grille forward to disengage the rear tabs.

3. Remove the wiper motor arm-to-connecting rod stop ring.

4. From under the instrument panel, disconnect the electrical connector from the wiper motor harness.

5. Remove the wiper motor-to-cowl screws and the wiper motor from the vehicle.

NOTE: If the motor has been run, be sure the motor is in the Park position before installing the wiper arms. To do this, turn the ignition switch On and cycle the motor 3–4 times. Turn the motor Off and allow the motor to return to the Park position.

6. To install, reverse the removal procedures. The wiper arms should be installed so that the blades are 0.98 in. (25mm) above and parallel to the windshield molding. If the motor has been run, be sure the motor is in the Park position before installing the wiper arms. To do this, turn the ignition switch On and cycle the motor 3–4 times. Turn the motor Off and allow the motor to return to the Park position.

REAR – VAN AND PATHFINDER

1. From the rear door, remove the wiper blade/arm as an assembly from the pivot. The arm is retained to the pivots by a nut; remove the nut and pull the arm straight off.

2. From inside the rear door, remove wiper motor cover plate.

3. Remove the wiper motor arm-to-connecting rod stop ring.

4. Disconnect the electrical connector from the rear wiper motor harness.

5. Remove the wiper motor-to-rear door screws and the wiper motor from the vehicle.

NOTE: If the wiper motor has been run, be sure the motor is in the Park position before installing the wiper arms. To do this, turn the ignition switch On and cycle the motor 3–4 times. Turn the motor Off and allow the motor to return to the Park position.

6. To install, reverse the removal procedures. The wiper arms should be installed so that the blades are 0.98 in. (25mm) above and parallel to the windshield molding.

WINDSHIELD/WIPER LINKAGE

Removal and Installation

Refer to the "Windshield/Wiper Motor, Removal and Installation" procedures in this section and replace the windshield/wiper linkage.

INSTRUMENT CLUSTER

Removal and Installation

1. Disconnect the negative battery terminal from the battery.

2. Remove the instrument cluster bezel screws and the bezel.

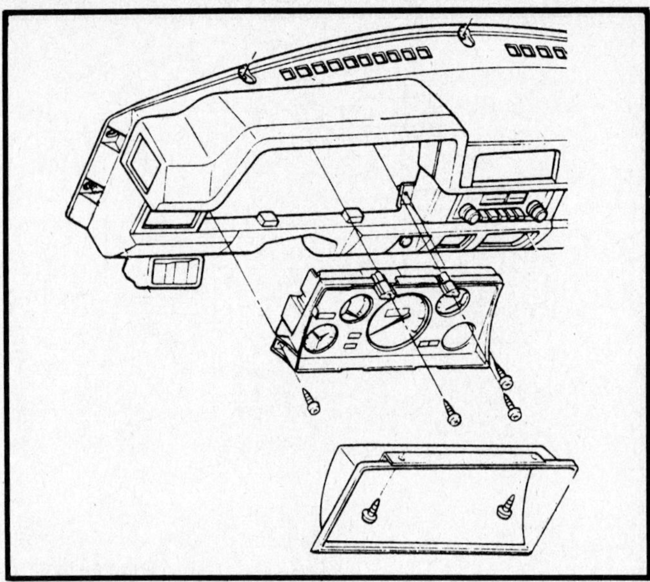

1984 and later cluster removal

3. Remove the instrument cluster-to-dash screws and pull the cluster assembly forward, then, disconnect the electrical connectors from the rear of the instrument cluster.

4. To install, reverse the removal procedures.

SPEEDOMETER

Removal and Installation

Refer to the "Instrument Cluster, Removal and Installation" procedures in this section and remove the instrument cluster, then, replace the speedometer.

SPEEDOMETER CABLE

Removal and Installation

1. Reach up under the instrument panel and disconnect the cable housing from the back of the speedometer. It is attached by a knurled knob which simply unscrews.

2. Pull the cable from the cable housing. If the cable is broken, the other half of the cable will have to be removed from the transmission end. Unscrew the retaining knob and remove the cable from the transmission extension housing.

3. To install, lubricate the cable with graphite powder and feed the cable into the housing. It is also usually necessary to unscrew the transmission connection and install the cable end to the gear, then, reconnect the housing to the transmission. Slip the cable end into the speedometer and reconnect the cable housing.

COOLING AND HEATING SYSTEM

Water Pump

Removal and Installation

1. Position a clean drain pan under the radiator, open the drain cock, remove the radiator cap and drain the engine coolant. If equipped with a diesel engine, remove the bypass hose from the pump.

NOTE: If equipped with a diesel engine, open the drain cocks on the engine. After draining the coolant, remove the thermostat coolant hose from the water pump.

2. Remove the upper radiator shroud screws and the shroud.

3. Loosen the alternator-to-bracket bolts, move the inward and remove the drive belt.

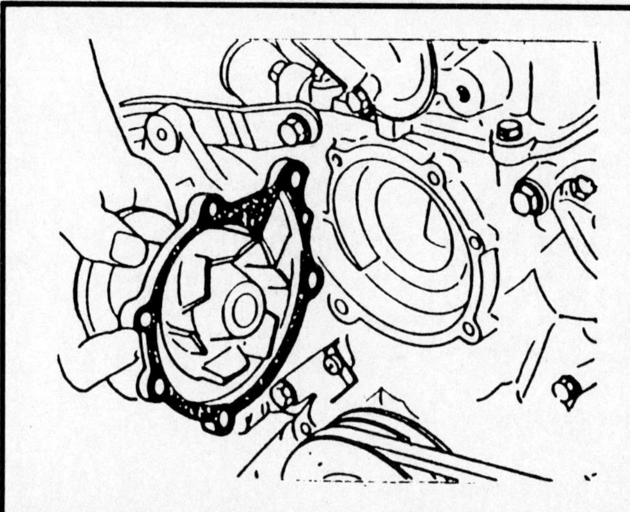

Removing the water pump

NOTE: If equipped with power steering, remove the drive belt.

4. Remove the fan-to-water pump bolts and the fan.
5. Remove the water pump-to-engine bolts and the pump with the fan pulley, coupling and gasket.
6. Using a putty knife, clean the gasket mounting surfaces.
7. To install, use a new gasket, sealant (if necessary) and reverse the removal procedures. Torque the water pump-to-engine bolts to 3–7 ft. lbs. (6mm bolts, Z-series), 7–12 ft. lbs. (8mm bolts, Z-series), 12–15 ft. lbs. (VG30i), 7–9 ft. lbs. (8mm bolts, diesel) or 14–18 ft. lbs. (10mm bolts, diesel). Adjust the drive belt tension. Refill the cooling system. Run the engine until normal operating temperatures are reached, then, inspect for leaks.

Thermostat

The factory-installed thermostat opening temperature is 180°F (USA) or 190°F (Canada). On the Z-series engines, the thermostat is located on the right, front-side of the intake manifold; on all other engines, the thermostat is located above the water pump.

Removal and Installation

1. Drain the engine coolant to a level below the thermostat housing.
2. Disconnect the coolant hose from the thermostat water outlet.
3. Remove the water outlet-to-thermostat housing bolts, gasket and thermostat.

NOTE:The thermostat spring must face the inside of the engine.

4. Using a putty knife, clean the gasket mounting surfaces.

NOTE: If the thermostat, on the Z-series engines, is equipped with an air bleed or jiggle valve, be sure to position it in the upward direction.

5. To install, use a new gasket, sealant (if necessary) and reverse the removal procedures. Torque the water outlet-to-thermostat housing bolts to 12–15 ft. lbs. (Z-series and VG30i engines) or 7–9 ft. lbs. (diesel engines).

Heater Core

Removal and Installation

WITH A/C

1. Disconnect the negative battery terminal from the battery.
2. Drain the cooling system to a level below the heater core.
3. Disconnect the heater hose from the engine.
4. Remove the console box and instrument assembly.

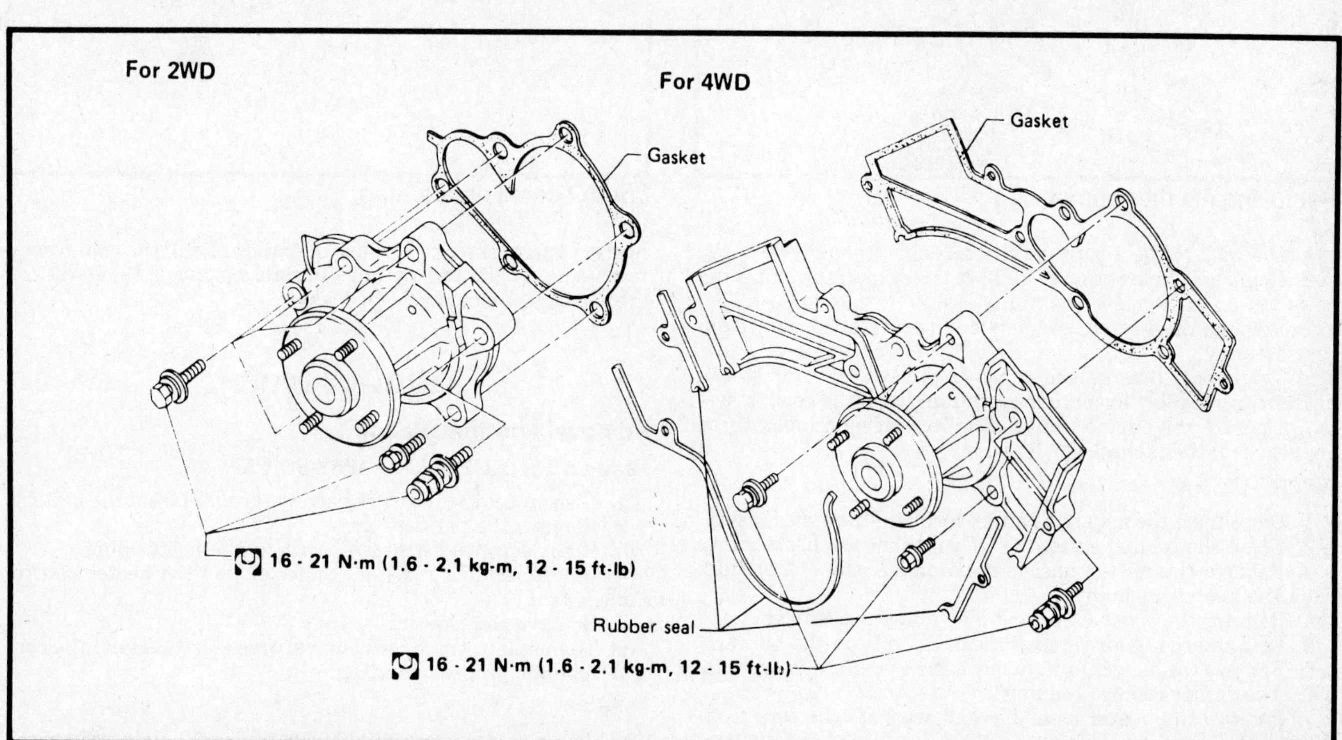

Exploded view of the water pump—VG30i (V6) engine

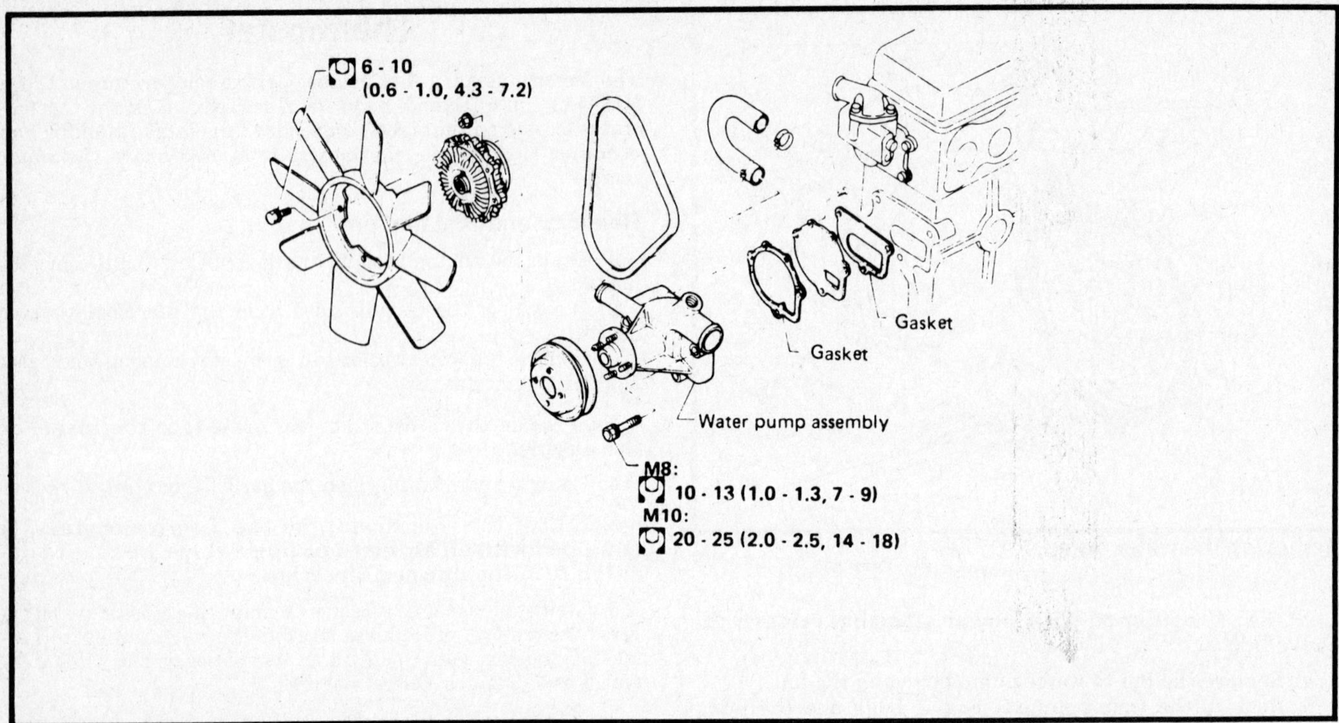

Exploded view of the water pump—diesel engine

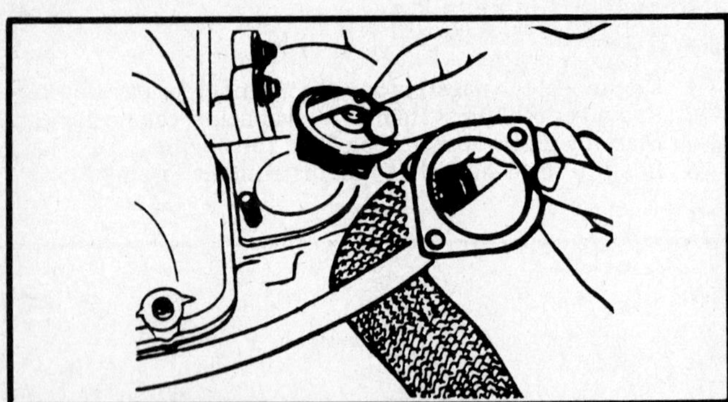

Removing the thermostat

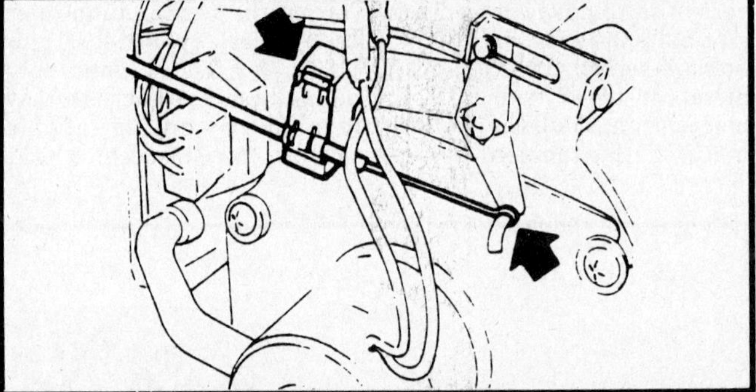

Control cable positioning

5. Disconnect the air intake control cable from the blower.
6. Remove the blower unit. Remove the evaporator unit nuts/bolts but do not remove the unit.
7. Remove the heater assembly and separate the core from the assembly.
8. To install, reverse the removal procedures. Adjust the heater control cable for proper operation. Refill the cooling system. Operate the engine until normal operating temperatures are reached, then, check for leaks.

WITHOUT A/C

1. Disconnect the negative battery terminal from the battery.
2. Drain the cooling system to a level below the heater core.
3. Remove the heater duct and disconnect the heater hose from the heater assembly.
4. Remove the console box and instrument assembly.
5. Disconnect the air intake control cable from the blower.
6. Remove the blower unit. Remove the evaporator unit nuts/bolts but do not remove the unit.
7. Remove the heater assembly and separate the core from the assembly.
8. To install, reverse the removal procedures. Adjust the heater control cable for proper operation. Refill the cooling system. Operate the engine until normal operating temperatures are reached, then, check for leaks.

Blower Motor

Removal and Installation

1982-85 PICKUPS AND 1987-88 VAN

1. Disconnect the negative battery terminal from the battery.
2. Remove the package tray.
3. If not equipped with A/C, remove the heater duct.
4. Disconnect the resistor connector and the heater control cable.
5. Remove the blower.
6. To install, reverse the removal procedures. Adjust the control cable for proper operation.

1986-88

The blower motor is accessible from under the right-side of the instrument panel.

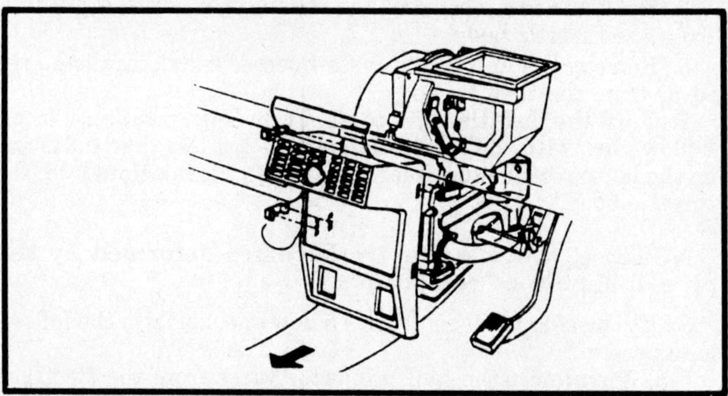
Removing the heater assembly front cover

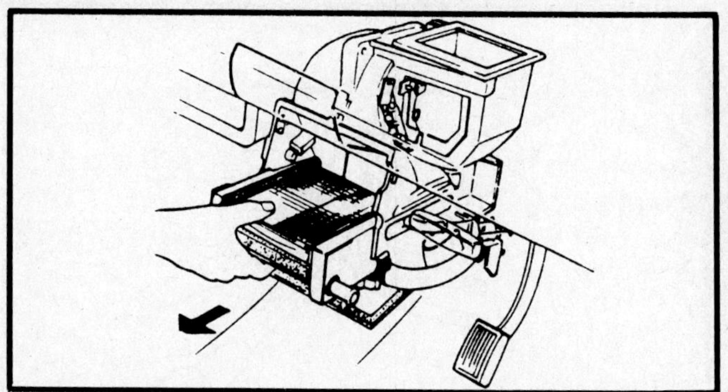
Removing the heater core

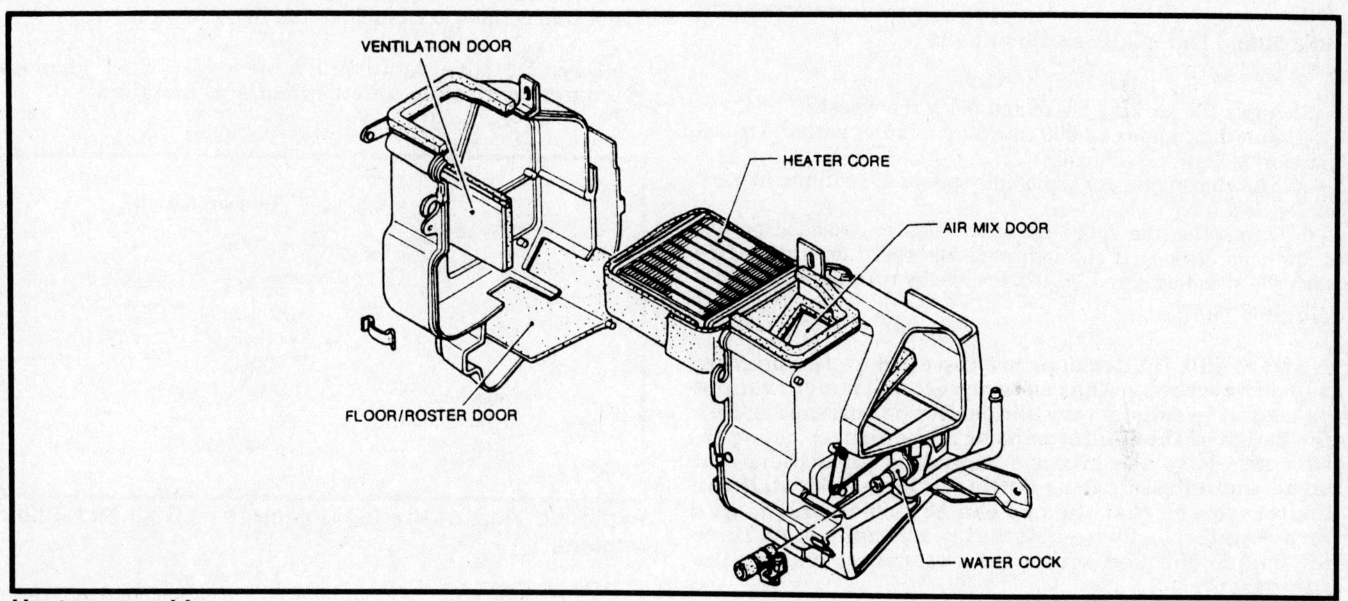

Heater assembly

1. Disconnect the electrical connector from the blower motor.
2. Remove the blower motor-to-heater unit screws and the blower motor from the unit.
3. To install, reverse the removal procedures.

FUEL SYSTEM

For calibration procedures, please refer to "Carburetors" in the Unit Repair section.

Carburetor

Removal and Installation

1. Remove the air cleaner.
2. Disconnect and label the fuel and vacuum lines from the carburetor.
3. Remove the throttle linkage.
4. Remove the carburetor-to-intake manifold nuts.
5. Remove the carburetor and the gasket from the manifold.

NOTE: The 1985 pickups are equipped with a mixture heater, located under the carburetor, be sure to replace it's gasket.

6. Remove and discard the gasket used between the carburetor and the manifold.
7. Using a putty knife, clean the gasket mounting surfaces.
8. To install, use new gaskets and reverse the removal procedures. Torque the carburetor-to-intake manifold nuts to 9–13 ft. lbs.

Adjustment

Refer to the Carburetor section of Unit Repair for adjustment and specifications.

IDLE SPEED AND AIR ADJUSTMENT

1. Connect a tachometer according to the manufacturer's instructions.
2. Turn all the accessories and lights Off. If equipped with power steering, make sure the wheels are in the straight ahead position.

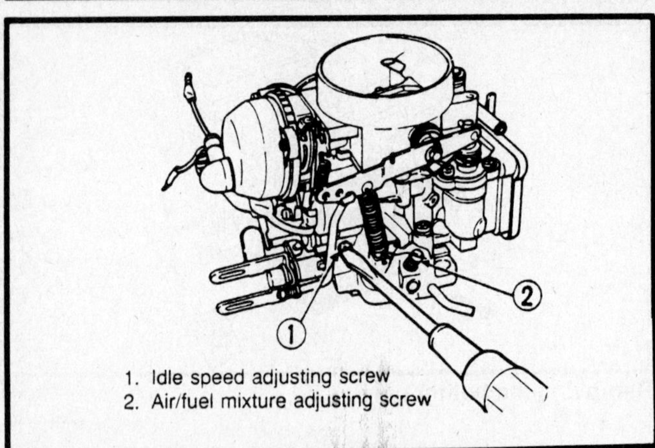

Idle speed and mixture adjustments

3. Apply the parking brake and block the wheels.
4. Run the engine at 2,000 rpm for 2 minutes with the transmission in Park or Neutral.
5. Run the engine at normal idle speed for 1 minute in Park or Neutral.
6. Check the idle speed using the figures provided on the underhood sticker. If the indicated idle speed does not agree with the specified speed, adjust the idle by turning the throttle adjusting screw.

NOTE: Idle limiter caps are installed on the mixture adjusting screws so that an incorrect adjustment cannot be made. If a satisfactory idle cannot be obtained within the range of the limiter caps or if the limiter caps prevent access to the mixture screws, remove them and make the adjustment as outlined above. Reinstall the limiter caps so that the cap can be turned only 1⁄8 of a turn counterclockwise before it reaches the stop. Have the engine checked with a CO meter after making the adjustment.

FUEL INJECTION

Relieve Pressure

1. From the fuse box, remove the fuel pump fuse.
2. Start the engine and allow it to run.
3. After the engine stalls, crank it 2-3 times to make sure the pressure is released.
4. Turn the ignition switch Off and replace the fuse.

INJECTORS

Removal and Installation

1. Refer to "Relieve Pressure" in this section and relieve the fuel pressure.
2. Drain about 1⅛ qt. (1L) of coolant from the engine.
3. From the throttle body, remove or disconnect the following items:
   a. Air cleaner.
   b. Electrical connectors from the throttle sensor, idle switch, fuel injectors, air flow meter and the Automatic Speed Control Device (ASCD), if equipped.
   c. Accelerator cable.
   d. Fuel and coolant hoses.
4. Remove the throttle body-to-intake manifold nuts and the throttle body.
5. Remove the rubber seal and the injector harness grommet from the throttle body.
6. Remove the injector cover-to-injector body screws and the cover from the throttle body.
7. Turn the throttle valve to the Fully Open position. Place a hollow pipe, with the inside diameter of not less than 0.217 in., on the bottom of the fuel injectors and tap the injectors from the throttle body.

NOTE: If the injector tip becomes deformed by the pipe, it should be replaced.

8. If replacing an injector with a new one, perform the following operation:
   a. Disconnect the faulty injector wires from the electrical connector, then, cut the injector wires from the metal terminals and pull the injector wiring from the harness tube.
   b. Using a new injector(s), install it into the harness tube and connect new terminals to the injector wires.

NOTE: Be sure to install a new electrical harness grommet every time a new injector is installed.

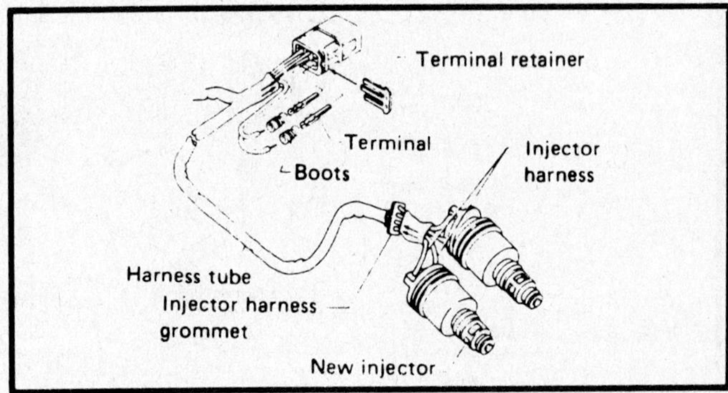

Exploded view of the fuel injectors—VG30i and Z42i engines

   c. Install the terminals into the electrical harness connector.
9. To install, use new O-rings (on the fuel injectors) and push the injectors into the throttle body until the O-rings are fully seated.

NOTE: Invert the throttle body to make sure the injector tips are properly seated.

10. Using silicone sealant, apply it to the injector harness grommet.

NOTE: An airtight seal is essential to ensure a stable and proper idling condition.

11. Using locking sealant, coat the injector cover screw threads, install the injector cover-to-throttle body screws. Torque the injector cover screws in a criss-cross pattern to 1.5–2.5 ft. lbs.
12. Using silicone sealant, coat the top of the throttle body and install the air cleaner rubber seal.

NOTE: Do not install the air cleaner until the air cleaner seal (silicone sealant) has hardened.

13. Install the throttle body and torque the throttle body-to-intake manifold nuts to 9–13 ft. lbs.
14. To complete the installation, reverse the removal procedures. Refill the cooling system. Start the engine, then, check for leaks and proper idling conditions. Stop the engine and check for dripping fuel on the throttle valve.

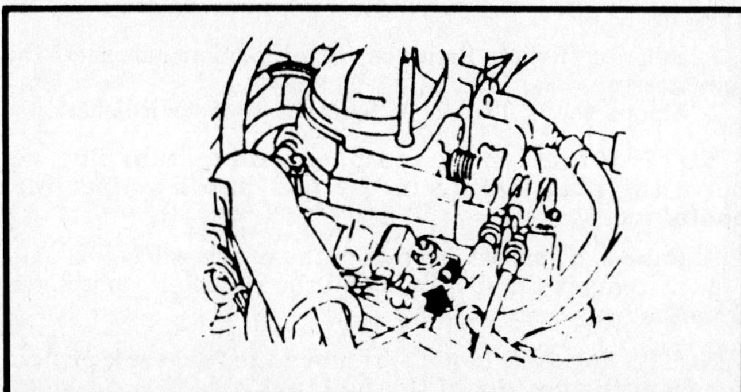

Location of the idle speed screw—VG30i engine—Z24i engine is similar

Adjustment

IDLE SPEED

1. Visually inspect the air cleaner for clogging, the hoses/ducts for leaks, the EGR valve operation, the electrical connectors, the gaskets, the throttle valve and throttle sensor operation and the AIV hose.
2. Set the parking brake and place the gear selector in "Neutral". Start the engine and allow it to reach normal operating temperatures.
3. Operate the engine, under no-load, for 2 minutes at about 2000 rpm.
4. Race the engine 2-3 times (under no-load) and operate it at idle speed for 1 minute.
5. If equipped with an A/T, place the gear selector in "Drive". Check the idle speed, it should be 750–850 rpm (VG30i, M/T), 850–950 rpm (Z24i, M/T), 650–750 rpm (VG30i, A/T) or 600–700 rpm (Z24i, A/T). If necessary, adjust the idle speed screw.
6. Using a timing light, check and/or adjust the ignition timing; it should be 10–14° BTDC (VG30i) or 3–7° BTDC. (except VG30i)

NOTE: If the ignition timing is not correct, turn the distributor to the correct value, then, reperform the idle speed adjustment until both values are correct.

Fuel Pump

MECHANICAL—1982-83

The fuel pump is a mechanically-operated, diaphragm-type driven by the fuel pump eccentric cam on the front of the camshaft. Design of the fuel pump permits disassembly, cleaning, and repair or replacement of defective parts.

Testing

1. Disconnect the line between the carburetor and the pump at the carburetor.
2. Connect a fuel pump pressure gauge into the line.
3. Start the engine. The pressure should be between 3.0–3.9 psi. There is usually enough gas in the float bowl to perform this test.
4. If the pressure is OK, perform a capacity test. Remove the gauge from the line. Use a graduated container to catch the gas from the fuel line. Fill the carburetor float bowl with gas. Run the engine for one minute at about 1,000 rpm. The pump should deliver 1,000cc in one minute or less.

Removal and Installation

1. Disconnect the two fuel lines from the fuel pump. Be sure to keep the line leading from the fuel tank up high to prevent the excessive loss of fuel.

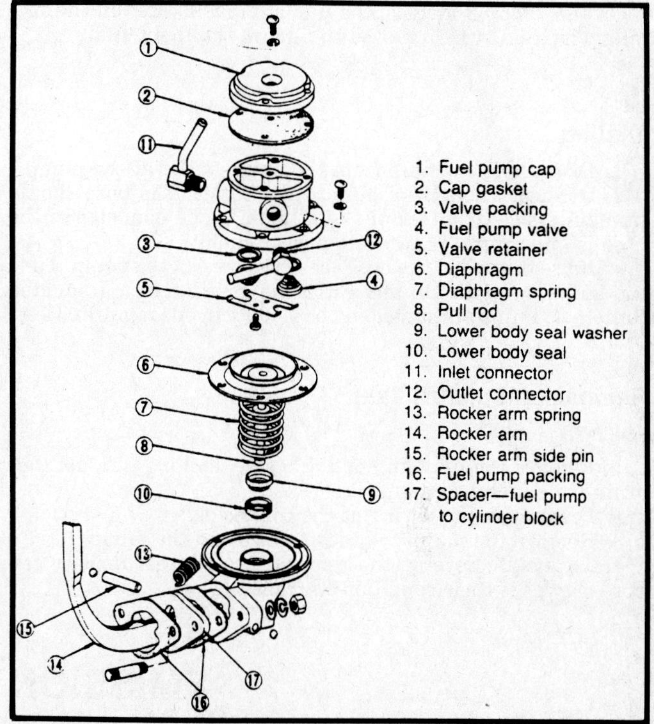

The mechanical fuel pump

2. Remove the fuel pump-to-engine nuts and the fuel pump assembly from the side of the engine.
3. Using a putty knife, clean the gasket mounting surfaces.
4. To install, use a new gasket, sealant and reverse the removal procedures.

ELECTRIC

On the 1982-85 models, the fuel pump is mounted to a bracket located on the right-side frame rail next to the fuel tank. There is a filter mounted in the body of the pump, which does not normally require service. The pump can be disassembled, if necessary, but all electronic parts within the body (one transistor, two diodes and three resistors) must be replaced as an assembly.

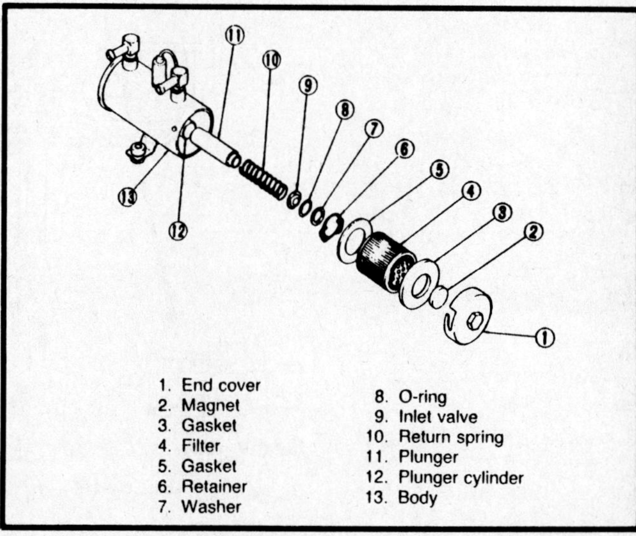

Exploded view of the electric fuel pump—1982-85

On the 1986-88 models, the fuel pump is located in the fuel tank which must be removed to remove the fuel pump.

Testing

1. Disconnect the hose from the pump outlet at the pump.
2. Connect a length of hose to the outlet. The hose should have an inside diameter of ¼ in. (6mm). The diameter of the hose is important for accurate measurements.
3. Raise the end of the hose above the level of the pump. Turn the ignition switch On and catch the gasoline in a graduated container. Pump output should be 1,400cc in one minute or less.

Removal and Installation

1982-85

1. Remove the inlet and outlet hoses, catching the fuel that drains in a metal container.
2. Disconnect the wiring at the connector.
3. Remove the pump-to-bracket bolts and the pump.
4. To install, reverse the removal procedures. Replace the hose clamps if their condition warrants.

1986-88

1. Refer to "Relieve Pressure" in this section and relieve the fuel pressure.
2. Siphon the fuel from the fuel tank to make it lighter.

NOTE: If fuel tank is equipped with a drain plug, remove the plug and drain the fuel into a proper fuel container.

3. Raise and support the rear of the vehicle safely.
4. Disconnect the fuel lines and the electrical connector(s) from the fuel pump assembly.

NOTE: For 4WD models, remove the fuel tank protector from the bottom of the fuel tank.

5. Remove the fuel tank filler tube-to-vehicle bolts (Pickups) or nuts (Van and Wagon) and the outer plate.
6. Remove the fuel tank-to-chassis connectors and lower the tank from the vehicle.
7. Remove the fuel pump assembly-to-tank screws and lift the assembly from the tank.
8. To install, use a new fuel pump assembly-to-tank O-ring and reverse the removal procedures. Torque the fuel pump assembly-to-tank screws to 18–24 inch lbs. and the fuel tank protectors-to-chassis bolts to 20–26 ft. lbs. Refill the fuel tank.

EMISSION CONTROLS

Crankcase Emission Control Systems

POSITIVE CRANKCASE VENTILATION (PCV) VALVE

A closed, positive crankcase ventilation system is employed on all vehicles. The system cycles crankcase fumes back into the intake manifold for burning with an fuel/air mixture. The oil filler cap is sealed; air is drawn from the air filter through a tube to the valve cover.

Removal and Installation

After every 12,000 miles or every year, perform the following services:

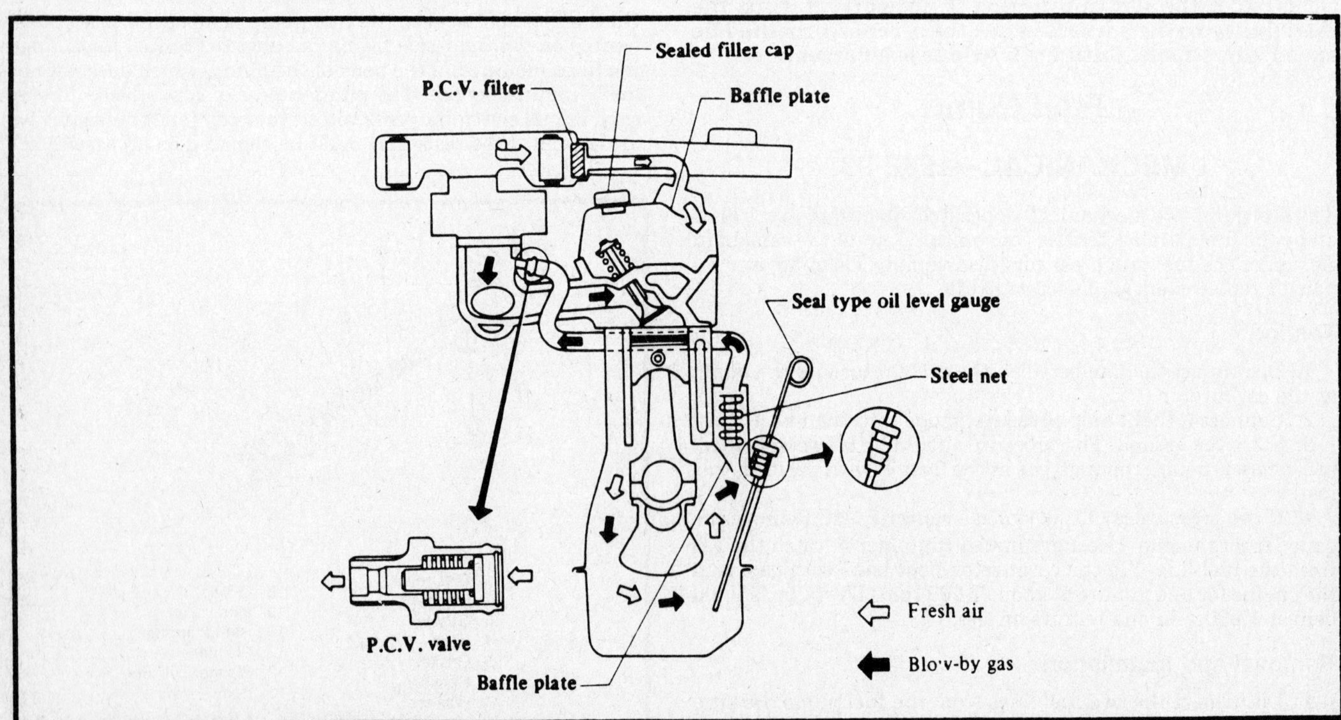

View of the crankcase emission control system

1. Check the condition of the hoses and connectors to ensure there is no leakage.
2. Disconnect the hoses and blow compressed air through them. When extreme blockage is encountered, replace the hose(s).
3. Check the PVC valve as follows:
a. Start the engine and allow it to idle.
b. Disconnect the ventilation hose from the PCV valve, allowing fresh air to be drawn into the manifold through the valve.

NOTE: The flow of air should produce an audible "hiss" and it should be possible to feel a strong vacuum when placing a finger over the valve inlet.

c. If the valve is clogged, replace it as it is not servicable. Replace the valve every 2 years.

Evaporative Emission Control System

The evaporative emission control system is used to reduce the amount of hydrocarbons which are emitted into the atmosphere. The reduction of hydrocarbons are accomplished through the equipment:
a. Sealed gas cap.
b. Fuel check valve.
c. Vapor vent line.
d. Carbon canister.
e. Vacuum signaling line.
f. Canister purge line.

CARBON CANISTER

The carbon canister stores the fuel vapor from the tank when the engine is not running. When the engine starts, vacuum carried by a vacuum signal line opens a purge valve on the top of the canister. Air is drawn through a filter on the bottom of the canister, through the charcoal, a nozzle in the purge valve and into the intake manifold.

Checking the Purge Valve

1. Disconnect the rubber hose which runs between the manifold and canister at the T-connector.
2. Blow into the open end of the hose and listen for leaks.
3. If there are leaks, remove the top cover of the purge valve and check for a dislocated or cracked diaphragm; replace the parts, as necessary.
4. At this time, the filter on the bottom of the canister should be inspected. It the filter is clogged, replace it. Inspection and replacement can be accomplished without removing the canister.

Removal and Installation

1. Disconnect and label the hoses from the top of the canister.
2. Loosen the canister from the bracket, then, remove the canister.
3. From the bottom of the canister, remove the filter.
4. To install, reverse the removal procedures.

FUEL CHECK VALVE

Removal and Installation

1. Disconnect the fuel vapor lines from the fuel check valve.
2. Remove the fuel check valve from its bracket.
3. To check the fuel check valve, perform the following inspection:
a. Blow through the fuel tank side of the fuel check valve; air should move through it with considerable resistance.
b. Blow through the carbon canister side of the fuel check valve; air should move smoothly through it.
4. To install, reverse the removal procedures.

Exhaust Emission Control System

AIR INDUCTION SYSTEM

The air induction system uses a reed valve mounted in the air cleaner to supply fresh air to the exhaust manifold to reduce the formation of Carbon Monoxide (CO) and Hydrocarbons (HC) in the exhaust gases. Some (1982-85) models use a twin valve, while other models use a single valve.

On the 1986-88 models, the reed valve is mounted on a separate air cleaner box. If the box is equipped with a vacuum cut solenoid, a 9-port reed valve is used.

Removal and Installation

1. Remove the air cleaner lid.

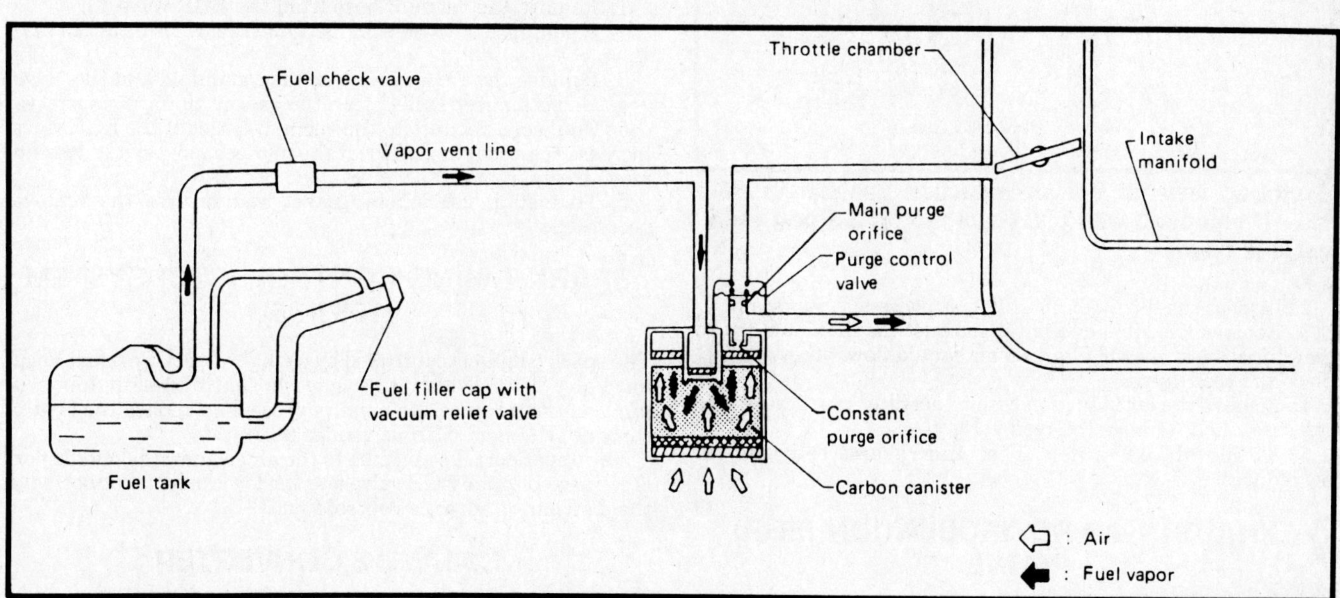

View of the evaporative emission control system

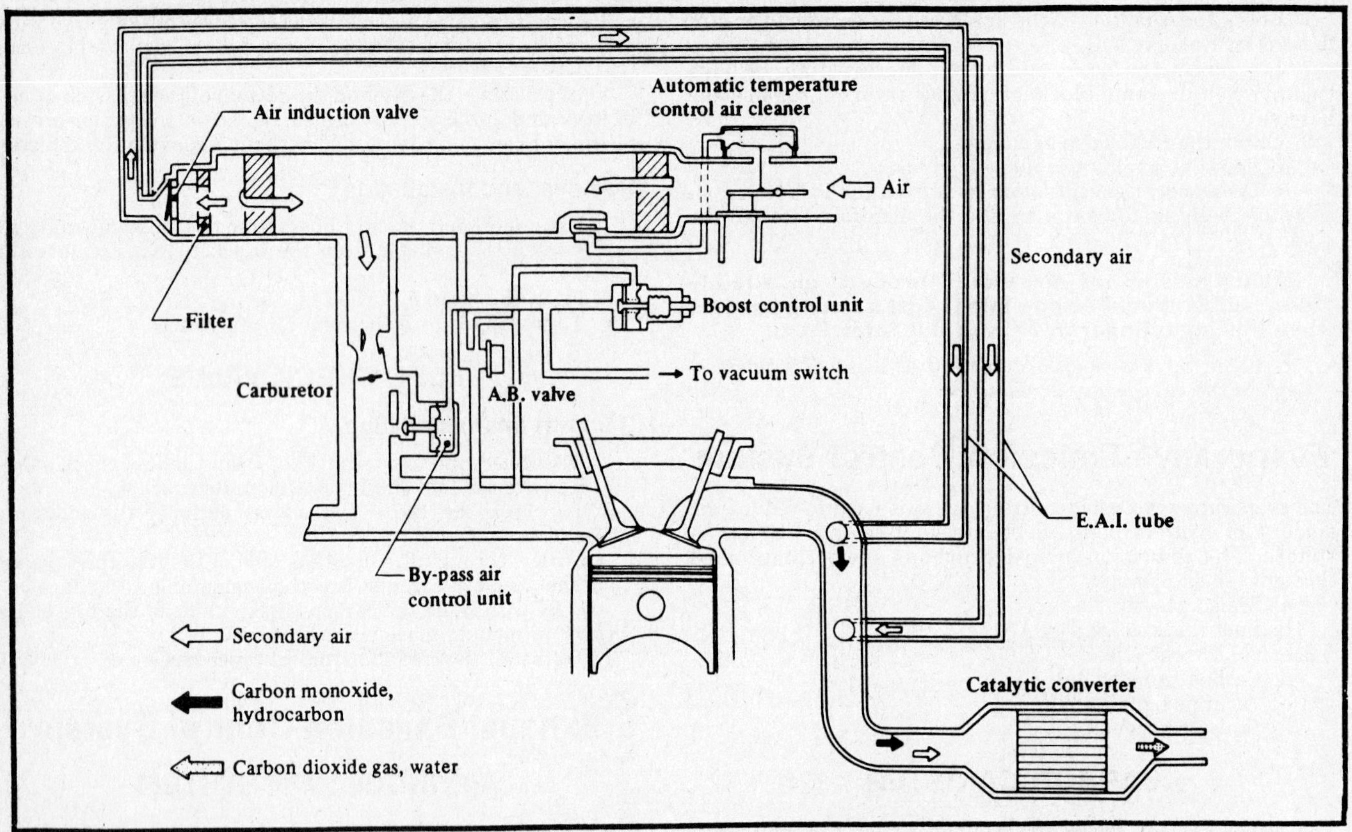

View of the air induction system (1982-85) – some models use twin chamber reed valves, while others use a single chamber

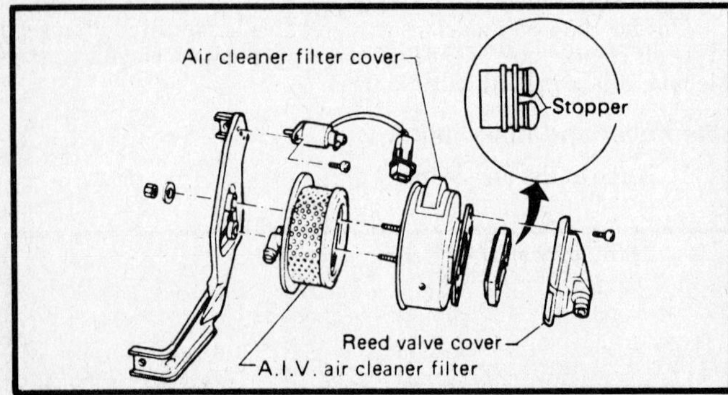

Exploded view of the air induction canister (1986-88) – if equipped with a vacuum motor, a 9-port reed valve is used

2. Inspect the air induction filter, if necessary, replace it.
3. Remove the air induction-to-exhaust manifold and try to blow air toward the air filter; no air should flow, otherwise, replace the reed valve.
4. Remove the air induction case-to-air filter case screws and the case, then, remove the reed valve.
5. To install, use a new filter and reverse the removal procedures.

EXHAUST GAS RECIRCULATION (EGR) VALVE

The EGR valve is installed in the intake manifold and is used to reduce Nitrous Oxides (NOx) in the exhaust gases. This is done by recirculating some exhaust gases into the engine to reduce the combustion temperature. The operation of the EGR is tied directly to the engine by a Venturi Vacuum Transducer (VVT) and a 3-port Thermal Vacuum Valve (TVV).

Removal and Installation

1. Remove the vacuum hose from the EGR valve.
2. If equipped with an exhaust tube, remove it from the EGR valve.
3. Remove the EGR valve-to-intake manifold and the valve.
4. Using a putty knife, clean the gasket mounting surfaces.
5. Connect a vacuum to the vacuum outlet of the EGR valve, increase the vacuum and see if the plunger moves; if it does not move freely, replace the valve.
6. To install, use a new gasket and reverse the removal procedures.

SPARK TIMING CONTROL (STC) SYSTEM (1982-85)

The spark timing is controlled by a single 3-port Thermal Vacuum Valve (TVV) which is designed to control distributor vacuum vacuum advance. Its main purpose is to reduce the Hydrocarbons (HC) and Nitrous Oxides (NOx).

The upper port if connected to the air cleaner, the middle port is connected to the EGR valve and the lower port is connected to the distributor advance control line.

CATAYLIC CONVERTER

All gasoline operated vehicles use a catalytic converter, which is

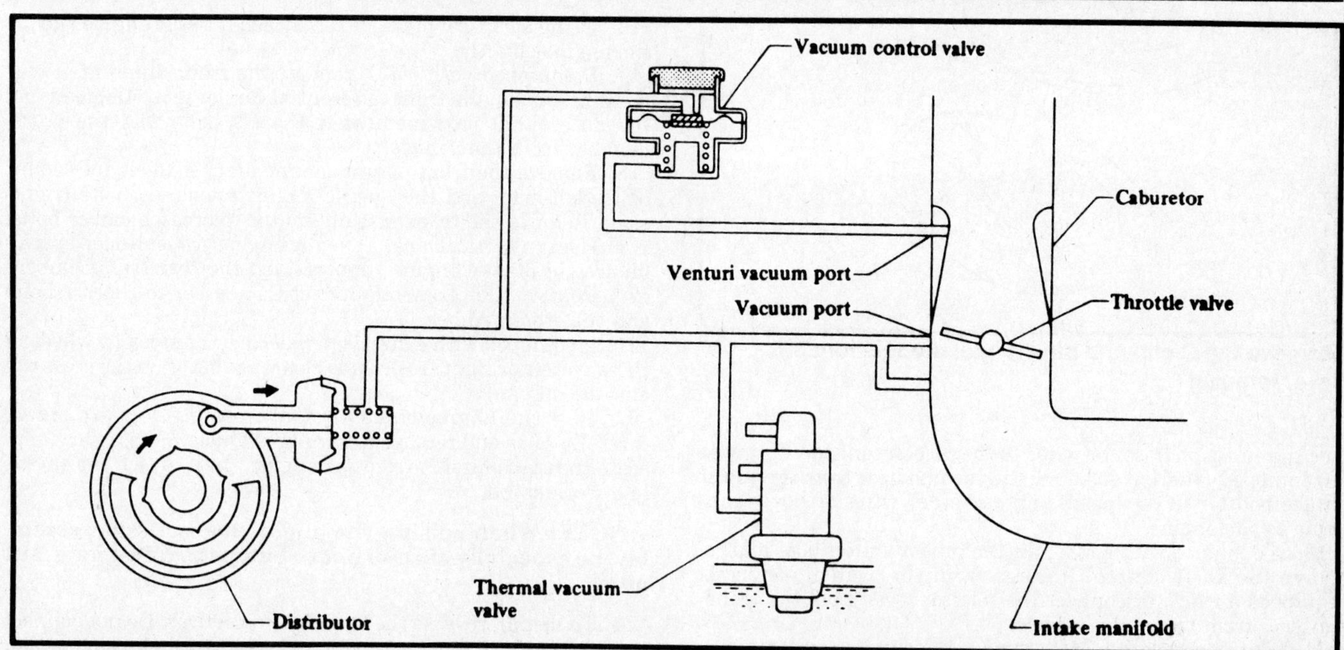

View of the Spark Timing Control

a muffler-shaped device installed in the exhaust system. The converter is filled with a monolithic substrate coated with small amounts of platinum and palladium. Through catalytic action, a chemical change converts Carbon Monoxide (CO), Hydrocarbons (HC) and Nitrous Oxides (NOx) into Carbon Dioxide (CO_2), Nitrogen gas (N_2) and water (H_2O).

Removal and Installation

1. Raise and support the vehicle safely.

NOTE: Be sure the exhaust system is cold before attempting to remove the catalytic converter.

2. If equipped, remove the catalytic converter shield.
3. Support the catalytic converter, then, remove the converter-to-front pipe bolts and the converter-to-rear pipe bolts. Remove the converter from the vehicle.
4. Using a putty knife, clean the gasket mounting surfaces.
5. To install, use new gaskets and reverse the removal procedures. Torque the contverter-to-exhaust pipes nuts/bolts to 23–31 ft. lbs.

ENGINE MECHANICAL

For overhaul information, please refer to "Engine Rebuilding" in the Unit Repair Section.

Engine

Removal and Installation

It is much easier to remove the engine and the transmission together as an assembly than to remove only the engine from the engine compartment. After the engine and transmission are removed from the vehicle, the two can be separated.

PICKUPS

1. Disconnect the negative battery terminal from the battery.

NOTE: On some vehicles, it may be necessary to remove the battery.

2. Using a scribing tool, mark the location of the hood hinges on the body (in order to facilitate installation) and remove the hood.

NOTE: If equipped with fuel injection, remove the fuel pump fuse from the fuse panel, operate the engine until it stalls, crank the engine to make sure it will not start.

3. Remove the air cleaner. Label and disconnect the electrical wiring and hoses which may be in the way. Using a shop rag, wrap it around the fuel line and disconnect it. If equipped, remove the splash pan from under the engine.

NOTE: Be sure to place a clean rag in the carburetor/throttle body to prevent dirt from entering the engine.

4. To remove the radiator, perform the following procedures:
   a. Drain the engine coolant into a clean container.
   b. Remove the upper and lower radiator hoses.
   c. If equipped with an A/T, disconnect and plug the transmission oil cooler lines from the radiator.
   d. Remove the radiator shroud and the radiator.
5. If equipped with A/C, loosen the idler pulley nut and the adjusting bolt, then, remove the compressor and move it aside; DO NOT disconnect the pressure hoses.
6. If equipped with P/S, remove the drive belt and the power steering pump, then, move it aside; DO NOT disconnect the pressure hoses. If equipped with a diesel engine, remove the power steering reservoir.
7. Disconnect the engine ground cable from the cylinder head. Disconnect the parking brake cable from the brake lever.
8. Disconnect the electrical leads from the starter, alternator, distributor, the high-tension ignition coil cable, the oil pressure and temperature sending units.
9. Disconnect the heater hose from the engine-side, accelerator cable from the carburetor/throttle body. Disconnect and la-

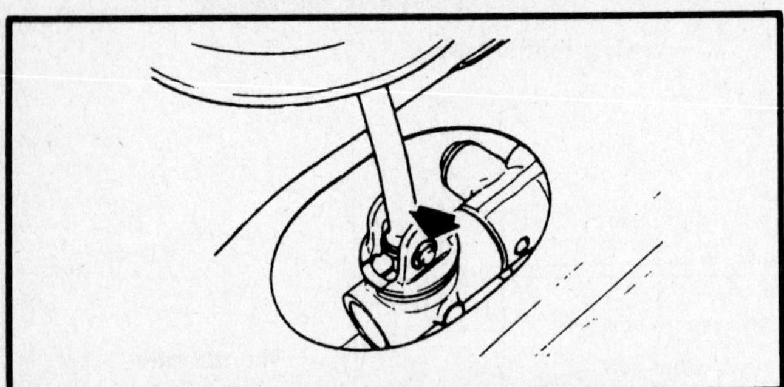

Remove the C-clip and pin on later models for shift lever removal

bel the emission hoses or wires to the carbon canister, air pump (if equipped), fuel cut solenoid; the vacuum hose from the power brake booster (if equipped) and any other wires or hoses running to the engine.

10. If equipped with a M/T, lift the rubber shifter boot and remove the shift control linkage from the transmission. If equipped an A/T, disconnect the selector lever from the transmission from under the vehicle.

11. If equipped with a M/T, remove the clutch slave cylinder-to-transmission bolts, the cylinder and the exhaust tube.

12. Disconnect the speedometer cable, the back-up light wiring and the neutral switch (if equipped) from the rear section of the transmission.

13. Disconnect the exhaust pipe(s) from the exhaust manifold(s).

14. Using a piece of chalk, make alignment marks on the driveshaft and rear differential flange for realignment purposes. If equipped with a center driveshaft bearing, disconnect the center bearing bracket-to-chassis bolts. Disconnect the driveshaft-to-differential flange, lower and pull the driveshaft from the transmission extension housing (2WD) or transfer case (4WD). Using a clean shop rag, plug the rear end of the transmission or transfer case to prevent fluid loss.

15. If equipped with 4WD, perform the following procedures:

a. Using a piece of chalk, make alignment marks on the front driveshaft-to-transfer case flanges and the front driveshaft-to-differential drive flanges for realignment purposes.

b. Remove the front driveshaft-to-transfer case drive flange bolts and the front driveshaft-to-front differential, then, remove the front driveshaft.

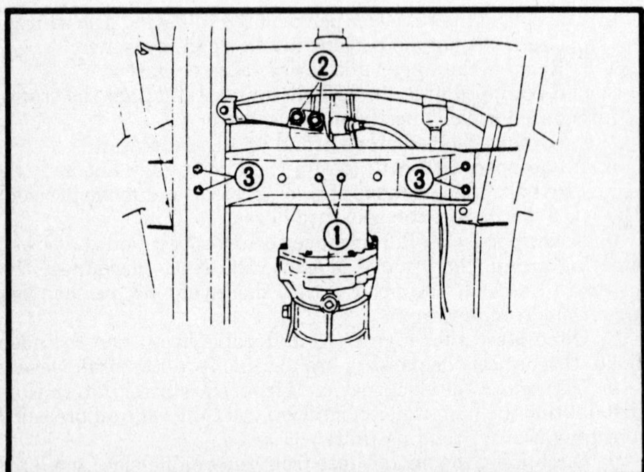

Engine and transmission cross member removal

16. Using a vertical lifting hoist, attach it to the engine and lift the engine slightly.

17. If equipped with 4WD, remove the front differential rear mounting bolts, the front differential carrier mounting bolt and the differential crossmember-to-chassis bolts and the crossmember from the vehicle.

18. Remove the front engine mount bracket-to-engine mount bolts (left-side) and the engine mount-to-chassis bolts (right-side). Remove the transmission mount-to-crossemember bolts.

19. Using a vertical hoist, take the engine/transmission assembly weight off the engine supports and the rear crossmember.

20. Remove the transmission crossmember-to-chassis bolts and the crossmember.

21. If equipped with a diesel engine, turn the steering wheel all the way (left or right) to provide clearance between the cross rod and the oil pan.

22. Pull the engine/transmission assembly forward, then, carefully raise and remove it from the vehicle. If necessary, separate the transmission from the engine, then, attach the engine to a work stand.

NOTE: When raising the engine/transmission assembly, be especially careful not to bump it against adjacent parts.

23. To install, reverse the removal procedures. Do not connect any parts to the engine or transmission until the engine and transmission are in place on the engine/transmission mounts and secured by the mounting bolts. Secure the rear support first, then, the front engine mounts, using the upper bolt hole as a guide. Refill the cooling system, the A/T with Dexron II®. Adjust the accelerator cable. Start the engine, allow it to reach normal operating temperatures and check for leaks.

NOTE: If equipped with a diesel engine, prime the fuel injection pump.

VAN

1. Disconnect the negative battery terminal from the battery.

2. Remove the fuel pump fuse from the fuse panel, operate the engine until it stalls, crank the engine to make sure it will not start.

3. Remove the air cleaner. Label and disconnect the electrical wiring and hoses which may be in the way. Using a shop rag, wrap it around the fuel line and disconnect it. If equipped, remove the splash pan from under the engine.

NOTE: Be sure to place a clean rag in the throttle body to prevent dirt from entering the engine.

4. Drain the engine coolant into a clean container. Remove the upper and lower radiator hoses. If equipped with an A/T, disconnect and plug the transmission oil cooler lines from the radiator.

5. If equipped with A/C, loosen the idler pulley nut and the adjusting bolt, then, remove the compressor and move it aside; DO NOT disconnect the pressure hoses.

6. If equipped with P/S, remove the drive belt and the power steering pump, then, move it aside; DO NOT disconnect the pressure hoses. If equipped with a diesel engine, remove the power steering reservoir.

7. Disconnect the engine ground cable from the cylinder head. Disconnect the parking brake cable from the brake lever.

8. Disconnect the electrical leads from the starter, alternator, distributor, the high-tension ignition coil cable, the oil pressure and temperature sending units.

9. Disconnect the heater hose from the engine-side and the accelerator cable from the throttle body. Disconnect and label the emission hoses or wires to the carbon canister, fuel cut solenoid; the vacuum hose from the power brake booster (if equipped) and any other wires or hoses running to the engine.

10. If equipped with a M/T, remove the shift control linkage

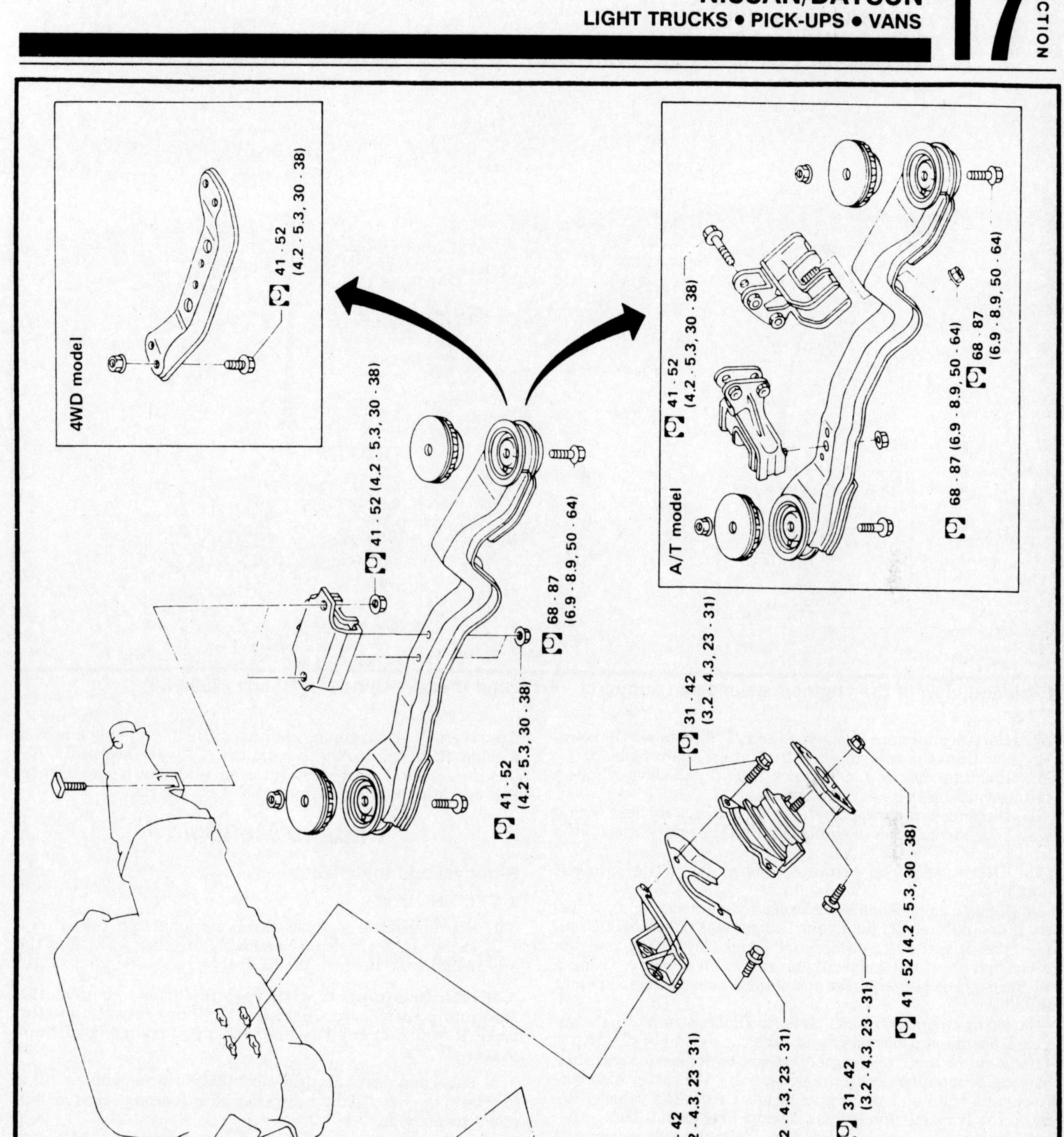

Exploded view of the engine/transmission supports—V6 engine—Pickups (1986-88)

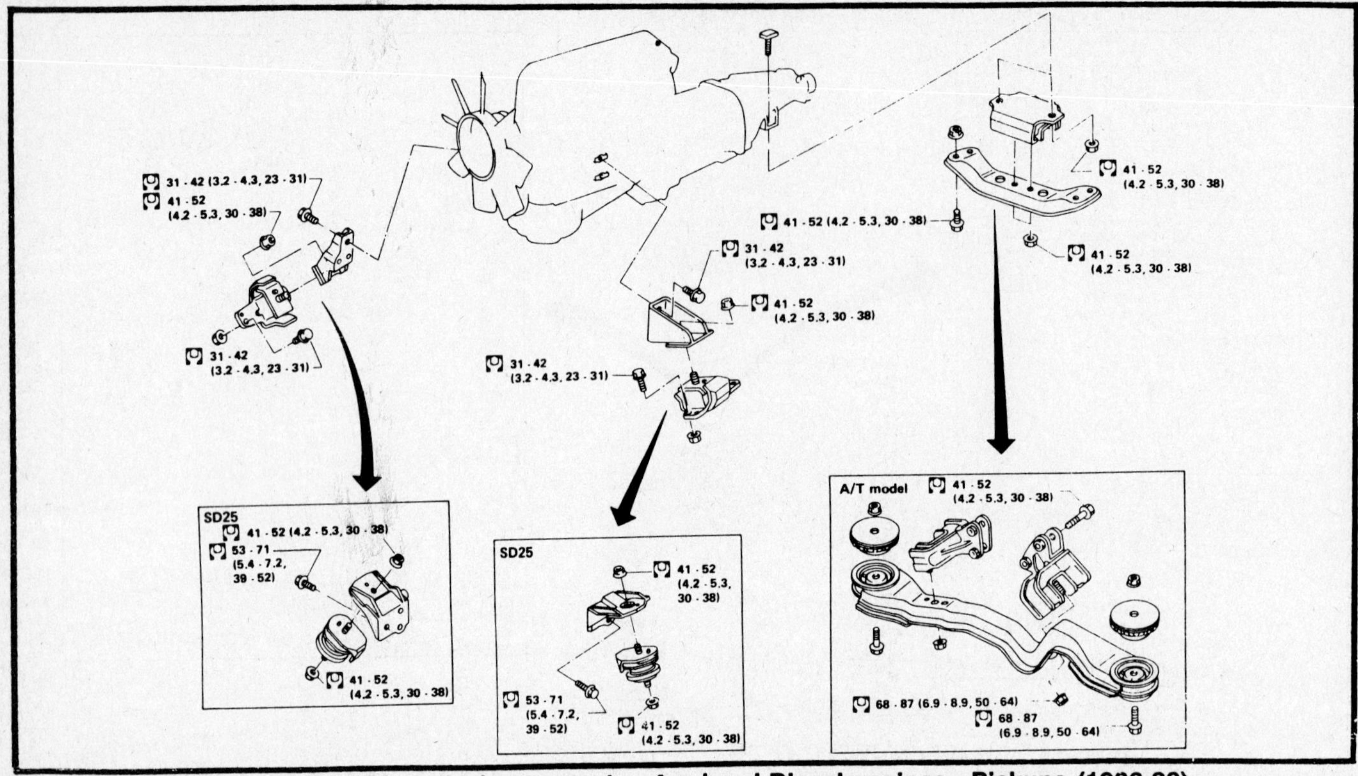

Exploded view of the engine/transmission supports—4-cyl and Diesel engines—Pickups (1986-88)

from the transmission. If equipped an A/T, disconnect the selector lever from the transmission from under the vehicle.

11. If equipped with a M/T, remove the clutch slave cylinder-to-transmission bolts and the cylinder.

12. Disconnect the speedometer cable, the back-up light wiring and the neutral switch (if equipped) from the rear section of the transmission.

13. Disconnect the exhaust pipe(s) from the exhaust manifold(s).

14. Using a piece of chalk, make alignment marks on the driveshaft and differential flange for realignment purposes. Disconnect the driveshaft-to-differential flange, lower and pull the driveshaft from the transmission extension housing. Using a clean shop rag, plug the rear end of the transmission to prevent fluid loss.

15. Using an under the vehicle engine hoist, attach it to the engine/transmission assembly and raise the assembly slightly.

16. Remove the front engine bracket-to-engine mount nuts, the engine mount-to-center member bolts, the center member-to-chassis bolts and the center member from the vehicle. Remove the transmission-to-rear support bracket nut/bolt.

17. Using an under the vehicle lift, lower the engine from the vehicle.

NOTE: It may be necessary to raise the vehicle to provide clearance to slide the engine/transmission from under the vehicle.

18. If necessary, separate the transmission from the engine, then, attach the engine to a work stand.

NOTE: When removing the engine/transmission assembly, be especially careful not to bump it against adjacent parts.

19. To install, reverse the removal procedures. Do not connect any parts to the engine or transmission until the engine and transmission are in place on the engine/transmission mounts and secured by the mounting bolts. Secure the rear support first, then, the front engine mounts, using the upper bolt hole as a guide. Refill the cooling system, the A/T with Dexron II®. Adjust the accelerator cable. Start the engine, allow it to reach normal operating temperatures and check for leaks.

Intake Manifold

Removal and Installation

4-CYL ENGINES

1. Disconnect the negative battery terminal from the battery.
2. Remove the air cleaner assembly together with all of the attending hoses. Remove the EGR tube.

NOTE: If equipped with fuel injection, remove the fuel pump fuse from the fuse panel, operate the engine until it stalls, crank the engine to make sure it will not start.

3. Label and disconnect the electrical wiring and hoses which may be in the way. Using a shop rag, wrap it around the fuel line and disconnect it.
4. Drain the engine coolant to a level below the thermostat housing, then, disconnect the upper coolant hose from the thermostat housing.
5. Disconnect the throttle linkage and vacuum lines from the carburetor/throttle body.

NOTE: The carburetor/throttle body can be removed from the manifold at this point or it can be removed as an assembly with the intake manifold.

6. Remove the carburetor/throttle body-to-intake manifold nuts, the carburetor/throttle body and the heater mixture (1986-88). Remove the intake manifold-to-engine bolts and the intake manifold.
7. Using a putty knife, clean the gasket mounting surfaces.
8. To install, use a new gaskets and reverse the removal procedures. Torque the intake manifold-to-engine bolts (working

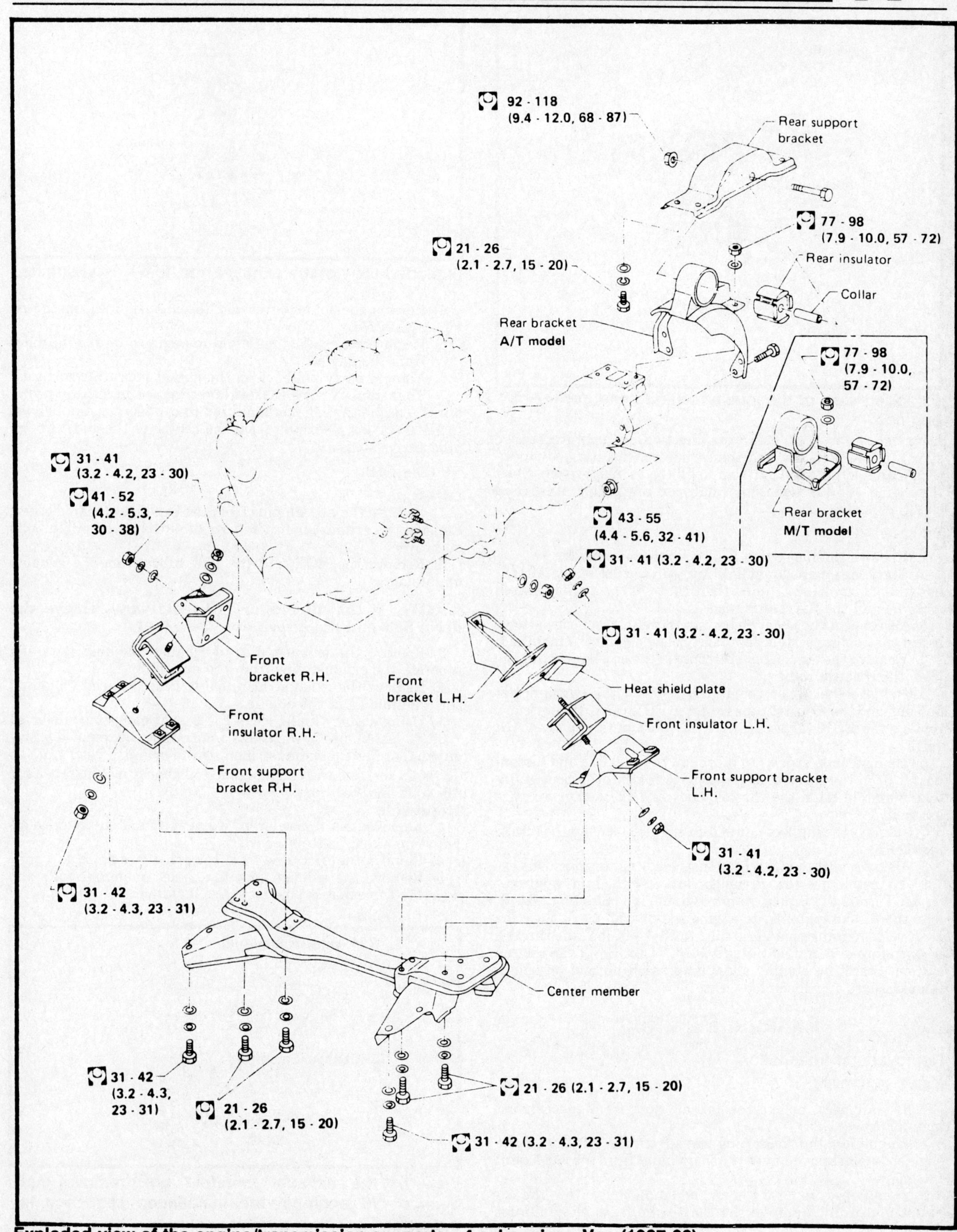

Exploded view of the engine/transmission supports—4-cyl engine—Van (1987-88)

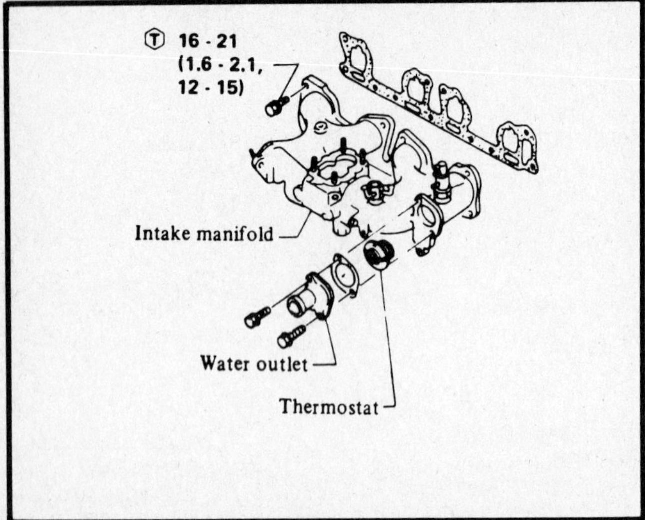

Exploded view of the intake manifold and gasket—Z-engines

from the center in an outwards direction—in two progressive steps) to 12–25 ft. lbs. and the carburetor/throttle body-to-intake manifold nuts 9–13 ft. lbs. Refill the cooling system. Start the engine, allow it to reach normal operating temperatures and check for leaks.

V6 ENGINE

1. Remove the fuel pump fuse from the fuse block.
2. Start the engine and allow it to run until it stalls. After it has stalled, crank it 2-3 times, then, turn Off the ignition switch and reinstall the fuel pump fuse.
3. Disconnect the negative battery terminal from the battery. Drain the cooling system to a level below the intake manifold.
4. Remove the air cleaner. Disconnect the accelerator linkage from the throttle body.
5. Remove the upper radiator hose from the water outlet housing and the exhaust tube from the EGR valve. If necessary, remove the EGR valve-to-intake manifold nuts and the EGR valve.
6. Using a shop rag, wrap it around the fuel line and disconnect it from the throttle body. Remove the throttle body-to-intake manifold nuts, the throttle body and the heater mixture assembly.
7. Remove the intake manifold-to-engine bolts and the intake manifold.
8. Using a putty knife, clean the gasket mounting surfaces.
9. To install, use new gaskets and reverse the removal procedures. Torque the intake manifold-to-engine bolts to 12–14 ft. lbs., the intake manifold-to-engine nuts to 17–20 ft. lbs., the EGR valve to intake manifold nuts to 13–17 ft. lbs., the throttle body-to-intake manifold nuts to 9–13 ft. lbs. Refill the cooling system. Start the engine, allow it to reach normal operating temperatures and check for leaks.

Exhaust Manifold

Removal and Installation

4-CYL ENGINES

1. If equipped, remove the hot air duct from the exhaust manifold cover.
2. Disconnect the spark plug wires from the left-side of the engine; if necessary, remove the spark plugs from the left-side of the engine.
3. If equipped, remove the air induction tubes from the exhaust manifold. Remove the EGR tube from the exhaust manifold.

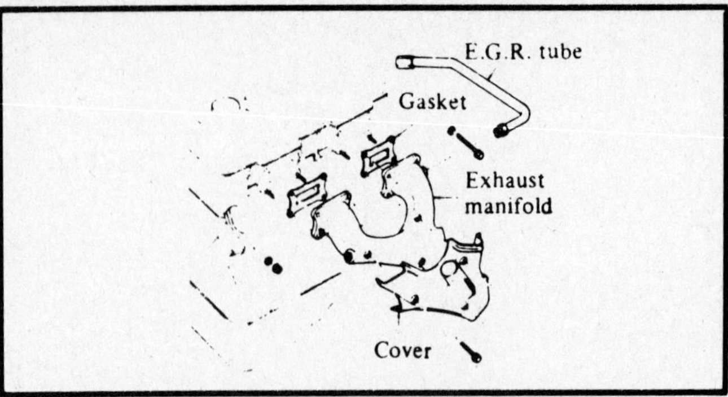

Exploded view of the exhaust manifold—4-cyl engine

4. Remove the hot air cover and the exhaust pipe from the exhaust manifold.
5. Remove the exhaust manifold-to-engine nuts and the manifold from the engine.
6. Using a putty knife, clean the gasket mounting surfaces.
7. To install, use new gaskets and reverse the removal procedures. Torque the exhaust manifold-to-cylinder head nuts/bolts to 12–15 ft. lbs. (working from the center to the ends) in two progressive steps.

V6 ENGINE

Left-Side

1. Remove the hot air tube from the exhaust manifold cover. Remove the exhaust manifold cover-to-exhaust manifold bolts and cover.
2. Remove the EGR and the AIR tubes from the exhaust manifold.

NOTE: If the alternator is in the way, remove the drive belt and the alternator.

3. Remove the exhaust pipe-to-exhaust manifold nuts and separate the exhaust pipe from the manifold.
4. Remove the exhaust manifold-to-cylinder head bolts and the manifold from the engine.
5. Using a putty knife, clean the gasket mounting surfaces.
6. To install, use new gaskets and reverse the removal procedures. Torque the exhaust manifold-to-cylinder head nuts to 13–16 ft. lbs. and the exhaust pipe-to-exhaust manifold bolts to 16–20 ft. lbs.

Right-side

1. Remove the upper/lower exhaust manifold cover-to-exhaust manifold bolts and covers.
2. Remove the AIR tube from the exhaust manifold.
3. Remove the exhaust pipe-to-exhaust manifold bolts and separate the exhaust pipe from the manifold.

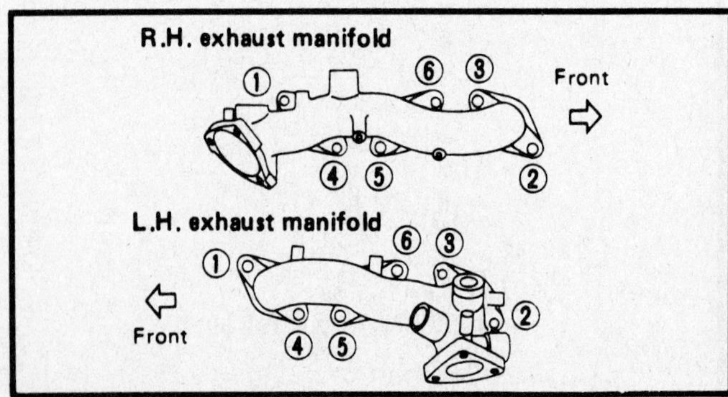

View of the exhaust manifold bolt removal sequence—V6 engines—the installation sequence is opposite

4. Remove the exhaust manifold-to-cylinder head bolts and the manifold from the engine.
5. Using a putty knife, clean the gasket mounting surfaces.
6. To install, use new gaskets and reverse the removal procedures. Torque the exhaust manifold-to-cylinder head nuts to 13–16 ft. lbs. and the exhaust pipe-to-exhaust manifold bolts to 16–20 ft. lbs.

Cylinder Head

Removal and Installation

4-CYL ENGINES

1. Refer to the "Intake Manifold" and "Exhaust Manifold, Removal and Installation" procedures in this section, then, remove the intake and exhaust manifolds.
2. Place a clean drain pan under the radiator and drain the engine coolant.
3. If equipped with a mechanical fuel pump, disconnect the fuel lines and remove the pump.
4. If equipped with P/S, disconnect the drive belt, then, remove the power steering pump and move it aside; do not disconnect the pressure hoses.
5. Remove the valve cover-to-engine bolts and the valve cover.
6. Remove the spark plugs to protect them from damage. Remove the valve cover.
7. Using a wrench on the crankshaft pulley bolt, rotate the crankshaft until the No. 1 cyl is on the TDC of its compression stroke.
8. Using paint or chalk, mark the camshaft sprocket-to-timing chain relationship; if this is done, it will not be necessary to locate the factory timing marks.

NOTE: If the timing chain is equipped with silver links, be sure to align the camshaft timing mark with the silver link.

9. Remove the camshaft sprocket-to-camshaft bolt and the camshaft sprocket. Using the Timing Chain tool No. KV10105800 or equivalent, wedge and support the timing chain; this will be necessary to keep the chain from falling into the front cover.
10. Remove the cylinder head-to-engine bolts and the cylinder head; be sure to remove the cylinder head-to-front cover bolts. It may be necessary to tap the head lightly with a copper or brass mallet to loosen it.
11. Using a putty knife, clean the gasket mounting surfaces. Inspect the cylinder head for warpage; the difference must be less than 0.0059 in.
12. To install the cylinder head, use a new gasket and torque the cylinder head-to-engine bolts (in order) to 51–58 ft. lbs. (1982), 58–65 ft. lbs. (1983) or 54–61 ft. lbs. (1984-88).

NOTE: When installing the cylinder head bolts, torque them in 3 steps: 1st – 20 ft. lbs., 2nd – 40 ft. lbs. and 3rd – final torque.

13. Install the camshaft sprocket together with the timing chain to the camshaft; make sure the timing marks are aligned. Torque the camshaft sprocket-to-camshaft bolt to 87–116 ft. lbs.
14. To complete the installation, reverse the removal procedures. It is always wise to drain the crankcase oil after the cylinder head has been installed to avoid coolant contamination. Start the engine and allow it to reach normal operating temperatures, then, check for leaks.

V6 ENGINE

Left-Side

1. Refer to the "Timing Belt, Removal and Installation", the "Exhaust Manifold, Removal and Installation" and the "Intake Manifold, Removal and Installation" procedures in this section,

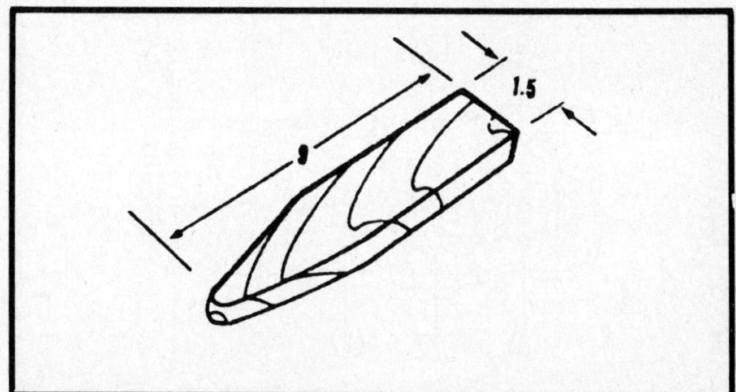

Dimensions for fabricating the wooden wedge used to support the timing chain

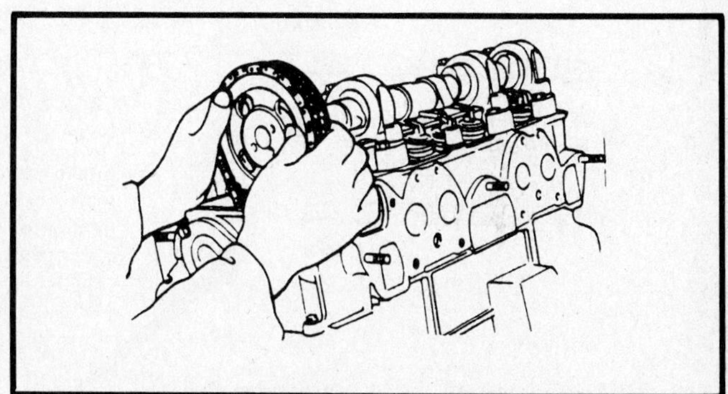
Removing the camshaft sprocket and chain

Support the timing chain with a wedge

Installing the camshaft sprocket

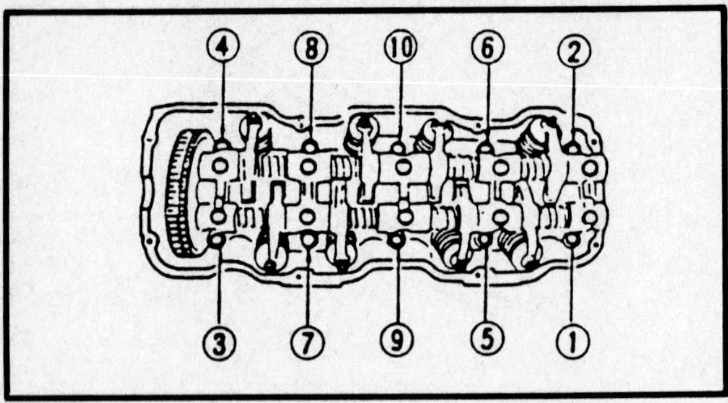

Z series engine head bolt loosening sequence

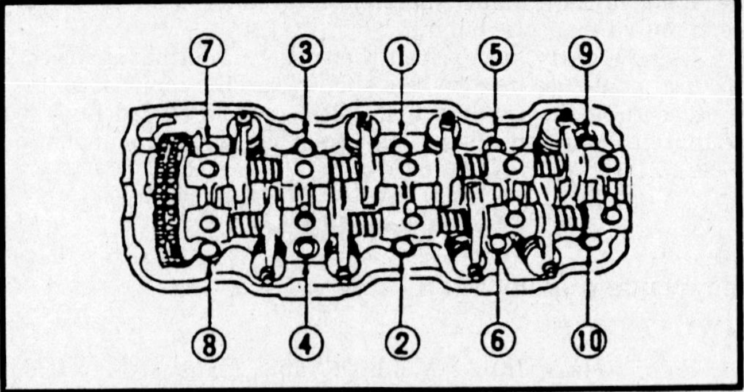

Z series engine head bolt tightening sequence

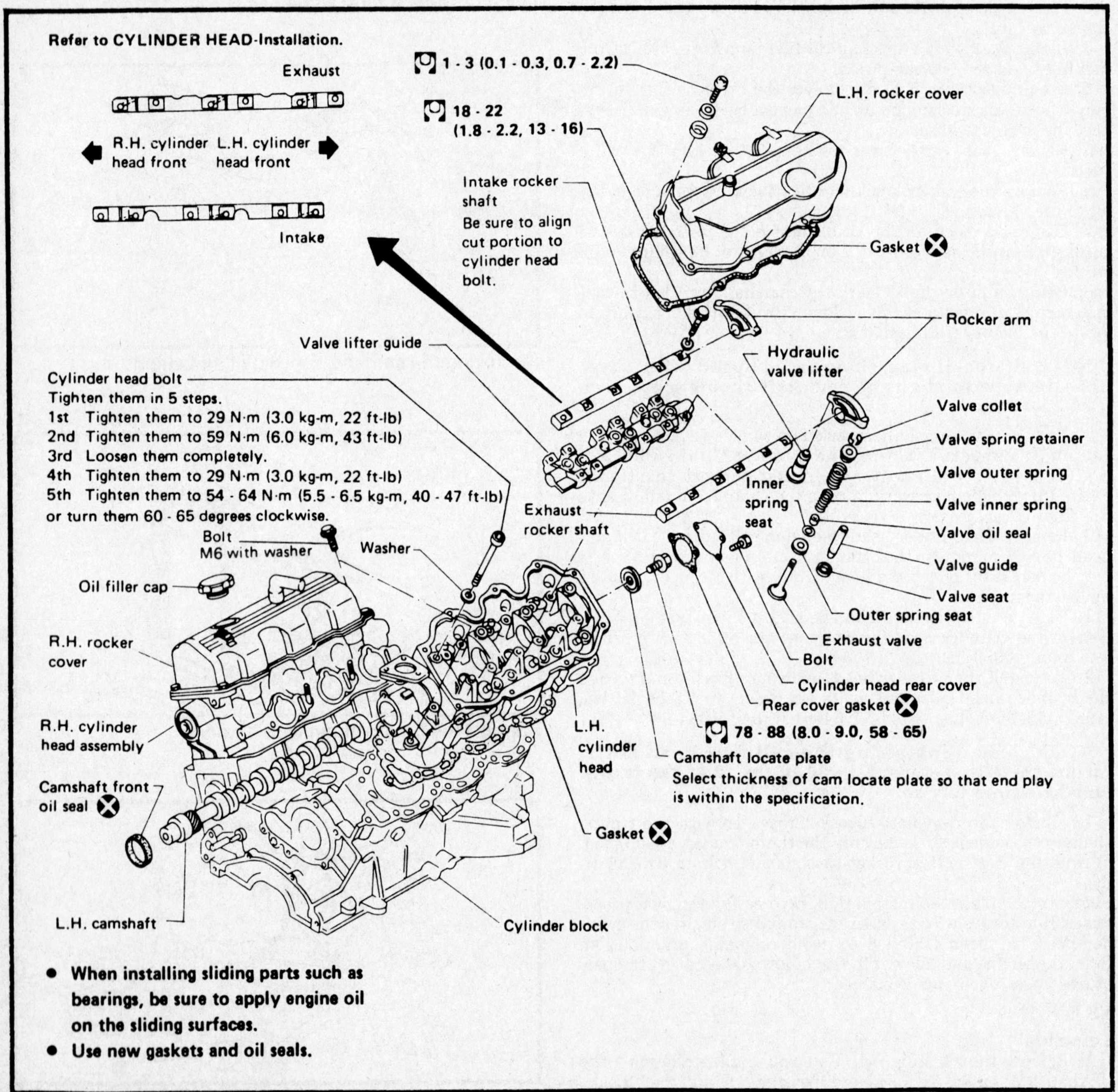

Refer to CYLINDER HEAD-Installation.

Exhaust

R.H. cylinder head front

L.H. cylinder head front

Intake

1 - 3 (0.1 - 0.3, 0.7 - 2.2)

L.H. rocker cover

18 - 22 (1.8 - 2.2, 13 - 16)

Intake rocker shaft
Be sure to align cut portion to cylinder head bolt.

Gasket ⊗

Rocker arm

Valve lifter guide

Hydraulic valve lifter

Cylinder head bolt
Tighten them in 5 steps.
1st Tighten them to 29 N·m (3.0 kg-m, 22 ft-lb)
2nd Tighten them to 59 N·m (6.0 kg-m, 43 ft-lb)
3rd Loosen them completely.
4th Tighten them to 29 N·m (3.0 kg-m, 22 ft-lb)
5th Tighten them to 54 - 64 N·m (5.5 - 6.5 kg-m, 40 - 47 ft-lb) or turn them 60 - 65 degrees clockwise.

Valve collet

Valve spring retainer

Valve outer spring

Inner spring seat

Valve inner spring

Exhaust rocker shaft

Valve oil seal

Bolt
M6 with washer

Washer

Valve guide

Oil filler cap

Valve seat

Outer spring seat

R.H. rocker cover

Exhaust valve

Bolt

Cylinder head rear cover

Rear cover gasket ⊗

R.H. cylinder head assembly

L.H. cylinder head

78 - 88 (8.0 - 9.0, 58 - 65)

Camshaft locate plate
Select thickness of cam locate plate so that end play is within the specification.

Camshaft front oil seal ⊗

Gasket ⊗

L.H. camshaft

Cylinder block

- **When installing sliding parts such as bearings, be sure to apply engine oil on the sliding surfaces.**
- **Use new gaskets and oil seals.**

Exploded view of the cylinder head assembly—V6 engine

then, remove the timing belt, the left exhaust manifold and the intake manifold.

NOTE: Before removing the timing belt, be sure to mark the position of the timing belt-to-camshaft sprockets and the timing belt-to-crankshaft sprocket, then, place an arrow on the timing belt in the direction or rotation. Do not rotate the crankshaft after the timing belt has been removed.

2. Remove the camshaft sprocket-to-camshaft bolt and the camshaft sprocket, then, remove the rear timing belt cover-to-cylinder head bolts.
3. Remove the distributor cap, then, using a piece of chalk, align the rotor-to-distributor housing and the distributor housing-to-cylinder head. Remove the distributor-to-cylinder head bolt and the distributor.
4. Remove the valve cover from the left cylinder head.

NOTE: It may be necessary to remove the valve lifter guide-to-cylinder head bolts and the valve lifter guide to provide access to the cylinder head bolts. When removing the valve lifter guide, be sure to secure the valve lifters with a safety wire, to keep them in their original positions.

5. Remove the cylinder head-to-engine bolts and the cylinder head.
6. Using a putty knife, clean the gasket mounting surfaces. Using a small power wire brush, clean the carbon from the piston depressions in the cylinder head.
7. Inspect the cylinder head for cracks and other flaws. Using a straight-edge and a feeler gauge, measure the cylinder head warpage. If the warpage exceeds 0.004 in. or there is other damage, repair or replace the cylinder head.

NOTE: If the cylinder head warpage is significant, requiring the head to be machined, submit it to a reputable automotive machine shop; be sure the cylinder head is disassembled before submitting it to a machine shop.

8. To install the cylinder head, use a new gasket and reverse the removal procedures. Torque the cylinder head-to-engine bolts (in sequence) in five steps: 1st – 22 ft. lbs., 2nd – 43 ft. lbs., 3rd – loosen all bolts, 4th – 22 ft. lbs. and 5th – 40–47 ft. lbs.
9. To complete the installation, use new gaskets and reverse the removal procedures. Torque the valve lifter guide-to-cylinder head bolts to 13–16 ft. lbs., the valve cover-to-cylinder head bolts to 9–25 inch lbs., the exhaust manifold-to-cylinder head nuts to 13–16 ft. lbs., the intake manifold-to-cylinder head nuts to 17–20 ft. lbs. or bolts to 12–14 ft. lbs. and the camshaft sprocket-to-camshaft nut to 58–65 ft. lbs. Refill the cooling system. Start the engine, allow it to reach normal operating temperatures and check for leaks.

Right-Side

1. Refer to the "Timing Belt, Removal and Installation", the "Exhaust Manifold, Removal and Installation" and the "Intake Manifold, Removal and Installation" procedures in this section, then, remove the timing belt, the right exhaust manifold and the intake manifold.

NOTE: Before removing the timing belt, be sure to mark the position of the timing belt-to-camshaft sprockets and the timing belt-to-crankshaft sprocket, then, place an arrow on the timing belt in the direction or rotation. Do not rotate the crankshaft after the timing belt has been removed.

2. Remove the camshaft sprocket-to-camshaft bolt and the camshaft sprocket, then, remove the rear timing belt cover-to-cylinder head bolts.
3. Remove the valve cover from the right cylinder head.

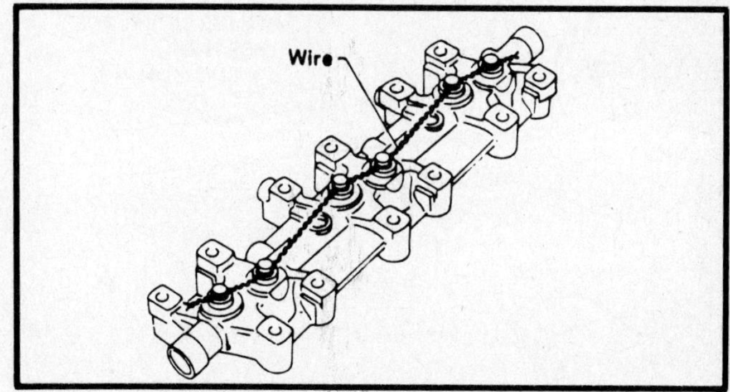

Using a wire to hold the valve lifter in place – V6 engine

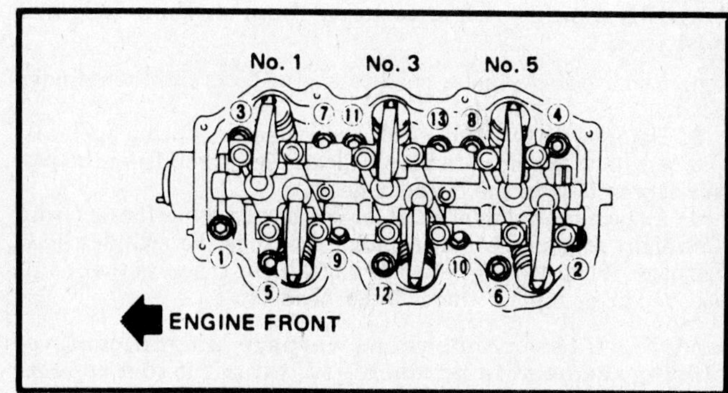

View of the left-side cylinder head removal sequence – V6 engine – the right-side is similar

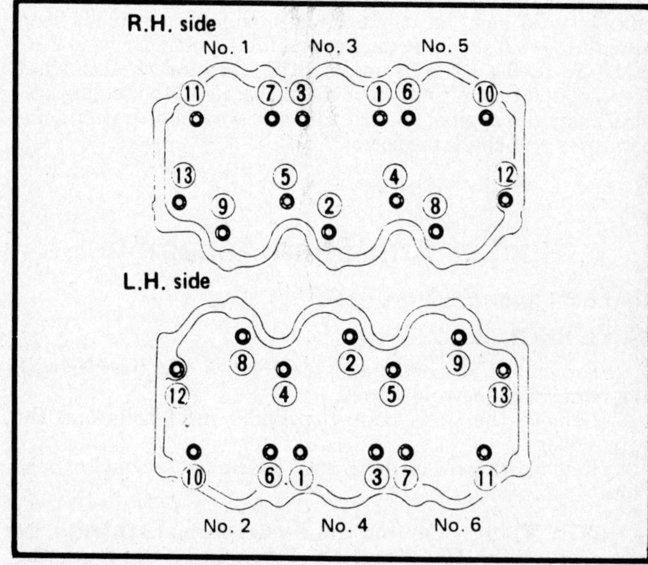

View of the cylinder head installation sequence – V6 engine

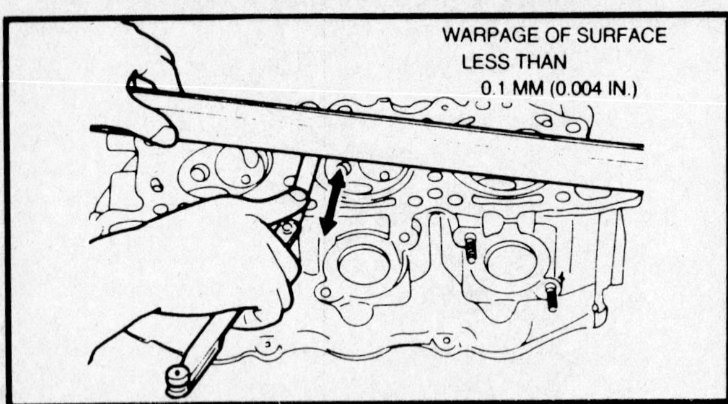

Using a straight edge and feeler gauge to measure the cylinder head distortion – V6 engine

NOTE: It may be necessary to remove the valve lifter guide-to-cylinder head bolts and the valve lifter guide to provide access to the cylinder head bolts. When removing the valve lifter guide, be sure to secure the valve lifters with a safety wire, to keep them in their original positions.

4. Remove the cylinder head-to-engine bolts and the cylinder head.
5. Using a putty knife, clean the gasket mounting surfaces. Using a small power wire brush, clean the carbon from the piston depressions in the cylinder head.
6. Inspect the cylinder head for cracks and other flaws. Using a straight-edge and a feeler gauge, measure the cylinder head warpage. If the warpage exceeds 0.004 in. or there is other damage, repair or replace the cylinder head.

NOTE: If the cylinder head warpage is significant, requiring the head to be machined, submit it to a reputable automotive machine shop; be sure the cylinder head is disassembled before submitting it to a machine shop.

7. To install the cylinder head, use a new gasket and reverse the removal procedures. Torque the cylinder head-to-engine bolts (in sequence) in five steps: 1st – 22 ft. lbs., 2nd – 43 ft. lbs., 3rd – loosen all bolts, 4th – 22 ft. lbs. and 5th – 40–47 ft. lbs.
8. To complete the installation, use new gaskets and reverse the removal procedures. Torque the valve lifter guide-to-cylinder head bolts to 13–16 ft. lbs., the valve cover-to-cylinder head bolts to 9–25 inch lbs., the exhaust manifold-to-cylinder head nuts to 13–16 ft. lbs., the intake manifold-to-cylinder head nuts to 17–20 ft. lbs. or bolts to 12–14 ft. lbs. and the camshaft sprocket-to-camshaft nut to 58–65 ft. lbs. Refill the cooling system. Start the engine, allow it to reach normal operating temperatures and check for leaks.

Rocker Arm/Shaft Assembly

Removal and Installation

4-CYL ENGINES

1. Disconnect any hoses and wires which may interfer with the removal of the valve cover.
2. Remove the valve cover-to-cylinder head bolts and the valve cover.
3. Remove the rocker arm/shaft assembly-to-cylinder head bolts.

NOTE: When removing the rocker/arm shaft bolts, do not remove the No. 1 and No. 5 bracket bolts from the rocker arm bracket or the rocker bracket will spring from the rocker shaft.

4. If separating the rocker arms from the rocker arm shafts, be sure to keep them in order for reinstallation purposes.
5. Using a putty knife, clean the gasket mounting surfaces.

NOTE: Be aware that the rocker arm shafts are different in construction and must be install in their original positions.

6. To install, use new gaskets, sealant (if necessary) and reverse the removal procedures. Torque the rocker arm/shaft assembly-to-cylinder head bolts to 11–18 ft. lbs. Adjust the valve clearances.

V6 ENGINE

1. Disconnect any hoses and wires which may interfer with the removal of the valve cover.
2. Remove the valve cover-to-cylinder head bolts and the valve cover.
3. Remove the rocker arm/shaft assemblies-to-cylinder head bolts and the rocker arm/shaft assemblies; if necessary, separate the rocker arms from the rocker arm shaft.

NOTE: If separating the rocker arms from the rocker arm shaft, be sure to keep them in order for reinstallation purposes.

4. Using a putty knife, clean the gasket mounting surfaces.

NOTE: Be aware that the rocker arm shafts are different in construction and must be install in their original positions.

5. To install, use new gaskets, sealant (if necessary) and reverse the removal procedures. Torque the rocker arm shaft-to-cylinder head bolts to 13–16 ft. lbs. and the valve cover-to-cylinder head bolts to 9–25 inch lbs.

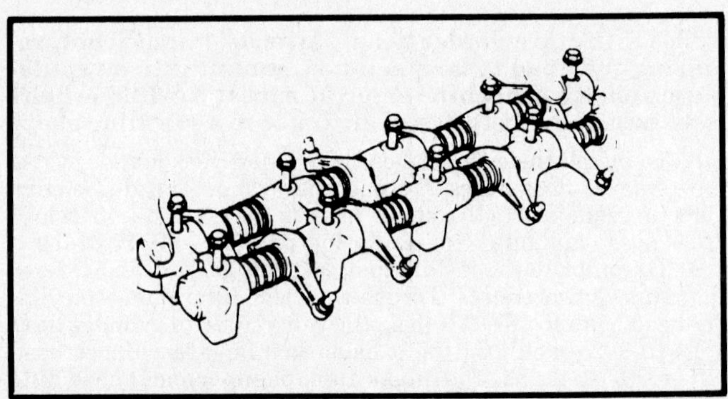

Z series engine rocker arm assembly

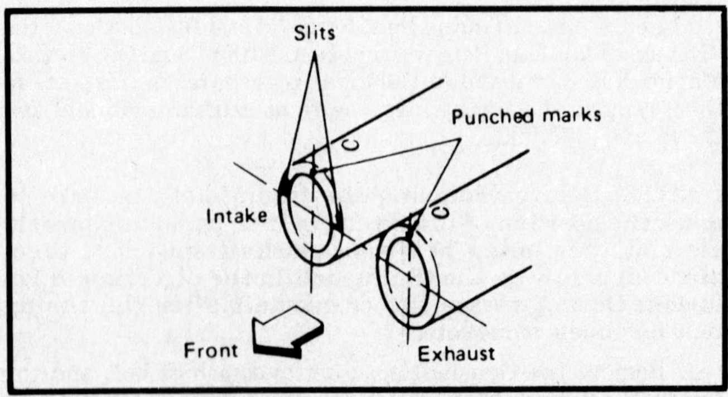

View of the rocker arm shaft positioning indicators – Z-series engines

Valve Arrangement

4-Cyl Engine

I-E-E-I-I-E-E-I (front-to-rear)

V6 Engine

Right-Side
E-I-E-I-E-I (front-to-rear)

Left-Side
I-E-I-E-I-E (front-to-rear)

4-Cyl Diesel Engine

E-I-I-E-E-I-I-E

Valve Adjustment – 4-Cyl

Procedure

1982 – Z22 ENGINES

1. Operate the engine until normal operating temperatures are reached and turn the engine Off.
2. Refer to the "Rocker Arm/Shaft, Removal and Installation" in this section and remove the valve cover.
3. Using a socket wrench on the crankshaft pulley bolt, rotate the crankshaft until the first cam lobe behind the camshaft timing chain sprocket is pointing straight down.

NOTE: If using the starter to rotate the crankshaft, be sure to disconnect the high tension wire from the coil(s) to prevent the engine from accidentally starting and spewing oil all over the engine compartment.

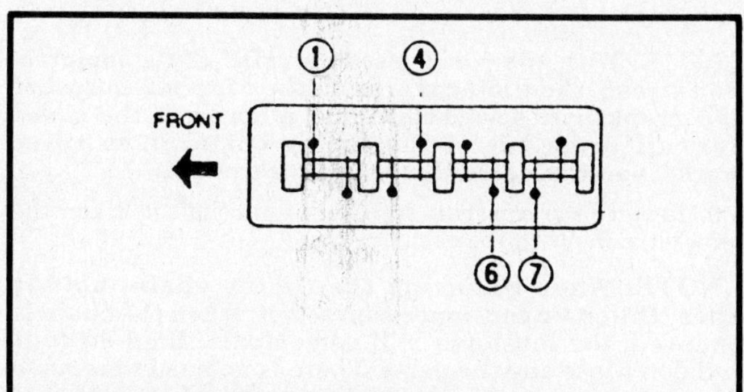

Primary adjustment on Z-engines – 1982

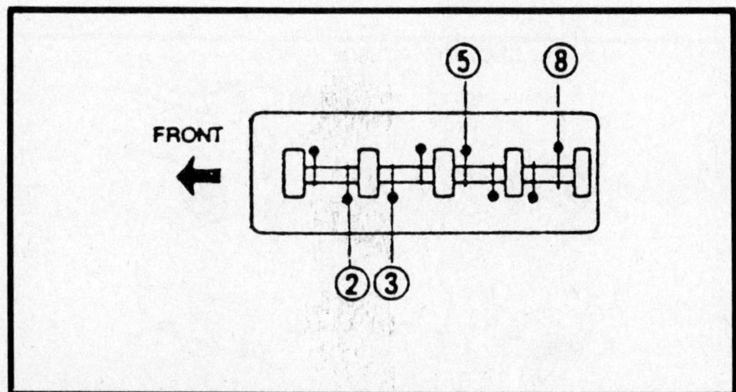

Secondary adjustment on Z-engines – 1982

CAUTION

Never attempt to turn the engine by using a wrench on the camshaft sprocket bolt; there is a 1:2 turning ratio between the camshaft and the crankshaft which will put a tremendous strain on the timing chain.

4. Using a wrench, a flat-bladed screwdriver and a feeler gauge, check and/or adjust valves No. 1, 4, 6 and 7 to 0.012 in.; the feeler gauge should pass between the valve stem end and the rocker arm screw with a very slight drag.
5. If the clearance is not within specified value, loosen the rocker arm lock nut and turn the rocker arm screw to obtain the proper clearance. After correct clearance is obtained, tighten the lock nut.
6. Rotate the crankshaft so the No. 1 cam lobe is pointing straight up, then, adjust valves No. 2, 3, 5 and 8 to 0.012 in.
7. Using a putty knife, clean the gasket mounting surfaces.
8. After adjustment, use new gaskets, sealant (if necessary) and reverse the removal procedures. Torque the lock nut to 12–16 ft. lbs.

1983-88 Z-SERIES ENGINES

NOTE: Adjustment should be made with the engine hot. Valve clearance is 0.012 in.

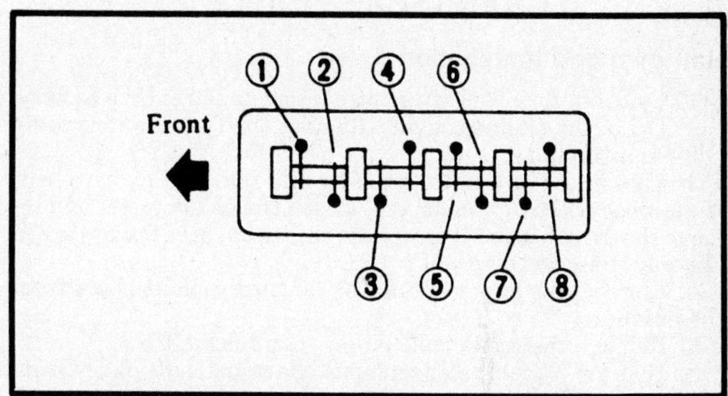

Valve arrangement on Z-engines – 1983-88

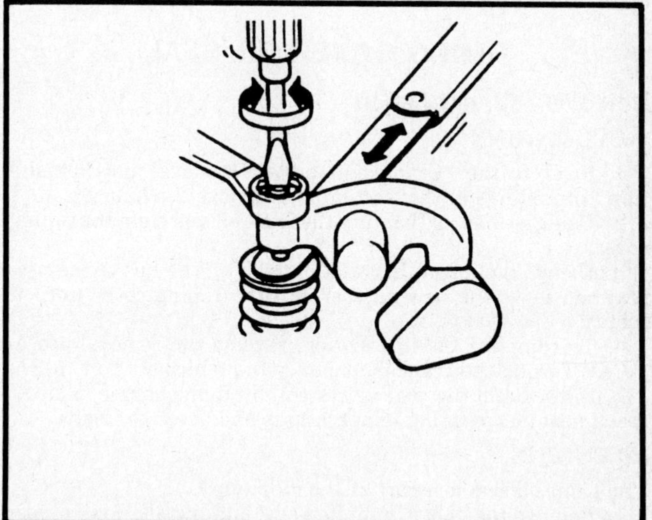
Adjusting the valves on Z-engines – 1983-88

1. Operate the engine until normal operating temperatures are reached, then, turn Off the engine.
2. Refer to the "Rocker Arm/Shaft, Removal and Installation" in this section and remove the valve cover.
3. Using a socket wrench on the crankshaft pulley bolt, rotate the crankshaft until the No. 1 cylinder is on the TDC of the compression stroke.

NOTE: To check for the No. 1 TDC position, remove the No. 1 spark plug, place you're thumb over the hole, rotate the crankshaft until the compression pressure can be felt in the cylinder.

4. Using a wrench, flat-bladed screwdriver and a feeler gauge, check and/or adjust the valves No. 1, 2, 4 and 6 to 0.012 in.
5. Rotate the crankshaft 180° to position the No. 4 cylinder on the TDC of its compression stroke.
6. With the No. 4 cylinder at the TDC of its compression stroke, adjust the valves No. 3, 5, 7 and 8 to 0.012 in.
7. Using a putty knife, clean the gasket mounting surfaces.
8. After adjustment, use new gaskets, sealant (if necessary) and reverse the removal procedures. Torque the lock nut to 12–16 ft. lbs.

Timing Sprockets and Chain

CRANKSHAFT PULLEY

Removal and Installation

1. Disconnect the negative battery terminal from the battery.
2. Drain the engine coolant. Remove the fan-to-water pump bolts and the fan.
3. Loosen the alternator adjuster and remove the drive belt; if equipped with A/C and/or P/S, loosen the belt adjuster and remove the drive belt(s). If any of the accessory drive pulleys are in the way, remove them.
4. Remove the upper and lower radiator coolant hoses from the engine.
5. Remove the crankshaft pulley-to-crankshaft bolt.
6. Using a Wheel Puller tool, pull the crankshaft pulley from the crankshaft.
7. To install, reverse the removal procedures. Torque the crankshaft pulley-to-crankshaft bolt to 87–116 ft. lbs. (Z-series) or nut to 90–98 ft. lbs. (V6). Refill the cooling system. Start the engine, allow it to reach normal operating temperatures and check for leaks.

TIMING COVER OIL SEAL

Removal and Installation

4-CYL ENGINE

1. Refer to the "Crankshaft pulley, Removal and Installation" procedures in this section and remove the pulley.
2. Using a small pry bar, pry the front oil seal from the timing cover.
3. Using an Oil Seal Installation tool, oil the lips of the new seal and drive the new oil seal into the timing cover until it seats.
4. To complete the installation, reverse the removal procedures. Torque the crankshaft pulley-to-crankshaft bolt to 87–116 ft. lbs. Refill the cooling system. Start the engine, allow it reach normal operating temperatures and check for leaks.

V6 ENGINE

The front oil seal is a part of the oil pump.

1. Refer to the "Oil Pump, Removal and Installation" procedures in this section and remove the oil pump.
2. Using a medimum size pry bar, pry the oil seal from the oil pump.
3. Using an Oil Seal Installation tool, lubricate the oil seal lips and drive the new oil seal into the oil pump.
4. To complete the installation, use new gaskets and reverse the removal procedures. Refill the crankcase with new oil and the cooling system with antifreeze.

TIMING CHAIN AND SPROCKET

Removal and Installation

4-CYL ENGINE

NOTE: Before attempting this procedure, rotate the crankshaft to position the No. 1 piston on the TDC of its compression stroke.

1. Disconnect the negative battery terminal from the battery. Drain the cooling system. Remove the upper and lower coolant hoses from the engine, then, the radiator.
2. Loosen the alternator adjusting bolt and remove the drive belt. Remove the alternator bracket-to-engine bolts and move the alternator aside. If equipped with A/C, remove the drive belt. If necessary, remove the A/C bracket-to-engine bolts, then, move the A/C compressor and bracket.
3. Remove the distributor.
4. Remove the oil pump-to-timing cover bolts, then, the oil pump and its drive spindle.
5. Remove the cooling fan-to-water pump bolts, the fan, the fan coupling (if equipped) and the water pump pulley.
6. Remove the crankshaft pulley-to-crankshaft bolt and the crankshaft pulley.
7. Remove the valve cover-to-cylinder head bolts, the valve cover, the timing cover-to-engine bolts, the front cover-to-oil pan bolts.
8. Cut the exposed timing cover-to-oil pan gasket from the oil pan gasket.

NOTE: With the No. 1 piston at TDC of its compression stroke, the timing marks on the camshaft sprocket and crankshaft sprocket should align with the silver links (if equipped) of the timing chain; if no silver marks, paint alignment marks on the chain.

9. Remove the camshaft sprocket-to-camshaft bolt and the sprocket along with the chain.

NOTE: When removing the timing chain, hold it where the chain tensioner contacts it. When the chain is removed, the tensioner will come apart. Hold on to it and don't lose any the parts. There is no need to remove the chain guide unless it is being replaced.

10. Inspect the timing chain for cracked links, wear and/or damage; if necessary, replace the chain.
11. Using a putty knife, clean the gasket mounting surfaces.

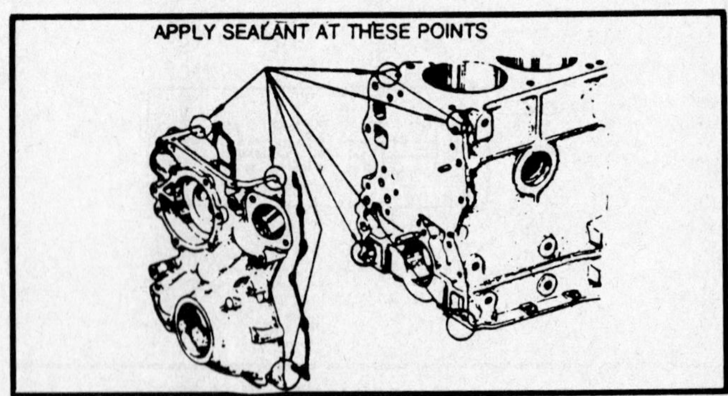

Gasoline engine front cover installation

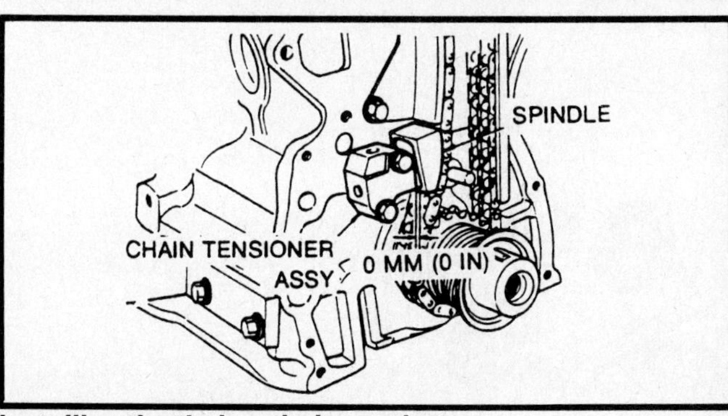

Installing the timing chain tensioner

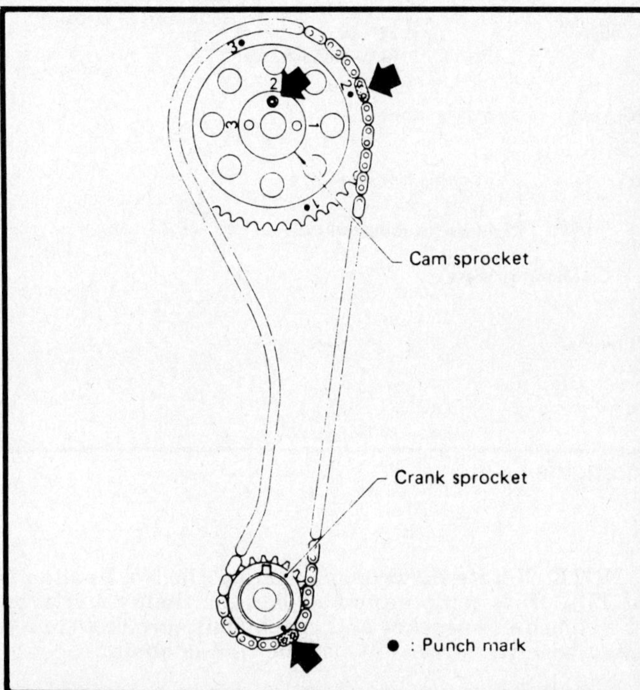

Assembled view of the timing marks—4-cylinder engines

Use the No. 2 mark and the hole to align the camshaft—Z20, Z22 and Z24 engines

NOTE: Whenever the timing cover is removed, it is a good idea to replace the oil seal.

12. To install, use new gaskets, sealant (if necessary) and reverse the removal procedures. Cut the portions needed from a new oil pan gasket and top front cover gasket.

NOTE: Before installing the oil pump, place the gasket over the shaft and make sure the drive spindle mark (faces) aligns with the oil pump hole.

13. Apply a light coating of oil to the crankshaft oil seal and carefully mount the timing cover to the front of the engine and install all of the mounting bolts. Torque the bolts to 7–12 ft. lbs. (8mm) or to 3–6 ft. lbs. (6mm), the oil pan-to-timing cover bolts to 4–7 ft. lbs., the camshaft sprocket-to-camshaft bolt to 87–116 ft. lbs. and the oil pump-to-timing cover bolts to 8–10 ft. lbs. Refill the cooling system. Check and/or adjust the ignition timing.

TIMING BELT AND SPROCKETS

Removal and Installation

V6 ENGINE

1. Disconnect the negative battery terminal from the battery and remove the spark plugs.
2. Place a clean drain pan under the radiator and drain the engine coolant into the pan.
3. Remove the radiator shroud, the fan-to-water pump bolts and the fan.
4. Disconnect the coolant hoses from the engine, then, remove the radiator from the vehicle.
5. Loosen and remove the alternator, the P/S (if equipped) and the A/C (if equipped) drive belts.
6. Using a socket wrench on the crankshaft bolt, rotate the crankshaft to position the No. 1 piston on the TDC of its compression stroke.

NOTE: Make sure the sprocket alignment marks are aligned with rear timing plate and the oil pump housing.

7. Remove the upper/lower timing belt covers-to-engine to engine bolts and the covers.
8. Using a piece of chalk or paint, mark the camshaft sprocket-to-timing belt and crankshaft sprocket-to-timing belt alignment marks; also, mark the direction of timing belt rotation (if reusing the belt).
9. Loosen the timing belt tensioner and remove the return spring. Remove the timing belt from the sprockets.
10. If removing the crankshaft sprocket, perform the following procedures:
    a. Remove the crankshaft pulley-to-crankshaft bolt.
    b. Using a Wheel Puller tool, press the crankshaft pulley from the crankshaft.
    c. Remove the crankshaft pulley plate and the crankshaft sprocket.

NOTE: It is good practice to remove the crankshaft oil seal when the crankshaft sprocket is removed.

11. If removing the camshaft sprocket(s), perform the following procedures:
    a. Remove the valve cover(s)-to-cylinder head bolts and the valve covers.
    b. Remove the camshaft sprocket-to-camshaft bolt and the camshaft sprocket.
12. Using a putty knife, clean the gasket mounting surfaces. Inspect the timing belt and the sprockets for cracks, wear and/or damage.
13. To install, align the timing marks, use new gaskets, sealant (if necessary) and reverse the removal procedures. Torque the camshaft sprocket(s)-to-camshaft bolt(s) to 58–65 ft. lbs., the crankshaft sprocket-to-crankshaft bolt to 90–98 ft. lbs., the timing cover-to-engine bolts to 26–42 inch lbs. Refill the cooling

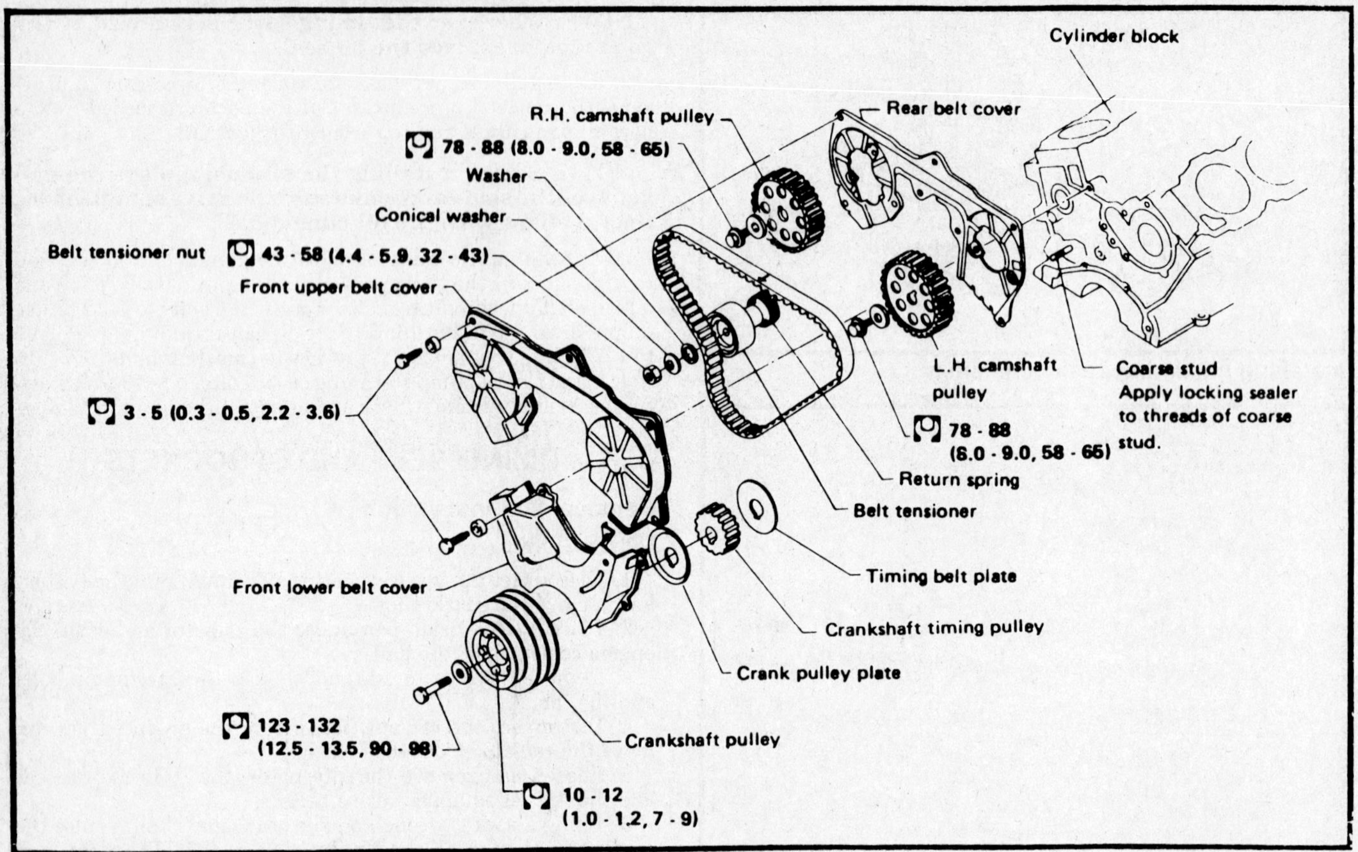

Exploded view of the timing belt and sprocket assembly – V6 engine

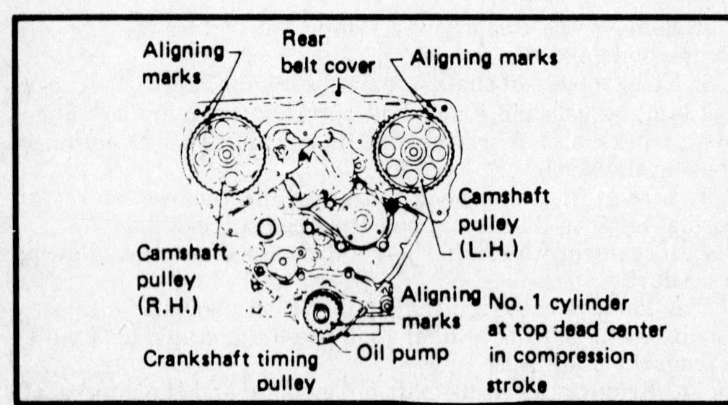

View of the camshaft and crankshaft sprocket timing marks – V6 engine

system. Start the engine, allow it to reach normal operating temperatures and check for leaks. Check and or adjust the ignition timing.

VALVE TIMING

Procedure

4-CYL ENGINE

1. Refer to the "Timing Chain and Sprocket, Removal and Installation" in this section, then, remove the valve cover the timing cover.

NOTE: Rotate the crankshaft until the No. 1 piston is at TDC of its compression stroke, the timing marks on the camshaft sprocket and crankshaft sprocket should align with the silver links of the timing chain.

2. If necessary, remove the camshaft sprocket-to-camshaft bolt and the sprocket along with the chain.

NOTE: When removing the timing chain, hold it where the chain tensioner contacts it. When the chain is removed, the tensioner will come apart. Hold on to it and don't lose any the parts. There is no need to remove the chain guide unless it is being replaced.

3. Position the camshaft sprocket with camshaft pin facing upwards. Position the crankshaft with the keyway facing upwards.
4. Align the timing chain silver links with the camshaft No. 2 punch mark and the crankshaft punch mark.
3. The No. 2 pin hole of the camshaft sprocket must align the camshaft pin.
4. To complete the installation, use new gaskets, sealant (if necessary) and reverse the removal procedures. Cut the portions needed from a new oil pan gasket and top front cover gasket.
5. Apply a light coating of oil to the crankshaft oil seal and carefully mount the timing cover to the front of the engine and install all of the mounting bolts. Torque the bolts to 7–12 ft. lbs. (8mm) or to 3–6 ft. lbs. (6mm), the oil pan-to-timing cover bolts to 4–7 ft. lbs., the camshaft sprocket-to-camshaft bolt to 87–116 ft. lbs. and the oil pump-to-timing cover bolts to 8–10 ft. lbs. Refill the cooling system. Check and/or adjust the ignition timing.

V6 ENGINE

1. Refer to the "Timing Belt and Sprockets, Removal and Installation" procedures in this section and remove the timing belt covers.
2. Using a socket wrench on the crankshaft bolt, rotate the crankshaft to position the No. 1 piston on the TDC of its compression stroke.

NOTE: Make sure the camshaft sprocket(s) punch mark is aligned with the marks on the rear timing plate and the crankshaft sprocket punch mark is aligned with oil pump housing mark.

3. If adjustment is necessary, loosen the timing belt tensioner and remove the timing belt from the sprockets.
4. To install, align the timing marks, use new gaskets, sealant (if necessary) and reverse the removal procedures. Torque the camshaft sprocket(s)-to-camshaft bolt(s) to 58–65 ft. lbs., the crankshaft sprocket-to-crankshaft bolt to 90–98 ft. lbs., the timing cover-to-engine bolts to 26–42 inch lbs. Refill the cooling system. Start the engine, allow it to reach normal operating temperatures and check for leaks. Check and or adjust the ignition timing.

Camshaft

Removal and Installation

4-CYL ENGINES

1. Refer to the "Rocker Arm/Shaft Assembly, Removal and Installation" procedures in this section, then, remove the rocker arm/shaft assembly.
2. Remove the camshaft from the cylinder head.

NOTE: Be sure to keep the disassembled parts in order for reinstallation purposes.

3. Inspect the camshaft for wear and/or damage, if necessary, replace the camshaft.

NOTE: When installing the camshaft, position it on the cylinder head with its dowel pin pointing upward.

4. To install, lubricate the camshaft and reverse the removal procedures. Torque the rocker arm/shaft assembly-to-cylinder head bolts to 11–18 ft. lbs., the camshaft sprocket-to-camshaft bolt to 87–116 ft. lbs. Readjust the valve clearances.

V6 ENGINES

1. Refer to the "Cylinder Head, Removal and Installation" procedures in this section and remove the cylinder head.

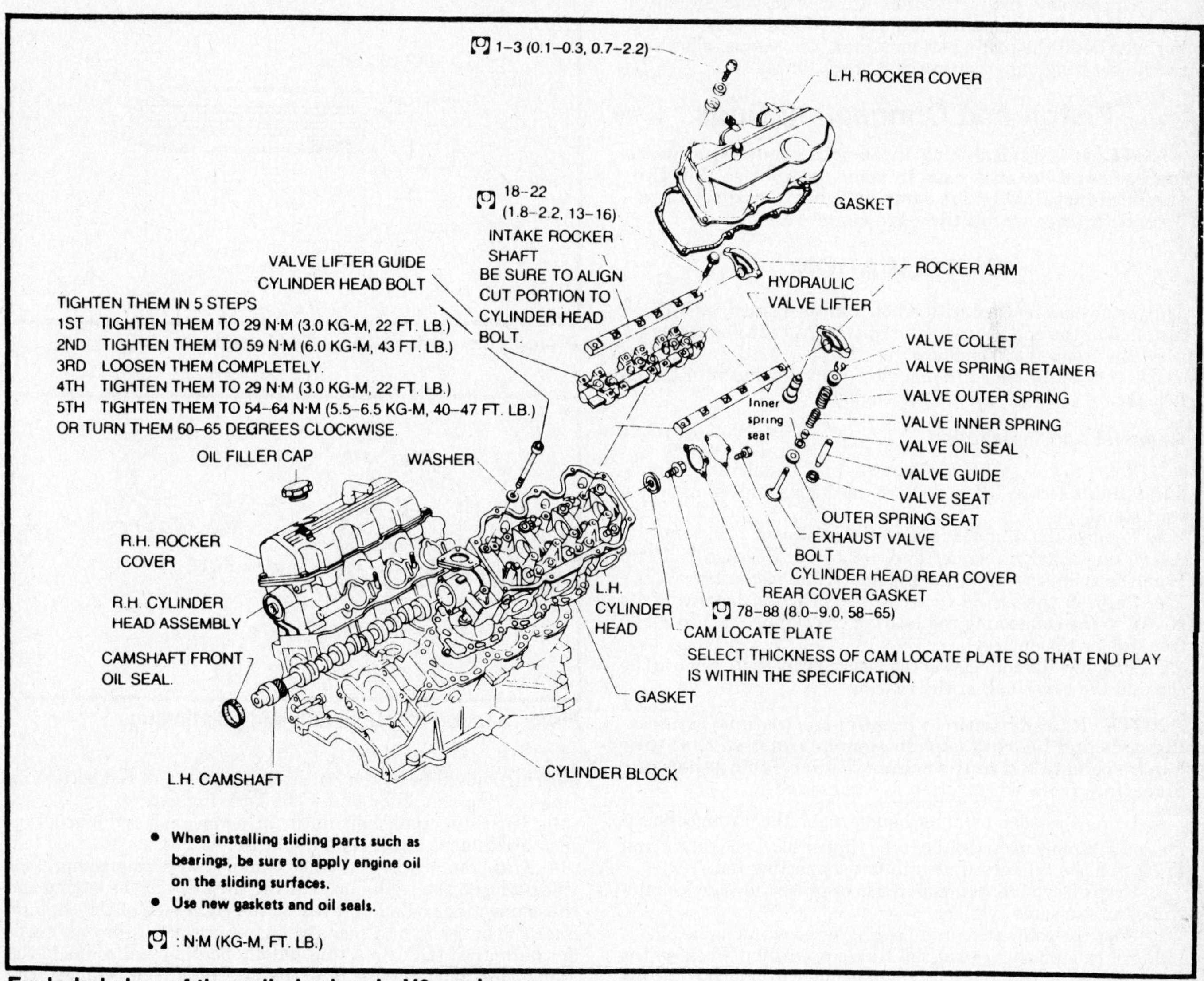

Exploded view of the cylinder head—V6 engine

2. Remove the rocker shafts with the rocker arms; loosen the bolts in two or three stages.
3. Remove the hydraulic valve lifters and lifter guide.

NOTE: Hold the valve lifters with a wire so they will not drop from the lifter guide. Place identification marks on the lifters to avoid mixing them up.

4. From the rear of the cylinder head, remove the cylinder head rear cover the camshaft bolt and the locating plate.
5. Remove the camshaft and the camshaft oil seal through the front of the cylinder head.
6. Using a putty knife, clean the gasket mounting surfaces.
7. To install the camshaft, perform the following procedures:
   a. Install the camshaft.
   b. Apply engine oil to the camshaft oil seal and install it in place.
   c. Adjust the camshaft end play with the correct locating plate.
8. Install the camshaft pulley(s).

NOTE: The right-side and the left-side camshaft pulleys are different parts. Install them in their correct positions. The right-side pulley has a "R3" identification mark and the left-side has an "L3".

9. To complete the installation, use new gaskets, sealant (if necessary) and reverse the removal procedures. Adjust the timing belt. Refill the cooling system. Start the engine, allow it to reach operating temperatures and check for leaks.

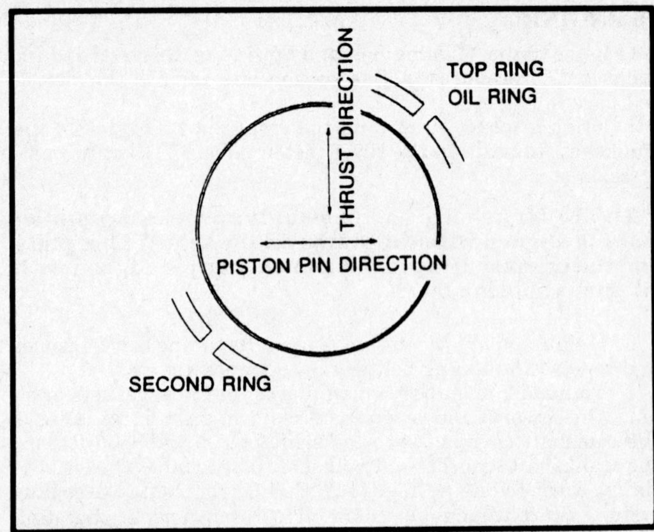

Arrangement of the piston ring gaps around the piston—4-cyl engines

Piston and Connecting Rods

NOTE: It is advisable to number the pistons, connecting rods and bearing caps in some manner so that they can be reinstalled in the same cylinder, facing the same direction from which they are removed.

IDENTIFICATION

The pistons are marked with a notch in the piston head. When installed in the engine, the notch markings are to be facing toward the front of the engine.

The connecting rods are installed in the engine with the oil hole facing the right-side of the engine.

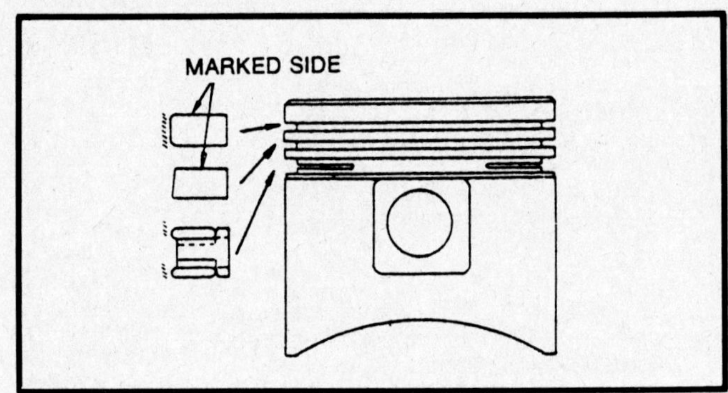

Piston ring installation—4-cyl engines

Removal and Installation

1. Refer to the "Engine, Removal and Installation" procedures in this section, then, remove the engine and secure it to a workstand.
2. Remove the cylinder head and the oil pan.
3. Using a Ridge Reamer tool, remove any carbon build up from the cylinder wall at the top end of the piston travel.
4. Position the piston to be removed at the bottom of its stroke so the connecting rod bearing cap can be reached easily from under the engine.
5. Unscrew the connecting rod bearing cap, then, remove the cap and the lower half of the bearing.

NOTE: It is advisable to number the pistons, connecting rods and bearing caps in some manner so that they can be reinstalled in the same cylinder, facing the same direction, from which they are removed.

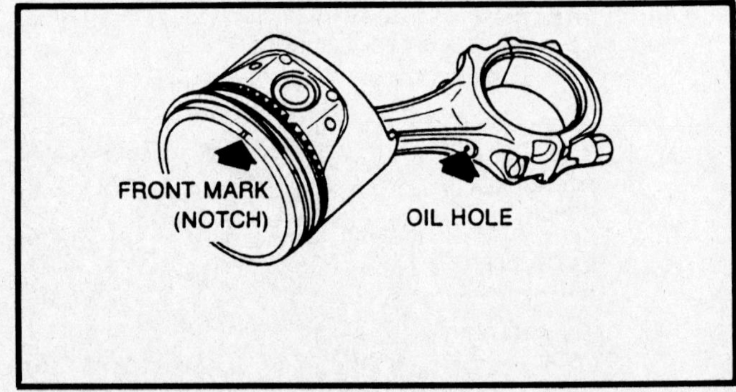

Piston and rod identification and positioning

6. Using a wooden hammer handle, push the piston/connecting rod assembly up and out of the cylinder block; be careful not to scratch the cylinder wall with the connecting rod.
7. Keep all cylinder components in order so they may be reinstalled in the same cylinder.
8. Coat the connecting rod bearing faces with engine oil.
9. Set the top ring gap at the 1 o'clock position. Position the 2nd ring gap at 180° opposite the top ring gap. The top oil ring rail gap should then be placed under the top ring gap, the expander ring should be at the 3 o'clock position and the bottom oil ring rail gap should be under the 2nd ring gap.
10. Turn the crankshaft until the connecting rod journal (of the particular cylinder) is brought to the TDC.
11. With the piston and rings clamped in a ring compressor (the notch on the piston head facing the front of the engine and the connecting rod oil hole facing the right-side of the engine), push the piston and the connecting rod assembly into the cylinder bore until the connecting rod big bearing end contacts the crankshaft journal. Use care not to scratch the cylinder wall with the connecting rod.

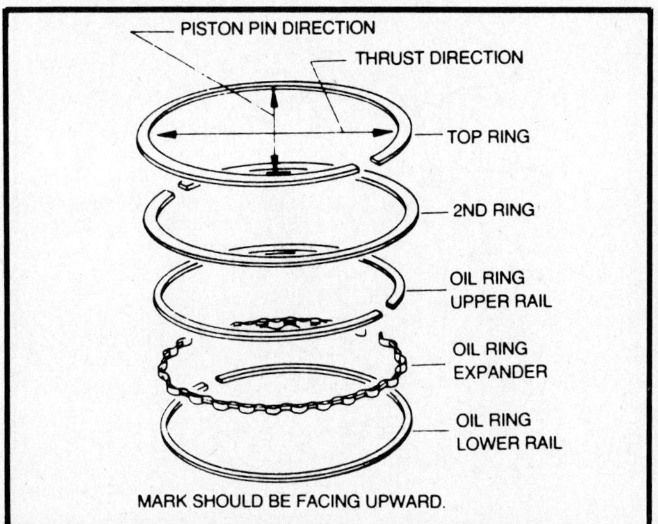

Exploded view of the piston rings—V6 engine

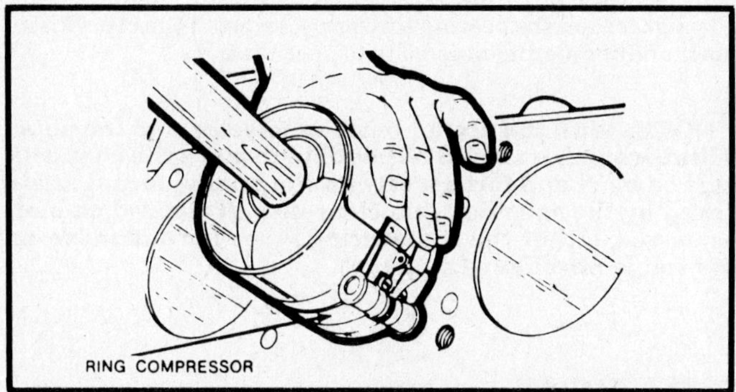

Using a ring compressor to install the piston/ring assemblies

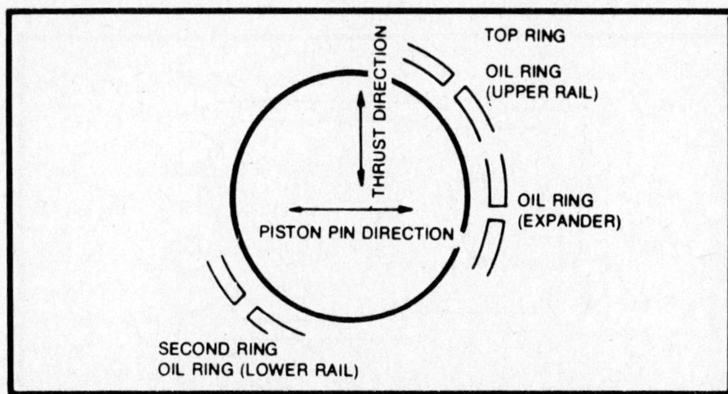

Location of the piston ring gaps—V6 engine

12. Push the piston down further, while turning the crankshaft, to the BDC. Align the connecting rod bearing cap with the connecting rod, then, torque the bearing cap to specifications.

NOTE: Be sure to use the Plastigage® method of checking the connecting rod-to-crankshaft bearing tolerances.

13. Install the other piston/connecting rod assemblies in the same order; be sure to turn the crankshaft after each installation to make sure there is no binding.

14. To complete the installation, use new gaskets, sealant (if necessary) and reverse the removal procedures. Start the engine, allow it to reach normal operating temperatures and check for leaks.

Connecting Rod and Main Bearings

Removal and Installation

Replacement bearings are available in standard and undersize (for reground crankshafts). The bearing-to-crankshaft clearance is checked using Plastigage® at either the top of bottom of each crank journal. The Plastigage® has a range of 0.001–0.003 in. (0.0254–0.0762mm).

1. Remove the bearing cap with the bearing shell. Completely clean the bearing shell and the crank journal, blow any oil from the oil hole in the crankshaft. Place the Plastigage® lengthwise, along the bottom center of the lower bearing shell. Install the cap with the shell and torque the bolt or nuts to specifications. DO NOT turn the crankshaft with the Plastigage® on the bearing.

2. Remove the bearing cap with the shell. The flattened Plastigage® will be found sticking to either the bearing shell or the crank journal. DO NOT remove it yet.

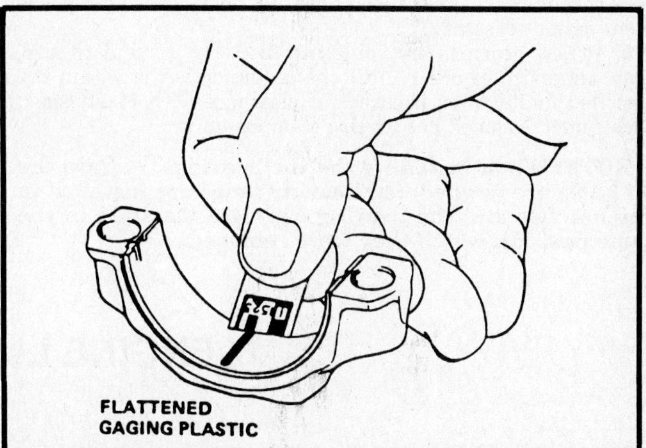

Plastigage® installed on the lower bearing shell

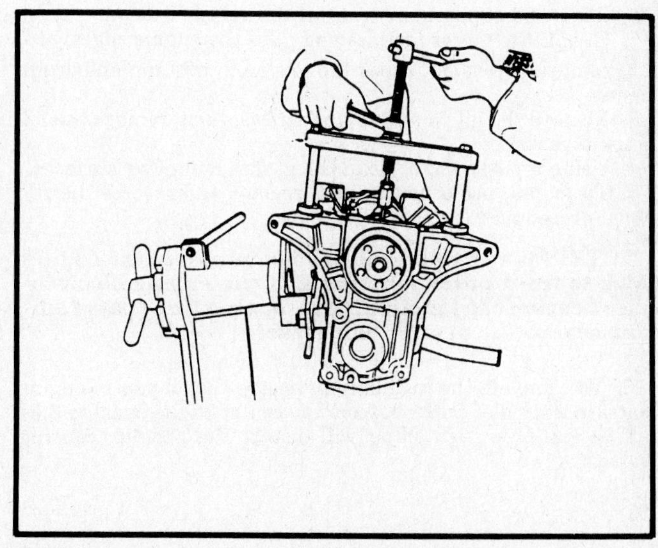

Removing the rear main bearing cap with a puller

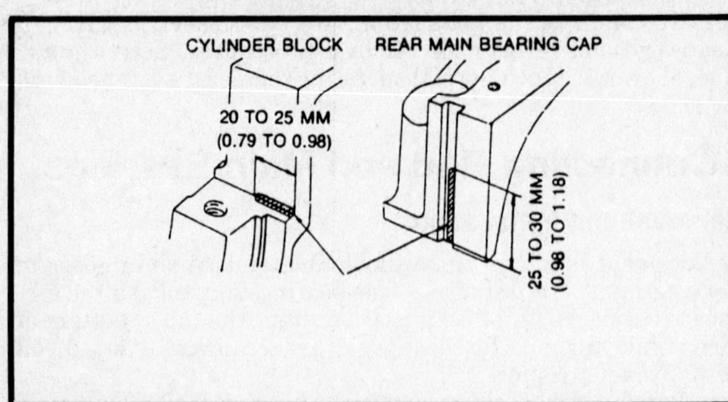

Application of sealer to the rear main bearing cap

3. Use the scale printed on the Plastigage® envelope to measure the flattened material at its widest point. The number within the scale which most closely corresponds to the width of the Plastigage® indicates the bearing clearance in thousandths of an inch.

4. Check the specification chart for the desired clearance. It is advisable to install a new bearing if the clearance exceeds 0.003 in. (0.0762mm); however, if the bearing is in good condition and is not being checked because of bearing noise, bearing replacement is not necessary.

5. If new bearings are being installed, try a standard size, each undersize in order until one is found that is within the specified limits when checked for clearance with Plastigage®; each undersize shell has its size stamped on it.

NOTE: When installing the the bearings, be sure the oil holes are aligned, the bearing tangs are installed in the notches and the bearing caps are installed in the same position which they were removed.

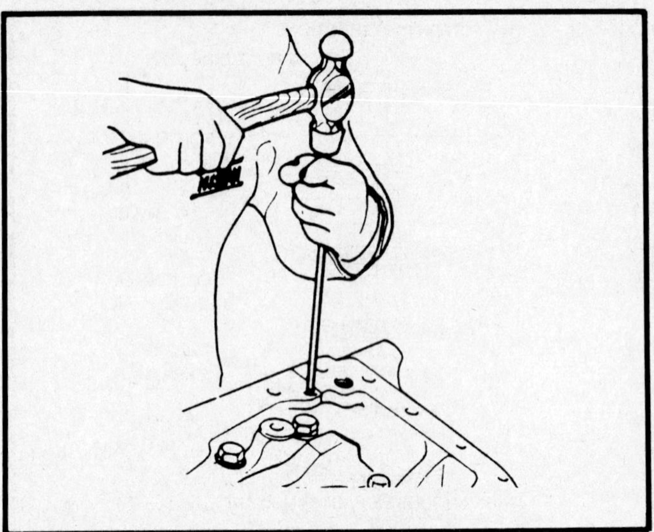
Installing the rear main bearing cap side seals

6. When the proper size shell is found, clean off the Plastigage®, oil the bearing throughly, reinstall the cap with its shell and torque the nuts/bolts to specifications.

NOTE: With the proper bearing selected and the nuts/bolts torqued, it should be possible to move the connecting rod back and forth freely on the crank journal as allowed by the specified end clearance. If the rod cannot be moved, either the rod bearing is too far undersize or the rod is misaligned.

ENGINE LUBRICATION

Oil Pan

Removal and Installation

1. Raise and support the front of the vehicle safely.
2. Unbolt the motor mounts and raise the engine slightly to gain removal clearance. Block the engine in position and drain the oil.
3. Remove the oil pan-to-engine screws, then, remove the oil pan and gasket.
4. Using a putty knife, clean the gasket mounting surfaces.
5. To install, use a new gasket, sealant and reverse the removal procedures.

NOTE: Apply a thin bead of silicone seal to the engine block-to-front cover junction and the engine block-to-main bearing cap junction, then, apply a thin coat of silicone seal to the new oil pan gasket.

6. To complete the installation, torque the oil pan-to-engine bolts (in a circular pattern, from the center to the ends) to 3.6–5.1 ft. lbs. Over tightening will distort the pan lip, causing leakage.

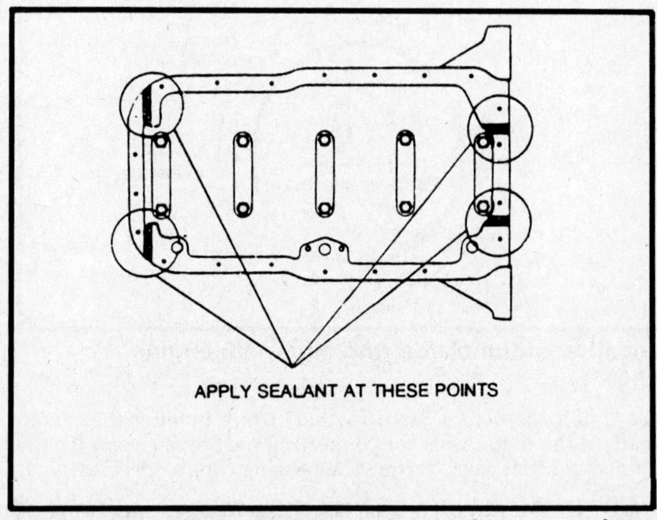

Apply a thin bead of silicone sealant to there areas before installation – 4-cyl engines

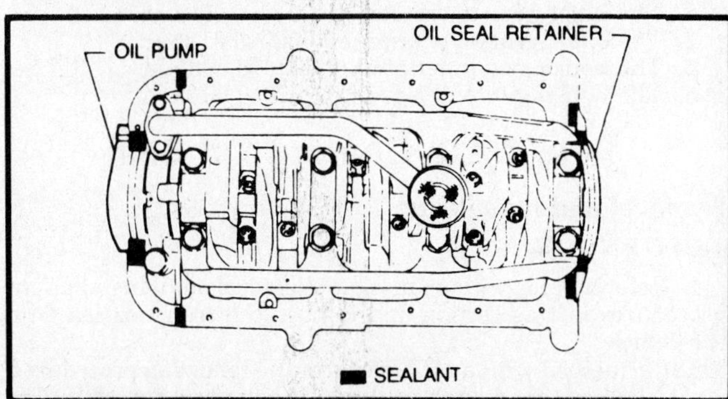

Apply sealant to these areas before installing the pan gasket on the block – V6 engines

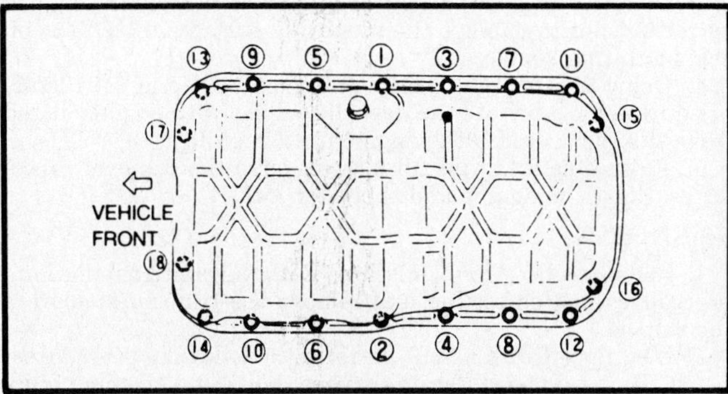

Oil pan bolt torque sequence – V6 engines

Oil Pump

Removal and Installation

4-CYL ENGINES

The oil pump is an external type, mounted to the right-side of the crankshaft pulley.

1. Rotate the crankshaft to position the No. 1 cylinder on the TDC of the compression stroke.
2. If equipped with a splash pan, remove it. If necessary, remove the stabilizer bar.
3. Remove the oil pump-to-housing bolts and the oil pump from the engine.

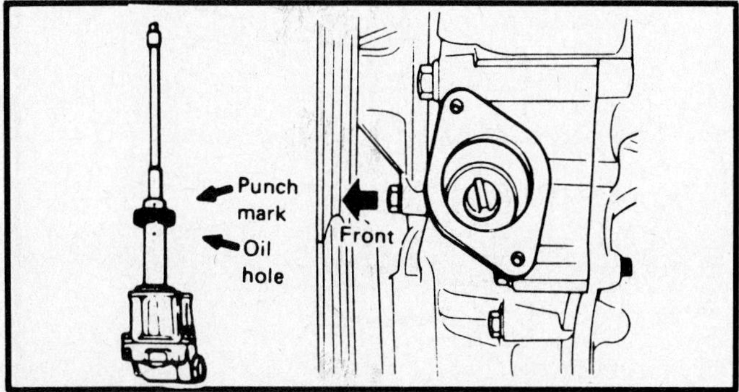

Aligning the oil pump marks before installing it into the housing – 4-cyl engines

4. Using a putty knife, clean the gasket mounting surfaces.
5. To install, use a new gasket, fill the oil pump with engine oil, align the drive spindle punch mark with the oil hole on the oil pump, then, insert the oil pump into the housing until the driveshaft tang fits into the distributor shaft notch. Torque the oil pump-to-engine housing bolts to 8–11 ft. lbs. Start the engine and check for leaks.

V6 ENGINES

The oil pump is mounted at the front of the engine behind the crankshaft pulley.

1. Raise and support the front of the vehicle safely. Drain the crankcase.
2. Refer to the "Oil Pan, Removal and Installation" and the "Timing Belt, Removal and Installation" procedures in this section, then, remove the oil pan and the timing belt.
3. Remove the crankshaft timing sprocket (it may be necessary to use a wheel puller) and the timing belt plate.

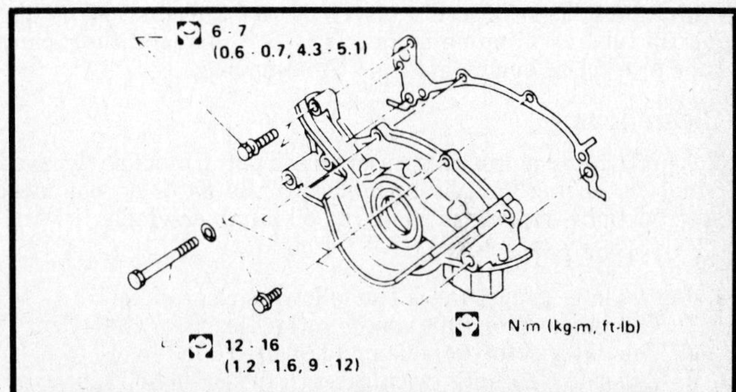

Exploded view of the oil pump – V6 (2WD) engine – 4WD is similar

4. Remove the oil pump strainer and the pickup tube from the oil pump.
5. Remove the oil pump-to-engine bolts and the oil pump from the engine.
6. Using a putty knife, clean the gasket mounting surfaces.

NOTE: When the oil pump is removed, it is a good idea to replace the oil seal.

7. To install, use new gaskets, silicone sealant, pack the oil pump cavity with petroleum jelly and reverse the removal procedures. Torque the oil pump-to-engine (6mm) bolts to 4.3–5.1 ft. lbs. (2WD) or 4.6–6.1 ft. lbs. (4WD), the oil pump-to-engine

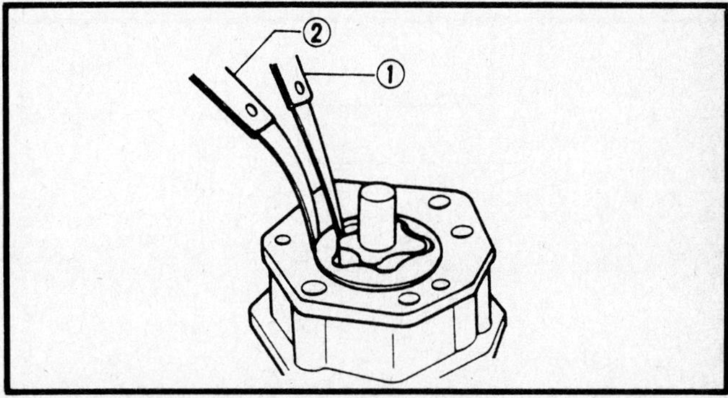

Inspecting the oil pump rotor clearances – 4-cyl engines

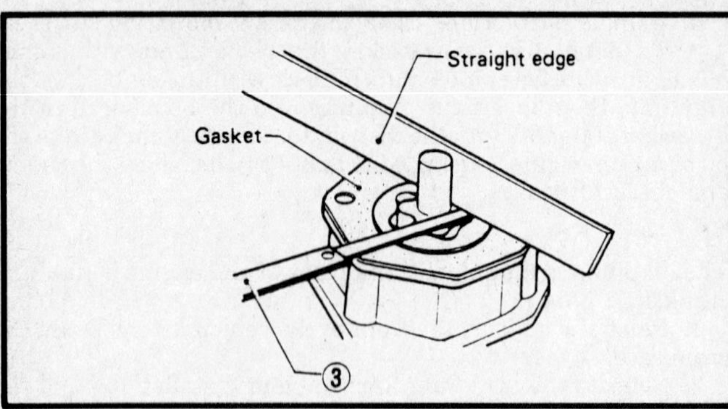

Inspecting the oil pump side clearance—4-cyl engines

(8mm) bolts to 9–12 ft. lbs. (2WD) or 16–22 ft. lbs. (4WD), the pickup tube-to-oil pump bolts to 12–15 ft. lbs. and the pickup tube bracket-to-engine bolt to 4.6–6.1 ft. lbs.

Clearances

To check the oil pump clearances, the oil pump must be removed from the engine and disassembled. If the parts do not meet specifications, replace them or the oil pump assembly.

4-CYL ENGINES

Using a feeler gauge, check the following clearances:

1. The inner rotor tip-to-outer rotor: less than 0.0047 in.
2. The outer rotor-to-housing: 0.0059–0.0083 in.
3. The side clearance (with gasket): 0.0016–0.0031 in.

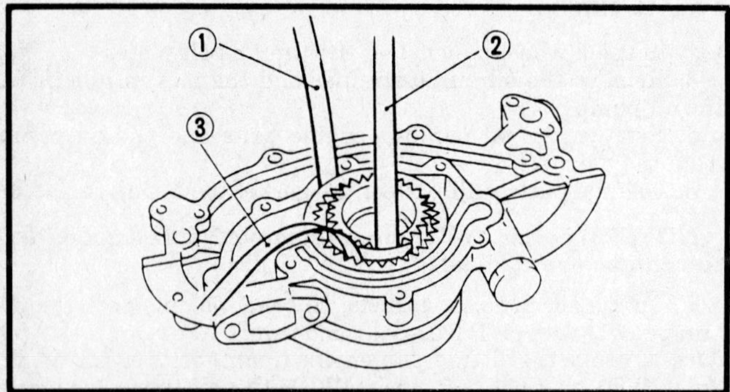

Inspecting the oil pump gear clearances—V6 engines

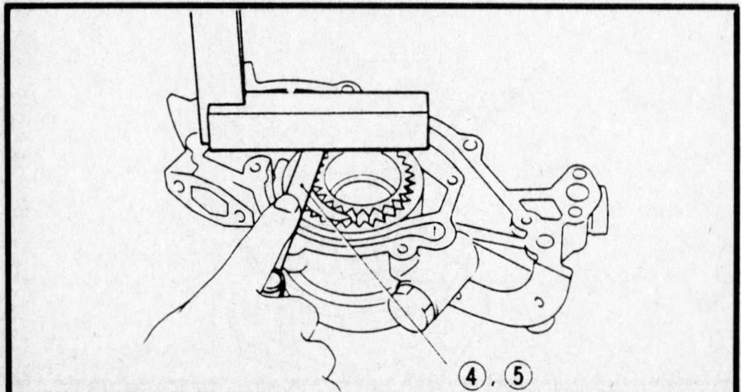

Inspecting the oil pump side clearances—V6 engines

V6 ENGINES

Using a feeler gauge, check the following clearances:

1. The pump body-to-outer gear: 0.0043–0.0079 in.
2. The inner gear-to-cressent: 0.0047–0.0091 in.
3. The outer gear-to-cressent: 0.0083–0.0126 in.
4. The housing-to-inner gear: 0.0020–0.0035 in.
5. The housing-to-outer gear: 0.0020–0.0043 in.

Rear Main Bearing Oil Seal

Removal and Installation

4-CYL ENGINE

1. Refer to the "Transmission, Removal and Installation" procedures in this section and remove the transmission from the vehicle.
2. If equipped with a M/T, perform the following procedures:
   a. Remove the clutch-to-flywheel bolts and the clutch assembly from the vehicle.
   b. Remove the flywheel-to-crankshaft bolts and the flywheel from the engine.
3. Using a small pry bar, pry the rear oil seal from the engine; be careful not to damage the mounting surfaces. Clean the oil seal mounting surfaces.
4. Using the Rear Oil Seal Installation tool No. KV10105500 or equivalent, lubricate the new oil seal lips with engine oil and drive the the seal into the engine until it seats.
5. To complete the installation, reverse the removal procedures. Start the engine and check for leaks.

V6 ENGINE

1. Refer to the "Transmission, Removal and Installation" procedures in this section and remove the transmission from the vehicle.
2. If equipped with a M/T, perform the following procedures:
   a. Remove the clutch-to-flywheel bolts and the clutch assembly from the vehicle.
   b. Remove the flywheel-to-crankshaft bolts and the flywheel from the engine.
3. Remove the oil seal retainer-to-engine bolts and the retainer from the engine.
4. Using a medium pry bar, pry the oil seal from the retainer; be careful not to damage the mounting surfaces. Clean the oil seal mounting surfaces.
5. Using the Rear Oil Seal Installation tool No. KV10105500 or equivalent, lubricate the new oil seal lips with engine oil and drive the the seal into the engine until it seats.
6. To complete the installation, new gaskets, sealant (if necessary) and reverse the removal procedures. Torque the oil seal retainer-to-engine bolts to 4.3–5.1 ft. lbs. Start the engine and check for leaks.

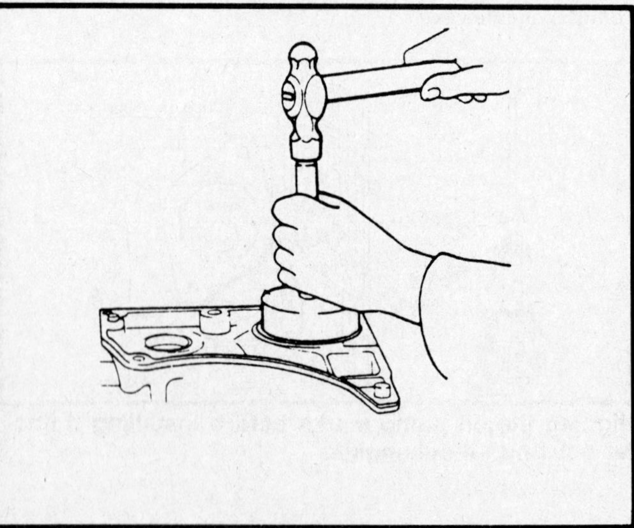
Installing the rear main seal

FRONT SUSPENSION

The Pickup front suspension is of an independent control arm type with torsion bar springs. The control arms are attached to a bracket which is welded to the frame at their inner pivot points and to the lower control arms. The torsion bar has splines on each end; the front-end is installed into the spring arm which is attached to the lower control arm and the rear-end is installed to the torsion bar anchor which is secured to the chassis frame. Fore-and-aft movement of the front suspension is controlled by a tension arm connected to the lower control arms at one end and mounted to the chassis frame at the forward end. The steering knuckle/spindle assembly is attached to the steering knuckle/spindle support by ball joints.

The Van front suspension is of a single (crossmember) type leaf spring which controls both sides of the vehicle.

1. Lock nut
2. Adjusting nut
3. Anchor arm
4. Dust cover

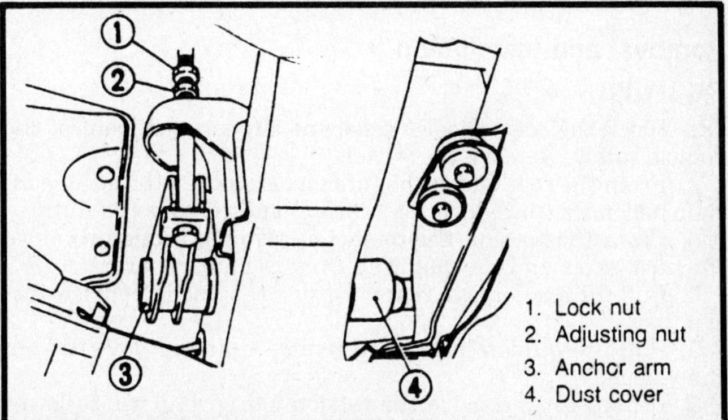

2-wheel drive torsion bar anchor

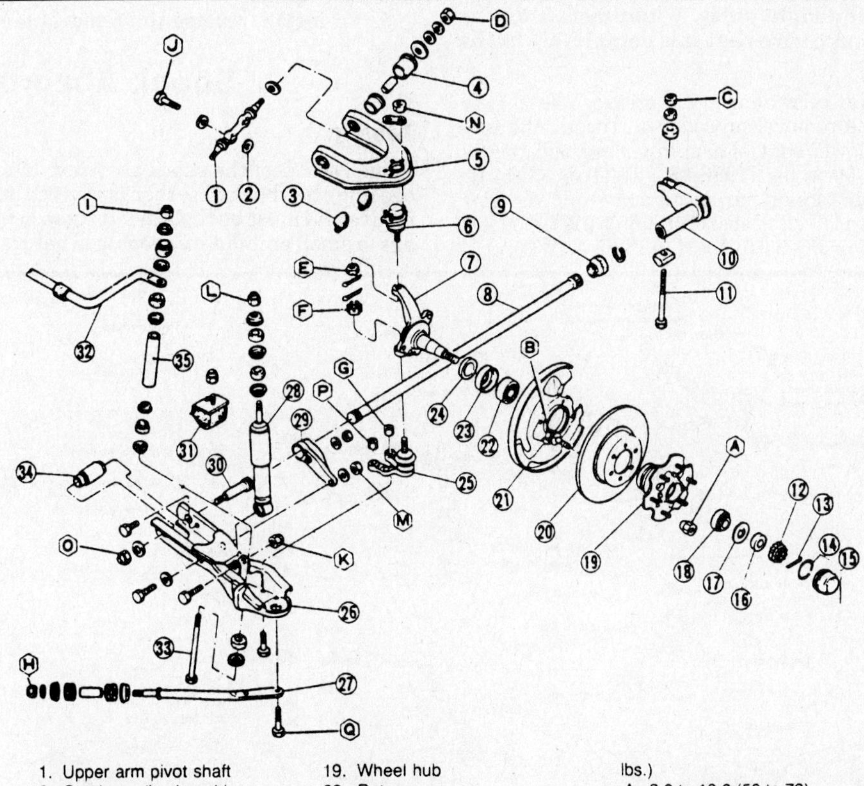

1. Upper arm pivot shaft
2. Camber adjusting shim
3. Rebound bumper
4. Bushing
5. Upper arm
6. Upper ball joint
7. Knuckle spindle
8. Torsion bar
9. Boot
10. Anchor arm
11. Anchor arm adjusting bolt
12. Adjusting nut
13. Cotter pin
14. O-ring
15. Hub cap
16. Spindle nut
17. Washer
18. Outer wheel bearing
19. Wheel hub
20. Rotor
21. Backing plate
22. Inner wheel bearing
23. Grease seal
24. Spacer
25. Lower ball joint
26. Lower arm
27. Tension rod (strut)
28. Shock absorber
29. Torque arm
30. Lower arm pivot shaft
31. Bumper stop
32. Stabilizer (optional)
33. Stabilizer connecting bolt
34. Lower arm bushing
35. Stabilizer collar
Tightening torque kg-m (ft. lbs.)
A. 8.0 to 10.0 (58 to 72)
B. 3.9 to 5.3 (28 to 38)
C. 3.1 to 4.1 (22 to 30)
D. 7.7 to 10.5 (56 to 76)
E. 8.0 to 10.0 (58 to 72)
F. 17.2 to 19.5 (124 to 141)
G. 3.9 to 5.3 (28 to 38)
H. 3.0 to 4.2 (22 to 30)
I. 1.6 to 2.2 (12 to 16)
J. 11.1 to 15.0 (90 to 108)
K. 3.1 to 4.1 (22 to 30)
L. 1.6 to 2.2 (12 to 16)
M. 2.7 to 3.7 (20 to 27)
N. 1.7 to 2.2 (12 to 16)
O. 11.1 to 15.0 (80 to 108)
P. 3.6 to 4.6 (26 to 33)
Q. 3.9 to 5.3 (28 to 38)

Exploded view of the front suspension system—2WD 1982-85

Spring

TORSION BAR

Removal and Installation

PICKUPS

1. Block the rear wheels. Raise and support the front of the vehicle safely. Remove the wheel.
2. From the rear end of the torsion bar, loosen the spring anchor bolt nuts (to reduce the tension) and remove the nuts.
3. From the torsion bar-to-anchor arm connection, remove the dust cover and the snapring from the anchor arm.
4. Pull the anchor arm rearward, disengaging it from the torsion bar.
5. Pull the torsion bar spring rearward and remove it from the vehicle.
6. If necessary, remove the torsion bar spring arm-to-lower control arm bolts/nuts and the spring arm from the vehicle.
7. Inspect the spring arm for wear, twist, bend or other damages; if necessary, replace it.

NOTE: The torsion bars are stamped with "L" and "R" indicating left and right sides. When installing the snapring, turn it to make sure that it is completely in the groove.

8. To install, coat the serrations with grease, use a new snapring and reverse the removal procedures. Torque the torsion bar spring arm-to-lower control arm inner nut/bolt to 26–33 ft. lbs. (1982-85), 37–50 ft. lbs. (1986-88 – 2WD) or 33–44 ft. lbs. (1986-88 – 4WD), the torsion bar spring arm-to-lower control arm outer nut/bolt to 20–27 ft. lbs. (1982-85 – 2WD), 37–50 ft. lbs. (1986-88 – 2WD) or 66–87 ft. lbs. (1986-88 – 4WD).
9. Lower the vehicle to the floor, bounce it a few times, allow the vehicle to come to rest, then, adjust the vehicle riding height. Adjust the anchor arm bolt until the "H" dimension is 4.88–5.08 in. (1982-83 – 2WD), 5.28–5.47 in. (1982-83 – 4WD), 4.45–4.61 in. (1984 – king cab) or 4.65–4.80 in. (1984 – regular cab), 5.04–5.20 in. (1985 – 2WD) or 2/09–2.24 in. (1985 – 4WD) and 4.37–4.53 in. (1986-88 – 2WD) or 1.73–1.89 in. (1986-88 – 4WD).

LEAF

Removal and Installation

1987-88 VAN

1. Refer to the "Lower Control Arm, Removal and Installation" procedures in this section and remove the lower control arm from one side.
2. From the opposite-side, loosen the leaf spring-to-lower control arm bolt.
3. Remove the leaf spring by sliding it from the opposite lower control arm.
4. Inspect the spring for wear and/or cracks; if necessary, replace the spring.
5. To install, reverse the removal procedures.

Shock Absorbers

Testing

Visually inspect the shock absorber. If there is evidence of leakage and the shock absorber is covered with oil, the shock is defective and must be replaced. If there is no sign of excessive leakage (a small amount of weeping is natural) bounce the vehicle at

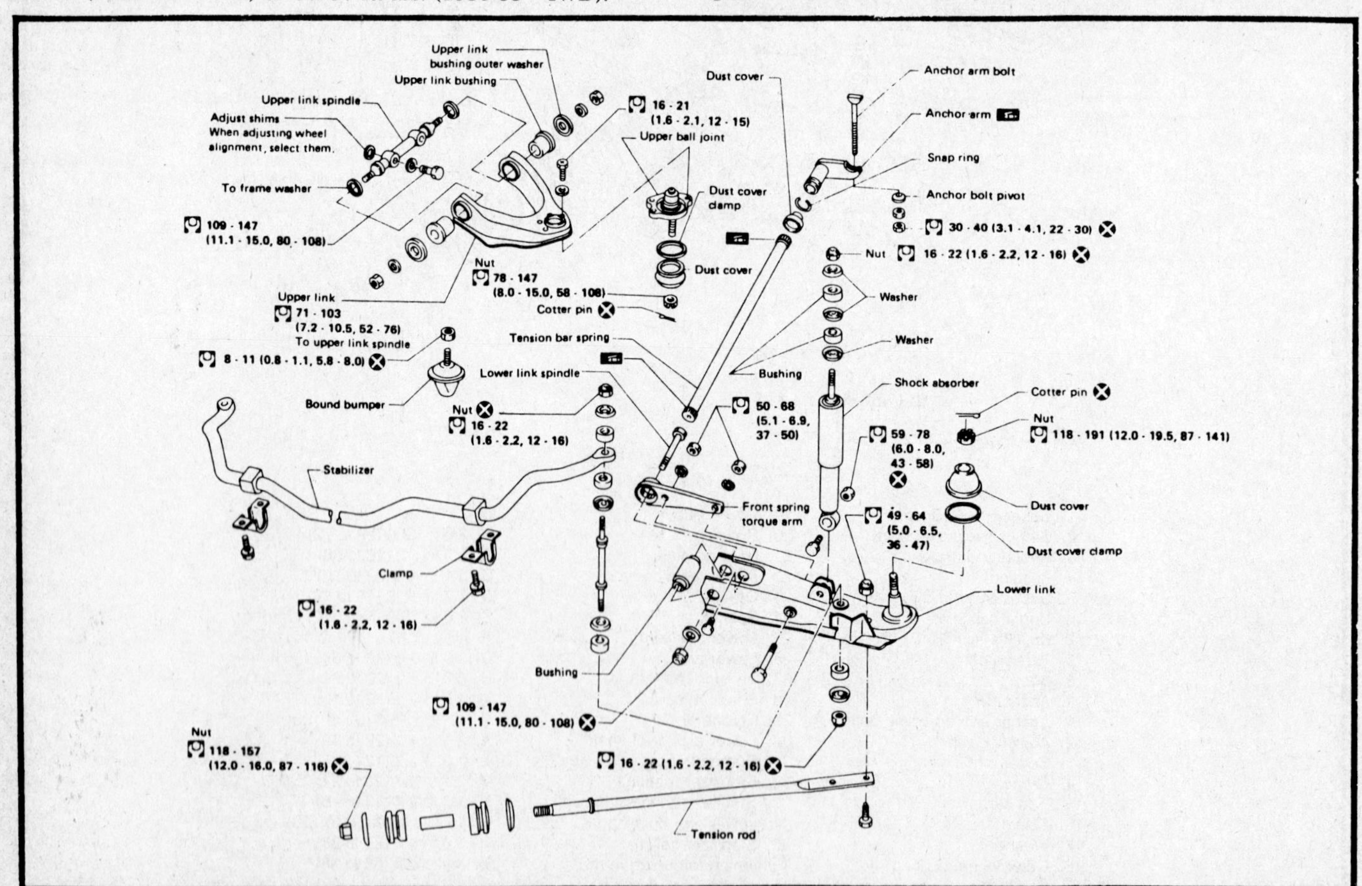

Exploded view of the front suspension system – 2WD Pickup (1986-88)

Exploded view of the front suspension system—4WD Pickup (1986-88)

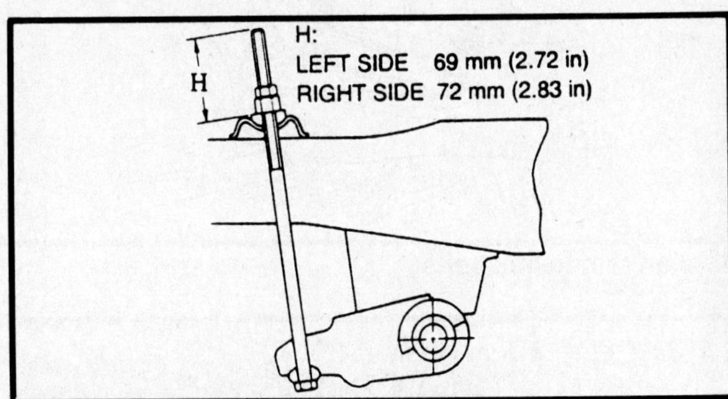

Anchor arm preliminary adjustment

one corner by pressing up and down on the fender or bumper. When you have the vehicle bouncing, stop and release the fender or bumper. The vehicle should stop bouncing after the first rebound. If the bouncing continues past the center point of the bounce more than once, the shock absorbers are worn and should be replaced.

Removal and Installation

1. Raise and support the front of the vehicle safely. Remove the wheel.
2. While holding the upper stem of the shock absorber, remove the shock absorber-to-chassis nut (Pickups) or nut/bolt (Van), washer and rubber bushing.
3. Remove the lower shock absorber-to-lower control arm nut/bolt (Pickups) or nut (Van) and the shock absorber from the vehicle.
4. To install, use new rubber bushings and reverse the removal procedures. Torque the shock absorber-to-lower control arm nut/bolt to 22–30 ft. lbs. (1982-83) or 43–58 ft. lbs. (1984-88) and the shock absorber-to-chassis nut to 12–16 ft. lbs. (Pickups) or nut/bolt to 22–30 ft. lbs. (Van)

Torsion bar spring anchor bolt

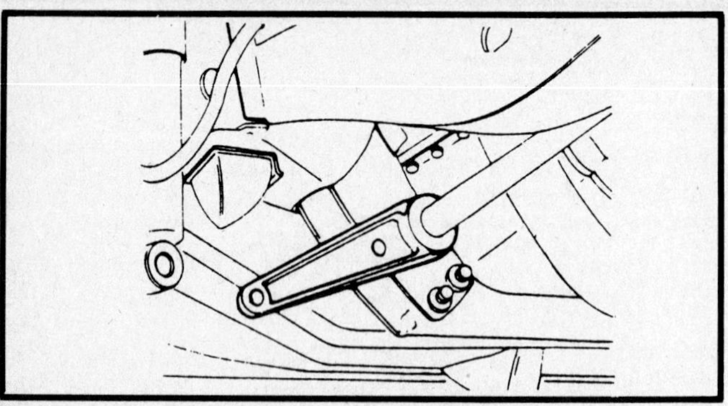

Torque arm-to-torsion bar attachment

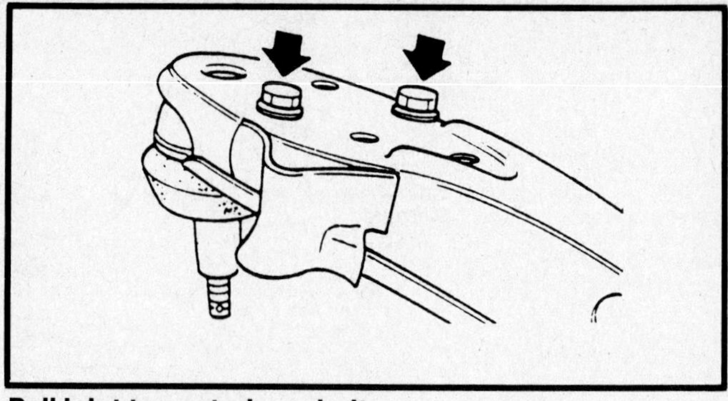

Ball joint-to-control arm bolts

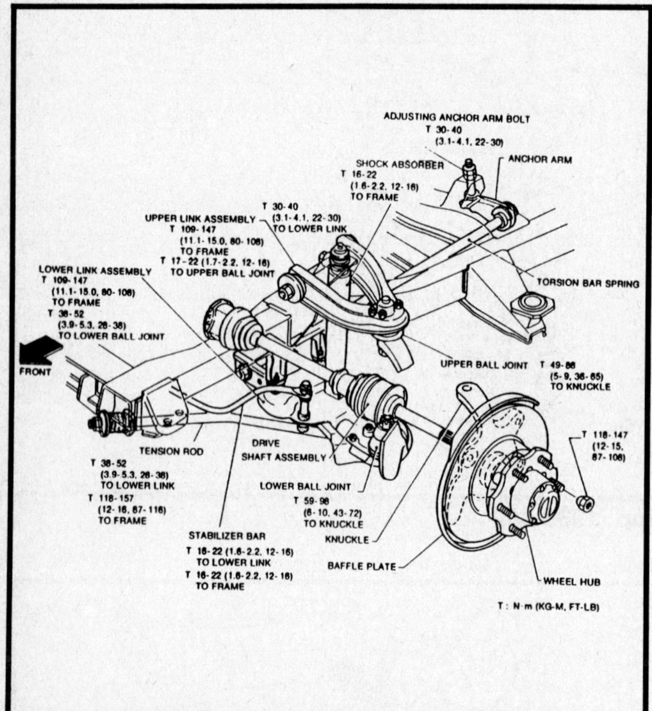

4-WD front suspension through 1983

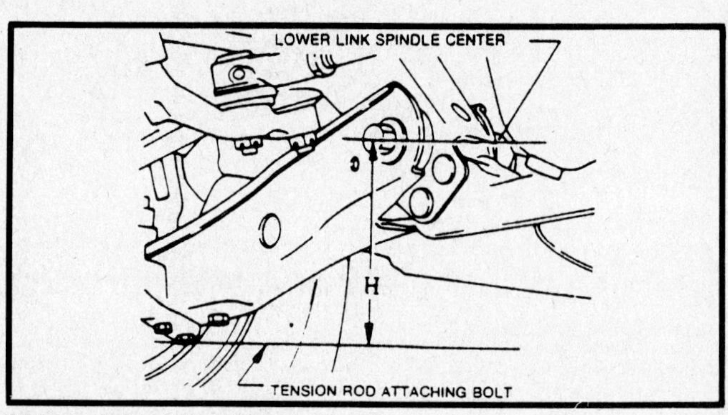

Ride height adjustment

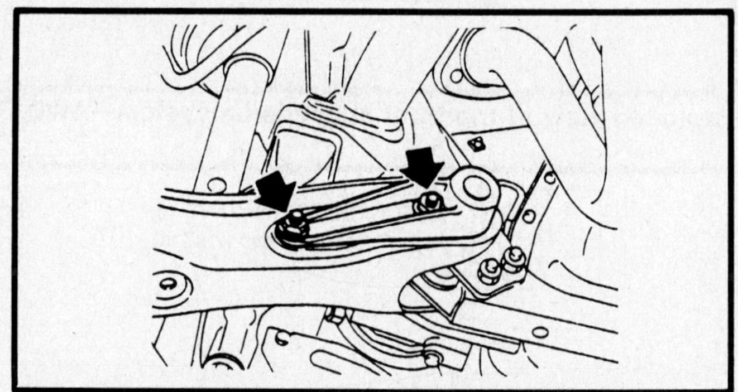

Torsion arm-to-link bolts

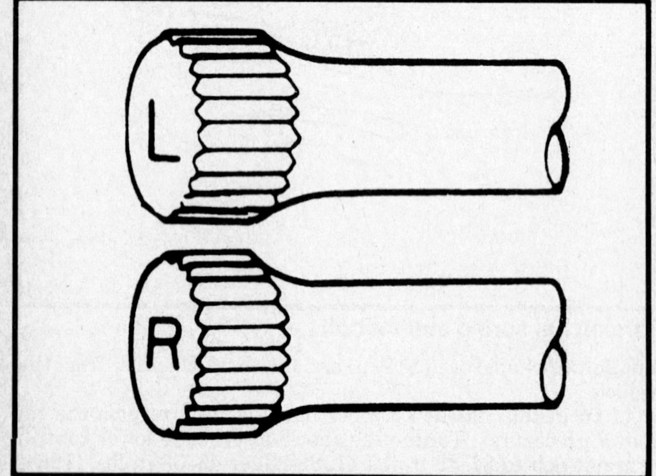

Torsion bar spring serrated ends. Note that they are marked and not interchangeable

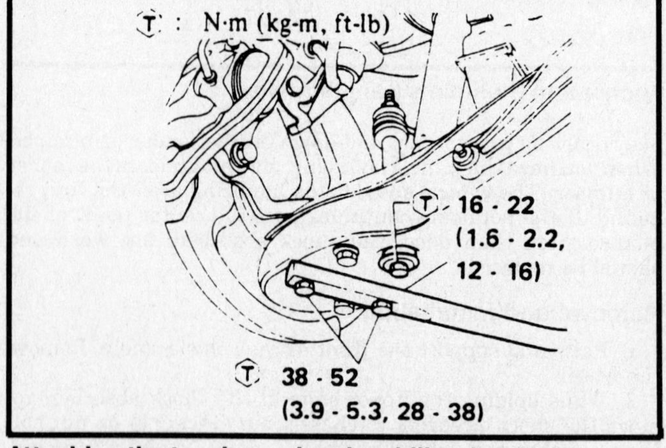

Attaching the tension rod and stabilizer bar to the lower control arm

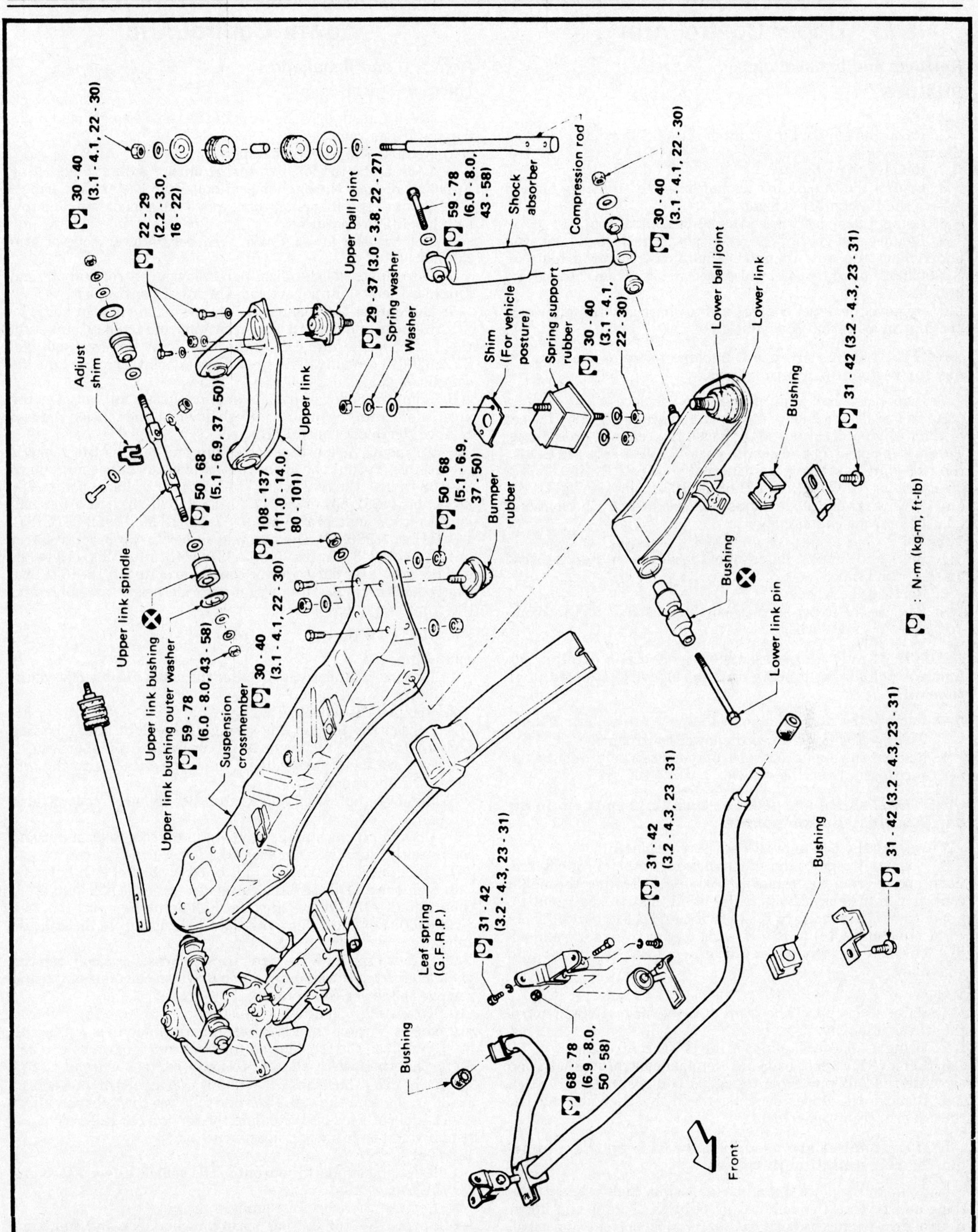
30 - 40 (3.1 - 4.1, 22 - 30)
22 - 29 (2.2 - 3.0, 16 - 22)
Adjust shim
Upper ball joint
29 - 37 (3.0 - 3.8, 22 - 27)
Spring washer
Washer
Upper link
50 - 68 (5.1 - 6.9, 37 - 50)
Upper link spindle
Upper link bushing
Upper link bushing outer washer
59 - 78 (6.0 - 8.0, 43 - 58)
Suspension crossmember
30 - 40 (3.1 - 4.1, 22 - 30)
108 - 137 (11.0 - 14.0, 80 - 101)
50 - 68 (5.1 - 6.9, 37 - 50)
Bumper rubber
59 - 78 (6.0 - 8.0, 43 - 58)
Shock absorber
Compression rod
30 - 40 (3.1 - 4.1, 22 - 30)
Shim (For vehicle posture)
Spring support rubber
30 - 40 (3.1 - 4.1, 22 - 30)
Lower ball joint
Lower link
31 - 42 (3.2 - 4.3, 23 - 31)
Bushing
Bushing
Lower link pin
: N·m (kg-m, ft-lb)
31 - 42 (3.2 - 4.3, 23 - 31)
31 - 42 (3.2 - 4.3, 23 - 31)
Leaf spring (G.F.R.P.)
31 - 42 (3.2 - 4.3, 23 - 31)
Bushing
31 - 42 (3.2 - 4.3, 23 - 31)
68 - 78 (6.9 - 8.0, 50 - 58)
Bushing
Front

Exploded view of the front suspension system—Van (1987–88)

Upper Control Arm

Removal and Installation

PICKUPS

1982-85

1. Raise and support the front of the vehicle safely placed on the frame rails.
2. Remove the wheels.
3. Loosen the torsion bar anchor lock and adjusting nuts to relieve the torsion bar tension.
4. Using a floor jack, raise the lower control arm.
5. Remove and discard the cotter pin from the ball joint stud and remove the nut. Using the Ball Joint Removal tool No. ST29020001 or equivalent, press the ball joint from the steering knuckle.
6. Remove the upper control arm-to-chassis bolts and the upper control arm from the vehicle.

NOTE: If shims are used, be sure to keep them in order for reinstallation purposes.

7. Inspect the ball joint, if necessary, replace it.
8. To install, use a new cotter pin, replace the shims (if used) in their original locations and reverse the removal procedures. Torque the upper control arm-to-chassis bolts to 80–108 ft. lbs., the ball joint-to-steering knuckle nut to 58–72 ft. lbs. (2WD), 36–65 ft. lbs. (4WD – 1982-83) or 58–108 ft. lbs. (4WD – 1984-85). Lower the vehicle and adjust the ride height. Check and/or adjust the front-end alignment.

1986-88

1. Raise and support the front of the vehicle on stands placed on the frame rails.
2. Remove the wheels.
3. Remove the upper shock absorber-to-chassis nut and compress the shock absorber.

NOTE: If may be necessary to loosen the torsion bar anchor lock and adjusting nuts to relieve the torsion bar tension.

4. Remove the upper ball joint-to-upper control arm bolts.
5. Using a floor jack, raise the lower control arm.
6. Remove the upper control arm-to-chassis bolts and the upper control arm from the vehicle.

NOTE: If shims are used, be sure to keep them in order for reinstallation purposes.

7. Inspect the ball joint, if necessary, replace it.
8. To install, replace the shims (if used) in their original locations and reverse the removal procedures. Torque the upper control arm-to-chassis bolts to 80–108 ft. lbs., the ball joint-to-upper control arm bolts to 12–15 ft. lbs. and the upper shock absorber-to-chassis nut to 12–16 ft. lbs. Lower the vehicle and adjust the ride height. Check and/or adjust the front-end alignment.

VAN

1. Raise and support the front of the vehicle safely. Remove the wheel assembly.
2. Using a floor jack, support the lower control arm.
3. Remove the upper ball joint-to-upper control arm bolts and separate the ball joint from the upper control arm.
4. Remove the upper control arm-to-chassis bolts and the control arm from the vehicle.

NOTE: If shims are used, be sure to keep them in order for reinstallation purposes.

5. To install, replace the shims (if used) in their original locations and reverse the removal procedures. Torque the upper control arm-to-chassis bolts to 37–50 ft. lbs. and the upper ball joint-to-upper control arm bolts to 16–22 ft. lbs. Check and/or adjust the front-end alignment.

Lower Control Arm

Removal and Installation

PICKUP – 2WD

1. Raise and support the front of the vehicle safely placed under the frame rails.
2. Remove the wheel assembly.
3. Loosen the torsion bar spring anchor lock and adjusting nuts and remove the anchor arm bolt from the anchor arm.
4. Remove the snapring, then, move the anchor arm and torsion bar fully rearward.
5. Remove the lower shock absorber-to-lower control arm nut/bolt.
6. Disconnect the stabilizer bar-to-lower control arm nut and separate the stabilizer bar from the lower control arm.
7. Disconnect the tension rod-to-lower control arm bolts.
8. Remove and discard the cotter pin from the ball joint stud, then, remove the nut. Using the Ball Joint Removal tool No. ST29020001 or equivalent, press the ball joint from the knuckle spindle.
9. Remove the lower control arm-to-chassis nut/bolt, tap the pivot shaft from the bushing. Push down on the tension rod and remove the lower control arm.
10. To install, use a new cotter pin and reverse the removal procedures. Torque the lower control arm-to-chassis nut/bolt to 80–108 ft. lbs., the tension rod-to-lower control arm bolt to 28–38 ft. lbs. (1982-85) or 36–47 ft. lbs. (1986-88), the lower ball joint-to-lower control arm nut to 87–123 ft. lbs. (1982-85) or 87–141 ft. lbs. (1986-88), the shock absorber-to-lower control arm nut/bolt to 22–30 ft. lbs. (1982-83) or 43–58 ft. lbs. (1984-88) and the stabilizer bar-to-lower control arm nut to 12–16 ft. lbs. Check and/or adjust the torsion bar ride height assembly and the front-end alignment.

PICKUP – 4WD

1982-83

1. Raise and support the front of the vehicle safely placed under the frame rails.
2. Remove the wheel assembly.
3. Loosen the torsion bar spring anchor lock and adjusting nuts and remove the anchor arm bolt from the anchor arm.
4. Remove the snapring, then, move the anchor arm and torsion bar fully rearward.
5. Remove the lower shock absorber-to-lower control arm nut/bolt.
6. Disconnect the stabilizer bar-to-lower control arm nut and separate the stabilizer bar from the lower control arm.
7. Disconnect the tension rod-to-lower control arm bolts.
8. Remove and discard the cotter pin from the ball joint stud, then, remove the nut. Using the Ball Joint Removal tool No. ST29020001 or equivalent, press the ball joint from the knuckle spindle.
9. Remove the lower control arm-to-chassis nut/bolt, tap the pivot shaft from the bushing. Push down on the tension rod and remove the lower control arm.
10. To install, use a new cotter pin and reverse the removal procedures. Torque the lower control arm-to-chassis nut/bolt to 80–108 ft. lbs., the tension rod-to-lower control arm bolt to 28–38 ft. lbs., the lower ball joint-to-lower control arm nut to 87–123 ft. lbs., the shock absorber-to-lower control arm nut/bolt to 22–30 ft. lbs. and the stabilizer bar-to-lower control arm nut to 12–16 ft. lbs. Check and/or adjust the torsion bar ride height assembly and the front-end alignment.

1984-88

1. Raise and support the front of the vehicle safely placed under the frame rails.
2. Remove the wheel assembly.
3. Loosen the torsion bar spring anchor lock and adjusting nuts and remove the anchor arm bolt from the anchor arm.
4. Remove the snapring, then, move the anchor arm and tor-

sion bar fully rearward.

5. Remove the lower shock absorber-to-lower control arm nut/bolt.

6. Disconnect the stabilizer bar-to-lower control arm nut and separate the stabilizer bar from the lower control arm.

7. Disconnect the compression rod-to-lower control arm bolts.

8. Remove and discard the cotter pin from the ball joint stud, then, remove the nut. Using the Ball Joint Removal tool No. ST29020001 or equivalent, press the ball joint from the knuckle spindle.

9. Remove the lower control arm-to-chassis nut/bolt, tap the pivot shaft from the bushing. Push down on the compression rod and remove the lower control arm.

10. To install, use a new cotter pin and reverse the removal procedures. Torque the lower control arm-to-chassis nut/bolt to 80–108 ft. lbs., the compression rod-to-lower control arm nut to 87–116 ft. lbs. (1984-85) or 87–108 ft. lbs. (1986-88), the lower ball joint-to-lower control arm nut to 87–123 ft. lbs. (1984-85) or 87–141 ft. lbs. (1986-88), the shock absorber-to-lower control arm nut/bolt to 43–58 ft. lbs. and the stabilizer bar-to-lower control arm nut to 12–16 ft. lbs. Check and/or adjust the torsion bar ride height assembly and the front-end alignment.

VAN

1. Raise and support the front of the vehicle safely.
2. Remove the wheel/tire assembly.
3. From the lower ball joint, remove the cotter pin (discard it), then, loosen the lower ball joint nut (do not remove it).
4. Remove the tie rod-to-steering knuckle nut, then, install the nut upside-down (to prevent damage to the nut). Using the Tie Rod Removal tool No. HT72520000 or equivalent, press the tie rod from the steering knuckle.
5. Using a floor jack, support the steering knuckle assembly.
6. Disconnect the brake caliper from the steering knuckle and support it on a wire; do not disconnect the brake hose.
7. Remove the upper ball joint-to-upper control arm bolts.
8. Using the Ball Joint Removal tool No. ST29020001 or equivalent, press the lower ball joint from the lower control arm. Remove the lower ball joint nut and the steering knuckle from the vehicle.
9. Remove the stabilizer bar brackets-to-lower control arm bolts and swing the stabilizer down (away) from the lower control arm.
10. Remove the shock absorber-to-lower control arm nut and the compression rod-to-lower control arm bolts, then, separate the shock absorber and compression rod from the lower control arm.
11. Lower the floor jack to take the spring pressure off the lower control arm.
12. Remove the leaf spring-to-lower control arm nut and support rubber.
13. Remove the lower control arm-to-suspension crossmember nut/bolt and the lower control arm.

NOTE: When installing the leaf spring and spring support rubber, be certain the washer does not protrude beyond the end surface of the leaf spring.

14. To install, reverse the removal procedures. Torque the lower control arm-to-suspension crossmember nut/bolt to 80–101 ft. lbs., the leaf spring-to-lower control arm nut to 22–27 ft. lbs., the stabilizer bar-to-lower control arm bolt to 23–31 ft. lbs., the upper ball joint-to-upper control arm bolts to 16–22 ft. lbs., the lower ball joint-to-steering knuckle nut to 124–141 ft. lbs., the tie rod-to-steering knuckle nut to 40–72 ft. lbs., the compression rod-to-lower control arm bolts to 22–30 ft. lbs. and the lower shock absorber-to-lower control arm nut to 22–30 ft. lbs. Check and/or adjust the front-end alignment.

Ball Joints

Inspection

The ball joint(s) should be replaced when play becomes excessive. The manufacturer does not publish specifications on just what constitutes excessive play, relying instead on a method of determining the force (in inch pounds) required to keep the ball joint turning. This method is not very helpful to the backyard mechanic since it involves removing the ball joint, which is what we are trying to avoid in the first place. An effective way to determine ball joint play is to raise the vehicle until the wheel is just a few inches off the ground and the ball joint is unloaded, which means not to jack directly under the ball joint. Place a long bar under the tire and move the wheel and tire assembly up and down; place one hand on top of the tire while you are doing this. If there is over 1/4 in. of play at the top of the tire, the ball joint is probably bad. This assuming that the wheel bearings are in good shape and properly adjusted. As a double check, have someone watch the ball joint while you move the tire up and down with the bar. If considerable play is seen, besides feeling play at the top of the wheel, the ball joints need to be replaced.

Removal and Installation

UPPER

1. Raise and support the front of the vehicle on stands placed on the frame rails.
2. Remove the wheel/tire assembly.

NOTE: On the Pickup models, it may be necessary to loosen the torsion bar anchor lock and adjusting nuts to relieve spring tension.

3. Place a floor jack under the steering knuckle and support it.
4. Remove and discard the cotter pin from the ball joint stud, then, loosen the nut. Using the Ball Joint Removal tool No. ST29020001 or equivalent, press the upper ball joint from the lower control arm. Remove the upper ball joint nut.
5. Remove the upper ball joint-to-upper control arm bolts and the ball joint from the vehicle.
6. To install, use a new ball joint, a new cotter pin and reverse the removal procedures. Torque upper ball joint-to-upper control arm bolts to 12–16 ft. lbs. and the upper ball-to-steering knuckle nut to 58–72 ft. lbs. (2WD Pickup – 1982-85), 36–65 ft. lbs. (4WD Pickup – 1982-83), 58–108 ft. lbs. (4WD Pickup – 1984-85), 58–108 ft. lbs. (Pickups – 1986-88) or 40–72 ft. lbs. (Van – 1987-88). Check and/or adjust the ride height and the front-end alignment.

LOWER

The lower control arm ball joint on the 2WD Pickup models (1986-88) is not removable; if the ball joint is defective, replace the lower control arm. For further information, please refer to the "Lower Control Arm, Removal and Installation" procedures in this section and replace the lower control arm.

1. Raise and support the front of the vehicle safely placed on the frame rails.
2. Remove the wheel/tire assembly.

NOTE: On the Pickup models, loosen the torsion bar spring anchor lock and adjusting nuts and remove the anchor arm bolt from the anchor arm. Remove the snapring, then move the anchor arm and torsion bar fully rearward. This procedure is to relieve the spring pressure on the lower control arm.

3. If equipped, it may be necessary to disconnect the stabilizer bar from the lower arm.
4. Disconnect the tension rod from the lower arm.
5. Remove the cotter pin (discard it) from the ball joint stud and loosen the nut.

6. Using the Ball Joint Separator tool No. ST29020001 or equivalent, press the ball joint from the steering knuckle.
7. Remove the lower ball joint-to-lower control arm bolts and the ball joint.
8. To install, use a new cotter pin and reverse the removal procedures. Torque the new ball joint-to-control arm bolts to 28–38 ft. lbs. (Pickups – 1982-85) or 35–45 ft. lbs. (4WD Pickup – 1986-88), the ball joint-to-steering knuckle nut to 87–123 ft. lbs. (2WD Pickup – 1982-85), 43–72 ft. lbs. (4WD Pickup – 1982-83), 87–123 ft. lbs. (4WD Pickup – 1984-85), 87–141 ft. lbs. (Pickups – 86-88) or 124–141 ft. lbs. (Van – 1987-88). Check and/or adjust the torsion bar ride height assembly and the front-end alignment.

Wheel Bearings

2WD MODELS

For 4WD model vehicles, please refer to the Front Drive Axle section.

Only the front wheel bearings require periodic service. The lubricant to use is high temperature disc brake wheel bearing grease meeting NLGI No.2 specifications. You will not need any special tools for this job, although the use of a torque wrench is strongly recommended for accurate measurement of bearing preload. The most important thing to remember when working with the wheel bearings is that although they are basically durable, in some ways they are remarkably fragile. Mishandling, grit, misalignment, scratches, improper preload, etc. will quickly destroy any roller bearing, no matter how well hardened during manufacture.

Removal and Installation PICKUP – 2WD

1. Loosen the wheel nuts, then, raise and support the front of the vehicle safely. Remove the wheel/tire assembly.
2. Remove the brake caliper-to-steering knuckle bolts and suspend the caliper on a wire.
3. Using 2 small pry bars, pry the grease cap from the wheel hub. Remove the cotter pin (discard it), the adjusting cap nut, the adjusting nut, the thrust washer and the outside wheel bearing. Pull the hub/disc assembly from the wheel spindle.

NOTE: It is not necessary to remove the disc from the hub.

3. Using a hammer and a brass drift, drive the inside wheel bearing, the grease seal (discard it) and the inside outer race, then, invert the hub/disc assembly and remove the outside outer race.
4. Using solvent clean all of the parts, then, allow them to air dry or blow them dry with compressed air.

NOTE: Do not use a cloth to dry the parts, you risk leaving bits of lint in the races.

5. Inspect the wheel bearings for wear, cracks, pits, burns, scoring or etc., if necessary, replaced them; do not mix old and new parts.
6. Using multi-purpose grease, coat the wheel bearing parts throughly.
7. Using the Wheel Bearing Race Installation tool No. KV401021S0 or equivalent, drive the races into the wheel hub until they seat.

NOTE: Use care not to cock the bearing cups in the hub. If they are not fully seated, the bearings will be impossible to adjust properly.

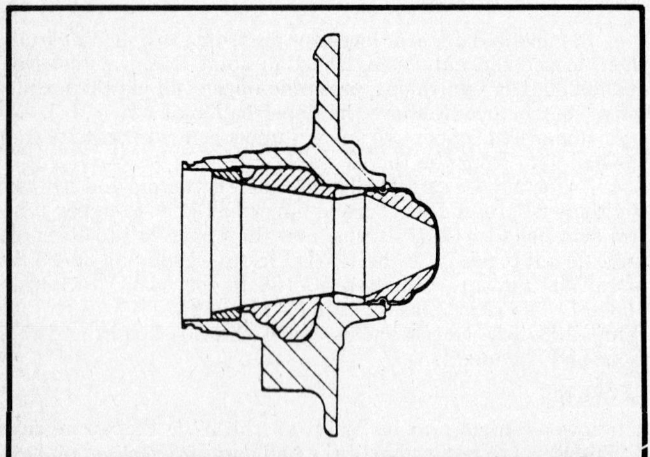

Fill the shaded portion of the hub and grease cap with wheel bearing grease. Also coat the cups with grease

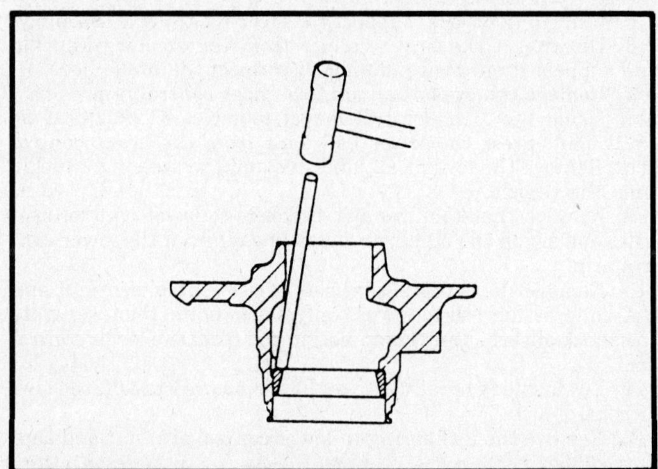

Drive worn bearing cups from the hub with a soft drift and hammer

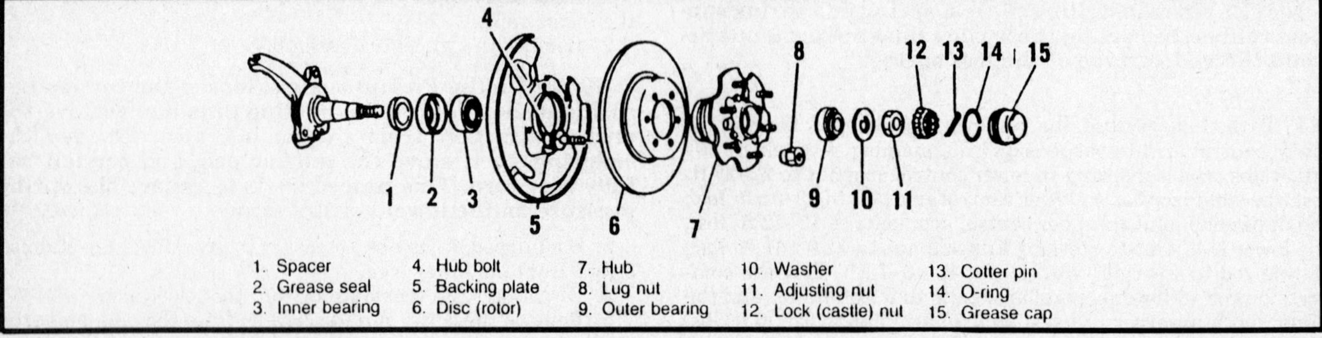

2-wheel drive hub and bearings

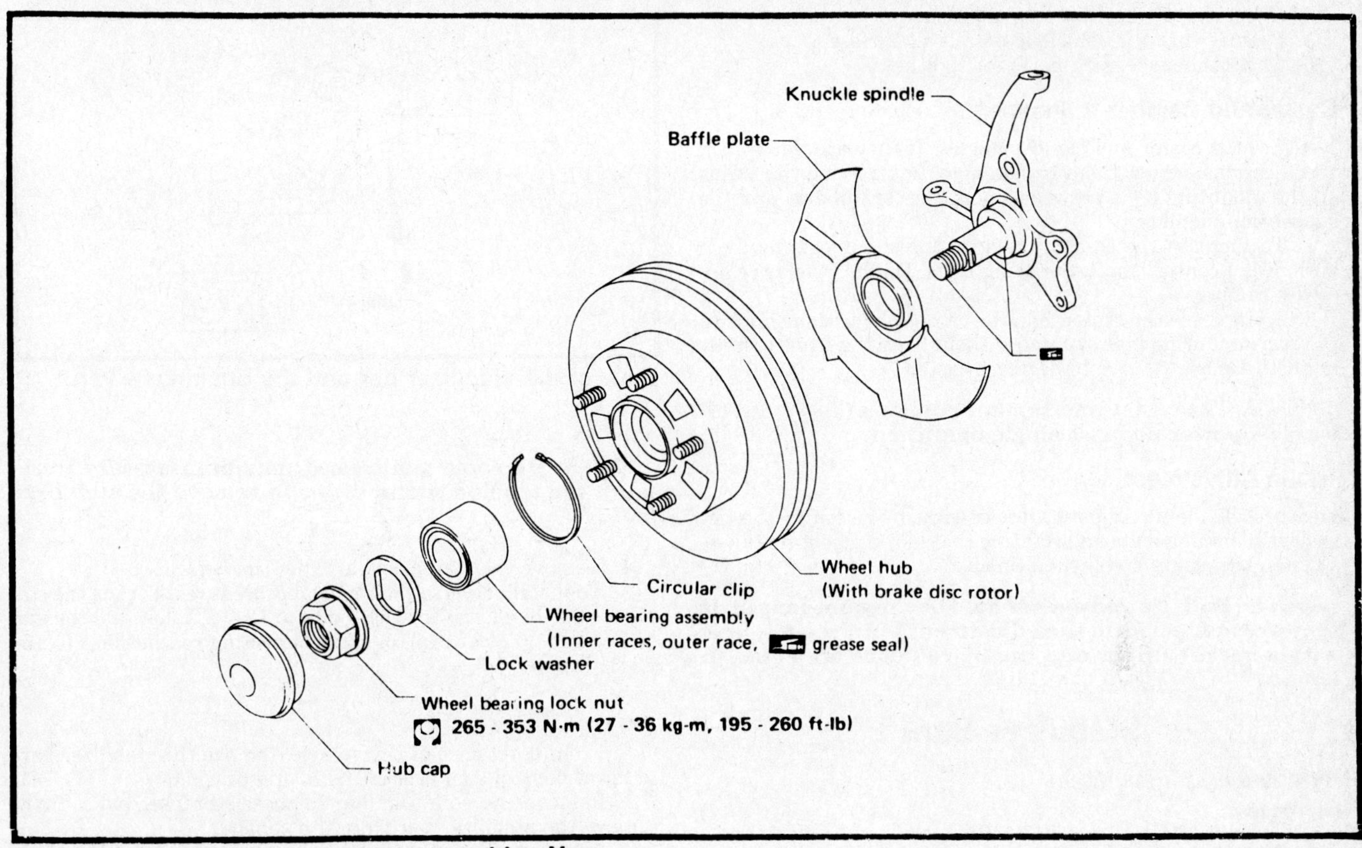

Exploded view of the front wheel assembly—Van

8. Using the multi-purpose grease, pack the internal areas of the hub and cups.
9. To pack the wheel bearing with grease, perform the following procedures:
   a. Place a large glob of grease into the palm of one hand.
   b. Using a rolling motion and push the wheel bearing; continue packing until the grease begins to ooze through the roller gaps.
10. Install the inner bearing into its cup in the hub. Drive the new grease seal (bearing side is indicated) into the wheel hub until it is flush.
11. To complete the installation, use a new cotter pin and reverse the removal procedures. Adjust the wheel bearing.

VAN

1. Loosen the wheel lug nuts. Raise and support the front of the vehicle safely. Remove the wheel/tire assembly.
2. Remove the caliper-to-steering knuckle bolts and the caliper. Using a wire, suspend the caliper from the vehicle; do not disconnect the brake hose from the caliper.
3. Remove the grease cap from the wheel hub.
4. Remove the wheel bearing nut and the lock washer. Pull the rotor/wheel hub from the spindle.
5. Remove the lock ring from the rotor/wheel hub.
6. Using a hydraulic press, press the wheel bearing and grease seal from the rotor/wheel hub assembly.
7. Using a new bearing, press it into the rotor/wheel hub assembly until it seats; use no more than 3 tons pressure. Install a new lock ring into the rotor/wheel hub.
8. To complete the installation, reverse the removal procedures. Torque the wheel bearing nut to 195–260 ft. lbs.

Adjustment

2WD PICKUPS

NOTE: The Van models do not require an adjustment procedure.

1. Raise and support the front of the vehicle safely. Remove the grease cup and the cotter pin and the adjusting nut retainer.

NOTE: If the wheel bearings have not been replaced, loosen the wheel bearing adjusting nut.

2. Using a torque wrench, torque the wheel bearing nut (while turning the wheel) to 22–29 ft. lbs.
3. Rotate the wheel hub a few more times to snug down the bearings.
4. Retighten the nut to 25–29 ft. lbs. Unscrew the adjusting nut 1/8 turn (45°). Install the lock nut (castellated nut) and snug it down against the adjusting nut until one of its grooves aligns with the a spindle hole.

NOTE: It is OK to tighten the adjusting nut up to 15° to allow the lock nut holes to align.

5. Install a new cotter pin, bending its ends around the lock nut.
6. Check the axial play of the wheel by shaking it back and forth. The bearing free-play should feel close to zero but the wheel should spin freely.

Alignment

Procedures

Front-end alignment measurements require the use of special equipment. Before measuring alignment or attempting to adjust it, always check the following points:

1. Be sure that the tires are properly inflated.
2. See that the wheels are properly balanced.
3. Check the ball joints to determine if they are worn or loose.

4. Check front wheel bearing adjustment.
5. Be sure that the vehicle is on a level surface.
6. Check all suspension parts for tightness.

Caster and Camber Adjustments

Measure the caster and camber angles. If they are not within specifications, adjust them by adding or subtracting the shims on the mounting bolts between the upper control arm and the suspension member:

1. To increase the camber, remove the shims equally from both of the control shaft mounting bolts. Do the reverse to decrease camber.
2. To increase the caster, add the camber adjusting shims to the rear mounting bolt or remove them from the front mounting bolt. Do the reverse to decrease caster.

NOTE: The caster and camber adjustments should always be performed in a single operation.

Toe-in Adjustment

Measure the toe-in. Adjust it, if necessary, by loosening the tie-rod end clamping bolts and rotating the tie-rod adjusting tubes. Tighten the clamp bolts when finished.

NOTE: Both tie-rod ends should be the same length. If they are not, perform the adjustment until the toe-in is within specifications and the tie-rod ends are equal in length.

Stabilizer Bars

Removal and Installation

PICKUPS

1. If equipped with a splash shield, remove it.
2. From both sides of the vehicle, remove the stabilizer bar-to-lower control arm connecting rod nut, bushings and tube.
3. Remove the stabilizer bar-to-chassis bracket bolts and brackets.

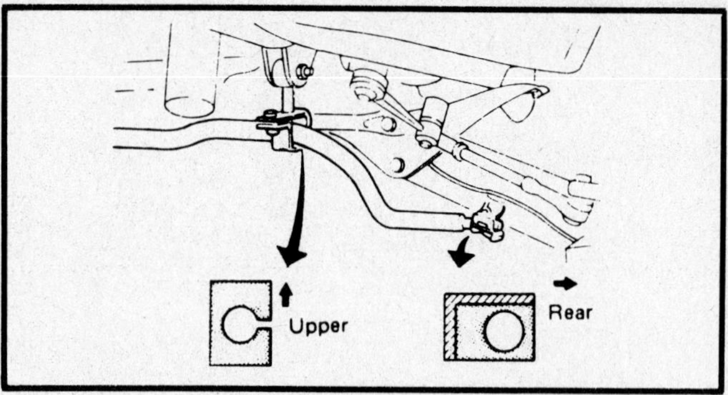

View of the stabilizer bar and the bushings—Van

NOTE: On some vehicles, it may be necessary to remove the tension rod in order to remove the stabilizer bar.

4. Remove the stabilizer bar from the vehicle.
5. To install, reverse the removal procedures. Torque the stabilizer bar-to-chassis bracket bolts to 12–16 ft. lbs. and the stabilizer bar-to-lower control arm connecting rod nut/bolt to 16–22 ft. lbs.

VAN

1. From both sides of the vehicle, remove the stabilizer bar-to-lower control arm bracket bolts and brackets.
2. Remove the stabilizer bar-to-chassis bracket bolts, then, remove the stabilizer bar from the vehicle.
3. Inspect the bushing for damage; replace them, if necessary.
4. To install, reverse the removal procedures. Torque the stabilizer bar-to-chassis bracket bolts to 23–31 ft. lbs. and the stabilizer bar-to-lower control arm bracket bolts to 23–31 ft. lbs.

STEERING GEAR AND LINKAGE

For overhaul information, please refer to "Steering" in the Unit Repair Section.

Manual Steering Gear

Manual steering gears are used on Pickups only.

Removal and Installation

1. Raise and support the front of the vehicle safely.
2. Remove the wormshaft-to-rubber coupling bolt.
3. Matchmark the idler arm and sector shaft and with the wheels in a straight ahead position, remove the idler arm-to-sector shaft nut.
4. Using the Steering Gear Arm Puller tool No. ST29020001 or equivalent, press the gear arm from the steering knuckle.
5. Remove the steering gear-to-chassis bolts and the steering gear from the vehicle.
6. To install, reverse the removal procedures. Torque the wormshaft coupling bolt to 29–36 ft. lbs. (1982-85) or 17–22 ft. lbs. (1986-88); the steering gear-to-gear arm nut to 94–108 ft. lbs. and the steering gear-to-frame bolts to 62–71 ft. lbs.

Adjustment

WORM GEAR PRELOAD

For this procedure, the steering gear must be removed from the and placed in a vise.

1. Using the Lock Nut Wrench tool No. KV481001500 or equivalent, loosen the lock nut.
2. Rotate the worm shaft a few times (in both directions) to settle the worm bearing and check the preload.
3. Using the Adjusting Plug Wrench tool No. KV48101400 or equivalent, the Torque Wrench tool No. ST3127S000 or equivalent, and the Adapter Socket tool No. KV48100700 or equivalent, check the worm bearing preload; it should be 3.5–5.2 inch lbs. (1982-83) or 1.7–5.2 inch lbs. (1984-88).
4. If necessary to adjust the worm gear preload, turn the adjusting plug and recheck the preload.
5. With the worm gear preload set, use the Adjusting Plug Wrench tool No. KV48101500 or equivalent, and the Lock Nut Wrench tool No. KV481001500 or equivalent, hold the adjusting plug and tighten the lock nut.

STEERING GEAR PRELOAD

1. Loosen the adjusting screw lock nut.
2. Rotate the worm shaft a few times (in both directions) to settle the worm bearing and check the preload.
3. Set the worm gear in the straight-ahead position.
4. Using the Torque Wrench tool No. ST3127S000 or equivalent, and the Adapter Socket tool No. KV48100700 or equiva-

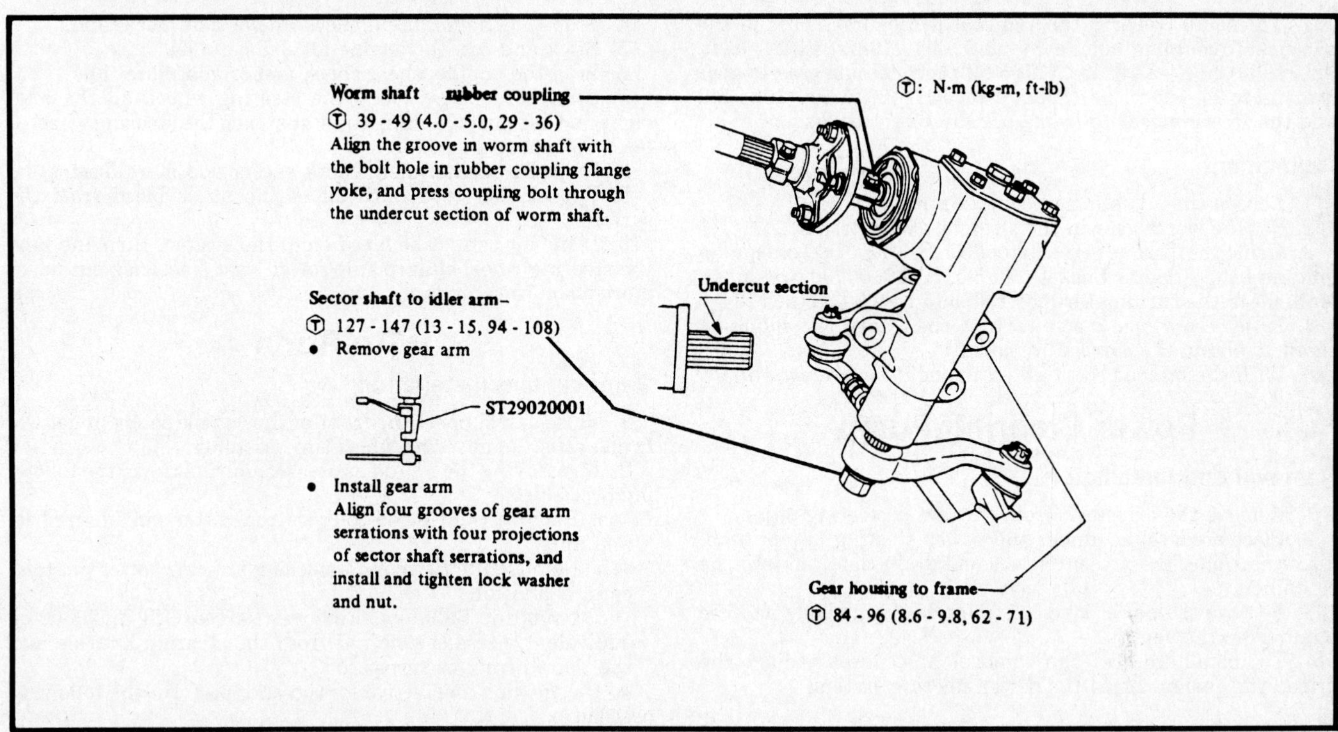

Manual steering gear removal and installation

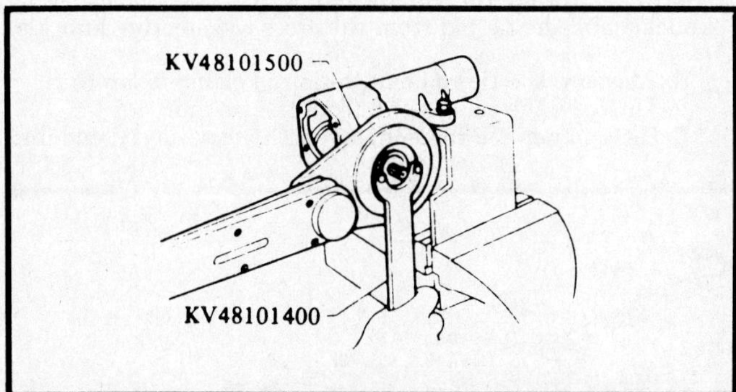

Adjusting the manual steering worm gear lock nut—Pickups

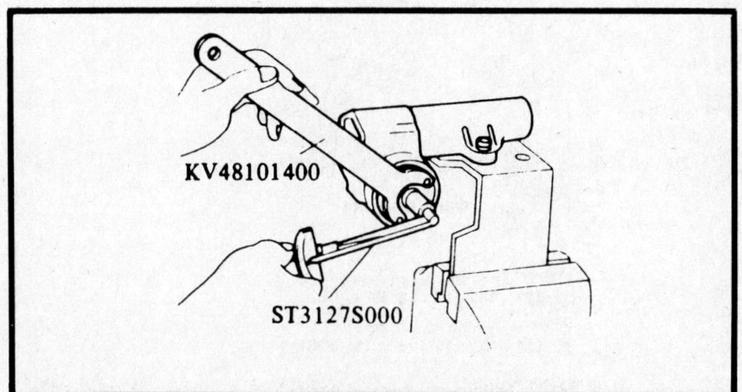

Adjusting the manual steering worm bearing preload—Pickups

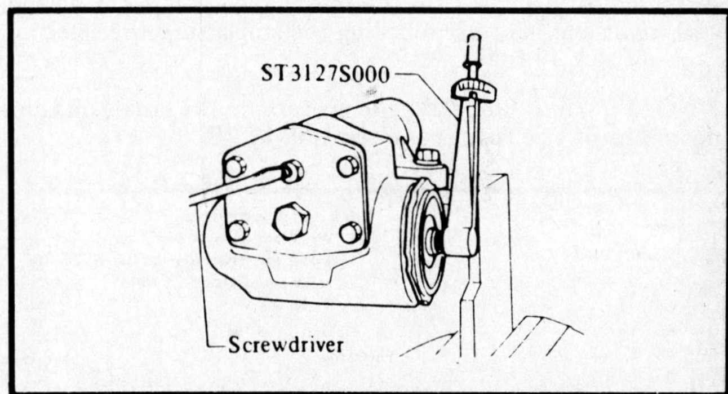

Adjusting the manual steering gear preload—Pickups

lent, check the worm gear preload; it should be 7.4–10.9 inch lbs. (new parts) or 5.2–8.7 inch lbs. (used parts).

5. If necessary, use a screwdriver, then, turn the adjusting screw to obtain the correct preload.
6. With the preload set, tighten the adjusting screw nut.

Power Steering Gear

Removal and Installation

1. Raise and support the front of the vehicle safely.
2. Remove the wormshaft-to-rubber coupling bolt.
3. Matchmark the idler arm and sector shaft and with the wheels in a straight-ahead position, remove the idler arm-to-sector shaft nut.
4. Disconnect the fluid lines from the gear, then, cap the lines and openings in the gear.
5. Using the Steering Gear Arm Puller tool ST29020001 or equivalent, press the gear arm from the steering knuckle.
6. Remove the steering gear-to-chassis bolts and the steering gear from the vehicle.

7. To install, reverse the removal procedures. Torque the wormshaft coupling bolt to 24–28 ft. lbs. (1982-84), 29–36 ft. lbs. (1985) or 17–22 ft. lbs. (1986-88); the steering gear-to-gear arm nut to 94–108 ft. lbs. (1982-83) or 101–130 ft. lbs. (1984-88) and the steering gear-to-frame bolts to 62–71 ft. lbs.

Adjustment

1. Loosen the adjusting screw lock nut.
2. Set the worm gear in the straight-ahead position.
3. Using the Torque Wrench tool No. ST3127S000 or equivalent, and the Adapter Socket tool No. KV48100700 or equivalent, check the turning torque; it should be 0.9–3.5 inch lbs.
4. If necessary, use a screwdriver, then, turn the adjusting screw to obtain the correct preload.
5. With the preload set, tighten the adjusting screw nut.

Power Steering Pump

Removal and Installation

1. Remove the drive belt from the power steering pump.
2. Place a container under the power steering pump, then, disconnect/plug the pressure lines and drain the fluid into the container.
3. Remove the power steering pump-to-engine bolts and the pump from the vehicle.
4. To install, reverse the removal procedures. Adjust the drive belt tension. Bleed the power steering system.

Bleeding System

1. Raise and support the front of the vehicle safely, with the wheels off the ground.
2. Check and add fluid to the reservoir (if necessary).
3. Start the engine. Turn the steering wheel quickly (all the way), right and left, just touching the stops; turn the steering wheel at least 10 times.

NOTE: When bleeding the system, make sure the temperature of the fluid reaches 140–176°F.

4. Stop the engine, then, check and/or add more fluid.
5. Start and run the engine for 3–5 seconds.
6. Stop the engine, then, check and/or add more fluid.
7. Start the engine. Turn the steering wheel (all the way) right and left, just touching the stops; turn the steering wheel at least 10 times.
8. Stop the engine, then, check and/or add more fluid.
9. Repeat the steps until all of the air is bleed from the system.
10. If the air cannot be bleed from the system, turn and hold the steering wheel at each stop for at least 5 seconds but never more than 15 seconds.

Tie Rods

Removal and Installation

1. Raise and support the front of the vehicle safely under the frame rails. Remove the wheel/tire assembly.
2. If removing the tie rod as an assembly, perform the following procedure:
   a. Remove the tie rod-to-cross rod cotter pin (discard it) and nut.
   b. Remove the tie rods-to-steering knuckle cotter pin (discard it) and nut.
   c. Using the Ball Joint Remover tool No. HT72520000 or equivalent, press the tie rod from the steering knuckle and the tie rod from the cross rod.
3. If removing a defective tie rod end, perform the following procedure:
   a. Remove the tie rod-to-cross rod/steering knuckle cotter pin (discard it) and nut.
   b. Loosen the tie rod end-to-tie rod clamp or lock nut.
   c. Using the Ball Joint Remover tool No. HT72520000 or equivalent, press the tie rod from the cross rod/steering knuckle and the tie rod from the cross rod/steering knuckle.
   d. Measure the tie rod end-to-tie rod clamp distance.
   e. Unscrew the tie rod end from the tie rod.
   f. Using a new tie rod end, screw the new tie rod end into

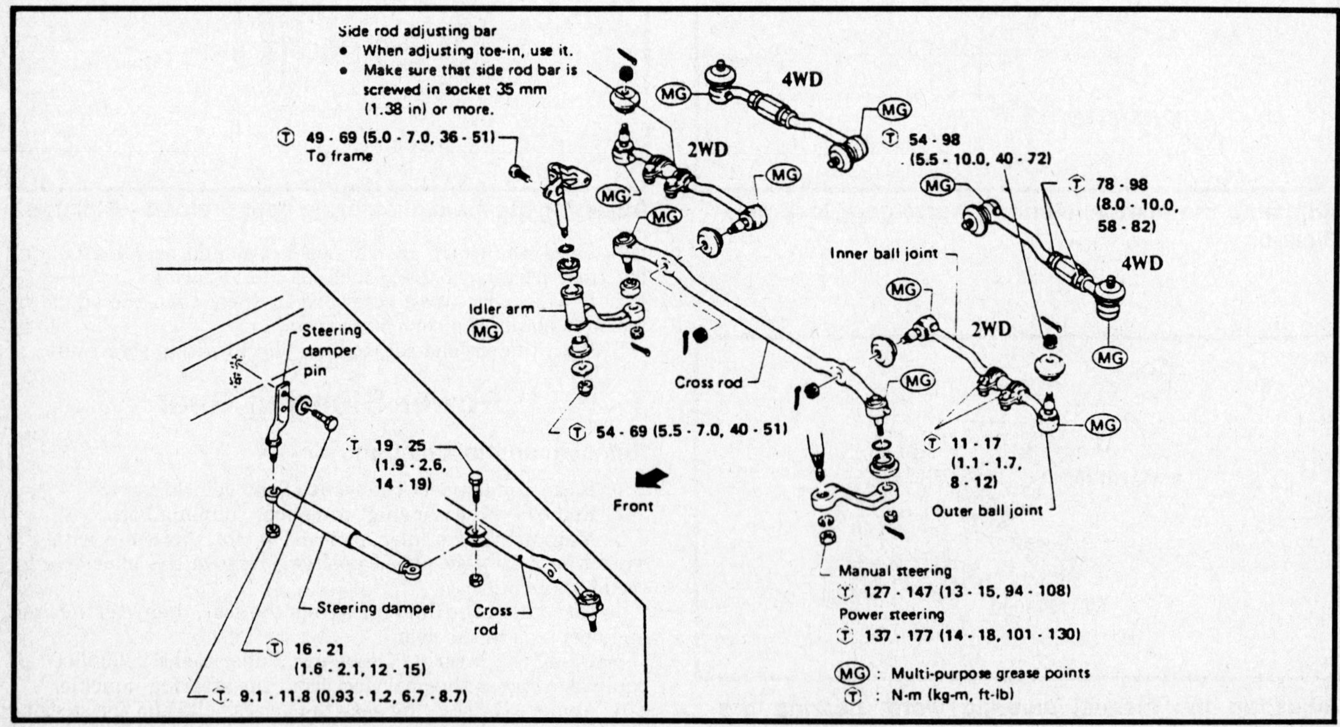

Steering linkage

the tie rod clamp until the measured distance is the same, then, torque the tie rod clamp bolt to 8–12 ft. lbs. (1982-85), 10–14 ft. lbs. (1986-88) or nut to 58–72 ft. lbs. (1984-88).

4. Inspect the tie rod ball joint for wear; if necessary, replace it.

5. To install, use new cotter pins and reverse the removal procedures. Torque the tie rod-to-steering knuckle nut to 40–72 ft. lbs. and the tie rod-to-cross rod nut to 40–72 ft. lbs. Check and/or adjust the front-end alignment.

Adjustment

This procedure should be performed only when adjusting the front-end alignment or replacing a defective tie rod end.

1. If replacing a defective tie rod end, perform the following procedure:

a. Remove the tie rod-to-cross rod or steering knuckle cotter pin (discard it) and the nut.

b. Loosen the tie rod end-to-tie rod clamp or lock nut.

c. Using the Ball Joint Remover tool No. HT72520000 or equivalent, press the tie rod from the cross rod or steering knuckle and the tie rod from the cross rod or steering knuckle.

d. Measure the tie rod end-to-tie rod clamp distance.

e. Unscrew the tie rod end from the tie rod.

f. Using a new tie rod end, screw the new tie rod end into the tie rod clamp until the measured distance is the same.

2. If performing the front-end alignment, perform the following procedure:

a. Loosen the tie rod end-to-tie rod clamp or lock nut.

b. Turn the adjusting sleeve to vary the length of the tie rod.

3. To complete the installation, torque the tie rod clamp bolt to 8–12 ft. lbs. (1982-85), 10–14 ft. lbs. (1986-88) or nut to 58–72 ft. lbs. (1984-88).

BRAKE SYSTEM

For brake system service and repair procedures not detailed below, refer to Brakes section in Unit Repair.

Master Cylinder

CAUTION

Be careful not to spill brake fluid on the painted surfaces of the vehicle; it will damage the paint.

Removal and Installation

1. Using a syringe, remove the brake fluid from the master cylinder.

2. Disconnect and plug the hydraulic lines at the master cylinder.

3. If equipped, disconnect the level warning switch connector from the master cylinder.

4. Remove the master cylinder mounting bolts, by performing one of the following procedures:

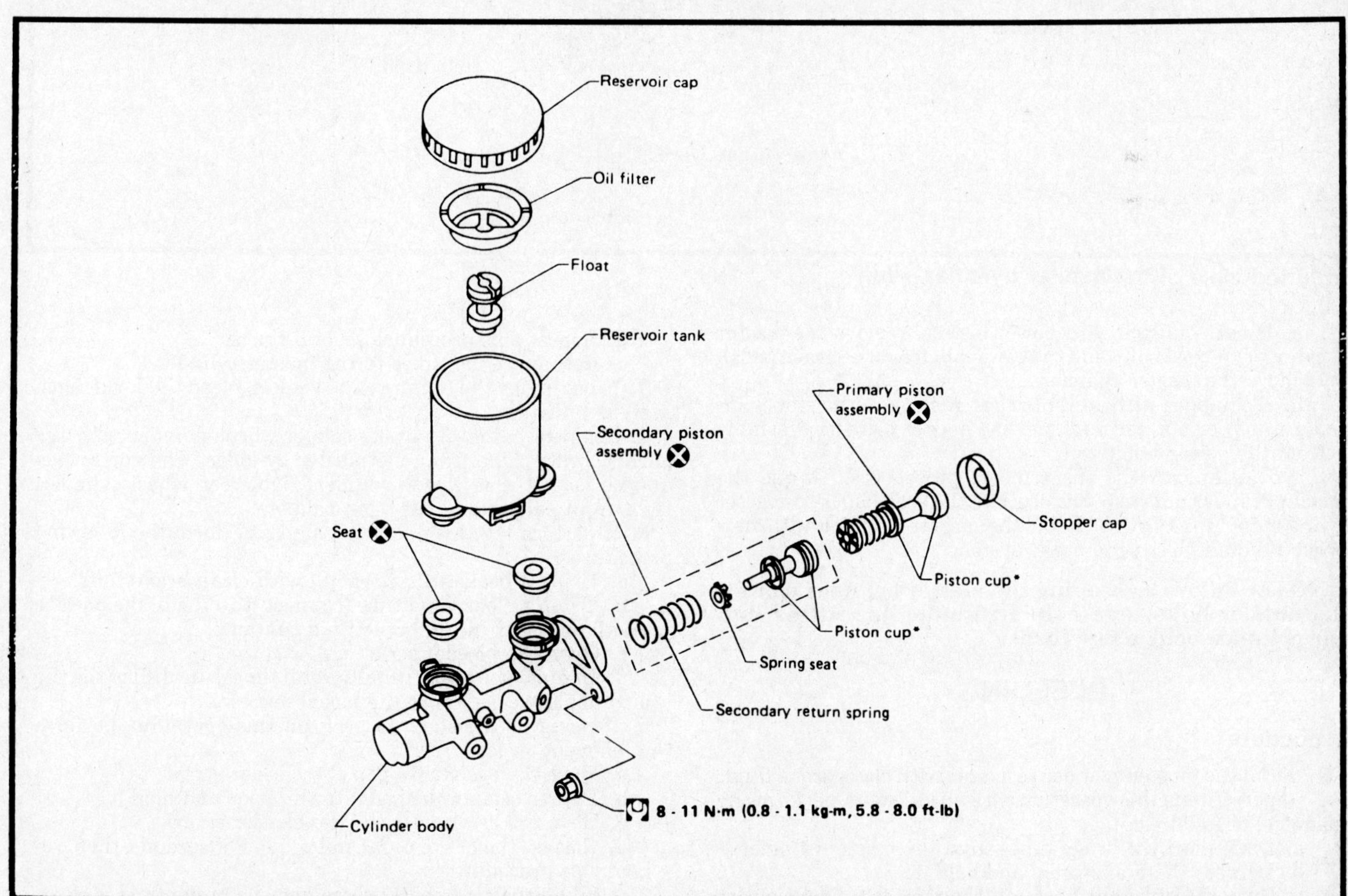

Exploded view of the master cylinder—Pickups (1986-88)—other years are similar

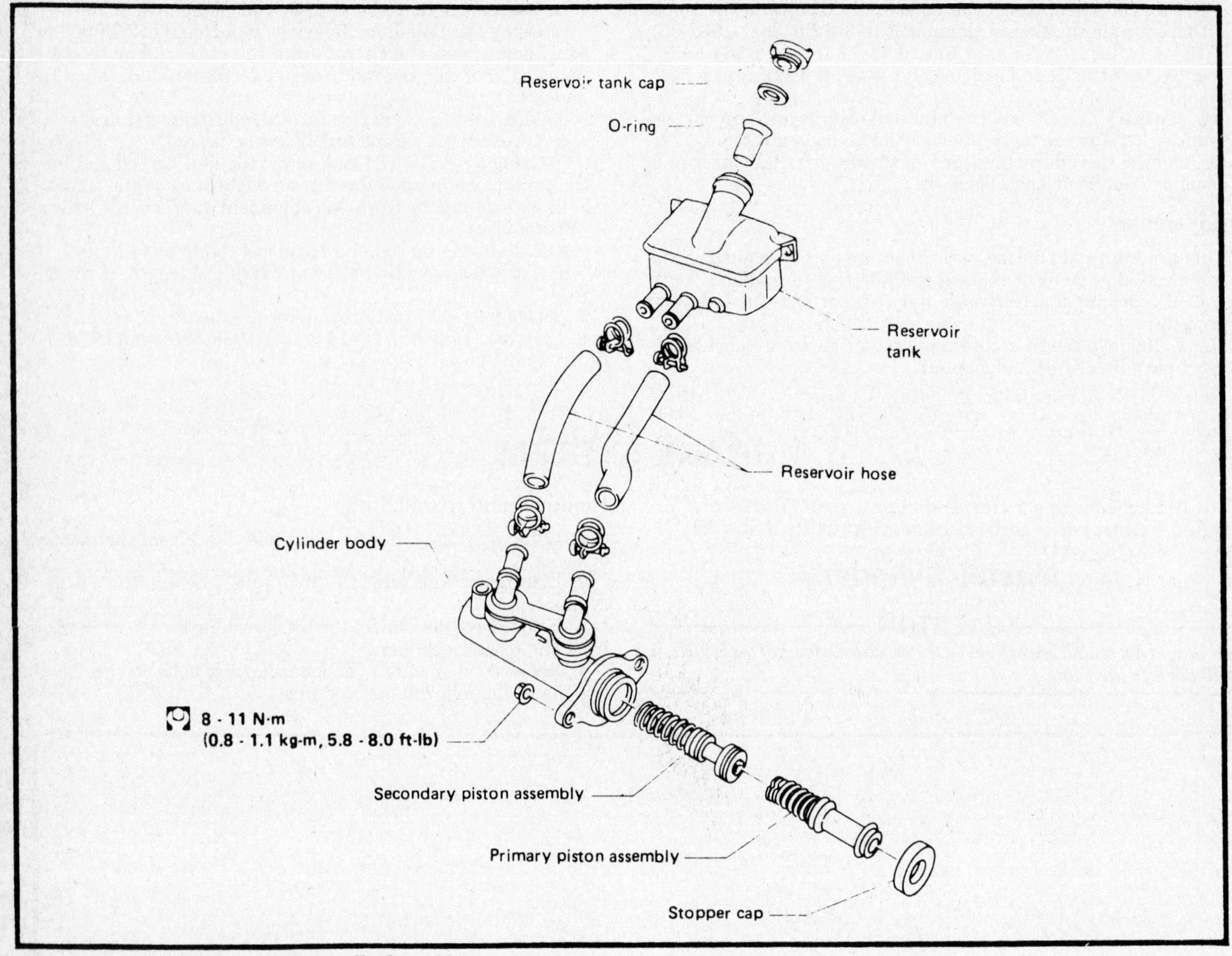

Exploded view of the master cylinder—Van

a. If not equipped with power brakes, remove the master cylinder-to-cowl bolts and the clevis pin from the brake pedal. Remove the master cylinder.

b. If equipped with power brakes, remove the master cylinder-to-power booster nuts and the master cylinder assembly from the power brake unit.

5. To install, reverse the removal procedures. Torque the master cylinder nuts to 6–8 ft. lbs. and the brake lines-to-master cylinder to 11–13 ft. lbs. Refill the master cylinder with new brake fluid and bleed the brake system.

NOTE: Before tightening the master cylinder mounting nuts or bolts, screw the hydraulic line fitting into the cylinder body a few turns.

BLEEDING

Procedure

1. Refill the master cylinder reservoir with clean brake fluid.
2. If performing this operation with an assistant, perform the following procedures:
   a. Disconnect the brake tubes from the master cylinder.
   b. Depress the brake pedal and hold it.
   c. Have the assistant block off the master cylinder outlet and hold it, then, release the brake pedal.
   d. Repeat this procedure several times.
   e. Reconnect the tubes to the master cylinder.
3. From under the center of the vehicle, bleed the Load Sensing Valve (LSV).
4. Begin bleeding the brake caliper/wheel cylinder with the longest brake tube from the master cylinder. The correct sequence is: left-rear wheel cylinder, right-rear wheel cylinder, right-front caliper and left-front caliper.
5. If performing this operation alone, perform the following procedures:
   a. Using a beaker, fill it ½ full with clean brake fluid.
   b. Using a clear vinyl tube, connect it to the brake bleeder and immerse it in the brake fluid container.
   c. Open the bleeder screw.
   d. Depress the brake pedal several times, until all of the the air bubbles cease. Close the bleeder screws.
6. If using an assistant to perform this operation, perform the following procedures:
   a. Have the assistant open the bleeder screw.
   b. Depress the brake pedal to the floor and hold it.
   c. Have the assistant close the bleeder screw.
   d. Release the brake pedal and wait a few seconds, then, repeat this procedure.
   e. When the air bubbles cease and the brake fluid is clear, proceed to the next wheel.

7. After the bleeding process is completed, be sure to place caps on the bleeder screws to prevent dirt entry.

Rear Wheel Cylinder

Removal and Installation

1. Raise and support the rear of the vehicle safely. Remove the wheel, brake drum and brake shoes.
2. Disconnect the brake tube from the rear of the wheel cylinder.
3. Remove the wheel cylinder-to-backing plate nuts and the wheel cylinder from the backing plate.
4. To install, reverse the removal procedures. Torque the wheel cylinder-to-backing plate nuts to 11–13 ft. lbs. (1982-83) or bolt to 3.9–5.4 ft. lbs. (1984-88). Bleed the brake hydraulic system.

Disc Brakes

Removal and Installation

1982-83

1. Raise and support the front of the vehicle safely. Remove the wheel/tire assembly.
2. Using a small pry bar, pry the spring clip from the caliper.
3. Using your finger, remove the brake pad pin springs.
4. Using a pair of pliers, remove the brake pad pins and the brake pads from the caliper.
5. Using a flat pry bar, insert it between the rotor and the caliper, then, pry the piston(s) back into the caliper; this procedure is to make clearance for the new brake pads.
6. Inspect the caliper for signs of fluid leakage; if necessary, replace or rebuild the caliper.
7. To install, use new brake pads and reverse the removal procedures.

1984-88

1. Raise and support the front of the vehicle safely. Remove the wheel/tire assembly.
2. Remove the bottom caliper-to-caliper support bolt and swing the caliper upward.
3. Remove the pad retainers, the inner/outer retainers and the brake pads.
4. Using a medium C-clamp and a block of wood, place the wood against the caliper piston(s), then, using the C-clamp

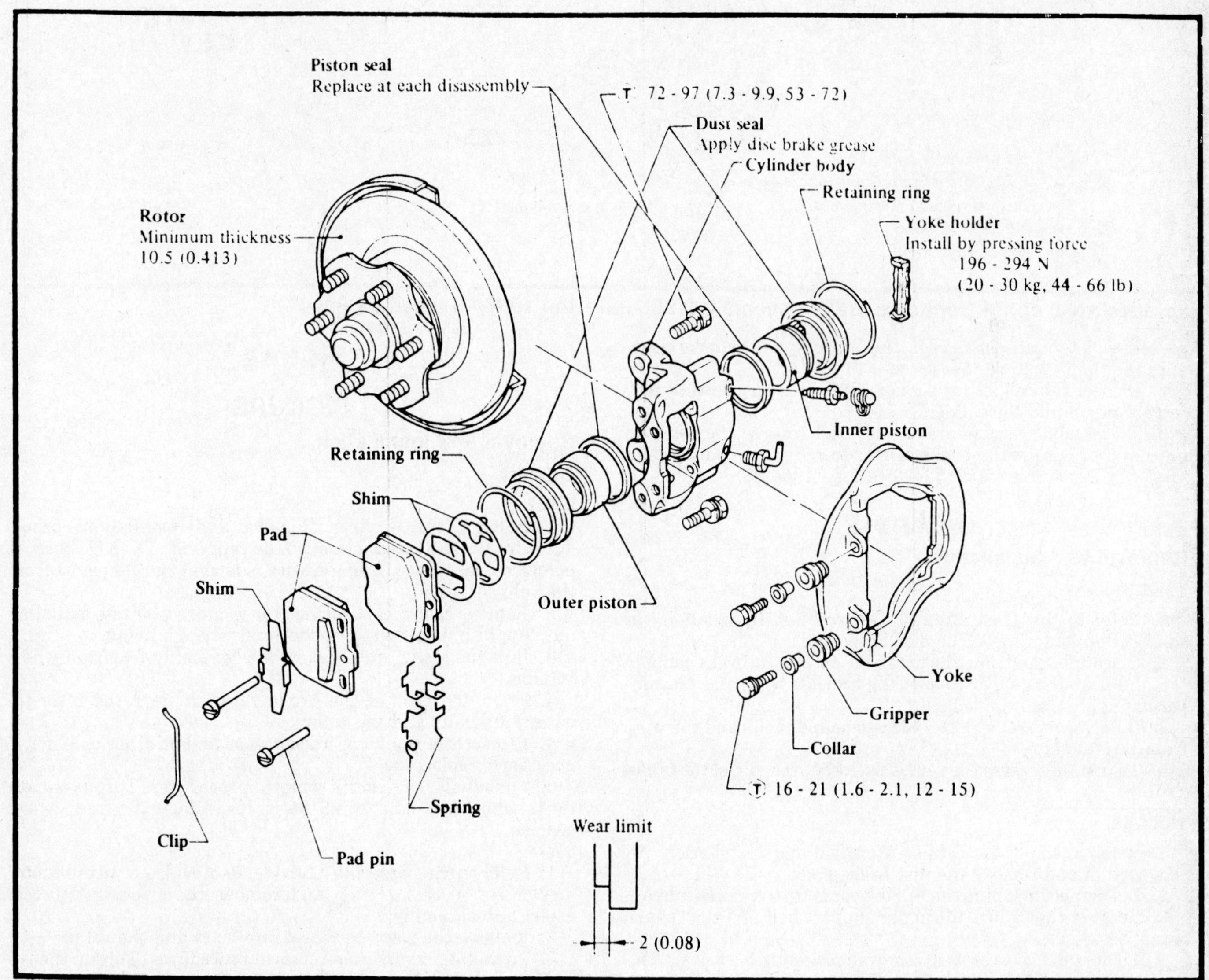

Exploded view of the front disc brake assembly (1982-83)

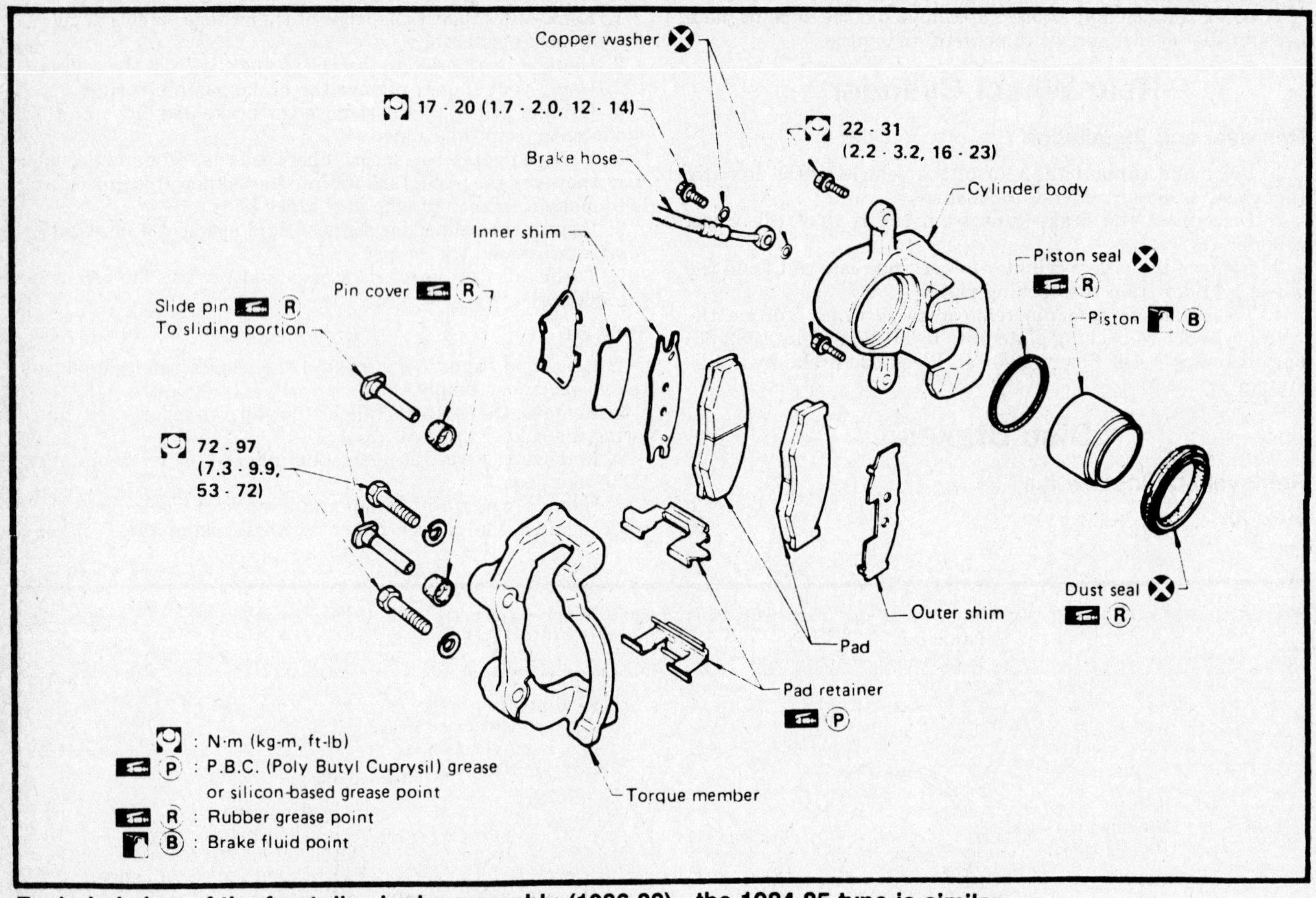

Exploded view of the front disc brake assembly (1986-88)—the 1984-85 type is similar

press the piston into the caliper; this procedure is to make clearance for the new brake pads.

5. Inspect the caliper for signs of fluid leakage; if necessary, replace or rebuild the caliper.

6. To install, use new brake pads and reverse the removal procedures. Torque the brake caliper-to-caliper support bolt to 16–23 ft. lbs. (1984-85) or 53–72 ft. lbs. (1986-88).

Calipers

Removal and Installation

1982-83

1. Refer to the "Disc Brakes, Removal and Installation" in this section and remove the disc brake pads.
2. Disconnect and plug the brake hose from the brake caliper.
3. Remove the caliper-to-steering knuckle bolts and the caliper assembly from the vehicle.
4. If necessary, remove the yoke-to-caliper bolts and the yoke from the caliper.
5. To install, reverse the removal procedures. Bleed the brake system.

1984-88

1. Refer to the "Disc Brakes, Removal and Installation" in this section and remove the disc brake pads.
2. Disconnect and plug the brake hose from the brake caliper.
3. Remove the caliper-to-caliper support bolt and the caliper from the vehicle.
4. To install, reverse the removal procedures. Torque the brake caliper-to-caliper support bolt to 16–23 ft. lbs. (1984-85) or 53–72 ft. lbs. (1986-88). Bleed the brake system.

Rotors

PICKUPS

Removal and Installation

1982-83

2WD

1. Refer to the "Caliper, Removal and Installation" procedures in this section and remove the caliper(s); DO NOT disconnect the brake hose. Using a wire, suspend the caliper(s) from the vehicle.
2. Remove the wheel bearing grease cup, cotter pin, adjusting nut cap, hub nut, thrust washer and wheel bearing.
3. Pull the wheel hub/brake rotor assembly from the wheel spindle.
4. From the rear of the brake rotor, remove the rotor-to-wheel hub bolts and the rotor.
5. Inspect the rotor for cracks, wear and/or other damage; if necessary, replace it.
6. To install, reverse the removal procedures. Torque the rotor-to-wheel hub bolts to 28–38 ft. lbs. Adjust the front wheel bearing.

4WD

1. Refer to the "Steering Knuckle, Removal and Installation" procedures in this section and remove the steering knuckle/wheel hub assembly.
2. Remove the rotor-to-wheel hub bolts and the rotor.
3. To install, reverse the removal procedures. Torque the rotor-to-wheel hub bolts to 28–38 ft. lbs., the wheel hub/rotor assembly-to-halfshaft to 108–145 ft. lbs. and the free-running hub

assembly-to-wheel hub Torx® bolts to 18–25 ft. lbs. Check and/or adjust the front wheel alignment.

1984-88

2WD

1. Refer to the "Caliper, Removal and Installation" procedures in this section and remove the calipers; DO NOT disconnect the brake hose. Using a wire, suspend the calipers from the vehicle.
2. Remove the caliper support-to-steering knuckle bolts and the caliper support.
3. Remove the wheel bearing grease cup, cotter pin, adjusting nut cap, hub nut, thrust washer and wheel bearing.
4. Pull the wheel hub/brake rotor assembly from the wheel spindle.
5. From the rear of the brake rotor, remove the rotor-to-wheel hub bolts and the rotor.
6. Inspect the rotor for cracks, wear and/or other damage; if necessary, replace it.
7. To install, use a new cotter pin and reverse the removal procedures. Torque the rotor-to-wheel hub bolts to 36–51 ft. lbs. and the wheel hub-to-spindle nut to 25–29 ft. lbs. Adjust the front wheel bearing preload. Check and/or adjust the front wheel alignment.

4WD

1. Raise and support the front of the vehicle safely under the axle case. Remove the wheel/tire assembly.
2. If equipped with a manual/free-running lock assembly, perform the following procedure:
   a. Remove the lock assembly-to-hub Torx® bolts.
   b. Pull the lock assembly from the wheel hub.
   c. From the halfshaft, remove the snapring and the drive clutch.
3. If equipped with a automatic/free-running lock assembly, perform the following procedure:
   a. Remove the lock assembly-to-hub Torx® bolts.
   b. Pull the lock assembly (with brake "A") from the wheel hub.
   c. From the halfshaft, remove the snapring, the washers and the brake "B".
4. From the halfshaft, remove the thrust washer, the snapring and the lock washer.

NOTE: To remove the lock washer (1984-85 4WD models), bend back the lock washer tabs. To remove the lock washer (1986-88 4WD models), remove the lock washer-to-lock nut screw(s).

5. Using the Lock Nut Socket Wrench tool No. KV40104300 or equivalent, remove the lock nut from the halfshaft.
6. Pull the wheel hub/rotor assembly from the steering knuckle.
7. Remove the rotor-to-wheel hub bolts and the rotor.
8. To install, reverse the removal procedures. Torque the rotor-to-wheel hub bolts to 36–51 ft. lbs., the lock washer-to-lock nut screw(s) to 9–14 inch lbs., the wheel hub/rotor assembly-to-halfshaft to 58–72 ft. lbs. and the free-running hub assembly-to-wheel hub Torx® bolts to 18–25 ft. lbs. Check and/or adjust the front wheel alignment.

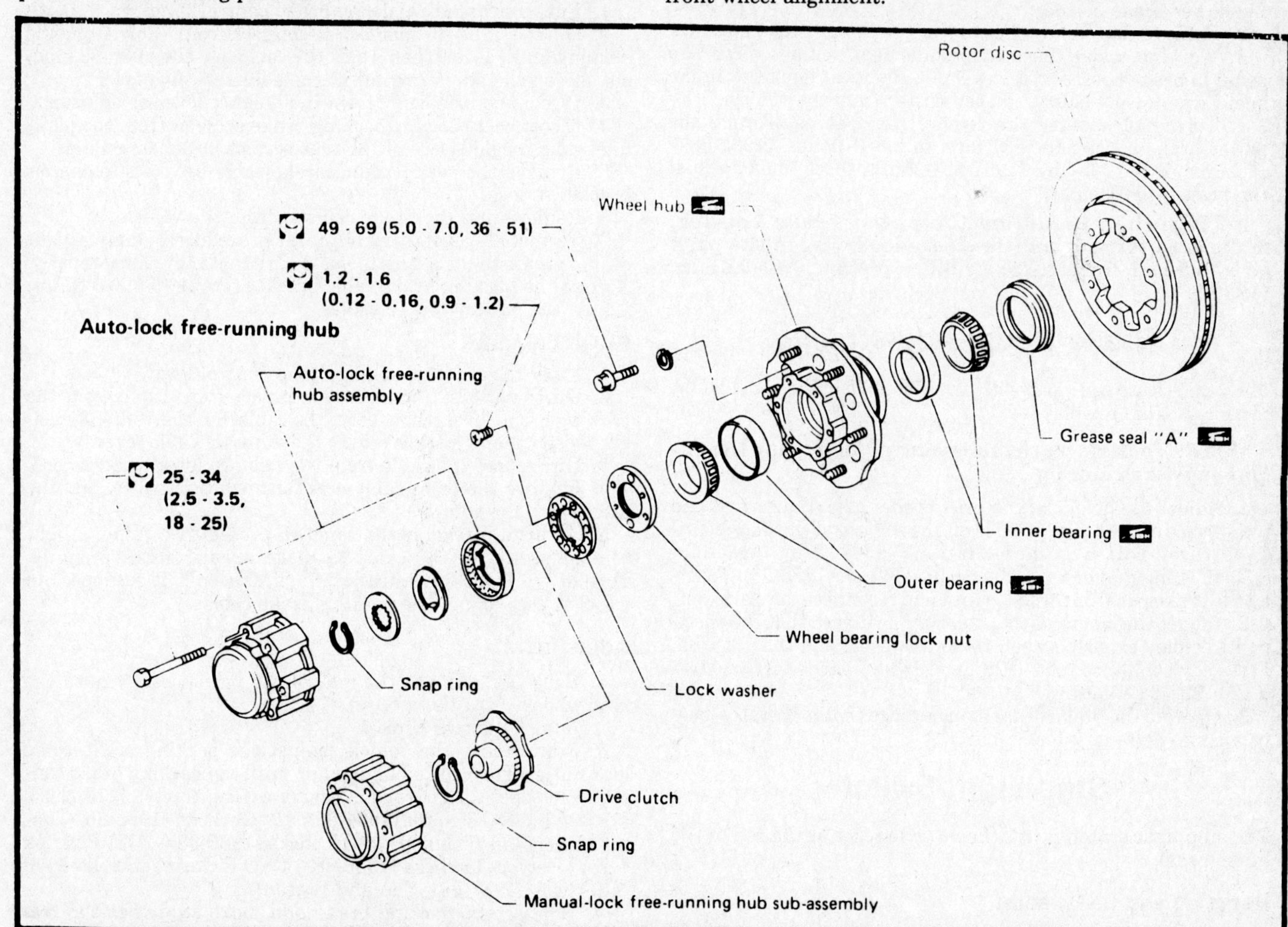

Exploded view of the front wheel hub assembly—4WD (1986-88)

Removal and Installation

1987-88 VAN

1. Refer to the "Caliper, Removal and Installation" procedures in this section and remove the calipers; DO NOT disconnect the brake hose. Using a wire, suspend the calipers from the vehicle.
2. Remove the caliper support-to-steering knuckle bolts and the caliper support from the vehicle.
3. Remove the wheel bearing grease cup, the hub nut and the lock washer.
4. Pull the wheel hub/brake rotor assembly from the wheel spindle.

NOTE: If replacing the wheel bearing, refer to "Wheel Bearings, Removal and Installation" procedures in this section and replace the wheel bearings.

5. Inspect the rotor for cracks, wear and/or other damage; if necessary, replace it.
6. To install, reverse the removal procedures. Torque the rotor/wheel hub assembly-to-spindle nut to 195–260 ft. lbs. Adjust the front wheel bearing.

Power Brake Boosters

Removal and Installation

1. Refer to the "Master Cylinder, Removal and Installation" procedures, in this section and remove the master cylinder from the power brake booster.
2. Remove the vacuum hose form the power brake booster.
3. Working under the instrument panel, remove the brake pedal-to-brake booster rod clevis pin. Remove the power brake booster mounting bolts and the booster from the vehicle.
4. To install, reverse the removal procedures. Torque the power brake booster-to-cowl nuts to 5.8–8 ft. lbs. (1982-88–Pickups) or 9–12 ft. lbs. (1987-88–Van). Check and/or adjust the brake pedal height.

NOTE: When installing the power brake booster, make sure there is a little clearance between the push rod end and the master cylinder piston; 0.40–0.41 in. (1986-88).

Brake Pedal Adjustment

The vehicles are equipped with an adjustable brake pedal push-rod for setting free-play.

NOTE: To perform the following adjustments, the engine must be running.

1. Adjust the height of the brake pedal push rod so that the top surface of the brake pedal is off the surface of the floor board (W/O rugs): 6.81–6.85 in. (1982-83), 6.93–7.32 in. (1984-85), 8.35–8.74 in. (1986-88–A/T) or 8.23–8.62 in. (1986-88). Tighten the brake pedal pushrod locknut and reconnect the clevis pin.
2. Adjust the length of the stop light switch so that the specified free-play exists between the brake pedal and the pushrod. Free-play should be 0.04–0.20 in. (1982-88–Pickups) or 0.04–0.12 (1987-88–Van).
3. Operate the brake pedal to make sure that it operates freely with no noise or interference.

Stop Light Switch

The stop light switch is attached to a bracket at the top of the brake pedal.

Removal and Installation

1. From under the dash, disconnect the electrical connector from the stop light switch.
2. Loosen and remove the lock nut from the stop light switch.
3. Unscrew the stop light switch from the brake pedal bracket.

NOTE: To adjust the stop light switch, the engine must be running.

4. To install, reverse the removal procedures. Perform the brake pedal height and free-play adjustments. Torque the stop light switch lock nut to 9–11 ft. lbs.

Adjustment

To perform this procedure the engine must be running.

1. Depress the brake pedal until push rod resistance is felt.
2. Using a 0.012–039 in. feeler guage, measure stop light switch-to-brake pedal gap.
3. If necessary, disconnect the electrical connector from the stop light switch, loosen the stop light switch lock nut and adjust the stop light switch.
4. After adjustment, torque the stop light switch lock nut to 9–12 ft. lbs.

Parking Brake

CABLE

Removal and Installation

REAR CABLE(S)

1. Fully release the parking brake control lever.
2. On the 1982-85 models, disconnect front cable from the parking brake lever, then, relax the cable. On the 1986-88 models, loosen the adjusting nut at the adjuster cable lever.
3. Disconnect the cable from the balance lever or adjuster.
4. Disconnect the rear parking brake cable(s) from the parking brake toggle levers of the rear service brake assemblies.
5. Remove the rear parking brake cable brackets-to-chassis bracket screws.
6. Remove parking brake cable(s) from the vehicle.
7. To install, reverse the removal procedures. Apply a light coat of grease to the cables to make sure that they slide properly. Torque the parking brake cable bracket screws to 5.8–8 ft. lbs. Adjust the parking brake cables.

FRONT CABLE

1. Fully release the parking brake control lever.
2. On the 1982-85 models, disconnect front cable from the parking brake lever, then, relax the cable. On the 1986-88 models, loosen the adjusting nut at the adjuster cable lever.
3. Disconnect the cable from the balance lever or adjuster.
4. Remove the front cable bracket-to-chassis bolt(s) and the cable from the vehicle.
5. To install, reverse the removal procedures. Apply a light coat of grease to the cable to make sure it slides properly. Torque the front cable bracket-to-chassis bolt (if equipped) to 5.8–8 ft. lbs. Adjust the parking brake cables.

Adjustment

1. Raise and support the rear of the vehicle safely until the rear wheels clear the ground.
2. Adjust the rear brakes.
3. From under the vehicle, adjust the parking brake cable lock nut(s). Turn the adjusting nut until the parking brake control lever operating stroke is (using 44 lbs. force): 6–10 clicks (1982-83), 13–16 clicks (1984-85), 10–12 clicks (1986-88–console lever–all Pickups), 10–12 clicks (1986-88–2WD Pickups, stick lever), 9–11 clicks (1986-88–4WD Pickups, stick lever) or 7–9 clicks (1987-88–Van and Wagon).
4. Release the parking brake and make sure that the rear wheels turn freely with no drag.
5. Lower the vehicle.

CLUTCH

The clutch is a hydraulically-operated single-plate, dry friction disc, diaphragm spring type.

The clutch is operated by a clutch pedal which is mechanically connected to a clutch master cylinder. When the pedal is depressed, the piston in the master cylinder is moved in the master cylinder bore. This movement compresses the fluid in the master cylinder causing hydraulic pressure which is transferred through a tube to the slave cylinder. The slave cylinder is mounted to the clutch housing with its piston connected to the clutch release lever. The hydraulic pressure in the slave cylinder forces the slave cylinder piston to travel out the cylinder bore and move the clutch release lever, disengaging the clutch.

Clutch Assembly

Removal and Installation

1. Refer to the "Manual Transmission, Removal and Installation" procedures in this section and remove the transmission.
2. Using a piece of chalk, paint or a center punch, mark the clutch assembly-to-flywheel relationship so it can be reassembled in the same position from which it is removed.
3. Using a Clutch Aligning Bar tool No. KV30100100 or equivalent, insert it into the clutch disc hub.

NOTE: The clutch alignment bar is available from your dealer or an auto parts store. It is important to support the weight of the clutch while the retaining bolts are being removed.

4. Loosen the clutch cover-to-flywheel bolts, one turn at a time in an alternating sequence, until the spring tension is relieved to avoid distorting or bending the clutch cover. Remove the clutch assembly.
5. Inspect the flywheel for scoring, roughness or signs of overheating. Light scoring may be cleaned up with emery cloth, but any deep grooves or scoring warrant replacement or refacing (if possible) of the flywheel. If the clutch facings or flywheel are oily, inspect the transmission front cover oil seal, the pilot bushing and engine rear seals, etc. for leakage; replace any leaking seals before replacing the clutch.
6. If the crankshaft pilot bushing is worn, replace it. Install it using a soft hammer. The factory-supplied part does not have to be oiled, but check the procedure if you are using an aftermarket part. Inspect the clutch cover for wear or scoring and replace it, if necessary.

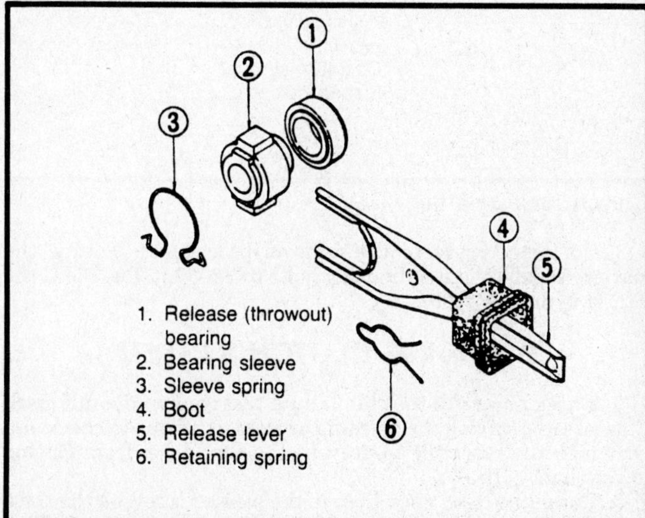

Clutch release mechanism

NOTE: The pressure plate and spring cannot be disassembled; Replace the clutch cover as an assembly.

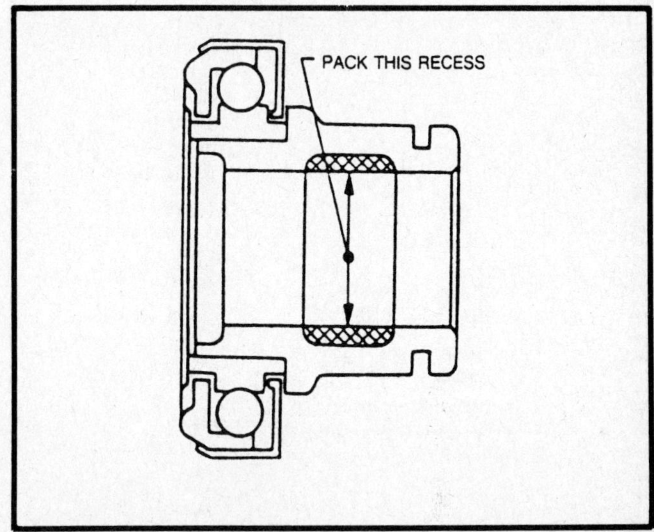

Coat the area indicated in the bearing sleeve with grease

7. Inspect the clutch release bearing. If it is rough or noisy, it should be replaced. The bearing can be removed from the sleeve with a puller; this requires a press to install the new bearing. After installation, coat the sleeve groove, the release lever contact surfaces, the pivot pin/sleeve and the release bearing-to-transmission contact surfaces with a light coat of grease. Be careful not to use too much grease, which will run at high temperatures and get onto the clutch facings. Reinstall the release bearing on the lever.
8. Apply a thin coat of grease to the pressure plate wire ring, diaphragm spring, clutch cover grooves and the pressure plate drive bosses.
9. Apply a thin coat of Lubriplate® to the splines in the driven plate. Slide the clutch disc onto the splines and move it back and forth several times. Remove the disc and wipe off the excess lubricant. Be very careful not to get any grease on the clutch facings.
10. Assemble the clutch cover and the clutch plate on the clutch alignment arbor.
11. To complete the installation, align the clutch assembly-to-flywheel alignment marks and reverse the removal procedures; three dowels are used to locate the clutch cover on the flywheel. Torque the clutch cover-to-flywheel bolts (in an alternating sequence, one turn at a time) to 12–15 ft. lbs. (1982-83) or 16–22 ft. lbs. (1984-88), the transmission-to-engine bolts to 29–36 ft. lbs. and the clutch slave cylinder-to-transmission bolts to 22–30 ft. lbs.

Pedal Height and Free-Play Adjustment

The pedal height is the distance from the top of the clutch pedal to the floor board (without the carpet).

The pedal free-play is the distance the clutch pedal pad moves from the released position to the point where resistance is felt.

lowing procedure:

a. From under the dash, loosen the pedal stopper lock nut.
b. Turn the pedal stopper until the specified pedal height is obtained: 6.73–6.97 in. (1982 – gasoline), 7.05–7.28 in. (1982 – diesel), 6.54–6.93 in. (1983 – gasoline), 6.85–7.24 in. (1983 – diesel), 7.05–7.44 in. (1984-85), 9.29–9.69 in. (1986-88 – 4 cyl and diesel), 8.94–9.33 in. (1986-88 – V6).

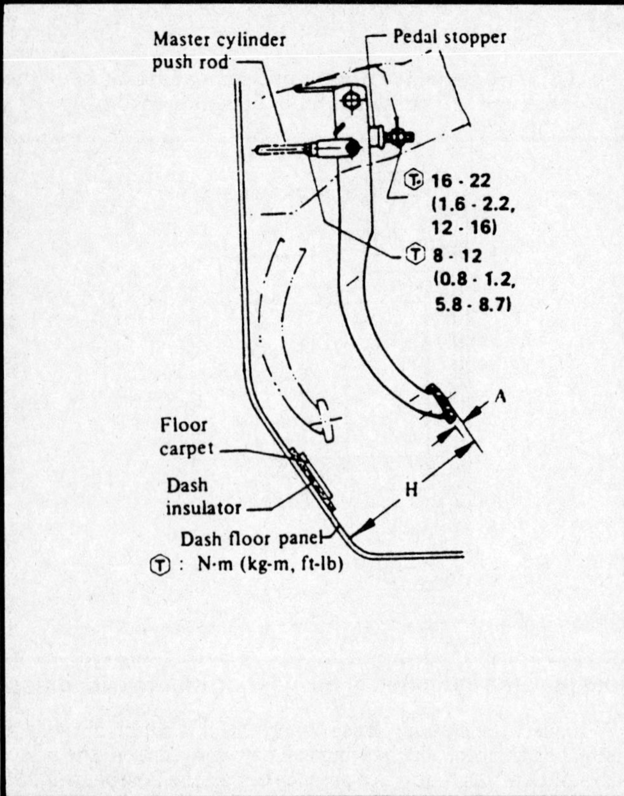

Clutch pedal adjustment: "A" is pedal free play, "H" is pedal height

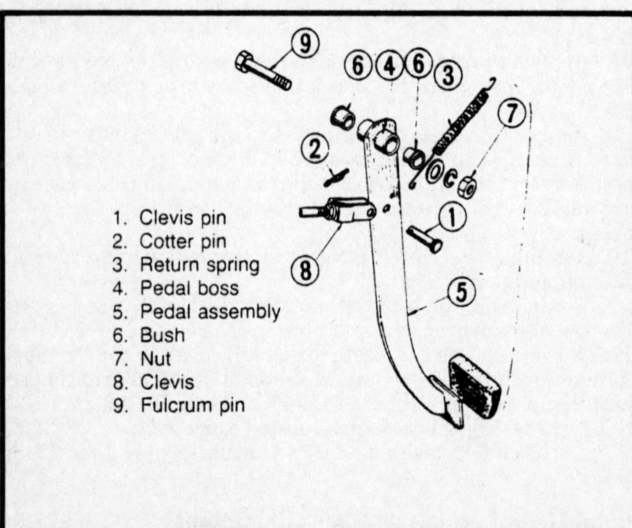

Clutch pedal assembly

c. After adjustment, torque the pedal stopper lock nut to 12–16 ft. lbs.

2. To adjust the pedal free-play, perform the following procedures:

a. Loosen the clutch pedal, pushrod locknut.

b. Using a ruler, measure the clutch pedal free-play.

c. Turn the clutch pedal push rod to the specified free-play is: 0.04–0.20 in. (1982-84 – Pickups) or 0.04–0.05 in. (1985-88 – Pickups) or 0.04–0.12 in. (1987-88 – Van).

d. After adjustment, torque the lock nut to 6–9 ft. lbs.

CLUTCH MASTER CYLINDER

On the Van models, the master cylinder is attached to a bracket located under the dash.

Removal and Installation

1. VAN: From under the dash, remove the clevis pin snap pin and pull the clevis pin from the clutch pedal.
2. Disconnect the clutch pedal arm from the pushrod clevis. Remove the dust cover (boot) from the master cylinder body and pushrod. It will not go through the cowl without tearing.
3. Disconnect and plug the hydraulic line from the clutch master cylinder.

NOTE: Take precautions to keep brake fluid from coming in contact with any painted surfaces.

4. PICKUP: Remove the master cylinder-to-cowl bolts and the master cylinder from the vehicle.
5. ALL: To install, reverse the removal procedures. Torque the clutch master cylinder-to-cowl bolts/nuts to 5.8–8.7 ft. lbs. (Pickups) or 12–14 ft. lbs. (Vans). Bleed the clutch hydraulic system.

SLAVE CYLINDER

Removal and Installation

ALL MODELS

1. Remove the slave cylinder-to-clutch housing bolts and the pushrod from the shift fork.
2. Disconnect and plug the hydraulic hose from the slave cylinder, then, remove the cylinder from the vehicle.

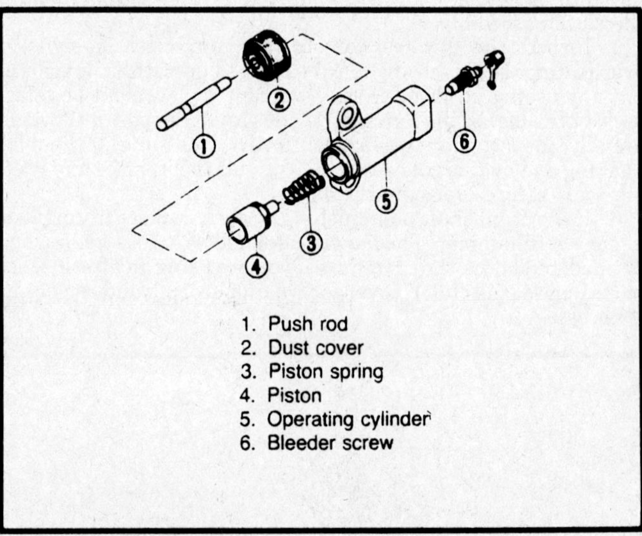

Clutch slave cylinder

3. To install, reverse the removal procedures. Torque the slave cylinder-to-clutch housing bolts to 22–30 ft. lbs. Bleed the clutch hydraulic system.

BLEEDING CLUTCH SYSTEM

1. Check and refill the clutch fluid reservoir to the full mark if necessary. During the bleeding process, continue to check and replenish the reservoir to prevent the fluid level from getting lower than ½ full.
2. Connect a clear vinyl hose to the bleeder screw on the slave cylinder. Immerse the other end of the hose in a clear jar ½ filled with brake fluid.

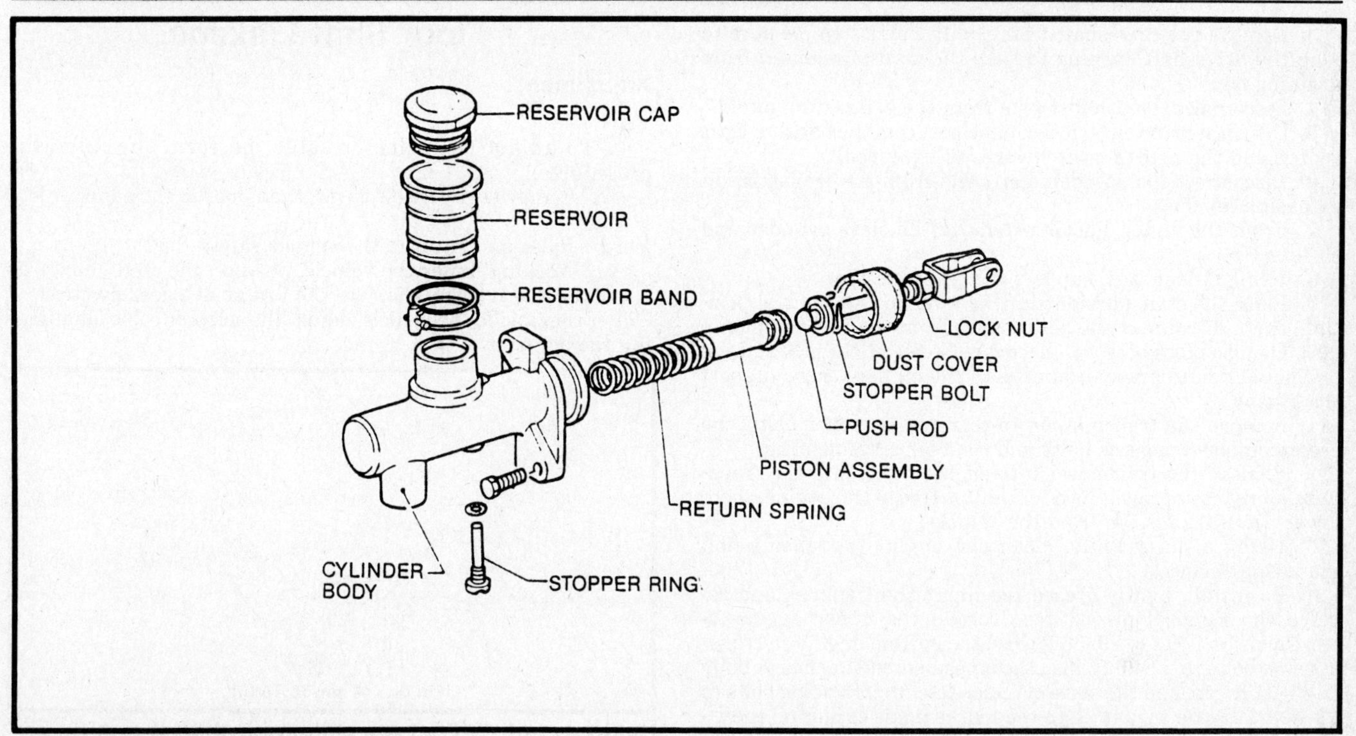

Disassembled view of master cylinder

3. Have an assistant pump the clutch pedal several times and hold it down. Loosen the bleeder screw slowly.
4. Tighten the bleeder screw and release the clutch pedal gradually. Repeat this operation until the air bubbles disappear from the brake fluid being expelled out through the bleeder screw.
5. When the air is completely removed, securely tighten the bleeder screw and replace the dust cap.
6. Check and refill the master cylinder reservoir as necessary.
7. Depress the clutch pedal several times to check the operation of the clutch and check for leaks.

MANUAL TRANSMISSION

For all overhaul procedures, please refer to "Manual Transmission" in the Unit Repair Section.

MANUAL TRANSMISSION ASSEMBLY

Removal and Installation

PICKUPS

1. Disconnect the negative battery terminal from the battery.
2. On the 1982-84 models, remove the accelerator wire. On the 1985 models, remove the parking brake cable.
3. Raise and support the vehicle safely.
4. Remove the driveshaft from the transmission (2WD) or transfer case (4WD); be sure to plug the driveshaft opening to keep the transmission/transfer case oil from draining out. If equipped with 4WD, remove the transfer case-to-front differential driveshaft; it may be necessary to remove the front differential carrier/crossmember.
5. If necessary, disconnect the exhaust pipe from the exhaust manifold.
6. Disconnect the electrical connectors from the back-up light switch and the neutral switch wires (if equipped).
7. Disconnect the speedometer cable from the transmission extension housing.
8. From the clutch housing, remove the slave cylinder and the starter.
9. Using a floor jack, support the transmission. On 4WD models, remove the transfer case-to-transmission bolts and the transfer case.
10. Place the transmission shifting lever in the Neutral position, then, remove the console box, the E-ring and the shift lever. On the 4WD models, remove the transfer case shift lever.
11. Using a block of wood, place it between a floor jack and the engine oil pan to prevent damage to the oil pan, then, support the engine.
12. Remove the transmission-to-rear crossmember bolts, the crossmember-to-chassis bolts and the rear crossmember.
13. Remove the transmission-to-engine bolts, pull the transmission rearward until the pilot shaft is free of the engine, then, lower the transmission from the vehicle.
14. Using a putty knife, clean the engine-to-transmission mounting surfaces.
15. To install, lightly grease the input shaft splines and reverse the removal procedures. Torque the upper engine-to-transmission bolts to 32–43 ft. lbs. (1982-84) or 29–36 ft. lbs. (1985-88), the bottom engine-to-transmission bolts to 6.5–8.7 ft. lbs. (1982-84 – 4 cyl, 1985-88 – Diesel), 22–29 ft. lbs. (1985 – 4 cyl, 1986-88 – V6) or 14–18 ft. lbs. (1986-88 – 4 cyl), the crossmember-to-chassis bolts to 23–31 ft. lbs. and the slave cylinder-to-clutch housing bolts to 22–30 ft. lbs. Be sure to align the marks made earlier on the U-joint and differential flange when installing the driveshaft, to maintain driveline balance.

VAN

1. Disconnect the negative battery terminal from the battery.
2. Raise and support the vehicle safely.

3. Remove the driveshaft from the transmission; be sure to plug the driveshaft opening to keep the transmission oil from draining out.
4. Disconnect the exhaust pipe from the exhaust manifold.
5. Disconnect the electrical connectors from the back-up light switch and the neutral switch wires (if equipped).
6. Disconnect the speedometer cable from the transmission extension housing.
7. From the clutch housing, remove the slave cylinder and the starter.
8. Using a floor jack, support the transmission.
9. Place the transmission shifting lever in the Neutral position, then, disconnect the shift cables from the transmission.
10. Using a block of wood, place it between a floor jack and the engine oil pan to prevent damage to the oil pan, then, support the engine.
11. Remove the transmission-to-rear crossmember bolts, the crossmember-to-chassis bolts and the rear crossmember.
12. Remove the transmission-to-engine bolts, pull the transmission rearward until the pilot shaft is free of the engine, then, lower the transmission from the vehicle.
13. Using a putty knife, clean the engine-to-transmission mounting surfaces.
14. To install, lightly grease the input shaft splines and reverse the removal procedures. Torque the upper engine-to-transmission bolts to 29–36 ft. lbs., the bottom engine-to-transmission bolts to 22–29 ft. lbs., the crossmember-to-chassis bolts to 23–31 ft. lbs. and the slave cylinder-to-clutch housing bolts to 22–30 ft. lbs. Be sure to align the marks made earlier on the U-joint and differential flange when installing the driveshaft, to maintain driveline balance.

Floor Shift Linkage

Adjustment

VAN

1. To adjust the selector cable, perform the following procedures:
   a. Remove the console cover, then, loosen the adjuster lock nut.
   b. Raise and support the vehicle safely.
   c. Working under the vehicle, position the shift change lever (on the transmission) to the 3rd or 4th gear position.
   d. From inside the vehicle, adjust the selector cable length using the adjuster.

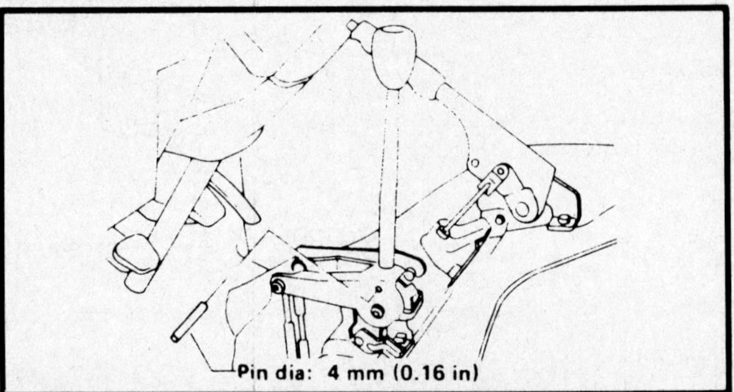

Using a pin to adjust the shift control lever and roller bearing—Van

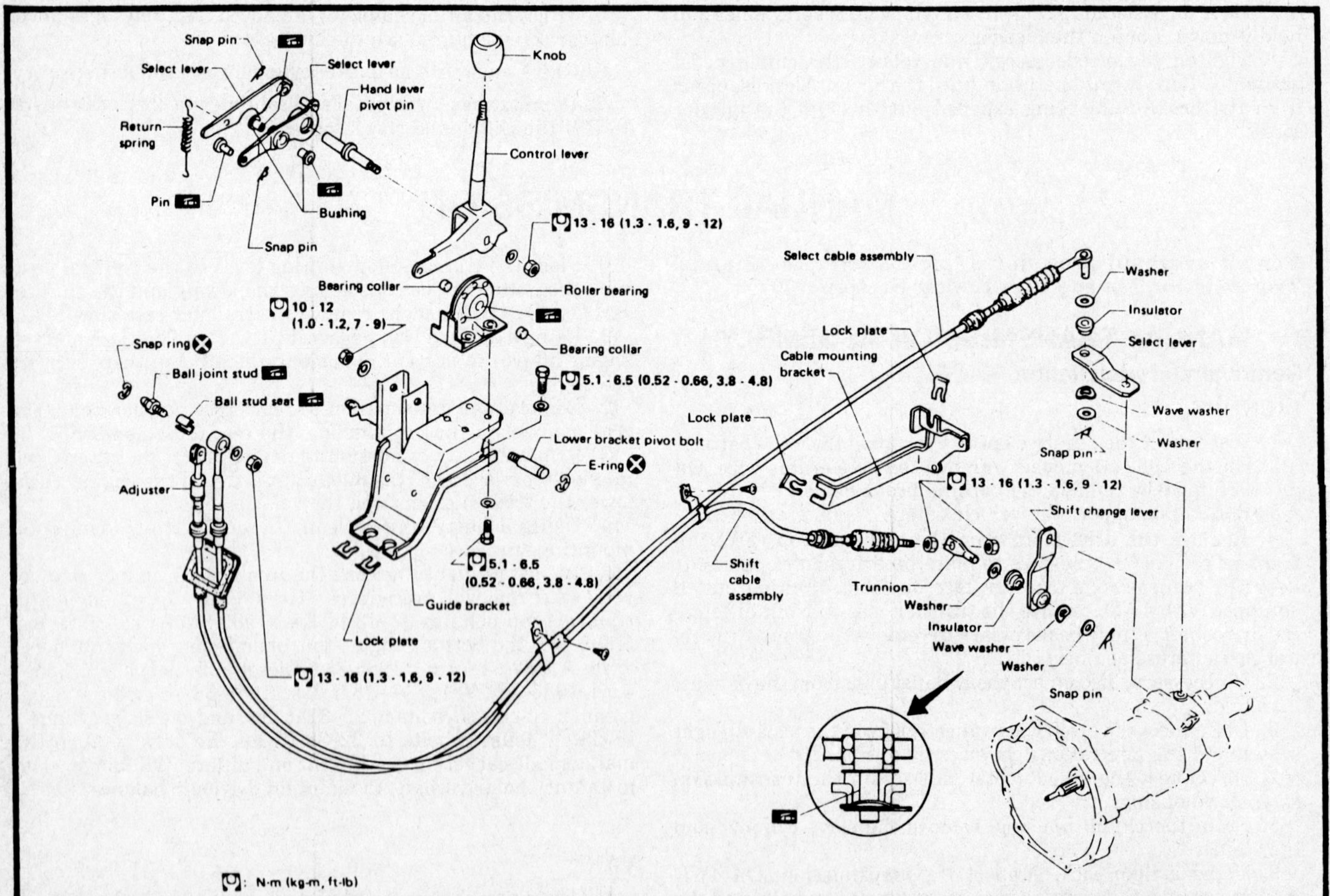

Exploded view of the shift change lever assembly—Van

e. After adjustment, tighten the adjuster lock nut.

2. To adjust the shifter cable, perform the following procedures:

a. From under the vehicle, loosen the trunnion-to-shift cable lock nut.

b. Remove the shift cable trunnion from the cross shaft.

c. Position the transmission cross shaft in the Neutral position.

d. Using a 0.16 in (4mm) pin, insert it (as vertical as possible) into the adjustment holes of both the control lever and roller bearing.

e. Adjust the trunnion position and install it into the cross shaft.

f. Torque the trunnion lock nut to 9–12 ft. lbs.

AUTOMATIC TRANSMISSION

AUTOMATIC TRANSMISSION ASSEMBLY

Removal and Installation

1. Disconnect the negative battery terminal from the battery.
2. Raise and support the vehicle safely.
3. Matchmark the driveshaft U-joint and differential flange, then, disconnect them from the differential. If the driveshaft is equipped with a center bearing, remove the center bearing bracket-to-chassis bolts and the driveshaft assembly. Plug the transmission extension housing to keep the fluid from leaking out.
4. Disconnect the exhaust pipe-to-exhaust manifold nuts and the pipe, then, discard the gasket.
5. Disconnect the shift linkage from the transmission.
6. Disconnect the neutral switch wires. Disconnect the vacuum hose from the diaphragm, the electrical connector from the downshift solenoid and the speedometer cable from the extension housing.

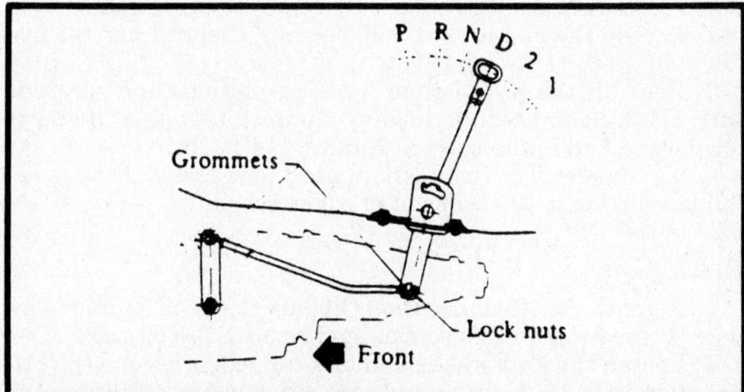

Automatic trans shift linkage

7. Remove the transmission fluid filler tube.
8. Using flare nut wrench, disconnect and plug the oil cooler lines from the transmission. Disconnect the governor tube from the converter housing/transmission case.
9. Using a floor jack and a block of wood (placed under the oil pan), support the engine. Using a transmission jack, support the transmission.

NOTE: When supporting the engine with a block of wood, do not position the wood under the oil drain plug.

10. Remove the torque converter housing dust cover. Using a piece of chalk, matchmark the converter with the drive plate for reassembly; the unit was balanced at the factory. Remove the torque converter-to-drive plate (flywheel) bolts; using a wrench on the crankshaft pulley bolt, rotate the crankshaft to expose the hidden torque converter bolts.
11. Remove the rear engine mount-to-crossmember bolts, the crossmember-to-chassis bolts and the crossmember.
12. Remove the starter electrical connectors, the starter-to-engine bolts and the starter.
13. Remove the transmission-to-engine bolts, then, slide the torque converter toward the transmission and secure it in place. Move the transmission rearward, lower and remove it from the vehicle.
14. Using a dial indicator, check the drive plate runout. Turn the crankshaft one full revolution. Maximum allowable runout is 0.020 in., if beyond specifications, replace the drive plate.
15. To install, use new gaskets (where necessary), align the torque converter-to-drive plate matchmarks and reverse the removal procedures.

NOTE: When installing the torque converter, be sure to align the notch in the converter with the projection on the oil pump.

16. To complete the installation, reverse the removal procedures. Torque the torque converter-to-drive plate bolts to 29–36 ft. lbs., then, rotate the engine a few turns to make sure the transmission rotates freely without binding. The upper engine-to-transmission bolt torque is 29-36 ft. lbs. (Pickups) or 22–36 ft. lbs. (Van) and the lower engine-to-transmission bolts to 20–24 ft. lbs. (Van). Check and/or refill the transmission with clean fluid. Adjust the shift linkage, the back-up light operation and the neutral switch.

Shift Linkage

Adjustment

1982-85

1. Loosen the control lever-to-linkage rod locknut.
2. Place the shift lever in "D" and the control lever on the transmission in the "D" detent position.
3. Tighten the locknut and move the shift lever through all positions making sure that the detent is felt in each position and the transmission responds properly to each gear selection. Make double certain that "Park" engages properly and holds the vehicle. If proper adjustment cannot be made in each detent, replace all shift lever and linkage grommets.

1986-88 – PICKUPS

2WD Floor Shift Models

1. Place the shift selector in the "P" position.
2. From under the vehicle, loosen the shift lever lock nuts.

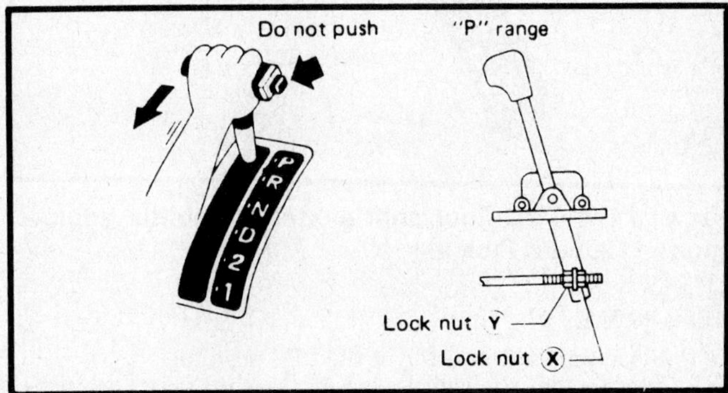

View of the 2WD floor shift model A/T shifter adjustment – 1986-88 Pickup

3. Tighten the rear lock nut "X" until it touches the trunnion; pulling the selector lever toward the "R" position (without pushing the button). Back off the rear lock nut "X" 1 revolution, adjust the front lock nut "Y" and torque the lock nuts to 5.8–8.0 ft. lbs.

4. After adjustment, move the selector lever through the ranges to make sure it moves smoothly.

2WD Column Shift Models

1. Place the shift selector in the "P" position.
2. From under the vehicle, loosen the shift lever lock nuts.
3. Tighten the front lock nut "A" until it touches the trunnion; pulling the selector lever toward the "R" position (without pushing the button). Back off the front lock nut "A" 2 revolutions, adjust the rear lock nut "B" and torque the lock nuts to 5.8–8.0 ft. lbs.
4. After adjustment, move the selector lever through the ranges to make sure it moves smoothly.

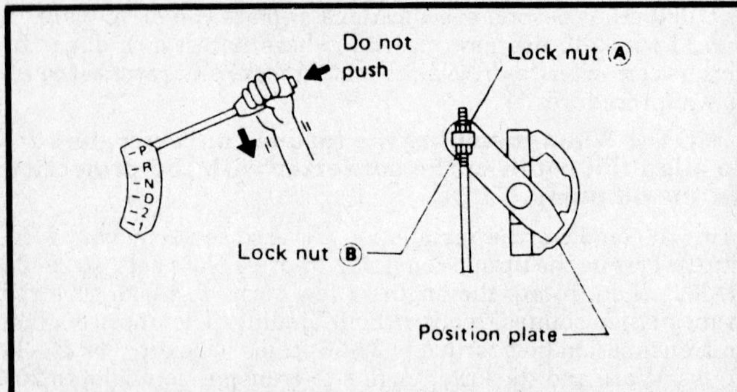

View of the 2WD column shift model A/T shifter adjustment – 1986-88 Pickup

4WD Floor Shift Models

1. Place the shift selector in the "P" position.
2. Remove the console cover.
3. Loosen the turn buckle lock nuts.
3. Tighten the turn buckle until it aligns with the inner cable; pulling the selector lever toward the "R" position (without pushing the button). Back off the turn buckle 1 revolution, torque the lock nuts to 3.3–4.3 ft. lbs.
4. After adjustment, move the selector lever through the ranges to make sure it moves smoothly.

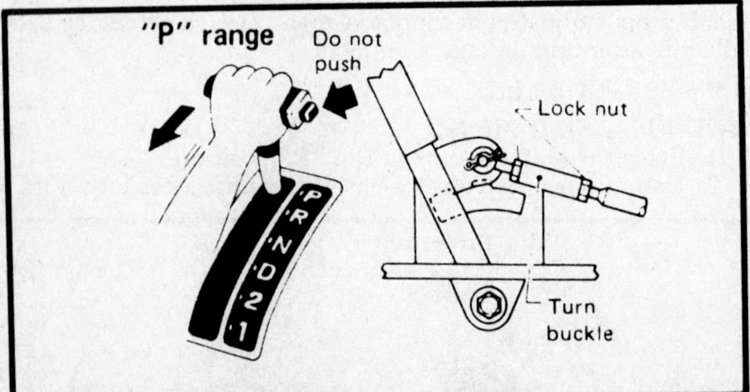

View of the 4WD floor shift model A/T shifter adjustment – 1986-88 Pickup

1987-88 VAN

1. Place the shift selector in the "P" position.
2. From under the vehicle, loosen the shift lever lock nuts.
3. Tighten the front lock nut "X" until it touches the trunnion; pulling the selector lever toward the "R" position (without pushing the button). Back off the front lock nut "X" ¼ revolution, adjust the rear lock nut "Y" and torque the lock nuts to 7–9 ft. lbs.
4. After adjustment, move the selector lever through the ranges to make sure it moves smoothly.

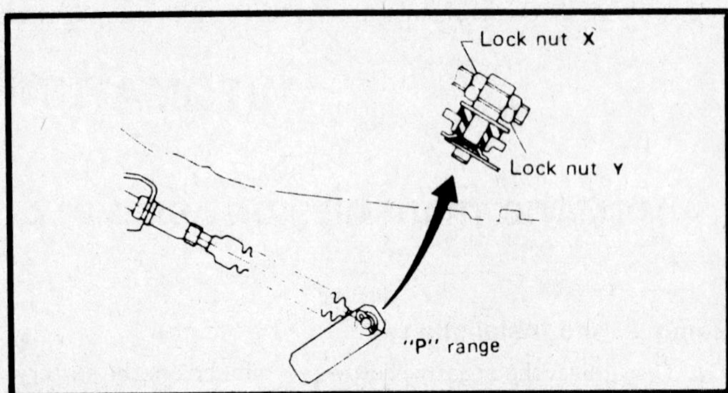

View of the floor shift model A/T shifter adjustment – 1987-88 Van

Band Adjustments

INTERMEDIATE

Procedure

1982-85

1. Refer to the "Transmission Oil Pan, Removal and Installation" procedures in this section and remove the oil pan.
2. Loosen the 2nd brake band lock nut, then, torque the piston stem to 9–11 ft. lbs.
3. Back off the piston stem 2 full revolutions and secure it with the lock nut. While holding the piston stem stationary, torque the 2nd brake band lock nut to 14 ft. lbs.
4. To complete the installation, use a new gasket, Dexron II® fluid and reverse the removal procedures.

1986-88

1. Refer to the "Transmission Oil Pan, Removal and Installation" procedures in this section and remove the oil pan.
2. Loosen the 2nd brake band lock nut, then, torque the piston stem to 9–11 ft. lbs.
3. Back off the piston stem 3 full revolutions and secure it with the lock nut. While holding the piston stem stationary, torque the 2nd brake band lock nut to 11–29 ft. lbs.
4. To complete the installation, use a new gasket, Dexron II® fluid and reverse the removal procedures.

OVERDRIVE

Procedure

1986-88

1. Remove the overdrive brake band-to-transmission cover bolts and cover.
2. Loosen the overdrive piston stem lock nut, then, torque the piston stem to 5.1–7.2 ft. lbs.
3. Back off the piston stem 2 full revolutions and secure it with the lock nut. While holding the piston stem stationary, torque the lock nut to 11–29 ft. lbs.
4. To complete the installation, use a new gasket and reverse the removal procedures.

Kickdown Switch

A kickdown switch is located inside the vehicle at the upper post of the accelerator pedal. It purpose is to provide transmission downshifting when the accelerator pedal is fully depressed; a click can be heard just before the pedal bottoms out.

Adjustment

With the ignition switch in the On position and the engine Off, when the accelerator pedal is depressed fully, the kick-down switch contacts should be closed and the downshift solenoid activated, emitting a clicking sound. If the components fail to operate in this manner, check for continuity first at the switch and then at the solenoid if the switch checks out as being satisfactory. Replace either of the components as necessary.

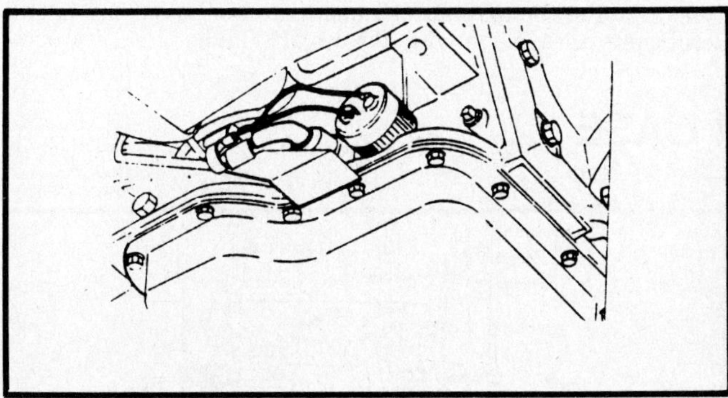

Downshift solenoid

Modulator

A vacuum modulator is used to help determine the shift patterns of the transmission.

Removal and Installation

1. Disconnect the vacuum hose from the vacuum modulator.

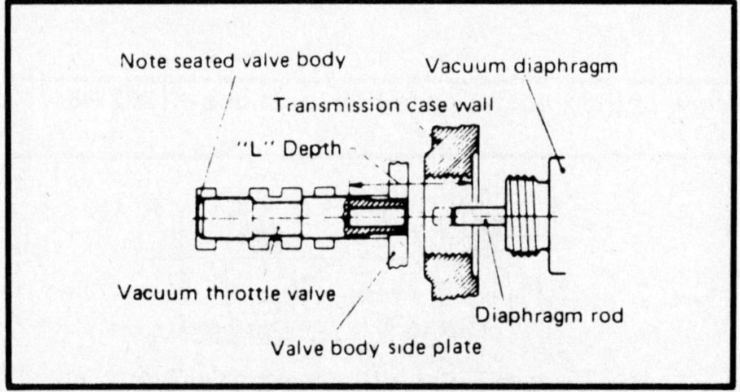

Cross-sectional view of the vacuum modulator—A/T

2. Unscrew and remove the vacuum modulator from the left-side of the transmission.
3. To install, use a new O-ring and reverse the removal procedures.

Adjustment

1. Remove the vacuum modulator from the transmission case.
2. Using a depth gauge, measure the "L" depth of the vacuum throttle valve.
3. Using an "L" depth chart, select the proper rod length.

Neutral Start Switch

The neutral safety switch is located on the transmission shift selector lever. The switch operates the back-up lights and controls the operation of the starter. The starter should only operate when the transmission is in Park or Neutral.

Removal and Installation

1. Disconnect the electrical connector from the neutral start switch.
2. Remove the shift selector lever-to-transmission nut and the shift lever.
3. Remove the neutral start switch-to-transmission screws and the switch.
4. To install, reverse the removal procedures and adjust the switch.

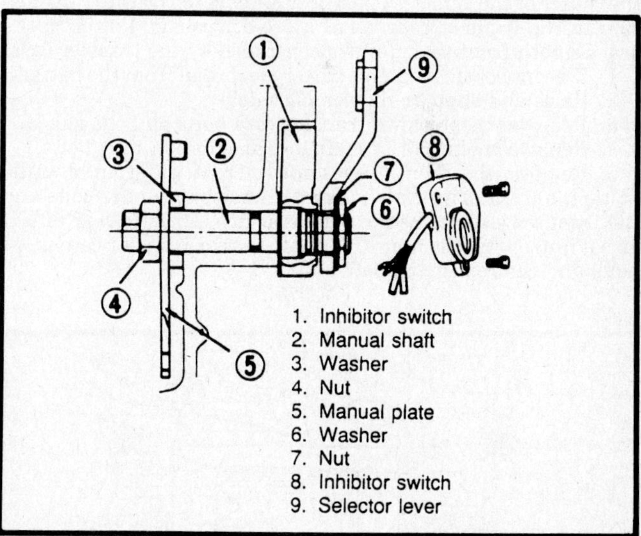

Neutral safety switch

Measured depth "L" mm (in)	Rod length mm (in)	Part number
Under 25.55 (1.0059)	29.0 (1.142)	31932-X0103
25.65 - 26.05 (1.0098 - 1.0256)	29.5 (1.161)	31932-X0104
26.15 - 26.55 (1.0295 - 1.0453)	30.0 (1.181)	31932-X0100
26.65 - 27.05 (1.0492 - 1.0650)	30.5 (1.201)	31932-X0102
Over 27.15 (1.0689)	31.0 (1.220)	31932-X0101

Vacuum modulator rod selection chart—A/T

Adjustment

1. Unscrew the securing nut of the shift selector lever and the switch-to-transmission screws.
2. Position the shift selector to the Neutral position (in vertical position and detent clicks). Move the switch slightly aside so that the screw hole will be aligned with the pin hole of the shift selector lever.
3. Using a 0.080 in. (2mm) diameter alignment pin, place it in the alignment holes of the neutral start switch and the shift selector lever.

NOTE: A No. 47 drill bit will substitute for the pin gauge.

4. Secure the switch body with the screws and pull out the pin.

NOTE: If the neutral safety switch does not perform satisfactorily after adjustment, replace it with a new one.

Oil Pan

Removal and Installation

1. Using a drain catch pan, position it under the transmission case.
2. Remove the oil pan-to-transmission bolts.

NOTE: When removing the bolts, do not remove all of them but do loosen them.

3. Using a mallet, hit one side of the pan, knocking it loose; allow the oil to drain from one corner, then, remove the remaining bolts and the pan.
4. Using a putty knife, clean the gasket mounting surfaces.
5. To install, use a new gasket and reverse the removal procedures. Torque the oil pan-to-transmission bolts 3.6–5.1 ft. lbs. Refill the transmission with Dexron II® fluid.

TRANSFER CASE

For all overhaul procedures, please refer to "Transfer Case" in the Unit Repair Section.

Transfer Case

Removal and Installation

1982-85

The 1982-85 model transfer case is a separate unit mounted in the center of the vehicle. The power is delivered by the transmission to the transfer case via of a pre-driveshaft. Power to the rear or both front/rear units is controlled by the transfer case.

1. Disconnect the negative battery terminal from the battery.
2. Raise and support the vehicle safely.
3. Remove the shield-to-transfer case bolts and the shield.
4. Remove the pre-driveshaft-to-transmission nuts/bolts.
5. Remove the front driveshaft-to-front differential nuts/bolts, the front driveshaft-to-front transfer case nuts/bolts and the front driveshaft. Remove the rear driveshaft-to-rear differential nuts/bolts, the rear driveshaft-to-rear transfer case nuts/bolts and the rear driveshaft.

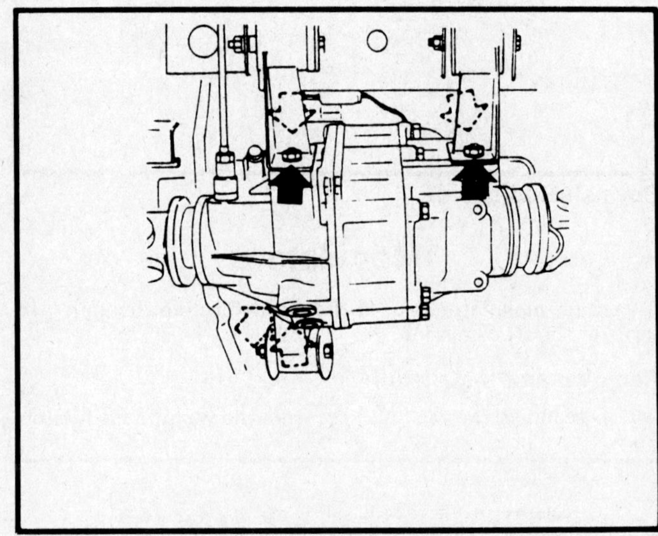

View of the transfer case bolt locations—1982-85

View of the transfer case shield bolt locations—1982-85

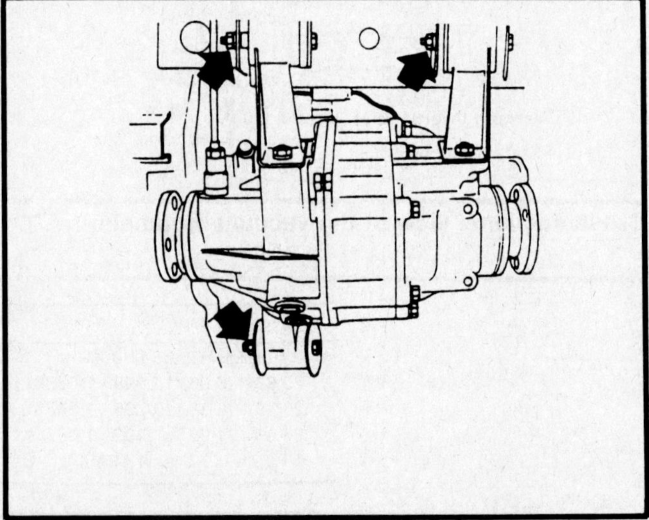

View of the transfer case insulator bolt locations—1982-85

6. Disconnect the 4WD switch wire and the speedometer cable.
7. Remove the exhaust pipe-to-exhaust manifold nuts and the exhaust pipe to catalytic converter nuts/bolts and the exhaust pipe.
8. Using a floor jack, support the transfer case.
9. Temporarily loosen the transfer case-to-chassis insulator bolts.
10. From the floor, remove the shift lever rubber boot.
11. Remove the transfer case-to-chassis bolts and the transfer case from the vehicle..
12. To install, reverse the removal procedures. Torque the transfer case-to-chassis bolts to 20–26 ft. lbs.

1986-88

The transfer case used on the 1986-88 vehicles are attached to the end of the transmission.

1. Raise and support the vehicle safely.
2. Place a drain pan under the transmission and transfer case, remove the drain plug and drain the oil from the cases.
3. Using a piece of chalk, make alignment marks on the transfer case and differential flanges.
4. Remove the front driveshaft-to-differential nuts/bolts, the front differential-to-transfer case nuts/bolts. Remove the rear driveshaft-to-differential nuts/bolts, the rear differential-to-transfer case nuts/bolts. Remove the differentials from the vehicle.
5. Remove the torsion bar springs from the front lower control arms.
6. Remove the crossmember-to-chassis bolts (located under the transfer case) and the crossmember.
7. From under the vehicle, remove the transfer control lever-to-transfer case nut, then, separate the lever from the transfer case.
8. Using a floor jack, support the transfer case.
9. Remove the transfer case-to-transmission bolts, move the transfer case rearward and lower it to the floor.
10. To install, reverse the removal procedures. Torque the transfer case-to-transmission bolts to 23–30 ft. lbs., the transfer control lever-to-transfer case nut to 18–22 ft. lbs., the crossmember-to-chassis bolt to 43–58 ft. lbs. Refill the transfer case and transmission with new fluid.

DRIVESHAFTS AND UNIVERSAL JOINTS

Driveshafts

FRONT

Removal and Installation

2WD PICKUP

The 2WD pickup is equipped with a 2-piece driveshaft and a center bearing.

1. Raise and support the vehicle safely. Using a piece of chalk, make alignment marks on the differential-to-driveshaft flange and the driveshaft-to-center bearing flange so the driveshaft can be reinstalled in the same position.
2. Remove the driveshaft-to-differential flange nuts/bolts and the driveshaft-to-center bearing flange nuts/bolts.
3. Lower and remove the rear driveshaft from the vehicle.
4. Remove the center bearing bracket-to-chassis bolts, the bracket and the front driveshaft from the vehicle.
5. Using a clean rag, plug the rear of the transmission to keep the oil from leaking out.
6. Using chalk, match-mark the driveshaft groove-to-center bearing flange. Remove the driveshaft-to-center bearing flange nut.

NOTE: It is a good idea to replace the transmission rear oil seal when the driveshaft is removed.

7. To install, align the match-marks and reverse the removal procedures. Torque the front driveshaft-to-center bearing nut to 145–174 ft. lbs. (nut/washer – 1982-85), 181–217 ft. lbs. (Model 3S63) or 174–203 ft. lbs. (Model 3S80), the driveshaft-to-differential flange nuts/bolts to 17–24 ft. lbs. (1982-85), 29–33 ft. lbs. (Model 3S63 – 1986-88) or 58–65 ft. lbs. (Model 3S80 – 1986-88), the center bearing bracket-to-chassis nuts/bolts to 12–16 ft. lbs. and the rear driveshaft-to-center bearing flange nuts/bolts to 17–24 ft. lbs. (1982-85), 29–33 ft. lbs. (Model 3S63 – 1986-88) or 58–65 ft. lbs. (Model 3S80 – 1986-88)

VAN

1. Raise and support the vehicle safely. Using a piece of chalk, make alignment marks on the differential-to-driveshaft flange so the driveshaft can be reinstalled in the same position.
2. Remove the driveshaft-to-differential flange nuts/bolts.
3. Lower and remove the driveshaft from the vehicle.
4. Using a clean rag, plug the rear of the transmission to keep the oil from leaking out.

NOTE: It is a good idea to replace the transmission rear oil seal when the driveshaft is removed.

5. To install, align the match-marks and reverse the removal procedures. Torque the driveshaft-to-differential flange nuts/bolts to 29–33 ft. lbs.

4WD

The 4WD 1982-85 pickups use 3 driveshafts: a primary (transmission-to-transfer case), a front and a rear; the 4WD 1986-88 pickups use 2 driveshafts.

Primary Driveshaft (1982-85)

1. Using a piece of chalk, make alignment marks on the primary driveshaft-to-transfer case flanges.
2. Remove the primary driveshaft-to-transfer case nuts/bolts, then, separate the driveshaft from the transfer case.
3. Remove the transfer case.
4. Pull the primary shaft from the transmission. Using a clean rag, plug the opening at the end of the transmission.
5. To install, align the match-marks and reverse the removal procedures. Torque the primary driveshaft-to-transfer case nuts/bolts to 25–33 ft. lbs. (1982-83) or 58–65 ft. lbs. (1984-85).

Front Driveshaft

1. Using a piece of chalk, make alignment marks on the front driveshaft-to-front differential flange and the front driveshaft-to-transfer case flange.
2. Remove the front driveshaft-to-front differential flange nuts/bolts and the front driveshaft flange.
3. Remove the front driveshaft from the vehicle.
4. To install, align the match-marks and reverse the removal procedures. Torque the front driveshaft-to-front differential flange and the front driveshaft-to-transfer case flange nuts/bolts to 25–33 ft. lbs. (1982-85) or 29–33 ft. lbs. (1986-88).

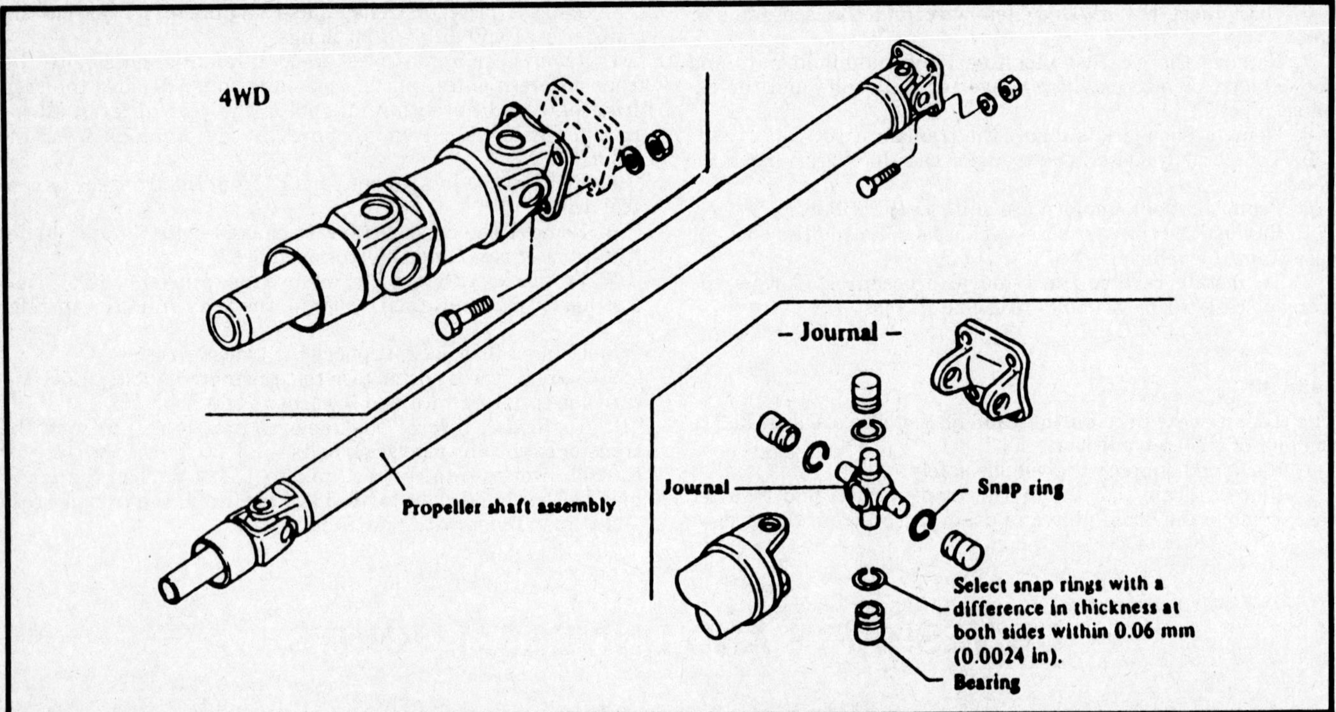

Front axle propellor shaft: the left insert shows the primary driveshaft which connects the transfer case with the transmission

CENTER BEARING 2WD PICKUP

The center bearing is a sealed unit which must be replaced as an assembly if defective.

Removal and Installation

1. Refer to the "Driveshaft, Removal and Installation" procedures in this section and remove the driveshaft assembly with the center bearing.
2. Using a piece of chalk, match-mark the center bearing flange-to-driveshaft flange, then, remove the nuts/bolts and separate the shafts.
3. Using a piece of chalk, match-mark the center bearing flange with the keyway slot of the driveshaft.
4. Remove the front driveshaft-to-center bearing flange nut, the companion flange, washer, the center bearing and the seal.
5. To install, use a new seal, position the center bearing with the "F" mark toward the front of the vehicle and reverse the removal procedures. Torque the companion flange-to-driveshaft nut to 181–217 ft. lbs. (flange type nut – 1982-85 or Model 3S63 – 1986-88) or 145–174 ft. lbs. (nut/washer – 1982-85 or Model 3S80 – 1986-88).

NOTE: Check that the center bearing rotates freely around the driveshaft.

5. To complete the installation, align the alignment marks and reverse the removal procedures. Torque the center bearing flange-to-rear driveshaft nuts/bolts to 17–24 ft. lbs. (1982-85 or Model 3S63 – 1986-88) or 58–65 ft. lbs. (Model 3S80 – 1986-88), the rear driveshaft-to-differential flange nuts/bolts to 17–24 ft. lbs. (1982-85), 29–30 ft. lbs. (Model 3S63 – 1986-88) or 58–65 ft. lbs. (Model 3S80 – 1986-88).

REAR

Removal and Installation

2WD PICKUP

1. Raise and support the vehicle safely. Using a piece of chalk, make alignment marks on the differential-to-driveshaft flange and the driveshaft-to-center bearing flange so the driveshaft can be reinstalled in the same position.
2. Remove the driveshaft-to-differential flange nuts/bolts and the driveshaft-to-center bearing flange nuts/bolts.
3. Lower and remove the rear driveshaft from the vehicle.
4. To install, align the match-marks and reverse the removal procedures. Torque the driveshaft-to-differential flange nuts/bolts to 17–24 ft. lbs. (1982-85), 29–33 ft. lbs. (Model 3S63 – 1986-88) or 58–65 ft. lbs. (Model 3S80 – 1986-88) and the driveshaft-to-center bearing flange nuts/bolts to 17–24 ft. lbs. (1982-85), 29–33 ft. lbs. (Model 3S63 – 1986-88) or 58–65 ft. lbs. (Model 3S80 – 1986-88).

4WD PICKUP

1. Using a piece of chalk, make alignment marks on the rear driveshaft-to-rear differential flange.
2. Remove the rear differential-to-driveshaft nuts/bolts.
3. Move the driveshaft rearward (disconnecting it from the transfer case), be sure to plug the rear of the transfer case to keep the oil from leaking from it.
4. To install, use a new transfer case oil seal, align the match-marks and reverse the removal procedures. Torque the driveshaft flange-to-differential flange nuts/bolts to 17–24 ft. lbs. (1982-85) or 58–65 ft. lbs. (1986-88).

Universal Joints

For service information, refer to the "U-Joint/CV-Joint" section in Unit Repair.

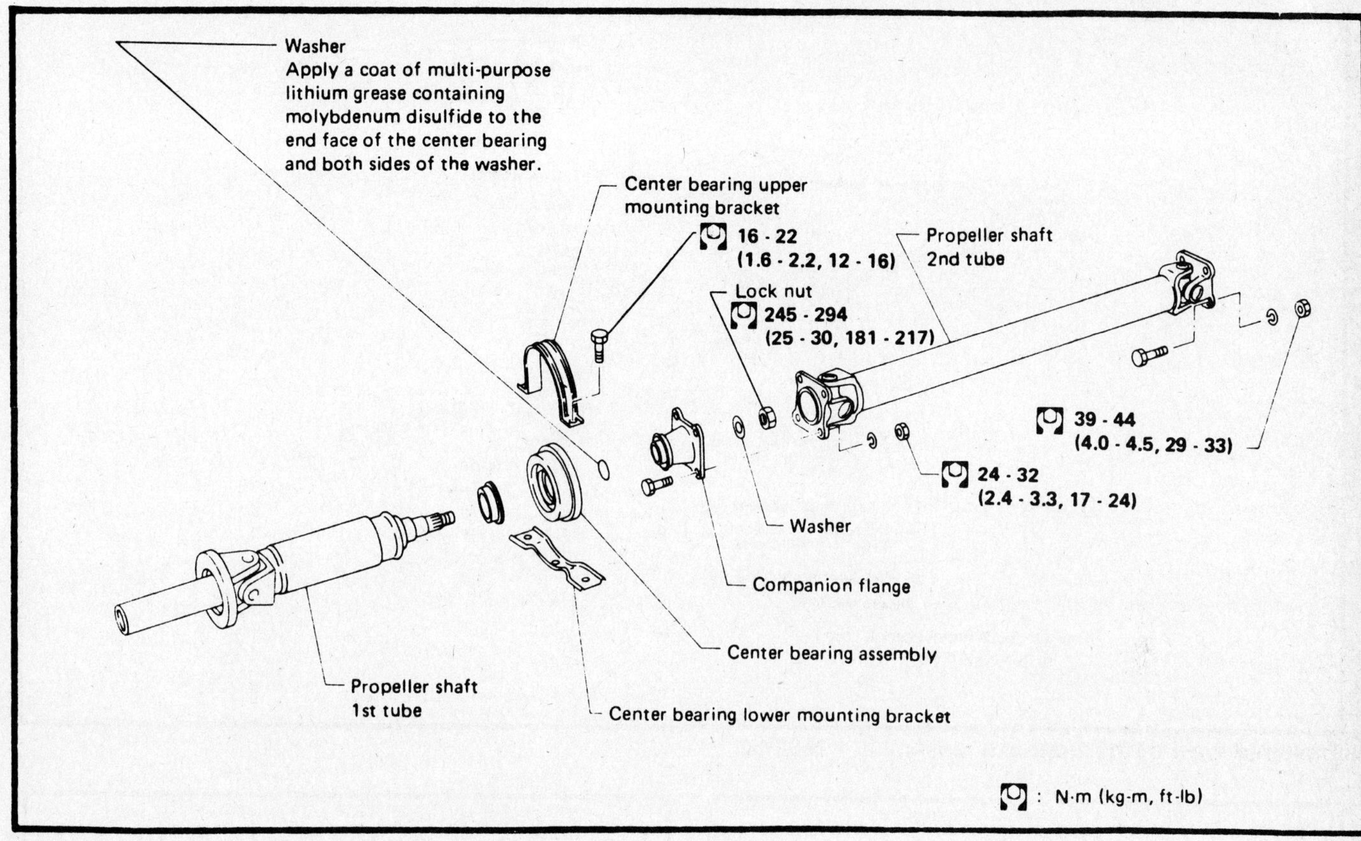

Exploded view of the 2WD driveshaft—typical

FRONT DRIVE AXLE—4WD

For overhaul information, refer to "Drive Axles" in the Unit Overhaul Section.

Locking Hubs

Removal and Installation

MANUAL

1. Remove the locking hub assembly-to-hub Torx® bolts.
2. Pull the locking hub assembly from the wheel hub.
3. From the halfshaft, remove the snapring and the drive clutch.
4. To install, reverse the removal procedures. Torque the locking hub-to-wheel hub Torx® bolts to 18–25 ft. lbs.

AUTOMATIC (1984-88)

1. Raise and support the front of the vehicle safely.
2. Remove the locking hub assembly-to-hub Torx® bolts.
3. Pull the locking hub assembly from the wheel hub.
4. From the halfshaft, remove the snapring and the washers.
5. To install, reverse the removal procedures. Torque the automatic hub-to-wheel hub Torx® bolts to 18–25 ft. lbs.

Halfshaft

Removal and Installation

1982-83

1. Refer to the "Locking Hubs, Removal and Installation" procedures in this section and remove the locking hubs.
2. Remove the snapring and the running hub.
3. Remove the front rebound bumper.
4. Remove the stabilizer bar-to-lower link bolt.
5. Remove the halfshaft-to-differential carrier bolts; DO NOT remove the rubber boots!
6. Pull the halfshaft from the wheel hub. It helps to turn the steering wheel to the right when pulling the right shaft and left when pulling the left shaft.

NOTE: Upon installation: Apply multi-purpose wheel bearing grease to the copper portion of the wheel bearing support and adjust the halfshaft axial end play by installing the proper thickness of snaprings on the end of the shaft.

7. To install, reverse the removal procedures. Torque the halfshaft-to-differential flange bolts to 20–27 ft. lbs., the locking hub-to-wheel hub bolts to 18–25 ft. lbs., the stabilizer bar-to-chassis bolts to 12–16 ft. lbs., the stabilizer bar-to-lower link bolt to 12–16 ft. lbs. and the wheel nuts to 87–108 ft. lbs.

1984-88

1. Refer to the "Locking Hubs, Removal and Installation" procedures in this section and remove the locking hubs.
2. Remove the snapring and drive clutch. Disconnect the tie-rod from the steering knuckle.
3. Remove the lower ball joint-to-lower control arm bolts; using a floor jack, support the lower control arm.
4. Remove the lower shock absorber-to-lower control arm nut/bolt.
5. Remove the halfshaft-to-differential carrier bolts and the halfshaft from the front axle.

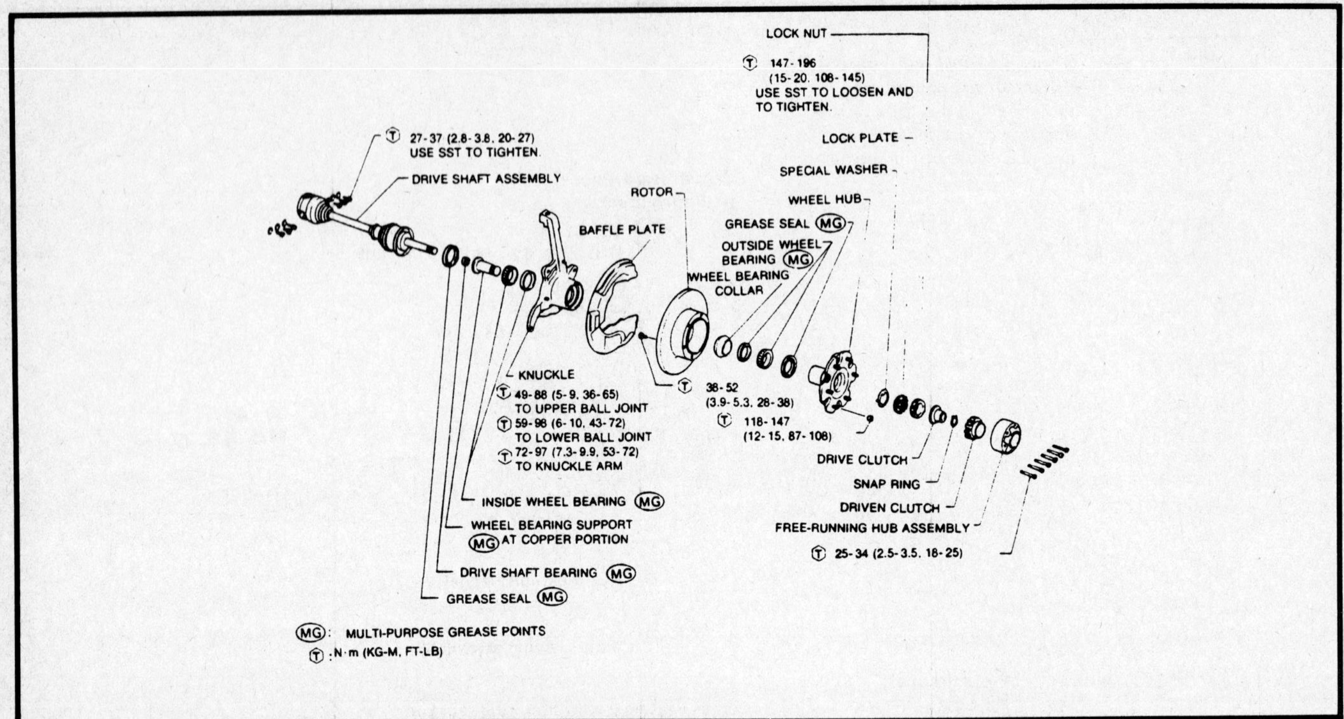

Exploded view of the front axle assembly—1982-83

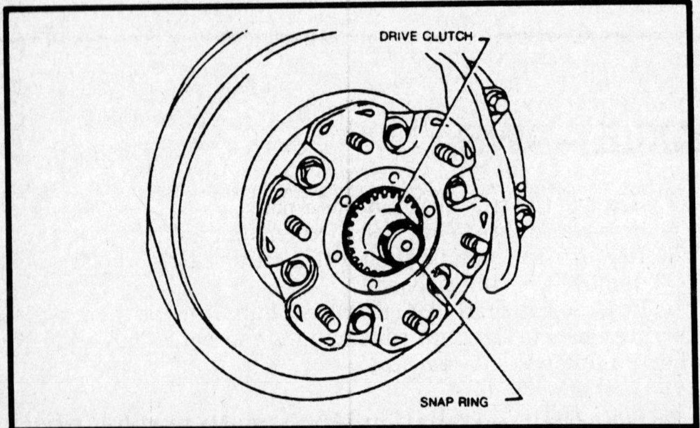

View of the free-running hub snap-ring and driven clutch—4WD 1982-83

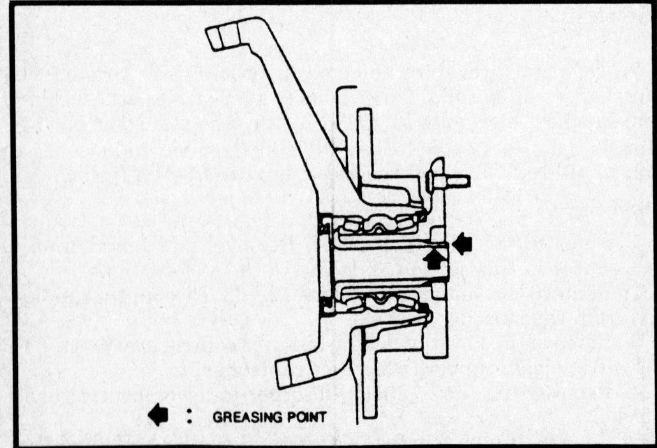

Copper wheel bearing support greasing locations

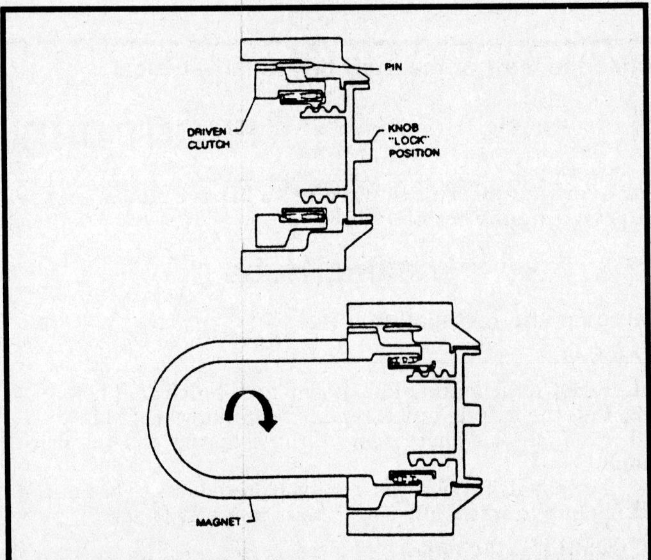

Hub removal sequence

6. Pull the halfshaft from the wheel hub. It helps to turn the steering wheel to the right when pulling the right shaft and left when pulling the left shaft.

NOTE: Upon installation, apply chassis lube to all bearing surfaces, make sure the spacer is in place and adjust the halfshaft end play (by using various thicknesses of snaprings) to 0.004–0.012 in.

7. To install, reverse the removal procedures. Torque the halfshaft-to-differential bolts to 20–27 ft. lbs. (1984-85) or 25–33 ft. lbs. (1986-88), the locking hub-to-wheel hub bolts to 18–25 ft. lbs., the lower ball joint-to-lower control arm nuts/bolts to 28–38 ft. lbs. (1984-85) or 35–45 ft. lbs. (1986-88).

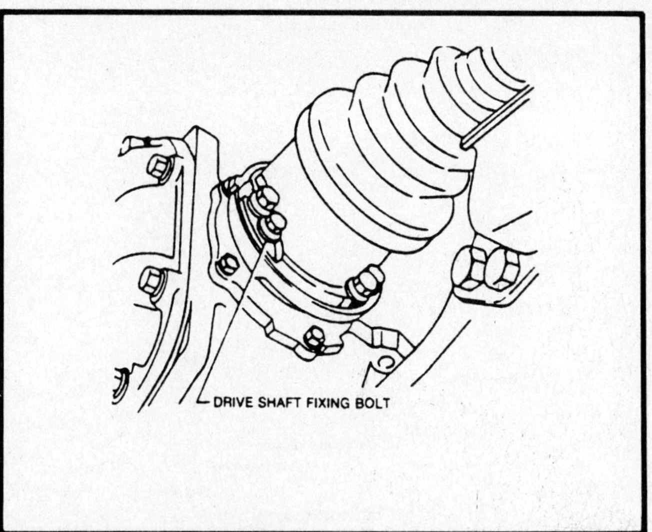

Axle shaft-to-carrier bolts

Differential Carrier

Removal and Installation

1. Refer to the "Halfshaft, Removal and Installation" procedures in this section and separate the halfshafts from the front differential.
2. Remove the front driveshaft from the front differential and transfer case.
3. On the 1982-85 pickups, perform the following procedures:
   a. Remove the differential-to-front mount insulator bracket nut/bolt.
   b. Remove the differential crossmember-to-chassis bolts.
   c. Lower the differential assembly from the vehicle.
4. On the 1986-88 pickups, perform the following procedures:
   a. Remove the engine-to-mount bolts.
   b. Raise and support the engine.
   c. Remove the differential support member-to-chassis bolts.
   d. Remove the differential-to-front mount insulator bracket nut/bolt.
   e. Lower the differential from the vehicle.
5. To install, reverse the removal procedures. Torque the differential-to-front insulator bracket nut/bolt to 52–71 ft. lbs. (1982-85) or 50–64 ft. lbs. (1986-88), the differential-to-front crossmember nuts to 37–50 ft. lbs. (1982-85) or 50–64 ft. lbs. (1986-88), the differential crossmember-to-chassis nuts/bolts to 52–71 ft. lbs. (1982-85). Inspect the front differential oil level.

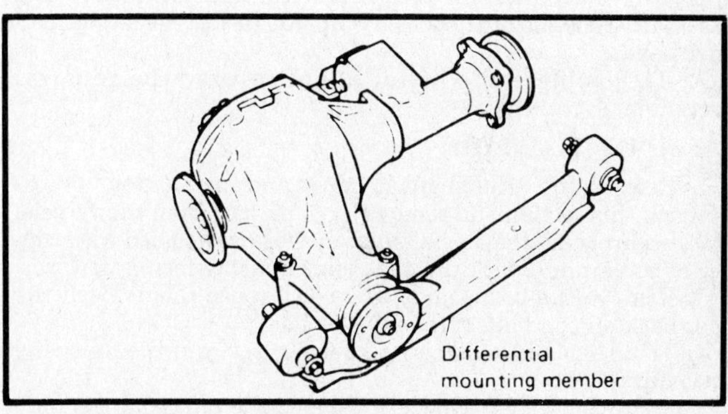

View of the front differential (1986-88)

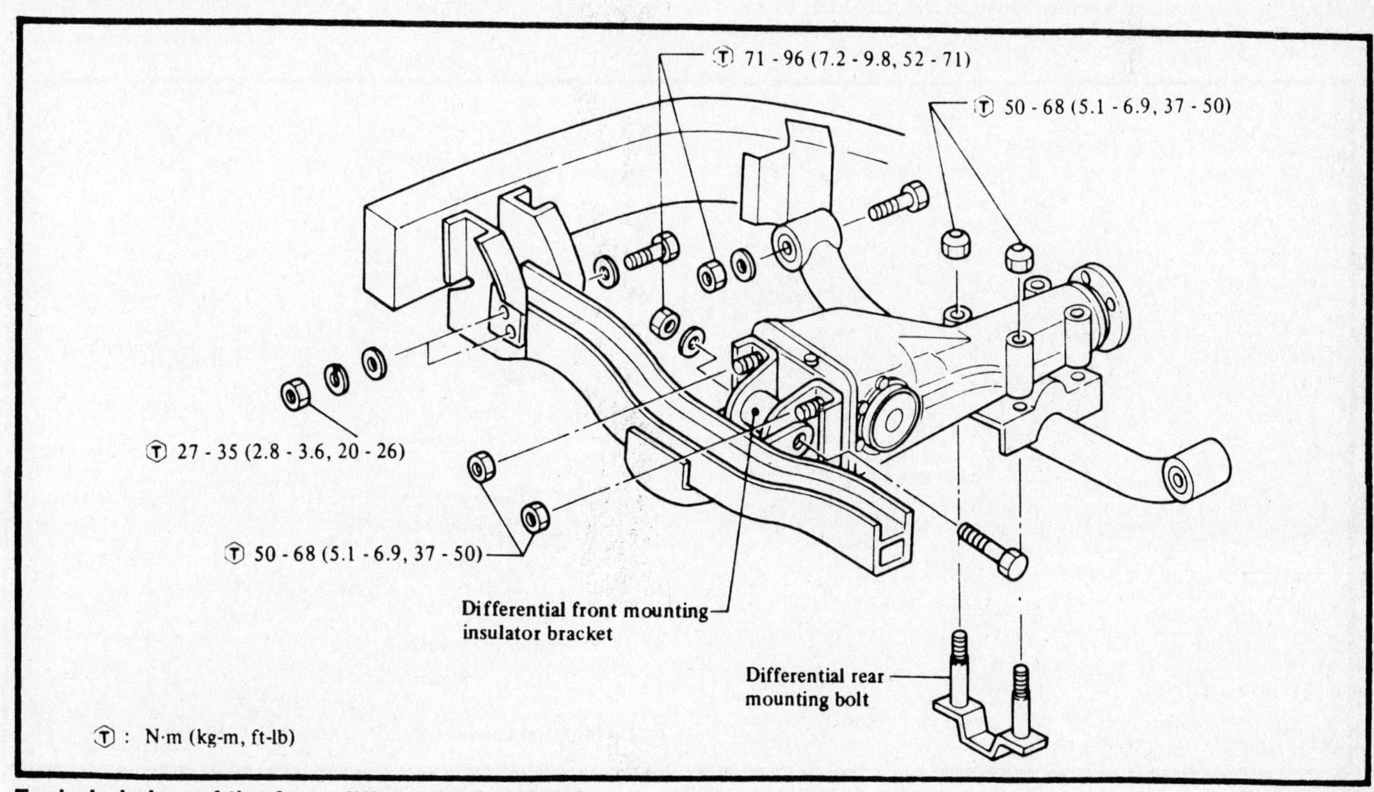

Exploded view of the front differential (1982-85)

Halfshaft Bearings

Removal and Installation

WHEEL SIDE

1. Refer to the "Halfshaft, Removal and Installation" procedures in this section and remove the halfshaft from the vehicle.
2. Remove the boot bands; DO NOT reuse them. Push the boot back on the halfshaft.
3. Using a piece of chalk, make alignment marks on the ball joint and halfshaft. The ball joint is of a non-disassembling design; it can be separated by lightly tapping it with a mallet.
4. Using solvent and compressed air, throughly clean all of the parts.
5. Inspect for ball joint and halfshaft spline damage and/or deformation; if necessary, replace the ball joint assembly or halfshaft.
6. To install, use multi-purpose grease to grease the halfshaft ball joint, make sure the ball joint moves freely. Using a mallet, align the match-marks and drive the ball joint onto the halfshaft. Slide the dust boot forward and install the large/small boot bands.
7. To complete the installation, reverse the removal procedures.

DIFFERENTIAL SIDE

1. Refer to the "Halfshaft, Removal and Installation" procedures in this section and remove the halfshaft from the vehicle.
2. Securely mount the halfshaft in a vise (jaws lined with copper or aluminum) with the slide joint housing facing upward.
3. Remove the boot bands; DO NOT reuse them. Push the boot back on the halfshaft.
4. To disassemble slide joint housing, perform the following procedures:
   a. On the 1982-85 models, remove the plug and the plug seal.
   b. On the 1986-88 models, strike the slide joint housing flange (with a mallet), forcing it toward the halfshaft, to dislodge the plug seal from the housing. Remove the internal snapring, then, discard the snapring and the plug seal.
   c. Move the slide joint housing downward on the halfshaft.
5. Using a piece of chalk, make alignment marks on the spider assembly and the halfshaft.

NOTE: The spider assembly is of a non-disassembling design.

6. Using an arbor or hydraulic press, press the spider assembly from the halfshaft; be sure to hold the halfshaft to keep it from dropping on the floor.
7. Inspect the spider assembly for needle bearing and washer damage; the halfshaft serrations for damage and the boot for fatigue, cracks and/or wear. If necessary, replaced the damaged part(s).

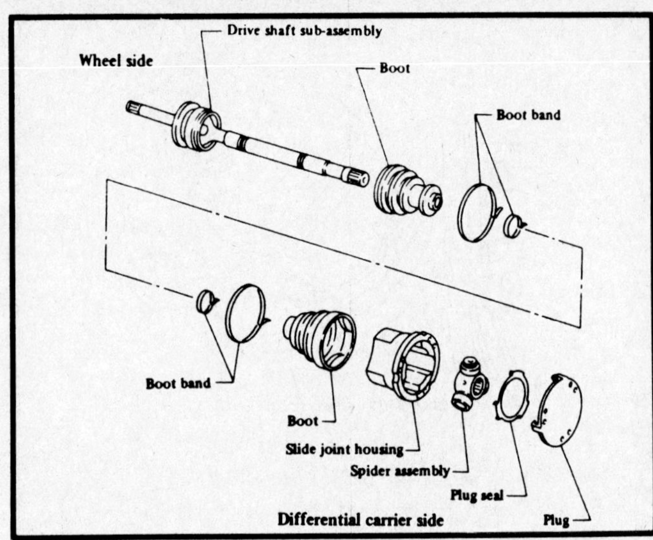

Exploded view of the halfshaft assembly (1982-85) –4WD

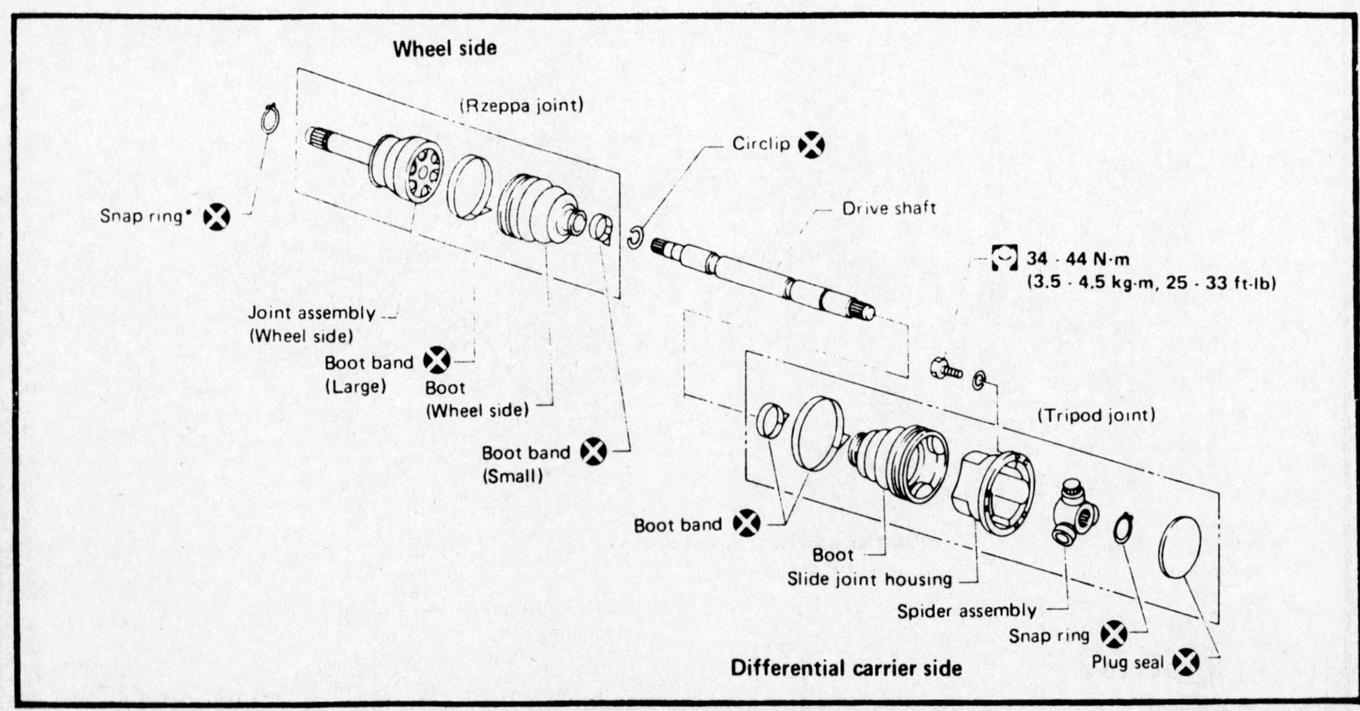

Exploded view of the halfshaft assembly (1986-88)–4WD

8. To install the spider assembly, perform the following procedures:

a. Align the spider assembly-to-halfshaft marks, then, press the spider assembly onto the halfshaft.

NOTE: If using a new spider assembly, be sure align (balance) it with the wheel-side joint.

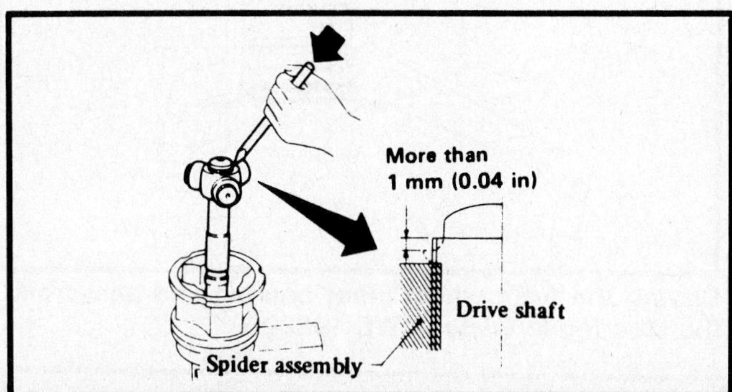

Using a center punch to caulk the spider assembly to the halfshaft (1982-85) – 4WD

b. Using a center punch, on the 1982-85 models, caulk the spider assembly (in 3 places) to the halfshaft; make sure there is at least 0.04 in. of halfshaft protruding beyond the spider assembly and the caulking is located on 2 serrations.

c. On the 1986-88 models, install a new snapring on the halfshaft.

9. Pack the slide joint housing with multi-grease, push the housing over the spider assembly, install the plug seal/plug (1982-85) or plug seal (1986-88).

NOTE: When installing the plug seal/plug (1982-85), coat the sealing edges with grease. When installing the plug seal (1986-88), coat the sealing edges with sealant.

10. On the 1982-85 models, install 3 dummy nuts/bolts to secure the plug seal to the slide joint housing.

11. Install the boot and the new boot bands.

12. To complete the installation, reverse the removal procedures. Check and/or adjust the front end alignment.

Wheel Bearings

Removal and Installation

1982-83

1. Refer to the "Steering Knuckle, Removal and Installation" procedures in this section and remove the steering knuckle.

2. Using a press, push the wheel bearing support from the wheel hub.

3. Using the Slide Hammer tool No. ST36230000 or equivalent, and the Rear Axle Stand tool No. KV40101000 or equivalent, pull the wheel hub/rotor assembly from the steering knuckle.

4. To replace the wheel bearings on the wheel hub, perform the following procedure:

a. Remove the rotor-to-wheel hub bolts and the rotor.

b. Remove the bearing collar and seal from the wheel hub.

c. Using a block of wood, knock the hub on a wooden block to move the outer bearing from the hub surface, then, use a press to remove the bearing from the wheel hub shaft. Remove the grease seal.

d. To install, use new grease seals, a new collar and reverse the removal procedures.

5. To replace the wheel bearing in the steering knuckle, perform the following procedure:

a. Using a brass drift and a hammer, drive the bearing races from the steering knuckle.

b. To install, press the bearing races into the steering knuckle until they seat.

c. Using multi-purpose grease, pack the inside of the steering knuckle.

d. Use a new grease seal, lubricate the seal lips and drive it into the steering knuckle until it is flush with the housing.

6. To complete the installation, reverse the removal procedures. Torque the locknut to 108–145 ft. lbs. Turn the hub several times (in both directions) to seat the bearings. Using a spring scale, check the preload to see that it falls between 2.2–9.5 ft. lbs. If not, adjust by replacing the collar with one of a different thickness, by the number stamped on the collar. The larger the number, the thicker the collar. When preload has been correctly set, secure the nut by bending the lockwasher tip.

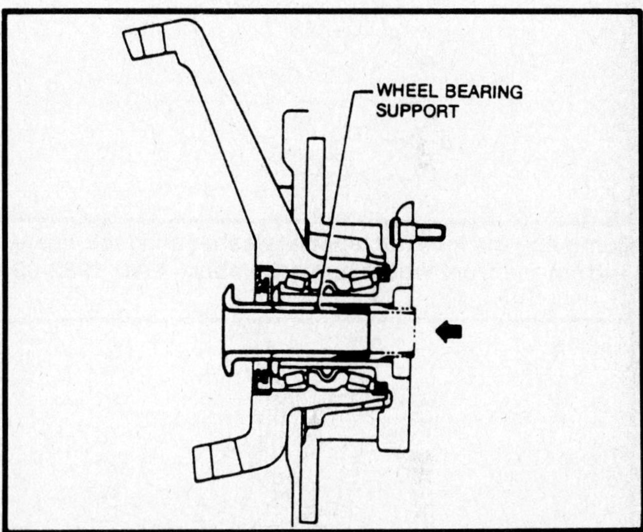

Cross-sectional view of the front wheel assembly –

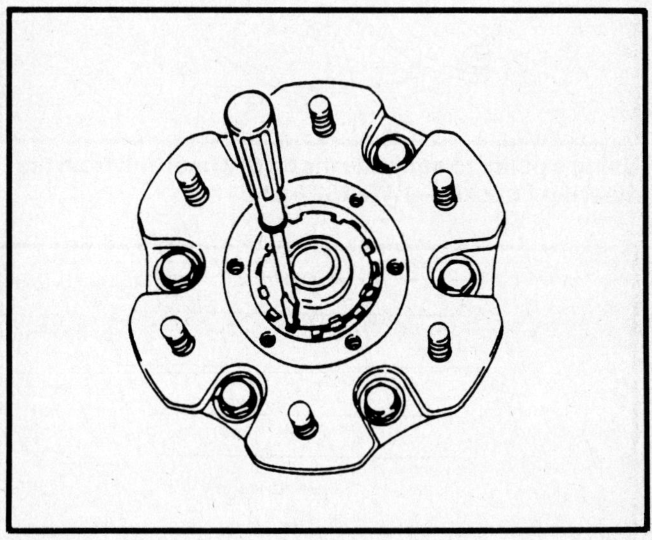

Unbending the front wheel lockwasher tab – 4WD 1982-83

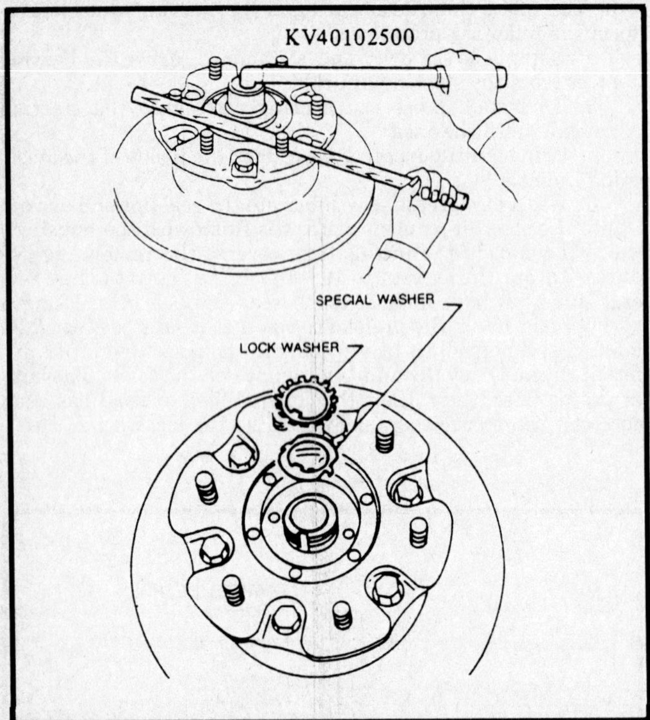

Removing the lock nut, special washer and lock washer from the front wheel hub assembly—4WD 1982-83

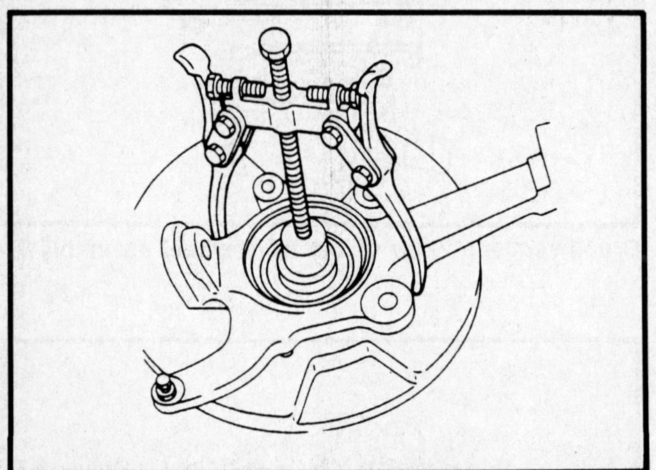
Using a puller to separate the front wheel hub from the steering knuckle—4WD 1982-83

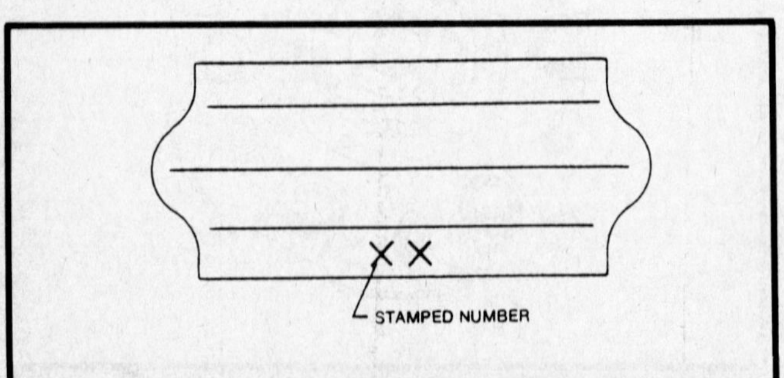

The front wheel bearing collars are stamped with a number to indicate the thickness—4WD 1982-83

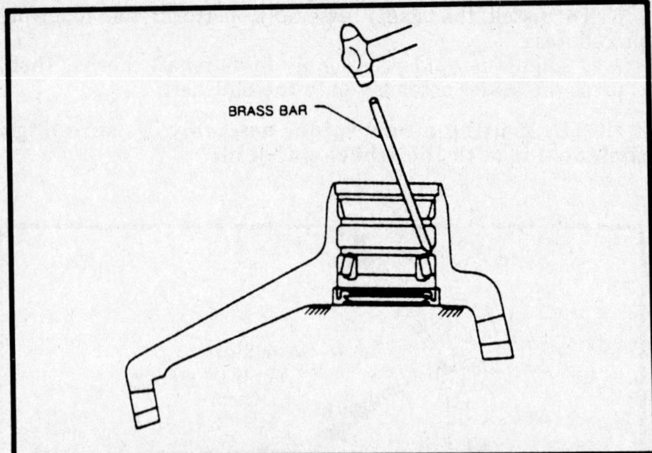

Driving the front wheel inner bearing and seal from the steering knuckle—4WD 1982-83

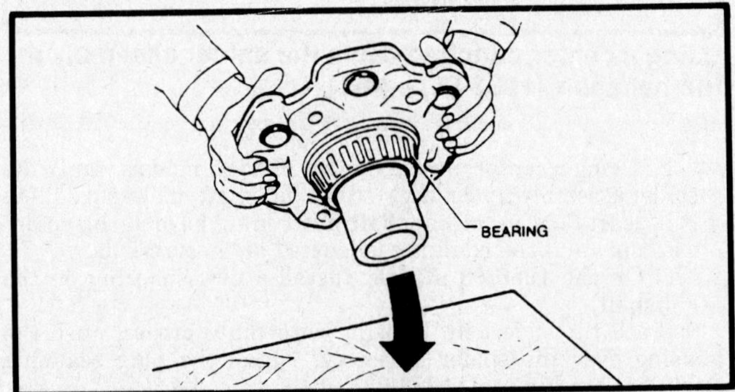

Using a wooden block to drive the outer bearing from the front wheel hub face—4WD 1982-83

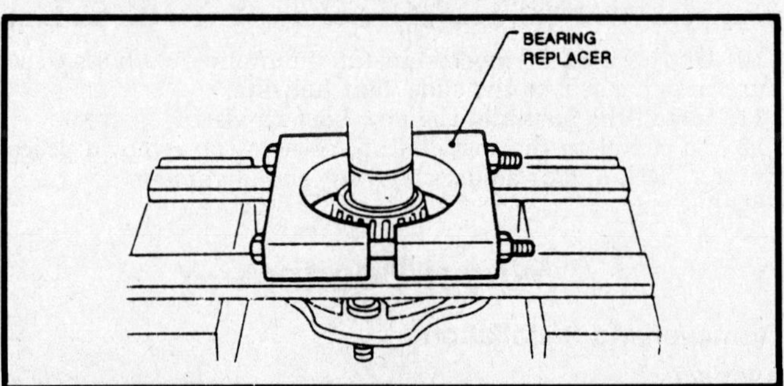

Using a press to remove the outer bearing from the front wheel hub—4WD 1982-83

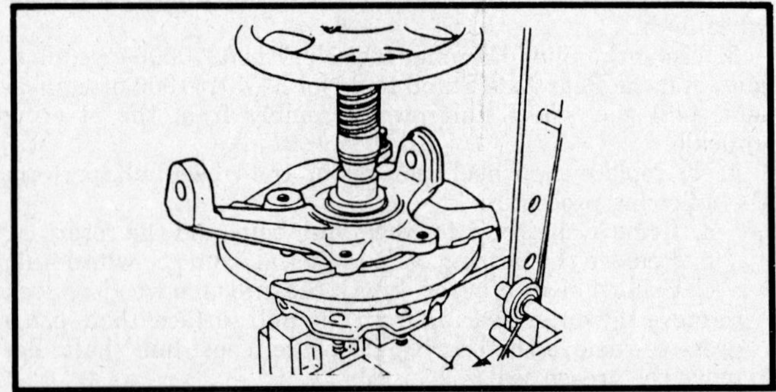
Using a press to install the outer bearing into the steering knuckle—4WD 1982-83

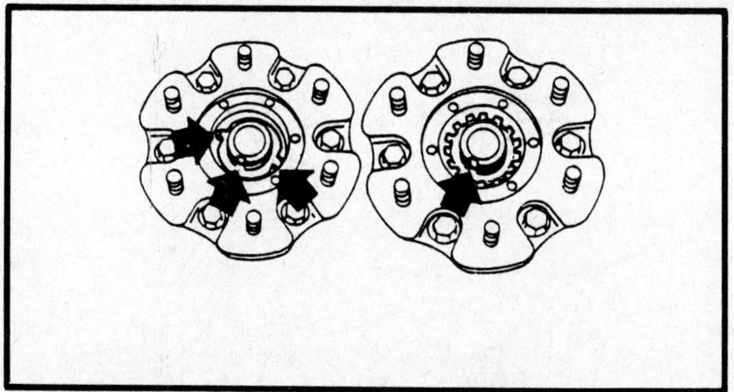

View of the proper positioning of the front wheel lock-washer and special washer—4WD 1982-83

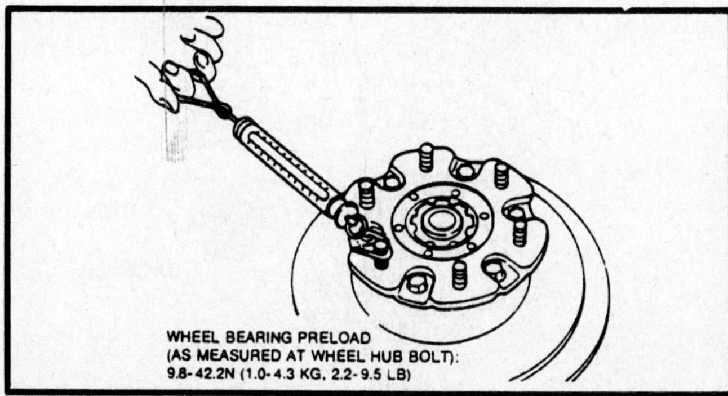

Using a spring scale to measure the front wheel assembly preload—4WD 1982-83

1984-88

1. Refer to the "Steering Knuckle, Removal and Installation" procedures in this section and remove the steering knuckle.
2. Using a brass bar, drive the inside wheel bearing race and grease seal from the wheel hub.
3. Invert the wheel hub, then, drive the outside wheel bearing race from the wheel hub.
4. Remove the needle bearing and grease seal from the rear of the steering knuckle.
5. Clean all of the parts in solvent and blow dry with compressed air.
6. Inspect the parts for damage and/or wear; if necessary, replace the damaged parts.
7. Using the Bearing Outer Race Driver Kit tool No. KV401021S0 or equivalent, drive the new bearing races into the wheel hub until they seat. Using multi-purpose grease, pack the inside of the wheel hub.
8. Force multi-purpose grease into each wheel bearing. Place the inside wheel bearing into the rear of the wheel hub, then, lubricate the new grease seal lips with grease and drive it into the wheel hub until it is flush with the wheel hub.
9. At the rear of the steering knuckle, lubricate and replace the needle bearing assembly. Install a new grease seal.
10. To install, reverse the removal procedures. Torque the wheel bearing lock nut to 58–72 ft. lbs. Adjust the wheel bearing preload. Check and/or adjust the front-end alignment.

Adjustment

1982-83

Refer to the "Wheel Bearing, Removal and Installation" procedures in this section and adjust the wheel bearing preload by replacing the collar with one of a different thickness.

1984-88

1. Raise and support the front of the vehicle safely. Remove the wheel/tire assembly.
2. Remove the locking hub, loosen the wheel bearing lock nut and retorque it to 58–72 ft. lbs.

NOTE: Before checking the wheel bearing preload, make sure the brake pads are not touching the brake disc.

3. Turn the wheel hub several times in both directions. Using a spring scale, measure the wheel bearing preload; it should be 1.59–4.72 lbs.
4. If the preload force is too light, turn the lock nut 15–30° and recheck the preload force.

NOTE: Repeat this procedure until the correct preload force is met.

5. When the correct preload force is met, bend the lock washer tab to secure the lock nut.
6. To complete the installation, reverse the removal procedures.

Steering Knuckle

Removal and Installation

1982-83

1. Block the rear wheels, then, raise and support the front of the vehicle safely.
2. Remove the wheel/tire assembly.
3. Remove the brake caliper and suspend it out of the way. DO NOT DISCONNECT THE BRAKE HOSE!
4. Using a Torx® wrench socket, remove the free-running hub assembly-to-wheel hub screws and the hub.
5. Using a pair of snapring pliers, remove the snapring from the halfshaft, then, remove the drive clutch from the halfshaft.
6. Using the Lock Nut Wrench Socket tool No. KV40102500 or equivalent, remove the lock nut (from the halfshaft), lock plate and thrust washer.
7. Remove the knuckle arm-to-steering knuckle bolts.
8. Loosen but do not remove the upper and lower ball joint nut/bolts.
9. Using a floor jack, support the lower control arm.
10. Remove the upper/lower ball joint-to-control arm nuts/bolts and the steering knuckle from the vehicle.

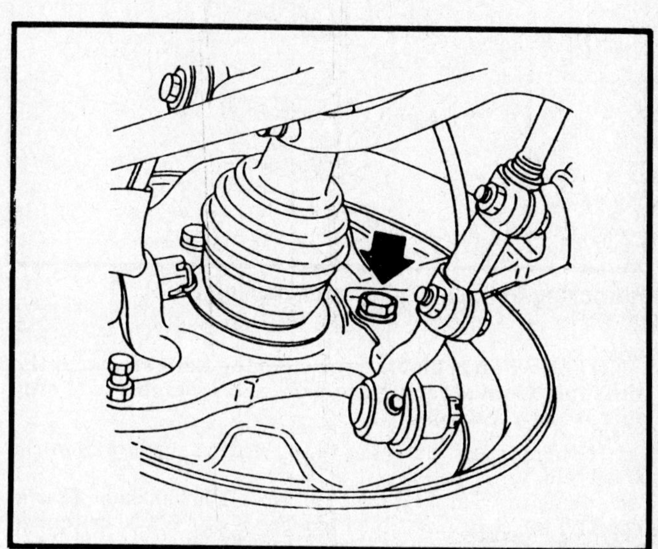

Knuckle arm attaching bolt

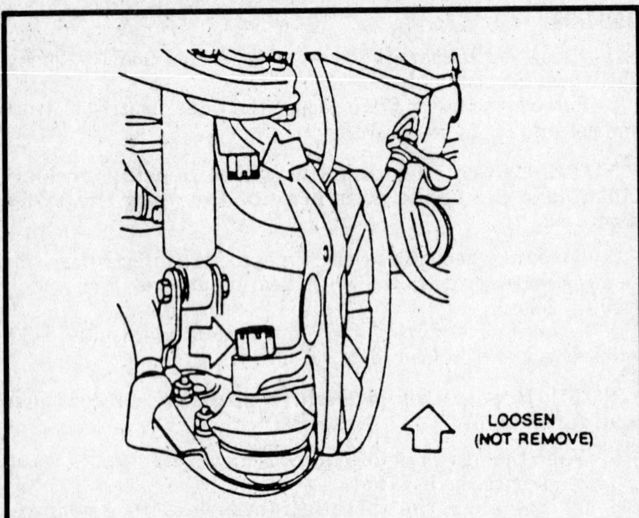

Upper and lower ball joint nuts

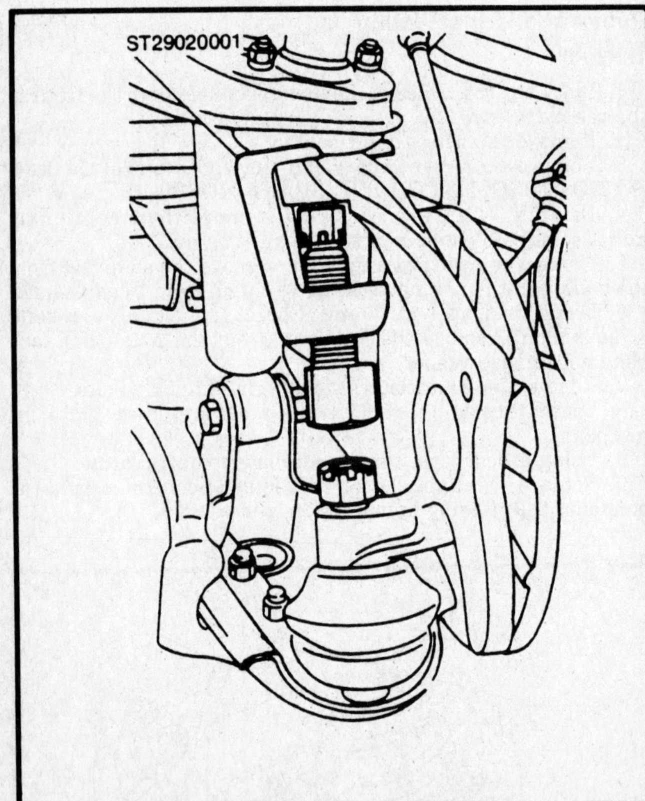

Removing the ball joint using a ball joint tool

NOTE: When removing the steering knuckle, push the halfshaft from steering knuckle/hub assembly and support it with a wire.

11. Using a press, push the wheel bearing support from the wheel hub.
12. Using the Slide Hammer tool No. ST36230000 or equivalent, and the Rear Axle Stand tool No. KV40101000 or equivalent, pull the wheel hub/rotor assembly from the steering knuckle.

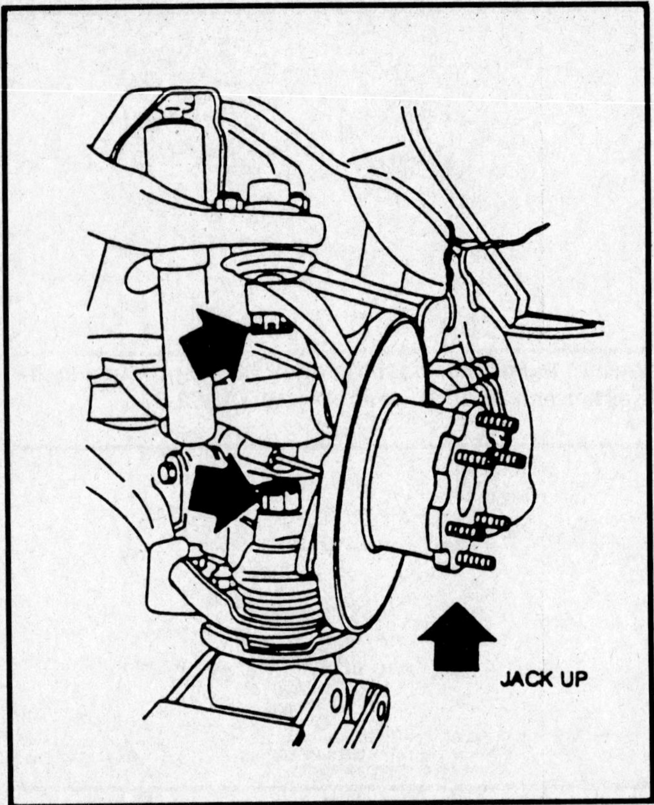

Removing the ball joint tightening nuts

13. To complete the installation, reverse the removal procedures. Torque the locknut to 108–145 ft. lbs. Turn the hub several times (in both directions) to seat the bearings. Using a spring scale, check the preload to see that it falls between 2.2–9.5 ft. lbs. If not, adjust by replacing the collar with one of a different thickness, by the number stamped on the collar. The larger the number, the thicker the collar. When preload has been correctly set, secure the nut by bending the lockwasher tab.

1984-88

1. Raise and support the front of the vehicle with jackstands under the frame rails.
2. Remove the front wheel assembly.
3. Remove the calipers and suspend them (on a wire) out of the way.
4. Remove the locking hub assembly-to-hub bolts and the assembly.
5. Using a pair of snapring pliers, remove the snapring from the halfshaft.
6. At the tie rod end, remove the cotter pin and loosen the tie rod-to-steering knuckle nut. Using the Ball Joint Removal tool No. HT72520000 or equivalent, separate the tie rod from the steering knuckle.
7. Remove the steering knuckle arm from the steering knuckle bolts.
8. Using a floor jack, support the lower control arm, then, remove the upper/lower ball joint-to-steering knuckle nuts or remove the upper/lower ball joint-to-steering knuckle cotter pins/nuts (loosen the ball joint nuts). Using the Ball Joint Removal tool No. HT2520000 or equivalent, press the ball joints from the steering knuckle.
9. Using a small pry bar, remove the snapring and lock washer from the front wheel hub.
10. Using the Lock Nut Wrench Socket tool No. KV40104300 or equivalent, remove the locknut from the front wheel hub.

11. Separate the front wheel hub/rotor disc from the steering knuckle.
12. Separate the front wheel hub from the brake rotor.
13. Inspect the wheel bearings; if necessary, replace them.
14. To install, reverse the removal procedures. Torque the steering knuckle arm-to-steering knuckle bolts to 53–72 ft. lbs., the upper ball joint-to-upper control arm nuts/bolts to 12–15 ft. lbs., the lower ball joint-to-lower control arm nuts/bolts to 28–38 ft. lbs., the upper ball joint-to-steering knuckle nut to 58–108 ft. lbs., the lower ball joint-to-steering knuckle nut to 87–123 ft. lbs., the wheel bearing lock nut to 58–72 ft. lbs. and the locking hub assembly to 18–25 ft. lbs. Adjust the wheel bearing preload.

REAR DRIVE AXLE

For overhaul information, refer to "Drive Axles" in the Unit Overhaul Section.

Axle Housing

Removal and Installation

PICKUPS

1. Block the front wheels.
2. Raise and support the rear of the vehicle safely located under the frame. Using a floor jack, position it under the differential and support its weight.
3. Remove the rear wheel/tire assemblies.
4. Using a piece of chalk, make alignment marks on the driveshaft and differential flanges. Remove the driveshaft-to-differential flange nuts/bolts and separate the driveshaft from the differential.
5. Remove the brake drum and disconnect the parking brake cable from the brake assembly.
6. Disconnect and plug the brake line from the wheel cylinders. Disconnect the brake line from the differential clips.
7. Remove the lower shock absorber-to-rear spring pad nut and separate the shock absorber from the rear spring pad.
8. Remove the rear spring pad-to-differential (U-bolt) nuts, the U-bolts and the spring pads.
9. With the rear differential disconnect from the vehicle, move the floor jack to pass it out through either side of the vehicle; pass it out above the springs.
10. To install, reverse the removal procedures. Torque the differential-to-rear spring pad (U-bolts) nuts to 65–72 ft. lbs., the lower shock absorber-to-rear spring pad nut to 12–16 ft. lbs. (1982-83) or 22–30 ft. lbs. (1984-88) and the driveshaft-to-differential flange nuts/bolts to 17–24 ft. lbs. (1982-83) or 25–33 ft. lbs. (1984-88). Adjust the parking brake. Bleed the rear brake system.

VAN

1. Block the front wheels.
2. Raise and support the rear of the vehicle safely located under the frame. Using a floor jack, position it under the differential and support its weight.
3. Remove the rear wheel/tire assemblies.

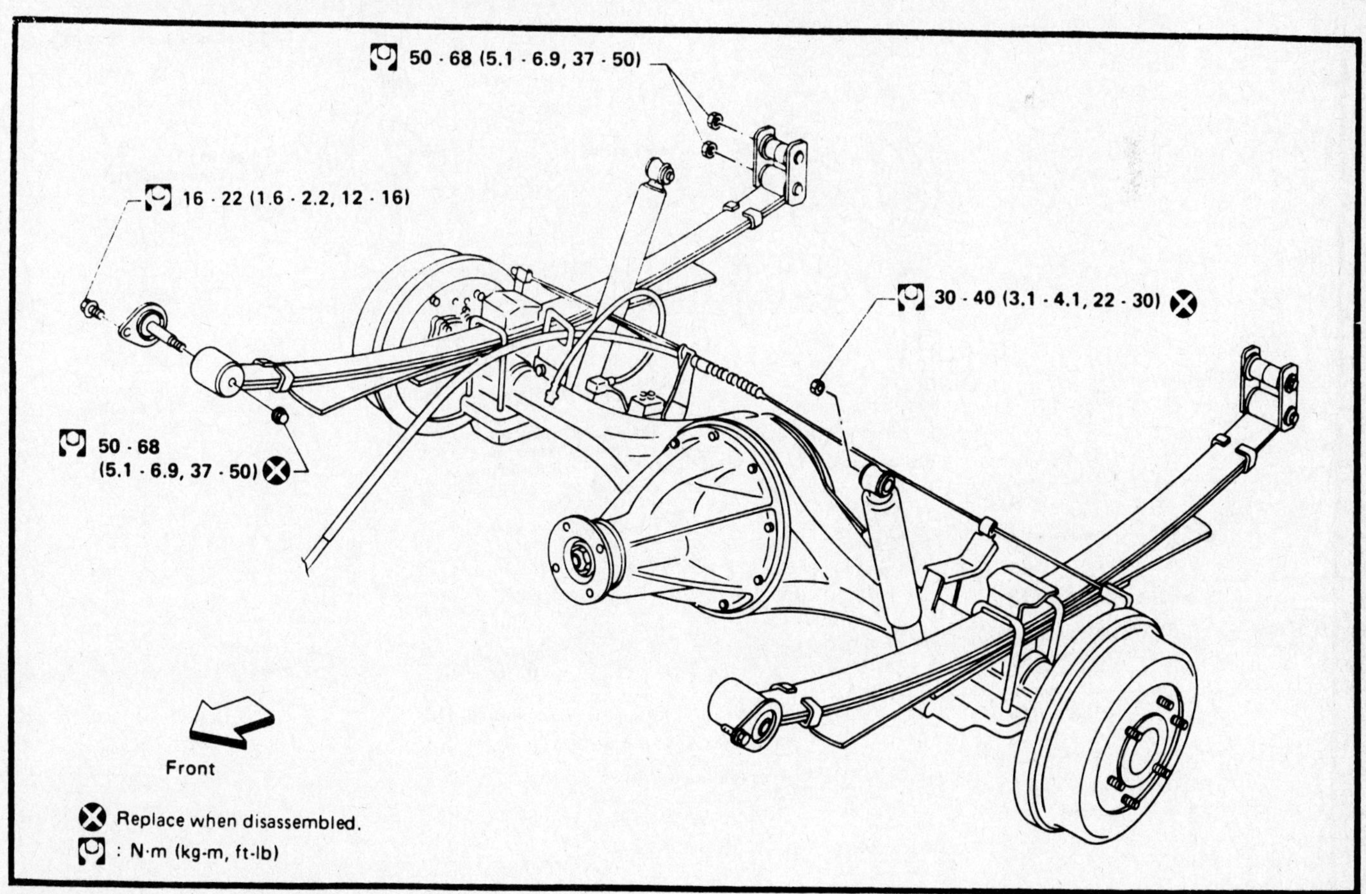

View of the rear differential—Pickups

4. Using a piece of chalk, make alignment marks on the driveshaft and differential flanges. Remove the driveshaft-to-differential flange nuts/bolts and separate the driveshaft from the differential.

5. Remove the brake drum and disconnect the parking brake cable from the brake assembly. On the Wagon, disconnect the parking brake cable from the equalizer.

6. Disconnect and plug the main brake line from the differential junction block.

7. Remove the stabilizer bar-to-chassis nuts/bolts and the stabilizer bar-to-differential nuts/bolts and the stabilizer bar from the vehicle.

8. Remove the upper shock absorber-to-chassis nut from inside the vehicle.

NOTE: The upper shock absorber nuts are located inside the vehicle.

9. Remove the panhard rod-to-chassis nut/bolt and lower the rod.

10. Remove the upper and lower links-to-chassis nuts/bolts, then, separate the links from the chassis supports.

11. Lower the differential. Remove the coil spring assemblies and the differential from the vehicle.

12. To install, temporarily tighten all of the links, lower the vehicle to the ground, bounce the vehicle several times and reverse the removal procedures. Torque the lower and upper links-to-chassis nuts/bolts to 80–94 ft. lbs., the shock absorber-to-chassis nuts/bolts to 12–18 ft. lbs., the panhard rod-to-chassis nut/bolt to 80–94 ft. lbs., the stabilizer bar-to-chassis nuts/bolts to 10–14 ft. lbs., the stabilizer bar-to-differential 5.8–7.2 ft. lbs. and the driveshaft-to-differential nuts/bolts to 25–33 ft. lbs.

Axle Shaft

Removal and Installation

PICKUPS

Single Rear Wheels

1. Block the front wheels. Raise and support the rear of the vehicle safely located under the frame rail. Using a floor jack, support the differential. Remove the rear wheel/tire assembly.

2. Remove the brake drum. Disconnect the parking brake cable from the brake shoes.

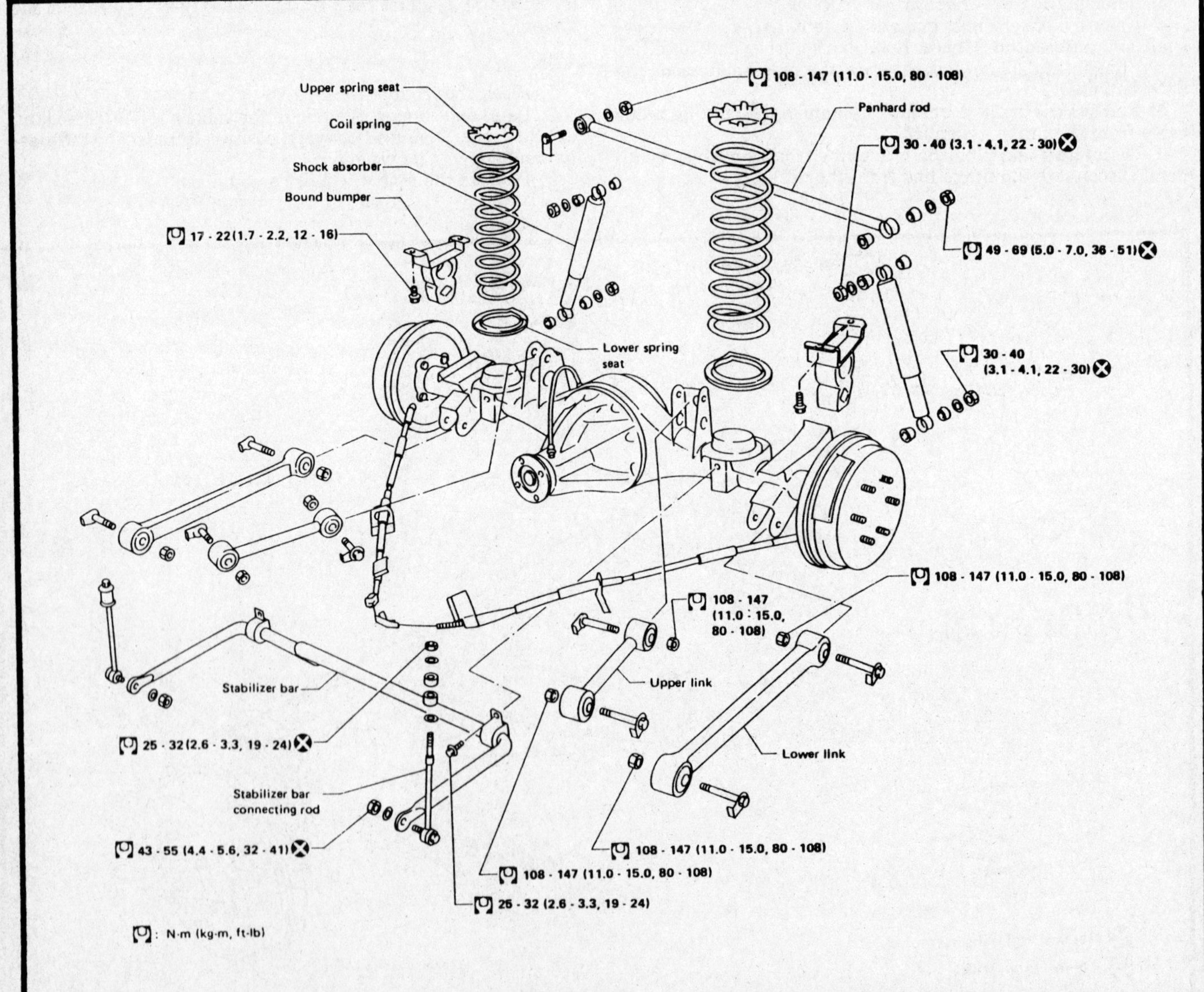

Exploded view of the rear differential—wagon. Van is similar

3. Disconnect and plug the brake tube from wheel cylinder.
4. From the rear of the backing plate, remove the backing plate-to-axle housing nuts.
5. Using the Rear Axle Stand tool No. KV40101000 or equivalent, and the Slide Hammer Puller tool No. ST36230000 or equivalent, pull the axle shaft/backing plate assembly from the axle housing.

Dual Rear Wheels

1. Block the front wheels. Raise and support the rear of the vehicle safely located under the frame rail. Using a floor jack, support the differential. Remove the rear wheel/tire assembly.
2. Remove the axle shaft-to-wheel hub bolts and pull the axle shaft from the axle housing.

NOTE: When removing the axle shaft, be careful not to damage the oil seal.

3. To install, reverse the removal procedures. Torque the axle shaft-to-wheel hub bolts to 42–55 ft. lbs. Check and/or adjust the axle shaft end-play.

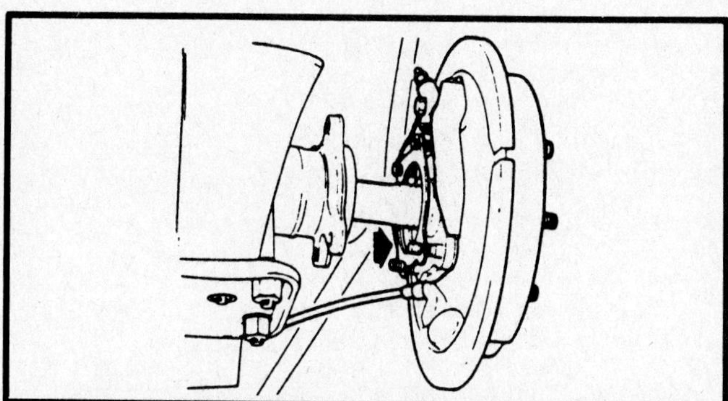

Axle shaft end play is adjusted by the addition or subtraction of shims behind the brake backing plate

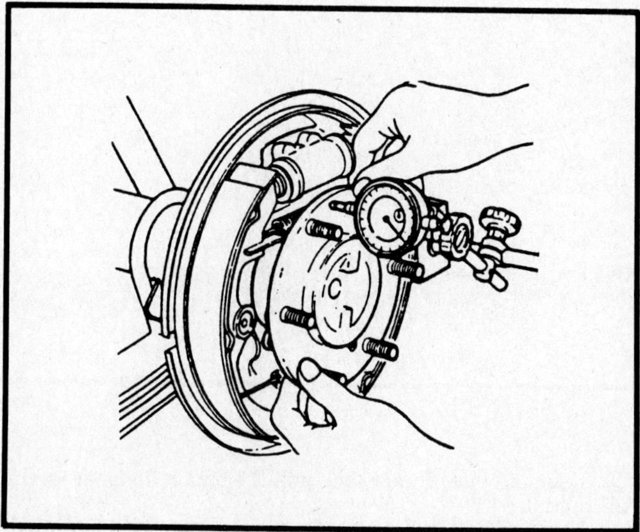

Measure the axial end-play with a dial indicator

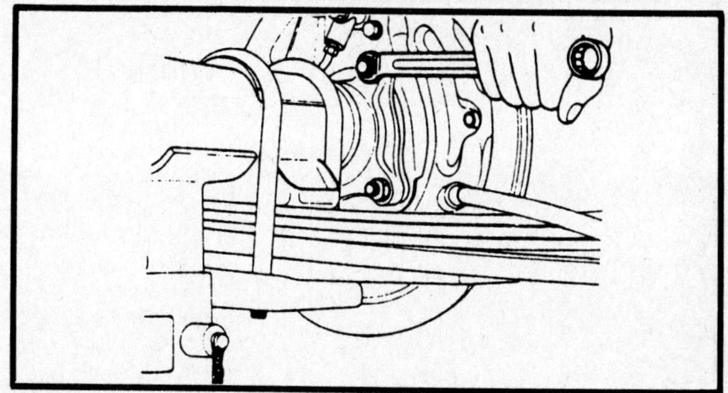

Disconnecting the brake backing plate from the axle housing

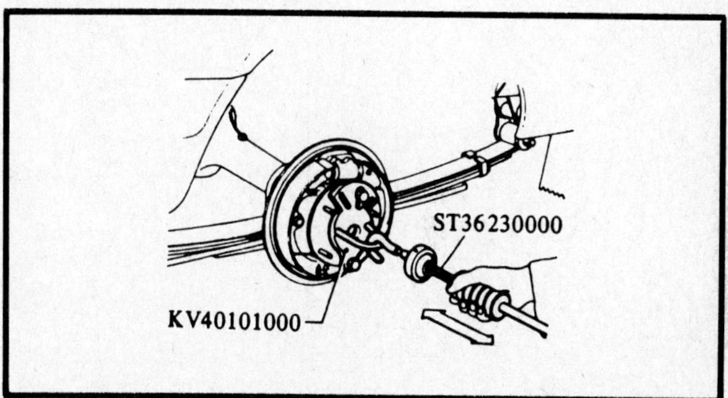

Removing the axle shaft/backing plate assembly from the axle housing—single rear wheel Pickup

VAN

1. Block the front wheels. Raise and support the rear of the vehicle safely located under the frame rail. Using a floor jack, support the differential. Remove the rear wheel/tire assembly.
2. Remove the brake drum. Disconnect the parking brake cable from the brake shoes.
3. Disconnect and plug the brake tube from wheel cylinder.
4. From the rear of the backing plate, remove the backing plate-to-axle housing nuts.
5. Using the Rear Axle Stand tool No. KV40101000 or equivalent, and the Slide Hammer Puller tool No. ST36230000 or equivalent, pull the axle shaft/backing plate assembly from the axle housing.

NOTE: When the axle shaft has been removed, the oil seal should be replaced.

6. To install, lubricate the oil seal lips and reverse the removal procedures. Torque the backing plate-to-axle housing nuts to 33–40 ft. lbs. Adjust the axle shaft end-play. Bleed the brake system.

Pinion Seal

Removal and Installation

PICKUPS

The pinion oil seal on Models H190 and C200 (1986-88) must not be replaced for they use a collapsible spacer.

1. Refer to the "Driveshaft, Removal and Installation" procedures in this section and remove the driveshaft.

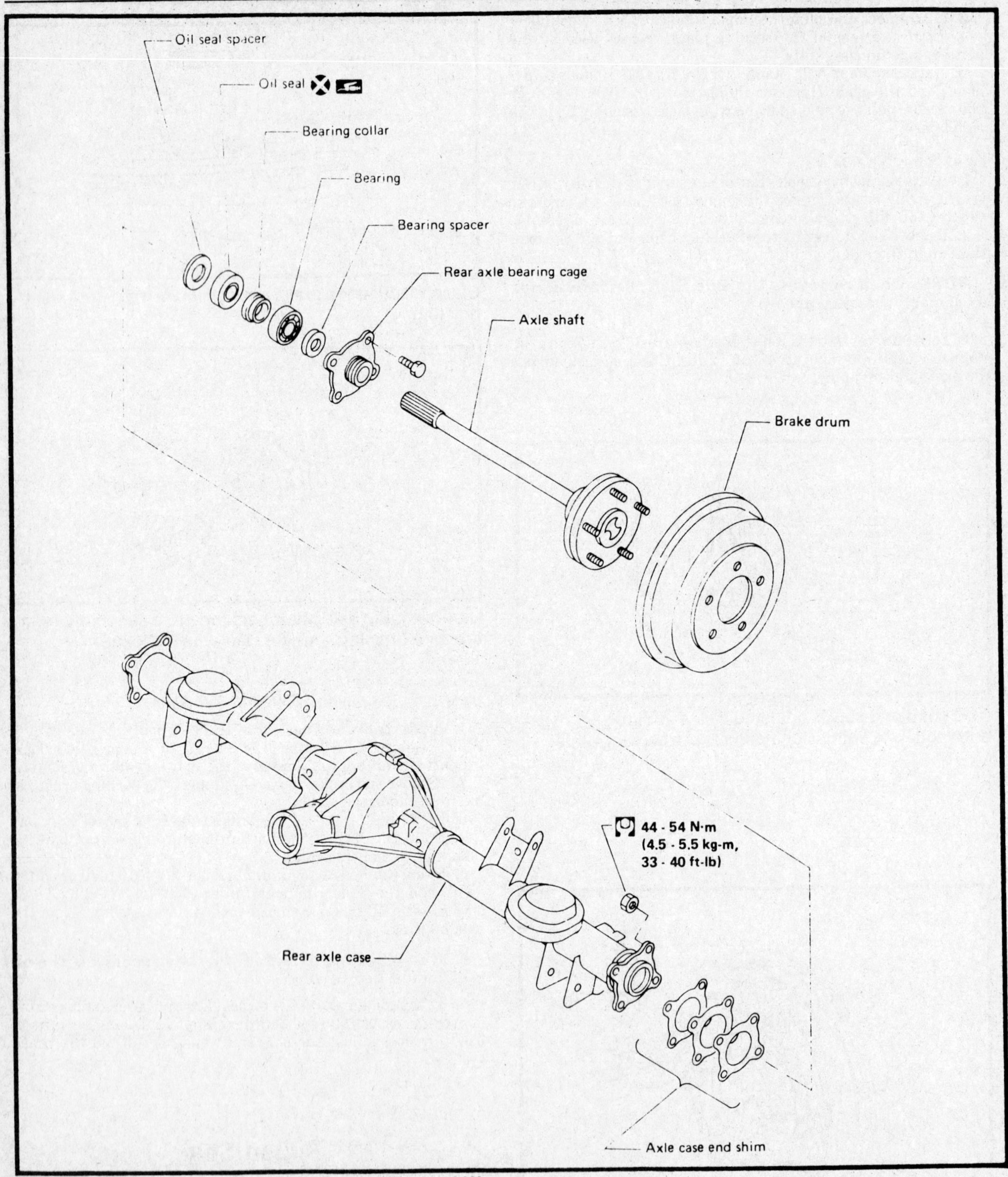

Exploded view of the rear axle assembly—Van and Wagon

2. Using a socket wrench and the Differential Flange Holding tool No. ST31530000 (all, except Model H233B—1986-88), KV38104700 (Model H233B—1986-88) or equivalent, hold the differential flange and the remove the differential pinion nut.

3. Using a Wheel Puller tool, pull the pinion flange from the differential.

4. Using a small pry bar, pry the oil seal from the differential.

5. Using the Oil Seal Driver tool No. ST30720000 (Model

R180 and H190), KV381025S0 (Model C200–1984-85) or equivalent, lubricate the new oil seal lips with multi-purpose grease and drive the new seal into the differential housing until it is flush the end of the housing.

6. Using a soft hammer, tap the pinion flange onto the pinion shaft.

7. Using a socket wrench and the Differential Flange Holding tool No. ST31530000 (all, except Model H233B–1986-88), KV38104700 (Model H233B–1986-88) or equivalent, hold the differential flange and torque the pinion flange nut to 123–145 ft. lbs. (Model R180), 94–217 ft. lbs. (Model H190 and C200–1984-85) or 145–181 ft. lbs. (Model H233B–1986-88).

8. To complete the installation, reverse the removal procedures.

VAN

1. Refer to the "Driveshaft, Removal and Installation" procedures in this section and remove the driveshaft.

2. Using a socket wrench and the Differential Flange Holding tool No. ST38060002 or equivalent, hold the differential flange and the remove the differential pinion nut.

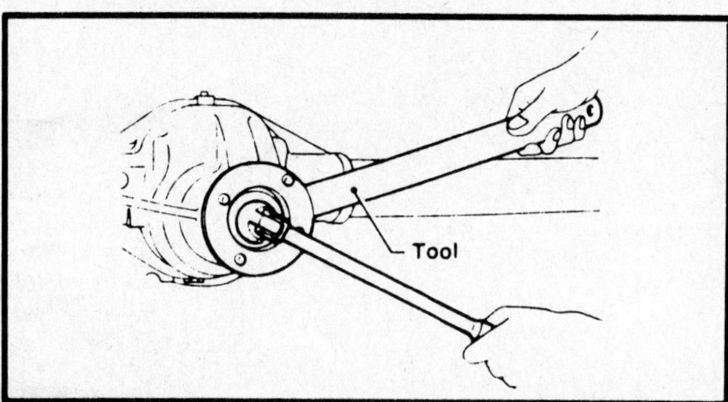

Replacing the differential pinion oil seal–Van and Wagon

3. Using a Wheel Puller tool, pull the pinion flange from the differential.

4. Using a small pry bar, pry the oil seal from the differential.

5. Using the Oil Seal Driver tool No. KV38100500 or equivalent, lubricate the new oil seal lips with multi-purpose grease and drive the new seal into the differential housing until it is flush the end of the housing.

6. Using a soft hammer, tap the pinion flange onto the pinion shaft.

7. Using a socket wrench and the Differential Flange Holding tool No. ST38060002 or equivalent, hold the differential flange and torque the pinion flange nut to 94 ft. lbs.

8. Turn the pinion flange, in both directions, several times to set the bearings. Using a small torque wrench, measure the pinion preload; it should be 9.5–14.8 inch lbs. If the preload value is not obtained, repeat the pinion torquing procedure.

Axle Shaft Seal

Removal and Installation

PICKUPS

Single Rear Wheels

NOTE: To replace the outer oil seal, refer to the "Wheel Bearings, Removal and Installation" procedures in this section and replace the outer oil seal.

1. Refer to the "Axle Shaft, Removal and Installation" procedures in this section and remove the axle shaft.

2. Using a small pry bar, pry the oil seal from the axle housing; do not reuse the old oil seal.

3. Using a mallet, lubricate the new oil seal and tap it into the axle housing.

4. To install, reverse the removal procedures. Adjust the axle shaft end-play. Torque the backing plate-to-axle housing nuts to 39–46 ft. lbs.

Dual Rear Wheels

1. Refer to the "Axle Shaft, Removal and Installation" procedures in this section and remove the axle shaft.

2. Remove the lockwasher-to-locknut screws and the lockwasher.

3. Using the Rear Axle Bearing Locknut Wrench tool No. KV40104400 (1984-85), KV40105400 (1986-88) or equivalent, remove the locknut from the wheel hub. Remove the outer wheel bearing with the brake drum assembly.

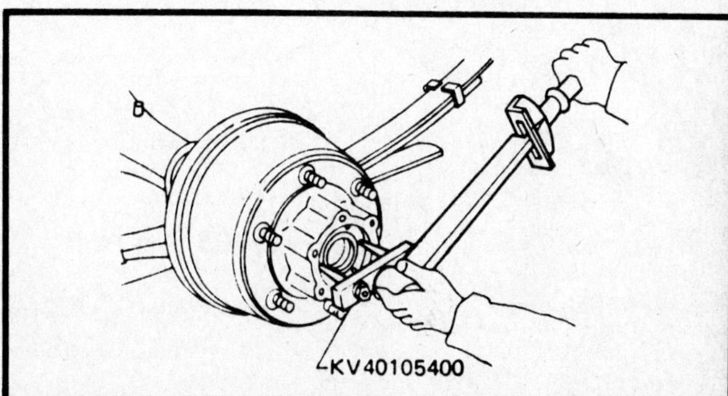

Removing the wheel bearing locknut from wheel hub–dual rear wheel pickup (1986-88)

4. Using a small pry bar, pry the oil seal from inside the axle housing and the oil seal from the rear of the wheel hub.

5. To install, lubricate the new seals and reverse the removal procedures. Torque the wheel hub locknut to 123–145 ft. lbs. Check and/or adjust the axle shaft preload.

VAN

1. Refer to the "Axle Shaft, Removal and Installation" procedures in this section and remove axle shaft.

2. Using a small pry bar, pry the oil seal from inside the axle housing.

3. Using multi-purpose grease, lubricate the new oil seal.

4. Using the Oil Seal Installation tool No. ST33190000 or equivalent, drive the new oil seal into the axle housing until it seats against the oil spacer.

5. To complete the installation, reverse the removal procedures.

Wheel Bearings

Removal and Installation

PICKUPS

Single Rear Wheels

1. Refer to the "Axle Shaft, Removal and Installation" procedures in this section and remove the axle shaft.

NOTE: When the axle shaft has been removed, it is a good idea to replace the oil seal.

2. Using a hammer and the drift punch at the rear of the backing plate, unbend and discard the lockwasher.

3. Using the Bearing Lock Nut Wrench tool No. ST36230000 or equivalent, remove the locknut from the rear of the backing plate.

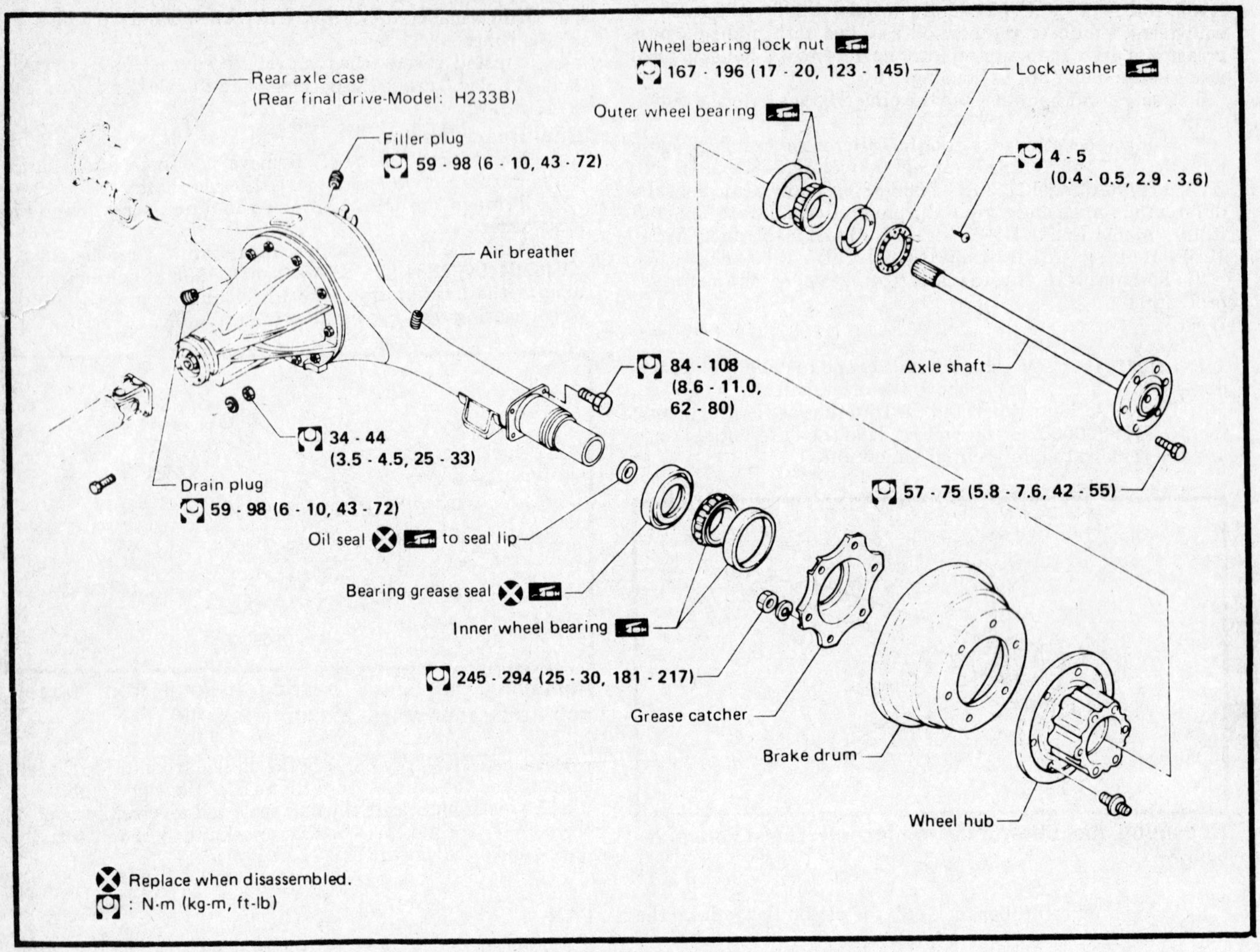

Rear axle case
(Rear final drive-Model: H233B)
Filler plug
59 - 98 (6 - 10, 43 - 72)
Air breather
Wheel bearing lock nut
167 - 196 (17 - 20, 123 - 145)
Lock washer
Outer wheel bearing
4 - 5
(0.4 - 0.5, 2.9 - 3.6)
Axle shaft
84 - 108
(8.6 - 11.0,
62 - 80)
34 - 44
(3.5 - 4.5, 25 - 33)
Drain plug
59 - 98 (6 - 10, 43 - 72)
Oil seal to seal lip
57 - 75 (5.8 - 7.6, 42 - 55)
Bearing grease seal
Inner wheel bearing
245 - 294 (25 - 30, 181 - 217)
Grease catcher
Brake drum
Wheel hub

Replace when disassembled.
: N·m (kg-m, ft-lb)

Exploded view of the rear axle assembly—dual rear wheel pickup

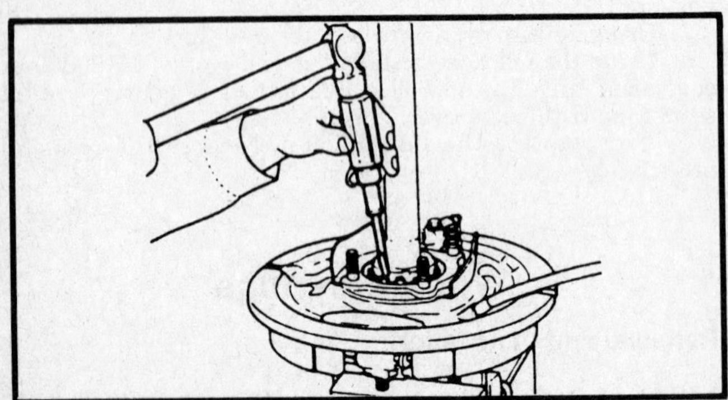

Unbend the lockwasher to remove the bearing locknut; use a new nut at installation

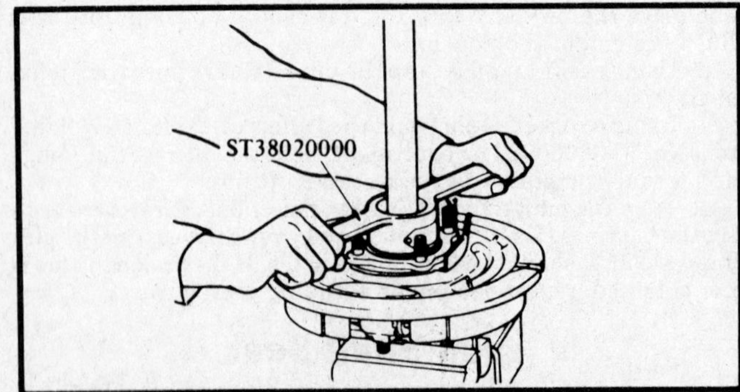

Removing the wheel bearing lock nut from the axle shaft/backing plate assembly—single rear wheel pickup

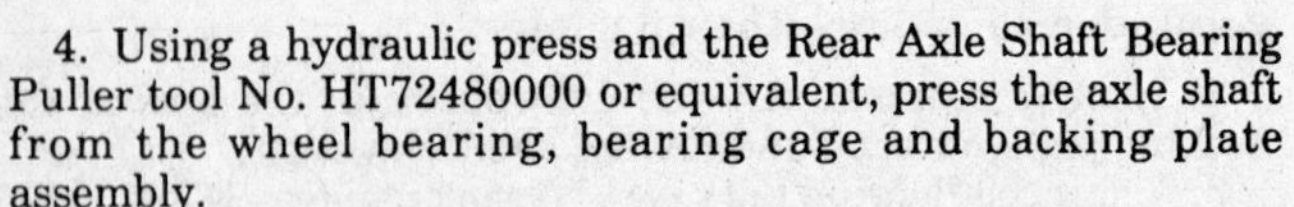

4. Using a hydraulic press and the Rear Axle Shaft Bearing Puller tool No. HT72480000 or equivalent, press the axle shaft from the wheel bearing, bearing cage and backing plate assembly.

5. Using a mallet and a brass drift, drive the bearing cage oil seal and the bearing outer race from the backing plate.

6. Using solvent and compressed air, clean and inspect the parts for damage; replace the damaged parts.

7. Using a mallet and a brass drift, lubricate with multi-purpose grease and install the bearing cage, the outer race and new oil seal.

8. Place the flat bearing lockwasher over the bearing, then,

Suzuki 18

INDEX

BEFORE SERVICING, SEE THE SAFETY NOTICE AT THE FRONT OF THE BOOK

ENGINE IDENTIFICATION CODES BY VIN NUMBER

Engine Cu. In. (liter)	Cylinders	1986	1987	1988
80.8 (1.3)	4	5	5	5

MODEL IDENTIFICATION
Suzuki Samurai

Year	Model Designation	Model Name
1986	Samurai JA Hardtop	Suzuki 4 Wheel Drive
	Samurai JA Convertible	Suzuki 4 Wheel Drive
	Samurai JX Hardtop	Suzuki 4 Wheel Drive
1987	Samurai JA Hardtop	Suzuki 4 Wheel Drive
	Samurai JA Convertible	Suzuki 4 Wheel Drive
	Samurai JX Hardtop	Suzuki 4 Wheel Drive
1988	Samurai JA Hardtop	Suzuki 4 Wheel Drive
	Samurai JA Convertible	Suzuki 4 Wheel Drive
	Samurai JX Hardtop	Suzuki 4 Wheel Drive

GENERAL ENGINE SPECIFICATIONS

Year	VIN	No. Cylinder Displacement cu. in. (liter)	Fuel System Type	Net Horsepower @ rpm	Net Torque @ rpm (ft.lbs.)	Bore × Stroke (in.)	Com-pression Ratio	Oil Pressure @ 2000 rpm
1986	5	4–80.8 (1.3)	2bbl	NA	NA	2.91 × 3.03	8.9:1	42–60
1987–88	5	4–80.8 (1.3)	2bbl	NA	NA	2.91 × 3.03	8.9:1	42–60

FIRING ORDER

To avoid confusion, replace spark plug wires one at a time.

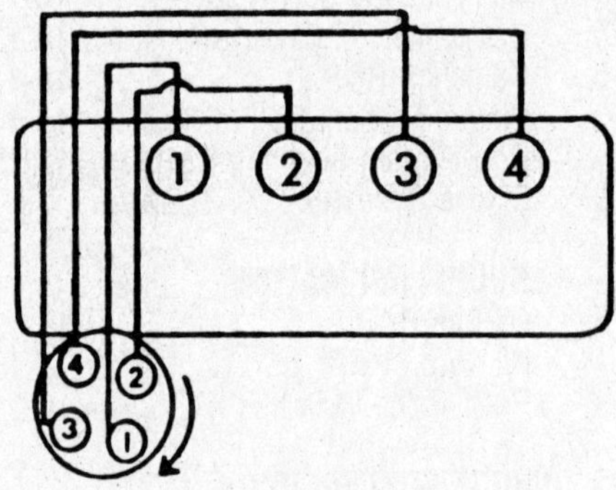

Firing order 1–3–4–2

GASOLINE ENGINE TUNE-UP SPECIFICATIONS

Year	VIN	No. Cylinder Displacement cu. in. (liter)	Spark Plugs Type	Spark Plugs Gap (in.)	Ignition Timing (deg.) MT	Ignition Timing (deg.) AT	Com-pression Pressure (psi)	Fuel Pump (psi)	Idle Speed (rpm) MT	Idle Speed (rpm) AT	Valve Clearance (mm) In.	Valve Clearance (mm) Ex.
1986	5	4–80.0 (1.3)	①	0.030	10	NA	199	NA	800	NA	0.13–0.17 ②	0.16–0.20 ③
1987	5	4–80.0 (1.3)	①	0.030	10	NA	199	NA	800	NA	0.13–0.17 ②	0.16–0.20 ③

GASOLINE ENGINE TUNE-UP SPECIFICATIONS

Year	VIN	No. Cylinder Displacement cu. in. (liter)	Spark Plugs Type	Spark Plugs Gap (in.)	Ignition Timing (deg.) MT	Ignition Timing (deg.) AT	Compression Pressure (psi)	Fuel Pump (psi)	Idle Speed (rpm) MT	Idle Speed (rpm) AT	Valve Clearance (mm) In.	Valve Clearance (mm) Ex.
1988	5	4–80.0 (1.3)	①	0.030	10	NA	199	NA	800	NA	0.13–0.17 ②	0.16–0.20 ③

NA Not Available

① Either NGK BPR5ES or Nippondenso W16EXR-U

② Specification is for cold engine. Hot engine-0.23–0.27

③ Specification is for cold engine. Hot engine-0.26–0.30

CAPACITIES

Year	Model	No. Cylinder Displacement cu. in. (liter)	Engine Crankcase with Filter	Engine Crankcase without Filter	Transmission (pts.) 4-Spd	Transmission (pts.) 5-Spd	Transmission (pts.) Auto.	Drive Axle (pts.)	Fuel Tank (gal.)	Cooling System (qts.)
1986	Samurai	4-80.8 (1.3)	3.5	3.0	NA	2.7	NA	3.2①	10.6	4.6
1987	Samurai	4-80.8 (1.3)	3.5	3.0	NA	2.7	NA	3.2①	10.6	4.6
1988	Samurai	4-80.8 (1.3)	3.5	3.0	NA	2.7	NA	3.2①	10.6	4.6

① Front differential 3.6 pints.

CRANKSHAFT AND CONNECTING ROD SPECIFICATIONS

All measurements are given in inches.

Year	VIN	No. Cylinder Displacement cu. in. (liter)	Crankshaft Main Brg. Journal Dia.	Crankshaft Main Brg. Oil Clearance	Crankshaft Shaft End-play	Crankshaft Thrust on No.	Connecting Rod Journal Diameter	Connecting Rod Oil Clearance	Connecting Rod Side Clearance
1986	5	4–80.8 (1.3)	1.7710–1.7716	.0008–.0016	.0044–.0122	3	1.6529–1.6535	.0012–.0019	.0039–.0078
1987	5	4–80.8 (1.3)	1.7710–1.7716	.0008–.0016	.0044–.0122	3	1.6529–1.6535	.0012–.0019	.0039–.0078
1988	5	4–80.8 (1.3)	1.7710–1.7716	.0008–.0016	.0044–.0122	3	1.6529–1.6535	.0012–.0019	.0039–.0078

VALVE SPECIFICATIONS

Year	VIN	No. Cylinder Displacement cu. in. (liter)	Seat Angle (deg.)	Face Angle (deg.)	Spring Test Pressure (lbs.)	Spring Installed Height (in.)	Stem-to-Guide Clearance (in.) Intake	Stem-to-Guide Clearance (in.) Exhaust	Stem Diameter (in.) Intake	Stem Diameter (in.) Exhaust
1986	5	4–80.8 (1.3)	45	45	NA	1.63	.0008–.0019	.0014–.0025	.2742–.2748	.2737–.2742
1987	5	4–80.8 (1.3)	45	45	NA	1.63	.0008–.0019	.0014–.0025	.2742–.2748	.2737–.2742
1988	5	4–80.8 (1.3)	45	45	NA	1.63	.0008–.0019	.0014–.0025	.2742–.2748	.2737–.2742

PISTON AND RING SPECIFICATIONS

All measurments are given in inches.

Year	VIN	No. Cylinder Displacement cu. in. (liter)	Piston Clearance	Ring Gap Top Compression	Ring Gap Bottom Compression	Ring Gap Oil Control	Ring Side Clearance Top Compression	Ring Side Clearance Bottom Compression	Ring Side Clearance Oil Control
1986	5	4-80.8 (1.3)	.0008–.0015	.0079–.0129	.0079–.0137	.0079–.0275	.0012–.0027	.0008–.0023	NA
1987	5	4-80.8 (1.3)	.0008–.0015	.0079–.0129	.0079–.0137	.0079–.0275	.0012–.0027	.0008–.0023	NA
1988	5	4-80.8 (1.3)	.0008–.0015	.0079–.0129	.0079–.0137	.0079–.0275	.0012–.0027	.0008–.0023	NA

NA—Not Available

TORQUE SPECIFICATIONS

All readings in ft. lbs.

Year	VIN	No. Cylinder Displacement cu. in. (liter)	Cylinder Head Bolts	Main Bearing Bolts	Rod Bearing Bolts	Crankshaft Pulley Bolts	Flywheel Bolts	Manifold Intake	Manifold Exhaust	Spark Plugs
1987	5	4-80.8 (1.3)	46–50	36–41	24–26	47–54①	41–47	13.5–20	13.5–20	14–21
1986	5	4-80.8 (1.3)	46–50	36–41	24–26	47–54①	41–47	13.5–20	13.5–20	14–21
1988	5	4-80.8 (1.3)	46–50	36–41	24–26	47–54①	41–47	13.5–20	13.5–20	14–21

① The specification is for the timing belt pulley. Torque the drive belt pulley bolt to 7.5–9.0 ft. lbs.

WHEEL ALIGNMENT

Year	Model	Caster Range (deg.)	Caster Preferred Setting (deg.)	Camber Range (deg.)	Camber Preferred Setting (deg.)	Toe-in (in.)	Steering Axis Inclination (deg.)
1986	Samurai	2½P–4½P	3½P	¼P–1¼P	1P	.08P–.24P	NA
1987	Samurai	2½P–4½P	3½P	¼P–1¼P	1P	.08P–.24P	NA
1988	Samurai	2½P–4½P	3½P	¼P–1¼P	1P	.08P–.24P	NA

NA Not Available

ENGINE ELECTRICAL

Refer to the Electrical Section for Alternator and Starter Overhaul.

Alternator

The charging system consists of an alternator with an IC integral voltage regulator. With the exception of belt tension, no adjustments are possible on this system.

Removal and Installation

1. Disconnect the negative battery cable.
2. Disconnect the wire coupler and white lead wire from the alternator.
3. Raise and support the vehicle safely.
4. Remove the brake pipe clamp from the radiator under cover and remove the cover.
5. Remove the alternator adjusting bolt and remove the drive belt.
6. Support the alternator and remove the pivot bolt.
7. Remove the alternator from under the vehicle.
8. Installation is the reverse of the removal procedure. Adjust the drive belt tension when finished.

Voltage Regulator

Removal and Installation

Alternators used on these vehicles are equipped with an internal voltage regulator. No adjustments are possible. Removal and Installation requires that the alternator be disassembled.

Refer to the Electrical Section in the Unit Repair Section for the procedure.

Starter

Removal and Installation

1. Disconnect the negative battery cable.
2. Raise and support the vehicle safely.
3. Disconnect the lead wire and battery cable from the starter motor.
4. Support the starter and remove the two mounting bolts.
5. Remove the starter.
6. Installation is the reverse of the removal procedure.

Distributor

Removal and Installation

1. Disconnect the negative battery cable.
2. Disconnect and tag the lead wires and vacuum hose at the distributor.
3. Remove and tag the spark plug wires at the distributor cap.
4. Unhook the distributor cap mounting clamps and remove the cap. Save the gasket that is between the distributor cap and housing for installation.
5. Remove the distributor mounting bolt and note the position of the rotor in relation to the engine.
6. Remove the distributor from the engine by lifting up on the housing of the distributor.
7. To install, place the distributor in the engine, aligning the rotor in the same position it was in before removal.

NOTE: If the engine was disturbed while the distributor was removed, remove the No. 1 spark plug and rotate the crankshaft in the normal direction of rotation until compression is felt at the spark plug hole. Continue rotating the engine in the same direction while observing the timing marks on the flywheel and bellhousing line up when No. 1 cylinder is at TDC. Install the distributor with the rotor lined up with the No. 1 lug on the distributor cap.

8. Install the distributor mounting bolt and distributor cap with gasket.
9. Connect the lead wires and vacuum hose on the distributor.
10. Install the spark plug wires in the distributor cap in the correct position. Connect the negative battery cable.
11. Run the engine and adjust the ignition timing to the correct specification.

TIMING LIGHT AND TACHOMETER CONNECTIONS

All timing lights and tachometers should be connected according to the manufacturers instructions.

IGNITION TIMING

Procedure

Two timing marks are located on the flywheel and one on the bellhousing. Access is obtained by removing the rubber plug on the bellhousing and rotating the distributor while observing the

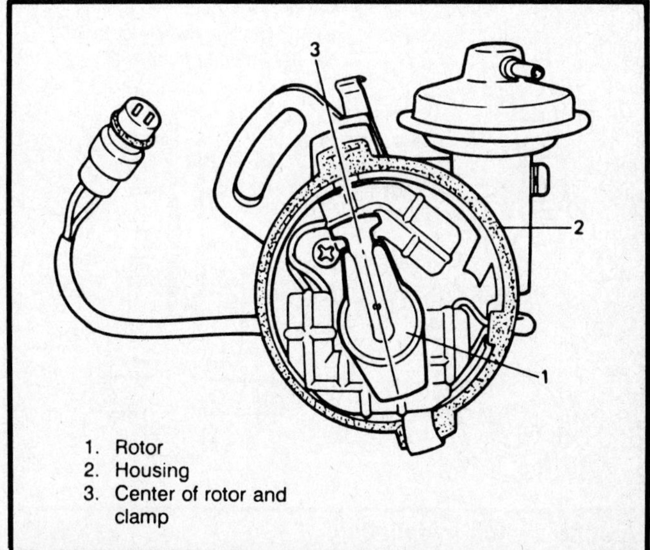

Distributor rotor position with engine in No. 1 firing position

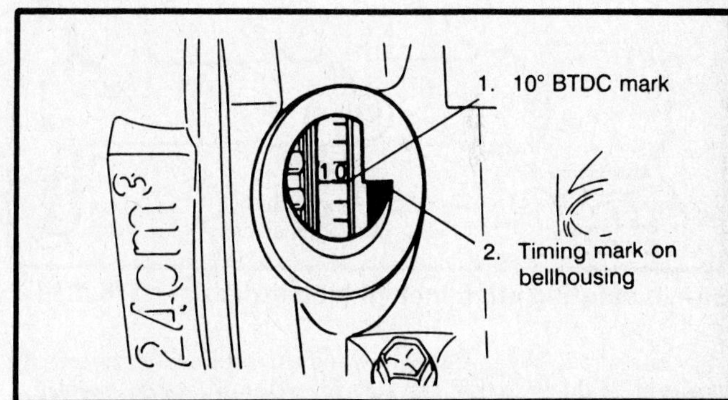

Timing marks are visible by removing rubber plug in top of bellhousing

mark alignment with a timing light while the engine is running. All vacuum controls on the distributor must remain connected while adjusting the ignition timing. Correct ignition timing is 10° BTDC at 800 RPM.

Electrical Controls

IGNITION SWITCH

Removal and Installation

1. Disconnect the negative battery cable.
2. Remove the lower instrument panel cover.
3. Loosen, but do not remove the two upper and four lower steering column mounting nuts and bolts. Lower and support the steering column.
4. Disconnect the wire connector at the ignition switch.
5. With the ignition switch in the OFF position, remove the mounting bolts and remove the switch.
6. To install, rotate the steering wheel until the slot in the steering shaft aligns with the hole in the steering column.
7. Install the switch in the OFF position, making sure that the lock bolt in the switch fits into the slot. Torque the bolts to 13–20 ft. lbs.

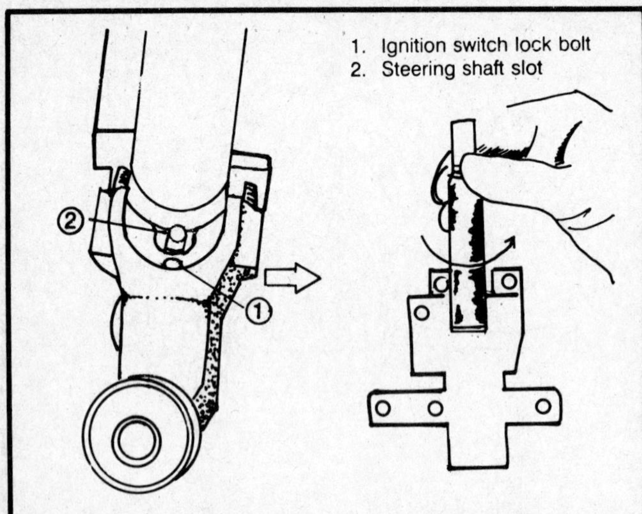

Ignition switch installation

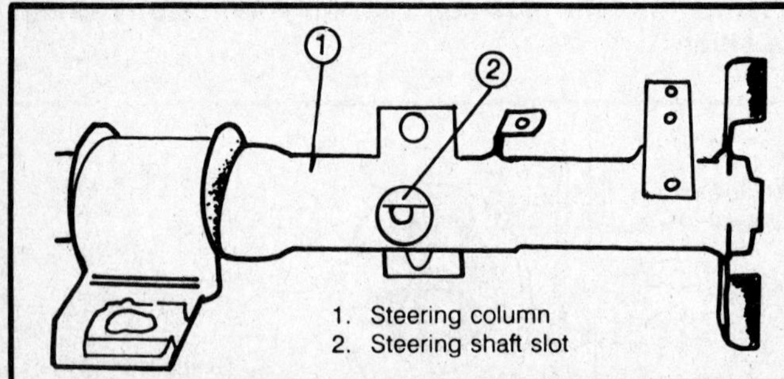

Slot in steering shaft that ignition switch must fit in to

8. Insert the key in the switch and turn the switch to the ON position. Make sure that the steering column rotates smoothly.
9. The remainder of the installation is the reverse of the removal procedure.

COMBINATION SWITCH

The Combination Switch incorporates the Turn Signal, W/Wiper, Dimmer and Headlight Switches into one switch.

Removal and Installation

1. Disconnect the negative battery cable.
2. Remove the center horn button by pulling outwards.
3. Remove the steering wheel retaining nut and remove the steering wheel by using puller 09944–3812 or equivalent.
4. Loosen, but do not remove the four lower steering column to firewall nuts and the two upper steering column to crossbrace screws.
5. Lower the steering column, remove the combination switch upper and lower cover screws and remove the covers.
6. Disconnect the wiring connectors from the back of the combination switch.
7. Remove the four combination switch mounting screws and remove the switch from the steering column.
8. Installation is the reverse of the removal

W/WIPER MOTOR

Removal and Installation

1. Disconnect the negative battery cable.

Removing combination switch

2. Remove the wiper linkage to wiper motor mounting nut.
3. Disconnect the wire connector from the wiper motor.
4. Remove the three wiper motor mounting screws and remove the wiper motor.
5. Installation is the reverse of the removal procedure.

INSTRUMENT CLUSTER

Removal and Installation

1. Disconnect the negative battery cable.
2. Remove the lower instrument panel cover.
3. Loosen, but do not remove the two upper and four lower steering column mounting nuts and bolts. Lower and support the steering column.
4. Remove the outer instrument cluster cover.
5. Remove the four instrument cluster mounting screws and slide the cluster outwards.
6. Disconnect the speedometer cable from the rear of the instrument cluster.
7. Disconnect and tag the wire connector from the rear of the instrument cluster.
8. Remove the instrument cluster.
9. Installation is the reverse of the removal procedure.

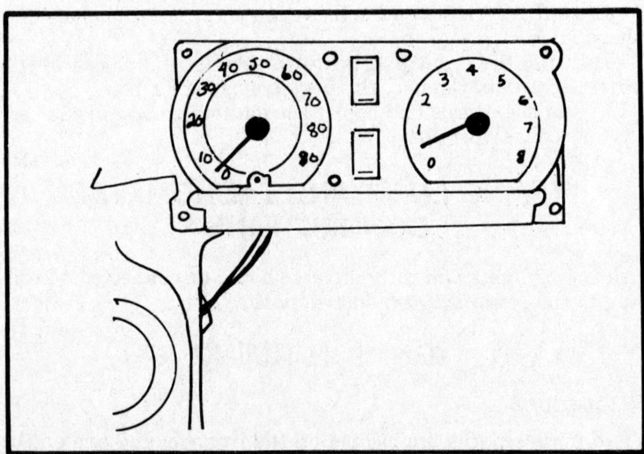

Instrument cluster mounting holes

SPEEDOMETER

Removal and Installation

1. Remove the instrument cluster.
2. Place the instrument cluster on a clean surface.
3. Remove the four instrument cluster bezel screws and remove the bezel.
4. Remove the front and rear speedometer mounting screws and nuts. Remove the speedometer.

NOTE: Use care when removing the rear speedometer mounting nuts. Damage to the printed circuit could occur, causing improper operation.

5. Installation is the reverse of the removal procedure.

COOLING AND HEATING SYSTEMS

Water Pump

Removal and Installation

1. Drain the cooling system.
2. Loosen the drive belt tension and remove the drive belt.
3. Remove the radiator fan shroud mounting bolts and cooling fan to water pump mounting nuts. Remove the shroud, fan and water pump pulley as an assembly.
4. Remove the four crankshaft pulley mounting bolts and remove the crankshaft pulley.

NOTE: The crankshaft pulley can be removed without removing the center crankshaft bolt.

5. Remove the timing belt cover mounting bolts and remove the cover.
6. Loosen the timing belt tensioner adjusting bolt and pivot nut. Hold the tensioner to loosen the timing belt and remove the belt from the camshaft pulley.

NOTE: Mark the position of the timing belt to the camshaft sprocket with chalk. If the timing belt position on the crankshaft is not disturbed, the belt can be later installed in the same position as removed without having to check the camshaft timing.

7. Remove the timing belt tensioner mounting bolts and remove the tensioner, plate and spring.
8. Remove the water pump mounting bolts and remove the water pump.
9. Clean and inspect the surface of the engine before installation.
10. Using a new gasket, install the new water pump on the engine. Torque the mounting bolts to 7–9 ft. lbs.
11. Install the rubber seals between the water pump to cylinder head and water pump to oil pump.
12. Install the timing belt tensioner plate, tensioner and spring.
13. Align the marks on the timing belt and camshaft sprocket. Install the timing belt in the same position on the camshaft sprocket as when removed.

NOTE: If the timing belt position on the crankshaft sprocket was disturbed, refer to Timing Belt and Sprockets Removal and Installation to correct the camshaft timing.

14. Adjust the timing belt so that there is no slack in the belt on the side opposite the tensioner. Torque the tensioner bolts to 7–8.5 ft. lbs.
15. Install the crankshaft and water pump pulleys. Torque the crankshaft and water pump pulley bolts to 7.5–9.0 ft. lbs.
16. Install the timing belt cover, cooling fan, shroud and drive belt. Adjust the drive belt tension.
17. Fill the cooling system, connect the negative battery cable, run the engine and check for leaks.

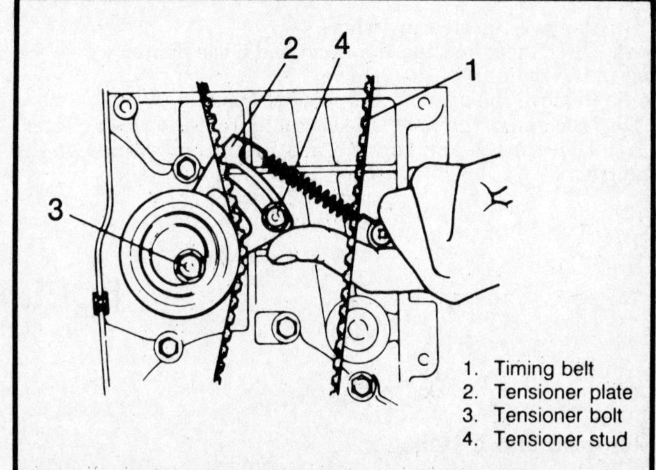

Releasing timing belt tension to remove belt

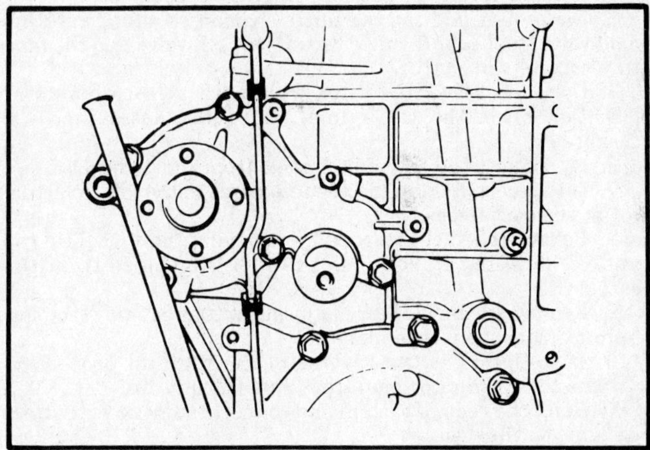

Water pump mounting

Thermostat

Removal and Installation

1. Drain the cooling system to below the thermostat.
2. Remove the upper radiator hose from the thermostat housing.
3. Remove the two thermostat housing bolts and remove the thermostat housing and thermostat.
4. Clean and inspect the surfaces of the housing and engine.
5. Install the new thermostat with the spring facing towards the engine.

6. Using a new gasket, install the thermostat housing on the engine.
7. Install the upper radiator hose on the housing.
8. Fill the cooling system, run the engine until it reaches normal operating temperature and check the thermostat operation.

Heater Core/Blower Motor

Removal and Installation

Removal and Installation procedures are the same for vehicles with or without air conditioning.

1. Disconnect the negative battery cable. Drain the cooling system.
2. Disconnect the inlet and outlet heater hoses from the heater core.
3. Remove the steering wheel.
4. Disconnect and tag the radio and cigar lighter wires. Remove the radio from the vehicle.
5. Remove the ashtray and mounting plate.
6. Disconnect the hood release cable from the release lever.
7. Disconnect and tag the heater control cables at the controls.
8. Remove the heater control knobs and remove the facing plate.
9. Remove the defroster and side ventilator hoses.
10. Disconnect the lead wires and the speedometer cable from the speedometer. Disconnect and tag the heater control wires.
11. Disconnect the wiring harness clamps from the instrument panel.
12. Remove the instrument panel mounting screws and remove the instrument panel.
13. Loosen the front door opening stop screws and remove the steering column holder.
14. Disconnect and tag the blower motor and resistor connections at the coupler.
15. Remove the heater assembly from the vehicle.

NOTE: If the blower motor is being replaced, remove the blower motor from the case and install the new motor.

16. Remove the clips holding the heater case together, separate the case and remove the heater core.
17. Installation is the reverse of the removal procedure. Use care during assembly not to tangle the wiring harness or pinch any hoses or cables.

FUEL SYSTEM

Carburetor

Removal and Installation

1. Disconnect the negative battery cable. Drain the cooling system.
2. Remove the air intake case from the carburetor.
3. Disconnect and tag the micro switches, switch vent solenoid valve, fuel cut off valve, vacuum switch valve and the mixture control valve (MCSV).
4. Disconnect the EGR valve bracket from the carburetor.
5. Disconnect the water inlet and outlet hoses from the carburetor.
6. Disconnect the accelerator cable from the carburetor.
7. Disconnect and tag the vacuum hoses to the idle up actuator at the carburtor.
8. Relieve the fuel pressure by removing the fuel filler cap and reinstalling it. Remove the fuel inlet hose from the carburetor.
9. Remove the carburetor mounting nuts and remove the carburetor from the intake manifold
10. Installation is the reverse of the removal procedure. Torque the carburetor mounting nuts to 20 ft. lbs.
11. Refill the cooling system and connect the negative battery cable when finished.

Fuel Pump

Removal and Installation

1. Disconnect the negative battery cable. Relieve the fuel pressure by removing the filler cap and reinstalling it.
2. Disconnect and tag the fuel inlet, outlet and return hoses from the fuel pump.

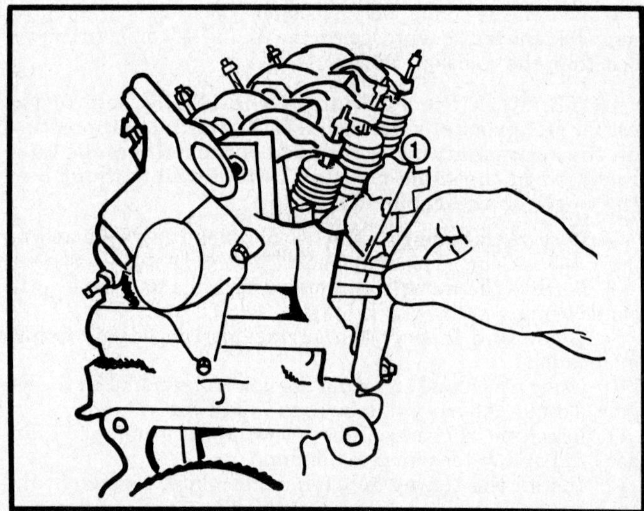

Installing fuel pump pushrod

3. Remove the fuel pump mounting bolts and remove the fuel pump.
4. Remove the fuel pump rod from the engine and lubricate it with engine oil before installation.
5. Install the lubricated pump rod in the engine and using a new gasket, install the fuel pump.
6. The remainder of the installation is the reverse of the removal procedure. Run the engine and check for fuel leaks when finished.

EMISSION CONTROLS

1986–88 Emission Controls and Separate Components

High Altitude Compensator (HAC)
Fuel Cut Solenoid
Electronic Control Module (ECM)
Air Control Actuator
Thermostatically Controlled Air Cleaner (TCAC)
Thermo Sensor
Vacuum Switching Valve (VSV)
Vacuum Transmitting Valve (VTV)
Secondary Throttle Valve
Idle Micro Switch
Vapor Storage Canister
Hot Idle Compensator
Three Way Solenoid Valve (TWSV)
Mixture Control Valve (MCV)
Mixture Control Solenoid Valve (MCSV)
Exhaust Gas Recirculation Valve (EGR)
Positive Crankcase Ventilation (PCV)
Bi-metal Vacuum Switching Valve (BVSV)
Oxygen Sensor
Catalytic Converter

Crankcase Emission Control Systems

PCV VALVE

Removal and Installation

The blow-by gases in the crankcase flow through the passages in the cylinder block and into the cylinder head. The oil particles are separated from the blow-by gases by the oil separator in the rocker cover. The gases are picked up by the PCV Valve and returned with fresh air into the intake manifold. The gases and fresh air are then burned together in the engine. The PCV Valve is replaced by removing the valve from the rocker cover, disconnecting the hose and replacing the hose on the new valve.

Evaporative Emission Control System

CHARCOAL CANISTER

Removal and Installation

The Charcoal Canister is used to store fuel vapors without allowing the vapors to enter the fuel system. The Charcoal Canister should not have to be removed from the vehicle but, it should be cleaned and the lines and filters inspected every 60,000 miles.

Exhaust Emission Control System

OXYGEN SENSOR

An Oxygen Sensor is located on the exhaust manifold to monitor the exhaust gas air/fuel ratio and send the information to the Electronic Control Module (ECM). The ECM then adjusts the air/fuel ratio to obtain the correct mixture. The Oxygen Sensor is replaced by disconnecting the wire and removing the oxygen sensor from the exhaust manifold.

EGR VALVE

The EGR system controls the exhaust emissions by recirculating the exhaust gases into the combustion chamber and burning them. The EGR Valve opens and closes in accordance with the vacuum at the EGR Modulator. The EGR Valve requires no maintenance however, the modulator that is installed on the EGR Valve vacuum line should be cleaned with compressed air every 60,000 miles. Should the EGR Valve need replacing, disconnect the hoses at the valve and remove the EGR Valve mounting bolts.

TROUBLESHOOTING

Symptoms

NOTE: Vacuum hoses and wiring connections are problems commonly found with emission systems. However, when diagnosing a system, all components of the system should be checked. Symptoms and solutions given, only pertain to the emission system. Other problems may exist with other non-emission systems that cause the same symptom.

Engine starts, but stalls

1. EGR valve hose damaged.
2. BVSV malfunction.

Rough idle or engine stalls

1. Vacuum hose disconnected or damaged.
2. Improper vacuum to EGR valve at idle.
3. EGR valve stuck open.
4. Faulty PCV system.

Hesitation or poor acceleration

1. EGR valve stuck.
2. EGR hose damaged.
3. EGR valve gasket damaged or misssing.

Excessive oil consumption

1. PCV line clogged.

Poor fuel mileage

1. Intake air temperature system faulty.
2. Exhaust gas recirculation system faulty.
3. Oxygen sensor system faulty.

Reset Maintenance Lamp

Procedure

The Maintenance Lamp is designed to come on every 60,000 miles. This indicates a need for emission system service. The lamp reset switch is located under the left side of the dashboard mounted on the steering column support. The lamp can be reset by moving the switch upwards and then downwards. If the light remains on after being reset, check the system.

ENGINE MECHANICAL

Refer to the Unit Repair Section for General Overhaul procedures.

Engine

Removal and Installation

1. Disconnect the battery cables, negative first and remove the battery from the vehicle.
2. Disconnect and tag the starter motor wire and battery cable from the starter.
3. Disconnect and tag the alternator wiring from the alternator.
4. Disconnect and tag the water temperature, thermal switch and ground cable wires on the intake manifold.
5. Disconnect and tag the carburetor wiring connectors. Remove the warm air hose.
6. Disconnect the breather hose at the air cleaner. Remove the air intake case and hose from the carburetor.
7. Disconnect the accelerator cable from the carburetor.
8. Disconnect and tag the vacuum hoses for the air cleaner and canister from the intake manifold.
9. Remove the fuel tank filler cap to relieve the fuel pressure. Reinstall the cap.
10. Disconnect and tag the fuel feed and return hoses at the fuel pump.
11. Disconnect the oil pressure and oxygen sensor wires at the connector.
12. Disconnect the back up light and fifth switch wires at the connector.
13. Disconnect the distributor lead wire at the connector. Remove the coil wire from the coil.
14. Drain the cooling system. Disconnect the upper and lower radiator hoses from the engine.
15. Remove the fan shroud and cooling fan mounting bolts and remove the fan and shroud together.
16. Remove the radiator mounting bolts and remove the radiator.
17. Disconnect the heater hoses from the heater core outlet pipe and intake manifold.
18. Disconnect the brake booster vacuum hose.
19. Disconnect the wire connector from the distributor gear case.
20. Remove the four gear shift lever boot mounting bolts and slide the boot upwards on the shifter.
21. Loosen the three gear shift lever mounting bolts and remove the lever.
22. Raise and support the vehicle safely.
23. Disconnect the clutch cable from the mounting bracket.
24. Remove the driveshaft from between the transfer case and the transmission. Drain the transmission oil.
25. Support the engine from the top with a chain type hoist or by other equivalent means. This will keep the engine from falling backwards during the next procedures.
26. With the engine safely supported from above, remove the center exhaust pipe mounting bracket and four transmission mounting bolts.
27. Remove the chassis brace from under the transmission.
28. Lower the vehicle and the engine support at the same speed. Keep the engine supported when the vehicle is lowered.
29. With the engine supported, remove the four engine mounting bolts and remove the engine from the vehicle.
30. Installation is the reverse of the removal procedure. Observe the following torques during installation: Engine mount bolts, 29–43 ft. lbs.; Transmission mount bolts, 13–20 ft. lbs.; Driveshaft bolts, 17–21 ft. lbs.

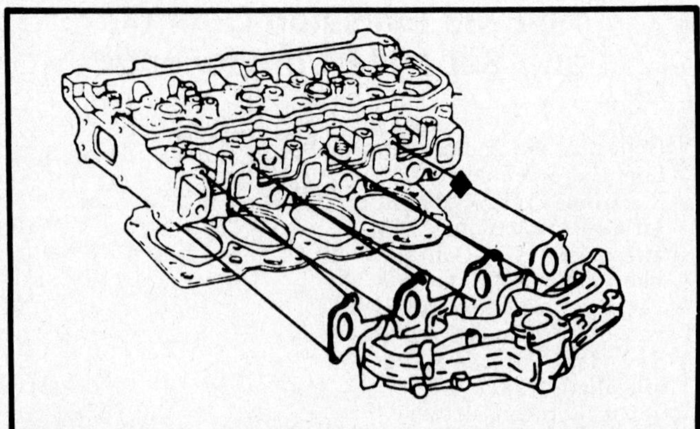

Intake manifold mounting

Intake Manifold

Removal and Installation

1. Disconnect the negative battery cable. Drain the cooling system.
2. Remove the air intake case from the carburetor.
3. Disconnect and tag the micro switches, switch vent solenoid valve, fuel cut off valve, vacuum switch valve and the mixture control valve (MCSV).
4. Disconnect the EGR valve bracket from the carburetor.
5. Disconnect the water inlet and outlet hoses from the carburetor.
6. Disconnect the accelerator cable from the carburetor.
7. Disconnect and tag the vacuum hoses to the idle up actuator at the carburetor.
8. Relieve the fuel pressure by removing the fuel filler cap and reinstalling it. Remove the fuel inlet hose from the carburetor.
9. Disconnect and tag the vacuum hoses and switch wires at the intake manifold.
10. Remove the upper radiator hose at the thermostat housing.
11. Remove the intake manifold mounting bolts and remove the manifold from the engine.
12. Clean and inspect the sealing surfaces of the intake manifold and cylinder head.
13. Using a new gasket, install the intake manifold and torque the bolts to 13–20 ft. lbs.
14. The remainder of the installation is the reverse of the removal procedure.
15. Check for vacuum, fuel and water leaks when finished.

Exhaust Manifold

Removal and Installation

1. Raise and support the vehicle safely.
2. Disconnect the exhaust pipe from the exhaust manifold.
3. Lower the vehicle.
4. Remove the hot air hose from the exhaust manifold heat shield.
5. Remove the heat shield from the manifold.
6. Remove the exhaust manifold mounting bolts and remove the manifold.
7. Clean and inspect the sealing surfaces of the manifold and cylinder head.

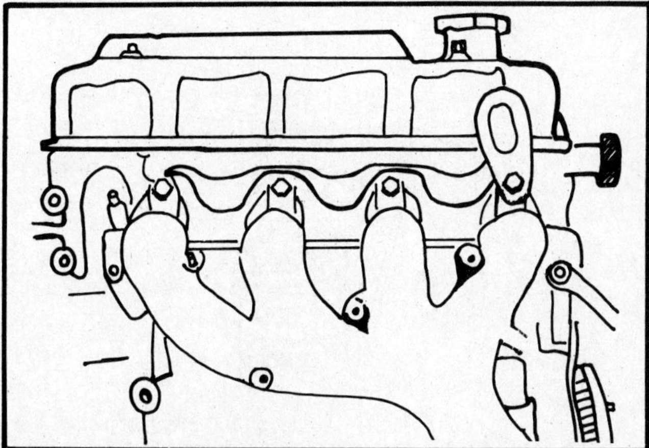

Exhaust manifold mounting

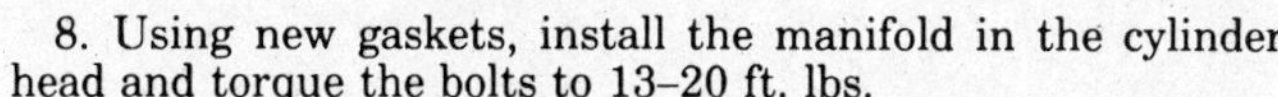

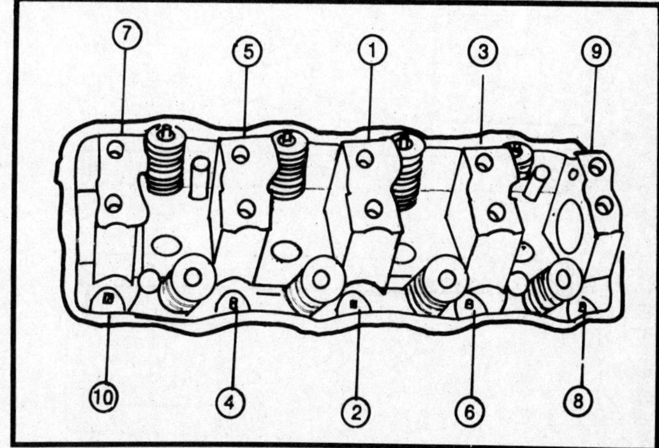

Cylinder head bolt torque sequence

8. Using new gaskets, install the manifold in the cylinder head and torque the bolts to 13–20 ft. lbs.
9. The remainder of the installation is the reverse of the removal procedure.
10. Check for exhaust leaks when finished.

Cylinder Head

Removal and Installation

1. Disconnect the negative battery cable. Drain the cooling system.
2. Raise and support the vehicle safely.
3. Disconnect the exhaust pipe from the exhaust manifold. Lower the vehicle.
4. Remove the timing belt cover. Remove the timing belt from the camshaft sprocket. Remove the upper rear timing belt cover.
5. Remove the intake manifold from the cylinder head.
6. Remove the rocker arm shaft mounting screws and slide the shafts out of the cylinder head while marking the position of the rocker arms and springs.
7. Remove the distributor, fuel pump and distributor housing from the rear of the cylinder head.
8. Starting with the outer bolts and working inward, remove the cylinder head mounting bolts.
9. Remove the cylinder head from the engine.
10. Remove any oil and water in the cylinder bores and on the top of the pistons.
11. Clean and inspect the sealing surfaces of the cylinder head and engine block.
12. If the cylinder head is being replaced, transfer the exhaust manifold and camshaft to the new cylinder head.
13. Lubricate the rocker arms and springs and install the rocker shafts in the cylinder head while positioning the rockers and springs in the same place as when removed.
14. Using a new gasket, install the cylinder head on the engine.
15. Torque the bolts to 20 ft. lbs. in the proper sequence. Retorque the bolts to 46–50 ft. lbs. also in the proper sequence.
16. Align the timing marks on the engine and timing belt sprockets and install the timing belt on the cylinder head.
17. Adjust the valve lash.

Refer to Valve Lash Adjustment for Procedures.

Install the distributor housing and fuel pump on the cylinder head.

18. Rotate the engine to the No. 1 firing position and install the distributor with the rotor pointing to the No. 1 lug on the distributor cap.
19. Install the intake manifold on the cylinder head.
20. Raise and support the vehicle safely.
21. Connect the exhaust pipe to the exhaust manifold. Lower the vehicle.
22. The remainder of the installation is the reverse of the removal procedure.
23. Check for water and fuel leaks when finished.

Rocker Arms and Shaft

Removal and Installation

1. Disconnect the negative battery cable.
2. Remove the rocker cover.
3. Loosen, but do not remove the valve lash adjusting screws in the rocker arms.
4. Remove the timing belt and gear from the camshaft.
5. Remove the rear timing belt cover from the cylinder head.
6. Loosen the rocker arm shafts mounting screws.

NOTE: The two rocker arm shafts are not identical and must be kept in the proper order for installation. If the shafts get mixed before installation, the intake rocker shaft has a 14 mm stepped end and the exhaust rocker shaft has a 13 mm stepped end. The stepped end of the intake rocker shaft faces the front of the engine and the stepped end of the exhaust rocker shaft faces the rear of the engine.

7. Remove the rocker arm shafts while separating the rocker arms and springs.
8. Keep all valve train parts in the order that they were removed in.
9. Apply engine oil to the rocker arms, springs and shafts and install the shafts, in the correct direction, into the cylinder head placing the rocker arms and springs on the shafts as they are installed.
10. With the rocker arms, springs and shafts installed, torque the rocker shaft mounting screws to 7–8.5 ft. lbs.
11. Install the upper timing belt cover on the cylinder head.
12. Install the camshaft timing belt gear.
13. Align the timing marks on the camshaft and crankshaft gears with the marks on the engine and install the timing belt and tensioner.
14. Adjust the belt tension to the correct specification and install the timing belt cover.
15. Adjust the valve lash.

Refer to Valve Lash Adjustment for Procedures.

16. The remainder of the installation is the reverse of the removal procedure.

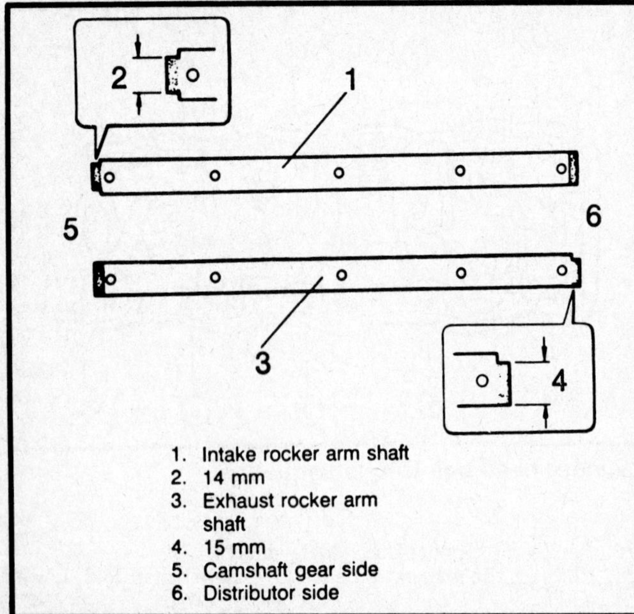

Identifying rocker arm shafts

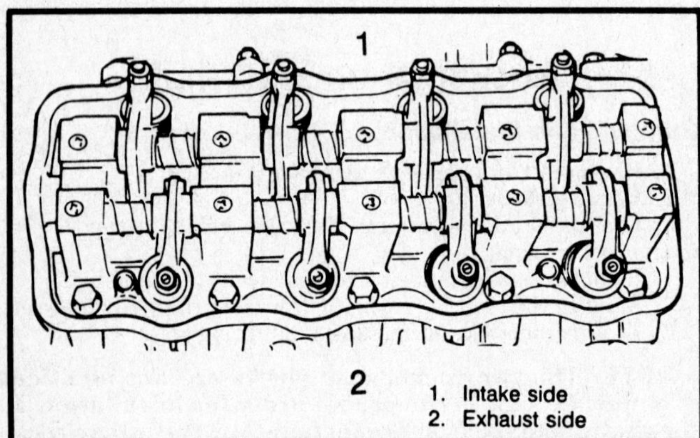

Position of rocker arm shafts, rocker arms and springs

Valve Adjustment

Procedure

Valve lash can be adjusted with the engine hot or cold. Specifications are provided for both adjustments.

1. Remove the rocker cover.
2. Remove the rubber plug from the transmission case to obtain access to the timing marks.
3. Rotate the crankshaft, in the normal direction of rotation, until the line under the "T" mark on the flywheel is in line with the mark on the transmission case.
4. Remove the distributor cap and confirm that the rotor is facing the No. 1 firing position. If the rotor is 180° away from No. 1, rotate the crankshaft one revolution and line up the timing marks on the flywheel.
5. With the engine in the No. 1 firing position, adjust No.1 and 2 intake valves and No. 1 and 3 exhaust valves.

NOTE: The valves are adjusted by loosening the lock nut on the valve adjuster and turning the adjusting screw to obtain the proper clearance. Once the proper clearance is obtained, the lock nut must be torqued to 11–13 ft. lbs. while holding the adjusting screw. Check the clearance after the lock nut is torqued. Clearance should be: Intake 0.13–0.17 mm HOT, 0.23–0.27 mm COLD. Exhaust 0.16–0.20 mm HOT, 0.26–0.30 mm COLD.

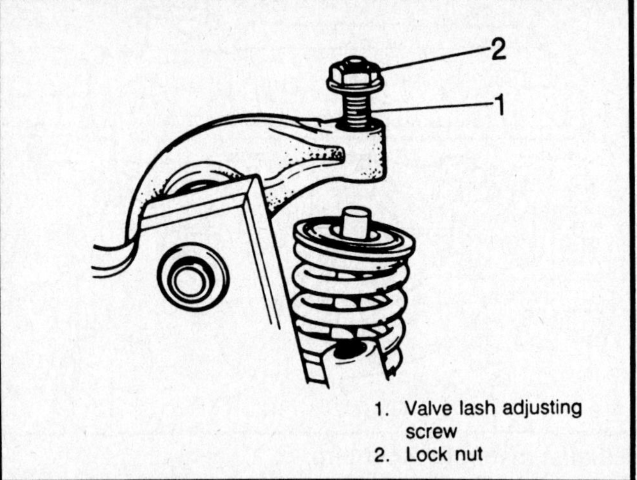

Valve lash adjusting screw and lock nut

6. Rotate the engine one revolution and adjust No. 3 and 4 intake valves and No. 2 and 4 exhaust valves.
7. Install the distributor cap and rocker cover using a new gasket.

Timing Belt and Sprockets

Removal and Installation

1. Disconnect the negative battery cable.
2. Loosen the drive belt tension and remove the drive belt.
3. Remove the radiator fan shroud mounting bolts and cooling fan to water pump mounting nuts and remove the shroud, fan and water pump pulley as an assembly.
4. Remove the four crankshaft drive belt pulley mounting bolts and remove the crankshaft pulley.

NOTE: The crankshaft drive belt pulley can be removed without removing the center crankshaft bolt.

5. Remove the timing belt cover mounting bolts and remove the cover.
6. Loosen the timing belt tensioner adjusting bolt and pivot nut. Hold the tensioner to loosen the timing belt and remove the belt from the camshaft and crankshaft pulleys.
7. Lock the camshaft with camshaft holding tool 09917–68210 or equivalent and remove the camshaft sprocket mounting bolt, sprocket and sprocket pin.
8. Hold the flywheel with a flywheel holding tool and remove the crankshaft sprocket bolt, sprocket and key.
9. To install, place the crankshaft sprocket with key on the crankshaft with the concave side of the sprocket facing the engine. Hold the flywheel with a holding tool, install and torque the bolt to 47–54 ft. lbs.
10. Place the camshaft sprocket pin in the sprocket and install the sprocket and bolt on the camshaft.
11. Using camshaft sprocket holding tool 09917–68210 or equivalent, torque the bolt to 41–46 ft. lbs.
12. Install the timing belt tensioner, plate and spring on the engine hand tight.
13. Remove the rocker cover. Loosen all valve adjusting screws

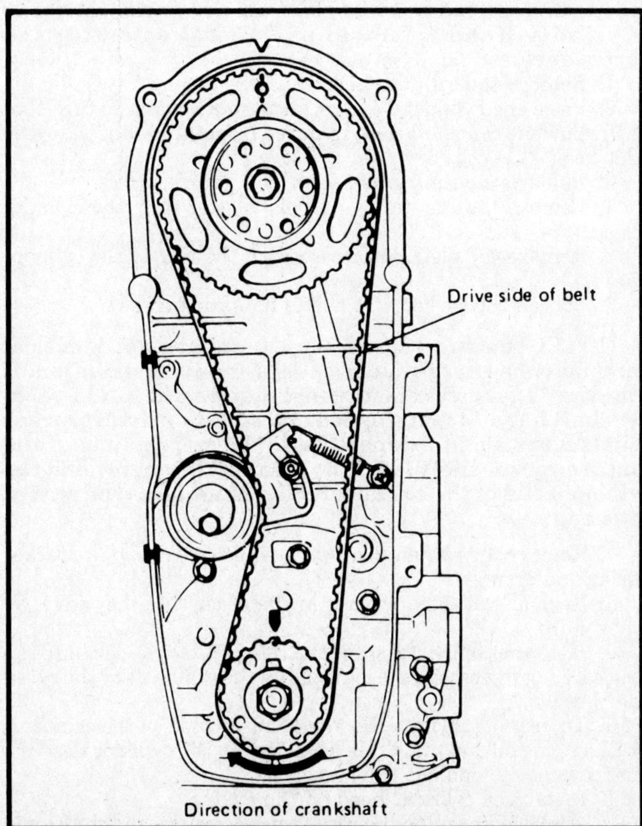

Timing belt installed with timing marks aligned

enough to permit free rotation of the camshaft without the rockers moving.

14. Rotate the camshaft to align the timing marks on the camshaft sprocket and marks on the upper rear timing belt cover.
15. Rotate the crankshaft to align the timing marks on the oil pump with the marks on the crankshaft pulley.
16. With the timing marks aligned, install and adjust the timing belt so that there is no slack in the belt on the side opposite the tensioner. Torque the tensioner bolts to 7–8.5 ft. lbs.
17. Install the crankshaft and water pump pulleys. Torque the crankshaft and water pump pulley bolts to 7.5–9.0 ft. lbs.
18. Install the timing belt cover, cooling fan, shroud and drive belt. Adjust the drive belt tension.
19. Adjust the valve lash.
20. The remainder of the installation is the reverse of the removal procedure.

Camshaft Oil Seal

Removal and Installation

1. Remove the timing belt and camshaft sprocket.
2. Remove the upper rear timing belt cover.
3. Insert a suitable tool between the camshaft and the oil seal and pull the seal outwards to remove it.

CAUTION

Use care when removing and installing the oil seal not to damage the camshaft or cylinder head sealing surfaces.

4. Clean and inspect the surfaces of the camshaft and cylinder head.
5. Using a seal driver, install the new seal over the camshaft and into the cylinder head, with the seal lip facing the cylinder head, to the same depth as the old seal.

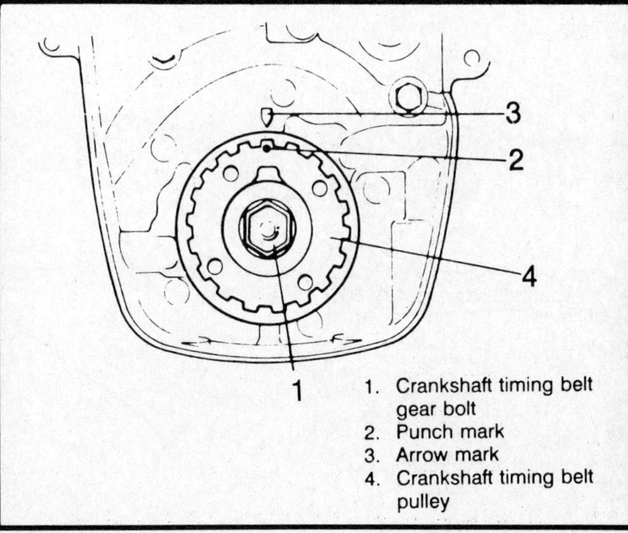

Crankshaft timing belt gear in line with mark on oil pump

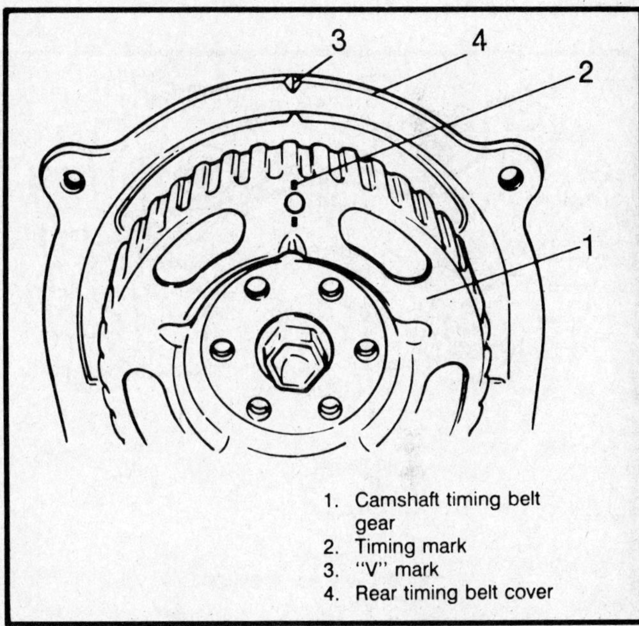

Camshaft timing belt gear in line with mark on rear timing belt cover

6. Install the upper rear timing belt cover.
7. Install the camshaft sprocket and timing belt.
8. Check the camshaft timing before installing the timing belt cover.
9. Run the engine and check for leaks when finished.

Crankshaft Oil Seal

Removal and Installation

1. Remove the timing belt and crankshaft sprocket.
2. Insert a suitable tool between the crankshaft and the oil seal and pull the seal outwards to remove it.

CAUTION

Use care when removing and installing the oil seal, not to damage the crankshaft or oil pump sealing surfaces.

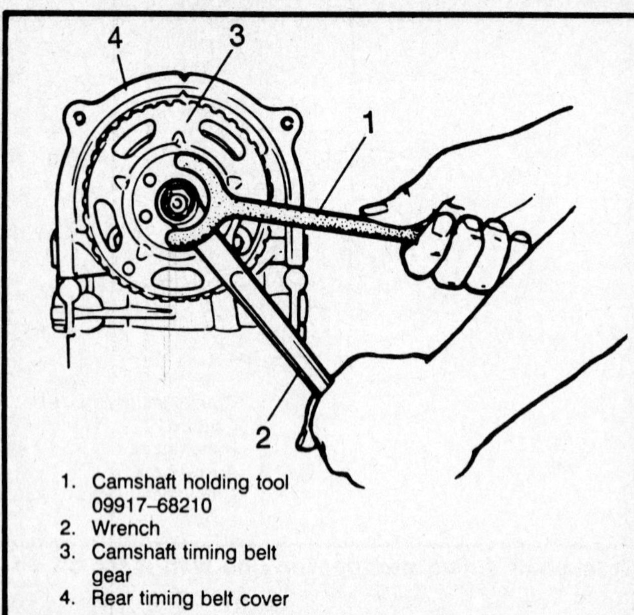

Removing camshaft timing belt gear

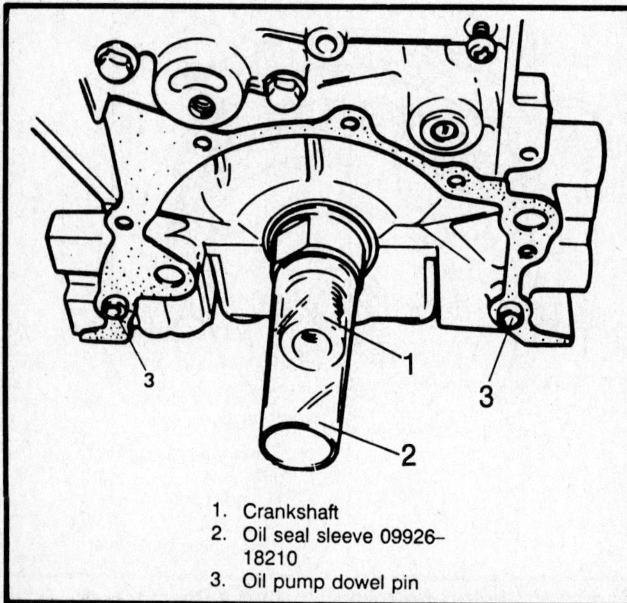

Oil seal sleeve installed on crankshaft snout

3. Clean and inspect the surfaces of the crankshaft and oil pump.
4. Install crankshaft sleeve 09926-18210 or equivalent over the crankshaft and using a seal driver, install the new seal over the crankshaft and into the oil pump, with the seal lip facing the oil pump, to the same depth as the old seal.
5. Install the crankshaft sprocket and timing belt.
6. Check the camshaft timing before installing the timing belt cover.
7. Run the engine and check for leaks when finished.

Camshaft

Removal and Installation

Removal and Installation of the camshaft requires that the cylinder head be removed from the engine. Refer to Cylinder Head Removal and Installation for the procedure.

1. Remove the cylinder head from the engine.
2. Place the cylinder head in a suitable holding fixture that will allow the camshaft to be removed from the rear of the cylinder head.
3. Remove the timing belt gear from the camshaft.
4. Remove the fuel pump and distributor from the cylinder head.
5. Remove the distributor case from the rear of the cylinder head.
6. Loosen the rocker arm shafts mounting screws.

NOTE: The two rocker arm shafts are not identical and must be kept in the proper order for installation. If the shafts get mixed before installation, the intake rocker shaft has a 14 mm stepped end and the exhaust rocker shaft has a 13 mm stepped end. The stepped end of the intake rocker shaft faces the front of the engine and the stepped end of the exhaust rocker shaft faces the rear of the engine.

7. Remove the rocker arm shafts while separating the rocker arms and springs.
8. Keep all valve train parts in the order that they were removed in.
9. Slide the camshaft out of the rear of the cylinder head using care not to damage the journals on the camshaft or the cylinder head.
10. To install, lubricate the lobes and journals of the camshaft with engine oil and install the camshaft in the cylinder head using care not to damage the journals.
11. Install the cylinder head on the engine.
12. Apply engine oil to the rocker arms, springs and shafts and install the shafts, in the correct direction, into the cylinder head placing the rocker arms and springs on the shafts as they are installed.
13. With the rocker arms, springs and shafts installed, torque the rocker shaft mounting screws to 7–8.5 ft. lbs.
14. Using new gaskets, install the distributor case, rocker cover and fuel pump on the cylinder head.
15. Install the upper timing belt cover and camshaft timing belt gear.
16. Align the timing marks on the camshaft and crankshaft gears with the marks on the engine and install the timing belt and tensioner.
17. Adjust the belt tension to the correct specification and install the timing belt cover.
18. Adjust the valve lash.
19. Install the distributor with the rotor facing the No. 1 spark plug wire lug on the distributor cap.
20. The remainder of the installation is the reverse of the removal procedure.

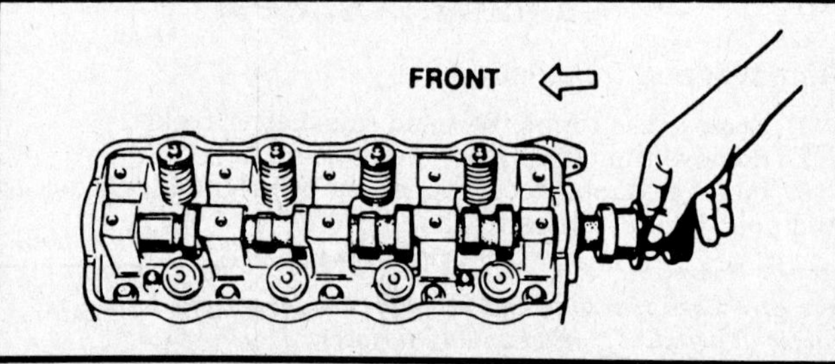

Installing camshaft in cylinder head

Piston and Connecting Rods

NOTE: Whenever pistons and connecting rods are removed or replaced, they must be marked to identify

which cylinder and which direction that they are installed.

IDENTIFICATION

Removal and Installation

NOTE: Remove the ridge at the top of the cylinder wall before removing. Replace the connecting rod caps on the connecting rod immediately after removal and inspect for cylinder number markings.

Connecting Rod and Main Bearings

Removal and Installation

Engine bearings are of the precision insert type. They are available for service in standard and various undersizes. Upper and lower bearing inserts may be different. Be careful to align holes. Do not obstruct any oil passages. Bearing inserts must not be shimmed. Do not touch the bearing surface of the insert with bare fingers. Skin oil and acids will etch the bearing surface. **Refer to the Unit Repair Section for General Procedures.**

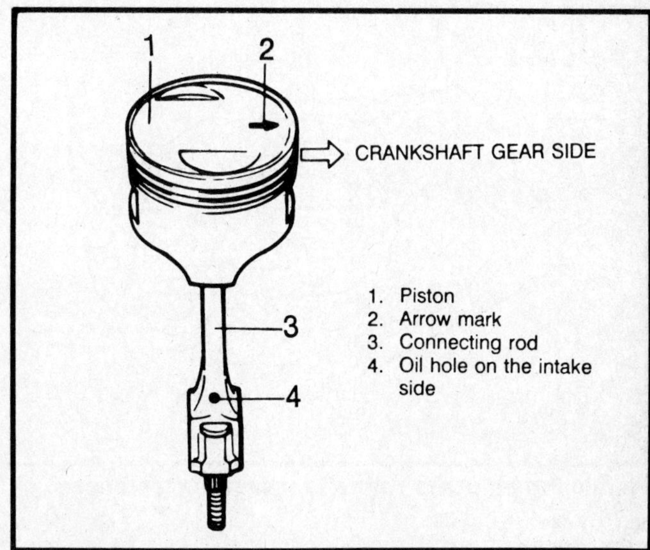

Piston and connecting rod positioning

ENGINE LUBRICATION

Oil Pan

Removal and Installation

1. Raise and support the vehicle safely. Drain the engine oil.
2. Remove the oil pan mounting nuts and bolts and remove the oil pan.
3. Clean and inspect the sealing surfaces of the oil pan, oil pump, crankshaft rear oil seal housing and engine block.
4. Using new gaskets, install the oil pan and torque the nuts and bolts to 7–8 ft. lbs.
5. Install a new oil filter and fill the engine with the proper engine oil.
6. Lower the vehicle, run the engine and check for leaks.

Oil Pump

Removal and Installation

1. Raise and support the vehicle safely. Drain the engine oil.
2. Remove the oil pan. Remove the right side front engine mount to oil pump bolt from the front of the oil pump.
3. Lower the vehicle.
4. Remove the timing belt and crankshaft gear from the engine.
5. Remove the dipstick and dipstick tube from the oil pump.
6. Remove the oil pump mounting bolts and remove the oil pump.
7. If the old oil pump is being reinstalled, inspect the sealing surface and oil seal. Replace if necessary.
8. Using a new gasket, install the oil pump on the engine and torque the mounting bolts to 7–8.5 ft. lbs. Install the dipstick tube and dipstick in the oil pump.
9. Install the timing belt, crankshaft gear and cover on the engine.
10. Check and adjust the camshaft timing, if necessary.
11. Raise and support the vehicle safely. Using new gaskets, install the oil pan and front engine mount to oil pump bolt. Torque the oil pan nuts and bolts and engine mount bolt to 7–8 ft. lbs.
12. Lower the vehicle. Fill the engine to the proper level with the proper engine oil.
13. Run the engine and check for leaks.

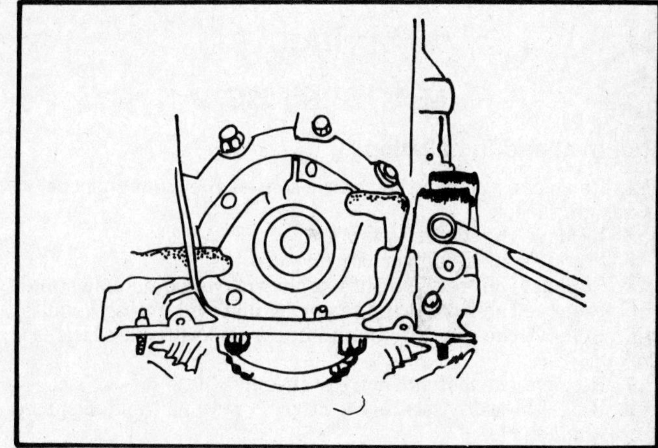

Oil pump mounting

Clearances

With the oil pump removed from the engine, certain clearances must be checked on the oil pump, if it is being reused.

RADIAL CLEARANCE

The radial clearance is the clearance between the outer oil pump rotor and the oil pump case. The maximum clearance is 0.0122 in. (.310 mm).

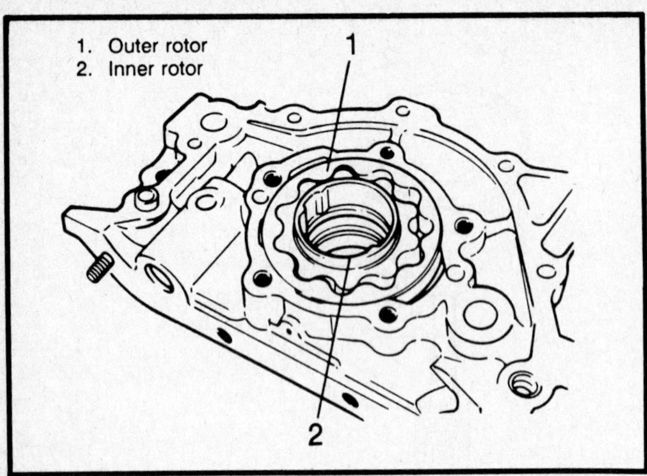

Identifying oil pump rotors to measure clearances

SIDE CLEARANCE

The side clearance is measured with a straight edge across the mounting surface of the oil pump. The measurement is taken between the inner oil pump rotor and the straight edge. The maximum clearance is 0.0059 in. (.15 mm).

Rear Crankshaft Oil Seal

Removal and Installation

1. Raise and support the vehicle safely.
2. Support the engine and remove the transmission from the vehicle.
3. Matchmark and remove the clutch assembly and flywheel.
4. Using a suitable tool, insert the tool between the crankshaft and seal. Pull the seal outwards to remove it. Use care not to damage the sealing surface of the crankshaft.
5. Clean and inspect the sealing surfaces of the crankshaft and seal housing.
6. Using a seal driver, install the new seal into the seal housing, with the lip of the seal facing the engine, to the same depth as the old seal.
7. Align the marks made during removal and install the flywheel and clutch assembly.
8. Install the transmission in the vehicle.
9. Lower the vehicle. Check the engine oil level. Run the engine and check for leaks when finished.

FRONT SUSPENSION

Springs

LEAF SPRINGS

Removal and Installation

1. Raise and support the vehicle so that the front suspension is hanging freely.
2. Remove the wheel assembly.
3. Remove the stabilizer bar pivot bolt.
4. Support the front axle assembly with an adjustable stand.
5. Remove the leaf spring to spring plate mounting U-bolts.
6. Remove the shackle pin and nut from the front of the leaf spring.
7. Remove the leaf spring rear through bolt.
8. Raise the axle assembly enough to remove the leaf spring from the vehicle.
9. Installation is the reverse of the removal procedure.
10. Torque leaf spring and stabilizer bar nuts and bolts to 51–65 ft. lbs.

Front Wheel Hub and Bearing

Removal and Installation

1. Raise and support the vehicle safely. Remove the wheel assembly.
2. Remove the brake caliper mounting bracket, with the caliper and brake line attached, from the mount and support it out of the way.

NOTE: Do not allow the caliper to hang on the brake hose. Support it by the mounting bracket.

3. Install two (8 mm) bolts into the threaded holes in the brake rotor and tighten them evenly. This will remove the rotor from the hub.
4. If the vehicle is equipped with locking hubs, remove the outer hub cover and internal circlip on the axle. Remove the locking hub from the vehicle.
5. If the vehicle is not equipped with locking hubs, remove the front axle shaft cap and circlip. Remove the drive flange from the axle shaft.
6. Straighten the bent lock washer and remove the hub nut and washer.
7. Remove the front wheel hub and bearing from the spindle.
8. Support the hub and bearing in a vise and remove the grease seal and outer race from the hub.
9. Clean and inspect the hub and bearing seats. Install the new bearing, race and grease seal in the same position.
10. Installation is the reverse of the removal procedure. When installing the hub nut and washer, torque the nut to 57 ft. lbs. Loosen the nut until the torque becomes Zero. Retorque the nut to 57 ft. lbs. This will apply the proper preload to the bearing.

Steering Knuckle

Removal and Installation

1. Remove the front wheel hub and bearing from the vehicle.
2. Loosen the upper and lower kingpin bolts, but do not remove the kingpins.
3. Remove the backing plate, caliper bracket and spindle.
4. Disconnect the tie rod end from the steering knuckle. Tie rod removal from the knuckle may require the use of a puller.
5. Remove the eight joint seal cover bolts and remove the cover, pad, oil seal and retainer from the knuckle.
6. Mark the upper and lower kingpins to determine the upper from the lower and remove them from the knuckle. Note the amount of shims under each kingpin and keep them in order for installation.
7. Remove the steering knuckle while noting the upper from the lower kingpin bearing positions during removal of the knuckle.

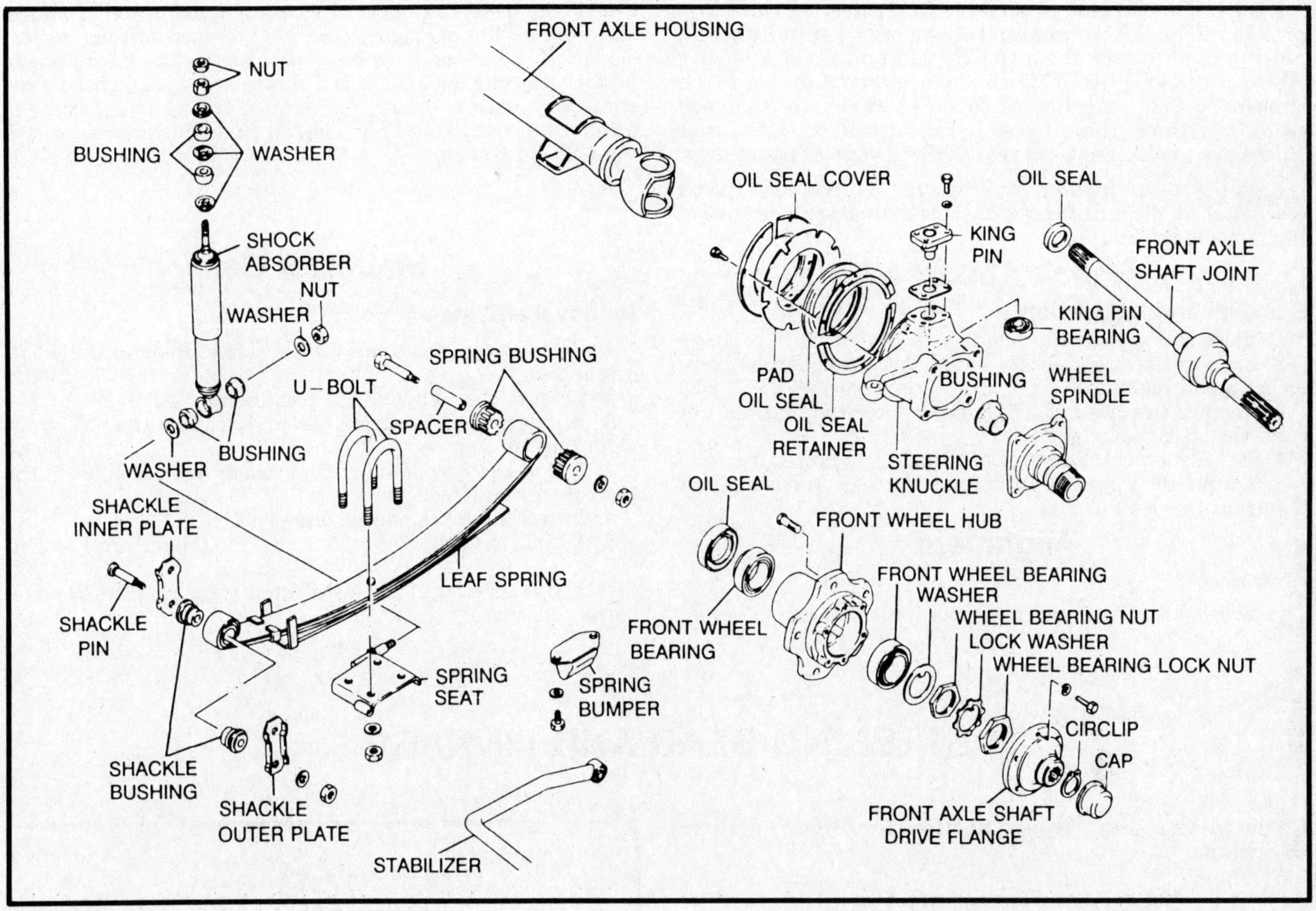

Front suspension-exploded view

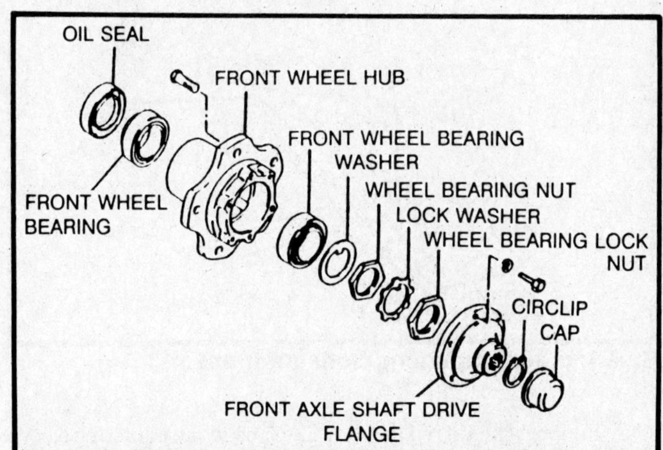

Front wheel hub and bearing-exploded view

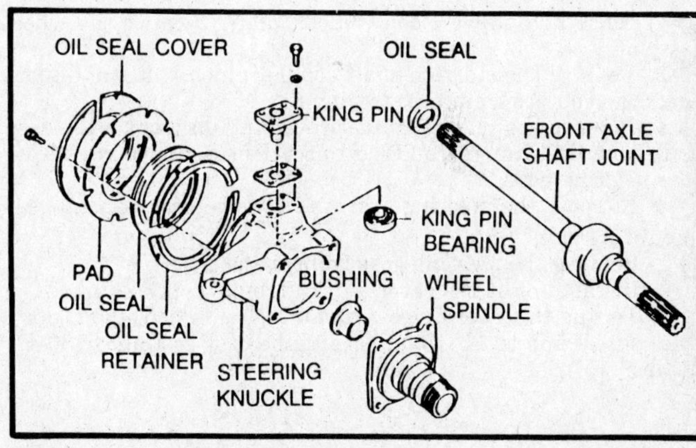

Steering knuckle, front axle and oil sealexploded view

8. Install the kingpin bearings in the new knuckle and install the knuckle on the vehicle.
9. The remainder of the installation is the reverse of the removal procedure.

King Pin and Bearing

Removal and Installation

Removal and installation of the king pin and bearing requires that the steering knuckle be removed from the vehicle. Refer to Steering Knuckle Removal and Installation for procedures.

1. Raise and support the vehicle safely.
2. Remove the steering knuckle from the vehicle.
3. Install the new kingpin bearings in the steering knuckle holding them in with grease.
4. Install the steering knuckle on the axle assembly.
5. Install the new kingpins in the knuckle, shim them correctly and torque the bolts to 14–21 ft. lbs.

NOTE: The correct procedure for installing the kingpins is to check the turning torque of the spindle while pulling it outwards from the tie rod end hole. A spring type gauge is required for this procedure. Correct force should be 2.20–3.96 lbs. of force required to turn the spindle without the oil seal being installed. Additional shims are available to correct the pressure, if necessary.

6. With the turning torque of the spindle correct and the oil seal installed, the remainder of the installation is the reverse of the removal procedure.

Shock Absorbers

Removal and Installation

1. Raise and support the vehicle safely.
2. Support the axle assembly and remove the upper shock absorber mounting nut.
3. Remove the lower shock absorber mounting nut and remove the shock absorber.
4. Installation is the reverse of the removal procedure.
5. Torque the upper mounting nut to 16–25 ft. lbs. and the lower nut to 23–40 ft. lbs.

Alignment

Procedures

The only adjustment possible on the front suspension is toe. Should the caster or camber be found to be out of specifications, the cause may be damaged, loose, bent, broken or worn suspension parts. Locate and repair any problems before attempting to perform the alignment. Toe is adjusted by loosening the tie rod adjusting sleeve lock nuts and rotating the adjusting sleeve to achieve the proper setting. Tighten the adjusting sleeve lock nuts when finished.

Stabilizer Bar

Removal and Installation

1. Raise and support the vehicle safely. Remove the wheel assemblies.
2. Remove the stabilizer bar pivot bolts.
3. Support the stabilizer bar and remove the two front mounting bracket.
4. Install the new stabilizer bar, using new bushings in the front mounting brackets.
5. Install the two stabilizer bar pivot bolts.
6. Torque the bolts to 51–65 ft. lbs. and the nuts to 13–20 ft. lbs.
7. The remainder of the installation is the reverse of the removal procedure.

STEERING GEAR AND LINKAGE

Refer to the Unit Repair Section for Steering Gear Overhaul.

Manual Steering Gear

Removal and Installation

1. Raise and support the vehicle safely. Remove the wheel assembly.
2. Remove the steering shaft coupler pinch bolt and disconnect the coupler from the steering box.
3. Remove the radiator under cover and disconnect the drag link from the pitman arm. Disconnect the steering damper from the steering gear.
4. Support the steering gear and remove the steering gear mounting bolts.
5. Remove the steering gear from the vehicle.
6. Installation is the reverse of the removal procedure.
7. Torque the steering gear mounting bolts to 51–65 ft. lbs., the coupler bolt to 11–18 ft. lbs. and the drag link nut to 30–50 ft. lbs.

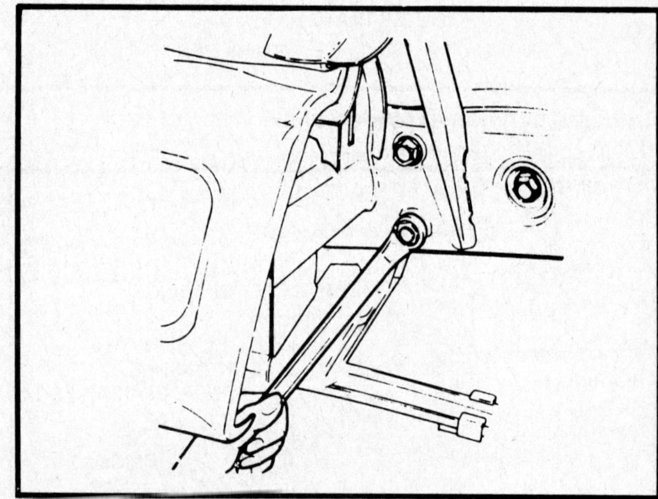

Steering gear mounting bolts on frame rail

Tie Rod

Removal and Installation

1. Raise and support the vehicle safely. Remove the wheel assemblies.
2. Disconnect the drag link from the tie rod.
3. Disconnect the outer tie rod ends from the steering knuckles.
4. Remove the tie rod from the vehicle.
5. Support the tie rod in a vise and loosen the adjusting sleeve lock nuts.
6. Remove the outer tie rod end from the tie rod counting the number of turns required to remove the tie rod end.
7. Install the tie rod end on the new tie rod the exact number of turns required to remove it.
8. Install the tie rod in the vehicle observing the following torques: Tie rod to drag link, 30–50 ft. lbs.; tie rod end nuts, 22–39 ft. lbs.
9. Check and adjust the toe when finished.

HYDRAULIC BRAKE SYSTEM

Refer to the Unit Repair Section for all overhaul procedures.

Master Cylinder

Removal and Installation

1. Disconnect and plug the two brake fluid lines at the master cylinder.
2. Remove the two master cylinder to booster attaching nuts and remove the master cylinder from the vehicle.
3. Remove the brake fluid from the reservoir. Remove the reservoir mounting screw and remove the reservoir from the master cylinder.
4. Remove the reservoir grommets from the master cylinder and install the grommets and the reservoir on the new master cylinder.
5. Fill the reservoir with an approved DOT 3 brake fluid and bench bleed the new master cylinder before installing it on the vehicle.
6. With the master cylinder installed on the vehicle, torque the mounting nuts to 7.5–11.5 ft. lbs.
7. Connect the fluid lines at the master cylinder.
8. Check and fill the reservoir. Bleed the brake system when finished.
9. Check the brake system before moving the vehicle.

BLEEDING

Procedure

1. Clean all dirt from around the master cylinder reservoir filler cap. If a bleeder tank is used, follow the manufacturer's instructions. Remove the filler cap and fill the master cylinder reservoir to the lower edge of the filler cap.
2. Clean off the bleeder connections at all of the wheel cylinders or disc brake calipers.
3. Attach the bleeder hose and fixture to the right rear wheel cylinder bleeder screw and place the end of the tube in a glass jar, submerged in brake fluid. Open the bleeder valve $^1/_2$–$^3/_4$ of a turn.
4. Have an assistant depress the brake pedal and allow it to return slowly.
5. Continue this pumping action to force any air out of the system. When bubbles cease to appear at the end of the bleeder hose, close the bleeder valve and remove the hose.
6. Check the level of the brake fluid in the master cylinder and add fluid, if necessary.
7. After the bleeding operation at each caliper or wheel cylinder has been completed, fill the master cylinder reservoir and replace the filler cap.

CAUTION

Never reuse brake fluid which has been removed from the lines through the bleeding process because it contains air bubbles and dirt.

Wheel Cylinder

Removal and Installation

1. Raise and support the vehicle safely. Remove the wheel assembly.
2. Remove the brake drum. Inspect the brake components for signs of damage from leaking brake fluid. Replace if necessary.
3. Disconnect and plug the brake line at the wheel cylinder.
4. Remove the two wheel cylinder mounting bolts and remove the wheel cylinder from the backing plate by spreading the brake shoes apart.

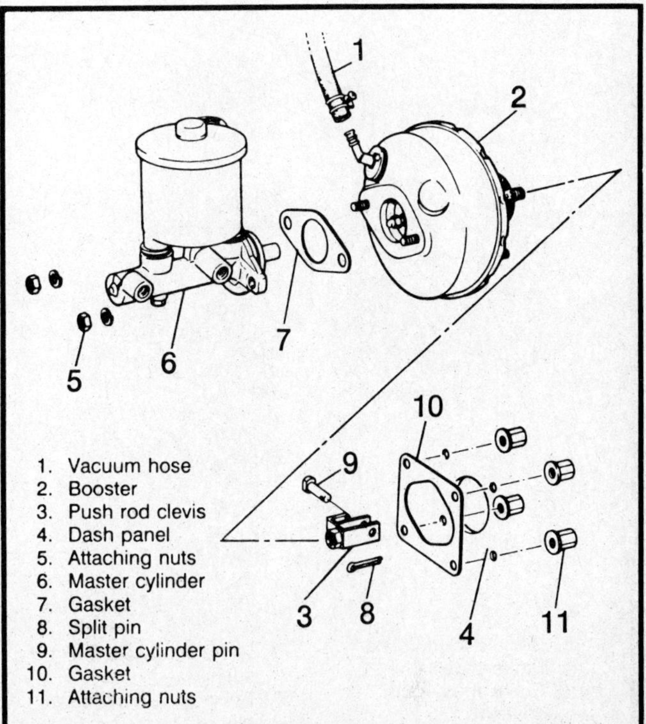

Brake master cylinder and power booster mounting

5. Spread the brake shoes apart and install the new wheel cylinder on the backing plate.
6. Torque the mounting bolts to 6–8.5 ft. lbs.
7. Install the brake line in the wheel cylinder and torque the flare nut to 10–13 ft. lbs.
8. Install the brake drum and wheel assembly. Bleed the the wheel cylinder.
9. Check the system operation before moving the vehicle.

Disc Brakes

Removal and Installation

1. Raise and support the vehicle safely. Remove the wheel assembly.
2. Remove the caliper anti-rattle clip.
3. Remove the caliper guide pins using a hexagon wrench.
4. Remove the brake pad end protectors.
5. Remove the caliper and support it safely out of the way. Do Not allow the caliper to hang on the brake line.
6. Replace the brake pads.
7. Using a suitable tool, push the caliper piston into the body of the caliper until it bottoms out.
8. Installation is the reverse of the removal procedure.
9. Pump the brake pedal until pressure is felt before moving the vehicle.

Calipers

Removal and Installation

1. Raise and support the vehicle safely. Remove the wheel assembly.
2. Disconnect and plug the brake fluid line at the caliper.

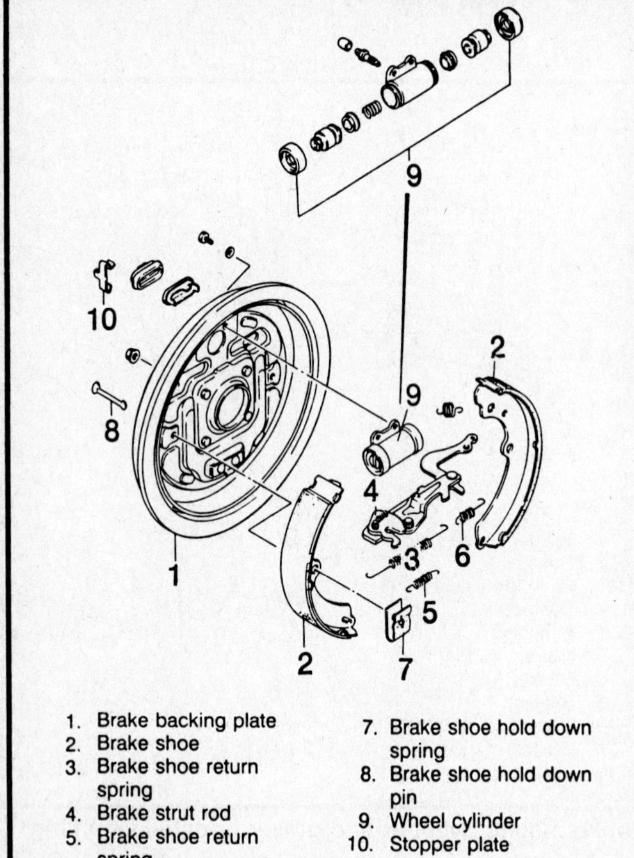

1. Brake backing plate
2. Brake shoe
3. Brake shoe return spring
4. Brake strut rod
5. Brake shoe return spring
6. Rod spring
7. Brake shoe hold down spring
8. Brake shoe hold down pin
9. Wheel cylinder
10. Stopper plate

Rear wheel cylinder and brake shoe exploded view

3. Remove the caliper anti-rattle clip.
4. Remove the caliper guide pins using a hexagon wrench.
5. Remove the brake pad end protectors.
6. Remove the caliper from the vehicle.
7. Install the new caliper over the brake pads and onto the mount.
8. Using new washers, connect the brake fluid line onto the caliper.
9. The remainder of the installation procedure is the reverse of the removal procedure.
10. Bleed the brake system when finished.

Rotors

Removal and Installation

1. Raise and support the vehicle safely. Remove the wheel assembly.
2. Remove the brake caliper mounting bracket, with the caliper and brake line attached, from the mount and support it out of the way.

NOTE: Do not allow the caliper to hang on the brake hose. Support it by the mounting bracket.

3. Install two bolts into the threaded holes in the brake rotor and tighten them evenly. This will remove the rotor from the hub.
4. Install the new brake rotor on the hub.
5. The remainder of the installation is the reverse of the removal procedure.

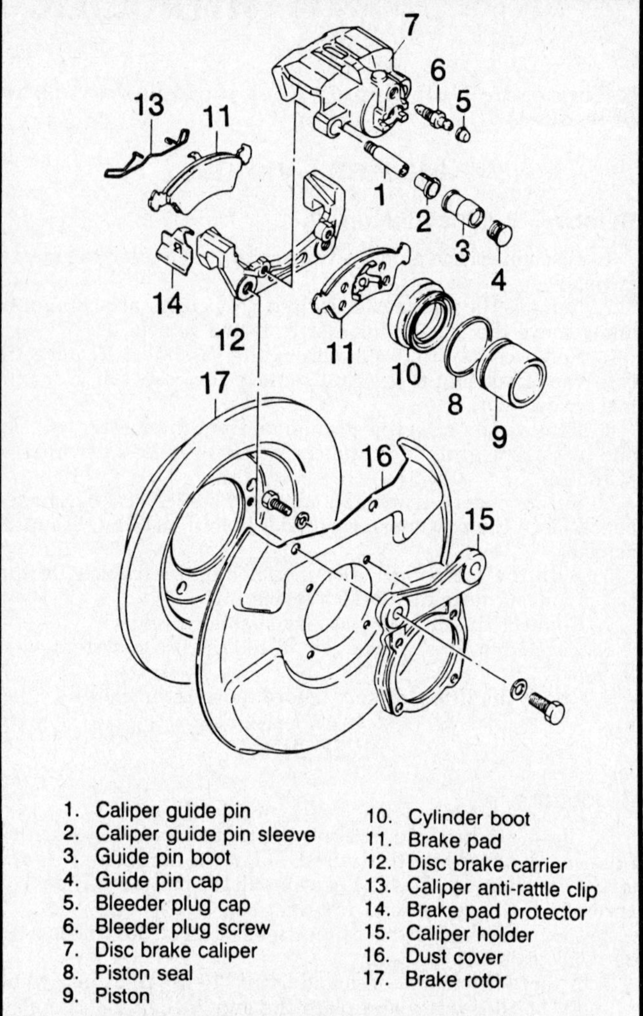

1. Caliper guide pin
2. Caliper guide pin sleeve
3. Guide pin boot
4. Guide pin cap
5. Bleeder plug cap
6. Bleeder plug screw
7. Disc brake caliper
8. Piston seal
9. Piston
10. Cylinder boot
11. Brake pad
12. Disc brake carrier
13. Caliper anti-rattle clip
14. Brake pad protector
15. Caliper holder
16. Dust cover
17. Brake rotor

Front brake caliper and brake pad exploded view

Power Brake Booster

VACUUM

Removal and Installation

1. Remove the master cylinder from the brake booster.
2. Disconnect the vacuum hose at the booster.
3. From inside the vehicle, disconnect the brake pedal pushrod from the booster.
4. Remove the brake booster mounting nuts and remove the booster from the vehicle.
5. Installation is the reverse of the removal procedure. Torque the booster mounting nuts to 7.5–11.5 ft. lbs.
6. Bleed the brake system when finished.

Brake Pedal Adjustment

Procedure

Whenever the brake pedal pushrod has been disconnected from the booster, the pedal height must be checked. The correct measurement from between the booster mounting surface and the center of the pushrod pin is 4.94–4.98 in. If the measurement is not correct, adjust the clevis pin on the brake pedal and/or bleed the brake system.

Stoplight Switch

Removal, Installation and Adjustment

1. Push the brake pedal down and remove the stoplight switch lock nut.
2. Disconnect the wire connector at the switch.
3. Remove the switch from the bracket.
4. Install the new switch on the bracket and adjust the switch so that there is 0.02–0.04 in. clearance between the switch and the brake pedal with the lock nut torqued to 7.5–10.5 ft. lbs. and the brake pedal in the normal position.

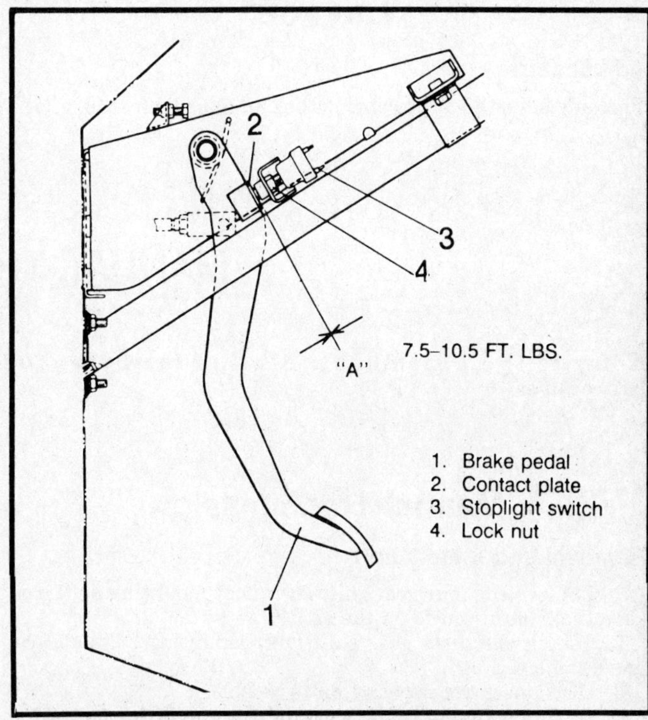

Brake pedal free play and stoplight switch

Parking Brake

CABLES

Removal and Installation

1. Raise and support the vehicle safely.
2. Disconnect the front cable from the parking brake handle by removing the cable through pin.
3. Remove the front cable from the bracket at the crossmember.
4. Disconnect the rear cables from the brake shoe levers by removing the pins.
5. Disconnect the front cable from the rear cables at the rear axle assembly by removing the pins.
6. Remove the rear cables from the brackets on the rear axle assembly.
7. Replace the necessary cable(s).
8. Installation is the reverse of the removal procedure.
9. Adjust the parking brake at the handle so that the rear wheels cannot be rotated by hand with the handle engaged 3–6 clicks.

CLUTCH

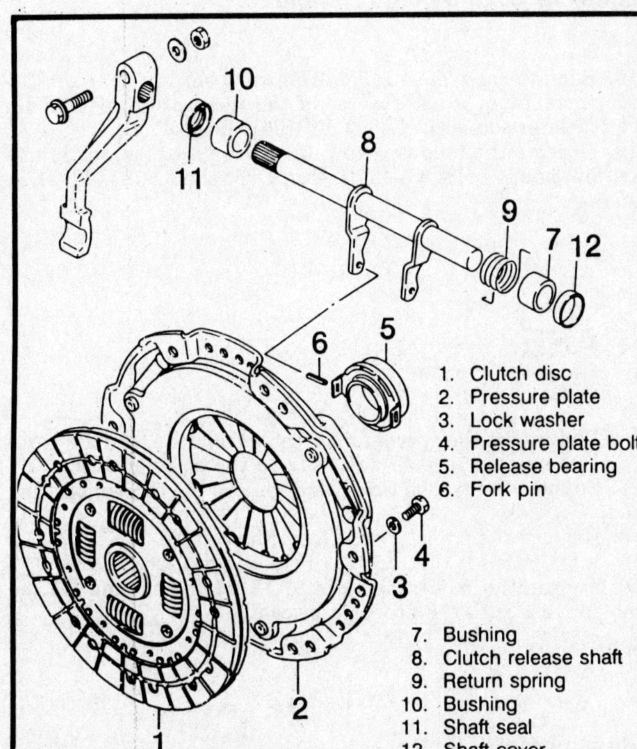

Clutch assembly and release bearing mechanism

Clutch Assembly

Removal and Installation

1. Raise and support the vehicle safely.
2. Support the engine and remove the transmission from the vehicle.
3. If the clutch assembly is being reused, matchmark the pressure plate to the flywheel to insure proper balance after reassembly.
4. Support the pressure plate and remove the six pressure plate to flywheel mounting bolts evenly.
5. Remove the pressure plate and clutch disc from the flywheel.
6. Inspect the condition of the flywheel, pressure plate and disc. Replace as necessary.
7. Remove the flywheel mounting bolts and remove the flywheel.
8. Install the new flywheel and torque the bolts to 41–47 ft. lbs.
9. Install the pressure plate and clutch disc with the large part of the hub on the disc facing the pressure plate.
10. Using a clutch disc alignment tool, align the clutch disc and evenly torque the pressure plate bolts to 13–20 ft. lbs.
11. Check the condition of the release bearing in the transmission and replace if necessary.
12. Install the transmission in the vehicle.
13. Check and adjust the clutch pedal height. Check the clutch operation when finished.

Adjustment

Refer to Linkage Adjustment for procedures.

LINKAGE

Adjustment

The only adjustment possible is the clutch pedal free play. The free play is adjusted at the release bearing arm. Clutch pedal free play should be between 0.8–1.1 in. If the free play cannot be adjusted to within the specification, check the condition of the release bearing arm, release bearing, pressure plate, clutch disc and/or clutch cable.

MANUAL TRANSMISSION

Refer to the Unit Repair Section for Overhaul Procedures.

Manual Transmission

Removal and Installation

1. Remove the four gear shift lever boot mounting bolts and slide the boot upwards on the shifter.
2. Loosen the three gear shift lever mounting bolts and remove the lever.
3. Disconnect the negative battery cable.
4. Disconnect and tag the backup light and fifth gear switch connector.
5. Disconnect and tag the starter motor wiring.
6. Remove the starter motor from the engine.
7. Remove the fuel line clamp from the transmission.
8. Raise and support the vehicle safely. Drain the transmission oil.
9. Disconnect the clutch cable from the transmission.
10. Matchmark and remove the driveshafts from the transmission to the transfer case and transfer case to front axle assembly.
11. Remove the lower bellhousing cover.
12. Support the transmission and remove the transmission to engine mounting bolts.
13. Remove the transmission cross brace.
14. Remove the center exhaust pipe.
15. Remove the rear transmission mount from the transmission and chassis.

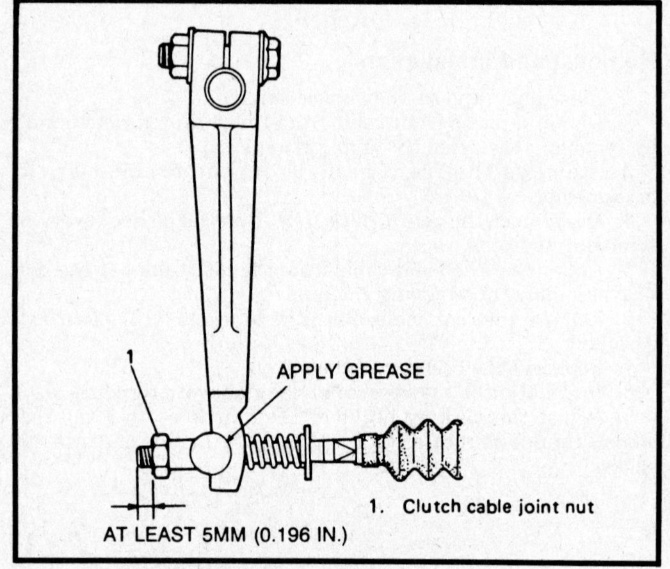

Adjusting point on clutch cable

16. Remove the transmission from the vehicle.
17. Installation is the reverse of the removal procedure. Fill the transmission with the an SAE 90W or 80W oil.
18. Observe the following torques during installation: Transmission mount bolts, 13–20 ft. lbs.; Driveshaft bolts, 17–21 ft. lbs.

TRANSFER CASE

Refer to the Unit Repair Section for Overhaul Procedures.

Transfer Case

Removal and Installation

1. Raise and support the vehicle safely. Drain the transfer case oil.
2. Matchmark and remove the transfer case driveshafts.
3. Remove the clamp from the transfer case lever boot and slide the boot up the lever.
4. Twist the lever guide counterclockwise while pushing down and remove the lever from the transfer case.
5. Disconnect the speedometer cable from the transfer case.
6. Disconnect the 4WD switch from the transfer case.
7. Support the transfer case and remove the three mounting nuts.
8. Remove the transfer case from the vehicle.
9. Installation is the reverse of the removal procedure.
10. Torque the mounting nuts to 18–25 ft. lbs. and fill the transfer case with the proper lubricant.

Linkage

Adjustments

No adjustments are possible on the transfer case linkage.

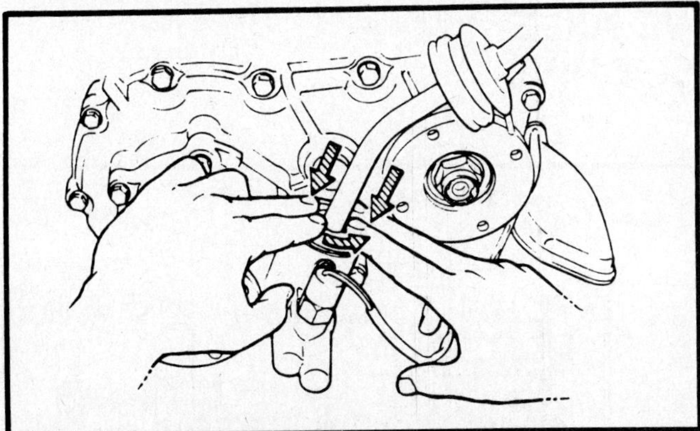

Removing control lever from transfer case

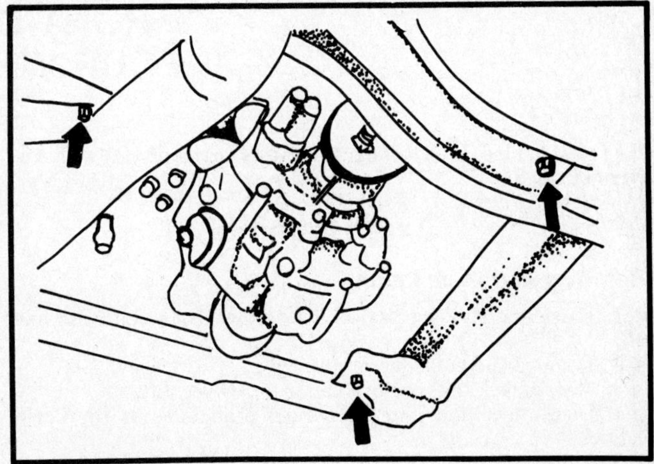

Transfer case mounting

DRIVE LINES AND UNIVERSAL JOINTS

Drive Lines

FRONT AND REAR

Removal and Installation

1. Raise and support the vehicle safely.
2. Matchmark the driveshafts to the yokes on the transfer case and differential.
3. Support the driveshaft and remove the attaching bolts.
4. Remove the driveshaft from the vehicle.
5. Install the drive shaft aligning the match marks.
6. Torque the mounting bolts to 17–21 ft. lbs.

INTERMEDIATE

Removal and Installation

1. Raise and support the vehicle safely.
2. Matchmark the driveshaft yoke to the transfer case flange.
3. Support the driveshaft and remove the attaching bolts.
4. Remove the driveshaft from the vehicle.
5. If the driveshaft comes apart at the middle, align the matchmarks when reassembling.
6. Install the driveshaft aligning the matchmarks and torque the bolts to 17–21 ft. lbs.

Universal Joints

Removal, Overhaul and Installation

1. Raise and support the vehicle safely. Remove the driveshaft.
2. If the front yoke is to be disassembled, matchmark the driveshaft and sliding splined yoke so that driveline balance is preserved upon reassembly. Remove the snap rings that retain the bearing caps.
3. Select two press components, with one small enough to pass through the yoke holes for the bearing caps and the other large enough to receive the bearing cap.
4. Use a vise or a press and position the small and large press components on either side of the U-joint. Press in on the smaller press component so that it presses the opposite bearing cap out of the yoke and into the larger press component. If the cap does not come all the way out, grasp it with a pair of pliers and work it out.
5. Reverse the position of the press components so that the smaller press component presses on the cross. Press the other bearing cap out of the yoke.
6. Repeat the procedure on the other bearings.
7. To install, grease the bearing caps and needles thoroughly if they are not pregreased. Start a new bearing cap into one side of the yoke. Position the cross in the yoke.

NOTE: Some U-joints have a grease fitting that must be installed in the joint before assembly. When installing the fitting, make sure that once the driveshaft is installed in the vehicle that the fitting is accessible to be greased at a later date.

8. Select two press components small enough to pass through the yoke holes. Put the press components against the cross and the cap and press the bearing cap ¼ in. below the surface of the yoke. If there is a sudden increase in the force needed to press the cap into place, or if the cross starts to bind, the bearings are cocked. They must be removed and restarted in the yoke. Failure to do so will cause premature bearing failure.
9. Install a new snap-ring.
10. Start the new bearing into the opposite side. Place a press component on it and press in until the opposite bearing contacts the snap ring.
11. Install a new snap ring. It may be necessary to grind the facing surface of the snap ring slightly to permit easier installation.
12. Install the other bearings in the same manner.
13. Check the joint for free movement. If binding exists, smack the yoke ears with a brass or plastic faced hammer to seat the bearing needles. If binding still exists, dissassemble the joint and check to see if the needles are in place. Do not strike the bearings unless the shaft is supported firmly. Do not install the driveshaft until free movement exists at all joints.

FRONT DRIVE AXLE FOUR WHEEL DRIVE

Refer to the Unit Repair Section for Overhaul Procedures.

Axle Housing

Removal and Installation

1. Raise and support the vehicle safely. Drain the front axle oil.
2. Remove the wheel assemblies.
3. Matchmark and remove the front driveshaft.
4. Disconnect and plug the brake fluid lines at the brake calipers.
5. Remove the housing to leaf spring U-bolts and nuts.
6. Slide the housing to one side while tilting the opposite side under the leaf spring.
7. Remove the housing from the vehicle.
8. Installation is the reverse of the removal procedure. Torque the housing U-bolt nuts to 43–57 ft. lbs.
9. Refill the differential with the proper lubricant and bleed the brake system when finished.

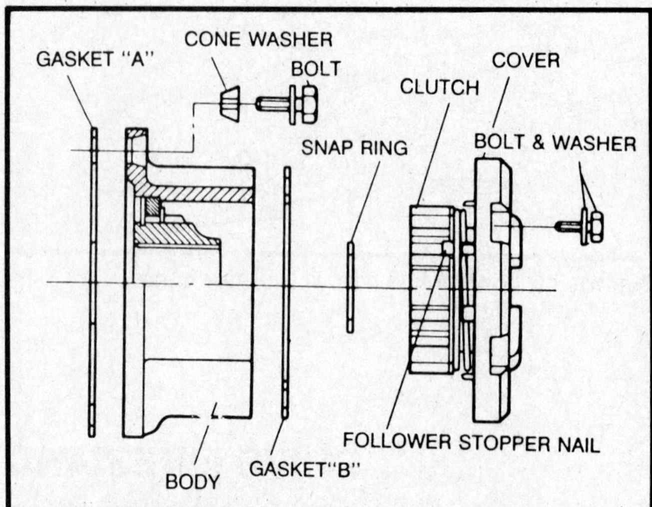

Locking hub-exploded view

Locking Hubs

Removal and Installation

1. Raise and support the vehicle safely.
2. Remove the six locking hub cover to hub body mounting bolts and remove the hub.
3. Remove the six body to steering knuckle bolts and remove the body.

NOTE: If the vehicle was not equipped with locking hubs, the axle shaft must be pulled out enough to install a snap ring in the outer groove on the axle. The snap ring comes with the kit to install locking hubs on the vehicle.

4. With the snap ring in place on the axle, use a new gasket and install the hub body to the steering knuckle. Torque the bolts to 14–21 ft. lbs.
5. Before installing the cover assembly on the hub body, place the triangle on the cover to the FREE position.
6. Align the teeth on the cover with the grooves in the body and install the cover with a new gasket in the body. Torque the bolts to 6–8.5 ft. lbs.
7. Check the operation of the locking hub in both the FREE and the LOCK positions.

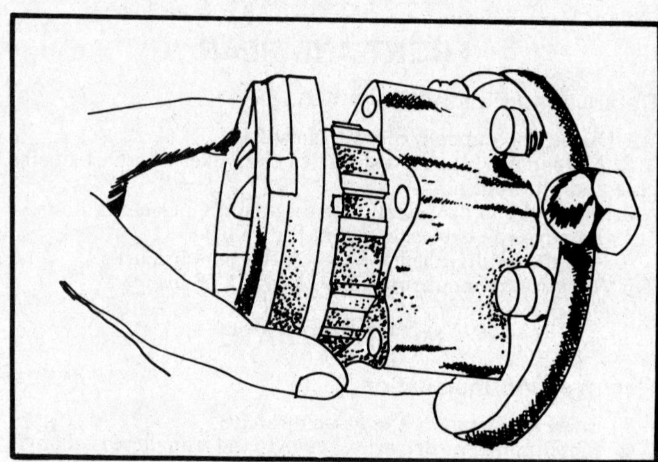
Install locking hub by aligning teeth

Axle Shaft

Removal and Installation

1. Raise and support the vehicle safely.
2. Drain the front axle oil.
3. Remove the brake caliper from the caliper bracket and support it safely out of the way. Do Not allow the caliper to hang on the brake hose.
4. Disconnect the tie rod end from the steering knuckle. Tie rod removal from the knuckle may require the use of a puller.
5. Remove the eight joint seal cover bolts and disconnect the cover, pad, oil seal and retainer from the knuckle.
6. Mark the upper and lower kingpins to determine the upper from the lower and remove them from the knuckle. Note the amount of shims under each kingpin and keep them in order for installation.
7. Remove the axle shaft from the housing with the steering knuckle attached.
8. Transfer the steering knuckle to the new axle.
9. Installation is the reverse of the removal procedure. Fill the axle with the proper lubricant when finished.
10. Observe the following torques during installation: Joint seal bolts, 6–8.5 ft. lbs.; Tie rod nut, 22–39 ft. lbs.; King pin bolts, 14–21 ft. lbs.

Axle Shaft Seal and/or Bearing

Removal and Installation

1. Raise and support the vehicle safely. Drain the front axle oil.
2. Remove the front wheel hub and bearing.
3. Support the hub and drive out the oil seal in the hub.
4. Using a seal driver, install the new seal in the hub until it is flush with the hub face. Apply a thin film of oil to the lip of the seal before installation in the vehicle.
5. Install the hub and bearing on the vehicle.

Removing front axle shaft with steering knuckle attached

Differential Carrier

Removal and Installation

1. Raise and support the vehicle safely. Drain the front axle oil.
2. Remove the wheel assemblies.
3. Remove the front axles enough to allow the carrier to be removed.
4. Matchmark and remove the front driveshaft.
5. Remove the carrier to housing mounting bolts and remove the carrier.
6. Installation is the reverse of the removal procedure.
7. Torque the carrier to housing bolts to 13–20 ft. lbs.
8. Fill the axle to the proper level with an SAE 90W or 80W oil.

Wheel Bearings

Removal and Installation

Refer to Front Wheel Hub and Bearing Removal and Installation for procedures.

Steering Knuckle

Removal and Installation

Refer to Steering Gear and Linkage in the front of this section.

REAR DRIVE AXLE

Refer to the Unit Repair Section for Overhaul Procedures.

Axle Housing

Removal and Installation

1. Raise and support the vehicle safely. Remove the rear wheel assemblies.
2. Remove the parking brake cables from the levers at the backing plates.
3. Disconnect the parking brake cables from the rear axle assembly.
4. Matchmark and remove the rear driveshaft.
5. Disconnect and plug the brake fluid line at the point where the line separates to the rear brakes.
6. Drain the rear axle housing oil.
7. Remove the housing to leaf spring U-bolts and nuts.
8. Slide the housing to one side while tilting the opposite side under the leaf spring.
9. Remove the housing from the vehicle.
10. Installation is the reverse of the removal procedure. Torque the housing U-bolt nuts to 43–57 ft. lbs.
11. Refill the differential with an SAE 90W or 80W lubricant and bleed the brake system when finished.

Axle Shaft

Removal and Installation

1. Check to make sure that the parking brake is not on.
2. Raise and support the vehicle safely. Remove the rear wheel assemblies.
3. Remove the rear brake drums. A slide hammer type puller may be necessary to remove the drums.
4. Disconnect the parking brake cables from the levers. Remove the parking brake lever stop plates.

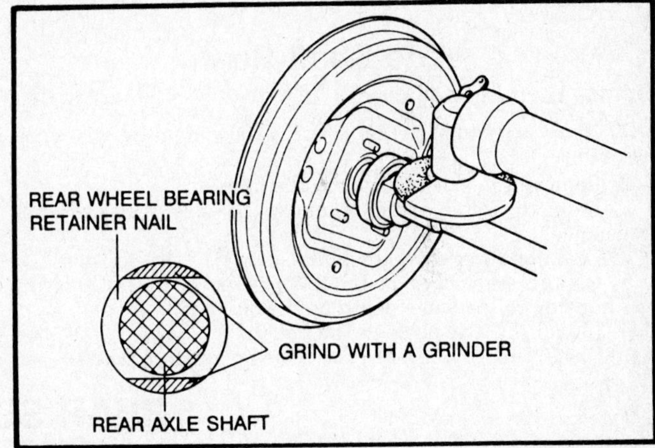

Grinding bearing retainer on rear axle to remove bearing

5. Disconnect and plug the brake lines at the wheel cylinders.
6. Remove the backing plate mounting bolts.
7. Remove the rear axles with the backing plates attached using a slide hammer type puller.
8. If the axle, axle bearing or backing plate is being replaced, support the axle in a vise with an additional support under the axle shaft next to the bearing.

CAUTION

Eye protection must be worn during the next 3 Steps. Failure do do so could cause injury.

9. With the axle supported properly, grind the top and bottom

of the axle bearing retainer to remove it without damaging the axle.

10. Using a chisel, finish removing the retainer from the axle shaft.
11. Using a press or suitable bearing puller, remove the axle bearing from the axle shaft.
12. Remove the backing plate from the axle shaft.
13. To install, place the backing plate on the axle shaft and using a press, install the bearing and retainer on the axle shaft.
14. Install the axle shaft in the housing.
15. The remainder of the installation is the reverse of the removal procedure.

Pinion Seal

Removal and Installation

1. Raise and support the vehicle safely.
2. Matchmark and remove the driveshaft.
3. Check the turning torque of the pinion before proceding. This is the torque that must be reached during installation of the pinion nut.
4. Using pinion flange holding tool 09939–4013 or equivalent, remove the pinion nut and washer.
5. Remove the pinion flange from the pinion gear.
6. Pry the pinion seal out of the differential carrier.
7. Clean and inspect the sealing surface of the carrier.
8. Using a seal driver, drive the new seal into the carrier until the flange on the seal is flush with the carrier.
9. With the seal installed, the pinion bearing preload must be set.
10. Tighten the pinion nut while holding the flange with tool 09939–4013, or equivalent until the turning torque is the same as before removal of the nut.
11. Align the matchmarks and install the drive shaft.
12. Check the level of the differential lubricant when finished.

Axle Shaft Seal

Removal and Installation

1. Raise and support the vehicle safely. Remove the wheel assembly.
2. Remove the axle shaft from the housing.
3. Using a suitable tool, remove the axle seal from the housing.
4. Clean and inspect the sealing surface of the housing.
5. Using a seal driver, install the new seal with the lip facing the housing to the same depth as the old seal.
6. Install the axle shaft in the housing.
7. Check the fluid level in the housing when finished.

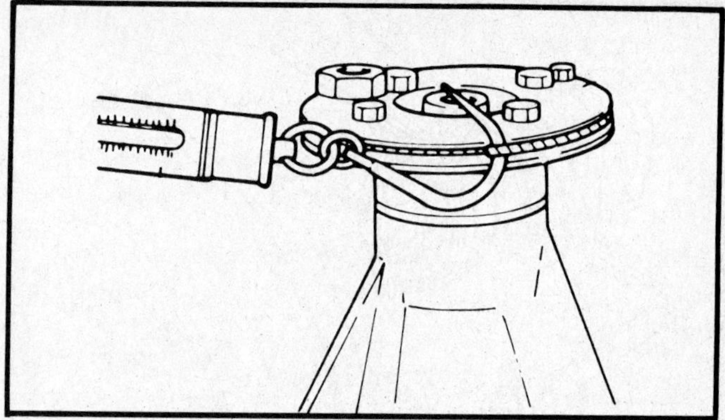

Checking turning torque of pinion gear in differential

Differential Carrier

Removal and Installation

1. Check to make sure that the parking brake is not on.
2. Raise and support the vehicle safely. Remove the rear wheel assemblies.
3. Remove the rear brake drums. A slide hammer type puller may be necessary to remove the drums.
4. Disconnect the parking brake cables from the levers. Remove the parking brake lever stop plates.
5. Disconnect and plug the brake lines at the wheel cylinders.
6. Remove the backing plate mounting bolts.
7. Remove the rear axles with the backing plates using a slide hammer type puller.
8. Matchmark and remove the rear driveshaft.
9. Drain the rear axle oil.
10. Remove the differential carrier case nuts and remove the differential from the housing.
11. Clean and inspect the sealing surfaces of the carrier and the housing.
12. Using a liquid gasket on the carrier, install the carrier in the housing and torque the nuts to 13–20 ft. lbs.
13. Fill the carrier to the proper level with Hypoid gear oil SAE 90 or 80.
14. The remainder of the installation is the reverse of the removal procedure.

Axle Shaft Bearings

Removal and Installation

Refer to Axle Shaft Removal and Installation for procedures.

REAR SUSPENSION

Leaf Spring

Removal and Installation

1. Raise and support the vehicle safely. Remove the wheel assembly.
2. Support the axle housing separately.
3. Disconnect the shock absorber and stabilizer bar from the shackle plate under the leaf spring.
4. Remove the axle housing U-bolts and nuts.
5. Raise the axle housing and remove the shackle plate.
6. Support the leaf spring and remove the front and rear leaf spring mounting bolts.
7. Remove the leaf spring.
8. Installation is the reverse of the removal procedure.
9. Observe the following torques during installation: Front leaf spring bolts, 33–50 ft. lbs.; Rear leaf spring bolts, 22–39 ft. lbs.; Stabilizer bar bolts, 16–25 ft. lbs.; Shock absorber nuts, 25–39 ft. lbs.

Shock Absorbers

Removal and Installation

1. Raise and support the vehicle safely. Remove the wheel assembly.
2. Support the rear axle assembly and remove the upper and lower shock absorber mounting bolts.
3. Remove the shock absorber.
4. Installation is the reverse of the removal procedure.
5. Torque the upper and lower mounting bolts to 25–39 ft. lbs.

Toyota 19

INDEX

BEFORE SERVICING, SEE THE SAFETY NOTICE AT THE FRONT OF THE BOOK

ENGINE IDENTIFICATION CODES BY VIN NUMBER

Engine Cu. In. (liter)	Cylinders	1982	1983	1984	1985	1986	1987	1988
144 (2.3)	4	22R	22R	22R	22R	22R	22R	22R
144 (2.3)	4	—	—	22R-E	22R-E	22R-E	22R-E	22R-E
144 (2.3)	4	—	—	—	22R-TE	22R-TE	22R-TE	22R-TE
134 (2.2)	4	L	L	—	—	—	—	—
149 (2.4)	4	—	—	2L	2L	2L	2L	2L
149 (2.4)	4	—	—	—	2L-T	2L-T	2L-T	2L-T
258 (4.2)	6	2F	2F	2F	2F	2F	2F	2F
122 (2.0)	4	—	3Y-E	3Y-E	—	—	—	—
122 (2.0)	4	—	—	—	3Y-EC	—	—	—
136 (2.2)	4	—	—	—	—	4Y-E	4Y-E	4Y-E

MODEL IDENTIFICATION

Model Name	Model Designation
RN34	Pickup
RN44	Pickup
RN44L-KH	Pickup
RN44L-3W	Cab & Chassis
SR-5 (Short Bed)	Pickup
SR-5 (Long Bed)	Pickup
SR-5 (Extra Cab, Long Bed)	Pickup
YR-21	Van
YR-22	Van
YR-27	Van
YR-29	Van
YR-31	Van
YR-32	Van
FJ-40	Land Cruiser

MODEL IDENTIFICATION

Model Name	Model Designation
FJ-43	Land Cruiser
FJ-45	Land Cruiser
FJ-60	Land Cruiser
FA-100	Land Cruiser
FA-115	Land Cruiser
RN-50	Pickup & 4-Runner
RN-55	Pickup & 4-Runner
RN-61	Pickup & 4-Runner
RN-66	Pickup & 4-Runner
RN-70	Pickup & 4-Runner
RN-75	Pickup & 4-Runner
LN-51	Pickup
LN-56	Pickup
LN-65	Pickup

GENERAL ENGINE SPECIFICATIONS

Year	Engine Type	Engine Displacement Cu. In. (cc)	Carburetor Type	Horsepower (@ rpm)	Torque @ rpm (ft. lbs.)	Bore × Stroke (in.)	Compression Ratio	Oil Pressure @ rpm (psi)
1982	22R	144.4 (2366)	2-bbl	96 @ 4800	93 @ 2800	3.62 × 3.50	9.0:1	36–71 @ 3000
	2F	258 (4230)	2-bbl	125 @ 3600	200 @ 1800	4.02 × 4.13	7.8:1	50–70 @ 2000
1983	22R	144.4 (2366)	2-bbl	100 @ 4800	93 @ 2800	3.62 × 3.50	9.0:1	36–71 @ 3000
	2F	258 (4230)	2-bbl	125 @ 3600	200 @ 1800	4.02 × 4.13	7.8:1	50–70 @ 2000
	3Y-E	121.9 (1998)	EFI	90 @ 4400	120 @ 3000	3.40 × 3.40	9.0:1	36–71 @ 3000

GENERAL ENGINE SPECIFICATIONS

Year	Engine Type	Engine Displacement Cu. In. (cc)	Carburetor Type	Horsepower (@ rpm)	Torque @ rpm (ft. lbs.)	Bore × Stroke (in.)	Compression Ratio	Oil Pressure @ rpm (psi)
1984	22R	144.4 (2366)	2-bbl	100 @ 4800	130 @ 2800	3.62 × 3.50	9.0:1	36–71 @ 3000
	2F	258 (4230)	2-bbl	125 @ 3600	200 @ 1800	4.02 × 4.13	7.8:1	50–70 @ 2000
	22R-E	144.4 (2366)	EFI	106 @ 4800	137 @ 2800	3.62 × 3.50	9.0:1	36–71 @ 3000
	3Y-E	121.9 (1998)	EFI	90 @ 4400	120 @ 3000	3.40 × 3.40	9.0:1	36–71 @ 3000
1985	22R	144.4 (2366)	2-bbl	103 @ 4800	133 @ 2800	3.62 × 3.50	9.0:1	36–71 @ 3000
	22R-E	144.4 (2366)	EFI	116 @ 4800	140 @ 2800	3.62 × 3.50	9.0:1	36–71 @ 3000
	22R-TE	144.4 (2366)	EFI ①	135 @ 4800	173 @ 2800	3.62 × 3.50	9.3:1	36–71 @ 3000
	2F	258 (4230)	2-bbl	125 @ 3600	200 @ 1800	4.02 × 4.13	7.8:1	50–70 @ 2000
	3Y-EC	121.9 (1998)	EFI	90 @ 4400	120 @ 3000	3.40 × 3.40	9.0:1	36–71 @ 3000
1986	22R	144.4 (2366)	2-bbl	103 @ 4800	133 @ 2800	3.62 × 3.50	9.0:1	36–71 @ 3000
	22R-E	144.4 (2366)	EFI	116 @ 4800	140 @ 2800	3.62 × 3.50	9.3:1	36–71 @ 3000
	22R-TE	144.4 (2366)	EFI ①	135 @ 4800	173 @ 2800	3.62 × 3.50	9.3:1	36–71 @ 3000
	2F	258 (4230)	2-bbl	125 @ 3600	200 @ 1800	3.70 × 4.00	8.3:1	50–70 @ 2000
	3B	258 (4230)	—	—	—	3.70 × 4.00	—	50–70 @ 2000
	2H	258 (4230)	—	—	—	3.70 × 4.00	—	50–70 @ 2000
	4Y-E	136.5 (2237)	EFI	101 @ 4000	132 @ 3000	3.58 × 3.40	8.8:1	50–70 @ 3000
1987-88	22R	144.4 (2366)	2-bbl	103 @ 4800	133 @ 2800	3.62 × 3.50	9.3:1	36–71 @ 3000
	22R-E	144.4 (2366)	EFI	116 @ 4800	140 @ 2800	3.62 × 3.50	9.3:1	36–71 @ 3000
	22R-TE	144.4 (2366)	EFI ①	135 @ 4800	173 @ 2800	3.62 × 3.50	7.5:1	36–71 @ 3000
	2F	258 (4230)	2-bbl	125 @ 3600	200 @ 1800	3.70 × 4.00	8.3:1	50–70 @ 2000
	3B	258 (4230)	—	—	—	3.70 × 4.00	—	50–70 @ 2000
	2H	258 (4230)	—	—	—	3.70 × 4.00	—	50–70 @ 2000
	4Y-E	136.5 (2237)	EFI	101 @ 4400	132 @ 3000	3.58 × 3.40	8.8:1	50–70 @ 3000

EFI—Electronic Fuel Injection
① Turbo

GASOLINE TUNE-UP SPECIFICATIONS

Year	Engine Type	Spark Plugs		Distributor		Ignition Timing (deg) ▲		Fuel Pump Pressure (psi)	Manifold Vacuum at Idle* in. Hg	Compression Pressure (psi) @ 250 rpm**	Idle Speed (rpm)		Valve Clearance (in.)	
		Type	Gap (in.)	Dwell (deg)	Gap (in.)	MT	AT				MT	AT	In	Ex
1982	22R	W16 EXR-U	0.032	Elec.	Elec.	8B	8B	2.1–4.3	15.8	156	700	750	0.008	0.012
	2F	W14 EXR-U	0.032	41	0.008–0.016	7B ④	—	2.1–4.3	—	149	650	—	0.008	0.014
1983	22R	W16 EXR-U	0.031	Elec.	Elec.	5B	5B	2.1–4.3	15.8	142–171	700	750	0.008	0.012
	2F	W14 EXR-U	0.031	41	0.008–0.016	7B ④	—	2.1–4.3	—	149	650	—	0.008	0.014
	3Y-E	P16R	0.043	Elec.	Elec.	8B ①④	8B ①	33–38	15.8	142–171	700	750	②	②
1984	22R	W16 EXR-U	0.031	Elec.	Elec.	5B	5B	2.1–4.3	15.8	142–171	700	750	0.008	0.012
	22R-E	W16 EXR-U	0.031	Elec.	Elec.	5B ③	—	36–38	15.8	142–171	750	—	0.008	0.012
	2F	W14 EXR-U	0.031	41	0.008–0.016	7B ④	—	2.1–4.3	—	149	650	—	0.008	0.014
	3Y-E	P16R	0.043	Elec.	Elec.	8B ①	8B ①	33–38	15.8	142–171	700	750	②	②

GASOLINE TUNE-UP SPECIFICATIONS

Year	Engine Type	Spark Plugs Type	Spark Plugs Gap (in.)	Distributor Dwell (deg)	Distributor Gap (in.)	Ignition Timing (deg) ▲ MT	Ignition Timing (deg) ▲ AT	Fuel Pump Pressure (psi)	Manifold Vacuum at Idle* in. Hg	Compression Pressure (psi) @ 250 rpm**	Idle Speed (rpm) MT	Idle Speed (rpm) AT	Valve Clearance (in.) In	Valve Clearance (in.) Ex
1985	22R	W16 EXR-U	0.031	Elec.	Elec.	0 ④	0 ④	2.1–4.3	15.8	142–171	700	750	0.008	0.012
	22R-E	W16 EXR-U	0.031	Elec.	Elec.	5B ③	—	36–38	15.8	142–171	750	—	0.008	0.012
	22R-TE	W16 EXR-U	0.031	Elec.	Elec.	5B ③	—	36–38	15.8	120–149	800	—	0.008	0.012
	2F	W14 EXR-U	0.031	41	0.008–0.016	7B ④	—	2.1–4.3	—	149	650	—	0.008	0.014
	3Y-EC	P16R	0.043	Elec.	Elec.	8B ①④	8B ①④	33–38	15.8	142–171	700	750	②	②
1986	22R	W16 EXR-U	0.031	Elec.	Elec.	0 ①④	0 ①④	2.1–4.3	15.8	142–171	700	750	0.008	0.012
	22R-E	W16 EXR-U	0.031	Elec.	Elec.	5B ③	—	36–38	15.8	142–171	750	—	0.008	0.012
	22R-TE	W16 EXR-U	0.031	Elec.	Elec.	5B ③	—	36–38	15.8	120–149	800	—	0.008	0.012
	2F	W14 EXR-U	0.031	41	0.008–0.016	7B ④	—	2.1–4.3	—	149	650	—	0.008	0.014
	4Y-E	P16R	0.043	Elec.	Elec.	12B ③	12B ③	27–31	15.8	128–178	700	750	②	②
1987	22R	W16 EXR-U	0.031	Elec.	Elec.	0 ①④	0 ①④	2.1–4.3	15.8	142–171	700	750	0.008	0.012
	22R-E	W16 EXR-U	0.031	Elec.	Elec.	5B ③	—	33–38	15.8	142–171	750	—	0.008	0.012
	22R-TE	W16 EXR-U	0.031	Elec.	Elec.	5B ③	—	33–38	15.8	142–171	800	—	0.008	0.012
	2F	W14 EXR-U	0.031	41	0.008–0.016	7B ④	—	2.1–4.3	—	149	650	—	0.008	0.014
	4Y-E	P16 R	0.043	Elec.	Elec.	12B ③	12B ③	27–31	15.8	128–178	700	750	②	②
1988	—See Underhood Sticker—													

NOTE: If these figures do not correspond to information given on the engine compartment decal, use the figures on the decal. They are current for the engine in your truck.

▲ With automatic transmission in D (drive) and manual transmission in Neutral
* These are the minimum readings you must obtain
** Look for uniformity among cylinders rather than specific pressure
① Vacuum advance OFF
② No adjustment is necessary
③ T terminal shorted
④ 950 rpm

FIRING ORDERS

NOTE: To avoid confusion, always replace the spark plug wires one at a time.

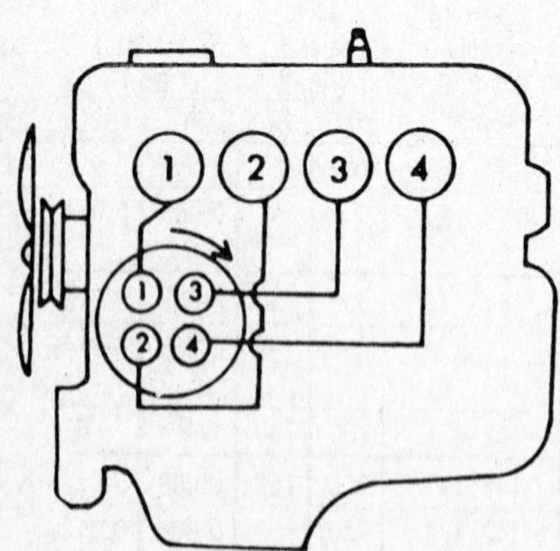

Engines 22R, 22R-E and 22R-TE
Firing order: 1-3-4-2

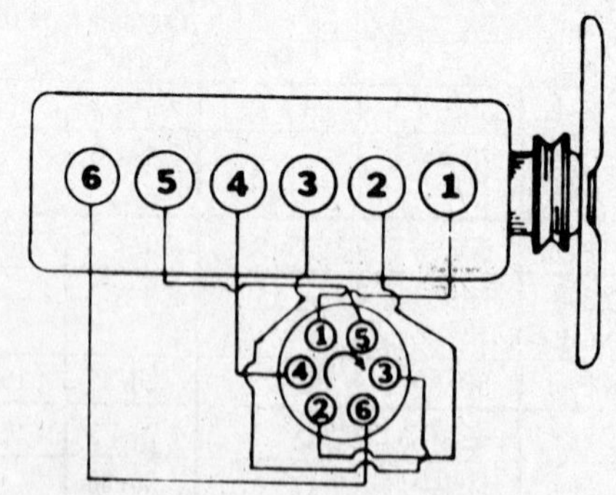

Engines 2F, 3B and 2H
Distributor rotation: Clockwise
Firing order: 1-5-3-6-2-4

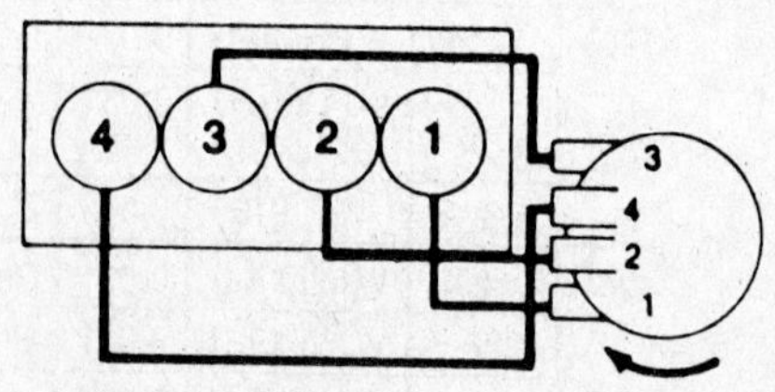

Engines 3Y-EC and 4Y-E
Firing order: 1-3-4-2

CRANKSHAFT AND CONNECTING ROD SPECIFICATIONS

(All measurements in inches)

Year	Engine Type	Crankshaft Main Brg Journal Dia	Crankshaft Main Brg Oil Clearance	Crankshaft Shaft End-Play	Crankshaft Thrust on No.	Connecting Rod Journal Diameter	Connecting Rod Oil Clearance	Connecting Rod Side Clearance
1982	22R	2.3614–2.3622	0.0006–0.0020	0.0008–0.0089	3	2.0862–2.0866	0.0008–0.0020	0.0008–0.0087
	2F	①	0.0008–0.0017	0.0024–0.0063	3	2.1252–2.1260	0.0008–0.0024	0.0043–0.0091
1983	22R	2.3614–2.3622	0.0006–0.0020	0.0008–0.0089	3	2.0862–2.0866	0.0008–0.0020	0.0008–0.0087
	2F	①	0.0008–0.0017	0.0024–0.0063	3	2.1252–2.1260	0.0008–0.0024	0.0043–0.0091
	3Y-E	2.2829–2.2835	0.0008–0.0020	0.0008–0.0087	3	1.8892–1.8898	0.0008–0.0020	0.0063–0.0123
1984	22R	2.3614–2.3622	0.0006–0.0020	0.0008–0.0089	3	2.0862–2.0866	0.0008–0.0020	0.0008–0.0087
	22R-E	2.3616–2.3622	0.0010–0.0022	0.0008–0.0087	3	2.0861–2.0866	0.0010–0.0022	0.0008–0.0087
	2F	①	0.0008–0.0017	0.0024–0.0063	3	2.1252–2.1260	0.0008–0.0024	0.0043–0.0091
	3Y-E	2.2829–2.2835	0.0008–0.0020	0.0008–0.0087	3	1.8892–1.8898	0.0008–0.0020	0.0063–0.0123
1985	22R	2.3616–2.3622	0.0010–0.0022	0.0008–0.0087	3	2.0861–2.0866	0.0010–0.0022	0.0008–0.0087
	22R-E	2.3616–2.3622	0.0010–0.0022	0.0008–0.0087	3	2.0861–2.0866	0.0010–0.0022	0.0008–0.0087
	22R-TE	2.3616–2.3622	0.0010–0.0022	0.0008–0.0087	3	2.0861–2.0866	0.0010–0.0022	0.0008–0.0087
	2F	①	0.0008–0.0017	0.0024–0.0063	3	2.1252–2.1260	0.0008–0.0024	0.0043–0.0091
	3Y-EC	2.2829–2.2835	0.0008–0.0020	0.0008–0.0087	3	1.8892–1.8898	0.0008–0.0020	0.0063–0.0123
1986	22R	2.3616–2.3622	0.0010–0.0022	0.0008–0.0087	3	2.0861–2.0866	0.0010–0.0022	0.0008–0.0087
	22R-E	2.3616–2.3622	0.0010–0.0022	0.0008–0.0087	3	2.0861–2.0866	0.0010–0.0022	0.0008–0.0087
	22R-TE	2.3616–2.3622	0.0010–0.0022	0.0008–0.0087	3	2.0861–2.0866	0.0010–0.0022	0.0008–0.0087
	2F,3B 2H	①	0.0008–0.0017	0.0024–0.0063	3	2.1252–2.1260	0.0008–0.0024	0.0043–0.0091
	4Y-E	2.2829–2.2835	0.0008–0.0020	0.0008–0.0087	3	1.8892–1.8898	0.0008–0.0020	0.0063–0.0123
1987-88	22R	2.3616–2.3622	0.0010–0.0022	0.0008–0.0087	3	2.0861–2.0866	0.0010–0.0022	0.0008–0.0087
	22R-E	2.3616–2.3622	0.0010–0.0022	0.0008–0.0087	3	2.0861–2.0866	0.0010–0.0022	0.0008–0.0087
	22R-TE	2.3616–2.3622	0.0010–0.0022	0.0008–0.0087	3	2.0861–2.0866	0.0010–0.0022	0.0008–0.0087
	2F, 3B 2H	①	0.0008–0.0017	0.0024–0.0063	3	2.1252–2.1260	0.0008–0.0024	0.0043–0.0091
	4Y-E	2.2829–2.2835	0.0008–0.0020	0.0008–0.0087	3	1.8892–1.8898	0.0008–0.0020	0.0063–0.0123

① No. 1—2.6367-2.6376; No. 2—2.6957-2.6967; No. 3—2.7548-2.7557; No. 4—2.8139-2.8148

VALVE SPECIFICATIONS

Year	Engine Type	Seat Angle (deg.)	Face Angle (deg.)	Spring Test Pressure (lbs.)	Spring Installed Height (in.)	Stem-to-Guide Clearance (in.)▲		Stem Diameter (in.)	
						Intake	Exhaust	Intake	Exhaust
1982	22R	45 ①	44.5	55.1	1.594	0.0008–0.0024	0.0012–0.0026	0.3145–0.3188	0.3136–0.3142
	2F	45	44.5	71.6	1.693	0.0012–0.0024	0.0016–0.0028	0.3140	0.3137
1983	22R	45 ①	44.5	55.1	1.594	0.0008–0.0024	0.0012–0.0026	0.3145–0.3188	0.3136–0.3142
	2F	45	44.5	71.6	1.693	0.0012–0.0024	0.0016–0.0028	0.3140	0.3137
	3Y-E	45 ①	44.5	64–77	1.598	0.0010–0.0024	0.0012–0.0026	0.3138–0.3144	0.3136–0.3142
1984	22R	45 ①	44.5	55.1	1.594	0.0008–0.0024	0.0012–0.0026	0.3145–0.3188	0.3136–0.3142
	22R-E	45 ①	44.5	64	1.594	0.0008–0.0012	0.0012–0.0028	0.3145–0.3188	0.3136–0.3142
	2F	45	44.5	71.6	1.693	0.0012–0.0024	0.0016–0.0028	0.3140	0.3137
	3Y-E	45 ①	44.5	64–77	1.598	0.0010–0.0024	0.0012–0.0026	0.3138–0.3144	0.3136–0.3142
1985	22R	45 ①	44.5	66	1.909 ②	0.0010–0.0024	0.0012–0.0026	0.3138–0.3144	0.3136–0.3142
	22R-E	45 ①	44.5	66	1.909 ②	0.0010–0.0024	0.0012–0.0026	0.3138–0.3144	0.3136–0.3142
	22R-TE	45 ①	44.5	66	1.909 ②	0.0010–0.0024	0.0012–0.0026	0.3138–0.3144	0.3136–0.3142
	2F	45	44.5	71.6	1.693	0.0012–0.0024	0.0016–0.0028	0.3140	0.3137
	3Y-E	45 ①	44.5	64–77	1.598	0.0010–0.0024	0.0012–0.0026	0.3138–0.3144	0.3136–0.3142
1986	22R	45 ①	44.5	66	1.909 ②	0.0010–0.0024	0.0012–0.0026	0.3138–0.3144	0.3136–0.3142
	22R-E	45 ①	44.5	66	1.909 ②	0.0010–0.0024	0.0012–0.0026	0.3138–0.3144	0.3136–0.3142
	22R-TE	45 ①	44.5	66	1.909 ②	0.0010–0.0024	0.0012–0.0026	0.3138–0.3144	0.3136–0.3142
	2F, 3B 2H	45	44.5	71.6	1.693	0.0012–0.0024	0.0016–0.0028	0.3140	0.3137
	4Y-E	45 ①	44.5	64–77	1.85 ②	0.0010–0.0024	0.0012–0.0026	0.3138–0.3144	0.3136–0.3142
1987–88	22R	45 ①	44.5	66	1.909 ②	0.0010–0.0024	0.0012–0.0026	0.3138–0.3144	0.3136–0.3142
	22R-E	45 ①	44.5	66	1.909 ②	0.0010–0.0024	0.0012–0.0026	0.3138–0.3144	0.3136–0.3142
	22R-TE	45 ①	44.5	66	1.909 ②	0.0010–0.0024	0.0012–0.0026	0.3138–0.3144	0.3136–0.3142

VALVE SPECIFICATIONS

Year	Engine Type	Seat Angle (deg.)	Face Angle (deg.)	Spring Test Pressure (lbs.)	Spring Installed Height (in.)	Stem-to-Guide Clearance (in.) ▲		Stem Diameter (in.)	
						Intake	Exhaust	Intake	Exhaust
1987–88	2F, 3B 2H	45	44.5	71.6	1.693	0.0012–0.0024	0.0016–0.0028	0.3140	0.3137
	4Y-E	45 ①	44.5	64–77	1.85 ②	0.0010–0.0024	0.0012–0.0026	0.3138–0.3144	0.3136–0.3142

▲ Valve guides are removable
① Blend the seat with 30° and 60° cutters to center the 45° portion on the valve face.
② Free Length

PISTON AND RING SPECIFICATIONS

(All measurements in inches)

Year	Engine Type	Piston Clearance 68°	Ring Gap			Ring Side Clearance (Ring to Land)		
			Top Compression	Bottom Compression	Oil Control	Top Compression	Bottom Compression	Oil Control
1982	22R	0.0020–0.0028	0.0094–0.0142	0.0071–0.0154	snug	0.0080 ①	0.0080 ①	snug
	2F	0.0012–0.0020	0.0079–0.0157	0.0079–0.0157	0.0118–0.0354	0.0012–0.0028	0.0008–0.0024	0.0016–0.0075
1983	3Y-E	0.0030–0.0037	0.0087–0.0185	0.0059–0.0165	0.0079–0.0323	0.0012–0.0028	0.0012–0.0028	0.0012–0.0028
	22R	0.0020–0.0028	0.0094–0.0142	0.0071–0.0154	snug	0.0080 ①	0.0080 ①	snug
	2F	0.0012–0.0020	0.0079–0.0157	0.0079–0.0157	0.0118–0.0354	0.0012–0.0028	0.0008–0.0024	0.0016–0.0075
1984	22R	0.0012–0.0020	0.0090–0.0150	0.0090–0.0150	0.0080–0.0320	0.0080 ①	0.0080 ①	snug
	3Y-E	0.0030–0.0037	0.0087–0.0185	0.0059–0.0165	0.0079–0.0323	0.0012–0.0028	0.0012–0.0028	0.0012–0.0028
	2F	0.0012–0.0020	0.0079–0.0157	0.0079–0.0157	0.0118–0.0354	0.0012–0.0028	0.0008–0.0024	0.0016–0.0075
1985	22R	0.0012–0.0020	0.0090–0.0150	0.0090–0.0150	0.0080–0.0320	0.0080 ①	0.0080 ①	snug
	22R-E	0.0012–0.0020	0.0090–0.0150	0.0090–0.0150	0.0080–0.0320	0.0080 ①	0.0080 ①	snug
	3Y-EC	0.0030–0.0037	0.0087–0.0185	0.0059–0.0165	0.0079–0.0323	0.0012–0.0028	0.0012–0.0028	0.0012–0.0028
	2F	0.0012–0.0020	0.0079–0.0157	0.0079–0.0157	0.0118–0.0354	0.0012–0.0028	0.0008–0.0024	0.0016–0.0075
1986	22R	0.0012–0.0020	0.0138–0.0224	0.0098–0.0185	0.0079–0.0323	0.0080 ①	0.0080 ①	0.0080 ①
	22R-E	0.0012–0.0020	0.0138–0.0224	0.0098–0.0185	0.0079–0.0323	0.0080 ①	0.0080 ①	0.0080 ①
	22R-TE	0.0022–0.0030	0.0138–0.0224	0.0098–0.0186	0.0079–0.0323	0.0080 ①	0.0080 ①	0.0080 ①

PISTON AND RING SPECIFICATIONS

(All measurements in inches)

Year	Engine Type	Piston Clearance 68°F	Ring Gap			Ring Side Clearance (Ring to Land)		
			Top Compression	Bottom Compression	Oil Control	Top Compression	Bottom Compression	Oil Control
1986	4Y-E	0.0026–0.0033	0.0091–0.0189	0.0063–0.0173	0.0051–0.0185	0.0012–0.0028	0.0012–0.0028	0.0012–0.0028
	2F	0.0012–0.0020	0.0079–0.0157	0.0079–0.0157	0.0118–0.0354	0.0012–0.0028	0.0008–0.0024	0.0016–0.0075
	3B	0.0012–0.0020	0.0079–0.0157	0.0079–0.0157	0.0118–0.0354	0.0012–0.0028	0.0008–0.0024	0.0016–0.0075
	2H	0.0012–0.0020	0.0079–0.0157	0.0079–0.0157	0.0118–0.0354	0.0012–0.0028	0.0008–0.0024	0.0016–0.0075
1987–88	22R	0.0008–0.0016	0.0098–0.0185	0.0236–0.0323	0.0079–0.0224	0.0080 ①	0.0080 ①	0.0080 ①
	22R-E	0.0008–0.0016	0.0098–0.0185	0.0236–0.0323	0.0079–0.0224	0.0080 ①	0.0080 ①	0.0080 ①
	22R-TE	0.0022–0.0030	0.0098–0.0185	0.0236–0.0323	0.0079–0.0224	0.0080 ①	0.0080 ①	0.0080 ①
	4Y-E	0.0026–0.0033	0.0091–0.0189	0.0063–0.0173	0.0051–0.0185	0.0012–0.0028	0.0012–0.0028	0.0012–0.0028
	3B	0.0012–0.0020	0.0079–0.0157	0.0079–0.0157	0.0118–0.0354	0.0012–0.0028	0.0008–0.0024	0.0016–0.0075
	2H	0.0012–0.0020	0.0079–0.0157	0.0079–0.0157	0.0118–0.0354	0.0012–0.0028	0.0008–0.0024	0.0016–0.0075
	2F	0.0012–0.0020	0.0079–0.0157	0.0079–0.0157	0.0118–0.0354	0.0012–0.0028	0.0008–0.0024	0.0016–0.0075

① Maximum

TORQUE SPECIFICATIONS

(All readings in ft. lbs.)

Year	Engine Type	Cylinder Head Bolts	Rod Bearing Bolts	Main Bearing Bolts	Crankshaft Pulley Bolt	Flywheel-to-Crankshaft Bolts	Manifolds	
							Intake	Exhaust
1982	2F	83–98	35–55	90–108 ①	116–145	59–62	28–37 ②	28–37 ②
	22R	53–63	40–47	69–83	120–130	73–86	13–19	29–36
1983	2F	83–98	35–55	90–108 ①	116–145	59–62	28–37 ②	28–37 ②
	22R	53–63	40–47	69–83	120–130	73–86	13–19	29–36
	3Y-E	④	36	58	80	61 ③	36	36
1984	2F	83–98	35–55	90–108 ①	116–145	59–62	28–37 ②	28–37 ②
	22R	55–63	40–47	69–83	120–130	73–86	13–19	29–36
	22R-E	58	46	76	116	80	14	33
	3Y-E	④	36	58	80	61 ③	36	36
1985	2F	83–98	35–55	90–108 ①	116–145	59–62	28–37 ②	28–37 ②
	22R	55–63	40–47	69–83	120–130	73–86	13–19	29–36
	22R-E	58	46	76	116	80	14	33
	3Y-E	④	36	58	80	61 ③	36	36

TORQUE SPECIFICATIONS

(All readings in ft. lbs.)

Year	Engine Type	Cylinder Head Bolts	Rod Bearing Bolts	Main Bearing Bolts	Crankshaft Pulley Bolt	Flywheel-to-Crankshaft Bolts	Manifolds Intake	Manifolds Exhaust
1986	3B, 2F, 2H	83–98	35–55	90–108 ①	116–145	59–62	28–37 ②	28–37 ②
	22R	58	46	76	116	80	14	33
	22R-E	58	46	76	116	80	14	33
	22R-TE	58	46	76	116	80	14	33
	4Y-E	④	36	58	116	61 ③	36	36
1987–88	3B, 2F, 2H	83–98	35–55	90–108 ①	116–145	59–62	28–37 ②	28–37 ②
	22R	58	51	76	116	80	14	33
	22R-E	58	51	76	116	80	14	33
	22R-TE	58	51	76	116	80	14	33
	4Y-E	④	36	58	116	61 ③	36	36

① Rear bearing—76–94 ft. lbs.
② California vehicles—37–51 ft. lbs.
③ 54 ft. lbs.: drive plate
④ 12 mm bolt: 14 ft. lbs.: 14 mm bolt; 65 ft. lbs.

CAPACITIES

Year	Model	Engine Type	Crankcase ▲ w/filter	Crankcase ▲ wo/filter	Transmission ▲ Manual	Transmission ▲ Automatic	Trans. Case▲	Differential ▲ Front	Differential ▲ Rear	Fuel Tank ■	Cooling System▲
1982	Pickup (Gasoline)	22R	5.0	4.0	2.1	6.7	1.7	2.4	1.8 ⑦	13.7 ⑤	8.9
	Pickup (Diesel)	L	6.1	5.1	1.9	—	—	—	1.8	16.0	11.1
	Land Cruiser	2F	8.4	7.4	⑧	—	2.6	2.2	2.2	22.2 ⑨	17.5 ⑩
1983	Pickup (Diesel)	L	6.1	5.1	1.9	—	—	—	1.8	16.0	11.1
	Pickup (Gasoline)	22R	5.0	4.0	⑪	6.9	1.7	2.3	1.8 ⑫	13.7 ⑤	8.9
	Land Cruiser	2F	8.4	7.4	⑧	—	2.6	2.2	2.2	22.2 ⑨	17.5 ⑩
	Van	3Y-E	3.7	3.2	2.3	6.9	—	—	1.3	15.9	7.5
1984	Pickup (Gasoline)	22R 22R-E	5.0	4.0	⑬	6.9	1.7	2.4	1.8 ⑫	13.7 ⑤	8.9
	Pickup (Diesel)	2L	6.0 ⑭	5.0 ⑭	⑮	—	1.7	2.3	1.8 ⑫	16.0	12.0
	Land Cruiser	2F	8.4	7.4	⑧	—	2.6	2.2	2.2	22.2 ⑨	17.5 ⑩
	Van	3Y-E	3.7	3.2	2.3	6.9	—	—	1.3	15.9	7.5
1985	Van	3Y-EC	3.7	3.2	2.3	6.9	—	—	1.3	15.9	7.5
	4 Runner (Gasoline)	22R 22R-E	4.0	4.9	③	—	1.7	2.4	2.3	②	8.9
	4 Runner (Diesel)	2L-T	6.1	5.1	3.2	—	1.7	2.4	2.3	②	10.4
	Pickup (Gasoline)	22R 22R-E 22R-TE	4.9	4.0	④	6.9	—	—	1.9	⑯	8.9
	Pickup (Diesel)	2L 2L-T	6.1	5.1	⑥	6.9	1.7	①	2.3	⑰	10.4
	Land Cruiser	2F,3B 2H	8.4	7.4	⑧	—	2.6	2.2	2.2	22.2 ⑨	17.5 ⑩

CAPACITIES

Year	Model	Engine Type	Crankcase ▲ w/filter	Crankcase ▲ wo/filter	Transmission ▲ Manual	Transmission ▲ Automatic	Trans. Case▲	Differential ▲ Front	Differential ▲ Rear	Fuel Tank ■	Cooling System▲
1986	Van	4Y-E	3.7	3.2	2.3	6.9	—	—	1.3	15.9	7.5
	4 Runner (Gasoline)	22R 22R-E	4.0	4.9	③	—	1.7	2.4	2.3	②	8.9
	4 Runner (Diesel)	2L-T	6.1	5.1	3.2	—	1.7	2.4	2.3	②	10.4
	Pickup (Gasoline)	22R 22T-E 22R-TE	4.9	4.0	④	6.9	—	—	1.9	⑯	8.9
	Pickup (Diesel)	2L 2L-T	6.1	5.1	⑥	6.9	1.7	①	2.3	⑰	10.4
	Land Cruiser	2F,3B 2H	8.4	7.4	⑧	—	2.6	2.2	2.2	22.2 ⑨	17.5 ⑩
1987-88	Van	4Y-E	3.7	3.2	2.3 ①	6.9	1.3	1.3	1.5 ⑥	13.2	⑳
	Pickup (Gasoline)	22R 22R-E 22R-TE	4.9	4.2	⑮	㉑	㉒	2.4	㉓	⑯	8.9
	Pickup (Diesel)	2L 2L-T	6.1	5.1	3.2	—	1.7	2.4	2.3	②	10.4
	4 Runner (Gasoline)	22R-E 22R-TE	4.9	4.2	4.1	—	㉒	2.4	㉓	②	8.9
	Land Cruiser	2F,3B 2H	8.4	7.4	⑧	—	2.6	2.2	2.2	22.2 ⑨	17.5 ⑩

▲ Measurements in quarts
■ Measurements in gallons
① 4WD: 2.7 qts.
② Std.—14.8; large—17.2
③ 22R engine—4.1; 22R-E—3.2
④ 4 speed—2.5; 5 speed (22R)—2.7; 5 speed (22R-E)—2.5
⑤ Long bed—16.1
⑥ 4WD: 2.0 qts.
⑦ ¾ Ton—1.9; 4 × 4—2.3
⑧ 3 speed—1.8; 4 speed—3.3; 5 speed—4.7
⑨ Station Wagon—23.8
⑩ 2-Door—19.9
Wagon—18.3
⑪ 4 sp: 2.1; 5 sp.: 1.9
⑫ 4 × 4; 2.3
⑬ W52: 2.7
W42: 2.9
G52: 2.3
⑭ Calif.: 7 w/filter; 6 w/o filter
⑮ 2WD: 2.5
4WD: 4.1
⑯ Short bed—13.7; long bed—17.2
⑰ Short bed—17.2; long bed (std.)—17.2; long bed (large)—19.3
⑱ 4 speed—2.5; 5 speed—2.3; 4WD—3.2
⑲ 4WD: 2.4
⑳ w/o rear heater, 2WD: 8.3 qts.
with rear heater, 2WD: 8.9 qts.
w/o rear heater, 4WD: 7.4 qts.
with rear heater, 4WD: 7.9 qts.
㉑ A43D: 6.9 qts.
A340E: 7.3 qts.
A340H: 10.9 qts.
㉒ 22R-E: 0.8 qts.
22R-TE: 1.2 qts.
㉓ 2WD; 7.5 in: 1.42 qts.
8 in: 1.9 qts.
4WD; 22R, 22R-E: 2.3 qts.
22R-TE: 2.5

WHEEL ALIGNMENT SPECIFICATIONS

Year	Model	Caster Range (deg)	Caster Preferred Setting (deg)	Camber Range (deg)	Camber Preferred Setting (deg)	Toe-In (in.)	Steering Axis Inclination (deg)
1982	Pick-up 2-WD	½P–½N	½P	1/12P–½P	1P	0.16–0.24 ① 0.04–0.12 ②	7
	Pick-up 4-WD	—	3½P	—	1P 9½P ①	0.12–0.20 ① 0–0.08 ②	—
	Land Cruiser	½P–1½P	1P	½P–1½P	1P	④	9½

WHEEL ALIGNMENT SPECIFICATIONS

Year	Model	Caster Range (deg)	Caster Preferred Setting (deg)	Camber Range (deg)	Camber Preferred Setting (deg)	Toe-In (in.)	Steering Axis Inclination (deg)
1983	Pick-up 2-WD Short	1/4P-1 3/4P	1P	1/2P-1/2P	1P	⑤	7°10′
	Long	1/4N-1 1/4P	1/2P	0-1P	1/2P	⑤	7°10′
	Pick-up 4-WD & 4 Runner	2 3/4P-4 1/4P	3 1/2P	1/4P-1 3/4P	3/4P	⑥	9°30′
	Van	1 1/3P-2 5/6P	2 1/12P	1/4N-1 1/4P	1/2P	-0.16-0.16	10°
	Land Cruiser	1/2P-1 1/2P	1P	1/2P-1 1/2P	1P	④	9 1/2
1984	Pick-up 2-WD Short	1/4P-1 3/4P	1P	1/2P-1/2P	1P	⑤	7°10′
	Long	1/4N-1 1/4P	1/2P	0-1P	1/2P	⑤	7°10′
	Pick-up 4-WD & 4 Runner	2 3/4P-4 1/4P	3 1/2P	1/4P-1 3/4P	3/4P	⑥	9°30′
	Van	1 1/3P-2 5/6P	2 1/12P	1/4N-1 1/4P	1/2P	-0.16-0.16	10°
	Land Cruiser	1/2P-1 1/2P	1P	1/2P-1 1/2P	1P	④	9 1/2
1985	Pick-up 2-WD Short	1/12N-1 5/12P	2/3P	1/4N-1 1/4P	1/2P	⑥	10°
	Long	5/12P-1 11/12P	1 1/6P	1/4N-1 1/4P	1/2P	0.08-0.16	10°
	Pick-up 4-WD & 4 Runner	1 1/4P-2 1/4P	1 3/4P	1/4P-1 3/4P	3/4P	⑥	—
	Van	1 11/12P-3 5/12P	2 2/3P	1/4N-1 1/4P	1/2P	-0.16-0.16	10°
	Land Cruiser	1/2P-1 1/2P	1P	1/2-1 1/2P	1P	④	9 1/2
1986	Pick-up 2-WD Short	1/12N-1 5/12P	2/3P	1/4N-1 1/4P	1/2P	⑥	10°
	Long	5/12P-1 11/12P	1 1/6P	1/4N-1 1/4P	1/2P	③	10°
	Pick-up 4-WD & 4 Runner	3/4P-2 1/4P	1 1/2P	1/12N-1 5/12P	2/3P	⑥	12°
	Van	2 1/4P-3 3/4P	3P	3/4N-3/4P	0	-0.04-0.04	10 1/2
	Land Cruiser	1/2P-1 1/2P	1P	1/2-1 1/2P	1P	④	9 1/2
1987-88	Pick-up 2-WD Short	1/12N-1 5/12P	2/3P	1/4N-1 1/4P	1/2P	⑥	10°
	Long	5/12P-1 11/12P	1 1/6P	1/4N-1 1/4P	1/2P	③	10°
	Pick-up 4-WD & 4 Runner	3/4P-2 1/4P	1 1/2P	1/12N-1 5/12P	2/3P	⑥	12°
	Van (2 WD)	2P-3P	2 1/2P	5/6N-5/6P	1/12P	-0.04-0.04	10 1/2

WHEEL ALIGNMENT SPECIFICATIONS

Year	Model	Caster Range (deg)	Caster Preferred Setting (deg)	Camber Range (deg)	Camber Preferred Setting (deg)	Toe-In (in.)	Steering Axis Inclination (deg)
1987-88	Van (4 WD)	2⅓P-3⅓P	2⅚P	⅓N-⅔P	⅙P	-0.04-0.04	12½
	Land Cruiser	½P-1½P	1P	½-1½P	1P	④	9½

① Bias Ply Tire
② Radial Ply Tire
③ Bias ply tires: 0.20-0.28 in.
Radial ply tires: 0.08-0.16 in.
④ Non Radial tires: 0.10-0.20
Radial tires: 0.04 out-0.04 in.
⑤ Bias ply tires: 0.16-0.24 in.
Radial tires: 0.04-0.12
⑥ Bias ply tires: 0.12-0.20 in.
Radial tires: 0-0.08 in.

ENGINE ELECTRICAL

Alternator

Precautions

1. Always observe proper polarity of the battery connections; be especially careful when jump-starting the vehicle.
2. Never ground or short out any alternator or alternator regulator terminals.
3. Never operate the alternator with any of its or the battery's leads disconnected.
4. Always remove the battery or disconnect its output lead while charging it.
5. Always disconnect the ground cable when replacing any electrical components.
6. Never subject the alternator to excessive heat or dampness if the engine is being steam-cleaned.
7. Never use arc-welding equipment with the alternator connected.

Removal and Installation

NOTE: On some models the alternator is mounted very low on the engine. On these models it may be necessary to remove the gravel shield and work from underneath the vehicle in order to gain access to the alternator.

1. Disconnect the negative battery terminal from the battery.
2. Remove the air cleaner, if necessary, to gain access to the alternator.
3. If equipped with an L, 2L or 2L-T engine (1984-88), remove the vacuum pump and the A/C compressor (DO NOT disconnect the pressure hoses).
4. On the 22R and 22R-E engines (1984), remove the vane pump pulley.
5. On the 22R, 22R-E and 22R-TE engines (1985-88), drain the engine coolant. If necessary, remove the under engine cover. If equipped with power steering, remove the water inlet pipe bolts and the water inlet hose from the engine.

NOTE: If equipped with A/C, it may be necessary to remove the No. 2 fan shroud.

6. Remove the nut or the wiring connector and the wire(s) from the alternator.
7. Remove the adjusting lock, the pivot and the adjusting bolt(s), then the drive belt from the alternator.
8. Remove the alternator attaching bolt and then withdraw the alternator from its bracket.
9. To install, reverse the removal procedures. Rotate the drive belt 8 revolutions (new belt) or 5 revolutions (used belt). Adjust the drive belt tension. Refill the cooling system, if it was drained.

Belt Tension Adjustment

Inspection and adjustment to the alternator drive belt should be performed every 30,000 miles or if the alternator has been removed.

1. Inspect the drive belt to see that it is not cracked or worn. Be sure that its surfaces are free of grease or oil.
2. If not using a belt tension gauge, push down on the belt halfway between the fan and the alternator pulleys, (or crankshaft pulley) with thumb pressure; belt deflection should be ⅜-½ in.
3. If using the Belt Tension Gauge tool No. BTG-20 (Nippondenso) or BT-33-73F (Borroughs) or equivalent, position it in the middle of the drive belt and check the belt tension; a new belt should be 170-180 lbs. (Van) or 100-150 lbs. (Truck), a used belt should be 95-135 lbs. (Van) or 60-100 lbs. (Truck).
4. If the belt tension requires adjustment, loosen the adjusting link bolt and move the alternator until the proper belt tension is obtained.

CAUTION

Do not overtighten the belt; damage to the alternator bearings could result.

5. Tighten the adjusting link bolt.

Voltage Regulator

Two types of voltage regulators are used: the Integrated Circuit (IC) and the Tirrill. The IC type is internally mounted in the alternator and is not adjustable. The Tirrill is externally mounted and is adjustable.

EXTERNAL TYPE-TIRRILL (1982-84)

Removal and Installation

1. Disconnect the negative battery terminal from the battery.
2. Disconnect the wiring harness.

NOTE: On Land Cruisers, disconnect the leads from their screw terminals after noting their position for installation.

3. Remove the retaining hardware and the regulator.
4. To install, reverse the removal procedures.

Adjustments

VOLTAGE

NOTE: Only external regulators used with gasoline engines are adjustable.

1. Disconnect the battery wire from the "B" terminal of the alternator. Remove the cover from the regulator assembly.
2. Using a voltmeter, connect the (+) positive lead to the "B" terminal of the alternator and the (−) negative lead to a ground.
3. Start the engine and gradually increase the engine speed to about 2000 rpm.
4. At this speed, the voltage reading should be 13.8–14.8V.
5. If the voltage does not fall within this range, a minor adjustment may be made to the adjusting arm by performing the following procedure:
   a. Disconnect the negative battery terminal from the battery.
   b. Remove the regulator cover.
   c. Using a pair of needle nose pliers, bend the adjusting arm very slightly.
   d. Replace the cover and battery terminal.
6. To install, reverse the removal procedures.

FIELD RELAY

NOTE: Only external regulators used with gasoline engines are adjustable. This adjustment does not apply to Land Cruisers.

1. Remove the cover from the regulator assembly.
2. Clean off the points with emery cloth if they are dirty and wash them with solvent.
3. The relay actuating voltage is 4.5–5.8V; adjust the point gap, as required, by bending the adjusting arm.
4. To install, reverse the removal procedures.

IC-INTEGRAL TYPE

Removal and Installation

NOTE: Refer the "Alternator, Removal and Installation" procedures, in this section and remove the alternator from the vehicle.

2F (1982-88), 22R AND 22R-E ENGINES (1982–84)

1. At the rear of the alternator, remove the retaining nuts, the terminal insulators and the noise suppression condenser.
2. Using a small pry bar, pry the rear end frame from the stator.
3. Remove the insulators from the rectifier holder studs.
4. Using a soldering iron, free the stator leads from the rectifier holder, then remove the holder from the alternator.

NOTE: The regulator is a part of the rectifier holder.

5. To install, reverse the removal procedures.

3Y-EC (1983-85), 4Y-E (1986-88) 22R, 22R-E and 22R-TE ENGINES (1985-88)

1. Remove the nut and the electrical terminal insulator from the rear of the alternator.
2. Remove the retaining nuts and the rear cover from the alternator.
3. Remove the retaining screws, the brush holder and the brush holder cover.
4. Remove the voltage regulator screws and the regulator from the alternator.
5. To install, reverse the removal procedures.

L, 2L AND 2L-T ENGINES (DIESEL)

1. Remove the brush holder cover retaining nuts, the insulator, the rubber washer and the cover from the alternator.
2. Remove the screw and disconnect the blue wire from the brush holder/IC regulator assembly.
3. Lift the brush holder/IC regulator assembly from the rectifier holder, then remove the screw and the wire from the assembly.
4. Remove the screws and separate the IC regulator from the brush holder.
5. To install, reverse the removal procedures.

Starter

OVERHAUL

For overhaul procedures, please refer to the "Electrical Section" in Unit Repair section and perform the necessary procedures.

Removal and Installation

1. If necessary, raise and support the front of the vehicle on jackstands.
2. Disconnect the negative battery terminal from the battery.

NOTE: On some 22R series engines equipped with an A/T, it may be necessary to remove the transmission oil filler tube.

3. Disconnect the wiring connectors and the wiring from the starter.
4. Remove the starter-to-engine bolts and the starter from the engine.
5. To install, reverse the removal procedures.

Distributor

Removal

2F AND 22R SERIES ENGINES

1. Label and disconnect the high tension cables from the spark plugs. Remove the high tension cable from the coil.
2. Remove the primary wire or the electrical connector and the vacuum line (if equipped) from the distributor. Remove the distributor cap spring clips or screws, then the cap.
3. Using a piece of chalk, match-mark the rotor-to-distributor housing and the distributor-to-engine block. This will aid in correct positioning of the distributor during installation.
4. Remove the distributor hold-down clamp bolt and the distributor from the engine.

NOTE: It is easier to install the distributor if the engine timing is not disturbed while it is removed. If the timing has been lost, see "Installation–Timing Disturbed".

3Y-EC AND 4Y-E ENGINES–TYPE IIA

1. Disconnect the negative battery terminal from the battery.
2. Remove the front-right seat from the vehicle.
3. Remove the engine service hole cover.
4. Disconnect the distributor vacuum advance hoses.
5. Disconnect the high tension cables from the spark plugs.
6. Using a piece of chalk, match-mark the rotor-to-distributor housing and the distributor housing-to-engine.
7. Remove the distributor-to-engine bolt and the distributor from the engine.

Installation – Timing Not Disturbed

ALL ENGINES

1. Insert the distributor into the engine block by aligning the matchmarks made during removal.
2. Engage the distributor drive with the oil pump drive shaft.
3. Install the distributor hold-down clamp, the cap, the high

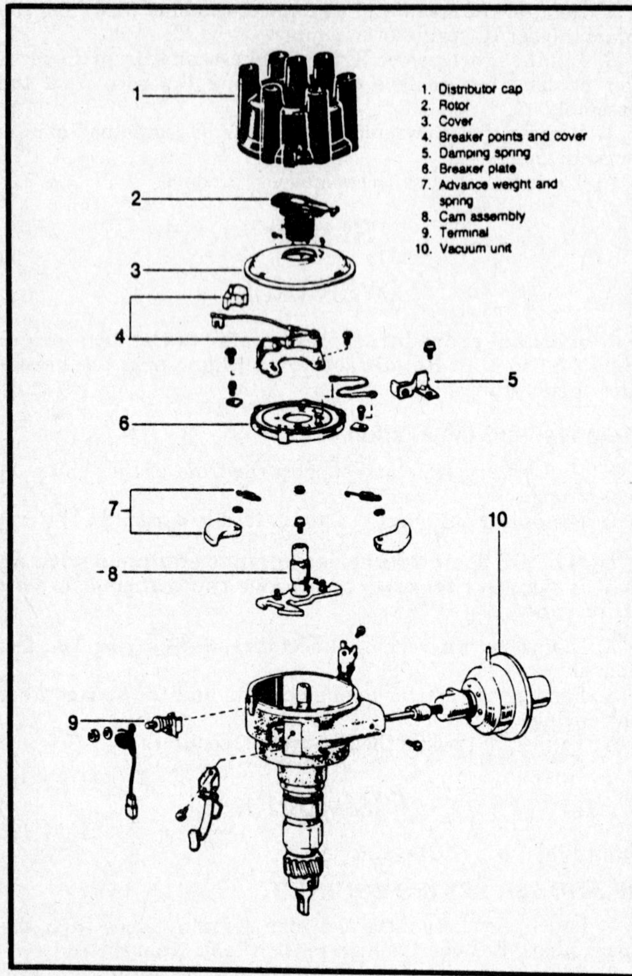

2F engine point type distributor

tension wire, the primary wire or the electrical connector and the vacuum line(s).

4. Install the spark plugs cables.

5. Start the engine, check and/or adjust the timing, then adjust the octane selector (if equipped).

Installation–Timing Disturbed

2F, 22R AND 22R-E ENGINES

If the engine has been cranked, dismantled or the timing otherwise lost, proceed as follows:

1. Determine the Top Dead Center (TDC) of the No. 1 cylinder's compression stroke by removing the spark plug from the No. 1 cylinder and placing a finger or a compression gauge over the spark plug hole.

NOTE: Using a wrench, turn the crankshaft until the compression pressure starts to build up. Continue cranking the engine until the timing marks indicate TDC (0°).

2. Turn the crankshaft to align the timing marks on the 2F (1982-88) and 22R (1982) engine to 8° BTDC, on the 22R engines (1983–84) to 5° BTDC, on the 22R-E and 22R-TE engines (1984-88) to 5° BTDC or on the 22R engines (1985–88) to 0° TDC.

3. Temporarily install the rotor on the distributor shaft so that the rotor is pointing toward the No. 1 terminal of the distributor cap.

4. Using a small screwdriver, align the slot on the distributor drive (oil pump driveshaft) with the key on the bottom of the distributor shaft.

5. Install the distributor in the block by rotating it slightly (no more than one gear tooth in either direction) until the driven gear meshes with the drive.

NOTE: Oil the distributor drive gear and the oil pump driveshaft end before installation.

6. Temporarily tighten the lock bolt.

7. Remove the rotor, then install the dust cover, the rotor and the distributor cap.

8. Install the primary wire or the electrical connector and the vacuum line(s).

9. Install the No. 1 cylinder spark plug. Connect the cables to the spark plugs in the proper order by using the labels made during the removal procedures. Install the high tension wire on the coil.

10. Start the engine and adjust the ignition timing.

3Y-EC AND 4Y-E ENGINES–TYPE IIA

1. Remove the No. 1 spark plug, place your finger over the opening and rotate the crankshaft (with a wrench) in the clockwise direction, until pressure is felt (this is TDC), then replace the spark plug.

NOTE: Make sure that the notch on the crankshaft pulley is aligned with the 0° mark on the timing plate.

2. Position the oil pump drive rotor slot 30° from the centerline.

3. On the distributor, align the groove on the housing with the pin of the driven gear (the drill mark side).

4. Insert the distributor by aligning the flange center with the bolt hole in the engine block.

5. Lightly tighten the hold-down bolt.

6. To complete the installation, reverse the removal procedures. Adjust the ignition timing.

TIMING LIGHT AND TACHOMETER CONNECTIONS

NOTE: The electronic ignition system is fully transistorized. A stationary magnetic pick-up coil (mounted in the distributor) and a toothed timing rotor (mounted on the distributor shaft) entirely replace the conventional breaker points and condenser. Because no mechanical contact exists between the pick-up coil and the timing rotor, the system is considered to be maintenance-free.

PRECAUTIONS–FULLY TRANSISTORIZED SYSTEM

1. If the engine will not start, DO NOT leave the ignition switch "ON" for more than 10 minutes.

2. Make sure that your test equipment is compatible to this system before making any connections.

3. Do not connect the tachometer positive lead to the distributor. Connect this lead only to the service connector (yellow) provided in the system.

4. Do not disconnect the battery with the engine running.

5. Do not allow the ignition coil terminals or service connector terminal to touch ground: Damage to the igniter or the ignition coil could result.

AIR GAP ADJUSTMENT

1. Remove the distributor cap, the rotor and the dust cover from the distributor.

2. Using the ignition switch, bump the engine until one of the timing rotor teeth aligns with the pick-up coil. Turn the ignition switch "OFF".

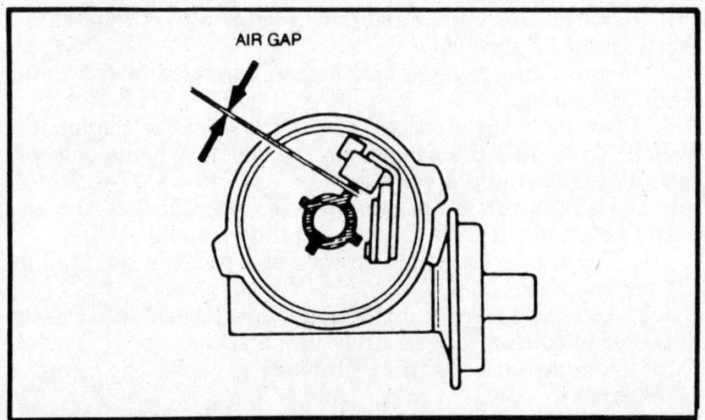

Check the air gap between the timing rotor and the pick-up call

3. Using a flat, brass feeler gauge, check the gap between the timing rotor tooth and the pick-up coil. If adjustment is needed, loosen (but do not remove) the pick-up coil attaching screws and move the pick-up coil as necessary to attain the specified clearance. Tighten the pick-up coil attaching screws and recheck the clearance.

4. Reinstall the dust cover, the rotor and the distributor cap.

IGNITION TIMING

Procedure

NOTE: The timing mark locations differ between the engines used in the Pickup and the 4-Runner (22R, 22R-E and 22R-TE), the Van (3Y-EC and 4Y-E) and the Land Cruiser (2F, 3B and 2H). On the 22R, 22R-E, 22R-TE, 3Y-EC and 4Y-E engines, the timing marks are located on the crankshaft pulley (painted notch) and the timing cover (plate). On the 2F, 3B & 2H engines, the timing marks are located on the flywheel (ball) and the bellhousing (pointer).

1. Set the parking brake and block the wheels.
2. Clean off the timing marks and mark them with chalk or paint. The crankshaft may have to rotated to find the marks.
3. Warm the engine to operating temperatures. Connect a tachometer to the engine, then, check and/or adjust the engine idle speed.

CAUTION

On the 22R, 22R-E and 22R-TE engines, connect the positive (+) tachometer terminal either to the negative (−) ignition coil terminal (Type III) or to the yellow service connector (Type IV). On the 3Y-EC and 4Y-E engines, connect the positive (+) tachometer to the service connector on the ignition coil/igniter (Type IIA) assembly. DO NOT connect it to the distributor side. Improper connections will damage the transistorized igniter.

NOTE: On the 4Y-E engine, use a service wire to short the "Engine Check Connector"

4. Turn "OFF" the engine and connect a timing light according to the manufacturer's directions.
5. On the 22R-E and 22R-TE engine, disconnect and short the "T" and the "E_1" (1986-88) connector of the engine check harness (near the front of the vehicle). On all other models, disconnect and plug the vacuum hose(s) from the distributor vacuum unit.

NOTE: If equipped with a High Altitude Compensation (HAC) system there are two vacuum hoses which connect to the distributor. Both must be disconnected and plugged. These systems require an extra step in the timing procedure, found at the end of this section.

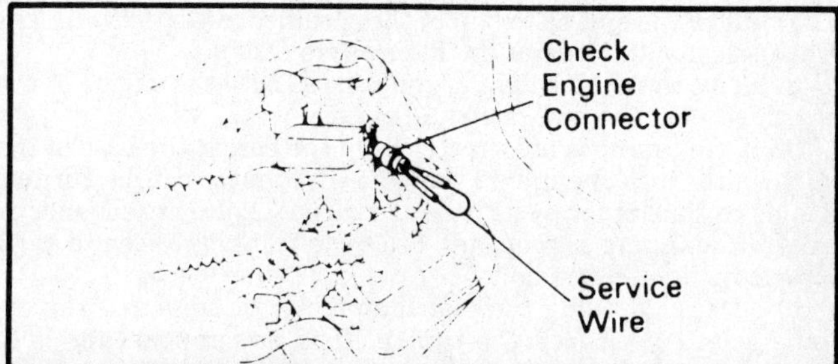

Inserting a jumper wire into the Check Engine Connector—4Y-E (1986-88) engine

View of the timing mark—2F, 3B and 2H engines

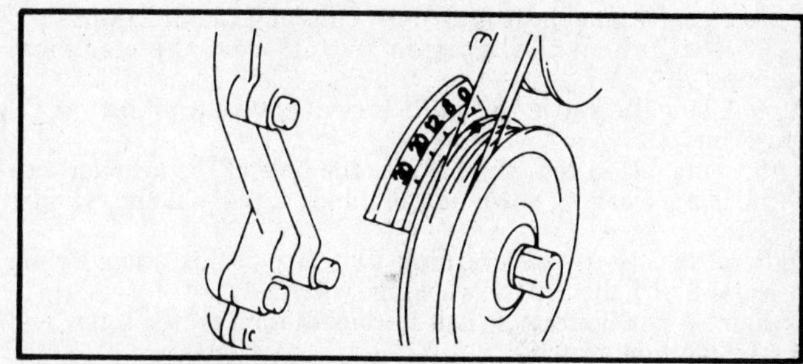

View of the timing marks used on the 3Y-EC (1983-85) and the 4Y-E (1986-88)

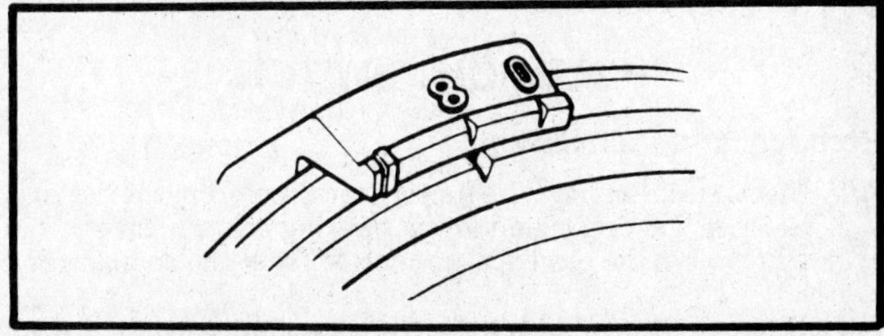

View of the timing marks used on the 22R, 22R-E and 22R-TE engines

6. Be sure that the timing light wires are clear of the fan and pulleys, then start the engine.

CAUTION

Keep your fingers, clothes, hair, tools and wires clear of the fan and fan belts. Run the engine only in a well-ventilated area.

7. Allow the engine to run at the specified idle speed with the shift selector in Neutral (M/T) or Drive (A/T).

8. Point the timing light at the marks. With the engine at the specified idle, the marks should align.

9. If the timing is incorrect, loosen the bolt at the base of the distributor just enough so that the distributor can be turned. Hold the distributor by its base and turn it slightly to advance or retard the timing as required. Once the marks are seen to align properly, tighten the bolt.

10. After tightening the distributor bolt or adjusting the octane selector, recheck the timing. It is not unusual for it to change during the tightening process. It may take 2–3 tries to get it perfect. Turn "OFF" the engine, then, disconnect the timing light and connect the vacuum line(s) at the distributor or the electrical "T" and "E_1" (1986-88) connector (22R-E and 22R-TE), except on engines with HAC.

11. On engines with HAC (identified in the Note earlier) after setting the initial timing, reconnect the vacuum hoses at the distributor. Recheck the timing.

12. If the advance is still low, pinch the hose between the HAC valve and the three way connector; it should now be to specifications. If not, the HAC valve should be checked for proper operation.

Instrument Panel Controls

IGNITION SWITCH

Removal and Installation

The ignition lock/switch is located behind the combination switch on the steering column.

1. Disconnect the negative battery terminal from the battery.
2. Remove the upper and lower steering column covers.
3. Disconnect the ignition switch from the electrical connector.
4. Using the key in the ignition switch, turn it to the "ACC" position.
5. Using a thin rod, place it into the hole of the cylinder lock housing. Pushing down on the thin rod, pull out the cylinder lock.
6. Remove the unlock warning switch-to-combination switch screws and the unlock warning switch.
7. Remove the ignition switch-to-combination switch screw and the ignition switch.
8. To install, push the ignition switch into the housing and install the screw. Using the key, install cylinder lock into the housing until the retaining tab locks it in place.
9. To complete the installation, reverse the removal procedures.

HEADLIGHT SWITCH

Removal and Installation

1. Disconnect the negative battery terminal from the battery.
2. Remove the upper and lower steering column covers.
3. Disconnect the electrical connector from the combination switch.
4. Remove the headlight switch-to-combination switch screws and the headlight switch from the combination switch.
5. To install, reverse the removal procedures.

COMBINATION SWITCH

The combination switch is composed of the turn signal, the headlight control, the dimmer, the hazard, the wiper and the washer switches.

Removal and Installation

1. Refer to the "Steering Wheel, Removal and Installation" procedures, in this section and remove the steering wheel.
2. Remove the upper and lower steering column shroud screws and the shrouds.
3. Remove the combination switch screws and the switch from the column.
4. Disconnect the electrical connector from the combination switch. To remove the wires from the electrical connector, perform the following procedures.
   a. Using a miniature screwdriver, insert it into the open end between the locking lugs and the terminal.
   b. Pry the locking lugs upward and pull the terminal out from the rear.
   c. To install the terminals, simply push them into the connector until they lock securely in place.
5. To complete the installation, reverse the removal procedures.

DIMMER SWITCH

For service information, refer to the "Combination Switch, Removal and Installation" procedures in this section and separate the dimmer switch from the combination switch.

TURN SIGNAL SWITCH

Removal and Installation

1. Disconnect negative battery terminal from the battery.
2. Remove the upper and the lower steering column shrouds.
3. Disconnect the combination switch electrical connector.
4. At the left-rear of the combination switch, remove the mounting screws and the turn signal switch.
5. If necessary to the remove the turn signal switch wires from the electrical connector, place a small screwdriver into the end of the connector, pry up on the retaining tab and pull the wire(s) from the connector.
6. To install, place the wire(s) into the electrical connector's slots, place a screwdriver behind the wire terminal and push the wire into the connector until the retaining tab locks it into place.
7. To complete the installation, reverse the removal procedures.

WINDSHIELD/WIPER SWITCH

Removal and Installation

FRONT

1. Disconnect negative battery terminal from the battery.
2. Remove the upper and the lower steering column shrouds.
3. Disconnect the combination switch electrical connector.
4. Remove the terminal from the horn contact.
5. To remove the windshield/wiper switch wires from the electrical connector, place a small screwdriver into the end of the connector, pry up on the retaining tab and pull the wire(s) from the connector.
6. Remove the windshield/wiper switch-to-combination switch screw and the switch.
7. To complete the installation, reverse the removal procedures. To install, place the wire(s) into the electrical connector's slots, place a screwdriver behind the wire terminal and push the wire into the connector until the retaining tab locks it into place.

REAR

If equipped with a rear wiper switch, it will be located in the center of the dash.

1. Using a small pry bar, pry the rear wiper switch from the center of the dash.

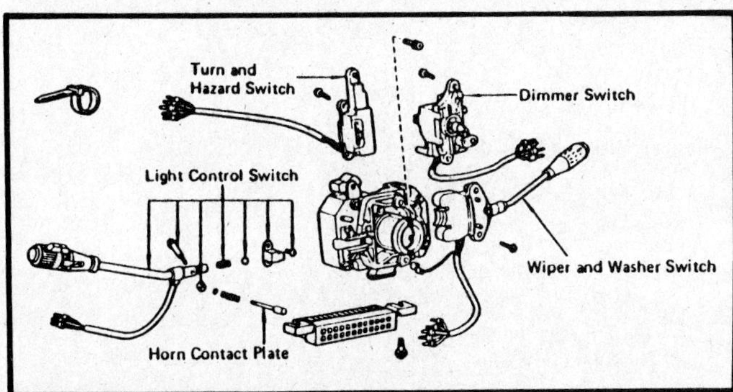

Exploded view of the combination switch

2. Disconnect the electical connector from the rear of the switch.
3. To install, reverse the removal procedures.

WINDSHIELD/WIPER MOTOR

Removal and Installation

PICKUPS, VAN AND 4-RUNNER

Front

1. Disconnect the wiring from the wiper motor. Remove the motor from the fire wall.
2. Remove the nut, then, pry the wiper link from the crank arm.
3. Remove the motor.
4. To install, reverse the removal procedures and inspect he operation.

Rear – Van and 4-Runner

1. At the rear of the vehicle, remove the wiper motor cover panel.
2. Remove the wiper arm from the wiper motor.
3. Disconnect the electrical connector from the wiper motor.
4. Remove the wiper motor-to-door bolts and the motor from the vehicle.
5. To install, reverse the removal procedures and inspect the operation.

LAND CRUISER

Except Station Wagon

1. Using a small pry bar, disconnect the wiper link from the motor.
2. Remove the rear motor bracket bolts.
3. Disconnect the wiper motor wiring.
4. Remove the wiper motor screws and withdraw the motor.
5. To install, reverse the removal procedures.

Station Wagon

NOTE: On these models, the wiper motor is removed with the linkage assembly.

1. Remove the wiper arm retaining nuts, then, the wiper arm/blade assemblies.
2. Remove both wiper arm pivot covers and the pivot-to-cowl attaching screws.
3. Remove the two service hole covers from the cowl area of the engine compartment.
4. Disconnect the wiring from the wiper motor.
5. From the engine compartment, remove the wiper motor plate-to-cowl screws. Withdraw the wiper motor and the linkage from the cowl panel as an assembly.
6. Pry the linkage from of the wiper motor.
7. To install, reverse the removal procedures.

WINDSHIELD/WIPER LINKAGE

Removal and Installation

PICKUPS, VAN AND 4-RUNNER

1. Refer to the "Wiper Motor, Removal and Installation" procedures, in this section and remove the motor.
2. Remove the wiper arms by removing their retaining nuts and working them off their shafts.
3. Remove the wiper shafts nuts/spacers and push the shafts down into the body cavity. Pull the linkage out of the cavity through the wiper motor hole.
4. To install, reverse the removal procedures.

LAND CRUISER

2-Door

1. Remove the wiper arm assemblies.
2. Remove the end plate from the pivot housing.
3. Remove the wiper motor with the linkage cable.
4. Separate the wiper motor and the transmission.
5. Remove the linkage cable.
6. To install, reverse the removal procedures.

Station Wagon

Refer to the "Engine, Removal and Installation" procedures, in this section and remove the linkage.

INSTRUMENT CLUSTER

Removal and Installation

PICKUP, VAN AND 4-RUNNER

1. Disconnect the negative battery terminal from the battery.
2. Remove the upper and lower steering column covers.
3. Remove the instrument trim panel screws and the panel.
4. Disconnect the speedometer cable from the speedometer.
5. Remove the instrument panel screws and pull the panel forward. Disconnect the electrical connectors from the back of the panel and remove the panel.
6. To install, reverse the removal procedures.

LAND CRUISER

1. Disconnect the negative battery terminal from the battery.
2. Disconnect the speedometer cable. Remove the instrument panel screws.
3. Loosen the steering column clamp by removing the attaching bolts.
4. Pull out the instrument panel and the speedometer, disconnect the electrical connectors and remove the panel.
5. To install, reverse the removal procedures.

SPEEDOMETER

Removal and Installation

1. Remove the instrument cluster and disconnect the cable from the speedometer.
2. Disconnect the other end of the speedometer cable from the transmission extension housing and pull the cable from its jacket at the transmission end.

NOTE: If the cable is being replace because it is broken, be sure to remove the both pieces of the broken cable.

3. Using graphite, lubricate the new speedometer cable and insert it into the cable jacket at the lower end.
4. Connect the speedometer cable to the transmission, then, to the instrument cluster.
5. To complete the installation, reverse the removal procedures.

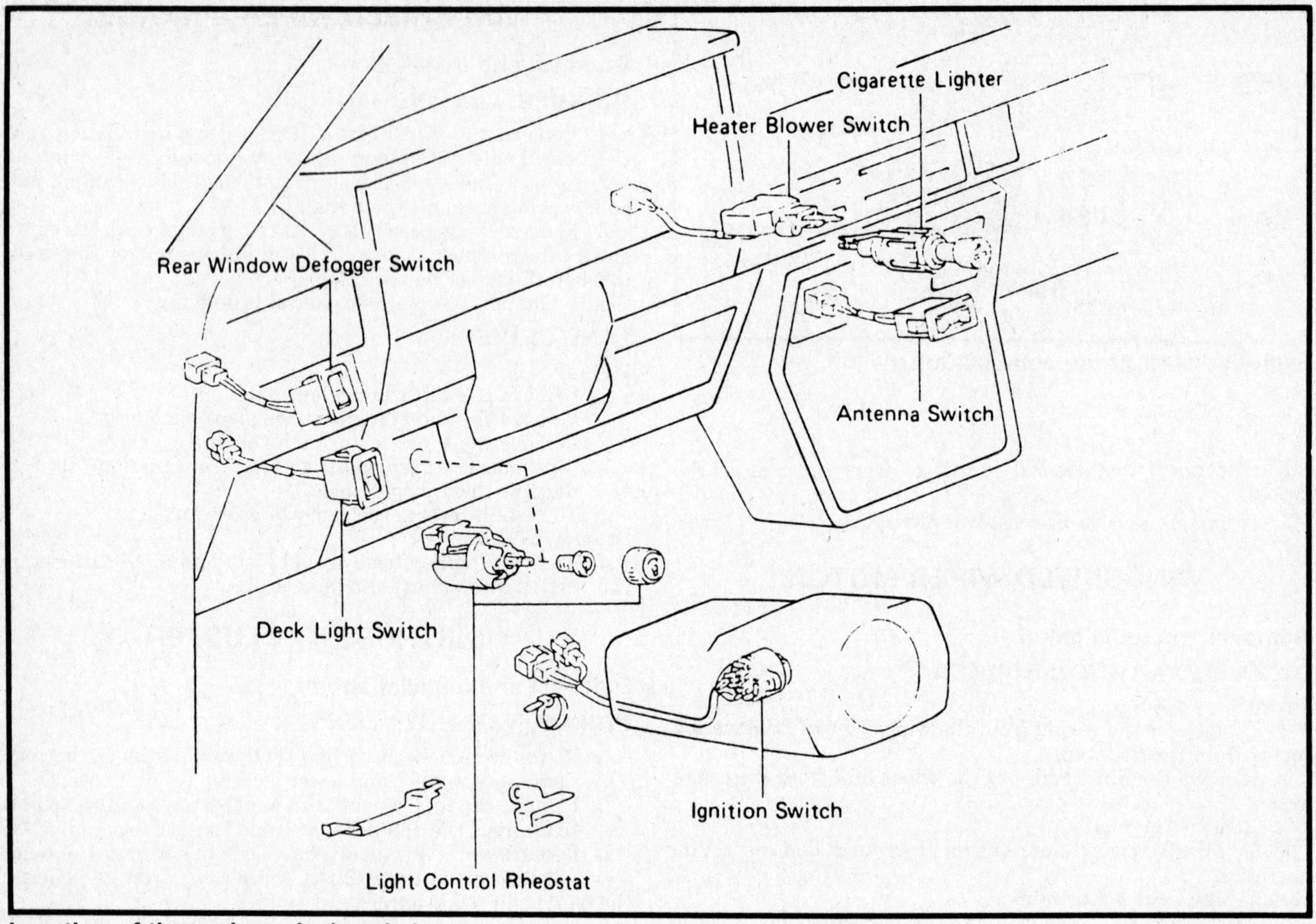

Cigarette Lighter
Heater Blower Switch
Rear Window Defogger Switch
Antenna Switch
Deck Light Switch
Ignition Switch
Light Control Rheostat

Location of the various dash switches

Wiper and Washer Switch
Turn Signal and Hazard Warning Switch
Headlight Dimmer Switch
Horn Contact Plate
Light Control Switch

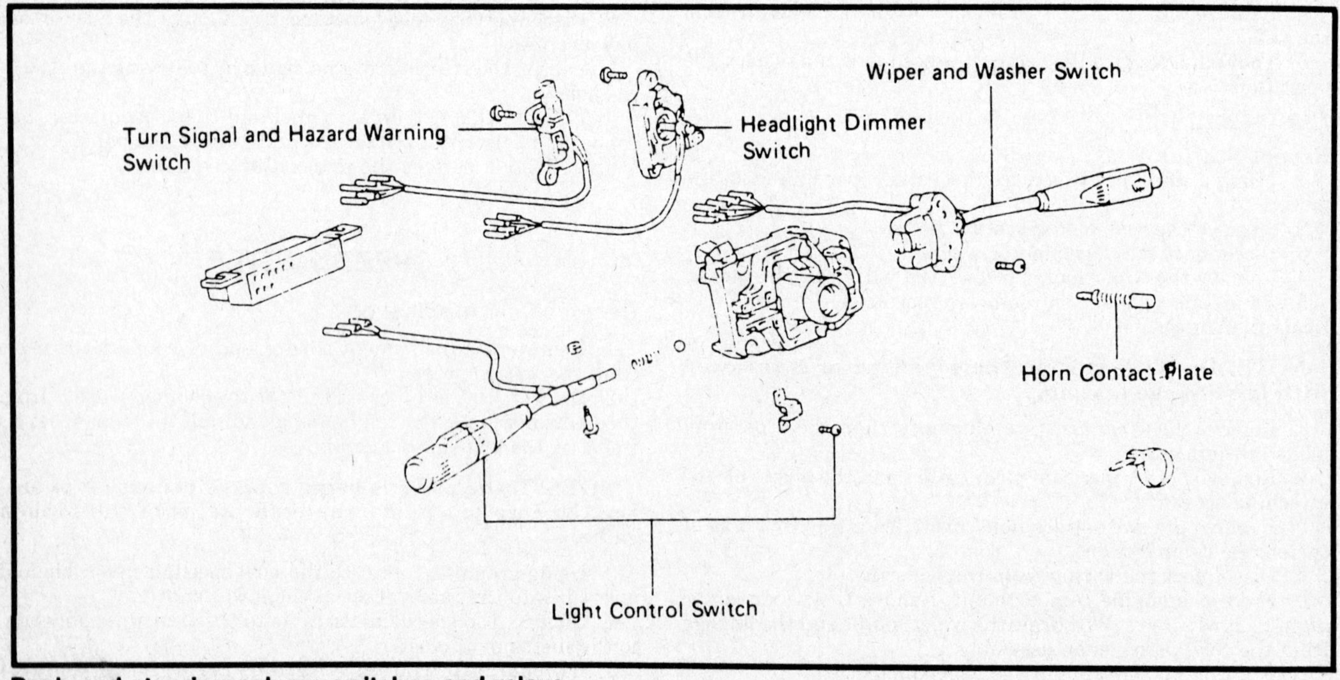

Dash and steering column switches and relays

COOLING AND HEATING SYSTEM

Water Pump

Removal and Installation

22R SERIES ENGINES

1. Drain the cooling system.
2. If equipped, remove the fan shroud bolts and the shroud.
3. Loosen the alternator adjusting link bolt and remove the drive belt, then, swing the alternator toward the engine.
4. If equipped with an air pump, air conditioning compressor or power steering pump drive belts, it may be necessary to loosen the adjusting bolt, remove the drive belt(s) and move the component(s) out of the way.
5. Remove the fan from the fluid coupling, the fluid coupling and pulley from the water pump, then, the water pump-to-engine bolts and the pump.

CAUTION

If the water pump is equipped with a fluid coupling, DO NOT tip the fluid coupling on its side, for the fluid will run out.

6. Using a putty knife, clean the gasket mounting surfaces.
7. To install, use a new gasket, sealant and reverse the removal procedures. Adjust the drive belt(s) tension. Refill the cooling system.

3Y-EC AND 4Y-EC ENGINE

1. Drain the cooling system. Disconnect the drive belt from the water pump.
2. Remove the fan from the fluid coupling and the fluid coupling/pulley from the water pump.
3. Remove the drive belt adjusting bar (from the water pump), the water pump-to-engine bolts and the water pump.
4. Using a putty knife, clean the gasket mounting surfaces.
5. To install, use a new gasket, sealant and reverse the removal procedures. Torque the water pump nuts/bolts to 13 ft. lbs., the drive belt adjusting bar to 29 ft. lbs., the pulley/fluid coupling-to-water pump nuts to 10 ft. lbs. and the fan-to-fluid coupling nuts to 10 ft. lbs. Adjust the drive belt tension. Refill the cooling system.

L, 2L AND 2L-T ENGINES

1. Refer to the "Front Cover, Removal and Installation" procedures, in this section and remove the front cover.
2. Drain the cooling system and remove the radiator.
3. Remove the timing belt tension spring.
4. Remove the mounting bolts, the spring bracket and the water pump.
5. Using a putty knife, clean the gasket mounting surfaces.
6. To install, use new gaskets, sealant and reverse the removal procedures. Torque the water pump bolts to 14 ft. lbs. Adjust the drive belts. Refill the cooling system.

Thermostat

Removal and Installation

22R SERIES ENGINES

1. Partially drain the cooling system to a level below the thermostat.

NOTE: Unless the upper radiator hose is positioned over one of the thermostat housing (water outlet) bolts, it is not necessary to detach the hose.

2. Remove the mounting bolts, the water outlet and the thermostat from the intake manifold.
3. Using a putty knife, clean the gasket mounting surfaces.

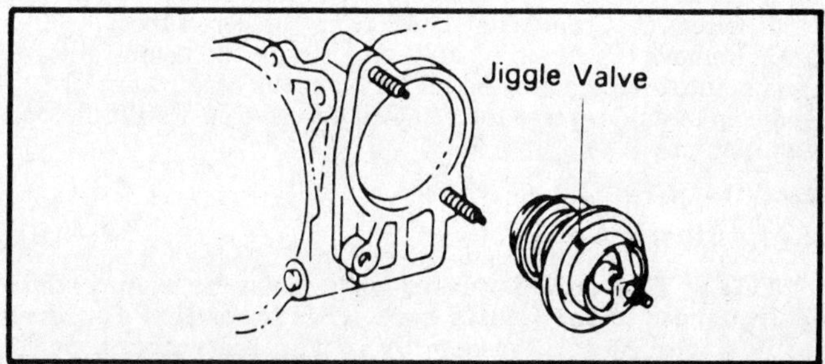

View of the thermostat installation position – 3Y-EC and 4Y-E engines

4. To install, use a new gasket, sealant and reverse the removal procedures. Refill the cooling system.

NOTE: When installing a new thermostat, be sure that the thermostat is positioned with the spring down.

3Y-EC AND 4Y-E ENGINE

1. Drain the cooling system to a level below the thermostat.
2. Disconnect the radiator outlet hose from the thermostat housing.
3. Remove the mounting bolts, the thermostat housing and the thermostat.
4. Using a putty knife, clean the gasket mounting surfaces.
5. To install, use a new gasket, sealant and reverse the removal procedures, making sure that the jiggle valve is placed at the upper-left position. Torque the thermostat housing to 9 ft. lbs. Refill the cooling system.

NOTE: When installing a new thermostat, be sure that the thermostat is positioned with the spring facing the engine block.

L, 2L AND 2L-T ENGINES

1. Drain the cooling system to a level below the thermostat.
2. Disconnect the radiator inlet hose from the thermostat housing.
3. Remove the mounting bolts, the thermostat housing and the thermostat.
4. Using a putty knife, clean the gasket mounting surfaces.
5. To install, use a new gasket, sealant and reverse the removal procedures. Refill the cooling system.

NOTE: When installing a new thermostat, be sure that the thermostat is positioned with the spring facing the engine block.

Heater Core

NOTE: On models equipped with A/C, the heater and the air conditioner are completely separate units. Be certain when working under the dashboard that only the heater hoses are disconnected.

CAUTION

The air conditioning hoses are under pressure; if disconnected, the escaping refrigerant will freeze any surface with which it comes in contact, including your skin and eyes.

Removal and Installation

PICKUPS, VAN AND 4-RUNNER

1. Disconnect the negative battery terminal from the battery.

2. Drain the cooling system.
3. Remove the glove box, the defroster hoses, the air damper, the air duct and the two side defroster ducts.
4. Remove the control unit from the instrument panel.
5. Disconnect the heater hoses from the core tubes.
6. Remove the retaining bolts and lift out the heater unit. At this point, the core may be pulled from the case.
7. To install, reverse the removal procedures. Refill the cooling system.

LAND CRUISER

Front Heater Core

NOTE: The entire heater unit must be removed to gain access to the heater core. This procedure requires almost complete disassembly of the instrument panel and lowering of the steering column.

1. Note the following points before proceeding:
   a. Be sure to tag any wiring which must be disconnected so that it may be correctly installed.
   b. As the fasteners are removed, arrange them so that they may be installed in their original locations.
   c. Do not force any parts to remove them; if a part cannot easily be removed, remove any additional fasteners which may have been initially overlooked.
   d. When disconnecting the coolant hoses, be careful not to damage the heater core tubes. Place a drain pan under the coolant hose connections before disconnecting the hoses.
2. Disconnect the negative battery terminal from the battery. Remove the glove box and the glove box door.
3. Remove the lower heater ducts. Remove the large heater duct from the passenger-side of the heater unit.
4. Remove the ductwork from behind the instrument panel. If equipped, remove the radio.
5. Disconnect the wiring connector from the right-side inner portion of the glove opening.
6. Remove the instrument panel pad. Remove the hood release lever. Disconnect the hand throttle control cable.
7. Remove the retaining screw from the left-side of the fuse block.
8. Remove the steering column-to-instrument panel attaching nuts and carefully lower the steering column. Tag and disconnect the wiring as necessary in order to lower the column assembly.
9. Disconnect the electrical connector from the rheostat located to the left of the steering column opening.
10. Remove the center dual outlet duct which is attached to the upper portion of the heater unit.
11. Remove the lower instrument panel. The fasteners are located in the following places:
   a. Left-side of the instrument panel: two at the left-side end and two at the left-lower end.
   b. Above the steering column: two.
   c. To the right of the steering column opening: two.
   d. Left-upper corner of the glove box opening: two.
   e. Left-lower corner of the glove box opening: one.
   f. Right-side of the instrument panel: two at the right-side end and two at the right-lower end.
12. Tag and disconnect the hoses from the heater unit. Remove the heater unit-to-firewall fasteners and the heater unit.
13. Remove the heater core-to-heater unit pipe clamps and the heater core retaining clamp, then, withdraw the heater core from the heater unit.
14. To install, reverse the removal procedures. Torque the steering column-to-instrument panel fasteners to 14–15 ft. lbs. Refill the cooling system.

Rear Heater Core

1. Turn off the water valve and disconnect both hoses from the rear heater core.
2. Disconnect the wiring from the rear heater.
3. Remove the mounting bolts and lift out the core.
4. To install, reverse the removal procedures. Refill the cooling system.

Blower Motor

Removal and Installation

PICKUPS, VAN (1983-88) AND 4-RUNNER (1985-88)

1. Disconnect the electrical connector from motor.
2. Remove the blower motor-to-case screws and lift the motor from the case.
3. To install, reverse the removal procedures. Make sure that the seal around the motor flange is in good condition.

LAND CRUISER

1. Disconnect the electrical connector from the blower motor.
2. Disconnect the flexible tube from the side of the blower motor.
3. Remove the blower motor fasteners and lower the blower motor out of the air inlet duct.
4. To install, reverse the removal procedures. During installation, be sure to position the motor so that the flexible tube can be attached to the motor.

GASOLINE FUEL SYSTEM

For calibration information, refer to the Unit Repair section.

Carburetor

Removal and Installation

1. Disconnect the negative battery terminal from the battery.
2. Label and disconnect the emission control hoses. Disconnect the air intake hose. Remove the mounting and butterfly nuts, then, lift the air cleaner from the carburetor.
3. If equipped with an A/T, disconnect the throttle cable or rod. Disconnect the fuel hose, the emission control hose, the PCV hose and the wiring connector(s) from the carburetor.
4. Disconnect the accelerator linkage and the choke pipe (if equipped).
5. On the 2F engines, disconnect the magnetic valve wire from the coil terminal and the choke cable from the carburetor.
6. Remove the carburetor-to-manifold nuts/bolts and lift it from the manifold.
7. Cover the open manifold with a clean cloth to prevent dirt and small objects from entering into the engine.
8. Using a putty knife, clean the gasket mounting surfaces.
9. To install, use a new gasket and reverse the removal procedures. After the engine has been started, check for fuel and vacuum leaks.

Adjustment

FLOAT LEVEL

All – Except 2F Engines

For this procedure, the air horn must be removed from the carburetor and the gasket removed from the air horn.

1. Position the air horn with the floats facing upward; allow the float to rest by itself.
2. Using tool No. SST 09240-00014 or equivalent, position it between the floats and the air horn; the measurement should be 0.386 in. If adjustment is necessary, bend the tang at point "A".
3. Using a vernier caliper, raise the float and measure the distance between the bottom of the float and the air horn; the distance should be 1.89 in. If adjustment is necessary, bend the tang at point "B".
4. After adjustment, replace the air horn onto the carburetor.

2F Engines

1. Remove The air horn from the carburetor. Invert the air horn and allow the float to hang towards the air horn.
2. With the air horn gasket removed, measure the distance between the float and the air hron, at the end of the float opposite the needle valve. The distance should be 0.295 in. If adjustment is necessary, remove tthe flat and bend the tab which is centered between the hinge pivot points. After the adjustment is completed, reinstall the float and recheck the steeing.
3. Lift upwards on the float and measure the distance between the needle valve push pin and the lip of the float. The distance should be 0.043 in. If adjustment is necessary, remove the float and bend the tabs located just inside of the hinge points. After the adjustment is completed, reinstall the float and recheck the setting.

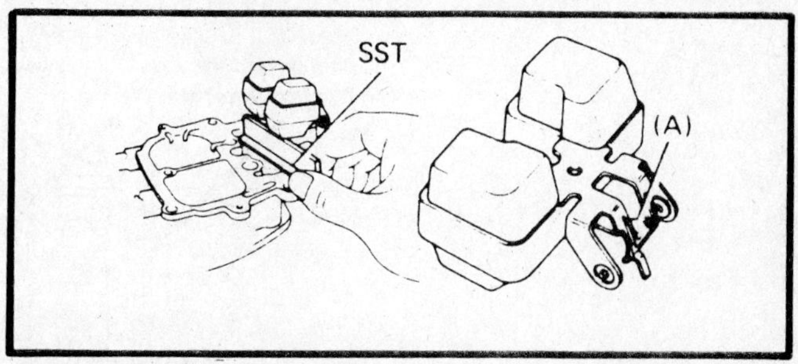

Using tool No. SST 09240-00014 to check the float raised position

Using a vernier caliper to check the float lowered position

Idle Speed and Mixture

2F ENGINES

NOTE: Idle mixture adjustments cannot be performed; these adjustments are preset at the factory.

The idle speed and mixture should be adjusted under the following conditions: the air cleaner must be installed, the choke fully opened, the transmission should be in Neutral (N), all accessories should be turned OFF, all vacuum lines should be connected and the ignition timing should be set to specification.

1. Start the engine and allow it to reach normal operating temperatures.
2. Check the float setting; the fuel level should be just about even with the spot on the sight glass. If the fuel level is too high or low, adjust the float level.
3. Connect a tachometer in accordance with its manufacturer's instructions. However, connect the tachometer positive (+) lead to the coil's (−) negative terminal or to the igniter's service connector (if provided).

CAUTION

DO NOT connect the tachometer to the distributor side; damage to the transistorized ignition could result. NEVER allow the tachometer terminal to touch ground for damage to the igniter or the ignition coil could result.

4. Using a pair of pliers, break the caps from the idle mixture screws. Turn the idle speed adjusting screw to obtain one of the following initial idle speeds: 2F–690 rpm (M/T).
5. Turn the idle mixture adjusting screw to increase the idle speed as much as is possible.
6. Next, turn the idle speed screw to again obtain the same idle speed figure given in Step 4.
7. If possible, turn the idle mixture screw to increase the idle speed again.
8. Repeat Steps 6 and 7 until the idle mixture adjusting screw will no longer increase the idle speed above the figure specified in Step 4.
9. Slowly turn the idle mixture screw clockwise, until the idle speed specified in the "Tune-Up Specifications" chart is reached (this makes the mixture leaner).
10. Disconnect the tachometer and install new idle mixture screw caps.

22R ENGINES

NOTE: The idle mixture screw is preset at the factory and adjustment should not be necessary.

The idle speed should be adjusted under the following conditions: the air cleaner must be installed, the choke fully opened, the transmission should be in Neutral (N), all accessories should be turned OFF, all vacuum lines should be connected and the ignition timing should be set to specification.

1. Start the engine and allow it to reach normal operating temperatures.
2. Check the float setting; the fuel level should be just about even with the spot on the sight glass. If the fuel level is too high or low, adjust the float level.
3. Connect a tachometer in accordance with its manufacturer's instructions. However, connect the tachometer positive (+) lead to the coil's (−) negative terminal or to the igniter's service connector (if provided).

CAUTION

DO NOT connect the tachometer to the distributor side; damage to the transistorized ignition could result. NEVER allow the tachometer terminal to touch ground for damage to the igniter or the ignition coil could result.

NOTE: If the idle mixture caps have been removed, turn the idle mixture screws to the fully closed position, then, open them 3½ turns.

4. Using a pair of pliers, break the caps from the idle speed adjusting screw. Turn the idle speed adjusting screw to obtain the correct idle speed: 700 rpm (M/T) or 750 rpm (A/T).

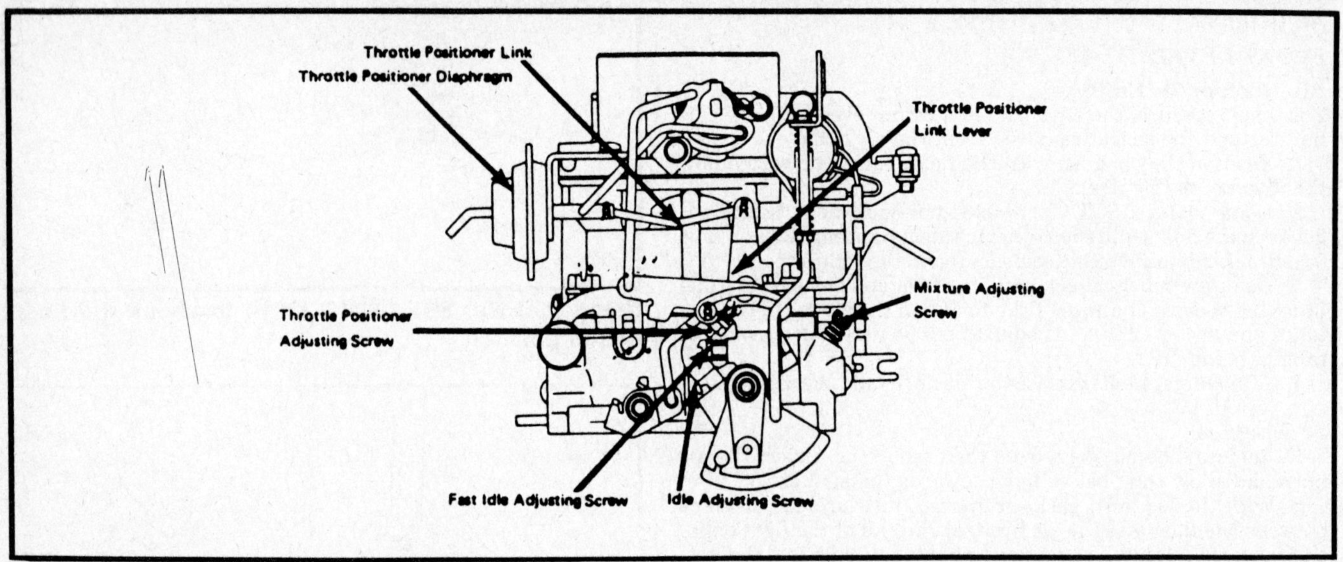

Carburetor adjusting screws—2F engine

5. Disconnect the tachometer and install new idle speed adjusting screw cap.

FUEL INJECTION

Relieve Pressure

1. Disconnect the negative battery terminal from the battery.
2. Allow the system enough time to bleed off the fuel pressure through the fuel return line.
3. Before disconnecting any fuel line component, place a rag under the item to catch any excess fuel.
4. After installation, install the negative battery terminal, turn ON the ignition switch and check for fuel leaks.

INJECTORS

Testing

Each injector may be tested for operation while on the engine, in two ways.

1. Use an mechanic's stethoscope and listen for a clicking at the injector.
2. Using an ohmmeter, check the continuity at each injector's terminal; the resistance should be 1.5–3.0Ω.

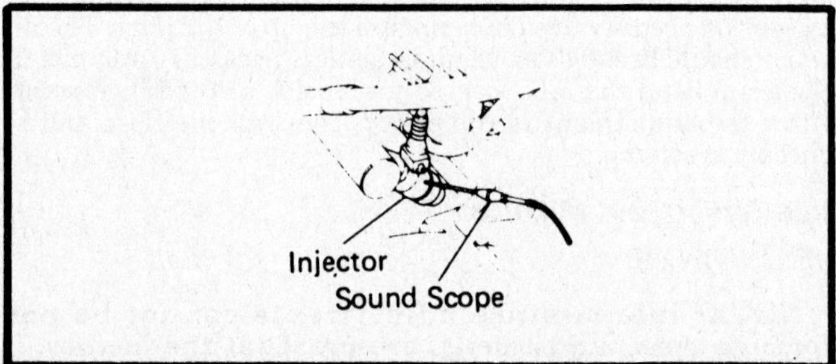

Listening to injector with a mechanic's stethescope

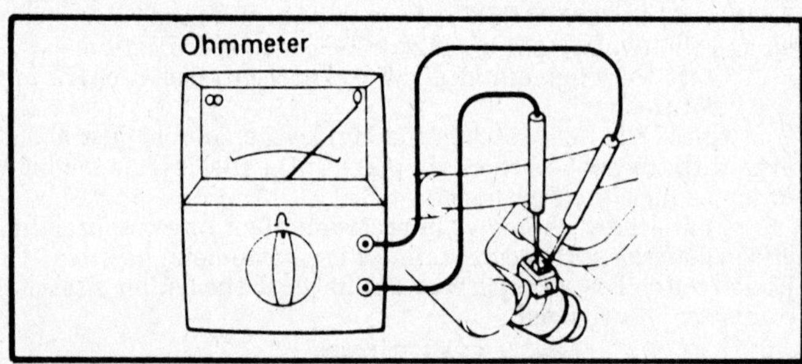

Testing the injector with an ohmmeter

Removal and Installation

1. Disconnect the negative battery terminal from the battery and the ground strap from the rear side of the engine.
2. Disconnect the accelerator wire. If equipped with an A/T, disconnect the throttle cable from the bracket and the clamp.
3. If not equipped with a 22R-TE engine, disconnect the No. 1 and No. 2 PCV hoses.
4. If equipped with a 22R-TE engine, disconnect the No. 2 PCV hose and the Vacuum Control Valve (VCV).
5. Disconnect the following items:
   a. Brake power booster hose.
   b. Air control valve hoses (P/S).
   c. Vacuum Switching Valve (VSV).
   d. Evaporative emission control hose.
   e. EGR vacuum hose and modulator.
   f. Pressure regulator hose (2WD).
   g. Fuel pressure-up (VSV) and hose.
   h. No. 1 and No. 2 air valve hose from the throttle body.
   i. No. 2 and No. 3 water by-pass hoses from the throttle body.
   j. Cold start injector wire.
   k. Throttle position wire.
6. Remove the following items:
   a. Cold start injector-to-plenum chamber bolt.
   b. No. 1 EGR pipe-to-plenum chamber bolts.
   c. Manifold stay-to-plenum chamber bolts.
   d. Fuel hose clamp, four bolts, two nuts and the bond strap.
   e. The plenum chamber with the throttle body and gaskets.
7. Disconnect the fuel return hose.
8. Disconnect the following wires:
   a. Auxiliary air valve wire.

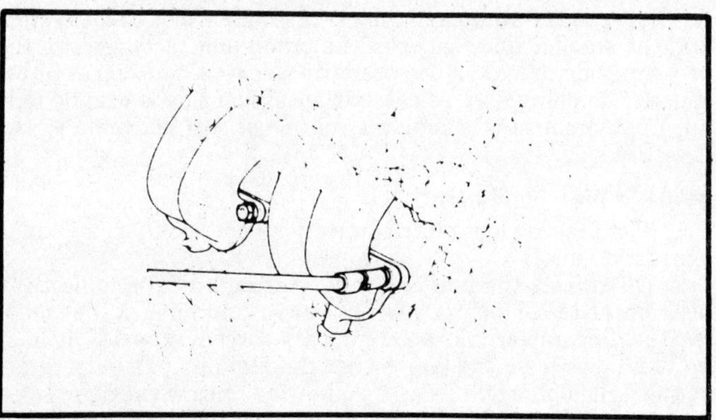

Injector removal

b. Knock sensor wire.
c. Oil pressure sender gauge/switch.
d. Starter wire (terminal 50).
e. Transmission wires.
f. Compressor wires (A/C).
g. Injector wires.
h. Water temperature sender gauge wire.
i. Overdrive temperature switch wire (A/T).
j. Oxygen sensor and igniter wire.
k. Vacuum Switching Valve (VSV) wire (A/C).
l. Cold start injector time switch wire.
m. Water temperature sensor wire.

9. Disconnect the fuel hose from the delivery pipe with the pulsation damper and gaskets.
10. Remove the injectors from the engine. Take care in handling the injectors. DO NOT DROP THEM! KEEP THEM AS CLEAN AS POSSIBLE!

NOTE: Injector performance tests are possible but special tools are required. If these tools are unavailable, use the test procedures above.

11. To install, use new O-rings and reverse the removal procedures. Torque the hold down bolts to 14 ft. lbs. Check for fuel leakage.

NOTE: Each injector should have four insulators. Prior to installation, coat the O-rings with clean gasoline. Prior to tightening the hold down bolts, make sure that the injector rotates smoothly in its bore. If not, the O-rings are twisted.

Adjustment

IDLE SPEED

The 22R-E, 22R-TE, 3Y-EC and 4Y-E engines are equipped with a computer activated, electronic fuel injection system. Prior to adjusting the idle speed, make sure that: The air cleaner is installed. All vacuum hoses are connected. All pipes and hoses in the air intake system are connected and in good condition. All fuel injection system wiring is connected and in good condition. The engine is at normal operating temperature. All accessories are OFF. Transmission in Neutral.

CAUTION

Not all tachometers are compatible with the fuel injection system; consult the tachometer manufacturer's recommendations before installing the tachometer. NEVER allow the tachometer terminal to touch ground for damage to the igniter or the ignition coil could result.

1. Connect the tachometer positive (+) lead to the coil's (−) negative terminal or to the igniter's service connector (if provided).
2. Race the engine at 2,500 rpm for 2 minutes.

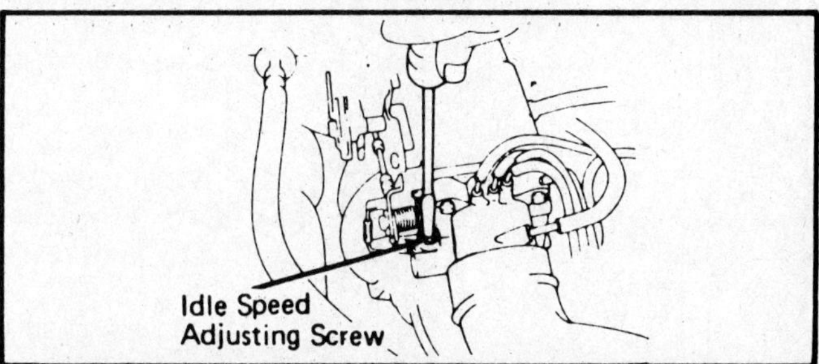

Adjusting the idle speed – 22R-E and 22R-TE engines

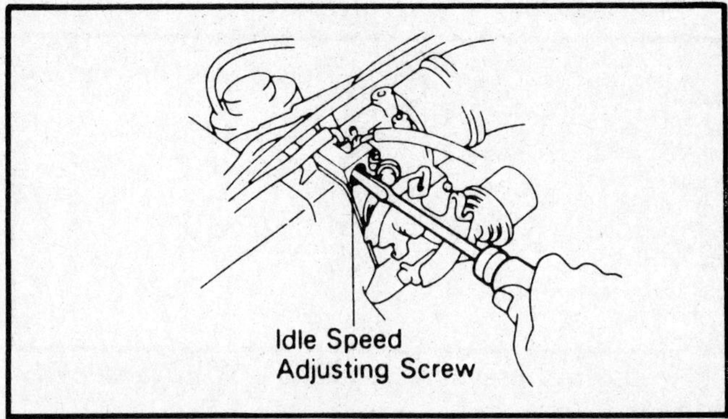

Adjusting the idle speed – 3Y-EC and 4Y-E engines

3. Run the engine at idle and turn the idle speed adjusting screw to obtain a the correct speed of: 700 rpm (M/T) or 750 rpm (A/T) for the 3Y-EC and 4Y-E engines; 750 rpm for 22R-E engines and 800 rpm for 22R-TE engines.
4. Disconnect and remove the tachometer.

Cold Start Injector

The EFI engines have a cold start injector located in the intake air chamber which aids in cold weather starting.

Removal and Installation

22R-E, 22R-TE, 3Y-EC AND 4Y-E ENGINES

1. Disconnect the negative battery cable and the cold start injector wire.
2. Place a shop towel or a container under the fuel delivery pipe and drain the fuel from the pipe.
3. Disconnect the fuel pipe from the cold start injector.
4. Remove the mounting bolts and the cold start injector from the intake air chamber.
5. To install, use new gaskets and reverse the removal procedures. Torque the injector bolts to 44–60 inch lbs.

Fuel Pressure Regulator

The fuel pressure regulator is located on the fuel delivery pipe of the EFI system, it maintains a constant fuel pressure in the injection system.

Removal and Installation

22R-E, 22R-TE, 3Y-EC AND 4Y-E ENGINES

NOTE: On the Van (3Y-EC and 4Y-E) models, raise and support the vehicle on jackstands.

1. Disconnect the vacuum sensing hose from the pressure regulator.

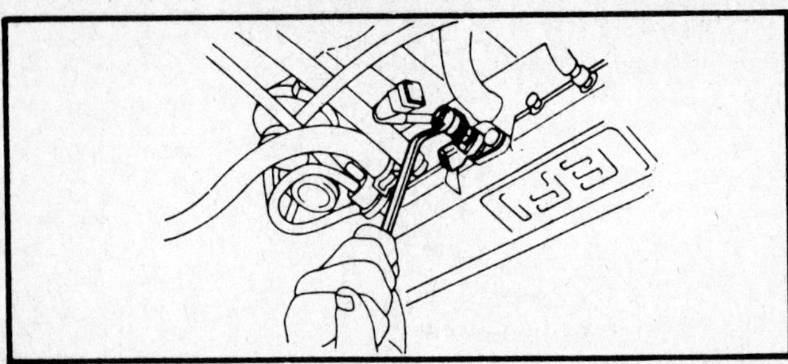

Removing the cold start valve—22R series, 3Y-EC and 4Y-E engines

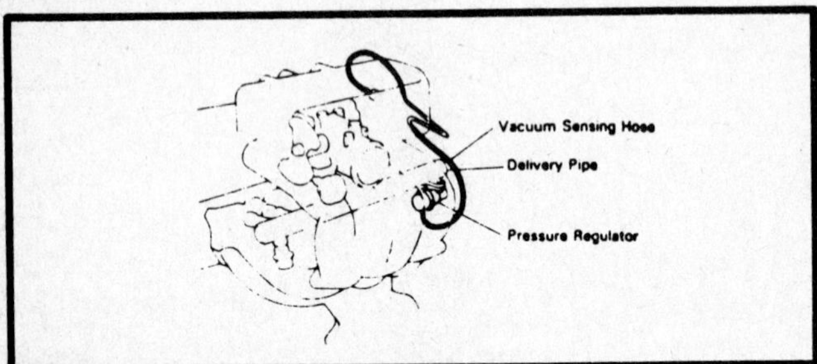

Removing the pressure regulator—3Y-EC and 4Y-E engines

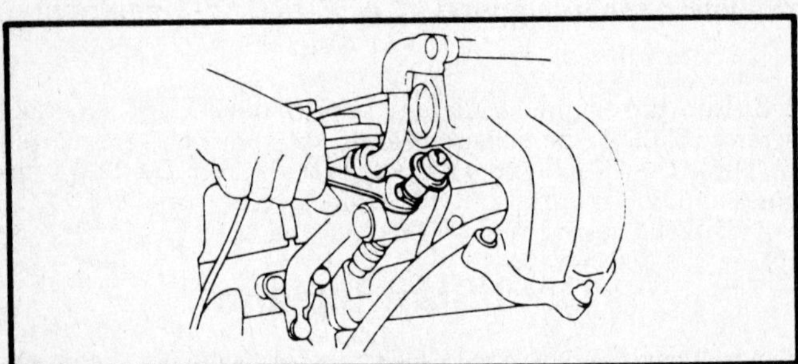

Removing the pressure regulator—22R series engines

NOTE: On the 22R-E and the 22R-TE engines, remove the No. 1 EGR pipe.

2. Place a shop towel or a container under the fuel hose connection and disconnect the fuel return hose from the regulator.
3. Remove the locknut (22R-E and 22R-TE) or the mounting bolts (3Y-EC and 4Y-E) and the pressure regulator from the fuel delivery pipe.
4. To install, reverse of removal. Torque the locknut to 22 ft. lbs. (22R-E and 22R-TE) or bolts to 44–60 inch lbs. (3Y-EC and 4Y-E). Start the engine and check for fuel leaks.

Fuel Pump

MECHANICAL

A mechanical fuel pump is used on all engines except the 3Y-EC, 4Y-E, 22R-E and 22R-TE engines. The mechanical fuel pump is actuated by an eccentric which is integral with the engine camshaft on 2F, 3B and 2H engines and bolted in front of the camshaft drive sprocket on the 22R engines.

Testing

Fuel pumps should always be tested on the vehicle. The larger line between the pump and tank is the suction side of the system and the smaller line, between the pump and carburetor is the pressure side. A leak in the pressure side would be apparent because of dripping fuel. A leak in the suction side is usually only apparent because of a reduced volume of fuel delivered to the pressure side.

LEAK TEST

1. Tighten any loose line connections and look for any kinks or restrictions.
2. Disconnect the fuel line at the carburetor. Disconnect the distributor-to-coil primary wire. Place a container at the end of the fuel line and crank the engine a few revolutions. If little or no fuel flows from the line, either the fuel pump is inoperative or the line is plugged. Blow through the lines with compressed air and try the test again. Reconnect the line.
3. If fuel flows in good volume, check the fuel pump pressure to be sure.

PRESSURE TEST

1. Attach a pressure gauge to the pressure side of the fuel line. On vehicles equipped with a vapor return system, squeeze off the return hose.
2. Run the engine at idle and note the reading on the gauge. Stop the engine and compare the reading with the specifications listed in the "Tune-Up Specifications" chart. If the pump is operating properly, the pressure will be as specified and will be constant at idle speed. If the pressure varies or is too high or low, the pump should be repaired or replaced, depending upon the pump type.
3. Remove the pressure gauge.

FLOW TEST

1. Disconnect the fuel line from the carburetor. Run the fuel line into a suitable measuring container.
2. Run the engine at idle until there is one pint of fuel in the container. One pint should be pumped in 30 seconds or less.
3. If the flow is below minimum, check for a restriction in the line.

Removal and Installation

22R ENGINES

1. Disconnect the negative battery terminal from the battery.

CAUTION

When working on the fuel system, do not smoke or work near any fire hazard. Keep gasoline off rubber or leather parts.

2. Drain the cooling system to a level below the upper radiator hose and remove the upper radiator hose.
3. Remove all three lines from the fuel pump, the mounting bolts, the fuel pump and the gasket.

NOTE: The fuel pump is not repairable. It must be replaced as a complete unit.

4. Using a putty knife, clean the gasket mounting surfaces.
5. To install, use a new gaskets and reverse the removal procedures. Refill the cooling system. Start the engine and check for leaks.

2F, 3B AND 2H ENGINES

1. Disconnect the negative battery terminal from the battery.
2. Remove and plug the fuel lines at fuel pump. Remove the fuel pump-to-engine bolts and the pump.

NOTE: If any new rubber hose must be used to repair the fuel line, be sure that it is gasoline-resistant.

3. Using a putty knife, clean the gasket mounting surfaces.
4. To install, use a new gasket and reverse the removal procedures. Start the engine and check for fuel leaks.

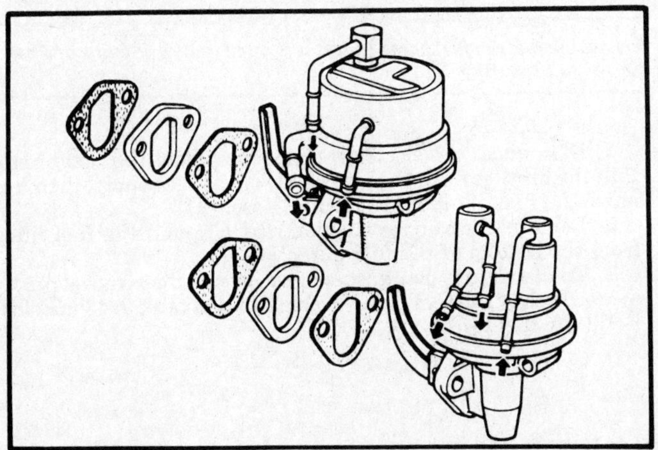

Exploded view of the mechanical fuel pumps—22R series engines—arrows indicate the fuel flow in and out of the pump

NOTE: The 2F, 3B and 2H engine mechanical fuel pump is rebuildable, depending upon the parts availability. If the fuel pump is to be rebuilt rather than replaced, follow the instructions supplied with the rebuilding kit.

ELECTRIC

An electric fuel pump is used on the 22R-E, 22R-TE, 3Y-EC and 4Y-E engines. The fuel pump is wired into the ignition switch and oil pressure switch circuits. In the event of an oil pressure loss, the fuel pump is turned OFF so that the engine will stall, thus preventing engine damage due to the oil pressure loss. The fuel pump will operate only when the ignition switch is turned to the START position and when the oil pressure is normal.

Operation Testing

1. Disconnect the electrical clip from the oil pressure switch.
2. Turn the ignition switch to the ON position (DO NOT start the engine).
3. Short the "Fp" and the " + B" terminals of the check connector. Check the cold start injector hose for pressure.
4. Check for a smooth flow of gasoline from the fuel filter outlet. If the pump is noisy, it is probably defective. If the pump does not run, check the pump resistor and relay.
5. Disconnect the jumper wire and reconnect the check connector. Turn the ignition switch OFF.

Pressure Testing

1. Disconnect the negative battery terminal from the battery and the wiring connector from the cold start injector.
2. Place a container or a shop towel near the end of the delivery tube.
3. Slowly loosen the cold start injector union bolt, then, remove the bolt and the gaskets. Drain the fuel line.
4. Using pressure gauge tool No. 09268–45011, connect it in line with the cold start injector. Reconnect the battery cable.
5. Short the "Fp" and " + B" terminals of the check connector wire. Turn the ignition switch to the ON position and measure to fuel pump pressure. It should be 33–38 psi. Turn the ignition switch OFF.

NOTE: If the pressure is high, replace the pressure regulator; if the pressure is low, check the hoses, the connections, the fuel pump, the fuel filter or the pressure regulator.

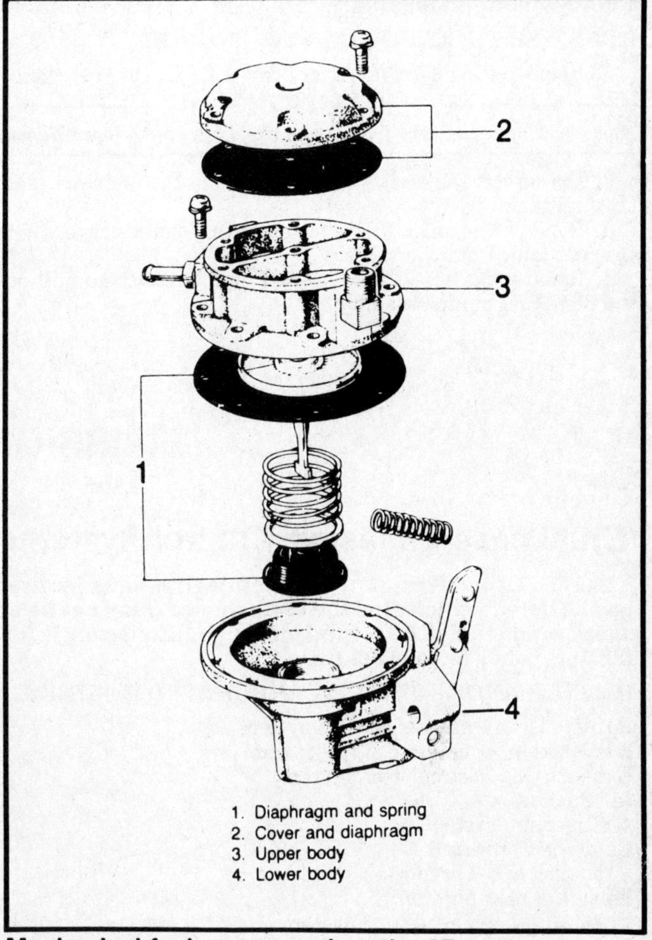

Mechanical fuel pump used on the 2F engine

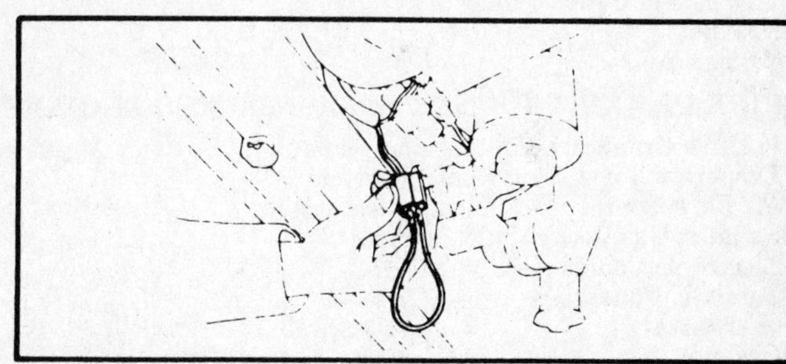

Shorting the Fp and +B terminals of the check connector—EFI system

6. Remove the jumper wire from the check connector. Start the engine. Disconnect and plug the vacuum sensing hose at the pressure regulator, then, measure the fuel pressure at idle. It should be 33–38 psi.
7. Reconnect the vacuum sensing hose to the pressure regulator. The pressure should now be 27–31 psi.; if not, check the vacuum hose and/or the pressure regulator.
8. Stop the engine and check that the fuel pressure remains at 21 psi. for 5 minutes. If not, check the fuel pump, the pressure regulator and/or the injectors.

Removal and Installation

22R-E, 22R-TE, 3Y-EC AND 4Y-E ENGINES

1. Remove the negative battery cable. Drain the fuel tank.

CAUTION

When working around the fuel system, avoid smoking or open flames.

2. Disconnect the electrical connector and the fuel lines from the fuel tank.
3. Remove the inlet tube and mounting bolts/straps, then, the fuel tank from the vehicle.
4. Remove the access plate-to-fuel tank bolts, then, pull out the plate/fuel pump assembly.

CAUTION

Do not operate the fuel pump unless it is immersed in gasoline and connected to its resistor.

5. Disconnect the electrical connectors from the fuel pump. Pull the bracket from the lower-side of the fuel pump, then, remove the fuel pump from the fuel hose.
6. Remove the rubber cushion, the clip and the fuel filter from the bottom of the fuel pump.
7. To install, use new gaskets and reverse the removal procedures. Torque the fuel pump bracket-to-fuel tank to 43 inch lbs. Refill the fuel tank.

EMISSION CONTROLS

Crankcase Emission Control Systems

NOTE: Other Emission Control devices may be used on the listed vehicles, or the same devices may not be on every engine. Refer to the Underhood Emission Information Label for applications.

PICK-UP AND 4 RUNNER CARBURETED ENGINES

Positive Crankcase Ventilation system
Evaporation Emission Control system
Exhaust Gas Recirculation system
Air Suction
Air Injection system
Catalytic Converter
(Monolith and Three-way)
Early Fuel Evaporation
Electronic Controlled Carburetor
Fuel Shut-off system
Spark Control system
Thermostatic Air Cleaner
Dashpot
Oxygen Sensor

PICK-UP AND 4 RUNNER FUEL INJECTED ENGINES

Positive Crankcase Ventilation system
Evaporation Emission Control system
Air Flow Controlled Fuel Injection system
Exhaust Gas Recirculation system
Electronic Control Unit
Catalytic Converter
(Three-way)
Dashpot

LAND CRUISER

Positive Crankcase Ventilation system
Evaporative Emission Control system
Exhaust Gas Recirculation system
Air Injection
Catalytic Converter
(Three-way)
Spark Control system
Thermostatic Air Cleaner
Dashpot
Qxygen Sensor
Deceleration Control system
High Altitude Compensator
Idle Control system

VAN

Positive Crankcase Ventilation system
Evaporative Emission Control system
Air Flow Controlled Fuel Injection
Exhaust Gas Recirculation system
Electronic Control Unit
Catalytic Converter
(Three-way)
Oxygen Sensor
Dashpot

POSITIVE CRANKCASE VENTILATION (PCV) VALVE

The Positive Crankcase Ventilation (PCV) system is used on all engines. Blow-by gases are routed from the crankcase to the intake manifold where they are combined with the air/fuel mixture and burned in the engine.

The PCV valve, located on top of the rocker arm cover, is used to prevent the crankcase gases from being ignited in the event of a backfire. It is connected to the intake manifold by a hose; it should be replaced every 30,000 miles.

Removal and Installation

1. Remove the PCV valve from the rocker arm cover.
2. Using a clean hose, attach it to the rocker arm side of the PCV valve.
3. Blow through the hose (from the cylinder head-side); air should pass freely.

CAUTION

DO NOT suck air through the valve, for ingested petroleum products inside the valve are harmful to the body.

4. Attach the clean hose to the intake manifold-side of the PCV valve.
5. Blow through the hose (from the intake manifold-side); air should have difficulty passing in this direction).

NOTE: If either test of the PCV valve fails, replace the valve.

6. Reinstall the PCV valve.

Evaporative Emission Control System

The system is used to prevent hydrocarbon emissions from entering the atmosphere due to evaporation in the fuel system.

CHARCOAL CANISTER—ALL MODELS

The charcoal canister serves as a fuel vapor storage reservoir, equipped with an internal check valve and as an integral part of the air filter. The canister should be replaced every 50,000 miles.

Removal and Installation

1. Disconnect and label the hoses from the charcoal canister.
2. Disconnect the canister from its mounting bracket and the canister from the vehicle.
3. Inspect the hoses for cracking or deterioration; replace the damaged hoses.
4. To install, use a new charcoal canister and reverse the removal procedures.

FUEL FILLER CAP

The fuel filler cap is of a closed circuit design using a check valve; its design allows air to flow in one direction (into the tank). Inspect the gasket and the cap for damage or deformation; if necessary, replace the cap.

EXTERNAL CHECK VALVE – VAN

The external check valve is a one-way, fuel vapor flow valve, located in the fuel line between the fuel tank and the charcoal canister; it is used as a fuel block incase of the roll-over situation.

Removal and Installation

1. Disconnect the fuel vapor hoses from the check valve.
2. Remove the check valve from the vehcile.
3. To inspect the valve, perform the following procedures:
   a. Blow through the fuel tank-side of the valve; air flow should open the valve with slight resistance.
   b. Blow through the charcoal canister-side of the valve; air flow should open the valve without resistance.
   c. If the test does not meet specifications, replace the valve.
4. To install, reverse the removal procedures.

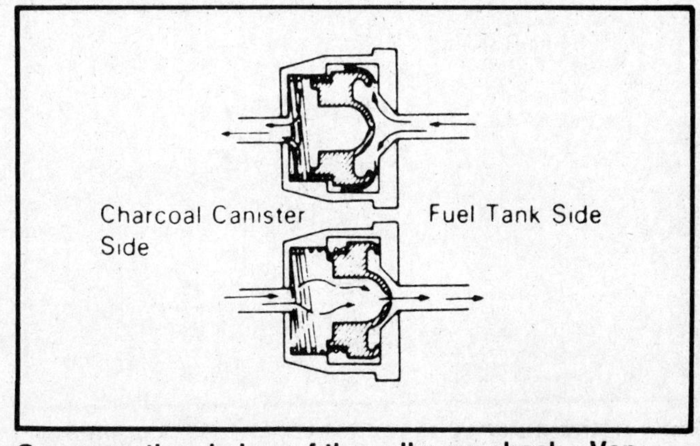

Cross-sectional view of the roll-over check – Van

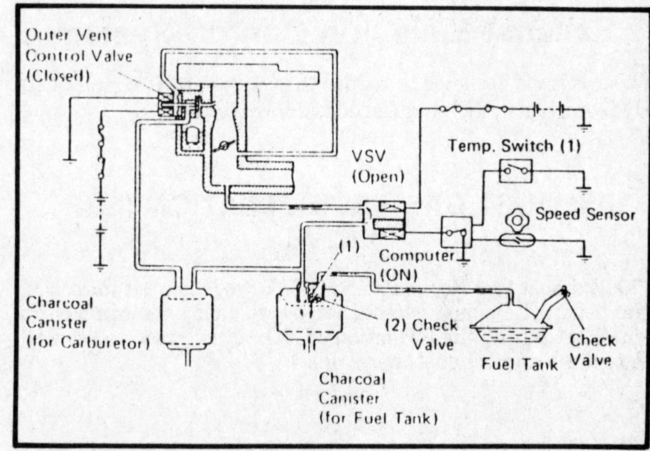

Cross-sectional view of the evaporative emission control system – 22R engine

VACUUM SWITCHING VALVE (VSV) – 22R ENGINES

The Vacuum Switching Valve (VSV) is used to block the flow of fuel vapors to the carburetor through a combination of voltage, temperature and speed.

Removal and Installation

1. Disconnect and label the hoses from the VSV.
2. Disconnect the electrical connector from the VSV.
3. Remove the VSV from its bracket.
4. To install, reverse the removal procedures.

Inspection

IGNITION SWITCH

1. Connect a 12V DC power source to the VSV electrical connectors.
2. Blow air through one of the ports; air should flow freely.
3. Remove the power source from the VSV electrical connectors.
4. Blow air through one of the ports; air should not flow.

SPEED SENSOR

The vehicle speed sensor blocks electical flow to the VSV during low speed operation.

1. Disconnect the bottom hose to the VSV.
2. Using a 3-way connector, connect a vacuum gauge between the VSV and the charcoal canister.

NOTE: The vacuum gauge hose must be long enough to reach the front seat.

3. Warm the engine. Drive the vehicle at speeds below 7 mph; the vacuum gauge should read zero.
4. Increase the speed to at least 16 mph; the vacuum gauge should read engine vacuum.
5. If a problem is found, replace the speed sensor of the VSV.

TEMPERATURE SWITCH

The temperature switch is located on the intake manifold; it controls the VSV operation by temperature alone.

1. Drain the engine coolant to a level below the temperature switch.
2. Remove the temperature switch from the intake manifold.
3. Cool the switch to a level below 109°F.
4. Using an ohmmeter, check that the switch has continuity.
5. Place the switch in water heated to 131°F and check the continuity of the switch; there should be no continuity.
6. If a problem is found, replace the switch.
7. Using electrically conductive sealant, coat the threads and reinstall the VSV in the intake manifold.

OUTER VENT CONTROL VALVE (VCV)

The outer Vent Control Valve (VCV) is attached to the side of the carburetor.

1. Disconnect the outer vent hose from the control valve and blow through the hose; the vent should be open.
2. Start the engine.
3. Blow through the hose again; the vent should be closed.
4. If a problem exists, replace the valve.

View of the outer vent control valve—22R engines

Exhaust Emission Control System

The system is designed to reduce the Oxides of Nitrogen (NOx), Hydrocarbons (HC) and Carbon Monoxide (CO).

EXHAUST GAS RECIRCULATION (EGR) VALVE

The Exhaust Gas Recirculation (EGR) valve is used to recirculate unburnt exhaust gases; thereby, reducing the combustion temperature and the formation of NOx. It is connected to both the intake and exhaust manifolds.

Removal and Installation

1. Disconnect and label the hoses to the EGR valve.
2. Remove the exhaust pipe-to-EGR valve tube.
3. Remove the EGR valve-to-intake manifold bolts and the EGR valve.
4. Clean the mating surfaces and inspect the valve.
5. To install, reverse the removal procedures.

CATALYTIC CONVERTER

The catalytic converter is located under the vehicle, between the exhaust manifold and the muffler. Its purpose it to convert HC, CO and NOx into CO_2, H_2O and N_2.

Removal and Installation

CAUTION

DO NOT perform this operation on a hot (or warm) engine. The catalyst temperatures may reach 1,700°F and can cause a severe burn.

1. Raise and support the vehicle on jackstands.
2. Remove the converter-to-exhaust pipe bolts, the converter and gaskets from the vehicle.

NOTE: On the 1982-83, 2-bbl models, remove the converter-to-vehicle rubber rings.

3. Using a putty knife, clean the gasket mounting surfaces.

NOTE: When installing the converter on the Van, be aware of the delta mark (on the underside) which indicates the front of the vehicle.

4. To install, use new gaskets and reverse the removal procedures. Torque the converter-to-exhaust pipe bolts to 32 ft. lbs.

GASOLINE ENGINE MECHANICAL

For engine overhaul procedures, refer to "Engine Rebuilding" in the Unit Repair Section.

Engines

Removal and Installation

2WD PICKUPS

1. Drain the cooling system, the engine and the transmission oil.
2. Disconnect and remove the battery from the vehicle. Remove the air cleaner, complete with the attendant hoses.
3. Scribe marks on the hood and its hinges to aid in alignment during installation, then, remove the hood.

NOTE: Do not remove the supports from the hood. If equipped with a windshield washer system, DO NOT remove the hoses from the hood.

4. Remove the radiator hoses, the fan shroud and the radiator.
5. If equipped with A/C, disconnect the compressor and move it aside without disconnect the hoses.

NOTE: If equipped with power steering, remove the drive belt, the bond cable from the bracket, the mounting bolts and the power steering pump, the move it aside without disconnecting the pressure hoses.

6. Remove the fan, the drive pulley and the drive belt. Remove the clamps, then the heater hoses from the engine. Remove the heater control cable from the water valve.
7. Remove the brake booster-to-intake manifold hose, the fuel hose(s) and the emission control hoses.

NOTE: If equipped with an A/T, remove the oil cooler lines from the radiator.

8. If equipped, remove the bond cables from the left-side of the engine and the parking brake bracket.
9. Remove the wiring from the alternator, the igniter-to-distributor, the fuel cut solenoid valve, the carburetor wires, the high tension cable from the igniter, the coolant temperature and oil pressure sending units.

NOTE: If equipped with an EFI system, remove the EGR valve from the plenum chamber, the plenum chamber from the bracket(s), the plenum chamber-to-intake manifold and the plenum chamber with the throttle body.

10. If equipped with a carburetor, remove the accelerator linkage from the carburetor.
11. Depending on the situation, perform one of the following procedures:
    a. If equipped with an A/T, remove the transmission linkage-to-shift lever.
    b. If equipped with a floor-mounted selector, disconnect the control rod from the transmission.
    c. If equipped with a column-mounted gear selector, remove the shifter rod.

12. Disconnect the wiring from the O_2 sensor (if equipped), the thermo switch, the vacuum switch, the VSV switch and etc. Remove the VSV bracket mounting bolts and lay the bracket on the engine.
13. If equipped with a M/T, use the shift lever remover tool No. 09305–20012 to remove the shift lever from the transmission. If equipped with an A/T, disconnect the throttle cable from the carburetor and the valve cover.
14. Raise and support the front of the vehicle on jackstands.
15. At the differential, place alignment marks on the drive shaft and the differential flanges. Remove the mounting bolts and pull the drive shaft from the transmission, then, plug the rear of the transmission with tool No. 09325–20010 or a clean rag to prevent fluid leakage.

NOTE: If equipped with a two piece driveshaft, remove the driveshaft's center bearing-to-frame bolts.

16. Disconnect the wires from the oil pressure switch and the oil pressure sending unit.
17. Disconnect the speedometer cable and the back-up switch wire from the transmission.
18. Disconnect the exhaust pipe from the catalytic converter (if equipped), the exhaust pipe clamp from the transmission housing and the exhaust pipe-to-manifold nuts.
19. Remove the bond cable from the right engine mount.
20. Remove the wires from the starter, the starter mounting bolts and the starter. Remove the clutch release cylinder (M/T) with the bracket and lay it aside.
21. Place a floor jack under the transmission with a block of wood between the transmission and the jack.
22. Remove the retaining screws and remove the parking brake equalizer support bracket. Disconnect the cable which runs between the lever and the equalizer.
23. Remove the bolts from the side and or the rear engine mounting bracket.
24. Attach a chain to the engine lifting brackets and a vertical hoist to the chain.
25. Remove the engine/transmission assembly from the vehicle.

NOTE: Make sure that the wiring and hoses are clear of the engine.

26. Remove the stiffener plate bolts, the mounting bolts and the transmission from the engine, then, support it on a workstand.
27. To install, reverse the removal procedures. Refill the cooling system, the engine and the transmission.

4WD PICKUPS AND 4-RUNNER

NOTE: Refer to the "Transmission and Transfer Case, Removal and Installation" procedures, in this section, then, remove the transfer case and the transmission from the vehicle.

CAUTION

Place a floor jack under the engine with a block of wood between the engine and the jack to prevent damage to front engine mounts.

1. Drain the cooling system, the engine, the transmission and the transfer case oil.
2. Disconnect and remove the battery from the vehicle. Remove the air cleaner, complete with the attendant hoses.
3. Scribe marks on the hood and its hinges to aid in alignment during installation, then remove the hood.

NOTE: Do not remove the supports from the hood. If equipped with a windshield washer system, DO NOT remove the hoses from the hood.

4. Remove the radiator hoses, the fan shroud, the oil cooler lines (A/T) and the radiator.
5. If equipped with A/C, disconnect the compressor and move it aside without disconnect the hoses.

NOTE: If equipped with power steering, remove the drive belt, the bond cable from the bracket, the mounting bolts and the power steering pump, the move it aside without disconnecting the pressure hoses.

6. Remove the fan, the drive pulley and the drive belt. Remove the clamps, then the heater hoses from the engine. Remove the heater control cable from the water valve.
7. Remove the brake booster-to-intake manifold hose, the fuel hose(s) and the emission control hoses.
8. Remove the bond cables (if equipped) from the left-side of the engine and the parking brake bracket.
9. Remove the wiring from the alternator, the igniter-to-distributor, the fuel cut solenoid valve, the carburetor wires (if equipped), the high tension cable from the igniter, the coolant temperature and oil pressure sending units.

NOTE: If equipped with an EFI system, remove the EGR valve from the plenum chamber, the plenum chamber from the bracket(s), the plenum chamber-to-intake manifold and the plenum chamber with the throttle body.

10. If equipped with a carburetor, remove the accelerator linkage from the carburetor.
11. Disconnect the wiring from the O_2 sensor (if equipped), the thermo switch, the vacuum switch, the VSV switch and etc. Remove the VSV bracket mounting bolts and lay the bracket on the engine.
12. If equipped with an A/T, disconnect the throttle cable from the carburetor and the valve cover.
13. Raise and support the front of the vehicle on jackstands.
14. Disconnect the wires from the oil pressure switch and the oil pressure sending unit.
15. Disconnect the exhaust pipe from the catalytic converter (if equipped) and the exhaust pipe-to-manifold nuts.
16. Remove the bond cable from the right engine mount.
17. Remove the wires from the starter, the starter mounting bolts and the starter. Remove the clutch release cylinder (M/T) with the bracket and lay it aside.
18. Remove the retaining screws and remove the parking brake equalizer support bracket. Disconnect the cable which runs between the lever and the equalizer.
19. Attach a chain to the engine lifting brackets and a vertical hoist to the chain.
20. Remove the engine from the vehicle and support it on a workstand.

CAUTION

When removing the engine, make sure that the wiring and hoses are clear of the engine.

21. To install, reverse the removal procedures. Refill the cooling system, the engine, the transmission and the transfer case.

LAND CRUISER AND WAGON

1. Scribe alignment marks on the hood and hinges, then remove the hood. Drain the cooling system and engine oil.
2. Remove the radiator grille mounting bolts and the grille.

NOTE: On station wagon models, remove the parking light assembly and wiring first.

3. Remove the hood latch support rod. Detach the hood latch assembly from the radiator upper bracket, then, remove the bracket.
4. Disconnect the heater and the radiator hoses from the radiator. Remove the radiator bolts and lift the radiator out of the vehicle.
5. Remove the heater hoses from the water valve and heater

box. Disconnect the temperature control cable from the water valve.

6. Remove the the battery cables and the battery. Remove the wires from the starter solenoid terminal.

7. Remove the fuel lines from the pump and the fuel filter assembly.

8. Disconnect the primary wire from the ignition coil.

9. On the column shift models, detach both intermediate rods from the shifter shafts.

10. Remove the air cleaner assembly complete with hoses, from its bracket. Remove the emission control system cables and hoses. Remove the multi-connector from the alternator.

11. Disconnect the hand throttle, the accelerator and the choke linkages from the carburetor.

12. If equipped with vacuum-assisted 4WD engagement, remove the control unit vacuum hose from its manifold fitting.

13. Disconnect the oil pressure and water temperature gauge sender's wiring.

14. Remove the downpipe from the exhaust manifold. Detach the parking brake cable from the intermediate lever.

15. Unbolt and remove the front driveshaft from the flange on the transfer case output shaft.

16. Remove both the left and right engine stone shields, then, the transmission skid-plate.

17. Remove the cotter pin and disconnect both the high and low-range shifter rods from their respective inner levers. Remove the high/low range shifter link lever and rod.

18. Disconnect the clutch release fork spring. Remove the clutch release cylinder from its mounting bracket at the rear of the engine.

19. If equipped with vacuum-assisted 4WD engagement, remove the clamp screws and withdraw the vacuum lines from the transfer case, control unit vacuum chamber.

20. Remove the 4WD indicator switch assembly.

21. Remove the speedometer cable from the transmission.

22. Disconnect the rear driveshaft from the transmission.

23. Detach the gearshift and the gear selector rods from the shift and the gear selector outer levers, respectively.

24. Remove the front and the rear engine mounts from the frame.

25. Install lifting hooks on the engine lift-points and connect to a vertical hoist.

26. Lift the engine slightly and toward the front, so the engine/transmission assembly clears the front of the vehicle.

27. To install, reverse the removal procedures. Refill the engine with coolant and lubricant.

VAN

1. Disconnect the negative battery terminal from the battery.

2. Remove the right seat and the engine service hole cover.

3. Drain the coolant from the radiator. Remove the reservoir tank, the heater hoses and the radiator.

4. Remove the air cleaner, the breather tube, the brake booster, the charcoal canister and the fuel hoses from the engine.

5. If equipped with power steering, remove the drive belt, the pulley, the woodruff key and the pump from the engine, then, move the pump aside.

NOTE: When removing the power steering pump, DO NOT disconnect the pressure lines unless it is absolutely necessary.

6. Disconnect the accelerator cable with the bracket from the throttle body.

7. Disconnect the following wiring connectors from the: water temperature sender, oil pressure switch, IIA unit, A/C compressor, idle-up (A/C), VSV (A/C), A/T, water temperature switch (A/T), alternator connector and wire, air flow meter, solenoid resistor and etc.

8. Remove the fan shroud, the fan, the fluid coupling and the water pump pulley.

9. From inside the vehicle, remove the center pillar cover, the seat belt retractor and cover, then, disconnect the electrical connectors from the ECU.

10. If equipped with A/C, remove the drive belt and the compressor mounting bolts, then, move the compressor aside.

11. Raise and support the vehicle on jackstands, about 3 ft. off the floor.

12. Drain the engine oil. Remove the driveshaft and the front exhaust pipe.

13. Remove the transmission selector and shift cables, then, the clutch release cylinder (M/T).

14. Disconnect the starter wires, the mounting bolts and the starter from the engine.

15. Remove the speedometer cable, the bond cable and the back-up light switch connector.

16. If equipped with a rear heater, disconnect the mode selector and the air mix damper cable from the damper. Disconnect the heater hoses to the rear heater unit.

17. Disconnect the bond cable(s) from the engine mount(s). Remove the engine under cover.

18. Disconnect the oil level sensor and the oil cooler hoses (A/T).

19. Place matchmarks on the front strut bar and the rear mounting nut. Remove the rear nut, the strut bar-to-lower control arm bolts and the strut.

20. Using an engine saddle, place it under the engine and support it. Place a floor jack under the transmission and support it.

NOTE: If equipped with a M/T, remove the engine rear mounting bracket from the body. If equipped with A/T, remove the engine mounting member-to-transmission through bolt.

21. Remove the engine mounts-to-body nuts/bolts and lower the engine/transmission assembly, then, remove the engine mounting member from the engine.

22. Remove the transmission from the engine.

23. To install, reverse the removal procedures. Refill the engine with oil and the cooling system with coolant.

Diesel Engines

Removal and Installation

L ENGINE (1982–83)

1. Scribe match-marks on the hood and the hood supports. Remove the hood.

2. Remove the batteries from the vehicle.

NOTE: Some models may require the removal of both batteries from the vehicle.

3. Drain the cooling system and remove the radiator, shroud and radiator hoses.

4. If the vehicle is equipped with A/C, remove the compressor drive belt, unbolt the compressor and tie the compressor out of the way. DO NOT disconnect the refrigerant lines from the compressor.

5. Remove the drive belt, the water pump pulley and the cooling fan.

6. Disconnect the two heater hoses from the left-side of the engine.

7. Disconnect the vacuum reservoir hose from the rear of the alternator.

8. Disconnect the vacuum hose from the "idle-up" unit, if the vehicle is equipped with air conditioning.

9. Disconnect the fuel hoses from the fuel injection pump.

10. Disconnect the wiring from the following components:

a. Alternator.
b. Thermo-switch.
c. Oil pressure switch.
d. No. 1 glow plug relay (terminal +B).
e. Starter.

NOTE: Mark these wires and tie them out of the way.

11. Disconnect the wiring from the left fender and the injection pump (accelerator wire). Also mark and tie these wires out of the way.
12. Using Toyota special service tool No. 09305–20012, or its equivalent, remove the transmission shift lever from inside the vehicle.
13. Raise and support the vehicle on jackstands.
14. Drain the engine oil. Remove the engine under-cover and remove the backup light switch wire.
15. Remove the engine shock absorber and the driveshaft from the vehicle.

NOTE: Mark the drive shaft and the companion flange so that the shaft may be reinstalled in its original position.

16. Remove the speedometer cable and the exhaust pipe clamp from the transmission housing, then the exhaust pipe mounting nuts from the exhaust manifold.
17. Remove the clutch release cylinder and lay the cylinder along-side the frame.
18. Remove the engine mounting bolts from each side of the engine.
19. Place a jack under the transmission to support it. Remove the rear mount bracket at the crossmember and the crossmember.
20. Attach the engine lifting device to the engine.

NOTE: Check that all wiring and hoses are clear of the engine/transmission assembly.

21. Carefully, raise the engine/transmission assembly out of the engine compartment, being especially careful not to damage the air conditioning compressor, if equipped.
22. Remove the starter and the transmission from the engine, then mount the engine securely to a workstand.
23. To install, reverse the removal procedures. Refill the cooling system, the engine oil and/or the transmission.

2L AND 2L-T ENGINES (1984-88)

NOTE: If equipped with 2WD, refer to the "Transmission, Removal and Installation" procedures, in this section and remove the transmission. If equipped with 4WD, refer to the "Transmission/Transfer Case, Removal and Installation" procedures, in this section and remove the transmission with the transfer case. DO NOT drain the fluid from the transmission or the transfer case.

1. Scribe match-marks on the hood and the hood supports, then, remove the hood.
2. Remove the negative battery terminal from the battery.
3. Drain the cooling system by opening the drain cocks at the radiator and the left-side of the engine block.
4. Remove the radiator hoses, the upper radiator shroud, the coolant reservoir hose, the mounting bolts and the radiator.

NOTE: If equipped with A/C, remove the lower radiator shroud.

5. If equipped with a 2L engine, remove the air cleaner.
6. Disconnect the accelerator cable from the fuel injection pump.
7. If equipped with A/C, remove the A/C vacuum hose from the VSV. Remove the drive belt, then the A/C compressor and move it aside. DO NOT disconnect the refrigerant lines from the compressor.
8. If equipped with a 2L-T engine, remove the turbocharger pressure hose from the pressure switch.
9. Disconnect the oil inlet hose from the vacuum pump.
10. Remove the inlet and the outlet fuel lines from the fuel injection pump.
11. Remove the wires or the electrical connectors from the following:
    a. The glow plug current sensor.
    b. The water temperature sensor.
    c. The glow plug resistor.
    d. The injection pump.
    e. The water temperature sender gauge.
    f. The starter.
    g. The engine ground cables.
    h. The oil pressure switch.
    i. The alternator.

NOTE: On California models, disconnect the throttle position sensor and the EVRV connectors. For 4WD models, disconnect the water temperature switch. Mark these wires and tie them out of the way.

12. Remove the engine splash shield.
13. If equipped with P/S, remove the drive belt, the mounting bolts and the pump, then, move the pump aside. DO NOT disconnect the power steering pressure hoses.
14. If equipped with 2WD, remove the engine mounting shock absorber from the crossmember.
15. Remove the engine mounting insulator-to-crossmember nuts and bolts.
16. Remove the exhaust pipe mounting nuts from the exhaust manifold.
17. Attach the engine lifting device to the engine.

NOTE: Check that all wiring and hoses are clear of the engine.

18. Carefully, raise the engine out of the engine compartment, being especially careful not to damage the A/C compressor, if equipped.
19. Remove the starter and mount the engine securely to a workstand.
20. To install, reverse the removal procedures. Refill the cooling system and the engine oil. Adjust the drive belts.

Intake Manifold

Removal and Installation

22R ENGINES

1. Disconnect the battery negative cable. Drain the engine coolant to a level below the carburetor.
2. Remove the air cleaner assembly, complete with hoses.
3. Label and disconnect the vacuum lines from the manifold and the carburetor.
4. Remove the fuel line, the accelerator linkage, the electrical leads and the coolant hoses from the carburetor.
5. Remove the coolant by-pass hose from the manifold.
6. Remove the air valve from the intake manifold.
7. Unbolt and remove the intake manifold, complete with carburetor and EGR valve.
8. Cover the cylinder head intake ports with a clean cloth.
9. Using a putty knife, clean the gasket mounting surfaces.
10. To install, use a new gasket and reverse the removal procedures. Torque the mounting nuts to 13–19 ft. lbs. Refill the cooling system.

NOTE: Tighten the bolts in several stages, working from the inside bolts outward.

22R-E AND 22R-TE ENGINES

1. Disconnect the battery negative terminal from the battery.
2. If equipped with a 22R-E engine, remove the air cleaner hose from the throttle body; if equipped with a 22R-TE engine, remove the turbocharger air tube from the throttle body. Drain the cooling system to a level below the throttle body.
3. From the throttle body, remove the fuel lines from the distribution rail, the accelerator linkage, the throttle position sen-

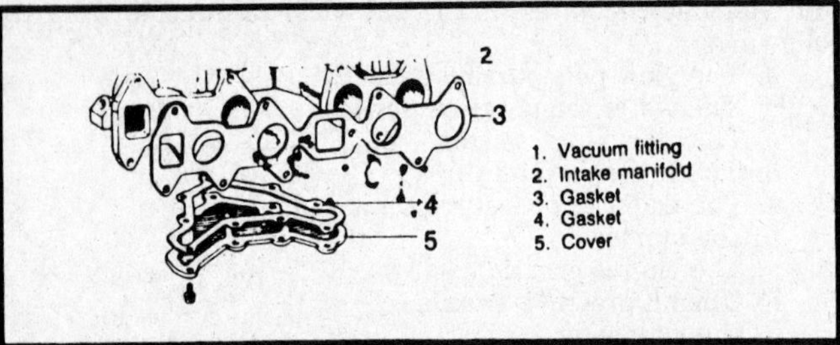

Exploded view of the intake manifold – 22R engine

sor, the electrical leads, the coolant hoses, the PCV hose and the emission control hoses.

4. Remove the throttle body with the air intake chamber from the intake manifold.
5. Remove the coolant by-pass hose from the intake manifold.
6. Remove the intake manifold with the EGR valve.
7. Cover the cylinder head intake ports with a clean cloth.
8. Using a putty knife, clean the gasket mounting surfaces.
9. To install, use a new gaskets and reverse the removal procedures. Torque the mounting nuts to 13–19 ft. lbs. Refill the cooling system.

NOTE: Tighten the bolts in several stages, working from the inside bolts outward.

Exhaust Manifold

Removal and Installation

22R AND 22R-E ENGINES

1. Remove the exhaust pipe flange bolts and disconnect the exhaust pipe from the manifold.

NOTE: On the 22R-E engine, disconnect the O_2 sensor wiring connector.

2. Remove the air cleaner tube from the heat stove. Remove the outer part of the heat stove.
3. Remove the mounting nuts, the exhaust insulator, the exhaust manifold with the air injection tube, then, separate the inner portion of the heat stove from the manifold.
4. To install, use new gaskets and reverse the removal procedures. Torque the retaining nuts to 29–36 ft. lbs. (working from the inside out) and the exhaust pipe flange nuts to 25–32 ft. lbs.

22R-TE ENGINE

1. Disconnect the negative battery terminal from the battery.
2. Place a clean drain pan under the radiator and drain the cooling system to a level below the turbocharger.
3. From the turbocharger outlet elbow, disconnect the O_2 sensor wire clamp and the connector.
4. To remove the turbocharger-to-intake plenum air tube, perform the following procedures:
   a. From the air tube, disconnect the No. 1 and 3 PCV hoses.
   b. From the turbocharger, disconnect the No. 1 and 2 water hoses.
   c. From the throttle body, loosen the air tube clamp.
   d. Remove the air tube-to-turbocharger nuts, the air tube and the gasket.
5. Remove the No. 1 air cleaner hose assembly and the No. 2 air cleaner-to-turbocharger hose.
6. Remove the turbocharger and exhaust manifold heat insulators.
7. From the turbocharger, remove the No. 3 water hose clamp and disconnect the hose.
8. Raise and support the front of the vehicle on jackstands.
9. To disconnect the exhaust pipe from the turbo outlet elbow, perform the following procedures:

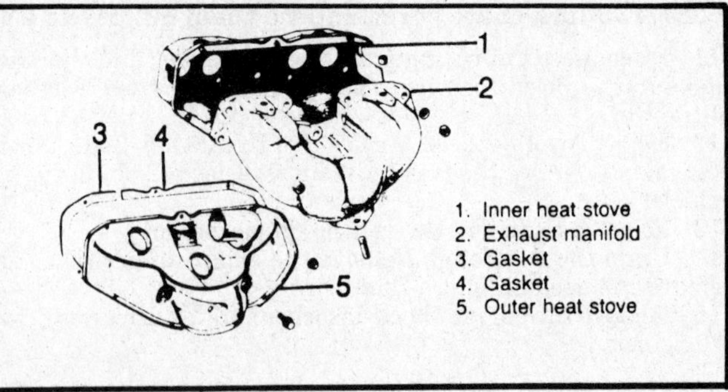

Exploded view of the exhaust manifold – 22R and 22R-E engines

   a. Remove the exhaust pipe-to-turbo outlet elbow nuts.
   b. Loosen the exhaust pipe-to-exhaust system clamp bolt/nut, then, disconnect the clamp.
   c. Disconnect the exhaust pipe from the turbo outlet elbow and remove the gasket.
10. Remove the turbocharger-to-engine stay bolts and the stay.
11. Remove the turbo oil pipe-to-turbocharger union bolt, then, separate the union and the two gaskets.
12. Remove the turbocharger oil pipe-to-turbocharger bolts, then separate the oil pipe and the gasket from the turbocharger.

NOTE: The turbocharger may be separated from the exhaust manifold or it may be removed with the exhaust manifold as an assembly.

13. Remove the exhaust manifold-to-cylinder head nuts, the turbocharger/exhaust manifold assembly and the gasket.
14. If necessary, remove the turbocharger-to-exhaust manifold bolts, the turbocharger and the gaskets.
15. Using a putty knife, clean the gasket mounting surfaces.

NOTE: When installing the new turbo-to-exhaust manifold gasket, make sure the gasket groove is positioned facing upward. After installing the turbocharger assembly, pour 20cc of new oil into the oil inlet hole, turn the impeller wheel (by hand) to splash oil on the bearing.

16. To install, use new gaskets and reverse the removal procedures. Torque the turbocharger-to-exhaust manifold nuts to 29 ft. lbs., the exhaust manifold-to-cylinder head nuts to 33 ft. lbs., the oil pipe union-to-turbocharger bolt to 20 ft. lbs., the oil pipe union-to-turbocharger nuts to 14 ft. lbs., the turbo stay-to-turbocharger bolts to 14 ft. lbs., the turbo stay-to-engine bolt to 29 ft. lbs., the exhaust pipe-to-turbo outlet elbow nuts to 32 ft. lbs. Refill the cooling system. Start the engine, allow it to reach operating temperatures and check for leaks.

Combination Manifold

Removal and Installation

2F, 3B AND 2H Engines

1. Remove the air cleaner assembly, complete with hoses.
2. Disconnect the accelerator and choke linkages, then the fuel and vacuum lines from the carburetor. Remove the hand throttle linkage.
3. Remove or move aside, any of the emission control system components which are in the way.
4. Disconnect the oil filter lines and remove the oil filter assembly from the intake manifold. Disconnect the solenoid valve wire from the ignition coil terminal. Remove the EGR tubes from the exhaust gas cooler, if equipped.
5. Remove the mounting bolts and the carburetor from the manifold.

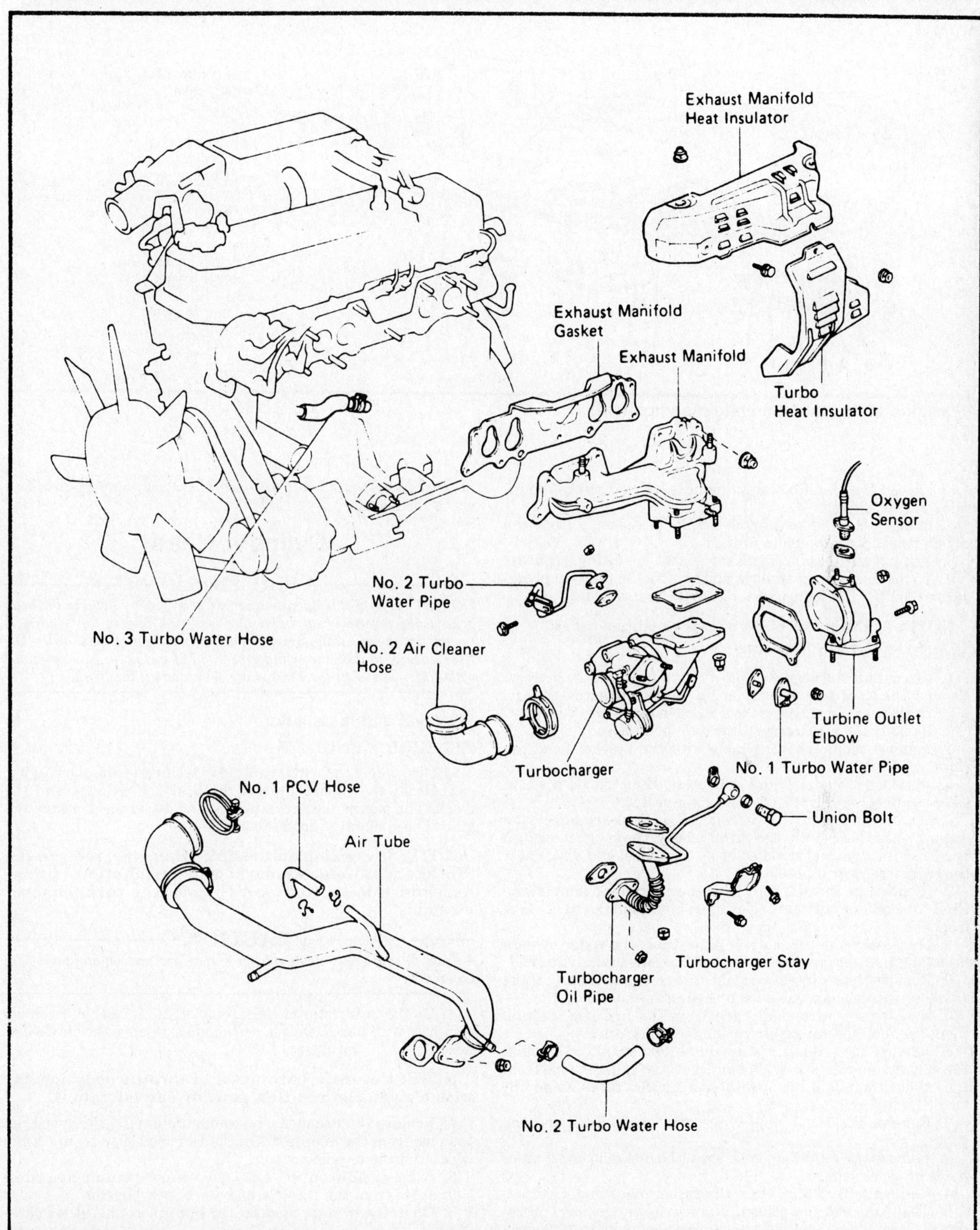

Exploded view of the turbocharger assembly—22R-TE engine

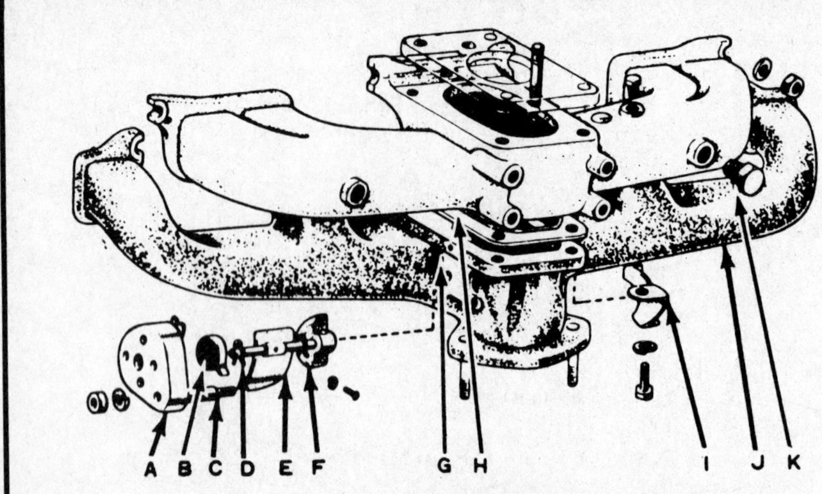

2F engine combination manifold components

6. Loosen the manifold retaining nuts, working from the inside out, in 2-3 steps.

7. Remove the intake/exhaust manifold assembly from the cylinder head as a complete unit.

8. Using a putty knife, clean the gasket mounting surfaces.

9. To install, use new gaskets and reverse the removal procedures. Tighten the bolts, working from the inside out.

NOTE: Tighten the bolts in two or three stages.

3Y-EC AND 4Y-E ENGINES

1. Disconnect the negative battery terminal from the battery. Remove the right seat and the engine service hole cover.

2. Drain the engine coolant to a level below the throttle body.

3. Remove the air cleaner-to-throttle body hose.

4. Remove the accelerator cable with the bracket from the throttle body.

5. Disconnect the air valve connector, the throttle position sensor connector and the O_2 sensor connector.

6. Disconnect the PCV hose from the air intake chamber, the water by-pass hoses from the throttle body, the booster vacuum hose and the charcoal canister hose, then label and disconnect the emission control hoses.

7. Remove the throttle body from the air intake chamber, the EGR tube union nut from the exhaust manifold, the EGR valve from the air intake chamber.

8. Disconnect the cold start injector tube, the water by-pass hoses and the pressure regulator hose from the intake manifold.

9. Remove the air intake chamber brackets and the air intake chamber with the air valve from the intake manifold.

10. Remove the wire clamp bolt from the fuel injector rail, then, the fuel injector rail from the fuel injectors.

11. Remove the exhaust manifold-to-intake manifold bracket, the exhaust manifold-to-engine bracket, the exhaust pipe from the exhaust manifold, the fuel inlet and outlet tubes union nut from the fuel rail.

12. Remove the spark plug wires, the spark plugs and the tubes.

13. Remove the retaining bolts, then, the intake/exhaust manifolds as an assembly.

14. Using a putty knife, clean the gasket mounting surfaces.

15. To install, use new gaskets and reverse the removal procedures. Torque the manifold-to-cylinder head bolts to 36 ft. lbs., the air intake chamber-to-intake manifold bolts to 9 ft. lbs. and the throttle body bolts to 9 ft. lbs. Refill the cooling system. Start the engine, allow it to reach operating temperatures and check for leaks.

Cylinder Head

CAUTION

DO NOT perform this operation on a warm engine. Remove the head bolts in the reverse of the tightening sequence. Loosen the head bolts evenly, not one at a time. Keep the pushrods in their original order. DO NOT attempt to slide the cylinder head off of the block, as it is located with dowel pins. Lift the head straight up and off the block.

Removal and Installation

22R SERIES ENGINES

1. Disconnect the battery negative terminal from the battery.

2. Drain the cooling system, both at the radiator and the block. The engine block drain is on the driver's side of the engine. The coolant, if good, may be reused.

NOTE: If working on the 22R-TE engine, refer to the "Intake Manifold, Removal and Installation" procedures in this section and remove the turbocharger assembly.

CAUTION

Be sure to drain the engine oil, for it may become contaminated with coolant.

3. On the carburetor models, remove the air cleaner assembly complete with hoses. On the EFI models, remove the air cleaner hose.

NOTE: Cover the carburetor or throttle body opening with a clean cloth so that nothing can fall into it.

4. Remove the exhaust pipe-to-manifold nuts, then separate the pipe from the manifold. On the EFI models, disconnect the wire from the oxygen sensor.

5. Label and disconnect all of the various vacuum and emission hoses from the throttle body or the carburetor.

6. On the carburetor models (1984-88), disconnect the following wire(s):

a. The Vacuum Switching Valve (VSV) for A/C.

b. The vacuum switch.

c. The VSV for the Evaporative Emission Control (EVAP).
d. The water temperature sender gauge.
e. The cold mixture heater.
f. The fuel cut solenoid valve.
g. The Electronic Air Control Valve (EACV).
h. The Vacuum Control Switch (VCS).

7. On the EFI models (1984-88), disconnect the following wire(s):

a. The cold start injector.
b. The throttle position sensor.
c. The water temperature sender gauge.
d. The temperature sensor.
e. The start injection time switch.
f. The Overdrive (OD) thermo switch (for A/T).
g. The injectors.
h. The air valve.

8. At the cylinder head cover, remove the PCV hose, the spark plug wire holders, the distributor wiring connector and the throttle cable (if equipped with an A/T). Remove the mounting nuts and seals, then, lift off the cylinder head cover.

CAUTION

Cover the oil return hole in the cylinder head to prevent objects from falling in.

9. Remove the upper radiator hose from the thermostat housing.

10. On the EFI models, remove the EGR valve from the chamber, the chamber-to-brace, the chamber-to-manifold nuts/bolts and the chamber with the throttle body.

11. At the distributor:

a. Match-mark the rotor-to-distributor housing and the distributor housing-to-engine block.

b. Disconnect the spark plug cables from the spark plugs (pull on the plug boot).

c. Disconnect the primary ignition wire from the distributor cap and the electrical connector from the housing.

d. Remove the distributor hold-down clamp, then, the distributor from the cylinder head with the high tension cables attached.

12. Remove the fuel hoses from the fuel pump, the mounting bolts, the fuel pump and the gaskets from the cylinder head.

13. Disconnect the bond cables from the front and the rear of the cylinder head, then the wire(s) from the carburetor and the thermo-switch.

NOTE: If equipped with P/S, remove the drive belt, the pulley, the pump and the bracket, then, move the pump aside without disconnecting the pressure hoses.

14. On the carburetor models, disconnect the following hoses:

a. The water by-pass hose from the intake manifold.
b. The heater inlet hose from the water valve.
c. The brake booster hose from the intake manifold.
d. The 2 fuel hoses from the pipes under the intake manifold.
e. On Calif. models, the hose from the air injection tube.
f. Label and disconnect the emission control hoses from the carburetor and the intake manifold that will interfere with the head removal.

15. On the EFI models, disconnect the following:

a. The No. 1 and No. 2 hoses at the PCV.
b. The air control valve hose.
c. The actuator (cruise control) hose.
d. The EGR vacuum modulator hose.
e. The No. 1 air valve hose from the throttle body.
f. The No. 2 air valve hose from the chamber.
g. The No. 2 and No. 3 water by-pass hoses from the throttle body.
h. The actuator's air control valve hose.
i. The pressure regulator hose for the actuator.
j. The cold start injection tube.
k. The Bi-metal Vacuum Switch Valve (BVSV) hoses.
l. The brake booster hose.

16. On the carburetor models, disconnect the accelerator linkage from the carburetor. If equipped with an A/T, disconnect the throttle cable from the carburetor.

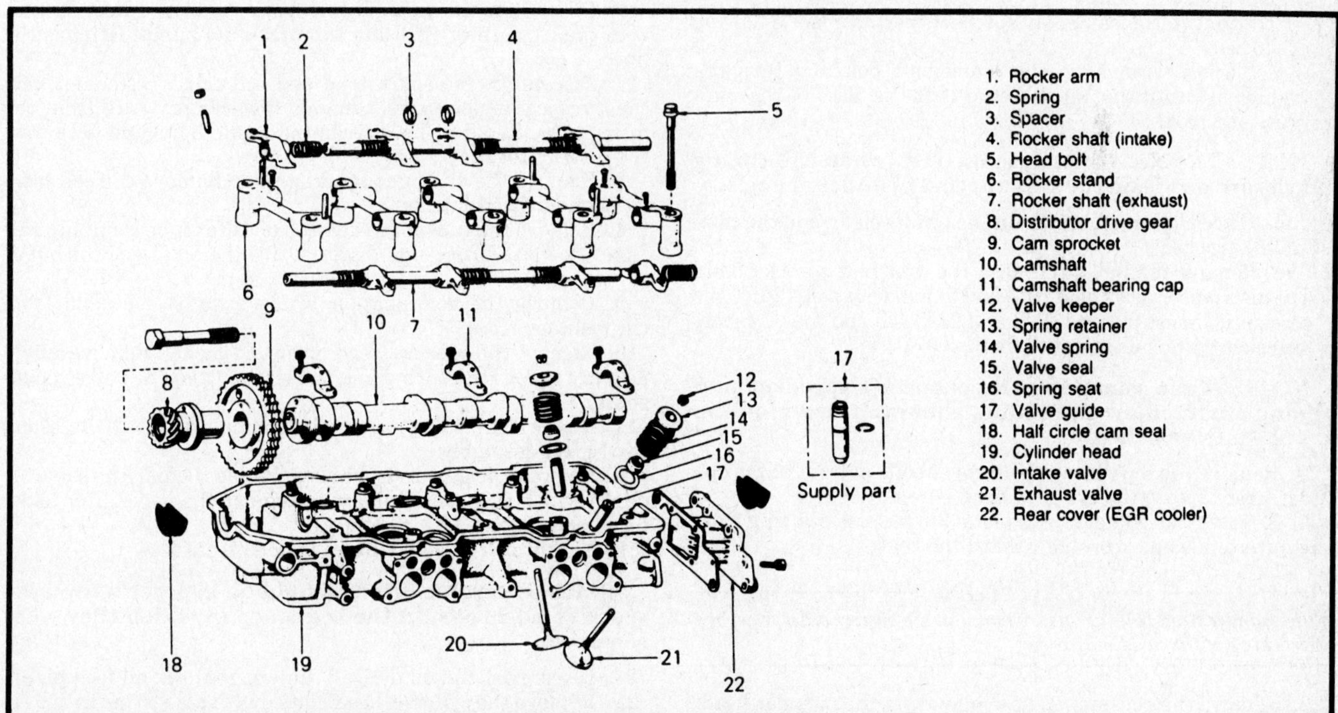

Exploded view of the cylinder head components—22R series engines

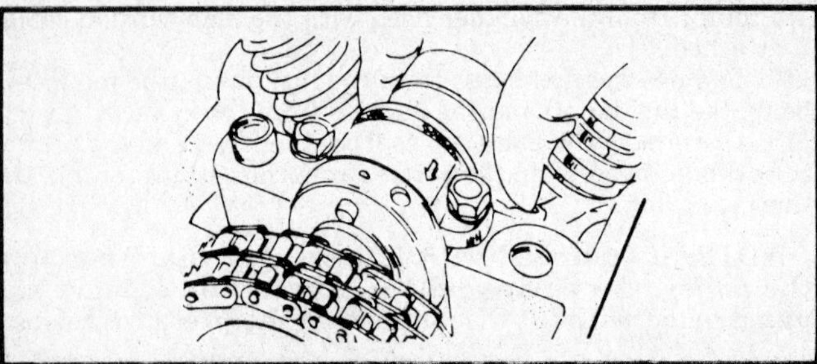

Rotate the camshaft so that the pin is at the top. Also note that the arrow on the camshaft bearing cap points to the front of the engine—22R series engines

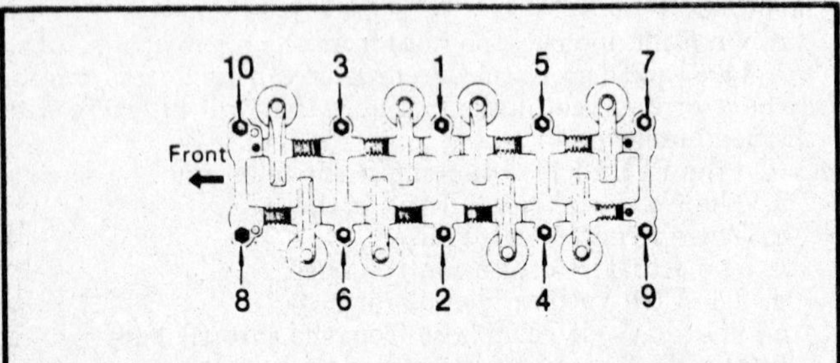

Cylinder head bolt torquing sequence—22R series engines

17. On the carburetor models (Federal and Canada), remove the air suction rear pipe.
18. On the EFI models, remove the pulsation damper, the fuel hose-to-delivery tube bolt and the fuel hose from the delivery tube. Disconnect the No. 4 by-pass hose from the air valve and the air valve from the intake manifold, then the by-pass hose from the intake manifold.
19. To remove the camshaft sprocket, perform the following procedures:
   a. Place a wrench on the crankshaft bolt and turn the crankshaft until the No. 1 piston is at the TDC of the compression stroke.

NOTE: The No. 1 piston is on TDC when the timing marks are on 0° and the valve of that cylinder are closed.

   b. Place alignment marks on the timing chain and the camshaft sprocket.
   c. Remove the half circle seal, the camshaft sprocket bolt, the distributor drive gear, the fuel pump drive cam (22R), the camshaft thrust plate (22R-E and 22R-TE) and the camshaft sprocket with the timing chain.

NOTE: When removing the camshaft sprocket and timing chain, allow the timing chain to remain on the crankshaft sprocket.

20. Remove the top timing chain cover bolt (in front of the cylinder head, before the cylinder head is removed.
21. Remove the cylinder head bolts (2-3 passes), starting from the outer ends and working toward the center.

CAUTION

If the cylinder head bolts are not removed in the correct order, warpage or cracking of the head may occur.

22. Remove the rocker arm assembly from the cylinder head. It may be necessary to use a small pry bar to loosen the rocker arm assembly.
23. Lift the cylinder head from the engine, place it on a workbench and support it on 2 blocks of wood.

CAUTION

DO NOT pry between the cylinder head gasket and the engine block.

24. To install, use new gaskets and reverse the removal procedures. Torque the cylinder head-to-engine block to 58 ft. lbs., the timing chain cover-to-cylinder head bolt to 9 ft. lbs., the camshaft sprocket-to-camshaft bolt to 58 ft. lbs., the intake manifold bolts to 14 ft. lbs., the exhaust manifold bolts to 33 ft. lbs. and the rocker arm cover to 7–12 ft. lbs. Replace the cooling system fluid and the engine oil. Adjust the valves, the drive belts, then, check and/or adjust the timing.

2F, 3B AND 2H ENGINES

1. Disconnect the negative battery terminal from the battery. Place a clean drain pan under the radiator and drain the cooling system.
2. Remove the air cleaner assembly, complete with its attendant hoses.
3. Detach the accelerator cable from the cylinder head cover support and the carburetor throttle arm.
4. Remove the choke cable and fuel lines from the carburetor. Remove the water hose bracket from the cylinder head cover.
5. Remove the clamps and the hoses from the water pump, then, the water valve. Disconnect the heater temperature control cable from the water valve.
6. Disconnect the PCV line from the cylinder head cover. Disconnect the vacuum lines, from the vacuum switching valve to the various components of the emission control system.
7. Position a drain pan under the engine, remove the oil pan drain plug and drain the engine oil. Remove the oil lines from the oil filter and the filter assembly from the manifold.
8. Detach the vacuum valve solenoid wire from the coil.
9. Disconnect any remaining lines from the carburetor and remove the carburetor from the manifold.
10. Remove the alternator adjusting link, then, the drivebelt and the alternator.
11. Disconnect the vacuum line from the distributor. Disconnect the carburetor fuel line from the fuel pump. Remove the line.
12. Disconnect the spark plug and coil cables, after marking their respective locations. Remove the primary wire from the distributor. Remove the distributor clamp bolts and withdraw the distributor.
13. Remove the oil gauge sending unit. Remove the coil from its cylinder head bracket.
14. Remove the fuel pump and the oil filter tube clamping bolt from the valve lifter (side) cover. Drive the oil filler tube out of the cylinder block.
15. Remove the combination intake/exhaust manifold from the cylinder block.
16. Remove the cylinder head cover and gasket. Remove the oil delivery union, the spring and the sleeve from the valve rocker shafts.
17. Remove the valve rocker shaft supports nuts/bolts, then, the rocker assembly.
18. Remove the pushrods, be sure to keep them in the same order in which they were removed. Remove the valve lifter (side) cover and gasket.
19. Withdraw the valve lifters from the block.

NOTE: The valve lifters should be kept with their respective pushrods, in the sequence in which they were removed.

20. Disconnect the oil delivery union from the oil feed pipe.
21. Remove the cylinder head bolts in 2–3 stages and in the reverse order of installation.
22. Lift off the cylinder head and the gasket.

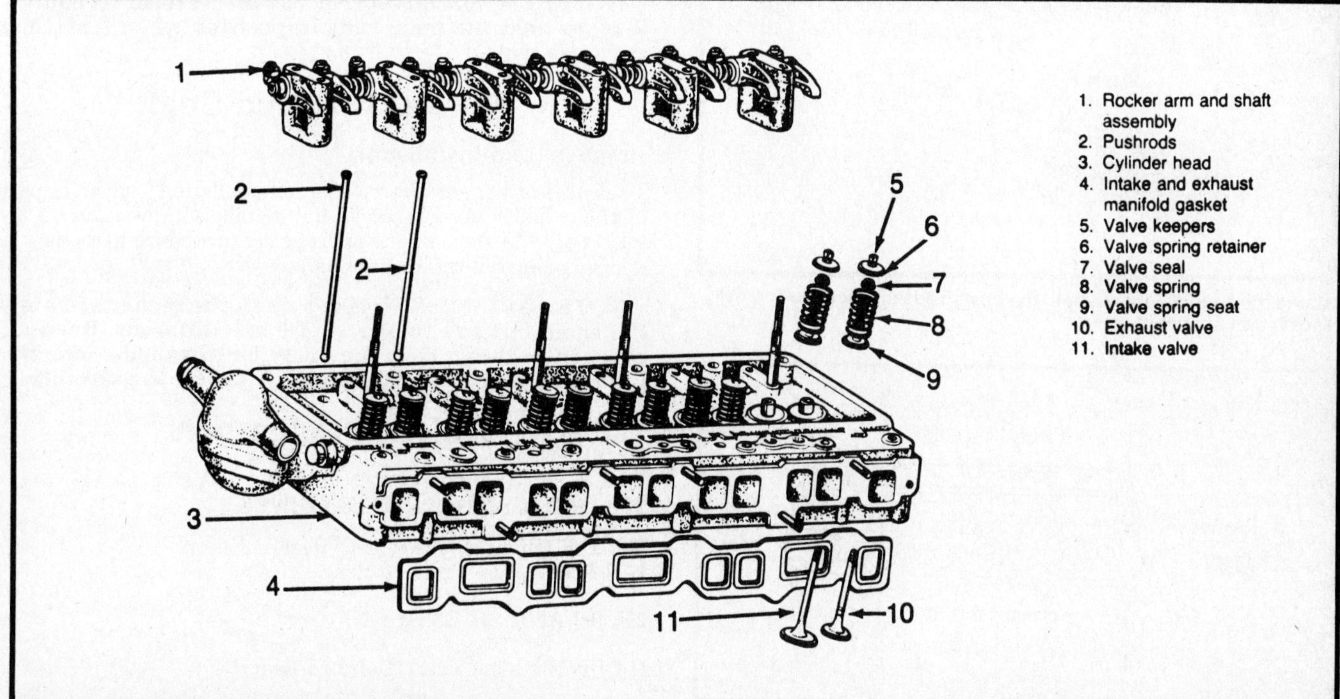

Cylinder head components – 2F engine

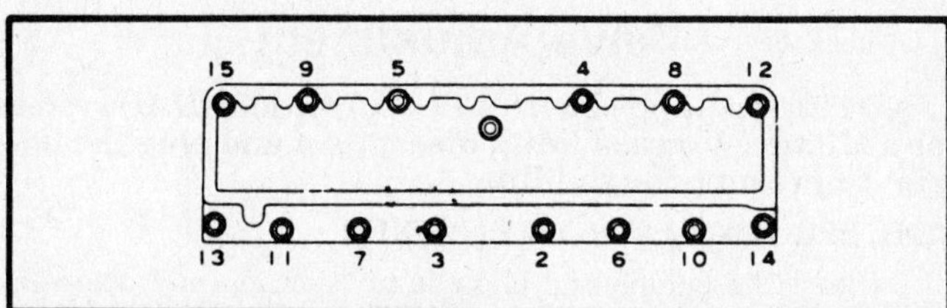

Cylinder head bolt tightening sequence – 2F engine

NOTE: Cylinder head service procedures are covered in the Unit Repair Section.

23. To install, use new gaskets and reverse the removal procedures. Torque the cylinder head bolts to 83–98 ft. lbs. (in 3 steps), the rocker assembly nuts/bolts to 25–30 ft. lbs. (10mm) or 14–22 ft. lbs. (8mm). Adjust the valves. Refill the cooling system. Check and/or adjust the timing. Start the engine, allow it to reach operating temperatures and check for leaks.

3Y-EC AND 4Y-E ENGINES

1. Disconnect the negative battery terminal from the battery.
2. Remove the right-front seat and the engine service hole cover.
3. Drain the engine coolant (at the radiator and the left-side of the engine) and the engine oil.
4. If equipped with P/S, perform the following:
   a. Remove the air hoses from the air control valve.
   b. Drain the fluid from the reservoir tank.
   c. Disconnect the return hose from the pump.
   d. Using the tool No. 09631-22020, or its equivalent, disconnect the pressure hose from the pump.
   e. Remove the drive belt, the pulley nut, the pulley, the woodruff key, the mounting bolts and the pump.
5. Remove the exhaust pipe and the bracket. Remove the air cleaner pipe and the hoses.
6. Disconnect the accelerator cable with the bracket from the throttle body.
7. Disconnect the water temperature sender gauge connector from the cylinder head.
8. Disconnect the following EFI connectors from the:
   a. The water thermo sensor.
   b. The start injector time switch.
   c. The cold start injector.
   d. The air valve.
   e. The throttle position sensor.
   f. The oxygen sensor.
   g. The water temperature switch (A/C).
9. Disconnect the following hoses from the:
   a. The radiator inlet.
   b. The radiator breather.
   c. The reserve tank.
   d. The heater outlet.
   e. The PCV.
   f. The water by-pass.
   g. The brake booster vacuum.
   h. The charcoal canister.
   i. Label and disconnect the emission control.
10. Remove the throttle body from the air intake chamber.
11. Remove the EGR valve nuts from the intake chamber and the exhaust manifold-to-EGR valve union.
12. Disconnect the cold start injector pipe, the water by-pass hoses and the pressure regulator hose.
13. Using a 12mm offset box wrench, remove the air intake chamber brackets, then, the chamber with the air valve.
14. Remove the wire clamp bolts and the injector connectors from the injectors.
15. Remove the exhaust manifold bracket, the heater pipe bracket, the fuel inlet pipe union bolt from the fuel filter and the fuel outlet hose.
16. Remove the spark plugs and the tubes.
17. Remove the cap nuts, the seal washers, the cylinder head cover and the gasket.
18. Remove the rocker arm shaft assembly nuts/bolts a little at

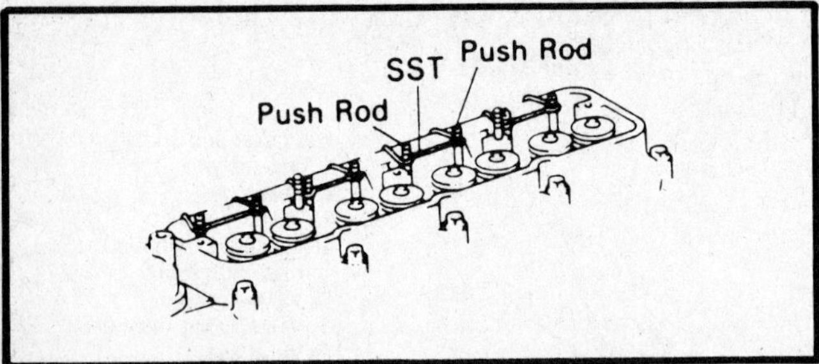

Using the special tools to hold the push rods in place, during the rocker arm installation

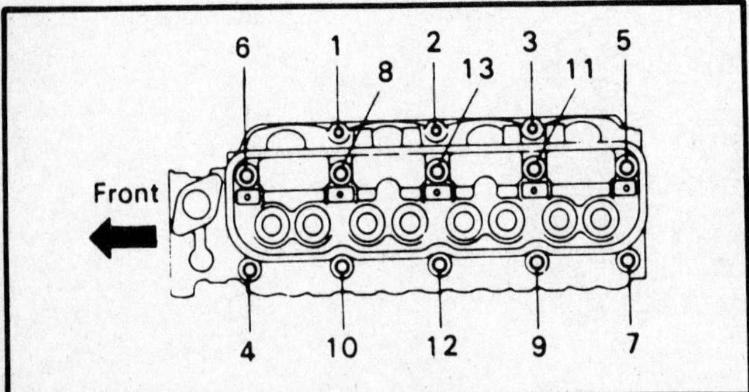

Cylinder head bolt removal sequence – 3Y-EC and 4Y-E engines

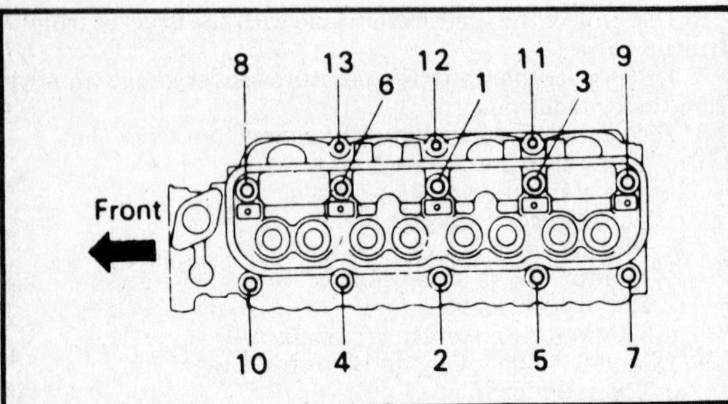

Cylinder head bolt tightening sequence – 3Y-EC and 4Y-E engines

a time, in 3–4 steps. Remove the push rods, keeping them in order.

19. Remove the cylinder head bolts, a little at a time, in 3 passes. Lift the cylinder head off of the dowels and place it on 2 blocks of wood.

CAUTION

If the cylinder head bolts are not removed correctly, warpage or cracking of the cylinder head may occur. If necessary to pry the cylinder head from the block, pry between the cylinder head and the block projection.

20. Remove the valve lifters from the cylinder block.
21. Using a putty knife, clean the gasket mounting surfaces.
22. To install, use new gaskets and reverse the removal procedures. Torque the cylinder head bolts (in 3 passes) to 65 ft. lbs. (14mm) or 14 ft. lbs. (12mm), the rocker arm shaft-to-cylinder head bolts (in 3 passes) to 17 ft. lbs., the spark plugs to 13 ft. lbs., the air intake chamber bolts to 9 ft. lbs., the throttle body-to-intake chamber to 9 ft. lbs. and the exhaust pipe-to-exhaust manifold to 29 ft. lbs. Adjust the drive belts. Refill the cooling system and the engine with oil. Check and/or adjust the timing.

NOTE: Use special tool No. 09270–71010, or its equivalent, to hold the push rods in position when installing the push rods.

Rocker Arm and Shaft

Removal and Installation

The valve rocker shaft removal and installation is given as part of the cylinder head removal and installation procedure. Perform only the steps of the appropriate procedure necessary to remove or install the rocker shafts.

NOTE: On the 22R series engines, the rocker arms are the same but the rocker shafts are different. Keep all parts in order so that they may be installed correctly. Lubricate all parts with engine oil prior to assembly.

Valve Arrangement

22R, 22R-E AND 22R-TE ENGINES

E-E-E-E (Right-side, Front-to-Rear)
I-I-I-I (Left-side, Front-to-Rear)

2F, 3B AND 2H ENGINES

E-I-I-E-E-I-I-E-E-I-I-E (Front-to-Rear)

3Y-EC AND 4Y-E ENGINES

E-I-I-E-E-I-I-E (Front-to-Rear)

Valve Adjustment

NOTE: If equipped with a Hot Air Intake (HAI) system or a Mixture Control (MC), disconnect and plug the hose(s) to prevent rough idling.

22R, 22R-E AND 22R-TE ENGINES

1. Start the engine and allow it to reach normal operating temperatures (above 175°F).
2. Stop the engine. Remove the air cleaner assembly, the hoses and the bracket, then any cables, hoses, wires and etc., which are attached to the valve cover. Remove the valve cover.
3. Set the No. 1 cylinder to TDC of the compression stroke. Place a wrench on the crankshaft pulley bolt and turn the engine until the notch on the crankshaft pulley is aligned with the 0° mark on the timing plate; the engine is at TDC.

NOTE: The rocker arms on cylinder No. 1 should be loose and the rocker arms on cylinder No. 4 should be tight.

CAUTION

DO NOT start the engine. Valve clearances are checked with the engine stopped to prevent hot oil from being splashed out by the timing chain.

4. With the engine "Hot", the valve clearances are 0.008 in. (intake) and 0.012 in. (exhaust).

NOTE: The clearance is measured with a feeler gauge between the valve stem and the adjusting screw.

5. To adjust the valve clearance, loosen the locknut and turn the adjusting screw until the specified clearance is obtained. Tighten the locknut and check the clearance again. Adjust the intake valves of No. 1 and 2 cylinders; the exhaust valves of No. 1 and 3 cylinders.
6. Turn the crankshaft one revolution (360°). Adjust the intake valves of No. 3 and 4 cylinders; the exhaust valves of No. 2 and 4 cylinders.

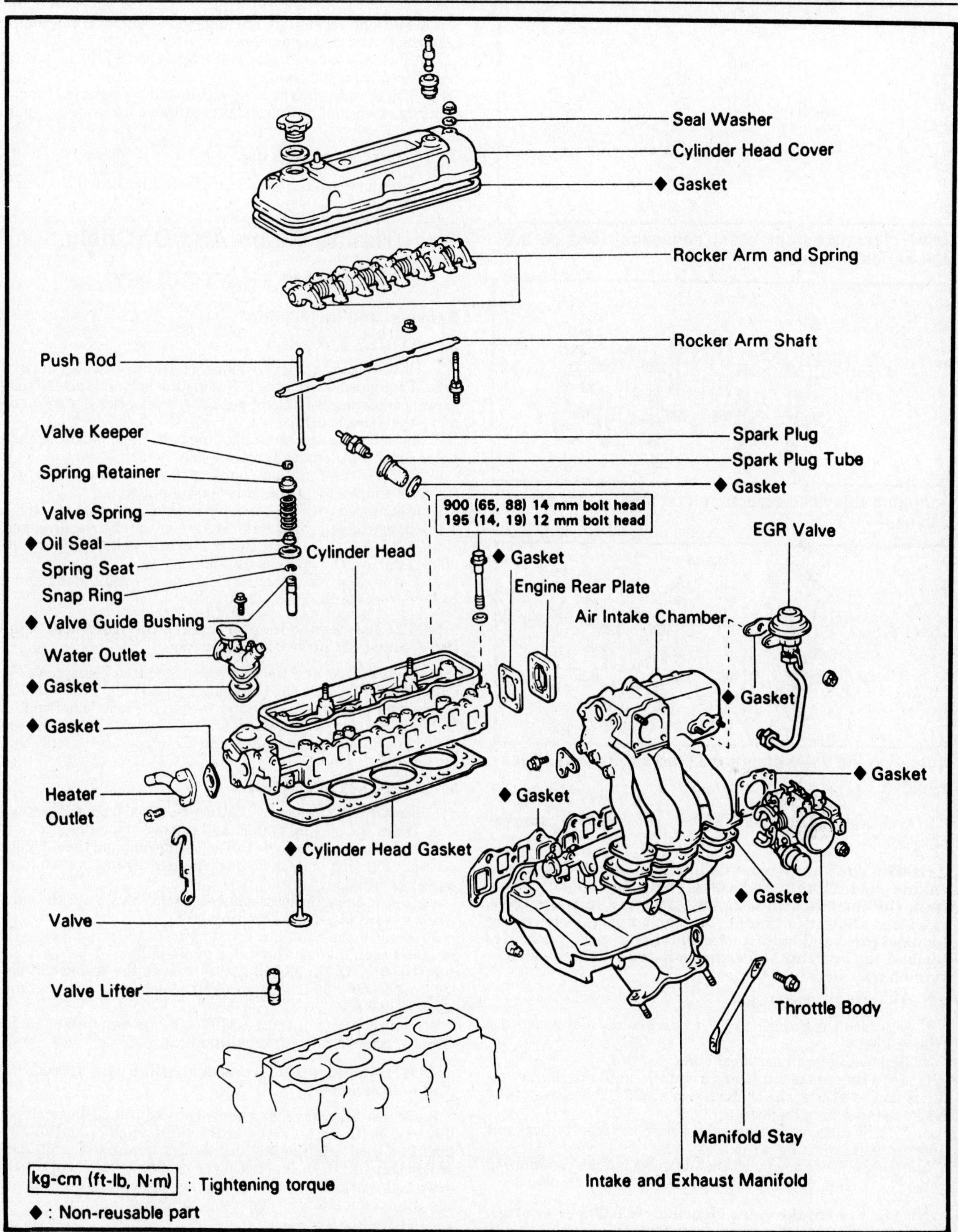
Seal Washer
Cylinder Head Cover
◆ Gasket
Rocker Arm and Spring
Rocker Arm Shaft
Push Rod
Valve Keeper
Spring Retainer
Valve Spring
◆ Oil Seal
Spring Seat
Snap Ring
◆ Valve Guide Bushing
Water Outlet
◆ Gasket
◆ Gasket
Heater Outlet
Valve
Valve Lifter
Cylinder Head
◆ Cylinder Head Gasket
Spark Plug
Spark Plug Tube
◆ Gasket
900 (65, 88) 14 mm bolt head
195 (14, 19) 12 mm bolt head
◆ Gasket
Engine Rear Plate
Air Intake Chamber
EGR Valve
◆ Gasket
◆ Gasket
◆ Gasket
◆ Gasket
Throttle Body
Manifold Stay
Intake and Exhaust Manifold
kg-cm (ft-lb, N·m) : Tightening torque
◆ : Non-reusable part

Exploded view of the cylinder head—3Y-EC and 4Y-E engines

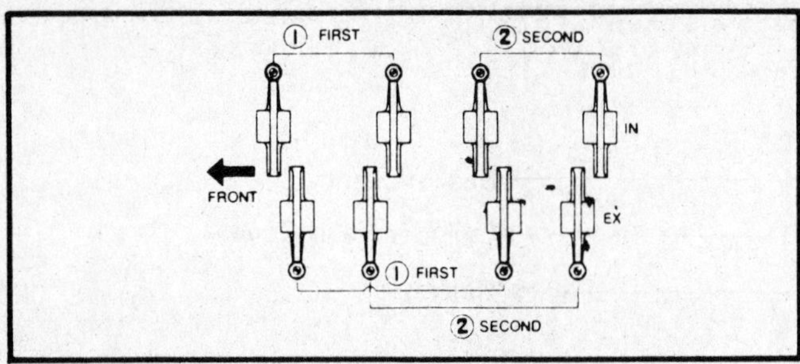

Valve clearance adjustment sequence used on the 22R series engines

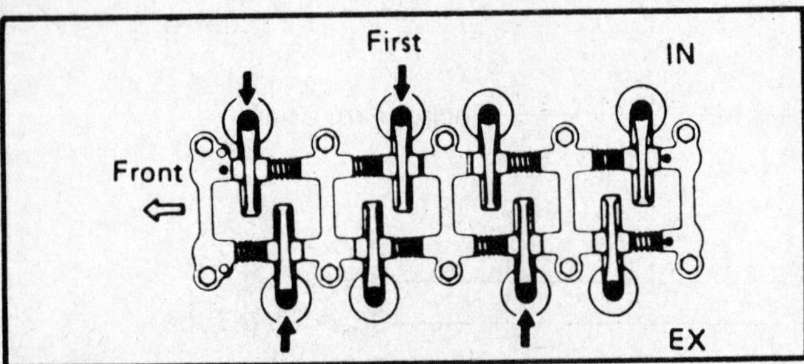

Adjusting the valve clearance (1st step) – 22R series engines

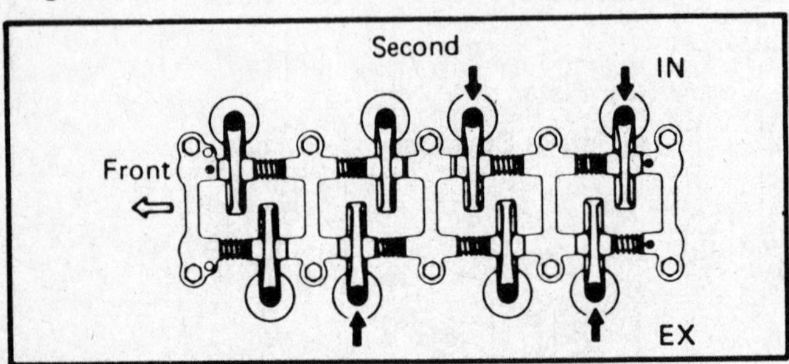

Adjusting the valve clearance (2nd step) – 22R series engines

7. To install the components, reverse the removal procedures.

NOTE: The valves must be initially adjusted with the engine cold. Obtain the valve clearance specification from the Specifications chart. After the initial engine start-up, allow the engine to reach normal operating temperature and adjust the valves as previously described to the "Hot" clearances listed in the specification chart.

2F, 3B AND 2H ENGINES

1. Operate the engine until it reaches normal operating temperatures.
2. Remove the cylinder head cover.
3. Turn the crankshaft (using a wrench) until the No. 1 cylinder is on the TDC of the compression stroke. The valves of the No. 1 cylinder must be loose.
4. To adjust the valve clearance, loosen the adjuster lock nut and turn the adjusting screw.
5. Using a feeler gauge, check and/or adjust the clearance of valve No. 1, 2, 3, 5, 7 and 9 (numbered from the front).

NOTE: The intake valve clearance is 0.008 in. (warm); the exhaust valve clearance is 0.014 in. (warm).

6. Using a wrench on the crankshaft pulley bolt, turn the crankshaft one revolution, aligning the 0° mark on the timing pulley with the timing pointer.
7. Adjust the clearance of valve No. 4, 6, 8, 10, 11 and 12 (numbered from the front).
8. With the adjustment complete, install the removed components by reversing the removal procedures. Check and/or adjust the timing.

3Y-EC AND 4Y-E ENGINES

The valve tappets of this engine are hydraulic; no adjustment is necessary.

Timing Gears And/Or Chain

CRANKSHAFT PULLEY

Removal and Installation

22R SERIES ENGINES

1. Disconnect the negative battery terminal from the battery.
2. If equipped, loosen the P/S adjusting bolt and the A/C compressor adjusting bolt, then, push the accessories inward to remove the drive belt(s).
3. Loosen the alternator adjusting bolt, then, push the alternator inward to remove the drive belt.
4. Remove the fan/fluid coupling-to-water pump bolts, the fan/fluid coupling and the water pump pulley.
5. If equipped with A/C, remove the No. 2 crankshaft pulley.
6. Using the following numbered tools, or their equivalents, No. 09213-70010 (to hold the crankshaft pulley) and 09330-00021, remove the crankshaft pulley bolt.
7. Using tool No. 09213-31021, or its equivalent and a wrench, remove the crankshaft pulley.

NOTE: It is a good idea to replace the front seal when the crankshaft pulley is removed.

8. To install, reverse the removal procedures. Using tools No. 09213-70010 (to hold the crankshaft pulley) and 09330-00021, or their equivalents, install and torque the crankshaft pulley bolt to 116 ft. lbs. Adjust the drive belt tension(s). Start the engine, allow it to reach normal operating temperatures and check for leaks.

3Y-EC AND 4Y-E ENGINES

1. Disconnect the negative battery terminal from the battery.
2. Drain the cooling system and remove the radiator.
3. If equipped, loosen the P/S adjusting bolt and the A/C compressor adjusting bolt, then, push the accessories inward to remove the drive belt(s).
4. Loosen the alternator adjusting bolt, then, push the alternator inward to remove the drive belt.
5. Remove the fan/fluid coupling-to-water pump bolts, the fan/fluid coupling and the water pump pulley.
6. Using tools No. 09213-70010 (to hold the crankshaft pulley) and 09330-00021, or their equivalents, remove the crankshaft pulley bolt.
7. Using tool No. 09213-31021, or its equivalent and a wrench, remove the crankshaft pulley.

NOTE: Replace the front seal when the crankshaft pulley is removed.

8. To install, reverse the removal procedures. Using tools No. 09213-70010 (to hold the crankshaft pulley) and 09330-00021,or their equivalents, install and torque the crankshaft pulley bolt to 116 ft. lbs. Refill the cooling system. Adjust the drive belt tension(s). Start the engine, allow it to reach normal operating temperatures and check for leaks.

L SERIES ENGINES

1. Disconnect the negative battery terminal from the battery.

2. Drain the cooling system and remove the radiator.
3. If equipped, loosen the P/S adjusting bolt and the A/C compressor adjusting bolt, then, push the accessories inward to remove the drive belt(s).
4. Loosen the alternator adjusting bolt, then, push the alternator inward to remove the drive belt.
5. Remove the fan/fluid coupling-to-water pump bolts, the fan/fluid coupling and the water pump pulley.
6. If equipped with A/C, remove the A/C pulley from the crankshaft pulley.
7. Using tools No. 09213-54012 (to hold the crankshaft pulley) and 09330-00020, or their equivalents, remove the crankshaft pulley bolt.
8. Using tool No. 09213-60017, or its equivalent and a wrench, remove the crankshaft pulley.

NOTE: It is a good idea to replace the front seal when the crankshaft pulley is removed.

9. Using tool No. 09214-60010, or its equivalent and a hammer, drive the pulley onto the crankshaft.
10. To install, reverse the removal procedures. Using tools No. 09213-54012 (to hold the crankshaft pulley) and 09330-00020, or their equivalents,install and torque the crankshaft pulley bolt to 116 ft. lbs.
11. If equipped with an A/C pulley, install it onto the crankshaft pulley. Refill the cooling system. Adjust the drive belt tension(s). Start the engine, allow it to reach normal operating temperatures and check for leaks.

2F, 3B AND 2H ENGINES

1. Place a clean drain pan under the radiator and drain the cooling system. Disconnect the negative battery cable.
2. Remove the headlight bezels and grille assembly.
3. Remove the upper and lower radiator hoses, the mounting bolts and the radiator.

NOTE: Remove the fan shroud, if equipped.

4. Loosen the drive belt adjusting link and remove the drive belt.
5. Remove the fan-to-water pump bolts and the fan.
6. Remove the crankshaft pulley-to-crankshaft nut. Using a Wheel Puller tool No. 09213-60016, or its equivalent, pull the crankshaft pulley from the crankshaft.
7. To install, use the tool No. 09214-60010, or its equivalent and a hammer, drive the crankshaft pulley onto the crankshaft. Torque the crankshaft pulley nut-to-crankshaft to 116–144 ft. lbs. and reverse the removal procedures. Adjust the drive belts and refill the cooling system.

Front Cover

Removal and Installation

22R, 22R-E AND 22R-TE

1. Refer to the "Cylinder Head, Removal and Installation" procedures, in this section and remove the cylinder head.
2. Remove the radiator hoses, the fan shroud, the transmission oil cooler hoses from the radiator (A/T), the coolant reservoir tube, the mounting bolts and the radiator.

NOTE: On the 2WD models (1982–83), remove the idler arm bracket from the frame, the pitman arm from the selector shaft and the crossmember (under the engine).

3. Remove the engine undercover and the engine mounting bolts, then, place a floor jack under the transmission and raise it 0.98 in. Remove the mounting nuts/bolts and the oil pan from the transmission.
4. Remove the fan from the water pump, the drive belts and the water pump pulley.
5. Remove the air pump, hoses and bracket, if equipped.
6. Remove the alternator adjuster bracket and move it towards the alternator.
7. Remove the center bolt on the crankshaft pulley. Using a Gear Puller tool No. 09213–31021 or its equivalent, remove the crankshaft pulley.
8. Remove the mounting bolts, the water bypass tube and the heater tube.
9. On the 1985-88 models, remove the alternator adjusting bracket bolt and move the bracket toward the alternator.
10. Remove the mounting bolts, the front cover and the gasket from the engine; it may be necessary to use a plastic hammer to loosen the front cover.
11. Using a putty knife, clean the gasket mounting surfaces.
12. To install, use new gaskets, sealant and reverse the removal procedures. Torque the front cover bolts to 9 ft. lbs. (8mm) or 29 ft. lbs. (10mm), the alternator adjusting bracket bolt to 9 ft. lbs., the oil pan bolts to 9 ft. lbs. and the crankshaft pulley bolt to 116 ft. lbs.

2F, 3B AND 2H ENGINES

1. Drain the cooling system and the engine oil. Disconnect the negative battery terminal from the battery.
2. Remove the air cleaner assembly, complete with hoses, from the bracket.
3. Remove the hood latch as well as its brace and support. Remove the headlight bezels and grille assembly.
4. Remove the upper and lower radiator hoses, the mounting bolts and the radiator.

NOTE: Remove the fan shroud, if equipped.

5. Loosen the drive belt adjusting link and remove the drive belt. Remove the alternator electrical connector, the retaining bolts and the alternator.
6. If equipped with an air injection pump, remove the hoses from the pump, the mounting bolts and the air pump.
7. Remove the fan and water pump as an assembly.
8. Remove the crankshaft pulley-to-crankshaft nut. Using a Wheel Puller tool No. 09213-60016, or its equivalent, pull the crankshaft pulley from the crankshaft.
9. Remove the gravel shield from under the engine and the front driveshaft.
10. Remove the front oil pan bolts, to gain access to the bottom of the timing chain cover.

NOTE: It may be necessary to insert a thin knife between the pan and the gasket in order to break the pan loose. Use care not to damage the gasket.

11. To install, use the tool No. 09214-60010, or its equivalent and a hammer, drive the crankshaft pulley onto the crankshaft and reverse the removal procedures. Torque the crankshaft pulley nut-to-crankshaft to 116–144 ft. lbs. and the front cover-to-engine bolts to 53–69 inch lbs. (6mm) or 12–17 ft. lbs. (10mm). Adjust the drive belts and refill the cooling system. Adjust the drive belts and refill the cooling system.

3Y-EC AND 4Y-E ENGINES

1. Disconnect the negative battery terminal from the battery. Drain the cooling system.
2. If equipped with an A/T, remove and plug the oil cooler lines at the radiator.
3. Remove the fan shroud, the radiator hoses, the coolant reservoir hose and the upper radiator bolt. Raise and support the front of the vehicle on jackstands. Remove the engine under cover, the mounting bolts and the radiator.
4. Remove the drive belts, the fan, the fluid coupling and the water pump pulley from the water pump.
5. Using the tools No. 09213–70010 and 09330–00020, or their equivalents, remove the crankshaft pulley center bolt. Using the Wheel Puller tool No. 09213-31021 or its equivalent, pull the crankshaft pulley from the crankshaft.

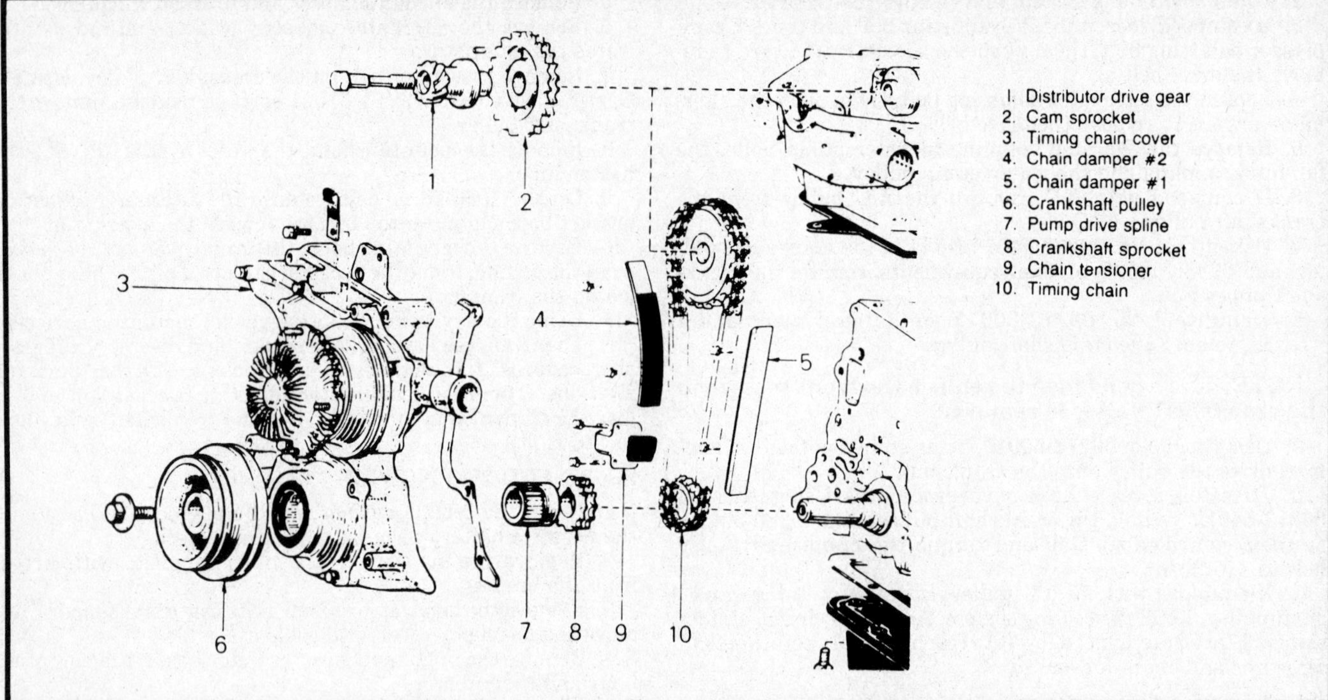

Exploded view of the timing cover and related components – 22R series engines

6. Remove the front cover mounting bolts. Using a small pry bar, lift the front cover from the engine.
7. Using a putty knife, clean the gasket mounting surfaces.
8. To install, use a new gasket, sealant and reverse the removal procedures. Using a soft faced hammer, drive the crankshaft pulley onto the crankshaft. Using the tools No. 09213-70010 and 09330-00020, or their equivalents, torque the crankshaft pulley bolt to 80 ft. lbs. Adjust the drive belts and refill the cooling system. Start the engine, allow it to reach normal operating temperatures and check for leaks.

FRONT COVER OIL SEAL

Removal and Installation

22R, 22R-E AND 22R-TE ENGINES

1. Refer to the "Front Cover, Removal and Installation" procedures, in this section and remove the crankshaft pulley.
2. Using a small pry bar, pry the oil seal from the oil pump housing.
3. Using the Seal Installation tool No. 09223-50010, or its equivalent, drive the new seal into the oil pump housing. Apply multi-purpose grease to the lip of the new seal.
4. To complete the installation, reverse the removal procedures.

3Y-EC AND 4Y-E ENGINES

Front Cover Removed

1. Using a drift punch and a hammer, drive the oil seal from the front cover.
2. Using the Seal Installation tool No. 09223-22010, or its equivalent and a hammer, drive the new oil seal into the front cover.
3. Apply grease to the lip of the new seal.

Front Cover Installed

1. Refer to the "Front Cover, Removal and Installation" procedures, in this section and remove the crankshaft pulley.
2. Using the Seal Removal tool No. 09308-10010 or its equivalent, pull the oil seal from the front cover.
3. Apply multi-purpose grease to the lip of the new seal.
4. Using the Seal Installation tool No. 09223-22010, or its equivalent and a hammer, drive the new oil seal into the front cover.
5. To complete the installation, reverse the removal procedures.

2F, 3B AND 2H ENGINES

1. Refer to the "Front Cover, Removal and Installation" procedures, in this section and remove the crankshaft pulley.
2. Using a small pry bar, pry the oil seal from the front cover.
3. Using the Seal Installation tool No. 09515-35010, or its equivalent, drive the new seal into the front cover. Apply multi-purpose grease to the lip of the new seal.
4. To complete the installation, reverse the removal procedures.

TIMING CHAIN AND TENSIONER

Removal and Installation

22R, 22R-E AND 22R-TE ENGINES

1. Refer to the "Cylinder Head" and the "Front Cover, Removal and Installation" procedures, in this section, then, remove the cylinder head and the front cover. Remove the oil pan.
2. Remove the chain from the damper and the cam sprocket together.

NOTE: If the chain and sprocket are worn, replace them, along with the crankshaft sprocket.

3. Using the Wheel Removal tool No. 09213-36020, or its equivalent, pull the crankshaft sprocket and pump drive spline as a unit.
4. Measure the chain tensioner for wear; if it is worn below 0.43 in., replace it as a unit.
5. Measure the chain dampers for wear; if measurements are

below the limit: 0.200 in. (Damper No. 1) and 0.180 in. (Damper No. 2), replace them.

6. After installing any necessary dampers or a new tensioner, turn the crankshaft by hand until the key is at TDC. If removed, slide the crankshaft sprocket over the key. Place the chain on the sprocket so that the single bright link is over the mark on the sprocket.

7. Position the cam sprocket in the chain so that the timing mark on the sprocket is located between the two bright links (1982–84) or aligned with the bright link (1985-88) of the chain.

8. Install the oil pump drive spline over the crankshaft key, if removed.

9. Turn the camshaft sprocket counterclockwise to take any slack out of the chain.

10. To complete the installation, use new gaskets, sealant and reverse the removal procedures.

3Y-EC AND 4Y-E ENGINES

1. Refer to the "Front Cover, Removal and Installation" procedures, in this section and remove the front cover.

NOTE: Using a tension gauge, measure the slack of the timing chain, it should be 0.531 in. at 22 lbs. pressure.

2. Remove the mounting bolts and the timing chain tensioner.

3. Install the crankshaft pulley on the crankshaft. Using tools No. 09213–70010 and 09330–00020, or their equivalents, to secure the crankshaft pulley, remove the camshaft mounting bolt with a socket wrench and remove the crankshaft pulley.

4. Using the wheel puller tool No. 09950–20015, or its equivalent, uniformly remove the camshaft sprocket with the crankshaft sprocket and chain.

5. Using a putty knife, clean the gasket mounting surfaces.

6. Upon installation, align the timing chain with the timing marks on the sprockets, then install the sprockets on their respective shafts.

7. To complete the installation, use new gaskets, sealant and reverse the removal procedures. Torque the camshaft mounting bolt to 67 ft. lbs., the timing chain tensioner bolts to 13 ft. lbs., the crankshaft pulley bolt to 80 ft. lbs. Adjust the drive belt tension and refill the cooling system. Check and/or adjust the engine timing.

TIMING GEARS

Removal and Installation

2F, 3B AND 2H ENGINES

NOTE: This procedure contains camshaft removal and installation.

1. Refer to the "Cylinder Head" and "Front Cover, Removal and Installation" procedures, in this section and remove the cylinder head and the front cover from the engine.

2. Remove the oil slinger from the crankshaft. Remove the camshaft thrust plate retaining bolts, by working through the holes provided in the camshaft timing gear.

3. Remove the camshaft through the front of the cylinder block. Support the camshaft while removing it, so the bearings or the lobes do not become damaged.

NOTE: The timing gear is a press-fit and cannot be removed without removing the camshaft.

4. Inspect the crankshaft timing gear. Replace it if it has worn or damaged teeth.

5. Remove the sliding key, then, pull the crankshaft timing gear from the crankshaft with a gear puller.

6. Use a large piece of pipe to drive the timing gear onto the crankshaft. Lightly and evenly tap the end of the pipe until the gear is in its original position.

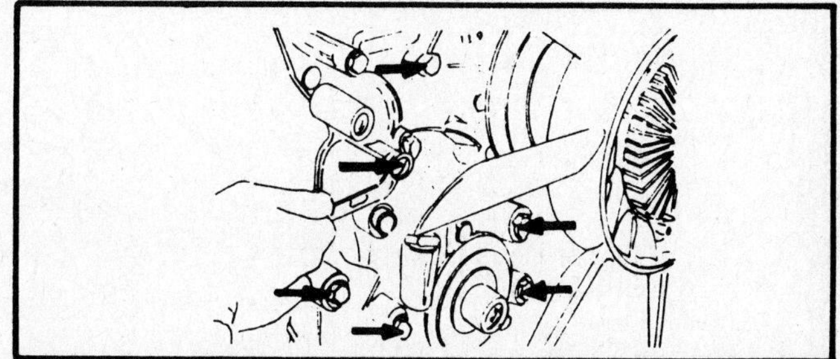

Removing the timing cover bolts – 22R series engines

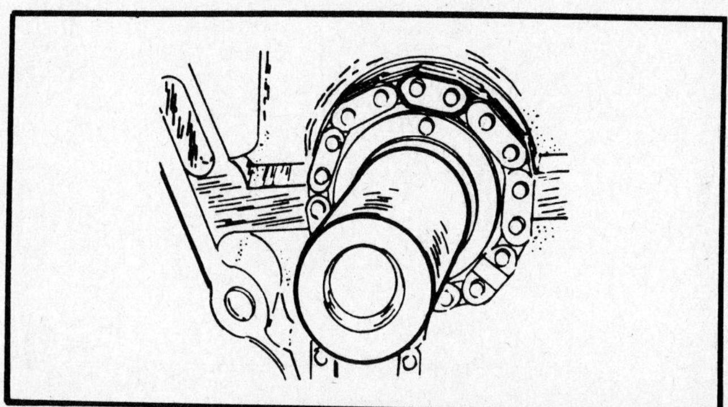

Aligning the crankshaft gear mark with the single bright link of the timing cover – 22R series engines.

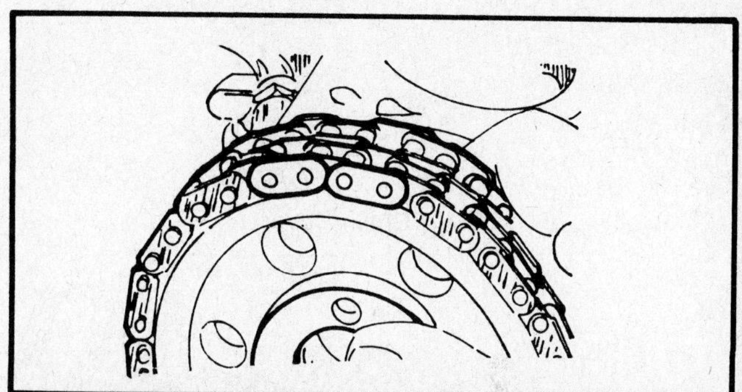

Aligning the camshaft sprocket mark between the two bright links of the timing chain – 22R series (1982-84) engines

Aligning the timing chain to the camshaft sprocket – 22R series (1985-88) engines

7. Apply a coat of engine oil to the camshaft journals and bearings, then, insert the camshaft into the block.

CAUTION

Use care not to damage the camshaft lobes, the bearings or the journals.

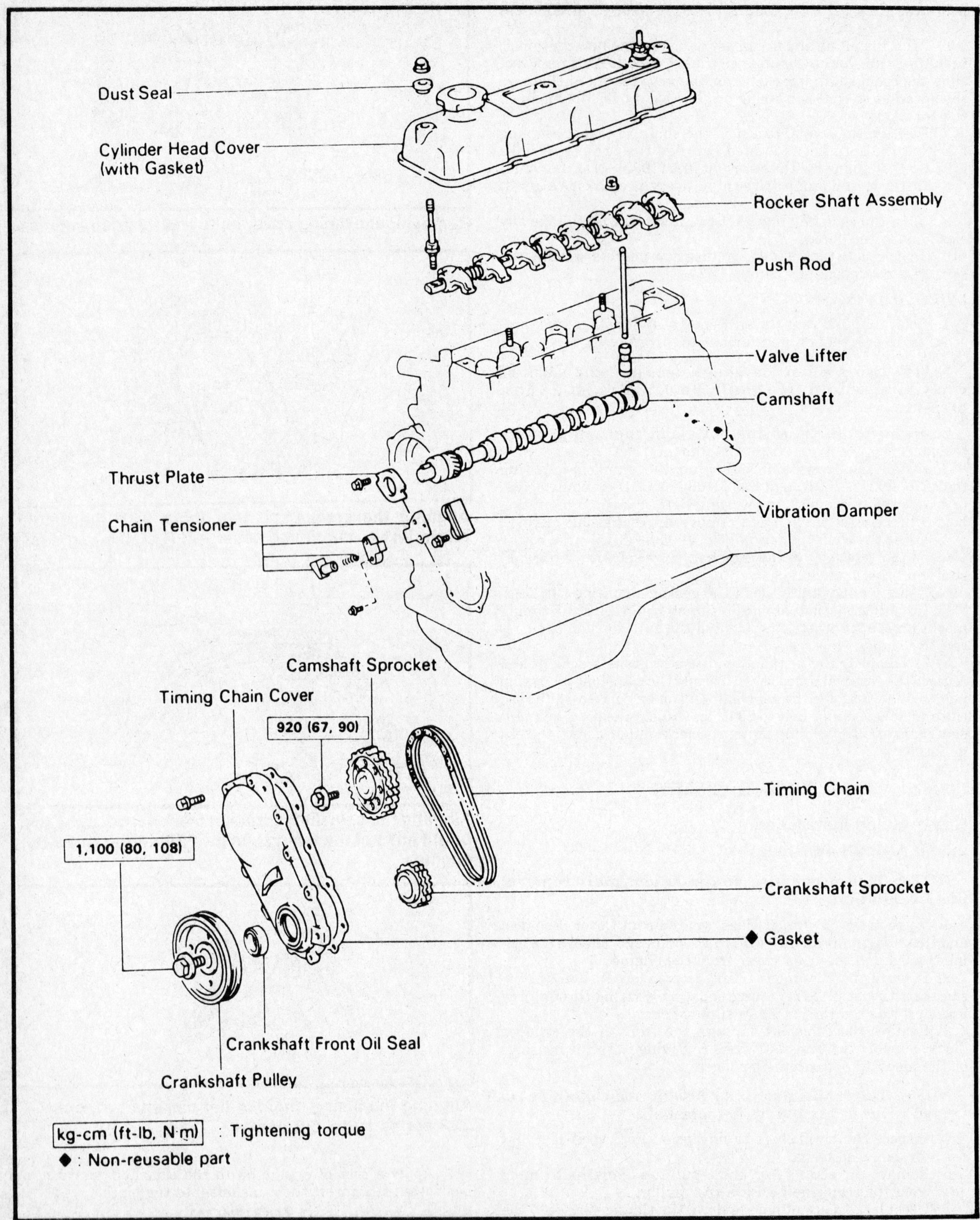

Exploded view of the timing chain and camshaft assembly—3Y-EC and 4Y-E engines

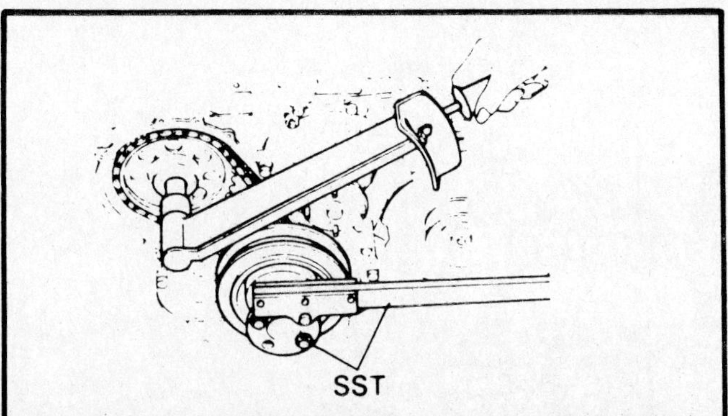

Removing and installing the camshaft sprocket bolt—3Y-EC and 4Y-E engines

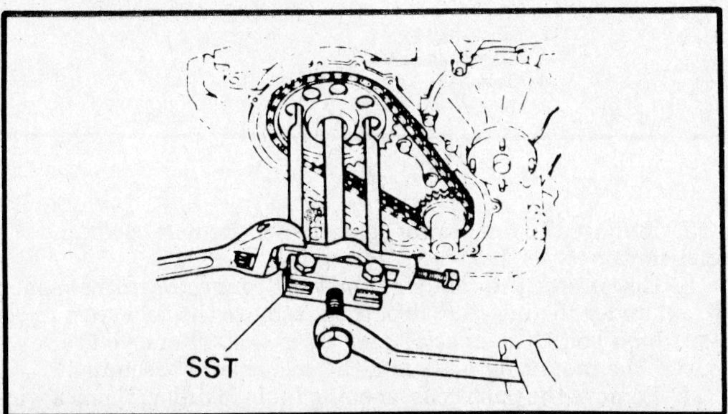

Removing the camshaft sprocket—3Y-EC and 4Y-E engines

8. Align the mating marks on the timing gears. Slip the camshaft into position. Torque the camshaft thrust plate bolts to 14.5 ft. lbs.

9. Using a feeler gauge, check the gear backlash, inserted between the crankshaft and the camshaft timing gears. The maximum backlash should be 0.002–0.005 in.; if it exceeds this, replace one or both of the gears, as required.

10. Using a dial indicator, check the gear run-out. Maximum run-out, for both gears, is 0.008 in.; if not, replace the gear.

11. Install the oil nozzle (if removed) by screwing it in place with a screwdriver and punching it in two places, to secure it.

NOTE: Be sure that the oil hole in the nozzle is pointed toward the timing gear before securing it.

12. To complete the installation, use new gaskets, sealant and reverse the removal procedures.

VALVE TIMING PROCEDURE

For the valve timing procedure, refer to the "Timing Chain and Gears, Removal and installation procedures in this section to verify the valve timing.

Camshaft

Rotate the engine so that the notch on the crankshaft pulley aligns with 0° mark on the timing plate and the No. 1 cylinder is at the TDC of the compression stroke. With the valve cover removed, the valves of the No. 1 cylinder must be closed.

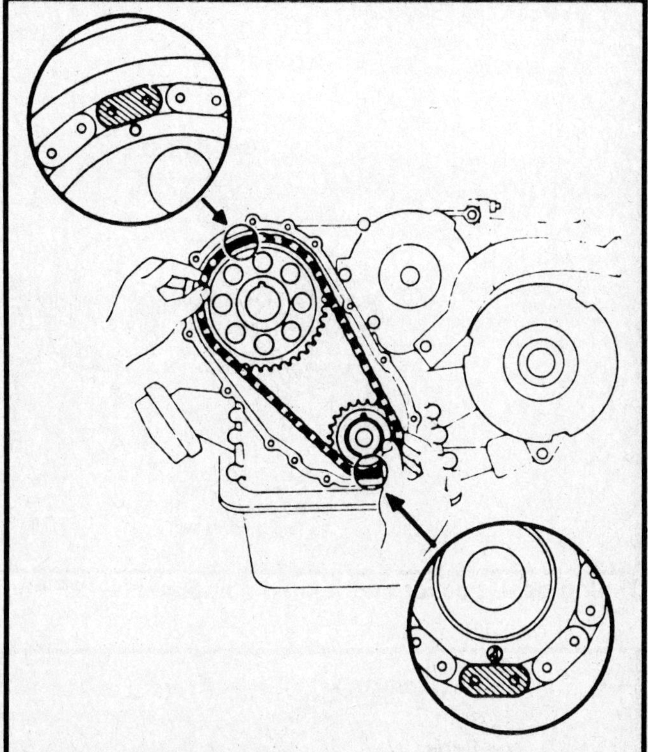

Aligning the timing chain with the sprocket timing marks—3Y-EC and 4Y-E engines

Removal and Installation

22R, 22R-E AND 22R-TE ENGINES

1. Refer to the "Cylinder Head, Removal and Installation" procedures, in this section and remove the cylinder head from the engine.

2. Remove the rocker arm assembly from the cylinder head.

NOTE: It may be necessary to use a small pry bar to lift the rocker arm assembly from the cylinder head.

3. Using a feeler gauge, measure the thrust bearing clearance at the front of the camshaft; the standard clearance is 0.003–0.007 in., it should not exceed 0.0098 in.

4. Remove the camshaft bearing caps and lift out the camshaft. Keep the bearings in order so that they may be installed in their original position.

5. Check the camshaft journal caps for damage. Clean all of the bearing surfaces, including the caps, cam journal and the cylinder head.

6. With the camshaft in place on the cylinder head, lay small strips of plastigage® on each of the camshaft journals (at the tops of the journals, facing front-to-rear).

7. Reinstall the journal caps in their original locations (arrows facing forward) and torque the caps to 13–16 ft. lbs.

8. Remove the journal caps and gauge the width of the plastigage® against the chart on the plastigage® package. Maximum journal clearance is 0.004 in. If the journal clearance is greater than specified, measure the cam journal diameters with a micrometer. If the diameter of any cam journal is less than specified, obtain a new camshaft and recheck the journal clearance. If the clearance is still excessive, the cylinder head must be replaced.

9. To complete the installation, use new gaskets, sealant and reverse the removal procedures. Refill the cooling system. Torque the camshaft bearing cap bolts to 14 ft. lbs., the cylinder

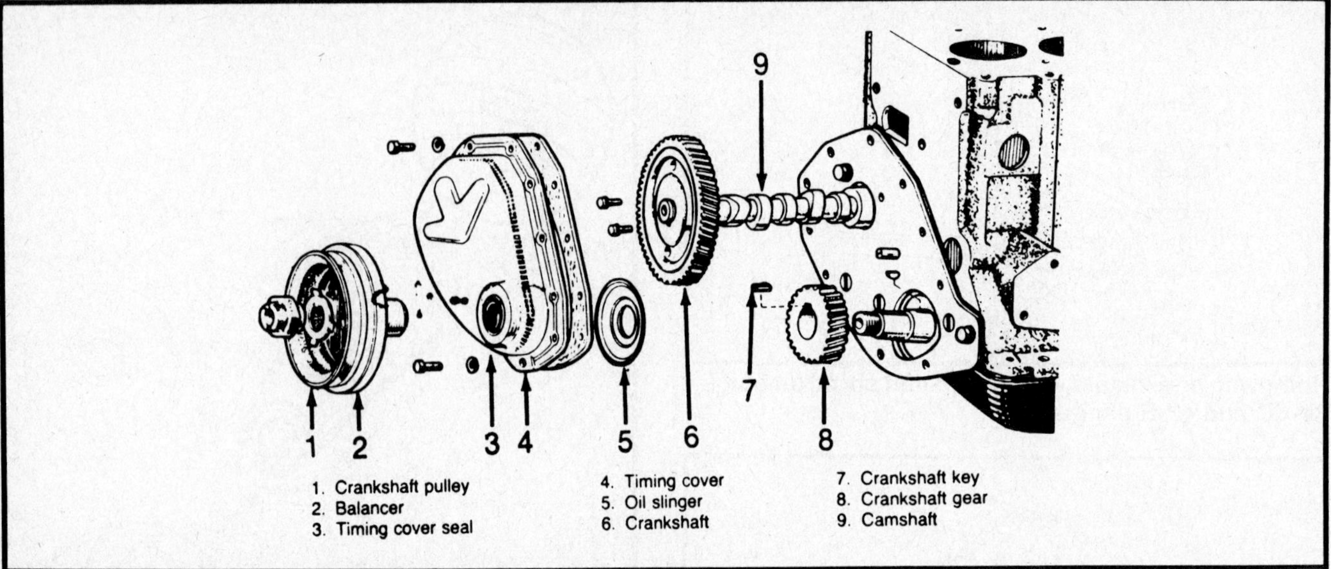

Timing gears, cover and related components—2F engines

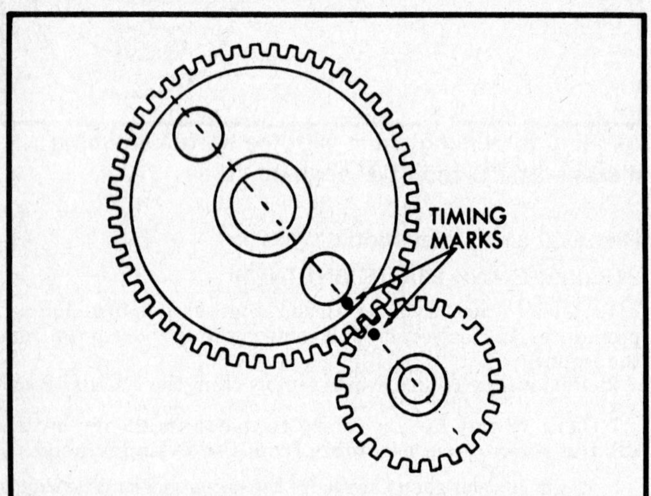

2F engines—align the camshaft and crankshaft gear marks

head-to-engine block to 58 ft. lbs., the timing chain cover-to-cylinder head bolt to 9 ft. lbs., the camshaft sprocket-to-camshaft bolt to 58 ft. lbs., the intake manifold bolts to 14 ft. lbs., the exhaust manifold bolts to 33 ft. lbs. and the rocker arm cover to 7–12 ft. lbs. Replace the cooling system fluid and the engine oil. Adjust the valves, the drive belts, then, check and/or adjust the timing.

NOTE: If a new cam is installed, use an assembly lube on the cam lobes and engine oil on the journals. Change the engine oil and filter.

2F, 3B AND 2H ENGINES

Refer to the "Timing Gear, Removal and Installation" procedures, in this section and remove the camshaft.

3Y-EC AND 4Y-E ENGINES

1. Refer to the "Timing Chain and Tensioner, Removal and Installation" procedures, in this section and remove the timing chain from the engine.
2. Remove the right-front seat, the service hole cover and the distributor (type IIA).
3. Disconnect the cold start injector connector, place a shop towel under the injector tube, then, remove the cold start injector union bolts, the injector and the gaskets. Remove the valve cover, the mounting bolts and the rocker arm assembly.
4. Remove the push rods, keeping them in order. Using a wire hook or a magnetic finger, remove the valve lifters, keeping them in order.
5. Remove the thrust plate mounting bolts and the plate.
6. While turning the camshaft, slowly pull it out through the front of the engine, making sure not to damage the bearings, the camshaft lobes or the camshaft bearing surfaces.
7. Install the thrust plate, the camshaft sprocket and bolt onto the camshaft. Using a feeler gauge, measure the thrust bearing clearance, it should be 0.0028–0.0087 in.; if the clearance exceeds 0.012 in., replace the thrust plate.
8. Using a micrometer, check the bearing diameters of the camshaft. Using an internal micrometer, check the camshaft bearing diameters on the engine block.
9. Using a putty knife, clean the gasket bearing surfaces.

NOTE: Before installing the valve lifters, coat them with oil.

10. To install, use new gaskets, sealant and reverse the removal procedures. Torque the camshaft thrust bearing plate bolts to 13 ft. lbs., the camshaft sprocket bolt to 67 ft. lbs., the timing chain tensioner bolts to 13 ft. lbs. and the crankshaft pulley bolt to 80 ft. lbs. Adjust the drive belts and refill the cooling system. Check and/or adjust the timing.

Piston and Connecting Rods

IDENTIFICATION

If no visible signs of piston/connecting rods direction or numbering are present, use a grease pencil, paint or etc. to mark the component. The components MUST BE installed in their original positions.

NOTE: The pistons have a notch (2F, 22R series) or a dot mark (3Y-EC and 4Y-E), indicating the front of the engine. Be sure to install them with the mark facing the front of the engine.

Removal and Installation

1. Refer to the "Cylinder Head" and the "Oil Pan, Removal and Installation" procedures, in this section and remove the cylinder head/oil pan from the engine.
2. Remove the oil pump (3Y-EC and 4Y-E) and the strainer.

NOTE: On the 22R series engines, it is not necessary to remove the oil pump.

3. Using a ridge reamer tool, remove the ridges from the top of the cylinder.
4. Measure the connecting rod side clearance.
5. Remove the connecting rod cap of the No. 1 cylinder and check the oil clearance with plastigage®. Record the clearance and compare with the specification chart; repeat this step for each connecting rod.
6. With the No. 1 connecting rod cap removed, install a short piece of rubber hose onto each connecting rod bolt (the hose must completely cover the bolt).
7. Using a wooden or plastic handle (an old hammer handle works well), carefully tap the piston/connecting rod assembly out of the cylinder. DO NOT use excessive force as this could damage the connecting rods. Repeat this step for each cylinder.

NOTE: When removing the piston/connecting rod assemblies, be sure to keep the parts in order for reassembly purposes.

8. To install the piston/connecting rod assemblies, place the assembly into the appropriate cylinders. Using a ring compressor, compress the piston rings. Using a hammer handle, drive the piston assembly into the cylinder bore; make sure that the connecting rod seat onto the crankshaft.

NOTE: The pistons have a notch (2F, 22R series) or a dot mark (3Y-EC and 4Y-E), indicating the front of the engine. Be sure to install them with the mark facing the front of the engine.

9. To complete the installation, use new gaskets, sealant and reverse the removal procedures. Torque the connecting rod cap bolts to 46 ft. lbs. (2F, 22R series) or 36 ft. lbs. (3Y-EC and 4Y-E), the oil strainer to 9 ft. lbs. (2F, 22R series) or 6 ft. lbs. (3Y-EC and 4Y-E), the oil pump bolts to 13 ft. lbs. and the oil pan bolts to 52 inch lbs. (2F, 22R series) or 9 ft. lbs. (3Y-EC and 4Y-E). Adjust the drive belt tensions, then refill the cooling system and the engine oil. Check and/or adjust the timing.

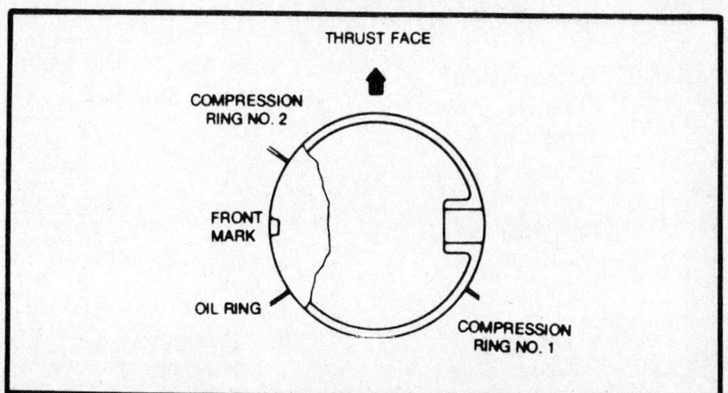

Ring gap staggering on the 22R series engines

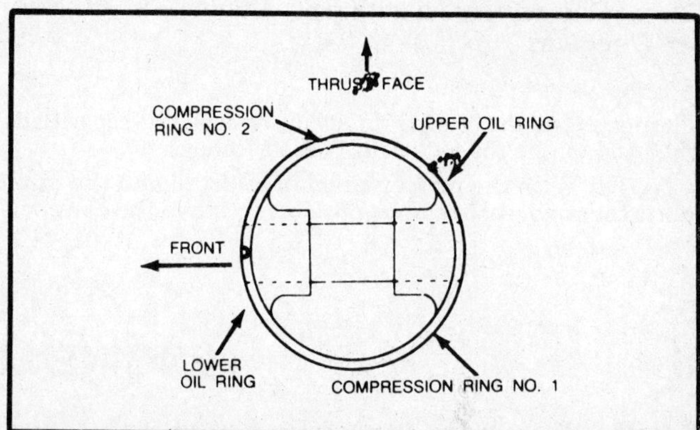

2F engines—after installing the piston rings, rotate each ring so that the ring gaps are positioned as shown. Failure to stagger the ring gaps will result in excesive oil consumption

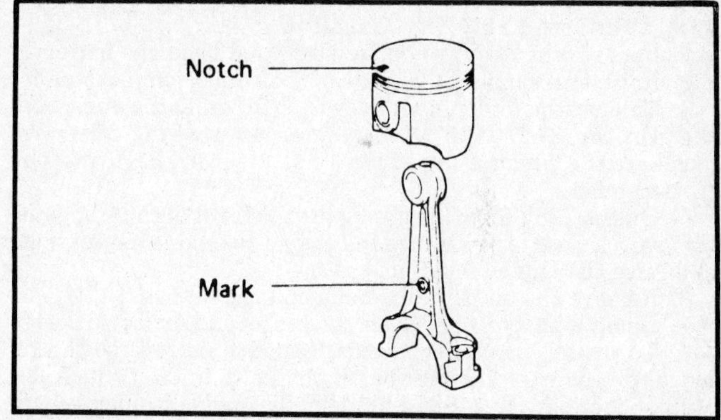

View of the piston and connecting rod—3Y-EC and 4Y-E engines

Connecting Rod and Main Bearings

Removal and Installation

Replacement bearings are available in standard and undersize (for reground crankshafts). The bearing-to-crankshaft clearance is checked using Plastigage® at either the top of bottom of each crank journal. The Plastigage® has a range of 0.001–0.003 in. (0.0254–0.0762mm).

1. Remove the bearing cap with the bearing shell. Completely clean the bearing shell and the crank journal, blow any oil fron the oil hole in the crankshaft.

Place the Plastigage® lengthwise, along the bottom center of the lower bearing shell. Install the cap with the shell and torque the bolt or nuts to specifications. DO NOT turn the crankshaft with the Plastigage® on the bearing.

2. Remove the bearing cap with the shell. The flattened Plastigage® will be found sticking to either the bearing shell or the crank journal. DO NOT remove it yet.
3. Use the scale printed on the Plastigage® envelope to measure the flattened material at its widest point. The number within the scale which most closely corresponds to the width of the Plastigage® indicates the bearing clearance in thousandths of an inch.
4. Check the specification chart for the desired clearance. It is advisable to install a new bearing if the clearance exceeds 0.003 in. (0.0762mm); however, it the bearing is in good condition and is not being checked because of bearing noise, bearing replacement is not necessary.
5. If new bearings are being installed, try a standard size, each undersize in order until one is found that is within the specified limits when checked for clearance with Plastigage®; each undersize shell has its size stamped on it.

NOTE: When installing the the bearings, be sure the oil holes are aligned, the bearing tangs are installed in the notches and the bearing caps are installed in the same position which they were removed.

6. When the proper size shell is found, clean off the

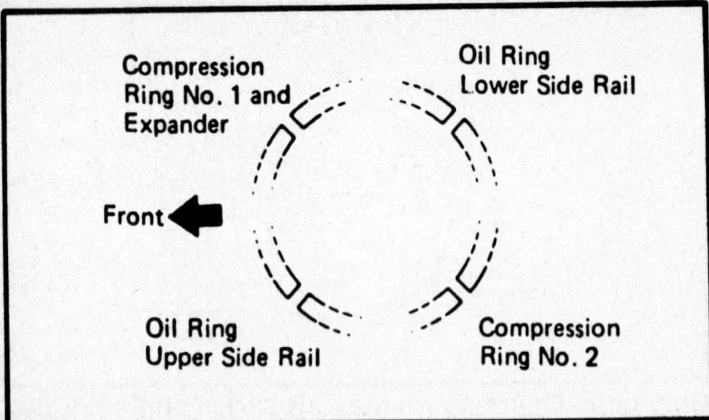

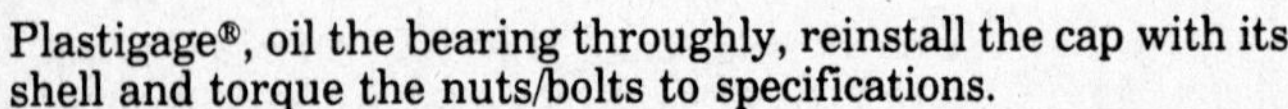
View of the compression ring positioning – 3Y-EC and 4Y-E engines

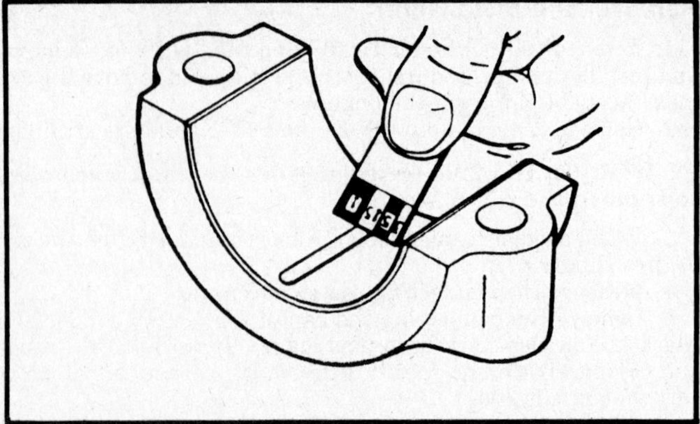
Using Plastigage® to determine the bearing clearance

Plastigage®, oil the bearing throughly, reinstall the cap with its shell and torque the nuts/bolts to specifications.

NOTE: With the proper bearing selected and the nuts/bolts torqued, it should be possible to move the connecting rod back and forth freely on the crank journal as allowed by the specified end clearance. If the rod cannot be moved, either the rod bearing is too far undersize or the rod is misaligned.

ENGINE LUBRICATION

Oil Pan

Removal and Installation

PICKUPS (2WD AND 4WD)

22R, 22R-E and 22R-TE – Gasoline

1. Remove the negative battery terminal from the battery.
2. Raise and support the front of the vehicle on jackstands.
3. Remove the under engine cover, then, drain the engine oil.
4. On the 2WD (1982–83), remove the steering idler arm bracket, the pitman arm from the selector shaft and the crossmember.
5. On the 1984-88 models, support the front of the transmission with a floor jack, remove the engine-to-engine mount bolts and raise the engine 0.980 in.
6. Remove the oil pan nuts/bolts and the oil pan.
7. Using a putty knife, clean the gasket mounting surfaces.
8. To install, use a new gasket, sealant and reverse the removal procedures. Torque the oil pan bolts to 33–70 inch lbs. (1982-83) or 9 ft. lbs. (1984-88). Refill the engine crankcase with oil.

2F, 3B AND 2H ENGINES

1. Disconnect the negative battery terminal from the battery.
2. Raise and support the front of the vehicle on jackstands.
3. Remove the under-engine skid plates, then, the flywheel side cover and undercover.
4. Disconnect the front driveshaft from the engine. Drain the engine oil.
5. Remove the oil pan bolts, the pan and gasket.
6. To install, use a new gasket, sealant and reverse the removal procedures. Refill the engine crankcase with oil.

3Y-EC AND 4Y-E ENGINES

1. Disconnect the negative battery terminal from the battery.
2. Raise and support the front of the vehicle on jackstands.
3. Remove the stiffener plates from both sides of the engine. Drain the engine oil.
4. Disconnect the oil level sensor electrical connector.
5. Remove the oil pan bolts and the pan.

NOTE: If necessary, use tool No. 09032-00100, or its equivalent and insert it between the oil pan and the cylinder block. Cut off the excessive sealant.

6. Using a putty knife, clean the gasket mounting surfaces.
7. To install, use a new gasket, sealant and reverse the removal procedures. Torque the oil pan bolts to 9 ft. lbs. Refill the crankcase with new oil.

Oil Pump

Removal and Installation

PICKUPS (2WD AND 4WD)

22R, 22R-E and 22R-TE – Gasoline

NOTE: When the oil pump has been removed from the engine, it is recommended that the new oil seal be installed.

1. Refer to the "Oil Pan, Removal and Installation" procedures, in this section, then, remove the oil pan and the oil strainer.
2. Remove the drive belts from the crankshaft pulley.
3. Remove the crankshaft pulley bolt. Using the Wheel Puller tool No. 09213-31021, or its equivalent, remove the crankshaft pulley.
4. Remove the mounting bolts and the oil pump assembly.

NOTE: Check the timing chain cover for excessive wear or damage. If necessary, replace the gears or pump body or cover. Unbolt the relief valve (the vertical bolt on the pump body when attached to the engine), then, check the piston, the oil passages and the sliding surfaces for burrs or scoring. Inspect the crankshaft front oil seal and replace if worn or damaged.

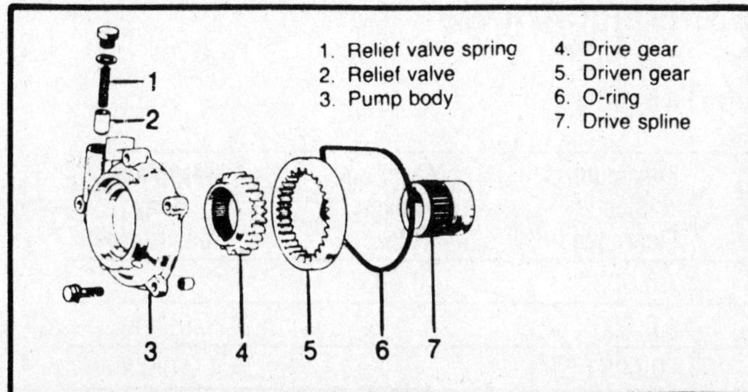

Exploded view of the oil pump – 22R series engines

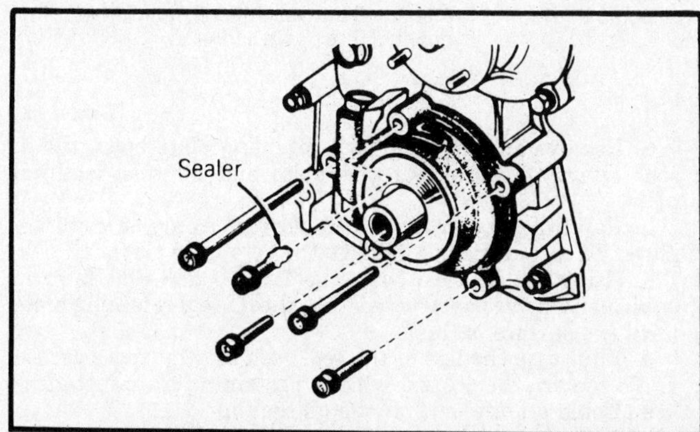

Oil pump installation – apply sealer to the upper mounting bolt as shown – 22R series engines

5. Using a putty knife, clean the gasket mounting surfaces.

NOTE: Before installing the oil pump, be sure to pack the oil pump cavity with petroleum jelly.

6. To install, use a new oil pump-to-front cover O-ring, a new oil pan gasket, sealant and reverse the removal procedures. Adjust the drive belts and refill the crankcase with engine oil.

NOTE: When installing the oil pump bolts, apply sealant to the upper bolt. Be sure to apply sealer to the corners of the oil pan gasket before installing the pan.

LAND CRUISER – 2F, 3B AND 2H ENGINES

NOTE: When the oil pump has been removed from the engine, it is recommended that the new oil seal be installed.

1. Refer to the "Oil Pan, Removal and Installation" procedures, in this section and remove the oil pan, the oil strainer and the union nuts on the oil pump pipe.
2. Remove the lock wire, the oil pump retaining bolt and the pipe from the engine.
3. Remove the oil pump cover and inspect the following parts for nicks, scoring, grooving and etc.: The pump cover, the drive/driven gears and the pump body.
4. If damage is excessive, replace the damaged parts or the complete pump.
5. To install, use new gaskets, sealant and reverse the removal procedures.

VAN – 3Y-EC AND 4Y-E ENGINES

1. Refer to the "Oil Pan, Removal and Installation" procedures, in this section and reverse the removal procedures.

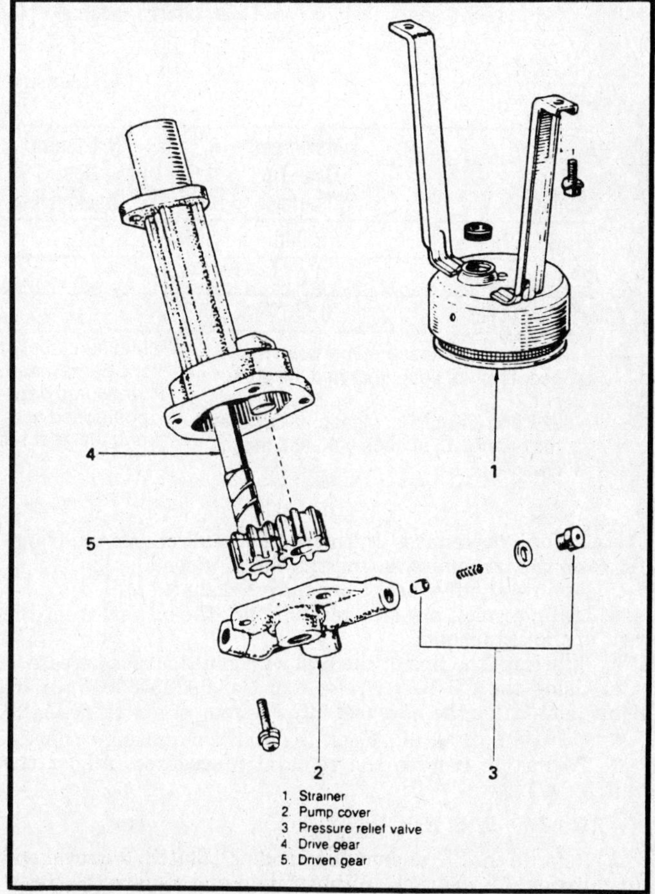

Exploded view of the 2F engine oil pump

2. Remove the oil pump mounting bolts, then pull out the pump assembly.
3. Using a putty knife, clean the gasket mounting surfaces.
4. To install, use new gaskets, sealant and reverse the removal procedures. Torque the oil pump bolts to 13 ft. lbs.

Rear Main Bearing Oil Seal

Removal and Installation

22R, 22R-E AND 22R-TE ENGINES

1. Refer to the "Transmission" and/or "Clutch, Removal and Installation" procedures, in this section and remove the transmission (with the torque converter for A/T) and the clutch assembly (if equipped). Remove the transfer case, if equipped.
2. Remove the flywheel or the flex plate from the crankshaft. Remove the cover plate from the rear of the engine.
3. Remove oil pan-to-oil seal retaining plate bolts, the oil seal retaining plate-to-engine bolts and oil seal retaining plate.
4. Carefully pry or drive the old seal from the retaining plate. Be careful not to damage the retaining plate.
5. Using the Oil Seal Driver tool No. 09223–41020, or its equivalent, drive the new seal into the oil seal retaining plate, until the surface is flush.
6. Lubricate the lips of the seal with multipurpose grease.
7. Using a putty knife, clean the gasket mounting surfaces.
8. To install, use new gaskets and reverse the removal procedures. Adjust the clutch (M/T).

2F, 3B AND 2H ENGINES

1. Refer to the "Transmission" and "Clutch, Removal and

OIL PUMP CLEARANCE SPECIFICATIONS

(All measurements in inches)

Engine	Maximum Gear Tip Clearance ①	Maximum Gear Backlash ②	Maximum Side Clearance ③	Maximum Cover Wear ④	Maximum Body Clearance ⑤
2F, 3B, 2H	0.008	0.037	0.006	0.006	—
22R, 22R-E, L	0.012	—	0.006	—	0.008
3Y-EC & 4Y-E	0.0079	—	0.0059	—	0.0079

① 2F Engines: Measured between the gear teeth of each gear and the pump body.
22R and L Engines: Measured between the gear teeth of each gear and the crescent.

② Measured between the gear teeth with the gears meshed together.

③ Measured between a straightedge positioned across the oil pump body and the gear face.

④ Measured between a straightedge positioned across the cover and the cover wear (gear contact) surface.

⑤ Measured between the oil pump driven gear and the pump body.

Installation" procedures, in this section and remove the transfer case, the transmission and the clutch assembly.

2. Remove the flywheel from the crankshaft.

3. Using a small pry bar, carefully pry the oil seal from the rear of the crankshaft.

4. Lubricate the lips of the seal with multipurpose grease.

5. Using the Oil Seal Driver tool No. 09223-60010, or its equivalent, drive the new seal into the rear of the crankshaft.

6. Using a putty knife, clean the gasket mounting surfaces.

7. To install, reverse the removal procedures. Adjust the clutch (M/T).

3Y-EC AND 4Y-E ENGINES

1. Refer to the "Transmission" and/or "Clutch, Removal and Installation" procedures, in this section and remove the transmission (with the torque converter for A/T) and the clutch assembly (if equipped). Remove the transfer case, if equipped.

2. Remove the flywheel or the flex plate from the crankshaft. Remove the cover plate from the rear of the engine.

3. To replace the oil seal with the retaining plate removed:

a. Remove oil pan-to-oil seal retaining plate bolts, the oil seal retaining plate-to-engine bolts and oil seal retaining plate.

b. Carefully pry or drive the old seal from the retaining plate. Be careful not to damage the retaining plate.

c. Using the Oil Seal Driver tool No. 09223-63010, or its equivalent, drive the new seal into the oil seal retaining plate, until the surface is flush.

d. Lubricate the lips of the seal with multipurpose grease.

4. To replace the oil seal with the retaining plate installed:

a. Using a knife, cut off the oil seal lip.

b. Using a small pry bar, pry the oil seal from the retaining plate.

c. Apply multi-purpose grease to the new oil seal.

d. Using the Oil Seal Driver tool No. 09223-63010, or equivalent, drive the new seal into the oil seal retaining plate until the surface is flush.

5. Using a putty knife, clean the gasket mounting surfaces.

6. To complete the installation, reverse the removal procedures. Adjust the clutch (M/T).

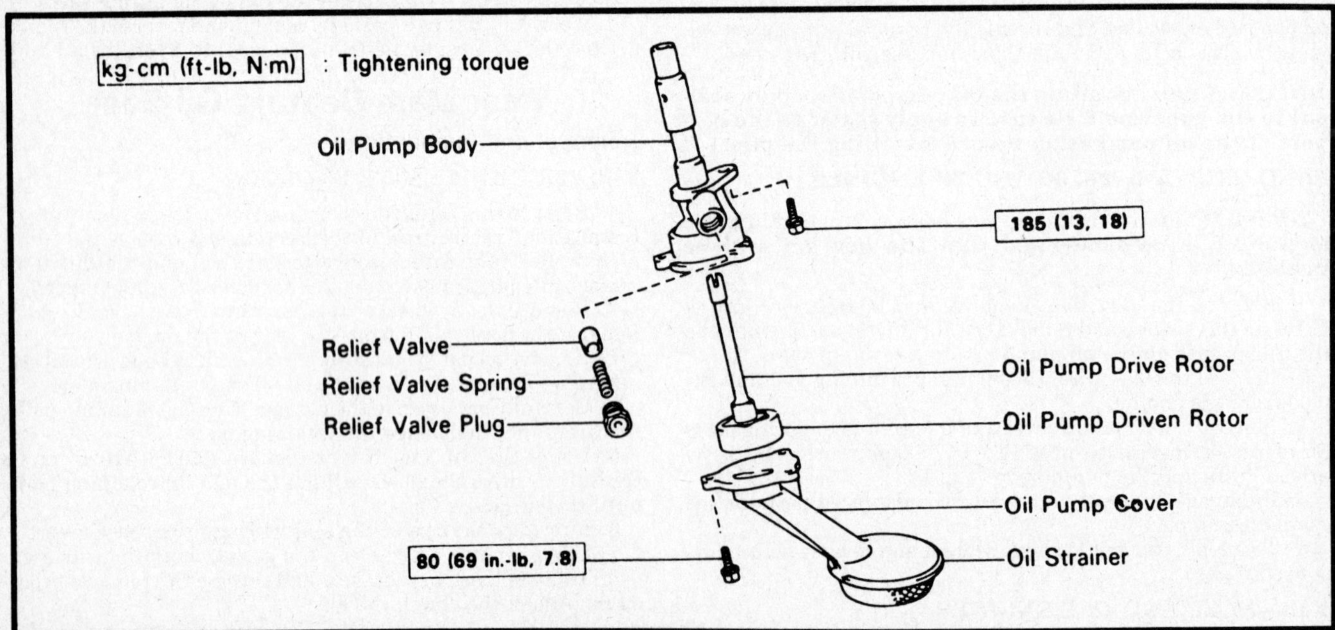

Exploded view of the oil pump—3Y-EC and 4Y-E engines

FRONT SUSPENSION

Spring

TORSION BAR

Removal and Installation

2WD PICKUP AND VAN

These models are equipped with a torsion bar front springs.

CAUTION

Great care must be taken to make sure springs are not mixed after removal. It is strongly suggested that before removal, each spring be marked with paint, showing front and rear of spring and from which side of the truck it was taken. If the springs are installed backwards or on the wrong sides of the truck, they could fracture. If replacing the springs, it is not necessary to mark them.

1. Raise and support the front of the vehicle on jackstands.
2. Slide the boot from the rear of torsion bar spring, then paint an alignment mark from the torsion bar spring onto the anchor arm and the torque arm. There are right and left identification marks on the rear end of the torsion bar springs.

CAUTION

Be sure to mark the front of spring from back of spring.

3. On the rear torsion bar spring holder, there is a long bolt that passes through the arm of the holder and up through the frame crossmember. REMOVE THE LOCKING NUT ONLY FROM THIS BOLT.
4. Using a small ruler, measure the length from the bottom of the remaining nut to the threaded tip of the bolt and record this measurement.
5. Place a jack under the rear torsion bar spring holder arm and raise the arm to remove the spring pressure from the long bolt. Remove the adjusting nut from the long bolt.
6. SLOWLY lower jack.
7. Remove the long bolt, the spacers, the anchor arm and the torsion bar spring. The torsion bar should be easily pulled out of the anchor and the torque arms.

NOTE: Inspect all parts for wear damage or cracks. Check the boots for rips and wear. Inspect the splined ends of the torsion bar spring and the splined holes in the rear holder and the front torque arm for damage. Replace as necessary.

8. To install, coat the splined ends of the torsion bar with multi-purpose grease.
9. If refitting the old torsion bars, perform the following:
   a. Slide the front of the torsion bar spring into the torque arm, making sure that the alignment marks are matched.
   b. Slide the anchor arm onto the rear of the torsion bar spring, making sure that the alignment marks are matched. Install the long bolt and it's spacers.
   c. Tighten the adjusting nut so that it is the same length as it was before removal.

NOTE: DO NOT install the lock nut.

10. When installing a new torsion bar spring, perform the following:
    a. Raise the front of the vehicle, replace the wheel/tire assembly, place a wooden block ($7\frac{1}{2}$ in. high) under the front

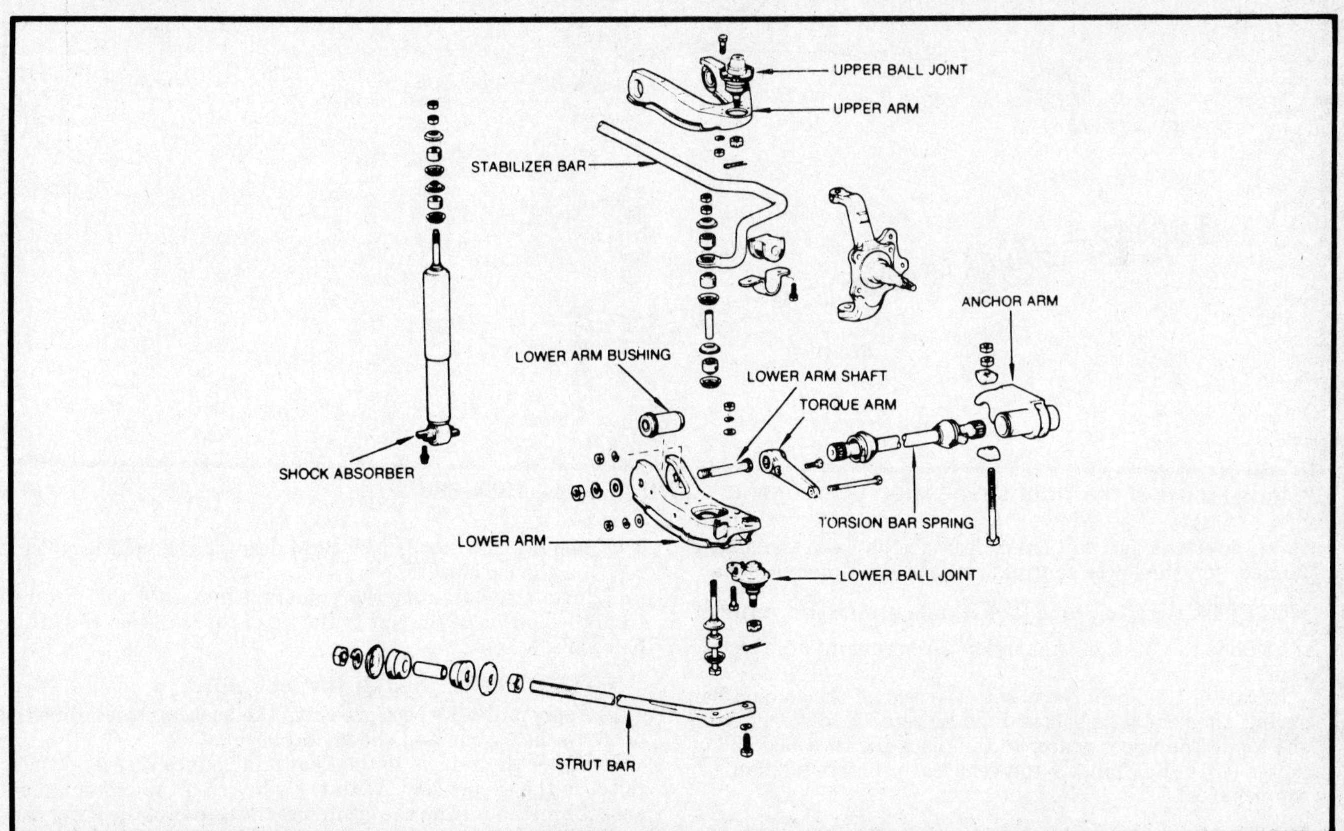

Exploded view of the front suspension components—2WD pickup—1982-83

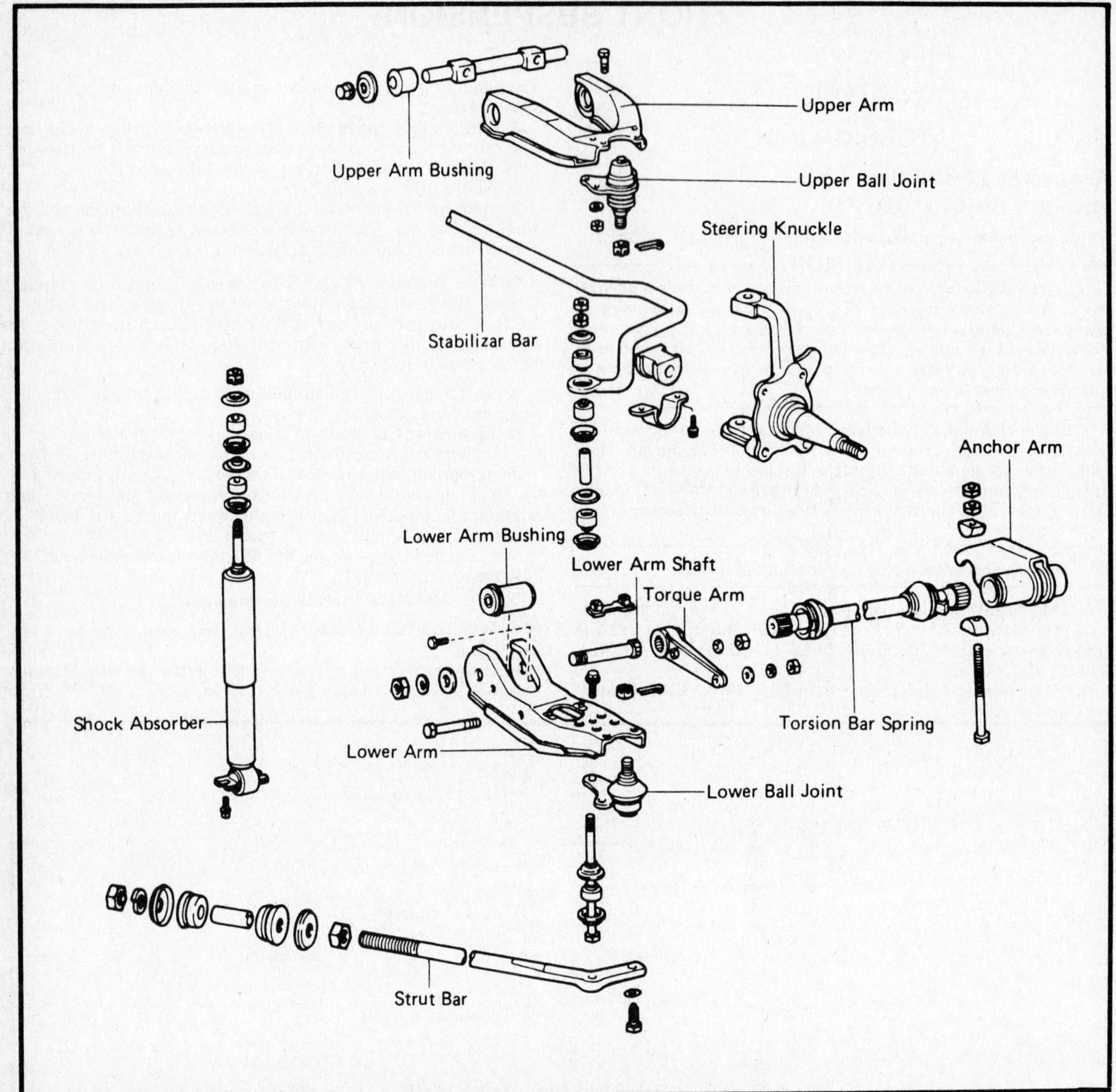

Exploded view of the front suspension components – 2WD pickup – 1984-88

tire. Lower the jack until the clearance between the spring bumper (on the lower control arm) and the frame is $\frac{1}{2}$ in.

NOTE: Be sure to place jackstands under the vehicle.

b. Slide the front of the torsion bar spring into the torque arm.

c. Install the anchor arm into the rear of the torsion bar spring, then the long bolt and the spacers. the distance from the top of the upper spacer to the tip of the threaded end of bolt is 0.310–1.100 in. ($\frac{1}{2}$ ton vehicles) or 0.430–1.220 in. ($\frac{3}{4}$ ton vehicles).

NOTE: Make sure the bolt and bottom spacer are snuggly in the holder arm while measuring.

d. Remove the wooden block and lower the vehicle until it rests on the jackstands.

e. Install and tighten the adjusting nut until the distance from the bottom of the nut to the tip of the threaded end of the bolt is 2.7–3.5 in.

NOTE: DO NOT install the lock nut.

11. Apply multi-purpose grease to the boot lips, then refit the boots to the torque and the anchor arms.

12. Lower the vehicle to the floor and bounce it several times to settle the suspension. With the wheels on the ground, measure the distance from the ground to the center of the lower control arm-to-frame shaft. Adjust the vehicle height using the adjusting nut on the anchor arm.

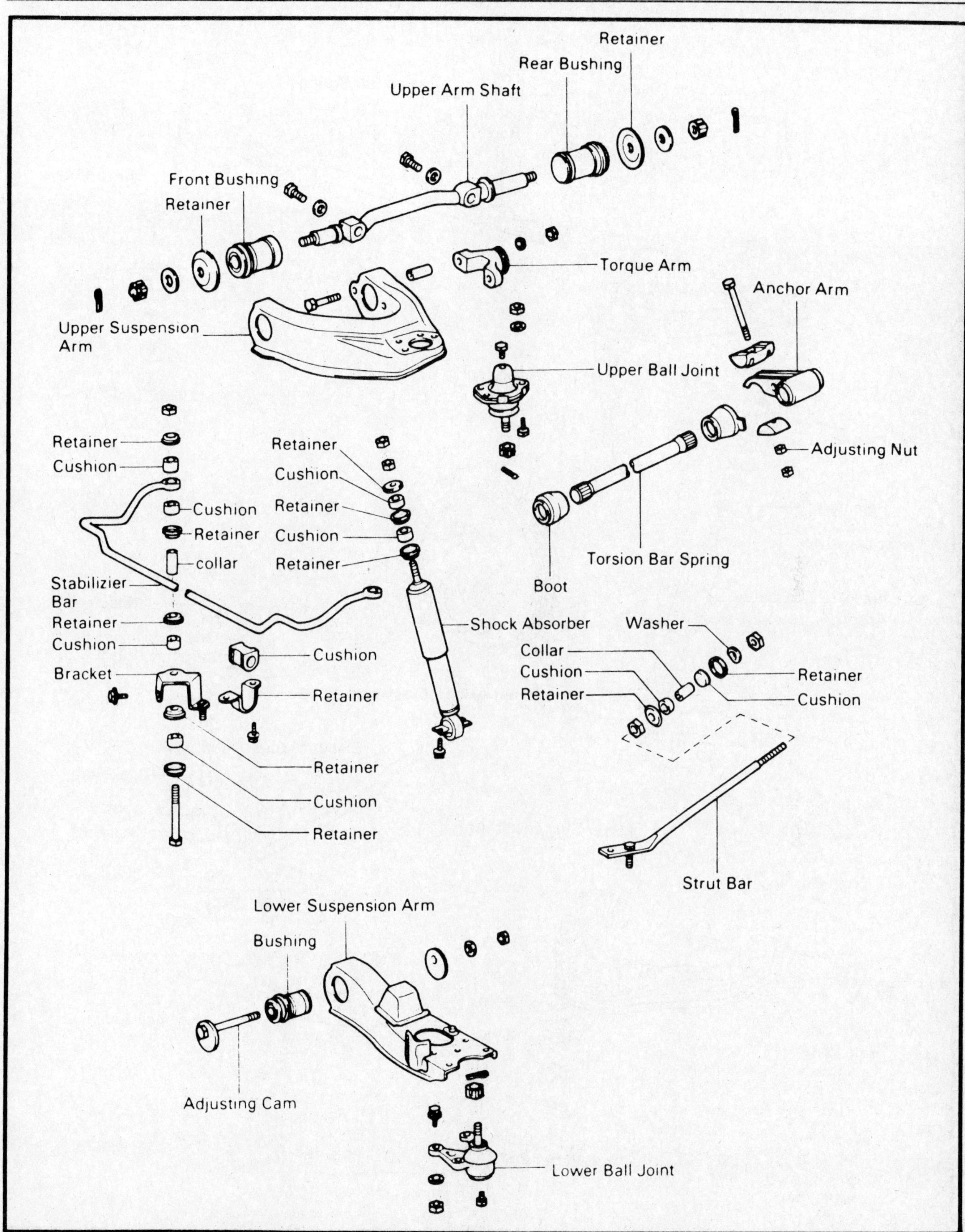

Exploded view of the front suspension system – Van 2WD

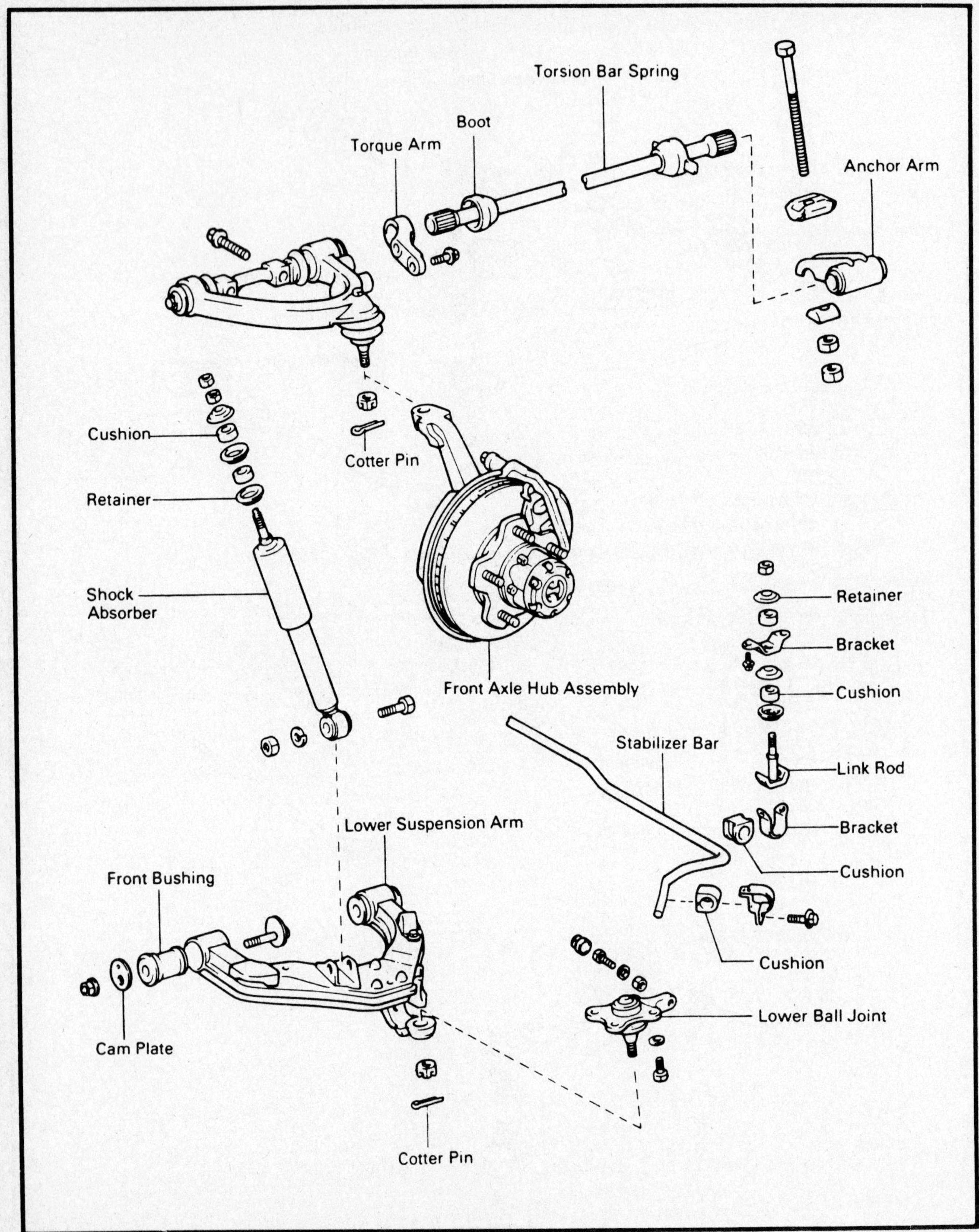

Exploded view of the front suspension system—Van 4WD

VEHICLE HEIGHT

Year	Model	Pay Load	Tire Size	Front Height (in.) (Unloaded)
1983	RN34	½ Ton	7.00-14-6PR	10.291
	RN44		E78-14 (B)	10.016
			ER78-14 (B)	9.866
			205/70 SR 14	9.512
	RN44L-KH	¾ Ton	7.50-14-6PR	10.961
	RN44L-3W C&C		7.50-14-6PR	10.961
	Van		P185/75 R 14	9.57
1984	Short Bed (Std)		7.00-14-6PR	10.59
			ER78-14	10.04
	Long Bed (std)		7.00-14-6PR	10.75
			ER78-14	10.20
	Long Bed (Soft Ride)		ER78-14	10.20
	Extra Cab (Soft Ride)		ER78-14	9.80
	Extra Cab (Std)		ER78-14	9.80
	¾ Ton		7.50-14-6PR	10.71
	C & C		7.50-14-6PR	10.83
	SR-5 (Short)		P195/75 R 14	9.76
			205/70 R 14	10.00
			ER78-14	10.00
	SR-5 (Long)		P195/75 R 14	9.96
			205/70 SR 14	10.20
			ER78-14	10.12
	Extra Cab SR5 (Long Bed)		P195/75 R 14	9.80
			205/70 SR 14	10.04
			ER78-14	9.96
	Van		P185/75 R 14	9.57
1985	Short Bed (Std)		7.00-14-6 PR	10.63
	Long Bed (Std)		7.00-14-6 PR	10.83
	Long Bed (Soft Ride)		P195/75 R 14	10.24
	Extra Cab (Soft Ride)		P195/75 R 14	9.84
	Extra Cab (Std)		P195/75 R 14	9.84
	1 Ton		185 R 14-LT8PR	10.31
	C & C		185 R 14-LT8PR	10.20
	Short Bed (SR-5)		P195/75 R 14	9.80
			205/70 SR 14	10.04
	Long Bed (SR-5)		P195/75 R 14	9.96
			205/70 SR 14	10.20
	Extra Cab SDR-5 (Long Bed)		P195/75 R 14	9.84

VEHICLE HEIGHT

Year	Model	Pay Load	Tire Size	Front Height (in.) (Unloaded)
1985			205/70 SR 14	10.08
	(Diesel) Short Bed (Std)		7.00-14–6PR	10.59
	Long Bed (Soft Ride)		P195/75 R 14	9.96
	Extra Cab (Soft Ride)		P195/75 R 14	9.80
	Extra Cab (Std)		P195/75 R 14	9.80
	Van		P185/75 R 14	9.57
1986	Short Bed (Std)		7.00-14–6PR	10.59
	Long Bed (Std)		7.00-14–6PR	10.83
	Long Bed (Soft Ride)		P195/75 R 14	10.83
	Extra Cab (Soft Ride)		P195/75 R 14	9.84
	Extra Cab (Std)		P195/75 R 14	9.84
	1 Ton		185 R 14-LT8PR	10.31
	C & C		185 R 14-LT8PR	10.28
	Short Bed (SR-5)		P195/75 R 14	9.88
	Long Bed (SR-5)		P195/75 R 14	9.96
			205/70 SR 14	10.20
	Extra Cab SR-5 (Long Bed)		P195/75 R 14	10.04
			205/70 SR 14	10.28
	(Diesel) Short Bed (Std)		7.00-14–6PR	10.59
	Long Bed (Soft Ride)		P195/75 R 14	9.96
	Extra Cab (Soft Ride)		P195/75 R 14	9.80
	Extra Cab (Std)		P195/75 R 14	9.80
	Van		P185/75 R 14	9.57
1987-88	½ Ton (Short)		7.00-14–6PR	10.59
			P195/75 R 14	9.88
	½ Ton (Long)		7.00-14–6PR	10.75
			P195/75 R 14	10.04
			205/70 SR 14	10.28
	½ Ton (Extra Long)		P195/75 R 14	10.04
	1 Ton		185 R 14LT–8PR	10.31
	C&C Long SRW		185 R 14LT–8PR	10.31
	Long DRW		185 R 14LT–6PR	10.28
	Super Long DRW		185 R 14LT–6PR	10.35
	Van		P205/75 R 14	10.09

NOTE: If, after achieving the correct vehicle height, the distance from the bottom of the adjusting nut to the top of the threaded end of the long bolt is not within 2.7–3.5 in., change the position of the anchor arm-to-tension bar spring spline and reassemble.

13. Install and torque the lock nut on the long bolt to 61 ft. lbs.

CAUTION

Make sure the adjusting nut does not move when tightening lock nut.

4WD VAN

These models are equipped with torsion bar front springs.

CAUTION

Great care must be taken to make sure springs are not mixed after removal. It is strongly suggested that before removal, each spring be marked with paint, showing front and rear of spring and from which side of the van it was taken. If the springs are installed backwards or on the wrong sides of the van, they could fracture. If replacing the springs, it is not necessary to mark them.

1. Raise and support the front of the vehicle on jackstands.
2. Using a piece of chalk, remove the boots, then, matchmark the torsion bar spring, the anchor arm and the torque arm.
3. Remove the lock nut.
4. Measure the protruding length of the adjusting arm bolt (from the nut to the end of the bolt).

NOTE: The adjusting arm bolt measurement is used as a reference to establish the chassis ground clearance.

5. Remove the adjusting nut, the anchor arm and the torsion bar spring.

NOTE: When installing the torsion bar springs, be sure to check the left/right indicating marks on the rear end of the springs; be careful not to interchange the springs.

6. Using molybdenum disulphide lithium base grease, apply a coat to the torsion bar spring splines.
7. If installing a used torsion bar spring, perform the following procedures:
   a. Align the matchmarks and install the torsion bar spring to the torque arm.
   b. Align the matchmarks and install the anchor arm to the torsion bar spring.
   c. Tighten the adjusting nut until the bolt protrusion is the same as it was before.
8. If installing a new torsion bar spring, perform the following procedures:
   a. Make sure the upper and lower arms rebound.
   b. Install the two boots onto the torsion bar spring.
   c. Install one end of the torsion bar spring to the torque arm.
   d. Install the torsion bar spring onto the opposite end of the anchor arm.
   e. Figner tighten the adjusting nut until the adjusting bolt protrudes about 1.570 in.
   f. Tighten the adjusting nut until the adjusting bolt protrudes about 2.480 in. (wagon) or 2.400 in. (van).
   g. Install the wheel(s) and remove the jackstands. Bounce the front of the vehicle to stablize the suspension.
9. To adjust the ground clearance, turn the adjusting nut until the center of the cam plate nut (located of the front end of the lower suspension arm) is 10.090 in. (wagon) or 9.940 in. (van) above the ground.
10. After adjusting the ground clearance, torque the lock nut to 58 ft. lbs., then, install the boots.

4WD PICKUP AND 4-RUNNER (1986-88)

These models are equipped with torsion bar front springs.

CAUTION

Great care must be taken to make sure springs are not mixed after removal. It is strongly suggested that before removal, each spring be marked with paint, showing front and rear of spring and from which side of the truck it was taken. If the springs are installed backwards or on the wrong sides of the truck, they could fracture. If replacing the springs, it is not necessary to mark them.

1. Raise and support the front of the vehicle on jackstands.
2. Using a piece of chalk, remove the boots. Matchmark the torsion bar spring, the anchor arm and the torque arm.
3. Remove the lock nut.
4. Measure the protruding length of the adjusting arm bolt (from the nut to the end of the bolt).

NOTE: The adjusting arm bolt measurement is used as a reference to establish the chassis ground clearance.

5. Remove the adjusting nut, the anchor arm and the torsion bar spring.

NOTE: When installing the torsion bar springs, be sure to check the left/right indicating marks on the rear end of the springs; be careful not to interchange the springs.

6. Using molybdenum disulphide lithium base grease, apply a coat to the torsion bar spring splines.
7. If installing a used torsion bar spring, perform the following procedures:
   a. Align the matchmarks, install the torsion bar spring to the torque arm.
   b. Align the matchmarks and install the anchor arm to the torsion bar spring.
   c. Tighten the adjusting nut until the bolt protrusion is the same as it was before.
8. If installing a new torsion bar spring, perform the following procedures:
   a. Make sure the upper and lower arms rebound.
   b. Install the two boots onto the torsion bar spring.
   c. Install one end of the torsion bar spring to the torque arm.
   d. Install the torsion bar spring onto the opposite end of the anchor arm.
   e. Finger tighten the adjusting nut until the adjusting bolt protrudes about 1.570 in.
   f. Tighten the adjusting nut until the adjusting bolt protrudes about 3.430 in.
   g. Install the wheel(s) and remove the jackstands. Bounce the front of the vehicle to stablize the suspension.
9. To adjust the ground clearance, turn the adjusting nut until the center of the cam plate nut (located of the front end of the lower suspension arm) about 11.220 in. above the ground.
10. After adjusting the ground clearance, torque the lock nut to 61 ft. lbs., then, install the boots.

LEAF

Removal and Installation

4WD PICKUP (1982-85)

1. Raise and support the front of vehicle with jackstands under the frame. Remove the wheel/tire assembly.

NOTE: DO NOT place the supports under the front axle housing.

2. Lower the axle housing until the tension is removed from the spring.
3. Remove the shock absorber-to-spring seat bolt and raise the shock, up and out of the way.
4. If removing the driver's side-front leaf spring, remove the

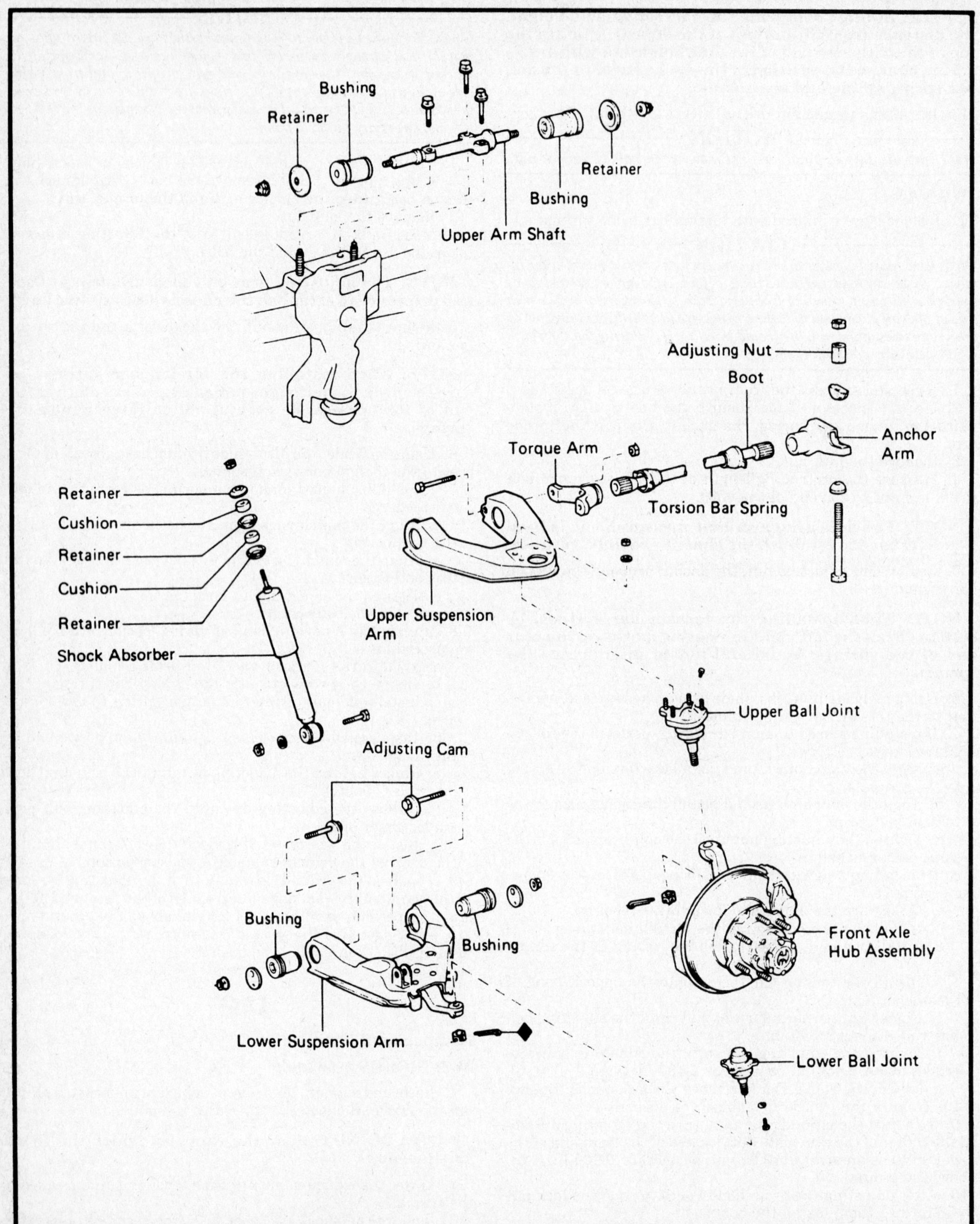

Exploded view of the front suspension system—4WD Pickup and 4-Runner

cotter pin from the end of the steering drag link at the axle housing. Remove the plug from the end of the drag link.

5. Remove stabilizer bar-to-axle housing nut, bolt, spacer and washer assemblies. Remove the stabilizer bar-to-frame mounting clamps.

6. Disconnect brake line from the brake backing plate. Drive out shim holding brake line to holder and withdraw brake line. Plug end of brake line running to master cylinder to prevent fluid loss.

7. Place a jack under the front axle housing and raise to put pressure on the leaf spring. Remove the U-bolt nuts, the spring seat, the U-bolts and the spring bumper. Disconnect the drag link from the steering knuckle arm.

8. Lower the jack enough to take the pressure off the leaf spring but allow it to support the axle housing.

9. Remove the hanger pin nut/bolt (at the front of the spring) and the shackle pin nut/bolt (at the rear of the spring), then carefully pry the spring from retainers.

NOTE: It may be necessary to lower the jack under the axle housing to remove spring.

10. To install, reverse the removal procedures. Torque the U-bolt nuts to 90 ft. lbs., the front hanger pin bolts to 8–11 ft. lbs., the front hanger pin nut to 67 ft. lbs., the rear shackle pin nuts to 67 ft. lbs., the shock absorber-to-body nuts to 19 ft. lbs., the shock absorber-to-spring seat bolt to 70 ft. lbs., the stabilizer bar clamps-to-frame bolts to 9 ft. lbs. and the stabilizer bar-to-axle housing nuts to 19 ft. lbs. Refill the brake master cylinder and bleed the system.

NOTE: Finger-tighten the hanger and the shackle pin nuts. Lower the vehicle to the floor and bounce it to stabilize the suspension.

Land Cruiser

Land Cruiser models are equipped with leaf springs in the front and rear. Thus, front spring removal is performed in almost the same manner as rear spring removal.

Refer to the "Rear Spring, Removal and Installation" procedures, in this section and remove the front spring in the same manner.

CAUTION

Be careful when raising or lowering the front suspension with a jack so as not to damage the steering system components.

Shock Absorbers

Removal and Installation

2WD PICKUP AND VAN

1. Raise and support the front of the vehicle on jackstands. Remove the wheel/tire assembly.

2. Unfasten the double nuts at the top end of the shock absorber. Remove the cushions and the cushion retainers.

3. Remove the shock absorber-to-lower control arm bolts.

4. Compress the shock absorber and remove it from the vehicle.

5. To install, reverse the removal procedures. Torque the shock absorber-to-lower control arm bolts to 13 ft. lbs. and the shock absorber-to-body nuts to 19 ft. lbs.

4WD PICKUP, 4-RUNNER AND 4WD VAN

1. Raise and support the front of the vehicle on jackstands. Remove the wheel/tire assembly.

2. Unfasten the double nuts at the top end of the shock absorber. Remove the cushions and the cushion retainers.

3. Remove the shock absorber-to-axle housing bolt.

4. Compress the shock absorber and remove it from the vehicle.

5. To install, reverse the removal procedures. Torque the shock absorber-to-axle housing bolt to 33 ft. lbs. (Pickup—1982–83) or shock absorber-to-lower suspension arm nut/bolt to 101 ft. lbs. (Pickup and 4-Runner) or 70 ft. lbs. (Van—1987-88) and the shock absorber-to-body nuts to 19 ft. lbs.

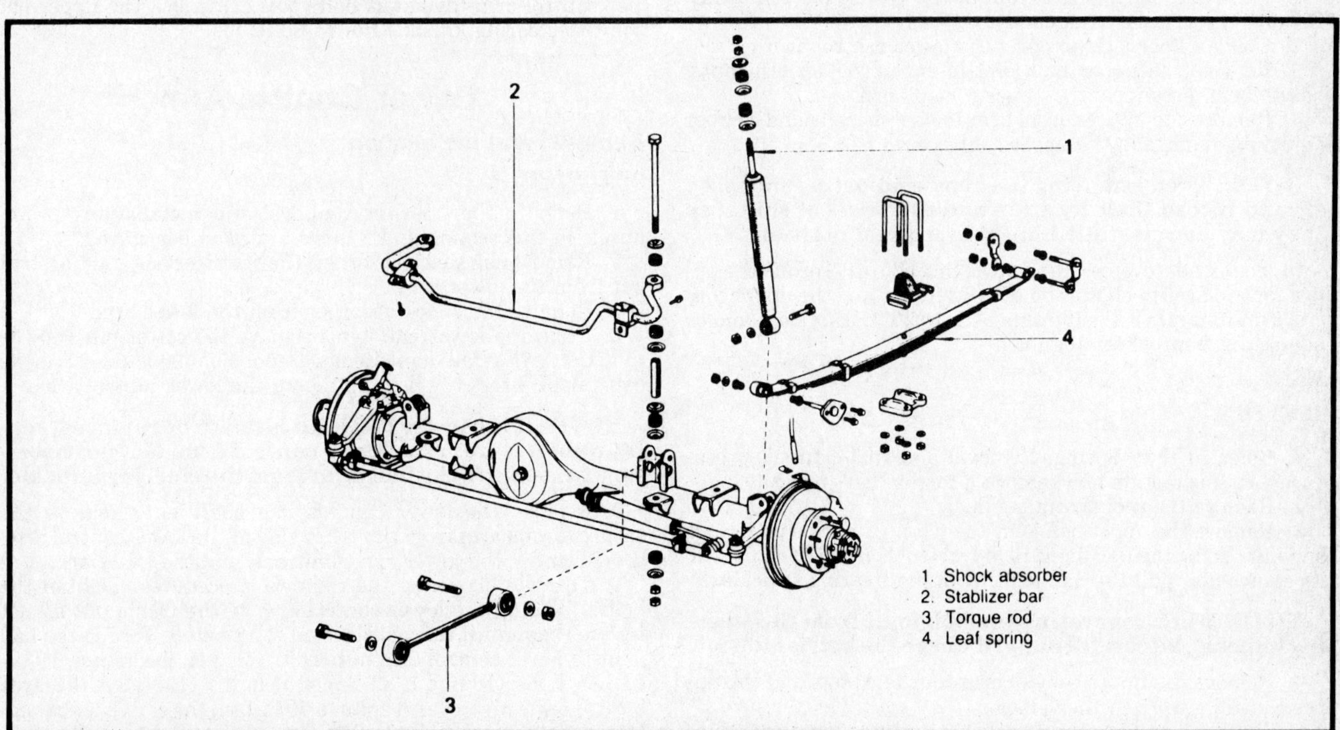

Front suspension components (4WD)—pick-up shown, Land Cruiser similar

LAND CRUISER

1. Raise and support the front of the vehicle on jackstands. Remove the wheel/tire assembly.

CAUTION

Be careful not to damage steering assembly when raising the front of the vehicle.

2. Remove mounting bolts from the top and the bottom of the shock and remove shock.
3. To install, reverse the removal procedures.

Upper Control Arm

Removal and Installation

2WD PICKUP (1982-86)

1. Raise and support the vehicle on jackstands. Remove the wheel/tire assembly.
2. Remove the caliper and suspend it from the frame.
3. Raise the lower control arm with a jack.
4. Remove the nut from the upper ball joint stud.
5. Using the Ball Joint Removal tool No. 09628–62011, or its equivalent, separate the ball joint from the steering knuckle. Be careful not to damage the ball joint boot.
6. Unbolt and remove the upper arm at the two bolts holding the inner shaft to the frame, taking note of the number and size of the aligning shims.
7. To install, reverse the removal procedures. Replace the shims in their original positions. Tighten fasteners but DO NOT torque them until the vehicle is on the ground.
8. Lower the vehicle to the ground and bounce it several times to align the suspension.
9. Torque the upper control arm-to-body bolts to 51–65 ft. lbs. (1982–83), 72 ft. lbs. (1984-86) and the upper ball joint-to-steering knuckle nut to 80 ft. lbs.

2WD PICKUP (1987-88), 4WD PICKUP AND 4-RUNNER

1. Raise and support the front of the vehicle on jackstands. Remove the wheel/tire assembly.
2. Using a floor jack, support the lower control arm.
3. Remove the upper ball joint-to-upper control arm nuts/bolts, then, disconnect the upper control arm.
4. Remove the upper conrol arm-to-chassis bolts and camber adjusting shims and the upper control arm.

NOTE: When removing the cambe adjusting shims, be sure to record their location and thickness of shims, so they may be reinstalled in their original positions.

5. To install, reverse the removal procedures. Torque the upper control arm-to-chassis bolts to 72 ft. lbs. and the upper control arm-to-upper ball joint nuts/bolts to 20 ft. lbs. Check and/or adjust the front wheel alignment.

VAN

1983-86

1. Refer to the "Spring, Removal and Installation" procedures, in this section and remove a torsion bar spring.
2. Remove the cool air intake duct.
3. Remove the upper ball joint-to-steering knuckle cotter pin and nut. Using the Ball Joint Removal tool No. 09628–62011, or its equivalent, pull the ball joint from the steering knuckle.

NOTE: When separating the ball joint from the steering knuckle, be careful not to damage the ball joint boot.

4. Remove the upper control arm-to-frame bolts and the upper control arm from the vehicle.
5. To install, reverse the removal procedures. Torque the upper control arm-to-frame rear bolt to 112 ft. lbs., the upper control arm-to-frame front bolt to 65 ft. lbs. and the ball joint-to-steering knuckle nut to 58 ft. lbs. Check the front end alignment.

2WD – 1987-88

1. Refer to the "Spring, Removal and Installation" procedures, in this section and remove a torsion bar spring.
2. Remove the cool air intake duct.
3. Remove the upper control arm-to-upper ball joint nuts/bolts and separate the upper control arm from the ball joint.
4. Remove the upper control arm-to-chassis bolts and the control arm from the vehicle.
5. To install, reverse the removal procedures. Torque the upper control arm-to-chassis bolts to 65 ft. lbs. (front) and 112 ft. lbs. (rear), then, the upper control arm-to-ball joint nuts/bolts to 22 ft. lbs. Check and/or adjust the front end alignment.

4WD – 1987-88

1. Refer to the "Spring, Removal and Installation" procedures, in this section and remove a torsion bar spring.
2. Remove the front-right seat and the console box. Disconnect the control and shift cables from the shift levers, then, remove the transmission/transfer shifting levers (with retainer).
3. Disconnect the parking brake cable from the brake lever, then, remove the parking brake lever assembly from the vehicle.
4. Disconnect the parking brake cable from the intermediate lever and remove it. Disconnect the shift cable from the transmission and remove it.
5. Remove the seat floor panel.
6. Remove the fan shroud, the radiator mounting bolts/nuts and move it aside; DO NOT drain the coolant.
7. Remove the shock absorber-to-frame nuts and disconnect the shock absorber from the frame.
8. From the upper ball joint, remove the cotter pin and the nut. Using the Ball Joint Removal tool No. 09628-62011, or its equivalent, press the ball joint from the steering knuckle.
9. Remove the upper control arm-to-chassis bolts and the arm from the vehicle.
10. To install, reverse the removal procedures. Torque the upper control arm-to-chassis bolts to 112 ft. lbs., the upper ball joint-to-steering knuckle nut to 83 ft. lbs.

Lower Control Arm

Removal and Installation

2WD PICKUP

1. Refer to the "Spring, Removal and Installation" procedures, in this section and remove a torsion bar spring.
2. Remove the shock absorber, the stablizer bar and the strut bar from the lower arm.
3. Remove the shock absorber from the lower arm.
4. From the lower ball joint, remove the cotter pin and the nut. Using the Ball Joint Removal tool No. 09628-62011, or its equivalent, press the ball joint from the lower control arm.

NOTE: If the lower ball joint is not to be replaced, simply unbolt it from the lower control arm. It is not necessary to separate the ball joint from the steering knuckle.

5. Remove the lower control arm shaft nut. Remove the spring torque arm from the other side of the lower control arm, then, remove the lower arm shaft bolt and the lower arm.
6. To install, reverse the removal procedures. Tighten the bolt(s) holding the lower control arm to the frame but do not torque them until the vehicle is on the ground. Torque the ball joint-to-lower control arm nuts/bolts to 18 ft. lbs. (8mm, 1982–83), 35 ft. lbs. (10mm, 1982–83) or 51 ft. lbs. (1984-88), the strut bar-to-lower control arm bolts to 70 ft. lbs., the stabilizer bar-to-lower control arm bolts to 9 ft. lbs., the lower shock absorber bolt to 13 ft. lbs., upper shock absorber bolt to 18 ft. lbs. and the

lower arm mounting nuts to 199 ft. lbs. (1982-85) or 166 ft. lbs. (1986-88). Check and/or adjust the front end alignment.

CAUTION

DO NOT torque the control arm bolts fully until the vehicle is lowered and bounced several times; if the bolts are tightened with the control arm(s) hanging, excessive bushing wear will result.

4WD PICKUP AND 4-RUNNER (1986-88)

1. Refer to the "Shock Absorber, Removal and Installation" procedures in this section and remove the shock absorber.
2. Disconnect the stabilizer bar from the lower suspension arm.
3. Remove the lower ball joint-to-lower control arm bolts, then, separate the control arm from the ball joint.
4. Using a piece of chalk, place match-marks on the front/rear adjusting cams.
5. Remove the nuts and adjusting cams and the lower control arms.
6. To install, reverse the removal procedures. Torque the lower ball joint-to-lower control arm bolts to 20 ft. lbs., the stabilizer bar-to-lower control arm bolts to 19 ft. lbs., the shock absorber-to-lower control arm nut/bolt to 101 ft. lbs.
7. Lower the vehicle to the ground, bounce it a few times, align the match-marks and torque the adjusting cam nuts to 203 ft. lbs. Check and/or adjust the front wheel alignment.

VAN

2WD (1983-88)

1. Raise and support the front of the vehicle on jackstands.
2. Remove the stablizer bar and the strut bar from the lower arm.
3. Remove the shock absorber from the lower arm. If necessary, disconnect the tie-rod end from the steering knuckle.
4. From the lower ball joint, remove the cotter pin and the nut. Using the Ball Joint Removal tool No. 09628-62011, or its equivalent, press the ball joint from the lower control arm.

NOTE: If the lower ball joint is not to be replaced, simply unbolt it from the lower control arm. It is not necessary to separate the ball joint from the steering knuckle.

5. Using a piece of chalk, match-mark the adjusting cam of the lower control arm.
6. Remove the adjusting cam, the nut and the lower control arm.
7. To install, reverse the removal procedures. Align the cam match-marks and finger tighten the nut. Torque the ball joint-to-lower control arm nuts/bolts to 49 ft. lbs., the lower ball joint-to-steering knuckle nut to 76 ft. lbs., the strut bar-to-lower control arm bolts to 49 ft. lbs., the stabilizer bar-to-lower control arm bolts to 9 ft. lbs., the tie-rod end-to-steering knuckle nut to 43 ft. lbs., the lower shock absorber bolt to 13 ft. lbs., upper shock absorber bolt to 19 ft. lbs. and the adjusting cam nut to 112 ft. lbs. (1983-86) or 152 ft. lbs. (1987-88). Check and/or adjust the front end alignment.

CAUTION

DO NOT torque the control arm bolts fully until the vehicle is lowered and bounced several times.

4WD (1987-88)

1. Raise and support the front of the vehicle on jackstands.
2. Remove the stablizer bar from the lower control arm.
3. Remove the shock absorber from the lower control arm.
4. From the lower ball joint, remove the cotter pin and the nut. Using the Ball Joint Removal tool No. 09628-62011, or its equivalent, press the ball joint from the lower control arm.

NOTE: If the lower ball joint is not to be replaced, simply unbolt it from the lower control arm. It is not necessary to separate the ball joint from the steering knuckle.

5. Using a piece of chalk, match-mark the adjusting cam of the lower control arm.
6. Remove the adjusting cam, the nut and the lower control arm.
7. To install, reverse the removal procedures. Align the cam match-marks and finger tighten the nut. Torque the ball joint-to-lower control arm nuts/bolts to 83 ft. lbs., the stabilizer bar-to-lower control arm bolts to 14 ft. lbs., the tie-rod end-to-steering knuckle nut to 43 ft. lbs., the lower shock absorber bolt to 70 ft. lbs. and the adjusting cam nut to 152 ft. lbs. Check and/or adjust the front end alignment.

CAUTION

DO NOT torque the control arm bolts fully until the vehicle is lowered and bounced several times.

Ball Joints

Inspection and Manufacturers Specs.

To check the lower ball joint for wear, raise the lower control arm and check for excess play. If the ball joints are within specifications and a looseness problem still exists, check the other suspension parts (wheel bearings, tie-rods and etc.). The bottom of the tire should not move more than 0.200 in. when the tire is pushed and pulled inward and outward. The tire should not move more than 0.090 in. up and down. If the play is greater than these figures, replace the ball joint. The upper ball joint should be replaced if a distinct looseness is felt when turning the ball joint stud with the steering knuckle removed.

Removal and Installation

1. Raise and support the vehicle on jackstands. Remove the wheel/tire assembly.
2. Support the lower control arm with a floor jack.
3. Remove the brake caliper and support it out of the way, with a wire.
4. Using the Ball Joint Removal tool No. 09611–22012, or its equivalent, separate the tie-rod end from the knuckle arm.
5. Using the Ball Joint Removal tool No. 09628–62011, or its equivalent, separate the upper or lower ball joint from the steering knuckle.

NOTE: Removal and installation will be easier if the bottom joint is removed first.

6. Remove the ball joint-to-control arm mounting bolts and separate the joint from the arm.
7. To install, reverse the removal procedures. Torque the ball joint-to-upper control arm bolts 20 ft. lbs. (2WD Pickup), 25 ft. lbs. (4WD Pickup) or 22 ft. lbs. (2WD Van), the upper ball joint-to-steering knuckle nut to 80 ft. lbs. (2WD Pickup), 105 ft. lbs. (4WD Pickup), 58 ft. lbs. (2WD Van) or 83 ft. lbs. (4WD Van), the ball joint-to-lower control arm bolts to 15–21 ft. lbs. (8mm, 1982–83), 29–39 ft. lbs. (10mm, 1982–83), 51 ft. lbs. (Pickup, 1984-88) or 49 ft. lbs. (Van), and the lower ball joint-to steering knuckle nut to 25 ft. lbs. (4WD Pickup – 1986), 43 ft. lbs. (4WD Pickup – 1987-88), 76 ft. lbs. (2WD Van) or 83 ft. lbs. (4WD Van – 1987-88).

NOTE: Be sure to grease the ball joints before moving the vehicle.

Wheel Bearings – 2WD Pickup and Van

For the 4WD models, refer to the "Front Wheel Bearing" in this section to perform the wheel bearing the adjustments, the removal and the installation procedures.

Removal and Installation

1. Raise and support the front of the vehicle on jackstands. Remove the wheel/tire assembly.
2. Remove the brake caliper (DO NOT disconnect the brake hose from the caliper) and suspend it on a wire.
3. Remove axle hub dust cap, the cotter pin, the nut lock, the adjusting nut, the thrust washer and the outer bearing, then pull the hub/disc assembly from the axle spindle.
4. Using a small pry bar, pry the oil seal from the rear of the disc/hub assembly, then remove the inner bearing.
5. Using a brass drift and a hammer, drive the bearing races from both sides of the disc/hub assembly.
6. Clean the parts in solvent (NOT gasoline) and blow dry with compressed air (DO NOT use a rag).
7. Using the palm of the hand, force multi-purpose into the bearings.
8. Using the installation tool No. 09608–30011 (Pickup) or 09608–30021 (Van), or their equivalents and a hammer, drive the outer bearing race(s) into the disc/hub assembly until it seats.
9. Place some grease inside the disc/hub assembly (between the races) and install the bearing into the rear of the hub. Coat the new oil seal with grease.
10. Using the installation tool No. 09608–30011 (Pickup) or 09608–30021 (Van), or their equivalents and a hammer, drive the new seal into the rear of the hub until it is flush.
11. To complete the installation, reverse the removal procedures and adjust the wheel bearing. Torque the brake caliper to 65 ft. lbs. (Pickup) or 61 ft. lbs. (Van).

Adjustment

1. Raise and support the front of the vehicle on jackstands.
2. Remove the wheel bearing grease cap, the cotter pin and the lock nut.
3. Tighten the wheel bearing adjust nut to 25 ft. lbs.
4. Turn the disc/hub assembly 2–3 times from left-to-right.
5. Loosen the adjusting, so there is 0.020–0.039 in. axial play.
6. Install the lock nut, the cotter pin and the grease cap.
7. Lower the vehicle and road test.

Alignment

Procedures

Front-end alignment measurements require the use of special equipment. Before measuring alignment or attempting to adjust it, always check the following points:

1. Be sure that the tires are properly inflated.
2. See that the wheels are properly balanced.
3. Check the ball joints to determine if they are worn or loose.
4. Check front wheel bearing adjustment.
5. Be sure that the vehicle is on a level surface.
6. Check all suspension parts for tightness.

Caster and Camber Adjustments

Measure the caster and camber angles. If they are not within specifications, adjust them by adding or subtracting the shims on the mounting bolts between the upper control arm and the suspension member:

1. To increase the camber, remove the shims equally from both of the control shaft mounting bolts. Do the reverse to decrease camber.
2. To increase the caster, add the camber adjusting shims to the rear mounting bolt or remove them from the front mounting bolt. Do the reverse to decrease caster.

NOTE: The caster and camber adjustments should always be performed in a single operation.

Toe-in Adjustment

Measure the toe-in. Adjust it, if necessary, by loosening the tie-rod end clamping bolts and rotating the tie-rod adjusting tubes. Tighten the clamp bolts when finished.

NOTE: Both tie-rod ends should be the same length. If they are not, perform the adjustment until the toe-in is within specifications and the tie-rod ends are equal in length.

Stabilizer Bars and Shafts

Removal and Installation

2WD PICKUP AND VAN

1. Refer to the "Spring, Removal and Installation" procedures, in this section and remove one of the torsion bar springs from the vehicle.
2. Remove the stabilizer bar-to-lower control arm nuts, the cushions and the bolts.

NOTE: Be sure to arrange the hardware as originally installed.

3. Remove the stabilizer bar-to-frame brackets and bushings and lower the stabilizer bar from the vehicle.
4. To install, reverse the removal procedures. Be sure to carefully inspect each bushing for damage and replace the bushing(s) (if necessary). Torque the stabilizer bar-to-lower control arm nuts to 9 ft. lbs. (Pickup) or 0.510–0.630 in. (Van) and the stabilizer bar-to-frame bracket bolts to 9 ft. lbs. (Pickup) or 14 ft. lbs. (Van). Adjust the tension bar spring and the vehicle heights.

NOTE: When torquing the stabilizer bar-to-lower control arm (on the Van), the distance from the end of the bolts to the top of the nut should be 0.510–0.630 in.

4WD PICKUP, 4-RUNNER AND LAND CRUISER

1. Remove the stabilizer bar-to-axle housing nuts, the cushions and the bolts.

NOTE: Be sure to arrange the hardware as originally installed.

2. Remove the stabilizer bar-to-frame brackets and bushings and lower the stabilizer bar from the vehicle.
3. To install, reverse the removal procedures. Be sure to carefully inspect each bushing for damage and replace the bushing(s) (if necessary). Torque all stabilizer bar-to-frame bracket bolts to 9 ft. lbs. and the stabilizer bar-to-axle housing nuts to 19 ft. lbs.

Strut Bar—2WD Pickup and Van

Removal and Installation

1. Raise and support the vehicle on jackstands.
2. Place match-marks on the strut bar-to-inner mounting nut at the frame bracket.
3. Remove the front mounting nut from the strut bar.
4. Remove the strut bar-to-lower control arm.
5. To install, reverse the removal procedures. Torque the strut bar-to-lower control arm bolts to 70 ft. lbs. (Pickup) or 49 ft. lbs. (Van) and the strut bar-to-frame bracket nut to 90 ft. lbs. Check the front-end alignment.

Torque Rod—4WD Pickup, 4-Runner and Land Cruiser

Removal and Installation

1. Raise and support the front of the vehicle on jackstands.
2. Remove the torque rod-to-axle housing nut/bolt.
3. Remove the torque rod-to-frame bracket nut/bolt.
4. Remove the torque rod from the vehicle.
5. To install, reverse the removal procedures. Torque the torque rod nuts and bolts to 105 ft. lbs.

STEERING GEAR AND LINKAGE

For overhaul information, refer to "Steering" in the Unit Repair Section of this manual.

Manual Steering Gear

Removal and Installation

2WD PICKUP

1. Remove the pitman arm-to-relay rod cotter pin and nut. Using the tool No. 09611-22012, or its equivalent, separate the relay rod from the pitman arm.
2. Match-mark the flexible steering coupling-to-steering gear, then remove the lock bolt and separate the steering coupling from the steering gear.
3. Remove the steering gear housing mounting bolts and the gear housing.
4. To install, reverse the removal procedures. Torque the housing-to-frame bolts to 37–43 ft. lbs. (1982–83) or 48 ft. lbs. (1984 and later), the pitman arm-to-relay rod nut 80–90 ft. lbs. (1982–83) or 67 ft. lbs. (1984-88) and the steering gear-to-coupling yoke to 15–20 ft. lbs.

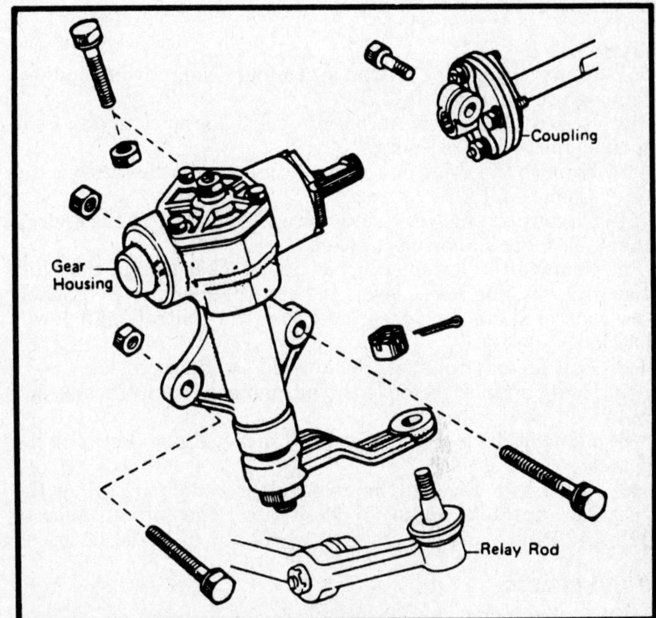

2WD pick-up manual steering gear

4WD PICKUP AND 4-RUNNER

1. Remove the stone shield from the gear housing, if equipped.
2. Match-mark the intermediate shaft-to-steering gear and disconnect them.
3. Remove the cotter pin and plug from the drag link.
4. Disconnect the drag link from the pitman arm.
5. Remove the pitman arm nut. Using the Puller tool No. 09610-55012, or its equivalent, separate the pitman arm from the steering gear.
6. Remove the steering gear housing-to-frame bolts and the gear housing.
7. To install, reverse the removal procedures. Torque the steering gear-to-frame bolts to 42 ft. lbs., the steering gear-to-intermediate bolts to 29 ft. lbs., the pitman arm-to-steering gear nut to 127 ft. lbs.

NOTE: When installing the drag link to the pitman arm, tighten the plug completely and loosen it $1^1/_3$ turns.

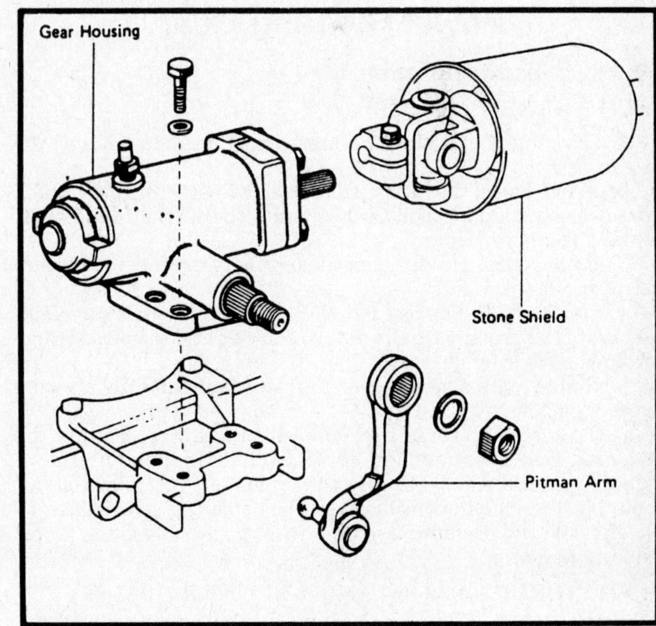

4WD pick-up manual steering gear

VAN

1. Match-mark the steering gear-to-intermediate shaft, then remove the coupling bolt.
2. At the pitman arm-to-drag link and the drag link-to-steering gear connections, remove the cotter pin and the mounting nut.
3. Using the tool No. 09610-20012, or its equivalent, separate the pitman arm from the steering gear, then separate the pitman arm from the drag link.
4. Remove the steering gear-to-frame bolts and the steering gear from the frame.
5. To install, reverse the removal procedures. Torque the steering gear-to-frame bolts to 70 ft. lbs., the steering gear-to-coupling bolt to 18 ft. lbs., the pitman arm-to-steering gear nut to 90 ft. lbs. and the pitman arm-to-drag link nut to 67 ft. lbs.

LAND CRUISER

55 Series

1. Remove the worm yokes from the worm and the main shaft.
2. Remove the intermediate shaft assembly.
3. Remove the Pitman arm from the sector shaft.
4. Remove the steering gear-to-frame bolts and the steering gear from the vehicle.
5. To install, reverse the removal procedures. Torque the Pitman arm to 119–141 ft. lbs.

NOTE: The intermediate shaft must be installed with the wheels in a straight ahead position and the steering wheel straight ahead.

40 Series

1. Remove the horn button assembly. Using a wheel puller, remove the steering wheel.
2. Remove the steering column jacket lower clamp and the turn signal switch assembly.
3. Remove the steering column access plate, then the carburetor and the oil filter.
4. Disconnect the No. 1 shift rod and select rod at the ends of the shift control and select levers.
5. Remove the lower shift control bracket clamp, the shift control lever, the select lever, the control shaft lower bracket, the control shaft low speed lever and the control shaft lower bracket.
6. Pull the control shaft out toward the driver's side.
7. Using a puller, remove the pitman arm from the steering gear.
8. Remove the steering gear box bracket cap and lift out the gear box.
9. To install, reverse the removal procedures. Torque the gear box bracket cap to 75–90 ft. lbs., the pitman arm to 120–140 ft. lbs. and the steering wheel nut to 30–50 ft. lbs.

Adjustments

Adjustments to the manual steering gear are not necessary during normal service. Adjustments are performed only as part of overhaul, which is covered in the Unit Repair section.

Power Steering Gear

Removal and Installation

2WD PICKUPS (1982-88)

1. Disconnect and plug the pressure line clamp bolts at the steering gear.
2. Match-mark the intermediate shaft-to-steering gear, then, remove the coupling bolt and separate the intermediate shaft from the steering gear.
3. Remove the pitman arm-to-steering gear and the pitman arm-to-relay rod nuts.
4. Using the Puller tool No. 09611–22012, or its equivalent, separate the pitman arm from the relay rod and the pitman arm from the steering gear.
5. Remove the steering gear-to-frame bolts and the steering gear from the vehicle.
6. To install, reverse the removal procedures. Torque the steering gear-to-frame bolts to 48 ft. lbs., the pitman arm-to-steering gear nut to 90 ft. lbs., the pitman arm-to-relay rod nut to 67 ft. lbs., the intermediate shaft-to-steering gear bolt to 19 ft. lbs. and the pressure line nuts to 33 ft. lbs. Bleed the power steering system.

4WD PICKUP (1982-88) AND 4-RUNNER (1985-88)

1. Remove the battery and the engine lower gravel shield.
2. Disconnect and plug the pressure lines at the steering gear.
3. Remove the steering gear stone shield.

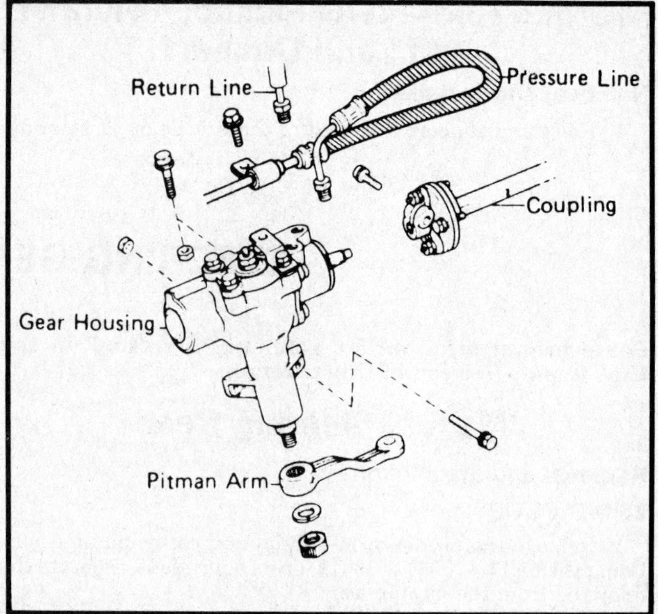

2WD pick-up power steering gear

4. Match-mark the intermediate shaft-to-steering gear, then remove coupling bolt and the intermediate shaft from the steering gear.
5. Remove the pitman arm-to-steering gear nut. Using the Puller tool No. 09610-5512, or its equivalent, separate the pitman arm from thesteering gear.
6. Remove the gear housing-to-frame bolts and the steering gear from the vehicle.
7. To install, reverse the removal procedures. Torque the steering gear-to-frame bolts to 42 ft. lbs., the pitman arm-to-steering gear nut to 127 ft. lbs., the intermediate shaft-to-steering gear bolt to 29 ft. lbs. and the pressure line union nuts to 33 ft. lbs. Bleed the power steering system.

VAN

1. Match-mark the intermediate shaft-to-steering gear, then, remove the intermediate shaft-to-steering gear coupling bolt.
2. Disconnect and plug the pressure lines at the steering gear.
3. Remove the pitman arm-to-steering gear nut. Using the Puller tool No. 09610–20012, or its equivalent, separate the pitman arm from the steering gear.
4. Remove the steering gear-to-frame bolts and the steering gear form the vehicle.
5. To install, reverse the removal procedures. Torque the steering gear-to-frame bolts to 78 ft. lbs., the pitman arm-to-steering gear nut to 90 ft. lbs., the intermediate shaft-to-steering gear bolt to 18 ft. lbs. and the pressure lines-to-steering gear to 33 ft. lbs. Bleed the power steering system.

LAND CRUISER

1. Disconnect the pressure lines from the steering gear.
2. Remove the intermediate shaft-to-steering gear bolt and the steering column-to-firewall bolts.
3. Loosen the steering column-to-dash bolts. Remove the pitman arm-to-steering gear nut.
4. Using a puller, separate the relay rod from the Pitman shaft and the Pitman arm from the steering gear.
5. Pull the steering column towards the passenger compartment to uncouple the steering shaft from the steering gear.
6. Remove the steering gear-to-frame bolts and the steering gear from the vehicle.

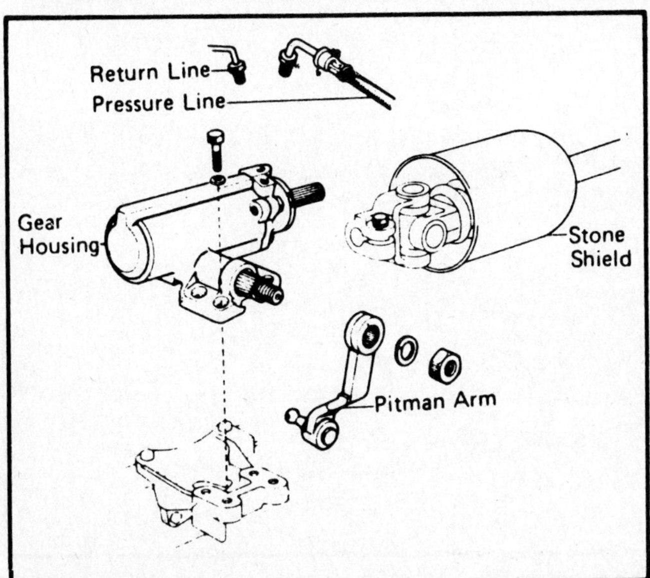

4WD pick-up power steering gear

7. To install, reverse the removal procedures. Torque the steering gear-to-frame bolts to 40–63 ft. lbs., the pitman arm-to-steering gear nut to 120–141 ft. lbs., the intermediate shaft-to-steering gear bolt to 22–32 ft. lbs., the pressure hose fitting to 29–36 ft. lbs. and the return hose fitting to 24–30 ft. lbs. Bleed the power steering system.

NOTE: During installation of the hydraulic lines, position each line clear of any surrounding components, then tighten the fittings.

Power Steering Pump

Removal and Installation

PICKUP, LAND CRUISER AND 4-RUNNER

NOTE: On the 1984-88 models (except diesel), disconnect the air hoses from the air control valve and the high tension wires from the distributor. On the diesel models, remove the engine under cover.

1. Loosen the power steering pump pulley nut.

NOTE: Use the drive belt as a brake to keep the pulley from rotating.

2. Place a container under the pump. Disconnect the return line and the pressure tube, then drain the fluid into the container.
3. Loosen the idler pulley nut and the adjusting bolt, then remove the drive belt.
4. Remove the drive pulley and the woodruff key from the pump shaft.
5. Remove the mounting bolts and the power steering pump from the vehicle.
6. To install, reverse the removal procedures. Torque the pump pulley mounting bolt to 29 ft. lbs. (gasoline) or 45 ft. lbs. (diesel), the pump pulley nut to 32 ft. lbs. and the pressure hoses to 33 ft. lbs. Adjust the drive belt tension. Bleed the power steering system.

VAN

1. Disconnect the air hoses from the air control valve of the power steering pump.
2. Drain the fluid from the power steering reservoir tank.
3. At the power steering pump, disconnect the return hose and the pressure tube.
4. Loosen the power steering pump adjusting bolt, then, remove the drive belt, the pulley and the woodruff key.
5. Remove the mounting bolts, the power steering pump and the bracket from the vehicle.
6. To install, reverse the removal procedures. Torque the power steering pump-to-engine bolts to 29 ft. lbs., the pulley set nut to 32 ft. lbs. and the pressure tube to 33 ft. lbs.

Bleeding System

1. Raise and support the front of the vehicle on jackstands.
2. Fill the pump reservoir with Dexron® automatic transmission fluid.
3. With the engine running, rotate the steering wheel from lock to lock several times. Add fluid as necessary.

NOTE: Perform the bleeding procedure until all of the air is bled from the system.

4. The fluid level should not have risen more than 0.200 in.; if it does, check the pump.

Steering Linkage

Removal and Installation

2WD PICKUP

1. Raise and support the front of the vehicle on jackstands.
2. Remove the front wheels.
3. Remove the pitman arm-to-relay rod nut. Using the Puller tool No. 09611-22012, or its equivalent, separate the pitman arm from the relay rod.
4. Remove the idler arm-to-relay rod cotter pin and nut bolts and remove the idler arm-to-frame bolts.
5. Remove the tie-rod end-to-knuckle arm and the tie-rod end-to-relay rod cotter pin and nut.
6. Using the Puller tool No. 09611-22012, or its equivalent, separate the tie-rod from the knuckle arm and from the relay rod.
7. To install, reverse the removal procedures. Torque the tie-rod end-to-knuckle arm, the tie-rod end-to-relay rod nut to 67 ft. lbs., the relay rod-to-pitman arm nut to 67 ft. lbs. and the relay rod-to-idler arm to 43 ft. lbs.

4WD PICKUP AND 4-RUNNER

1. Raise and support the vehicle on jackstands. Remove the front wheels.
2. Remove tie-rod end-to-knuckle arm and the tie-rod-to-steering damper cotter pins and nuts. Remove the steering damper-to-axle housing nut, retainer and cushion; be sure to note the order of the cushions and retainers.
3. Using the Puller tool No. 09611-22012, or it equivalent, separate the steering damper from the tie-rod andthe tie-rod ends from the knuckle arms. Remove the tie-rod and the steering damper from the vehicle.
4. At both ends of the drag link, remove the cotter pin. Using a prybar, remove the plug from both ends of the drag link.

NOTE: The cap may be tight, a wrench or pliers may have to be used to turn the prybar.

5. When the cap is removed, dislodge the spring seat, spring and outer socket holder inside the drag link by working the steering knuckle back and forth. The steering knuckle socket in the drag link can now be removed.

NOTE: Be sure to note the order in which the spring seat, the spring and the outer socket are removed from the drag link.

6. To install, reverse the removal procedures. Torque the

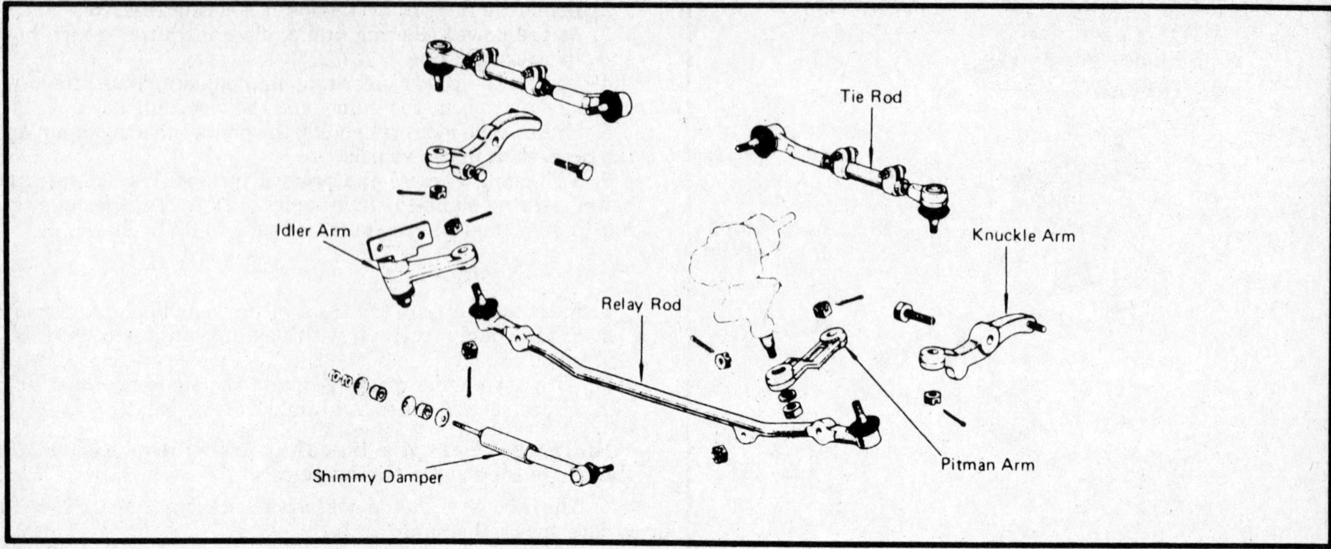

Exploded view of the steering linkage – 2WD pickup – 1982-88

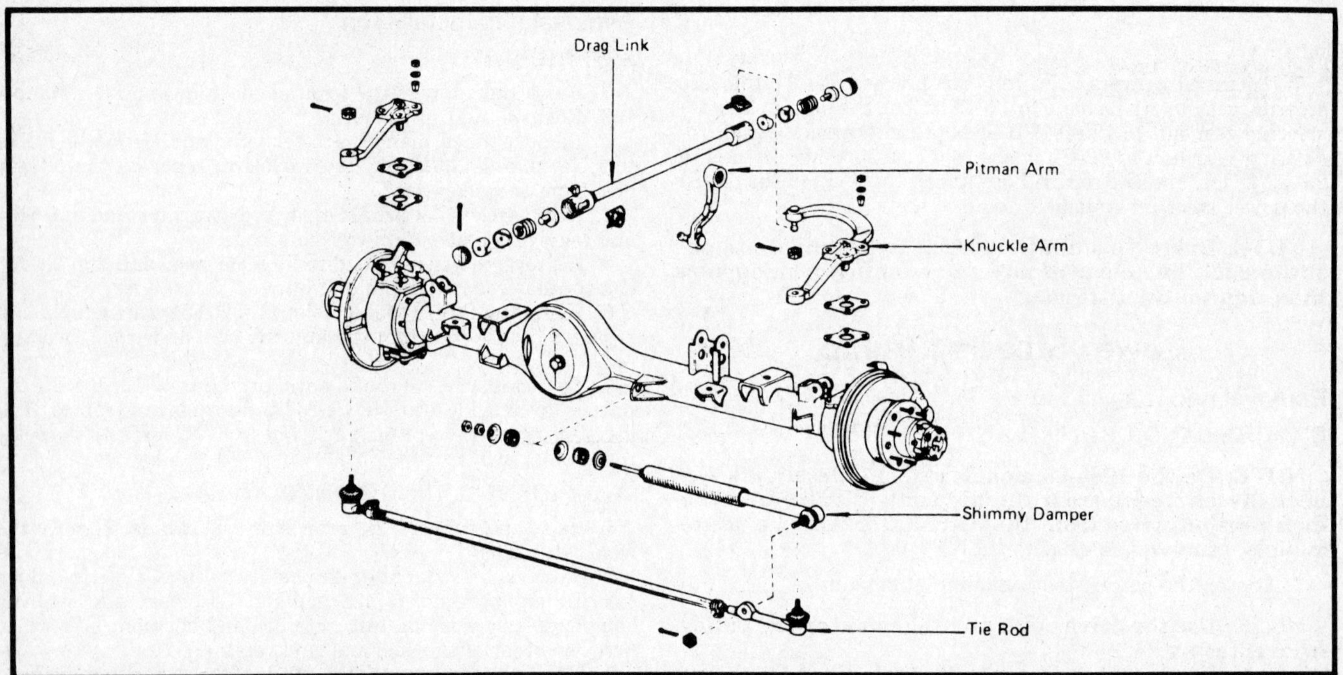

4WD Pick-up and 4-Runner steering linkage

steering damper-to-axle housing nut to 9 ft. lbs., the tie-rod end-to-steering knuckle arm to 67 ft. lbs. and the steering damper-to-tie-rod end to 43 ft. lbs.

NOTE: Be sure to grease drag link ends at their grease nipples. When installing drag link end caps, tighten the plugs completely and loosen them $1^1/_3$ turns.

VAN

1. Raise and support the front of the vehicle on jackstands. Remove the wheel/tire assemblies.

NOTE: Before removing any component in the steering system, remove the cotter pin and the retaining nut first.

2. Using the Puller tool No. 09611–22012, or its equivalent, separate the drag link from the pitman arm.
3. Using the Puller tool No. 09628–62011, or its equivalent, separate the tie-rod ends from the relay rod, the relay rod from the center arm, the center arm from the center arm bracket and the tie-rod end from the knuckle arm.
4. Remove the idler arm-to-frame bolts and the idler arm from the vehicle.
5. To install, reverse the removal procedures. Torque the drag link-to-pitman arm nut to 67 ft. lbs., the drag link-to-center arm nut to 43 ft. lbs., the center arm-to-center arm bracket nut to 67 ft. lbs., the relay rod-to-idler arm nut to 43 ft. lbs., the relay rod-to-tie-rod end nut to 43 ft. lbs., the tie-rod end-to-knuckle arm nut to 43 ft. lbs., the idler arm-to-frame bolts to 58 ft. lbs. and the center arm bracket-to-frame bolts to 58 ft. lbs.

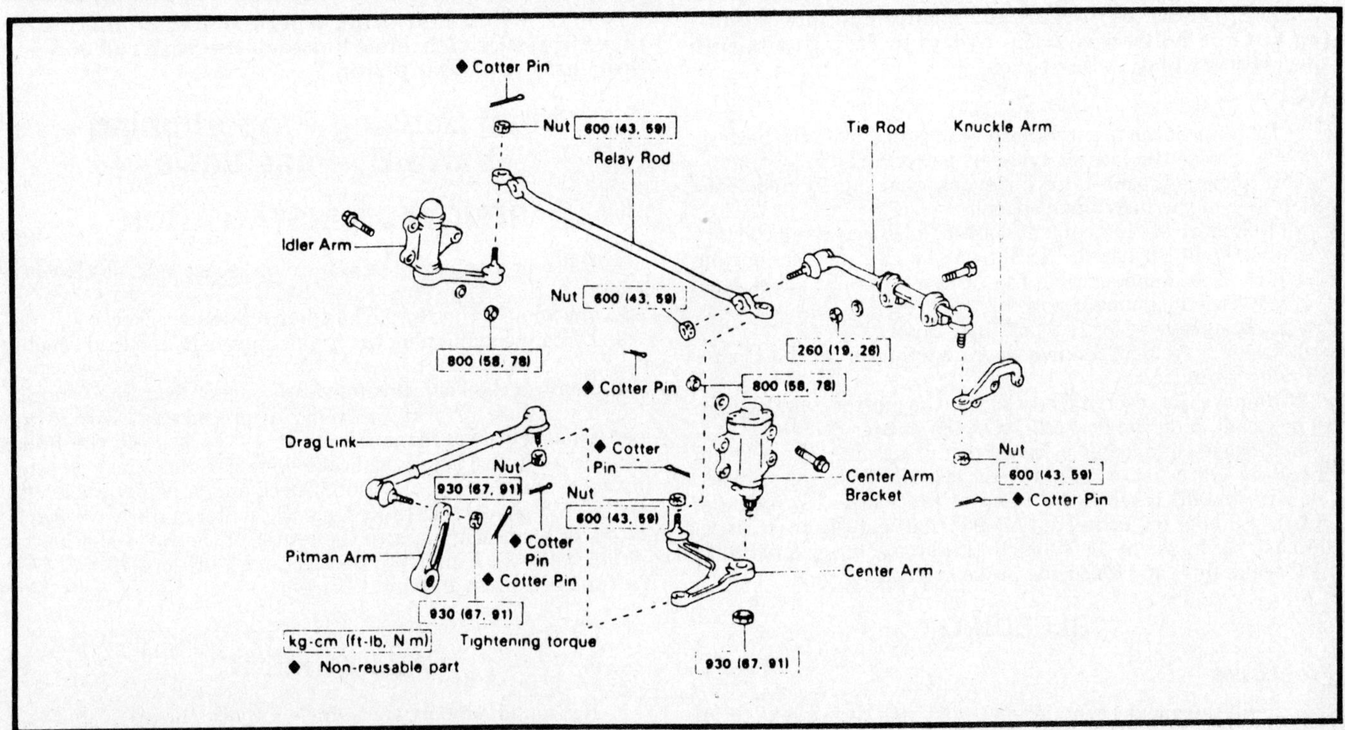

Exploded view of the steering linkage—Van

LAND CRUISER

1. Raise and support the front of the vehicle on jackstands. Remove the wheel/tire assemblies.
2. Remove the pitman arm-to-steering gear nut.

NOTE: Punch match-marks on the Pitman arm-to-steering gear to aid reinstallation.

3. Using a puller tool, remove the pitman arm from the steering gear.
4. Disconnect the drag link from the center arm with a tie-rod puller. Remove the drag link with the Pitman arm.
5. Using a puller tool, disconnect the tie-rod ends from the steering knuckle.
6. Disconnect the relay rod ends from the center arm. Remove the tie-rod/relay rod assembly.
7. Disconnect the steering damper from the front crossmember bracket.
8. Remove the center arm mounting nut. Using a puller tool, remove the center arm, complete with damper.
9. Remove the skid plate and the center arm-to-frame bracket.
10. To install, reverse the removal procedures. Torque the pitman arm-to-steering gear bolt to 120–140 ft. lbs. Lubricate all of the rod ends and damper ends with multipurpose grease. Check and/or adjust the alignment.

NOTE: When installing the pitman arm to the steering gear, be sure to align the match-marks.

BRAKE SYSTEM

For overhaul information, refer to "Brakes" in the Unit Repair Section of this manual.

Master Cylinder

CAUTION

Be careful not to spill brake fluid on the painted surfaces of the vehicle; it will damage the paint.

Removal and Installation

PICKUPS, 4-RUNNER AND LAND CRUISER

1. Using a syringe, remove the brake fluid from the master cylinder.
2. Disconnect and plug the hydraulic lines at the master cylinder.
3. If equipped, disconnect the level warning switch connector from the master cylinder.
4. Remove the master cylinder mounting bolts, by performing one of the following procedures:
   a. If not equipped with power brakes, remove the master cylinder-to-cowl bolts and the clevis pin from the brake pedal. Remove the master cylinder.
   b. On other models with power brakes, remove the master cylinder-to-power booster nuts and the master cylinder assembly from the power brake unit.
5. To install, reverse the removal procedures. Torque the master cylinder mounting bolts to 9 ft. lbs. and the brake lines-to-master cylinder to 11 ft. lbs. Refill the master cylinder with new brake fluid and bleed the brake system.

NOTE: Before tightening the master cylinder mounting nuts or bolts, screw the hydraulic line fitting into the cylinder body a few turns.

VAN

1. Disconnect the negative battery terminal from the battery.
2. To expose the master cylinder, perform the following:
   a. Remove the master cylinder reservoir cap, located at the left-side of the instrument panel.
   b. Remove the instrument cluster finish panel and the lower cluster finish panel. Disconnect the electrical connectors and the speedometer cable from the instrument panel, then remove the instrument panel.
   c. Remove the No. 1, 2 and 3 air ducts.
3. Using a syringe, remove the brake fluid from the master cylinder reservoir.
4. Remove the reservoir hoses from the master cylinder. Disconnect and plug the brake lines at the master cylinder.
5. Remove the master cylinder mounting nuts, the vacuum check valve bracket and the master cylinder from the vehicle.
6. To install, reverse the removal procedures. Torque the master cylinder mounting nuts to 9 ft. lbs. and the brake lines-to-master cylinder to 11 ft. lbs. Refill the master cylinder with new brake fluid and bleed the brake system.

BLEEDING

Procedure

1. Refill the master cylinder reservoir with clean brake fluid.
2. If equipped with a 2WD (½ ton) or a 4WD (22R-TE engine), perform the following procedure:
   a. Disconnect the brake tubes from the master cylinder.
   b. Depress the brake pedal and hold it.
   c. Have an assistant block off the outlet and hold it, then release the brake pedal.
   d. Repeat this procedure several times.
   e. Reconnect the tubes to the master cylinder.
3. Begin bleeding the brake cylinder/disc with the longest brake tube from the master cylinder.
4. If performing this operation alone, perform the following procedures:
   a. Using a beaker, fill it ½ full with clean brake fluid.
   b. Using a clear vinyl tube, connect it to the brake bleeder and immerse it in the brake fluid container.
   c. Open the bleeder screw.
   d. Depress the brake pedal several times, until all of the the air bubbles cease. Close the bleeder screws.
5. If using an assistant to perform this operation, perform the following procedures:
   a. Have the assistant open the bleeder screw.
   b. Depress the brake pedal to the floor and hold it.
   c. Have the assistant close the bleeder screw.
   d. Release the brake pedal and wait a few seconds, then, repeat this procedure.
   e. When the air bubbles cease and the brake fluid is clear, proceed to the next wheel.

Power Brake Boosters

Removal and Installation

1. Refer to the "Master Cylinder, Removal and Installation" procedures, in this section and remove the master cylinder from the power brake booster.
2. Remove the vacuum hose form the power brake booster.
3. Working under the instrument panel, remove the brake pedal-to-brake booster rod clevis pin. Remove the power brake booster mounting bolts and the booster from the vehicle.
4. To install, reverse the removal procedures. Torque the power brake booster nuts to 9 ft. lbs. Check and/or adjust the brake pedal height.

NOTE: When installing a new booster, make sure there is a little clearance between the push rod end and the master cylinder piston.

Load Sensing Proportioning Valve/By-Pass Valve

REMOVAL & INSTALLATION

1. Raise and support the vehicle on jackstands, so that it is level.
2. Disconnect the No. 2 shackle from the bracket.
3. Disconnect and plug the brake lines from the load sensing valve.
4. Remove the load sensing valve bracket from the frame.
5. To install, reverse the removal procedures. Torque the load sensing valve-to-frame bolts to 14 ft. lbs. and the brake tubes to 11 ft. lbs. Bleed the brake system. Adjust the load sensing valve and the rear axle load. Check and/or adjust the length of the No. 2 shackle (distance from the center of the No. 2 shackle-to-shackle bracket bolt to the center of the No. 1 shackle-to-spring bolt): 3.07 in. (2WD Pickup and Van) or 4.72 in. (4WD Pickup, 4-Runner and Land Cruiser).

ADJUSTMENT

1. Raise and support the vehicle on jackstands, so that it is level.
2. Check and/or adjust the rear axle load: 1,323 lbs. (¾ ton: 1982–83), 1,150 lbs. (FJ40, Land Cruiser), 1,200 lbs. (FJ60, Land Cruiser), 1,543 lbs. (2WD Pickup: 1984-88, Van: 1983-88), 1,433 lbs. (4WD Pick-up: 1982–83) or 1,653 lbs. (4WD Pickup: 1984-88, 4-Runner: 1985-88).
3. Using the Pressure Gauge tool No. 09705–29017, or its equivalent (1982–83) or 09709–29017, or its equivalent (1984-88), install one (in the brake line) at the front wheel and one at the rear wheel.
4. Depress the brake pedal, raising the front pressure to 365 psi. (Land Cruiser), 711 psi. (Pickups, Van, 4-Runner), then check the rear brake pressure. The rear brake pressure should be 148–205 psi. (Land Cruiser), 398–540 psi. (Pickups: 1982–83, Van: 1983-88), 455–597 psi. (2WD Pickup: 1984-88) or 441–589 psi. (4WD Pickup: 1984-88, 4-Runner: 1985-88).

NOTE: When checking the fluid pressure, depress the pedal ONLY once and record the pressures within 2 seconds; NEVER depress it twice.

5. Depress the brake pedal, raising the front pressure to 835 psi. (Land Cruiser), 1,138 psi. (Pickups: 1982–83) or 1,422 psi. (Pickups: 1984-88, Van: 1983-88, 4-Runner: 1985-88), then, check the rear brake pressure. The rear brake pressure should be 312–411 psi. (Land Cruiser), 526–726 psi. (Pickups: 1982–83), 512–712 psi. (Van: 1983-88), 696–896 psi. (2WD Pickup: 1984-88) or 682–882 psi. (4WD Pickup: 1984-88, 4-Runner: 1985-88).
6. If the pressures do not fall within the specifications, perform the following:
   a. Remove the No. 2 shackle from the shackle bracket. Loosen the lock nut and adjust the length of the No. 2 shackle (distance from the center of the No. 2 shackle-to-shackle bracket bolt to the center of the No. 1 shackle-to-spring bolt): 2.83–3.31 in. (2WD) or 4.49–4.96 in. (4WD).

NOTE: When adjusting the No. 2 shackle length, lengthening the distance decreases the pressure and shortening the distance increases the pressure.

   b. If the pressure cannot be adjusted with the No. 2 shackle, raise or lower the valve body.

NOTE: When adjusting the valve body, lowering the valve lowers the pressure and raising the valve increases the pressure.

c. After adjusting the valve body, adjust the length of the No. 2 shackle. If the adjustment cannot be accurately made, inspect the valve body.

NOTE: With the valve body installed in it's correct position, the distance between the valve body and the spring should be 0.040 in.

Parking Brake

DRIVE SHAFT—LAND CRUISER

Adjustment

Land Cruiser models use a separate drum brake assembly, operating on the driveshaft, to serve as a parking brake. Adjust it as follows:

1. Push the parking brake lever all the way in, so that the brake is released.
2. Raise and support the rear of the vehicle on jackstands.
3. Turn the parking brake adjustment shaft, located at the bottom of the parking brake backing plate, counterclockwise until the shoes seat against the drum.
4. Back the adjuster off one notch.
5. Apply the parking brake; the drum should be locked. Release the brake; the drum should rotate freely.

NOTE: If the drum does not rotate freely with the brake off, loosen the adjuster one more notch.

6. Adjust the turnbuckles on the parking brake intermediate levers and the adjusting nuts on the end of the parking brake cables, so that 7–12 notches are required to apply the parking brake.

CABLE

Adjustment

PICKUPS (1982-88) AND 4-RUNNER (1985-88)

1. Make sure that the rear brakes are properly adjusted.
2. Pull the parking brake lever out as far as it will go, counting the number of notches heard in the travel: 10–16 notches (2WD) or 7–15 notches (4WD).
3. If these standards are not met, proceed as follows:

2WD Pickup

1. Working under the truck, tighten the adjusting nut at the equalizer until the travel is within limits and there is no drag at the rear shoes.
2. Apply the parking brake several times and again check that there is no drag with the brake released.

4WD Pickup and 4-Runner

1. Working under the truck, tighten the bellcrank stopper screw until the play at the rear brake links is gone, then loosen the nut one full turn. Tighten the locknut.
2. Tighten one of the adjusting nuts on the intermediate lever while loosening the other, until the travel is correct. Tighten the two locknuts.
3. Confirm that the bellcrank is in contact with the backing plate.

VAN

NOTE: The rear brake shoe clearance should be adjusted before adjusting the parking brake.

1. Raise and support the rear of the vehicle on jackstands.
2. Remove the shift knob and the console box.
3. At the parking brake handle, loosen the cable locknut. Pull the hand brake UP 7–9 clicks.
4. Turn the adjust nut until the rear wheels can no longer be turned, then, tighten the locknut.
5. Install the console and the shift knob.

CLUTCH

Clutch Assembly

HYDRAULIC

Removal and Installation

1. Refer to the "Manual Transmission and Transfer Case, Removal and Installation" procedures, in this section and remove the transmission from the engine.
2. Stamp or chalk matchmarks on the clutch cover and flywheel, indicating their relationship.
3. Loosen the clutch cover-to-flywheel retaining bolts one turn at a time. The pressure on the clutch disc must be released GRADUALLY.
4. Remove the clutch cover-to-flywheel bolts. Remove the clutch cover and the clutch disc.
5. If the clutch release bearing is to be replaced, perform the following:
   a. Remove the bearing retaining clip(s), the bearing and hub.
   b. Remove the release fork and the boot.
   c. The bearing is press fitted to the hub.

NOTE: In some cases, the bearing is available with the hub. If this is not the case, have the bearing replaced using a hydraulic press. Using other means to replace the bearing could result in personal injury.

   d. Clean all parts and lightly grease the input shaft splines and all of the contact points.
   e. Install the bearing/hub assembly, the fork, the boot and the retaining clip(s) in their original locations.
6. Inspect the flywheel surface for cracks, heat scoring (blue marks) and warpage. If oil is present on the flywheel surface, this indicates that either the engine rear oil seal or the transmission front oil seal is leaking. If necessary, refer to the appropriate section for seal replacement.

NOTE: Before installing any new parts, make sure that they are clean. During installation, do not get grease or oil on any of the components, as this will shorten clutch life considerably.

7. Using the Alignment tool No. 09301-20020 or its equivalent, position the clutch disc against the flywheel. (Pickups and Vans: The short side of the splined section faces the flywheel; Land Cruisers: The long side of the splined section faces the flywheel).

8. Install the clutch cover over the disc and install the bolts loosely. Align the pressure plate-to-flywheel matchmarks. If a new or rebuilt clutch cover assembly is installed, use the matchmark on the old cover assembly as a reference. Torque the pressure plate-to-flywheel bolts to 14 ft. lbs. (using a criss-cross pattern).

CLUTCH PEDAL HEIGHT

Adjustment

The pedal height measurement is gauged from the angled section of the floorboard to the center of the clutch pedal pad. Refer to the accompanying specification chart to determine the recommended pedal height.

If necessary, adjust the pedal height by loosening the locknut and turning the pedal stop bolt which is located above the pedal towards the drivers seat. Tighten the locknut after the adjustment.

CLUTCH MASTER CYLINDER

Removal and Installation

CAUTION

Brake fluid dissolves paint. DO NOT allow it to drip onto the body when removing the master cylinder.

PICKUPS AND LAND CRUISER

1. Disconnect the master cylinder pushrod pin from the top of the clutch pedal.
2. Using the tool No. 09751–36011, or its equivalent, remove the hydraulic line from the master cylinder, being careful not to damage the compression fitting.
3. Remove the master cylinder-to-cowl nuts/ bolts.
4. To install, reverse the removal procedures. Partially tighten the hydraulic line before tightening the master cylinder mounting nut(s). Torque the nuts/bolts to 9 ft. lbs. Bleed the clutch system. Adjust the push rod play clearance.

VANS

1. Disconnect the negative battery terminal from the battery.
2. Remove the reservoir cap from the cluster finish panel, the mounting screws, then, pull the cluster finish panel forward and remove it.
3. Remove the mounting screws and pull the instrument pan-

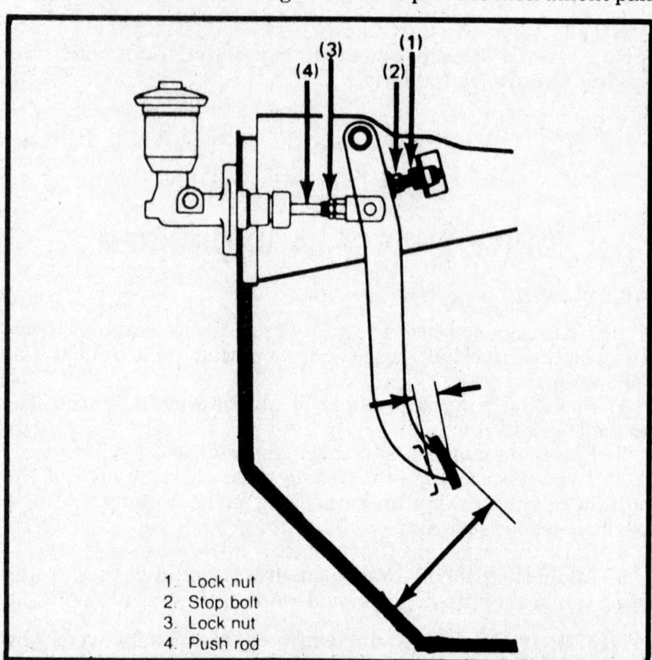

Clutch pedal adjustment points—typical. The distance between the ends of the long arrow is the pedal height. The distance between the two short arrows is the pedal free-play. Push rod play is only a small movement of the pedal—Pick-ups

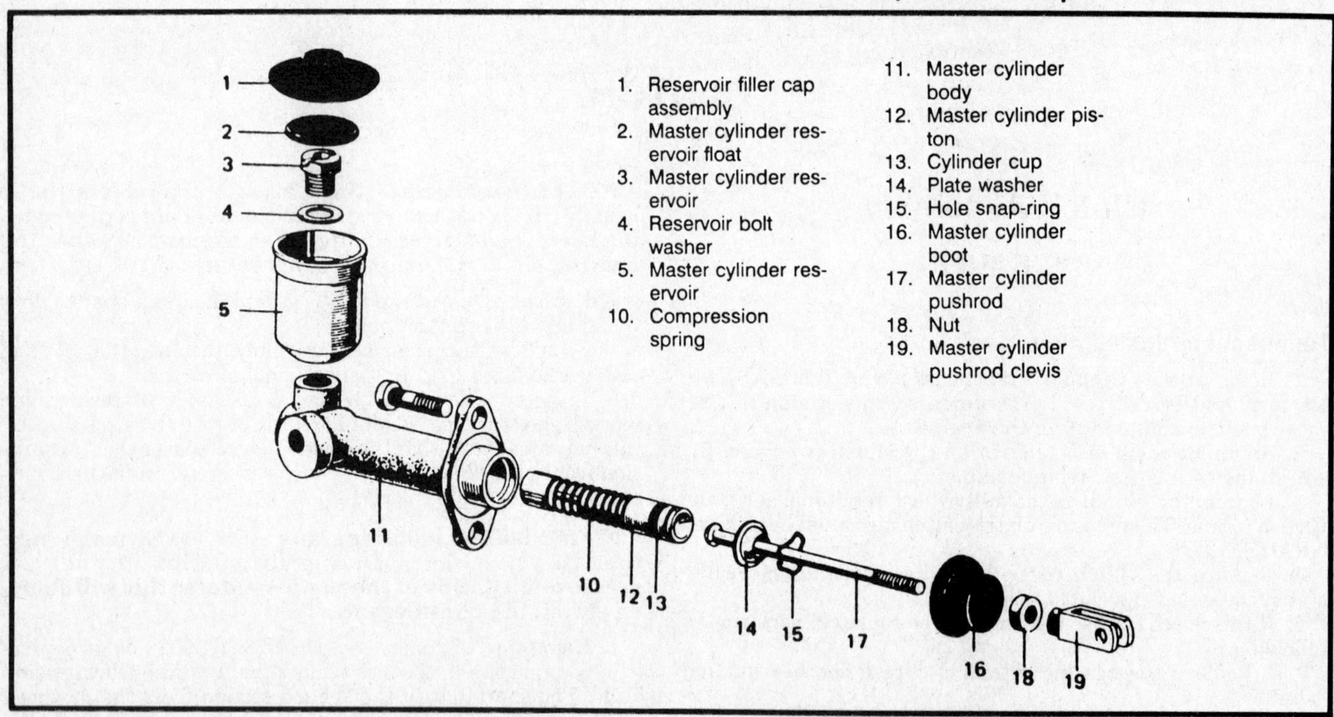

Clutch master cylinder exploded view—typical

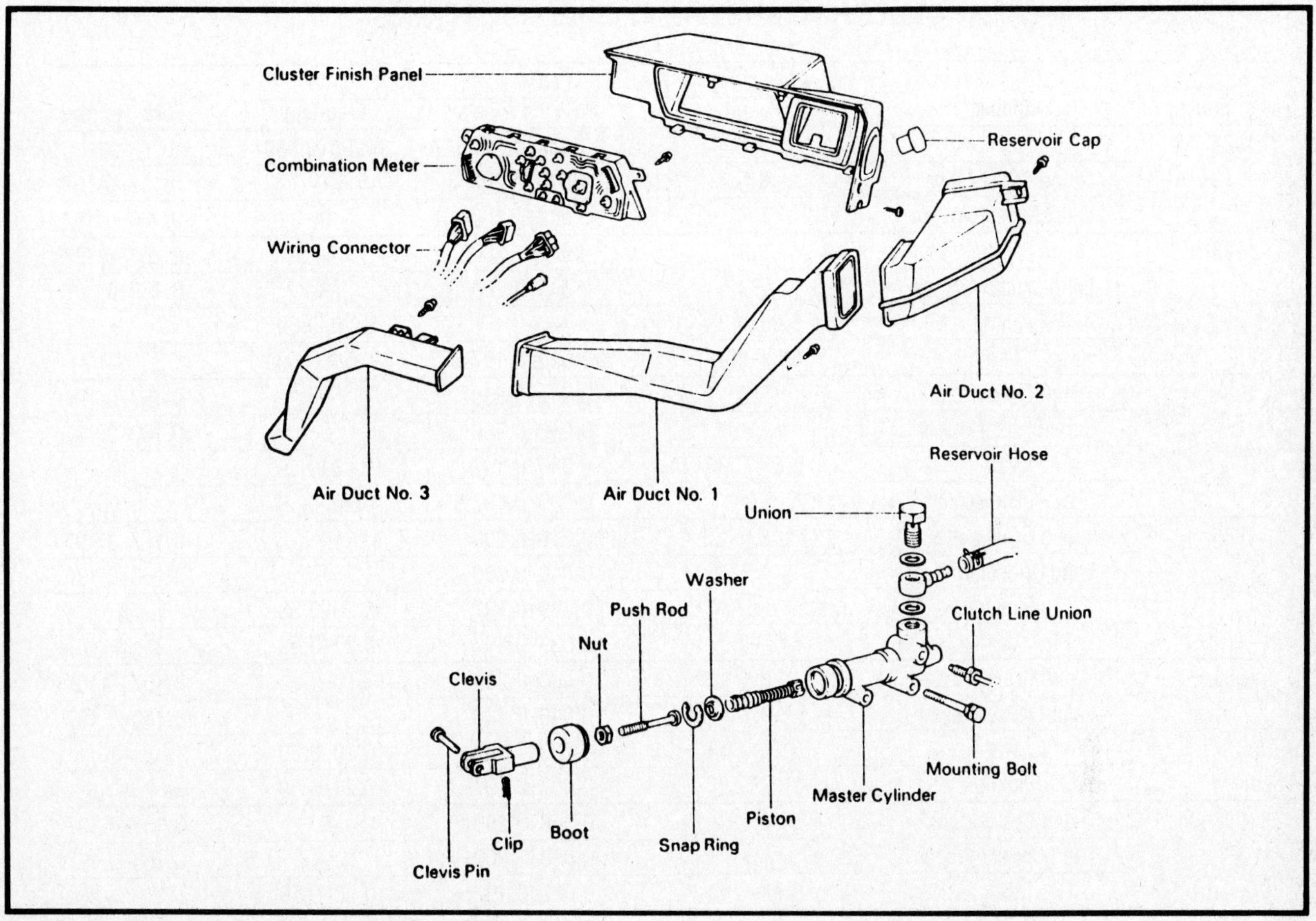

Removing the clutch master cylinder—Vans

el forward, then, disconnect the speedometer and the electrical connectors form it.

4. Remove the No. 3, the No. 1 and the No. 2 air ducts.
5. Disconnect and plug the reservoir hose at the master cylinder. Using the tool No. 09751-36011, disconnect the clutch line union.
6. Remove the mounting bolts and the master cylinder.
7. To install, reverse the removal procedures. Bleed the clutch system. Adjust the clutch pedal.

Adjustment

PUSH ROD

The pedal push rod play is the distance between the clutch master cylinder piston and the pedal pushrod located above the pedal towards the firewall. Since it is nearly impossible to measure this distance at the source, it must be measured at the pedal pad, preferably with a dial indicator gauge. Refer to the accompanying specification chart to determine the recommended play.

If necessary, adjust the pedal play by loosening the pedal pushrod locknut and turning the pushrod. Tighten the locknut after the adjustment.

FREE-PLAY

The free-play measurement is the total travel of the clutch pedal from the fully released position to where resistance is felt as the pedal is pushed downward. Refer to the accompanying specification chart to determine the recommended pedal free play.

If the clutch pedal free play is incorrect, perform the previous clutch adjustments then bleed the system according to the procedure which follows. If a pedal free-play dimension is not listed for your model, perform the previous clutch adjustments and disregard the pedal free-play measurement.

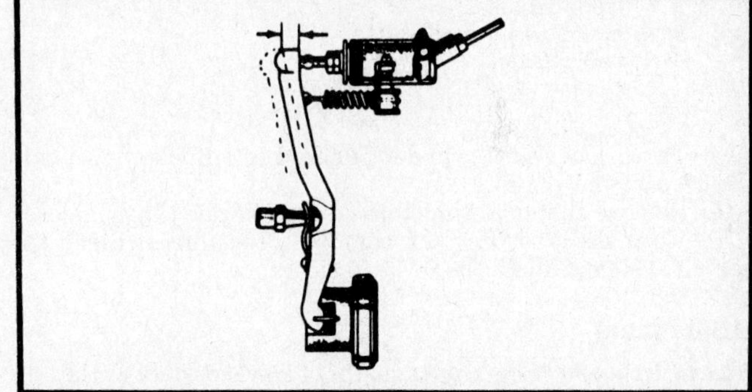

Measuring the fork tip end-play—typical

SLAVE CYLINDER

Removal and Installation

1. Raise and support the front of the vehicle on jackstands.
2. If equipped, remove the tension spring on the clutch fork.
3. Using the tool No. 09751-36011, remove the hydraulic line from the release cylinder. Be careful not to damage the fitting.

CLUTCH ADJUSTMENT SPECIFICATIONS

Year	Model	Pedal Height	Pedal Push Rod Play	Pedal Free-Play	Fork Tip Play
1982	Pickup	6.0–6.4	0.040–0.200	0.200–0.600	
	Land Cruiser 2 dr.	8.5	0.040–0.200	—	0.157–0.197
	Land Cruiser Wagon	7.7	0.040–0.200	—	0.160–0.197
1983	Land Cruiser 2 dr.	8.5	0.040–0.200	—	0.157–0.197
	Land Cruiser Wagon	7.7	0.040–0.200	—	0.160–0.197
	Pickup	5.98–6.38	—	0.20–0.59	③
	Van	6.57–6.97 ①	0.039–0.197	0.20–0.59	②
1984	Land Cruiser 2 dr.	8.5	0.040–0.200	—	0.157–0.197
	Land Cruiser Wagon	7.7	0.040–0.200	—	0.160–0.197
	Van	6.57–6.97 ①	0.039–0.197	0.20–0.59	②
	Pickup	5.94	0.039–0.197	0.20–0.59	③
1985	Land Cruiser 2 dr.	8.5	0.040–0.200	—	0.157–0.197
	Land Cruiser Wagon	7.7	0.040–0.200	—	0.160–0.197
	Pickup	5.67 ①	0.039–0.197	0.20–0.59	⑤
	Van	6.57–6.97 ①	0.039–0.197	0.20–0.59	②
1986	Land Cruiser 2 dr.	8.5	0.040–0.200	—	0.157–0.197
	Land Cruiser Wagon	7.7	0.040–0.200	—	0.160–0.197
	Van	6.73–7.13	0.039–0.197	0.20–0.59	②
	Pickup	5.67 ①	0.039–0.197	0.20–0.59	②
1987–88	Land Cruiser 2 dr.	8.5	0.040–0.200	—	0.157–0.197
	Land Cruiser Wagon	7.7	0.040–0.200	—	0.160–0.197
	Van	6.73–7.13	0.039–0.197	0.20–0.59	②
	Pickup	6.12 ①	0.039–0.197	0.20–0.59	②

① From asphalt sheet
② Self adjusting
③ With power brakes
④ Without power breaks
⑤ Non adjustable

4. Turn the release cylinder pushrod in sufficiently to gain clearance from the fork.
5. Remove the mounting bolts and withdraw the cylinder.
6. To install, reverse the removal procedures. Bleed the clutch system. Adjust the fork tip clearance.

Adjustment

The fork tip play is the total amount of travel evident at the outer end of the clutch release fork where the fork comes in contact with the release cylinder pushrod. Refer to the accompanying specification chart to determine the recommended fork tip play.

The fork tip play is adjusted by loosening the release cylinder pushrod locknut and effectively increasing or decreasing the pushrod length as required.

NOTE: Some models do not have adjustable release cylinder pushrods. These models are identified by having no adjustment nuts on the pushrod.

BLEEDING SYSTEM

NOTE: This procedure may be utilized when either the clutch master or release cylinder has been removed or if any of the hydraulic lines have been disturbed.

CAUTION

DO NOT spill brake fluid on the body of the vehicle as it will destroy the paint.

1. Fill the master cylinder reservoir with brake fluid.
2. Remove the cap and loosen the bleeder screw on the clutch release cylinder. Cover the hole with your finger.
3. Have an assistant pump the clutch pedal several times. Take your finger off the hole while the pedal is being depressed so that the air in the system can be released. Put your finger back on the hole and release the pedal.
4. When fluid pressure can be felt (with your finger) tighten the bleeder screw.
5. Place a short length of hose over the bleeder screw and the other end in a jar half full of clean brake fluid.
6. Depress the clutch pedal and loosen the bleeder screw. Allow the fluid to flow into the jar.
7. Tighten the plug, then release the clutch pedal.
8. Repeat this procedure until no air bubbles are visible in the bleeder tube.
9. When there are no more air bubbles in the system, tighten the plug fully with the pedal depressed. Replace the plastic cap.
10. Refill the master cylinder to the correct level with brake fluid. Check the system for leaks.

MANUAL TRANSMISSION

For overhaul procedures, refer to the Manual Transmission section in the Unit Repair Section.

Removal and Installation

2WD PICKUP AND VAN

1. Disconnect the negative battery terminals (L) or terminal (2L and 2L-T).
2. If equipped with a floorshifter (Pickup), perform the following:
   a. Remove the center floor console, if equipped.
   b. Remove the shift lever handle, then the floor mat or carpet along with the shift lever boot in order to gain access to the shift lever.
   c. Using the shift lever removal tool No. 09305–20012, remove the shift lever.

NOTE: On the pickup (1984-88) models, remove the boot and the shift lever from inside the vehicle.

3. Raise and support the vehicle on jackstands. Drain the transmission fluid.
4. Chalk matchmarks on the driveshaft flange and the differential pinion flange to indicate their relationships; these marks must be aligned during installation.
5. Remove the driveshaft flange bolts and the center support bearing-to-frame bolts (if equipped with a 2-piece driveshaft). Lower the driveshaft out of the vehicle. Using tool No. 09325–20010, or its equivalent (Pickup), insert it into the end of the transmission to prevent oil leakage.
6. On the Van models, disconnect the shift and the select cables from the select outer levers, the clips and the cables.
7. Disconnect the back-up lamp switch electrical connector, and the speedometer cable from the transmission, then tie the cable out of the way.
8. Disconnect the wiring at the starter. Remove the starter mounting bolts and lower the starter out of the vehicle.
9. Remove the exhaust pipe clamp and the exhaust pipe.
10. If the hydraulic line from the clutch release cylinder is clamped to the frame, remove the clamp retaining bolt. Remove the release cylinder mounting bolts and the fork spring (if equipped). Tie the release cylinder out of the way.

NOTE: It is not necessary to disconnect the hydraulic line from the release cylinder.

11. On column shift vehicles, disconnect the shift selector linkage at the transmission and remove the transmission cross shafts.
12. Support the rear of the transmission with a jack and remove the transmission-to-crossmember bolts, the crossmember-to-frame bolts and the crossmember from the vehicle.

NOTE: When removing the crossmember, raise the rear of the transmission SLIGHTLY, just enough to take the weight off of the crossmember.

13. Place a support under the engine with a wooden block (3/4 in. thick) between the support and the engine oil pan.

CAUTION

The wooden block and support should be no more than about 1/4 in. away from the engine so that when the engine is lowered, damage will not occur to any underhood components. If possible, shim the support so that the wooden block touches the engine.

14. Remove the transmission-to-engine bolts, draw the transmission rearward and down, away from the engine.

NOTE: When removing the transmission, be careful not to damage the extension housing dust deflector.

15. To install, reverse the removal procedures. Torque transmission-to-engine bolts to 53 ft. lbs., the stiffener plate bolts to 27 ft. lbs., the transmission mount/bracket bolts to 19 ft. lbs., the rear engine mount bracket-to-crossmember bolts to 9 ft. lbs., the exhaust pipe-to-manifold bolts to 29 ft. lbs., the upper exhaust pipe bracket-to-clutch housing bolts to 27 ft. lbs., the lower exhaust pipe bracket-to-clutch housing bolts to 51 ft. lbs., the lower starter bolt/release cylinder tube bracket bolt to 29 ft. lbs., the clutch release cylinder bolts to 9 ft. lbs. Refill the transmission.

4WD PICKUP (INCLUDING TRANSFER CASE)

1. Disconnect the negative battery terminals (L) or terminal (2L and 2L-T). Remove the starter upper mounting bolt.
2. Working inside the vehicle, pull up the shift lever boot and pull out the shift lever, using tool No. 09305–20012, or its equivalent. If equipped with a 22R-E (1984-88) engine, pull up the shift lever boot, then, remove the mounting bolts and pull out the shift lever.

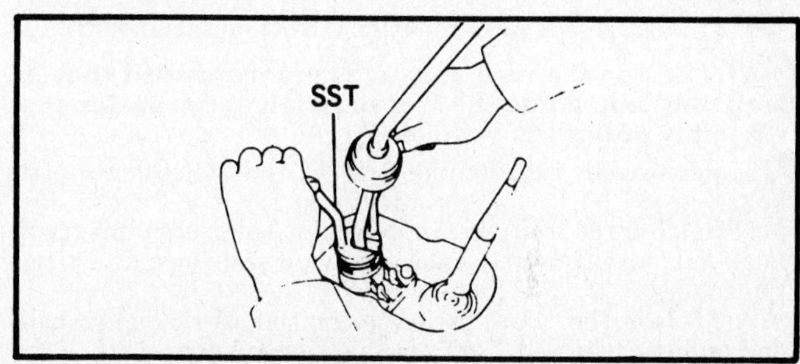

Using tool 09305-20012 to remove the shift lever

3. Using needle nose pliers, remove the transfer case shift lever snap ring and the shift lever.
4. Raise and support the vehicle on jackstands.

NOTE: Because of space limitations, it may be necessary to raise both the front and rear of the vehicle. If this is done, place jackstands under both axles as follows: On the outside of the U-bolts at the front axle; on the inside of the U-bolts at the rear axle.

5. Drain the lubricant from both the transmission and the transfer case.
6. Chalk matchmarks on the driveshaft flanges and the differential pinion flanges to indicate their relationships. These marks must be aligned during installation.
7. Remove the driveshaft mounting bolts and remove the front driveshaft assembly.

NOTE: DO NOT disassemble the front driveshaft to remove it.

8. Using a piece of chalk, place matchmarks on the rear driveshaft and the slip yoke to indicate their relationships; these marks must be aligned during installation.
9. Remove the mounting bolts from the rearward flange of the rear driveshaft. Lower the driveshaft out of the vehicle. Remove the mounting bolts from the slip yoke flange, then, remove the flange and yoke assembly.
10. Unbolt the clutch release cylinder and tie it out of the way.

NOTE: It is not necessary to disconnect the hydraulic line from the clutch release cylinder.

11. Disconnect the starter motor electrical connectors. Remove the starter bolts and lower the starter from the vehicle.

12. At the transfer case, disconnect the speedometer cable (tie it out of the way), the back-up light switch connector and the 4WD indicator switch connector.
13. Disconnect the exhaust pipe clamp and the exhaust pipe from the transmission housing.
14. Remove the clutch release cylinder and the tube bracket, then, move the cylinder aside.

NOTE: When removing the clutch release cylinder, DO NOT disassemble the hydraulic line from the cylinder.

15. Remove the crossmember-to-transfer case mounting bolts. Using a jack, raise the transmission and transfer case assembly SLIGHTLY off of the crossmember. Remove the crossmember-to-frame attaching bolts and remove the crossmember.
16. Place a support under the engine oil pan, with a wooden block (3/4 in. thick) between the support and the engine oil pan.

CAUTION

The wooden block and support should be no more than about 1/4 in. away from the engine so that when the engine is lowered, damage will not occur to any underhood components. If possible, shim the support so that the wooden block touches the engine.

17. Lower the jack until the engine rests on the support.

NOTE: For the next step, it is recommended that an assistant help guide the transmission and transfer case assembly out of the vehicle.

18. Remove the exhaust pipe bracket and the stiffener plate bolts.
19. Remove the transmission-to-engine bolts, draw the transmission/transfer case assembly rearward and down away from the engine.
20. Remove the transmission-to-transfer case adapter bolts and pull the transfer case from the transmission.
21. To install, use new gaskets and reverse the removal procedures. Torque transmission-to-engine bolts to 53 ft. lbs., the stiffener plate bolts to 27 ft. lbs., the transmission mount/bracket bolts to 19 ft. lbs., the rear engine mount bracket-to-crossmember bolts to 9 ft. lbs., the crossmember-to-frame bolts to 70 ft. lbs., the exhaust pipe-to-manifold bolts to 29 ft. lbs., the upper exhaust pipe bracket-to-clutch housing bolts to 27 ft. lbs., the lower exhaust pipe bracket-to-clutch housing bolts to 51 ft. lbs., the lower starter bolt/release cylinder tube bracket bolt to 29 ft. lbs., the clutch release cylinder bolts to 9 ft. lbs. Refill the transmission.

LAND CRUISER

1. Disconnect the negative battery terminals from the battery.
2. Remove the entrance scuff plates from the floor of the interior.
3. Remove both side trim panels from beneath the instrument panel.
4. Remove the center heater duct and the front floor mat or carpet.
5. Remove the handles from both shift levers and the transmission tunnel cover along with the shift lever boots.
6. Disconnect the wiring from both the back-up lamp switch and the 4WD indicator (if equipped).
7. Using the tool No. 09305–55010, or its equivalent, remove the transmission shift lever.
8. Raise and support the vehicle on jackstands. Remove the transfer case skid plate.
9. Disconnect the speedometer cable from the transfer case and tie it out of the way.
10. Using chalk, place matchmarks on the driveshaft flanges and the differential pinion flanges to indicate their relationships; these marks must be aligned during installation.
11. Remove the driveshaft flanges mounting bolts and the driveshaft assemblies.
12. Disconnect the starter electrical connectors, the mounting bolts and the starter from the vehicle.
13. Remove the clutch release cylinder and move it out of the way.

NOTE: It is not necessary to disconnect the hydraulic line from the release cylinder.

14. Drain the lubricant from both the transmission and the transfer case. Remove the tachometer sensor, if equipped.
15. Remove the crossmember-to-transfer case mounting bolts. Using a jack, raise the transmission and transfer case assembly SLIGHTLY off the crossmember. Remove the crossmember-to-frame attaching bolts and the crossmember.
16. Place a support under the engine oil pan, with a wooden block (3/4 in. thick) between the support and the engine oil pan.

CAUTION

The wooden block and support should be no more than about 1/4 in. away from the engine so that when the engine is lowered, damage will not occur to any underhood components. If possible, shim the support so that the wooden block touches the engine.

17. Lower the jack until the engine rests on the support.

NOTE: For the next step, it is recommended that an assistant help guide the transmission and transfer case assembly out of the vehicle.

18. Remove the exhaust pipe bracket and the stiffener plate bolts.
19. Remove the transmission-to-engine bolts, then, draw the transmission/transfer case assembly rearward and down away from the engine.
20. To separate the transfer case from the transmission, remove the transfer case mounting bolts and slide the transfer case off the transmission.
21. To install, reverse the removal procedures. Torque transmission-to-engine bolts to 53 ft. lbs., the stiffener plate bolts to 27 ft. lbs., the transmission mount/bracket bolts to 19 ft. lbs., the rear engine mount bracket-to-crossmember bolts to 9 ft. lbs., the exhaust pipe-to-manifold bolts to 29 ft. lbs., the upper exhaust pipe bracket-to-clutch housing bolts to 27 ft. lbs., the lower exhaust pipe bracket-to-clutch housing bolts to 51 ft. lbs., the lower starter bolt/release cylinder tube bracket bolt to 29 ft. lbs., the clutch release cylinder bolts to 9 ft. lbs. Refill the transmission.

Linkage

Adjustment

PICKUP AND LAND CRUISER

Column Shifter

The only adjustments which may be performed on the column shift linkages are for the length of the column-to-transmission rods. Adjust these so that the transmission operates smoothly.

Floor Shifter

All models equipped with a floor shifter have internally-mounted shift linkages. On older models, the linkage is contained in the side cover which is bolted on the transmission case.

VAN

1. Remove the console box and loosen the adjusting lock nut.
2. Place the shift lever in the Neutral position.
3. Using a 0.200 in. dia. guide pin, insert it into the neutral adjust service hole; adjust the length of the cable by turning the adjusting nut.
4. After adjustment, remove the guide pin and reinstall the console box.

AUTOMATIC TRANSMISSION

For further overhaul information, refer to "Chilton's Automatic Transmission Manual".

Automatic Transmission

Description

The A43D is a fully automatic 4-speed transmission. The 4th speed of this transmission is an overdrive 0.688:1 ratio, which offers improved gasoline mileage by lowering the engine rpm at highway speeds. The hydraulic circuit of the overdrive mode is electrically controlled. The main electrical components include the following:

1. A dash mounted overdrive control switch.
2. A dash mounted "OVERDRIVE-OFF" indicator lamp.
3. A transmission mounted solenoid.
4. An engine mounted thermo-switch which prevents overdrive engagement until the engine coolant temperature reaches 131°F.

Removal

1. Disconnect the negative battery terminal from the battery. On the Pickup, remove the air cleaner assembly.
2. Disconnect the transmission throttle cable from the carburetor linkage (Pickup) or the throttle body (Van).
3. Raise and support the vehicle on jackstands. Drain the transmission fluid.
4. Disconnect the wiring connectors (near the starter) for the neutral start switch and the back-up light switch. If equipped, disconnect the solenoid (overdrive) switch wiring at the same location.
5. Disconnect the starter wiring at the starter. Remove the mounting bolts and the starter from the engine.
6. Chalk matchmarks on the rear driveshaft flange and the differential pinion flange. These marks must be aligned during installation.
7. Unbolt the rear driveshaft flange. If the vehicle has a two-piece driveshaft, remove the center bearing bracket-to-frame bolts. Remove the driveshaft from the vehicle.
8. Disconnect the speedometer cable (tie it out of the way) and the shift linkage from the transmission.
9. Disconnect the transmission oil cooler lines at the transmission.
10. Disconnect the exhaust pipe clamp and remove the oil filler tube.
11. Support the transmission, using a jack with a wooden block placed between the jack and the transmission pan. Raise the transmission, just enough to take the weight off of the rear mount.
12. On the Pickup models, remove the rear engine mount with the bracket and the engine under cover (pickups), to gain access to the engine crankshaft pulley. On the Van models, remove the fuel tank mounting bolts and support the fuel tank; remove the transmission mount through bolt.
13. Place a wooden block (or blocks) between the engine oil pan and the front frame crossmember.

CAUTION

The wooden block(s) should be no more than about 1/4 in. away from the engine so that when the engine is lowered, damage will not occur to any underhood components.

14. Slowly, lower the transmission until the engine rests on the wooden block.
15. Remove the rubber plug(s) from the service holes located at the rear of the engine in order to gain access to the torque convertor bolts.
16. Rotate the crankshaft (to remove the torque convertor bolts) to access the bolts through the service holes.
17. Obtain a bolt of the same dimensions as the torque convertor bolts. Cut the head off of the bolt and hacksaw a screwdriver slot in the bolt opposite the threaded end.

NOTE: This modified bolt is used as a guidepin. Two guides pins are needed to properly install the transmission.

18. Thread the guide pin into one of the torque convertor bolt holes. The guide pin will help keep the convertor with the transmission.
19. Remove the stiffener plates from the transmission.
20. Remove the transmission-to-engine bolts, then carefully move the transmission rearward by prying on the guide pin through the service hole.

CAUTION

As the transmission moves away from the engine about 1/8 in., feed wire through the front of the transmission and secure the wire in order to keep the convertor attached to the transmission. Also, try to keep the nose of the transmission pointed upward SLIGHTLY to help keep the convertor in place.

21. Pull the transmission rearward and lower it (front end down) out of the vehicle.

CAUTION

Do not allow the attached cables to catch on any components during removal.

22. With the transmission out of the vehicle, remove the torque convertor as follows:
    a. Place a drain pan under the front of the transmission.
    b. Pull the convertor straight off of the transmission and allow the fluid to drain.

Installation

1. Apply a coat of multi-purpose grease to the torque convertor stub shaft and the corresponding pilot hole in the flywheel.
2. Install the torque convertor into the front of the transmission. Push inward on the torque convertor while rotating it to completely couple the torque convertor to the transmission.
3. To make sure that the convertor is properly installed, measure the distance between the torque convertor mounting lugs and the front mounting face of the transmission. The proper distance is 0.080 in.
4. Install guide pins into two opposite mounting lugs of the torque convertor.
5. Raise the transmission to the engine, align the transmission with the engine alignment dowels and position the convertor guide pins into the mounting holes of the flywheel.
6. Install and tighten the transmission-to-engine mounting bolts. Torque the bolts to 47 ft. lbs.
7. Remove the convertor guide pins and install the convertor mounting bolts. Rotate the crankshaft as necessary to gain access to the guide pins and bolts through the service holes. Evenly, tighten the convertor mounting bolts to 13 ft. lbs. Install the rubber plugs into the access holes.
8. Install the engine undercover. Raise the transmission slightly and remove the wood block(s) from beneath the engine oil pan.
9. Install the transmission crossmember. Torque the crossmember-to-frame bolts to 26–36 ft. lbs.
10. Lower the transmission onto the crossmember and install the transmission mounting bolts. Torque the bolts to 19 ft. lbs.
11. Install the oil filler tube and connect the exhaust pipe clamp.

12. Connect the oil cooler lines to the transmission and torque the fittings to 25 ft. lbs.

13. To complete the installation, reverse the removal procedures. Adjust the transmission throttle cable. Refill the transmission with Dexron®II fluid. Road test the vehicle and check for leaks.

Shift Linkage

Adjustment

1. Loosen the adjustment nut on the transmission connecting rod (1982–83) or the shift cable (1984-88).
2. Push the manual lever of the transmission fully forward (1982–83) or rearward (1984-88).
3. Move the manual lever back three (1982–83) or two (1984-88) notches, which is the Neutral position.
4. Set the gearshift selector lever in it's Neutral position.
5. Apply a slight amount of forward pressure on the selector lever (towards the Reverse position) and tighten the connecting rod (1982–83) or the shift cable (1984-88) adjustment nut.

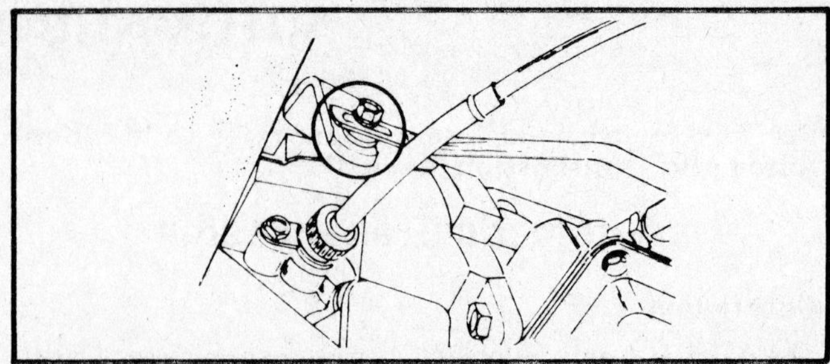

Loosen the nut to adjust the shift linkage – automatic transmission

Throttle Linkage

Adjustment

1. Remove the air cleaner assembly.
2. Push the accelerator to the floor and check that the throttle valve opens fully; if not, adjust the accelerator link, so that it does.
3. Push back the rubber boot from the throttle cable which runs down to the transmission. Loosen the throttle cable adjustment nuts so that the cable housing can be adjusted.
4. Fully open the carburetor throttle by having an assistant press the accelerator all the way to the floor.
5. Adjust the cable housing so that, with the throttle wide open, the distance between the outer cable end rubber cap to the inner cable stopper is 0–0.04 in.
6. Tighten the nuts and double check the adjustment. Install the rubber boot and the air cleaner.

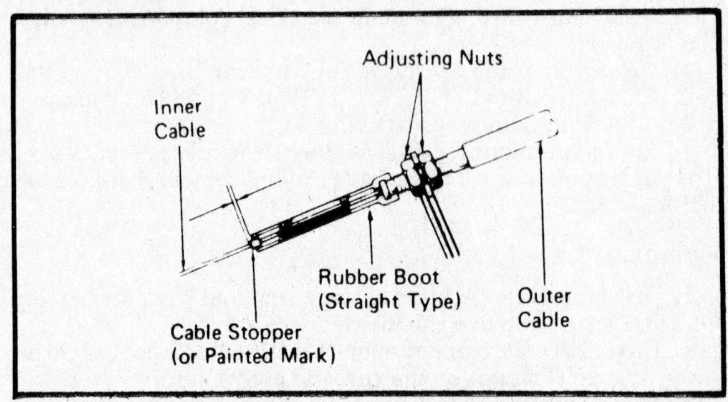

Throttle control cable adjustment – automatic transmission

Neutral Start Switch

Adjustment

The neutral safety switch prevents the vehicle from starting unless the gearshift selector is in either the Park or Neutral positions. If the vehicle will start in these positions, adjustment of the switch is required.

1982–83

1. Loosen the Neutral Start Switch bolt.
2. Place the gearshift selector lever in the Neutral position.
3. Align the shaft groove of the switch with the neutral Basic line. Hold the switch in this position and tighten the switch bolt to 35–60 inch lbs.

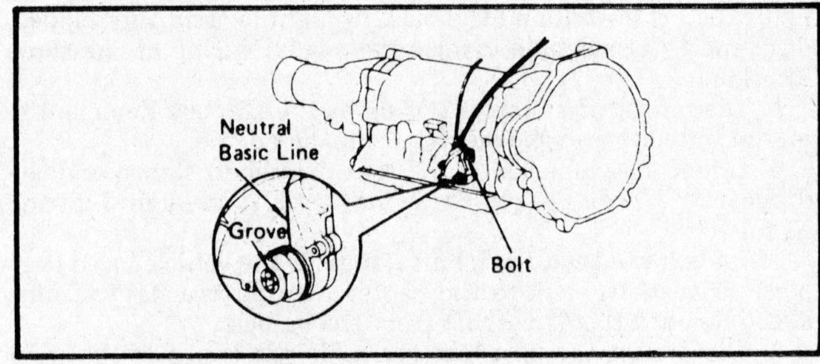

Neutral safety switch adjustment – 1982-83

1984-88

1. Loosen the Neutral Start Switch bolt.
2. Place the selector lever in the Neutral position.
3. Disconnect the wires from the neutral start switch.
4. Connect an ohmmeter between the terminals of the switch.
5. Adjust the switch until there is continuity between the N and B terminals.
6. Reconnect the wires. Torque the bolt to 48 inch lbs.

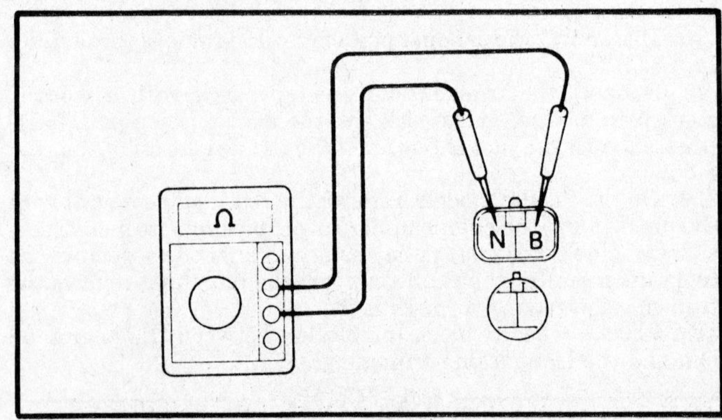

Checking the neutral start switch continuity – 1984-88

Oil Pan and Strainer

Removal and Installation

1. Raise and support the front of the vehicle on jackstands.
2. Place a container under the transmission drain plug and drain the transmission fluid.
3. Remove the pan securing bolts, the pan and the gasket.
4. The pan may be washed in solvent for cleaning but must be absolutely dry when it is reinstalled. DO NOT wipe it out with a rag or you will risk leaving bits of lint inside the transmission.

5. Using a small pry bar, remove the oil tube (covering the oil strainer pan). Remove the oil strainer pan and the strainer. Clean the oil strainer.

6. Remove all traces of the old gasket from the pan and the transmission.

7. To install, use a new gasket(s) and reverse the removal procedures. Torque the oil strainer pan to 48 inch lbs. and the transmission pan to 39 inch lbs. Refill the transmission with Dexron®II fluid.

CAUTION

The pan bolts break easily if overtightened.

TRANSFER CASE

For overhaul information, refer to "Transfer Cases" in the Unit Repair Section of this manual.

DRIVE LINES AND UNIVERSAL JOINTS

REAR

Removal and Installation

2WD STANDARD BED PICKUP AND VAN

1. Raise and support the rear of the vehicle on jackstands.

2. Paint a mating mark on the two halves of the rear universal joint flange.

3. Remove the bolts which hold the rear flange together.

4. Remove the splined end of the driveshaft from the transmission.

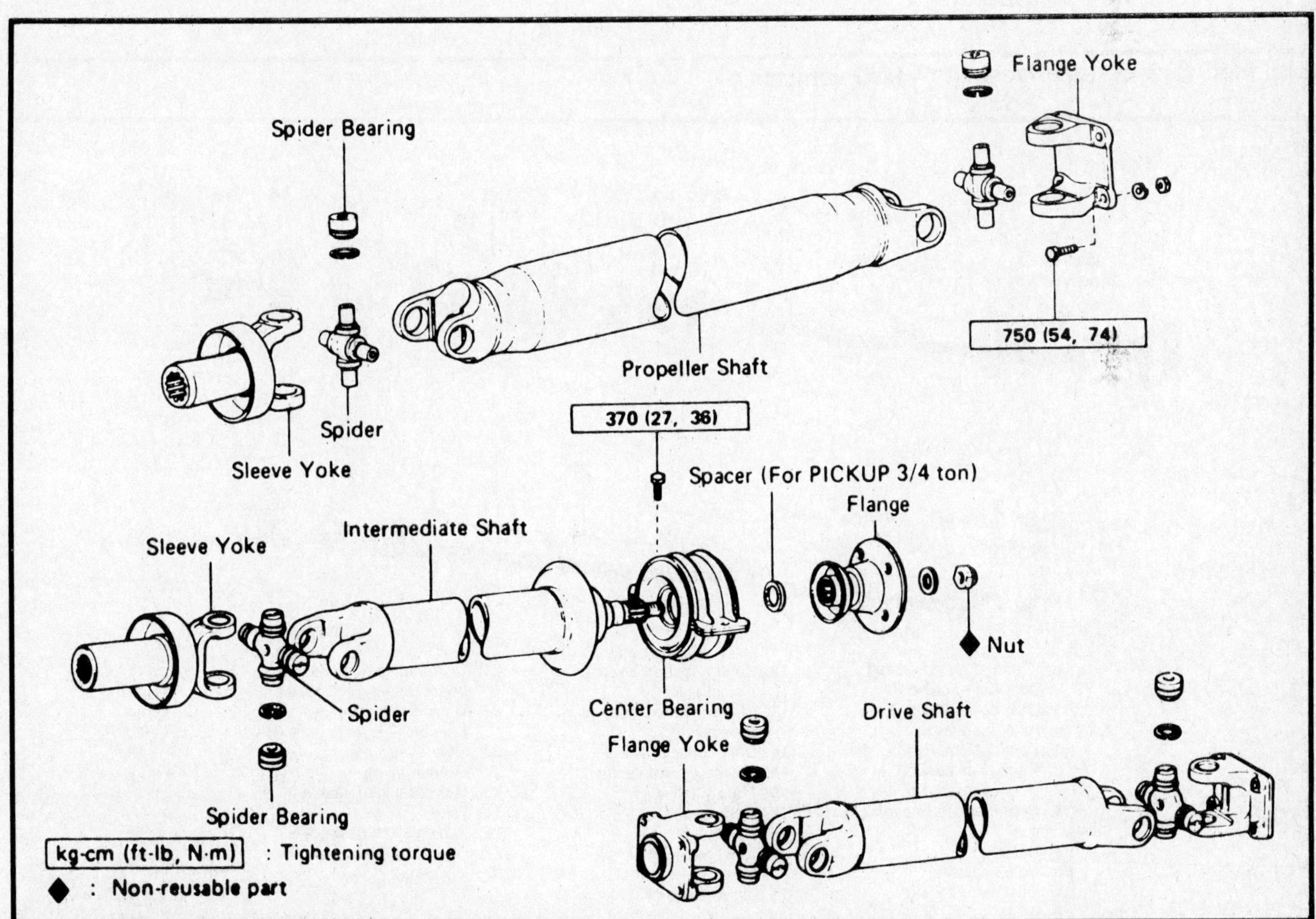

Exploded view of the driveshafts—2WD vehicles

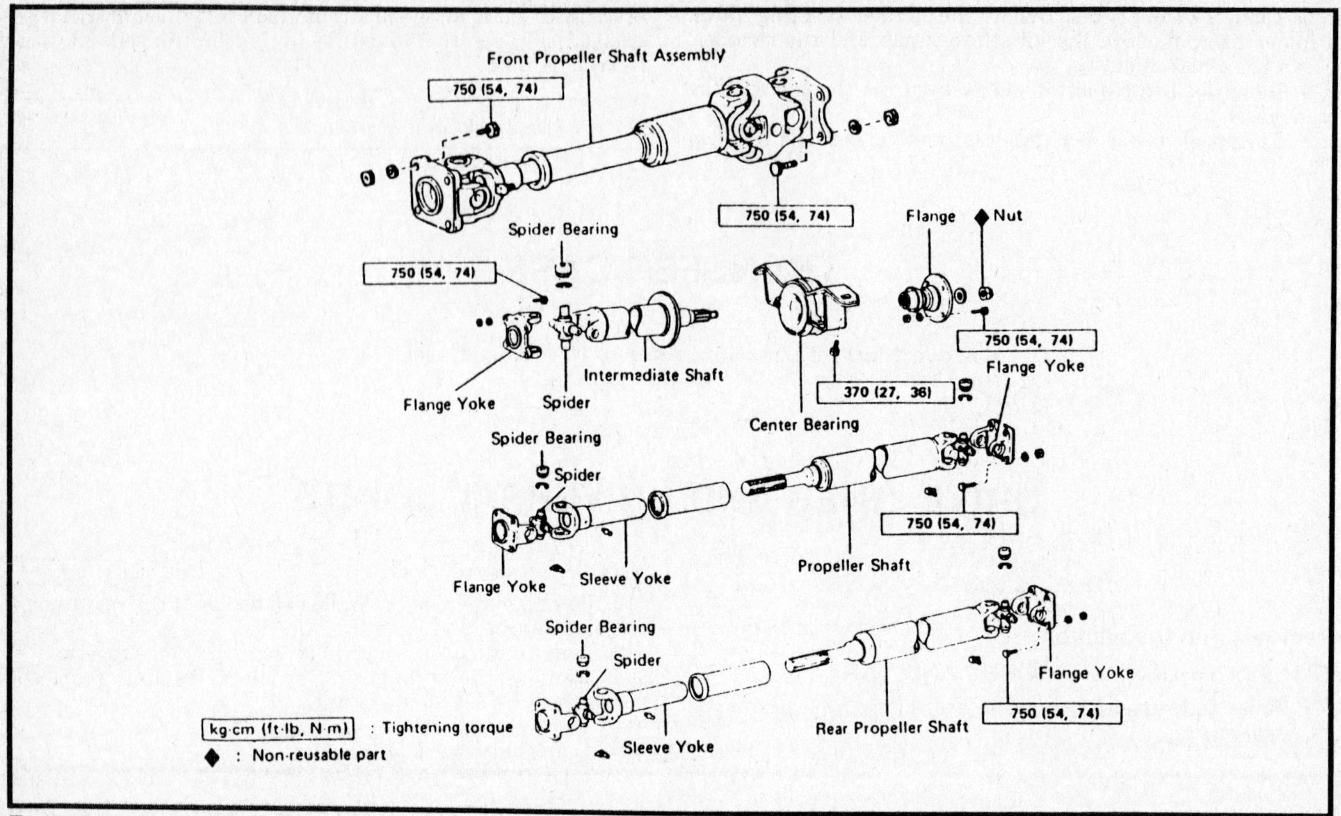

Exploded view of the driveshafts—4WD vehicles

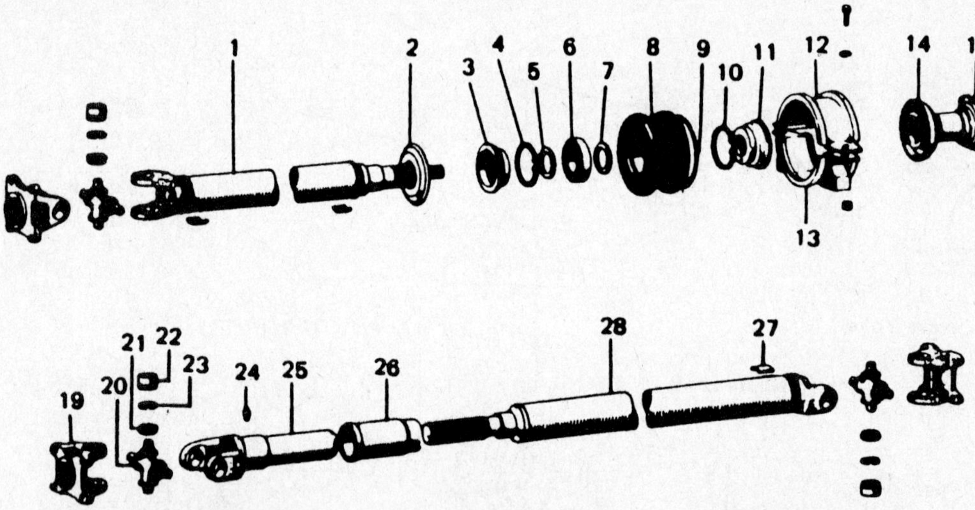

1. Intermediate driveshaft
2. Dust deflector No. 1
3. Dust deflector No. 2
4. Hole snap-ring
5. Dust deflector No. 3
6. Radial ball bearing
7. Dust deflector No. 4
8. Center support bearing cushion
9. Set ring
10. Hole snap-ring
11. Dust deflector No. 2
12. Center support bearing housing No. 1
13. Center support bearing housing No. 2
14. Dust deflector No. 1
15. Universal joint flange
16. Plate washer
17. Castle nut
18. Cotter pin
19. Universal joint flange yoke
20. Universal joint spider
21. Universal joint spider bearing seal
22. Universal joint spider bearing
23. Hole snap-ring
24. Grease fitting
25. Universal joint sleeve yoke
26. Sliding shaft dust cover
27. Balance piece
28. Driveshaft

Exploded view of a two-piece driveshaft assembly—typical

NOTE: Plug the end of the transmission with a rag or dummy flange to avoid losing transmission oil.

5. Remove the driveshaft from under the truck.
6. To install, reverse the removal procedures. Grease the splined end of the shaft before installing. Torque bolts to 31 ft. lbs. (Van) or 54 ft. lbs. (Pickup).

2WD LONG BED PICKUP

1. Raise and support the rear of the vehicle on jackstands.
2. Paint mating marks on all six flange halves.
3. Remove the bolts attaching the rear universal joint flange to the drive pinion flange.
4. Drop the rear section of the shaft slightly and pull the unit out of the center bearing sleeve yoke.
5. Remove the center bearing support from the crossmember.
6. Unbolt the driveshaft flange from the rear of the transmission and remove driveshaft along with center bearing support.
7. To install, align the matchmarks and reverse the removal procedures. Torque the flange bolts to 54 ft. lbs.

4WD PICKUP–ALL

1. Raise and support the whole vehicle off the ground and on jackstands.
2. Match-mark all driveshaft flanges BEFORE removing the bolts.
3. Unbolt the rear driveshaft flange from the rear pinion flange.
4. Unbolt the rear driveshaft flange from the rear transfer case flange and remove driveshaft.
5. Repeat steps 3 and 4 on front driveshaft.
6. To install, reverse the removal procedures. Torque the flange bolts to 54 ft. lbs. and the center support-to-frame bolts to 27 ft. lbs.

NOTE: For the 4 × 4 Long Bed Pickups, see above for rear driveshaft removal and installation.

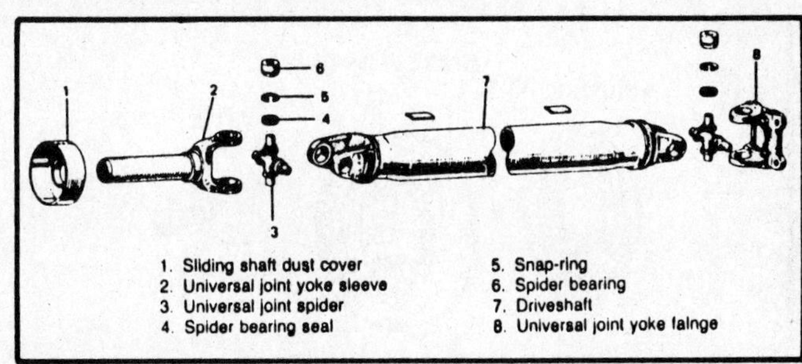

Exploded view of a one-piece driveshaft assembly—typical

LAND CRUISER

1. Raise and support the vehicle on jackstands.
2. Match-mark all driveshaft flanges BEFORE removing the bolts.
3. Unfasten the bolts which secure the universal joint flange to the differential pinion flange.
4. Perform Step 2 for the U-joint-to-transfer case flange bolts.
5. Withdraw the driveshaft from beneath the vehicle.
6. Repeat steps 3–5 on the front driveshaft.
7. To install, reverse the removal procedures.

NOTE: Lubricate the U-joints and sliding joints with multipurpose grease before installation.

Universal Joints

For service information, refer to the "U-Joint/CV-Joint" section in Unit Repair.

FRONT DRIVE AXLE—4WD

For overhaul information, refer to the Unit Overhaul Section.

Locking Hubs

Removal and Installation

AUTOMATIC

1. If equipped with free-wheeling hubs, turn the hub control handle to the FREE position.
2. Remove the hub cover bolts and pull off the cover.
3. If equipped with automatic locking hubs, remove the axle bolt with the washer.
4. Using snap ring pliers, remove the snap-ring from the axle shaft.
5. Remove the hub body mounting nuts.
6. Remove the cone washers from the hub body mounting studs by tapping on the washer slits with a tapered punch.
7. Remove the hub body from the axle hub.
8. Apply multi-purpose grease to the inner hub splines.
9. To install, use new gaskets and reverse the removal procedures. Torque the hub body-to-axle hub nuts to 23 ft. lbs., the plate washer/bolt to 13 ft. lbs. (auto. locking hub) and the hub cover-to-hub body bolts to 7 ft. lbs.

NOTE: To install the snap-ring onto the axle shaft, install a bolt into the axle shaft, pull it out and install the snap ring.

Axle Shaft

Removal and Installation

4WD PICKUP AND 4-RUNNER

1. Refer to the "Free Wheeling/Locking Hub, Removal and Installation" procedures, in this section and the remove the hub (with the flange) from the axle hub.
2. Raise and support the front of the vehicle on jackstands. Remove the wheel/tire assembly.
3. Disconnect and plug the brake line from the caliper. Remove the caliper from the axle hub.
4. Using a drift punch and a hammer, drive the lock washer tabs away from the lock nut.
5. Using a 2 in. socket, remove the locknut from the axle shaft. Remove the lock washer, the adjusting nut, the thrust washer, the outer bearing and the axle hub/disc assembly from the vehicle.
6. Remove the knuckle spindle bolts, the dust seal and the dust cover. Using a brass bar and a hammer, tap the steering spindle from the steering knuckle.
7. Turn the axle shaft until a flat spot on the outer shaft is in the upper position, then pull the axle shaft from the steering knuckle.
8. Using a slide hammer, pull the oil seal from the axle housing.

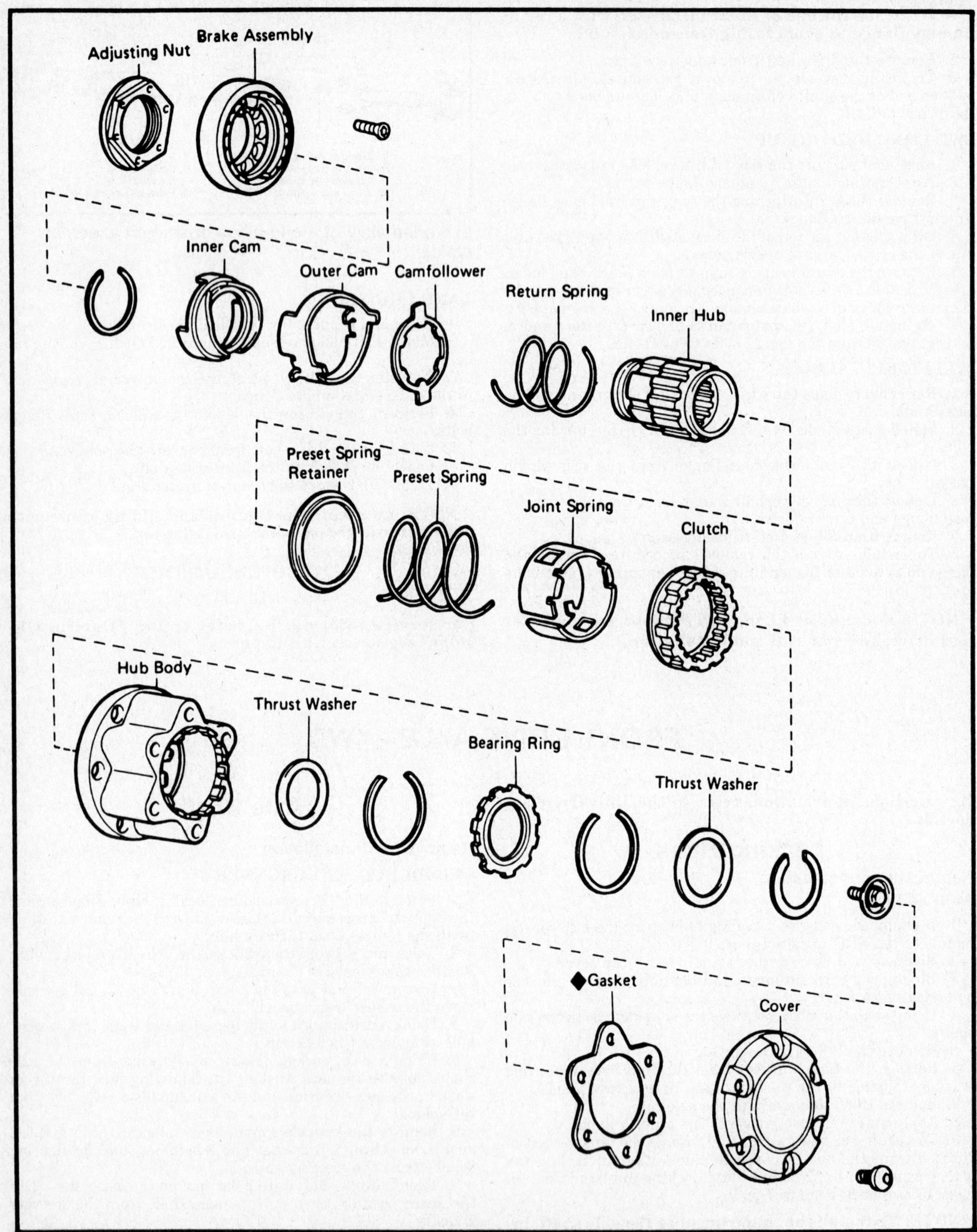

Exploded view of the automatic locking hub—4WD vehicles

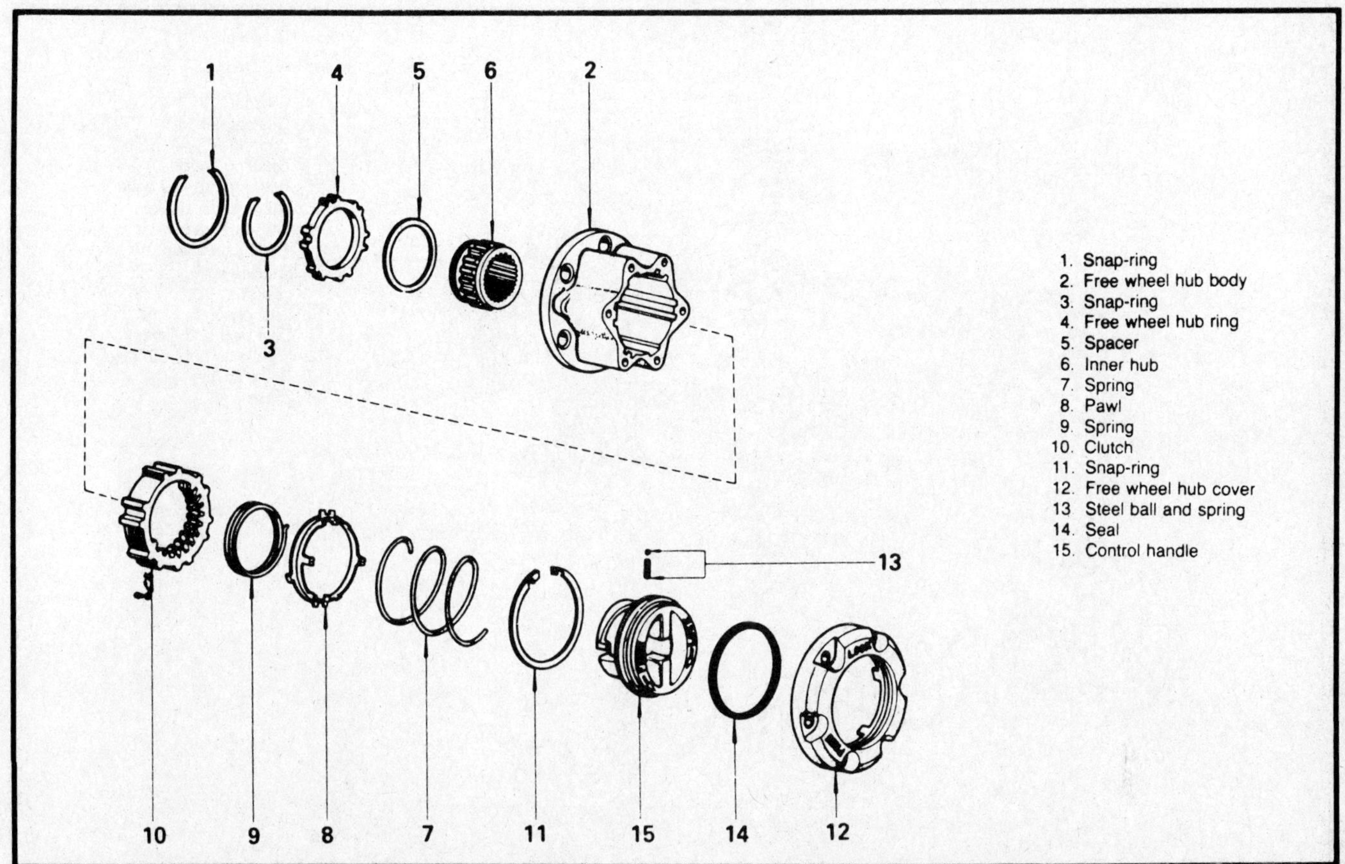

Exploded view of a free-wheeling hub assembly

9. Using a clean shop towel, wipe the from inside the steering knuckle housing and the axle shaft.

10. Using the oil seal installation tool No. 09618–60010, or its equivalent, drive a new oil seal into the axle housing until it seats. Install the axle shaft into the axle housing.

11. Using multi-purpose grease, fill the steering knuckle cavity to about $^{3}/_{4}$ full.

12. To complete the installation, use seals/gaskets and reverse the removal procedures. Torque the steering spindle-to-steering knuckle bolts to 38 ft. lbs., the axle hub adjusting nut to 18 ft. lbs., the axle hub locknut to 33 ft. lbs., the free wheel/locking hub nuts to 23 ft. lbs. and the brake caliper to 65 ft. lbs.

NOTE: To install the wheel bearings with the axle hub, torque the adjusting nut to 43 ft. lbs., turn the axle hub (back and forth, several times), loosen the nut and retorque the adjusting nut to 18 ft. lbs.

LAND CRUISER

1. Raise and support the vehicle on jackstands. Remove the wheel/tire assembly.

2. Plug the brake master cylinder reservoir to prevent brake fluid leakage from the disconnected brake flexible hose.

3. Remove the outer axle shaft flange cap (automatic locking hub) or the hub cover bolts and the cover (free wheel locking hub) and the shaft snap-ring from the axle hub.

4. Remove the outer axle shaft flange (automatic locking hub) or the hub ring (free wheel locking hub)-to-axle hub bolts, then alternately, screw two service bolts into the shaft flange or hub ring and remove the shaft flange or the hub ring with it's gasket.

5. Remove the brake drum set screws and the brake drum. If equipped with disc brakes, remove the caliper and disc.

6. Straighten the lockwasher and remove the front wheel bearing adjusting nuts with front wheel adjusting nut wrench or similar tool.

7. Remove the front axle hub together with its claw washer, bearings and oil seal.

8. Remove the clip and disconnect the brake flexible hose from the brake tube.

9. Cut and remove the lock wire, then remove the brake backing plate-to-steering knuckle bolts. Remove the brake backing plate together with the brake shoes, the tension springs and the wheel cylinder as an assembly.

10. Using a soft mallet, lightly, tap the steering knuckle spindle and remove the spindle with it's gasket.

NOTE: When removing the steering knuckle spindle on a vehicle equipped with the ball joint type axle shaft joint, be prepared for the disconnection of the outer axle shaft from the joint. Prevent the shaft joint ball from falling from the joint.

11. If equipped with the ball type axle shaft joint, slide the inner front axle shaft out of the axle housing. If equipped with the Birfield constant velocity joint type of axle shaft joint, remove the entire axle shaft assembly from the axle housing.

12. Using a bearing puller, remove the bushing from inside of knuckle spindle and the axle housing oil seal. Using a metal tube as a seating tool, drive oil seal into the axle housing and the new bushing into the knuckle spindle.

NOTE: If equipped with the ball joint type axle joint, install the inner axle with its proper spacer in position until the splines are fully meshed with the differential. If equipped with the Birfield constant velocity joint axle

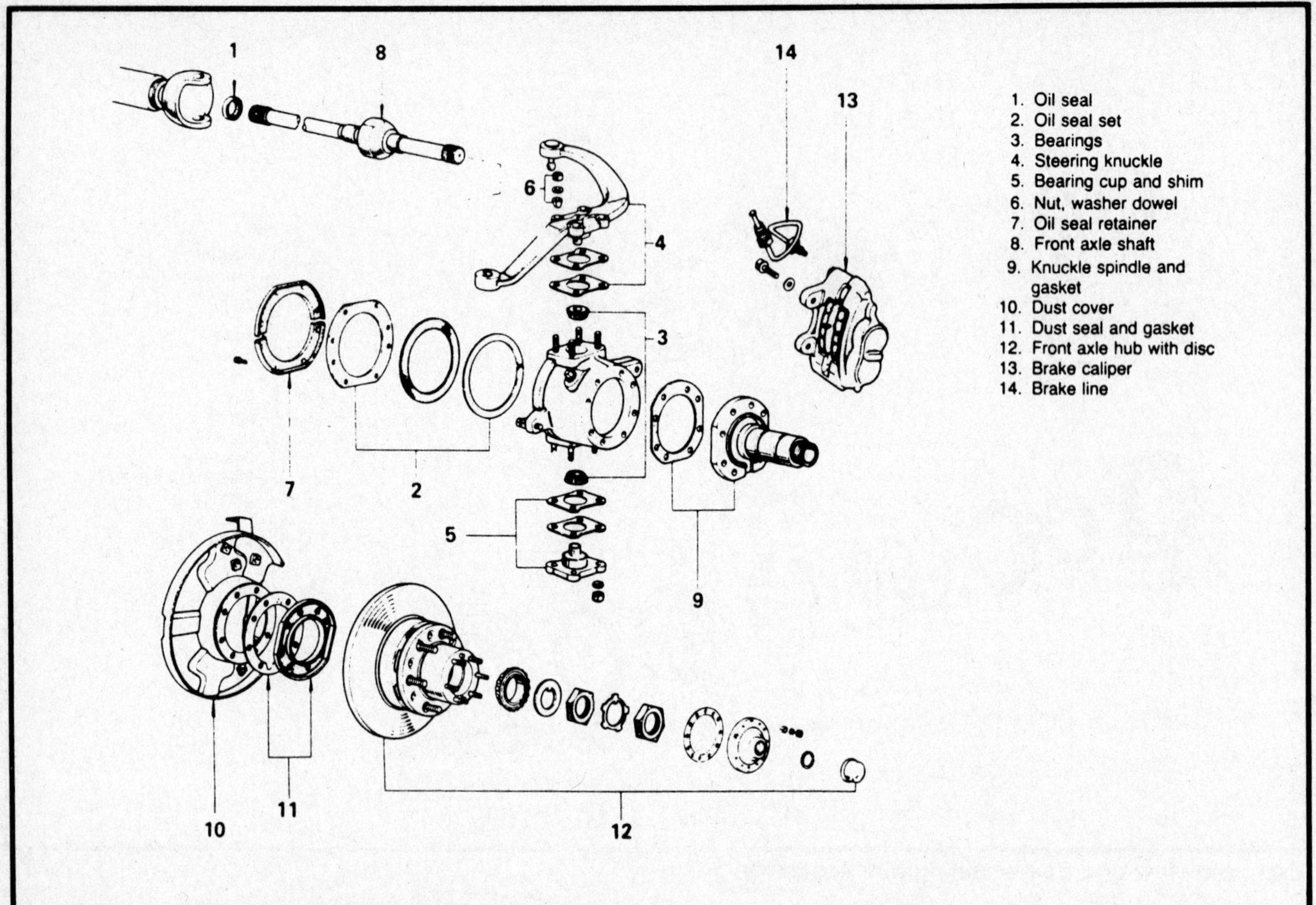

Front axle and steering knuckle (4WD) – pick-up illustrated, Land Cruiser similar

joint, install the axle into the housing and rotate the axle shaft until its splines mesh with the differential. Fill the steering knuckle about $^3/_4$ full with grease and place the joint ball on the inner shaft end.

13. To complete the installation, reverse the removal procedures. Adjust the wheel bearing preload.

Differential Carrier

Removal and Installation

1. Refer to the "Front Axle Shaft, Removal and Installation" procedures, in this section and remove the front axle shafts from the axle housing.
2. Drain the lubricant from the differential.
3. Match-mark the front driveshaft flange to the differential flange. Remove the mounting bolts and separate the driveshaft from the differential.
4. Remove the carrier retaining nuts and pull the carrier assembly out of the differential housing.
5. To install, use new gaskets and reverse the removal procedures. Torque the differential-to-axle nuts to 19 ft. lbs. and the front driveshaft flange-to-differential flange nuts/bolts to 54 ft. lbs. Refill the axle with 80W-90 gear oil to a level of 1/4 in. below the fill hole.

NOTE: Before installing the carrier, apply a thin coat of liquid or silicone sealer to the carrier housing gasket and to the carrier side face of each carrier retaining nut.

Axle Shaft Bearings

This procedure is used for 4WD front wheel bearings.

Removal and Installation

1. Refer to the "Free-Wheeling and Automatic Locking Hubs, Removal and Installation" procedures, in this section and remove the hubs.
2. Using a small pry bar, pry the grease seal from the rear of the disc/hub assembly, then remove the inner bearing from the assembly.
3. Using a shop cloth, wipe the grease from inside the disc/hub assembly.
4. Using a brass drift, drive the outer bearing races from each side of the disc/hub assembly.
5. Using solvent (NOT gasoline), clean all of the parts and blow dry with compressed air.
6. Using the bearing installation tool No. 09608-35013, or its equivalent, drive the outer races into the disc/hub assembly until they seat against the shoulder.
7. Using multi-purpose grease, coat the area between the races and pack the bearings.
8. Place the inner bearing into the rear of the disc/hub assembly. Using the installation tool No. 09608-35013, or its equivalent, drive a new grease seal into the rear of the disc/hub assembly until it is flush with the housing.
9. Install the disc/hub assembly onto the axle shaft, the outer bearing, the thrust washer and the adjusting nut.

10. To adjust the bearing preload, perform the following:
a. Using tool No. 09607–60020, or its equivalent, torque the adjusting nut to 43 ft. lbs.
b. Turn the disc/hub assembly 2–3 times, from the left to the right.
c. Loosen the adjusting nut until it can be turned by hand.
d. Retorque the adjusting nut to 18 ft. lbs.
e. Install the lock washer and the lock nut. Torque the lock nut to 33 ft. lbs.
f. Check that the bearing has no play.
g. Using a spring gauge, connect it to a wheel stud, the gauge should be held horizontal, then measure the rotating force, it should be 6–12 lbs.
11. To complete the installation, reverse the removal procedures.

Steering Knuckle

Removal and Installation

2WD PICKUP AND VAN

1. Raise and support the front of the vehicle on jackstands. Remove the wheel/tire assembly.
2. Remove the brake caliper (DO NOT disconnect the brake hose from the caliper) and suspend it on a wire.
3. Remove axle hub dust cap, the cotter pin, the nut lock, the adjusting nut, the thrust washer and the outer bearing, then pull the hub/disc assembly from the axle spindle.
4. Remove the backing plate cotter pins and the mounting nuts or bolts, then the backing plate.
5. Remove steering knuckle arm from the back of the steering knuckle.
6. Remove the nuts, the retainers and the bushings, then the shock absorber from the lower control arm.
7. Support the lower arm with a jack and raise to put pressure on spring.

CAUTION

Be careful not to unbalance vehicle support stands when jacking up lower arm.

8. Remove cotter pins, then the upper and lower ball joint nuts. Using the ball joint removal tool No. 09628–62010, or its equivalent (1982–83) or 09628–62011, or its equivalent (1984-88), separate the ball joints from the steering knuckle.
9. Remove the steering knuckle from the vehicle.

NOTE: Whenever the hub/disc assembly is removed from the vehicle, it is good practice to replace the grease seal.

10. To install, reverse the removal procedures. Torque the upper ball joint nut to 80 ft. lbs. (Pickup) or 58 ft. lbs. (Van), the lower ball joint nut to 105 ft. lbs. (Pickup) or 76 ft. lbs., the steering knuckle arm-to-steering knuckle bolts to 80 ft. lbs. (Pickup) or 61 ft. lbs. (Van), the shock absorber-to-lower control arm nuts to 19 ft. lbs. and the backing plate-to-steering knuckle bolts to 80 ft. lbs. (Pickup) or 61 ft. lbs. (Van). Adjust the wheel bearing.

4WD PICKUP AND LAND CRUISER

1. Refer to the "Front Axle Shaft, Removal and Installation" procedures, in this section and remove the front axle.
2. Remove the oil seal retainer and the oil seal set from the rear of the steering knuckle.
3. At the drag link end of the steering knuckle arm, remove the cotter pin. Using a screwdriver, remove the plug from the drag link, then disconnect the drag link from the steering knuckle arm.
4. Remove the tie-rod-to-steering knuckle, cotter pin and nut. Using the Ball Joint Removal tool No. 09611–22012, or its equivalent, separate the tie-rod from the steering knuckle arm..
5. Remove the steering knuckle arm-to-steering knuckle (top) nuts and the steering knuckle-to-bearing cap (bottom) nuts. Using a tapered punch, tap the cone washers slits and remove the washers.

CAUTION

DO NOT tap on the bearings.

NOTE: DO NOT mix or lose the upper and lower bearing cap shims.

6. Using the bearing removal tool No. 09606–60020, or its equivalent (without a collar), press the steering knuckle arm with the shims from the steering knuckle.
7. Using the bearing removal tool No. 09606–60020, or its equivalent (without a collar), press the bearing cap with the shims from the steering knuckle.
8. Remove the steering knuckle from the vehicle.
9. To install the steering knuckle, use tool No. 09606–60020, or its equivalent, (with a collar) to support the upper inner bearing. Using a hammer, tap the steering knuckle arm into the bearing inner race.
10. Invert the tool No. 09606–60020, or its equivalent, to support the lower bearing inner race. Using a hammer, tap the bearing cap into the bearing inner race.

NOTE: When installing the drag link-to-steering knuckle arm, torque the plug all the way, then loosen it $1\frac{1}{3}$ turns and secure it with the cotter pin.

11. To install, use gaskets, seals, pack the steering knuckle with multi-purpose grease and reverse the removal procedures. Torque the steering knuckle arm-to-steering knuckle nuts to 71 ft. lbs., the bearing cap-to-steering knuckle nuts to 71 ft. lbs., the tie-rod-to-steering knuckle arm nut to 67 ft. lbs., the axle

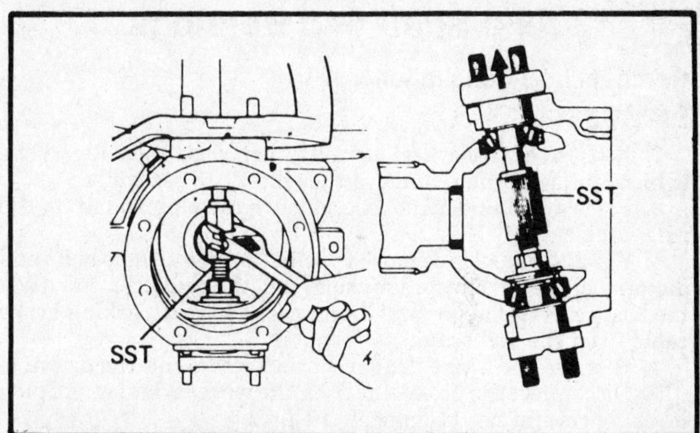

Removing the steering knuckle arm from the steering knuckle – 4WD vehicles

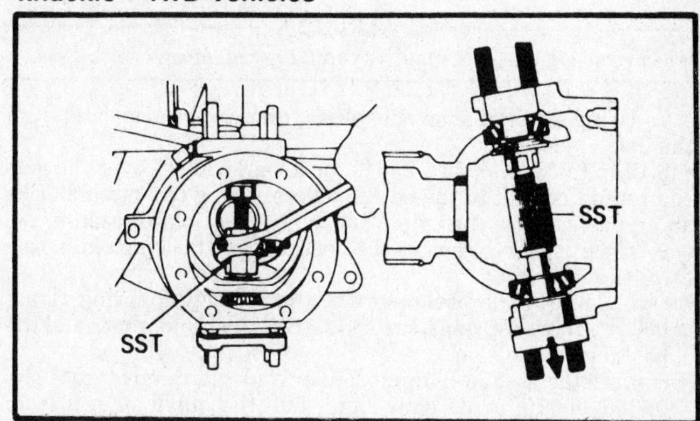

Removing the bearing cap from the steering knuckle – 4WD vehicles

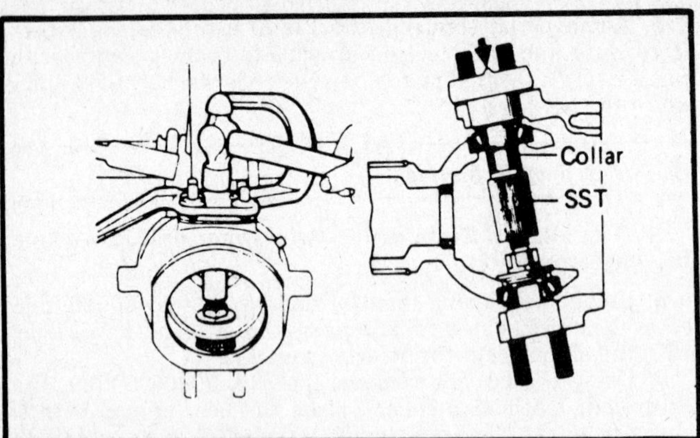

Installing the steering knuckle arm to the steering knuckle – 4WD vehicles

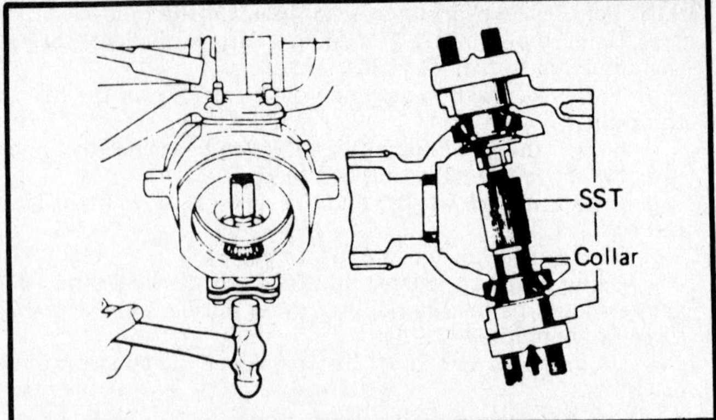

Installing the bearing cap to the steering knuckle – 4WD vehicles

spindle-to-steering knuckle bolts to 38 ft. lbs. Adjust the wheel bearing preload.

NOTE: To test the knuckle bearing preload, attach a spring scale to the tie-rod end hole (at a right angle) in the steering knuckle arm. The force required to move the knuckle from side to side should be 4–8 lbs. (Pickup, 1982–83), 6.6–13 lbs. (Pickup, 1984-88) or 4–5 lbs. (Land Cruiser). If the preload is not correct, adjust by replacing shims.

REAR DRIVE AXLE

For overhaul information, refer to "Drive Axles" in the Unit Repair Section.

Axle Shaft and Bearings

Removal and Installation

PICKUPS

1. Loosen the rear wheel lug nuts, then raise and support the vehicle on jackstands. Remove the wheel/tire assembly.
2. Place a pan under the axle, remove the plug and drain the axle housing.
3. For 2WD models, remove the clip/clamp-to-frame bolts and disconnect the parking brake cable from the equalizer. For 4WD models, remove the pin and disconnect the rear parking brake cable from the bell crank.
4. Remove the brake drum securing screw and the drum.
5. Disconnect the brake line from the wheel cylinder and plug it, being careful not to damage the fitting.
6. Remove the brake backing plate-to-axle housing nuts and pull the backing plate with the axle from the axle housing.

CAUTION

When removing the axle shaft, be careful not to damage the oil seal.

7. Using a pair of snap ring pliers, remove the snap ring from the axle shaft.
8. Slip tool No. 09521–25011, or its equivalent, over the axle shaft and fasten it to the backing plate. Using two metal blocks and a press, press the axle from the backing plate assembly.
9. If necessary to remove the bearing from backing plate, perform the following:
   a. Remove the brake spring, the retracting spring clamp bolt, the lower springs, the shoe strut, the brake shoes and the parking brake lever.
   b. Using a slide hammer puller and the removal tool No. 09308–00010, or its equivalent, pull the outer oil seal from the backing plate.
   c. Using the removal tools No. 09228–44010 and 09608–30011, or their equivalents, press the bearing from the backing plate.
   d. Using the installation tools No. 09515–30010 and 09608–35013, or their equivalents, press the new bearing into the backing plate.
   e. Using the installation tool No. 09608–30011, or its equivalent, press the new oil seal into the backing plate.
   f. Reassemble the brake components to the backing plate.
10. Using a slide hammer and the removal tool No. 09308–00010, or its equivalent, pull the oil seal from the axle housing.
11. Using the installation tool and a hammer, drive a new oil seal into the axle housing.
12. Using a press and the installation tool No. 09515–30010, or its equivalent, press the axle shaft into the backing plate and the bearing retainer. Using snap-ring pliers, install the snap-ring onto the axle shaft.
13. Using a putty knife, clean the gasket mounting surfaces.
14. To complete the installation, reverse the removal proce-

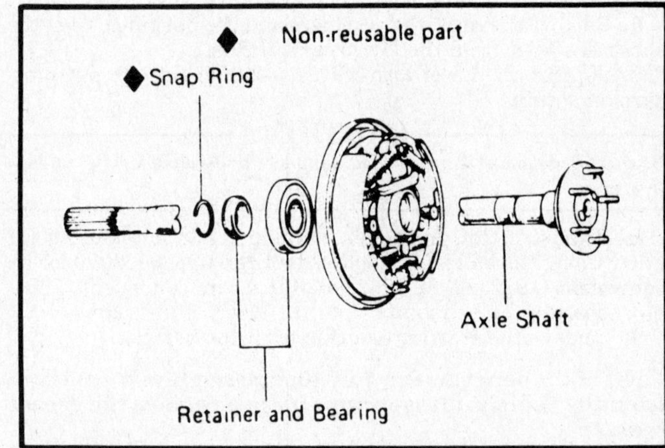

Exploded view of the rear axle assembly – Pick-ups and 4-Runner

dures. Torque the backing plate-to-axle housing nuts to 51 ft. lbs. Adjust the brake shoe clearance and bleed the brake system. Refill the axle housing with SAE 90W GL5 gear oil.

LAND CRUISER

Semi-Floating Type Differential

1. Loosen the rear wheel nuts. Raise and support the rear axle housing on jackstands. Remove the wheel/tire assembly.
2. Place a pan under the axle, remove the plug and drain the oil from the differential.
3. Remove the brake drum and related parts, as follows:
   a. Remove the cover from the back of the differential housing.
   b. Remove the pin from the differential pinion shaft.
   c. Withdraw the pinion shaft and it's spacer from the case.
   d. Use a mallet to tap the rear axle shaft toward the differential, then remove the C-lock from the axle shaft.
   e. Withdraw the axle shaft from the housing.
4. Using a bearing puller, remove axle bearing and oil seal together from the axle housing. Using a metal tube and a hammer, drive the bearing and the seal into the housing until they seat.

CAUTION

DO NOT mix the parts of the left and right axle shaft assemblies.

5. To complete the installation, reverse the removal procedures. Refill the axle housing with SAE 90W GL5 gear oil.

NOTE: After installing the axle shaft, C-lock, spacer and pinion shaft, measure the clearance between the axle shaft and the pinion shaft spacer with a feeler gauge. The clearance should fall between 0.0024–0.0181 in. If the clearance is not within specifications, use one of the following spacers to adjust it:

a. 1.172–1.173 in.
b. 1.188–1.189 in.
c. 1.204–1.205 in.

Full Floating Type Differential

1. Loosen the rear wheel nuts. Raise and support the rear axle housing on jackstands. Remove the wheel/tire assembly.
2. Place a pan under the axle, remove the plug and drain the oil from the differential.
3. Remove the rear axle shaft plate nuts.
4. Remove the cone washers from the mounting studs by tapping the slits of the washers with a tapered punch.
5. Install bolts into the two unused holes of the axle shaft plate.
6. Tighten the bolts to draw the axle shaft assembly out of the housing.
7. To install, use a new gasket, sealant and reverse the removal procedures. Torque the axle shaft nuts to 21–25 ft. lbs.

VAN

1. Loosen the rear wheel nuts. Raise and support the rear axle housing on jackstands. Remove the wheel/tire assembly.
2. Working through the hole in the axle flange, remove the backing plate-to-axle housing bolts.
3. Using a slide hammer puller and removal tool No. 09520-00031, or its equivalent, pull the axle shaft from the housing.
4. Using a grinder, grind down the inner bearing retainer on the axle shaft. Using a chisel and a hammer, cut off the retainer and remove it from the shaft.
5. Using a arbor press and the removal tool 09527-21011, or its equivalent, press the bearing from the axle shaft.
6. Using a slide hammer puller and the removal tool 09308-00010, or its equivalent, pull the oil seal from the axle housing.
7. Lubricate the new oil seal with multi-purpose grease. Using the installation tool No. 09517-30010, or its equivalent and a hammer, drive the new oil seal into the axle housing to a depth of 0.236 in.

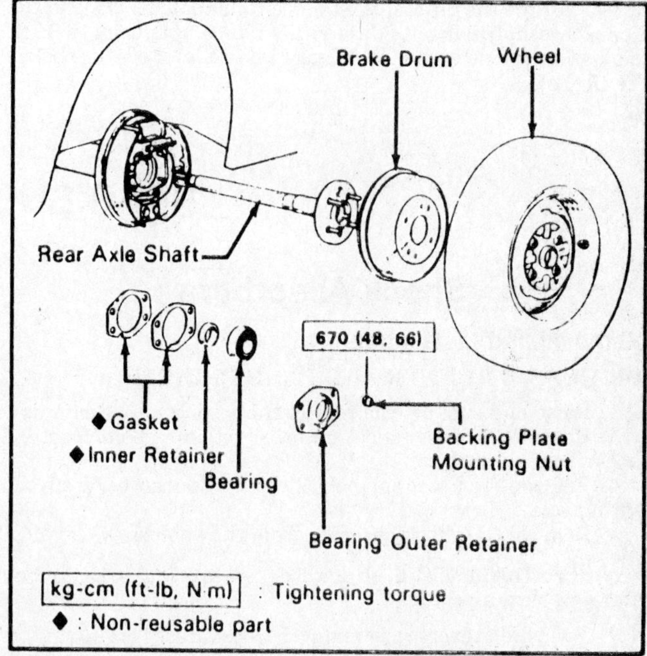

Exploded view of the rear axle assembly—Van

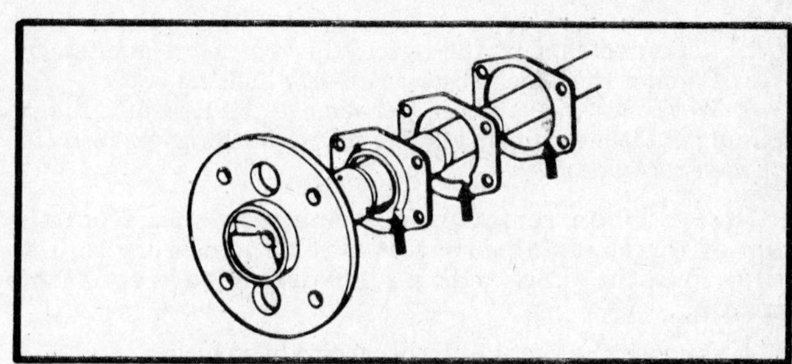

Aligning the gaskets and retainer of the axle shaft—Van

8. To install, use new gaskets and reverse the removal procedures. Torque the axle retainer-to-housing bolts to 48 ft. lbs.

Differential Carrier

Removal and Installation

PICKUPS, 4-RUNNER AND LAND CRUISER

Refer to the "Differential, Removal and Installation" procedures, listed in the "Front Drive Axle" section, of this section and remove the differential.

VAN

1. Refer to the "Front Axle Shaft, Removal and Installation" procedures, in this section and remove the front axle shafts from the axle housing.
2. Drain the lubricant from the differential.
3. Match-mark the front driveshaft flange to the differential flange. Remove the mounting bolts and separate the driveshaft from the differential.
4. Remove the carrier retaining nuts and pull the carrier assembly out of the differential housing.
5. To install, use new gaskets and reverse the removal proce-

dures. Torque the differential-to-axle nuts to 23 ft. lbs. and the front driveshaft flange-to-differential flange nuts/bolts to 31 ft. lbs. Refill the axle with 80W–90 gear oil to a level of ¼ in. below the fill hole.

NOTE: Before installing the carrier, apply a thin coat of liquid or silicone sealer to the carrier housing gasket and to the carrier side face of each carrier retaining nut.

REAR SUSPENSION

Shock Absorbers

Removal and Installation

PICKUPS, 4-RUNNER AND LAND CRUISER

1. Raise and support the rear of the vehicle on jackstands.
3. Remove the upper shock absorber retaining bolts from the upper frame member.
4. Remove the lower end bolt of the shock absorber from the spring seat.
5. Remove the shock absorber from the vehicle.

NOTE: Inspect the shock for wear, leaks or other signs of damage.

6. To install, reverse the removal procedures. Torque the upper bolt to 19 ft. lbs. (2WD) or 47 ft. lbs. (4WD) and the lower bolt to 19 ft. lbs. (2WD) or 47 ft. lbs. (4WD).

VAN

1. Raise and support the rear of the vehicle on jackstands.
2. Remove the shock absorber-to-axle housing bolt.
3. Working inside the vehicle, remove the lock nut, the retaining nut, the retainers and the rubber bushings from the top of the shock absorber.

NOTE: When removing the retaining nut, from the top of the shock absorber, it may be necessary to hold the top of the shock with a screwdriver, to keep it from turning.

4. Remove the shock absorber from the vehicle.
5. To install, reverse the removal procedures. Torque the shock absorber-to-body nut to 16–24 ft. lbs. and the shock absorber-to-axle housing bolt to 27 ft. lbs.

Coil Spring – Van

Removal and Installation

1. Raise and support the rear of the vehicle with jackstands under the frame. Support the axle housing with a floor jack. Remove the wheel/tire assembly.
2. Remove the shock absorber-to-axle housing bolt.
3. Remove the stabilizer-to-axle housing bar bushing bracket bolts.
4. Remove the lateral control arm-to-axle housing nut and disconnect the lateral control arm.
5. Lower the floor jack, then remove the coil spring(s) and the insulators.

NOTE: While lowering the axle housing, be careful not to snag the brake line of the parking brake cable.

6. To install, reverse the removal procedures. Torque the shock absorber bolt to 27 ft. lbs., the lateral control arm-to-axle housing nut to 43 ft. lbs. and the stabilizer-to-axle housing bolts to 27 ft. lbs.

NOTE: Before tightening the lateral control arm and the stabilizer nuts/bolts, bounce the vehicle to stabilize the suspension.

Leaf Spring – Except Van

Removal and Installation

1. Raise and support the rear of the vehicle with jackstands under the frame. Support the axle housing with a floor jack. Remove the wheel/tire assembly.
2. Lower the floor jack to take the tension off of the spring. Remove the shock absorber mounting nuts/bolts and the shock absorber.
3. On the Land Cruiser models, perform the following:
   a. Remove the cotter pins and the nuts from the lower end of the stabilizer link.
   b. Detach the link from the axle housing.
4. Remove the spring-to-axle housing U-bolt nuts, the spring seat (2WD) or spring bumper (4WD) and the U-bolt.
5. At the front of the spring, remove the hanger pin bolt. Disconnect the spring from the bracket.
6. Remove the spring shackle retaining nuts and the spring shackle inner plate, then carefully pry out the spring shackle with a pry bar.
7. Remove the spring from the vehicle.

CAUTION

Use care not to damage the hydraulic brake line or the parking brake cable.

8. To install, perform the following procedure:
   a. Install the rubber bushings in the eye of the spring.
   b. Align the eye of the spring with the spring hanger bracket and drive the pin through the bracket holes and rubber bushings.

NOTE: Use soapy water as lubricant (if necessary), to aid in pin installation. Never use oil or grease.

   c. Finger-tighten the spring hanger nuts/bolts.
   d. Install the rubber bushings in the spring eye at the opposite end of the spring.
   e. Raise the free end of the spring. Install the spring shackle through the bushings and the bracket.
   f. Install the shackle inner plate and finger-tighten the retaining nuts.
   g. Center the bolt head in the hole which is provided in the spring seat on the axle housing.
   h. Fit the U-bolts over the axle housing. Install the lower spring seat (2WD) or spring bumper (4WD) and the nuts.
9. To complete the installation, reverse the removal procedures. Torque the U-bolt nuts to 72 ft. lbs. (2WD) or 90 ft. lbs. (4WD), the hanger pin-to-frame nut to 67 ft. lbs., the shackle pin nuts to 67 ft. lbs., the shock absorber bolts to 19 ft. lbs. (2WD) or 47 ft. lbs. (4WD).

NOTE: When installing the U-bolts, tighten the nuts so that the length of the bolts are equal.

Rear Control Arms – Van

Removal and Installation

1. Raise and support the rear of the vehicle, with jackstands

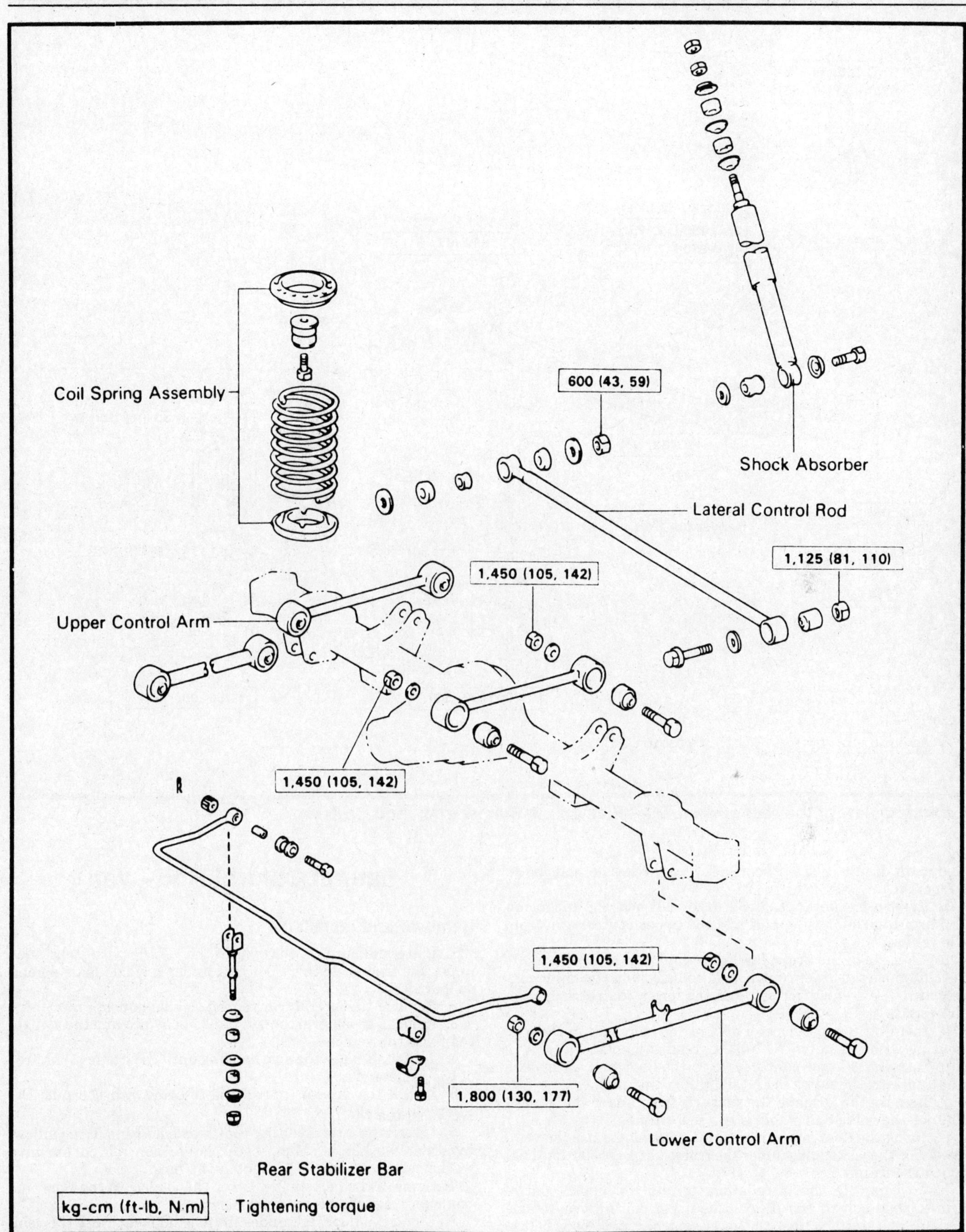

Exploded view of the rear suspension—Van

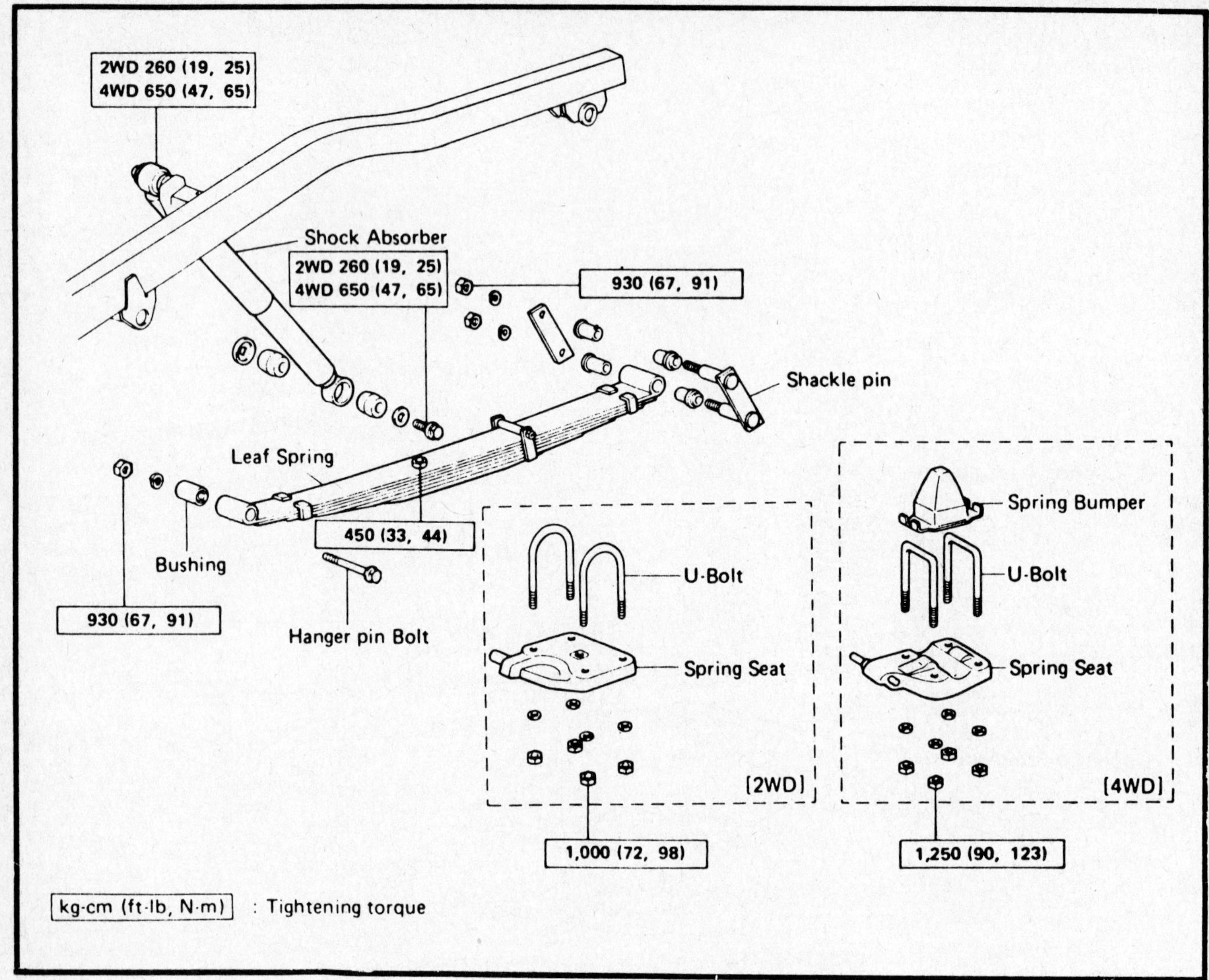

Exploded view of the rear suspension—Pick-ups, 4-Runner and Land Cruiser

under the frame. Place a floor jack under the axle housing to support it.

2. Remove the upper control arm-to-body bolt, the upper control arm-to-axle housing bolt and the upper control arm from the vehicle.

3. Disconnect the brake line from the lower control arm.

4. Remove the lower control arm-to-body bolt, the lower control arm-to-axle housing bolt and the lower control arm from the vehicle.

5. Install the upper control arm to the body and to the axle housing with the nuts. DO NOT tighten the nuts.

6. Install the lower control arm to the body and to the axle housing with the nuts. DO NOT tighten the nuts.

7. Remove the jack and the supports from under the vehicle. Bounce the vehicle to stabilize the suspension.

8. Using the floor jack under the axle housing, raise the vehicle. Place the jackstands under the frame but DO NOT let them touch the frame.

9. To complete the installation, torque the upper control arm-to-body bolt to 105 ft. lbs., the upper control arm-to-axle housing bolt to 105 ft. lbs., the lower control arm-to-body bolt to 130 ft. lbs. and the lower control arm-to-axle housing bolt to 105 ft. lbs.

Lateral Control Rod—Van

Removal and Installation

1. Raise and support the rear of the vehicle with jackstands under the frame. Place a floor jack under the axle housing and support it.

2. Remove the lateral control rod-to-axle housing nut.

3. Remove the lateral control rod-to-body nut and the control rod from the vehicle.

4. To install, raise the axle housing until the frame is just free of the jackstands.

5. Install the lateral control rod-to-body with the nut. DO NOT tighten the nut.

6. Install the lateral control rod-to-axle housing in the following order: washer, bushing, spacer, lateral control rod, bushing, washer and nut. DO NOT tighten the nut.

7. Remove the jackstands, lower the vehicle to the floor and bounce it to stabilize the suspension.

8. Using the floor jack under the axle housing, raise the vehicle. Torque the lateral control rod-to-body nut to 81 ft. lbs. and the lateral control rod-to-axle housing nut to 43 ft. lbs.

Electrical System
Import Trucks

INDEX

ALTERNATORS AND REGULATORS

STARTING SYSTEMS

ELECTRONIC IGNITION SYSTEMS

ELECTRONIC FUEL INJECTION IGNITION SYSTEMS

ELECTRICAL

Test Instruments

OHMMETER

An ohmmeter is used to measure electrical resistance in a unit or circuit. The ohmmeter has a self-contained power supply. In use, it is connected across (or in parallel with) the terminals of the unit being tested.

AMMETER

An ammeter is used to measure current (amount of electricity) flowing through a unit, or circuit. Ammeters are always connected in the line (in series) with the unit or circuit being tested.

VOLTMETER

A voltmeter is used to measure voltage (electrical pressure) pushing the current through a unit, or circuit. The meter is connected across the terminals of the unit being tested.

Alternator Testing

IS IT THE ALTERNATOR OR THE VOLTAGE REGULATOR?

The first step in diagnosing troubles of the charging system, is to identify the source of failure. Does the fault lie in the alternator or the regulator? The next move depends upon preference or necessity; either repair or replace the offending unit.

Alternator output is controlled by the amount of current supplied to the field circuit of the system.

The alternator is capable of producing substantial current at idle speed. Higher maximum output is also a possibility. This presents a potential danger when testing. As a precaution, a field rheostat should be used in the field circuit when making the following isolation test. The field rheostat permits positive control of the amount of current allowed to pass through the field circuit during the isolation test. Unregulated alternator capacity could ruin the unit.

NOTE: Most manufacturers of precision gauges offer special test connectors, in sets, that will adapt to the leads and connections of any charging system.

There are certain precautionary measures that apply to alternator tests in general. These items are listed in detail to avoid repetition when testing each make of alternator and to encourage a habit of good test procedure.

1. Check alternator drive belt for condition and tension.
2. Disconnect battery cables, check physical, chemical and electrical condition of battery.
3. Be absolutely sure of polarity before connecting any battery in the circuit. Reversed polarity will ruin the diodes.
4. Never use a battery charger to start the engine.
5. Disconnect both battery cables when making a battery recharge hook-up.
6. Be sure of polarity connections when using a booster battery for starting.
7. Never ground the alternator output or battery terminal.
8. Never ground the field circuit between alternator and regulator.
9. Never run any alternator on an open circuit with the field energized.
10. Never try to polarize an alternator, unless directed by the manufacturer of the alternator.
11. Do not attempt to motor an alternator.
12. The regulator cover must be in place when taking voltage limiter readings.

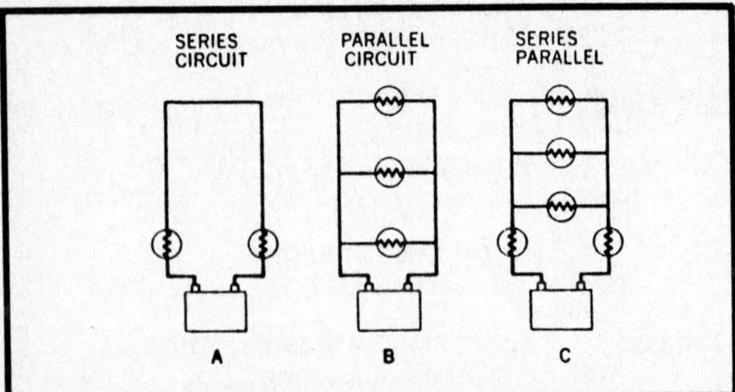

Basic electrical circuits

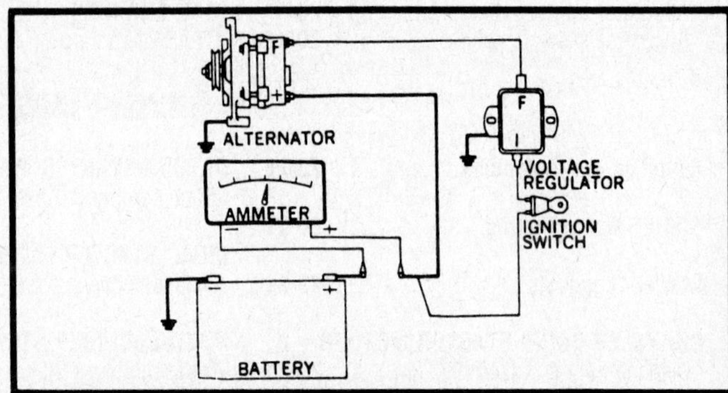

Ammeter connected to test wire

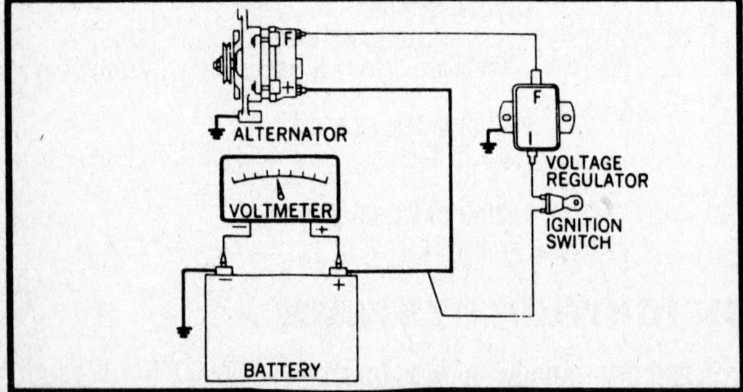

Voltmeter connected in parallel circuit

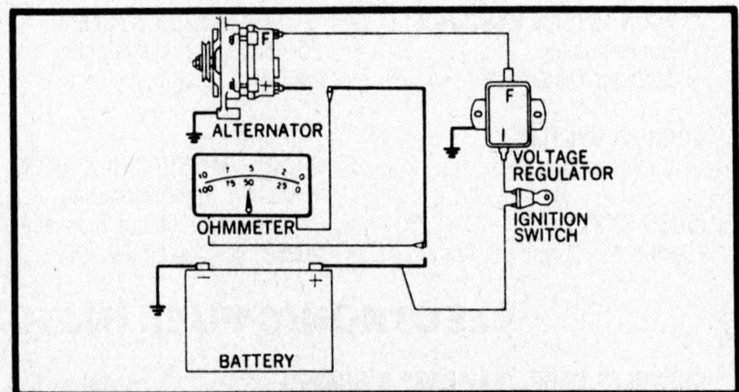

Ohmmeter connected to test wire resistance

13. The ignition switch must be in the OFF position when removing or installing the regulator cover.

14. Use insulated tools only to make adjustments to the regulator.

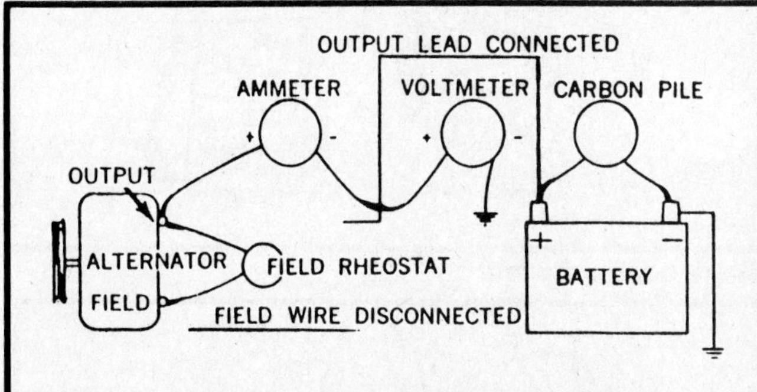

Checking current output of the charging system

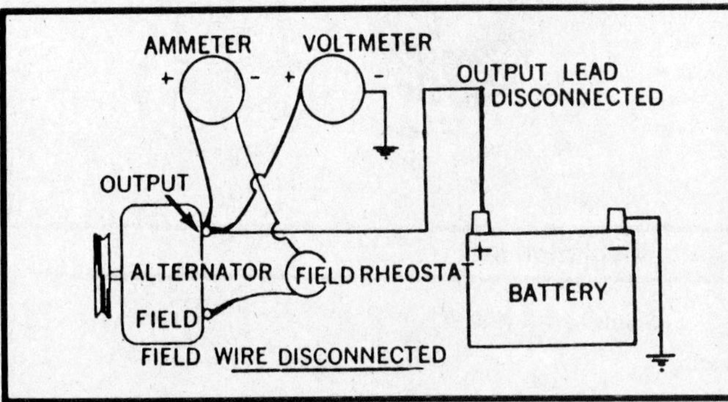

Checking field current draw

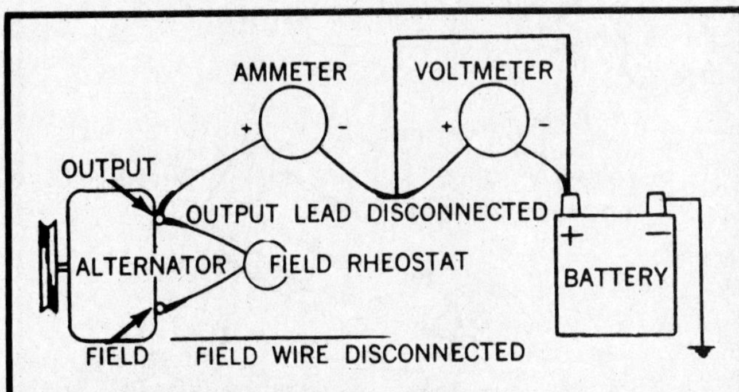

Checking charging system resistance

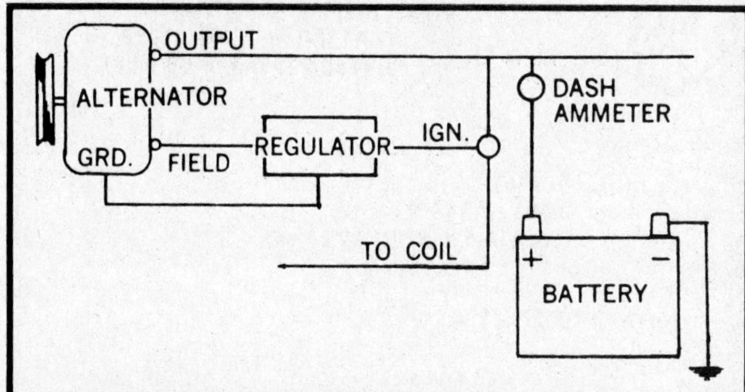

Alternator system with ammeter in the circuit

15. When making engine idle speed adjustments, always consider potential load factors that influence engine rpm. To compensate for electrical load, switch on the lights, radio, heater, air conditioner, etc.

DIAGNOSIS OF CHARGING SYSTEM

LOW OR NO CHARGING

1. Blown fuse.
2. Broken or loose fan belt.
3. Voltage regulator not working.
4. Brushes sticking.
5. Slip ring dirty.
6. Open circuit.
7. Bad wiring connections.
8. Bad diode rectifier.
9. High resistance in charging circuit.
10. Voltage regulator needs adjusting.
11. Grounded stator.
12. May be open rectifiers (check all three phases).
13. If rectifiers are found blown or open, check capacitor.

NOISY UNIT

1. Damaged rotor bearings.
2. Poor alignment of unit.
3. Broken or loose belt.
4. Open diode rectifiers.

REGULATOR POINTS BURNED OR STUCK

1. Regulator set too high.
2. Poor ground connections.
3. Shorted generator field.
4. Regulator air gap incorrect.

Datsun Charging System

ALTERNATOR

Disassembly

1. On diesel engine models only, remove the vacuum pump.

2. Remove the through bolts and separate the front cover from the rear cover.

3. Place the rear cover side of the rotor in a vise and remove the pulley nut and pulley.

4. Remove the screws from the bearing retainer.

5. Remove the attaching nuts and take out the stator assembly.

6. Use a bearing puller or a press and pull the rear bearing from the rotor assembly.

NOTE: The bearing cannot be reused and must be replaced with a new one.

7. To remove the stator, disconnect the stator coil lead wires from the diode terminals, using a soldering iron.

8. On diesel engine models, check the oil seal for leakage. If replacement is needed, pry out the old seal, apply engine oil to the new seal and install in position.

ROTOR

Testing And Inspection

1. Using an ohmmeter, check for continuity at the slip end rings. If there is no continuity, replace the rotor.

2. Using an ohmmeter, make an insulation test. Check for continuity between the slip ring and the rotor core. If continuity exists, replace the rotor.

3. Measure the slip ring outer diameter for wear. Mimimum diameter is 1.18 in. (30mm).

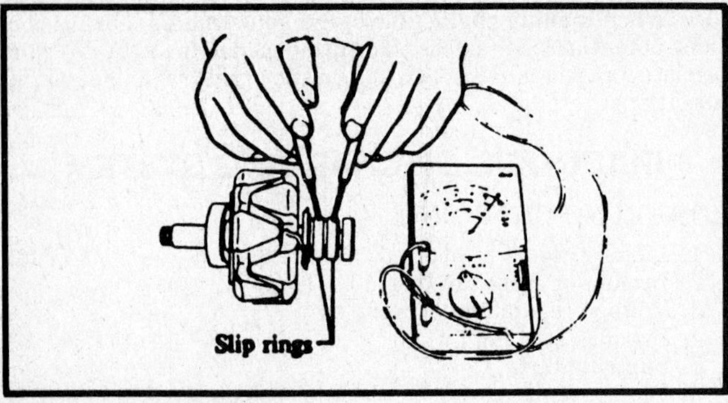

Rotor test at slip rings

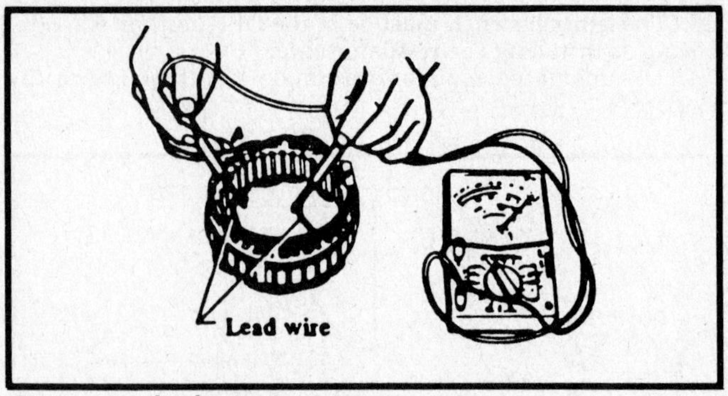

Lead wire

Stator continuity test

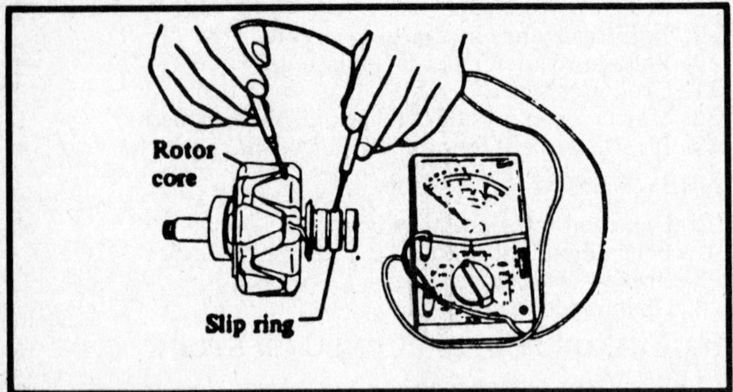

Rotor insulation test

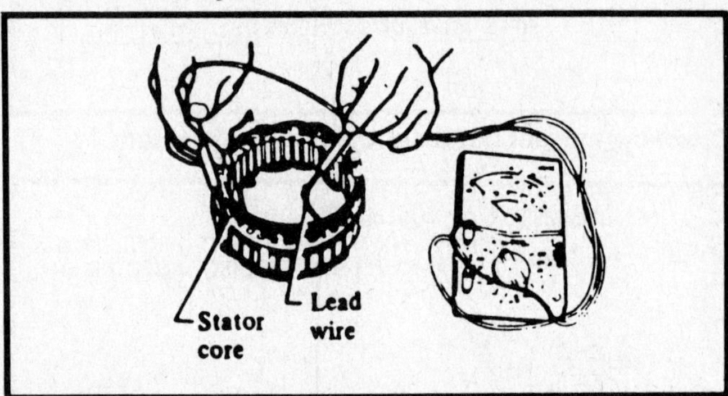

Stator insulation test

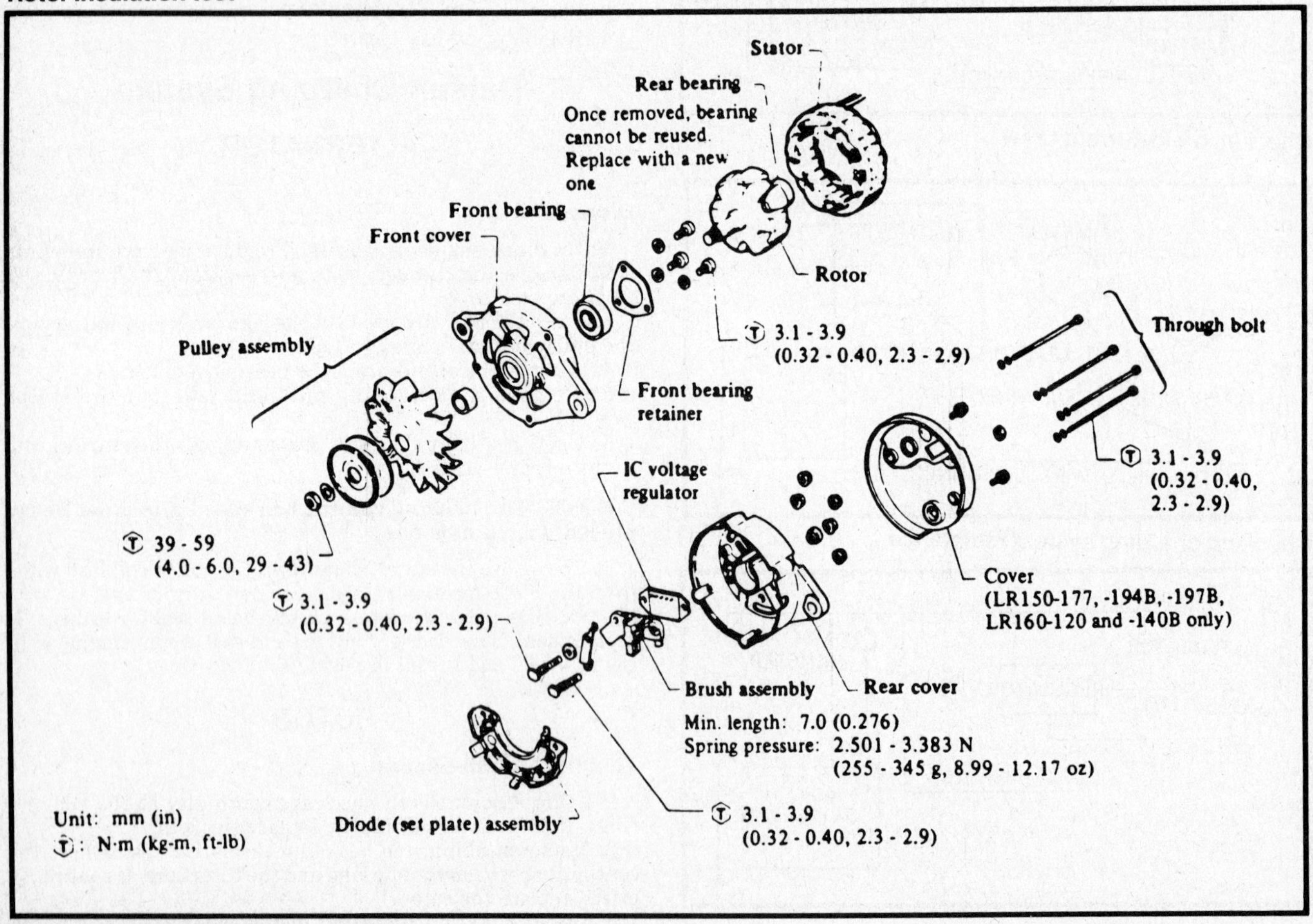

Stator
Rear bearing
Once removed, bearing cannot be reused. Replace with a new one
Front bearing
Front cover
Rotor
Pulley assembly
Ⓣ 3.1 - 3.9 (0.32 - 0.40, 2.3 - 2.9)
Through bolt
Front bearing retainer
Ⓣ 3.1 - 3.9 (0.32 - 0.40, 2.3 - 2.9)
IC voltage regulator
Ⓣ 39 - 59 (4.0 - 6.0, 29 - 43)
Cover (LR150-177, -194B, -197B, LR160-120 and -140B only)
Ⓣ 3.1 - 3.9 (0.32 - 0.40, 2.3 - 2.9)
Brush assembly
Rear cover
Min. length: 7.0 (0.276)
Spring pressure: 2.501 - 3.383 N (255 - 345 g, 8.99 - 12.17 oz)
Unit: mm (in)
Ⓣ: N·m (kg-m, ft-lb)
Diode (set plate) assembly
Ⓣ 3.1 - 3.9 (0.32 - 0.40, 2.3 - 2.9)

Datsun gasoline alternator—typical

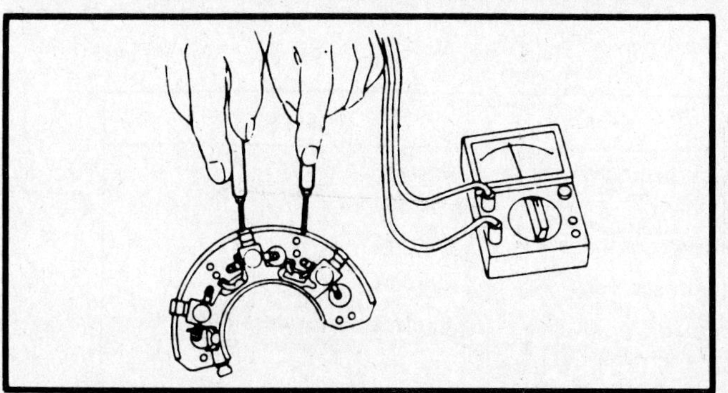

Positive diode test

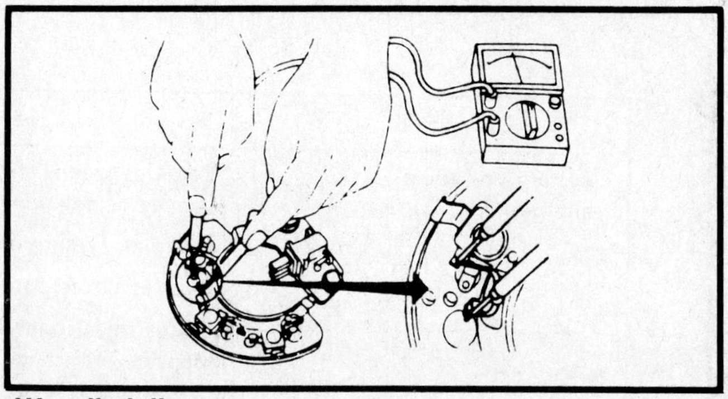

Wear limit line

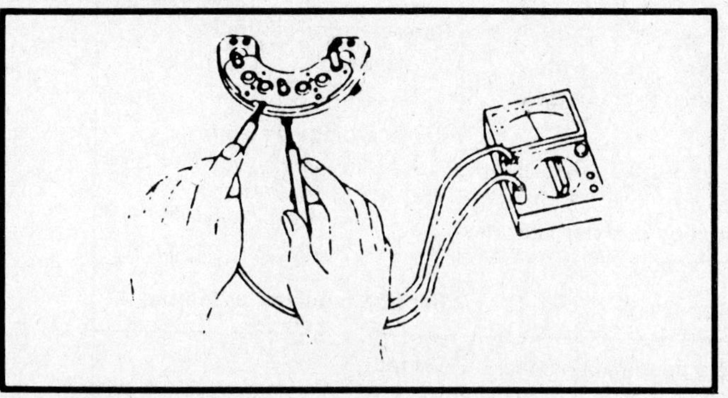

Negative diode test

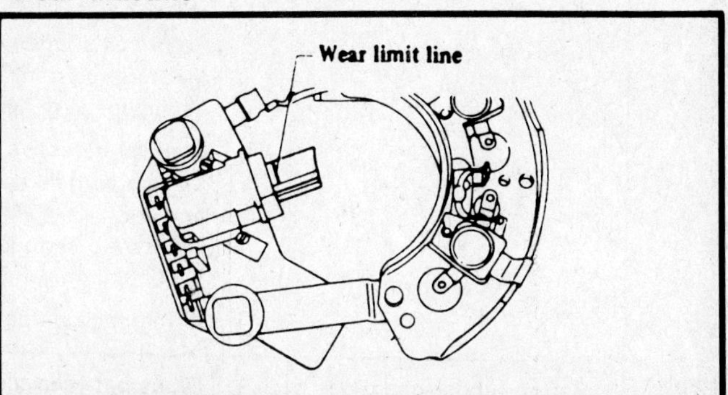

Brush wear limit line

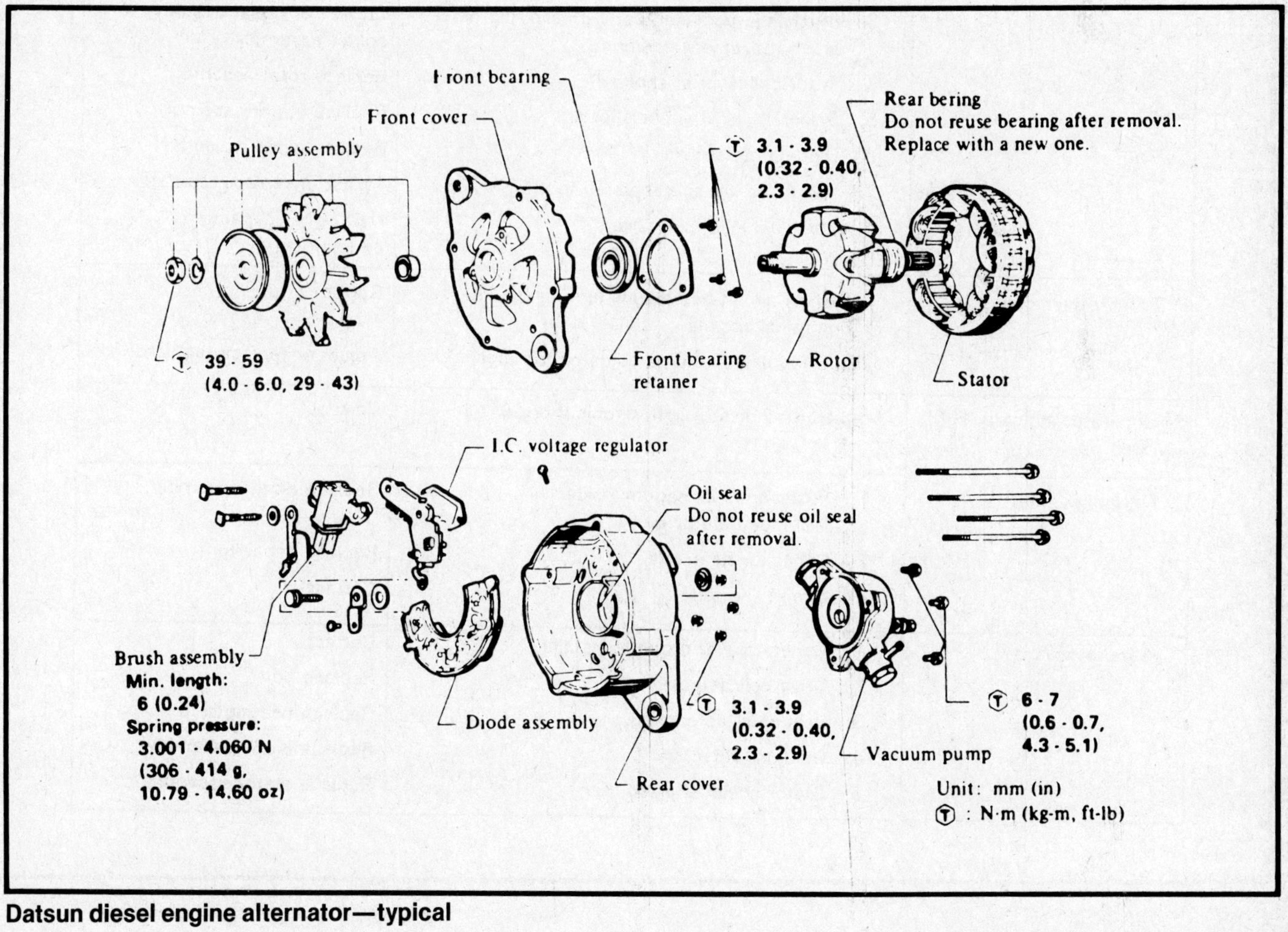

Front bearing
Front cover
Pulley assembly
Rear bering
Do not reuse bearing after removal.
Replace with a new one.
Ⓣ 3.1 - 3.9
(0.32 - 0.40,
2.3 - 2.9)
Ⓣ 39 - 59
(4.0 - 6.0, 29 - 43)
Front bearing
retainer
Rotor
Stator
I.C. voltage regulator
Oil seal
Do not reuse oil seal
after removal.
Brush assembly
Min. length:
6 (0.24)
Spring pressure:
3.001 - 4.060 N
(306 - 414 g,
10.79 - 14.60 oz)
Diode assembly
Ⓣ 3.1 - 3.9
(0.32 - 0.40,
2.3 - 2.9)
Rear cover
Vacuum pump
Ⓣ 6 - 7
(0.6 - 0.7,
4.3 - 5.1)
Unit: mm (in)
Ⓣ : N·m (kg-m, ft-lb)

Datsun diesel engine alternator—typical

Complaint	Cause	Correction
Battery not being charged	1. Cable between terminals broken or connector defective	Correct
	2. Charging system not properly grounded	Correct
	3. Brushes not in contact with slip ring	Correct
	4. Stator coil(s) open or burned Measure resistance across terminals at connectors between diode cover and stator coil leads.	Replace stator assembly
	5. Rotor coil(s) open or burned Measure resistance across F and E with connector at generator side disconnected	Replace rotor assembly
	6. Diode(s) defective Make a continuity test across B-N, B-E and N-E. Diodes are in good condition if tester indicates continuity only in one direction.	Replace diode assembly
	7. IC regulator defective	Replace regulator assembly
Battery under-charging	1. Wires between terminals poorly connected	Correct
	2. Drive belt slipping	Correct or replace belt
	3. Brushes in poor contact with slip ring or brush movement unsmooth	Correct or replace brush holder assembly
	4. Rotor coil layer(s) shorted	Replace rotor assembly
	5. Stator coil(s) open or shorted	Replace stator assembly
	6. Diode(s) defective	Replace diode assembly
	7. Regulated voltage adjusted too low	Adjust or replace regulator
	8. Electrical load excessive	Use higher capacity generator
Battery over-charging	1. Short circuit between B terminal and F terminal circuits	Correct
	2. IC regulated voltage adjusted too high	Adjust or replace regulator
Generator indicator light turns on	Generator indicator light circuit shorted	Correct
Fuse blows out	1. Positive (+) or negative side (–) diode defective	Replace diode assembly
	2. Capacitor defective	Replace capacitor
	3. Circuit shorted	Correct
Generator noisy	1. Generator not properly installed	Correct
	2. Drive belt defective	Replace belt
	3. Bearing(s) defective	Replace bearing(s)
	4. Diode(s) defective	Replace diode assembly
	5. Stator coil(s) shorted	Replace stator assembly

STATOR

Testing And Inspection

1. Using an ohmmeter, make a continuity test between the stator lead wires. If there is no lead wires, replace the stator.
2. Using an ohmmeter. make an insulation test between the stator core and the lead wire. If the continuity exists, replace the stator.

DIODE

Testing And Inspection

1. Using an ohmmeter, perform a continuity test on diodes in both directions.
2. Replace diodes as necessary.

BRUSH

Inspection

1. Check for smooth movement of the brush and clean the brush holder if necessary.
2. Check for brush wear by looking at the wear limit line on the brush and replace if necessary.

ALTERNATOR

Assembly

1. Assembly of the alternator is the reverse of disassembly with the following instructions: Solder each stator coil lead wire to the diode assembly terminal as quickly as possible. When soldering the brush lead wire, position the brush so that it extends 0.43 in. from the brush holder and wrap the coil lead wire at least 1.5 times around the terminal groove. Solder the outside of the terminal.
2. Tighten the pulley nut to 29–43 ft. lbs.
3. Before installing the front and rear sides of the alternator, push the brush up and retain the brush by inserting a wire from the outside into a lift hole. After installing the front and rear sides of the alternator, pull the brush lift by pushing towards the center.

NOTE: Do not pull brush lift by pushing towards the outside of the cover as it will damage the slip ring as it slides.

Isuzu Charging System

Troubleshooting

1. Measure the resistance between F and E terminals (rotor coil resistance): The rotor coil circuit is normal if resistance measured across the terminals is 5 ohms. If resistance is higher than 5 ohms, the trouble is poor contact between the brushes and commutator. If no continuity exists between terminals F and E, the trouble is either an open coil rotor circuit, brush sticking or a broken lead wire. If resistance is lower than 5 ohms, it may be an indication of rotor coil layer short or the circuit being grounded.
2. Test the rectifying diodes in the following manner: Connect the positive (+) lead of a tester to the the alternator N terminal and the tester negative (−) lead to the alternator A terminal. If there exists a continuity between terminals, it indicates that one or more of the three diodes in the positive side are shorted. Connect the positive (+) lead of a tester to the alternator E terminal and the tester negative (-) lead to the alternator N terminal. If there exists a continuity, it indicates that one or more of the three diodes in the negative side are shorted.

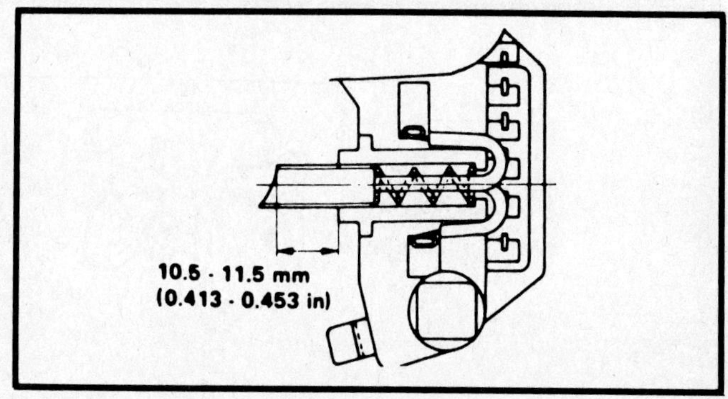

Positioning the brush in the holder

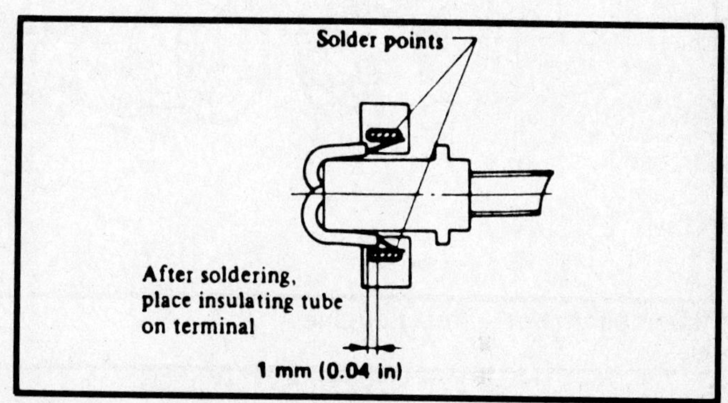

Soldering the brush lead wires

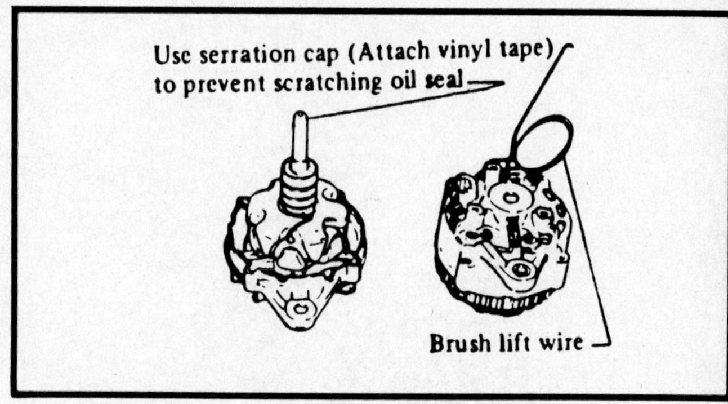

Insert a brush lift wire—gasoline engine

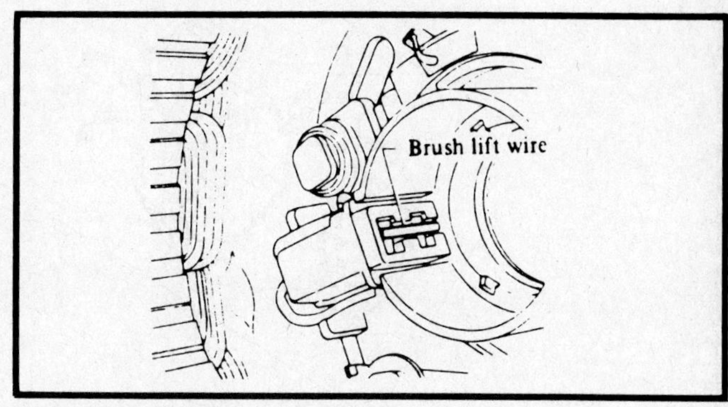

Internal view of the brush lift wire

1. Vacuum pump
2. Cover
3. Brush
4. Through bolt
5. Pulley assembly
6. Pulley nut
7. Pulley
8. Fan
9. Rotor assembly
10. Spacer
11. Ball bearing
12. Rotor
13. Front cover assembly
14. Front cover
15. Ball bearing
16. Bearing retainer
17. Screw
18. Terminal bolt and nut
19. Lead wire
20. Rear cover
21. Stator
22. Diode
23. Holder plate
24. Brush holder
25. IC regulator assembly
26. Lead wire

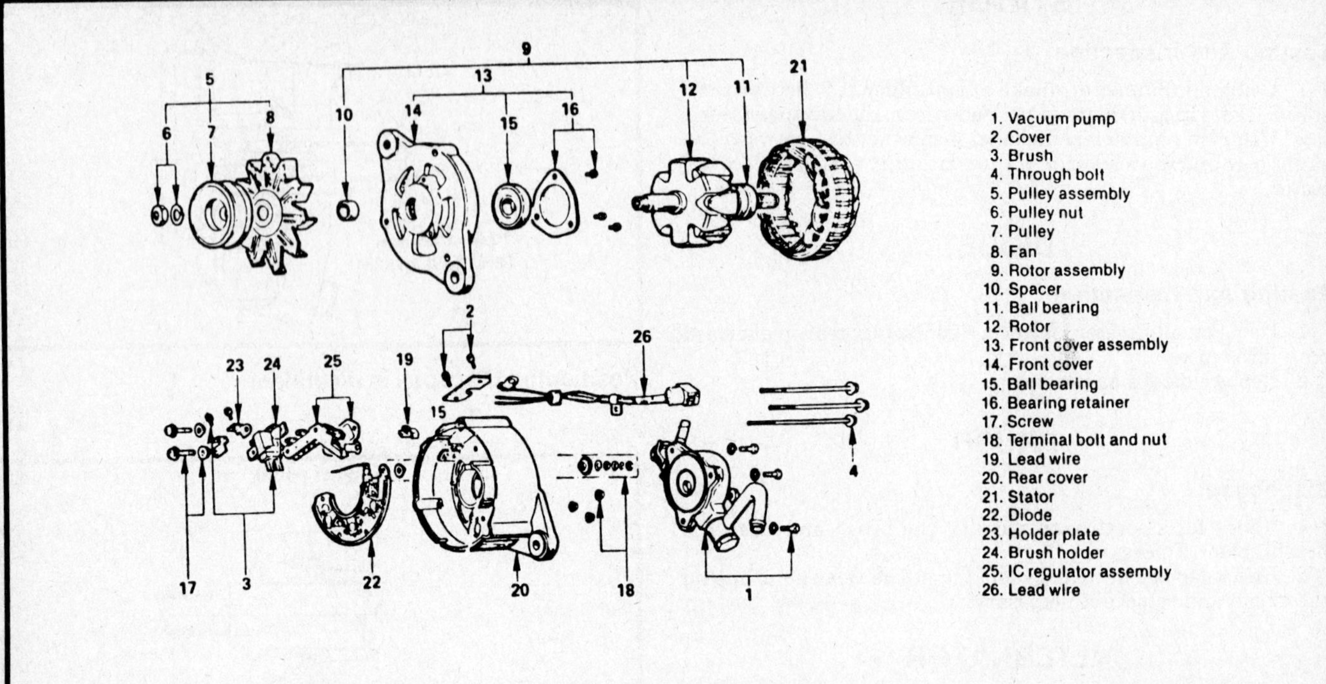

Isuzu alternator—diesel engine

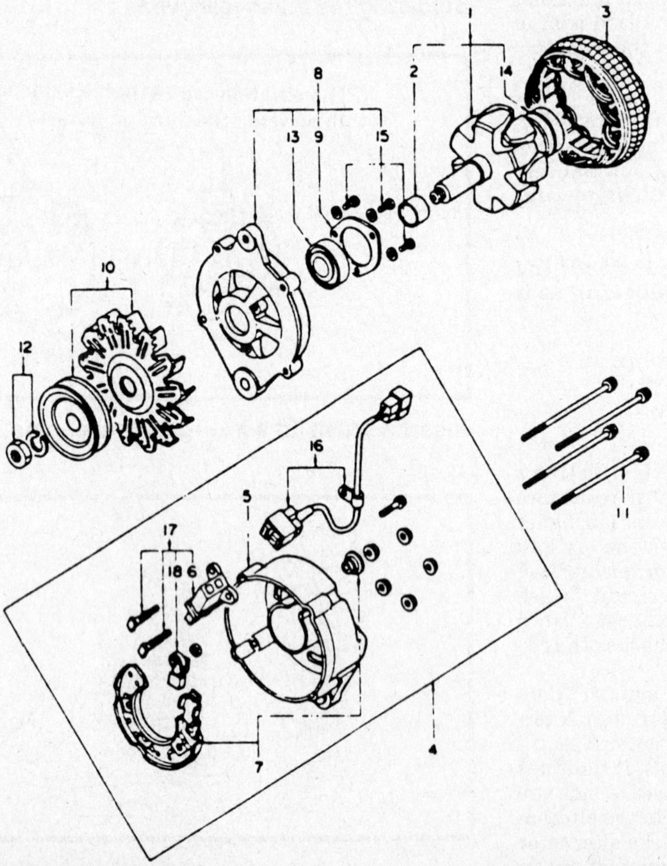

1. Rotor asm.
2. Spacer
3. Stator ams.
4. Cover ams.
5. Rear cover
6. Holder
7. Diode ams.
8. Cover asm.
9. Retainer
10. Pulley ams.
11. Through bolt
12. Nut ams.
13. Bearing
14. Bearing
15. Screw kit
16. Wire asm.
17. Brush and Condenser asm.
18. Condenser asm.

Isuzu alternator—gasoline engine

ALTERNATOR

Disassembly

GASOLINE ENGINE MODELS

1. Remove the through bolts and disconnect the lead wires at the connector.
2. Separate the alternator assembly into front and rear sections. The stator should be on the rear side.
3. Carefulley clamp the rotor in a vise and remove the pulley nut, then remove the pulley fan and rotor.
4. Remove the bearing retainer screws, then remove the ball bearing.
5. Remove the rear side nuts, then remove the stator from the rear cover together with the diodes, brush and capacitor.
6. Unsolder the diode to stator coil connections, then separate the diodes from the stator together with the brush and capacitor.
7. Remove the screws retaining the brush holder, then remove the diodes, brush and capacitor.

ROTOR

Testing

1. Using an ohmmeter, check for continuity at the slip end rings. If there is no continuity, replace the rotor.
2. Using an ohmmeter, make an insulation test. Check for continuity between the slip ring and the rotor core. If continuity exists, replace the rotor.
3. Measure the slip ring outer diameter for wear. Mimimum diameter is 1.18 in. (30mm).

STATOR

Testing

1. Using an ohmmeter, make a continuity test between the stator lead wires. If there is no continuity, replace the stator.
2. Using an ohmmeter, make an insulation test between the stator core and the lead wire. If the continuity exists, replace the stator.

DIODE

Testing

1. Using and ohmmeter, perform a continuity test on diodes in both directions.
2. Replace as necessary.

BRUSH

Inspection

1. Check for smooth movement of the brush and clean the brush holder if necessary.
2. Check for brush wear by looking at the wear limit line on the brush and replace if necessary.

ALTERNATOR

Assembly

GASOLINE ENGINE MODELS

1. Assembly of the alternator is the reverse of disassembly with the following instructions:
2. Before assembling the front and rear sections. insert a wire into the hole in the rear face of the rear cover from the outboard side to support the brush in the raised position, then insert the front section to which the rotor is assembled

ALTERNATOR

Disassembly

DIESEL ENGINE MODELS

1. If so equipped, remove the vacuum pump attaching bolts, then hold the center plate and remove the vacuum pump in direction in line with the rotor shaft.
2. Remove the brush cover and the brush attaching bolts, then remove the brush from the holder.
3. Remove the through bolts and separate the body into front and rear sections.

NOTE: When separating, be careful so that the stator coils do not come off the rear cover. Do not damage the oil seal when removing the rear cover. Taping the splines could provide some protection.

4. Carefully clamp the rotor assembly in a vise and remove the pulley nut.

Disassembled view of vacuum pump

Across terminals		BTA (Positive side (+) diodes)	
	Tester pin	Positive side	Negative side
U.V.W.	Positive side		No continuity
	Negative side	Continuity	
Across terminals		**E (Negative side (–) diodes)**	
	Tester pin	Positive side	Negative side
U.V.W.	Positive side		No continuity
	Negative side	Continuity	

Diode test chart

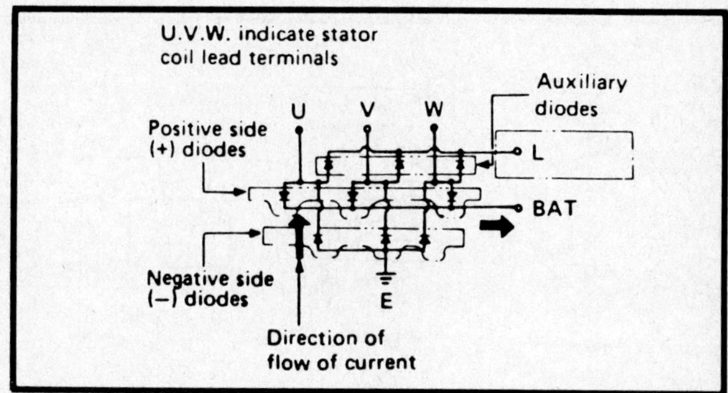

Testing diodes

5. Separate the pulley front cover and rotor, then remove the spacer and ball bearing.
6. Remove the bearing retaining screws from the front cover, then remove the bearing.
7. Remove the terminal bolt and nut, then remove the lead wire.
8. Remove the nuts securing the B terminal and diode holder, then remove the screw inside the stator. Separate the stator and rear cover.

NOTE: Observe the position of the insulation washers for reassembly.

9. Remove the stator, then separate the diodes from the stator by melting the solder on the stator coil, diode and 'N' terminal leads. When melting the solder, hold the lead wire with long nose pliers to prevent heat from being transferred to the diodes.
10. Remove the holder plate and brush holder.
11. Melt away the solder on the IC holder plate terminal, then remove the IC regulator assembly.
12. If necessary, the vacuum pump may be disassembled by removing the center plate, exposing the rotor and vane.

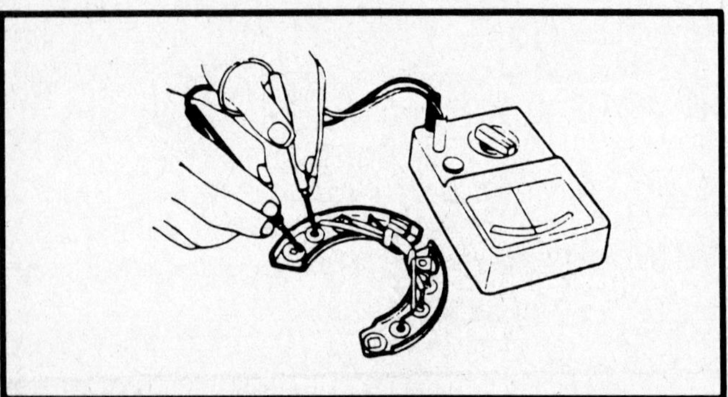

Testing diodes with an ohmmeter

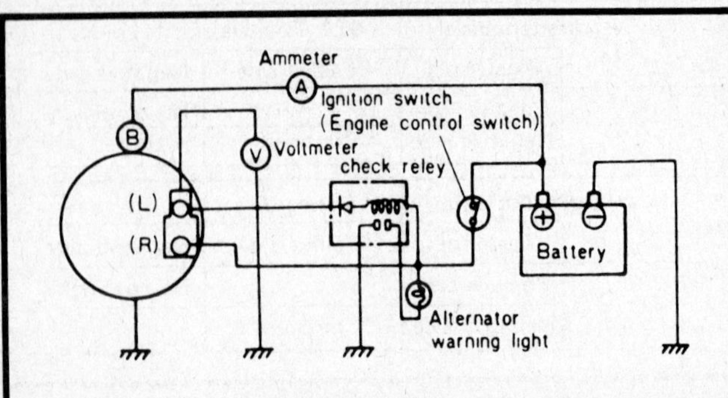

Checking charging system

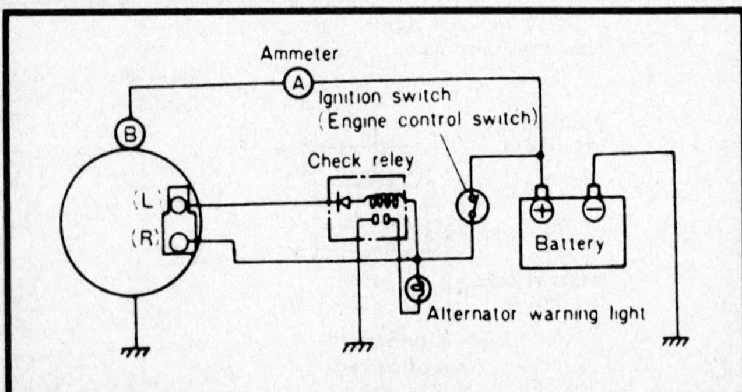

Checking regulated voltage with no-load

ROTOR

Testing

1. Using an ohmmeter, check for continuity at the slip end rings. If there is no continuity, replace the rotor.
2. Using an ohmmeter, make an insulation test. Check for continuity between the slip ring and the rotor core. If continuity exists, replace the rotor.
3. Measure the slip ring outer diameter for wear. Mimimum diameter is 1.18 in. (30mm).

STATOR

Testing

1. Using an ohmmeter, make a continuity test between the stator lead wires. If there is no continuity, replace the stator.
2. Using an ohmmeter, make an insulation test between the stator core and the lead wire. If the continuity exists, replace the stator.

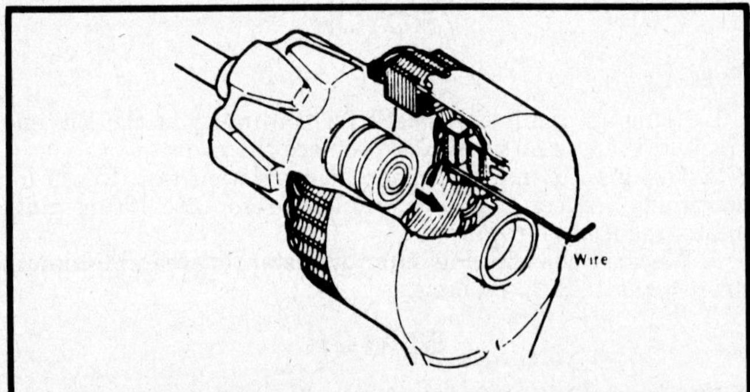

Insert a wire during assembly to avoid brush damage

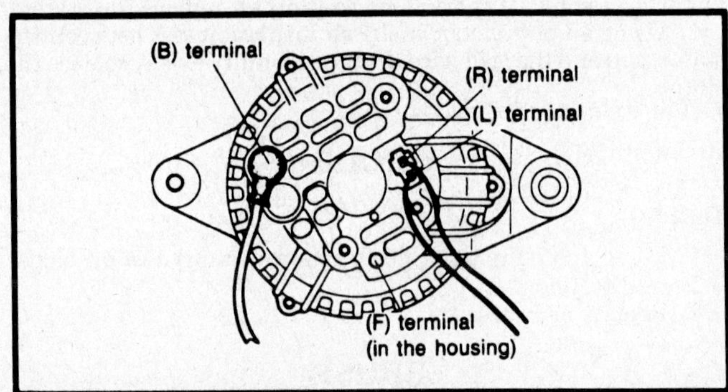

Mazda alternator terminal location

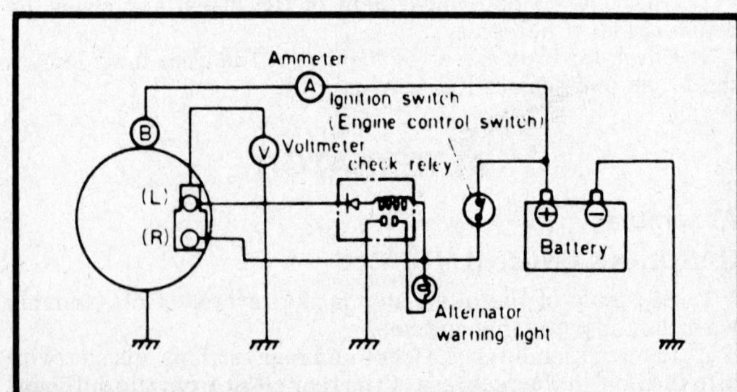

Checking output current

DIODE

Testing

1. Using and ohmmeter, perform a continuity test on diodes in both directions.
2. Replace as necessary.

BRUSH

Inspection

1. Check for smooth movement of the brush and clean the brush holder if necessary.
2. Check for brush wear by looking at the wear limit line on the brush and replace if necessary.

ALTERNATOR

Assembly

DIESEL ENGINE MODEL

1. Assembly of the alternator is the reverse of disassembly with the following instructions: Resolder the IC regulator lead wires. To prevent heat from being transfered to the diodes, use long nose pliers to hold the stator coil leads and diode leads and solder as quickly as posible.
2. Carefully clamp the rotor in a vise and torque the pulley nut to 33–43 ft. lbs.
3. Place some type of guide bar through the holes in the front cover and rear cover flange for alignment, then install the through bolts. Make sure the brush is installed in the brush holder correctly. If the vacuum pump was disassembled, position the rotor, with the serrated boss turned up, on the center plate and housing. Install the vanes into the slits in the rotor. The vanes should be installed with the camfered side turned outward. Install the housing, making sure the O-ring is not projected beyond the slot in the center plate. If the holes in the housing and center plate are not in alignment, adjust by turning the housing slightly, then tighten the three retaining bolts. Add engine oil (around 5 cc) through the filler port, then check that the pulley can be turned smoothly by hand.

Mazda/Courier Charging System

ALTERNATOR

Inspection and Circuit Evaluation

1982-84

1. Connect an ammeter and voltmeter to the charging system.
2. Turn the ignition switch "OFF".
3. Read the voltmeter connected between the "L" terminal and ground, if the alternator is normal the voltage should be zero (0 V).
4. Turn the ignition switch "ON" and read the voltmeter. The voltage should be less than battery voltage, in the 1–3 V range. If the voltage is zero, either the alternator or wiring is bad. If the the voltage is near battery voltage, connect the "F" terminal to ground and read the voltmeter. if the voltage drops lower than the battery voltage, the IC regulator may be faulty.

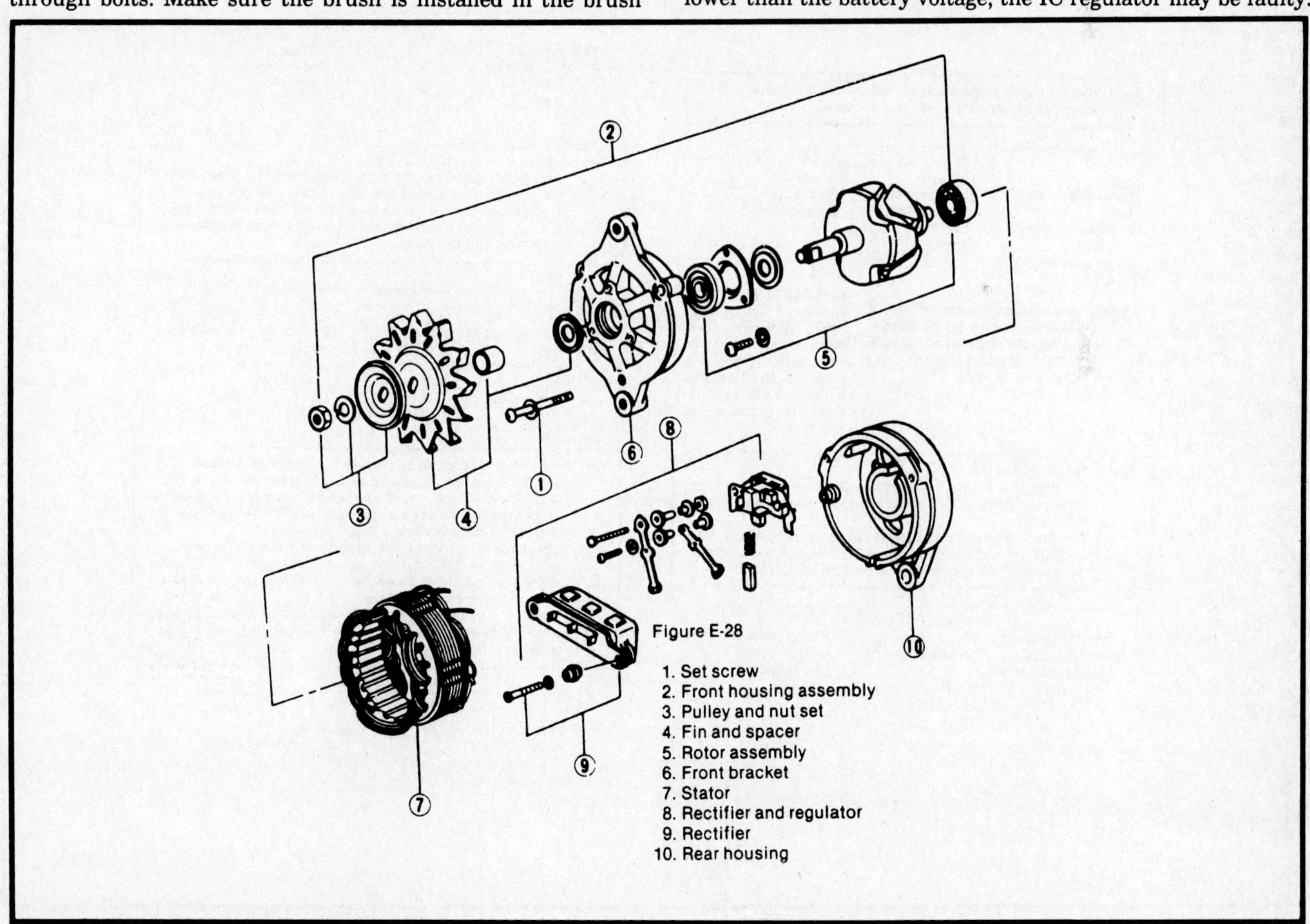

Mazda Alternator—Gasoline engine—1979-84

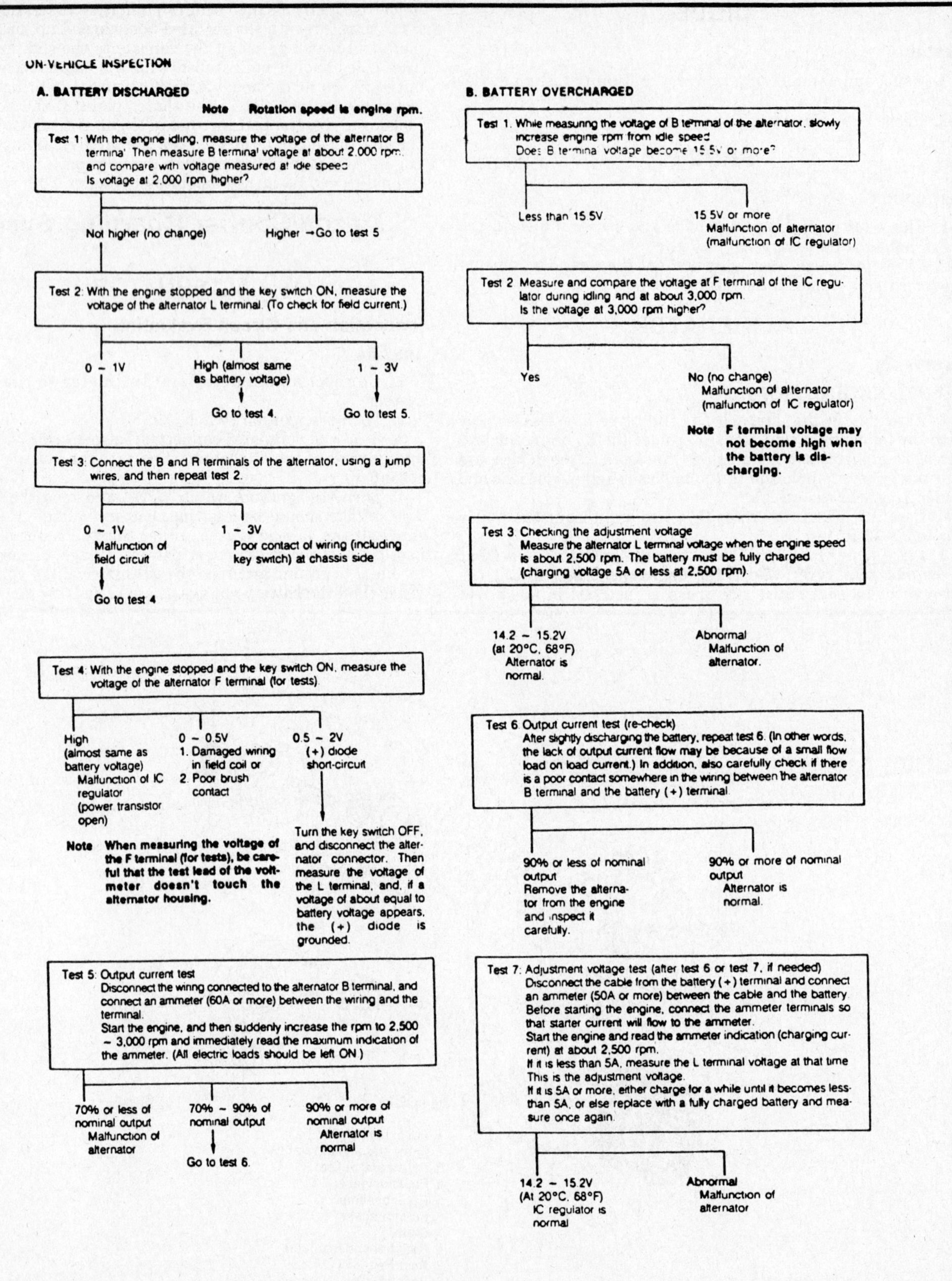

ON-VEHICLE INSPECTION
A. BATTERY DISCHARGED
Note Rotation speed is engine rpm.
Test 1: With the engine idling, measure the voltage of the alternator B terminal. Then measure B terminal voltage at about 2,000 rpm, and compare with voltage measured at idle speed. Is voltage at 2,000 rpm higher?
Not higher (no change)
Higher → Go to test 5
Test 2: With the engine stopped and the key switch ON, measure the voltage of the alternator L terminal. (To check for field current.)
0 ~ 1V
High (almost same as battery voltage)
Go to test 4.
1 ~ 3V
Go to test 5.
Test 3: Connect the B and R terminals of the alternator, using a jump wires, and then repeat test 2.
0 ~ 1V
Malfunction of field circuit
Go to test 4
1 ~ 3V
Poor contact of wiring (including key switch) at chassis side
Test 4: With the engine stopped and the key switch ON, measure the voltage of the alternator F terminal (for tests).
High (almost same as battery voltage)
Malfunction of IC regulator (power transistor open)
0 ~ 0.5V
1. Damaged wiring in field coil or
2. Poor brush contact
0.5 ~ 2V
(+) diode short-circuit
Turn the key switch OFF, and disconnect the alternator connector. Then measure the voltage of the L terminal, and, if a voltage of about equal to battery voltage appears, the (+) diode is grounded.
Note When measuring the voltage of the F terminal (for tests), be careful that the test lead of the voltmeter doesn't touch the alternator housing.
Test 5: Output current test
Disconnect the wiring connected to the alternator B terminal, and connect an ammeter (60A or more) between the wiring and the terminal.
Start the engine, and then suddenly increase the rpm to 2,500 ~ 3,000 rpm and immediately read the maximum indication of the ammeter. (All electric loads should be left ON.)
70% or less of nominal output
Malfunction of alternator
70% ~ 90% of nominal output
Go to test 6.
90% or more of nominal output
Alternator is normal
B. BATTERY OVERCHARGED
Test 1. While measuring the voltage of B terminal of the alternator, slowly increase engine rpm from idle speed
Does B terminal voltage become 15.5V or more?
Less than 15.5V
15.5V or more
Malfunction of alternator (malfunction of IC regulator)
Test 2 Measure and compare the voltage at F terminal of the IC regulator during idling and at about 3,000 rpm.
Is the voltage at 3,000 rpm higher?
Yes
No (no change)
Malfunction of alternator (malfunction of IC regulator)
Note F terminal voltage may not become high when the battery is discharging.
Test 3 Checking the adjustment voltage
Measure the alternator L terminal voltage when the engine speed is about 2,500 rpm. The battery must be fully charged (charging voltage 5A or less at 2,500 rpm).
14.2 ~ 15.2V (at 20°C, 68°F)
Alternator is normal.
Abnormal
Malfunction of alternator.
Test 6 Output current test (re-check)
After slightly discharging the battery, repeat test 6. (In other words, the lack of output current flow may be because of a small flow load on load current.) In addition, also carefully check if there is a poor contact somewhere in the wiring between the alternator B terminal and the battery (+) terminal.
90% or less of nominal output
Remove the alternator from the engine and inspect it carefully.
90% or more of nominal output
Alternator is normal.
Test 7: Adjustment voltage test (after test 6 or test 7, if needed)
Disconnect the cable from the battery (+) terminal and connect an ammeter (50A or more) between the cable and the battery. Before starting the engine, connect the ammeter terminals so that starter current will flow to the ammeter.
Start the engine and read the ammeter indication (charging current) at about 2,500 rpm.
If it is less than 5A, measure the L terminal voltage at that time. This is the adjustment voltage.
If it is 5A or more, either charge for a while until it becomes less than 5A, or else replace with a fully charged battery and measure once again.
14.2 ~ 15.2V (At 20°C, 68°F)
IC regulator is normal
Abnormal
Malfunction of alternator

On vehicle tests

Checking Regulated Voltage With No Load

1. Disconnect the wiring connected to alternator terminal"B".
2. Connect an ammeter (more than 40 A) between the alternator terminal "B" and the battery positive terminal.
3. Connect a voltmeter between alternator terminal "L" and ground.
4. Start the engine and increase the engine speed to approximately 2,000 rpm. Turn off all unnecessary electrical loads and read the value shown on the ammeter.
5. When the amperage in Step 4 is less than 5 amp., read the voltage (regulated voltage) of terminal "L". The regulated should be 14.1–14.7 V.

Checking Output Current

1. Disconnect the wiring connected to the alternator terminal "B".
2. Connect an ammeter (more than 40 amp) between the alternator terminal "B" and the battery positive terminal.
3. Start the engine and increase the engine speed to more than 2,500 rpm and read the maximum value shown on the ammeter. Apply all electrical loads. If the value shown on the ammeter is more than 90% of the rated output, the alternator is normal.

ALTERNATOR

Disassembly And Assembly

DIESEL ENGINE MODELS

1. Remove the vacuum pump.
2. Remove the retaining screw and remove the end cover from the top of the housing.
3. Remove the screws and remove the IC regulator and brush holder.
4. Remove the front and rear bracket assembly.
5. Carefully place the rotor in a vise and remove the pulley nut. Remove the pulley and fan assembly.
6. Remove the front bracket, rotor, rear bracket and stator.

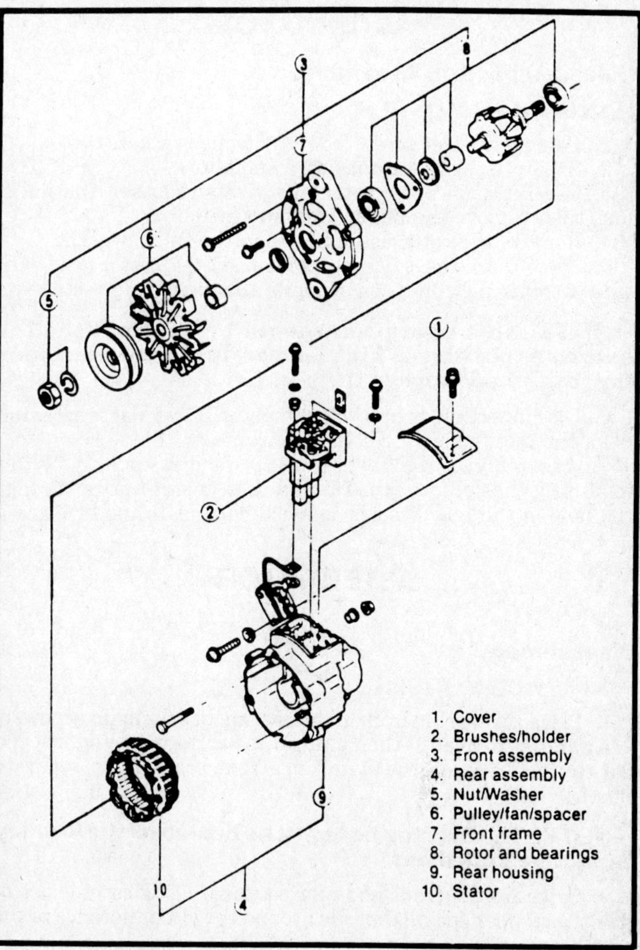

Mazda Alternator—Diesel engine—1982-84

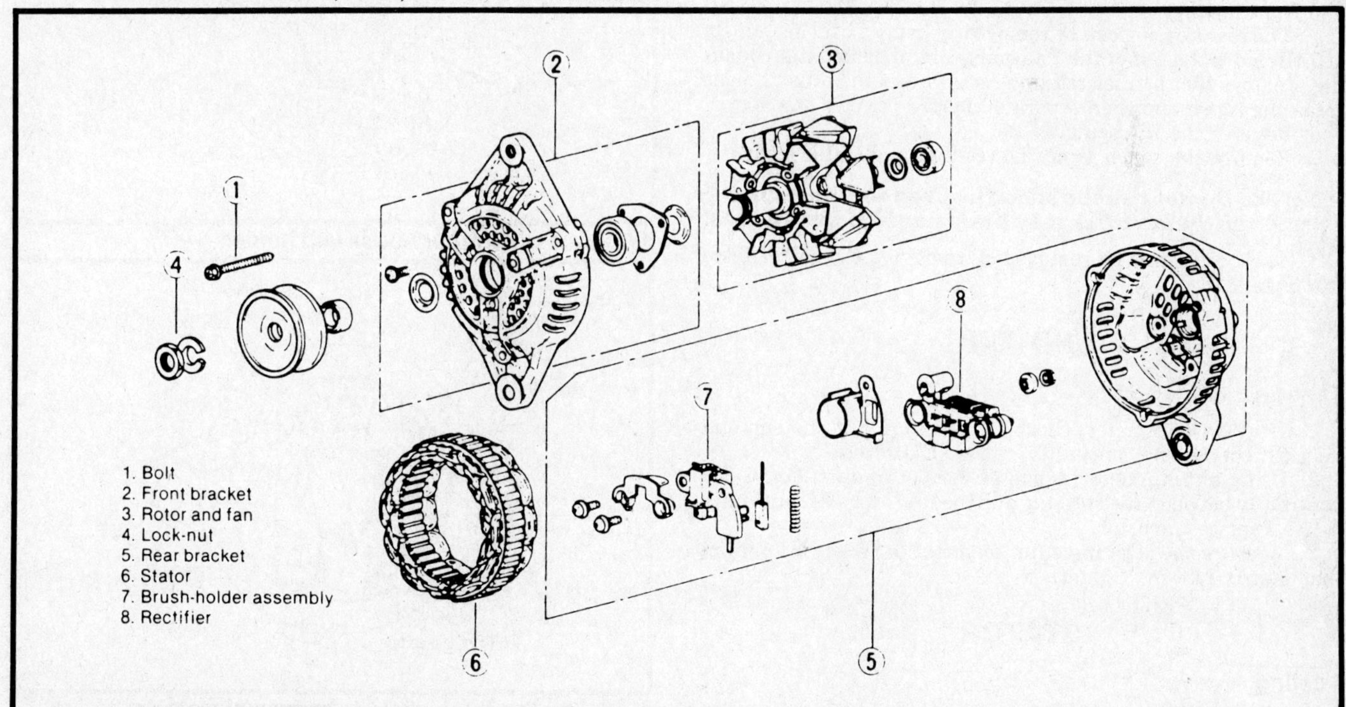

Mazda alternator—1986-88

ALTERNATOR

Disassembly And Assembly

GAS ENGINE MODELS

1. Remove the set screw from the front bracket.
2. Separate the front housing assembly.
3. Carefully place the rotor in a vise and loosen the pulley nut, then remove the pulley and fan assembly.
4. Remove the rotor assembly, then the front bracket.
5. Disconnect the soldered portion of the stator lead wire with a soldering iron, then separate the stator and rectifier.

NOTE: This operation should be accomplished as quickly as possible as high temperature from the soldering iron could damage the rectifier.

6. Disconnect the brush holder and the IC regulator assembly from the rectifier with a soldering iron.
7. Assembly is the reverse order of disassembly. When mounting the rotor on the rear bracket, insert a wire through the hole in the rear bracket to avoid damage to the brushes.

ALTERNATOR

Disassembly

1986-88 ALL MODELS

1. Place a soldering iron on the bearing box for approximately 3–4 minutes to heat it, then pull out the three bolts and insert a flat tip tool between the stator and front bracket and separate them.

NOTE: The bearing box must be heated or the bearing cannot be pulled out.

2. Separate the front and rear sections, being careful not to lose the stopper spring that fits around the circumference of the rear bearing.
3. Remove the pulley nut, then disassemble the pulley, rotor and front bracket.
4. The rear bearing can be removed by using a bearing puller.
5. Remove the nut of the B terminal and the insulation bushing. Remove the rectifier retaining screws and the brush holder retaining screw and then separate the rear bracket and stator.
6. Remove the IC regulator.
7. Remove the solder from the rectifier and stator leads.

NOTE: Do not use the soldering iron for more than 5 seconds as the rectifier may be damaged if overheated.

8. The brush may be removed by removing the solder from the pigtail.

ROTOR

Testing

1. Using an ohmmeter, check for continuity at the slip end rings. If there is no continuity, replace the rotor.
2. Using an ohmmeter, make an insulation test. Check for continuity between the slip ring and the rotor core. If continuity exists, replace the rotor.
3. Measure the slip ring outer diameter for wear. Mimimum diameter is 1.18 in. (30mm).

STATOR

Testing

1. Using an ohmmeter, make a continuity test between the stator lead wires. If there is no continuity, replace the stator.
2. Using an ohmmeter, make an insulation test between the stator core and the lead wire. If the continuity exists, replace the stator.

DIODE

Testing

1. Using and ohmmeter, perform a continuity test on diodes in both directions.
2. Replace as necessary.

BRUSHES

Inspection

1. Check for smooth movement of the brush and clean the brush holder if necessary.
2. Check for brush wear by looking at the wear limit line on the brush and replace if necessary.

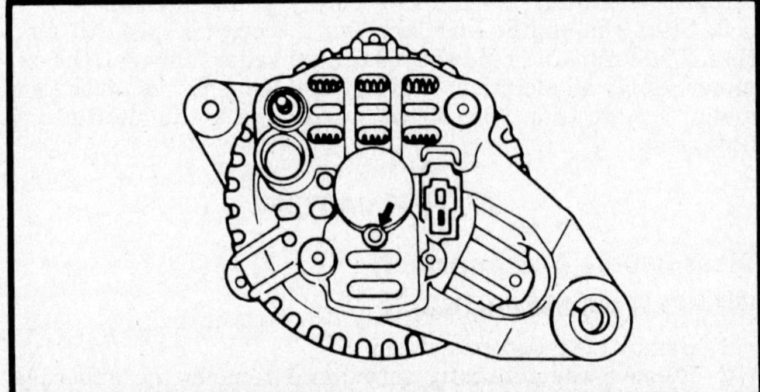

Hole for pushing wire through for reassembly

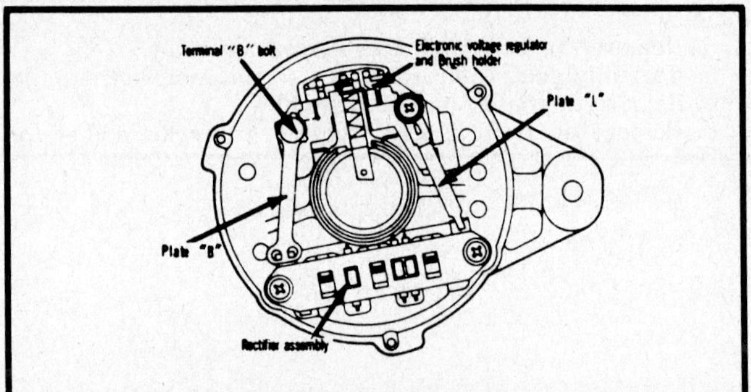

Location of rectifier and brush holder

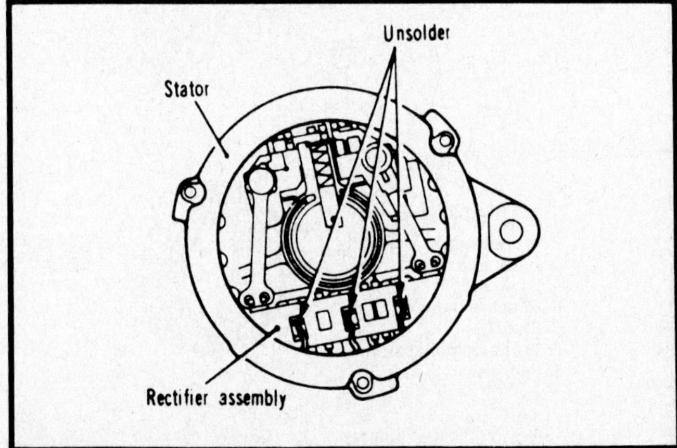

Unsolder the three wires to remove the stator assembly

ALTERNATOR

Assembly

1. Assembly of the alternator is the reverse of disassembly with the following instructions:

2. When installing the front bearing, use a socket which exactly fits the outer race of the bearing, then use a hand press or vise and press the bearing in evenly. When pressing the rear bearing on, first heat the rear bracket, then press it so that the groove at the bearing circumference is at the slip ring side. When soldering a new brush, solder the pigtail so that the wear limit line of the brush projects 0.079–0.118 in. out from the end of the brush holder. Fit the stopper spring into the eccentric groove of the rear bearing circumference. The protruding part of the spring should be fit into the deepest part of the groove. This makes assembly much easier.

3. Before assembly, use a finger to push the brush into the brush holder, then pass a wire through the hole in the brush holder and secure the brush into position. After reassembly, manually turn the pulley to make sure that the rotor turns easily.

Chrysler Corp. Arrow, Ram 50, Ram Raider Charging System

ALTERNATOR

Disassembly

1982-86 GASOLINE ENGINE MODELS

1. Remove alternator from vehicle.
2. Remove the three through bolts from the alternator body.
3. Insert an appropriate pry tool between the front bracket and stator. Pry the front bracket away from the stator. Remove the front bracket along with the rotor.

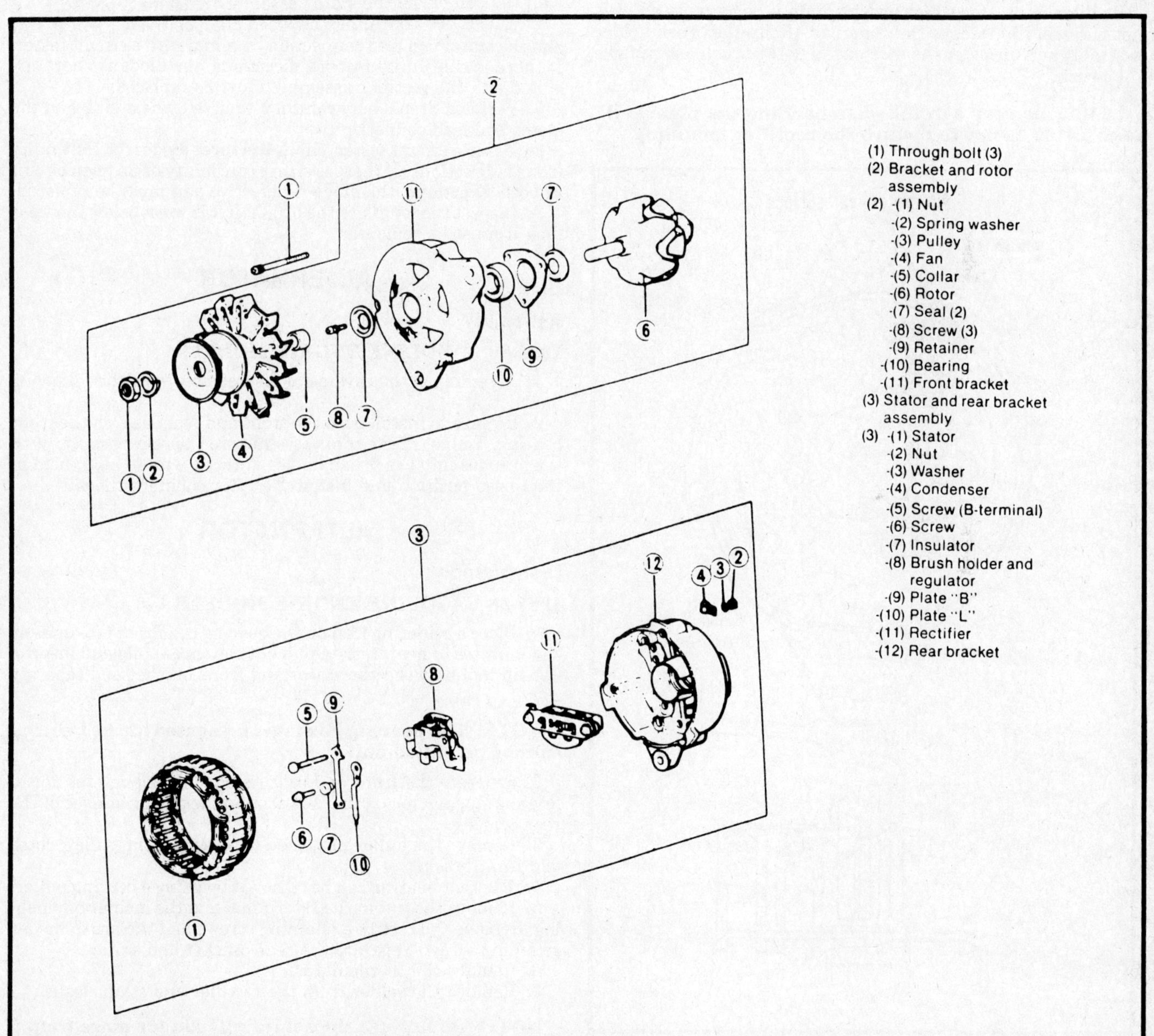

Arrow/Ram 50/Raider—1982–86 gasoline engine

NOTE: If the Tool is inserted too deeply, the stator coil might be damaged.

4. Hold the rotor in a vise and remove the pulley nut. Then remove the pulley, fan, spacer and seal. Remove the rotor from the front bracket and remove the seal.
5. Unsolder the rectifier from the stator coil lead wires and remove the stator assembly.

NOTE: Make sure the solder is removed quickly (in less than five seconds). If a diode is heated to more than 150°C, it might be damaged.

6. Remove the condenser from terminal "B".
7. Unsolder the plates "B" and "L" from the rectifier assembly.
8. Remove the mounting screw and terminal "B" bolt and remove the electronic voltage regulator and brush holder. The regulator and brush holder cannot be separated.
9. Remove the rectifier assembly.
10. When only a brush or brush spring is to be replaced, it is not necessary to remove the stator, etc. Raise the brush holder assembly and unsolder the wire pigtail of the brush and remove the brush.

NOTE: Be very careful when bending the plates "B" and "L" so as not to disturb the rectifier moulding.

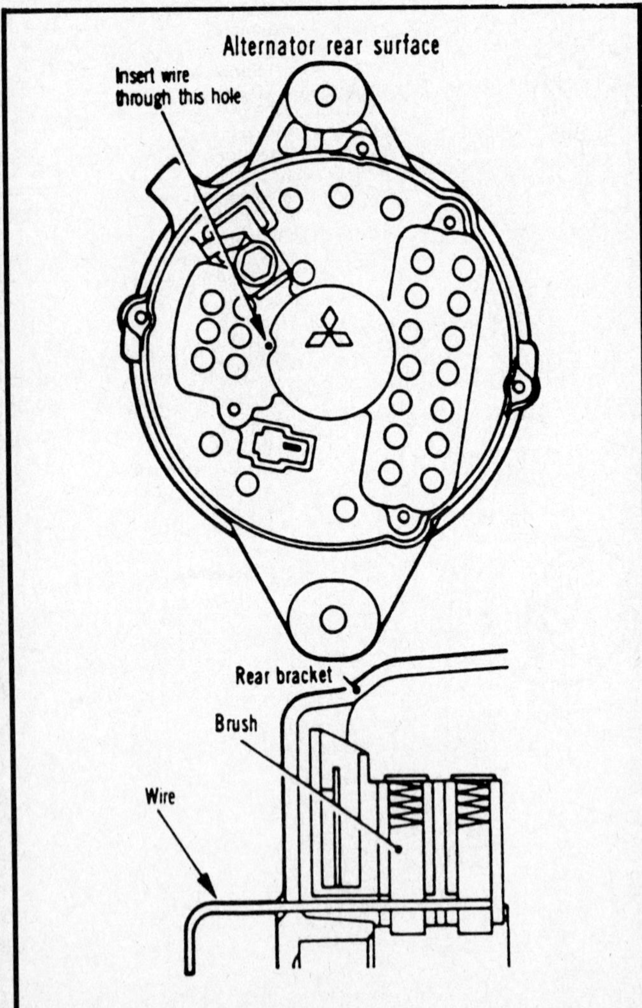

Insert a wire to hold the brushes

ALTERNATOR CIRCUITS

Testing And Inspection

1. Check the outside circumference of the slip ring for dirtiness and roughness. Clean or polish with armature paper, if required. A badly damaged slip ring or a slip ring worn down beyond the service limit should also be replaced. The service limit for the slip ring outside diameter is 1.268 in.
2. Check for continuity between the field coil and slip ring. If there is not continuity, the field coil is defective and the rotor must be replaced.
3. Check for continuity between the slip ring and the shaft (or core). If there is continuity, the rotor assembly must be replaced.
4. Check for continuity between the leads of the stator coil. If there is no continuity, the stator coil is defective.
5. Check for an open circuit between the stator coil leads and the stator core. If there is continuity between the stator core and the coil leads, the stator assembly must be replaced.
6. Check for continuity between the positive (+) heat sink and the stator coil lead connection terminal with a circuit tester. If there is continuity in both directions, the diode is short circuited and the rectifier assembly must be replaced.
7. Perform Step 6 between the negative (-) heat sink and the stator coil lead connection.
8. Using a circuit tester, check the three diodes for continuity in both directions. If there is either continuity or an open circuit in both directions, the diode is defective and must be replaced.
9. Inspect the length of the brush. If it is worn below the wear line, it must be replaced.

ALTERNATOR

Assembly

1982-86 GASOLINE ENGINE MODELS

1. Assembly is the reverse of disassembly with the following instructions:
2. Be sure to install both the front and rear seals on the front bearing. To install the rotor assembly in the rear bracket, push the brushes into the brush holder, insert a wire to hold them in the raised position and install the rotor. Remove the wire.

ALTERNATOR

Disassembly

1987-88 GASOLINE ENGINE MODELS

1. Place a soldering iron on the bearing box for approximately 3–4 minutes to heat it, then pull out the three bolts and insert a flat tip tool between the stator and front bracket and separate them.

NOTE: The bearing box must be heated or the bearing cannot be pulled out.

2. Separate the front and rear sections, being careful not to lose the stopper spring that fits around the circumference of the rear bearing.
3. Remove the pulley nut, then disassemble the pulley, rotor and front bracket.
4. The rear bearing can be removed by using a bearing puller.
5. Remove the nut of the B terminal and the insulation bushing. Remove the rectifier retaining screws and the brush holder retaining screw. Separate the rear bracket and stator.
6. Remove the IC regulator.
7. Remove the solder from the rectifier and stator leads.

NOTE: Do not use the soldering iron for more than 5 seconds as the rectifier may be damaged if overheated.

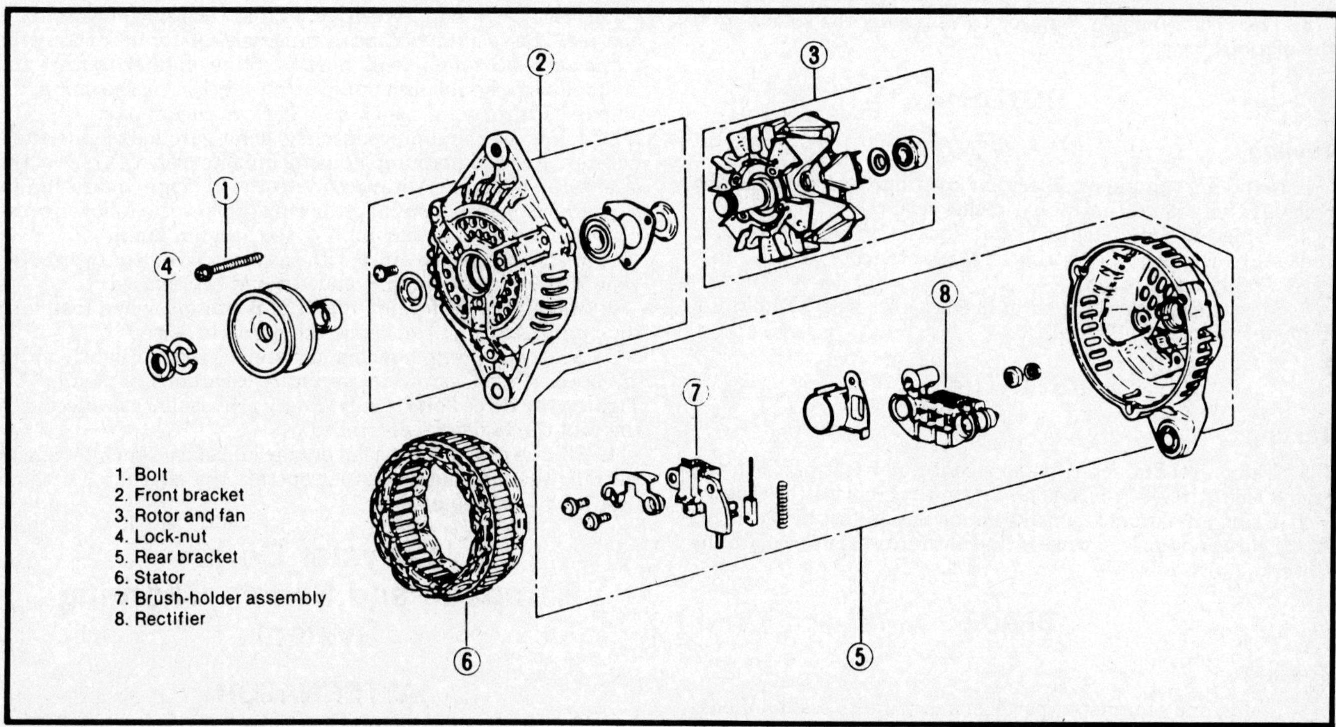

Ram 50/Raider alternator—1987–88

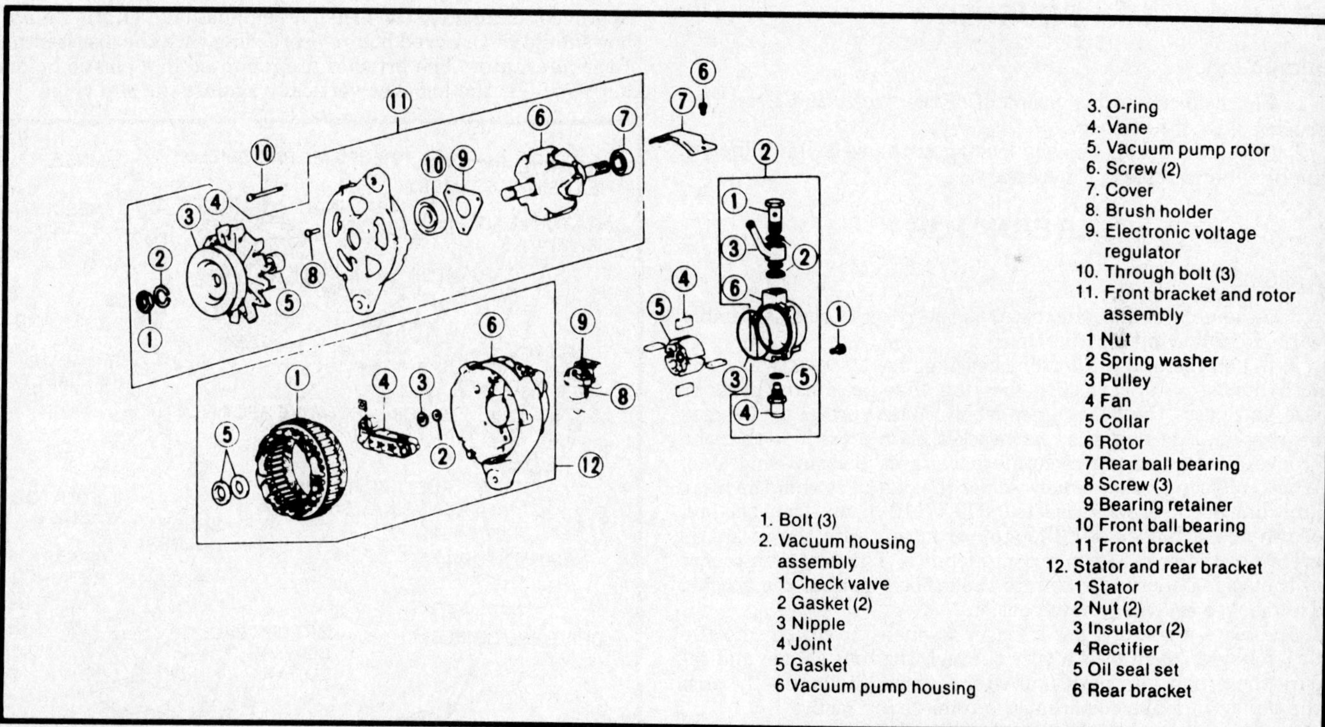

Arrow/Ram 50/Raider—diesel alternator

8. The brush may be removed by removing the solder from the pigtail.

ROTOR

Testing

1. Using an ohmmeter, check for continuity at the slip end rings. If there is no continuity, replace the rotor.
2. Using an ohmmeter, make an insulation test. Check for continuity between the slip ring and the rotor core. If continuity exists, replace the rotor.
3. Measure the slip ring outer diameter for wear. Mimimum diameter is 1.18 in. (30mm).

STATOR

Testing

1. Using an ohmmeter, make a continuity test between the stator lead wires. If there is no continuity, replace the stator.
2. Using an ohmmeter, make an insulation test between the stator core and the lead wire. If the continuity exists, replace the stator.

DIODE

Testing

1. Using and ohmmeter, perform a continuity test on diodes in both directions.
2. Replace as necessary.

BRUSHES

Inspection

1. Check for smooth movement of the brush and clean the brush holder if necessary.
2. Check for brush wear by looking at the wear limit line on the brush and replace if necessary.

ALTERNATOR

Assembly

1. Assembly of the alternator is the reverse of disassembly with the following instructions:
2. When installing the front bearing, use a socket which exactly fits the outer race of the bearing, then use a hand press or vise and press the bearing in evenly. When pressing the rear bearing on, first heat the rear bracket, then press it so that the groove at the bearing circumference is at the slip ring side. When soldering a new brush, solder the pigtail so that the wear limit line of the brush projects 0.079–0.118 in. out from the end of the brush holder. Fit the stopper spring into the eccentric groove of the rear bearing circumference. The protruding part of the spring should be fit into the deepest part of the groove. This makes assembly much easier.
3. Before assembly, use a finger to push the brush into the brush holder, then pass a wire through the hole shown and secure the brush into position. After reassembly, manually turn the pulley to make sure that the rotor turns easily.

ALTERNATOR

Disassembly And Assembly

DIESEL ENGINE MODELS

The alternator on the diesel engine models is the same as used on the gasoline engine models, except that the rear end of the rotor shaft is longer. Mounted on the end of the rotor shaft is a small vacuum pump, which generates vacuum for the brake booster. The vacuum pump is a vane type. Oil for lubricating the pump passes through an oil hose from the oil filter bracket and is supplied to the vacuum pump. After lubricating the pump, the oil passes through a return hose back to the oil pan.
Follow the Overhaul procedure above for gasoline engine alternators. The vacuum pump housing unbolts from the rear of the alternator housing. Always replace the O-ring. Grease the O-ring groove before installing the ring. Follow the following precautions below when assembling the vacuum pump:

1. Install the pump vanes with the rounded end outward. Any vane with worn or chipped ends should be replaced.
2. Make sure no foreign material is present when installing the pump. Any dirt can cause the pump to seize.
3. When the pump housing is installed, push it lightly in the direction of the arrow to minimize clearance at point "A". Tighten the three bolts evenly. Pump performance is affected by the way the housing is installed.
4. Fill the pump with clean engine oil before bench testing or running the alternator. Do not operate the alternator without first lubing the pump.

Chrysler Corp. Rampage and Scamp Charging System

ALTERNATOR

Disassembly and Assembly

CHRYSLER UNITS

To prevent damage to the brush assemblies (114 and 117 amp), they should be removed before proceeding with the disassembly of the alternator. The brushes are mounted in a plastic holder that positions the brushes vertically against the slip rings.

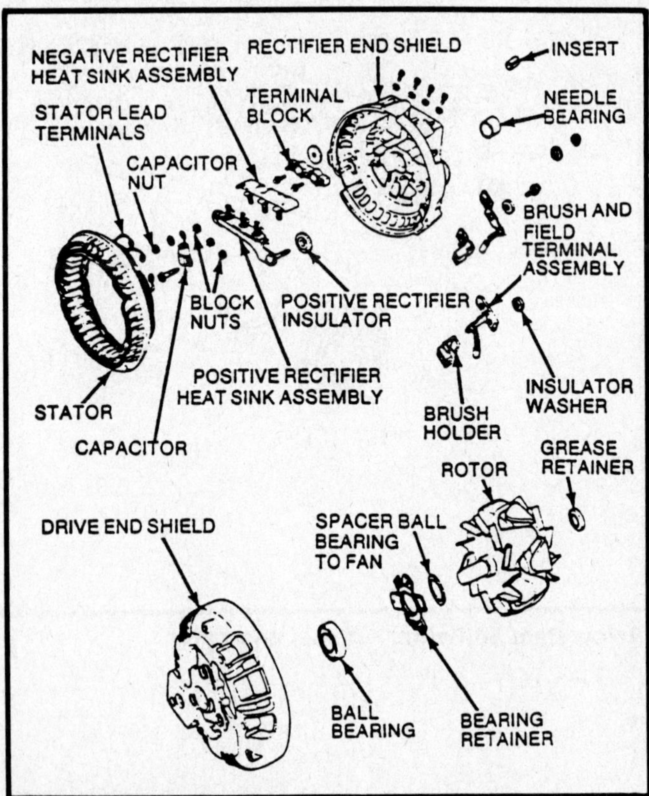

Scamp/Rampage—Chrysler built alternator

1. Remove the retaining screw, flat washer, nylon washer and field terminal and carefully lift the plastic holder containing the spring and brush assembly from the end housing.

2. The ground brush (60 amp) is positioned horizontally against the slip ring and is retained in the holder that is integral with the end housing. Remove the retaining screw and lift the clip, spring and brush assembly from the end housing. The stator is laminated, so don't burr the stator or end housings.

3. Remove the through bolts and pry between the stator and drive end housing with a suitable tool. Carefully separate the drive end housing, pulley and rotor assembly from the stator and rectifier housing assembly.

4. The pulley is an interference fit on the rotor shaft. Remove with a puller and special adapters.

5. Remove the three nuts and washers and, while supporting the end frame, tap the rotor shaft with a plastic hammer and separate the rotor and end housing.

6. The drive end ball bearing is an interference fit with the rotor shaft. Remove the bearing with puller and adapters.

NOTE: Further dismantling of the rotor is not advisable, as the remainder of the rotor assembly is not serviced separately.

7. Remove the DC output terminal nuts and washers and remove terminal screw and inside capacitor (on units so equipped).

8. Remove the insulator.

NOTE: Positive rectifiers are pressed into the heat sink and negative rectifiers in the end housing. When removing the rectifiers it is necessary to support the end housing and the heat sink in order to prevent damage to the castings. Another caution is in order relative to the diode rectifiers. Don't subject them to unnecessary jolting. Heavy vibration or shock may ruin them. Cut rectifier wire at point of crimp. Support rectifier housing. The factory tool is cut away and slotted to fit over the wires and around the bosses in the housing. Be sure that the bore of the tool completely surrounds the rectifier, then press the rectifier out of the housing. The roller bearing in the rectifier end frame is a press fit. To protect the end housing, it is necessary to support the housing with a tool when pressing out the bearing.

9. To assemble, support the heat sink or rectifier end housing on circular plate.

10. Check rectifier identification to be sure the correct rectifier is being used. The part numbers are stamped on the case of the rectifier. They are also marked red for positive and black for negative.

11. Start the new rectifier into the casting and press it in squarely. Do not start rectifier with a hammer or it will be ruined.

12. Crimp the new rectifier wire to the wires disconnected at removal or solder using a heat sink with rosin core solder.

13. Support the end housing on tool so that the notch in the support tool will clear the raised section of the heat sink, then press the bearing into position with tool SP-3381, or equivalent. New bearings are prelubricated, additional lubrication is not required.

14. Insert the drive end bearing in the drive end housing and install the bearing plate, washers and nuts to hold the bearing in place.

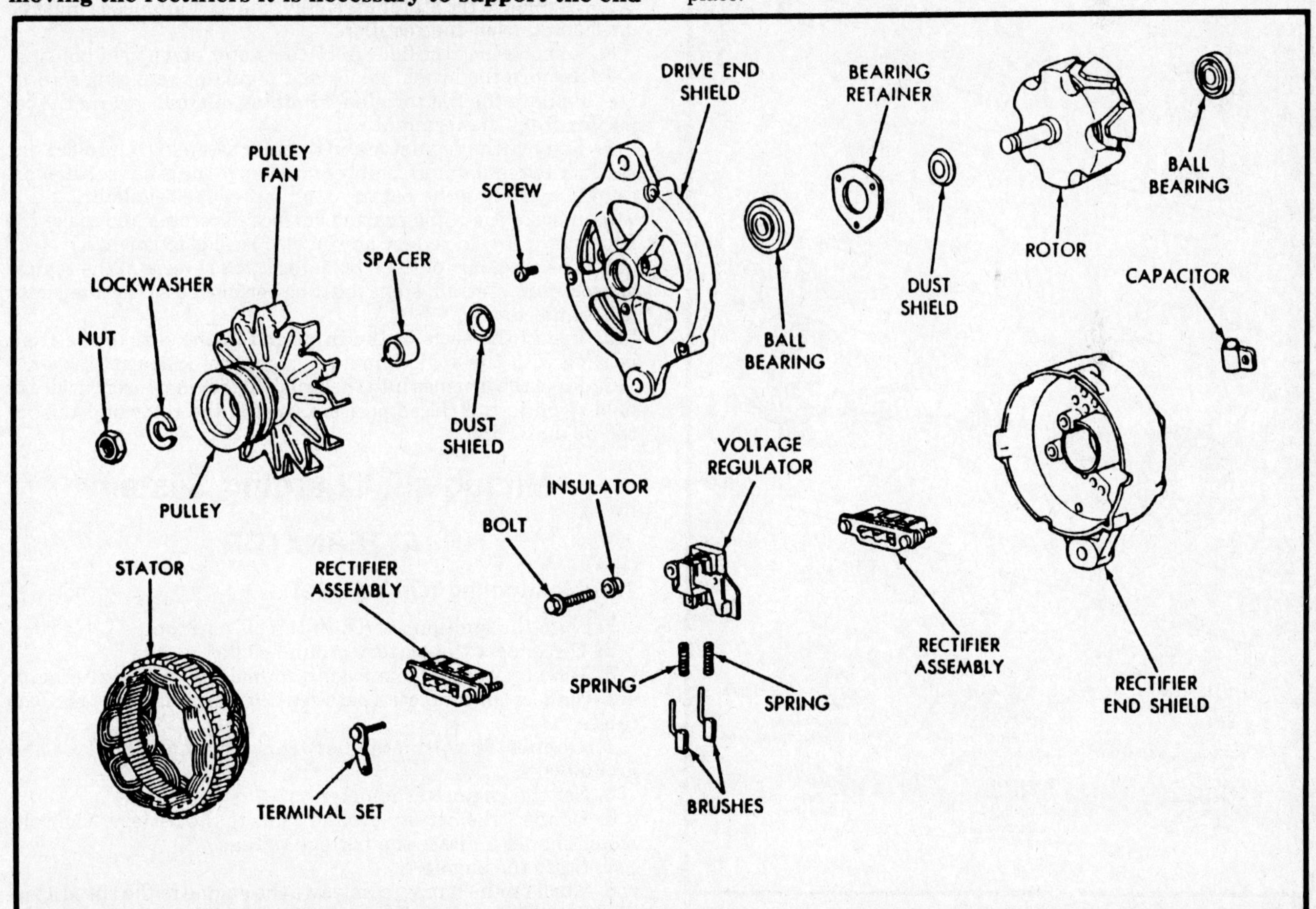

Scamp/Rampage—Mitsubishi built alternator

15. Position the bearing and drive end housing on the rotor shaft and, while supporting the base of the rotor shaft, press the bearing and housing in position on the rotor shaft with an arbor press and arbor tool. Be careful that there is no cocking of the bearing at installation; or damage will result. Press the bearing on the rotor shaft until the bearing contacts the shoulder on the rotor shaft.
16. Install pulley on rotor shaft. Shaft of rotor must be supported so that all pressing force is on the pulley hub and rotor shaft. Do not exceed 6800 lbs. pressure. Pulley hub should just contact bearing inner race.
17. Some alternators will be found to have the capacitor mounted internally. Be sure the heat sink insulator is in place.
18. Install the output terminal screw with the capacitor attached through the heat sink and end housing.
19. Install insulating washers, lockwashers and locknuts.
20. Make sure the heat sink and insulator are in place and tighten the locknut.
21. Position the stator on the rectifier end housing. Be sure that all of the rectifier connectors and phase leads are free of interference with the rotor fan blades and that the capacitor (internally mounted) lead has clearance.

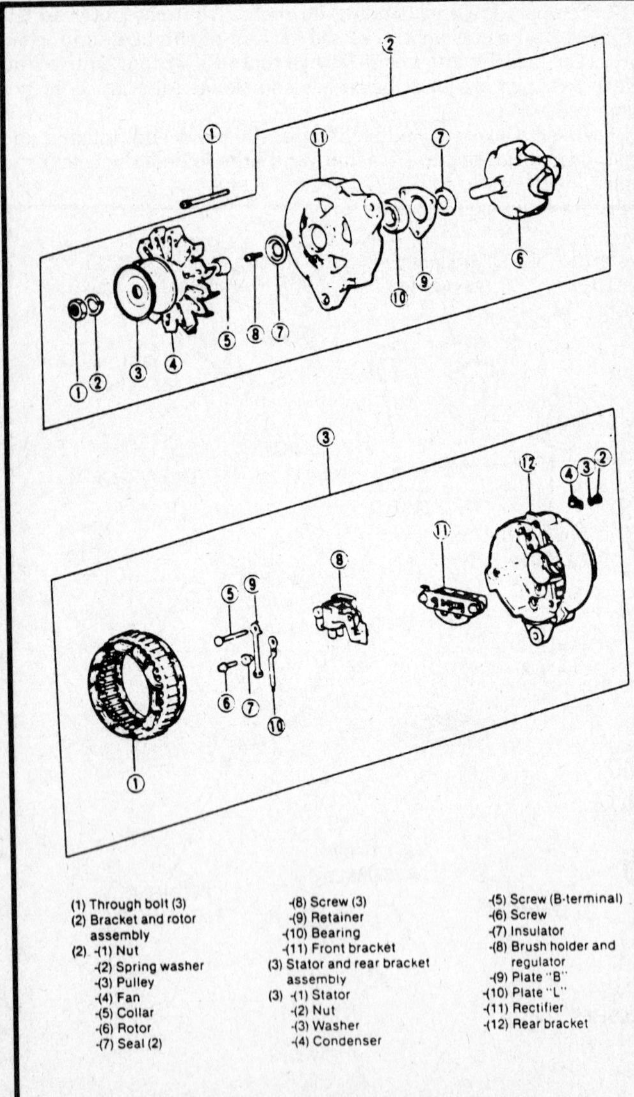

Mitsubishi alternator—gasoline engine

22. Position the rotor assembly in the rectifier end housing. Align the through bolt holes in the stator with both end housings.
23. Enter stator shaft in the rectifier end housing bearing, compress stator and both end housings manually and install through bolts, washers and nuts.
24. Install the insulated brush and terminal attaching screw.
25. Install the ground screw and attaching screw.
26. Rotate pulley slowly to be sure the rotor fan blades do not hit the rectifier and stator connectors.

ALTERNATOR

Disassembly And Assembly

MITSUBSHI UNITS

1. Place the alternator in a vise or similar holding fixture, mark the body components and remove the three through body bolts.
2. Pry between the stator and the drive end shield and carefully separate the drive end plate, the pulley and the rotor assembly from the stator and rectifier end shield assembly.
3. Carefully clamp the rotor and remove the pulley nut from the end of the shaft. Remove the pulley, the pulley fan, the pulley fan spacer and the alternator drive end shield from the rotor shaft.
4. The front bearing can be removed from the front drive housing by the removal of the dust seals, front and rear, the three bearing retainer screws, the retainer, exposing the bearing so that it can be tapped from the drive housing.
5. To remove the stator assembly, the six stator leads must be unsoldered from the rectifiers.
6. Remove the rectifiers from the stator end shield housing.
7. Remove the brush holder and regulator retaining screw.
8. Remove the Bat terminal retaining nut and remove the capacitor from the terminal.
9. Remove the regulator and rectifier assembly. Unsolder one rectifier to regulator assembly and remove the other rectifier assembly by sliding the battery stud out of the regulator.
10. Inspect the rotor bearing surface for scores and make the necessary off vehicle test on the electrical components.
11. The assembly of the alternator is the reverse of the removal procedure. Certain steps must be performed as the alternator is assembled.
12. Install the seals in the front and in the rear of the front bearing with the angled lip away from the bearing.
13. Push the brushes into the brush holder and insert a wire to hold them in the raised position. Install the rotor and remove the holding wire.

Mitsubishi Charging System

ALTERNATOR

Troubleshooting (On Vehicle)

1. Place the ignition switch in the off position.
2. Disconnect the battery ground cable.
3. Disconnect the cable from terminal "B" of the alternator and connect an ammeter between the terminal "B" and the cable.
4. Connect a voltmeter between terminal "B" (+) and ground (-).
5. Set the engine tachometer.
6. Connect the battery ground cable to the battery. The voltmeter should indicate the battery voltage.
7. Start the engine.
8. Turn on the lamps, accelerate the engine to the speed specified and measure the output current. Check it against the specifications.

ALTERNATOR

Disassembly

GASOLINE ENGINE MODELS

1. Remove alternator from vehicle.
2. Remove the three through bolts from the alternator body.
3. Insert an appropriate pry tool between the front bracket and stator. Pry the front bracket away from the stator. Remove the front bracket along with the rotor.

NOTE: If the tool is inserted too deeply, the stator coil might be damaged.

4. Hold the rotor in a vise and remove the pulley nut. Then remove the pulley, fan, spacer and seal. Remove the rotor from the front bracket and remove the seal.
5. Unsolder the rectifier from the stator coil lead wires and remove the stator assembly.

NOTE: Make sure the solder is removed quickly (in less than five seconds). If a diode is heated to more than 150°C, it might be damaged.

6. Remove the condenser from terminal "B".
7. Unsolder the plates "B" and "L" from the rectifier assembly.
8. Remove the mounting screw and terminal "B" bolt and remove the electronic voltage regulator and brush holder. The regulator and brush holder cannot be separated.
9. Remove the rectifier assembly.
10. When only a brush or brush spring is to be replaced, it is not necessary to remove the stator, etc. Raise the brush holder assembly and unsolder the wire pigtail of the brush and remove the brush.

NOTE: Be very careful when bending the plates "B" and "L" so as not to disturb the rectifier moulding.

Testing & Inspection

1. Check the outside circumference of the slip ring for dirtiness and roughness. Clean or polish with armature paper, if required. A badly damaged slip ring or a slip ring worn down beyond the service limit should also be replaced. The service limit for the slip ring outside diameter is 1.268 in.
2. Check for continuity between the field coil and slip ring. If there is not continuity, the field coil is defective and the rotor must be replaced.
3. Check for continuity between the slip ring and the shaft (or core). If there is continuity, the rotor assembly must be replaced.
4. Check for continuity between the leads of the stator coil. If there is no continuity, the stator coil is defective.
5. Check for an open circuit between the stator coil leads and the stator core. If there is continuity between the stator core and the coil leads, the stator assembly must be replaced.

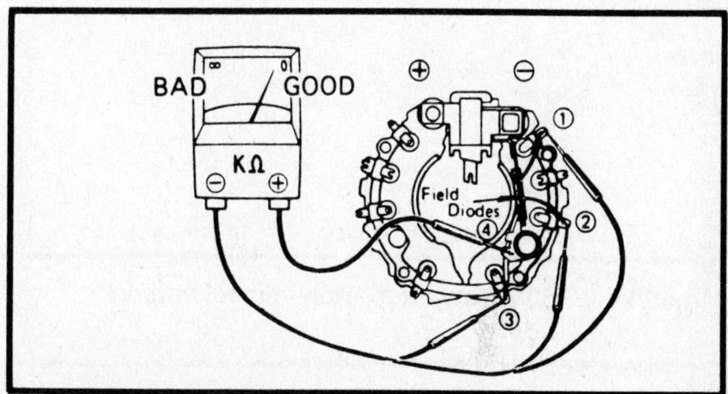

Field diode test

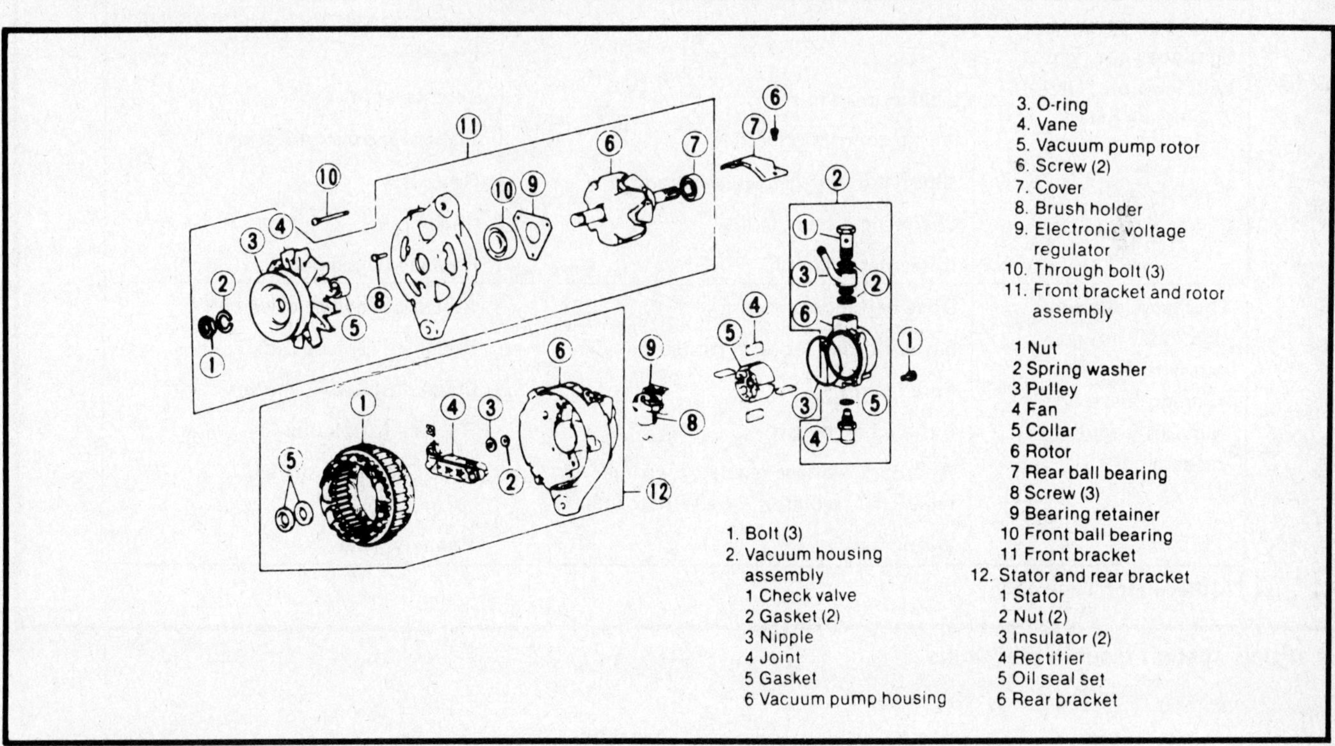

Mitsubishi alternator—diesel engine

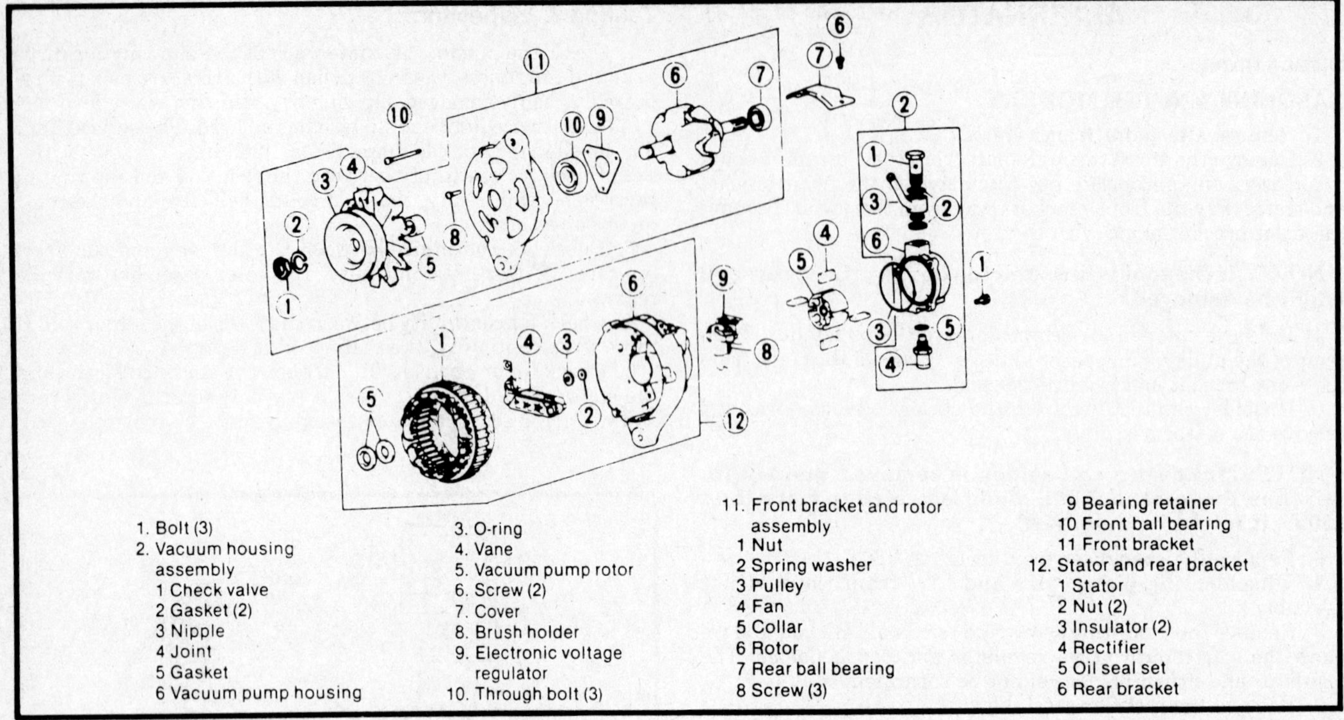

Mitsubishi/D-50 Arrow alternator—diesel engine

Problem	Possible cause	Remedy
Discharge warning light does not light with ignition "ON" and engine off	Fuse blown	Check "GAUGES" and "ENGINE"* fuses
	Light burned out	Replace light
	Wiring connection loose	Tighten loose connections
	Alternator voltage regulator faulty	Regulator
	Charge light relay faulty*	Check relay
	IC regulator faulty*	Replace IC regulator
Discharge warning light does not go out with engine running (battery requires frequent recharging)	Drive belt loose or worn	Adjust or replace drive belt
	Battery cables loose, corroded or worn	Repair or replace cables
	Fuse blown	Check "ENGINE" fuse
	Fusible link blown	Replace fusible link
	Alternator voltage regulator, charge light relay*, IC regulator* or alternator faulty	Check charging system
	Wiring faulty	Repair wiring

*IC Regulator Type only

Charging system trouble diagnosis

6. Check for continuity between the positive (+) heat sink and the stator coil lead connection terminal with a circuit tester. If there is continuity in both directions, the diode is short circuited and the rectifier assembly must be replaced.

7. Perform Step 6 between the negative (-) heat sink and the stator coil lead connection.

8. Using a circuit tester, check the three diodes for continuity in both directions. If there is either continuity or an open circuit in both directions, the diode is defective and must be replaced.

9. Measure the length of the brush. If it is worn below 0.315 in., it must be replaced.

ALTERNATOR

Assembly

GASOLINE ENGINE MODELS

1. Assembly is the reverse of disassembly with the following instructions:

2. Be sure to install both the front and rear seals on the front bearing. To install the rotor assembly in the rear bracket, push the brushes into the brush holder, insert a wire to hold them in the raised position and install the rotor. Remove the wire.

Problem	Possible cause	Remedy
Discharge warning light does not light with ignition ON and engine off	Fuse blown	Check "CHARGE" and "IGN" fuses
	Light burned out	Replace light
	Wiring connection loose	Tighten loose connections
	IC regulator faulty	Replace IC regulator
Discharge warning light does not go out with engine running (battery requires frequent recharging)	Drive belt loose or worn	Adjust or replace drive belt
	Battery cables loose, corroded or worn	Repair or replace cables
	Fuse blown	Check "ENGINE" fuse
	Fusible link blown	Replace fusible link
	IC regulator or alternator faulty	Check charging system
	Wiring faulty	Repair wiring

Problem	Possible cause	Remedy
Charge warning light does not light with starter switch at "ON" and engine not running	Fuse blown	Check "ENGINE", "IGN" and "CHARGE" fuse
	Light burned out	Replace light
	Wiring connection loose	Tighten loose connections
	Charge light relay	Check relay
	IC regulator faulty	Replace IC regulator
Charge warning light does not go out with engine running (battery requires frequent recharging)	Drive belt loose or worn	Adjust or replace drive belt
	Battery cables loose, corroded or worn	Repair or replace cables
	Fuse blown	Check "ENGINE" fuse
	Fusible link blown	Replace fusible link
	Alternator regulator, charge light relay, IC regulator or alternator faulty	Check charging system
	Wiring faulty	Repair wiring

Charging system trouble diagnosis

ALTERNATOR

Disassembly And Assembly

DIESEL ENGINE MODELS

The alternator on the turbo diesel models is the same as on the 2,555cc gasoline engine, except that the rear end of the rotor shaft is longer. Mounted on the end of the rotor shaft is a small vacuum pump, which generates vacuum for the brake booster. The vacuum pump is a vane type. Oil for lubricating the pump passes through an oil hose from the oil filter bracket and is supplied to the vacuum pump. After lubricating the pump, the oil passes through a return hose back to the oil pan.

Follow the Overhaul procedure above for gasoline engine alternators. The vacuum pump housing unbolts from the rear of the alternator housing. Always replace the O-ring. Grease the O-ring groove before installing the ring. Follow the following precautions below when assembling the vacuum pump.

Assembly

1. Install the pump vanes with the rounded end outward. Any vane with worn or chipped ends should be replaced.
2. Make sure no foreign material is present when installing the pump. Any dirt can cause the pump to seize.
3. When the pump housing is installed, push it lightly to minimize clearance at point "A". Tighten the three bolts evenly. Pump performance is affected by the way the housing is installed.
4. Fill the pump with clean engine oil before bench testing or running the alternator. Do not operate the alternator without first lubing the pump.

Toyota Charging System

Alternator

Disassembly

1982–84

1. Remove the three through bolts and pry the drive end from the stator. Do not pry the coil wires.
2. Place the drive end frame in a soft jaw vise and remove the pulley nut spring washer, space collar, pulley, fan and space collar.
3. Remove the rotor from the drive end frame.
4. Using a puller, remove the rear bearing from the rotor shaft.
5. Remove the four nuts and terminal insulators.
6. Remove the noise suppression condenser.
7. Remove the rear end cover and rear end frame from the stator.
8. Remove the insulators from the rectifier holder studs.
9. Hold the rectifier terminal with long nose pliers and unsolder the leads. Perform this step quickly as excessive heat can damage the rectifier.
10. On the 40 amp. alternator, unsolder the wire to the brush holder.

Testing And Inspection

1. Using an ohmmeter, check for continuity between the slip rings of the rotor. Standard resistance: 40 amp. alternator or the TIRRILL Regulator Type, should be 3.9–4.1 ohms; 55 amp. alternator or the IC Regulator Type, should be 2.8–3.0 ohms. If there is no continuity, replace the rotor.
2. Check the positive rectifier by using an ohmmeter and connecting the positive (+) lead to the rectifier holder and the negative (-) lead to the rectifier terminal. If there is no continuity, replace the rectifier assembly with brush.
3. Check the negative rectifier by using an ohmmeter and connecting the positive (+) lead to the rectifier terminal and the negative (-) lead to the rectifier holder. If there is no continuity, replace the rectifier with brush.
4. Using an ohmmeter, connect the positve (+) lead to the No.4 lead of the field diodes and the negative (-) lead to the Nos.1, 2 and 3 leads of the field diodes. If there is no continuity, replace the rectifier assembly with brush.

Assembly

1. Hold the rectifier terminal with long nose pliers and solder each stator lead to the rectifier. Protect the rectifiers from heat.
2. Place the two insulators on the positive (+) side of the rear end frame.
3. Install the rear end frame on the rectifier holder and check that the wires are not touching the case.
4. Place the rear end cover on the rear end frame.
5. Place the two insulators on the positive (+) side studs.
6. Install the four nuts on the studs.
7. On the 55 amp. alternator or the IC Regulator Type, mount the noise surpression condenser on the stud and connect the lead wire to the "B" terminal of the alternator.
8. Install the front bearing in the drive end frame, then install the three screws.
9. Press the rear bearing onto the rotor shaft.
10. Slide the spacer collar, then the drive end frame onto the rotor shaft.
11. Place the rotor in a soft jaw vise, then slide the spacer, fan, pulley and spacer collar on the rotor shaft. Tighten the nut to 37–47 ft. lbs.
12. Before installing the rotor on the rectifier end frame, bend the rectifier lead wires back to clear the rotor, then using a curved tool, push the wires in as far as they will go and hold them in place by inserting a stiff wire through the access hole in the end frame.
13. Install the drive end frame onto the rectifier end frame by inserting the rear bearing on the rotor shaft into the rear end frame.
14. Install the three through bolts.
15. Remove the wire from the access hole and make sure the rotor rotates smoothly.

ALTERNATOR

Disassembly

1985–86 GASOLINE ENGINE MODELS

1. Remove the nut and terminal insulator, then remove the three nuts and end cover.
2. Remove the two screws then remove the brush holder and brush holder cover.
3. Remove the three screws and remove the IC regulator.
4. Remove the four screws and remove the rectifier holder.
5. Remove the terminal insulator.
6. To remove the pulley and nut, use Tool No. 09820–63010, or its equivalent to perform the following procedure: Hold the tool at point "A" with a torque wrench, then tighten at point "B" clockwise to 29 ft. lbs. Confirm that the tool "A" is secured to the pulley shaft. Grip tool "C" in a vise and then install the alternator to special tool "C". To loosen the pulley nut turn the tool "A".

CAUTION

To prevent damage to the rotor shaft, do not loosen the pulley nut more than one-half turn.

7. Turn the tool at point "B" and remove all the tool components. Remove the pulley nut and the pulley.
8. Remove the four nuts from the rear end frame, then using a puller, tool No. 09286–46011 or equivalent, remove the rear end frame.

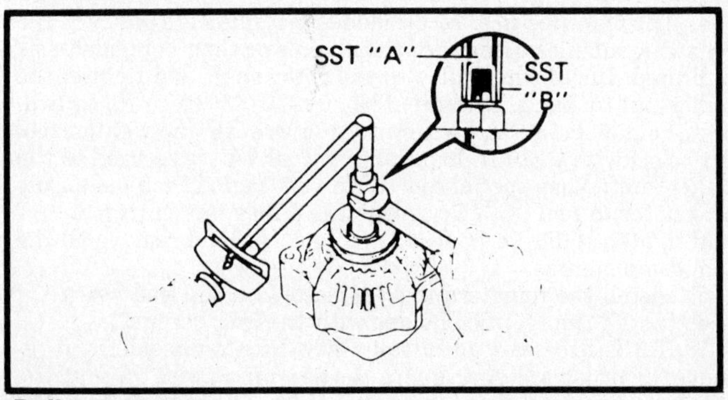

Pulley removal

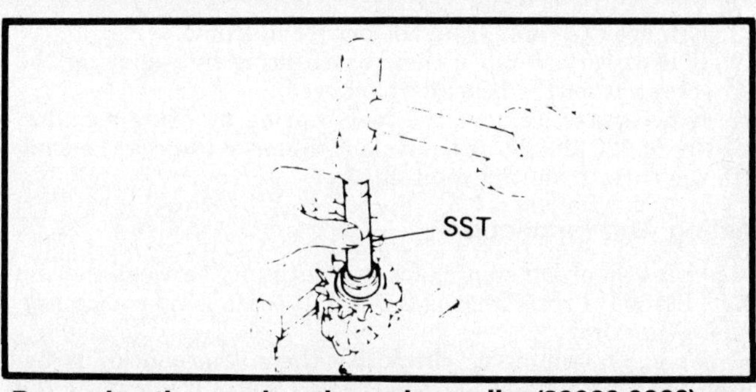

Removing the rear bearing using puller (09820-0020) or equivalent

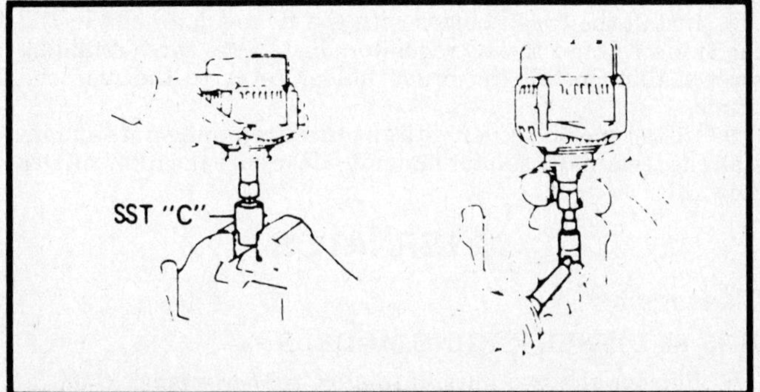

Pulley removal

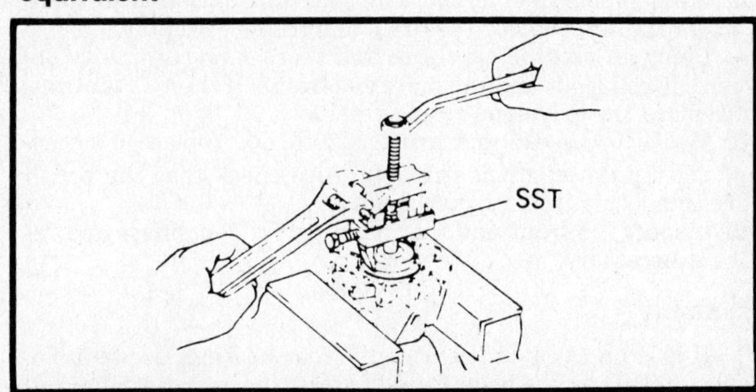

Installing the rear bearing using tool (09825-76010) or equivalent

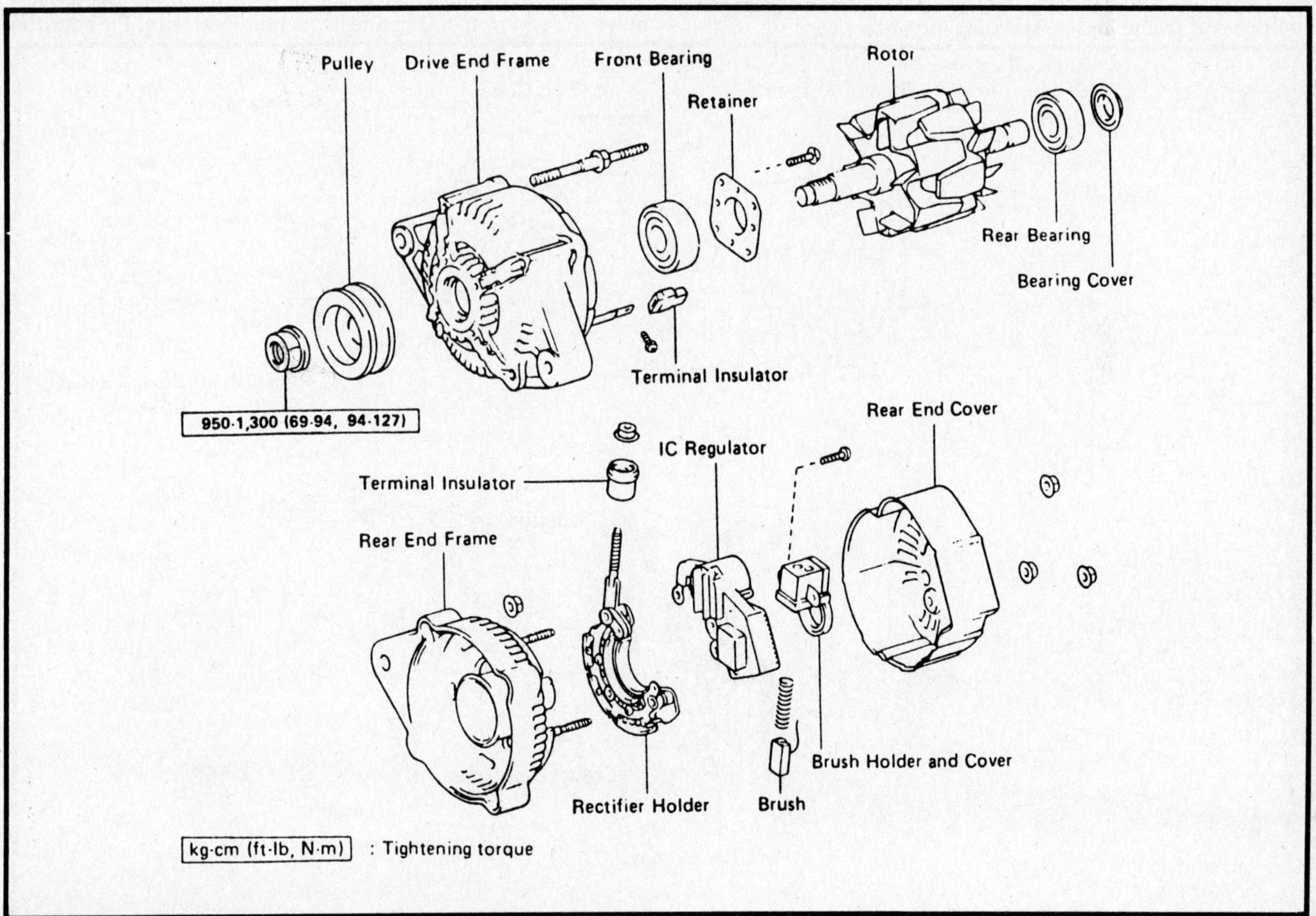

Pulley
Drive End Frame
Front Bearing
Retainer
Rotor
Rear Bearing
Bearing Cover
Terminal Insulator
950-1,300 (69-94, 94-127)
Rear End Cover
IC Regulator
Terminal Insulator
Rear End Frame
Brush Holder and Cover
Rectifier Holder
Brush
kg-cm (ft-lb, N·m) : Tightening torque

Toyota alternator—gas engine, 1985 and later

9. Remove the rotor from the drive end frame.
10. If necessary, remove the front bearing by removing the four screws from the bearing retainer.
11. If necessary, remove the rear bearing by using a puller, tool No. 09820–00020 or equivalent. Remove the rear bearing with the cover from the rotor shaft.

Testing And Inspection

1. Using an ohmmeter, check for continuity between the slip rings. Standard resistance is 2.8–3.0. If there is no continuity, replace the rotor.
2. Using an ohmmeter, check that there is no continuity between the slip ring and rotor. If there is continuity, replace the rotor.
3. Using an ohmmeter, check all leads for continuity. If there is no continuity, replace the drive end frame assembly.
4. Using an ohmmeter, check that there is no continuity between the coil leads and the drive end frame. If there is continuity, replace the drive end frame assembly.
5. Measure the exposed brush length and replace if necessary. Minimum length is 0.177 in. Also check that the brush moves smoothly in the brush holder.
6. Inspect the front and rear bearings for roughness and replace if necessary.

Assembly

1. If it is necessary to replace the rear bearing, use tool No. 09285–76010, or equivalent and install the rear bearing and cover onto the rotor shaft.
2. Install the rotor to the drive end frame.
3. Using a plastic hammer, lightly tap the rear end frame on the drive end frame and install the four nuts.
4. The manufacturer recommends installing the pulley in the following manner using the special tools or their equivalents as indicated: Install the pulley to the rotor shaft and tighten the pulley nut by hand. Using tool No. 09820–63010, or its equivalent, hold at point "A" with a torque wrench and tighten tool "B" clockwise to 29 ft. lbs. Confirm tool "A" is secured to the pulley shaft. Grip special tool "C" in a vise and then install the alternator to tool "C". To torque the pulley nut, turn tool "A" and tighten to 69–94 ft. lbs. Turn tool "B" and remove all the tool components.
5. Install the four terminal insulators on the lead wires.
6. Install the rectifier holder with the four screws.
7. If it is necessary to install a new brush, unsolder and remove the brush and spring. Put the new brush wire through the spring and insert it into the brush holder. Solder the wire to the brush holder and cut off any excess.
8. Install the brush holder with the IC regulator and install the two screws to the IC regulator. Install the three retaining screws, then install the brush holder cover to the rear end frame.
9. Install the end cover with the three retaining nuts and install the terminal insulator and nut. Make sure the rotor rotates smoothly.

ALTERNATOR

Disassembly

1985–86 DIESEL ENGINE MODELS

1. Remove the two nuts, insulator, rubber washer, then remove the brush holder cover.
2. Remove the brush holder and IC regulator as follows: Remove the screw and disconnect the blue lead wire. Pull out the

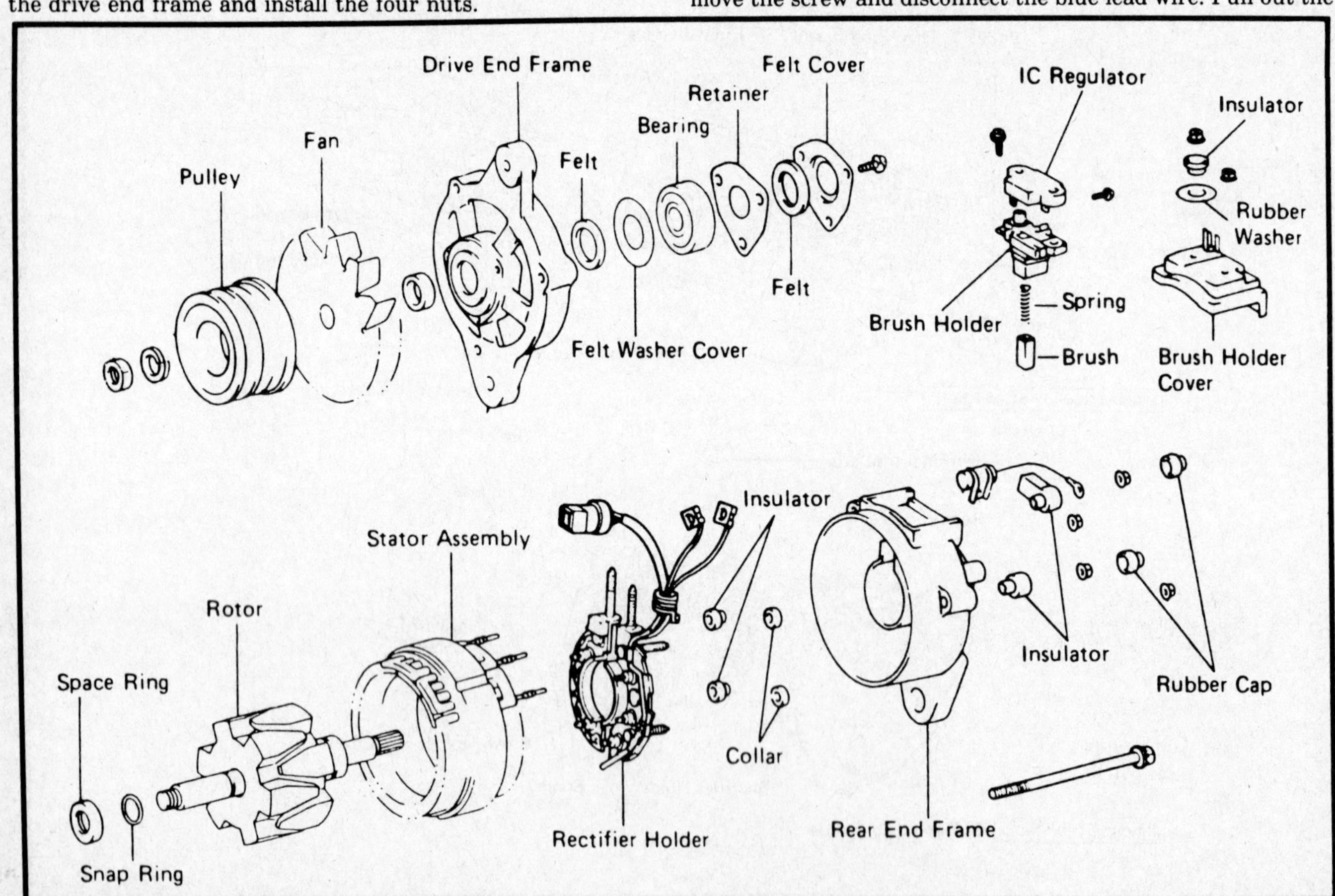

Toyota alternator—diesel engine, 1985 and later

brush holder with the IC regulator from the rectifier holder. Remove the screw and disconnect the lead wire from the brush holder. Remove the two screws and separate the IC regulator and brush holder.

3. Remove the three through bolts and remove the end frame with the rotor.

NOTE: It may be necessary to lightly tap the rotor shaft with a plastic hammer.

4. Mount the rotor in a soft jaw vise and remove the pulley nut, spring washer, puley and fan.

5. Using a socket wrench and press, press out the rotor, spacer ring and collar. Remove the snap ring from the rotor shaft.

6. Remove the two rubber caps, four nuts, two terminal insulators, then remove the stator with the rectifier holder.

7. Hold the rectifier terminal with needle nose pliers and unsolder the stator leads from the rectifier holder. Perform this step quickly as excessive heat can damage the rectifiers.

Testing And Inspection

1. Using an ohmmeter, check that there is no continuity between the slip rings on the rotor. Standard resistance is 2.9.

2. Using an ohmmeter, check that there is no continuity between the slip ring and rotor. If there is no continuity, replace the rotor.

3. Inspect the stator for an open circuit by using an ohmmeter and checking that there is no continuity between the coil leads.

NOTE: At this time, the meeting wires should be connected with solder. If there is no continuity, replace the stator.

4. Measure the brush length. Standard length: 0.790 in.; Minimum length: 0.217 in.

5. Inspect the bearing for roughness and replace if necessary.

Assembly

1. If it is necessary to replace the bearing, remove the three retaining bolts, felt cover, felt, retainer, bearing, washer and felt. Install the bearing and related parts in the reverse order of removal and if necessary, lightly tap the bearing with a plastic hammer to install.

2. Hold the rectifier terminal with needle nose pliers and solder each stator lead to the rectifier holder. Protect the rectifiers from excessive heat.

3. Assemble the rectifier end frame and rectifier holder as follows:

a. Place the two inner terminal insulators on the positive side studs.

b. Place the collars on the negative side studs.

c. Install the rectifier end frame on the rectifier holder and check that the wires are not touching the case.

d. Place the two outer terminal insulators on the positive side studs.

e. Install the lead wire of the noise suppression condenser on the positive side studs, if so equipped.

f. Install the four nuts on the studs.

g. Install the two rubber caps on the positive side studs.

4. Install the snap ring in the rotor shaft groove and install the space ring on the rotor shaft, then using a press, press in the rotor. Install the spacer collar.

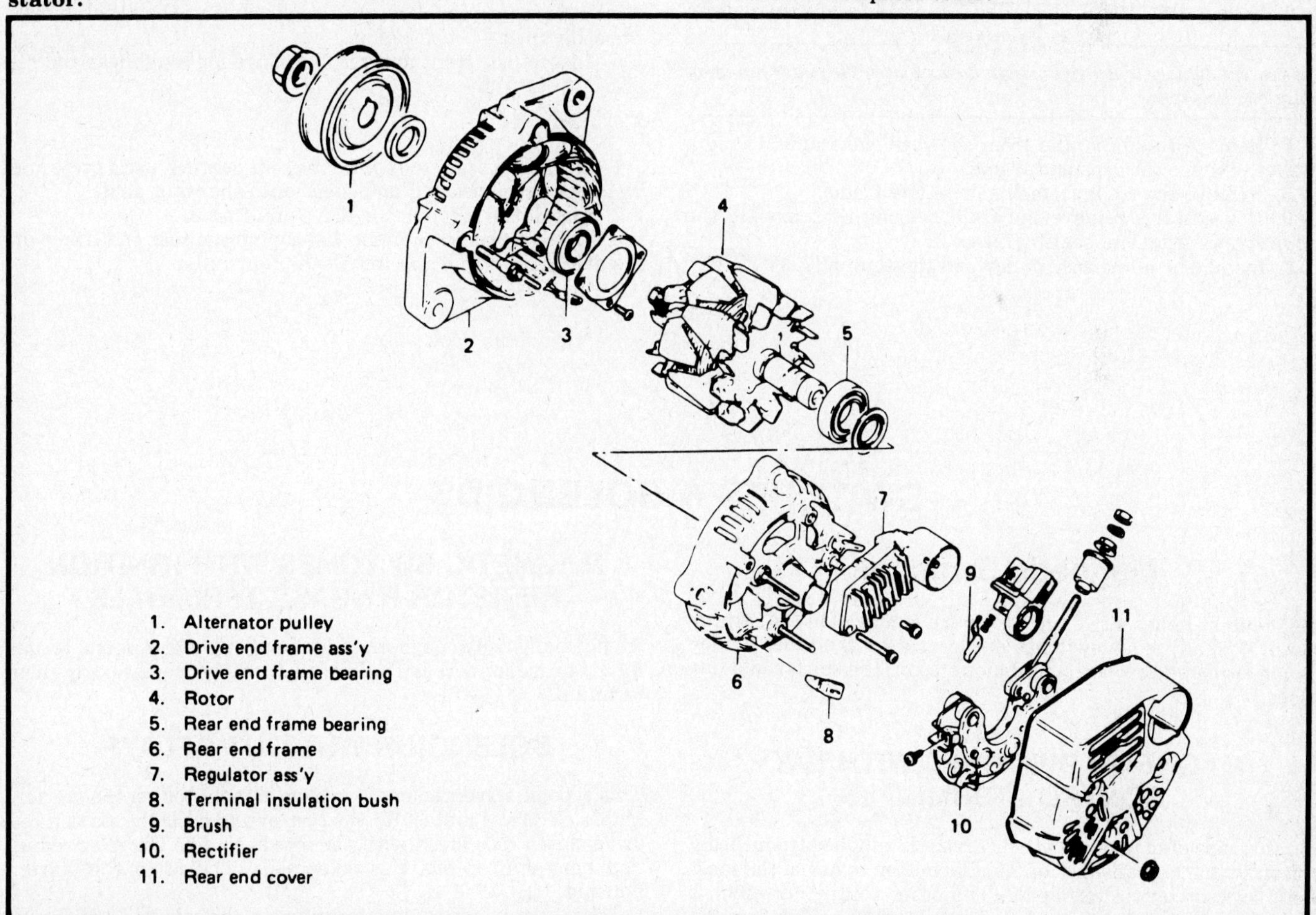

Suzuki alternator

5. Mount the rotor in a soft jaw vise, then slide the fan, pulley and spring washer onto the shaft. Torque the nut to 65 ft. lbs.

6. Assemble the drive end frame and rectifier end frame and install the three through bolts. Make sure the rotor rotates smoothly.

7. If it is necessary to install a new brush, unsolder and remove the brush and spring. Insert the new brush wire through the spring and install the brush in the brush holder. Solder the wire to the brush holder at the standard length of 0.790 in. and cut off the excess wire.

8. Install the IC regulator on the brush holder with the two retaining screws and connect the white lead wire to the terminal of the IC regulator with the screw. Install the brush holder and blue lead wire with the screw.

9. Place the cover on the rectifier end frame and place the terminal insulator and rubber washer on terminal B. Install the two retaining nuts.

Suzuki Samurai Charging System

ALTERNATOR

Disassembly

1. Remove the nut and terminal insulator, then remove the three nuts and end cover.
2. Remove the two screws, then remove the brush holder and brush holder cover.
3. Remove the three screws and remove the IC regulator.
4. Remove the four screws and remove the rectifier holder.
5. Remove the terminal insulator.
6. Loosen the alternator pulley nut and take off the pulley.

CAUTION

To prevent damage to the rotor shaft, do not loosen the pulley nut more than one-half turn.

7. Remove the four nuts from the rear end frame. Using a puller, remove the rear end frame.
8. Remove the rotor from the drive end frame.
9. If necessary, remove the front bearing by removing the four screws from the bearing retainer.
4. Install the alternator pulley and tighten to 37–47 ft. lbs.
5. Install the four terminal insulators on the lead wires.
6. Install the rectifier holder with the four screws.
7. If it is necessary to install a new brush, unsolder and remove the brush and spring. Put the new brush wire through the spring and insert it into the brush holder. Solder the wire to the brush holder and cut off any excess.
8. Install the brush holder with the IC regulator and install the two screws to the IC regulator. Install the three retaining screws, then install the brush holder cover to the rear end frame.
9. Install the end cover with the three retaining nuts and install the terminal insulator and nut. Make sure the rotor rotates smoothly.
10. If necessary, remove the rear bearing by using a puller.Remove the rear bearing with the cover from the rotor shaft.

Testing & Inspection

1. Using an ohmmeter, check for continuity between the slip rings. Standard resistance is 2.8–3.0. If there is no continuity, replace the rotor.
2. Using an ohmmeter, check that there is no continuity between the slip ring and rotor. If there is continuity, replace the rotor.
3. Using an ohmmeter, check all leads for continuity. If there is no continuity, replace the drive end frame assembly.
4. Using an ohmmeter, check for continuity between the coil leads and the drive end frame. If there is continuity, replace the drive end frame assembly.
5. Measure the exposed brush length and replace, if necesary. Minimum length is 0.200 in. Also check that the brush moves smoothly in the brush holder.
6. Inspect the front and rear bearings for roughness and replace, if necessary.

Assembly

1. If it is necessary to replace the rear bearing, use a press and install the rear bearing and cover onto the rotor shaft.
2. Install the rotor to the drive end frame.
3. Using a plastic hammer, lightly tap the rear end frame on the drive end frame and install the four nuts.

SWITCHES & SOLENOIDS

Magnetic Switches

Magnetic switches serve only to make contact for the starter motor. Usually, such switches are located on the inner fender panel, although they are found mounted on the starter in a few cases.

MAGNETIC SWITCHES WITH TWO CONTROL TERMINALS

On this type of magnetic switch current is supplied from the ignition switch or transmission neutral button to one of the magnetic switch control terminals. The other control terminal is connected to the transmission neutral safety switch (on the transmission) where it is grounded.

MAGNETIC SWITCHES WITH IGNITION RESISTOR BY-PASS TERMINALS

All normally use a magnetic switch with a single control terminal. The second terminal is an ignition resistor by-pass terminal.

SOLENOIDS WITHOUT RELAYS

This type of starter solenoid is always mounted on the starter. Makes electrical contact for the starter and pulls the starter and drive clutch into mesh with the flywheel. The Chrysler reduction gear starter has this solenoid embodied in the starter housing.

There is only one control terminal on the solenoid and the ignition by-pass terminal is usually marked R or IGN, if it is used.

SOLENOIDS WITH SEPARATE RELAYS

The solenoid itself is always mounted on the starter. In addition to making contact for the starter, it also pulls the starter drive clutch gear into mesh with the flywheel. A single control terminal is used on the solenoid itself. The relay is usually found mounted to the inner fender panel or on the firewall.

SOLENOIDS WITH BUILT-IN RELAYS

These units are always mounted on the starter and are connected, through linkage, to the starter drive clutch. The relay portion is built into and integral with the front end of the solenoid assembly.

NEUTRAL SAFETY SWITCHES

The purpose of the neutral safety switch is to prevent the starter from cranking the engine except when the transmission is in neutral or park.

On some trucks, the neutral safety switch is located on the transmission. It serves to ground the solenoid or magnetic switch, whichever is used.

On other trucks, the neutral safety switch is located on the steering column, where it contacts the shift mechanism within the steering column, or on the shift linkage when a console is used.

Some manual transmission models have a clutch linkage safety switch to prevent starter operation unless the clutch pedal is depressed.

On most trucks, the neutral safety switch and the backup light switch are combined into a single switch mechanism.

Troubleshooting Neutral Safety Switches Quick Test

If the starter fails to function and the neutral safety switch is to be checked, a jumper can be placed across its terminals. If the starter then functions, the safety switch is defective.

In the case of neutral safety switches with one wire, the wire must be grounded for testing purposes. If the starter works with the wire grounded, the switch is defective.

NEUTRAL SAFETY SWITCH/BACK-UP LIGHT SWITCH

When the neutral safety switch is built in combination with the back-up light switch, the quickest way to determine which terminals are for the back-up lights is to take a test lamp/jumper wire and cross from a hot wire to a neutral wire. The wires which light the back-up lamps should be ignored when testing the neutral safety switch. Once the back-up light wires have been located, jump the other pair of wires to test the neutral safety switch. If the starter functions only when the jumper is placed across these two wires, the neutral safety switch is defective or requires adjustment.

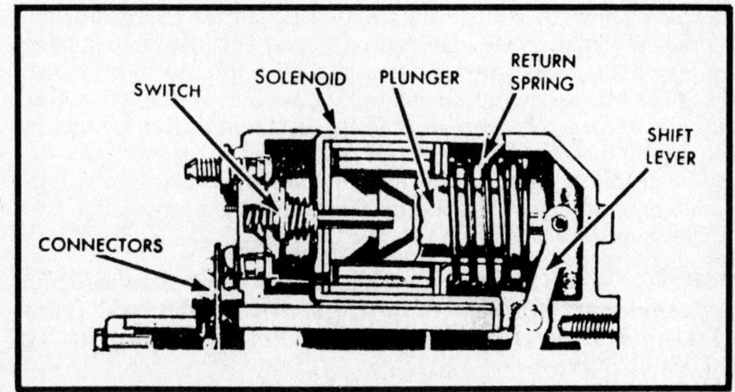

Starter solenoid mounted on starter motor

STARTING SYSTEMS

Starter Motor Testing

The starter circuit should be divided and tested in four separate phases:

1. Cranking voltage check
2. Amperage draw
3. Voltage drop on grounded side
4. Voltage drop on battery side

NOTE: The battery must be in good condition for this test to have significance. To accurately check battery condition, use equipment designed to measure its capacity under a load. Instructions accompanying the equipment should be followed.

CRANKING VOLTAGE

Connect voltmeter leads to prods tapped into the battery posts (observe polarity and reverse meter leads if necessary). Remove the high tension wire from the distributor cap and ground it to prevent engine starting. With electronic ignition, disconnect the control box harness from the distributor. Turn the key to the

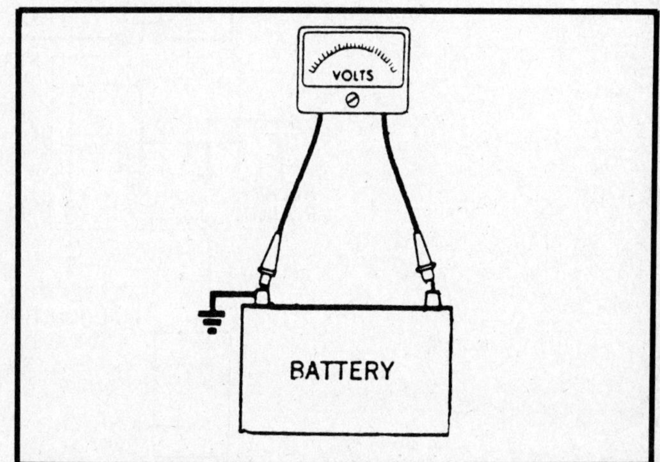

Voltmeter connected to battery for cranking voltage test

START position. Observe both voltmeter reading and cranking speed. The cranking speed should be even and at a satisfactory rate of speed, with a voltmeter reading of at least 9.6 volts for 12 volt systems.

AMPERAGE DRAW

The amount of current the starter motor draws is usually (but not always) associated with the mechanical problems involved in cranking the engine. (Mechanical trouble in the engine, frozen or worn starter parts, misaligned starter or starter components, etc.) Because starter motor amperage draw is directly influenced by anything restricting the free turning of the engine, or starter, it is important that the engine and all components be at operating temperatures.

To measure starter current draw, remove the high tension wire from the center of the distributor cap and ground it. With electronic ignition, disconnect the control box harness from the distributor. A very simple and inexpensive starter current indicator is available. This indicator is an induction type gauge and shows, without disconnecting any wires, starter current draw.

Place the yoke of the meter directly over the insulated starter supply cable (cable must be straight for a minimum of 2 in.). Close the starter switch for about 20 seconds, watch the meter dial and record the average reading. If the indicator swings in the wrong direction, reverse the position of the meter.

The cranking amperage draw can vary from 150 to 400 amperes, depending on the engine size, engine compression and starter type.

NOTE: When starter specifications are not available, average starter draw amperage can be derived from testing a like starter unit, known to be operating satisfactorily.

More accurate equipment is available from many manufacturers. This equipment consists of a combination voltmeter, ammeter and carbon pile rheostat. When using this equipment, follow the equipment manufacturer's procedures and recommendations.

High amperage and lazy performance would suggest an excessively tight engine, friction in the starter or starter drive, grounded starter field or armature.

Normal amperage and lazy performance suggest high resistance, or possibly poor connections somewhere in the starter circuit.

Low amperage and lazy or no performance suggest battery condition poor, bad cables or connections along the line.

VOLTAGE DROP ON GROUNDED SIDE

With a voltmeter on the 3 volt scale and without disconnecting any wires, connect negative test lead of the voltmeter to a prod secured in the grounded battery post. The positive test lead is connected to a cleaned, bare metal portion of the starter motor housing. Close the starter switch and note the voltmeter reading. If the reading is the same as battery reading, the ground circuit is open somewhere between the battery and the starter. In many cases, the reading will be very small. The reading shown will indicate voltage drop (loss) between battery ground post and starter housing. The drop should not exceed 0.2 volt. If the voltage drop is above the specified amount, the next step is to isolate and correct the cause. It can be a bad cable or connection anywhere in the battery-to-starter ground circuit. A check of this type should progress along the various points of possible trouble between the battery ground post and the starter motor housing until the trouble spot has been located.

VOLTAGE DROP ON BATTERY SIDE

Bad starter cranking may result from poor connections or faulty components of the battery or hot phase of the starter motor circuit. To check this phase of the circuit, without disconnecting any wires, connect one lead of a voltmeter to a prod secured in the hot post of the battery and the other voltmeter lead to the

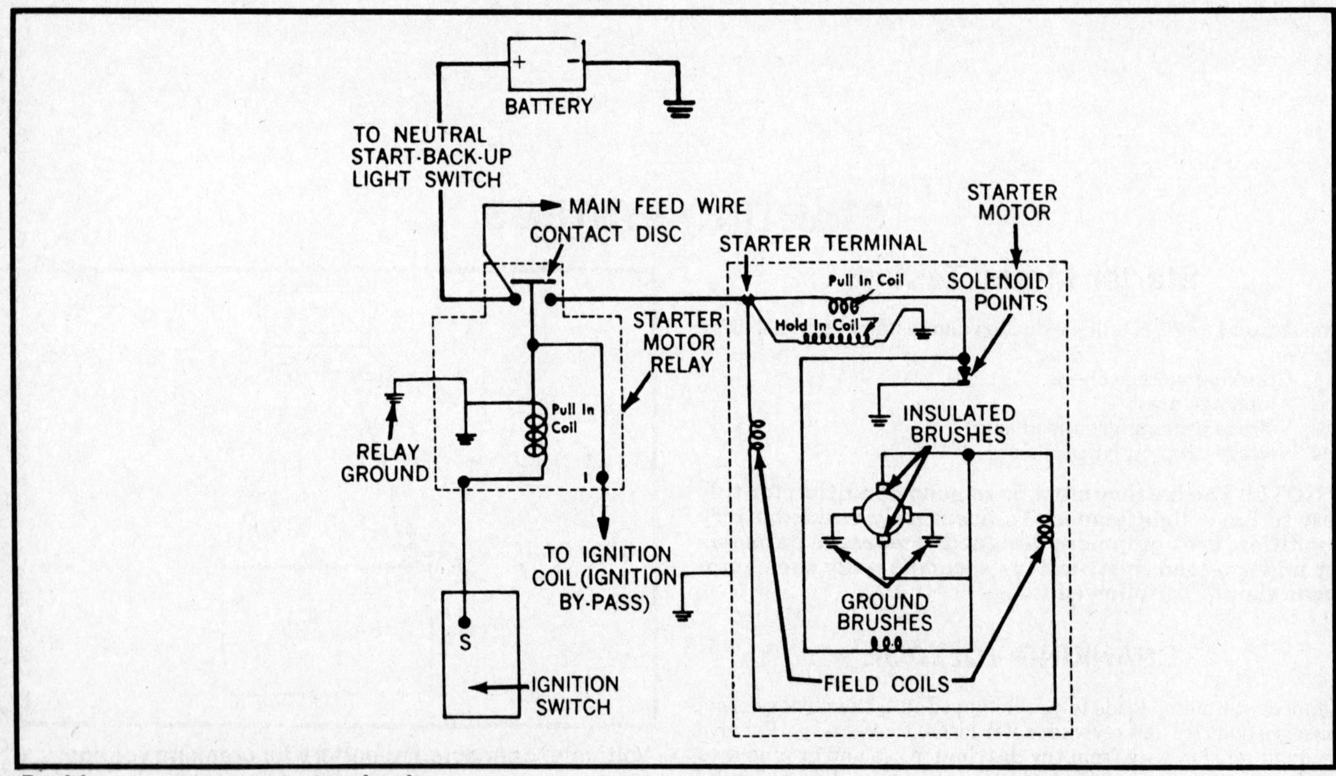

Positive engagement starter circuits

field terminal of the starting motor. The meter should be set to the 16–20 volt scale. Before closing the starter switch, the voltmeter reading will be that of the battery. After closing the starter switch, change the selector on the voltmeter to the 3 volt scale. With a jumper wire between the relay battery terminal and the relay starter switch terminal, crank the engine. If the starting motor cranks the engine, the relay (solenoid) is operating.

While the engine is being cranked, watch the voltmeter. It should not register more than 0.5 volt. If more than this, check each part of the circuit for voltage drop to isolate the trouble, (high resistance).

Without disturbing the voltmeter-to-battery hook-up, move the free voltmeter lead to the battery terminal of the relay (solenoid) and crank the engine. The voltmeter should show no more than 0.1 volt.

If this reading is correct, move the same voltmeter lead to the starting motor terminal of the relay (solenoid). While the engine is being cranked, the voltmeter should show no more than 0.3 volt. If it does, the trouble lies in the relay.

If the reading is correct, the trouble is in the cable or connections between the relay and the starting motor.

Diagnosis

STARTER WON'T CRANK ENGINE

1. Dead battery.
2. Open starter circuit, such as:
   a. Broken or loose battery cables.
   b. Inoperative starter motor solenoid.
   c. Broken or loose wire from starter switch to solenoid.
   d. Poor solenoid or starter ground.
   e. Bad starter switch.
3. Defective starter internal circuit, such as:
   a. Dirty or burnt commutator.
   b. Stuck, worn or broken brushes.
   c. Open or shorted armature.
   d. Open or grounded fields.
4. Starter motor mechanical faults, such as:
   a. Jammed armature end bearings.
   b. Bad bearing, allowing armature to rub fields.
   c. Bent shaft.
   d. Broken starter housing.
   e. Bad starter worm or drive mechanism.
   f. Bad starter drive or flywheel driven gear.
5. Engine hard or impossible to crank such as:
   a. Hydrostatic lock caused by water or other liquid in combustion chamber.
   b. Crankshaft seizing in bearings.
   c. Piston or ring seizing.
   d. Bent or broken connecting rod.
   e. Seizing of connecting rod bearing.
   f. Flywheel jammed or broken.

STARTER SPINS FREE, WON'T ENGAGE

1. Sticking or broken drive mechanism.

Chrysler Corp. Scamp And Rampage Starter System

BOSCH AND NIPPON DENSO STARTERS

Disassembly And Assembly

1. Position the assembly in the proper holding fixture. Disconnect the field coil wire from the solenoid terminal.

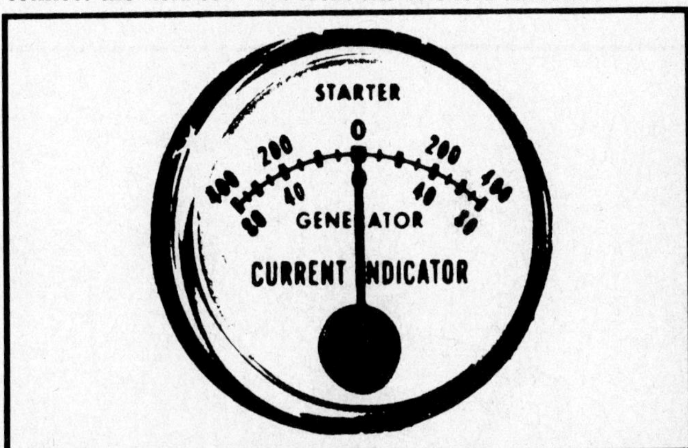

Starter current indicator

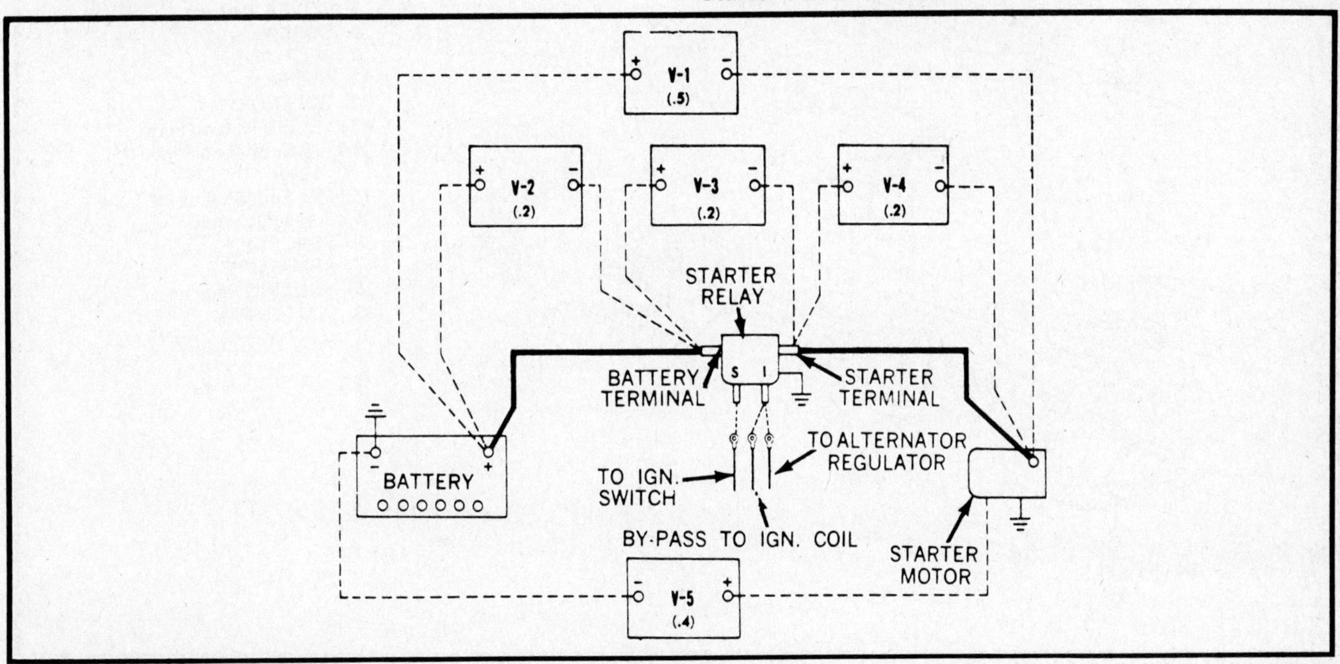

Starter cable resistance tests

2. Remove the solenoid mounting screws (and the solenoid onBosch starters, when used with automatic transmission equipped vehicles) and work the solenoid and/or plunger off the shift fork.
3. On Nippon Denso units, remove the bearing cover, armature shaft lock, washer, spring and seal.
4. On Bosch units, remove the two screws holding down the end shield bearing cap and remove the cap and washers.
5. Remove the through bolts and the commutator end frame cover. Remove the two brushes and the brush plate. Slide the field frame off over the armature.
6. Take out the shift lever pivot bolt. Take off the rubber gasket and metal plate.
7. For the Bosch (automatic transmission) and all Nippon Denso units, remove the armature assembly and shift lever from the drive end housing. For the Bosch (manual transmission) press the stop collar off the snapring, remove the snapring, remove the clutch assembly and remove the drive end housing from the armature.
8. For all except the Bosch (manual transmission), press the stop collar off the snapring, then remove the snapring, stop collar and clutch.
9. Brushes that are worn more than one half the length of new brushes, or are oil soaked, should be replaced. New brushes are $^{11}/_{16}$ in. long.
10. Do not immerse the starter clutch unit in cleaning solvent. Solvent will wash the lubricant from the clutch.
11. Place the drive unit on the armature shaft and while holding the armature, rotate the pinion. The drive pinion should rotate smoothly in one direction only. The pinion may not rotate easily, but as long as it rotates smoothly, it is in good condition. If the clutch unit does not function properly or if the pinion is worn, chipped or burred, replace the unit.
12. Assembly is the reverse of the disassembly procedure. Lubricate the armature shaft and splines with oil.
13. On all except the Bosch (manual transmission), install the clutch, stop collar, lock ring and shaft fork on the armature. On the Bosch (manual transmission), install the drive end housing on the armature, then install the clutch, stop collar and snapring on the armature.
14. On all except the Bosch (manual transmission), install the armature assembly and shift fork in the drive end housing. On Bosch units, install the shim and armature shaft lock. Check the end play. It should be 0.002–0.021 in.

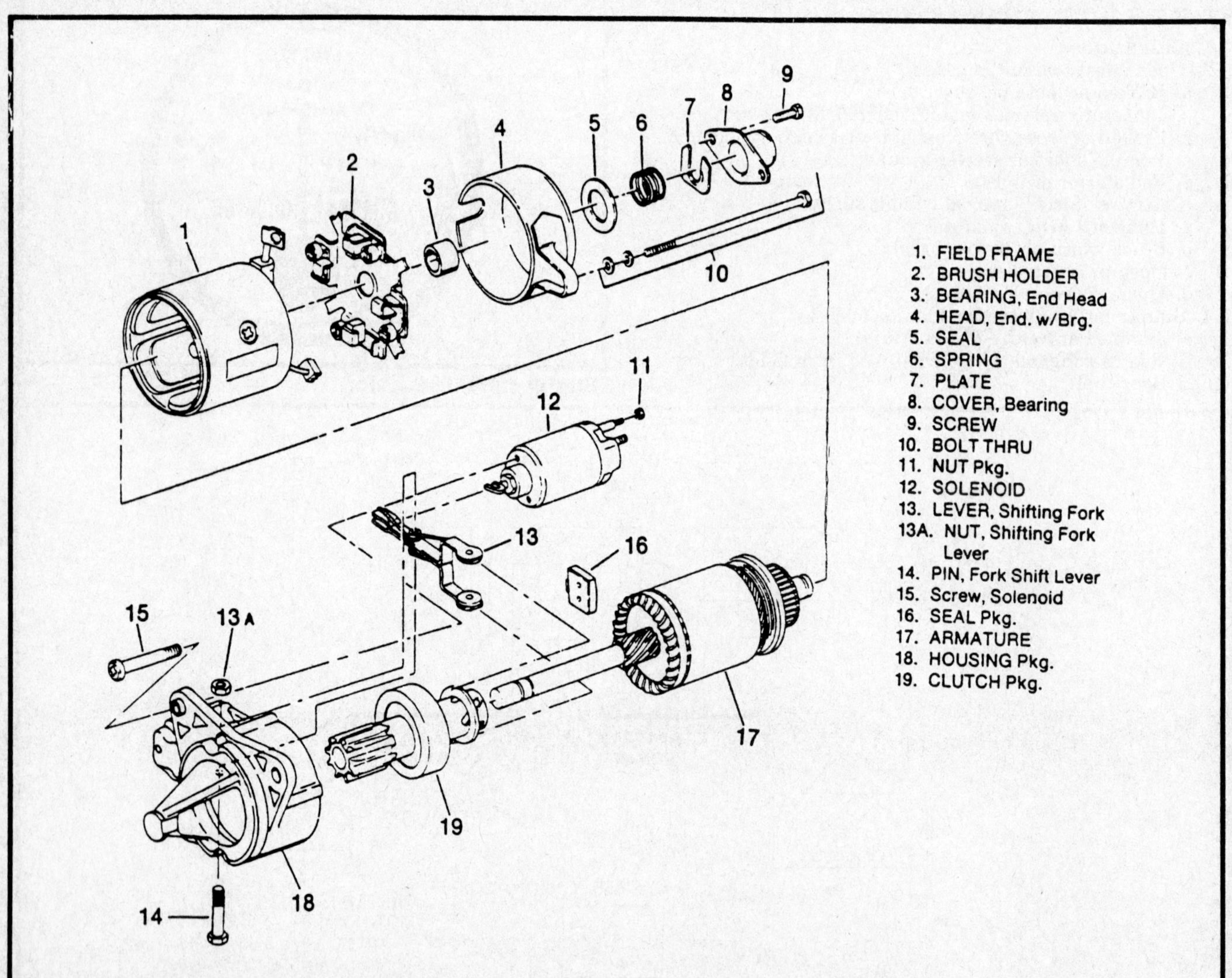

Rampage/Scamp with Nippondenso starter—1.7L engine with manual transmission

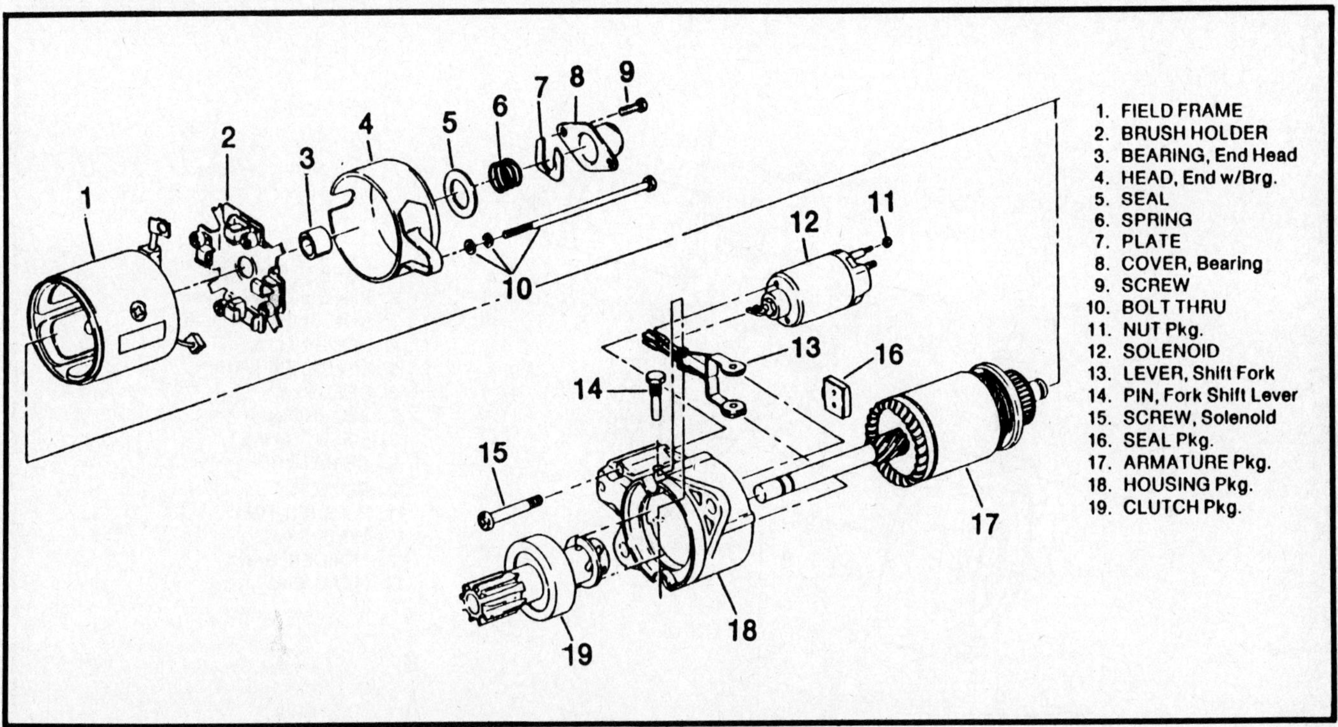

1. FIELD FRAME
2. BRUSH HOLDER
3. BEARING, End Head
4. HEAD, End w/Brg.
5. SEAL
6. SPRING
7. PLATE
8. COVER, Bearing
9. SCREW
10. BOLT THRU
11. NUT Pkg.
12. SOLENOID
13. LEVER, Shift Fork
14. PIN, Fork Shift Lever
15. SCREW, Solenoid
16. SEAL Pkg.
17. ARMATURE Pkg.
18. HOUSING Pkg.
19. CLUTCH Pkg.

Rampage/Scamp with Nippondenso starter— except 1.7L engine with manual transmission

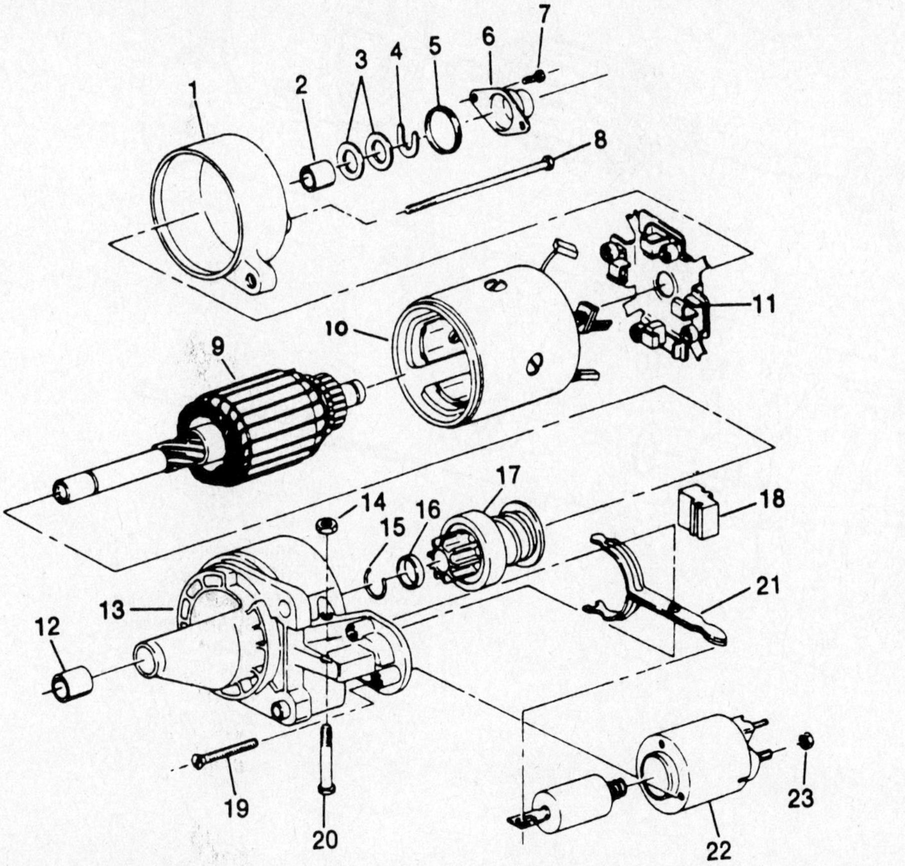

1. HEAD, End
2. BEARING, End Head
3. SHIM PKG.
4. WASHER, Retaining
5. SEAL
6. COVER, Bearing
7. SCREW, Bearing Cover
8. BOLT THRU
9. ARMATURE
10. FIELD FRAME
11. BRUSH HOLDER
12. BEARING, Housing
13. HOUSING
14. NUT, Fork shift Lever
15. SNAP RING
16. SEAL
17. CLUTCH
18. SEAL
19. SCREW, Solenoid
20. PIN, Shift Fork Lever
21. LEVER, Shift Fork
22. SOLENOID
23. NUT, Connecting Terminal

Rampage/Scamp with Bosch starter—1.7L,2.2L engine with automatic transmission

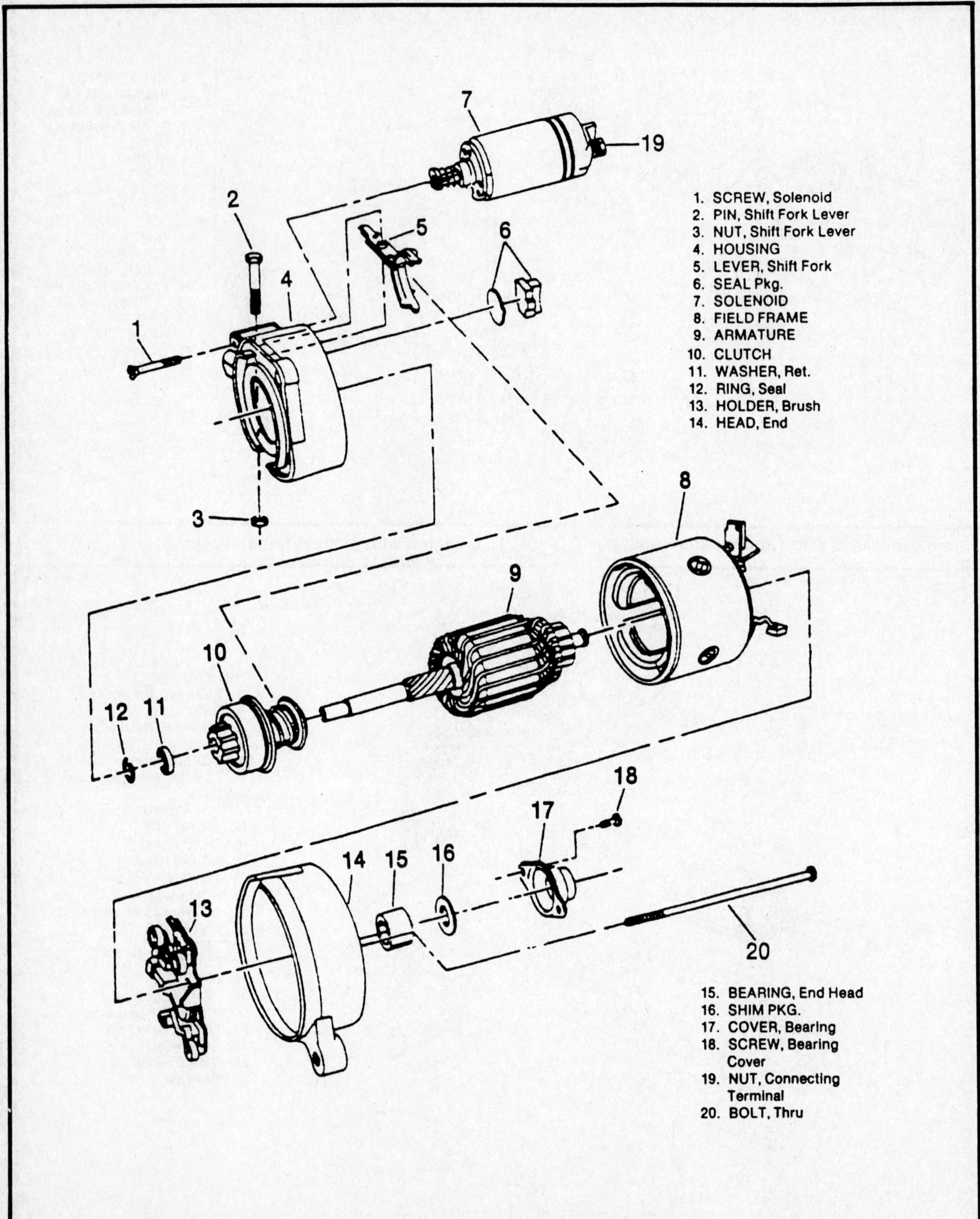

Rampage/Scamp with Bosch starter—1.7L engine with manual transmission

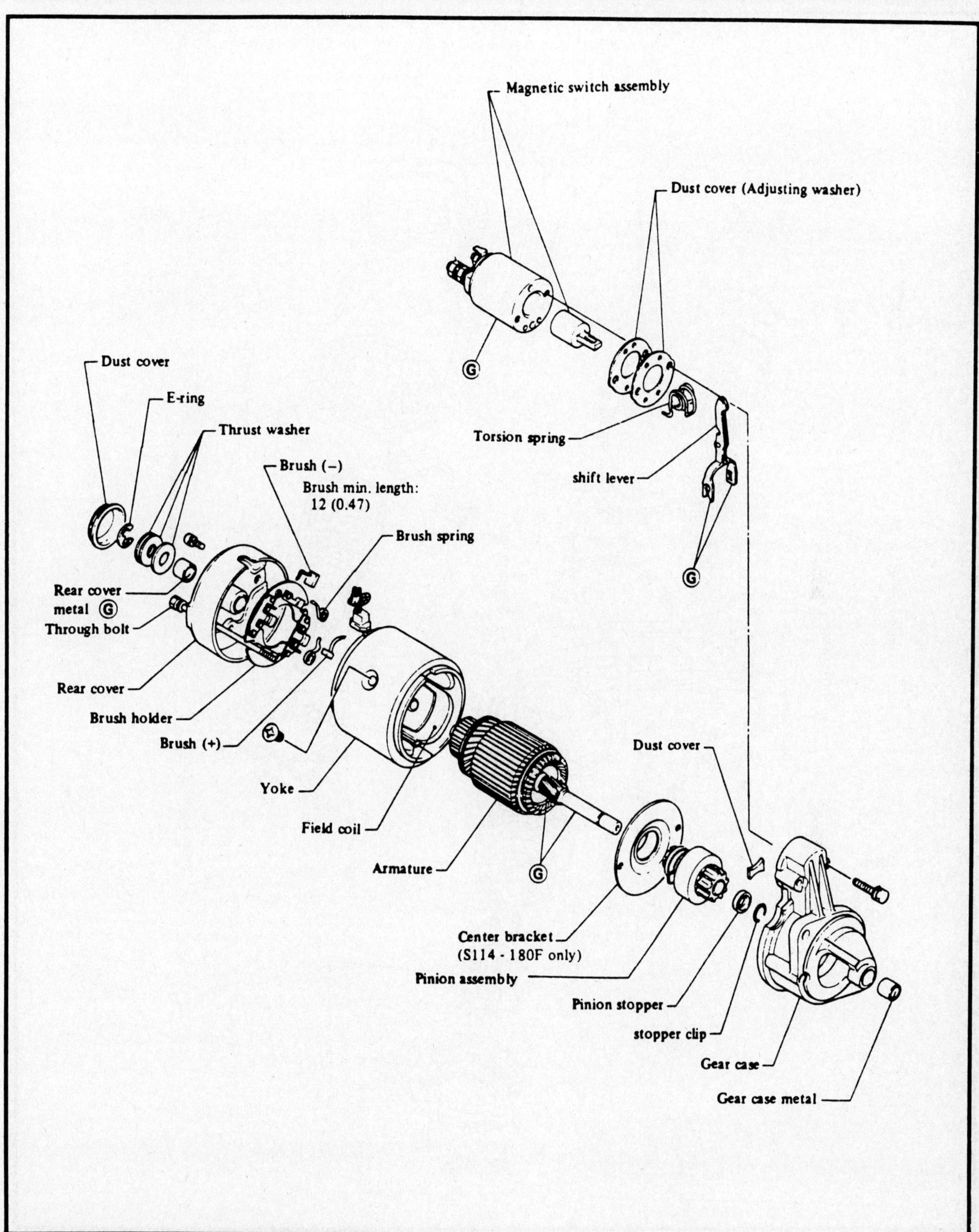

Datsun Non Reduction gear starter—typical

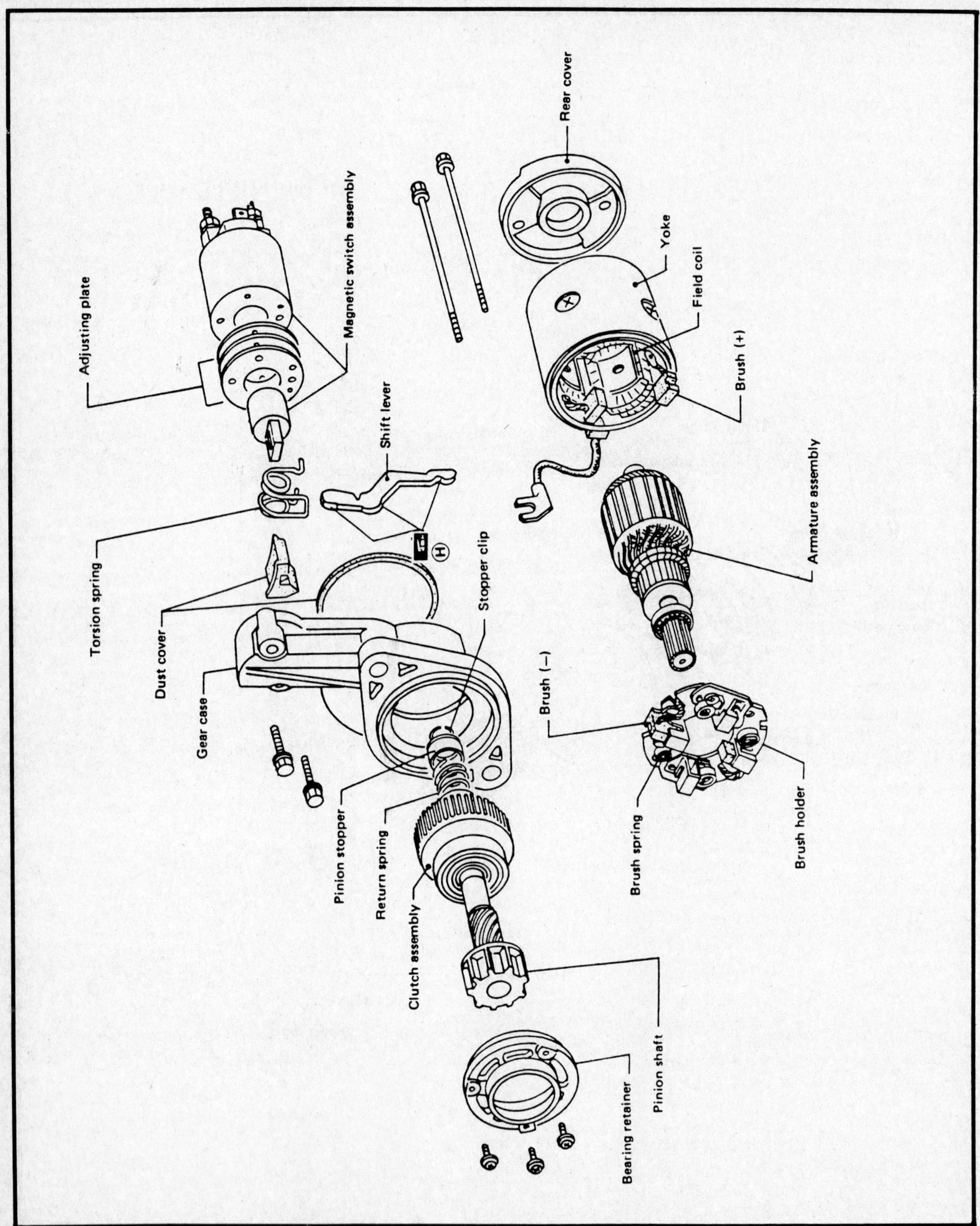

Datsun Reduction gear starter—typical

Datsun Starting System

NON-REDUCTION GEAR TYPE STARTER

Brush Replacement

1. With the starter out of the vehicle, remove the bolts holding the solenoid to the top of the starter and remove the solenoid.
2. To remove the brushes, remove the two thru-bolts and the two rear cover attaching screws and remove the rear cover.
3. Disconnect the electrical leads and remove the brushes.
4. Install the brushes in the reverse order of removal.

REDUCTION GEAR TYPE STARTER

1. Remove the starter. Remove the solenoid.
2. Remove the through bolts and the rear cover. The rear cover can be pried off, but be careful not to damage the O-ring.
3. Remove the starter housing, armature and brush holder from the center housing. They can be removed as an assembly.
4. Remove the positive side brush from its holder. The positive brush is insulated from the brush holder and its lead wire is connected to the field coil.
5. Carefully lift the negative brush from the commutator and remove it from the holder.
6. Installation is the reverse of the removal procedure.

NON-REDUCTION GEAR TYPE STARTER DRIVE

Replacement

1. With the starter motor removed from the vehicle, remove the solenoid from the starter.
2. Remove the two thru-bolts and separate the gear from the yoke housing.
3. Remove the pinion stopper clip and the pinion stopper.
4. Slide the starter drive off the armature shaft.
5. Install the starter drive and reassemble the starter in the reverse order of removal.

REDUCTION GEAR TYPE STARTER DRIVE

Replacement

1. Remove the starter.
2. Remove the solenoid and the shift lever.
3. Remove the bolts securing the center housing to the front cover and separate the parts.
4. Remove the gears and starter drive.
5. Installation is the reverse of the removal procedure.

Isuzu Starting System

STARTER BRUSHES

Replacement

1. With the starter out of the vehicle, remove the bolts holding the solenoid to the top of the starter and remove the solenoid.
2. To remove the brushes, remove the two through-bolts and the two rear cover attaching screws and remove the rear cover.
3. Disconnect the brushes, electrical leads and remove the brushes.
4. Install the brushes in the reverse order of removal.

STARTER DRIVE

Replacement

1. With the starter motor removed from the vehicle, remove the solenoid from the starter.
2. Remove the two through bolts and separate the gear case from the yoke housing.
3. Remove the pinion stopper clip and the pinion stopper.
4. Slide the starter drive off the armature shaft.
5. Install the starter drive and reassemble the starter in the reverse order of removal.

Mazda/Courier Starting System

STARTER BRUSHES

Replacement

1. Remove the starter. Remove the two screws attaching the brush end bearing cover and remove the bearing cover.
2. Remove the through bolts.
3. Remove the C washer, washer and spring from the brush end of the armature shaft.
4. Pull the brush end cover from the starter frame.
5. Unsolder the two brushes from the field terminals an slide the brush holder from the armature shaft.
6. Cut the two brush wires at the brush holder and solder two new brushes to the brush holder.
7. Install the brush holder on the armature shaft and install the brushes in the brush holder.
8. Install the brush end cover on the starter frame and be sure that the ear tabs of the brush holder are aligned with the through-bolt holes.
9. Install the through bolts.
10. Install the rubber gasket, spring, washer and C washer on the armature shaft.
11. Install the brush end bearing cover on the brush end cover and install the two screws. If the brush holder tabs are not aligned with the through bolts, the bearing cover screws cannot be installed.

SOLENOID

Replacement

1. Remove the starter from the engine.
2. Disconnect the field strap from the solenoid terminal.
3. Remove the two solenoid attaching screws.
4. Disengage the solenoid plunger from the shift fork and remove the solenoid.
5. Install the solenoid on the drive end housing, making sure that the solenoid plunger hook is engaged with the shift fork.
6. Apply 12 volts to the solenoid "S" terminal and measure the clearance between the starter drive and the stop-ring retainer. It should be 0.080–0.200 in. If not, remove the solenoid and adjust the clearance by inserting an adjusting shim between the solenoid body and drive end housing.
7. Check the solenoid for proper operation and install the starter.
8. Check the operation of the starter.

STARTER

Disassembly And Assembly

1. Remove the starter from the engine.
2. Disconnect the field strap from the solenoid.
3. Remove the screws attaching the solenoid to the drive end housing. Disengage the solenoid plunger hook from the shift fork and remove the solenoid.

1. Lead wire
2. Through bolt
3. Yoke
4. Brush and brush holder
5. Armature
6. Screw
7. Drive side housing
8. Two pinions
9. Overrunning clutch and retainer
10. Return spring
11. Steel ball

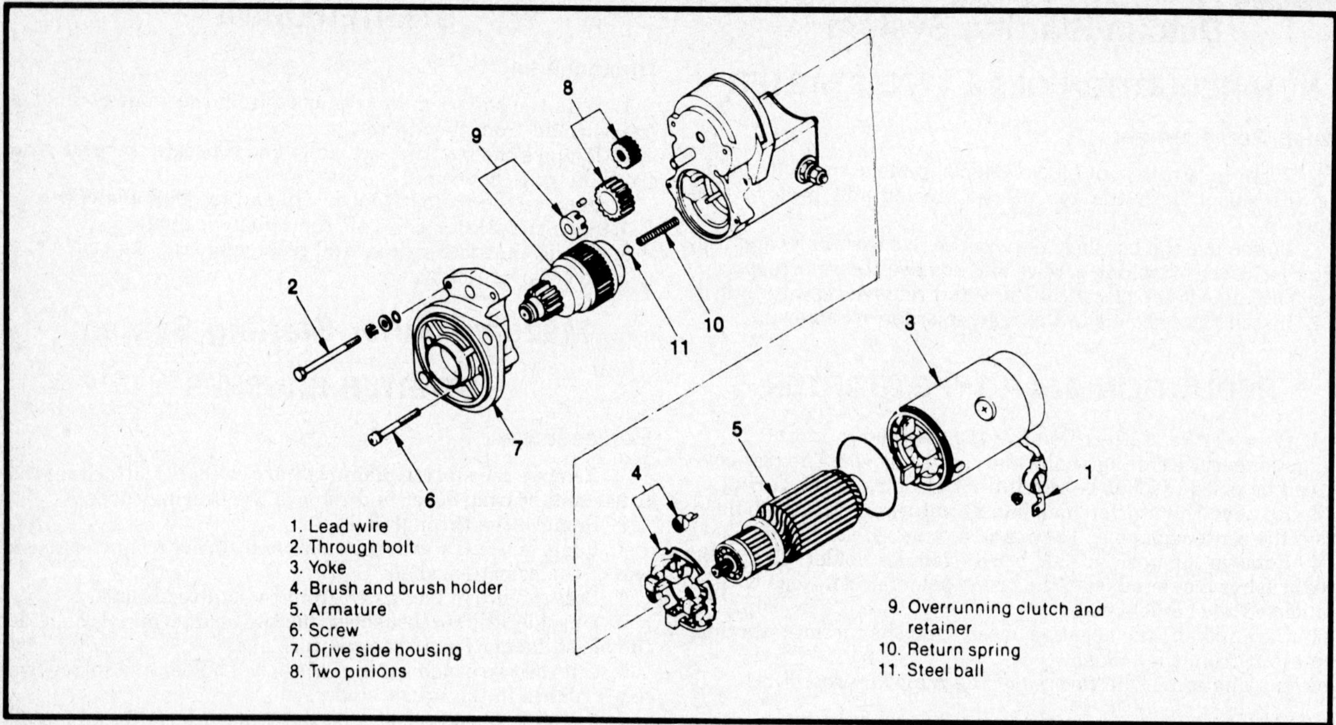

Isuzu starter—diesel engine

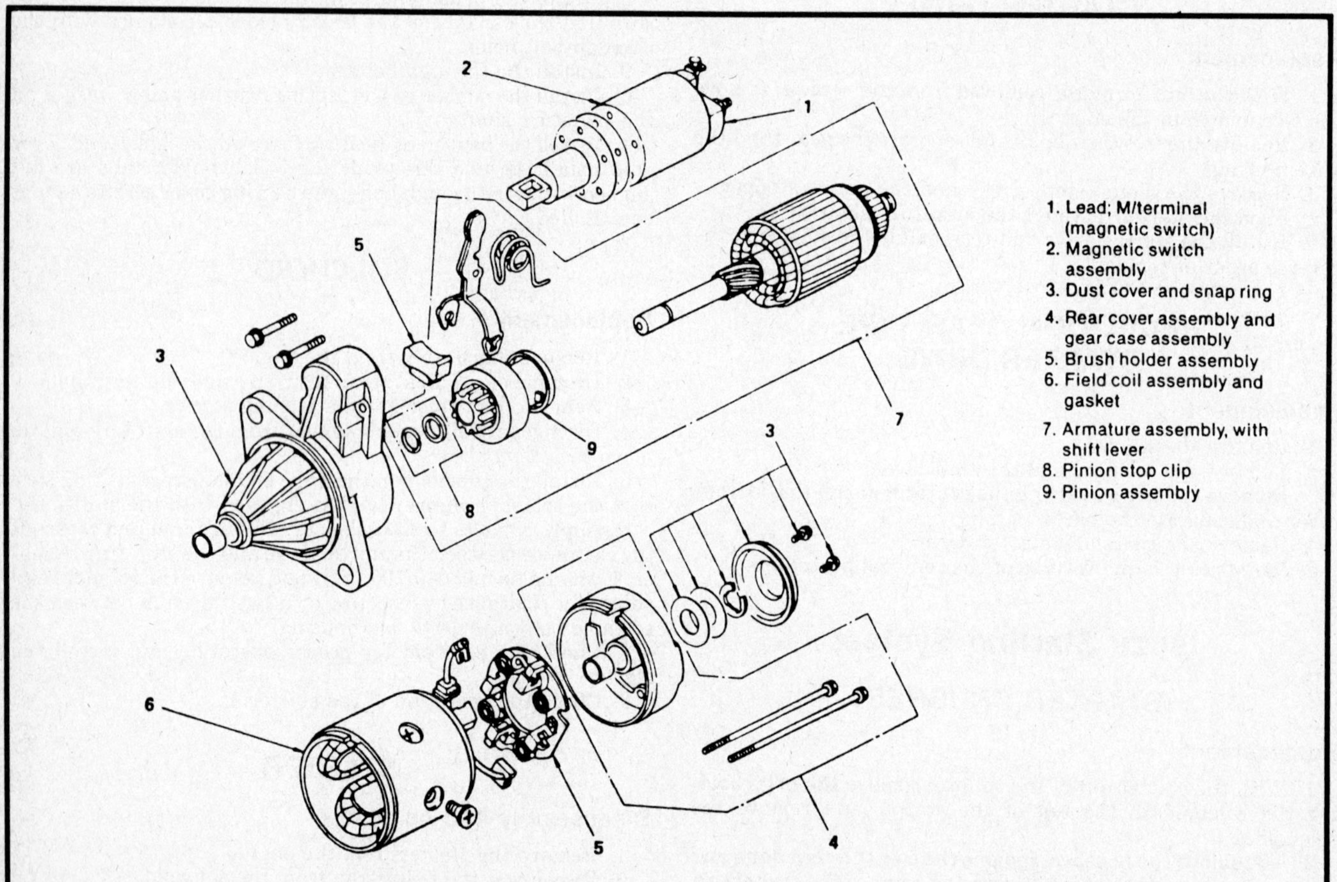

1. Lead; M/terminal (magnetic switch)
2. Magnetic switch assembly
3. Dust cover and snap ring
4. Rear cover assembly and gear case assembly
5. Brush holder assembly
6. Field coil assembly and gasket
7. Armature assembly, with shift lever
8. Pinion stop clip
9. Pinion assembly

Isuzu starter—gasoline engine

4. Remove the shift fork pivot bolt, nut and lockwasher.
5. Remove the through bolts and separate the drive end housing from the starter frame. At the same time, disengage the shift fork from the drive assembly.
6. Remove the two screws attaching the brush end bearing cover to the brush end cover.
7. Remove the C washer, washer and spring from the brush end of the armature shaft.
8. Pull the brush end cover from the starter frame.
9. Slide the armature from the starter frame and brushes.
10. Slide the drive stop-ring retainer toward the armature and remove the stop-ring. Slide the retainer and drive assembly off the armature shaft.
11. Remove the field brushes from the brush holder and separate the brush holder from the starter frame.
12. Position the drive assembly on the armature shaft.
13. Position the drive stop-ring retainer on the armature shaft and install the drive stop-ring. Slide the stop-ring retainer over the stop-ring to secure the stop-ring on the shaft.
14. Position the armature in the starter frame. Install the brush holder on the armature and starter frame. Install the brushes in the brush holder.
15. Install the drive end housing on the armature shaft and starter housing. Engage the shift fork with the starter drive assembly as the drive end housing is moved toward the starter frame.
16. Install the brush end cover on the starter frame making sure that the rear tabs of the brush holder are aligned with the through-bolt holes.
17. Install the through-bolts.
18. Install the rubber washer, spring, washer and C-washer on the armature shaft at the brush end. Install the brush end bearing cover on the brush end cover and install the attaching screws. If the brush end cover is not properly positioned, the bearing cover screws cannot be installed.
19. Align the shift fork with the pivot bolt hole and install the pivot bolt, lockwasher and nut. Tighten the nut securely.
20. Position the solenoid on the drive end housing. Be sure that the solenoid plunger hook is engaged with the shift fork.
21. Install the two solenoid retaining screws and washers.
22. Apply 12 volts to the solenoid "S" terminal (ground the "M" terminal) and check the clearance between the starter drive and the stop-ring retainer. The clearance should be 0.080–0.200 in. If not, the solenoid plunger is not properly adjusted. The clearance can be adjusted by inserting an adjusting shim between the solenoid body and drive end housing.
23. Install the field strap and tighten the nut.
24. Install the starter. Check the operation of the starter.

Mitsubishi, Arrow, Ram 50, Ram Raider Starting System

DIRECT DRIVE TYPE STARTER DRIVE, SOLENOID AND BRUSHES

Replacement

1. Remove the wire connecting the starter solenoid to the starter.
2. Remove the two screws holding the starter solenoid on the starter drive housing and remove the solenoid.
3. Remove the two long through bolts at the rear of the starter and separate the armature yoke from the armature.
4. Carefully remove the armature and the starter drive engagement lever from the front bracket, noting the way they are positioned along with the attendant spring and spring retainer.
5. Loosen the two screws and remove the rear bracket.
6. Tap the stopper ring at the end of the drive gear engagement shaft in towards the drive gear to expose the snapring. Remove the snapring.
7. Pull the stopper, drive gear and overrunning clutch from the end of the shaft.
8. Inspect the pinion and spline teeth for wear or damage. If the engagement teeth are damaged, visually check the flywheel ring gear through the starter hole to insure that it is not damaged. It will be necessary to turn the engine over by hand to completely inspect the ring gear.

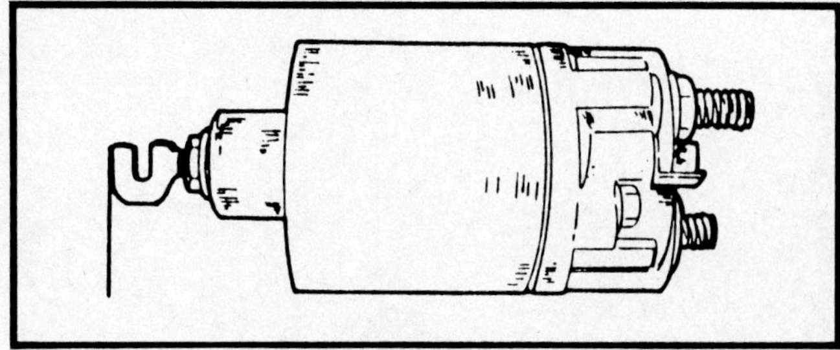

Starter solenoid plunger adjustment—adjust to 0.8 in.

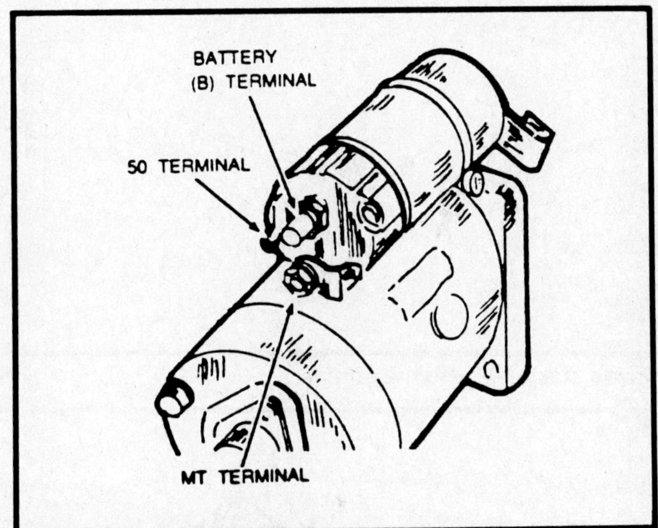

Starter solenoid terminals

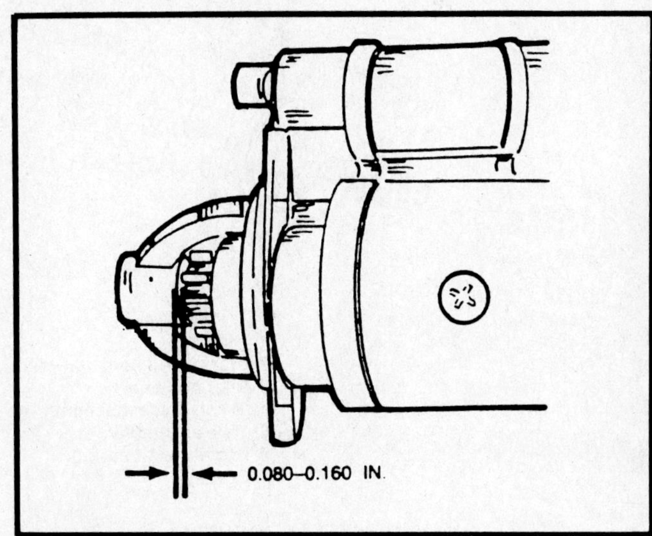

Starter drive and clearance

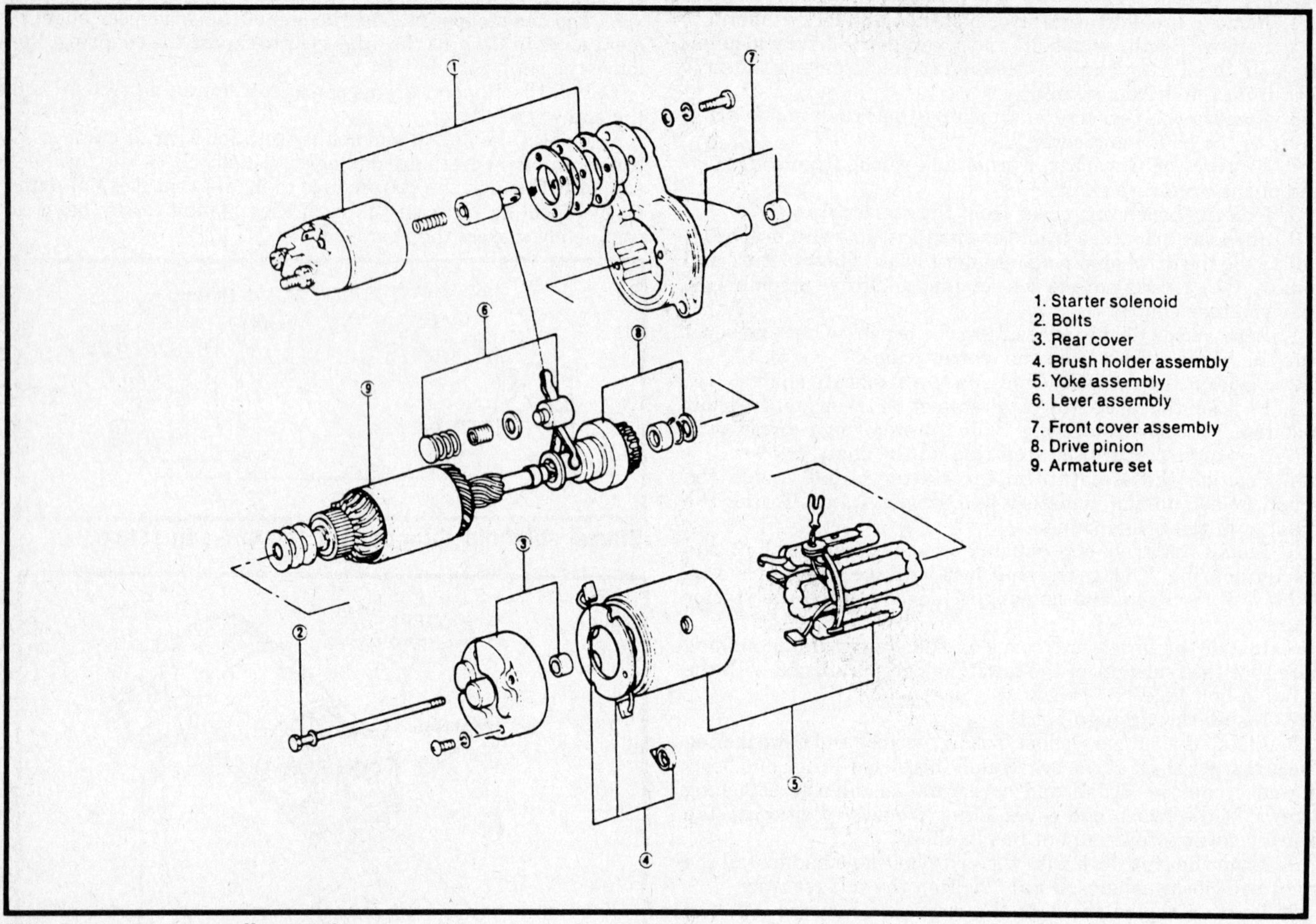

1. Starter solenoid
2. Bolts
3. Rear cover
4. Brush holder assembly
5. Yoke assembly
6. Lever assembly
7. Front cover assembly
8. Drive pinion
9. Armature set

Mazda starter—gasoline engine

1. Glow switch
2. Starter solenoid
3. Rear housing
4. Brush holder assembly
5. Yoke assembly
6. Armature & bearing
7. Cover
8. Center bracket
9. Drive pinion
10. Pinion shaft
11. Gear
12. Lever & spring
13. Over running clutch
14. Front housing assembly

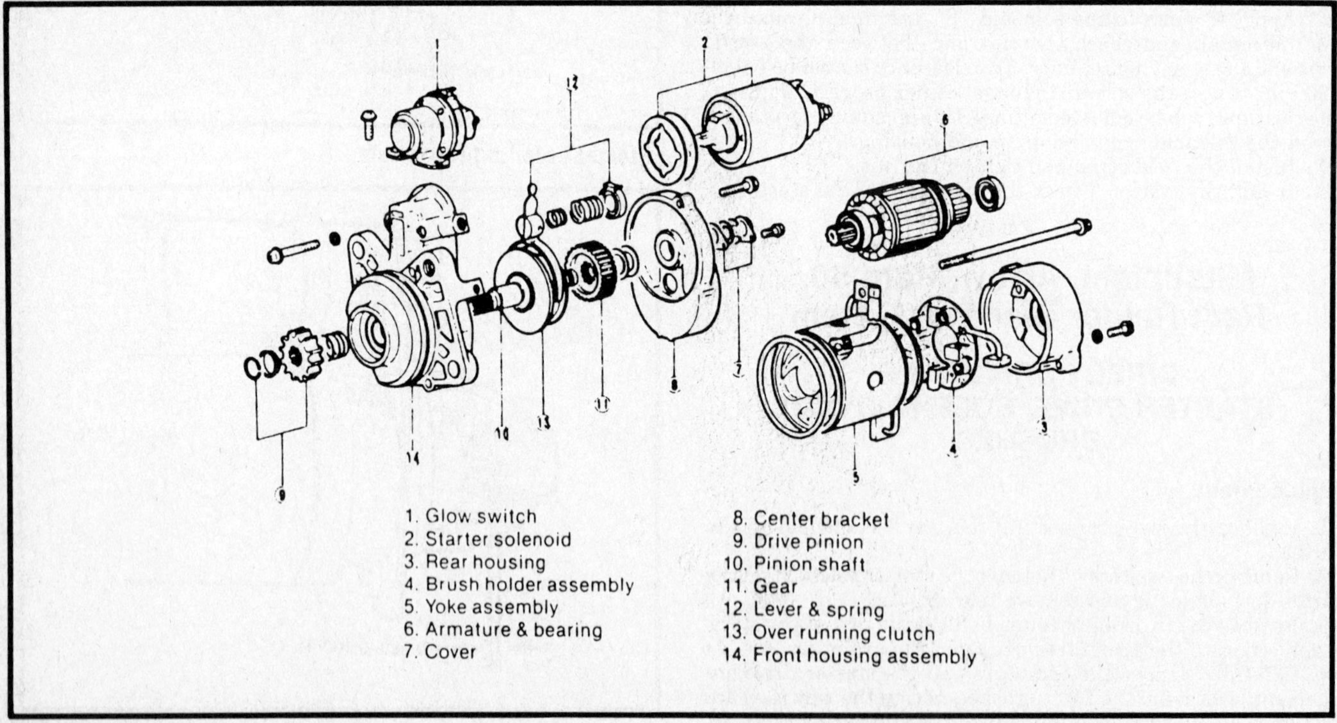

Mazda starter—diesel engine

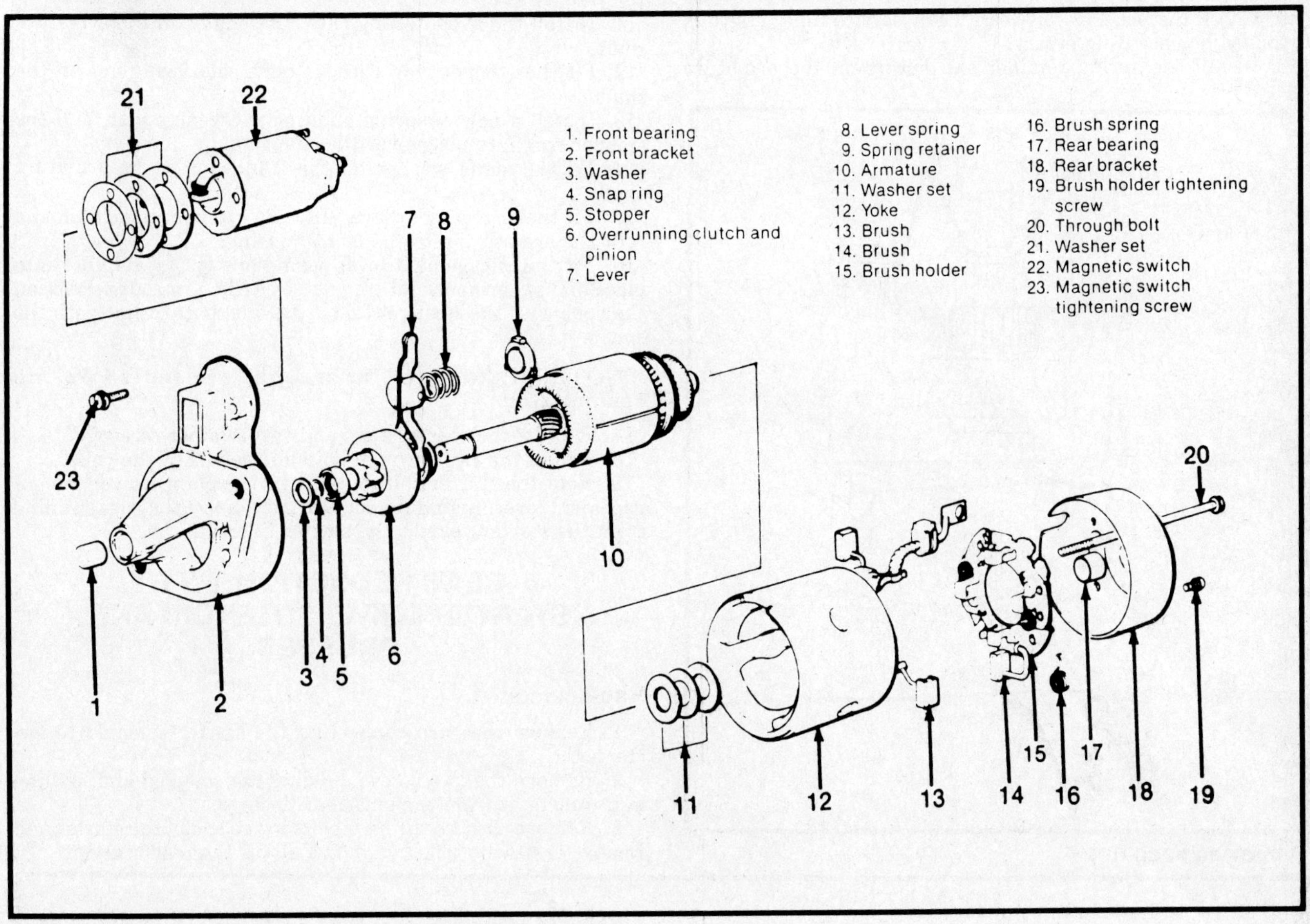

1. Front bearing
2. Front bracket
3. Washer
4. Snap ring
5. Stopper
6. Overrunning clutch and pinion
7. Lever
8. Lever spring
9. Spring retainer
10. Armature
11. Washer set
12. Yoke
13. Brush
14. Brush
15. Brush holder
16. Brush spring
17. Rear bearing
18. Rear bracket
19. Brush holder tightening screw
20. Through bolt
21. Washer set
22. Magnetic switch
23. Magnetic switch tightening screw

Mitsubishi/Arrow/Ram 50/Raider direct drive starter

SOLENOID
SHIFT FORK
BEARING
DRIVE END HOUSING
DRIVE ASSEMBLY
STOP RING RETAINER
STOP RING
ARMATURE
BRUSH HOLDER
POLE SHOE
C-WASHER
SPRING
WASHER
FIELD COILS
STARTER FRAME
BEARING COVER
BEARING
BRUSH END COVER
THROUGH BOLT
BRUSH SPRING
BRUSH

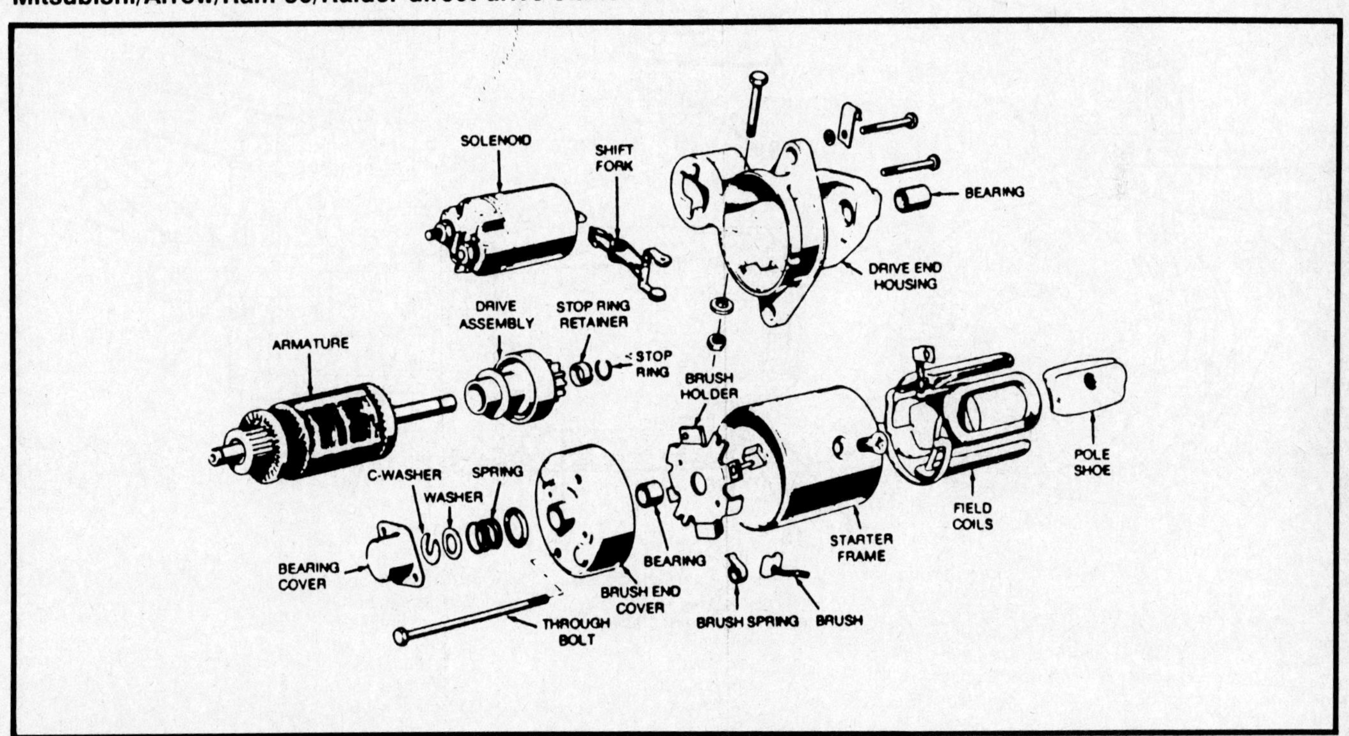

Courier starter—exploded view

9. Check the brushes for wear. Their service limit length is 0.453 in. Replace if necessary.

10. Install the spring retainer and spring on the armature shaft.

Snap ring
Stopper
Removing snap ring

11. Install the overrunning clutch assembly on the armature shaft.

12. Fit the stopper ring with its open side facing out on the shaft.

13. Install a new snapring and, using a gear puller, pull the stopper ring into place over the snapring.

14. Fit the small washer on the front end of the armature shaft.

15. Fit the engagement lever into the overrunning clutch and refit the armature into the front housing.

16. Fit the engagement lever spring and spring retainer into place and slide the armature yoke over the armature. Position the yoke with the spring retainer cut-out space in line with the spring retainer.

NOTE: Make sure the brushes are seated on the commutator.

17. Replace the rear bracket and two retainer screws.

18. Install the two through bolts in the end of the yoke.

19. Refit the starter solenoid, fitting the plunger over the engagement lever. Install the screws and connect the wire running from the starter yoke to the starter solenoid.

GEAR REDUCTION TYPE STARTER DRIVE, SOLENOID AND BRUSHES

Replacement

1. Remove the wire connecting the starter solenoid to the starter.

2. Remove the two screws holding the solenoid and, pulling out, unhook it from the engagement lever.

3. Remove the two through bolts in the end of the starter and remove the two bracket screws. Pull off the rear bracket.

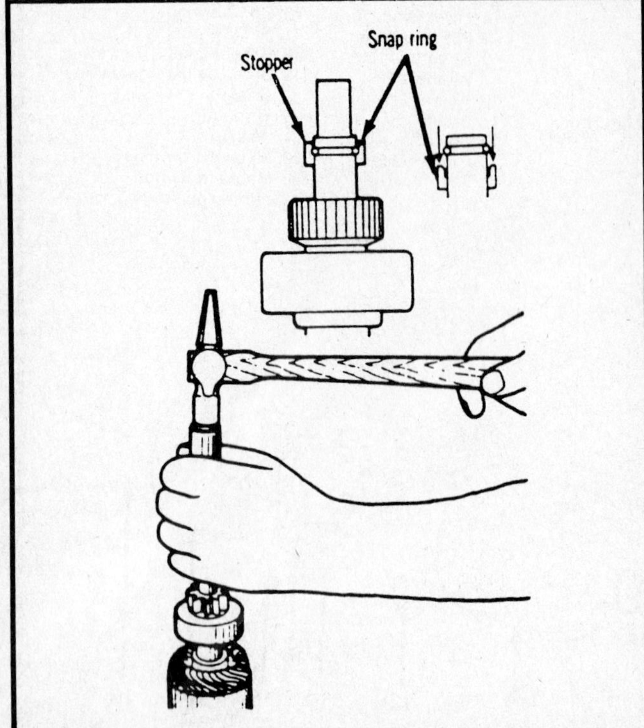

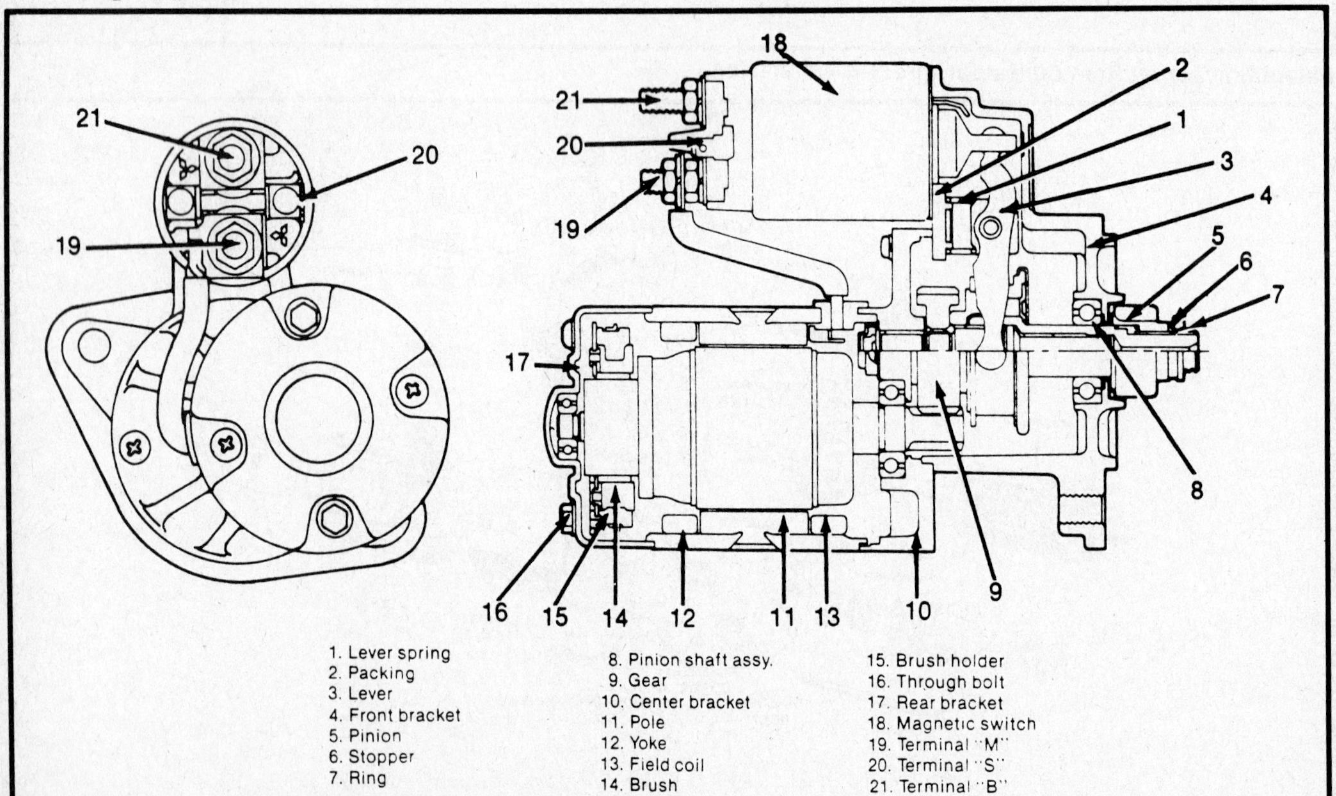

21
20
19
18
2
1
3
4
5
6
7
8
9
17
16
15
14
12
11
13
10
1. Lever spring
2. Packing
3. Lever
4. Front bracket
5. Pinion
6. Stopper
7. Ring
8. Pinion shaft assy.
9. Gear
10. Center bracket
11. Pole
12. Yoke
13. Field coil
14. Brush
15. Brush holder
16. Through bolt
17. Rear bracket
18. Magnetic switch
19. Terminal "M"
20. Terminal "S"
21. Terminal "B"
Mitsubishi/Arrow/Ram 50/Raider gear reduction starter

NOTE: Since the conical spring washer is contained in the rear bracket, be sure to take it out.

4. Remove the yoke and brush holder assembly while pulling the brush upward.
5. Pull the armature assembly out of the mounting bracket.
6. In the side of the mounting bracket that the armature fits into, there is a small dust cap held by two screws. Remove it and remove the snapring and washer under it.
7. Remove the remaining bolts in the mounting bracket and split the reduction case.

NOTE: Several washers will come out when the case is split. These adjust the end play for the pinion shaft. Do not lose them.

8. Remove the reduction gear, lever and lever spring from the front bracket.
9. Using a brass drift or deep socket, knock the stopper ring on the end of the shaft in toward the pinion. Remove the snapring. Remove the stopper, pinion and pinion shaft assembly.
10. Remove the ball bearings at both ends of the armature.

NOTE: The ball bearings are pressed in the front bracket and are not replaceable. Replace them together with the bracket.

11. Inspect the pinion and spline teeth for wear or damage. If the engagement teeth are damaged, visually check the flywheel ring gear through the starter hole to insure that it is not damaged also. It will be necessary to turn the engine over by hand to completely inspect the ring gear.
12. Check the brushes for wear. Their service limit length is 0.453 in. Replace if necessary.
13. Assembly is the reverse of disassembly. Be sure to replace all adjusting and thrust washers. When replacing the rear bracket, fit the conical spring pinion washer with its convex side facing out. Make sure that the brushes seat themselves on the commutator.

Toyota Starting System

DIRECT DRIVE TYPE STARTER DRIVE

Replacement

1. Remove the field coil lead from the solenoid terminal.
2. Remove the solenoid retaining screws. Remove the solenoid by tilting it upward and withdrawing it.
3. Remove the through bolts, then the drive housing from the field frame.
4. Remove the end frame cap screws, the cap, the C-lock and the washer from the commutator end frame. Remove the commutator end frame from the field frame.
5. Withdraw the brushes from their holder if they are to be replaced.

NOTE: Check the brush length against the specifications. Replace the brushes with new ones if required.

6. Remove the armature assembly through the front of the field frame.

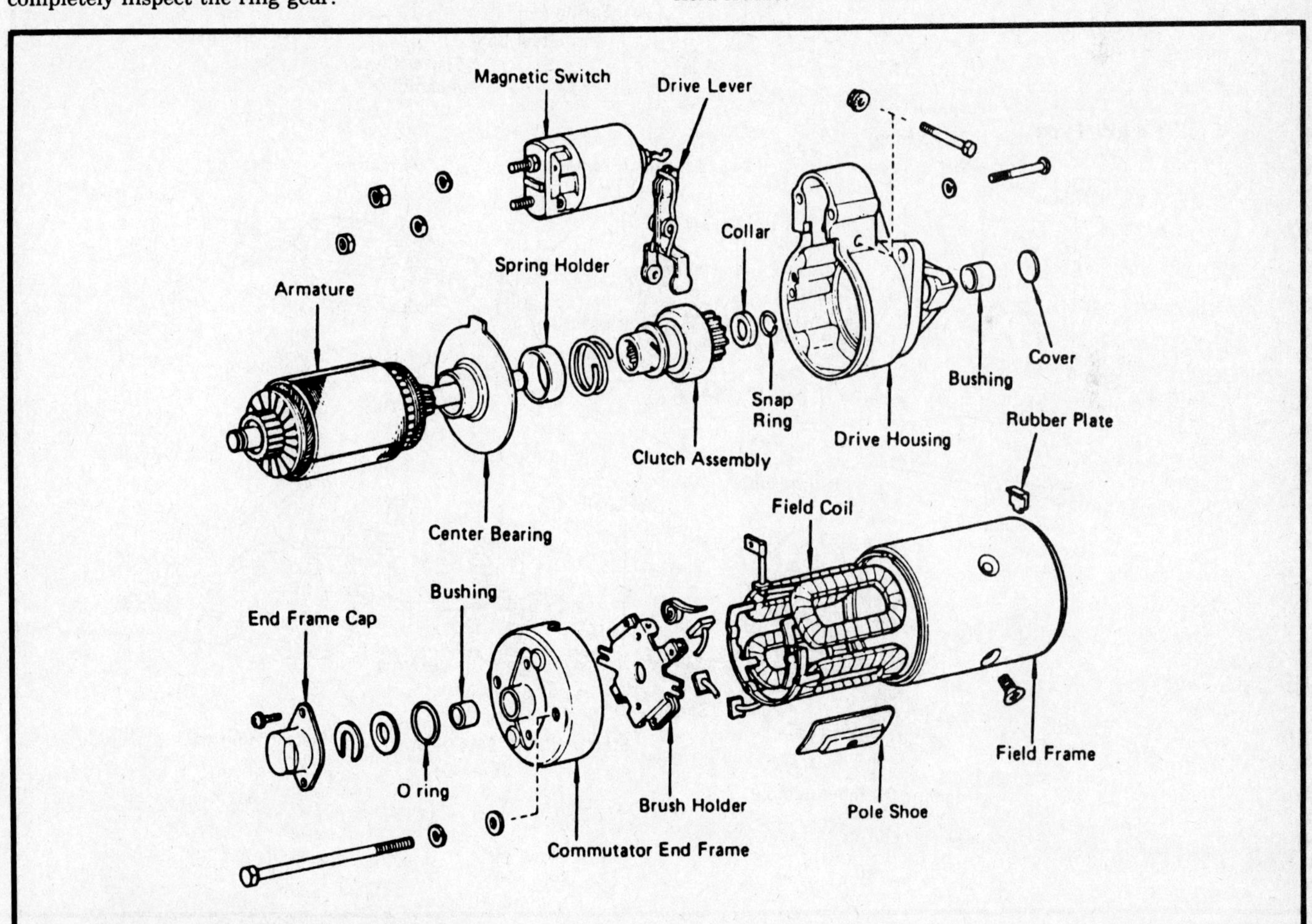

Toyota—direct drive starter—typical

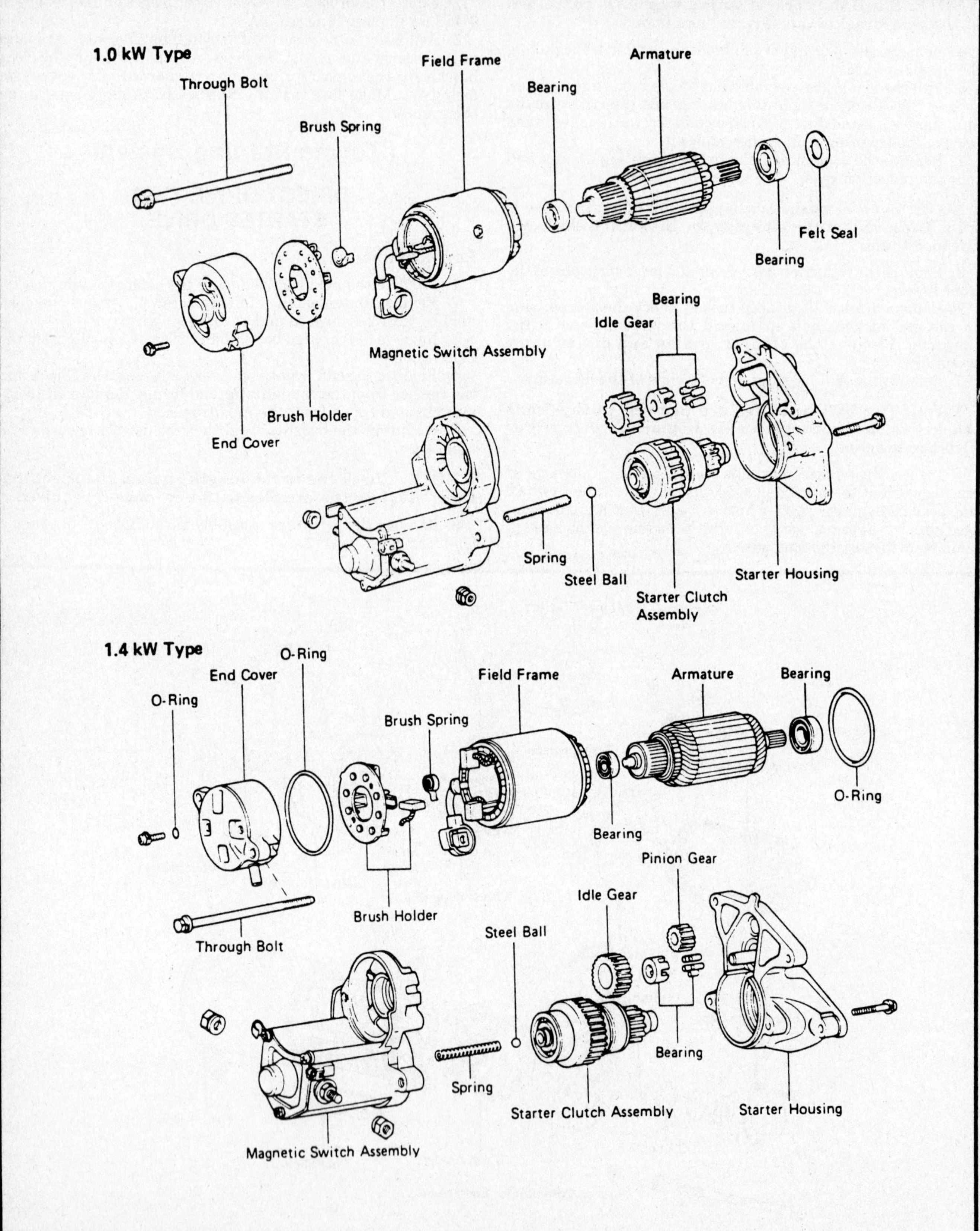

Toyota reduction type starter

7. Place the armature vertically on a block of wood with the clutch assembly facing upwards.

8. Using a 14mm socket and a hammer, drive the stop collar (on the shaft) toward the armature to expose the snap ring.

9. Remove the snap ring, the stop collar and the drive assembly from the shaft.

10. To assemble, reverse the disassembly procedures. Pack the end bearing cover with multipurpose grease before installing it.

REDUCTION TYPE STARTER DRIVE

Repalcement

NOTE: The starter must be removed from the vehicle, in order to perform this operation.

1. Remove the starter housing-to-field frame bolts and the starter housing-to-solenoid bolts, then separate the starter housing from the solenoid/field frame assembly.

2. On the 1.0 kw type, withdraw the clutch and idler gear. On the 1.4 kw, withdraw the pinion gear, the idler gear and the clutch.

3. To install, grease the moving parts and reverse the removal procedures.

Volkswagen Starting System

NOTE: A new type of starter has been installed on some models that are equipped with a manual transmission. The new style starter is not interchangeable with the old design.

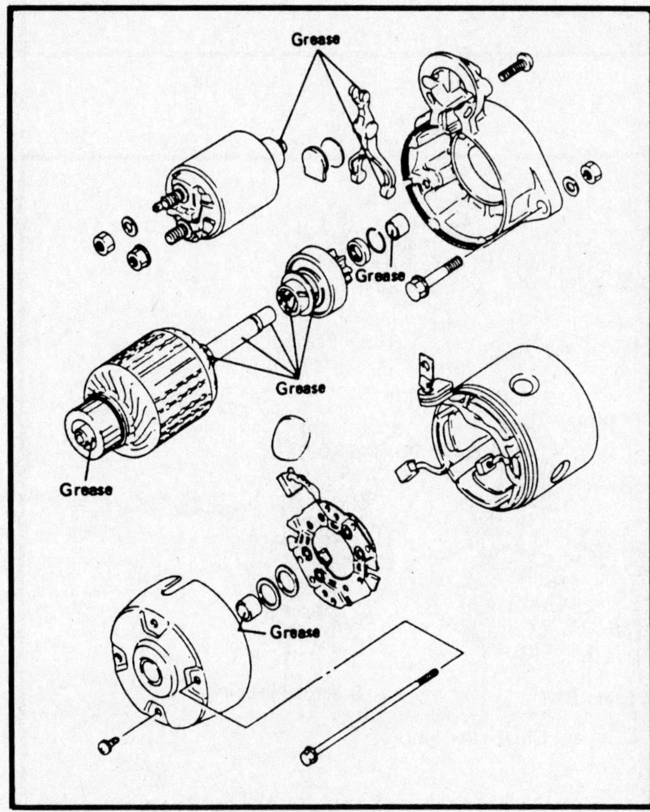

Suzuki starter motor greasing points

3. Take out the two retaining screws on the mounting bracket and pull out the solenoid after it has been unhooked from the operating lever.

4. Installation is the reverse of removal. In order to facilitate engagement of the lever, the pinion should be pulled out as far as possible when inserting the solenoid.

Suzuki Samurai Starting System

STARTER MOTOR

Dissassembly And Assembly

1. Remove the nut securing the end of the field coil lead to the terminal on the head of the magnetic switch.

2. Remove the two magnetic switch mounting screws and remove the switch from the motor body.

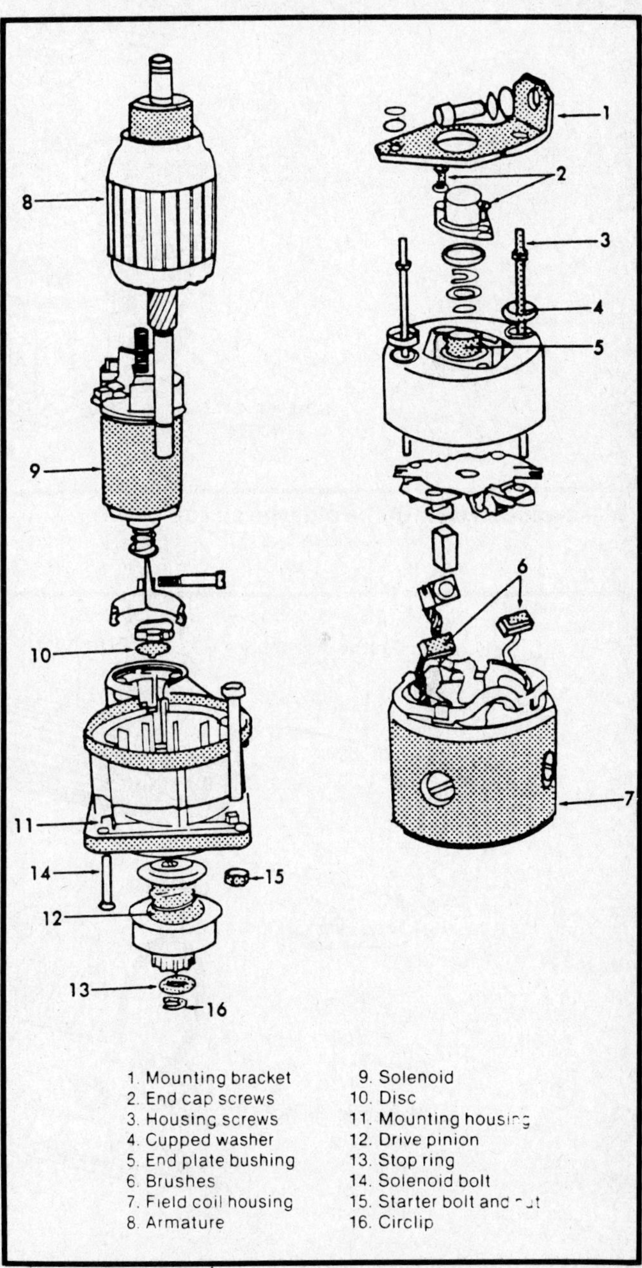

VW—exploded view of the new type starter

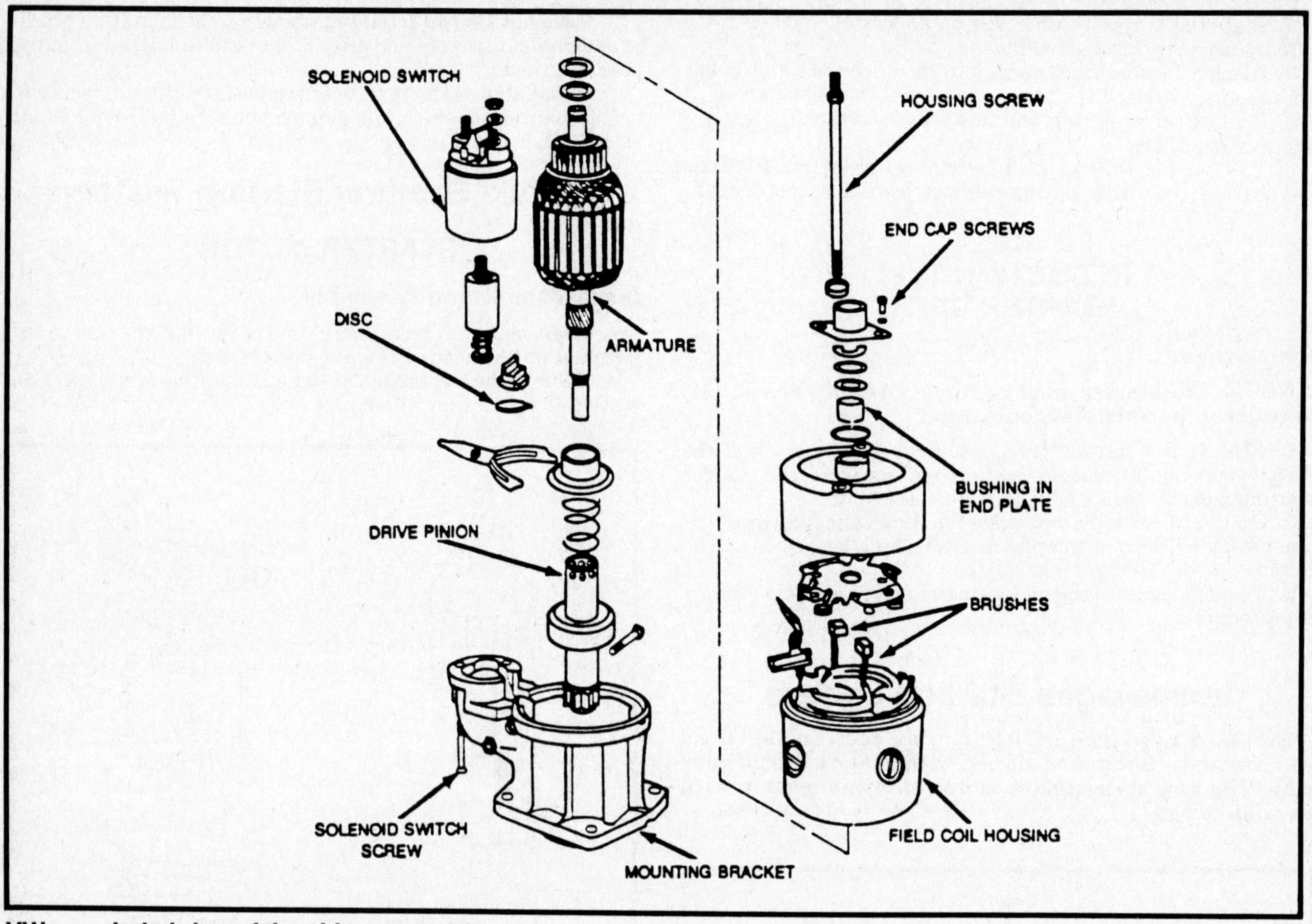

SOLENOID SWITCH
HOUSING SCREW
END CAP SCREWS
DISC
ARMATURE
BUSHING IN END PLATE
DRIVE PINION
BRUSHES
SOLENOID SWITCH SCREW
FIELD COIL HOUSING
MOUNTING BRACKET

VW—exploded view of the old type starter

Field Frame Assembly
Armature
Felt Seal
Brush Spring
Brush Holder
Pinion Gear
Idler Gear
O-ring
Magnetic Switch Assembly
Steel Ball
Starter Housing
Clutch Assembly

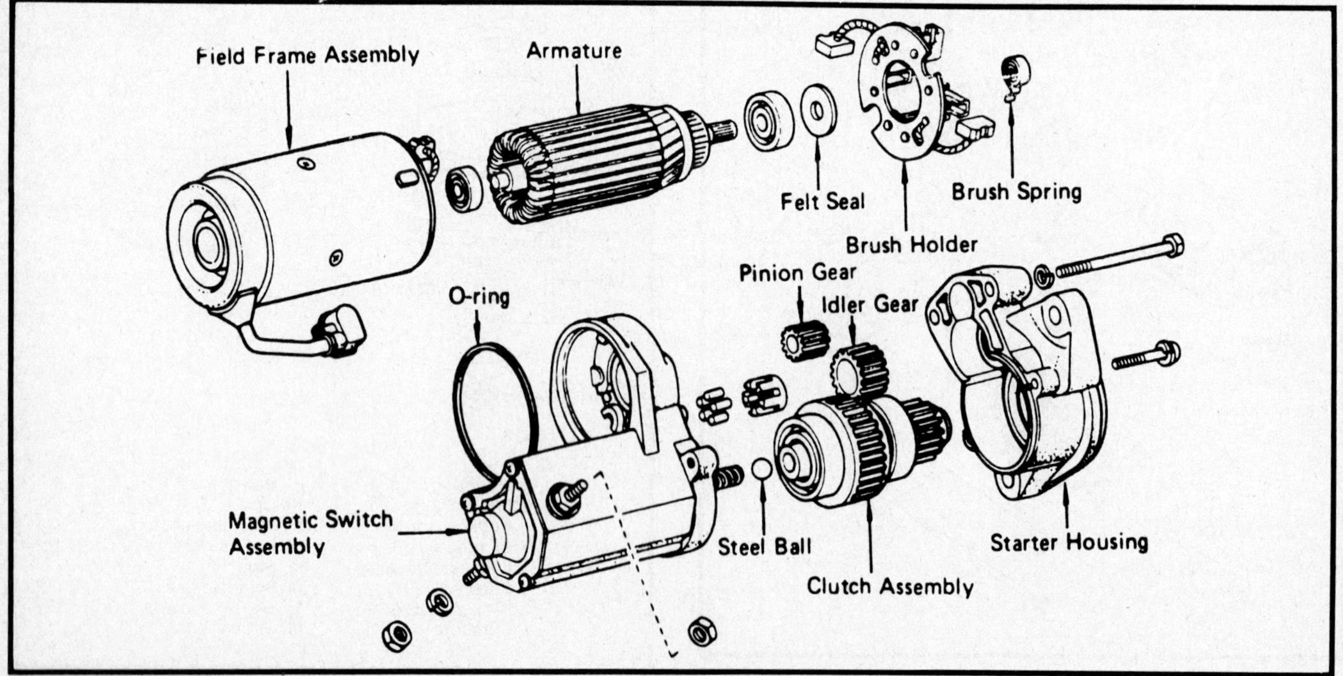

Toyota—diesel engine starter

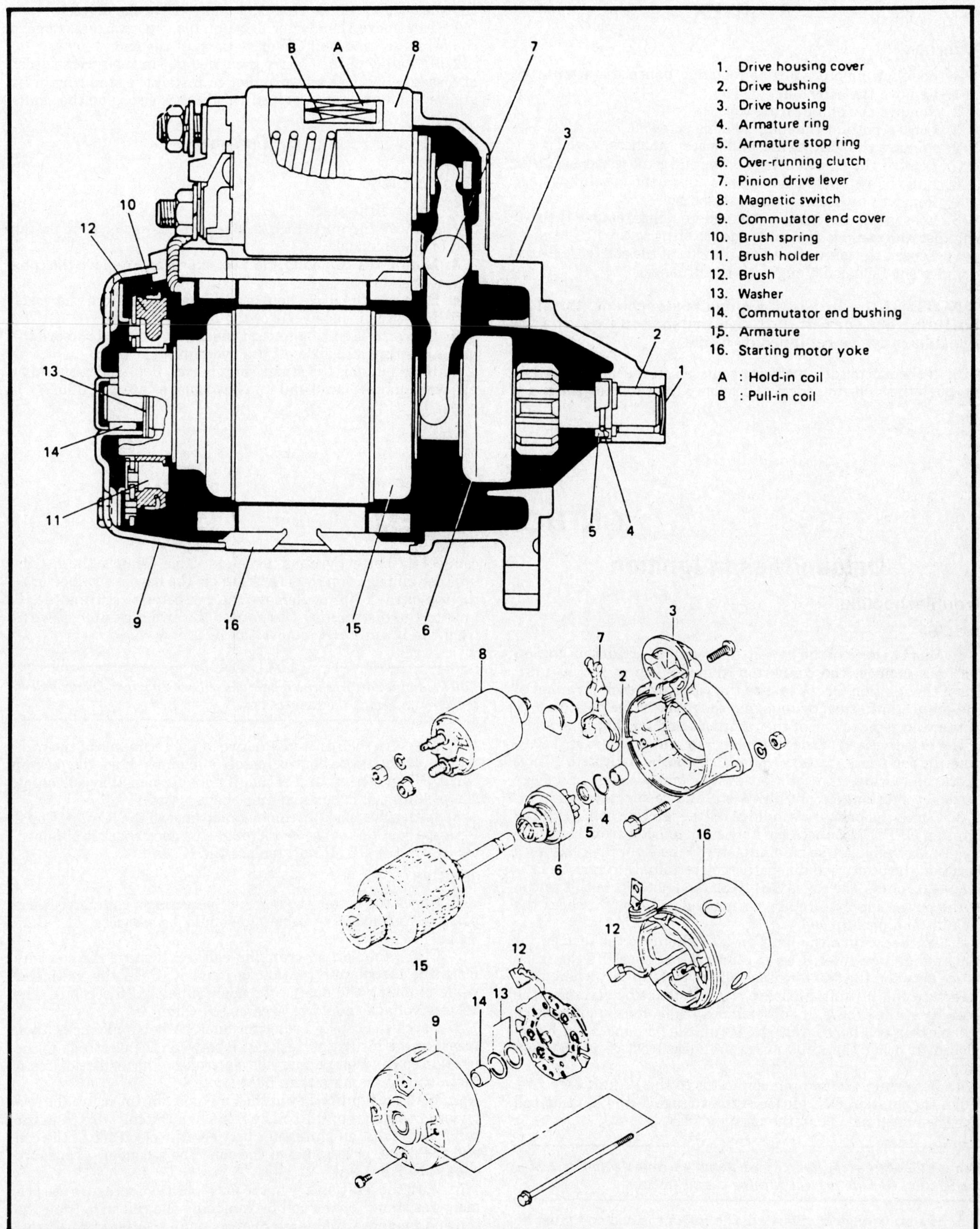
1. Drive housing cover
2. Drive bushing
3. Drive housing
4. Armature ring
5. Armature stop ring
6. Over-running clutch
7. Pinion drive lever
8. Magnetic switch
9. Commutator end cover
10. Brush spring
11. Brush holder
12. Brush
13. Washer
14. Commutator end bushing
15. Armature
16. Starting motor yoke
A : Hold-in coil
B : Pull-in coil

Suzuki starter motor

STARTER

Overhaul

Use the following procedure to replace brushes or starter drive.

1. Remove the solenoid.
2. Remove the end bearing cap.
3. Loosen both of the long housing screws.
4. Remove the lockwasher and spacer washers.
5. Remove the long housing screws and remove the end cover.
6. Pull the two field coil brushes out of the brush housing.
7. Remove the brush housing assembly.
8. Loosen the nut on the solenoid housing, remove the sealing disc and remove the solenoid operating lever.
9. Loosen the large screws on the side of the starter body and remove the field coil along with the brushes.

NOTE: If the brushes require replacement, the field coil and brushes and/or the brush housing and its brushes must be replaced as a unit.

10. If the starter drive is being replaced on the new type starter, push the stop-ring down and remove the circlip on the end of the shaft. Remove the stop-ring and remove the drive.
11. To remove the starter drive on old type starters, remove the armature and pull the drive unit off the end.
12. Assembly of the starter is carried out in the reverse order of disassembly. Use a gear puller to install the stop-ring in its groove (on models so equipped). Use a new circlip on the shaft.

SOLENOID

Replacement

1. Remove the starter.
2. Remove the nut which secures the connector strip on the end of the solenoid.
3. Loosen the two bolts and two screws and remove the commutator end cover.
4. Separate the drive housing and armature from the yoke.
5. Draw the brushes out of the holder.
6. Draw the stop ring toward the clutch side and remove the armature ring and slide off the overrunning clutch.
7. Installation is the reverse of removal. Replace brushes that are worn more than 0.450 in. New brushes are 0.670 in.

IGNITION SYSTEM

Datsun/Nissan Ignition

Troubleshooting

1982-85

1. Make a check of the power supply circuit. Turn the ignition OFF. Disconnect the connector from the top of the IC unit. Turn the ignition ON. Measure the voltage at each terminal of the connector in turn by touching the probe of the positive lead of the voltmeter to one of the terminals and touching the probe of the negative lead of the voltmeter to a ground, such as the engine. In each case, battery voltage should be indicated. If not, check all wiring, the ignition switch and all connectors for breaks, corrosion, discontinuity, etc. and repair as necessary.
2. Check the primary windings off the ignition coil. Turn the ignition OFF. Disconnect the harness connector from the negative coil terminals. Use an ohmmeter to measure the resistance between the positive and negative coil terminals. If resistance is 0.84–1.02 ohms, the coil is OK. Replace, if not within this range. If the power supply, circuits, wiring and coil are OK, check the IC unit and pick-up coil.
3. To check, turn the ignition OFF. Remove the distributor cap and ignition rotor. Use an ohmmeter to measure the resistance between the two terminals of the pick-up coil, where they attach to the IC unit. Measure the resistance by reversing the polarity of the probes. If approximately 400 ohms are indicated, the pick-up coil is OK, but the IC unit is bad and must be replaced. If other than 400 ohms are measured, go to the next step.
4. Be certain the two pin connector to the IC unit is secure. Turn the ignition ON. Measure the voltage at the ignition coil negative terminal. Turn the ignition OFF.

CAUTION

Remove the tester probe from the coil negative terminal before switching the ignition OFF, to prevent burning out the tester.

5. If zero voltage is indicated, the IC unit is bad and must be replaced. If battery voltage is indicated, proceed.
6. Remove the IC unit from the distributor as follows: Disconnect the battery ground (negative) cable. Remove the distributor cap and ignition rotor. Disconnect the harness connector at the top of the IC unit. Remove the two screws securing the IC unit to the distributor. Disconnect the two pick-up coil wires from the IC unit and remove the IC unit.

CAUTION

Pull the connectors free with a pair of needlenosed pliers. Do not pull on the wires to detach the connectors.

7. Measure the resistance between the terminals of the pick-up coil. It should be approximately 400 ohms. If so, the pick-up coil is OK and the IC unit is bad. If not approximately 400 ohms, the pick-up coil is bad and must be replaced.
8. With a new pick-up coil installed, install the IC unit. Check for a spark at one of the spark plugs. If a good spark is obtained, the IC unit is OK. If not, replace the IC unit.

1986–88

1. Check the battery voltage by connecting a voltmeter to the positive and negative cables it should be between 11.5–12.5 volts.
2. Check the battery cranking voltage. Remove the coil wire from the distributor cap and ground it. Read the voltmeter while cranking the engine for approximately 15 seconds. The battery voltage should be greater 9.6 volts.
3. Check the cap and rotor for dust, carbon and cracks, then measure the insulation resistance between the electrode to the ignition coil and spark plug side electrodes. The insulation resistance should be more than 50M Ω.
4. With the ignition key in the OFF position, measure the secondary resistance of the coil by removing the coil wire from the coil and connect an ohmmeter between the electrode of the coil and the negative terminal of the coil. The secondary resistance should be 0.8–1.0 Ω.
5. With the ignition key in the OFF position, measure the primary resistance of the coil by removing the coil wire from the coil and connect an ohmmeter between the positive and negative terminals of the coil. The secondary resistance should be 7.6–11.4k Ω.

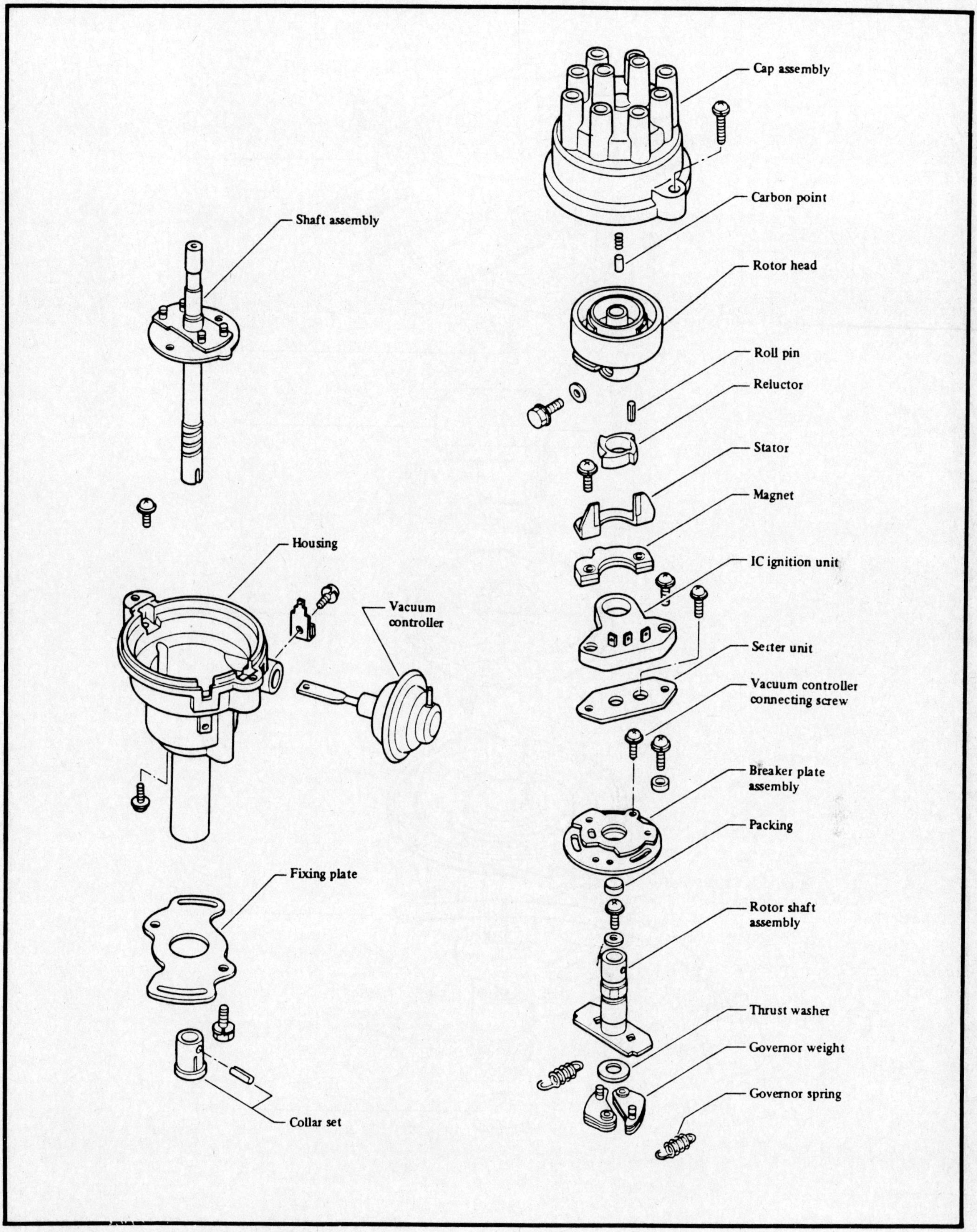

Cap assembly

Carbon point

Shaft assembly

Rotor head

Roll pin

Reluctor

Stator

Magnet

Housing

IC ignition unit

Vacuum
controller

Setter unit

Vacuum controller
connecting screw

Breaker plate
assembly

Packing

Fixing plate

Rotor shaft
assembly

Thrust washer

Governor weight

Governor spring

Collar set

Datsun/Nissan distributor—1982–85

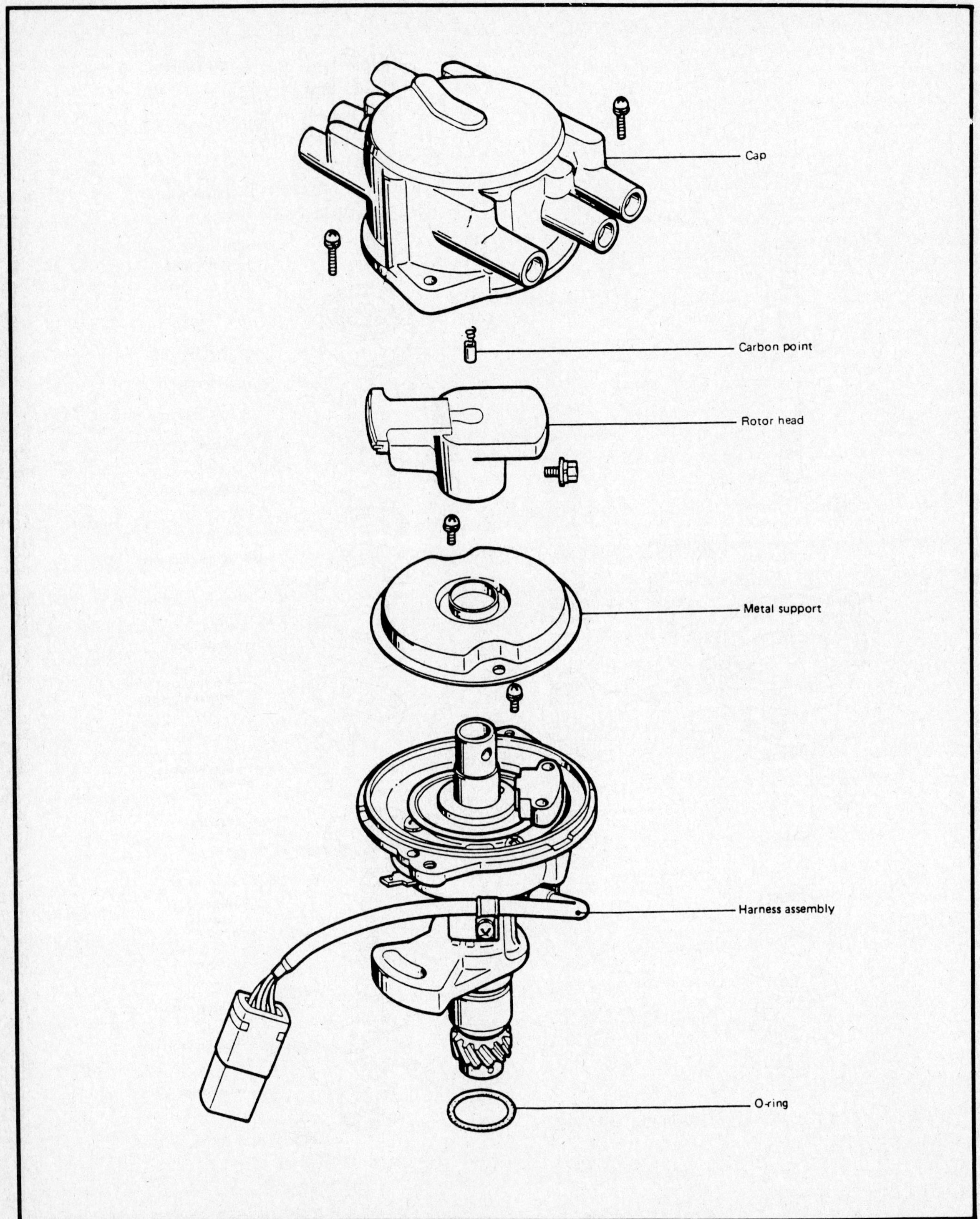

Datsun/Nissan distributor—1986–88 VG30i V6 engine

DISTRIBUTOR

Disassembly

1982-85

1. Remove the distributor cap and rotor haed.
2. Pry the reluctor from the shaft.
3. Remove the IC ignition and setter unit.
4. Remove the stator and magnet.
5. Remove the vacuum control assembly.
6. Remove the breaker plate.
7. Mark the housing and fixing plate and remove the fixing plate.
8. Remove the collar.
9. Remove the bearing retainer attaching bolts.
10. Remove the rotor shaft and drive shaft.
11. Mark the rotor shaft and the drive shaft, then remove the packing from the top of the rotor shaft and remove the rotor shaft.
12. Mark one of the governor springs and its bracket. Also mark one of the governor weights and its pivot pins.
13. Unhook and remove the governor springs.
14. Remove the governor weights and apply grease to the weights, after disassembly.
15. Assembly is the reverse order of disassembly with the following precautions:
    a. Make sure all match marks are aligned when assembling.
    b. Make sure the reluctor is properly installed and always use a new roll pin.
    c. Apply grease to the top rotor shaft as required.
    d. Make sure the air gap is between 0.012–0.020 in.

DISTRIBUTOR

Disassembly

1986–88

On these models the only servicable parts are the distributor cap, rotor and the metal support plate under the rotor.

Courier Ignition

Troubleshooting

An accurate ohmmeter, a jumper wire and a 3.4 watt test light will be needed to troubleshoot the electronic ignition. Before suspecting the module or pickup coil, inspect all connections for breaks, improper hookups, shorts, or corrosion. Repair any faults before proceeding.

1. Check for a spark at the coil high tension lead: Remove the coil high tension lead from the distributor and position it approximately ¼ in. from the engine block or other suitable ground. Hold the lead with a pair of insulated pliers and a heavy glove. Crank the engine and check for a spark. If the spark is good and consistent, inspect the cap and rotor. If the spark is weak or nonexistent, replace the high tension lead, clean and tighten all connections and retest. If the spark is still weak, go to the next step.
2. Check the coil primary resistance: Connect an ohmmeter across the coil primary terminals and read the resistance on the low scale. Resistance should measure approximately 0.9 ± 0.09 ohms @ 68°F. If the reading is far different, replace the coil.
3. Check the coil secondary resistance: Connect an ohmmeter across the distributor side of the coil and the coil center tower. Read the resistance on the high scale of the meter. Resistance should measure 6,800–9,200 ohms @ 70°F. If the resistance is much higher (30,000–40,000 ohms), replace the coil.

NOTE: The armature gap is not adjustable.

5. Using the ohmmeter, measure the pickup coil resistance.

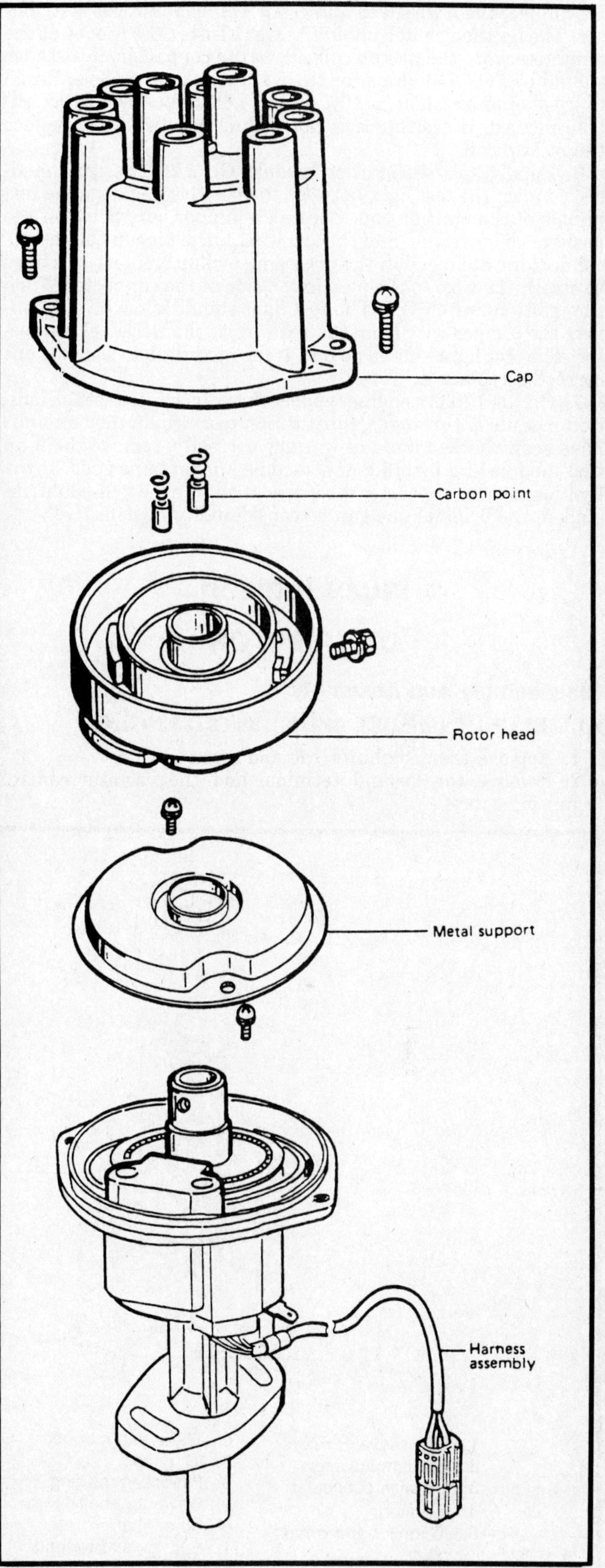

Datsun/Nissan distributor—1986–88 Z24i 4 cyl. engine

Disconnect the 2 wire (red and green) connector at the distributor. The ignition switch should be OFF. Insert the probes of the ohmmeter into the pickup coil side of the connector. Resistance should be 760–840 ohms for the 2,299cc engine models. Resistance should be 1,050 ± 10% ohms @ 68°F for the 1,970cc engine models. If resistance is not within specifications, replace the pickup coil.

6. Finally, test the ignition module. On 2,299cc engine models, connect the test light between the positive and negative terminals of the ignition coil. Connect a jumper wire between the positive coil terminal and the red wire of the pickup coil (at the connector unplugged in the preceding pickup coil test). Be sure to attach the wire to the pickup coil side of the connector. Turn the ignition switch ON. The test light should come on. Disconnect the jumper wire from the red wire at the electrical connector. The test light should go out. If the module does not test out correctly, replace it.

7. On the 1,970cc engine models, the only way to test the ignition module is through a substitution test. If all other systems have been checked and are working correctly, remove the ignition module and install a new module known to be good. If the ignition system operates properly with the new module installed, the original one can be considered to be defective.

Isuzu Ignition

DISTRIBUTOR

Disassembly And Assembly

ALL EXCEPT (MODEL 4ZD1) 138 CID ENGINE

1. Remove the distributor cap and rotor.
2. Remove the ground terminal and the vacuum control mounting screw.
3. Pry loose the retractor outer cover and insert a suitable tool into the lower side of the retractor and pull the retractor free.
4. Break away the caulking on the gear set and remove the pin, collar and ring.
5. Remove the governor shaft, then remove the weight and springs from the shaft.
6. To assemble, reverse the disassembly procedures with the following precautions:
   a. When attaching the governor spring to the shaft spring hanger pin, the smaller tapered ends of the spring (both ends) should be secured to the lower side of the hook.
   b. When installing the rotor shaft, align the rotor shaft notches and the shaft notches.
   c. When installing the pin collar and ring, after driving in a new pin, peen both ends of the pin in a vise. Replace the old O-ring with as new one.
   d. When installing the IC igniter and breaker plate assembly, carefully align the scribe marks on the breaker plate assembly and the housing.
   e. When installing the retractor, the roll pin notch and the retractor notch must be parallel when the roll pin is inserted into the retractor.
   f. Apply vacuum and make sure the vacuum advance moves.
   g. Use a feeler gauge and measure the air gap between the pick-up coil projections. The air gap should be 0.0012–0.020 in. Move the igniter to adjust.

Disassembly and Assembly

ALL (MODEL 4ZD1) 138 CID ENGINES

1. Remove the cap seal and rotor.
2. Remove the ignitor covers.
3. Remove the screw and snap ring and pull out the vacuum advance.

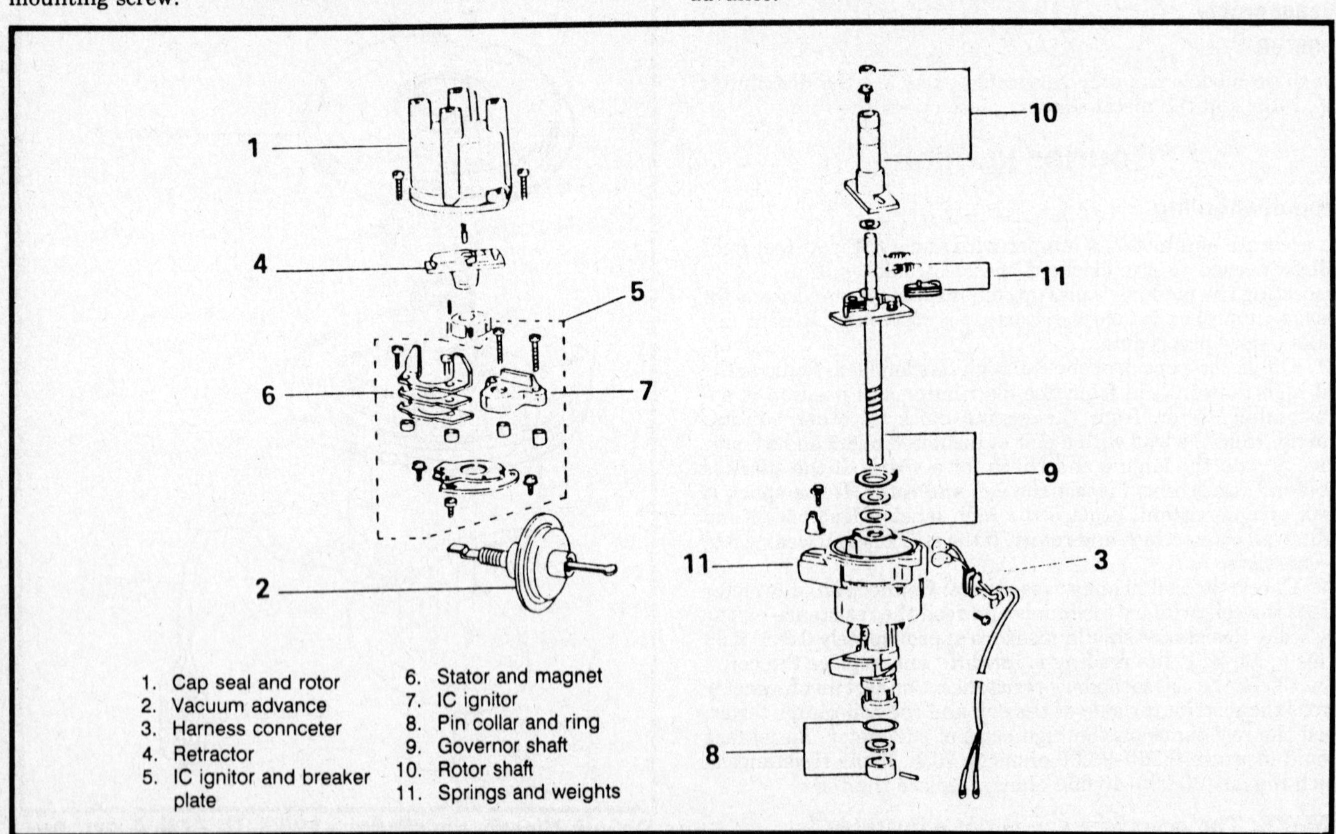

Isuzu All With (Model 4ZD1) 138 c.u. in. Engine

4. Remove the pin collar and governor shaft as follows:
a. Using a drill and grinding stone, grind the pin and drive it out with a punch and hammer.
b. Remove the two springs from the signal rotor.
5. Remove the cap from the signal rotor and remove the screw from the governor shaft.
6. To assemble, reverse the disassembly procedures with the following precautions:
a. When attaching the weight to the governor shaft, align the "10" mark with the stopper.
b. When attaching the signal rotor to the governor shaft, apply grease to the top of the signal rotor and seal it with the cover.
c. When assembling the governor shaft to the distributor housing, apply oil to the shaft and washer.
d. When installing a new collar, select the washer cap to make the clearance between the collar and the housing from 0.15–0.5mm.
7. When installing the pin, collar and ring, peen both ends of the pin in a vise. Replace the old O-ring with as new one.
8. Apply vacuum and make sure the vacuum advance moves.
9. Use a non-magnetic feeler gauge and measure the air gap between the pick-up coil projections. The air gap should be 0.008–0.016 in. Move the igniter to adjust.

Mazda Ignition

TROUBLESHOOTING IGNITION SYSTEM

1982-85

An accurate ohmmeter, a jumper wire and a 3.4 watt test light is needed to troubleshoot the electronic ignition system. Before proceeding with troubleshooting, make sure that all connections are tight and all wiring is intact.

1. Check for spark at the coil high tension lead by removing the lead from the distributor cap and holding it about $^1/_4$ in. from the engine block or other good ground. Use a heavy rubber glove or non-conductive clamp, such as a fuse puller or clothes pin, to hold the wire. Crank the engine and check for spark. If a good spark is noted, check the cap and rotor; if the spark is weak or nonexistent, replace the high tension lead, clean and tighten the connections and retest. If a weak spark is still noted, proceed to Step 2.
2. Check the coil primary resistance. Connect an ohmmeter across the coil primary terminals and check resistance on the low scale. Resistance should be 0.81–0.98 Ω @ 70°F. If not, replace the coil.
3. Check the coil secondary resistance. Connect an ohmmeter across the distributor side of the coil and the coil center tower. Read resistance on the high scale. Resistance should be 6,800–9,200 Ω @ 70°F. If resistance is much higher (30,000–40,000 Ω), replace the coil.
4. Next, remove the distributor cap and rotor. Crank the engine until a spoke on the rotor is aligned with the pick-up coil contact. Use a flat non-magnetic feeler gauge to check the gap. Gap should be 0.008–0.024 in. The gap is not adjustable. On these models, gap is corrected by parts replacement.
5. Using an ohmmeter, check the pick-up coil resistance. Disconnect the 2-wire (red and green) connector at the distributor. The ignition switch should be in the OFF position. Insert the probes of the ohmmeter in the pick-up coil side of the connector. Resistance should be 1,050 Ω ± 10%. If not, replace the pick-up coil.
6. Finally, test the ignition module. The only way to test the module is to substitute a known good module in its place.

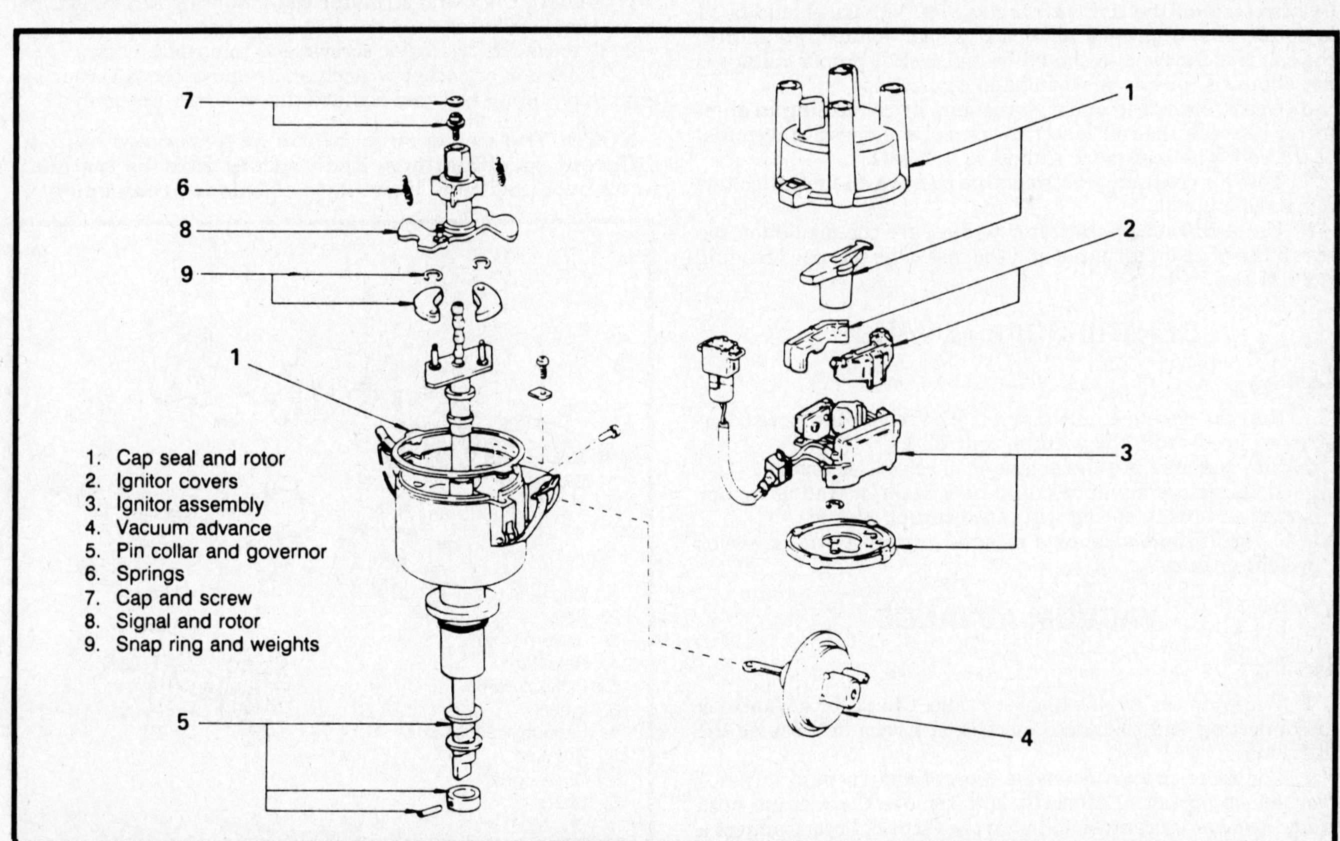

Isuzu All Except (Model 4ZD1) 138 c.u. in. Engine

TROUBLESHOOTING IGNITION SYSTEM

1986–88

1. Remove the high voltage cable from the center tower of the distributor and hold the end of the cable at a point $^3/_{16}$–$^3/_8$ in. away from a good engine ground. In this condition, crank the engine with the starter and look for a spark at the coil high voltage cable.

CAUTION

Be sure there are no fuel leaks before performing this test.

2. If there is a spark at the coil secondary wire, it should be constant and bright blue in color. If it is, continue to crank the engine and while slowly moving the the coil secondary wire away from the ground, look for arching at the coil tower. If arcing occurs, replace the coil. If the spark is weak, not constant or there is no spark, proceed to stap 3.

If the spark is good or there is no arcing at the coil tower, the ignition system is producing the necessary high secondary voltage. However, make sure that this voltage is getting to the spark plugs by checking the distributor rotor, cap, spark plug wires and spark plugs. If they are OK, the igniton system is not the reason why the engine will not start. It will be necessary to check the fuel system and engine mechanical items.

3. Turn the ignition switch on and measure the voltage at the negative (-) coil terminal. The voltage should be the same as battery voltage. If it is 3 volts or less, the IC distributor is defective. If there is no voltage, check for an open circuit in the coil or wiring.

4. With the key on, use a special jumper wire and momemtarily touch the negative (-) terminal of the coil to ground while holding the the coil secondary wire ¼ in. from a good engine ground. A spark should be obtained.

5. If no spark was obtained, check for voltage at the positive (+) terminal of the coil with the key on. Voltage should be at least 12 volts or battery voltage. If proper voltage is obtained, the coil is defective and should be replaced. If proper voltage is not obtained, check the wiring and connections.

6. Check the coil secondary resistance by connecting an ohmmeter between the coil center tower and the negative terminal of the coil. The resistance should be 6–30k Ω.

7. Test for continuity between the positive and negative terminals of the coil.

8. Use a 500 meg ohm tester to measure the insulation between the primary terminal and the case. The standard reading is 10 M Ω.

CENTRIFUGAL ADVANCE

Testing

1. Run the engine at idle and remove the vacuum hose (non-stripped hose) from the vacuum controller.

2. Slowly accelerate the engine to check for advance.

a. Excessive advance could be a deteriorated governor spring. A broken spring will cause abrupt advance.

b. Insufficient advance or no advance could be the governor weight or cam.

VACUUM ADVANCE

Testing

1. Warm up the engine and let it idle. Check for advance by disconnecting and then reconnecting the vacuum hose at the distributor.

2. For more precise determination of the vacuum advance mechanism operating properly, is to remove the vacuum hose from the advance control and plug the vacuum hose. Connect a vacuum pump to the advance control and install a timing light.

3. Run the engine at idle and slowly apply vacuum pressure to check for advance.

a. Excessive advance could be a deteriorated or sagging vacuum controller spring. A broken spring will cause abrupt advance.

b. Insufficient advance or no advance could be a breaker plate in faulty operation or a broken diaphragm.

DISTRIBUTOR

Disassembly And Assembly

1982–85

1. Loosen the screws and remove the distributor cap.
2. Loosen the screws and remove the rotor.
3. Loosen the governor set attaching bolt and remove the governor set.
4. Loosen the pick-up coil and igniter attaching screws. Remove the pick-up coil, the ignitor assembly and gasket from the distributor housing.
5. Remove the vacuum control unit attaching screws and remove the vacuum control.
6. Loosen the signal plate attaching screws and remove the signal plate.
7. Loosen the plate attaching screws and remove the plate.
8. Drive the lock pin out of the driven gear with a punch and remove the gear and washers.
9. Remove the shaft through the top of the distributor housing.
10. Assembly is the reverse of the disassembly procedure.

Disassembly And Assembly

1986–88

1. Remove the two distributor cap mounting screws and remove the distributor cap.
2. Remove the two rotor screws and remove the rotor.
3. Use a box or socket wrench and remove the governor assembly retaining bolt and remove the governor assembly.

NOTE: The two springs of the governor are built to different specifications. Each spring must be installed in its own position. Make note of this for reassembly.

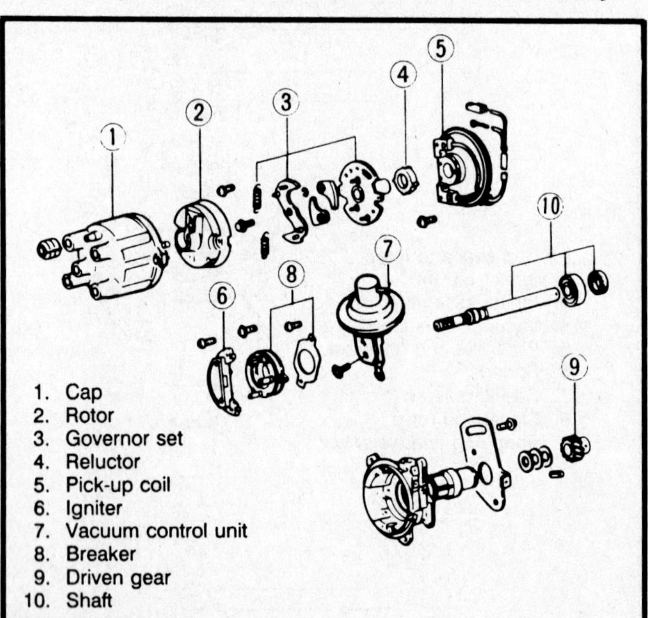

Mazda distributor—1986–88

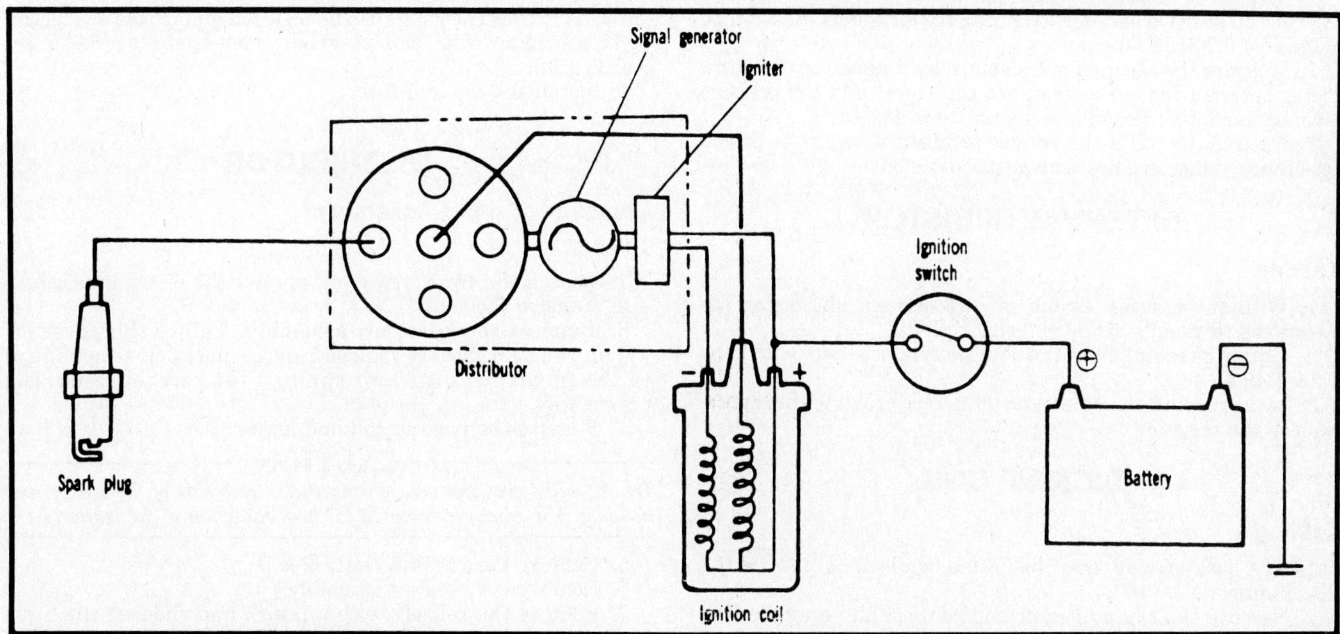

Electronic ignition system—1982-83

4. Remove the wire clamp screw and remove the clamp.
5. Remove the two pick-up coil and IC igniter tightening screws and remove the pick-up coil and IC igniter simultaneously.
6. Remove the two governor vacuum chamber screws and remove the governor vacuum chamber.
7. Remove the two breaker assembly screws and remove the breaker assembly. Keep the breaker assembly clean.
8. Remove the two bearing retainer plate screws and remove the bearing retainer.
9. Make alignment marks on the gear and shaft for reassembly.
10. Drive out the distributor drive gear pin with a punch and remove the drive gear.
11. Remove the distributor shaft and bearing assembly.
12. Remove the distributor housing seal.
13. Remove the two governor springs.

NOTE: The two springs of the governor are built to different specifications. Each spring must be installed in its own position. Make note of this for reassembly.

14. Remove the governor centrifugal plate and the governor weight.
15. Installation is the reverse of removal.

Mitsubishi Pick-up and Montero Ignition

IGNITION SYSTEM TESTING WITH ENGINE RUNNING

Troubleshooting

1982–83

1. Start the engine, allow to idle until the normal operating temperature is reached.
2. Check the ignition timing, adjust if necessary.
3. Visually check electrical connections for frayed insulation or bare wires. Make sure all plug-in connectors are clean and tight. Check the spark plug and coil wires for cracking, crossfiring, corroded terminals, continuity and resistance. Check the distributor cap for cracks or carbon tracking. Check any suspect parts. Check the spark plugs for foiling, nonfiring and correct gap.
4. If none of the checks have solved the problem, or the car fails to start, proceed to the following tests.

IGNITION SYSTEM TESTING ENGINE DOES NOT RUN

Troubleshooting

1982-83

1. Remove the coil wire from the distributor cap tower. Hold the end of the wire with insulated pliers.
2. Locate the end of the wire about $\frac{1}{4}$ in. away from the cylinder head and crank the engine with the starter.
3. Observe the spark or no spark condition. If a spark is produced, the IC igniter and ignition coil may be considered in good condition.
4. Remove the distributor cap and check it for cracks, carbon tracking or dirt.
5. Check the rotor for wear. Replace as necessary.
6. If no spark is produced, a defective control unit (internal), pick-up coil, ignition coil or faulty wiring may be the problem.

IGNITION COIL

If the the earlier test produces no spark, the ignition coil could be at fault. The fastest way to check is by substituting a known good coil. If a coil is not on hand, proceed with one or more of the following tests:

1. With the ignition switch in the ON position, measure the voltage at the negative terminal of the ignition coil. If zero volts are shown, there is an open circuit in the coil.
2. Check the ignition coil resistance. If the engine will run, allow it to reach normal operating temperature (the ignition coil should be hot). Shut off the engine and disconnect the high tension lead (coil wire) from the coil tower.
3. Measure primary resistance with an ohmmeter, connect-

ing the coil positive and negative primary terminals. Resistance should be 0.7–0.85 Ω.

4. Measure the secondary resistance by connecting the ohmmeter between the contacts in the coil tower and the positive primary terminal. Resistance should be 9–11k Ω.

5. Replace the coil if the voltage tests show zero volts or the resistance values are not within specifications.

EXTERNAL RESISTOR

Testing

1. With the ignition switch off, connect an ohmmeter between the terminals of the external resistor.
2. Obtain a reading from the ohmmeter. Resistance should be 1.22–1.49 Ω.
3. If the reading on the ohmmeter is zero or not within specs, replace the resistor.

PICK-UP COIL

Testing

1. The pick-up coil may be tested while mounted in the distributor.
2. Remove the cap and rotor and connect an ohmmeter between the two terminals of the pick-up coil.
3. Replace the pick-up coil if the resistance is not within these limits: 920–1.120 Ω,.

PICK-UP COIL

Replacement

NOTE: The distributor must be removed from the engine.

1. Remove the distributor cap and rotor.
2. Remove the center mounting bolt (screw) and remove the governor assembly.

NOTE: Take care not to mix up the governor springs. They must be installed in the same position.

3. Remove the reluctor. Remove the two mounting screws and take out the pick-up coil and IC igniter. Carefully, pull the igniter from the pick-up coil.
4. Installation of the new pick-up coil is the reverse of the removal procedure.

RELUCTOR GAP

Checking

The reluctor gap is non-adjustable and can only be checked. Doing so is not a matter of routine maintenance, but usually is necessary only if the distributor is overhauled. However, too tight a fit between the signal rotor and the pickup stator could cause rotation of the distributor to damage the parts involved or produce an incorrect signal. Check the fit as described below and replace the stator and rotor to correct known deficiencies.

In some cases, severe wear or incorrect original manufacturing tolerances in the distributor bearings could cause wear of these two pieces that resembles damage due to too tight a fit. However, in this case, the appropriate gap would exist between the rotor and stator and there would be excessive play in the distributor shaft.

1. Remove the distributor cap. Remove the rotor.
2. Rotate the engine using a wrench on the front pulley, until the three vertical stator pieces line up with three of the rotor lobes.
3. Using a non-magnetic (brass, plastic, or wood) feeler gauge of 0.008 in. thickness, insert it straight between the stator and rotor. As long as the gauge can be inserted and moved easily, the parts are okay. The gap may be wider than the 0.008 in. specification.
4. Install the cap and rotor.

DISTRIBUTOR

Disassembly And Assembly

1982-83

1. Loosen the two screws and remove the distributor cap.
2. Remove the rotor.
3. Remove the governor assembly. Before the governor weights and springs are removed, make marks on either one of of the governor pins and springs for reference during reassembly.
4. Remove the pick-up coil and igniter.

CAUTION

Do not wipe away the grease from the reverse side of the igniter and housing. The grease is required for heat radiation of the ignitor.

5. Remove the vacuum controller.
6. Remove the breaker assembly.
7. Remove the roll pin with a punch and slide off the drive gear.
8. Assembly is the reverse of the disassembly procedure with the following precautions:
   a. When assembling the gear to the shaft, align the punch mark on the gear with the mating mark on the housing. Make sure the notched portion of the shaft end is positioned properly and then install the pin.
   b. After the governor assembly has been installed, turn the shaft to confirm that the projection of the signal rotor does not touch the stator.

IGNITION SYSTEM

Troubleshooting

1984–88

Mitsubishi trucks use either Mitsubishi or Nippon Denso type distributors between 1984–88. The following troubleshooting chart applies to both:

MITSUBISHI TYPE DISTRIBUTOR

Disassembly And Assembly

1984–88

1. Clamp the distributor in a soft jawed vise.
2. Pull off the rotor.
3. Remove the two vacuum controller attaching screws, remove the link and remove the vacuum controller.
4. Remove the two screws and the igniter.
5. Remove the black lead wire.
6. Remove the signal rotor shaft tightening screw and the two breaker plate retaining screws. Remove the rotor shaft and and breaker plate.
7. Remove the signal rotor shaft from the signal rotor.
8. Remove the two spring retainers with pliers and then remove the two governor springs.
9. Remove the two governor weights.
10. Mark the location of the drive gear on the distributor shaft.
11. Drive out the roll pin with a punch and remove the drive gear and washer.
12. Remove the distributor shaft from the housing.
13. Assembly is the reverse of disassembly. Adjust the air gap between the signal rotor and the pick-up of the ignitor to 0.031 in.

NIPPON DENSO TYPE DISTRIBUTOR

Disassembly And Assembly

1. Clamp the distributor in a soft jawed vise.
2. Pull off the rotor.
3. Remove the vacuum controller attaching screw. Remove the link and the vacuum controller.
4. Remove the two screws from the igniter.
5. Remove the two screws and signal generator with the ignitor.
6. Remove the two breaker plate retaining screws and remove the breaker plate.
7. Remove the signal rotor shaft from the signal rotor.
8. Remove the two spring retainers with pliers and then remove the two governor springs.
9. Assembly is the reverse of disassembly. Adjust the air gap between the signal rotor and the signal generator to 0.008–0.015 in.

Toyota Ignition System

TROUBLESHOOTING

An accurate ohmmeter and voltmeter are needed to troubleshoot this system. The numbers in the diagram correspond to the numbers of the following troubleshooting steps. Be sure to perform each step in order.

IGNITION COIL

Testing

PRIMARY CIRCUIT

Using an ohmmeter, check between the positive (+) and negative (−) primary terminals of the ignition coil. The resistance (cold) should be, 0.4–0.5 ohms (1982–84, type III), 0.4–0.5 ohms (1985 and later, 22R engine), 0.8–1.1 ohms (1983–84, type IV), 0.5–0.7 ohms (1985 and later, 22R-E engine) or 1.2–1.5 ohms (1983 and later, 3Y-EC engine).

Testing

SECONDARY CIRCUIT

Using an ohmmeter, check between the (+) primary terminal and the high tension terminal. The resistance (cold) should be 8.5–11.5k Ω for 1982–84, type III engines, 10.7–14.5k Ω 1983–84, type IV engines, 8.5–11.5k Ω 1985 and later, 22R engines, 11.4–15.6k Ω 1985 and later, 22R-E engines, or 7.5–10.5k Ω for 1983 and later, 3Y-EC engines. The insulation resistance between the positive (+) primary terminal and the ignition coil case should be infinite.

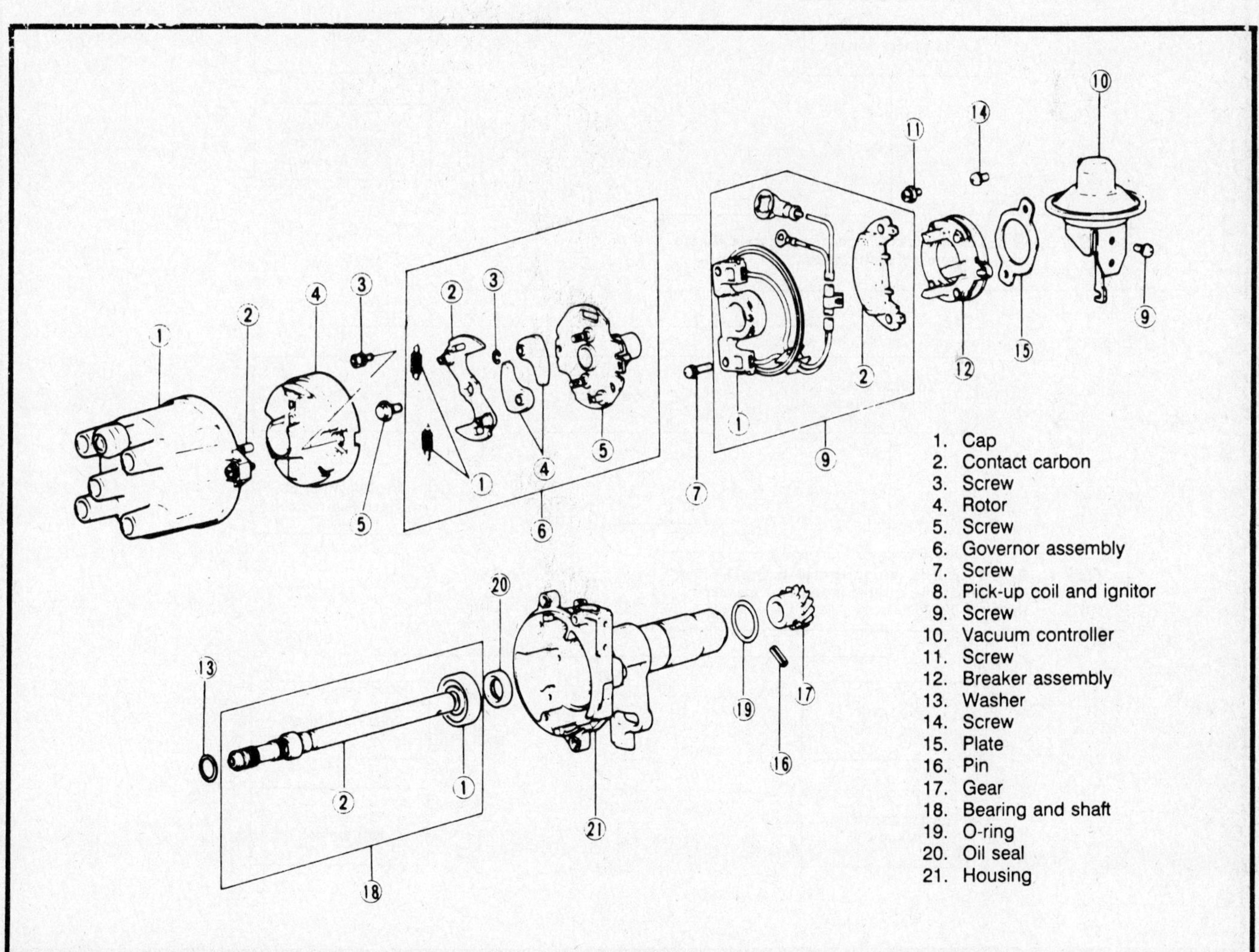

Mitsubishi distributor—1982-83

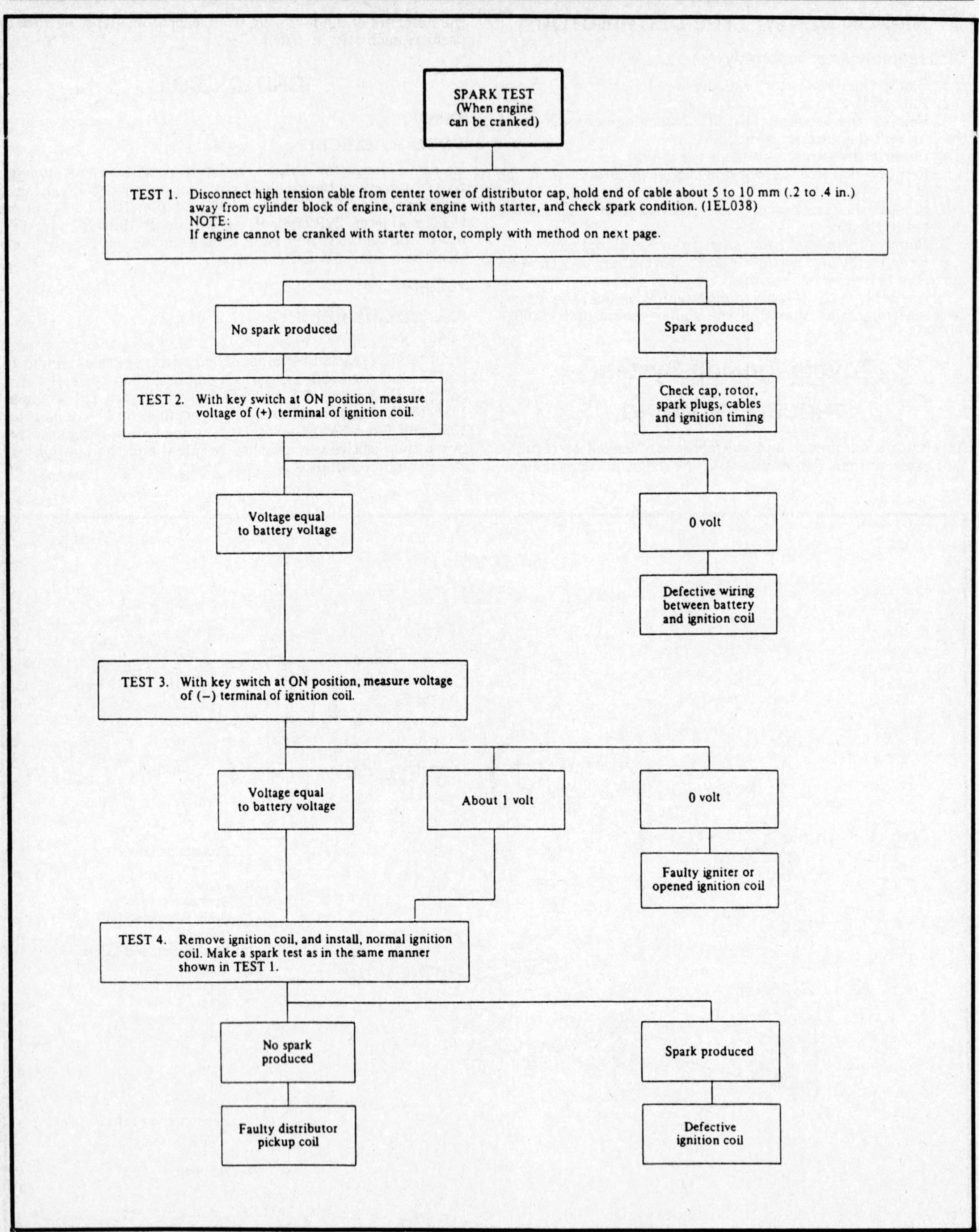
SPARK TEST
(When engine can be cranked)
TEST 1. Disconnect high tension cable from center tower of distributor cap, hold end of cable about 5 to 10 mm (.2 to .4 in.) away from cylinder block of engine, crank engine with starter, and check spark condition. (1EL038)
NOTE:
If engine cannot be cranked with starter motor, comply with method on next page.
No spark produced
Spark produced
TEST 2. With key switch at ON position, measure voltage of (+) terminal of ignition coil.
Check cap, rotor, spark plugs, cables and ignition timing
Voltage equal to battery voltage
0 volt
Defective wiring between battery and ignition coil
TEST 3. With key switch at ON position, measure voltage of (−) terminal of ignition coil.
Voltage equal to battery voltage
About 1 volt
0 volt
Faulty igniter or opened ignition coil
TEST 4. Remove ignition coil, and install, normal ignition coil. Make a spark test as in the same manner shown in TEST 1.
No spark produced
Spark produced
Faulty distributor pickup coil
Defective ignition coil

Mitsubishi troubleshooting—1984–88

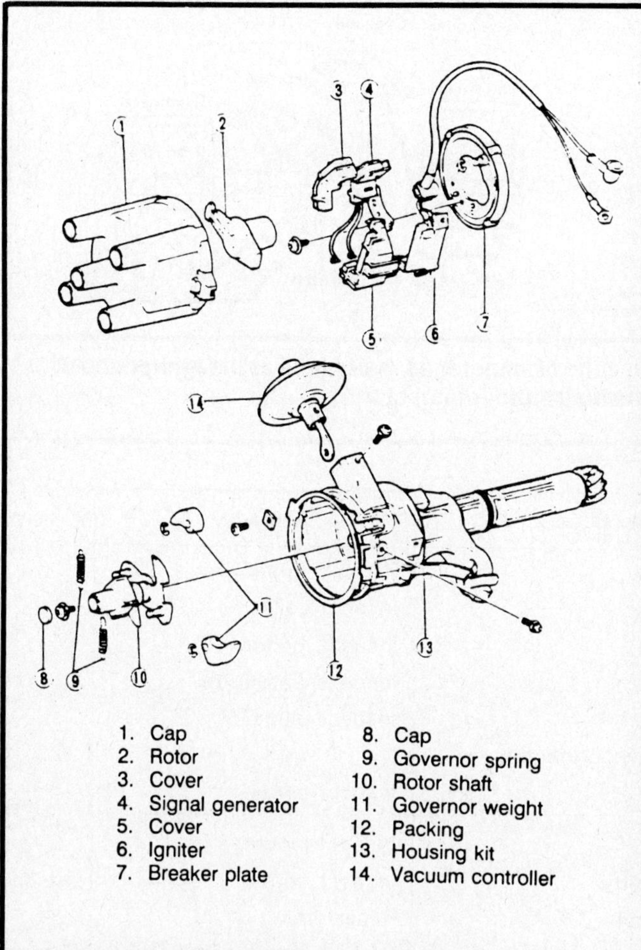

Nippon Denso type distributor—1984-88

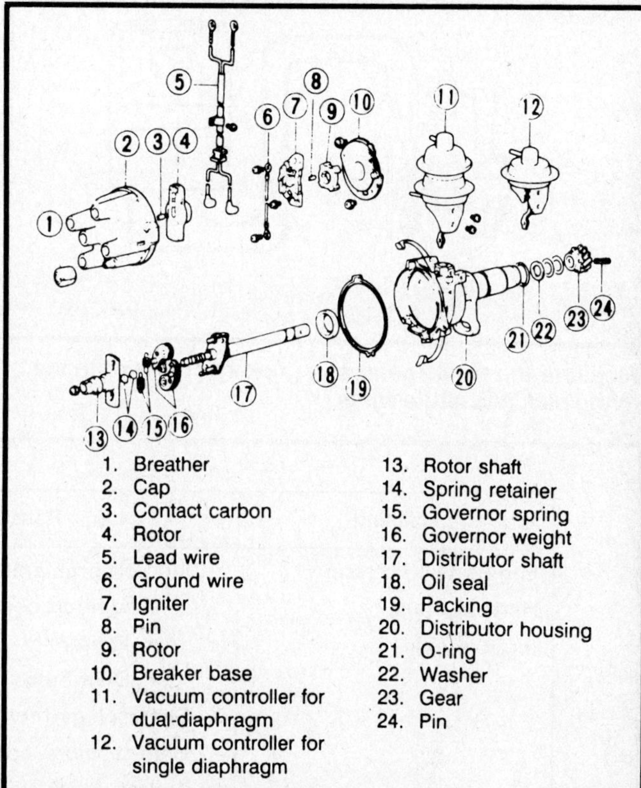

Mitsubishi type distributor—1984-88

AIR GAP

Adjustment

1. Remove the distributor cap and ignition rotor.
2. Check the air gap between the timing rotor spoke and the pick-up coil.
3. When aligned, the air gap should be 0.008–0.016 in.

SIGNAL GENERATOR

Testing

1. Unplug the electrical connector at the distributor.
2. Connect one ohmmeter lead to the white wire and the other lead to the pink wire.
3. The resistance of the signal generator should be 140–180 Ω.

POWER TRANSISTOR/IGNITOR

Testing

ALL MODELS (1982)
22R ENGINE (1985 AND LATER)

1. Turn the ignition switch ON.
2. Connect the positive (+) voltmeter lead to the yellow connector of the igniter and the negative (−) voltmeter lead to the body ground. The voltage should measure 12 volts.
3. Unplug the electrical connector form the distributor.
4. Using a 1.5V dry cell battery, connect the positive (+) terminal to the pink wire and the negative (−) terminal to the white wire. The voltage reading should be 8–10 volts for all 1982 models and 1985 and later 22R engines. If not, replace the igniter.

CAUTION

DO NOT apply voltage to the igniter for more than 5 seconds or the power transistor may be destroyed.

5. Turn the ignition switch OFF.

Testing

1983-84 TYPE III AND IV SYSTEMS
1983 AND LATER TYPE IIA, VAN SYSTEMS
1985 AND LATER 22R-E ENGINE SYSTEMS

1. Turn the ignition switch ON.
2. Connect the positive (+) voltmeter lead to the ignition coil negative (−) terminal and the negative (−) voltmeter lead to the body ground. The voltage should measure 12 volts.
3. Unplug the electrical connector form the distributor.

NOTE: On the Van and Type IIA systems, DO NOT disconnect the electrical connector at the distributor.

4. Using a 1.5V dry cell battery, connect the positive (+) terminal to the pink wire and the negative (−) terminal to the white wire. The voltage should 8–10 volts - type III, 5–8 volts - type IV, 0–3 volts - type IIA, Van, or 5–8 volts - 22R-E, 1985 and later); if not, replace the igniter.

CAUTION

DO NOT apply voltage to the igniter for more than 5 seconds or the power transistor may be destroyed.

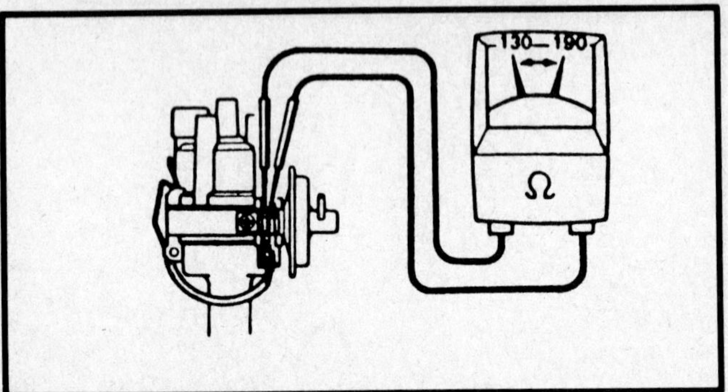

Measure the signal generator (pick-up coil) resistance at the pink and white wires

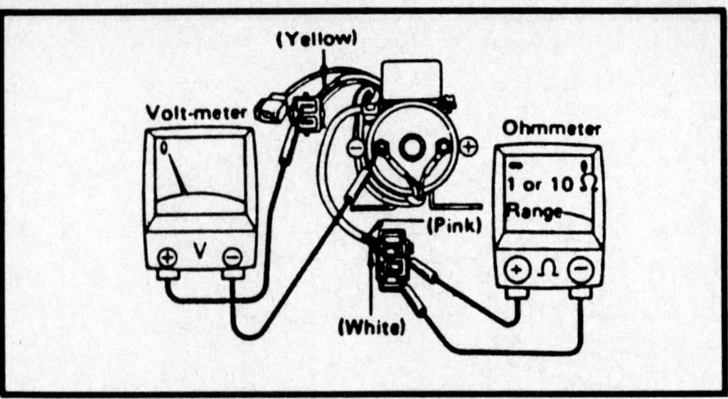

Use the ohmmeter as resistance at the igniter end of the distributor connector

Problem	Possible cause	Remedy
Engine will not start/ Hard to start (cranks ok)	Ignition problems • Ignition coil • Igniter • Distributor Spark plugs faulty High-tension cords disconnected or broken	Perform spark test Inspect coil Inspect igniter Inspect distributor Inspect plugs Inspect cords
Rough idle or stalls	Spark plugs faulty High-tension cords faulty Incorrect ignition timing Ignition problems • Ignition coil • Igniter • Distributor	Inspect plugs Inspect cords Reset timing Perform spark test Inspect coil Inspect igniter Inspect distributor
Engine hesitates/ Poor acceleration	Spark plugs faulty High-tension cords faulty Incorrect ignition timing	Inspect plugs Inspect cords Reset timing
Engine dieseling (22R) (runs after ignition switch is turned off)	Fuel cut system faulty	Repair fuel cut system
Muffler explosion (after fire) all the time	Incorrect ignition timing	Reset timing
Engine backfires	Incorrect ignition timing	Reset timing
Poor gasoline mileage	Spark plugs faulty Incorrect ignition timing	Inspect plugs Reset timing
Engine overheats	Incorrect ignition timing	Reset timing

Ignition system trouble diagnosis

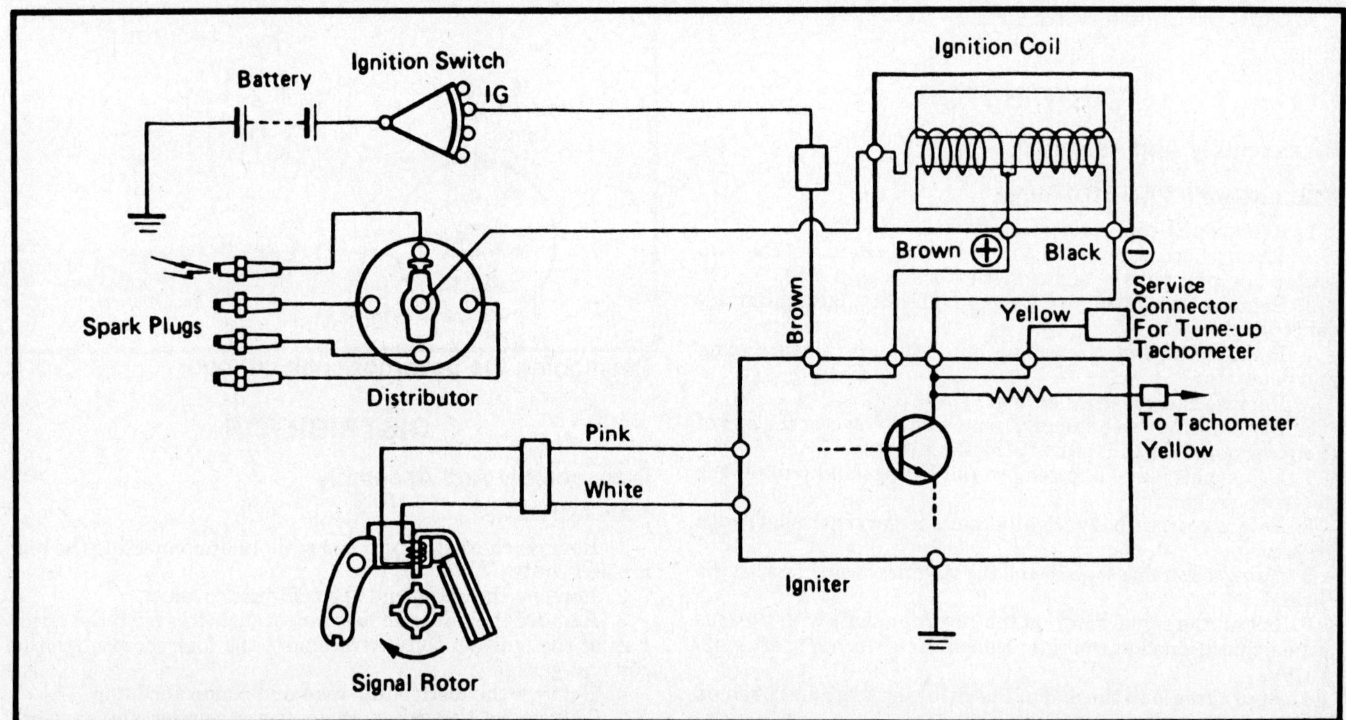

Toyota ignition system circuit—1982–84

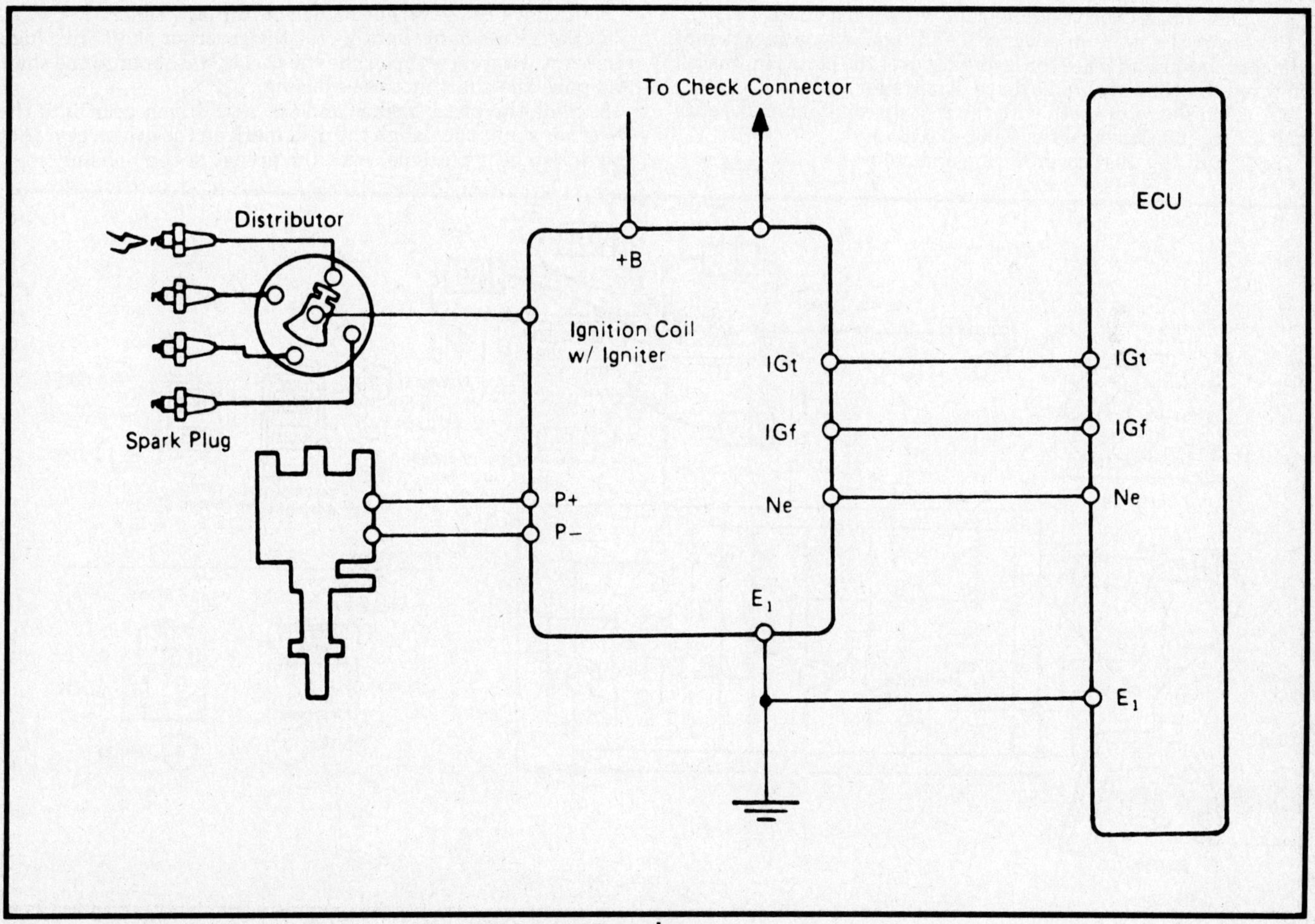

To Check Connector
ECU
Distributor
+B
Ignition Coil w/ Igniter
IGt
IGt
IGf
IGf
Spark Plug
P+
P–
Ne
Ne
E_1
E_1

Electronic Spark Advance (ESA)—1985 and later 22RE engine

5. Turn the ignition switch OFF.

DISTRIBUTOR

Disassembly And Assembly

ALL EXCEPT VAN MODELS

1. Remove the cap, rotor, dust cover and O-ring.
2. Remove the screw and ground strap. Remove the two screws and pull out the signal generator (pick-up coil).
3. Remove the screw and E-ring. Pull out the vacuum advance diaphragm.
4. Remove the two screws and pull out the staionary plate and generator.
5. Remove the governor springs.
6. Pry out the grease stopper, remove the screws at the end of the governor shaft and pull off the signal rotor.
7. Use a suitable tool to remove the E-rings and pull off the governor weights.
8. Before reassembling, lightly coat the governor shaft with grease.
9. Using a suitable tool, install the governor weights with the E-rings.
10. Install the signal rotor on the governor shaft with the cut-out part positioned at the right side of the governor shaft stopper pin.
11. Apply grease to the end of the governor shaft and push on the grease stopper.
12. Install the governor springs.
13. Fit the four clips on the breaker plate into the housing slots, then install the two hold-clips with two screws.
14. Insert the vacuum advance diaphragm with a gasket into the distributor and place the lever hole over the plate pin. Install and tighten the vacuum advance diaphragm screw.
15. Align the rotor tooth with the pick-up coil, then make sure the air gap measurement is 0.008–0.016 in.
16. Install the dust cover O-ring and rotor.

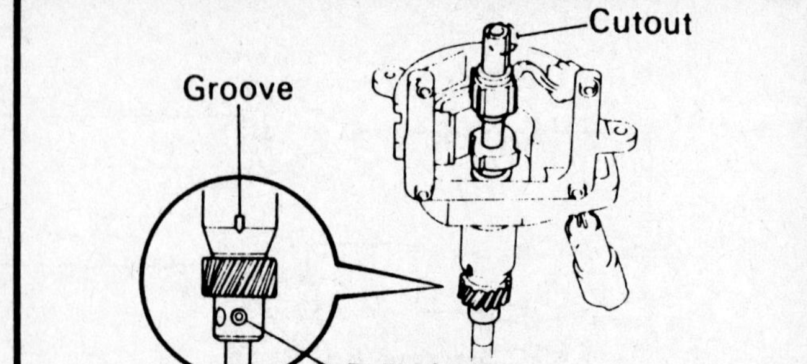

Positioning the governor shaft cut-out

DISTRIBUTOR

Disassembly And Assembly

VAN MODELS

1. Remove the distributor cap without disconnecting the high tension cords.
2. Remove the rotor and the coil dust cover.
3. Remove the nuts and disconnect the wires from the terminals of the ignition coil, then remove the four screws, ignition coil and gasket.
4. Remove the distributor wire and connector lamp.
5. To remove the driven gear, use a grinder and carefully grind the head off the pin, then with a punch and a hammer, tap out the pin. Remove the drive gear and plate washer.
6. Remove the governor shaft and thrust washer.
7. Before assemby, lightly coat the governor shaft with high temperature grease, then slide the thrust washer onto the shaft and push the shaft into the housing.
8. Slide the plate washer and the new driven gear onto the governor shaft, then align the drill mark on the driven gear (not the driven gear pin hole) with the groove of the housing.

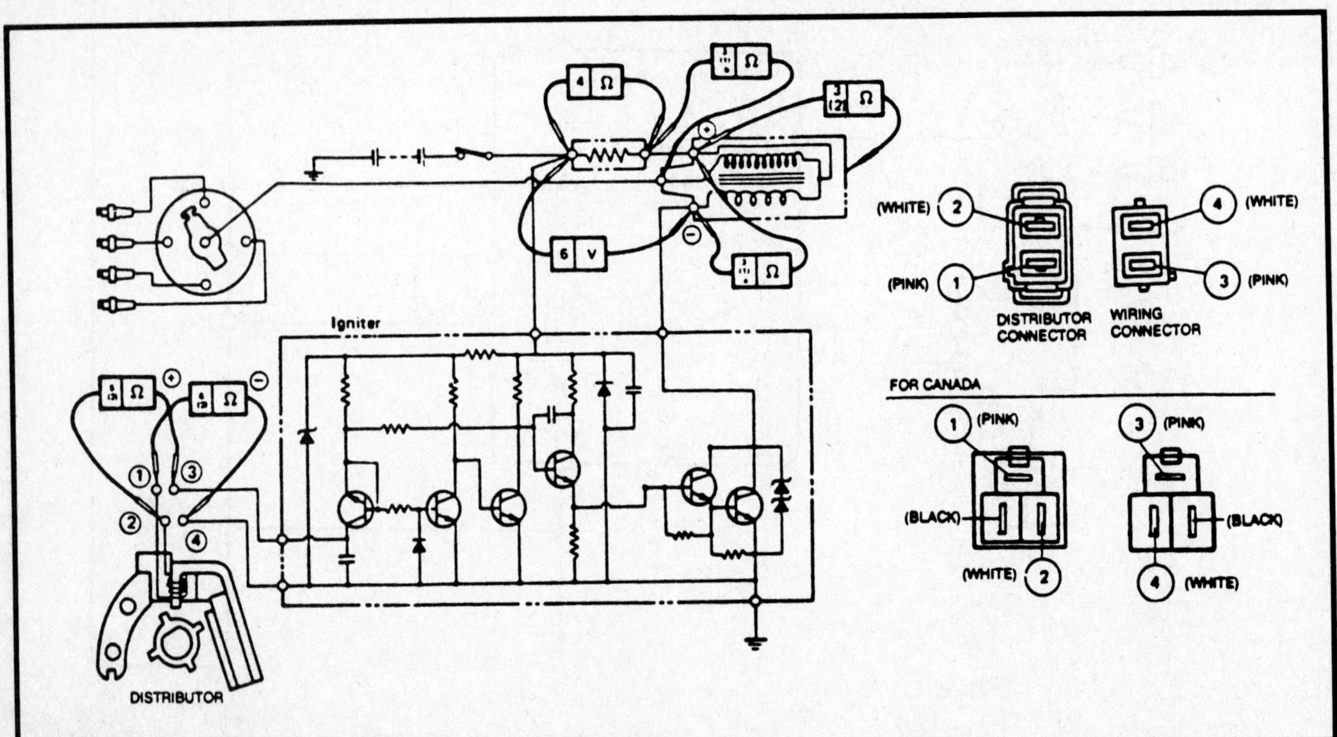

Fully transistorized ignition system troubleshooting

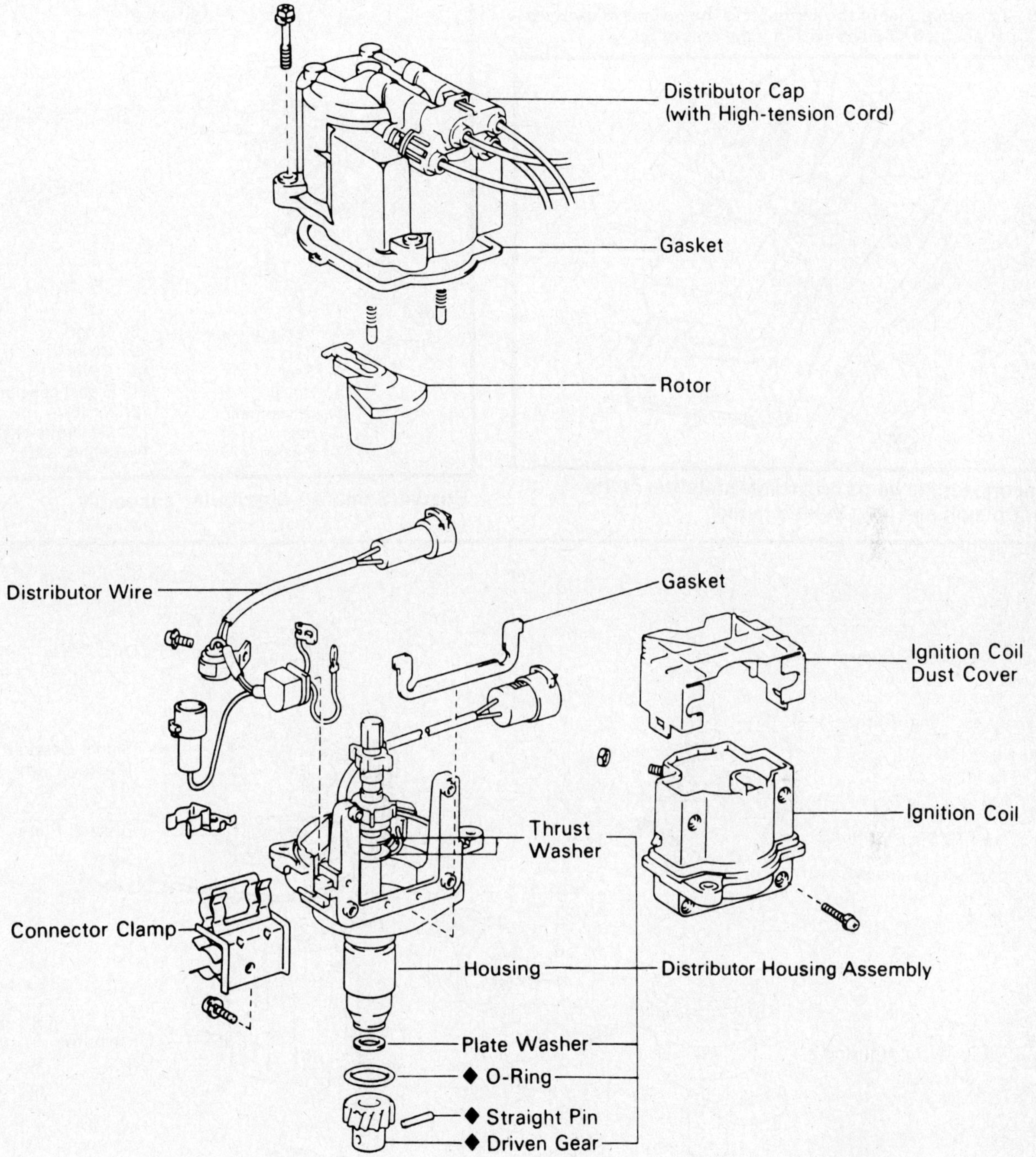

Toyota distributor—all vans

NOTE: Make sure the governor shaft cutout is positioned properly.

9. Install a new pin and measure the governor shaft thrust clearance. If clearance is not within 0.0059–0.0197 in., adjust with thrust washers, which are available. Secure the ends of the pin in a vise.

10. The remainder of the assembly is the reverse of disassembly. Coat the new O-rings with a light coat of oil.

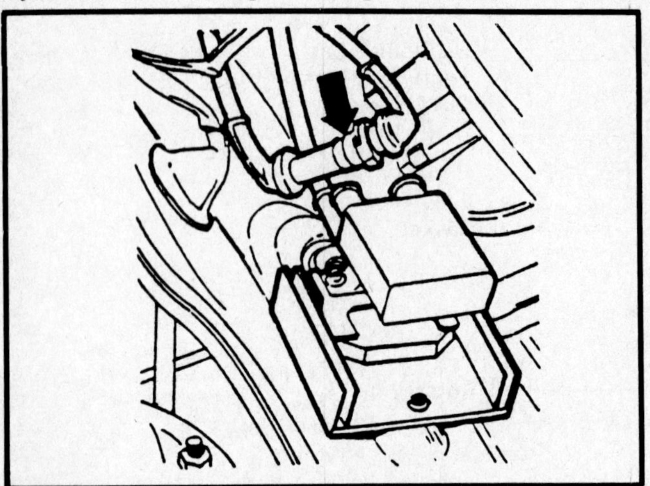

Disconnect the plugs on the idle stabilizer at the control unit and plug them together

1. Vacuum controller
2. Cap
3. Seal
4. Housing
5. Driven gear
6. Pin
7. O-ring
8. Rotor
9. Cover
10. Cover
11. Signal generator
12. Ignitor
13. Generator base plate
14. Signal; rotor

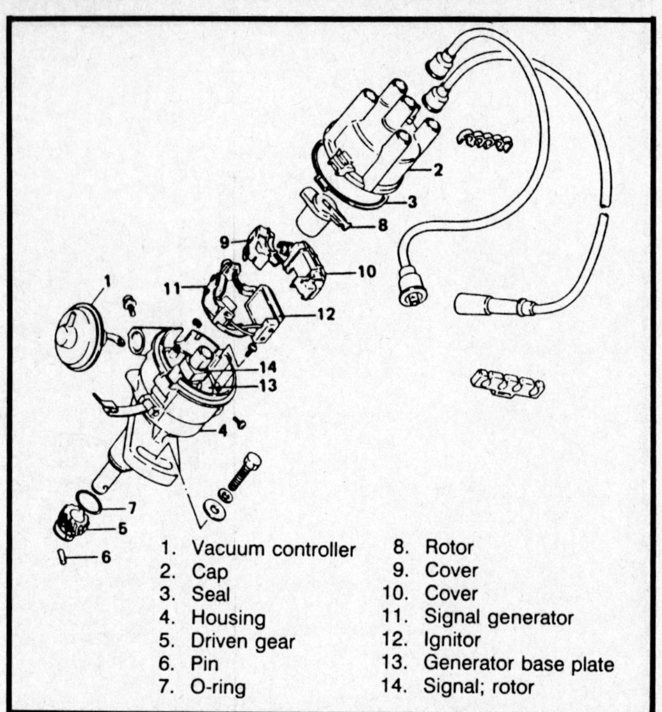

Suzuki(Samurai) distributor assembly

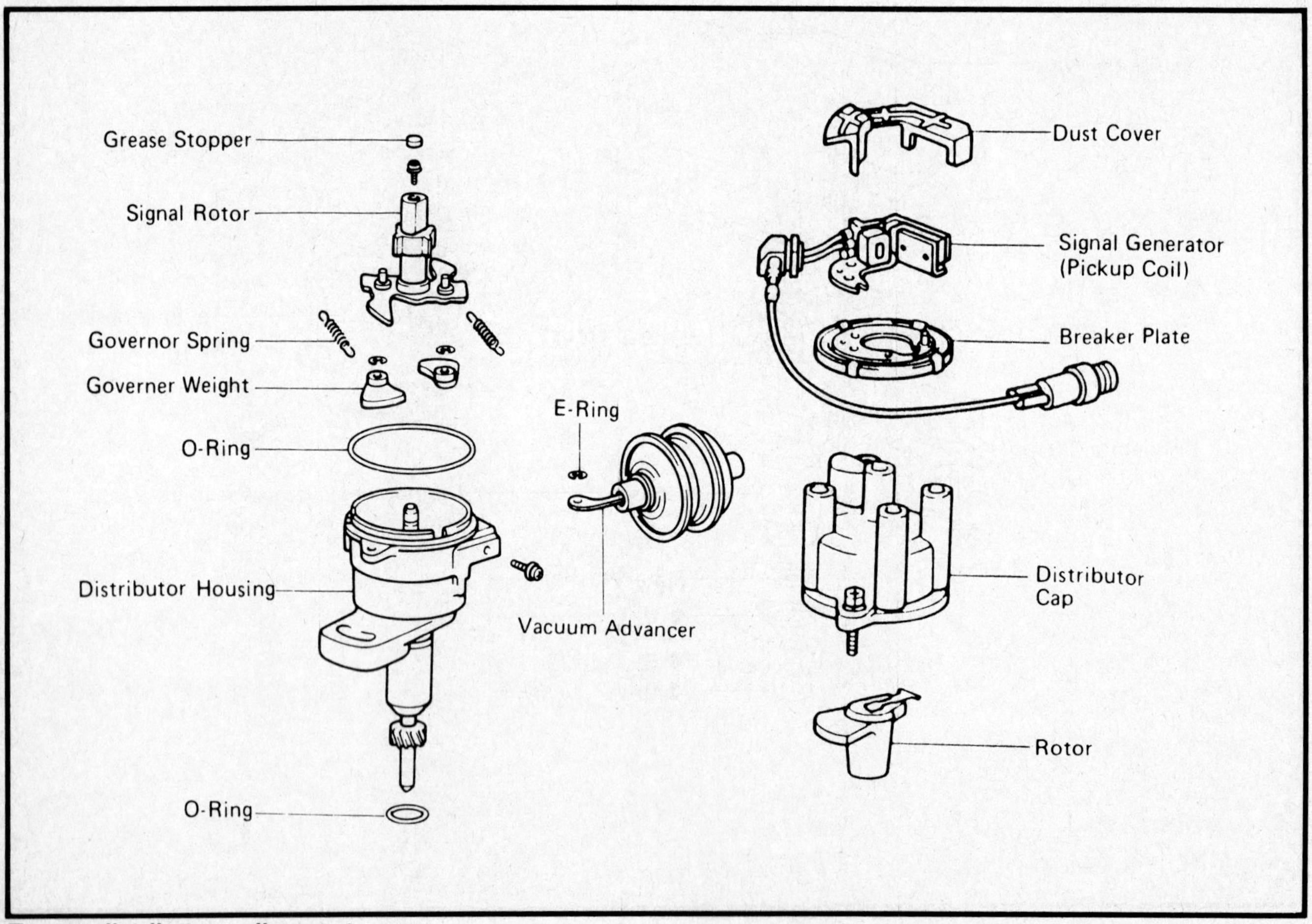

Grease Stopper
Signal Rotor
Governor Spring
Governer Weight
O-Ring
Distributor Housing
O-Ring
E-Ring
Vacuum Advancer
Dust Cover
Signal Generator
(Pickup Coil)
Breaker Plate
Distributor
Cap
Rotor

Toyota distributor—all except vans

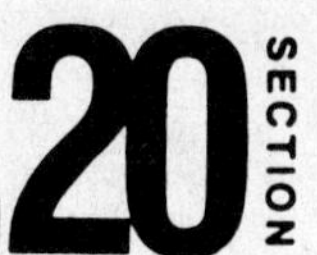

Volkswagon Ignition

IGNITION COIL

Testing

A defective Hall Switch operated ignition coil cannot be checked with standard coil testing equipment. If there is no high tension current and all other components of the ignition system check out, see if a spark from the coil wire to the distributor cap ia present by unplugging the coil wire at the distributor, holding the end of it with insulated pliers about ½ inch from ground (engine block, etc.) and turning over the engine. If a weak or no spark is obtained, try replacing the coil.

HALL SWITCH PICKUP UNIT

Testing

1. Check for voltage on positive terminal (15) of the ignition coil. There should be voltage with the ignition ON.
2. Ground a high tension coil wire.
3. Connect a test light (4 to 24 volts) between positive terminal (15) and negative terminal (1).
4. Crank the engine with the starter for approximately 5 seconds. The test light should flicker. If not, replace the ignition distributor.

IGNITION CONTROL UNIT

Testing

1. Disconnect the plugs at the control unit and connect the plugs to each other.
2. Turn the ignition switch on and make sure there is current at positive terminal (15) of the ignition coil. Turn the ignition OFF.
3. Disconnect the high tension wire between the ignition coil and the distributor at the distributor.
4. Disconnect the wire plug between the control unit and the distributor at the distributor.
5. Connect the positive (+) terminal of the voltmeter to negative terminal (1) of the ignition coil and the negative (-) terminal to ground.
6. Turn the ignition ON. There should be a voltage reading of at least 12 volts. If voltage drops below 12 volts in one second, turn off the ignition. The control unit is defective and will have to be replaced.
7. Disconnect the green wire where it connects to the distributor and ground the wire. Turn the ignition switch ON. The voltmeter should read about 12 volts. Disconnect the ground wire. The voltage should drop to 6 volts. If not, replace the control unit. Turn off the ignition.
8. Connect the terminals of the voltmeter to the outer connector of the control unit. Connect the positive (+) lead to the red wire and the negative (-) lead to the brown wire. Switch on the ignition. The voltmeter should read about 10 volts. If not, replace the control unit.

IDLE STABILIZER

Testing

The idle stabilizer is located on top of the ignition control unit. The idle stabilizer controls idle speed by either advancing or retarding the distributor timing in accordance with engine load (air conditioner on, lights on, etc.). If idle speed is erratic or if the engine fails to start, try bypassing the idle stabilizer by disconnecting the two plugs at the idle stabilizer and plugging them together. If idle improves, the idle stabilizer should probably be replaced.

Suzuki (Samurai) Ignition

IGNITION COIL

Testing

1. Disconnect the negative battery cable.

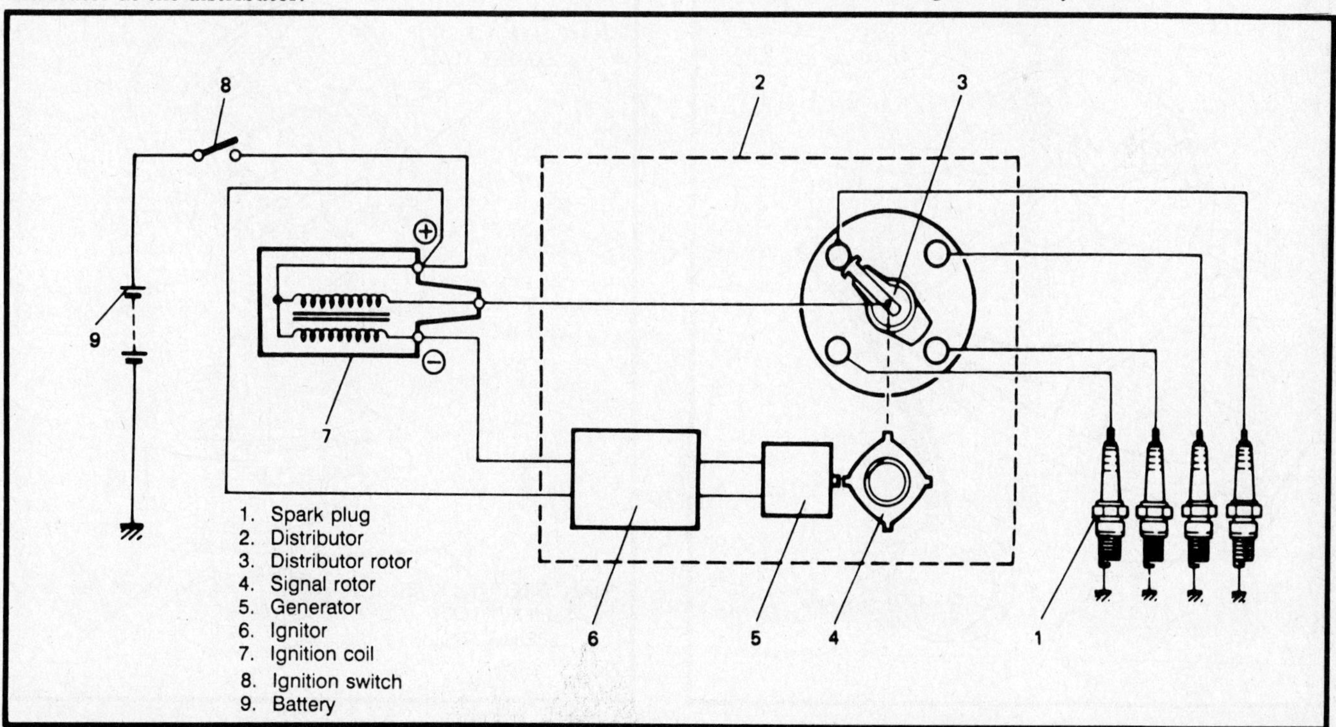

Suzuki(Samural) ignition system circuit

2. Disconnect the lead wires and the high tension wire from the ignition coil.

3. Remove the coil and with the use of an ohmmeter measure the primary coil resistance between the positive (+) and negative (-) terminals. The reading should be 1.35–1.65 Ω.

4. Measure the secondary coil resistance between the positive (+) terminal and the high tension terminal. The reading should be 11.0–14.5 k Ω.

SIGNAL ROTOR AIR GAP

Adjustment

1. Remove the distributor cap and rotor.

2. Measure the air gap between the signal rotor tooth and the generator.

3. If the air gap is not between 0.008–0.016 in., adjust it as follows:

a. Remove the distributor and then the ignitor.

b. Loosen the two screws securing the generator.

c. Using a suitable tool, move the generator and adjust the air gap.

d. Tighten the two screws and recheck the air gap.

e. Install the ignitor, rotor and distributor cap, then install the distributor.

GENERATOR

Testing

1. Disconnect the negative battery cable.

2. Remove the distributor then the ignitor.

3. Remove the dust cover from the ignitor.

4. Disconnect the red and white wires from the ignitor and connect an ohmmeter between the two wires. The resistance should be between 130–190 Ω. If not, replace the generator.

IGNITOR

Testing

1. Disconnect the negative battery cable.

2. Remove the distributor then the ignitor and generator.

3. Remove the dust cover from the ignitor.

4. Disconnect the red and white wires from the ignitor.Connect an ohmmeter, a bulb and a 12 volt battery to the ignitor. Set the ohmmeter at 1-10 ohm range. Touch the negative (-) prod of the ohmmeter to the red terminal of the ignitor and touch the positive (+) terminal of the prod to the white terminal. If the bulb lights, it indicates that the ignitor is satisfactory. If not, replace the ignitor.

CAUTION

This test should be performed within two or three seconds or damage to the ignitor could result.

5. After installing the generator and ignitor on the distributor, adjust the air gap.

ELECTRONIC FUEL INJECTION IGNITION SYSTEMS

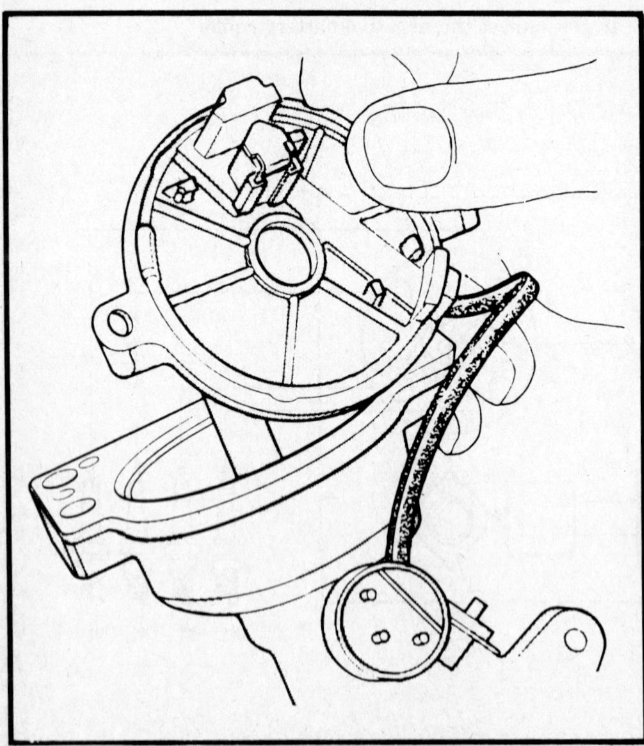

Hall Effect pick-up removal—2.2L engine

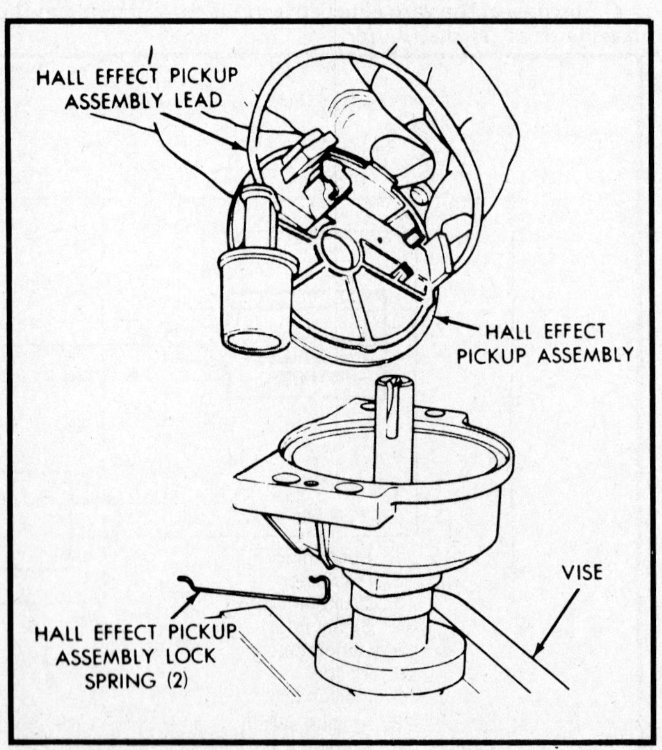

Hall Effect pick-up removal—1.7L engine

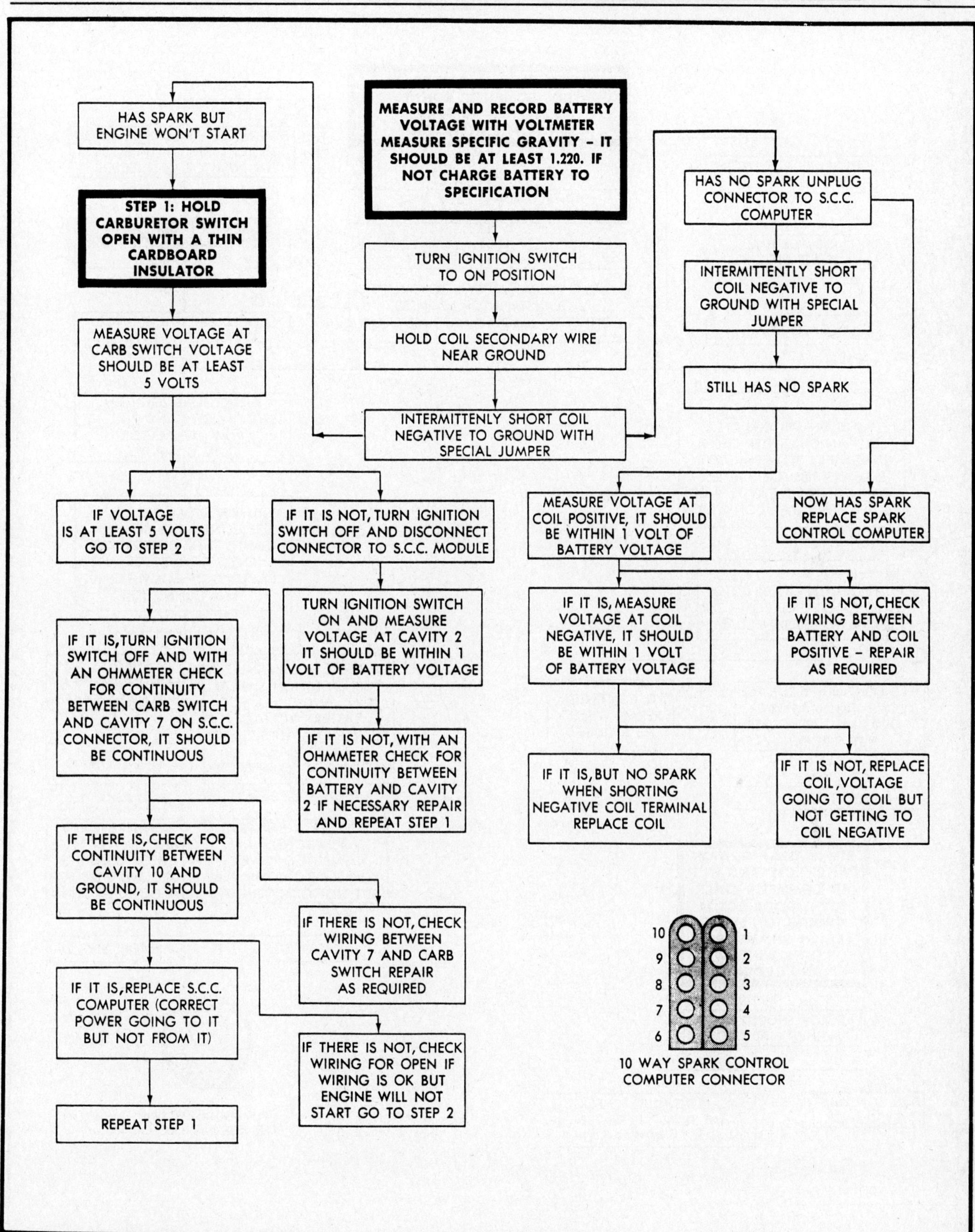
HAS SPARK BUT ENGINE WON'T START
STEP 1: HOLD CARBURETOR SWITCH OPEN WITH A THIN CARDBOARD INSULATOR
MEASURE VOLTAGE AT CARB SWITCH VOLTAGE SHOULD BE AT LEAST 5 VOLTS
IF VOLTAGE IS AT LEAST 5 VOLTS GO TO STEP 2
IF IT IS NOT, TURN IGNITION SWITCH OFF AND DISCONNECT CONNECTOR TO S.C.C. MODULE
IF IT IS, TURN IGNITION SWITCH OFF AND WITH AN OHMMETER CHECK FOR CONTINUITY BETWEEN CARB SWITCH AND CAVITY 7 ON S.C.C. CONNECTOR, IT SHOULD BE CONTINUOUS
TURN IGNITION SWITCH ON AND MEASURE VOLTAGE AT CAVITY 2 IT SHOULD BE WITHIN 1 VOLT OF BATTERY VOLTAGE
IF IT IS NOT, WITH AN OHMMETER CHECK FOR CONTINUITY BETWEEN BATTERY AND CAVITY 2 IF NECESSARY REPAIR AND REPEAT STEP 1
IF THERE IS, CHECK FOR CONTINUITY BETWEEN CAVITY 10 AND GROUND, IT SHOULD BE CONTINUOUS
IF THERE IS NOT, CHECK WIRING BETWEEN CAVITY 7 AND CARB SWITCH REPAIR AS REQUIRED
IF IT IS, REPLACE S.C.C. COMPUTER (CORRECT POWER GOING TO IT BUT NOT FROM IT)
IF THERE IS NOT, CHECK WIRING FOR OPEN IF WIRING IS OK BUT ENGINE WILL NOT START GO TO STEP 2
REPEAT STEP 1
MEASURE AND RECORD BATTERY VOLTAGE WITH VOLTMETER MEASURE SPECIFIC GRAVITY - IT SHOULD BE AT LEAST 1.220. IF NOT CHARGE BATTERY TO SPECIFICATION
TURN IGNITION SWITCH TO ON POSITION
HOLD COIL SECONDARY WIRE NEAR GROUND
INTERMITTENLY SHORT COIL NEGATIVE TO GROUND WITH SPECIAL JUMPER
HAS NO SPARK UNPLUG CONNECTOR TO S.C.C. COMPUTER
INTERMITTENTLY SHORT COIL NEGATIVE TO GROUND WITH SPECIAL JUMPER
STILL HAS NO SPARK
NOW HAS SPARK REPLACE SPARK CONTROL COMPUTER
MEASURE VOLTAGE AT COIL POSITIVE, IT SHOULD BE WITHIN 1 VOLT OF BATTERY VOLTAGE
IF IT IS, MEASURE VOLTAGE AT COIL NEGATIVE, IT SHOULD BE WITHIN 1 VOLT OF BATTERY VOLTAGE
IF IT IS NOT, CHECK WIRING BETWEEN BATTERY AND COIL POSITIVE - REPAIR AS REQUIRED
IF IT IS, BUT NO SPARK WHEN SHORTING NEGATIVE COIL TERMINAL REPLACE COIL
IF IT IS NOT, REPLACE COIL, VOLTAGE GOING TO COIL BUT NOT GETTING TO COIL NEGATIVE
10
9
8
7
6
1
2
3
4
5
10 WAY SPARK CONTROL COMPUTER CONNECTOR

Hall Effect Electronic Spark Advance System diagnosis—part 1 of 2

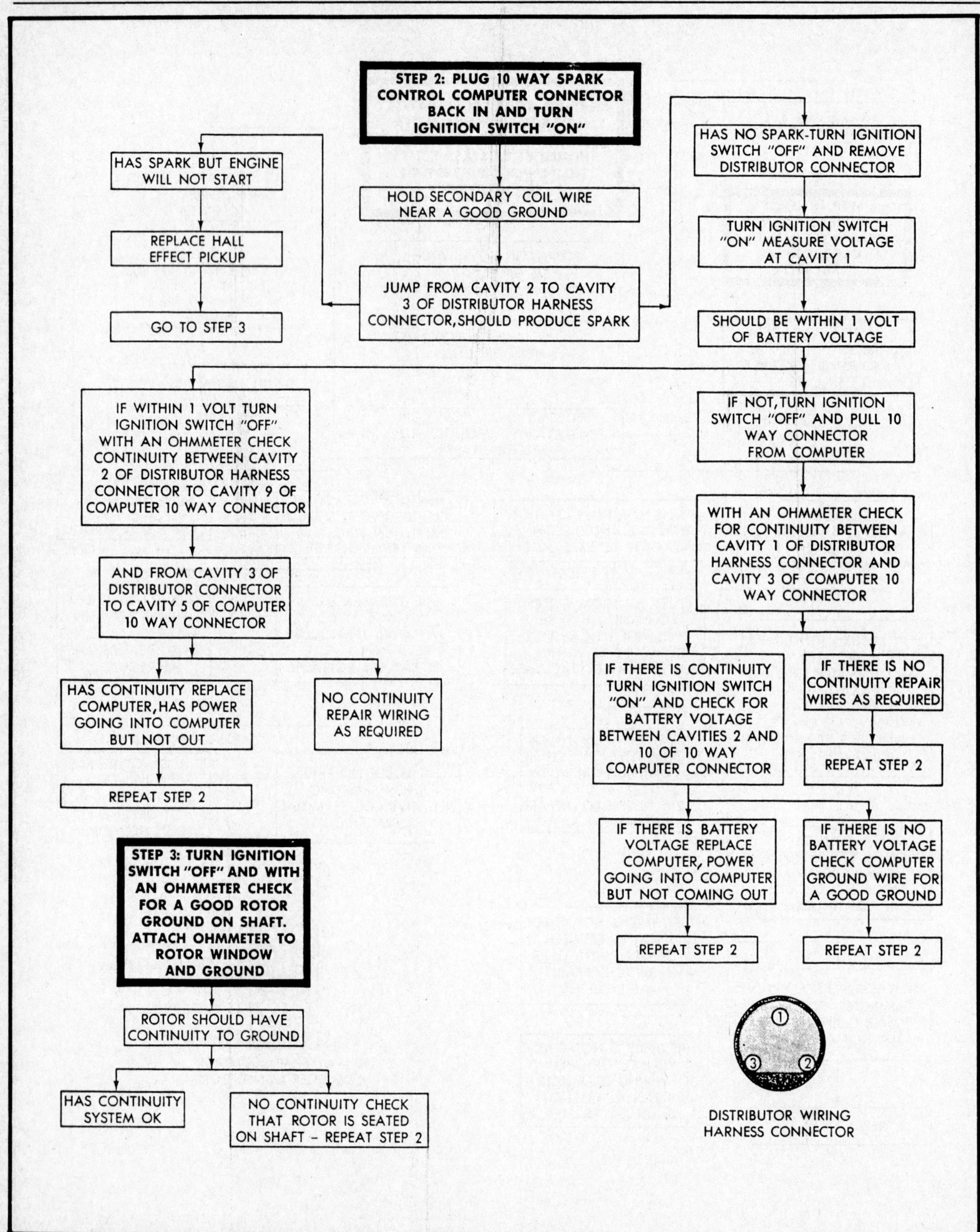
STEP 2: PLUG 10 WAY SPARK CONTROL COMPUTER CONNECTOR BACK IN AND TURN IGNITION SWITCH "ON"
HOLD SECONDARY COIL WIRE NEAR A GOOD GROUND
JUMP FROM CAVITY 2 TO CAVITY 3 OF DISTRIBUTOR HARNESS CONNECTOR, SHOULD PRODUCE SPARK
HAS SPARK BUT ENGINE WILL NOT START
REPLACE HALL EFFECT PICKUP
GO TO STEP 3
HAS NO SPARK-TURN IGNITION SWITCH "OFF" AND REMOVE DISTRIBUTOR CONNECTOR
TURN IGNITION SWITCH "ON" MEASURE VOLTAGE AT CAVITY 1
SHOULD BE WITHIN 1 VOLT OF BATTERY VOLTAGE
IF WITHIN 1 VOLT TURN IGNITION SWITCH "OFF" WITH AN OHMMETER CHECK CONTINUITY BETWEEN CAVITY 2 OF DISTRIBUTOR HARNESS CONNECTOR TO CAVITY 9 OF COMPUTER 10 WAY CONNECTOR
AND FROM CAVITY 3 OF DISTRIBUTOR CONNECTOR TO CAVITY 5 OF COMPUTER 10 WAY CONNECTOR
HAS CONTINUITY REPLACE COMPUTER, HAS POWER GOING INTO COMPUTER BUT NOT OUT
REPEAT STEP 2
NO CONTINUITY REPAIR WIRING AS REQUIRED
IF NOT, TURN IGNITION SWITCH "OFF" AND PULL 10 WAY CONNECTOR FROM COMPUTER
WITH AN OHMMETER CHECK FOR CONTINUITY BETWEEN CAVITY 1 OF DISTRIBUTOR HARNESS CONNECTOR AND CAVITY 3 OF COMPUTER 10 WAY CONNECTOR
IF THERE IS CONTINUITY TURN IGNITION SWITCH "ON" AND CHECK FOR BATTERY VOLTAGE BETWEEN CAVITIES 2 AND 10 OF 10 WAY COMPUTER CONNECTOR
IF THERE IS NO CONTINUITY REPAIR WIRES AS REQUIRED
REPEAT STEP 2
IF THERE IS BATTERY VOLTAGE REPLACE COMPUTER, POWER GOING INTO COMPUTER BUT NOT COMING OUT
REPEAT STEP 2
IF THERE IS NO BATTERY VOLTAGE CHECK COMPUTER GROUND WIRE FOR A GOOD GROUND
REPEAT STEP 2
STEP 3: TURN IGNITION SWITCH "OFF" AND WITH AN OHMMETER CHECK FOR A GOOD ROTOR GROUND ON SHAFT. ATTACH OHMMETER TO ROTOR WINDOW AND GROUND
ROTOR SHOULD HAVE CONTINUITY TO GROUND
HAS CONTINUITY SYSTEM OK
NO CONTINUITY CHECK THAT ROTOR IS SEATED ON SHAFT – REPEAT STEP 2
1
3
2
DISTRIBUTOR WIRING HARNESS CONNECTOR

Hall Effect Electronic Spark Advance System diagnosis—part 2 of 2

Chrysler Corp. Rampage And Scamp Models

IGNITION SYSTEMS

1.7 AND 2.2 LITER ENGINES

The Electronic Fuel Control System used on these engines consist of a Spark Control Computer, various sensors and a specially calibrated carburetor.

The Spark Control Computer is the center of the entire system. It gives the capability of igniting the fuel mixture according to different modes of engine operation by delivering an infinite amount of variable advance curves. The computer determines the exact instant when ignition is required and then signals the ignition coil to produce the electrical impulses which fire the spark plugs.

A Hall Effect Pickup, located in the distributor on these engines, supplies the basic timing signal to the computer. Also, the computer can determine from this signal engine speed (RPM)

HALL EFFECT PICKUP

Replacement

1. Remove the splash shield retaining screws and remove the splash shield on the 1.7 L engine.
2. Loosen the distributor cap retaining screws and lift off the distributor cap.
3. Remove the rotor from the shaft.
4. Remove the Hall Effect Pickup assembly from the distributor housing by removing the retaining springs on the 1.7L or the retaining clips on the 2.2L.
5. When placing the Hall Effect Pickup assembly into the housing make sure the lead retainer is in the locating hole properly before attaching the distributor cap.
6. Install the rotor with the ESA stamped on the top.
7. Install the cap and the shield assembly.

IGNITION SYSTEM

2.6 ENGINE

This system consists of the battery, ignition switch, ignition coil, IC igniter (electronic control unit), built into the distributor, spark plugs and intercomponent wiring. Primary current is switched by the IC ignitor in response to timing signals produced by a distributor magnetic pickup.

The distributor consists of a power distributing section, signal generator, IC igniter, advance mechanism and drive section. The signal generator is a small size magneto generator which produces signal for driving the IC ignitor. The distributor operates by using this signal as an ignition timing signal.

The distributor is equipped with both centrifugal and vacuum advance mechanisms.

A centrifugal advance mechanism, located below the rotor assembly, has governor weights that move inward or outward with changes in the engine speed. As engine speed increases, the weights move outward and cause the reluctor to rotate ahead of the distributor shaft, thus advancing the ignition timing.

The vacuum advance has a spring loaded diaphragm connected to the breaker assembly. The diaphragm is actuated against the spring pressure by carburetor vacuum pressure. When the vacuum increases, the diaphragm causes the movable breaker assembly to pivot in a direction opposite to distributor rotation, advancing the ignition timing

Troubleshooting

1. Remove the high voltage cable from the center tower of the distributor and hold the end of the cable at a point $^{3}/_{16}$–$^{3}/_{8}$ in. away from a good engine ground. In this condition, crank the engine with the starter and look for a spark at the coil high voltage cable.

CAUTION

Be sure there are no fuel leaks before performing this test.

2. If there is a spark at the coil secondary wire, it must be constant and bright blue in color. If it is, continue to crank the engine and while slowly moving the the coil secondary wire away from the ground, look for arching at the coil tower. If arcing occurs, replace the coil. If the spark is weak, not constant or there is no spark, proceed to step 3.

If the spark is good or there is no arcing at the coil tower, the ignition system is producing the necessary high secondary voltage. However, make sure that this voltage is getting to the spark plugs by checking the distributor rotor, cap, spark plug wires and spark plugs. If they are OK, then the igniton system is not the reason why the engine will not start. It will be necessary to check the fuel system and engine mechanical items.

3. Turn the ignition switch ON and measure the voltage at the negative coil terminal. The voltage should be the same as battery voltage. If it is 3 volts or less, the IC distributor is defective. If there is no voltage, check for an open circuit in the coil or wiring
4. With the key ON, use a special jumper wire and momemtarily touch the negative (-) terminal of the coil to ground while holding the the coil secondary wire ¼ in. from a good engine ground. A spark should be obtained.
5. If no spark was obtained, check for voltage at the positive (+) terminal of the coil with the key ON. Voltage should be at least 12 volts or battery voltage. If proper voltage is obtained, the coil is defective and should be replaced. If proper voltage is not obtained, check the wiring and connections.

CENTRIFUGAL ADVANCE

Testing

1. Run the engine at idle and remove the vacuum hose (non-stripped hose) from the vacuum controller.
2. Slowly accelerate the engine to check for advance.
   a. Excessive advance could be a deteriorated governor spring. A broken spring will cause abrupt advance.
   b. Insufficient advance or no advance could be the governor weight or cam.

VACUUM ADVANCE

Testing

1. Set the engine speed at 2,500 rpm. Check for advance by disconnecting and then reconnecting the vacuum hose at the distributor.
2. For more precise determination of whether the vacuum advance mechanism is operating properly, remove the vacuum hose from the distributor and connect a vacuum pump, tool No.C-4207, or equivalent to the advance.
3. Run the engine at idle and slowly apply vacuum pressure to check for advance.
   a. Excessive advance could be a deteriorated or sagging vacuum controller spring. A broken spring will cause abrupt advance.
   b. Insufficient advance or no advance could be a breaker plate in faulty operation or a broken diaphragm.

DISTRIBUTOR

Disassembly And Assembly

1. Remove the two distributor cap mounting screws and remove the distributor cap.

2. Remove the two rotor screws and remove the rotor.
3. Use a box or socket wrench and remove the governor assembly retaining bolt. Remove the governor assembly.

NOTE: The two springs of the governor are built to different specifications. Each spring must be installed in its own position. Make note of this for reassembly.

4. Remove the wire clamp screw and remove the clamp.
5. Remove the two pick-up coil and IC igniter tightening screws and remove the pick-up coil and IC igniter simultaneously.
6. Remove the two governor vacuum chamber screws and remove the governor vacuum chamber.
7. Remove the two breaker assembly screws and remove the breaker assembly. Keep the breaker assembly clean.
8. Remove the two bearing retainer plate screws and remove the bearing retainer.
9. Make alignment marks on the gear and shaft for reassembly.
10. Drive out the distributor drive gear pin with a punch and remove the drive gear.
11. Remove the distributor shaft and bearing assembly.
12. Remove the distributor housing seal.
13. Remove the two governor springs.

NOTE: The two springs of the governor are built to different specifications. Each spring must be installed in its own position. Make note of this for reassembly.

14. Remove the governor centrifugal plate and the governor weight.
15. Installation is the reverse of removal.

Chrysler Corp. Arrow, Ram 50, Ram Raider

FUEL INJECTION IGNITION SYSTEM

Troubleshooting

1982-83 MITSUBISHI AND NIPPON DENSO TYPE WITH ENGINE RUNNING

NOTE: All 1982–85 models use a Mitsubishi type distribiutor. Beginning in 1986, the distributor could be either a Mitsubishi or a Nippon Denso type distributor.

1. Start the engine, allow to idle until the normal operating temperature is reached.
2. Check the ignition timing, adjust if necessary.
3. Visually check electrical connections for frayed insulation or bare wires. Make sure all plug-in connectors are clean and tight. Check the spark plug and coil wires for cracking, crossfiring, corroded terminals, continuity and resistance. Check the distributor cap for cracks or carbon tracking. Check any suspect parts. Check the spark plugs for fouling, nonfiring and correct gap.
4. If none of the checks have solved the problem, or the car fails to start, proceed to the following tests.

ENGINE DOES NOT RUN

1. Remove the coil wire from the distributor cap tower. Hold the end of the wire with insulated pliers.

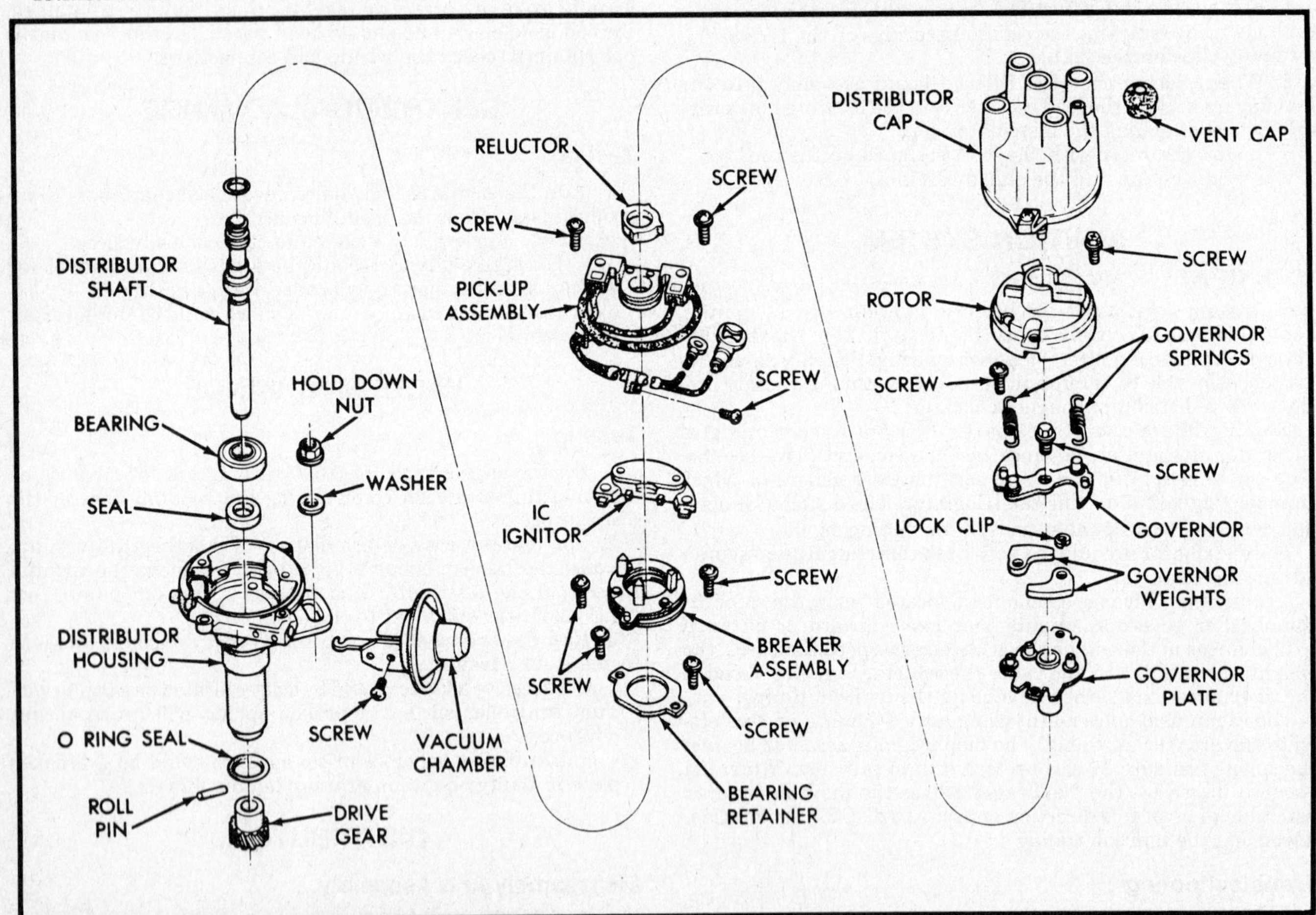

Exploded view of the distributor—2.6 Liter engine

2. Locate the end of the wire about 1/4 in. away from the cylinder head and crank the engine with the starter.

3. Observe the spark or no spark condition. If a spark is produced, the IC igniter and ignition coil may be considered in good condition.

4. Remove the distributor cap and check it for cracks, carbon tracking or dirt. Check the rotor for wear. Replace as necessary.

5. If no sparks are produced, a defective control unit (internal), pick-up coil, ignition coil or faulty wiring may be the problem.

IGNITION COIL

Testing

If the the earlier test produces no spark, the ignition coil could be at fault. The fastest way to check is by substituting a known good coil. If a coil is not on hand, proceed with one or more of the following tests:

1. With the ignition switch in the ON position, measure the voltage at the negative terminal of the ignition coil. If zero volts are shown, there is an open circuit in the coil.

2. Check the ignition coil resistance. If the engine will run, allow it to reach normal operating temperature (the ignition coil should be hot). Shut off the engine and disconnect the high tension lead (coil wire) from the coil tower.

3. Measure primary resistance with an ohmmeter, connecting the coil negative and positive primary terminals. Resistance should be 0.7–0.85 Ω.

4. Measure the secondary resistance by connecting the ohmmeter between the contacts in the coil tower and the positive primary terminal. Resistance should be 9–11k Ω.

5. Replace the coil if the voltage tests show zero volts or the resistances are not within specifications.

EXTERNAL RESISTOR

Testing

1. With the ignition switch off, connect an ohmmeter between the terminals of the external resistor.

2. Obtain a reading from the ohmmeter. Resistance should be 1.22–1.49 Ω.

3. If the reading on the ohmmeter is zero or not within specs, replace the resistor.

PICK-UP COIL

Testing

1. The pick-up coil may be tested while mounted in the distributor.

2. Remove the cap and rotor and connect an ohmmeter between the two terminals of the pick-up coil.

3. Replace the pick-up coil if the resistance is not within these limits: 920–1.120 Ω.

PICK-UP COIL

Replacement

NOTE: The distributor must be removed from the engine.

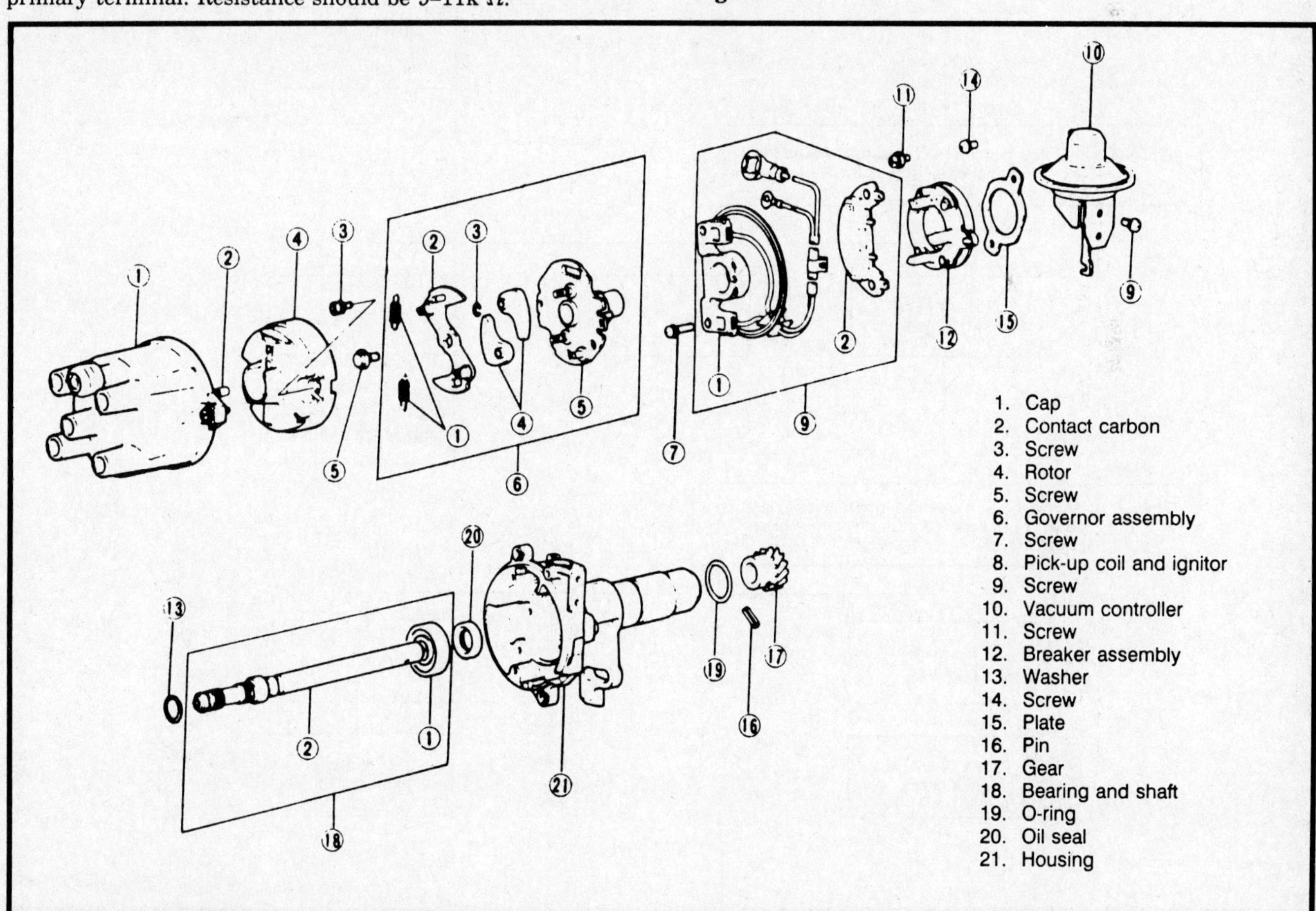

Mitsubishi type distributor—1982-83

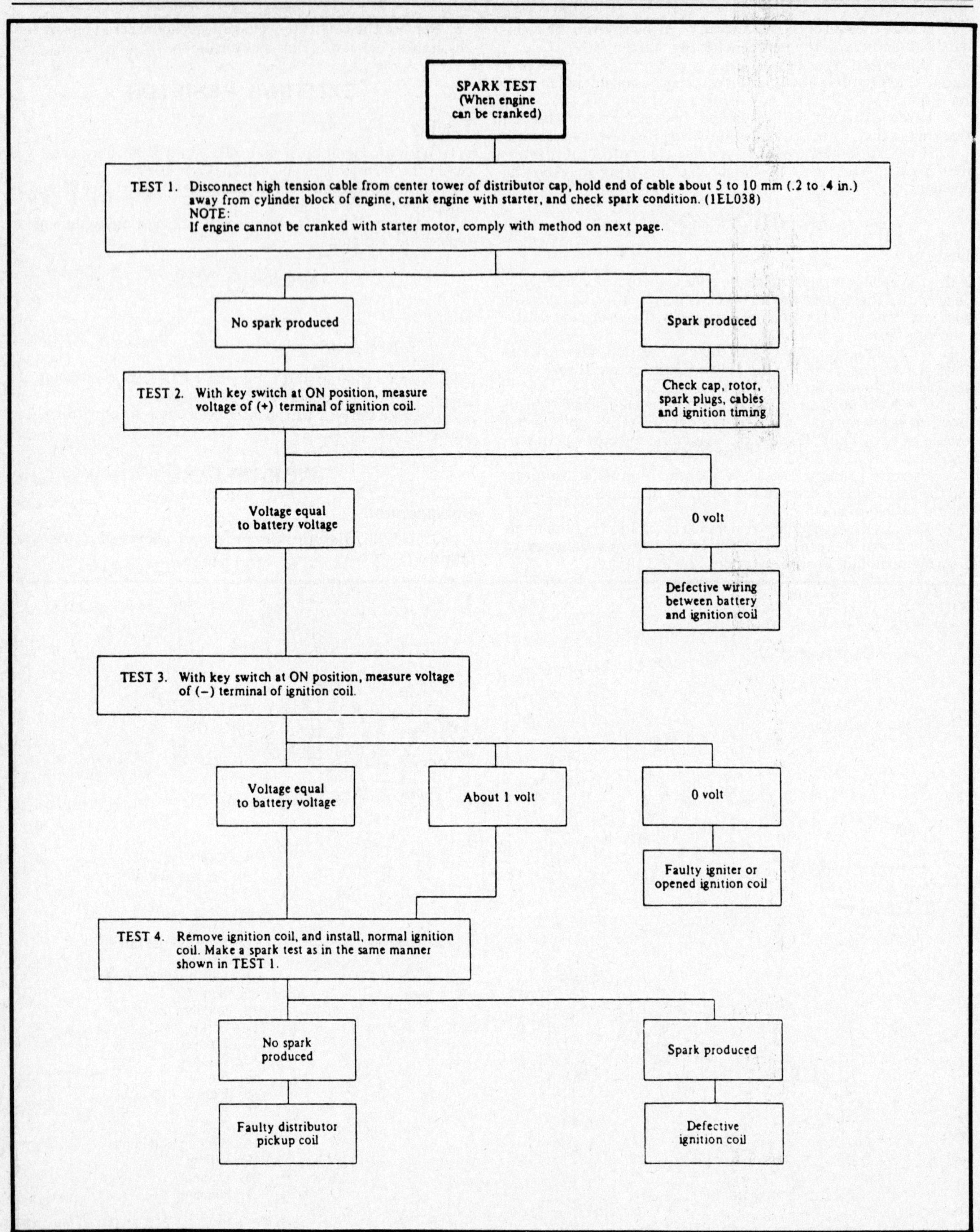
SPARK TEST (When engine can be cranked)
TEST 1. Disconnect high tension cable from center tower of distributor cap, hold end of cable about 5 to 10 mm (.2 to .4 in.) away from cylinder block of engine, crank engine with starter, and check spark condition. (1EL038)
NOTE:
If engine cannot be cranked with starter motor, comply with method on next page.
No spark produced
Spark produced
Check cap, rotor, spark plugs, cables and ignition timing
TEST 2. With key switch at ON position, measure voltage of (+) terminal of ignition coil.
Voltage equal to battery voltage
0 volt
Defective wiring between battery and ignition coil
TEST 3. With key switch at ON position, measure voltage of (−) terminal of ignition coil.
Voltage equal to battery voltage
About 1 volt
0 volt
Faulty igniter or opened ignition coil
TEST 4. Remove ignition coil, and install, normal ignition coil. Make a spark test as in the same manner shown in TEST 1.
No spark produced
Spark produced
Faulty distributor pickup coil
Defective ignition coil

1. Remove the distributor cap and rotor.
2. Remove the center mounting bolt (screw) and remove the governor assembly. Take care not to mix up the governor springs. They must be installed in the same position. Remove the reluctor.
3. Remove the two mounting screws and take out the pick-up coil and IC igniter. Carefully pull the igniter from the pick-up coil.
4. Installation of the new pick-up coil is the reverse of the removal.

RELUCTOR GAP

Inspection

The reluctor gap can only be checked. Doing so is not a matter of routine maintenance, but usually is necessary only if the distributor is overhauled. However, too tight a fit between the signal rotor and the pickup stator could cause rotation of the distributor to damage the parts involved or produce an incorrect signal.

In some cases, severe wear or incorrect original manufacturing tolerances in the distributor bearings could cause wear of these two pieces that resembles damage due to too tight a fit. However, in this case, the appropriate gap would exist between the rotor and stator and there would be excessive play in the distributor shaft.

DISTRIBUTOR

Disassembly And Assembly

1. Remove the distributor cap. Remove the rotor.
2. Rotate the engine using a wrench on the front pulley, until the three vertical stator pieces line up with three of the rotor lobes.
3. Using a non-magnetic (brass, plastic, or wood) feeler gauge of 0.008 in. thickness and insert it straight between the stator and rotor. As long as the gauge can be inserted and moved easily, the parts are okay. The gap may be wider than the 0.008 in. specification.
4. Install the cap and rotor.

DISTRIBUTOR

Disassembly And Assembly

1982-83

1. Loosen the two screws and remove the distributor cap.
2. Remove the rotor.
3. Remove the governor assembly. Before the governor weights and springs are removed, make marks on either one of of the governor pins and springs for reference during reassembly.
4. Remove the pick-up coil and igniter.

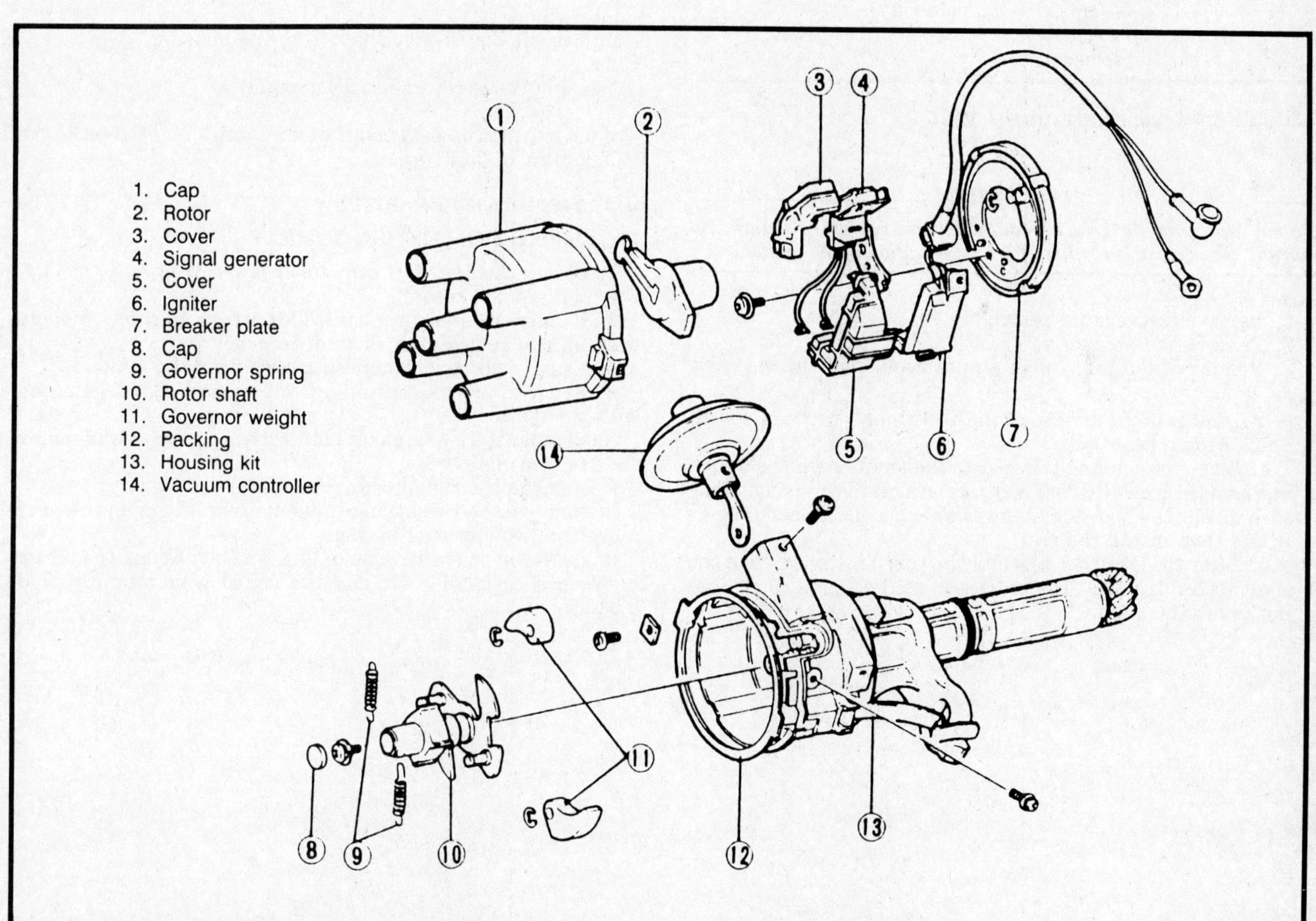

Nippon Denso type distributor—1984-88

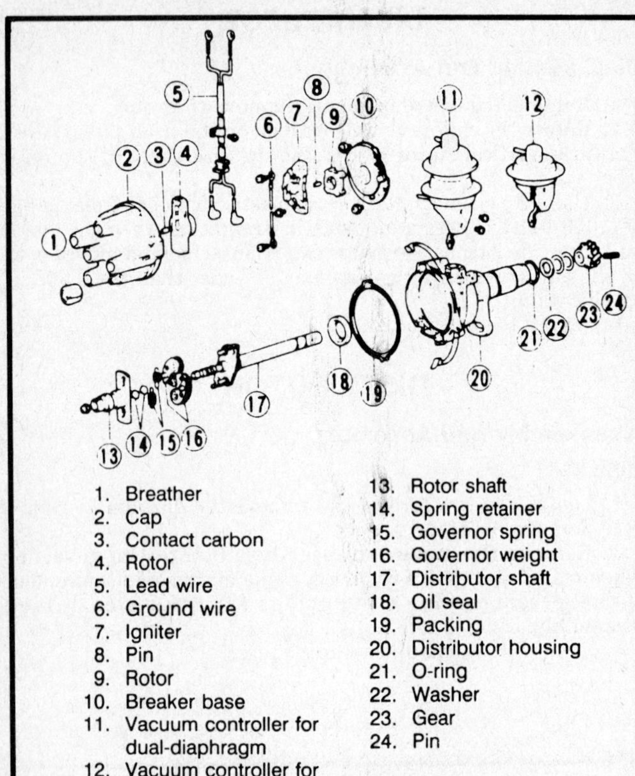

Mitsubishi type distributor—1984-88

CAUTION

Do not wipe away the grease from the reverse side of the igniter and housing. The grease is required for heat radiation of the ignitor.

5. Remove the vacuum controller.
6. Remove the breaker assembly.
7. Remove the roll pin with a punch and slide off the drive gear.
8. Assembly is the reverse of the disassembly procedure with the following precautions:
   a. When assembling the gear to the shaft, align the punch mark on the gear with the mating mark on the housing. Make sure the notched portion of the shaft end is positioned properly and then install the pin.
   b. After the governor assembly has been installed, turn the shaft to confirm that the projection of the signal rotor does not touch the stator.

IGNITION SYSTEM

Troubleshooting

1984-88

These vehicle models use either a Mitsubishi or Nippon Denso type distributor. The following troubleshooting chart applies to both.

DISTRIBUTOR

Disassembly And Assembly

1984-88 MITSUBISHI TYPE

1. Clamp the distributor in a soft jawed vise.
2. Pull off the rotor.
3. Remove the two vacuum controller attaching screws, remove the link and remove the vacuum controller.
4. Remove the two retaining screws and the igniter.
5. Remove the black lead wire.
6. Remove the signal rotor shaft tightening screw and the two breaker plate retaining screws and remove the rotor shaft and and breaker plate.
7. Remove the signal rotor shaft from the signal rotor.
8. Remove the two spring retainers with pliers and then remove the two governor springs.
9. Remove the two governor weights.
10. Mark the location of the drive gear on the distributor shaft.
11. Drive out the roll pin with a punch and remove the drive gear and washer.
12. Remove the distributor shaft from the housing.
13. Assembly is the reverse of disassembly.
14. Adjust the air gap between the signal rotor and the pick-up of the ignitor to 0.031 in.

Disassembly And Assembly

1984-88 NIPPON DENSO TYPE

1. Clamp the distributor in a soft jawed vise.
2. Pull off the rotor.
3. Remove the vacuum controller attaching screw. Remove the link and remove the vacuum controller.
4. Remove the two retaining screws from the igniter.
5. Remove the two retaining screws and signal generator with the ignitor.
6. Remove the two breaker plate retaining screws and remove the breaker plate.
7. Remove the signal rotor shaft from the signal rotor.
8. Remove the two spring retainers with pliers and then remove the two governor springs.
9. Assembly is the reverse of disassembly. Adjust the air gap between the signal rotor and the signal generator to 0.008–0.015 in.

Brakes Import Trucks 21

INDEX

HYDRAULIC SYSTEM SERVICE

DRUM BRAKE SERVICE

DISC BRAKE SERVICE

PARKING BRAKE SERVICE

POWER BRAKE BOOSTER SERVICE

Brakes

IMPORT CARDS AND LIGHT TRUCKS

NOTICE: Should state inspection regulations exceed manufacturer's specifications for lining or rotor/drum reserve, the state inspection regulation specification **must** be used.

Year, Make, Model	Brake Shoe Minimum Lining Thickness	Brake Drum Diameter Standard Size	Brake Drum Diameter Machine To	Brake Pad Minimum Lining Thickness	Brake Rotor Min. Thickness Machine To	Brake Rotor Min. Thickness Discard At	Brake Rotor Variation From Parallelism	Brake Rotor Runout T.I.R.	Caliper Mounting Bolts Torque (ft-lbs)	Caliper Bridge, Pin or Key Bolts Torque (ft-lbs)	Wheel Lugs or Nuts Torque (ft-lbs)	Wheel Bearing Setting STEP 1 Tighten Spindle Nut (ft-lbs)	Wheel Bearing Setting STEP 2 Back Off Retorque (in-lbs)	Wheel Bearing Setting STEP 3 Lock, or Back Off and Lock
CHRYSLER/PLYMOUTH														
79-82 Arrow Pickup	.040	9.500	9.550	.040	—	.720	—	.006	51-65	—	51-58	21.7	48	Step 2
DATSUN/NISSAN														
82-83 720 Pickup	.059	10.000	10.055	.080	—	.413	.0012	.006	53-72	12-15	87-108	25-29†	Skip	1/6 Turn
84-86 720 Pickup single whl.	.059	10.000	10.060	.080	—	.787	.0012★	.0028	53-72	16-23	87-108	25-29•	Skip	1/8 Turn
dual whl.	.059	8.660	8.720	.080	—	.787	.0012★	.0028	53-72	16-23	87-108■	25-29•	Skip	1/8 Turn
86-87 D21 Pickup 2 W.D. w/4 cyl. gas eng.	.059	10.240	10.300	.079	—	.787	—	.0028	53-72	16-23	87-108	25-29	45°	15°
exc./4 cyl. gas. eng. w/8.66" rear brakes	.059	8.660	8.720	.079	—	.945	—	.0028	53-72	16-23	87-108■	25-29	45°	15°
w/10" rear brakes	.059	10.000	10.060	.079	—	.945	—	.0028	53-72	16-23	87-108	25-29	45°	15°
w/10.24" rear brakes	.059	10.240	10.300	.079	—	.945	—	.0028	53-72	16-23	87-108	25-29	45°	15°
4/W.D.	.059	10.240	10.300	.079	—	.945	—	.0028	53-72	16-23	87-108	58-72	12	15°-30°
87 Pathfinder	.059	10.000	10.060	.079	—	.945	—	.0028	53-72	16-23	87-108	58-72	12	15°-30°
87 Vanette	.059	10.240	10.300	.079	—	.945	—	.0028	53-72	16-23	72-87	NOT ADJUSTABLE		

Chrysler/Plymouth notes:

■ w/aluminum wheels; 58-72 ft/lbs.
• w/aluminum wheels; 65-80 ft/lbs.
‡ 1984-87 58-72 ft/lbs.

Datsun/Nissan notes:

★ 1985-86—.0008"
†† 1985-86—28-38 ft/lbs.
† 2 WD only; 4 WD 108-145 ft/lbs.
□ 1983—.0028"
• 2 WD only; 4 WD 58-72 ft/lbs.—loosen— + 15°-30°
■ Front shown, rear; 84 159-188 ft/lbs. 1985-87 exc. Alum. wheel 166-203 ft/lbs., Alum. wheel 58-72 ft/lbs.
▲ 1987 72-87 ft/lbs.

IMPORT CARS AND LIGHT TRUCKS

NOTICE: Should state inspection regulations exceed manufacturer's specifications for lining or rotor/drum reserve, the state inspection regulation specification **must** be used.

Year, Make, Model	Brake Shoe: Minimum Lining Thickness	Brake Drum Diameter: Standard Size	Brake Drum Diameter: Machine To	Brake Pad: Minimum Lining Thickness	Brake Rotor Min. Thickness: Machine To	Brake Rotor Min. Thickness: Discard At	Brake Rotor: Variation From Parallelism	Brake Rotor: Runout T.I.R.	Caliper: Mounting Bolts Torque (ft-lbs)	Caliper: Bridge, Pin or Key Bolts Torque (ft-lbs)	Wheel: Lugs or Nuts Torque (ft-lbs)	Wheel Bearing Setting STEP 1: Tighten Spindle Nut (ft-lbs)	Wheel Bearing Setting STEP 2: Back Off Retorque (in-lbs)	Wheel Bearing Setting STEP 3: Lock, or Back Off and Lock
DODGE														
79-82 D-50, Ram-50 Pickup	.040	9.500	9.550	.040	—	.720	—	.006	51-65	—	51-58	21.7	48	Step 2
83-86 Ram-50														
w/9½" rear brake	.040	9.500	9.570	.040	—	.720	—	.006	51-65	—	51-57	21.7††	69.6	Step 2
w/10" rear brake	.040	10.000	10.070	.040	—	.720	—	.006	51-65★	—	51-57	94-145†	216	30°
87 Raider	.040	10.000	10.079	.040	—	.724	—	.0059	58-72	—	72-87	94-145	150	30°-40°
87 Ram 50 (4x2)	.040	10.000	10.079	.079	—	.803	—	.0059	58-72	—	87-101	22	72	Skip
(4x4)	.040	10.000	10.079	.079	—	.803	—	.0059	58-72	—	87-101	94-145	150	30°-40°

□ Caliper to adapter shown, adapter to caliper 29-36 ft/lbs.
■ w/aluminum wheels; 58-72 ft/lbs.
† 4 WD
†† 2 WD
• w/aluminum wheels; 65-80 ft/lbs.
★ 1985-86 4 WD 58-72 ft/lbs.
‡ 1984-87 58-72 ft/lbs.

Year, Make, Model	Brake Shoe: Minimum Lining Thickness	Brake Drum Diameter: Standard Size	Brake Drum Diameter: Machine To	Brake Pad: Minimum Lining Thickness	Brake Rotor Min. Thickness: Machine To	Brake Rotor Min. Thickness: Discard At	Brake Rotor: Variation From Parallelism	Brake Rotor: Runout T.I.R.	Caliper: Mounting Bolts Torque (ft-lbs)	Caliper: Bridge, Pin or Key Bolts Torque (ft-lbs)	Wheel: Lugs or Nuts Torque (ft-lbs)	Wheel Bearing Setting STEP 1: Tighten Spindle Nut (ft-lbs)	Wheel Bearing Setting STEP 2: Back Off Retorque (in-lbs)	Wheel Bearing Setting STEP 3: Lock, or Back Off and Lock
ISUZU														
81-83 Pickup	.039	10.000	10.039	.039	.453	.437	.003	.005	64	15	65	22	Handtight	1.8-2.6□
81-84 I-Mark	.039	9.000	9.040	.067	.354	.338	—	.006	36	—	50†	22	Handtight	Step 2
84-86 Trooper II	.039	10.000	10.039	.039	.668	.654	.0012	.005	62-65	22-25	58-80†	22	Handtight	2.2■□
84-87 Pickup	.039	10.000	10.039	.039	.668	.654	.0012	.005	62-65	22-25	58-80†	22	Handtight	2.2■□
87 Trooper II	.039	10.000	10.039	.039	.826	.811	—	—	—	—	—	—	—	—

† w/aluminum whls. 90 ft/lbs.
□ Radial pull in lbs. at lug nuts.
■ 4x2 shown, 4x4-3.3

IMPORT CARDS AND LIGHT TRUCKS

NOTICE: Should state inspection regulations exceed manufacturer's specifications for lining or rotor/drum reserve, the state inspection regulation specification **must** be used.

Year, Make, Model	Brake Shoe: Minimum Lining Thickness	Brake Drum Diameter: Standard Size	Brake Drum Diameter: Machine To	Brake Pad: Minimum Lining Thickness	Brake Rotor Min. Thickness: Machine To	Brake Rotor Min. Thickness: Discard At	Brake Rotor: Variation From Parallelism	Brake Rotor: Runout T.I.R.	Caliper: Mounting Bolts Torque (ft-lbs)	Caliper: Bridge, Pin or Key Bolts Torque (ft-lbs)	Wheel: Lugs or Nuts Torque (ft-lbs)	Wheel Bearing Setting STEP 1: Tighten Spindle Nut (ft-lbs)	Wheel Bearing Setting STEP 2: Back Off Retorque (in-lbs)	Wheel Bearing Setting STEP 3: Lock, or Back Off and Lock
LUV-CHEVROLET														
81-82	.059	10.000	10.059	.236	.668	.653	.003	.005	64	15	65	22■	Handtight	Step 2

■ Wheel bearing adjustment for 2 WD only

Year, Make, Model	Brake Shoe: Minimum Lining Thickness	Brake Drum Diameter: Standard Size	Brake Drum Diameter: Machine To	Brake Pad: Minimum Lining Thickness	Brake Rotor Min. Thickness: Machine To	Brake Rotor Min. Thickness: Discard At	Brake Rotor: Variation From Parallelism	Brake Rotor: Runout T.I.R.	Caliper: Mounting Bolts Torque (ft-lbs)	Caliper: Bridge, Pin or Key Bolts Torque (ft-lbs)	Wheel: Lugs or Nuts Torque (ft-lbs)	Wheel Bearing Setting STEP 1: Tighten Spindle Nut (ft-lbs)	Wheel Bearing Setting STEP 2: Back Off Retorque (in-lbs)	Wheel Bearing Setting STEP 3: Lock, or Back Off and Lock
MAZDA														
77-83 B1800/B2000 Pickup	.040	10.236	10.275	.276■	—	.433	—	.004	40-47	—	58-65	SEAT	1.3-2.4□	Step 2
82-83 B2200 Pickup	.040	10.236	10.275	.276■	—	.748	—	.004	40-47	—	58-65	SEAT	1.3-2.4□	Step 2
84 B2200 Pickup	.040	10.236	10.275	.040	—	.748	—	.004	40-47	—	58-65	18-22	Handtight	1.3-2.5□
84 B2000 Pickup	.040	10.236	10.275	.040	—	.433	—	.004	40-47	—	58-65	18-22	Handtight	1.3-2.5□
86-87 B2000 Pickup	.040	10.240	10.310	.118	—	.710	—	.002	65-80	23-30	87-108	14-22	Handtight	1.3-2.4□
87 B2200, 2600 Pickup 4x2	.040	10.240	10.300	.118	—	.710	—	.006	65-80	23-30	65-87†	14-22	Handtight	1.3-2.4□
4x4	.040	10.240	10.300	.118	—	.790	—	.006	65-80	23-30	65-87†	14-22	Handtight	1.3-2.6□

■ Measurement of shoe & lining
□ Radial pull in lbs. at lug nuts.
* Upper bolt: 11-18 ft/lbs., Lower bolt: 15-22 ft/lbs.
† Design wheel shown; styled wheel 87-108 ft/lbs.

Year, Make, Model	Brake Shoe: Minimum Lining Thickness	Brake Drum Diameter: Standard Size	Brake Drum Diameter: Machine To	Brake Pad: Minimum Lining Thickness	Brake Rotor Min. Thickness: Machine To	Brake Rotor Min. Thickness: Discard At	Brake Rotor: Variation From Parallelism	Brake Rotor: Runout T.I.R.	Caliper: Mounting Bolts Torque (ft-lbs)	Caliper: Bridge, Pin or Key Bolts Torque (ft-lbs)	Wheel: Lugs or Nuts Torque (ft-lbs)	Wheel Bearing Setting STEP 1: Tighten Spindle Nut (ft-lbs)	Wheel Bearing Setting STEP 2: Back Off Retorque (in-lbs)	Wheel Bearing Setting STEP 3: Lock, or Back Off and Lock
MITSUBISHI														
83-86 Pickup w/9½" rear brakes	.040	9.500	9.550	.040	—	.720	—	.006	51-65	—	51-57	21.7■	69.6	Step 2
w/10" rear brakes	.040	10.000	10.070	.040	—	.720	—	.006	51-65□	—	51-57	94-145•	216	30°
83-86 Montero	.040	10.000	10.040	.040	—	.720	—	.006	51-65□	—	72-87*	95-145	216	30°
87 Pickup 4x2	.040	10.000	10.070	.040	—	.803	—	.006	58-72	29-36	87-101	22	72	Step 2
4x4	.040	10.000	10.070	.040	—	.803	—	.006	58-72	29-36	87-101	94-145	216	30°-40°
87 Montero	.040	10.000	10.040	.040	—	.724	—	.006	58-72	—	72-87	94-145	216	30°-40°
87 Van Wagon	.040	10.000	10.080	.079	—	.803	—	.006	59-74	30-37	87-101	22	72	Step 2

† w/aluminum wheels; 57-72 ft/lbs.
■ 2 WD
• 4 WD.
†† w/aluminum wheels; (1984-87) 65-80 ft/lbs. (1983) 57-72 ft/lbs.
+ w/aluminum wheels; 66-81 ft/lbs.
□ 1985-86 58-72 ft/lbs.
* 1983; 50-57 ft/lbs.

IMPORT CARDS AND LIGHT TRUCKS

NOTICE: Should state inspection regulations exceed manufacturer's specifications for lining or rotor/drum reserve, the state inspection regulation specification **must** be used.

Year, Make, Model	Brake Shoe: Minimum Lining Thickness	Brake Drum Diameter: Standard Size	Brake Drum Diameter: Machine To	Brake Pad: Minimum Lining Thickness	Brake Rotor Min. Thickness: Machine To	Brake Rotor Min. Thickness: Discard At	Brake Rotor: Variation From Parallelism	Brake Rotor: Runout T.I.R.	Caliper: Mounting Bolts Torque (ft-lbs)	Caliper: Bridge, Pin or Key Bolts Torque (ft-lbs)	Wheel: Lugs or Nuts Torque (ft-lbs)	Wheel Bearing Setting STEP 1: Tighten Spindle Nut (ft-lbs)	STEP 2: Back Off Retorque (in-lbs)	STEP 3: Lock, or Back Off and Lock
SUZUKI														
86–87 Samurai	.120■	8.660	8.740	.236■	—	.334	—	.006	51–72	18–21	36–57	Not Adjustable		

■ Measurement of shoe & lining

Year, Make, Model	Brake Shoe: Minimum Lining Thickness	Brake Drum Diameter: Standard Size	Brake Drum Diameter: Machine To	Brake Pad: Minimum Lining Thickness	Brake Rotor Min. Thickness: Machine To	Brake Rotor Min. Thickness: Discard At	Brake Rotor: Variation From Parallelism	Brake Rotor: Runout T.I.R.	Caliper: Mounting Bolts Torque (ft-lbs)	Caliper: Bridge, Pin or Key Bolts Torque (ft-lbs)	Wheel: Lugs or Nuts Torque (ft-lbs)	Wheel Bearing Setting STEP 1: Tighten Spindle Nut (ft-lbs)	STEP 2: Back Off Retorque (in-lbs)	STEP 3: Lock, or Back Off and Lock
TOYOTA														
75–83 Pickup 2 W.D. (4x2)	.040	10.000	10.060	.040	—	.453	—	.006	68–86	—	66–86	22	Handtight	1.3–3.8■
75–84 Land Cruiser	.060	11.610	11.650	.040	—	.748	—	.005	52–76	—	66–86	43	35–60	6.2–12.6■
79–83 4x4 Pickup	.040	10.000	10.060	.040	—	.453	—	.006	55–75	—	66–86	43	35–60	6.2–12.6■
79–83 4x2 Cab & Chassis	.040	10.000	10.060	.040	—	.748	—	.006	80–126	29–39	66–86	22	Handtight	1.3–3.8■
84 Pickup 2 W.D. (4x2)	.040	10.000	10.060	.040	—	.827	—	.006	73–86	62–68	76	25	Handtight	1.3–4.0■
84–85 Pickup 4x4	.040	10.000	10.060	.040	—	.453	—	.006	55–75	—	76	43	Handtight	18 ft/lbs.•
84–86 VanWagon	.040	10.000	10.060	.040	—	.748	—	.006	61	14	76	21	Handtight	.8–1.9■
85–87 Pickup 2 W.D. (4x2) 1/2 ton	.040	10.000	10.060	.040	—	.827	—	.006	80	65	76	25	Handtight	1.3–4.0■
1 ton, Heavy	.040	10.000	10.060	.040	—	.945	—	.006	80▲	29	76+	25	Handtight	1.3–4.0■‡
86 Pickup 4x4	.060	11.614	11.654	.040	—	.748	—	.006	90	—	76	43	Handtight	6.2–12.6■
87 Pickup 4x4	.040	11.614	11.693	.040	—	.748	—	.006	90	—	76	43	Handtight	6.2–12.6■
87 VanWagon 4x2	.040	10.000	10.079	.040	—	.748	—	.006	77	14	76	21	Handtight	.8–1.9■
4x4	.040	10.000	10.079	.118	—	.945	—	.006	61	27	76	43	Handtight	11 ft/lbs.

■ Radial pull in lbs. at lug nuts.
• torque locknut to 33 ft/lbs., brg. preload; 2.2–8.6 lbs.
‡ 1987 w/dual rear wheels 0.9–2.2 lbs.
† 1987 34 ft/lbs.
▲ 1987 90 ft/lbs.
+ 1987 w/dual rear wheels, rear wheel 140 ft/lbs.
□ 14" wheel shown, 13" wheel 51–65 ft/lbs.

Year, Make, Model	Brake Shoe: Minimum Lining Thickness	Brake Drum Diameter: Standard Size	Brake Drum Diameter: Machine To	Brake Pad: Minimum Lining Thickness	Brake Rotor Min. Thickness: Machine To	Brake Rotor Min. Thickness: Discard At	Brake Rotor: Variation From Parallelism	Brake Rotor: Runout T.I.R.	Caliper: Mounting Bolts Torque (ft-lbs)	Caliper: Bridge, Pin or Key Bolts Torque (ft-lbs)	Wheel: Lugs or Nuts Torque (ft-lbs)	Wheel Bearing Setting STEP 1: Tighten Spindle Nut (ft-lbs)	STEP 2: Back Off Retorque (in-lbs)	STEP 3: Lock, or Back Off and Lock
VOLKSWAGEN														
80–85 Vanagon	.098	9.921	9.960	.078	.452	.433	—	.004 ■	115	—	123	Snug-Up	Handtight	Step 2
82–84 Rabbit Pickup	.098	7.874	7.894	.250†	.413	.393	—	.002 8	50	30	87	■	—	—
86–87 Vanagon	.098	9.921	9.960	.079	—	.512	—	.004 61	26	—	123	Snug-Up	Handtight	Step 2

■ Seat brg. while turning wheel, back off nut until thrust washer can be moved slightly by screwdriver w/finger pressure, lock.
* .098 riveted; .059 bonded
• Design 38 or 39
† Measurement of shoe & lining
□ w/self locking bolt 50 ft/lbs.

HYDRAULIC BRAKE SYSTEM TROUBLE DIAGNOSIS

Condition	Possible Cause	Correction
Insufficient brakes	1. Improper brake adjustment.	1. Adjust brakes.
	2. Worn lining.	2. Replace brake lining and adjust brakes.
	3. Sticking brakes.	3. Lubricate brake pivots and support platforms.
	4. Brake valve pressure low.	4. Inspect for leaks and obstructed brake lines.
	5. Slack adjuster to diaphragm rod not adjusted properly.	5. Adjust slack adjuster.
	6. Master cylinder low on brake fluid.	6. Fill master cylinder and inspect for leaks.
Brakes apply slowly	1. Improper brake adjustment or lack of lubrication.	1. Adjust brakes and lubricate linkage.
	2. Low air pressure.	2. Check belt tension and compressor for output. Adjust as necessary.
	3. Brake valve delivery pressure low.	3. Check valve pressure and clean or replace as necessary.
	4. Excessive leakage with brakes applied.	4. Inspect all fittings and lines for leaks and repair as necessary.
	5. Restriction in brake line or hose.	5. Clean or replace brake line or hose.
Spongy pedal	1. Air in hydraulic system.	1. Fill and bleed hydraulic system.
	2. Swollen rubber parts due to contaminated brake fluid.	2. Clean hydraulic system and recondition wheel cylinders and master cylinder.
	3. Improper brake shoe adjustment.	3. Adjust brakes.
	4. Brake fluid with low boiling point.	4. Flush hydraulic system and refill with proper brake fluid.
	5. Brake drums ground excessively.	5. Replace brake drums.
Erratic brakes	1. Linings soaked with grease or brake fluid.	1. Correct the leak and replace brake lining.
	2. Primary and secondary shoes mounted in wrong position.	2. Match the primary and secondary shoes and mount in proper position.
Chattering brakes	1. Improper adjustment of brake shoes.	1. Adjust brakes.
	2. Loose front wheel bearings.	2. Clean, pack and adjust wheel bearings.
	3. Hard spots in brake drums.	3. Grind or replace brake drums.
	4. Out-of-round brake drums.	4. Grind or replace brake drums.
	5. Grease or brake fluid on lining.	5. Correct leak and replace brake lining.
Squealing brakes	1. Incorrect lining.	1. Install correct lining.
	2. Distorted brakedrum.	2. Grind or replace brake drum.
	3. Bent brake support plate.	3. Replace brake support plate.
	4. Bent brake shoes.	4. Replace brake shoes.
	5. Foreign material embedded in brake lining.	5. Replace brake shoes.
	6. Dust or dirt in brake drum.	6. Use compressed air and blow out drums and support plate and shoes.
	7. Shoes dragging on support plate.	7. Sand support plate platforms and lubricate.
	8. Loose support plate.	8. Tighten support plate attaching nuts.
	9. Loose anchor bolts.	9. Tighten anchor bolts.
	10. Loose lining on brake shoes or improperly ground lining.	10. Replace brake shoes and cam-grind lining.
Brakes fading	1. Improper brake adjustment.	1. Adjust brakes correctly.
	2. Improper brake lining.	2. Replace brake lining.
	3. Improper type of brake fluid.	3. Drain, flush and refill hydraulic system.
	4. Brake drums ground excessively.	4. Replace brake drums.
Dragging brakes	1. Improper brake adjustment.	1. Correct adjust brakes.
	2. Distorted cylinder cups.	2. Recondition or replace cylinder.
	3. Brake shoe seized on anchor bolt.	3. Clean and lubricate anchor bolt.
	4. Broken brake shoe return spring.	4. Replace brake shoe return spring.
	5. Loose anchor bolt.	5. Adjust and tighten anchor bolt.
	6. Distorted brake shoe.	6. Replace defective brake shoes.
	7. Loose wheel bearings.	7. Lubricate and adjust wheel bearings.

HYDRAULIC BRAKE SYSTEM TROUBLE DIAGNOSIS

Condition	Possible Cause	Correction
Dragging brakes	8. Obstruction in brake line. 9. Swollen cups in wheel cylinder or master cylinder. 10. Master cylinder linkage improperly adjusted.	8. Clean or replace brake line. 9. Recondition wheel or master cylinder. 10. Correctly adjust master cylinder linkage.
Hard pedal	1. Incorrect brake lining. 2. Incorrect brake adjustment. 3. Frozen brake pedal linkage. 4. Restricted brake line or hose.	1. Install matched brake lining. 2. Adjust brakes and check fluid. 3. Free up and lubricate brake linkage. 4. Clean out or replace brake line hose.
Wheel locks	1. Loose or torn brake lining. 2. Incorrect wheel bearing adjustment. 3. Wheel cylinder cups sticking. 4. Saturated brake lining.	1. Replace brake lining. 2. Clean, pack and adjust wheel bearings. 3. Recondition or replace the wheel cylinder. 4. Reline front, rear or all four brakes.
Brakes fade (high speed)	1. Improper brake adjustment. 2. Distorted or out of round brake drums. 3. Overheated brake drums. 4. Incorrect brake fluid (low boiling temperature). 5. Saturated brake lining.	1. Adjust brakes and check fluid. 2. Grind or replace the drums. 3. Inspect for dragging brakes. 4. Drain flush and refill and bleed the hydraulic brake system. 5. Reline brakes as necessary.

HYDRAULIC SYSTEM SERVICE

Basic Hydraulic System

The hydraulic system controls the braking operation and consists of a master cylinder, hydraulic lines and hoses, control valves and calipers and/or wheel cylinders. When the brake pedal is depressed, the master cylinder forces brake fluid to the calipers and/or cylinders, via lines and hoses. Sliding rubber seals contain the fluid and prevent leakage.

Return springs in the master cylinder help the brake pedal return to the original unapplied position. Check valves (in most cases) regulate the return flow of the fluid to the master cylinder. Other valves, such as the metering valve, proportioning valve, or combination valve, regulate the flow of fluid to the caliper/wheel cylinder, to achieve efficient braking.

Single Braking Systems

On single brake systems, the master cylinder has only one piston which operates all of the wheel cylinders. The single brake system is confined to over the road vehicles above 10000 lbs. GVW, industrial and construction equipment.

Dual Braking Systems

The "dual"system differs from the "single" system by employing a "tandem" master cylinder, essentially two master cylinders (usually) formed by aligning two separate pistons and fluid reservoirs into one cylinder bore. Dual brake lines "split" the calipers and/or wheel cylinders into two groups, each actuated by a separate master cylinder piston. In event of failure of one of the "dual" systems, the other should provide enough braking power to safely stop the vehicle. The dual system usually includes a red warning light on the instrument panel which is activated by a pressure differential valve. The valve is sensitive to any loss of hydraulic pressure that might result from a braking failure on either side of the system.

Light trucks are equipped with either a front/rear wheel "split" or a diagonally "split" system. On front/rear systems, the front wheels are connected to one circuit while the rear wheels are connected to the other circuit. Diagonally split systems have diagonally opposite wheels connected to each circuit. Medium and heavy trucks may use the front/rear split or, if equipped with two wheel cylinders per wheel, each circuit will operate one cylinder per wheel.

General Information

Servicing the hydraulic brake system is chiefly a matter of adjustments, replacement of worn or damaged parts and correcting the damage caused by grit, dirt or contaminated brake fluid. Always make sure the brake system is clean and tightly sealed when a brake job is completed and that only approved heavy duty brake fluid is used.

The approved heavy duty type brake fluid retains the correct consistency throughout the widest range of temperature variation, will not affect rubber cups, helps protect the metal parts of the brake system against failure and assures long trouble free brake operation.

Never use brake fluid from a container that has been used for any other liquid. Mineral oil, alcohol, antifreeze, or cleaning solvents, even in very small quantities, will contaminate brake fluid. Contaminated brake fluid will cause piston cups and the valve(s) in the master cylinder to swell or deteriorate.

Brake adjustment is required after installation of new or relined brake shoes. Adjustment is also necessary whenever excessive travel of pedal is needed to start braking action.

LOW PEDAL

Normal brake lining wear reduces pedal reserve. Low pedal reserve may also be caused by the lack of brake fluid in the master cylinder. The wear condition may be compensated for by a minor brake adjustment. Check fluid level in master cylinder and add as required.

FLUID LOSS

If the master cylinder requires constant addition of hydraulic fluid, fluid may be leaking past the piston cups in the master cylinder or brake cylinders, the hydraulic lines; hoses or connections may be loose or broken. Loose connections should be tightened, or other necessary repairs or parts replacement made and the hydraulic brake system bled.

FLUID CONTAMINATION

To determine if contamination exists in the brake fluid, as indicated by swollen, deteriorated rubber cups, the following tests can be made.

Place a small amount of the drained brake fluid into a small clear glass bottle. Separation of the fluid into distinct layers will indicate mineral oil content. Be safe and discard old brake fluid that has been bled from the system. Fluid drained from the bleeding operation may contain dirt particles or other contamination and should not be reused.

BRAKE ADJUSTMENT

Self adjusting brakes usually do not require manual adjustment but in the event of a brake reline it may be advisable to make the initial adjustment manually to speed up adjusting time.

AUTOMATIC ADJUSTER CHECK

Raise and safely support the vehicle, have a helper in the driver's seat to apply brakes. Remove the plug from the adjustment slot to observe adjuster star wheel. Then, to exclude possibility of maximum adjustment which is, the adjuster refuses to operate because the closest possible adjustment has been reached; the star wheel should be backed off approximately 30 notches. It will be necessary to hold adjuster lever away from star wheel to allow backing off of the adjustment.

Spin the wheel and brake drum in reverse direction and apply brakes vigorously. This will provide the necessary inertia to cause the secondary brake shoe to leave the anchor. The wrap up effect will move the secondary shoe, and a cable or link will pull the adjuster lever away from the starwheel teeth. Upon release of brake pedal, the lever should snap back in position, turning star wheel. Thus, a definite rotation of adjuster star wheel can be observed if automatic adjuster is working properly. If by the described procedure one or more automatic adjusters do not function properly, the respective drum must be removed for adjuster servicing.

HYDRAULIC LINE REPAIR

Steel tubing is used in the hydraulic lines between the master cylinder and the front brake tube connector, and between the rear brake tube connector and the rear brake cylinders. Flexible hoses connect the brake tube to the front brake cylinders or calipers and to the rear brake tube connector.

When replacing hydraulic brake tubing, hoses, or connectors, tighten all connections securely. After replacement, bleed the brake system at the wheel cylinders or calipers and at the booster, if equipped with a bleeder screw.

BRAKE TUBE

If a section of the brake tube becomes damaged, the entire section should be replaced with tubing of the same type, size, shape, and length. Copper tubing should not be used in the hydraulic system. When bending brake tubing to fit the frame or rearaxle contours, be careful not to kink or crack the tube.

All brake tubing should be double flared to provide good leak proof connections. Always clean the inside of a new brake tube with clean isopropyl alcohol.

BRAKE HOSE

A flexible brake hose should be replaced if it shows signs of softening, cracking, or other damage.

When installing a new brake hose, position the hose to avoid contact with other vehicle components.

Hydraulic Control Valves

PRESSURE DIFFERENTIAL VALVE

Also known as a "warning valve", "dash-lamp valve" or "system effectiveness indicator". The valve activates a panel warning lamp in event of pressure loss failure. As pressure fails in one "split" system, the other system's normal pressure causes a piston in the switch to compress a spring and move until an electrical circuit is completed lighting the dash lamp. On some vehicles the spring balanced piston automatically recenters when the brake pedal is released, thus flashing the warning lamp only during brake application. On other vehicles the lamp will stay on until the cause of pressure loss is corrected.

Valves (pressure differential, metering or proportioning) may be located separately, but are usually part of a combination valve. On some brake systems the valve and switch are part of the master cylinder.

Resetting Valves

The pressure differential valve on many vehicles (equipped with a combination valve) will re-center automatically upon brake application after repairs to the system are completed. Other systems require manual resetting. Repair system as required, open a bleeder screw in the half of the system that did not fail. Turn on the ignition to light the warning lamp and slowly depress the brake pedal until the lamp goes out. If too much pressure is applied the piston will go to the other side and the procedure will have to be reversed by opening a bleeder screw in the opposite half of the system.

METERING VALVE

Often used on vehicles equipped with front disc and rear drum brakes, the metering valve improves braking balance during light brake applications by preventing application of the front disc brakes until pressure is built-up in the hydraulic system. The built up hydraulic pressure overcomes the tension of the rear brake shoe return springs. Thus, when the front brake pads contact the rotor the rear brakes shoes move outward to contact the brake drum at the same time.

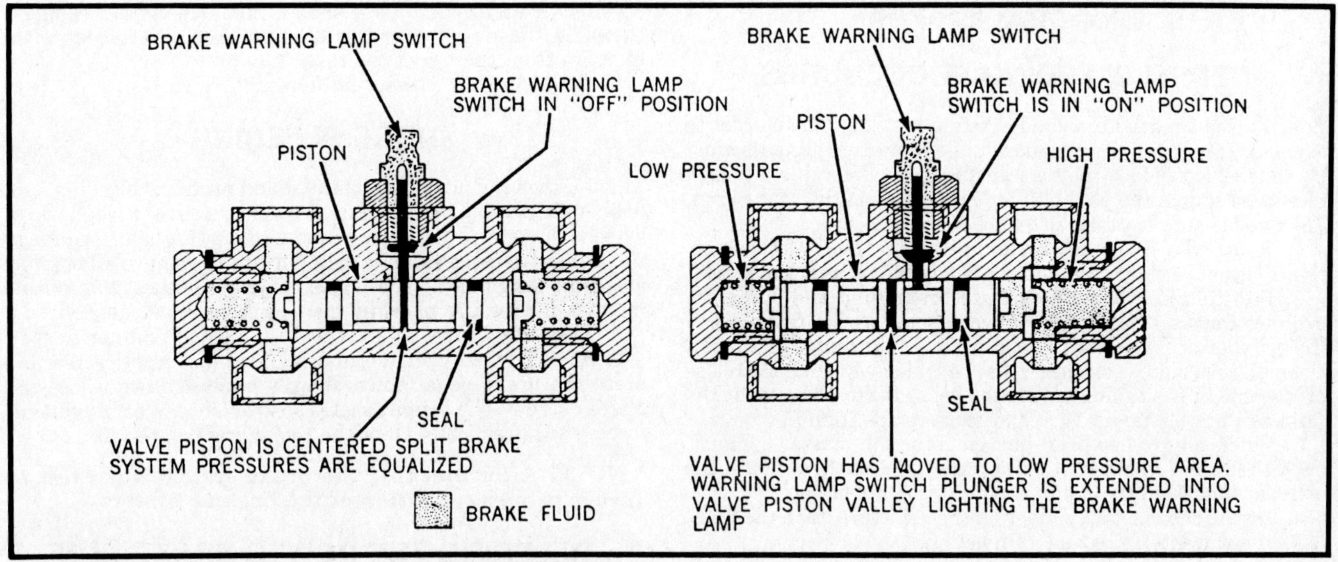

Differential valve system with split hydraulic brakes

The metering valve should be inspected whenever the brakes are serviced. A slight amount of moisture inside the boot does not indicate a defective valve, however a great deal of fluid indicates a worn valve and replacement is indicated. Make sure to install the brake lines in the correct ports when installing a new valve, crossed lines will cause the rear brakes to drag.

If a pressure bleeder is used to bleed a hydraulic system that includes a metering valve, the valve stem (inside the boot on some valves) must either be pushed in or pulled out, depending upon the type of valve. Never apply excessive pressure that might damage the valve. Never use a solid block or clamp to force the valve open. If the valve must be blocked, rig the stem with a yieldable spring load and take care not to exert more than normal pressure.

If the brakes are to be bled manually using the brake pedal, the pressure developed is sufficient to overcome the metering valve and the stem need not be pushed in or pulled out.

PROPORTIONING VALVE

Used on vehicles equipped with front disc and rear drum brakes, the proportioning valve is installed in the line(s) to the rear drum brakes, and in a split system, below the pressure differential valve. By reducing pressure to the rear drum brakes, the valve helps to prevent premature lock-up during severe brake application and provides better braking balance.

Whenever the brakes are serviced, the valve should be inspected. To check valve operation, install hydraulic gauges ahead and behind the valve and determine that it has an operative transition point above which rear brake pressure is proportioned. If the valve is leaking replacement is required. Make sure the valve port marked "R" is connected to the rear brake line(s).

COMBINATION VALVE

A valve combining two or three functions (metering, proportioning, and/or brake warning) may be used. The combination valve is usually mounted under the hood close to the master cylinder, where the brake lines can be easily routed to the front and rear wheels. The combination valve is a non-serviceable unit, and if found to be malfunctioning, must be replaced as a unit.

Master Cylinder Service

CLEANING AND INSPECTION

Thoroughly clean the master cylinder and any other parts to be reused in clean alcohol. DO NOT USE PETROLEUM PRODUCTS FOR CLEANING. If the bore is not badly scored, rusted or corroded, it is possible to rebuild the master cylinder in some cases. A slight bit of honing is permissible to clean up and smooth out the bore. A master cylinder rebuilding kit and fresh fluid should be used. If the cylinder bore is badly pitted or corroded, or if it has been rebuilt before, the master cylinder should be replaced with a new one. Do not hone or repair a scratched or pitted bore of an aluminum master cylinder. Replace the master cylinder. Be sure to note the relative positions of all the parts, paying particular attention to the way the rubber cups are facing. Lubricate all new rubber parts with brake fluid or brake system assembly lubricant.

Cast Iron Bore Cleanup

Crocus cloth or an approved cylinder hone should be used to remove lightly pitted, scored, or corroded areas from the bore. Brake fluid can be used as a lubricant while honing lightly. The master cylinder should be replaced if it cannot be cleaned up readily. After using the crocus cloth or a hone, the master cylinder should be thoroughly washed in clean alcohol or brake fluid to remove all dust and grit. If alcohol is used, dry parts thoroughly before reinstalling. Other solvents should not be used. Check the clearance between the bore wall and the piston (primary piston of a dual system master cylinder) it should be as follows. If a narrow $\frac{1}{8}$ in. to $\frac{1}{4}$ in. wide. If a 0.006 in. feeler gauge can be inserted between the wall and a new piston, the clearance is excessive, and the master cylinder should be replaced. The maximum clearance allowed for units containing pistons without replenishing holes is 0.009 in.

Aluminum Bore Cleanup

Inspect the bore for scoring, corrosion and pitting. If the bore is scored or badly pitted and corroded the assembly should be replaced. Under no conditions should the bore be cleaned with an abrasive material. This will remove the wear and corrosion resistant anodized surface. Clean the bore with a clean piece of cloth around a wooden dowel and wash thoroughly with alcohol. Do not confuse bore discoloration or staining with corrosion.

Bleeding Brakes

BENCH BLEEDING PROCEDURES

Bench bleed the master cylinder before installation. In order to expel air trapped in the cylinder, tandem master cylinders must be bench bled before they are installed on the vehicle. Bench bleeding reduces the possibility of air getting in the brake lines. Follow this simple procedure for bench bleeding:

1. Route two shortened brake lines from the outlet connection(s) into the fluid reservoir(s), below the normal fluid level.
2. Fill the reservoir(s) with fresh brake fluid and pump the cylinder until air bubbles no longer appear in the reservoir. If the cylinder does not have a check valve at the outlet port, use a clean piece of rubber or plastic, or the end of your finger to close off the end of the tubing during the back stroke. Otherwise, the fluid will merely pump back and forth in the tubing.
3. When all air has been purged from the master cylinder, bend the tubes up out of the fluid, and remove them. Refill the cylinder and securely install the master cylinder cap.
4. Install the master cylinder on the vehicle. Attach the lines, but do not tighten the tube connection.
5. Force out any air that might have been trapped in the connection by slowly depressing the pedal several times. Tighten the nut slightly before releasing pedal, and loosen before depressing each time. Catch the fluid in a rag to avoid damaging car finish. DO NOT BOTTOM THE PISTON. Tighten the connections when air bubbles are no longer present in the fluid. Make sure the master cylinder is adequately filled with brake fluid.

MANUAL BLEEDING

Bleed the longest line first on the individual system (i.e. front/rear split or diagonally front wheel, opposite side rear wheel split. If a single system, the right rear is usually the longest.) being serviced. During the complete bleeding operation, do not allow the reservoir to run dry. Keep the master cylinder reservoirs filled with the specified brake fluid. Never use brake fluid that has been drained from the hydraulic system.

1. Bleed the master cylinder at the outlet port side of the system being serviced.

NOTE: On a master cylinder without bleed screws, loosen the master cylinder to hydraulic line nut. Operate the brake pedal slowly until the brake fluid at the outlet connection is free of bubbles, then tighten the tube nut to the specified torque. Do not use the secondary piston stop screw located on the bottom of the master cylinder to bleed the brake system. Loosening or removing this screw could result in damage to the secondary piston or stop screw. Operate the brake pedal slowly until the brake fluid at the outlet connection is free of air bubbles, then tighten the bleed screw.

2. Position a suitable size (usually $^3/_8$ in.) box wrench on the bleeder fitting on the cylinder or caliper to be bled. Attach a rubber drain tube to the bleeder fitting. The end of the tube should fit snugly around the bleeder fitting.
3. Submerge the free end of the tube in a container partially filled with clean brake fluid, and loosen the bleeder fitting approximately $^3/_4$ turn.
4. Push the brake pedal down slowly thru its full travel. Close the bleeder fitting, then return the pedal to the full released position. Repeat this operation until air bubbles cease to appear at the submerged end of the bleeder tube.
5. When the fluid is completely free of air bubbles, close the bleeder fitting and remove the bleeder tube.
6. Repeat this procedure at the brake cylinder or caliper on the other side of the split system. Refill the master cylinder reservoir after each cylinder or caliper is bled. When the bleeding is complete, the master cylinder fluid level should be filled to within $^1/_4$ in. from the top of the reservoirs.
7. Centralize the pressure differential valve.

SURGE BLEEDING

This method includes both manual and pressure bleeding, and deliberately creates a churning (higher pressure) turbulence in wheel cylinders so that any remaining air can be drawn off in the form of aerated fluid. It is important to remove all possible air before surging, this method is never used unless the routine manual or pressure bleeding method proves inadequate.

1. Bleed the brakes at all wheels in a usual manner.
2. At each wheel cylinder, in turn, open the bleeder screw and press the brake pedal down sharply several times. Close the bleeder screw. The action creates a turbulence in each cylinder, forcing out practically all of the remaining trapped air.

NOTE: After bleeding the brake system, road test to insure proper operation of the braking system.

BLEEDING THE POWER BRAKE UNIT

On power booster equipped vehicles, the engine should be turned off and the power system purged of vacuum or compressed air by depressing the brake pedal several times. After bleeding the master cylinder, bleed the power brake unit (if equipped with a bleeder screw).

Pressure multiplying type power units often have bleeder screws to remove the air trapped within the unit. If the unit has more that one bleeder screw, bleed the one at the pressure (main) cylinder first and the control valve second. When bleeding, manually close the bleeder screw before the pedal is allowed to back stroke each time.

Wheel Cylinders and Calipers

DRUM BRAKE WHEEL CYLINDER

The wheel cylinder performs in response to the master cylinder. It receives fluid from the hydraulic hose through its inlet port. As the pressure increases the wheel cylinder cups and pistons are forced apart. As a result, the hydraulic pressure is converted into mechanical force acting on the brake shoes. The wheel cylinder size may vary from front to rear. The variation in wheel cylinder size (diameter) is one of the factors controlling the distribution of braking force in a vehicle. Larger diameter wheel cylinders are normally specified for the front brakes of front engine passenger cars equipped with drum brakes. Bleeder screws are provided to remove air or vapor trapped in the system.

Three types of wheel cylinders are normally used with drum brakes.

Single Piston or "Single-end" Type

A single piston wheel cylinder has only one cup, piston, and dust boot and spring. It may also contain a cup filler or cup expander.

Double Piston or "Double-end" Straight Bore Type

The double piston, straight bore type is most commonly used. This type carries two opposed pistons, two cups and two boots.

Double Piston or "Double-end" Step Bore Type

This type is used on some of the non-servo brakes and has the same components as the straight bore type. Two different sized dust boots, cups, and pistons are used. Opposed pistons of different diameters exert different amounts of force.

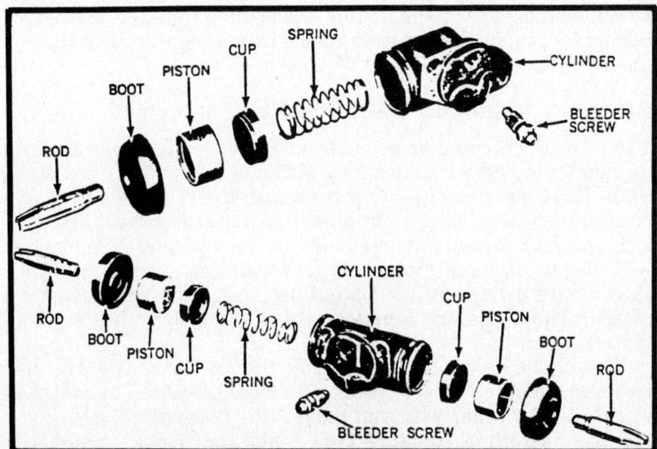

Typical wheel cylinder—exploded view

SERVICE PROCEDURES

Wheel cylinders may need reconditioning or replacement whenever the brake shoes are replaced or when required to correct a leak condition. On many designs, the wheel cylinders can be diassembled without removing them from the backing plate. On some designs, however, the cylinder is mounted in an indention in the backing plate or a cylinder piston stop is welded to the backing plate. When servicing brakes of this type, the cylinder must be removed from the backing plate before being disassembled.

Diagnostic Inspection and Cleaning

Leaks which coat the boot and the cylinder with fluid, or result in a dropped reservoir fluid level, or dampen and stain the brake linings are dangerous. Such leaks can cause the brakes to "grab" or fail and should be immediately corrected. A leakage, not immediately apparent, can be detected by pulling back the cylinder boot. A small amount of fluid seepage dampening the interior of the boot is normal, however a dripping boot is not. Unless other conditions causing a brake to pull, grab, or drag becomes obvious, the wheel cylinder is a suspect and should be included in general reconditioning.

Cylinder binding may be caused by rust, deposits, grime, or swollen cups due to fluid contamination, or by a cup wedged into an excessive piston clearance. If the clearance between the pistons and the bore wall exceeds allowable values, a condition called "heel drag" may exist. It can result in rapid cup wear and can cause the pistons to retract very slowly when the brakes are released.

A ring of a hard, crystal like substance is sometimes noticed in the cylinder bore where the piston stops after the brakes are released.

Some front wheel cylinders have a baffle located between the opposed pistons. The baffle contains a small hole which causes the cylinder to act as a fluid shock absorber damping servo brake shoes as they become energized. These cylinders cannot be honed and should be replaced if the bore is pitted or corroded.

Hydraulic system parts should not be allowed to come in contact with oil or grease, neither should those be handled with greasy hands. Even a trace of any petroleum based product is sufficient to cause damage to the rubber parts.

RECONDITIONING DRUM BRAKE WHEEL CYLINDERS

It is a common practice to recondition a drum brake wheel cylinder without dismounting it, however some brakes are equipped with external piston stops which prevent disassembly unless the cylinder is removed. In order to dismount, remove the shoe springs and spread the shoes apart, disconnect the brake line, remove the mounting bolts or retaining clips, and pull the cylinder free.

Most wheel cylinders are attached to the backing plate with bolts and are easily removed for service or replacement. In recent years, some GM vehicles use a retaining clip for this purpose. To remove this type cylinder, use a special service tool, or insert $^1/_8$ in. diameter or less awls or pins into the slots between wheel cylinder pilot and retainer locking tabs. Bend both tabs away at the same time until tabs spring over the shoulder, releasing cylinder. Discard the old retainer.

To replace the wheel cylinder, use a new retainer and the following procedure.

1. Hold wheel cylinder against backing plate by inserting a block between the wheel cylinder and axle shaft flange.
2. Position wheel cylinder retainer clip so the tabs will be away from and in horizontal position with the backing plate when installing.
3. Press new retaining clip over wheel cylinder abutment and into position using 1 $^1/_8$ in. 12 point socket. The retainer is in place when the tabs are snapped under the retainer abutment. Examine closely to be sure both retainer tabs are properly engaged.

Another variation of retainer clip is used on some imported vehicles. The retainer usually consists of two or three separate pieces which when slid together will lock themselves and the wheel cylinder in place. The retainers can be carefully removed without incurring damage which allows them to be reused. If they are damaged or corroded, however, they must be replaced.

Pull the protective dust boots off the cylinder. Internal parts should slide out, or be picked out easily. Parts can be driven out with a wooden dowel, or blown out at low pressure by applying compressed air to the fluid inlet port. Parts which cannot be removed easily indicate they are damaged beyond repair and the cylinder should be replaced.

Clean the cylinder and the parts in alcohol and/or brake fluid. (Do not use gasoline or other petroleum based products.) Use only lint free wiping cloths. Crocus cloth can be used to clean minute scratches, signs of rust, corrosion or discoloration from the cylinder bore and pistons. Slide the cloth in a circular rather than a lengthwise motion. A clean up hone may be used. After a cylinder has been honed, inspect it for excessive piston clearance and remove any burrs formed on the edge of fluid intake or bleeder screw ports.

NOTE: Do not rebuild aluminum cylinders. A cylinder that does not clean up at 0.002 in. should be discarded and a new cylinder installed. (Black stains on the cylinder walls are caused by the piston cups and will do no harm.)

Assemble the cylinder with the internal parts, making sure that the cylinder wall is wet with brake fluid. Insert the cups and pistons from each end of a double end cylinder; do not slide them through the cylinder. Cup lips should always face inward.

Disc Brake Caliper

An integral part of the caliper, the caliper bore(s) contains the piston(s) that direct thrust against the brake pads supported within the caliper. Since all braking forces (pad application force) are applied on each side of the rotor with no self energization, the cylinder and piston are large in comparison to a drum brake wheel cylinder.

FIXED CALIPER TYPE

A fixed type caliper is mounted solidly to the spindle bracket.

Pistons are located on both sides of the rotor, in inboard and outboard caliper halves. Fluid passes between caliper halves through an external crossover tube or through internal passages. A bleeder screw is located in the inboard caliper half. A dust boot protecting each cylinder fits in a circumferential groove on the piston.

FLOATING CALIPER TYPE

Floating or sliding calipers are free to move in a fixed bracket or support.

The piston is located only on the inboard side of the caliper housing, which straddles the rotor. The cylinder piston applies the inboard brake shoe directly, and simultaneously hydraulic pressure slides the caliper in a clamping action which forces the caliper to apply the outboard brake shoe.

The actual applying movement is small. The unit merely grips during application, relaxes upon release, and the shoes do not retract an appreciable distance from the rotor. The fluid inlet port and the bleeder screw are located n the inboard side of the caliper. A dust boot is fitted into a circumferential groove on the piston and into a recess at or near the outer end of the cylinder bore.

HYDRAULIC SEAL ARRANGEMENTS

Seal arrangements at the caliper pistons vary depending upon the brake manufacturer. Three makes of fixed caliper brakes, Bendix, Budd, and Delco-Moraine, use a ring seal which fits in a circumferential groove on the piston.

A fixed seal is now commonly used in brake calipers. During the very small applying movement of the piston, the elasticity of the fixed seal permits some deflection in the cylinder groove. The seal deflects as the brakes are applied and relaxes as the brakes are released, retracting the piston a small amount. Some GM types have a rolling seal that retracts the piston slightly further to reduce pad rubbing friction.

A scratched piston, nicked seal, or a sludge or varnish deposit which lifts the sealing edge away from the piston will cause a fluid leak. A serious leak could develop if calipers are not reconditioned when new pads are installed. Then dust and road grime, gradually accumulating behind the dust boot, could be carried into the seal when the piston is shoved inward to accommodate new thick linings. Old seals may have taken a "set," thus preventing proper seating in the retainer groove and on the piston. Therefore, when reconditioning calipers, new seals should be installed.

Service Procedures

Before servicing, syphon or syringe about $^2/_3$ of the fluid from the master cylinder reservoir do not allow the, fluid level to fall below the cylinder intake port. To prevent a gravity loss of fluid, plug the brake line after disconnecting from the caliper. To recondition, remove the caliper from the vehicle, allow the unit to drain, and remove the brake shoes. For benchwork, clamp the caliper housing in a soft jaw vice. On fixed-caliper types, remove the bridge bolts and separate the caliper into halves. Remove the sealing O-rings at cross-over points, if the unit has internal fluid passages across the halves.

Whenever required, use special tools to remove pistons, dust boots, and seals. If compressed air is used, apply it gradually, gently ease the pistons from the cylinders, and trap them in a clean cloth; do not allow them to pop out. Take care to avoid pinching hands or fingers.

While removing stroking type seals and boots, work lip of boot from the groove in the caliper. After the boot is free, pull the piston, and strip the seal and boot from the piston.

While removing fixed position (rectangular ring) seals and boots, pull the piston through the boot. Do not use a metal tool which would scratch the piston. Use a small pointed wooden or plastic tool to lift the boots and seals from the grooves in the cylinder bore.

Cleaning, Inspection, and Installation

Use only alcohol and/or brake fluid and a lint free wiping cloth to clean the caliper and parts. Other solvents should not be used. Blow out passages with compressed air. Always wear eye protection when using compressed air or cleaning calipers.

To correct minor imperfections in the cylinder bore, polish with a fine grade of crocus cloth working in a circular rather than a lengthwise motion. Do not use any form of abrasive on a plated piston. Discard a piston which is pitted or has signs of plating wear.

Inspect the new seal. It should lie flat and be round. If it has suffered a distorted "set" during its shelf life, do not use it. Lubricate the cylinder wall and parts with brake fluid.

While installing stroking type seals and boots, stretch the boot and the seal over the piston and seat them in position.

Use special alignment tools for inserting lip cup seals. Be sure the seal does not twist or roll.

Where the boot lip is retained inside the cylinder bore the following method works well.

1. Lubricate bottom inside edge of piston and brake seal in caliper with brake fluid.
2. Pull boot over bottom end of piston so that boot is positioned on bottom of piston with lip about $^1/_4$ in. up from bottom end.
3. Hold piston suspended over bore.
4. Insert back boot lip into groove in caliper.
5. Then tuck the sides of boot into groove and work forward until only one bulge remains.
6. Tuck the final bulge into front of the groove.
7. Then push the piston carefully through the seal and boot to the bottom of the bore. The inside of the boot should slide on the piston and come to rest in the boot groove.
8. If the boot lip is retained outside the cylinder bore, first stretch boot over the piston and seat it in its groove, then press the piston through the seal. Fully depress the piston. You'll need 50 to 100 pounds force to fasten the boot lip in place. On some designs, it is necessary to use a wooden drift or a special tool to seat the metal boot in the caliper counterbore below the face of the caliper.

INSTALLING FIXED CALIPER BRIDGE BOLTS

If the caliper contains internal fluid cross-over passages, be sure to install the new O-ring seals at joints. Install high tensile strength bridge bolts on the mated caliper halves. Never replace the bridge bolts with ordinary standard hardware bolts.

Brake Disc (Rotor)

ROTOR RUNOUT

Manufacturers differ widely on permissible runout, but too much can sometimes be felt as a pulsation at the brake pedal. A wobble pump effect is created when a rotor is not perfectly smooth and the pad hits the high spots forcing fluid back into the master cylinder. This alternating pressure causes a pulsating feeling which can be felt at the pedal when the brakes are applied. This excessive runout also causes the brakes to be out of adjustment because disc brakes are self adjusting, they are designed so that the pads drag on the rotor at all times and therefore automatically compensate for wear. To check the actual runout of the rotor, first tighten the wheel spindle nut to a snug bearing adjustment, end play removed. Fasten a dial indicator on the suspension at a convenient place so that the indicator stylus contacts the rotor face approximately one in. from its outer edge. Set the dial at zero. Check the total indictor reading while turning the rotor one full revolution. If the rotor is warped beyond the runout specification, it is likely that it can be successfully remachined.

Lateral Runout: A wobbly movement of the rotor from side to side at it rotates. Excessive lateral runout causes the rotor faces to knock bac the disc pads and can result in chatter, excessive pedal travel, pumping or fighting pedal and vibration during the breaking action.

Parallelism (lack of): Refers to the amount of variation in the thickness of the rotor. Excessive variation can cause pedal vibration or fight, front end vibrations and possible "grab" during the braking action; a condition comparable to an "out-of-round brake drum." Check parallelism with a micrometer, "mike" the thickness at eight or more equally spaced points, equally distant from the outer edge of the rotor, preferrably at mid-points of the braking surface. Parallelism then is the amount of variation between maximum and minimum measurements.

Surface of Micro-inch finish, flatness, smoothness: Different from parallelism, these terms refer to the degree of perfection of the flat surface on each side of the rotor, that is, the minute hills, valleys and swirls inherent in machining the surface. In a visual inspection, the remachined surface should have a fine ground polish with, at most, only a faint trace of nondirectional swirls.

Disc Brake Surface Refinishing

To meet mandated brake system performance requirements, semi-metallic brake linings have been used for several years in some vehicle applications. In order to maintain the proper performance, it is important to correctly service these semi-metallic brake components as outlined in the following procedures.

Service Recommendations

1. Semi-metallic linings should be replaced with semi-metallic service linings, equal to the original equipment specifications.
2. Routine replacement of the disc pads does not require rotor refinishing, unless damage or extreme wear to the rotor has occurred.
3. Rotor refinishing should only be required if non-parallelism, excessive runout, rotor damage or scoring of the rotor surface has occurred.
4. If refinishing is necessary, the semi-metallic brake pads require a micro- inch surface refinish like new vehicle rotor specifications (10 to 50 micro-inches with non-directional swirl patterns).
5. The recommended procedure for obtaining this finish is outlined in the following chart.

ROTOR REFINISHING

Procedure	Rough Cut	Finish Cut
Spindle Speed	150 RPM	150 RPM
Depth of Cut Per Side	.005″	.002″
Tool Cross Feed Per Rev.	.006″.010″	.002″ Max.
Vibration Dampener	Yes	Yes
Swirl Pattern-120 GRIT	No	Yes

6. When refinishing brake rotors for semi-metallic linings, the following is important;
   a. The brake lathe must be in good working order and have the capability to produce the intended surface finish.
   b. Use the correct tool feed and arbor speeds. Too fast a speed or too deep a cut can result in a rough finish.
   c. Cutting tools must be sharp.
   d. Adapters must be clean and free of nicks.
   e. Lathe finish cuts should be further improved and made non-directional by dressing the rotor surface with a sanding disc power tool, such as AMMCO model 8350 Safe Swirl Disc Rotor Grinder or its equivalaent.
   f. Rotor surfaces are to be refinished to 10 to 50 microinches.
7. To become familiar with the required surface finish, drag the fingernail over the surface of a new rotor from parts stock or on a new vehicle. If your brake equipment cannot produce this smooth-a-finish when correctly used, contact the equipment manufacturer for corrective instructions.
8. When installing new rotors from service stock, do not refinish the surface as these parts are to the recommended finish. It also is not required to refinish a rotor on a vehicle which has a smooth finish.

Drum Brake Service

Basic Service

CAUTION

Do not blow the brake dust out of the drums with compressed air or lung power; always use a damp cloth, a vacuum unit and soft brush to gather the dust particles into a container for disposal. Use a nose/mouth protective cover Brake linings contain asbestos, a known cancer causing substance. Dispose of the residue safely.

NOTE: Never work on a vehicle supported only by a jack. Use a hydraulic lift and/or jack stands to support the vehicle safely.

Check For Leaks

Press the brake pedal to ensure that there are no leaks in the hydraulic system. If the pedal does not remain hard and drops to the end of its pedal travel, an internal or external fluid leakage is indicated in the master cylinder, hoses, wheel cylinders, or brake calipers. When performing this test, the engine should be running, if equipped with power brakes. With power brakes, it is normal for the pedal to drop slightly when the engine starts. If the pedal continues to drop, a leak in the system is indicated.

Drum Inspection

Check the drums for any cracks, scores, grooves, or out-of-round conditions. Slight scores can be removed with fine emery cloth, while extensive scoring requires machining the drum on a suitable drum lathe.

If the friction surface of the brake drum is scored or otherwise damaged beyond the allowable machining specification, it will require replacement. After machining, the drum diameter must not exceed the diameter specification cast on the drum or 0.060 in. (1.5mm) over the original nominal diameter. Carefully look for signs of grease, oil or brake fluid on the drum assembly and repair as required.

Rebuild the Wheel Cylinders

It is always a good practice to rebuild or replace the wheel cylinder when relining the brakes. This helps to assure a properly operating brake system and to prevent premature leakage of brake fluid past the cups and piston seals.

Clean and Lubricate

With the brake parts off, clean the backing plate with a damp cloth to avoid raising any asbestos dust and dispose of the rag after use. Clean any rust with a wire brush. File smooth any ridges or rough edges on the contact points of the backing plate. Lubricate the contact points with an approved brake lubricant. Clean and lightly lubricate the adjuster threads and screw the adjuster all the way together to facilitate reassembly of the brake components. If the wheel bearings are available, wash in solvent and repack with lubricant. Check the backing plate retaining bolts for tightness.

Reassemble And Install The Brake Shoes

Reassemble the brake shoes in the reverse order of their removal. Make sure all parts are in their proper position and that both brake shoes are properly positioned at either end of the adjuster assembly. Also, both brake shoes should correctly engage the wheel cylinder push rod and parking brake links, if equipped. With the brake shoes and components in position, measure the inside of the drum diameter and adjust the brake shoes to match the diameter with a brake shoe pre-set measuring tool. Install the brake drum and make final brake adjustment, as required. Install the remaining components and torque to specifications.

BLEED AND ROAD TEST

Bleed the air from the hydraulic system to insure a high, hard pedal and road test the vehicle. Self-adjusting mechanisms are activated by the application of the brake pedal when the vehicle is driven in reverse, driven forward or when the parking brake is applied. Be sure the road test course includes enough stops, enough traveling in reverse, and the use of the parking brake assembly, to allow the self adjusters to perform the proper adjustment on all wheels.

DRUM BRAKE SERVICE

INDEX TO DRUM BRAKE TYPES

Courier/Mazda	Type 1,2
Datsun	Type 3,4
D50/Arrow/ Mitsubishi	Type 5,6
LUV/Isuzu	Type 5,7
Toyota	Type 3,5,6
VW	Type 6,8

Type 1 Dual Cylinders, Dual Pistons—Manual Adjusters

Two dual piston wheel cylinders are used in each rear wheel brake assembly. The dual pistons act together to expand both the shoes equally against the brake drum when hydraulic fluid pressure is applied through the brake pedal and master cylinder.

The shoes and linings are interchangeable as are the brake shoe retracting springs.

Removal & Installation

1. Raise the vehicle. Remove the wheel and tire assembly. Remove the brake drum. Remove the brake drum attaching screws and install them into the tapped holes in the brake drum. Turn these screws in evenly to force the brake drum away from the wheel hub and remove the brake drum. Back off adjustment, if necessary, for drum removal.
2. Remove the brake shoe retracting springs.
3. Remove the shoe retaining spring guide pins and retaining spring by holding the guide pin to the backing plate and compressing and turning the retaining spring 90 degrees to release it from the guide pin.
4. Remove the parking brake link.
5. Disengage the parking brake cable from the parking brake lever.
6. Lubricate the threads of the adjusting screws, mating surfaces of the shoe webs and the brake backing plate ledges with a small amount of Lubriplate.
7. Position the parking brake lever on the rear shoe and install its retaining clip. Hold the rear brake shoe assembly near the brake backing plate and install the eye of the parking brake cable on the parking brake operating lever.
8. Position both brake shoes to the backing plate, install the parking brake link between the two shoes and then engage the brake shoes with the slots in the wheel cylinder pistons and adjusting screws.
9. Install the shoe retaining spring guide pins. Position the retaining springs over the guide pins. Depress the retaining springs and turn them 90 degrees to lock the retaining springs in place.
10. Install the brake shoe retracting springs, being careful not to bend the hooks or stretch the springs beyond the attaching points.
11. Install the brake drum.
12. Install the wheel and tire. Torque the wheel stud nuts to 58–65 ft. lbs.
13. Adjust the brakes.
14. Lower the vehicle and check the brakes for proper operation.

Adjustment

The brake drums should be at normal room temperature when the brake shoes are adjusted. If the shoes are adjusted when the drums are hot and expanded, the shoes may drag as the drums cool and contract.

A brake adjustment re-establishes the brake lining-to-drum clearance and compensates for normal lining wear.

The two-cylinder brake assembly brake shoes are adjusted by turning adjusting wheels reached through slots in the backing plate.

The brake adjustment is made with the vehicle raised. Check the brake drag by rotating the drum in the direction of forward rotation as the adjustment is made. Be sure that the parking brake is fully released by disconnecting the equalizer clevis pin.

EXCEPT MAZDA

1. Remove the adjusting slot covers from the backing plate.
2. Turn the lower wheel cylinder adjusting wheel inside the hole to expand the brake shoe until it locks against the brake drum.
3. Back off the adjusting screw (5 notches) so that the drum rotates freely without drag.
4. Repeat the above procedure on the upper wheel cylinder. Connect the parking brake equalizer clevis pin and recheck parking brake adjustment.
5. Replace the adjusting hole covers.
6. After the brake shoes on each wheel have been adjusted, test drive the vehicle to check for equal brake action. Readjust, if necessary.

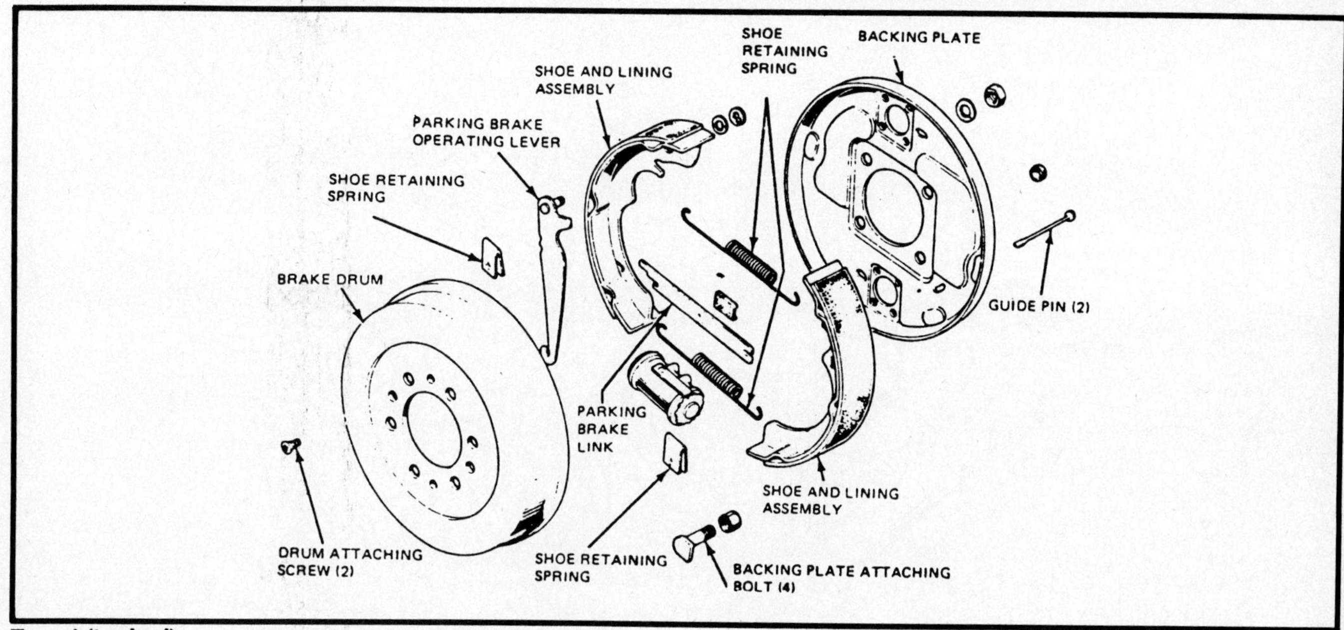

Type 1 (typical)

MAZDA

1. If the shoe retaining spring has been removed, first retract the pushrod fully (drum removed).
2. Raise and support the rear of the truck. The wheels must be free to turn.
3. Make sure the parking brake is fully released.
4. Remove the two adjusting hole plugs from the brake backing plate.
5. An arrow stamped on the backing plate indicates the direction to turn the adjuster starwheel to expand the shoes. Insert a brake spoon through the adjuster hole and turn the starwheel until the brakes are locked.
6. Insert a drift through the other adjuster hole. Use the drift to hold the pole lever of the self-adjuster firmly. Back off the starwheel three or four notches; the wheel should rotate freely (no drag).
7. Repeat the adjustment on the other wheel. Make sure the adjustment is exactly the same. Road test for equal brake action and readjust as necessary.

Type 2 Single Cylinder, Dual Pistons—Automatic Adjuster

A dual piston wheel cylinder is used in each rear wheel brake assembly. The dual pistons act together to expand both the shoes equally against the brake drum when hydraulic fluid pressure is applied through the brake pedal and master cylinder.

The shoes and linings are interchangeable as are the brake shoe retracting springs.

Removal & Installation

1. Raise the vehicle. Remove the wheel and tire assembly. Remove the brake drum attaching screws and install them into the tapped holes in the brake drum. Turn these screws in evenly to force the brake drum away from the wheel hub and remove the brake drum.
2. Remove the brake shoe retracting springs.
3. Remove the shoe retaining spring guide pins and retaining spring by holding the guide pin to the backing plate and compressing and turning the retaining spring 90 degrees to release it from the guide pin.
4. Remove the parking brake link.
5. Disengage the parking brake cable from the parking brake lever.
6. Lubricate the threads of the adjusting screws, mating surfaces of the shoe webs and the brake backing plate ledges with a small amount of Lubriplate®.
7. Position the parking brake lever on the rear shoe and install its retaining clip. Hold the rear brake shoe assembly near the brake backing plate and install the eye of the parking brake cable on the parking brake operating lever.
8. Position both brake shoes to the backing plate, install the operating strut between the two shoes and then engage the brake shoes with the slots in the wheel cylinder pistons and adjusting screws.
9. Install the shoe retaining spring guide pins. Position the retaining springs over the guide pins. Depress the retaining springs and turn them 90 degrees to lock the retaining springs in place.
10. Install the brake shoe retracting springs, being careful not to bend the hooks or stretch the springs beyond the attaching points.
11. Install the brake drum.
12. Adjust the brakes.
13. Install the wheel and tire. Torque the wheel stud nuts to 58–65 ft. lbs.
14. Lower the vehicle and check the brakes for proper operation.

Adjustment

The brake drums should be at normal room temperature, when the brake shoes are adjusted. If the shoes are adjusted when the drums are hot and expanded, the shoes may drag as the drums cool and contract.

The rear brakes are self-adjusting and require a manual adjustment only after the brake shoes have been replaced, or when the length of the adjusting rod has been changed while performing some other service operation. To adjust the rear brake shoes, proceed as follows:

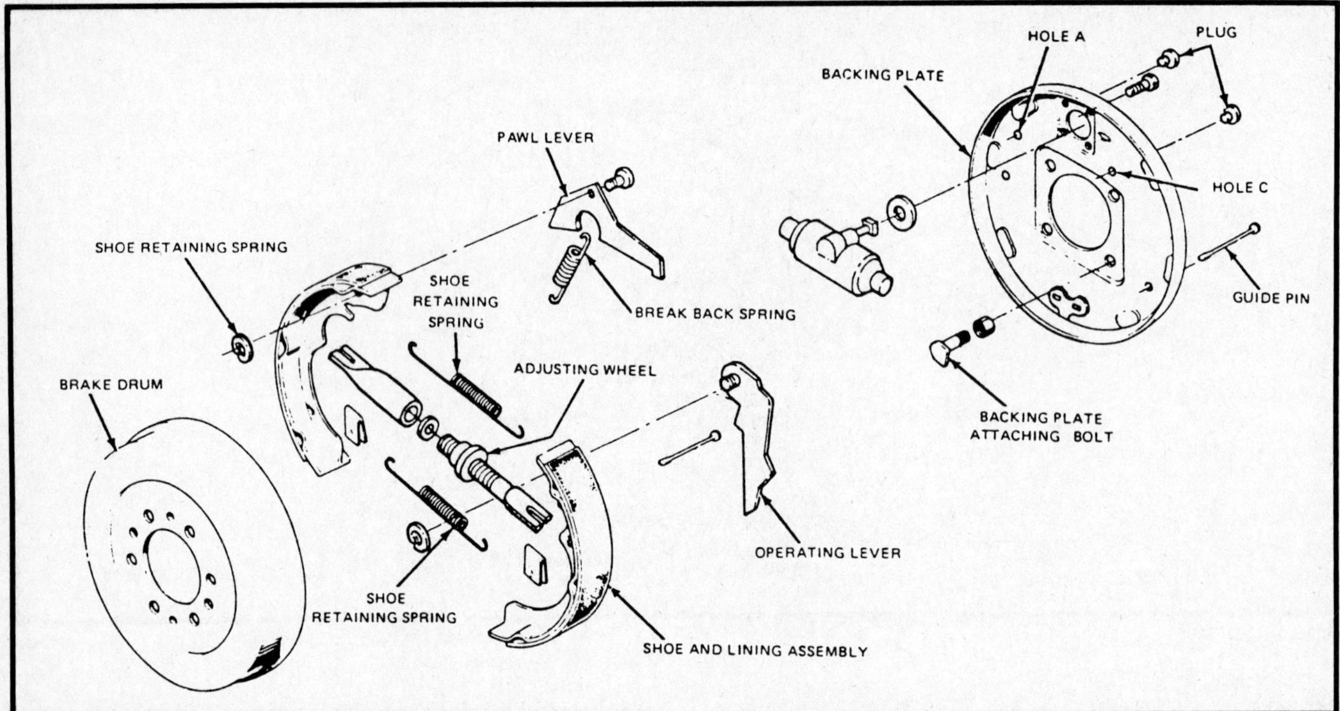

Type 2 (typical)

NOTE: When the shoe retaining spring is removed or installed, retract the push rod fully.

1. Jack up the rear end of the vehicle until the wheels are free to turn. Then, support with stands.
2. Make sure that the parking brake is fully released.
3. Remove the two shoe adjusting hole plugs from the back of the backing plate.
4. Insert a screwdriver into the star wheel of the adjuster through the hole and turn the star wheel toward the arrow direction marked on the backing plate until the wheel is locked.
5. Through the hole, hold the pole lever of the self-adjuster with a suitable drift and back off the adjusting wheel about 3 or 4 notches so that the drum rotates freely without drag.
6. Repeat the above adjustment on the other rear wheel. The adjustments must be the same on both rear wheels.
7. After the brake shoes on each wheel have been adjusted, test drive the vehicle to check for equal brake action. Readjust, if necessary.

Type 3 Non-Servo—Manual Adjuster

This brake consists of non-servo forward and reverse shoes with a double-end type wheel cylinder. The shoes anchor upon the slotted adjusting screws which permit them a sliding self centering action. Brakes are mounted with cylinder and adjuster horizontally, or with the cylinder at the top and the adjuster at the bottom.

Removal & Installation

1. Raise the front/rear of the vehicle and support it on jackstands. Remove the tire and wheel.
2. Remove the drums (some vehicles may require special pullers).
3. Detach both retracting springs.
4. Remove the hold-down springs and lift the brake shoes from the backing plate. On the rear wheels, unhook the parking brake cable from parking brake lever before shoe removal.
5. Clean and lubricate the backing plate as detailed earlier.
6. Check the wheel cylinder for frozen pistons or fluid leaks. If any are found, rebuild or replace the cylinder. Disassemble the adjusters and clean and lubricate them.
7. Install the parking brake lever on a new reverse shoe (only on rear wheel brakes).
8. Place new brake shoes on the backing plate and attach the hold-down springs. Slots in the adjusting screws must be slanted toward the center of the assembly. The ends of the shoes should engage the wheel cylinder piston slots, and the adjuster slots. If the adjuster screw ends have a slot with a bevel on one side, make sure the bevel lines up with the bevel on the shoe web. The end of the shoe with a slot for the parking strut should be installed near the wheel cylinder.
9. Hook the parking brake lever on the parking brake cable and then install the parking brake strut.
10. Install the heavier retracting spring between the toe or cylinder ends of the brake shoes.
11. Attach the lighter retracting spring to the heel or anchor ends of the shoes.
12. Replace the drums, bleed and adjust the assembly and road test the car.

Adjustment

Insert an adjusting spoon or a small screwdriver through the adjusting hole in the backing plate and expand the shoe assembly by revolving the notched adjusting wheel in a clockwise direction when facing the end of the wheel cylinder. Adjust the shoe until a heavy drag is felt when turning the wheel and drum; then, back off the adjustment until the wheel spins freely. Adjust one shoe at a time and repeat this procedure at all brake shoes.

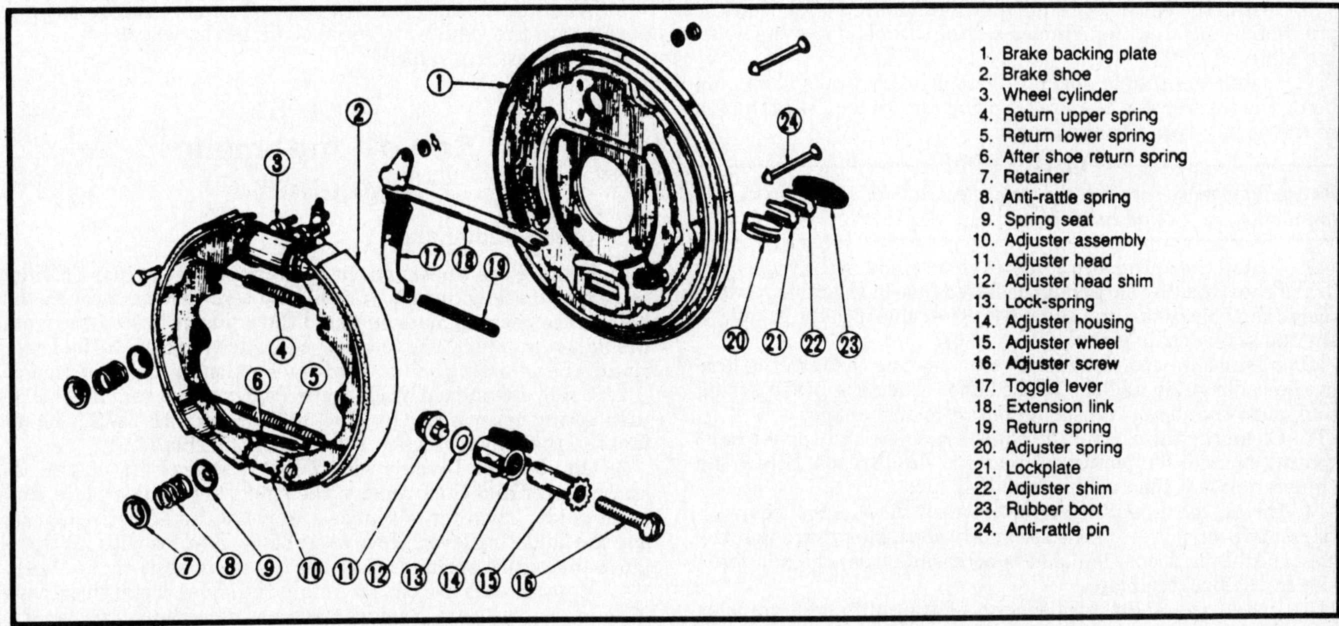

Type 3 (typical)

Type 4 Servo—Automatic Adjuster

Removal & Installation

1. Raise and safely support the vehicle. Remove the brake drum.
2. Place the hollow end of a brake spring service tool (available at auto parts stores) on the brake shoe anchor pin and twist it to disengage one of the brake retracting springs. Repeat this operation to remove the other spring.

CAUTION

Be careful the springs do not slip off the tool during removal, as they could cause personal injury.

3. Reach behind the brake backing plate and place a finger on the end of one of the brake hold-down spring mounting pins. Using a pair of pliers, grasp the washer on the top of the hold-down spring which corresponds to the pin that you are holding. Push down on the pliers and turn them 90° to align the slot in the washer with the head on the spring mounting pin. Remove the spring and washer and repeat this operation on the hold-down spring on the other brake shoe.
4. Place the tip of a prybar on the top of the brake adjusting screw and move the brake adjusting lever. When there is enough slack in the automatic adjuster cable, disconnect the loop on the top of the cable from the anchor. Grasp the top of each brake shoe and move it outward to disengage it from the wheel cylinder (and parking brake link on rear wheels). When the brake shoes are clear, lift them from the backing plate. Twist the shoes slightly and the automatic adjuster assembly will disassemble itself.
5. If you are working on rear brakes, grasp the end of the brake cable spring with a pair of pliers and, using the brake lever as a fulcrum, pull the end of the spring away from the lever. Disengage the cable from the brake lever.
6. Transfer the parking brake lever from the old secondary shoe to the new one. This is accomplished by spreading the bottom of the horseshoe clip and disengaging the lever. Position the lever on the new secondary shoe and install the spring washer and the horseshoe clip. Close the bottom of the clip after installing it. Grasp the metal tip of the parking brake cable with a pair of pliers. Position a pair of side cutter pliers on the end of the cable coil spring and, using the pliers as a fulcrum, pull the coil spring back with the side cutters. Position the cable in the parking brake lever.

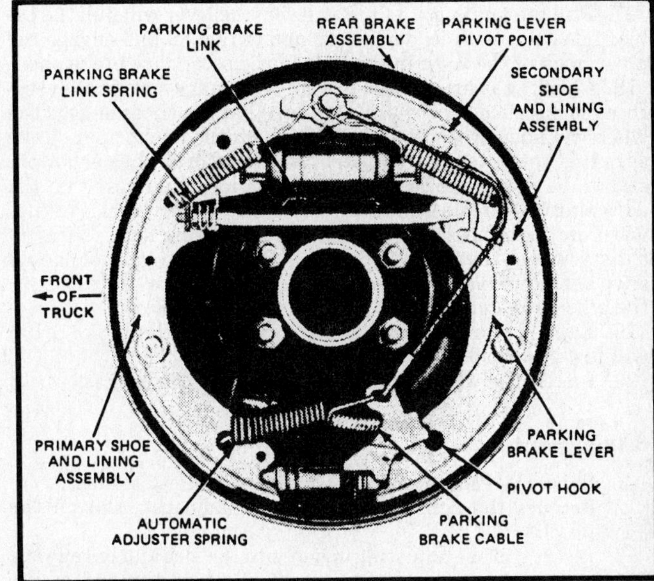

Type 4 (typical)

7. Apply a light coating of high-temperature grease to the brake shoe contact points on the backing plate. Position the primary brake shoe on the front of the backing plate and install the hold-down spring and washer over the mounting pin. Install the secondary shoe on the rear of the backing plate.
8. Install the parking brake link between the notch in the primary brake shoe and the notch in the parking brake lever.

9. Install the automatic adjuster cable loop end on the anchor pin. Make sure that the crimped side of the loop faces the backing plate.

10. Install the return spring in the primary brake shoe and, using the tapered end of a brake spring service tool, slide the top of the spring onto the anchor pin.

CAUTION

Be careful to make sure that the spring does not slip off the tool during installation, as it could cause injury.

11. Install the automatic adjuster cable guide in the secondary brake shoe, making sure that the flared hole in the cable guide is inside the hole in the brake shoe. Fit the cable into the groove in the top of the cable guide.

12. Install the secondary shoe return spring through the hole in the cable guide and the brake shoe. Using the brake spring tool, slide the top of the spring onto the anchor pin.

13. Clean the threads on the adjusting screw and apply a light coating of high-temperature grease to the threads. Screw the adjuster closed, then open it one-half turn.

14. Install the adjusting screw between the brake shoes with the starwheel nearest to the secondary shoe. Make sure that the starwheel is in a position that is accessible from the adjusting slot in the backing plate.

15. Install the short hooked end of the automatic adjuster spring in the proper hole in the primary brake shoe.

16. Connect the hooked end of the automatic adjuster cable and the free end of the automatic adjuster spring in the slot in the top of the automatic adjuster lever.

17. Pull the automatic adjuster lever (the lever will pull the cable and spring with it) downward and to the left and engage the pivot hook of the lever in the hole in the secondary brake shoe.

18. Check the entire brake assembly to make sure that everything is installed properly. Make sure that the shoes engage the wheel cylinder properly and are flush on the anchor pin. Make sure that the automatic adjuster cable is flush on the anchor pin and in the slot on the back of the cable guide. Make sure that the adjusting lever rests on the adjusting screw starwheel. Pull upward on the adjusting cable until the adjusting lever is free of the starwheel, then release the cable. The adjusting lever should snap back into place on the adjusting screw starwheel and turn the wheel one tooth.

19. Expand the brake adjusting screw until the brake drum will just fit over the brake shoes.

20. Install the wheel and drum and adjust the brakes.

Adjustment

1. Raise the vehicle and support it with safety stands.

2. Remove the rubber plug from the adjusting slot on the backing plate.

3. Insert a brake adjusting spoon into the slot and engage the lowest possible tooth on the starwheel. Move the end of the brake spoon downward to move the starwheel upward and expand the adjusting screw. Repeat this operation until the brakes lock the wheel.

4. Insert a small prybar or piece of firm wire (coat-hanger wire) into the adjusting slot and push the automatic adjuster lever out and free of the starwheel on the adjusting screw.

5. Holding the adjusting lever out of the way, engage the topmost tooth possible on the starwheel with a brake adjusting spoon. Move the end of the adjusting spoon upward to move the adjusting screw starwheel downward and contract the adjusting screw. Back off the adjusting screw starwheel until the wheel spins freely with the minimum of drag. Keep track of the number of turns the starwheel is backed off.

6. Repeat this operation for the other side. When backing off the brakes on the other side, the adjusting lever must be backed off the same number of turns to prevent side-to-side brake pull.

7. Repeat this operation on the other set of brakes.

8. When the brakes are adjusted, make several stops, while backing up the vehicle, to equalize all of the wheels.

9. Road-test the vehicle.

Type 5 Servo—Automatic Adjuster

Removal & Installation

1. Remove the wheel and the brake drum. If the drum cannot be removed easily, insert a flat-bladed screwdriver through the hole in the backing plate and hold the adjuster lever away from the adjuster. Then, use another screwdriver to turn the lower side of the adjusting bolt toward you and loosen the adjustment.

2. Using a standard brake return spring tool, remove the return spring or springs. On 1985-86 Toyotas with 2WD, this refers the the two springs at the tops of the shoes only.

3. On 1985-86 Toyotas with 2WD, first push up on the adjusting lever and then remove the cable, shoe guide plate, and cable guide. Then, on all models, remove the adjusting spring and the adjusting lever. Now, on 1985-86 Toyotas with 2WD, remove the return springs located at the lower ends of the shoes.

4. Many models use clips to retain the shoes. Turn these clips 90° and remove them. Remove the brake shoes and, if necessary, remaining parts of the adjusting assembly. Then remove the cable from the parking brake lever.

5. Installation is the reverse of removal with the following notes: Grease those ares of the backing plate where the brake shoes will ride as brakes are applied and released.

6. On most models, after the primary shoes have been installed, install the parking brake cable. On 1985-86 Toyotas with 2WD, first install the brake cable and connect it to the parking brake lever; then, install the rear shoe. Make sure to secure the hold-down springs and clips on those models using them. Set the adjuster assembly, then secure the secondary shoes on all models but 1985-86 Toyota 2WD.

NOTE: When setting the adjuster, grease the threaded area on the adjuster assembly and make sure it turns smoothly.

7. Except on the 1985-86 Toyota 2WD, install the primary shoe return springs, adjusting cable and the secondary shoe return springs in the given order. On those Toyota models, install the two adjustment tension springs located at the lower ends of the shoes (one runs between the shoes and the other from one shoe to the backing plate).

NOTE: The springs for the primary shoe and secondary shoe are different colors. Do not mix them, as they are different lengths.

8. On other models, skip to the Step 10. On 1985-86 Toyota with 2WD, grease the threads of the adjuster and the ends with high temperature grease. Then, spread the shoes apart with a screwdriver and install the adjuster. Now, install the shoe guide plate, cable guide, and adjusting cable. Finally, install the front and rear return springs between the tops of the two shoes and the post between the two shoes at the top.

9. Install the tension spring to the rear shoe. Then, hook the adjusting lever to the cable and install the adjusting lever. Hook the tensioning spring to the adjusting lever.

10. To check the adjuster assembly operation: pull the adjuster cable toward you to see if the adjuster lever goes into mesh with the next tooth on the adjuster wheel. Make sure that when the cable is released, the adjuster lever returns to its original position after the adjuster wheel has moved a tooth ahead. On the 1985-86 Toyota with 2WD, loosen the adjustment all the way to permit easy installation of the brake drum. Install the drum and wheel. Then, complete the brake adjustment by backing the vehicle up and applying the brakes hard several times.

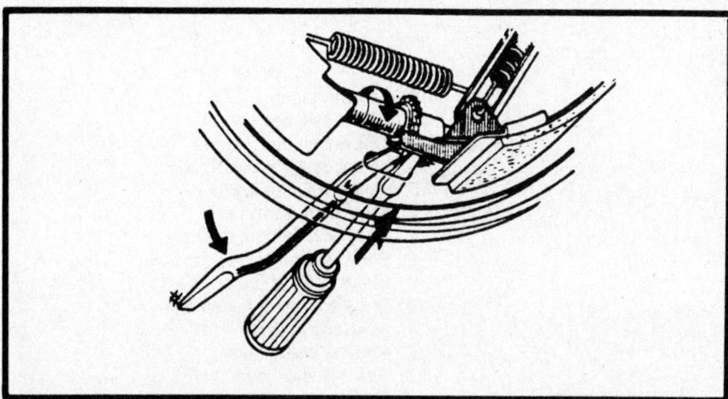

Loosening the brake adjustment on Toyota duo servo rear drum brakes

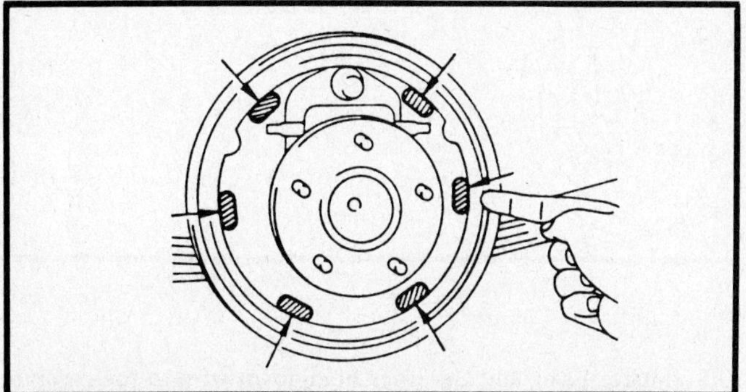

Grease the backing plate for Toyota duo-servo 2WD rear brakes as shown

11. On all models, bleed the system as necessary.

Adjustment

1. During reassembly of the rear brake shoes on the remaining models, manually adjust the automatic adjuster so that shoe to drum clearance is no more than 2.5mm (0.1 in.). An excessive clearance will cause malfunction of the adjuster.
2. After installation is complete, operate the vehicle in reverse and apply the brakes so that the adjuster will equalize.

Type 6 Leading-Trailing—Automatic Adjuster

Removal & Installation

1. Raise and safely support the vehicle.
2. Remove the rear wheel and brake drum.
3. Remove the shoe return spring(s) from the two brake shoes. Remove the two brake shoe hold-down springs.
4. Remove the shoes and adjuster as an assembly. Disconnect the parking brake cable from the lever.
5. The wheel cylinder may be removed for servicing if necessary.
6. Transfer the parking brake lever and adjuster lever to the new trailing shoe.
7. Clean and lubricate the adjuster. Assemble the shoes and adjuster as in removal.
8. Lubricate the backing plate shoe contact points.
9. Connect the parking brake cable. Install the brake shoes and adjuster to the backing plate with the holddown pins and springs. Install the return spring(s).
10. Turn adjuster until the brake drum can be installed and

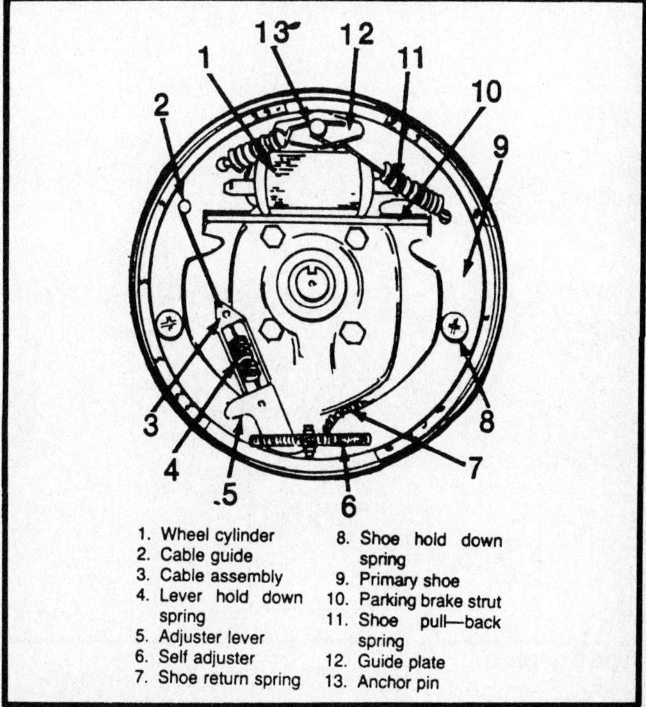

Type 5 (typical)

turned with a slight drag. Remove drum and back off adjuster until the drum can be turned with no drag.
11. Install wheel and bleed brakes, if necessary.

Adjustment

The brakes are self-adjusting. Operate the vehicle in reverse while applying brakes, stop the vehicle and apply parking brake. Repeat the procedure several times until the adjusters equalize.

Type 7 Non-Servo—Automatic Adjuster

Removal & Installation

1. Raise and safely support the vehicle. Remove the brake drums.
2. Unhook the brake drum return springs from the anchor pin using a brake tool and remove the springs.
3. Remove the brake shoe hold-down springs using pliers. Depress the spring retainer while rotating it 90° to align the slot in the retainer with the flanged end of the pin.
4. Remove the self-adjuster cable assembly by disconnecting the spring at the adjuster lever and removing the cable end from the anchor pin. Remove the guide plate from the anchor pin.
5. Remove the adjuster lever and the lever hold-down wire from the shoe pivot.
6. Separate the shoes from the wheel cylinder pushrods.
7. Separate the primary and secondary brake shoes, adjuster, return spring, and parking brake strut assemblies.

NOTE: If the brake shoes are to be reinstalled, be sure to identify them so that they can be reinstalled in their original positions.

8. Separate the parking brake lever and the rear cable. Remove the clip and washer and remove the parking brake lever from the secondary shoe.

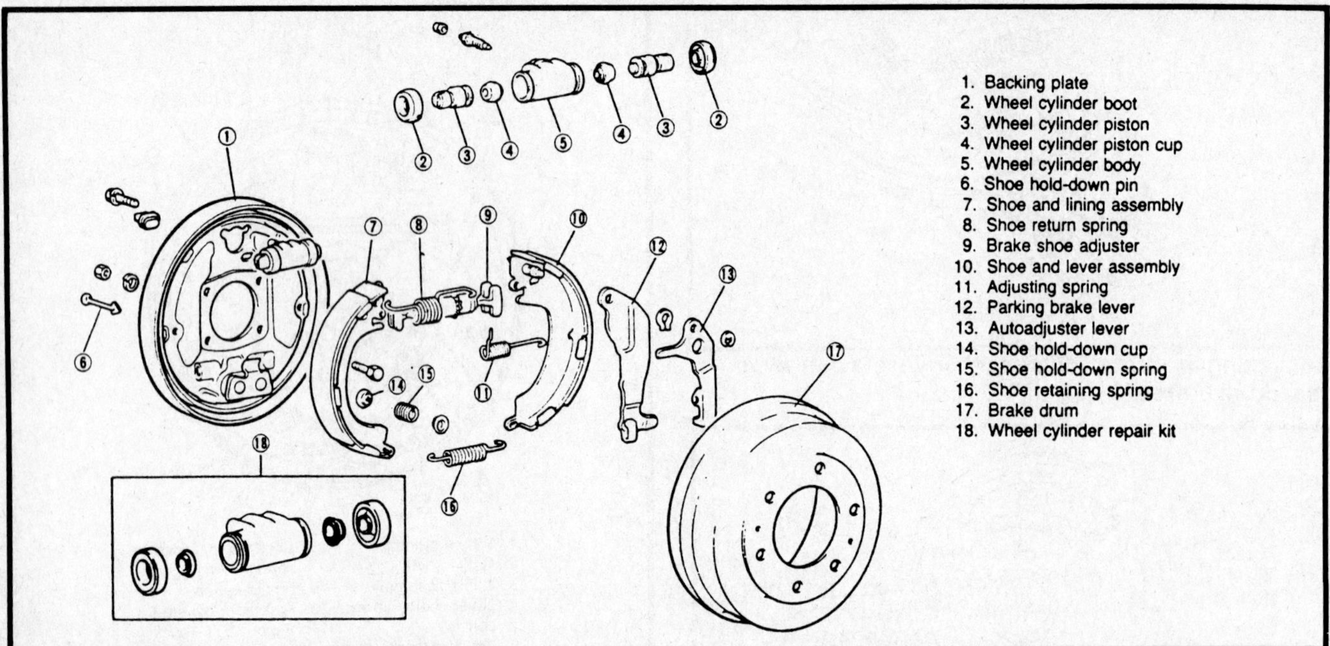

Type 6 (typical)

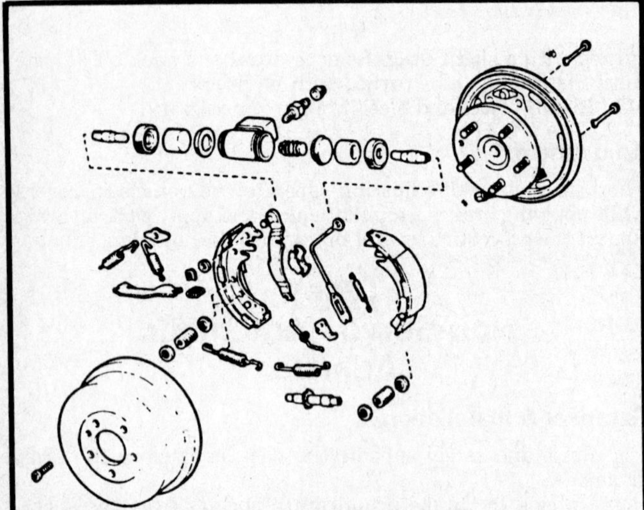

Exploded view of '85–'86 Toyota 2WD rear brake system

9. Lubricate the parking brake cable with Lubriplate®.
10. Assemble the parking brake lever to the secondary shoe and then assemble the parking brake cable to the lever.
11. Before installation, make sure that the adjusting screw is clean, lubricated and operable.
12. Connect the brake shoes together with bottom return spring and then place the adjuster screw into position. The adjuster screw is installed with the starwheel nearest to the secondary shoe.
13. Assemble the parking brake strut with the spring on the primary shoe end, and assemble the shoes to the wheel cylinder pushrods.
14. Install the shoe hold-down springs using a pair of pliers. Compress the springs and rotate the retainers 90°.
15. Install the guide plate on the anchor pin. Assemble the self-adjuster lever and the lever hold-down wire to the secondary shoe pivot pin. Place the adjuster cable over the anchor pin, route the cable around the shoe shield and then attach the spring at the opposite end to the adjuster lever.
16. Install the return springs using a brake tool.
17. Pry the shoes away from the backing plate and lubricate the shoe contact areas with a thin coat of Lubriplate®.
18. Check the operation of the parking brake. Do not step on the brake pedal.
19. Using a piece of fine (400 grit) sandpaper, evenly rough the surface of the brake linings before installing the brake drums. Do this for the linings on both wheels.
20. Install the brake drum and adjust the brake shoes.

Adjustment

1. With the brake drum removed, remove actuator from the starwheel on the rear brakes.
2. Turn the starwheel until the brake drum slides over the brake shoes with a slight drag.
3. Turn the starwheel on the rear brakes 1¼ turns to retract the shoes.
4. Install the brake drums and wheels and lower the vehicle.
5. Perform the final adjustment by making a number of forward and reverse stops, applying the brakes with a firm pedal effort until a satisfactory brake pedal height and straight-line braking is achieved.

Type 8 Non-Servo—Manual Adjuster

This brake consists of non-servo forward and reverse shoes with a double-ended wheel cylinder. The shoes are held in position by an anchor plate and are manually adjusted.

Removal & Installation

1. Raise the rear of the vehicle and support it with jackstands. Remove the tire and wheel assembly.

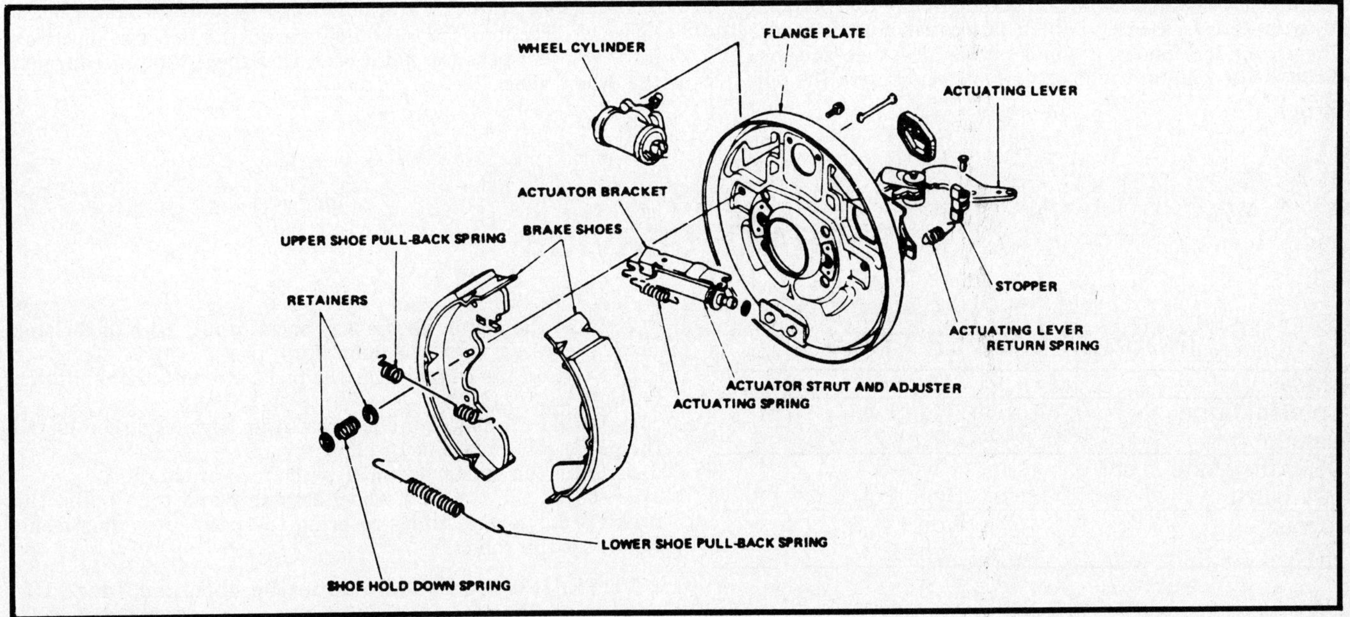

Type 7 (typical)

2. Remove the plug from the brake adjusting hole. Using a small prybar or other suitable tool, release the brake shoes by rotating the shoe adjuster downward on the right side of the vehicle and upward on the left side of the vehicle.
3. Remove the brake drum.
4. Remove the parking brake cable from the parking brake lever by compressing the cable return spring.
5. Remove the shoe-to-anchor springs located at the bottom.
6. Remove the brake shoe hold-down clips and pins.
7. Remove the adjuster screw assembly by spreading the shoes apart making sure that the adjuster screw is fully backed off.
8. Pull the reverse shoe away from the anchor plate to release the tension on the upper return spring. Disengage the shoe and remove the spring. To facilitate the reassembly operation, note how the upper return spring is positioned on the shoe and how it is connected to the hole in the anchor plate.
9. Remove the forward shoe in the same manner as above.
10. Inspect the wheel cylinder and recondition or replace if necessary.
11. Clean and inspect the adjuster screw assembly. Apply a thin coat of lubricant to the adjuster threads.
12. Inspect the old springs. If old springs are damaged or have been overheated, they should be replaced. Indications of overheated springs are paint discoloration or distortion.
13. Lubricate the bosses on the anchor plate which make contact with the brake shoe tabs.
14. Remove the parking brake lever and attach the parking brake lever to the web of a new reverse shoe.
15. Position the upper return spring on the forward shoe and hook the other end of the spring into the hole in the backing plate.
16. Rotate the shoe outward with the upper part of the shoe against the wheel cylinder piston and insert the bottom part of the shoe under the anchor plate.
17. Repeat the above procedure for the reverse shoe.
18. With the adjuster screw fully retracted, position the straight forked end of the adjuster screw assembly on the parking brake lever. Make sure that the spring lock on the adjuster screw is on the outside and away from the adjusting hole.
19. Rotate the bottom of the forward shoe off the anchor plate and insert the curved fork end of the adjuster screw assembly into the web on the forward shoe.

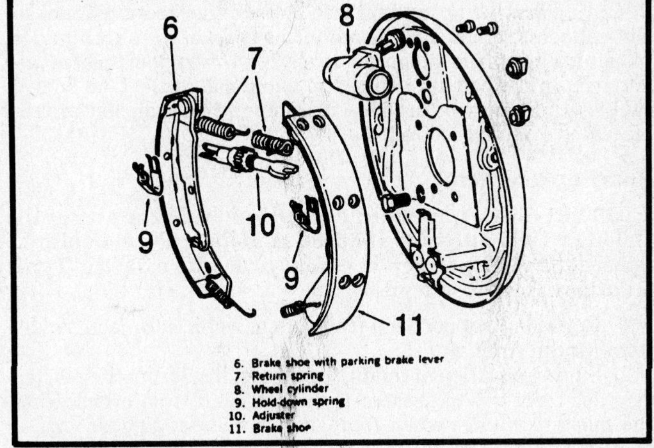

Type 8 (typical)

NOTE: Make sure that the curved portion of the forked end is facing downward and that the spring lock is on the outside and away from the adjusting hole.

20. Insert the pins for the hold-down clips through the backing plate and web of the shoes. Install the hold-down clips.
21. Install the shoe-to-anchor springs.
22. Compress the brake cable return spring and attach the cable to the bottom of the parking brake lever.
23. Install the brake drum.
24. Install the wheel and tire assembly.
25. Adjust the brakes.
26. Bleed the system and road test the car.

Adjustment

Adjust the brakes through the adjusting hole located in the

backing plate. Adjustment is made manually by spreading the adjuster screw assembly which is located directly under the wheel cylinder. Insert a small prybar or other suitable tool through the hole in the backing plate and rotate the adjuster wheel clockwise until the brakes drag as you turn the wheel in a forward direction. Turn the adjuster in the opposite direction until you just pass the point of drag. Repeat the procedure on the other wheel.

DISC BRAKE SERVICE

INDEX TO CALIPER TYPES

Model	Types
Courier/Mazda	Type 1, 4
Datsun	Type 2
D50/Arrow Mitsubishi	Type 3
LUV/Isuzu	Type 1, 4
Toyota	Type 1, 4, 5
VW	Type 2, 3

Type 1 Akebono, Girling, Etc. Sliding Caliper

This unit is a single piston, one-piece caliper that slides on a mounting bracket or frame which bolts to the steering knuckle. The caliper is retained in the mounting bracket by caliper guides (retaining keys) and support springs. Narrow support plates under each brake pad are utilized to eliminate rattle. One or two caliper guides may be used— —it is imperative that they are replaced as originally found.

Pad Replacement

NOTE: This procedure applies to Mazda trucks through 1984 only. On 1985–86 models, a Type 4 caliper is used. See the pad replacement procedure for the Type 4 caliper for these models.

1. Raise and support the front of the vehicle on jackstands. Remove the front wheel.
2. Siphon a sufficient quantity of brake fluid from the master cylinder reservoir to prevent the brake fluid from overflowing the master cylinder when removing or installing pads. This is necessary as the piston must be forced into the cylinder bore to provide sufficient clearance to remove the pads.
3. Remove the clips or pins that hold the caliper guides in position.
4. Lightly tap out the guides— —there may only be one, so remember the correct positioning.
5. Lift the caliper off of the mounting bracket. It may be necessary to rock it back and forth a bit in order to seat the piston so it will clear the brake pads. Position the caliper out of the way and support it with wire so it doesn't hang by the brake lines.
6. Remove the brake pads from the mounting bracket. *Do not remove the support springs.*
7. A support plate is under each pad; they are not interchangeable and must be replaced correctly. Remove the support plates.
8. Inspect the brake disc (rotor) as detailed in the appropriate section.
9. Inspect the caliper and piston assembly for breaks, cracks or other damage. Overhaul or replace the caliper as necessary.
10. Replace the support plates in their *original* positions.
11. Place the new pads in the support bracket over the support springs.
12. Push the piston all the way back into its bore (a C-clamp may be necessary for this operation).
13. Position the caliper over the pads and onto the mounting bracket.
14. Install the caliper guides (retaining keys) and then install the guide retaining pins or clips.
15. Refill the master cylinder with fresh brake fluid.
16. Install the tire and wheel assembly and then pump the brake pedal several times to bring the pads into adjustment. Road test the vehicle.

NOTE: If a firm pedal cannot be obtained, bleed the system as detailed in "Bleeding the Brakes".

Type 2 Girling/Annette Sliding Yoke Caliper

This unit is a double piston, one-piece caliper. The cylinder body contains two pistons, back-to-back, in a thru-bore. The cylinder body is bolted to the steering knuckle, with both pistons inboard of the rotor. A yoke, which slides on the cylinder body, is installed over the rotor and the caliper.

When the brakes are applied, hydraulic pressure forces the pistons apart in the double ended bore. The piston closest to the rotor applies force directly to the inboard pad. The other piston applies force to the yoke, which transmits the force to the outer pad, creating a friction force on each side of the rotor.

One variation has a yoke that floats on guide pins screwed into the cylinder body.

Some designs incorporate parking brake mechanisms which are actuated by a lever and cam working between the piston and the yoke. The yokes do not have to be removed to replace the brake pads.

Pad Replacement

1. Raise and support the front of the vehicle on jackstands. Remove the wheel.
2. Siphon a sufficient quantity of brake fluid from the master cylinder reservoir to prevent the brake fluid from overflowing the master cylinder when removing or installing new pads. This is necessary as the piston must be forced into the cylinder bore to provide sufficient clearance to remove the pads.
3. Disconnect the brake pad lining wear indicator if so equipped.
4. Remove the dust cover and/or anti-rattle (damper) clip if so equipped.
5. Lift off the wire clip(s) which hold the guide pins or retaining pin in place.
6. Remove the upper guide pin and the two hanger springs. Carefully tap out the lower guide pin.

CAUTION

The lower guide pin usually contains an anti-rattle coil spring, be careful not to lose this spring. If a retaining pin is used, pull the pin out and remove the two hanger springs.

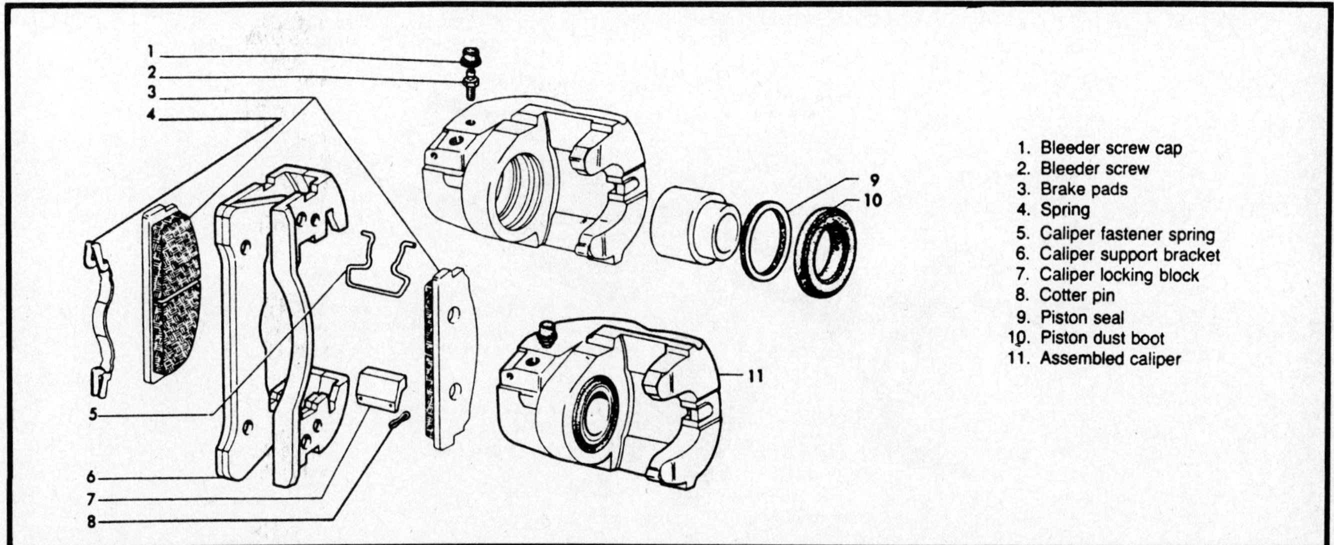

Type 1 caliper (typical)

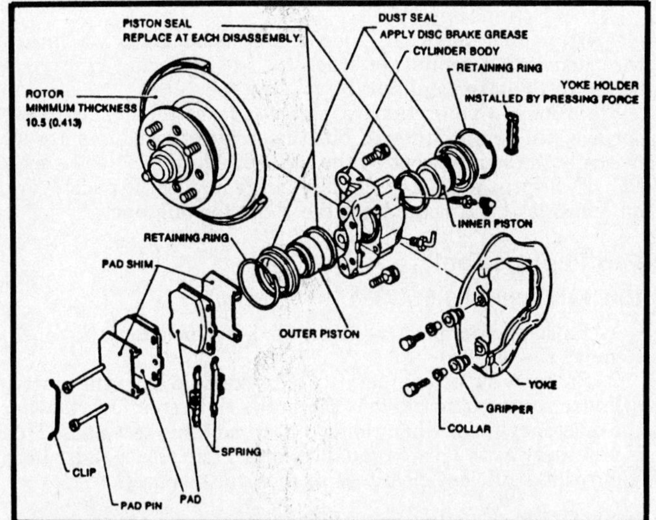

Type 2 caliper (typical)

7. Slide the yoke outward and remove the outer brake pad and the anti-noise shim (if so equipped).
8. Slide the yoke inward and repeat Step 7.
9. Check the rotor as detailed in the appropriate section.
10. Inspect the caliper and piston assembly for breaks, cracks or other damage. Overhaul or replace the caliper as necessary.
11. Push the piston next to the rotor back into the cylinder bore until the end of the piston is flush with the boot retaining ring.

CAUTION

If the piston is pushed further than this, the seal will be damaged and the caliper assembly will have to be overhauled.

12. Retract the piston farthest from the rotor by pulling the yoke toward the outside of the vehicle.
13. Install the outboard pad. Anti-noise shims (if so equipped) must be located on the plate side of the pad with the triangular cutout pointing toward the top of the caliper.
14. Install the inboard pad with the shims (if so equipped) in the correct position.
15. Replace the lower guide pin and the anti-rattle coil spring.
16. Hook the hanger springs under the pin and over the brake pads.
17. Install the upper guide pin over the ends of the hanger springs.

NOTE: If a single two-sided retaining pin is used, install the pin and then install the hanger springs as in Steps 16–17.

18. Insert the wire clip locks into the holes in the guide pins or retaining pin.
19. Refill the master cylinder with fresh brake fluid.
20. Install the tire and wheel assembly. Pump the brake pedal several times to bring the pads into adjustment. Road test the vehicle. If a firm pedal cannot be obtained, refer to "Bleeding the Brakes".

Type 3 Kelsey-Hayes Floating Caliper

This unit is a single piston, one-piece caliper which floats on two guide pins screwed into the adapter (anchor plate). The adaptor, in turn, is held to the steering knuckle with two bolts. As the brake pads wear, the caliper floats along the adapter and guide pins during braking.

Pad Replacement

1. Raise the front of the vehicle and support it with jackstands. Remove the wheel.
2. Siphon some brake fluid from the master cylinder reservoir to prevent its overflowing when the piston is retracted into the cylinder bore.
3. Disconnect the brake pad warning indicator if so equipped.
4. Using a pair of needlenose pliers or the like, remove the anti-rattle springs.
5. Using an Allen wrench, back out the two guide pins that attach the caliper to the anchor plate.

NOTE: When replacing pads only, it is not necessary to remove the guide pins completely from the rubber bushings, as they may be difficult to reinstall.

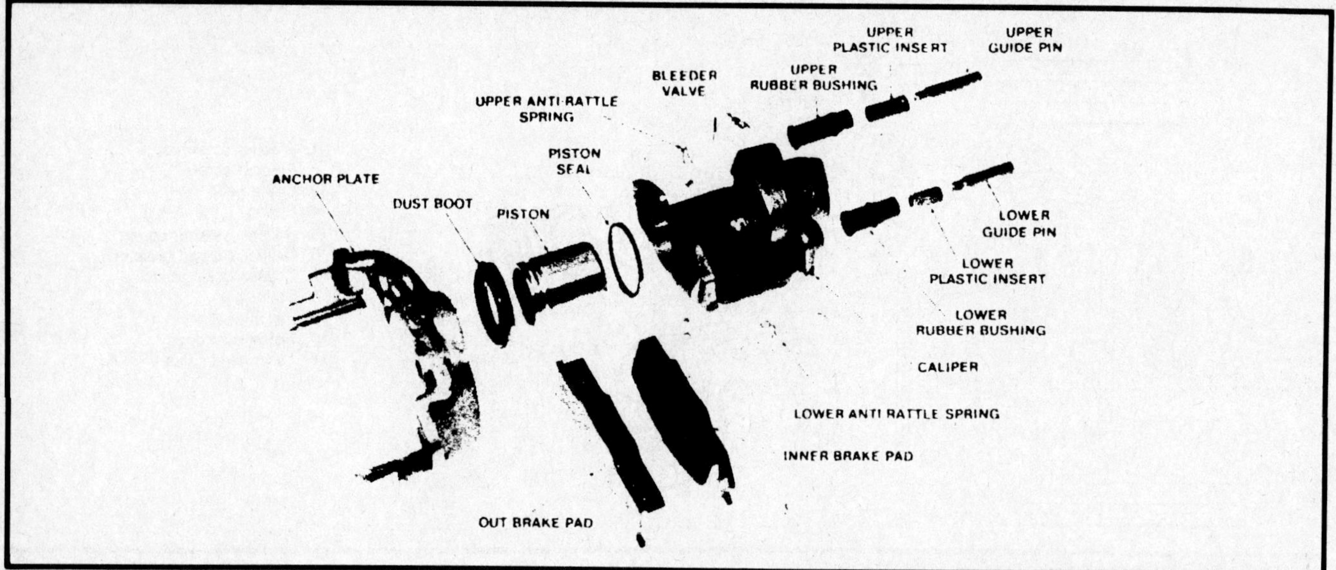

Type 3 caliper (typical)

6. Lift off the caliper and position it out of the way with some wire— —you need not remove the brake lines.

CAUTION

Never allow the caliper to hang by its brake lines.

7. Slide the outer pad out of the anchor plate and then remove the inner pad. Check the rotor as detailed in the appropriate section. Check the caliper for fluid leaks or cracked boots. If any damage is found, the caliper will require overhauling or replacement.

8. Carefully clean the anchor plate with a wire brush or some other abrasive material. Install the new brake pads into position on the anchor plate. The inner pad usually has chamfered edges.

NOTE: When replacing brake pads, always replace both pads on both sides of the vehicle. Mixed pads will cause uneven braking.

9. Slowly and carefully push the piston into its bore until it's bottomed and then position the caliper onto the anchor plate. Install the guide pins and tighten them to 25–30 ft. lbs.

NOTE: The upper guide pin is usually longer than the lower one.

CAUTION

Use extreme care so as not to cross-thread the guide pins when tightening.

10. Install the anti-rattle springs between the anchor plate and brake pads ears. The loops on the springs should be positioned inboard.

11. Fill the reservoir with brake fluid and pump the brake pedal several times to set the piston. It should not be necessary to bleed the system; however, if a firm pedal cannot be obtained, the system must be bled.

12. Install the wheel and lower the vehicle.

Type 4
Ate, Girling, Etc.
Floating Caliper

Although similar in many respects to a sliding caliper, this single piston unit floats on guide pins and bushings which are threaded into a mounting bracket. The mounting bracket is bolted to the steering knuckle.

Variations in pad retainers, shims, anti-rattle and retaining springs will be encountered but the service procedures are all basically the same except on the 1985–86 Mazda. Note the position of all springs, clips or shims when removing the pads. Work on one side at a time and use the other for reference.

Pad Replacement

EXCEPT 1985–86 MAZDA

1. Raise and support the front of the vehicle on jackstands. Remove the wheel.

2. Siphon a sufficient quantity of brake fluid from the master cylinder reservoir to prevent the brake fluid from overflowing the master cylinder when removing or installing new pads. This is necessary as the piston must be forced into the cylinder bore to provide sufficient clearance to remove the pads.

NOTE: Make sure you perform the next step on each caliper with the opposite caliper fully assembled. If you try to do both sides simultaneously, you may force once piston out of its caliper as you depress the other into the bore.

3. Grasp the caliper from behind and pull it toward you. This will push the piston back into the cylinder bore. If it is too difficult to depress the piston into the bore this way, use a flat, soft object such as a hammer handle to depress the piston directly after you have removed the pads (Step 8).

4. Disconnect the brake pad lining wear indicator if so equipped. Remove any anti-rattle springs or clips if so equipped.

NOTE: Depending on the model and year of the particular caliper, you may not have to remove it entirely to get at the brake pads. If the caliper is the "swing" type, it will have sufficient clearance and brake hose length to permit you to pivot it upward on the upper guide bolt. On these calipers, remove the lower guide bolt, pivot the caliper on the upper bolt and swing it upward exposing the brake pads. If this method is employed, skip to Step 7.

5. Remove the caliper guide pins.

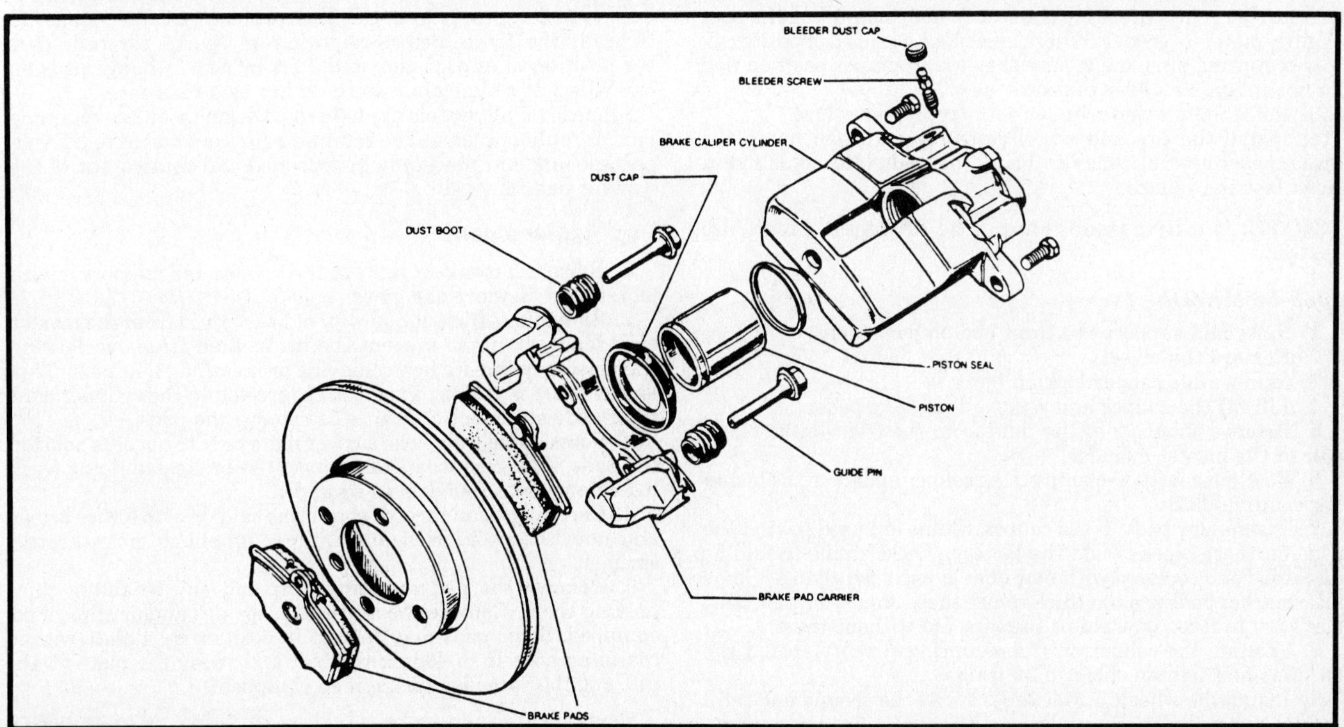

Type 4 caliper (typical)

Exploded view of the components that must be removed to replace brake pads—Toyota PD60 caliper, used on later model two wheel drive pickups

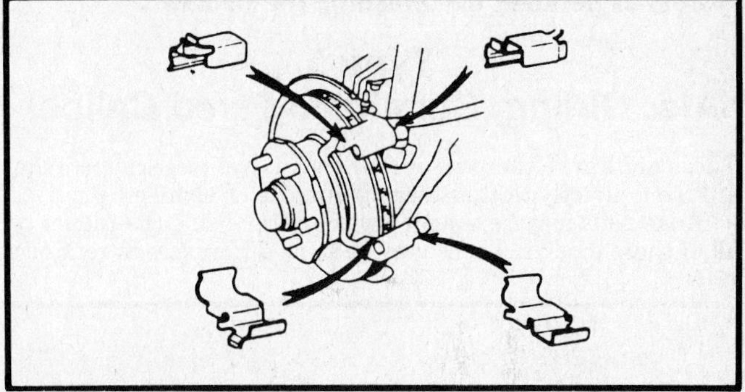

Exploded view of components to be removed/replaced when replacing brake pads on Toyota FS17 type calipers

6. Remove the caliper from the rotor by slowly sliding it out and away from the rotor. Position the caliper out of the way and support it with wire so that it doesn't hang by the brake line.

7. On models equipped with anti-rattle springs, remove them. Slide the outboard pad out of the adapter.

8. Remove the inboard pad. Remove any shims or shields behind the pads and note their positions. Remove any support plates (clips) that may be present. If the piston was not depressed back into the caliper in Step 3, do it now.

9. Install the anti-rattle hardware and then the pads (in their proper positions!). On Toyotas with PD60 type calipers, install the anti squeal shim onto the surface of the piston. On Toyotas with the FS17 type calipers, replace the single, outboard anti-squeal shim with a new one, facing it toward the rear of the outboard pad. Toyota recommends that the pad support plates or clips used on their disc brakes be replaced with the pads. Note that on FS17 type calipers, anti-rattle springs are used and must be installed last.

10. Install any pad shims or heat shields.

11. Reposition the caliper and install the guide pin(s) carefully so as to avoid damaging the rubber boots. On Toyota PD60 calipers, torque the guide pins to 29 ft. lbs. On Toyota FS17 type calipers, torque the pin to 65 ft. lbs.

Installing the anti-squeal shim onto the caliper piston of Toyota PD60 type disc brakes

NOTE: If the caliper is the "swing" type, you need only pivot it back into position and install the lower guide pin.

12. Check to make sure rubber boots are securely seated in their grooves. Make sure they are not bulged out with entrapped air and that they are nowhere pinched. If necessary, relieve air

pressure by gently breaking the seal on one end-pulling the boot slightly out of its groove. Where hole plugs are used opposite caliper mounting pins, make sure they are in proper position and do not retain air under pressure, also.

13. Refill the master cylinder with fresh brake fluid.
14. Install the tire and wheel assembly and then pump the brake pedal several times to bring the pads into adjustment. Road test the vehicle.

NOTE: If a firm pedal cannot be obtained, bleed the system.

1985–86 MAZDA

1. Raise and support the front end on jackstands.
2. Remove the wheels.
3. Remove the caliper lockpin bolts.
4. Lift off the caliper and remove the brake pads.
5. Remove about $^1/_2$ of the fluid from the front brake reservoir of the master cylinder.
6. Position a large C-clamp on the caliper and force the piston back into its bore.
7. Install new pads in the caliper. Shims are used behind the pads on these trucks from the factory. These shims should be discarded and replaced with new ones at each pad change. Some aftermarket pads are too thick to use these shims. In that case, don't try to force new shims in place. Do without them.
8. Position the caliper on the mounting support, install the lockpins and tighten them to 30 ft. lbs.
9. Install the wheels, lower the truck to the ground and refill the master cylinder. Pump the brake pedal a few times to restore pressure.

NOTE: If a firm pedal cannot be obtained, bleed the system as detailed in "Bleeding the Brakes".

Type 5
Ate, Girling, Sumitomo Fixed Caliper

These units are either two or four piston, two-piece calipers that are fixed directly to the steering knuckle or spindle.

Brake pads may be changed without removing the caliper on all of these models. There may be some differences in retainers or anti-rattle springs from the illustrations, but all versions are basically the same. Before removing any parts, carefully note the position of any springs, retainers or clips. Change pads on one wheel at a time and use the other as a reference.

All pads on all models are held in position by either retaining pins or retainer plates. The retainer plates are bolted to the caliper housing and need only be loosened and rotated out of the way for pad removal.

Pad Replacement

1. Raise the front (or rear) of the vehicle and support it with jackstands. Remove the wheel.
2. Siphon a sufficient quantity of brake fluid from the master cylinder reservoir to prevent the brake fluid from overflowing the master cylinder when removing or installing new pads. This is necessary as the pistons must be forced into the cylinder bore to provide sufficient clearance to remove the pads.
3. Some models may use a cover plate over the access hole for the pads, if so, remove it. Disconnect the brake pad lining wear indicator wire on models so equipped.
4. Carefully clean the exterior of the caliper with a wire brush and note the position of any dampening shims or anti-rattle springs.
5. Remove the pad retaining pins and any retaining clips holding them. Remove the anti-rattle springs and/or clips, if so equipped. Some pads may be held in position by a plate with a retaining bolt. If so, loosen the bolt and swing the plate away. Lift out the spreader spring if so equipped.

NOTE: It is a good idea to remove one retaining spring or plate and then remove the anti-rattle springs or spreader spring. Remove the second retaining pin or plate last.

6. Force the old pads away from the rotor for easy withdrawal and remove the pads from the caliper.
7. If so equipped, remove the lower anti-rattle springs and dampening shims using needlenose pliers.
8. Check the brake disc (rotor) as detailed in the appropriate section.
9. Examine the dust boot for cracks or damage and push the pistons back into the cylinder bores. If the pistons are frozen or if the caliper is leaking hydraulic fluid, it must be overhauled.

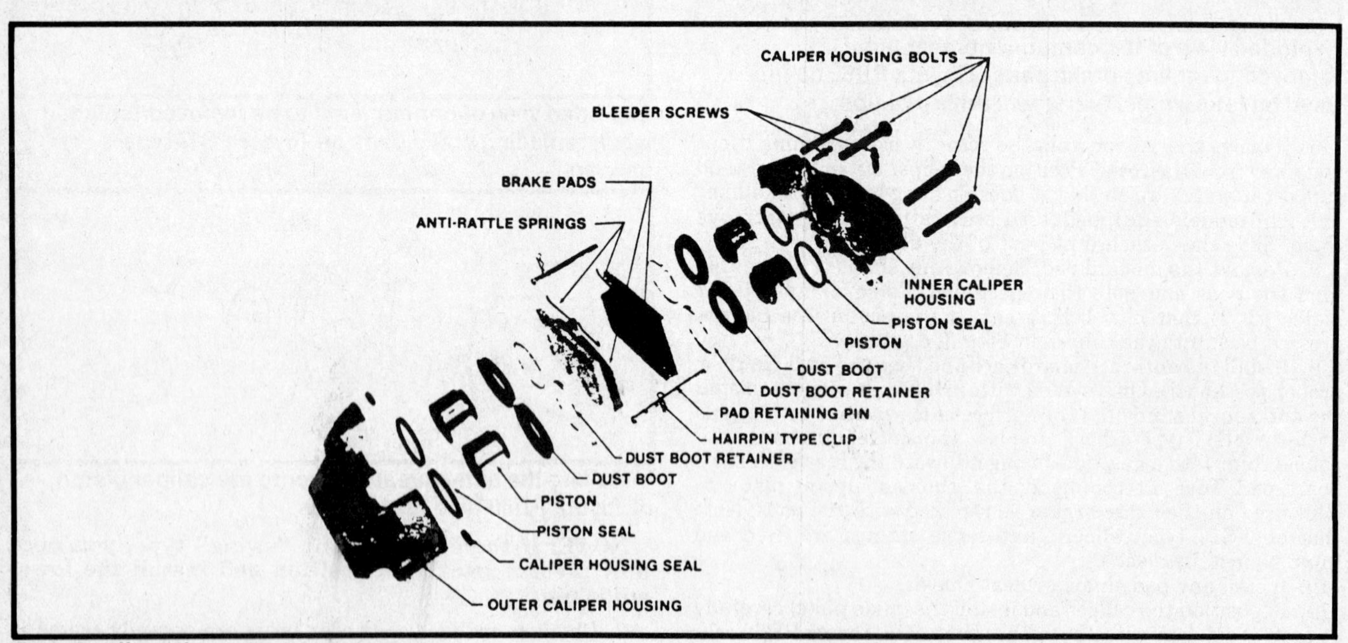

Type 5 caliper (four-piston, typical)

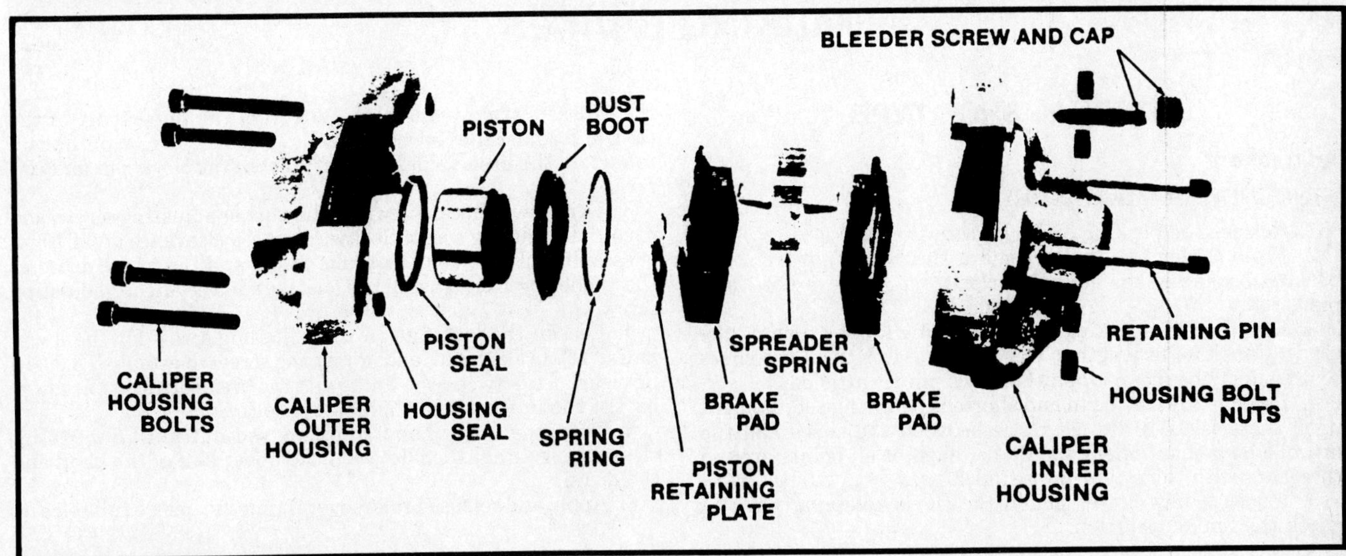

Type 5 caliper (two-piston, typical)

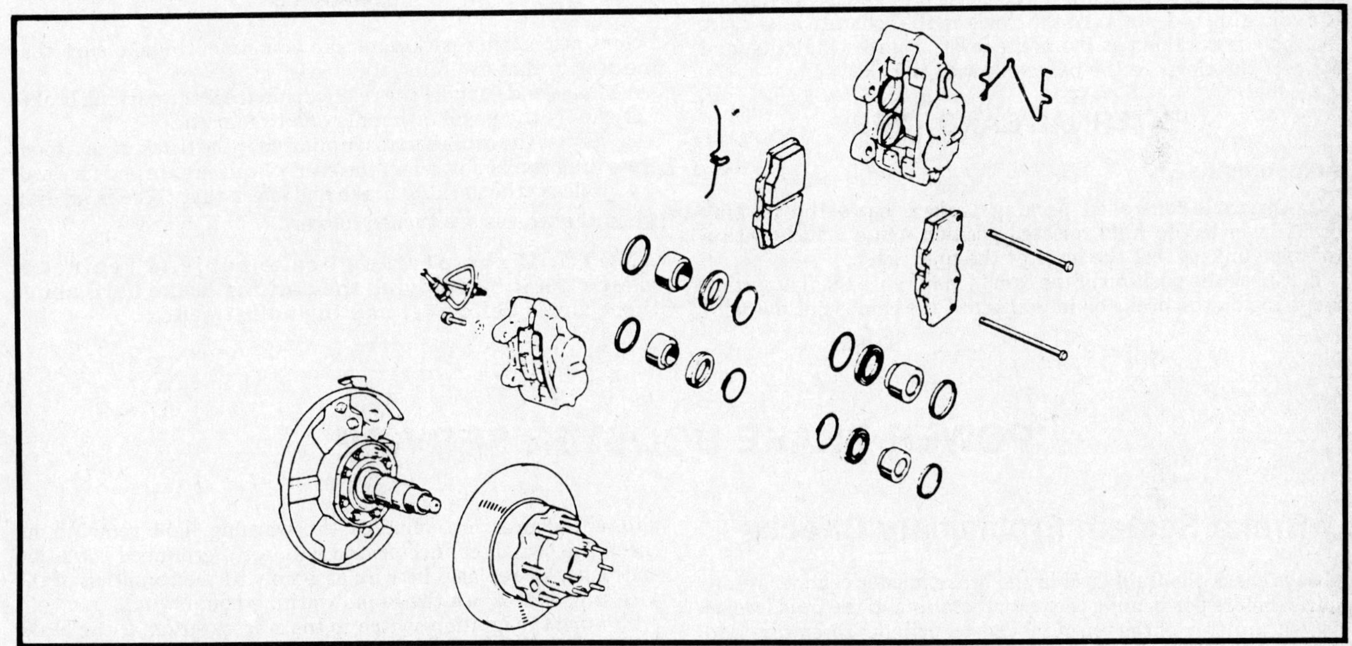
Exploded view of Toyoto S12 + 8 type disc brake caliper, used on late model four wheel drive trucks

10. Install the anti-rattle spring or damping shims and slip the new pads into the caliper. If damping shims are used, be sure that the directional arrow on the shims face the forward rotation of the rotor.
11. Install one pad retaining pin and hairpin clip. Position the anti-rattle springs and/or spreader spring and then install the other pad retaining pin and clip.
12. Refill the master cylinder to the correct level with the proper brake fluid.
13. Replace the wheel and lower the vehicle. Pump the brake pedal several times to bring the pads into correct adjustment. Road test the vehicle. If a firm pedal cannot be obtained, the system will require bleeding.

PARKING BRAKES

INTERNAL SHOE TYPE

Adjustment

NINE INCH DIAMETER DRUM

1. Release the parking brake lever in the cab.
2. From under the truck, remove the cotter pin from the parking brake linkage adjusting clevis pin. Remove the clevis pin.
3. Lengthen the parking brake adjusting link by turning the clevis. Continue to lengthen the adjusting link until the shoes seat against the drum when the clevis pin is installed.
4. Remove the clevis pin and shorten the linkage adjustment until there is 0.010 in. clearance between the shoes and the drum. The measurement should be taken at all points around the drum with the clevis pin installed.
5. Install a new cotter pin in the clevis retaining pin and check the brake operation.

Twelve Inch Diameter Drum

There is no internal adjustment on this brake. Adjustment is made on the linkage. Remove the clevis pin, loosen the nuts on the adjusting rod, and turn the clevis on the rod until a $^1/_4$–$^3/_8$ in. free play is obtained at the brake lever. Tighten the nuts, and connect the clevis to the bellcrank with the clevis pin.

EXTERNAL BAND TYPE

Adjustment

1. On cable-controlled parking brakes, move the parking brake lever to the fully released position. On a vehicle with a rod-type linkage, set the lever at the first notch.
2. Check the position of the cam to make sure the flat portion is resting on the brake band bracket. If the cam is not flat with the bracket, remove the clevis pin from the upper part of the cam, and adjust the clevis rod to allow the flat portion of the cam to rest on the brake band bracket. Install the clevis pin and cotter pin.
3. Remove the lock wire from the anchor adjusting screw, and turn the adjusting screw clockwise until a clearance of 0.010 in. is established between the brake lining and the brake drum at the anchor bracket. Install the lock wire in the anchor adjusting screw.
4. Loosen the lock nut on the adjusting screw for the lower half of the brake band, and adjust the screw to establish a 0.010 in. clearance between the lining and the brake drum at the lower half of the brake band. Tighten the lock nut.
5. Turn the upper band adjusting rod nut until a 0.010 in. clearance is established between the upper half of the band and the drum.
6. Apply and release brake several times to insure full release.

PARKING BRAKE INCLUDED WITH REAR BRAKES

Before attempting parking brake adjustment, make sure that the rear brakes are fully adjusted.

1. Raise and support the rear axle. Release the parking brake.
2. Apply the pedal or handle one to four clicks.
3. Adjust the cable equalizer nut under the truck until a moderate drag can be felt when the rear wheels are turned forward.
4. Release the parking brake and check that there is no drag when the wheels are turned forward.

NOTE: If the parking brake cable is replaced, prestretch it by applying the parking brake hard about three times before attempting adjustment.

POWER BRAKE BOOSTER SERVICE

Brake System Preliminary Checks

Always check the fluid level in the brake master cylinder reservoir(s) before performing the test procedures. If the fluid level is not within $^1/_4$ in. of the top of the master cylinder reservoirs, add the specified brake fluid.

Push the brake pedal down as far as it will go. If the pedal travels more than halfway between the released position and the floor, adjust the brakes. If the vehicle is equipped with automatic brake adjusters, serveral sharp brake applications while backing up may be necessary to adjust the brakes.

Road test the vehicle and apply the brakes at a speed of about 20 mph to see if the vehicle stops evenly. If not, the brakes should be adjusted. Perform the road test only when the brakes will apply and the vehicle can be safely stopped.

DUAL BRAKE WARNING LIGHT SYSTEM TESTS

1. Turn the ignition switch to the ACC or ON position. If the light on the brake warning lamp remains on, the condition may be caused by a shorted or broken switch, grounded switch wires or the differential pressure valve is not centered. Centralize the differential pressure valve. If the warning light remains on, check the switch connector and wire for a grounded condition and repair or replace the wire assembly. If the condition of the wire is good, replace the brake warning lamp switch.
2. Turn the ignition switch to the start position. If the brake warning lamp does not light, check the light and wiring and replace or repair wiring as necessary. When both brake systems are functioning normally, the equal pressure at the pressure differential valve during brake pedal application keeps the valve centered. The brake warning light will be on only when the ignition key is in the start position.
3. If the brake warning lamp does not light when a pressure differential condition exists in the brake system, the warning lamp may be burned out, the warning lamp switch is inoperative or the switch to lamp wiring has an open circuit. Check the bulb and replace it, if required. Check the switch to lamp wires for an open circuit and repair or replace them, if required. If the warning lamp still does not light, replace the switch.

POWER BRAKE FUNCTION

Testing

With the engine stopped, eliminate all vacuum from the system by pumping the brake pedal several times. Then push the pedal down as far as it will go, and note the effort required to hold it in this position. If the pedal gradually moves downward under this pressure, the hydraulic system is leaking and should be checked by a hydraulic pressure test.

With the brake pedal still pushed down, start the engine. If the vacuum system is operating properly, the pedal will move downward. If the pedal position does not change, the vacuum system is not operating properly and should be checked by a vacuum test.

VACUUM BOOSTER CHECK VALVE

Testing

Disconnect the line from the bottom of the vacuum check valve, and connect a vacuum gauge to the valve. Start the engine, run it at idle speed, and check the reading on the vacuum gauge.

The gauge should register 17–19 in. Hg. with standard transmission and 14–15 in. Hg. in Drive range if equipped with an automatic transmission. Stop the engine and note the rate of vacuum drop. If the vacuum drops more than one in. Hg. in 15 seconds, the check valve is leaking. If the vacuum reading does not reach 18 in. Hg. or is unsteady, an engine tuneup is needed.

Remove the gauge and reconnect the vacuum line to the check valve.

BENDIX PISTON TYPE VACUUM BOOSTER

Testing

Disconnect the vacuum line from the booster end plate. Install a tee fitting in the end plate, and connect a vacuum gauge (no. 1) and vacuum line to the fitting. Install a second vacuum gauge (no. 2) in place of the pipe plug in the booster control valve body.

Start the engine, and note the vacuum reading on both gauges. If both gauges do not register manifold vacuum, air is leaking into the vacuum system. If both gauges register manifold vacuum, stop the engine and note the rate of vacuum drop on both gauges. If the drop exceeds one in. Hg. in 15 seconds on either gauge, air is leaking into the vacuum system. Tighten all vacuum connections and repeat the test. If leakage still exists, the leak may be localized as follows:

1. Disconnect the vacuum line and gauge no. 1 from the booster.
2. Connect vacuum gauge no. 1 directly to the vacuum line. Start the engine and note the gauge reading. Stop the engine and check the rate of vacuum drop. If gauge no. 1 does not register manifold vacuum, or if the vacuum drop exceeds 1 in. Hg. in 15 seconds, the leak is in the vacuum line or check valve connections.
3. Reconnect vacuum gauge no. 1 and the vacuum line to the tee fitting. Start the engine, and run it at idle speed for one minute. Depress the brake pedal sufficiently to cause vacuum gauge no. 2 to read from zero to 1 in. Hg. Gauge no. 1 should register manifold vacuum of 17–19 in. Hg. with standard transmission and 14–16 in. Hg. in Drive range if equipped with an automatic transmission. If the drop of vacuum on gauge no. 2 is slow, the air cleaner, or air cleaner line, may be plugged. Inspect and if necessary, clean the air cleaner.
4. Release the brake pedal and observe the action of gauge no. 2. Upon releasing the pedal, the vacuum gauge must register increasing vacuum until manifold vacuum is reached. The rate of increase must be smooth, with no lag or slowness in the return to manifold vacuum. If the gauge readings are not as outlined, the booster is not operating properly and should be removed and overhauled.

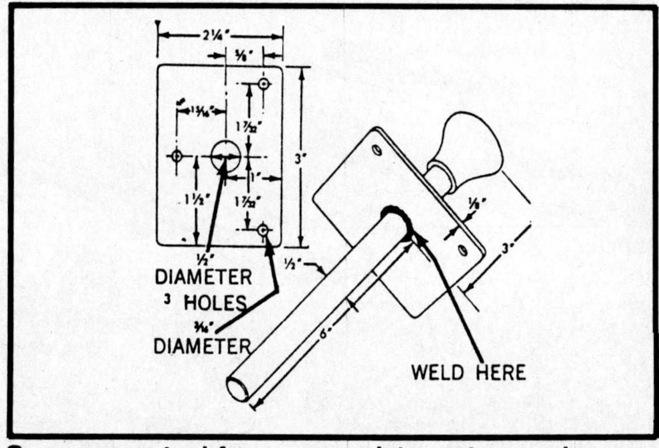

Compressor tool for vacuum piston return spring

DIAGRAGM TYPE VACUUM BOOSTER

Testing

This procedure can be used to test all diaphragm boosters which are equipped with a pipe thread outlet on the atmosphere portion of the diaphragm chamber.

Remove the pipe plug from the rear half of the booster chamber, and install a vacuum gauge. Start the engine and run it at idle speed. The gauge should register 18–21 in. Hg.

1. With the engine running, depress the brake pedal with enough pressure to show a zero reading on the vacuum gauge. Hold the pedal in the applied position for one minute. Any downward movement of the pedal during this time indicates a brake fluid leak. Any kickback (upward movement) of the pedal indicates brake fluid is leaking past the hydraulic piston check valve.
2. With the engine running, push down on the brake pedal with sufficient pressure to show a zero reading on the vacuum gauge. Hold the pedal down, and shut the engine off. Maintain pedal position for one minute. A kickback of the pedal indicates a vacuum leak in the vacuum check valve, in the vacuum line connections, or in the booster.

VACUUM—HYDRAULIC BOOSTER SYSTEMS

Bleeding

1. Eliminate vacuum in the booster by depressing the brake pedal several times while the engine is not running.
2. On trucks not equipped with reservoir tanks, disconnect the manifold tube at the booster side of the manifold check valve (engine not running).
3. Alternately loosen the brake tube at each unit until all air is expelled. Booster slave-cylinder is bled first.

CAUTION

Where air pressure brake bleeding equipment is used to bleed brakes, do not use more than 25–30 psi.

NOTE: A piston stop is provided in the slave cylinder to eliminate the possibility of damaging the return spring while bleeding the system. This damage occurs only when bleeding the brakes with a vacuum present in the booster system.

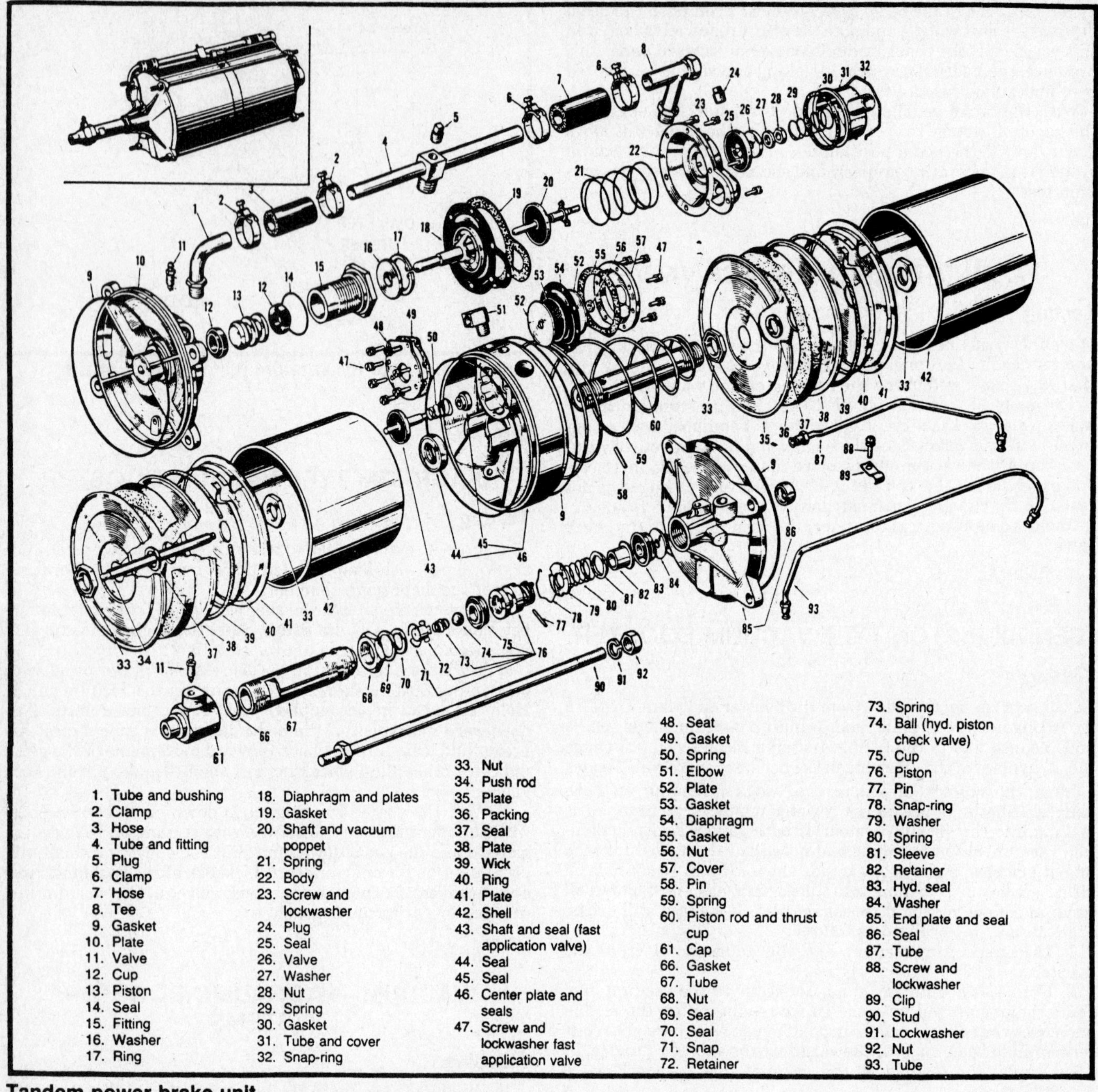

Tandem power brake unit

Hydraulic Tandem Brake Unit

Disassembly

1. Disconnect hydraulic and vacuum by-pass tube from valve body.
2. Remove control valve air inlet fitting from control valve body.
3. Remove control valve body and valve parts from end plate.
4. Make a special tool.

NOTE: If this is to be a regular service this tool is recommended. For one time or emergency, a vise, C-clamps, and a guide tube 10 in. long may be used.

5. Insert tool through end plate opening, and force vacuum cylinder piston forward.
6. Attach flange of tool to end plate with three valve body cover screws.
7. Loosen slave cylinder check nut, and remove slave cylinder.
8. Compress push rod pin retaining spring, remove retainer pin, then remove hydraulic piston from push rod.
9. Hold end cap in a vise, and remove hydraulic cylinder from cap.
10. Loosen vacuum hose clamps, then slide both hoses on the vacuum tube toward center plate.
11. Remove hydraulic by-pass tube from rear end plate, then

remove return spring compression tool from end plate.

12. Remove the nuts and studs from power cylinder, then disassemble end plates, cylinder shells and center plate assembly.

13. Force center plate and vacuum piston together, and insert a rod through hole in piston rod to hold piston return spring in the compressed position.

14. Place assembly ring over piston, then remove piston assembly, but keep piston parts assembled in assembly ring. After vacuum tubes and tee fittings have been removed from center plate, position plate on a flat surface.

15. Remove fast application valve cover.

16. To disassemble the diaphragm assembly, hold valve shaft with a screwdriver, and remove nut.

17. Lift retainer and diaphragm off valve shaft.

18. Turn center plate upside down, then remove valve seat plate screws and plate, gasket, valve, and spring from center plate.

19. Position front end plate assembly on a flat surface with flat side down.

20. Remove the O-ring seal, snap-ring and retainer washer, push rod seal spring and flange washer, push rod rubber cup seal, and guide washer from end plate.

21. Drive push rod leather seal out of end plate.

22. Position end plate in a holding fixture, then remove hydraulic valve fitting with a 1 $^7/_8$ in. socket wrench.

23. Push hydraulic piston out of valve fitting, and remove gasket from fittings.

NOTE: Clean all metal parts in a suitable cleaning fluid. After cleaning, wash all the hydraulic system parts in alcohol. Examine the bore of the cylinder shells for rust and corrosion, and polish with fine steel wool or crocus cloth if necessary. If the cylinders are badly pitted or scored, install new cylinders. If felt type wicks are worn, replace them with cotton type wicks.

CAUTION

Use overhaul kit and install ALL parts contained. Do not gamble on ANY old parts that the kit replaces.

Assembly

1. Install nut on piston rod with flat side of nut upward.

2. Position larger diameter piston plate on piston rod with chamfered side of hole at top. Guide rubber seal ring over threads of piston rod.

3. Place assembly ring on a flat surface, then install leather packing, with lip side upward; and smaller diameter piston plate with chamfered side of hole downward in the ring.

4. Cut a new piece of wick to the required length, then place it against inner face of leather packing lip.

5. Assemble expander ring against wick with gripper points upward, and hook notched end of spring under the clip near opposite end of spring. Position cut of retainer plate over loop of the spring.

6. Hold piston parts in the assembly ring, assemble them on end of piston rod, then install nut on tip of piston assembly. Tighten nut until it is flush with end of rod. Stake nuts securely at two places.

7. Clamp staked nut firmly in a vise, and tighten nut on opposite side of piston plate solidly against piston plate.

8. Press the fast application valve stem and push rod seals into center plate. The application valve seal must be flush with bottom of hole. The push rod seal should rest against the shoulder of center plate. Position center plate. Then place valve spring on top of seal with the small end at top.

9. Install the bullet-nosed tool at threaded end of valve shaft, and insert valve shaft through seal. Position gasket on center plate.

10. Place valve seat plate, with seat side downward, on gasket, and install screws and lockwashers.

11. Turn center plate over. Place lower diaphragm plate on valve shaft with rounded edge at top, then place diaphragm gasket at top of plate. Position diaphragm on top of gasket so screw holes and the bypass hole index with the identical holes in center plate.

12. Install the other diaphragm plate with rounded edge facing diaphragm.

13. Install valve shaft nut on valve shaft. Use a screw driver to prevent shaft from turning, and tighten nut. Stake nut securely at opposite points.

14. Position cover gasket and cover plate, then install screw and lockwashers.

15. Place piston return spring over piston rod with small end of spring at bottom.

16. Carefully guide piston rod through leather seal in center plate, with piston stop flanges of center plate facing upward. Press center plate down against spring, and insert a rod in piston rod. Thread piston rod nut on piston rod, with flat side of nut upward to limit of threads.

17. If forward piston was disassembled to replace leather piston packing, cotton wicking, or other parts, assemble the piston parts in the ring and turn assembly ring over.

18. Remove larger piston plate and O-ring seal.

19. With assembly ring still in place, guide the remaining piston parts over end of push rod and against piston nut. Carefully install O-ring seal over threads of piston rod.

20. Place the larger diameter piston plate on piston rod with chamfered side of hole toward O-ring seal.

21. Assemble large end of push rod in end of piston rod and install retainer pin. Install piston rod nut on end of piston rod with flat side downward. Tighten nut until it is flush with face of piston rod, then stake nut securely at opposite points.

22. Hold piston rod nut in a vise or with a wrench, and tighten inner nut securely against piston. Care must be exercised when tightening inner nut to prevent expander spring retainer plate from shifting.

23. Remove assembly ring, then remove rod holding return spring compressed. Install a new copper gasket in end cap.

24. The hydraulic cylinder must be assembled with milled flats next to end cap. Tighten hydraulic cylinder solidly in end cap, then thread check nut on hydraulic cylinder up to the limit of the threads.

25. Install check nut seal (if used) in groove or cylinder tube. Install bleeder screw in cap.

26. Press push rod leather seal into hydraulic cylinder bore of front end plate from inner side of plate with lip of seal toward outer end of the plate. Install push rod seal parts.

27. The chamfered side of stop washer is down, lip of cup is up, flat side of washer is next to cup, and small end of spring is down. Place washer against spring. Install snap-ring in inner groove of end plate.

28. Install stop washer with flat side in control valve hydraulic fitting. Install stop washer retaining ring.

29. Dip hydraulic piston cups in brake fluid, and assemble them on the hydraulic piston with lips of cups positioned away from each other. Insert piston into the fitting with open end of piston toward stop washer.

30. Install a new gasket on the hydraulic fitting (copper gasket on fitting without the groove, and a rubber seal gasket on fitting with the groove). Install the hydraulic fitting in end plate with a 1 $^7/_8$ in. socket wrench. Tighten fitting equipped with a rubber gasket firmly, and fitting equipped with a copper gasket to 324–330 ft. lbs.

31. Assemble vacuum control parts in control body. Install a new lead washer.

32. Hold slave cylinder end cap in a vise, and thread cylinder into end plate. Install T-fitting and tubes on center plate.

33. Position an end plate gasket on the plate, place cylinder shell on end plate, and coat interior of cylinder with vacuum cylinder oil.

34. Dip cylinder piston on packing in vacuum cylinder oil and allow the excess oil to drain off the wickings.
35. Position a gasket on ledge of center plate, then carefully guide push rod through seal in front end plate. At the same time, align the vacuum tube in end plate with vacuum tube on center plate. Slide hose in place to contact the two vacuum tubes.
36. Position a new gasket at center plate ledge.
37. Coat the interior of cylinder shell with vacuum cylinder oil, then tip cylinder at a 45 degree angle to prevent damage to the piston leather packing.
38. Carefully push the cylinder over piston and onto center plate.
39. Place a new gasket on ledge of end plate, then install end plate on cylinder, aligning end plate vacuum tube and center plate tube. Install cylinder studs and tighten nuts evenly.
40. To assemble the hydraulic piston parts, place large end of spring in retainer cup, then install check ball in piston body behind spring.
41. Dip piston cup in brake fluid, then install it on piston with lip of cup toward check ball.
42. Position the vacuum hoses on tubes, and tighten hose clamps firmly.
43. Connect hydraulic by-pass tube to front and rear end plate.
44. Remove slave cylinder from end plates, then insert and attach return spring compressing tool.
45. Assemble hydraulic piston on push rod.
46. Make certain lock ring is positioned over the retainer pin. Install hydraulic gasket in the plate. Carefully guide the hydraulic cylinder over piston cup, and thread cylinder into end plate.
47. Adjust cylinder 7 ¾ in., measuring between points shown in illustration.
48. Align bleeder screw in end cap with bleeder screw in control valve.
49. Remove spring compressing tool. After cylinder length adjustment is completed, tighten cylinder check nut solidly.
50. Install guide pins, made from 8–32 × 2 ½ in. machine screws with the heads cut off, in end plate.
51. Install diaphragm with diaphragm stem inserted into hydraulic control piston hole. Place diaphragm return spring and control valve body on top of diaphragm.
52. Remove guide pins, one at a time, and replace each guide pin with an attaching screw and a new lock washer. Tighten screws progressively and firmly.
53. Install air inlet fitting in control body, then install retainer.
54. Install vacuum by-pass tube.
55. Inspect assembly to see that all bolts, nut, screws, washers and plugs are in place, and that all tubes, clamps, and fittings are firmly tightened.

Installation

1. Position assembly on mounting brackets, and install attaching bolts.
2. Tighten bolts firmly.
3. Connect stop light wires and hydraulic lines to stop light switch.
4. Attach vacuum hose to booster.
5. Connect master cylinder hydraulic line to booster control valve.
6. Connect wheel cylinder hydraulic line to booster end cap.
7. Attach air inlet hose to control valve air inlet fitting, then check and tighten connections.
8. Remove lubricating plugs from end and center plates.
9. Add vacuum cylinder oil to level of filler holes, install plugs, then bleed hydraulic system.

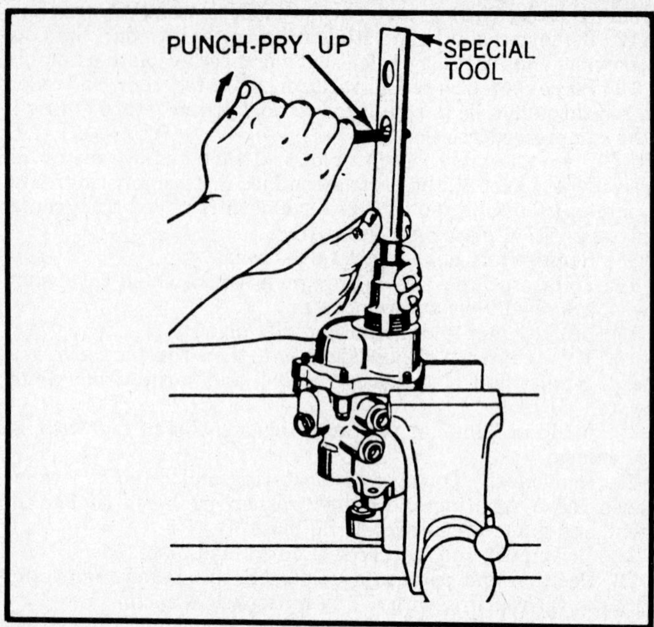

Removing the booster pedal rod—Bendix hydro boost

Bendix Hydro-Boost

The Bendix Hydro-Boost uses the hydraulic pressure supplied by the power steering pump to provide a power assist to brake application.

Disassembly

1. Place the booster in a vise with the bracket end up. Using a hammer and chisel, cut the bracket nut that holds the linkage bracket to the booster assembly. The nut should be cut at the open slot in the booster cover threads. Care must be exercised to avoid damage to the threads. Spread the nut and remove the bracket.
2. Remove the pedal boot by pulling if off over the pedal rod eyelet.
3. Position pedal rod removing tool around the pedal rod. The tool should be resting on the booster cover. Insert a punch through the pedal rod from the lower side of the special tool. Push the punch through until it rests on the higher side of the tool. Push up on the punch to shear the pedal rod retainer; remove the pedal rod.
4. Remove the grommet from the groove near the end of the pedal rod and from the groove in the input rod.
5. Disengage the tabs of the spring retainer from the ledge inside the opening near the master cylinder mounting flange of the booster. Remove the retainer and piston return spring from the opening.
6. Pull straight out on the output push rod to remove the push rod and push rod retainer from inside the booster piston.
7. Press in on the spool plug, and insert a small punch into the hole on top of the housing. This unseats one side of the spool plug snap-ring from the groove in the bore. Remove the snap-ring.
8. Remove the spool plug from the bore with a pair of pliers. Remove the O-ring from the plug and discard. Remove the spool spring from the bore.
9. Place the booster cover in a soft-faced vise and remove the cover retaining bolts. Remove the booster assembly from the vise and separate the booster cover from the housing. Remove the large seal ring and discard.
10. Press in on the end of the spool assembly, and use a spiral

snap-ring removing tool to remove the snap-ring from the forward groove in the spool. Discard the snap-ring.

11. Remove the input rod and piston assembly, and the spool assembly from the booster housing.

12. Remove the input rod seals from the input rod end, and the piston seal from the piston bore in the housing. Discard the seals.

13. Remove the plunger, seat, spacer and ball from the accumulator valve bore in the flange of the booster housing. Remove the O-ring from the seat and discard.

14. Thread a screw extractor into the opening in the check valve in the bottom of the accumulator valve bore, and remove the check valve from the bottom of the bore. Discard the check valve and O-ring.

NOTE: Using a screw extractor damages the seat in the check valve. A new check valve, O-ring and valve must be installed whenever the check valve is removed from the accumulator valve bore.

15. Using a ¼ or a 5/16 in. spiral flute type screw extractor, remove the tube seats from the booster ports.

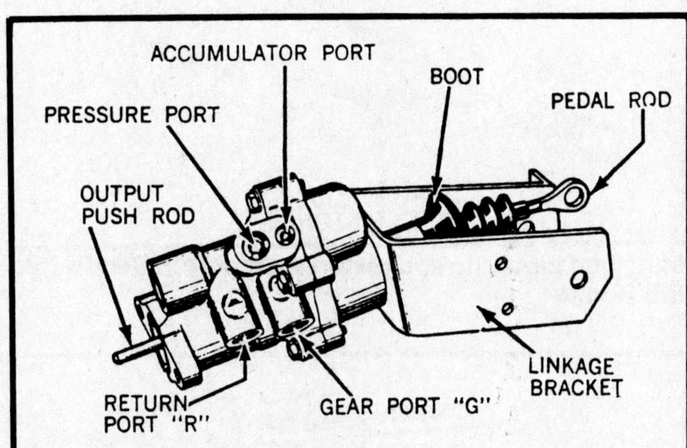

Typical Bendrix hydro boost

Cleaning & Inspection

1. Clean all parts in a suitable solvent.

2. Inspect the valve spool and the valve spool bore for any damage or ware. Discoloration of the spool or bore is normal,

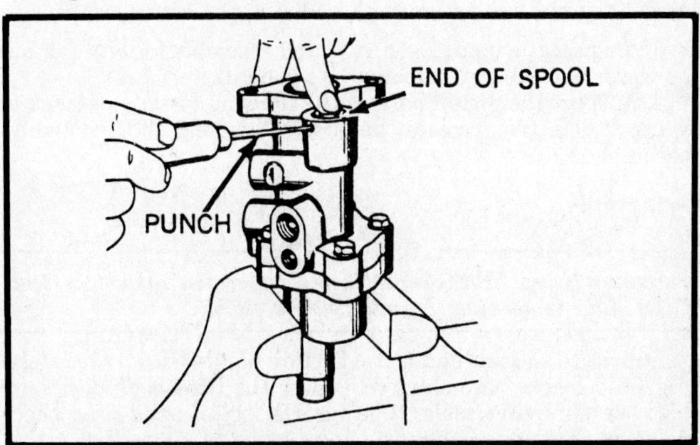

Removing the spool plug from the Bendix hydro boost

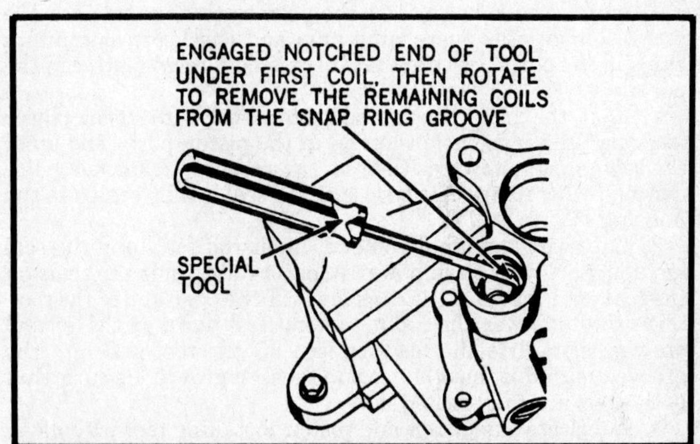

Removing spiral snap ring Bendix hydro boost

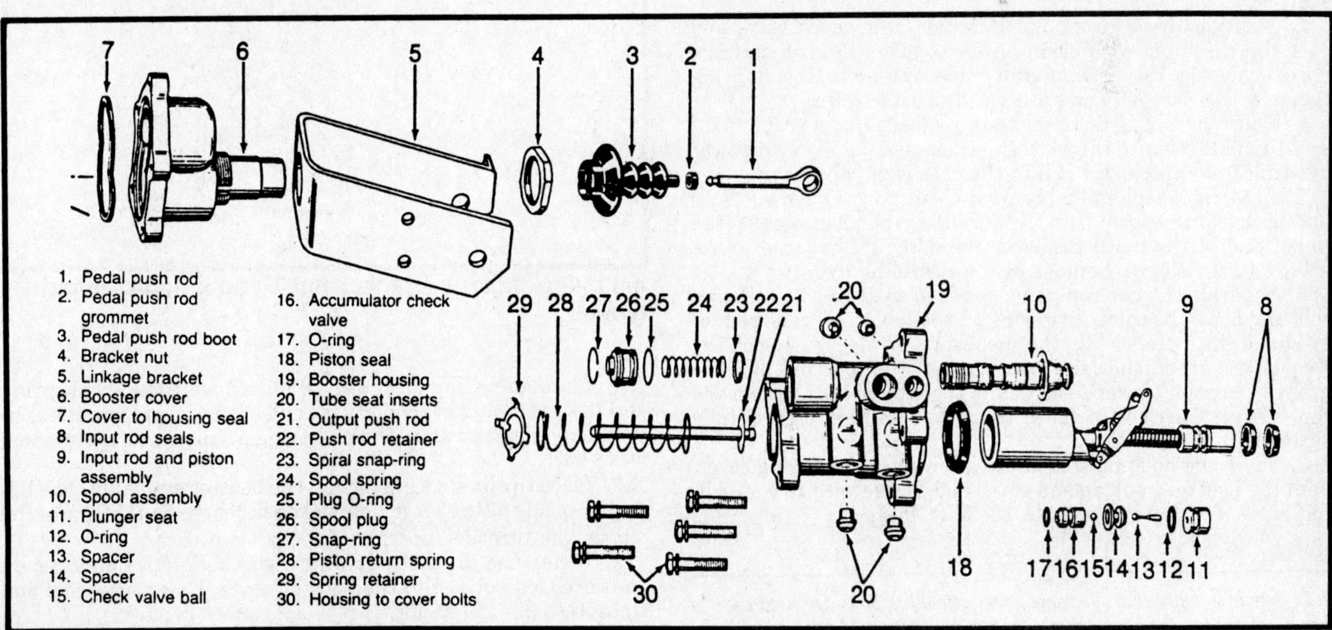

Exploded view of Bendix hydro boost

particulary in the grooves. If any damage is noted, replace the valve spool and housing.

NOTE: The clearance between the valve spool and the bore is very important. Because of this, the valve spool and housing are to be replaced only as an assembly.

3. Inspect the input rod and piston assembly for any damage or ware. Replace any defective components.
4. Inspect the piston bore in the housing for any damage or ware. If defective, replace the booster housing and spool valve assembly.

Assembly

CAUTION

Parts must be kept VERY clean. If there is any reason to doubt the cleanliness of the components, re-wash before assembly.

Lubricate all seals and metal friction points with power steering fluid before assembly. Whenever the booster is disassembled, be sure that seals, tube inserts, spiral snap-ring, check valve and ball are replaced.

1. Position a tube seat in each booster port and screw a spare tube nut in each port to press the seat down into the port. Do not tighten the tube nuts in the port as this may deface the seats. Remove the spare tube nuts and check for aluminium chips in the ports. Be sure that there is no foreign matter in the ports.
2. Coat the piston bore and piston seal with clean power steering fluid. Assemble the seal in the piston bore. The lip of the seal must be towards the rear (away from the master cylinder mounting flange). Be sure that the seal is fully seated in the housing.
3. Lubricate the input rod end, input rod seals and the seal installer tool with clean power steering fluid. Slide the seals on the tool with the lip of the cups towards the open end of the tool. Slide the tool over the input rod end end down to the second groove; then slide the forward seal off the tool and into the groove. Assemble the other seal in the first groove. Be sure, that both seals are fully seated.
4. Lubricate the piston and piston installing tool with clean power steering fluid. Insert the large end of the tool into the piston and the tool and piston into the piston bore, through the seal.
5. Position the O-ring on the accumulator check valve and coat the assembly with clean power steering fluid. Insert the check valve in the accumulator valve recess in the housing flange. Place the ball and spacer in the same recess.
6. Place the O-ring on the changing valve plunger seat and insert the plunger into the seat. Dip the assembly in clean power steering fluid and insert it into the changing valve recess.
7. Coat the spool assembly with clean power steering fluid and insert in the spool bore. Be sure that the pivot pins on the upper end of the input rod lever assembly are engaged in the groove in the sleeve. Remove piston installing tool.
8. Separate the two components of the snap-ring installation tool and place the spiral snap-ring on the tool. Insert the rounded end of the installer into the spool bore. While pressing on the rear of the spool, slide the snap-ring off the tool and into the groove near the forward end of the spool by pressing in on the tool sleeve. Check to be sure that the retaining ring is fully seated.
9. Place the housing seal in the groove in the housing cover. Join the booster housing and cover and secure with five attaching bolts. Tighten the bolts to 18–26 ft. lbs.

CAUTION

It is very important that the same cover attaching bolts are used as they are designed for the booster only. If they are damaged replace with the same part numbers.

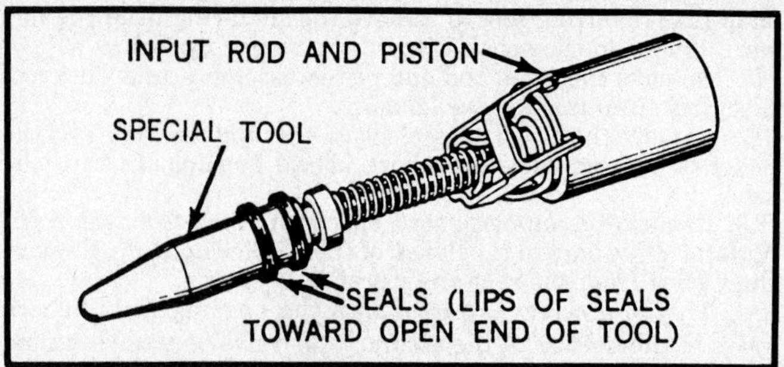

Installing input rod seals Bendix hydro boost

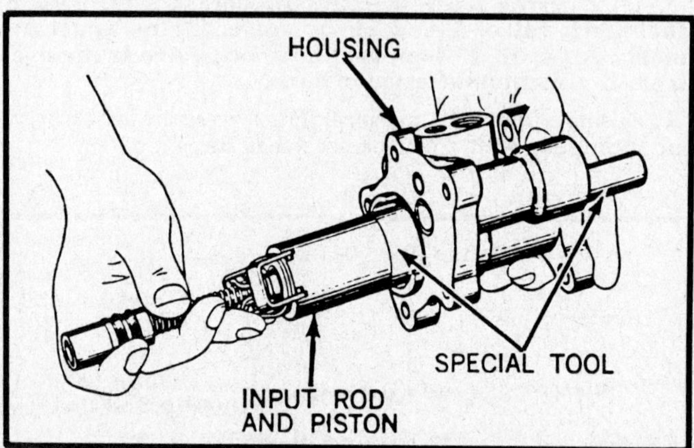

Installing input rod and piston assembly in Bendix hydro boost

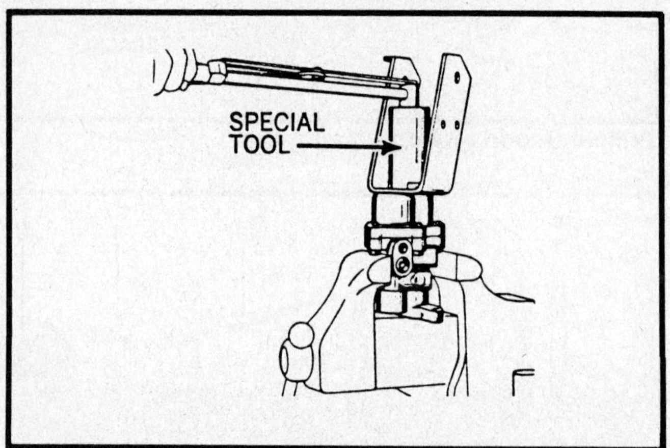

Installing linkage bracket nut Bendix hydro boost—typical

10. Place an O-ring on the spool plug. Insert the spool spring and the spool plug in the forward end of the spool bore. Press in on the plug and position the snap-ring in its groove in the spool valve bore.
11. Place the linkage bracket on the booster assembly. The tab on the inside of the large hole in the bracket should fit into the slot in the threaded portion of the booster cover.
12. Install the bracket nut with a staking groove outward on the threaded portion to the booster cover. Use special tool and tighten to 95–120 ft. lbs.
13. Insert a small punch into the staking groove of the nut, at the slot in the booster cover, and with a hammer stake the nut

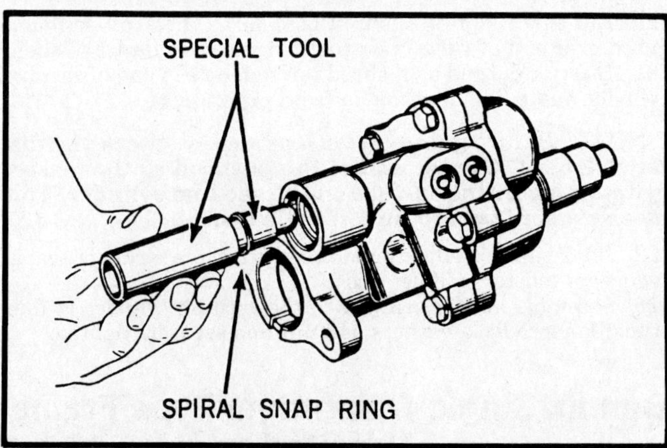

Installing spiral snap ring Bendix hydro boost

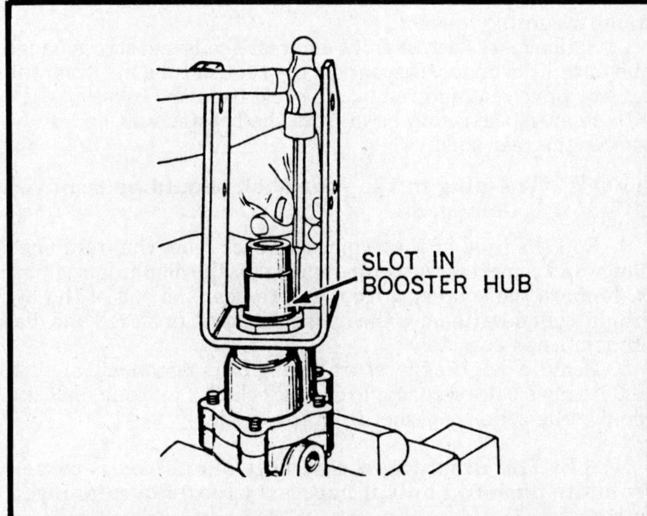

Staking linkage bracket nut Bendix hydro boost

in place. Be sure that the threads on the nut are deformed so the nut will not loosen.

14. Position a new boot and grommet on the pedal rod. Moisten the grommet and insert the grommet end of the pedal rod into the input rod of the booster. When the grommet is fully seated, the pedal rod will rotate freely.
15. Install the boot on the booster cover.

Bendix Master Vac

Removal

1. Disconnect clevis at brake pedal to push rod.
2. Remove vacuum hoses from power cylinder.
3. Disconnect hydraulic line from master cylinder.
4. Remove the four attaching nuts and lock washers that hold the unit to the firewall. Remove the power brake unit.

Disassembly

1. Remove four master cylinder to vacuum cylinder attaching nuts and washers.
2. Separate master cylinder from vacuum cylinder, then remove the rubber seal from the outer groove at end of master cylinder.
3. Remove the push rod from the power section. (Do not disturb adjusting screw.)
4. Remove push rod boot and valve operating rod.
5. Scribe alignment marks across the rear shell and vacuum cylinder. Remove all but two of the end plate attaching screws (opposite each other). Hold down on the rear shell while removing the two remaining screws to prevent the piston return spring from expanding.
6. Scribe a mark across the face of the piston, to index the mark on the rear shell, and remove rear shell with vacuum piston and piston return spring.
7. Remove vacuum hose from vacuum piston and from vacuum tube on inside of rear shell. Separate rear shell from vacuum piston.
8. Remove air cleaner and vacuum tube assembly, and air filter from the rear shell.
9. Spring the felt retaining ring enough to disengage ring from grooves in bosses on rear piston plate.
10. Remove piston felt and expander ring from piston assembly.
11. Remove six piston plate attaching screws and separate front piston plate and piston packing from piston plate.
12. Remove valve return spring, floating control valve and diaphragm assembly, valve spring and diaphragm plate. Separate floating control valve spring-retainer and control valve diaphragm from control valve.
13. Remove rubber reaction disc and shim (if present) from front piston plate.

NOTE: Do not remove the valve operating rod and valve plunger from the rear piston plate unless it is necessary to replace defective parts. Normally, the next two Steps can be omitted.

14. When it is necessary to replace the valve operating rod or valve plunger, remove valve rod seal from groove in piston plate and pull seal over end of rod.
15. Hold piston with valve plunger side down and inject alcohol into valve plunger through opening around valve rod. This will wet the rubber lock in the plunger. Then drive or pry valve plunger off the valve rod.

NOTE: If master cylinder is not to be rebuilt, omit Steps 16–19.

16. Remove snap-ring from groove in base at end of master cylinder.
17. Remove piston assembly, primary cup, retainer spring, and check-valve from master cylinder.
18. Remove filler cap and gasket from master cylinder body.
19. Remove secondary cup from master cylinder piston.

Cleaning Note

After disassembly, cleaning of all metal parts in satisfactory commercial cleaner solvent is recommended. Use only alcohol or Declene on rubber parts or parts containing rubber. After cleaning and drying, metal parts should be rewashed in clean alcohol or Declene before assembly.

Assembly

Steps 1–5 apply to a completely disassembled master cylinder. Otherwise, omit Steps 1–5.

1. Coat bore of master cylinder with brake fluid.
2. Dip secondary cup in brake fluid and install on master cylinder piston.
3. Dip other piston parts in brake fluid and assemble the piston. Install piston.
4. Install snap-ring into groove of cylinder.
5. Use new gasket and install filler cap.
6. Assemble valve rod seal on rod and insert valve rod through the piston. Dip valve plunger in alcohol and assemble to

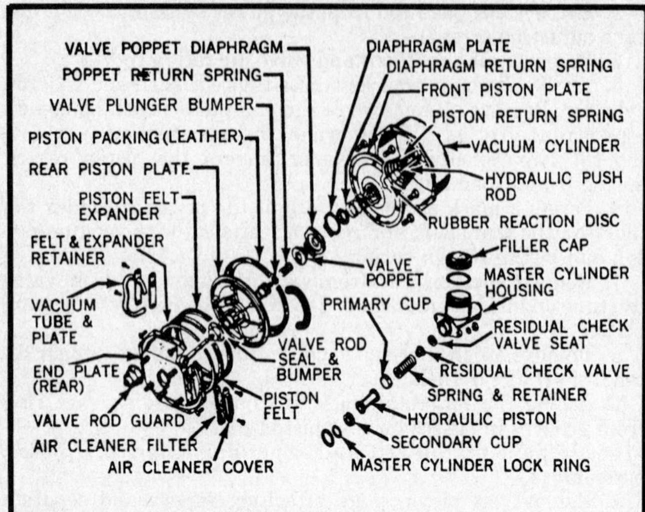

bendix master vac unit

ball end of valve rod. Be sure ball end of rod is locked in place in plunger.

7. Assemble floating control valve diaphragm over end of floating control valve. Be sure disphragm is in recess of floating control valve. Press control valve spring retainer over end of control valve and diaphragm.

8. Clamp valve operating rod in a vise with rear piston plate up. Lay leather piston packing on rear piston plate with lip of leather over edge of piston plate.

9. Install floating control valve return spring over end of valve plunger.

10. Assemble diaphragm plate to diaphragm and assemble floating control valve with diaphragm in recess of rear piston plate.

11. Install floating control valve spring over retainer. Align and assemble front piston plate with rear piston plate. Center the floating control valve spring on front piston plate and center valve plunger stem in hole of piston.

12. Holding front and rear piston plates together, loosely install six piston plate cap screws.

13. Install shim and rubber reaction disc in recess at center of front piston plate.

NOTE: A piston assembling ring is handy in assembling the piston.

14. Place the assembling tool over piston packing, turn piston assembly upside down and assemble the expander ring against inside lip of leather packing. Saturate felt with vacuum cylinder oil or shock absorber fluid, type A. Then assemble in expander ring. Assemble retainer ring over bosses on rear piston plate. Be sure retainer is anchored in grooves of piston plate.

15. Assemble air cleaner filter over vacuum tube of air cleaner and attach air cleaner shell in position with screws.

16. Slide vacuum hose onto vacuum inlet tube of piston and align hose to lay flat against piston.

17. Wipe a coat of vacuum cylinder oil on bore of cylinder. Remove assembling ring from vacuum piston and coat leather piston packing with vacuum cylinder oil.

18. Install rear shell over end of valve operating rod and attach vacuum hose to tube end on each side of end plate.

19. Center small diameter end of piston return spring in vacuum cylinder. Center large diameter of spring on piston. Check alignment mark on piston with marks on vacuum cylinder and rear shell, compress spring and install two attaching screws at opposite sides to hold rear shell and cylinder together. Now, install balance of screws and tighten evenly.

20. Dip small end of pushrod boot in alcohol and assemble guard over end of valve operating rod and over flange of shell.

21. Insert large end of pushrod through hole in end of vacuum cylinder and guide into hole of front piston plate.

NOTE: Before going on with assembly, check the distance from the outer end of the pushrod to the master cylinder mounting surface on the vacuum cylinder. This measurement should be 1.195–1.200 in.

22. After pushrod adjustment is correct, replace rubber seal in groove on master cylinder body.

23. Assemble master cylinder to the vacuum cylinder at four studs. Replace lock washers and nut and securely tighten.

Bendix Single Diaphragm Type Frame Mounted

Disassembly

1. Remove the booster unit and hydraulic cylinder from frame mounting bracket.

2. Scribe marks across front and rear shells and across flange of hydraulic cylinder. Disconnect the control tube nut from the control valve seat and remove the seal from the tube.

3. Remove the clamp band from the booster unit and disassemble the rear shell.

NOTE: The plug in the rear shell should be removed only if it is damaged.

4. Roll the bead of the diaphragm back from the front shell flange and compress the return spring for the diaphragm slightly. Remove the snap-ring from groove near the end of the hydraulic cylinder. Remove the hydraulic parts, push rod and diaphragm as an assembly.

5. Remove diaphragm return spring from piston end of push rod. Remove bolts securing hydraulic cylinder to front shell and remove the cylinder gasket from the shell.

NOTE: The diaphragm assembly should be removed from the push rod only if necessary to remove damaged parts.

6. Remove the retaining ring from groove in hydraulic piston and press the retaining pin from hole in push rod and piston. Remove the cup from the piston and if a new seal is to be installed in end of push rod, remove old push rod seal.

NOTE: Be careful to avoid damaging push rod. Carefully slide the seal retainer, seal, O-ring, guide bearing, retainer washer and snap-ring from push rod.

7. Scribe marks across the flanges of valve body and housing and remove the four attaching bolts. Remove the valve body and remove cups from the control valve piston.

Assembly

1. Install check valve, spring, washer and snap-ring in hydraulic cylinder end fitting. Next assemble O-ring seal and end fitting on the hydraulic cylinder.

2. Install cups, back to back, on control valve piston. Then assemble piston, diaphragm retainer and valve diaphragm.

NOTE: Make sure inner bead of diaphragm is seated in the piston groove.

3. Install the spring retainer, with the flange down, on the spring in the valve body. Install the piston and diaphragm assembly on the retainer and press the outer bead of the diaphragm into the groove in the valve body.

4. Coat the valve piston with clean brake fluid and assemble the piston in the control valve cylinder bore. Align the scribe

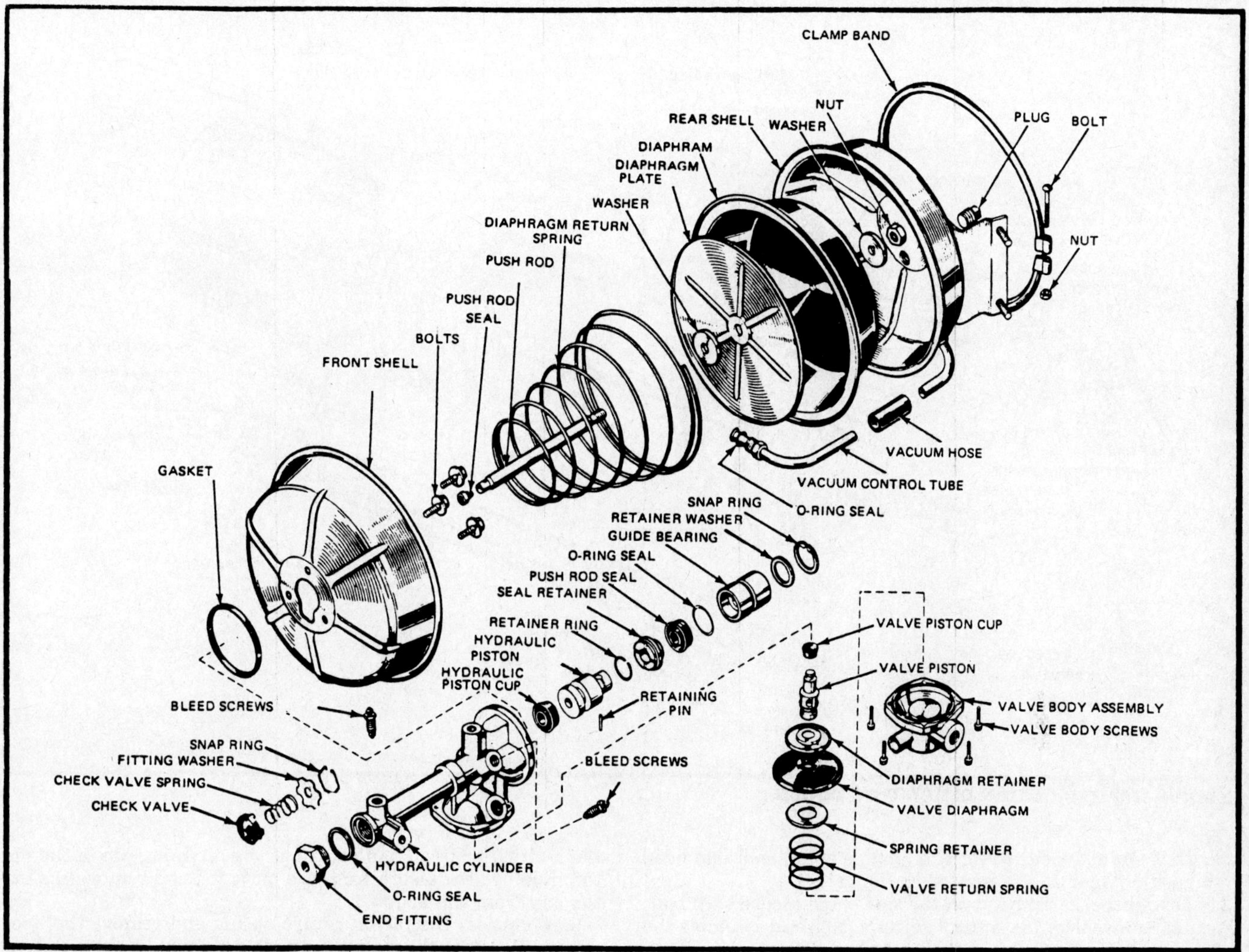

CLAMP BAND
NUT
REAR SHELL
WASHER
PLUG
BOLT
DIAPHRAGM
DIAPHRAGM PLATE
WASHER
NUT
DIAPHRAGM RETURN SPRING
PUSH ROD
PUSH ROD SEAL
BOLTS
FRONT SHELL
VACUUM HOSE
GASKET
VACUUM CONTROL TUBE
SNAP RING
O-RING SEAL
RETAINER WASHER
GUIDE BEARING
O-RING SEAL
PUSH ROD SEAL
SEAL RETAINER
VALVE PISTON CUP
RETAINER RING
HYDRAULIC PISTON
VALVE PISTON
HYDRAULIC PISTON CUP
VALVE BODY ASSEMBLY
RETAINING PIN
VALVE BODY SCREWS
BLEED SCREWS
SNAP RING
FITTING WASHER
BLEED SCREWS
CHECK VALVE SPRING
DIAPHRAGM RETAINER
CHECK VALVE
VALVE DIAPHRAGM
SPRING RETAINER
HYDRAULIC CYLINDER
VALVE RETURN SPRING
O-RING SEAL
END FITTING

Bendix single diaphragm frame mounted booster

marks on the valve cylinder body and housing and attach with bolts. Torque bolts to 40–60 inch lbs.

5. If installing new seal on push rod, place new seal on clean block of wood, with the rubber side down. Place the push rod vertically on the seal stem and strike the threaded end with a soft mallet to seat the seal stem in the push rod.

NOTE: Make sure the shoulders of the push rod and seal are in contact.

6. Slide snap-ring, retaining washer, guide bearing with O-ring seal in outer groove of guide, seal cup and seal retainer on push rod.

7. Attach the piston to the push rod with retaining ring and pin. Dip the piston cup in the clean brake fluid and install on piston.

8. Install new gasket in groove at flange end of hydraulic cylinder and install cylinder on front shell with the hold down bolts.

9. Install the diaphragm return spring, with the large coil first, against the diaphragm plate. Lubricate the cylinder bore with clean brake fluid and carefully insert the piston, cups and seals into cylinder bore. Roll back the edge of the diaphragm and press against the diaphragm to compress the return slightly. When push rod and parts are installed all the way into the cylinder bore, install the retaining snap-ring.

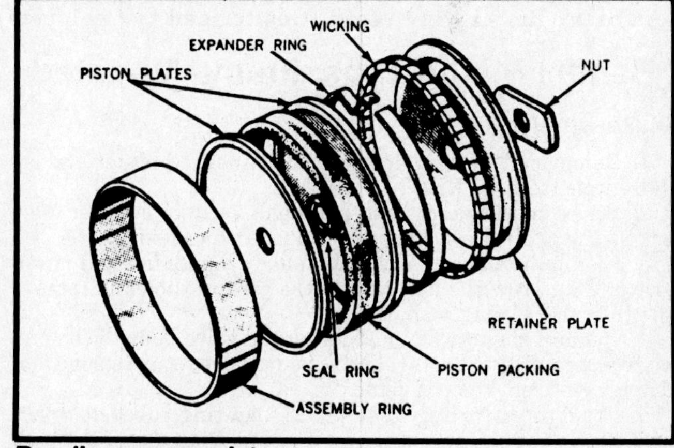

Bendix vacuum piston

NOTE: Be sure the snap-ring is seated properly before releasing pressure on the spring.

10. Coat both sides of the diaphragm lightly with talcum powder or silicone lubricant. Align scribe marks made on front and

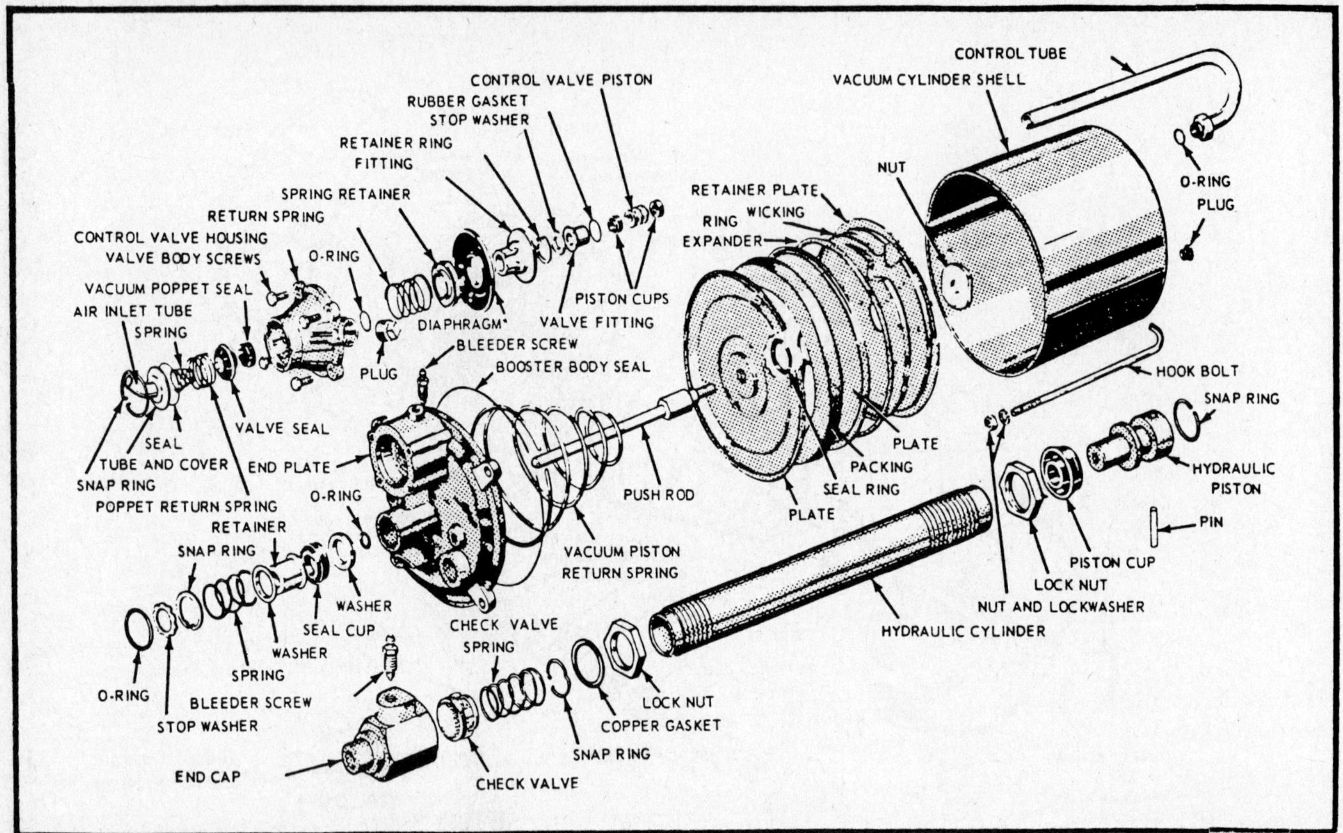

Bendix frame mounted piston type booster

rear shells and press the rear shell flange and diaphragm bead into position against the front shell flange.

11. Install the clamp band on the shells and secure with bolt. Install a new seal on the control vacuum tube and assemble the tube and hose onto the rear shell tube and tighten nut.

12. Reinstall on vehicle and check for vacuum leaks and road test to check for proper operation.

NOTE: Be sure to bleed all air from hydraulic cylinder and brake lines before attempting to road test vehicle.

Bendix Piston Type, Frame Mounted

Disassembly

1. Remove all vacuum and hydraulic lines to booster and remove unit from vehicle.
2. Scribe marks across end plate and vacuum cylinder, also across the control valve body and flange on the end plate.
3. Clamp the end nut of the hydraulic cylinder in a soft jawed vise and unscrew the lock nut on the control tube and remove the tube and O-ring seal.
4. Remove the four bolts securing the valve body to the end plate and remove the control valve body, valve return spring and diaphragm from the end plate.
5. From the valve body remove the snap-ring, tube and cover, gasket, the two poppet return springs and the valve seal. From the valve housing remove the valve poppet seal.
6. Remove the four hook bolts that hold the shell to the end plate and separate the shell from the end plate.
7. Compress the return spring and hold in place with two hook type clamps.
8. Loosen the lock nut on the hydraulic cylinder and separate the cylinder from the end plate. Remove the retaining ring from the hydraulic piston and press out the retaining pin in the piston. Remove the piston from the push rod and remove the piston cup from the piston.
9. Compress the piston return spring and remove the hook clamps. Separate the piston and push rod assembly from the end plate, and remove the return spring from the push rod.
10. From the end plate remove the seal O-ring, stop washer, snap-ring, spring, sleeve, retainer, seal cup, push rod washer and small seal O-ring. On the opposite of the end plate remove the large seal O-ring.
11. From the control valve opening in the end plate, remove the retaining snap-ring, piston stop washer and valve fitting. Remove the O-ring seal from the valve fitting.
12. Remove the hydraulic piston from the valve fitting and remove the piston cups from the piston.
13. To prevent damaging the push rod when disassembling the vacuum power piston, clamp the push rod in a soft jawed vise. Next remove the nut, piston felt retainer, packing ring, packing wick, rear plate, packing, front plate and washer from the push rod.
14. To remove the end cap on hydraulic cylinder, loosen the lock nut on the cylinder and remove the cap. Remove the seal O-ring, snap-ring, check valve spring and residual pressure check valve from the end cap.

Assembly

1. Assemble the residual pressure check valve, check valve spring, snap-ring and seal O-ring in the end cap. Screw the end cap on the cylinder tube until the tube bottoms in the cap and lock in place with the lock nut.
2. Make a vacuum piston assembly ring by cutting a one in. wide section from an old cylinder shell of the proper size. Install the flat washer over the threaded end of the push rod, then in-

stall the front piston plate on the rod with the chamfered side of the hole away from the washer. Guide the O-ring seal over the threads of the push rod.

3. Place the assembly ring over the piston plate and install the leather packing with the lip of the packing up. Install the rear piston plate keeping the chamfered side of the hole next to the seal.

4. Cut the packing wick to the required length and saturate with a good quality oil. Install the wick against the inner lip of the leather packing.

5. Install the packing expander ring inside the wick with the gripping point up. Put the notch, at the loop end of the ring, under the clip on the opposite end of the ring. Install the piston retainer with the cut-out portion over the loop of the expander ring.

6. Install the nut on the threaded end of the push rod and tighten securely.

NOTE: Be careful the piston retainer does not shift when tightening the nut. Also leave the assembly ring in place until ready to install the piston assembly in the cylinder.

7. Install in the center bore of the end plate the O-ring seal, push rod washer, cup retainer, sleeve, spring, snap-ring, piston stop washer and seal O-ring.

NOTE: Make sure the snap-ring is seated fully, in the groove in the bore of the end plate.

8. Install the valve piston cups, back to back, on the control valve piston. Dip the piston assembly in clean brake fluid and install in the valve fitting with the hole end of the piston first. Install a new O-ring on the valve fitting and insert the fitting into the control valve bore in the end plate. Install the piston stop washer and snap-ring in the bore.

9. Install the piston return spring over the push rod with the small end next to the piston. Slide the end plate over the end of the push rod. Compress the return spring slightly to project the push rod approximately 2 in. through the end plate, and hold in place with two hook type clamps. Install the hydraulic piston on the end of the push rod and attach with the retainer pin. Slide the snap-ring into its groove to hold the pin in place.

10. Dip the piston cup in clean brake fluid and install the cup on the piston with the lip away from the end plate. Next dip the piston assembly in clean brake fluid and coat the inside of the hydraulic cylinder with fluid. Guide the hydraulic cylinder over the piston being careful not to turn the lip of the seal cup backwards when installing.

11. Screw the hydraulic cylinder into the end plate until the cylinder bottoms. Then back off the cylinder until the bleeder screw in the end cap aligns with the bleeder screw in the end plate and tighten the lock nut. Compress the return spring and remove the hook clamps.

12. In the groove in the end plate install the large O-ring seal. Coat the inside of the vacuum cylinder with a good quality oil. Remove the assembly ring from the piston and insert the piston into the cylinder.

NOTE: Tip the piston 45 degrees or more when sliding it into the cylinder. This will make it easier to install the piston. Align the scribe marks on the end plate and cylinder shell and install the hook bolts, lock washers and nuts. Tighten the nuts a little at a time to avoid warping the end plate or the cylinder shell.

13. Install the valve diaphragm and spring retainer on the diaphragm plate. Install the valve poppet seal over the end of the valve seal and place the assembly in the valve body.

14. Install the poppet return springs with the small end of the small spring over the button on the valve seal. In the recess in the valve body, install the O-ring seal and attach the tube and cover with the snap-ring.

15. In the groove in the control vacuum port of the valve body install the small O-ring seal.

16. Install the valve diaphragm and spring retainer assembly on the end plate flange and position the control valve return spring on the retainer. Position the control valve housing on the spring and secure with the four hold down bolts.

NOTE: Be sure to align the scribe marks made on the housing and end plate before assembling the housing to the end plate.

17. Install the O-ring seal on the end of the vacuum tube and install the tube with one end in the control valve body and the other end secured to the rear of the shell with the tube nut.

18. Install the unit on the vehicle and check for vacuum leaks and road test for proper operation of unit.

NOTE: Be sure to bleed all air from the hydraulic cylinder and brake lines before road testing the vehicle.

Bendix Dual Diaphragm Type

This unit features a direct pedal connection to a vacuum unit mounted on the firewall, with the master cylinder directly mounted to booster.

The booster chamber contains two diaphragms and is under constant engine vacuum. When brakes are applied, the control valve is opened to allow atmospheric pressure behind both diaphragms. This provides the power boost to the master cylinder.

This vacuum-suspended system provides reserve against fade. Pedal linkages are eliminated, no additional vacuum storage tanks are needed.

NOTE: Do not attempt to diasassemble the booster. It is serviced only by the dealer.

Bendix Tandem Diaphragm Type Frame Mounted

Disassembly

1. Remove all hydraulic and vacuum lines attached to booster and hydraulic cylinder. Then remove the unit from frame brackets and remove from vehicle.

2. Scribe marks across both clamp rings onto the shell surfaces, also across top of hydraulic cylinder flange onto the front shell. Scribe marks across control valve body and housing below hydraulic cylinder.

3. Disconnect the control tube and nut from control valve port and remove the three hose clamps and tee. Remove the seal ring from the control tube.

4. Remove the rear clamping ring and remove the rear shell.

5. Remove the front clamping ring and separate the front, center and rear shells and remove the diaphragm assemblies.

6. Clamp the hydraulic cylinder in a soft jawed vice being careful to avoid damaging cylinder.

7. Press on the spring retainer to compress the diaphragm return spring and remove the three bolts that hold the hydraulic cylinder to the front shell and support plate. Then carefully release the pressure on the return spring and pull the push rod and hydraulic piston from the cylinder.

8. Remove the return spring from the piston end of the push rod.

NOTE: Do not remove the spring retainer except to replace damaged parts.

9. Remove the snap-ring from the groove in the piston and press plunger pin from the hole in the piston and push rod.

10. Remove the piston, snap-ring, seal retainer, push rod cup, push rod bearing and support plate and piston stop from the push rod.

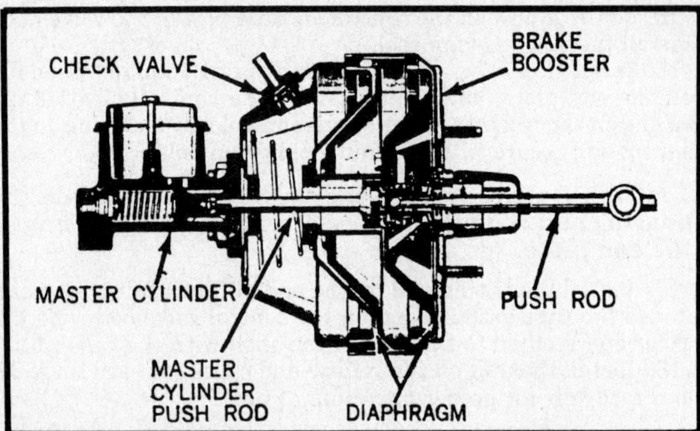

Cutaway view of brake booster and master cylinder

11. Remove the cup from the piston and the O-ring from the groove in the push rod bearing.
12. Remove the end fitting from the hydraulic cylinder and remove the snap-ring from the end cap. Disassemble the residual pressure check valve.
13. Remove the end fitting seal from the push rod being careful not to damage the push rod.
14. Clamp the nut, on the push rod seat end of the rear shaft, in a vise and remove by unscrewing the shaft. Remove the assembly from the vise and remove the front diaphragm and diaphragm plate from the shaft.
15. Slide center shells off the shaft and remove the O-ring seal from its groove in the hub of the center shells.
16. Clamp the nut on the rear shaft and remove by unscrewing the shaft. Remove the nut, washer, rear diaphragm, diaphragm plate and washer from the shaft.
17. Remove the valve body and control valve from the valve housing.
18. Remove the cups from the control valve piston and slide the control valve diaphragm and retainer off the opposite end of the piston.

Cleaning and Inspection

Clean all metal parts in clean metal parts cleaner. Discard any old parts that are to be replaced with new ones. Clean all hydraulic parts in clean brake fluid. Check the diaphragms for cracks, tears and kinks and replace any diaphragms that are questionable. Inspect all metal and plastic parts for nicks, cracks, scores or burrs and replace any damaged parts. Check the shells for cracked or broken welds, dents or cracks. DO NOT attempt to disassemble the center shell assembly. Inspect the hydraulic cylinder bore and valve body bore for any surface damage. Remove deposits, pitted areas or light scores with crocus cloth. Replace the part if it can not be cleaned up with crocus cloth.

Assembly

1. Install the valve piston cups back to back in the grooves on the control valve piston.
2. Slide the valve diaphragm retainer, with the flange side first, onto the other end of the piston. Wet the inside of the valve diaphragm with alcohol and slide it over the end of the piston and seat it against the retainer. Install the spring retainer on the hub of the valve diaphragm with the flange side away from the diaphragm.
3. Install the control valve piston and diaphragm assembly on the return spring. Position the spring around the vacuum poppet guides in the valve body and press the bead of the diaphragm firmly into the groove on the flange of the valve body.
4. Dip the control valve piston and cups into clean brake fluid and install them into the control valve bore in the hydraulic cylinder. Align the scribe marks on the valve body and housing and attach with four bolts. Tighten the bolts to 40–60 inch lbs.
5. Assemble the washer, rear diaphragm plate, diaphragm and washer onto the rear shaft with the holes in the shaft towards the diaphragm.
6. Install the nut on the end of the shaft and tighten to 10–15 ft. lbs. Stake the nut in two places to prevent any movement.
7. Install the O-ring seal in its groove inside the hub of the center shells. With a silicone lubricant, coat the seal and bearing and the outer surface of the rear shaft.
8. Insert the front end of the rear shaft through the middle of the center shells.
9. Install the washer, front diaphragm and diaphragm plate on the end of the shaft. Screw on retaining nut and tighten to 10–15 ft. lbs. Stake the nut in two places to prevent any movement.
10. To install a new push rod seal, in end of push rod, place new seal face down on a clean block of wood. Place the push rod uptight on the seal stem and strike end of rod with a soft mallet to seat the seal.

NOTE: Be sure that the shoulders of the seal and push rod are in contact.

11. Dip all hydraulic parts, push rod and push rod bearing in clean brake fluid. Install the support plate and piston stop assembly, push rod bearing, with O-ring in its groove, push rod cup and seal retainer on the push rod.
12. Install the snap-ring on the piston but not in its groove. Attach the piston to the push rod with the plunger pin and then slide the snap-ring into its groove in the piston.
13. Dip the piston cup in brake fluid and install on the piston with the open flared end away from the piston.
14. Install the residual pressure check valve in the end fitting, then install the check valve spring and washer in the end fitting and secure with the snap-ring.
15. Install the gasket onto the end fitting and screw into the hydraulic cylinder and tighten to 50–85 ft. lbs.
16. Install the O-ring seal in groove around the hydraulic cylinder flange.
17. Slide the small end of the diaphragm return spring over the piston end of the push rod. Lubricate the piston and cylinder bore with clean brake fluid.
18. Bottom the small end of the return spring against the spring retainer on the push rod and place the large coil of the spring in the front shell with the piston through the hole in the shell.
19. With the return slightly compressed, guide the piston, seal retainer, push rod cup, and push rod bearing into the cylinder bore. Seat the cylinder flange against the front shell, make sure the O-ring is in place. Place the support plate and stop plate on the opposite side of the shell and secure the stop assembly and front shell to the cylinder with the three securing bolts. Release the pressure on the spring.
20. On the front and rear diaphragm beads put a light coat of talcum powder or silicone lubricant.
21. Guide the rear shaft onto the push rod and align the scribe marks made on the front shell flanges. Press the shells together and seat the bead of the diaphragm all the way around in the shell flanges.
22. Install the clamp ring on the shell falnges and align the scribe marks. Tighten the clamp screw to 30–40 inch lbs.
23. Align the scribe marks on the rear shells and press them together making sure the diaphragm bead is in the shell flange all the way around. Install the clamp ring, aligning the marks, and tighten the clamp bolt to 30–40 inch lbs.
24. Install the hose tee to the control tube on the rear shell and to hose nipple on the center shell.
25. Install the seal ring on the end of the control tube and nut assembly and attach the tube to the hose tee with a hose clamp. Screw the nut onto the control valve port and tighten to 80–120 inch lbs.

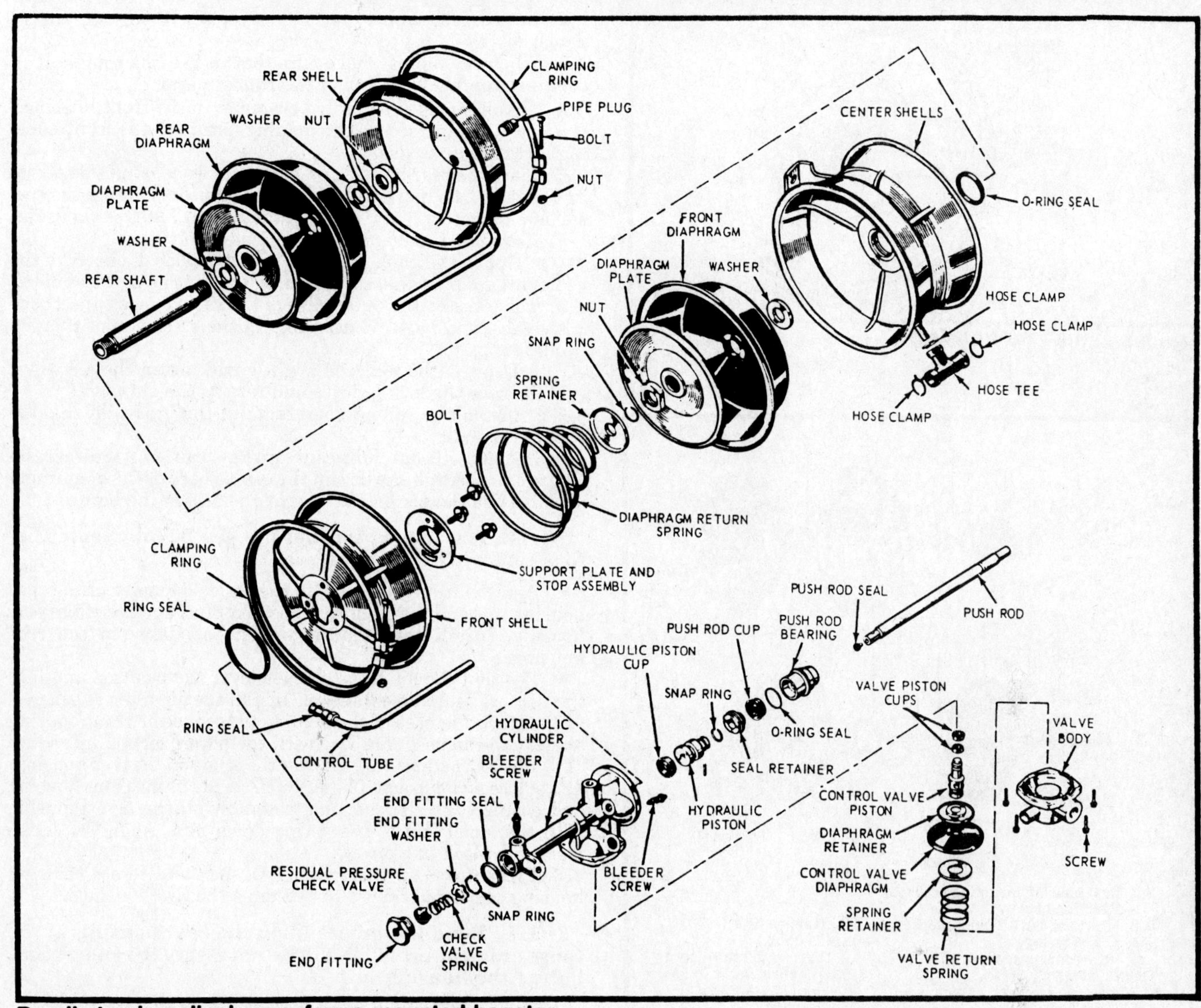

Bendix tandem diaphragm frame mounted booster

26. Install unit on vehicle and test for vacuum leaks and road test for proper operation.

NOTE: Be sure to bleed hydraulic cylinder of all air before attempting to road test vehicle.

Bendix Single Diaphragm Booster

Disassembly

1. Scribe a line across the front and rear housings for reassembly.
2. Pull the piston rod from the front housing and remove the seal.
3. Attach a holding fixture to the front housing and clamp the base in a vise with the power section up.
4. Loosen the locknut and remove the pushrod device and locknut.
5. Remove the mounting bracket from the rear housing.
6. Remove the dust boot retainer, dust boot and silencer from the diaphragm plate extension.
7. The edge of the rear housing contains twelve lances. Four of these lances (one in each quadrant) are deeper than the other lances. The metal that forms the four deep lances must be partially straightened so that the lances will clear the cutouts in the front housing.

NOTE: If the metal tabs that form the deep lances crack or break during straightening, the housing must be replaced.

8. Place a spanner wrench over the studs on the rear housing and attach with nuts and washers.
9. Press down on the spanner wrench and rotate the rear housing clockwise to separate the two housings.

NOTE: It may be necessary to tap the rear housing lightly with a plastic hammer to loosen.

10. Lift the rear housing assembly from the unit.
11. Use a small screwdriver and carefully remove the air filter element from the diaphragm plate extension.
12. Separate the diaphragm plate assembly from the rear housing and disassemble the plate assembly.

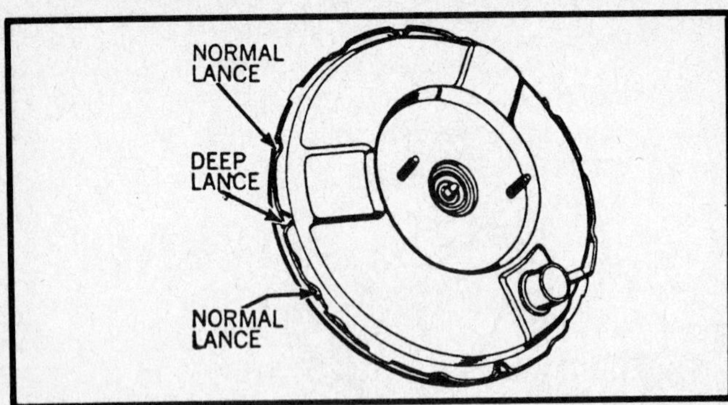

Lances in the rear housing

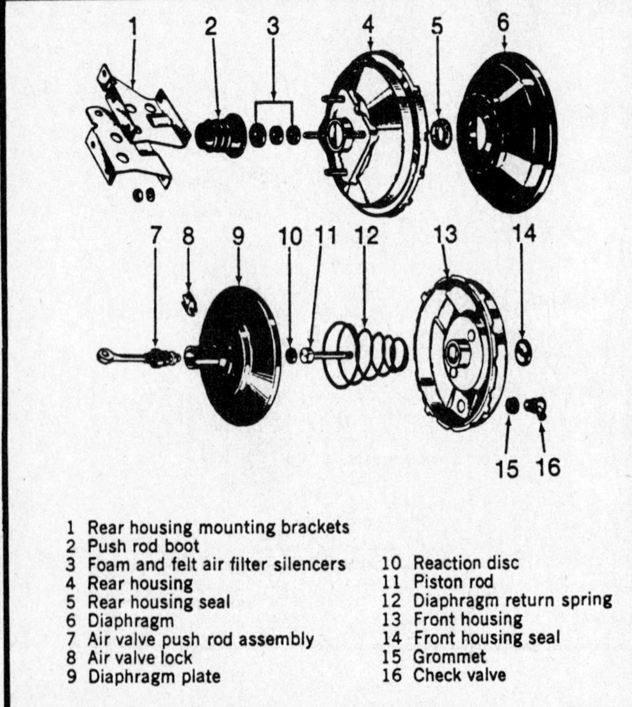

Bendix single diaphragm booster

13. Remove the rolling diaphragm from the groove in the diaphragm plate hub.

NOTE: Protect the diaphragm from oil, and nicks.

14. Hold the diaphragm plate in a horizontal position and depress the push rod approximately $^1/_{16}$ in. and rotate the piston so the air valve lock will fall from its location. Remove the air valve pushrod assembly and the reaction disc.
15. If a new seal is needed, support the outer surface of the rear housing and drive out the seal with a suitable tool.

NOTE: Do not reuse old seal once it has been removed.

16. Remove the check valve and grommet from the front housing and discard.
18. Remove the front housing from the holding fixture.

Assembly

1. Use clean brake fluid and thoroughly clean all reusable brake parts.
2. Inspect all rubber parts and replace if nicked, cut or damaged.
3. When rebuilding, make sure that no grease or mineral oil comes in contact with any of the rubber parts.
4. Install a new check valve grommet in the front housing.
5. Position and secure the holding fixture to the front housing and place in a vise.
6. Place the rear housing on a block of wood, stud side down, and position the housing seal in the center hole. Using the special installing tool seat the seal in the recess of the rear housing.
7. Assemble the diaphragm plate assembly:
   a. Apply a silicone lubricant to the outside diameter of the diaphragm plate and extension, to the bearing surfaces of the air valve and to the outer edge of the valve poppet. Insert the air valve and pushrod assembly in the extension of the diaphragm plate.
   b. Depress the pushrod slightly and install the air valve. Make sure the lock indexes and retains the air valve.
   c. Install the rolling diaphragm in the groove of the diaphragm plate.
   d. Apply silicone lubricant to the surface of the reaction disc and position the disc in the center bore of the diaphragm plate. Use the piston rod to seat the disc in the bore.

NOTE: It is important that the disc be fully seated before removing the piston rod.

8. Apply silicone lubricant to the inside diameter of the rear housing seal and the diaphragm bead contact surface of the rear housing. Install the diaphragm plate assembly in the rear housing.
9. Position the air filter element over the pushrod and into the diaphragm plate extension. Install the air filter retainer.
10. Attach the base of the holding fixture to the front housing and clamp the base in a vise with the power section up.
11. Place a spanner wrench over the studs on the rear housing.
12. Place a diaphragm plate return spring in the front housing and position the rear housing assembly on the front housing with the small end of the spring downward. Align the scribe marks and lock in place.
13. Press down on the spanner wrench and rotate the rear housing counterclockwise to assemble the two housings.

NOTE: Bend the lances in on the rear housing. If the tangs crack or break, it will be necessary to replace that half of the housing.

14. Remove the spanner wrench from the rear shell.
15. Install the air silencer over the push rod end, then the boot retainer.
16. On vehicles with a clevis type push rod, install the locknut and clevis.
17. Install the mounting bracket to the rear shell, if so equipped.
18. Remove the cylinder from the vise and remove the holding fixture.
19. Apply silicone lubricant to the piston rod and guide the rod into the center bore of the diaphragm plate until it is fully seated.

NOTE: Keep the lubricant away from the rounded end of the rod.

20. Press the seal into the front housing until it is bottomed in the recess of the housing.

Midland Ross Diaphragm Type

The self-contained booster assembly is mounted on the engine side of the firewall. It is connected directly to the brake pedal. This booster is not equipped with a separate vacuum tank.

The master cylinder is attached to the forward side of the

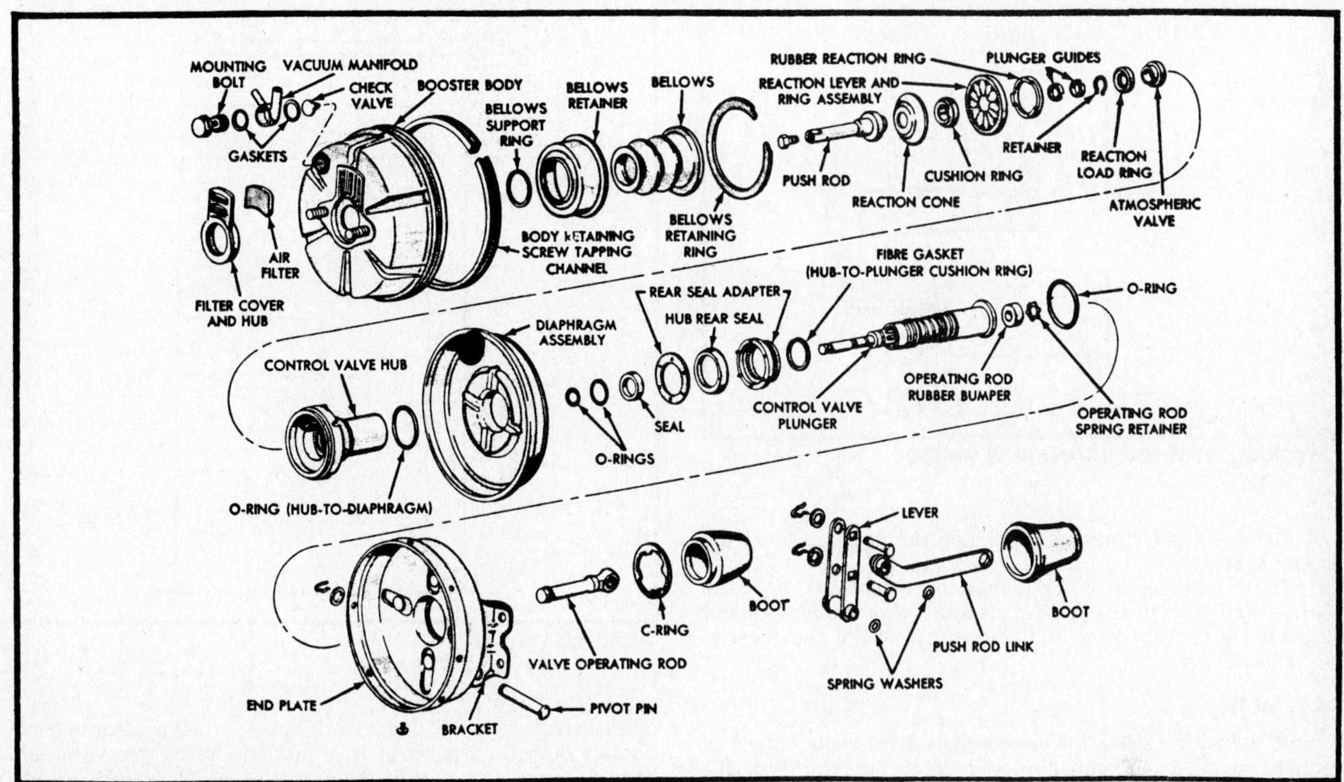

Disassembled view of booster

booster. The balance of the hydraulic brake system is identical to other standard service brakes.

Booster Repairs

1. Separate master cylinder from booster body.
2. Remove air filter cover and hub and the filter from the booster body.
3. Remove the vacuum manifold mounting bolt, manifold, gaskets and vacuum check valve from the booster body.
4. Disconnect the valve operating rod from the lever by removing its retaining clip, washers, and pivot pin.
5. Disconnect the lever from the booster end plate brackets by removing its retaining clip, washers, and pivot pin.
6. Remove two brackets from the end plate.
7. Remove the rubber boot from the valve operating rod.
8. To remove the bellows, control valve, and diaphragm assemblies, remove large C-ring that holds the rear seal adapter assembly to the booster end plate.
9. Scribe matching lines on the booster body and the end plate. Then remove the ten retaining screws. Tap the outside of the plate with a soft hammer and separate the plate from the booster body.
10. Push the bellows assembly into the vacuum chamber and remove the bellows, control valve, and diaphragm as an assembly from the booster body.
11. Remove the outer O-ring from the control valve hub.
12. To disassemble the bellows, pushrod, and control valve assemblies, remove the large bellows retaining ring, bellows, bellows retainer, and support ring from the diaphragm and valve assembly.
13. Remove the retainer and support ring from the bellows.
14. Remove pushrod assembly, the reaction lever and ring assembly, and the rubber reaction ring from the control valve hub.
15. Remove the reaction cone and cushion ring from the pushrod assembly. Then disassemble the reaction levers from the ring.

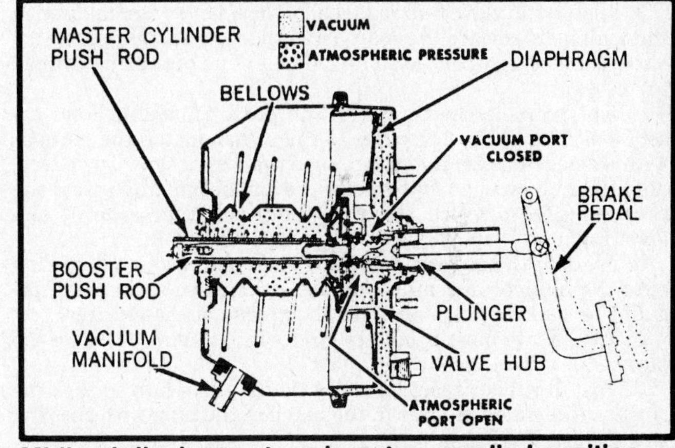

Midland diaphragm type booster—applied position

16. Remove the two plastic plunger guides from the control valve plunger. Then remove the retainer that holds the reaction load ring and atmospheric valve on the control valve hub.
17. Slide the reaction load ring and atmospheric valve from the control valve hub.
18. Separate the control valve hub and the plunger assembly from the diaphragm by sliding the plunger and rear seal adapter from the rear of the hub. Then remove the hub outer O-ring from the front side of the diaphragm.
19. To disassemble the control valve plunger, remove the hub rear seal adapter from the valve plunger assembly, and remove the seal from the adapter.

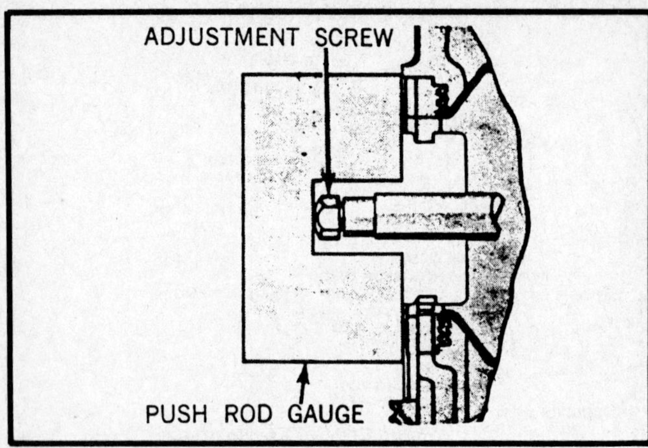

Checking pushrod screw with gauge

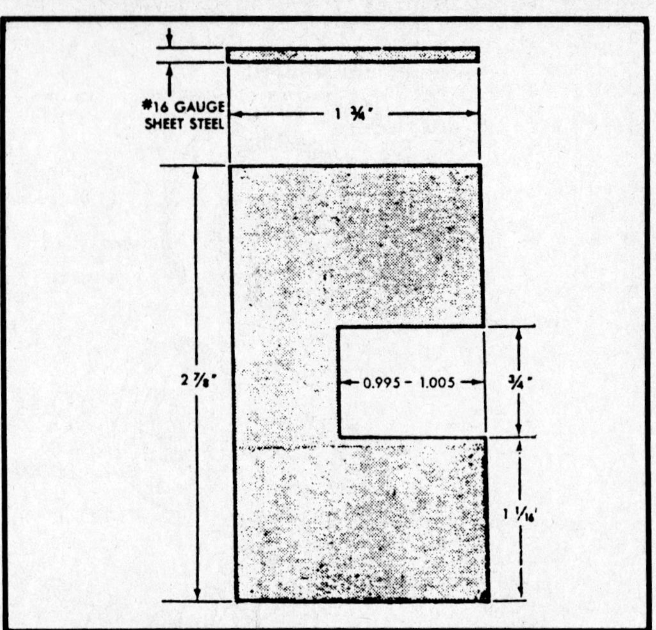

Pushrod gauge

20. Remove the O-rings, the seal, and the fiber gaskets from the plunger.
21. If the plunger assembly needs to be replaced, hold the plunger and pull out the valve operating rod with pliers. Do not separate the operating rod and plunger unless the plunger is to be replaced.

Assembly

1. If valve operating rod was removed for replacement of plunger, install a new rubber bumper and spring retainer on the rod before installing it on the replacement plunger. Then push the rod firmly until it bottoms in the plunger.
2. Install fiber gaskets, plunger seal, and the two O-rings on the plunger assembly.
3. Install the valve hub rear seal in the adapter assembly with the sealing lip toward the rear. Then slide the adapter assembly onto the plunger with the small diameter end of the hub toward the rear.
4. To assemble the control valve, pushrod, and bellows assemblies, install the hub outer O-ring. Then install the plunger with the seal adapter and the hub on the diaphragm. To do this, hold the hub on the front side of the diaphragm and insert the plunger assembly in the hub from the rear side of the diaphragm.
5. Install atmospheric valve and then the reaction load ring onto the plunger and hub. Compress the valve spring, and install the load ring retainer into the groove of the plunger.
6. Install two plastic plunger guides into their grooves on the plunger.
7. Install rubber reaction ring into the valve hub so that the ring locating knob indexes in the notch in the hub, with the ring tips toward the front.
8. Assemble the reaction lever and ring assembly, and install the assembly into the valve hub.
9. Install the reaction cone and cushion ring on the pushrod. Then install the pushrod assembly on the valve hub so that the plunger indexes in the rod.
10. Assemble the bellows, retainer, and support ring. The ring should be positioned on the middle fold of the bellows.
11. Position the bellows assembly on the diaphragm, and secure it with the retaining ring. Make sure the retaining ring is fully seated.
12. Install the bellows, control valve, and diaphragm assemblies with a screwdriver, moving the booster body retaining screw tapping channel just enough to provide a new surface for the self-tapping attaching screws.
13. Install the diaphragm, the control valve components, and the bellows as an assembly into the booster body. (Be sure the lip of the diaphragm is evenly positioned on the retaining radius of the booster body.) Pull the front lip of the bellows through the booster body, and position it around the outer groove of the body.
14. Install O-ring in the front side of the end plate, and locate the plate on the booster body. Align the scribed lines, compress the two assemblies together with a clamp. Then install all ten self-tapping attaching screws.
15. Install the large C-ring onto the rear seal adapter at the rear side of the end plate.

Pushrod Adjustment

The pushrod has an adjusting screw to maintain the correct relationship between the control valve plunger and the master cylinder piston after the booster is completely assembled. If this screw is not properly adjusted, the brakes may drag.

To check adjustment of the screw, make a gauge to the dimensions shown. Place this gauge against the master cylinder mounting surface of the booster body. The pushrod screw should be adjusted so that the end of the screw just touches the inner edge of the slot in the gauge.

Booster Installation

1. Install rubber boot on the valve operating rod.
2. Position the two mounting brackets on the end plate, and install on retaining nuts.
3. Connect the lever assembly to the lower end of the mounting brackets with its pivot pin. Then install the spring washer and retaining clip.
4. Connect the valve operating rod to the upper end of the lever with its pivot pin, washer, and retaining clip.
5. Install the vacuum check valve, the vacuum manifold, the two gaskets, and the mounting bolt. Torque the mounting bolt to 8–10 ft. lbs.

Midland Diaphragm Type Frame Mounted

The Midland frame mounted booster is a remote type, without mechanical operation, utilizing vacuum to boost the hydraulic pressure between master and wheel cylinder.

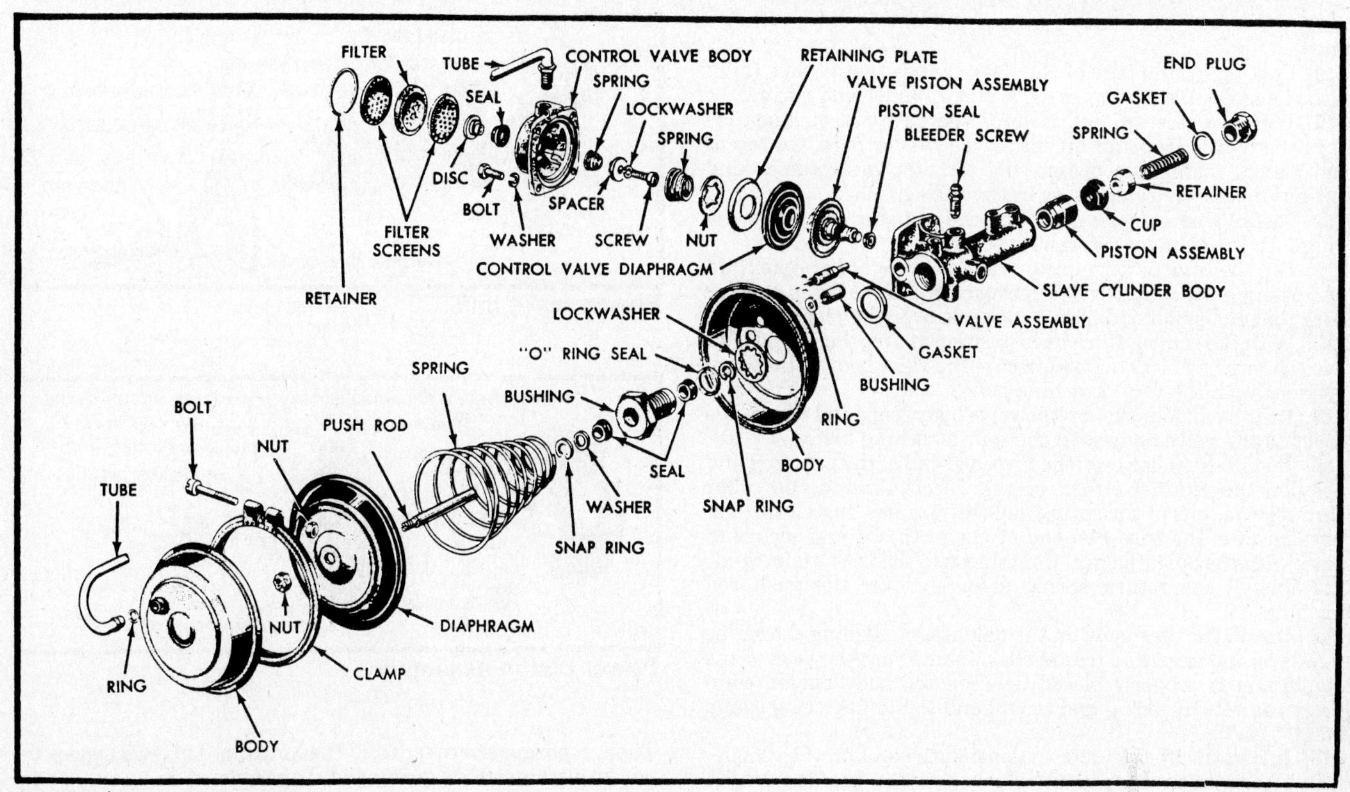

Midland vacuum booster

Removal

1. Remove all hydraulic lines from the booster unit hydraulic cylinder.
2. Remove all vacuum lines from the booster unit and remove the support bracket bolts.
3. Remove the unit from the vehicle and place on a clean work bench.

Disassembly

1. Remove the control tube from the control valve body and the rear body.
2. Scribe marks across the diaphragm body and across the flanges of the slave cylinder body and the control valve body.
3. Remove the body clamp carefully, and remove the rear body and diaphragm with the return spring.
4. Remove the push rod, spring retainer and collar from the return spring.
5. Scribe a line across the valve body cover and the valve body, and remove the valve body cover and gasket.
6. Remove the valve body, spring, and the piston and diaphragm assembly from the slave cylinder.
7. From the end of the slave cylinder remove the end plug, copper gasket, spring, spring seat and spring retainer.
8. Remove the piston cup and piston assembly from the cylinder.

NOTE: If the assembly does not fall free from the cylinder it may be pushed out by inserting the push rod through the bushing.

9. From the hydraulic piston remove the check valve, check valve retainer and the return spring.
10. Hold the cylinder in a soft jawed vise and remove the push rod bushing, lockwasher and front body.
11. Remove the gasket, rubber seal and transfer bushing from the slave cylinder body. From the bushing remove the two push rod bushing snap-rings, and remove the washer and two seals. From the outside of the push rod bushing remove the O-ring seal.
12. From the lower end of the control valve piston remove the seal, also remove the seal from the piston boss.
13. Remove the retaining nut from the piston boss and remove the diaphragm plate and control valve diaphragm.
14. Remove the screw, lockwasher, spacer, spring, disc., and the seal from the control valve body.

Assembly

1. Install new spring in the control valve body and assemble the spring and spacer in the valve body. Secure with the screw and locknut.
2. Secure the control valve diaphragm and plate in place with the attaching nut.
3. On the control valve piston install the piston seal.
4. In the hydraulic piston install the check valve spring, check valve and retainer, making sure that the valve floats free in the bore and does not bind.
5. On the front end of the slave cylinder body, install the transfer bushing, seal and gasket.
6. In the push rod bushing install the push rod seals, washer and snap-rings.

NOTE: Install the push rod seals with the open end of the seal towards the slave cylinder body. Install the lockwasher over the end of the rod bushing and install the bushing seal.

7. With the slave cylinder mounted in a vise, position the front body over the end of the cylinder, inserting the transfer bushing in the front body.
8. Thread push rod bushing in place and tighten securely,

making sure the front body seats squarely on the slave cylinder body.

9. Coat the piston bore of the slave cylinder with brake fluid, also the hydraulic piston, seals, spring retainer and spring.

10. With the recessed end towards the push rod bushing, install the hydraulic piston in the slave cylinder bore. On top of the piston, install the piston cup, large spring retainer and spring. Install the spring seat in the spring coils.

11. Install a new copper gasket on the end plug and screw the plug into the cylinder tightening securely.

12. Dip the control valve piston and diaphragm in brake fluid and position the control valve spring on the diaphragm, making sure that the small end of the spring is over the piston boss.

13. With the control valve body positioned over the spring, and with the scribe marks aligned, secure the valve body to the slave cylinder with the four attaching bolts.

14. Install a new gasket on the valve body cover and secure the cover to the valve body with the four attaching bolts.

15. Install the collar over the threaded end of the push rod and position the retainer on the spring. Insert the rod and collar through the coils of the spring and the retainer. Install the diaphragm over the threaded end of the push rod and secure in place with the push rod nut. Coat the push rod with brake fluid.

16. Install the return spring assembly over the push rod bushing.

17. Install the rear body on the diaphragm aligning the scribe marks on the front and rear shells. Making sure the bead of the diaphragm is properly placed between the body halves, compress the return spring and install and tighten the ring clamp band.

18. Install the by-pass tube and install the unit on the vehicle.

19. Check the unit for vacuum leaks and road test the vehicle for proper operation of the unit.

NOTE: Bleed all air from the hydraulic cylinder and lines before road testing the vehicle.

Kelsey-Hayes Diaphragm Type

IDENTIFICATION

The Kelsey-Hayes power brake unit can be identified by the twistlock method of locking the housing and cover together, plus the white-colored vacuum check valve assembly.

Removal

1. With engine off, apply brakes several times to equalize internal brake pressure.
2. Disconnect hydraulic line from master cylinder.
3. Disconnect vacuum hose from power brake check valve.
4. Disconnect power brake from brake pedal (under instrument panel).
5. Disconnect power brake unit from dash panel.
6. Remove power brake and master cylinder assembly from the vehicle.

Disassembly

1. Separate master cylinder from power brake unit.
2. Remove master cylinder pushrod and air cleaner plate.
3. Mount the power unit in a vise with the master cylinder attaching studs up.
4. Scribe an index line across the housing and cover for reassembly reference.
5. Pry out the housing lock. Do not damage the lock, as it must be used at assembly.
6. Remove check valve from cover by prying out of rubber grommet.
7. Place parking brake flange holding tool over the master cylinder mounting studs.
8. Rotate the tool and cover in a counterclockwise direction.

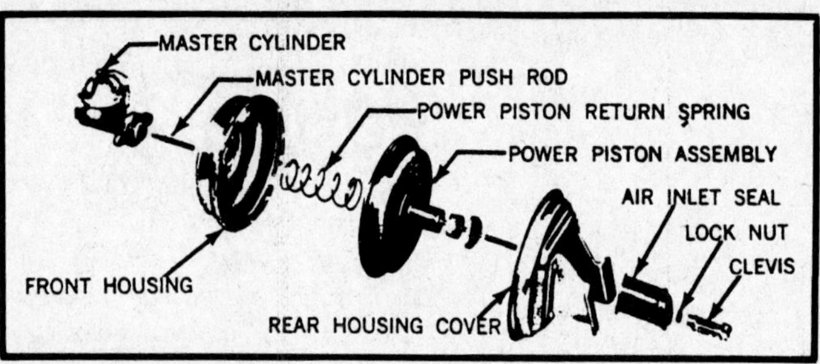

Power brake unit

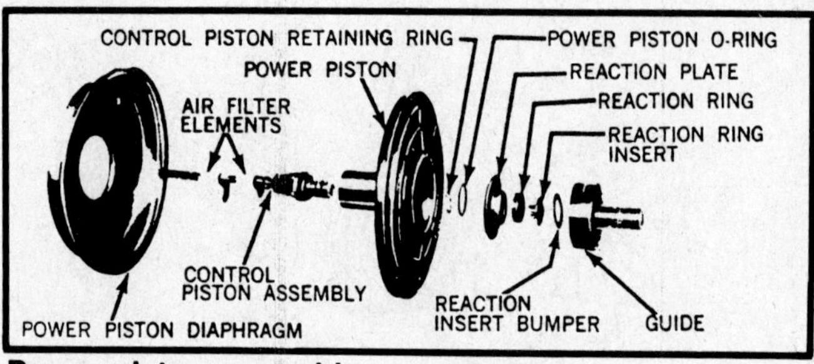

Power piston assembly

Then, separate the cover from the housing. This will expose the power piston return spring and diaphragm.

9. Lift out the power piston return spring. Remove the brake unit from the vise.
10. Remove power piston by slowly lifting the piston straight up.
11. Remove air cleaner, guide seal and seal retainer from the cover.
12. Remove the block seal from the center hole of the housing, using a blunt drift. (Don't scratch the bore of the housing, it could cause a vacuum leak.)

Power Piston Disassembly

1. Remove power piston diaphragm from the power piston. Keep it clean.
2. Remove screws that attach the plastic guide to the power piston. Remove guide and place to one side.
3. Remove the power piston square seal ring, reaction ring insert, reaction ring and reaction plate.
4. Depress operating rod slightly, then remove the Truarc snap-ring.
5. Remove control piston by pulling the operating rod.
6. Remove the O-ring seal from the end of the control piston.
7. Remove the filter elements and dust felt from the control piston rod.

Cleaning and Inspection

Thoroughly wash all metal parts in a suitable solvent and dry with compressed air. The power diaphragm, plastic power piston and guide should be washed in a mild soap and water solution. Blow dust and all cleaning material out of internal passages. All rubber parts should be replaced, regardless of condition. Install new air filters at assembly. Inspect all parts for scoring, pits, dents or nicks. Small imperfections can be smoothed out with crocus cloth. Replace all badly damaged parts.

Assembly

When assembling, be sure that all rubber parts, except the diaphragm and the reaction ring are lubricated with silicone grease.

1. Install control piston O-ring onto the piston.
2. Lubricate and install the control piston into the power piston. Install the Truarc snap-ring into its groove. Wipe all lubricant off the end of the control piston.
3. Install air filter elements and felt seal over the pushrod and down past the retaining shoulder on the rod. Install the power piston square seal ring into its groove.
4. Install the reaction plate in the power piston. Align the three holes with those in the power piston.
5. Install the rubber reaction ring in the reaction plate. Do not lubricate this ring.
6. Lubricate outer diameter of the reaction insert and install in the reaction ring.
7. Install reaction insert bumper into the guide.
8. Place guide on the power piston, align the holes with the aligning points on the power piston. Install retaining screws and torque to 80–100 inch lbs.
9. Install diaphragm on power piston; be sure that the diaphragm is correctly seated in the power piston groove.
10. With the housing blocked to prevent damage, install the block seal in the housing.
11. Install a new cover seal on the retainer and lubricate thoroughly, inside and out, with silicone grease, then install in the cover bore. Install new air filter.
12. Lubricate check valve grommet and install the vacuum check valve.
13. Mount the power unit in a vise, with master cylinder attaching studs up.
14. Apply a light coating of silicone grease to the bead, outer edge only, of the power piston diaphragm.
15. Install the power piston assembly in the housing with the operating rod down.
16. Install the power piston return spring into the flange of the guide.
17. Place the cover over the return spring and press down on the cover. At the same time, pilot the guide through the seal.
18. Rotate the cover to lock it to the housing. Be sure the scribe lines are in correct index and that the diaphragm is not pinched during assembly.
19. Install the housing lock on one of the long tangs of the housing.
20. Remove the power unit from the vise.
21. Install the master cylinder push-rod and air cleaner plate, then install the master cylinder on the studs. Install attaching nuts and washers. Torque to 200 inch lbs.

Installation

1. Install the power brake seal to the firewall.
2. Install power brake unit onto firewall and torque the attaching nuts to 200 inch lbs.
3. Install pushrod to brake pedal attaching bolt. Torque to 30 ft. lbs.
4. Install vacuum hose onto the power brake unit.
5. Attach the hydraulic tube and fill the master cylinder. Bleed hydraulic system.
6. Adjust stop light switch if necessary.

Hydro-Max Electro Hydraulic Brake Booster

OPERATION

1982-83

Beneath the booster a vane type pump is attached and is integral with a 12 volt DC electric motor. If the vehicle engine was not operating or a hose or belt was broken the pump and motor would serve as a reserve power source to provide boost pressure. The electric pump draws fluid from the low pressure side of the booster piston and delivers it to the high pressure side. The electric pump provides one-half of the primary system pressure.

ELECTRICAL CONTROL CIRCUITS

The electric pump operation is controlled by a relay which is operated by a flow switch located in the booster outlet to sense the fluid flow. A pedal switch also controls the electric pump operation whenever the brake pedal is depressed and the engine is not operating. The system is monitored by two dash mounted telltale lamps and a buzzer. The two lamps will be marked to:

1. Warn of failure of the primary system.
2. Warn of failure of the reserve system.
3. To make the driver aware that the reserve is in operation, the dash lamp will light and the buzzer will sound. The monitoring system is controlled by a solid state module, and two in line diodes. The plug in module is not repairable and must be replaced as a unit.

WARNING MODES

The function of the system warning devices, tell-tales and alarm buzzer, under different vehicle operational modes are indicated in the Electro-Hydraulic Pump Diagnosis Chart.

ELECTRO-HYDRAULIC PUMP

Diagnosis

1. The pump and tell-tale light does not come on when the brake pedal is depressed with the engine off:
   a. Check the brake pedal switch.
   b. Check for electrical continuity through the pump flow switch.
   c. Check for voltage to the ignition side of the relay coil.
   d. Check for voltage at the battery connection to the relay coil.
   d. Check for voltage at the battery connection to the relay.
   e. Check for an open at the ignition diode.
   f. Check for voltage at the pump terminal at the relay.
2. The engine is off and the pump is operating but the light is not on when the brake pedal is depressed.
   a. Check the voltage at the warning light bulb.
   b. Replace the bulb.
3. The engine and the pump are off, but when the brake pedal is depressed, the light is on.
   a. Check the voltage at the pump motor.
   b. Replace pump.
4. The accessories, radio, heater, wipers etc. operate when the brake pedal is depressed and the engine off.
   a. Check the ignition diode for a short.
5. The pump and warning light stay on after the engine is started.
   a. Check for air in the boost systems.
   b. Check to see if the flow switch is shorted or in the stuck position.
   c. Check to see if the relay is in the closed position.

Hydro-Max

1984-88

The main features of the new style Hydro-Max system are as follows;

1. All front brakes are dual piston, disc brakes of the Dayton/Walther design.
2. The parking brake is actuated by a spring/ramp assembly, located on the rear wheel backing plate and controlled by hydraulic pressure from the Hydro-Max pump, through a parking brake control in the cab of the vehicle.
3. The hydraulic brake system is a vertically split system,

Electro-Hydraulic Pump Diagnosis

Mode	Tell-Tale #1①	Tell-Tale #2②	Buzzer
Engine off—ignition off No brake apply Brake apply	 off on	 off off	 off on
Engine off—ignition on with or without brake apply—(bulb check)	on	on	on
Engine off—ignition on start with or without brake apply	on	on	on
Engine on with or without brake apply	off	off	off
Engine on—primary boost interrupted with or without brake apply	on	on	on
Engine on—open circuit in EH pump motor with or without brake apply	off	on	off

①Brake ②Brake Elect. Hyd. Boost

DIAGNOSIS OF EH PUMP

Problem	Possible Cause	Correction
Excessive Pump Noise (gurgle, chatter, etc.)	Trapped air in pump.	Depress brake pedal lightly with the engine off for thirty seconds and release. Recheck and should the problem persist, repeat above procedure after a three minute waiting period.①
Inoperative pump	Non-functioning motor.	1. Check electrical connection between motor lead wire and wiring harness. If loose, corroded, or disconnected, clean and secure connection. 2. Check grounding of pump housing to booster. The pump housing must be securely bolted to the booster to properly ground the motor. 3. Replace EH Pump
	Low or no voltage at motor connection of wiring harness.	1. Check condition of battery and battery terminals.Correct an abnormally low battery condition and/or clean battery terminals if necessary. 2. Check electrical leads at battery terminal of starter or ignition bus bar—not corroded or loose.
Oil leak at booster and EH pump mating surface.	Damaged or missing O-rings at pressure and/or return port.	Replace two O-rings.
Oil leak from pump end plate	damaged or missing end plate seal.	Replace EH pump assembly.
Oil leak from EH pump motor	Damaged shaft seal.	Replace EH pump assembly.

①This noise will diminish upon continued use of the brakes under normal driving conditions.

with the front disc brakes as one system and the rear brakes as the other system, except on tandem equipped vehicles.

4. The tandem vehicle brakes are split with the front disc and one of the wheel cylinders of the forward axle as one system and the second wheel cylinder of the forward axle and the total rear axle as the second system.

5. The hydraulic brake pump and reservoir is completely separate from the power steering system and uses Dexron®II A/T fluid for operation of the in-wheel parking brake system. Brake fluid is used in the two brake systems.

6. Seals are located between the master cylinder and the booster, along with spacing, making it impossible for the two fluids to mix. A vent is provided between the two units to for normal fluid "weepage".

DAYTON/WALTHER DISC BRAKES

The Dayton/Walther disc brakes are dual piston, sliding caliper units, using semi-metallic, asbestos-free disc pads, interchangable from right to left and from outer to inner. One common caliper is used on both the right and left sides with the bleed screw port located at the top of each caliper.

Removal

NOTE: Disc pads should be replaced when the lining is worn to a minimum thickness of 0.032 in. (0.794mm) above the pad plate, unless state or local vehicle inspection codes dictates otherwise.

1. Remove approximately ⅔ of the brake fluid from the reservoir of the master cylinder for the front brake system.
2. Raise the vehicle and support safely. Remove the wheel assembly to expose the caliper.
3. Remove the two bolts and the spring retainer from the bottom end of the caliper.
4. Remove the bolt at the top end of the caliper support and remove the key from between the caliper and the support rails by sliding it from, the assembly.
5. With the caliper resting on the lower rail, rotate the upper end up and away from the upper rail and lift the assembly from the rotor.
6. Do not allow the caliper to hang by the jounce hydraulic line. Either disconnect the line or hang the caliper from the frame with a piece of wire.
7. Remove the lining from the caliper, starting with the pad farthest from the pistons.
8. If the disc pads are to be replaced only, use a block of wood and a C-clamp to push the pistons back into the calipers.
9. Install the disc pads and calipers in the reverse order of the removal procedure.

CALIPERS

Disassembly

1. With the caliper removed from the vehicle and the hose removed, clean the assembly with isopropyl alcohol or brake fluid.

CAUTION

Do not use mineral based cleaning solvents to clean the assembly. Damage to the new rubber parts can occur due to the solvent not being completely cleaned from the assembly.

2. Place a shop towel covered wooden block under the caliper pistons and direct compressed air into the fluid port to slowly push the pistons from their bores in the caliper.

CAUTION

Do not place fingers on the front of the pistons to catch or protect them during the removal. Personal injury could occur when thee pistons are blown from the caliper bores.

3. Remove and discard the piston boots.
4. Use a pointed piece of wood or plastic to remove the piston seals from the groove in the caliper bores. Discard the seals. Do not use metal tools as damage to the bore could occur.
5. Examine the pistons, the piston bores and calipers for damage, nicks, scoring , corrosion or extreme wear.

NOTE: The piston outer surface is the primary sealing surface in the caliper assembly and must not be refinished by any means nor should abrasives be used.

Assembly

1. Clean all parts in isopropyl alcohol or brake fluid. Dry with filtered compressed air.
2. Dip the new piston seal in brake fluid and install it into the groove in the cylinder bore. Gently work the seal around with a finger until it is properly seated in the groove.

CAUTION

Be sure the seal is not twisted or rolled in its groove.

3. Install the dust boot into its cylinder groove in the same manner as the piston seal was installed.
4. Coat or dip the piston in brake fluid and using a small flat plastic or wooden tool, gradually work the dust boot around the piston.
5. Press the piston straight into the caliper bore until it bottoms. The boot internal diameter should slide up the piston as the piston is pushed into the caliper bore and slide into position in the boot groove of the piston.
6. Install the second piston in the same manner as the first piston was installed.
7. Upon completion, the caliper is ready to be re-installed on the axle, along with the disc pads.

SPIDER, HUB AND ROTOR ASSEMBLY

The spider, hub and rotor assembly can be inspected for damages, scores or abnormal wear and replaced as required.

Hydraulic Booster (Dual Power)

Disassembly

1. Pull the piston rod out with a twisting motion.

NOTE: It is advised that this be done over a large open container as the fluid must be drained from the booster.

2. Secure the booster in a vise by clamping across the body flange (flow switch up).
3. Remove the flow switch and the flow switch O-ring seal.
4. Insert a suitable pry tool under the lip of the cap, and pry the cap free. Be careful not to bend or distort the cap.

CAUTION

The piston return spring is under a considerable load. Exercise caution when removing the cap as spring pressure may forcibly expel the support plate, cylinder seal, and expander, resulting in personal injury.

5. Remove the O-ring from the cap.
6. Remove the support plate, cylinder seal, and seal expander.
7. Remove the return spring and the piston.
8. Remove the double lip seal from the narrow end of the booster body.
9. Remove the seal from the power piston.
10. Clean all parts, thoroughly, and check for excessive wear or damage. Replace parts as necessary.

NOTE: The manufacturer states specifically that internal parts of surfaces are NOT to be remachined. DO NOT use abrasives to remove surface defects.

Assembly

1. Secure the booster in a vise with the large bore up.
2. Lubricate the piston seal, and install it on the power piston.
3. Install the piston in the booster body bore. Press the piston to bottom in the bore. Be careful not to roll the seal.
4. Install the return spring.
5. Lubricate the inside and outside diameters of the cylinder seal.
6. Assemble the O-ring seal, support plate, cylinder seal, and seal expander against the cap in the order in which they are to be installed.
7. Position this assembly over the booster and on the return spring.
8. Push the cap down until the extensions on the cap contact the booster casting, and tap into place using a rubber or plastic mallet.

NOTE: Make sure that the cap is flush with the casting.

9. Install the flow switch with a new O-ring.

NOTE: If the original flow switch shows signs of leakage, discard it and replace it with a new switch.

10. Install the piston rod and gauge the length of the rod.

NOTE: It is advised that the gauging procedure be performed after any hard parts have been replaced, or if any components of the vacuum booster have been replaced.

Gauging the Piston Rod

1. Press down on the piston to be sure that all internal parts are bottomed in the booster.
2. Using special tool J–28675 or any suitable push rod height gauge, check the extended length of the piston rod to determine whether, or not, it falls within limits.
3. If it has been determined that the extended length of the piston push rod does not fall within limits, then select a rod of suitable length from among the six rods available, each of a differnt length. (See Piston Rod Chart).
4. Repeat the gauging procedure for each piston rod which is used in selecting one of proper length.

Engine Rebuilding
Import Trucks

This section describes, in detail, the procedures involved in rebuilding a typical engine. The procedures are basically identical to those used in rebuilding engines of nearly all design and configurations.

The section is divided into two parts. The first, Cylinder Head Reconditioning, assumes that the cylinder head is removed from the engine, all manifolds are removed, and the cylinder head is on a workbench. The camshaft should be removed from overhead cam cylinder heads. The second section, Cylinder Block Reconditioning, covers the block, pistons, connecting rods and crankshaft. It is assumed that the engine is mounted on a work stand, and the cylinder head and all accessories are removed.

Procedures are identified as follows:

Unmarked—Basic procedures that must be performed in order to successfully complete the rebuilding process.

Starred (*)—Procedures that should be performed to ensure maximum performance and engine life.

Double starred (**)—Procedures that may be performed to increase engine performance and reliability.

In many cases, a choice of methods is also provided. Methods are identified in the same manner as procedures. The choice of method for a procedure is at the discretion of the user.

The tools required for the basic rebuilding procedure should, with minor exceptions, be those included in a mechanic's tool kit. An accurate torque wrench, and a dial indicator (reading in thousandths) mounted on a universal base should be available. Special tools, where required, all are readily available from the major tool suppliers. The services of a competent automotive machine shop must also be readily available.

When assembling the engine, any parts that will be in frictional contact must be prelubricated, to provide protection on initial start-up. Any product specifically formulated for this purpose may be used. NOTE: *Do not use engine oil.* Where semi-permanent (locked but removable) installation of bolts or nuts is desired, threads should be cleaned and coated with Loctite® or a similar product (non-hardening).

Aluminum has become increasingly popular for use in engines, due to its low weight and excellent heat transfer characteristics. The following precautions must be observed when handling aluminum engine parts:

—Never hot-tank aluminum parts.

—Remove all aluminum parts (identification tags, etc.) from engine parts before hot-tanking (otherwise they will be removed during the process).

—Always coat threads lightly with engine oil or anti-seize compounds before installation, to prevent seizure.

—Never over-torque bolts or spark plugs in aluminum threads. Should stripping occur, threads can be restored using any of a number of thread repair kits available (see next section).

Magnaflux and Zyglo are inspection techniques used to locate material flaws, such as stress cracks. Magnafluxing coats the part with fine magnetic particles, and subjects the part to a magnetic field. Cracks cause breaks in the magnetic field, which are outlined by the particles. Since Magnaflux is a magnetic process, it is applicable only to ferrous materials. The Zyglo process coats the material with a fluorescent dye penetrant, and then subjects it to blacklight inspection, under which cracks glow brightly. Parts made of any material may be tested using Zyglo. While Magnaflux and Zyglo are excellent for general inspection, and locating hidden defects, specific checks of suspected cracks may be made at lower cost and more readily using spot check dye. The dye is sprayed onto the suspected area, wiped off, and the area is then sprayed with a developer. Cracks then will show up brightly. Spot check dyes will only indicate surface cracks; therefore, structural cracks below the surface may escape detection. When questionable, the part should be tested using Magnaflux or Zyglo.

REPAIRING DAMAGED THREADS

Several methods of repairing damaged threads are available. Heli-Coil® (shown here), Keenserts® and Microdot® are among the most widely used. All involve basically the same principle—drilling out stripped threads, tapping the hole and installing a prewound insert— making welding, plugging and oversize fasteners unnecessary.

Two types of thread repair inserts are usually supplied—a standard type for most Inch Coarse, Inch Fine, Metric Coarse and Metric Fine thread sizes and a spark plug type to fit most spark plug port sizes. Consult the individual manufacturer's catalog to determine exact applications. Typical thread repair kits will contain a selection of prewound threaded inserts, a tap (corresponding to the outside diameter threads of the insert) and an installation tool. Most manufacturers also supply blister-packed thread repair inserts separately and a master kit with a variety of taps and inserts plus installation tools.

Before effecting a repair to a threaded hole, remove any snapped, broken or damaged bolts or studs. Penetrating oil can be used to free frozen threads; the offending item can be removed with locking pliers or with a screw or stud extractor. After the hole is clear, the thread can be repaired as follows.

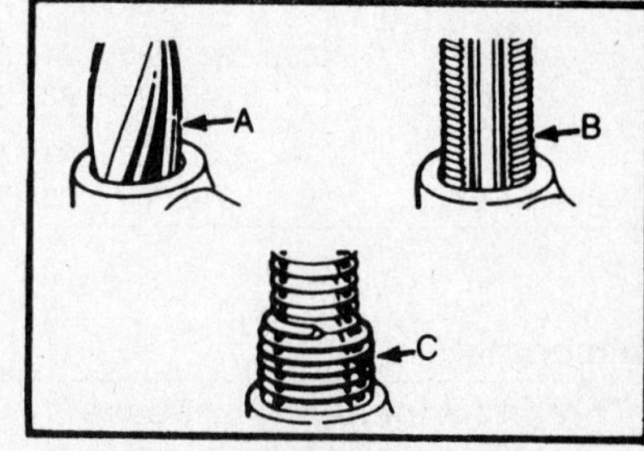

A. Drill out the damaged threads with the specified drill. Drill completely through the hole or to the bottom of a blind hole.

B. With the tap supplied tap the hole to receive the threaded insert. Keep the tap well oiled and back it out frequently to avoid clogging the threads.

C. Screw the threaded insert onto the installation tool until the tang engages the slot. Screw the insert into the tapped hole until it is ¼–½ turn below the top surface. After installation, break the tang off with a hammer and punch.

STANDARD TORQUE SPECIFICATIONS AND CAPSCREW MARKINGS

Newton-Meter has been designated as the world standard for measuring torque and will gradually replace the foot-pound and kilogram-meter torque measuring standard. Torquing tools are still being manufactured with foot-pounds and kilogram-meter scales, along with the new Newton-Meter standard. To assist the repairman, foot-pounds, kilogram-meter and Newton-Meter are listed in the following charts, and should be followed as applicable.

U.S. BOLTS

SAE Grade Number	1 or 2			5			6 or 7			8		
Capscrew Head Markings Manufacturer's marks may vary. Three-line markings on heads below indicate SAE Grade 5. 	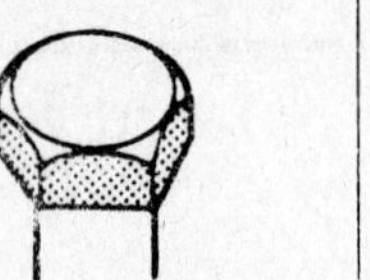						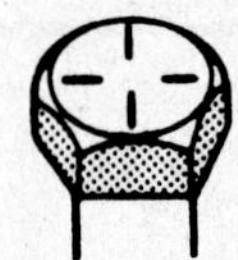			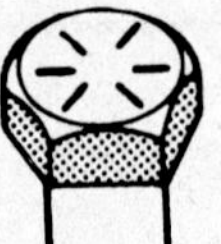		
Usage	Used Frequently			Used Frequently			Used at Times			Used at Times		
Quality of Material	Indeterminate			Minimum Commercial			Medium Commercial			Best Commercial		
Capacity Body Size	**Torque**			**Torque**			**Torque**			**Torque**		
(inches)-(thread)	Ft-Lb	kgm	Nm	Ft-Lb	kgm	Nm	Ft-Lb	kgm	Nm	Ft-Lb	kgm	Nm
1/4-20	5	0.6915	6.7791	8	1.1064	10.8465	10	1.3630	13.5582	12	1.6596	16.2698
-28	6	0.8298	8.1349	10	1.3830	13.5582				14	1.9362	18.9815
5/16-18	11	1.5213	14.9140	17	2.3511	23.0489	19	2.6277	25.7605	24	3.3192	32.5396
-24	13	1.7979	17.6256	19	2.6277	25.7605				27	3.7341	36.6071
3/8-16	18	2.4894	24.4047	31	4.2873	42.0304	34	4.7022	46.0978	44	6.0852	59.6560
-24	20	2.7660	27.1164	35	4.8405	47.4536				49	6.7767	66.4351
7/16-14	28	3.8132	37.9629	49	6.7767	66.4351	55	7.6065	74.5700	70	9.6810	94.9073
-20	30	4.1490	40.6745	55	7.6065	74 5700				78	10.7874	105.7538
1/2-13	39	5.3937	52.8769	75	10.3725	101.6863	85	11.7555	115.2445	105	14.5215	142.3609
-20	41	5.6703	55.5885	85	11.7555	115.2445				120	16.5860	162.6960
9/16-12	51	7.0533	69.1467	110	15.2130	149.1380	120	16.5960	162.6960	155	21.4365	210.1490
-18	55	7.6065	74.5700	120	16.5960	162.6960				170	23.5110	230.4860
5/8-11	83	11.4789	112.5329	150	20.7450	203.3700	167	23.0961	226.4186	210	29.0430	284.7180
-18	95	13.1385	128.8027	170	23.5110	230.4860				240	33.1920	325.3920
3/4-10	105	14.5215	142.3609	270	37.3410	366.0660	280	38.7240	379.6240	375	51.8625	508.4250
-16	115	15.9045	155.9170	295	40.7985	399.9610				420	58.0860	568.4360
7/8-9	160	22.1280	216.9280	395	54.6285	535.5410	440	60.8520	596.5520	605	83.6715	820.2590
-14	175	24.2025	237.2650	435	60.1605	589.7730				675	93.3525	915.1650
1-8	236	32.5005	318.6130	590	81.5970	799.9220	660	91.2780	894.8280	910	125.8530	1233.7780
-14	250	34.5750	338.9500	660	91.2780	849.8280				990	136.9170	1342.2420

METRIC BOLTS

Description	Torque ft-lbs. (Nm)			
Thread for general purposes (size x pitch (mm)	**Head Mark 4**		**Head Mark 7**	
6 x 1.0	2.2 to 2.9	(3.0 to 3.9)	3.6 to 5.8	(4.9 to 7.8)
8 x 1.25	5.8 to 8.7	(7.9 to 12)	9.4 to 14	(13 to 19)
10 x 1.25	12 to 17	(16 to 23)	20 to 29	(27 to 39)
12 x 1.25	21 to 32	(29 to 43)	35 to 53	(47 to 72)
14 x 1.5	35 to 52	(48 to 70)	57 to 85	(77 to 110)
16 x 1.5	51 to 77	(67 to 100)	90 to 120	(130 to 160)
18 x 1.5	74 to 110	(100 to 150)	130 to 170	(180 to 230)
20 x 1.5	110 to 140	(150 to 190)	190 to 240	(160 to 320)
22 x 1.5	150 to 190	(200 to 260)	250 to 320	(340 to 430)
24 x 1.5	190 to 240	(260 to 320)	310 to 410	(420 to 550)

CAUTION: Bolts threaded into aluminum require much less torque

NOTE: This engine rebuilding section is a guide to accepted rebuilding procedures. Typical examples of standard rebuilding procedures are illustrated.

CYLINDER HEAD RECONDITIONING

Procedure	Method
Identify the valves:	Invert the cylinder head, and number the valve faces front to rear, using a permanent felt-tip marker.
Remove the rocker arms (OHV engines only):	Remove the rocker arms with shaft(s) or balls and nuts. Wire the sets of rockers, balls and nuts together, and identify according to the corresponding valve.
Remove the camshaft (OHC engines only):	See the engine service procedures earlier in this book for details concerning specific engines.
Remove the valves and springs:	Using an appropriate valve spring compressor (depending on the configuration of the cylinder head), compress the valve springs. Lift out the keepers with needlenose pliers, release the compressor, and remove the valve, spring, and spring retainer.
Remove glow plugs and fuel injectors (Diesel engines only):	Label and remove all fuel injectors and glow plugs from the head. Glow plugs unscrew. See the appropriate car section for injector removal. Inspect glow plugs for bulges, cracks or signs of melting. Clean injector tips with a steel brush, then inspect for evidence of melting.
Remove pre-combustion chamber inserts (Diesel engines only): 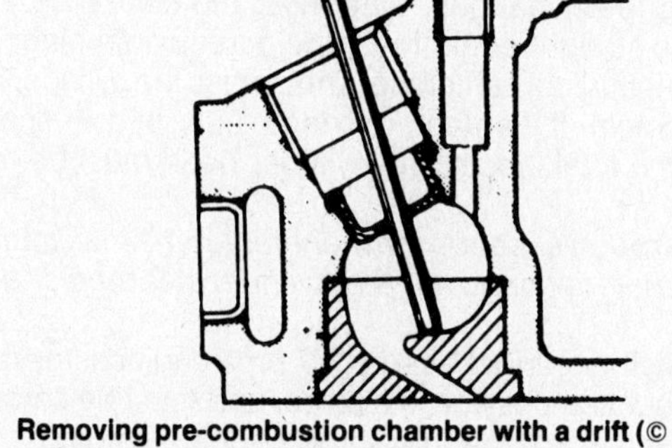 **Removing pre-combustion chamber with a drift (© G.M. Corp.)	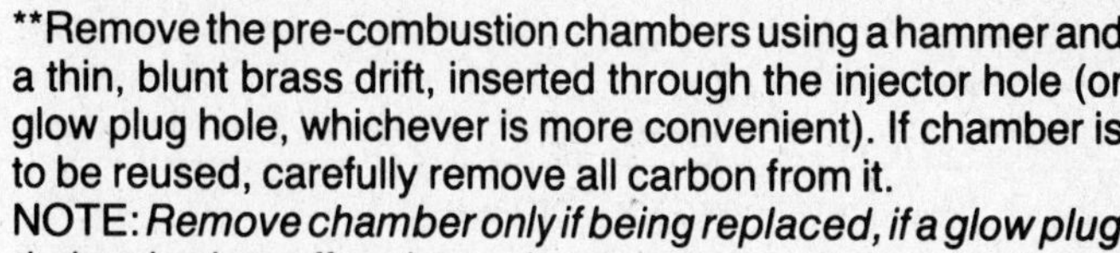 **Remove the pre-combustion chambers using a hammer and a thin, blunt brass drift, inserted through the injector hole (or glow plug hole, whichever is more convenient). If chamber is to be reused, carefully remove all carbon from it. NOTE: *Remove chamber only if being replaced, if a glow plug tip has broken off and must be removed, or if chamber is obviously damaged or loose.*
Check the valve stem-to-guide clearance: 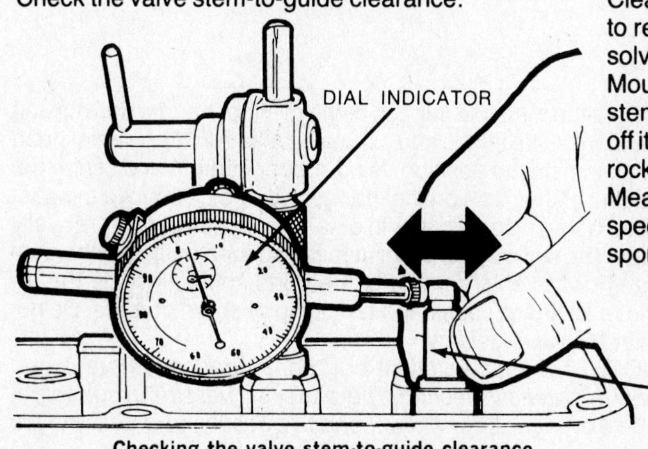 **Checking the valve stem-to-guide clearance**	Clean the valve stem with lacquer thinner or a similar solvent to remove all gum and varnish. Clean the valve guides using solvent and an expanding wire-type valve guide cleaner. Mount a dial indicator so that the stem is at 90° to the valve stem, as close to the valve guide as possible. Move the valve off its seat, and measure the valve guide-to-stem clearance by rocking the stem back and forth to actuate the dial indicator. Measure the valve stems using a micrometer, and compare to specifications, to determine whether stem or guide wear is responsible for excessive clearance.

CYLINDER HEAD RECONDITIONING

Procedure	Method
De-carbon the cylinder head and valves: 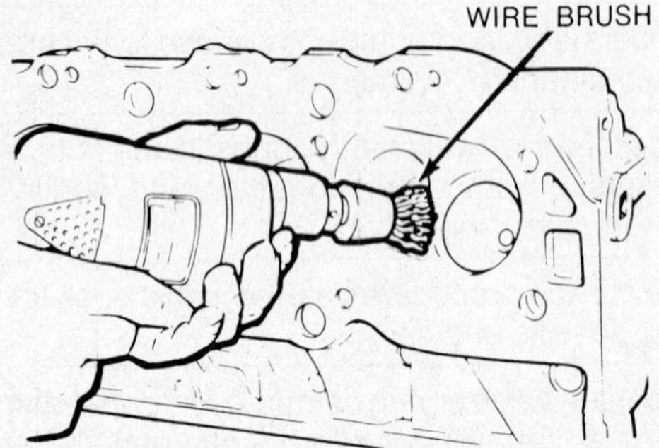 Removing carbon from the cylinder head	Chip carbon away from the valve heads, combustion chambers, and ports, using a chisel made of hardwood. Remove the remaining deposits with a stiff wire brush. NOTE: *Ensure that the deposits are actually removed, rather than burnished.*
Hot-tank the cylinder head (cast iron heads only): CAUTION: *Do not hot-tank aluminum parts.*	Have the cylinder head hot-tanked to remove grease, corrosion, and scale from the water passages. NOTE: *In the case of overhead cam cylinder heads, consult the operator to determine whether the camshaft bearings will be damaged by the caustic solution.*
Degrease the remaining cylinder head parts:	Using solvent (i.e., Gunk), clean the rockers, rocker shaft(s) (where applicable), rocker balls and nuts, springs, spring retainers, and keepers. Do not remove the protective coating from the springs.
Check the cylinder head for warpage: 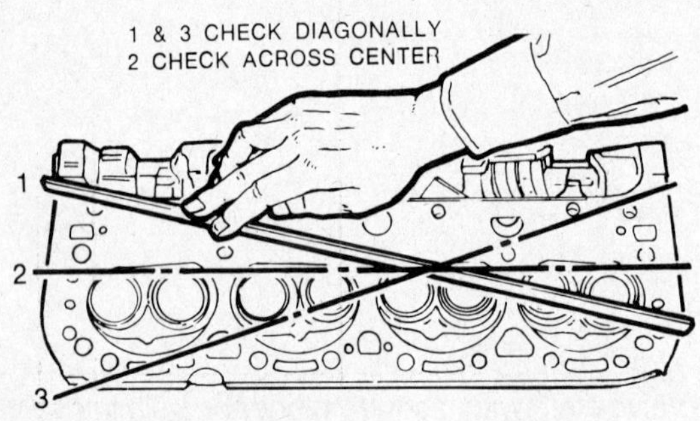 Checking cylinder head for warpage	Place a straight-edge across the gasket surface of the cylinder head. Using feeler gauges, determine the clearance at the center of the straight-edge. Measure across both diagonals, along the longitudinal centerline, and across the cylinder head at several points. If warpage exceeds .003′ in a 6′ span, or .006′ over the total length, the cylinder head must be resurfaced. NOTE: *If warpage exceeds the manufacturer's maximum tolerance for material removal, the cylinder head must be replaced.* When milling the cylinder heads of V-type engines, the intake manifold mounting position is altered, and must be corrected by milling the manifold flange a proportionate amount.
**Porting and gasket matching:	**Coat the manifold flanges of the cylinder head with Prussian blue dye. Glue intake and exhaust gaskets to the cylinder head in their installed position using rubber cement and scribe the outline of the ports on the manifold flanges. Remove the gaskets. Using a small cutter in a hand-held power tool gradually taper the walls of the port out to the scribed outline of the gasket. Further enlargement of the ports should include the removal of sharp edges and radiusing of sharp corners. Do not alter the valve guides. NOTE: *The most efficient port configuration is determined only by extensive testing. Therefore, it is best to consult someone experienced with the head in question to determine the optimum alterations.*

CYLINDER HEAD RECONDITIONING

Procedure	Method
*Knurling the valve guides:	*Valve guides which are not excessively worn or distorted may, in some cases, be knurled rather than replaced. Knurling is a process in which metal is displaced and raised, thereby reducing clearance. Knurling also provides excellent oil control. The possibility of knurling rather than replacing valve guides should be discussed with a machinist.

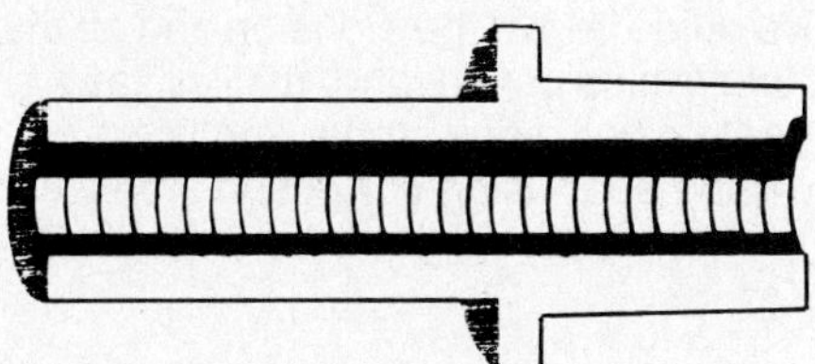

Cut-away view of a knurled valve guide

Procedure	Method
Replacing the valve guides: NOTE: *Valve guides should only be replaced if damaged or if an oversize valve stem is not available.*	Depending on the type of cylinder head, valve guides may be pressed, hammered, or shrunk in. In cases where the guides are shrunk into the head, replacement should be left to an equipped machine shop. In other cases, the guides are replaced as follows: Press or tap the valve guides out of the head using a stepped drift (see illustration). Determine the height above the boss that the guide must extend, and obtain a stack of washers, their I.D. similar to the guide's O.D., of that height. Place the stack of washers on the guide, and insert the guide into the boss. NOTE: *Valve guides are often tapered or beveled for installation.* Using the stepped installation tool (see illustration), press or tap the guides into position. Ream the guides according to the size of the valve stem.

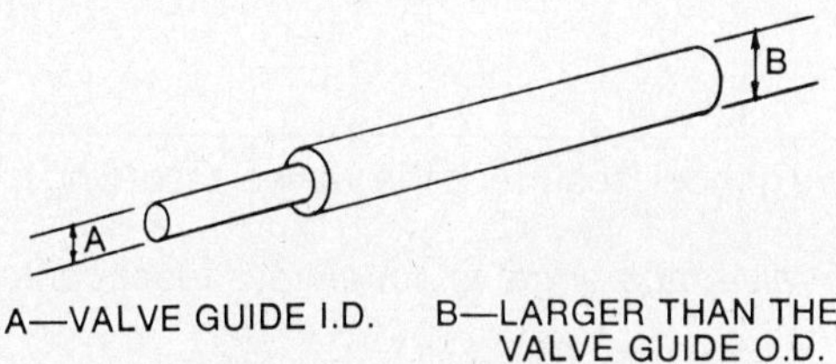

Valve guide removal tool

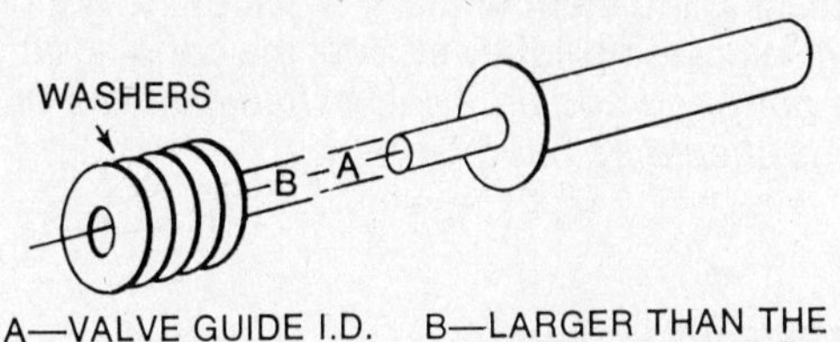

Valve guide installation tool (with washers used for installation)

Procedure	Method
Replacing valve seat inserts:	Replacement of valve seat inserts which are worn beyond resurfacing or broken, if feasible, must be done by a machine shop.
Resurfacing the valve seats using reamers:	Select a reamer of the correct seat angle, slightly larger than the diameter of the valve seat, and assemble it with a pilot of the correct size. Install the pilot into the valve guide, and using steady pressure, turn the reamer clockwise. CAUTION: *Do not turn the reamer counterclockwise.* Remove only as much material as necessary to clean the seat. Check the concentricity of the seat (see below). If the dye method is not used, coat the valve face with Prussian blue dye, install and rotate it on the valve seat. Using the dye marked area as a centering guide, center and narrow the valve seat to specifications with correction cutters. NOTE: *When no specifications are available, minimum seat width for exhaust valves should be 5/64", intake valves 1/16".* After making correction cuts, check the position of the valve seat on the valve face using Prussian blue dye. NOTE: *Do not cut induction hardened seats; they must be ground.*

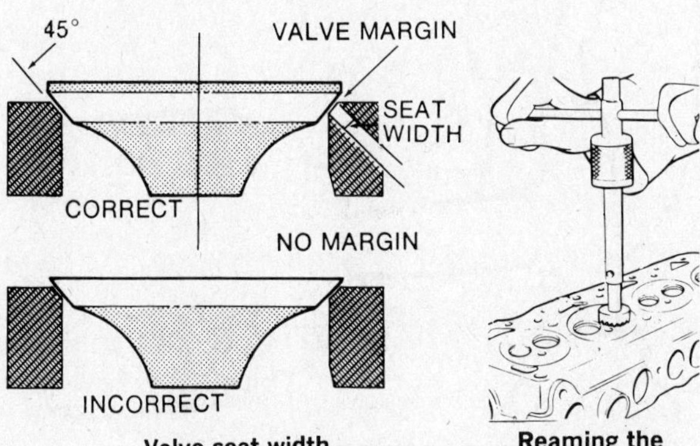

Valve seat width and centering

Reaming the valve seat

CYLINDER HEAD RECONDITIONING

Procedure	Method
*Resurfacing the valve seats using a grinder:	*Select a pilot of the correct size, and a coarse stone of the correct seat angle. Lubricate the pilot if necessary, and install the tool in the valve guide. Move the stone on and off the seat at approximately two cycles per second, until all flaws are removed from the seat. Install a fine stone, and finish the seat. Center and narrow the seat using correction stones, as described above.
Resurfacing (grinding) the valve face:	Using a valve grinder, resurface the valves according to specifications. CAUTION: *Valve face angle is not always identical to valve seat angle.* A minimum margin of 1/32″ should remain after grinding the valve. The valve stem top should also be squared and resurfaced, by placing the stem in the V-block of the grinder, and turning it while pressing lightly against the grinding wheel. NOTE: *Do not grind sodium filled exhaust valves on a machine. These should be hand lapped.*

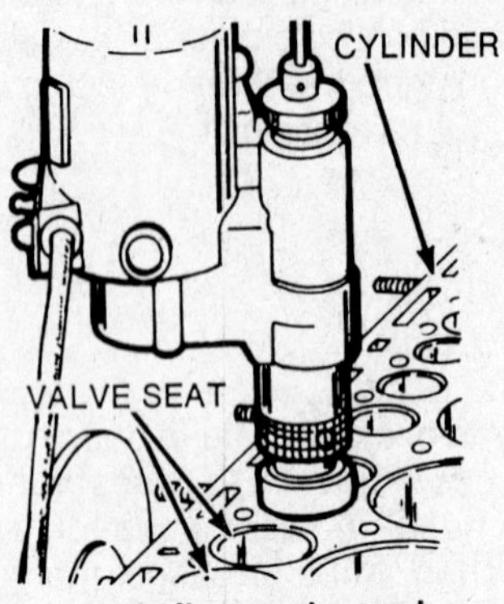

Grinding a valve seat

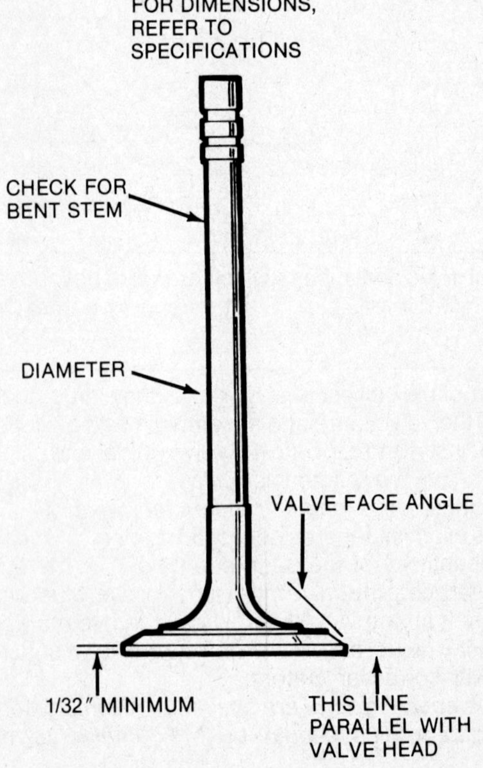

Critical valve dimensions

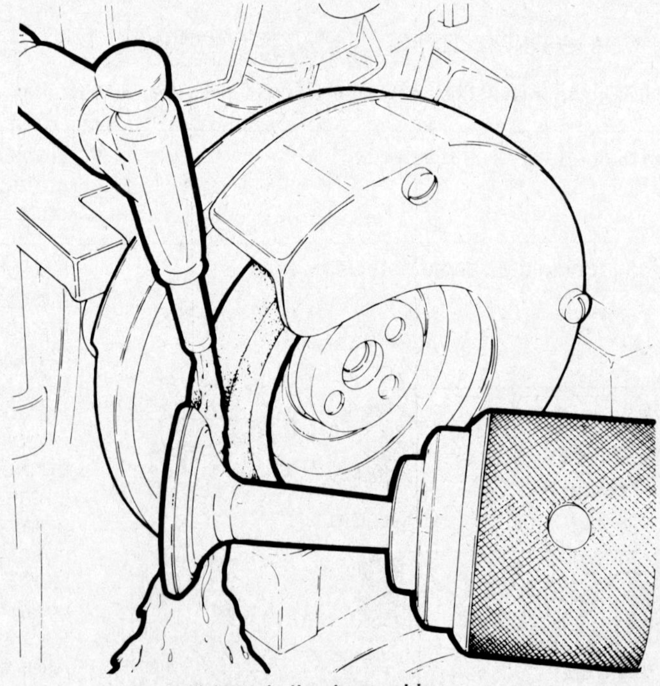
Valve grinding by machine

CYLINDER HEAD RECONDITIONING

Procedure	Method
Checking the valve seat concentricity:	Coat the valve face with Prussian blue dye, install the valve, and rotate it on the valve seat. If the entire seat becomes coated, and the valve is known to be concentric, the seat is concentric. *Install the dial gauge pilot into the guide, and rest the arm on the valve seat. Zero the gauge, and rotate the arm around the seat. Run-out should not exceed .002″.
*Lapping the valves: NOTE: *Valve lapping is done to ensure efficient sealing of resurfaced valves and seats.*	*Invert the cylinder head, lightly lubricate the valve stems, and install the valves in the head as numbered. Coat valve seats with fine grinding compound, and attach the lapping tool suction cup to a valve head. NOTE: *Moisten the suction cup.* Rotate the tool between the palms, changing position and lifting the tool often to prevent grooving. Lap the valve until a smooth, polished seat is evident. Remove the valve and tool, and rinse away all traces of grinding compound. **Fasten a suction cup to a piece of drill rod, and mount the rod in a hand drill. Proceed as above, using the hand drill as a lapping tool. CAUTION: *Due to the higher speeds involved when using the hand drill, care must be exercised to avoid grooving the seat.* Lift the tool and change direction of rotation often.
Check the valve springs:	Place the spring on a flat surface next to a square. Measure the height of the spring, and rotate it against the edge of the square to measure distortion. If spring height varies (by comparison) by more than 1/16″ or if distortion exceeds 1/16″, replace the spring. **In addition to evaluating the spring as above, test the spring pressure at the installed and compressed (installed height minus valve lift) height using a valve spring tester. Springs used on small displacement engines (up to 3 liters) should be ∓ 1 lb. of all other springs in either position. A tolerance of ∓ 5 lbs. is permissible on larger engines.

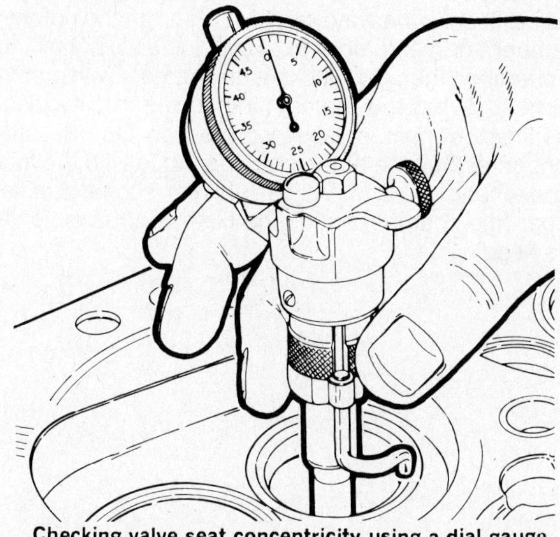

Checking valve seat concentricity using a dial gauge

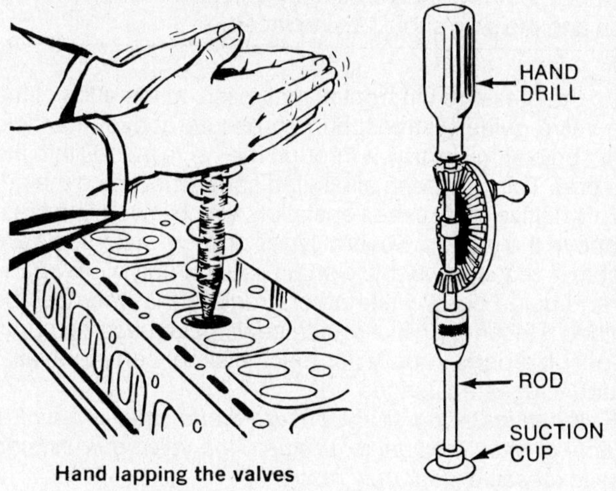

Hand lapping the valves

Home made mechanical valve lapping tool

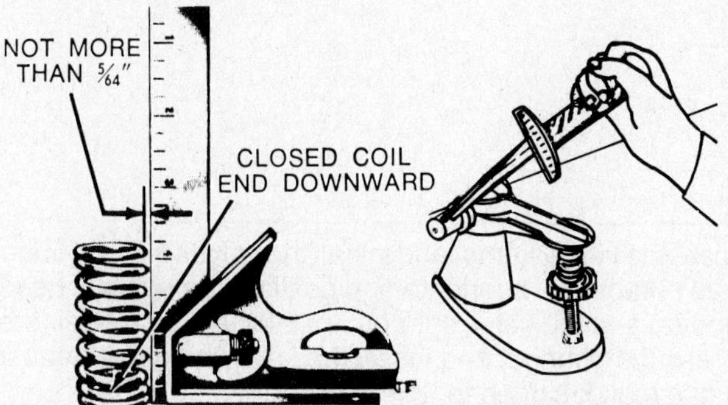

Checking valve spring free length and squareness

Measuring valve spring test pressure

CYLINDER HEAD RECONDITIONING

Procedure	Method
Install pre-combustion chambers (Diesel engines only)	Pre-combustion chambers are press-fit into the head. The chambers will fit only one way: on G.M. V8, align the notches in the chamber and head; on 1.8L 4 cyl., install lock ball into groove in chamber, then align lock ball in chamber with groove in cylinder head. Press the chamber into the head. Fit a piece of metal against the chamber face for protection. On 1.8L, after installation, grind the face of the chamber flush with the face of the cylinder head. On G.M. V8, use a 1¼ in. socket to install the chamber (the chamber should be flush ± .003 in. to the face of the head).

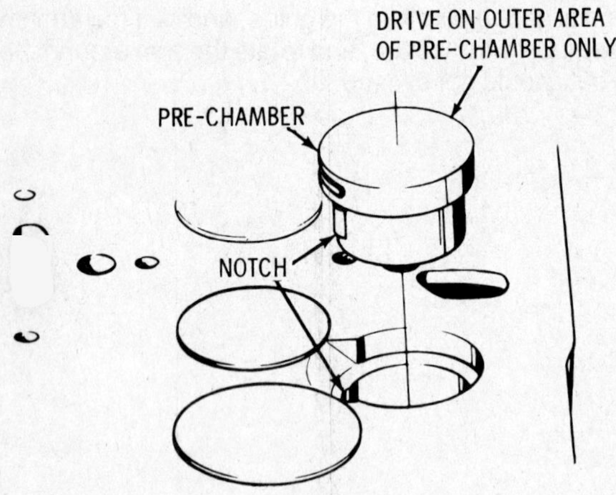

Align the notches to install the pre-combustion chamber

Procedure	Method
Install fuel injectors and glow plugs (Diesel engines)	Before installing glow plugs, check for continuity across plug terminals and body. If no continuity exists, the heater wire is broken and the plug should be replaced.
*Install valve stem seals:	*Due to the pressure differential that exists at the ends of the intake valve guides (atmospheric pressure above, manifold vacuum below), oil is drawn through the valve guides into the intake port. This has been alleviated somewhat since the addition of positive crankcase ventilation, which lowers the pressure above the guides. Several types of valve stem seals are available to reduce blow-by. Certain seals simply slip over the stem and guide boss, while others require that the boss be machined. Recently, Teflon guide seals have become popular. Consult a parts supplier or machinist concerning availability and suggested usages. NOTE: *When installing seals, ensure that a small amount of oil is able to pass the seal to lubricate the valve guides; otherwise, excessive wear may result.*

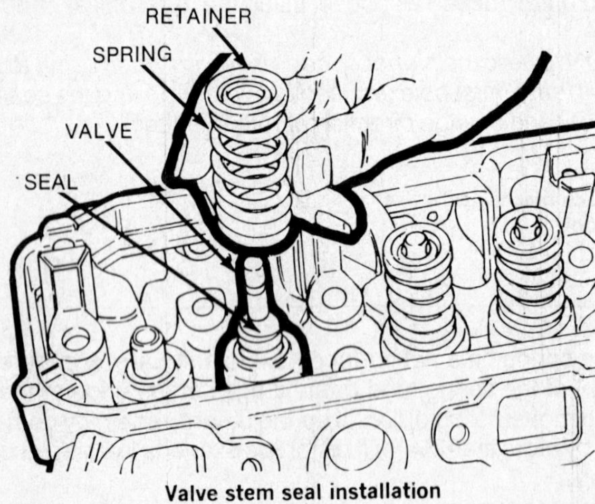

Valve stem seal installation

Procedure	Method
Install the valves:	Lubricate the valve stems, and install the valves in the cylinder head as numbered. Lubricate and position the seals (if used, see above) and the valve springs. Install the spring retainers, compress the springs, and insert the keys using needlenose pliers or a tool designed for this purpose. NOTE: *Retain the keys with wheel bearing grease during installation.*

CYLINDER HEAD RECONDITIONING

Procedure	Method
Check valve spring installed height: 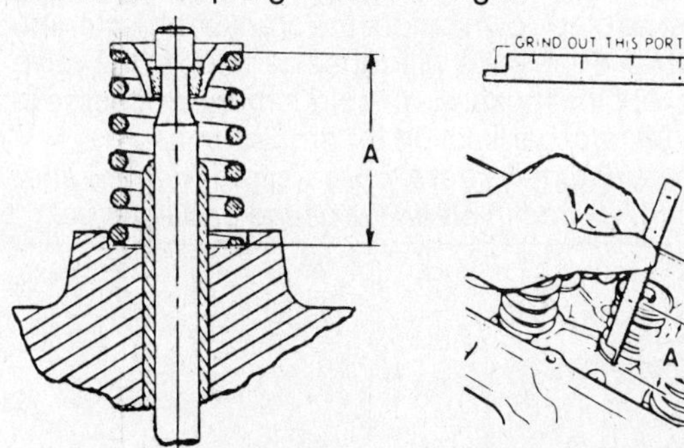 Valve spring installed height dimension; Measuring valve spring installed height	Measure the distance between the spring pad and the lower edge of the spring retainer, and compare to specifications. If the installed height is incorrect, add shim washers between the spring pad and the spring. CAUTION: *Use only washers designed for this purpose.*
Install the camshaft (OHC engines only) and check end play:	See the engine service procedures earlier in this book for details concerning specific engines.
Inspect the rocker arms, balls, studs, and nuts (OHV engines only): 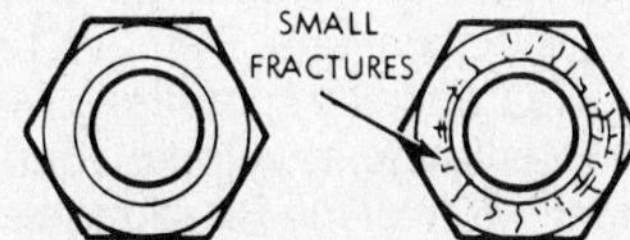 Stress cracks in the rocker nuts	Visually inspect the rocker arms, balls, studs, and nuts for cracks, galling, burning, scoring or wear. If all parts are intact, liberally lubricate the rocker arms and balls, and install them on the cylinder head. If wear is noted on a rocker arm at the point of valve contact, grind it smooth and square, removing as little material as possible. Replace the rocker arm if excessively worn. If a rocker stud shows signs of wear, it must be replaced (see below). If a rocker nut shows stress cracks, replace it. If an exhaust ball is galled or burned, substitute the intake ball from the same cylinder (if it is intact), and install a new intake ball. NOTE: *Avoid using new rocker balls on exhaust valves.*
Replacing rocker studs (OHV engines only): 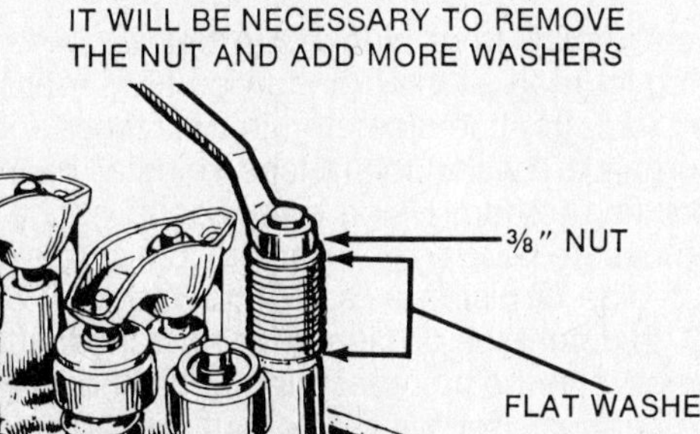 Extracting a pressed-in rocker stud	In order to remove a threaded stud, lock two nuts on the stud, and unscrew the stud using the lower nut. Coat the lower threads of the new stud with Loctite®, and install. Two alternative methods are available for replacing pressed in studs. Remove the damaged stud using a stack of washers and a nut (see illustration). In the first, the boss is reamed .005–.006" oversize, and an oversize stud pressed in. Control the stud extension over the boss using washers, in the same manner as valve guides. Before installing the stud, coat it with white lead and grease. To retain the stud more positively drill a hole through the stud and boss, and install a roll pin. In the second method, the boss is tapped, and a threaded stud installed. Retain the stud using Loctite® Stud and Bearing Mount. 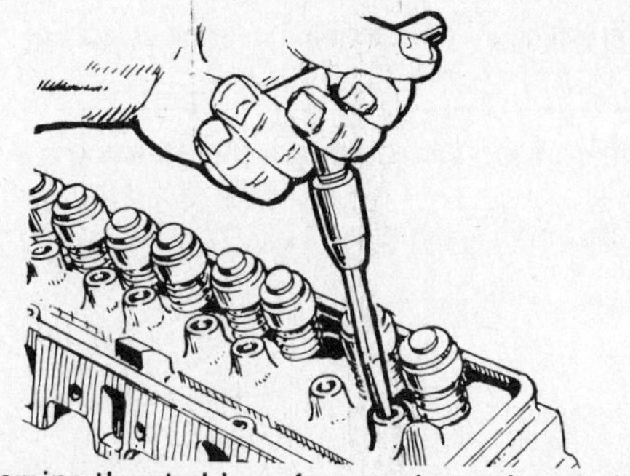 Reaming the stud bore for oversize rocker studs

CYLINDER HEAD RECONDITIONING

Procedure	Method
Bleed the hydraulic lifters (diesel engines only):	After the cylinder heads are installed on G.M. V8 diesels, the valve lifters must be bled down before the crankshaft is turned. Failure to bleed down the lifters will cause damage to the valve train. See diesel engine rocker arm replacement procedure in Oldsmobile 88, 98, etc. car section for procedures. NOTE: *When installing new lifters, prime by working the lifter plunger while submerged in clean kerosene or diesel fuel.*

CYLINDER BLOCK RECONDITIONING

Procedure	Method
Checking the main bearing clearance:	Invert engine, and remove cap from the bearing to be checked. Using a clean, dry rag, thoroughly clean all oil from crankshaft journal and bearing insert. NOTE: *Plastigage is soluble in oil; therefore, oil on the journal or bearing could result in erroneous readings.* Place a piece of Plastigage along the full length of journal, reinstall cap, and torque to specifications. Remove bearing cap, and determine bearing clearance by comparing width of Plastigage to the scale on Plastigage envelope. Journal taper is determined by comparing width of the Plastigage strip near its ends. Rotate crankshaft 90° and retest, to determine journal eccentricity. NOTE: *Do not rotate crankshaft with Plastigage installed.* If bearing insert and journal appear intact, and are within tolerances, no further main bearing service is required. If bearing or journal appear defective, cause of failure should be determined before replacement. *Remove crankshaft from block (see below). Measure the main bearing journals at each end twice (90° apart) using a micrometer, to determine diameter, journal taper and eccentricity. If journals are within tolerances, reinstall bearing caps at their specified torque. Using a telescope gauge and micrometer, measure bearing I.D. parallel to piston axis and at 30° on each side of piston axis. Subtract journal O.D. from bearing I.D. to determine oil clearance. If crankshaft journals appear defective, or do no meet tolerances, there is no need to measure bearings; for the crankshaft will require grinding and/or undersize bearings will be required. If bearing appears defective, cause for failure should be determined prior to replacement.
Checking the connecting rod bearing clearance:	Connecting rod bearing clearance is checked in the same manner as main bearing clearance, using Plastigage. Before removing the crankshaft, connecting rod side clearance also should be measured and recorded. *Checking connecting rod bearing clearance, using a micrometer, is identical to checking main bearing clearance. If no other service is required, the piston and rod assemblies need not be removed.

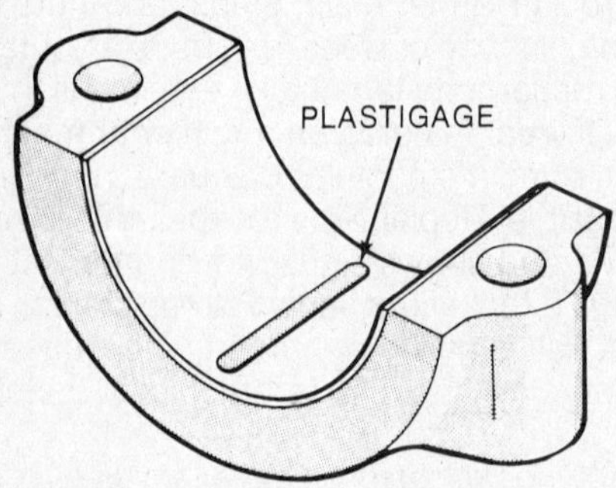

Plastigage® installed on the lower bearing shell

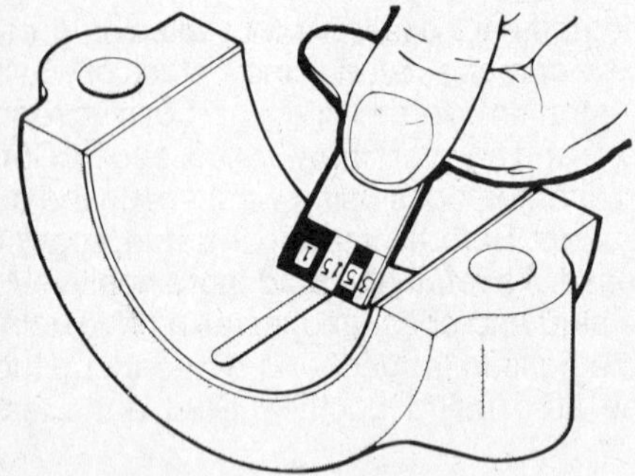
Measuring Plastigage® to determine bearing clearance

CYLINDER HEAD RECONDITIONING

Procedure	Method
Inspect the rocker shaft(s) and rocker arms (OHV engines only):	Remove rocker arms, springs and washers from rocker shaft. NOTE: *Lay out parts in the order as they are removed.* Inspect rocker arms for pitting or wear on the valve contact point, or excessive bushing wear. Bushings need only be replaced if wear is excessive, because the rocker arm normally contacts the shaft at one point only. Grind the valve contact point of rocker arm smooth if necessary, removing as little material as possible. If excessive material must be removed to smooth and square the arm, it should be replaced. Clean out all oil holes and passages in rocker shaft. If shaft is grooved or worn, replace it. Lubricate and assemble the rocker shaft.
Inspect the camshaft bushings and the camshaft (OHC engines):	See next section.
Inspect the pushrods (OHV engines only):	Remove the pushrods, and, if hollow, clean out the oil passages using fine wire. Roll each pushrod over a piece of clean glass. If a distinct clicking sound is heard as the pushrod rolls, the rod is bent, and must be replaced. *The length of all pushrods must be equal. Measure the length of the pushrods, compare to specifications, and replace as necessary.
Inspect the valve lifters (OHV engines only):	Remove lifters from their bores, and remove gum and varnish, using solvent. Clean walls of lifter bores. Check lifters for concave wear as illustrated. If face is worn concave, replace lifter, and carefully inspect the camshaft. Lightly lubricate lifter and insert it into its bore. If play is excessive, an oversize lifter must be installed (where possible). Consult a machinist concerning feasibility. If play is satisfactory, remove, lubricate, and reinstall the lifter. NOTE: *1981 and later G.M. diesel V8 valve lifters have roller cam followers. Check these for smooth operation and wear. The roller should rotate freely, but without excessive play. Check the rollers for missing or broken needle bearings. If the roller is pitted or rough, check the camshaft lobe for wear.*
*Testing hydraulic lifter leak down (OHV gasoline engines only):	Submerge lifter in a container of kerosene. Chuck a used pushrod or its equivalent into a drill press. Position container of kerosene so pushrod acts on the lifter plunger. Pump lifter with the drill press, until resistance increases. Pump several more times to bleed any air out of lifter. Apply very firm, constant pressure to the lifter, and observe rate at which fluid bleeds out of lifter. If the fluid bleeds very quickly (less than 15 seconds), lifter is defective. If the time exceeds 60 seconds, lifter is sticking. In either case, recondition or replace lifter. If lifter is operating properly (leak down time 15–60 seconds), lubricate and install it.

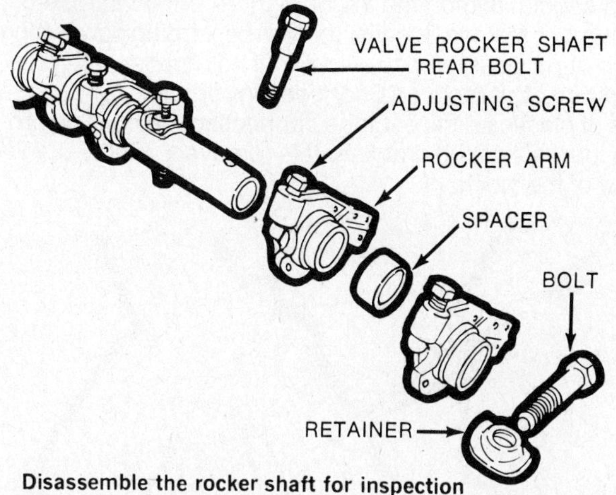

Disassemble the rocker shaft for inspection

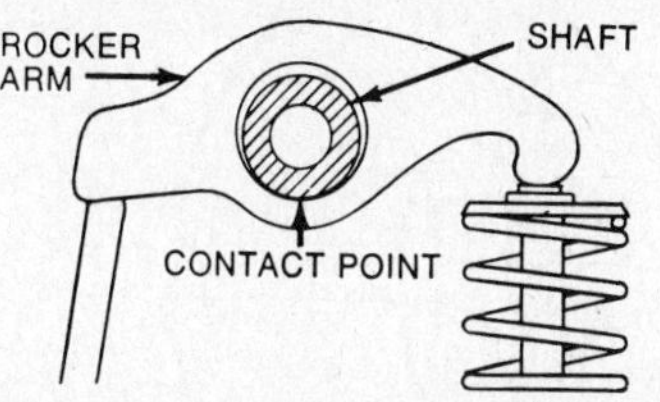

Rocker arm-to-rocker shaft contact area

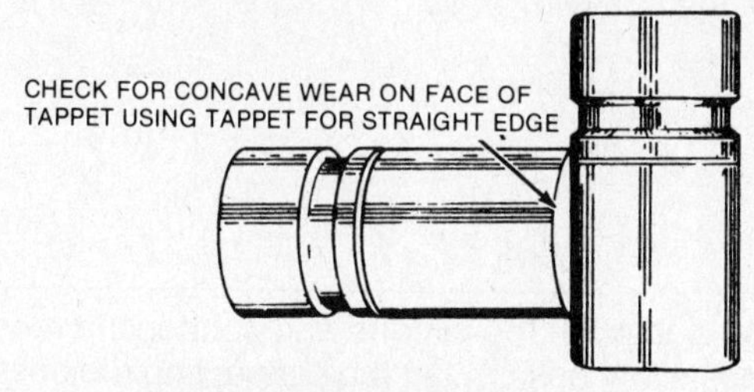

Checking the lifter face

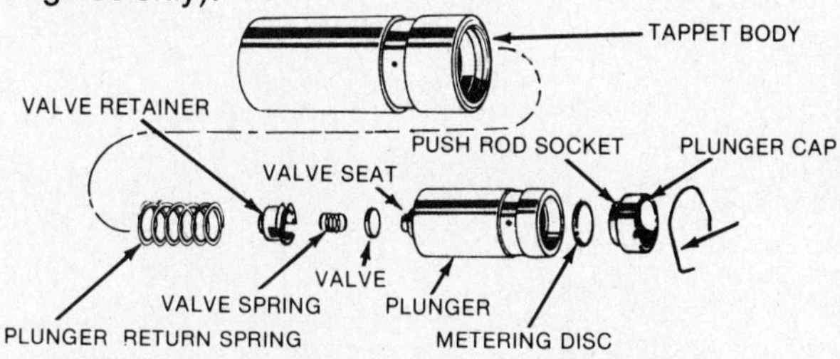

Typical exploded view of hydraulic valve lifter

CYLINDER BLOCK RECONDITIONING

Procedure	Method
Removing the crankshaft:	Using a punch, mark the corresponding main bearing caps and saddles according to position (i.e., one punch on the front main cap and saddle, two on the second, three on the third, etc.). Using number stamps, identify the corresponding connecting rods and caps, according to cylinder (if no numbers are present). Remove the main and connecting rod caps, and place sleeves of plastic tubing over the connecting rod bolts, to protect the journals as the crankshaft is removed. Lift the crankshaft out of the block.

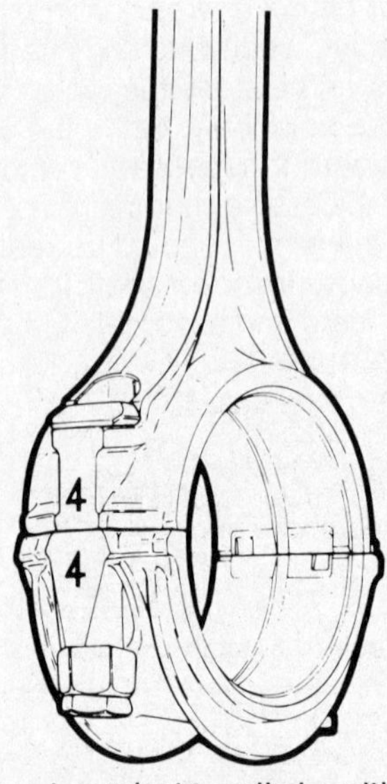

Connecting rod matched to cylinder with a number stamp

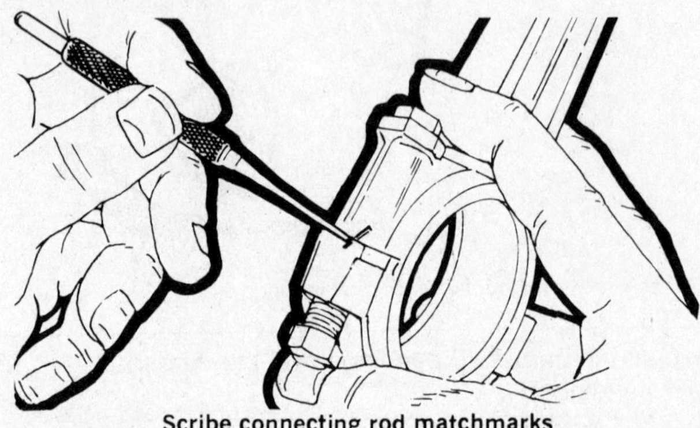
Scribe connecting rod matchmarks

Procedure	Method
Remove the ridge from the top of the cylinder:	In order to facilitate removal of the piston and connecting rod, the ridge at the top of the cylinder (unworn area; see illustration) must be removed. Place the piston at the bottom of the bore, and cover it with a rag. Cut the ridge away using a ridge reamer, exercising extreme care to avoid cutting to deeply. Remove the rag, and remove cuttings that remain on the piston. CAUTION: *If the ridge is not removed, and new rings are installed, damage to rings will result.*

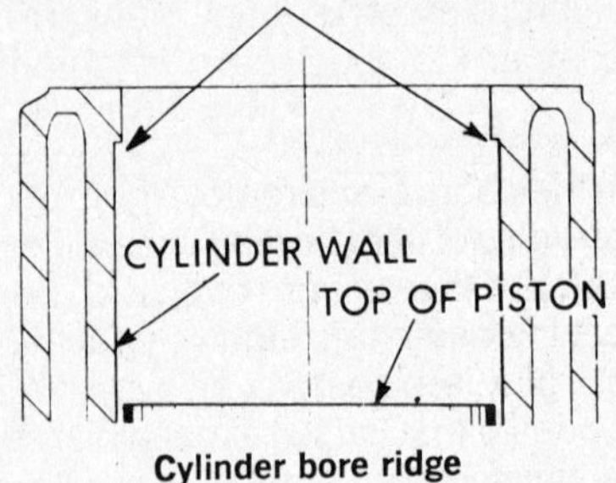

Cylinder bore ridge

Procedure	Method
Removing the piston and connecting rod:	Invert the engine, and push the pistons and connecting rods out of the cylinders. If necessary, tap the connecting rod boss with a wooden hammer handle, to force the piston out. CAUTION: *Do not attempt to force the piston past the cylinder ridge* (see above).

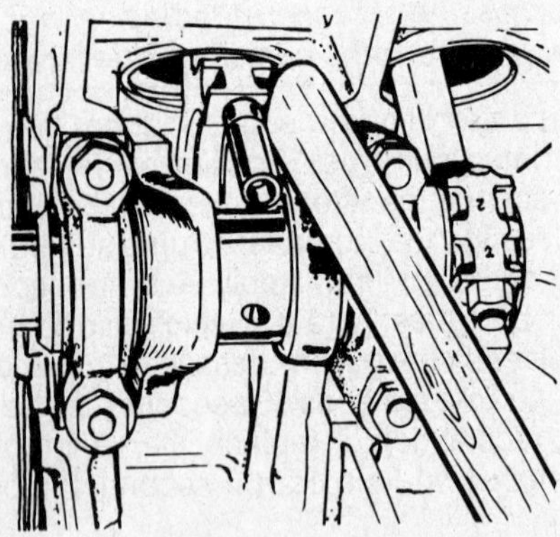
Removing the piston

CYLINDER BLOCK RECONDITIONING

Procedure	Method
Service the crankshaft:	Ensure that all oil holes and passages in the crankshaft are open and free of sludge. If necessary, have the crankshaft ground to the largest possible undersize. **Have the crankshaft Magnafluxed, to locate stress cracks. Consult a machinist concerning additional service procedures, such as surface hardening (e.g., nitriding, Tuftriding) to improve wear characteristics, cross drilling and chamfering the oil holes to improve lubrication, and balancing.
Removing freeze plugs:	Drill a small hole in the middle of the freeze plugs. Thread a large sheet metal screw into the hole and remove the plug with a slide hammer.
Remove the oil gallery plugs:	Threaded plugs should be removed using an appropriate (usually square) wrench. To remove soft, pressed in plugs, drill a hole in the plug, and thread in a sheet metal screw. Pull the plug out by the screw using pliers.
Hot-tank the block: NOTE: *Do not hot-tank aluminum parts.*	Have the block hot-tanked to remove grease, corrosion, and scale from the water jackets. NOTE: *Consult the operator to determine whether the camshaft bearings will be damaged during the hot-tank process.*
Check the block for cracks:	Visually inspect the block for cracks or chips. The most common locations are as follows: Adjacent to freeze plugs. Between the cylinders and water jackets. Adjacent to the main bearing saddles. At the extreme bottom of the cylinders. Check only suspected cracks using spot check dye (see introduction). If a crack is located, consult a machinist concerning possible repairs. **Magnaflux the block to locate hidden cracks. If cracks are located, consult a machinist about feasibility of repair.
Install the oil gallery plugs and freeze plugs:	Coat freeze plugs with sealer and tap into position using a piece of pipe, slightly smaller than the plug, as a driver. To ensure retention, stake the edges of the plugs. Coat threaded oil gallery plugs with sealer and install. Drive replacement soft plugs into block using a large drift as a driver. *Rather than reinstalling lead plugs, drill and tap the holes, and install threaded plugs.
*Check the deck height:	*The deck height is the distance from the crankshaft centerline to the block deck. To measure, invert the engine, and install the crankshaft, retaining it with the center main cap. Measure the distance from the crankshaft journal to the block deck, parallel to the cylinder centerline. Measure the diameter of the end (front and rear) main journals, parallel to the centerline of the cylinders, divide the diameter in half, and subtract it from the previous measurement. The results of the front and rear measurements should be identical. If the difference exceeds .005″, the deck height should be corrected. NOTE: *Block deck height and warpage should be corrected at the same time.*

CYLINDER BLOCK RECONDITIONING

Procedure	Method
Clean and inspect the pistons and connecting rods:	Using a ring expander, remove the rings from the piston. Remove the retaining rings (if so equipped) and remove piston pin. NOTE: *If the piston pin must be pressed out, determine the proper method and use the proper tools; otherwise the piston will distort.* Clean the ring grooves using an appropriate tool, exercising care to avoid cutting too deeply. Thoroughly clean all carbon and varnish from the piston with solvent. CAUTION: *Do not use a wire brush or caustic solvent on pistons.* Inspect the pistons for scuffing, scoring, cracks, pitting, or excessive ring groove wear. If wear is evident, the piston must be replaced. Check the connecting rod length by measuring the rod from the inside of the large end to the inside of the small end using calipers (see illustration). All connecting rods should be equal length. Replace any rod that differs from the others in the engine. *Have the connecting rod alignment checked in an alignment fixture by a machinist. Replace any twisted or bent rods. *Magnaflux the connecting rods to locate stress cracks. If cracks are found, replace the connecting rod.

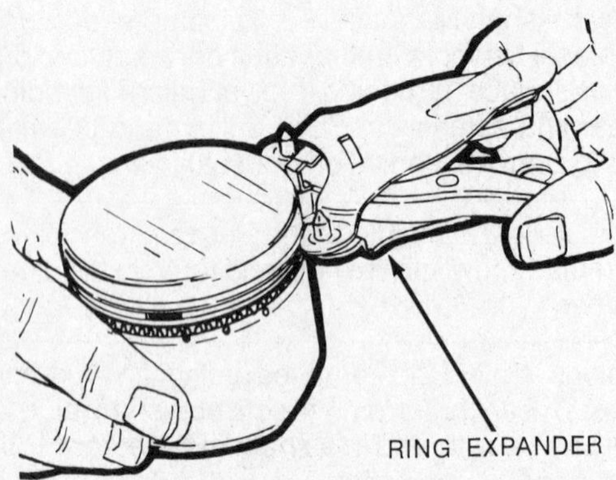

Removing the piston rings

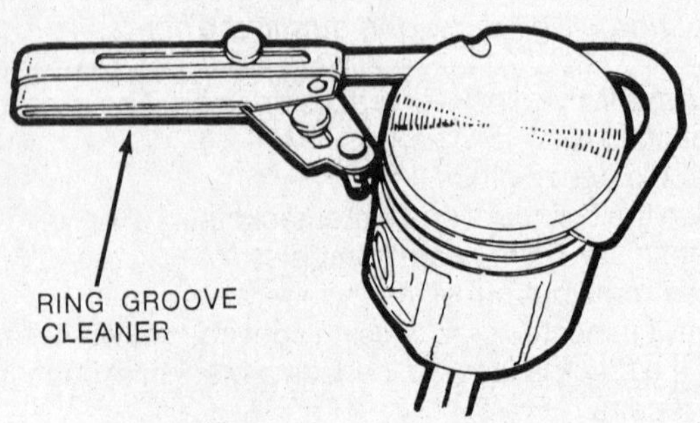

Cleaning the piston ring grooves

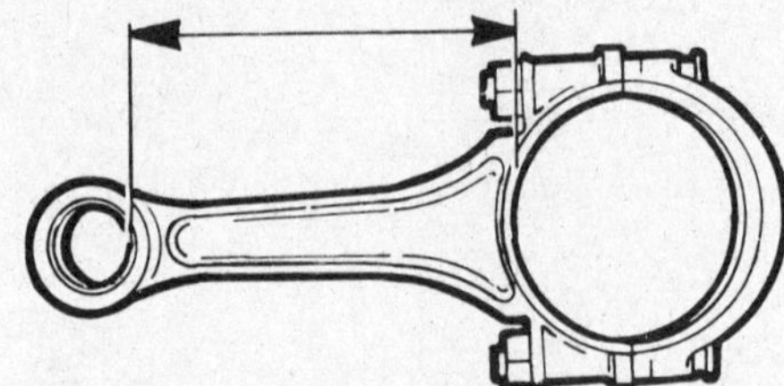
Check the connecting rod length (arrow)

Procedure	Method
Fit the pistons to the cylinders:	Using a telescope gauge and micrometer, or a dial gauge, measure the cylinder bore diameter perpendicular to the piston pin, 2½° below the deck. Measure the piston perpendicular to its pin on the skirt. The difference between the two measurements is the piston clearance. If the clearance is within specifications or slightly below (after boring or honing), finish honing is all that is required. If the clearance is excessive, try to obtain a slightly larger piston to bring clearance within specifications. Where this is not possible, obtain the first oversize piston, and hone (or if necessary, bore) the cylinder to size.

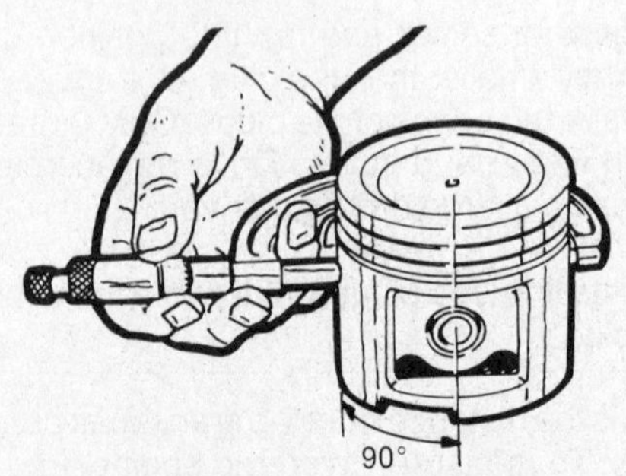

Measuring the piston prior to fitting

Procedure	Method
Assemble the pistons and connecting rods:	Inspect piston pin, connecting rod small end bushing, and piston bore for galling, scoring, or excessive wear. If evident, replace defective part(s). Measure the I.D. of the piston boss and connecting rod small end, and the O.D. of the piston pin. I within specifications, assemble piston pin and rod. CAUTION: *If piston pin must be pressed in, determine the proper method and use the proper tools; otherwise the piston will distort.*

CYLINDER BLOCK RECONDITIONING

Procedure	Method
Check the block deck for warpage:	Using a straightedge and feeler gauges, check the block deck for warpage in the same manner that the cylinder head is checked (see Cylinder Head Reconditioning). If warpage exceeds specifications, have the deck resurfaced. NOTE: *In certain cases a specification for total material removal (Cylinder head and block deck) is provided. This specification must not be exceeded.*
Check the bore diameter and surface:	Visually inspect the cylinder bores for roughness, scoring, or scuffing. If evident, the cylinder bore must be bored or honed oversize to eliminate imperfections, and the smallest possible oversize piston used. The new pistons should be given to the machinist with the block, so that the cylinders can be bored or honed exactly to the piston size (plus clearance). If no flaws are evident, measure the bore diameter using a telescope gauge and micrometer, or dial guage, parallel and perpendicular to the engine centerline, at the top (below the ridge) and bottom of the bore. Subtract the bottom measurements from the top to determine taper, and the parallel to the centerline measurements from the perpendicular measurements to determine eccentricity. If the measurements are not within specifications, the cylinder must be bored or honed, and an oversize piston installed. If the measurements are within specifications the cylinder may be used as is, with only finish honing (see below). NOTE: *Prior to boring, check the block deck warpage, height and bearing alignment.* CAUTION: *The 4 cyl. 140 G.M. engine cylinder walls are impregnated with silicone. Boring or honing can be done only by a shop with the proper equipment.*

Measuring the cylinder bore with a dial gauge

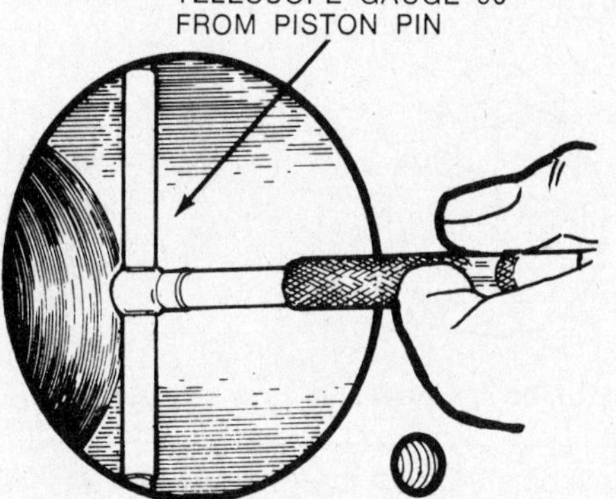

Measuring cylinder bore with a telescope gauge

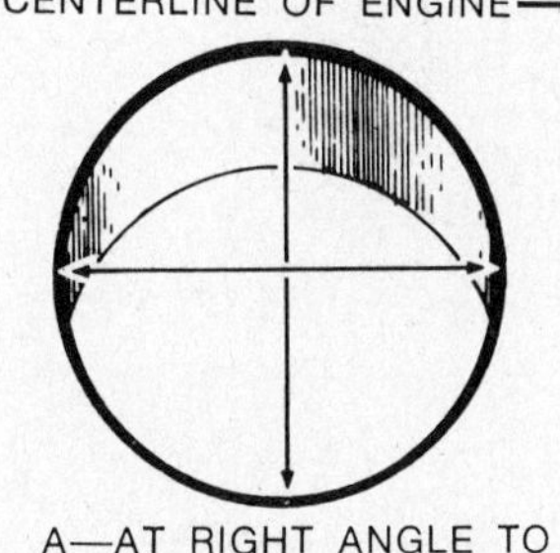

Cylinder bore measuring points

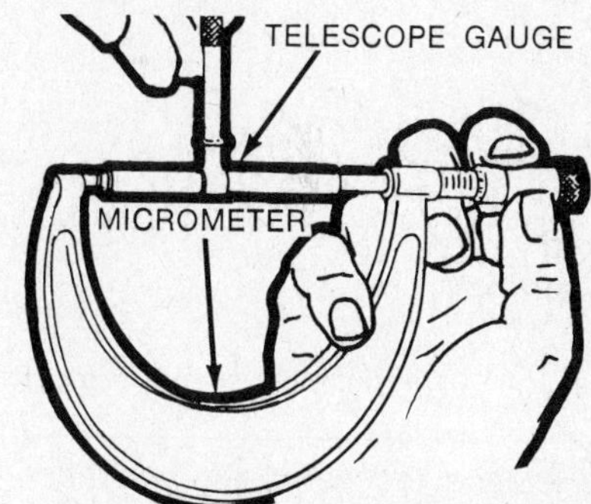

Determining cylinder bore by measuring telescope gauge with a micrometer

Procedure	Method
Check the cylinder block bearing alignment:	Remove the upper bearing inserts. Place a straightedge in the bearing saddles along the centerline of the crankshaft. If clearance exists between the straightedge and the center saddle, the block must be alignbored.

Checking main bearing saddle alignment

CYLINDER BLOCK RECONDITIONING

Procedure	Method
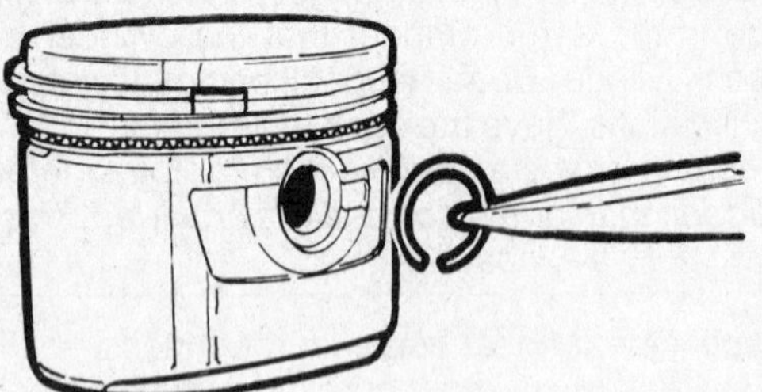 Installing piston pin lock rings	Install the lock rings; ensure that they seat properly. If the parts are not within specifications, determine the service method for the type of engine. In some cases, piston and pin are serviced as an assembly when either is defective. Others specify reaming the piston and connecting rods for an oversize pin. If the connecting rod bushing is worn, it may in many cases be replaced. Reaming the piston and replacing the rod bushing are machine shop operations.
Clean and inspect the camshaft: 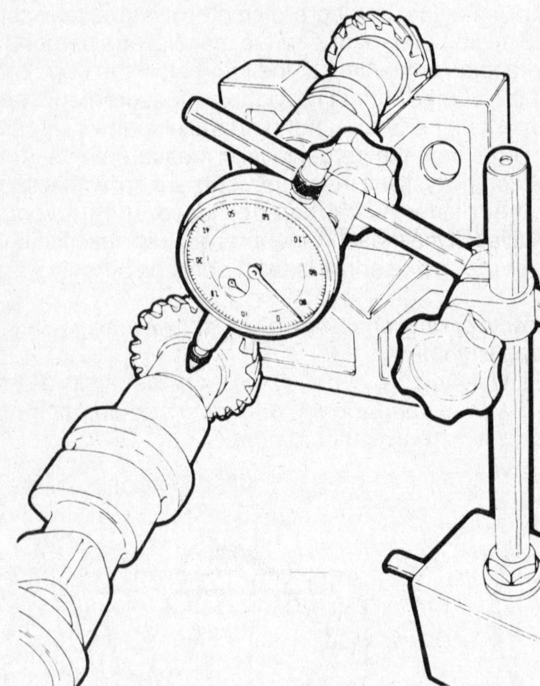 Checking the camshaft for straightness	Degrease the camshaft, using solvent, and clean out all oil holes. Visually inspect cam lobes and bearing journals for excessive wear. If a lobe is questionable, check all lobes as indicated below. If a journal or lobe is worn, the camshaft must be reground or replaced. NOTE: *If a journal is worn, there is a good chance that the bushings are worn.* If lobes and journals appear intact, place the front and rear journals in V-blocks, and rest a dial indicator on the center journal. Rotate the camshaft to check straightness. If deviation exceeds .001°, replace the camshaft. *Check the camshaft lobes with a micrometer, by measuring the lobes from the nose to base and again at 90° (see illustration). The lift is determined by subtracting the second measurement from the first. If all exhaust lobes and all intake lobes are not identical, the camshaft must be reground or replaced. 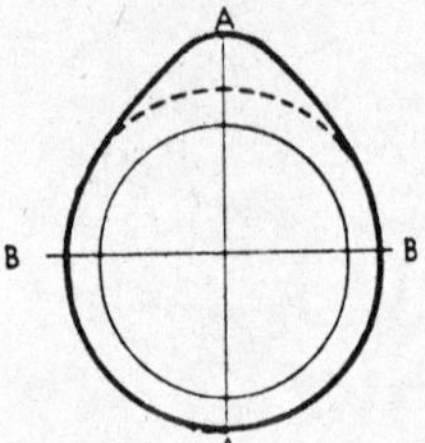 Camshaft lobe measurement
Replace the camshaft bearings (OHV engines only): 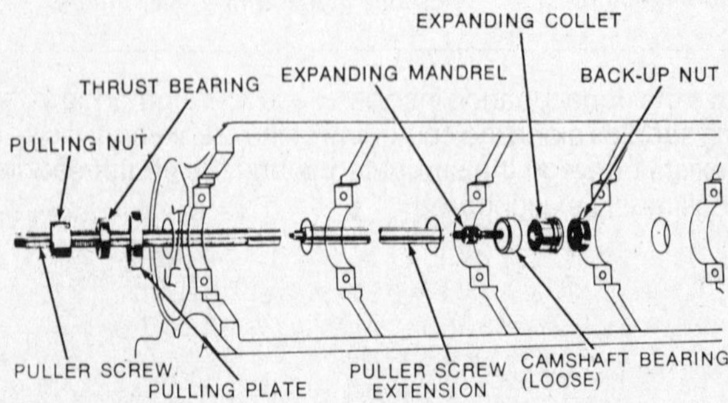 Camshaft removal and installation tool (typical)	If excessive wear is indicated, or if the engine is being completely rebuilt, camshaft bearings should be replaced as follows: Drive the camshaft rear plug from the block. Assemble the removal puller with its shoulder on the bearing to be removed. Gradually tighten the puller nut until bearing is removed. Remove remaining bearings, leaving the front and rear for last. To remove front and rear bearings, reverse position of the tool, so as to pull the bearings in toward the center of the block. Leave the tool in this position, pilot the new front and rear bearings on the installer, and pull them into position: Return the tool to its original position and pull remaining bearings into postion. NOTE: *Ensure that oil holes align when installing bearings.* Replace camshaft rear plug, and stake it into position to aid retention.

CYLINDER BLOCK RECONDITIONING

Procedure	Method
Finish hone the cylinders: 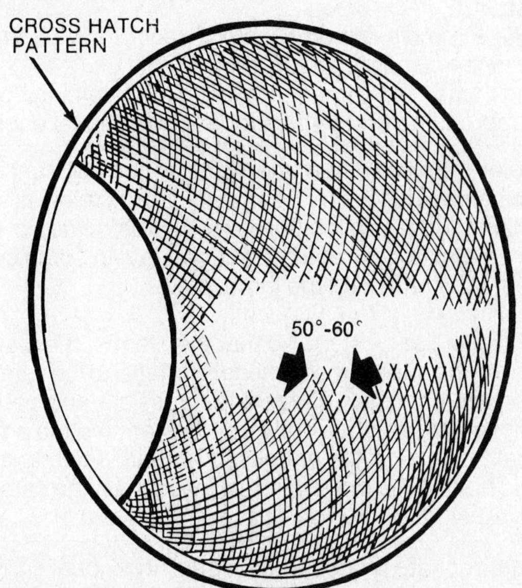	Chuck a flexible drive hone into a power drill, and insert it into the cylinder. Start the hone, and move it up and down the cylinder at a rate which will produce approximately a 60° crosshatch pattern (see illustration). NOTE: *Do not extend the hone below the cylinder bore.* After developing the pattern, remove the hone and recheck piston fit. Wash the cylinders with a detergent and water solution to remove abrasive dust, dry, and wipe several times with a rag soaked in engine oil.
Check piston ring end-gap: 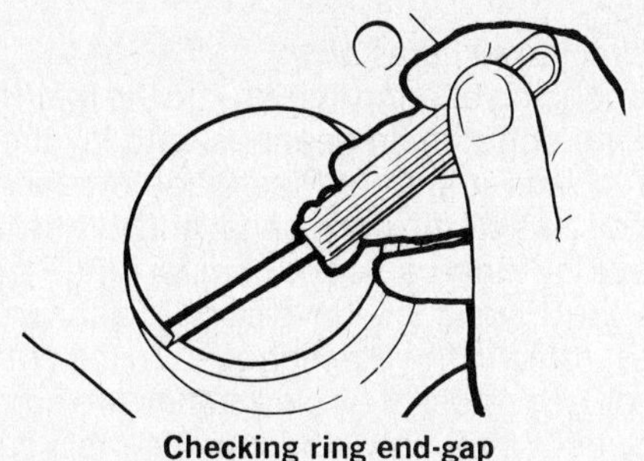 Checking ring end-gap	Compress the piston rings to be used in a cylinder, one at a time, into that cylinder, and press them approximately 1″ below the deck with an inverted piston. Using feeler gauges, measure the ring end-gap, and compare to specifications. Pull the ring out of the cylinder and file the ends with a fine file to obtain proper clearance. CAUTION: *If inadequate ring end-gap is utilized, ring breakage will result.*
Install the piston rings: 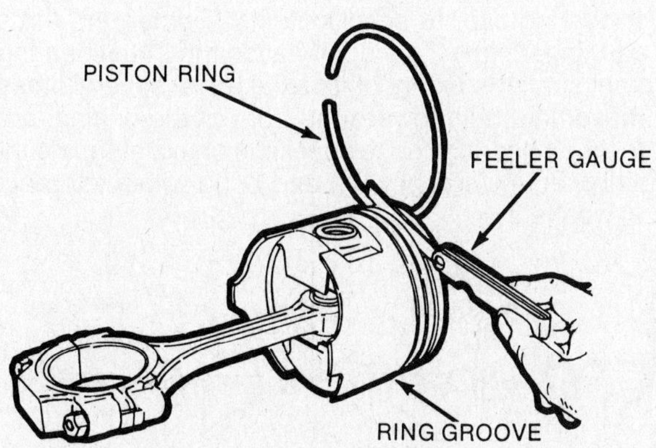 Checking ring side clearance	Inspect the ring grooves in the piston for excessive wear or taper. If necessary, recut the groove(s) for use with an overwidth ring or a standard ring and spacer. If the groove is worn uniformly, overwidth rings, or standard rings and spacers may be installed without recutting. Roll the outside of the ring around the groove to check for burrs or deposits. If any are found, remove with a fine file. Hold the ring in the groove, and measure side clearance. If necessary, correct as indicated above. NOTE: *Always install any additional spacers above the piston ring.* The ring groove must be deep enough to allow the ring to seat below the lands (see illustration). In many cases, a "go-no-go" depth gauge will be provided with the piston rings. Shallow grooves may be corrected by recutting, while deep grooves require some type of filler or expander behind the piston. Consult the piston ring supplier concerning the suggested method. Install the rings on the piston, lowest ring first, using a ring expander. NOTE: *Position the ring markings as specified by the manufacturer (see car section).*

CYLINDER BLOCK RECONDITIONING

Procedure	Method
Install the camshaft (OHV engines only):	Liberally lubricate the camshaft lobes and journals, and install the camshaft. CAUTION: *Exercise extreme care to avoid damaging the bearings when inserting the camshaft.* Install and tighten the camshaft thrust plate retaining bolts. See the appropriate procedures for each individual engine.
Check camshaft end-play (OHV engines only):	Using feeler gauges, determine whether the clearance between the camshaft boss (or gear) and backing plate is within specifications. Install shims behind the thrust plate, or reposition the camshaft gear and retest end-play. In some cases, adjustment is by replacing the thrust plate. *Mount a dial indicator stand so that the stem of the dial indicator rests on the nose of the camshaft, parallel to the camshaft axis. Push the camshaft as far in as possible and zero the gauge. Move the camshaft outward to determine the amount of camshaft endplay. If the endplay is not within tolerance, install shims behind the thrust plate, or reposition the camshaft gear and retest.
Install the rear main seal (where applicable):	See the appropriate procedures for each individual engine.
Install the crankshaft:	Thoroughly clean the main bearing saddles and caps. Place the upper halves of the bearing inserts on the saddles and press into position. NOTE: *Ensure that the oil holes align.* Press the corresponding bearing inserts into the main bearing caps. Lubricate the upper main bearings, and lay the crankshaft in position. Place a strip of Plastigage on each of the crankshaft journals, install the main caps, and torque to specifications. Remove the main caps, and compare the Plastigage to the scale on the Plastigage envelope. If clearances are within tolerances, remove the Plastigage, turn the crankshaft 90°, wipe off all oil and retest. If all clearances are correct, remove all Plastigage, thoroughly lubricate the main caps and bearing journals, and install the main caps. If clearances are not within tolerance, the upper bearing inserts may be removed, without removing the crankshaft, using a bearing roll out pin (see illustration). Roll in a bearing that will provide proper clearance, and retest. Torque all main caps, excluding the thrust bearing cap, to specifications. Tighten the thrust bearing cap finger tight. To properly align the thrust bearing, pry the crankshaft the extent of its axial travel several times, the last movement held toward the front of the engine, and torque the thrust bearing cap to specifications. Determine the crankshaft end-play (see below), and bring within tolerance with thrust washers.

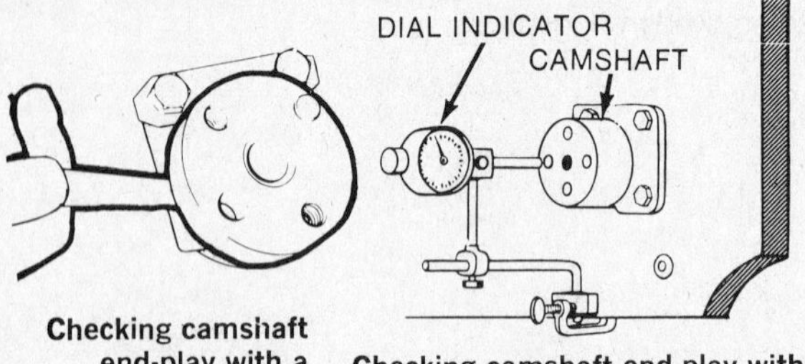

Checking camshaft end-play with a feeler gauge

Checking camshaft end-play with a dial indicator

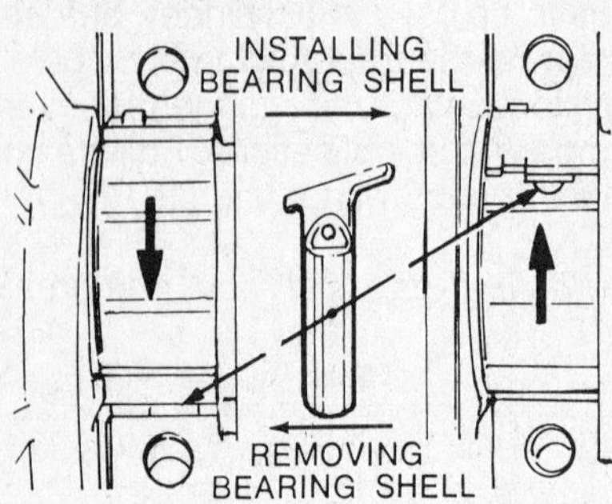

Removal and installation of upper bearing insert using a roll-out pin

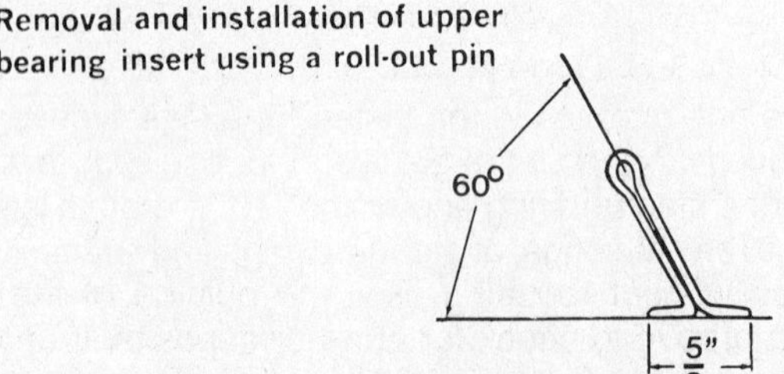

Home-made bearing roll-out pin

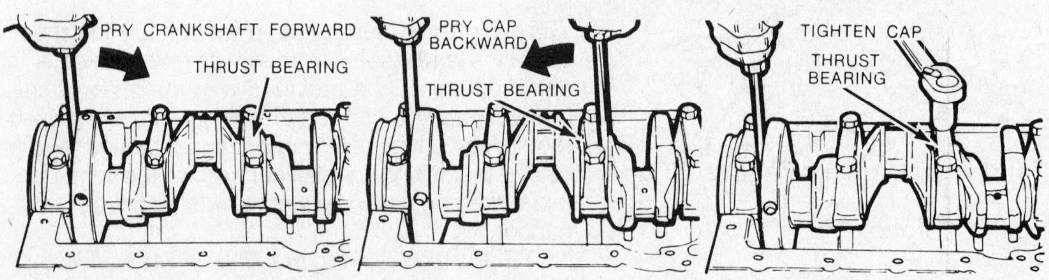

Aligning the thrust bearing

CYLINDER BLOCK RECONDITIONING

Procedure	Method
Measure crankshaft end-play:	Mount a dial indicator stand on the front of the block, with the dial indicator stem resting on the nose of the crankshaft, parallel to the crankshaft axis. Pry the crankshaft the extent of its travel rearward, and zero the indicator. Pry the crankshaft forward and record crankshaft end-play. NOTE: *Crankshaft end-play also may be measured at the thrust bearing, using feeler gauges* (see illustration).

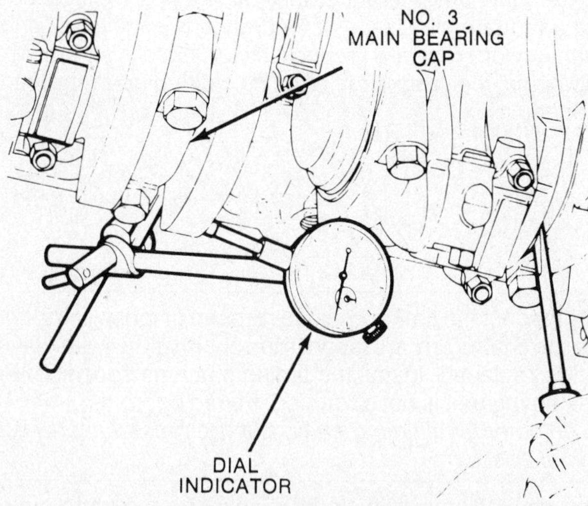

Checking crankshaft end-play with a dial indicator

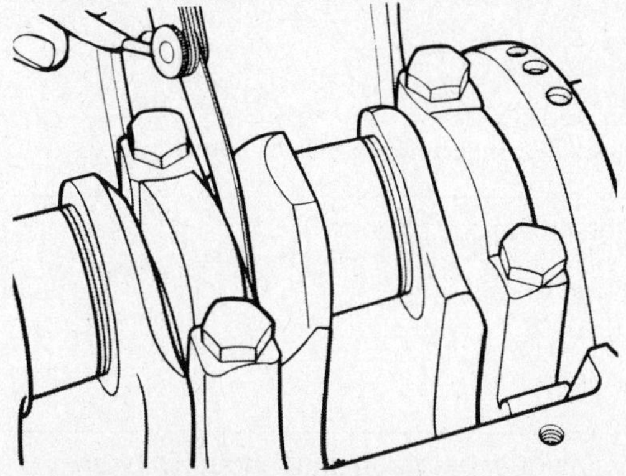
Checking crankshaft end-play with a feeler gauge

Procedure	Method
Install the pistons:	Press the upper connecting rod bearing halves into the connecting rods, and the lower halves into the connecting rod caps. Position the piston ring gaps according to specifications (see car section), and lubricate the pistons. Install a ring compressor on a piston, and press two long (8″) pieces of plastic tubing over the rod bolts. Using the tubes as a guide, press the pistons into the bores and onto the crankshaft with a wooden hammer handle. After seating the rod on the crankshaft journal, remove the tubes and install the cap finger tight. Install the remaining pistons in the same manner. Invert the engine and check the bearing clearance at two points (90° apart) on each journal with Plastigage. NOTE: *Do not turn the crankshaft with Plastigage installed.* If clearance is within tolerances, remove *all* Plastigage, thoroughly lubricate the journals, and torque the rod caps to specifications. If clearance is not within specifications, install different thickness bearing inserts and recheck. CAUTION: *Never shim or file the connecting rods or caps.* Always install plastic tube sleeves over the rod bolts when the caps are not installed, to protect the crankshaft journals.

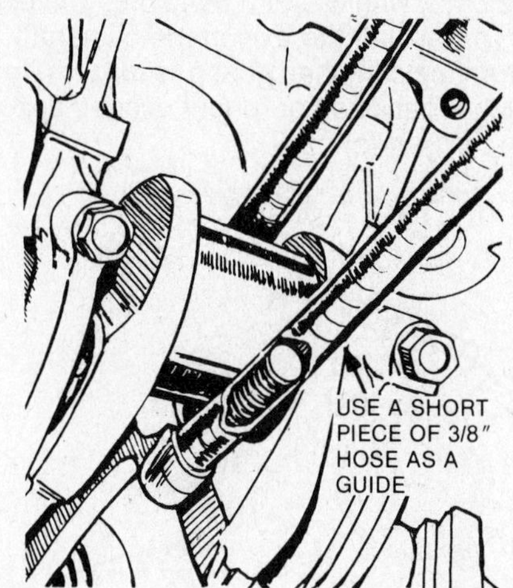

Tubing used to protect crankshaft journals and cylinder walls during piston installation

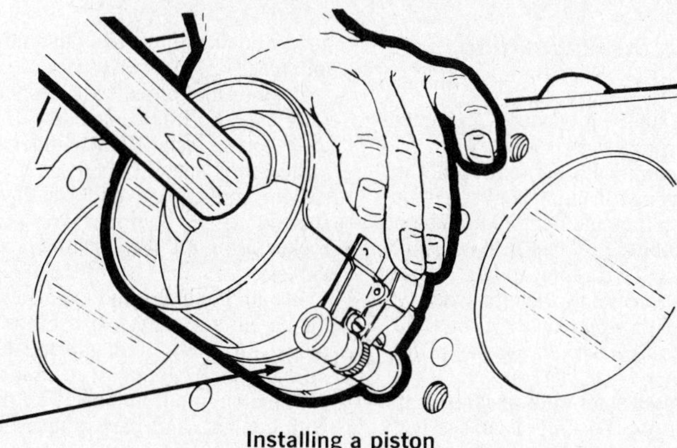

Installing a piston

CYLINDER BLOCK RECONDITIONING

Procedure	Method
Check connecting rod side clearance: 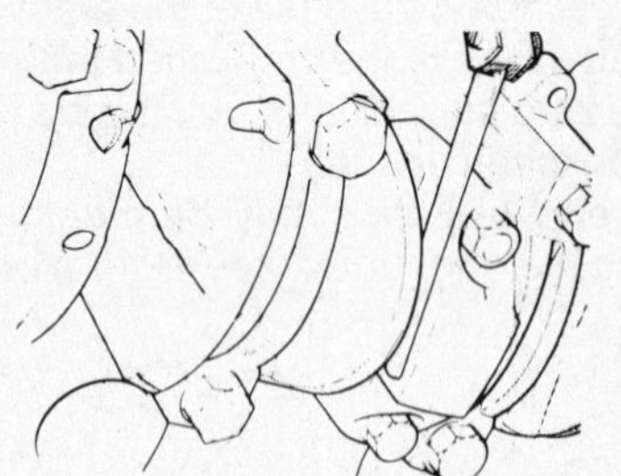 Checking connecting rod side clearance	Determine the clearance between the sides of the connecting rods and the crankshaft, using feeler gauges. If clearance is below the minimum tolerance, the rod may be machined to provide adequate clearance. If clearance is excessive, substitute an unworn rod, and recheck. If clearance is still outside specifications, the crankshaft must be welded and reground, or replaced.
Inspect the timing chain (or belt):	Visually inspect the timing chain for broken or loose links, and replace the chain if any are found. If the chain will flex sideways, it must be replaced. Install the timing chain as specified. Be sure the timing belt is not stretched, frayed or broken. NOTE: *If the original timing chain is to be reused, install it in its original position.*
Check timing gear backlash and runout (OHV engines):  Checking camshaft gear backlash	Mount a dial indicator with its stem resting on a tooth of the camshaft gear (as illustrated). Rotate the gear until all slack is removed, and zero the indicator. Rotate the gear in the opposite direction until slack is removed, and record gear backlash. Mount the indicator with its stem resting on the edge of the camshaft gear, parallel to the axis of the camshaft. Zero the indicator, and turn the camshaft gear one full turn, recording the runout. If either backlash or runout exceed specifications, replace the worn gear(s).  Checking camshaft gear runout

Completing the Rebuilding Process

Following the above procedures, complete the rebuilding process as follows:

Fill the oil pump with oil, to prevent cavitating (sucking air) on initial engine start up. Install the oil pump and the pickup tube on the engine. Coat the oil pan gasket as necessary, and install the gasket and the oil pan. Mount the flywheel and the crankshaft vibration damper or pulley on the crankshaft. NOTE: *Always use new bolts when installing the flywheel.* Inspect the clutch shaft pilot bushing in the crankshaft. If the bushing is excessively worn, remove it with an expanding puller and a slide hammer, and tap a new bushing into place.

Position the engine, cylinder head side up. Lubricate the lifters, and install them into their bores. Install the cylinder head, and torque it as specified. Insert the pushrods (where applicable), and install the rocker shaft(s) (if so equipped) or position the rocker arms on the pushrods. Adjust the valves.

Install the intake and exhaust manifolds, the carburetor(s), the distributor and spark plugs. Adjust the point gap and the static ignition timing. Mount all accessories and install the engine in the car. Fill the radiator with coolant, and the crankcase with high quality engine oil.

Break-in Procedure

Start the engine, and allow it to run at low speed for a few minutes, while checking for leaks. Stop the engine, check the oil level, and fill as necessary. Restart the engine, and fill the cooling system to capacity. Check the point dwell angle and adjust the ignition timing and the valves. Run the engine at low to medium speed (800–2500 rpm) for approximately ½ hour, and retorque the cylinder head bolts. Road test the car, and check again for leaks.

Follow the manufacturer's recommended engine break-in procedure and maintenance schedule for new engines.

Carburetor Service
Import Trucks

23

INDEX

CARBURETOR IDENTIFICATION

All carburetors are identified by code numbers, either stamped on the attaching flange side, the main body or on a metal tag retained by a bowl cover screw. This identification number is important in order to obtain the correct carburetor replacement or parts and to properly adjust the carburetor when matched to a specific engine.

Carburetor Overhaul Tips

When the carburetor is disassembled, wash all parts (except diaphragms, electric choke units, pump plunger, and any other plastic, leather, fiber, or rubber parts) in clean carburetor solvent. Do not leave parts in the solvent any longer than is necessary to sufficiently loosen the deposits. Excessive cleaning may remove the special finish from the float bowl and choke valve bodies, leaving these parts unfit for service. Rinse all parts in clean solvent and blow them dry with compressed air or allow them to air dry. Wipe clean all cork, plastic, leather, and fiber parts with a clean, lint-free cloth.

Blow out all passages and jets with compressed air and be sure that there are no restrictions or blockages. Never use wire or similar tools to clean jets, fuel passages, or air bleeds. Clean all jets and valves separately to avoid accidental interchange. Check all parts for wear or damage. If wear or damage is found, replace the defective parts. Especially check the following:

1. Check the float needle and seat for wear. If wear is found, replace the complete assembly.
2. Check the float hinge pin for wear and the float(s) for dents or distortion. Replace the float if fuel has leaked into it.
3. Check the throttle and choke shaft bores for wear or an out-of-round condition. Damage or wear to the throttle arm, shaft, or shaft bore will often require replacement of the throttle body. These parts require a close tolerance of fit. Wear may allow air leakage, which could affect starting and idling.

NOTE: Throttle shafts and bushings are not included in overhaul kits. They can be purchased separately.

4. Inspect the idle mixture adjusting needles for burrs or grooves. Any such condition requires replacement of the needle, since you will not be able to obtain a satisfactory idle.

5. Test the accelerator pump check valves. They should pass air one way but not the other. Test for proper seating by blowing and sucking on the valve. Replace the valve if necessary. If the valve is satisfactory, wash the valve again to remove breath moisture.

6. Check the bowl cover for warped surfaces with a straight edge.

7. Closely inspect the valves and seats for wear and damage, replacing as necessary.

8. After the carburetor is assembled, check the choke valve for freedom of operation.

Carburetor overhaul kits are recommended for each overhaul. These kits contain all gaskets and new parts to replace those that deteriorate most rapidly. Failure to replace all parts supplied with the kit (especially gaskets) can result in poor performance later.

After cleaning and checking all components, reassemble the carburetor, using new parts and referring to the exploded view. When reassembling, make sure that all screws and jets are tight in their seats, but do not overtighten as the tips will be distorted. Tighten all screws gradually, in rotation. Do not tighten needle valves into their seats. Uneven jetting will result. Always use new gaskets. Be sure to adjust the float level, following the instructions contained in the rebuilding kit, when reassembling.

CHRYSLER/MITSUBISHI CARBURETORS

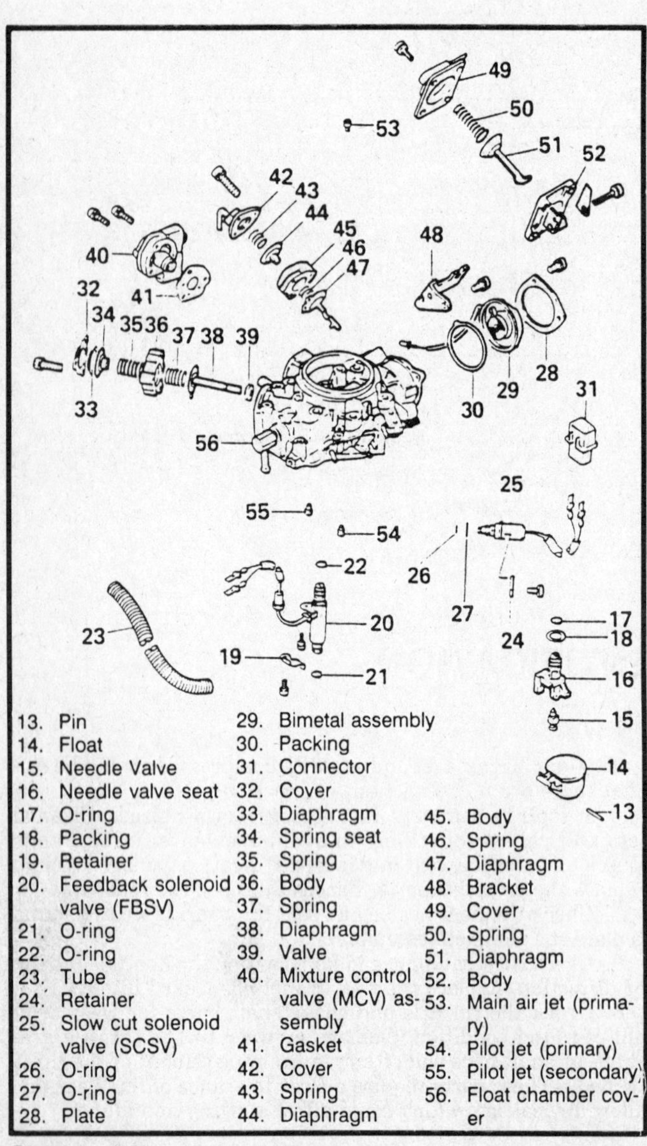

Chrysler/Mitsubishi exploded view – upper half typical

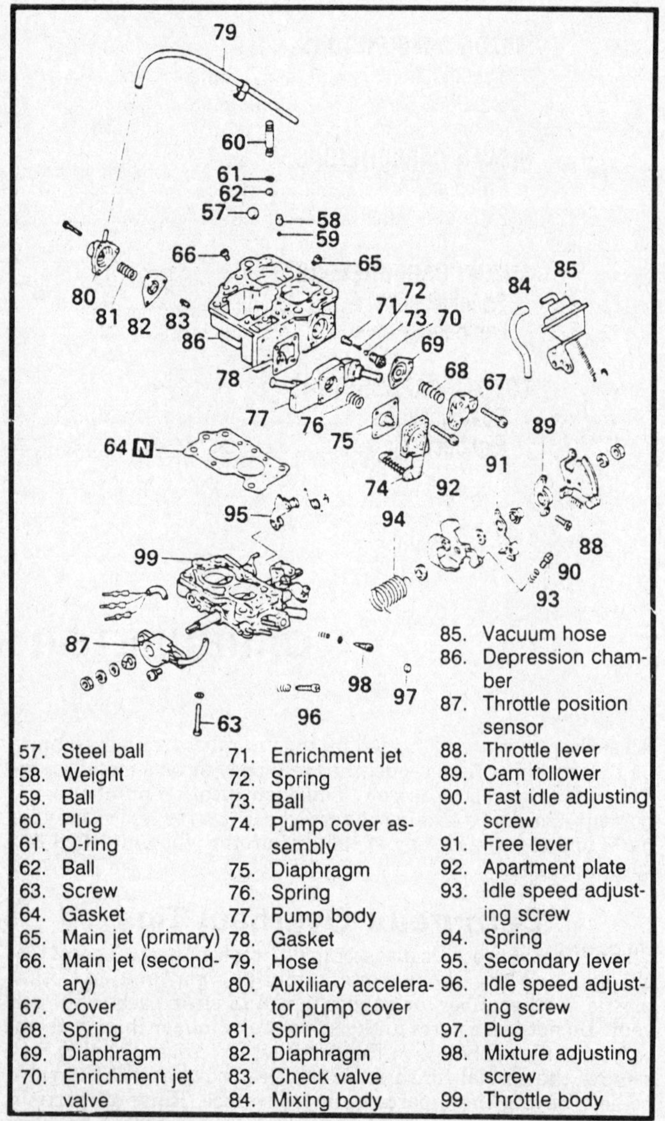

Chrysler/Mitsubishi exploded view – lower half typical

CHRYSLER/MITSUBISHI CARBURETORS

(All measurements in inches or degrees)

Year	Carburetor Number	Float Level	Fast Idle Opening ①	Choke Valve
1983	DIDTA-117	.0394	12°	②
	DIDTA-121	.0394	12°	②
	DIDTA-118	.0394	13°	②
	DIDTA-106	.0394	13°	②
	DIDTA-107	.0394	14°	②
	DIDTA-115	.0394	12°	②
	DIDTA-116	.0394	13°	②
	DIDTA-104	.0394	13°	②
	DIDTA-105	.0394	14°	②
1984	DIDTA-177	.0394	12°	②
	DIDTA-179	.0394	12°	②
	DIDTA-178	.0394	13°	②
	DIDTA-182	.0394	13°	②
	DIDTA-183	.0394	14°	②
	DIDTA-165	.0394	12°	②
	DIDTA-166	.0394	13°	②
	DIDTA-167	.0394	12°	②
	DIDTA-168	.0394	13°	②
	DIDTA-169	.0394	14°	②
	DIDTA-170	.0394	13.5°	②
	DIDTA-171	.0394	14.5°	②
	DIDTA-175	.0394	12°	②
	DIDTA-176	.0394	13°	②
	DIDTA-180	.0394	13°	②
	DIDTA-181	.0394	14°	②
	DIDTA-184	.0394	13.5°	②
	DIDTA-185	.0394	14.5°	②
	DIDTA-186	.0394	13.5°	②
	DIDTA-187	.0394	14.5°	②
1985	DIDTF-205	.0394	.025	②
	DIDTF-206	.0394	.028	②
	DIDTF-207	.0394	.028	②
	DIDTF-208	.0394	.031	②
	DIDTA-209	.0394	.028	②
	DIDTA-210	.0394	.031	②
1986	DIDTA-209	.0394	.028°	②
	DIDTA-210	.0394	.031°	②
	DIDTF-205	.0394	.025°	②
	DIDTF-206	.0394	.028°	②
	DIDTF-207	.0394	.028°	②
	DIDTF-208	.0394	.031°	②
1987-88	DIDEF-400	.0394	—	②
	DIDEF-401	.0394	—	②
	DIDEF-402	.0394	—	②

CHRYSLER/MITSUBISHI CARBURETORS

(All measurements in inches or degrees)

Year	Carburetor Number	Float Level	Fast Idle Opening ①	Choke Valve
1987-88	DIDEF-403	.0394	—	②
	DIDEF-404	.0394	—	②
	DIDEF-405	.0394	—	②
	DIDEF-406	.0394	—	②
	DIDEF-407	.0394	—	②
	DIDEF-410	.0394	—	②
	DIDEF-411	.0394	—	②
	DIDEF-412	.0394	—	②
	DIDEF-413	.0394	—	②

① @ 73°F
② Align marks on choke pinion and cam lever

ISUZU CARBURETORS

ISUZU CARBURETORS Stromberg Models

(All numbers are OEM jet numbers unless otherwise specified)

Year	Carburetor Number	Main Jet		Main Air Bleed		Slow Jet		Slow Jet Air Bleed		Float Level (in.)	Power Jet
		Primary	Secondary	Primary	Secondary	Primary	Secondary	Primary	Secondary		
1982	DCH340-227	114	170	120	70	50	100	150	100	.059	50
	DCH340-228	114	170	120	70	50	100	150	100	.059	50
	DFP340-3	93	180	100	90	53	125	120	130	.059	—
	DFP340-4	93	180	100	90	53	125	120	130	.059	—
	DCR384	108	170	85	60	50	100	160	0	.059	—
	DFP384	88	170	100	60	52	100	150	0	.059	—
1983	DCH340-227	114	170	120	70	50	100	150	100	.059	50
	DCH340-228	114	170	120	70	50	100	150	100	.059	50
	DFP340-3	93	180	100	90	53	125	120	130	.059	—
	DFP340-4	93	180	100	90	53	125	120	130	.059	—
	DCR384	108	170	85	60	50	100	160	0	.059	—
	DFP384	88	170	100	60	52	100	150	0	.059	—
1984	DCH340-227	114	170	120	70	50	100	150	100	.059	50
	DCH340-228	114	170	120	70	50	100	150	100	.059	50
	DFP340-3	93	180	100	90	53	125	120	130	.059	—
	DFP340-4	93	180	100	90	53	125	120	130	.059	—
	DCR384	108	170	85	60	50	100	160	0	.059	—
	DFP384	88	170	100	60	52	100	150	0	.059	—
1985	DCH340-227	114	170	120	70	50	100	150	100	.059	50
	DCH340-228	114	170	120	70	50	100	150	100	.059	50
	DFP340-3	93	180	100	90	53	125	120	130	.059	—
	DFP340-4	93	180	100	90	53	125	120	130	.059	—
	DCR384	108	170	85	60	50	100	160	0	.059	—
	DFP384	88	170	100	60	52	100	150	0	.059	—

ISUZU CARBURETORS
Stromberg Models

(All numbers are OEM jet numbers unless otherwise specified)

Year	Carburetor Number	Main Jet Primary	Main Jet Secondary	Main Air Bleed Primary	Main Air Bleed Secondary	Slow Jet Primary	Slow Jet Secondary	Slow Jet Air Bleed Primary	Slow Jet Air Bleed Secondary	Float Level (in.)	Power Jet
1986	DCH340-227	114	170	120	70	50	100	150	100	.059	50
	DCH340-228	114	170	120	70	50	100	150	100	.059	50
	DFP340-3	93	180	100	90	53	125	120	130	.059	—
	DFP340-4	93	180	100	90	53	125	120	130	.059	—
	DCR384	108	170	85	60	50	100	160	0	.059	—
	DFP384	88	170	100	60	52	100	150	0	.059	—
1987-88	DCH340-227	114	170	120	70	50	100	150	100	.059	50
	DCH340-228	114	170	120	70	50	100	150	100	.059	50
	DFP340-3	93	180	100	90	53	125	120	130	.059	—
	DFP340-4	93	180	100	90	53	125	120	130	.059	—
	DCR384	108	170	85	60	50	100	160	0	.059	—
	DFP384	88	170	100	60	52	100	150	0	.059	—

NOTE: Throttle valve opening angle is 16 degrees on all models

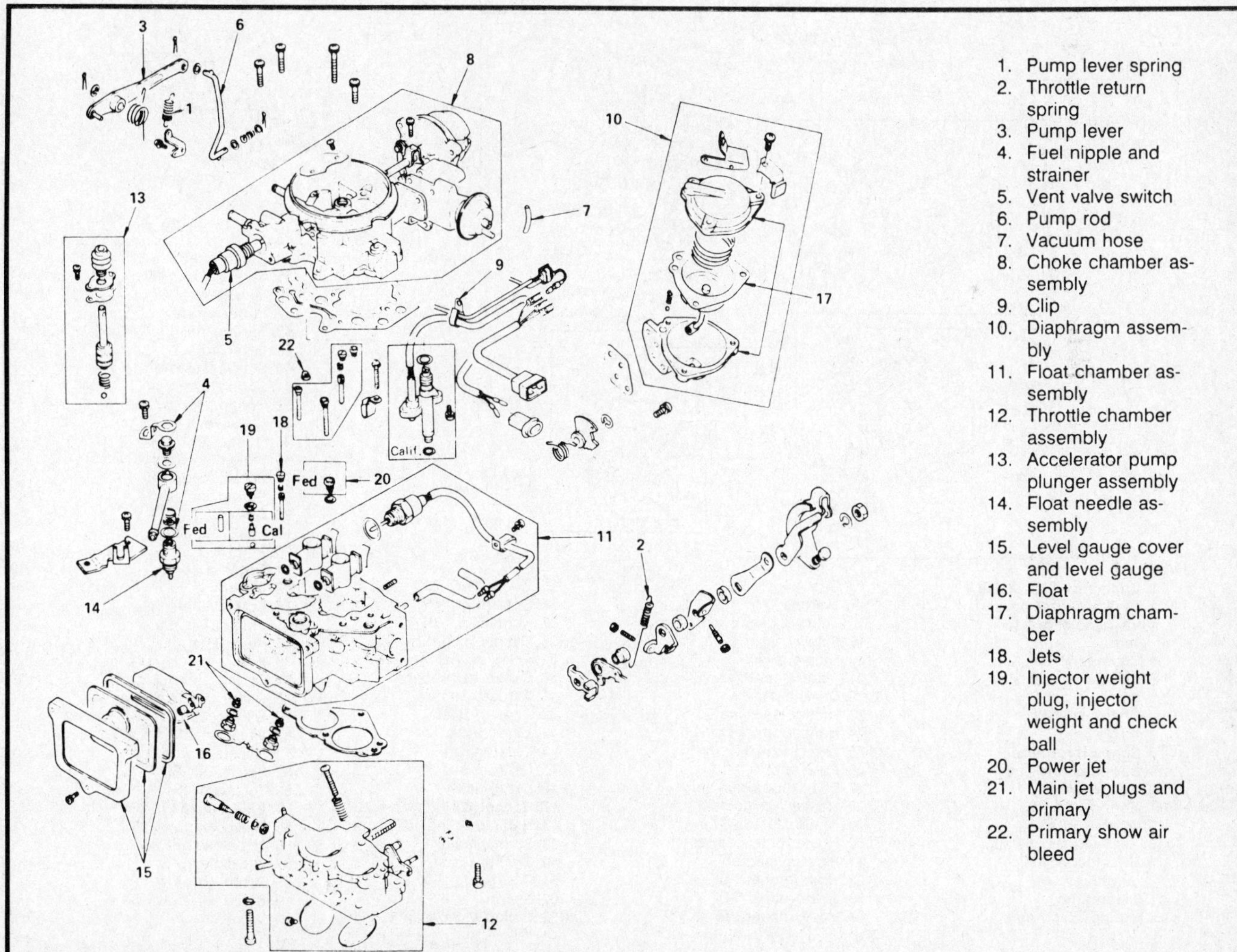

Exploded view of the DCR384/DFP384 carburetor

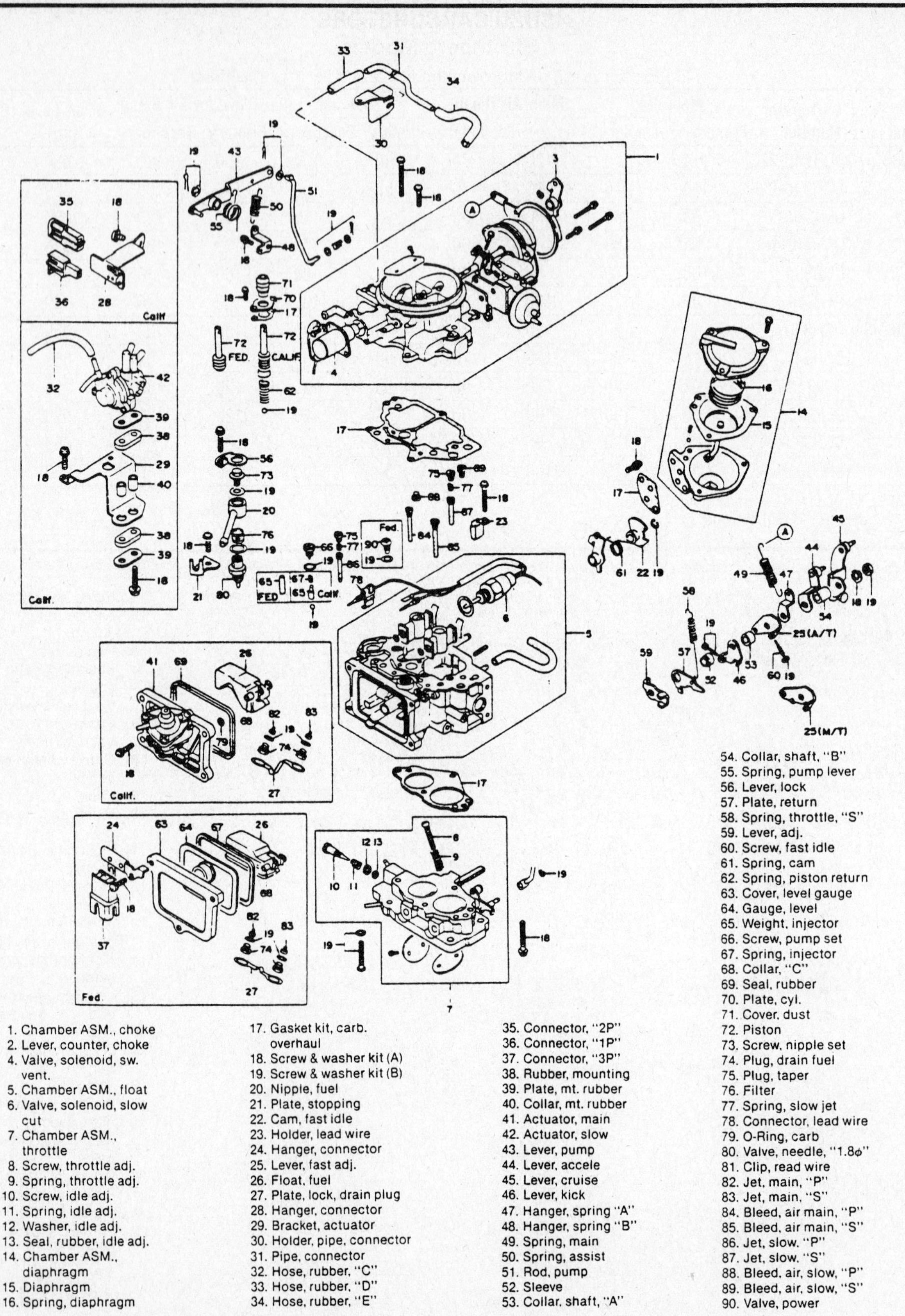
1. Chamber ASM., choke
2. Lever, counter, choke
4. Valve, solenoid, sw. vent.
5. Chamber ASM., float
6. Valve, solenoid, slow cut
7. Chamber ASM., throttle
8. Screw, throttle adj.
9. Spring, throttle adj.
10. Screw, idle adj.
11. Spring, idle adj.
12. Washer, idle adj.
13. Seal, rubber, idle adj.
14. Chamber ASM., diaphragm
15. Diaphragm
16. Spring, diaphragm
17. Gasket kit, carb. overhaul
18. Screw & washer kit (A)
19. Screw & washer kit (B)
20. Nipple, fuel
21. Plate, stopping
22. Cam, fast idle
23. Holder, lead wire
24. Hanger, connector
25. Lever, fast adj.
26. Float, fuel
27. Plate, lock, drain plug
28. Hanger, connector
29. Bracket, actuator
30. Holder, pipe, connector
31. Pipe, connector
32. Hose, rubber, "C"
33. Hose, rubber, "D"
34. Hose, rubber, "E"
35. Connector, "2P"
36. Connector, "1P"
37. Connector, "3P"
38. Rubber, mounting
39. Plate, mt. rubber
40. Collar, mt. rubber
41. Actuator, main
42. Actuator, slow
43. Lever, pump
44. Lever, accele
45. Lever, cruise
46. Lever, kick
47. Hanger, spring "A"
48. Hanger, spring "B"
49. Spring, main
50. Spring, assist
51. Rod, pump
52. Sleeve
53. Collar, shaft, "A"
54. Collar, shaft, "B"
55. Spring, pump lever
56. Lever, lock
57. Plate, return
58. Spring, throttle, "S"
59. Lever, adj.
60. Screw, fast idle
61. Spring, cam
62. Spring, piston return
63. Cover, level gauge
64. Gauge, level
65. Weight, injector
66. Screw, pump set
67. Spring, injector
68. Collar, "C"
69. Seal, rubber
70. Plate, cyl.
71. Cover, dust
72. Piston
73. Screw, nipple set
74. Plug, drain fuel
75. Plug, taper
76. Filter
77. Spring, slow jet
78. Connector, lead wire
79. O-Ring, carb
80. Valve, needle, "1.8φ"
81. Clip, read wire
82. Jet, main, "P"
83. Jet, main, "S"
84. Bleed, air main, "P"
85. Bleed, air main, "S"
86. Jet, slow, "P"
87. Jet, slow, "S"
88. Bleed, air, slow, "P"
89. Bleed, air, slow, "S"
90. Valve, power

Exploded view of Stromberg DCH340 carburetor

MAZDA CARBURETORS

MAZDA CARBURETORS

(All measurements in inches)

Year	Engine (cc)	Fast Idle Cam	Float Level	Choke Valve Opening	Choke Diaphragm	Choke Unloader	Secondary Throttle Valve
1982	1970	0.051–0.059	0.335	0.016–0.028 ③	0.047–0.067 ②	0.079–0.099	0.256
	1998	0.029–0.044	0.453–0.492	0.023–0.039	0.066–0.084	0.107–0.141	0.289–0.325
	2555	0.033–0.041	0.457–0.496 ⑦	0.024–0.045	0.067–0.085	0.110–0.143	0.289–0.325
1983	1970	0.051–0.059	0.335	0.016–0.028 ③	0.047–0.067 ②	0.079–0.099	0.256
	1998	0.029–0.044	0.453–0.492	0.023–0.039	0.066–0.084	0.107–0.141	0.289–0.325
	2555	0.033–0.041	0.457–0.496 ⑦	0.024–0.045	0.067–0.085	0.110–0.143	0.289–0.325
1984	1970	0.051–0.059	0.335	0.016–0.028 ③	0.047–0.067 ②	0.079–0.099	0.256
	1998	0.029–0.044	0.453–0.492	0.023–0.039	0.066–0.084	0.107–0.141	0.289–0.325
	2555	0.033–0.041	0.457–0.496 ⑦	0.024–0.045	0.067–0.085	0.110–0.143	0.289–0.325
1985	1970	0.051–0.059	0.335	0.016–0.028 ③	0.047–0.067 ②	0.079–0.099	0.256
	1998	0.029–0.044	0.453–0.492	0.023–0.039	0.066–0.084	0.107–0.141	0.289–0.325
	2555	0.033–0.041	0.457–0.496 ⑦	0.024–0.045	0.067–0.085	0.110–0.143	0.289–0.325
1986	1970	0.051–0.059	0.335	0.016–0.028 ③	0.047–0.067 ②	0.079–0.099	0.256
	1998	0.029–0.044	0.453–0.492	0.023–0.039	0.066–0.084	0.107–0.141	0.289–0.325
	2555	0.033–0.041	0.457–0.496 ⑦	0.024–0.045	0.067–0.085	0.110–0.143	0.289–0.325
1987-88	1970	0.051–0.059	0.335	0.016–0.028 ③	0.047–0.067 ②	0.079–0.099	0.256
	1998	0.029–0.044	0.453–0.492	0.023–0.039	0.066–0.084	0.107–0.141	0.289–0.325
	2555	0.033–0.041	0.457–0.496 ⑦	0.024–0.045	0.067–0.085	0.110–0.143	0.289–0.325

① On 2nd step of fast idle cam
② California models: .065-.085
③ California models: .024-.036
⑦ Auto. Trans. 0.421-0.461

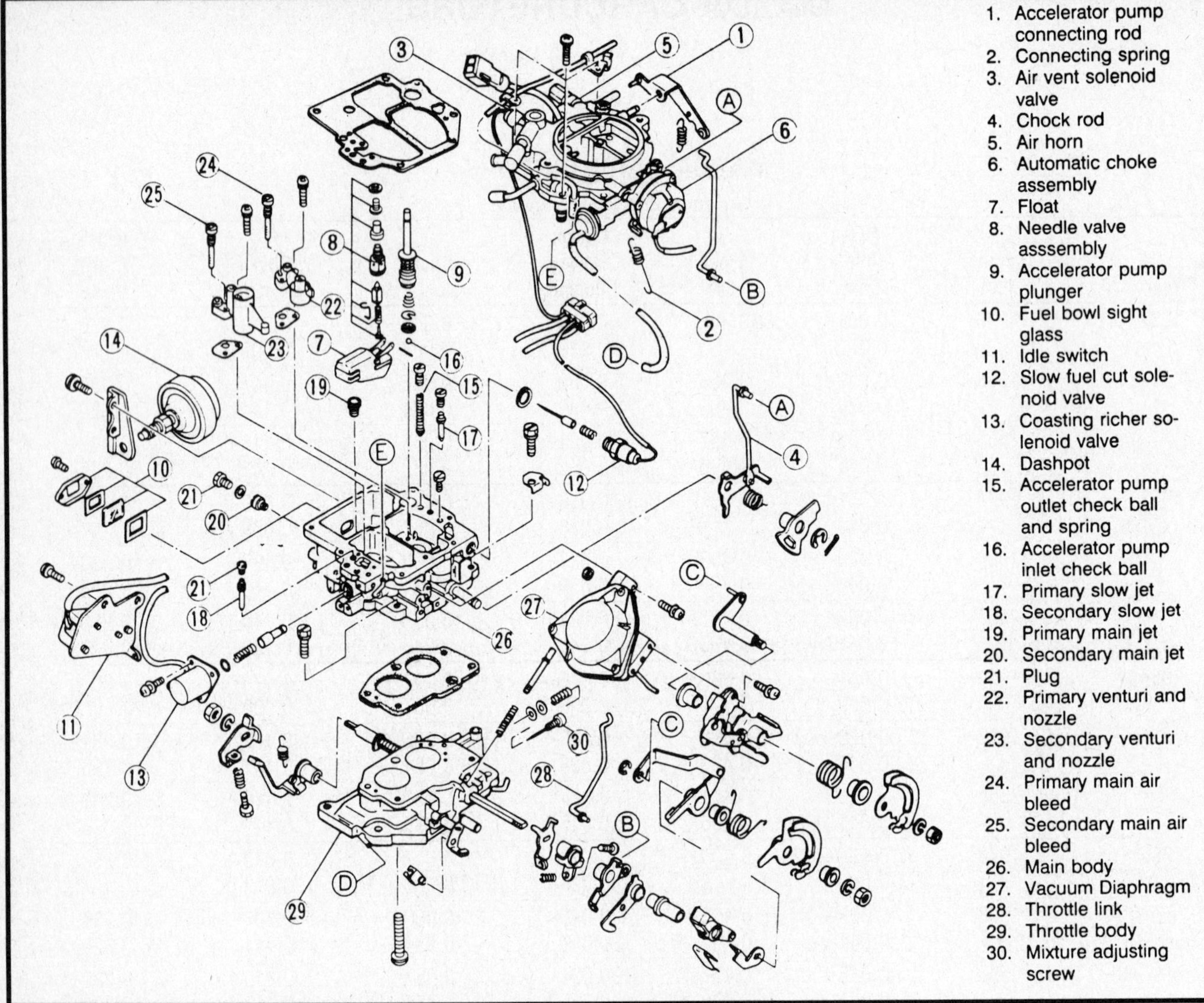

Exploded view of the Mazda 2555cc engine carburetor, others similar

NISSAN (DATSUN) CARBURETORS

NISSAN (DATSUN) CARBURETORS

(All measurements in inches)

Year	Engine	Carburetor Number	Fuel Level	Throttle Valve Gap ①		Vacuum Break ②	Choke Unloader	Dashpot Adjustment (rpm)
				MT	AT			
1982	Z24	DFP384-3 ③	.910	.0280–.0335	.0343–.0398	.1220–.1457	.0807–.1122	1700–1900
		DFP384-4 ③	.910	.0280–.0335	.0343–.0398	.1220–.1457	.0807–.1122	1400–1600
		DFP384-12 ③	.910	.0280–.0335	.0343–.0398	.1220–.1457	.0807–.1122	1700–1900
		DCR384-3	.910	.0280–.0335	.0343–.0398	.0965– ④ .1201	.0807–.1122	1400–1600

NISSAN (DATSUN) CARBURETORS

(All measurements in inches)

Year	Engine	Carburetor Number	Fuel Level	Throttle Valve Gap ① MT	Throttle Valve Gap ① AT	Vacuum Break ②	Choke Unloader	Dashpot Adjustment (rpm)
1982		DCR384-4	.910	.0280–.0335	.0343–.0398	.0965–.1201	.0807–.1122	1400–1600
		CDR384-5 ⑤	.910	.0280–.0335	.0343–.0398	.0913–.1150	.0807–.1122	1400–1600
		DCR384-6 ⑤	.910	.0280–.0335	.0343–.0398	.0913–.1150	.0807–.1122	1400–1600
		DCR384-11A	.910	.0280–.0335	.0343–.0398	.0965–.1201	.0807–.1122	1400–1600
		DCR384-15 ⑤	.910	.0280–.0335	.0343–.0398	.0965–.1201	.0807–.1122	1400–1600
		DCR384-21A	.910	.0280–.0335	.0343–.0398	.0965–.1201	.0807–.1122	1400–1600
		DCR384-25 ⑤	.910	.0280–.0335	.0343–.0398	.0965–.1201	.0807–.1122	1400–1600
	Z20	DCR342-8	.910	.0299–.0354	.0343–.0398	.0965– ④ .1201	0807–.1122	1400–1600
1983	Z24	DFP384-3 ③	.910	.0280–.0335	.0343–.0398	.1220–.1457	.0807–.1122	1700–1900
		DFP384-4 ③	.910	.0280–.0335	.0343–.0398	.1220–.1457	.0807–.1122	1400–1600
		DFP384-12 ③	.910	.0280–.0335	.0343–.0398	.1220–.1457	.0807–.1122	1700–1900
		DCR384-3	.910	.0280–.0335	.0343–.0398	.0965– ④ .1201	0807–.1122	1400–1600
		DCR384-4	.910	.0280–.0335	.0343–.0398	.0965–.1201	.0807–.1122	1400–1600
		CDR384-5 ⑤	.910	.0280–.0335	.0343–.0398	.0913–.1150	.0807–.1122	1400–1600
		DCR384-6 ⑤	.910	.0280–.0335	.0343–.0398	.0913–.1150	.0807–.1122	1400–1600
		DCR384-11A	.910	.0280–.0335	.0343–.0398	.0965–.1201	.0807–.1122	1400–1600
		DCR384-15 ⑤	.910	.0280–.0335	.0343–.0398	.0965–.1201	.0807–.1122	1400–1600
		DCR384-21A	.910	.0280–.0335	.0343–.0398	.0965–.1201	.0807–.1122	1400–1600
		DCR384-25 ⑤	.910	.0280–.0335	.0343–.0398	.0965–.1201	.0807–.1122	1400–1600
	Z20	DCR342-8	.910	.0299–.0354	.0343–.0398	.0965– ④ .1201	0807–.1122	1400–1600
1984	Z24	DFP384-3 ③	.910	.0280–.0335	.0343–.0398	.1220–.1457	.0807–.1122	1700–1900
		DFP384-4 ③	.910	.0280–.0335	.0343–.0398	.1220–.1457	.0807–.1122	1400–1600
		DFP384-12 ③	.910	.0280–.0335	.0343–.0398	.1220–.1457	.0807–.1122	1700–1900
		DCR384-3	.910	.0280–.0335	.0343–.0398	.0965– ④ .1201	.0807–.1122	1400–1600

NISSAN (DATSUN) CARBURETORS

(All measurements in inches)

Year	Engine	Carburetor Number	Fuel Level	Throttle Valve Gap ①		Vacuum Break ②	Choke Unloader	Dashpot Adjustment (rpm)
				MT	AT			
1984		DCR384-4	.910	.0280–.0335	.0343–.0398	.0965–.1201	.0807–.1122	1400–1600
		CDR384-5 ⑤	.910	.0280–.0335	.0343–.0398	.0913–.1150	.0807–.1122	1400–1600
		DCR384-6 ⑤	.910	.0280–.0335	.0343–.0398	.0913–.1150	.0807–.1122	1400–1600
		DCR384-11A	.910	.0280–.0335	.0343–.0398	.0965–.1201	.0807–.1122	1400–1600
		DCR384-15 ⑤	.910	.0280–.0335	.0343–.0398	.0965–.1201	.0807–.1122	1400–1600
		DCR384-21A	.910	.0280–.0335	.0343–.0398	.0965–.1201	.0807–.1122	1400–1600
		DCR384-25 ⑤	.910	.0280–.0335	.0343–.0398	.0965–.1201	.0807–.1122	1400–1600
	Z20	DCR342-8	.910	.0299–.0354	.0343–.0398	.0965–.1201 ④	.0807–.1122	1400–1600
1985	Z24	DFP384-3 ③	.910	.0280–.0335	.0343–.0398	.1220–.1457	.0807–.1122	1700–1900
		DFP384-4 ③	.910	.0280–.0335	.0343–.0398	.1220–.1457	.0807–.1122	1400–1600
		DFP384-12 ③	.910	.0280–.0335	.0343–.0398	.1220–.1457	.0807–.1122	1700–1900
		DCR384-3	.910	.0280–.0335	.0343–.0398	.0965–.1201 ④	.0807–.1122	1400–1600
		DCR384-4	.910	.0280–.0335	.0343–.0398	.0965–.1201	.0807–.1122	1400–1600
		CDR384-5 ⑤	.910	.0280–.0335	.0343–.0398	.0913–.1150	.0807–.1122	1400–1600
		DCR384-6 ⑤	.910	.0280–.0335	.0343–.0398	.0913–.1150	.0807–.1122	1400–1600
		DCR384-11A	.910	.0280–.0335	.0343–.0398	.0965–.1201	.0807–.1122	1400–1600
		DCR384-15 ⑤	.910	.0280–.0335	.0343–.0398	.0965–.1201	.0807–.1122	1400–1600
		DCR384-21A	.910	.0280–.0335	.0343–.0398	.0965–.1201	.0807–.1122	1400–1600
		DCR384-25 ⑤	.910	.0280–.0335	.0343–.0398	.0965–.1201	.0807–.1122	1400–1600
	Z20	DCR342-8	.910	.0299–.0354	.0343–.0398	.0965–.1201 ④	.0807–.1122	1400–1600
1986	Z24	DFP384-3 ③	.910	.0280–.0335	.0343–.0398	.1220–.1457	.0807–.1122	1700–1900
		DFP384-4 ③	.910	.0280–.0335	.0343–.0398	.1220–.1457	.0807–.1122	1400–1600
		DFP384-12 ③	.910	.0280–.0335	.0343–.0398	.1220–.1457	.0807–.1122	1700–1900
		DCR384-3	.910	.0280–.0335	.0343–.0398	.0965–.1201 ④	.0807–.1122	1400–1600

NISSAN (DATSUN) CARBURETORS

(All measurements in inches)

Year	Engine	Carburetor Number	Fuel Level	Throttle Valve Gap ①		Vacuum Break ②	Choke Unloader	Dashpot Adjustment (rpm)
				MT	AT			
1986		DCR384-4	.910	.0280–.0335	.0343–.0398	.0965–.1201	.0807–.1122	1400–1600
		CDR384-5 ⑤	.910	.0280–.0335	.0343–.0398	.0913–.1150	.0807–.1122	1400–1600
		DCR384-6 ⑤	.910	.0280–.0335	.0343–.0398	.0913–.1150	.0807–.1122	1400–1600
		DCR384-11A	.910	.0280–.0335	.0343–.0398	.0965–.1201	.0807–.1122	1400–1600
		DCR384-15 ⑤	.910	.0280–.0335	.0343–.0398	.0965–.1201	.0807–.1122	1400–1600
		DCR384-21A	.910	.0280–.0335	.0343–.0398	.0965–.1201	.0807–.1122	1400–1600
		DCR384-25 ⑤	.910	.0280–.0335	.0343–.0398	.0965–.1201	.0807–.1122	1400–1600
	Z20	DCR342-8	.910	.0299–.0354	.0343–.0398	.0965– ④ .1201	.0807–.1122	1400–1600
1987-88	Z24	DFP384-3 ③	.910	.0280–.0335	.0343–.0398	.1220–.1457	.0807–.1122	1700–1900
		DFP384-4 ③	.910	.0280–.0335	.0343–.0398	.1220–.1457	.0807–.1122	1400–1600
		DFP384-12 ③	.910	.0280–.0335	.0343–.0398	.1220–.1457	.0807–.1122	1700–1900
		DCR384-3	.910	.0280–.0335	.0343–.0398	.0965– ④ .1201	.0807–.1122	1400–1600
		DCR384-4	.910	.0280–.0335	.0343–.0398	.0965–.1201	.0807–.1122	1400–1600
		CDR384-5 ⑤	.910	.0280–.0335	.0343–.0398	.0913–.1150	.0807–.1122	1400–1600
		DCR384-6 ⑤	.910	.0280–.0335	.0343–.0398	.0913–.1150	.0807–.1122	1400–1600
		DCR384-11A	.910	.0280–.0335	.0343–.0398	.0965–.1201	.0807–.1122	1400–1600
		DCR384-15 ⑤	.910	.0280–.0335	.0343–.0398	.0965–.1201	.0807–.1122	1400–1600
		DCR384-21A	.910	.0280–.0335	.0343–.0398	.0965–.1201	.0807–.1122	1400–1600
		DCR384-25 ⑤	.910	.0280–.0335	.0343–.0398	.0965–.1201	.0807–.1122	1400–1600
	Z20	DCR342-8	.910	.0299–.0354	.0343–.0398	.0965– ④ .1201	.0807–.1122	1400–1600

MT Manual Transmission
AT Automatic Transmission
① Second step of fast idle cam
② Above 68°F
③ California Models
④ MPG Models: .1031–.1268
⑤ Canadian Models

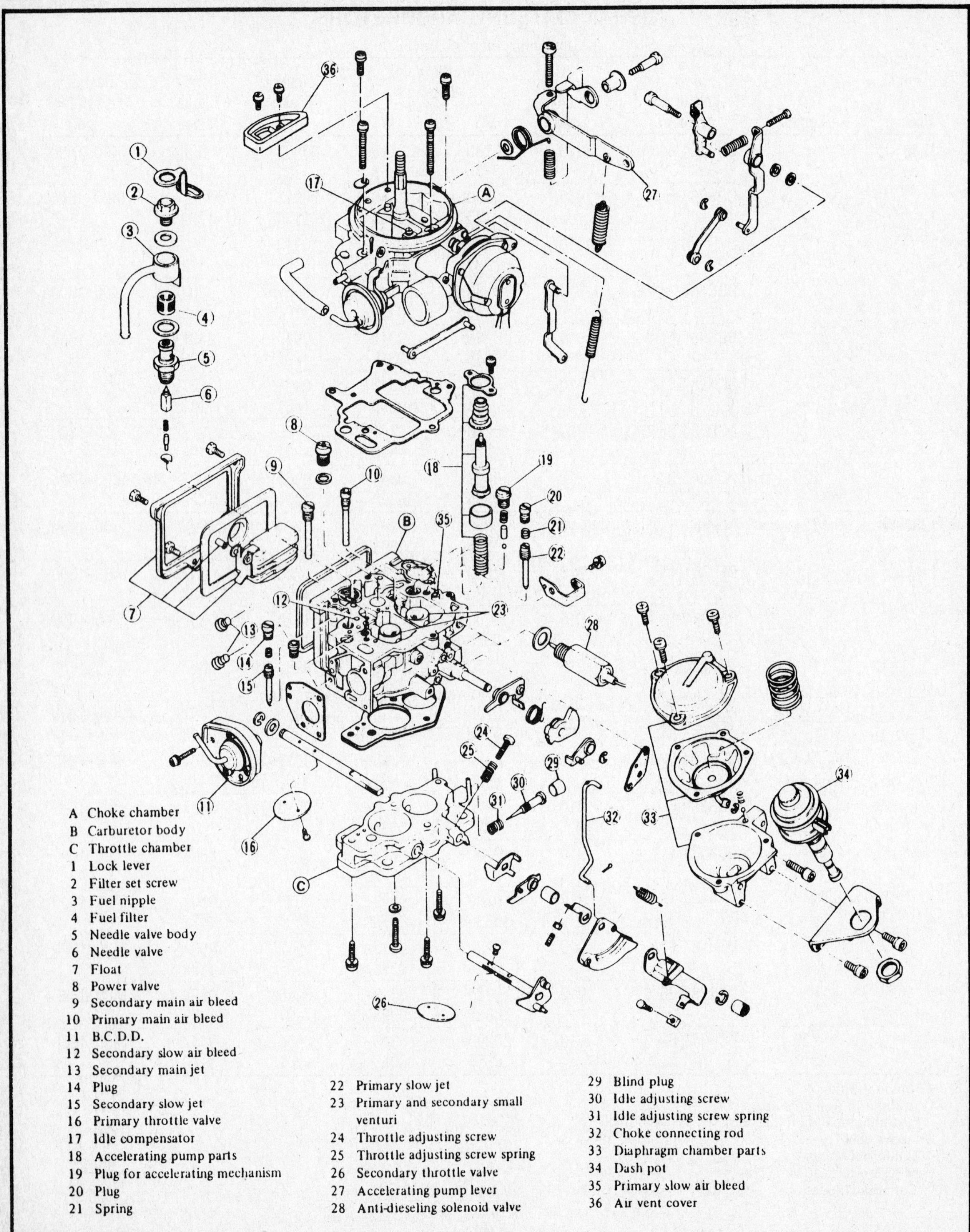
A Choke chamber
B Carburetor body
C Throttle chamber
1 Lock lever
2 Filter set screw
3 Fuel nipple
4 Fuel filter
5 Needle valve body
6 Needle valve
7 Float
8 Power valve
9 Secondary main air bleed
10 Primary main air bleed
11 B.C.D.D.
12 Secondary slow air bleed
13 Secondary main jet
14 Plug
15 Secondary slow jet
16 Primary throttle valve
17 Idle compensator
18 Accelerating pump parts
19 Plug for accelerating mechanism
20 Plug
21 Spring
22 Primary slow jet
23 Primary and secondary small venturi
24 Throttle adjusting screw
25 Throttle adjusting screw spring
26 Secondary throttle valve
27 Accelerating pump lever
28 Anti-dieseling solenoid valve
29 Blind plug
30 Idle adjusting screw
31 Idle adjusting screw spring
32 Choke connecting rod
33 Diaphragm chamber parts
34 Dash pot
35 Primary slow air bleed
36 Air vent cover

Exploded view of the Nissan (Datsun) DCR series carburetor

SUZUKI CARBURETORS

SUZUKI CARBURETORS

(All measurements in inches)

Year	Carburetor Number	Float Level	Idle-Up Speed (rpm)	Fast Idle Clearance	Choke Valve Clearance
1987–88	All	0.31	900–1000	0.10–0.12	0.13–0.14 ①

① With 30–50 cm Hg vacuum applied

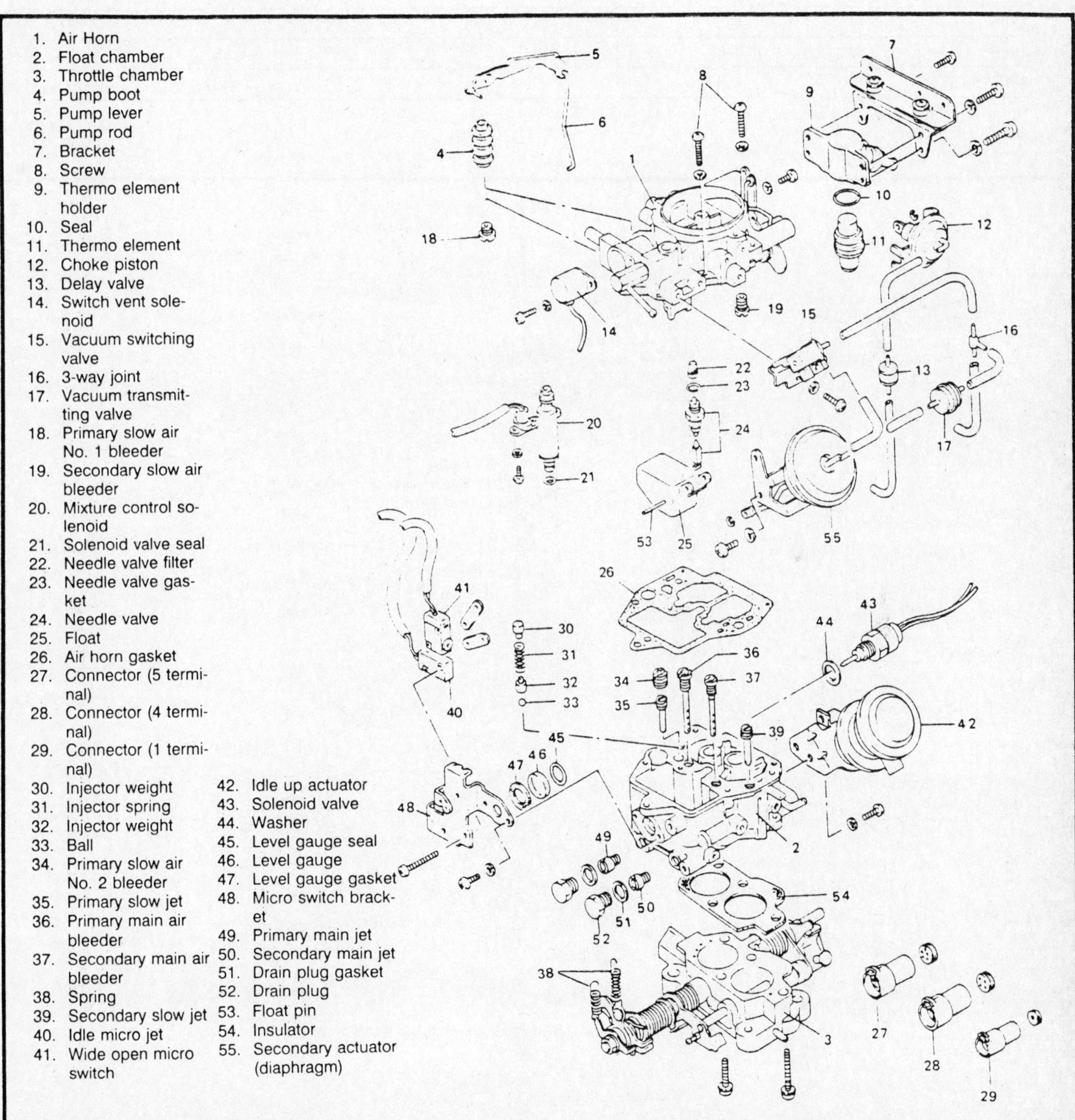

Exploded view of the Suzuki carburetor

TOYOTA CARBURETORS

TOYOTA CARBURETORS

(All measurements in inches or degrees)

Year	Carburetor Number	Float Level	Throttle Valve Angle	Secondary Touch Angle	Fast Idle Angle	Choke Unloader Angle	Idle Mixture Screw ①
1982	All	1.89	90°	50°	24°	45°	2 1/2
1983	All	1.89	90°	59°	22°	50°	4
1984	All	1.89	90°	59°	22°	50°	4 1/2
1985	All	1.89	90°	59°	23°	45°	3 1/2
1986	All	1.89	90°	59°	23°	45°	3 1/2
1987-88	All	1.89	90°	59°	23°	45°	3 1/2

Note: Angle specifications for use with angle degree tool
① Turns out

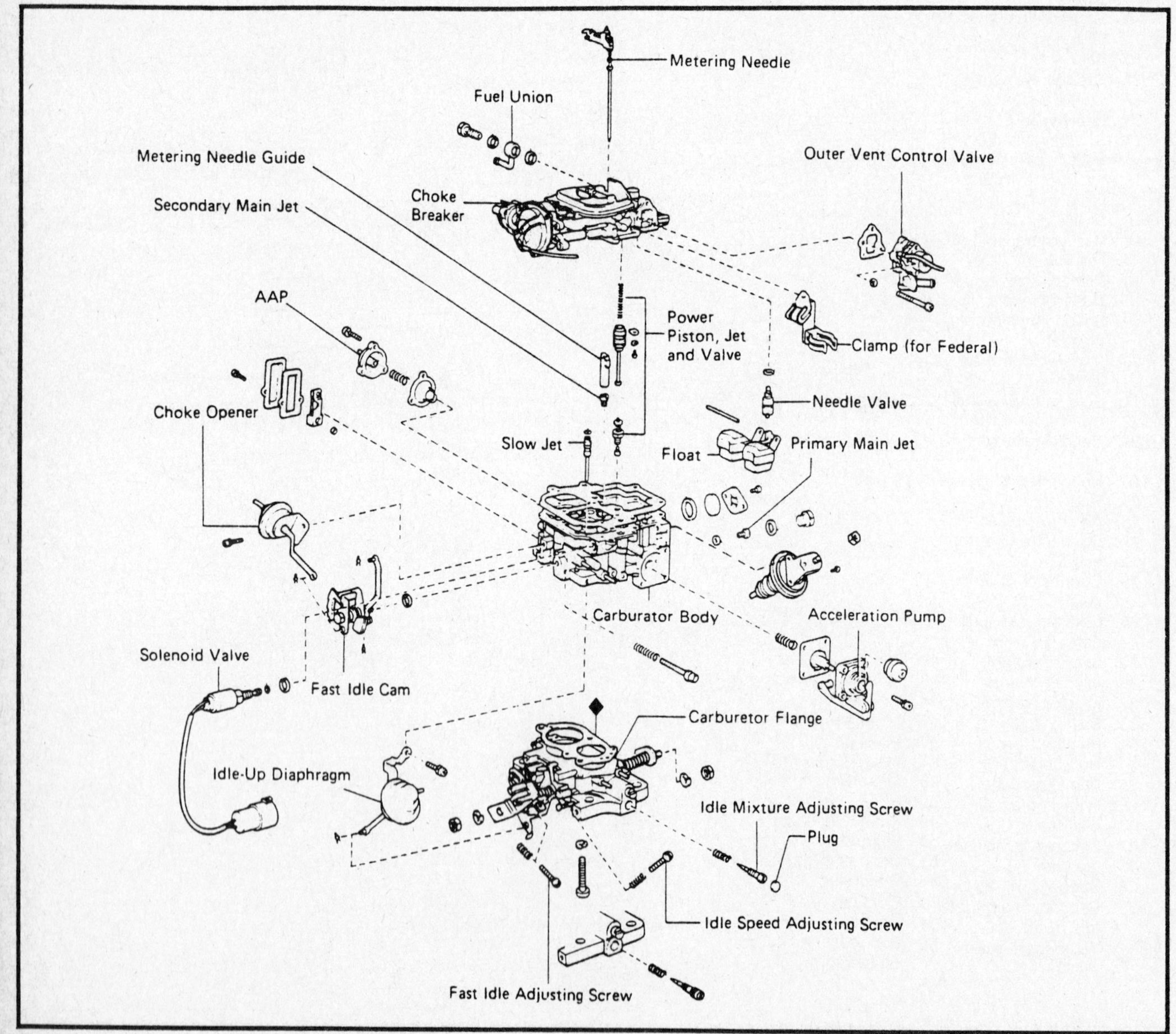

Exploded view of the Toyota carburetor

Steering Gears
Import Trucks

24

INDEX

DATSUN/NISSAN

Manual Steering Gear

Disassembly

1. Place the steering gear in a vise using tool KV48100301 or its equivalent.
2. Set the worm gear in a straight ahead position.
3. Remove the sector shaft cover retaining bolts.
4. Pull the sector shaft out, being careful not to damage the oil seal. Make sure the worm gear is set in a straight ahead position and do not remove the shaft needle bearings from the steering gear housing.
5. Remove the sector shaft cover, then if necessary the sector shaft oil seal.
6. Loosen the adjusting plug lock nut using tool K48101500 or its equivalent.
7. Draw out the worm gear with the worm bearing.

CAUTION

Be careful not to allow the ball nut to run down to either end of the worm or damage to the ball guides may result.

8. Remove the seal from the adjusting plug using the appropriate tool.

Assembly and Adjustment

NOTE: Before reassembly, clean and lubricate all parts with gear fluid and fill the space between the sealing lips of the new sector shaft and adjusting plug oil seals with the recommended multi-purpose grease.

1. Position the worm gear assembly with the worm bearing assembly in the gear housing.
2. Install the adjusting plug using tool KV4801400.
3. Adjust the worm bearing preload.
   a. Rotate the worm shaft a few turns in both directions to set worm bearing.
   b. Adjust the worm bearing preload by turning the adjusting plug in the tighten direction to 1.7–5.2 inch lbs.
4. Apply suitable sealant around the lock nut inner surface.
5. Tighten the locknut using the appropriate tools. Recheck the worm bearing preload.
6. Select a suitable adjusting shim and adjust the end play between the sector shaft and the adjusting screw (0.0004–0.0012 in.).
7. Coat the seal face with gear fluid, then press the oil seal to the steering gear housing using the appropriate tool.
8. Install the sector cover on the adjusting screw with the sector shaft.
9. Set the worm gear in a straight ahead position.
10. Insert the sector shaft and sector cover assembly with gasket into the gear housing, using care not to scratch the oil seal.
11. Tighten the sector cover to gear housing bolts to 11–18 ft. lbs.
12. Pour the recommended gear oil into through the filler hole and install the filler plug.
13. Tighten the adjusting screw so that the gear preload is within specification.

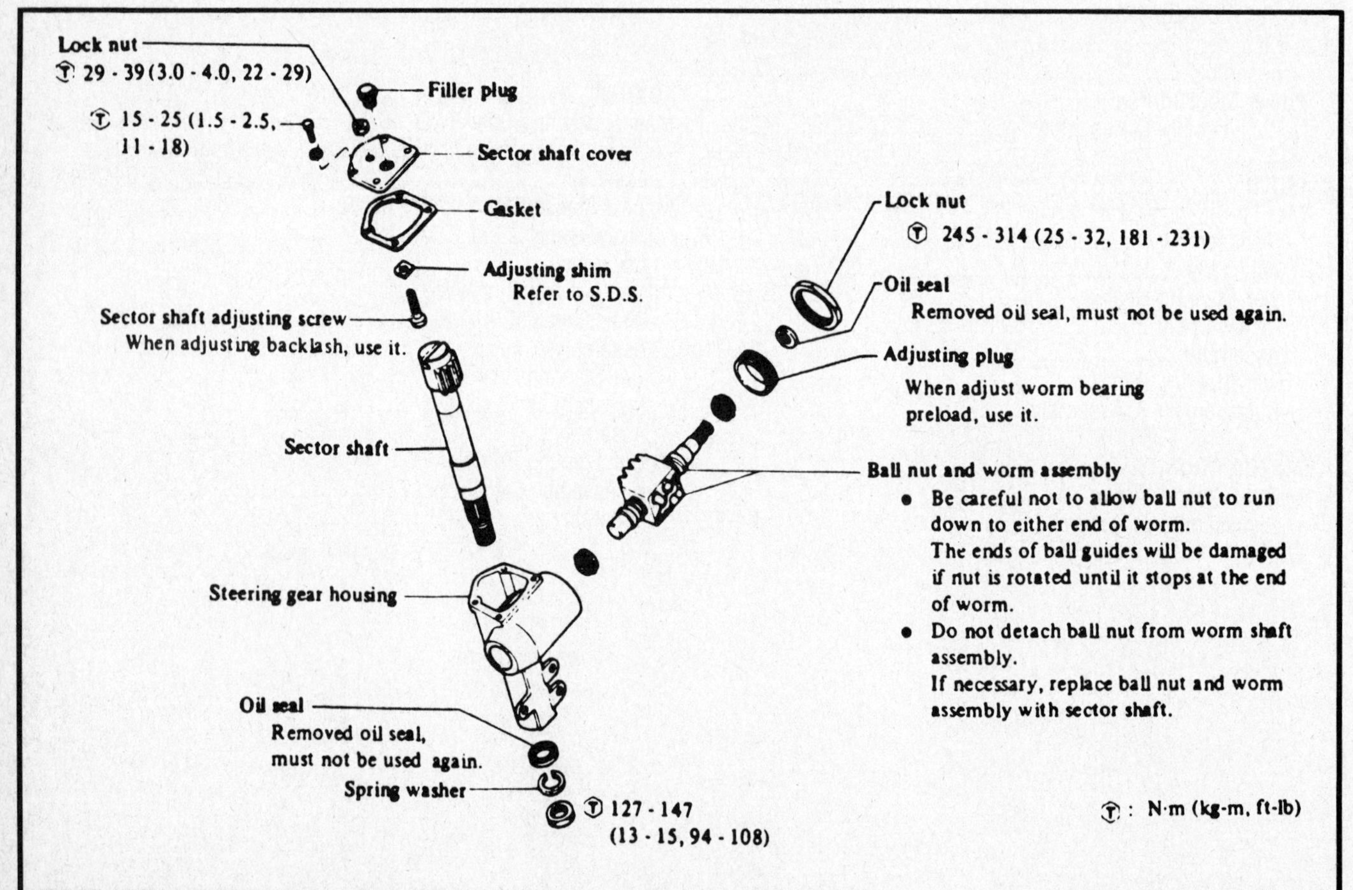

Datsun manual steering gear—typical

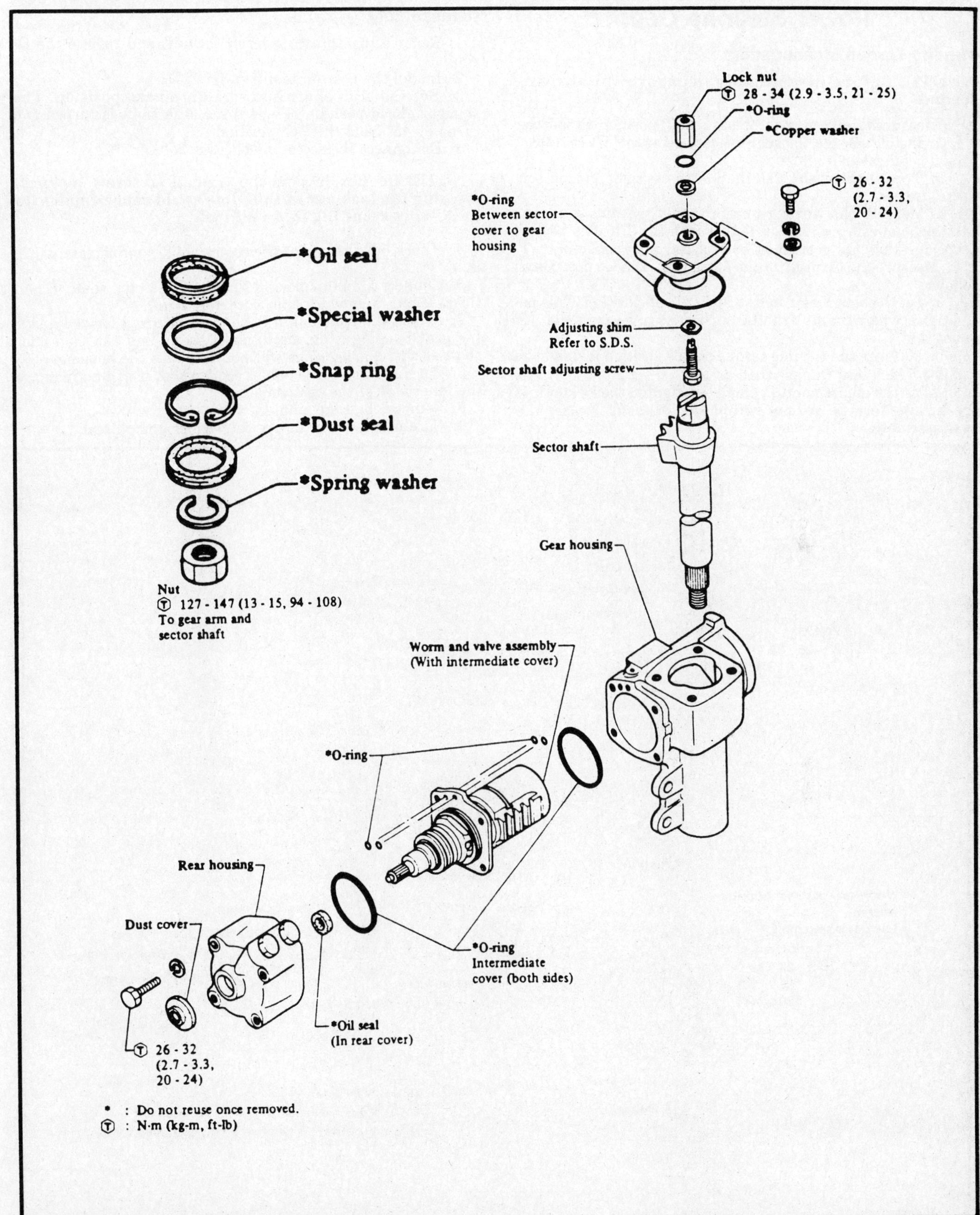
Lock nut
Ⓣ 28 - 34 (2.9 - 3.5, 21 - 25)
*O-ring
*Copper washer
Ⓣ 26 - 32 (2.7 - 3.3, 20 - 24)
*O-ring
Between sector cover to gear housing
*Oil seal
*Special washer
*Snap ring
*Dust seal
*Spring washer
Nut
Ⓣ 127 - 147 (13 - 15, 94 - 108)
To gear arm and sector shaft
Adjusting shim
Refer to S.D.S.
Sector shaft adjusting screw
Sector shaft
Gear housing
Worm and valve assembly
(With intermediate cover)
*O-ring
Rear housing
Dust cover
*O-ring
Intermediate cover (both sides)
*Oil seal
(In rear cover)
Ⓣ 26 - 32
(2.7 - 3.3,
20 - 24)
* : Do not reuse once removed.
Ⓣ : N·m (kg-m, ft-lb)

Datsun power steering gear—1982-83

Power Steering Gear

Turning Torque Measurement

NOTE: Before disassembly, measure the turning torque.

1. Measure the turning torque at a 360° position as follows:
   a. Install the steering gear in a vise using tool KV48100301 or its equivalent.
   b. Turn the stub shaft all the way to the right and left several times.
   c. Measure the turning torque at 360° position from the straight ahead position. (6.1–10.4 inch lbs.). If it is beyond specification, the gear must be replaced as an assembly.
2. Measure the turning torque at a straight ahead position as follows:
   a. Set the worm gear in a straight ahead position. This position is where the stub shaft is turned 1.9 turns from the lock position.
   b. Measure the turning torque at this position it should be 0.9–3.5 inch lbs., (higher than at 360°).
3. After the adjustment is completed, tighten the lock nut. If the turning torques are not within specifications, replace the gear assembly.

Disassembly

1. Remove the adjusting screw locknut and replace the O-ring.
2. Install the gear on tool KV48100301.
3. Set the stub shaft in a straight ahead position. The straight ahead position is where the stub shaft is turned two turns by 45° from the lock position.
4. Disconnect the sector shaft cover bolt.

NOTE: Do not loosen the adjusting screw locknut. Turning the lock nut at this time could cause damage to the O-ring resulting in an oil leak.

5. Knock out the end of the sector shaft approximately 0.79 in..
6. Connect a roll of plastic film to the sector shaft. (1mm thick, length and width approximately 8 in.).
7. Attach the plastic film to the two bearings located inside the gear housing while simultaneously pulling out the sector shaft so that the bearings will not drop into the housing.
8. Carefully pry out the dust seal so that it will not damage the inner side of the gear housing.
9. Remove the snap ring.
10. Carefully remove the special washer and oil seal.

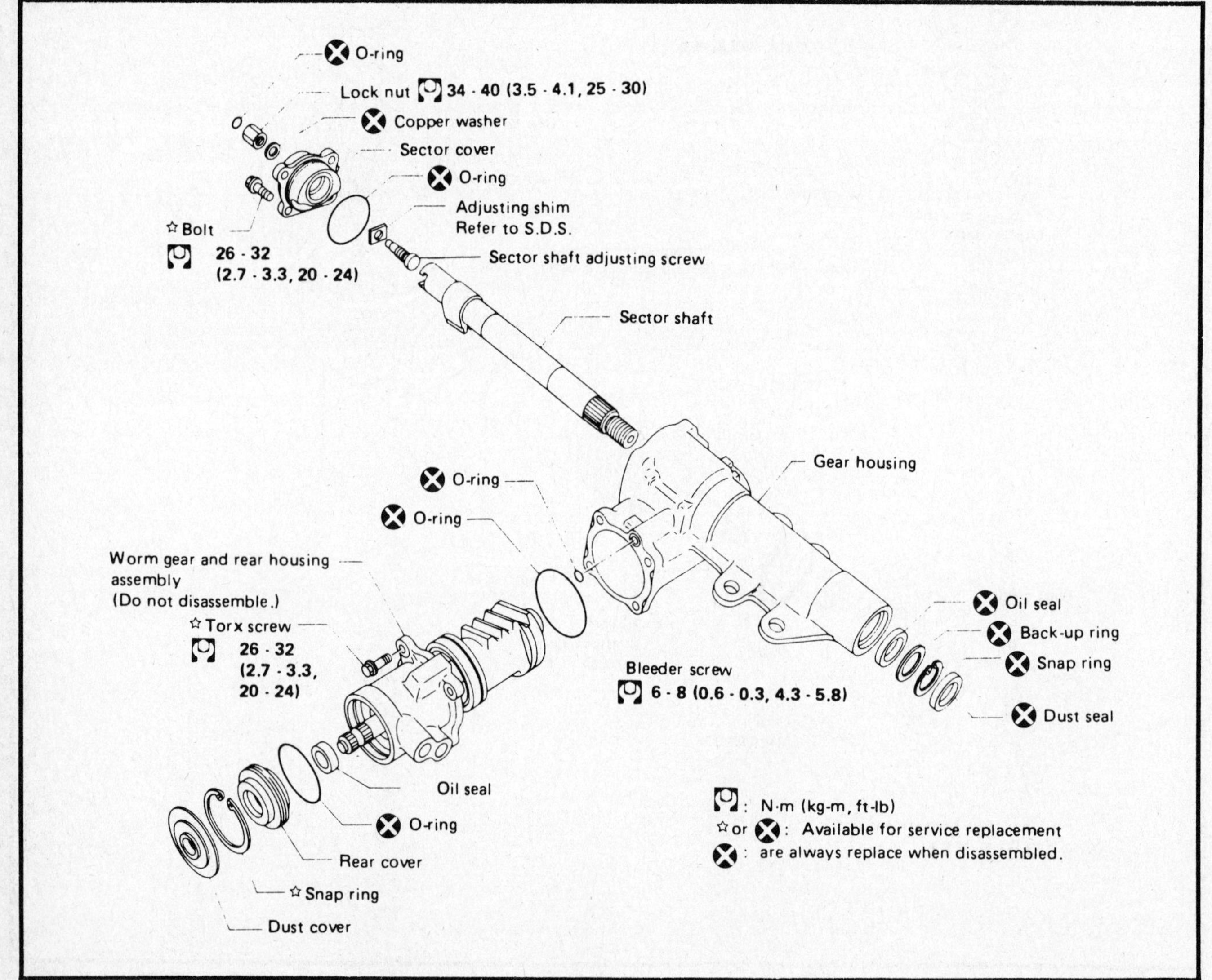

Datsun power steering gear—(Model PB48S), 1986–88

11. Remove the O-ring.
12. Remove the torx screws, then remove the rear housing together with the worm gear assembly.

NOTE: When the worm assembly is removed, the piston may turn and come off under its own weight. Hold the piston to prevent it from turning. If piston to rear housing clearance exceeds 1.77 in. after loosening, the recirculating ball will be out of groove of worm; do not reinstall the piston but replace the entire assembly.

13. Remove the O-rings.
14. Remove the snap ring, then the rear cover.
15. Remove the O-ring then the oil seal.

Assembly

1. Apply a thin coat of vaseline to a new adjusting screw lock nut O-ring and insert it into the groove.
2. Apply a thin coat of vaseline to the new oil seal and dust seal then press in the new seal and the special washer.
3. Install a new snap ring into the gear housing. Turn the snap ring to make sure it fits into the groove and always install the snap ring with its rounded edges facing the oil seal.
4. Press in a new dust seal.
5. Apply a thin coat of vaseline to a new O-ring then fit the O-ring into the sector shaft cover.
6. Set the piston rack at a straight ahead position. Turn the piston rack about 10° to 15° toward yourself. This is for smooth insertion of the sector gear.
7. Wrap vinyl tape around serration area of sector shaft to prevent damage to the oil seal lip during insertion.
8. With the plastic film wraped around the sector shaft as in Step 7 of disassembly, insert the sector shaft into the gear housing. Gradually remove the plastic film being careful not to drop the bearings into the gear housing.
9. Tighten the sector shaft cover bolts to 20–24 ft. lbs. in a criss-cross pattern.
10. At this time check the turning torque and steering gear preload as described earlier. If there is a great difference between the values before and after disassembly, it will be necessary to replace the assembly.
11. Apply a thin coat of vaseline to new rear housing O-ring then install.
12. Gradually insert the worm gear and rear housing assembly into the gear housing, being careful not to damage the oil seal and O-rings.
13. Install and tighten the torx screws in a criss-cross pattern to 20–24 ft. lbs.
14. Install a new O-ring and oil seal.
15. Install the rear cover then the snap ring. Turn the snap ring to make sure it fits into the groove and always install the snap ring with its rounded edge facing the rear cover.

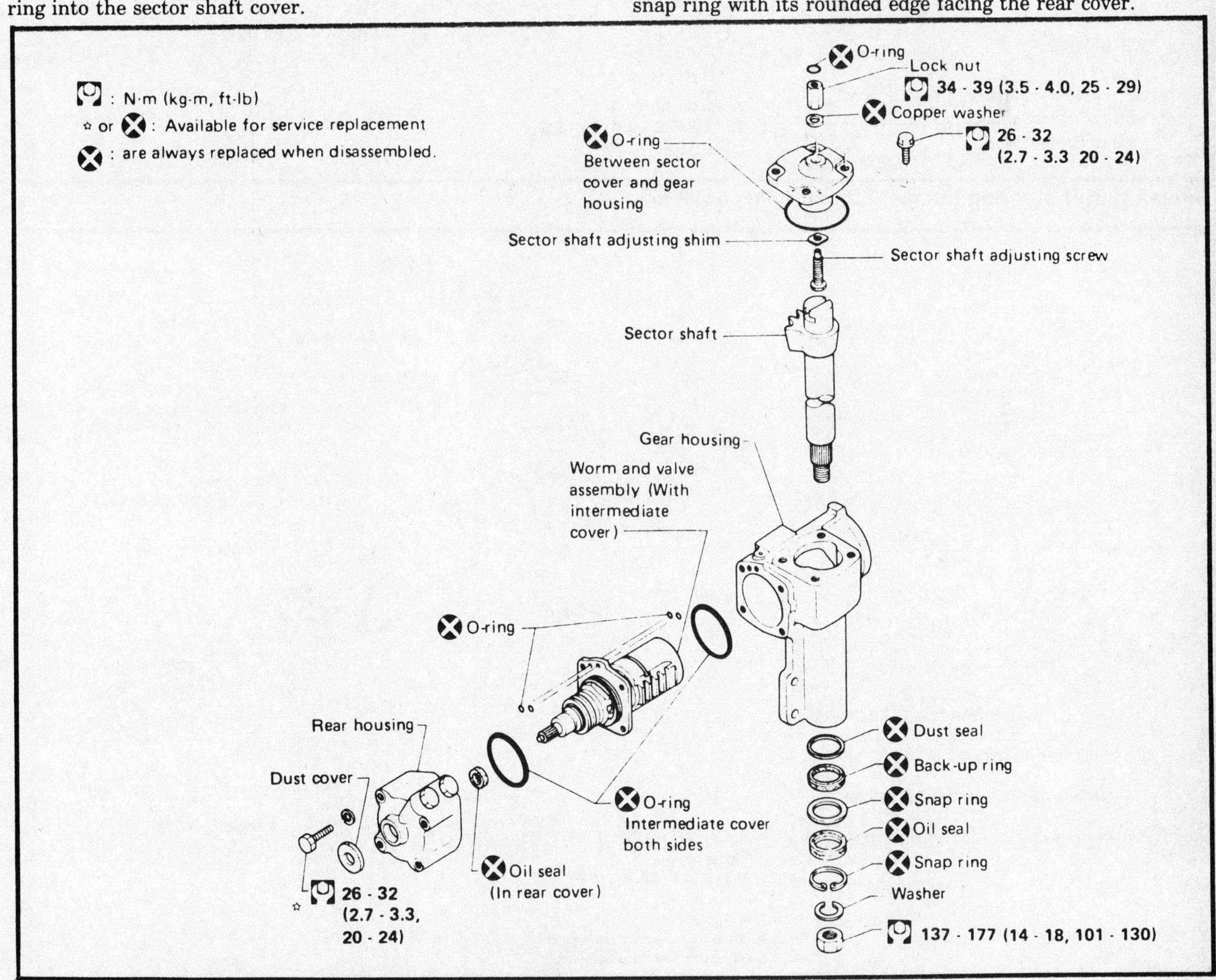

Datsun power steering gear – (Model PB56S), 1986–88

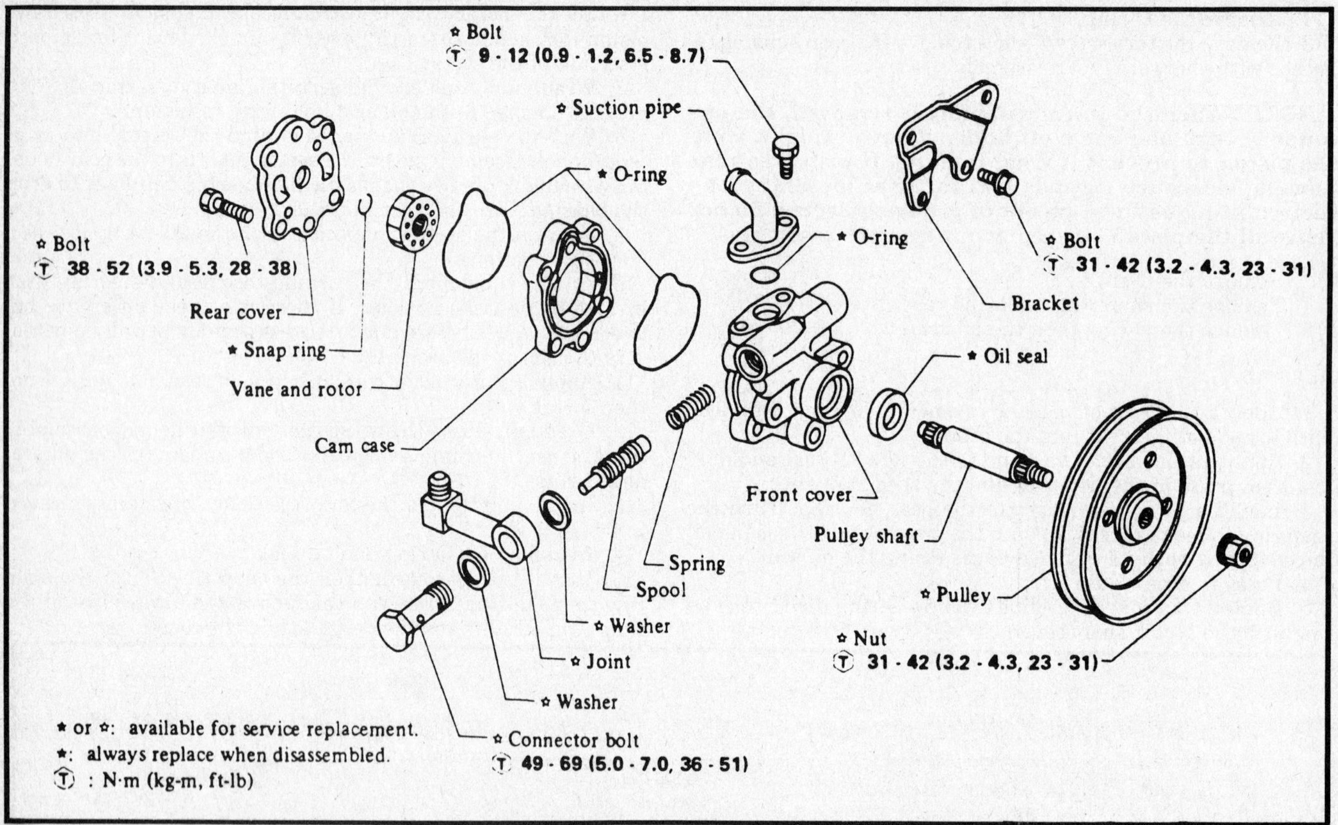

☆ Bolt
Ⓣ 9 - 12 (0.9 - 1.2, 6.5 - 8.7)
☆ Suction pipe
★ O-ring
☆ Bolt
Ⓣ 38 - 52 (3.9 - 5.3, 28 - 38)
Rear cover
★ Snap ring
Vane and rotor
Cam case
★ O-ring
☆ Bolt
Ⓣ 31 - 42 (3.2 - 4.3, 23 - 31)
Bracket
★ Oil seal
Front cover
Pulley shaft
Spring
Spool
☆ Washer
☆ Joint
☆ Washer
☆ Connector bolt
Ⓣ 49 - 69 (5.0 - 7.0, 36 - 51)
☆ Pulley
☆ Nut
Ⓣ 31 - 42 (3.2 - 4.3, 23 - 31)
★ or ☆: available for service replacement.
★: always replace when disassembled.
Ⓣ : N·m (kg-m, ft-lb)

Nissan power steering pump—SD25 engine, 1984–85

Gear housing
★ Dust seal
★ Snap ring
☆ Back-up ring
Sector shaft
★ Oil seal
Sector shaft adjusting screw
Worm gear and rear housing assembly (Do not disassemble)
☆ Adjusting screw Refer to S.D.S.
☆ Torx screw
Ⓣ 26 - 32 (2.7 - 3.3, 20 - 24)
★ O-ring
★ O-ring
★ O-ring
Sector cover
☆ Bolt Ⓣ 26 - 32 (2.7 - 3.3, 20 - 24)
★ Copper washer
☆ Lock nut Ⓣ 28 - 34 (2.9 - 3.5, 21 - 25)
★ O-ring
★ Oil seal
★ O-ring
Rear cover
★ Snap ring
Dust cover
Bleeder screw
Ⓣ 6 - 8 (0.6 - 0.8, 4.3 - 5.8)
Ⓣ : N·m (kg-m, ft-lb)
★ or ☆: available for service replacement
★: always replace when disassembled.

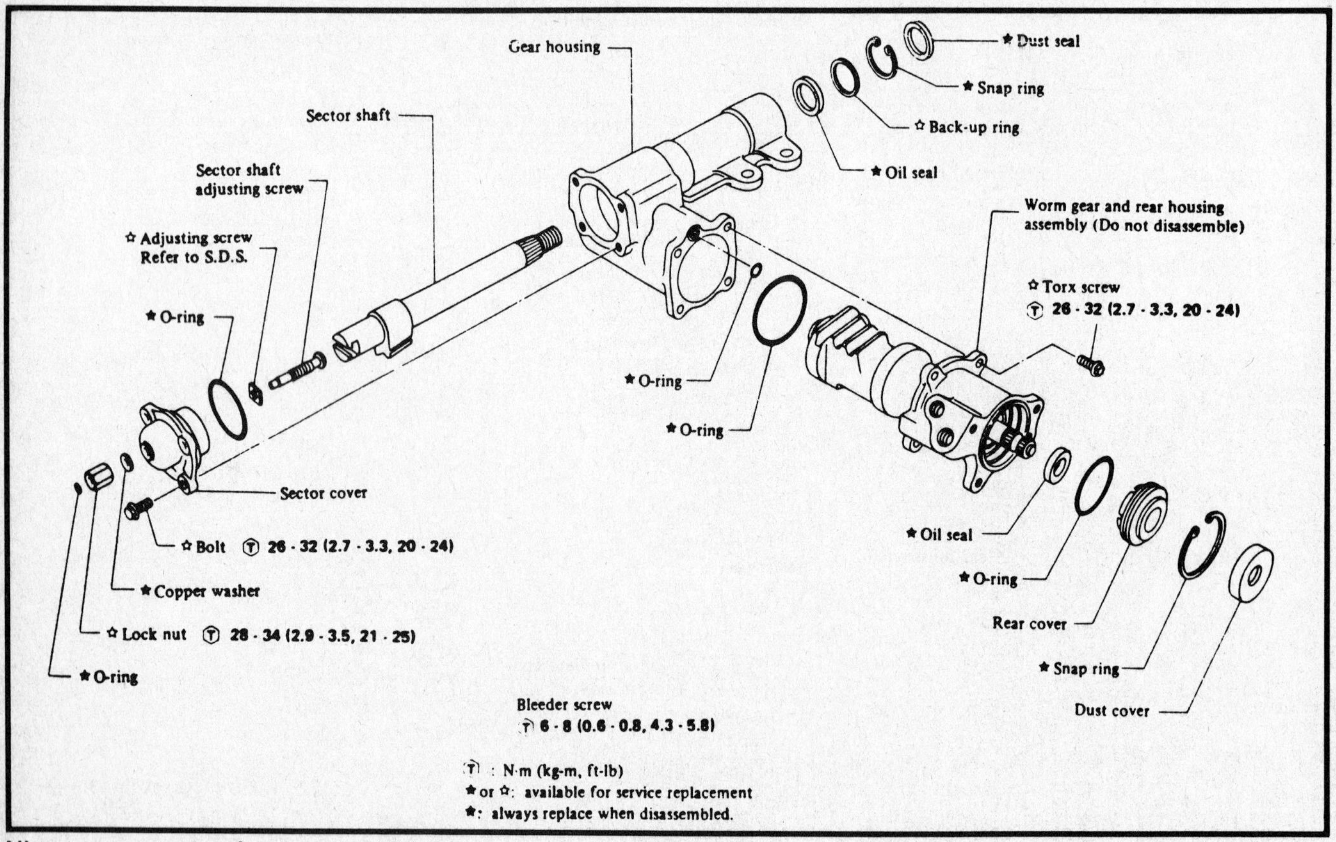

Nissan power steering gear—1984–85

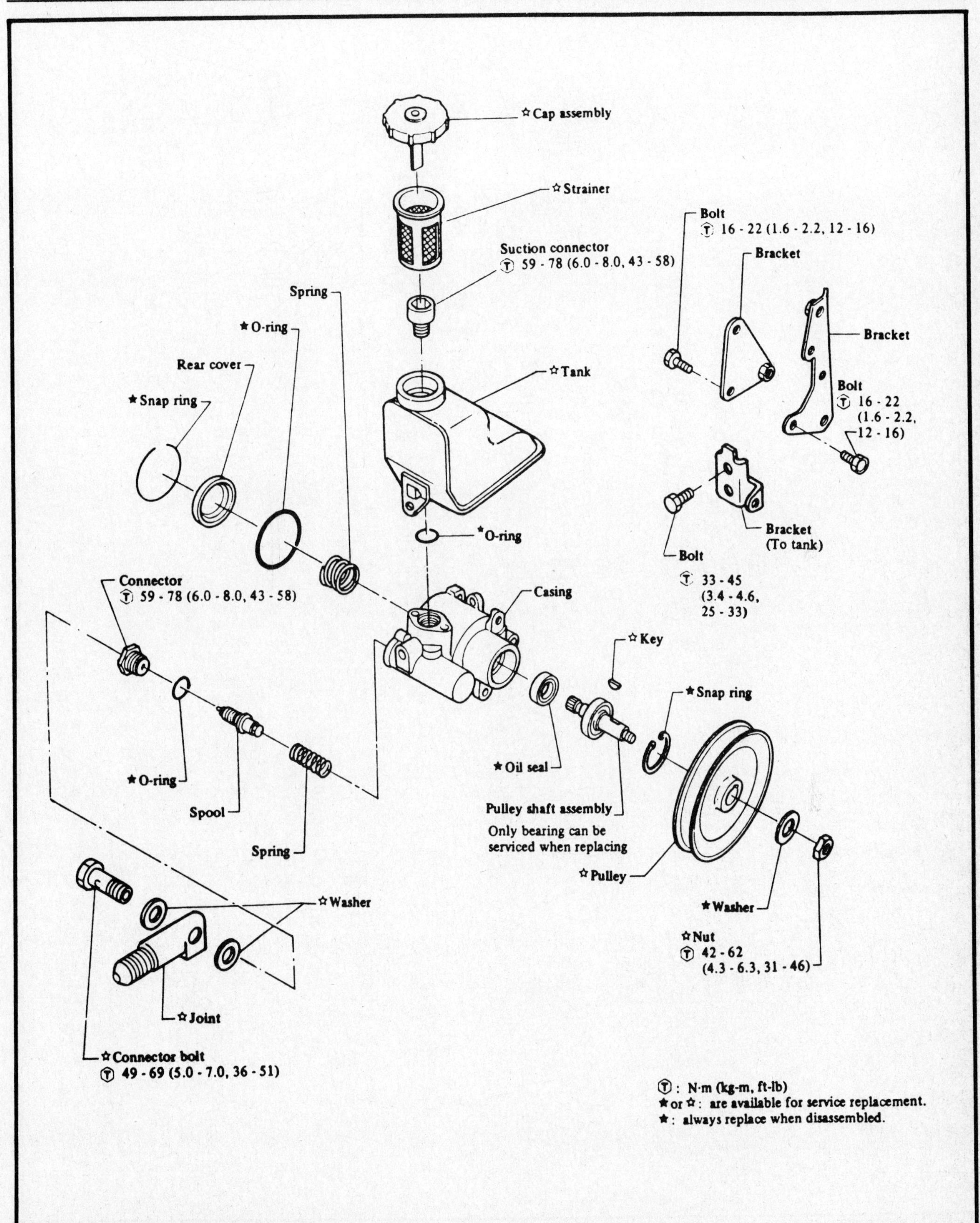
☆Cap assembly
☆Strainer
Bolt
Ⓣ 16 - 22 (1.6 - 2.2, 12 - 16)
Bracket
Suction connector
Ⓣ 59 - 78 (6.0 - 8.0, 43 - 58)
Spring
★O-ring
Bracket
Rear cover
☆Tank
Bolt
Ⓣ 16 - 22
(1.6 - 2.2,
12 - 16)
★Snap ring
*O-ring
Bracket
(To tank)
Bolt
Ⓣ 33 - 45
(3.4 - 4.6,
25 - 33)
Connector
Ⓣ 59 - 78 (6.0 - 8.0, 43 - 58)
Casing
☆Key
★Snap ring
★Oil seal
★O-ring
Spool
Pulley shaft assembly
Only bearing can be
serviced when replacing
Spring
☆Pulley
☆Washer
★Washer
☆Nut
Ⓣ 42 - 62
(4.3 - 6.3, 31 - 46)
☆Joint
☆Connector bolt
Ⓣ 49 - 69 (5.0 - 7.0, 36 - 51)
Ⓣ: N·m (kg-m, ft-lb)
★or ☆: are available for service replacement.
★: always replace when disassembled.

Datsun/Nissan power steering gear—1982–85

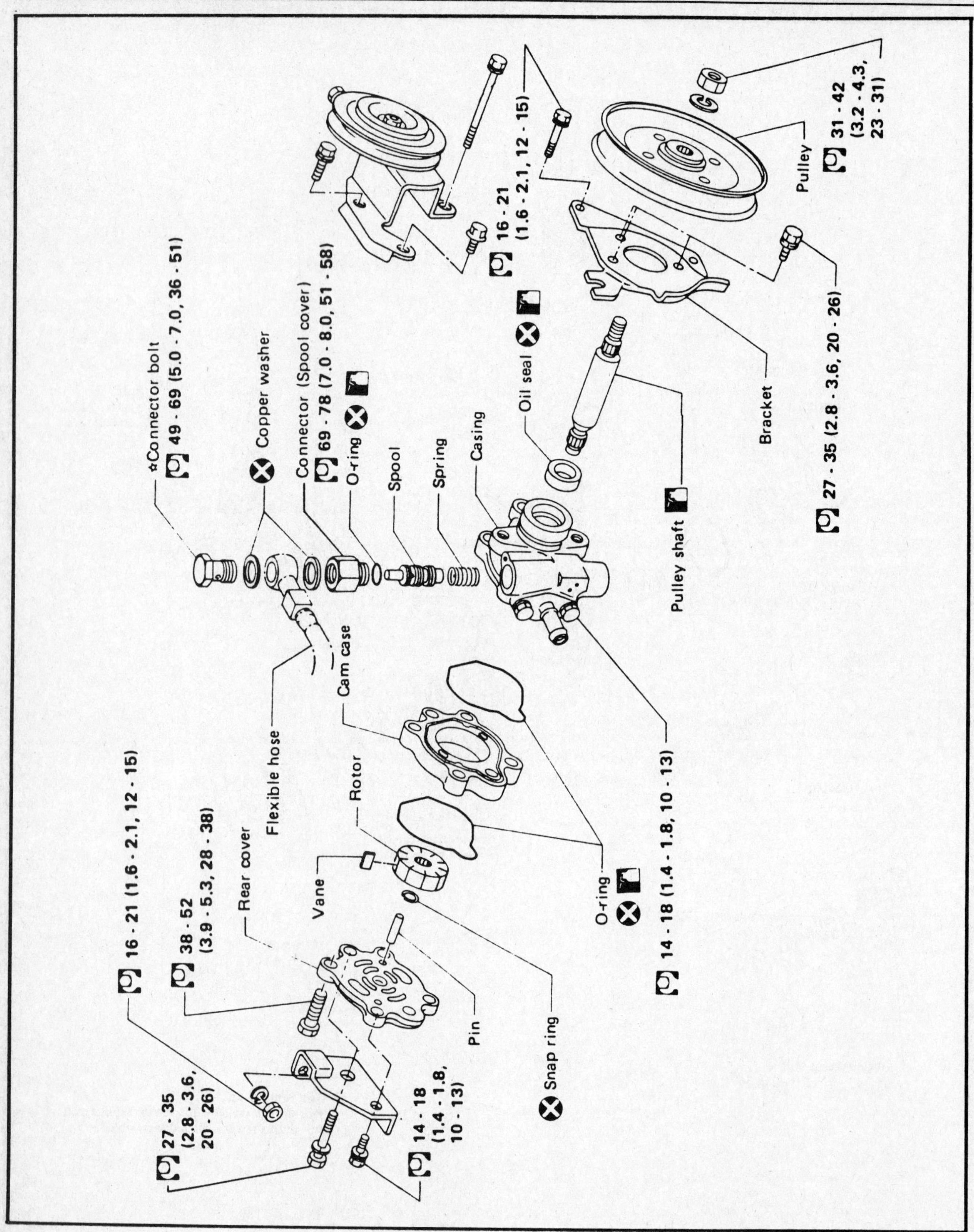

Nissan power steering pump—with Z engine, 1986–88

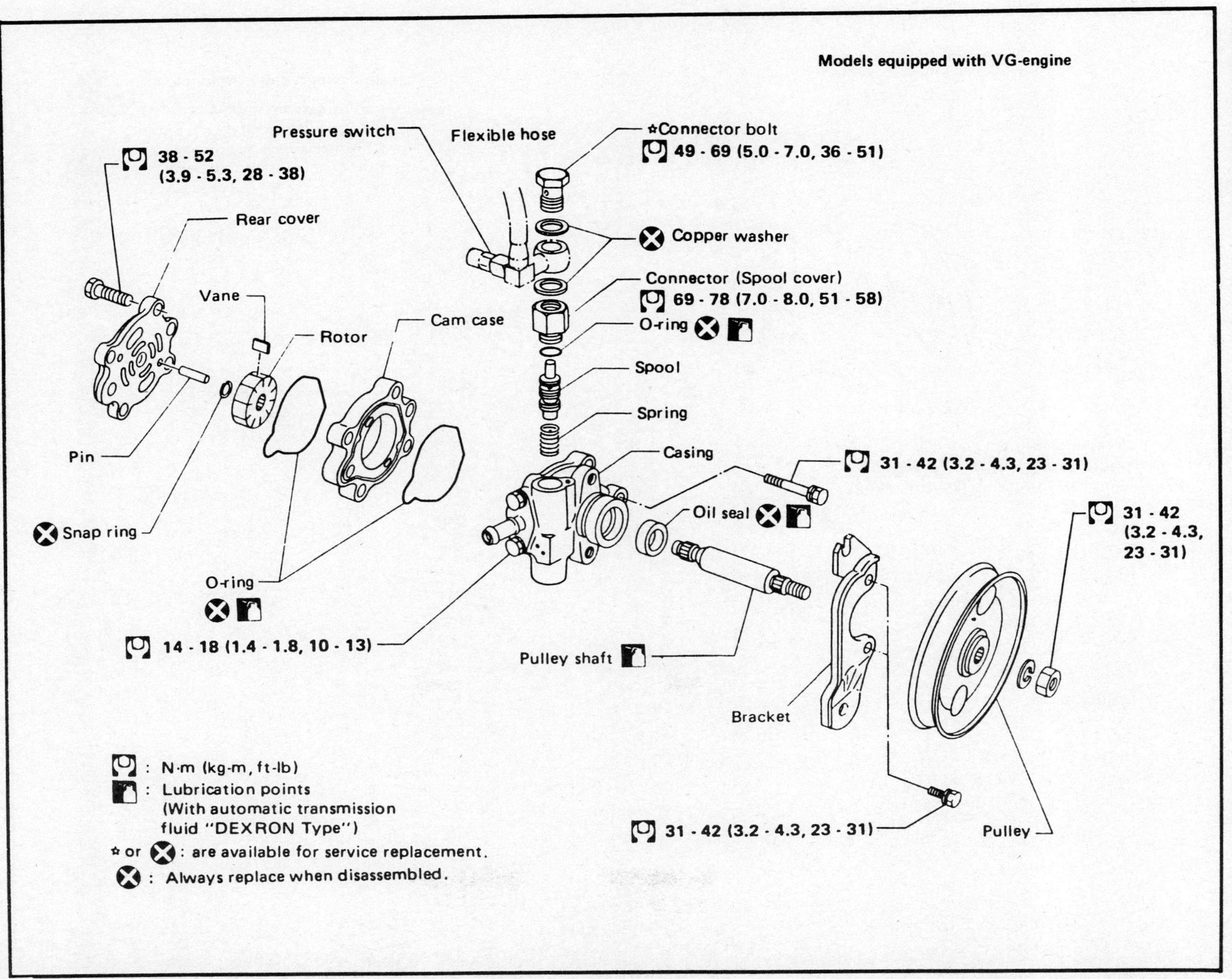
Models equipped with VG-engine
Pressure switch
Flexible hose
☆Connector bolt
49 - 69 (5.0 - 7.0, 36 - 51)
38 - 52
(3.9 - 5.3, 28 - 38)
Rear cover
Copper washer
Connector (Spool cover)
69 - 78 (7.0 - 8.0, 51 - 58)
Vane
Rotor
Cam case
O-ring
Spool
Spring
Pin
Casing
31 - 42 (3.2 - 4.3, 23 - 31)
Oil seal
31 - 42
(3.2 - 4.3,
23 - 31)
Snap ring
O-ring
14 - 18 (1.4 - 1.8, 10 - 13)
Pulley shaft
Bracket
: N·m (kg-m, ft-lb)
: Lubrication points
(With automatic transmission
fluid "DEXRON Type")
☆ or : are available for service replacement.
: Always replace when disassembled.
31 - 42 (3.2 - 4.3, 23 - 31)
Pulley

Nissan power steering pump—with VG engine, 1986–88

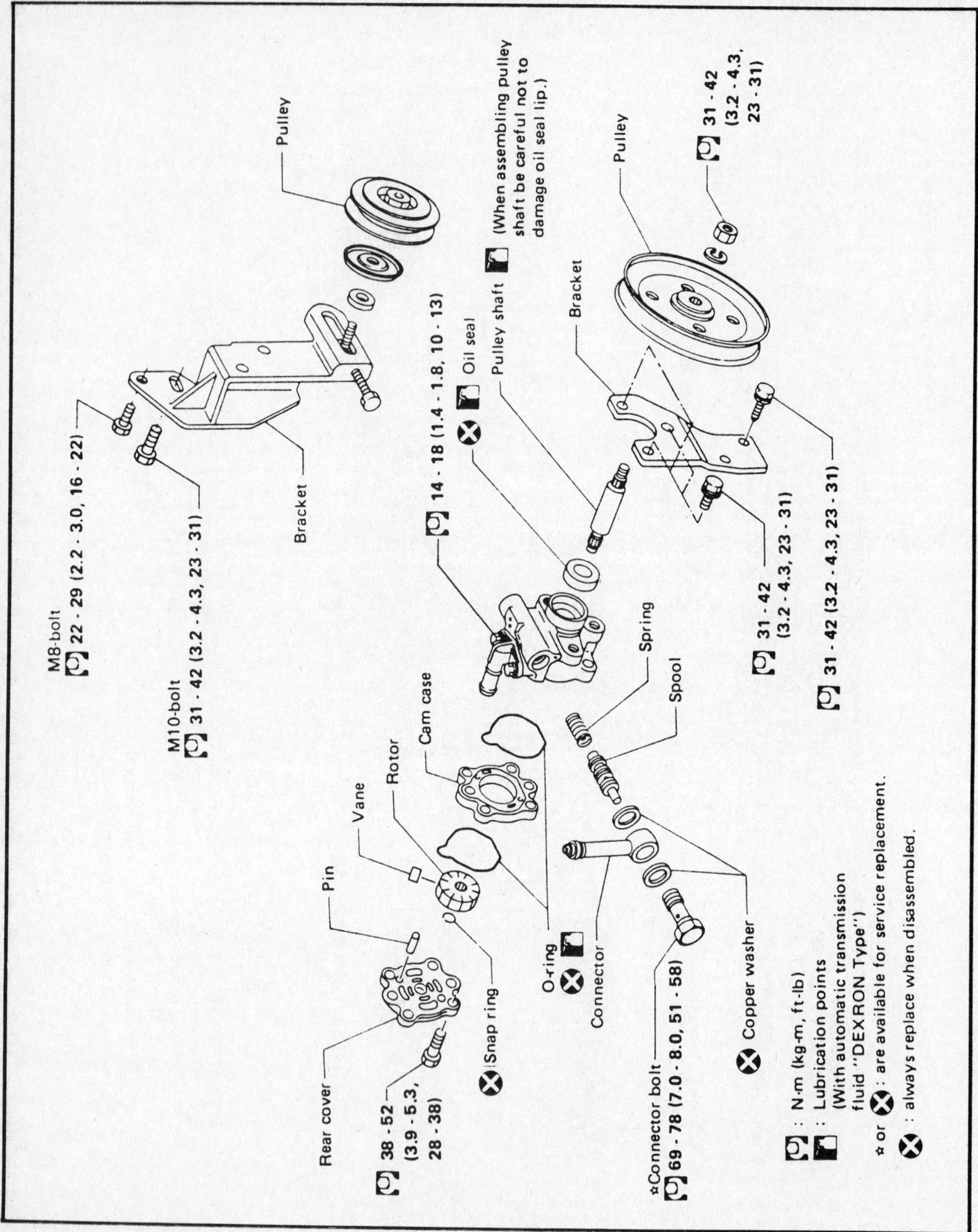
M8-bolt
22 - 29 (2.2 - 3.0, 16 - 22)
M10-bolt
31 - 42 (3.2 - 4.3, 23 - 31)
Bracket
Pulley
14 - 18 (1.4 - 1.8, 10 - 13)
Oil seal
Pulley shaft
(When assembling pulley shaft be careful not to damage oil seal lip.)
Bracket
Pulley
31 - 42 (3.2 - 4.3, 23 - 31)
Cam case
Rotor
Vane
Pin
Spring
Spool
31 - 42 (3.2 - 4.3, 23 - 31)
31 - 42 (3.2 - 4.3, 23 - 31)
Rear cover
38 - 52 (3.9 - 5.3, 28 - 38)
Snap ring
O-ring
Connector
Copper washer
☆Connector bolt
69 - 78 (7.0 - 8.0, 51 - 58)
: N·m (kg-m, ft-lb)
: Lubrication points (With automatic transmission fluid "DEXRON Type")
☆ or : are available for service replacement.
: always replace when disassembled.

Nissan power steering pump—with SD engine, 1986–88

16. Select suitable adjusting shims and adjust the end play between the sector shaft and adjusting screw. End play should be 0.0004–0.0012 in.

Power Steering Pump

Disassembly

1982–83

1. Remove the pulley and use new washer upon reassembly.
2. Remove the cap assembly.
3. Remove the tank and O-ring.
4. Remove the connector bolt, washers and joint.
5. Remove the connector then remove the O-ring.
6. Remove the rear O-ring as follows: With the tank and tank O-ring removed, remove the bracket, snap ring, rear cover and spring then remove the O-ring.

NOTE: Do not turn the rear cover side of the housing downwards, otherwise the side plate may fall. If dropped do not attempt to reassemble them, rather replace the oil pump assembly.

7. Replace the pulley shaft oil seal as follows: With the pulley removed remove the snap ring, then remove the pulley shaft assembly. Remove the oil seal.

Assembly

1. Clean all disassembled parts in a suitable cleaning solvent.
2. Always use new washers, seals and O-rings and coat all O-rings with a thin coat of vaseline before installing.
3. Install a new O-ring then install the tank. Temporarily tighten the bolt and then after the pump is installed on the vehicle then tighten the bolt securely.
4. Install the cap and strainer.
5. Install a new rear cover O-ring.
6. Install the spring and press the rear cover with a hydraulic press so that the snap ring can be installed.
7. Install a new snap ring then install the bracket.
8. Install a new pulley shaft oil seal, using a suitable tool.
9. Install the pulley shaft assembly by adjusting with a screwdriver until the rotor comes to the center position.
10. Install a new snap ring, then install the pulley.
11. Install the connector and O-ring, then install the connector bolt washers and joint. Tighten the bolt to 36–51 ft. lbs.

Disassembly

1984 AND LATER

1. Remove the pulley.
2. Remove the tank.
3. Make match marks then remove the rear cover.
4. Remove the O-rings from the cam case making sure that the vane does not come off of the rotor.
5. Remove the snap ring, then pull pulley shaft out.
6. Install the cam case and rear cover, then remove the oil seal being careful not to damage the casing.
7. Remove the connector without dropping the spool.

Assembly

1. Assembly of the oil pump is the reverse of disassembly. Before installing O-rings and oil seals, apply a thin coat of power steering fluid to them.

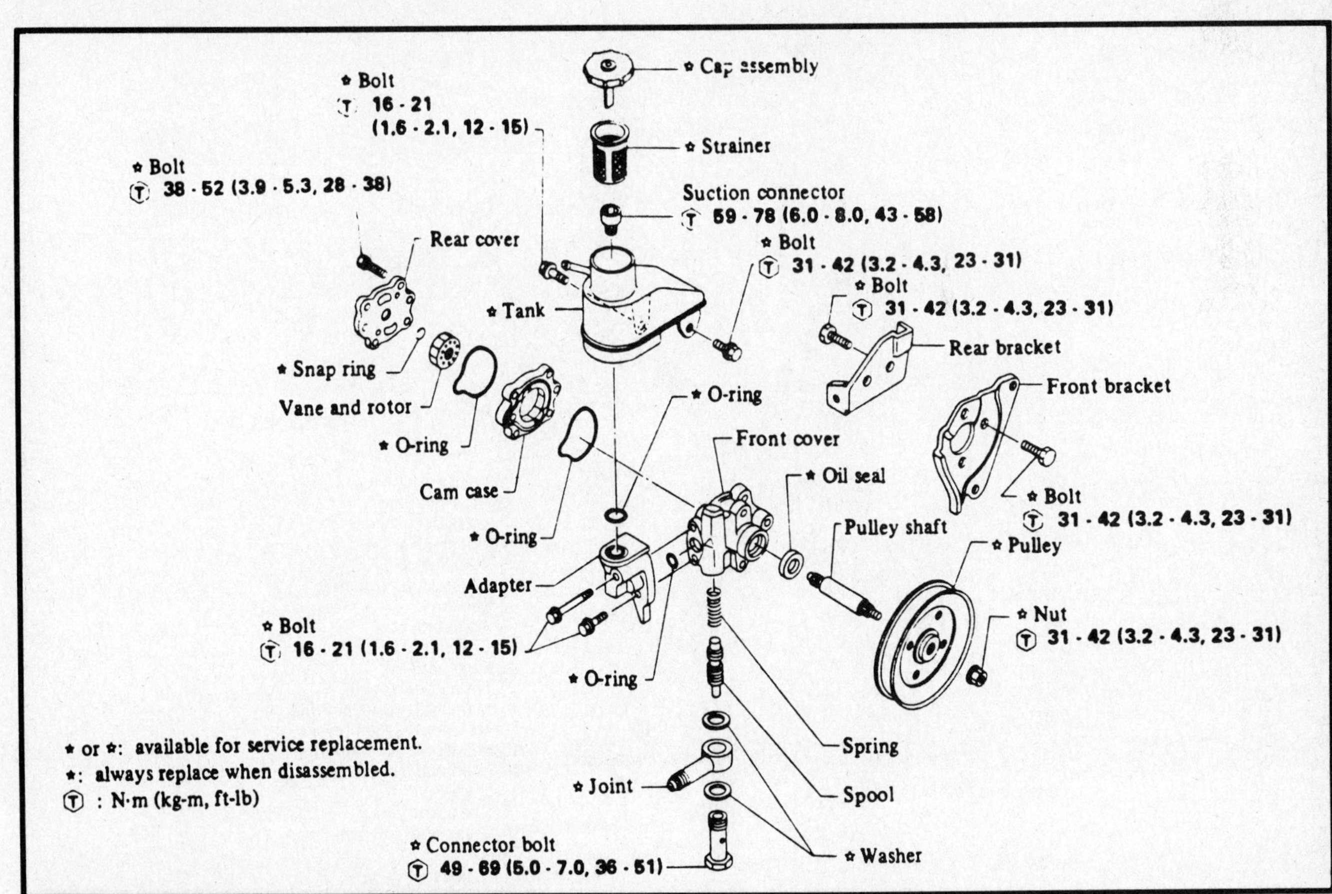

Power steering pump—Z24 engine—1984-85

CHRYSLER CORP.
ARROW, RAM 50, RAM RAIDER

Manual Steering Gear

Disassembly

1. Remove the gear box from the vehicle.
2. Remove the nut holding the Pitman arm on the cross shaft and using a gear puller, pull the arm from the shaft.
3. Before disassembling any further, record the starting preload of the mainshaft as a guide for reassembly.
4. Loosen the lock nut on the cross shaft adjusting bolt and turn the bolt slightly counterclockwise. Remove the cover bolts.
5. Lift the cover up slightly and turn the adjusting bolt in until it unfastens from the cover and remove the cover.
6. Turn the cross shaft until its teeth will fit through the cover hole and pull it out of the gear housing.

NOTE: Use care not to damage the cross shaft splines and the oil seal when removing the cross shaft.

7. Measure the main shaft starting preload with the cross shaft removed.
8. Loosen the end cover attaching bolts and remove the end cover and shim.

NOTE: Keep the shim for reassembly.

9. Gently pull out the main shaft, ball nut assembly and the bearings.

NOTE: Never attempt to disassemble the main shaft and ball nut assembly.

Assembly

1. Check the component parts for wear or damage. Make sure the ball nut slides easily on the mainshaft. There should not be excessive free play. Never allow the ball not to run entirely to the end of its travel, or it could be damaged.
2. Insert the main shaft assembly into the gear housing. Hold the main shaft horizontally.
3. Install the oil seal after applying a small amount of grease to its lip.
4. Install the gasket, shim and gasket end cover to the housing. Tighten the four end cover bolts to 11–45 ft.lb. Use sealant on both the cover gasket and the bolt threads.
5. Measure the main shaft preload. It should be between 3–4.8 ft.lb. If not, adjust by replacing the shim with a thicker or thinner shim. Shims come in thicknesses from 0.0020 to 0.0200 in.
6. Fit the adjusting bolt and shim in the top of the cross shaft and, using a feeler gauge, check the clearance between the adjusting bolt head and the cross shaft. Clearance should be 0–0.002. If not, replace the shim.
7. Insert the cross shaft into the gear housing. Be sure to align the teeth on both shafts in the center of their travel.

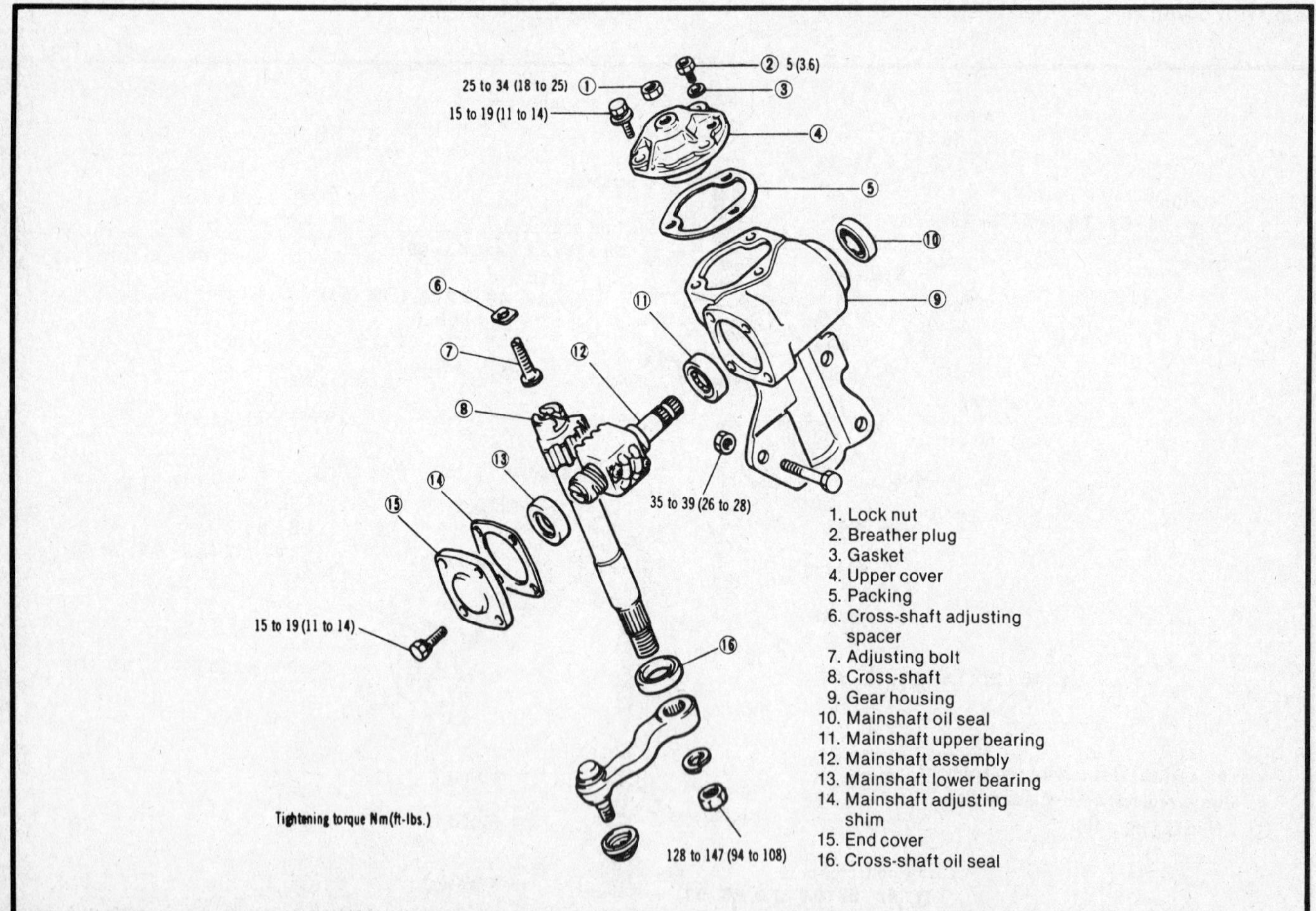

Arrow, Ram 50, Ram Raider manual steering gear

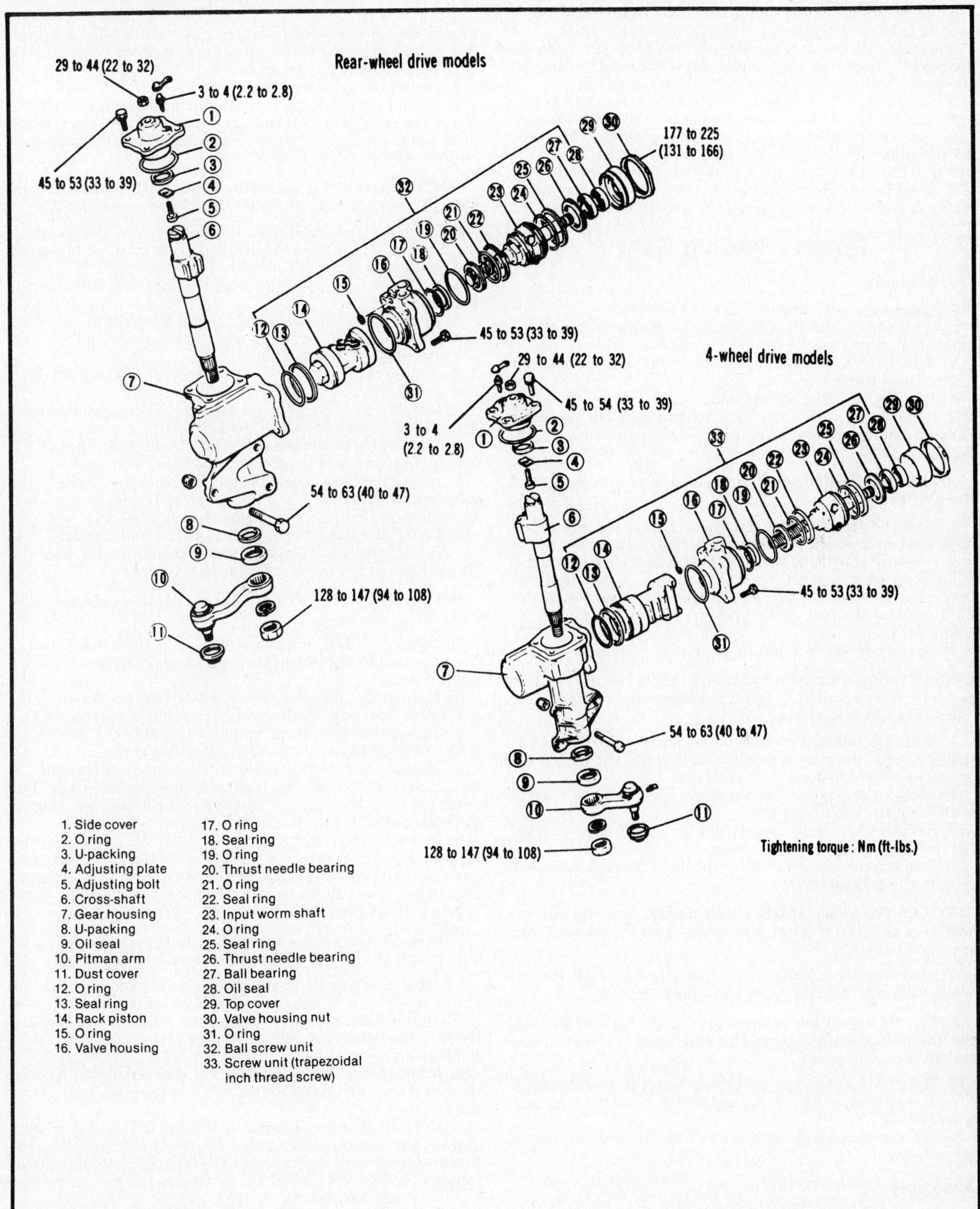
Rear-wheel drive models
29 to 44 (22 to 32)
3 to 4 (2.2 to 2.8)
45 to 53 (33 to 39)
177 to 225
(131 to 166)
45 to 53 (33 to 39)
54 to 63 (40 to 47)
128 to 147 (94 to 108)
4-wheel drive models
29 to 44 (22 to 32)
45 to 54 (33 to 39)
3 to 4
(2.2 to 2.8)
45 to 53 (33 to 39)
54 to 63 (40 to 47)
128 to 147 (94 to 108)
Tightening torque: Nm (ft-lbs.)
1. Side cover
2. O ring
3. U-packing
4. Adjusting plate
5. Adjusting bolt
6. Cross-shaft
7. Gear housing
8. U-packing
9. Oil seal
10. Pitman arm
11. Dust cover
12. O ring
13. Seal ring
14. Rack piston
15. O ring
16. Valve housing
17. O ring
18. Seal ring
19. O ring
20. Thrust needle bearing
21. O ring
22. Seal ring
23. Input worm shaft
24. O ring
25. Seal ring
26. Thrust needle bearing
27. Ball bearing
28. Oil seal
29. Top cover
30. Valve housing nut
31. O ring
32. Ball screw unit
33. Screw unit (trapezoidal inch thread screw)

Arrow, Ram50, Ram Raider power steering gear

8. Install the cover and torque the bolts to 11–14 ft.lb. Apply sealant to the cover gasket and the threads of the bolts.
9. Verify that the unit works smoothly, then screw the adjusting bolt in and out of the cover two or three times to adjust the cross shaft into proper mesh with the main shaft.
10. Loosen the adjusting bolt, making sure there is no free play at the mainshaft center position. Backlash should be 0–0.002 in.
11. Test the main shaft preload. Starting torque should be 5.7–7.4 ft.lb.
12. Fill the unit with multipurpose gear oil and install the pitman arm. Its two match marks should align with the match mark on the cross shaft. Tighten the nut to 94–109 ft.lb.

Power Steering Gear

Disassembly

1. Loosen the adjusting lock nut and remove it.
2. With the gear in neutral position, tap the bottom of the cross shaft with a plastic hammer to remove the cross shaft.
3. Remove the side cover bolts and screw in the adjusting bolt two or three turns.
4. Remove the valve housing nut.
5. Remove the valve housing bolts and take out the valve housing and rack piston, holding the rack piston to avoid turning it.

NOTE: Be careful not to let the rack piston fall off of the shaft.

6. Hold the valve housing in a vise and move the rack piston up and down to check the backlash between the groove of the rack piston and the balls. Measure the backlash after fully tightening the rack piston on the shaft and then loosening it two turns. Service limit is 0.008 in. If backlash exceeds the service limit, replace the ball screw unit and the rack piston as an assembly.
7. To remove the rack piston, turn it counterclockwise.

NOTE: There are twenty-six steel balls in the rack piston which will probably fall out when removed from the shaft. Do not lose them.

8. To disassemble the rack piston, remove the circular holder, the circulator, the steel balls, the seal ring and the O-ring. Do not disassemble the rack piston end cap.
9. Loosen the top cover and remove it and the input worm shaft from the valve housing.
10. Remove worm shaft thrust plate, thrust needle roller bearing, two seal rings and two O-rings.
11. Screw in the adjusting bolt at the tip of the cross shaft and remove the side cover.

NOTE: There are thirty-three needle bearing rollers which may fall out when the cross shaft is removed. Do not lose them.

12. Remove the following parts from the side cover: O-ring, needle bearings, adjusting bolt and adjusting plate.

NOTE: If no oil leaks through the threads of the adjusting bolt, do not remove the sealing at the rear of the needle bearing seat.

13. Remove the seal ring and O-ring from the valve housing.
14. To remove the ball bearing and oil seal in the top cover, use a brass drift.
15. Remove the oil seal and seal ring from the gear box using a screwdriver.

Assembly

1. Clean and inspect all parts for wear or damage. Always use new gaskets and oil seals and coat indicated parts with Dexron®II before installing.
2. Apply a thin coat of multipurpose grease to the bearing race in the side cover and insert the thirty-three roller bearings. Apply a dab of grease to bottom of the side cover. Be careful not to disturb the needle bearings.
3. Install the side cover O-ring.
4. With the adjusting bolt and adjusting plate inserted in the top of the cross shaft, measure the clearance between the bolt head and the cross shaft. It should be from 0 to 0.002 in. Adjust clearance by replacing shim plate.

NOTE: Install the adjusting plate with its chamfered side in contact with the surface of the cross shaft.

5. Align the cross shaft with the side cover and install. Attach them by tightening the adjusting bolt. Take care not to disturb the needle bearings while installing the cross shaft. Make sure not to damage the oil seal. Tighten the adjusting bolt lock nut temporarily.
6. To assemble the top cover, apply a thin coat of multipurpose grease to the lip of the oil seal and press fit it in the cover.
7. Press fit the ball bearing.
8. Apply a thin coat of multipurpose grease on the gear box oil seal and install it.
9. Install the O-ring first and then the seal ring on the input worm shaft. Lubricate with Dexron® II.
10. Install the thrust plate, thrust needle bearing and the thrust plate in the order given on the input worm shaft.
11. Install the O-rings and the seal ring into their seats in the valve housing without using undue force. The seal ring should be compressed into a heart shape when fit.
12. Install the input worm shaft in the valve housing.
13. Install the thrust plate, needle roller bearing and the thrust plate in the given order in the top cover.

NOTE: Install the thinner thrust plate on the top cover side.

14. Temporarily tighten the top cover to the valve housing. Take care not to disturb the thrust plate and needle roller bearing in the top cover.
15. Tighten the top cover bolts to 12–16 inch lbs. Turn the input worm shaft and check for smooth rotation and noise.
16. Tighten the valve housing nut to 130–166 ft. lb. Do not allow the top cover to rotate while tightening the nut.
17. Measure the starting preload of the input worm shaft. It should be from 3–5 inch lbs. If not, adjust by tightening or loosening the valve housing nut. Install the O-ring and seal ring on the rack piston in the given order.
18. Insert the rack piston in the input worm shaft until the piston reaches the end of its travel. Rotate the input shaft and align the ball running surface on the worm with the ball insertion holes. Insert nineteen balls into the hole, pushing them lightly with a brass rod.

NOTE: Do not rotate the worm shaft on rack piston at this point or the balls might enter other grooves.

19. After installing all nineteen of the balls, make sure the last ball is about ½ in. below the end of the rack piston. If there is more than a ½ in. clearance, it probably means one or more of the balls has fallen into a different worm groove. Remove the assembly and begin again.
20. Insert the remaining seven balls in the circulator, holding them in place with grease. Fit the circulator in place and tighten the screws.
21. Hold the gear box in a vise and install the ball screw unit. Tighten the valve housing to 33–40 ft. lb. After installation, rotate the input worm shaft to move the rack piston to the neutral (center) position. Be careful not to damage the seal ring when installing the rack piston.
22. Install the cross shaft assembly (with side cover) in to the gear box and tighten the side cover to 33–40 ft. lb. When installing the cross shaft, apply a thin coat of ATF to the teeth and

shaft of the rack piston and multipurpose grease to the oil seal lip. Do not rotate the side cover during installation or risk damage to the O-ring. It might be a good idea to wrap tape around the splined end of the cross shaft to prevent damage to the seals.

23. Measure the total starting torque of the input worm shaft to neutral position (center). Make sure the ball screw operates smoothly through its entire travel. Starting torque should be between 4–6 inch lbs. Tighten the valve housing nut to 130–166 ft.lb. Measure the preload after tightening.

24. Install the pitman arm on the cross shaft aligning the slit in the end of the shaft with the two slits on the pitman arm. Tighten the pitman nut to 94–109 ft.lb.

25. After tightening the pitman arm, measure the distance between the center of the frame mounting bolt hole closest to the pitman arm and the inner surface of the pitman arm. This length should be about 0.77 in.

Power Steering Pump

Disassembly and Assembly

SEPARATE RESERVOIR TYPE

1. Remove the pulley bracket with a gear puller.
2. Loosen and remove the suction port assembly.
3. Remove the pressure hose fitting assembly.
4. Remove the end plate retaining ring by inserting a small punch in the 0.13 in. diameter hole in the housing opposite the flow control valve hole. Compress the retaining ring with the punch and remove it by inserting a small pry tool under the ring and twisting.
5. Remove the end plate and the end plate O-ring. The end plate is spring loaded and should pop out. If it sticks, rocking it from side to side should free it.

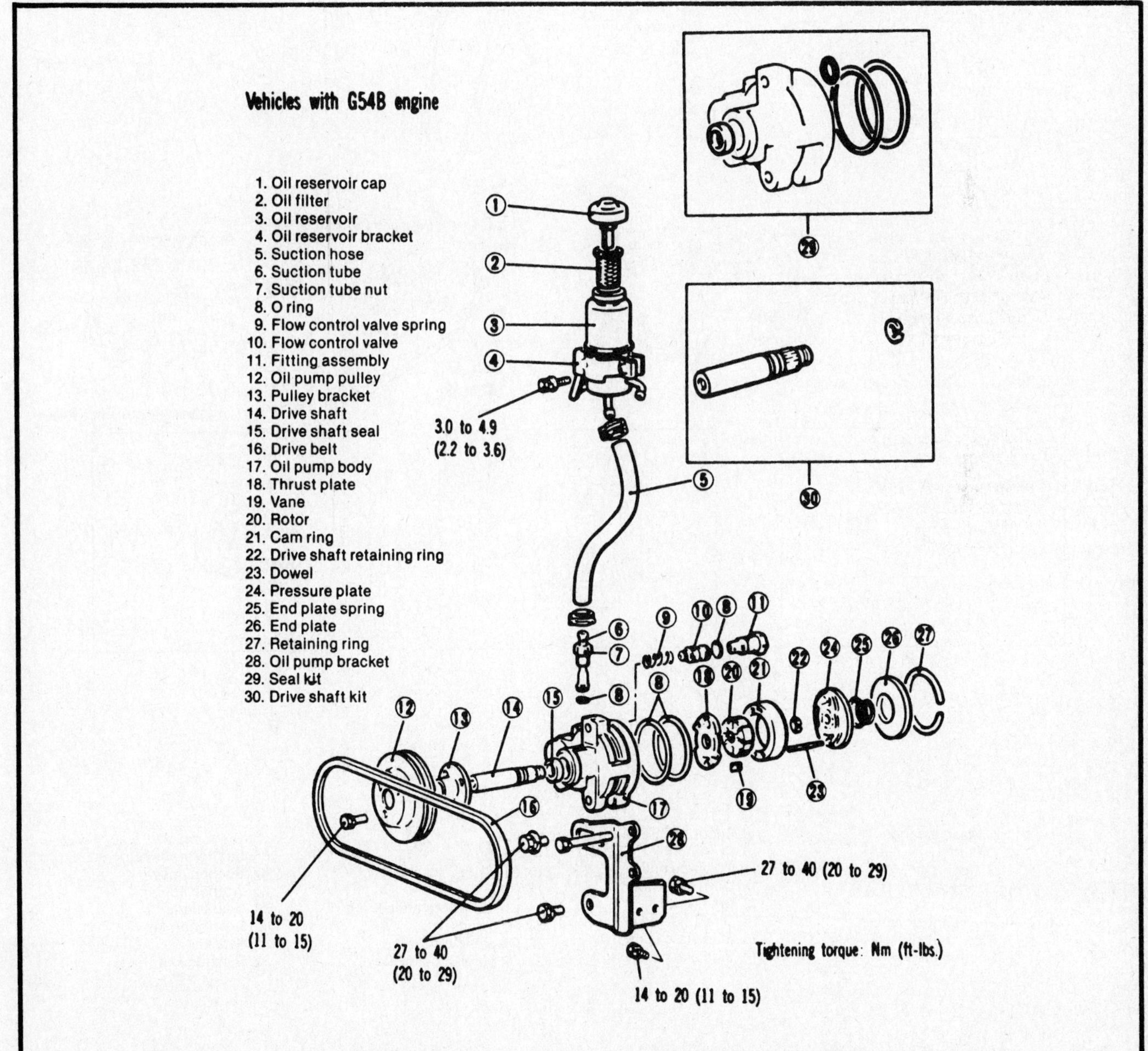

Arrow, Ram50, Ram Raider power steering pump—1982–86 with the GB4B (155.9) engine

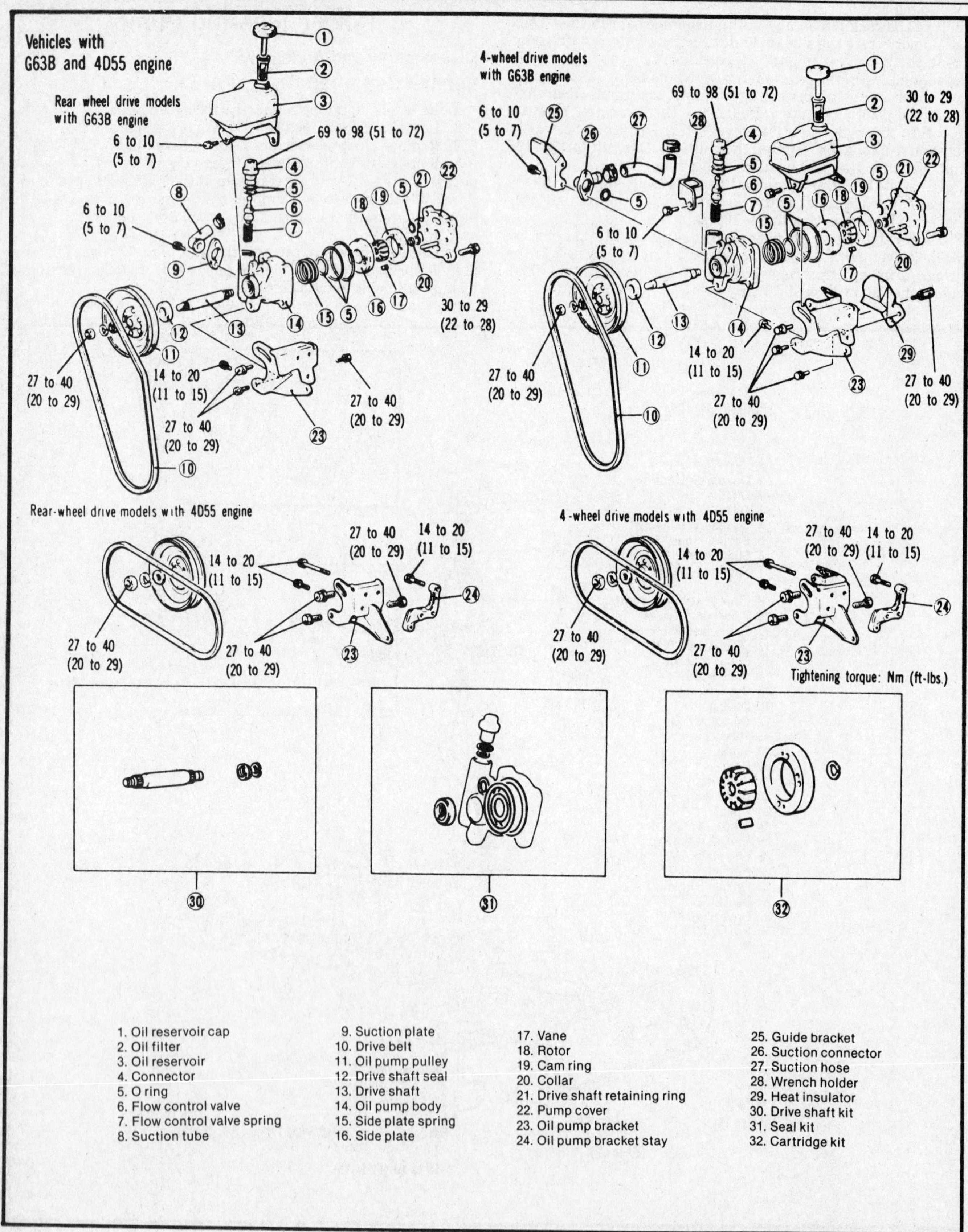
Vehicles with
G63B and 4D55 engine
Rear wheel drive models
with G63B engine
4-wheel drive models
with G63B engine
Rear-wheel drive models with 4D55 engine
4-wheel drive models with 4D55 engine
Tightening torque: Nm (ft-lbs.)
6 to 10
(5 to 7)
69 to 98 (51 to 72)
30 to 29
(22 to 28)
14 to 20
(11 to 15)
27 to 40
(20 to 29)
1. Oil reservoir cap
2. Oil filter
3. Oil reservoir
4. Connector
5. O ring
6. Flow control valve
7. Flow control valve spring
8. Suction tube
9. Suction plate
10. Drive belt
11. Oil pump pulley
12. Drive shaft seal
13. Drive shaft
14. Oil pump body
15. Side plate spring
16. Side plate
17. Vane
18. Rotor
19. Cam ring
20. Collar
21. Drive shaft retaining ring
22. Pump cover
23. Oil pump bracket
24. Oil pump bracket stay
25. Guide bracket
26. Suction connector
27. Suction hose
28. Wrench holder
29. Heat insulator
30. Drive shaft kit
31. Seal kit
32. Cartridge kit

Arrow, Ram50, Ram Raider power steering pump—1982–86 with the G635 (121.9) and 4D55 (143.2) engine

6. Turn the pump over and allow the flow control valve and the valve spring to fall out.
7. With the end cover O-ring removed, tap lightly on the end of the driveshaft to free the pressure plate.
8. Remove the pressure plate, driveshaft, pump ring, vanes and rotor.

NOTE: Do not remove the welch plug. If it is cracked or otherwise damaged, replace the whole housing.

9. Remove the driveshaft retaining ring.
10. Remove the rotor and thrust plate from the driveshaft and both dowel pins from the housing.
11. Pry the driveshaft seal out of the housing, being careful not to damage the housing, discard the shaft seal.
12. Clean all parts and inspect them for wear or damage.
13. Install new driveshaft seal using a seal installer with a press or hammer.

NOTE: Only use as much force as necessary to seat the seal.

14. Lubricate the pressure plate O-ring with Dexron® II or its equivalent and install it in the third groove from the rear of the housing.
15. Insert both dowel pins in the housing.
16. Assemble the driveshaft, thrust plate and rotor, then fit a new snap ring on the driveshaft. The rotor must have its countersunk side toward the thrust plate.
17. Lubricate the oil seal and driveshaft with Dexron® II or its equivalent and insert the driveshaft in the housing. Be sure to align the dowel pins with the thrust plate so as not to damage the oil seal lip.
18. Install the pump ring on the dowel pins with the arrow in the pump ring facing the rear of the housing.
19. Insert all ten vanes in the rotor slots with their rounded edges outward. They should slide freely in the rotor.

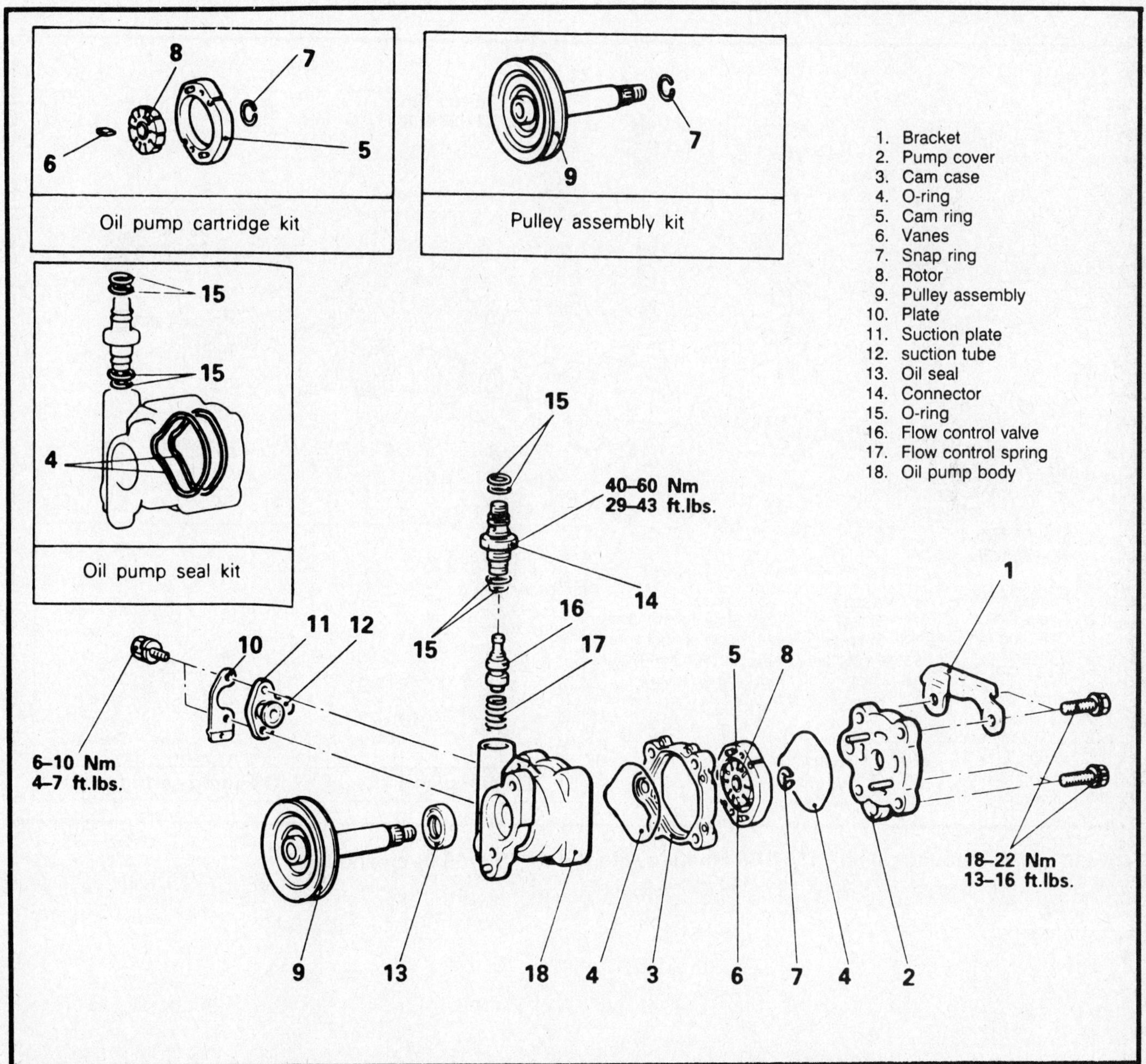

Ram Raider power steering pump—1987–88 pick-up with the G63B (121.9) and G54B (155.9) engine

20. Lubricate the pressure plate and install with O-ring on the dowel pins with the circular depression which holds the spring toward the rear of the housing. The pressure plate must be pressed about 0.06 in. over the O-ring to seat properly.
21. Fit the end plate O-ring in the second groove from the rear of the housing.
22. Install the end plate spring in the groove provided in the pressure plate.
23. Lubricate the end plate to avoid damage to the O-ring and press it into the housing. Fit the end plate retaining ring.
24. Be sure to bleed the system (refer to bleeding procedure).

RESERVOIR ON PUMP TYPE

1. Remove the oil reservoir.
2. Hold the pump in a vise, loosen the pump cover bolts and remove the cover.
3. Remove the following parts from the pump body: cam ring, vanes, O-ring, side plate assembly and the shaft assembly which includes the shaft, rotor, side plate, collar and snap ring.
4. Remove the shaft assembly snap ring and remove the collar, rotor side plate.
5. Remove the oil seal with a small pry tool. Remove the suction connector.
6. Remove the connector at the top of the pump body and remove the flow control valve assembly and flow control spring.
7. Assembly is the reverse of disassembly with the following instructions:
   a. Clean and check all parts for wear. Always use new gaskets and lubricate all parts with Dexron®II before assembling.
   b. Note the proper direction when installing the side plate, rotor and collar.
   c. When installing the cam ring, the countersunk holes at the end of the vanes face toward the cover.
   d. Fit the vanes with their rounded sides pointed out.
   e. Bleed the system.

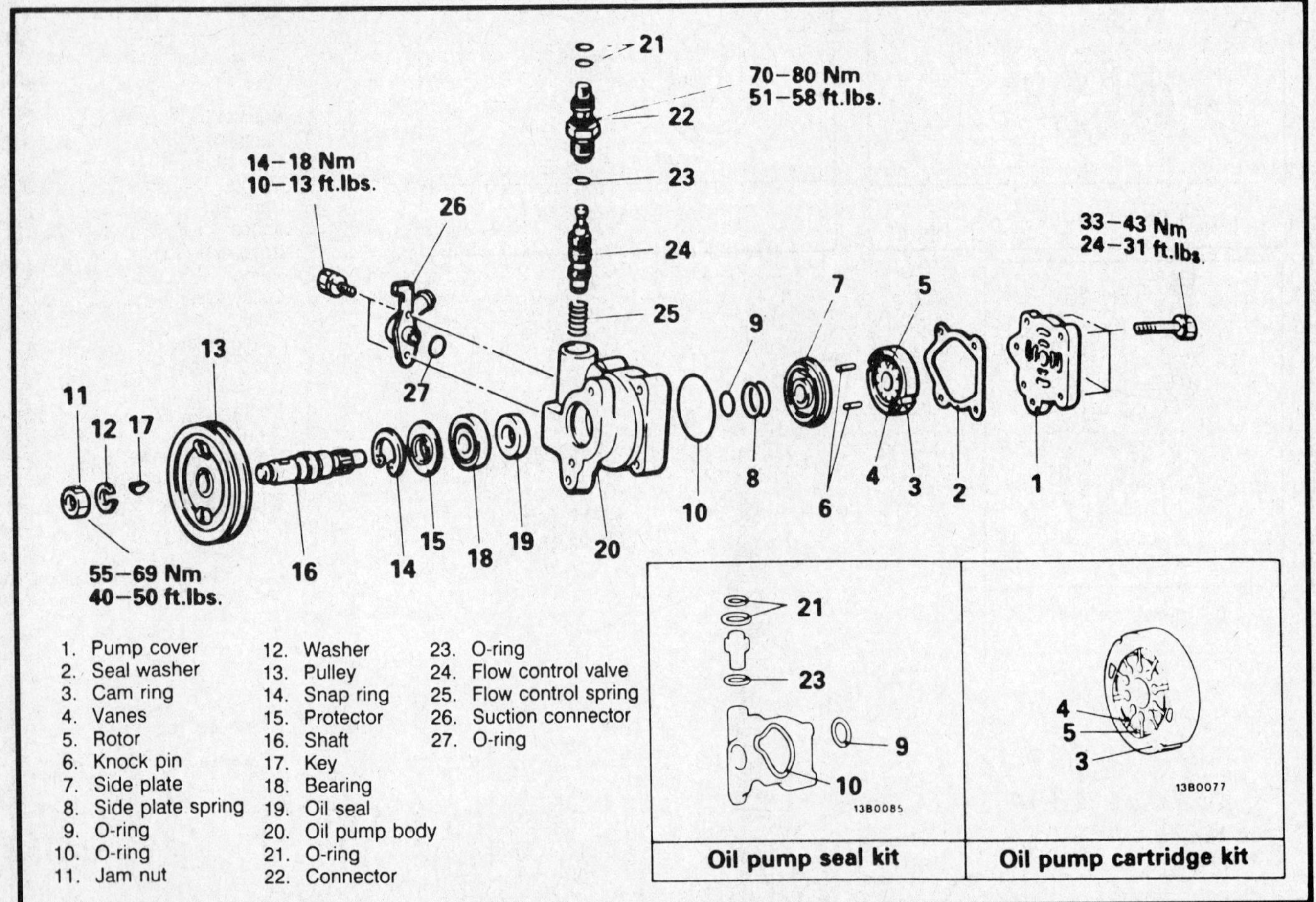

Ram50 power steering pump—1987–88 Montero with the G54B (155.9) engine

ISUZU

Manual Steering Gear

Disassembly

1. Remove the lock nut on the side cover.
2. Turn the adjusting screw counter-clockwise slightly, then remove the side cover fixiing bolt.
3. Turn the adjusting screw clockwise with the side cover kept from turning and remove the side cover.
4. Remove the gasket, adjusting screw and adjusting shim.
5. Hold the sector shaft in the straight ahead position and remove it from the gear box. Do not drive the sector shaft off the gear box with a hammer or any impact tools.
6. Remove the lock nut using special tool J-29753 or equivalent.
7. Remove the end cover using special tool J-7624 or equivalent then remove the oil seal and O-ring.
8. Remove the ball nut and worm shaft, always holding it in the horizontal position so that the ball-nut will not slide out.
9. Remove the bearings oil seal and bushings.

Assembly

Assembly of the steering gear is the reverse of disassembly with the following instructions:

1. When installing the end cover tape the splines so that you do not damage the oil seal, then adjust the bearing preload to 0.22–0.43 ft. lbs.,using special tool socket J-29754 or equivalent.
2. Torque the lock nut to 116–145 ft. lbs., then recheck the bearing preload.
3. When installing the sector shaft, align the center tooth of the ball nut with that of the sector shaft.
4. When installing the shim, adjust the clearance and check that the adjust screw slides freely. Clearance should be 0.004 in.
5. Before installing the side cover and gasket, apply a liquid sealer to the joining face of each part.
6. Install the locknut and adjust the backlash between the sector gear and ball nut as follows: Set the sector shaft in a straight ahead position. Using the adjusting screw, adjust the backlash to 0.36–0.72 ft. lbs. Torque the adjusting screw lock nut to 14–22 ft. lbs.

Power Steering Gear

Disassembly

1. Remove the dust cover, retaining ring and back up ring.
2. Clean the faces of the stub shaft extended outward and plug the hose fitting on the inlet side, then remove the oil seal by applying compressed air through the hole in the outlet side.
3. Remove the adjusting screw lock nut and turn the adjusting screw counter-clockwise to remove the preload between the sector gear and the rack piston, then remove the top cover bolts.
4. Hold the top cover stationary, turn the adjusting screw clockwise to raise and free the cover, then remove the cover.
5. Remove the O-ring and needle bearing.

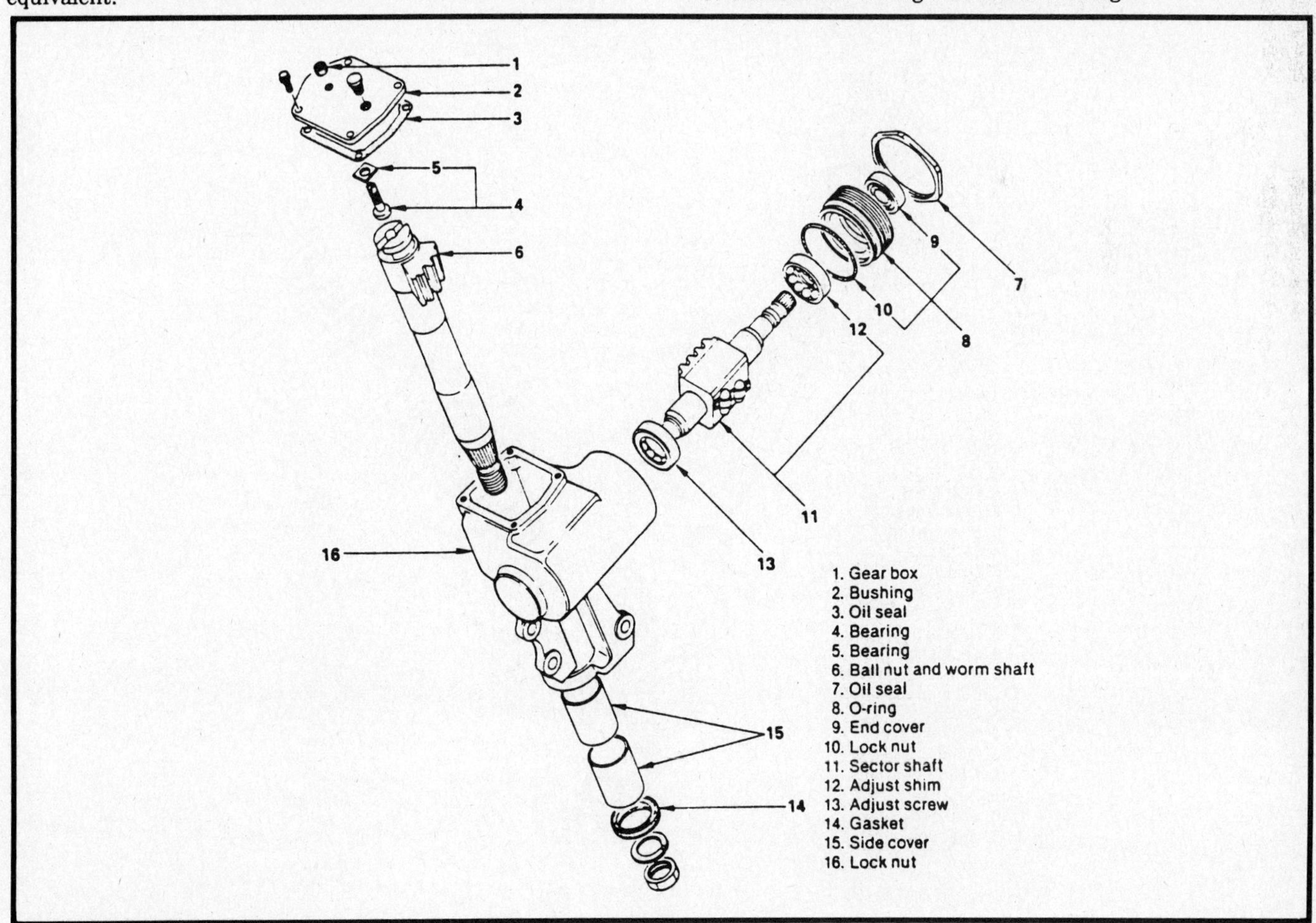

Isuzu manual steering gear

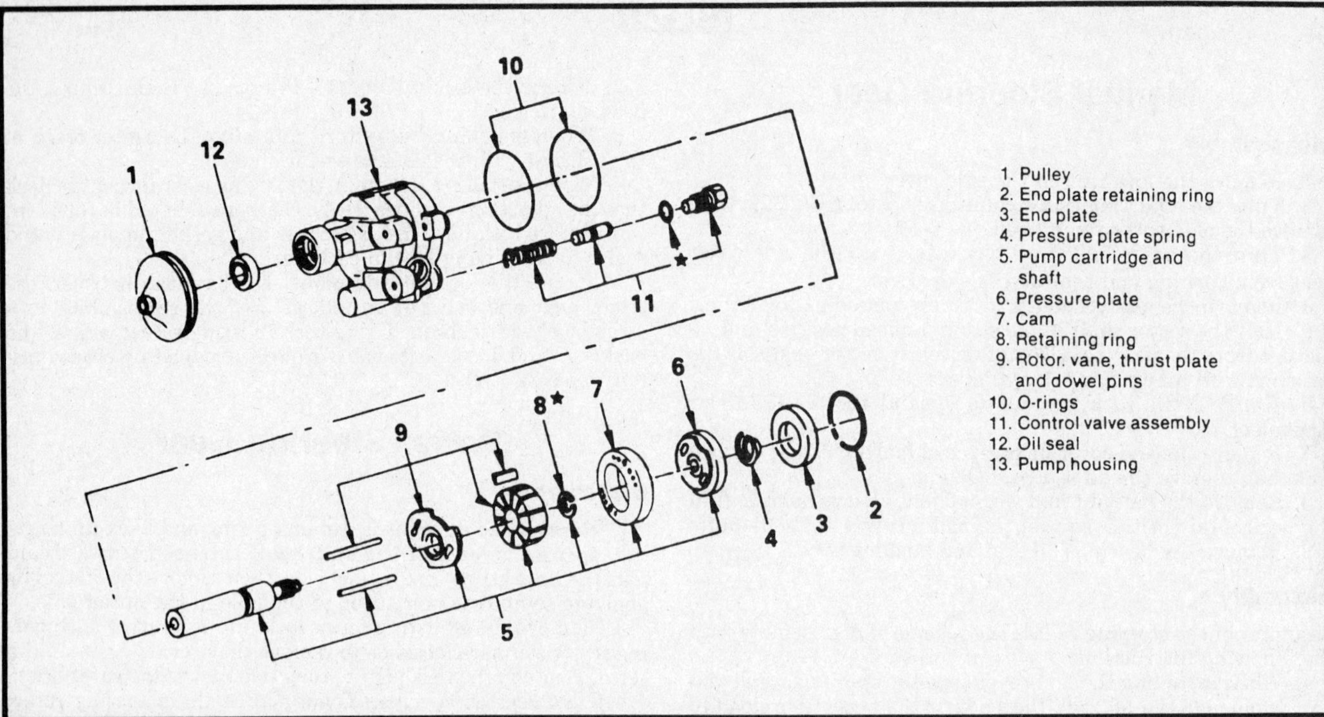

10
13
12
1
11
6
8★
7
9
4
3
2
5
★
1. Pulley
2. End plate retaining ring
3. End plate
4. Pressure plate spring
5. Pump cartridge and shaft
6. Pressure plate
7. Cam
8. Retaining ring
9. Rotor, vane, thrust plate and dowel pins
10. O-rings
11. Control valve assembly
12. Oil seal
13. Pump housing

Isuzu power steering pump—all except (4ZD1) 138 c.u. engine

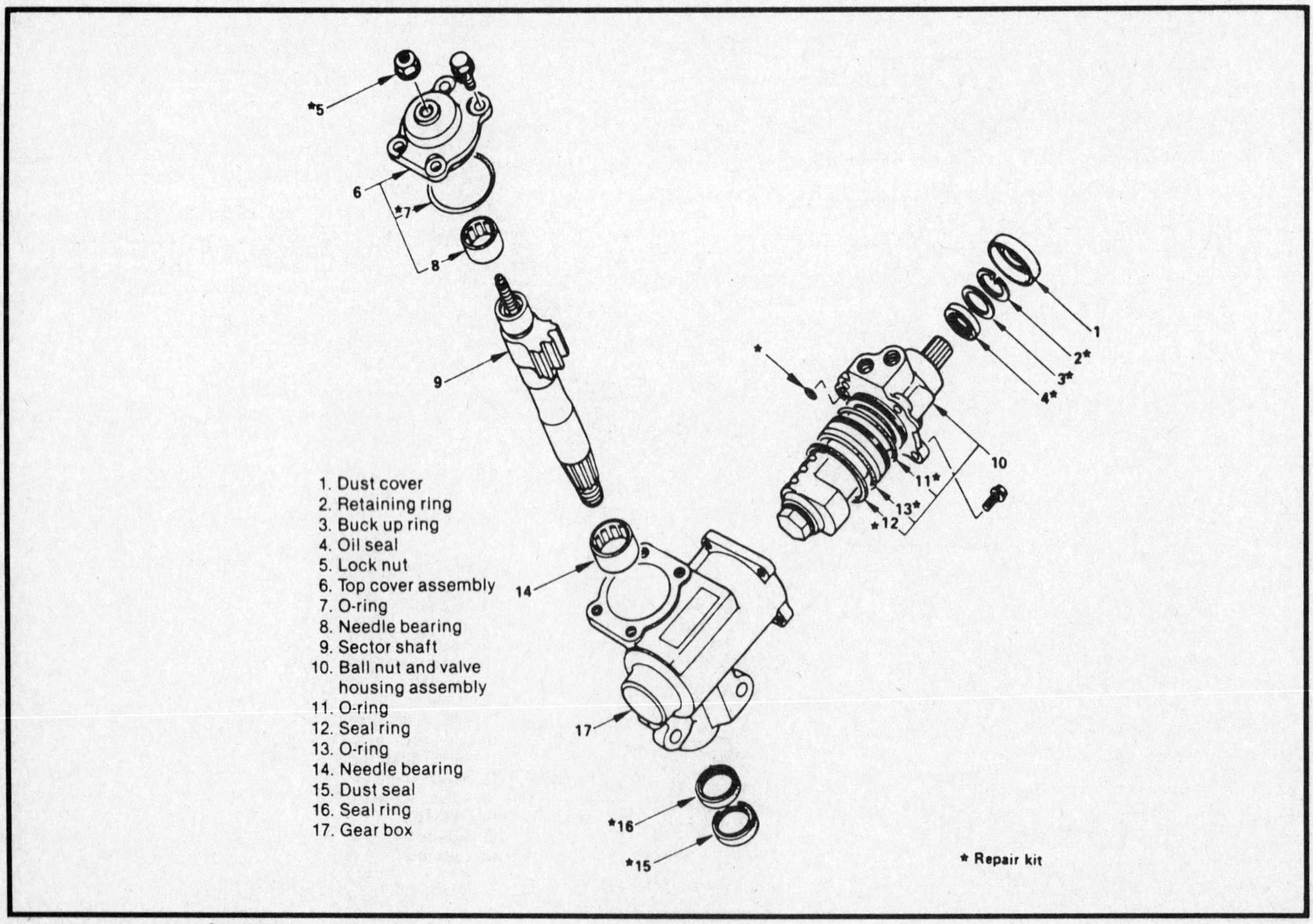

*5
6
*7
8
9
*
1
2*
3*
4*
10
11*
13*
*12
14
17
*16
*15
1. Dust cover
2. Retaining ring
3. Buck up ring
4. Oil seal
5. Lock nut
6. Top cover assembly
7. O-ring
8. Needle bearing
9. Sector shaft
10. Ball nut and valve housing assembly
11. O-ring
12. Seal ring
13. O-ring
14. Needle bearing
15. Dust seal
16. Seal ring
17. Gear box
* Repair kit

Isuzu power steering gear

6. Bring the stub shaft into a straight ahead position and remove the sector shaft.

NOTE: Do not use a hammer or any impact tools to remove the sector shaft.

7. Remove the ball nut and valve housing assembly.

NOTE: Always keep the ball nut and valve housing assembly in the horizontal position, or the rack piston will fall off onto the end of the worm, causing the rack piston to slip out of the worm shaft and the balls to fall out.

4. Remove the remainder of the seals and bearings.

Assembly

NOTE: Before reassembly apply a thin coat of grease to the lips of all seals and O-rings.

1. Install the seal ring and dust seal the the gear box.
2. Install the needle bearing into the housing.
3. Install the two O-rings and the seal ring onto the ball nut and valve assembly.
4. Install the ball nut and valve assembly and tighten the valve housing retaining bolts to 27–30 ft. lbs.

NOTE: Be careful not to drop the O-ring fitted to the oil passage in the valve housing. Refer to the note in Step 7 of disassembly.

5. Install the oil seal using special tool J-26508, then install the back up ring and retaining ring. Turn the face with the rounded edge (outer circumference) to the oil seal.
6. Install the dust cover.
7. Tape the sector shaft serration to protect the seal ring from damage, then align the center tooth of the ball nut with that of the sector shaft and install the sector shaft.
8. Install the needle bearing, O-ring and top cover. Tighten the top cover bolts to 27–30 ft. lbs.
9. Install the lock nut and adjust the backlash between the sector gear and ball nut as follows: Set the sector shaft in a straight ahead position. Using the adjusting screw, adjust the backlash to 3.4–5.6 ft. lbs. Tighten the lock nut to 25–35 ft. lbs.

Power Steering Pump

Disassembly and Assembly

ALL EXCEPT MODEL 4ZD1, 138 CID ENGINE

1. Remove the pulley.
2. Remove the end plate retaining ring then remove the end plate.
3. Remove the pressure plate spring.
4. Remove the pump cartridge and shaft.
5. Remove the pressure plate.
6. Remove the cam.
7. Remove the retaining ring, then remove the rotor vane thrust plate and dowel pins.
8. Remove the O-rings from the pump housing.
9. Remove the control valve assembly.
10. Remove the oil seal from the housing.
11. Assembly is the reverse of removal with the following instructions:
    a. When installing the oil seal to the housing, use special tool J-29755-3.

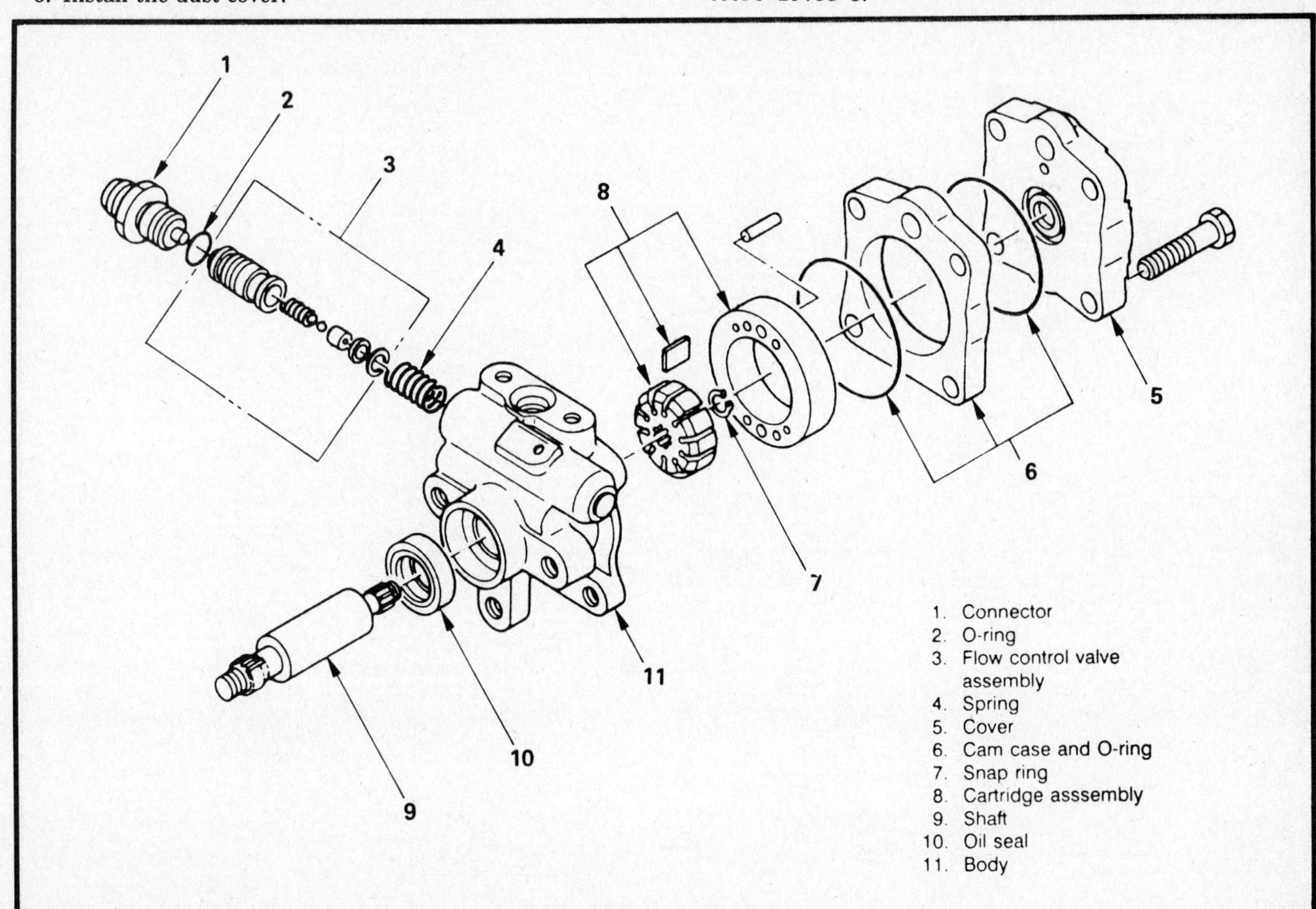

Isuzu power steering pump—(4ZD1) 138 c.u. engine

b. When installing the shaft and pump cartridge, install the vanes with the curved face in contact with the inner wall of the cam. Also set the side plate in the correct position.

c. Install the end plate retaining ring with the spring drawn in by a press.

d. Use a press to install the pulley.

MODEL 4ZD1, 138 CID ENGINE

1. Remove the pulley.
2. Remove the connector, O-ring, flow control valve assembly and spring from the body.
3. Remove the snap ring, then remove the cartridge asembly, shaft and oil seal.
4. Assembly is the reverse of removal with the following instructions:

a. When installing the oil seal to the body use a suitable bar tool.

b. When installing the cartridge assembly, install the rotor, cam ring and vane in the proper sequence. Place the rotor so that the specified mark turns up. Align the holes of the cam ring to the slots of the body and turn the face with clearance around douel up. The round end of the vane should be matched to the inner surface of the cam ring.

c. When installing the spacer and snap ring, make sure the outer diameter of the snap ring is less than 0.038 in.

MAZDA/COURIER

Manual Steering Gear

Disassembly and Assembly

1982-88

1. Remove the pitman arm nut and washer and remove the pitman arm using a puller, then remove the seal.
2. Remove the lock nut and bolt, then remove the side cover and gasket.
3. Remove the adjusting shim and adjusting screw, then pull out the sector shaft while keeping it in the middle position.
4. Remove the lock nut with special tool 49 1391 580 or its equivalent.
5. Remove the oil seal and the adjusting nut with special tool 49 UB39 585 or its equivalent.
6. Remove the bearing then the worm ball nut and the bearing at the end of the ball nut.
7. Assemble in the reverse order of disassembly with the following instructions:

a. Apply grease or oil to the lips of all oil seals.

b. Preload of the worm ball nut is 0.5–1.0 lb., using a pull scale (without sector). If an adjustment is to be made loosen

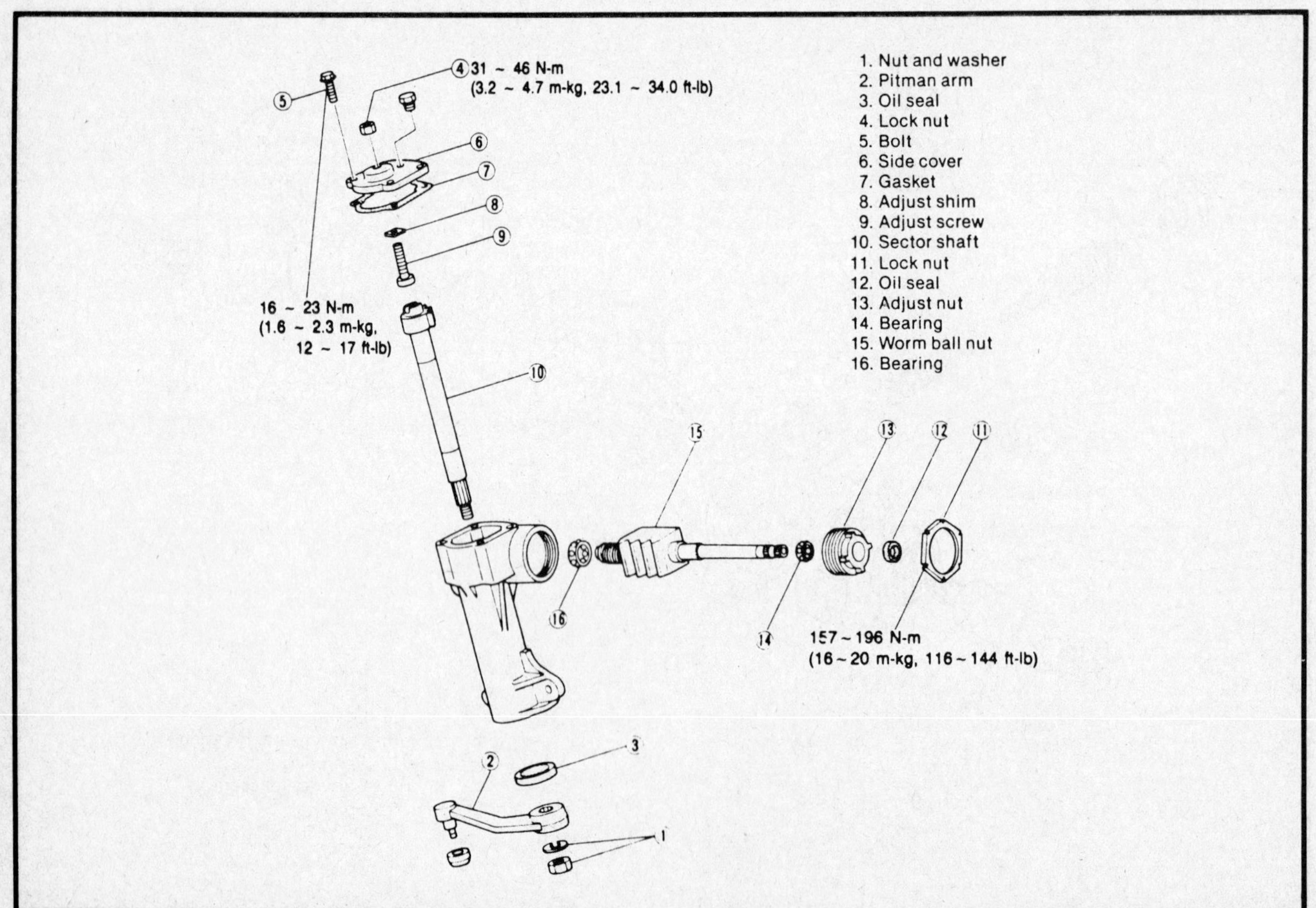

Mazda/Courier manual steering gear—1982 and later

the locknut and adjust with the adjusting screw. Tighten the locknut to 116–144 ft. lbs.

c. Set the adjusting screw and shim, in the "T" groove on the top of the sector shaft and measure the clearance in the axial direction. If the clearance is more than 0.004 in., adjust by selecting the proper size shim.

d. When installing the sector shaft, make sure the teeth of the sector shaft mesh with the center part of the teeth of the worm ball nut. The side cover tightening torque is 12–17 ft. lbs.

e. The pitman arm attaching nut torque is 108–130 ft. lbs.

f. Adjust the backlash while keeping the steering gear in the straight forward position. Backlash: 0mm

Power Steering Gear

Disassembly and Assembly

1. Plug the openings of all pipe installation fittings and clean the exterior of the gear assembly.
2. Remove the lock nut and bolts from the side cover, then remove the O-ring.
3. Remove the sector shaft dust cover and oil seal.
4. Remove the dust cover, snap ring, washer and oil seal then remove the valve and piston assembly.
5. Remove the O-ring and piston seal ring.
6. Assemble in the reverse order of disassembly with the following instructions.
   a. Apply grease or oil to the lips of all oil seals.
   b. Its a good idea to apply a sealing agent to the adjusting screws after adjustments are made.
   c. Position the worm shaft with the vehicle in the straight ahead position and then set the sector shaft adjustment screw so that the preload at that position is 2.2 lb. or less. Tighten the adjustment screw lock nut to 25–35 ft. lbs. The preload at the straight ahead position must be 0.4–0.9 lb. higher than when the steering wheel is turned 360° to the left or right.
   d. Tighten the side cover bolts to 29–36 ft. lbs.

Power Steering Pump

Disassembly and Assembly

ALL EXCEPT 1987–88 MODEL B2600

1. Before disassembly, plug the pipe installation hole, then clean the exterior of the pump assembly.
2. Secure the pump in a vise.
3. Remove the nut, washer and oil tank.
4. Remove the two through bolts and remove the rear body.
5. Remove the rubber O-ring, the cam ring and the rotor and vanes.
6. Remove the pressure plate. Remove the small and large O-rings, then remove the front body.
7. Compress the clip in the front body using snap ring pliers then remove from the groove using the appropriate tool.
8. Remove the bearing and drive shaft, retaining ring and oil seal.
9. Remove the control valve O-ring and seal.
10. Assembly is the reverse of disassembly with the following instructions:
    a. Before assembly, apply automatic transmission fluid

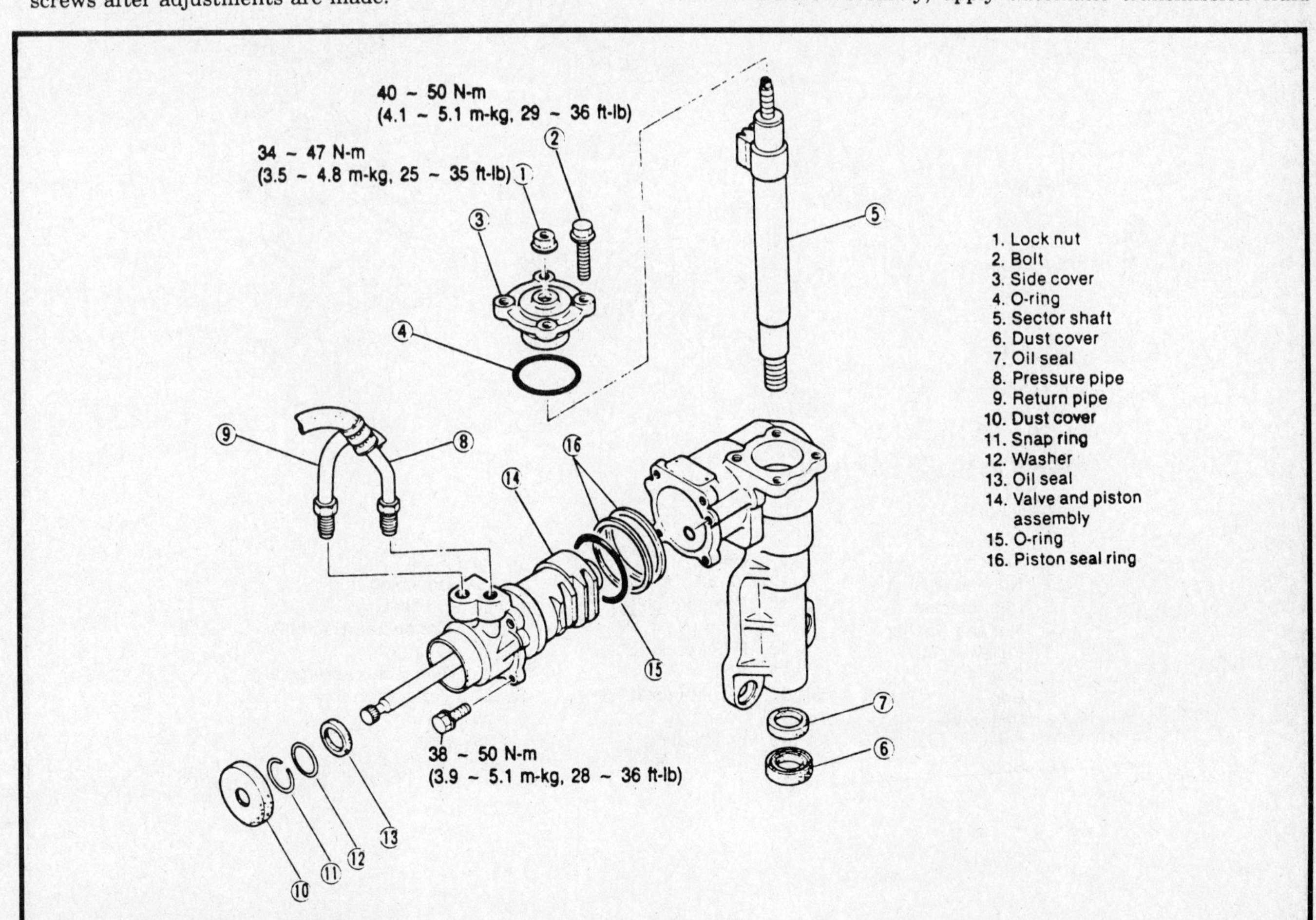

Mazda/Courier power steering gear

Type F to the vanes, rotor and control valve. Also apply a lithium base grease to the lip of the oil seal.

b. Attach the vanes to the rotor so that the rounded end contacts the cam.

c. When installing the oil seal, use a press and a piece of pipe with an outer diameter of 1.102 in., inner diameter 0.079 in. to press the oil seal in.

1987–88 MODEL B2600

1. Before disassembly, plug the pipe installation hole, then clean the exterior of the pump assembly.
2. Secure the pump in a vise.
3. Disassemble in the numbered order.
4. Assembly is the reverse of disassembly with the following instructions:

a. Before assembly, apply AFT type F or Dexron II to the vanes, rotor and control valve.

b. Apply lithium base grease to the lip of the oil seal.

c. Use a new seal kit when assembling.

d. Torque the pulley installation nut to 29–43 ft. lbs.

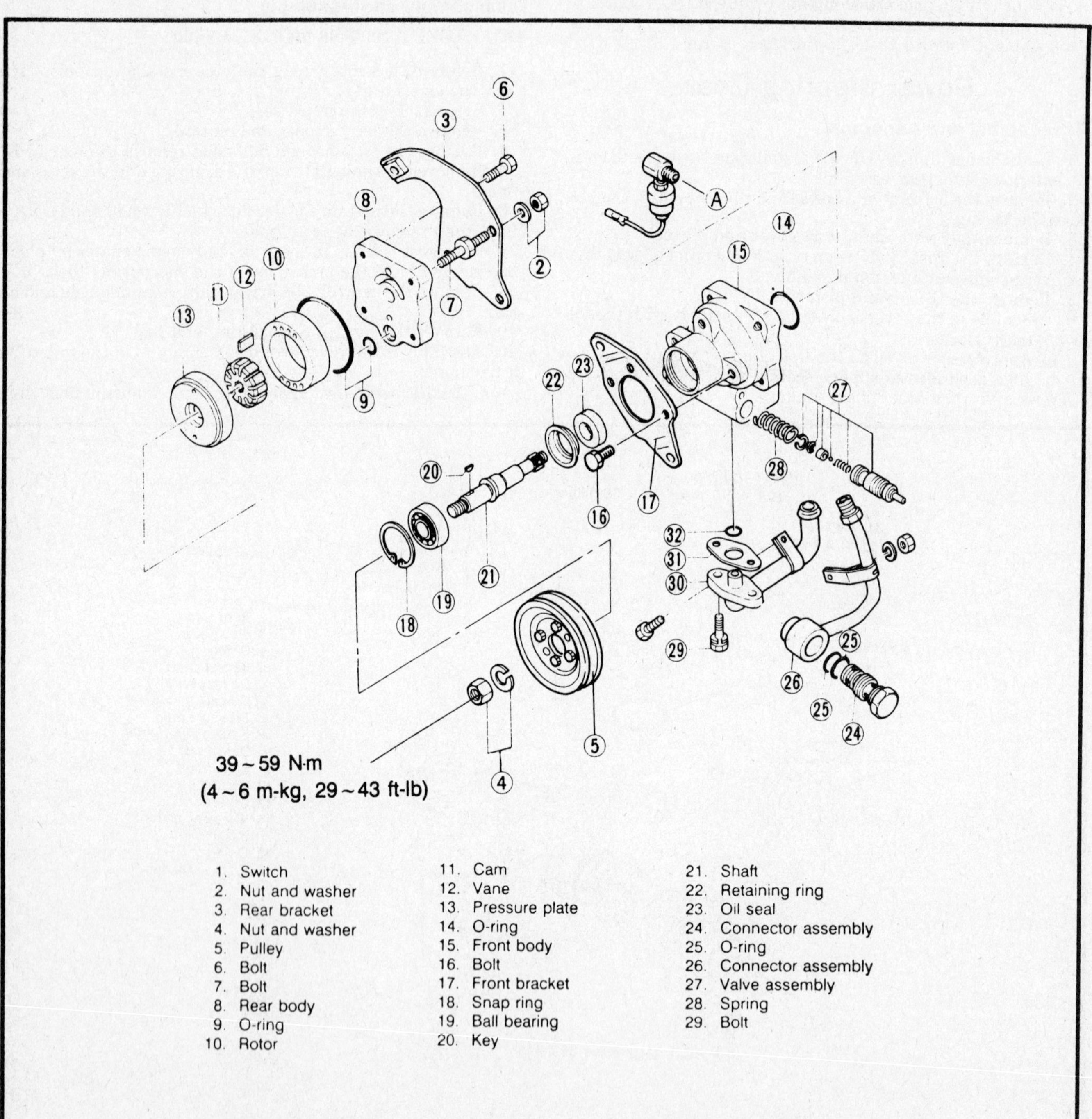

Mazda power steering pump—1987–88 Model B2600

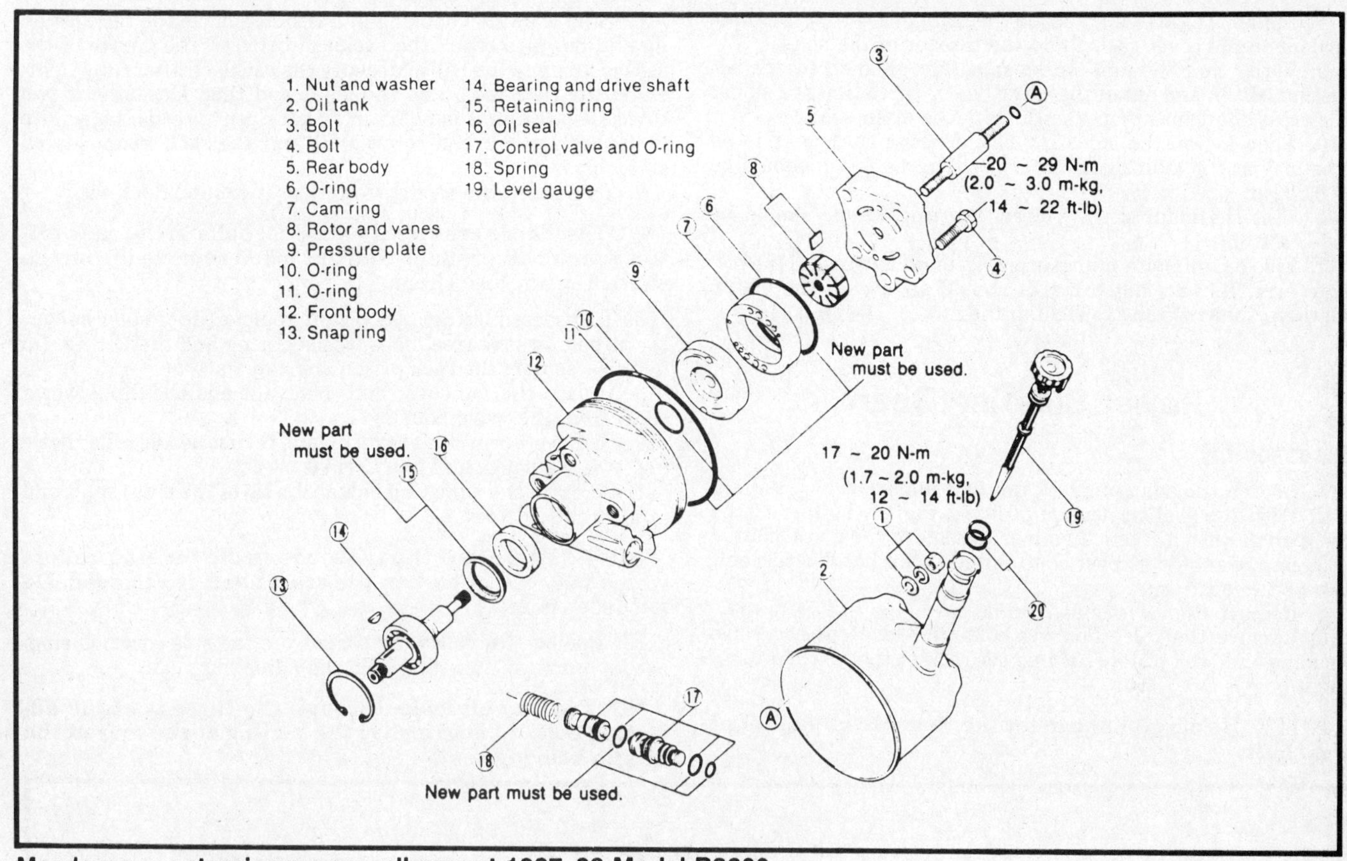

Mazda power steering pump—all except 1987–88 Model B2600

MITSUBISHI PICK-UP AND MONTERO

Manual Steering Gear

Disassembly

1. Remove the gear box from the vehicle.
2. Remove the nut holding the pitman arm on the cross shaft and using a gear puller, pull the arm from the shaft.
3. Before disassembling any further, record the starting preload of the mainshaft as a guide for reassembly.
4. Loosen the lock nut on the cross shaft adjusting bolt and turn the bolt slightly counterclockwise. Remove the cover bolts.
5. Lift the cover up slightly and turn the adjusting bolt in until it unfastens from the cover and remove the cover.
6. Turn the cross shaft until its teeth will fit through the cover hole and pull it out of the gear housing.

NOTE: Use care not to damage the cross shaft splines and the oil seal when removing the cross shaft.

7. Measure the main shaft starting preload with the cross shaft removed.
8. Loosen the end cover attaching bolts and remove the end cover and shim.

NOTE: Keep the shim for reassembly.

9. Gently pull out the main shaft, ball nut assembly and the bearings.

NOTE: Never attempt to disassemble the main shaft and ball nut assembly.

Assembly

1. Check the component parts for wear or damage. Make sure the ball nut slides easily on the mainshaft. There should not be excessive free play. Never allow the ball not to run entirely to the end of its travel, or it could be damaged.
2. Insert the main shaft assembly into the gear housing. Hold the main shaft horizontally.
3. Install the oil seal after applying a small amount of grease to its lip.
4. Install the gasket, shim and gasket end cover to the housing. Tighten the four end cover bolts to 11–45 ft. lb. Use sealant on both the cover gasket and the bolt threads.
5. Measure the main shaft preload. It should be between 3–4.8 ft. lb. If not, adjust it replacing the shim with a thicker or thinner shim. Shims come in thicknesses from 0.0020 to 0.0200 in.
6. Fit the adjusting bolt and shim in the top of the cross shaft and, using a feeler gauge, check the clearance between the adjusting bolt head and the cross shaft. Clearance should be 0–0.002. If not, replace the shim.
7. Insert the cross shaft into the gear housing. Be sure to align the teeth on both shafts in the center of their travel.

8. Install the cover and torque the bolts to 11–14 ft.lb. Apply sealant to the cover gasket and the threads of the bolts.

9. Verify that the unit works smoothly, then screw the adjusting bolt in and out of the cover two or three times to adjust the cross shaft into proper mesh with the main shaft.

10. Then loosen the adjusting bolt, making sure there is no free play at the mainshaft center position. Backlash should be 0–0.002 in.

11. Test the main shaft preload. Starting torque should be 5.7–7.4 ft.lb.

12. Fill the unit with multipurpose gear oil and install the pitman arm. Its two match marks should align with the match mark on the cross shaft. Tighten the nut to 94–109 ft.lb.

Power Steering Gear

Disassembly

1. Loosen the adjusting lock nut and remove it.
2. With the gear in neutral position, tap the bottom of the cross shaft with a plastic hammer to remove the cross shaft.
3. Remove the side cover bolts and screw in the adjusting bolt two or three turns.
4. Remove the valve housing nut.
5. Remove the valve housing bolts and take out the valve housing and rack piston, holding the rack piston to avoid turning it.

NOTE: Be careful not to let the rack piston fall off of the shaft.

6. Hold the valve housing in a vise and move the rack piston up and down to check the backlash between the groove of the rack piston and the balls. Measure the backlash after fully tightening the rack piston on the shaft and then loosening it two turns. Service limit is 0.008 in. If backlash exceeds the service limit, replace the ball screw unit and the rack piston as an assembly.
7. To remove the rack piston, turn it counterclockwise.

NOTE: There are twenty-six steel balls in the rack piston which will probably fall out when removed from the shaft. Do not lose them.

8. To disassemble the rack piston, remove the circular holder, the circulator, the steel balls, the seal ring and the O-ring. Do not disassemble the rack piston end cap.
9. Loosen the top cover and remove it and the input worm shaft from the valve housing.
10. Remove worm shaft thrust plate, thrust needle roller bearing, two seal rings and two O-rings.
11. Screw in the adjusting bolt at the tip of the cross shaft and remove the side cover.

NOTE: There are thirty-three needle bearing rollers which may fall out when the cross shaft is removed. Do not lose them.

12. Remove the following parts from the side cover: O-ring, needle bearings, adjusting bolt and adjusting plate.

NOTE: If no oil leaks through the threads of the adjusting bolt, do not remove the sealing at the rear of the needle bearing seat.

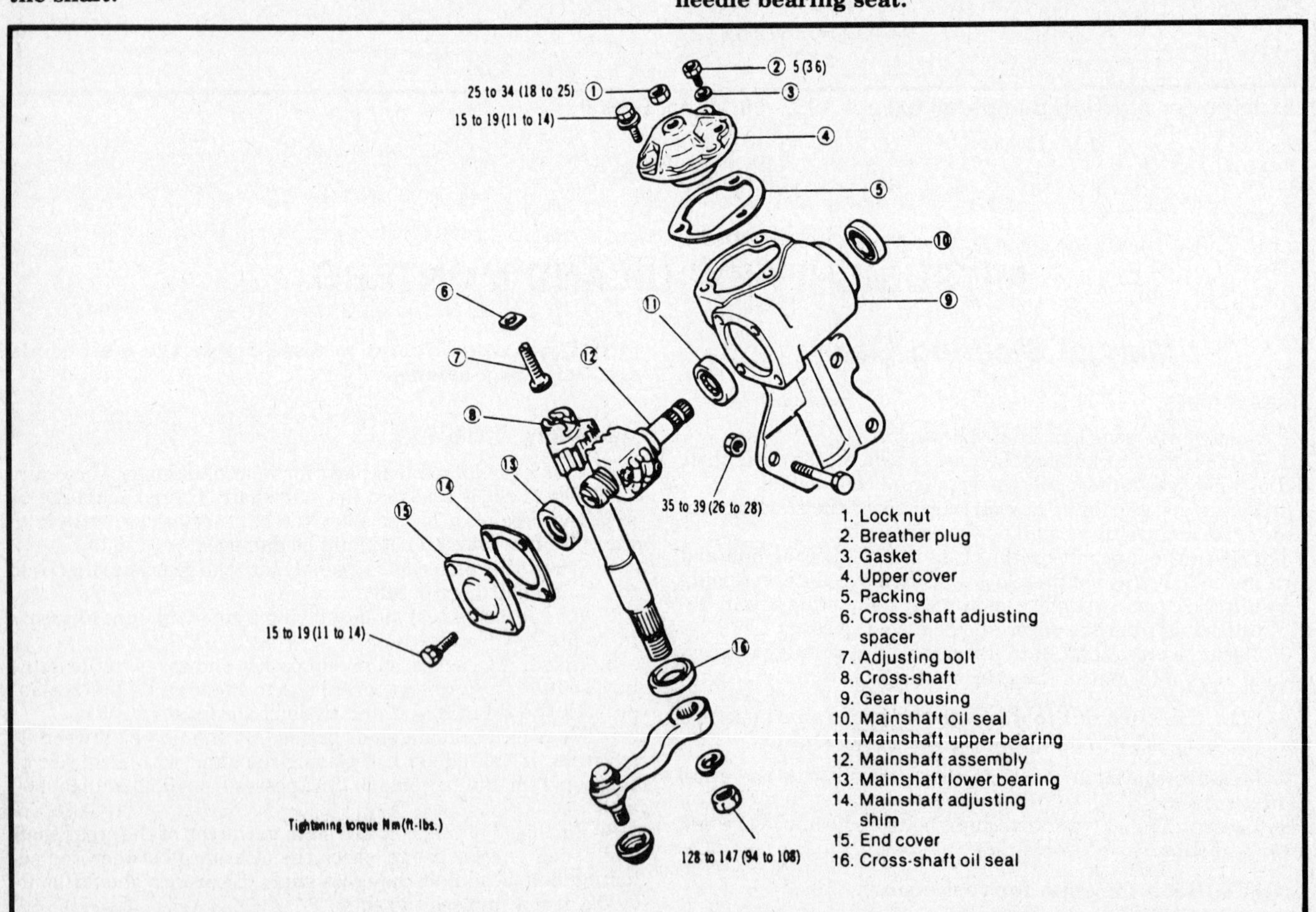

Mitsubishi manual steering gear

13. Remove the seal ring and O-ring from the valve housing.
14. To remove the ball bearing and oil seal in the top cover, use a brass drift.
15. Remove the oil seal and seal ring from the gear box using a screwdriver.

Assembly

1. Clean and inspect all parts for wear or damage. Always use new gaskets and oil seals and coat indicated parts with Dexron®II before installing.
2. Apply a thin coat of multipurpose grease to the bearing race in the side cover and insert the thirty-three roller bearings. Apply a dab of grease to bottom of the side cover. Be careful not to disturb the needle bearings.
3. Install the side cover O-ring.
4. With the adjusting bolt and adjusting plate inserted in the top of the cross shaft, measure the clearance between the bolt head and the cross shaft. It should be from 0 to 0.002 in. Adjust clearance by replacing shim plate.

NOTE: Install the adjusting plate with its chamfered side in contact with the surface of the cross shaft.

5. Align the cross shaft with the side cover and install. Attach them by tightening the adjusting bolt. Take care not to disturb

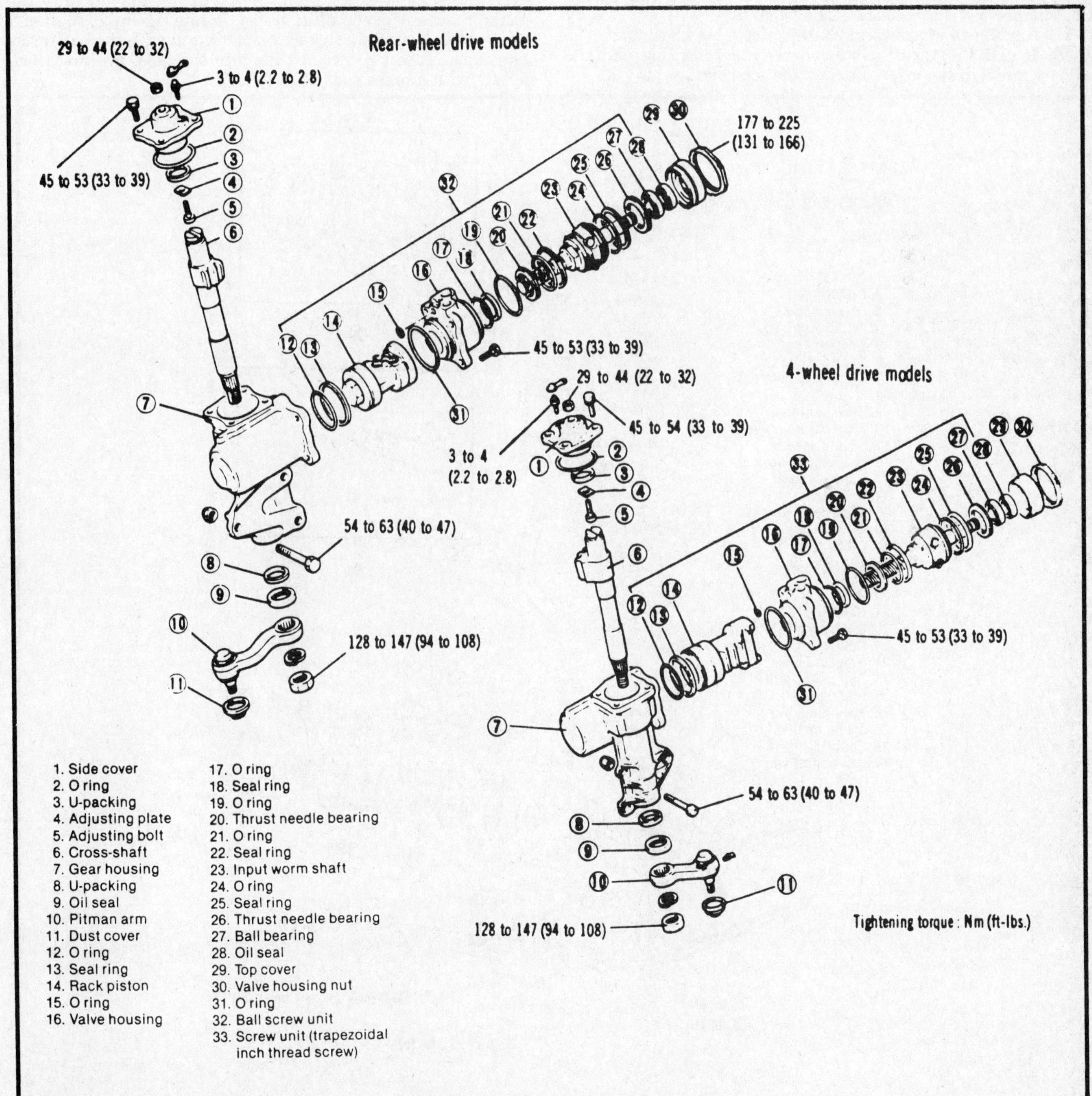

Mitsubishi power steering gear

the needle bearings while installing the cross shaft. Make sure you don't damage the oil seal. Tighten the adjusting bolt lock nut temporarily.

6. To assemble the top cover, apply a thin coat of multipurpose grease to the lip of the oil seal and press fit it in the cover.

7. Press fit the ball bearing.

8. Apply a thin coat of multipurpose grease on the gear box oil seal and install it.

9. Install the O-ring first and then the seal ring on the input worm shaft. Lubricate with Dexron® II.

10. Install the thrust plate, thrust needle bearing and the thrust plate in the order given on the input worm shaft.

11. Install the O-rings and the seal ring into their seats in the valve housing without using undue force. The seal ring should be compressed into a heart shape when fit.

12. Install the input worm shaft in the valve housing.

13. Install the thrust plate, needle roller bearing and the thrust plate in the given order in the top cover.

NOTE: Install the thinner thrust plate on the top cover side.

14. Temporarily tighten the top cover to the valve housing. Take care not to disturb the thrust plate and needle roller bearing in the top cover.

15. Tighten the top cover bolts to 12–16 inch lbs. Turn the input worm shaft and check for smooth rotation and noise.

16. Tighten the valve housing nut to 130–166 ft. lb. Do not allow the top cover to rotate while tightening the nut.

17. Measure the starting preload of the input worm shaft. It should be from 3–5 inch lbs. If not, adjust by tightening or loosening the valve housing nut. Install the O-ring and seal ring on the rack piston in the given order.

18. Insert the rack piston in the input worm shaft until the piston reaches the end of its travel. Rotate the input shaft and align the ball running surface on the worm with the ball insertion holes. Insert nineteen balls into the hole, pushing them lightly with a brass rod.

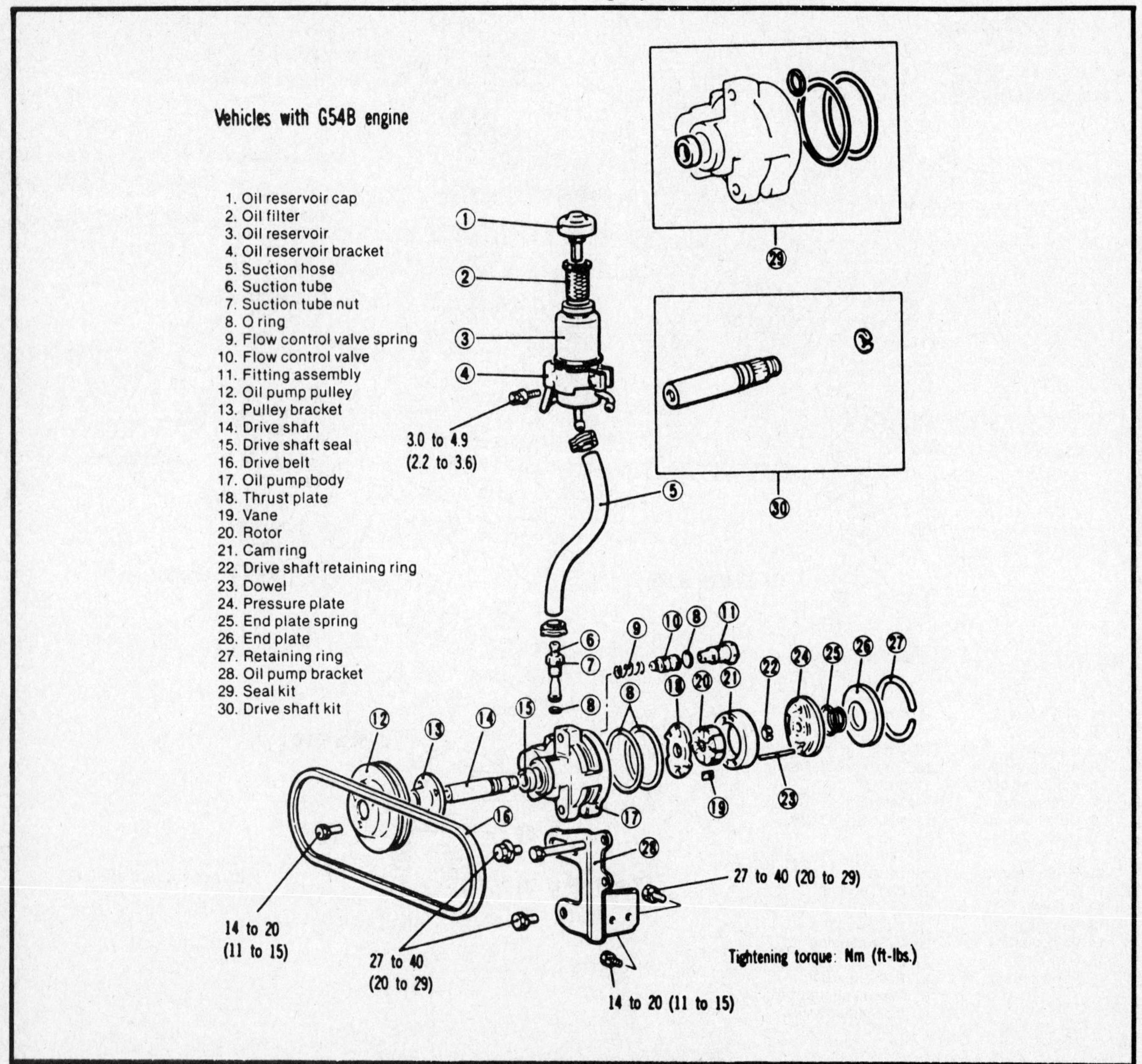

Mitsubishi power steering pump—1982-86 with the GB4B (155.9) engine

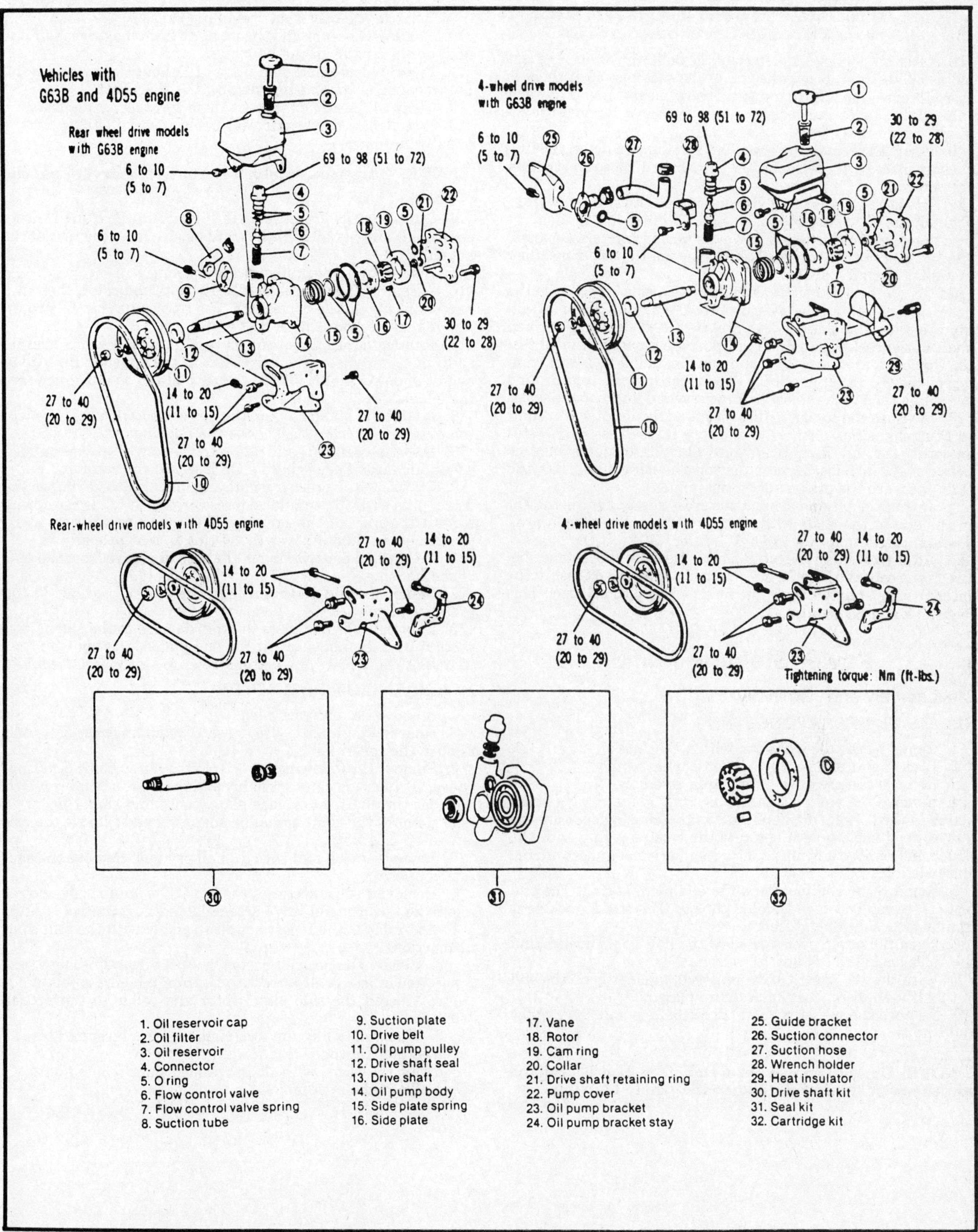

Mitsubishi power steering pump–1982-86 with the G635 (121.9) and 4D55 (143.2) engine

NOTE: Do not rotate the worm shaft on rack piston at this point or the balls might enter other grooves.

19. After installing all nineteen of the balls, make sure the last ball is about ½ in. below the end of the rack piston. If there is more than a ½ in. clearance, it probably means one or more of the balls has fallen into a different worm groove. Remove the assembly and begin again.

20. Insert the remaining seven balls in the circulator, holding them in place with grease. Fit the circulator in place and tighten the screws.

21. Hold the gear box in a vise and install the ball screw unit. Tighten the valve housing to 33–40 ft. lb. After installation, rotate the input worm shaft to move the rack piston to the neutral (center) position. Be careful not to damage the seal ring when installing the rack piston.

22. Install the cross shaft assembly (with side cover) in to the gear box and tighten the side cover to 33–40 ft. lb. When installing the cross shaft, apply a thin coat of ATF to the teeth and shaft of the rack piston and multipurpose grease to the oil seal lip. Do not rotate the side cover during installation or risk damage to the O-ring. It might be a good idea to wrap tape around the splined end of the cross shaft to prevent damage to the seals.

23. Measure the total starting torque of the input worm shaft to neutral position (center). Make sure the ball screw operates smoothly through its entire travel. Starting torque should be between 4–6 inch lbs. Tighten the valve housing nut to 130–166 ft.lb. Measure the preload after tightening.

24. Install the pitman arm on the cross shaft aligning the slit in the end of the shaft with the two slits on the pitman arm. Tighten the pitman nut to 94–109 ft.lb.

25. After tightening the pitman arm, measure the distance between the center of the frame mounting bolt hole closest to the pitman arm and the inner surface of the pitman arm. This length should be about 0.77 in.

Power Steering Pump

Disassembly and Assembly

SEPARATE RESERVOIR TYPE

1. Remove the pulley bracket with a gear puller.
2. Loosen and remove the suction port assembly.
3. Remove the pressure hose fitting assembly.
4. Remove the end plate retaining ring by inserting a small punch in the 0.13 in. diameter hole in the housing opposite the flow control valve hole. Compress the retaining ring with the punch and remove it by inserting a small pry tool under the ring and twisting.
5. Remove the end plate and the end plate O-ring. The end plate is spring loaded and should pop out. If it sticks, rocking it from side to side should free it.
6. Turn the pump over and allow the flow control valve and the valve spring to fall out.
7. With the end cover O-ring removed, tap lightly on the end of the driveshaft to free the pressure plate.
8. Remove the pressure plate, driveshaft, pump ring, vanes and rotor.

NOTE: Do not remove the welch plug. If it is cracked or otherwise damaged, replace the whole housing.

9. Remove the driveshaft retaining ring.
10. Remove the rotor and thrust plate from the driveshaft and both dowel pins from the housing.
11. Pry the driveshaft seal out of the housing, being careful not to damage the housing, discard the shaft seal.
12. Clean all parts and inspect them for wear or damage.
13. Install new driveshaft seal using a seal installer with a press or hammer.

NOTE: Only use as much force as necessary to seat the seal.

14. Lubricate the pressure plate O-ring with Dexron® II or its equivalent and install it in the third groove from the rear of the housing.
15. Insert both dowel pins in the housing.
16. Assemble the driveshaft, thrust plate and rotor, then fit a new snap ring on the driveshaft. The rotor must have its countersunk side toward the thrust plate.
17. Lubricate the oil seal and driveshaft with Dexron® II or its equivalent and insert the driveshaft in the housing. Be sure to align the dowel pins with the thrust plate so as not to damage the oil seal lip.
18. Install the pump ring on the dowel pins with the arrow in the pump ring facing the rear of the housing.
19. Insert all ten vanes in the rotor slots with their rounded edges outward. They should slide freely in the rotor.
20. Lubricate the pressure plate and install with O-ring on the dowel pins with the circular depression which holds the spring toward the rear of the housing. The pressure plate must be pressed about 0.06 in. over the O-ring to seat properly.
21. Fit the end plate O-ring in the second groove from the rear of the housing.
22. Install the end plate spring in the groove provided in the pressure plate.
23. Lubricate the end plate to avoid damage to the O-ring and press it into the housing. Fit the end plate retaining ring.
24. Be sure to bleed the system (refer to bleeding procedure).

RESERVOIR ON PUMP TYPE

1. Remove the oil reservoir.
2. Hold the pump in a vise, loosen the pump cover bolts and remove the cover.
3. Remove the following parts from the pump body: cam ring, vanes, O-ring, side plate assembly and the shaft assembly which includes the shaft, rotor, side plate, collar and snap ring.
4. Remove the shaft assembly snap ring and remove the collar, rotor side plate.
5. Remove the oil seal with a small pry tool. Remove the suction connector.
6. Remove the connector at the top of the pump body and remove the flow control valve assembly and flow control spring.
7. Assembly is the reverse of disassembly with the following instructions:
   a. Clean and check all parts for wear. Always use new gaskets and lubricate all parts with Dexron®II before assembling.
   b. Install the side plate, rotor and collar in the proper direction.
   c. When installing the cam ring, the countersunk holes at the end of the vanes face toward the cover.
   d. Fit the vanes with their rounded sides pointed out.
   e. Bleed the system.

TOYOTA

Manual Steering Gear

Disassembly

1. Remove the oil filler plug and drain the gear oil.
2. Using a puller, remove the pitman arm from the sector shaft.
3. Remove the adjusting screw lock nut and three retaining bolts from the end cover.
4. Remove the end cover by tightening the adjusting screw.
5. Pull the sector shaft from the housing.

NOTE: On some later models remove the needle bearings from the housing at this time.

6. Using special tool 09617-30040 or equivalent, remove the locknut.
7. Using special tool 09616-22010 or equivalent, remove the bearing adjusting screw.
8. Carefully pull the worm shaft out of the gear housing.

NOTE: Never attempt to disassemble the ball nut from the steering worm shaft.

Assembly

1. Inspect the worm bearings, bearing races and oil seal and if a problem is suspected, replace them.
2. If it is necessary to replace the oil seal, remove it with an appropriate prying tool, then using special tool 09620-30010 or equivalent, install a new seal.
3. If it is necessary to replace the outer race in the gear housing use special tool 09612-65013 or equivalent to remove it, then use special tool 09620-30010 or equivalent to install a new one.
4. If it is necessary to replace the outer race from the adjusting nut, perform the following: Remove the oil seal with an appropriate prying tool. Using special tool 09612-30012 or equivalent remove the outer race from the nut. Using special tool 09620-30010 or equivalent, install a new race and then a new seal into the nut.
5. If necessary remove the inner races from the shaft with a press, then using special tool 09620-30010 or equivalent, press new ones into the shaft.
6. Measure the shaft thrust clearance with a feeler gauge. The maximum clearance should be less than 0.0020 in. If necessary, install a new thrust washer between the sector shaft and the adjusting screw to provide the minimum clearance.
7. Apply MP grease to the bushing needle, roller bearings and oil seals.
8. Place the worm bearings on the shaft and insert the shaft into the housing.
9. Install the bearing adjusting screw and using special tool 09616-22010 or equivalent, gradually tighten the adjusting screw until it is snug.
10. Using a torque wrench and the same special tool, measure the bearing preload in both directions. Turn the adjusting screw until the preload is correct. Preload (starting): 2.6–3.5 inch lbs. Hold the adjusting screw in position then tighten the lock nut to 108 ft. lbs. Recheck preload. Apply MP grease to the needle rollers and install them into the housing.

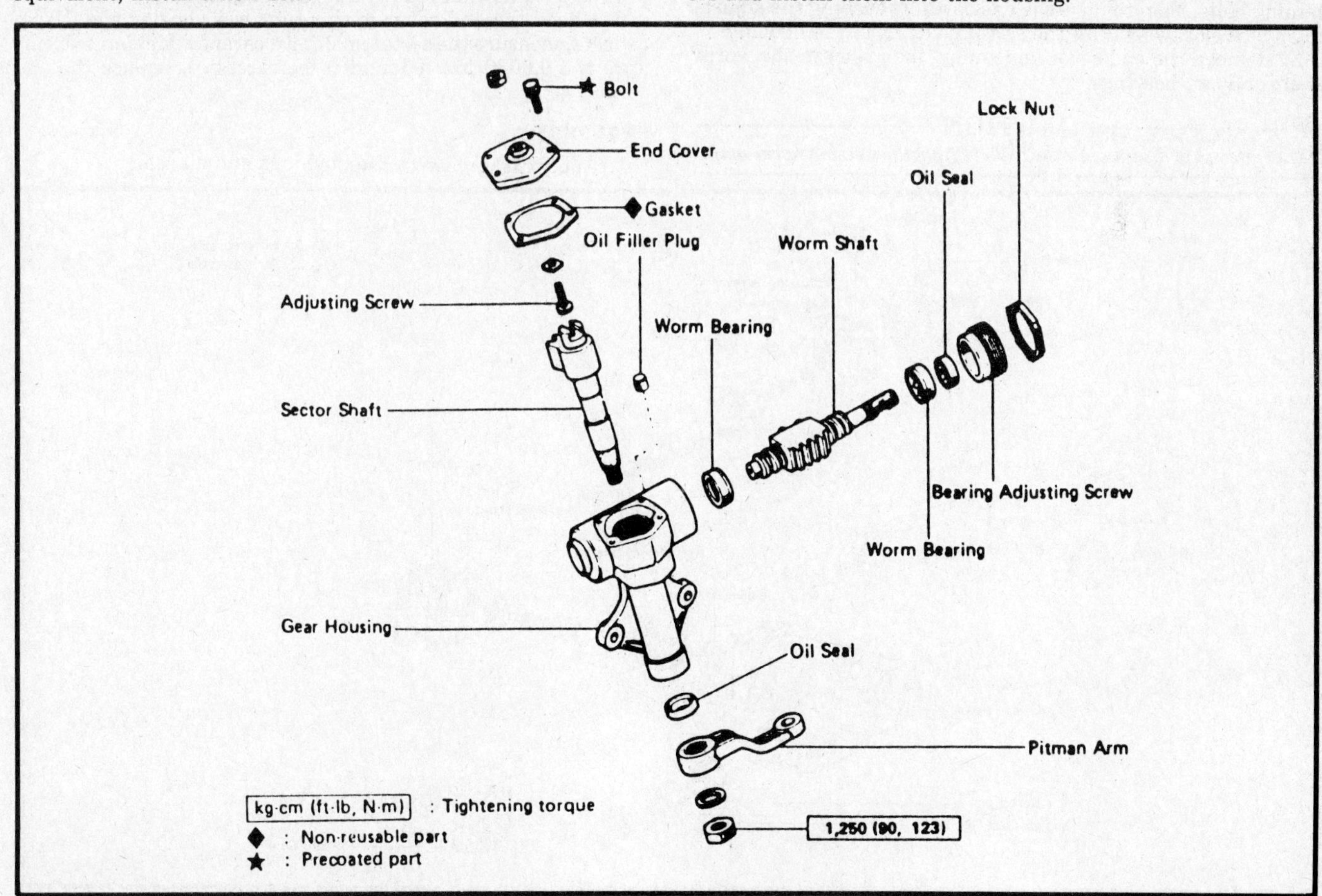

Toyota manual steering gear—2WD

11. Install the adjusting screw and thrust washer onto the sector shaft, then set the ball nut at the center of the worm shaft. Insert the sector shaft into the gear housing so that the center teeth mesh together.
12. Apply liquid sealer to the gasket and end cover and install the end cover. Loosen the adjusting screw as far as possible, then torque the four cover bolts to 13 ft. lb.
13. Place the worm shaft in the neutral position by counting the total shaft rotations, then turning the shaft half of that number. Place the matchmarks on the wormshaft and housing to show the neutral position.
14. Using a torque wrench and special tool, turn the adjusting screw while measuring the preload until it is correct. Make sure the worm shaft is in the neutral position. Preload: 6.9–9.1 inch lbs.
15. Apply liquid sealer to the locknut, then hold the screw with a screwdriver and tighten the lock nut to 18 ft. lbs. Recheck the preload.
16. Measure the sector shaft backlash. There should be no backlash within 100 degrees of the right and left sides from the neutral position.
17. Install the pitman arm and replenish with gear oil. Install the filler plug.

Manual Steering Gear (4WD)

Disassembly

1982–85

1. Remove the filler plug and drain the steering gear oil.
2. Remove the adjusting screw locknut and four end cover retaining bolts, then remove the end cover by turning the adjusting screw clockwise. Pull the sector shaft from the housing.
3. Remove the end cover and shims, then remove the worm shaft and two bearings.

CAUTION

Do not attempt to disassemble the ball nut from the steering worm shaft.

Inspection

1. If it is necessary to replace the oil seal in the end cover, pry out the old seal, then using special tool 09620-30010 or equivalent, install the new oil seal.
2. If it is necessary to replace the outer race in the end cover, use special tool 09612-65013 or equivalent to remove and then to install a new one.
3. If it is necessary to replace the outer race in the gear housing, use special tool 09612-65013 to remove and then install a new one.
4. If necessary, replace the inner race on the worm shaft by removing with a press, then using special tool 09620-30010 or equivalent, press the inner races into the shaft.
5. Measure the thrust clearance with a feeler gauge and if necessary, install a new thrust washer to provide minimum clearance between the sector shaft and the adjusting screw. Maximum clearance: 0.0020 in.
6. Measure the shaft outer diameter. Minimum: 1.2579 in.
7. Using calipers, measure the sector shaft oil clearance and if necessary replace the bushings. Maximum: 0.0039 in.
8. If necessary, replace the bushing and oil seal as follows:
   a. Using special tool 09308-00010 or equivalent, remove the oil seal.
   b. Using special tool 09307-12010 or equivalent and a press, remove the two bushings together in the same direction.
   c. Using the same special tool and a press, install the inner and outer bushings.
   d. Hone the inner surface of the bushings until the standard oil clearance of 0.0004–0.0024 in. is obtained between the bushings and the sector shaft.
   e. Install a new oil seal to the gear housing.
9. Check the end cover bushing for wear or damage. Using calipers, measure the sector shaft oil clearance. Maximum clearance is : 0.0039 in., if found to be excessive, replace the end cover.

Assembly

1. Apply MP grease to the bushings and oil seal.

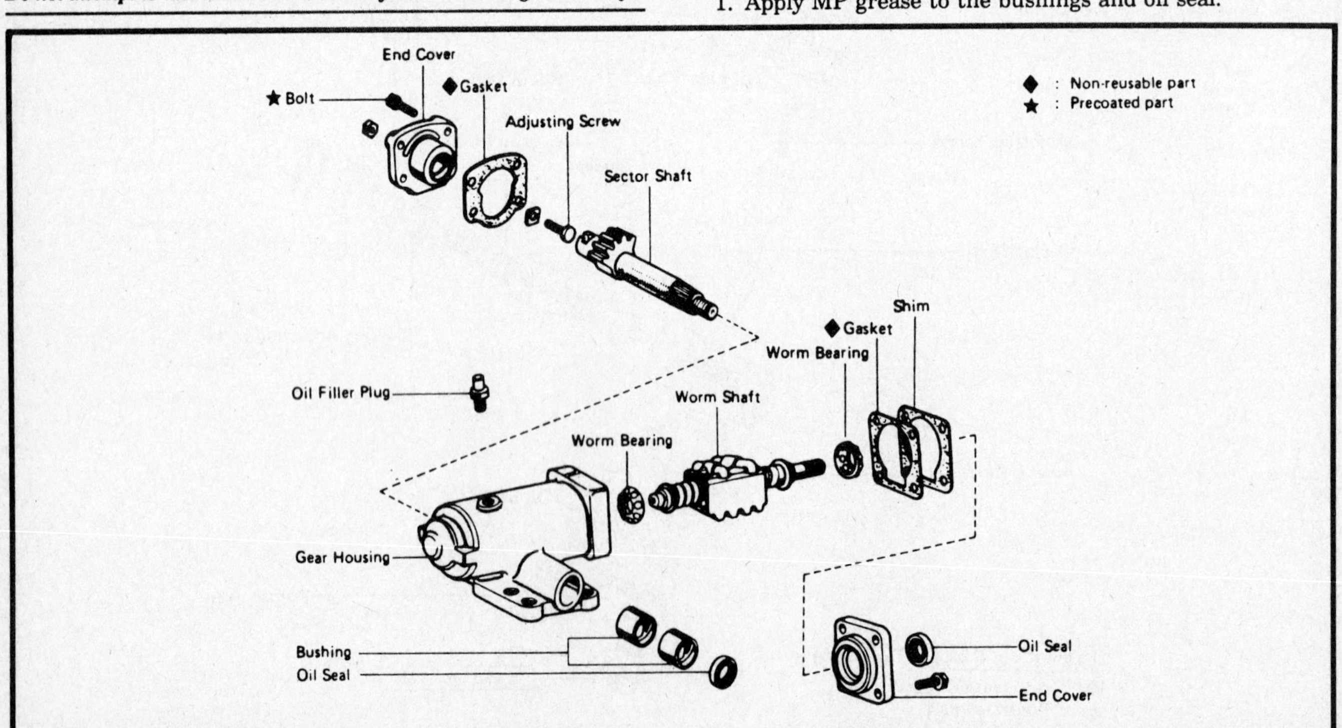

Toyota manual steering gear—4WD—1982–85

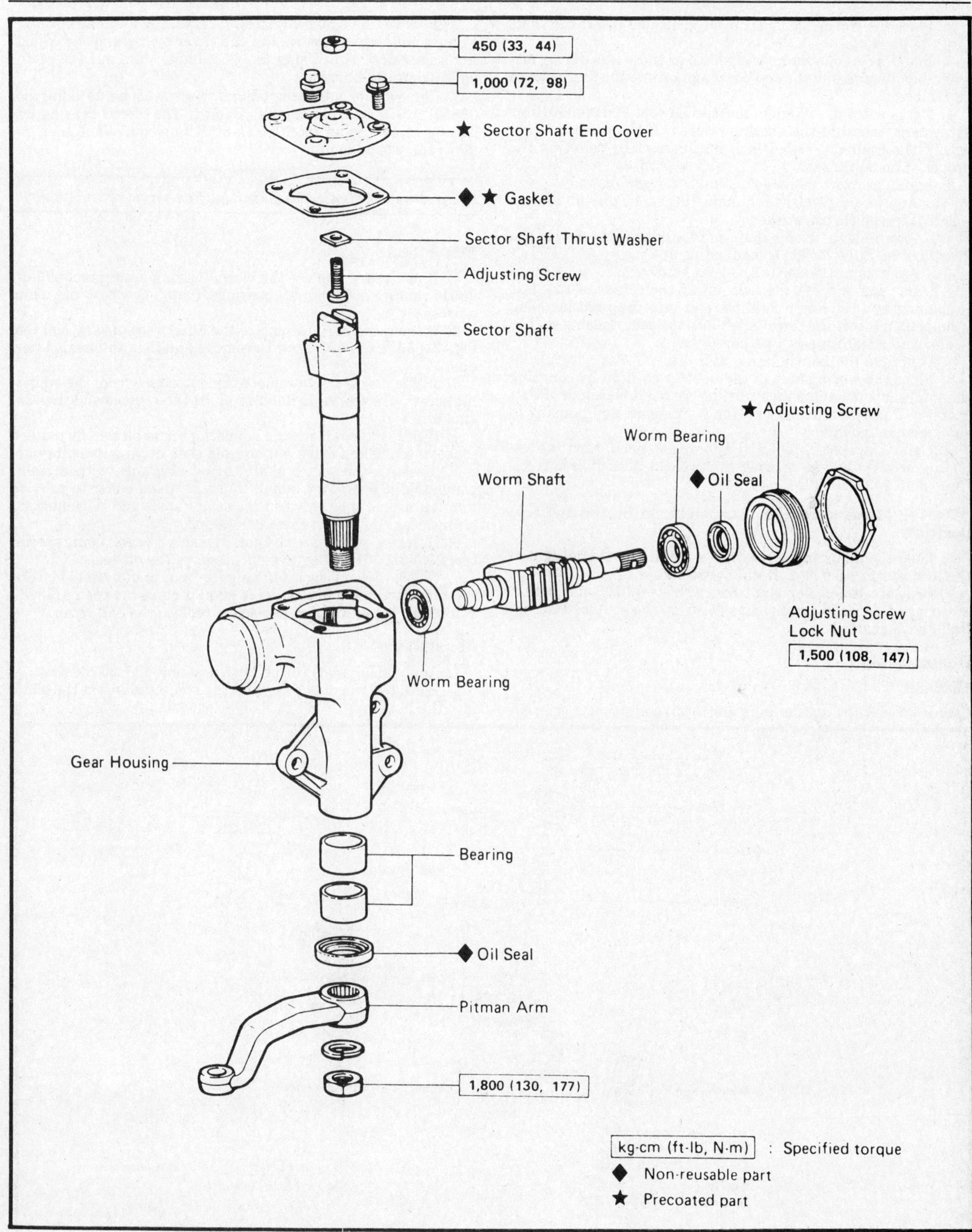

Toyota manual steering gear – 4WD – 1986–88

2. Place the worm bearings on the shaft and insert the shaft into the housing.

3. Install the same number of shims as there was during disassembly, then install the end cover and torque the four bolts to 29 ft. lbs.

4. Using a torque wrench and special tool 09616–00010 or equivalent, measure the bearing preload. If the preload is not within the limit of 3.0–5.6 inch lbs., correct by selecting the proper shim thickness.

5. Install the sector shaft and end cover as follows:

a. Apply liquid sealer to the adjusting screw threads and insert it in the thrust washer.

b. Assemble the sector shaft and the adjusting screw to the end cover. Fully loosen the adjusting screw.

c. Apply liquid sealer to the gear housing.

d. Set and support the ball nut at the center of the gear housing by inserting a suitable tool into the breather plug hole, then insert the sector shaft into the gear housing so that the center teeth mesh together.

e. Torque the four bolts to 29 ft. lbs.

6. Place the worm shaft in the neutral position by counting the total shaft rotations then turning the shaft back half of that number. Place matchmarks on the worm shaft and housing to show neutral position.

7. Using the special tool and a torque wrench, turn the adjusting screw while measuring the preload until it is correct. Preload: 6.9–9.5 inch lb.

NOTE: Make sure the wormshaft is in the neutral position.

8. Hold the adjusting screw with a suitable tool and tighten the lock nut to 31 ft. lbs. Recheck preload.

9. Measure the sector shaft backlash (0–0.0106 in.) within 100 degrees of the left and right sides from the neutral position. Refill with gear oil.

Disassembly

1986–88

1. Remove the breather plug and drain the steering gear oil.

2. Remove the adjusting screw locknut and four end cover retaining bolts, then remove the end cover by turning the adjusting screw clockwise. Using plastic hammer, tap out the sector shaft from the housing.

3. Remove worm bearing adjusting screw lock nut using tool 09617–60010 or equivalent.4. Remove the worm bearing adjusting screw, using tool 09617–60010 or equivalent then remove the worm shaft.

CAUTION

Do not attempt to disassemble the ball nut from the steering worm shaft.

Inspection

1. If necessary, replace the worm bearing. Using tool 09950–20017 remove both the side bearings. Install new bearings using a press.

2. If it is necessary to replace the outer race, use special tool 09612–65014 or equivalent to remove and then to install a new one.

3. If it is necessary to replace the outer race from the adjusting screw, use special tool 09612–65014 to remove and then install a new one.

4. If necessary replace the adjusting screw oil seal by using a socket wrench and driving it out and then driving in a new one.

5. Measure the sector shaft thrust clearance with a feeler gauge and if necessary install a new thrust washer to provide minimum clearance between the sector shaft and the adjusting screw. Maximum clearance: 0.0020 in.

6. If necessary replace the gear housing oil seal, using special tool 09308–00010 or equivalent, remove the oil seal.

7. Check the end cover bushing for wear or damage. Measure the bushing inside diameter. It should be in between 1.2598–1.2608 in. If found to be excessive, replace the end cover.

Assembly

1. Apply MP grease to the bushings and oil seal.

2. Place the worm bearings on the shaft and insert the shaft into the housing.

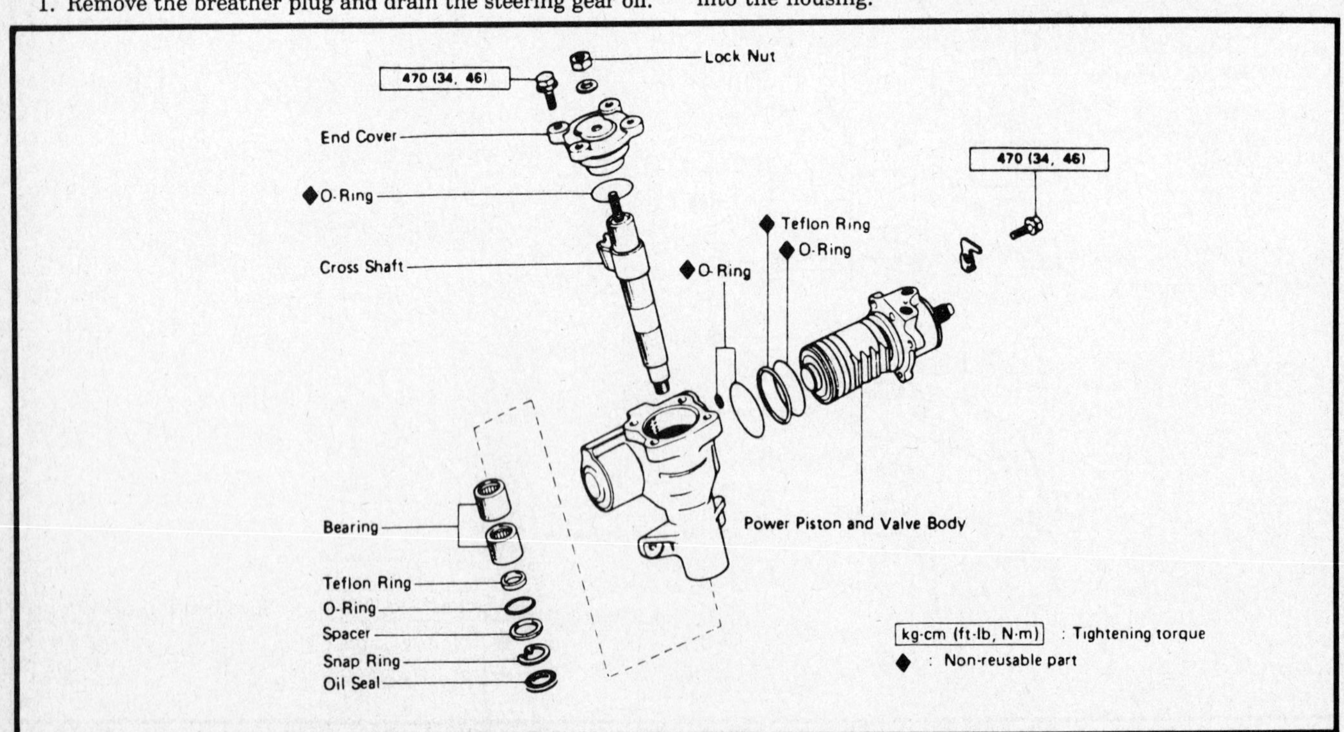

Toyota power steering gear—2WD—1982–85

3. Apply liquid sealer to the adjusting screw threads and tighten the adjusting screw until it is snug, using tool 09616–00010 or equivalent.

4. Using a torque wrench and special tool 09616–00010 or equivalent, measure the bearing preload in both directions. If the preload is not within the limit of 3.0–4.3 inch lbs., correct by turning the adjusting screw.

5. Hold the adjusting screw in position and tighten the lock nut to 108 ft. lbs. Recheck bearing preload.

6. Install the sector shaft and end cover as follows:

a. Apply liquid sealer to the adjusting screw threads and insert it in the thrust washer.

b. Install the adjusting screw and the thrust washer onto the sector shaft.

c. Set and support the ball nut at the center of the gear housing by inserting a suitable tool into the housing, then insert the sector shaft into the gear housing so that the center teeth mesh together.

e. Apply liquid sealer to the gasket and the end cover and install the end cover over the gasket. Loosen the adjusting screw as far as possible and torque the four cover bolts to 72 ft. lbs.

7. Place the worm shaft in the neutral position by counting the total shaft rotations then turning the shaft back half of that number. Place matchmarks on the worm shaft and housing to show neutral position.

8. Using the special tool and a torque wrench, turn the adjusting screw while measuring the preload until it is correct. Preload: 6.9–9.5 inch lb.

NOTE: Make sure the wormshaft is in the neutral position.

8. Hold the adjusting screw with a suitable tool and tighten the lock nut to 33 ft. lbs. Recheck preload.

9. Measure the sector shaft backlash (0–0.0106 in.) within 100 degrees of the left and right sides from the neutral position. Refill with gear oil.

Power Steering Gear (2WD)

Disassembly

1982–85

1. Remove the adjusting screw lock nut from the end cover and the four bolts, then screw in the adjusting screw until the cover comes off.

2. Tap on the cross shaft end with a plastic hammer and pull out the cross shaft.

3. Remove the four cap screws from the housing. Hold the power piston nut so it cannot move and turn the wormshaft clockwise, then withdraw the valve body and power piston assembly.

CAUTION

Make sure the power piston nut does not come off the worm shaft.

Inspection

1. Mount the valve body in a vise, then using a dial indicator, check the ball clearance. Move the worm gear up and down. The maximum ball clearance is 0.0059 in. If the clearance is excessive, the power control valve assembly must be replaced.

2. Clamp the cross shaft in a vise, then using a dial indicator check the end play. The end play should be 0.0012–0.0020 in. If necessary, adjust end play as follows: Use a chisel and a hammer and remove the lock nut stake. Using special tool 09630–00011 or its equivalent, loosen the lock nut. Adjust the adjusting screw for the correct end play and tighten the lock nut. Stake the lock nut.

3. Replace the Teflon ring and needle roller bearings as follows:

a. Pry out the old seal from the pitman arm end of the housing.

b. Remove the snap ring using snap ring pliers.

c. Remove the metal spacer, Teflon ring and O-ring.

d. Using special tool 09630–00011 or equivalent, drive out the bearings.

e. Using the same special tool, install the top bearing with the long flange out. Drive the bearing in flush with the inside casting surface.

f. Install the lower bearing with the long flange out. The special tool will bottom and correctly position the bearing.

g. Install the O-ring and metal spacer.

h. Using snap ring pliers, install the snap ring.

i. Form the seal into a heart shape and install it by hand, then using the same special tool as above form the seal, then drive the oil seal into the gear housing.

Assembly

1. Install two new O-rings and insert the valve body into the housing. Torque the bolts in a diagonal pattern to 34 ft. lbs.

2. Inspect the worm shaft bearing as follows: Using special tool 09630–00011 or its equivalent, remove the lock nut and the bearing cap. Remove the worm bearing and O-ring, then install a new O-ring and bearing cap.

3. Adjust the worm bearing preload as follows: Using special tool 09630–00011, tighten the bearing cap until the preload is correct. Using special tool 09616–00010 or its equivalent and a torque wrench, check the preload of the bearing. Preload should be 3.5–5.6 in. lb. Hold the power piston nut to prevent it from turning. Tighten the lock nut while holding the bearing cap to 36 ft. lbs. Recheck the preload.

4. Install a new O-ring on the end cover.

5. Assemble the cross shaft to the end cover and fully loosen the adjusting screw.

6. Set the worm gear at the center of the gear housing, then insert and push the cross shaft into the gear housing so that the center teeth mesh together.

7. Install the four cap bolts and torque the four cap bolts in a diagonal pattern to 34 ft. lbs.

8. Turn the worm shaft to full lock in both directions and determine the exact center.

9. Adjust the total preload as follows: Install special tool 09616–00010 or its equivalent and a torque wrench, on the center worm shaft. Turn the adjusting screw while measuring the preload until it is correct. Total preload: (Add worm preload), 1.7–2.6 inch lbs.

10. Install a new washer, then install and tighten the lock nut to 34 ft. lbs.

11. Recheck the total preload.

Disassembly

1986–88

1. Remove the adjusting screw lock nut from the end cover and the four bolts, then screw in the adjusting screw until the cover comes off.

2. Tap on the cross shaft end with a plastic hammer and pull out the cross shaft.

3. Remove the four cap screws from the housing. Hold the power piston nut so it cannot move and turn the wormshaft clockwise, then withdraw the valve body and power piston assembly. Remove the O-ring.

CAUTION

Make sure the power piston nut does not come off the worm shaft.

4. Mount the valve body on special tool 9630–00011 and clamp the tool in a vise. Pull out the power piston nut without loosing the ball.

5. Hold the adjusting screw and remove the lock nut and bearing.

6. Remove the O-ring.
7. Remove the worm shaft, thrust bearing, plate washer, teflon ring and the O-ring.

Inspection

1. Mount the valve body in a vise, then using a dial indicator, check the ball clearance. Move the worm gear up and down. The maximum ball clearance is 0.0059 in. If the clearance is excessive, the power control valve assembly must be replaced.
2. Clamp the cross shaft in a vise, then using a dial indicator check the end play. The end play should be 0.0012–0.0020 in. If necessary, adjust end play as follows: Use a chisel and a hammer and remove the lock nut stake. Using special tool 09630–00011 or its equivalent, loosen the lock nut. Adjust the adjusting screw for the correct end play and tighten the lock nut. Stake the lock nut.
3. Replace the Teflon ring and needle roller bearings as follows:
   a. Pry out the old seal from the pitman arm end of the housing.
   b. Remove the snap ring using snap ring pliers.
   c. Remove the metal spacer, Teflon ring and O-ring.
   d. Using special tool 09630–00011 or equivalent, drive out the bearings.
   e. Using the same special tool, install the top bearing with the long flange out. Drive the bearing in flush with the inside casting surface.
   f. Install the lower bearing with the long flange out. The special tool will bottom and correctly position the bearing.
   g. Install the O-ring and metal spacer.
   h. Using snap ring pliers, install the snap ring.
   i. Form the seal into a heart shape and install it by hand, then using the same special tool as above form the seal, then drive the oil seal into the gear housing.

Assembly

1. Coat all parts with power steering fluid.
2. Mount the valve body using tool 09630–00011 in a vise and install a new O-ring. Form the new teflon ring into a heart shape and install it by hand. Install it using tool 09630–00011.
3. Install the worm shaft with the thrust bearing and the plate washer to the valve body.
4. Install the O-ring and bearing to the control valve.
5. Using special tool 09630–00011 or its equivalent, install and temporarily tighten the adjusting screw and the lock nut.
6. Install the power piston nut and balls as follows:
   a. Clean all parts with power steering fluid.
   b. Insert the power piston nut about 0.59 in. from the worm shaft end and align the ball transfer surface with the ball hole.
   c. Insert the balls one at a time into the holes and turn the worm shaft a little with each insertion. Then securely insert the 33 balls into the piston.
   d. Install the eleven new balls into the ball guide and apply MP grease to the ball guide lips so the balls do not fall out.
   e. Install the ball guide to the power piston nut.
   f. Using tool 09060–20010, install the ball guide clamp and torque to 26 inch lbs. Make sure the power piston nut rotates smoothly.
7. Install the two O-rings to the gear housing and valve body.

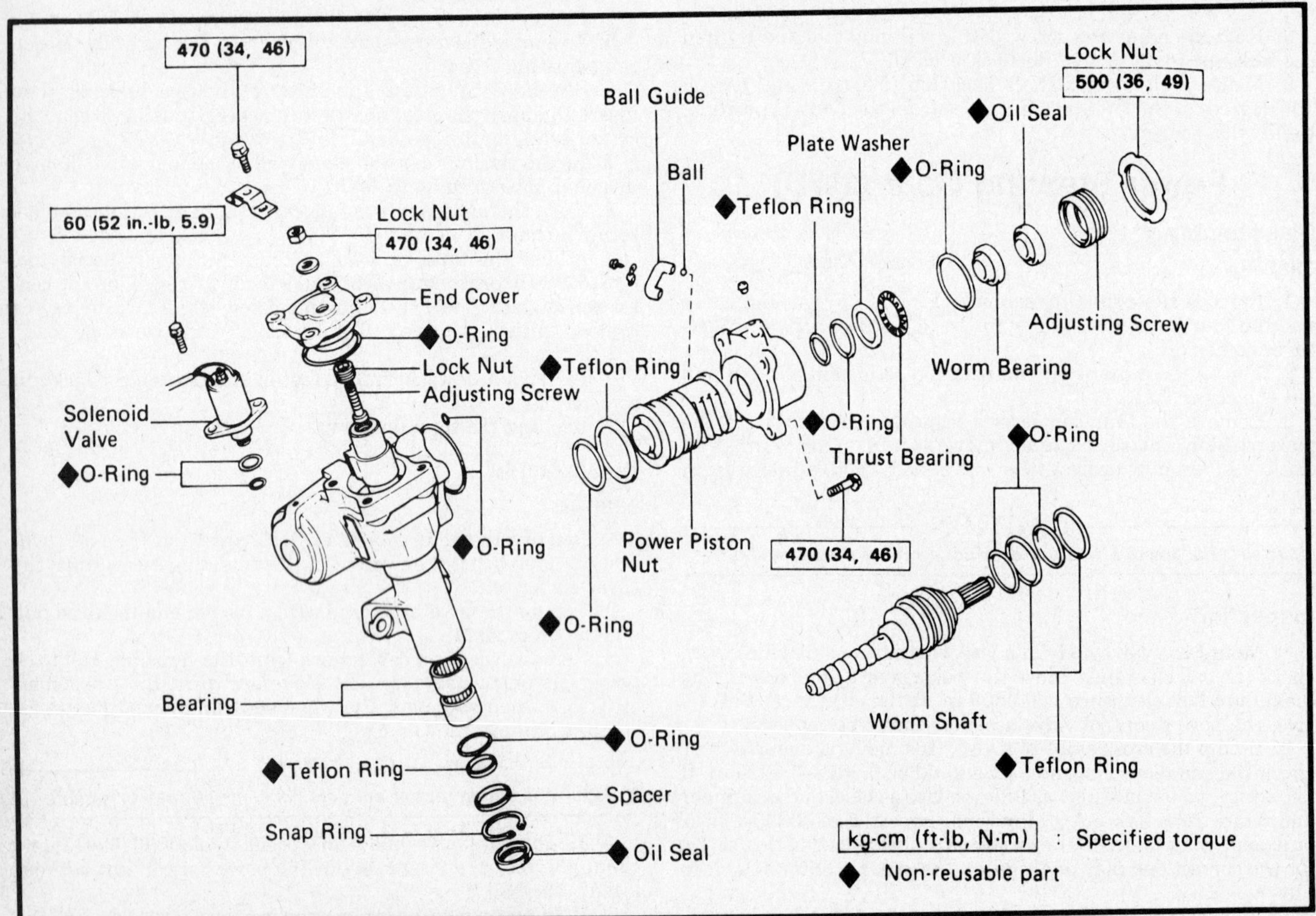

Toyota power steering gear—2WD—1986–88

Mount the gear housing in the special tool and clamp the tool in a vise. Install the worm gear valve body assembly and torque the four bolts to 34 ft. lbs.

8. Adjust the worm bearing preload as follows: Using special tool 09630–00011, tighten the adjusting screw. Turn the worm shaft to the right and the left and snug down the bearing. Slightly loosen the adjusting screw then tighten until the preload is correct. Using special tool 09616–00010 or its equivalent and a torque wrench, check the preload of the bearing. Preload should be 3.5–5.6 inch lb. Hold the power piston nut to prevent it from turning. Tighten the lock nut while holding the adjusting nut to 36 ft. lbs. Recheck the preload.

9. Install a new O-ring on the end cover.

10. Assemble the cross shaft to the end cover and fully loosen the adjusting screw.

11. Set the worm gear at the center of the gear housing, then insert and push the cross shaft into the gear housing so that the center teeth mesh together.

12. Install the four cap bolts and torque the four cap bolts in a diagonal pattern to 34 ft. lbs.

13. Turn the worm shaft to full lock in both directions and determine the exact center.

14. Adjust the total preload as follows: Install special tool 09616–00010 or its equivalent and a torque wrench, on the center worm shaft. Turn the adjusting screw while measuring the preload until it is correct. Total preload: (Add worm preload), 1.7–2.6 inch lbs.

15. Install a new washer, then install and tighten the lock nut to 34 ft. lbs.

16. Recheck the total preload.

Power Steering Gear (4WD)

Disassembly

1982–85

1. Remove the adjusting screw lock nut from the end cover and the four bolts, then screw in the adjusting screw until the cover comes off.

2. Tap on the cross shaft end with a plastic hammer and pull out the cross shaft.

3. Remove the four cap screws from the housing. Hold the power piston nut so it cannot move and turn the wormshaft clockwise, then withdraw the valve body and power piston assembly. Make sure the power piston nut does not come off the worm shaft.

Inspection

1. Mount the valve body in a vise, then using a dial indicator, check the ball clearance. Move the worm gear up and down. The maximum ball clearance is 0.0059 in. If the clearance is excessive, the power control valve assembly must be replaced.

2. Clamp the cross shaft in a vise, then using a dial indicator check the end play. The end play should be 0.0012–0.0020 in. If necessary, adjust end play as follows: Use a chisel and a hammer and remove the lock nut stake. Using special tool 09630–00011 or its equivalent, loosen the lock nut. Adjust the adjusting screw for the correct end play and tighten the lock nut. Stake the lock nut.

3. Replace the Teflon ring and needle roller bearings as follows: Pry out the old seal from the pitman arm end of the hous-

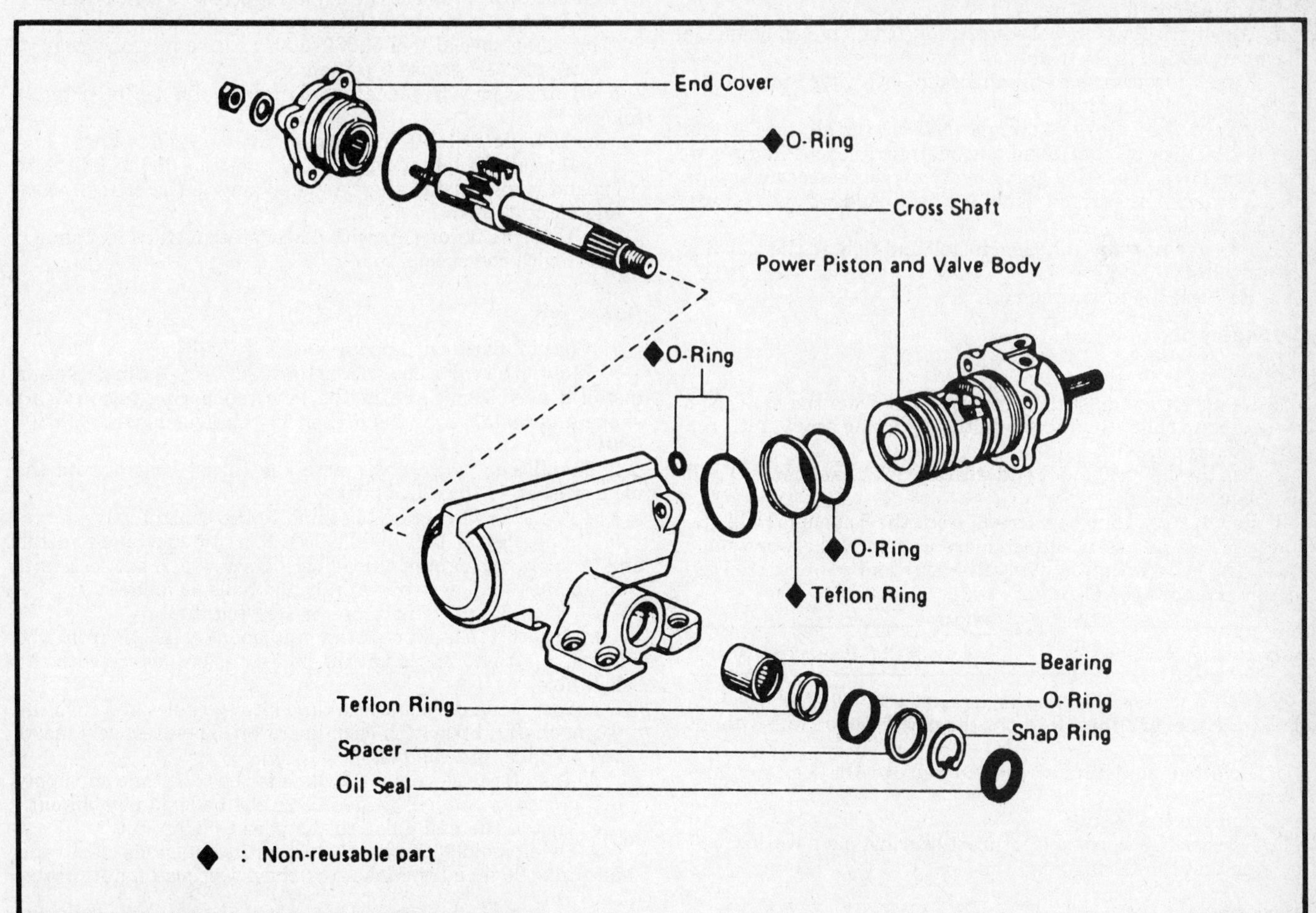

Toyota power steering gear—4WD—1982–85

ing. Remove the snap ring using snap ring pliers. Remove the metal spacer, Teflon ring and O-ring. Using special tool 09630–00011 or equivalent, drive out the bearing. Using special tool 09631–60010 or its equivalent, install a new bearing so that it is positioned 0.929 in. away from the housing inner end surface. Install a new Teflon ring together with a new O-ring to the special tool above, then install to the gear housing using the tool. Install the metal spacer. Using snap ring pliers, install the snap ring. Using tool 09630–00011 form the seal, then drive the seal into the gear housing, using tool 09631–600010.

Assembly

1. Install two new O-rings and insert the valve body into the housing. Torque the bolts in a diagonal pattern to 34 ft. lbs.
2. Inspect the worm shaft bearing as follows: Using special tool 09630–00011 or its equivalent, remove the lock nut and the bearing cap. Remove the worm bearing and O-ring, then install a new O-ring and bearing cap.
3. Adjust the worm bearing preload as follows: Using special tool 09630–00011, tighten the bearing cap until the preload is orrect. Using special tool 09616–00010 or its equivalent and a torque wrench, check the preload of the bearing. Preload should be 3.5–5.6 inch lb. Hold the power piston nut to prevent it from turning. Tighten the lock nut while holding the bearing cap to 36 ft. lbs. Recheck the preload.
4. Install a new O-ring on the end cover.
5. Assemble the cross shaft to the end cover and fully loosen the adjusting screw.
6. Set the worm gear at the center of the gear housing, then insert and push the cross shaft into the gear housing so that the center teeth mesh together.
7. Install the four cap bolts and torque the four cap bolts in a diagonal pattern to 34 ft. lbs.
8. Turn the worm shaft to full lock in both directions and determine the exact center.
9. Adjust the total preload as follows: Install special tool 09616–00010 or its equivalent and a torque wrench, on the center worm shaft. Turn the adjusting screw while measuring the preload until it is correct. Total preload: (Add worm preload), 1.7–2.6 in. lbs.
10. Install a new washer, then install and tighten the lock nut to 34 ft. lbs.
11. Recheck the total preload.

Disassembly

1986–88

1. Remove the adjusting screw lock nut from the end cover and the four bolts, then screw in the adjusting screw until the cover comes off.
2. Tap on the cross shaft end with a plastic hammer and pull out the cross shaft.
3. Remove the four cap screws from the housing. Hold the power piston nut so it cannot move and turn the wormshaft clockwise, then withdraw the valve body and power piston assembly. Remove the O-ring.

CAUTION

Make sure the power piston nut does not come off the worm shaft.

4. Mount the valve body on special tool 9630–00011 and clamp the tool in a vise. Pull out the power piston nut without loosing the ball.
5. Hold the adjusting screw and remove the lock nut and bearing.
6. Remove the O-ring.
7. Remove the worm shaft, thrust bearing, plate washer, teflon ring and the O-ring.

Inspection

1. Mount the valve body in a vise, then using a dial indicator, check the ball clearance. Move the worm gear up and down. The maximum ball clearance is 0.0059 in. If the clearance is excessive, the power control valve assembly must be replaced.
2. Clamp the cross shaft in a vise, then using a dial indicator check the end play. The end play should be 0.0012–0.0020 in. If necessary, adjust end play as follows: Use a chisel and a hammer and remove the lock nut stake. Using special tool 09630–00011 or its equivalent, loosen the lock nut. Adjust the adjusting screw for the correct end play and tighten the lock nut. Stake the lock nut.
3. Replace the Teflon ring and needle roller bearings as follows:
   a. Pry out the old seal from the pitman arm end of the housing.
   b. Remove the snap ring using snap ring pliers.
   c. Remove the metal spacer, Teflon ring and O-ring.
   d. Using a brass bar and hammer, drive out the upper bearing.
   e. Using special tool 09630–00011 or equivalent, press out the lower bearing.
   f. Using the same special tool, press in the top bearing so that it aligns with the housing end surface.
   g. Using special tool 09630–00011, install the bearing so that it is positioned 0.909 in. away from the housing inner end surface.
   h. Install a new O-ring.
   i. Form the seal into a heart shape and install it by hand.
   j. Install the metal spacer.
   k. Using snap ring pliers, install the snap ring.
   l. Using special tool 09630–00011, drive in a new seal.
4. If necessary, replace the adjusting screw oil seal as follows:
   a. Using a suitable tool drive out the oil seal.
   b. Using special tool 09630–00011, drive in a new seal.
   c. Apply MP grease top the lip.
5. If necessary, replace the control valve teflon ring as follows:
   a. Using a suitable tool remove the two teflon rings.
   b. Install the teflon ring to the special tool 09630–00011, to expand it and install the expanded ring to the control valve and snug it down by hand.
   c. Coat the teflon ring with power steering fluid and snug it down with the special tool

Assembly

1. Coat all parts with power steering fluid.
2. Mount the valve body using tool 09630–00011 in a vise and install a new O-ring. Form the new teflon ring into a heart shape and install it by hand then install it using tool 09630–00011.
3. Install the worm shaft with the thrust bearing and the plate washer to the valve body.
4. Install the O-ring and bearing to the control valve.
5. Using special tool 09630–00011 or its equivalent install and temporarily tighten the adjusting screw and the lock nut.
6. Install the power piston nut and balls as follows:
   a. Clean all parts with power steering fluid.
   b. Insert the power piston nut about 0.59 in. from the worm shaft end and align the ball transfer surface with the ball hole.
   c. Insert the balls one at a time into the holes and turn the worm shaft a little with each insertion. Then securely insert the 33 balls into the piston.
   d. Install the eleven new balls into the ball guide and apply MP grease to the ball guide lips so the balls do not fall out.
   e. Install the ball guide to the power piston nut.
   f. Using tool 09060–20010, install the ball guide clamp and torque to 26 inch lbs. Make sure the power piston nut rotates smoothly.
7. Install the two O-rings to the gear housing and valve body. Mount the gear housing in the special tool and clamp the tool in

a vise. Install the worm gear valve body assembly and torque the four bolts to 34 ft. lbs.

3. Adjust the worm bearing preload as follows: Using special tool 09630–00011, tighten the adjusting screw. Turn the worm shaft to the right and the left and snug down the bearing. Slightly loosen the adjusting screw then tighten until the preload is correct. Using special tool 09616–00010 or its equivalent and a torque wrench, check the preload of the bearing. Preload should be 3.5–5.6 inch lb. Hold the power piston nut to prevent it from turning. Tighten the lock nut while holding the adjusting nut to 36 ft. lbs. Recheck the preload.

4. Install a new O-ring on the end cover.

5. Assemble the cross shaft to the end cover and fully loosen the adjusting screw.

6. Set the worm gear at the center of the gear housing, then insert and push the cross shaft into the gear housing so that the center teeth mesh together.

7. Install the four cap bolts and torque the four cap bolts in a diagonal pattern to 34 ft. lbs.

8. Turn the worm shaft to full lock in both directions and determine the exact center.

9. Adjust the total preload as follows: Install special tool 09616–00010 or its equivalent and a torque wrench, on the center worm shaft. Turn the adjusting screw while measuring the preload until it is correct. Total preload: (Add worm preload), 1.7–2.6 inch lbs.

10. Install a new washer, then install and tighten the lock nut to 34 ft. lbs.

11. Recheck the total preload.

Power Steering Pump

Disassembly

1982–88

1. Clamp the pump in a vise.
2. Remove the air control valve from the rear housing on the 22R–E engine only.
3. Remove the suction port union from the rear housing.
4. Place matchmarks on the front and rear housing.
5. Remove the four front housing bolts, then using a plastic hammer, tap off the front housing. Be careful that the vane plates, rotor and cam ring do not fall out.
6. Remove the cam ring, rotor and vane plates without scratching them.
7. Remove the rotor shaft as follows: Clamp the front housing in a vise. Pry off the oil seal using a chisel and a hammer. Remove the snap ring using snap ring pliers. Using a plastic hammer, lightly tap the rotor shaft out of the front housing.
8. Using a plastic hammer, tap the bottom end of the rear housing and remove the rear plate and spring.

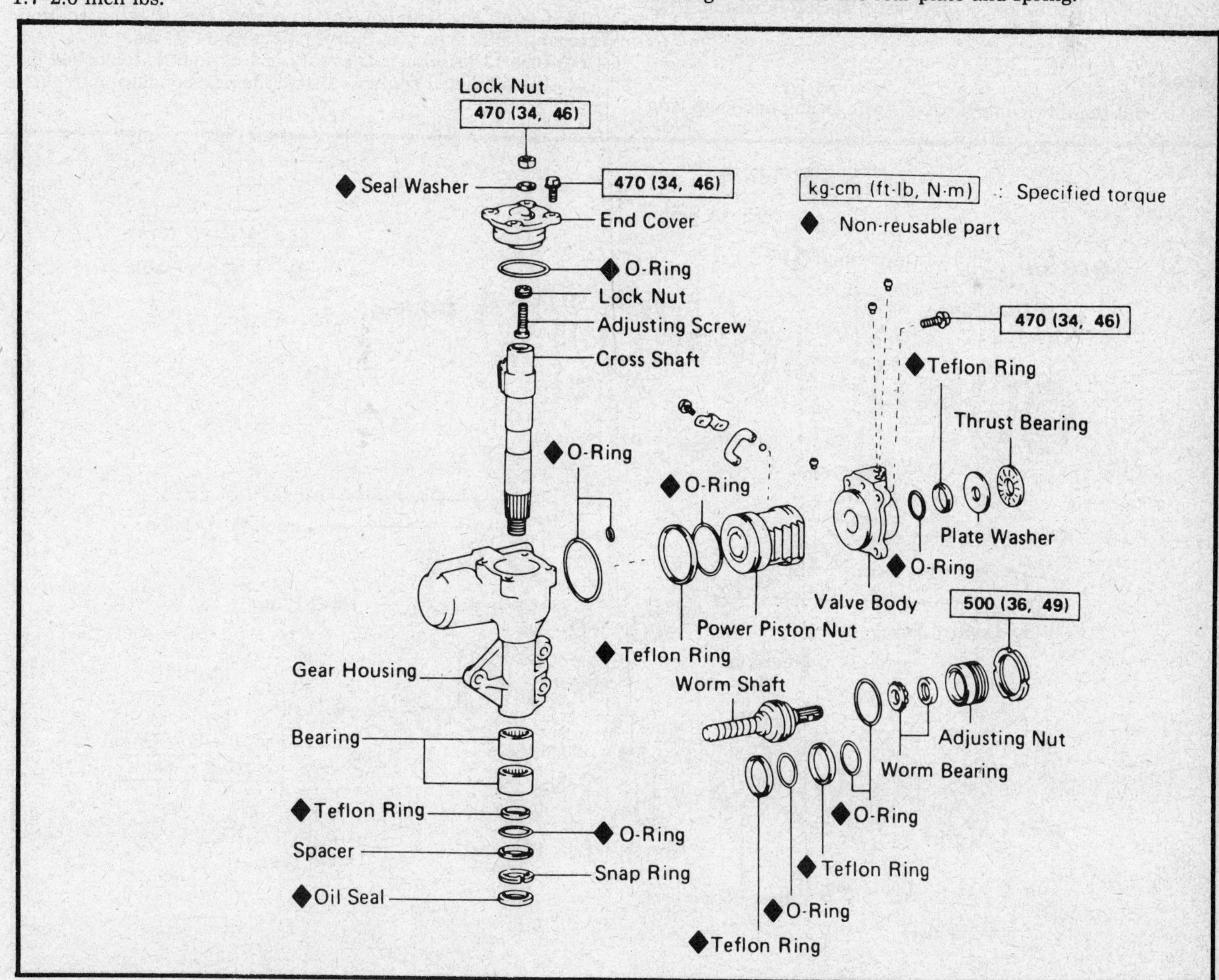

Toyota power steering gear—4WD—1986–88

9. Remove the flow control valve as follows: Temporarily loosen the bolt to the plug. Push the bolt and remove the snap ring with snap ring pliers. Pull out the bolt and remove the plug. Remove the spring and flow control valve by hand. Remove the pressure port union.

Inspection

1. Check the front housing bushing for wear or damage. If wear or damage is found, the entire housing must be replaced.
2. Check the oil clearance between the bushing and rotor shaft. Maximum oil clearance is 0.0028 in.
3. If necessary, replace the rotor shaft bearing as follows: Using snap ring pliers, remove the snap ring. Using a press, press out the old bearing and press in the new one. Using the snap ring pliers, install the snap ring.
4. Measure the cam ring thickness. Check that the difference between the rotor and cam ring is less than the maximum 0.0024 in. If the difference is excessive, replace the cam ring with one having the same letter as the rotor.
5. Check the vane plates for wear or scratches.
6. Measure the clearance between the vane plate and the rotor groove. Maximum clearance is 0.0024 in.
7. Check the flow control valve for wear or damage. If necessary, replace the valve with one having the same letter on the rear housing.
8. Check that the flow control valve spring is within 1.85–1.97 in. If not replace it.

Assembly

1. Install the flow control valve, spring, plug and snap ring.

NOTE: Make sure the letter inscribed on the flow control valve matches the letter stamped on the rear of the pump body.

2. Install the pressure port union and torque to 51 ft. lbs.
3. Install the rotor shaft to the front housing by tapping it with a plastic hammer.
4. Install the snap ring to the front housing using snap ring pliers.
5. Apply a light coat of MP grease to the oil seal lip, then using special tool 09608-300011 and a hammer, install the oil seal.
6. Install the O-ring.
7. Align the fluid passages of the cam ring and front housing, and install the cam ring.
8. Install the rotor with the camfered end facing toward the front.

NOTE: Be sure the letters inscribed on the cam ring and rotor match.

9. Install the vane plates with the round end facing outward.
10. Align the fluid passages of the rear plate and cam ring and install the rear plate with the spring. Place the spring on the rear plate.
11. Align the matchmarks on the front and rear housing and assemble them. Tighten the the front and rear housing mounting bolts by hand.
12. Clamp the rear housing in a vise, then tighten the four housing bolts evenly in 3 or 4 passes to 34 ft. lbs.
13. Insert the union to the rear housing and tighten to 9 ft. lbs.
14. Install the air control valve to the rear housing and tighten to 27 ft. lbs.

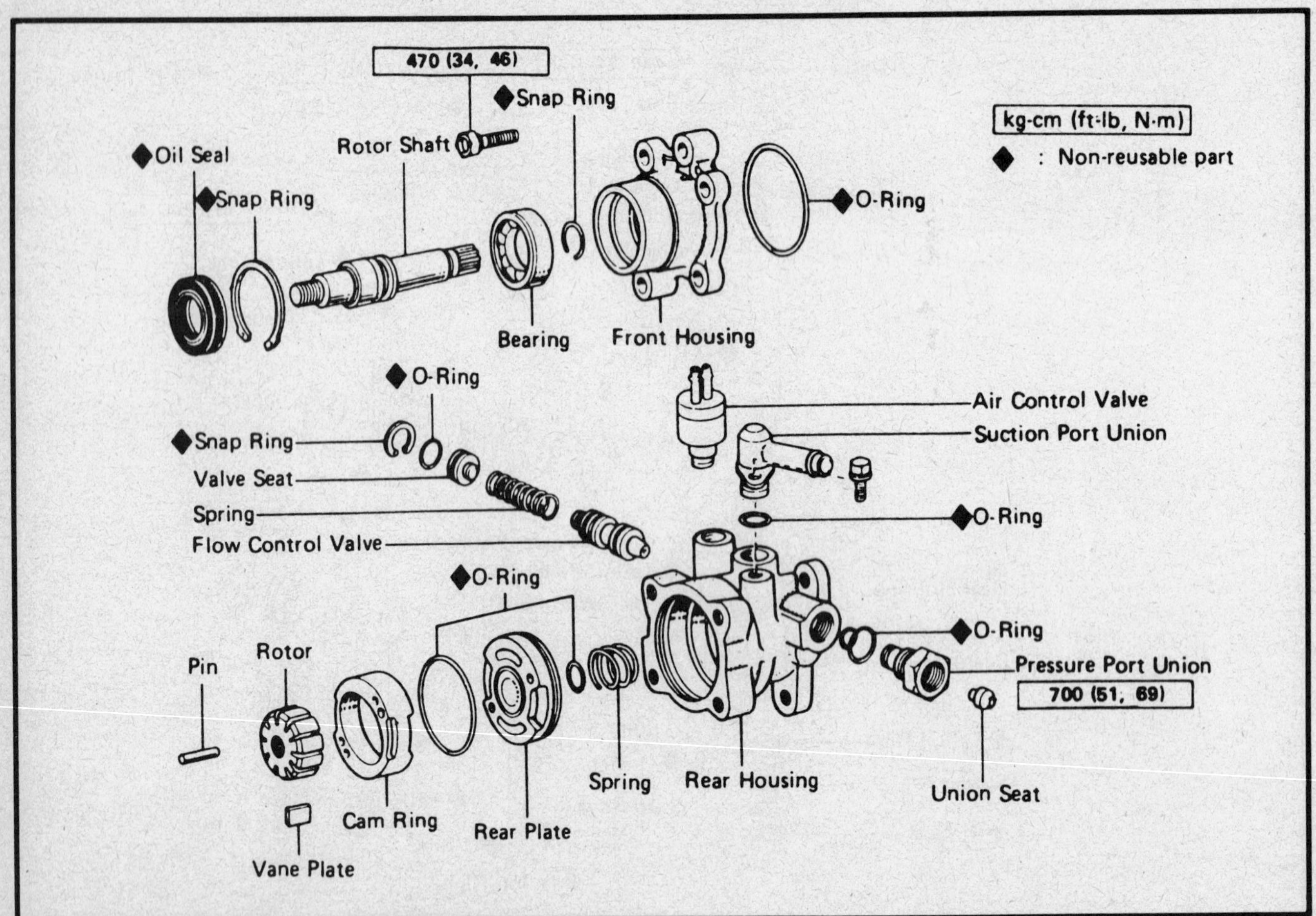

Toyota power steering pump—1981 88 pick up

Suspensions
Import Trucks

FRONT SUSPENSION TROUBLE DIAGNOSIS

UNEVEN TIRE WEAR

1. Tire pressure's low
2. Excessive camber
3. Tires out of balance
4. Tires overloaded
5. Out of round tires and rims
6. Caster incorrect
7. Toe-in incorrect
8. High speed driving into turns
9. Unequal tire size
10. Improper tracking
11. Bent or worn steering and suspension components

STEERING WHEEL SPOKE POSITION NOT PROPERLY CENTERED

1. Steering gear set off "high-spot"
2. Improper toe-in
3. Relationship between lengths of tie-rods not equal
4. Bent steering components
5. Steering wheel improperly placed on steering shaft

HARD STEERING

1. Tire pressure low
2. Wheel spindle bent
3. Steering assembly binding or maladjusted
4. Tie rod ends tight
5. Caster excessive
6. Kingpins or ball joints too tight
7. Lack of lubrication to steering and suspension units.

SHIMMY

1. Tire pressure incorrect
2. Tires of unequal size
3. Loose wheel bearings
4. Loose steering arms or steering gear adjustment
5. Steering gear loose on frame
6. Loose or broken steering linkage rods or internal adjustment parts
7. Spring shackles loose
8. Ball joints or kingpins and bushings worn
9. Front end alignment out of specifications
10. Wheels and tires out of balance
11. Wheels and tires out of round or loose on hub
12. Shock absorbers worn out.
13. U-bolts loose on axle to spring.
14. Worn or out-of-round brake drum or rotor (shimmy felt upon brake application)

WANDER OR WEAVE

1. Tire pressure incorrect
2. Tires of unequal size
3. Bent spindle
4. Wheel bearings loose or worn
5. Kingpins worn or bent
6. Kingpins tight in steering knuckle or bushings
7. Steering gear assembly too tight or too loose
8. Too little caster
9. Too much or too little chamber
10. Too much or too little toe-in
11. Front axle bent or shifted
12. Springs broken
13. Frame diamond shaped
14. Rear axle housing shifted or bent
15. Steering linkage tight or binding
16. Lack of lubrication to front suspension or steering linkage
17. Defective power steering assembly

FRONT END RIDES HARD

1. Improper tire pressure
2. Springs broken or too stiff
3. Shock absorbers too stiff or malfunctioning
4. Front end alignment incorrect
5. Loose suspension components

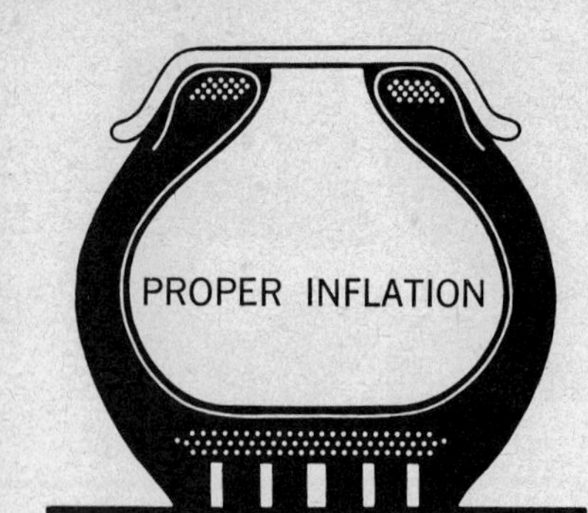

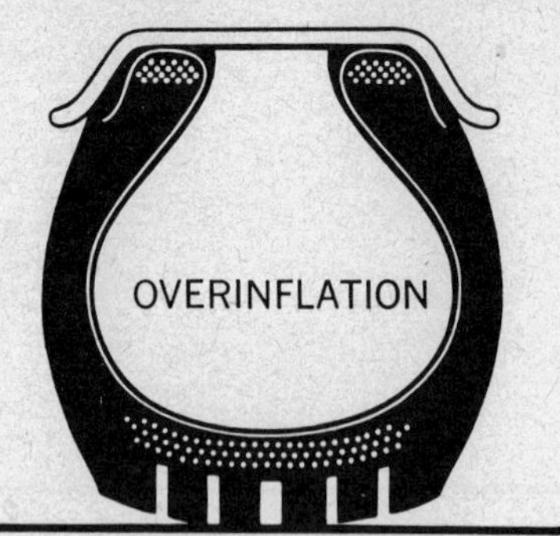

Comparison of normal, under and over tire inflation and effect on the tire tread

VEHICLE STEERS TO ONE SIDE AT ALL TIMES

1. Incorrect caster setting
2. Incorrect camber setting
3. Incorrect kingpin inclination or wheel support angle
4. Unequal tire pressure or tire size
5. One side brake drag
6. Unequal shock absorber control
7. Bent or damaged steering and suspension components
8. Uneven or weak spring condition, front or rear
9. Broken center or shackle bolts
10. Frame bent causing improper tracking

NOISY FRONT END

1. Lack of, or improper lubrication
2. Loose steering linkage
3. Loose suspension parts
4. Loose brake parts
5. Worn universal (FWD)
6. Worn differential (FWD)
7. Loose sheet metal

LUBRICATION LEAKING INTO DRUM OR ON ROTOR

1. Excessive differential lubricant (FWD)
2. Clogged axle housing vent (FWD)
3. Damage or worn universal driveshaft oil seal (FWD)
4. Loose steering knuckle flange bearings (FWD)
5. Defective outer seal
6. Rough spindle to oil seal surface
7. Wheel bearings overpacked or use of wrong lubricant
8. Clogged oil slinger drain
9. Cracked steering knuckle outer flange

EXCESSIVE TIRE WEAR

1. Incorrect wheel alignment
2. Failure to rotate tires
3. Improper tire inflation
4. Overload or improperly loaded vehicle
5. High tire temperature operation
6. Excessive speed, quick starts and quick stops
7. Bent suspension, frame or wheel parts
8. Tires out of balance

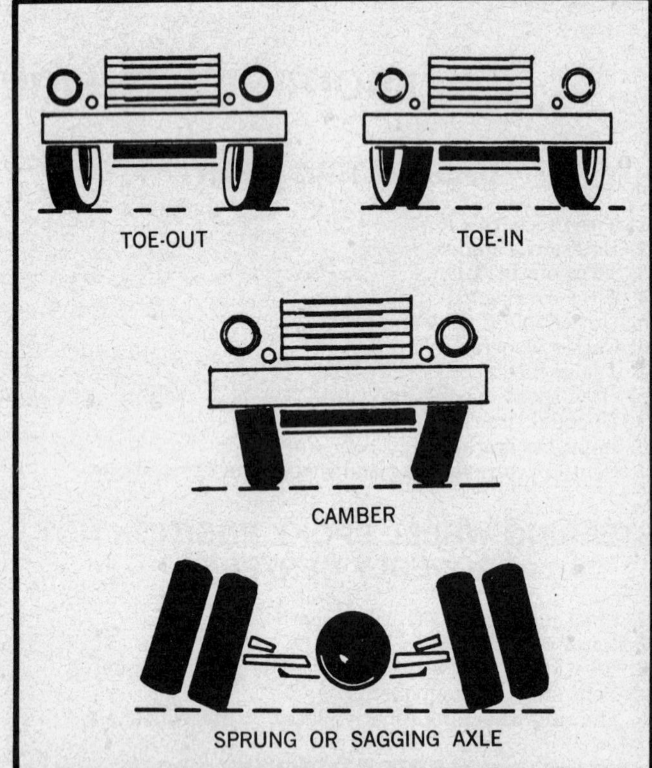

Exaggerated views of alignment problems

9. Uneven brake application
10. Excessive hard turning of tandem and spread axle wheels

Wheel Alignment

For a truck to have safe steering control with a minimum of tire wear, certain established rules must be followed. These rules fix the values of planes, angles and radii relative to each other and to truck and tire dimensions. Some factors are built in, with no provision for adjustment; others are adjustable within limits. The entire system depends upon all value factors, separately and combined. It is therefore difficult to change some of the established settings without influencing others.

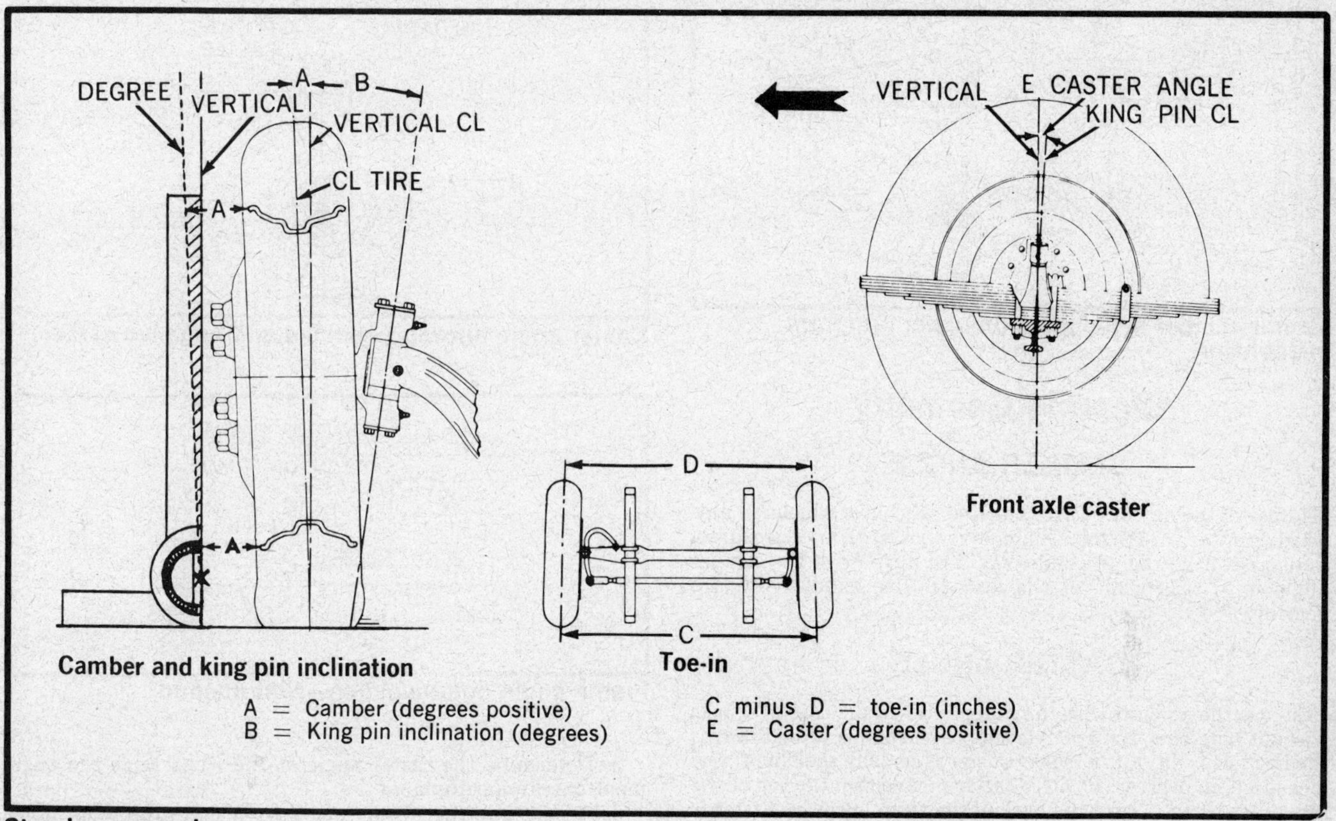

Steering geometry

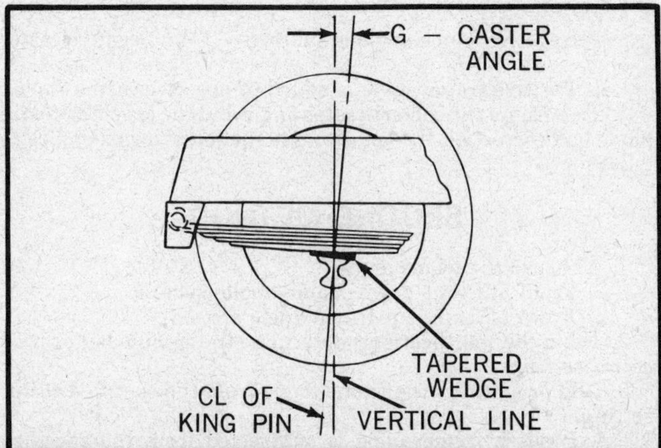

Use of tapered wedge between the axle and spring to adjust caster angle

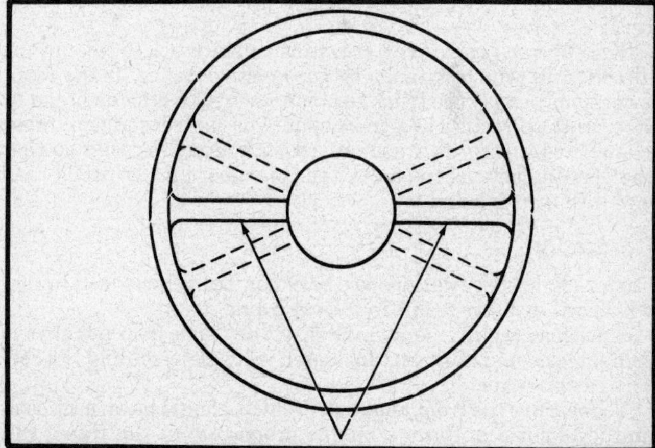
Steering wheel position

This system is called steering geometry or wheel alignment and requires a complete check of all the factors involved. Definitions of these factors and the effect each one has on the truck are given in the following paragraphs. For adjustment data relative to each separate truck and year, refer to the individual truck sections.

STEERING WHEEL POSITION

Always check steering wheel alignment in conjunction with and at the same time as toe-in. In fact, the steering wheel spoke position, with the truck on a straight section of highway, may be the first indication of front end misalignment.

If the truck has been wrecked, or indicates any evidence of steering gear or linkage disturbance, the Pitman arm should be disconnected from the sector shaft. The steering wheel (or gear) should be turned from extreme right to extreme left to determine the halfway point in its turning scope. This will be the spot on the gear that is in action during straight ahead driving and in which position the steering gear should be adjusted. With the steering wheel in the straight-ahead position and the steering gear adjusted to zero lash status, reconnect the Pitman arm.

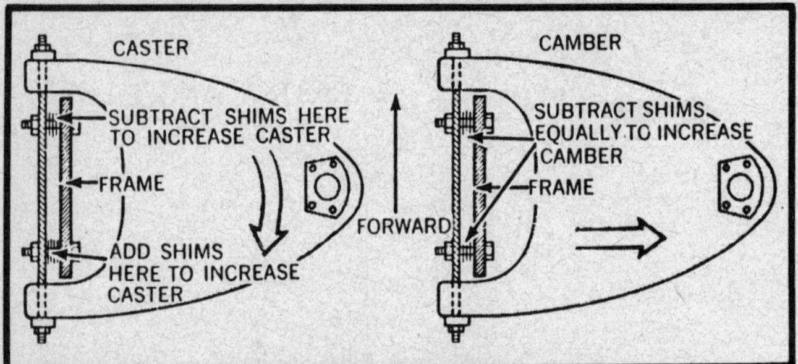

Caster-camber adjustment on upper arm front suspension

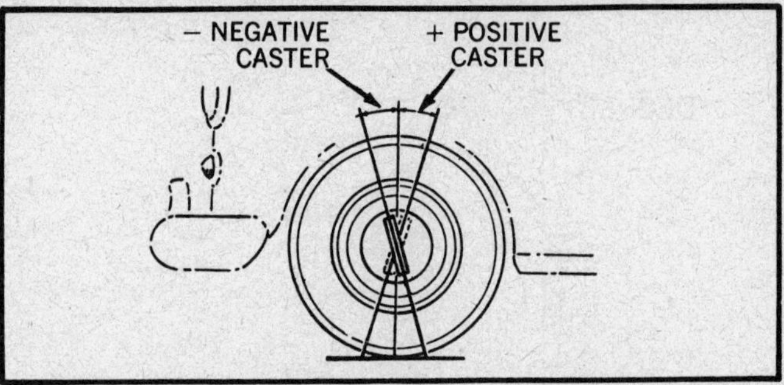

Caster angle showing positive and negative caster

Steering Geometry

CAMBER ANGLE

Camber is the amount that the front wheels are inclined outward or inward at the top. Chamber is spoken of, and measured, in degrees from the perpendicular. The purpose of the camber angle is to take some of the load off the spindle outboard bearing.

CASTER ANGLE

Caster is the amount that the kingpin (or in the case of trucks without king-pins, the knuckle support pivots) is tilted towards the back or front of the truck. Caster is usually spoken of, and measured, in degrees. Positive caster means that the top of the kingpin is tilted toward the back of the truck. Positive caster is indicated by the sign "+".

Negative caster is exactly the opposite; the top of the kingpin is tilted toward the front of the truck. This is generally indicated by the sign "-". Negative caster is sometimes referred to as reverse caster.

The effect of positive caster is to cause the truck to steer in the direction in which it tends to go. Positive caster in the front wheels may cause the truck to steer down off a crowned road or steer in the direction of a cross wind. For this reason, a number of our modern trucks are arranged with negative caster so that the opposite is true; the truck tends to steer up a crowned road and into a cross wind.

Correction

Caster angle specifications are based on the vehicle load limits, which will usually result in a level frame.

Since load requirements may vary, the frame does not always remain level and must be considered when determining the correct caster angle.

To measure the from angle, the vehicle should be on a smooth and level surface. Place a bubble protractor on the frame rail and measure the degree of frame tilt and in what direction, either front or rear.

Two methods of determining caster angles are used. The first method is to determine the caster angle from the wheel with alignment equipment, and the second method is to obtain the desired caster angle from the specification charts. The frame angle is then added to or subtracted fro the caster angles as necessary. The two methods are outlined. Examples and diagrams are provided for use by the repairman to assist in determining the proper caste angle to use.

FIRST METHOD

1. Determine the frame angle.
   a. Frame high at rear–frame angle is negative.
   b. Frame low at rear–frame angle is positive.

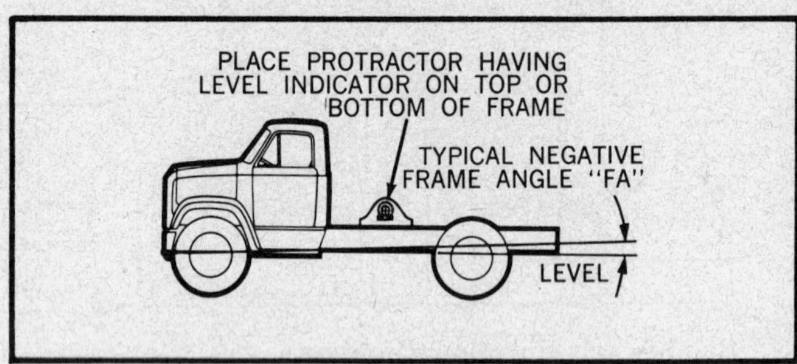

Frame angle determination—first method

2. Determine the caster angle at the wheel with the alignment checking equipment.
3. Add or subtract frame angle from or to the determined caster angle.
   a. Negative frame angle is added to positive caster angle.
   b. Positive frame angle is subtracted from positive caster angle.
   c. Negative frame angle is subtracted from negative caster angle.
   d. Positive frame angle is added to negative caster angle.
4. Determine the correct caster angle and the specified caster angle and correct on the vehicle. Use the following examples as guides.

SECOND METHOD

1. Measure the frame angle.
   a. Front of frame down–frame angle positive.
   b. Front of frame up–frame angle negative
2. From the specifications, determine the specified or desired caster setting.
3. Add or subtract the frame angle from the specified caster setting.
   a. Positive frame angle is subtracted from the specified setting.
   b. Negative frame angle is added to the specified caster setting.
4. Using wheel alignment equipment, obtain the measured caster angle from the wheel and determine the corrected specified setting, using the following examples as guides.

ANGLE OF KINGPIN INCLINATION

In addition to the caster angle, the kingpins (or knuckle support pivots) are also inclined toward each other at the top. This angle is known as kingpin inclination and is usually spoken of, and measured, in degrees.

The effect of kingpin inclination is to cause the wheels to steer in a straight line, regardless of outside forces such as crowned

EXAMPLE NO. 1 (FRAME LOWER AT REAR—POSITIVE)

Measured wheel caster angle	+2°
Frame angle	3°
Actual caster angle (Frame at zero degrees)	−1°
Specifications (desired)	+2°
Necessary degrees to change	+3°

REFER TO EXAMPLE 1

WHEEL CL
CA +2°
FRONT
POSITIVE FA
FRAME 0°
FA 3°

ACTUAL CASTER ANGLE = −1° @ 0° FA

WHEEL CL
CA-2°
FRONT
NEGATIVE
FRAME 0°
FA 2°

ACTUAL CASTER ANGLE = −4° @ 0° FA

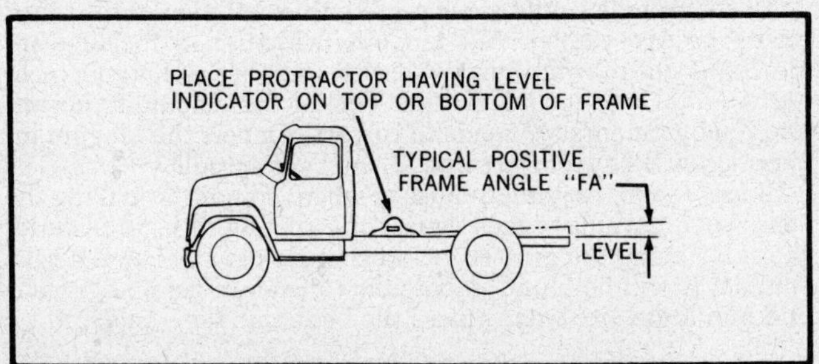

Frame angle determination—second method

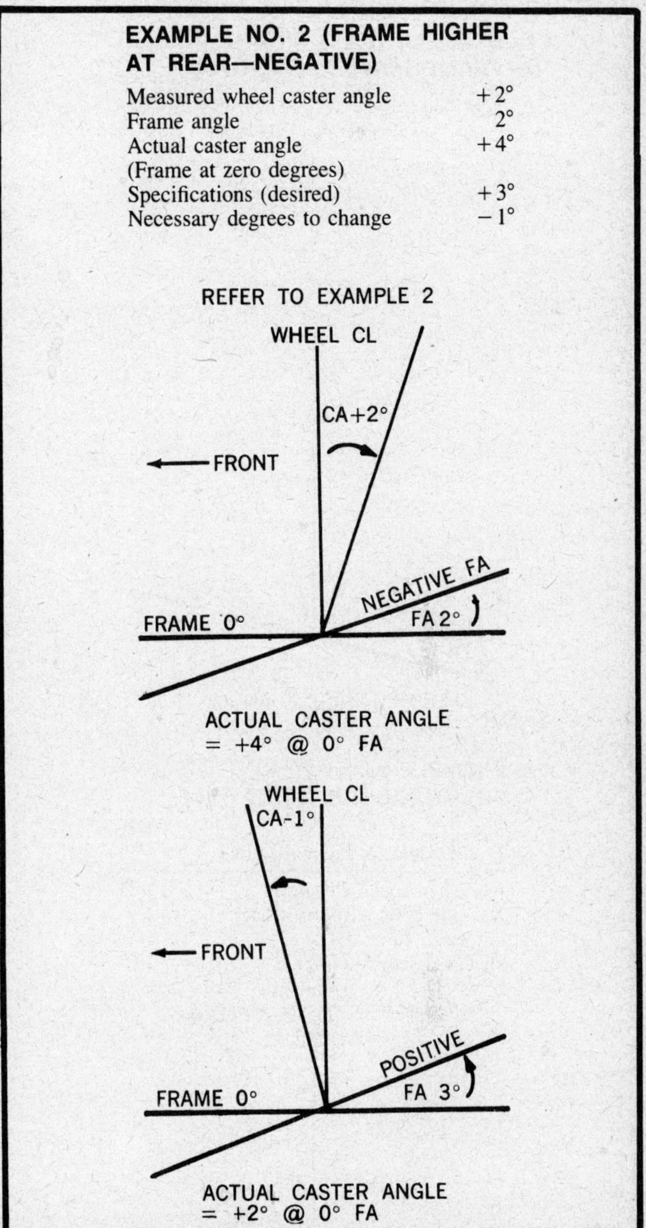

EXAMPLE NO. 2 (FRAME HIGHER AT REAR—NEGATIVE)

Measured wheel caster angle	+2°
Frame angle	2°
Actual caster angle (Frame at zero degrees)	+4°
Specifications (desired)	+3°
Necessary degrees to change	−1°

roads, cross winds, etc., which may tend to make it steer at a tangent. As the spindle is moved from extreme right to extreme left it apparently rises and falls. Notice that it reaches its highest position when the wheels are in the straight-ahead position. In actual operation, the spindle cannot rise and fall because because the wheel is in constant contact with the ground.

Therefore, the truck itself will rise at the extreme right turn and come to its lowest point at the straight-ahead position, and again rise for an extreme left turn. The weight of the truck will tend to cause the wheels to come to the straight-ahead position, which is the lowest position of the truck itself.

INCLUDED ANGLE

Included angle is the name given to that angle which includes kingpin inclination and camber. It is the relationship between the centerline of the wheel and the centerline of the kingpin (or the knuckle support pivots). This angle is build into the knuckle

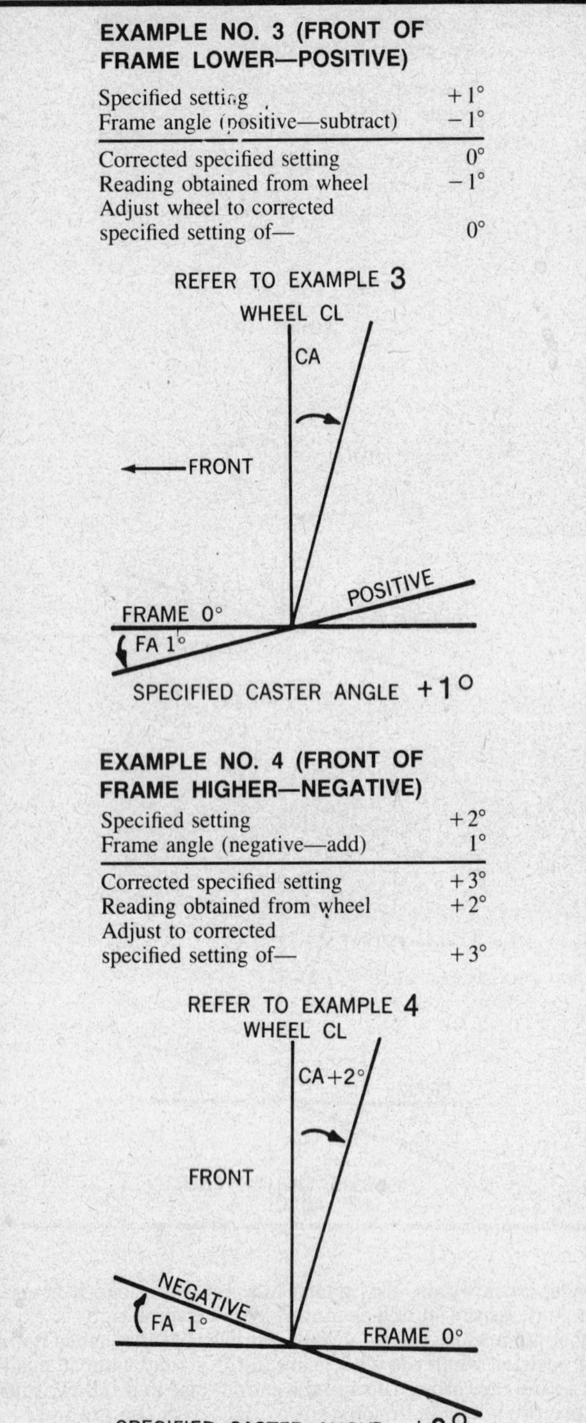

EXAMPLE NO. 3 (FRONT OF FRAME LOWER—POSITIVE)

Specified setting	+1°
Frame angle (positive—subtract)	−1°
Corrected specified setting	0°
Reading obtained from wheel	−1°
Adjust wheel to corrected specified setting of—	0°

EXAMPLE NO. 4 (FRONT OF FRAME HIGHER—NEGATIVE)

Specified setting	+2°
Frame angle (negative—add)	1°
Corrected specified setting	+3°
Reading obtained from wheel	+2°
Adjust to corrected specified setting of—	+3°

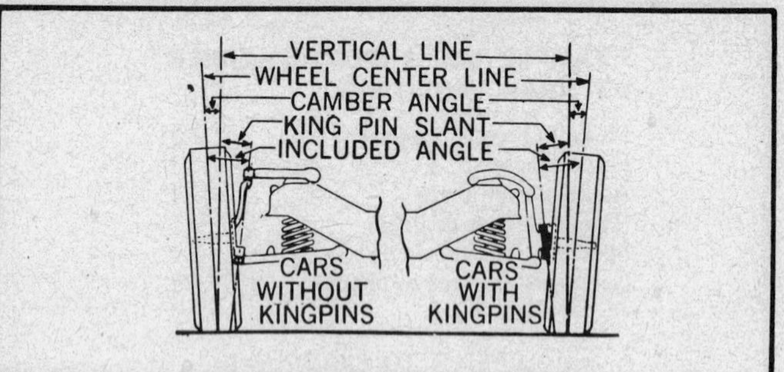

Camber, king pin slant and included angle

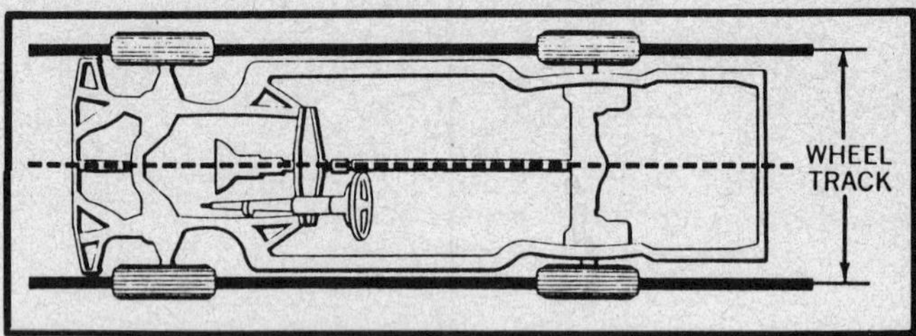

Typical parallel wheel track

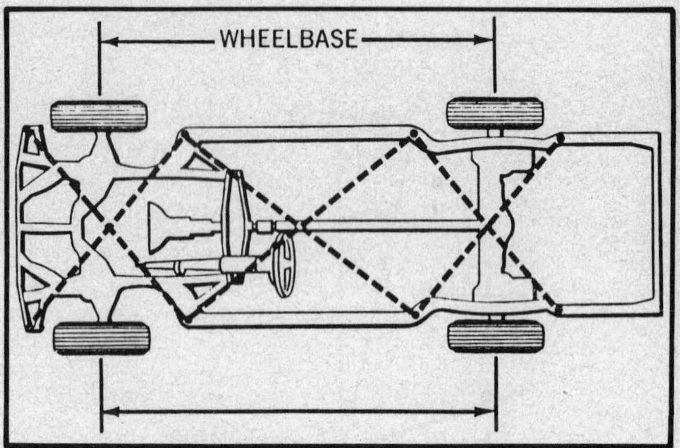

Measuring corresponding points of frame

(spindle) forging and will remain constant throughout the life of the truck, unless the spindle itself is damaged.

When checking a truck on the front end stand, always measure kingpin inclination as well as camber unless some provision is made on the stand for checking condition of the spindle. Where no such provision is made, add the kingpin inclination inclination to the camber for each side of the truck. These totals should be exactly the same, regardless of how far from the norm the readings may be.

For example, the left side of the truck checks 5 1/2° kingpin inclination and 1° positive camber–total 6 1/2°. Since both sides check exactly the same for the included angle, it is unlikely that both spindles, in this instance, are bent. Adjusting to correct for camber will automatically set correct kingpin inclination.

A bent spindle would show up like this: left side of the truck has 3/4° positive camber, 5 1/4° kingpin inclination–6° included angle. Right side of truck has 1 1/4° positive camber, 6° kingpin inclination–total 7 1/4° included angle. One of these spindles is bent and if adjustments are made to correct camber, the kingpin inclination will be incorrect due to the bent spindle.

Since the most common cause of a bent spindle is striking the curb when parking, which causes the spindle to bend upward, the side having the greater included angle usually has the bent spindle. It will be found impossible to achieve good alignment and minimum tire wear unless the bent spindle is replaced.

TOE-IN

Toe-in is the amount that the front wheels are closer together at

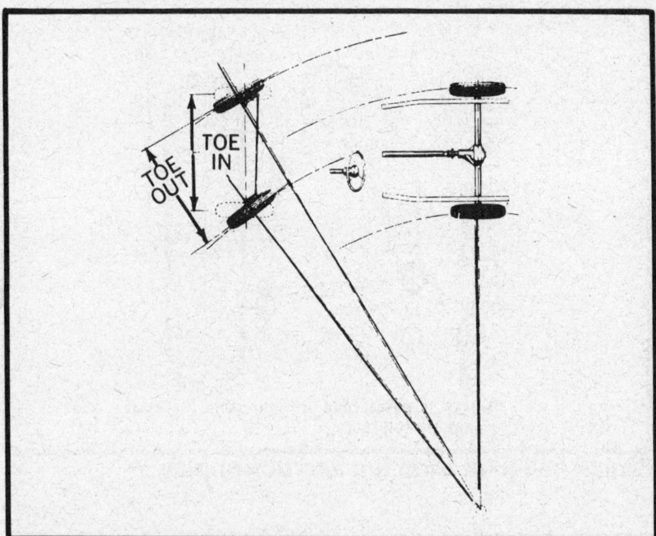

Steering geometry on turns

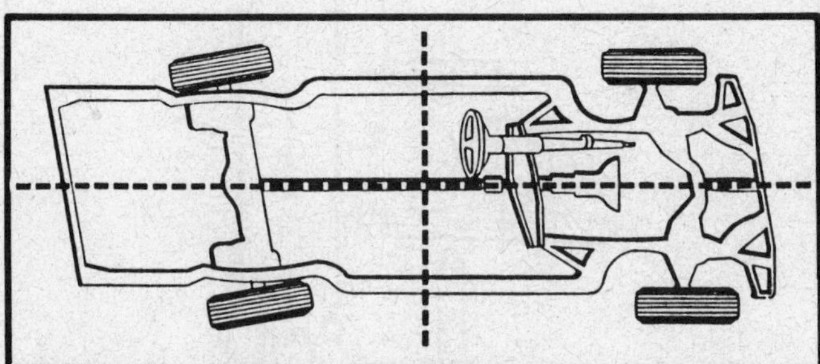
Bent frame, diamond shaped

the front than they are at the back. This dimension is usually spoken of, and measured, in inches or fractions of inches.

Generally speaking, the wheels are toed-in because they are cambered. When a truck operates with 0° camber it will be found to operate with zero toe-in. As the required camber increases, so does the toe-in. The reason for this is that the cambered wheel tends to steer in the direction in which it is cambered. Therefore it is necessary to overcome this tendency of the wheel by compensating very slightly in the direction opposite to that in which it tends to roll. Caster and camber both have an effect on toe-in. Therefore toe-in is the last thing on the front end which should be corrected.

TOE-OUT STEERING RADIUS

When a truck is steered into a turn, the outside wheel of the vehicle scribes a much larger circle than the inside wheel. Therefore, the outside wheel must be steered to a somewhat less angle than the inside wheel. This difference in the angle is often called toe-out.

The change in angle from toe-in in the straight-ahead position to toe-out in the turn is caused by the relative position of the steering arms to the kingpin and to each other.

If a line were drawn from the center of the kingpin through the center of the steering arm-tie rod attaching hole at each wheel, these lines would be found to cross almost exactly in the center of the rear axle.

If the front end angles, including toe-in, are set correctly, and the toe-out is found to be incorrect, one or both of the steering arms are bent.

TRACKING

While tracking is more a function of the rear axle and frame, it is difficult to align the front suspension when the truck does not track straight. Tracking means that the centerline of the rear axle follows exactly the path of the centerline of the front axle when the truck is moving in a straight line.

On trucks that have equal tread, front and rear, the rear tires will follow in exactly the thread of the front tires, when moving in a straight line. However, there are many trucks whose rear tread is wider than the front tread. On such trucks, the rear axle tread will straddle the front axle tread an equal amount on both sides, when moving in a straight line.

Perhaps the easiest way to check a truck for tracking is to stand directly in back of it and watch it more in a straight line down the street. If the observer will stand as near to the center of the truck as possible, he can readily observe, even with the difference in perspective between the front and rear wheels, whether or not they are tracking properly. If the truck is found to track incorrectly, the difficulty will be found in either the frame or in the rear axle alignment.

Another more accurate method to check tracking is to park the truck on a level floor and drop a plumb-line from the extreme outer edge of the front suspension lower A-frame. Use the same drop point on each side of the truck. Make a chalk lie where the plumb-line strikes the floor. Do the same with the rear axle, selecting a point on the rear axle housing for the plumb-line.

Measure diagonally from the left rear mark to the right front mark and from the right rear mark to the left front mark. These two diagonal measurements should be exactly the same. A ¼ in. variation is acceptable.

If the diagonal measurements taken are different, measure from the right rear mark to the right front mark and from the left rear to the left front. These two measurements should also be the same within ¼ in..

If the diagonal measurements are different, but the longitudinal measurements are the same, the frame is swayed (diamond shaped).

However, in the event that the diagonal measurements are unequal and the longitudinal measurements are also unequal, and the truck is tracking incorrectly, the rear axle is misaligned.

If the diagonal and longitudinal measurements are both unequal, but the truck appears to track correctly on the street, a kneeback is indicated.

NOTE: A kneeback means that one complete side of the front suspension is bent back. This is often caused by crimping the front wheels against the curb when parking the vehicle, then starting up without straightening the wheels out.

Suspension And Ball Joint System

When checking the suspension and ball joints, it is advisable to follow the manufacturer's recommendations. For all practical purposes, however, the following general procedures are applicable.

SUSPENSION SYSTEM

Inspection

This check is made with the ball joints fully loaded, so that suspension elements other than the ball joints may be checked.
When the front spring or torsion bar is supported by lower control arm, the jackstand should be located under the front crossmember or frame.
When the front spring is supported by the upper control arm, the jackstand should be located under the lower control arm.

Vertical or horizontal movement at the road wheel should not exceed the following:

1. Up to and including 16 in. – ¼ in. movement.
2. 16 to 18 in. – ⅓ in. movement.
3. More than 18 in. – ½ in. movement.

Ball Joint

Inspection

When checking the ball joints for any wear, they must be free of any load.

When the front spring or torsion bar is supported by the lower control arm, the jackstand should be positioned under the lower control arm.

When the front spring is supported by the upper control arm, the jackstand should be located under the front crossmember or frame.

Replace the upper ball joint if any noticeable play is present in the joint when the spring is supported by the upper control arm; If the sideplay (horizontal motion) of the wheel, when rocked, exceed specifications; or if the up and down (vertical motion) exceed specifications.

WHEEL BEARING AND SEAL

Replacement

NOTE: Refer to individual truck section for oil filled hub service.

1. Place jack under lower suspension arm. Remove hub cover

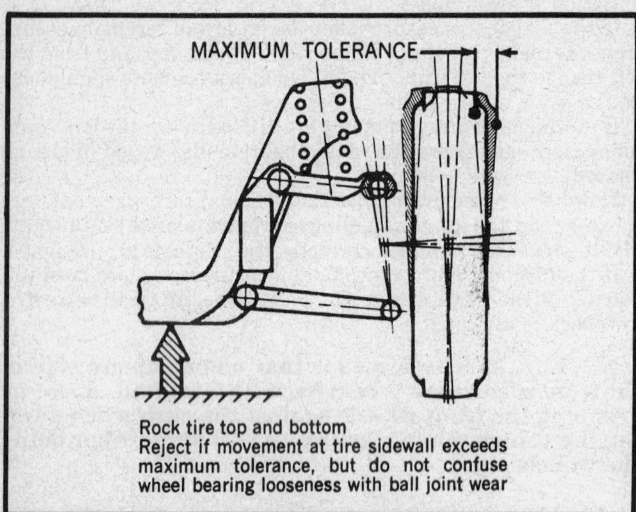
MAXIMUM TOLERANCE
Rock tire top and bottom
Reject if movement at tire sidewall exceeds maximum tolerance, but do not confuse wheel bearing looseness with ball joint wear

Check ball joint radial (side play)

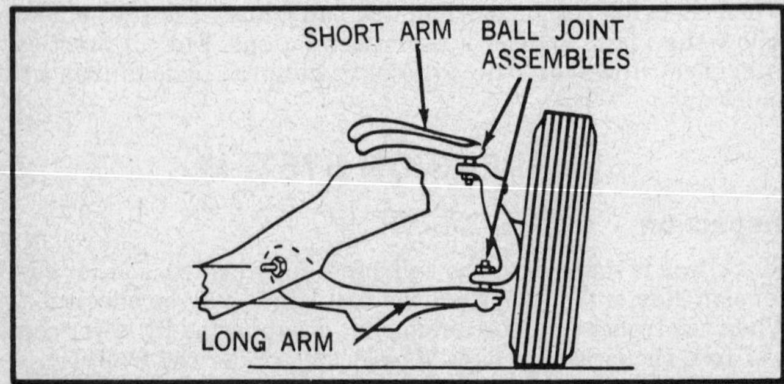
SHORT ARM
BALL JOINT ASSEMBLIES
LONG ARM

Use of control arms and ball joints for independent suspension

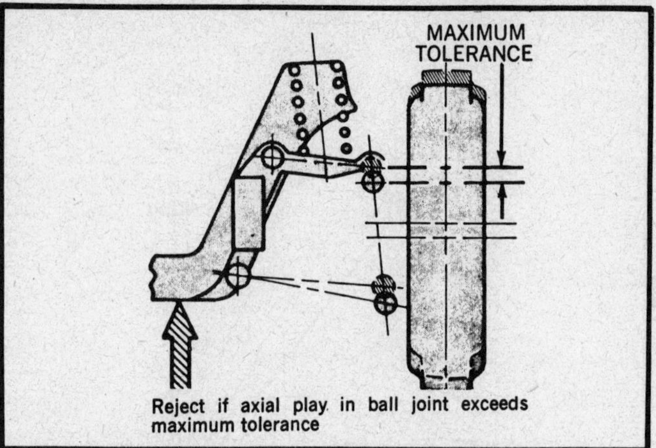
MAXIMUM TOLERANCE
Reject if axial play in ball joint exceeds maximum tolerance

Check ball joint axial (up and down) play

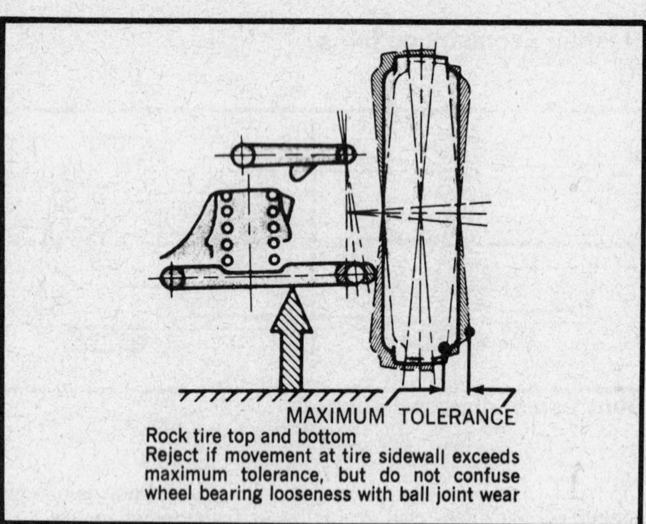
MAXIMUM TOLERANCE
Rock tire top and bottom
Reject if movement at tire sidewall exceeds maximum tolerance, but do not confuse wheel bearing looseness with ball joint wear

Maximum tolerance

and grease cap. Remove spindle nut, keyed washer and outer bearing. Slide off hub and drum.

NOTE: In some cases, drum removal may require loosening of brake adjustment.

2. At this point, brakes and drums should be inspected for their condition.
3. With hub and drum on bench, remove seal and inner bearing. Thoroughly clean all parts. Drive out inner and outer races of roller type. Use care not to mar the bearing surfaces.
4. Pack bearings with approved lubricant. When replacing cups, use a bearing race driver if possible. If a punch is used, make sure it is blunt and then drive parts in every carefully to avoid cocking the bearings.
5. Install new grease seal in hub. Assemble hub and drum on spindle and replace the outer bearing, key washer and nut.
6. A common method of adjustment is to tighten to zero clearance and then back off to first cotter pin castellation. Some manufacturers recommend tightening to approximately 10 to 12 ft. lbs., then backing off nut ⅙ turn. If cotter pin hole does not line up, loosen slightly.
7. Readjust brake if necessary and install grease cap and hub cover. Remove jack.

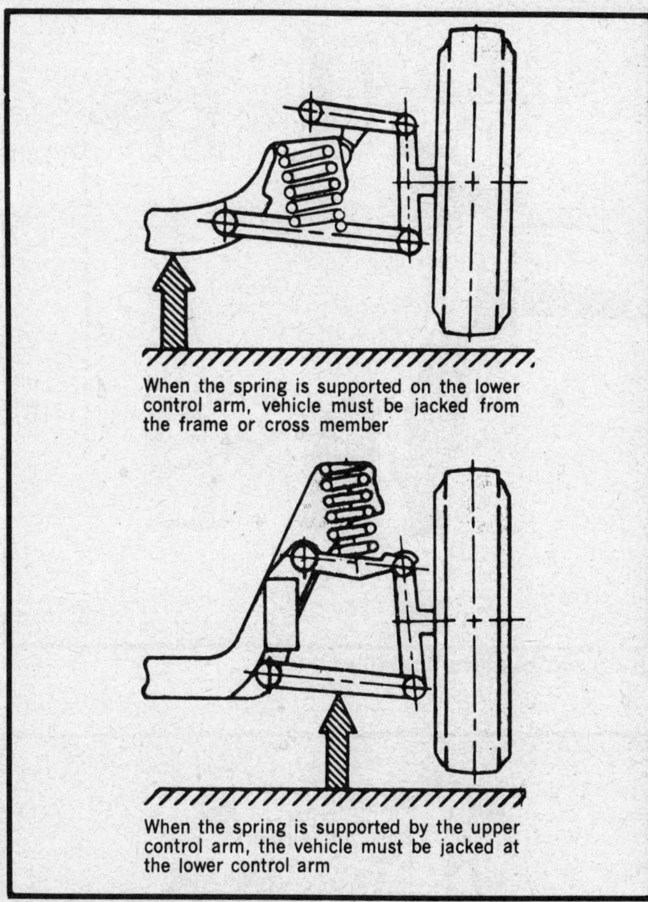
When the spring is supported on the lower control arm, vehicle must be jacked from the frame or cross member
When the spring is supported by the upper control arm, the vehicle must be jacked at the lower control arm

Steering and suspension jacking procedure

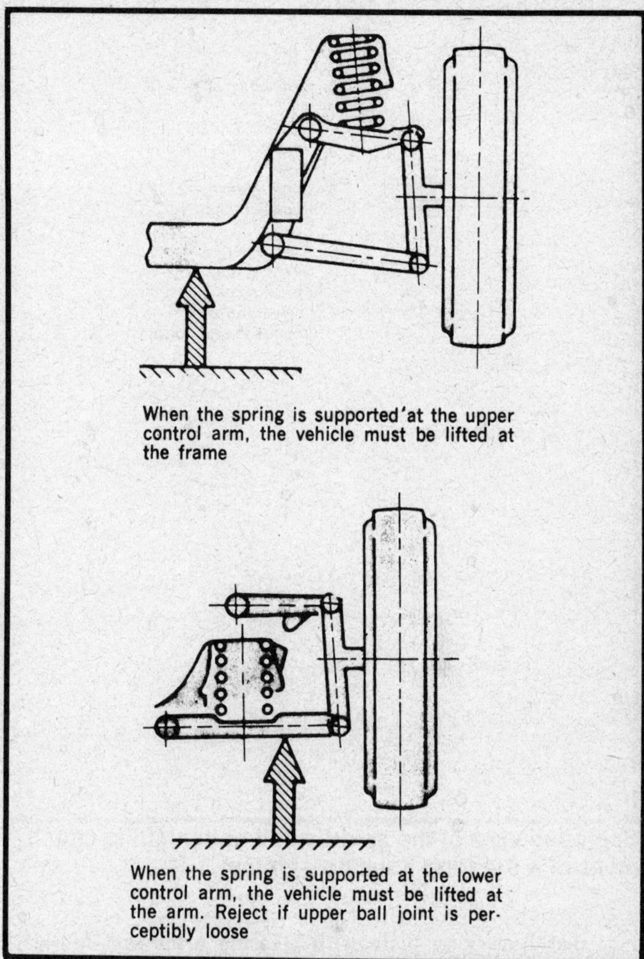
When the spring is supported at the upper control arm, the vehicle must be lifted at the frame
When the spring is supported at the lower control arm, the vehicle must be lifted at the arm. Reject if upper ball joint is perceptibly loose

The bearing and seal replacement procedure is the same as for the drum brakes

NOTE: When disc brakes are used on the front wheels, the calipers must be removed before the rotors can be taken from the spindle. Hang the calipers by wire from the frame rail so the weight of the caliper is not on the brake hose. The bearing and seal replacement procedure is the same as for the drum brakes.

KINGPIN AND BUSHING

Kingpins and bushings can be placed in two general classes:
1. With bushings in knuckle.
2. With bushings in spindle.

Replacement

1. Jack up the truck and remove the hub as described in the wheel bearing section. Remove the backing plate to knuckle bolts and lift assembly, with brakes, from the knuckle. Suspend it with a piece of wire to prevent damage to brake hose.
2. Drive out lock pin or bolt. with a sharp punch, remove top welch plug. Drive pin and lower welch plug down through knuckle and support.

NOTE: Remove top and bottom threaded plugs with wrench.

3. Drive bushings from the spindle and replace them. Be sure, when driving new bushing, that grease holes line up with those in knuckle.
4. Align and ream bushings to a snug running fit for the new kingpin.

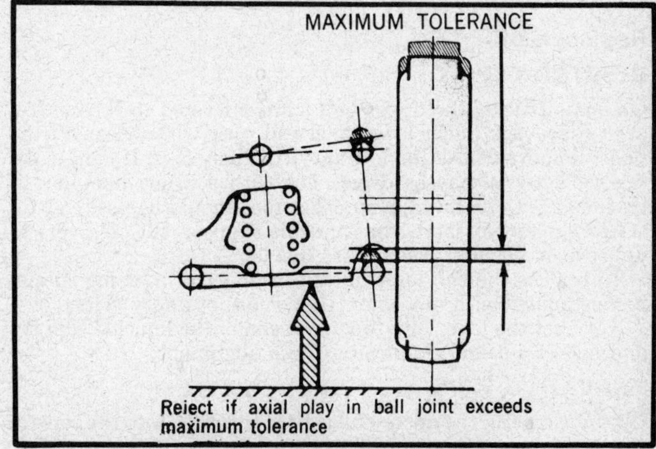
MAXIMUM TOLERANCE
Reject if axial play in ball joint exceeds maximum tolerance

Check ball joint axial (up and down) play

5. Insert the kingpin through the top of the spindle, support, thrust bearing (with shims to control vertical play) and into the spindle bottom. Keep the kingpin in proper rotation so that the lockpin can be inserted. Install lockpin or bolt. Install upper and lower welch plugs.

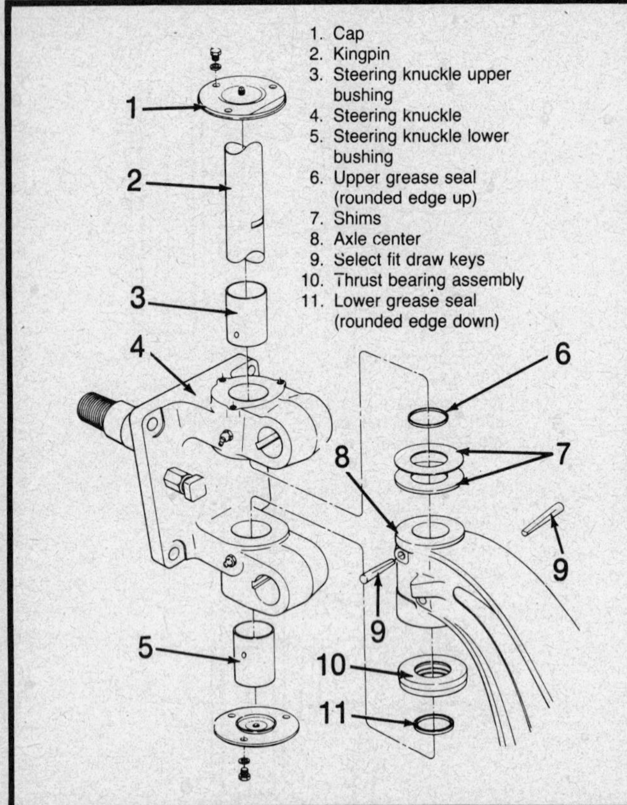

Exploded view of the spindle bolt and bushing attachment of a steering knuckle—typical

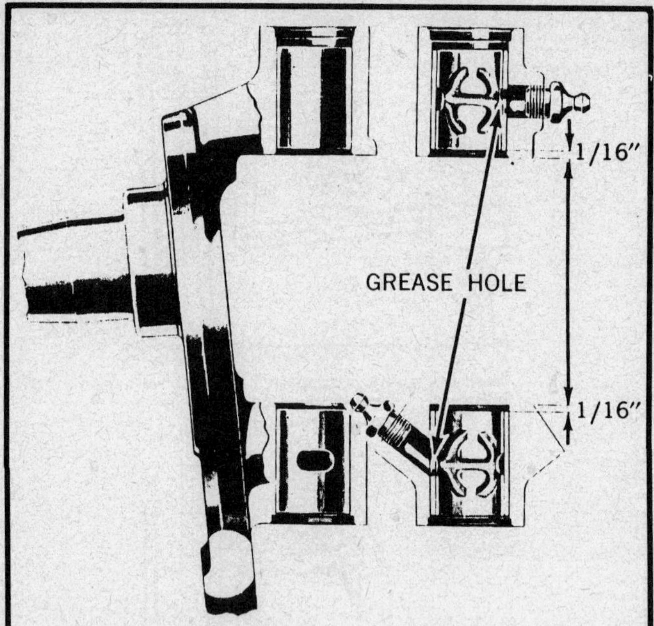

King pin bushins installed

6. Install backing plate with steering arms and lubricate properly.
7. Install hubs, drums and wheels, then remove jack.

UPPER BALL JOINT

Replacement

RIVETED TYPE

On some trucks, the upper ball joint is riveted to the control arm. Place jack under lower arm and raise wheel clear off the floor. Remove wheel. Remove nut from ball joint. If joint is being replaced, it may be driven out with a heavy hammer. If threads are to be saved, a spreader tool should be used.

After removing joint from knuckle support, cut off rivets at upper arm. Drilling rivets eases this job.

To replace the ball joint: install in upper arm, using special bolts supplied with new joint. Do not use ordinary bolts.

Next, set the taper into the upper end of the knuckle support and install nut and cotter pin. Check alignment.

THREADED TYPE

On some trucks, the upper ball joint is threaded into the control arm.

Place jack under lower control arm and relieve load on torsion bar. Raise wheel clear of floor. Remove wheel. Remove nut from ball joint. If ball joint is being replaced, it may be driven out with a heavy hammer. If threads are to be saved, use a spreader tool.

After removing from knuckle support, the ball joint can be unscrewed from the support arm. Special tools are recommended for this operation.

When replacing the ball joint, be sure to engage the threads into the control arm squarely. Torque to 125 ft. lbs. If this torque cannot be obtained, check for bad threads in arm or on joint. Install new balloon seal.

Place joint in knuckle and install nut. Reload torsion bar (if so equipped) and reset height.

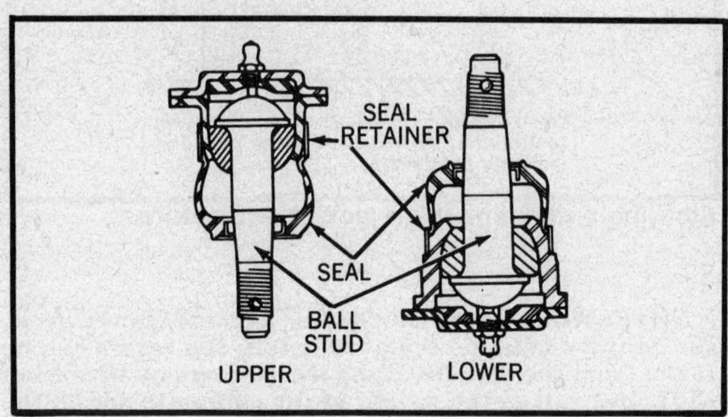

Typical ball joint assemblies

LOWER BALL JOINT

Removal and Installation

PRESSED TYPE

These ball joints are pressed into support arms. To replace pressed-in units, it is necessary to remove the front spring and support arm.

After removing wheel and drum, loosen nut slightly at ball joint taper and hammer lightly around area to loosen. If new ball joints are being installed, it is not necessary to protect the threads.

Place support arm in an arbor press with a suitable tool and press ball joint from the arm.

Install ball joint by reversing the pressing procedure.

NOTE: Special tools of the C-clamp type are available and an be used n some trucks to avoid removal of front spring and support arm.

INTEGRAL TYPE

On some trucks, the lower ball joint is integral with the steering arm and is not serviced separately. To service this unit, remove the upper arm bumper. Raise truck so that the front suspension is under no load. If jacks are used, a support must be placed between the jack and K-member.

1. Remove the wheel and drum assembly. Remove the two lower bolts holding the steering arm to the backing plate.
2. Disconnect tie-rod end from the steering arm. Do not damage seal.
3. Remove the ball joint stud from the lower control arm. A spreading tool will aid in this operation.
4. Install new seal on ball joint. Bolt the steering arm to the backing plate. Insert the ball joint into control arm and torque nut.
5. Connect the tie-rod end. Install drum and wheel.

TIRE REPLACEMENT

Specialized tools and equipment have been designed for use in the replacement of a tire on multipiece rims. The manufacturers instructions should be followed in the use of the machines in the amounting and dismounting of tires to avoid personal injury.

For the safety of the repairman, the word "D.I.P." should be remembered when working with tires and wheels.

1. D–DEFLATE–The tire before working on it.
2. I–INSPECT–The rim, rings, lug holes and tires for damage and proper sealing.
3. P–PROTECT–Yourself by placing the tire and wheel assembly in a cage before inflating.

Tire safety. Remember the word D.I.P.

STRUT SUSPENSION

Design

In a conventional front suspension, the wheel is attached to a spindle, which is in turn connected to upper and lower control arms through upper and lower ball joints. A coil spring between the control arms (sometimes on top of the upper arm) supports the weight of the vehicle and a shock absorber controls rebound and dampens oscillations. In a MacPherson strut type suspension, the strut performs a shock dampening function like a shock absorber, but unlike a conventional shock absorber the strut is a structural part of the vehicle's suspension.

The strut assembly usually contains a spring seat to retain the coil spring that supports the vehicle's weight. The shock absorber is built into the body of the strut housing. The strut is normally attached at the bottom to the lower control arm and at the top to the car body. The upper mount usually features a bearing that permits the coil spring to rotate as the wheels turn for smoother steering. The entire design eliminates the need for the upper control arm, upper ball joint and many of the conventional suspension bushings. The lower ball joint is no longer a load carrying unit, because it is isolated from the weight of the vehicle.

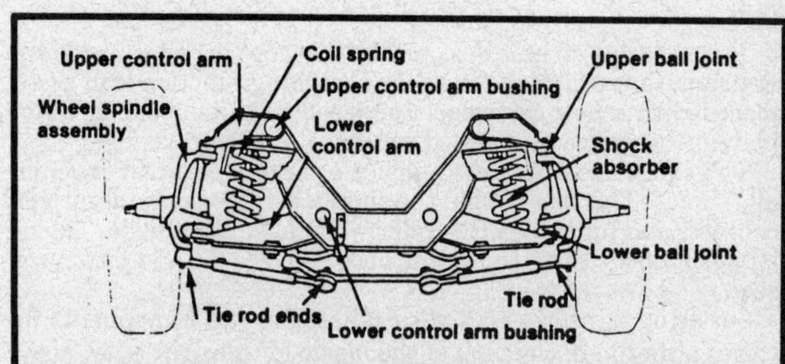

Conventional upper and lower arm suspension

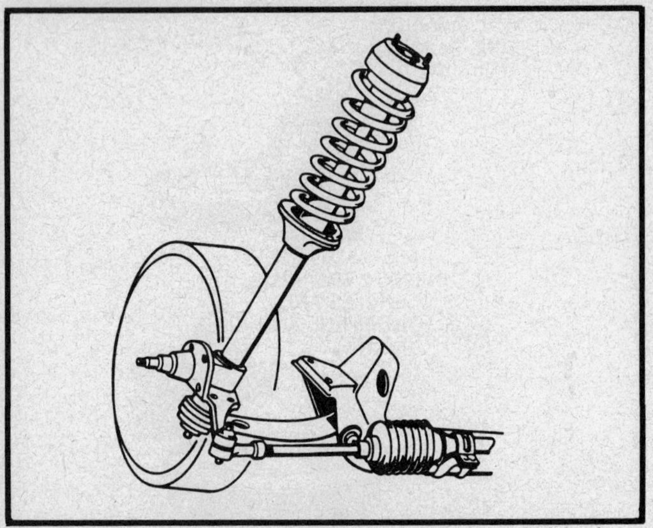
Strut with concentric coil spring (rear wheel drive)

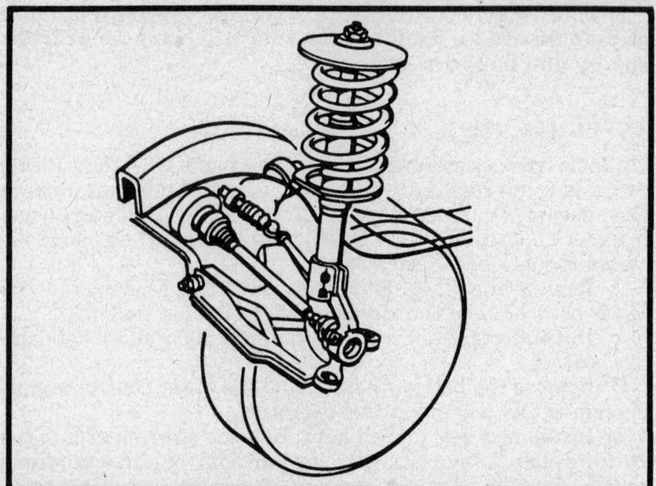
Strut with concentric coil spring

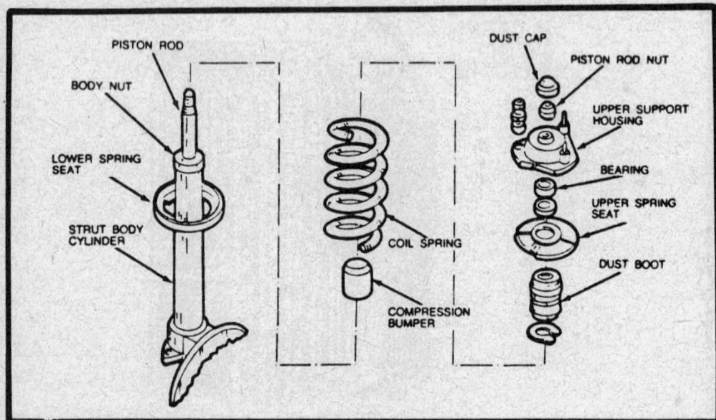

Exploded view of a typical strut

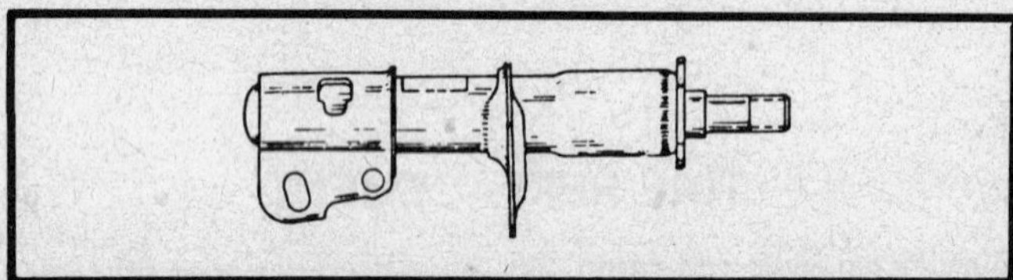
A sealed strut has no body nut and is servicable by replacement

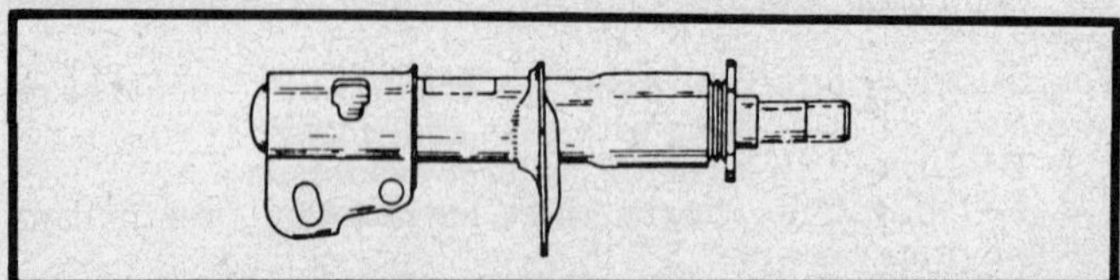
Serviceable struts have removable body nut to allow replacement of the strut cartridge

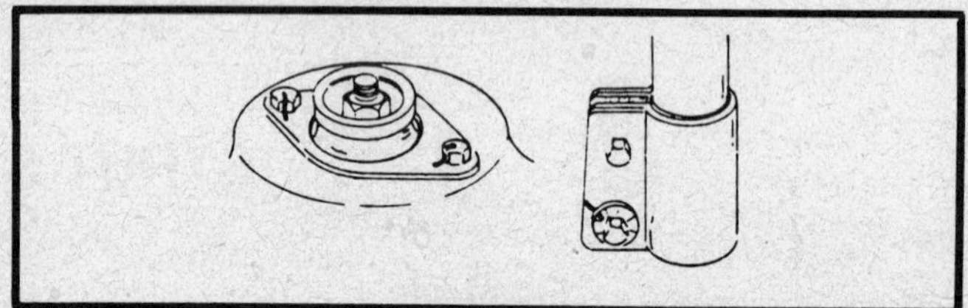

Serviceability

Struts fall into 2 broad categories; serviceable and sealed units. A sealed strut is designed so that the top closure of the strut assembly is permanently sealed. There is no access to the shock absorber cartridge inside the strut housing and no means of replacing the cartridge. It is necessary to replace the entire strut unit.

A serviceable strut is designed so that the cartridge inside the housing, that provides the shock absorbing function, can be replaced with a new cartridge. Serviceable struts use a threaded body nut in place of a sealed cap to retain the cartridge.

The shock absorber device inside a serviceable strut is generally "wet." This means that the shock absorber contains oil that contacts and lubricates the inner wall of the strut body. The oil is sealed inside the strut by the body nut, O-ring and piston rod seal.

Servicing a "wet" strut with the equivalent components involves a thorough cleaning of the inside of the strut body, absolute cleanliness and great care in reassembly.

Cartridge inserts were developed to simplify servicing "wet" struts. The insert is a factory sealed replacement for the strut shock absorber. The replacement cartridge is simply substituted for the original shock absorber cartridge and retained with the body nut, avoiding the near laboratory-like conditions required to service a "wet" strut with "wet" service components.

Sealed, OEM units can also be serviced by replacement with an aftermarket unit, that will permit future servicing by cartridge replacement.

Wheel Alignment

It is not always necessary to re-align the wheels after struts are serviced. If care is taken matchmarking affected components and in reassembling, alignment may be unaffected. However, if wheels were not in proper alignment prior to service, or if the entire strut assembly was replaced, a wheel alignment check should be made. Generally, only camber is adjustable, and then only within a narrow range.

Do not attempt to bend components to correct wheel alignment.

Since the majority of OEM struts are serviced by replacement, most manufacturers recommend wheel alignment following strut replacement.

Transfer Cases
Import Trucks
26

INDEX

TRANSFER CASE SERVICE

Trouble Analysis

SLIPS OUT OF GEAR (HIGH–LOW)

1. Shifting poppet spring weak.
2. Bearing broken or worn.
3. Shifting fork bent.
4. Improper control rod adjustment.

SLIPS OUT OF FRONT WHEEL DRIVE

1. Shifting poppet spring weak or broken.
2. Bearing worn or broken.
3. Excessive shaft end-play.
4. Shifting fork bent.

HARD SHIFTING

1. Lack of lubricant.
2. Shift lever binding on shaft.
3. Shifting poppet ball scored.
4. Shifting fork bent.
5. Low tire pressure.

BACKLASH

1. Companion yoke loose.
2. Transfer case loose on mounts.
3. Internal parts excessively worn.

NOISY

1. Low lubricant level.
2. Bearings improperly adjusted or excessively worn.
3. Gears worn or damaged.
4. Improper alignment of driveshafts or U-joints.

OIL LEAKAGE

1. Excessive amount of lubricant in case.
2. Vent clogged.
3. Gaskets or seals leaking.
4. Bearings loose or damaged.
5. Driveshaft yoke mating surfaces scored.

OVERHEATING

1. Excessive or insufficient amount of lubricant.
2. Bearing adjustment too tight.

CLEANING & INSPECTION

During overhaul, all components of the transfer case (except bearing assemblies) should be thoroughly cleaned with solvent and dried with air pressure prior to inspection and reassembly. Be sure all gasket sealing material is cleaned off of the case, cover plates and mounting flanges.

Bearing Cleaning

Proper cleaning of bearings is of utmost importance. Bearings should always be cleaned separately from other parts.

Soak all bearing assemblies in clean solvent or fuel oil. Bearings should never be cleaned in a hot solution tank. Wash the bearings in solvent until all old lubricant is loosened. Hold races so that bearings will not rotate; then clean bearings with a soft bristled brush until all dirt has been removed. Remove loose particles of dirt by tapping bearing flat against a block of wood. Rinse bearings in clean solvent; then blow bearings dry with air pressure.

CAUTION

Do not spin bearings while drying.

After drying, rotate each bearing slowly while examining balls or rollers for roughness, damage, or excessive wear. Replace all bearings that are not in first class condition. After cleaning and inspecting bearings lubricate generously with recommended lubricant, then wrap each bearing in clean paper until ready for reassembly.

INSPECTION

1. Inspect all parts for discoloration or warpage.
2. Examine all gears and splines for chipped, worn, broken or nicked teeth. Small nicks or burrs may be removed with a fine abrasive stone.
3. Inspect the breather assembly to make sure that it is open and not damaged.
4. Check all threaded parts for damaged, stripped, or crossed threads.
5. Replace all gaskets, oil seals and snap-rings.
6. Inspect housings, retainers and covers for cracks or other damage. Replace the damaged parts.
7. Inspect keys and keyways for condition and fit.
8. Inspect shift forks for wear, distortion or any other damage.
9. Check detent ball springs for free length, compressed length, distortion or collapsed coils.
10. Check bearing fit on their respective shafts and in their bores or cups. Inspect bearings, shafts and cups for wear.

NOTE: If either the bearings or cups are worn or damaged, it is advisable to replace both parts.

11. Inspect all bearing rollers or balls for pitting or galling.
12. Examine detent balls for corrosion or brinneling. If shift bar detents show wear, replace them.
13. Replace all worn or damaged parts. When assembling the transfer case, coat all moving parts with recommended lubricant.

Chrysler/Mitsubishi Transfer Case

SERVICING

Disassembly, Inspection and Assembly

NOTE: The transfer case has been removed from the transmission in the following procedure.

1. Remove the two 4WD switches from the case. Take out the steel balls behind the switches.
2. Remove the speedometer sleeve clamp and the speedometer sleeve assembly,
3. Remove the rear cover, gasket, wave spring and spacer.
4. Take a $^{3}/_{16}$ in. punch and drive out the spring pin that retains the H–L shift fork. Remove the two threaded plugs and remove the poppet springs and balls.
5. Pull out the H–L shift rail. Take out the interlock plunger.
6. Remove the rear bearing snap-ring from the rear output shaft. Remove the chain cover, oil guide and side cover.
7. Remove the countershaft locking plate and remove the countershaft. Remove the counter gear assembly through the side cover opening. The gear assembly consists of gear, spacers, needle bearings and thrust washers.
8. Remove the snap-ring, the two spring retainers and the spring from the 2–4WD shift rail.
9. Remove the front output shaft, the rear output shaft and the chain (as an assembly) from the transfer case.
10. Remove the 2–4WD shift rail. Remove the H–L shift fork and clutch sleeve. Remove the needle bearing from the input gear.
11. Remove the snap-ring retaining the input gear assembly and remove the input gear assembly.

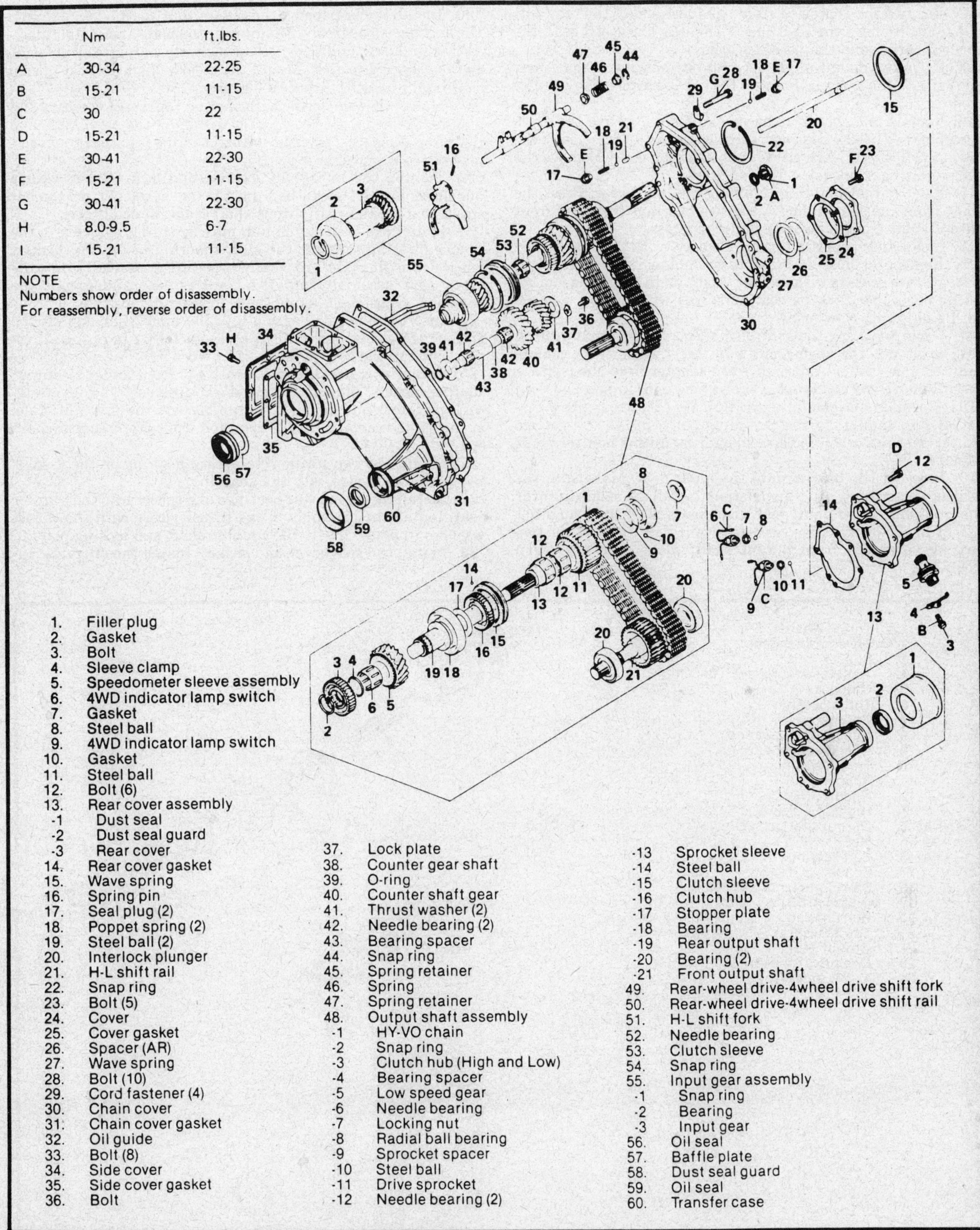

	Nm	ft.lbs.
A	30-34	22-25
B	15-21	11-15
C	30	22
D	15-21	11-15
E	30-41	22-30
F	15-21	11-15
G	30-41	22-30
H	8.0-9.5	6-7
I	15-21	11-15

NOTE
Numbers show order of disassembly.
For reassembly, reverse order of disassembly.

1. Filler plug
2. Gasket
3. Bolt
4. Sleeve clamp
5. Speedometer sleeve assembly
6. 4WD indicator lamp switch
7. Gasket
8. Steel ball
9. 4WD indicator lamp switch
10. Gasket
11. Steel ball
12. Bolt (6)
13. Rear cover assembly
    - -1 Dust seal
    - -2 Dust seal guard
    - -3 Rear cover
14. Rear cover gasket
15. Wave spring
16. Spring pin
17. Seal plug (2)
18. Poppet spring (2)
19. Steel ball (2)
20. Interlock plunger
21. H-L shift rail
22. Snap ring
23. Bolt (5)
24. Cover
25. Cover gasket
26. Spacer (AR)
27. Wave spring
28. Bolt (10)
29. Cord fastener (4)
30. Chain cover
31. Chain cover gasket
32. Oil guide
33. Bolt (8)
34. Side cover
35. Side cover gasket
36. Bolt
37. Lock plate
38. Counter gear shaft
39. O-ring
40. Counter shaft gear
41. Thrust washer (2)
42. Needle bearing (2)
43. Bearing spacer
44. Snap ring
45. Spring retainer
46. Spring
47. Spring retainer
48. Output shaft assembly
    - -1 HY-VO chain
    - -2 Snap ring
    - -3 Clutch hub (High and Low)
    - -4 Bearing spacer
    - -5 Low speed gear
    - -6 Needle bearing
    - -7 Locking nut
    - -8 Radial ball bearing
    - -9 Sprocket spacer
    - -10 Steel ball
    - -11 Drive sprocket
    - -12 Needle bearing (2)
    - -13 Sprocket sleeve
    - -14 Steel ball
    - -15 Clutch sleeve
    - -16 Clutch hub
    - -17 Stopper plate
    - -18 Bearing
    - -19 Rear output shaft
    - -20 Bearing (2)
    - -21 Front output shaft
49. Rear-wheel drive-4wheel drive shift fork
50. Rear-wheel drive-4wheel drive shift rail
51. H-L shift fork
52. Needle bearing
53. Clutch sleeve
54. Snap ring
55. Input gear assembly
    - -1 Snap ring
    - -2 Bearing
    - -3 Input gear
56. Oil seal
57. Baffle plate
58. Dust seal guard
59. Oil seal
60. Transfer case

Exploded view of Chrysler Mitsubishi transfer case

12. Remove the snap-ring from the front end of the rear output shaft. Remove the H–L clutch hub, the low speed gear, the thrust bearing and the needle bearing.

13. Raise the detent of the locknut on the rear output shaft and remove the locknut. Remove the rear bearing using a puller or press.

14. Remove the sprocket spacer and balls. Remove the drive sprocket, two needle bearings, sprocket sleeve and steel ball. Remove the 2–4WD clutch sleeve, hub and stop plate. Remove the bearing using a suitable puller or press.

15. Remove the snap-ring retaining the input gear. Press the shaft from the gear. Remove the two bearings from the front output shaft using a suitable puller or press.

16. Clean and inspect all parts. Replace worn parts as necessary. Replace all oil seals. When reassembling the transfer case, coat the new gaskets with sealant. Apply oil to all sliding and rotating parts, pack the oil seal lip spaces with grease. Replace spring pins with new ones.

17. When replacing the control shaft oil seal or input gear oil seal, drive out the spring pin from the transmission control shaft change shifter and remove the adapter from the transfer case. Remove the seals and press fit new ones in position.

18. Assemble the adapter to the transfer case using a new gasket. Before tightening the mounting bolts, install the change shifter over the control shaft. Adapter mounting bolt torque is 22–30 ft. lbs.

19. Press fit the bearing into the input gear. Make sure the bearing turns freely after installation. Install the snap-ring over the front end of the input gear. Use the thickest snap-ring that will fit in the groove (five sizes are available). Press fit the two bearings over the front output shaft, make sure they turn freely.

20. Install the bearing on the rear output shaft and make sure the bearing turns freely. Mount the stop plate and install the 2–4WD clutch hub and sleeve. Make sure they are installed facing in the proper direction. Mount the steel ball on the rear output shaft and mount the sprocket sleeve.

21. Mount the two needle berarings on the sprocket sleeve and mouint the drive sprocket. After installing the steel balls and the sprocket spacer, press fit the ball bearing into the inner race, make sure it moves freely.

22. Tighten the mainshaft locknut and lock the tab with a punch. Mount the needle bearing, the thrust washer and the low speed gear on the rear output shaft from the front end.

23. Mount the H–L clutch hub making sure it is facing in the proper direction. Mount the H–L snapring using the thickest one that will fit in the groove (five sizes are available). Insert the input gear assembly into the transfer case and mount the snapring. Once again using the thickest ring possible.

24. Insert the needle bearing into the input gear. Mount the H–L clutch sleeve and shift fork (sleeve facing in proper direction). Install the 2–4WD shift rail.

25. Securely engage the chain with the front and rear output shaft sprockets. Assemble the 2–4WD clutch sleeve with the 2–4WD shift fork and install the assembly over the shift rail while, at the same time, mount the rear and front input shafts, chain etc.

26. Mount the two spring retainers and spring on the 2–4WD shift rail and secure with the snapring.

27. Install the two needle bearings and spacer into the counter gear. Install the assembly in the transfer case with the thrust washers in place. Insert the counter shaft and locking plate.

28. Install the side cover and gasket. Install the oil guide. In-

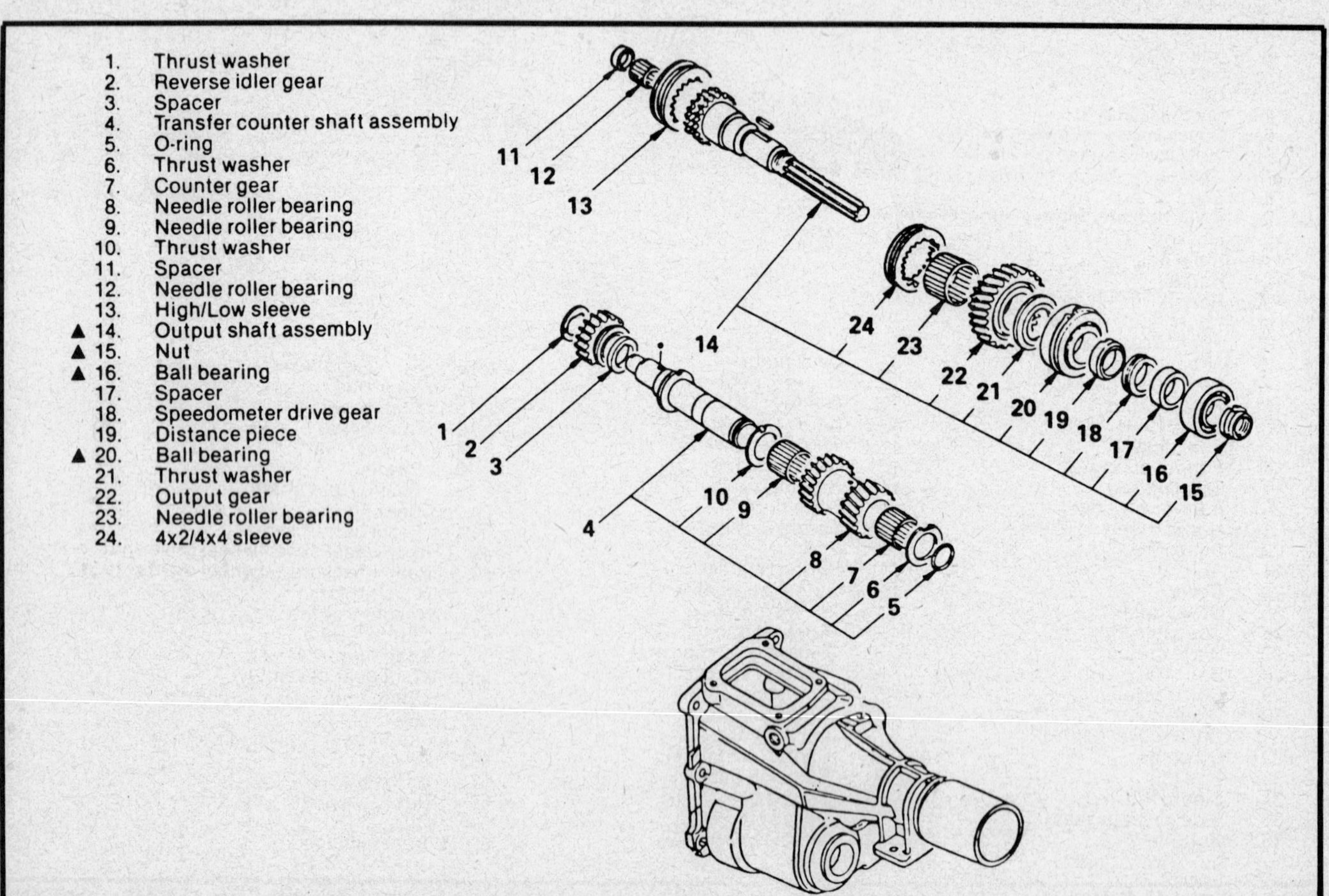

Toyota transfer case used with 5 speed MSG transmission

stall the chain cover and gasket and make sure that the oilguide end fits in the chain cover opening.

29. Fit the snapring in the groove of the rear output shaft bearing. Insert the interlock plunger. Insert the H–L shift rail and pass it through the shift fork. The shift fork must be to the 4WD side or the shift rail cannot be inserted.

30. Mount the two poppet balls and two springs and mount the seal plug. The smaller end of the spring goes toward the ball.

31. Align the H–L shift fork and rail holes and install the spring pin. Install the spring pin with its center slit placed on the center line of the shift rail.

32. Mount the spacer on the rear end of the rear output shaft bearing and install the rear cover and gasket. Check endplay and use a thicker or thinner spacer as needed.

33. Mount the wave spring washer on the rear end of the front output shaft rear bearing and install the cover and gasket. Install the speedometer sleeve assembly and secure. Install the switches and balls. Mount the neutral plungers and springs in the hole on top of the adapter and tighten the seal plug. Install the steel ball, resistance spring and plug.

Isuzu Transfer Case

SERVICING

Disassembly and Inspection

NOTE: The transfer case has been removed from the transmission for the following procedure.

1. Remove the three bolts retaining the lock plate.
2. Remove the distance piece below the lock plate.
3. Lightly tap the transfer countershaft assembly out through the fitting hole in the case.
4. From the transfer countershaft, remove the O-ring, thrust washer, countergear, needle roller bearings, and thrust washer.
5. Remove the spacer, needle roller bearing and the High/Low sleeve from the outputshaft.
6. Expand the rear output shaft front bearing snap ring and remove the output shaft assembly foreward.

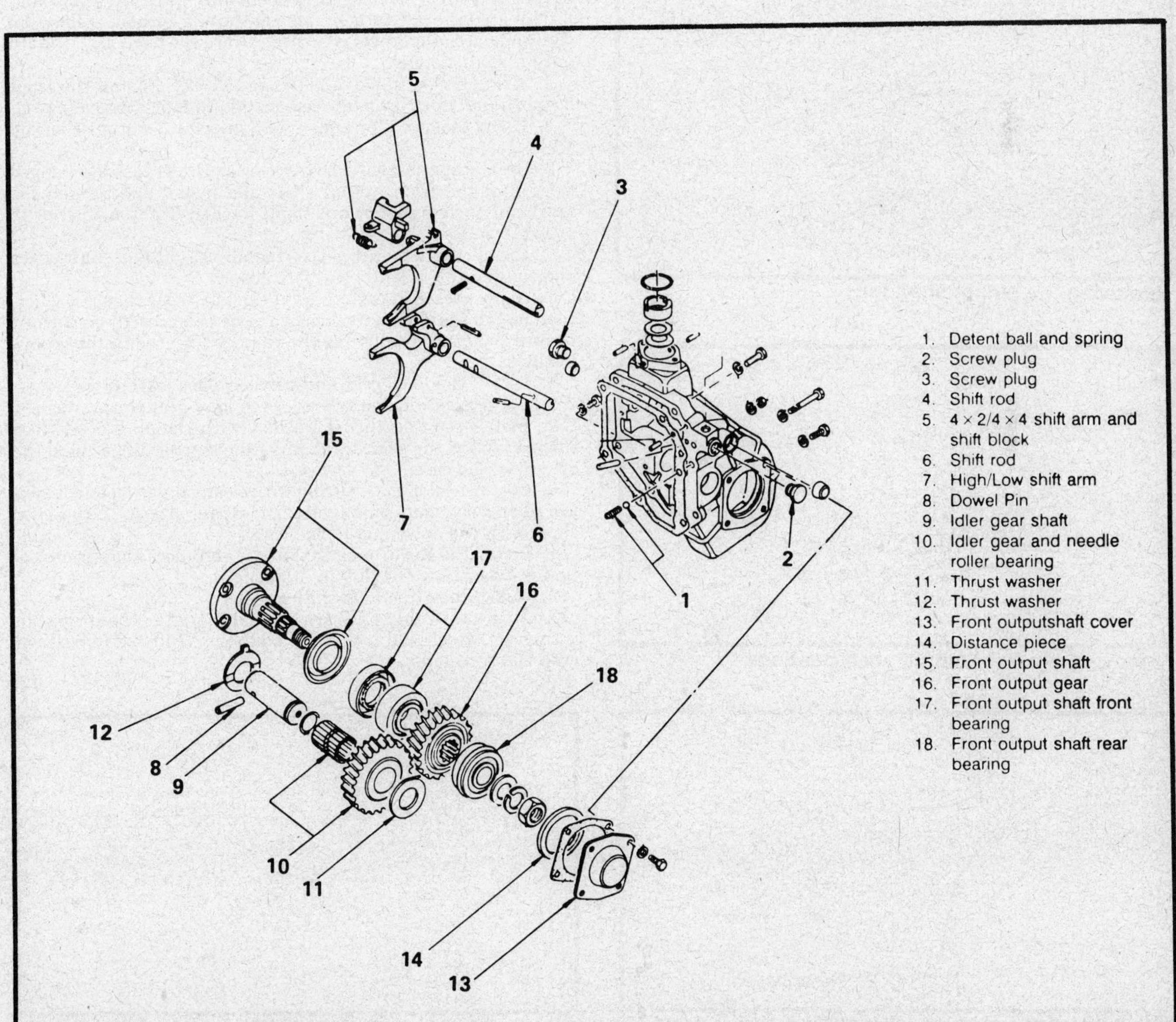

Transfer side case—exploded view

7. Remove the 1⅝ in. (41mm) nut from the output shaft.
8. Using a bench press and special tool J-22912-01 or equivalent, press the bearing off of the front of the input shaft.
9. Remove the spacer, speedometer drive gear, and the distance piece.
10. Using a bench press and special tool J-22912-01 or equivalent, press the bearing off of the center of the input shaft.
11. Remove the thrust washer, output gear, needle roller bearing and the 4×2/4×4 sleeve.

TRANSFER SIDE CASE

Dissassembly and Inspection

1. Remove the detent spring and detent ball.
2. Remove the two screw plugs.
3. Remove the spring pin from the shift arm and drive the shift rod toward the output side of the case, remove the shift rods.

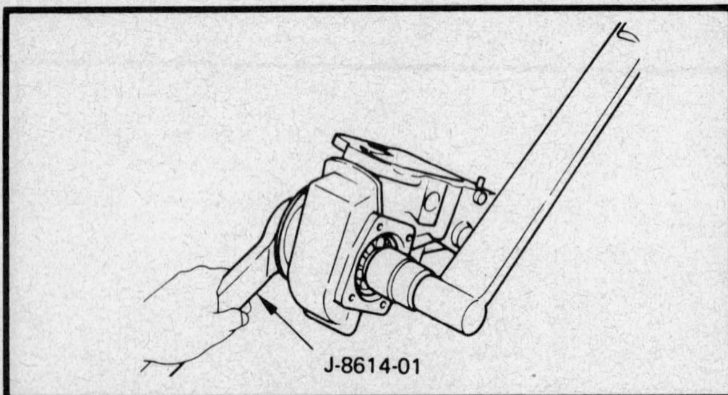

Removing the output shaft nut

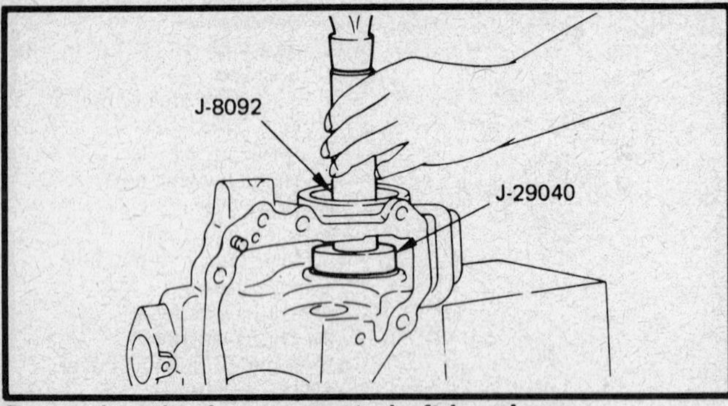

Removing the front output shaft bearings

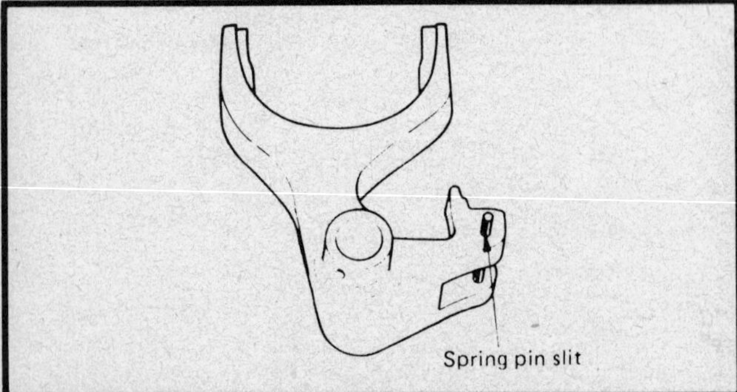

High/Low shift rod and spring pin location

4. Remove the 4×2/4×4 shift arm and shift block.
5. Remove the High/Low shift arm.
6. Remove the dowel pin.
7. Force the idler gear shaft by turning in the 8mm bolt in the threaded hole at the end of the idler shaft, then remove the thrust washers, idler gear and needle bearing.
8. Remove the two thrust washers.
9. Remove the front output shaft cover, then remove the distance piece
10. Set the special tool J-8614-01 or equivalent, to the flanged portion of the front output shaft and loosen and remove the shaft nut spring washer and plain washer.
11. Remove the front output gear.
12. Using special tools J-29040 and J-8092, remove the front output shaft front and rear bearings

TRANSFER SIDE CASE

Reassembly

1. Using special tools J-29040 and J-8092, install the front output shaft rear bearing deep enough to touch the snap ring.
2. Install the output gear, so that the end without splines (on the inner circumference) is turned toward the front side (toward output shaft flange).
3. Using special tools J-29040 and J-8092, install the front output shaft front bearing deep enough to touch the snap ring.
4. Using tool J-29037 and J-8092 install the output shaft oil seal.
5. Set the special tool J-8614-01 or equivalent, to the flanged portion of the front output shaft and install and tighten the shaft nut spring washer and plain washer. Tighten the nut to 101–116 ft. lbs.
6. Install the distance piece. Install the output shaft cover and tighten the bolts to 18–22 ft. lbs.
7. Apply grease to both faces of the idler gear thrust washer, then install the thrust washer, with the oil grooved face turned toward the gear, by aligning the stopper finger with the groove in the case.
8. Install the idler gear and needle roller bearing.
9. Apply grease to both faces of the idler gear thrust washer, then install the 2nd thrust washer, with the oil grooved face turned toward the gear, by aligning the stopper finger with the groove in the case.
10. Coat the idler shaft O-ring with clean engine oil and install the idler gear shaft by aligning the dowel groove in the idler shaft with the dowel pin hole.
11. Install the dowel pin into the case and check that its projection is within 0.355–0.433 in. (9–11mm).
12. Install the High/Low shift arm.
13. Attach the range shift arm so that the slit in the spring pin is turned. Attach and secure the shift arm shift rod in position with the spring pin.

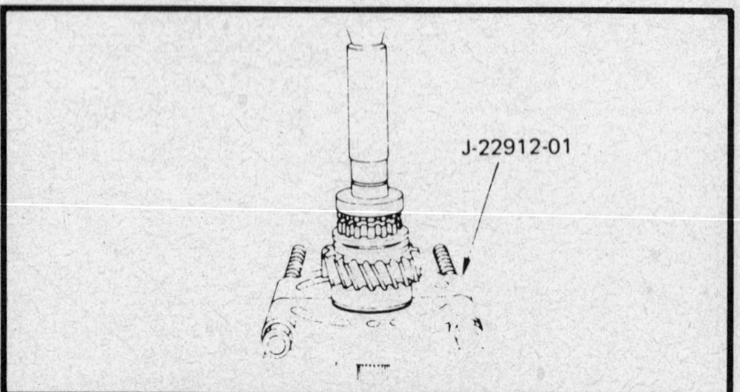

Installing the output shaft front bearing

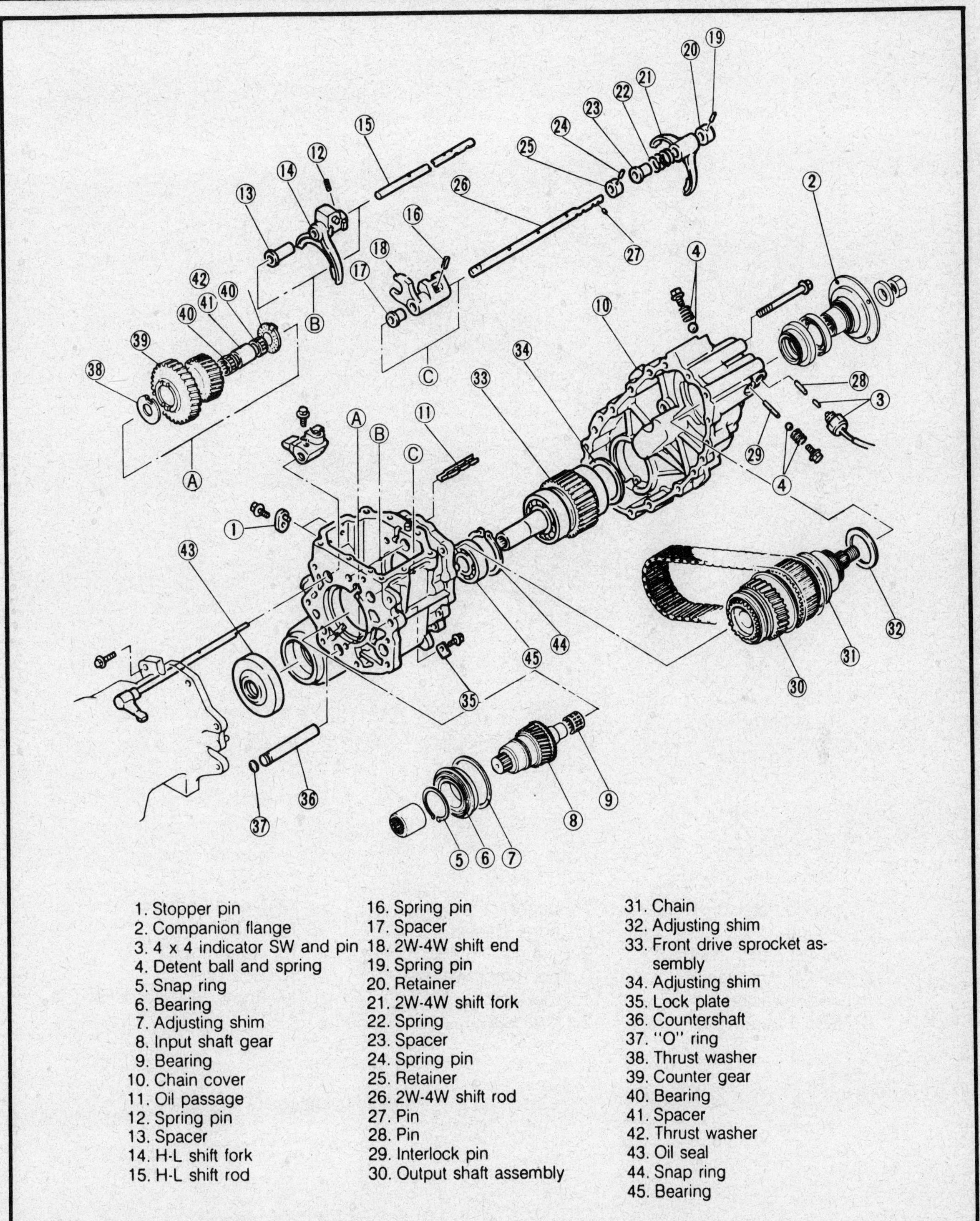
1. Stopper pin
2. Companion flange
3. 4 x 4 indicator SW and pin
4. Detent ball and spring
5. Snap ring
6. Bearing
7. Adjusting shim
8. Input shaft gear
9. Bearing
10. Chain cover
11. Oil passage
12. Spring pin
13. Spacer
14. H-L shift fork
15. H-L shift rod
16. Spring pin
17. Spacer
18. 2W-4W shift end
19. Spring pin
20. Retainer
21. 2W-4W shift fork
22. Spring
23. Spacer
24. Spring pin
25. Retainer
26. 2W-4W shift rod
27. Pin
28. Pin
29. Interlock pin
30. Output shaft assembly
31. Chain
32. Adjusting shim
33. Front drive sprocket assembly
34. Adjusting shim
35. Lock plate
36. Countershaft
37. "O" ring
38. Thrust washer
39. Counter gear
40. Bearing
41. Spacer
42. Thrust washer
43. Oil seal
44. Snap ring
45. Bearing

Exploded view of the Mazda transfer case

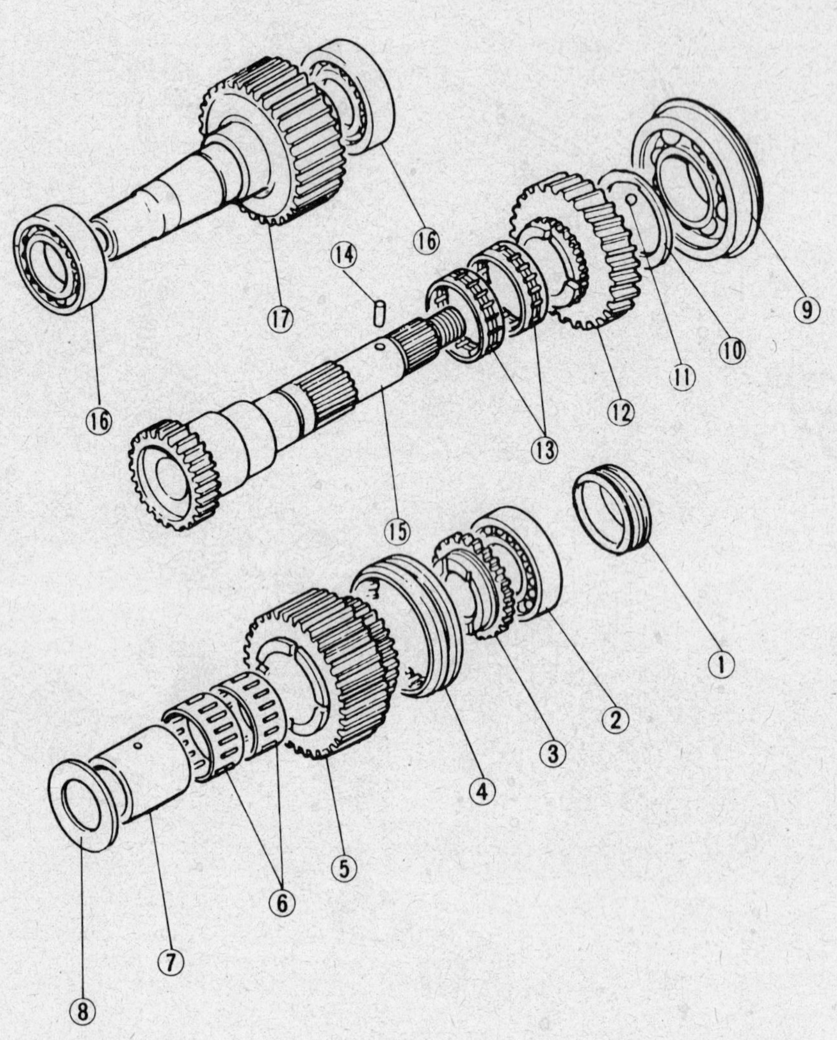

1. Speedometer drive gear
2. Bearing
3. 2W-4W clutch hub
4. 2W-4W hub sleeve
5. Drive sprocket
6. Needle bearing
7. Spacer
8. Thrust washer
9. Bearing
10. Thrust lock washer
11. Steel ball
12. Low gear
13. Needle bearing
14. Knock pin
15. Output shaft
16. Bearing
17. Front drive sprocket

Exploded view of the Mazda transfer case output shaft

14. Assemble the shift arm with the shift block, then attach the gear lock release spring.
15. Insert the interlock pin, the shift rod detent ball and the detent spring in the case. Insert and secure the shift arm, the shift block and the shift rod in position with the spring pin.
16. Install the screw plugs and tighten to 33–40 ft. lbs.
17. Install the detent spring and detent ball.

TRANSFER CASE

Assembly

1. Attach the 4×2/4×4 sleeve, so that the side with the chamfering is turned to the rear.
2. Install the needle roller bearing.
3. Install the output gear.
4. Attach the thrust washer, so that the oil groove is turned to the front.
5. Using bearing installer tool J-22912-01 or equivalent, attach the output shaft front bearing to the output shaft, so that the snap ring groove is turned to the rear.
6. Install the distance piece, speedometer drive gear, and spacer onto the output shaft.
7. Using bearing installer tool J-22912-01 or equivalent, press the output shaft rear bearing onto the output shaft so that the face of the seal is turned to the rear.
8. Install the nut and tighten to 101–116 ft. lbs.
9. Install the output shaft assembly into the transfer case, insert the snap ring on the transfer case into the groove in the output shaft front bearing.
10. Assemble the components onto the countershaft; thrust washer, needle roller bearing, counter gear, needle roller bearing, thrust washer, and O-ring.
11. Install the counter shaft assembly in the case.
12. Install the range shaft sleeve on the output shaft, so that the end of the sleeve with the heavy chamfering on the outer circumference is turned toward the front.

Mazda Transfer Case

SERVICING

Disassembly and Inspection

NOTE: The transfer case has been removed from the transmission for the following procedure.

1. Remove the two stopper pins.
2. Hold the companion flange with special tool 49 S120 710 "coupling flange holder" and remove the companion flange nut.
3. Remove the companion flange by lightly tapping the backside with a plastic hammer.
4. Remove the 4×4 indicator switch, pin, plugs, detent springs and balls.
5. Remove the speedometer drive gear.
6. Remove the snap ring from the end of the input shaft.
7. Using special tool, 49 0839 425C or equivalent, remove the outer bearing.
8. Position the flat section of the input shaft gear toward the countershaft gear, then, remove the input shaft gear and bearing.
9. Using a plastic hammer, separate the chain cover from the transfer case and remove the chain cover.

NOTE: Lift the chain cover vertically to prevent damaging the shift rods.

10. Remove the speedometer drive gear from the output shaft, then, remove the knock pin and bearing.
11. Remove the oil passage by lightly tapping with a plastic hammer.
12. Tap out the spring pin and remove the High/Low shift rod, spacer and shift fork.
13. Tap out the spring pin and remove the 2W-4W shift rod assembly, spacer and 2W-4W shift end.
14. Tap out the spring pins and remove the retainers, 2W-4W shift fork, spring and spacer. Remove the pin for the 4×4 indicator switch from the rod.
15. Using a magnet, remove the pin and interlock pin from the chain cover.
16. Set the input gear on the output shaft.
17. Remove the output shaft and the front drive sprocket from the transfer case housing by lightly tapping on the input shaft gear and the front drive sprocket with a plastic hammer.
18. Remove the input shaft gear from the transfer case housing.
19. Remove the lock plate.
20. Tap out the countershaft gear support using a punch and hammer.
21. Re move the counter gear and thrust washers.
22. Remove the needle bearings and spacer from the countershaft gear.
23. Remove the O-ring from the countershaft.
24. Using a press and special tool 49 G030 370, press the output shaft assembly apart.
25. Remove the parts from the output shaft in the sequence shown below.

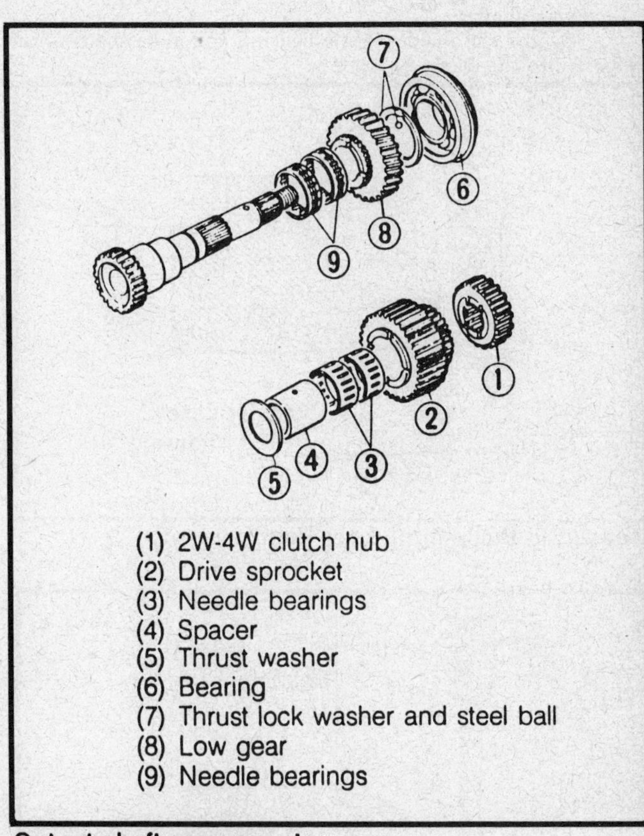

Output shaft components

26. Using bearing puller set 49 0839 425C or equivalent, remove the bearings from both sides of the front drive sprocket.
27. Remove the oil seals.
28. Remove the snap ring.
29. Using special tool 49 F401 331 or equivalent, press the front sprocket bearing out of the housing.

TRANSFER CASE

Assembly

1. Using tool 49 0727 415 or equivalent, press the front drive sprocket bearing into the transfer case housing. Install the snap ring and secure the bearing.
2. Apply oil to the lip of the oil seal and install the seal into the transfer case housing, using tool 49 0727 415 or equivalent.
3. Apply oil to the lip of the oil seal and install the seal into the chain cover, using tool 49 0727 415 or equivalent.
4. Using tool 49 0727 415 or equivalent, press the bearings on both sides of the friont drive sprocket. Press the bearings until they stop.
5. Install the lower gear on the output shaft. Lubricate the needle bearing assembly with oil and set it on the shaft.
6. Set the steel ball in the shaft, and install the thrust lock washer.
7. Using special tool 49 0727 415 or equivalent, press the bearing on the output shaft.
8. Install the counter gear as follows:
   a. While lubricating the contact surface of the thrust washer and the housing, install the washer so that the dished (convex) part of the washer sets down into the housing.
   b. Lubricate the needle bearings with oil, then install them and the spacer in the counter gear.
   c. Install the couner gear in the housing.
   d. Lubricate a new O-ring with oil and install it on the countershaft.
   e. Center the inside needle bearing and slide the counter shaft into the case.

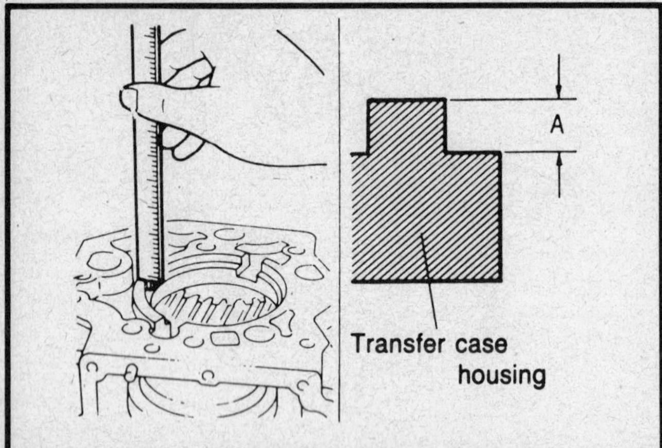

Measuring the bearing bore depth

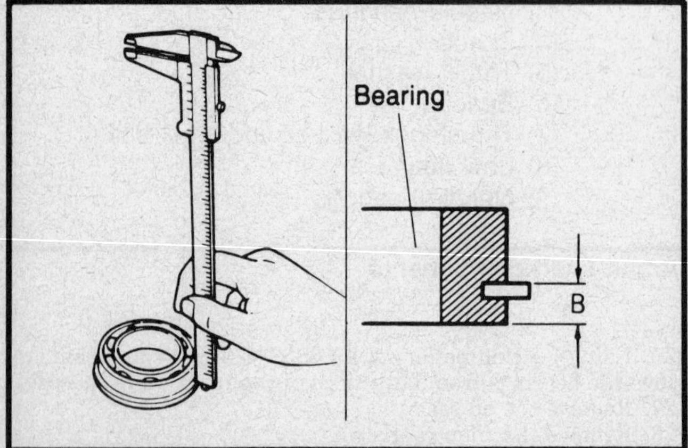

Measuring the bearing height

   f. Install the lock plate and tighten the bolt to 14–19 ft. lbs.
9. Install the input shaft as follows:
   a. Measure the bearing bore depth "A" of the housing with
   b. Measure the height "B" of the bearing clip with vernier calipers and a surface plate.
   c. Calculate the difference between measurement "A" and "B" to determine the clearance. The formula looks like this:

Difference (Clearance) = A - B

   d. Select and install the proper shim to obtain a clearance of 0–0.004 in. (0–0.1mm).

Adjusting shim thickness:		mm (in)
0.7 (0.28)	0.8 (0.032)	0.9 (0.035)
1.0 (0.039)	1.1 (0.043)	1.2 (0.047)

   e. Using tool 49 0727 415 or equivalent, press the bearing onto the input shaft gear. Install the snap ring.
   f. Install the input shaft assembly in the housing by lightly tapping the outer race of the bearing with a plastic hammer.
10. Install the needle bearing and the High/Low hub sleeve onto the input shaft.

NOTE: To identify the High/Low sleeve from the 2W-4W sleeve, the thickness of the High/Low hub sleeve is 0.83 in. (21mm) and the 2W–4W hub sleeve is 0.71 in. (18mm).

11. Install the output shaft in the housing by lightly tapping the outer race of the bearing with a plastic hammer.
12. Set the thrust washer on the output shaft.
13. Lubricate the needle bearings with oil and install them onto the drive sprocket along with the spacer.
14. Install the chain on the drive sprocket assembly and the front drive sprocket, and expand the chain using special tool 49 S231 395 to set the center to center distance for easy installation into the housing.

NOTE: Be careful not to overtighten the chain expansion tool.

15. Install the front drive sprocket assembly into the housing by lightly tapping it with a plastic hammer, while keeping the chain horizontal. After installing, check that the chain rotates smoothly.
16. Using tool 49 0500 330 or equivalent, tap in the 2W–4W clutch hub.
17. Install the 2W–4W shift fork onto the shift rod as follows:
   a. Slide the retainer on the shift rod and secure it with the spring pin.
   b. Install the 0.79 in. (20mm) spacer, spring, 2W–4W shift fork and the other retainer.
   c. Secure the retainer with the spring pin.

Adjusting shim thickness:		mm (in)
0.5 (0.020)	0.6 (0.024)	0.7 (0.028)
0.8 (0.031)	0.9 (0.035)	1.0 (0.039)
1.1 (0.043)	1.2 (0.047)	1.3 (0.051)
1.4 (0.055)	1.5 (0.059)	1.6 (0.063)
1.7 (0.067)		

18. Assemble the 2W–4W hub sleeve to the shift fork and insert them to the transfer case housing.
19. Set the 2W–4W shift fork and the 0.79 in. (20mm) spacer into the case and slide the shift rod assembly through it.

20. Secure the 2W–4W shift end to the rod with the spring pin.
21. Install the High/Low shift fork, 1.46 in. (37mm) spacer, and the rod in the transfer case housing.
22. Secure the High/Low shift fork with the spring pin.
23. Install the bearing on the output shaft.
24. Measure the bearing height and the bearing bore depth for the output shaft using the shim selector gauge set tool 49 U017 3A0.
25. Put the two pieces of the gauge set together and measure the clearance.
26. Select the proper adjusting shim to adjust the clearance to 0–0.004 in. (0–0.1mm).
27. Repeat the procedures above and select the correct size shim(s) for the front drive sprocket.
28. Apply grease to the adjusting shims selected and place them in the chain cover.
29. Install the knock pin in the output shaft and install the speedometer drive gear.
30. Install the oil passage in the case.
31. Apply grease to the ball (A/T only), pin and interlock pin and install them in the chain cover.
32. Apply grease to the pin and install it in the 2W–4W shift rod.
33. Apply RTV to the mating surface of the chain cover and set the cover on the housing.
34. Apply sealant to the threads of the bolts and tighten to 14–19 ft. lbs.
35. Apply sealant to the threads of the plugs. Install the balls, springs and plugs. Tighten the plugs to 14–19 ft. lbs.
36. Install the pin and the 4 × 4 indicator switch and tighten to tighten to 18–25 ft. lbs.
37. Install the speedometer gear and tighten the hold down bolt to 69–95 in. lbs.

Measuring for shim selection

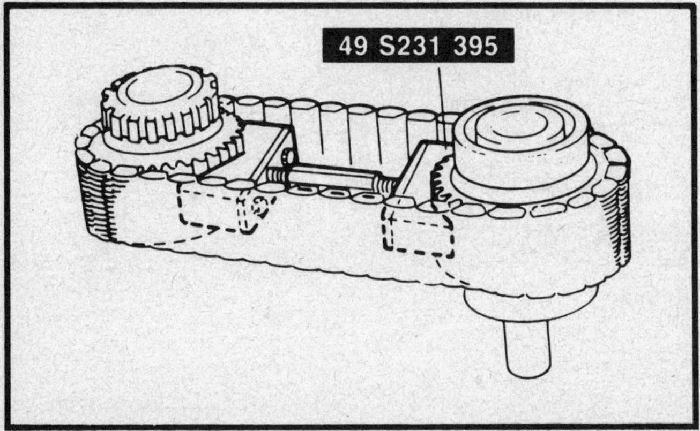

Using tool to install the chain onto the drive sprockets

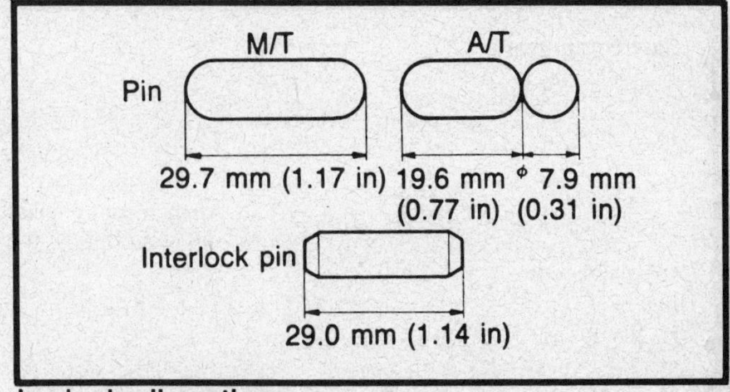

Lock pin dimentions

38. Check that the transfer case shifts smoothly using a screwdriver to move the shift forks.
39. Install the companion flanges as follows:
   a. Apply sealant to the splines of the companion flange.
   b. Install the companion flange on the shaft by lightly tapping with a plastic hammer.
   c. Use a new locknut and tighten the flange. Hold the flange with special tool 49 S120 710 or equivalent, then torque to 94–130 ft lbs.
40. Apply sealant to the contact surfaces of the stopper pins and install them with new "O" rings.

Nissan/Datsun Transfer Case

SERVICING (1982-85 MODELS)

Disassembly and Inspection

SHIFTING FORKS & FORK RODS

NOTE: The transfer case has been removed from the vehicle.

1. Wipe off all dirt and grease from the transfer case. Drain the lubricant, if not already done.
2. Move the shift lever to the 4L and 2H positions, then remove the driveshaft companion flange locknuts. Remove the companion flanges and the 4WD switch.
3. Remove the front cover from the transfer case. Remove the FR driveshaft and needle bearings.
4. Remove the snap-ring retaining the FR shift fork and remove the FR shift fork, spacer and coupling sleeve.
5. Remove the snap-ring retaining the coupling sleeve hub and remove the hub.
6. Remove the bolts that attach the front and back transfer case halves together. Tap the front case half away from the rear with a soft faced hammer. Do not pry the cases apart.
7. Remove the pin that retains the shift cross shaft. The pin is retained by a nut. Remove the nut and carefully drive the pin out with a soft drift. Remove the shift cross shaft and lever.
8. Remove the check ball plug, spring and ball. Drive out the High & Low shift fork retaining pin. Tap the rear of the driveshaft assembly and remove it with the High & Low shift fork and counter gear assembly. The main gear assembly can now be removed. Take care not to drop the counter gear needle bearing when removing the gear.
9. Remove the front shim from the transfer case. Remove the High & Low and FR shift fork rods, interlock plunger, steel ball and check spring.
10. If servicing is necessary, secure the FR fork rod and carefully drive out the retaining pin, the fork rod bracket can now be removed. Insert an M8 bolt into the shift fork and tighten the nut to eliminate the shift fork spring tension. Remove the retaining snap-ring.

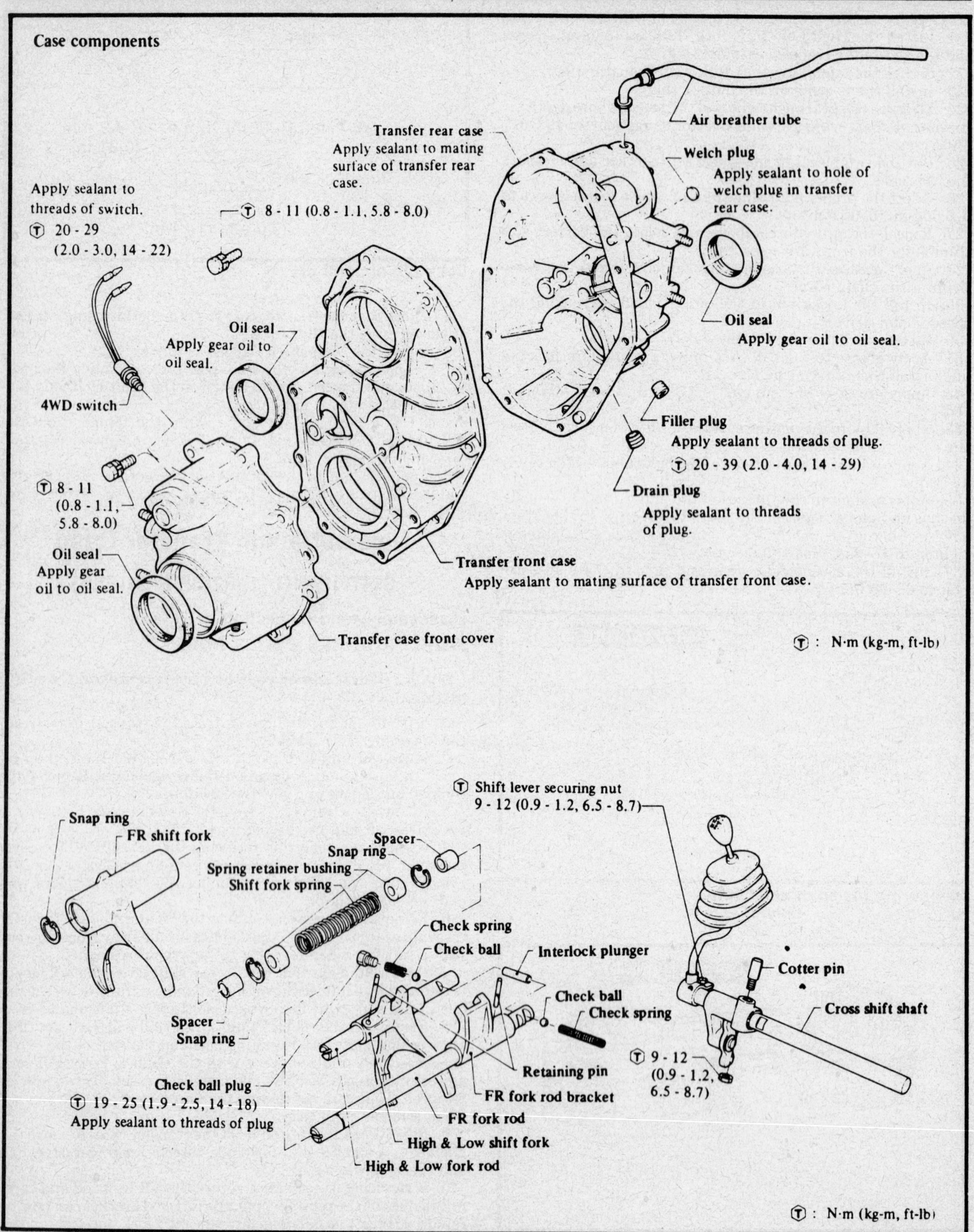
Case components
Air breather tube
Transfer rear case
Apply sealant to mating surface of transfer rear case.
Welch plug
Apply sealant to hole of welch plug in transfer rear case.
Apply sealant to threads of switch.
Ⓣ 20 - 29 (2.0 - 3.0, 14 - 22)
Ⓣ 8 - 11 (0.8 - 1.1, 5.8 - 8.0)
Oil seal
Apply gear oil to oil seal.
Oil seal
Apply gear oil to oil seal.
4WD switch
Filler plug
Apply sealant to threads of plug.
Ⓣ 20 - 39 (2.0 - 4.0, 14 - 29)
Drain plug
Apply sealant to threads of plug.
Ⓣ 8 - 11 (0.8 - 1.1, 5.8 - 8.0)
Oil seal
Apply gear oil to oil seal.
Transfer front case
Apply sealant to mating surface of transfer front case.
Transfer case front cover
Ⓣ : N·m (kg-m, ft-lb)
Ⓣ Shift lever securing nut 9 - 12 (0.9 - 1.2, 6.5 - 8.7)
Snap ring
FR shift fork
Spacer
Snap ring
Spring retainer bushing
Shift fork spring
Check spring
Check ball
Interlock plunger
Cotter pin
Check ball
Check spring
Cross shift shaft
Spacer
Snap ring
Retaining pin
Ⓣ 9 - 12 (0.9 - 1.2, 6.5 - 8.7)
Check ball plug
Ⓣ 19 - 25 (1.9 - 2.5, 14 - 18)
Apply sealant to threads of plug
FR fork rod bracket
FR fork rod
High & Low shift fork
High & Low fork rod
Ⓣ : N·m (kg-m, ft-lb)

Nissan/Datsun transfer case and shift control parts—1982–85

11. Remove the spring retaining bushings and shift fork spring. Separate the spring retainer bushing and spring.
12 .Clean all parts with solvent and check for wear and damage. Replace as necessary.
13. Install the breather cover (if removed). Install the main gear asembly carefully by tapping into position.
14. Drive out the FR shift fork freeze plug to enable shift fork installation.
Install the check spring and ball in the rear transfer case half. Take care not to lose the check ball as spring pressure will force it out of the bore.
15. Install the High & Low shift fork into the coupling sleeve. Install the retaining pin. Install the FR fork rod and the interlocking pin. Secure the FR fork rod bracket to the fork rod with the retaining pin.
16. Assemble the snap-ring, spring retainer bushings and shift fork spring to the FR shift fork. Insert an M8 bolt into the bushing and tighten the nut to eliminate spring tension. Install the other retaining snap-ring and remove the M8 bolt.
17. Lubricate and install a new O-ring to the countershaft and then install the countershaft assembly. Raise the counter gear assembly slightly and install the rear driveshaft assembly making sure the gear teeth mesh.
18. Install the companion flange on the rear end of the driveshaft assembly and tighten the nut finger tight.
19. Install the High & Low fork rod and secure with the retaining pin. Apply sealant to the freeze plug bore edges and install a new freeze plug. Install the check ball and spring. Tighten the check ball retaining bolt to 14–18 ft. lbs. after applying sealer to the threads.
20. Install the coupling sleeve hub and snap-ring. Check end play. The end play should be between 0–0.0079 in. Snap-rings of different thicknesses are available to control the end play.
21. Install the shift lever. Install the shift cross shaft. Apply grease to the main gear front shims and transfer case thrust washer and install them to the front half of the transfer case. Be sure the mating surfaces of the case halves are clean. Apply a bead of sealant to the mating edge and install the front half of the transfer case. Tap with a soft hammer to seat if necessary.
22. Tighten the mounting bolts to 5–8 ft. lbs.
23. Install the spacer, FR shift fork assembly with the coupling sleeve and secure with snap-ring.
24. Lubricate the pilot needle bearing and place in position. Install the FR driveshaft to the transfer case driveshaft. Clean the mating surfaces of the cases. Apply sealant to the extension case surface and install the cover (5–8 ft. lbs.). Install the companion flanges. Tighten the new flange locknuts to 87–101 ft. lbs. Install the 4WD switch to 14–22 ft. lbs.

GEARS AND SHAFTS

Inspection and Endplay

1. Check all parts for excessive wear, chips or cracks. Replace as necessary.
2. Measure the endplay before and after disassembling the driveshaft. If excessive endplay is present, disassemble shaft and check for worn parts.
3. Standard endplay: High gear & Low gear; 0.0039–0.0079. Coupling sleeve hub; 0–0.0079.

COUNTER GEAR & MAIN GEAR

Disassembly and Assembly

1. Refer to the previous Shifter Fork procedure and remove the transfer case driveshaft assembly, counter gear assembly, forks and fork rods.
2. Remove the main gear and breather assembly from the rear case half. Remove the main gear front bearing and/or rear bearing with a press, if service is necessary. Remove the needle bearings, center spacer and end spacers from the counter gear for cleaning and any required servicing.
3. Press on the front and rear bearings. Install the breather cover and main gear. Apply grease to the needle bearings and spacers and assemble them in the counter gear. 28 needle bearings are used, 14 at each end.
4. Reassembly in reverse order of removal.

LOW GEAR

Disassembly and Assembly

1. Press off the front bearing from the driveshaft. Remove the thrust washer and steel ball.
2. Remove the Low gear and needle bearings. Replace parts as required.
3. Lubricate the needle bearings with gear oil and install the needle bearings, coupling sleeve and Low gear.
4. Apply grease to the steel ball and thrust washer and install them on the Low gear. Press on the front bearing while holding the Low gear so that the trust washer will not drop out of position.

NOTE: If internal parts (i.e. thrust washers, bearings, gears etc.) are replace, check clearances and adjust as necessary using the correct shim(s) to reduce excessive play.

HIGH GEAR

Disassembly and Assembly

1. Remove the speedometer drive gear. Remove the spacer and steel ball. Press off the rear driveshaft bearing. Remove the thrust washer and steel ball.
2. Remove the high gear, needle bearings and coupling sleeve. Replace parts as required.
3. Lubricate the needle bearings with gear oil and install the bearings and High gear on the shaft.
4. Apply grease to the steel ball and thrust washer and place them on the high gear. Press the bearing onto the shaft. Hold the gear while pressing on the bearing to make sure the thrust washer does not fall.
5. Install the driveshaft spacer. Apply grease to the steel ball and install ball and speedometer drive gear.

NOTE: After servicing components, assemble the unit as described under Shifting Rods and Forks.

SERVICING (1986-87 MODELS)

Disassembly

NOTE: Transfer case has been removed from the vehicle.

1. While holding the companion flange with tool ST38060002, remove the companion flange nut.
2. Remove the rear case.
3. Remove the companion flange with tool ST33051001 or equivalent.
4. Remove the oil cover and oil gutter.
5. Remove the snap ring from the 2–4 shift rod.
6. Remove the bolts securing the bearing retainer. This is necessary to remove the mainshaft from the center case.
7. Remove the bolts securing the center case to the front case and then separate the center case from the front case.
8. Measure the end play of the low gear, if its beyond 0.0079–0.0256 in. (0.2–0.65mm), check the low gear and the L & H hub for wear.

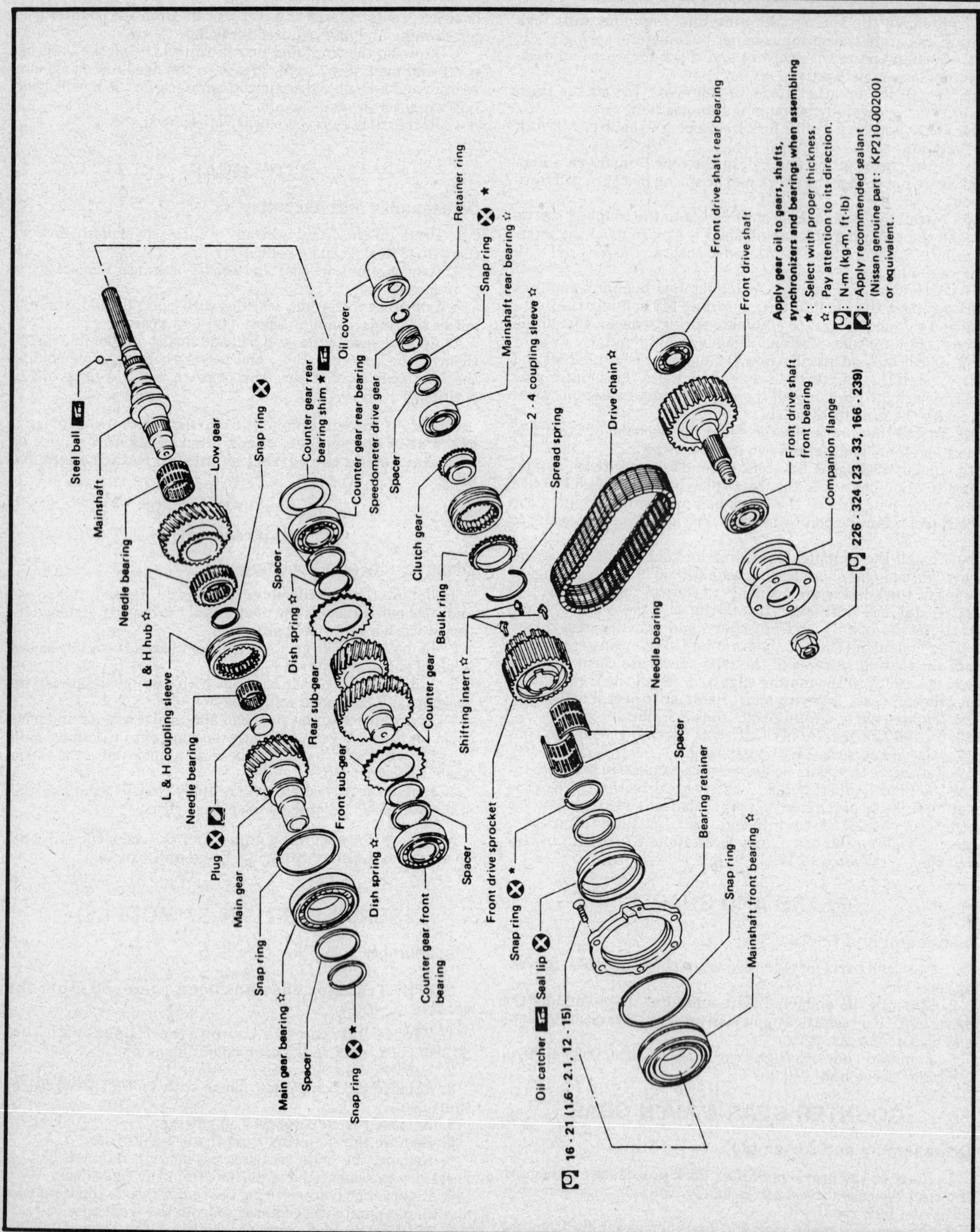

Nissan/Datsun transfer case gear components—1986–87

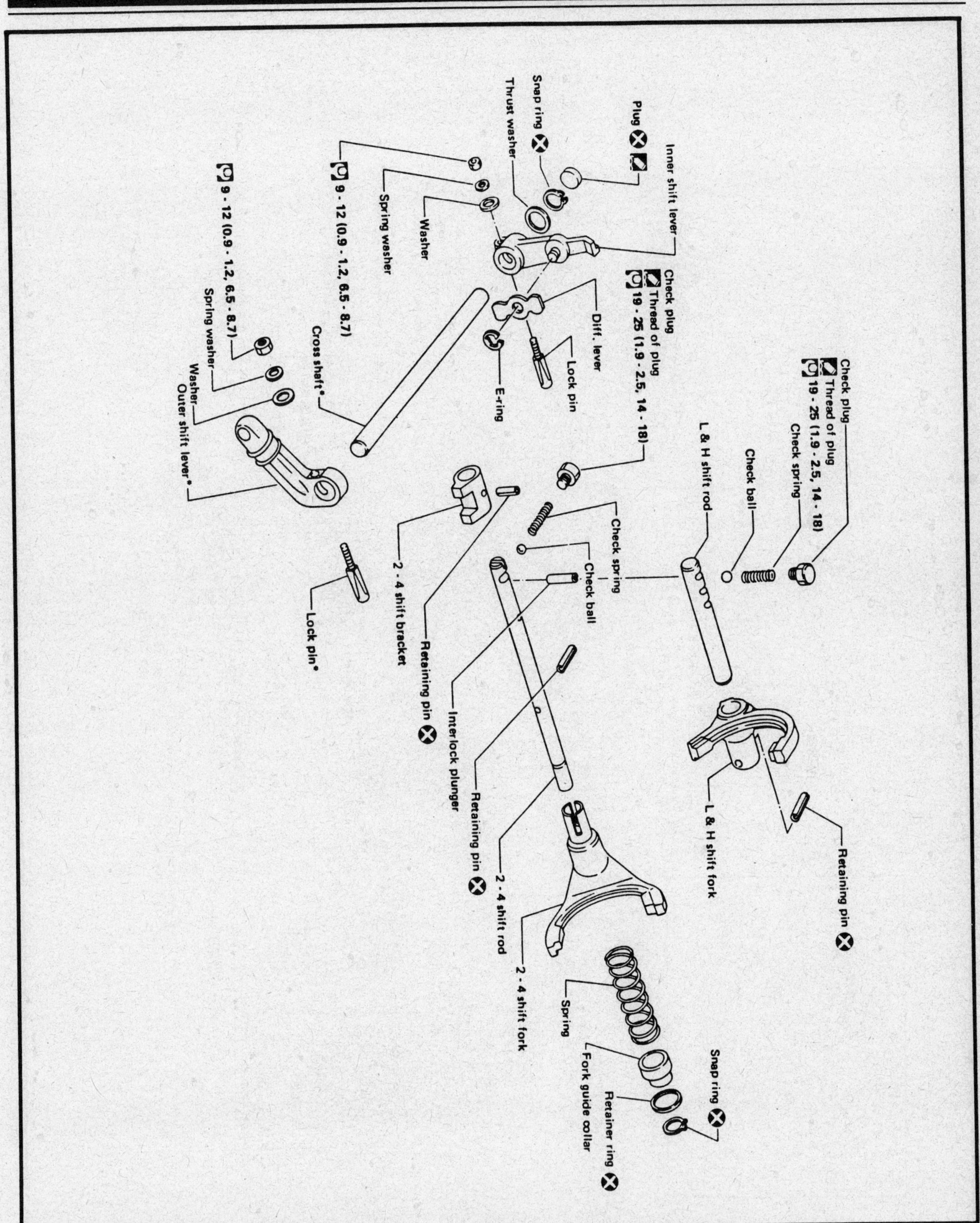
Check plug
Thread of plug
19 - 25 (1.9 - 2.5, 14 - 18)
Check spring
Check ball
L & H shift rod
Plug
Snap ring
Thrust washer
Inner shift lever
Check plug
Thread of plug
19 - 25 (1.9 - 2.5, 14 - 18)
9 - 12 (0.9 - 1.2, 6.5 - 8.7)
Spring washer
Washer
Diff. lever
Lock pin
E-ring
Cross shaft*
9 - 12 (0.9 - 1.2, 6.5 - 8.7)
Spring washer
Washer
Outer shift lever*
Check spring
Check ball
2 - 4 shift bracket
Lock pin*
Retaining pin
Interlock plunger
Retaining pin
2 - 4 shift rod
L & H shift fork
Retaining pin
2 - 4 shift fork
Spring
Fork guide collar
Retainer ring
Snap ring

Nissan/Datsun transfer case shift components—1986–87

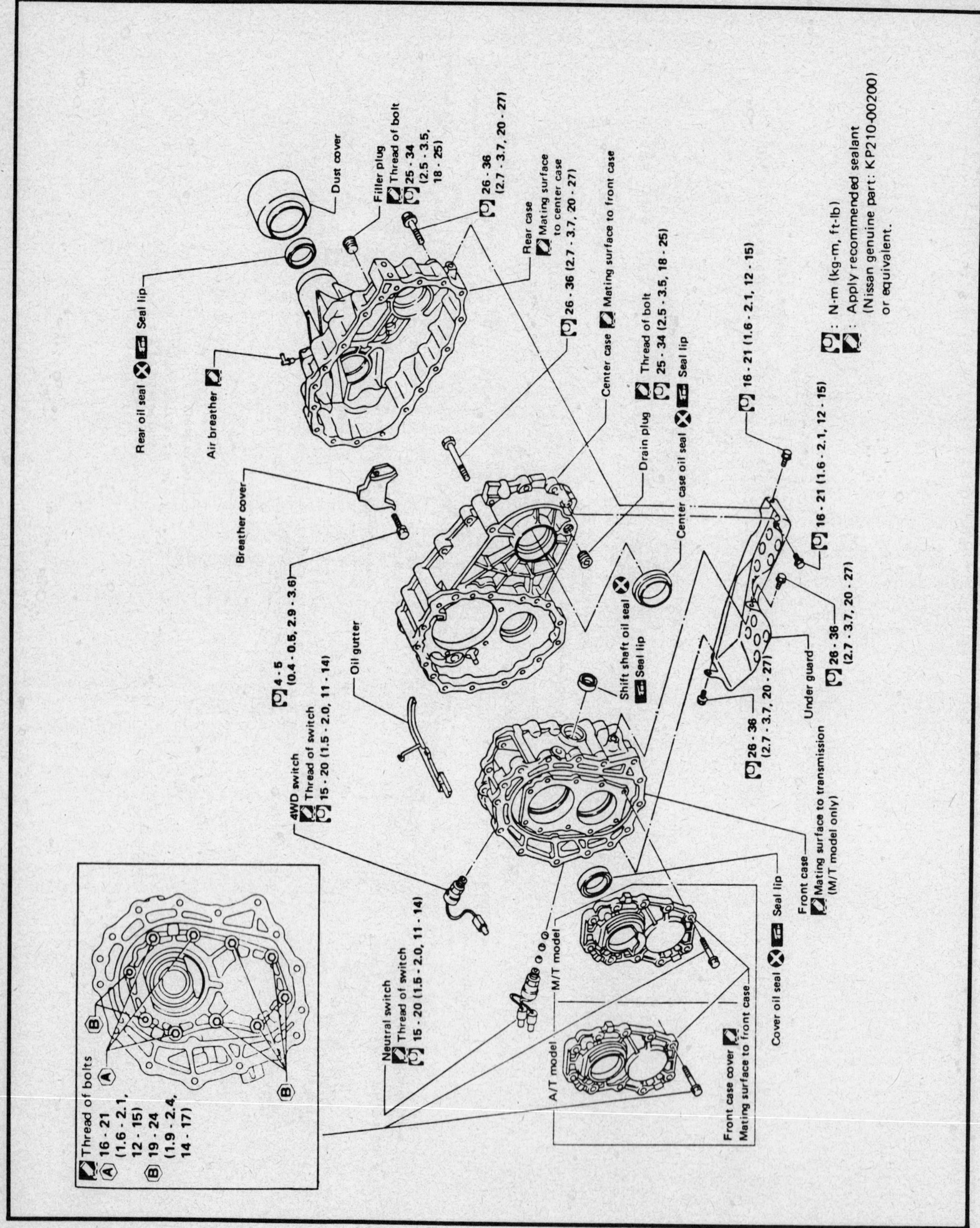

Nissan/Datsun transfer case gear case—1986–87

9. Disassemble the center case assembly as follows:
a. Remove the snap ring from the mainshaft.
b. Pull out the low gear with the L & H hub.
c. Remove the needle bearing of low gear.
d. Make sure the direction of the drive chain before removing it. (It must be reinstalled in the same direction.) Check whether the spring part of the drive chain is installed on the front or rear side.
e. Remove the mainshaft, front drive and drive chain as a set by tapping the front end of the mainshaft and the front drive shaft alternately. Be careful not to bend the drive chain.
10. Disassemble the front case assembly as follows:
a. Remove the switches, check plugs, check springs and check balls.
b. Remove the outer shift lever.
c. Remove the lock pin of the inner shift lever and drive out the cross shaft with plug.
d. Remove the 2–4 shift rod.
e. Remove the L & H shift rod and fork assembly with coupling sleeve.
f. Remove the needle bearing from the main gear.
g. Remove the bolts securing the front case cover and then remove the case.
h. Remove the counter gear by tapping lighty.
i. Remove the main gear by tapping lightly.

MAINSHAFT

Dissassembly

1. Check the end play of the front drive sprocket with a dial indicator. If the end play is beyond 0.008–0.020 in. (0.2–0.5mm), check the front drive sprocket and clutch gear for wear.
2. Remove the retaining ring, speedometer drive gear and the steel ball.
3. Remove the snap ring and spacer.
4. Press out the front drive sprocket with mainshaft rear bearing and clutch gear together.
5. Remove the needle bearing.
6. Remove the bearing retainer and then remove the snap ring and spacer.
7. Press the mainshaft front bearing from the mainshaft.

Assembly

1. Press the front bearing onto the mainshaft.
2. Install the spacer.
3. Select the proper snap ring from the chart to allow a clearance of 0–0.0059 in. (0–0.15mm) between the snap ring.
4. Install the mainshaft in the case as assemble the case as described below.

TRANSFER CASE

Assembly

1. Assemble the front case as follows:
a. Install the main gear assembly by tapping lightly.
b. Apply sealant to the mating surface and bolts of the front case cover and install it on the front case. Coat the ten bolts with sealant, then tighten the bolts: (A)12–15 ft. lbs. (B)14–17 ft. lbs.

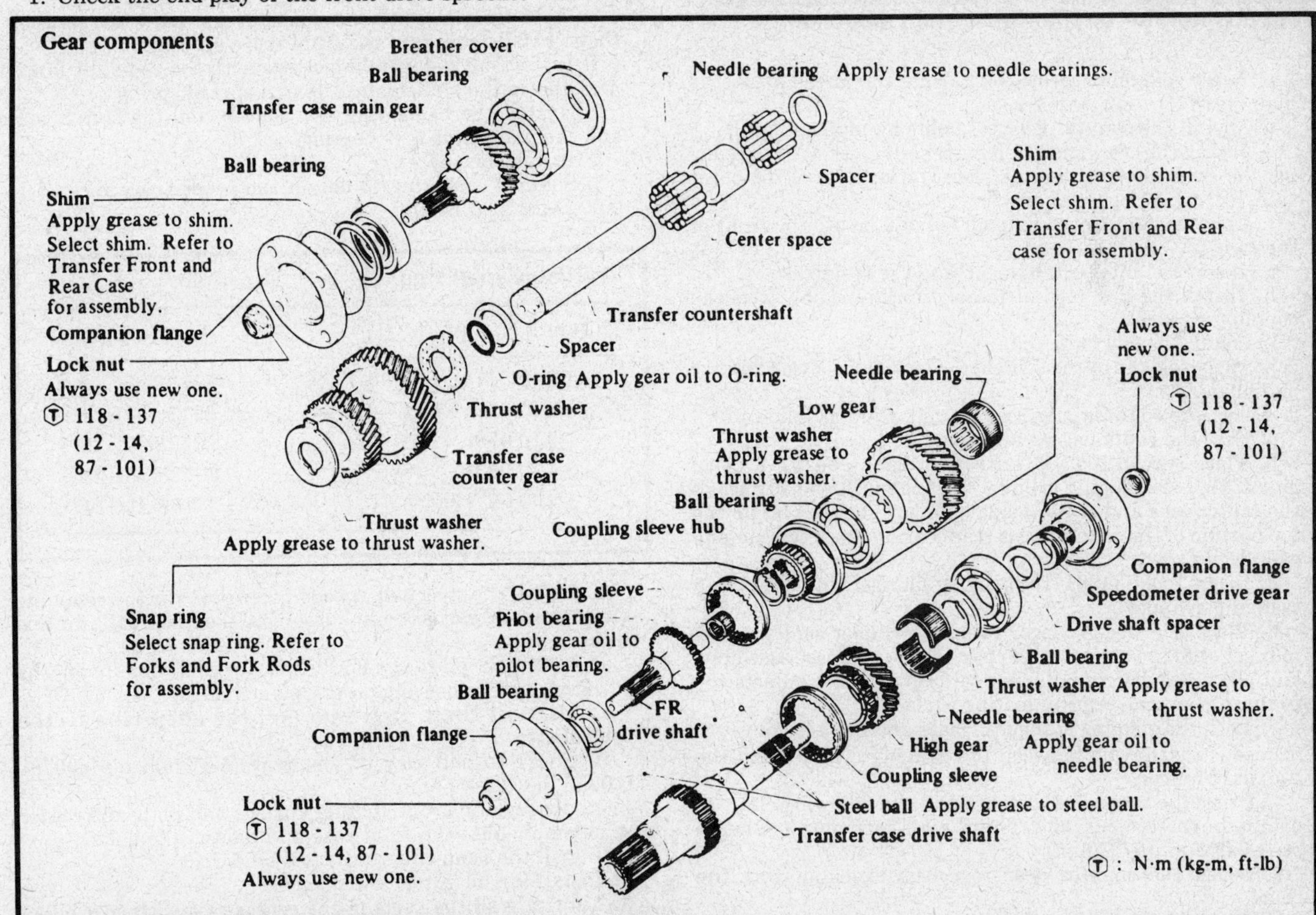

Nissan/Datsun transfer case gear components—1982–85

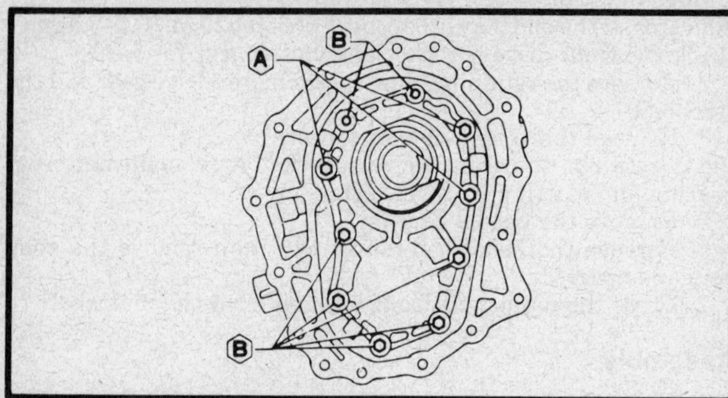

Front cover bolt locations

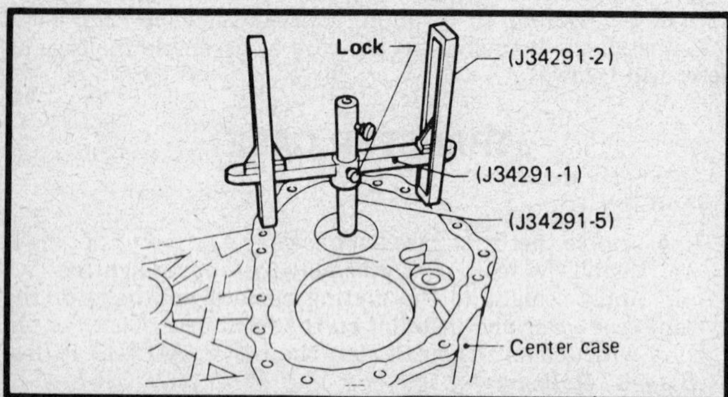

Tool position for counter gear shim selection

c. Apply gear oil to the needle bearing and install it into the main gear.

d. Install the counter gear assembly by tapping lightly.

e. Install the cross shaft and inner shift lever. When replacing the cross shaft, outer shift lever or lock pin of the outer shift lever, replace them as a set.

f. Apply sealant to the plug and install it into the front of the case.

g. Insert the interlock plunger into the front case.

h. Install the L & H shift rod and fork assembly with the coupling sleeve.

i. Install the 2–4 shift rod.

j. Apply sealant to the switches, check balls, check springs and plugs.

2. Select the counter gear rear bearing shim as follows:

a. Seat the counter gear assembly.

b. Place special tools J34291-1 (bridge), J34291-2 (legs) and J34291-5 (gauging cylinder) on the machined surface of the center case and allow the gauging cylinder to rest on the top portion of the counter gear rear bearing. Lock the gauging cylinder in place.

c. Insert tool J34291-15 (gauging plunger) into J34291-5 (gauging cylinder).

d. Place the bridge, legs, gauging cylinder and gauging plunger onto the machined surface of the front case assembly, and allow the gauging plunger to drop until it contacts the counter gear rear bearing mating surface.

e. Lock the gauging plunger in place and use a feeler gauge to meausure the gap between the gauging cylinder and the gauging plunger.

f. Using the measured distance and the following chart to obtain the correct shim size. The counter gear end play should be 0–0.008 in. (0–0.2mm)

g. Select the counter gear rear bearing shim from the chart.

3. Place a suitable shim on the counter gear rear bearing with grease.

Counter gear rear bearing shim:

Thickness mm (in)	Part number
0.1 (0.004)	33112-C6900
0.2 (0.008)	33112-C6901
0.3 (0.012)	33112-C6902
0.4 (0.016)	33112-C6903
0.5 (0.020)	33112-33G00
0.6 (0.024)	33112-33G01

4. Apply gear oil to each part of the front case.

5. Assemble the center case assembly as follows:

a. Apply gear oil to the mainshaft front bearing and install the mainshaft on the center case by tapping lightly.

b. Install the bearing retainer.

c. Put the drive chain onto the front drive sprocket and the front drive shaft, and then put them in the center case. **The chain must be installed in its original position as described during disassembly.**

d. Install the front driveshaft by tapping lightly.

e. Apply gear oil to the needle bearings, and while rotating them install them into the front drive sprocket.

f. Install the 2–4 coupling sleeve with the 2–4 shift fork.

g. Insert the shifting inserts and spread spring.

h. Install the baulk ring and then install the clutch gear and the mainshaft rear bearing.

i. Install the spacer.

j. Select a snap ring to obtain the proper clearance of 0–0.0059 in. (0–0.15mm)

Available snap ring

Thickness mm (in)	Part number
1.8 (0.071)	33138-33G20
1.9 (0.075)	33138-33G21
2.0 (0.079)	33138-33G22
2.1 (0.083)	33138-33G23
2.2 (0.087)	33138-33G24

k. Install the steel ball, speedometer gear and the retaining ring. The steel ball is the smallest of all the check balls for this unit.

l. Apply gear oil to the needle bearing and then install the low gear and its bearing on the mainshaft.

m. Install the L & H hub and the snap ring to the mainshaft.

n. Check to end play of low gear, it should be 0.0079–0.0256 in. (0.2–0.65mm).

6. Apply sealant to the mating surface and place the center case assembly onto the front case and tighten the bolts.

7. Install the snap ring to the 2–4 shift rod.

8. Install the oil gutter and oil cover.

9. Lubricate all the parts in the center case with gear oil.

10. Apply sealant to the mating surface, install the rear case to the center case and tighten the bolts.

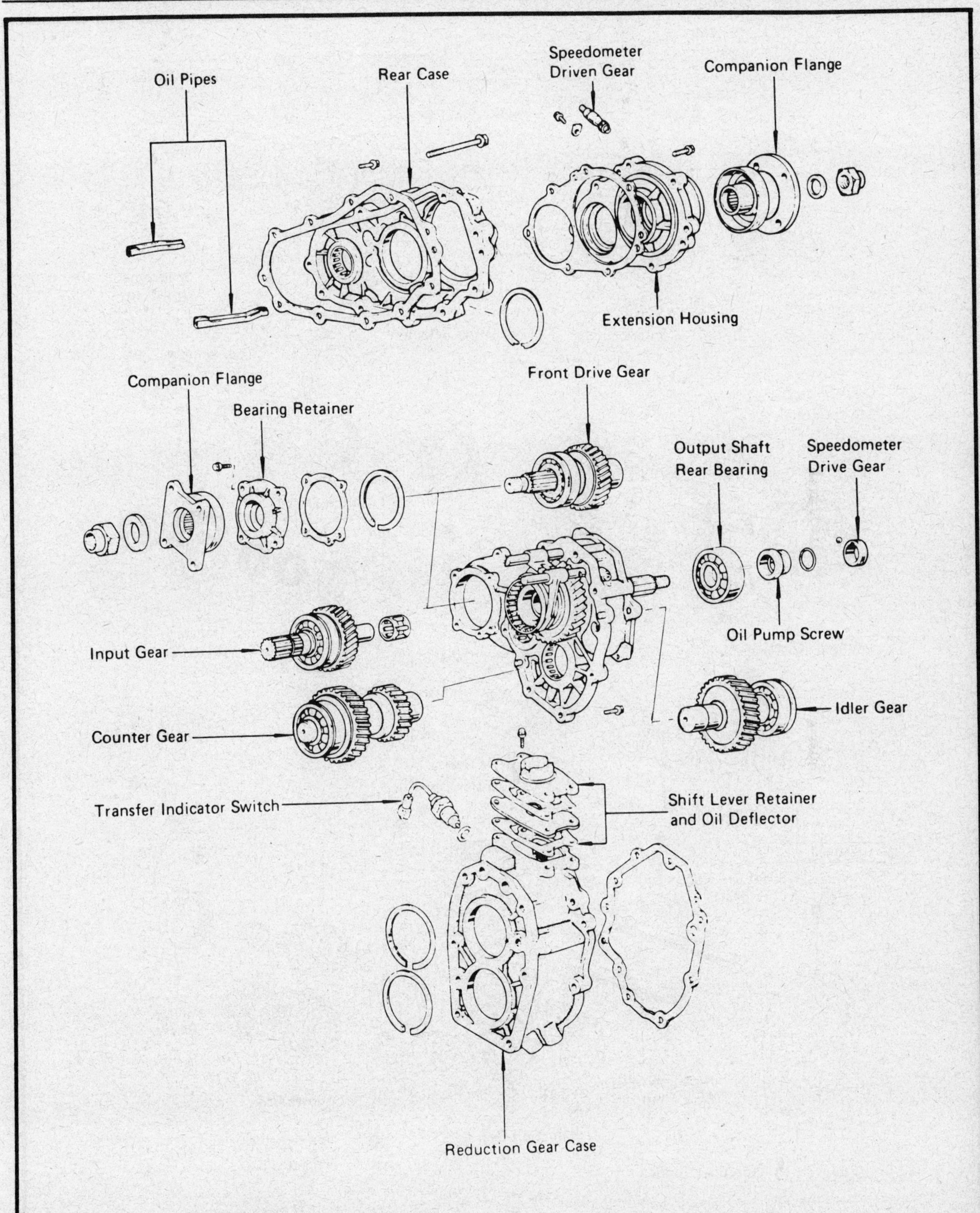
Oil Pipes
Rear Case
Speedometer
Driven Gear
Companion Flange
Extension Housing
Companion Flange
Bearing Retainer
Front Drive Gear
Output Shaft
Rear Bearing
Speedometer
Drive Gear
Oil Pump Screw
Input Gear
Idler Gear
Counter Gear
Transfer Indicator Switch
Shift Lever Retainer
and Oil Deflector
Reduction Gear Case

Toyota transfer case components

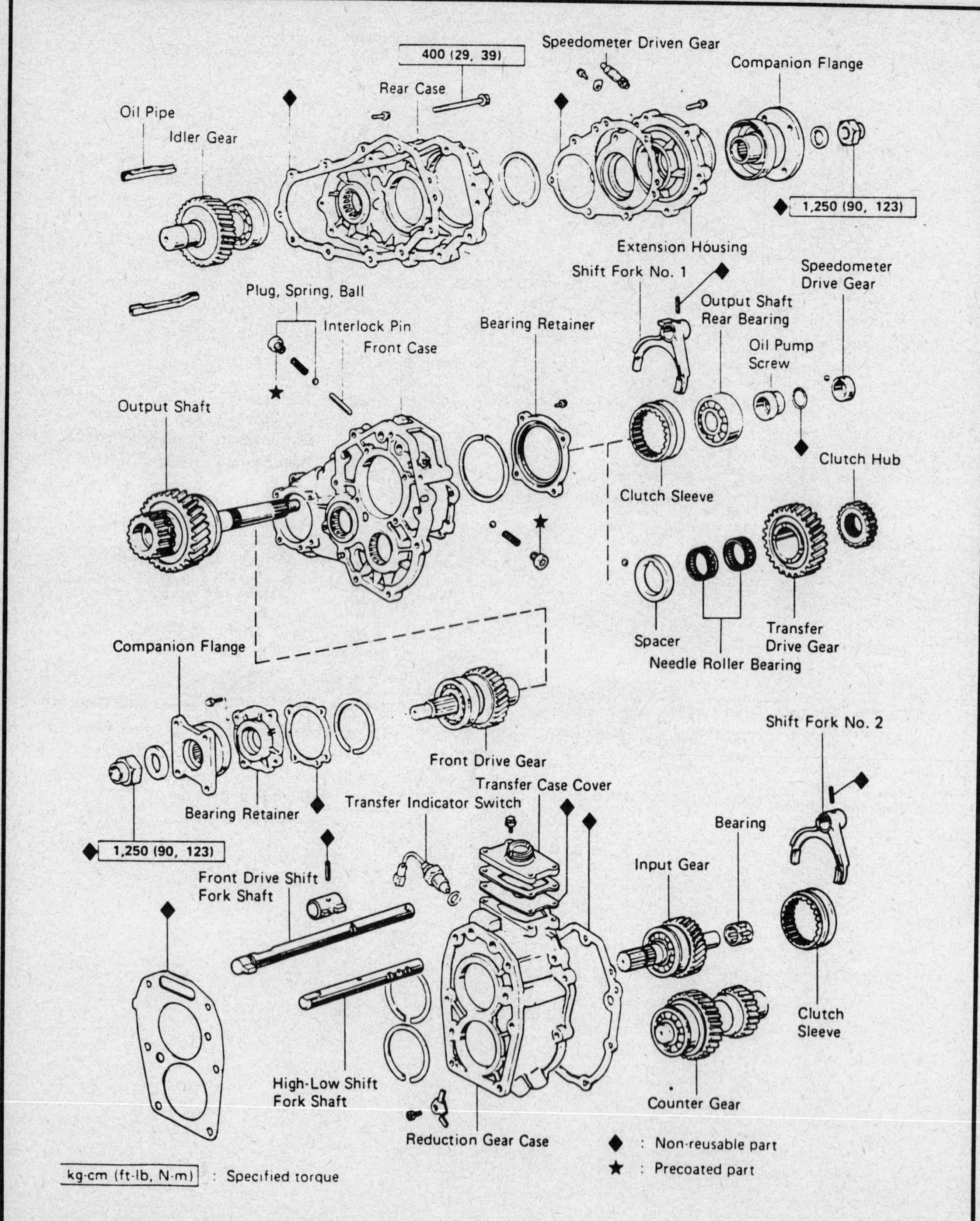
400 (29, 39)
Speedometer Driven Gear
Companion Flange
Rear Case
Oil Pipe
Idler Gear
1,250 (90, 123)
Extension Housing
Shift Fork No. 1
Speedometer
Drive Gear
Plug, Spring, Ball
Output Shaft
Rear Bearing
Interlock Pin
Bearing Retainer
Oil Pump
Screw
Front Case
Output Shaft
Clutch Hub
Clutch Sleeve
Spacer
Transfer
Drive Gear
Needle Roller Bearing
Companion Flange
Shift Fork No. 2
Front Drive Gear
Transfer Case Cover
Transfer Indicator Switch
Bearing Retainer
Bearing
1,250 (90, 123)
Input Gear
Front Drive Shift
Fork Shaft
Clutch
Sleeve
High-Low Shift
Fork Shaft
Counter Gear
Reduction Gear Case
◆ : Non-reusable part
★ : Precoated part
kg-cm (ft-lb, N·m) : Specified torque

Toyota transfer case assembly with torque valves

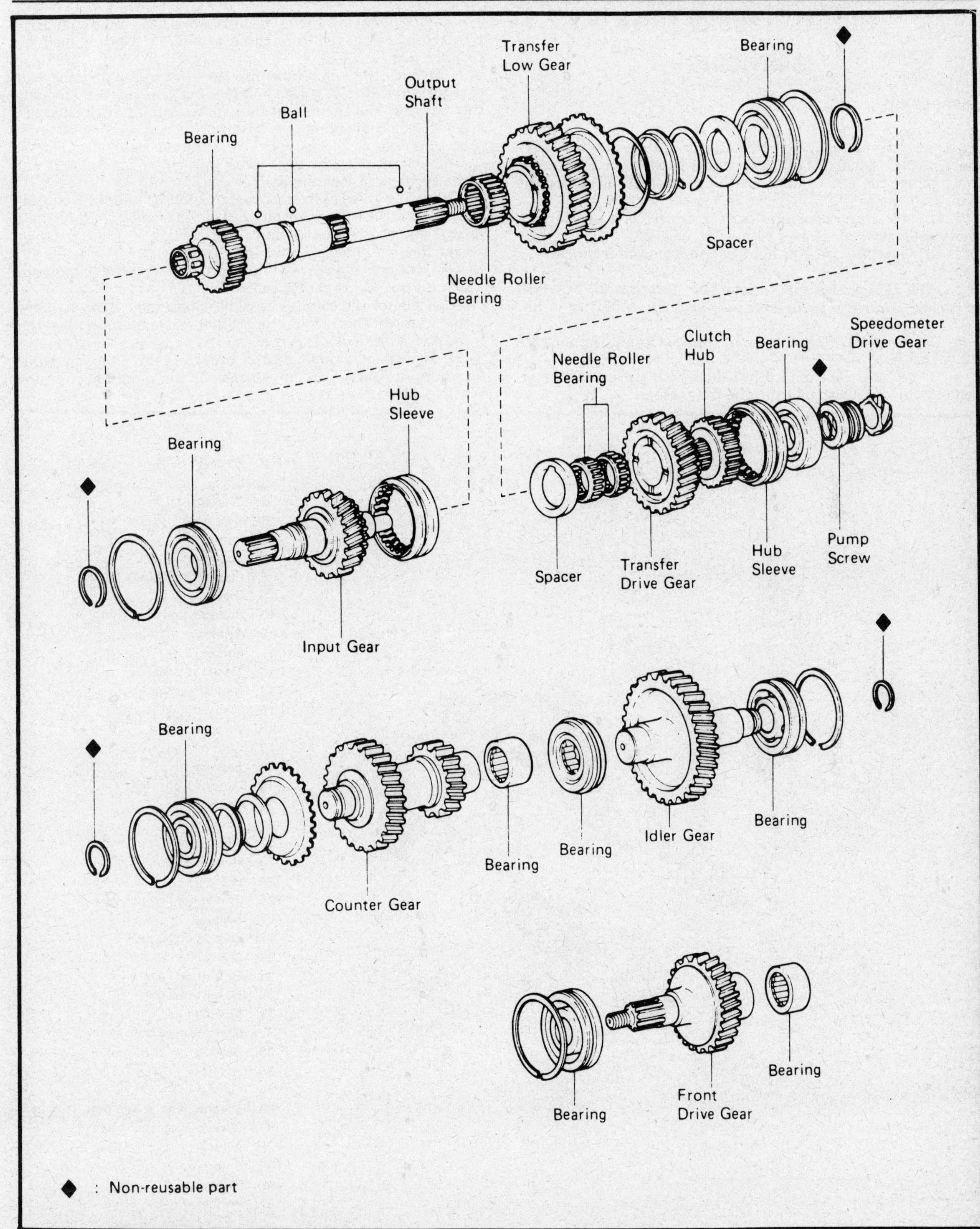

Toyota transfer case gear assemblies

Suzuki Transfer Case

SERVICING

Disassembly

1. Remove the three flanges; one from the input shaft, one from the front and rear output shafts. Lock the flange with special tool No. 09930-40113, so that it will not turn, and loosen and remove the nut holding the flange to the shaft. Draw the flange off the shaft.
2. Loosen the speedometer drive gear case bolt and remove the speedometer drive gear case with the gear.
3. Remove the indicator light switch from the front case.

NOTE: Be careful not to lose the switch ball. The ball is larger than the interlock ball and the locating balls.

4. Remove the bolts securing the transfer front case, and take off the case.
5. By tapping the front output shaft with a plastic hammer, remove the output shaft from the fron case.
6. After removing the oil seal, remove the circlip and drive the bearing out of the front case by using the bearing installer tool No. 09913-76010.
7. Remove the bolts fastening the center case and the rear case together. Do not loosen bolt No. 1 at this point! By tapping the rear case and the output rear shaft with a plastic hammer, separate the center and rear case.
8. Disassemble the components of the center case as follows:
   a. Loosen the gear shift locating spring plug and take out the spring and locating ball.
   b. Using spring pin remover, tool 09922-85811 or equivalent, drive the two spring pins out of the front drive shift shaft No.1 and the reduction shift shaft No.2.
   c. Remove the forks and shift shafts.
   d. Hammer the rear output shaft with a plastic hammer to drive it out of the center case.
   e. Pull out the counter gear, bearings and spacer. Remove the counter shaft from the center case by loosening the counter shaft lock plate bolt.
   f. Remove the input shaft f rom the center case by hammering the thick part of the case or the input shaft center with a plastic hammer.

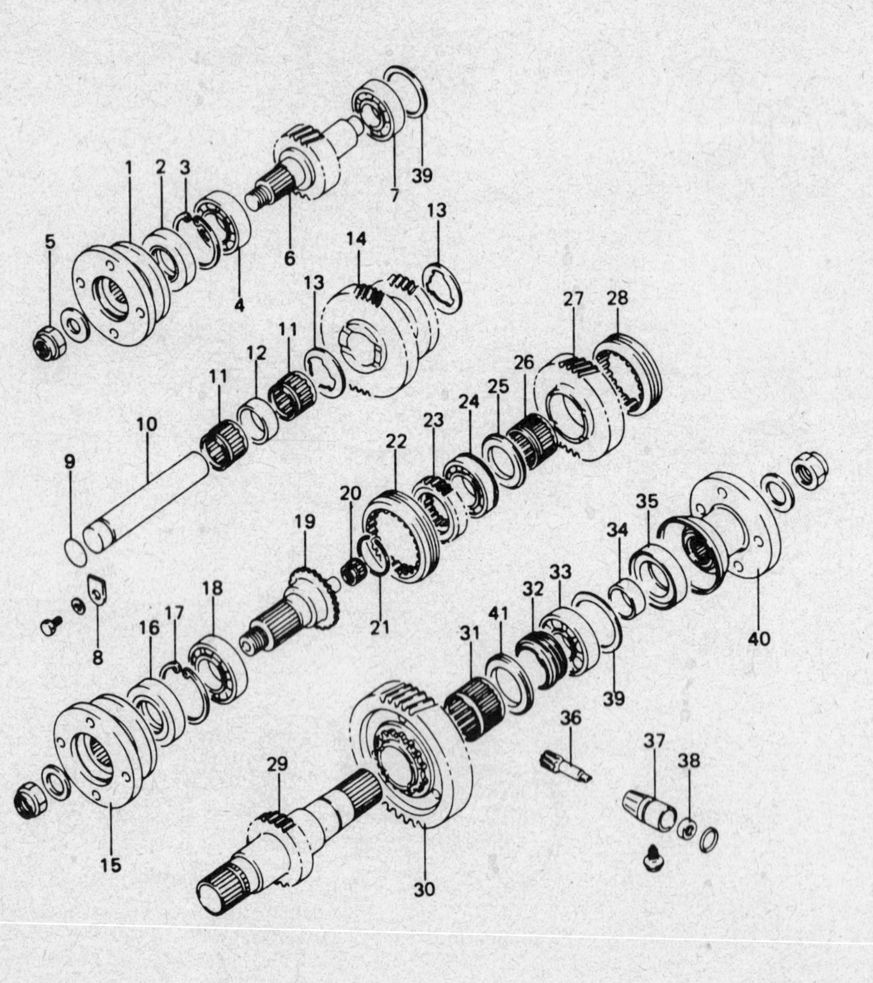

1. Flange
2. Oil seal
3. Circlip
4. Bearing
5. Nut
6. Input shaft
7. Bearing
8. Counter shaft lock plate
9. O-ring
10. Counter shaft
11. Bearing
12. Spacer
13. Thrust washer
14. Counter gear
15. Flange
16. Oil seal
17. Circlip
18. Bearing
19. Output front shaft
20. Bearing
21. Circlip
22. Sleeve
23. Hub
24. Bearing
25. Thrust washer
26. Bearing
27. Output high gear
28. Sleeve
29. Output rear shaft
30. Output low gear
31. Bearing
32. Speedometer drive gear
33. Bearing
34. Retainer
35. Oil seal
36. Speedometer driven gear
37. Speedometer gear case
38. Oil seal
39. Shim
40. Flange
41. Washer

Exploded view of the Suzuki transfer case components

g. Remove the output shaft rear bearing and retainer together by using a bearing puller. After removing the bearing, speedometer gear, thrust washer, the output low gear and the needle roller bearing can be removed.

Location of the No. 1 bolt on the center case

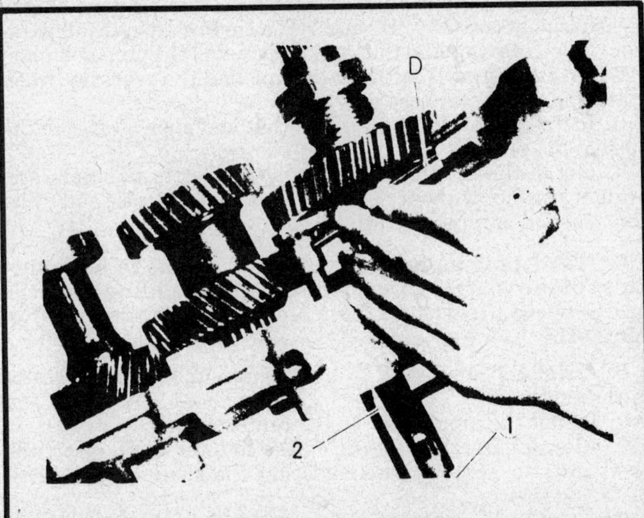

Spring pin removal from the shift shafts

h. Remove the front drive clutch hub circlip and pull the clutch hub off the shaft by using a bearing puller and puller attachment, special tool 09926-58010 or equivalent.

NOTE: Be careful to prevent damage to the needle roller bearing in the output rear shaft when removing the clutch hub.

i. Remove the front bearing by using the bearing puller and puller attachment, special tool 09926-58010 or equivalent.

NOTE: Be careful to prevent damage to the needle roller bearing in the output rear shaft when removing the clutch hub.

j. When the input shaft is removed or the center case and rear case are separated, the input bearings may come off. In such a case, the bearings can be removed from the shaft by using a bearing puller.

k. When the input shaft is removed, the front bearing may be left in the case. In this case, after removing the oil seal and circlip, the bearing can be taken out of the case using the bearing installer tool No. 09913-75810.

9. When the center case and the rear case are separated, the input shaft may be left in the rear case. In this case, remove the input shaft from the rear case by hammering the thick part of the case with a plastic hammer.

Reassembly

All parts to be used in reassembly must be perfectly clean. Oil or grease sliding and rubbing surfaces of the transfer case components with gear oil just before reassembling them. Oil seals, O-rings, and gaskets must be in perfect condition.

1. Press fit the bearings onto both sides of the input shaft by using bearing installer No. 09913-84510.
2. Install the component parts onto the output shaft in the following order:

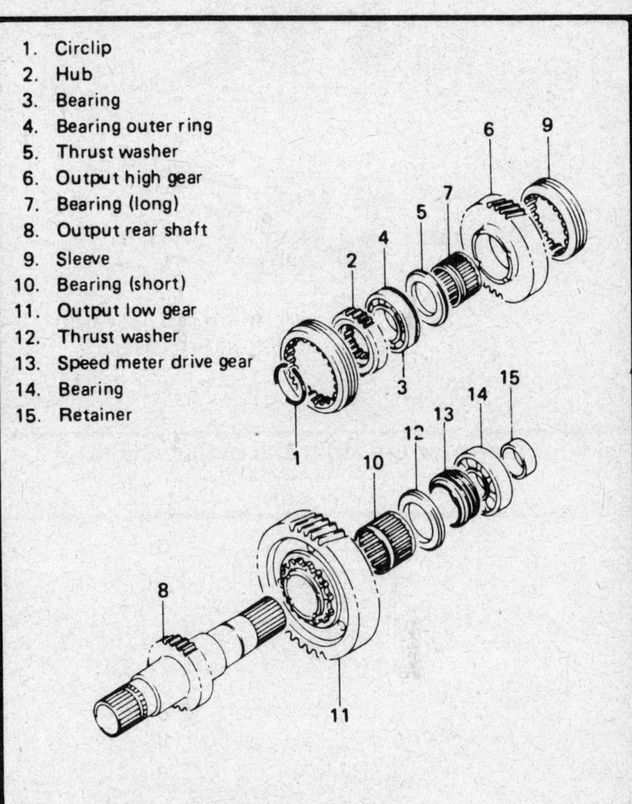

Output shaft components

a. After installing the (long) bearing, high gear and the thrust washer, press- fit the bearing, and then install the hub using the bearing installer, tool No. 09913-84510.

b. Fit the circlip securely to the groove in the shaft.

c. After installing the sleeve, (short) bearing, low gear and the thrust washer, press-fit the speedometer gear by using the bearing installer tool No. 09913-84510.

d. Press fit the bearing and the retainer by using the bearing installer tool No. 09913-84510.

3. Perform the shim adjustment of the input and output shafts. Clearance in the thrust direction of both the input and putput shafts is adjusted by putting shims between the input shaft rear bearing and the rear case for the input shaft and between the output shaft rear bearing and the rear case for the output shaft.

As the thrust clearance is specified as follows, determine the shim thickness to meet specification according to the following procedures.

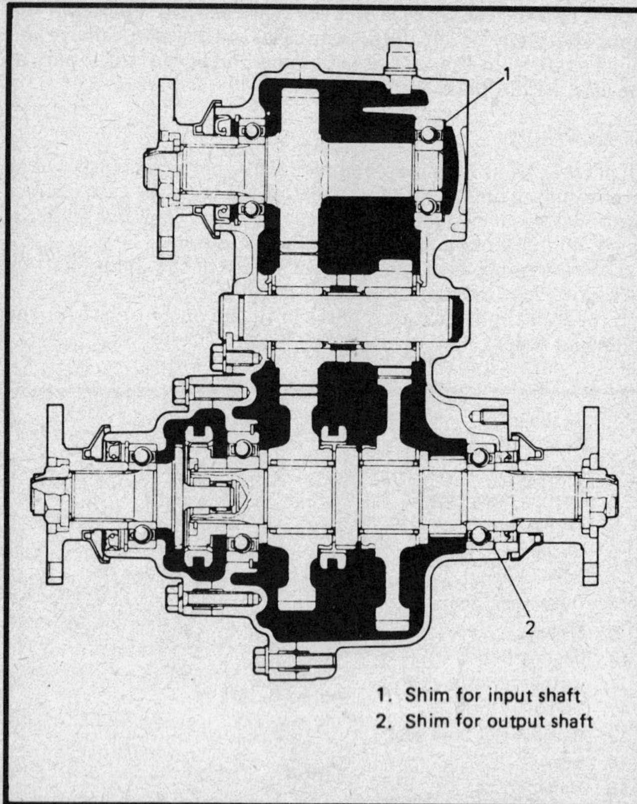

Shim locations for the input and output shafts

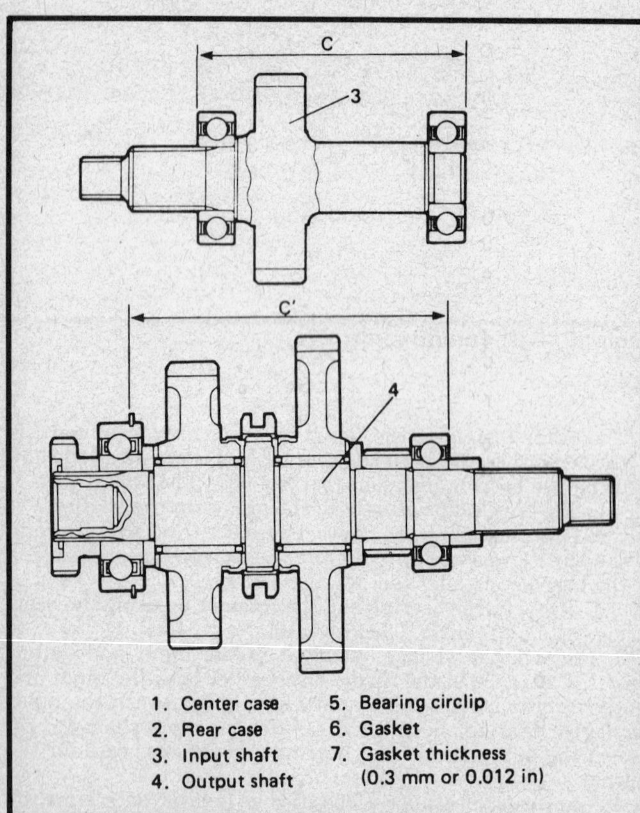

Input and output shaft measurements

Thrust clearance specifi‹ation:
0.002–0.006 in. (0.05–0.15mm)

4. Make the input shaft measurements as follows:
   a. With vernier calipers and a straight edge, take measurement "A" of the rear case as shown in the illustration.
   b. Take measurement "B" of the center case with the bearing circlip installed.
   c. Take measurement "C" (between the bearing inner races) of the input shaft with the bearings installed.
   d. Using measurements obtained in steps a thru c and the equation described below, calculate shim thickness which is necessary for the proper thrust clearance.

Thrust clearance =
("A" + "B" + Gasket thickness) - "C"

As the above equation holds for the thrust clearance and gasket thickness is specified as 0.3mm and the thrust clearance as 0.05–0.15mm, the shim thickness is calculated by the following equation:

Shim thickness =
("A" + "B" + 0.3mm) - ("C" + 0.05–0.15mm)

   e. When the proper thickness is determined, select the proper shim(s) from among the following shim sizes and use them between the input shaft and the rear bearing and the rear case when matching the center case and the rear case.

Avaiable shim thickness: 0.1, 0.3, 0.5mm

5. Shim the output shaft the same as the inputshaft, take measurements of "A", "B" and "C" as indicated in the illustration. Calculate the shim thickness and install the proper shim(s) between the output shaft rear bearing and the rear case when matching the center case and rear case
6. Install the oil seal in the rear case and apply grease to the oil seal lip.
7. Install the counter shaft thrust washer to the rear case, bringing its face without depressions against the case and fit its bent portion securely into the groove in the case.

NOTE: Apply an ample amount of grease to both surfaces of the washer so as to lubricate the sliding surfaces and prevent the washer from moving out of place or slipping off.

8. Install the input shaft front bearing, circlip and the oil seal in the center case.
9. Install the input shaft to the center case.
10. After greasing the O-ring on the counter shaft, insert the shaft into the center case and secure the shaft with the lock plate and bolt.

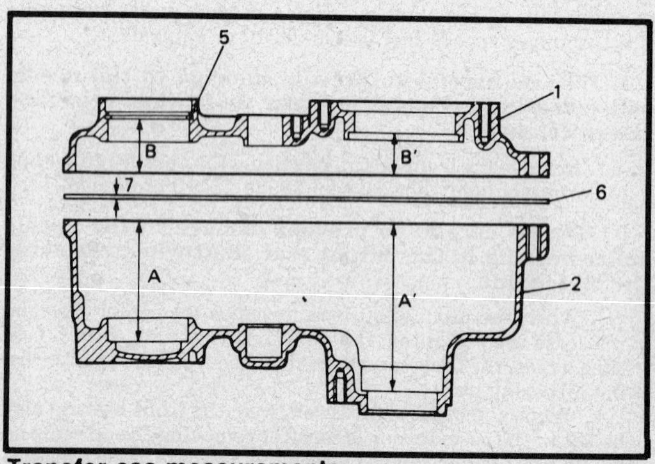

Transfer cas measurements

11. Install the counter shafty thrust washer to the center case. For installation, apply an ample amount of grease to both faces of the washer so as to lubricate the sliding surfaces and prevent it from moving out of place or slipping off and bring its face without depressions against the center case, and fit its bent portion into the groove in the case securely.
12. Install the needle roller bearings, spacer and the counter gear on the counter shaft.
13. Install the output shaft assembly to the center case.
14. When installing the front drive shift shaft and the reduction shift shaft in the center case, install the spring, ball, shafty, ball, shaft, ball, spring, and plug in that order.
15. Fit the forks on the shift shafts and lock them with spring pins. Forks should be fitted in their original positions.
16. Check the center case (or the rear case) to ensure that it is provided with two dowel pins.
17. Put the gasket on the center case. Bring the rear case and the center case into alignment and apply uniform force gradually all around the rear case with a plastc hammer. Tighten the center case securing bolts to 9.5–16.5 ft. lbs.
18. Apply grease to the front output shaft rear bearing.
19. Install the bearing, circlip and oil seal to the front case. Apply grease to the oil seal lip and install the front output shaft using the bearing installer tool No. 09913-76010.
20. Put a new gasket on the center case.
21. Check that the two dowel pins are posioned in the front case.
22. Install the front case to the center case.
23. When installing the speedometer gear and its gear case in the rear case, apply grease to the O-ring and the oil seal lip, and align the bolt holes in the rear case and the drive gear case.
24. Install the 4WD ball and switch. Then clamp the switch lead wire properly.
25. Install the propeller shaft flanges and tighten the nuts to 80–108 ft. lbs., then calk the nuts to prevent them from loosening.
26. Install the Transfer case in the vehicle.

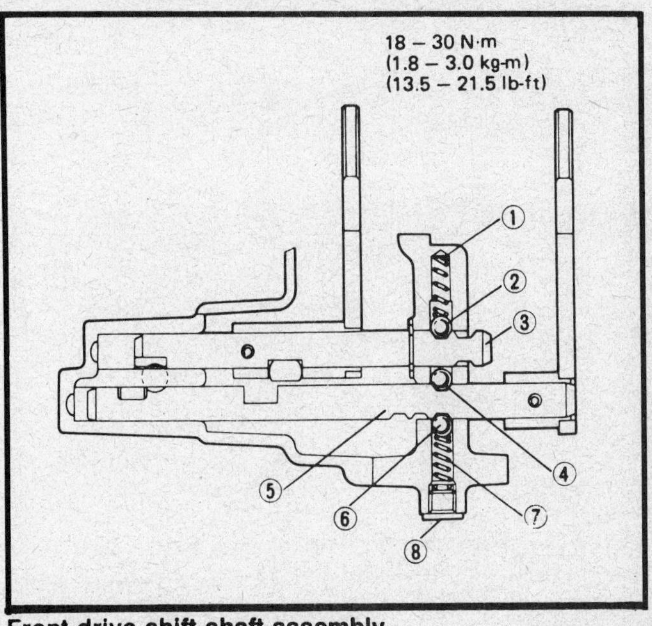

Front drive shift shaft assembly

Toyota Transfer Case

SERVICING

Disassembly, Inspection and Assembly

1. Remove the front and rear companion flanges
2. Remove the extension housing. Remove the speedometer drive gear, steel ball, oil pump screw and bearing.
3. Remove the rear case half with the idler gear in position while holding the front half so that the clutch hub and steel ball do not fall out.
4. Remove the idler gear from the rear case.
5. Remove the front bearing retainer and front drive gear.
6. Remove the two oil pipes. Remove shift fork No. 1 and clutch sleeve.
7. Remove the clutch hub and transfer drive gear. Remove the needle roller bearing, No. 2 spacer and steel ball. On models equipped with the 22R engine, remove the transfer case cover and shift lever retainer.
8. Remove the screw cover plugs, springs and locking balls from both sides of the case.
9. Remove the spring pins that retain the shifting forks and remove the front drive fork shaft. Remove the interlocking pin and the high–low fork.
10. Remove the front case, tap lightly with a plastic hammer if necessary.
11. Remove the No.2 fork, clutch sleeve, and needle roller bearing from the input shaft.
12. Remove the input gear and counter gear from the reduction gear case. Remove the output shaft from the front case.
13. Check the oil and thrust clearance of the transfer low gear: Oil clearance between the gear and shaft with needle bearing installed; 0.0004–0.0022 in. Thrust clearance with spacer and bearing installed; 0.0039–0.0098 in.
14. Check the clearance of the thrust drive gear: Oil clearance between gear and shaft with needle bearing installed: 0.004–0.0020 in. Thrust clearance with clutch hub and spacer installed: 0.0035–0.0106 in.
15. Measure the clearance of the shift forks and clutch sleeves: Max.is 0.039 in.
16. Inspect all parts and bearings, replace as necessary. If bearing replacement is indicated, press the bearing from the shaft. When installing a bearing, use the thickest snap ring that will allow minimum end play.
17. Inspect all oil seals and replace as necessary.
18. Reassembly begins with the installation of the output shaft to the front case. Install the front bearing retainer and torque the mounting bolts to 9 ft. lbs.
19. Install the input gear and counter gear to the reduction gear case. Install the roller bearing on the input shaft.
20. Install the No. 2 hub sleeve and No. 2 shift fork on the input shaft.
21. Install the reduction gear case and new gasket to the front case. Torque the bolts to 29 ft. lbs. Two different length bolts are used, be sure to install in correct position.
22. Install the front drive gear. Install the bearing retainer and new gasket. Torque the bolts to 14 ft. lbs.
23. Install the high–low shift fork, the interlock pin and front drive shift fork shaft. Install the slotted spring pins. Install the balls, springs and side plugs. Tighten the plugs to 9 ft. lbs.
24. Install the locking ball and No. 2 spacer. Install the needle roller bearing, transfer low gear and clutch hub.
25. Install No. 1 shift fork and hub sleeve. Install the oil pipes.
26. Install the idler gear to the rear case and install the rear case with a new gasket. Tighten the bolts to 29 ft. lbs. Be sure the bolts are install in the correct position, two different lengths are used.
27. Install the bearing, oil; pump screw, locking ball and speedometer drive gear. Install the extension housing with a new gasket. Torque the bolts to 29 ft. lbs.
28. On vehicles equipped with the 22R engine, install the transfer case cover and shift lever retainer.
29. Install the front and rear flanges (90 ft. lbs.). Install the indicator switch and speedometer driven gear.

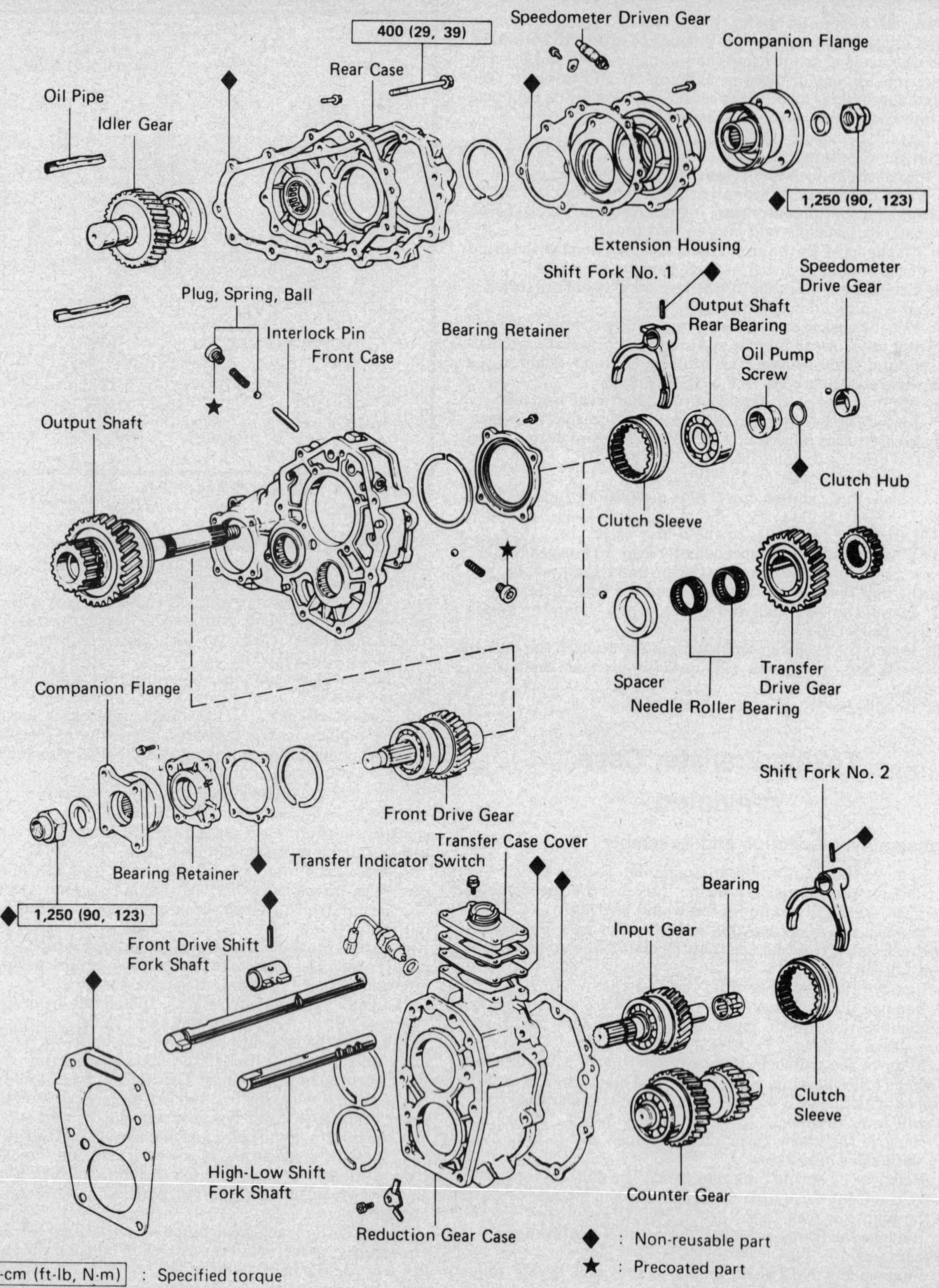

Toyota transfer case components torque values

Drive Axles Import Trucks 27

INDEX

The drive axle must transmit power through 90°. To accomplish this, straight cut bevel gears or spiral bevel gears were used. This type of gear is satisfactory for differential side gears, but since the centerline of the gears must intersect, they rapidly became unsuited for ring and pinion gears. The lowering of the driveshaft brought about a variation of the bevel gear, which is called the hypoid gear. This type of gear does not require a meeting of the gear centerlines and can therefore be underslung, relative to the centerline of the ring gear.

Gear Ratios

The drive axle of a vehicle is said to have a certain axle ratio. This number (usually a whole number and a decimal fraction) is actually a comparison of the number of gear teeth on the ring gear and the pinion gear. For example, a 4:11 rear means that theoretically, there are 4:11 teeth on the ring gear and one tooth on the pinion. Actually, on a 4:11 rear, there are 37 teeth on the ring gear and nine teeth on the pinion gear. By dividing the number of teeth on the pinion gear into the number of teeth on the ring gear, the numerical axle ratio (4:11) is obtained. This also provides a good method of ascertaining exactly which axle ratio one is dealing with.

Differential Operation

The differential is an arrangement of gears that permits the wheels to turn at different speeds when cornering and divides the torque between the axle shafts. The differential gears are mounted on a pinion shaft and the gears are free to rotate on this shaft. The pinion shaft is fitted in a bore in the differential case and is at right angles to the axle shafts.

Power flow through the differential is as follows. The drive pinion, which is turned by the driveshaft, turns the ring gear. The ring gear, which is bolted to the differential case, rotates the case. The differential pinion forces the pinion gears against the side gears. In cases where both wheels have equal traction, the pinion gears do not rotate on the pinion shaft, because the input force of the pinion gear is divided equally between the two side gears. Consequently the pinion gears revolve with the pinion shaft, although they do not revolve on the pinion shaft itself.

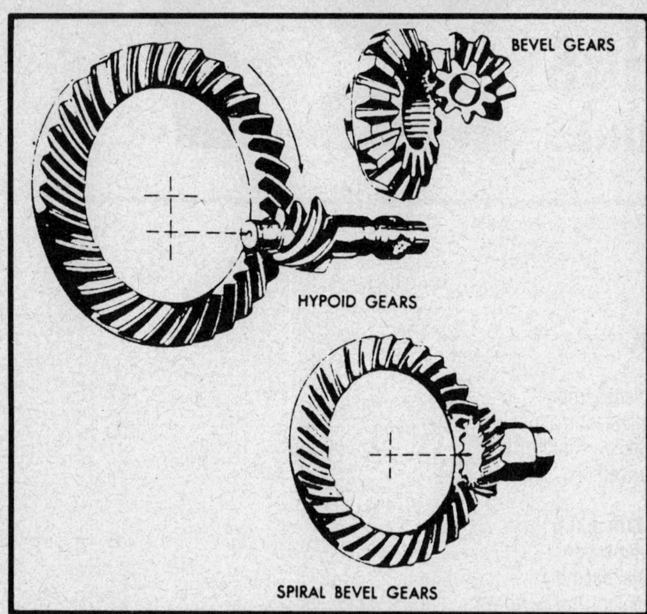

Hypoid and Bevel gear applications

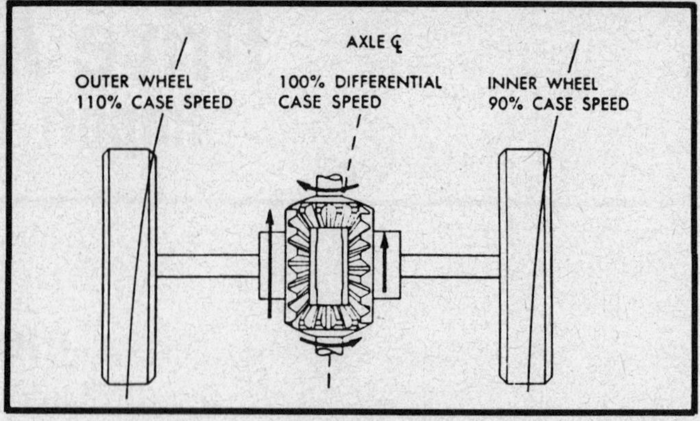

Differential action during cornering

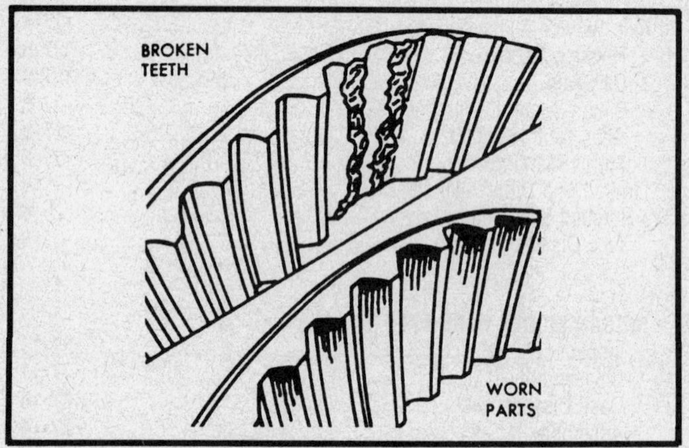

Two types of damage which cause gear noise

The side gears, which are splined to the axle shafts, and meshed with the pinion gears, rotate the axle shafts.

When it becomes necessary to turn a corner, the differential becomes effective and allows the axle shafts to rotate at different speeds. As the inner wheel slows down, the side gear splined to the inner wheel axle shaft also slows down. The pinion gears act as balancing levers by maintaining equal tooth loads to both gears while allowing unequal speeds of rotation at the axle shafts. If the vehicle speed remains constant, and the inner wheel slows down to 90 percent of vehicle speeds, the outer wheel will speed up to 110 percent.

DIFFERENTIAL DIAGNOSIS

The most essential part of rear axle service is proper diagnosis of the problem. Bent or broken axle shafts or broken gears pose little problem, but isolating an axle noise and correctly interpreting the problem can be extremely difficult, even for an experienced mechanic.

Any gear driven unit will produce a certain amount of noise, therefore, a specific diagnosis for each individual unit is the best practice. Acceptable or normal noise can be classified as a slight noise heard only at certain speeds or under unusual conditions. This noise tends to reach a peak at 40–60 mph depending on the road condition, load, gear ratio and tire size. Frequently, other noises are mistakenly diagnosed as coming from the rear axle. Vehicle noises from tires, transmission, driveshaft, U-joints and front and rear wheel bearings will often be mistaken as emanating from the rear axle. Raising the tire pressure to eliminate tire noise (although this will not silence mud or snow treads), listening for noise at varying speeds and road conditions and listening for noise at drive and coast conditions will aid in diagnosing alleged rear axle noises.

External Noise Elimination

It is advisable to make a thorough road test to determine whether the noise originates in the rear axle or whether it originates from the tires, engine transmission, wheel bearings or road surface. Noise originating from other places cannot be corrected by overhauling the rear axle.

Road Noise

Brick roads or rough surfaced concrete, may cause a noise which can be mistaken as coming from the rear axle. Driving on a different type of road (smooth asphalt or dirt) will determine whether the road is the cause of the noise. Road noise is usually the same on drive or coast conditions.

Tire Noise

Tire noise can be mistaken as rear axle noises, even though the tires on the front are at fault. Snow tread and mud tread tires or tires worn unevenly will frequently cause vibrations which seem to originate elsewhere; temporarily, and for test purposes only, inflate the tires to 40–50 lbs. This will significantly alter the noise produced by the tires, but will not alter noise from the rear axle. Noises from the rear axle will normally cease at speeds below 30 mph on coast, while tire noise will continue at lower tone as vehicle speed is decreased. The rear axle noise will usually change from drive conditions to coast conditions, while tire noise will not. Do not forget to lower the tire pressure to normal after the test is complete.

Engine and Transmission Noise

Engine and transmission noises also seem to originate in the rear axle. Road test the vehicle and determine at which speeds the noise is most pronounced. Stop the vehicle in a quiet place to avoid interfering noises. With the transmission in neutral, run the engine slowly through the engine speeds corresponding to the vehicle speed at which the noise was most noticeable. If a similar noise was produced with the vehicle standing still, the noise is not in the rear axle, but somewhere in the engine or transmission.

Front Wheel Bearing Noise

Front wheel bearing noises, sometimes confused with rear axle noises, will not change when comparing drive and coast conditions. While holding the vehicle speed steady, lightly apply the footbrake. This will often cause wheel bearing noise to lessen, as some of the weight is taken off the bearing. Front wheel bearings are easily checked by jacking up the wheels and spinning the wheels. Shaking the wheels will also determine if the wheel bearings are excessively loose.

Rear Axle Noises

If a logical test of the vehicle shows that the noise is not caused by external items, it can be assumed that the noise originates from the rear axle. The rear axle should be tested on a smooth level road to avoid road noise. It is not advisable to test the axle by jacking up the rear wheels and running the vehicle.

True rear axle noises generally fall into two classes; gear noise and bearing noises, and can be caused by a faulty driveshaft, faulty wheel bearings, worn differential or pinion shaft bearings, U-joint misalignment, worn differential side gears and pinions, or mismatched, improperly adjusted, or scored ring and pinion gears.

Rear Wheel Bearing Noise

A rough rear wheel bearing causes a vibration or growl which will continue with the vehicle coasting or in neutral. A brinelled rear wheel bearing will also cause a knock or click approximately every two revolutions of the rear wheel, due to the fact that the bearing rollers do not travel at the same speed as the rear wheel and axle. Jack up the rear wheels and spin the wheel slowly, listening for signs of a rough or brinelled wheel bearing.

Differential Side Gear & Pinion Noise

Differential side gears and pinions seldom cause noise since their movement is relatively slight on straight ahead driving. Noise produced by these gears will be more noticeable on turns.

Pinion Bearing Noise

Pinion bearing failures can be distinguished by their speed of rotation, which is higher than side bearings or axle bearings. Rough or brinelled pinion bearings cause a continuous low pitch whirring or scraping noise beginning at low speeds.

Side Bearing Noise

Side bearings produce a constant rough noise, which is slower than the pinion bearing noise. Side bearing noise may also fluctuate in the above rear wheel bearing test.

Gear Noise

Two basic types of gear noise exist. First is the type produced by bent or broken gear teeth which have been forcibly damaged. The noise from this type of damage is audible over the entire speed range. Scoring or damage to the hypoid gear teeth generally results from insufficient lubricant, improper lubricant, improper breaking, insufficient gear backlash, improper ring and pinion gear alignment or loss of torque on the drive pinion nut. If not corrected, the scoring will lead to eventual erosion or fracture of the gear teeth. Hypoid gear tooth fracture can also be caused by extended overloading of the gear set (fatigue fracture) or by shock overloading (sudden failure). Differential and side gears rarely give trouble, but common causes of differential failure are shock loading, extended overloading and differential pinion seizure at the cross-shaft, resulting from excessive wheel spin and consequent lubricant breakdown.

The second type of gear noise pertains to the mesh pattern between the ring and pinion gears. This type of abnormal gear noise can be recognized as a cycling pitch or whine audible in either drive, float or coast conditions. Gear noises can be recognized as they tend to peak out in a narrow speed range and remain constant in pitch, whereas bearing noises tend to vary in pitch with vehicle speeds. Noises produced by the ring and pinion gears will generally follow the pattern below.

BEARING DIAGNOSIS

This section will help in the diagnosis of bearing failure and the causes. Bearing diagnosis can be very helpful in determining the cause of rear axle failure.

When disassembling a rear axle, the general condition of all bearings should be noted and classified where possible. Proper recognition of the cause will help in correcting the problem and avoiding a repetition of the failure. Some of the common causes of bearing failure are:

1. Abuse during assembly or disassembly.
2. Improper assembly methods.
3. Improper or inadequate lubrication.
4. Bearing contact with dirt or water.
5. Wear caused by dirt or metal chips.
6. Corrosion or rust.
7. Seizing due to overloading.
8. Overheating.
9. Frettage of the bearing seats.
10. Brinelling from impact or shock loading.
11. Manufacturing defects.
12. Pitting due to fatigue.

To avoid damage to the bearing from improper handling, it is best to treat a used bearing the same as a new bearing. Always work in a clean area with clean tools. Remove all outside dirt from the housing before exposing a bearing and clean all bearing seats before installing a bearing.

CAUTION

Never spin a bearing, either by hand or with compressed air, as this will lead to almost certain bearing failure.

COMPONENT FAILURE DIAGNOSIS

Scoring & Seizure of Spider and Pinion Gears

The spider arms and pinion gears were badly discolored by heat, caused by the unit operating for a long time after the initial scoring took place. The most probable cause of this type of failure is excessive wheelspin, particularly in off-road or icy road conditions. Other possible causes are inadequate lubrication or overstress. Friction causes the hardened areas to overheat, score, and eventually to seize. The best way to prevent this problem is to avoid wheelspin and overloading under rough terrain or poor traction conditions.

SHOCK FRACTURE

These differential pinion and side gears show a grainy structure which indicates a shock fracture. This type of damage occurs instantaneously. The usual cause is a sudden excessive load, as might be caused by sudden clutch engagement at high engine speed. Another cause is a rapidly spinning wheel suddenly reaching a good traction area. This failure can be prevented by proper clutch operation, and by avoiding wheelspin and overloading under rough terrain or poor traction conditions.

FATIGUE FRACTURE OF THE DIFFERENTIAL SIDE GEARS

This damage occurs in stages. An initial stress caused a crack, and repeated stresses caused complete failure. Some of the gear teeth were broken off in the later stages. The failures can be seen best at points A and B. All differential gears should be checked when this type of failure is found, very often the other gears will be in the initial stages of failure and must be replaced. This is most often caused by abuse such as sudden clutch engagement or incorrect two-speed axle operation, combined with overloading.

SCORED AND SCUFFED GEAR TEETH

This wear pattern is a result of the gear running without enough lubrication between the tooth surfaces. Either poor quality gear lube or low lubrication level can cause this condition. Excessive torque input to the rear can also cause this wear since it will break down even the best of gear lube. Changing gear lube at regular recommended intervals and keeping excessive torque input to a minimum will usually prevent this problem.

FATIGUE FRACTURED PINION GEAR

This type of fracture develops over a period of time. The fracture works through the gear tooth until the tooth is not strong enough to support the load applied. Failure happens and a section of the tooth breaks away. Continued use of pitted gears is the usual cause of this type of gear failure. As the gear pits, the support area is reduced and must carry the entire load of the gear tooth. As this continues the gear tooth fatigues and the final result is failure of the gear. To prevent this problem the ring and pinion must be replaced if there is any pitting on the gears.

MISALIGNMENT FATIGUE FRACTURE

This problem comes from misalignment in the axle shaft. This kind of failure can also happen when the axle shaft breaks. If twisted, bent or sprung axle shaft are are not replaced after they are damaged, this kind of failure to the side gears can occur. Bent axle housing can also cause this to happen. In most cases, this type of failure is not instantaneous. It tends to happen over a period of time. The usual cause of this type of failure is abusive operation of the vehicle and severe overloading.

OVERHEATED GEAR SET

This problem can be caused by one of three, or any combination of the following circumstances. The causes are low gear lubricant level; improper gear lubricant; or infrequent lubricant change. When one or more of these conditions is present in the rear, it causes the lubricant to break down and allows the gear surface to build up heat because of increased friction. In the failure shown, the gears became so hot the pinion bearing fused to the pinion gear and the pinion gear teeth became distorted. To prevent this problem a good quality gear lubricant must be used in the rear to prevent the breakdown of lubricant under a heavy load.

FRACTURE GEAR TEETH

This problem is caused by improper gear adjustment. The picture on the left shows the result of excessive backlash between the ring and pinion gear. Such backlash allows overloading of the heel section of the gear; gear fracture will follow. The picture on the right shows the result of too little backlash thus allowing the toe section of the gear to overload and become fractured. The best way to eliminate this problem is to correctly adjust the ring and piston gears, when necessary, according to specifications.

TWISTED AXLE SHAFT

This problem with the axle comes from abusive and/or extremely severe operation of the vehicle. This is only the first stage of failure where the axle shaft has only twisted, but has not yet started to crack. At this stage the shaft should be replaced. If it is not, the shaft will continue to twist and eventually will break. When this happens it will almost certainly damage other axle parts. To eliminate this problem, the shaft should be replaced if found to be twisted. The driver of the vehicle should be informed to adopt better driving procedures.

PITTED PINION TEETH

This problem is the result of extremely high pressure on the gear teeth due to severe use. The pitting located at the heel end of the pinion gear teeth happens when overloading of the pinion moves the pinion out of its proper position relative to the ring gear. The result is a concentrated area of contact on the heel part of the gear teeth which will break down the oil film, and thus allow the pinion teeth to pit. Sometimes the ring gear will appear to be undamaged. This is because ring gear damage might not be visible to the naked eye; but the contour of the gear teeth will have changed. The ring and pin‹chion gears must be replaced as a pair, or early failure will occur. The best way to eliminate this problem is to use good quality gear lube. The more severely the vehicle is used the better quality the gear lube should be.

SCUFFED GEAR TEETH ON THE COAST SIDE ONLY

This wear can be caused by two different things. The first is worn pinion bearing which allows excessive end play in the pin‹chion gear. The result is incorrect contact between the ring and pinion gear teeth on the coast side. This allows excessive pressure to build up on the gear teeth and will break down the oil film, resulting in scoring of the teeth. The second cause is hard, abusive driving in vehicles equipped with a manual transmission. This usually happens when going down a steep grade at high speed and slowing the vehicle by using the clutch to break the speed. The best way to eliminate this problem is to replace the pin‹chion bearing if worn and recommend good driving procedures.

Types of Drive Axles

FULL FLOATING AXLES

Support of the vehicle and the payload weight is by the axle housing. The wheels are driven by splined shafts which "float" within the axle housing.

SEMI-FLOATING AXLE

This axle design provides for the support of the payload and vehicle weight to be carried by the axle shaft through the wheel bearings to the axle housing.

SINGLE REDUCTION AXLE

Final drive ratio is obtained by the use of a single ring gear and pinion set. This type is used for most light and medium duty applications.

AXLE SERVICE & INSPECTION

Cleaning Bearings

Proper bearing cleaning is important. Bearings should always be cleaned separately from other rear axle parts.

1. Soak all bearings in clean kerosene or diesel fuel oil.

CAUTION

Ordinary gasoline should not be used. Bearings should not be cleaned in hot solution tank.

2. Slush bearings in cleaning solution until all oil lubricant is loosened. Brush bearings with soft bristled brush until ALL dirt has been removed. Remove loose particles of dirt by striking flat against a wood block.
3. Rinse bearings in clean fluid. While holding races to prevent rotation, blow dry with compressed air.

CAUTION

Do not spin bearings while drying.

4. After bearings have been inspected, lubricate thoroughly with regular axle lubricant; then wrap each bearing in clean cloth until ready to use.

Cleaning Parts

Immerse all parts in suitable cleaning fluid and clean thorough-

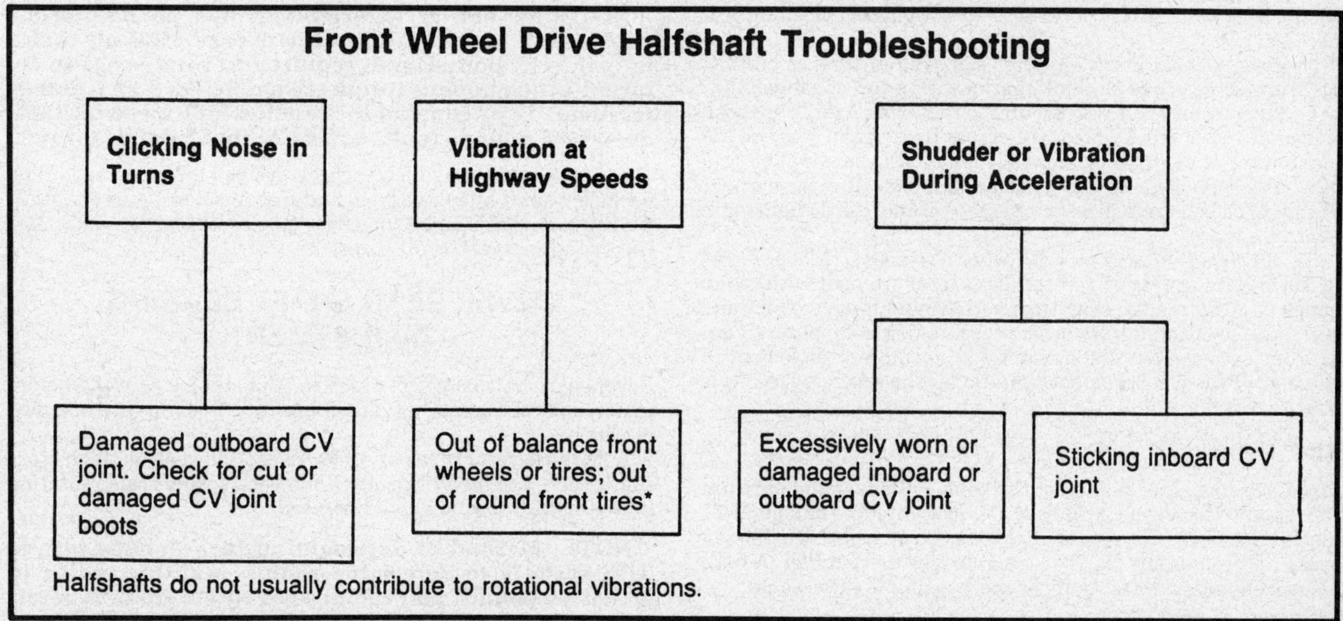
Front Wheel Drive Halfshaft Troubleshooting
Clicking Noise in Turns
Vibration at Highway Speeds
Shudder or Vibration During Acceleration
Damaged outboard CV joint. Check for cut or damaged CV joint boots
Out of balance front wheels or tires; out of round front tires*
Excessively worn or damaged inboard or outboard CV joint
Sticking inboard CV joint
Halfshafts do not usually contribute to rotational vibrations.

ly. Use a stiff bristle brush as required to remove foreign deposits. Clean all lubricant passages or channels in pinion cage, carrier, caps and retainers. Make certain that interior of housing is thoroughly cleaned. Clean vent plugs and breathers.

Small parts such as cap screws, bolts, studs, nuts etc., should be cleaned thoroughly.

Inspection

Magna Flux all steel parts, except ball and roller bearings, to detect presence of wear and cracks.

Bearings

Rotate each bearing and check to see if the rollers are worn, chipped, rough or in any other way damaged. Check the cage to see if it is in any way damaged. If either the bearing rollers or the cage are damaged the bearing must be replaced.

Gears

Examine drive gear and drive pinion, differential pinions and differential side gears carefully, for damaged teeth, worn spots in surface hardening, distortion and where drive gear is attached to differential case with rivets, inspect rivets for looseness, replace loose rivets. Check radial clearances between differential side gears and differential case. Check fit of differential pinions on spider.

Differential Case

Inspect case for cracks, distortion or damage, if in good condition, thoroughly clean case and cover; then assemble case with bolts and mount in lathe centers of "V" block stand. If lathe is not available, install differential side bearings and mount case in differential carrier. Install dial indicator and check differential case run out.

Differential case with drive gear installed is checked in the same manner, except that dial indicator reading must be taken at gear instead of at case flange.

Whenever run-out exceeds limits, it may be corrected as later described under "Repair" in this section. However, the support case used in the 2 speed axle cannot be repaired and should be replaced with new case.

Axle Shafts

Examine splined end of axle shaft for twisted or cracked splines, twisted shaft, and worn dowel holes in flange. Install new shafts if necessary.

Install axle shaft assembly in lathe centers and check shaft run-out with dial indicator so that indicator shaft end contacts inner surface of flange near outer edge of flange and check flange run-out.

Shims

Carefully inspect shims for uniform thickness. Where various thickness of shims are used in a pack, it is recommended that the thickest shims be used between the thin shims.

Thrust Washers

Replace all thrust washers.

Spider

Carefully inspect spider arms for wear or defects.

Differential Pinion Bushings

Examine bushings (when used) for excessive wear, looseness, or damage. Check fit or gears on spider for excessive clearance.

Axle Housing Sleeves

Sleeves showing damaged threads, wear, or other damage should be replaced if hydraulic press is available, otherwise replace housing.

HOUSING CHECK

Before Removal

A check for bent axle housing can be made with unit in vehicle; however, conventional alignment instruments can be used if available.

1. Raise rear axle with a jack until wheels clear floor. Block up axle under each spring seat.
2. Check wheel bearing adjustment and adjust if necessary,

then check wheels for looseness and tighten wheel nuts if necessary.

3. Place a chalk mark on outer side wall of tires at bottom. Measure across tires at chalk marks with a toe-in gauge.

4. Turn wheels half-way around so that chalk marks are positioned at top of wheel. Measure across tires again. If measurement at top is 1/8" or more, smaller than measurement at bottom of wheels, axle housing has sagged and is bent. If measurement at top exceeds bottom dimension by 1/8" or more, axle housing is bent at ends.

5. Turn chalk marks on both wheels so that marks are level with axle and at rear of vehicle. Take measurement with toe-in gauge at chalk marks; then turn both chalk marks to front and level with axle and take another measurement. If measurement at front exceeds rear dimension by 1/8" or more, axle is bent to the rear. If the measurement condition is the reverse, the axle is bent forward.

After Removal

Place two straightedges across the housing flanges and measure the distance between the ends of the straightedges at a point 11 inches from the tube center. Relocate the straightedge 180 degrees and remeasure. If the straightedges are parallel in both measurements within 3/32 inch, the housing is serviceable.

GENERAL REPAIR

Oil Seal Contact Surfaces

Surface of parts, contacted by oil seals must be free of corrosion, pits and grooves. When abrasive cleaning fails to clean up the seal contact surface and restore smooth finish, a new part must be installed.

OIL SEAL

Removal

Oil seals can be removed with a drift pin. When removing a seal, be careful that it does not become cocked and result in damage to the retainer. Clean surface of retainer carefully, so that seal will seat properly in retainer.

Installation

Coat outer surface of seal retainer with a light coat of sealer, to prevent lubricant leaks. Carefully start seal in retainer. Cutting, scratching, or curling of lip of seal seriously impairs its efficiency and usually results in premature replacement. Lip of seal should be coated with a high temperature grease containing zinc oxide to help prevent scoring and damage to parts during installation.

Seals must always be installed so that seal lip is toward the lubricant.

PINION BEARING ADJUSTMENTS (PRE-LOAD)

Pinion bearing must be adjusted for pre-load before assembly is installed in carrier.

Do not install oil seal until after adjustment is made. Installation of seal would produce false rotating torque.

Cage Type

1. With pinion bearings, and adjusting spacers (or shims) installed in cage, check bearing contact by rotating cage.

2. Using a press, apply pressure (approx. 20,000 lbs.) to outer bearing.

3. Wrap soft wire around cage and pull on horizontal line with spring scale. Rotating (not starting) torque should be within limits recommended by manufacturer.

NOTE: Method of determining inch pounds torque with scale is to determine radius of cage. Multiply radius in inches by pounds pull required to rotate cage to determine inch-pounds torque. Example: An 8-inch diameter divided by 2 equals 4-inch radius. Multiply 4-inch (radius) by 5 pounds (pull) equals 20 inch pounds torque.

4. If press is not available, check preload torque by installing propeller shaft yoke, washer, and nut and torque to specifications; then check as previously explained. Remove yoke after correct adjustment is obtained.

BEVEL GEAR SHAFT BEARING ADJUSTMENT

Bevel gear shaft bearings must be adjusted for pre-load before pinion and cage assembly and differential assembly are installed in carrier.

1. Wrap several turns of soft wire around gear teeth on cross shaft, then pull on a horizontal line with spring scale. Rotating (not starting) torque should be used.

NOTE: Method of determining inch-pounds torque with scale is to determine radius. Multiply radius in inches by pounds pull required to rotate shaft to determine inch-pounds torque. Example: An 8-inch diameter divided by 2 equals 4-inch radius times 5 pounds (pull) equals 20 inch pounds torque.

2. Remove or add shims from under cage or cap opposite bevel gear to obtain specified bearing pre-load.

3. When making bevel gear and pinion tooth contact or backlash adjustments it is sometimes necessary to remove or add shims from one side.

NOTE: Always remove or add an equal thickness to the opposite side so to maintain correct pre-load.

GEAR TOOTH CONTACT AND BACKLASH

Pinion Depth Measurement Methods

Methods of adjusting pinions to obtain the proper depths will vary with the axle type and the manufacturers recommendations. Pinion depth settings and gear teeth contact may be determined by the use of pinion setting gauges or by the use of marking dye on the gear teeth.

When using the gauge method, backlash is established after the pinion has been properly set. With the dye method, backlash is obtained first, then the proper pinion tooth contact is established.

The pinion gauge method can be a direct reading micrometer, mounted on or through an arbor bar, set in adapter discs and located in the side carrier bearing cup locations on the differential housing and held in place by the bearing cup caps. The arbor bar coincides and represents the center line of the axle shafts. A reading is taken by the mounted micrometer, from the arbor bar to the head of the pinion to determine the need to add to or remove shims from the shim pack total, to adjust the pinion to the proper nominal assembly dimension or standard pinion depth.

Another method using the arbor bar and discs, is the use of a gauge block with a spring loaded plunger and a thumb screw to lock the plunger upon expansion. A micrometer is used to measure the gauge block after the plunger has been allowed to expand between the arbor bar and the pinion head. As in the mounted micrometer procedure, the shim pack thickness is determined by the reading obtained.

A third method is the use of a gauge block tool, installed in the housing in place of the pinion gear, and a large arbor bar placed in the axle housing differential bearing seats and tightened securely. A measurement is taken between the arbor bar and the pinion tool by either a feeler gauge or the use of individual shims

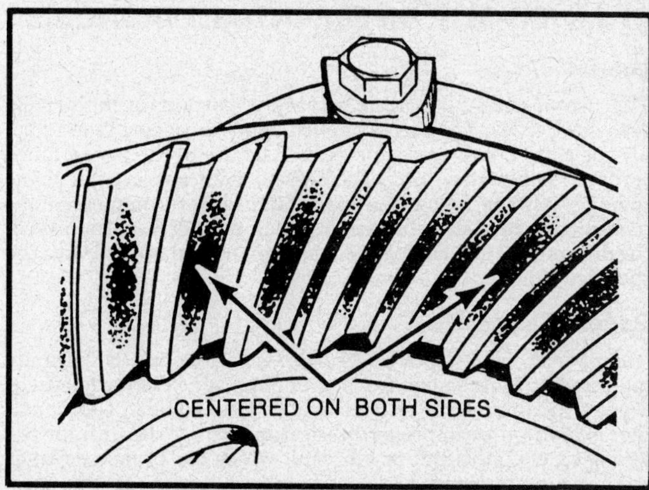

Gear tooth pattern showing load centered on gear tooth

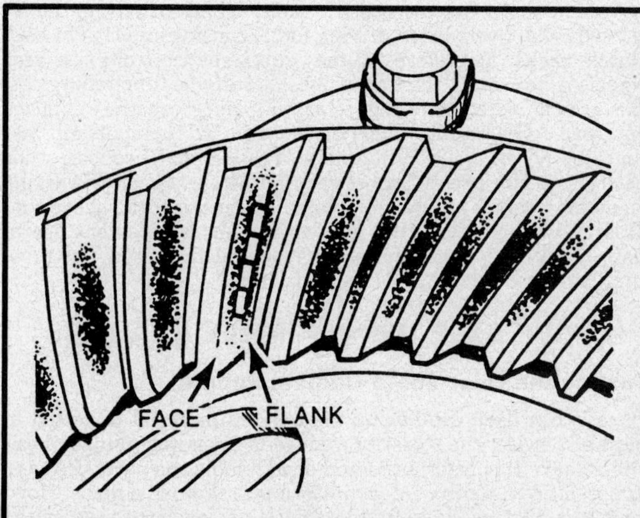

Gear tooth face and flank showing oval gear tooth contact pattern

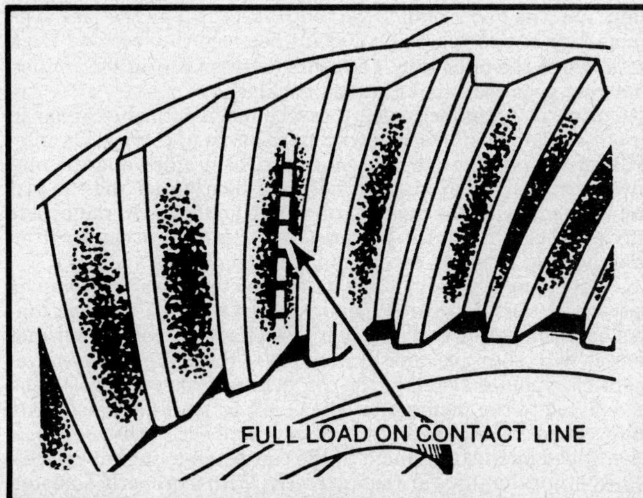

Gear tooth pattern showing load centered on gear tooth

from the shim pack. This measurement represents the shim pack needed for a zero marked pinion.

Setting New Pinion (Without Gauge)

Whenever a pinion setting gauge is not available, the approximate thickness of the pinion shim pack at the rear pinion bearing cup, change the sign of the marking (individual variation distance) on the *new* pin‹chion (plus to minus or minus to plus), then add the variation of the old pinion (sign unchanged) which will determine the amount the original shim pack must be changed when installing a new pinion.

On those types of axles where the shims are located between the pinion cage and differential carrier, change the sign of the marking (individual variation distance) on the *old* pinion (plus to minus or minus to plus), then add variation of the new pinion (sign unchanged) which will determine how much the original shim pack must be altered when installing a new pinion.

When the approximate thickness of shim pack has been determined, final check of gear tooth contact must be made using dye method.

Gear Tooth Contact (Dye)

Gear tooth contact cannot be successfully accomplished until pinion and bevel gear bearings are in proper adjustment and gear backlash is within specified limits.

Check for proper tooth contact by painting a few teeth of bevel gear with marking dye. Turn pinion in direction of normal rotation, then check tooth impression on bevel gear.

Gear Backlash

Gears that have been in extended service, form running contacts due to wear of teeth; therefore the original shim pack (between pinion cage and carrier) should be maintained when checking backlash. If backlash exceeds maximum tolerance, reduce backlash only in the amount that will avoid overlap of worn tooth section. Smoothness and roughness can be noted by rotating bevel gear.

If a slight overlap is present at worn tooth section, rotation will be rough.

If new gears are installed, check backlash with dial indicator.

Backlash is increased by moving bevel gear away from pinion, and may be decreased by moving bevel gear toward pin‹chion.

When the drive gear is attached to the differential, backlash is accomplished is differential bearing adjusting rings. It should be remembered that when one ring is tightened, the opposite ring must be loosened an equal amount to maintain previously established bearing adjustment.

On axles where the bevel gear is supported by cross shaft, backlash is accomplished by adding or removing shims under bearing cages.

Terms Used

Certain dimensions must be determined when using the pinion setting gauge:

1. *Nominal Assembly Dimension.* (standard pinion depth) This dimension (varying with axle model) is the distance between the center line of the drive gear (or differential carrier bore) and the end of the drive pinion. This dimension may be marked on the pin‹chion or listed on the Nominal Assembly Dimension and Adapter Disc chart.
2. *Individual Variation Distance,* (pinion depth variance) This dimension is a plus or minus variation of the *Nominal Assembly Dimension* on each individual pinion which may be caused by manufacturing variations.
3. *Corrected Nominal Dimension* (desired pinion depth) This dimension is the *Nominal Assembly Dimension* plus or minus the *Individual Variation Distance.*
4. *Corrected Micrometer Distance is the Corrected Nominal Dimension* less the thickness of the gauge set step plate (0.400 in.) mounted on end of pinion.

5. *Initial Micrometer Reading* is the dimension taken by micrometer to the gauge step plate.

6. *Shim Pack Correction* is determined by the difference between the *Corrected Micrometer Distance* and the *Initial Micrometer Reading,* and represents the amount of shim pack to be added or removed as later explained.

7. *Measured Pinion Depth.* This measurement is the distance between the axle center line and the top of the pin‹chion gear. If a step plate or other type gauge tool is used, this measurement is included in the total.

MARKINGS ON THE PINION AND DRIVE GEARS

Drive gears and pinions are tested at the time of manufacture to detect machining variances and to obtain desirable tooth contact and quietness. When the correct setting is achieved, the gears are considered matched and a set of numbers, along with other identifying marks are etched on the gear set.

A + (plus) or – (minus) sign is used, followed by a digit to represent the factory setting where the tooth contact and quietness were the best. This is called the *Pinion Depth Variance* or *Individual Variation Distance.*

If the pinion is marked +5 for example, this means the distance from the pinion gear rear face to the axle shaft center line is .005 in. more than the standard setting, and if the pinion gear is marked -5, this means that the distance is 0.005 in. less than the standard setting. To move the pinion to the standard setting, compensating for the variation, shims must be either added to subtracted from the total shim pack, located under the rear pinion bearing cup, between the pinion cage and the differential carrier, or under the rear pinion bearing, depending upon the differential model being serviced.

The procedures to follow in the adjustment of the pinion and drive gears are outlined in the respective differential model disassembly and assembly chapters.

As a rule of thumb on the addition or removal of shims for the pinion depth adjustment, draw a diagram as shown and determine which way the pinion must be moved to obtain the desired pinion depth.

STANDARD TORQUE SPECIFICATIONS AND CAPSCREW MARKINGS

Because of the varied bolt sizes used in the many models of differentials, the torque specifications are not always available to the technician for a specific bolt. By determining the grade of bolt, size, and thread, the proper torque limit can be found in the following chart.

Limited-Slip Differential Operation

Limited-slip differentials provide driving force to the wheel with the best traction before the other wheel begins to spin. This is accomplished through clutch plates or cones. The clutch plates or cones are located between the side gears and inner wall of the differential case. When they are squeezed together through spring tension and outward force from the side gears, three reactions occur. Resistance on the side gears causes more torque to be exerted on the clutch packs or clutch cones. Rapid one-wheel spin cannot occur, because the side gear is forced to turn at the same speed as the case. Most important, with the side gear and the differential case turning at the same speed, the other wheel is forced to rotate in the same direction and at the same speed as the differential case. Thus driving force is applied to the wheel with the better traction.

LIMITED-SLIP DIFFERENTIAL DIAGNOSIS

Lubrication

The use of proper lubricant is very important in limited-slip type drive axles. The forces applied when cornering tend to apply the clutch pack or clutch cones. The use of the wrong lubricant can cause the clutch surfaces to grab and chatter while turning. Always follow the manufacturer's recommendations regarding drive axle lubrication. When chatter is encountered, the differential lubricant should be drained and refilled with the specified lubricant.

General Diagnosis

Improper operation of a limited-slip type rear axle is generally indicated by clutch slippage or grabbing, which will sometimes produce a whirring or chatter sound. Occasionally, this condition is induced by improper lubrication. Check the unit for the wrong type of lubricant or lubricant which has broken down or become contaminated. Replace the lubricant with the type specified by the manufacturer.

During normal operation, i.e., straight-ahead driving, both wheels are rotating at equal speeds, and the driving force is distributed equally between both wheels. When cornering, the inside wheel delivers extra driving force, causing slippage in both clutch packs. Therefore, if the wheel rotation of both rear wheels is not equal, the unit will constantly be functioning as if the vehicle were cornering. This will cause constant slippage and lead to eventual failure of the unit. It is important that there be no excessive differences in wheel and tire size, wear pattern, or tire pressures between both rear wheels. Swerving on acceleration is an indication of one or more of the above conditions. Before attempting an overhaul or replacement operation, check both rear wheels for identical tire sizes, tire pressure, tire tread depth, and wear pattern.

DRIVE AXLE DISASSEMBLY ANALYSIS

Testing the Gear Tooth Contact Pattern

Once it has been established that the differential is indeed in need of service, the worst procedure is to simply plunge ahead and remove the differential and disassemble the parts. Prior to disassembly, a tooth contact pattern test should be made. However, it is worthwhile to first know the nomenclature associated with hypoid gear teeth.

The thick end of the tooth is called the heel and the thin end of the tooth is called the toe. The base half of the tooth is called the flank and the other end of the tooth is known as the face. The imaginary line at the halfway point between the face and flank is known as the pitch line. The space between the meshed pinion and ring gear tooth is known as backlash.

A gear tooth contact pattern can be made with the carrier in or out of the housing depending on the type of carrier. On integral carrier models, the lubricant must be drained and the rear cover removed. The ring gear will now be exposed and the test can be made with the carrier still in the housing. On removable carrier models, drain the lubricant and remove the carrier from the housing. The test can be made on the bench.

Unlike simple spur gears, hypoid gear teeth leave a complex pattern on the ring gear. When hypoid gears turn, the line contact between pinion and ring gear teeth has the same wiping motion as with spur gear teeth. Because of the complicated movement of hypoid gear teeth, the contact area takes an oval shape as opposed to the rectangular shape left by spur gear teeth. Actually, the tooth contact test shows where each gear tooth has been wiped by the movement of the contact line, so that you can tell whether the gears are set correctly. With a properly adjusted ring and pinion (with properly adjusted pinion depth and backlash) the tooth contact will be close to center. In this case, the load is borne by the strongest part of the tooth. If the gear set-

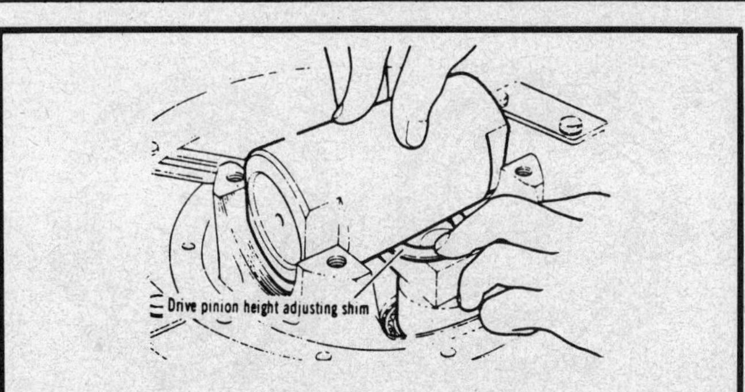

Select drive pinion height adjusting shims

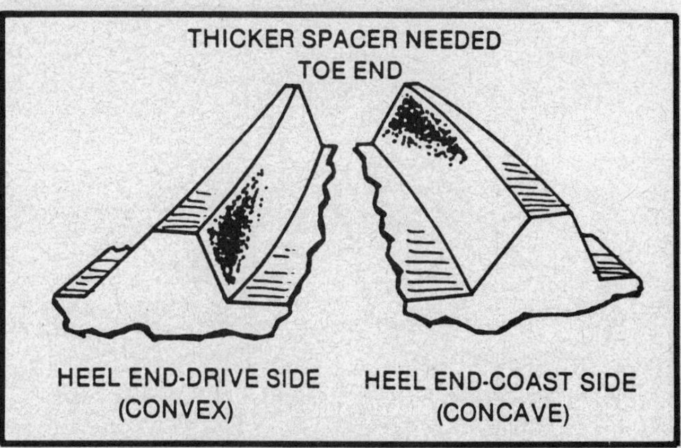

Tooth contact patterns high on the tooth side

ting is off, the contact line may reach any part of the edge of a tooth, and the metal will be overloaded at that point. When overload occurs, rapid deterioration of the gears will follow.

PREPARING THE TEST

Coat the drive gear teeth with a metallic base artists' oil color such as zinc white or titanium white. The tooth coating material must be smooth and firm enough to spread without running. A consistency somewhat like toothpaste works well. If it is necessary to thicken the material, add a small amount of cup grease.

NOTE: Prussian blue dye does not work well, since the blue tends to smear the pattern.

Thoroughly clean the ring gear and pinion before applying the testing material. Any gear lube left on the teeth will make the pattern quite unreadable. Coat the drive and coast sides of all the ring gear teeth, but leave the pinion gear teeth clean. Do not apply the coating too thickly as the pattern will be smeared.

Because the axle gears are normally easy to rotate, turning resistance must be applied to produce pressure between the pinion and ring gear teeth to make a legible pattern. On a removable carrier type axle, insert a suitable pry bar between the carrier housing and the differential case rim. Apply the load squarely against the case rim while prying out against the upper or lower section of the carrier housing. On integral carrier models, apply the parking brake to a point where it requires approximately 50 ft.lbs. to turn the pinion with a torque wrench. Since the shape and position of the contact pattern will vary, depending on the load, try to use the same load for each test or the results can be misleading. This is especially true when testing after an overhaul.

Once the gears have a load applied, obtain a tooth contact pattern by rotating the ring gear and pinion one complete turn in each direction. This will produce a constant pattern on the coast and drive side of each tooth. Do not rotate the ring gear more than one revolution in each direction as this will tend to obscure the pattern.

NOTE: If the pattern does not look right on the first try, try again.

Making a good gear tooth test takes a little practice; so if it is not right, try again.

INTERPRETING GEAR TOOTH CONTACT PATTERNS

The tooth contact pattern should be the same on every tooth. If the pattern shows heavy and light areas on different teeth, check the ring gear and differential case for excessive run-out.

NOTE: Run-out can be cured in many cases by removing the ring gear from the case, rotating it 90° or 180°, and remounting it.

Since you can only apply test load pressure to the gears, the contact pattern will be less distinct toward the tooth ends. But, when the ring gear and pinion are under operating loads in the vehicle, the tooth contact area spreads out, especially towards the heel end of the tooth. For this reason, do not try to "get by" with a tooth contact pattern that is centered, but favors the heel end of the teeth. This will only lead to overloading at the heel ends of the gear teeth. On the other hand, a contact pattern which is reasonably centered, but favors the toe end of the teeth, is acceptable.

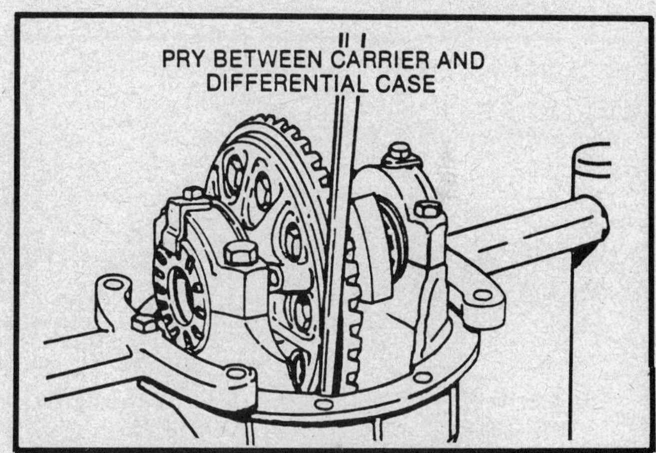

Applying a load to the differential case

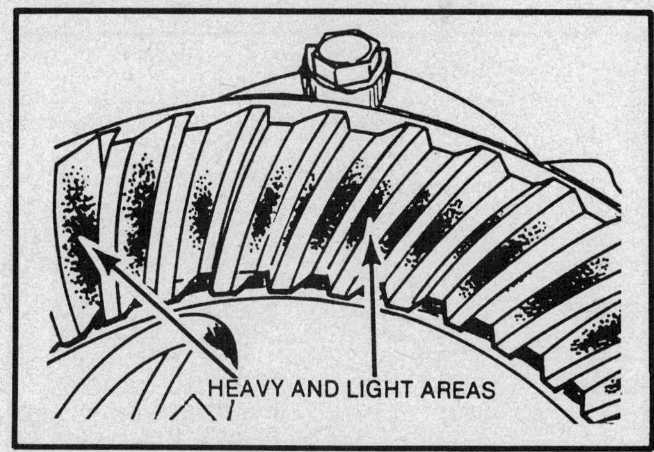

Excessive run-out will cause an uneven pattern

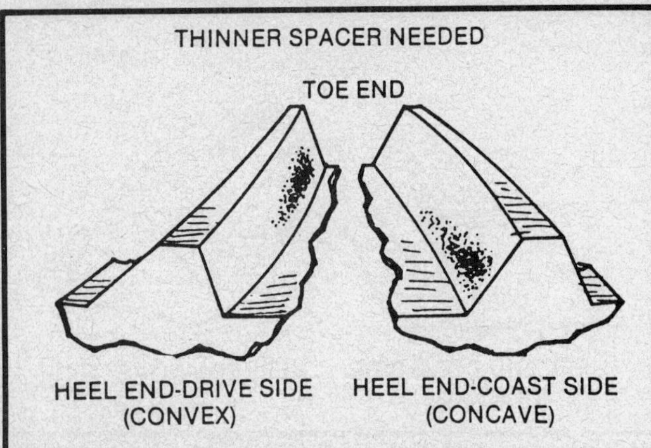

Gear contact pattern low on tooth side

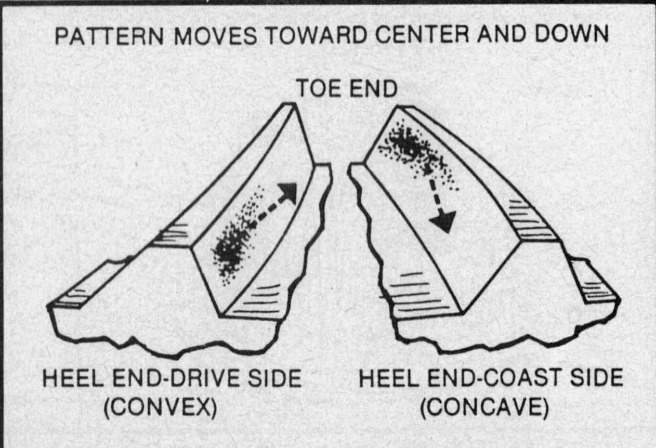

A thicker spacer moves the pattern in and down

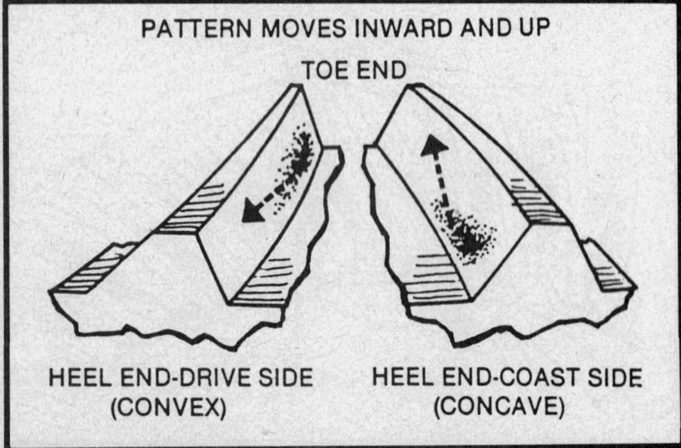

A thinner spacer will move the pattern up and inward

Assuming that the tooth contact pattern is even on all teeth, the main problems is to get the most distinct part of the pattern centered on both the teeth. The contact patterns should be nearly opposite each other on both sides of each tooth. In some cases, the pattern will be centered on the drive side and off center on the coast side, or vice versa. The off center pattern can be moved to a more acceptable position by slightly altering the backlash.

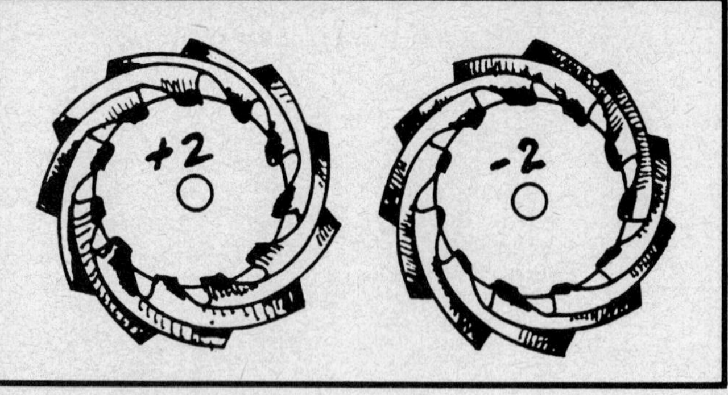

One example of pinion markings

This procedure will not seriously affect the other pattern. More often, however, the pattern will be off center on both sides of the teeth. The basic cause of this condition is an improperly adjusted pinion.

ADJUSTING PINION DEPTH

It is necessary to understand that an incorrect pinion depth setting moves the contact pattern away from the center on both sides of the tooth in opposite directions. This means that when you install a thicker or thinner washer under the pinion head you bring the pattern into the center of the tooth from opposite ends.

When the contact pattern is high on the heel end of the drive side and low on the toe end of the coast side, a thicker washer is needed to bring the pinion in, toward the center of the drive gear. Increasing the thickness of the spacer washer will bring the pattern in, toward the center of the drive gear teeth, and also will move the pattern down from the tooth face. However, this movement is less than the in-or-out movement.

When tooth contact is low on the toe end of the drive side and high on the heel end of the coast side, the pinion must be moved out, by installing a thinner washer under the pinion head. This will move the pattern inward toward the center, and will also result in slight movement of the pattern up from the tooth flank.

A factory service facility will use special tools and gauge blocks to determine the thickness of the spacer under the pinion head. In the absence of such specialized equipment, the following procedure may be used. Bear in mind that with the "hit-or-miss" method, each time you are wrong with the pinion depth, the unit must be disassembled, the spacer thickness changed, and the unit must be completely set up again.

Gather a handful of spacers to cover any thickness and several collapsible pinion spacers (if the unit uses them). Assemble the unit. If the original gear set is being reused, and the tooth contact pattern is reasonably correct, install a new spacer of the same thickness as the old one. This will provide a reasonable starting point. If the gear contact pattern test indicates a need for movement of the pinion, use a new spacer 0.001–0.002 in. thicker or thinner, depending on the direction the pinion must go. If a new gear set is being used, the thickness of the spacer will have to be determined in the following manner. Compare the markings on the old and new pinion. It will usually be marked with a number preceded by a plus (+) or minus (–) sign. This number indicates the production deviation from the nominal pinion, which are known as "zero pinions." In service, zero pinions are rare. Assume that the old pinion is marked with a plus two (+2). Assume that the new pinion is marked with a +3. By comparing the pinion markings, find the numerical difference between the two pinions, in this case +1. With a micrometer, measure the thickness of the original spacer. We will assume that the older spacer is 0.030 in. thick. If the numerical difference between pinions is a positive number (+1) the spacer should be 0.001 in. thinner than the original spacer, or 0.029 in.

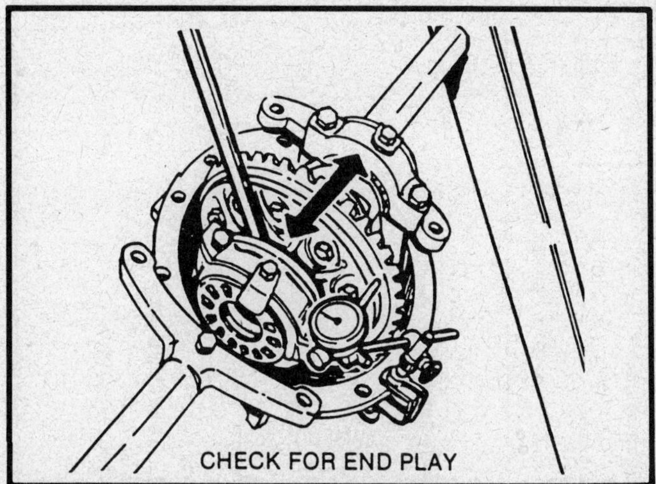

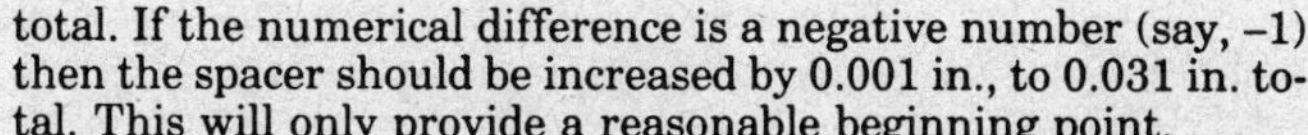

Checking differential bearing end-play

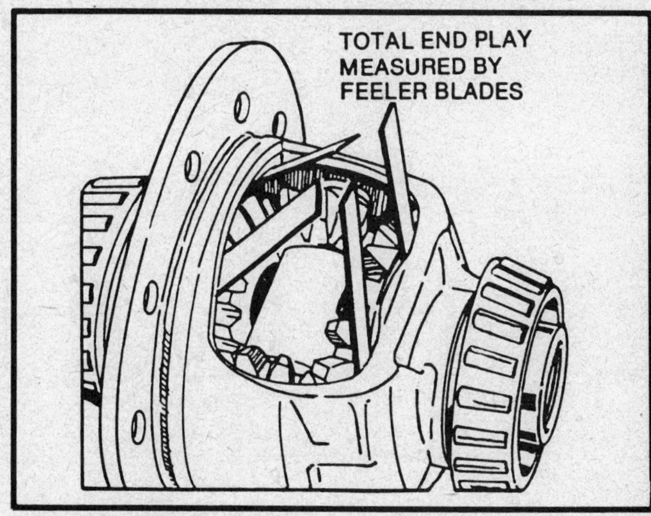

Checking total differential end-play

total. If the numerical difference is a negative number (say, –1) then the spacer should be increased by 0.001 in., to 0.031 in. total. This will only provide a reasonable beginning point.

It is rare that this method works out the first time. Assemble the pinion, differential, and ring gear with the spacer of calculated thickness. The side bearing preload, backlash, pinion nut torque, and pinion rotating torque must all be set correctly. Obtain a gear tooth pattern on the ring gear teeth and analyze the results. Small deviations from the acceptable pattern can usually be made by varying the backlash within the limits of specifications. If the gear tooth contact pattern is off, the unit must be disassembled and another spacer installed. This spacer must be of suitable thickness to compensate for the contact pattern test.

NOTE: Without special tools, there is absolutely no way of determining exactly how much to increase or decrease the thickness of the pinion shim; it must be estimated.

After estimating the thickness of the new shim, assemble the unit again, setting all preloads and backlash. Check the contact pattern again and act accordingly. If the unit uses a collapsible spacer, be sure a new one is installed each time it is disassembled. Crushed spacers can not be used again. It is well to note that the unit may have to be assembled and disassembled several times before an acceptable contact pattern is obtained.

Adjusting Backlash

The tooth contact pattern can be altered slightly, by varying the backlash adjustment within the limits of the specifications. The backlash adjustment can be used to alter a pattern which is slightly off center on either side of the tooth, but should not be used as a substitute for pinion depth adjustment. This adjustment must always be made after the pinion depth has been adjusted.

Nissan

Model H190

Pre-Disassembly Inspection

1. Check backlash of ring gear with a dial indicator at several points. If it is not within specification, 0.0059–0.0079 in., adjust as needed.
2. Check runout of ring gear with a dial indicator. If it is over specification (0.0031 in.), hypoid gear set or differential case should be replaced.

NOTE: When backlash varies excessively in different places, the variance may have resulted from foreign matter caught between ring gear and differential case.

3. Check tooth contact.
4. Check backlash of side gear. Using a thickness gauge, measure clearance between side gear and differential case. If it is not within specification, adjust it by selecting side gear thrust washer .0305–.0364 in.

TOOTH CONTACT

Gear tooth contact pattern check is necessary to verify correct relationship between ring gear and drive pinion.

Hypoid gear set which are not positioned properly may be noisy, or have short life or both. With a pattern check, the most desirable contact for low noise level and long life can be assured.

1. Thoroughly clean ring gear and drive pinion teeth.
2. Sparingly apply a mixture of powdered ferric oxide and oil or equivalent to 3 or 4 teeth of ring gear drive side.
3. Hold companion flange steady by hand and rotate the ring gear in both directions.

Disassembly

1. Put match marks on one side of side bearing cap with paint or punch to ensure that it is replaced in proper position during reassembly.

NOTE: Bearing caps are line-bored during manufacture and should be put back in their original places.

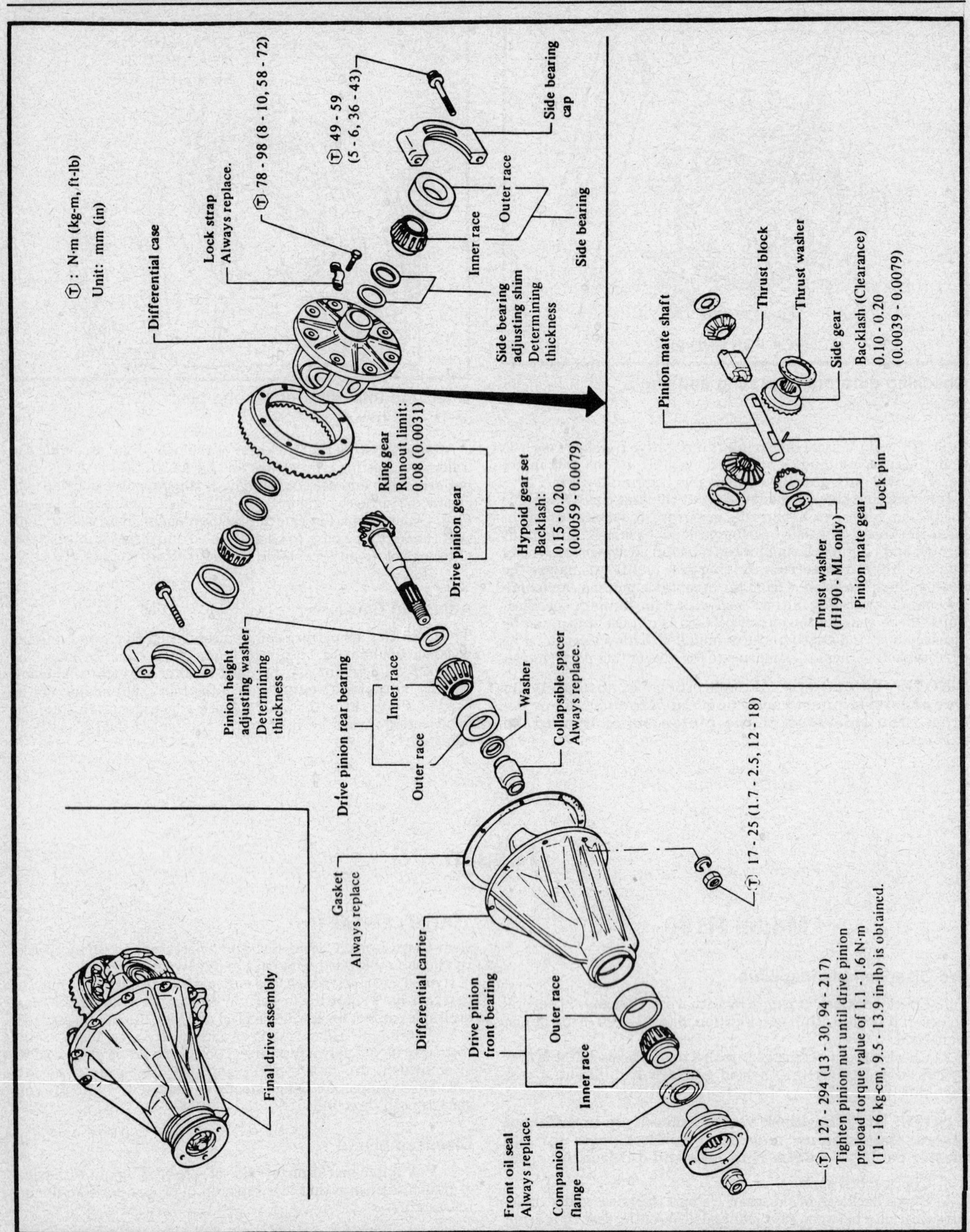
Ⓣ : N·m (kg-m, ft-lb)
Unit: mm (in)
Differential case
Lock strap
Always replace.
Ⓣ 78 - 98 (8 - 10, 58 - 72)
Ⓣ 49 - 59
(5 - 6, 36 - 43)
Side bearing cap
Outer race
Inner race
Side bearing
Side bearing adjusting shim
Determining thickness
Thrust block
Thrust washer
Pinion mate shaft
Side gear
Backlash (Clearance)
0.10 - 0.20
(0.0039 - 0.0079)
Lock pin
Pinion mate gear
Thrust washer
(H190 - ML only)
Ring gear
Runout limit:
0.08 (0.0031)
Hypoid gear set
Backlash:
0.15 - 0.20
(0.0059 - 0.0079)
Drive pinion gear
Pinion height adjusting washer
Determining thickness
Drive pinion rear bearing
Inner race
Outer race
Washer
Collapsible spacer
Always replace.
Ⓣ 17 - 25 (1.7 - 2.5, 12 - 18)
Gasket
Always replace
Differential carrier
Drive pinion front bearing
Outer race
Inner race
Front oil seal
Always replace.
Companion flange
Final drive assembly
Ⓣ 127 - 294 (13 - 30, 94 - 217)
Tighten pinion nut until drive pinion preload torque value of 1.1 - 1.6 N·m (11 - 16 kg-cm, 9.5 - 13.9 in-lb) is obtained.

Differential carrier—Model H190-ML, H190A

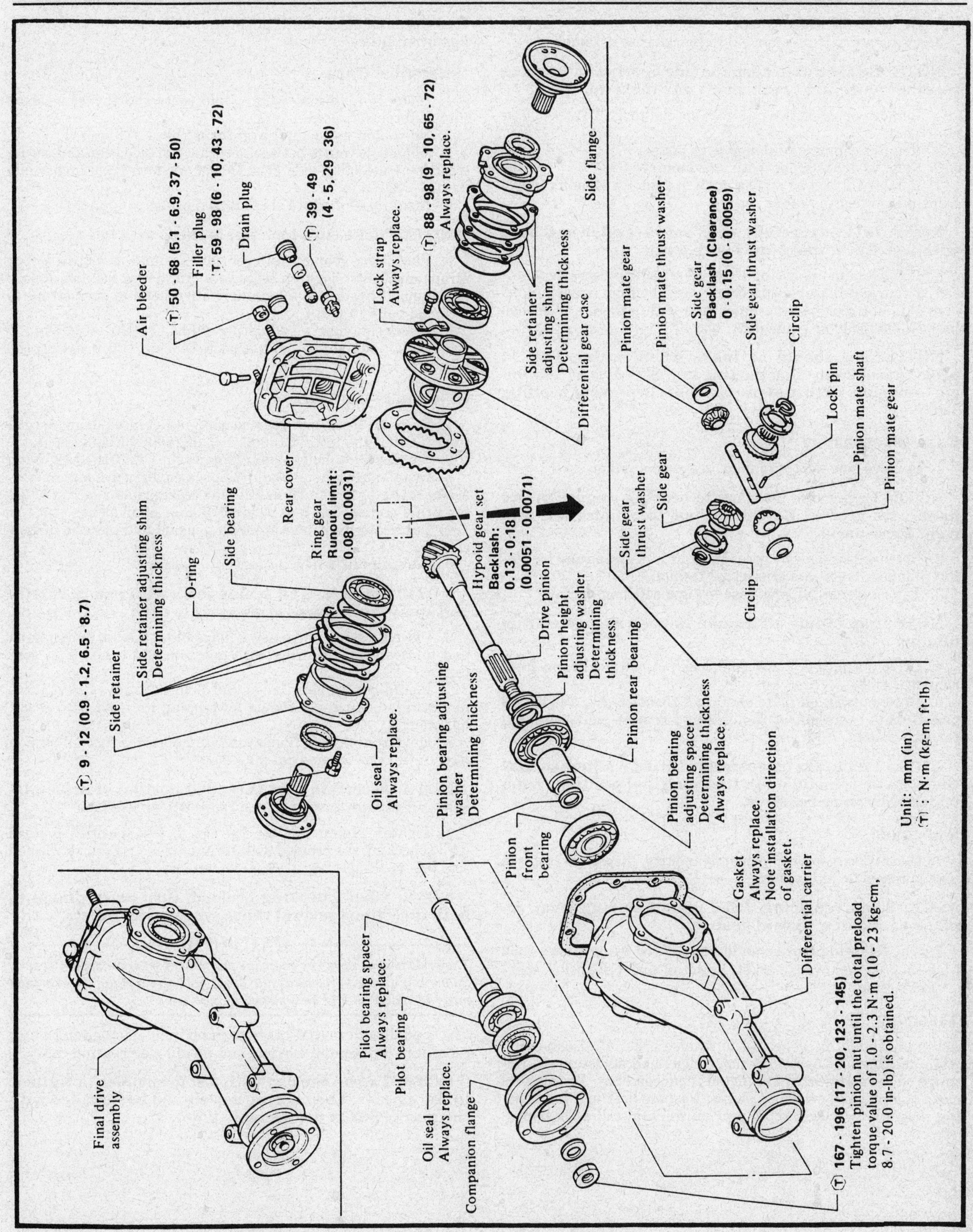
(T) 9 - 12 (0.9 - 1.2, 6.5 - 8.7)
Side retainer
Side retainer adjusting shim
Determining thickness
O-ring
Side bearing
Rear cover
Ring gear
Runout limit:
0.08 (0.0031)
Air bleeder
(T) 50 - 68 (5.1 - 6.9, 37 - 50)
Filler plug
(T) 59 - 98 (6 - 10, 43 - 72)
Drain plug
(T) 39 - 49
(4 - 5, 29 - 36)
Lock strap
Always replace.
(T) 88 - 98 (9 - 10, 65 - 72)
Always replace.
Side flange
Side retainer
adjusting shim
Determining thickness
Differential gear case
Pinion mate gear
Pinion mate thrust washer
Side gear
Backlash (Clearance)
0 - 0.15 (0 - 0.0059)
Side gear thrust washer
Circlip
Lock pin
Pinion mate shaft
Pinion mate gear
Side gear
thrust washer
Side gear
Circlip
Hypoid gear set
Backlash:
0.13 - 0.18
(0.0051 - 0.0071)
Drive pinion
Pinion height
adjusting washer
Determining
thickness
Pinion rear bearing
Oil seal
Always replace.
Pinion bearing adjusting
washer
Determining thickness
Pinion
front
bearing
Pinion bearing
adjusting spacer
Determining thickness
Always replace.
Gasket
Always replace.
Note installation direction
of gasket.
Differential carrier
Unit: mm (in)
(T) : N·m (kg-m, ft-lb)
Final drive
assembly
Pilot bearing spacer
Always replace.
Pilot bearing
Oil seal
Always replace.
Companion flange
(T) 167 - 196 (17 - 20, 123 - 145)
Tighten pinion nut until the total preload
torque value of 1.0 - 2.3 N·m (10 - 23 kg-cm,
8.7 - 20.0 in-lb) is obtained.

Exploded view of a Datsun/Nissan R180 drive axle

2. Remove side bearing caps.
3. Using a pry bar, remove differential case assembly.

NOTE: Be careful to keep the side bearing outer races together with inner race, don't mix them up.

4. Remove drive pinion nut with special tool ST31530000 or equivalent.
5. Remove companion flange with puller.
6. Remove drive pinion with soft hammer.
7. Remove oil seal by prying up with a large awl, and remove front pinion bearing inner race.

NOTE: Do this carefully so as not to scratch seal bore with awl. Cover end of awl with a rag.

8. Remove pinion bearing outer race using a brass drift.
9. Remove collapsible spacer and washer from drive pinion.
10. Pull out rear bearing inner race with a press and special tool ST30031000 or equivalent.

NOTE: Care should be taken when setting Tool in press to make sure that parting line of Tool is a right angle to support fixture of press. This is to prevent bending Tool.

Case Disassembly

1. Remove side bearing inner race with a puller.

NOTE: To prevent damage to bearing, engage puller paws with groove. Be careful not to confuse left and right hand parts.

2. Remove ring gear by spreading out lock straps and loosening ring gear bolts in a criss-cross fashion.
3. Tap ring gear off gear case using a soft hammer.

NOTE: Tap evenly all around to keep ring gear from binding.

4. Drive out pinion mate shaft lock pin, with drift pin from ring gear side.
5. Draw out pinion mate shaft and thrust block, and rotate pinion mate gears out of the case and remove side gears and thrust washers.

NOTE: Put marks on gears and thrust washers so that they can be reinstalled in their original positions from which they were removed.

Inspection

1. Clean disassembled parts completely. Repair or replace any damaged or faulty parts.

NOTE; When replacing drive pinion or ring gear, replace with a new hypoid gear set.

2. The following parts should be replaced by new ones each time they are removed. Gasket. Front oil seal. Collapsible spacer. Lock strap.

Assembly

Assembly should be done in the reverse order of disassembly, while making any necessary inspections and adjustments. Arrange shims and washers to install them correctly. Thoroughly clean the surfaces on which shims, washers bearings and bearing caps are installed. Apply gear oil when installing bearings. Pack recommended multi-purpose grease into cavity between lips when fitting oil seal.

Differential Case

1. Install pinion mate gears, side gears and thrust washers into differential case.
2. Fit pinion mate shaft and thrust block.
3. Adjust clearance between rear face of side gear and thrust washer by selecting side gear thrust washer. Clearance limits 0.0039–0.0079 in.
4. Install pinion mate shaft lock pin using a punch.

NOTE: Make sure lock pin is flush with case.

5. Place ring gear on differential case and install new lock straps and bolts. Tighten bolts in a criss-cross fashion, lightly tapping bolt head with a hammer. Then bend up lock straps to lock the bolts in place.
6. Select side bearing adjusting shims, 0.0020–0.0197 in.
7. Install the shims behind each bearing and press on the bearings, using a press.

Differential Carrier

1. Press fit front and rear bearing outer races using special tools ST3061100, ST30613000, ST30621000 or equivalent.
2. Select pinion height adjusting washer, 0.1016–0.1252 in.
3. Install pinion height adjusting washer in drive pinion, bevel side toward gear, and press fit rear bearing inner race in it, using press and special tool ST30901000 or equivalent.
4. Lubricate front bearing with gear oil and place it in gear carrier.
5. Carefully fit a new oil seal into carrier.

NOTE: Make sure oil seal is flush with end of carrier and apply multi-purpose grease into cavity between lips.

6. Place a washer and a new collapsible spacer on drive pinion and lubricate rear bearing with gear oil, and insert it in gear carrier.
7. Install companion flange and hold it firmly. Insert drive pinion into companion flange by tapping its head with a soft hammer.
8. Hold companion flange and temporarily tighten pinion nut, until there is no axial play.

NOTE: Ascertain that threaded portion of drive pinion and pinion nut are free from oil or grease.

9. Tighten pinion nut by degrees to the specified preload while checking the preload with torque wrench. Preload with oil seal 9.5–13.9 inch lbs.

NOTE: When checking preload, turn drive pinion in both directions several times set bearing rollers.

CAUTION

The preload is achieved by using the permanent set of collapsible spacer. So here, if an over-preload results from excessive turning of the pinion nut, the spacer should be replaced by new one.

10. Install differential case assembly and side bearing outer races into differential carrier, and install side bearing cap.

NOTE: Tap on the cap with a soft hammer to settle it in the carrier. The bearing cap should be installed with the marks put at disassembly aligned.

ISUZU

Removal

1. Raise and safely support the vehicle.
2. Remove both wheel covers, wheel and tire assemblies, and brake drums.
3. Disconnect brake pipes at both rear wheel cylinders. Cover ends of pipes to prevent entry of foreign material into system.
4. Remove four through bolts from each end-flange.
5. Disengage axle shafts from carrier assembly and partially withdraw shafts from axle tube. It is not necessary to completely remove axle shafts. Move only enough to allow the differential to be removed.
6. Disconnect the propeller shaft at the companion flange and remove propeller shaft.
7. Remove eight nuts and two bolts mounting the differential carrier and case assembly to the axle housing.
8. Remove the carrier and case assembly and take to bench. On some bench operations, it may be advantageous to use a holding fixture. Tool J–21533 or equivalent is an available tool that works well for this purpose.

DISASSEMBLY

NOTE: Before disassembling, make a pattern check of the ring gear and pinion.

1. Mark the side bearing caps for reinstallation in the same position.
2. Remove the nuts and bearing caps, then remove the differential case and ring gear assembly. Keep the right and left side bearing races in separate groups for reinstallation in same positions.
3. Remove the differential side bearings from the case by using puller J–22888 and plug J–8107–2 or equivalent. Carefully record the thickness of each side bearing and each shim pack removed for later use in reassembly and keep separated.

NOTE: Puller arms must not pull against roller cage. Use care to position legs against inner race. As bearing is being removed, check for free rotation of bearing. If bearing does not rotate freely, check position of puller legs.

4. Remove the ring gear bolts and separate the ring gear from the differential case.

NOTE: Use care when removing ring gear to prevent damage to differential case or ring gear. Do not force a chisel or other tools between the joining faces.

5. Drive out the pinion shaft lock pin with a long drift. It may be necessary to first remove caulking in the lock pin with a 5mm drill.
6. Remove the pinion shaft with a drift and take out the thrust block, pinion gears, side gears and thrust washers from the differential case.
7. Remove the pinion nut by use of Holder, J–8614–11 or equivalent. Save the pinion nut for pinion bearing preload adjustment procedure.
8. Remove companion flange by use of Nut J–8614–2, and

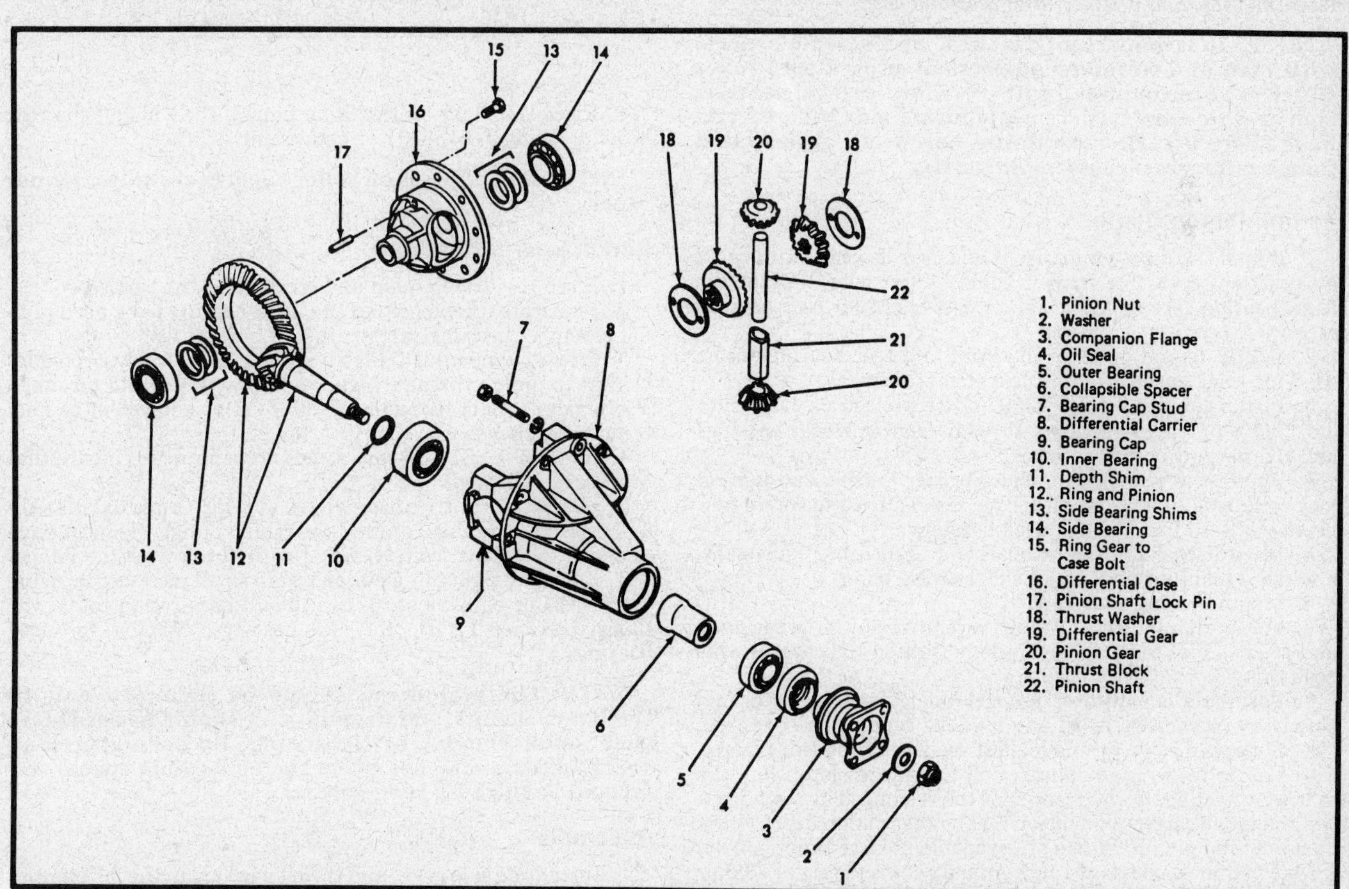

LUV/Isuzu rear axle assembly

Screw J-8614-3 or equivalent. Install nut onto screw; position nut into J-8614-11 or equivalent and rotate 45 degrees to locking position. Turn screw to draw companion flange off of the drive pinion splines.

9. Hold a soft metal rod against the end of the drive pinion. Drive the pinion from the carrier by using a hammer against the metal rod. The outer (front) bearing will fall loose in the carrier, while the inner (rear) bearing will remain pressed on the drive pinion. Both races will remain in the carrier bores.

10. Remove a rear bearing from the drive pinion by use of a press and tool J-22912-01 or equivalent.

11. Remove the oil seal and then drive the two outer races from the carrier by use of a drift.

Inspection

1. Wash the bearings in a suitable solvent. Then examine bearings carefully for wear, separation, cracks, seizure and other abnormal conditions. Replace bearings as necessary.

2. Check the ring gear and drive pinion teeth for wear, chipping, cracks, pitting, and abnormal contact. Check the drive pinion splines for cracks, distortion and step wear. Replace parts if needed. Ring gears and pinions come only in matched sets. If either item is defective, both parts must be replaced.

3. Check the pinion gears and side gears for wear, chipped teeth and separation, and replace if needed.

4. Check and replace the thrust blocks and thrust washers, if worn.

5. Check the lock pin for bending, dents and other abnormal conditions. Replace if necessary.

6. Check the side gear-to-axle shaft fit. Also check the fit of the pinion shaft to pinion gears.

7. Examine the contact surfaces between side gears and differential case, and between ring gear and case.

NOTE: It is important to clean and assemble parts with care and to follow adjustment procedures. Axles which are contaminated with dirt or other foreign material, or which are incorrectly adjusted may be noisy and have short life. Be sure to use new seals, gaskets and flange nuts when reassembling axle.

Setting Pinion Depth

1. Install the drive pinion front and rear bearing outer races into carrier bores. Use Drive Handle J-8092 with J-24256 for front bearing race and J-24252 or equivalent for rear bearing race.

2. Lubricate and position the front and rear bearings to be used for final assembly into their respective races.

3. Install gauging plate J-23597-7 and preload stud and pilot J-23597-9 or their equivalent through front and rear bearings and tighten nut snugly.

4. Rotate the bearings to insure proper seating and tighten lock nut until 20 inch lbs. of torque are required to rotate new bearings; 8-10 inch lbs. for used bearings.

5. Place discs J-23597-8 onto arbor J-23597-1 or equivalent, and place tool into position in side bearing bores.

6. Install bearing caps snugly.

7. Mount dial indicator J-8001 or equivalent on arbor post, and preload dial one-half revolution. Tighten indicator in this position.

8. Position the indicator plunger on the gauge plate, and slowly swing across until the highest reading is obtained. "Zero" the indicator on the highest reading of the gauge plate.

9. Carefully swing the plunger off the gauge plate. Note the indicator reading. Recheck to verify the reading. The reading on the dial is the correct dimension for the rear pinion depth shim, on a nominal pinion. Shims are available in sizes ranging from 2.18-2.56mm (0.086-0.101 in.). An indicator reading of .000 or 0.03mm (0.001 in.) requires shims of 2.54 and 2.57mm (0.100 and 0.101 in.), respectively.

10. Examine the head of the drive pinion. The pinion depth code is stamped by chemical ink and is in the lower position of the three numbers. The number indicates a necessary change in the pinion mounting distance. A plus number indicates the need for a greater mounting distance (which can be achieved by decreasing the shim thickness). A minus number indicates the need for a smaller mounting distance (which can be achieved by increasing the shim thickness). If examination reveals no pinion depth code, the pinion is "nominal". Use the chart to determine the proper shim variation to compensate for plus or minus markings.

Pinion Depth Code Number	Alter the Shim Thickness as Determined by Dial Indicator Reading, as Follows:
+10	Subtract 0.13 mm (.005")
+ 8	Subtract 0.10 mm (.004")
+ 6	Subtract 0.08 mm (.003")
+ 4	Subtract 0.05 mm (.002")
+ 2	Subtract 0.03 mm (.001")
0	Use Indicator Reading
− 2	Add 0.03 mm (.001")
− 4	Add 0.05 mm (.002")
− 6	Add 0.08 mm (.003")
− 8	Add 0.10 mm (.004")
−10	Add 0.13 mm (.005")

11. Place the shim on the drive pinion, then install the rear bearing, using J-6133-01 or equivalent.

NOTE: Do not press on roller cage. Press only on inner race.

Pinion Bearing Preload

1. Place the drive pinion and spacer into the carrier.

2. Lubricate, then position the front bearing to be used in final assembly into the carrier. Install new oil seal.

3. Mount companion flange to drive pinion. Apply hypoid lubricant to pinion threads. Install new pinion nut and torque to 115 N;pdm (85 lb. ft.), using J-8614-11 or equivalent to hold companion flange.

4. Remove J-8614-11 and rotate drive pinion to insure that bearings are seated.

5. Wind a small amount of string (approximately 4+ +-+ +6 windings) around the pinion flange. Connect scale to string. Note the scale reading required to rotate the flange.

6. Continue tightening pinion nut in small increments, using J-8614-11 or equivalent, until the pull required to rotate the flange becomes 17 lbs. for new bearings, 7-9 lbs. for used bearings.

NOTE: The pinion nut should be tightened only in small increments, and the pull scale should be used after each small amount of tightening. Exceeding preload specifications may compress the collapsible spacer too far and require its replacement.

Assembly

1. Install the side gears and thrust washers in the differential case.

2. Position the pinion gears 180 degrees apart. Roll gears into

position, making sure they are in alignment, to allow installation of the pinion shaft.

3. Place the thrust block between the pinion gears, and drive the pinion shaft into position. Make sure that the lock pin hole in cross shaft aligns with the hole in the case.

4. Measure the amount of backlash between the differential gears and the pinion gears. If the backlash is greater than 0.8mm (0.003 in.), make the necessary adjustment with the thrust washers, available in thicknesses of 1.04, 1.14, 1.24 and 1.35mm (0.041, 0.045, 0.049 and 0.053 in.). Increasing washer thickness will decrease backlash. Decreasing washer thickness will increase backlash.

5. Install lock pin into cross shaft and caulk its end to prevent loosening.

6. Clean and apply primer to the bolts. Apply Loctite or equivalent to the threaded portion of the bolts. Install the ring gear in position on the differential case. Tighten the bolts in diagonal sequence to 80–87 ft. lbs.

SIDE BEARING PRELOAD/INITIAL BACKLASH SETTING

If the original side bearings, differential case, ring and pinion, and differential carrier are being reused, and if the pattern check taken before removal showed proper tooth contact, the original shims (or new shims of the same dimension) may be reinstalled in their respective positions.

If new side bearings only are being installed, and if the pattern check taken before removal showed proper tooth contact, this alternate procedure of shim selection may be used: Measure the new bearing with a micrometer, and compare its thickness with the original bearing. If the new bearing is thicker, subtract the numerical difference between new and old bearing from the original shim pack. If the new bearing is thinner, add the numerical difference between old and new bearing to the original shim pack.

If new bearings and/or differential case, ring and pinion, or differential carrier are being installed, new shims will have to be selected for installation behind side bearings.

1. Install the side bearings to be used in final assembly onto the differential case. Do not install shims at this time. Use J-24244 or equivalent for the first bearing installation.

2. Support case on plug J-8107-2 or equivalent for opposite bearing installation.

3. Mount the case into carrier bores.

4. Move the ring gear tightly against the carrier on the ring gear side, away from the drive pinion, and hold in this position. Using a feeler gauge just thick enough to produce a slight drag, carefully measure the clearance between the bearing and differential carrier on the side opposite the ring gear. Record the result.

5. To determine the proper shims for installation, use the following procedure: A predetermined dimension of 0.05mm (0.002 in.) is always needed to establish proper preload. Therefore, add 0.05mm (0.002 in.) (for proper preload) to the clearance measured in Step 4. This will give the necessary combined total thickness of both shim packs. For example, if the measure clearance was 1.12mm (0.044 in.), the combined shims packs would be 1.12 + 0.05 = 1.17mm (0.044 + 0.002 = 0.046 in.). Divide the total dimension into two shim packs, so that the numerical difference between the packs equals the numerical difference between the original shim packs. For example, if the original packs measured 1.02 and 0.41mm (0.040 and 0.016 in.), the difference between them was 1.02 – 0.41 = 0.61mm (0.040 – 0.016 = 0.024 in.). If the new combined shim packs are to total 1.17mm (0.046 in.), the individual shim packs would measure 0.89 and 0.28mm (0.035 and 0.011 in.). The difference between 0.89 and 0.28mm (0.035 and 0.011 in.), is 0.61mm (0.024 in.); the same numerical difference as between the original packs.

6. Remove the case from the carrier. Carefully remove both side bearings. Install shims as determined in Step 5 behind each bearing, install bearings onto case.

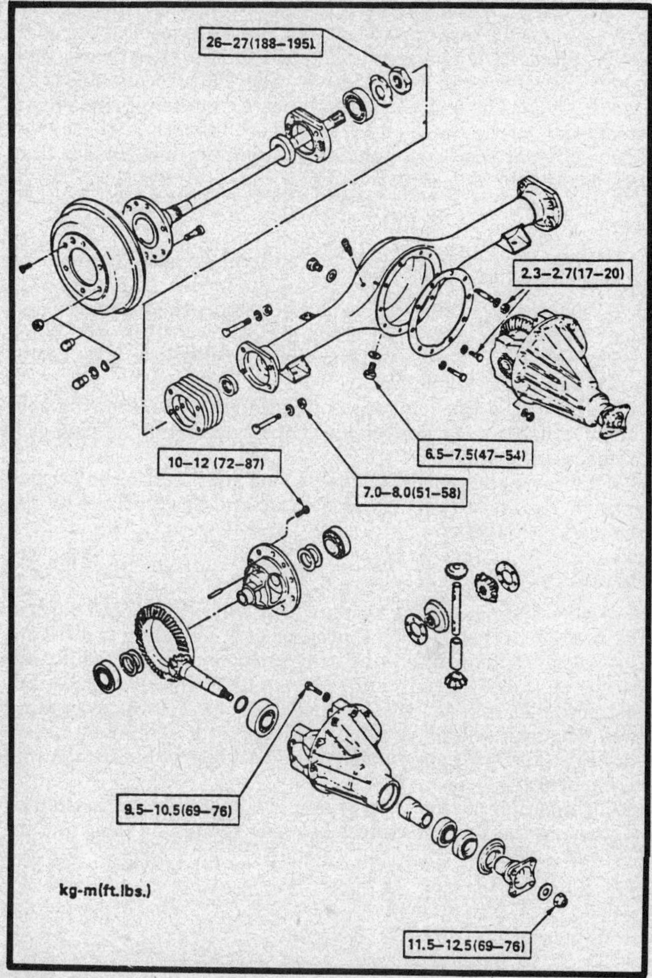

Isuzu/LUV drive axle torque specifications

7. Install case onto carrier, tapping carefully into place. Install side bearing caps in original position. Tighten to 75 ft. lbs.

8. Measure the run-out of the ring gear. If the run-out exceeds 0.05mm (0.002 in.), correct by cleaning or replacement of parts.

9. Mount a dial indicator against the ring gear teeth. Make sure indicator button is perpendicular to tooth travel. Measure backlash in three locations. Backlash should be 0.13–0.18mm (0.005–0.007 in.).

10. If backlash is not within limits, the shims behind each side bearing will have to be adjusted. In order to maintain proper preload, whenever the backlash is adjusted, the total thickness of both shim packs must not be changed. Therefore, if it is necessary to increase one shim pack, the opposite shim pack must be decreased the same amount.

11. To increase backlash, the right side bearing shim must be increased, and the left side decreased.

12. To decrease backlash, the right side shim must be decreased, while the left side is increased. Backlash changes approximately 0.05mm (0.002 in.) for each 0.08mm (0.003 in.) shim change.

Gear Tooth Pattern Check

Prior to final assembly of the differential, a Gear Tooth Contact Pattern Check is necessary to verify the correct relationship between ring gear and drive pinion. Gear sets which are not positioned properly may be noisy, or have short life, or both. With a pattern check, the most desirable contact between ring gear and drive pinion for low noise level and long life can be assured.

The side of the ring gear tooth which curves outward, or is convex, is referred to as the "drive" side. The concave side is the "coast" side. The end of the tooth nearest center of ring gear is referred to as the "toe" end. The end of the tooth farthest away from center is the "heel" end. Toe end of tooth is smaller than heel end.

Test

1. Wipe oil out of carrier and carefully clean each tooth of ring gear.
2. Use gear marking compound and apply this mixture sparingly to all ring gear teeth using a medium stiff brush. When properly used, the area of pinion tooth contact will be visible when hand load is applied.
3. Hand load the companion flange and rotate the ring gear one revolution in each direction. Excessive turning of ring gear is not recommended.
4. Observe the pattern made on ring gear teeth. The contact pattern should be centrally located up and down on the face of the ring gear teeth.

Adjustments

Two adjustments can be made which will affect tooth contact pattern: (1) backlash, and (2) position of drive pinion in differential carrier. The effects of bearing preloads are not readily apparent on (hand loaded) tooth pattern tests; however, these adjustments should be within specifications before proceeding with backlash and drive pinion adjustments. It may be necessary to adjust both pinion depth and backlash to obtain the correct pattern.

The position of the drive pinion is adjusted by increasing or decreasing the shim thickness between the pinion head and inner race of rear bearing. The shim is used in the differential to compensate for manufacturing tolerances. Increasing shim thickness will move the pinion closer to centerline of the ring gear. Decreasing shim thickness will move pinion farther away from centerline of the ring gear.

Backlash is adjusted by means of the side bearing adjusting shims which moves the entire case and ring gear assembly closer to, or farther from the drive pinion. (The adjusting shims are also used to set side bearing preload.) To increase backlash, increase right shim and decrease left shim an equal amount. To decrease backlash, decrease right shim and increase left shim an equal amount.

Installation

1. Clean the faces of the rear axle case and differential carrier and apply a thin coat of liquid gasket and install the gasket.
2. Mount the differential case and carrier assembly to the rear axle case and tighten the nuts to 24 N;pdm (18 lb. ft.).
3. Install the axle shaft assemblies.
4. Connect the companion flange with the propeller shaft and tighten the bolts to 18 ft. lbs.

NOTE: This propeller shaft to pinion flange fastener is an important attaching part in that it could affect the perform‹chance of vital components and systems, and/or could result in major repair expense. It must be replaced with one of the same part number or with an equivalent part if replacement becomes necessary. Do not use a replacement part of lesser quality or substitute design. Torque values must be used as specified during reassembly to assure proper retention of this part.

5. Fill the rear axle case with hypoid gear lubricant, to just below the filler hole.

MAZDA

Inspection

An inspection of the adjustments and parts as the carrier is disassembled can assist in learning the cause of the trouble and in determining what corrections are needed.

Mount the carrier in a holding fixture. Wipe the lubricant from the internal working parts and visually inspect them for damage. Rotate the gears to see if there is any roughness which could indicate worn or damaged bearings or chipped gears. Look carefully at the surface of the gear teeth for any scoring, flaking, or signs of abnormal wear.

Mark the ring gear at four points at approx. 90° intervals and mount a dial indicator to the carrier flange. Check to see that the backlash at one of the marked points is 0–0.008 in. or for 1986 models 0–0.004 in. Also check the backlashes at other three marked points and make sure that the difference between the maximum and minimum backlashes is less than 0.0028 in.

If no obvious misadjustment or damage is noted, inspect the gear tooth contact. Coat the gear teeth with special compound available, or red lead. Too fluid a mixture will run and smear. Too dry a mixture cannot be squeezed out from between the teeth. Rotate the ring gear back and forth (use a box wrench on the ring gear attaching bolts for a lever), until a clean tooth contact pattern is obtained.

Certain types of gear tooth contact patterns on the ring gear indicate incorrect adjustment. A noise condition caused by incorrect adjustment can often be corrected by readjusting the gears. Gear tooth runout can be detected by an erratic pattern on the teeth. If ring gear runout is suspected, mount a dial indicator to measure the runout of the back face of the ring gear.

Servicing

1. Remove the carrier from the differential.
2. Mount the carrier in a holding fixture.
3. Apply identification punch marks on the carrier, the differential bearing cap and the adjusters for accurate reassembly.
4. Remove the adjuster lock plates.
5. Loosen the bolts securing the bearing cap and slowly back off the adjuster slightly to relieve the preload.
6. Remove the nuts, bearing caps and adjusters. Keep each bearing cap with its own adjuster.
7. Lift out the differential assembly and keep each bearing outer race with its own bearing.
8. If the differential bearings are to be replaced, remove them using a puller.
9. Remove the bolts and washers retaining the ring gear to the case.
10. Remove the ring gear.
11. Position the assembly in a vise and remove the lock pin with a suitable punch.
12. Remove the pinion shaft and the thrust block.
13. Rotate the differential pinion gears 90 degrees and remove.
14. Remove the differential side gears and thrust washers.
15. Using a holding tool, steady the companion flange and remove the nut.

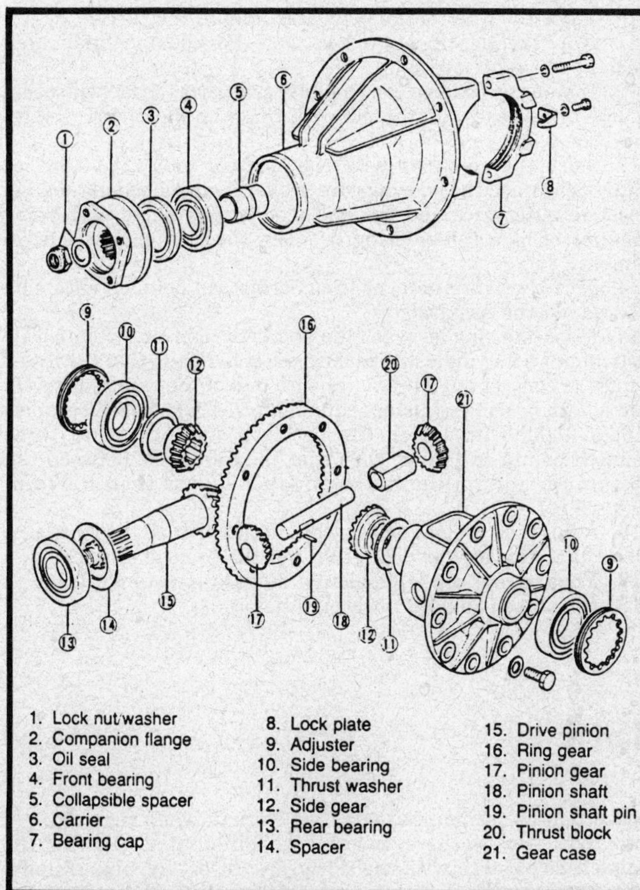

Mazda rear axle assembly

16. Remove the companion flange.
17. Remove the drive pinion and rear bearing from the carrier, which may require tapping with a plastic or rubber mallet. Guide the pinion to avoid damage to the teeth.
18. Remove the oil seal and the front bearing.
19. The pinion bearing outer races (cups) can be removed from the carrier by using a drift in the slots provided for the purpose.
20. Remove the bearing from the pinion using suitable equipment.
21. With the carrier completely apart, check the drive pinion for damaged or worn teeth, damaged bearing journals or splines. Inspect the ring gear again for worn or chipped teeth. If any of the above conditions are found, replace both drive pinion and ring gear as these are only available in sets.
22. Before reassembly of the carrier, inspect bearing cones and cups and replace any showing wear, flaking or damage. Replace only in sets.

NOTE: Do not use an old cup with a new bearing or an old bearing with a new cup. If this is done, damage will result.

23. Check the companion flange carefully for cracks or worn splines. If either exist, the part should be replaced. Check for rough or scratched oil seal contact surface. If only slight scratches appear, it may be possible to repair with crocus cloth. Otherwise, replace it. Be sure to use a new oil seal when reassembling the carrier. Reassemble the components in the reverse order.

Pinion Depth

If you use the same pinion and ring gear, the shim combination found on the pinion may prove satisfactory provided other things are equal.

Individual differences in machining the carrier casting and the gear set require a shim or shims between the pinion rear bearing and the pinion gear to locate the pinion for correct tooth contact with the ring gear.

NOTE: Special tools are required to check and adjust the pinion depth, these include a drive pinion model (49 8531 565), a pinion height adjustment gauge body (49 0727 570) and a gauge block (40 0305 555) or their equivalents. The original factory installed spacers are of the correct thickness to adjust for individual variations in both the carrier casting dimension and in the original gear set dimension. To select the correct spacer thickness when installing a new gear set, follow these steps:

1. Fit the spacer, rear bearing and Collar B (49 8531 568) onto the drive pinion model. Secure the collar with an O-ring and install in the assembly in the carrier.
2. Attach the front bearing, Collar A (49 8351 567), companion flange, washer and nut to the drive pinion model. Use the same spacer and nut which were removed at disassembly. Be careful to install Collars A and B in their correct position facing in the correct direction.
3. Tighten the nut until the drive pinion model can be turned by hand without any apparant play.
4. Install a dial indicator on the pinion height adjustment gauge body. Place the gauge block on top of the drive pinion model and then set the pinion height adjustment gauge body on top of the gauge block.
5. Place the measuring probe of the dial indicator so that it contacts the location where the side bearing is installed in the carrier. Zero and set up the indicator to measure the lowest point. Measure both the left and right sides.
6. Add the two values (right and left side readings) and divide the total by 2. From this result, subtract the result obtained by dividing the number inscribed on the end surface of the drive pinion by 100. (If there is no figure inscribed, use 0). The resulting figure is the pinion height adjustment value.
7. For example, if the measured results obtained are 0.06mm and 0.04mm and the figure inscribed on the end of the drive pinion is -2 the following formula would be used. Thus a spacer which is 0.07mm thicker than the one now used is required. Select the spacer thickness that is closest to requirement.
8. Install the selected spacer on the pinion shaft (facing in the proper direction) and press the bearing on the pinion shaft.
9. Install the drive pinion, spacer, front bearing, collapsible spoacer and companion flange in the carrier (remove the measuring tools first) and temporarily tighten the locknut. DO NOT install the pinion seal at this time.
10. Adjust the pinion bearing preload at this time.
11. After preload measurements are taken install the pinion seal. Coat the drive flange and seal surface with "moly" grease. Install the flangeand a NEW locknut. Tighten the locknut to torque measurement taken when establishing the required preload.

Pinion Bearing Preload

1. Install the correctly "shimmed" pinion shaft in the carrier with the spacer, flange and nut but NO pinion seal.
2. Turn the flange by hand to seat the bearing.
3. Use a torque wrench to tighten the locknut. Tighten slowly until the required preload drag of 7.8–12.2 inch lbs. is reached with a locknut torque of 94–130 ft. lbs.
4. If the specified preload cannot be maintained within the locknut tightening range, install a new collapsible spacer and repeat the process.
5. Remove the locknut and flange. Install the pinion seal, flange and NEW locknut. Tighten the locknut to the ft. lb. torque giving the correct preload.

Differential Assembly

1. Install the thrust washer on each differential side gear and install these in the case.
2. Through the openings of the case, insert each of two pinion gears exactly 180 degrees opposite each other.
3. Rotate the gears 90 degrees so the pinion shaft holes of the case align with the holes in the two pinion gears.
4. Insert the pinion shaft through the case and pinion gears.
5. Check the backlash of the side gear and pinion gear. The backlash should not exceed 0.008 or 0.004 on 1986 models. If it exceeds this, adjustment can be made with the side gear thrust washers.
6. After adjustment, remove the pinion shaft and install the thrust block so the hole is centered between the differential pinion gears. Reinstall the pinion shaft into the case until the lock pin hole in the pinion shaft is in exact alignment with the hole in the case.
7. Install the lock pin to secure the pinion shaft. Stake the lock pin into position with a punch to prevent it from working out.
8. Install the ring gear on the case and tighten the bolts to the specification listed at the end of this Part.
9. Install each differential bearing to the case using T72J-4221 or equivalent by press or with a hammer. Install the outer races to their respective bearing.
10. Place the differential gear assembly in the carrier.
11. Note the identification marks on the adjusters and install each to its respective side.
12. Install the bearing caps making sure that the identification marks on the caps correspond with those on the carrier and install the bolts.
13. Turn the adjusters with the spanner tool T72J-4067 or equivalent until the bearings are properly positioned in their respective outer race and the end play is eliminated with some amount of backlash existing between the ring gear and drive pinion.
14. Slightly tighten one of the bearing cap bolts on each side and adjust the backlash.
15. Mark the ring gear at four points at approx. 90° intervals and mount a dial indicator to the carrier flange so that the feeler comes in contact at right angles with one of the ring gear teeth. Turn both bearing adjusters equally until the backlash becomes 0.0075–0.0083 in. Check the backlashes at the other three marked points and make sure that the difference between the maximum and minimum backlashes is less than 0.07mm (0.0028 in).
16. Adjust the preload taking care not to disturb the backlash. Use a dial indicator and carefully set the preload at 0.0045.
17. The bearing cap bolts should be tightened to 45 ft. lbs.
18. Install the adjuster lock plates.

MITSUBISHI

Overhaul

Differential overhaul requires many special tools and access to a range of preload shims and other dealer equipment. If you have never overhauled a rear axle assembly before, it would be wise to let a specialist perform this operation.

1. Remove the lock bolts and plates holding the side bearing nut in place.
2. Remove the side bearing nuts with the special adjusting spanner no. MB990201.
3. Remove the carrier caps and pry out the differential.
4. Pull off the differential side bearings.

NOTE: Be sure to keep the right and left bearings and shims separated.

5. Loosen the ring gear mounting bolts in diagonal sequence. Remove the ring gear.
6. Drive the pinion shaft lock pin out from the rear of the ring gear using a punch, and remove the pinion shaft.
7. Remove the side gears with their spacers. Keep left and right side gears and spacers separate.
8. Hold the end yoke and remove the pinion lock nut.
9. Remove the end yoke.
10. Tap the end of the drive pinion shaft with a plastic hammer and force out the drive pinion along with its adjusting shim, the rear inner race, the drive pinion spacer and the preload adjusting shim. The rear bearing inner race can be pressed off the pinion shaft.
11. Remove the front and rear pinion bearing outer races. The front race should be removed with its oil seal.

NOTE: Do not reuse the old oil seal. If the unit is to be assembled using no replacement parts except oil seals, the same spacers and shims can generally be used. If either pinion bearing or ring gear and drive pinion are being replaced, new shims should be used. Only replace the drive pinion and ring gear in matched sets.

12. Assemble the side gears in the differential case. Install the spacers in the same positions they were in when removed.
13. With the washers, insert both differential gears at the same time to mesh with the side gears. Insert the pinion shaft.
14. Measure the backlash of the differential pinion gears and the side gears. Backlash should be within 0.002–0.005 in. If not, replace the side gear spacers with the appropriate ones listed below.
15. Align the differential drive pinion shaft with the lock pin hole in the differential case and drive the pin in from the rear of the case. Stake the pin with a small pointed punch to secure it.
16. Remove the old adhesive from the ring gear mounting bolts and apply new adhesive. Snug up all bolts then tighten them on a crisscross pattern of 58–65 ft.lb.

NOTE: To allow the adhesive to set on the bolt threads, keep the unit stationary for about an hour.

17. Press the front and rear bearing outer races into the gear carrier.

CAUTION

Make sure that the races do not tilt and that they sit fully in the case.

18. Look at the top face of the drive pinion (gear side). If there is an etched number, such as −0, −1, −2, +1, +2, etc., complete step 17. If not, skip step 19 and go on to step 20.
19. Insert a shim between the drive pinion and rear bearing. If the original gear set is being replaced, the original shims may be used. If a new gear set is being installed, calculate the shim dimension in the following manner. Assuming the pinion height before disassembly is correct, subtract the new pinion variation marking (on the pinion head) from the old pinion variation marking. If the answer is positive, add shims in the corresponding amount. If the answer is negative, subract shims in the corresponding amount. This will produce a reasonable starting point for assembly. If the shim choice is proved incorrect, the entire pinion must be disassembled, and the shim changed accordingly. The etched marking on the face of the pinion represents a positive or negative variation from the standard in millimeters.

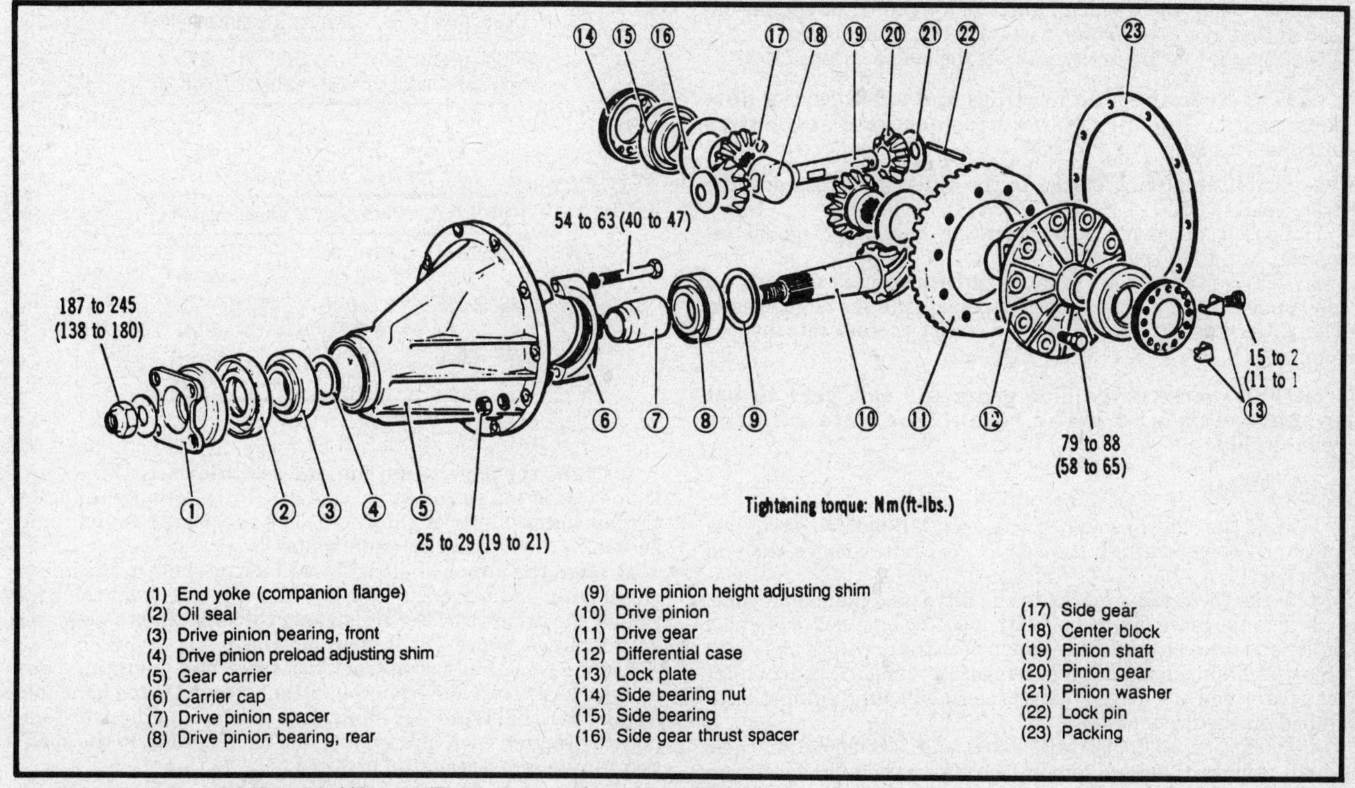

Exploded view of Mitsubisi/Arrow/D-50 rear axle assembly

NOTE: If the original gear set is being reused in the differential case, the original shims may be used.

20. If the drive pinion has no marking on its gear side face, it will be necessary to obtain two dealer special tools: MB990819 and MB990552. Install parts marked 1,6,2,7,3,4, and 5 in the illustration labeled "Measuring pinion height (clearance)" with special tool MB990819 into the carrier case. Gradually tighten the nut to produce 6–9 in. lbs. without the oil seal. Fit special tool MB990552 in the differential caps and replace the caps on the case. Measure the clearance between the two special tools (see illustration) and select a shim of an equivalent thickness to the clearance to make the pinion height within tolerance of ±0.0012 in.

NOTE: If the pinion height has to be adjusted by more than 0.0650 in. use two shims including one 0.0118 in. thick.

21. Install the selected shim between the drive pinion and the rear bearing. Press the bearing onto the drive pinion shaft.
22. Assemble the drive pinion in the case and torque the pinion nut gradually to 137–180 ft.lb. Check the pinion preload. With oil seal, it should be between 9–11 in. lbs. Without the oil seal, it should be 6–9 in. lbs. The preload shim selection ranges from 0.0118–0.0917 in.
23. If you have not already done so, apply a thin coat of grease to the drive pinion oil seal and insert it in the case. Refit the yoke and tighten to 137–180 ft.lb.
24. Press the side bearings into the differential case and fit the case into the carrier.
25. Install the carrier caps with their mating marks in line with the marks on the carriers and finger tighten the four set bolts.
26. Install the side bearing nuts, and tighten the carrier cap bolts to 40–47 ft.lb.
27. Screw in the side bearing nuts to adjust the standard backlash value. Each nut should be tightened to 11 lbs. Repeatedly loosen and tighten the bearing nuts to insure smooth operation, then tighten them until they become hard to turn.
28. Attach a dial indicator to the ring gear teeth and make certain the backlash is between 0.005–0.007 in.

NOTE: If the backlash is less than the limit, loosen the bearing nut on the back side of the ring gear and tighten the bearing nut on the teeth side by the same amount.

29. After adjusting backlash, tighten the bearing nuts $^1/_2$ pitch.

NOTE: One pitch is the space between two adjacent holes on the side of the bearing nut.

30. Again measure the backlash and install a one or two pronged lock plate whichever lines up with the bearing nut holes. Tighten the lock plate bolts to 11–16 ft.lb.
31. Measure the ring gear runout in four or more spots. Runout should be 0.002 in. or less.
32. Make a ring gear tooth pattern check.
33. Apply gear oil to all moving parts and use sealant when assembling. Install the packing with the embossed portion at about 3 o'clock position on the axle housing.
34. Fit the differential and tighten the mounting nuts to 18–22 ft.lb.
35. Be sure to fill the rear axle with about 3 pints of gear oil before testing.

D50 Arrow

Case Disassembly

1. Remove the lock plate, and then remove the side bearing nut using special tool (MB990201) or equivalent.
2. Remove the carrier cap. Then remove the differential case

assembly using the wooden handle of a hammer or similar object so that gears and other parts will not be damaged.

3. Using a bearing puller pull off the side bearing.

NOTE: Keep the side bearings and side bearing nuts separate, so that they do not become mixed at the time of reassembly.

4. Make the mating marks to the differential case and the drive gear.

5. Loosen the drive gear mounting bolts in diagonal sequence, and then remove.

6. Remove the lock pin from the drive gear back side using a long punch. Then pull out the pinion shaft and the pinion gears. The side gears with the side gear thrust spacers can then be removed.

NOTE: The removed side gears and side gear thrust spacers, left and right, should be retained for reassembly.

Drive Pinion

1. Hold the end yoke with special tool (MB990850) or equivalent and after removing the self-locking nut, remove the end yoke.

2. Make the mating marks to the drive pinion and end yoke.

3. Tap the drive pinion end with a plastic hammer or a wheel puller and force out the drive pinion with the drive pinion height adjusting shim, drive pinion bearing (rear) inner race, drive pinion spacer and the drive pinion preload adjusting shim still installed on the drive pinion.

4. Using special tools (MB990339 and MB990648 or their equal) remove the drive pinion bearing (rear) inner race from the drive pinion. Remove the drive pinion height adjusting shim at the same time.

NOTE: The drive pinion height adjusting shim should be retained for reassembly.

5. Remove the drive pinion bearing (front and rear) outer race. When removing drive pinion bearing (front) outer race, remove oil seal and drive pinion bearing (front) inner race at the same time.

NOTE: The removed oil seal should not be reused.

Inspection

1. Check differential gear tooth contact. Replace any gear that is worn or damaged.

2. Check the bearing race curvature for discoloration caused by seizure, and rough surface. Replace any bearing that is defective.

3. Install the side gear onto the splined end of the axle shaft. Check for looseness of the axle shaft spline using a dial indicator on the side gear.

4. Check the differential pinion and pinion shaft for wear or seizure.

Assembly & Adjustment Differential Case

1. Install the side gear thrust spacers in their original positions behind the side gears. Then assemble the side gears (left and right) in the differential case.

2. With pinion washers attached to the pinion gears, insert the both pinion gears at the same time and mesh with the side gears by rotating the pinion gears.

3. Complete the temporary assembly of the differential gears by inserting the pinion shaft.

Description	Service Limit mm (in.)
Axle shaft spline looseness	0.6 (.024)

Description	Standard Value mm (in.)
Pinion gear and side gear backlash	0.051 to 0.127 (.002 to .005)

TYPES OF SIDE GEAR THRUST SPACER

Part No.	Thickness of Spacer mm (in.)	
MB092034	0.8–0.08 —0.17	(.0315—.0031 —.0067)
MB092035	0.8–0.18 —0.27	(.0315—.0071 —.0106)
MB092036	0.8—0 —0.07	(.0315—0 —.0028)

4. Check the pinion gear and side gear backlash. If the backlash exceeds the repair limit, adjust it by selecting a side gear thrust spacer of proper thickness. The backlash, left and right, should be adjusted to an equal value.

5. Align the pinion shaft with the lock pin hole in the differential case, and drive the lock pin into the hole from the back side of the drive gear. Securely stake the lock pin at two places with a punch to prevent it from moving.

6. Remove old adhesive from the drive gear mounting bolts using a wire brush and from the internal thread using hand tap. Apply "LOCTITE 271" or equivalent anaerobic adhesive. Temporarily tighten each bolt evenly, and then tighten to the specified torque in a criss-cross fashion.

NOTE: Keep the differential stationary to harden the anaerobic adhesive for half an hour to one hour.

Adjusting Drive Pinion Height

1. Press the drive pinion bearing (front and rear) outer races into the gear carrier using special tools (MB990934, MB990936 and MB990938) or their equal. Use great care so that the outer race does not tilt and be sure the race bottoms in its bore in the gear carrier.

2. Install the drive pinion bearings and special tool (MB990819) or equivalent. Gradually tighten with the nut until the drive pinion preload becomes within 6 to 9 inch lbs.

CAUTION

When installing the washer, apply a thin coat of grease on the washer.

3. Mount the special tool (MB990552) or equivalent in the side bearing seat of the gear carrier, and then select a drive pinion height adjusting shim of a thickness which corresponds to the gap between the special tools (MB990552 and MB990819) or their equal.

NOTE: Be sure to clean the side bearing seat thoroughly. When mounting the special tool (MB990552) or equivalent, be sure that the cut-out sections are in the position shown in the illustration, and also confirm that the tool is in close contact with the side bearing seat.

4. Install the selected drive pinion height adjusting shim between the drive pinion and the drive pinion bearing (rear). Using special tool (MB990802) or equivalent, press the drive pinion bearing (rear) onto the drive pinion.

5. If the gear set is to be replaced, install new shims of the same thickness as the shims previously used on the drive pinion.

CAUTION

In determining the thickness of the shim pack, the amount of compression of the shim pack and wear of the bearing (when the old bearing is reused) should be taken into account.

Adjusting Drive Pinion Preload

1. Insert drive pinion preload adjusting shim between drive pinion spacer and drive pinion bearing (front). Tighten end yoke to specified torque, to obtain standard preload 9–11 inch lbs. with seal, 6–9 inch lbs. no seal. If preload is wrong, install a preload adjusting shim of a different thickness until preload is in the standard value.

NOTE: Beside the drive pinion preload adjusting shims, the drive pinion spacers may be used for adjustment.

2. After completion of the drive pinion preload adjustment, remove the end yoke. Apply a thin coat of grease to the periphery of the oil seal, and drive it into the gear carrier using special tool (MB990031) or equivalent.
3. Next apply grease (cotaining 50% or more of molybdenum disulfide) to the oil seal lip contact surface of the end yoke shaft, insert the end yoke, and tighten the self-locking nut to the specified torque.

Side Bearing

1. Press in the side bearing inner race to the differential case using special tool (MB990802) or equivalent.
2. Place differential case assembly into gear carrier. Line up the mating mark on gear carrier with that on carrier cap, and tighten set bolts for tightening bearing cap to gear carrier with fingers. Then install side bearing nut, and tighten it on carrier cap to the specified torque 40–47 ft. lbs.
3. Screw in the side bearing nut on each side of drive gear using the special tool (MB990201) or equivalent to adjust the standard backlash value. Make sure the side bearing nuts are tightened to 11 lbs. at end of special tool. Turn the bearing nuts in and out several times until they operate smoothly, then tighten them to the proper torque.
4. Apply a dial indicator to the drive gear tooth, and make certain that backlash is within the standard value.

NOTE: If the backlash is smaller than the standard value, loosen the side bearing nut on the back side of the drive gear and tighten the side bearing nut on the teeth side by the same amount.

5. After adjustment, tighten side bearing nut on both sides by a half pitch to give preload on side bearings. One pitch means space between two adjacent holes on the side of the side bearing nuts.

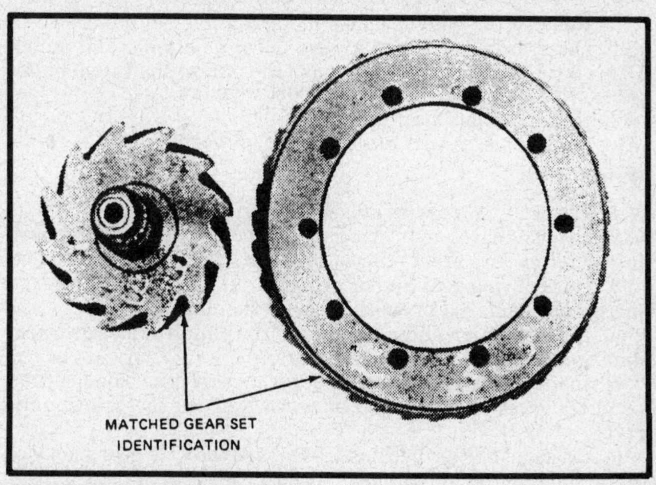

Pinion and ring markings

6. Measure the backlash again to ensure that it is within the standard value. Choose a lock plate of proper type, and tighten it to the specified torque 11–15 ft. lbs.

Drive Gear

1. Apply a dial indicator to the back of the drive gear and measure the amount of runout. Maximum Runout .002 in.

CAUTION

Measure the runout at 4 or more points.

2. If the runout exceeds the repair limit, change the mounting position of drive gear to differential case and measure the runout again. If the runout is still excessive, replace drive gear or the differential case as necessary.

Installation

During installation, observe the following items:
1. Apply gear oil to bearing and gear slide surfaces.
2. Apply a semi-drying sealer to axle housing and gasket.
3. Install carrier into axle assembly. Torque to 19–21 ft. lbs.
4. Install axle shafts.
5. Fill differential with SAE 80W-90 gear oil.

TOYOTA

NOTE: If the differential is noisy, perform the following pre-inspection before disassembly to determine the cause of the noise.

1. Check ring gear runout. If the runout is greater than maximum, install a new ring gear. Maximum runout: ½ ton and ¾ ton; 0.0028 in.: C&C and 4×4; 0.0039 in.
2. Check ring gear backlash. If the backlash is not within specification, adjust the side bearing preload or repair as necessary. Backlash: 0.0051–0.0071 in.
3. Check the tooth contact.
4. Using a torque meter, measure the total preload. Total preload (Starting): Drive pinion preload plus 3.5–5.2 inch lb.

Disassembly

1. Remove differential case and ring gear. Put alignment marks on the bearing cap and differential carrier. Remove two adjusting nut locks.
2. Remove two bearing caps and two adjusting nuts. Remove the bearing outer races. Remove the differential case from the carrier.
3. Remove companion flange, oil seal and front bearing.
4. Remove drive pinion from differential carrier.
5. Remove drive pinion rear bearing using a universal puller.
6. Remove front and rear drive pinion bearing outer race, using a hammer and punch.
7. Remove ring gear from differential case.
8. Remove the ring gear set bolts and lock plates.
9. Using a brass bar and hammer, tap on the ring gear to separate it from the differential case.

CAUTION

Be careful not to damage the side bearing.

10. Remove the side bearings using a universal puller.
11. Disassemble differential case using a hammer and punch. Drive out the straight pin. Remove the pinion shaft, two pinion gears, two side gears and two thrust washers.
12. Inspect differential case parts.
13. Replace parts that are damaged or worn.

Inspection

1. Clean all parts with solvent.
2. Inspect drive pinion bearings and outer races. If the bearing or outer race are damaged or worn, replace them as a set.
3. Inspect ring gear and drive pinion. If the ring gear or drive pinion are damaged or worn, replace them as a set.
4. Inspect pinion and side gears. If the pinion or side gears are damaged or worn, replace the gears.
5. Inspect side bearings and outer races. If the side bearings or outer races are damaged or worn, replace the bearing and race.
6. Check side gear backlash. Measure the side gear backlash while holding one pinion gear toward the case. Standard backlash: 0.0020–0.0079 in. If the backlash is out of specification, install the correct thrust washers.

Assembly

½ & ¾ TON

1. Adjust drive pinion protrusion. Install the bearings and adjusting gauge (tool 09530–30012 and 09536–30030 or equivalent) in the differential carrier in the following order: Rear bearing. Base rod. Drive pinion front bearing. Collar. Flange. Nut. Base rod head. Bolt.

NOTE: Tighten the bolt only to the point where the drive pinion gear has no play.

2. Place the master gauge on the differential carrier.
3. Align the marks and install the bearing caps. Torque the bearing cap bolts 51–65 ft. lbs.
4. Select a washer that can just be inserted into the clearance between the master gauge and the base rod. Washer thickness 0.0878–1.075 in. Remove the adjusting gauge.
5. Install rear bearing and washer on drive pinion using a press.

NOTE: The chamfered end of the washer should face toward the gear.

6. Coat the bearings with gear oil and install the drive pinion into the carrier.
7. Install new bearing spacer, front bearing and oil slinger.
8. Install new oil seal. Apply multipurpose grease to the oil seal.
9. Install companion seal.
10. Tighten drive pinion nut and adjust preload. Coat threads of a new nut with multipurpose grease. Torque nut to 80 ft. lbs. Turn the companion flange several times to snug down the bearing.
11. Using a torque meter, measure the preload of the backlash between the drive pinion and ring gear. Preload: If preload is greater than specification, replace the bearing spacer. If preload is less than specification, retighten the nut 5–10° at a time until the specified preload is reached. If the maximum torque is exceeded while retightening the nut, replace the bearing spacer and repeat the preload procedure. Do not back off pinion nut to reduce the preload. Maximum torque: 173 ft. lb.
12. Using a dial indicator, measure the longitudinal and latitudinal deviation of the companion flange.

CAB CHASSIS AND 4×4

1. Adjust drive pinion preload. Install the bearings, spacer, shim and adjusting gauge etc. into the differential carrier.

NOTE: Do not install the oil seal. Do not install the shim for drive pinion height.

2. Using a wrench to hold the collar, tighten the nut. Torque the nut 123–151 ft. lbs.
3. Using a torque meter, measure the preload.
4. Adjust drive pinion protrusion. Place the master gauge on the differential carrier. Align the marks and install the bearing caps. Torque the bearing cap bolts, 51–65 ft. lbs.
5. Select a washer than can just be inserted into the clearance between the master gauge and the base rod. Remove the adjusting gauge.
6. Using a press and special tool 09506–30011 or equivalent, press the washer and rear bearing on the drive pinion.

NOTE: The chamfered end of the washer should face the gear.

7. Install drive pinion, bearing spacer, shim, front bearing and washer in differential carrier. Coat the bearings with gear oil.
8. Install new oil seal.
9. Install companion flange.
10. Place the bearing outer races on their respective bearings. Make sure left and right races are not interchanged. Install the case in the carrier.
11. Install the adjusting nuts on their respective carrier. Make sure the nuts are threaded properly.

NOTE: Make sure that there is backlash between the gear and drive pinion.

12. Install the adjusting nuts. Align the marks on the cap and carrier. Screw in the two bearing cap bolts two or three turns and press down the bearing cap by hand.

NOTE: If the bearing cap does not fit tightly on the carrier, the adjusting nut threads are not threaded properly. Reinstall adjusting nuts if necessary.

13. To adjust side bearing preload tighten the bearing cap bolts until the spring washers are slightly compressed. Using an adjusting nut wrench special tool 09504–00010 or equivalent, tighten the adjusting nut on the ring gear side until the ring gear has a backlash of about 0.008 in.
14. Using an adjusting nut wrench, firmly tighten the adjusting nut on the drive pinion side.
15. Check the ring gear backlash. If tightening the adjusting nut creates ring gear backlash, loosen the nut so that backlash is eliminated.
16. Place a dial indicator on the top of the bearing cap on the ring gear side.
17. Adjust the side bearing for zero preload by tightening the other adjusting nut until the pointer on the indicator begins to move.
18. Tighten the adjusting nut 1 to 1½ notches from the zero preload position.
19. Using a dial indicator and adjusting nut wrench, adjust the ring gear backlash until the backlash is within specification. Backlash: 0.0051–0.0071 in.

NOTE: The backlash is adjusted by turning the left and right adjusting nuts equal amounts. For example, loosen the nut on the left side one notch and tighten the nut on the right side one notch.

20. Torque the bearing cap bolts 51–65 ft. lbs.
21. Recheck the ring gear backlash.
22. Measure the total preload. Total preload (Starting): Drive pinion preload plus 3.5–5.2 inch lb.
24. Inspect tooth contact between ring gear and drive pinion. Adjust if needed.
25. Stake the drive pinion nut.
26. Install the adjusting nut locks.
27. Install differential carrier assembly in the axle housing.
28. Install axle shafts.
29. Connect the driveshaft.
30. Fill differential with SAE 80W–90 gear oil.

Manual Transmissions
Import Trucks

28

INDEX

MANUAL TRANSMISSION SERVICE

Sequence of Diagnosis

In order to determine the problems that may exist in a transmission, a systematic diagnosis procedure should be followed to locate and repair the malfunction.

1. Consult with the owner or operator to identify the problem.
2. Road test, whenever possible with the owner or operator, to verify the problem is within the transmission and not caused by a related component.
3. Verify that all controls are operating properly and in good condition.
4. With the unit removed from the vehicle, inspect it prior to the disassembly.
5. During the disassembly, inspect the varied parts to locate the source of the problem.
6. Replace companion gears to defective or worn gears. Do not re-install a part that does not have a long service life remaining.
7. make any modifications or changes as recommended by the manufacturer.

Diagnosis & Troubleshooting

Noises with Transmission in Neutral

1. Misalignment of transmission.
2. Worn flywheel pilot bearing.
3. Worn or scored countershaft bearings.
4. Worn or rough reverse idler gear.
5. Sprung or worn countershaft.
6. Excessive backlash in gears.
7. Worn mainshaft pilot bearing.
8. Scuffed gear tooth contact surface.
9. Insufficient lubrication.
10. Use of incorrect grade of lubricant.

Noises with Transmission in Gear

1. Worn or rough mainshaft rear bearing.
2. Rough, chipped or tapered sliding gear teeth.
3. Noisy speedometer gears.
4. Excessive end play of mainshaft gears.
5. Refer to conditions listed above under noises with transmission in neutral.

Growling, Humming and Grinding

1. Pitted, chipped or cracked gears.
2. Damaged gears or chips in lubricant from failed power-Take-off.
3. Excessive gear wear from high mileage or overloading.

Hissing, Thumping and Bumping

1. Bad bearings on way to failure.
2. Broken bearings and retainers.

Metallic Rattles

1. Engine torsional vibration.
2. Clutch disc assembly worn or without torsional vibration dampers.
3. Engine idle speed too low.
4. Rough engine idle.
5. Excessive backlash in power-take-off mounting.

Squealing, Gear Whine and Gear Seizure

1. One of the free-running gears seizing on thrust-face or fluted diameter momentarily, then letting go.
2. Whine of excessive backlash in mating gears or improper shimming of power-take-off unit.

Walking or Jumping out of Gear

CAUSES OUTSIDE TRANSMISSION

1. Improperly positioned forward remote control which limits full travel forward and backward from the remote neutral position.
2. Improper adjustment or length shift rods or linkage that limits travel of forward remote from neutral position.
3. Loose bell cranks, sloppy ball and socket joints.
4. Shift rods, cables, etc., too spongy, flexible, or not secured properly at both ends.
5. Worn or loose engine mounts if forward unit is mounted to frame.
6. Forward remote mount too flimsy, loose on frame, etc.
7. Set screws loose at remote control joints.
8. Air shift system partially inoperative.
9. Transmission and engine out of alignment either vertically or horizontally.

CAUSES INSIDE TRANSMISSION

1. Shift tower or cover loose or interlock balls or pins worn or springs broken.
2. Shift fork pads not square with shift rod bore.
3. Shift rod poppet springs broken.
4. Shift rod poppet notches worn.
5. Shift rod bent or sprung out of line.
6. Shift fork pads or groove in sliding gear or collar worn excessively.
7. Shift fork pads not square with rod bore.
8. Worn taper on gear teeth, spacers or bearings.
9. Backing rings or retaining rings not installed properly on rear unit curvic rings on gears.

Hard Shifting

PRELIMINARY INVESTIGATION

1. Not enough clutch pedal free-play.
2. Worn or inoperative clutch hydraulic cylinder.
3. Worn or loose clutch shaft, levers.
4. Worn or loose throwout bearing or carrier.
5. Low air pressure to main auxiliary unit shift cylinder.
6. Air leaks in cylinders, control lines or cab control valve.
7. Improper remote control function.
8. No lubricant in remote control units.
9. No lubricant in (or grease fittings on) U-joints or swivels of remote controls.

UNSYNCHRONIZED (CONSTANT MESH) TRANSMISSIONS

1. Lack of lubricant or wrong lubricant used causing buildup of sticky varnish and sludge deposits on splines of shaft and gears.
2. Sliding clutch gears tight on splines of shaft.
3. Clutch teeth burred over, chipped or badly mutilated due to improper shifting.
4. Driver not familiar with proper shifting procedure for this transmission. Also includes proper shifting if used with 2-speed axle, auxiliary, etc.
5. Clutch or drive gear pilot bearing seized, rough, or dragging.
6. Clutch brake engaging too soon when clutch pedal is depressed.

SYNCHRONIZED TRANSMISSION

1. Badly worn or bent shift rods.

2. Loose or flimsy remote controls, spongy or flexible rods and/or cables preventing full application of force to hold and synchronize gears.
3. Further, driver may not be able to feel the synchronizer action which usually results in a snap-type shift.
4. Synchronizer bronze or aluminum rings worn or steel chips imbedded in rings prevent proper synchronization.
5. Damaged synchronizer such as broken poppet springs, poppets jammed, loose or broken blocker pins.
6. Free running gears, seized or galled on either the thrust face or diameters.

Sticking in Gear

1. Clutch not releasing.
2. Inoperative slave power units.
3. Sliding clutch gears tight on splines.
4. Chips wedged between or under splines of shaft and gear.
5. Improper adjustment, excessive wear or lost motion in shifter linkage.
6. Clutch brake set too high on clutch pedal locking gears behind hopping guard.

Crash Shifting or Raking Gears

SYNCHRONIZED TRANSMISSIONS

1. Raking of gears during manual shift may be caused by a defective synchronizer or improper shifting technique for synchronized transmission.
2. Occurs with cold, heavy oil, but synchronizer begins to work properly when transmission oil reaches normal operating temperature.
3. Heavy oil prevents the synchronizer cone from breaking through oil film and doing job properly.
4. Glazing of synchronizer cones due to use of E.P. addition in multi-purpose axle lubricant.
5. Synchronizer cones worn smooth causing loss of clutching action: Failure to control engine speed drop-off during upshift. Failure to bring engine speed nearly up to governor speed when driver shifting. Attempted shifting without using clutch.
6. Blocker pin detents worn resulting in loss of blocker action.
7. Blocker pins loose, broken or turned over.

Oil Leaks

1. Oil level too high.
2. Wrong lubricant in unit.
3. Non-shielded bearing used at front or rear bearing cap (where applicable.)
4. Seals (if used) defective or omitted from bearing cap, wrong type seal used, etc.
5. Screwback threads in bearing caps off location, worn out, or filled with varnish, sludge, dirt, etc.
6. Transmission breather omitted, plugged internally, etc.
7. Capscrews loose, omitted or missing from remote control, shifter housing, bearing caps, P.T.O. or covers, etc.
8. Welch "seal" plugs loose or missing entirely from machine openings in case.
9. Oil drain-back openings in bearing caps or case plugged with varnish, dirt, covered with gasket material, etc.
10. Broken gaskets, gaskets shifted or squeezed out of position, pieces still under bearing caps, clutch housing, P.T.O. and covers, etc.
11. Cracks or holes in castings.
12. Drain plug loose.
13. Also possibility that oil leakage could be from engine.
14. Internal O-ring worn in air cylinders, leaking air into transmission, pressurizing transmission.

Vibration

ORIGINATING IN TRANSMISSION

1. Sprung mainshafts and countershaft.
2. Gears that have seized to shaft and broken loose.
3. Bearings that are extremely worn allowing rotating shafts to oscillate from intended centers.

ORIGINATING ELSEWHERE BUT APPARENTLY IN TRANSMISSION

1. Drive lines out of static or dynamic balance.
2. Out of phase, wrong drive line working angles.
3. Worn crosses and bearings in U-joints.
4. Loose mounting or worn center bearings.
5. Worn and pitted teeth on ring gear and pinion of driving axle(s).
6. Wheels out of balance.
7. Warped parking brake drum or disc.

Bearing Failure

1. Dirt, always abrasive enters through seals, breathers, dirty containers.
2. Lapping action of fine steel particles from balls and raceways.
3. Entry of chips from hammers, chisels, punches during disassembly and assembly.
4. Bearing jammed with chip(s) may turn on shaft or in housing.
5. Brinnelling, ball depressions, spalling.
6. Excessive looseness under load scrubs shaft and bearing bore.
7. Failure due to heat: Failure of lubricant circulation. Lubricant deterioration or low level. Radically tight bearing caused by expansion of inner race when mounted on shaft or compression of outer race when pressed into housing. Off-square mounting producing heat at retainers.

Transfer Case

DIAGNOSIS & TROUBLESHOOTING

Slips Out of Gear (High-Low)

1. Shifting poppet spring weak.
2. Bearing broken or worn.
3. Shifting fork bent.
4. Improper control rod adjustment.

Slips Out of Front Wheel Drive

1. Shifting poppet spring weak or broken.
2. Bearing worn or broken.
3. Excessive shaft end-play.
4. Shifting fork bent.

Hard Shifting

1. Lack of lubricant.
2. Shift lever binding on shaft.
3. Shifting poppet ball scored.
4. Shifting fork bent.
5. Low tire pressure.

Backlash

1. Companion yoke loose.
2. Transfer case loose on mounts.
3. Internal parts excessively worn.

Noisy

1. Low lubricant level.
2. Bearings improperly adjusted or excessively worn.

3. Gears worn or damaged.
4. Improper alignment of driveshafts or U-joints.

Oil Leakage

1. Excessive amount of lubricant in case.
2. Vent clogged.
3. Gaskets or seals leaking.
4. Bearings loose or damaged.
5. Driveshaft yoke mating surfaces scored.

Overheating

1. Excessive or insufficient amount of lubricant.
2. Bearing adjustment too tight.

CLEANING COMPONENTS

Cleanliness of parts, tools, and work area is of the utmost importance. All transmission components (except bearing assemblies) should be cleaned in cleaning solvent and dried with compressed air before any inspection or work is begun. Great care should be taken when cleaning bearings. Bearings should always be cleaned separately from other parts in clean cleaning solvent and not gasoline. They must never be cleaned in a hot solution tank. It is advisable that they be soaked in cleaning fluid and then tapped against a block of wood in order to free any solidified lubricant that may be trapped inside. Rinse bearings thoroughly in clean solvent and then dry them with moisture-free compressed air being careful not to spin the bearings with the air stream. Rotate each bearing slowly and inspect rollers or balls for any signs of excessive wear, roughness, or damage. Those bearings not in excellent condition must be replaced. If they pass this inspection, they should be dipped in clean oil and wrapped in clean lintless cloth to protect them until installation.

INSPECTION OF COMPONENTS

All parts must be completely and carefully inspected and replaced for any signs of wear, stress, discoloration or warpage due to excessive heat. Whenever available, the magna flux process should be used on all parts except roller and ball bearings, to detect small cracks unseen by the eye. Inspect the breather assembly to see that it is not clogged or damaged and check all threaded parts for stripped or cross threads. Oil passages must be cleared of obstructions by the use of air pressure or brass rods and all gaskets, oil seals, lock wires, cotter pins, and snap rings are to be replaced. Small nicks or burrs in gears or splines can be removed with a fine abrasive stone. It is important that any housings or covers having cracks or other damage should be replaced and not welded. Synchronizers, not in excellent condition, must be replaced. The bronze synchronizer cone should be checked for wear or for any steel chips that may have become imbedded in it. Springs must be inspected for free length, compressed length, distortion, or collapsed coils.

NOTE: The splines on many clutch gears, mainshafts, etc., are equipped with a machined relief called a "hopping guard". With the clutch gear engaged, the mating gear is free to slip into this notch, preventing the two gears from separating or "walking out of gear" under various load conditions. This is not a worn or chipped gear. Do not grind or discard the gear.

Check all shafts for spline wear or damage. If the mainshaft 1st and reverse sliding gear or clutch hub have worn into the sides of the splines, the shaft should be replaced. Shift forks, shift rods, interlock balls and pins must be replaced if scored, worn, distorted or damaged.

NISSAN

4 Speed

Disassembly

This transmission is constructed in three sections: clutch housing, transmission housing and extension housing. There are no case cover plates. There is a cast iron adapter plate between the transmission and extension housings.

1. Remove the clutch housing dust cover. Remove the retaining spring, release bearing sleeve and lever.
2. Remove the backup light/neutral safety switch.
3. Unbolt and remove the clutch housing, rapping with a soft hammer if necessary. Remove the gasket, mainshaft bearing shim, and countershaft bearing shim.
4. Remove the speedometer pinion sleeve.
5. Remove the striker rod pin from the rod. Separate the striker rod from the shift lever bracket.
6. Unbolt and remove the rear extension. It may be necessary to rap the housing with a soft hammer.
7. Remove the mainshaft bearing snap-ring.
8. Remove the adapter plate and gear assembly from the transmission case.
9. Punch out the shift fork retaining pins. Remove the shift rod snap-rings. Remove the detent plugs, springs and balls from the adapter plate. Remove the shift rods, being careful not to lose the interlock balls.
10. Remove the snap-ring, speedometer drive gear and locating ball.
11. Remove the nut, lockwasher, thrust washer, reverse hub and reverse gear.
12. Remove the snap-ring and countershaft reverse gear. Remove the snap-ring, reverse idler gear, thrust washer and needle bearing.
13. Support the gear assembly while rapping on the rear of the mainshaft with a soft hammer.
14. Remove the setscrew from the adapter plate. Remove the shaft nut, spring washer, plain washer and reverse idler shaft.
15. Remove the bearing retainer and the mainshaft rear bushing.
16. To disassemble the mainshaft (rear section), remove the front snap-ring, third/fourth synchronizer assembly, third gear and needle bearing. From the rear, remove the thrust washer, locating ball, first gear, needle bearing, first gear bushing, first/second synchronizer assembly, second gear, and needle bearing.
17. To disassemble the clutch shaft, remove the snap-ring and bearing spacer and press off the bearing.
18. To disassemble the countershaft, press off the front bearing. Press off the rear bearing, press off the gears and remove the keys.
19. Remove the retaining pin, control arm pin and shift control arm from the rear of the extension housing.

Assembly

1. Place the O-ring in the front cover. Install the front cover to the clutch housing with a press. Put in the front cover oil seal.
2. Install the rear extension oil seal.
3. Assemble the first/second and third/fourth synchronizer assemblies. Make sure that the ring gaps are not both on the same side of the unit.

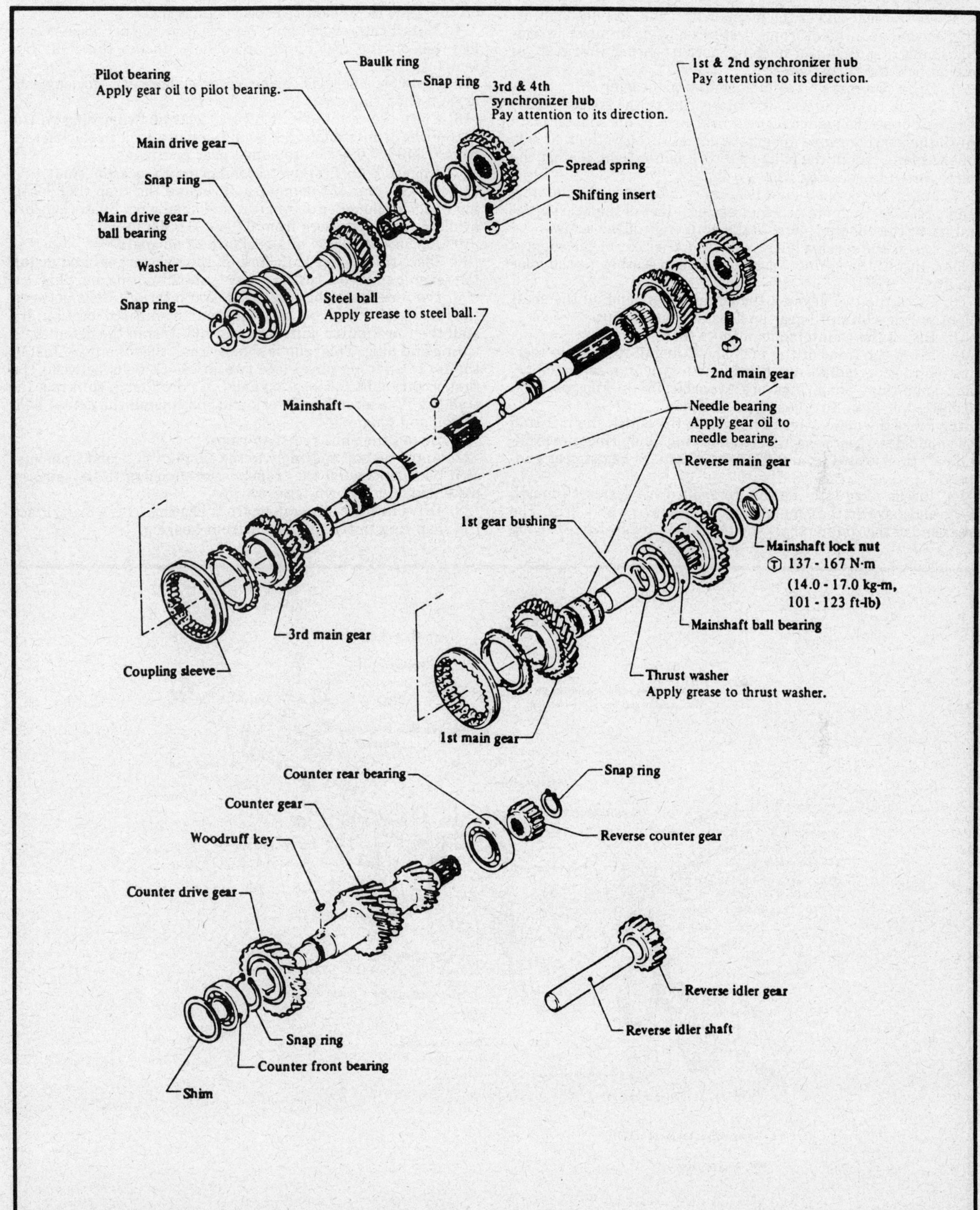

Datsun/Nissan 4 speed transmission gear assemblies

4. On the rear end of the mainshaft, install the needle bearing, second gear, baulk ring, first/second synchronizer assembly, baulk ring, first gear bushing, needle bearing, first gear, locating ball and thrust washer.

5. Drive or press on the mainshaft rear bearing.

6. Install the countershaft rear bearing to the adapter plate. Drive or press the mainshaft rear bearing into the adapter plate until the bearing snap-ring groove comes through the rear side of the plate. Install the snap-ring. If it is not tight against the plate, press the bearing back in slightly.

7. Insert the countershaft bearing ring between the countershaft rear bearing and bearing retainer. Install the bearing retainer to the adapter plate. Stake both ends of the screws.

8. Insert the reverse idler shaft from the rear of the adapter plate. Install the spring washer and plain washer to the idler shaft.

9. Place the two keys on the countershaft and oil the shaft lightly. Press on third gear and install a snap-ring.

10. Install the countershaft into its rear bearing.

11. From the front of the mainshaft, install the needle bearing, third gear, baulk ring, third/fourth synchronizer assembly and snap-ring. Snap-rings are available in thicknesses from 0.0561–0.0640 in. to adjust gear end-play.

12. Press the main drive bearing onto the clutch shaft. Install the main drive gear spacer and a snap-ring. Snap-rings are available in thicknesses from 0.0710–0.0820 in. to adjust gear end-play.

13. Insert a key into the countershaft drive gear with fourth gear and drive on the countershaft fourth gear with a drift. The rear end of the countershaft should be held steady while driving on the gear, to prevent rear bearing damage.

14. Install the reverse hub, reverse gear, thrust washer, and lock tab on the rear of the mainshaft. Install the shaft nut temporarily.

15. Install the needle bearing, reverse idler gear, thrust washer, and snap-ring.

16. Place the countershaft reverse gear and snap-ring on the rear of the countershaft. Snap-rings are available in thicknesses from 0.0433–0.0590 in. to adjust gear end-play.

17. Engage both first and second gears to lock the shaft.

18. On the rear of the mainshaft, install the snap-ring, locating ball, speedometer drive gear, and snap-ring. Snap-rings are available in thicknesses from 0.0433–0.0590 in.

19. Recheck end-play and backlash of all gears.

20. Place the reverse shift fork on the reverse gear and install the reverse shift rod. Install the detent ball, spring and plug. Install the fork retaining pin. Place two interlock balls between the reverse shift rod and the third/fourth shift rod location. Install the third/fourth shift fork and rod. Install the detent ball, spring and plug. This plug is shorter than the other two. Install the fork retaining pin. Place two interlock balls between the first/second shift rod location and the third/fourth shift rod. Install the first/second shift fork and rod. Install the detent ball, spring and plug.

21. Install the shift rod snap-rings.

22. Apply sealant sparingly to the adapter plate and transmission housing. Install the transmission housing to the adapter plate and bolt it down temporarily.

23. Drive in the countershaft front bearing with a drift. Place the snap-ring in the mainshaft front bearing.

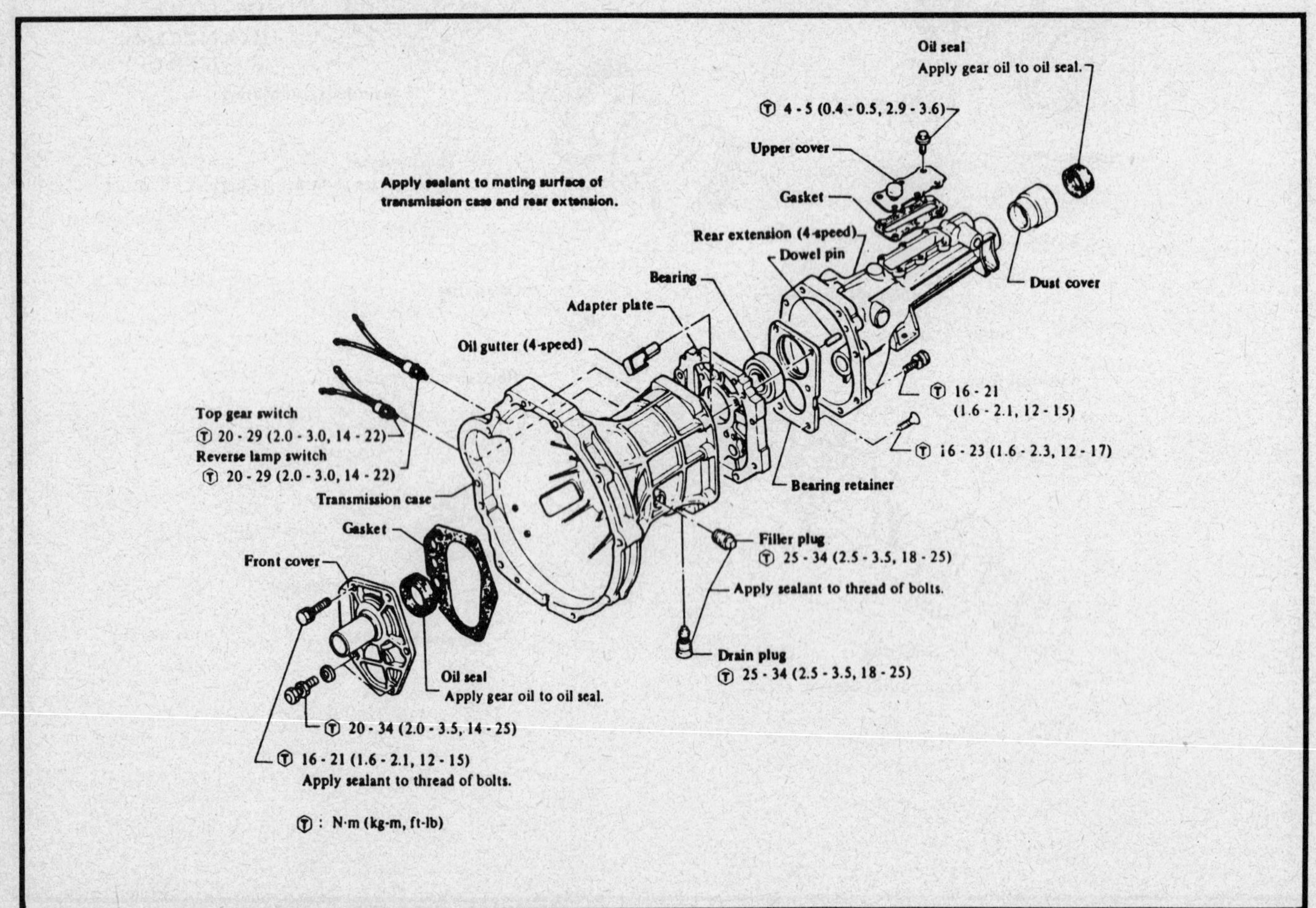

Datsun/Nissan 4 speed transmission case assembly

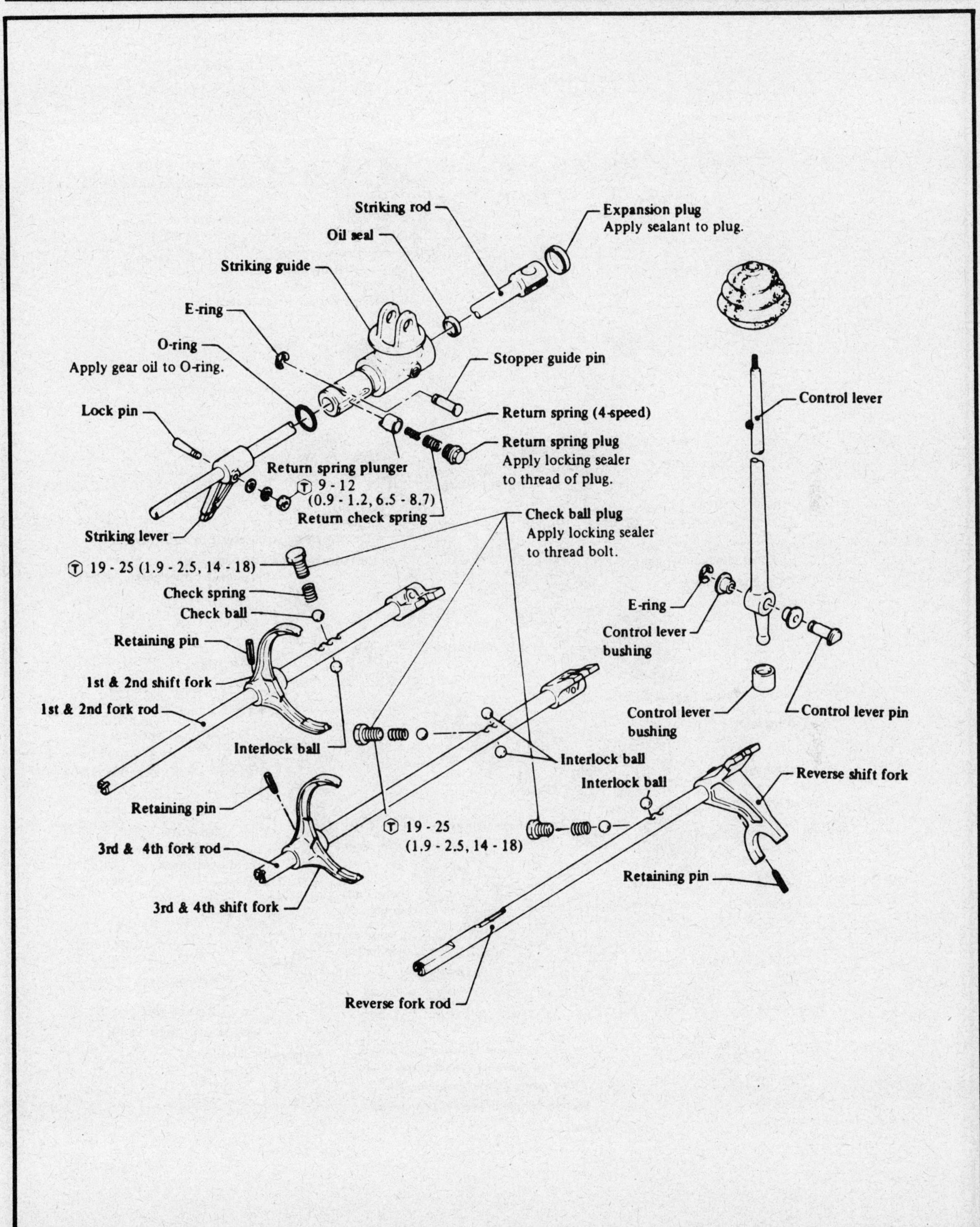
Striking rod
Expansion plug
Apply sealant to plug.
Oil seal
Striking guide
E-ring
O-ring
Apply gear oil to O-ring.
Stopper guide pin
Control lever
Lock pin
Return spring (4-speed)
Return spring plug
Apply locking sealer
to thread of plug.
Return spring plunger
Ⓣ 9 - 12
(0.9 - 1.2, 6.5 - 8.7)
Return check spring
Striking lever
Check ball plug
Apply locking sealer
to thread bolt.
Ⓣ 19 - 25 (1.9 - 2.5, 14 - 18)
Check spring
Check ball
E-ring
Retaining pin
Control lever
bushing
1st & 2nd shift fork
1st & 2nd fork rod
Control lever
bushing
Control lever pin
Interlock ball
Interlock ball
Interlock ball
Reverse shift fork
Retaining pin
Ⓣ 19 - 25
(1.9 - 2.5, 14 - 18)
3rd & 4th fork rod
Retaining pin
3rd & 4th shift fork
Reverse fork rod

Datsun/Nissan 4 speed transmission forks and shifter assemblies

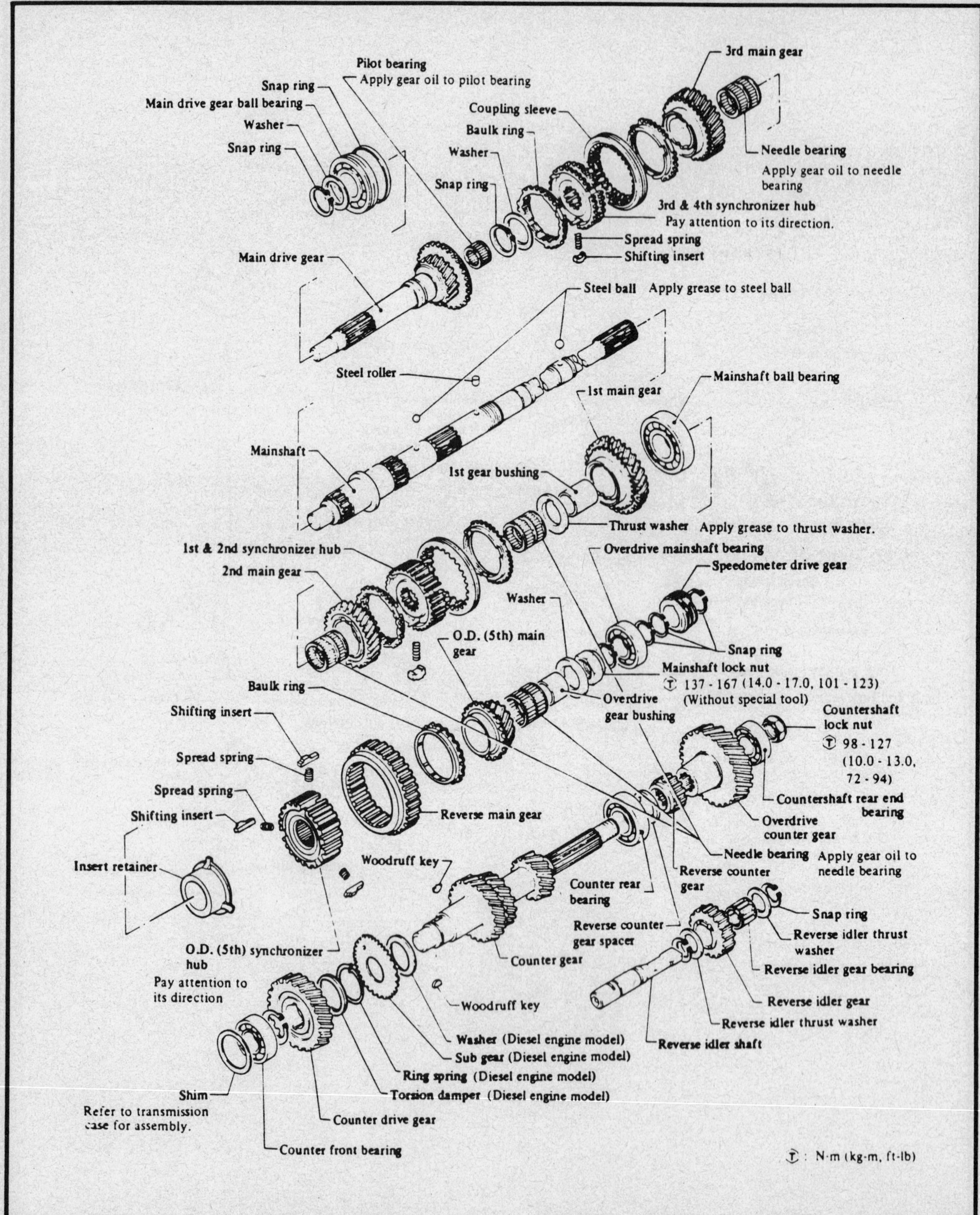

Datsun/Nissan 5 speed transmission gear assemblies

24. Apply sealant sparingly to the adapter plate and extension housing. Align the shift rods in the neutral positions. Position the striker rod to the shift rods and bolt down the extension housing.
25. Insert the striker rod pin, connect the rod to the shift lever bracket and install the striker rod pin retaining ring. Replace the shift control arm.
26. To select the proper mainshaft bearing shim, first measure the amount the bearing protrudes from the front of the transmission case. Then measure the depth of the bearing recess in the rear of the clutch housing. Required shim thickness is found by subtracting, the difference is required shim size. Shims are available in thicknesses of 0.0551 and 0.0630 in.
27. To select the proper countershaft front bearing shim, measure the amount that the bearing is recessed into the transmission case. Shim thickness should equal this measurement. Shims are available in thicknesses from 0.0157 to 0.0394 in.
28. Apply sealant sparingly to the clutch and transmission housing mating surfaces.
29. Replace the clutch operating mechanism.
30. Install the shift lever temporarily and check shifting action.

5 Speed

This transmission is similar to the 4 speed transmission (Model F4W71B). The overhaul can be accomplished by following the outline for the disassembly and assembly of the 4 speed.

Servo type synchromesh is used, instead of the Borg Warner type in the four speed. Shift linkage and interlock arrangements are the same, except the reverse shift rod also operates fifth gear. Most service procedures are identical to those for the four speed unit.

Those unique to the five-speed follow:

Disassembly

To disassemble the synchronizers, remove the circlip, synchronizer ring, thrust block, brake band, and anchor block. Be careful not to mix parts of the different synchronizer assemblies.

Assembly

1. The synchronizer assemblies for second, third, and fourth are identical. When assembling the first gear synchronizer, be sure to install the 0.0866 in. thick brake band at the bottom.
2. When assembling the mainshaft, select a third gear synchronizer hub snap-ring to minimize hub end-play. Snap-rings are available in thicknesses of 0.061–0.630 in., 0.0591–0.0610 in. and 0.0571–0.0591 in. The synchronizer hub must be installed with the longer boss to the rear.
3. When reassembling the gear train, install the mainshaft, countershaft, and gears to the adapter plate. Hold the rear nut and force the front nut against it to a torque of 217 ft. lbs. for 1979 models and 123 ft. lbs. for 1980 and later models. Select a snap-ring to minimize end-play of the fifth gear bearing at the rear of the mainshaft. Snap-rings are available in thicknesses from 0.0433–0.0551 in.

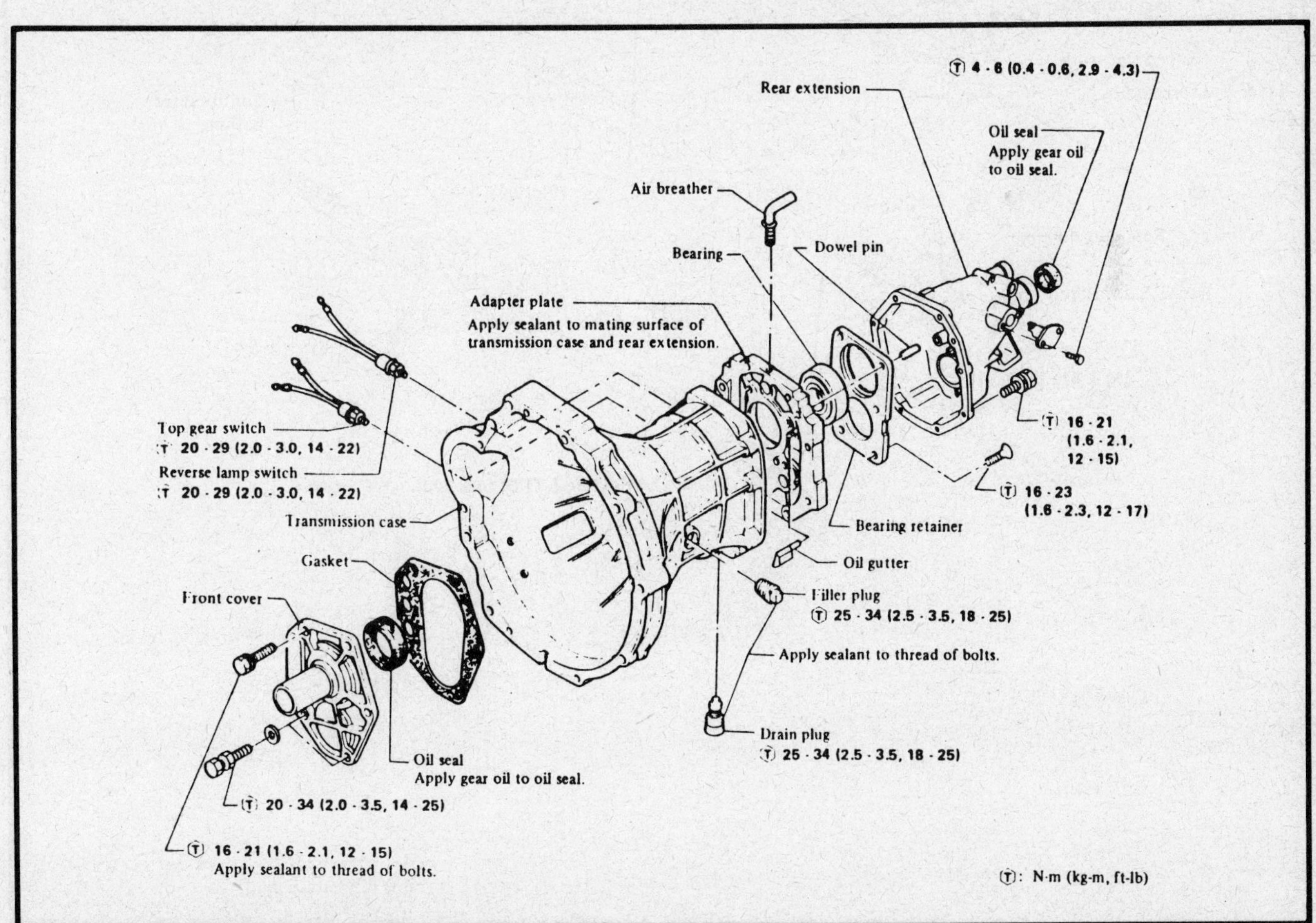

Datsun/Nissan 5 speed transmission case assembly

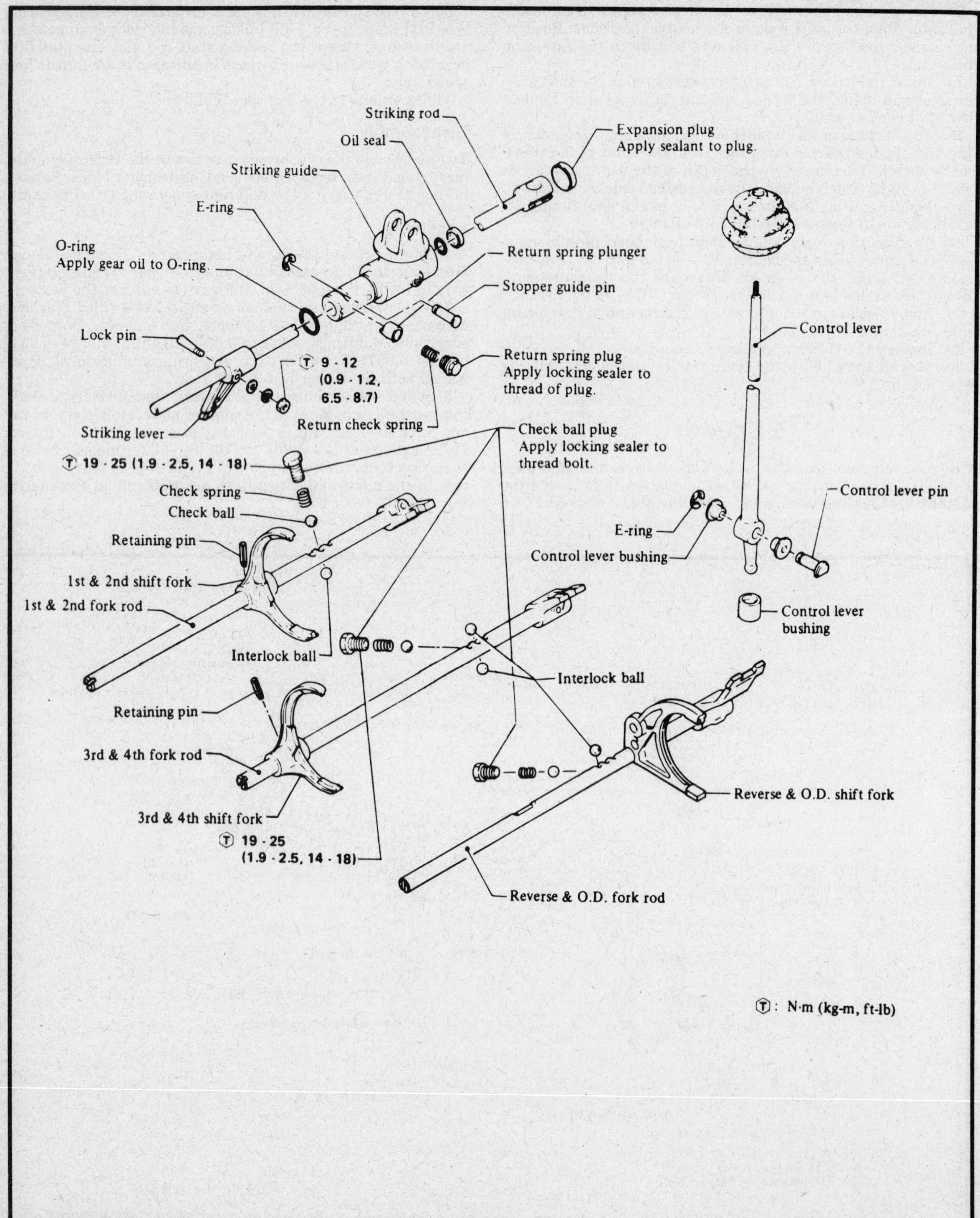
Striking rod
Oil seal
Striking guide
E-ring
O-ring
Apply gear oil to O-ring.
Expansion plug
Apply sealant to plug.
Return spring plunger
Stopper guide pin
Lock pin
Control lever
Ⓣ 9 - 12
(0.9 - 1.2,
6.5 - 8.7)
Return spring plug
Apply locking sealer to
thread of plug.
Return check spring
Striking lever
Check ball plug
Apply locking sealer to
thread bolt.
Ⓣ 19 - 25 (1.9 - 2.5, 14 - 18)
Check spring
Check ball
Control lever pin
E-ring
Retaining pin
Control lever bushing
1st & 2nd shift fork
1st & 2nd fork rod
Control lever
bushing
Interlock ball
Interlock ball
Retaining pin
3rd & 4th fork rod
Reverse & O.D. shift fork
3rd & 4th shift fork
Ⓣ 19 - 25
(1.9 - 2.5, 14 - 18)
Reverse & O.D. fork rod
Ⓣ: N·m (kg-m, ft-lb)

Datsun/Nissan 5 speed transmission forks and shifter assemblies

ISUZU

4 Speed

Disassembly

1. Remove the boot, clutch fork and throwout bearing.
2. Remove bearing retainer, gasket and spring washer.
3. Remove the speedometer gear and bushing.
4. Remove the shifter cover and gasket.
5. Remove the back-up switch on California vehicles and both back-up and CRS switches on all others.
6. Remove the rear extension and gasket.
7. Remove the thrust washers and reverse idler gear.
8. Remove the snap-rings, speedometer drive gear and key from the mainshaft.
9. Remove the spring pin from the reverse shifter fork and reverse gear.
10. Remove the snap-ring from the outer circumference of the clutch gear shaft ball bearing.
11. Remove the center support assembly from the transmission case.
12. Drive out the spring pins from the third and fourth and first and second shift forks.

NOTE: When removing the spring pin, hold a round bar against the end of the shifter rods to prevent damage.

13. Remove the detent spring plate from the center support, then remove the detent springs and balls.
14. Remove the first and second and the third and fourth shifter rods from the center support, then remove the shifter forks.
15. Remove the reverse shifter rod forward as it is fitted with a stopper pin.

NOTE: Be careful not to lose the detent interlock plugs located between the shifter rods in the center support.

16. Move both synchronizers rearward to prevent turning of the mainshaft.

NOTE: It may be necessary to tap the synchronizers with the hammer handle to get them engaged.

17. Remove the locknut and washer from the mainshaft.
18. Remove the nut, washer countershaft reverse gear and collar from the rear of the countergear.
19. Remove the center support countergear bearing snap-ring.
20. Remove the center support.
21. Separate the clutch gear, needle bearings and blocker ring from the mainshaft assembly.
22. Press the rear bearing from the mainshaft.
23. Remove the thrust washer, 1st speed gear, needle roller bearing, a collar and blocker ring.
24. Remove the 1st and 2nd gear synchronizer assembly.
25. Remove the 2nd gear, blocker ring and needle roller bearing from the mainshaft.
26. Remove the snap-ring, 3rd and 4th synchronizer assembly and blocker ring from the mainshaft.

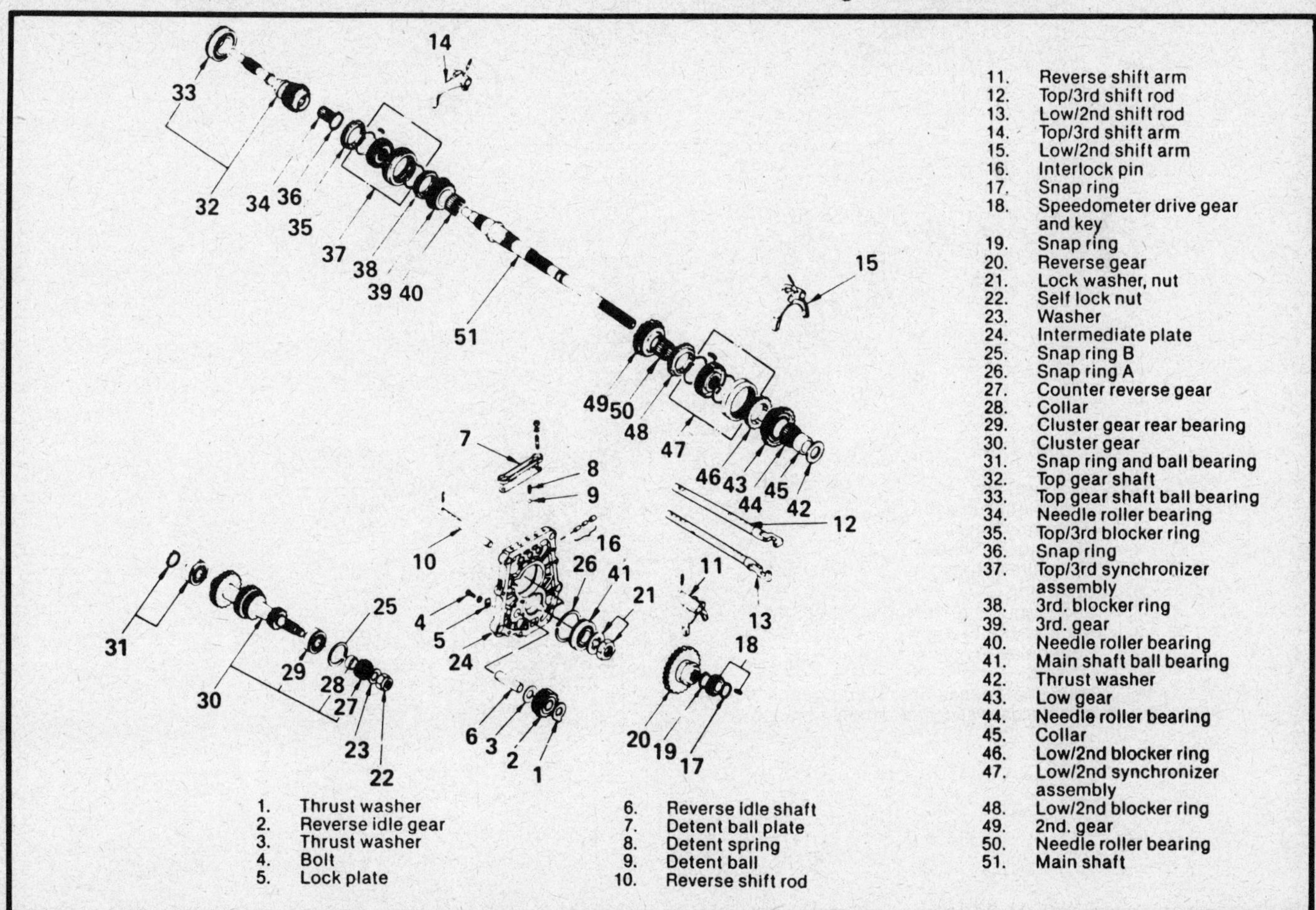

Isuzu/LUV 4 speed transmission gear assemblies

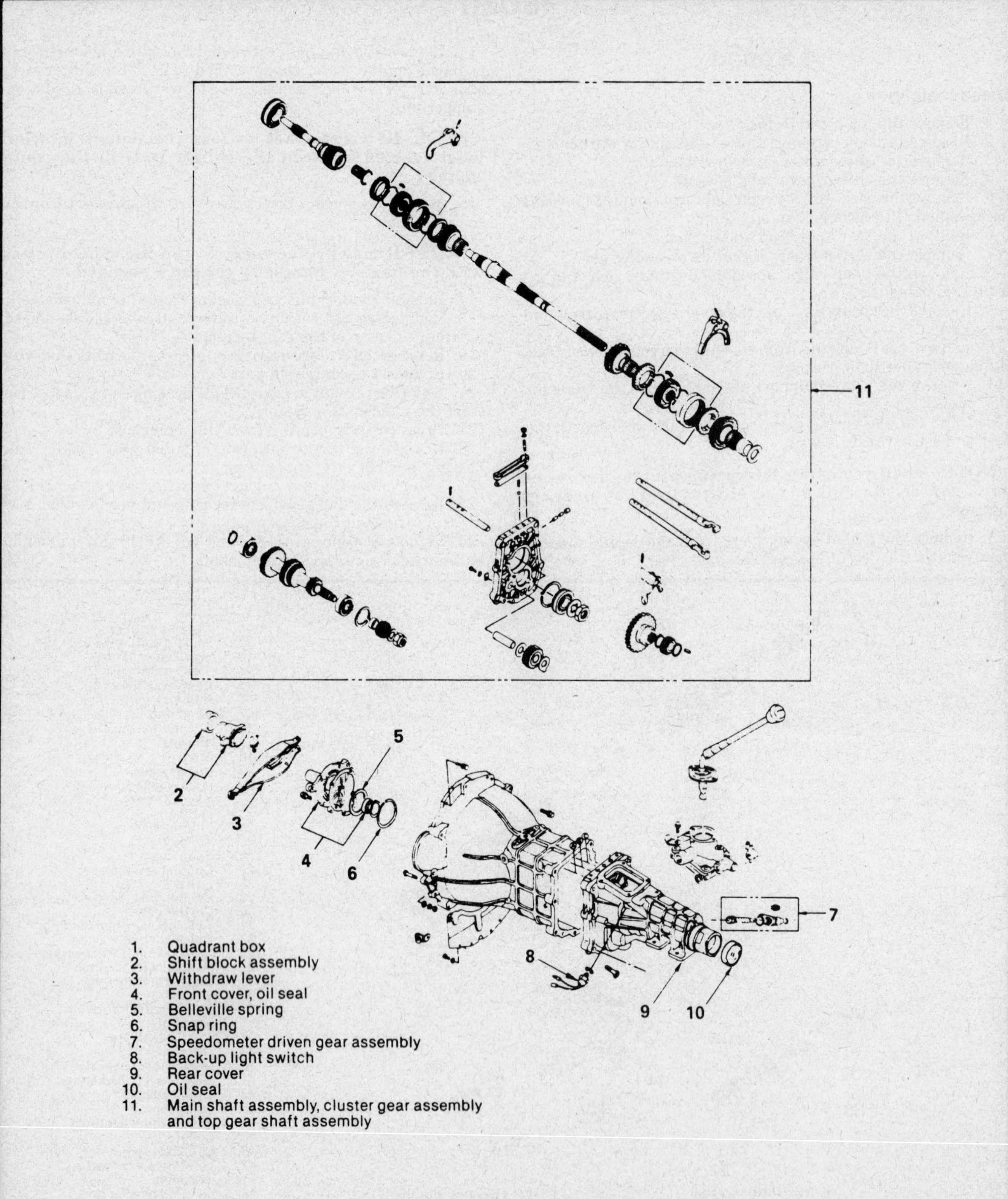

Isuzu/LUV 4 speed transmission major components

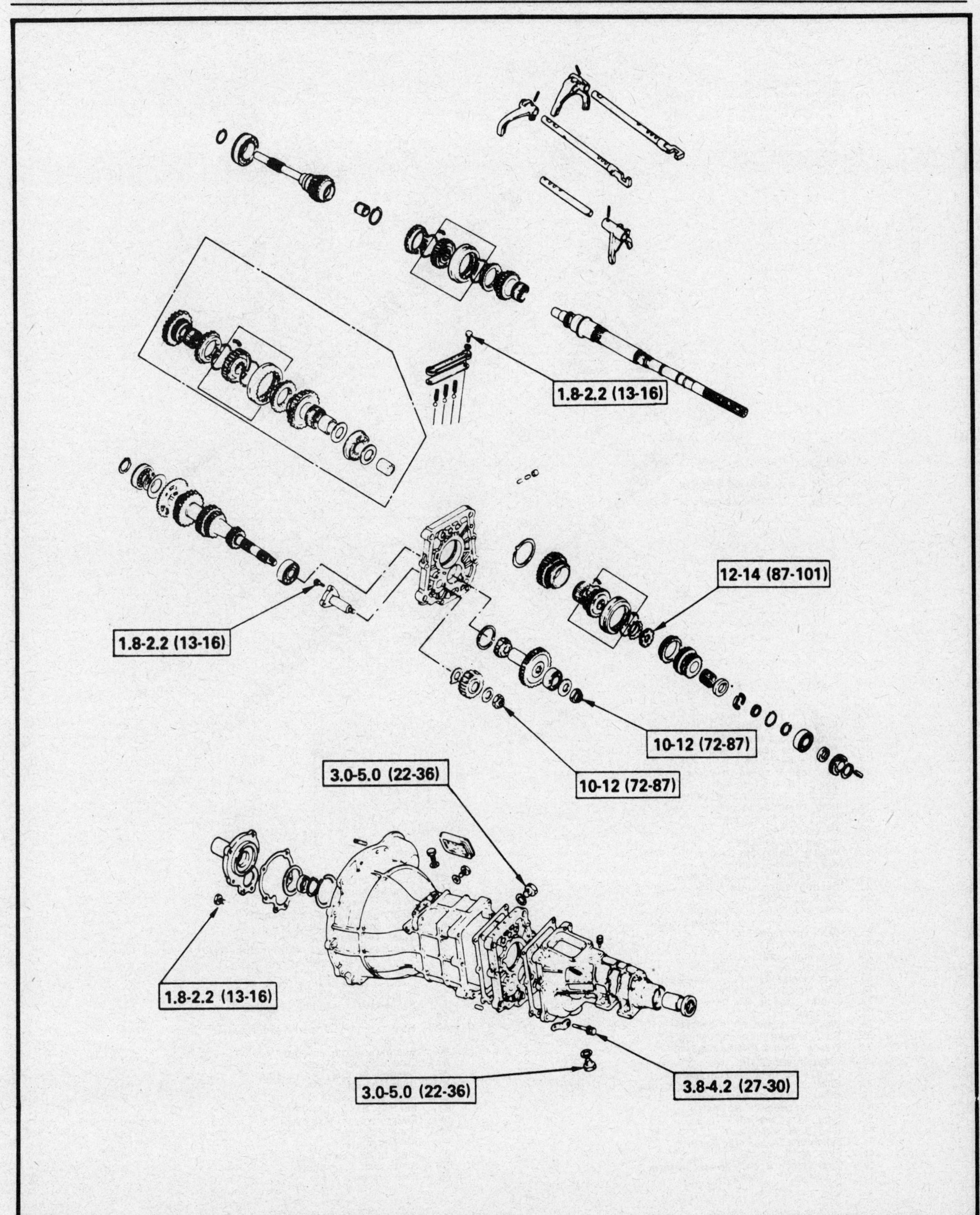

Isuzu/LUV 5 speed transmission gear assemblies torque values

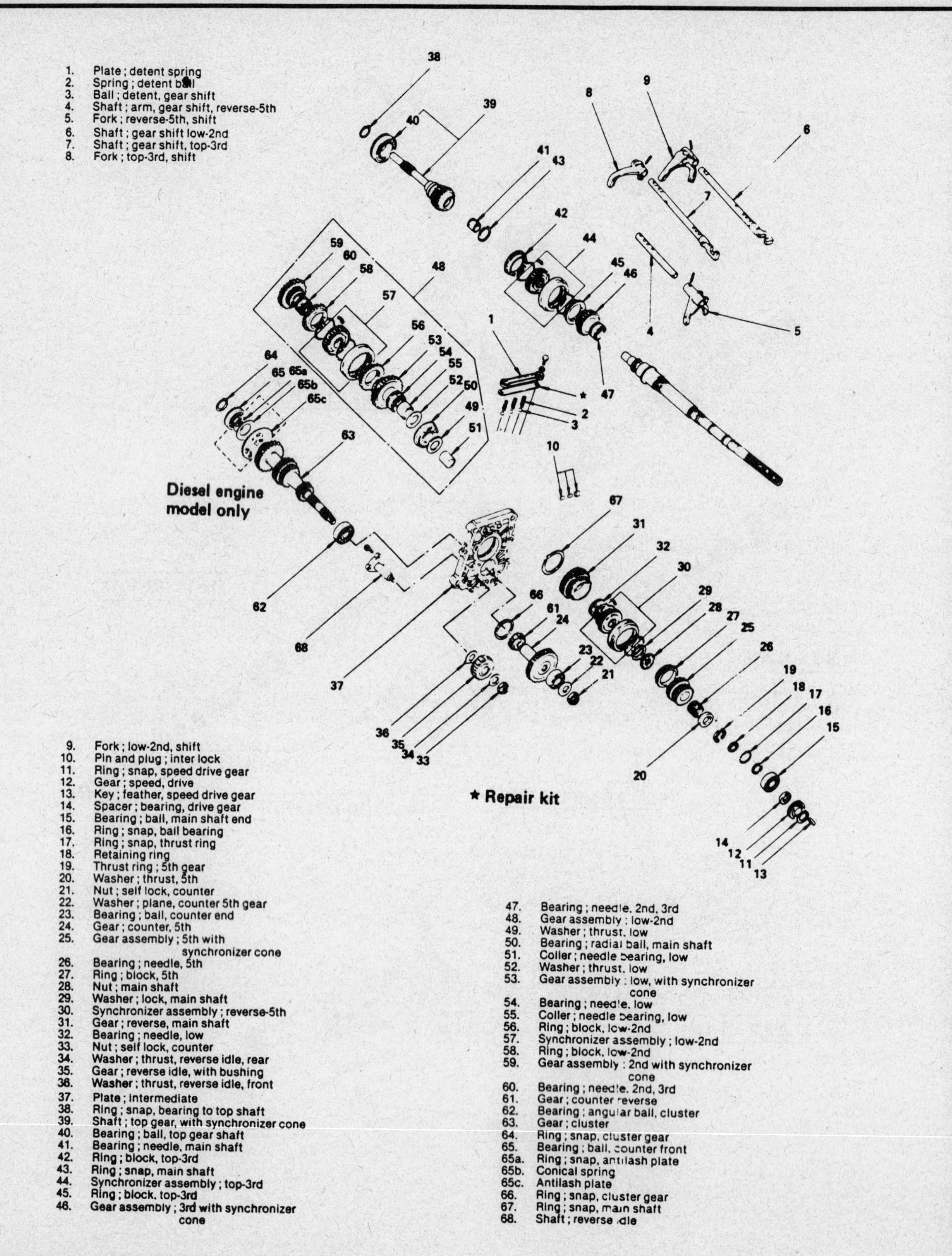
1. Plate ; detent spring
2. Spring ; detent ball
3. Ball ; detent, gear shift
4. Shaft ; arm, gear shift, reverse-5th
5. Fork ; reverse-5th, shift
6. Shaft ; gear shift low-2nd
7. Shaft ; gear shift, top-3rd
8. Fork ; top-3rd, shift
9. Fork ; low-2nd, shift
10. Pin and plug ; inter lock
11. Ring ; snap, speed drive gear
12. Gear ; speed, drive
13. Key ; feather, speed drive gear
14. Spacer ; bearing, drive gear
15. Bearing ; ball, main shaft end
16. Ring ; snap, ball bearing
17. Ring ; snap, thrust ring
18. Retaining ring
19. Thrust ring ; 5th gear
20. Washer ; thrust, 5th
21. Nut ; self lock, counter
22. Washer ; plane, counter 5th gear
23. Bearing ; ball, counter end
24. Gear ; counter, 5th
25. Gear assembly ; 5th with synchronizer cone
26. Bearing ; needle, 5th
27. Ring ; block, 5th
28. Nut ; main shaft
29. Washer ; lock, main shaft
30. Synchronizer assembly ; reverse-5th
31. Gear ; reverse, main shaft
32. Bearing ; needle, low
33. Nut ; self lock, counter
34. Washer ; thrust, reverse idle, rear
35. Gear ; reverse idle, with bushing
36. Washer ; thrust, reverse idle, front
37. Plate ; intermediate
38. Ring ; snap, bearing to top shaft
39. Shaft ; top gear, with synchronizer cone
40. Bearing ; ball, top gear shaft
41. Bearing ; needle, main shaft
42. Ring ; block, top-3rd
43. Ring ; snap, main shaft
44. Synchronizer assembly ; top-3rd
45. Ring ; block, top-3rd
46. Gear assembly ; 3rd with synchronizer cone
47. Bearing ; needle, 2nd, 3rd
48. Gear assembly ; low-2nd
49. Washer ; thrust, low
50. Bearing ; radial ball, main shaft
51. Coller ; needle bearing, low
52. Washer ; thrust, low
53. Gear assembly ; low, with synchronizer cone
54. Bearing ; needle, low
55. Coller ; needle bearing, low
56. Ring ; block, low-2nd
57. Synchronizer assembly ; low-2nd
58. Ring ; block, low-2nd
59. Gear assembly ; 2nd with synchronizer cone
60. Bearing ; needle, 2nd, 3rd
61. Gear ; counter reverse
62. Bearing ; angular ball, cluster
63. Gear ; cluster
64. Ring ; snap, cluster gear
65. Bearing ; ball, counter front
65a. Ring ; snap, antilash plate
65b. Conical spring
65c. Antilash plate
66. Ring ; snap, cluster gear
67. Ring ; snap, main shaft
68. Shaft ; reverse idle
Diesel engine model only
★ Repair kit

Isuzu/LUV 5 speed transmission gear assemblies

27. Remove the 3rd gear and needle bearings.
28. Remove the snap-ring and press off the clutch bearing and countergear bearing from the shaft.

Assembly

1. Stand the front of the mainshaft upward and install the 3rd speed gear and needle roller bearing with the tapered side of the gear facing the front of the mainshaft.
2. Install a blocker ring with the clutching teeth upward over the synchronizing surface of the 3rd speed gear.
3. If it is necessary to reassemble the synchronizer assembly, turn the face of the synchronizer hub with the heavy boss to the face of the sleeve with the light chamfering on the outer rim.
4. Fit the keys into the key groove and position the synchronizer springs into the hole in the side face of the hub.
5. Install the 3rd and 4th synchronizer assembly on the mainshaft with the face of the sleeve with the light chamfer rearward.
6. Turn the rear of the mainshaft upward and install the 2nd speed gear and needle roller bearing on the mainshaft with the tapered surface of the gear facing the rear of the mainshaft.
7. Install a blocker ring with the clutching teeth downward over the synchronizing surface of the 2nd speed gear.
8. Install the 1st and 2nd synchronizer assembly with the chamfer on the sleeve facing the front of the mainshaft.
9. Install a blocker ring with the clutching teeth rearward.
10. Install the collar, needle roller bearing and 1st speed gear on the mainshaft.

NOTE: The tapered side of the gear should be facing the front of the mainshaft.

11. Install the 1st speed gear thrust washer on the mainshaft with the grooved side facing 1st gear.
12. Press the rear bearing on the mainshaft with the snap-ring groove facing the front of the mainshaft.
13. If removed, press the ball bearing on the clutch gearshaft with the snap-ring groove on the bearing facing the front of the transmission. Install the snap-ring on the clutch gear shaft.
14. Assemble the needle roller bearing, blocker ring and clutch gear to the front of the mainshaft.
15. If removed, press on the countergear ball bearing with the snap-ring groove facing the rear of the transmission.
16. If removed, install the snap-rings in the inner circumference of the mainshaft and countergear holes of the center support.
17. If removed, insert the idler gear shaft with the lock plate groove side into the center support from the rear, then install the lock plate.
18. Mesh the countergear with the mainshaft assembly and install a holding tool on the mainshaft and countergear.
19. Install the center support.
20. Press the center support onto the shaft until the countergear bearing is brought into contact with its snap-ring.
21. Expand the countergear bearing snap-ring and press the center support further until the mainshaft and countergear snap-rings are fitted into their grooves.
22. Remove the holding tool from the mainshaft and countergear.
23. Move both synchronizers rearward to prevent turning of the mainshaft.
24. Install the collar, countershaft reverse gear, washer and nut on the rear of the countergear.

NOTE: Install the locknut so that the chamfered side is facing the lock washer.

25. Install the locknut and lock washer on the mainshaft.

NOTE: Install the locknut so that the chamfered side is facing the lockwasher.

26. Apply grease to the two detent plugs and insert them into their detent holes from the middle hole of the center support.
27. Install the 1st and 2nd shifter forks and the 3rd and 4th into their grooves in the synchronizer assembly.
28. Install 3rd and 4th shifter rod from the rear of the center support through the middle hole and into the 1st and 2nd, 3rd and 4th shifter forks. Align the spring pin hole in the shifter fork with the hole in the shifter rod.

NOTE: Identify the 3rd and 4th shifter rod by the two detent grooves on the side of the rod.

29. Install the 1st and 2nd shifter rod from the rear of the center support through the 1st and 2nd shifter fork and align the hole in the rod to the hole in the shifter fork.
30. If removed, install the stopper pin in the reverse shifter rod and the front of the center support.
31. Install the two spring pins in the 1st/2nd and 3rd/4th shifter forks.
32. Install the detent balls, spring, gasket and retainer on the center support.
33. Install the center support assembly and gasket.
34. Assemble the reverse shifter fork to the reverse gear and install these parts into position from the rear side of the mainshaft, then connect them to the reverse shifter rod.
35. Install the spring pin in the reverse shifter fork.
36. Install the thrust washer and reverse idler gear on the idler shaft.

NOTE: The reverse idler gear should be installed with undercut teeth forward.

37. Install the speedometer drive gear snap-ring and key on the mainshaft.
38. Install a new oil seal in the rear extension.
39. Apply grease to the outer thrust washer of the reverse idler shaft and insert it in the rear extensions.
40. Install the rear extension and gasket.
41. Install the back-up lamp switch and CRS switch.
42. Install the shifter cover and gasket.
43. Install the oil O-ring to the speedometer drive gear and install the gear.
44. Install the front bearing retainer seal.
45. Install a snap-ring in the outer circumference of the clutch gear bearing.
46. Apply grease to the bearing retainer spring washer and place it in the bearing retainer with the dished face turned to the bearing outer race.
47. Install the bearing retainer to the front of the transmission case.

NOTE: The shorter bolts are used on countergear front bearing side of the bearing retainer.

48. Install the ball stud to the bearing retainer.
49. Install the boot clutch fork and throwout bearing, then install the retaining spring.

MAZDA

4 Speed

Disassembly

The clutch housing, split transmission case, and extension housing are all made of aluminum.

1. Drain the oil.
2. Remove the clutch housing, bearing retainer, release bearing, and release fork.
3. Remove the speedometer shaft sleeve and driven gear.
4. Remove the extension housing.
5. Remove the back-up light switch.
6. Separate the case halves. Do not pry apart.
7. Measure gear backlash. The backlash for all gears should be 0.004–0.008 in.
8. Remove the countergear set from the right-hand half of the case.
9. Use a magnet to remove the ball from the second countergear bearing.
10. Withdraw the input and the output shafts as a unit.
11. Use a punch to drive the three slotted spring pins out of the shift forks and shift fork shafts.

NOTE: The slotted pin cannot always be fully removed from the first/second shift fork; however, the shift fork can still be withdrawn. Do not try to force the pin out, as damage to the transmission case could result.

12. Remove the case cover and the three detent balls and springs.
13. Remove the shift fork shafts in the following order: First/second shaft. Pin. Reverse shift fork shaft. Third/fourth shaft. Pin.
14. Measure the thrust clearance of the reverse idler gear. The specified clearance is 0.002–0.020 in.
15. Remove the idler shaft. Remove the gear and washer.
16. Measure the thrust clearance of the gears on the output shaft: 1st, 2nd, 5th; 0.006–0.010 in. 3rd; 0.006–0.012 in. Reverse; 0.008–0.012 in. 5th gear is optiona.
17. Disassemble the components of the output shaft. Five-speed transmissions have an extra gearset and related parts. Replace the front bearing, if it is rough or noisy. Use a drift and a press. Remove the snap-ring first. For bearing installation, replacement snap-rings are available in a range of sizes 0.0925–0.1024 in. to obtain minimum axial play between the input shaft and the bearing.

Assembly

1. Assemble the components of the synchronizer hubs, and the output shaft.
2. Install the rear bushing on the output shaft, being careful to install it in the proper direction.
3. Install the ball into the groove of the bushing and slide the bushing over the shaft.

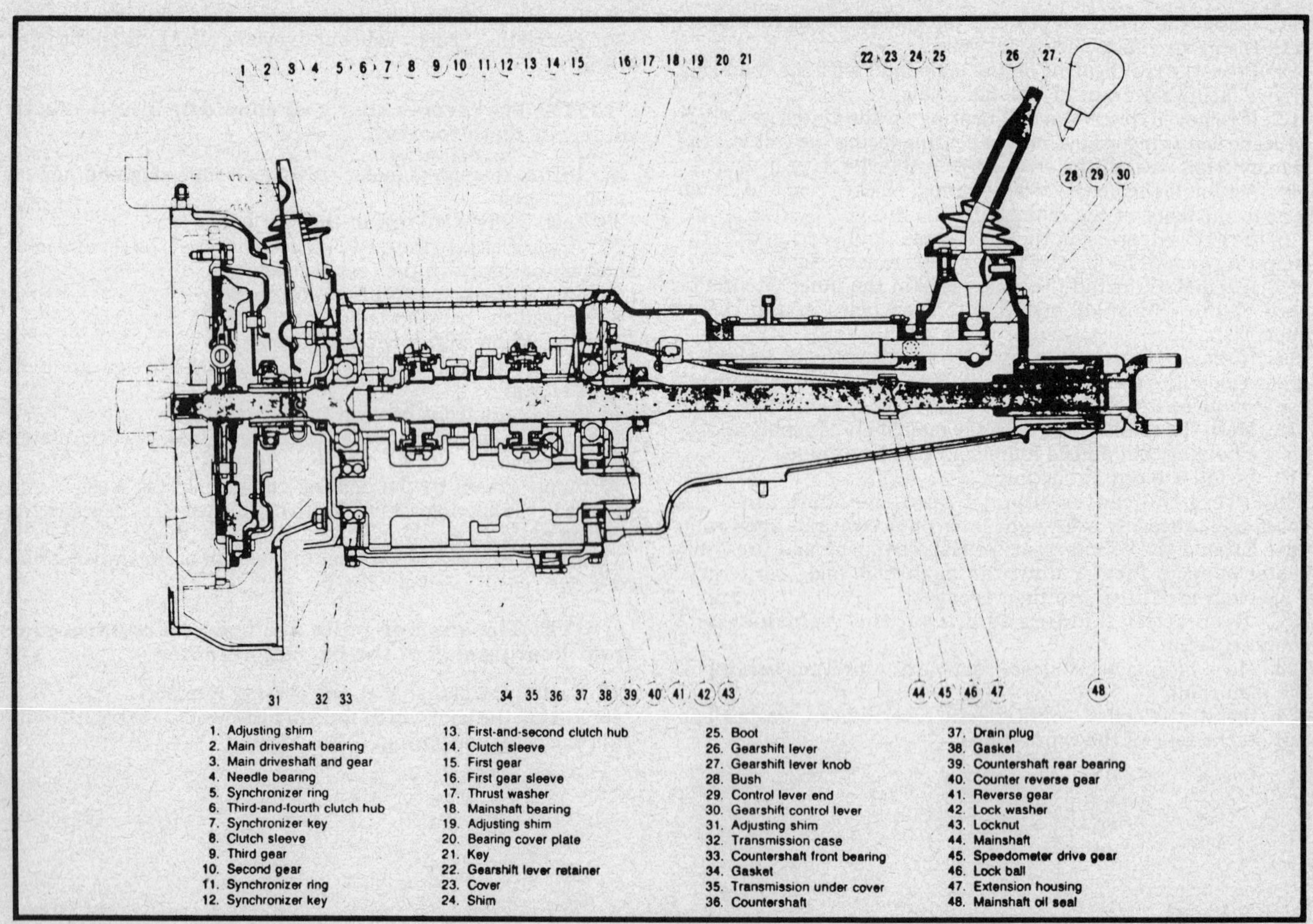

Cross section of Mazda/Courier 4-speed without intermediate housing

4. Install the needle roller bearing, reverse gear, the ball and the reverse gear synchronizer hub.

5. Install the following items on the output shaft of the four-speed transmission, in the order indicated: Large-diameter reverse gear spacer. Long spacer. Shims.

6. Install the following items on the output shaft of the five-speed transmission in the order indicated: Ball. Fifth gear synchronizer ring. Fifth gear. Needle roller bearing. Bushing. Rear support ball bearing.

7. Install the shims and the nut on the end of the output shaft.

NOTE: If the original nut is being used, change the number of shims to alter the locking portion of the nut.

8. Check the thrust clearance of each gear.

9. Working from the rear of the output shaft, install 3rd gear, synchronizer, spacer, and 3rd/4th synchronizer hub (should face forward).

10. Select a snap-ring to obtain a thrust clearance of less than 0.002 in. for the 3rd/4th synchronizer hub.

11. Assemble the following from the rear of the output shaft: Snap-ring. Key. Speedometer drive gear. Snap-ring.

12. Check thrust clearance of gears.

13. Install the fork and shaft assembly in the transmission case.

14. Insert the straight pins in the grooves on either side of the third/fourth shift shaft.

15. Assemble the first/second gear shaft and fork.

16. Perform Step 11 for the reverse shift fork shaft.

17. Insert the three detent balls, followed by their springs.

18. Place the cover gasket on the case and install the cover.

19. Use a punch to drive a slotted spring pin into each shift fork to secure it.

20. Assemble the input and output shafts.

21. Install the shift forks into their respective grooves on the input/output shaft assembly.

22. Install the shaft assembly in the right-hand half of the transmission case, so that the snap-ring is positioned firmly against the front surface of the transmission case.

23. Apply grease to the countergear rear bearing lockball. Insert the ball into the hole in the rear bearing outer race.

24. Place the countergear assembly into the right-hand half of the transmission case. Mate the lockball with the hole in the transmission case. Place the bearing snap-ring firmly against the front surface of the transmission case.

25. Install the reverse idler gear.

26. Install the washers, so that their protrusions align with the grooves in the transmission case.

27. Install the shaft into the case and through the gears and washers.

28. Align the grooves in the idler shaft with the hole in the shaft boss. Install the retaining bolt and washer into the boss.

29. Apply a light coating of liquid sealer over the joint surfaces of the transmission case halves.

CAUTION

Do not apply sealer to the ½ in. hole for the back-up light switch.

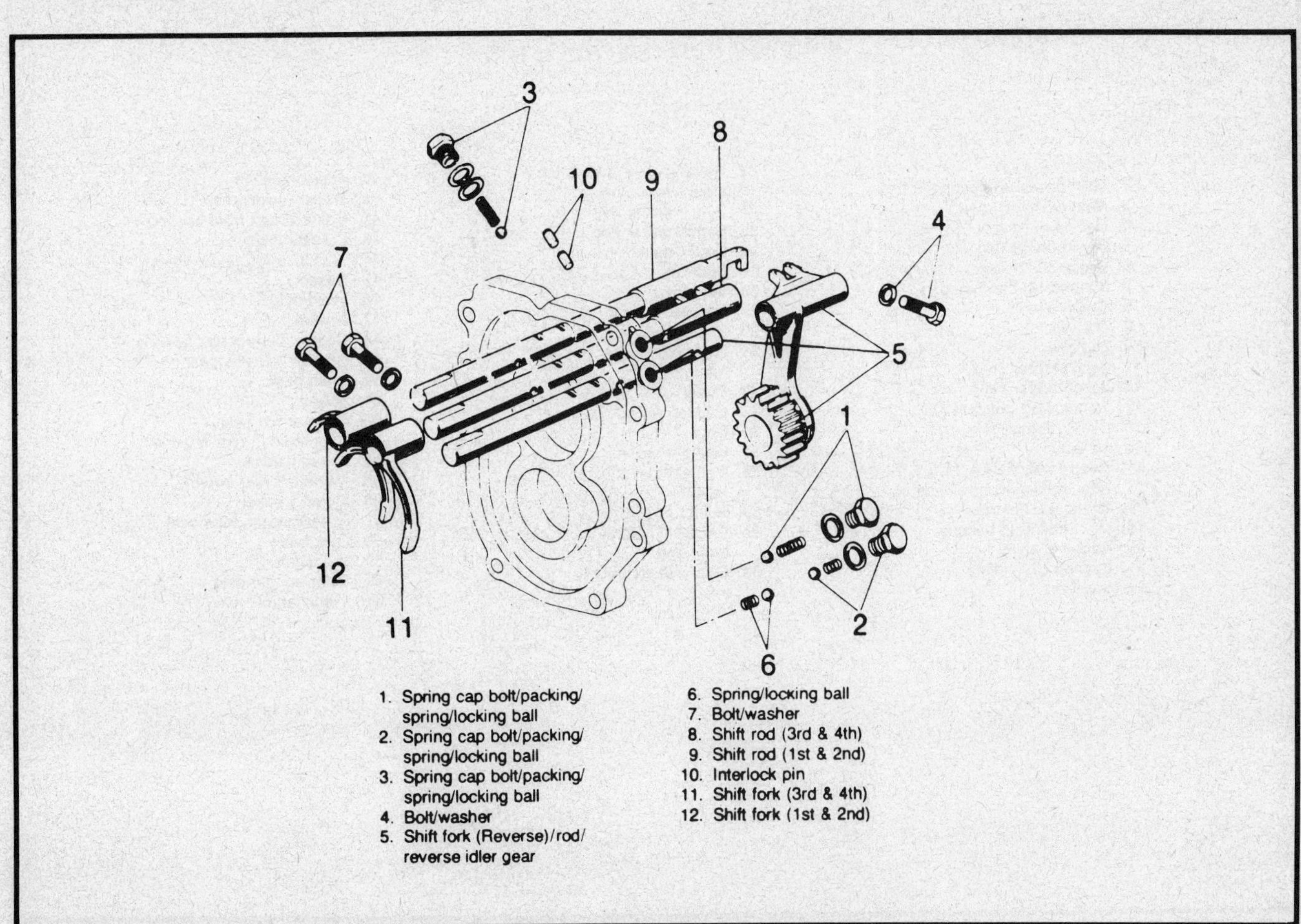

Exploded view of shift selector rods and forks, 4- speed with intermediate housing

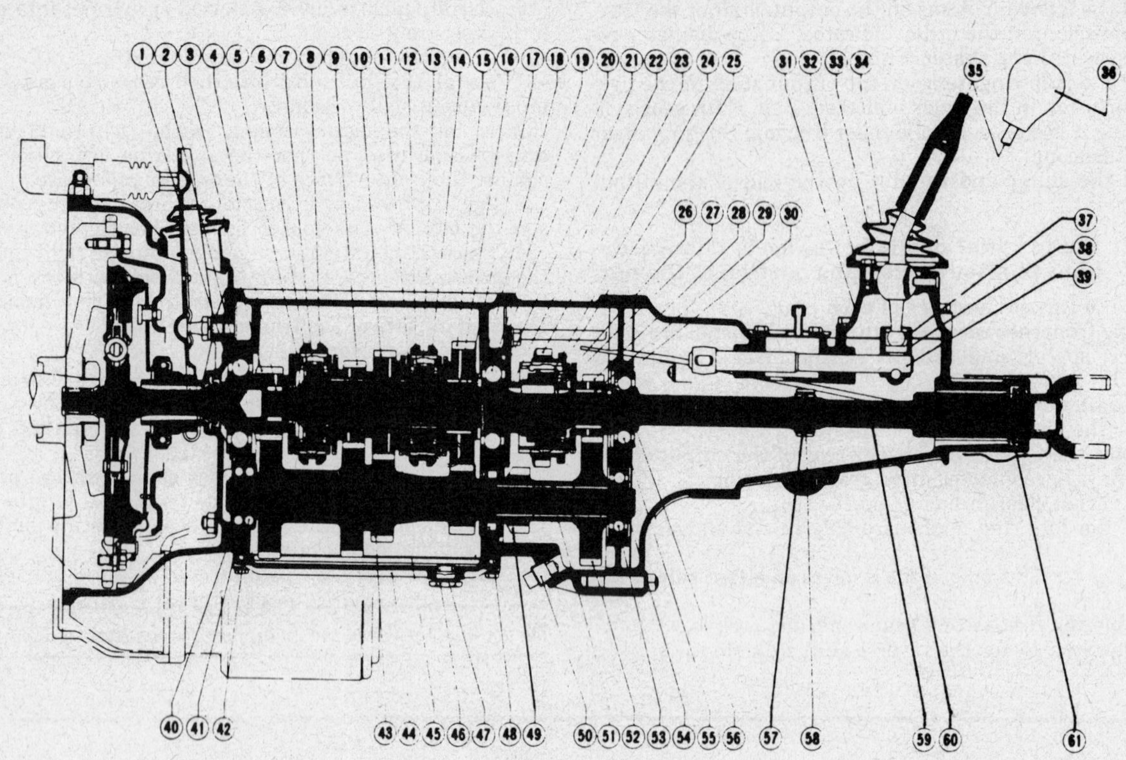

1. Adjusting shim
2. Main driveshaft bearing
3. Main driveshaft gear
4. Needle bearing
5. Synchronizer ring
6. Synchronizer key
7. 3rd-and-4th clutch hub
8. Clutch sleeve
9. 3rd gear
10. 2nd gear
11. Synchronizer ring
12. Synchronizer key
13. 1st-and-2nd clutch hub
14. Clutch sleeve
15. 1st gear
16. Needle bearing
17. Needle bearing inner race
18. Thrust washer
19. Mainshaft front bearing
20. Adjusting shim
21. Bearing cover plate
22. Spacer
23. Reverse gear and clutch sleeve assembly
24. Synchronizer key
25. Synchronizer ring
26. Lock washer
27. Locknut
28. 5th gear
29. Needle bearing
30. Thrust washer
31. Gearshift lever retainer
32. Cover
33. Gasket
34. Boot
35. Gearshift lever
36. Gearshift lever knob
37. Bush
38. Gearshift control lever end
39. Gearshift control lever
40. Adjusting shim
41. Transmission case
42. Countershaft front bearing
43. Countershaft
44. Transmission under cover
45. Gasket
46. Drain plug
47. Gasket
48. Countershaft center bearing
49. Counter reverse gear
50. Drain plug
51. Spacer
52. Counter 5th gear
53. Countershaft rear bearing
54. Thrust washer
55. Mainshaft rear bearing
56. Thrust washer
57. Speedometer drive gear
58. Lock ball
59. Mainshaft
60. Extension housng
61. Mainshaft oil seal

Cross section Mazda 5-speed

30. Align the transmission case locating pins with their holes and assemble the halves of the case.

NOTE: There are four different bolt lengths, do not install the wrong bolt in the wrong hole.

31. Insert the ball, spring, and washer in the back-up light switch hole. Screw in the switch assembly.
32. Install the gasket and bolt the extension housing to the rear of the transmission.
33. Install the speedometer shaft sleeve and drive gear.
34. Apply grease to the conical springs. Install one spring over the input shaft bearing and the other over the countershaft bearing. Install the spacer over the countershaft bearing spring, after coating the spacer with grease.
35. Install the gasket and the clutch housing.

5 Speed

Disassembly

1. Pull the release fork outward until the spring clip of the fork releases from the ball pivot.
2. Remove the fork and release bearing.
3. Remove the clutch housing shim and gasket.
4. Remove the gearshift lever retainer and gasket.
5. Remove the spring and steel ball, select lock spindle and spring from the gearshift lever retainer.
6. Remove the extension housing with the control lever end down to the left as far as it will go.
7. Remove the control lever end, key and control rod.
8. Remove the lock plate and speedometer gear.
9. Remove the back-up light switch.
10. Remove the snap-ring and slide the speedometer drive gear from the mainshaft.
11. Remove the bottom cover and gasket.
12. Remove the shift rod ends.
13. Remove the rear bearing housing.
14. Remove the snap-ring and remove the mainshaft rear bearing, thrust washer and race.
15. Using the puller, remove the washer and countershaft rear bearing.
16. Remove the counter fifth gear.
17. Remove the intermediate housing.
18. Remove the springs and shift locking balls.
19. Remove the two blind covers and gaskets from the case.
20. Remove the reverse/fifth shift rod, fork and interlock pin.
21. Remove the first/second and third/fourth shift forks, rods and interlock pins.
22. Remove the snap-ring and slide the washer, fifth gear and synchronizer ring from the mainshaft. Also, remove the steel ball and needle bearing.
23. Lock the rotation of the mainshaft with second and reverse.
24. Remove the locknut and slide the reverse/fifth clutch hub and sleeve assembly, synchronizer ring, reverse gear and needle bearing from the mainshaft.
25. Remove the spacer and counter reverse gear from the countershaft.
26. Remove the reverse idler gear, thrust washers and shaft from the transmission case.
27. Remove the bearing rear cover plate.
28. Remove the snap-ring from the front end of the countershaft and install Mazda tool number 49 0839 445 synchronizer ring holder or its equivalent between the fourth synchronizer ring and the synchromesh gear on the main driveshaft.
29. Remove the countershaft front bearing.
30. Remove the adjusting shim from the countershaft front bearing bore.
31. Remove the countershaft center bearing outer race.
32. With a special puller and attachment, remove the mainshaft front bearing, thrust washer and inner race along with the adjusting shim from the mainshaft front bearing bore.
33. Remove the snap-ring, and remove the main driveshaft bearing.
34. Remove the countershaft center bearing inner race with the puller.
35. Separate the input shaft from the mainshaft and remove the input shaft.
36. Remove the synchronizer ring and needle bearing from the input shaft.
37. Remove the mainshaft assembly.
38. Remove the first/second and third/fourth shift forks from the case.
39. Remove the snap-ring and slide the third/fourth clutch hub and sleeve assembly, synchronizer ring and third gear from the mainshaft.
40. Remove the thrust washer, first gear and needle bearing from the rear of the mainshaft.
41. Press out the needle bearing inner race, synchronizer ring, first and second clutch hub, sleeve assembly, synchronizer ring and second gear from the mainshaft.

Assembly

1. Install the third/fourth clutch hub into the sleeve, place the three keys into the clutch hub slots and install the springs onto the hub.
2. Assemble the first/second and reverse/fifth clutch hub and sleeve.
3. Install the needle bearing, second gear, synchronizer ring, and first/second clutch assembly on the rear section of the mainshaft.
4. Press on the first gear needle bearing inner race.
5. Install the third gear and synchronizer ring onto the front section of the mainshaft.
6. Install the third/fourth clutch assembly onto the mainshaft.
7. Install the snap-ring on the mainshaft.
8. Install the needle bearing, synchronizer ring, first gear and thrust washer on the mainshaft.
9. Install the mainshaft assembly.
10. Install the needle bearing on the front end of the mainshaft.
11. Install the first/second and third/fourth shift forks in their respective clutch sleeves.
12. Check the mainshaft bearing end-play. Check the depth of the mainshaft bearing bore in the case. Measure the mainshaft bearing height. The difference indicates the required adjusting shim to give a total end-play of less than 0.0039 in.
13. Install the synchronizer ring holder tool between the fourth synchronizer ring and the synchromesh gear on the input shaft.
14. Position the shims and mainshaft bearing in the bore and install with a press.
15. Install the input shaft bearing in the same way.
16. Check the countershaft front bearing end-play in the same way as the mainshaft bearing end-play.
17. Install the front bearing snap-ring.
18. Press the countershaft center bearing into position.
19. Install the bearing cover plate.
20. Install the reverse idler gearshaft, thrust washers and reverse idler gear.
21. Install the counter reverse gear and spacer on the rear end on the countershaft.
22. Install the thrust washer and press the needle bearing inner race of the reverse gear on the mainshaft.
23. Install the needle bearing, reverse gear, synchronizer ring, reverse/fifth clutch assembly and new mainshaft locknut on the mainshaft.
24. Lock the mainshaft with the second and reverse gears. Tighten the locknut.

25. Install the needle bearing, synchronizer ring and fifth gear on the mainshaft.
26. Install the thrust washer, steel ball and snap-ring on the mainshaft.
27. Check the thrust washer-to-snap-ring clearance. It should be 0.0039–0.0118 in.
28. Install the first/second shift rod through the holes in the case and fork.
29. Install the interlock pin with a special installer and guide.
30. Install the third/fourth shift rod through the holes in the case and fork.
31. Align the holes and install the lockbolts of each shift fork and rod.
32. Install the interlock pin as above.
33. Position the reverse/fifth shift fork on the clutch sleeve and install the shift rod.
34. Tighten the lockbolt.
35. Install the three shift locking balls, springs and cap bolts.
36. Place the third/fourth clutch sleeve in third gear.
37. Check the clearance between the synchronizer key and the exposed edge of the synchronizer ring with a feeler gauge. The gap should be 0.026–0.079 in. Adjust by varying thrust washers.
38. Install the two blind covers and gaskets.
39. Install the undercover and gasket.
40. Apply a thin coat of sealer to the mating edges and install the intermediate housing on the transmission case. Align the lockbolt holes of the housing and reverse idler gearshaft, install and tighten the lockbolt.
41. Position the counter fifth gear and bearing to the rear end of the countershaft and install with a press.
42. Install the thrust washer and snap-ring.
43. Check the clearance between the washer and snap-ring. Clearance should be less than 0.0039 in.
44. Install the mainshaft rear bearing.
45. Install the thrust washer and snap-ring.
46. Check the thrust washer-to-snap-ring clearance. Clearance should be less than 0.0059 in.
47. Apply a thin coat of sealing agent to the mating surfaces and install the bearing housing on the intermediate housing.
48. Install the shift rod ends on their respective rods.
49. Install the speedometer drive gear and steel ball on the mainshaft. Secure it with a snap-ring.
50. Install a speedometer driven gear assembly on the extension housing and secure it with the bolt and lock plate.
51. Insert the control rod through the holes from the front side of the extension housing.
52. Align the key and insert the control lever end in the control rod.
53. Install the bolt and tighten it to 20–30 ft. lbs.
54. Install the back-up light switch.
55. Place the gasket on the case and install the extension housing with the control lever end down and as far to the left as it will go.
56. Insert the select lock spindle and spring from the underside of the shift lever retainer.
57. Install the steel ball and spring in alignment with the spindle groove and install the spring cap bolt.
58. Install the gearshift lever retainer and gasket on the extension housing.
59. Check the bearing end-play. Measure the depth of the bearing bore in the housing. Measure the height of the bearing protrusion. The difference indicates the thickness of the shim needed. The end-play should be less than 0.0039 in.
60. Place the gasket on the front side of the case. Apply lubricant to the lip of the oil seal and install the clutch housing on the case.
61. Install the release bearing and fork on the clutch housing.

Mazda 4 & 5 Speed (1982-84)

On models equipped with a 5 speed transmission, the disassembly and assembly of the rear extension housing, selector levers and forks are completed in the same manner as the 4 speed transmission. After this has been done, the added housing can be removed by taking out the retaining bolts. The housing will have to be lightly tapped with a soft-faced hammer. The removal of the housing exposes the 5th/reverse synchronizer assembly, the reverse countergear, the countershaft and mainshaft bearings. The bearings are pulled from the shafts and then the gears can be removed. The assembly is in the reverse of the removal procedure.

Disassembly

1. Remove the throwout bearing and fork from the clutch housing. Remove the front transmission cover, shim and gasket. Remove the snap-ring from the maindrive shaft.
2. Remove the gearshift lever retainer and gasket from the extension housing. Unbolt and remove the extension housing by sliding the housing off the mainshaft with the control lever end laid down to the left as far as possible.
3. Unbolt and remove the control lever end and rod from the extension housing.
4. Remove the speedometer driven gear and the back-up light switch.
5. Remove the snap-ring retaining the speedometer drive gear on the main shaft. Slide the gear off of the mainshaft. Remove the lock ball.
6. Use an appropriate pusher tool and remove the transmission case from the intermediate bearing housing plate.
7. Remove the bearing from the case. remove the front bearing from the countershaft using a suitable puller.
8. Remove the three spring cap bolts and remove the springs and shift locking balls. Remove the reverse shift rod, fork assembly and reverse gear from the bearing housing. Remove each shift fork mounting spring pin and push the shift rods rearward out of the housing. Remove the rods and forks. Remove the reverse shift rod locking ball and retaining pins from the bearing housing.
9. Remove the reverse gear and key from the mainshaft. Remove the snap ring from the rear end of the countershaft and slide the reverse counter gear off.
10. Remove the bearing cover and the reverse idler gear from the bearing housing.
11. Use a "soft" brass or copper hammer and tap the rear ends of the mainshaft and countershaft lightly and in turn until they can be removed from the bearing housing.
12. Remove the bearings from the housing. Remove the thrust washer, first gear, sleeve and synchronizer ring from the mainshaft.
13. Remove the snap-ring from the front of the mainshaft. Press the third and fourth clutch hub and sleeve assembly, synchronizer ring and third gear from the front of the mainshaft. Press the first and second clutch hub and sleeve assembly, synchronizer ring and second gear from the rear of the mainshaft.
14. Clean and inspect all parts. Replace as necessary.

Assembly

1. Assemble the third and fourth, first and second clutches by installing the clutch hub into the sleeve, positioning the three keys in the slots and installing the retainer springs.
2. Install the third gear and synchronizer ring onto the front of the mainshaft. Install the third and fourth clutch hub assembly onto the mainshaft. Be sure the hub is facing in the proper direction. Fit the retaining snap-ring in position.
3. Install the second gear and synchronizer ring onto the rear section of the mainshaft. Press the first and second clutch assembly onto the mainshaft. Install the synchronizer ring, first gear with sleeve and the thrust washer onto the mainshaft.
4. Install the main driveshaft and needle bearing to the mainshaft.
5. Check the countershaft rear bearing and mainshaft bear-

ing clearances. Clearance should be less than 0.0039 in. Shims are available in 0.0039 and 0.118 in. sizes. Press each bearing and shim into position in the bearing housing.

6. Press the countershaft and mainshaft assemblies in position on the bearing housing.

7. Install the reverse idler gear shaft and bearing cover to the bearing housing. Install the reverse gear and key onto the mainshaft. When installing the reverse gears, both gears should be fitted so that the chamfer on the teeth face rearward. Tighten the locknut to 125–150 ft. lbs. Bend the lock tab on the washer. Install the countershaft reverse gear and secure with snap-ring.

8. Insert the spring and ball into the bearing housing. Push down on the ball with a suitable tool and install the reverse shift rod, shift lever and reverse idler gear at the same time.

9. Install the first and second shift fork and the third and fourth shift fork over the clutch sleeves. Install the shift fork rods, align the mounting holes and secure with new spring pins. Install the pins with the split parallel to the shift fork mounting rod.

10. Install the shift locking balls and springs in their respective positions and secure with the retaining bolt.

11. Apply a thin coat of sealer to both sides of the bearing housing and mount the bearing housing in position on the transmission case.

12. Install the speedometer drive gear and steel ball on the mainshaft, secure them with the snap-ring.

13. Install the mainshaft and countershaft ball bearings.

14. Install the speedometer driven gear assembly to the extension housing. Insert the shift control lever through the holes from the front side of the extension housing. Install the control lever end to the control lever and tighten the mounting bolt to 20–25 ft. lbs.

15. Mount the back-up light switch on the extension housing. Apply a thin coat of sealer to the extension housing mounting flange and install the housing onto the bearing housing. Be sure the control lever is laid over to the left as far as possible when installing the extension housing. Install the gearshift lever retainer and gasket.

16. Lubricate the front oil seal and install the front cover on the transmission. The front bearing should have less than 0.004 play when the front cover is installed. Shims of 0.006 and 0.012 in. are available for adjustment purposes.

17. Install the throwout bearing fork and bearing and install the transmission.

Mazda 4 & 5 Speed (1986-88)

The 4 and 5 speed transmissions are basically the same, with an added housing located between the adapter plate and the rear extension housing, to carry the 5th and reverse gears. Added roller bearings are used in the housing to prevent shaft misalignment.

Disassembly

1. Remove the throwout bearing return spring, throwout bearing, and the release fork.
2. Remove the bearing housing.
3. Remove the input shaft and countershaft snap-rings.
4. Remove the floorshift lever retainer, complete with gasket.
5. Unfasten the cap bolt and withdraw the spring, steel ball, select lock pin and spring from the retainer.
6. Remove the extension housing. Turn the control lever as far left as it will go and slide the extension housing off the output shaft.
7. Remove the spring seat and spring from the end of the shift control lever.
8. Loosen the spring cap and withdraw the spring and plunger from their bore.
9. Remove the control rod and boss from the extension housing.
10. Remove the speedometer driven gear. Remove the back-up light switch.
11. Remove the speedometer drive gear.
12. Tap the front ends of the input shaft and countershaft with a plastic hammer; then remove the intermediate housing assembly from the transmission case.
13. Remove the three cap bolts; then withdraw the springs and lockballs.
14. Remove the reverse shift rod, reverse idler gear, and shift lever.
15. Remove the setscrews from all the shift forks and push the shift rods rearward to remove them. Remove the shift forks.
16. Withdraw the reverse shift rod lockball, spring, and interlock pins from the intermediate housing.
17. Remove reverse gear and key from the output shaft.
18. Remove the reverse countergear.
19. Remove the countershaft and output shaft from the intermediate housing.
20. Remove the bearings from the intermediate housing and transmission case.
21. Remove the snap-ring from the output shaft.
22. Slide the third/fourth clutch hub, sleeve, synchronizer ring, and third gear off the output shaft.
23. Remove the thrust washer, first gear, sleeve, synchronizer ring, and second gear from the rear of the output shaft.

Assembly

1. Install the third/fourth synchronizer clutch hub on the sleeve. Place the three synchronizer keys in the clutch hub key slots. Install the key springs with their open ends 120° apart.
2. Install third gear and the synchronizer ring on the front of the output shaft. Install the third/fourth clutch hub assembly on the output shaft. Be sure that the larger boss faces the front of the shaft.
3. Secure the gear and synchronizer with the snap-ring.
4. Perform Step 1 to the first/second synchronizer assembly.
5. Position the synchronizer ring on second gear. Slide second gear on the output shaft so that the synchronizer ring faces the rear of the shaft.
6. Install the first/second clutch hub assembly on the output shaft so that its oil grooves face the front of the shaft. Engage the keys in the notches on the second gear synchronizer ring.

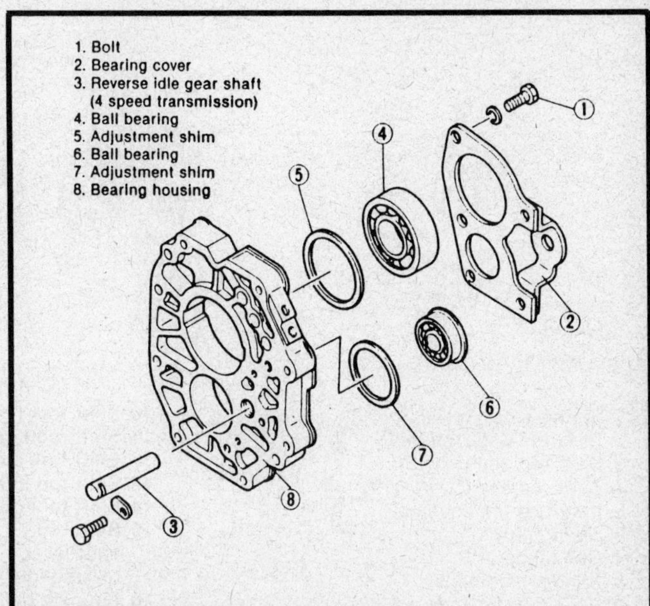

Mazda 4 & 5 speed extension bearing parts

1. Control lever
2. Control rod end
3. Oil passage
4. Speedometer driven gear
5. Back up lamp switch
6. Oil seal
7. Extension housing
8. Pin
9. Holder
10. Shim
11. Wave washer
12. Cover } 4 speed
13. Gasket } transmission

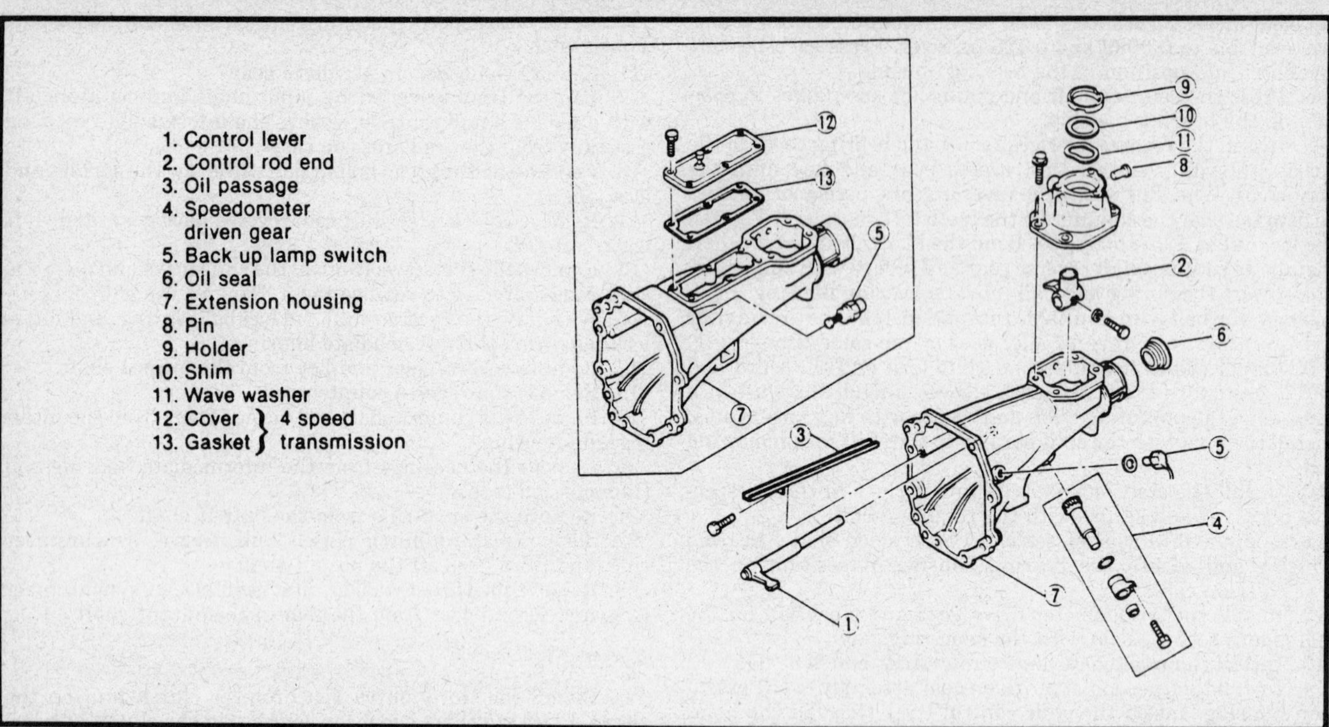

Mazda 4 & 5 speed extension housing parts

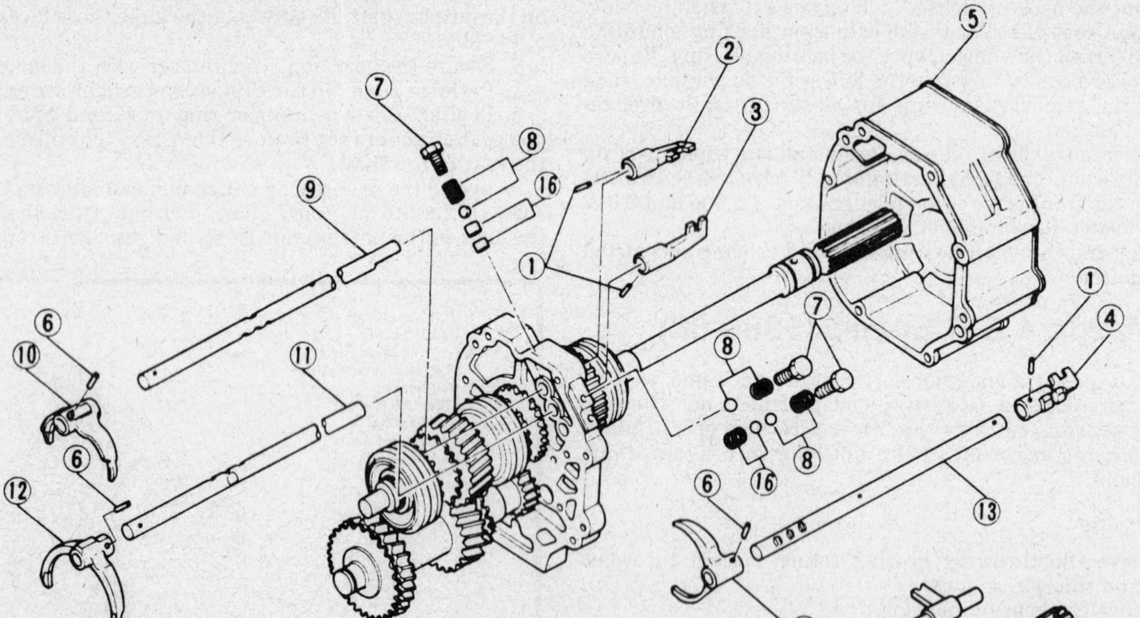

1. Spring pins } 5 speed transmission
2. Shift rod end (1st/2nd) } 5 speed transmission
3. Shift rod end (3rd/4th) } 5 speed transmission
4. Shift rod end (5th/reverse) } 5 speed transmission
5. Intermediate housing
6. Spring pins
7. Cap plugs
8. Springs and balls
9. Shift rod (1st/2nd)
10. Shift fork (1st/2nd)
11. Shift rod (3rd/4th)
12. Shift fork (3rd/4th)
13. Shift rod (5th/reverse) } 5 speed transmission
14. Shift fork (5th/reverse) } 5 speed transmission
15. Shift rod, shift lever, reverse idle gear } 4 speed transmission
16. Springs, balls, interlock pins

Mazda 4 & 5 speed shift forks and rods

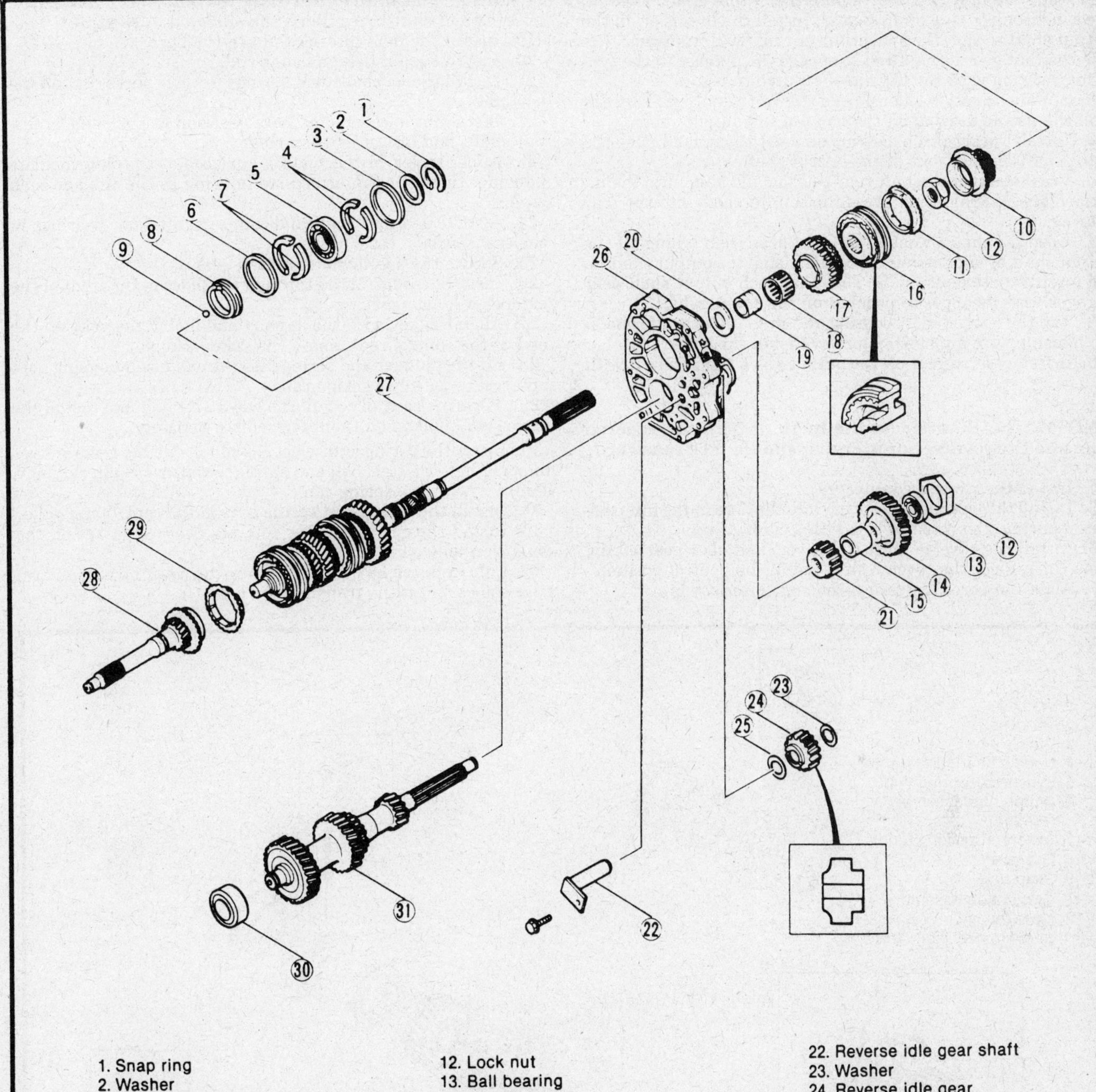

1. Snap ring
2. Washer
3. Retaining ring
4. C washers
5. Ball bearing
6. Retaining ring
7. C washers
8. Thrust lock washer
9. Ball
10. 5th gear
11. Synchronizer ring
12. Lock nut
13. Ball bearing
14. Counter gear
15. Spacer
16. Clutch hub assembly (5th/reverse)
17. Reverse gear
18. Needle bearing
19. Inner race
20. Washer
21. Counter reverse gear
22. Reverse idle gear shaft
23. Washer
24. Reverse idle gear
25. Washer
26. Bearing housing assembly
27. Main shaft and gear assembly
28. Main drive gear
29. Synchronizer ring
30. Ball bearing
31. Counter shaft gear

Mazda 5 speed main and countershaft assemblies

7. Slide the first gear sleeve onto the output shaft. Position the synchronizer ring on first gear. Install the first gear on the output shaft so that the synchronizer ring faces frontward. Rotate the first gear as required to engage the notches in the synchronizer ring with the keys in the clutch hub.
8. Slip the thrust washer on the rear of the output shaft. Install the needle bearing on the front of the output shaft.
9. Install the synchronizer ring on fourth gear and install the input shaft on the front of the output shaft.
10. Press the countershaft rear bearing and shim into the intermediate housing, then press the countershaft into the rear bearing.
11. Keep the thrust washer and first gear from falling off the output shaft by supporting the shaft. Install the output shaft on the intermediate housing. Be sure that each output shaft gear engages with its opposite number on the countershaft.
12. Tap the output shaft bearing and shim into the intermediate housing with a plastic hammer. Install the cover.
13. Install reverse gear on the output shaft and secure it with its key.

NOTE: The chamfer on the teeth of both the reverse gear and the reverse countergear should face rearward.

14. Install the reverse countergear.
15. Install the lockball and spring into the bore in the intermediate housing. Depress the ball with a screwdriver.
16. Install the reverse shift rod, lever, and idler gear at the same time. Place the reverse shift rod in the neutral position.
17. Align the bores and insert the shift interlock pin.
18. Install the third/fourth shift rod into the intermediate housing and shift bores. Place the shift rod in Neutral.
19. Install the next interlock pin in the bore.
20. Install the first/second shift rod.
21. Install the lockballs and springs in their bores. Install the cap bolt.
22. Install the speedometer drive gear and lockball on the output shaft, and install its snap-ring.
23. Apply sealer to the mating surfaces of the intermediate housing. Install the intermediate housing in the transmission case.
24. Install the input shaft and countershaft front bearings in the transmission case.
25. Secure the speedometer driven gear.
26. Install the control rod through the holes in the front of the extension housing.
27. Align the key with the keyway and install the yoke on the end of the control rod. Install the yoke lockbolt.
28. Fit the plunger and spring into the extension housing bore and secure with the spring cap.
29. Turn the control rod all the way to the left and install the extension housing on the intermediate housing.
30. Insert the spring and select lockpin inside the gearshift retainer. Align the steel ball and spring with the lockpin slot, and secure it with the spring cap.
31. Install the spring and spring seat in the control rod yoke.
32. Install the gearshift lever retainer over its gasket on the extension housing.
33. Lubricate the lip of the front bearing cover oil seal and secure the cover on the transmission case.

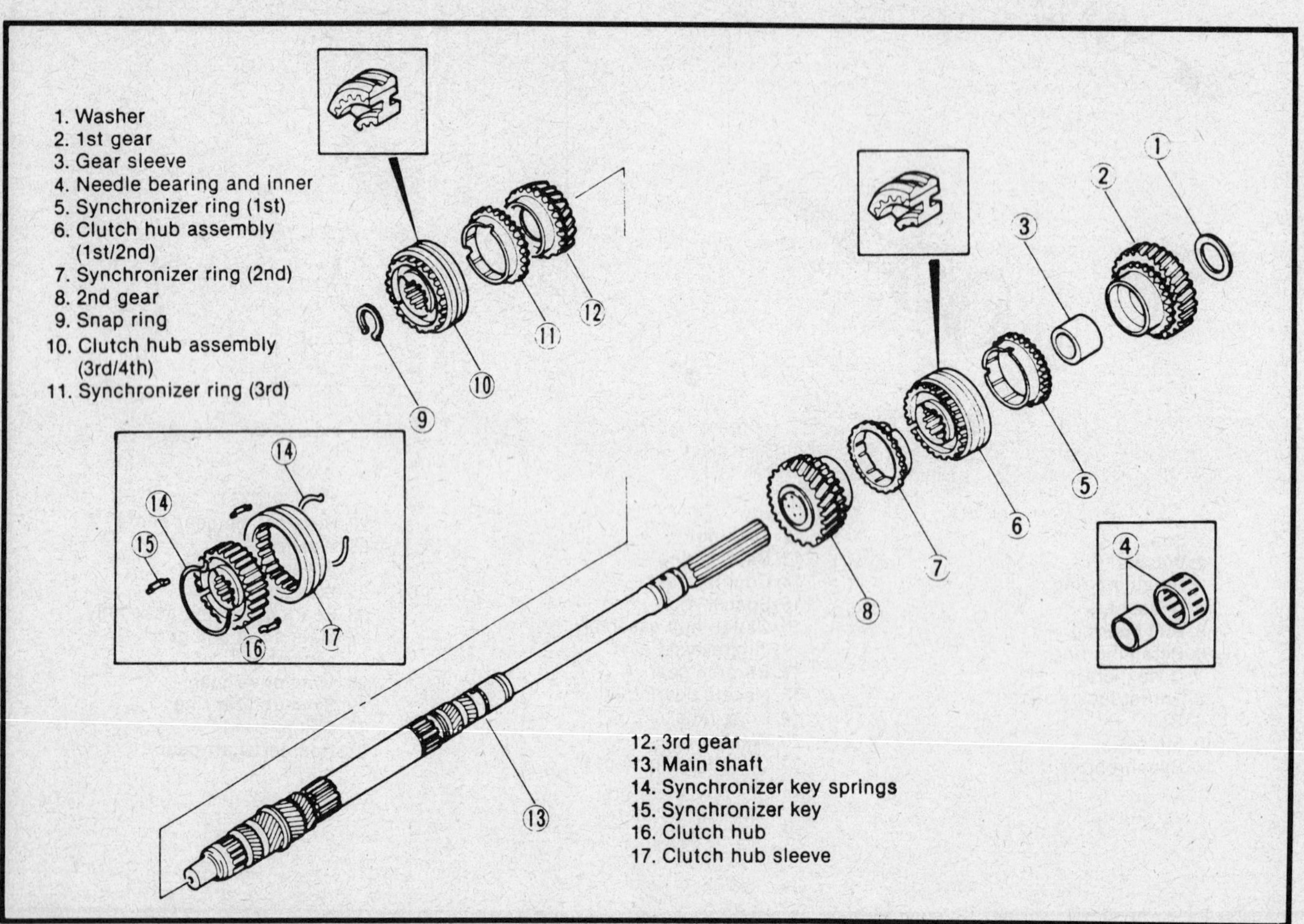

Mazda 4 & 5 speed mainshaft parts

34. Check the clearance between the front bearing cover and bearing. It should be less than 0.006 in. If it is not within specifications insert additional adjusting shims. The shims are available in 0.006 in. or 0.012 in. sizes.

35. Install the throwout bearing, return spring and release fork.

NOTE: On 5 Speed transmissions, the disassembly and assembly of the rear extension housing, selector levers and forks are completed in the same manner as the 4 speed transmission. After this has been done, the added housing can be removed by taking out the retaining bolts. The housing will have to be lightly tapped with a soft-faced hammer. The removal of the housing exposes the 5th/reverse synchronizer assembly, the reverse countergear, the countershaft and mainshaft bearings. The bearings are pulled from the shafts and then the gears can be removed. The assembly is in the reverse of the removal procedure.

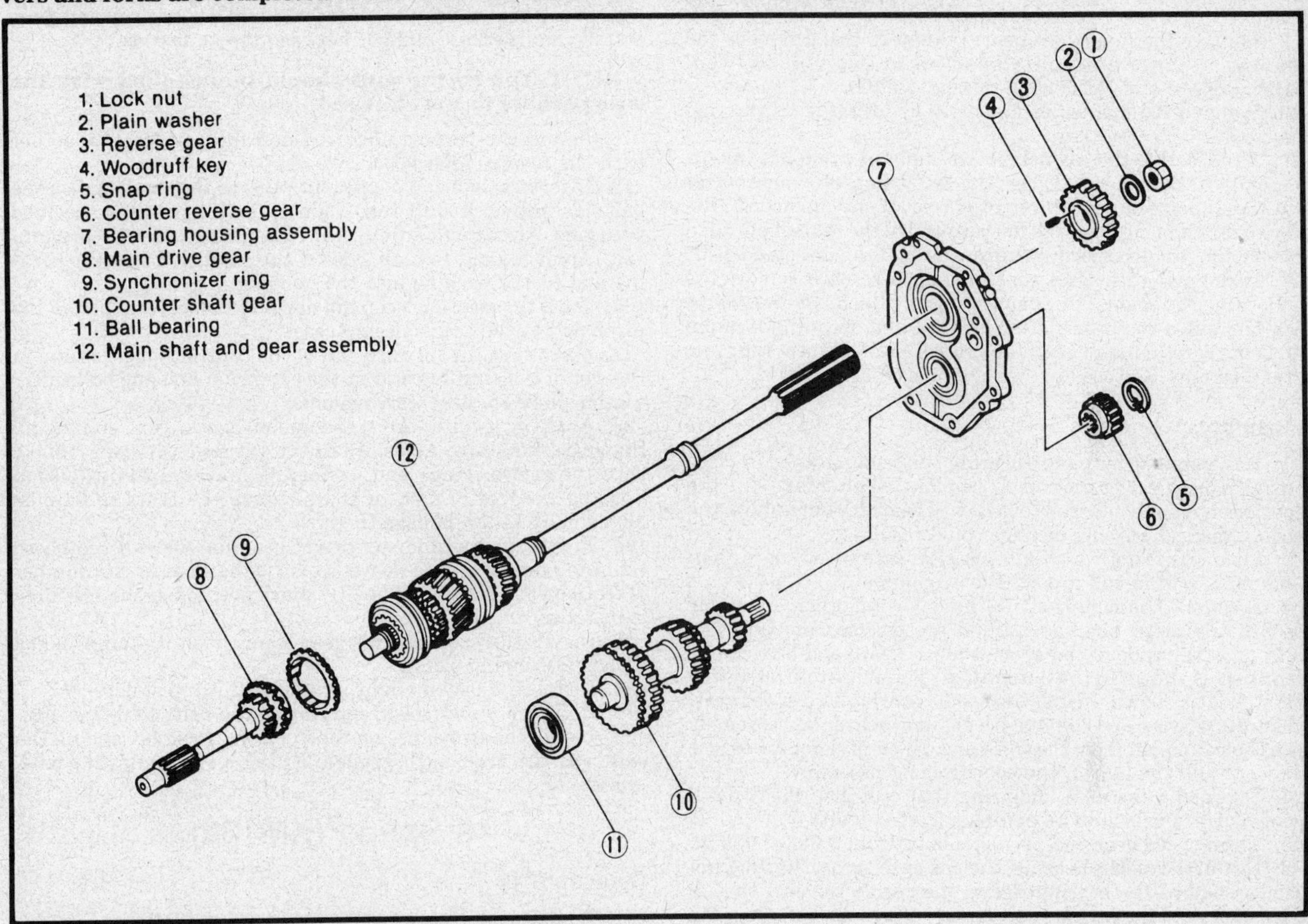

Mazda 4 speed main and countershaft assemblies

MITSUBISHI/CHRYSLER CORP.

4 Speed (KM130)

Disassembly

1. Remove the undercover.
2. Remove the back-up light switch. Be careful not to lose the steel ball.
3. Remove the speedometer gear sleeve clamp and remove the speedometer driven gear and sleeve assembly from the extension housing assembly.
4. Remove the extension housing bolts. Turn the shift lever to the left and pull off the extension housing.
5. Loosen the three poppet plugs, then remove the three poppet springs and the three steel balls.
6. Place the 1st/2nd speed shift rod in Neutral position.
7. Remove the reverse shift rail and fork assembly together with the reverse idler gear.
8. Using a $^{3}/_{16}$ in. punch, drive off the 3rd/4th and 1st/2nd speed shift fork spring pins. Push each shift rod toward the rear of the transmission case and remove the shift forks. Remember to remove the interlock plunger.
9. Remove the snap-ring from the rear end of the counter gear and then remove the reverse counter gear.
10. Unlock the mainshaft locknut and remove the locknut. The locknut can be loosened by double-engaging the 3rd speed gear and the 1st speed gear.
11. Remove the reverse gear from the mainshaft.
12. Remove the five attaching screws and then remove the rear bearing retainer.
13. Remove the front bearing retainer.

14. With the counter gear pressed to the rear, remove the rear bearing snap-ring. Then using a bearing puller remove the rear counter bearing.
15. Remove the snap-ring from the front counter bearing. Pull off the bearing with a bearing puller.
16. Pull the counter gear out of the case.
17. Remove the main drive pinion from the front of the case. To remove the bearing from the main drive pinion, remove the two snap-rings and then remove the bearing with a bearing puller.
18. Remove the mainshaft bearing snap-ring and remove the bearing using a dual post bearing puller (special tool MD998056-10 and MD998056 or equivalents).
19. Remove the mainshaft assembly by lifting it up through the case.
20. Disassemble the mainshaft assembly in the following order: Pull off the 1st speed gear, the 1st/2nd speed synchronizer and the 2nd speed gear toward the rear of the mainshaft. Remove the snap-ring from the forward end of the mainshaft, then remove the 3rd/4th speed synchronizer and the 3rd speed gear.
21. If removing the shift control shaft assembly, remove the pin locking the gear shifter using a $^{3}/_{16}$ in. punch. To remove the lock pin, press the gear shifter forward and drive the lock pin off, being careful not to bend the control shaft. Inspect the parts after cleaning. Replace any worn, damaged or defective.

Assembly

1. If the main drive pinion bearing has been removed, replace it using a pipe fit over the end of the pinion shaft. Make sure the pipe does not apply pressure on the ball bearings but only on the bearing race, or bearing damage could result.
2. Fit a snap-ring which gives a clearance of no more than 0–0.002 in. and install it on the drive pinion.
3. Assemble the mainshaft in the following order: Assemble the 3rd/4th speed and the 1st/2nd speed synchronizers. The front and rear ends of the synchronizer sleeve and hub can be identified as shown in the illustration. The synchronizer spring is installed as shown. Install the needle bearing, 3rd speed gear, synchronizer ring and the 3rd/4th speed synchronizer assembly onto the mainshaft from the front end. Be careful not to confuse the front and the rear of the synchronizer assembly.
4. Select and install a snap-ring that will give the 3rd/4th speed synchronizer hub an end-play from 0–0.003 in.
5. Third speed gear end-play should be from 0.002–0.008 in.
6. Install the needle bearing, the 2nd speed gear, the synchronizer assembly, the bearing sleeve, the needle bearing, the 1st speed gear, and the bearing spacer onto the mainshaft from the rear end.
7. Push the bearing spacer forward and check the 1st and 2nd speed gear end-play. Clearance should be within 0.002–0.008 in.
8. Insert the mainshaft assembly into the transmission case and fit the mainshaft center bearing using a bearing driver. Hold the forward end of the mainshaft by hand at the front of the case.
9. Install the needle bearing and the synchronizer ring, then insert the main drive pinion assembly into the case from the front.
10. Insert the countershaft gear into the case. With a snap-ring fitted to the countershaft front needle bearing, drive the bearing into the case by hammering on the outer race of the bearing.
11. Fit a snap-ring to the countershaft rear ball bearing and then install the bearing with a bearing installer.
12. Install the front bearing retainer. When installing the retainer, install a spacer that will give a clearance of 0.0–0.004 in. Apply sealant to both sides of the front bearing retainer packing and apply gear oil to the oil seal lip. Install packing and oil seal.
13. Install the rear bearing retainer and its five screws. It is suggested that each screw head be staked with a pointed punch to prevent them from coming loose.
14. Install the reverse gear on the mainshaft and tighten the locknut to 73–94 ft. lbs. Lock the nut at the notch of the mainshaft.
15. Install the spacer and counter reverse gear to the counter gear rear end.
16. Install a snap-ring of the proper size so that the reverse counter gear and play will be from 0.0–0.003 in.
17. Install the 3rd/4th and 1st/2nd speed shift forks into their respective synchronizer sleeves. Insert each shift rod from the rear of the case. Lock the shift forks and rod with spring pins, install the interlock plunger between the shift rods.

NOTE: The spring pins should be installed with the slits parallel to the shift rod.

18. Install the reverse shift rod and fork assembly together with the reverse idler gear.
19. Insert the ball and poppet spring with the small end on the ball side into each shift rod. Tighten the plugs to the specified positions. After installation, seal each plug head with sealant.
20. Apply sealant to both sides of the extension housing packing and fit the packing into the housing.
21. Turn the gear shift control down to the left and install the extension to the transmission case.
22. Make sure the forward end of the control finger is snug in the slot of the shift lug and fit the extension housing bolts after coating their threads with sealant.
23. Apply gear oil to the speedometer driven gear and install the gear and sleeve assembly in the extension housing. Make sure the sleeve flange and its mating areas on the extension housing are free of dirt, or it will cause the gears to be misaligned and could damage them.
24. Rotate the speedometer driven gear and sleeve assembly so that the number on the sleeve, which is the same as the number of teeth on the gear, is in the "U" mark position as the assembly is installed.
25. Install the speedometer gear clamp with its tongs in the sleeve positioning slots.
26. Install the backup light switch with its steel ball.
27. Refit the under cover and torque the bolts to 6–7 ft. lbs.
28. Install the transmission control lever assembly and fill the gear shifter area with grease. Fill the transmission with lubricant.

5 Speed (KM132)

Disassembly

1. Remove the clutch release bearing and carrier.
2. Remove the spring pin and the clutch control shaft. Remove the felt, return spring and clutch shift arm.
3. Remove the case cover.
4. Remove the back-up light switch.
5. Remove the extension housing.
6. Remove the speedometer drive gear.
7. Remove the ball bearing from the mainshaft rear end.
8. Loosen three poppet spring plugs, then remove three poppet springs and three balls.
9. Remove the 3–4 and 1–2 speed shift fork spring pins. Pull off each shift rail toward the rear of the transmission case, then remove the shift fork. Remove the interlock plunger.
10. Remove the overtop and reverse shift forks spring pins, shift rails and forks.
11. Loosen the locknuts (mainshaft and countershaft rear ends).
12. Pull off the counter overtop gear and the ball bearing at the same time using a puller. Remove the spacer and the counter reverse gear.
13. Remove the overtop gear and sleeve from the mainshaft. Remove the overtop synchronizer assembly and spacer.
14. Remove the reverse idler gear.
15. Remove the rear bearing retainer.

16. Drive the reverse idler gear shaft from inside the case.
17. Remove the front bearing retainer.
18. With the counter gear pressed to the rear, remove the rear bearing snap-ring. Remove the counter rear bearing.
19. Remove the counter front bearing.
20. Remove the counter gear from the inside of the case.
21. Remove the main drive pinion from the front of the case. Remove the main drive pinion bearing.
22. Remove the mainshaft bearing snap-ring. Remove the ball bearing.
23. Pull the mainshaft assembly from the case.
24. Disassemble the mainshaft in the following order: Remove the 1st gear, the 1–2 speed synchronizer and the 2nd speed gear toward the rear of the mainshaft. Remove the snap-ring from the forward end of the mainshaft. Remove the 3–4 speed synchronizer and the 3rd gear.
25. Disassemble the extension housing: Remove the lock plate and the speedometer driven gear. Remove the plug, spring and neutral return plunger.

When removing the control shaft assembly, pull off the lock pin locking the gear shifter. To remove the lock pin, press the gear shifter forward and pull it off.

Assembly

1. Install the ball bearing on the main drive pinion. Install a selective snap-ring so that there will be 0–0.002 in. clearance between the snap-ring and the bearing. Thickness of snap-ring—0.0906 in.; 0.0925 in.; 0.0945 in.; 0.0965 in.; 0.0984 in. Identification color—White; None; Red; Blue; Yellow.
2. Install the mainshaft in the following order: Assemble the 3–4 speed and 1–2 speed synchronizers. Be sure the synchronizer assemblies are installed facing in the proper direction. Install the needle bearing, the 3rd speed gear, the synchronizer ring, and the 3–4 speed synchronizer assembly on to the mainshaft from the front end. Select and install a snap-ring of proper size so that the 3–4 speed synchronizer hub end-play will be 0–0.003 in. Check the 3rd gear end-play (0.0016–0.0079 in.). Install the needle bearing, the 2nd speed gear, the synchronizer assembly, the bearing sleeve, the needle bearing, the 1st speed gear, and the bearing spacer on the mainshaft from the rear. With the bearing spacer pressed forward, check the 2nd and 1st gear end-play (0.0016–0.0079 in.).
3. Install the mainshaft into the transmission case and drive in the mainshaft center bearing.
4. Install the needle bearing and the synchronizer ring. Install the main drive pinion assembly into the case from the front.
5. Install the countershaft gear into the case. Drive the front bearing into the case.
6. Install the snap-ring on the countershaft rear bearing.
7. Install the front bearing retainer. Select and install a spacer of proper size so that the clearance will be 0–0.0039 in. Replace the front bearing retainer oil seal.
8. Install the rear bearing retainer.
9. Install the reverse idler gear shaft.
10. Install the needle bearing, the reverse idler gear and the thrust washer. Check the reverse idler gear end-play (0.0047–0.0110 in.). Install the thrust washer with the ground side toward the gear side.

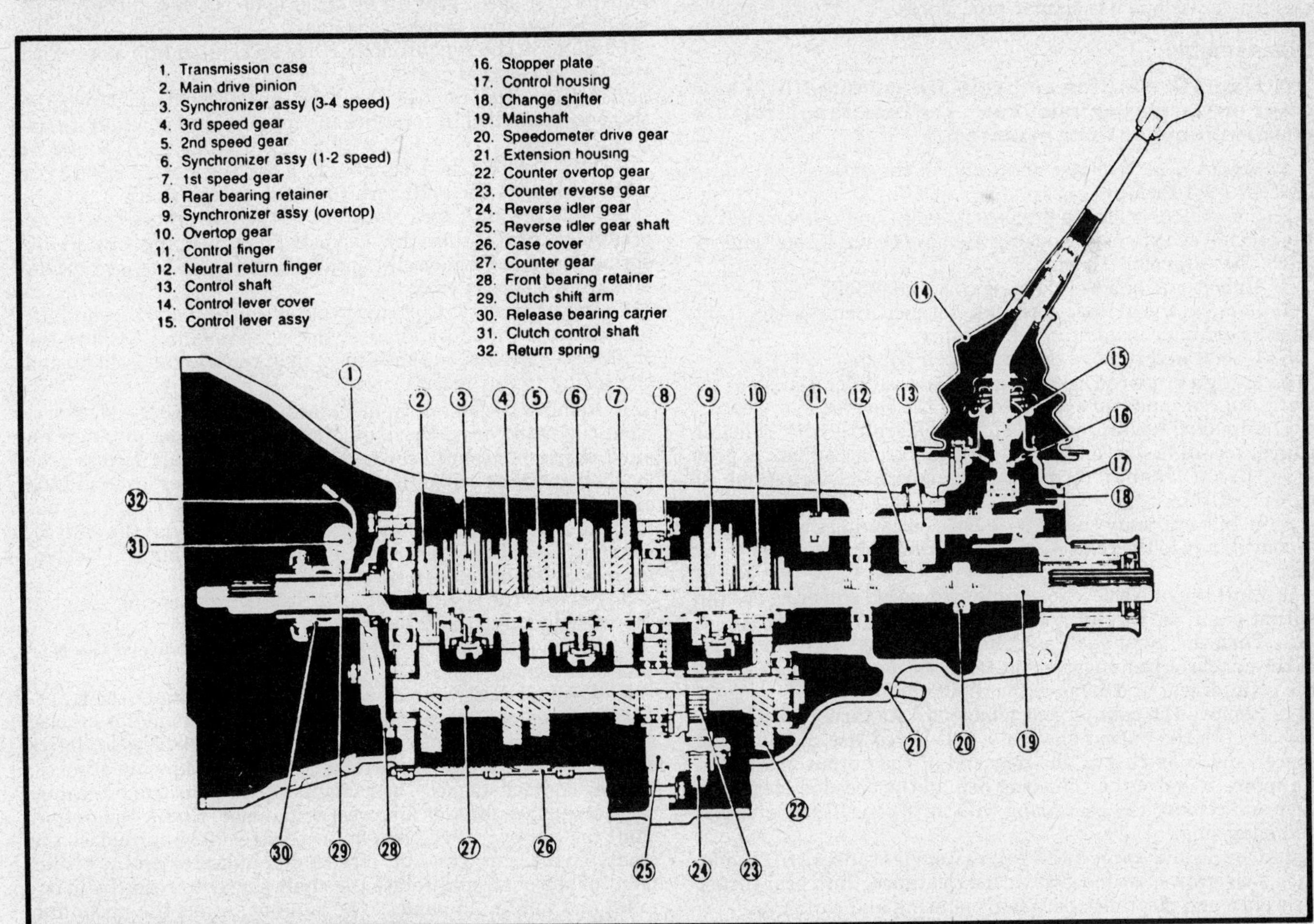

Cross section of 5-speed transmission, model KM 132

11. Assemble the overtop synchronizer.
12. Install the spacer, the stop plate, the overtop synchronizer assembly, the overtop gear bearing sleeve, the needle bearing, the synchronizer ring and the overtop gear in the written order on to the mainshaft from the rear end. Check the overtop gear end-play.
13. Install the spacer, the counter reverse gear, the spacer, the counter overtop gear and the ball bearing on to the countershaft gear from the rear end.
14. Insert the 3–4 and 1–2 speed shift forks into respective synchronizer sleeves. Insert each shift rail from the rear of the case. Lock the shift forks and rails with spring pins. Install an interlock plunger between shift rails. The pin should be installed with the slit in the axial direction of the shift rail.
15. Insert the ball and poppet spring into each shift rail. Install the poppet spring with the small end on the ball side.
16. Install the ball bearing on to the rear end of the mainshaft.
17. Install the speedometer drive gear.
18. Install the extension housing. Turn the change shifter fully down to the left. Make sure the forward end of the control finger is snugly fitted in the slot of the shift lug.
19. Install the neutral return plungers, the spring, and resistance spring and ball. Tighten each plug till its top is flush with the boss top surface.
20. Install the speedometer driven gear sleeve into the extension housing and into mesh with the drive gear.
21. Install the back-up light switch. Remember the steel ball.
22. Install the under cover.
23. Insert the clutch control shaft. Install the packing (felt), the return spring and the clutch shift arm. The spring pin should be installed in such a manner that the slip will be at right angles with the axis of the control shaft.
24. Install the transmission control lever assembly. Fill the gear shifter area with grease.
25. After reassembly, rotate the drive pinion to see if it rotates smoothly.

TOYOTA

4 & 5 Speed (L Series)

The following procedures are for a L Series 4 speed, other L Series transmissions use similar procedures.

Disassembly

NOTE: The shifting controls are mounted in a side cover on the transmission case. The remote controls are either column or floor mounted.

1. Remove speedometer drive unit in the extension housing (Except 4 × 4 Pick-up).
2. Some models have a driveshaft flange and crimped nut at the end of the extension housing. Remove them. Unbolt and remove the extension housing.
3. Unbolt and remove the case cover assembly.
4. Remove the release fork and bearing. Remove the front bearing retainer inside the bell housing.
5. Unbolt and remove the clutch bell housing.
6. Using a brass rod, gently tap the reverse idler gear shaft toward the rear and remove it. Remove the reverse idler gear.
7. Check the countergear thrust clearance with a feeler gauge, record the reading, then pick the proper adjusting gear side thrust washer to obtain the specified clearance of 0.004–0.010 in.
8. Using a dummy shaft, drive out the countershaft and the Woodruff key to the rear. Allow the countergear to drop into the case.
9. Shift the hub sleeve toward the top speed and draw out the output shaft. Be careful not to lose the synchronizer ring.
10. Turn the input shaft assembly so that one of the flat sides of the synchronizer engagement teeth on the input shaft clears the countergear and remove the input shaft.
11. Remove the countergear along with its thrust washers.
12. Secure the output shaft in a soft-jawed vise. Remove the spacer and snap-ring at the rear end of the output shaft if so equipped. Remove the snap-ring behind the speedometer drive gear and remove the gear along with its Woodruff key and second snap-ring.
13. Check and record the following clearances: first gear thrust clearance, second gear thrust clearance, third gear thrust clearance and clearance between snap-ring and clutch hub.
14. Remove the snap-ring holding the clutch hub in place and remove clutch hub and third speed gear.
15. Remove the snap-ring behind the rear bearing and press the bearing off the shaft with the first speed gear. Be careful not to lose the small locking ball. Do not attempt to force the bearing and first speed gear off by striking on the end of the output shaft, or you may damage the shaft.
16. Remove the synchronizer rings and clutch hub along with reverse and second gears.
17. Loosen and remove the back-up light switch. Move the third and fourth shift fork into the fourth speed position (to the front).
18. Using a long drift punch, drive out the slotted spring pin which connects the shift fork to the shift fork shaft.
19. Slide the shift fork shaft out of the rear of the case cover gradually, preventing the lockball from popping out under spring tension. Remove the lockball, spring and two interlock pins from the case cover.
20. Drive the slotted spring pin out of the first and second shift fork and the shift fork shaft in the same manner. Remove the shift fork shaft and the shift fork, then remove the lockball and the spring from the case cover.
21. Remove the shift arm pivot locknut. Remove the shift arm from the case cover. Drive out the slotted spring pin, and remove the reverse shift head and the shift fork shaft. Remove the lockball and the spring. Remove the selector outer lever and the selector lever shaft.
22. Remove the shift lever shaft lockbolt, slide out the shift lever shaft from the case cover. Be careful to prevent the lockball from popping out under spring tension.
23. Remove the sliding shift lever, lockball and spring. Remove the wire and shift lever lockbolt.
24. Remove the shift and selector lever shaft toward the rear side of the case.
25. Wash all disassembled parts thoroughly. Check the transmission case, case cover and the extension housing for cracks; check the bearing fitting portions and gasket surfaces for burrs and nicks. Check the output shaft splines, snap-ring grooves, bearing contact surfaces, bearing fitting portions and oil seal lip contact surface for wear, scores, or damage. Check the output shaft for run-out. If the run-out exceeds 0.0024 in. replace the shaft. To measure run-out, place a dial indicator on the center point of the shaft and rotate the shaft slowly to read the maximum and minimum values. The run-out equals the maximum value minus the minimum value divided by two. Check the bearings for roughness and wear. Check for noise or damage by ro-

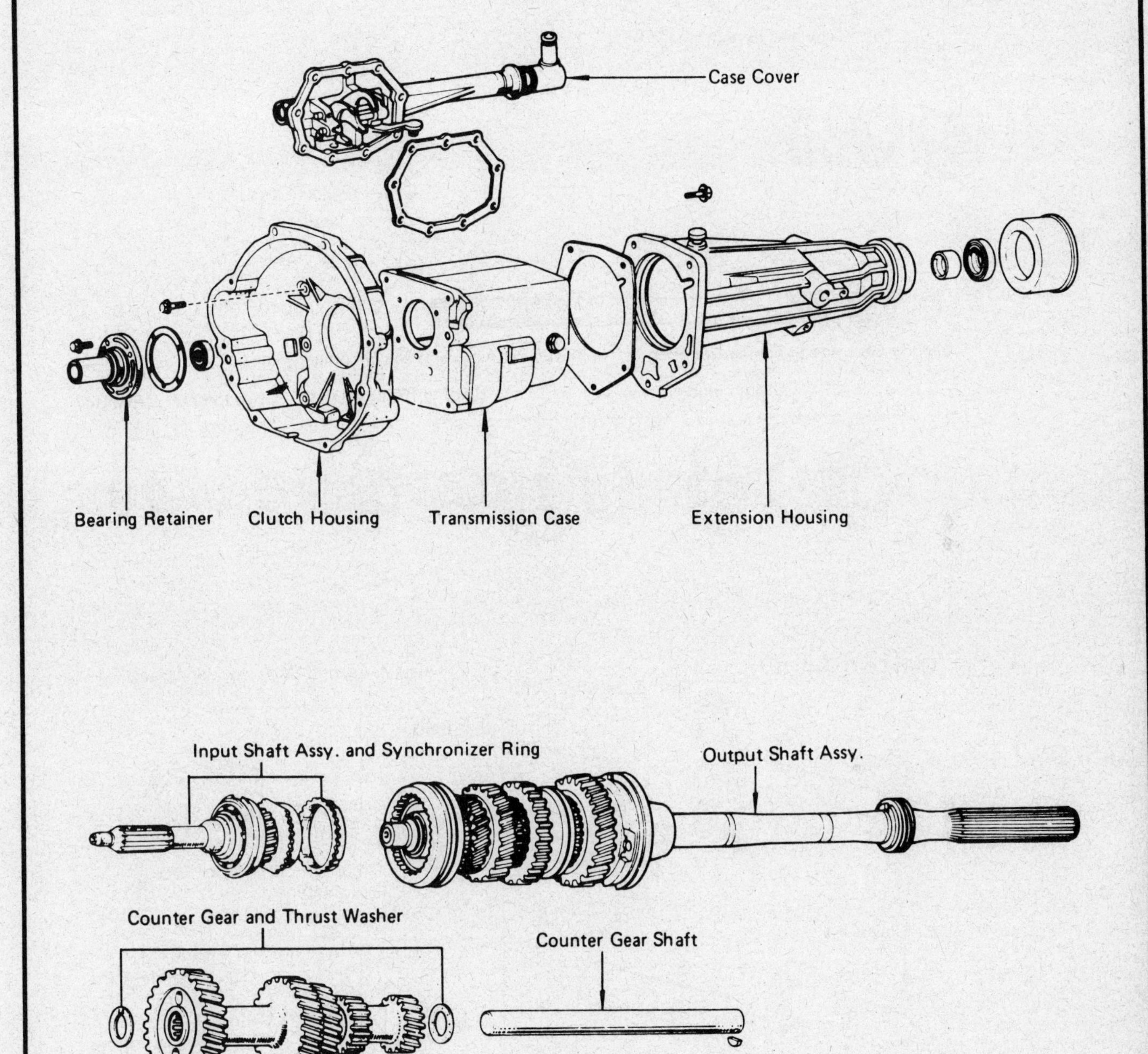

Toyota L-series transmission

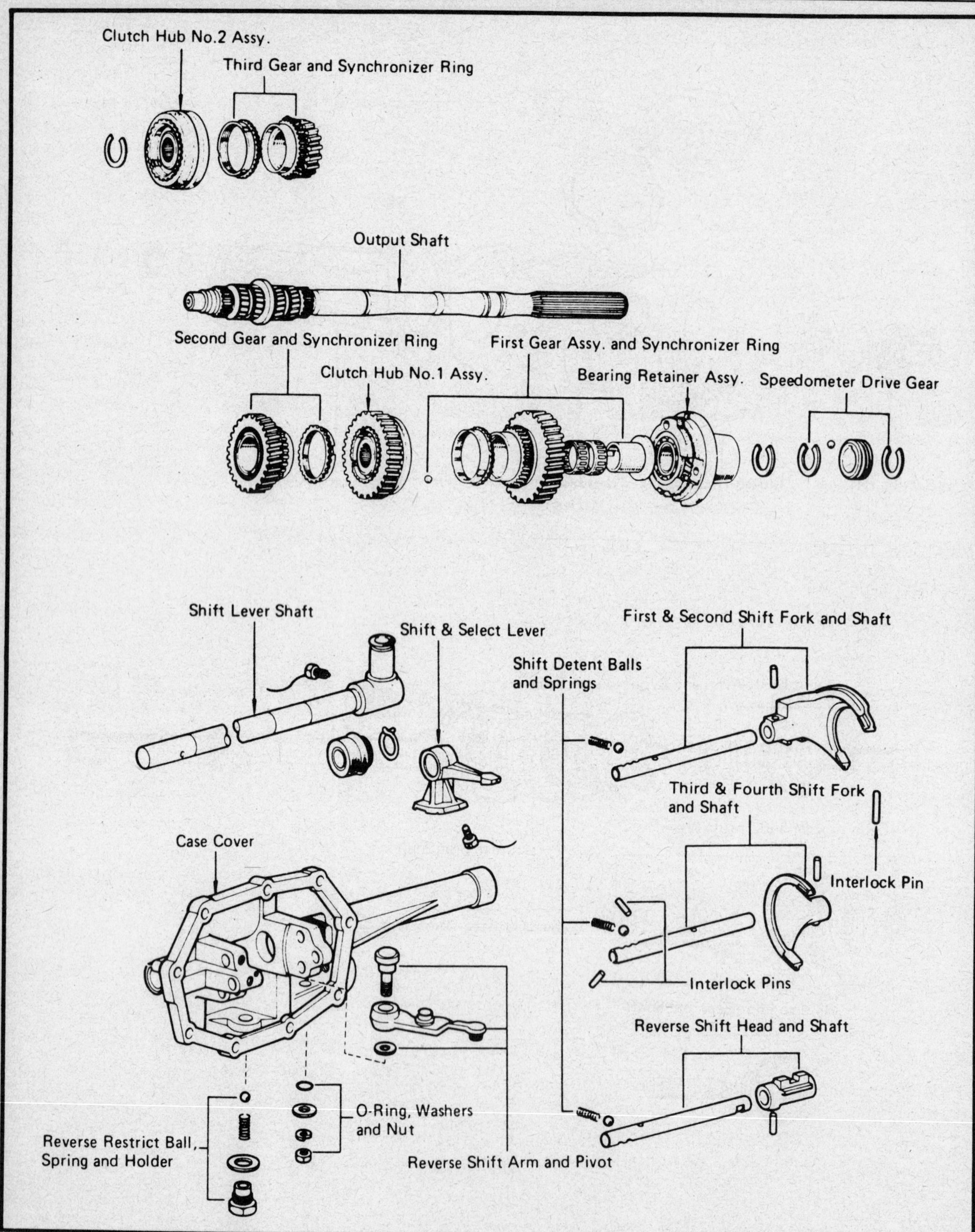
Clutch Hub No.2 Assy.
Third Gear and Synchronizer Ring
Output Shaft
Second Gear and Synchronizer Ring
First Gear Assy. and Synchronizer Ring
Clutch Hub No.1 Assy.
Bearing Retainer Assy.
Speedometer Drive Gear
Shift Lever Shaft
Shift & Select Lever
First & Second Shift Fork and Shaft
Shift Detent Balls
and Springs
Third & Fourth Shift Fork
and Shaft
Case Cover
Interlock Pin
Interlock Pins
Reverse Shift Head and Shaft
O-Ring, Washers
and Nut
Reverse Restrict Ball,
Spring and Holder
Reverse Shift Arm and Pivot

Toyota L-series transmission

tating the bearing after applying a few drops of oil. To remove the input shaft bearing, remove the shaft snap-ring with a snap-ring expander, then remove the bearing from the input shaft with a puller. Check the bushings and the bearing rollers for abnormal wear. If the wear is excessive, replace the busings or the bearing rollers. Inspect the extension housing bushing for wear or scoring. To replace the bushing, press the bushing out of the extension housing to the front side. To install, align the oil grooves of the bushing and the extension housing, and press the bushing into the housing. After installing the bushing, ream the bushing to fit the outer diameter of the universal joint sleeve yoke.

26. Gear Backlash: Input shaft gear to countergear: 0.004 in. Third gear to countergear: 0.004–0.008 in. Second gear to countergear: 0.004–0.008 in. First gear to countergear: 0.004–0.008 in. Reverse idler gear to countergear: 0.004–0.008 in. Reverse idler gear to reverse gear: 0.004– + 0.008 in.

Assembly

Assembly is performed in the following order:

NOTE: Always install new gaskets, apply liquid sealer or gasket cement when assembling. Apply a thin coating of transmission lubricant on all parts before installation. Thrust clearances of gears and bearings are important factors for smooth shifting. Therefore, select and assemble thrust washers, snap-rings and spacers of proper thickness.

1. If the shifting hubs have been disassembled, reassemble them by: Install the two shifting springs in the inner hub with the spring ends 120° apart, so that the spring tension on each shifting key will be uniform. Place the three shifting keys into the clutch hub key slots and onto the shifting springs. The shifting keys for each hub are of different sizes. The keys with the shorter straddle length should be installed on the third and fourth gear synchronizer unit. Slide the hub sleeve onto the clutch hub. The clutch hubs and the hub sleeves of the gear are matched, and should be kept together as an assembly for smooth operation.

NOTE: The hubs fit into the clutch sleeves directionally, that is, they must fit into the clutch sleeves facing a certain way.

2. Install the second gear and its synchronizer ring on the output shaft. Install the first and second gear clutch hub behind second gear. Be sure to align the grooves in the synchronizer ring with the shift keys in the clutch hub. Place the small steel lockball in its slot on the output shaft.
3. Oil and place the roller bearings on the bushing. Slide the bushing into the first speed gear with the collared end of the bushing butting the flat side of the gear. Fit the synchronizer ring on the other side of the gear and insert the gear on the output shaft. Take care to fit the notch in the bushing over the steel lockball and align the notches in the synchronizer ring with those in the clutch hub.
4. Press the bearing retainer assembly on the output shaft. Check the gears for smooth rotation. Select a snap-ring that will give 0–0.006 in. clearance on the output shaft and install. Five different snap-ring thicknesses are available.
5. Check the second and first gear thrust clearances. The allowable limits are 0.004–0.010 in.
6. Install first speedometer snap-ring and Woodruff key on the output shaft and install speedometer gear and second snap-ring.
7. Oil and install the third speed gear on the front of the output shaft. Fit its synchronizer ring and install the clutch hub, making sure to align the grooves in the synchronizer with the keys in the clutch hub.
8. Select a snap-ring that will give an allowable thrust clearance of 0–0.006 in. between the hub end and the snap-ring. Fit the snap-ring.
9. Measure the thrust clearance of the third speed gear. Allowable limit for clearance is 0.004–0.010 in.
10. Assemble the countergear by placing the spacers and greased roller bearings in both ends and fitting a tube or rod that is the exact length of the countergear with the thrust washers on its ends and fit it into the countergear.
11. Referring to the thrust measurement on the countergear when disassembling, select thrust washers that give an allowable clearance of 0.004–0.010 in. Adjust clearance by replacing the rear thrust washer.
12. Install the thrust washers on the ends of the countergear. Rear thrust washers are identified by Number 1, 2, 3 or 4 stamped on their outside face. Be sure to install the washers with their protruding groove facing out.
13. Place the countergear assembly into the case with the notches in the thrust washers facing up and align the notches with the case grooves.
14. Allow the countergear to drop down into the case. Do not replace the countergear shaft at this point.
15. Install the input shaft in the same manner of removal, aligning one of the flat sides of the clutch hub with the large countershaft gear and, using a brass drift, drive the input shaft bearing into the case, tapping it around the outer ball race.
16. Fit the synchronizer ring on the input shaft. Shift the clutch hub on the end of the output shaft forward.
17. Fit the output shaft into the case, making sure the slotted spring pin in the bearing retainer aligns with its groove in the case, and align the grooves in the synchronizer ring with the clutch hub keys.
18. Oil the countershaft. Raise the countergear assembly so that it aligns with the case holes and, making sure the thrust washers are in place, insert the countergear shaft from the rear of the case with the Woodruff key slot at the rear. The countergear shaft will push the tube out of the case. Install the Woodruff key and fit it into its slot in the case.
19. Install the reverse idler gear with its toothed end facing forward. Slide the reverse idler gear shaft in with its Woodruff key slot end facing the rear. Install the Woodruff key and tap the shaft in so that the key is in its seat in the case.
20. Install the front bearing retainer. Be sure to align the oil seal slot in the retainer with the oil hole in the case. Coat the bolt threads with sealer and tighten to 5–6 ft. lbs.
21. Install the clutch bell housing. Coat the bolt threads with sealer and tighten to 37–50 ft. lbs.
22. Install clutch release fork assembly.
23. Apply grease to the extension housing rear oil seal and install the extension housing. Be careful not to damage the oil seal on the output shaft when assembling.
24. Coat the extension housing bolts with sealer and tighten to 22–32 ft. lbs.
25. Oil the speedometer gear assembly and fasten to the extension housing.
26. To assemble the transmission case cover, install the shift arm pivot onto the reverse shift arm, and insert into the case.
27. Assemble the shift and selector lever shaft together with the shift and selector lever, and secure the bolt with a wire.
28. Insert the reverse shift fork shaft compression spring and lockball into the case, and insert the fork shaft from the rear side, then secure the shift head with a new slotted spring pin.
29. Align the fork shaft positioning groove with the shift interlock pin groove.
30. Align the reverse shift arm knob with the reverse shift fork shaft, and install the O-ring, washer and nut onto the shift arm pivot. Insert the shift interlock pin into the rear side of the case cover and the compression spring and lockball into the front side, and assemble the shift fork together with the first and second shift fork shaft. Secure the shift fork with a new slotted spring pin.

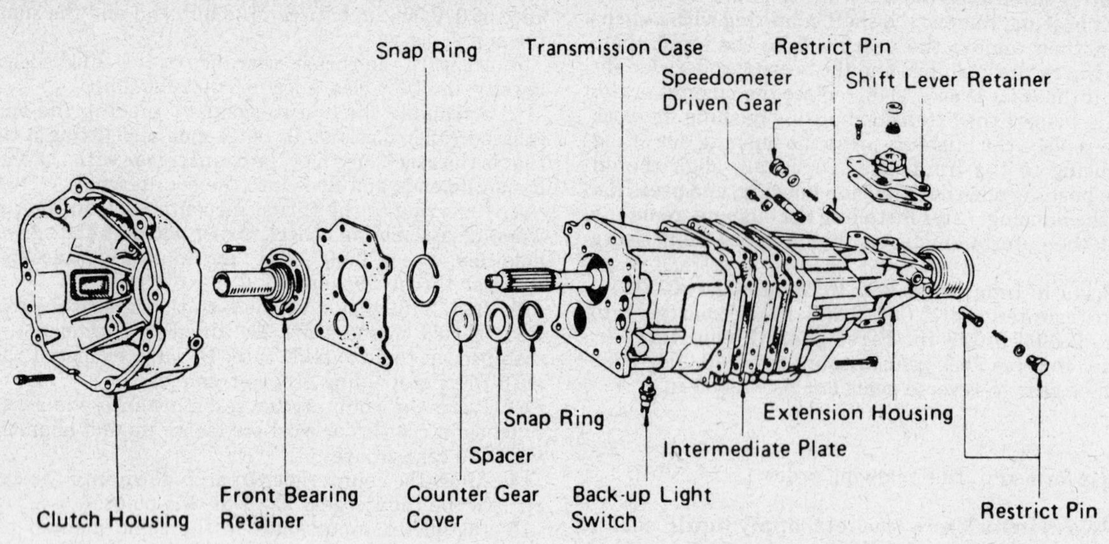
Snap Ring
Transmission Case
Restrict Pin
Speedometer Driven Gear
Shift Lever Retainer
Snap Ring
Spacer
Extension Housing
Intermediate Plate
Front Bearing Retainer
Counter Gear Cover
Back-up Light Switch
Clutch Housing
Restrict Pin

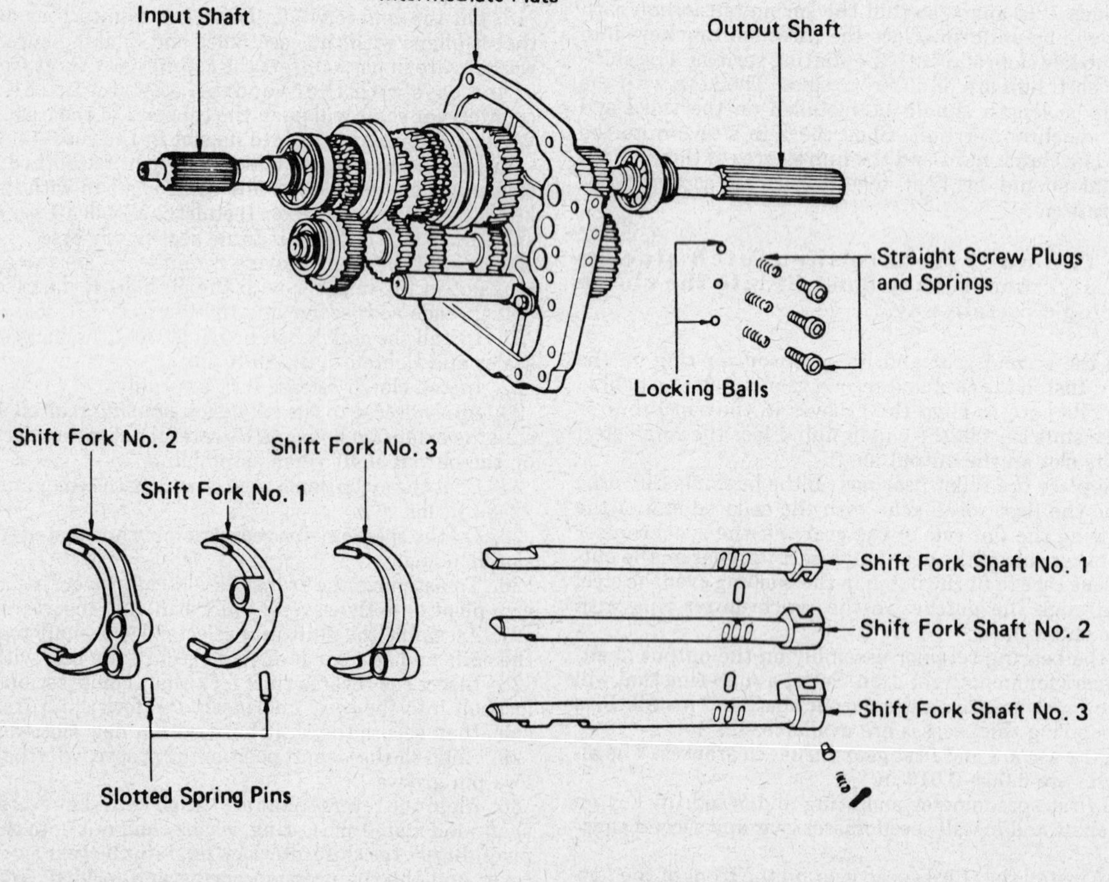
Intermediate Plate
Input Shaft
Output Shaft
Straight Screw Plugs and Springs
Locking Balls
Shift Fork No. 2
Shift Fork No. 3
Shift Fork No. 1
Shift Fork Shaft No. 1
Shift Fork Shaft No. 2
Shift Fork Shaft No. 3
Slotted Spring Pins

Toyota W-series transmission

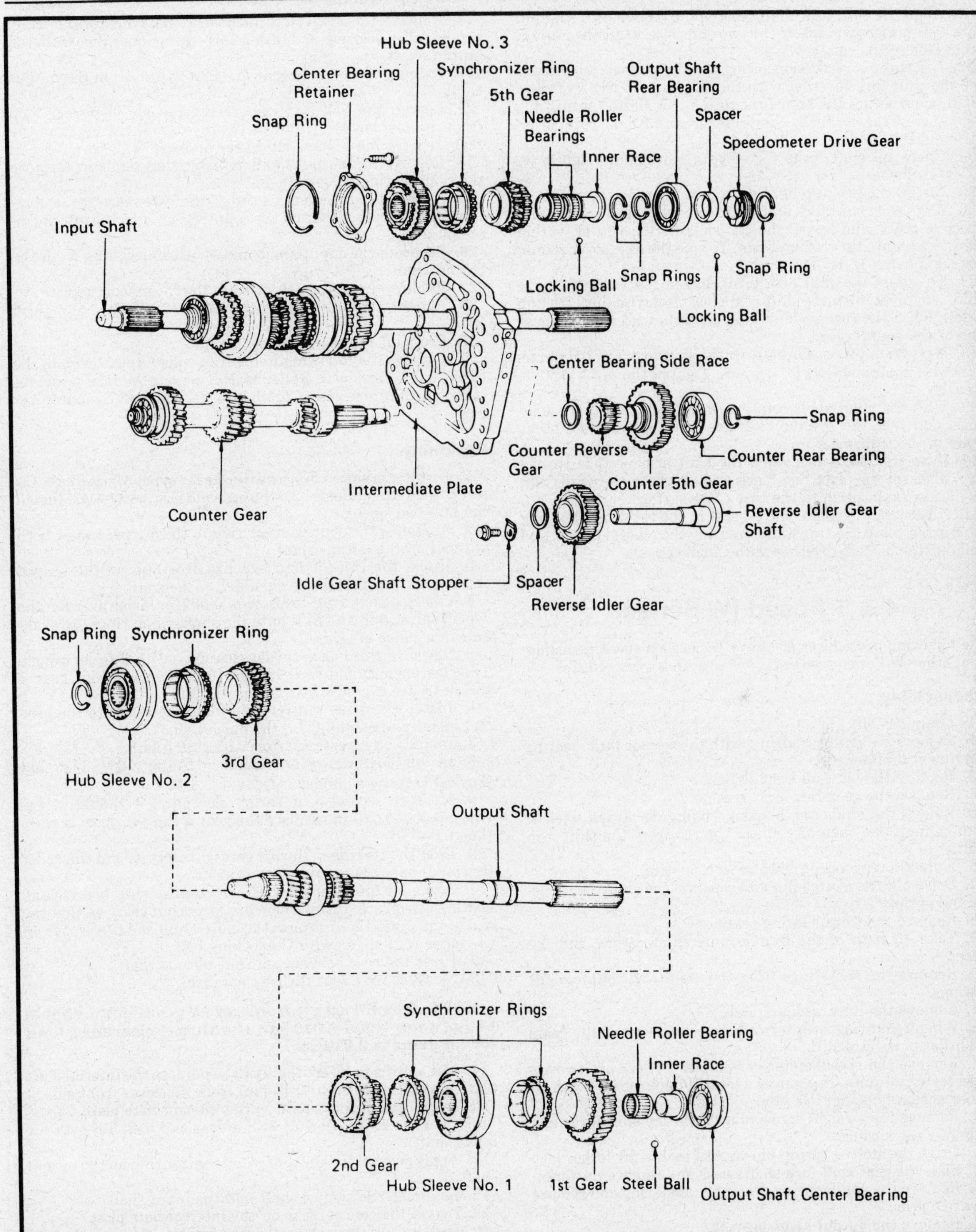
Hub Sleeve No. 3
Center Bearing Retainer
Synchronizer Ring
Output Shaft Rear Bearing
5th Gear
Snap Ring
Needle Roller Bearings
Spacer
Speedometer Drive Gear
Inner Race
Input Shaft
Locking Ball
Snap Rings
Snap Ring
Locking Ball
Center Bearing Side Race
Snap Ring
Counter Reverse Gear
Counter Rear Bearing
Counter 5th Gear
Intermediate Plate
Counter Gear
Reverse Idler Gear Shaft
Idle Gear Shaft Stopper
Spacer
Reverse Idler Gear
Snap Ring
Synchronizer Ring
3rd Gear
Hub Sleeve No. 2
Output Shaft
Synchronizer Rings
Needle Roller Bearing
Inner Race
2nd Gear
Hub Sleeve No. 1
1st Gear
Steel Ball
Output Shaft Center Bearing

Toyota W-series transmission

31. Align the shift fork shaft positioning groove with the shift interlock pin groove. Insert the two shift interlock pins into the front side of the case cover.
32. Insert the compression spring and the lockball, and assemble the shift fork together with the third and fourth shift fork shaft, then secure the shift fork with a new slotted spring pin.
33. Install the lockball, compression spring and reverse restricting ball holder.
34. Check all shift forks for smooth movement. Tighten to 27–32 ft. lbs.
35. Install the back-up light switch on the case cover.
36. Align each shift fork and the reverse shift arm with the respective gears, and install the transmission case cover, within the gasket, onto the transmission. Torque the case cover retaining bolts to 11–16 ft. lbs.
37. To adjust the shift arm pivot, loosen the locknut on the shift arm pivot, turn the shift arm pivot clockwise until friction is felt, when the reverse idler gear contacts with the first gear and/or the countergear.
38. Next from this position, turn the shift arm pivot counterclockwise approximately 90 degrees. Tighten the pivot locknut securely.
39. With the input shaft rotating, make sure that there is no noise and that the reverse idler gear does not contact other gears in the transmission.
40. If no friction is felt when the shift arm pivot is turned clockwise, set the pivot line mark at 60 degrees rearward from its horizontal position to the case cover surface.
41. If necessary, replace the oil seal in the extension housing after assembling the transmission using the oil seal puller, and pull out the oil seal together with the dust seal.

4 & 5 Speed (W Series)

The following procedures are for a W Series 5 speed transmission, other W Series transmissions use similar procedures.

Disassembly

1. Drain the oil.
2. Remove the clutch housing, with the release fork, bearing and hub still attached.
3. Remove the back-up light switch.
4. Remove the gearshift lever retainer.
5. Rotate the shift rod housing counterclockwise (viewed from behind) and then disconnect the rod from the shift fork shafts.
6. Unbolt and remove the extension housing.
7. Drive out the slotted pin and separate the shift rod, housing and spring.
8. Remove the front bearing retainer.
9. Take off both of the front countershaft covers, and the spacer.
10. Remove the snap-rings from the input and countershaft bearings.
11. Remove the intermediate plate.
12. When removing the intermediate plate, leave all the gears and other parts attached.
13. Remove the speedometer driven gear. There are two reverse restrictor pins. The pins are located underneath plugs on the extension housing.
14. Remove the straight screw plugs from the shift forks and withdraw the springs.
15. Drive the slotted spring pins out of each shift fork.
16. Slide the gear shift fork shafts back and remove the forks.
17. Remove the speedometer drive gear snap-ring and remove the drive gear.
18. Remove the output shaft bearing.
19. Remove the countershaft bearing.
20. Remove the fifth and reverse gears from the countershaft.
21. Remove the snap-ring, fifth gear, its synchronizer ring, needle roller bearing, and fifth gear bearing inner race from the output shaft.
22. Remove the reverse gear and clutch hub from the output shaft.
23. Loosen the bolt and remove the reverse idler gear stop from the rear cover. Withdraw the reverse idler shaft from the rear; remove the reverse idler gear and spacer.
24. Remove the output shaft rear bearing retainer. Remove the rear bearing snap-ring.
25. Push the countergear bearing outer race rearward, and remove the bearing. Separate the countergear from the intermediate plate.
26. Separate the input shaft and synchronizer ring from the output shaft.
27. Remove the output shaft from the intermediate plate.
28. Remove the hub and synchronizer ring, followed by third gear.
29. Press off the rear bearing.
30. Remove the following items from the output shaft, in the order listed: First gear. Roller bearing with inner race. Synchronizer ring. Reverse gear. Clutch hub. Second gear. Synchronizer ring.

Assembly

1. Install the sleeve over the third gear synchronizer hub. Insert the three shift keys into the hub and sleeve keyways. Install the hub two springs.
2. Assemble the synchronizer ring to third gear, and fit both of them on the output shaft.
3. Insert the third/fourth synchronizer hub on the output shaft, until it contacts the shoulder of the shaft.
4. Select a snap-ring to provide 0.002 in. axial play for the synchronizer hub and fit it onto the shaft. Snap-rings are available in a range of sizes.
5. Measure third gear thrust clearance with a feeler gauge. The clearance should be 0.004–0.010 in. Replace third gear if the clearance exceeds the limit of 0.010 in.
6. Install the synchronizer ring for second gear to the gear and install the assembly on the output shaft.
7. Install the reverse gear over its clutch hub.
8. Install the reverse gear and hub on the output shaft so that they contact the shoulder.
9. Measure second gear thrust clearance; it should be between 0.004–0.010 in. Replace the gear if the clearance is more than 0.010 in.
10. Coat the locking ball with grease. Insert it, and the roller bearing inner race, on the output shaft.
11. Assemble first gear with its synchronizer ring, bearing and bearing inner race. Install them on the output shaft, so that the end of the inner race contacts the clutch hub and the groove on the inner race aligns with the locking ball.
12. Press the rear bearing onto the output shaft.
13. Measure first gear thrust clearance.

NOTE: The thrust clearance of all gears in the should be between 0.006–0.010 in.; the thrust clearance limit for all gears is 0.012 in.

14. Use a press to insert the straight pin into the intermediate plate, until it protrudes $^1/_4$–$^5/_{16}$ in. from the cover front side.
15. Install the output shaft on the intermediate plate.
16. Coat the roller bearing with grease and install it over the input shaft.
17. Apply gear oil to the front synchronizer ring on the output shaft.
18. Assemble the output shaft and the input shaft.
19. Install the countergear on the intermediate plate.
20. Install the cylindrical roller bearing into the intermediate plate, and then install the spacer.
21. Assemble the output shaft and countergear, then fit them

through the holes in the intermediate plate. Push them in until the snap-ring sticks out beyond the intermediate plate. Install the snap-ring and then push the shafts back until the snap-ring is flush with the intermediate plate surface.

22. Install the shaft through the reverse idler gear. Insert the end of the shaft into the end of the intermediate plate.

23. Install the spacer on the idler shaft and secure it with a snap-ring.

24. Lock the reverse idler shaft on the intermediate plate with its stop. Check the reverse idler gear thrust clearance, it should be 0.006–0.010 in.

25. Install the reverse clutch hub on the reverse gear.

26. Install the three shift keys into the hub keyways and secure them with the two springs and a snap-ring.

27. Slide the reverse gear hub over the output shaft until it registers against the inner race of the intermediate plate bearing.

28. Insert the inner race lockball into the output shaft bore, after greasing it so that it can't fall out.

29. Assemble fifth gear, its synchronizer ring, needle roller bearing, and race. Slide the assembly onto the output shaft until the inner bear face rests against the reverse clutch hub. Be sure that the inner race groove is aligned with the lockball.

30. Secure fifth gear with a snap-ring.

31. Measure fifth gear thrust clearance; it should be 0.004–0.010 in. The thrust clearance limit is 0.012 in.

32. Install the countershaft reverse gear so that it just rests against the bearing inner race. Install the countershaft fifth gear and then install the countershaft bearing with a brass drift.

33. Install a snap-ring on the countershaft; select a snap-ring from one of the four available sizes.

34. Install a snap-ring on the output shaft, and drive its bearing into place with a brass drift. Coat the bearing with grease first.

35. Install the spacer, ball, and speedometer drive gear on the output shaft.

36. Install the three shift forks in their hub sleeve grooves. Install the first and third shift fork shafts and secure them with their interlock pins. Install the second shift fork shaft next.

NOTE: Place each shift fork shaft in Neutral during assembly.

37. Secure the shift fork shafts to the end cover by inserting the lockballs into their bores, followed by the lockball springs.

38. Use a new gasket between the transmission case and the intermediate plate. Slide the case into place.

39. Fit snap-rings on the input shaft and countershaft front bearings.

40. Install the shift lever housing on the end of the shifter shaft. Slide the shifter shaft into the extension housing and secure it with a slotted spring pin.

41. Install a new gasket and slide the extension housing into place, until there is about an inch of clearance between it and the intermediate plate.

42. Rotate the shift lever housing clockwise (as viewed from the rear) to engage the shifter shaft with the selector lever and the shift fork shaft.

43. Slide the extension housing the rest of the way.

44. Install the spacer and then the countershaft end covers.

45. Align the front bearing retainer gasket with the oil holes. Install the bearing retainer over the gasket.

46. Bolt the clutch housing onto the front of the transmission case.

47. Fit the restrictor pins and springs into their extension housing bores.

48. Install the shift lever retainer over the oil baffle on the extension housing.

49. Install the shift lever conical spring, large side down, and install the ball seat in the shift lever retainer.

50. Attach the shift lever retainer to the extension housing.

51. Install the speedometer driven gear.

52. Install the back-up light switch.

53. Check to see that the input shaft has no more than 0.020 in. end-play. Put the transmission in Neutral and see if the output shaft can be rotated freely by hand.

5 Speed (G52)

Disassembly

1. Remove the back-up light switch, speedometer driven gear, shift lever retainer and shift lever restrictor pins. Remove the clutch housing from the transmission.

2. From the side of the transfer case, remove the Torx headed plug, the spring and ball. Remove the Torx plug from the back of the transfer adapter. Remove the shift lever housing set bolt and lock washer and remove the shift lever shaft and housing.

3. Remove the transfer adapter mounting bolts and the adapter.

4. Remove the front transmission mainshaft bearing retainer and the two snap rings.

5. Separate the intermediate mounting plate and gear assemblies from the transmission case.

6. Secure the intermediate plate and gear assemblies in a vise. Use blocks to prevent clamping directly on the aluminum intermediate plate.

7. Use a Torx socket and remove the four plugs from the side of the intermediate plate. Remove the springs and ball from behind the plugs.

8. Remove the slotted spring pins using a pin punch and hammer. Remove the two E-rings from the shift shafts. Pull No. 4 shift fork shaft from the intermediate plate. Catch the locking balls and interlocking pin and remove the shift fork shaft No. 4 and No. 3 shift fork.

9. Pull out No. 5 shift fork shaft and remove it with the reverse shift head.

10. Pull out No. 3 shift fork shaft and No. 1 shift fork shaft from the intermediate plate. Pull out shift fork shaft No. 2 and remove shift fork No. 2 and No. 1.

11. Remove the reverse idler gear shaft stopper and remove the idler gear and shaft.

12. Remove the reverse shift arm from the reverse shift arm bracket.

13. Measure the 5th gear clearance on the countershaft. Clearance should be 0.0039–0.118 in.

14. Remove the 5th gear synchronizer ring, needle bearings and fifth gear from the countershaft by engaging the gear and using a hammer and chisel to loosen the staked nut. Remove the nut, disengage the gear and, using a puller, remove the gear splined No. 5 synchronizer assembly, needle bearing and 5th gear from the countershaft.

15. Remove the spacer and ball from the countershaft. Remove the two bolts and the reverse shift arm bracket. Use a Torx socket and remove the rear bearing retainer.

16. Remove the snap ring from the main output shaft and remove the output shaft, countershaft and input shaft as an assembly. Separate the output shaft and needle bearings (14) from the input shaft. Remove the countershaft rear bearing from the intermediate plate. Remove the sleeve from the output shaft using an appropriate puller. Measure each gear thrust clearance, maximum clearance is 0.0098 in.

17. Press off the fifth gear, rear bearing and first gear assemblies after removing the retaining snap ring. Remove the locking ball.

18. Press off the No. 1 synchronizer assembly and second gear. Remove the needle bearing. Remove the snap ring and press off No. 2 synchronizer assembly and 3rd gear. Remove the needle bearing.

19. Inspect all parts and replace as necessary. Required clearances follow: Output flange thickness; 0.1890 in. Inner race flange thickness; 0.1571 in. Output shaft journal thickness–2nd

gear; 1.4954 in. 3rd gear; 1.3773 in.: Shaft out-of-round; 0.0020 in.: Synchronizer ring clearance; 0.0039–0.079 in.: Shift forks to hub sleeves; 0.039 in. max.

Assembly

1. Replace the grease retainers as necessary. Check and replace the input shaft and the countershaft front bearings if necessary. Select a snap ring that will allow the minimum axial play.
2. Assemble the gears and synchronizers in the reverse order of removal. Make sure the synchronizers are installed facing in the proper direction. Use snap rings that will allow a minimum of axial play. Check clearances of all gears, synchronizers and bearings.
3. After the input, output and countershafts are ready for installation (reverse order of removal): Install the output shaft into the intermediate plate by pulling on the output shaft and tapping on the intermediate plate with a soft hammer.
4. Apply MP grease to the needle bearings and install them in position on the input shaft. Install the input shaft to the output shaft with the synchronizer ring slots aligned with the shifting keys.
5. Install the countershaft and bearing to the intermediate plate. Install the output shaft snap ring flush with the intermediate plate. Install the rear bearing retainer on the intermediate plate. Tighten the retainers to 13 ft. lbs. Install the reverse shift arm bracket. Install the ball and spacer on the countershaft and install the fifth gear with hub and needle bearings. Install the synchronizer assembly with the ring slots aligned with the shifting keys. Engage the gear and install the locknut. Torque the locknut to 87 ft. lbs. and stake the locknut. Disengage the gears. Check fifth gear thrust clearance.
6. Install the reverse shift arm to the pivot of the reverse shift arm bracket.
7. Install the reverse idler gear and shaft. Align the reverse shift arm shoe with the reverse idler gear groove and insert the reverse idler gear shaft into the intermediate plate. Install the gear shaft stopper and tighten the retaining bolt to 13 ft. lbs.
8. Position No. 1 and No. 2 shift forks into the grooves of their respective hub sleeves and install the No. 2 fork shaft through the forks and intermediate plate. Apply MP grease to the interlock pins and install the pins into the forks and intermediate plate.
9. Install the interlock pin in No. 1 shift shaft hole. Install the shift shaft through fork No. 1 and the intermediate plate. Install the interlock pin into the intermediate plate.
10. Install the interlock pin to the head of shift shaft No. 3. Install the shaft through the reverse shift arm and the intermediate plate.
11. Install the reverse shift head into fork shaft No. 5. Install fork shaft No. 5 to the intermediate plate and put the reverse shift head onto shift fork shaft No. 3.
12. Install the locking ball into the reverse shift head hole. Shift the No. 3 synchronizer hub sleeve to the 5th speed position. Place shift fork No. 3 into the groove of hub sleeve No. 3 and install fork shaft No. 4 to shift fork No. 4 and the reverse shift arm. Install the locking ball into the intermediate plate and insert fork shaft No. 4 to the intermediate plate.
13. Shift fork shaft No. 1 to the 1st speed position. Forks No. 2, No. 3, No. 4 and No. 5 should not move. Install the slotted retainer spring pins into each shift fork, reverse shift arm and reverse shift head. Install the two fork shaft E-rings. Apply sealer to the locking ball cover screw plugs. Install the locking balls, springs and screw plugs with a Torx socket and tighten to 14 ft. lbs. The short spring goes in the bottom of the intermediate plate.
14. Mount the intermediate plate and gear assemblies to the transmission. Align each bearing outer race, each fork end and reverse idler shaft with the case installation holes, tap with a plastic hammer if necessary to help with alignment. Install the two bearing snap rings.
15. Install the front bearing retainer with a new gasket after applying sealer to the mounting bolts. Tighten the bolts to 12 ft. lbs.
16. Install a new gasket on the intermediate plate. Install the transfer adapter and eight mounting bolts, torque the bolts to 27 ft. lbs. Insert the shift lever housing to the transfer adapter and connect the shift fork shafts. Insert the shift lever shaft to the transfer adapter and shift lever housing. Install and torque the shift lever housing bolt, torque to 28 ft. lbs. Install the front Torx plug cover, tighten to 27 ft. lbs.
17. Install the side locking ball, spring and screw plug. Apply sealer to the plug before installation, torque to 14 ft. lbs.
18. After installing the extension housing or transfer adapter, check to see that the input and output shafts rotate smoothly. Check to see that shifting can be made smoothly in all positions.
19. Install the black restrict pin on the reverse gear/5th gear side. Install the other restrict pin and torque both to 20 ft. lbs.
20. Install the clutch housing and torque the bolts to 27 ft, lbs. Install the shift lever retainer and new gasket. Tighten to 13 ft. lbs.
21. Install the back-up light switch (27 ft. lbs.). Install the release fork and bearing and install the transmission.

Land Cruiser 3 Speed

Disassembly

1. Remove the transfer case shift lever guide, cotter pin, and lockbolt. Remove the shift lever and linkage; do not lose the link lever shoe.
2. Remove the back-up light switch and gasket from the transmission cover.
3. Remove the transfer case cover, complete with gasket. Remove the power take-off cover and gasket.
4. Straighten out the tabs on the input shaft nut lockwasher and remove the nut. Slide the spacer off.

NOTE: Lock the power take-off drive gear with a wooden block or brass drift to keep the shaft from turning while the nut is being removed.

5. Loosen the five bolts which secure the transfer case to the transmission case and separate the cases with a puller. Hold the power take-off drive gear, spacer, and input gear, so that they don't drop out.
6. Unfasten the bolt and remove the gear selector outer lever.
7. Unfasten the bolts and remove the transmission case cover, complete with gasket.
8. Loosen the bolts and remove the front bearing retainer, with gasket, from the transmission case.
9. Drive the shift fork shaft out toward the front of the case with a hammer and a brass drift. Use care not to lose the fork balls, springs and pin.
10. Withdraw the first/reverse shift fork and the second/third shift fork from the transmission case. Remove the lockballs and springs.
11. Drive the countershaft rearward with a brass drift. Remove the countershaft Woodruff key.

NOTE: The countergear should remain in the case.

12. Remove the input shaft and bearing with a puller. Install the puller on the front of the input shaft.
13. Use a hammer and a brass drift to drive the output shaft rearward until the output shaft bearing clears the case. Do not pound on the output shaft; tap it lightly.
14. Separate the bearing from the output shaft with a puller.
15. Remove the output shaft and the related components from the transmission case.
16. Use a snap-ring expander to remove the snap-ring from the front of the output shaft. Slide the synchronizer clutch hub,

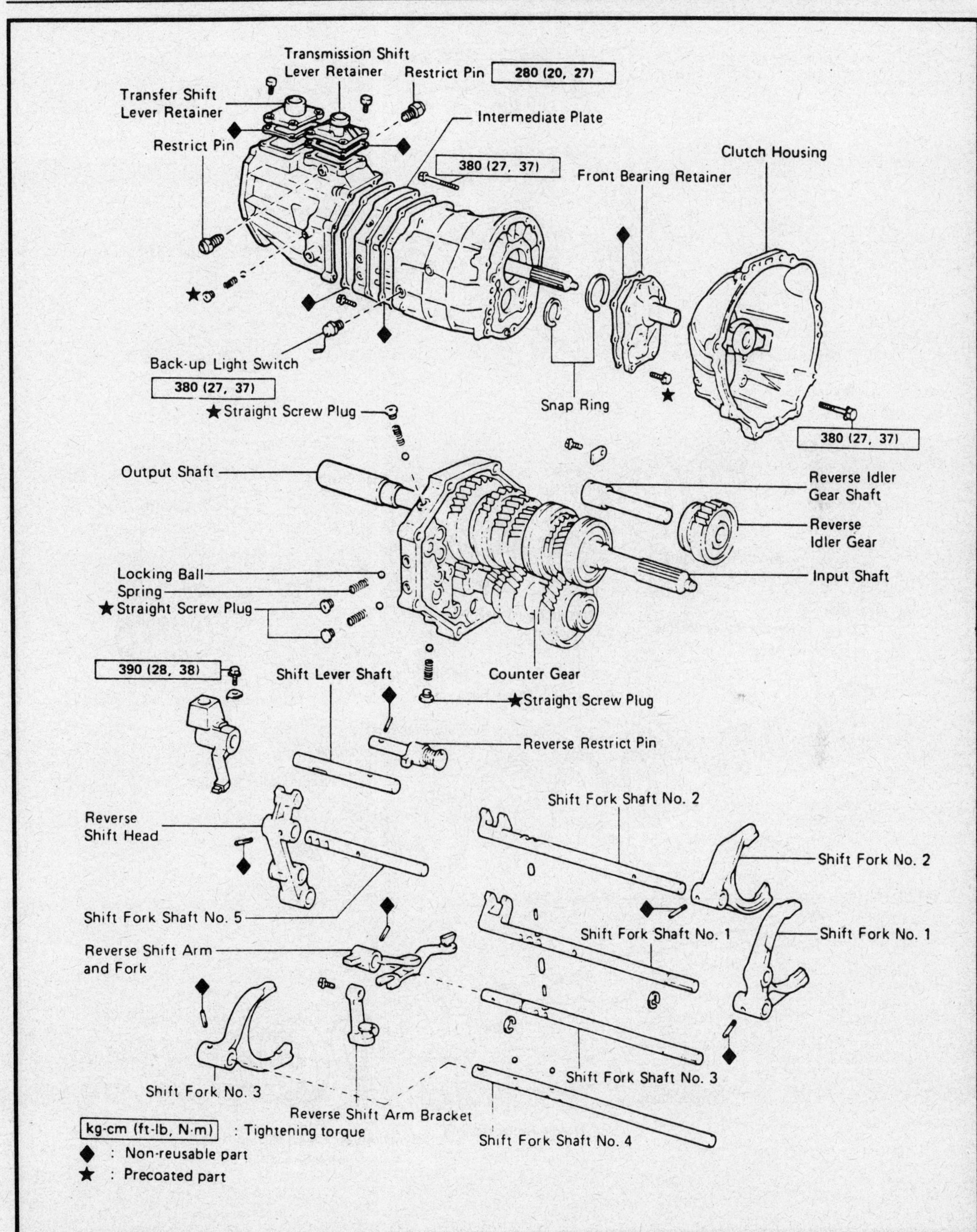
Transmission Shift
Lever Retainer
Restrict Pin
280 (20, 27)
Transfer Shift
Lever Retainer
Restrict Pin
Intermediate Plate
380 (27, 37)
Clutch Housing
Front Bearing Retainer
Back-up Light Switch
380 (27, 37)
★Straight Screw Plug
Snap Ring
380 (27, 37)
Output Shaft
Reverse Idler
Gear Shaft
Reverse
Idler Gear
Input Shaft
Locking Ball
Spring
★Straight Screw Plug
390 (28, 38)
Shift Lever Shaft
Counter Gear
★Straight Screw Plug
Reverse Restrict Pin
Shift Fork Shaft No. 2
Reverse
Shift Head
Shift Fork No. 2
Shift Fork Shaft No. 5
Shift Fork Shaft No. 1
Shift Fork No. 1
Reverse Shift Arm
and Fork
Shift Fork Shaft No. 3
Shift Fork No. 3
Reverse Shift Arm Bracket
Shift Fork Shaft No. 4
kg-cm (ft-lb, N·m) : Tightening torque
◆ : Non-reusable part
★ : Precoated part

Toyota G-series transmission

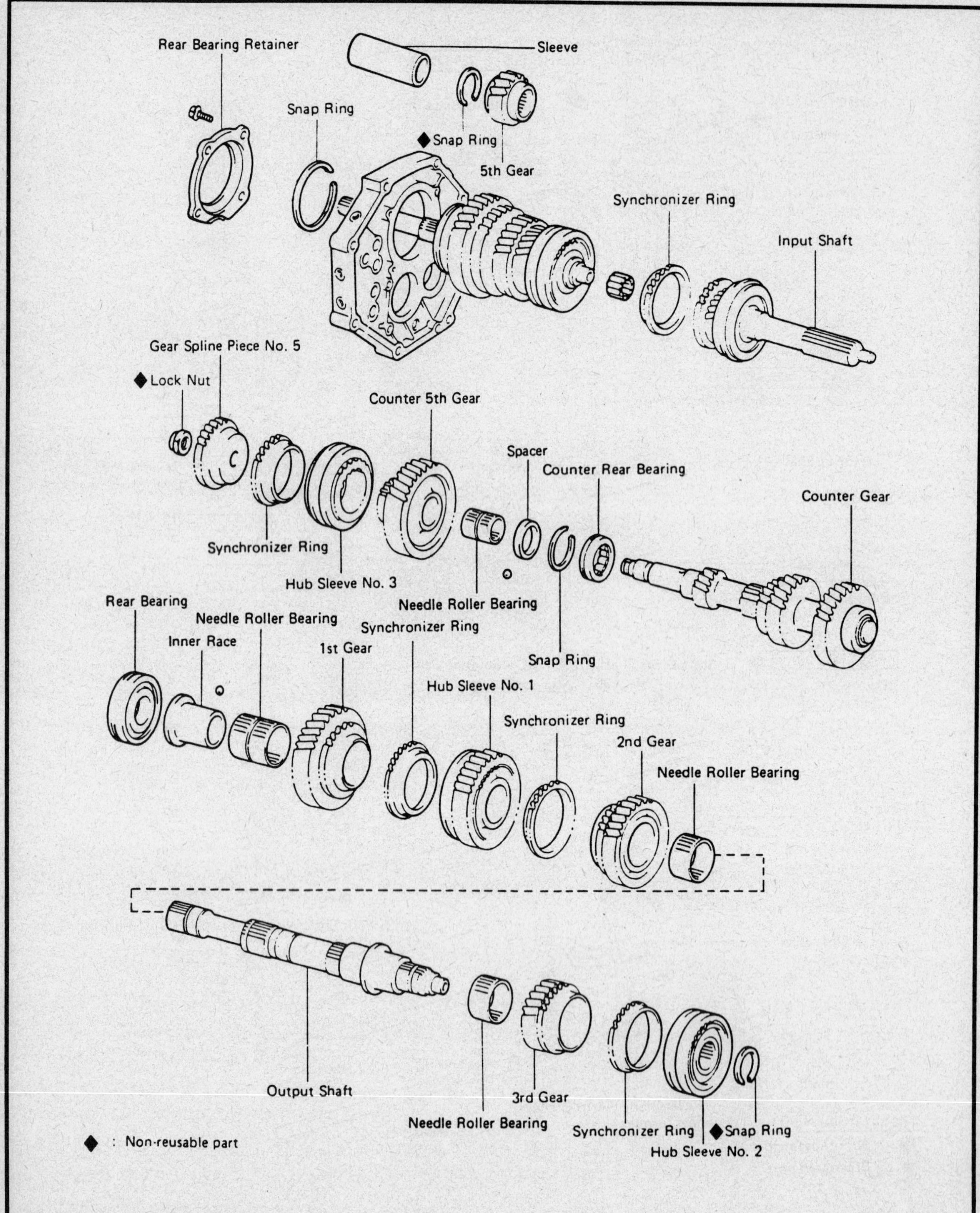
Rear Bearing Retainer
Sleeve
Snap Ring
◆Snap Ring
5th Gear
Synchronizer Ring
Input Shaft
Gear Spline Piece No. 5
◆Lock Nut
Counter 5th Gear
Spacer
Counter Rear Bearing
Counter Gear
Synchronizer Ring
Hub Sleeve No. 3
Needle Roller Bearing
Rear Bearing
Needle Roller Bearing
Inner Race
1st Gear
Synchronizer Ring
Snap Ring
Hub Sleeve No. 1
Synchronizer Ring
2nd Gear
Needle Roller Bearing
Output Shaft
3rd Gear
Needle Roller Bearing
Synchronizer Ring
◆Snap Ring
Hub Sleeve No. 2
◆ : Non-reusable part

Toyota G-series transmission

sleeve, synchronizer ring, second gear, and the first/reverse gearset off of the shaft.

17. Remove the countershaft drive gear, spacer, roller bearing, and washers. Note the placement of the gear thrust washers. Use care not to lose the rollers.

18. Drive the reverse idler gear shaft rearward and remove its Woodruff key.

19. Remove the reverse idler gear, rollers and thrust washers from the case.

20. Gear Backlash: Input shaft gear-to-countershaft drive gear: 0.004 in. Second-to-countergear: 0.004 in. First/reverse gear-to-countergear: 0.008 in. Countergear-to-reverse idler gear: 0.008 in. Reverse gear-to-reverse idler gear: 0.008 in. Synchronizer ring-to-gear: 0.039 in.

Assembly

NOTE: Use new gaskets, oil seals, and dust seals. Coat the gaskets with sealer.

1. Apply a light coating of gear oil to all components, prior to assembly.
2. Grease the bore of the reverse idler gear. Insert the bearing rollers and washer in the bore.
3. Install the reverse idler gear and the two thrust washers into the case. Drive the reverse idler gear shaft through the case, by gently tapping it into place from behind. Lock the shaft into place with the Woodruff key.
4. Grease the bore of the countershaft drive gear and fit its spacer. Install the rollers in the bore and hold them in place with a heavy coating of grease. Install the washers in the bore.
5. Place the countershaft drive gear, thrust washer, and side thrust washers in the case.
6. If the bearing was removed from the input shaft, press it into place on the shaft.
7. Select a snap-ring that will give the input shaft minimum end-play, and install it on the shaft.
8. Grease bore of the input shaft, install the rollers, and then fit the snap-ring.
9. Carefully drive the input shaft assembly and bearing into the transmission case.
10. Lift the countershaft drive gear up and install the countershaft from the rear of the case. Secure the countershaft with its Woodruff key.
11. Use a feeler gauge to measure the countershaft thrust clearance; it should be 0.002–0.008 in. Select a countergear side thrust washer of the proper size to obtain the specified thrust clearance.
12. Install the two synchronizer shifting key springs into the clutch hub, so that the open ends are 120° apart. Place the three shifting keys into the clutch hub key slots.
13. Slide the clutch hub sleeve into the clutch hub.
14. Fit second gear, its synchronizer ring, and the synchronizer assembly on the output shaft. Check second gear thrust clearance with a feeler gauge. It should be 0.003–0.009 in.
15. Working from the rear, slide the first/reverse gearset on the output shaft.
16. Install the output shaft assembly in the transmission case. Using a suitable brass drift, install the rear bearing over the output shaft and into the case.
17. Install both shift forks and retain them with their balls and lockpins.
18. Depress the shift fork lockballs with a screwdriver, then drive the shift fork shaft through the case, and into shift forks.
19. Install a new O-ring on the shift fork shaft and lock it in place with its pin.
20. Coat the front bearing retainer with liquid sealer and install the bearing retainer over it.
21. Install a suitable size pipe over the transmission output shaft. Place the transfer case input gear, power take-off drive gear, and the spacers over the pipe, which should be projecting through the transfer case.
22. Coat a new gasket with liquid sealer and install.
23. Install the transfer case on the transmission case. Be sure to install the two short bolts from the inside of the transfer case.
24. Install the bearing over the end of the transmission output shaft and into the transfer case with a drift.
25. Install the transfer case input shaft spacer.
26. Install the transfer case cover over its gasket.
27. Coat the gasket with liquid sealer and install the power take-off cover.
28. Install the back-up light switch and gasket.
29. Install the transfer front drive fork and its gasket on the transfer case extension housing.

4 Speed

Disassembly

1. Remove the transfer case shift lever guide, cotter pin, and lockbolt. Remove the shift lever and linkage, do not lose the link lever shoe.
2. Remove the back-up light switch and gasket from the transmission cover.
3. Remove the transfer case cover, complete with gasket. Remove the power take-off cover and gasket.
4. Straighten out the tabs on the input shaft nut lockwasher and remove the nut. Slide the spacer off.

NOTE: Lock the power take-off drive gear with a wooden block or brass drift to keep the shaft from turning while the nut is being removed.

5. Loosen the five bolts which secure the transfer case to the transmission case and separate the cases with a puller. Hold the power take-off drive gear, spacer, and input gear, so that they don't drop out.
6. Remove the transfer case input shaft gear stop from the transmission rear bearing retainer.
7. Remove the rear bearing retainer and gasket.
8. Remove the front bearing retainer and gasket.
9. Remove the input shaft and front bearing from the case with a puller.

NOTE: Prior to removing the input shaft, align the slot in the input shaft with the countershaft drive gear.

10. Remove the synchronizer ring.
11. Use an expander to remove the snap-ring on the output shaft rear bearing. Remove the bearing with a puller.
12. Withdraw the output shaft and gearset from the transmission case.
13. Straighten out the tabs on the countershaft front bearing retainer and remove the bolts; then remove the retainer and lockwasher.
14. Remove the front countershaft bearing. Remove the bearing spacer. Remove the rear countershaft bearing.
15. Remove the countershaft.
16. Remove the reverse shift arm pivot and shift arm.
17. Install a puller on the reverse idler shaft, and pull the gear shaft and key from the transmission case. Remove the reverse idler gear from the case.
18. Slide the first gear and its thrust washer off the back end of the output shaft.
19. Remove the snap-ring from the front of the output shaft; then remove the clutch hub, sleeve, synchronizer ring, and third gear from the shaft.
20. Remove the snap-ring and slide second gear and thrust washer off the shaft.
21. Slide the reverse gear synchronizer ring off the output shaft.
22. Press the countershaft drive gear off of the countershaft. Remove the Woodruff key and spacer from the shaft.
23. Repeat Step 22 for the third gear and Woodruff key.

24. Move the shift forks into neutral. Drive the slotted spring pin out of the third/fourth shift fork with a long drift.
25. Without using excessive force, drive the third/fourth shift fork shaft and plug forward with a brass drift. Remove the shift fork, lockball, and spring.
26. Drive the spring pins out of the reverse shift fork and boss with a long pin punch.
27. Remove the plug from the rear of the transmission case. Drive the first/second shift fork shaft forward with a brass drift. Remove the shift fork, boss, lockball, and spring.
28. Drive the spring pins out of the reverse shift fork and boss. Loosen and remove the tapered screw plugs from the transmission cover; then push the interlock rollers out with a long drift.
29. Remove the cotter pin, spring, and lockball from the shift fork boss.
30. Remove the C-washer, then withdraw the reverse return spring and plunger from the boss.
31. Gear Backlash: Input gear-to-countershaft drivegear: 0.004 in. Third gear-to-countershaft gear: 0.004 in. Second gear-to-countershaft gear: 0.004 in. First gear-to-countershaft gear: 0.004 in. Reverse gear-to-reverse idler gear: 0.005 in.

Assembly

1. Apply a light coating of gear oil to all components, prior to assembly.
2. Place the reverse idler gear in the case with its fork groove facing forward.
3. Align the Woodruff key, groove, and slot. Carefully drive the reverse idler shaft through the holes in the case, and into the gear.

NOTE: If you install new bushings in the idler gear, be sure that their openings are at least 90° apart.

4. Adjust the reverse idler gear position by trunging the shaft arm pivot to obtain a distance of 4.49 in. between the outer rear of the transmission case and the reverse idler gear. Move the gear to neutral, the distance between the front end of the gear and outer rear of the transmission case should now be 2.71 in. Adjust by rotating the shift arm pivot.
5. Install the Woodruff key into the groove of the countershaft and align its keyway with the countershaft third gear. Place the gear on the shaft with the long hub facing forward.
6. Slide the spacer on the countershaft and press its drivegear on, in a similar manner to third gear (Step 5), with its long hub facing rearward.
7. Place the countershaft assembly into the transmission case and install the countershaft rear bearing with a press. Install the snap-ring over the end of the countershaft.
8. Install the front bearing spacer, protruded end forward, on the countershaft. Press the front bearing on, until its snap-ring registers firmly against the transmission case.

CAUTION

Apply pressure to the outer bearing race only, to prevent damage to the bearing.

9. Place the bearing retainer and lockwasher on the front of the countershaft.
10. Slide second gear on the output shaft so that its synchronizer outer ring faces rearward. Select a snap-ring so that second gear has a thrust clearance of 0.004–0.012 in.
11. Slide third gear on the output shaft, so that its synchronizer cone faces forward.
12. Install the two synchronizer shifting key springs into the clutch hub, so that the open ends are 120° apart. Place the three shifting keys into the clutch hub key slots.
13. Slide the clutch hub sleeve into the clutch hub.
14. Install the synchronizer ring and slide the synchronizer assembly over the output shaft. The grooves should face the rear.
15. Select a snap-ring to provide 0.008 in. thrust clearance for the clutch hub.
16. Slide the reverse gear synchronizer ring over the output shaft. Check the ring for smooth movement.
17. Slide first gear on the output shaft.
18. Place the output shaft assembly in the transmission case.
19. Fit the first gear thrust washer on the output shaft. Align the slot in the thrust washer with the output shaft pin.
20. Install the output shaft rear bearing with a press. Be sure to apply pressure on the bearing outer race only. Install the rear bearing and its gasket.
21. Press-fit the bearing on the input shaft. Grease the bearing rollers and install all 18 in the input shaft.
22. Place the input shaft in the transmission case, so that the synchronizer ring keyways align with the shift keys. Install the output shaft bearing spacer in the output shaft.

CAUTION

Be sure the bearing rollers or the spacer do not fall into the transmission case during installation.

23. Install the input shaft bearing retainer and gasket.

NOTE: Make sure that all shift fork shafts are in neutral during the shift fork shaft assembly steps, below.

24. Install the spring and return plunger in the reverse shift boss. Secure them with the C-washer. Install the ball and spring then secure them with a cotter pin.
25. Place the reverse shift fork and boss in the transmission cover, its bore, shift fork and into its boss, while depressing the lockball with a screwdriver.
26. Slide the reverse shift fork shaft through the front of the cover. Install the fork lock-spring and ball in the cover.
27. Align the holes and drive the slotted spring pin through the reverse shift fork and boss to secure them to the shaft.
28. Coat the roller with grease and install it into the interlock hole in the cover.
29. Place the first/second shift boss and fork into the cover. Install the first/second shift fork shaft and spacer from the front of the cover, after fitting its pin, and while depressing the lockball with a screwdriver.
30. Secure the first/second shift fork and boss with their slotted spring pins. Install another roller into the hole in the cover.
31. Install the third/fourth shift fork lock-spring and ball in the shift fork. Install the shift fork and shaft in the cover and secure them with a slotted spring pin.
32. Check the shift fork assembly for smooth operation. Install the plugs.
33. Install a suitable size pipe over the transmission output shaft. Place the transfer case input gear, power take-off drive gear, and the spacers over the pipe, which should be projecting through the transfer case.
34. Coat a new gasket with liquid sealer and install.
35. Install the transfer case on the transmission case. Be sure to install the two short bolts from the inside of the transfer case.
36. Remove the pipe from the output shaft and transfer case.
37. Install the bearing over the end of the transmission output shaft and into the transfer case with a drift.
38. Install the transfer case input shaft spacer.
39. Install the transfer case cover over its gasket.
40. Coat the gasket with liquid sealer and install the power take-off cover.
41. Install the back-up light switch and gasket.
42. Install the transfer front drive fork and its gasket on the transfer case extension housing.

HONING CYLINDERS

Operation	Unit	Time
Hone or Deglaze Cylinders	per cyl	.2
Remove Cylinder Ridge	per cyl	.2

CYLINDER SLEEVES, INSTALL

(Includes Finishing to any oversize required.)

Operation	Unit	Time
Pass Cars & Lt. Trucks	one	2.8
2 or 3 sleeves	per cyl	2.5
4 or more sleeves	per cyl	2.1
Angle Block	one	3.8
2 or 3 sleeves	per cyl	3.1
4 or more sleeves	per cyl	2.3
Trucks to 5″ Dia	One	3.2
2 or 3 sleeves	per cyl	3.1
4 or more sleeves	per cyl	2.3
Sleeves over 5″ Dia		(Special Quote)

Note: Engine in chassis and extra charge.

ENGINE BLOCK CLEAN & DEGREASE OR STEAM CLEAN

Operation	Time
Small blocks	1.9
Large blocks	2.4

PISTONS, RINGS, PINS & BEARINGS OPERATIONS

Fit Pins

Includes: Disassembly, hone, fitting, assembly and align rod. per rod .3

Operation	Unit	Time
Align Rods	each	.1
Clean Piston & Install Rings	each	.2
Grind Piston:		
Pass cars & lt. trucks	each	.4
Med. & H.D. trucks	each	.5
Regroove Piston Top Ring Land		
Pass cars & lt. trucks	each	.3
Med. & H.D. trucks	each	.4
Expand or Knurl Pistons	each	.3

CRANKSHAFT OPERATIONS

(Shaft Removed)

Crankshaft Grind (Connecting Rod Throws)

Operation	Unit	Time
1 con. rod throw		.8
2 con. rod throws	both	1.2
3. con. rod throws	All	1.6
4 con. rod throws	All	1.8
6 con. rod throws	All	2.0
8 con. rod throws	All	2.8

Crankshaft Grind (Main Bearing Throws)

Operation	Unit	Time
2 main brg. throws	both	1.2
3 main brg. throws	All	1.8
4 main brg. throws	All	2.0
5 main brg. throws	All	2.2
6 main brg. throws	All	2.4
7 main brg. throws	All	2.6

Crankshaft Grind (Connecting Rod & Main Bearing Throws)

Operation	Time
4 con. rod and 2 main brg. throws	2.5
4 con. rod and 3 main brg. throws	3.2
4 con. rod and 4 main brg. throws	3.4
4 con. rod and 5 main brg. throws	3.6
6 con. rod and 3 main brg. throws	3.2
6 con. rod and 4 main brg. throws	3.4
6 con. rod and 7 main brg. throws	4.4
8 con. rod and 4 main brg. throws	4.2
8 con. rod and 5 main brg. throws	4.9

(in Chassis)

Rod Journals Grind

Operation	Unit	Time
Pass car & lt. truck	one	4.0
Additional journals	each	2.0
Med. & H.D. trucks	one	5.0
Additional journals	each	2.5
Throws over 2½″ dia.		(Special Quote)

Crankshaft Micro Finish

Operation	Time
Pass car & lt. truck	1.2
Med. & H.D. trucks	2.0

CAMSHAFT AND GEAR OPERATIONS

Operation	Time
Camshaft Gear, Press off and Renew	.5
Camshaft Bearings, Renew and Align Bore	
1 or 2 Bearings	2.0
3 Bearings	2.3
4 Bearings	2.7
5 Bearings	3.1
6 Bearings	3.8
7 Bearings	4.6

CLUTCH AND FLYWHEEL OPERATIONS

Operation	Type	Time
Adjust Clutch Pressure Plate Levers	(Finger Type)	.6
	(Diaphragm Type)	.7
Clutch Disc Facings, Install		.5
Recondition Clutch Pressure Plate	(Finger Type)	1.2
	(Diaphragm Type)	1.5
Resurface clutch pressure plate, add		.6

Flywheel, Reface (Grind)

Operation	Time
Flat up to 13″	1.2
14″	1.4
15″ to 17″	2.3
Concave-stepped up to 11″	1.4
12″ & 13″	2.0
14″	2.2
15″ to 17″	2.4

Flywheel Ring Gear, Renew

Operation	Time
Shrink	.7
Weld	1.1
Machine	2.0

REAR AXLE OPERATIONS

Operation	Unit	Time
Rear Axle Bearings, Press off and Renew		
All exec below	each	.4
Chrysler products	each	.5
Pinion Shaft Rear Bearing Press off And Renew	each	.4

MAGNAFLUX OPERATIONS

Cylinder Heads

Operation	Unit	Time
Flat head - 4 cyl	each	1.5
6 cyl.	each	1.7
V8	each	1.5
O.H.V. - 4 cyl	each	1.8
6 cyl	each	2.0
V8	each	1.8

Engine Blocks

Operation	Time
4 cyl	2.0
6 cyl	2.5
V8	3.0
Camshaft caps add	1.0

Crankshafts

Operation	Time
4 cyl	1.5
6 cyl	1.7
V8	2.0

BRAKE SYSTEM OPERATIONS

Resurface Disc Brake Rotor .... each .9

Resurface Brake Drums:
- Pass car and Lt. trucks .... each .5
- Heavy Truck up to 16½" dia. .... per in. .2
- Over 16½" dia. .... per in. .3

Remove Hub and Press into New Drum .... each .5

Press in New Hub and True-up Drum .... each .6

Reline Brake Shoes (Riveted):
- Pass cars & Light trucks .... each .1
- Heavy trucks to 3¼" dia. .... each .2
- over 3¼" dia. .... each .3

Cam Grind Brake Shoes .... each .2

Emergency Brake Bands Install:
- Light Trucks .... each .4
- Med. & H.D. Trucks .... each .6

FRONT SUSPENSION OPERATIONS

Fit King Bolts and Install Bushings:
- Up to 1" dia. .... pair .6
- Over 1" to 1⅛" dia. .... pair .8
- Over 1⅛" dia. .... pair 1.0

Fit King Bolts and Install Bushings:
- Volkswagen .... pair 1.3
- Fiat & M.G. (Stepped) .... pair 1.3
- Mercedes Benz .... pair 1.8
- Volvo .... pair 1.8

Tapered Spindles .... pair 2.0

CYLINDER HEAD & VALVE OPERATIONS

Resurface (Grind) Cylinder Head:
- Pass cars & trucks—4 cyl 1.0
- 6 cyl 1.5
- V8—each 1.0
- Diesel Engines .... (Time Quote)
- Grinding over .030 add .... per cyl. .2
- Grinding to Specific Size Request, add .... per cyl. .2

Special Tool Cut Volkswagen Head—Per Cyl 2

Overhaul Cylinder Head:

Includes: Disassemble, clean, reface valves, reseat head, grinding valves to seats, reassemble ready for installation.
- Pass car engines. 4 cyl. 1.6
- 6 cyl 2.3
- V8 .... each 1.6
- F-heads .... each 1.2
- Volkswagen .... each 1.2
- H.D. truck engines, 6 cyl 2.8
- V6 .... each 1.6
- V8 .... each 1.8
- All Diesel engines .... (Time Quote)

NOTE: EXTRA CHARGE TO BE ADDED FOR RESEATING STELLITE VALVE SEATS OR REFACING STELLITE VALVES.

Cylinder Head Clean and Degrease
- Four cyl .... each .4
- Six cyl .... each .5
- V6 .... pair .6
- V8 .... pair .8

Heli Coil, Install .... one 1.0
- Additional .... each .6

VALVE RESEATING

(Includes: Cleaning Valve Ports.)

Grind 1 or 2 Iron or Steel Seats:
- Up to 2⁷⁄₁₆" ID. .... each .4

Grind 3 or More Seats, Add .... each .1

Grind 1 or 2 Iron or Steel Seats:
- Over 2⁷⁄₁₆" ID. .... each .5

Grind 3 or More Seats, Add .... each .2

Grind One Stellite Seat .... each .6

Grind 2 or More Stellite Seats, Add .... each .3

Grind All Import Car Seats .... each .7

Note: Service charge to shop add 7

VALVE GUIDE REAMING

Valve Guides, Ream for Oversize Stems
- Pass cars and Lt. trucks .... One .1
- Eight .6
- Twelve .8
- Sixteen .9
- Med. and H.D. Trucks .... each .2

Valve Guides, Knurl
- Each 3

Valve Guides, Bronze Wall
- Each 6

VALVE SEAT RINGS

Install Steel or Cast Iron Valve Seat Rings
- 1 seat up to 2" ID .... each .8
- Additional seats, add .... each .5
- Complete sets .... each .4
- Seats over 2" ID .... (Special Quote)

NOTE: If Stellite seat rings are installed add charges for grinding.

VALVE ROCKER ARMS AND STUDS

Reface Valve Rocker Arms .... each .1

Remove and Replace One Stud (Drill) 8
- 4 or more studs (drill) addtnl, add .... each .4

Remove and Replace One Stud (Pull) 4
- 4 or more studs (pull) addtnl, add .... each .2

VALVE REFACING

(Includes: Cleaning Valves.)

Reface Valves up to ⅜" stem .... each .1
- Over ⅜" stem .... each .2

Reface Stellite Valves .... each .3

Reface Valves over ½" Stem .... (Special Quote)

Reface Valve Tappets .... each .1

ENGINE BLOCK OPERATIONS

RESURFACE ENGINE BLOCK

- 4 cyl 2.0
- 6 cyl 3.0
- V8-each side 2.0

REBORING CYLINDERS:

Note: Boring blocks to customers specifications, or blocks with hard sleeves, add additional charges:

Passenger Car & Lt. Truck .... one 2.0
- Additional cylinders .... each 1.0

Med. and H.D. Trucks up to 4½" Cyl .... one 2.5
- Additional cylinders .... each 1.5

Over 5" Cylinder .... (Special Quote)

Chilton's LABOR CALCULATOR

For dollar rates ending with 50 cents or 1.00 add to the appropriate rate column.

TIME	.50 per hr.	$1.00 per hr.	$10.00 per hr.	$12.00 per hr.	$14.00 per hr.	$16.00 per hr.	$18.00 per hr.	$20.00 per hr.	$22.00 per hr.	$24.00 per hr.	$26.00 per hr.	$28.00 per hr.	$30.00 per hr.	$32.00 per hr.	$34.00 per hr.	$36.00 per hr.	$38.00 per hr.	$40.00 per hr.	$42.00 per hr.	$44.00 per hr.	$46.00 per hr.	$48.00 per hr.	$50.00 per hr.	$55.00 per hr.
.1	.05	.10	$1.00	$1.20	$1.40	$1.60	$1.80	$2.00	$2.20	$2.40	$2.60	$2.80	$3.00	$3.20	$3.40	$3.60	$3.80	$4.00	$4.20	$4.40	$4.60	$4.80	$5.00	$5.50
.2	.10	.20	2.00	2.40	2.80	3.20	3.60	4.00	4.40	4.80	5.20	5.60	6.00	6.40	6.80	7.20	7.60	8.00	8.40	8.80	9.20	9.60	10.00	11.00
.3	.15	.30	3.00	3.60	4.20	4.80	5.40	6.00	6.60	7.20	7.80	8.40	9.00	9.60	10.20	10.80	11.40	12.00	12.60	13.20	13.80	14.40	15.00	16.50
.4	.20	.40	4.00	4.80	5.60	6.40	7.20	8.00	8.80	9.60	10.40	11.20	12.00	12.80	13.60	14.40	15.20	16.00	16.80	17.60	18.40	19.20	20.00	22.00
.5	.25	.50	5.00	6.00	7.00	8.00	9.00	10.00	11.00	12.00	13.00	14.00	15.00	16.00	17.00	18.00	19.00	20.00	21.00	22.00	23.00	24.00	25.00	27.50
.6	.30	.60	6.00	7.20	8.40	9.60	10.80	12.00	13.20	14.40	15.60	16.80	18.00	19.20	20.40	21.60	22.80	24.00	25.20	26.40	27.60	28.80	30.00	33.00
.7	.35	.70	7.00	8.40	9.80	11.20	12.60	14.00	15.40	16.80	18.20	19.60	21.00	22.40	23.80	25.20	26.60	28.00	29.40	30.80	32.20	33.60	35.00	38.50
.8	.40	.80	8.00	9.60	11.20	12.80	14.40	16.00	17.60	19.20	20.80	22.40	24.00	25.60	27.20	28.80	30.40	32.00	33.60	35.20	36.80	38.40	40.00	44.00
.9	.45	.90	9.00	10.80	12.60	14.40	16.20	18.00	19.80	21.60	23.40	25.20	27.00	28.80	30.60	32.40	34.20	36.00	37.80	39.60	41.40	43.20	45.00	49.50
1.0	.50	1.00	10.00	12.00	14.00	16.00	18.00	20.00	22.00	24.00	26.00	28.00	30.00	32.00	34.00	36.00	38.00	40.00	42.00	44.00	46.00	48.00	50.00	55.00
1.1	.55	1.10	11.00	13.20	15.40	17.60	19.80	22.00	24.20	26.40	28.60	30.80	33.00	35.20	37.40	39.60	41.80	44.00	46.20	48.40	50.60	52.80	55.00	60.50
1.2	.60	1.20	12.00	14.40	16.80	19.20	21.60	24.00	26.40	28.80	31.20	33.60	36.00	38.40	40.80	43.20	45.60	48.00	50.40	52.80	55.20	57.60	60.00	66.00
1.3	.65	1.30	13.00	15.60	18.20	20.80	23.40	26.00	28.60	31.20	33.80	36.40	39.00	41.60	44.20	46.80	49.40	52.00	54.60	57.20	59.80	62.40	65.00	71.50
1.4	.70	1.40	14.00	16.80	19.60	22.40	25.20	28.00	30.80	33.60	36.40	39.20	42.00	44.80	47.60	50.40	53.20	56.00	58.80	61.60	64.40	67.20	70.00	77.00
1.5	.75	1.50	15.00	18.00	21.00	24.00	27.00	30.00	33.00	36.00	39.00	42.00	45.00	48.00	51.00	54.00	57.00	60.00	63.00	66.00	69.00	72.00	75.00	82.50
1.6	.80	1.60	16.00	19.20	22.40	25.60	28.80	32.00	35.20	38.40	41.60	44.80	48.00	51.20	54.40	57.60	60.80	64.00	67.20	70.40	73.60	76.80	80.00	88.00
1.7	.85	1.70	17.00	20.40	23.80	27.20	30.60	34.00	37.40	40.80	44.20	47.60	51.00	54.40	57.80	61.20	64.60	68.00	71.40	74.80	78.20	81.60	85.00	93.50
1.8	.90	1.80	18.00	21.60	25.20	28.80	32.40	36.00	39.60	43.20	46.80	50.40	54.00	57.60	61.20	64.80	68.40	72.00	75.60	79.20	82.80	86.40	90.00	99.00
1.9	.95	1.90	19.00	22.80	26.60	30.40	34.20	38.00	41.80	45.60	49.40	53.20	57.00	60.80	64.60	68.40	72.20	76.00	79.80	83.60	87.40	91.20	95.00	104.50
2.0	1.00	2.00	20.00	24.00	28.00	32.00	36.00	40.00	44.00	48.00	52.00	56.00	60.00	64.00	68.00	72.00	76.00	80.00	84.00	88.00	92.00	96.00	100.00	110.00
2.1	1.05	2.10	21.00	25.20	29.40	33.60	37.80	42.00	46.20	50.40	54.60	58.80	63.00	67.20	71.40	75.60	79.80	84.00	88.20	92.40	96.60	100.80	105.00	115.50
2.2	1.10	2.20	22.00	26.40	30.80	35.20	39.60	44.00	48.40	52.80	57.20	61.60	66.00	70.40	74.80	79.20	83.60	88.00	92.40	96.80	101.20	105.60	110.00	121.00
2.3	1.15	2.30	23.00	27.60	32.20	36.80	41.40	46.00	50.60	55.20	59.80	64.40	69.00	73.60	78.20	82.80	87.40	92.00	96.60	101.20	105.80	110.40	115.00	126.50
2.4	1.20	2.40	24.00	28.80	33.60	38.40	43.20	48.00	52.80	57.60	62.40	67.20	72.00	76.80	81.60	86.40	91.20	96.00	100.80	105.60	110.40	115.20	120.00	132.00
2.5	1.25	2.50	25.00	30.00	35.00	40.00	45.00	50.00	55.00	60.00	65.00	70.00	75.00	80.00	85.00	90.00	95.00	100.00	105.00	110.00	115.00	120.00	125.00	137.50
2.6	1.30	2.60	26.00	31.20	36.40	41.60	46.80	52.00	57.20	62.40	67.60	72.80	78.00	83.20	88.40	93.60	98.80	104.00	109.20	114.40	119.60	124.80	130.00	143.00
2.7	1.35	2.70	27.00	32.40	37.80	43.20	48.60	54.00	59.40	64.80	70.20	75.60	81.00	86.40	91.80	97.20	102.60	108.00	113.40	118.80	124.20	129.60	135.00	148.50
2.8	1.40	2.80	28.00	33.60	39.20	44.80	50.40	56.00	61.60	67.20	72.80	78.40	84.00	89.60	95.20	100.80	106.40	112.00	117.60	123.20	128.80	134.40	140.00	154.00
2.9	1.45	2.90	29.00	34.80	40.60	46.40	52.20	58.00	63.80	69.60	75.40	81.20	87.00	92.80	98.60	104.40	110.20	116.00	121.80	127.60	133.40	139.20	145.00	159.50
3.0	1.50	3.00	30.00	36.00	42.00	48.00	54.00	60.00	66.00	72.00	78.00	84.00	90.00	96.00	102.00	108.00	114.00	120.00	126.00	132.00	138.00	144.00	150.00	165.00
3.1	1.55	3.10	31.00	37.20	43.40	49.60	55.80	62.00	68.20	74.40	80.60	86.80	93.00	99.20	105.40	111.60	117.80	124.00	130.20	136.40	142.60	148.80	155.00	170.50
3.2	1.60	3.20	32.00	38.40	44.80	51.20	57.60	64.00	70.40	76.80	83.20	89.60	96.00	102.40	108.80	115.20	121.60	128.00	134.40	140.80	147.20	153.60	160.00	176.00
3.3	1.65	3.30	33.00	39.60	46.20	52.80	59.40	66.00	72.60	79.20	85.80	92.40	99.00	105.60	112.20	118.80	125.40	132.00	138.60	145.20	151.80	158.40	165.00	181.50
3.4	1.70	3.40	34.00	40.80	47.60	54.40	61.20	68.00	74.80	81.60	88.40	95.20	102.00	108.80	115.60	122.40	129.20	136.00	142.80	149.60	156.40	163.20	170.00	187.00
3.5	1.75	3.50	35.00	42.00	49.00	56.00	63.00	70.00	77.00	84.00	91.00	98.00	105.00	112.00	119.00	126.00	133.00	140.00	147.00	154.00	161.00	168.00	175.00	192.50
3.6	1.80	3.60	36.00	43.20	50.40	57.60	64.80	72.00	79.20	86.40	93.60	100.80	108.00	115.20	122.40	129.60	136.80	144.00	151.20	158.40	165.60	172.80	180.00	198.00
3.7	1.85	3.70	37.00	44.40	51.80	59.20	66.60	74.00	81.40	88.80	96.20	103.60	111.00	118.40	125.80	133.20	140.60	148.00	155.40	162.80	170.20	177.60	185.00	203.50
3.8	1.90	3.80	38.00	45.60	53.20	60.80	68.40	76.00	83.60	91.20	98.80	106.40	114.00	121.60	129.20	136.80	144.40	152.00	159.60	167.20	174.80	182.40	190.00	209.00
3.9	1.95	3.90	39.00	46.80	54.60	62.40	70.20	78.00	85.80	93.60	101.40	109.20	117.00	124.80	132.60	140.40	148.20	156.00	163.80	171.60	179.40	187.20	195.00	214.50
4.0	2.00	4.00	40.00	48.00	56.00	64.00	72.00	80.00	88.00	96.00	104.00	112.00	120.00	128.00	136.00	144.00	152.00	160.00	168.00	176.00	184.00	192.00	200.00	220.00
4.1	2.05	4.10	41.00	49.20	57.40	65.60	73.80	82.00	90.20	98.40	106.60	114.80	123.00	131.20	139.40	147.60	155.80	164.00	172.20	180.40	188.60	196.80	205.00	225.50
4.2	2.10	4.20	42.00	50.40	58.80	67.20	75.60	84.00	92.40	100.80	109.20	117.60	126.00	134.40	142.80	151.20	159.60	168.00	176.40	184.80	193.20	201.60	210.00	231.00
4.3	2.15	4.30	43.00	51.60	60.20	68.80	77.40	86.00	94.60	103.20	111.80	120.40	129.00	137.60	146.20	154.80	163.40	172.00	180.60	189.20	197.80	206.40	215.00	236.50
4.4	2.20	4.40	44.00	52.80	61.60	70.40	79.20	88.00	96.80	105.60	114.40	123.20	132.00	140.80	149.60	158.40	167.20	176.00	184.80	193.60	202.40	211.20	220.00	242.00
4.5	2.25	4.50	45.00	54.00	63.00	72.00	81.00	90.00	99.00	108.00	117.00	126.00	135.00	144.00	153.00	162.00	171.00	180.00	189.00	198.00	207.00	216.00	225.00	247.50
4.6	2.30	4.60	46.00	55.20	64.40	73.60	82.80	92.00	101.20	110.40	119.60	128.80	138.00	147.20	156.40	165.60	174.80	184.00	193.20	202.40	211.60	220.80	230.00	253.00
4.7	2.35	4.70	47.00	56.40	65.80	75.20	84.60	94.00	103.40	112.80	122.20	131.60	141.00	150.40	159.80	169.20	178.60	188.00	197.40	206.80	216.20	225.60	235.00	258.50
4.8	2.40	4.80	48.00	57.60	67.20	76.80	86.40	96.00	105.60	115.20	124.80	134.40	144.00	153.60	163.20	172.80	182.40	192.00	201.60	211.20	220.80	230.40	240.00	264.00
4.9	2.45	4.90	49.00	58.80	68.60	78.40	88.20	98.00	107.80	117.60	127.40	137.20	147.00	156.80	166.60	176.40	186.20	196.00	205.80	215.60	225.40	235.20	245.00	269.50
5.0	2.50	5.00	50.00	60.00	70.00	80.00	90.00	100.00	110.00	120.00	130.00	140.00	150.00	160.00	170.00	180.00	190.00	200.00	210.00	220.00	230.00	240.00	250.00	275.00
5.1	2.55	5.10	51.00	61.20	71.40	81.60	91.80	102.00	112.20	122.40	132.60	142.80	153.00	163.20	173.40	183.60	193.80	204.00	214.20	224.40	234.60	244.80	255.00	280.50
5.2	2.60	5.20	52.00	62.40	72.80	83.20	93.60	104.00	114.40	124.80	135.20	145.60	156.00	166.40	176.80	187.20	197.60	208.00	218.40	228.80	239.20	249.60	260.00	286.00
5.3	2.65	5.30	53.00	63.60	74.20	84.80	95.40	106.00	116.60	127.20	137.80	148.40	159.00	169.60	180.20	190.80	201.40	212.00	222.60	233.20	243.80	254.40	265.00	291.50
5.4	2.70	5.40	54.00	64.80	75.60	86.40	97.20	108.00	118.80	129.60	140.40	151.20	162.00	172.80	183.60	194.40	205.20	216.00	226.80	237.60	248.40	259.20	270.00	297.00
5.5	2.75	5.50	55.00	66.00	77.00	88.00	99.00	110.00	121.00	132.00	143.00	154.00	165.00	176.00	187.00	198.00	209.00	220.00	231.00	242.00	253.00	264.00	275.00	302.50

Chilton's LABOR CALCULATOR

For dollar rates ending with 50 cents or 1.00 add to the appropriate rate column.

TIME	.50 per hr.	$1.00 per hr.	$10.00 per hr.	$12.00 per hr.	$14.00 per hr.	$16.00 per hr.	$18.00 per hr.	$20.00 per hr.	$22.00 per hr.	$24.00 per hr.	$26.00 per hr.	$28.00 per hr.	$30.00 per hr.	$32.00 per hr.	$34.00 per hr.	$36.00 per hr.	$38.00 per hr.	$40.00 per hr.	$42.00 per hr.	$44.00 per hr.	$46.00 per hr.	$48.00 per hr.	$50.00 per hr.	$55.00 per hr.
5.6	2.80	5.60	56.00	67.20	78.40	89.60	100.80	112.00	123.20	134.40	145.60	156.80	168.00	179.20	190.40	201.60	212.80	224.00	235.20	246.40	257.60	268.80	280.00	308.00
5.7	2.85	5.70	57.00	68.40	79.80	91.20	102.60	114.00	125.40	136.80	148.20	159.60	171.00	182.40	193.80	205.20	216.60	228.00	239.40	250.80	262.20	273.60	285.00	313.50
5.8	2.90	5.80	58.00	69.60	81.20	92.80	104.40	116.00	127.60	139.20	150.80	162.40	174.00	185.60	197.20	208.80	220.40	232.00	243.60	255.20	266.80	278.40	290.00	319.00
5.9	2.95	5.90	59.00	70.80	82.60	94.40	106.20	118.00	129.80	141.60	153.40	165.20	177.00	188.80	200.60	212.40	244.20	236.00	247.80	259.60	271.40	283.20	295.00	324.50
6.0	3.00	6.00	60.00	72.00	84.00	96.00	108.00	120.00	132.00	144.00	156.00	168.00	180.00	192.00	204.00	216.00	228.00	240.00	252.00	264.00	276.00	288.00	300.00	330.00
6.1	3.05	6.10	61.00	73.20	85.40	97.60	109.80	122.00	134.20	146.40	158.60	170.80	183.00	195.20	207.40	219.60	231.80	244.00	256.20	268.40	280.60	292.80	305.00	335.50
6.2	3.10	6.20	62.00	74.40	86.80	99.20	111.60	124.00	136.40	148.80	161.20	173.60	186.00	198.40	210.80	223.20	235.60	248.00	260.40	272.80	285.20	297.60	310.00	341.00
6.3	3.15	6.30	63.00	75.60	88.20	100.80	113.40	126.00	138.60	151.20	163.80	176.40	189.00	201.60	214.20	226.80	239.40	252.00	264.60	277.20	289.80	302.40	315.00	346.50
6.4	3.20	6.40	64.00	76.80	89.60	102.40	115.20	128 00	140.80	153.60	166.40	179.20	192.00	204.80	217.60	230.40	243.20	256.00	268.80	281.60	294.40	307.20	320.00	352.00
6.5	3.25	6.50	65.00	78.00	91.00	104.00	117.00	130.00	143.00	156.00	169.00	182.00	195.00	208.00	221.00	234.00	247.00	260.00	273.00	286.00	299.00	312.00	325.00	357.50
6.6	3.30	6.60	66.00	79.20	92.40	105.60	118.80	132.00	145.20	158.40	171.60	184.80	198.00	211.20	224.40	237.60	250.80	264.00	277.20	290.40	303.60	316.80	330.00	363.00
6.7	3.35	6.70	67.00	80.40	93.80	107.20	120.60	134.00	147.40	160.80	174.20	187.60	201.00	214.40	227.80	241.20	254.60	268.00	281.40	294.80	308.20	321.60	335.00	368.50
6.8	3.40	6.80	68.00	81.60	95.20	108.80	122.40	136.00	149.60	163.20	176.80	190.40	204.00	217.60	231.20	244.80	258.40	272.00	285.60	299.20	312.80	326.40	340.00	374.00
6.9	3.45	6.90	69.00	82.80	96.60	110.40	124.20	138.00	151.80	165.60	179.40	193.20	207.00	220.80	234.60	248.40	262.20	276.00	289.80	303.60	317.40	331.20	345.00	379.50
7.0	3.50	7.00	70.00	84.00	98.00	112.00	126.00	140.00	154.00	168.00	182.00	196.00	210.00	224.00	238.00	252.00	266.00	280.00	294.00	308.00	322.00	336.00	350.00	385.00
7.1	3.55	7.10	71.00	85.20	99.40	113.60	127.80	142.00	156.20	170.40	184.60	198.80	213.00	227.20	241.40	255.60	269.80	284.00	298.20	312.40	326.60	340.80	355.00	390.50
7.2	3.60	7.20	72.00	86.40	100.80	115.20	129.60	144.00	158.40	172.80	187.20	201.60	216.00	230.40	244.80	259.20	273.60	288.00	302.40	316.80	331.20	345.60	360.00	396.00
7.3	3.65	7.30	73.00	87.60	102.20	116.80	131.40	146.00	160.60	175.20	189.80	204.40	219.00	233.60	248.20	262.80	277.40	292.00	306.60	321.20	335.80	350.40	365.00	401.50
7.4	3.70	7.40	74.00	88.80	103.60	118.40	133.20	148.00	162.80	177.60	192.40	207.20	222.00	236.80	251.60	266.40	281.20	296.00	310.80	325.60	340.40	355.20	370.00	407.00
7.5	3.75	7.50	75.00	90.00	105.00	120.00	135.00	150.00	165.00	180.00	195.00	210.00	225.00	240.00	255.00	270.00	285.00	300.00	315.00	330.00	345.00	360.00	375.00	412.50
7.6	3.80	7.60	76.00	91.20	106.40	121.60	136.80	152.00	167.20	182.40	197.60	212.80	228.00	243.20	258.40	273.60	288.80	304.00	319.20	334.40	349.60	364.80	380.00	418.00
7.7	3.85	7.70	77.00	92.40	107.80	123.20	138.60	154.00	169.40	184.80	200.20	215.60	231.00	246.40	261.80	277.20	292.60	308.00	323.40	338.80	354.20	369.60	385.00	423.50
7.8	3.90	7.80	78.00	93.60	109.20	124.80	140.40	156.00	171.60	187.20	202.80	218.40	234.00	249.60	265.20	280.80	296.40	312.00	327.60	343.20	358.80	374.40	390.00	429.00
7.9	3.95	7.90	79.00	94.80	110.60	126.40	142.20	158.00	173.80	189.60	205.40	221.20	237.00	252.80	268.60	284.40	300.20	316.00	331.80	347.60	363.40	379.20	395.00	434.50
8.0	4.00	8.00	80.00	96.00	112.00	128.00	144.00	160.00	176.00	192.00	208.00	224.00	240.00	256.00	272.00	288.00	304.00	320.00	336.00	352.00	368.00	384.00	400.00	440.00
8.1	4.05	8.10	81.00	97.20	113.40	129.60	145.80	162.00	178.20	194.40	210.60	226.80	243.00	259.20	275.40	291.60	307.80	324.00	340.20	356.40	372.60	388.80	405.00	445.50
8.2	4.10	8.20	82.00	98.40	114.80	131.20	147.60	164.00	180.40	196.80	213.20	229.60	246.00	262.40	278.80	295.20	311.60	328.00	344.40	360.80	377.20	393.60	410.00	451.00
8.3	4.15	8.30	83.00	99.60	116.20	132.80	149.40	166.00	182.60	199.20	215.80	232.40	249.00	265.60	282.20	298.80	315.80	332.00	348.60	365.20	381.80	398.40	415.00	456.50
8.4	4.20	8.40	84.00	100.80	117.60	134.40	151.20	168.00	184.80	201.60	218.40	235.20	252.00	268.80	285.60	302.40	319.20	336.00	352.80	369.60	386.40	403.20	420.00	462.00
8.5	4.25	8.50	85.00	102.00	119.00	136.00	153.00	170.00	187.00	204.00	221.00	238.00	255.00	272.00	289.00	306.00	323.00	340.00	357.00	374.00	391.00	408.00	425.00	467.50
8.6	4.30	8.60	86.00	103.20	120.40	137.60	154.80	172.00	189.20	206.40	223.60	240.80	258.00	275.20	292.40	309.60	326.80	344.00	361.20	378.40	395.60	412.80	430.00	473.00
8.7	4.35	8.70	87.00	104.40	121.80	139.20	156.60	174.00	191.40	208.80	226.20	243.60	261.00	278.40	295.80	313.20	330.60	348.00	365.40	382.80	400.20	417.60	435.00	478.50
8.8	4.40	8.80	88.00	105.60	123.20	140.80	158.40	176.00	193.60	211.20	228.80	246.40	264.00	281.60	299.20	316.80	334.40	352.00	369.60	387.20	404.80	422.40	440.00	484.00
8.9	4.45	8.90	89.00	106.80	124.60	142.40	160.20	178.00	195.80	213.60	231.40	249.20	267.00	284.80	302.60	320.40	338.20	356.00	373.80	391.60	409.40	427.20	445.00	489.50
9.0	4.50	9.00	90.00	108.00	126.00	144.00	162.00	180.00	198.00	216.00	234.00	252.00	270.00	288.00	306.00	324.00	342.00	360.00	378.00	396.00	414.00	432.00	450.00	495.00
9.1	4.55	9.10	91.00	109.20	127.40	145.60	163.80	182.00	200.20	218.40	236.60	254.80	273.00	291.20	309.40	327.60	345.80	364.00	382.20	400.40	418.60	436.80	455.00	500.50
9.2	4.60	9.20	92.00	110.40	128.80	147.20	165.60	184.00	202.40	220.80	239.20	257.60	276.00	294.40	312.80	331.20	349.60	368.00	386.40	404.80	423.20	441.60	460.00	506.00
9.3	4.65	9.30	93.00	111.60	130.20	148.80	167.40	186.00	204.60	223.20	241.80	260.40	279.00	297.60	316.20	334.80	353.40	372.00	390.60	409.20	427.80	446.40	465.00	511.50
9.4	4.70	9.40	94.00	112.80	131.60	150.40	169.20	188.00	206.80	225.60	244.40	263.20	282.00	300.80	319.60	338.40	357.20	376.00	394.80	413.60	432.40	451.20	470.00	517.00
9.5	4.75	9.50	95.00	114.00	133.00	152.00	171.00	190.00	209.00	228.00	247.00	266.00	285.00	304.00	323.00	342.00	361.00	380.00	399.00	418.00	437.00	456.00	475.00	522.50
9.6	4.80	9.60	96.00	115.20	134.40	153.60	172.80	192.00	211.20	230.40	249.60	268.80	288.00	307.20	326.40	345.60	364.80	384.00	403.20	422.40	441.60	460.80	480.00	528.00
9.7	4.85	9.70	97.00	116.40	135.80	155.20	174.60	194.00	213.40	232.80	252.20	271.60	291.00	310.40	329.80	349.20	368.60	388.00	407.40	426.80	446.20	465.60	485.00	533.50
9.8	4.90	9.80	98.00	117.60	137.20	156.80	176.40	196.00	215.60	235.20	254.80	274.40	294.00	313.60	333.20	352.80	372.40	392.00	411.60	431.20	450.80	470.40	490.00	539.00
9.9	4.95	9.90	99.00	118.80	138.60	158.40	178.20	198.00	217.80	237.60	257.40	277.20	297.00	316.80	336.60	356.40	376.20	396.00	415.80	435.60	455.40	475.20	495.00	544.50
10.0	5.00	10.00	100.00	120.00	140.00	160.00	180.00	200.00	220.00	240.00	260.00	280.00	300.00	320.00	340.00	360.00	380.00	400.00	420.00	440.00	460.00	480.00	500.00	550.00
11.0	5.50	11.00	110.00	132.00	154.00	176.00	198.00	220.00	242.00	264.00	286.00	308.00	330.00	352.00	374.00	396.00	418.00	440.00	462.00	484.00	506.00	528.00	550.00	605.00
12.0	6.00	12.00	120.00	144.00	168.00	192.00	216.00	240.00	264.00	288.00	312.00	336.00	360.00	384.00	408.00	432.00	456.00	480.00	504.00	528.00	552.00	576.00	600.00	660.00
13.0	6.50	13.00	130.00	156.00	182.00	208.00	234.00	260.00	286.00	312.00	338.00	364.00	390.00	416.00	442.00	468.00	494.00	520.00	546.00	572.00	598.00	624.00	650.00	715.00
14.0	7.00	14.00	140.00	168.00	196.00	224.00	252.00	280.00	308.00	336.00	364.00	392.00	420.00	448.00	476.00	504.00	532.00	560.00	588.00	616.00	644.00	672.00	700.00	770.00
15.0	7.50	15.00	150.00	180.00	210.00	240.00	270.00	300.00	330.00	360.00	390.00	420.00	450.00	480.00	510.00	540.00	570.00	600.00	630.00	660.00	690.00	720.00	750.00	825.00
16.0	8.00	16.00	160.00	192.00	224.00	256.00	288.00	320.00	352.00	384.00	416.00	448.00	480.00	512.00	544.00	576.00	608.00	640.00	672.00	704.00	736.00	768.00	800.00	880.00
17.0	8.50	17.00	170.00	204.00	238.00	272.00	306.00	340.00	374.00	408.00	442.00	476.00	510.00	544.00	578.00	612.00	646.00	680.00	714.00	748.00	782.00	816.00	850.00	935.00
18.0	9.00	18.00	180.00	216.00	252.00	288.00	324.00	360.00	396.00	432.00	468.00	504.00	540.00	576.00	612.00	648.00	684.00	720.00	756.00	792.00	828.00	864.00	900.00	990.00
19.0	9.50	19.00	190.00	228.00	266.00	304.00	342.00	380.00	418.00	456.00	494.00	532.00	570.00	608.00	646.00	684.00	722.00	760.00	798.00	836.00	874.00	912.00	950.00	1045.00
20.0	10.00	20.00	200.00	240.00	280.00	320.00	360.00	400.00	440.00	480.00	520.00	560.00	600.00	640.00	680.00	720.00	760.00	800.00	840.00	880.00	920.00	960.00	1000.00	1100.00

Truck Labor Guide 30

CONTENTS

DOMESTIC TRUCKS

IMPORT TRUCKS

This section covers Labor Guide data on standard production line, gasoline and diesel powered vehicles. The time shown does not include interference items unless specified. Where these items cause additional labor, times should be adjusted accordingly.

Chevrolet/GMC Ser 10–30 • 1500 • 3500

GROUP INDEX

ALPHABETICAL INDEX

LABOR 1 TUNE UP 1 LABOR

(Factory Time)	Chilton Time
Compression Test	
Four	
S-series	.6
Astro	.9
Six	.9
V-6	
Vans-Astro	.9
All other models	.7
V-8	1.4
Diesel	1.3

Engine Tune Up, (Electronic Ignition)

Includes: Test battery and clean connections. Tighten manifold and carburetor mounting bolts. Check engine compression, clean and adjust or renew spark plugs. Test resistance of spark plug cables. Inspect distributor cap and rotor. Adjust distributor air gap. Check vacuum advance operation. Reset ignition timing. Adjust idle mixture and idle speed. Service air cleaner. Inspect and adjust drive belts. Inspect choke operation and adjust or free up. Check operation of EGR valve.

(Factory Time)	Chilton Time
Four–1984-88	
S-series	1.5
Astro	1.8
Six–1984-88	
Vans	2.5
All other models	2.3
V-6–1984-88	
Vans-Astro	2.3
All other models	2.0
V-8–1984-88	
Vans	3.4
All other models	3.0
w/A.C. add	.5

LABOR 2 IGNITION SYSTEM 2 LABOR

GASOLINE ENGINES

(Factory Time)	Chilton Time
Spark Plugs, Clean and Reset or Renew	
Vans-Astro	
Four (.6)	.8
Six (.4)	•.8
V-6 (.6)	.8
V-8 (.9)	1.3
All Other Models	
Four (.3)	.5
Six (.3)	.6
V-6 (.4)	.6
V-8 (.6)	.9
•w/A.C. add (.5)	.5
Ignition Timing, Reset	
All models (.3)	.5

Distributor, Renew

Includes: Reset ignition timing.

(Factory Time)	Chilton Time
Vans-Astro	
Four (.6)	.9
Six (.3)	•.9
V-6 (.8)	1.1
V-8 (.6)	1.1
All Other Models	
Four	
eng code A (.3)	.5
eng code Y (.6)	.9
eng code E (.6)	.9
Six (.6)	.8
V-6 (.6)	1.0
V-8 (.4)	.6
•w/A.C. add (.5)	.5

Distributor, R&R and Recondition

Includes: Reset ignition timing.

(Factory Time)	Chilton Time
Vans-Astro	
Four (.9)	1.5
Six (.5)	•1.4
V-6 (1.1)	1.8
V-8 (.8)	1.6
All Other Models	
Four	
eng code A (.6)	1.0
eng code Y (.9)	1.5
eng code E (.9)	1.5
Six (.8)	1.5
V-6 (.9)	1.5
V-8 (.9)	1.1
•w/A.C. add (.5)	.5

Distributor Points and Condenser, Renew

Includes: Adjust dwell and timing.

(Factory Time)	Chilton Time
Vans	
Six (.6)	.8
V-8 (.7)	.9
All Other Models	
Six (.4)	.6
V-8 (.5)	.7
Distributor Cap and/or Rotor, Renew	
Vans-Astro	
Four (.3)	.5
Six (.4)	•.6
V-6 (.5)	.7
V-8 (.5)	.7
All Other Models	
All engs (.3)	.5
•w/A.C. add (.5)	.5

Ignition Coil, Renew

Includes: Test coil.

(Factory Time)	Chilton Time
Four	
eng code Y (2.0)	2.8
eng code E (.6)	.9
eng code A (.3)	.5
Six (.6)	•.8
V-6	
S-series (.7)	1.0
Vans-Astro (.5)	.8
All other models (.4)	.7
V-8 (.5)	.8
•w/A.C. add (.5)	.5

Vacuum Advance Assembly, Renew

Includes: Adjust dwell and timing.

(Factory Time)	Chilton Time
Vans	
Six (.7)	•1.1
V-6 (.3)	.6
V-8 (1.0)	1.4
All Other Models	
Four	
eng code A (.4)	.7
eng code Y (.6)	.9
eng code E (.6)	.9
Six (.5)	.6
V-6 (.6)	.9
V-8 (.4)	.8
•w/A.C. add (.5)	.5
Vacuum Advance Solenoid, Renew	
All models (.2)	.3

(Factory Time)	Chilton Time
Spark Plug Wires, Renew	
Vans	
Six (.3)	•.7
V-6 (.3)	.6
V-8 (.7)	1.2
All Other Models	
Four	
S-series (.3)	.5
Astro (.5)	.7
Six (.5)	.6
V-6 (.5)	.8
V-8 (.5)	.8
•w/A.C. add (.5)	.5
Ignition Switch, Renew	
All models (.6)	1.0
Ignition Switch Lock Cylinder, Renew	
All models (.4)	.7
w/Tilt whl add (.1)	.1
Recode cyl add (.3)	.3
Vans, add	.2

ELECTRONIC IGNITION

(Factory Time)	Chilton Time
Distributor Module, Renew	
Vans	
Six (.3)	•.7
V-6 (.5)	.8
V-8 (.5)	.8
All Other Models	
Four (.3)	.6
Six (.3)	.6
V-6 (.6)	.9
V-8 (.3)	.6
•w/A.C. add (.5)	.5
Distributor Hall Effect Switch, Renew	
S-series (.5)	.8
Astro (.7)	1.0
ESC Detonation Sensor, Renew (Knock Sensor)	
10-30 Series (.7)	1.0
All other models (.6)	.9
ESC Module, Renew	
S-series (.9)	1.2
All other models (.5)	.7
Distributor Capacitor and/or Module Wiring Harness, Renew	
Vans	
Six (.4)	.8
V-6 (.5)	.8
V-8 (.5)	.9

LABOR 2 IGNITION SYSTEM 2 LABOR

(Factory Time) Chilton Time

All Other Models
Four (.4) .7
Six (.4) .7
V-6 (.6) .8
V-8 (.5) .7
*w/A.C. add (.5) .5

Distributor Pick-Up Coil and/or Pole Piece, Renew
Includes: R&R distributor and reset ignition timing.
Vans
Six (.5) *1.1
V-6 (.8) 1.3
V-8 (.8) 1.3
All Other Models
Four
eng code A (.3) .6
eng code Y (1.0) 1.5

(Factory Time) Chilton Time

Six (.5) .7
V-6
S-series (.7) 1.1
Astro (.9) 1.3
V-8 (.6) .8
*w/A.C. add (.5) .5

DIESEL IGNITION COMPONENTS

Coolant Fast Idle Temperature Switch, Renew
All models (.3) .4

Glow Plug Relay, Renew
Vans (.4) .6
All other models (.2) .3

Fast Idle Solenoid, Renew
Vans (.5) .7
All other models (.3) .4

(Factory Time) Chilton Time

Glow Plugs, Renew
All models
Four (.5) .7
V-8
one .4
one-each bank .7
all-both banks 1.3

Glow Plug Module, Renew
All models (.3) .5

Glow Plug Control Switch, Renew
Vans (.5) .7
All other models (.3) .4

Fast Idle Relay, Renew
All models (.3) .4

Starter Lockout Relay, Renew
All models (.2) .3

LABOR 3 FUEL SYSTEM 3 LABOR

(Factory Time) Chilton Time

GASOLINE ENGINES

Fuel Pump, Test
Includes: Disconnect line at carburetor, attach pressure gauge.
All models .3

Carburetor, Adjust (On Truck)
Vans
Curb & Fast Idle (.5) .6
Vacuum Break (.4) .5
Complete (1.3) 1.8

Accelerator Pump Dual Capacity Solenoid, Renew
Vans (.8) 1.1

Choke Coil, Cover and/or Gasket, Renew
Vans (1.1) 1.5

Fast Idle Solenoid, Renew
Vans (.6) .8

Fast Idle Actuator Vacuum Switching Valve, Renew
Vans (.3) .5

Fast Idle Actuator, Renew
Vans (.3) .5

Throttle Return Control Actuator, Renew
Vans (.5) .7

Carburetor, Renew
Includes: Necessary adjustments.
S-series
Rochester (.6) 1.0
Isuzu (.8) 1.2
Astro (1.2) 1.7
Vans (1.0) 1.4
All other models (.6) 1.0
To perform C.C.C. system test add (.5) 1.0

Carburetor, R&R and Clean or Recondition
Includes: Necessary adjustments.
Vans
1 bbl (2.5) 3.2
2 bbl (2.5) 3.2
4 bbl (2.7) 3.5
All Other Models
1 bbl (2.3) 3.0
2 bbl (2.3) 3.0
4 bbl (2.5) 3.2
To perform C.C.C. system test add (.5) 1.0

Needle Valve and Seat, Renew
Includes: R&R carb air horn and floats. Adjust idle speed.

(Factory Time) Chilton Time

Vans
1 bbl (1.1) 1.5
2 bbl (.8) 1.2
4 bbl (.9) 1.3
S-series
Rochester (.9) 1.3
Isuzu (.8) 1.2
All Other Models
1 bbl (.5) .9
2 bbl (.7) 1.0
4 bbl (.8) 1.1
To perform C.C.C. system test add (.5) 1.0

Fuel Filter, Renew
Vans (.5) .6
All other models (.3) .4

Anti-Dieseling or Idle Stop Solenoid, Renew
S-series (.5) .7
Vans (.4) .5
All other models (.2) .3

Automatic Choke Vacuum Diaphragm, Renew (One)
S-series-Astro
Rochester (.6) .8
Isuzu (.9) 1.2
Vans (.9) 1.2
All other models (.4) .6

Carburetor Base Gasket EFE Heater, Renew
S-series (.6) 1.0

Fuel Pump, Renew
Four (.6) *.9
Six (.5) .7
V-6 (.6) *.9
V-8 (1.0) 1.4
w/A.I.R. add (.3) .3
*Astro, add .4

Fuel Tank, Renew
Includes: Drain and refill tank.
Cab Mount
All models (.5) 1.0
Frame Mount
side tank-each (1.2) 1.7
Pick-Ups (1.0) 1.6
Vans (1.0) 1.6
Suburban & Blazer (.9) 1.4
Jimmy (.9) 1.4
S-series
rear (1.1) 1.7
left (1.3) 1.9

(Factory Time) Chilton Time

Astro (1.3) 1.9
w/Fuel tank shield add (.3) .4

Fuel Gauge (Tank), Renew
Includes: Drain and refill tank.
Cab Mounted Tank
All models (.5) .9
Frame Mounted Tank
side tank-each (1.0) 1.5
Pick-Ups (1.3) 1.9
Vans (1.1) 1.7
Suburban & Blazer (.9) 1.3
Jimmy (.9) 1.3
S-series
rear (1.3) 1.8
left (1.5) 2.0
Astro (1.5) 2.0
w/Fuel tank shield add (.3) .4

Fuel Gauge (Dash), Renew
1984-86
S-series (.3) .5
Astro (.9) 1.4
All other models (.5) .9
1987-88
S-series-Astro (.9) 1.4
Vans (.8) 1.3
All other models (.4) .9

Intake Manifold, Renew
Six
Vans (2.7) 3.9
All other models (1.2) 1.8
w/P.S. add (.5) .5

Intake and Exhaust Manifold Gaskets, Renew
Six
Vans (2.5) 3.6
All other models (1.4) 2.0
w/P.S. add (.5) .5

Intake Manifold or Gasket, Renew
Four
eng code A (1.7) 2.5
eng code Y (1.9) 2.7
eng code E
S-series (2.3) 3.2
Astro (2.2) 3.1
w/Cruise control add .2
Six–All models (2.7) 3.9
V-6
S-series (3.9) 5.5
Astro (2.2) 3.1
exc Vans (2.1) 3.0
Vans (2.3) 3.3

LABOR 3 FUEL SYSTEM 3 LABOR

(Factory Time)	Chilton Time
w/A.C. add (.2)	.2
w/C.C.C. add (.2)	.2
V-8–454 eng	
All models (2.0)	2.7
V-8–All other engs	
exc Vans (1.7)	2.5
Vans (2.7)	3.9
w/A.C. add (.2)	.2
Renew manif add (.3)	.5

FUEL INJECTION

(Factory Time)	Chilton Time
Throttle Body, R&R or Renew	
Astro (.9)	1.3
S-series (.6)	1.1
All other models (.3)	.5
Renew throttle body kit add (.3)	.3
Renew fuel meter body add (.3)	.3
Throttle Body Fuel Meter Assy., and/or Gasket, Renew	
Astro (.6)	.8
S-series (.4)	.6
All other models (.6)	.8
Idle Air Control Valve, Renew	
Astro (.7)	1.0
S-series (.5)	.8
All other models (.5)	.8
Throttle Body Injector and/or Gasket, Renew	
Astro-one (.6)	.8
both (.6)	.9
S-series-one (.8)	1.2
both (.9)	1.3
All other models	
one (.4)	.6
both (.4)	.7
Minimum Idle Speed, Adjust	
Astro (.9)	1.2
S-series (.5)	.8
Vans (.7)	1.0
All other models (.3)	.4
Fuel Pressure Regulator and/or Gaskets, Renew	
Vans-Astro (.7)	1.3
S-series (.7)	1.1
All other models (.5)	.7
Fuel Pump, Renew (In Tank)	
Left Tank	
S-series (1.7)	2.3
All other models (1.3)	1.8
Rear Tank	
S-series (1.5)	2.0
All other models (1.2)	1.7
Fuel Pump Relay, Renew	
Astro (.7)	.9
S-series (.5)	.7
All other models (.5)	.7

DIESEL ENGINE

(Factory Time)	Chilton Time
Air Cleaner, Service	
All models (.2)	.4
Air Intake Crossover, Renew	
All models (.3)	.5
Fuel Filter, Renew	
All models (.2)	.4
Idle Speed, Adjust	
All models (.2)	.4
Injection Timing, Check and Adjust	
All models (.5)	.9
Throttle Position Sensor, Renew	
All models (.5)	.7
Fuel Solenoid, Renew	
Vans (2.0)	*2.7
All other models (.5)	.7
*w/A.C. add (.2)	.2
Cold Advance Solenoid, Renew	
Vans (2.1)	*2.8
All other models (.6)	.8
*w/A.C. add (.2)	.2
Fuel Injection Head Seal, Renew	
Includes: Renew head and drive shaft seals. Renew governor weight retaining ring.	
All models	
5.7L eng (3.3)	4.7
6.2L eng	
Vans (4.0)	5.3
All other models (3.2)	4.1
Fuel Injection Pump, Renew	
Includes: Pressure and electrical tests. Adjust timing.	
All models	
2.2L eng (1.9)	2.7
5.7L eng (2.6)	3.5
6.2L eng	
Vans (3.8)	*4.9
All other models (3.3)	4.4
*w/A.C. add (.2)	.2
Fuel Return Lines (At Nozzles), Renew	
All models-one side (.3)	.5
both sides (.4)	.7
return hose (.2)	.3
w/A.C. add (.2)	.2
High Pressure Fuel Lines, Renew	
Includes: Flush lines.	
Four-one (.4)	.7
all (.5)	.8
V-8-one (1.2)	1.5
one-each bank (1.4)	1.7
all-both banks (1.5)	2.5
w/A.C. add (.2)	.2
Injector Nozzle and/or Seal, Renew	
Four	
one or all (.6)	1.0
V-8-one (.8)	1.2
one-each bank (1.0)	1.4
all-both banks (1.5)	3.0
w/A.C. add (.2)	.2
Clean nozzles add-each	.2
Fuel Supply Pump, Renew	
All models (.5)	.7
w/A.C. add (.2)	.2
Fuel Injection Pump Throttle Shaft Seal, Renew	
All models	
5.7L eng (.9)	1.3
6.2L eng	
Vans (2.0)	*2.5
All other models (1.7)	2.3
*w/A.C. add (.2)	.2
Injection Pump Adapter and/or Seal, Renew	
All models	
5.7L eng (1.9)	2.4
Locate new timing mark add (.1)	.1
Vacuum Pump, Renew	
Vans (1.2)	1.6
All other models (.3)	.6
Intake Manifold or Gasket, Renew	
All models	
2.2L eng (.7)	1.2
5.7L eng (2.7)	3.5
6.2L eng (1.4)	2.0
Renew manif add (.2)	.5

LABOR 3A EMISSION CONTROLS 3A LABOR

GASOLINE ENGINES

(Factory Time)	Chilton Time
Emission Control Check	
Includes: Check and adjust engine idle speed, mixture and ignition timing.	
All models	.6

CRANKCASE EMISSION

(Factory Time)	Chilton Time
Positive Crankcase Ventilation Valve, Renew	
All models (.2)	.3
Crankcase Vent Filter, Renew	
All models (.2)	.3

AIR INJECTION REACTOR TYPE

(Factory Time)	Chilton Time
A.I.R. Air Pump Cleaner, Renew	
All models (.2)	.4
Air Pump, Renew	
Four (.4)	*.6
Six (.6)	.8
V-6 (.4)	*.7
V-8 (.8)	1.0
*Astro add	.2
Air Pump Relief Valve, Renew	
Six (.8)	1.0
V-8 (1.0)	1.2
Diverter or Gulp Valve, Renew	
Vans-Astro (.4)	.6
All other models (.2)	.4
Check Valve, Renew (One)	
Vans (.4)	.6
All other models (.2)	.4
each adtnl	.1
Combustion Pipes and/or Extensions, Renew	
Vans	
Six (.6)	.9
V-8-one (.6)	.9
both (.8)	1.2
All Other Models	
Four (.6)	1.0
Six (.5)	.8
V-6-each (.3)	.6
V-8-one (.3)	.6
both (.5)	.9
Vacuum Delay Valve, Renew	
All models (.3)	.4
Deceleration Valve, Renew	
All models (.3)	.4

LABOR 3A EMISSION CONTROLS 3A LABOR

(Factory Time) — Chilton Time

CONTROLLED COMBUSTION TYPE

Air Cleaner Vacuum Motor, Renew
Vans-Astro (.6) 8
All other models (.3) 6

Air Cleaner Temperature Sensor, Renew
Vans-Astro (.4) 5
All other models (.3) 4

EGR/EFE Thermal Vacuum Switch, Renew
Vans-Astro (.4) 6
All other models (.3) 5

EVAPORATIVE EMISSION TYPE

Charcoal Canister, Renew
Vans (.7) 1.0
All other models (.2) 4

Canister Purge Thermal Vacuum Switch, Renew
exc Vans (.3) 4
Vans-Astro (.5) 6

TRANSMISSION CONTROLLED SPARK

Transmission Controlled Spark Solenoid, Renew
Vans (.4) 5
All other models (.2) 3

Thermostatic Vacuum Switch or Temperature Switch, Renew
Vans (.5) 6
All other models (.3) 4

Controlled Spark Relay, Renew (On Firewall)
All models (.2) 3

Thermal Vacuum Switch, Renew
All models (.3) 4

EXHAUST GAS RECIRCULATION SYSTEM

E.G.R. Valve, Renew
Four
eng code A (.8) 1.1
eng code Y (.3) 5
eng code E
Astro (.9) 1.2
S-series (.5) 8
Vans (.5) 8
Diesel
5.7L eng (.6) 1.0
6.2L eng (.2) 4
All other models (.3) 5

E.G.R. Vacuum Delay Valve, Renew
S-series (.2) 3

EARLY FUEL EVAPORATION SYSTEM

E.F.E. Valve, Renew
Six (.3) 6
V-6 & V-8 (.6) 1.0
dual exhaust (.5) 9

E.F.E. Actuator and Rod Assy., Renew
All models (.3) 6

E.F.E. Vacuum Check Valve, Renew
All models (.2) 3

COMPUTER COMMAND CONTROL SYSTEM (C.C.C.)

Computer Command Control System Performance Check
All models (.5) 1.0

Throttle Position Sensor, Adjust
Does not include system performance check.
All models (.4) 9

Manifold Absolute Pressure Sensor, Renew
Does not include system performance check.
S-series (.4) 6
All other models (.5) 7

Engine Speed Sensor, Renew
Does not include system performance check.
Vans (.7) 9
All other models (.5) 7

Calpak, Renew
Does not include system performance check.
All models (.5) 7

Electronic Control Module, Renew
Does not include system performance check.
All models (.5) 6

Mixture Control Solenoid, Renew
Does not include system performance check.
Vans-Astro (1.4) 1.8
All other models-2 bbl (1.1) 1.4
4 bbl (1.2) 1.5

Prom, Renew
Does not include system performance check.
All models (.5) 8

Coolant Temperature Sensor, Renew
Does not include system performance check.
Vans-Astro (.7) 9
All other models (.5) 6

Oxygen Sensor, Renew
Does not include system performance check.
All models (.5) 7

Barometric Sensor, Renew
Does not include system performance check.
All models (.5) 7

Manifold Differential Pressure Sensor, Renew
Does not include system performance check.
All models (.5) 7

Throttle Position Sensor, Renew
Does not include system performance check.
Vans-Astro (1.3) 1.7
All other models-2 bbl (1.1) 1.4
4 bbl (1.2) 1.5

Idle Speed Control Motor, Renew
Does not include system performance check.
All models (.5) 8

Air Control/Air Switching Valve, Renew
Does not include system performance check.
All models (.6) 8

E.G.R. Vacuum Control Solenoid, Renew
Does not include system performance check.
All models (.6) 8

Vehicle Speed Sensor, Renew
Does not include system performance check.
All models (1.0) 1.5

E.G.R. Bleed Control Solenoid, Renew
Does not include system performance check.
Vans-Astro (.5) 7
All other models (.4) 6

EFE/EGR Relay, Renew
Does not include system performance check.
All models (.3) 4

Tachometer Filter, Renew
Does not include system performance check.
All models (.3) 3

COASTING RICHER SYSTEM (C.R.S.)

Engine Speed Sensor, Renew
S-series (.3) 4

Accelerator Switch, Renew
S-series (.3) 4

Clutch Switch, Renew
S-series (.3) 4

Transmission Switch, Renew
S-series (.4) 7

Coasting Valve Solenoid, Renew
S-series (.3) 4

DIESEL ENGINE

Crankcase Depression Regulator Valve, Renew
Vans (.5) 7
All other models (.3) 4

Crankcase Ventilation Filter, Renew
All models (.3) 4

E.G.R. Valve and/or Gasket, Renew
All models
5.7L eng (.6) 1.0
6.2L eng (.2) 4

E.G.R. Control Valve Solenoid, Renew
Vans (.5) 7
All other models (.2) 3

E.P.R. Valve, Renew
Vans (.3) 4
All other models (.6) 8

E.P.R. Control Valve Switch, Renew
All models (.5) 7

E.P.R. Control Valve Solenoid, Renew
Vans (.7) 1.0
All other models (.5) 7

Vacuum Regulator Valve, Renew
Vans (.8) 1.1
All other models (.5) 7

LABOR 4 ALTERNATOR AND REGULATOR 4 LABOR

(Factory Time) — Chilton Time

Delcotron Circuits, Test
Includes: Test battery, regulator and Delcotron output.
All models 6

Alternator Drive Belt, Renew
Four
eng code A (.2) 3
w/P.S. add (.2) 2
eng code E (.2) 3
eng code S (.2) 3
w/A.C. add (.1) 1

LABOR 4 ALTERNATOR AND REGULATOR 4 LABOR

(Factory Time)	Chilton Time
Six–exc Vans (.2)	.3
Vans (.4)	.5
w/AIR add (.2)	.2
V-6 (.2)	.3
w/AIR add (.1)	.1
V-8–exc Vans (.2)	.3
Vans (.3)	.4
w/AIR add (.2)	.2
Diesel (.2)	.3

Delcotron, Renew

Includes: Transfer fan and pulley.

(Factory Time)	Chilton Time
Four–	
eng code A (.6)	.8
eng code Y (.3)	.5
eng code E (.3)	.5
Six–exc Vans (.4)	.6
Vans (.6)	.8
V-6	
Astro (.7)	.9
All other models (.5)	.7
V8–exc Vans (.6)	.8
Vans (.8)	1.0
Diesel–exc Vans (.4)	.6
Vans (.7)	1.0

Add circuit test if performed.

Delcotron, R&R and Recondition

Includes: Complete disassembly, replace parts as required, reassemble.

(Factory Time)	Chilton Time
Four–	
eng code A (1.5)	2.2
eng code Y (1.3)	2.0
eng code E (1.1)	2.0
Six–exc Vans (1.2)	1.8
Vans (1.3)	1.9
V-6	
Astro (1.3)	2.2
All other models (1.1)	1.8
V-8–exc Vans (1.2)	2.0
Vans (1.4)	2.2
Diesel–exc Vans (1.3)	2.0
Vans (1.8)	2.7

Add circuit test if performed.

Delcotron Bearings, Renew (Both)

Includes: R&R Delcotron, separate end frames.

(Factory Time)	Chilton Time
Four–	
eng code A (.8)	1.1
eng code Y (.6)	1.0
eng code E (.6)	1.0
Six–exc Vans (.6)	.9
Vans (.7)	1.0
V-6	
Astro (.8)	1.1
All other models (.6)	1.0
V-8–exc Vans (.6)	.9
Vans (.8)	1.1
Diesel–exc Vans (.6)	.9
Vans (1.0)	1.4

Voltage Regulator, Test and Renew

Includes: Disassemble and reassemble Delcotron.

(Factory Time)	Chilton Time
Four–	
eng code A (.7)	1.0
eng code Y (.6)	1.1
eng code E (.6)	1.1
Six–exc Vans (.5)	.8
Vans (.6)	.9
V-6	
Astro (.8)	1.2
All other models (.6)	1.1
V-8–exc Vans (.6)	.9
Vans (.8)	1.1
Diesel–exc Vans (.6)	1.0
Vans (1.0)	1.4

Voltmeter, Renew

(Factory Time)	Chilton Time
1984-86	
S-series (.3)	.6
Astro (.9)	1.4
All other models (.6)	1.0
1987-88	
S-series-Astro (.9)	1.4
Vans (.8)	1.3
All other models (.7)	1.2

LABOR 5 STARTING SYSTEM 5 LABOR

Starter Draw Test (On Truck)

(Factory Time)	Chilton Time
All models	.3

Starter, Renew

(Factory Time)	Chilton Time
Four	
eng code A (.6)	1.0
eng code Y (.8)	1.2
eng code E	
4X2 (.7)	1.0
4X4 (1.6)	2.1
Six (.4)	.7
V-6	
4X2 (.6)	1.0
4X4 (1.1)	1.5
V-8 (.6)	.8
Diesel (.8)	1.1

Add draw test if performed.

Starter, R&R and Recondition

Includes: Turn down armature.

(Factory Time)	Chilton Time
Four	
eng code A (1.5)	2.3
eng code Y (2.0)	2.8
eng code E	
4X2 (1.5)	2.3
4X4 (2.4)	3.4
Six (1.2)	2.0
V-6	
4X2 (1.5)	2.3
4X4 (2.0)	2.8
V-8 (1.5)	2.1
Diesel (1.6)	2.2
Renew field coils add (.2)	.5

Add draw test if performed.

Starter Solenoid, Renew

Includes: R&R starter.

(Factory Time)	Chilton Time
Four	
eng code A (.6)	1.0
eng code Y (.9)	1.3
eng code E	
4X2 (.8)	1.1
4X4 (1.6)	2.2
Six (.5)	.8
V-6	
4X2 (.6)	1.0
4X4 (1.1)	1.5
V-8 (.7)	.9
Diesel (.8)	1.1

Starter Drive, Renew

Includes: R&R starter.

(Factory Time)	Chilton Time
Four	
eng code A (.8)	1.2
eng code Y (1.0)	1.4
eng code E	
4X2 (.9)	1.2
4X4 (1.8)	2.4
Six (.7)	1.0
V-6	
4X2 (.8)	1.2
4X4 (1.4)	1.8
V-8 (.8)	1.1
Diesel (1.0)	1.3

Battery Cables, Renew

(Factory Time)	Chilton Time
Positive–exc Vans (.3)	.4
Vans (.5)	.6
Negative (.2)	.3
batt to batt	
Vans (.7)	1.0
All other models (.3)	.4

LABOR 6 BRAKE SYSTEM 6 LABOR

Brakes, Adjust (Minor)

Includes: Adjust brake shoes, fill master cylinder.

(Factory Time)	Chilton Time
two wheels	.4

Bleed Brakes (Four Wheels)

Includes: Fill master cylinder.

(Factory Time)	Chilton Time
All models (.4)	.6

Brake Pedal Free Play, Adjust

(Factory Time)	Chilton Time
All models	.3

Brake Shoes and/or Pads, Renew

Includes: Install new or exchange shoes or pads, adjust service and hand brake. Bleed system.

(Factory Time)	Chilton Time
With Single Rear Wheels	
front-disc (.9)	1.2
rear-drum (1.0)	1.7
All four wheels	2.8
With Dual Rear Wheels	
front-disc (.9)	1.2
rear-drum (2.1)	3.0
All four wheels	4.0
Resurface brake rotor add, each	.9
Resurface brake drum add, each	.5

Brake Drum, Renew (One)

(Factory Time)	Chilton Time
w/Single rear wheels (.3)	.6
w/Dual rear wheels (1.0)	1.4

Free-Up or Renew Brake Self Adjusting Units (One)

(Factory Time)	Chilton Time
w/Single rear wheels (.4)	.7
w/Dual rear wheels (.7)	1.0

LABOR 6 BRAKE SYSTEM 6 LABOR

(Factory Time) — Chilton Time

Brake Combination Valve and/or Switch, Renew
Includes: Bleed system.
Vans (.8) 1.1
All other models
w/2 wheel drive (.7) 1.0
w/4 wheel drive (.7) 1.0

BRAKE HYDRAULIC SYSTEM

Wheel Cylinder, Renew
Includes: Bleed system.
With Single Rear Wheels
one (.8) 1.3
both (1.1) 1.8
With Dual Rear Wheels
one (1.0) 1.7
both (1.8) 2.6

Wheel Cylinder, R&R and Recondition
Includes: Home cylinder and bleed system.
With Single Rear Wheels
one (1.0) 1.6
both (1.5) 2.4
With Dual Rear Wheels
one (1.2) 2.0
both (2.2) 3.2

Brake Hose, Renew
Includes: Bleed system.
All models-front-one (.5) 8
rear-one (.5) 8

Master Cylinder, Renew
Includes: Bleed system.
All models (.6) 1.0

Master Cylinder, R&R and Recondition
All models (1.4) 1.8

POWER BRAKES

Vacuum Power Brake Booster, Renew
S-series (1.2) 1.8
All other models (.6) 1.0

Vacuum Power Brake Booster, R&R and Recondition
S-series
single (1.7) 2.5
tandem (1.8) 2.6
All other models
single (1.1) 1.8
tandem (1.3) 2.0

Brake Booster Check Valve, Renew
All models (.3) 3

Hydraulic Brake Booster, Renew
Vans (1.2) 1.7
All other models (1.1) 1.6

Hydraulic Brake Booster, R&R and Recondition
Vans (1.8) 2.7
All other models (1.5) 2.4

COMBINATIONS

Add to Brakes, Renew

See Machine Shop Operations

(Factory Time) — Chilton Time

RENEW WHEEL CYLINDER
Each (.3) 4

REBUILD WHEEL CYLINDER
Each (.3) 6

REBUILD CALIPER ASSEMBLY
Each (.5) 5

RENEW BRAKE HOSE
Each 3

RENEW REAR WHEEL GREASE SEALS
Semi-floating axle
one (.2) 3
Full-floating axle
one (.3) 4

RENEW BRAKE DRUM (ONE)
With single rear whls (.4) 5
With dual rear whls (.5) 6

REPACK FRONT WHEEL BEARINGS (BOTH WHEELS)
All models (.6) 6

RENEW DISC BRAKE ROTOR
Each-w/2 whl drive (.3) 5
Each-w/4 whl drive (.6) 8

(Factory Time) — Chilton Time

Hydra-Boost Pump, Renew
All models (.9) 1.3
w/A.C. add (.2) 2

Hydra-Boost Pump, R&R and Recondition
All models (1.3) 1.9
w/A.C. add (.2) 2

Hydra-Boost Pump Line, Renew
All models-one (.5) 7

Hydra-Boost Pump Drive Belt, Renew
All models (.2) 3

Accumulator (Hydra-Boost), R&R or Renew
All models (.3) 7

DISC BRAKES

Brake Shoes and/or Pads, Renew
Includes: Install new or exchange shoes or pads, adjust service and hand brake. Bleed system.
With Single Rear Wheels
front-disc (.9) 1.2
rear-drum (1.0) 1.7
All four wheels 2.8

(Factory Time) — Chilton Time

With Dual Rear Wheels
front-disc (.9) 1.2
rear-drum (2.1) 3.0
All four wheels 4.0
Resurface brake rotor add, each 9
Resurface brake drum add, each 6

Disc Brake Pads, Renew
Includes: Install new disc brake pads only.
All models (.9) 1.2

Disc Brake Rotor, Renew
With Two Wheel Drive
All models-one (.7) 1.0
both (1.2) 1.8
With Four Wheel Drive
S-series-one (.5) 8
both (.8) 1.4
All other models-one (1.0) 1.2
both (1.8) 2.1

Caliper Assembly, Renew
Includes: Bleed system.
All models-one (.7) 1.1
both (1.1) 1.7

Caliper Assembly, R&R and Recondition
Includes: Bleed system.
All models-one (1.2) 1.6
both (2.1) 2.5

PARKING BRAKE

Parking Brake, Adjust
10-30 series (.8) 1.0
All other models (.3) 4

Parking Brake Equalizer, Renew
10-30 series (.9) 1.2
All other models (.3) 6

Parking Brake Control Assembly, Renew
S-series (1.0) 1.7
Vans (.9) 1.5
Astro (1.6) 2.3
All other models (.6) 9
w/Diesel eng add 4

Parking Brake Cables, Renew
Front
All models (.6) 1.0
Intermediate
All models (.3) 5
Rear-one
with single rear whls (.7) 1.0
with dual rear whls (.9) 1.2

ANTI-SKID BRAKE SYSTEM (ABS)

Electronic Brake Control Module, Renew
All models (.3) 4

Brake Pressure Modulator Valve, Renew
Includes: Bleed brakes.
All models (.4) 7

LABOR 7 COOLING SYSTEM 7 LABOR

(Factory Time) — Chilton Time

Winterize Cooling System
Includes: Run engine to check for leaks, tighten all hose connections. Test radiator and pressure cap, drain radiator and engine block. Add anti-freeze and refill coolant.
All models 8

Thermostat, Renew
All models
Gas engine (.4) 5
Diesel engine (.6) 8
Vans-w/A.C. add (.5) 5

(Factory Time) — Chilton Time

Radiator Assembly, R&R or Renew
Gasoline Engines
All models-w/M.T. (.6) 1.0
w/A.T. (.8) 1.2

Diesel Engines
All models-w/M.T. (.8) 1.2
w/A.T. (1.0) 1.4
w/Eng oil cooler add (.2) 2
w/A.C. add (.3) 3
Renew side tank add

(Factory Time) — Chilton Time

one side (.7) 1.0
both sides (1.2) 1.7

ADD THESE OPERATIONS TO RADIATOR R&R

Boil & Repair 1.5
Rod Clean 1.9
Repair Core 1.3
Renew Tank 1.6
Renew Trans. Oil Cooler 1.9
Recore Radiator 1.7

LABOR 7 COOLING SYSTEM 7 LABOR

(Factory Time)	Chilton Time
Radiator Hoses, Renew	
Vans-Astro	
upper (.4)	.5
lower (.6)	.6
both (.8)	1.0
All other models	
upper (.3)	.4
lower (.4)	.5
both (.5)	.7
by-pass (.3)	*.5
*Vans-Astro add	.3
Fan Blade or Clutch Assy., Renew	
Gas (.4)	.6
Diesel (.6)	.8
Fan Belt, Renew	
All models-one (.2)	.3
each adtnl (.2)	.3
If necessary to R&R fan pulley add (.2)	.3
Water Pump, Renew	
Four–	
eng code A (.9)	1.3
eng code Y (.9)	1.5
eng code E	
S-series (.9)	1.3
Astro (.9)	1.3
Six (1.2)	1.8
V-6	
S-series (1.2)	2.0
Astro (1.1)	1.9
V-8–exc Vans (.8)	1.5
Vans (1.1)	1.7

(Factory Time)	Chilton Time
Diesel	
2.2L eng (1.1)	1.9
5.7L eng (1.0)	1.8
6.2L eng	
exc Vans (1.6)	2.4
Vans (2.2)	3.0
w/P.S. add (.2)	.2
w/A.C. add (.5)	.5
w/A.I.R. add (.3)	.3
Water Jacket Expansion Plugs, Renew (Engine Block)	
All models-each (.3)	.5
Note: If necessary to R&R any component to gain access to plug, add appropriate time.	
Temperature Gauge (Engine Unit), Renew	
All models (.3)	.4
Temperature Gauge (Dash Unit), Renew	
1984-86	
exc Vans (.6)	1.0
Vans (.5)	1.0
S-series (.3)	.6
Astro (.9)	1.4
1987-88	
S-series-Astro (.9)	1.4
Vans (.8)	1.3
All other models (.7)	1.2
Heater Hoses, Renew	
Includes: Drain coolant at hose.	
All models-each (.4)	.5
Auxiliary Heater Hoses, Renew (One or All)	
Includes: Drain coolant at hose.	
All models (1.8)	2.4

(Factory Time)	Chilton Time
Hot Water Shut Off Valve, Renew (Auxiliary Heater)	
All models (.7)	1.1
Heater Core, R&R or Renew	
Without Air Conditioning	
Vans (2.1)	4.0
Astro (1.2)	2.3
All other models	
Gas (.8)	1.5
Diesel (1.7)	3.3
With Air Conditioning	
Vans-Astro (2.7)	5.0
S-series (1.5)	3.5
All other models	
Gas (1.4)	2.5
Diesel (2.6)	5.0
ADD THESE OPERATIONS TO HEATER CORE R&R	
Boil & Repair	1.2
Repair Core	.9
Recore	1.2
Heater Blower Motor, Renew	
Astro (.6)	1.0
All other models (.3)	.5
w/Diesel eng (1.0)	1.5
Heater Blower Motor Switch, Renew	
All models (.4)	.7
Heater Blower Motor Resistor, Renew	
All models (.2)	.4
Heater Control Assembly, Renew	
All models (.5)	.9

LABOR 8 EXHAUST SYSTEM 8 LABOR

(Factory Time)	Chilton Time
Muffler, Renew	
All models	
single exh-each (.6)	.9
dual exh	
right (.7)	1.0
left (.8)	1.1
Tail Pipe, Renew	
All models-each (.5)	.9
Catalytic Converter, Renew	
S-series (.9)	1.3
All other models (.6)	1.0
Front Exhaust Pipe, Renew	
All models	
right side (.7)	.9
left side (.6)	.9
Crossover Exhaust Pipe, Renew	
S-series (1.2)	1.6
All other models (.5)	.8
Front Exhaust Pipe, Renew (To Converter)	
S-series (.6)	1.0
All other models (.4)	.7
Rear Exhaust Pipe, Renew	
All models	
right side (.4)	.9
left side (1.0)	1.3
crossover (.7)	1.3
Intermediate Exhaust Pipe, Renew	
All models (.4)	.7

(Factory Time)	Chilton Time
Resonator and Pipe Assy., Renew	
All models (.4)	.6
E.F.E. Valve (Heat Riser), Renew	
Six (.3)	.6
V-6 & V-8-single exh (.6)	1.0
dual exh (.5)	.9
E.F.E. Actuator and Rod Assy., Renew	
All models (.3)	.6
Exhaust Manifold, Renew	
Four–	
eng codes A-Y (1.0)	1.5
w/A.C. add (.8)	.8
w/P.S. add (.4)	.4
eng code E	
S-series (.7)	1.1
Astro (.9)	1.3
w/A.C. add (.4)	.4
Six–exc Vans (1.1)	1.6
Vans (2.5)	3.6
w/P.S. add (.5)	.5
w/A.I.R. add (.6)	.6
V-6–	
S-series	
right side (.6)	1.0
left side (.9)	1.5
Astro	
right side (1.0)	1.7
left side (.7)	1.5
exc Vans	
right side (.7)	1.1
left side (1.0)	1.5

(Factory Time)	Chilton Time
Vans	
right side (.8)	1.2
left side (1.0)	1.5
w/A.C. add (.3)	.3
w/P.S. add (.3)	.3
w/C.C.C. add (.3)	.3
V-8–454 eng	
right side (1.6)	2.3
left side (1.4)	2.0
w/A.C. add (.5)	.5
V-8–All other engs	
exc Vans-right side (.6)	1.0
left side (1.0)	1.5
Vans-right side (1.0)	1.5
left side (1.0)	1.5
w/P.S. add (.2)	.2
w/A.C. add (.7)	.7
w/A.I.R. add (.2)	.2
Diesel	
2.2L eng (.7)	1.2
5.7L eng	
right side (.9)	1.3
left side (.7)	1.1
6.2L eng	
right side (1.1)	1.6
left side (1.3)	1.8
COMBINATIONS	
Muffler, Exhaust and Tail Pipe, Renew	
Four (1.2)	1.7
Six (1.3)	1.9
V-6 (.7)	1.2
V-8-one side (1.1)	1.6

(Factory Time) Chilton Time

Note: On all front suspension operations alignment charges must be added if performed. Time given does not include alignment.

Check Alignment of Front End
All models.................... .5
Note: Deduct if alignment is performed.

Toe-In, Adjust
All models (.4).................... .6

Align Front End
Includes: Adjust front wheel bearings.
S-series
4X2 (.7).................... 1.4
4X4 (1.1).................... 2.0
All other models (1.1).................... 2.0

Front Wheel Bearings, Clean and Repack
Two Wheel Drive
one wheel (.7).................... .8
both wheels (1.1).................... 1.4
Four Wheel Drive
one wheel (1.2).................... 1.4
both wheels (2.2).................... 2.5

Front Wheel Grease Seal, Renew
Two Wheel Drive
one wheel (.7).................... .7
both wheels (1.1).................... 1.2
Four Wheel Drive
one wheel (1.2).................... 1.3
both wheels (2.2).................... 2.4

Front Wheel Bearings and Cups, Renew
Two Wheel Drive
one wheel (.7).................... .9
both wheels (1.1).................... 1.5
Four Wheel Drive
one wheel (1.2).................... 1.5
both wheels (2.2).................... 2.6

Front Wheel Bearing and Hub Assy., Renew
S-series-4X4
one side (.8).................... 1.1
both sides (1.4).................... 2.0
Renew inner seal add
one (.4).................... .4
both (.6).................... .6

Front Shock Absorber, Renew
S-series 4X4
one (.5).................... .7
both (.7).................... 1.1
All other models-one (.3).................... .5
both (.4).................... .8

Steering Arm and Knuckle (Integral), Renew
Add alignment charges.
Two Wheel Drive
S-series-one (1.2).................... 1.6
both (2.2).................... 3.0
All other models-one (1.0).................... 1.3
both (1.8).................... 2.5

Steering Knuckle, Renew
Add alignment charges.
Four Wheel Drive
S-series
one (1.2).................... 1.6
both (2.2).................... 3.0
All other models-one (1.2).................... 1.6
both (2.1).................... 2.9

Lower Control Arm Assy., Renew
Add alignment charges.
S-series-4X2-one (1.1).................... 1.6
both (2.1).................... 3.1
4X4-one (1.5).................... 2.0
both (2.8).................... 3.8
All other models-one (.9).................... 1.3
both (1.7).................... 2.5

(Factory Time) Chilton Time

Lower Control Arm Bushings and Shaft, Renew
Add alignment charges.
S-series-4X2-one side (1.2).................... 1.9
both sides (2.3).................... 3.5
4X4-one side (1.4).................... 2.1
both sides (2.5).................... 4.0
Astro-one side (1.2).................... 1.9
both sides (2.3).................... 3.5
All other models-one side (.9).................... 1.5
both sides (1.7).................... 2.9

Upper Control Arm Assy., Renew
Add alignment charges.
S-series-4X2-one (.8).................... 1.3
both (1.2).................... 2.2
4X4-one (.9).................... 1.4
both (1.7).................... 2.7
All other models-one (.6).................... 1.1
both (1.1).................... 2.1

Upper Control Arm Bushings and Shaft, Renew
Add alignment charges.
S-series-one side (1.1).................... 1.7
both sides (2.0).................... 3.0
Astro-one side (1.0).................... 1.6
both sides (1.8).................... 2.8
All other models-one side (.7).................... 1.4
both sides (1.3).................... 2.7

Upper Ball Joint, Renew
Add alignment charges.
S-series-4X4
one (.9).................... 1.3
both (1.6).................... 2.4
All other models-one (.7).................... 1.1
both (1.2).................... 2.1

Lower Ball Joint, Renew
Add alignment charges.
S-series-4X4
one (1.1).................... 1.5
both (2.0).................... 2.8
All models-one (.7).................... 1.2
both (1.2).................... 2.3

Ball Joints or King Pins (Upper and Lower), Renew
Four Wheel Drive
All models-one side (1.8).................... 2.4
both sides (3.5).................... 4.7

Front Spring, Renew
Coil
All models-one (.8).................... 1.2
both (1.4).................... 2.3
Leaf
All models-one (.8).................... 1.4
both (1.5).................... 2.7

Front Spring Shackle or Pin, Renew
All models-one (.3).................... .5
both (.5).................... .9

Front Stabilizer Shaft, Renew
All models (.6).................... .9

Front Stabilizer Shaft Bushings, Renew
All models-one (.4).................... .7
both (.5).................... .8

FOUR WHEEL DRIVE

K-10-20-30 SERIES

Steering Knuckle Spindle Bearings, Renew
All models-one (1.1).................... 1.4
both (2.1).................... 2.7
Renew spindle add,
each (.1).................... .2
Renew knuckle add,
each (.5).................... .6

(Factory Time) Chilton Time

Front Wheel Hub, Renew
All models-one (.6).................... .9
both (1.1).................... 1.7

Free Wheeling Hub Control Mechanism, Recondition
All models-one (.3).................... .5
both (.5).................... .8
Recond add each (.5).................... .6

Front Axle Shaft Oil Seals, Renew
All models-one (3.0).................... 4.0
both (3.1).................... 4.3

Front Differential Housing Assy., Renew
Includes: R&R drive shaft, transfer all parts as required. Bleed brakes and make all necessary adjustments.
All models (7.4).................... 10.0

Front Drive Axle Differential Case, R&R or Renew
All models
Corp axle (3.4).................... 4.2
Dana axle (4.4).................... 5.4

Ring Gear and Pinion Set, Renew
Includes: R&R differential case.
All models
Corp axle (4.3).................... 5.4
Dana axle (5.5).................... 6.9

Pinion Bearings, Renew
Includes: R&R differential case.
All models
Corp axle (4.0).................... 5.5
Dana axle (5.2).................... 6.6

Differenetial Side Bearings, Renew
Includes: R&R differential case.
All models
Corp axle (3.3).................... 4.4
Dana axle (4.1).................... 5.6

Front Axle Housing Cover and/or Gasket, Renew
All models (.4).................... .7

Pinion Shaft Oil Seal, Renew
All models (.5).................... .9

Front Drive Shaft, R&R or Renew
All models (.4).................... .6
w/Transfer case shield add (.1).................... .1

Front Propeller Shaft U-Joints, Renew
All models
front (.6).................... .9
rear (1.1).................... 1.5
both (1.3).................... 2.0
w/Transfer case shield add (.1).................... .1

Front Axle Shaft and/or Universal Joint, Renew (One Side)
All models (1.2).................... 1.7
Renew inner shaft add.................... .4
Renew outer shaft add.................... .4
Renew U-Joint add.................... .4
Renew spindle brg add.................... .1

Front Drive Axle, R&R or Renew
All models-one (1.1).................... 1.5
both (2.0).................... 2.8
Renew or recond outer
C.V. Joint add-each (.6).................... .6
Renew or recond inner
C.V. Joint add-each (.4).................... .4
Renew shaft add-each (.3).................... .3

S-SERIES

Front Torsion Bar, Adjust
S-Series (.3).................... .5

Front Torsion Bar, Renew
S-Series-one side (.8).................... 1.2
both sides (1.1).................... 1.6
w/Skid plate add (.2).................... .2

LABOR 9 FRONT SUSPENSION 9 LABOR

(Factory Time)	Chilton Time
Torsion Bar Pivot Arm, Renew	
S-Series–one side (.5)	.7
both sides (.7)	1.1
w/Skid plate add (.2)	.2
Torsion Bar Support Crossmember, Renew	
S-Series (1.0)	1.5
w/Skid plate add (.2)	.2
Front Differential Vacuum Locking Actuator, Renew	
S-series (.2)	.5
Front Differential Locking Cable, Renew	
S-series (.4)	.6
w/Skid plate add (.1)	.1
Front Propeller Shaft U-Joints, Renew	
S-series	
front (.6)	.9
rear (1.1)	1.5
both (1.3)	2.0
Front Propeller Shaft Assy., Renew	
S-series (.4)	.6
w/Transfer case shield add	.1
Output Shaft, Renew	
S-Series	
right side (1.5)	2.1
left side (1.3)	1.8
both sides (2.7)	3.8
Renew shaft seal add each (.2)	.2
Drive Axle Assy., R&R or Renew	
S-Series	
one (1.1)	1.5
both (1.9)	2.6
Renew axle shaft, add each (.5)	.5
Renew C/V joint boot or seal, add each side (.4)	.4
Renew outer C/V joint, add each (.3)	.3
Renew D.O. joint, add each (.3)	.3
Repack or Recond joints, add	
inner (.4)	.4
outer (.6)	.6
Front Differential Cover or Gasket, Renew	
All models (.4)	.6
Differential Pinion Shaft Oil Seal and/or Flange, Renew	
All models (3.7)	5.2
Differential Output Shaft Tube Assy., R&R or Renew	
All models (1.4)	1.9
Renew output shaft seal add (.1)	.1
Renew pilot brg add (.2)	.2
Renew shaft assy add (.1)	.1
Recond tube assy add (.3)	.3
Differential Carrier Assy., Remove & Install	
All models (3.1)	4.3
Renew pinion shaft and/or side pinion gears add (.4)	.4
Renew side brgs add (1.0)	1.0
Renew pinion brgs add (1.7)	1.7
Renew ring and pinion assy, add (1.6)	1.6
Renew case add (1.2)	1.2
Renew carrier add (1.8)	1.8
Renew output shaft brgs add (.9)	.9
Renew mount bushs add (.2)	.2
Recond complete add (2.2)	3.0
Recond tube add (.3)	.3

LABOR 10 STEERING LINKAGE 10 LABOR

(Factory Time)	Chilton Time
Tie Rods or Tie Rod Ends, Renew	
Includes: Reset toe-in.	
Two Wheel Drive	
one (.7)	.9
both (.9)	1.4
Four Wheel Drive	
one (.8)	1.1
both (1.0)	1.6
Idler Arm, Renew	
All models (.7)	1.0
4X4 add	.2
Drag Link, Renew	
All models (.4)	.9
Intermediate Rod, Renew	
Includes: Reset toe-in.	
Vans-Astro (.7)	1.2
All other models (.9)	1.3
S-series 4X4 add	.2
Pitman Arm, Renew	
10-30 Series 4X4 (.9)	1.3
All other models (.5)	.8
S-series 4X4 add	.2
Steering Knuckle Arm, Renew	
Includes: Reset toe-in.	
All models–one (.9)	1.3
both (1.1)	1.7
Steering Damper, Renew	
All models (.3)	.6
S-series 4X4 add	.2
Idler Arm Bracket and Bushing, Renew	
All models (.4)	.8

LABOR 11 STEERING GEAR 11 LABOR

(Factory Time)	Chilton Time
STANDARD STEERING	
Steering Wheel, Renew	
All models (.3)	.4
Upper Mast Jacket Bearing, Renew	
All models–std column (.8)	1.4
tilt column (.9)	1.6
w/Cruise control add (.2)	.2
Steering Column Shift Bowl, Renew	
All models	
std colm (1.4)	2.0
tilt colm (1.7)	2.3
Steering Shaft Lower Coupling (Pot Joint), Renew	
Includes: R&R intermediate shaft.	
S-series (.4)	.7
w/P.S. add (.3)	.3
All other models (.6)	1.0
Flexible Coupling (Rag Joint), Renew	
All models (.6)	1.0
Steering Column Lock Actuator Parts, Renew	
All models	
std colm (.8)	1.4
tilt colm (.9)	1.6
w/Cruise control add (.2)	.2
Steering Gear, Adjust (On Truck)	
All models (.4)	.6
Steering Gear, R&R or Renew	
All models (.6)	1.0
S-series 4X4 add	.2
Steering Gear, R&R and Recondition	
Includes: Disassemble, renew necessary parts, reassemble and adjust.	
All models (1.5)	2.4
S-series 4X4 add	.2
Pitman Shaft Seal, Renew	
Does not require gear R&R.	
All models (.9)	1.4
S-series 4X4 add	.2
POWER STEERING	
Trouble Shoot Power Steering	
Includes: Test pump and system pressure. Check pounds pull on steering wheel and check for leaks.	
All models	.5
Power Steering Belt, Renew	
All models (.2)	.4
Power Steering Gear, R&R or Renew	
S-series (.6)	1.1
Astro (1.0)	1.5
All other models (.8)	1.3
Power Steering Gear, R&R and Recondition	
S-series (1.6)	2.5
Astro (2.0)	3.2
All other models (1.8)	3.0
Valve Body, Recondition	
Includes: R&R gear assy.	
S-series (.9)	1.4
Astro (1.3)	1.8
All other models (1.2)	1.8
Adjuster Plug, Recondition	
Includes: R&R gear assy.	
S-series (.8)	1.2
Astro (1.2)	1.7
All other models (1.0)	1.5
Rack Piston Assy., Recondition	
Includes: R&R gear assy.	
S-series (1.0)	1.5
Astro (1.4)	1.9
All other models (1.2)	1.8
Power Steering Pump, R&R or Renew	
All models (.8)	1.2
w/A.C. add (.2)	.2

LABOR 11 STEERING GEAR 11 LABOR

	(Factory Time)	Chilton Time
Vans-w/Diesel eng add		.2
w/Hyd. Brake Booster add		.1
Power Steering Pump, R&R and Recondition		
All models	(1.2)	1.8
w/A.C. add	(.2)	.2
Vans-w/Diesel eng add		.2
w/Hyd. Brake Booster add		.1
Power Steering Reservoir and/or 'O' Ring Seal, Renew		
All models	(1.0)	1.4
w/A.C. add	(.2)	.2
Vans-w/Diesel eng add		.2
w/Hyd. Brake Booster add		.1
Pump Flow Control Valve, Renew		
S-series	(.3)	.7
All other models	(.6)	1.0
w/A.C. add	(.2)	.2
Power Steering Hoses, Renew		
All models		
pressure	(.4)	.6
return	(.5)	.8
w/A.C. add	(.2)	.2
w/Hyd. Brake Booster add		.1

LABOR 12 CYLINDER HEAD & VALVE SYSTEM 12 LABOR

	(Factory Time)	Chilton Time
GASOLINE ENGINES		
Compression Test		
Four		.6
Six		.9
V-6		.9
V-8		1.4
Cylinder Head Gasket, Renew		
Includes: Clean carbon and make all necessary adjustments.		
Four		
eng code A	(3.4)	4.7
eng code Y	(3.7)	5.1
eng code E		
S-series	(4.0)	5.6
Astro	(4.4)	6.2
w/Cruise control add		.2
w/A.C. add	(.8)	.8
w/P.S. add	(.4)	.4
Six-exc Vans	(3.0)	4.3
Vans	(4.2)	6.0
w/P.S. add	(.4)	.4
w/A.C. add	(.5)	.5
w/A.I.R. add	(.6)	.6
w/P.A.I.R. add		.6
V-6-		
S-series-Astro		
one	(5.7)	8.1
both	(7.6)	10.8
All other models		
one	(4.2)	6.0
both	(6.5)	9.2
w/A.C. add	(.5)	.5
w/P.S. add	(.5)	.5
w/C.C.C. add	(.3)	.3
V-8-454 eng		
one	(5.2)	7.5
both	(7.1)	10.2
V-8-all other engs		
exc Vans-one	(4.5)	6.2
both	(6.4)	8.8
Vans-left	(4.8)	6.9
right	(5.6)	8.1
both	(7.0)	10.4
w/P.S. add	(.2)	.2
w/A.C. add	(.7)	.7
w/A.I.R. add	(.2)	.2
Cylinder Head, Renew		
Includes: Transfer all components, reface valves, clean carbon.		
Four		
eng code A	(5.7)	7.9
eng code Y	(6.2)	8.7
eng code E		
S-series	(5.5)	7.7
Astro	(5.7)	8.0
w/Cruise control add		.2
w/A.C. add	(.8)	.8
w/P.S. add	(.4)	.4
Six-exc Vans	(5.9)	8.5
Vans	(6.2)	8.9
w/P.S. add	(.4)	.4
w/A.C. add	(.5)	.5
w/A.I.R. add	(.6)	.6
w/P.A.I.R. add		.6
V-6-		
S-series-Astro		
one	(6.5)	9.2
both	(9.0)	12.8
All other models		
one	(5.0)	7.1
both	(7.6)	10.8
w/A.C. add	(.5)	.5
w/P.S. add	(.5)	.5
w/C.C.C. add	(.3)	.3
V-8-454 eng		
one	(6.2)	8.9
both	(9.2)	13.3
V-8-all other engs		
exc Vans-one	(5.4)	7.4
both	(8.1)	11.1
Vans-left	(5.6)	8.1
right	(6.5)	9.4
both	(8.8)	12.7
w/P.S. add	(.2)	.2
w/A.C. add	(.7)	.7
w/A.I.R. add	(.2)	.2
Clean Carbon and Grind Valves		
Includes: R&R cylinder heads, grind valves and seats. Minor tune up.		
Four		
eng code A	(5.2)	7.3
eng code Y	(5.3)	7.4
eng code E		
S-series	(5.6)	8.0
Astro	(6.0)	8.5
w/Cruise control add		.2
w/A.C. add	(.8)	.8
w/P.S. add	(.4)	.4
Six-exc Vans	(5.6)	8.1
Vans	(5.9)	8.5
w/P.S. add	(.4)	.4
w/A.C. add	(.5)	.5
w/A.I.R. add	(.6)	.6
w/P.A.I.R. add		.6
V-6-		
S-series-Astro		
one side	(7.0)	9.9
both sides	(9.4)	13.3
All other models		
one side	(5.3)	7.5
both sides	(7.8)	11.1
w/A.C. add	(.5)	.5
w/P.S. add	(.5)	.5
w/C.C.C add	(.3)	.3
V-8-454 eng		
one bank	(6.5)	9.4
both banks	(9.5)	13.7
V-8-all other engs		
exc Vans-one bank	(5.8)	8.0
both banks	(8.8)	12.1
Vans-left bank	(6.1)	8.8
right bank	(6.9)	10.0
both banks	(9.6)	13.9
w/P.S. add	(.2)	.2
w/A.C. add	(.7)	.7
w/A.I.R. add	(.2)	.2
Valves, Adjust		
Six	(.5)	1.4
V-8	(.8)	1.9
w/A.C. add		.7
w/P.A.I.R. add		.6
Valve Cover Gasket, Renew		
Four		
eng code A	(.4)	.7
eng code Y	(.6)	.9
eng code E		
S-series	(.9)	1.3
Astro	(1.4)	2.0
Six-exc Vans	(.7)	.9
Vans	(1.1)	1.6
w/A.I.R. add	(.3)	.3
w/P.A.I.R. add		.6
V-6-		
S-series-Astro		
one side	(.9)	1.3
both sides	(1.8)	2.6
exc Vans		
right side	(.7)	1.0
left side	(.3)	.5
both sides	(.9)	1.4

COMBINATIONS

Add to Valve Job

See Machine Shop Operations

	(Factory Time)	Chilton Time
GASOLINE ENGINES		
DRAIN, EVACUATE & RECHARGE AIR CONDITIONING SYSTEM		
All models	(.5)	1.0
ROCKER ARM STUD, RENEW		
Each	(.3)	.3
HYDRAULIC VALVE LIFTERS, DISASSEMBLE AND CLEAN		
Each		.2
DISTRIBUTOR, RECONDITION		
All models	(.5)	.9
CARBURETOR, RECONDITION		
1 BBL	(1.0)	1.0
2 BBL	(1.0)	1.2
4 BBL	(.8)	1.5
VALVE GUIDES, REAM OVERSIZE		
Each	(.1)	.1

(Factory Time)	Chilton Time
Vans	
right side (.9)	1.3
left side (.5)	.8
both sides (1.1)	1.7
w/A.C. add (.3)	.3
w/C.C.C. add (.3)	.3
V-8-454 eng	
one (.6)	.8
both (1.1)	1.5
V-8-all other engs	
exc Vans-one (.6)	.8
both (1.0)	1.3
Vans-right (1.5)	2.1
left (.8)	1.1
both (1.9)	2.7
w/A.C. add (.7)	.7
w/A.I.R. add (.2)	.2

Push Rod Side Cover Gasket, Renew

(Factory Time)	Chilton Time
Four	
eng code E	
S-series (1.6)	2.2
Astro (1.8)	2.5
Six-exc Vans	
front (.5)	.7
rear (.3)	.4
both (.7)	1.0
Vans	
front (.7)	1.0
rear (.3)	.4
both (1.0)	1.4

Valve Push Rods and/or Rocker Arms, Renew

(Factory Time)	Chilton Time
Four	
eng code A-all (.9)	1.2
eng code Y-all (1.0)	1.4
eng code E	
S-series-all (1.4)	2.0
Astro-all (1.9)	2.7
Six-exc Vans	
one or two (.5)	*.8
three or more (.7)	*1.2
w/A.I.R. add (.3)	.3
w/P.A.I.R. add	.6
Vans	
one cyl (1.3)	1.9
all cyls (1.7)	2.4
V-6-	
S-series-Astro	
one cyl (1.0)	1.5
one cyl-each side (1.8)	2.7
exc Vans	
one cyl-right side (.9)	1.4
one cyl-left side (.5)	1.0
one cyl-both sides (1.2)	1.9
Vans	
one cyl-right side (1.1)	1.7
one cyl-left side (.7)	1.2
one cyl-each side (1.4)	2.2
each adtnl cyl	.1
w/A.C. add (.3)	.3
w/C.C.C. add (.3)	.3
V-8-454 eng	
one cyl (.8)	1.1
one cyl-each bank (1.4)	2.0
all-both banks (1.9)	2.7
V-8-all other engs	
exc Vans	
one cyl (.8)	1.1
one cyl-each bank (1.4)	1.9
all cyls-both banks (1.9)	2.6
Vans	
one cyl-right bank (1.7)	2.5
one cyl-left bank (1.1)	1.6
one cyl-both banks (2.3)	3.3
all cyls-both banks (2.8)	4.0
w/A.C. add (.7)	.7
w/A.I.R. add (.2)	.2

Valve Lifters, Renew

Includes: R&R intake manifold on V-6 & V-8 engs. Make all necessary adjustments.

(Factory Time)	Chilton Time
Four	
eng code E	
S-series-all (3.1)	4.3
Astro-all (3.3)	4.6
Six-exc Vans-one (1.0)	1.4
all (1.5)	2.0
Vans-one cyl (1.9)	2.7
all cyls (2.7)	3.9
w/A.I.R. add (.3)	.3
w/P.A.I.R. add	.6
V-6-	
S-series	
one cyl (4.1)	6.0
one cyl-each side (4.2)	6.2
all cyls-both sides (4.7)	6.9
Astro	
one cyl (3.0)	4.4
one cyl-each side (3.3)	4.8
all cyls-both sides (3.8)	5.5
All other models	
one cyl (2.6)	3.8
one cyl-each side (2.8)	4.1
all cyls-both sides (3.3)	4.8
w/A.C. add (.3)	.3
w/C.C.C. add (.3)	.3
V-8-454 eng	
one cyl (2.5)	3.6
all cycls (3.5)	5.0
V-8-all other engs	
exc Vans-one cyl (2.8)	3.8
all cyls (3.4)	4.6
Vans-one cyl (3.2)	4.6
one cyl-each bank (3.6)	5.2
all cyls-both banks (4.2)	6.0
w/A.C. add (.7)	.7
w/A.I.R. add (.2)	.2

Valve Springs or Valve Stem Oil Seals, Renew (Head on Truck)

(Factory Time)	Chilton Time
Four	
eng code A	
one cyl (.8)	1.3
all cyls (1.4)	2.2
eng code Y	
one cyl (1.1)	1.6
all cyls (2.0)	3.0
eng code E	
S-series	
one cyl (1.3)	1.9
all cyls (2.2)	3.1
Astro	
one cyl (1.8)	2.6
all cyls (2.7)	3.8
Six-exc Vans	
one cyl (.7)	1.1
all cyls (1.2)	2.1
Vans	
one cyl (1.4)	2.0
all cyls (2.6)	3.8
w/A.I.R. add (.3)	.3
w/P.A.I.R. add	.6
V-6	
S-series-Astro	
one cyl (1.3)	1.9
one cyl-each side (2.3)	3.4
all cyls-both sides (3.6)	5.3
All other models	
one cyl-right side (1.4)	2.0
one cyl-left side (1.0)	1.5
one cyl-each side (2.0)	2.9
all cyls-both sides (3.2)	4.7
V-8-454 eng	
one cyl (1.1)	1.6
all cyls (3.7)	5.3
V-8-all other engs	
exc Vans	
one cyl (1.1)	1.5
all cyls (3.6)	5.0
Vans	
one cyl-right bank (2.1)	3.0
one cyl-left bank (1.4)	2.0
one cyl-each bank (3.0)	4.3
all cyls-both banks (4.7)	6.8
w/A.C. add (.7)	.7
w/A.I.R. add (.2)	.2

Valve Rocker Arm Stud, Renew (One)

Includes: Drain and refill cooling system.

(Factory Time)	Chilton Time
Four	
eng code E	
S-series (1.0)	1.5
Astro (1.5)	2.2
Six-exc Vans (.7)	1.0
Vans (1.5)	2.1
w/P.A.I.R. add	.6
V-6	
S-series-Astro (1.3)	1.8
All other models	
right side (1.3)	1.8
left side (.9)	1.4
w/A.C. add (.3)	.3
w/C.C.C. add (.3)	.3
V-8-454 eng (.8)	1.1
V-8-all other engs	
exc Vans (1.1)	1.5
Vans (.8)	1.1
each adtnl-all engs (.3)	.3
w/A.C. add (.2)	.2
w/A.I.R. add (.3)	.3

DIESEL ENGINE

Compression Test

(Factory Time)	Chilton Time
All models	1.3

Cylinder Head Gasket, Renew

Includes: R&R injector pump and lines. R&R intake manifold and disconnect exhaust manifolds. Clean gasket surfaces, bleed litters and adjust timing. Drain and refill cooling system.

(Factory Time)	Chilton Time
All models-5.7L eng	
right side (5.0)	6.1
left side (4.9)	6.0
both sides (7.2)	9.1
6.2L eng	
one side (5.8)	8.0
both sides (8.1)	11.2
2.2L eng (2.6)	3.8
w/A.C. add (.3)	.3
Vans-w/A.C. add (2.0)	2.0

Cylinder Head, Renew

Includes: R&R injector pump and lines. R&R intake manifold and disconnect exhaust manifolds. Clean gasket surfaces. Transfer parts, reface valves. Bleed lifters and adjust timing. Drain and refill cooling system.

(Factory Time)	Chilton Time
All models-5.7L eng	
right side (5.5)	6.9
left side (5.4)	6.8
both sides (8.1)	10.7
6.2L eng	
one side (6.8)	9.5
both sides (9.6)	13.3
2.2L eng (3.9)	5.7
w/A.C. add (.3)	.3
Vans-w/A.C. add (2.0)	2.0

Clean Carbon and Grind Valves

Includes: R&R injector pump and lines. R&R cylinder heads, clean carbon. Recondition valves and valve seats. Check and adjust valve stem length. Bleed lifters, drain and refill cooling system.

(Factory Time)	Chilton Time
All models-5.7L eng	
right side (5.4)	7.2
left side (5.3)	7.1
both sides (9.1)	12.6

LABOR 12 CYLINDER HEAD & VALVE SYSTEM 12 LABOR

(Factory Time)	Chilton Time
6.2L eng	
one side (7.1)	9.8
both sides (10.4)	14.4
2.2L eng (3.9)	5.7
w/A.C. add (.3)	.3
Vans-w/A.C. add (2.0)	2.0

Rocker Arm Cover or Gasket, Renew

Includes: R&R injector pump and lines.

(Factory Time)	Chilton Time
All models-5.7L eng	
one side (2.0)	2.6
both sides (2.2)	2.9
6.2L eng	
one side (2.6)	3.6
both sides (3.1)	4.3
2.2L eng (.4)	.6
Vans-w/A.C. add (2.0)	2.0

Valve Spring or Valve Stem Oil Seals, Renew (Head on Truck)

Includes: R&R injector pump and lines.

(Factory Time)	Chilton Time
All models-5.7L eng	
one (2.2)	3.1
one-each bank (2.6)	3.7
each adtnl(.3)	.3
6.2L eng	
one cyl (3.0)	4.2
one cyl-each side (3.9)	5.4
each adtnl cyl (.4)	.4
2.2L eng	
one cyl (.8)	1.2
all cyls (1.3)	2.0
Vans-w/A.C. add (2.0)	2.0

Rocker Arm and/or Push Rod, Renew

Includes: R&R injector pump and lines.

(Factory Time)	Chilton Time
All models-5.7L eng	
one cyl (2.1)	3.0
one cyl-each side (2.5)	3.5
each adtnl cyl (.1)	.1
6.2L eng	
one cyl (2.7)	3.7
one cyl-each side (3.3)	4.6
each adtnl cyl (.1)	.1
2.2L eng	
one or all (.7)	1.2
Vans-w/A.C. add (2.0)	2.0

Valve Lifters, Renew

Includes: R&R fuel injection pump and lines.

(Factory Time)	Chilton Time
All models-5.7L eng	
one cyl (3.2)	4.2
one cyl-each side (3.5)	4.5
each adtnl cyl (.1)	.2
6.2L eng-exc Vans	
one cyl (3.4)	4.7
one cyl-each side (4.6)	6.4
each adtnl cyl (.1)	.2
Vans	
one cyl (6.7)	9.3
one cyl-each side (8.8)	12.2
each adtnl cyl (.1)	.1
2.2L eng-all (6.9)	10.0
w/A.C. add (.8)	.8
w/P.S. add (.3)	.3
Vans-w/A.C. add (2.0)	2.0

Push Rod Side Cover Gasket, Renew

(Factory Time)	Chilton Time
All models	
2.2L eng (1.1)	1.5

Valve Clearance, Adjust

(Factory Time)	Chilton Time
All models	
2.2L eng (.6)	1.0

LABOR 13 ENGINE ASSEMBLY & MOUNTS 13 LABOR

GASOLINE ENGINES

Engine Assembly, R&R

Does not include transfer of any parts or equipment.

(Factory Time)	Chilton Time
Four	5.0
w/A.C. add	.9
w/P.S. add	.4
w/A.T. add	.3
w/Cruise control add	.2
w/Skid plate add	.3
Six-exc Vans	5.1
Vans	7.7
w/P.S. add	.5
w/A.C. add	1.3
w/A.I.R. add	.5
w/P.A.I.R. add	.6
V-6	
S-series	
4X2	5.5
4X4	*6.7
*w/M.T. add	2.0
Astro	6.9
exc Vans	4.9
Vans	5.9
w/P.S. add	.3
w/C.C.C. add	.6
w/A.T. add	.4
w/A.C. add	
Vans	1.1
Astro	.9
All other models	.4
V-8-454 eng	6.2
V-8-all other engs	
exc Vans	6.2
Vans	8.6
w/A.C. add	.4
w/P.S. add	.3
w/A.I.R. add	.4
w/M.T. add	.5
w/A.T. add	.3
Vans with A.C. add	1.7

Engine Assembly, Renew

Includes: R&R engine and transmission assy. Transfer all component parts not supplied with replacement engine. Minor tune up.

(Factory Time)	Chilton Time
Four	
eng code Y	
4X2 (5.4)	8.0
4X4 (8.4)	12.0
w/A.C. add	.4
w/P.S. add	.4
eng code E	
S-series	
4X2 (4.8)	7.0
4X4 (5.6)	8.1
Astro (6.6)	9.6
w/A.C. add	.9
w/P.S. add	.3
w/A.T. add	.3
w/Cruise control add	.2
w/Skid plate add	.3
Six-exc Vans (4.1)	8.2
Vans (5.5)	9.6
w/P.S. add (.4)	.5
w/A.C. add (1.3)	1.3
w/A.I.R. add (.4)	.5
w/P.A.I.R. add	.6
V-6	
S-series	
4X2 (6.2)	9.0
4X4 (7.1)	*10.2
*w/M.T. add	2.0
Astro (7.2)	10.4
exc Vans (5.8)	8.4
Vans (6.5)	9.4
w/P.S. add (.3)	.3
w/C.C.C. add (.6)	.6
w/A.T. add (.4)	.4
w/A.C. add	
Vans (1.1)	1.1
Astro (.9)	.9
All other models (.4)	.4
V-8-454 eng (6.9)	9.3
V-8-all other engs	
exc Vans (6.0)	8.2
Vans (7.8)	11.3
w/A.C. add (.4)	.4
w/P.S. add (.3)	.3
w/A.I.R. add (.4)	.4
w/M.T. add (.5)	.5
w/A.T. add (.3)	.3
Vans with A.C. add (1.7)	1.7

Cylinder Block, Renew (w/Internal Parts Less Head(s) and Oil Pan)

Includes: R&R engine and transmission assy. Transfer all components parts not supplied with replacement engine. Clean carbon, grind valves. Minor tune up.

(Factory Time)	Chilton Time
Four	
eng code A	
4X2 (8.0)	12.0
4X4 (8.9)	13.0
eng code Y	
4X2 (9.9)	14.5
4X4 (13.1)	19.0
w/A.C. add (.4)	.4
w/P.S. add (.4)	.4
eng code E	
S-series	
4X2 (9.0)	13.0
4X4 (9.9)	14.4
Astro (10.9)	15.8
w/A.C. add	.9
w/P.S. add	.3
w/A.T. add	.3
w/Cruise control add	.2
w/Skid plate add	.3
Six-exc Vans (9.1)	15.0
Vans (11.0)	17.3
w/P.S. add (.4)	.5
w/A.C. add (1.3)	1.3
w/A.I.R. add (.4)	.5
w/P.A.I.R. add	.6
V-6	
S-series	
4X2 (11.7)	16.9
4X4 (12.5)	*18.1
*w/M.T. add	2.0
Astro (13.1)	19.0
exc Vans (11.6)	16.8
Vans (12.4)	17.9
w/P.S. add (.3)	.3
w/C.C.C. add (.6)	.6
w/A.T. add (.4)	.4
w/A.C. add	
Vans (1.1)	1.1
Astro (.9)	.9
All other models (.4)	.4

LABOR 13 ENGINE ASSEMBLY & MOUNTS 13 LABOR

(Factory Time)	Chilton Time
V-8–454 eng (14.9)	20.1
V-8–all other engs	
exc Vans (14.2)	19.5
Vans (15.0)	21.7
w/A.C. add (.4)	.4
w/P.S. add (.3)	.3
w/A.I.R. add (.4)	.4
w/M.T. add (.5)	.5
w/A.T. add (.3)	.3
Vans with A.C. add (1.7)	1.7

Cylinder Block, Renew (w/Pistons, Rings and Bearings)

Includes: R&R engine and transmission assy. Transfer all component parts not supplied with replacement engine. Clean carbon, grind valves. Minor tune up.

(Factory Time)	Chilton Time
Four	
eng code E	
S-series	
4X2 (11.3)	16.4
4X4 (12.1)	17.5
Astro (13.1)	19.0
w/A.C. add	.9
w/P.S. add	.3
w/A.T. add	.3
w/Cruise control add	.2
w/Skid plate add	.3
Six–exc Vans (12.4)	17.0
Vans (13.3)	19.6
w/P.S. add (.4)	.5
w/A.C. add (1.3)	1.3
w/A.I.R. add (.4)	.5
w/P.A.I.R. add	.6
V-6	
S-series	
4X2 (14.1)	20.5
4X4 (14.9)	*21.6
*w/M.T. add	2.0
Astro (16.0)	23.2
exc Vans (14.5)	21.0
Vans (15.3)	22.2
w/P.S. add (.3)	.3
w/C.C.C. add (.6)	.6
w/A.T. add (.4)	.4
w/A.C. add	
Vans (1.1)	1.1
Astro (.9)	.9
All other models (.4)	.4
V-8–454 eng (17.7)	23.8
V-8–all other engs	
exc Vans (17.0)	23.4
Vans (17.8)	25.8
w/A.C. add (.4)	.4
w/P.S. add (.3)	.3
w/A.I.R. add (.4)	.4
w/M.T. add (.5)	.5
w/A.T. add (.3)	.3
Vans with A.C. add (1.7)	1.7

Engine Assy., R&R and Recondition

Includes: Rebore block, install new pistons, rings, rod and main bearings. Clean carbon, grind valves. Tune engine.

(Factory Time)	Chilton Time
Four	
eng code A	
4X2 (13.2)	19.7
4X4 (14.1)	21.0
eng code Y	
4X2 (16.0)	23.8
4X4 (18.6)	27.7
w/A.C. add (.4)	.4
w/P.S. add (.4)	.4
eng code E	
S-series	
4X2 (13.5)	19.5
4X4 (14.4)	20.8
Astro (15.4)	22.3
w/A.C. add	.9
w/P.S. add	.3
w/A.T. add	.3
w/Cruise control add	.2
w/Skid plate add	.3
Six–exc Vans (25.0)	32.0
Vans (27.6)	34.6
w/P.S. add (.4)	.5
w/A.C. add (1.3)	1.3
w/A.I.R. add (.4)	.5
w/P.A.I.R. add	.6
V-6	
S-series	
4X2 (20.7)	28.4
4X4 (22.2)	*29.5
*w/M.T. add	2.0
Astro (23.4)	31.5
exc Vans (20.9)	28.8
Vans (21.7)	29.2
w/P.S. add (.3)	.3
w/C.C.C. add (.6)	.6
w/A.T. add (.4)	.4
w/A.C. add	
Vans (1.1)	1.1
Astro (.9)	.9
All other models (.4)	.4
V-8–454 eng (32.5)	41.9
V-8–all other engs	
exc Vans (30.7)	43.5
Vans (32.2)	45.0
w/A.C. add (.4)	.4
w/P.S. add (.3)	.3
w/A.I.R. add (.4)	.4
w/M.T. add (.5)	.5
w/A.T. add (.3)	.3
Vans with A.C. add (1.7)	1.7

Engine Mounts, Renew

(Factory Time)	Chilton Time
Front	
Four–one (.5)	.7
both (.7)	1.0
Six–exc Vans–one (.5)	1.1
both (.8)	1.4
Vans–one (.9)	1.3
both (1.2)	1.6
V-6	
S-series	
one (1.0)	1.4
both (1.4)	1.9
All other models	
one (.8)	1.1
both (1.2)	1.7
V-8–all engines	
one (.8)	1.3
both (1.2)	1.9
Rear	
All models (.4)	.7

DIESEL ENGINE

Engine Assembly, Remove & Install

Does not include transfer of any parts or equipment.

(Factory Time)	Chilton Time
All models	5.0
w/A.C. add	1.2
w/A.T. add	.8

Engine Assembly, Renew (Universal)

Includes: R&R engine assembly. Transfer all component parts not supplied with replacement engine. Make all necessary adjustments.

(Factory Time)	Chilton Time
All models	
5.7L eng	20.0
6.2L eng	22.0
w/A.C. add	1.2
w/A.T. add	.8

Cylinder Block, Renew (Partial)

Includes: Transfer all component parts not supplied with replacement block. Clean carbon, grind valves. Make all necessary adjustments.

(Factory Time)	Chilton Time
All models	
2.2L eng (11.1)	18.0
5.7L eng	21.3
6.2L eng	
Vans (17.4)	29.5
All other models (15.5)	27.6
w/A.C. add	1.2
w/A.T. add	.8

Engine Assembly, R&R and Recondition

Includes: Rebore block, install new pistons, rings, rod and main bearings. Clean carbon, grind valves. Make all necessary adjustments.

(Factory Time)	Chilton Time
All models	
2.2L eng	27.3
5.7L eng	37.2
6.2L eng	40.0
w/A.C. add	1.2
w/A.T. add	.8

Engine Assembly, Recondition (In Truck)

Includes: Expand or renew pistons, install new rings, pins, rod and main bearings. Clean carbon, grind valves. Make all necessary adjustments.

(Factory Time)	Chilton Time
All models	
2.2L eng	20.1
5.7L eng	28.5
6.2L eng	32.9
w/A.C. add (.3)	.3

Engine Mounts, Renew

(Factory Time)	Chilton Time
Front	
All models–5.7L eng	
one (.5)	.8
both (.6)	1.0
6.2L eng	
one (.7)	1.0
both (1.1)	1.5
2.2L eng	
one (1.0)	1.4
both (1.8)	2.6
Rear	
All models (.4)	.6

LABOR 14 PISTONS, RINGS & BEARINGS 14 LABOR

GASOLINE ENGINES

Rings, Renew (See Engine Combinations)

Includes: Remove cylinder top ridge, deglaze cylinder walls, replace rod bearings, clean carbon from cylinder heads. Clean piston and ring grooves. Minor tune up.

(Factory Time)	Chilton Time
Four	
eng code A	
one cyl (5.9)	8.5
each adtnl cyl	.7
4X4 add (.9)	.9
eng code Y	
one cyl (6.9)	10.0
each adtnl cyl	.7
4X4 add (.4)	.4
w/A.C. add (.4)	.4
w/P.S. add (.4)	.4
eng code E	
S-series	
4X2–one cyl (7.3)	10.5

(Factory Time)	Chilton Time
4X4-one cyl (9.0)	13.0
Astro-one cyl (6.9)	10.0
each adtnl cyl	.7
w/A.C. add	.6
w/P.S. add	.1
w/Cruise control add	.2
w/A.T. add	.2
w/Skid plate add	.3
Six–exc Vans-one (4.7)	6.9
all (6.7)	10.3
Vans-one (6.6)	9.5
all (8.4)	12.1
w/P.S. add (.4)	.5
w/A.C. add (.5)	.5
w/A.I.R. add (.6)	.6
w/P.A.I.R. add	.6
V-6	
S-series-Astro	
one cyl (8.4)	12.2
one cyl-each side (10.2)	14.8
all cyls-both sides (12.1)	17.5
All other models	
one cyl (6.6)	9.5
one cyl-each side (8.8)	12.8
all cyls-both sides (10.7)	15.5
w/A.C. add (.5)	.5
w/P.S. add (.5)	.5
w/C.C.C. add (.3)	.3
V-8–454 eng-one (6.6)	9.1
all (10.9)	14.8
V-8–all other engs	
exc Vans-one (6.1)	8.4
all (10.8)	14.9
Vans-one cyl (7.7)	11.1
all cyls (12.7)	18.4
w/A.C. add (.7)	.7
w/P.S. add (.2)	.2
w/A.I.R. add (.2)	.2

Piston or Connecting Rod, Renew

Includes: Remove cylinder top ridge, deglaze cylinder walls, replace rod bearings, clean carbon from cylinder heads. Minor tune up.

(Factory Time)	Chilton Time
Four	
eng code A	
one cyl (6.3)	9.1
each adtnl cyl	.7
4X4 add (.9)	.9
eng code Y	
one cyl (7.3)	10.5
each adtnl cyl	.7
4X4 add (.4)	.4
w/A.C. add (.4)	.4
w/P.S. add (.4)	.4
eng code E	
S-series	
4X2-one cyl (7.5)	10.8
4X4-one cyl (9.2)	13.3
Astro-one cyl (7.1)	10.3
each adtnl cyl	.7
w/A.C. add	.6
w/P.S. add	.1
w/Cruise control add	.2
w/A.T. add	.2
w/Skid plate add	.3
Six–exc Vans-one (4.7)	7.2
all (6.7)	11.8
Vans-one (6.8)	9.8
all (9.4)	13.9
w/P.S. add (.4)	.5
w/A.C. add (.5)	.5
w/A.I.R. add (.6)	.6
w/P.A.I.R. add	.6
V-6	
S-series-Astro	
one cyl (8.4)	12.5
one cyl-each side (10.2)	15.4
all cyls-both sides (12.8)	19.3
All other models	
one cyl (6.6)	9.8

COMBINATIONS

Add to Engine Work
See Machine Shop Operations

GASOLINE ENGINES

(Factory Time)	Chilton Time
DRAIN, EVACUATE AND RECHARGE AIR CONDITIONING SYSTEM	
All models (.5)	1.0
ROCKER ARM STUD, RENEW	
Each (.3)	.3
HYDRAULIC VALVE LIFTERS, DISASSEMBLE AND CLEAN	
Each	.2
DISTRIBUTOR, RECONDITION	
All models (.5)	.9
CARBURETOR, RECONDITION	
1 BBL (1.0)	1.0
2 BBL (1.0)	1.2
4 BBL (.8)	1.5
VALVE GUIDES, REAM OVERSIZE	
Each (.1)	.1
DEGLAZE CYLINDER WALLS	
Each (.1)	.1
REMOVE CYLINDER TOP RIDGE	
Each (.1)	.1
VALVES, RECONDITION	
Four (1.8)	2.5
Six (2.1)	3.0
V-6 (2.0)	3.0
V-8 (2.7)	3.5
PLASTIGAUGE BEARINGS	
Each (.1)	.1
OIL PUMP, RECONDITION	
All models	.6
w/P.S. add (.2)	.2
w/C.C.C. add (.2)	.2
OIL FILTER, RENEW	
Four (.3)	.4
Six (.2)	.3
V-6 (.3)	.4
V-8 (.3)	.4

(Factory Time)	Chilton Time
one cyl-each side (8.8)	13.4
all cyls-both sides (13.3)	17.3
w/A.C. add (.5)	.5
w/P.S. add (.5)	.5
w/C.C.C. add (.3)	.3
V-8–454 eng-one (6.6)	9.4
all (10.9)	17.2
V-8–all other engs	
exc Vans-one (6.1)	8.7
all (10.8)	17.3
Vans-one cyl (7.9)	11.4
all cyls (13.8)	20.8
w/A.C. add (.7)	.7
w/P.S. add (.2)	.2
w/A.I.R. add (.2)	.2

Connecting Rod Bearings, Renew

(Factory Time)	Chilton Time
Four	
eng code A (4.8)	6.7
eng code Y	
4X2 (5.7)	8.0
4X4 (4.7)	6.5
w/A.C. add (.4)	.4
w/P.S. add (.4)	.4
eng code E	
S-series	
4X2 (3.8)	5.5
4X4 (5.4)	7.8
Astro (2.9)	4.2
w/P.S. add	.1
w/A.T. add	.2
w/Skid plate add	.2
Six–one (2.2)	2.8
all (3.1)	4.9
w/A.C. add (.7)	.7
V-6	
S-series	
4X2 (6.4)	9.4
4X4 (4.9)	7.3
All other models (3.4)	4.9
w/A.C. add (.2)	.2
w/P.S. add (.2)	.2
w/C.C.C. add (.2)	.2
w/A.T. add (.3)	.3
V-8–454 eng-one (1.8)	2.8
all (3.9)	5.4
V-8–all other engs	
All models-one (1.4)	2.0
all (3.4)	4.9
w/M.T. add (.2)	.2

DIESEL ENGINE

Rings, Renew (See Engine Combinations)

Includes: Remove cylinder to ridge, deglaze cylinder walls. Clean piston and ring grooves. Make all necessary adjustments.

(Factory Time)	Chilton Time
All models	
2.2L eng (10.0)	14.5
w/A.C. add (.8)	.8
w/P.S. add (.3)	.3
5.7L eng (10.6)	14.0
6.2L eng (15.4)	21.5
w/A.C. add (.3)	.3

Piston or Connecting Rod, Renew

Includes: Remove cylinder top ridge, deglaze cylinder walls. Make all necessary adjustments.

(Factory Time)	Chilton Time
All models	
2.2L eng (10.0)	16.3
w/A.C. add (.8)	.8
w/P.S. add (.3)	.3
5.7L eng (10.7)	16.8
6.2L eng (16.5)	23.9
w/A.C. add (.3)	.3

Connecting Rod Bearings, Renew

Includes: Raise engine and clean oil pump screen.

(Factory Time)	Chilton Time
All models	
2.2L eng (7.5)	10.8
w/A.C. add (.8)	.8
w/P.S. add (.3)	.3
5.7L eng (4.0)	5.6
6.2L eng	
Vans (5.6)	7.8
All other models (4.0)	5.8

GASOLINE ENGINES

Crankshaft and Main Bearings, Renew

Includes: R&R engine, plastigauge bearings.

(Factory Time)	Chilton Time
Four	
eng code A	
4X2 (7.8)	11.3
4X4 (8.9)	12.9
eng code Y	
4X2 (7.8)	11.5
4X4 (10.4)	15.0
w/A.C. add (.4)	.4
w/P.S. add (.4)	.4
eng code E	
S-series	
4X2 (6.4)	9.3
4X4 (7.3)	10.6
Astro (8.3)	12.0
w/A.C. add	.9
w/P.S. add	.3
w/A.T. add	.3
w/Cruise control add	.2
w/Skid plate add	.3
Six–exc Vans (6.5)	8.4
Vans (9.3)	13.4
w/P.S. add (.4)	.5
w/A.C. add (1.2)	1.2
w/A.I.R. add (.3)	.5
w/P.A.I.R. add	.6
V-6	
S-series	
4X2 (8.5)	12.3
4X4 (9.0)	*13.0
*w/M.T. add	2.0
Astro (10.2)	14.8
exc Vans (9.1)	13.2
Vans (9.7)	14.0
w/P.S. add (.3)	.3
w/C.C.C. add (.6)	.6
w/A.T. add (.4)	.4
w/A.C. add	
Vans (1.1)	1.1
Astro (.9)	.9
All other models (.4)	.4
V-8–454 eng (9.2)	12.4
V-8–all other engs	
exc Vans (8.8)	12.3
Vans (10.3)	14.8
w/A.C. add (.4)	.4
w/P.S. add (.3)	.3
w/A.I.R. add (.4)	.4
w/M.T. add (.5)	.5
w/A.T. add (.3)	.3
Vans with A.C. add (1.7)	1.7

Main Bearings, Renew

Includes: Plastigauge bearings.

(Factory Time)	Chilton Time
Four	
eng code A (5.2)	7.5
eng code Y	
4X2 (5.8)	8.4
4X4 (4.7)	6.8
w/A.C. add (.4)	.4
w/P.S. add (.4)	.4
eng code E	
S-series	
4X2 (4.0)	5.8
4X4 (5.6)	8.1
Astro (3.1)	4.5
w/P.S. add	.1
w/A.T. add	.2
w/Skid plate	.2
Six–exc Vans (3.3)	4.9
Vans (4.3)	6.2
V-6	
S-series	
4X2 (6.1)	9.5
4X4 (4.9)	7.8
All other models (3.1)	4.5
w/A.C. add (.2)	.2
w/P.S. add (.2)	.2
w/C.C.C. add (.2)	.2
w/A.T. add (.3)	.3
V-8–454 eng (3.2)	5.0
V-8–all other engs	
All models (3.9)	5.6
w/M.T. add (.2)	.2

Rear Main Bearing Oil Seal, Renew

(Factory Time)	Chilton Time
Four	
eng code A (4.1)	*6.3
eng code Y	
4X2 (6.7)	*9.7
4X4 (9.2)	*13.3
w/A.C. add (.4)	.4
w/P.S. add (.4)	.4
eng code E	
S-series	
4X2 (2.4)	3.5
4X4 (3.4)	5.0
Astro (2.1)	3.2
w/Skid plate add	.3
w/A.T. add (.3)	.3
w/M.T. add (.4)	.4
Six–exc Vans (1.6)	2.7
Vans (2.2)	3.2
w/A.C. add (.7)	.7
V-6	
S-series	
Full Circle Type	
4X2 (7.3)	10.5
4X4 (7.8)	*11.3
w/A.C. add (.2)	.2
w/P.S. add (.2)	.2
w/C.C.C. add (.6)	.6
*w/M.T. add	2.0
Split Lip Type	
4X2 (3.0)	4.5
4X4 (3.6)	5.5
w/A.T. add (.4)	.4
Vans-Astro	
w/M.T. (2.2)	3.2
w/A.T. (2.9)	4.2
All other models	
4X2	
w/M.T. (2.5)	3.6
w/A.T. (2.3)	3.3
4X4	
w/M.T. (3.1)	4.5
w/A.T. (2.7)	3.9
V-8–454 eng (2.0)	3.3
V-8–all other engs	
4X2	
w/M.T. (2.1)	3.0
w/A.T. (2.2)	3.1
4X4	
w/M.T. (2.9)	4.2
w/A.T. (2.6)	3.7

*Includes R&R engine.

Harmonic Balancer (Vibration Damper), Renew

Includes: Renew timing cover oil seal.

(Factory Time)	Chilton Time
Four	
eng code A (.9)	1.5
eng code Y (.7)	1.4
eng code E (.5)	1.1
w/A.C. add (.2)	.2
w/P.S. add (.2)	.2
Six–exc Vans (.8)	1.2
Vans (1.1)	1.5
w/P.S. add (.2)	.2
w/A.C. add (.2)	.2
w/A.I.R. add (.2)	.2
V-6	
All models (.8)	1.3
w/A.C. add (.2)	.2
w/P.S. add (.2)	.2
V-8–454 eng (1.2)	1.6
V-8–all other engs	
All models (1.0)	1.5
w/A.C. add (.2)	.2
w/P.S. add (.2)	.2
w/A.I.R. add (.2)	.2

DIESEL ENGINE

Crankshaft and Main Bearings, Renew

Includes: R&R engine, plastigauge bearings.

(Factory Time)	Chilton Time
All models	
2.2L eng (8.9)	13.0
w/A.C. add (.8)	.8
w/P.S. add (.3)	.3
5.7L eng (7.5)	10.9
6.2L eng	
Vans (13.4)	19.5
All other models (8.5)	12.3
w/A.C. add (.3)	.3
w/A.T. add	.8

Main Bearings, Renew

Includes: Plastigauge bearings.

(Factory Time)	Chilton Time
All models	
2.2L eng (7.9)	11.4
w/A.C. add (.8)	.8
w/P.S. add (.3)	.3
5.7L eng (3.5)	5.4
6.2L eng	
Vans (4.9)	7.0
All other models (3.5)	5.0

Main and Rod Bearings, Renew

Includes: Check all bearing clearance.

(Factory Time)	Chilton Time
All models	
2.2L eng (9.1)	12.6
w/A.C. add (.8)	.8
w/P.S. add (.3)	.3
5.7L eng (5.1)	7.8
6.2L eng	
Vans (7.3)	9.4
All other models (5.3)	7.4

Rear Main Bearing Oil Seals, Renew or Repack (Upper and Lower)

Includes: R&R oil pan and rear main bearing cap.

(Factory Time)	Chilton Time
All models	
2.2L eng (1.9)	2.8
5.7L eng (2.8)	4.0
6.2L eng	
Vans (3.7)	5.4
All other models (2.5)	3.6

Harmonic Balancer (Vibration Damper), Renew

(Factory Time)	Chilton Time
All models	
5.7L eng (.9)	1.3
6.2L eng	
Vans (1.2)	1.6
All other models (.8)	1.2
w/A.C. add (.4)	.4

Crankshaft Front Oil Seal, Renew

(Factory Time)	Chilton Time
All models	
5.7L eng (1.0)	1.5
6.2L eng	
Vans (1.2)	1.8
All other models (.8)	1.4
w/A.C. add (.4)	.4

GASOLINE ENGINES

Timing Cover Oil Seal, Renew

(Factory Time)	Chilton Time
Four	
eng code A (.9)	1.7
eng code Y (.7)	1.6
eng code E (.5)	1.2
w/A.C. add (.2)	.2
w/P.S. add (.2)	.2
Six–exc Vans (.8)	1.4
Vans (1.1)	1.6
w/P.S. add (.2)	.2
w/A.C. add (.2)	.2
w/A.I.R. add (.2)	.2
V-6	
All models (.8)	1.4
w/A.C. add (.2)	.2
w/P.S. add (.2)	.2
V-8–454 eng (1.2)	1.6
V-8–all other engs	
All models (1.0)	1.6
w/A.C. add (.2)	.2
w/P.S. add (.2)	.2
w/A.I.R. add (.2)	.2

Timing Cover Gasket, Renew

Includes: Renew oil seal.

(Factory Time)	Chilton Time
Four	
eng code A (5.6)	8.0
eng code Y (1.7)	2.5
eng code E (1.3)	2.0
w/A.C. add (.4)	.4
w/P.S. add (.4)	.4
Six–all models (1.5)	2.1
w/P.S. add (.2)	.2
w/A.C. add (.2)	.2
w/A.I.R. add (.2)	.2
V-6	
S-series (2.0)	3.0
Astro (2.9)	4.2
exc Vans (2.4)	3.4
Vans (3.4)	4.9
w/A.C. add (.2)	.2
w/P.S. add (.3)	.3
V-8–454 eng (2.2)	2.8
V-8–all other engs	
exc Vans (2.0)	3.0
Vans (2.7)	3.9
w/A.C. add (.5)	.5
w/P.S. add (.2)	.2
w/A.I.R. add (.3)	.3
Vans w/A.C. add (1.2)	1.2

Timing Chain, Renew

Includes: R&R engine front cover.

(Factory Time)	Chilton Time
Four	
eng code A (5.7)	8.5
eng code Y (2.0)	3.0
w/A.C. add (.4)	.4
w/P.S. add (.4)	.4
V-6	
S-series (2.3)	3.5
Astro (3.0)	4.7
exc Vans (2.5)	3.9
Vans (3.5)	5.4
w/A.C. add (.2)	.2
w/P.S. add (.3)	.3
V-8–454 eng (2.6)	3.3
V-8–all other engs	
exc Vans (2.2)	3.5
Vans (3.0)	4.4
w/A.C. add (.5)	.5
w/P.S. add (.2)	.2
w/A.I.R. add (.3)	.3
Vans w/A.C. add (1.2)	1.2

Camshaft, Renew

Includes: R&R engine and front cover, where required.

(Factory Time)	Chilton Time
Four	
eng code A (1.0)	1.5
eng code Y (4.0)	6.0
eng code E	
S-series (4.7)	6.8
Astro (6.0)	8.7
w/A.C. add	.5
w/P.S. add	.3
w/A.T. add	.1
Six–exc Vans (3.9)	6.0
Vans (4.7)	7.0
w/P.S. add (.4)	.5
w/A.C. add (1.0)	1.0
w/A.I.R. add (.4)	.5
w/P.A.I.R. add	.6
V-6	
S-series (5.1)	8.5
Astro (5.7)	8.8
exc Vans (5.0)	7.2
Vans (7.5)	10.8
w/C.C.C. add (.3)	.3
w/A.C. add (.3)	.3
w/P.S. add (.3)	.3
V-8–454 eng (6.2)	9.3
V-8–all other engs	
exc Vans (4.9)	8.0
Vans (6.7)	9.5
w/A.C. add (.6)	.6
w/P.S. add (.4)	.4
w/A.I.R. add (.4)	.4

Camshaft Timing Gear, Renew

(Factory Time)	Chilton Time
Four	
eng code A (.5)	.9
eng code Y (2.0)	3.0
eng code E	
S-series (4.7)	6.8
Astro (6.0)	8.7
w/A.C. add	.5
w/P.S. add	.3
w/A.T. add	.1
Renew crank gear add	.2
V-6	
S-series (2.3)	3.5
Astro (3.0)	4.7
exc Vans (2.5)	3.9
Vans (3.5)	5.4
w/A.C. add (.2)	.2
w/P.S. add (.3)	.3

DIESEL ENGINE

Timing Cover or Gasket, Renew

Includes: R&R fan blade, crankshaft pulley and balancer. Drain and refill oil and coolant.

(Factory Time)	Chilton Time
All models	
2.2L eng (2.5)	3.6
5.7L eng (2.3)	3.3
6.2L eng (4.3)	6.2
w/A.C. add (.4)	.4

Timing Cover Oil Seal, Renew

Includes: R&R fan blade, crankshaft pulley and balancer. Drain and refill oil and coolant.

(Factory Time)	Chilton Time
All models	
2.2L eng (1.1)	2.0
5.7L eng (1.0)	1.6
6.2L eng	
Vans (1.2)	2.0
All other models (.8)	1.5
w/A.C. add (.4)	.4

Camshaft Gear and/or Timing Chain, Renew

Includes: R&R fan blades, crankshaft pulley and balancer. Drain and refill oil and coolant.

(Factory Time)	Chilton Time
All models	
5.7L eng (3.6)	4.8
6.2L eng (4.5)	6.7
w/A.C. add (.4)	.4

Injector Pump Drive Gear, Renew

Includes: R&R timing gear and chain. R&R intake manifold and lifters. Drain and refill oil and coolant, where required.

(Factory Time)	Chilton Time
All models	
2.2L eng (.9)	1.5
5.7L eng (5.2)	7.2
6.2L eng (4.4)	6.6
w/A.C. add (.4)	.4

Camshaft, Renew

Includes: R&R radiator, front cover, fuel pump, timing gear and chain. R&R injector pump, intake manifold and lifters. Disconnect exhaust system. Drain and refill oil and coolant. Make all necessary adjustments.

(Factory Time)	Chilton Time
All models	
2.2L eng (6.9)	10.0
w/A.C. add (.6)	.6
w/P.S. add (.3)	.3
5.7L eng (6.5)	10.8
6.2L eng (12.0)	17.4
w/A.C. add (2.0)	2.0
w/A.T. add (.3)	.3

Camshaft Bearings, Renew

Includes: R&R radiator, front cover, fuel pump, timing gear and chain. R&R injector pump, intake manifold and lifters. Disconnect exhaust system. Drain and refill oil and coolant. Make all necessary adjustments.

(Factory Time)	Chilton Time
All models	
5.7L eng (9.5)	14.6
w/A.C. add (.2)	.2

Camshaft Rear Bearing Plug, Renew

Note: Use appropriate labor operation for removal of necessary components to gain access to plug.

(Factory Time)	Chilton Time
All models (.3)	.6

Camshaft Timing Gear, Renew

(Factory Time)	Chilton Time
All models	
2.2L eng (.9)	1.6
w/A.C. add (.1)	.1

Crankshaft Timing Gear, Renew

(Factory Time)	Chilton Time
All models	
2.2L eng (.9)	1.6
w/A.C. add (.1)	.1

Camshaft Idler Pulley, Renew

(Factory Time)	Chilton Time
All models	
2.2L eng (.4)	.6
w/A.C. add (.1)	.1

Camshaft Drive Belt, Renew

(Factory Time)	Chilton Time
All models	
2.2L eng (.8)	1.5
w/A.C. add (.1)	.1

Camshaft Drive Belt Covers and/or Gaskets, Renew

(Factory Time)	Chilton Time
All models	
2.2L eng	
upper (.3)	.5
lower or both (.6)	1.0
w/A.C. add (.1)	.1

LABOR 17 ENGINE OILING SYSTEM 17 LABOR

GASOLINE ENGINE

Oil Pan and/or Gasket, Renew

(Factory Time)	Chilton Time
Four	
eng code A (3.7)	5.5
eng code Y	
4X2 (4.3)	6.2
4X4 (3.2)	4.6
w/A.C. add (.4)	.4
w/P.S. add (.4)	.4
eng code E	
S-series	
4X2 (2.5)	3.6
4X4 (4.1)	6.0
Astro (1.6)	2.3
w/A.T. add	.2
w/Skid plate add	.3
Six–exc Vans (1.4)	2.4
Vans (1.8)	2.6
w/A.C. add (.7)	.7
V-6	
S-series	
4X2 (4.9)	7.3
4X4 (3.4)	5.1
All other models (1.7)	2.5
w/A.C. add (.2)	.2
w/P.S. add (.2)	.2
w/C.C.C. add (.2)	.2
w/A.T. add (.3)	.3
V-8–454 eng (1.4)	2.5
V-8–all other engs (1.1)	1.6
w/M.T. add (.2)	.2

Pressure Test Engine Bearings (Pan Off)

(Factory Time)	Chilton Time
All models	1.0

Oil Pump, Renew

(Factory Time)	Chilton Time
Four	
eng code A (3.8)	5.7
eng code Y	
4X2 (4.4)	6.4
4X4 (3.4)	4.8
w/A.C. add (.4)	.4
w/P.S. add (.4)	.4
eng code E	
S-series	
4X2 (2.7)	3.9
4X4 (4.2)	6.2
Astro (1.7)	2.5
w/A.T. add	.2
w/Skid plate add	.3
Six–exc Vans (1.5)	2.6
Vans (1.9)	2.8
w/A.C. add (.7)	.7
V-6	
S-series	
4X2 (4.9)	7.5
4X4 (3.4)	5.3
All other models (1.8)	2.7
w/A.C. add (.2)	.2
w/P.S. add (.2)	.2
w/C.C.C. add (.2)	.2
w/A.T. add (.3)	.3
V-8–454 eng (1.5)	2.7
V-8–all other engs (1.2)	1.8
w/M.T. add (.2)	.2

Oil Pressure Gauge (Dash), Renew

(Factory Time)	Chilton Time
1984-86	
S-series (.3)	.5
Astro (.9)	1.4
All other models (.6)	1.0
1987-88	
S-series (.9)	1.4
Astro (.9)	1.4
All other models (.7)	1.2

Oil Pressure Gauge (Engine Unit), Renew

(Factory Time)	Chilton Time
All models (.2)	.5
w/A.C. add (.2)	.2
w/Cruise control add (.4)	.4

Oil Filter By-Pass Valve, Renew

(Factory Time)	Chilton Time
Four–eng code Y (.3)	.4
Six (.2)	.3
V-6 (.3)	.4
V-8 (.3)	.4

Oil Filter Element, Renew

(Factory Time)	Chilton Time
Four (.3)	.4
Six (.2)	.3
V-6 (.3)	.4
V-8 (.3)	.4

DIESEL ENGINE

Oil Pan and/or Gasket, Renew

Includes: Raise engine, R&R and clean oil pump screen.

(Factory Time)	Chilton Time
All models	
2.2L eng (.7)	1.2
5.7L eng (2.1)	3.0
6.2L eng	
Vans (3.2)	4.6
All other models (2.0)	2.9
w/M.T. add (.3)	.3

Pressure Test Engine Bearings (Pan Off)

(Factory Time)	Chilton Time
All models	1.0

Oil Pump, Renew

Includes: Raise engine, R&R and clean oil pump screen.

(Factory Time)	Chilton Time
All models	
2.2L eng (5.9)	8.5
w/A.C. add (.6)	.6
w/P.S. add (.3)	.3
5.7L eng (2.2)	3.2
6.2L eng	
Vans (3.2)	4.8
All other models (2.1)	3.1
w/M.T. add (.3)	.3

Oil Pump, R&R and Recondition

Includes: Raise engine, R&R and clean oil pump screen.

(Factory Time)	Chilton Time
All models	
5.7L eng (2.4)	3.4

Oil Pressure Sending Unit, Renew

(Factory Time)	Chilton Time
All models	
5.7L eng (.3)	.5
6.2L eng (1.4)	1.8

Oil Filter Element, Renew

(Factory Time)	Chilton Time
All models (.3)	.4

Crankcase and/or Gasket, Renew

(Factory Time)	Chilton Time
All models	
2.2L eng (5.8)	8.4
w/A.C. add (.6)	.6
w/P.S. add (.3)	.3

LABOR 18 CLUTCH & FLYWHEEL 18 LABOR

Clutch Pedal Free Play, Adjust

(Factory Time)	Chilton Time
All models (.3)	.4

Bleed Clutch Hydraulic System

(Factory Time)	Chilton Time
All models (.5)	.6

Clutch Master Cylinder, Renew

Includes: Bleed system.

(Factory Time)	Chilton Time
10-30 Series (.5)	.8
All other models (.8)	1.2
Recond cyl add (.2)	.4

Clutch Slave (Actuator) Cylinder, Renew

Includes: Bleed system.

(Factory Time)	Chilton Time
All models (.6)	1.0
Recond cyl add (.2)	.4

Clutch Assembly, Renew

Includes: R&R trans and adjust clutch free play.

(Factory Time)	Chilton Time
10-30 Series	
2 WD (2.5)	3.5
4 WD (3.0)	4.2
Vans-Astro	
All models (2.0)	2.8
S-series	
Four (2.7)	3.7
V-6	
2 WD (2.2)	3.0
4 WD (3.5)	4.9
w/Skid plate add (.3)	.3
w/Catalytic converter add (.4)	.4
w/Power take off add (.3)	.3
Renew pilot brg add (.2)	.2

Clutch Release Bearing, Fork and/or Ball Stud, Renew

Includes: R&R trans, and adjust clutch free play.

(Factory Time)	Chilton Time
10-30 Series	
2 WD (2.0)	2.8
4 WD (2.5)	3.5
Vans-Astro	
All models (1.5)	2.1
S-series	
Four (2.3)	3.2
V-6	
2 WD (1.9)	2.6
4 WD (2.8)	3.9
Renew fork assy add (.3)	.3
w/Skid plate add (.3)	.3
w/Catalytic converter add (.4)	.4
w/Power take off add (.3)	.3

Clutch Cross Shaft Assy., Renew

Includes: Raise vehicle and adjust linkage.

(Factory Time)	Chilton Time
All models (.4)	.9

Flywheel, Renew

Includes: R&R transmission.

(Factory Time)	Chilton Time
10-30 Series	
2 WD (2.7)	3.7
4 WD (3.2)	4.4
Vans-Astro	
All models (2.2)	3.0
S-series	
Four (2.9)	4.0
V-6	
2 WD (2.3)	3.2
4 WD (3.7)	5.1
Renew pilot brg add (.2)	.2
w/Skid plate add (.3)	.3
w/Catalytic converter add (.3)	.4
w/Power take off add (.3)	.3
Renew ring gear add	.5

LABOR 19 STANDARD TRANSMISSION 19 LABOR

(Factory Time) Chilton Time

Transmission Assy., R&R or Renew

Includes: Raise vehicle and perform necessary adjustments. Transfer all attaching parts.

3 Speed

2 WD (1.6) 2.2
4 WD (1.4) 1.9

4 Speed

10-30 Series
Muncie
2 WD (2.1) 2.9
4 WD (2.5) 3.5
Muncie Getrag
2 WD (2.3) 3.2
4 WD (2.5) 3.5
Vans
Muncie-Warner (1.7) 2.3
Astro
Muncie (1.5) 2.0

S-series
Isuzu
Four (2.3) 3.2
V-6
2 WD (1.9) 2.6
4 WD (2.9) 4.0
New Process-Warner
2 WD (1.4) 1.9
4 WD (2.9) 4.0

5 Speed

10-30 Series
2 WD (2.3) 3.2
4 WD (2.5) 3.5
Astro
All models (1.3) 1.8
S-series
Four
2 WD (1.4) 1.9
4 WD (2.3) 3.2
V-6
2 WD (1.4) 1.9
4 WD (2.8) 3.9
w/Skid plate add (.3) 3
w/Catalytic converter add (.4) 4
w/Power take off add (.3) 3

Transmission Assy., R&R and Recondition

Includes: Raise vehicle and perform all necessary adjustments.

3 Speed

2 WD (3.6) 5.0
4 WD (3.4) 4.7

4 Speed

10-30 Series
Muncie
2 WD (4.7) 6.5
4 WD (5.2) 7.2
Muncie Getrag
2 WD (5.0) 7.0
4 WD (5.2) 7.2

Vans
Muncie-Warner (3.6) 5.0
Astro
Muncie (3.3) 4.6
S-series
Isuzu
Four (4.2) 6.7
V-6
2 WD (3.8) 5.3
4 WD (4.6) 6.4
New Process-Warner
2 WD (3.2) 4.4
4 WD (4.6) 6.4

Astro
All models (3.3) 4.6
S-series
2 WD (3.4) 4.7
4 WD (4.8) 6.7
w/Skid plate add (.3) 3
w/Catalytic converter add (.4) 4
w/Power take off add (.3) 3

Transmission Shift Cover, Renew or Recondition

Includes: Raise vehicle and adjust linkage.

3 Speed

exc Vans (.7) 1.3
Vans (.6) 1.0
Recond cover add (.3) 5

4 Speed

Saginaw (1.9) 2.6
New Process (.6) 1.0
Isuzu (.5) 9
Warner (.8) *1.4
Muncie
10-30 Series (1.4) 2.0
Astro (.6) 8
*Recond add (.6) 8

5 Speed

S-series (.8) *1.4
Astro (1.8) 2.5
*Recond add (.6) 8

Transmission Rear Oil Seal, Renew

Includes: Raise vehicle, R&R drive shaft.
All models (.5) 9
Renew bush add (.1) 1

Speedometer Driven Gear, Renew

All models (.3) 6

Speedometer Drive Gear, Renew

4 Speed

All models (.9) 1.4

5 Speed

Astro (1.8) 2.5

LABOR 20 TRANSFER CASE 20 LABOR

(Factory Time) Chilton Time

Transfer Case Assy., R&R or Renew

Dana (3.1) 4.5
New Process Model 241 (1.3) 2.0
New Process Model 208 (1.3) 2.0
New Process Model 207 (1.4) 2.1
New Process Model 205 (1.4) 2.1
New Process Model 203 (2.5) 3.8
w/Power take off add (.3) 3
w/Skid plate add (.3) 3

Transfer Case Assy., R&R and Recondition

Dana (5.2) 7.1
New Process Model 241 (3.5) 5.6
New Process Model 208 (3.5) 5.6
New Process Model 207 (3.4) 5.5
New Process Model 205 (3.9) 6.0
New Process Model 203 (6.8) 8.7
w/Power take off add (.3) 3
w/Skid plate add (.3) 3

New Process Model 241

front (.5) 9
rear (.3) 6

New Process Model 208

front (.5) 9
rear (.3) 6

New Process Model 207

front (.5) 9
rear (.4) 7

New Process Model 205

front (1.1) 1.7
rear (.6) 1.0

New Process Model 203

front (.8) 1.4
rear (.7) 1.3

Transfer Case Oil Seals, Renew

Dana

front (1.1) 1.7
rear (.6) 1.0

Transfer Case Power Take Off Cover Gasket, Renew

All models (.4) 7

Transfer Case Rear Output Shaft Housing Gasket, Renew

All models-New Process
Model 241 (.5) 8
Model 208 (.5) 8
Model 207 (.6) 1.0
Model 205 (.8) 1.2

Transfer Case Speedometer Drive Gear, Renew

New Process Model 241 (.5) 7
New Process Model 208 (.5) 7
New Process Model 207 (.6) 1.0
New Process Model 205 (.8) 1.1
New Process Model 203 (.9) 1.2

Rear Output Shaft Housing, Renew

All models-New Process
Model 241 (.5) 9
Model 208 (.5) 9
Model 207 (.6) 1.0
Model 205 (.8) 1.4

LABOR 21 SHIFT LINKAGE 21 LABOR

(Factory Time) Chilton Time

STANDARD

Shift Linkage, Adjust
All models (.3) 4

Gearshift Control Lever, Renew
All models-column mount (.2) 4
floor mount (.3) 6

Transfer Case Gearshift Lever, Renew
New Process Model 205 (.4) 6
New Process Model 203 (.3) 5

Transfer Case Shifter Assy., Renew
New Process Model 203 (1.4) 2.1

Gearshift Control Rods, Renew
All models-one (.4) 6
two (.5) 9

Gear Shift Tube and/or Levers, Renew
exc Vans (1.7) 2.5
Vans (1.4) 2.2

AUTOMATIC

Linkage, Adjust
All models
Neutral Safety Switch (.2) 3
Shift Indicator Needle (.2) 3
Shift Linkage (.3) 4
T.V. Cable (.4) 5

Shift Linkage, Adjust (w/Diesel Eng)
All models
Fast idle speed (.2) 3
Throttle rod/T.V. cable (.5) 6

Trans vacuum valve (.5) 6
Complete (.6) 1.0

Note: Does not apply to Vans with THM 400 trans.

Column Shift Selector Lever, Renew
All models (.2) 3

Shift Control Rods, Renew
Includes: Necessary adjustments.
All models-one (.4) 5

Cross Shaft Assembly, Renew
Includes: Necessary adjustments.
All models (.3) 6

Shift Indicator Needle, Renew
All models (.6) 1.0

LABOR 23 AUTOMATIC TRANSMISSION 23 LABOR

(Factory Time) Chilton Time

TURBO HYDRA-MATIC - 180

ON CAR SERVICES

Drain & Refill Unit
All models 1.0

Oil Pressure Check
All models 5

Check Unit for Oil Leaks
Includes: Clean and dry outside of case and run unit to determine point of leak.
All models 9

Neutral Safety Switch, Renew
All models (.3) 5

Shift Linkage, Adjust
All models
Neutral Safety Switch (.2) 3
Shift Indicator Needle (.3) 4
Shift Linkage (.3) 4
T.V. Cable (.4) 5

Vacuum Modulator, Renew
All models (.4) 5

Speedometer Driven Gear, Renew
All models (1.0) 1.7

Torque Converter Clutch Switches, Renew
All models
Third Clutch (.6) 8

Detent Cable, Adjust
All models (.2) 4

Detent Cable, Renew
All models (.5) 9

Detent Valve, Renew
Includes: R&R oil pan and valve body, servo cover and reinforcement plate.
All models (1.6) 2.2

Extension Housing or Gasket, Renew
All models (1.1) 1.6
Renew bushing add (.2) 2

Extension Housing Rear Oil Seal, Renew
All models (.5) 7

Governor Assembly, Renew
Includes: R&R drive shaft and extension housing.
All models (1.0) 1.6
Recond governor hub add (.1) 3

Oil Pan Gasket, Renew
All models (.6) 1.0

Governor Pressure Switch and/or Electrical Connector, Renew
Includes: R&R oil pan.
All models (.6) 1.1

Converter Clutch Solenoid Assy., Renew
Includes: R&R oil pan.
All models (.7) 1.2

Low Band Servo, Renew
Includes: R&R oil pan, reinforcement plate, servo cover and valve body. Adjust servo.
All models (1.1) 1.6
Recond servo add (.1) 2

Valve Body Assembly, Renew
Includes: R&R oil pan, reinforcement plate, screen and servo cover.
All models (1.0) 1.5

Valve Body Assy., R&R and Recondition
Includes: R&R oil pan, reinforcement plate, screen and servo cover. Replace parts as required.
All models (1.6) 2.2

Parking Pawl, Renew
Includes: R&R oil pan and extension housing.
All models (1.1) 1.9

Transmission Mount, Renew
All models
rear (.4) 6

SERVICES REQUIRING R&R

Transmission Assy., R&R or Renew
Includes: R&R converter and front pump seal.
S-series (3.2) 4.6

Transmission and Converter Assy., R&R and Recondition
Includes: Disassemble trans, inspect and replace parts as required. Make all necessary adjustments. Road test.
S-series (6.6) 10.0

Transmission Assembly, Reseal
Includes: R&R transmission and install all new gaskets and seals.
S-series 7.1

Transmission Assembly, Recondition (Off Truck)
All models (3.0) 5.4

Front Pump Oil Seal, Renew
Includes: R&R converter and seal.
S-series (2.6) 3.8

Torque Converter, Renew
S-series (3.2) 4.6

Flywheel (Flexplate), Renew
S-series (3.4) 4.9

Front Oil Pump, Renew
S-series (3.6) 5.2
Renew pump bushing add (.3) 3
Renew conver housing bushing add (.2) 2

Front Oil Pump, R&R and Recondition
S-series (4.2) 6.1
Renew pump bushing add (.3) 3
Renew cover housing bushing add (.2) 2

Apply and Actuator Valve and/or Bushing, Renew
Includes: R&R trans, converter and oil pump.
S-series (3.1) 4.5

Second and Third Clutch Assemblies, Renew
Includes: R&R trans and converter.
S-series (3.5) 5.1
Overhaul second clutch add (.5) 5
Overhaul third clutch add (.4) 4
R&R planetary carrier and reaction sun gear add (.6) 6
Renew sun gear drum bushing add (.3) 3

Low Band, Renew
Includes: R&R trans and converter, housing, pump valve body and servo. Remove second and third clutch assys., extension housing and speedometer drive and driven gears. Remove governor body and hub sun gear, planetary carrier and modulator.
S-series (4.4) 6.4
Recond valve body add (.6) 7
Recond oil pump add (.6) 8
Recond low servo add (.1) 2
Renew parking pawl rod add (.1) 1
Renew selector shaft seal add (.1) 1

(Factory Time) Chilton Time

Record second clutch add (.5) 6
Recond third clutch add (.4) 5
Renew reaction sun gear and drum bushing add (.3) 4
Recond gov and hub add (.1) 2
Renew bushings add-each 1

TURBO HYDRA-MATIC 200C

ON TRUCK SERVICES

Drain & Refill Unit
All models 9

Oil Pressure Check
All models (.5) 7

Check Unit For Oil Leaks
Includes: Clean and dry outside of case and run unit to determine point of leak.
All models 9

Neutral Safety Switch, Renew
All models (.3) 4

Throttle Valve Control Cable and/or 'O' Ring, Renew
Includes: Adjust cable.
All models (.5) 8

Speedometer Driven Gear and/or Seal, Renew
All models (.3) 5

Transmission Rear Oil Seal, Renew
Includes: R&R driveshaft.
All models (.4) 8

Torque Converter Clutch Switches, Renew
All models
Brake (.2) 4
Thermal Vacuum (.3) 5
Temp Indicator (.3) 5

Governor Assy., R&R or Renew
Includes: Renew governor seal.
All models (1.1) 1.7

Governor Assy., R&R and Recondition
Includes: Clean and inspect governor, renew seal and gear.
All models (1.3) 2.0

Oil Pan and/or Gasket, Renew
Includes: Clean pan and service screen.
All models (.6) 9

Manual Shaft Seal and/or Detent Lever, Renew
Includes: R&R oil pan.
All models (.7) 1.1

Valve Body Assembly, Renew
Includes: R&R oil pan and renew filter.
All models (.9) 1.5

Valve Body Assy., R&R and Recondition
Includes: R&R oil pan and renew filter. Disassemble, clean, inspect and free all valves. Replace parts as required.
All models (1.6) 2.8

Intermediate Servo Assy., R&R or Renew
All models (1.1) 1.7
Recond servo add (.2) 2

Parking Pawl, Shaft, Rod or Spring, Renew
Includes: R&R oil pan.
All models (1.3) 2.0

1-2 Accumulator Piston and/or Spring, R&R or Renew
Includes: R&R oil pan.
All models (.9) 1.4
Recond accumulator add (.2) 2

SERVICES REQUIRING R&R

Transmission Assembly, R&R or Renew
All models
4X2 (2.6) 3.7
4X4 (3.2) 4.6

Transmission and Converter, R&R and Recondition
Includes: Disassemble transmission completely, including valve body. Clean and inspect all parts. Renew all parts as required. Make all necessary adjustments. Road test.
All models
4X2 (6.2) 11.2
4X4 (6.8) 11.8

Transmission Assy., R&R and Reseal
Includes: Install all new gaskets and seals.
All models 6.5
4X2 .... 6.5
4X4 .... 7.0

Flywheel (Flexplate), Renew
Includes: R&R transmission.
All models
4X2 (2.8) 3.9
4X4 (3.4) 4.8

Torque Converter, Renew
Includes: R&R transmission.
All models
4X2 (2.6) 3.8
4X4 (3.2) 4.7

Front Pump Oil Seal, Renew
Includes: R&R transmission.
All models
4X2 (2.6) 3.8
4X4 (3.2) 4.7

Front Pump Assy., Renew or Recondition
Includes: R&R transmission.
All models
4X2 (3.0) 4.3
4X4 (3.6) 5.2
Recond front pump add (.5) 8
Renew bushing add (.1) 1

Converter Clutch Solenoid Assy., Renew
Includes: R&R transmission, converter and oil pump.
All models
4X2 (2.6) 4.0
4X4 (3.2) 4.9

Apply and Actuator Valves and/or Bushing, Renew
Includes: R&R transmission, converter and oil pump.
All models
4X2 (2.6) 4.0
4X4 (3.2) 4.9

Direct, Forward Clutches and Intermediate Band, Renew
Includes: R&R transmission, converter, pump and seal, oil pan, valve body and servo.
All models
4X2 (3.4) 4.9
4X4 (4.0) 5.8
Recond valve body add (.7) 1.0
Recond oil pump add (.5) 8
Recond servo add (.2) 2
Recond direct clutch add (.3) 4
Recond forward clutch add (.4) 5
Renew bushings add-each (.1) 1

Output Carrier, Sun Gear and Drive Shell, R&R or Renew
Includes: R&R transmission, converter, pump and seal, oil pan, valve body, direct and forward clutches, intermediate band and servo.
All models
4X2 (3.5) 5.5
4X4 (4.1) 5.9
Recond valve body add (.7) 1.0
Recond oil pump add (.5) 8
Recond servo add (.2) 2
Recond direct clutch add (.3) 4
Recond forward clutch add (.4) 5
Recond sun gear and drum, add (.3) 4
Renew output shaft add (.7) 1.0
Renew bushings add-each (.1) 1

TURBO HYDRA-MATIC '350'

ON TRUCK SERVICE

Drain and Refill Unit
All models (.5) 1.0

Oil Pressure Check
All models (.5) 7

Check Unit for Leaks
Includes: Clean and dry outside of case and run unit to determine point of leak.
All models 9

Vacuum Modulator, Renew
w/2 whl drive (.3) 4
w/4 whl drive (.5) 6

Detent Valve Control Cable or Seal, Renew
All models (.5) 9

Speedometer Drive Gear, Renew
Includes: R&R extension housing.
w/2 whl drive (.7) 1.2
w/4 whl drive (.6) 1.1

Speedometer Driven Gear, Renew
All models (.3) 5

Governor Assy., R&R or Renew
Includes: R&R cover and gasket.
All models (.4) 6

Governor Assy., R&R and Recondition
Includes: R&R cover and gasket.
All models (.6) 1.1

Extension Housing Rear Oil Seal, Renew
Includes: R&R drive shaft.
exc Vans (.5) 8
Vans (.4) 7

Torque Converter Clutch Brake Switch, Renew
All models (.2) 4

Torque Converter Clutch Thermal Vacuum Switch, Renew
All models (.3) 5

Torque Converter Clutch Vacuum Delay Valve, Renew
All models (.2) 3

Engine Low Vacuum Switch, Renew
All models (.2) 4

High Vacuum Switch, Renew
All models (.3) 5

Oil Pan and/or Gasket, Renew
Includes: Clean oil pan and service screen.
All models (.6) 1.0

Parking Pawl, Renew
Includes: R&R oil pan.
All models (1.4) 1.9

Intermediate Servo, Renew
Includes: R&R oil pan, valve body and adjust servo.
All models (.8) 1.4
Recond servo add (.2) 2

(Factory Time) Chilton Time

Governor Pressure Switch and/or Electrical Connector, Renew
Includes: R&R oil pan.
All models (.6) 1.1

Auxiliary Valve Body and/or Apply Valve, Renew
Includes: R&R oil pan.
All models (.9) 1.4
Renew body gskt add (.2) 2

Converter Clutch Solenoid, Renew
Includes: R&R oil pan.
All models (.6) 1.1

Intermediate Clutch Accumulator, Renew
All models (.7) 1.2

Valve Body Assy., R&R or Renew
Includes: R&R oil pan and vacuum modulator, clean pan and strainer.
All models (.8) 1.6

Valve Body, R&R and Recondition
Includes: R&R oil pan and vacuum modulator, clean pan and strainer. Disassemble, clean, inspect, free all valves. Replace parts as required.
All models (1.4) 2.4

SERVICES REQUIRING R&R

Transmission, R&R or Renew
2 whl drive (2.0) 3.6
4 whl drive (4.3) 6.1
w/Skid plate add (.3) 3
Pressure check converter add (.2) 2

Transmission and Converter, R&R and Recondition
Includes: Disassemble trans including valve body, clean, inspect and replace parts as required.
2 whl drive (6.3) 10.0
4 whl drive (8.3) 12.3
w/Skid plate add (.3) 3
Pressure check converter add (.2) 2

Transmission Assembly, Reseal
Includes: R&R transmission and renew all seals and gaskets.
2 whl drive (3.5) 5.5
4 whl drive (5.3) 8.1
w/Skid plate add (.3) 3

Front Pump Seal, Renew
Includes: R&R transmission.
2 whl drive (2.1) 3.7
4 whl drive (4.0) 6.4
w/Skid plate add (.3) 3

Flywheel (Flexplate), Renew
Includes: R&R transmission.
2 whl drive (2.2) 3.8
4 whl drive (4.0) 6.4
w/Skid plate add (.3) 3

Torque Converter, Renew
Includes: R&R transmission and check end play of converter.
2 whl drive (2.0) 3.6
4 whl drive (4.4) 6.7
w/Skid plate add (.3) 3

Forward, Direct or Intermediate Clutch, R&R or Renew
Includes: R&R transmission, converter and pump seal, intermediate, direct and forward clutches, oil pan, valve body and intermediate servo piston.
2 whl drive (3.2) 5.7
4 whl drive (5.2) 7.4
w/Skid plate add (.3) 3

(Factory Time) Chilton Time

Forward, Direct or Intermediate Clutch, R&R and Recondition
Includes: R&R transmission, converter and pump seal, intermediate, direct and forward clutches, oil pan, valve body and intermediate servo piston.
2 whl drive (3.6) 6.4
4 whl drive (6.1) 8.8
w/Skid plate add (.3) 3

Front Oil Pump, Renew
Includes: R&R transmission, converter and pump seal.
2 whl drive (2.2) 3.9
4 whl drive (4.5) 6.6
w/Skid plate add (.3) 3

Front Oil Pump, R&R and Recondition
Includes: R&R transmission, converter and pump seal.
2 whl drive (2.7) 4.8
4 whl drive (5.0) 7.3
w/Skid plate add (.3) 3

Low and Reverse Clutch Piston Assembly, R&R or Renew
Includes: R&R trans, converter, pump and seal, intermediate clutch, oil pan, valve body, intermediate servo piston, direct and forward clutches, intermediate band, output carrier, sungear and drive shell, extension housing, speedometer drive gears, governor, output ring gear, low and reverse roller clutch support, reaction carrier and output shell.
2 whl drive (3.6) 6.4
4 whl drive (5.7) 8.1
w/Skid plate add (.3) 3

Low and Reverse Clutch Piston Assembly, R&R and Recondition
Includes: R&R trans, converter, pump and seal, intermediate clutch, oil pan, valve body, intermediate servo piston, direct and forward clutches, intermediate band, output carrier, sungear and drive shell, extension housing, speedometer drive gears, governor, output ring gear, low and reverse roller clutch support, reaction carrier and output shell.
2 whl drive (3.8) 6.8
4 whl drive (6.2) 8.9
w/Skid plate add (.3) 3

Intermediate Band, Renew
Includes: R&R transmission, converter and pump seal, intermediate clutch, oil pan, valve body and intermediate servo piston.
2 whl drive (3.4) 6.1
4 whl drive (5.2) 7.6
w/Skid plate add (.3) 3

TURBO HYDRA-MATIC '400'

ON TRUCK SERVICES

Drain and Refill Unit
All models (.5) 1.0

Oil Pressure Check
All models (.5) 7

Check Unit for Leaks
Includes: Clean and dry outside of case and run unit to determine point of leak.
All models 9

Vacuum Modulator, Renew
w/2 whl drive (.3) 4
w/4 whl drive (.5) 6

Detent Solenoid, Renew or Adjust
Includes: R&R oil pan.
All models (.7) 1.1

(Factory Time) Chilton Time

Down Shift Control Switch, Renew
All models (.2) 4

Detent Solenoid Connector, Renew
Includes: R&R oil pan.
All models (.7) 1.1

Speedometer Drive Gear, Renew
Includes: R&R extension housing.
All models (.8) 1.5

Speedometer Driven Gear, Renew
All models (.3) 5

Governor Assy., R&R or Renew
Includes: R&R cover and gasket.
w/2 whl drive (.5) 8
w/4 whl drive (1.4) 1.9

Governor Assy., R&R and Recondition
Includes: R&R cover and gasket.
w/2 whl drive (.8) 1.1
w/4 whl drive (1.7) 2.4

Extension Housing Rear Oil Seal, Renew
Includes: R&R drive shaft.
All models (.5) 1.0

Oil Pan and/or Gasket, Renew
Includes: Clean oil pan and service screen.
All models (.6) 1.0

Parking Pawl, Renew
Includes: R&R oil pan.
All models (.8) 1.5

Servos, Renew or Recondition
Includes: R&R oil pan, detent solenoid, servo cover and valve body. Adjust servo.
All models-front (1.2) 1.8
rear (1.5) 2.1

Pressure Regulator Valve, Renew
Includes: R&R oil pan.
All models (.8) 1.4

Valve Body Assy., R&R or Renew
Includes: R&R oil pan and vacuum modulator, clean pan and strainer.
All models (.8) 1.6

Valve Body, R&R and Recondition
Includes: R&R oil pan and vacuum modulator, clean pan and strainer. Disassemble, clean, inspect, free all valves. Replace parts as required.
All models (1.3) 2.6

SERVICES REQUIRING R&R

Transmission, R&R or Renew
2 whl drive (2.8) 3.7
4 whl drive (3.6) 4.7
w/Skid plate add (.3) 3

Transmission and Converter, R&R and Recondition
Includes: Disassemble trans including valve body, clean, inspect and replace parts as required.
2 whl drive (8.1) 11.2
4 whl drive (8.8) 12.5
w/Skid plate add (.3) 3
Pressure check converter add (.2) 2

Transmission Assembly, Reseal
Includes: R&R transmission and renew all seals and gaskets.
2 whl drive (3.6) 6.9
4 whl drive (5.6) 8.2
w/Skid plate add (.3) 3

Front Pump Seal, Renew
Includes: R&R transmission.

(Factory Time) — Chilton Time

2 whl drive (2.9)........................... 3.8
4 whl drive (3.7)........................... 4.9
w/Skid plate add (.3)........................... .3

Flywheel (Flexplate), Renew
Includes: R&R transmission.
2 whl drive (3.0)........................... 3.9
4 whl drive (3.8)........................... 5.0
w/Skid plate add (.3)........................... .3

Torque Converter, Renew
Includes: R&R transmission and check end play of converter.
2 whl drive (2.9)........................... 3.8
4 whl drive (3.6)........................... 4.7
w/Skid plate add (.3)........................... .3

Front Oil Pump, Renew
Includes: R&R transmission and converter.
2 whl drive (3.0)........................... 3.9
4 whl drive (3.7)........................... 4.9
w/Skid plate add (.3)........................... .3

Front Oil Pump, R&R and Recondition
Includes: R&R transmission and converter.
2 whl drive (3.5)........................... 4.6
4 whl drive (4.2)........................... 5.5
w/Skid plate add (.3)........................... .3

Forward, Direct or Intermediate Clutch, R&R or Renew
Includes: R&R transmission, converter, oil pan, oil pump and seal.
2 whl drive (3.5)........................... 4.6
4 whl drive (4.2)........................... 5.5
w/Skid plate add (.3)........................... .3

Forward, Direct or Intermediate Clutch, R&R and Recondition
Includes: R&R transmission, converter, oil pan, oil pump and seal, forward clutch, sun gear shaft, front brake band and adjust end play.
2 whl drive (4.1)........................... 5.4
4 whl drive (4.8)........................... 6.3
w/Skid plate add (.3)........................... .3

Center Support and Gear Unit Assy., Renew
Includes: R&R transmission, converter, pump and seal, forward clutch, front brake band, valve body, case extension, speedometer driven gear. Check end play.
2 whl drive (4.3)........................... 5.7
4 whl drive (5.0)........................... 6.6
w/Skid plate add (.3)........................... .3

Center Support and Gear Unit Assy., R&R and Recondition
Includes: R&R transmission, converter, pump and seal, forward clutch, front brake band, valve body, case extension, speedometer driven gear. Check end play.
2 whl drive (4.9)........................... 6.5
4 whl drive (5.6)........................... 7.4
w/Skid plate add (.3)........................... .3

TURBO HYDRA-MATIC 700-R4

ON TRUCK SERVICES

Drain & Refill Unit
All models........................... .9

Oil Pressure Check
All models (.5)........................... .7

Check Unit For Oil Leaks
Includes: Clean and dry outside of case and run unit to determine point of leak.
All models........................... .9

Neutral Safety Switch, Renew
All models (.3)........................... .4

Shift Linkage, Adjust
All models (.4)........................... .6

Torque Converter Clutch Switches, Renew
All models
Brake (.2)........................... .4
Thermal Vacuum (.3)........................... .5
Temp Indicator (.3)........................... .5

Detent Valve Control Cable and/or 'O' Ring, Renew
Includes: Adjust cable.
All models (.7)........................... .9

Speedometer Driven Gear and/or Seal, Renew
All models (.3)........................... .5

Extension Housing Rear Oil Seal, Renew
Includes: R&R driveshaft.
All models (.4)........................... .8

Governor Cover and/or Seal, Renew
S-series
4 WD (1.0)........................... 1.4
All other models (.3)........................... .5

Governor Assembly, R&R or Renew
S-series
4 WD (1.0)........................... 1.4
All other models (.4)........................... .7

Governor Assy., R&R and Recondition
S-series
4 WD (1.2)........................... 1.7
All other models (.6)........................... 1.0

Oil Pan and/or Gasket, Renew
Vans (.8)........................... 1.1
All other models (.6)........................... .9
w/Skid plate add (.3)........................... .3

Governor Pressure Switch, Renew
Includes: R&R oil pan.
Vans (.8)........................... 1.3
All other models (.6)........................... 1.1
w/Skid plate add (.3)........................... .3

Converter Clutch Solenoid, Renew
Includes: R&R oil pan.
Vans (.8)........................... 1.3
All other models (.6)........................... 1.1
w/Skid plate add (.3)........................... .3

Valve Body Assembly, Renew
Includes: R&R oil pan and renew filter.
Vans-K-series (1.0)........................... 1.7
All other models (.8)........................... 1.5
w/Skid plate add (.3)........................... .3

Valve Body Assy., R&R and Recondition
Includes: R&R oil pan and renew filter. Disassemble, clean, inspect and free all valves. Replace parts as required.
Vans-K-series (1.9)........................... 2.7
All other models (1.7)........................... 2.5
w/Skid plate add (.3)........................... .3

2-4 Servo Assy., R&R or Renew
S-series (1.4)........................... 1.9
All other models (.5)........................... 1.0
w/Skid plate add (.3)........................... .3
Recond servo add (.2)........................... .3

Parking Pawl, Shaft, Rod or Spring, Renew
Includes: R&R oil pan.
Vans (.9)........................... 1.4
All other models (.6)........................... 1.1
Renew pawl add (.5)........................... .5
w/Skid plate add (.3)........................... .3

1-2 Accumulator Piston and/or Spring, Renew
Includes: R&R oil pan.
All models (.8)........................... 1.5

w/Skid plate add (.3)........................... .3
Recond add (.1)........................... .2

SERVICES REQUIRING R&R

Transmission Assy., R&R or Renew
2 whl drive (2.2)........................... 3.1
4 whl drive (4.0)........................... 5.8
w/Skid plate add (.3)........................... .3

Transmission and Converter, R&R and Recondition
Includes: Disassemble transmission completely, including valve body and overhaul unit. Clean and inspect all parts. Renew all parts as required. Make all necessary adjustments. Road test.
2 whl drive (6.3)........................... 12.0
4 whl drive (7.1)........................... 15.0
w/Skid plate add (.3)........................... .3
Clean and leak check
converter add (.2)........................... .4
Check end play add (.2)........................... .3

Transmission Assy., R&R and Reseal
Includes: Install all new gaskets and seals.
2 whl drive........................... 4.7
4 whl drive........................... 7.4
w/Skid plate add........................... .3

Flywheel (Flexplate), Renew
Includes: R&R transmission.
2 whl drive (2.4)........................... 3.3
4 whl drive (4.2)........................... 6.0
w/Skid plate add (.3)........................... .3

Torque Converter, Renew
Includes: R&R transmission.
2 whl drive (2.1)........................... 2.9
4 whl drive (3.9)........................... 5.6
w/Skid plate add (.3)........................... .3

Front Pump Oil Seal, Renew
Includes: R&R transmission.
2 whl drive (2.1)........................... 3.0
4 whl drive (3.9)........................... 5.6
w/Skid plate add (.3)........................... .3

Front Pump Assy., Renew or Recondition
Includes: R&R transmission.
2 whl drive (2.7)........................... 4.0
4 whl drive (4.5)........................... 6.5
w/Skid plate add (.3)........................... .3
Recond front pump add (.5)........................... .6
Renew bushing add (.1)........................... .1

Input Drum, Reverse and Input Clutch, Renew
Includes: R&R transmission.
2 whl drive (3.2)........................... 4.6
4 whl drive (5.0)........................... 7.2
w/Skid plate add (.3)........................... .3
Recond valve body add (.4)........................... .5
Recond front pump add (.5)........................... .6
Renew bushings add-each (.1)........................... .1

Reaction Gear Set, Renew
Includes: R&R transmission.
2 whl drive (3.5)........................... 5.2
4 whl drive (5.3)........................... 7.6
w/Skid plate add (.3)........................... .3
Recond valve body add (.4)........................... .5
Recond front pump add (.5)........................... .6
Renew input clutch drum add (.2)........................... .3
Recond reaction gear set add (.2)........................... .2
Renew bushings add-each (.1)........................... .1

LABOR 23 AUTOMATIC TRANSMISSION 23 LABOR

(Factory Time) Chilton Time

Low and Reverse Clutch Piston Assy., Renew
Includes: R&R transmission.

	Chilton Time
2 whl drive (3.7)	5.7
4 whl drive (5.5)	7.9
w/Skid plate add (.3)	.3
Recond valve body add (.4)	.5
Recond front pump add (.5)	.6
Recond reverse clutch add (.4)	.5
Recond input clutch add (.4)	.5
Renew input clutch drum add (.2)	.2
Recond reaction gear set add (.2)	.3
Recond low and reverse clutch add (.1)	.2
Recond reverse piston add (.3)	.4
Recond gov or renew gear add (.2)	.3
Renew gov bushing add (.4)	.5
Renew bushings add-each (.1)	.1

LABOR 25 U-JOINTS & DRIVESHAFT 25 LABOR

(Factory Time) Chilton Time

Universal Joints, Renew

	Chilton Time
All models-one (.6)	1.0
each adtnl (.3)	.4

Drive Shaft, R&R or Renew
One Piece Shaft

	Chilton Time
All models (.3)	.5

Two Piece Shaft

	Chilton Time
front shaft (.4)	.7
rear shaft (.3)	.5

Center Support Bearing, Renew

	Chilton Time
All models (.5)	1.0

Driveshaft Slip Joint, Renew

	Chilton Time
All models (.6)	.9

LABOR 26 REAR AXLE 26 LABOR

(Factory Time) Chilton Time

Rear Axle, Drain and Refill

	Chilton Time
All models	.6

Rear Axle Housing Cover Gasket, Renew

	Chilton Time
All models (.4)	.6

Rear Wheel Hub Assembly, Renew

	Chilton Time
All models-one side (.8)	1.1
both sides (1.4)	1.8
w/Dual whls add-each side	.1

Rear Wheel Hub Oil Seal, Renew

	Chilton Time
All models-one side (.6)	.9
both sides (1.0)	1.6
w/Dual whls add-each side	.1

Axle Shaft, Renew

	Chilton Time
Semi-Floating Axle	
one (.6)	.9
both (.8)	1.2
Full Floating Axle	
one (.3)	.6
both (.5)	.8

Axle Shaft Oil Seal, Renew

	Chilton Time
Semi-Floating Axle	
one (.6)	1.1
both (.8)	1.4
Full Floating Axle	
one (.7)	1.1
both (1.2)	1.6
w/Dual whls add, each side (.1)	.1

Axle Shaft Bearing, Renew

	Chilton Time
Semi-Floating Axle	
one (.7)	1.1
both (.9)	1.4
Full Floating Axle	
one (.9)	1.4
both (1.6)	2.7
w/Dual whls add-each side	.1

Pinion Shaft Oil Seal, Renew
Includes: Renew pinion flange if necessary.

	Chilton Time
All models	
Semi-Floating (.5)	.8
Full Floating (.7)	1.1

Differential Case, Renew

	Chilton Time
Standard	
Semi-Floating (2.0)	3.1
Full Floating (2.2)	3.3
Limited Slip (Semi-Floating)	
Eaton Case (2.4)	3.5
exc Eaton Case (2.6)	3.7
Limited Slip (Full Floating)	
Eaton Case (2.4)	3.5
exc Eaton Case (2.1)	3.2

Ring and Pinion Gears, Renew

	Chilton Time
Semi-Floating Axle (2.4)	4.1
Full Floating Axle (2.8)	4.6
Recond diff case add	
std (.3)	.5
limited slip (.7)	1.0

Pinion Bearings, Renew
Note: Does not require case removal on semi-floating axles.

	Chilton Time
Semi-Floating Axle (2.2)	3.1
Full Floating Axle (1.9)	2.8
Renew side brgs add (.3)	.5

Limited Slip Clutch Plates, Renew

	Chilton Time
Semi-Floating Axle	
Eaton Case (2.4)	3.5
exc Eaton Case (1.1)	2.0
S-series (1.2)	2.1
Full Floating Axle	
Eaton Case (2.4)	3.5
exc Eaton Case (2.3)	3.4

Side Bearings, Renew

	Chilton Time
Semi-Floating Axle (1.9)	2.6
Full Floating Axle (1.8)	2.5

Rear Axle Housing, Renew

	Chilton Time
Semi-Floating Axle (4.5)	6.1
Full Floating Axle (5.1)	6.7
w/Dual whls add (.2)	.4

Differential Assy., Renew (Complete)
Includes: Transfer parts as required. Bleed brake system.

	Chilton Time
All models (2.1)	3.5

LABOR 27 REAR SUSPENSION 27 LABOR

(Factory Time) Chilton Time

Rear Spring, Renew

	Chilton Time
S-series-one (.7)	1.1
both (1.2)	2.0
Vans-Astro-one (.9)	1.3
both (1.5)	2.1
All other models-one (.7)	1.1
both (.9)	1.5
w/Aux fuel tank add (.6)	.6
w/Dual whls add-each side	.1
w/Skid plate add (.3)	.3
Recond add-each side	.5

Rear Spring Shackle and/or Bushing, Renew

	Chilton Time
S-series-one (.4)	.6
both (.6)	1.0
All other models-one (.5)	.7
both (.7)	1.1

Rear Spring Eye Bushing, Renew

	Chilton Time
All models-one side (.9)	1.3
both sides (1.2)	1.8
w/Dual whls add-each side	.1
w/Skid plate add (.3)	.3

Rear Shock Absorber, Renew

	Chilton Time
All models-one (.3)	.5
both (.4)	.8

Rear Stabilizer Bar, Renew

	Chilton Time
C-models (.4)	.5
S-series (.6)	.8

(Factory Time) Chilton Time

Note: If more than one item requires replacement where evacuation and discharging the system is already included in the operation, deduct 1.0 hour for each additional item to the times listed.

Drain, Evacuate and Recharge System
All models (.5) 1.0

Leak Test
Includes: Check all lines and connections.
All models 6

Refrigerant, Add Partial Charge
All models 6

Compressor Belt, Renew
All models (.2) 5
If necessary to R&R fan pulley,
add (.3) 3
w/P.S. add (.2) 2
w/AIR add (.2) 2

COMPRESSOR - 6 CYLINDER AXIAL

Compressor Assembly, Renew
Includes: Transfer all necessary attaching parts. Evacuate and charge system.
Six (2.0) 3.1
V-8-exc Vans (1.9) 3.0
Vans (2.3) 3.4

Compressor Assy., R&R and Recondition
Includes: Complete disassembly and overhaul, making all checks and gauging operations. Evacuate and charge system.
Six (3.8) 6.3
V-8-exc Vans (3.8) 6.2
Vans (4.2) 6.8

Compressor Clutch Hub and Drive Plate, Renew
Includes: Check air gap. Does not include R&R compressor.
Six (.8) 1.1
V-8-exc Vans (.5) 8
Vans (.8) 1.1

Compressor Pulley and/or Bearing, Renew
Includes: R&R hub and drive plate.
Six (.9) 1.2
V-8-exc Vans (.6) 9
Vans (.9) 1.2

Compressor Clutch Holding Coil, Renew
Includes: R&R hub and drive plate, pulley and bearing.
Six (1.0) 1.4
V-8-exc Vans (.6) 1.1
Vans (1.0) 1.4

Compressor Shaft Seal Kit, Renew
Includes: R&R clutch hub and drive plate. Evacuate and charge system.
Six (1.7) 2.8
V-8-exc Vans (1.5) 2.6
Vans (1.7) 2.8

Compressor Rear Head, Oil Pump Gears and/or Rear Reed Assembly, Renew
Includes: R&R compressor. R&R rear head and rear reed plate assy. Clean and test parts. Add oil. Evacuate and charge system.
Six (2.0) 3.4
V-8-exc Vans (1.9) 3.3
Vans (2.4) 3.8

Compressor Front Head and/or Front Reed Assembly, Renew
Includes: R&R compressor. R&R rear head and reed plate assy. Disassemble shell to internal mechanism and front head assy. R&R front valve and reed plate and shaft seal assy. Clean and inspect parts. Add oil. Evacuate and charge system.
Six (2.7) 4.5
V-8-exc Vans (2.5) 4.3
Vans (3.1) 4.9

Internal Cylinder and Piston Assy., Renew
Includes: R&R compressor, disassemble, clean and inspect parts. Install new pre-assembled cylinder, pistons and wobble plate unit. Evacuate and charge system.
Six (2.7) 4.3
V-8-exc Vans (2.5) 4.2
Vans (3.1) 4.8

COMPRESSOR - 4 CYLINDER RADIAL

Compressor Assembly, Renew
Includes: Transfer all necessary attaching parts. Evacuate and charge system.
Astro-Vans (1.5) 2.5
All other models (1.0) 2.0

Compressor Clutch Hub and Drive Plate, Renew
Includes: Check air gap. Does not include R&R compressor.
All models (.5) 8

Compressor Rotor and/or Bearing, Renew
Astro-Vans (1.4) 2.3
All other models (.6) 1.0
Add time to evacuate and charge system if required.

Compressor Clutch Coil and/or Pulley Rim, Renew
Astro-Vans (1.4) 2.3
All other models (.6) 8
Add time to evacuate and charge system if required.

Compressor Shaft Seal Kit, Renew
Includes: R&R clutch hub and drive plate. Evacuate and charge system.
All models (1.3) 2.5

Compressor Front Bearing, Front Head and/or Seal, Renew
Includes: R&R clutch hub and drive plate, rotor, pulley and coil. Evacuate and charge system.
Astro-Vans (2.0) 3.0
All other models (1.5) 2.8

Compressor Outer Shell and/or 'O' Rings, Renew
Includes: R&R compressor. R&R clutch hub and drive plate, rotor, pulley and coil. Evacuate and charge system.
Astro-Vans (2.1) 3.2
All other models (1.7) 2.9

Compressor Discharge Valve Plate Assy., Renew
Includes: R&R compressor. R&R clutch hub and drive plate, rotor, pulley and coil. Evacuate and charge system.
Astro-Vans (2.2) 3.4
All other models (1.8) 2.9
Renew two or more valves add (.1) 2

Compressor Cylinder and Shaft Assy., Renew
Includes: R&R compressor. Transfer clutch hub, drive plate, rotor, pulley, and coil. Inspect front head. Add oil. Evacuate and charge system.
Astro-Vans (2.3) 3.5
All other models (1.9) 3.0

COMPRESSOR ASSEMBLY DA-6

Compressor Assembly, Renew
Includes: Transfer parts as required. Evacuate and charge system.
Vans-Astro (1.3) 2.4
All other models (1.0) 2.0

Compressor Clutch Plate and Hub Assy., Renew
Includes: R&R hub and drive plate assy. Check air gap.
Vans-Astro (.4) 7
All other models (.3) 6

Compressor Clutch Coil and/or Pulley Rim, Renew
Includes: R&R hub and drive plate assy.
Vans-Astro (1.0) 1.5
All other models (.8) 1.3
Add time to evacuate and charge system if required.

Compressor Rotor and/or Bearing, Renew
Includes: R&R hub and drive plate assy.
Vans-Astro (.9) 1.4
All other models (.7) 1.2
Add time to evacuate and charge system if required.

Compressor Shaft Seal Kit, Renew
Includes: Evacuate and charge system.
Vans-Astro (1.2) 2.6
All other models (1.1) 2.5

Compressor Front Head and/or Seal, Renew
Includes: R&R compressor. R&R clutch and pulley assy. R&R shaft seal assy. Clean and inspect parts. Evacuate and charge system.
Vans-Astro (1.6) 3.0
All other models (1.4) 2.8

Compressor Cylinder and Shaft Assy., Renew
Includes: R&R compressor. R&R clutch and pulley assy. R&R shaft seal assy., remove and transfer front head assy. R&R compressor shell and 'O' rings. R&R compressor valve plates. Clean and inspect parts. Evacuate and charge system.
Vans-Astro (2.3) 3.7
All other models (1.9) 3.3

Compressor Relief Valve, Renew
Includes: Evacuate and charge system.
exc Vans (.9) 1.5
Vans-Astro (1.4) 2.0

Condenser, Renew
Includes: Evacuate and charge system.
S-series (1.3) 2.8
exc Vans (1.5) 3.1
Vans-Astro (1.3) 2.8
w/Aux oil cooler add (.3) 3

Evaporator Assembly, Renew
Includes: Evacuate and charge system.
Front Unit
S-series (1.4) 2.8
exc Vans (1.1) 2.5
Vans-Astro (1.8) 3.5
w/Diesel eng
exc Vans (1.1) 2.5
Vans (2.0) 4.5

Rear Unit
exc Vans (1.6) 3.6
Vans (1.9) 4.3

Accumulator, Renew
Includes: Evacuate and charge system.
All models (.9) 1.5

Expansion Tube (Orifice), Renew
Includes: Evacuate and charge system.
All models (.7) 1.4

LABOR 28 AIR CONDITIONING 28 LABOR

(Factory Time) — Chilton Time

Pressure Cycling Switch, Renew
All models (.2) 3

Receiver - Dehydrator, Renew
Includes: Evacuate and charge system.
Vans (1.4) 2.2

Sight Glass and/or 'O' Ring, Renew
Includes: Evacuate and charge system.
Vans (.8) 2.0

Expansion Valve, Renew
Includes: Evacuate and charge system.
All models (1.2) 1.7

Expansion Tube and Screen, Clean and Inspect or Renew
Includes: Evacuate and charge system.
All models (.9) 1.5

A.C. Blower Motor, Renew
Front Unit
Gas Engine
S-series (.3) 5
Astro (.6) 1.0
exc Vans (.2) 5
Vans (.3) 6
Diesel Eng
Vans (.5) 8
All other models (2.4) *4.0
Rear Unit
All models (.6) 1.1
*Includes evacuate and charge A.C. system.

Blower Motor Switch, Renew
Front unit (.5) 9
Rear unit (.4) 8

Temperature Control Assy., Renew
All models (.5) 9

Blower Motor Resistor, Renew
Front unit (.2) .... &7.4
Rear unit (.3) .... *.5
*R&R seat add 2
†1987-88 C & K models add 4

Blower Motor Relay, Renew
All models (.3) 5

Air Conditioning Hoses, Renew
Includes: Evacuate and charge system.
Condenser Outlet
Astro (1.1) 2.2
Comp to Condenser
exc Vans (1.1) 2.2
Vans (1.3) 2.4
Condenser to Receiver-Dehydrator
Vans (1.4) 2.5
Receiver-Dehydrator to Exp Valve
Vans (1.6) 2.7
Condenser to Evaporator
S-series (.8) 1.7
w/Front A.C. (1.3) 2.4
w/Rear A.C. (1.5) 2.6

Hose, Muffler and Comp Manifold Assy.
exc Suburban
w/Rear A.C. (1.3) 2.4
Suburban-w/Rear A.C. (1.0) 2.1
Front to Rear Unit (Under Floor)
exc Vans-one or both (1.4) 2.6
Vans-one or both (1.5) 2.7
Astro-one or both (1.5) 2.7
Hose and Plate Assy.–Pillar to Overhead
Series 10-20-Rear Unit (1.3) 2.5
Chevy Van-Rear Unit (1.5) 2.7
Sport Van-Rear Unit (1.7) 2.9
Beauville-Rear Unit (2.9) 4.1

LABOR 30 HEAD AND PARKING LAMPS 30 LABOR

(Factory Time) — Chilton Time

Aim Headlamps
two 4
four 6

Headlamp Sealed Beam Bulb, Renew
All models-each (.2) 3

Turn Signal or Parking Lamp Assy., Renew
All models-each (.2) 4

Side Marker Lamp Assy., Renew
All models-each (.2) 3

Tail and Stop Lamp Assy., Renew
Includes: Back-up and/or marker lamp assy. on combination units.
All models-each (.3) 4

License Lamp Assy., Renew
All models-each (.2) 3

Roof Marker Lamp Assy., Renew
All models-each (.2) 3

Reflectors, Renew
All models-each 2

LABOR 31 WINDSHIELD WIPER & SPEEDOMETER 31 LABOR

(Factory Time) — Chilton Time

Windshield Wiper Motor, Renew
S-series (.5) 7
exc Vans (.7) 1.0
Vans (.9) 1.2
Recond motor add (.3) 5

Wiper Transmission, Renew (One Side)
All models (.6) 8

Wiper Switch, Renew
std whl (1.2) 1.7
tilt whl (1.0) 1.5

Delay Wiper Controller Assy., Renew
All models (.5) 7

Windshield Washer Pump Assy., Renew
All models (.3) 4

Intermittant Wiper Controller Assy., Renew
S-series (.3) 5
All other models (.5) 8

Pulse Wiper Control Module, Renew
S-series (.6) 8
All other models (.3) 5

Windshield Washer Pump Valve, Renew
All models (.2) 4

Speedometer Head, R&R or Renew
1984-86
S-series (.4) 8
exc Vans (.6) 1.0
Vans (.5) 9
Astro (.7) 1.2
1987-88
S-series-Astro (.7) 1.2
exc Vans (.4) 7
Vans (.6) 1.0
Reset odometer add 2

Speedometer Cable and Casing, Renew
1984-86
upper cable (.4) 6
lower cable (.3) 5
one piece cable
conv cab (.4) 6
All other models (.7) 1.1
1987-88
One Piece Cable
Astro (.7) 1.1
All other models (.8) 1.2

LABOR 32 LIGHT SWITCHES & WIRING 32 LABOR

(Factory Time) — Chilton Time

Headlamp Switch, Renew
S-series (.4) 7
exc Vans (.5) 8
Vans-Astro (.3) 6

Headlamp Dimmer Switch, Renew
S-series (.6) 9
Vans-Astro (.4) 7
All other models (.5) 8

Turn Signal and Hazard Warning Switch, Renew
All models (.7) 1.1
w/Tilt whl add 2

Back-Up Lamp and Park/Neutral Switch, Renew
S-series (.4) 6
All other models (.3) 5

Starter Safety Switch, Renew
w/A.T.-column mount (.3) 5
w/M.T.-clutch mount (.2) 4

Back-Up Lamp Switch, Renew
w/A.T. (.3) 5
w/M.T.-floor shift (.2) 4
w/M.T.-column shift (.3) 5

LABOR 32 LIGHT SWITCHES & WIRING 32 LABOR

	(Factory Time)	Chilton Time
Stop Light Switch, Renew		
All models	(.2)	.3
Parking Brake Lamp Switch, Renew		
S-series	(.4)	.6
All other models	(.2)	.4
Turn Signal or Hazard Warning Flasher, Renew		
S-series	(.4)	.5
All other models	(.2)	.3
Horn, Renew		
All models	(.2)	.4

LABOR 34 CRUISE CONTROL 34 LABOR

	(Factory Time)	Chilton Time
Regulator Assembly (Transducer), Renew		
Includes: Adjust.		
exc Vans	(.4)	.8
Vans	(.5)	.9
Engagement Switch, Renew		
All models	(.4)	.6
Cruise Control Release Switch, Renew		
All models		
Brake	(.4)	.5
Clutch	(.4)	.5
Cruise Control Servo, Renew		
exc Vans	(.3)	.5
Vans-Astro	(.5)	.7
Renew bracket add	(.1)	.2
Vacuum Hoses, Renew		
exc Vans	(.2)	.3
Vans-Astro	(.4)	.6
Cruise Control Cable or Chain, Renew		
Vans-Astro	(.5)	.7
All other models	(.3)	.5
Cruise Control Vacuum Regulator Valve, Renew		
(w/Diesel eng)		
All models	(.2)	.3
Cruise Control Resume Solenoid, Renew		
All models	(.2)	.3
Cruise Control Module, Renew		
Astro	(.5)	.7
All other models	(.3)	.5
Cruise Control Speed Sensor, Renew		
S-series-Vans-Astro	(.6)	.9
All other models	(.7)	1.0
Cruise Control Check Valve, Renew		
All models	(.2)	.4
Cruise Control Stepper Motor, Renew		
All models	(.4)	.6

GROUP INDEX

ALPHABETICAL INDEX

MODEL IDENTIFICATION CHART

B 100 - DODGE TRADESMAN VAN

B 100 - DODGE SPORTSMAN WAGON

B 200 - DODGE TRADESMAN VAN

B 200 - DODGE SPORTSMAN WAGON

B 300 - DODGE TRADESMAN VAN

B 300 - DODGE SPORTSMAN WAGON

PB 100 - PLYMOUTH VOYAGER WAGON

PB 200 - PLYMOUTH VOYAGER WAGON

PB 300 - PLYMOUTH VOYAGER WAGON

CB 300 - FRONT SECTION - KARY VAN

CB 400 - FRONT SECTION - KARY VAN

AW 100 - RAMCHARGER - 4 WHEEL DRIVE

PW 100 - TRAILDUSTER - 4 WHEEL DRIVE

AD 100 - RAMCHARGER - 2 WHEEL DRIVE

AD 150 - SPORT UTILITY - 2 WHEEL DRIVE

PD 100 - TRAILDUSTER - 2 WHEEL DRIVE

D 100 - DODGE PICK-UP - 2 WHEEL DRIVE

D 150 - DODGE PICK-UP - 2 WHEEL DRIVE

D 200 - DODGE PICK-UP - 2 WHEEL DRIVE

RD 200 - DODGE RAIL-TRACK - 2 WHEEL DRIVE

D 300 - DODGE PICK-UP - 2 WHEEL DRIVE

W 100 - DODGE PICK-UP - 4 WHEEL DRIVE

AW 150 - SPORT UTILITY - 4 WHEEL DRIVE

W 200 - DODGE PICK-UP - 4 WHEEL DRIVE

W 300 - DODGE PICK-UP - 4 WHEEL DRIVE

W 400 - DODGE PICK-UP - 4 WHEEL DRIVE

LABOR 1 TUNE UP 1 LABOR

(Factory Time) Chilton Time

Compression Test
Six(.6).. .9
V-8-318-360 engs (.7)...................... 1.0

Engine Tune Up, (Electronic Ignition)
Includes: Test battery and clean connections. Tighten manifold and carburetor mounting bolts. Check engine compression, clean and adjust or renew spark plugs. Test resistance of spark plug wires. Inspect distributor cap and rotor. Adjust distributor air gap. Check vacuum advance operation. Reset ignition timing. Adjust idle mixture and idle speed. Service carburetor air cleaner. Inspect crankcase ventilation system. Inspect and adjust drive belts. Inspect and adjust drive belts. Inspect choke operation, adjust or free up as necessary. Check operation of E.G.R. valve.
Six.. 2.8
V-8-318-360 engs 3.2
w/A.C. add 6

LABOR 2 IGNITION SYSTEM 2 LABOR

(Factory Time) Chilton Time

Spark Plugs, Clean and Reset or Renew
Six(.4).. .7
V-8-318-360 eng (.5)......................... .8

Ignition Timing, Reset
B-PB-CB Models (.5).................. .7
All other models (.3)...................... .5

Distributor, Renew
Includes: Adjust ignition timing and renew oil seal if required.
Six-B-PB-CB Models (.7).................. 1.0
All other models (.6)...................... .9
V-8-318-360 engs
B-PB-CB Models (.7).................. 1.0
All other models (.6)...................... .9

Distributor, R&R and Recondition
Includes: Adjust ignition timing and renew oil seal if required.
Six-B-PB-CB Models (1.4)................ 2.0
All other models (1.3)...................... 1.9
V-8-318-360 engs
B-PB-CB Models (1.4)................ 2.0
All other models (1.3)...................... 1.9

Distributor Pick-Up Plate and Coil Assembly, Renew
Includes: R&R distributor, reset ignition timing.
Six-B-PB-CB Models (.9).................. 1.3
All other models (.8)...................... 1.2
V-8-318-360 engs
B-PB-CB Models (.9).................. 1.3
All other models (.8)...................... 1.2

Electronic Distributor Reluctor, Renew
Includes: R&R distributor and reset ignition timing.
Six-B-PB-CB Models (.8).................. 1.2
All other models (.7)...................... 1.1
V-8-318-360 engs
B-PB-CB Models (.8).................. 1.2
All other models (.7)...................... 1.1

Vacuum Control Unit, Renew
Includes: R&R distributor and reset ignition timing.
Six-B-PB-CB Models (.8).................. 1.2
All other models (.7)...................... 1.1
V-8-318-360 engs
B-PB-CB Models (.8).................. 1.2
All other models (.7)...................... 1.1

Distributor Cap and/or Rotor, Renew
B-PB-CB Models (.4).................. .5
All other models (.3)...................... .4

Electronic Ignition Control Unit, Renew
B-PB-CB Models (.3).................. .5
All other models (.2)...................... .4

Spark Control Computer, Renew
B-PB-CB models (.7).................. 1.1
All other models (.6)...................... 1.0

Ignition Cables, Renew
Six(.5).. .8
V-8-318-360 engs (.6)...................... .9

Ignition Coil, Renew
B-PB-CB Models (.4).................. .6
All other models (.3)...................... .5

Electronic Ignition Ballast Resistor, Renew
B-PB-CB Models (.3).................. .5
All other models (.2)...................... .4

Ignition Switch, Renew
Includes: Renew lock cylinder if required.
1984-88
std colm (.7)................................ 1.2
tilt colm (.4)................................ .7

LABOR 3 FUEL SYSTEM 3 LABOR

(Factory Time) Chilton Time

Fuel Pump, Test
Includes: Disconnect line at carburetor, attach pressure gauge.
All models .3

Carburetor, Adjust (On Truck)
All models (.6) .8

Air Cleaner Vacuum Diaphragm, Renew
All models (.3) .5

Air Cleaner Vacuum Sensor, Renew
All models (.3) .5

Coolant Temperature Sensor/Switch, Renew
B-PB-CB models (.4) .6
All other models (.3) .5

Carburetor, Renew
Includes: All necessary adjustments.
1 bbl (.7) 1.1
2 bbl (.7) 1.1
4 bbl (.8) 1.2

Carburetor, R&R and Clean or Recondition
Includes: All necessary adjustments.
Holly-1 bbl (1.9) 2.5
Carter-2 bbl (2.3) 3.1
Holly-2 bbl (1.9) 2.5
Carter-4 bbl (2.6) 3.5
Rochester-4 bbl 3.5

Fuel Pump, Renew
Six–B-PB-CB Models (.6) .9
All other models (.5) .8
V-8–318-360 engs (.5) .8
Add pump test if performed.

Fuel Tank, Renew
Includes: Drain and refill, test and renew tank gauge if necessary.
Main Tank
frame mount (1.0) 1.5
cab mount (.7) 1.2
plastic tank (1.0) 1.5
Auxiliary Tank
cab mount (1.2) 1.7
frame mount (1.0) 1.5
w/Skid plate add (.3) .3
w/Towing pkg add .5

Fuel Gauge (Tank), Renew
Main Tank
frame mount (.7) 1.2
cab mount (.5) .9
plastic tank (1.0) 1.4
Auxiliary Tank
cab mount (.5) .9
frame mount (.6) 1.0
w/Skid plate add (.3) .3
w/Towing pkg add .5

Fuel Gauge (Dash), Renew
1984-88 (.6) 1.1

Intake and Exhaust Manifold Gaskets, Renew
Six
B-PB-CB Models (2.0) 3.0
All other models (1.8) 2.8
w/A.C. add (.4) .4
Renew manif add .5

Intake Manifold Gasket, Renew
V-8
318-360 engs (2.5) 3.5
w/A.C. add (.4) .4
w/Air inj add .6
Renew manif add .5

LABOR 3A EMISSION CONTROLS 3A LABOR

(Factory Time) Chilton Time

CRANKCASE EMISSION

Positive Crankcase Ventilation Valve, Renew
All models (.2) .3

EVAPORATIVE EMISSION

Vapor Canister, Renew
All models (.3) .5

Vapor Canister Hoses, Renew
All models-one (.2) .3

Vapor Canister Filter, Renew
All models (.2) .3

Vapor Separator, Renew
All models (.9) 1.2

AIR INJECTION SYSTEM

Air Pump, Renew
Six (.9) 1.2
V-8 (.8) 1.1

Aspirator, Renew
All models (.3) .4

Diverter/Control Valve, Renew
Six (.3) .6
V-8 (.4) .7

Injection Tube and Check Valve Assy., Renew
Six (.4) .7
V-8 (.5) .8

Orifice Spark Advance Control Valve, Renew
All models (.2) .4

HEATED AIR SYSTEM

Air Cleaner Vacuum Diaphragm, Renew
1984-88 (.3) .5

Air Cleaner Vacuum Sensor, Renew
1984-88 (.3) .5

EXHAUST GAS RECIRCULATION SYSTEM

E.G.R. Valve, Renew
Six (.4) .6
V-8 (.5) .7

E.G.R. Coolant Control Valve, Renew
All models (.3) .5

E.G.R. Vacuum Amplifier, Renew
All models (.3) .5

E.G.R. Time Delay Timer, Renew
All models (.2) .4

E.G.R. Time Delay Solenoid, Renew
All models (.2) .4

Change Temperature Switch, Renew
All models (.2) .3

Coolant Vacuum Switch Valve, Renew
All models (.3) .4

Spark Advance Delay Valve, Renew
All models (.2) .3

E.G.R. Purge Control Solenoid Bank, Renew
All models (.2) .3

E.F.C. SYSTEM

Oxygen Sensor, Renew
All models (.3) .5

Emission Maintenance Reminder Module, Renew
All models (.2) .4

Electronic Speed Switch, Renew
All models (.3) .4

LABOR 4 ALTERNATOR AND REGULATOR 4 LABOR

(Factory Time) Chilton Time

Alternator Circuits, Test
Includes: Test battery, regulator and alternator output.
All models .6

Alternator, Renew
Six(.7) 1.2
V-8–318-360 engs
B-PB-CB Models (.9) 1.4
All other models (.7) 1.2
Add circuit test if performed.

Alternator, R&R and Recondition
Six(2.0) 3.1
V-8–318-360 engs
B-PB-CB Models (2.2) 3.3
All other models (2.0) 3.1
Add circuit test if performed.

Alternator Drive End Frame Bearing, Renew
Six(1.0) 1.5
V-8–318-360 engs
B-PB-CB Models (1.2) 1.7
All other models (1.0) 1.5
Renew rear brg add .2

Voltage Regulator, Test and Renew
All models (.3) .6

Alternator Gauge, Renew
1984-88 (.6) 1.1

LABOR 5 STARTING SYSTEM 5 LABOR

(Factory Time) Chilton Time

Starter Draw Test (On Truck)
All models 3

Starter, Renew
Six(.6) 1.0
V-8-318-360 engs (.7) 1.2
Add draw test if performed.

Starter, R&R and Recondition
Six(1.8) 2.7
V-8-318-360 engs (1.9) 2.8
Renew field coils add 5
Add draw test if performed.

Starter Drive, Renew
Includes: R&R starter.
Six(1.1) 1.5
V-8-318-360 engs (1.2) 1.7

Starter Solenoid, Renew
Includes: R&R starter.
Six(1.1) 1.5
V-8-318-360 engs (1.2) 1.7

Starter Relay, Renew
All models (.3) 5

Battery Cables, Renew
All models-positive (.4) 6
ground (.3) 4
starter to relay (.3) 5

LABOR 6 BRAKE SYSTEM 6 LABOR

(Factory Time) Chilton Time

Brakes, Adjust (Minor)
Includes: Adjust brakes, fill master cylinder.
two wheels 5
four wheels 8

Brake Pedal Free Play, Adjust
All models 4

Bleed Brakes (Four Wheels)
Includes: Fill master cylinder.
All models (.4) 6

Brake Drum and Hub Assy., Renew
Includes: Repack and/or renew wheel bearings.
front-one (1.0) 1.6
rear-one (.8) 1.4
w/Dual rear whls add 3

Rear Brake Drum, Renew (One)
All models
semi-floating axle (.3) 6
full floating axle (1.8) 2.3
w/Dual rear whls add (.2) 3

Brake System Indicator Switch, Renew
All models (.3) 5

Brake Shoes and/or Pads, Renew
Includes: Install new or exchange shoes or pads. Service adjusters. Adjust service and hand brake. Bleed system.
front-disc (.6) 1.2
rear-drum
semi-floating axle (.7) 1.4
full floating axle (1.5) 2.5
All four wheels
semi-floating axle 2.5
full floating axle 4.4
Resurface brake rotor add, each 1.0
Resurface brake drum add, each 6

BRAKE HYDRAULIC SYSTEM

Wheel Cylinder, Renew (Disc Brakes)
rear-one (1.1) 1.5
both (2.1) 2.9
w/Dual rear whls add 3

Wheel Cylinder, R&R and Recondition (Disc Brakes)
Includes: Hone cylinder, bleed brake system.
rear-one (1.4) 1.8
both (2.7) 3.5
w/Dual rear whls add 3

Brake Hose, Renew (Flex)
Includes: Bleed brake system.
front-one (.4) 6
rear (.5) 7

COMBINATIONS

Add to Brakes, Renew
See Machine Shop Operations

(Factory Time) Chilton Time

RENEW WHEEL CYLINDER
Each (.3) 4

REBUILD WHEEL CYLINDER
Each 6

RENEW BRAKE HOSE
Each (.4) 5

REBUILD CALIPER ASSEMBLY
Each (.4) 6

RENEW BRAKE DRUM
Front
Each 3
Rear
Full Floating Axle-each 3
Semi-FLoating Axle-each 1.0

RENEW DISC BRAKE ROTOR
Each (.3) 4

RENEW REAR WHEEL GREASE SEALS OR BEARINGS
Full Floating Axle-each 2
Semi-Floating Axle-each 8

RENEW FRONT WHEEL BEARINGS
(One Wheel) one or both
Drum Brakes 2
Disc Brakes 4

FRONT WHEEL BEARINGS, REPACK OR RENEW SEALS
(Both Wheels)
Drum Brakes 4
Disc Brakes 8

(Factory Time) Chilton Time

Master Cylinder, Renew
Includes: Bleed brake system.
Cast Iron (.4) 8
Aluminum
w/Manual brks (.6) 1.0
w/Power brks (.4) 8

Master Cylinder, R&R and Recondition
Includes: Bleed brake system.
Cast Iron 1.5
Aluminum
w/Manual brks 1.7
w/Power brks 1.5

Brake System Combination Valve, Renew
Includes: Bleed brake system.
B-PB-CB models (.9) 1.3
All other models (.8) 1.2

POWER BRAKES

Power Brake Unit, Renew
All models (.5) 1.1
w/A.C. add (.1) 3

Power Brake Check Valve, Renew
All models (.2) 4

Power Brake Vacuum Hose, Renew
All models (.3) 4

DISC BRAKES

Brake Shoes and/or Pads, Renew
Includes: Install new or exchange shoes or pads. Service adjusters. Adjust service and hand brake. Bleed system.
front-disc (.6) 1.2
rear-drum
semi-floating axle (.7) 1.4
full floating axle (1.5) 2.5
All four wheels
semi-floating axle 2.5
full floating axle 4.4
Resurface brake rotor add, each 1.0
Resurface brake drum add, each 6

Disc Brake Pads, Renew
Includes: Install new disc brake pads only.
All models (.6) 1.2

Disc Brake Rotor (w/Hub), Renew (One)
Includes: Repack and/or renew bearings.
2 WD
All models (.8) 1.4
4 WD
44 FBJ front axle (1.1) 2.0
60 F front axle (.9) 1.7

Disc Brake Caliper, Renew (One)
Includes: Bleed front brake lines only.
All models (.5) 1.0

LABOR 6 BRAKE SYSTEM 6 LABOR

(Factory Time) Chilton Time

Disc Brake Caliper, R&R and Recondition (One)
Includes: Renew parts as required, bleed front brake lines only.
All models (.8) 1.6

PARKING BRAKE

Parking Brake, Adjust
All models (.3) 5

Parking Brake Lever Assembly, Renew
All models (.6) 9

Parking Brake Cables, Renew
Front
All models (.6) 8

Intermediate
All models (.3) 5
Rear
2 wd-each (.6) 8
4 wd-each (1.0) 1.4
w/Dual rear whls add 3

LABOR 7 COOLING SYSTEM 7 LABOR

(Factory Time) Chilton Time

Winterize Cooling System
Includes: Run engine to check for leaks, tighten all hose connections. Test radiator and pressure cap, drain radiator and engine block. Add anti-freeze and refill coolant.
All models 5

Thermostat, Renew
All models (.5) 8
w/A.C. add (.3) 3

Radiator Assembly, R&R or Renew
B-PB-CB Models (1.0) 1.5
All other models (.7) 1.3
w/A.C. add (.4) 5
w/A.T. add (.1) 2

ADD THESE OPERATIONS TO RADIATOR R&R

Boil & Repair 1.5
Rod Clean 1.9
Repair Core 1.3
Renew Tank 1.6
Renew Trans. Oil Cooler 1.9
Recore Radiator 1.7

Radiator Hoses, Renew
All models-upper (.3) 5
lower (.4) 6
by-pass (.5) 7

Fan Belt, Renew
All models (.3) 5
w/Air inj add (.1) 1

Fluid Fan Drive Unit, Renew
B-PB-CB Models
w/225-318-360 engs (.8) 1.1
All other models
w/225-318-360 engs (.5) 7

Idler Pulley, Renew
All models (.3) 5

Fan Pulley, Renew
All models (.3) 5
w/A.C. add (.3) 3

Coolant Reserve Tank, Renew
All models (.2) 3

Water Pump, Renew
Six–1984-88
B-PB-CB Models (.9) 1.4
D-AD-PD Models (.7) 1.3
AW-PW-W Models (1.0) 1.6
w/A.C. add (.3) 3
V-8–318-360 engs
B-PB-CB Models
1984-88
wo/A.C. (1.3) 1.8
w/A.C. (1.8) 2.6
w/P.S. add (.2) 2
w/100 Amp alt add (.6) 6
AD-PD-D-W Models
1984-88 (1.1) 1.5
w/A.C. add (.4) 6
w/P.S. add (.2) 2
w/Air inj add (.2) 2

Water Jacket Expansion Plugs, Renew Engine Block
Six–All models
left side-one (1.9) 2.3
V-8–318-360 engs
All models
front-right or left-one (.6) 1.1
center-right or left-one (.6) 1.1
rear-right side (.5) 1.0
rear-left side (.8) 1.2

Water Jacket Expansion Plugs, Renew Cylinder Head
V-8–318-360 engs
front-one-all models (.3) 6
Rear-one
B-PB-CB Models (.3) 6
All other models (3.1) 4.2

Temperature Gauge (Engine Unit), Renew
All models (.3) 5

Temperature Gauge (Dash Unit), Renew
1984-88 (.6) 1.1

Heater Core, R&R or Renew
Without Air Conditioning
Front
B-PB-CB Models
1984-88 (.7) 1.6
All other models
1984-88 (1.3) 2.2
Rear
1984-88-All models (.8) 1.5
With Air Conditioning
Front
B-PB-CB Models
1984-88 (2.7) *5.0
All other models
1984-88 (2.1) *4.0
Rear
1984-88-All models (1.5) *3.0
*Includes Recharge A.C. System.

ADD THESE OPERATIONS TO HEATER CORE R&R

Boil & Repair 1.2
Repair Core 9
Recore 1.2

Heater Water Valve, Renew
All models
w/Heater (.4) 7
w/A.C. (.5) 8

Heater Hoses, Renew
All models-one or both (.4) 6

Heater Blower Motor, Renew
Front
1984-88-All models (.5) 9
Rear
1984-88-All models (.4) 9

Heater Blower Motor Resistor, Renew
All models (.3) 5

Heater Blower Motor Switch, Renew
B-PB-CB Models
1984-88 (.4) 6
All other models
1984-88 (.4) 6

Heater Temperature Control Assembly, Renew
All models (.5) 8

LABOR 8 EXHAUST SYSTEM 8 LABOR

(Factory Time) Chilton Time

Muffler, Renew
All models (.7) 1.1

Tail Pipe, Renew
All models (.4) 7

Exhaust Pipe, Renew
Six(.6) 1.0
V-8–318-360 engs (.8) 1.2

Exhaust Pipe Extension, Renew
All models (.7) 1.1

Catalytic Converter, Renew
All models (.6) 1.1

Catalytic Converter Heat Shield, Renew
upper (.6) 9
lower (.2) 4
intermediate (.2) 5

Exhaust Manifold Heat Control Valve, Recondition
Six(2.7) 3.4
w/A.C. add (.3) 3
V-8–318-360 engs (1.2) 1.9

LABOR 8 EXHAUST SYSTEM 8 LABOR

(Factory Time) Chilton Time

Intake and Exhaust Manifold Gaskets, Renew
Six
B-PB-CB Models (2.0)................ 3.0
All other models (1.8).................... 2.8
w/A.C. add (.4)................................ .4
Renew manif add 5

Exhaust Manifold or Gaskets, Renew
Six
B-PB-CB Models
1984-88 (2.1)................................ 2.7
D-AD-PD Models
1984-88 (1.9)................................ 2.5
W-AW-PW Models
1984-88 (1.9)................................ 2.5
V-8–1984-88-318-360 engs
right side (.5) 1.1
left side (.7)................................ 1.3

COMBINATIONS

Muffler, Exhaust and Tail Pipe, Renew
Six... 1.6
V-8 .... 1.8

Muffler and Tail Pipe, Renew
All models.................................... 1.2

LABOR 9 FRONT SUSPENSION 9 LABOR

(Factory Time) Chilton Time

Note: On all front suspension operations alignment charges must be added if performed. Time given does not include alignment.

Check Alignment of Front End
All models..................................... .8
Note: Deduct if alignment is performed.

Toe-In, Adjust
All models..................................... .7

Align Front End
Includes: Adjust front wheel bearings.
All models (1.0) 1.5

Wheels, Balance
one.. .5
each adtnl...................................... .3

Front Wheel Bearings, Clean and Repack (Both Wheels)
All models
w/Drum Brakes.......................... 1.0
w/Disc Brakes........................... 1.5
w/4 wd.. 2.0

Front Wheel Bearings and Cups, Renew (One Wheel)
Drum Brakes (.6)......................... .9
Disc Brakes
w/2 wd (.7)............................ 1.1
w/4 wd (1.2)........................... 1.7

Front Wheel Grease Seals, Renew (One Wheel)
All models
w/2 wd (.6) 8
w/4 wd (1.1) 1.5

Front Shock Absorbers, Renew
1984-88–one (.3)........................... .6
both (.5) 9

Steering Knuckle, Renew (One)
w/2 WD
1984-88 (1.1)................................. 1.7
w/4 WD
1984-88
w/44 FBJ Axle (1.5) 2.1
w/60 F Axle (1.2)...................... 1.8

Lower Control Arm, Renew (One)
Add alignment charges.
1984-88 (1.3).................................. 1.9

Lower Ball Joint, Renew (One)
Add alignment charges.
1984-88
w/2 wd (1.4) 2.0
w/4 wd (1.9) 2.7

Lower Control Arm Strut Bushings, Renew (One Side)
Add alignment charges.
1984-88 (.3).................................... .6

Lower Control Arm Bushings, Renew (One Side)
Add alignment charges.
1984-88 (1.5)................................ 2.3

Upper Control Arm, Renew (One)
Includes: Align front end.
1984-88 (1.9)................................ 2.7

Upper Ball Joint, Renew (One)
Add alignment charges.
1984-88
w/2 wd (.9) 1.4
w/44 FBJ Axle (2.0) 3.2
w/60 F Axle (1.8)...................... 3.0

Upper Control Arm Bushings, Renew (One Side)
Includes: Align front end.
1984-88 (1.8)................................ 2.6

Front Sway Bar Bushings, Renew (One or All)
D-AD-PD 150
D-RD 250
D350-450 models (.6) 8
All other models (.4).................. .6

Front Sway Bar, Renew
All models (.4) 6

Front Spring, Renew (One)
Coil
1984-88 (1.0)................................ 1.4
Leaf
1984-88 (.7).................................. 1.1

Front Spring Shackle, Renew (One)
Includes: Renew bushings.
1984-88
right side (.7) 1.0
left side (.5)................................ .8

FOUR WHEEL DRIVE

Front Axle Shaft, R&R or Renew (One or Both–One Side)
1984-88
44 FBJ Axle (1.2)........................ 1.8
60 F Axle (1.3)........................... 1.9
Recond U-Joint add-each 2

Front Axle Inner Oil Seals, Renew (Both Sides)
1984-88
44 FBJ Axle (4.1)........................ 6.0
60 F Axle (3.5)........................... 5.0

Front Axle Shaft Spindle, Renew
All models
44 FBJ Axle (.9)........................ 1.3
60F Axle (.8).............................. 1.2

Locking Hub Assy., Renew or Recondition
All models
44 FBJ Axle
Spicer (.5)................................ .9
Auto (.4)................................... .8
60F Axle
Dualmatic (.2) 5

Vacuum Shift Motor, Renew
All models (.2) 3

Inner Axle Shaft or Bearing, Renew
Includes: Renew shift collar.
All models (.9) 1.2

Intermediate Axle Shaft, Renew
Includes: Renew inner and outer bearings and seal.
All models (.7) 1.0

Drive Pinion Oil Seal, Renew
1984-88 (.5).................................... .9

Front Axle Housing Cover and/or Gasket, Renew or Reseal
All models (.4) 8

Front Drive Shaft, Renew (Transfer Case To Front Axle)
1984-88 (.4).................................... .7
w/Skid plate add (.3)....................... .3

Front Drive Shaft Universal Joint, Renew At Transfer Case
Dana-CV Type (.8)...................... 1.3
Saginaw-CV Type (1.3) 2.0
At Front Axle(.6) 1.0

Front Axle Shaft Outer Oil Seal, Renew
44 FBJ Axle-one (.7).................. 1.0
60 F Axle-one (.9)....................... 1.2

Front Axle Assy., R&R or Renew
Includes: Renew oil seals, transfer axle shafts and brake assemblies.
All models
44 FBJ Axle (3.8)........................ 5.6
60 F Axle (3.7)........................... 5.5
Renew axle shafts add-each 5

Differential Side Bearings, Renew
Includes: R&R ring and pinion, if necessary. Renew axle inner oil seals and adjust side bearing preload and backlash.
All models
44 FBJ Axle (5.5)........................ 8.1
60 F Axle (4.9)........................... 7.2

Differential Case, Renew
Includes: R&R ring and pinion, if necessary. Renew bearings and gears. Renew pinion seal and axle inner oil seals. Adjust backlash.
All models
44 FBJ Axle (5.8)........................ 8.5
60 F Axle (5.4)........................... 7.9

LABOR 9 FRONT SUSPENSION 9 LABOR

(Factory Time) Chilton Time

Differential Side Gears, Renew

Includes: Renew axle inner oil seals if required.

All models

44 FBJ Axle (4.5) 6.6

60 F Axle (3.8) 5.5

Ring Gear and Pinion Set, Renew

Includes: Renew pinion bearing, side bearings and all seals. Make all necessary adjustments.

All models

44 FBJ Axle (6.5) 9.6

60 F Axle (5.8) 8.5

Renew diff case add (.3) 5

LABOR 10 STEERING LINKAGE 10 LABOR

(Factory Time) Chilton Time

Tie Rods or Tie Rod Ends, Renew

Includes: Reset toe-in.

1984-88-each (.7) 1.0

Steering Knuckle Arm, Renew (One)

w/2 wd

1984-88 (1.1) 1.5

w/4 wd

1984-88 (.6) 9

Center Link, Renew

B-PB-CB Models

1984-88 (.6) 8

All other models

1984-88 (.4) 6

Idler Arm, Renew

1984-88-one (.3) 5

both (.5) 7

Pitman Arm, Renew

B-PB-CB Models

1984-88 (.4) 7

All other models

1984-88 (.5) 8

Drag Link, Renew

B-PB-CB models (.3) 6

All other models (.5) 8

LABOR 11 STEERING GEAR 11 LABOR

(Factory Time) Chilton Time

STANDARD STEERING

Steering Gear, Adjust (On Truck)

All models (.9) 1.1

Steering Gear Assembly, Renew

B-PB-CB Models

1984-88 (1.3) 1.9

D-AD-PD-RD Models

1984-88 (.6) 1.2

Steering Gear Assy., R&R and Recondition

Includes: Disassemble, renew necessary parts, reassemble and adjust.

B-PB-CB Models

1984-88 (1.9) 2.9

D-AD-PD-RD Models

1984-88 (1.3) 2.2

Steering Column Mast Jacket, Renew

Does not include painting.

B-PB-CB Models

1984-88

column shift (1.3) 2.0

floor shift (1.1) 1.6

All other models

1984-88

column shift (1.6) 2.4

floor shift (1.1) 1.6

Tilt Column

All models (2.3) 3.3

Upper Mast Jacket Bearing, Renew

All models

w/Std column (.5) 1.0

w/Tilt column (1.1) 1.5

Steering Column Shift Housing, Renew

All models

w/Std column (.9) 1.5

w/Tilt column (2.2) 3.3

Steering Gear Cross Shaft Oil Seal, Renew

All models (.8) 1.4

Steering Wheel, R&R or Renew

All models (.3) 5

POWER STEERING

Trouble Shoot Power Steering

Includes: Test pump and system pressure. Check pounds pull on steering wheel and check for leaks.

All models 5

Power Steering Belt, Renew

All models (.3) 5

w/Air inj add (.1) 1

w/A.C. add (.1) 1

Power Steering Gear Assy., Renew

B-PB-CB Models

1984-88 (1.2) 1.7

All other models

1984-88 (1.1) 1.6

Power Steering Gear, R&R and Recondition

B-PB-CB Models

1984-88 (2.7) 3.9

All other models

1984-88 (2.2) 3.2

Power Steering Gear Assy., Renew (w/ Remanufactured Unit)

B-PB-CB Models

1984-88 (1.2) 1.7

Steering Gear Cross Shaft Oil Seals, Renew (Inner and Outer)

B-PB-CB Models

1984-88 (.9) 1.6

All other models

1984-88 (1.2) 1.9

Gear Control Valve Assy., Renew

B-PB-CB Models

1984-88 (.5) 9

All other models

1984-88 (1.5) 2.2

Pressure Control Valve, Renew

B-PB-CB Models

1984-88 (.4) 8

Power Steering Pump, Test and Renew

Includes: Transfer or renew pulley.

B-PB-CB Models

1984-88 (1.1) 1.5

All other models

1984-88 (.9) 1.4

w/Air inj add (.2) 2

Power Steering Pump, R&R and Recondition

B-PB-CB Models

1984-88 (1.6) 2.5

All other models

1984-88 (1.1) 2.3

w/Air inj add (.2) 2

Pump Flow Control Valve, Test and Clean or Renew

B-PB-CB models (1.1) 1.6

All other models (.9) 1.3

w/Air inj add (.2) 2

Power Steering Pump Reservoir and/or Seals, Renew

B-PB-CB models (.8) 1.1

All other models (.7) 1.0

w/Air inj add (.2) 2

Pump Drive Shaft Oil Seal, Renew

All models (.9) 1.3

w/Air inj add (.2) 2

Power Steering Hoses, Renew

All models

pressure-each (.4) 7

return-each (.3) 6

LABOR 12 CYLINDER HEAD & VALVE SYSTEM 12 LABOR

(Factory Time)	Chilton Time
Compression Test	
Six(.6)	.9
V-8	
318-360 engs (.7)	1.0
Cylinder Head Gasket, Renew	
Includes: Clean gasket surfaces, clean carbon, make all necessary adjustments.	
Six	
B-PB-CB Models	
1984-88 (3.6)	5.0
All other models	
1984-88 (2.5)	4.0
V-8–318-360 engs	
B-PB-CB Models	
1984-88-one (3.7)	4.5
both (4.9)	6.6
All other models	
1984-88-one (3.1)	4.3
both (4.2)	5.9
w/100 Amp alt add (.6)	.6
w/Air inj add (.6)	.6
w/A.C. add (.4)	.4
w/P.S. add (.2)	.2
Cylinder Head, Renew	
Includes: Transfer all parts, reface valves, make all necessary adjustments.	
Six	
B-PB-CB Models	
1984-88 (5.9)	8.2
All other models	
1984-88 (5.0)	7.0
V-8–318-360 engs	
B-PB-CB Models	
1984-88-one (5.0)	6.5
both (7.4)	9.6
All other models	
one (4.2)	6.3
both (6.7)	8.9
w/100 Amp alt add (.6)	.6
w/Air inj add (.6)	.6
w/A.C. add (.4)	.4
w/P.S. add (.2)	.2
Clean Carbon and Grind Valves	
Includes: R&R cylinder heads, clean gasket surfaces, clean carbon, reface valves and seats. Minor tune up.	
Six	
B-PB-CB Models	
1984-88 (5.4)	7.8
All other models	
1984-88 (4.9)	7.8
V-8–318-360 engs	
B-PB-CB Models	
1984-88 (7.0)	10.6

COMBINATIONS

Add to Valve Job

See Machine Shop Operations

GASOLINE ENGINES

(Factory Time)	Chilton Time
DRAIN, EVACUATE AND RECHARGE AIR CONDITIONING SYSTEM	
All Models	1.4
ROCKER ARMS & SHAFT ASSY., DISASSEMBLE AND CLEAN OR RECONDITION	
Six (.5)	.6
V-8-one side (.5)	.6
both sides (.9)	1.1
HYDRAULIC VALVE LIFTERS, DISASSEMBLE AND CLEAN	
Each	.2
DISTRIBUTOR, RECONDITION	
All Models (.7)	1.0
CARBURETOR, RECONDITION	
1 BBL (.9)	1.4
2 BBL (1.1)	1.6
4 BBL (1.6)	2.1
VALVE GUIDES, REAM OVERSIZE	
Each (.2)	.3
VALVES, RECONDITION (ALL)	
Cylinder Head Removed	
Six (2.2)	3.0
V-8 (2.7)	4.0

(Factory Time)	Chilton Time
All other models	
1984-88 (6.2)	9.9
w/100 Amp alt add (.6)	.6
w/Air inj add (.6)	.6
w/A.C. add (.4)	.4
w/P.S. add (.2)	.2
Valves, Adjust	
Six	
B-PB-CB Models (.8)	1.2
All other models (.7)	1.1
Valve Cover Gasket, Renew	
Six	
B-PB-CB Models	
1984-88 (.9)	1.2
All other models	
1984-88 (.8)	1.1

(Factory Time)	Chilton Time
V-8–318-360 engs	
B-PB-CB Models	
1984-88-one (.5)	.8
both (.8)	1.2
All other models	
1984-88-one (.5)	.8
both (.8)	1.2
w/Air inj add (.2)	.2
Valve Push Rod and/or Rocker Arm, Renew	
Six	
B-PB-CB Models	
1984-88-one or all (1.1)	1.7
All other models	
1984-88-one or all (.9)	1.5
V-8–318-360 engs	
B-PB-CB Models	
1984-88-one side (.7)	1.1
both sides (1.0)	2.1
All other models	
1984-88-one side (.6)	.9
both sides (.9)	1.6
w/Air inj add (.5)	.5
Valve Tappets, Renew (SEE NOTE)	
Includes: R&R cylinder head on 6 cyl engine, where required.	
Six	
B-PB-CB Models	
1984-88-one (1.6)	2.1
each adtnl (.1)	.1
All other models	
1984-88-one (1.5)	2.0
each adtnl (.1)	.1
V-8–318-360 engs-all models	
1984-88-one (1.0)	3.1
one-each bank (1.5)	3.6
all-both banks (2.4)	4.4
w/A.C. add (.2)	.2
w/Air add (.2)	.2

NOTE: Factory time for V-8 engines is based on using magnetic tool through push rod opening to remove lifters. Chilton experience finds it better and safer to R&R intake manifold, since the lifters have a tendency to stick in the block and sometimes come apart.

(Factory Time)	Chilton Time
Valve Spring and/or Valve Stem Oil Seals, Renew (Head on Truck)	
Six–1984-88	
All models-one (1.0)	1.4
all (2.6)	3.6
V-8–318-360 engs-all models	
1984-88-one (1.1)	1.5
one-each bank (1.7)	2.4
all-both banks (4.4)	5.2
w/Air add (.2)	.2

LABOR 13 ENGINE ASSEMBLY & MOUNTS 13 LABOR

(Factory Time)	Chilton Time
Engine Assembly, R&R	
Does not include transfer of any parts or equipment.	
Six	
B-PB-CB Models	
1984-88-w/M.T.	8.7
w/A.T.	7.8
All other models	
1984-88-w/M.T.	7.8
w/A.T.	6.6
V-8–318-360 engs	
B-PB-CB Models	
1984-88-w/M.T.	9.6
w/A.T.	9.2
All other models	
1984-88-w/M.T.	7.7
w/A.T.	6.5
w/P.S. add (.2)	.2
w/Skid plate add (.3)	.3
w/Air inj add (.3)	.3
Six–w/A.C. add (1.0)	1.0
V-8–w/A.C. add (1.7)	*1.7

*Includes recharge A.C. system.

(Factory Time)	Chilton Time
(G) Rebuilt Engine Assembly, Renew (w/Cyl. Head(s) and Oil Pan)	
Includes: R&R engine assy. Transfer all component parts not supplied with replacement engine.	
Six	
B-PB-CB models	
1984-88-w/M.T.	11.7
w/A.T.	10.8
All other models	
1984-88-w/M.T.	10.8
w/A.T.	9.6

LABOR 13 ENGINE ASSEMBLY & MOUNTS 13 LABOR

(Factory Time)	Chilton Time
V-8	
318-360 engs	
B-PB-CB models	
1984-88-w/M.T.	12.6
w/A.T.	12.2
All other models	
1984-88-w/M.T.	10.7
w/A.T.	9.5
w/A.C. add	1.0
w/P.S. add	.2
w/Air inj add	.3
w/Skid plate add	.3
w/Air inj add (.3)	.3
Six–w/A.C. add (1.0)	1.0
V-8–w/A.C. add	*1.7

*Includes: Recharge A.C. system.

Short Engine Assy., Renew (w/All Internal Parts Less Cylinder Head(s) and Oil Pan)

Includes: R&R engine, transfer all component parts not supplied with replacement engine. Clean carbon, grind valves. Tune engine.

(Factory Time)	Chilton Time
Six	
B-PB-CB Models	
1984-88-w/M.T. (12.7)	18.5
w/A.T. (11.8)	17.6
All other models	
1984-88-w/M.T. (10.3)	16.6
w/A.T. (9.1)	15.7
V-8–318-360 engs	
B-PB-CB Models	
1984-88-w/M.T. (13.7)	21.0
w/A.T. (12.6)	20.1
All other models	
1984-88-w/M.T. (13.4)	19.2
w/A.T. (12.5)	18.3
w/P.S. add (.2)	.2
w/Skid plate add (.3)	.3
w/Air inj add (.3)	.3
Six–w/A.C. add (1.0)	1.0
V-8–w/A.C. add (1.7)	*1.7

*Includes recharge A.C. system.

Cylinder Block, Renew (w/Pistons and Rings)

Includes: R&R engine, transfer all component parts not supplied with replacement engine, clean carbon, grind valves. Tune engine.

(Factory Time)	Chilton Time
Six	
B-PB-CB Models	
1984-88-w/M.T. (15.5)	22.7
w/A.T. (14.7)	21.8
All other models	
1984-88-w/M.T. (14.6)	21.6
w/A.T. (13.7)	20.7
w/P.S. add (.2)	.2
w/Skid plate add (.3)	.3
w/Air inj add (.3)	.3
Six–w/A.C. add (1.0)	1.0
V-8–w/A.C. add (1.7)	*1.7

*Includes recharge A.C. system.

Engine Assembly, R&R and Recondition

Includes: Rebore block, install new pistons, rings, rod and main bearings. Clean carbon, grind valves. Tune engine.

(Factory Time)	Chilton Time
Six	
B-PB-CB Models	
1984-88-w/M.T. (30.0)	35.2
w/A.T. (29.1)	34.3
All other models	
1984-88-w/M.T. (28.6)	33.0
w/A.T. (27.4)	32.6
V-8–318-360 engs	
B-PB-CB Models	
1984-88-w/M.T. (36.3)	41.5
w/A.T. (35.9)	40.1
All other models	
1984-88-w/M.T. (33.7)	38.9
w/A.T. (32.5)	37.7
w/P.S. add (.2)	.2
w/Skid plate add (.3)	.3
w/Air inj add (.3)	.3
Six–w/A.C. add (1.0)	1.0
V-8–w/A.C. add (1.7)	*1.7

*Includes recharge A.C. system.

Engine Mounts, Renew

(Factory Time)	Chilton Time
Front	
Six–all models	
1984-88-one (.4)	1.0
V-8–318-360 engs	
B-PB-CB Models	
1984-88-one (.9)	1.2
All other models	
1984-88-one (.3)	.5
Rear	
Six–1984-88 (.5)	1.0
V-8	
B-PB-CB Models	
1984-88 (.6)	1.0
All other models	
1984-88 (1.0)	1.4

LABOR 14 PISTONS, RINGS & BEARINGS 14 LABOR

Rings, Renew (See Engine Combinations)

Includes: R&R pistons, remove cylinder top ridge, hone cylinder walls.

(Factory Time)	Chilton Time
Six	
B-PB-CB Models	
1984-88 (6.8)	9.5
All other models	
1984-88 (6.9)	10.1
V-8–318-360 engs	
B-PB-CB Models	
1984-88 (9.6)	13.4
All other models	
1984-88 (9.1)	13.0
w/100 Amp alt add (.6)	.6
w/Air inj add (.6)	.6
w/A.C. add (.2)	.2

Pistons (w/Pin), Renew

Includes: Remove cylinder top ridge, hone cylinder walls, renew connecting rod bearings if required.

(Factory Time)	Chilton Time
Six	
B-PB-CB Models	
1984-88 (8.5)	11.3
All other models	
1984-88 (9.2)	12.0
V-8–318-360 engs	
B-PB-CB Models	
1984-88 (12.1)	15.8
All other models	
1984-88 (10.5)	12.9
w/100 Amp alt add (.6)	.6
w/Air inj add (.6)	.6
w/A.C. add (.2)	.2

COMBINATIONS

Add to Engine Work

See Machine Shop Operations

GASOLINE ENGINES

(Factory Time)	Chilton Time
DRAIN, EVACUATE AND RECHARGE AIR CONDITIONING SYSTEM	
All models	1.4
ROCKER ARMS & SHAFT ASSY., DISASSEMBLE AND CLEAN OR RECONDITION	
Six (.5)	.6
V-8-one side (.5)	.6
both sides (.9)	1.1
HYDRAULIC VALVE LIFTERS, DISASSEMBLE AND CLEAN	
Each	.2
DISTRIBUTOR, RECONDITION	
All Models (.7)	1.0
CARBURETOR, RECONDITION	
1 BBL (.9)	1.4
2 BBL (1.1)	1.6
4 BBL (1.6)	2.1
VALVE GUIDES, REAM OVERSIZE	
Each (.2)	.3
VALVE, RECONDITION (ALL)	
Cylinder Head Removed	
Six (2.2)	3.0
V-8 (2.7)	4.0
DEGLAZE CYLINDER WALLS	
Each (.1)	.2
REMOVE CYLINDER TOP RIDGE	
Each (.1)	.1
PLASTIGAUGE BEARINGS	
Each (.1)	.1
OIL PUMP, RECONDITION	
Six (.2)	.4
V-8 (.2)	.4
OIL FILTER ELEMENT, RENEW	
All Models (.2)	.3

LABOR 14 PISTONS, RINGS & BEARINGS 14 LABOR

(Factory Time)	Chilton Time
Connecting Rod Bearings, Renew	
Six	
B-PB-CB Models	
1984-88–one (1.6)	2.3
all (2.6)	4.5
All other models	
1984-88–one (2.3)	3.3
all (3.3)	5.9
V-8–318-360 engs	
B-PB-CB Models	
1984-88–one (2.4)	3.6
all (3.8)	6.6
All other models	
1984-88–one (1.3)	2.4
all (2.7)	5.1

LABOR 15 CRANKSHAFT & DAMPER 15 LABOR

(Factory Time)	Chilton Time
Crankshaft and Main Bearings, Renew	
Includes: R&R engine assembly, plastigauge all bearings.	
Six	
B-PB-CB Models	
1984-88–w/M.T. (10.1)	13.6
w/A.T. (9.2)	12.7
All other models	
1984-88–w/M.T. (6.6)	10.4
w/A.T. (6.1)	9.6
V-8–318-360 engs	
B-PB-CB Models	
1984-88–w/M.T. (9.6)	14.7
w/A.T. (8.7)	14.2
All other models	
1984-88–w/M.T. (8.4)	12.2
w/A.T. (7.9)	11.0
w/P.S. add (.2)	.2
w/Skid plate add (.3)	.3
V-8–w/A.C. add (1.7)	*1.7
*Includes recharge A.C. system.	
Main Bearings, Renew	
Includes: Plastigauge bearings.	
Six	
B-PB-CB Models	
1984-88–one (2.7)	3.9
all (4.2)	6.0
All other models	
1984-88–one (1.6)	4.0
all (3.2)	5.4
V-8–318-360 engs	
B-PB-CB Models	
1984-88–one (2.6)	3.7
all (3.2)	5.7
All other models	
1984-88–one (1.8)	3.2
all (3.2)	4.5
Rod and Main Bearings, Renew	
Includes: Plastigauge bearings.	
Six	
B-PB-CB Models	
1984-88 (6.0)	7.8
All other models	
1984-88 (4.2)	7.2
V-8–318-360 engs	
B-PB-CB Models	
1984-88 (5.6)	8.1
All other models	
1984-88 (4.5)	6.9
Rear Main Bearing Oil Seals, Renew (Upper & Lower)	
Six	
B-PB-CB Models	
1984-88 (1.4)	2.0
All other models	
1984-88 (1.6)	2.5
V-8–318-360 engs	
B-PB-CB Models	
1984-88 (1.9)	2.7
All other models	
1984-88 (1.4)	2.0
NOTE: Upper seal removed with special tool. If necessary to R&R crankshaft, use Crankshaft and Main Bearings, Renew.	
Vibration Damper, Renew	
Six	
B-PB-CB Models	
1984-88 (.9)	1.4
D-AD-PD Models	
1984-88 (.8)	1.2
W-AW-PW Models	
1984-88 (.8)	1.4
V-8–318-360 engs	
B-PB-CB Models	
1984-88 (.7)	1.3
All other models	
1984-88 (.6)	1.2
w/A.C. add (.2)	.2
w/P.S. add (.1)	.1
Crankshaft Pulley, Renew	
All models	
1984-88 (.5)	.9
w/A.C. add (.2)	.2
w/P.S. add (.1)	.1

LABOR 16 CAMSHAFT & TIMING GEARS 16 LABOR

(Factory Time)	Chilton Time
Timing Chain Case Cover Gasket, Renew	
Six	
All models	
1984-88 (1.4)	2.5
V-8–318-360 engs	
B-PB-CB Models	
1984-88 (2.0)	2.9
All other models	
1984-88 (1.8)	2.6
w/P.S. add (.2)	.2
w/A.C. add (.2)	.2
w/100 Amp alt add (.5)	.5
w/Air inj add (.2)	.2
Timing Chain Case Cover Oil Seal, Renew	
Six	
B-PB-CB Models	
1984-88 (1.1)	1.7
D-AD-PD Models	
1984-88 (.9)	1.2
W-AW-PW Models	
1984-88 (.9)	1.2
V-8–318-360 engs	
All models	
1984-88 (.9)	1.3
w/P.S. add (.2)	.2
w/A.C. add (.4)	.4
Timing Chain or Gear, Renew	
Includes: Renew cover oil seal and crankshaft gear if necessary.	
Six	
1984-88 (2.2)	2.9
V-8–318-360 engs	
B-PB-CB Models	
1984-88 (2.4)	3.5
All other models	
1984-88 (2.3)	3.0
w/P.S. add (.2)	.2
w/A.C. add (.4)	.4
w/100 Amp alt add (.5)	.5
w/Air inj add (.2)	.2
Camshaft, Renew	
Includes: Renew valve tappets and adjust valve clearance when required.	
Six	
All models	
1984-88 (4.4)	6.4
w/A.C. add (.8)	.8
V-8–318-360 engs	
B-PB-CB Models	
1984-88 (5.3)	7.6
All other models	
1984-88 (4.7)	7.1
w/A.C. add (.8)	.8
w/P.S. add (.2)	.2
w/100 Amp alt add (.5)	.5
w/Air inj add (.8)	.8
Camshaft Bearings, Renew	
(Engine Removed and Disassembled)	
All models (2.0)	2.6

LABOR 17 ENGINE OILING SYSTEM 17 LABOR

(Factory Time)	Chilton Time
Oil Pan or Gasket, Renew	
Six	
B-PB-CB Models	
1984-88 (1.1)	1.7
All other models	
1984-88 (1.4)	2.0
V-8-318-360 engs	
B-PB-CB Models	
1984-88 (1.4)	2.0
All other models	
1984-88 (1.0)	1.6
Oil Pump, Renew	
Six	
B-PB-CB models	
1984-88 (.6)	1.2
All other models	
1984-88 (.8)	1.3
V-8-318-360 engs	
B-PB-CB Models	
1984-88 (1.7)	2.3
All other models	
1984-88 (1.1)	1.8
Oil Pump, R&R and Recondition	
Six	
B-PB-CB Models	
1984-88 (.8)	1.5
All other models	
1984-88 (1.4)	1.8
V-8-318-360 engs	
B-PB-CB Models	
1984-88 (2.1)	2.7
All other models	
1984-88 (1.6)	2.2
Pressure Test Engine Bearings (Pan Off)	
All models	1.2
Oil Pressure Gauge (Dash), Renew	
1984-88 (.6)	1.1
Oil Pressure Gauge (Engine), Renew	
All models (.4)	.6
Oil Filter Element, Renew	
All models (.2)	.3

LABOR 18 CLUTCH & FLYWHEEL 18 LABOR

(Factory Time)	Chilton Time
Clutch Pedal Free Play, Adjust	
All models (.3)	.5
Bleed Clutch Hydraulic System	
All models	.4
Clutch Master Cylinder, Renew	
Includes: Bleed system.	
All models (.5)	.8
Recond cyl add	.4
Clutch Slave Cylinder, Renew	
Includes: Bleed system.	
All models (.4)	.6
Recond cyl add	.4
Clutch Assembly, Renew	
4 Speed	
w/2 wheel drive (2.9)	4.1
w/4 wheel drive (3.9)	5.1
w/Skid plate add (.3)	.3
w/P.T.O. add (.3)	.5
Clutch Release Bearing, Renew	
4 Speed	
w/2 wheel drive (2.5)	3.9
w/4 wheel drive (3.5)	4.9
w/Skid plate add (.3)	.3
w/P.T.O. add (.3)	.5
Clutch Release Fork, Renew	
4 Speed	
B-PB-CB Models (.3)	.6
D-AD-PD-RD Models (.8)	1.2
W-AW-PW Models (.4)	.7
Clutch Torque Shaft, Renew	
Includes: Renew bearings.	
B-PB-CB Models (.3)	.6
All other models (.5)	.9
Flywheel Assembly, Renew	
4 Speed	
1984-88	
w/Overdrive (2.8)	3.9
w/NP-435-445 and 2/wd (3.0)	4.2
w/NP-435-445 and 4/wd (4.3)	6.0
Renew ring gear add (.6)	.6
w/Skid plate add (.3)	.3

LABOR 19 STANDARD TRANSMISSION 19 LABOR

(Factory Time)	Chilton Time
Transmission Assy., R&R or Renew	
4 Speed	
O/Drive 4	
B-models (1.4)	2.0
AD-D models (1.6)	2.2
NP-435-445	
w/2 wheel drive (2.2)	3.0
w/4 wheel drive (3.5)	4.9
w/Skid plate add (.3)	.3
w/P.T.O. add (.3)	.5
Renew assy add (.4)	.6
Transmission Assy., R&R and Recondition	
4 Speed	
O/Drive 4	
B-models (4.3)	6.0
AD-D models (4.5)	6.3
NP-435-445	
w/2 wheel drive (5.4)	7.5
w/4 wheel drive (6.4)	8.5
w/Skid plate add (.3)	.3
w/P.T.O. add (.3)	.5
Transmission, Recondition (Off Truck)	
Overdrive 4 (2.9)	3.9
NP-435-445 (2.7)	3.6
Transmission Front Oil Seal, Renew	
Includes: R&R transmission.	
4 Speed	
O/Drive 4	
B-models (1.6)	2.2
AD-D models (1.8)	2.4
NP-435-445	
w/2 wheel drive (2.8)	4.2
w/4 wheel drive (3.8)	5.2
w/Skid plate add (.3)	.3
w/P.T.O. add (.3)	.5
Extension Housing Oil Seal, Renew	
All models (.5)	.7
Speedometer Drive Pinion, Renew	
All models (.3)	.6

LABOR 20 TRANSFER CASE 20 LABOR

(Factory Time)	Chilton Time
Transfer Case Assy., R&R or Renew	
All models (1.3)	1.8
w/Skid plate add (.3)	.3
Transfer Case Assy., R&R and Recondition	
All models	
NP 208 (4.5)	6.6
NP 205 (4.6)	6.7
w/Skid plate add (.3)	.3
Transfer Case Adapter, Renew	
All models (1.5)	2.1
w/Skid plate add (.3)	.3
Transfer Case Adapter Gasket, Renew	
All models (1.2)	1.7
w/Skid plate add (.3)	.3
Transfer Case Shift Lever, Renew	
All models (.2)	.4
Rear Output Shaft Seal, Renew	
All models (1.2)	1.6
Transfer Case Shift Rod, Renew	
All models-one (.3)	.5
both (.4)	.7
Transfer Case Front Yoke, Renew	
All models (.4)	.7

LABOR 20 TRANSFER CASE 20 LABOR

(Factory Time) Chilton Time

Front Output Shaft Bearing and/or Gasket, Renew
All models (1.2) 1.6
w/Skid plate add (.3) 3

Speedometer Drive Pinion, Renew
All models (.8) 1.1

(Factory Time) Chilton Time

Power Take Off Assy., R&R or Renew
1984-88 (1.4) 2.5

Power Take Off Assy., R&R and Recondition
1984-88 (3.1) 4.9

(Factory Time) Chilton Time

Power Take Off Mounting Gasket, Renew
1984-88 (1.3) 2.4

Power Take Off Cover Gasket, Renew
1984-88 (.4) 7

Power Take Off Control Cable, Renew
1984-88 (.6) 1.0

LABOR 21 SHIFT LINKAGE 21 LABOR

(Factory Time) Chilton Time

STANDARD

Shift Linkage, Adjust
All models (.3) 5

Gearshift Lever, Renew
All models
Overdrive (.2) 4
NP435-445 (.5) 7

Gearshift Control Rod and/or Swivels, Renew
All models-one (.3) 4

(Factory Time) Chilton Time

Gearshift Mechanism, Renew (4 Speed)
All models-w/Overdrive (.6) 1.1

AUTOMATIC

Throttle Linkage, Adjust
All models (.3) 5

Gearshift Lever, Renew
All models (.4) 6

(Factory Time) Chilton Time

Gearshift Control Rod, Renew
All models (.4) 6

Gear Selector Indicator, Renew
All models
inst panel mount (.7) 1.0
column mount (.2) 4

Steering Column Shift Housing, Renew
1984-88
w/Std column (.9) 1.5
w/Tilt column (2.2) 3.3

LABOR 23 AUTOMATIC TRANSMISSION 23 LABOR

(Factory Time) Chilton Time

ON TRUCK SERVICES

Drain and Refill Unit
All models 1.0

Oil Pressure Test
Note: Using 3 pressure test points.
All models 1.5

Check Unit For Oil Leaks
Includes: Clean and dry outside of case and run unit to determine point of leak.
All models 1.0

Neutral Safety Switch, Renew
All models (.3) 4

Oil Cooler Lines, Renew
Includes: Cut and form to size.
All models-one (.6) 1.0

Transmission Auxiliary Oil Cooler, Renew
All models (.7) 1.2

Throttle Linkage, Adjust
All models (.3) 5

Kickdown Band, Adjust
All models (.3) 5

Throttle Valve Lever Shaft Seal, Renew
All models (.3) 7

Valve Body Manual Lever Shaft Seal, Renew
All models (.4) 8

Extension Housing Oil Seal, Renew
All models (.5) 1.1

Extension Housing or Adapter Gasket, Renew
All models
w/2 wheel drive (1.4) 2.0
w/4 wheel drive (1.9) 2.5
w/Skid plate add (.3) 3

Governor Assy., R&R or Recondition
Includes: R&R extension housing.
All models
w/2 wheel drive (1.8) 2.5
w/4 wheel drive (2.3) 3.0
w/Skid plate add (.3) 3

(Factory Time) Chilton Time

Parking Lock Sprag, Renew
Includes: R&R extension housing.
All models
w/2 wheel drive (1.3) 2.2
w/4 wheel drive (1.8) 2.4
w/Skid plate add (.3) 3

Output Shaft Bearing and Oil Seal, Renew
Includes: R&R extension housing.
All models
w/2 wheel drive (1.4) 2.3
w/4 wheel drive (1.9) 2.5
w/Skid plate add (.3) 3

Oil Pan Gasket, Renew
All models (.5) 1.0

Oil Filter, Renew
All models (.6) 1.1

Parking Lock Sprag Control Rod, Renew
Includes: R&R oil pan and remove valve body.
All models (.9) 1.5

Accumulator Piston, Renew or Recondition
Includes: R&R oil pan and adjust band.
All models (1.1) 1.7

Kickdown Servo, Renew or Recondition
Includes: R&R oil pan and adjust band.
All models (.9) 1.5

Reverse Servo, Renew or Recondition
Includes: R&R oil pan and adjust band.
All models (.8) 1.4

Valve Body Assembly, Renew
Includes: R&R oil pan and replace filter.
All models (.9) 1.5

Valve Body Assy., R&R and Recondition
Includes: R&R oil pan and replace filter. Disassemble, clean, inspect, free all valves. Replace parts as required.
All models (1.7) 2.4

Bands, Adjust
Includes: R&R oil pan.
All models
reverse & kickdown (.6) 1.2

(Factory Time) Chilton Time

SERVICES REQUIRING R&R

Transmission Assembly, Remove and Reinstall
B-PB-CB Models
1984-88 (2.0) 4.7
D-AD-PD-RD Models
1984-88 (2.3) 5.0
W-AW-PW Models
1984-88 (4.1) 6.9
Renew trans add (.4) 5
Flush converter and lines add (.5) 7
w/Skid plate add (.3) 3

Transmission Assembly, Renew (w/Remanufactured Unit)
Includes: Remove and install all necessary interfering parts. Transfer all parts not supplied with replacement unit. Road test.
B-PB-CB Models
1984-88 (2.3) 5.2
D-AD-PD-RD Models
1984-88 (2.6) 5.5
W-AW-PW Models
1984-88 (4.5) 7.4
Pressure test governor add (.7) 1.1
w/Skid plate add (.3) 3

Transmission Assembly, Reseal
Includes: R&R trans and renew all seals and gaskets.
B-PB-CB Models
1984-88 (4.2) 6.8
D-AD-PD-RD Models
1984-88 (4.5) 7.1
W-AW-PW Models
1984-88 (6.3) 8.9
w/Skid plate add (.3) 3

Transmission and Converter, R&R and Recondition
Includes: Disassemble trans including valve body, clean, inspect and replace parts as required.
B-PB-CB Models
1984-88 (6.5) 11.8
D-AD-PD-RD Models
1984-88 (6.8) 12.1

LABOR 23 AUTOMATIC TRANSMISSION 23 LABOR

(Factory Time) — Chilton Time

W-AW-PW Models
1984-88 (8.6) 13.9
w/Skid plate add (.3) 3
Flush converter and lines add (.5) 7

Torque Converter, Renew
Includes: R&R transmission.
B-PB-CB Models
1984-88 (2.2) 5.1
D-AD-PD-RD Models
1984-88 (2.5) 5.4
W-AW-PW Models
1984-88 (4.3) 7.3
w/Skid plate add (.3) 3

Kickdown Band, Renew
Includes: R&R transmission.
B-PB-CB Models
1984-88 (2.7) 6.1
D-AD-PD-RD Models
1984-88 (3.0) 6.4
W-AW-PW Models
1984-88 (4.8) 8.3
w/Skid plate add (.3) 3

Reverse Band, Renew
Includes: R&R transmission.
B-PB-CB Models
1984-88 (3.1) 6.7
D-AD-PD-RD Models
1984-88 (3.4) 7.0
W-AW-PW Models
1984-88 (5.2) 8.9
w/Skid plate add (.3) 3

Transmission Case, Renew
Includes: R&R transmission.
B-PB-CB Models
1984-88 (3.9) 7.7
D-AD-PD-RD Models
1984-88 (4.2) 8.0
W-AW-PW Models
1984-88 (6.0) 9.9
w/Skid plate add (.3) 3

Front Pump Assembly, Renew or Recondition
Includes: R&R trans, replace reaction shaft if necessary.
B-PB-CB Models
1984-88 (2.6) 5.9
D-AD-PD-RD Models
1984-88 (2.9) 6.2
W-AW-PW Models
1984-88 (4.7) 8.1
w/Skid plate add (.3) 3

Front Pump Oil Seal, Renew
Includes: R&R transmission.
B-PB-CB Models
1984-88 (2.2) 5.1
D-AD-PD-RD Models
1984-88 (2.5) 5.4
W-AW-PW Models
1984-88 (4.3) 7.3
w/Skid plate add (.3) 3

LABOR 25 U-JOINTS & DRIVESHAFT 25 LABOR

(Factory Time) — Chilton Time

Drive Shaft, R&R or Renew
All Models
trans to rear axle (.4) 7
center bearing
to rear axle (.4) 7
transfer case to front axle (.5) 8
transfer case to rear axle (.4) 7
trans to center brg (1.2) 1.7
w/Skid plate add (.3) 3

Universal Joints, Renew or Recondition
Includes: R&R drive shaft.
All Models
Single Piece Shaft
(without center bearing)
trans to rear axle (.6) 9
at rear axle (.5) 8
transfer case to rear axle (.5) 8
transfer case to
rear axle (.9) 1.2
(transfer case to front axle)
Dana CV Type (.8) 1.3
Saginaw CV Type (1.5) 2.0
at front axle (.6) 9

Two Piece Shaft
trans to center brg (.9) 1.2
center brg to rear
axle (.6) 9
at rear axle (.5) 8
w/Skid plate add (.3) 3

Drive Shaft Center Bearing, Renew
Includes: Renew insulator if necessary.
All models (1.1) 1.5

Universal Joint Ball and Socket Assy., Renew
Front shaft-Saginaw
C/V type (1.3) 1.7
w/Skid plate add (.2) 3

Universal Joint Center Yoke or Flange, Renew
Front shaft-Saginaw
C/V type (1.3) 1.7
w/Skid plate add (.2) 3

LABOR 26 REAR AXLE 26 LABOR

(Factory Time) — Chilton Time

Differential, Drain & Refill
All models 6

Rear Axle Housing Cover, Renew or Reseal
All models (.4) 6

Axle Shaft, Renew
Includes: Renew outer oil seal, bearing and gasket on 8³⁄₈ - 9¹⁄₄ axles.
8¹⁄₄ - 8³⁄₈ - 9¹⁄₄ Axles
1984-88-one (.7) 1.0
Spicer 60 - 70 Axle
1984-88-one (.5) 8

Axle Shaft Bearing, Renew
Includes: Renew oil seal.
8¹⁄₄ - 8³⁄₈ - 9¹⁄₄ Axles
1984-88-one (.6) 9

Axle Shaft Oil Seal, Renew
8¹⁄₄ - 8³⁄₈ - 9¹⁄₄ Axles
1984-88-one (.6) 9

Pinion Shaft Oil Seal, Renew
All models (.6) 1.0

Rear Axle Housing, Renew
Includes: Renew pinion oil seal, inner and outer axle shaft or wheel bearing oil seals and gaskets.
8¹⁄₄ - 8³⁄₈ - 9¹⁄₄ Axles
All models (4.2) 6.3
Spicer 60 - 70 Axles
All models (5.7) 8.5

Differential Carrier Assembly, Renew
Note: Assembly includes axle housing.
8¹⁄₄ - 8³⁄₈ - 9¹⁄₄ Axles
All models (2.0) 3.1
Spicer 60 - 70 Axles
All models (3.0) 4.6

Differential Side Bearings, Renew
Includes: Renew pinion oil seal and adjust backlash.
8¹⁄₄ - 8³⁄₈ - 9¹⁄₄ Axles
All models (1.5) 2.5
Spicer 60 - 70 Axles
All models (3.1) 4.6
Renew pinion bearings, add (.9) 1.4

Differential Case, Renew
Includes: Renew ring gear and pinion, bearings and side gears if necessary.
8¹⁄₄ - 8³⁄₈ - 9¹⁄₄ Axles
Std & Sure Grip
All models (3.0) 4.5
Spicer 60 - 70 Axles
All models (3.6) 5.4

Differential Side Gears, Renew
Includes: Renew axle shaft oil seals.
8¹⁄₄ - 8³⁄₈ - 9¹⁄₄ Axles
All models (1.1) 2.0
Spicer 60 - 70 Axles
All models (1.4) 3.0

Ring Gear and Pinion Set, Renew
Includes: Renew wheel bearing or inner axle shaft oil seals, pinion oil seal and gaskets.
8¹⁄₄ - 8³⁄₈ - 9¹⁄₄ Axles
All models (3.7) 7.0
Spicer 60 - 70 Axles
All models (3.7) 7.0
Renew side bearings add (.3) 7

LABOR 27 REAR SUSPENSION 27 LABOR

(Factory Time) Chilton Time

Rear Spring, Renew
All models-one (.5) 9
both (1.0) 1.7
w/Aux. rear spring add,
each (.5) 5
w/Skid plate add (.3) 3

Auxiliary Rear Spring, Renew
All models-one (.7) 1.5

Rear Spring Shackle, Renew
Includes: Renew bushings.
B-PB-CB Models
one (.3) 7
All other models
one (.6) 1.0
w/Skid plate add (.3) 3

Rear Shock Absorbers, Renew
All models-one (.2) 4
both (.4) 6

LABOR 28 AIR CONDITIONING 28 LABOR

(Factory Time) Chilton Time

Note: If more than one item requires replacement where evacuation and discharging the system is already included in the operation, deduct 1.0 hour for each additional item to the times listed.

Drain, Evacuate, Leak Test and Charge System
All models 1.7

Partial Charge
Includes: Leak test.
All models
w/Front unit (.6) 1.1
w/Front and rear unit (.9) 1.4

Performance Test
All models 8

Vacuum Leak Test
All models 9

ON TRUCK SERVICES

Compressor Belt, Renew
B-PB-CB Models (.4) 6
All other models (.3) 5
w/Air inj add (.1) 1
w/P.S. add (.1) 1

Compressor Clutch Field Coil, Renew
Includes: Renew pulley w/Hub, if necessary.
B-PB-CB Models
w/C-171 comp (.5) 9
All other models (.5) 9

Compressor Clutch Assembly, Renew
B-PB-CB Models
w/C-171 comp (.5) 8
All other models (.5) 8

C-171 COMP

Compressor Assembly, Renew
Includes: Transfer parts as required. Pressure test and charge system.
Six
All models (1.8) 3.2
V-8
B-PB-CB models (2.1) 3.5
All other models (1.7) 3.1
w/Rear A.C. add (.3) 3

Compressor Front Cover and/or Seal, Renew
Includes: Pressure test and charge system.
Six
All models (2.2) 3.5
V-8
B-PB-CB models (2.5) 3.8
All other models (2.1) 3.4

Compressor Rear Cover and/or Seal, Renew
Includes: Pressure test and charge system.
Six
All models (2.1) 3.4
V-8
B-PB-CB models (2.4) 3.7
All other models (2.0) 3.3

Compressor Center Seal, Renew
Includes: Pressure test and charge system.
Six
All models (2.3) 3.6
V-8
B-PB-CB models (2.6) 3.9
All other models (2.2) 3.5

Compressor Shaft Gas Seal, Renew
Includes: Pressure test and charge system.
Six
All models (2.2) 3.5
V-8
B-PB-CB models (2.5) 3.8
All other models (2.1) 3.4

Expansion Valve, Renew
Includes: Pressure test and charge system.
B-PB-CB Models
front unit (1.1) 2.0
rear unit (1.9) 2.8
All other models (1.0) 1.9

Receiver Drier, Renew
Includes: Add partial charge, leak test and charge system.
B-PB-CB Models
w/Front unit (1.1) 1.9
w/Front and rear unit (1.5) 2.3
All other models (1.1) 1.9

Low Pressure Cut Off Switch, Renew
Includes: Evacuate and charge system.
B-PB-CB Models
w/Front unit (1.0) 1.8
w/Front and rear unit (1.3) 2.1
All other models (1.0) 1.8

Clutch Cycling (Thermostatic Control) Switch, Renew
All models (.3) 5

Condenser Assembly, Renew
Includes: Add partial charge, leak test and charge system.
B-PB-CB Models
w/Front unit (1.6) 2.5
w/Front and rear unit (1.9) 3.0
All other models (1.2) 2.2
Renew receiver drier add 2

Evaporator Coil, Renew
Includes: Add partial charge, leak test and charge system.
B-PB-CB Models
Front Unit
1984-88 (2.9) 5.4
Front Unit-Front and Rear
Unit Equipped
1984-88 (3.2) 6.0
Rear Unit (1.6) 2.8
All other models (2.3) 4.7

Blower Motor, Renew
B-PB-CB Models
1984-88
Front (.9) 1.5
Rear (.4) 9
All other models
1984-88 (.4) 9

Blower Motor Resistor, Renew
All models (.3) 4

Blower Motor Switch, Renew
All models
Front unit (.5) 9
Rear unit (.3) 6

Temperature Control Assembly, Renew
B-PB-CB Models
1984-88 (.6) 1.0
All other models
1984-88 (.5) 9

A.C. Push Button Vacuum Switch, Renew
All models (.6) 1.0

Air Conditioning Hoses, Renew
Includes: Evacuate and charge system.
SUCTION ASSY
B-PB Models (1.2) *2.0
All other models (1.1) 1.9
DISCHARGE ASSY
All models (1.1) *1.9
REAR UNIT TUBE ASSY
B-PB Models (3.7) 5.0
SUCTION HOSE
Rear unit to rear evap. (1.3) 2.1
DISCHARGE HOSE
Rear unit to rear evap. (1.3) 2.1
SUCTION HOSE
Rear unit to front tube (1.3) 2.1
DISCHARGE HOSE
Rear unit to front tube (1.3) 2.1
*w/Rear A.C. add (.3) 3
Renew receiver drier add 2

LABOR 30 HEAD AND PARKING LAMPS 30 LABOR

(Factory Time) Chilton Time

Aim Headlamps
two 4
four 6

Headlamp Sealed Beam Bulb, Renew
Does not include aim headlamps.
All models-one (.3) 3

Parking Lamp or Turn Signal Lamp Lens or Bulb, Renew
All models-one (.2) 3

Tail and Stop Lamp Lens or Bulb, Renew
All models-one (.2) 3

Reflectors, Renew
All models-one (.2) 2

LABOR 31 WINDSHIELD WIPER & SPEEDOMETER 31 LABOR

(Factory Time) Chilton Time

Windshield Wiper Motor, Renew
B-PB-CB Models
1984-88 (.8) 1.2
All other models
1984-88 (.6) 1.1

Windshield Wiper Pivot, Renew
All models-one (.5) 7

Wiper Link, Renew
All models-one (.5) 8

Wiper Switch, Renew
B-PB-CB Models
1984-86 (.3) 7
1987-88
std colm (.8) 1.2
tilt colm (1.2) 1.6
All other models
1984-88 (.4) 6

Wiper Delay Control Module, Renew
All models (.3) 5

Windshield Washer Pump, Renew
All models (.3) 5

Speedometer Head, R&R or Renew
B-PB-CB Models
1984-88 (.3) 6
All other models
1984-88 (.4) 7
Reset odometer add 2

Speedometer Cable and Casing, Renew
All models-each (.5) 7

LABOR 32 LIGHT SWITCHES & WIRING 32 LABOR

(Factory Time) Chilton Time

Headlamp Switch, Renew
1984-88 (.4) 7

Headlamp Dimmer Switch, Renew
All models (.3) 5

Back-Up Lamp Switch, Renew
(w/Manual Trans)
All models (.3) 4

Neutral Safety Switch, Renew
All models (.3) 4

Stop Light Switch, Renew
All models (.3) 4
w/Cruise control add (.1) 1

Turn Signal Switch, Renew
1984-88
w/Std column (.5) 9
w/Tilt column (.9) 1.4

Turn Signal or Hazard Warning Flasher, Renew
All models (.2) 3

LABOR 34 CRUISE CONTROL 34 LABOR

(Factory Time) Chilton Time

Cruise Control Servo, Renew
All models (.2) 6

Cruise Control Cable, Renew
All models (.3) 5

Cruise Control Vacuum Hoses, Renew
All models (.2) 3

Cruise Control Switch (Turn Signal Lever), Renew
1984-88
w/Std column (.5) 9
w/Tilt column (.9) 1.4

Cruise Control Cut-Off Safety Switch, Renew
All models (.3) 4

Dodge Rampage/Plymouth Scamp—Front Drive Pick-Ups

GROUP INDEX

ALPHABETICAL INDEX

LABOR — SERVICE BAY OPERATIONS — LABOR

(Factory Time) Chilton Time

COOLING

Winterize Cooling System
Includes: Run engine to check for leaks, tighten all hose connections. Test radiator and pressure cap, drain radiator and engine block. Add anti-freeze and refill system.
All models 5

Thermostat, Renew
All models (.4) 6

Radiator Hoses, Renew
All models-upper (.3) 4
lower (.5) 6

Drive Belt, Adjust
All models-one 3
each adtnl 1

FUEL

Carburetor Air Cleaner, Service
All models (.3) 3

Carburetor Float Level, Adjust
All models (.7) 1.1

Fuel Filter, Renew
All models
in line (.2) 3
in tank (.5) 8

BRAKES

Brakes, Adjust (Minor)
Includes: Adjust brakes, fill master cylinder.
two wheels 4

Bleed Brakes (Four Wheels)
Includes: Fill master cylinder.
All models (.4) 6

Parking Brake, Adjust
All models (.3) 4

LUBRICATION SERVICE

Lubricate Chassis, Change Oil & Filter
Includes: Inspect and correct all fluid levels.
All models 6
Install grease fittings add 1

Lubricate Chassis
Includes: Inspect and correct all fluid levels.
All models 4
Install grease fittings add 1

Engine Oil & Filter, Change
Includes: Inspect and correct all fluid levels.
All models 4

WHEELS

Wheel, Renew
one 5

Wheel, Balance
one 3
each adtnl 2

Wheels, Rotate (All)
All models 5

ELECTRICAL

Aim Headlamps
All models (.3) 4

Headlamp Sealed Beam Bulb, Renew
Does not include aim headlamps.
All models-each (.2) 3

Battery Cables, Renew
All models-ground (.2) 2
positive (.5) 6

Headlamp Switch, Renew
All models (.3) 4

Headlamp Dimmer Switch, Renew (Column Mounted)
All models (.3) 6

Stop Light Switch, Renew
All models (.3) 4
w/Cruise control add (.1) 1

Back-Up Lamp Switch, Renew (w/Manual Trans)
All models (.2) 4

Neutral Safety Switch, Renew
All models (.3) 4

Turn Signal Switch, Renew
All models (.5) 1.0

License Lamp Lens, Renew
All models (.2) 2

Tail Lamp Lens, Renew
All models-one (.2) 3

Side Marker Lamp Assy., Renew
All models (.2) 3

License Lamp Assembly, Renew
All models (.2) 2

Turn Signal or Hazard Warning Flasher, Renew
All models (.2) 3

Horn Relay, Renew
All models (.2) 3

Horns, Renew
All models-one (.2) 4

LABOR — 1 TUNE UP 1 — LABOR

(Factory Time) Chilton Time

Compression Test
All models 6

Engine Tune Up, (Electronic Ignition)
Includes: Test battery and clean connections. Tighten manifold and carburetor mounting bolts. Check engine compression, clean and adjust or renew spark plugs. Test resistance of spark plug cables. Inspect distributor cap and rotor. Adjust air gap. Check vacuum advance operation. Reset ignition timing. Adjust idle mixture and idle speed. Service air cleaner. Inspect and adjust drive belts. Inspect choke operation and adjust or free up. Check operation of EGR valve.
All models 1.5

LABOR — 2 IGNITION SYSTEM 2 — LABOR

(Factory Time) Chilton Time

Spark Plugs, Clean and Reset or Renew
All models (.5) 6

Ignition Timing, Reset
All models (.3) 4

Spark Control Computer, Renew
All models (.3) 1.0

Distributor, Renew
Includes: Reset ignition timing.
All models (.4) 6

Distributor, R&R and Recondition
Includes: Reset ignition timing.
All models (.9) 1.5

Distributor Pick-Up Plate and Coil Assy., Renew
Includes: R&R distributor and reset ignition timing.
All models (.5) 8

Distributor Pick-Up Plate and Coil Assy., Renew (Hall Effect)
Does not require R&R of distributor.
All models (.3) 6

Vacuum Advance Unit, Renew
Includes: R&R distributor and reset ignition timing.
All models (.6) 9

Distributor Cap, Renew
All models (.2) 4

Ignition Coil, Renew
All models (.2) 4

Ignition Cables, Renew
All models (.2) 5

Ignition Switch, Renew
All models (.4) 8

Ignition Key Buzzer Switch, Renew
All models (.3) 5

Ignition Key Warning Buzzer, Renew
All models (.2) 3

Ignition Lock Housing, Renew
Does not include painting.
All models (.9) 1.6

LABOR 3 FUEL SYSTEM 3 LABOR

(Factory Time) Chilton Time

Fuel Pump, Test
Includes: Disconnect line at carburetor, attach pressure gauge.
All models 3

Carburetor Air Cleaner, Service
All models (.3) 3

Heated Air Door Sensor, Renew
All models (.2) 3

Automatic Choke, Renew
All models (.7) 1.0

Choke Vacuum Kick, Adjust
All models (.2) 3

Choke Vacuum Kick Diaphragm, Renew
All models (.2) 4

Accelerator Pump, Renew
All models (.4) 8

Needle Valve and Seat, Renew
Includes: Adjust float level and idle speed and mixture.
All models (.7) 1.1

Carburetor Assembly, Renew
Includes: All necessary adjustments.
All models (.8) 1.2

Carburetor, R&R and Clean or Recondition
Includes: All necessary adjustments.
All models (1.6) 2.4

Fuel Filter, Renew
All models
in line (.2) 3
in tank (.5) 8

Fuel Pump, Renew
All models (.5) 9
Add pump test if performed.

Fuel Tank, Renew
Includes: Drain and refill tank.
All models (.9) 1.5

Fuel Gauge (Dash), Renew
All models (.2) 5

Fuel Gauge (Tank), Renew
All models (.6) 1.0

Intake Manifold, Renew
All models (2.0) 3.7

Intake and Exhaust Manifold Gaskets, Renew
All models (1.9) 3.5

LABOR 3A EMISSION CONTROLS 3A LABOR

(Factory Time) Chilton Time

AIR INJECTION SYSTEM

Air Pump, Renew
All models (.5) 7

Injection Tube and Check Valve Assy., Renew
All models
ex manif mount (.5) 8
to conv
one or both (.4) 6

Air Pump Diverter/Switching Valve, Renew
All models (.4) 7

Aspirator, Renew
All models (.2) 4

Aspirator Tube, Renew
All models (.7) 1.0

Orifice Spark Advance Control Valve, Renew
All models (.3) 5

EVAPORATIVE EMISSION

Vapor Canister, Renew
All models (.4) 6

Vapor Canister Filter, Renew
All models (.2) 3

CRANKCASE EMISSION

Crankcase Vent Valve, Renew
All models (.2) 3

Crankcase Vent Hose, Renew
All models-one (.2) 2

E.G.R. SYSTEM

E.G.R. Valve, Renew
All models (.6) 8

E.G.R. Coolant Valve, Renew (CCEGR)
All models-one (.3) 5

Coolant Controlled Engine Vacuum Switch, Renew (CCEVS)
All models (.3) 5

HEATED INLET AIR SYSTEM

Carburetor Air Cleaner, Service
All models (.3) 3

Heated Air Door Sensor, Renew
All models-one (.2) 3

EFC SYSTEM

Oxygen Sensor, Renew
All models (.2) 4

LABOR 4 ALTERNATOR AND REGULATOR 4 LABOR

(Factory Time) Chilton Time

Alternator Circuits, Test
Includes: Test battery, regulator and alternator output.
All models 6

Alternator Assy., Renew
Includes: Transfer pulley if required.
All models (.8) 1.2
w/A.C. add (.5) 5
Add circuit test if performed.

Alternator, R&R and Recondition
Includes: Test and disassemble, renew parts as required.
All models (1.5) 2.1
w/A.C. add (.5) 5

Alternator Front Bearing or Retainer, Renew
Includes: R&R alternator.
All models (.8) 1.3
w/A.C. add (.5) 5
Renew rear brg. add 2

Alternator Regulator, Test and Renew
All models
External type (.2) 6

Alternator Gauge, Renew
All models (.2) 5

Instrument Cluster Voltage Limiter, Renew
All models (.2) 5

LABOR 5 STARTING SYSTEM 5 LABOR

(Factory Time) Chilton Time

Starter Draw Test (On Truck)
All models 3

Starter Assembly, Renew
Includes: Test starter relay, starter solenoid and amperage draw.
All models (1.0) 1.6

Starter, R&R and Recondition
Includes: Test relay, starter solenoid and amperage draw. Turn down armature.
All models (1.5) 2.5
Renew field coils add (.4) 5

Starter Drive, Renew
Includes: R&R starter.
All models (1.6) 2.0

Starter Solenoid, Renew
Includes: R&R starter.
All models (1.1) 1.8

LABOR 5 STARTING SYSTEM 5 LABOR

	(Factory Time)	Chilton Time
Starter Relay, Renew		
All models	(.2)	.3
Neutral Safety Switch, Renew		
All models	(.3)	.4
Ignition Switch, Renew		
All models	(.4)	.8
Battery Cables, Renew		
All models-ground	(.2)	.2
positive	(.5)	.6

LABOR 6 BRAKE SYSTEM 6 LABOR

	(Factory Time)	Chilton Time
Brake Pedal Free Play, Adjust		
All models		.3
Brakes, Adjust (Minor)		
Includes: Adjust brakes, fill master cylinder.		
two wheels		.4
Bleed Brakes (Four Wheels)		
Includes: Fill master cylinder.		
All models	(.4)	.6
Brake Shoes and/or Pads, Renew		
Includes: Install new or exchange shoes or pads, adjust service and hand brake. Bleed system.		
All models		
Front-disc	(.5)	.8
Rear-drum	(.8)	1.5
All four wheels		2.2
Resurface rotor, add-each		.9
Resurface brake drum, add-each		.5
Rear Brake Drum, Renew		
All models-one	(.5)	.6

BRAKE HYDRAULIC SYSTEM

	(Factory Time)	Chilton Time
Wheel Cylinder, Renew		
Includes: Bleed system.		
All models-one	(.7)	1.1
both	(1.3)	2.1
Wheel Cylinder, R&R and Recondition		
Includes: Hone cylinder and bleed system.		
All models-one		1.2
both		2.3
Brake Hose, Renew (Flex)		
Includes: Bleed system.		
All models-front-one	(.4)	.8
rear-one	(.4)	.8
Master Cylinder, Renew		
Includes: Bleed complete system.		
All models	(.5)	.9
Master Cylinder, R&R and Recondition		
Includes: Bleed complete system.		
All models		1.6

COMBINATIONS

Add to Brakes, Renew

See Machine Shop Operations

	(Factory Time)	Chilton Time
RENEW WHEEL CYLINDER		
Each	(.3)	.3
REBUILD WHEEL CYLINDER		
Each		.4
REBUILD CALIPER ASSEMBLY		
Each		.5
RENEW MASTER CYLINDER		
All models	(.5)	.6
REBUILD MASTER CYLINDER		
All models		.8
RENEW BRAKE HOSE		
Each	(.3)	.3
RENEW REAR WHEEL GREASE SEALS		
One side	(.2)	.3
RENEW BRAKE DRUM		
Each	(.3)	.3
RENEW DISC BRAKE ROTOR		
Each	(.2)	.2
DISC BRAKE ROTOR STUDS, RENEW		
Each		.1

	(Factory Time)	Chilton Time
Master Cylinder Reservoir, Renew		
Includes: Bleed complete system.		
All models	(.6)	1.0
Brake System Combination Valve, Renew		
Includes: Bleed complete system.		
All models	(.7)	1.0
Load Sensing Proportioning Valve, Renew		
Includes: Adjust valve and bleed brakes.		
All models	(.7)	1.1

POWER BRAKES

	(Factory Time)	Chilton Time
Brake Booster Assembly, Renew		
All models	(.8)	1.2
Brake Booster Check Valve, Renew		
All models	(.2)	.2

DISC BRAKES

	(Factory Time)	Chilton Time
Brake Shoes and/or Pads, Renew		
Includes: Install new or exchange shoes or pads, adjust service and hand brake. Bleed system.		
All models		
Front-disc	(.5)	.8
Rear-drum	(.8)	1.5
All four wheels		2.2
Resurface rotor, add-each		.9
Resurface brake drum, add-each		.5
Disc Brake Rotor w/Hub, Renew		
All models-each	(1.0)	1.4
Disc Brake Rotor, Renew		
All models	(.3)	.6
Caliper Assembly, Renew		
Includes: Bleed system.		
All models-each	(.5)	.9
Caliper Assembly, R&R and Recondition		
Includes: Bleed system.		
All models-each	(.8)	1.4

PARKING BRAKE

	(Factory Time)	Chilton Time
Parking Brake, Adjust		
All models	(.3)	.4
Parking Brake Warning Lamp Switch, Renew		
All models	(.2)	.3
Parking Brake Lever, Renew		
All models	(.4)	.7
Parking Brake Cables, Renew		
All models-front	(.7)	1.0
rear-each	(.4)	.6

LABOR 7 COOLING SYSTEM 7 LABOR

	(Factory Time)	Chilton Time
Winterize Cooling System		
Includes: Run engine to check for leaks, tighten all hose connections. Test radiator and pressure cap, drain radiator and engine block. Add anti-freeze and refill system.		
All models		.5
Thermostat, Renew		
All models	(.4)	.6
Radiator Assembly, R&R or Renew		
Includes: Drain and refill coolant.		
All models	(.5)	.9
w/A.T. add	(.1)	.1

ADD THESE OPERATIONS TO RADIATOR R&R

	(Factory Time)	Chilton Time
Boil & Repair		1.5
Rod Clean		1.9
Repair Core		1.3
Renew Tank		1.6
Renew Trans. Oil Cooler		1.9
Recore Radiator		1.7
Coolant Reserve Tank, Renew		
All models	(.5)	.7
Radiator Fan Motor, Renew		
All models	(.4)	.5
Radiator Fan Motor Relay, Renew		
All models	(.2)	.3
Radiator Fan Switch, Renew		
All models	(.3)	.6
Radiator Hoses, Renew		
All models-upper	(.3)	.4
lower	(.5)	.6
Water Pump, Renew		
Includes: Drain and refill coolant.		
All models	(1.1)	1.6
w/A.C. add	(.5)	.7

LABOR 7 COOLING SYSTEM 7 LABOR

(Factory Time) Chilton Time

Drive Belt, Adjust
All models-one 3
each adtnl 1

Drive Belt, Renew
All models
A.C. (.2) 3
Fan & Alter (.3) 4
P/Str (.5) 6

Transaxle Auxiliary Oil Cooler, Renew
All models (.3) 6

Temperature Gauge (Engine Unit), Renew
All models (.3) 4

Heater Hoses, Renew
All models-one (.4) 4
both (.5) 6

Heater Core, R&R or Renew
All models-wo/A.C. (1.0) 1.7
w/A.C. (2.5) *4.2
*Includes recharge A.C. system.

ADD THESE OPERATIONS TO HEATER CORE R&R
Boil & Repair 1.2
Repair Core 9
Recore 1.2

Heater Control Assembly, Renew
All models (.4) 7

Heater Blower Motor, Renew
All models (.4) 6

Heater Blower Motor Resistor, Renew
All models (.2) 3

Heater Blower Motor Switch, Renew
All models (.4) 7

Water Valve, Renew (w/A.C.)
All models (.3) 5

LABOR 8 EXHAUST SYSTEM 8 LABOR

(Factory Time) Chilton Time

Muffler, Renew
All models (.4) 8
Cut exhaust pipe add 2

Catalytic Converter, Renew
All models-one (.7) 9

Exhaust Pipe Extension, Renew
All models (.6) 1.0

Exhaust Pipe, Renew
All models (.7) 1.1
Cut at muffler add 2

Intake and Exhaust Manifold Gaskets, Renew
All models (1.9) 3.5

Exhaust Manifold, Renew
All models (2.7) 3.7

Exhaust Pipe Flange Gasket, Renew
All models (.4) 6

COMBINATIONS

Muffler, Exhaust and Tail Pipe, Renew
All models (1.0) 1.5

LABOR 9 FRONT SUSPENSION 9 LABOR

(Factory Time) Chilton Time

Note: On all front suspension operations alignment charges must be added if performed. Time given does not include alignment.

Wheel, Renew
one (.3) 5

Wheels, Rotate (All)
All models 5

Wheel, Balance
one 3
each adtnl 2

Check Alignment of Front End
All models 5
Note: Deduct if alignment is performed.

Toe-Out, Adjust
All models 6

Align Front End
Includes: Adjust camber, toe-out and center steering wheel.
All models (.8) 1.4

Steering Knuckle, Renew (One)
Add alignment charges.
All models (1.0) 1.6

Front Strut Assembly, R&R or Renew (One)
Add alignment charges.
All models (.8) 1.4

Lower Control Arm, Renew (One)
Add alignment charges.
All models (1.1) 1.6

Lower Ball Joint, Renew (One)
Includes: Reset toe-in.
All models (.8) 1.2

Front Coil Spring or Strut Bearing, Renew (One)
Add alignment charges.
All models (.8) 1.5

Steering Knuckle Bearing, Renew (One) (Wheel Bearing)
All models (1.2) 1.6

Front Sway Bar, Renew
All models (.4) 7

Front Suspension Strut (Dual Path) Mount Assy., Renew
Includes: Renew bearing.
1984-88 (.8) 1.5

K-Frame Assembly, Renew
Add alignment charges.
All models (2.5) 4.0

Drive Shaft Boot, Renew
Includes: Clean and lubricate C/V joint.
All models
one-inner or outer (.7) 1.0
both-one side (1.0) 1.4

Renew shaft seal, add
right side (.1) 1
left side (.3) 3

Drive Shaft C/V Joint, Renew
All models
one-inner or outer (.7) 1.0
both-one side (1.0) 1.4
inter shaft U-joint (.6) 1.0
Renew shaft seal, add
right side (.1) 1
left side (.3) 3

Front Wheel Drive Shaft Assy., Renew
All models
inter spline yoke (.6) 1.0
inter stub shaft (.6) 1.0
all others-each (1.0) 1.4
Renew shaft seal, add
right side (.1) 1
left side (.3) 3

Intermediate Shaft Support Bearing, Renew
All models-each (.6) 1.0

Drive Shaft Oil Seal, Renew
All models
right side (.5) 8
left side (.7) 1.1

LABOR 11 STEERING GEAR 11 LABOR

(Factory Time) Chilton Time

Tie Rod Ends, Renew
Includes: Adjust toe, replace tie rod if necessary.
All models
outer-one (.9) 1.2

Inner and Outer
w/P.S.-one (1.9) 2.5

STANDARD STEERING

Horn Contact, Renew
All models (.2) 3

LABOR 11 STEERING GEAR 11 LABOR

(Factory Time)	Chilton Time
Steering Wheel, Renew	
All models (.2)	.3
Steering Column Jacket, Renew	
Does not include painting.	
All models (1.0)	1.9
Upper Mast Jacket Bearing, Renew	
Includes: Replace insulators if necessary.	
All models (.8)	1.7
Steering Column Lower Shaft Bearing, Renew	
Includes: Replace support if necessary.	
All models (.4)	.7
Steering Column Shaft, Renew	
All models (.8)	2.0
Steering Column Flexible Coupling, Renew	
All models (.5)	.9
Steering Gear Assembly, Renew	
All models (1.7)	3.0

POWER STEERING

(Factory Time)	Chilton Time
Power Steering Pump Pressure Check	
All models	.5
Power Steering Pump Belt, Renew	
All models (.5)	.6
w/A.C. add (.1)	.1
Power Steering Gear Assembly, Renew	
All models (2.3)	3.1
Steering Gear Oil Seals, Renew	
Includes: R&R gear assy. and reset toe-in.	
All models (3.5)	5.1
Upper and Lower Valve Pinion Seals, Renew	
All models (1.4)	2.0
Renew brgs add (.3)	.5
Power Steering Pump, Renew	
Includes: Test pump and transfer pulley.	
All models (1.2)	1.9
Power Steering Pump, R&R and Recondition	
All models (1.5)	2.8
Pump Flow Control Valve, Test and Clean or Renew	
All models (.6)	1.0
Power Steering Reservoir or Seals, Renew	
All models (.9)	1.4
Pump Drive Shaft Oil Seal, Renew	
All models (1.1)	1.9
Power Steering Hoses, Renew	
All models-each (.4)	.5

LABOR 12 CYLINDER HEAD & VALVE SYSTEM 12 LABOR

(Factory Time)	Chilton Time
Compression Test	
All models	.6
Cylinder Head Gasket, Renew	
Includes: Clean carbon.	
All models (3.4)	4.8
w/A.C. add (.1)	.1
w/Air inj add (.2)	.2
Cylinder Head, Renew	
Includes: Transfer all necessary parts. Clean carbon. Make all necessary adjustments.	
All models (5.3)	8.0
w/A.C. add (.1)	.1
w/Air inj add (.2)	.2
Clean Carbon and Grind Valves	
Includes: R&R cylinder head, adjust valve clearance when required. Minor engine tune up.	
All models (4.8)	6.8
w/A.C. add (.1)	.1
w/Air inj add (.2)	.2
Cylinder Head Cover Gasket, Renew or Reseal	
All models (.8)	1.1
Valve Rocker Arms or Shaft, Renew	
All models (1.2)	1.6
Valve Springs and/or Valve Stem Oil Seals, Renew (Head on Car)	
All models (1.9)	2.9
Valve Tappets, Renew	
All models-one (1.0)	1.5
all (1.9)	2.9

LABOR 13 ENGINE ASSEMBLY & MOUNTS 13 LABOR

(Factory Time)	Chilton Time
Engine Assembly, Remove and Install	
Includes: R&R engine and transmission as a unit.	
Does not include transfer of any parts or equipment.	
All models	4.5
w/A.C. add (.5)	.5
w/Air inj add (.3)	.3
Short Engine Assembly, Renew (w/All Internal Parts Less Cyl. Head and Oil Pan)	
Includes: R&R engine and transmission as a unit. Transfer all necessary parts not supplied with replacement engine. Clean carbon, grind valves. Minor tune up.	
All models (9.1)	15.0
w/A.C. add (.5)	.5
w/Air inj add (.3)	.3
Engine Assy., R&R and Recondition	
Includes: Rebore block, install new pistons, rings, rod and main bearings. Clean carbon, grind valves, replace valve stem oil seals. Tune engine.	
All models (17.8)	22.6
w/A.C. add (.5)	.5
w/Air inj add (.3)	.3
Engine Support, Renew	
All models	
Engine-right side (.3)	.5
left side (.3)	.5
center (.4)	.6
Trans/Axle	
Roll rod (.3)	.5

LABOR 14 PISTONS, RINGS & BEARINGS 14 LABOR

COMBINATIONS

Add to Engine Work

DRAIN, EVACUATE & RECHARGE AIR CONDITIONING SYSTEM
All models.......... 1.4

DISTRIBUTOR, RECONDITION
All models (.7).......... .7

CARBURETOR, RECONDITION
All models.......... 2.0

RECONDITION CYL. HEAD (HEAD REMOVED)
All models (1.4).......... 2.0

See Machine Shop Operations

CAMSHAFT, RENEW (HEAD DISASSEMBLED)
All models (.1).......... .2

DEGLAZE CYLINDER WALLS
Each (.1).......... .1

REMOVE CYLINDER TOP RIDGE
Each (.1).......... .1

VALVES, RECONDITION (HEAD REMOVED)
All models (1.4).......... 2.0

MAIN BEARINGS, RENEW (PAN REMOVED)
All models (.9).......... 1.4

OIL PUMP, RENEW
All models (.2).......... .3

OIL FILTER ELEMENT, RENEW
All models (.2).......... .3

(Factory Time) — Chilton Time

Rings, Renew (See Engine Combinations)
Includes: Replace connecting rod bearings, deglaze cylinder walls, clean carbon. Minor tune up.
All models
one cyl (4.6).......... 6.9
all cyls (5.9).......... 8.1
w/A.C. add (.2).......... .2
w/Air inj add (.2).......... .2

Pistons or Connecting Rods, Renew
Includes: Replace rings and connecting rod bearings, deglaze cylinder walls, clean carbon. Minor tune up.
All models
one cyl (4.9).......... 7.2
all cyls (7.0).......... 9.3
w/A.C. add (.2).......... .2
w/Air inj add (.2).......... .2

Connecting Rod Bearings, Renew
All models (2.1).......... 3.0

LABOR 15 CRANKSHAFT & DAMPER 15 LABOR

(Factory Time) — Chilton Time

Crankshaft and Main Bearings, Renew
Includes: R&R engine assy.
All models (6.7).......... 11.2
w/A.C. add (.2).......... .2
w/P.S. add (.3).......... .3

Main Bearings, Renew (All)
Includes: R&R engine assy.
All models (7.0).......... 11.0
w/A.C. add (.2).......... .2
w/P.S. add (.3).......... .3

Main and Rod Bearings, Renew (All)
Includes: R&R engine assy.
All models (7.7).......... 12.0
w/A.C. add (.2).......... .2
w/P.S. add (.3).......... .3

Rear Main Bearing Oil Seals, Renew (Complete)
All models (3.5).......... 5.4
w/Cruise control add (.2).......... .2

Crankshaft Rear Bearing Oil Seal Retainer, Renew
Includes: Replace oil seal, complete.
All models (4.1).......... 6.3
w/Cruise control add (.2).......... .2

Crankshaft Front Oil Seal, Renew
All models (1.3).......... 2.0
w/A.C. add (.2).......... .2
w/P.S. add (.2).......... .2

Crankshaft Pulley, Renew
All models (.5).......... .8
w/A.C. add (.1).......... .1
w/P.S. add (.1).......... .1

LABOR 16 CAMSHAFT & TIMING GEARS 16 LABOR

(Factory Time) — Chilton Time

Intermediate Shaft, Renew
All models (1.3).......... 2.5
w/A.C. add (.2).......... .2
w/P.S. add (.1).......... .1

Intermediate Shaft Oil Seal, Renew
All models (1.1).......... 1.8
w/A.C. add (.2).......... .2
w/P.S. add (.2).......... .2

Intermediate Shaft Sprocket, Renew
All models (1.7).......... 2.7
w/A.C. add (.5).......... .5
w/P.S. add (.2).......... .2
w/Air inj add (.2).......... .2

Camshaft, Renew
All models (1.7).......... 2.8
Renew valve springs add (1.1).......... 1.1

Camshaft Sprocket, Renew
Includes: Replace cover oil seal.
All models (1.7).......... 2.4
w/A.C. add (.5).......... .5
w/P.S. add (.2).......... .2
w/Air inj add (.2).......... .2

Timing Belt, Renew
All models (1.6).......... 2.3
w/A.C. add (.5).......... .5
w/P.S. add (.2).......... .2
w/Air inj add (.1).......... .1

Timing Belt Cover, Renew
All models-upper (.2).......... .4
lower (.6).......... 1.0
w/A.C. add (.2).......... .2
w/P.S. add (.1).......... .1

Timing Belt Tensioner, Renew
All models (.9).......... 1.5
w/A.C. add (.2).......... .2
w/P.S. add (.2).......... .2

Camshaft Oil Seal, Renew
All models-front (.7).......... 1.1
rear (.4).......... .8

LABOR 17 ENGINE OILING SYSTEM 17 LABOR

(Factory Time) — Chilton Time

Oil Pan or Gasket, Renew
All models (1.0).......... 1.4

Pressure Test Engine Bearings (Pan Off)
All models.......... 1.0

Oil Pump, Renew
All models (1.3).......... 1.7

Oil Pump, R&R and Recondition
All models (1.7).......... 2.2

Oil Pressure Gauge (Engine), Renew
All models (.3).......... .4

Oil Filter Element, Renew
All models (.2).......... .3

LABOR 18 CLUTCH & FLYWHEEL 18 LABOR

	(Factory Time)	Chilton Time
Clutch Assembly, Renew		
All models	(3.3)	4.6
Renew input seal add	(.2)	.2
w/Cruise control add	(.2)	.2
Clutch Release Bearing, Renew		
All models	(3.2)	4.4
w/Cruise control add	(.2)	.2
Clutch Self Adjusting Mechanism, Renew		
All models	(.3)	.6
Clutch Release Cable, Renew		
All models	(.3)	.5
Flywheel, Renew		
All models	(3.4)	4.7
w/Cruise control add	(.2)	.2
Renew ring gear add		.5

LABOR 19 STANDARD TRANSMISSION 19 LABOR

	(Factory Time)	Chilton Time
Front Wheel Drive Shaft Assy., Renew		
All models-each	(1.0)	1.5
Renew shaft seal, add		
right side	(.1)	.1
left side	(.3)	.3
Drive Shaft Boot, Renew		
Includes: Clean and lubricate C/V joint.		
All models		
one-inner or outer	(.7)	1.0
both-one side	(1.0)	1.4
Renew shaft seal, add		
right side	(.1)	.1
left side	(.3)	.3
Drive Shaft C/V Joint, Renew		
All models		
one-inner or outer	(.7)	1.0
both-one side	(1.0)	1.4
Renew shaft seal, add		
right side	(.1)	.1
left side	(.3)	.3
Drive Shaft Oil Seal, Renew		
All models-right side	(.5)	.7
left side	(.8)	1.1
Manual Trans/Axle, Remove & Install		
Does not include transfer of any parts or equipment.		
All models	(3.1)	4.3
Manual Trans/Axle Assy., Renew		
Includes: Transfer all necessary parts not supplied with replacement unit.		
All models	(3.5)	4.9
Manual Trans/Axle Assy., R&R and Recondition (Complete)		
All models		
w/A460	(5.6)	8.0
w/A465	(5.9)	8.5

LABOR 21 SHIFT LINKAGE 21 LABOR

	(Factory Time)	Chilton Time
MANUAL		
Gearshift Control Rod and/or Swivel, Renew		
All models	(.3)	.4
Crossover Rod, Renew		
All models	(.3)	.4
Gearshift Lever, Renew		
All models-floor shift	(.4)	.6
Gearshift Mechanism, Renew		
All models	(.6)	.9
w/Console add	(.1)	.1
Gearshift Selector Tube Assy., Renew		
All models	(.4)	.6
Selector Shaft Seal, Renew		
All models	(.8)	1.1
Trans/Axle Selector Shaft, Renew		
All models	(1.3)	1.7
AUTOMATIC		
Throttle Linkage, Adjust		
All models	(.2)	.4
Gearshift Lever, Renew		
All models	(.3)	.5
Gearshift Mechanism, Renew		
Includes: Replace knob and push button if necessary.		
All models	(.5)	.8
Gearshift Control Cable, Renew		
All models	(.7)	1.0
Throttle Lever Control Cable, Renew		
Includes: Adjust cable.		
All models	(.3)	.6

LABOR 23 AUTOMATIC TRANSMISSION 23 LABOR

	(Factory Time)	Chilton Time
ON CAR SERVICES		
Drain & Refill Unit		
All models		.6
Oil Pressure Check		
All models		.8
Check Unit For Oil Leaks		
Includes: Clean and dry outside of case and run unit to determine point of leak.		
All models		.8
Neutral Safety Switch, Renew		
All models	(.3)	.4
Oil Cooler Lines, Renew		
Includes: Cut and form to size.		
All models	(.4)	.6
Throttle Linkage, Adjust		
All models	(.2)	.4
Kickdown Band, Adjust		
All models	(.2)	.4
Throttle Valve Lever Shaft Seal, Renew		
All models	(.5)	.8
Valve Body Manual Lever Shaft Seal, Renew		
All models	(.3)	.6
Differential Gear Cover, Renew		
All models	(.8)	1.2
Drive Shaft Boot, Renew		
Includes: Clean and lubricate C/V joint.		
All models		
one-inner or outer	(.7)	1.0
both-one side	(1.0)	1.4
Renew shaft seal, add		
right side	(.1)	.1
left side	(.3)	.3
Drive Shaft C/V Joint, Renew		
All models		
one-inner or outer	(.7)	1.0
both-one side	(1.0)	1.4
inter shaft U-joint	(.6)	1.0
Renew shaft seal, add		
right side	(.1)	.1
left side	(.3)	.3
Front Wheel Drive Shaft Assy., Renew		
All models		
inter spline yoke	(.6)	1.0
inter stub shaft	(.6)	1.0
all others-each	(1.0)	1.4
Renew shaft seal, add		
right side	(.1)	.1
left side	(.3)	.3
Intermediate Shaft Support Bearing, Renew		
All models-each	(.6)	1.0

LABOR 23 AUTOMATIC TRANSMISSION 23 LABOR

(Factory Time) Chilton Time

Drive Shaft Seal, Renew
All models-right side (.5) 8
left side (.8) 1.1

Transfer Gear Cover, Renew
All models (.5) 7

Governor Assy., Renew or Recondition
Includes: R&R oil pan.
All models (1.3) 2.4

Governor Support and Parking Gear, Renew
Includes: R&R oil pan.
All models (1.9) 2.9

Oil Pan and/or Gasket, Renew
All models (.6) 1.2

Oil Filter, Renew
Includes: R&R oil pan.
All models (.7) 1.4

Parking Lock Sprag, Renew
Includes: R&R oil pan.
All models (1.5) 2.6

Accumulator Piston, Renew or Recondition
Includes: R&R oil pan.
All models (1.1) 2.2

Kickdown Servo, Renew
Includes: R&R oil pan.
All models (1.4) 2.5

Reverse Servo, Renew
Includes: R&R oil pan.
All models (1.2) 2.2

Valve Body, Renew
Includes: R&R oil pan and renew filter.
All models (1.0) 2.1

Valve Body, R&R and Recondition
Includes: R&R oil pan and renew filter.
All models (1.7) 3.2

SERVICES REQUIRING R&R

Trans/Axle Assy., Remove & Install
All models (3.1) 4.5

Trans/Axle Assembly, Reseal
Includes: R&R trans axle and renew all seals and gaskets.
All models (5.0) 7.0

Trans/Axle Assembly, Renew
Includes: Remove and install all necessary interfering parts. Transfer any parts not supplied with replacement unit. Road test.
All models (3.5) 4.9

Trans/Axle Assy., R&R and Recondition
Includes: Disassemble complete, clean, inspect and replace all parts as required.
All models (9.4) 12.7
Flush converter and cooler lines, add (.5) 5

Kickdown Band, Renew
All models (4.0) 6.2

Reverse Band, Renew
All models (4.2) 6.5

Trans/Axle Case, Renew
All models (7.7) 10.0

Front and Rear Clutch Seals, Renew
All models (4.2) 6.5

Torque Converter, Renew
All models (3.3) 5.2

Torque Converter Drive Plate, Renew (With Ring Gear)
All models (3.3) 5.2

Front Oil Pump, Renew
All models (3.7) 6.0

Front Oil Pump Seal, Renew
All models (3.3) 5.2

Reaction Shaft and/or Bushing, Renew
Includes: Renew front pump if necessary.
All models (3.7) 6.0

LABOR 26 REAR AXLE AND SUSPENSION 26 LABOR

(Factory Time) Chilton Time

Rear Wheel Bearing, Renew or Repack
Includes: Replace bearing cups and grease seal.
All models-each (.6) 9

Rear Wheel Grease Seal, Renew
All models-each (.4) 7

Rear Spring, Renew
All models-one (.6) 9
both (1.1) 1.7

Rear Shock Absorbers, Renew
All models-one (.3) 4
both (.4) 6

Rear Spring Bushing and/or Shackle, Renew
All models-one (.4) 6

Stub Axle Spindle, Renew
All models-one (.5) 8

Rear Spring Hanger, Renew
All models-one (.7) 1.1

LABOR 28 AIR CONDITIONING 28 LABOR

(Factory Time) Chilton Time

Note: If more than one item requires replacement where evacuation and discharging the system is already included in the operation, deduct 1.0 hour for each additional item to the times listed.

Drain, Evacuate, Leak Test and Charge System
All models 1.0

Partial Charge
Includes: Leak test.
All models (.6) 6

Performance Test
All models 8

Vacuum Leak Test
All models 8

Compressor Drive Belt, Renew
All models (.2) 3

C-171 COMPRESSOR

Compressor Clutch Field Coil, Renew
Includes: Replace pulley w/hub if necessary.
All models (.6) 9

Compressor Clutch Pulley (W/Hub), Renew
All models (.4) 7

Compressor Clutch Assembly, Renew
All models (.6) 9

Compressor Assembly, Renew
Includes: Pressure test and charge system.
All models (1.4) 2.5

Compressor Front Cover or Seal, Renew
Includes: R&R compressor. Pressure test and charge system.
All models (2.1) 3.4

Compressor Rear Cover or Seal, Renew
Includes: R&R compressor. Pressure test and charge system.
All models (2.0) 3.3

Compressor Center Seal, Renew
Includes: R&R compressor. Pressure test and charge system.
All models (2.2) 3.5

Compressor Shaft Gas Seal, Renew
Includes: R&R compressor. Pressure test and charge system.
All models (2.1) 3.4

Expansion Valve, Renew
Includes: Pressure test and charge system.
All models (1.0) 1.7

Receiver Dryer, Renew
Includes: Add partial charge, leak test and charge system.
All models (.9) 1.6

Low Pressure Cut Off Switch, Renew
Includes: Charge system.
All models (.9) 1.4

Clutch Cycling (Thermostatic Control) Switch, Renew
All models (.3) 6

Condenser Assembly, Renew
Includes: Add partial charge, leak test and charge system.
All models (1.5) 2.2

LABOR 28 AIR CONDITIONING 28 LABOR

(Factory Time) Chilton Time

Temperature Control Assembly, Renew
All models (.4) 7

Push Button Vacuum Switch, Renew
All models (.5) 9

Temperature Control Cable, Renew
All models (.6) 9

Vacuum Hose Control Assy., Renew
All models
main assy (2.0) 3.0

Evaporator Coil, Renew
Includes: Add partial charge, leak test and charge system.
All models (2.7) 3.9

Vacuum Actuator, Renew
All models
outside air door (.3) 6
heater/defroster door (.3) 6
A/C mode door (.6) 1.0

Blower Motor, Renew
All models (.6) 9

Blower Motor Resistor, Renew
All models (.3) 4

Blower Motor Switch, Renew
All models (.4) 8

Air Conditioning Hoses, Renew
Includes: Add partial charge, leak test and charge system.
All models-one (1.1) 1.5
each adtnl (.3) 5

LABOR 30 HEAD AND PARKING LAMPS 30 LABOR

(Factory Time) Chilton Time

Aim Headlamps
All models (.3) 4

Headlamp Sealed Beam Bulb, Renew
Does not include aim headlamps.
All models-each (.2) 3

Side Marker Lamp Assy., Renew
All models (.2) 3

License Lamp Assembly, Renew
All models (.2) 2

License Lamp Lens, Renew
All models (.2) 2

Tail Lamp Lens, Renew
All models-one (.2) 3

LABOR 31 WINDSHIELD WIPER & SPEEDOMETER 31 LABOR

(Factory Time) Chilton Time

Windshield Wiper Motor, Renew
All models (.4) 7

Windshield Wiper Switch, Renew
All models (.4) 9

Wiper Pivot, Renew (One)
All models (.3) 5

Wiper Links, Renew
All models (.3) 6

Windshield Washer Pump, Renew
All models (.3) 4

Speedometer Head, R&R or Renew
Does not include reset odometer.
All models (.4) 7

Speedometer Cable and Casing, Renew
All models
speed control to trans (.2) 6
speed control to speedo (.3) 6
trans to speedo (.4) 9

Speedometer Cable (Inner), Renew or Lubricate
All models
speed control to trans (.2) 5
speed control to speedo (.3) 5
trans to speedo (.3) 7

Speedometer Drive Pinion, Renew
Includes: Replace oil seal.
All models (.2) 4

Radio, R&R
All models (.3) 7

LABOR 32 LIGHT SWITCHES & WIRING 32 LABOR

(Factory Time) Chilton Time

Headlamp Switch, Renew
All models (.3) 4

Headlamp Dimmer Switch, Renew (Column Mounted)
All models (.3) 6

Stop Light Switch, Renew
All models (.3) 4
w/Cruise control add (.1) 1

Back-Up Lamp Switch, Renew (w/Manual Trans)
All models (.2) 4

Neutral Safety Switch, Renew
All models (.3) 4

Turn Signal Switch, Renew
All models (.5) 1.0

Turn Signal or Hazard Warning Flasher, Renew
All models (.2) 3

Horn Relay, Renew
All models (.2) 3

Horns, Renew
All models-one (.2) 4

LABOR 34 CRUISE CONTROL 34 LABOR

(Factory Time) Chilton Time

Speed Control Switch (Turn Signal Lever), Renew
All models (.3) 6

Speed Control Servo Assy., Renew
All models (.3) 5

Speed Control Cable, Renew
All models (.4) 6

Speed Control Vacuum Hose, Renew
All models (.2) 3

Cruise Control Clutch Safety Cut-Out Switch, Renew
All models (.3) 4

Dodge Ram Van • Caravan • Plymouth Voyager

GROUP INDEX

ALPHABETICAL INDEX

LABOR — SERVICE BAY OPERATIONS — LABOR

(Factory Time) — Chilton Time

COOLING

Winterize Cooling System

Includes: Run engine to check for leaks, tighten all hose connections. Test radiator and pressure cap, drain radiator and engine block. Add anti-freeze and refill system.

All models 5

Thermostat, Renew

1984-88 (.4) 5

Drive Belts, Adjust

All models-one 2
each adtnl 1

Drive Belts, Renew

1984-88
Water Pump
2.6L eng (.3) 3
Fan & alter (.2) .... *.3
Air pump (.3) 4
Pow str (.4) .... *.6
P.S. & A.C. (.2) .... *.3
A.C. (.2) 3
*w/A.C. add (.1) 1

Radiator Hoses, Renew

1984-88-upper (.3) 4
lower (.4) 6

FUEL

Carburetor Air Cleaner, Service

All models 3

Carburetor, Adjust (On Car)

Includes: Adjust idle mixture and idle speed. Check and reset ignition timing.

All models
Holly 2 bbl 6
All others 5

Automatic Choke, Renew

1984-88 (.7) 1.0

Carburetor Choke Vacuum Kick, Adjust

1984-88
Holly (.2) 4

BRAKES

Brake Pedal Free Play, Adjust

All models 3

Brakes, Adjust (Minor)

Includes: Adjust brake shoes, fill master cylinder.

two wheels 4

Bleed Brakes (Four Wheels)

Includes: Add fluid.

All models (.4) 6

Parking Brake, Adjust

All models 4

LUBRICATION SERVICE

Lubricate Chassis, Change Oil & Filter

Includes: Inspect and correct all fluid levels.

All models 6
Install grease fittings add 1

Engine Oil & Filter, Change

Includes: Inspect and correct all fluid levels.

All models 4

Lubricate Chassis

Includes: Inspect and correct all fluid levels.

All models 4
Install grease fittings add 1

WHEELS

Wheels, Balance

one 3
each adtnl 2

Wheel, Renew

one 5

Wheels, Rotate (All)

All models 5

ELECTRICAL

Aim Headlamps

two 4
four 6

Headlamp Sealed Beam Bulb, Renew

Does not include aim headlamps.

All models-each (.2) 3

License Lamp Lens, Renew

All models (.2) 2

License Lamp Assembly, Renew

All models (.2) 3

Turn Signal and Parking Lamp Assy., Renew

All models (.2) 4

Tail Lamp Assembly, Renew

1984-86 (.5) 8
1987-88 (.2) 4

Side Marker Lamp Assy., Renew

All models-each (.2) 3

Turn Signal or Hazard Warning Flasher, Renew

All models (.2) 3

Horn Relay, Renew

All models (.2) 3

Horn, Renew

All models-one (.2) 4

Battery Cables, Renew

All models
positive (.5) 6
negative (.2) 2

LABOR — 1 TUNE UP 1 — LABOR

(Factory Time) — Chilton Time

Compression Test

Four–1984-88 6
V-6–1978-88 8

Engine Tune Up, (Electronic Ignition)

Includes: Test battery and clean connections. Tighten manifold and carburetor mounting bolts. Check engine compression, clean and adjust or renew spark plugs. Test resistance of spark plug cables. Inspect distributor cap and rotor, reluctor and pick up plate. Check vacuum advance operation. Reset ignition timing. Adjust idle mixture and idle speed. Service air cleaner. Inspect crankcase ventilation system. Inspect and adjust drive belts. Inspect choke operation and adjust or free up. Check operation of EGR valve.

Four–1984-88 .... 1.5
V-6–1987-88 .... 1.8

LABOR — 2 IGNITION SYSTEM 2 — LABOR

(Factory Time) — Chilton Time

Spark Plugs, Clean and Reset or Renew

1984-88-Four (.5) 6
V-6 8

Ignition Timing, Reset

1984-88 (.3) 4

Spark Control Computer, Renew (SCC)

1984-88 (.3) 1.0

Electronic Control Unit, Renew

1984-88
2.6L eng (.3) 5

Distributor Assembly, Renew

Includes: Reset ignition timing.

1984-88-Four (.4) 6
V-6 (.5) 7

Distributor, R&R and Recondition

Includes: Reset ignition timing.

1984-88-Four (.9) 1.5
V-6 (1.0) 1.6

Distributor Pick-Up Plate and Coil Assy., Renew (Hall Effect)

Does not require R&R of distributor.

1984-88
2.2L & 2.5L engs (.3) 6

Distributor Pick-Up Set, Renew

Does not require R&R of distributor.

1984-88
2.6L eng (.5) 7

Distributor Ignitor Set, Renew

Does not require R&R of distributor.

1984-88
2.6L eng (.4) 6

Distributor Breaker Assy., Renew

Does not require R&R of distributor.

1984-88
2.6L eng (.4) 6

LABOR 2 IGNITION SYSTEM 2 LABOR

(Factory Time) Chilton Time

Distributor Reluctor and Governor Assy., Renew
Does not require R&R of distributor.
1984-88
2.6L eng (.3) 5

Distributor Vacuum Advance Control Unit, Renew
Does not require R&R of distributor.
1984-88
2.6L eng (.6) 9

Distributor Cap and/or Rotor, Renew
1984-88 (.2) 4

Ignition Coil, Renew
1984-88 (.2) 4

Ignition Cables, Renew
1984-88 (.2) 4

Ignition Switch, Renew
1984-88
std column (.4) 8
tilt column (.4) 9

Ignition Key Warning Buzzer, Renew
1984-88 (.2) 3

Ignition Switch Time Delay Relay, Renew
1984-88 (.2) 3

Ignition Key Buzzer/Chime Switch, Renew
1984-88
std column (.6) 1.2
tilt column (.5) 1.0

Ignition Lock Housing, Renew
1984-88-std colm (.8) 1.3
Tilt Column
console shift (1.1) 1.7
column shift (.8) 1.3

LABOR 3 FUEL SYSTEM 3 LABOR

(Factory Time) Chilton Time

Fuel Pump, Test
All models 3

Carburetor Air Cleaner, Service
All models 3

Carburetor Idle Speed and Mixture, Adjust
Includes: Check and reset ignition timing.
All models
Holly-2 bbl 6
All others 5

Idle Solenoid, Renew
1984-88 (.4) 6

Coolant Temperature Sensor/Switch, Renew
1984-88 (.2) 4

Throttle Position Sensor (Potentometer), Renew
1984-88
Four (.2) 3
V-6 (.3) 4

Choke Vacuum Kick, Adjust
1984-88 (.2) 3

Choke Vacuum Kick Diaphragm, Renew
1984-88 (.2) 4

Accelerator Pump, Renew
1984-88
Holly (.4) 8
All others (.8) 1.1

Heated Air Door Sensor, Renew
1984-88 (.2) 3

Carburetor Assembly, Renew
Includes: All necessary adjustments.
1984-88
Holly (.8) 1.3
All others (.7) 1.2

Carburetor, R&R and Clean or Recondition
Includes: All necessary adjustments.
1984-88
Holly (1.2) 2.4
All others (2.5) 3.5

Carburetor Needle and Seat, Renew
Includes: Adjust float level, idle speed and mixture.
1984-88
Holly (.7) 1.1
All others (1.1) 1.5

Fuel Filter, Renew
1984-88
in line (.2) 3
in tank (.5) 8

Fuel Pump, Renew
1984-88 (.4) 7
Add pump test if performed.

Fuel Tank, Renew
1984-88 (.9) 1.4

Fuel Gauge (Tank Unit), Renew
1984-88 (.6) 1.0

Fuel Gauge (Dash Unit), Renew
1984-88 (.5) 9

Intake Manifold or Gasket, Renew
1984-88
2.2L & 2.5L engs (2.0) 3.7
2.6L eng (1.9) 3.0
Renew manif add (.2) 5

Intake and Exhaust Manifold Gaskets, Renew
1984-88
2.2L & 2.5L engs (1.9) 3.5

Two Piece Intake Manifold Gaskets, Renew
1987-88
1987-88
3.0L eng-upper (.6) 9
lower (1.3) 1.7
Renew manif add-each (.2) 3

ELECTRONIC FUEL INJECTION

Throttle Body, Renew
1987-88-Four (.8) 1.2
V-6 (.4) 7

Fuel Pressure Regulator, Renew
1987-88-Four (.2) 4
V-6 (.7) 1.0

Fuel Pump, Renew
1987-88-Four (.7) 1.0
V-6 (.7) 1.0

Fuel Pump Relay, Renew
1987-88 (.3) 4

Automatic Idle Speed Assy., Renew
1987-88
motor (.3) 5
adapter (.3) 5

Fuel Injector, Renew
1987-88
Four-one (.3) 5
V-6-one (.8) 1.2
each adtnl (.1) 2

Throttle Body Temperature Sensor, Renew
1987-88 (.2) 4

Fuel Injector Rail, Renew
1987-88 (.8) 1.1

Throttle Position Sensor (Potentiometer), Renew
1987-88-Four (.2) 3
V-6 (.3) 4

M.A.P. Sensor, Renew
1987-88 (.4) 6

Single Module Engine Controller, Renew
1987-88 (.3) 4

LABOR 3A EMISSION CONTROLS 3A LABOR

(Factory Time) Chilton Time

CRANKCASE EMISSION

Crankcase Vent Valve, Renew
1984-88 (.2) 3

AIR INJECTION SYSTEM

Air Pump, Renew
1984-88
2.2L & 2.5L engs (.4) 7

Injection Tube and Check Valve Assy., Renew
1984-88-2.2L & 2.5L engs
ex manif mount (.5) 8
to conv
one or both (.4) 6
EFI engs
to conv (.5) 8

Aspirator Valve, Renew
1984-88 (.2) 4
w/EFI add (.1) 1

Air Pump Diverter/Switching Valve, Renew
1984-88
2.2L & 2.5L engs (.3) 5

Aspirator Silencer, Renew
1984-88 (.2) 3

LABOR 3A EMISSION CONTROLS 3A LABOR

	(Factory Time)	Chilton Time
Enrichment Solenoid Valve, Renew		
1984-88		
2.6L eng	(.3)	.4
Jet Air Control Valve, Renew		
1984-88	(.5)	.7
Jet Mixture Solenoid Valve, Renew		
1984-88		
2.6L eng	(.4)	.6
Deceleration Solenoid Valve, Renew		
1984-88		
2.6L eng	(.3)	.6
Thermal Check Valve, Renew		
1986-88		
2.6L eng	(.2)	.3
Air Switching Valve, Renew		
1986-88		
2.6L eng	(.4)	.5
Distributor/Air Switching Valve Solenoid Assy., Renew		
1984-88	(.2)	.3
Intake Air Temperature Sensor, Renew		
1984-88	(.2)	.3

EVAPORATIVE EMISSION

	(Factory Time)	Chilton Time
Vapor Canister, Renew		
1984-88	(.3)	.4
Vapor Canister Filter, Renew		
1984-88	(.2)	.3
Vapor Canister Valve, Renew		
1985-88	(.2)	.3

E.G.R. SYSTEM

	(Factory Time)	Chilton Time
Coolant Vacuum Switch, Renew (CCEVS)		
1984-88	(.3)	.4
Exhaust Gas Recirculation Control Valve, Renew		
1984-88		
2.2L & 2.5L engs	(.6)	.7
2.6L eng	(.4)	.5
E.G.R. and Purge Control Solenoid Bank, Renew		
1984-88	(.2)	.3
Coolant Vacuum Switch/Valve, Renew (CCEGR)		
1984-88-one	(.3)	.5
both	(.4)	.6

EFE SYSTEM

	(Factory Time)	Chilton Time
Oxygen Sensor, Renew		
1984-88		
2.2L & 2.5L engs	(.2)	.4
2.6L eng	(.5)	.7
3.0L eng	(.4)	.6
High Altitude Compensator, Renew		
1984-88	(.3)	.5

HEATED INLET AIR SYSTEM

	(Factory Time)	Chilton Time
Carburetor Air Cleaner, Service		
1984-88		.3
Air Cleaner Vacuum Sensor, Renew		
1984-88-one	(.2)	.3
Heated Air Door Sensor, Renew		
1984-88		
2.6L eng	(.2)	.3

PULSE AIR SYSTEM

	(Factory Time)	Chilton Time
Pulse Air Feeder, Renew		
1984-88	(.6)	.9
Pulse Air Feeder Tube, Renew		
1984-88	(.7)	1.1
EFI eng	(.4)	.6

LABOR 4 ALTERNATOR AND REGULATOR 4 LABOR

	(Factory Time)	Chilton Time
Alternator Circuits, Test		
Includes: Test battery, regulator and alternator output.		
All models		.6
Alternator Drive Belt, Renew		
1984-88	(.2)	.3
w/A.C. add	(.1)	.1
Alternator Assembly, Renew		
Includes: Transfer pulley if required.		
1984-88	(.8)	1.2
w/A.C. add	(.3)	.3
Add circuit test if performed.		
Alternator, R&R and Recondition		
Includes: Test and disassemble.		
1984-88	(1.5)	2.1
w/A.C. add	(.3)	.3
Alternator Front Bearing or Retainer, Renew		
1984-88	(.8)	1.1
w/A.C. add	(.3)	.3
Renew rear brg add		.2
Voltage Regulator, Test and Renew		
1984-88		
external type	(.3)	.5
internal type	(1.0)	*1.6
*w/A.C. add	(.3)	.3
Alternator Gauge, Renew		
1984-88	(.3)	.6
Gauge Alert Module, Renew		
1984-88	(.7)	1.1

LABOR 5 STARTING SYSTEM 5 LABOR

	(Factory Time)	Chilton Time
Starter Draw Test (On Truck)		
All models		.3
Starter Assy., Renew		
Includes: Test starter relay, starter solenoid and amperage draw.		
1984-88		
2.2L & 2.5L engs	(1.0)	1.3
2.6L & 3.0L engs	(.6)	1.0
Starter, R&R and Recondition		
Includes: Turn down armature.		
1984-88		
2.2L & 2.5L engs		2.8
2.6L & 3.0L engs		2.5
Renew field coils add	(.5)	.5
Starter Drive, Renew		
Includes: R&R starter.		
1984-88		
2.2L & 2.5L engs	(1.4)	1.8
2.6L & 3.0L engs	(.8)	1.1
Starter Solenoid or Switch, Renew		
Includes: R&R starter.		
1984-88		
2.2L & 2.5L engs	(1.0)	1.4
2.6L & 3.0L engs	(1.0)	1.4
Starter Relay, Renew		
1984-88	(.2)	.3
Neutral Start and Back-Up Lamp Switch, Renew		
1984-88	(.3)	.4
Ignition Switch, Renew		
1984-88		
std column	(.4)	.8
tilt column	(.4)	.9
Battery Cables, Renew		
1984-88		
positive	(.5)	.6
negative	(.2)	.2

LABOR 6 BRAKE SYSTEM 6 LABOR

	(Factory Time)	Chilton Time
Brake Pedal Free Play, Adjust		
All models		.3
Brakes, Adjust (Minor)		
Includes: Adjust brake shoes, fill master cylinder.		
two wheels		.4
Bleed Brakes (Four Wheels)		
Includes: Add fluid.		
All models	(.4)	.6

LABOR 6 BRAKE SYSTEM 6 LABOR

(Factory Time) Chilton Time

Brake Shoes and/or Pads, Renew
Includes: Install new or exchange brake shoes or pads. Adjust service and hand brake. Bleed system.
1984-88-front-disc (.5) 8
rear-drum (.8) 1.5
all four wheels (1.3) 2.2
Resurface disc rotor, add-each 9
Resurface brake drum, add-each 5

Rear Brake Drum, Renew (One)
1984-88 (.5) 6

BRAKE HYDRAULIC SYSTEM

Wheel Cylinder, Renew
Includes: Bleed system.
1984-88-one (.7) 1.1
both (1.3) 2.1

Wheel Cylinder, R&R and Rebuild
Includes: Hone cylinder and bleed system.
1984-88-one 1.2
both 2.3

Brake Hose, Renew (Flex)
Includes: Bleed system.
1984-88-front-one (.4) 8
rear-one (.4) 8

Master Cylinder, Renew
Includes: Bleed complete system.
1984-88 (.5) 9

Master Cylinder, R&R and Rebuild
Includes: Bleed complete system.
1984-88 .... 1.6

Master Cylinder Reservoir, Renew
Includes: Bleed complete system.
1984-88 (.6) 1.0

Brake System, Flush and Refill
All models 1.2

POWER BRAKES

Brake Booster Assembly, Renew
1984-88 (.8) 1.2

Brake Booster Check Valve, Renew
1984-88 (.2) 2

COMBINATIONS

Add to Brakes, Renew

See Machine Shop Operations

(Factory Time) Chilton Time

RENEW WHEEL CYLINDER
Each 3

REBUILD WHEEL CYLINDER
Each 4

REBUILD CALIPER ASSEMBLY
Each 5

RENEW MASTER CYLINDER
All models 6

REBUILD MASTER CYLINDER
All models 8

RENEW BRAKE HOSE
Each 3

RENEW REAR WHEEL GREASE SEALS
One side 3

RENEW DISC BRAKE ROTOR
Each 2

RENEW BRAKE DRUM
Each 3

DISC BRAKE ROTOR STUDS, RENEW
Each 1

(Factory Time) Chilton Time

DISC BRAKES

Disc Brake Pads, Renew
Includes: Install new disc brake pads only.
1984-88 (.5) 8

Disc Brake Rotor, Renew
1984-88-one (.3) 6

Disc Brake Rotor and Hub, Renew
1984-88-one (1.0) 1.4

Caliper Assembly, Renew
Includes: Bleed system.
1984-88-one (.5) 9
both 1.7

Caliper Assy., R&R and Recondition
Includes: Bleed system.
1984-88-one (.8) 1.4
both 2.7

Brake System Combination Valve, Renew
Includes: Bleed complete system.
1984-88 (1.2) 1.5

Load Sensing Proportioning Valve, Renew
Includes: Adjust valve and bleed brakes.
1984-88 (.7) 1.0

PARKING BRAKE

Parking Brake, Adjust
1984-88 (.3) 4

Parking Brake Warning Lamp Switch, Renew
1984-88 (.8) 1.1

Parking Brake Control, Renew
1984-88 (.9) 1.4

Parking Brake Cables, Renew
Includes: Adjust parking brake.
1984-88-front (.5) 7
intermediate (.3) 5
rear-each (.6) 8
assembly (1.0) 1.5

LABOR 7 COOLING SYSTEM 7 LABOR

(Factory Time) Chilton Time

Winterize Cooling System
Includes: Run engine to check for leaks, tighten all hose connections. Test radiator and pressure cap. Drain radiator and engine block. Add anti-freeze and refill system.
All models 5

Thermostat, Renew
1984-88 (.4) 6

Radiator Assembly, R&R or Renew
1984-88 (.5) 9
w/A.T. add (.1) 1

ADD THESE OPERATIONS TO RADIATOR R&R

Boil & Repair 1.5
Rod Clean 1.9
Repair Core 1.3
Renew Tank 1.6
Renew Trans. Oil Cooler 1.9
Recore Radiator 1.7

Fan Blades, Renew
1984-88 (.2) 5

Drive Belts, Renew
1984-88
Water Pump
2.6L eng (.3) 4
Fan & alter (.2) .... *.3
Pow str (.4) .... *.6
A.C. (.2) 3
Air pump (.3) 4
P.S. & A.C. (.2) .... *.3
*w/A.C. add (.1) 1

Drive Belts, Adjust
All models-one 2
each adtnl 1

Radiator Hoses, Renew
1984-88-upper (.3) 4
lower (.4) 6

Water Pump, Renew
1984-88
2.2L & 2.5L engs (1.0) 1.6
2.6L eng (.7) 1.2
3.0L eng (1.5) 2.2
w/A.C. add 5

Coolant Temperature Sensor/Switch, Renew
1984-88 (.2) 3

Radiator Fan Coolant Sensor, Renew
1984-88 (.2) 3

Radiator Fan Motor, Renew
1984-88-wo/A.C. (.4) 5
w/A.C. (.4) 5

Radiator Fan Switch, Renew
1984-88 (.3) 6

Radiator Fan Motor Relay, Renew
1984-88 (.2) 3

Transaxle Auxiliary Oil Cooler, Renew
1984-88 (.5) 9

Water Jacket Expansion Plugs, Renew (Cylinder Block)
1984-88
2.6L & 3.0L engs
right side
front (.7) 1.0
center or rear (1.1) 1.5

LABOR 7 COOLING SYSTEM 7 LABOR

	(Factory Time)	Chilton Time
left side		
upper front or center	(2.1)	3.0
lower front or center	(.3)	.5
rear	(1.0)	1.4
2.2L & 2.5L engs		
left side		
front	(.7)	1.0
rear	(.4)	.6
right side		
front or center	(.6)	.9
rear	(1.0)	1.4
w/P.S. add	(.3)	.3
w/Pulse air add	(.6)	.6
Water Jacket Expansion Plugs, Renew (Cylinder Head)		
1984-88		
2.2L & 2.5L engs		
front	(.6)	.9
rear	(.8)	1.1
2.6L eng		
rear	(.5)	.7
Temperature Gauge (Dash Unit), Renew		
1984-88	(.3)	.6
Temperature Gauge (Engine Unit), Renew		
1984-88		
sending unit	(.2)	.4
light switch	(.2)	.4
Heater Hoses, Renew		
1984-88-one	(.4)	.4
each adtnl	(.1)	.2
Heater Water Valve, Renew (Front Heater)		
1984-88-w/A.C.	(.3)	.5
Heater Control Assembly, Renew (Front Heater)		
1984-88-wo/A.C.	(.4)	.7
w/A.C.	(.3)	.6
Vacuum Switch (Push Button), Renew		
1984-88-w/A.C.	(.4)	.7
w/Console add	(.2)	.2
Blower Motor Switch, Renew (Front Heater)		
1984-88-wo/A.C.	(.4)	.7
w/A.C.	(.5)	.8
w/Console add	(.2)	.2
Heater Core, R&R or Renew (Front Heater)		
1984-88-wo/A.C.	(1.8)	3.5
w/A.C.	(2.4)	*5.5

*Includes: Recharge A.C. system.

ADD THESE OPERATIONS TO HEATER CORE R&R

	Chilton Time
Boil & Repair	1.2
Repair Core	.9
Recore	1.2

	(Factory Time)	Chilton Time
Heater Blower Motor, Renew (Front Heater)		
1984-88-wo/A.C.	(.4)	.6
w/A.C.	(.6)	1.2
Blower Motor Resistor, Renew (Front Heater)		
1984-88-wo/A.C.	(.2)	.3
w/A.C.	(.2)	.4
Rear Heater Coolant Line, Renew		
1987-88	(.4)	.5
Rear Heater Water Valve, Renew		
1987-88	(.9)	1.2
Rear Heater Control Assembly, Renew		
1987-88	(.3)	.5
Rear Heater Blower Motor Switch, Renew		
1987-88	(.4)	.6
Rear Heater Blower Motor, Renew		
1987-88	(.7)	1.1
Rear Heater Blower Motor Resistor, Renew		
1987-88	(.5)	.7
Rear Heater Blower Fan, Renew		
1987-88	(.9)	1.3
Rear Heater Core, R&R or Renew		
1987-88	(.7)	1.3

LABOR 8 EXHAUST SYSTEM 8 LABOR

	(Factory Time)	Chilton Time
Muffler, Renew		
1984-88	(.4)	.7
Cut exhaust pipe add	(.2)	.2
Exhaust Pipe, Renew		
1984-88	(.7)	1.1
Cut at muffler add	(.2)	.2
Exhaust Pipe Extension, Renew		
1984-88	(.6)	1.0
Tail Pipe, Renew		
1984-88	(.4)	.6
Cut at muffler add	(.2)	.2
Catalytic Converter, Renew		
1984-88		
exh pipe mount	(.7)	.9
manif mount	(.9)	1.3
Exhaust Manifold or Gasket, Renew		
1984-88		
2.2L & 2.5L engs	(2.7)	3.7
2.6L eng	(.7)	1.2
3.0L eng		
Front	(.6)	1.0
Rear	(.8)	1.2

COMBINATIONS

	(Factory Time)	Chilton Time
Exhaust System, Renew (Complete)		
1984-88		1.5

LABOR 9 FRONT SUSPENSION 9 LABOR

Note: On all front suspension operations alignment charges must be added if performed. Time given does not include alignment.

	(Factory Time)	Chilton Time
Wheel, Renew		
one		.5
Wheels, Rotate (All)		
All models		.5
Wheels, Balance		
one		.3
each adtnl		.2
Check Alignment of Front End		
All models		.5
Note: Deduct if alignment is performed.		
Toe-Out, Adjust		
All models		.6
Align Front End		
Includes: Adjust camber, toe, car height and center steering wheel.		
All models	(.8)	1.4
Steering Knuckle Bearing, Renew (Wheel Bearing)		
Add alignment charges.		
1984-88-one	(1.2)	1.6
both	(2.3)	3.0
Steering Knuckle, Renew (One)		
Add alignment charges.		
1984-88	(1.0)	1.6
Front Strut Assy., R&R or Renew		
Add alignment charges.		
1984-88-one	(1.1)	1.4
both	(2.0)	2.7
Lower Control Arm Assy., Renew		
Includes: Reset toe-in.		
1984-88-one	(1.1)	1.6
Lower Ball Joint, Renew (One)		
Add alignment charges.		
1984-88	(.8)	1.2
Lower Control Arm Strut Bushings, Renew		
Add alignment charges.		
1984-88-one side	(.6)	.9
Front Coil Spring, Renew		
Includes: R&R front strut.		
Add alignment charges.		
1984-88-one	(.8)	1.5
both	(1.5)	2.8
Front Sway Bar, Renew		
1984-88	(.4)	.7
Sway Bar Bracket and Bushings, Renew		
1984-88-both	(.5)	.9
Front Suspension Strut (Dual Path) Mount Assy., Renew		
Includes: Renew bearing.		
1984-88	(.8)	1.5
K-Frame Assembly, Renew		
Add alignment charges.		
All models	(2.5)	4.0
Drive Shaft Boot, Renew		
Includes: Clean and lubricate C/V joint.		
All models		
1984-88		
one-inner or outer	(.7)	1.0
both-one side	(1.0)	1.4
Renew shaft seal, add		
right side	(.1)	.1
left side	(.3)	.3

LABOR 9 FRONT SUSPENSION 9 LABOR

(Factory Time) Chilton Time

Drive Shaft C/V Joint, Renew
All models
1984-88
one-inner or outer (.7) 1.0
both-one side (1.0) 1.4
inter shaft U-joint (.6) 1.0
Renew shaft seal, add
right side (.1) 1
left side (.3) 3

Front Wheel Drive Shaft Assy., Renew
All models
1984-88
inter spline yoke (.6) 1.0
inter stub shaft (.6) 1.0
all others-each (1.0) 1.4
Renew shaft seal, add
right side (.1) 1
left side (.3) 3

Intermediate Shaft Support Bearing, Renew
1984-88-each (.6) 1.0

Drive Shaft Oil Seal, Renew
All models
1984-88
right side (.5) 8
left side (.7) 1.1

LABOR 11 STEERING GEAR 11 LABOR

(Factory Time) Chilton Time

Tie Rods or Tie Rod Ends, Renew
Includes: Reset toe-out.
1984-88
outer-one (.9) 1.2
inner & outer-w/P.S.
one side (1.9) 2.5

STANDARD STEERING

Horn Contact Cable and Ring, Renew
1984-88 (.2) 4

Horn Switch, Renew
1984-88 (.2) 3

Steering Wheel, Renew
1984-88 (.2) 3

Steering Column Jacket, Renew
Does not include painting.
1984-88
Std Column
console shift (1.1) 1.8
column shift (1.5) 2.3
Tilt Column
console shift (1.5) 2.6
column shift (1.6) 2.8

Upper Mast Jacket Bearing, Renew
Includes: Replace insulators if necessary.
1984-88
std column (.4) 9
tilt column (1.2) 2.0

Steering Column Gear Shift Tube, Renew
1984-88
std column (1.3) 2.1
tilt column (1.8) 2.6

Steering Column Lower Shaft Bearing, Renew
Includes: Replace support if necessary.
1984-88
Std Column
console shift (.8) 1.6
column shift (.9) 1.7
Tilt Column
console shift (.6) 1.0
column shift (.6) 1.0

Steering Gear Assy., R&R or Renew
1984-88 (1.6) 3.0

POWER STEERING

Power Steering Pump Pressure Check
All models 5

Power Steering Pump Belt, Renew
1984-88 (.4) 6
P.S. & A.C. belt (.2) 3
w/A.C. add (.1) 1
w/Air inj add (.1) 1

Power Steering Gear Assy., R&R or Renew
Includes: Reset toe-in.
1984-88 (1.9) 3.1

Steering Gear Oil Seals, Renew (All)
Includes: R&R gear assy. and reset toe-in.
1984-88 (3.1) 5.1

Upper and Lower Valve Pinion Seals, Renew
1984-88 (1.4) 2.0
Renew brgs add (.3) 5

Power Steering Pump, Renew
Includes: Test pump and transfer pulley.
1984-86
2.2L & 2.5L engs (1.0) 1.4
2.6L eng (.8) 1.2
1987-88
2.2L & 2.5L engs (1.2) 1.6
2.6L eng (.8) 1.2

Power Steering Pump, R&R and Recondition
1984-88
2.2L & 2.5L engs (1.6) 2.3
2.6L eng (1.3) 2.0

Pump Flow Control Valve, Test and Clean or Renew
1984-88
2.2L & 2.5L engs (.6) 1.0
2.6L eng (.7) 1.1

Power Steering Reservoir or Seals, Renew
1984-86 (.7) 1.1
1987-88
2.2L & 2.5L engs (1.3) 1.8
2.6L eng (.7) 1.1

Pump Drive Shaft Oil Seal, Renew
1984-86
2.2L & 2.5L engs (.9) 1.4
2.6L eng (.7) 1.1
1987-88
2.2L & 2.5L engs (1.3) 1.8
2.6L eng (.7) 1.1

Power Steering Hoses, Renew
1984-88-each (.4) 5

LABOR 12 CYLINDER HEAD & VALVE SYSTEM 12 LABOR

(Factory Time) Chilton Time

Compression Test
Four-1984-88 6
V-6-1987-88 8

Cylinder Head Gasket, Renew
Includes: Clean carbon.
1984-88
2.2L & 2.5L engs (3.4) 4.8
2.6L eng (2.8) 4.5
3.0L eng
front (2.8) 3.9
rear (2.8) 3.9
both (3.7) 5.2
w/P.S. add (.2) 2
w/Air inj add (.2) 2

Cylinder Head, Renew
Includes: Transfer parts as required. Clean carbon, make all necessary adjustments.
1984-88
2.2L & 2.5L engs (5.3) 8.0

COMBINATIONS

Add To Valve Job
See Machine Shop Operations

(Factory Time) Chilton Time

DRAIN, EVACUATE & RECHARGE AIR CONDITIONING SYSTEM
All models 1.0

CARBURETOR, RECONDITION
Holly (.5) 9

DISTRIBUTOR, RECONDITION
All models (.7) 7

RECONDITION CYL. HEAD (HEAD REMOVED)
2.2L eng (1.4) 2.0
2.5L eng (1.4) 2.0
3.0L eng (3.6) 4.8

CAMSHAFT, RENEW (HEAD DISASSEMBLED)
OHC engs (.1) 2

REMOVE CYLINDER TOP RIDGE
Each (.1) 1

RENEW OIL PUMP
All engs (.2) 3

ROD BEARINGS, RENEW (PAN REMOVED)
Four (.7) 1.2
V-6 .... 1.8

DEGLAZE CYLINDER WALLS
Each (.1) 1

PLASTIGAUGE BEARINGS
Each (.1) 1

OIL FILTER ELEMENT, RENEW
All models (.3) 3

LABOR 12 CYLINDER HEAD & VALVE SYSTEM 12 LABOR

(Factory Time) Chilton Time

2.6L eng (4.7) 7.4
3.0L eng
front (4.3) 6.0
rear (4.3) 6.0
both (6.0) 8.4
w/P.S. add (.2) 2
w/Air inj add (.2) 2

Clean Carbon and Grind Valves

Includes: R&R cylinder head. Reface valves and seats. Minor tune up.

1984-88
2.2L & 2.5L engs (4.8) 6.8
2.6L eng (5.4) 8.0
3.0L eng
front (3.7) 5.2
rear (3.7) 5.2
both (6.5) 9.1
w/P.S. add (.2) 2
w/Air inj add (.2) 2

Cylinder Head Cover Gasket, Renew or Reseal

1984-88
2.2L & 2.5L engs (.8) 1.1
2.6L eng (.4) 6
3.0L eng
front (.3) 5
rear (.4) 6

Valve Rocker Arms or Shafts, Renew

1984-88
2.2L & 2.5L engs
all arms (1.2) 1.6
2.6L eng-one shaft (1.0) 1.4
both shafts (1.1) 1.7
3.0L eng
one head (.9) 1.3
both heads (1.8) 2.5

Valve Tappets, Renew

1984-88
2.2L & 2.5L engs
one (1.0) 1.4
each adtnl (.1) 1
3.0L eng
one bank (.8) 1.2
both banks (1.6) 2.4

Valve Tappets, Adjust

1984-88
2.6L eng (.9) 1.5

Jet Valves, Renew

1984-88
2.6L eng-one or all (.9) 1.1

Valve Springs and/or Valve Stem Oil Seals, Renew

1984-88
2.2L & 2.5L engs
one (1.2) 1.5
all (1.9) 2.9
2.6L eng (4.7) *6.0
*w/Head on car 3.5

LABOR 13 ENGINE ASSEMBLY & MOUNTS 13 LABOR

(Factory Time) Chilton Time

Engine Assembly, Remove & Install

Includes: R&R engine and transmission as a unit. Does not include transfer of any parts or equipment.

1984-88
2.2L & 2.5L engs 6.0
2.6L eng 5.2
3.0L eng 6.5
w/A.C. add 5
w/P.S. add 2

Short Engine Assembly, Renew (w/All Internal Parts Less Cyl. Head and Oil Pan)

Includes: R&R engine and transmission as a unit. Transfer all necessary parts not supplied with replacement engine. Clean carbon, grind valves. Minor tune up.

1984-88
2.2L & 2.5L engs (9.1) 15.0
2.6L eng (9.4) 15.5
3.0L eng (10.8) 17.2
w/A.C. add (.5) 5
w/P.S. add (.2) 2

(P) Engine Assy., R&R and Recondition (Complete)

Includes: Rebore block, install new pistons, rings, rod and main bearings. Clean carbon, grind valves. Replace valve stem oil seals. Tune engine.

1984-88
2.2L & 2.5L engs (17.8) 25.2
2.6L eng (17.0) 23.4
3.0L eng (19.5) 28.2
w/A.C. add (.5) 5
w/P.S. add (.2) 2

Engine Assembly, Recondition (In Car)

Includes: Expand or renew pistons, install rings, pins, rod and main bearings. Clean carbon, grind valves. Tune engine.

1984-88
2.2L & 2.5L engs (15.2) 20.8
2.6L eng (14.4) 19.0
3.0L eng (15.8) 22.3
w/P.S. add (.2) 2

Engine Support, Renew

1984-88-right side (.3) 5
left side (.3) 5
center (.4) 6
Trans/Axle
Roll rod (.2) 5

LABOR 14 PISTONS, RINGS & BEARINGS 14 LABOR

(Factory Time) Chilton Time

Rings, Renew (See Engine Combinations)

Includes: Replace connecting rod bearings, deglaze cylinder walls, clean carbon. Minor tune up.

1984-88
2.2L & 2.5L engs
one cyl (4.6) 6.9
all cyls (5.9) 8.1
2.6L eng-one cyl (4.1) 6.3
all cyls (5.7) 8.0
3.0L eng
one cyl (4.4) 6.1
one cyl-each bank (5.4) 7.5
all cyls-both banks (7.7) 10.7
w/P.S. add (.2) 2
w/Air inj add (.2) 2

Pistons or Connecting Rods, Renew

Includes: Replace connecting rod bearings and piston rings, deglaze cylinder walls. Clean carbon from cylinder head.

1984-88
2.2L & 2.5L engs
one cyl (4.9) 7.2
all cyls (6.1) 9.3

COMBINATIONS

Add To Engine Work

See Machine Shop Operations

(Factory Time) Chilton Time

DRAIN, EVACUATE & RECHARGE AIR CONDITIONING SYSTEM
All models 1.0

CARBURETOR, RECONDITION
Holly (.5) 9

DISTRIBUTOR, RECONDITION
All models (.7) 7

R&R CYLINDER HEAD (ENGINE REMOVED)
Four 1.5

CONNECTING ROD, RENEW (ENGINE DISASSEMBLED)
Each 4

RECONDITION CYL. HEAD (HEAD REMOVED)
2.2L eng (1.4) 2.0
2.5L engs (1.4) 2.0
3.0L eng (3.6) 4.8

CAMSHAFT, RENEW (HEAD DISASSEMBLED)
OHC engs (.1) 2

REMOVE CYLINDER TOP RIDGE
Each (.1) 1

RENEW OIL PUMP
All engs (.2) 3

ROD BEARINGS, RENEW (PAN REMOVED)
Four (.7) 1.2
V-6 .... 1.8

DEGLAZE CYLINDER WALLS
Each (.1) 1

PLASTIGAUGE BEARINGS
Each (.1) 1

OIL FILTER ELEMENT, RENEW
All models (.3) 3

LABOR 14 PISTONS, RINGS & BEARINGS 14 LABOR

(Factory Time) Chilton Time

2.6L eng-one cyl (4.7) ... 6.6
all cyls (7.2) ... 9.2
3.0L eng
one cyl (4.4) ... 6.4
one cyl-each bank (5.4) ... 8.1
all cyls-both banks (7.8) ... 12.5
w/P.S. add (.2) 2
w/Air inj add (.2) 2

Connecting Rod Bearings, Renew
1984-88
2.2L & 2.5L engs (2.1) ... 3.0
2.6L eng (1.2) ... 2.2
3.0L eng (2.4) ... 3.4

LABOR 15 CRANKSHAFT & DAMPER 15 LABOR

(Factory Time) Chilton Time

Crankshaft and Main Bearings, Renew
Includes: R&R engine assembly.
1984-88
2.2L & 2.5L engs (6.7) ... 11.2
2.6L eng (7.6) ... 12.1
3.0L eng (6.5) ... 10.0
w/A.C. add (.5) 5
w/P.S. add (.2) 2

Main Bearings, Renew
1984-88
2.2L & 2.5L engs
No 2-3 or 4 (1.8) ... 2.8
No 1 (3.0) ... 4.0
No 5 (5.6) ... 8.8
all (7.0) ... 11.0
No. 5 brg. w/A520-A555
Trans/axle add (.3) 3
2.6L eng (2.2) ... 3.0
3.0L eng (2.0) ... 2.8

Main and Rod Bearings, Renew
1984-88
2.6L eng (2.9) ... 4.2
3.0L eng (3.1) ... 4.6

Rear Main Bearing Oil Seals, Renew (Complete)
1984-88
2.2L & 2.5L engs (3.0) ... 5.4
2.6L eng-w/A.T. (3.2) ... 5.5
3.0L eng (3.0) ... 5.4
w/A520-A555
Trans/axle add (.3) 3

Crankshaft Pulley, Renew
1984-88
2.2L & 2.5L engs (.5) 7
2.6L eng (.4) 6
3.0L eng (.4) 6
w/A.C. add (.1) 1
w/P.S. add (.1) 1

Crankshaft Front Oil Seal, Renew
1984-88
2.2L & 2.5L engs (1.3) ... 2.0
3.0L eng (1.4) ... 2.1
w/A.C. add (.2) 2
w/P.S. add (.2) 2

LABOR 16 CAMSHAFT & TIMING GEARS 16 LABOR

(Factory Time) Chilton Time

Timing Chain or Belt Case/Cover, Renew
Includes: Renew gasket.
1984-88
2.2L & 2.5L engs
upper cover (.2) 4
lower cover (.6) ... 1.0
2.6L eng (3.2) ... 4.5
3.0L eng
lower cover (1.0) ... 1.3
upper cover-one (.2) 4
w/A.C. add (.5) 5
w/P.S. add (.1) 1

Timing Belt, Renew
1984-88
2.2L & 2.5L engs (1.6) ... 2.3
3.0L eng (1.3) ... 2.0
w/A.C. add (.5) 5
w/P.S. add (.2) 2

Balance Shafts Chain and/or Sprockets, Renew
1986-88
2.5L eng (2.4) ... 3.4
w/A.C. add (.6) 6
w/P.S. add (.1) 1
Renew carrier add (.6) 6

Timing Chain, Renew
Includes: Renew cover seal.
1984-88
2.6L eng
cam drive (3.6) ... 5.0
shaft drive (3.4) ... 4.8
w/A.C. add (.2) 2
w/P.S. add (.1) 1

Timing Chain, Adjust
1984-88
2.6L eng (.4) 8

Timing Chain Guide, Renew
1984-88
2.6L eng-cam drive
right or left (3.2) ... 4.6
silent shaft-upper (3.2) ... 4.6
lower (3.2) ... 4.6
w/A.C. add (.2) 2
w/P.S. add (.1) 1

Timing Chain Tensioner, Renew
1984-88
2.6L eng (3.5) ... 4.9
w/A.C. add (.2) 2
w/P.S. add (.1) 1

Timing Belt Tensioner, Renew
1984-88
2.2L & 2.5L engs (.9) ... 1.5
3.0L eng (1.2) ... 1.8
w/A.C. add (.6) 6

Timing Chain Cover Oil Seal, Renew
1984-88
2.6L eng (.5) 9
w/P.S. add (.1) 1

Camshaft Sprocket, Renew
Includes: Renew cover oil seal, timing chain and crankshaft sprocket, where required.
1984-88
2.2L & 2.5L engs (1.7) ... 2.4
2.6L eng (3.6) ... 5.0
3.0L eng
front head (1.7) ... 2.4
rear head (1.7) ... 2.4
w/A.C. add (.2) 2
w/P.S. add (.2) 2

Camshaft Oil Seal, Renew
1984-88
2.2L & 2.5L engs (.7) ... 1.1
2.2-2.6L eng-rear (.4) 8

Camshaft, Renew
1984-88
2.2L & 2.5L engs (1.7) ... *2.8
2.6L eng (1.6) ... 2.2
3.0L eng
front head (2.1) ... 2.9
rear head (2.1) ... 2.9
*Renew valve springs add (1.1) ... 1.1

Camshaft Distributor Drive Gear, Renew
1984-88
2.6L eng (.7) ... 1.1

Intermediate Shaft, Renew
1984-88
2.2L & 2.5L engs (1.3) ... 2.5
w/A.C. add (.2) 2

Silent Shaft Sprocket, Renew
1984-88
2.6L eng-one or both (3.4) ... 4.7
w/A.C. add (.2) 2
w/P.S. add (.1) 1

Intermediate Shaft Sprocket, Renew
1984-88
2.2L & 2.5L engs (1.7) ... 2.7
w/A.C. add (.2) 2
w/P.S. add (.2) 2

Silent Shaft, Renew
1984-88
2.6L eng-right (4.0) ... 5.6
left (5.0) ... 7.0
both (5.3) ... 7.5
w/A.C. add (.4) 4
w/P.S. add (.1) 1

Intermediate Shaft Oil Seal, Renew
1984-88
2.2L & 2.5L engs (1.1) ... 1.8
w/A.C. add (.2) 2
w/P.S. add (.2) 2

LABOR 17 ENGINE OILING SYSTEM 17 LABOR

(Factory Time) — Chilton Time

Oil Pan or Gasket, Renew or Reseal
1984-88
2.2L & 2.5L engs (1.0)...... 1.4
2.6L eng (.6)...... 1.0
3.0L eng (1.0)...... 1.4

Pressure Test Engine Bearings (Pan Off)
All models...... 1.0

Oil Pump, Renew
1984-88
2.2L & 2.5L engs (1.3)...... 1.7
2.6L eng (3.8)...... 5.2
3.0L eng (2.0)...... 2.8
w/A.C. add (.2)...... .2
w/P.S. add (.1)...... .1

Oil Pump, R&R and Recondition
1984-88
2.2L eng (1.7)...... 2.2

Oil Pressure Relief Valve Spring, Renew
1984-88
2.2L & 2.5L engs (1.6)...... 2.2
2.6L eng (3.4)...... 4.7
3.0L eng (1.1)...... 1.5

Oil Pressure Gauge (Engine Unit), Renew
1984-88 (.2)...... .4

Oil Pressure Gauge (Dash), Renew
1984-88 (.3)...... .6

Oil Filter Element, Renew
1984-88 (.2)...... .3

LABOR 18 CLUTCH & FLYWHEEL 18 LABOR

(Factory Time) — Chilton Time

Clutch Self-Adjusting Mechanism, Renew
1984-88 (.3)...... .6

Clutch Release Cable, Renew
1984-88 (.4)...... .5

Clutch Release Lever and/or Seal, Renew
1984-88 (.5)...... .8

Clutch Release Bearing or Fork, Renew
1984-88 (2.8)...... 3.8
w/A520-A555
Trans/axle add (.3)...... .3

Clutch Assembly, Renew
1984-88 (2.9)...... 4.0
w/A520-A555
Trans/axle add (.3)...... .3
Renew input seal add (.2)...... .2

Flywheel, Renew
1984-88 (3.0)...... 4.2
w/A520-A555
Trans/axle add (.3)...... .3

LABOR 19 STANDARD TRANSMISSION 19 LABOR

(Factory Time) — Chilton Time

Drive Shaft Boot, Renew
Includes: Clean and lubricate C/V joint.
1984-88
one-inner or outer (.7)...... 1.0
both-one side (1.0)...... 1.4
Renew shaft seal, add
right side (.1)...... .1
left side (.3)...... .3

Drive Shaft C/V Joint, Renew
1984-88
one-inner or outer (.7)...... 1.0
both-one side (1.0)...... 1.4
Renew shaft seal, add
right side (.1)...... .1
left side (.3)...... .3

Front Wheel Drive Shaft Assy., Renew
1984-88-each (1.0)...... 1.4
Renew shaft seal, add
right side (.1)...... .1
left side (.3)...... .3

Drive Shaft Oil Seal, Renew
1984-88-right (.5)...... .8
left (.7)...... 1.1

Manual Trans/Axle Assembly, Remove & Install
Does not include transfer of any parts.
1984-88 (2.7)...... 3.7
w/A520-A555
Trans/axle add (.3)...... .3
Renew assy add (.4)...... .6

Manual Trans/Axle Assy., R&R and Recondition (Complete)
1984-88 (5.5)...... 8.0
w/A520-A555
Trans/axle add (.3)...... .3
Renew ring gear and pinion add (.7)...... 1.5
Renew clutch assy add (.2)...... .2

Manual Trans/Axle Assy., Recondition (Off Car)
1984-88
A460 (2.5)...... 3.9
A465-A525 (2.8)...... 4.2
A520-A555 (3.2)...... 4.5

LABOR 21 SHIFT LINKAGE 21 LABOR

(Factory Time) — Chilton Time

MANUAL

Gearshift Linkage, Adjust
1984-88 (.2)...... .4

Gearshift Lever, Renew
1984-88 (.4)...... .6

Gearshift Control Rod and/or Swivel, Renew
1984-88 (.3)...... .4

Gearshift Mechanism, Renew
1984-88
cable shift (.7)...... 1.1

Selector Shaft Seal, Renew
1984-88 (.8)...... 1.1

Trans/Axle Selector Shaft, Renew
1984-88 (1.3)...... 1.7

Gearshift Selector Cable, Renew
1984-88 (.9)...... 1.4

Gearshift Crossover Cable, Renew
1984-88 (.8)...... 1.3

AUTOMATIC

Throttle Linkage, Adjust
1984-88 (.2)...... .4

Selector Lever, Renew
1984-88 (.3)...... .4

Gearshift Mechanism, Renew
1984-88 (.4)...... .8

Gearshift Control Cable, Renew
1984-88 (.5)...... .8

Throttle Lever Control Cable, Renew
1984-88 (.3)...... .6

Gear Selector Dial, Renew
1984-88 (.7)...... 1.1

LABOR 23 AUTOMATIC TRANSMISSION 23 LABOR

(Factory Time) — Chilton Time

ON CAR SERVICES

Drain & Refill Unit
All models...... .6

Oil Pressure Check
All models...... .8

Check Unit For Oil Leaks
Includes: Clean and dry outside of case and run unit to determine point of leak.

LABOR 23 AUTOMATIC TRANSMISSION 23 LABOR

(Factory Time)	Chilton Time
All models	.9
Neutral Safety Switch, Renew	
All models (.3)	.4
Transmission Auxiliary Oil Cooler, Renew	
1984-88 (.5)	.9
Oil Cooler Lines, Renew	
Includes: Cut and form to size.	
1984-88 (.4)	.6
Throttle Linkage, Adjust	
1984-88 (.2)	.4
Kickdown Band, Adjust	
1984-88 (.2)	.4
Throttle Valve Lever Shaft Seal, Renew	
1984-88 (.5)	.8
Valve Body Manual Lever Shaft Seal, Renew	
1984-88 (.3)	.6
Differential Gear Cover, Renew or Reseal	
1984-88 (.8)	1.2
Drive Shaft Boot, Renew	
Includes: Clean and lubricate C/V joint.	
All models	
1984-88	
one-inner or outer (.7)	1.0
both-one side (1.0)	1.4
Renew shaft seal, add	
right side (.1)	.1
left side (.3)	.3
Drive Shaft C/V Joint, Renew	
All models	
1984-88	
one-inner or outer (.7)	1.0
both-one side (1.0)	1.4
inter shaft U-joint (.6)	1.0
Renew shaft seal, add	
right side (.1)	.1
left side (.3)	.3
Front Wheel Drive Shaft Assy., Renew	
All models	
1984-88	
inter spline yoke (.6)	1.0
inter stub shaft (.6)	1.0
all others-each (1.0)	1.4
Renew shaft seal, add	
right side (.1)	.1
left side (.3)	.3
Intermediate Shaft Support Bearing, Renew	
1984-88-each (.6)	1.0
Drive Shaft Seal, Renew	
1984-88-right side (.5)	.8
left side (.7)	1.1
Transfer Gear Cover, Renew or Reseal	
1984-88 (.5)	.7
Transfer Gear, Renew	
Includes: R&R cover, renew bearing.	
1984-88 (1.0)	1.3
Governor Assy., Renew or Recondition	
Includes: R&R oil pan.	
1984-88 (1.3)	2.4
Governor Support and Parking Gear, Renew	
Includes: R&R oil pan.	
1984-88 (1.9)	2.9
Oil Pan and/or Gasket, Renew	
1984-88 (.6)	1.2
Oil Filter Element, Renew	
Includes: R&R oil pan.	
1984-88 (.7)	1.4
Parking Lock Sprag, Renew	
Includes: R&R oil pan.	
1984-88 (1.5)	2.6
Accumulator Piston, Renew or Recondition	
Includes: R&R oil pan.	
1984-88 (1.1)	2.2
Kickdown Servo, Renew	
Includes: R&R oil pan.	
1984-88 (1.4)	2.5
Reverse Servo, Renew	
Includes: R&R oil pan.	
1984-88 (1.2)	2.2
Valve Body, Renew	
Includes: R&R oil pan.	
1984-88 (1.0)	2.1
Valve Body, R&R and Recondition	
Includes: R&R oil pan and renew filter.	
1984-88 (1.7)	3.2
SERVICES REQUIRING R&R	
Trans/Axle Assy., Remove & Install	
1984-88	
2.2L & 2.5L engs (2.7)	3.7
2.6L eng (3.0)	4.1
3.0L eng (2.7)	3.7
Renew assy add (.4)	.6
Trans/Axle Assembly, Reseal	
Includes: R&R trans/axle and renew all seals and gaskets.	
1984-88	
2.2L & 2.5L engs (5.4)	7.0
2.6L eng (5.6)	7.4
3.0L eng (5.4)	7.0
Trans/Axle Assy., R&R and Recondition	
Includes: Disassemble complete, clean, inspect and replace all parts as required.	
1984-88	
2.2L & 2.5L engs	12.5
2.6L eng	12.9
3.0L eng	12.5
Flush conv and cooler lines add	.5
Kickdown Band, Renew	
1984-88	
2.2L & 2.5L engs (4.0)	4.9
2.6L eng (4.3)	5.3
3.0L eng (4.0)	4.9
Reverse Band, Renew	
1984-88	
2.2L & 2.5L engs (4.2)	5.2
2.6L eng (4.5)	5.6
3.0L eng (4.2)	5.2
Trans/Axle Case, Renew	
1984-88	
2.2L & 2.5L engs (7.7)	10.0
2.6L eng (8.0)	10.4
3.0L eng (7.7)	10.0
Front and Rear Clutch Seals, Renew	
1984-88	
2.2L & 2.5L engs (4.2)	5.2
2.6L eng (4.5)	5.6
3.0L eng (4.2)	5.2
Torque Converter, Renew	
1984-88	
2.2L & 2.5L engs (3.3)	4.0
2.6L eng (3.6)	4.4
3.0L eng (3.3)	4.0
Torque Converter Drive Plate, Renew (w/ Ring Gear)	
1984-88	
2.2L & 2.5L engs (3.3)	4.0
2.6L eng (3.6)	4.4
3.0L eng (3.3)	4.0
Front Oil Pump, Renew	
1984-88	
2.2L & 2.5L engs (3.7)	4.5
2.6L eng (4.0)	4.9
3.0L eng (3.7)	4.5
Front Pump Oil Seal, Renew	
1984-88	
2.2L & 2.5L engs (3.3)	4.0
2.6L eng (3.6)	4.4
3.0L eng (3.3)	4.0
Reaction Shaft and/or Bushing, Renew	
Includes: Renew front pump if necessary.	
1984-88	
2.2L & 2.5L eng (3.7)	4.5
2.6L eng (4.0)	4.9
3.0L eng (3.7)	4.5
Trans/Axle Differential Assy., Recondition	
Includes: R&R trans/axle, completely recondition differential assembly only.	
1984-88	
2.2L & 2.5L engs (6.6)	9.0
2.6L eng (6.9)	9.4
3.0L eng (6.6)	9.0

LABOR 26 REAR AXLE AND SUSPENSION 26 LABOR

(Factory Time)	Chilton Time
Rear Wheel Bearings, Renew or Repack	
1984-88-one side (.6)	.9
both sides (1.1)	1.7
Rear Wheel Grease Seal, Renew	
1984-88-one side (.4)	.7
Rear Shock Absorbers, Renew	
1984-88-one (.3)	.5
both (.4)	.7
Rear Springs, Renew	
1984-88-one (.9)	1.2
both (1.6)	2.2
Lower Control Arm Bushings, Renew	
1984-88-one side (.6)	1.0
Stub Axle Spindle, Renew	
1984-88-each (.5)	.7
Rear Wheel Mounting Studs, Renew	
1984-88-one (.5)	.8
each adtnl	.1
Rear Spring Shackle, Renew	
1984-88-one (.4)	.6
Rear Spring Bushing, Renew	
1984-88-each (.4)	.6
Rear Spring Front Hanger, Renew	
1984-88-one (.7)	1.1

LABOR 28 AIR CONDITIONING 28 LABOR

(Factory Time) — Chilton Time

Note: If more than one item requires replacement where evacuation and discharging the system is already included in the operation, deduct 1.0 hour for each additional item to the times listed.

Drain, Evacuate, Leak Test and Charge System
All models........ 1.0

Partial Charge
Includes: Leak test.
All models (.4)........ .6

Performance Test
All models........ .8

Vacuum Leak Test
All models........ .8

Compressor Drive Belt, Renew
1984-88 (.2)........ .3

C-171 COMPRESSOR

Compressor Assembly, Renew
Includes: Transfer parts as required. Pressure test and charge system.
1984-88
2.2L & 2.5L engs (1.4)........ 2.5
2.6L eng (1.9)........ 3.0
3.0L eng (1.4)........ 2.5

Compressor Clutch Field Coil, Renew
1984-88
2.2L & 2.5L engs (.6)........ .9
2.6L eng (.9)........ 1.4
3.0L eng (.6)........ .9

Compressor Clutch Pulley (w/Hub), Renew
1984-88
2.2L & 2.5L engs (.4)........ .5
2.6L eng (.7)........ 1.0
3.0L eng (.4)........ .5

Compressor Clutch Assembly, Renew
1984-88
2.2L & 2.5L engs (.6)........ .8
2.6L eng (.9)........ 1.3
3.0L eng (.6)........ .8

(Factory Time) — Chilton Time

Compressor Front Cover Seal, Renew
Includes: R&R compressor. Pressure test and charge system.
1984-88
2.2L & 2.5L engs (1.8)........ 3.1
2.6L eng (2.3)........ 3.6
3.0L eng (1.8)........ 3.1

Compressor Rear Cover Seal, Renew
Includes: R&R compressor. Pressure test and charge system.
1984-88
2.2L & 2.5L engs (1.7)........ 3.0
2.6L eng (2.2)........ 3.5
3.0L eng (1.7)........ 3.0

Compressor Center Seal, Renew
Includes: R&R compressor. Pressure test and charge system.
1984-88
2.2L & 2.5L engs (1.9)........ 3.2
2.6L eng (2.4)........ 3.7
3.0L eng (1.9)........ 3.2

Compressor Shaft Gas Seal, Renew
Includes: R&R compressor. Pressure test and charge system.
1984-88
2.2L & 2.5L engs (1.8)........ 3.1
2.6L eng (2.3)........ 3.6
3.0L eng (1.8)........ 3.1

Expansion Valve, Renew
Includes: Pressure test and charge system.
1984-88 (1.0)........ 1.7
Renew receiver drier add........ .2

Receiver Drier, Renew
Includes: Add partial charge, leak test and charge system.
1984-88 (.9)........ 1.6

Low Pressure Cut Off Switch, Renew
Includes: Charge system.
1984-88 (.9)........ 1.4

Clutch Cycling (Thermostatic Control) Switch, Renew
1984-88 (.3)........ .6
pressure activated (.2)........ .4

(Factory Time) — Chilton Time

Condenser Assembly, Renew
Includes: Add partial charge, leak test and charge system.
1984-88 (1.1)........ 2.0
Renew receiver drier add........ .2

Evaporator Coil, Renew
Includes: Add partial charge, leak test and charge system.
1984-88
Front (2.8)........ 4.5
Rear (1.7)........ 3.5

Temperature Control Assembly, Renew
1984-88 (.4)........ .7

Push Button Vacuum Switch, Renew
1984-88 (.4)........ .7

Blower Motor Switch, Renew
1984-88 (.4)........ .7

Temperature Control Cable, Renew
1984-88 (1.2)........ 1.8

Blower Motor, Renew
1984-88 (.6)........ 1.2

Blower Motor Resistor, Renew
1984-88 (.2)........ .4

Vacuum Actuators, Renew
1984-88
outside air door (.2)........ .4
heater/defroster door (.3)........ .6
A/C mode door (.8)........ 1.5

Air Conditioning Hoses, Renew
Includes: Add partial charge, leak test and charge system.
1984-88
Suction Hose
2.2L & 2.5L engs (1.1)........ 1.5
2.6L eng (1.3)........ 1.7
3.0L eng (1.1)........ 1.5
Discharge Hose
2.2L eng (1.1)........ 1.5
2.6L eng (1.3)........ 1.7
3.0L eng (1.1)........ 1.5
Renew receiver drier add........ .2

LABOR 30 HEAD AND PARKING LAMPS 30 LABOR

(Factory Time) — Chilton Time

Aim Headlamps
two........ .4
four........ .6

Headlamp Sealed Beam Bulb, Renew
Does not include aim headlamp.
All models-each (.2)........ .3

(Factory Time) — Chilton Time

License Lamp Lens, Renew
All models (.2)........ .2

License Lamp Assembly, Renew
1984-88 (.2)........ .3

Turn Signal and Parking Lamp Assy., Renew
All models (.2)........ .3

(Factory Time) — Chilton Time

Tail Lamp Assembly, Renew
1984-86 (.5)........ .8
1987-88 (.2)........ .4

Side Marker Lamp Assy., Renew
All models-each (.2)........ .3

LABOR 31 WINDSHIELD WIPER & SPEEDOMETER 31 LABOR

(Factory Time) — Chilton Time

Windshield Wiper Motor, Renew
1984-88 (.4)........ .6

Wiper/Washer Switch Assy., Renew
1984-88
std column (.8)........ 1.2
tilt column (1.1)........ 1.5

Rear Window Wiper/Washer Switch, Renew
1984-88 (.5)........ .7

(Factory Time) — Chilton Time

Rear Window Wiper Motor, Renew
1984-88 (.3)........ .5

Washer Pump, Renew
1984-88
front (.3)........ .4
rear (.7)........ 1.0

Wiper Link Assembly, Renew
1984-88 (.5)........ .7

(Factory Time) — Chilton Time

Windshield Wiper Pivot, Renew
1984-88-one (.4)........ .6

Intermittent Wiper Control Module, Renew
1984-88 (.2)........ .4

Speedometer Head, R&R or Renew
Does not include reset odometer.
1984-88 (.6)........ 1.1
Reset odometer add........ .2

LABOR 31 WINDSHIELD WIPER & SPEEDOMETER 31 LABOR

	(Factory Time)	Chilton Time
Speedometer Cable and Casing, Renew		
1984-88		
upper	(.3)	.6
lower	(.5)	.9
one piece	(.6)	1.0
Speedometer Cable (Inner), Renew or Lubricate		
1984-88		
upper	(.3)	.5
lower	(.4)	.8
one piece	(.4)	.8
trans to speedo	(.3)	.5
Speedometer Drive Pinion, Renew		
Includes: Renew oil seal.		
1984-88	(.3)	.4
Radio, R&R		
1984-88	(.3)	.7

LABOR 32 LIGHT SWITCHES & WIRING 32 LABOR

	(Factory Time)	Chilton Time
Headlamp Switch, Renew		
1984-88	(.5)	.7
Headlamp Dimmer Switch, Renew		
1984-88	(.3)	.6
Back-Up Lamp Switch, Renew		
(w/Manual Trans)		
1984-88	(.2)	.4
Neutral Safety Switch, Renew		
1984-88	(.3)	.4
Stop Light Switch, Renew		
1984-88	(.3)	.4
w/Cruise control add	(.1)	.1
Parking Brake Warning Lamp Switch, Renew		
1984-88	(.8)	1.1
Turn Signal Switch, Renew		
1984-88		
std column	(.6)	1.0
tilt column	(.8)	1.5
Turn Signal or Hazard Warning Flasher, Renew		
1984-88	(.2)	.3
Horn, Renew		
1984-88-one	(.2)	.4
Horn Relay, Renew		
1984-88	(.2)	.3
Horn Switch, Renew		
1984-88	(.2)	.3
Wiring Harness, Renew		
1984-88		
Main harness to dash	(2.7)	4.5
Body harness	(1.3)	2.5
Intermediate harness	(.9)	1.7

LABOR 34 CRUISE CONTROL 34 LABOR

	(Factory Time)	Chilton Time
Speed Control Servo Assy., Renew		
1984-88	(.3)	.5
Speed Control Cable, Renew		
1984-88	(.4)	.6
Speed Control Turn Signal Lever Switch, Renew		
1984-88		
std column	(.5)	.9
tilt column	(1.0)	1.5
Speed Control Wiring Harness, Renew		
1984-88	(.3)	.6
Speed Control Safety (Cut-Out) Switch, Renew		
1984-88	(.3)	.4
(G) Electronic Speed Control Module, Renew		
1985-88	(.3)	.4

GROUP INDEX

ALPHABETICAL INDEX

LABOR 1 TUNE UP 1 LABOR

(Factory Time) Chilton Time

Compression Test
Four 5
V-6 7

Engine Tune Up, (Electronic Ignition)
Includes: Test battery and clean connections. Tighten manifold and carburetor mounting bolts. Check engine compression, clean and adjust or renew spark plugs. Test resistance of spark plug cables. Inspect distributor cap and rotor. Check vacuum advance operation. Reset ignition timing. Adjust idle mixture and idle speed. Service carburetor air cleaner. Inspect crankcase ventilation system. Inspect and adjust drive belts. Inspect choke operation and adjust or free up. Check operation of EGR valve.
Four 1.5
V-6 .... 1.8

LABOR 2 IGNITION SYSTEM 2 LABOR

(Factory Time) Chilton Time

Spark Plugs, Clean and Reset or Renew
Four (.3) 4
V-6 (.5) 6

Ignition Timing, Reset
All models (.3) 5

Distributor, Renew
Includes: Reset ignition timing and renew oil seal if required.
Four (.5) 8
V-6 (.5) 8

Distributor, R&R and Recondition
Includes: Reset ignition timing.
Four (1.0) 1.5
V-6 (1.0) 1.5

Distributor Pick-Up Plate and Coil Assembly, Renew
Includes: R&R distributor, reset ignition timing.
Four (.5) 1.0
V-6 (.5) 1.0
w/Dual coil add (.1) 1

Electronic Distributor Reluctor, Renew
Includes: R&R distributor and reset ignition timing.
Four (.5) 1.0
V-6 (.5) 1.0

Vacuum Control Unit, Renew
Includes: R&R distributor and reset ignition timing.
Four (.5) 9
V-6 (.5) 9

Distributor Cap and/or Rotor, Renew
All models (.3) 4

Electronic Ignition Control Unit, Renew
All models (.2) 4

Spark Control Computer, Renew
All models (.2) 4

Ignition Coil, Renew
All models (.3) 5

Electronic Ignition Ballast Resistor, Renew
All models (.2) 4

Ignition Switch, Renew
All models
std colm (.7) 1.2
tilt colm (.4) 7

LABOR 3 FUEL SYSTEM 3 LABOR

(Factory Time) Chilton Time

Fuel Pump, Test
Includes: Disconnect line at carburetor, attach pressure gauge.
All models 3

Carburetor, Adjust (On Truck)
All models (.6) 8

Air Cleaner Vacuum Diaphragm, Renew
All models (.2) 3

Air Cleaner Vacuum Sensor, Renew
All models (.2) 3

Coolant Temperature Sensor/Switch, Renew
All models (.3) 4

Choke Vacuum Kick, Adjust
All models (.2) 3

Choke Vacuum Kick, Renew
All models (.2) 4

Accelerator Pump, Renew
All models (.4) 8

Needle Valve and Seat, Renew
Includes: Reset float level.
All models (.4) 7

Choke Control Switch, Renew
All models (.2) 4

Carburetor, Renew
Includes: All necessary adjustments.
All models
Holly 2 bbl (.6) 1.0

Carburetor, R&R and Clean or Recondition
Includes: All necessary adjustments.
All models
Holly 2 bbl (1.5) 2.4

Fuel Pump, Renew
Four (.5) 7
V-6 (.5) 7
Add pump test if performed.

Fuel Tank, Renew
Includes: Drain and refill tank, transfer or renew tank gauge.
All models (1.0) 1.4

Fuel Gauge (Tank Unit), Renew
All models (1.0) 1.4

Fuel Gauge (Dash Unit), Renew
All models (.6) 1.1

Intake and Exhaust Manifold Gaskets, Renew
Four (1.8) 2.5
Renew intake manif add 4

Intake Manifold Gaskets, Renew
V-6 (1.5) 2.1
w/A.C. add (.2) 2
w/AIR inj add (.3) 3
Renew manif add 5

LABOR 3A EMISSION CONTROLS 3A LABOR

(Factory Time) Chilton Time

CRANKCASE EMISSION

Positive Crankcase Ventilation Valve, Renew
All models (.2) 3

EVAPORATIVE EMISSION

Vapor Canister or Filter, Renew
All models (.2) 3

AIR INJECTION SYSTEM

Air Pump, Renew
Four (.4) 7
V-6 (.3) 6

LABOR 3A EMISSION CONTROLS 3A LABOR

	(Factory Time)	Chilton Time
Aspirator, Renew		
All models	(.2)	.4
Diverter/Control Valve, Renew		
Four	(.2)	.3
V-6	(.3)	.4
Injection Tube and Check Valve Assy., Renew		
Four	(.7)	1.0
V-6	(.6)	.9
Orifice Spark Advance Control Valve, Renew		
All models	(.2)	.4

HEATED AIR SYSTEM

	(Factory Time)	Chilton Time
Air Cleaner Vacuum Diaphragm, Renew		
All models	(.2)	.3
Air Cleaner Vacuum Sensor, Renew		
All models	(.2)	.3

EXHAUST GAS RECIRCULATION SYSTEM

	(Factory Time)	Chilton Time
E.G.R. Valve, Renew		
Four	(.7)	1.0
V-6	(.3)	.5
Coolant Vacuum Switch Valve, Renew		
All models	(.2)	.3
Idle/EGR Speed Switch Timer, Renew		
All models	(.2)	.4
E.G.R. Vacuum Amplifier, Renew		
All models	(.2)	.4
Change Temperature Switch, Renew		
All models	(.2)	.3

E.F.C. SYSTEM

	(Factory Time)	Chilton Time
Oxygen Sensor, Renew		
All models	(.2)	.4
Carburetor Solenoid, Renew		
All models	(.2)	.3

LABOR 4 ALTERNATOR AND REGULATOR 4 LABOR

Alternator Circuits, Test

Includes: Test battery, regulator and alternator output.

	(Factory Time)	Chilton Time
All models		.6
Alternator, Renew		
Four	(1.0)	1.3
V-6	(.7)	1.0

Add circuit test if performed.

	(Factory Time)	Chilton Time
Alternator, R&R and Recondition		
Four		2.3
V-6		2.0

Add circuit test if performed.

	(Factory Time)	Chilton Time
Alternator Drive End Frame Bearing, Renew		
Four	(.8)	1.1
V-6	(.6)	.9
Renew rear brg add		.2
Voltage Regulator, Test and Renew		
All models	(.3)	.6
Alternator Gauge, Renew		
All models	(.6)	1.1

LABOR 5 STARTING SYSTEM 5 LABOR

	(Factory Time)	Chilton Time
Starter Draw Test (On Truck)		
All models		.3
Starter, Renew		
Four	(.9)	1.2
V-6	(.6)	.9
Starter, R&R and Recondition		
Four	(1.9)	2.6
V-6	(1.6)	2.3
Renew field coils add		.5

Add draw test if performed.

Starter Drive, Renew

Includes: R&R starter.

	(Factory Time)	Chilton Time
Four	(1.2)	1.5
V-6	(.9)	1.2

Starter Solenoid, Renew

Includes: R&R starter.

	(Factory Time)	Chilton Time
Four	(1.2)	1.5
V-6	(.9)	1.2
Dual Pick-Up Start Run Relay, Renew		
All models	(.3)	.4
Battery Cables, Renew		
All models-positive	(.3)	.4
negative	(.2)	.3
Battery Terminals, Clean		
All models		.3

LABOR 6 BRAKE SYSTEM 6 LABOR

Brakes, Adjust (Minor)

Includes: Adjust brakes, fill master cylinder.

	(Factory Time)	Chilton Time
two wheels		.5
Brake Pedal Free Play, Adjust		
All models		.4

Bleed Brakes (Four Wheels)

Includes: Fill master cylinder.

	(Factory Time)	Chilton Time
All models	(.4)	.6
Rear Brake Drum, Renew		
All models-one	(.3)	.6

Brake Shoes and/or Pads, Renew

Includes: Install new or exchange brake shoes or pads. Service adjusters. Adjust service and hand brake. Bleed system.

	(Factory Time)	Chilton Time
All models		
front-disc	(.6)	1.1
rear-drum	(.7)	1.4
all four wheels		2.3
Resurface brake rotor add, each		.9
Resurface brake drum add, each		.5

COMBINATIONS

Add to Brakes, Renew

See Machine Shop Operations

	(Factory Time)	Chilton Time
RENEW WHEEL CYLINDER		
Each		.2
REBUILD WHEEL CYLINDER		
Each		.3
RENEW BRAKE HOSE		
Each		.3
REBUILD CALIPER ASSEMBLY		
Each		.5
RENEW BRAKE DRUM		
Each		.3
RENEW DISC BRAKE ROTOR		
Each		.4
RENEW REAR WHEEL GREASE SEALS OR BEARINGS		
Each side		.2
FRONT WHEEL BEARINGS, CLEAN AND REPACK (BOTH WHEELS)		
All models		.6
DISC BRAKE ROTOR STUD, RENEW		
Each		.1

LABOR 6 BRAKE SYSTEM 6 LABOR

(Factory Time) Chilton Time

BRAKE HYDRAULIC SYSTEM

Wheel Cylinders, Renew
Includes: Bleed brake system.
All models-one (.8) 1.3
both (1.5) 2.4

Wheel Cylinders, R&R and Recondition
Includes: Bleed brake system.
All models-one 1.5
both 2.8

Brake Hose, Renew (Flex)
Includes: Bleed system.
All models
front-one (.4) 6
rear-one (.5) 7

Master Cylinder, Renew
Includes: Bleed brake system.
All models
w/Manual brks (.6) 1.0
w/Power brks (.4) 8

Master Cylinder, R&R and Recondition
Includes: Bleed brake system.
All models
w/Manual brks 1.7
w/Power brks 1.5

Brake System Combination Valve, Renew
Includes: Bleed brake system.
All models (.8) 1.2

POWER BRAKES

Power Brake Unit, Renew
All models (1.0) 1.4

Power Brake Check Valve, Renew
All models (.2) 3

DISC BRAKES

Brake Shoes and/or Pads, Renew
Includes: Install new or exchange brake shoes or pads. Service adjusters. Adjust service and hand brake. Bleed system.
All models
front-disc (.6) 1.1
rear-drum (.7) 1.4
all four wheels 2.3
Resurface brake rotor add, each 9
Resurface brake drum add, each 5

Disc Brake Pads, Renew
Includes: Install new disc brake pads only.
All models (.6) 1.1

Disc Brake Rotor (w/Hub), Renew (One)
All models
7¼ axle (.5) 7
8¼ axle (.8) 1.1

Disc Brake Caliper Assy., Renew
Includes: Bleed front brake lines only.
All models-one (.5) 8
both 1.5

Caliper Assy., R&R and Recondition
Includes: Bleed front brake lines only.
All models-one (.8) 1.3
both 2.5

PARKING BRAKE

Parking Brake, Adjust
All models (.3) 5

Parking Brake Lever Assembly, Renew
All models (.5) 9

Parking Brake Cables, Renew
All models
front (.6) 8
intermediate (.3) 5
rear (.6) 8

LABOR 7 COOLING SYSTEM 7 LABOR

(Factory Time) Chilton Time

Winterize Cooling System
Includes: Run engine to check for leaks, tighten all hose connections. Test radiator and pressure cap, drain radiator and engine block. Add anti-freeze and refill system.
All models 5

Thermostat, Renew
All models (.5) 6
w/A.C. add (.1) 1

Radiator Assembly, R&R or Renew
All models (.7) 1.3
w/A.T. add (.1) 1
w/Aux trans cooler add (.1) 1

ADD THESE OPERATIONS TO RADIATOR R&R

Boil & Repair 1.5
Rod Clean 1.9
Repair Core 1.3
Renew Tank 1.6
Renew Trans. Oil Cooler 1.9
Recore Radiator 1.7

Radiator Hoses, Renew
All models
upper (.3) 5
lower (.4) 6
by-pass (.3) .... *.5
*w/Air inj add (.1) 1

Fan Belt, Renew
All models (.2) 3

Fluid Fan Drive, Renew
All models (.5) 7
w/Air inj add (.1) 1

Water Pump, Renew
Four (1.1) 1.6
V-6 (1.1) 1.5
w/A.C. add (.4) 4
w/P.S. add (.2) 2
w/Air inj add (.2) 2

Water Jacket Expansion Plugs, Renew Engine BLock
Four
Front
right side-one (.6) 9
all (1.0) 1.7
Left side
upper (.9) 1.3
lower (.5) 8
V-6
Side
front or center (.6) 1.1
right rear (.8) 1.0
left rear (.8) 1.2
Front
right or left (.4) 7
Engine Rear
w/A.T. (2.9) 4.0

Water Jacket Expansion Plugs, Renew Cylinder Head
V-6
front-one (.3) 6
rear (3.1) 4.2

Temperature Gauge (Engine Unit), Renew
All models (.3) 5

Temperature Gauge (Dash Unit), Renew
All models (.6) 1.1

Heater Core, R&R or Renew
All models
wo/A.C. (1.3) 2.2
w/A.C. (2.1) *4.0
*Includes: Recharge A.C. system.

ADD THESE OPERATIONS TO HEATER CORE R&R

Boil & Repair 1.2
Repair Core 9
Recore 1.2

Heater Water Valve, Renew
All models (.4) 6

Heater Blower Motor, Renew
All models (.4) 9

Heater Blower Motor Resistor, Renew
All models (.3) 5

Heater Blower Motor Switch, Renew
All models (.5) 8

Temperature Control Assembly, Renew
All models
wo/A.C. (.3) 5
w/A.C. (.5) 8

LABOR 8 EXHAUST SYSTEM 8 LABOR

(Factory Time) — Chilton Time

Muffler, Renew
All models (.5) 8

Tail Pipe, Renew
All models (.4) 7

Exhaust Pipe, Renew
Four (.6) 1.0
V-6 (.8) 1.2

Exhaust Pipe Extension, Renew
All models (.7) 1.1

Catalytic Converter, Renew
All models (.9) 1.1

Catalytic Converter Heat Shield, Renew
All models
upper (.6) 9
lower (.2) 4

Exhaust Manifold Heat Control Valve, Recondition
V-6 (1.0) 1.7

Intake and Exhaust Manifold Gaskets, Renew
Four (1.8) 2.5
Renew manif add 5

Exhaust Manifold Gaskets, Renew
V-6
right side (.4) 1.1
left side (.7) 1.3

COMBINATIONS

Muffler, Exhaust and Tail Pipe, Renew
Four 2.0
V-6 .... 2.1

Muffler and Tail Pipe, Renew
All models 1.2

LABOR 9 FRONT SUSPENSION 9 LABOR

(Factory Time) — Chilton Time

Note: On all front suspension operations alignment charges must be added if performed. Time given goes not include alignment.

Check Alignment of Front End
All models 5
Note: Deduct if alignment is performed.

Toe-In, Adjust
All models (.4) 6

Align Front End
Includes: Adjust front wheel bearings.
All models (.8) 1.5

Wheels, Balance
one 5
each adtnl 3

Front Wheel Bearings, Clean and Repack (Both Wheels)
2 WD models 1.5
4 WD models 2.0

Front Wheel Bearings and Cups, Renew
All models
one side (.6) 8
both sides (1.1) 1.5

Steering Knuckle, Renew
7¼ axle (.8) 1.1
8¼ axle (1.1) 1.5

Lower Control Arm, Renew
Add alignment charges.
4X2 models (1.5) 2.0
4X4 models (.7) 1.0

Lower Control Arm Bushings, Renew
Add alignment charges.
4X2 models (1.5) 2.2

Lower Ball Joint, Renew
Add alignment charges.
4X2 models (1.4) 1.9

Upper Control Arm, Renew
Add alignment charges.
4X2 models (1.9) 2.6
4X4 models (1.7) 2.3

Upper Ball Joint, Renew
Add alignment charges.
4X2 models (.9) 1.2

Upper Control Arm Bushings, Renew
Add alignment charges.
4X2 models (1.0) 1.4

Front Sway Bar, Renew
All models (.4) 6

Front Sway Bar Links, Renew
All models-one (.3) 4
both (.4) 6

Front Sway Bar Bushings, Renew
All models
one or all (.4) 6

Torsion Bar, Renew
All models-one (.3) 4
both (.5) 7

Front Coil Spring, Renew
Add alignment charges.
All models (1.4) 1.9

FOUR WHEEL DRIVE

Front Axle Housing Cover, Renew or Reseal
All models (.4) 6

Front Axle Shaft, Renew
All models
one or both-one side (.4) 6

Drive Shaft Boot, Renew
All models
one or both-one side (.6) 9

Front Axle Shaft Spindle, Renew
All models (.7) 1.0

Vacuum Shift Motor, Renew
All models (.4) 5

Front Axle Housing, Renew
All models (4.0) 5.4

LABOR 10 STEERING LINKAGE 10 LABOR

(Factory Time) — Chilton Time

Tie Rods or Tie Rod Ends, Renew
Includes: Reset toe-in.
All models-each (.7) 1.0

Steering Knuckle Arm, Renew
All models-one (1.1) 1.5

Center Link, Renew
All models (.4) 6

Idler Arm, Renew
All models (.3) 5

Pitman Arm, Renew
All models (.4) 7

LABOR 11 STEERING GEAR 11 LABOR

(Factory Time) — Chilton Time

STANDARD STEERING

Steering Wheel, Renew
All models (.2) 4

Upper Mast Jacket Bearing, Renew
All models
Standard Column (.5) 1.0
Tilt Column (1.1) 1.5

Steering Column Shift Housing, Renew
All models
Standard Column (.9) 1.5
Tilt Column (2.2) 3.3

Steering Column Mast Jacket, Renew
Does not include painting.
All models
Standard Column
column shift (1.6) 2.4
floor shift (1.1) 1.6
Tilt Column
All models (2.3) 3.3

Steering Gear Assembly, Renew
All models (.6) 1.2

POWER STEERING

Trouble Shoot Power Steering
Includes: Test pump and system pressure. Check pounds pull on steering wheel and check for leaks.
All models 5

Power Steering Belt, Renew
All models (.2) 3
w/A.C. add (.1) 1
w/Air inj add (.1) 1

LABOR 11 STEERING GEAR 11 LABOR

(Factory Time) — Chilton Time

Power Steering Gear Assy., Renew
4X2 models (1.3) 2.0
4X4 models (.9) 1.5

Steering Gear Oil Seals, Renew (All)
Includes: R&R gear assy. Reset toe-in.
All models (2.4) 4.0
Renew housing add (.1) 1

Upper and Lower Valve Pinion Seals, Renew
All models (1.4) 2.0
Renew pinion brgs add (.3) 5

Power Steering Pump, Test and Renew
All models (.9) 1.4
w/Air inj add (.2) 2

Power Steering Pump, R&R and Recondition
All models (1.4) 1.9
w/Air inj add (.2) 2

Pump Flow Control Valve, Test and Clean or Renew
All models (.9) 1.3
w/Air inj add (.2) 2

Power Steering Reservoir and/or Seals, Renew
All models (.7) 1.0
w/Air inj add (.2) 2

Pump Drive Shaft Oil Seal, Renew
All models (.9) 1.3
w/Air inj add (.2) 2

Power Steering Hoses, Renew
All models
pressure (.4) 7
return (.3) 6

LABOR 12 CYLINDER HEAD & VALVE SYSTEM 12 LABOR

(Factory Time) — Chilton Time

Compression Test
Four 5
V-6 7

Cylinder Head Gasket, Renew
Includes: Clean gasket surfaces, clean carbon, make all necessary adjustments.
Four (3.4) 4.8
V-6-one side (2.8) 4.0
both sides (3.8) 5.5
w/A.C. add (.2) 2
w/Air inj add (.4) 4
w/100 amp alter add (.6) 6
w/P.S. add (.2) 2

Cylinder Head, Renew
Includes: Transfer all parts, reface valves, make all necessary adjustments.
Four (4.7) 8.0
V-6-one side (3.8) 5.5
both sides (6.1) 8.8
w/A.C. add (.2) 2
w/Air inj add (.4) 4
w/100 amp alter add (.6) 6
w/P.S. add (.2) 2

Clean Carbon and Grind Valves
Includes: R&R cylinder head(s), clean gasket surfaces, clean carbon, reface valves and seats. Minor tune up.
Four (4.2) 6.8
V-6-one side (3.1) 4.5
both sides (6.2) 8.9

COMBINATIONS

Add to Valve Job

See Machine Shop Operations

(Factory Time) — Chilton Time

DRAIN, EVACUATE AND RECHARGE AIR CONDITIONING SYSTEM
All models 1.0

ROCKER ARM SHAFT ASSY., DISASSEMBLE AND CLEAN OR RECONDITION
V-6-one side 5
both sides 9

HYDRAULIC VALVE LIFTERS, DISASSEMBLE AND CLEAN
Each 2

DISTRIBUTOR, RECONDITION
All models 1.0

VALVE GUIDES, REAM OVERSIZE
Each 3

VALVES, RECONDITION (HEAD REMOVED)
Four 2.0
V-6 .... 3.0

CARBURETOR, RECONDITION
All models 1.5

(Factory Time) — Chilton Time

w/A.C. add (.2) 2
w/Air inj add (.4) 4
w/100 amp alter add (.6) 6
w/P.S. add (.2) 2

Valve Cover Gasket, Renew
Four (.6) 1.0
V-6-one (.4) 6
both (.7) 1.0
w/Air inj add (.2) 2

Valve Push Rods and/or Rocker Arms, Renew
V-6-one cyl (.5) 8
one cyl-each side (.8) 1.4
all cyls-both sides (.9) 1.7
w/Air inj add (.2) 2

Valve Tappets (Lifters), Renew
Four-all (1.7) 2.5
V-6-one cyl (1.0) 1.5
one cyl-each side (1.4) 2.0
all cyls-both sides (2.3) 3.3
w/A.C. add (.2) 2
w/Air inj add (.2) 2

Valve Springs and/or Valve Stem Oil Seals, Renew (Head on Truck)
Four-all (1.8) 2.9
V-6-one cyl (1.1) 1.6
one cyl-each side (1.6) 2.3
all cyls-both sides (4.0) 5.8
w/Air inj add (.2) 2

LABOR 13 ENGINE ASSEMBLY & MOUNTS 13 LABOR

(Factory Time) — Chilton Time

Engine Assembly, Remove & Install
Does not include transfer of any parts or equipment.
Four 4.6
V-6 .... 6.0
w/P.S. add 3
w/M.T. add 1.9
w/A.C. add 1.0
w/Air inj add 2

Short Engine Assy., Renew (w/All Internal Parts Less Cylinder Head(s) and Oil Pan)
Includes: R&R engine assy. Transfer all component parts not supplied with replacement engine. Tune up.
Four (7.3) 13.0
V-6 (8.6) 14.5
w/P.S. add (.3) 3
w/M.T. add (1.9) 1.9
w/A.C. add (1.0) 1.0
w/Air inj add (.2) 2
Recond valves add
Four 2.0
V-6 .... 3.0

Engine Assembly, R&R and Recondition
Includes: Rebore block, install new pistons, rings, pins, rod and main bearings. Clean carbon, grind valves. Tune engine.
Four (14.2) 21.3
V-6 (19.9) 28.6
w/P.S. add (.3) 3
w/M.T. add (1.9) 1.9
w/A.C. add (1.0) 1.0
w/Air inj add (.2) 2

Engine Mounts, Renew
Front
V-6-each (.3) 5

LABOR 14 PISTONS, RINGS & BEARINGS 14 LABOR

(Factory Time)	Chilton Time
Rings, Renew	
(See Engine Combinations)	
Includes: Remove cylinder top ridge, deglaze cylinder walls.	
Four-one cyl (5.1)	6.9
all cyls (6.3)	8.1
V-6-one cyl (5.1)	7.3
all cyls (9.5)	
w/A.C. add (.2)	.2
w/Air inj add (.1)	.1
w/100 amp alter add (.6)	.6
Pistons or Connecting Rods, Renew	
Includes: Remove cylinder top ridge, deglaze cylinder walls.	
Four-one cyl (5.4)	7.2
all cyls (7.5)	9.3
V-6-one cyl (5.4)	7.6
all cyls (11.3)	15.6
w/A.C. add (.2)	.2
w/Air inj add (.1)	.1
w/100 amp alter add (.6)	.6
Connecting Rod Bearings, Renew	
Four (2.1)	3.0
V-6 (2.3)	3.5

COMBINATIONS

Add to Engine Work

See Machine Shop Operations

(Factory Time)	Chilton Time
DRAIN, EVACUATE AND RECHARGE AIR CONDITIONING SYSTEM	
All models	1.0
ROCKER ARMS & SHAFT ASSY., DISASSEMBLE AND CLEAN OR RECONDITION	
V-6-one side	.5
both sides	.9
HYDRAULIC VALVE LIFTERS, DISASSEMBLE AND CLEAN	
Each	.2
DISTRIBUTOR, RECONDITION	
All models	1.0
CARBURETOR, RECONDITION	
All models	1.2
VALVE GUIDES, REAM OVERSIZE	
Each	.3
VALVES, RECONDITION (ALL)	
Cylinder Head Removed	
Four	2.0
V-6	3.0
DEGLAZE CYLINDER WALLS	
Each	.2
REMOVE CYLINDER TOP RIDGE	
Each	.1
PLASTIGAUGE BEARINGS	
Each	.1
OIL PUMP, RECONDITION	
V-6	.4
OIL FILTER ELEMENT, RENEW	
All models	.3

LABOR 15 CRANKSHAFT & DAMPER 15 LABOR

(Factory Time)	Chilton Time
Crankshaft and Main Bearings, Renew	
Includes: R&R engine assy, plastigauge all bearings.	
Four (6.7)	11.2
V-6 (7.9)	12.0
w/P.S. add (.3)	.3
w/M.T. add (.5)	.5
w/Air inj add (.2)	.2
w/100 amp alter add (.2)	.2
w/A.C. add (1.0)	1.0
Main Bearings, Renew	
Includes: Plastigauge bearings.	
Four	
No. 2-3-4 (1.8)	2.8
No. 1 (3.0)	4.0
No. 5 (5.6)	8.8
V-6 (2.6)	4.0
Rod and Main Bearings, Renew	
V-6 (3.6)	5.8
Rear Main Bearing Oil Seals, Renew (Upper and Lower)	
Four	
w/M.T. (3.0)	5.4
V-6 (1.4)	3.0
Vibration Damper or Pulley, Renew	
V-6 (.6)	1.0
w/P.S. add (.1)	.1

LABOR 16 CAMSHAFT & TIMING GEARS 16 LABOR

(Factory Time)	Chilton Time
Timing Belt Cover, Renew	
Four	
upper (.2)	.4
lower (.6)	1.0
Timing Belt, Renew	
Four (1.1)	1.7
w/P.S. add (.1)	.1
w/A.C. add (.2)	.2
Timing Belt Tensioner, Renew	
Four (.9)	1.5
w/P.S. add (.2)	.2
w/A.C. add (.2)	.2
Camshaft Seals, Renew	
Four	
front (.7)	1.1
rear (.9)	1.3
Timing Chain Case Cover Gasket, Renew	
Includes: Renew oil seal.	
V-6 (1.8)	2.6
w/P.S. add (.2)	.2
w/A.C. add (.4)	.4
Timing Chain, Renew	
V-6 (2.3)	3.0
w/P.S. add (.2)	.2
w/A.C. add (.4)	.4
Timing Cover Oil Seal, Renew	
Four (1.3)	2.0
V-6 (.9)	1.3
w/P.S. add (.2)	.2
w/A.C. add (.4)	.4
Camshaft, Renew	
Four (1.7)	2.8
V-6 (3.9)	7.0
w/P.S. add (.2)	.2
w/Aux trans cooler add (.3)	.3
w/A.C. add (.8)	.8
w/Air inj add (.2)	.2
w/100 amp alter add (.5)	.5

LABOR 17 ENGINE OILING SYSTEM 17 LABOR

(Factory Time)	Chilton Time
Oil Pan and/or Gasket, Renew	
Four (.9)	1.4
V-6 (1.0)	1.5
Pressure Test Engine Bearings (Pan Off)	
All models	1.0
Oil Pump, Renew	
Four (1.2)	1.7
V-6 (1.1)	1.7
Oil Pump, R&R and Recondition	
Four (1.7)	2.2
Oil Pressure Gauge (Dash Unit), Renew	
All models (.6)	1.1
Oil Pressure Gauge (Engine Unit), Renew	
All models	
w/Gauge (.4)	.6
w/Light (.2)	.3
Oil Filter Element, Renew	
All models (.2)	.3

LABOR 18 CLUTCH & FLYWHEEL 18 LABOR

(Factory Time) — Chilton Time

Clutch Pedal Free Play, Adjust
All models (.3) 5

Bleed Clutch Hydraulic System
All models 4

Clutch Master Cylinder, Renew
Includes: Bleed system.
All models (.4) 6
Recond cyl add 4

Clutch Slave Cylinder, Renew
Includes: Bleed system.
All models (.4) 6
Recond cyl add 4

Clutch Assembly, Renew
5 Speed
All models (2.1) 3.0
w/Two piece shaft add (.2) 2
w/Skid plate add 3

Clutch Release Bearing, Renew
5 Speed
All models (1.9) 2.7
w/Two piece shaft add (.2) 2
w/Skid plate add 3

Clutch Release Fork, Renew
5 Speed
All models (2.1) 2.9
w/Two piece shaft add (.2) 2
w/Skid plate add 3

Clutch Torque Shaft, Renew
Includes: Renew bearings.
All models (.5) 8

Flywheel, Renew
5 Speed
All models (2.0) 3.3
Renew pilot brg add (.2) 2
Renew ring gear add (.3) 5
w/Two piece shaft add (.2) 2
w/Skid plate add 3

LABOR 19 STANDARD TRANSMISSION 19 LABOR

(Factory Time) — Chilton Time

Transmission Assy., R&R or Renew
5 Speed
NP2500
4X2 (1.2) 1.7
4X4 (1.9) 2.7
Renew assy add (.2) 4
w/Skid plate add (.1) 3

Transmission Assy., R&R and Recondition
5 Speed
NP2500
4X2 (4.4) 6.1
4X4 (5.1) 7.1
w/Skid plate add (.1) 3

Transmission Assembly, Recondition (Off Truck)
5 Speed
NP2500 (3.2) 4.5

Transmission Front Oil Seal, Renew
Includes: R&R transmission.
5 Speed
NP2500
4X2 (1.5) 2.0
4X4 (2.2) 3.0
w/Skid plate add (.1) 3

Speedometer Drive Pinion, Renew
All models (.3) 6

LABOR 21 SHIFT LINKAGE 21 LABOR

(Factory Time) — Chilton Time

STANDARD

Shift Linkage, Adjust
All models (.3) 5

Gearshift Lever, Renew
All models (.4) 6

AUTOMATIC

Throttle Linkage, Adjust
All models (.3) 5

Gearshift Lever, Renew
All models (.3) 5

Gearshift Control Rod, Renew
All models (.4) 6

Gear Selector Indicator, Renew
All models (.5) 8

Steering Column Shift Housing, Renew
All models
w/Std column (.9) 1.5
w/Tilt column (2.2) 3.3

LABOR 23 AUTOMATIC TRANSMISSION 23 LABOR

(Factory Time) — Chilton Time

ON TRUCK SERVICES

Drain and Refill Unit
All models 1.0

Oil Pressure Test
Note: Using 3 pressure test points.
All models 1.5

Check Unit for Oil Leaks
Includes: Clean and dry outside of case and run unit to determine point of leak.
All models 1.0

Neutral Safety Switch, Renew
All models (.3) 4

Oil Cooler Lines, Renew
Includes: Cut and form to size.
All models-one (.6) 1.0

Transmission Auxiliary Oil Cooler, Renew
All models (.7) 1.2

Throttle Linkage, Adjust
All models (.3) 5

Kickdown Band, Adjust
All models (.3) 5

Throttle Valve Lever Shaft Seal, Renew
All models (.3) 7

Valve Body Manual Lever Shaft Seal, Renew
All models (.4) 8

Extension Housing Oil Seal, Renew
All models (.5) 1.1

Extension Housing or Adapter Gasket, Renew
All models (1.4) 2.0

Governor Assy., R&R or Renew
Includes: R&R extension housing.
All models (1.6) 2.5

Parking Lock Sprag, Renew
Includes: R&R extension housing.
All models (1.3) 2.2

Output Shaft Bearing and/or Oil Seal, Renew
Includes: R&R extension housing.
All models (1.4) 2.3

Oil Pan and/or Gasket, Renew
All models (.5) 1.0

Parking Lock Sprag Control Rod, Renew
Includes: R&R oil pan and remove valve body.
All models (.9) 1.5

Accumulator Piston, Renew or Recondition
Includes: R&R oil pan and adjust band.
All models (1.1) 1.7

Kickdown Servo, Renew or Recondition
Includes: R&R oil pan and adjust band.
All models (.9) 1.5

Reverse Servo, Renew or Recondition
Includes: R&R oil pan and adjust band.
All models (.8) 1.4

Valve Body Assembly, Renew
Includes: R&R oil pan and renew filter.
All models (.9) 1.5

Valve Body Assy., R&R and Recondition
Includes: R&R oil pan and replace filter. Disassemble, clean, inspect, free all valves. Replace parts as required.
All models (1.7) 2.4

LABOR 23 AUTOMATIC TRANSMISSION 23 LABOR

(Factory Time) Chilton Time

Bands, Adjust

Includes: R&R oil pan.

All models
- reverse (.6) 1.2
- kickdown (.6) 1.2

Torque Converter Lock Up Solenoid, Renew

Includes: R&R oil pan.

All models (1.2) 1.8

SERVICES REQUIRING R&R

Transmission Assembly, Remove and Reinstall

All models (2.3) 3.2
Renew trans add (.4) 5
Flush conver and lines add (.5) 5

Transmission Assembly, Renew (w/ Remanufactured Unit)

Includes: Remove and install all necessary interfering parts. Transfer all parts not supplied with replacement unit. Road test.

All models (2.6) 3.6

Transmission Assembly, Reseal

Includes: R&R trans and renew all seals and gaskets.

All models (4.5) 6.0

Transmission and Converter, R&R and Recondition

Includes: Disassemble trans including valve body, clean, inspect and replace parts as required.

All models (6.8) 9.5

Torque Converter, Renew

Includes: R&R transmission.

All models (2.5) 3.5

Kickdown Band, Renew

Includes: R&R transmission.

All models (3.0) 4.2

Reverse Band, Renew

Includes: R&R transmission.

All models (3.4) 4.7

Transmission Case, Renew

Includes: R&R transmission.

All models (4.2) 5.8

Front Pump Assembly, Renew or Recondition

Includes: R&R transmission. Renew reaction shaft if necessary.

All models (2.9) 4.0

Front Pump Oil Seal, Renew

Includes: R&R transmission.

All models (2.5) 3.5

LABOR 25 U-JOINTS & DRIVESHAFT 25 LABOR

(Factory Time) Chilton Time

Drive Shaft, R&R or Renew

All models
- trans to rear axle (.4) 6
- center brg to rear axle (.4) 6
- transfer case to front axle (.5) 8
- trans to center brg (1.2) 1.5

Universal Joints, Renew or Recondition

SINGLE PIECE SHAFT
- at rear axle (.5) 7
- trans rear-to rear axle (.6) 9
- both (1.2) 1.5

TWO PIECE SHAFT
- trans to center brg (.7) 1.0
- center brg to rear axle (.7) 1.0
- at rear axle (.5) 7
- center brg to rear axle-all (1.2) 1.6
- both shafts-all three (1.4) 2.0

Center Bearing, Renew

All models (.8) 1.1

LABOR 26 REAR AXLE 26 LABOR

(Factory Time) Chilton Time

Differential, Drain & Refill

All models 6

Rear Axle Housing Cover, Renew or Reseal

All models (.4) 6

Rear Axle Shaft, Renew

All models (.7) 1.0

Axle Shaft Bearing, Renew

All models (.6) 9

Axle Shaft Oil Seal, Renew

All models (.6) 9

Pinion Shaft Oil Seal, Renew

All models (.4) 6

Differential Backlash, Adjust

All models
- 7¼ axle (1.1) 1.5
- 8¼ axle (1.3) 1.8

Rear Axle Housing, Renew

Includes: Renew pinion oil seal, inner and outer axle shaft or wheel bearing oil seals and gaskets.

All models (4.2) 6.3

Rear Axle Assembly, Renew

Includes: Renew oil seals and gaskets. Transfer axle shafts and brake assemblies.

All models (2.0) 3.1

Differential Side Bearings, Renew

Includes: Adjust backlash and renew axle shaft oil seals.

All models (1.5) 2.5

Differential Case, Renew

Includes: Renew side bearings and thrust washers, side gears if necessary.

All models (3.0) 4.5

Differential Side Gears, Renew

Includes: Renew axle shaft oil seals.

All models (1.1) 2.0

Ring Gear and Pinion Set, Renew

Includes: Renew wheel bearing or inner axle shaft oil seals, pinion oil seal and gaskets.

All models (2.7) 4.0
Renew side bearings add (.3) 5

LABOR 27 REAR SUSPENSION 27 LABOR

(Factory Time) Chilton Time

Rear Spring, Renew

All models-right (.5) 7
- left (.6) 8
- both (1.1) 1.5

Auxiliary Rear Spring, Renew

All models-one (.7) 1.0

Rear Spring Shackle, Renew

Includes: Renew bushings.

All models-one side (.6) 1.0

Rear Shock Absorbers, Renew

All models-one (.2) 4
- both (.4) 6

LABOR 28 AIR CONDITIONING 28 LABOR

	(Factory Time)	Chilton Time
Note: If more than one item requires replacement where evacuation and discharging the system is already included in the operation, deduct 1.0 hour for each additional item to the times listed.		
Drain, Evacuate, Leak Test and Charge System		
All models		1.0
Partial Charge		
Includes: Leak test.		
All models		.6
Compressor Belt, Renew		
All models	(.2)	.3
w/Air inj add	(.1)	.1
w/P.S. add	(.1)	.1
Compressor Clutch Field Coil, Renew		
Includes: Renew pulley w/Hub if necessary.		
All models	(.5)	.9
Compressor Clutch Assembly, Renew		
All models	(.5)	.8
Compressor Assembly, Renew		
Includes: Transfer parts as required. Pressure test and charge system.		
Four	(1.3)	2.7
V-6	(1.7)	3.1
Compressor Front Cover and/or Seal, Renew		
Includes: Pressure test and charge system.		
Four	(1.7)	3.0
V-6	(2.1)	3.4
Compressor Rear Cover and/or Seal, Renew		
Includes: Pressure test and charge system.		
Four	(1.6)	2.9
V-6	(2.0)	3.3
Compressor Center Seal, Renew		
Includes: Pressure test and charge system.		
Four	(1.8)	3.1
V-6	(2.2)	3.5
Compressor Shaft Gas Seal, Renew		
Includes: Pressure test and charge system.		
Four	(1.7)	3.0
V-6	(2.1)	3.4
Expansion Valve, Renew		
Includes: Pressure test and charge system.		
All models	(1.1)	2.0
Renew receiver drier add	(.2)	.2
Receiver Drier, Renew		
Includes: Add partial charge, leak test and charge system.		
All models	(1.1)	1.9
Low Pressure Cut Off Switch, Renew		
Includes: Pressure test and charge system.		
All models	(1.0)	1.8
Clutch Cycling (Thermostatic Control) Switch, Renew		
All models	(.3)	.5
Condenser Assembly, Renew		
Includes: Add partial charge, leak test and charge system.		
All models	(1.4)	2.2
Renew receiver drier add	(.2)	.2
Evaporator Coil, Renew		
Includes: Add partial charge, leak test and charge system.		
All models	(2.3)	4.7
Blower Motor, Renew		
All models	(.4)	.9
Blower Motor Resistor, Renew		
All models	(.3)	.4
Blower Motor Switch, Renew		
All models	(.5)	.9
Temperature Control Assembly, Renew		
All models	(.5)	.9
A.C. Push Button Switch, Renew		
All models	(.6)	1.0
Air Conditioning Hoses, Renew		
Includes: Pressure test and charge system.		
All models		
suction/liquid line	(1.1)	1.9
discharge/liquid line	(1.1)	1.9
Renew receiver drier add	(.2)	.2

LABOR 30 HEAD AND PARKING LAMPS 30 LABOR

	(Factory Time)	Chilton Time
Aim Headlamps		
two		.4
four		.6
Headlamp Sealed Beam Bulb, Renew		
Does not include aim headlamp.		
All models-one	(.3)	.3
Parking Lamp Lens or Bulb, Renew		
All models-one	(.2)	.3
Turn Signal Lamp Lens or Bulb, Renew		
All models-one	(.2)	.3
Tail and Stop Lamp Lens or Bulb, Renew		
All models-one	(.2)	.3
Back-Up Lamp Lens or Bulb, Renew		
All models-one	(.2)	.3
License Lamp Lens or Bulb, Renew		
All models-one	(.2)	.3
Reflectors, Renew		
All models-one	(.2)	.2

LABOR 31 WINDSHIELD WIPER & SPEEDOMETER 31 LABOR

	(Factory Time)	Chilton Time
Windshield Wiper Motor, Renew		
All models	(.4)	.6
Windshield Wiper Pivot, Renew		
All models-one	(.5)	.8
Wiper Links, Renew		
All models-one or both	(.5)	.8
Windshield Wiper and Washer Switch, Renew		
All models		
Std column	(.8)	1.2
Tilt column	(1.2)	1.7
Wiper Delay Control Module, Renew		
All models	(.3)	.5
Windshield Washer Pump, Renew		
All models	(.3)	.5
Speedometer Head, R&R or Renew		
All models	(.4)	.7
Reset odometer add		.2
Speedometer Cable and Casing, Renew		
All models		
lower	(.3)	.6
upper	(.4)	.7
one piece	(.4)	.7

LABOR 32 LIGHT SWITCHES & WIRING 32 LABOR

	(Factory Time)	Chilton Time
Headlamp Switch, Renew		
All models	(.4)	.6
Back-Up Lamp Switch, Renew (w/Manual Trans)		
All models	(.3)	.4
Headlamp Dimmer Switch, Renew		
All models	(.3)	.5

LABOR 32 LIGHT SWITCHES & WIRING 32 LABOR

(Factory Time)	Chilton Time
Neutral Safety Switch, Renew	
All models (.3)	.4
Parking Brake Warning Lamp Switch, Renew	
All models (.3)	.4
Stop Light Switch, Renew	
All models (.3)	.4
w/Cruise control add (.1)	.1
Turn Signal Switch, Renew	
All models	
Std column (.5)	.9
Tilt column (.9)	1.4
Turn Signal or Hazard Warning Flasher, Renew	
All models (.2)	.3

LABOR 34 CRUISE CONTROL 34 LABOR

(Factory Time)	Chilton Time
Cruise Control Servo, Renew	
All models (.2)	.4
Cruise Control Cable, Renew	
All models (.2)	.4
Cruise Control Vacuum Hoses, Renew	
All models (.2)	.3
Cruise Control Switch (Turn Signal Lever), Renew	
All models	
Std column (.5)	.9
Tilt column (.9)	1.4
Cruise Control Cut-Off Safety Switch, Renew	
All models (.3)	.4

Ford • F Series • Aerostar • Vans • Bronco I • II • Pick-Ups

GROUP INDEX

ALPHABETICAL INDEX

LABOR 1 TUNE UP 1 LABOR

(Factory Time)	Chilton Time
Compression Test	
Four	.5
Six	.6
V-6	.7
V-8	.9

Engine Tune Up, (Electronic Ignition)

Includes: Test battery and clean connections. Tighten manifold and carburetor mounting bolts. Check engine compression, clean and adjust or renew spark plugs. Test resistance of spark plug cables. Inspect distributor cap and rotor. Adjust air gap. Reset ignition timing. Adjust idle mixture and idle speed. Service air cleaner. Inspect and adjust drive belts. Inspect choke operation and adjust or free up. Check operation of EGR valve.

(Factory Time)	Chilton Time
Four	1.5
Six	2.1
V-6	2.0
V-8	2.7
w/A.C. add	.6

LABOR 2 IGNITION SYSTEM 2 LABOR

(Factory Time)	Chilton Time
Spark Plugs, Clean and Reset or Renew	
RANGER-BRONCO	
Four (.4)	.6
Six (.4)	.6
V-6 (.6)	.8
V-8 (.6)	.8
AEROSTAR	
Four (.5)	.7
V-6	
2.8L eng (1.0)	1.4
3.0L eng (1.8)	2.5
ECONOLINE-Six (.5)	.7
V-8 (.7)	1.0
F100-350-Six (.4)	.8
V-6 (.4)	.6
V-8 (.6)	.8
Ignition Timing, Reset	
All models (.3)	.4

Distributor, R&R or Renew

Includes: Reset ignition timing.

(Factory Time)	Chilton Time
RANGER (.8)	1.1
AEROSTAR	
Four (.6)	1.0
V-6 (.8)	1.3
BRONCO (.4)	.8
BRONCO II (.8)	1.1
ECONOLINE (.5)	.9
F100-350-Six (.5)	.9
V-6 (.5)	.9
V-8 (.6)	1.0
Renew vac. diaph add	.2

Distributor, R&R and Recondition

Includes: Reset ignition timing.

(Factory Time)	Chilton Time
BRONCO-Six (1.2)	1.7
V-8 (1.5)	2.0
ECONOLINE-Six (1.4)	1.9
V-8 (1.6)	2.1
F100-350-Six (1.2)	1.7
V-6 (1.5)	2.0
V-8 (1.7)	2.2
Distributor Cap and/or Rotor, Renew	
RANGER (.5)	.6
BRONCO (.3)	.5
ECONOLINE (.4)	.6
F100-350 (.3)	.5
AEROSTAR (.4)	.6
Distributor Vacuum Control Valve, Renew	
All models (.3)	.5

Ignition Coil, Renew

Includes: Test.

(Factory Time)	Chilton Time
AEROSTAR (.3)	.5
RANGER (.4)	.5
BRONCO I & II (.4)	.5
ECONOLINE (.5)	.6
F100-350 (.4)	.5
Profile Ignition Pick-Up Sensor, Renew	
All models	
Dura-Spark (.5)	.8
Test system add	.3
Ignition Maintenance Warning Module, Renew or Reset	
All models (.4)	.6
Ignition Module Assembly, Renew	
All models	
Dura-Spark II (.2)	.4
TFI (.5)	.7
Perform system test add (.3)	.3
Distributor Armature, Renew	
All models (.3)	.6

Distributor Stator, Renew

Includes: R&R armature.

(Factory Time)	Chilton Time
All models (.7)	.9
Renew TFI module add	.2
Test system add (.3)	.3

Ignition Cables, Renew

Includes: Test wiring.

(Factory Time)	Chilton Time
AEROSTAR	
Four (.5)	.7
V-6	
2.8L eng (.7)	1.0
3.0L eng (1.6)	2.1
RANGER (.6)	.8
BRONCO (.5)	.7
ECONOLINE (.5)	.8
F100-350 (.4)	.7
Ignition Switch, Renew	
All models (.3)	.7

LABOR 3 FUEL SYSTEM 3 LABOR

GASOLINE ENGINES

Fuel Pump, Test

Includes: Disconnect line at carburetor, attach pressure gauge.

(Factory Time)	Chilton Time
All models	
mechanical	.4
electric	.5
Fuel Filter, Renew	
RANGER-BRONCO (.3)	.4
AEROSTAR	
Four (.7)	.9
V-6	
2.8L (.3)	.4
3.0L (.6)	.8
ECONOLINE-Six (.4)	.5
V-8 (.3)	.4
F100-350	
Six (.4)	.5
V-8 (.3)	.4
Carburetor, Adjust (On Truck)	
All models (.3)	.4

Carburetor, R&R or Renew

Includes: Necessary adjustments.

(Factory Time)	Chilton Time
RANGER-BRONCO I & II	
Four (.4)	.7
Six (.5)	.9
V-6 (.6)	1.0
V-8 (.6)	1.0
AEROSTAR	
V-6 (.7)	1.1
ECONOLINE-Six (.7)	1.2
V-8 (1.0)	1.5
F100-350-Six (.5)	.9
V-6 (.5)	.9
V-8 (.8)	1.2

Carburetor, R&R and Clean or Recondition

Includes: Necessary adjustments.

(Factory Time)	Chilton Time
RANGER-BRONCO I & II	
Four (1.2)	1.8
Six (1.3)	2.0
V-6 (2.2)	3.0
V-8	
2150-2V (1.6)	2.4
2150-2V FB (2.6)	3.9
AEROSTAR	
V-6 (2.3)	3.4
ECONOLINE-Six (1.5)	2.0
V-8	
2150-2V (1.6)	2.4
2150-2V FB (2.2)	3.3
4160 4V (2.8)	4.2
F100-350-Six (1.1)	1.7
V-6 (1.3)	2.2
V-8-2 bbl	
w/Auto choke (1.8)	2.5
w/Manual choke (1.3)	1.9
4 bbl	
Motorcraft (1.8)	2.5
Holly (2.6)	3.9
Mechanical Fuel Pump, R&R or Renew	
RANGER-Four (.3)	.5
V-6 (.5)	.8

(Factory Time)	Chilton Time
AEROSTAR	
V-6 (.8)	1.1
BRONCO	
Six (.5)	.8
V-8 (.7)	1.0
ECONOLINE	
Six (.4)	.7
V-8	
Gas (.7)	1.0
Diesel (.5)	.8
F100-350	
Six (.4)	.7
V-8 (.7)	1.0

Add pump test if performed.

Fuel Tank, Renew

(Factory Time)	Chilton Time
RANGER	
aft tank (.9)	1.4
mid tank (1.2)	1.8
AEROSTAR (1.2)	1.8
BRONCO (1.0)	1.5
BRONCO II	
1984 (2.1)	3.0
1985-88 (1.2)	1.8
ECONOLINE	
aft tank (.9)	1.5
mid tank (1.2)	2.0
F100-350	
aft tank (.9)	1.5
mid tank (1.2)	2.0

Auxiliary Fuel Tank, R&R or Renew

(Factory Time)	Chilton Time
BRONCO (.7)	1.3
ECONOLINE (.9)	1.5
F100-350 (.9)	1.5

Fuel Gauge (Tank), Renew

(Factory Time)	Chilton Time
RANGER	
aft tank (.9)	1.4
mid tank (1.2)	1.8
AEROSTAR (1.2)	1.8
BRONCO	
aft tank (.9)	1.3
mid tank (.7)	1.1
BRONCO II	
1984 (2.1)	3.0
1985-88 (1.1)	1.9
ECONOLINE	
rear mounted (.3)	.6
side mounted (1.1)	1.9
aft tank (.8)	1.4
mid tank (1.1)	1.9
F100-350	
cab mounted (.3)	.6
rear mounted (1.1)	1.9
side mounted (.5)	.9

Fuel Gauge (Dash), Renew

(Factory Time)	Chilton Time
RANGER (.6)	1.0
AEROSTAR (.6)	1.0
BRONCO (.6)	1.0
BRONCO II (.6)	1.0
ECONOLINE (.5)	.9
F100-350 (.5)	.9

Intake Manifold or Gaskets, Renew

(Factory Time)	Chilton Time
RANGER-BRONCO I & II	
Four	
2.0-2.3 OHC L engs (1.2)	2.0
w/P.S. add (.2)	.2
Six	
1984 & later (3.4)	4.7
V-6 (2.8)	3.8
V-8 (1.9)	2.7
ECONOLINE-Six	
1984 & later (3.4)	4.9
V-8	
302-351 engs (1.6)	2.2
460 eng (2.3)	3.3
F100-350	
Six	
1984 & later (3.4)	4.7
V-6 (2.3)	3.3
V-8-1984	
255-302 351W engs (1.5)	2.2
351M-400 engs (1.9)	2.7
460 eng (2.0)	2.5
1985-88	
351 eng	
F-Series-Bronco (2.3)	3.2
Econoline (3.2)	4.5
w/Dual Thermactor	
F-Series (3.7)	5.2
Econoline (4.6)	6.5
460 eng	
F-Series (3.7)	5.2
Econoline (4.6)	6.5
Renew manif add (.4)	.5

ELECTRONIC FUEL INJECTION (EFI)

Fuel Injection Manifold Assy., Renew (Fuel Rail)

(Factory Time)	Chilton Time
Four	
Ranger (.8)	1.2
Aerostar (.9)	1.3
Six	
F-series-Bronco (1.9)	2.6
Econoline (2.1)	2.9
V-6	
2.9L eng (1.2)	1.7
3.0L eng (1.1)	1.6
V-8	
5.0L eng	
two piece	
right (1.3)	1.8
left (.8)	1.3
both (1.7)	2.8
one piece	
F-series (1.8)	2.5
Econoline (2.2)	3.0

Air Intake Charge Throttle Body, Renew

(Factory Time)	Chilton Time
Four (.6)	1.0
Six	
F-series-Bronco (.7)	1.1
Econoline (1.0)	1.4
V-6	
2.9L eng (.6)	1.0
3.0L eng (1.1)	1.5
V-8	
F-series-Bronco (1.0)	1.4
Econoline (1.1)	1.5

Fuel Charging Wiring Assy., Renew

(Factory Time)	Chilton Time
Four (.3)	.6
Six (1.6)	2.2
V-6 (1.2)	1.7
V-8	
F-series-Bronco (1.2)	1.7
Econoline (1.7)	2.3

Fuel Pressure Regulator, Renew

(Factory Time)	Chilton Time
Four (1.0)	1.5
Six (1.8)	2.5
V-6	
2.9L eng (.3)	.6
3.0L eng (.5)	.8
V-8 (.8)	1.3

Electric Fuel Pump, Renew

(Factory Time)	Chilton Time
Ranger-Bronco II (.6)	.8
All other models (.5)	.7
Test pump add (.4)	.4

Fuel Injectors, Renew

(Factory Time)	Chilton Time
Four	
Ranger-one (1.2)	1.6
all (1.3)	1.8
Aerostar-one (1.4)	1.9
all (1.5)	2.1
Six	
F-series-Bronco	
one (2.0)	2.7
all (2.2)	3.0
Econoline	
one (2.3)	3.2
all (2.5)	3.5
V-6	
2.9L eng-one (1.4)	1.9
all (1.6)	2.2
3.0L eng-one (1.1)	1.5
all (1.2)	1.7
V-8	
F-series-Bronco	
one (1.9)	2.6
all (2.1)	2.9
Econoline	
one (2.2)	3.0
all (2.4)	3.3

Intake Manifold and/or Gasket, Renew

(Factory Time)	Chilton Time
Four	
2.3L EFI	
upper (1.1)	1.5
lower (2.2)	3.1
V-6	
2.9L eng	
upper (1.0)	1.4
lower (2.2)	3.1
3.0L eng (3.4)	4.7
Six	
F-series-Bronco (2.6)	3.6
Econoline (2.9)	4.0
V-8	
5.8L eng	
F-series-Bronco	
upper (1.1)	1.5
lower (3.0)	4.2
Econoline	
upper (1.6)	2.2
lower (3.5)	4.9
w/A.C. add (.2)	.2
w/Cruise control add (.1)	.1
w/P.S. add (.2)	.2

DIESEL ENGINE

Glow Plugs, Renew

(Factory Time)	Chilton Time
Four-one (.2)	.4
all (.3)	.7
V-8-one (.4)	.6
all (.8)	1.2

Glow Plug Module, Renew

(Factory Time)	Chilton Time
Four (.3)	.4

Glow Plug Relay, Renew

(Factory Time)	Chilton Time
Econoline (.4)	.6
All other models (.3)	.4

Fuel/Water Separator, Renew

(Factory Time)	Chilton Time
V-8	
F series (.6)	.8
Econoline (.8)	1.0

Fuel Pump, Renew

(Factory Time)	Chilton Time
V-8	
All models (.5)	.7

Fuel Filter Element, Renew

(Factory Time)	Chilton Time
All models	
Four & V-8 (.3)	.4

Intake Manifold and or Gaskets, Renew

(Factory Time)	Chilton Time
Four	
2.2L eng (1.4)	2.2
2.3L eng (2.4)	3.3
V-8	
F series (2.9)	4.0
Econoline (4.5)	6.3
Renew manif add (.2)	.5

Fuel Injection Pump Nozzles, Renew

(Factory Time)	Chilton Time
Four-2.3L eng	
one (.8)	1.1
each adtnl (.2)	.2
all (1.2)	1.7

LABOR 3 FUEL SYSTEM 3 LABOR

(Factory Time) Chilton Time

V-8
one (.7) ... 1.0
each adtnl (.5) 6
all (1.7) ... 2.4

Fuel Injection Pump, Renew
Four
2.2L eng (1.6) ... 2.4
2.3L eng (1.4) ... 1.9

V-8
F series (2.0) ... 2.7
Econoline (3.7) ... 5.0

Injection Pump Drive Gear, Renew
Four
2.2L eng (1.9) ... 2.9
2.3L eng (1.2) ... 2.0

V-8
F series (1.8) ... 2.5
Econoline (3.4) ... 4.7

Turbocharger Assy., R&R or Renew
Four
2.3L eng (1.7) ... 2.5
Renew wastegate actuator add (.2) 2

LABOR 3A EMISSION CONTROLS 3A LABOR

(Factory Time) Chilton Time

Emission Control Check
Includes: Check and adjust engine idle speed and mixture, reset ignition timing. Check PCV valve.
All models (.4) 6

CRANKCASE EMISSION

Positive Crankcase Ventilation Valve, Clean or Renew
All models-clean (.4) 5
renew (.2) 3

EVAPORATIVE EMISSION TYPE

Canister, Renew
Bronco (.2) 4
Econoline (.2) 4
F100-350 (.4) 6

Vapor Separator, Renew
Bronco (.2) 4
Econoline (.2) 4
F100-350
cab mounted (.2) 4
frame mounted (.3) 5

CONTROLLED COMBUSTION TYPE

Air Cleaner Motor, Renew
All models (.2) 3

Air Cleaner Sensor, Renew
All models (.2) 3

THERMACTOR TYPE

Thermactor Air Pump, Renew
Four (.3) 5
V-6 (.5) ... *.7
Six (.3) 5
V-8-302-351 W engs (.4) 7
351M, 400 engs (.7) ... 1.0
460 eng (.5) 8
*Aerostar add 2

Thermactor Drive Belt, Renew
All models (.3) 5

Anti-Backfire Valve, Renew
All models (.3) 4

Relief Valve, Renew
All models (.3) 4

Thermactor Air By-Pass Valve, Renew
All models (.4) 7

TRANSMISSION CONTROLLED SPARK

Controlled Spark Solenoid, Renew
All models (.2) 3

Thermostatic Vacuum Switch, Renew
All models (.2) 3

Temperature Switch, Renew
All models (.3) 5

Spark Relay, Renew
All models (.2) 3

Transmission Controlled Spark Switch, Renew
All models (.3) 5

E.G.R. TYPE

E.G.R. Valve, Renew
Four (.3) ... *.5
Six (.4) 6
V-6
2.8L (.3) 5
2.9L (.5) 7
V-8 (.3) 5
*Aerostar add 2

E.G.R. Switch, Renew
All models (.3) 4

Vacuum Switch, Renew
All models (.3) 4

Air Supply Pump, Renew
All models (.3) 4

Thermostatic Exhaust Control Valve, Renew
Econoline-Six (1.7) ... 2.4
F100-350-Six (1.5) ... 2.2

ELECTRONIC EMISSION CONTROL

EEC System, Test
BRONCO (.7) ... 1.0

EGR Cooler, Renew
Does not include system test.
BRONCO (.6) ... 1.0

Power Relay, Renew
Does not include system test.
BRONCO (.3) 4

Calibrator Assembly, Renew
Does not include system test.
BRONCO (.2) 4

Processor Assembly, Renew
Does not include system test.
BRONCO (.3) 6

Feedback Carburetor Actuator, Renew
Does not include system test.
BRONCO (.3) 4

Exhaust Gas Oxygen Sensor, Renew
Does not include system test.
BRONCO (.4) 7

Barometric Manifold Absolute Pressure Sensor, Renew
Does not include system test.
BRONCO (.3) 5

Thermactor Air Bypass and Air Diverter Solenoid, Renew
Does not include system test.
BRONCO (.3) 5

MCU SYSTEM

MCU System, Test
All models (.4) 6

Oxygen Sensor, Renew
Does not include system test.
All models (.3) 7

Thermactor Air Valve, Renew
Does not include system test.
All models (.5) 7

Ported Vacuum Switch, Renew
Does not include system test.
All models (.1) 2

Fuel Control Solenoid, Renew
Does not include system test.
All models (.1) 2

E.G.R. Valve, Renew
Does not include system test.
All models (.3) 4

TAB/TAD Solenoid, Renew
Does not include system test.
All models (.1) 2

Canister Purge Solenoid, Renew
Does not include system test.
All models (.1) 2

Vacuum Switch, Renew
Does not include system test.
All models (.3) 4

MCU/ECU Module, Renew
Does not include system test.
All models (.3) 5

Low Temperature Switch, Renew (Electric or Vacuum)
Does not include system test.
All models
2 port (.4) 5
3 port (.3) 4

Feedback Carburetor Actuator, Renew
Does not include system test.
All models (.4) 6

Solenoid, Renew
Does not include system test.
All models-one (.3) 4

Mid Temperature Switch, Renew (Electric or Vacuum)
Does not include system test.
All models (.3) 4

Throttle Positioner Assembly, Renew
Does not include system test.
All models (.3) 4

ELECTRONIC ENGINE CONTROL IV

E.E.C. System, Test
All models (.6) ... 1.0

LABOR 3A EMISSION CONTROLS 3A LABOR

(Factory Time) — Chilton Time

Throttle Position Sensor, Renew
Does not include system test.
Four
All models (.6) 8
V-6
All models (.3) 5
Six
Econoline (.4) 6
All other models (.2) 4
V-8
Econoline (.4) 6
All other models (.3) 5

Idle Tracking Switch, Renew
Does not include system test.
All models (.2) 4

Air Change Temperature Sensor, Renew
Does not include system test.
All models (.1) 3

Exhaust Gas Oxygen Sensor, Renew
Does not include system test.
Four
All models (.2) 4
V-6
All models (.1) 3
Six
Econoline (.2) 4
All other models (.1) 3
V-8
All models (.2) 5

Knock Sensor, Renew
Does not include system test.
All models (.2) 4

Processor Assembly, Renew
Does not include system test.
All models (.2) 3

Electronic Control Power Relay, Renew
Does not include system test.
Four
All models (.1) 3
V-6
All models (.2) 4
Six & V-8
All models (.1) 3

Choke Cover, Renew
Does not include system test.
V-6
All models (.6) 1.0

E.G.R. Shut-Off Solenoid, Renew
Does not include system test.
Econoline (.2) 3
All other models (.1) 2

Fuel Pump Relay, Renew
Does not include system test.
Four
All models (.1) 2

Fuel Pump Inertia Switch Assy., Renew
Does not include system test.
Four
All models (.1) 2

Throttle Positioner Assembly, Renew
Does not include system test.
All models
Six (.5) 7
V-6 (.4) 6

Fuel Injector Assembly, Renew
Does not include system test.
Four
Ranger-one (.7) 9
all (.8) 1.3
Aerostar-one (1.1) 1.3
all (1.2) 1.7

Knock Sensor, Renew
Does not include system test.
All models
Four (.1) 3
V-6 (.1) 3

Air Change Temperature Sensor, Renew
Does not include system test.
V-6
All models (.1) 3

Canister Purge Valve, Renew
Does not include system test.
V-6
All models (.1) 2
Six
Econoline (.2) 3
All other models (.1) 2
V-8
All models (.2) 3

Engine Coolant Temperature Sensor, Renew
Does not include system test.
All models (.2) 4

Feedback Control Solenoid, Renew
Does not include system test.
V-6
All models (.3) 4
Six
Econoline (.4) 6
All other models (.2) 3
V-8
Econoline (.3) 4
All other models (.5) 7

Manifold Absolute Pressure Sensor, Renew
Does not include system test.
All models (.1) 3

E.G.R. Valve Position Sensor, Renew
Does not include system test.
All models (.2) 4

Thermactor Air Diverter Valve, Renew
Does not include system test.
Econoline (.3) 5
All other models (.2) 4

Thick Film Ignition Module, Renew
Does not include system test.
Four
All models (.4) 6
V-6
All models (.5) 7
Six & V-8
Econoline (.4) 6
All other models (.3) 4

Thermactor Air By-Pass Valve, Renew
Does not include system test.
All models (.2) 3

E.G.R. Valve, Renew
Does not include system test.
Four
Ranger (.3) 4
Aerostar (.5) 7
V-6
All models (.2) 4
V-8
Econoline (.4) 6
All other models (.3) 5

E.G.R. On-Off Solenoid, Renew
Does not include system test.
All models (.2) 3

Throttle Kicker Actuator, Renew
Does not include system test.
All models (.3) 4

Tab/Tad Solenoids, Renew
Does not include system test.
All models (.2) 3

E.G.R. Control Solenoids, Renew
Does not include system test.
All models (.2) 3

Throttle Kicker Solenoid, Renew
Does not include system test.
All models (.2) 3

Profile Ignition Pick-Up Sensor, Renew
Does not include system test.
Econoline (.6) 8
All other models (.5) 7

LABOR 4 ALTERNATOR AND REGULATOR 4 LABOR

(Factory Time) — Chilton Time

Alternator Circuits, Test
Includes: Test battery, regulator and alternator output.
All models (.4) 6

Alternator, R&R or Renew
Four (.4) 7
Six
Econoline (1.1) 1.5
All other models (.4) 7
V-6
2.8L-2.9L engs (.5) 9
3.0L eng (1.0) 1.5
V-8
Econoline-w/460 eng (1.2) *1.6
All other models (.5) 9
*w/Dual Therm. pumps add 5
Renew regulator add 2
Renew brushes add 3
Renew drive brg add 3
Renew end brg add 2
Renew rectifier assy add 4
Renew stator assy add 4

Alternator Regulator, Renew (External)
All models (.3) 5
Add circuit test if performed.

Ammeter, Renew
All models (.5) 9

Instrument Cluster Voltage Regulator, Renew
All models (.5) 7

LABOR 5 STARTING SYSTEM 5 LABOR

(Factory Time) Chilton Time

Starter Draw Test (On Truck)
All models (.3) .3

Starter, R&R or Renew
Gas Engines
All models (.4) .7
Diesel Engines
Four (.8) 1.1
V-8 (.6) .9

Renew brushes add
TK .5
Motorcraft .6
Delco .2
Renew starter drive add
TK .6
Motorcraft .2
Delco .4

Recond complete add
TK 1.5
Motorcraft & Delco 1.0
Renew field coils add .5
Add draw test if performed.

Starter Solenoid Relay, Renew
All models (.3) .5

Battery Cables, Renew
All models-each (.3) .4

LABOR 6 BRAKE SYSTEM 6 LABOR

(Factory Time) Chilton Time

Brake Pedal Free Play, Adjust
All models (.3) .4

Brakes, Adjust (Minor)
Includes: Adjust brakes, fill master cylinder.
two wheels .4
four wheels .7

Bleed Brakes (Four Wheels)
Includes: Fill master cylinder.
All models (.3) .6

Brake Shoes, Renew
Includes: Install new or exchange shoes, service self adjustors. Adjust service and hand brake. Bleed system.
BRONCO-front (1.5) 2.0
rear (1.3) 1.8
All four wheels (2.2) 3.7
ECONOLINE-F100-350
front (1.1) 1.5
rear (1.7) 2.2
All four wheels (2.3) 3.5
F100-350 4X4
front (1.3) 1.8
rear (1.7) 2.2
All four wheels (2.5) 3.7
Resurface brake drum add, each .5

Brake Shoes and/or Pads, Renew
Includes: Install new or exchange brake shoes or pads. Adjust service and hand brake. Bleed system.
All models
front-disc (.7) 1.1
rear-drum (.9) *1.8
All four wheels (1.3) 2.8
*w/Full floating axle add .6
Resurface brake rotor add, each .9
Resurface brake drum add, each .5

Front Brake Drum and Hub Assy., Renew
BRONCO-one (.7) .9
both (1.2) 1.6
ECONOLINE-one (.5) .8
both (.7) 1.1
F100-350-one (.5) .8
both (.8) 1.2

Rear Brake Drum, Renew
All models
Semi-Floating Axle
one (.4) .6
both (.6) .9
Ford Axle (Full Floating)
one (.4) .6
both (.6) .9
Dana Axle (Full Floating)
one (.7) 1.1
both (1.1) 1.9

Brake Pressure Warning Light Switch, Renew
All models (.3) .5

COMBINATIONS

Add to Brakes, Renew

See Machine Shop Operations

(Factory Time) Chilton Time

RENEW WHEEL CYLINDER
Each (.3) .4
REBUILD WHEEL CYLINDER
Each (.3) .6
REBUILD CALIPER ASSEMBLY
Each (.5) .8
RENEW MASTER CYLINDER
All models (.4) .7
REBUILD MASTER CYLINDER
All models 1.3
RENEW BRAKE HOSE
Each (.3) .3
RENEW REAR WHEEL GREASE SEALS
One side (.2) .4
FRONT WHEEL BEARINGS, REPACK OR RENEW SEALS (BOTH WHEELS)
Drum brakes (.3) .6
Disc brakes (.4) .7
4X4 (.6) .8
RENEW BRAKE DRUM
Each (.2) .3
RENEW DISC BRAKE ROTOR
4X2 (.2) .3
4X4 (.3) .5

(Factory Time) Chilton Time

BRAKE HYDRAULIC SYSTEM

Wheel Cylinder, Renew
Includes: Bleed system.
Front
BRONCO-one (1.1) 1.5
both (2.1) 2.9
ECONOLINE, F100-350
one (.9) 1.3
both (1.7) 2.5
F100-250 4X4
one (1.0) 1.4
both (1.9) 2.7
Rear
RANGER-AEROSTAR-one (.8) 1.4
both (1.5) 2.6
BRONCO-one (1.0) 1.5
both (1.9) 2.9
ECONOLINE, F-SERIES 4X2
one (1.2) 1.6
both (2.3) 3.0
F-SERIES 4X4
one (1.2) 1.9
both (2.3) 3.3

(Factory Time) Chilton Time

Wheel Cylinder, R&R and Recondition
Includes: Hone cylinder and bleed system.
Front
BRONCO-one (1.1) 1.8
both (2.1) 3.5
ECONOLINE, F100-350 F-SERIES 4X2
one (.9) 1.6
both (1.7) 3.1
F-SERIES F100-250 4X4
one (1.0) 1.7
both (1.9) 3.3
Rear
RANGER-AEROSTAR-one (.8) 1.6
both (1.5) 3.0
BRONCO-one (1.0) 1.8
both (1.9) 3.5
ECONOLINE, F-SERIES 4X2
one (1.2) 1.9
both (2.3) 3.7
F-SERIES 4X4
one (1.2) 2.2
both (2.3) 3.6

Brake Hose, Renew
Includes: Bleed system.
Front
RANGER-AEROSTAR-one (.5) .8
both (.6) 1.0
BRONCO, F100-350, F100-250 4X4
one (.5) .8
both (.6) 1.0
ECONOLINE 100-350
one (.6) .9
both (.8) 1.1
Rear
RANGER-AEROSTAR-one (.5) .8
BRONCO, F100-250 4X4
one (.5) .8
ECONOLINE 100-350, F100-350
one (.6) .9

Master Cylinder, Renew
Includes: Bleed complete system.
Aerostar (.7) 1.1
All other models
wo/Booster (.6) 1.0
w/Booster (.5) .9

Master Cylinder, R&R and Recondition
Includes: Hone cylinder and bleed complete system.
Aerostar (1.0) 1.6
All other models
wo/Booster (.8) 1.5
w/Booster (.7) 1.4

Vacuum Pump, Renew (w/Diesel Eng)
ECONOLINE-F-series (.6) .9
All other models (.4) .6

Brake Differential Valve, R&R or Renew
Includes: Bleed complete system and transfer switch.
All models (.7) 1.2

LABOR 6 BRAKE SYSTEM 6 LABOR

(Factory Time)	Chilton Time
POWER BRAKES	
Power Brake Booster, R&R or Renew	
Aerostar (1.0)	1.5
All other models (.6)	1.1
w/Cruise control add (.2)	.2
DISC BRAKES	
Brake Shoes and/or Pads, Renew	
Includes: Install new or exchange brake shoes or pads. Adjust service and hand brake. Bleed system.	
All models	
front-disc (.7)	1.1
rear-drum (.9)	*1.8
All four wheels (1.3)	2.8
*w/Full floating axle add	.6
Resurface brake rotor add, each	.9
Resurface brake drum add, each	.5
Disc Brake Rotor, Renew	
Includes: Renew front wheel bearings and grease retainer and repack bearings.	
4X2 models	
one (.6)	.9
both (1.0)	1.6
4X4 models	
Ranger-Bronco II	
one (.5)	.8
both (.8)	1.4
F-Series-Bronco	
one (.7)	1.0
both (1.1)	1.8
w/8 lug whl add	
each side	.1
Caliper Assembly, Renew	
Includes: Bleed complete system.	
All models	
one (.6)	1.0
both (.9)	1.4
w/8 lug whl add	
each side	.1
Caliper Assembly, R&R and Recondition	
Includes: Bleed complete system.	
All models	
Single Piston	
one (.8)	1.5
both (1.2)	2.4
Dual Piston	
one (.9)	1.6
both (1.3)	2.5
w/8 lug whl add	
each side	.1
PARKING BRAKE	
Parking Brake, Adjust	
All models (.3)	.5
Parking Brake Control, Renew	
AEROSTAR (.4)	.7
RANGER-BRONCO II (.5)	.8
ECONOLINE (.6)	.9
F-SERIES-BRONCO (.6)	.9
Parking Brake Cable, Renew	
Front–All models (.7)	1.0
Rear	
Semi-Floating Axle	
one (.5)	.8
both (.8)	1.1
Dana Full Floating Axle	
one (.8)	1.1
both (1.4)	2.0
Ford Full Floating Axle	
one (.6)	.9
both (.9)	1.4

LABOR 7 COOLING SYSTEM 7 LABOR

(Factory Time)	Chilton Time
Winterize Cooling System	
Includes: Run engine to check for leaks, tighten all hose connections. Test radiator and pressure cap, drain radiator and engine block. Add anti-freeze and refill system.	
All models	.5
Thermostat, Renew	
Gas Engines	
Four (.5)	.6
Six (.4)	.6
V-6 (.6)	.9
V-8 (.9)	1.0
Diesel Engines	
Four (.7)	.9
V-8 (1.1)	1.4
Radiator Assembly, R&R or Renew	
Includes: Drain and refill cooling system.	
RANGER-AEROSTAR	
Gas (.6)	1.0
Diesel (.7)	1.1
BRONCO I & II	
Six (.9)	1.5
V-6 (.6)	1.0
V-8 (.6)	1.0
ECONOLINE-Six (1.1)	1.7
V-8 (.6)	1.2
Diesel (.9)	1.5
F100-350	
Six (.9)	1.5
V-8 (.6)	1.0
Diesel (1.4)	2.0
ADD THESE OPERATIONS TO RADIATOR R&R	
Boil & Repair	1.5
Rod Clean	1.9
Repair Core	1.3
Renew Tank	1.6
Renew Trans. Oil Cooler	1.9
Renew Side Tank	.7
Recore Radiator	1.7
Radiator Hoses, Renew	
RANGER-BRONCO II-upper (.3)	.4
lower (.4)	.5
both (.5)	.6
ALL OTHER MODELS	
upper (.4)	.5
lower (.4)	.5
both (.5)	.7
Water Pump, Renew	
RANGER-BRONCO II	
Four (1.2)	1.7
w/A.C. add (.3)	.3
w/P.S. add (.2)	.2
V-6 (1.4)	2.0
w/A.C. add (.4)	.4
Diesel	
2.2L eng (1.1)	1.7
2.3L eng (1.6)	2.3
AEROSTAR	
Four (1.1)	1.7
V-6 (1.3)	2.0
w/A.C. add (.3)	.3
w/P.S. add (.2)	.2
BRONCO-Six (.9)	1.5
V-6 (1.4)	2.0
w/A.C. add (.4)	.4
V-8 (1.4)	1.9
w/A.C. add (.2)	.2
ECONOLINE	
1984	
Six (1.0)	1.6
V-8 (1.5)	2.1
Diesel (1.4)	2.0
1985-88	
Six (1.3)	2.0
w/A.C. add (.2)	.2
V-8	
302-351 engs (1.3)	2.0
w/Dual Therm add (1.0)	1.4
460 eng (2.3)	3.4
Diesel (2.5)	3.7
w/A.C. add (.3)	.3
F100-350-Six (1.0)	1.6
V-6 (1.1)	1.7
V-8	
302-351W engs (1.3)	2.0
351M-400 engs (1.3)	2.0
w/Dual Therm add (.5)	.7
460 eng (1.9)	2.7
Diesel (1.9)	2.7
w/P.S. add	.3
w/A.C. add	.3
Fan Blade, Renew	
V-8-Diesel (.7)	1.0
All other engs	
wo/Viscous drive (.4)	.6
w/Viscous drive (.5)	.7
Drive Belt, Adjust	
All models-one (.3)	.4
each adtnl (.2)	.3
Vacuum Pump Drive Belt, Renew	
All models (.3)	.4
Serpentine Drive Belt, Renew	
Econoline (.4)	.6
All other models (.3)	.5
Thermactor Drive Belt, Renew	
All models (.3)	.4
Temperature Gauge (Engine), Renew	
All models (.3)	.5
Temperature Gauge (Dash), Renew	
All models (.6)	1.0
Water Jacket Expansion Plugs, Renew (Side of Block)	
All models-each	.5
Add time to gain accessibility.	
Heater Core, R&R or Renew	
Without Air Conditioning	
AEROSTAR-Main (.6)	1.0
Auxiliary (.8)	1.4
RANGER (.5)	.9
BRONCO (.8)	1.6
BRONCO II (.5)	.9
ECONOLINE-Main (1.1)	1.0
Auxiliary (.8)	1.4
F100-350 (.8)	1.6
WITH AIR CONDITIONING	
Econoline (1.1)	2.0
All other models (.5)	1.1

LABOR 7 COOLING SYSTEM 7 LABOR

(Factory Time)	Chilton Time
ADD THESE OPERATIONS TO HEATER CORE R&R	
Boil & Repair	1.2
Repair Core	.9
Recore	1.2
Heater Water Control Valve, Renew	
All models (.3)	.6
Heater Blower Motor, Renew	
AEROSTAR-Main (.5)	.9
Auxiliary (.4)	.7
RANGER (.5)	.7
BRONCO (.5)	.7
ECONOLINE-Main (.3)	.6
Auxiliary (.6)	.9
F100-350 (.3)	.6
Heater Control Assembly, Renew	
All models (.6)	1.1
Heater Blower Motor Switch, Renew	
AEROSTAR	
main (.6)	.9
front (.6)	.9
rear (.4)	.6
RANGER (.5)	.9
BRONCO (.4)	.7
BRONCO II (.5)	.9
ECONOLINE (.3)	.6
F100-350 (.4)	.7
Heater Blower Motor Resistor, Renew	
RANGER, BRONCO (.3)	.6
ECONOLINE-Main (.3)	.6
Auxiliary (.5)	.8
F100-350 (.4)	.7
AEROSTAR-Main (.3)	.6
Auxiliary (.5)	.8

LABOR 8 EXHAUST SYSTEM 8 LABOR

(Factory Time)	Chilton Time
Catalytic Converter, Renew	
1984	
Four (.6)	.9
Six (.8)	1.2
V-6 (.8)	1.2
V-8 (.9)	1.6
1985-88	
Ranger-Bronco II'	
Aerostar	
Four (.5)	.8
V-6 (.9)	1.4
All other models	
Six (1.6)	2.2
V-8 (1.8)	2.5
Muffler, Renew	
1984	
RANGER-AEROSTAR	
Four (.4)	.7
V-6 (.6)	.9
Diesel (.5)	.8
BRONCO, F100-250 4X4 (.8)	1.4
BRONCO II (.6)	.9
ECONOLINE (.8)	1.4
F100-350	
Std W/B wo/Catalyst (.8)	1.4
w/Catalyst (.8)	1.4
Long W/B (.8)	1.4
V-6 (.7)	1.0
1985-88	
Ranger-Bronco II	
Four	
Gas (.4)	.7
Diesel (.5)	.8
V-6 (.8)	1.2
F-series-Bronco-Econoline	
Six (.8)	1.2
V-8	
302-351 engs (.8)	1.2
460 eng (.6)	.9
Diesel (.5)	.8
Aerostar	
Four (.5)	.8
V-6	
2.8L eng (.6)	.9
3.0L eng (.4)	.7
Intermediate Exhaust Pipe, Renew	
1984	
RANGER-AEROSTAR	
All models (.7)	1.2
BRONCO, F100-250 4X4	
Six (.5)	1.1
V-8 (.8)	1.4
BRONCO II (.7)	1.0
ECONOLINE-Six (.6)	1.2
V-8 (.9)	1.5
F100-350-Six (.6)	1.2
V-6 (.6)	.9
V-8-351M-400 engs	
Std W/B wo/Catalyst (1.6)	2.3
w/Catalyst (1.9)	2.6
Long W/B (.8)	1.4
460 eng-one (.7)	1.3
both (1.0)	1.9
Diesel (.6)	1.0
1985-88	
Ranger	
Four	
Gas (.7)	1.0
Diesel (.6)	.9
F-series-Bronco-Econoline	
Six (.6)	.9
V-8 (.7)	1.0
Diesel (.6)	.9
Aerostar	
Four (.8)	1.1
V-6	
2.8L eng (.7)	1.0
3.0L eng (.8)	1.1
Tail Pipe, Renew	
BRONCO (.5)	.7
ECONOLINE (.5)	.7
F100-350 (.4)	.6
Exhaust Manifold, Renew	
Four	
Gas	
2.0L eng (.9)	1.5
2.3L eng (1.4)	2.0
Diesel	
2.2L eng (.9)	1.6
2.3L eng (2.4)	3.4
Six	
1984 & later (3.1)	4.4
V-6	
2.8L eng	
Ranger-Bronco II	
right (1.5)	2.1
left (1.4)	2.0
both (2.4)	3.6
Aerostar	
right (1.1)	1.5
left (.8)	1.1
both (1.5)	2.1
2.9L eng	
right (1.4)	2.0
left (1.8)	2.5
both (2.9)	4.0
3.0L eng	
right (1.6)	2.2
left (1.9)	2.6
both (2.5)	3.5
V-8	
302-351W engs	
one side (.7)	1.1
both sides (1.1)	1.9
w/Dual Therm Pumps	
right (1.4)	1.9
left (1.7)	2.4
both (2.7)	3.8
351M-400 engs	
one side (.8)	1.3
both sides (1.2)	2.3
460 eng-F-series	
one side (1.3)	1.8
both sides (2.2)	3.0
460 eng-Econoline	
right side (2.7)	3.8
left side (1.5)	2.1
both sides (3.8)	5.3
Diesel	
right side (1.7)	2.3
left side (1.6)	2.2
both sides (2.6)	3.8
* w/A.C. add (.3)	.3

COMBINATIONS

	Chilton Time
Muffler, Exhaust and Tail Pipe, Renew	
RANGER	1.1
BRONCO	1.9
ECONOLINE	1.9
F100-350-one side	1.8
both sides	2.7

LABOR 9 FRONT SUSPENSION 9 LABOR

Note: On all front suspension operations alignment charges must be added if performed. Time given does not include alignment.

(Factory Time)	Chilton Time
Check Alignment of Front End	
All models (.5)	.6
Note: Deduct if alignment is performed.	
Toe-In, Adjust	
All models (.4)	.7

(Factory Time)	Chilton Time
Align Front End	
Includes: Adjust front wheel bearings.	
Aerostar (1.2)	1.5
All other models (1.9)	2.5
Front Wheel Bearings, Clean and Repack (Both Wheels)	
drum brakes	1.0
disc brakes	1.4
4 wheel drive	2.5
Front Wheel Bearings and Cups, Renew (One Wheel)	
Drum Brakes	
Bronco, F100-250 4X4 (.8)	1.1
Econoline, F100-150 (.6)	.9
F250-350 (.7)	1.0
Disc Brakes	
4X2	
All models (.7)	1.1
4X4	
Ranger-Bronco II (.7)	1.1
F-series-Bronco (.8)	1.2
Front Wheel Grease Seal, Renew (One Wheel)	
Drum Brakes	
Bronco (.6)	.8
Econoline (.4)	.6
F100-250 4X4 (.5)	.7
Disc Brakes	
4X2	
Ranger-Aerostar (.5)	.8
F-series-Bronco (.6)	.9
Econoline (.6)	.9
4X4	
Ranger-Bronco II (.5)	.8
F-series-Bronco (.7)	1.0
Front Shock Absorber or Bushings, Renew	
All models-one (.4)	.6
both (.5)	.8
Upper Control Arms, Renew	
Add alignment charges.	
Aerostar-one (1.0)	1.3
both (1.5)	2.0
Upper Control Arm Bushings, Renew	
Add alignment charges.	
Aerostar-one side (1.6)	2.2
both sides (2.5)	3.4
Lower Control Arms, Renew	
Add alignment charges.	
Aerostar-one side (1.5)	2.0
both sides (2.4)	3.2
Front Axle 'I' Beam, Renew	
Includes: R&R wheels and brake backing plates.	
Add alignment charges.	
STAMPED AXLE 4X2	
one side (2.3)	3.1
both sides (3.9)	5.3
FORGED AXLE 4X2	
one side (1.8)	2.4
both sides (2.7)	3.6
Renew ball joints	
add-each (.2)	.3
Renew pivot bushings	
add-each (.2)	.3
Front Spindle Assembly, Renew	
CONTROL ARM AXLE	
one side (1.4)	1.9
both sides (1.9)	2.9
STAMPED AXLE 4X2	
one side (1.6)	2.1
both sides (2.3)	3.1
FORGED AXLE 4X2	
one side (1.4)	1.9
both sides (1.9)	2.5
STAMPED AXLE 4X4	
one side (.6)	.9
both sides (.9)	1.3
FORGED AXLE 4X4	
one side (1.4)	1.9
both sides (1.9)	2.5
Rebush spindle, add	
each side (.4)	.5
Renew needle brgs, add	
each (.1)	.2
Steering Shock Absorber, Renew	
BRONCO, F100-250 4X4 (.3)	.6
Track Bar Assembly, Renew	
BRONCO, F100-250 4X4 (.6)	1.0
Radius Arm, Renew	
All models-one (1.4)	1.9
both (2.1)	2.8
Radius Arm Bushings, Renew	
Add alignment charges if required.	
All models-each side	1.0
Front Spring, Renew	
AEROSTAR	
one (.9)	1.2
both (1.6)	2.1
4X2	
All models	
one (.4)	.7
both (.7)	1.3
4X4	
Ranger-Bronco II	
one (.4)	.7
both (.7)	1.3
F series-Bronco	
one (.7)	1.1
both (1.1)	2.0
Renew tie bolt	
add-each (.5)	.5
Front Stabilizer Bushings, Renew	
All models (.5)	.8
Front Stabilizer Bar, Renew	
All models (.6)	.9
Ball Joints, Renew	
Add alignment charges if required.	
4X4 models-each side	2.0
FRONT WHEEL DRIVE	
Front Axle Housing and Differential Assy., R&R (Complete)	
Includes: Drain and refill axle, R&R wheels, hubs and axle shafts. Road test.	
BRONCO (3.9)	5.4
F100 (3.7)	5.2
F250 (2.8)	4.2
Front Axle Housing, Renew (One Piece Assy)	
Includes: R&R housing and differential assy. Transfer all parts. Adjust ring gear and pinion.	
Does not include disassembly of differential case.	
BRONCO (8.0)	9.6
F100 (7.4)	9.0
F250 (7.2)	9.0
Axle Housing Cover or Gasket, Renew	
All models (.5)	.7
Front Axle Arm (Beam), Renew (Independent Front Suspension)	
w/coil springs	
left side (3.8)	5.1
right side (2.9)	3.9
both sides (5.9)	7.9
w/leaf springs	
left side (3.8)	5.1
right side (3.0)	4.0
both sides (6.1)	8.2
monobeam (4.8)	6.5
Renew ball joints	
add-each (.2)	.3
Renew pivot bushings	
add-each (.2)	.3
Front Axle Shaft, Renew	
Bolted Shaft 4X4	
Ranger-Bronco II	
left (.6)	.8
right (1.2)	1.6
both (1.6)	2.1
F-series-Bronco	
left (.6)	.8
right (.9)	1.2
both (1.3)	1.8
C-Clip Shaft	
F-series-Bronco	
left (.6)	.8
right (1.2)	1.6
both (1.6)	2.1
Stamped Axle	
Ranger-Bronco II	
one (.7)	.9
both (1.4)	1.8
F-series-Bronco	
left (.8)	1.0
right (.9)	1.2
both (1.4)	1.9
MonoBeam	
one (.8)	1.0
both (1.3)	1.8
O/haul or renew U-Joints,	
add-each (.3)	.3
Front Axle Housing Oil Seals, Renew	
Bolted Shaft 4X4	
Ranger-Bronco II	
left (.6)	.9
right (1.2)	1.7
both (1.6)	2.2
F-series-Bronco	
left (.7)	.9
right (.9)	1.3
both (1.4)	2.0
C-Clip Shaft	
F-series-Bronco	
left (.6)	.9
right (1.2)	1.7
both (1.6)	2.2
Stamped Axle	
Ranger-Bronco II	
left (.7)	1.0
right (2.1)	2.8
both (2.1)	2.9
F-series-Bronco	
left (.8)	1.1
right (2.2)	2.9
both (2.3)	3.0
Monobeam	
one (3.4)	4.5
both (3.4)	4.5
Steering Knuckle, Renew	
Add alignment charges.	
Stamped Axle 4X4	
one side (2.4)	3.1
both sides (4.3)	5.5
Monobeam 4X4	
one side (1.7)	2.2
both sides (2.9)	3.8
Renew king pin add,	
each (.1)	.2
Renew brg and cup add,	
each (.1)	.1
Front Axle Pinion Oil Seal, Renew	
All models (.6)	1.0
Front Axle Pivot Bushings, Renew	
All models-one side (.5)	.8
both sides (.7)	1.3

LABOR 9 FRONT SUSPENSION 9 LABOR

(Factory Time) Chilton Time

Front Drive Shaft, R&R
All models (.5) 7
Recond U-Joint, Add
one (.3) 4
all (.5) 6

Differential Carrier, R&R or Reseal
All models
w/coil springs (2.3) 3.2
w/leaf springs (2.4) 3.3
w/monobeam (3.6) 5.0

Ring Gear Backlash, Adjust
All models
w/coil springs (3.1) 4.3
w/leaf springs (3.2) 4.4
w/monobeam (4.4) 6.1

Ring Gear and Pinion Set, Renew
All models
w/coil springs (3.9) 5.4
w/leaf springs (4.0) 5.6
w/monobeam (5.2) 7.2
Renew pinion brgs add (.2) 4
Recond diff assy add (.2) 5

Differential Case, Renew
All models
w/coil springs
std (3.2) 4.5
locker (3.5) 4.9
w/leaf springs
std (3.3) 4.6
locker (3.6) 5.0
w/monobeam
std (4.5) 6.3
locker (4.8) 6.7
Renew diff brgs add (.2) 4

LABOR 10 STEERING LINKAGE 10 LABOR

(Factory Time) Chilton Time

Tie Rod Ends, Renew (One Side)
Includes: Reset toe-in.
All models (.8) 1.1

Tie Rod, Renew (One)
Includes: Reset toe-in.
All models (.8) 1.2

Drag Link, Renew
Does not require toe-in adjustment.
All models (.5) 9

Pitman Arm, Renew
All models (.5) 9

Front Spindle Arm, Renew
Includes: R&R wheel hub and brake drum/rotor where required. Reset toe-in.
BRONCO-Part Time Hub
one (1.0) 1.4
both (1.9) 2.7
Full Time Hub
one (.9) 1.3
both (1.6) 2.4
ECONOLINE-one (.6) 1.0
both (1.0) 1.8
F100-350-one (1.1) 1.5
both (1.6) 2.2
F100-350 4X4
Part Time Hub-one (1.0) 1.4
both (1.9) 2.7
Full Time Hub-one (.9) 1.3
both (1.6) 2.4

LABOR 11 STEERING GEAR 11 LABOR

(Factory Time) Chilton Time

STANDARD

Steering Wheel, Renew
All models (.3) 5

Upper Mast Jacket Bearing, Renew
All models
std colm (.5) 9
tilt colm (.6) 1.0

Steering Column Lock Actuator, Renew
All models
std colm (1.0) 1.5
tilt colm (.9) 1.4

Steering Gear, Adjust (On Truck)
Includes: Bearing preload and gear mesh adjustments.
All models (.6) 1.0

Steering Gear, R&R or Renew
All models (.7) 1.2

Steering Gear, R&R and Recondition
Includes: Disassemble, renew necessary parts, reassemble and adjust.
All models (1.4) 2.2

POWER STEERING

Trouble Shoot Power Steering
Includes: Test pump and system pressure. Check pounds pull on steering wheel and check for leaks.
All models (.7) 1.0

Power Steering Belt, Renew
Four
Gas (.3) 5
Diesel (.3) 5
Six (.5) 7
V-6 (.3) 5
V-8
302-351 engs (.4) 6
460 eng (.8) 1.0
Diesel (.4) 6

Power Steering Gear, R&R or Renew
All models (.8) 1.4

Power Steering Gear, R&R and Recondition
Includes: Disassemble, renew necessary parts, reassemble and adjust.
ECONOLINE
Saginaw (2.5) 4.2
XR50 (2.2) 3.9
All other models (2.2) 3.8

Power Steering Cylinder Assembly, R&R or Renew
ECONOLINE (1.6) 2.1
F250 4X4 (.7) 1.1

Power Steering Pump, R&R or Renew
Includes: Transfer pulley where required.
Aerostar-Four (1.1) 1.5
V-6
2.8L (1.0) 1.4
3.0L (.9) 1.3
All other models
Four
Gas (.7) 1.0
Diesel
2.2L eng (.8) 1.2
2.3L eng (1.2) 1.6
Six (.6) 1.0
V-6 (.8) 1.2
V-8
302-351W engs (.6) 1.0
351M-400 engs (.8) 1.3
460 eng (.5) 1.0
Diesel (1.0) 1.4

Power Steering Pump, R&R and Recondition
Aerostar-Four (1.5) 2.3
V-6
2.8L (1.4) 2.2
3.0L (1.3) 2.1
All other models
Four
Gas (1.1) 1.8
Diesel
2.2L eng (1.2) 2.0
2.3L eng (1.6) 2.4
Six (1.1) 1.8
V-6 (1.3) 2.2
V-8
302-351W engs (1.1) 1.8
351M-400 engs (1.4) 2.0
460 eng (1.0) 1.8
Diesel (1.6) 2.2

Power Steering Pump Shaft Seal, Renew
Includes: R&R pump.
Aerostar-Four (1.2) 1.7
V-6
2.8L (1.1) 1.6
3.0L (1.0) 1.5
All other models
Four
Gas (.7) 1.2
Diesel
2.2L eng (.9) 1.4
2.3L eng (1.3) 1.8
Six (.7) 1.2
V-6 (.9) 1.4
V-8
302-351W engs (.6) 1.2
351M-400 engs (.9) 1.5
460 eng (.6) 1.2
Diesel (1.1) 1.6

LABOR 11 STEERING GEAR 11 LABOR

(Factory Time) — Chilton Time

Power Steering Control Valve, R&R or Renew
ECONOLINE (2.0) 2.7
F250 4X4 (.9) 1.3

Power Steering Control Valve, R&R and Clean or Recondition
ECONOLINE (2.8) 3.9
F250 4X4 (1.7) 2.4

Power Steering Hoses, Renew
AEROSTAR
pressure (.5) 7
return (.4) 6
BRONCO, F100-250 4X4
pressure (.4) 6
return (.5) 7
ECONOLINE-Six (.7) 1.0
V-8 (.8) 1.1
RANGER, F100-350
pressure (.4) 6
return (.4) 6
cooling (.3) 5
V-8-Diesel
cooling (.5) 7
return (.7) 9
pressure (.6) 8

RACK AND PINION STEERING

Steering Gear, R&R or Renew
All models
manual (.8) 1.3
power (1.0) 1.6
Purge system add (.3) 3

Steering Gear, R&R and Recondition
All models
manual (2.4) 3.8
power (3.0) 4.8
Purge system add (.3) 3

Steering Gear, Adjust (On Truck)
All models (.3) 5

Tie Rod Ball Joint Sockets and Bellows, Renew
All models
manual (1.2) 1.9
power (1.5) 2.4
Purge system add (.3) 3

Input Shaft and Valve Assy., Recondition
All models
manual (1.4) 2.2
power (1.6) 2.5
Purge system add (.3) 3

LABOR 12 CYLINDER HEAD & VALVE SYSTEM 12 LABOR

(Factory Time) — Chilton Time

GASOLINE ENGINES

Compression Test
Four 5
Six 6
V-6 7
V-8 9

Cylinder Head Gasket, Renew
Includes: Check cylinder head and block flatness. Clean carbon and make all necessary adjustments.
RANGER-BRONCO II
Four
2.0L eng (3.7) 5.1
2.3L eng (4.3) 6.0
V-6
2.8L eng
one side (4.3) 6.0
both sides (5.3) 7.4
2.9L eng
one side (3.6) 5.0
both sides (4.8) 6.7
AEROSTAR
Four (4.4) 6.1
V-6
2.8L eng
one side (4.4) 6.1
both sides (5.7) 7.9
3.0L eng
one side (5.0) 7.0
both sides (7.3) 10.2
ECONOLINE
Six
wo/EFI (3.4) 4.7
w/EFI (5.2) 7.2
V-8
5.0L eng
wo/EFI
one side (3.1) 4.3
both sides (4.4) 6.1
w/EFI
one side (6.3) 8.8
both sides (8.6) 12.0
5.8L eng
one side (5.2) 7.2
both sides (7.5) 10.5
5.8L-7.5L engs
w/Dual Thermactor
one side (7.3) 10.2
both sides (9.7) 13.5
F-series-BRONCO
Six
wo/EFI (2.8) 3.9
w/EFI (4.6) 6.4

COMBINATIONS

Add to Valve Job

(Factory Time) — Chilton Time

DRAIN, EVACUATE & RECHARGE AIR CONDITIONING SYSTEM
All models (.7) 1.5

ROCKER ARMS OR SHAFT ASSY. DISASSEMBLE AND CLEAN OR RECONDITION
Six (.6) 1.0
V-8-One side (.5) 7
Both sides (1.0) 1.3

HYDRAULIC VALVE LIFTERS, DISASSEMBLE AND CLEAN
Each (.2) 2

ROCKER ARM STUD, RENEW
Each (.3) 3

DISTRIBUTOR, RECONDITION
All models (.7) 1.0

CARBURETOR, RECONDITION
1 BBL (.9) 1.2
2 BBL (1.0) 1.3
4 BBL
Ford (1.0) 1.5
Holly (1.3) 2.0

VALVE GUIDES, REAM OVERSIZE
Each (.1) 2

VALVE SEAT INSERT, RENEW
DIESEL
V-8-one (.2) 3
each adtnl (.2) 2

VALVE GUIDES, RENEW
DIESEL
V-8-one (.5) 6
each adtnl (.5) 5

(Factory Time) — Chilton Time

V-8
5.0L eng
wo/EFI
one side (3.1) 4.3
both sides (4.4) 6.1
w/EFI
one side (5.0) 7.0
both sides (6.8) 9.5
5.8L eng
one side (4.7) 6.5
both sides (6.5) 9.1
5.8L-7.5L engs
w/Dual Thermactor
one side (5.5) 7.7
both sides (7.1) 9.9

Cylinder Head, Renew
Includes: Transfer all components, clean carbon. Reface valves, check valve spring tension, assembled height and valve head runout.
RANGER-BRONCO II
Four
2.0L eng (5.6) 7.8
2.3L eng (6.2) 8.6
V-6
2.8L eng
one side (5.3) 7.4
both sides (8.1) 11.3
2.9L eng
one side (4.6) 6.4
both sides (6.9) 9.6
AEROSTAR
Four (6.3) 8.8
V-6
2.8L eng
one side (5.4) 7.5
both sides (7.8) 10.9
3.0L eng
one side (6.0) 8.4
both sides (9.4) 13.1
ECONOLINE
Six
wo/EFI (6.3) 8.8
w/EFI (8.1) 11.3
V-8
5.0L eng
wo/EFI
one side (4.5) 6.3
both sides (7.2) 10.0

(Factory Time)	Chilton Time
w/EFI	
one side (7.7)	10.7
both sides (11.4)	15.9
5.8L eng	
one side (6.6)	9.2
both sides (10.3)	14.4
5.8L-7.5L engs	
w/Dual Thermactor	
one side (8.7)	12.1
both sides (12.5)	17.5
F-series-BRONCO	
Six	
wo/EFI (5.7)	7.9
w/EFI (7.5)	10.5
V-8	
5.0L eng	
wo/EFI	
one side (4.5)	6.3
both sides (7.2)	10.0
w/EFI	
one side (6.4)	8.9
both sides (9.6)	13.4
5.8L eng	
one side (6.1)	8.5
both sides (9.3)	13.0
5.8L-7.5L engs	
w/Dual Thermactor	
one side (6.9)	9.6
both sides (9.9)	13.8

Clean Carbon and Grind Valves

Includes: R&R cylinder heads, check valve spring tension, valve seat and head runout, stem to guide clearance and spring assembled height. Minor tune up.

(Factory Time)	Chilton Time
RANGER-BRONCO II	
Four	
2.0L eng (6.3)	8.8
2.3L eng (6.9)	9.6
V-6	
2.8L eng	
one side (5.8)	8.1
both sides (8.4)	11.7
2.9L eng	
one side (5.1)	7.1
one side (7.9)	11.0
AEROSTAR	
Four (7.0)	9.8
V-6	
2.8L eng	
one side (5.9)	8.2
both sides (8.8)	12.3
3.0L eng	
one side (6.4)	8.9
both sides (10.1)	14.1
ECONOLINE	
Six	
wo/EFI (6.1)	8.5
w/EFI (7.9)	11.0
V-8	
5.0L eng	
wo/EFI	
one side (4.8)	6.7
both sides (7.8)	10.9
w/EFI	
one side (8.0)	11.2
both sides (12.0)	16.8
5.8L eng	
one side (6.9)	9.6
both sides (10.9)	15.2
5.8L-7.5L engs	
w/Dual Thermactor	
one side (9.0)	12.6
both sides (13.1)	18.3
F-series-BRONCO	
Six	
wo/EFI (5.5)	7.7
w/EFI (7.3)	10.2
V-8	
5.0L eng	
wo/EFI	
one side (4.8)	6.7
both sides (7.8)	10.9
w/EFI	
one side (6.7)	9.3
both sides (10.2)	14.2
5.8L eng	
one side (6.4)	8.9
both sides (9.9)	13.8
5.8L-7.5L engs	
w/Dual Thermactor	
one side (7.2)	10.0
both sides (10.5)	14.7

Rocker Arm Cover or Gasket, Renew

(Factory Time)	Chilton Time
RANGER-BRONCO II	
Four	
2.0L eng (.7)	1.0
2.3L eng (1.3)	1.8
V-6	
2.8L eng	
one side (.8)	1.1
both sides (1.2)	1.7
2.9L eng	
one side (.9)	1.3
both sides (1.6)	2.3
AEROSTAR	
Four (1.2)	1.7
V-6	
2.8L eng	
one side (1.3)	1.9
both sides (2.5)	3.6
3.0L eng	
one side (1.5)	2.2
both sides (2.8)	4.0
ECONOLINE	
Six	
wo/EFI (1.0)	1.5
w/EFI (2.1)	3.0
V-8	
5.0L eng	
wo/EFI	
right side (.8)	1.2
left side (.6)	.9
both sides (1.0)	1.5
w/EFI	
right side (2.2)	3.1
left side (1.2)	1.7
both sides (2.9)	4.1
5.8L eng	
right side (.8)	1.2
left side (.6)	.9
both sides (1.0)	1.5
5.8L-7.5L engs	
w/Dual Thermactor	
right side (2.5)	3.6
left side (1.5)	2.2
both sides (3.5)	5.0
F-series-BRONCO	
Six	
wo/EFI (.9)	1.3
w/EFI (1.7)	2.4
V-8	
5.0L eng	
wo/EFI	
right side (.7)	1.0
left side (.5)	.8
both sides (.9)	1.3
w/EFI	
right side (1.5)	2.2
left side (.8)	1.2
both sides (1.9)	2.7
5.8L eng	
right side (.7)	1.0
left side (.5)	.8
both sides (.9)	1.3
5.8L-7.5L engs	
w/Dual Thermactor	
right side (1.7)	2.4
left side (1.0)	1.5
both sides (2.4)	3.4

Rocker Arm Shaft Assy., Recondition

Includes: R&R rocker arm cover.

(Factory Time)	Chilton Time
BRONCO-Six (1.1)	1.6

Valve Push Rod and/or Rocker Arm, Renew

Includes: R&R rocker arm cover.

(Factory Time)	Chilton Time
RANGER-BRONCO II	
Four	
2.0L eng-one (.8)	1.2
all (1.1)	1.6
2.3L eng-one (1.8)	2.6
all (2.3)	3.3
V-6	
2.8L eng	
one side (1.3)	1.9
both sides (2.2)	3.1
2.9L eng	
one side (1.2)	1.7
both sides (2.2)	3.1
AEROSTAR	
Four-one (1.3)	1.9
all (1.6)	2.3
V-6	
2.8L eng	
one side (1.8)	2.6
both sides (3.5)	5.0
3.0L eng	
one side (1.8)	2.6
both sides (3.4)	4.8
ECONOLINE	
Six	
wo/EFI-one (1.1)	1.6
all (1.4)	2.0
w/EFI-one (2.2)	3.1
all (2.5)	3.6
V-8	
5.0L eng	
wo/EFI	
one side (1.0)	1.5
both sides (1.4)	2.0
w/EFI	
right side (2.4)	3.4
left side (1.4)	2.0
both sides (3.3)	4.7
5.8L eng	
one side (1.0)	1.5
both sides (1.4)	2.0
5.8L-7.5L engs	
w/Dual Thermactor	
right side (2.7)	3.8
left side (1.7)	2.4
both sides (3.9)	5.5
F-series-BRONCO	
Six	
wo/EFI-one (1.0)	1.5
all (1.8)	2.6
w/EFI-one (1.8)	2.6
all (2.1)	3.0
V-8	
5.0L eng	
wo/EFI	
one side (.9)	1.3
both sides (1.3)	1.9
w/EFI	
right side (1.7)	2.4
left side (1.0)	1.5
both sides (2.3)	3.3
5.8L eng	
one side (.9)	1.3
both sides (1.3)	1.9

(Factory Time) Chilton Time

5.8L-7.5L engs
w/Dual Thermactor
right side (1.9) 2.7
left side (1.2) 1.7
both sides (2.8) 4.0

Valve Tappets, Renew (All)

Includes: R&R intake manifold where required. Adjust carburetor and ignition timing.

RANGER-BRONCO II
Four
2.0L eng (1.2) 1.7
2.3L eng (1.6) 2.3
V-6
2.8L eng (5.6) 7.9
2.9L eng (5.0) 7.1
AEROSTAR
Four (5.0) 7.1
V-6
2.8L eng (6.4) 9.0
3.0L eng (4.2) 5.9
ECONOLINE
Six
wo/EFI (2.1) 3.0
w/EFI (3.0) 4.3
V-8
5.0L eng
wo/EFI (4.3) 6.1
w/EFI (4.8) 6.8
5.8L eng (4.3) 6.1
5.8L-7.5L engs
w/Dual Thermactor (6.5) 9.2
F-series-BRONCO
Six
wo/EFI (1.7) 2.4
w/EFI (2.6) 3.7
V-8
5.0L eng
wo/EFI (2.8) 4.0
w/EFI (4.3) 6.1
5.8L eng (3.8) 5.4
5.8L-7.5L engs
w/Dual Thermactor (4.9) 6.9

Valve Spring or Valve Stem Oil Seals, Renew (Head on Truck)

Includes: R&R rocker arms or assy. and adjust valves, if adjustable.

RANGER-BRONCO II
Four
2.0L eng-one (.9) 1.3
all (1.9) 2.7
2.3L eng-one (1.5) 2.2
all (2.7) 3.8
V-6
2.8L eng
one side (1.7) 2.4
both sides (3.0) 4.2
2.9L eng
one side (2.0) 2.9
both sides (3.8) 5.4
AEROSTAR
Four-one (1.4) 2.0
all (2.6) 3.7
V-6
2.8L eng
one side (2.2) 3.1
both sides (4.3) 6.1
3.0L eng
one side (2.6) 3.7
both sides (5.0) 7.1
ECONOLINE
Six
wo/EFI-one (1.2) 1.7
all (2.8) 4.0
w/EFI-one (2.3) 3.3
all (3.9) 5.5
V-8
5.0L eng
wo/EFI
one side (2.0) 2.9
both sides (3.4) 4.8

(Factory Time) Chilton Time

w/EFI
right side (3.4) 4.8
left side (2.4) 3.4
both sides (5.3) 7.5
5.8L eng
one side (2.0) 2.9
both sides (3.4) 4.8
5.8L-7.5L engs
w/Dual Thermactor
right side (3.7) 5.2
left side (2.7) 3.8
both sides (5.9) 8.3
F-series-BRONCO
Six
wo/EFI-one (1.1) 1.6
all (2.7) 3.8
w/EFI-one (1.9) 2.7
all (3.5) 5.0
5.0L eng
wo/EFI
one side (1.9) 2.7
both sides (3.3) 4.7
w/EFI
right side (2.7) 3.8
left side (2.0) 2.9
both sides (4.3) 6.1
5.8L eng
one side (1.9) 2.7
both sides (3.3) 4.7
5.8L-7.5L engs
w/Dual Thermactor
right side (2.9) 4.1
left side (2.2) 3.1
both sides (4.8) 6.8
one-each side (1.1) 1.5
all-both sides (2.8) 3.5

Valve Clearance, Adjust
FOUR 1.8
V-6 2.7

DIESEL ENGINE

Compression Test
FOUR 1.0
V-8 1.8

Cylinder Head Gasket, Renew
Four
2.2L eng (2.8) 3.9
2.3L eng (4.2) 5.8
V-8
F series
right side (6.9) 9.6
left side (6.3) 8.8
both sides (9.6) 13.4
Econoline
right side (9.2) 12.8
left side (9.4) 11.7
both sides (12.0) 16.8
w/A.C. add (.4) .4
w/P.S. add (.5) .5

Cylinder Head, Renew

Includes: Transfer all components. Clean, replace and lap valves. Make all necessary adjustments.

Four
2.2L eng (4.4) 6.1
2.3L eng (6.4) 8.9
V-8
F series
right side (8.4) 11.7
left side (7.8) 10.9
both sides (12.5) 17.5
Econoline
right side (10.7) 14.9
left side (9.9) 13.8
both sides (14.9) 20.8
w/A.C. add (.4) .4
w/P.S. add (.5) .5

(Factory Time) Chilton Time

Clean Carbon and Grind Valves

Includes: R&R cylinder head. Reface valves and seats. Make all necessary adjustments.

Four
2.2L eng (5.9) 8.0
2.3L eng (6.7) 9.4
V-8
F series
right side (8.8) 12.3
left side (8.2) 11.4
both sides (13.3) 18.6
Econoline
right side (11.1) 15.5
left side (10.3) 14.4
both sides (15.7) 21.9
w/A.C. add (.4) .4
w/P.S. add (.5) .5

Rocker Arm Cover and/or Gasket, Renew
Four
2.2L eng (.4) .7
2.3L eng (.5) .8
V-8
F series
right side (.8) 1.1
left side (.6) .9
both sides (1.1) 1.7
Econoline
right side (1.7) 2.3
left side (.9) 1.2
both sides (2.1) 2.9

Valve Push Rods and/or Rocker Arms, Renew
Four
2.2L eng-one (.7) 1.2
all (.9) 1.6
2.3L eng-one (.7) 1.0
all (1.2) 1.7
V-8
F series
right side (1.1) 1.5
left side (.9) 1.3
both sides (1.6) 2.4
Econoline
right side (2.0) 2.8
left side (1.2) 1.6
both sides (2.6) 3.6

Note: If nece to tilt eng to renew rods for # 3 & 5 cyls add&.2.0

Valve Springs and/or Valve Stem Oil Seals, Renew (Head on Truck)
Four
2.2L eng-one (.9) 1.6
all (1.4) 2.4
2.3L eng-one (.7) 1.1
all (1.7) 2.4
V-8
F series
one cyl (1.1) 1.5
one cyl-each side (1.7) 2.3
all cyls-both sides (4.0) 5.6
Econoline
right side (3.2) 4.4
left side (2.4) 3.3
both sides (5.0) 7.0

Valve Tappets, Renew
Four
2.2L eng
all (6.1) 8.8
V-8
F series
one cyl (2.9) 4.2
all cyls-one side (3.2) 4.6
all cyls-both sides (4.0) 5.8
Econoline
one cyl (4.5) 6.3
all cyls-both sides (5.5) 7.7
w/A.C. add (.4) .4
w/P.S. add (.5) .5

LABOR 13 ENGINE ASSEMBLY & MOUNTS 13 LABOR

(Factory Time) Chilton Time

GASOLINE ENGINES

Engine Assembly, Remove & Install

Includes: R&R hood and radiator, adjust carburetor and linkage.

Does not include transfer of any parts or equipment.

RANGER–BRONCO II

	Chilton Time
Four	
2.0L eng (3.1)	4.3
2.3L eng	
w/M.T. (4.5)	6.3
w/A.T. (3.4)	4.7
V-6	
2.8L eng	
4X2	
w/M.T. (4.8)	6.7
w/A.T. (5.2)	7.2
4X4	
w/M.T. (5.1)	7.0
w/A.T. (5.3)	7.4
2.9L eng	
4X2 or 4X4	
w/M.T. (4.3)	6.0
w/A.T. (4.3)	6.0
AEROSTAR	
Four	
w/M.T. (5.8)	8.1
w/A.T. (5.9)	8.3
V-6	
2.8L eng (5.9)	8.3
3.0L eng (6.1)	8.5
ECONOLINE	
Six	
wo/EFI (6.8)	9.5
w/EFI (7.2)	10.0
V-8	
5.0L-5.8L engs	
wo/EFI (5.3)	7.4
w/EFI (6.3)	8.8
7.5L eng (6.2)	8.6
F-series-BRONCO	
4X2	
Six	
wo/EFI (4.5)	6.3
w/EFI (6.6)	9.2
V-8	
5.0L-5.8L engs	
w/M.T. (3.5)	4.9
w/A.T. (4.6)	6.4
7.5L eng (4.6)	6.4
4X4	
Six	
wo/EFI	
w/M.T. (3.9)	5.4
w/A.T. (4.2)	5.8
w/EFI	
w/M.T. (6.5)	9.1
w/A.T. (6.6)	9.2
V-8	
5.0L-5.8L engs	
w/M.T. (3.6)	5.0
w/A.T. (4.7)	6.5
7.5L eng (4.7)	6.5
w/P.S. add (.4)	.4
w/A.C. add (.6)	.6

Engine Assembly, Replace With New or Rebuilt Unit (With Cyl. Heads and Oil Pan)

Includes: R&R hood and radiator. R&R engine assembly, transfer all necessary parts, fuel and electrical units. Tune engine. Road test.

RANGER-BRONCO II

	Chilton Time
Four	
2.0L eng (5.2)	7.2
2.3L eng	
w/M.T. (7.0)	9.8
w/A.T. (5.9)	8.2
V-6	
2.8L eng	
4X2	
w/M.T. (7.1)	9.9
w/A.T. (7.5)	10.5
4X4	
w/M.T. (7.4)	10.3
w/A.T. (7.6)	10.6
2.9L eng	
4X2 or 4X4	
w/M.T. (6.8)	9.5
w/A.T. (6.8)	9.5
AEROSTAR	
Four	
w/M.T. (8.3)	11.6
w/A.T. (8.4)	11.8
V-6	
2.8L eng (8.4)	11.8
3.0L eng (8.6)	12.0
ECONOLINE	
Six	
wo/EFI (10.2)	14.2
w/EFI (10.6)	14.8
V-8	
5.0L-5.8L engs	
wo/EFI (7.6)	10.6
w/EFI (8.6)	12.0
7.5L eng (8.5)	11.8
F-series-BRONCO	
4X2	
Six	
wo/EFI (6.8)	9.5
w/EFI (8.9)	12.4
V-8	
5.0L-5.8L engs	
w/M.T. (5.8)	8.1
w/A.T. (6.9)	9.6
7.5L eng (6.9)	9.6
4X4	
Six	
wo/EFI	
w/M.T. (6.2)	8.6
w/A.T. (6.5)	9.1
w/EFI	
w/M.T. (8.8)	12.3
w/A.T. (8.9)	12.5
V-8	
5.0L-5.8L engs	
w/M.T. (5.9)	8.2
w/A.T. (7.0)	9.8
7.5L eng (7.0)	9.8
w/P.S. add (.4)	.4
w/A.C. add (.6)	.6

Cylinder Assembly, Renew (w/All Internal Parts Less Head(s) and Oil Pan)

Includes: R&R hood and radiator. R&R engine, transfer all component parts not supplied with replacement engine, clean carbon, grind valves, Minor tune up. Road test.

RANGER-BRONCO II

	Chilton Time
Four	
2.0L eng (9.7)	13.5
2.3L eng	
w/M.T. (11.3)	15.8
w/A.T. (10.2)	14.2
V-6	
2.8L eng	
4X2	
w/M.T. (12.4)	17.3
w/A.T. (12.8)	17.9
4X4	
w/M.T. (12.7)	17.7
w/A.T. (12.9)	18.0
2.9L eng	
4X2 or 4X4	
w/M.T. (12.2)	17.0
w/A.T. (12.2)	17.0
AEROSTAR	
Four	
w/M.T. (12.6)	17.6
w/A.T. (12.7)	17.8
V-6	
2.8L eng (13.3)	18.6
3.0L eng (14.0)	19.6
ECONOLINE	
Six	
wo/EFI (13.2)	18.4
w/EFI (13.6)	19.0
V-8	
5.0L-5.8L engs	
wo/EFI (14.9)	20.8
w/EFI (15.9)	22.2
7.5L eng (14.9)	20.8
F-series-BRONCO	
4X2	
Six	
wo/EFI (10.9)	15.2
w/EFI (13.0)	18.2
V-8	
5.0L-5.8L engs	
w/M.T. (13.1)	18.3
w/A.T. (14.2)	19.8
7.5L eng (14.2)	19.8
4X4	
Six	
wo/EFI	
w/M.T. (10.3)	14.4
w/A.T. (10.6)	14.8
w/EFI	
w/M.T. (12.9)	18.0
w/A.T. (13.0)	18.2
V-8	
5.0L-5.8L engs	
w/M.T. (13.2)	18.4
w/A.T. (14.3)	20.0
7.5L eng (13.4)	18.7
w/P.S. add (.4)	.4
w/A.C. add (.6)	.6

Engine Assembly, R&R and Recondition (Complete)

Includes: R&R hood and radiator. Rebore block, install new pistons, rings, rod and main bearings. Clean carbon, grind valves. Tune engine. Road test.

RANGER-BRONCO II

	Chilton Time
Four	
2.0L eng (15.6)	22.4
2.3L eng	
w/M.T. (16.6)	23.9
w/A.T. (15.5)	22.3
V-6	
2.8L eng	
4X2	
w/M.T. (19.0)	27.3
w/A.T. (19.4)	27.9
4X4	
w/M.T. (19.3)	27.7
w/A.T. (19.5)	28.0
2.9L eng	
4X2 or 4X4	
w/M.T. (18.7)	26.9
w/A.T. (18.7)	26.9
AEROSTAR	
Four	
w/M.T. (17.9)	25.7
w/A.T. (18.0)	25.9
V-6	
2.8L eng (20.1)	28.9
3.0L eng (20.3)	29.2
ECONOLINE	
Six	
wo/EFI (21.4)	30.8
w/EFI (21.8)	31.3

LABOR 13 ENGINE ASSEMBLY & MOUNTS 13 LABOR

(Factory Time) Chilton Time

V-8
5.0L-5.8L engs
wo/EFI (22.6) 32.5
w/EFI (23.6) 33.9
7.5L eng (24.0) 34.5
F-series-BRONCO
4X2
Six
wo/EFI (19.1) 27.5
w/EFI (21.2) 30.5
V-8
5.0L-5.8L engs
w/M.T. (20.8) 29.9
w/A.T. (21.9) 31.5
7.5L eng (22.4) 32.2
4X4
Six
wo/EFI
w/M.T. (18.5) 26.6
w/A.T. (18.8) 27.0
w/EFI
w/M.T. (21.1) 30.3
w/A.T. (21.2) 30.5
V-8
5.0L-5.8L engs
w/M.T. (20.9) 30.0
w/A.T. (22.0) 31.6
7.5L eng (22.5) 32.4
w/P.S. add (.4) 4
w/A.C. add (.6) 6

Engine Mounts, Renew
RANGER-BRONCO II
FRONT
Four
2.0L eng
one (.4) 6
both (.5) 9
2.3L eng
one (1.4) 1.9
both (1.5) 2.0
V-6
2.8L eng
one (.4) 6
both (.5) 9
2.9L eng
one (.6) 9
both (.8) 1.2
AEROSTAR
Four
one (1.4) 1.9
both (1.5) 2.0
V-6
2.8L eng
one (.7) 1.0
both (.9) 1.3

3.0L eng
right (.5) 7
left (.8) 1.2
both (.9) 1.4
ECONOLINE
Six
one (.4) 6
both (.5) 9
V-8
5.0L eng
one (1.0) 1.5
both (1.1) 1.7
5.8L eng
one (.8) 1.2
both (1.0) 1.5
7.5L eng
right (.7) 1.0
left (.5) 7
both (.8) 1.4
F-series-BRONCO
Six
one (.4) 6
both (.5) 9
V-8
5.0L-5.8L engs
one (.4) 6
both (.6) 1.0
7.5L eng
one (.4) 6
both (.6) 9
Rear
Ranger (.4) 6
Bronco (.6) 8
Aerostar (.5) 7
Econoline (.4) 7
F100-350 (.6) 8

DIESEL ENGINE

Engine Assembly, Remove & Install
Includes: R&R hood and radiator. Does not include transfer of any parts or equipment.
Four
2.2L eng (3.7) 5.1
2.3L eng (4.6) 6.5
w/A.C. add (.4) 4
w/P.S. add (.5) 5
V-8
F series (6.2) 8.6
w/A.T. add (.6) 6
4X4 add (.2) 2
Econoline (7.1) 9.9
w/A.C. add
F series (.3) 3
Econoline (1.0) 1.0

Cylinder Assembly, Renew (w/All Internal Parts Less Head(s) and Oil Pan)
Includes: R&R hood and radiator. R&R engine, transfer all component parts not supplied with replacement engine. Clean carbon, grind valves. Make all necessary adjustments.
Four
2.2L eng (12.6) 17.3
2.3L eng (11.6) 16.5
w/A.C. add (.4) 4
w/P.S. add (.5) 5
V-8
F series (19.6) 27.4
w/A.T. add (.6) 6
4X4 add (.2) 2
Econoline (20.5) 28.7
w/A.C. add
F series (.3) 3
Econoline (1.0) 1.0

Engine Assembly, R&R and Recondition (Complete)
Includes: R&R hood and radiator. Install new cylinder sleeves, pistons, rings, rod and main bearings. Clean carbon, grind valves. Make all necessary adjustments.
Four
2.2L eng (17.7) 24.7
2.3L eng (16.6) 23.5
w/A.C. add (.4) 4
w/P.S. add (.5) 5
V-8
F series (27.2) 38.0
w/A.T. add (.6) 6
4X4 add (.2) 2
Econoline (28.0) 39.2
w/A.C. add
F series (.3) 3
Econoline (1.0) 1.0

Engine Mounts, Renew
Front
Four–one (.6) 8
both (.9) 1.2
V-8
F series
right (1.8) 2.4
left (1.6) 2.1
both (1.9) 2.6
Econoline
right (1.9) 2.5
left (1.8) 2.3
both (2.1) 2.8
Rear
Four (.4) 6
V-8 (.4) 6

LABOR 14 PISTONS, RINGS & BEARINGS 14 LABOR

(Factory Time) Chilton Time

GASOLINE ENGINES

Rings, Renew (All)
Includes: Remove cylinder top ridge, deglaze cylinder walls, replace rod bearings, clean carbon. Minor tune up.
RANGER-BRONCO II
Four
2.0L eng (8.2) 11.4
2.3L eng (7.9) 11.0
V-6
2.8L eng (10.8) 15.1
2.9L eng
4X2 (10.8) 15.1
4X4 (11.7) 16.3

AEROSTAR
Four (8.0) 11.2
V-6
2.8L eng (10.7) 14.9
3.0L eng (11.0) 15.4
ECONOLINE
Six
wo/EFI (8.3) 11.6
w/EFI (12.7) 17.7
V-8
5.0L eng
wo/EFI (11.8) 16.5
w/EFI (14.2) 19.8
5.8L eng (11.8) 16.5
5.8L-7.5L engs
w/Dual Thermactor (13.7) 19.1

F-series-BRONCO
Six
wo/EFI (7.5) 10.5
w/EFI (9.2) 12.8
V-8
5.0L eng
wo/EFI
4X2 (10.2) 14.2
4X4 (13.4) 18.7
w/EFI
4X2 (13.2) 18.4
4X4 (13.4) 18.7
5.8L-7.5L engs
w/Dual Thermactor
4X2 (11.8) 16.5
4X4 (11.8) 16.5

(Factory Time) Chilton Time

Piston or Connecting Rod, Renew (One)

Includes: Remove cylinder top ridge, deglaze cylinder walls, replace rod bearings, clean carbon. Minor tune up.

RANGER-BRONCO II

	Chilton Time
Four	
2.0L eng (7.2)	10.0
2.3L eng (7.3)	10.2
V-6	
2.8L eng (7.9)	11.0
2.9L eng	
4X2 (7.1)	9.9
4X4 (8.0)	11.2
AEROSTAR	
Four (7.3)	10.2
V-6	
2.8L eng (7.3)	10.2
3.0L eng (7.1)	9.9
ECONOLINE	
Six	
wo/EFI (6.3)	8.8
w/EFI (10.5)	14.7
V-8	
5.0L eng	
wo/EFI (8.1)	11.3
w/EFI (11.1)	15.5
5.8L eng (8.1)	11.3
5.8L-7.5L engs	
w/Dual Thermactor (9.9)	13.8
F-series-BRONCO	
Six	
wo/EFI (5.4)	7.5
w/EFI (7.2)	10.0
V-8	
5.0L eng	
wo/EFI	
4X2 (5.6)	7.8
4X4 (8.4)	11.7
w/EFI	
4X2 (8.1)	11.3
4X4 (8.4)	11.7
5.8L-7.5L engs	
w/Dual Thermactor	
4X2 (7.6)	10.6
4X4 (7.6)	10.6

Connecting Rod Bearings, Renew

Includes: R&R oil pan, plastigauge and install new bearings. Clean oil pump pick up tube and screen. Renew oil filter.

RANGER-BRONCO II

	Chilton Time
Four	
2.0L eng (3.2)	4.4
2.3L eng	
4X2 (3.3)	4.6
4X4 (3.9)	5.4
V-6	
2.8L eng	
w/M.T. (4.4)	6.1
w/A.T. (4.6)	6.4
2.9L eng (4.7)	6.5
AEROSTAR	
Four (2.6)	3.6
V-6	
2.8L eng (3.2)	4.4
3.0L eng (2.9)	4.0
ECONOLINE	
Six	
wo/EFI (3.9)	5.4
w/EFI (5.1)	7.1
V-8	
5.0L-5.8L engs (6.3)	8.8
7.5L eng (4.3)	6.0
F-Series-BRONCO	
Six	
wo/EFI (3.7)	5.1
w/EFI (4.6)	6.4
V-8	
5.0L-5.8L engs	
4X2	
w/M.T. (5.1)	7.1
w/A.T. (5.3)	7.4
4X4	
w/M.T. (5.7)	7.9
w/A.T. (5.9)	8.2
7.5L eng	
4X2	
w/M.T. (3.9)	5.4
w/A.T. (4.1)	5.7
4X4	
w/M.T. (4.5)	6.3
w/A.T. (4.7)	6.5

COMBINATIONS

Add to Engine Work

(Factory Time)	Chilton Time
DRAIN, EVACUATE & RECHARGE AIR CONDITIONING SYSTEM	
All models (.7)	1.5
ROCKER ARMS OR SHAFT ASSY. DISASSEMBLE AND CLEAN OR RECONDITION	
Six (.6)	1.0
V-8-One side (.5)	.7
Both sides (1.0)	1.3
HYDRAULIC VALVE LIFTERS, DISASSEMBLE AND CLEAN	
Each (.2)	.2
ROCKER ARM STUD, RENEW	
Each (.3)	.3
DISTRIBUTOR, RECONDITION	
All models (.7)	1.0
CARBURETOR, RECONDITION	
1 BBL (.9)	1.2
2 BBL (1.0)	1.3
4 BBL	
Ford (1.0)	1.5
Holly (1.3)	2.0
TIMING CHAIN, RENEW (COVER REMOVED)	
All models (.3)	.5
VALVE GUIDES, REAM OVERSIZE	
Each (.1)	.2
DEGLAZE CYLINDER WALLS	
Each (.1)	.2
REMOVE CYLINDER TOP RIDGE	
Each (.1)	.1
MAIN BEARINGS, RENEW (PAN REMOVED)	
Four (1.9)	2.9
Six (1.6)	2.5
V-6 (1.5)	2.0
V-8 (1.9)	2.9
PLASTIGAUGE BEARINGS	
Each (.1)	.1
OIL PUMP, RECONDITION	
All models (.4)	.6
OIL FILTER ELEMENT, RENEW	
All models (.3)	.4

DIESEL ENGINE

Rings, Renew (All)

Includes: Remove cylinder top ridge, deglaze cylinder walls, replace rod bearings, clean carbon. Make all necessary adjustments.

(Factory Time)	Chilton Time
Four	
2.2L eng (8.8)	12.3
2.3L eng (8.8)	12.3
V-8	
F series (15.6)	22.6
Econoline (16.2)	23.4
w/A.C. add	
F series (.3)	.3
Econoline (1.0)	1.0

Piston or Connecting Rod, Renew (One)

Includes: Remove cylinder top ridge, deglaze cylinder wall, replace rod bearing, clean carbon. Make all necessary adjustments.

	Chilton Time
Four	
2.2L eng (7.9)	11.0
2.3L eng (7.7)	11.0
V-8	
F series (12.4)	17.9
Econoline (13.0)	18.8
w/A.C. add	
F series (.3)	.3
Econoline (1.0)	1.0

Connecting Rod Bearings, Renew

	Chilton Time
Four	
2.2L eng (4.2)	6.0
2.3L eng (3.7)	5.2
V-8	
F series	
4X2 (4.9)	7.1
4X4 (5.2)	7.5
Econoline (5.4)	7.8

GASOLINE ENGINES

Crankshaft and Main Bearings, Renew

Includes: R&R hood and radiator. R&R engine, check all bearing clearances.

(Factory Time)	Chilton Time
RANGER-BRONCO II	
Four	
2.0L eng (6.9)	9.7
2.3L eng	
w/M.T. (7.9)	11.0
w/A.T. (6.8)	9.5
V-6	
2.8L eng	
4X2	
w/M.T. (8.2)	11.4
w/A.T. (8.6)	12.0
4X4	
w/M.T. (8.5)	11.9
w/A.T. (8.7)	12.1
2.9L eng	
4X2 or 4X4	
w/M.T. (7.9)	11.0
w/A.T. (7.9)	11.0
AEROSTAR	
Four	
w/M.T. (9.2)	12.9
w/A.T. (9.3)	13.0
V-6	
2.8L eng (9.3)	13.0
3.0L eng (9.6)	13.4
ECONOLINE	
Six	
wo/EFI (10.9)	15.2
w/EFI (11.3)	15.8
V-8	
5.0L-5.8L engs	
wo/EFI (9.1)	12.7
w/EFI (10.1)	14.1
7.5L eng (10.2)	14.3
F-series-BRONCO	
4X2	
Six	
wo/EFI (8.6)	12.0
w/EFI (10.7)	15.0
V-8	
5.0L-5.8L engs	
w/M.T. (7.3)	10.2
w/A.T. (8.4)	11.7
7.5L eng (8.6)	12.0
4X4	
Six	
wo/EFI	
w/M.T. (8.0)	11.2
w/A.T. (8.3)	11.6
w/EFI	
w/M.T. (10.6)	14.8
w/A.T. (10.7)	15.0
V-8	
5.0L-5.8L engs	
w/M.T. (7.4)	10.3
w/A.T. (8.5)	11.9
7.5L eng (8.7)	12.1

Main Bearings, Renew

Includes: R&R oil pan, plastigauge and install new main bearings. Recondition oil pump and renew oil filter.

(Factory Time)	Chilton Time
RANGER-BRONCO II	
Four	
2.0L eng (4.1)	5.7
2.3L eng	
4X2 (4.2)	5.9
4X4 (4.8)	6.7
V-6	
2.8L eng	
w/M.T. (8.0)	11.2
w/A.T. (8.4)	11.7
AEROSTAR	
Four (3.5)	4.9
V-6	
2.8L eng	
w/M.T. (9.4)	13.1
w/A.T. (9.8)	13.7
3.0L eng	
w/M.T. (8.7)	12.1
w/A.T. (9.0)	12.6
ECONOLINE	
Six	
wo/EFI (4.1)	5.7
w/EFI (5.3)	7.4
V-8	
5.0L-5.8L engs (6.4)	8.9
7.5L eng (4.4)	6.1
F-series-BRONCO	
Six (3.9)	5.4
V-8	
4X2	
5.0L-5.8L engs	
w/M.T. (5.2)	7.2
w/A.T. (5.4)	7.5
4X4	
w/M.T. (5.8)	8.1
w/A.T. (6.0)	8.4
7.5L eng	
4X2	
w/M.T. (4.0)	5.6
w/A.T. (4.2)	5.8
4X4	
w/M.T. (4.6)	6.4
w/A.T. (4.8)	6.7

Main and Rod Bearings, Renew

Includes: R&R oil pan, plastigauge and install new rod and main bearings. Recondition oil pump and renew oil filter.

(Factory Time)	Chilton Time
RANGER-BRONCO II	
Four	
2.0L eng (5.1)	7.1
2.3L eng	
4X2 (5.2)	7.3
4X4 (5.8)	8.1
V-6	
2.8L eng	
w/M.T. (9.0)	12.6
w/A.T. (9.4)	13.1
AEROSTAR	
Four (4.5)	6.3
V-6	
2.8L eng	
w/M.T. (10.4)	14.5
w/A.T. (10.8)	15.1
3.0L eng	
w/M.T. (10.2)	14.2
w/A.T. (10.5)	14.7
ECONOLINE	
Six	
wo/EFI (5.5)	7.7
w/EFI (6.7)	9.3
V-8	
5.0L-5.8L engs (8.2)	11.4
7.5L eng (6.2)	8.6
F-series-BRONCO	
Six (5.3)	7.4
V-8	
4X2	
5.0L-5.8L engs	
w/M.T. (7.0)	9.8
w/A.T. (7.2)	10.0
4X4	
w/M.T. (7.6)	10.6
w/A.T. (7.8)	10.9
7.5L eng	
4X2	
w/M.T. (5.8)	8.1
w/A.T. (6.0)	8.4
4X4	
w/M.T. (6.4)	8.9
w/A.T. (6.6)	9.2

Rear Main Bearing Oil Seal, Renew (Upper & Lower)
Split Lip or Full Circle Type

Includes: R&R transmission on all 6 cyl models. Includes R&R oil pan on all V-8 models.

(Factory Time)	Chilton Time
RANGER-BRONCO II	
4X2	
Four	
2.0L eng (2.1)	2.9
2.3L eng	
w/M.T. (2.0)	2.8
w/A.T. (2.6)	3.6
V-6	
2.8L eng	
w/M.T. (3.3)	4.6
w/A.T. (3.5)	4.9
2.9L eng	
w/M.T. (2.4)	3.4
w/A.T. (2.6)	3.6
4X4	
Four	
TK (3.3)	4.6
MMC5 (3.5)	4.9
V-6 (4.2)	6.0
AEROSTAR	
Four	
w/M.T. (2.0)	2.8
w/A.T. (2.6)	3.6
V-6	
w/M.T. (2.4)	3.4
w/A.T. (2.6)	3.6
ECONOLINE	
Six	
3 Spd (1.8)	2.5
4 Spd (2.0)	2.8
C-6 (2.7)	3.7
AOD (2.6)	3.6
V-8	
5.0L-5.8L engs (2.7)	3.7
7.5L eng (2.7)	3.7
F-series-BRONCO	
4X2	
Six	
3 Spd (1.8)	2.5
4 Spd (2.5)	3.5
C-5 (2.3)	3.2
C-6 (2.3)	3.2
AOD (2.9)	4.0
V-8	
M.T. (2.6)	3.6
C-6 (2.7)	3.7
AOD (2.9)	4.0
4X4	
Six	
w/M.T. (4.2)	5.9
w/A.T. (4.0)	5.6
V-8 (4.3)	6.0

Crankshaft Front Oil Seal, Renew

Does not require R&R of front cover on V-6 & V-8 engines.

(Factory Time)	Chilton Time
RANGER-BRONCO II	
Four	
2.0L eng	
Crank (1.7)	2.4
Cam (1.7)	2.4
Aux (1.8)	2.5
All (2.0)	2.8
2.3L eng	
Crank (1.6)	2.2
Cam (1.5)	2.1
Aux (1.5)	2.1
All (1.9)	2.6
V-6	
2.8L eng	
w/M.T. (1.0)	1.4
w/A.T. (1.1)	1.5
2.9L eng (1.4)	1.9

LABOR 15 CRANKSHAFT & DAMPER 15 LABOR

(Factory Time)	Chilton Time
AEROSTAR	
Four	
Crank (1.6)	2.2
Cam (1.5)	2.1
All (1.9)	2.6
V-6	
2.8L eng	
w/M.T. (1.0)	1.4
w/A.T. (1.1)	1.5
3.0L eng (.9)	1.3
ECONOLINE	
Six (1.1)	1.5
V-8	
5.0L eng (1.7)	2.3
5.8L eng (1.8)	2.4
7.5L eng (4.4)	6.1
F-series-BRONCO	
Six (1.1)	1.5
V-8	
5.0L-5.8L engs (1.2)	1.6
7.5L engs (3.0)	4.2

DIESEL ENGINE

Crankshaft and Main Bearings, Renew

Includes: R&R engine assy., check all bearing clearances.

(Factory Time)	Chilton Time
Four	
2.2L eng (7.4)	10.7
2.3L eng (8.0)	11.6
V-8	
F series (12.7)	18.4
w/A.T. add (.6)	.6
4X4 add (.2)	.2
Econoline (13.6)	19.7
w/A.C. add	
F series (.3)	.3
Econoline (1.0)	1.0

Main Bearings, Renew

Includes: Check all bearing clearances.

(Factory Time)	Chilton Time
Four	
2.2L eng (5.0)	7.0
2.3L eng (4.6)	6.6
V-8	
F series	
4X2 (5.6)	8.1
4X4 (6.0)	8.7
Econoline (6.1)	8.8

Main and Rod Bearings, Renew

Includes: Check all bearing clearances.

(Factory Time)	Chilton Time
Four	
2.2L eng (6.0)	8.2
2.3L eng (5.6)	7.8
V-8	
F series	
4X2 (7.7)	11.1
4X4 (8.1)	11.7
Econoline (8.2)	11.2

Crankshaft Front Oil Seal, Renew

(Factory Time)	Chilton Time
Four	
both sides (7.9)	11.0
2.3L eng (1.7)	2.5
V-8	
F series (1.6)	2.5
Econoline (1.2)	1.8
w/A.C. add (.4)	.4
w/P.S. add (.5)	.5

Crankshaft Rear Oil Seal, Renew

(Factory Time)	Chilton Time
Four	
2.2L eng (1.9)	2.7
2.3L eng	
4X2 (1.7)	2.7
4X4 (3.5)	5.0
V-8	
F series	
4X2-w/M.T. (3.3)	4.8
w/A.T. (3.0)	4.3
4X4-w/M.T. (4.3)	6.2
w/A.T. (4.0)	6.0
Econoline (3.1)	4.5

Crankshaft and/or Camshaft Sprockets, Renew

(Factory Time)	Chilton Time
Four	
2.2L eng (1.9)	2.7
2.3L eng (1.1)	1.6
V-8	
F series (4.1)	5.9
Econoline (4.7)	6.8
w/A.C. add (.4)	.4
w/P.S. add (.5)	.5

Vibration Damper or Pulley, Renew

(Factory Time)	Chilton Time
Four	
2.2L eng (.8)	1.2
2.3L eng (.4)	.7
V-8	
F series (1.5)	2.1
Econoline (1.1)	1.5
w/A.C. add (.1)	.1

LABOR 16 CAMSHAFT & TIMING GEARS 16 LABOR

GASOLINE ENGINES

Timing Case Cover, Gasket or Oil Seal, Renew

Includes: R&R radiator. Does not require oil pan removal on 6 cyl (200) or 302 CID engines.

(Factory Time)	Chilton Time
RANGER-BRONCO II	
Four	
2.0L eng (2.0)	2.8
2.3L eng (1.9)	2.6
V-6	
2.8L eng (4.6)	6.4
2.9L eng (4.6)	6.4
AEROSTAR	
Four (1.9)	2.6
V-6 (4.8)	6.7
ECONOLINE	
Six (2.7)	3.7
V-8	
5.0L eng (3.1)	4.3
5.8L engs (3.4)	4.7
5.8-7.5L engs	
w/Dual Thermactor (4.4)	6.1
F-series-BRONCO	
Six (2.6)	3.6
V-8	
5.0L-5.8L engs (2.5)	3.5
5.8L-7.5L engs	
w/Dual Thermactor (3.0)	4.2

Timing Belt, Renew

(Factory Time)	Chilton Time
RANGER-AEROSTAR	
Four	
2.0L eng (1.6)	2.5
2.3L eng (1.3)	2.2
w/P.S. add (.2)	.2
w/A.C. add (.3)	.3

Timing Chain or Gears, Renew (SIX)

Includes: R&R timing case cover and radiator, renew gears or chain. Reset ignition timing.

(Factory Time)	Chilton Time
BRONCO-Six (2.7)	3.9
ECONOLINE-Six (3.5)	5.4
F100-350	
Six (2.7)	4.0

CRANKSHAFT GEAR ONLY. FOR CAMSHAFT FIBER GEAR USE CAMSHAFT, RENEW

Timing Chain or Gears, Renew (V-6 & V-8)

Includes: R&R timing case cover and radiator. Renew gears or chain. Reset ignition timing.

(Factory Time)	Chilton Time
RANGER-BRONCO	
V-6	
2.9L eng (4.4)	4.9
AEROSTAR	
V-6	
3.0L eng (4.2)	7.2
F-series-BRONCO	
V-8	
5.0L-5.8L engs (2.7)	4.0
5.8L-7.5L engs	
w/Dual Thermactor (3.1)	4.7
ECONOLINE	
V-8	
5.0L eng (3.5)	4.8
5.8L eng (3.7)	5.2
5.8L-7.5L engs	
w/Dual Thermactor (4.5)	6.6

Camshaft or Camshaft Gear, Renew

Includes: R&R radiator, timing case cover. Adjust carburetor and ignition timing.

(Factory Time)	Chilton Time
RANGER-BRONCO	
Four	
2.0L eng (2.2)	3.0
2.3L eng (4.2)	5.9
V-6	
2.8L eng	
w/M.T. (8.9)	12.5
w/A.T. (9.1)	12.7
2.9L eng (8.0)	11.2
AEROSTAR	
Four (5.4)	7.5
V-6	
2.8L eng (9.4)	13.1
3.0L eng (6.9)	9.7
ECONOLINE	
Six	
wo/EFI (6.6)	9.2
w/EFI (6.3)	8.8
V-8	
5.0L eng	
wo/EFI (5.6)	7.8
w/EFI (8.1)	11.3
5.8L eng (6.1)	8.5
5.8L-7.5L engs	
w/Dual Thermactor (9.7)	13.5
F-series-BRONCO	
Six	
wo/EFI (5.9)	8.2
w/EFI (6.1)	8.5
V-8	
5.0L eng	
wo/EFI (5.2)	7.3
w/EFI (6.7)	9.4
5.8L-7.5L engs (7.5)	10.5
5.8L eng	
w/Dual Thermactor (10.9)	15.2

LABOR 16 CAMSHAFT & TIMING GEARS 16 LABOR

(Factory Time) Chilton Time

Camshaft Bearings, Renew

Includes: R&R hood, radiator and engine assembly where required. R&R camshaft and renew bearings. Adjust carburetor and ignition timing.

RANGER-BRONCO II	
Four	
2.0L eng (2.7)	4.1
w/P.S. add (.2)	.2
w/A.C. add (.3)	.3
V-8	
F series (3.1)	4.5
Econoline (3.1)	4.5
w/A.C. add (.4)	.4
w/P.S. add (.5)	.5

Camshaft, Renew

Four	
2.2L eng (6.1)	8.8
2.3L eng (1.5)	2.2
V-8	
F series (11.6)	16.8
Econoline (11.7)	17.0
w/A.C. add	
F series (.3)	.3
Econoline (1.0)	1.0

Camshaft and/or Crankshaft Sprockets, Renew

Four	
2.2L eng (1.9)	2.7
2.3L eng (1.1)	1.6
V-8	
F series (3.3)	4.7
Econoline (3.3)	4.7
w/A.C. add (.4)	.4
w/P.S. add (.5)	.5

Camshaft Idler Gear, Renew

Four	
2.2L eng (2.0)	2.7
2.3L eng (1.0)	1.5
w/A.C. add (.4)	.4
w/P.S. add (.5)	.5

Timing Belt, Renew

Four	
2.3L eng (1.0)	1.5

DIESEL ENGINE

Timing Cover Gasket, Renew

Four	
2.2L eng (5.5)	7.9
2.3L eng (2.0)	3.0

LABOR 17 ENGINE OILING SYSTEM 17 LABOR

(Factory Time) Chilton Time

GASOLINE ENGINES

Oil Pan or Gasket, Renew

Includes: Clean oil pick up tube and screen. Renew oil filter.

RANGER-BRONCO II	
Four	
2.0L eng (2.2)	3.0
2.3L eng	
4X2 (2.3)	3.2
4X4 (2.9)	4.0
V-6	
2.8L eng	
w/M.T. (3.4)	4.7
w/A.T. (3.6)	5.0
2.9L eng (3.3)	4.6
AEROSTAR	
Four (1.6)	2.2
V-6	
2.8L eng (2.2)	3.0
3.0L eng (1.4)	1.9
ECONOLINE	
Six	
wo/EFI (2.5)	3.5
w/EFI (3.7)	5.1
V-8	
5.0L-5.8L engs (4.5)	6.3
7.5L eng (2.5)	3.5
F-Series-BRONCO	
Six	
wo/EFI (2.3)	3.2
w/EFI (3.2)	4.4
V-8	
5.0L-5.8L engs	
4X2	
w/M.T. (3.3)	4.6
w/A.T. (3.5)	4.9
4X4	
w/M.T. (3.9)	5.4
w/A.T. (4.1)	5.7
7.5L eng	
4X2	
w/M.T. (2.1)	2.9
w/A.T. (2.3)	3.2
4X4	
w/M.T. (2.7)	3.7
w/A.T. (2.9)	4.0

Oil Pump, R&R or Renew

Includes: R&R oil pan, clean oil pump pick up tube and screen. Renew oil filter.

RANGER-BRONCO II	
Four	
2.0L eng (2.4)	3.3
2.3L eng	
4X2 (2.4)	3.3
4X4 (3.0)	4.2
V-6	
2.8L eng	
w/M.T. (3.5)	4.9
w/A.T. (3.7)	5.1
2.9L eng (3.4)	4.7
AEROSTAR	
Four (1.7)	2.3
V-6	
2.8L eng (2.3)	3.2
3.0L eng (1.5)	2.1
ECONOLINE	
Six	
wo/EFI (2.6)	3.6
w/EFI (3.8)	5.3
V-8	
5.0L-5.8L engs (4.6)	6.4
7.5L eng (2.6)	3.6
F-Series-BRONCO	
Six	
wo/EFI (2.4)	3.3
w/EFI (3.3)	4.6
V-8	
5.0L-5.8L engs	
4X2	
w/M.T. (3.4)	4.7
w/A.T. (3.6)	5.0
4X4	
w/M.T. (4.0)	5.6
w/A.T. (4.2)	5.8
7.5L eng	
4X2	
w/M.T. (2.2)	3.0
w/A.T. (2.4)	3.3
4X4	
w/M.T. (2.8)	3.9
w/A.T. (3.0)	4.2
Recond pump add (.4)	.5

Pressure Test Engine Bearings (Pan Off)

All models	1.0

Oil Pressure Gauge (Engine), Renew

All models (.3)	.5

Oil Pressure Gauge (Dash), Renew

RANGER (.6)	1.0
BRONCO (.4)	.7
BRONCO II (.6)	1.0
AEROSTAR (.6)	1.0
ECONOLINE (.5)	.8
F100-350 (.5)	1.0

Oil Filter Element, Renew

All models (.3)	.4

DIESEL ENGINE

Oil Pan and/or Gasket, Renew

Four	
2.2L eng (3.2)	4.5
2.3L eng	
4X2 (1.6)	2.2
4X4 (2.7)	3.7
V-8	
F series	3.6
4X2 (2.6)	3.6
4X4 (3.1)	4.3
Econoline (3.3)	4.7

Pressure Test Engine Bearings (Pan Off)

All models	1.0

Oil Pump, Renew

Four	
2.2L eng (3.4)	4.8
2.3L eng (1.4)	1.9
V-8	
F series	
4X2 (2.8)	3.9
4X4 (3.3)	4.6
Econoline (3.5)	5.0
Recond pump add	.5

Oil Cooler Assembly, Renew

V-8	
F-series (2.5)	3.4
Econoline (1.9)	2.5

Oil Filter Element, Renew

All models (.3)	.4

LABOR 18 CLUTCH & FLYWHEEL 18 LABOR

(Factory Time)	Chilton Time
Clutch Pedal Free Play, Adjust	
All models (.3)	.4
Clutch Master Cylinder Control Assy., Renew	
RANGER (.6)	1.0

Clutch Assembly, Renew

Includes: R&R trans and transfer case as a unit. Adjust clutch pedal free play.

(Factory Time)	Chilton Time
RANGER-BRONCO II	
4X2	
4 Speed	
Four (2.0)	2.7
V-6 (2.5)	3.4
5 Speed	
Four	
Gas (2.1)	2.8
Diesel (1.7)	2.3
V-6 (2.3)	3.1
4X4	
4 Speed	
Four (2.9)	3.9
V-6 (3.8)	5.2
5 Speed	
V-6 (3.6)	4.9
AEROSTAR	
Four-TK-5 (2.0)	2.8
V-6-TK-5 (2.3)	3.1
BRONCO	
3 Speed (3.1)	4.1
4 Speed	
Warner T-18 (4.1)	5.4
SROD (3.3)	4.3
New Process 435 (4.2)	5.5
TOD (3.9)	5.4
5 Speed	
TK-5 (3.8)	4.9
ECONOLINE	
3 Speed (1.4)	2.7
4 Speed (2.3)	3.5
4 Speed O.D. (1.6)	2.9
4 Speed	
New Process 435 (2.4)	3.6
F100-350 4X2	
3 Speed (1.5)	2.4
4 Speed	
Overdrive (1.6)	2.5
SROD (1.6)	2.5
TOD (2.6)	3.6
Warner T-18 (2.4)	3.5
Warner T-19 (3.0)	4.0
New Process 435 (2.4)	3.5
F100-350 4X4	
4 Speed	
TOD (3.9)	5.3
Warner T-18 (4.1)	5.4
New Process 435 (4.2)	5.5
SROD (3.3)	4.3
Warner T-19 (3.9)	5.1
w/Skid plate add (.2)	.3
w/Full carpet add (.7)	1.0
w/P.T.O. add (.6)	.8
w/Coupling shaft add (.2)	.3

Clutch Release Bearing, Renew

Includes: R&R trans and transfer case as a unit. Adjust clutch pedal free play.

(Factory Time)	Chilton Time
RANGER-BRONCO II	
4X2	
4 Speed	
Four (1.7)	2.3
V-6 (2.1)	3.0
5 Speed	
Four	
Gas (1.7)	2.4
Diesel (1.3)	1.9
V-6 (1.9)	2.7
4X4	
4 Speed	
Four (2.5)	3.5
V-6 (3.4)	4.8
5 Speed	
V-6 (3.6)	4.5
AEROSTAR	
Four-TK-5 (2.7)	3.7
V-6-TK-5 (2.7)	3.7
BRONCO	
3 Speed (2.4)	3.4
4 Speed	
Warner T-18 (3.4)	4.7
New Process 435 (3.5)	4.8
SROD (2.6)	3.6
TOD (2.6)	3.6
5 Speed	
TK-5 (2.6)	4.8
ECONOLINE	
3 Speed (.8)	2.0
4 Speed (1.7)	2.6
4 Speed O.D. (1.0)	2.0
4 Speed	
New Process 435 (1.7)	2.8
F100-350 4X2	
3 Speed (.8)	1.7
4 Speed	
Overdrive (1.0)	1.8
SROD (.9)	1.8
TOD (1.6)	2.2
Warner T-18 (1.7)	2.8
Warner T-19 (1.7)	2.8
New Process 435 (1.7)	2.8
F100-350 4X4	
4 Speed	
TOD (3.3)	4.5
Warner T-18 (3.4)	4.7
New Process 435 (3.5)	4.8
SROD (2.6)	3.6
Warner T-19 (3.1)	4.5
w/Skid plate add (.2)	.3
w/Full carpet add (.7)	1.0
w/P.T.O. add (.6)	.8
w/Coupling shaft add (.2)	.3

Flywheel, Renew

Includes: R&R trans and transfer case as a unit. R&R clutch and adjust free play.

(Factory Time)	Chilton Time
RANGER-BRONCO II	
4X2	
4 Speed	
Four (2.3)	3.0
V-6 (2.8)	3.7
5 Speed	
Four	
Gas (2.1)	3.1
Diesel (2.0)	2.6
V-6 (2.6)	3.4
4X4	
4 Speed	
Four (3.2)	4.2
V-6 (4.1)	5.5
5 Speed	
V-6 (3.9)	5.2
AEROSTAR	
Four-TK-5 (1.2)	3.1
V-6-TK-5 (2.8)	3.7
BRONCO	
3 Speed (3.2)	4.4
4 Speed	
Warner T-18 (4.2)	5.7
SROD (3.4)	4.6
New Process 435 (4.4)	5.8
5 Speed	
TK-5 (4.0)	5.2
ECONOLINE	
3 Speed (1.5)	3.0
4 Speed (2.4)	3.8
4 Speed O.D. (1.6)	3.2
4 Speed	
New Process 435 (2.5)	3.9
F100-350 4X2	
3 Speed	
column shift (2.3)	3.6
floor shift (1.7)	3.0
4 Speed	
Overdrive (1.8)	2.8
SROD (1.7)	2.8
TOD (2.4)	3.3
Warner T-18 (2.5)	3.8
Warner T-19 (4.0)	5.4
New Process 435 (2.5)	3.8
F100-350 4X4	
4 Speed	
TOD (4.1)	5.6
Warner T-18 (4.2)	5.7
New Process 435 (4.3)	5.8
SROD (3.4)	4.6
Warner T-19 (4.2)	5.4
w/Skid plate add (.2)	.3
w/Full carpet add (.7)	1.0
Renew ring gear add (.2)	.4
w/P.T.O. add (.6)	.8
w/Coupling shaft add (.2)	.3

LABOR 19 STANDARD TRANSMISSION 19 LABOR

Transmission Assy., Remove and Reinstall

Includes: R&R transmission and transfer case as a unit.

(Factory Time)	Chilton Time
RANGER-BRONCO II	
4X2	
4 Speed	
Four (1.7)	2.4
V-6 (2.2)	3.1
5 Speed	
Four	
Gas (1.8)	2.5
Diesel (1.4)	2.0
V-6 (2.0)	2.8
4X4	
4 Speed	
Four (2.6)	3.6
V-6 (3.5)	4.9
5 Speed	
V-6 (3.3)	4.6
AEROSTAR	
Four-TK-5 (1.7)	2.5
V-6-TK-5 (2.0)	2.8
BRONCO	
3 Speed (2.4)	3.2
4 Speed	
Warner T-18 (3.4)	4.5
SROD (2.6)	3.4
New Process 435 (3.5)	4.6
TOD (3.2)	4.4
5 Speed	
TK-5 (3.5)	4.6
ECONOLINE	
3 speed (.8)	1.8
4 speed (1.7)	2.6
4 speed O.D. (.9)	1.8
4 Speed	
New Process 435 (1.7)	2.6
F100-350 4X2	
3 Speed (.8)	1.5

LABOR 19 STANDARD TRANSMISSION 19 LABOR

(Factory Time)	Chilton Time
4 Speed	
Overdrive (.9)	1.6
SROD (.9)	1.6
TOD (1.9)	2.6
Warner T-18 (1.7)	2.6
Warner T-19 (2.2)	3.0
New Process 435 (1.7)	2.6
F100-350 4X4	
4 Speed	
TOD (3.2)	4.4
Warner T-18 (3.4)	4.5
New Process 435 (3.5)	4.6
SROD (2.6)	3.4
Warner T-19 (3.1)	4.3
w/Skid plate add (.2)	.3
w/Full carpet add (.7)	1.0
w/P.T.O. add (.6)	.8
w/Coupling shaft add (.2)	.3

Transmission Assy., R&R and Recondition

Includes: R&R trans and transfer case as a unit. Separate and overhaul transmission only.

(Factory Time)	Chilton Time
RANGER-BRONCO II	
4X2	
4 Speed	
Four (3.9)	5.4
V-6 (4.4)	6.1
5 Speed	
Four	
Gas (6.1)	8.5
Diesel (5.7)	7.9
V-6 (6.3)	8.8
4X4	
4 Speed	
Four (4.8)	6.7
V-6 (5.7)	7.9
5 Speed	
V-6 (7.6)	10.6
AEROSTAR	
Four-TK-5 (6.0)	8.4
V-6-TK-5 (6.3)	8.8
BRONCO	
3 Speed (4.5)	6.1
4 Speed	
Warner T-18 (5.3)	7.3
SROD (4.4)	6.1
New Process 435 (5.5)	7.6
TOD (5.1)	7.1
5 Speed	
TK-5 (7.8)	10.9
ECONOLINE	
3 Speed (2.9)	4.5
4 Speed O.D. (3.6)	5.0
4 Speed	
New Process 435 (3.9)	5.5
F100-350 4X2	
3 Speed (2.9)	4.0
4 Speed	
Overdrive (2.8)	3.9
SROD (2.7)	3.8
TOD (3.8)	5.3
Warner T-18 (3.6)	4.9
New Process 435 (3.7)	5.1
F100-350 4X4	
4 Speed	
TOD (5.0)	7.0
Warner T-18 (5.2)	7.2
New Process 435 (5.5)	7.6
SROD (4.4)	6.1
Warner T-19 (5.0)	7.0
w/Skid plate add (.2)	.3
w/Full carpet add (.7)	1.0
w/P.T.O. add (.6)	.8
w/Coupling shaft add (.2)	.3

Transmission, Recondition (Off Truck)

(Factory Time)	Chilton Time
3 Speed (2.1)	3.2
4 Speed	
TOD (1.8)	2.5
New Process (2.2)	3.4
Warner (1.9)	3.0
Overdrive (2.3)	3.4
SROD (1.9)	3.0
TK (2.2)	3.0
5 Speed	
TK-5 (4.3)	6.0
MMC5 (4.2)	5.9

Extension Housing, Bearing Retainer or Gasket, Renew

Includes: Renew oil seal.

(Factory Time)	Chilton Time
All models 4X2	
3 Speed (1.2)	1.7
4 Speed-O/D (1.3)	1.8
4 Speed-TOD (1.3)	1.8
4 Speed-SROD (1.4)	1.9
4 Speed-TK (1.2)	1.7
4 Speed-Warner T-19 (1.1)	1.7
4 Speed-Warner T-18 (1.3)	1.8
New Process 435 (1.2)	1.8
5 Speed-TK (1.2)	1.7
4X4	
TK (2.2)	2.8
TOD (2.2)	2.8
MMC5 (2.2)	2.8
Warner T-18 (2.3)	3.0
New Process 435 (2.3)	3.0
Warner T-19 (2.0)	2.8
w/Coupling shaft add (.2)	.3

Transmission Rear Oil Seal and/or Bushing, Renew

(Factory Time)	Chilton Time
BRONCO (.7)	1.0
All other models (.5)	.8
w/Coupling shaft add (.2)	.3

TRANSFER CASE

Transfer Case Assembly, R&R or Renew

(Factory Time)	Chilton Time
All models (1.8)	2.5
Renew assy add	.5
w/P.T.O. add (.6)	.8
w/Coupling shaft add (.2)	.3

Transfer Case, R&R and Recondition

Includes: R&R trans and/or transfer case. Separate units and overhaul transfer case only.

(Factory Time)	Chilton Time
All models	
New Process 203	
Full Time (5.0)	8.3
New Process 205	
Part Time (4.3)	6.0
New Process 208	
Part Time (4.7)	6.4
Borg Warner 1345-1356	
Part Time (3.8)	5.3
Borg Warner 1350	
Part Time (3.8)	5.3
w/P.T.O. add (.6)	.8
w/Coupling shaft add (.2)	.3

LABOR 21 SHIFT LINKAGE 21 LABOR

STANDARD

Shift Linkage, Adjust

(Factory Time)	Chilton Time
All models (.3)	.4

Gear Shift Tube Assy., Renew (3 SPEED)

(Factory Time)	Chilton Time
Bronco (.5)	1.1
ECONOLINE (.6)	1.1
F100-250 (1.1)	1.7

Gear Shift Rods, Renew

Includes: Adjust shift linkage.

(Factory Time)	Chilton Time
BRONCO (.4)	.7
ECONOLINE-3 spd (.5)	.7
F100-250-3 spd (.5)	.7

Transfer Case Control Lever, Renew

(Factory Time)	Chilton Time
All models (.5)	.7

AUTOMATIC

Manual Shift Linkage, Adjust

Includes: Adjust neutral safety switch.

(Factory Time)	Chilton Time
All models	
C-4 (.2)	.6
C-5 (.4)	.6
C-6 (.3)	.6
AOD (.3)	.6
A4LD (.3)	.6

Gear Shift Tube Assembly, Renew

(Factory Time)	Chilton Time
F100-350 (.7)	1.5

Gear Selector Lever, Renew

(Factory Time)	Chilton Time
All models (.3)	.5

LABOR 23 AUTOMATIC TRANSMISSION 23 LABOR

ON TRUCK SERVICES

Drain and Refill Unit

(Factory Time)	Chilton Time
All models (.7)	.7

Oil Pressure Check

(Factory Time)	Chilton Time
All models (.3)	.5

Check Unit for Oil Leaks

Includes: Clean and dry outside of case, run unit to determine point of leak.

(Factory Time)	Chilton Time
All models (.7)	.9

Neutral Safety Switch, Renew

(Factory Time)	Chilton Time
All models (.3)	.4

Vacuum Modulator, Renew

(Factory Time)	Chilton Time
All models (.4)	.6

Vacuum Modulator, Adjust

Includes: Pressure check.

(Factory Time)	Chilton Time
All models (.5)	.9

(Factory Time) Chilton Time

Manual and Throttle Linkage, Adjust

Includes: Adjust dashpot, idle speed and accelerate pedal height if adjustable.

All models (.4) 7

Front Servo, Recondition

Includes: Adjust band.

RANGER-AEROSTAR
C-3 (.4) 7
C-5 (.6) 1.1
A4LD (.6) 1.1
BRONCO-C-4 (.7) 1.3
BRONCO II-C-5 (.6) 1.1
ECONOLINE, F100-350
C-4 (.6) 1.1
C-5 (.6) 1.1
C-6 (1.0) 1.9
AOD (1.0) 1.5

Rear Servo, Recondition

RANGER-C-5 (.5) 1.0
BRONCO-C-4 (.7) 1.3
ECONOLINE, F100-350
C-4 (.5) 1.0
AOD (1.0) 1.5

Extension Housing and/or Gasket, Renew

C-3 (.9) 1.5
C-5
4X2 (.9) 1.5
4X4 (1.0) 1.6
C-6
4X2 (1.0) 1.6
4X4 (2.2) 3.0
AOD (1.5) 2.3
A4LD (1.5) 2.3
w/Coupling shaft add (.2) 2

Extension Housing Rear Oil Seal, Renew

All models (.5) 8
w/Coupling shaft add (.2) 2

Front Band, Adjust

Includes: R&R oil pan and renew gasket on MX-FMX.

C-3 (.3) 7
C-4 (.3) 7
C-5 (.3) 7
C-6 (.2) 6
A4LD (.3) 7

Rear Band, Adjust

A4LD (.2) 6
C-4 (.2) 6
C-5 (.2) 6

Front and Rear Bands, Adjust

Includes: R&R oil pan and renew gasket on MX-FMX.

A4LD (.3) 9
C-4 (.3) 9
C-5 (.3) 9

Oil Pan or Gasket, Renew

A4LD (.9) 1.2
C-3 (.7) 1.2
C-5 (.7) 1.2
C-4 & C-6-exc below (.6) 1.1
C-6-w/460 eng (1.2) 1.7
AOD (.7) 1.2

Valve Body Assembly, Renew

Includes: R&R oil pan.

A4LD (1.2) 1.7
C-3 (1.0) 1.5
C-5 (.9) 1.5
C-4 & C-6-exc below (1.1) 1.5
C-6-w/460 eng (1.7) 2.2
AOD (1.3) 1.9

Valve Body Assy., R&R and Recondition

Includes: R&R oil pan and replace filter. Disassemble, clean, inspect, free all valves. Replace parts as required.

A4LD (1.7) 2.5
C-3 (1.5) 2.5
C-4 (1.7) 2.5
C-5 (1.4) 2.5
C-6-exc below (1.6) 2.4
C-6-w/460 eng (2.2) 3.0
AOD (1.7) 3.0

Parking Pawl, Renew

Includes: R&R oil pan or trans assy., as required.

A4LD
4X2 (1.0) 1.6
4X4 (2.4) 3.2
C-3 (1.0) 1.6
C-5
4X2 (3.4) 4.5
4X4 (5.0) 6.7
C-6
4X2 (3.9) 5.2
4X4 (5.3) 7.1
AOD (1.5) 2.4
w/Coupling shaft add (.2) 2

Governor and Counterweight Assy., Renew

Includes: Road test.

C-3 (1.0) 1.7
C-5
4X2 (3.4) 4.7
4X4 (5.0) 7.0
C-6
4X2 (3.9) 5.3
4X4 (5.3) 7.4
AOD (1.7) 2.6
w/Coupling shaft add (.2) 2

Governor (Less Counterweight), Renew

Includes: Road test.

C-4 (1.6) 2.4
C-3 (.9) 1.6
C-5
4X2 (1.3) 1.9
4X4 (2.3) 3.2
C-6
4X2 (1.2) 1.7
4X4 (2.2) 3.1
AOD (1.6) 2.5
A4LD
4X2 (1.0) 1.6
4X4 (1.8) 2.6
w/Coupling shaft add (.2) 2

SERVICES REQUIRING R&R

Transmission Assembly, R&R

Includes: R&R transmission and converter assembly. Drain and refill unit. Adjust linkage.

RANGER-AEROSTAR
C-3 (2.3) 4.0
C-5
4X2 (2.3) 4.0
4X4 (3.9) 5.4
A4LD
4X2 (2.2) 3.1
4X4 (3.9) 5.4
BRONCO (4.9) 6.9
BRONCO II 4X4 (3.9) 5.4
ECONOLINE (2.7) 4.8
F100-350 4X2
C-4 (2.9) 5.0
C-5 (2.4) 4.2
C-6-exc below (3.4) 5.5
C-6-w/460 eng (4.1) 6.2
AOD (2.9) 4.4
F100-150 4X4 (4.9) 6.9
F250-350 4X4 (4.2) 6.2
w/Skid plate add (.2) 3
w/P.T.O. add (.6) 8
w/Coupling shaft add (.2) 3

Transmission and Converter Assy., R&R and Recondition

Includes: Drain and refill unit. Disassemble trans including valve body, clean, inspect and replace parts as required. Adjust linkage. Road test.

RANGER-AEROSTAR
C-3 (6.3) 11.5
C-5
4X2 (6.4) 11.5
4X4 (8.0) 12.4
A4LD
4X2 (9.1) 12.3
4X4 (10.8) 14.5
BRONCO (9.1) 13.9
BRONCO II 4X4 (8.0) 12.4
ECONOLINE (6.9) 12.0
F100-350 4X2
C-4 (7.1) 12.3
C-5 (6.5) 11.3
C-6-exc below (6.7) 12.0
AOD (7.8) 12.5
F100-150 4X4 (9.1) 13.9
F250-350 4X4 (8.4) 13.4
Clean and check converter add (.5) .. .5
Flush oil cooler and lines add (.2) 2
w/Skid plate add (.2) 3
w/P.T.O. add (.6) 8
w/Coupling shaft add (.2) 3

Transmission Assembly, Renew

Includes: R&R transmission, transfer all necessary parts. Drain and refill unit. Adjust linkage. Road test.

RANGER-AEROSTAR
C-3 (2.5) 4.5
C-5
4X2 (2.8) 4.5
4X4 (4.4) 6.0
A4LD
4X2 (2.7) 3.7
4X4 (4.4) 6.0
BRONCO (5.4) 7.4
BRONCO II 4X4 (4.1) 6.0
ECONOLINE (3.2) 5.3
F100-350 4X2
C-4 (3.4) 5.5
C-5 (2.9) 5.0
C-6-exc below (3.9) 6.0
C-6-w/460 eng (4.6) 6.7
AOD (3.4) 5.5
F100-150 4X4 (5.4) 7.4
F250-350 4X4 (4.7) 6.7
w/Skid plate add (.2) 3
w/P.T.O. add (.6) 8
w/Coupling shaft add (.2) 3

Transmission Assembly, Reseal

Includes: R&R transmission, drain and refill unit. Renew all seals and gaskets. Adjust linkage. Road test.

RANGER-AEROSTAR
C-3 (4.1) 6.0
C-5
4X2 (4.1) 6.0
4X4 (5.7) 7.4
A4LD
4X2 (4.0) 5.1
4X4 (5.7) 7.4
BRONCO (6.7) 8.2
BRONCO II 4X4 .... 7.4
ECONOLINE (4.5) 6.5
F100-350 4X2
C-4 (4.7) 6.8
C-5 (4.4) 6.5
C-6-exc below (5.2) 7.3
C-6-w/460 eng (5.9) 8.0
AOD 6.0

(Factory Time)	Chilton Time
F100-150 4X4 (6.7)	8.2
F250-350 4X4 (6.0)	7.7
w/Skid plate add (.2)	.3
w/P.T.O. add (.6)	.8
w/Coupling shaft add (.2)	.3

Torque Converter, Renew

Includes: R&R transmission. Drain and refill unit. Adjust linkage. Road test.

(Factory Time)	Chilton Time
RANGER-AEROSTAR	
C-3 (2.8)	3.7
C-5	
4X2 (2.8)	3.7
4X4 (4.4)	5.9
A4LD	
4X2 (2.7)	3.6
4X4 (4.4)	5.9
BRONCO (5.0)	6.7
BRONCO II 4X4 (4.4)	5.9
ECONOLINE (2.8)	3.7
F100-350 4X2	
C-4 (3.0)	4.0
C-5 (2.9)	3.9
C-6-exc below (3.5)	4.7
C-6-w/460 eng (4.2)	5.6
AOD (3.0)	4.0
F100-150 4X4 (5.0)	6.7
F250-350 4X4 (4.3)	5.8
w/Skid plate add (.2)	.3
w/P.T.O. add (.6)	.8
w/Coupliong shaft add (.2)	.3

Bands, Renew (One or Both)

Includes: R&R transmission. Drain and refill unit. Renew gaskets and seals as necessary. Adjust linkage. Road test.

(Factory Time)	Chilton Time
RANGER	
C-3 (3.8)	5.5
C-5	
4X2 (3.6)	5.3
4X4 (5.2)	8.0
BRONCO	
C-4 (6.2)	8.3
C-6 (6.6)	8.7
BRONCO II 4X4 (5.2)	8.0
ECONOLINE	
C-4 (4.0)	6.5
C-6 (4.4)	6.9
F100-350 4X2	
C-4 (4.2)	6.3
C-5 (3.7)	6.4
C-6-exc below (5.1)	7.3
C-6-w/460 eng (5.8)	8.0
F100-150 4X4 (6.6)	8.7
F250-350 4X4 (5.9)	8.2
w/Skid plate add (.2)	.3
w/P.T.O. add (.6)	.8
w/Coupling shaft add (.2)	3

Front Oil Pump Seal, Renew

Includes: R&R transmission. Drain and refill unit. Adjust linkage. Road test.

(Factory Time)	Chilton Time
RANGER-AEROSTAR	
C-3 (2.4)	4.2
C-5	
4X2 (2.4)	4.2
4X4 (4.0)	6.2
A4LD	
4X2 (2.8)	3.8
4X4 (4.5)	6.1
BRONCO (5.0)	7.1
BRONCO II 4X4 (4.0)	6.2
ECONOLINE (2.8)	4.9
F100-350 4X2	
C-4 (3.0)	5.2
C-5 (2.5)	4.3
C-6-exc below (3.5)	5.7
C-6-w/460 eng (4.2)	6.4
AOD (3.0)	4.6
F100-150 4X4 (5.0)	7.1
F250-350 4X4 (4.3)	6.6
w/Skid plate add (.2)	.3
w/P.T.O. add (.6)	.8
w/Coupling shaft add (.2)	.3

Front Oil Pump, R&R and Recondition

Includes: R&R transmission. Drain and refill unit. Renew gaskets and seals as necessary. Adjust linkage. Road test.

(Factory Time)	Chilton Time
RANGER-AEROSTAR	
C-3 (2.9)	4.0
C-5	
4X2 (2.9)	4.0
4X4 (4.6)	6.4
A4LD	
4X2 (2.8)	3.9
4X4 (4.5)	6.3
BRONCO	
C-4 (5.6)	7.8
C-6 (6.1)	8.5
BRONCO II 4X4 (4.6)	6.4
ECONOLINE	
C-4 (3.4)	4.7
C-6 (3.9)	5.4
F100-350 4X2	
C-4 (3.6)	5.0
C-5 (3.1)	4.3
C-6-exc below (4.6)	6.4
C-6-w/460 eng (5.3)	7.4
AOD (3.5)	4.9
F100-150 4X4 (6.1)	8.5
F250-350 4X4 (5.4)	7.5
w/Skid plate add (.2)	.3
w/P.T.O. add (.6)	.6
w/Coupling shaft add (.2)	.3

Flywheel and Ring Gear Assy., Renew

Includes: R&R transmission. Drain and refill unit. Adjust linkage. Road test.

(Factory Time)	Chilton Time
RANGER-AEROSTAR	
C-3 (2.6)	4.3
C-5	
4X2 (2.6)	4.3
4X4 (4.2)	6.5
A4LD	
4X2 (2.5)	3.4
4X4 (4.2)	5.7
BRONCO (5.2)	7.4
BRONCO II 4X4 (4.2)	6.5
ECONOLINE (3.0)	5.3
F100-350 4X2	
C-4 (3.2)	5.5
C-5 (2.7)	4.7
C-6-exc below (3.7)	6.0
C-6-w/460 eng (4.4)	6.7
AOD (3.2)	4.8
F100-150 4X4 (5.2)	7.4
F250-350 4X4 (4.5)	6.7
w/Skid plate add (.2)	.3
w/P.T.O. add (.6)	.8
w/Coupling shaft add (.2)	.3

Parking Pawl, Renew

Includes: R&R transmission. Drain and refill unit. Renew gaskets and seals as necessary. Adjust linkage. Road test.

(Factory Time)	Chilton Time
BRONCO	
C-4 (6.3)	8.7
C-6 (6.6)	9.0
ECONOLINE	
C-4 (4.1)	6.3
C-6 (4.4)	6.6
F100-350 4X2	
C-4 (4.3)	6.8
C-5 (3.8)	6.6
C-6-exc below (5.1)	7.3
C-6-w/460 eng (5.8)	8.0
AOD (3.3)	4.9
F100-150 4X4 (6.6)	8.7
F250-350 4X4 (5.9)	8.0
w/Skid plate add (.2)	.3
w/P.T.O. add (.6)	.8
w/Coupling shaft add (.2)	.3

LABOR 25 U-JOINTS & DRIVESHAFT 25 LABOR

Drive Shaft, Renew

(Factory Time)	Chilton Time
RANGER-BRONCO (.4)	.6
AEROSTAR (.4)	.6
F-series-ECONOLINE	
wo/Coupling shaft (.3)	.5
w/Coupling shaft (.6)	.8
Recond U-Joints add,	
4X2	
RANGER-each (.4)	.5
AEROSTAR-each (.3)	.4
F-series-ECONOLINE	
wo/Coupling shaft	
each (.4)	.5
w/Coupling shaft	
each (.4)	.5
4X4	
Single Cardan	
each (.4)	.5
Double Cardan	
each (.6)	.8
Install yoke seal kit	
add-each (.1)	.1

Drive Shaft Center Support Bearing, Renew

(Factory Time)	Chilton Time
All models (.8)	1.2

LABOR 26 REAR AXLE 26 LABOR

(Factory Time)	Chilton Time
Rear Axle, Drain and Refill	
All models (.5)	.6
Axle Housing Cover or Gasket, Renew (Integral Type)	
All models (.5)	.6
Axle Shaft, Renew	
All models	
Removable Carrier	
one (.5)	.8
both (.8)	1.3
Integral Carrier	
one (.7)	1.0
both (.9)	1.4
Rear Wheel Bearing or Oil Seal, Renew (One Wheel)	
All models	
6.75 axle (.6)	.9
7.5 axle (.6)	.9
ball bearing (.6)	.9
roller brg	
Ford-Dana (.7)	1.0
Dana 250 (.9)	1.3
tapered roller brg (.7)	1.0
full floating axle (.7)	1.0
Rear Axle Shaft Gasket or Outer Oil Seal, Renew	
All models	
Semi-Floating Axle	
one side (.5)	.7
both sides (.6)	.9
Dana Full Floating Axle	
one side (.4)	.6
both sides (.6)	.9
Ford Full Floating Axle	
one side (.3)	.5
both sides (.5)	.8
Integral Carrier	
one side (.8)	1.1
both sides (1.2)	1.6
Removable Carrier	
one side (.6)	.9
both sides (.9)	1.3
Pinion Shaft Oil Seal, Renew	
All models (1.0)	1.4

INTEGRAL CARRIER

Rear Axle Housing, Renew

Includes: Drain and refill axle. R&R wheels, hubs and axle shafts. Renew inner oil seals, remove brake backing plates without disconnecting brake lines. Transfer all parts and adjust ring gear and pinion. Does not include disassembly of differential assembly.

(Factory Time)	Chilton Time
All models	
Ford 7.5 (3.5)	5.0
Dana 60 Semi-Float (6.6)	9.5
Dana 60-61 Full Float (6.9)	10.0
Dana 70 (6.3)	9.1
w/Dual whls add (.3)	.5

Ring Gear and Pinion, Adjust

Includes: Drain and refill axle. Adjust ring and pinion backlash. Road test.

(Factory Time)	Chilton Time
All models	
std axle (1.5)	2.2
limited slip/Trac-Lok (1.8)	2.6

Ring and Pinion Gear, Renew

Includes: Drain and refill axle. Adjust backlash. Road test.

(Factory Time)	Chilton Time
All models	
Ford axle (2.4)	4.0
Dana axle (2.1)	3.5
w/Limited slip add (.1)	.2
Renew pinion brgs and cups add (.6)	.8
Recond diff assy add	
Ford 7.5 (.4)	.6
Dana-std (.5)	.7
Trac-Lok 2 pinion (.6)	.8
Trac-Lok 4 pinion (.7)	1.0

REMOVABLE CARRIER

Differential Carrier, Remove & Install

Includes: Remove or renew axle shafts. Drain and refill axle. Renew oil seal and housing gasket.

(Factory Time)	Chilton Time
All models	
one piece shaft (1.7)	2.5
two piece shaft (1.8)	2.7
Adjust ring gear add (.2)	.3
Check case run out add (.3)	.4
Renew ring gear & pinion add	
std (1.1)	1.5
limited slip/Trac-Lok (2.0)	2.9
Renew pinion brg cups add (.2)	.3
Renew case add (1.0)	1.4
Renew diff brg add (.2)	.3

LABOR 27 REAR SUSPENSION 27 LABOR

(Factory Time)	Chilton Time
Rear Spring, Renew	
4 lug wheel	
Aerostar	
one (.5)	.8
both (.8)	1.4
All other models	
one (.9)	1.3
both (1.6)	2.4
5 lug wheel	
one (1.0)	1.5
both (1.8)	2.8
8 lug wheel	
one (1.1)	1.6
both (1.9)	3.0
Renew spring bushings	
add-each (.2)	.2
Rear Spring Shackle and/or Bushing, Renew	
RANGER-one (1.0)	1.5
both (1.6)	2.6
ALL OTHER MODELS	
one (.8)	1.2
both (1.2)	2.1
Rear Shock Absorbers, Renew	
All models-one (.3)	.6
both (.4)	.8
Rear Stabilizer Bar, Renew	
All models (.5)	.9
Upper Control Arm Bushings, Renew	
Aerostar	
one side (.7)	1.0
both sides (1.1)	1.7

LABOR 28 AIR CONDITIONING 28 LABOR

Note: If more than one item requires replacement where evacuation and discharging the system is already included in the operation, deduct 1.0 hour for each additional item to the times listed.

Drain, Evacuate and Recharge System

Includes: Check for leaks.

(Factory Time)	Chilton Time
All models (.7)	1.2
Pressure Test System	
All models	.8
Compressor Belt, Renew	
Four (.5)	.7
All other engs (.3)	.6

Compressor Assembly, Renew

Includes: Evacuate and charge system.

(Factory Time)	Chilton Time
Four	
Gas	
2.0L eng (2.0)	3.0
2.3L eng	
Ranger (2.1)	3.1
Aerostar (2.6)	3.7
Diesel	
2.3L eng (1.5)	2.3
Six (1.8)	2.5
V-6	
Ranger-Bronco II (1.5)	2.3
Aerostar (1.9)	2.7
V-8	
Gas (1.6)	2.3
Diesel (1.8)	2.5
Recond comp add (1.2)	1.5

Compressor Shaft Seal Kit, Renew

Includes: Evacuate and charge system.

(Factory Time)	Chilton Time
Four	
Gas	
2.0L eng (2.5)	3.5
2.3L eng	
Ranger (2.5)	3.4
Aerostar (3.1)	4.2
Diesel (2.2)	3.0
Six (1.9)	2.6
V-6	
2.8L-2.9L eng (1.9)	2.8
3.0L eng (2.2)	3.0
V-8	
Gas (1.8)	2.5
Diesel (2.1)	2.9

LABOR 28 AIR CONDITIONING 28 LABOR

(Factory Time)	Chilton Time
Condenser Assembly, Renew	
Includes: Evacuate and charge system.	
RANGER (.9)	2.0
AEROSTAR (1.0)	2.0
BRONCO (1.1)	2.3
BRONCO II (.9)	2.0
ECONOLINE (1.3)	2.7
F100-350 (1.1)	2.4
Expansion Valve, Renew	
Includes: Evacuate and charge system.	
All models	
std (1.0)	1.7
aux	2.0
Evaporator Core, Renew	
Includes: Evacuate and charge system.	
RANGER (1.4)	2.7
AEROSTAR (1.5)	2.9
BRONCO (1.2)	2.4
BRONCO II (1.4)	2.7
ECONOLINE	
std (2.3)	3.6
aux (1.9)	3.2
F100-350	
1984 & later (1.2)	2.4
Dehydrator Receiver Tank, Renew	
Includes: Evacuate and charge system.	
ECONOLINE (1.2)	1.9
Accumulator Assembly, Renew	
Includes: Evacuate and charge system.	
RANGER-BRONCO II (.9)	1.5
AEROSTAR (1.3)	1.8
BRONCO-F100-350 (1.0)	1.6
Orifice Valve, Renew	
Includes: Evacuate and charge system.	
RANGER-BRONCO II (1.0)	1.7
AEROSTAR	
main (1.0)	1.5
auxiliary (1.2)	1.8
BRONCO-F100-350 (.9)	1.4
Blower Motor, Renew	
RANGER (.5)	.9
AEROSTAR	
main (.4)	.7
auxiliary (.4)	.7
BRONCO	
1984 & later (.3)	.6
BRONCO II (.5)	.9
ECONOLINE	
std (.5)	.9
aux (.6)	1.0
F100-350	
1984 & later (.3)	.6
Blower Motor Switch, Renew	
RANGER (.5)	.7
AEROSTAR (.6)	.9
BRONCO (.5)	.7
ECONOLINE (.3)	.6
F100-350 (.4)	.7
Evaporator Thermostatic Switch, Renew	
BRONCO (.6)	1.0
ECONOLINE (.3)	.6
F100-350 (.7)	1.2
A/C Clutch Cycling Pressure Switch Assy., Renew	
All models (.2)	.4
Compressor Service Valve or Gasket, Renew	
Includes: Evacuate and charge system.	
All models (.7)	1.2
Air Conditioning Hoses, Renew	
Includes: Evacuate and charge system.	
All models-one (.8)	1.7
each adtnl (.3)	.5

LABOR 30 HEAD AND PARKING LAMPS 30 LABOR

(Factory Time)	Chilton Time
Aim Headlamps	
two	.4
four	.6
Headlamp Sealed Beam Bulb, Renew	
All models-each (.2)	.3
Parking Lamp Assembly, Renew	
RANGER (.2)	.3
AEROSTAR (.3)	.4
BRONCO-ECONOLINE (.2)	.3
F100-350 (.3)	.5
Rear Lamp Assembly, Renew	
All models (.2)	.3
License Lamp Assembly, Renew	
All models (.3)	.4
Reflector, Renew	
All models-each	.2

LABOR 31 WINDSHIELD WIPER & SPEEDOMETER 31 LABOR

(Factory Time)	Chilton Time
Wiper Motor, Renew	
RANGER-BRONCO II (.4)	.6
AEROSTAR	
front (.9)	1.4
rear (.7)	1.1
BRONCO (.9)	1.4
ECONOLINE (.9)	*1.4
F100-350 (.9)	1.4
*w/Cruise control add (.3)	.3
Wiper Switch, Renew	
Aerostar	
front (.5)	.8
rear (.5)	.8
All other models	
front (.4)	.6
rear (.2)	.4
Wiper Pivot, Renew	
RANGER-BRONCO II-one (.4)	.7
both (.5)	.9
BRONCO-each (.8)	1.1
AERSTAR-both (.4)	.7
ECONOLINE (.6)	.9
F100-350-each (.8)	1.1
Washer Pump, Renew	
Aerostar	
front (.6)	.9
rear (.3)	.5
All other models-front (.3)	.4
rear (.8)	1.1
Windshield Wiper Governor Assy., Renew	
Aerostar (.5)	.7
All other models (.4)	.6
Electronic Instrument Cluster Assy., R&R or Renew	
AEROSTAR (.5)	.9
Renew multi-gauge display add (.6)	.7
Renew elec. speedo add (.6)	.7
Renew tripminder add (.6)	.7
Renew message center add (.6)	.7
Renew printed circuit add (.5)	.6
Speedometer Head, R&R or Renew	
All models	
Standard (.6)	1.2
Electronic (.7)	1.3
Reset odometer add	.2
Speedometer Cable and Casing, Renew	
RANGER-BRONCO II (.4)	.7
AEROSTAR (.4)	.7
BRONCO	
one piece (.5)	.9
upper (.6)	1.1
lower (.4)	.7
ECONOLINE	
wo/Sensor (.4)	.7
w/Sensor-each (.3)	.5
one piece (.7)	1.3
upper or lower (.5)	.9
w/V-8 Diesel (.8)	1.3
F100-350 (.5)	.9
Speedometer Cable (Inner), Renew or Lubricate	
RANGER-BRONCO II (.4)	.7
AEROSTAR (.4)	.7
BRONCO	
one piece (.4)	.8
upper (.6)	1.0
lower (.4)	.6
ECONOLINE	
one piece (.6)	1.1
upper (.6)	1.1
lower (.4)	.7
w/V-8 Diesel	
upper (.9)	1.4
lower (.7)	1.2
F100-350 (.5)	.8

LABOR 32 LIGHT SWITCHES & WIRING 32 LABOR

(Factory Time)	Chilton Time
Headlamp Switch, Renew	
All models (.4)	.6
Headlamp Dimmer Switch, Renew	
All models	
floor mount (.3)	.5
column mount (.5)	.9
Turn Signal Switch Assy., Renew	
RANGER (.4)	1.0
AEROSTAR (.7)	1.0
BRONCO-std whl (.6)	1.1
tilt whl (.7)	1.2
BRONCO II-std whl (.5)	1.1
tilt whl (.6)	1.2
ECONOLINE-std whl (.6)	1.2
tilt whl (.7)	1.3
F100-350-std whl (.6)	1.1
tilt whl (.7)	1.2
Turn Signal or Hazard Warning Flasher, Renew	
ECONOLINE (.4)	.6
All other models (.3)	.4
Stop Light Switch, Renew	
All models (.3)	.5
Emergency Flasher Switch Assy., Renew	
BRONCO (.3)	.6
Parking Brake Indicator Lamp Switch, Renew	
All models (.3)	.4
Back-Up Lamp Switch, Renew (w/Manual Trans)	
All models (.3)	.4
Neutral Safety Switch, Renew	
All models (.3)	.4
Horns, Renew	
All models-each (.2)	.3
Horn Relay, Renew	
All models (.3)	.4

LABOR 34 CRUISE CONTROL 34 LABOR

(Factory Time)	Chilton Time
Cruise Control System Diagnosis	
All models (.4)	.6
Cruise Control Chain/Cable, Renew	
All models (.2)	.4
Speed Control Servo Assy., Renew	
All models (.3)	.5
Road test add (.3)	.3
Speed Control Relay, Renew	
All models (.3)	.5
Speed Control Sensor Assy., Renew	
All models (.2)	*.4
Road test add (.3)	.3
*Econoline	
w/V-8 Diesel add	.3
Speed Control Amplifier Assy., Renew	
All models (.2)	.3
Road test add (.3)	.3
Speed Control Actuator Switch Assy., Renew	
All models (.3)	.6
Road test add (.3)	.3
Speed Control Metering (Dump) Valve, Renew	
All models (.1)	.3
Speed Control Clutch Switch, Renew	
All models (.3)	.4
Road test add (.3)	.3

Jeep Vehicles

GROUP INDEX

ALPHABETICAL INDEX

LABOR SERVICE BAY OPERATIONS LABOR

(Factory Time) Chilton Time

COOLING

(M) Winterize Cooling System
Includes: Run engine to check for leaks, tighten all hose connections. Test radiator and pressure cap, drain radiator and engine block. Add antifreeze and refill system.
All models 5

(M) Thermostat, Renew
All models (.5) 6

(M) Radiator Hoses, Renew
All models
upper (.4).... .5
lower (.5).... .6

FUEL

(M) Carburetor Air Cleaner, Service
All models.... .3

(M) Carburetor, Adjust (On Truck)
All models.... .4

BRAKES

(G) Brake Pedal Free Play, Adjust
All models.... .4

(G) Brakes, Adjust (Minor)
two wheels.... .4

(G) Bleed Brakes (Four Wheels)
Includes: Fill master cylinder.
All models (.4) 5

(M) Parking Brake, Adjust
All models (.3) 4

LUBRICATION SERVICE

(M) Lubricate Chassis, Change Oil & Filter
Includes: Inspect and correct all fluid levels.
All models.... .6
Install grease fittings add 1

(M) Lubricate Chassis
Includes: Inspect and correct all fluid levels.
All models.... .4
Install grease fittings add 1

(M) Engine Oil & Filter, Change
Includes: Inspect and correct all fluid levels.
All models.... .4

WHEELS

(M) Wheel, Renew
one.... .5

(G) Wheel, Balance
one.... .3
each adtnl.... .2

(G) Front Wheel Bearings, Clean and Repack (Both Wheels)
w/Disc brakes.... 1.2
w/4 whl drive.... 2.3

(M) Front Wheel Bearings, Adjust
All models.... .4

ELECTRICAL

(G) Aim Headlamps
two.... .4
four.... .6

(M) Headlamp Sealed Beam Bulb, Renew
All models-one.... .3
each adtnl.... .2

(M) Park and Turn Signal Lamp Lens or Bulb, Renew
All models-one (.3).... .4

(M) Tail Lamp Lens or Bulb, Renew
All models-one (.3).... .4

(M) License Lamp Assembly, Renew
All models-one (.3).... .4

LABOR 1 TUNE UP 1 LABOR

(Factory Time) Chilton Time

(G) Compression Test
Four (.4) 5
Six (.4) 6
V-6 (.6).... .7
V-8 (.7).... .9

(G) Engine Tune Up (Electronic Ignition)
Includes: Test battery and clean connections. Tighten manifold and carburetor mounting bolts. Check engine compression, clean and adjust or renew spark plugs. Test resistance of spark plug cables. Inspect distributor cap and rotor. Adjust air gap. Check vacuum advance operation. Reset ignition timing. Adjust idle mixture and idle speed. Service air cleaner. Inspect crankcase ventilation system. Inspect and adjust drive belts. Inspect choke operation and adjust or free up. Check operation of EGR valve.
Four–1984-88 (2.0).... 2.8
Six–1984-88 (1.4).... 2.0
V-6–1984-88 (2.1).... 3.0
V-8–1984-88 (1.9).... 2.5
w/A.C. add 6

LABOR 2 IGNITION SYSTEM 2 LABOR

(Factory Time) Chilton Time

(G) Ignition Coil, Renew
All models (.3) 5

(G) Ignition Control Unit, Renew
All models (.5) 7

(G) Spark Knock Sensor, Renew
All models (.3) 5

(G) Distributor Cap and/or Rotor, Renew
All models (.3) 5

(G) Ignition Switch, Renew
All models (.4) 7

(G) Spark Plugs, Clean & Reset or Renew
Four (.3) 4
Six (.3) 5
V-6 (.5) 6
V-8 (.6).... .8

(G) Ignition Timing, Reset
CJ/Scrambler
Four (.5).... .6
Six (.2).... .3
All other models (.3).... .4

(G) Distributor Assy., R&R or Renew
Includes: Reset ignition timing.
All models (.5) 7
Renew driven gear add (1.0).... 1.0

(G) Distributor, R&R and Recondition
Includes: Reset ignition timing.
All models (.9) 1.3

(G) Distributor Sensor, Renew
All models (.5) 7

(G) Distributor Trigger Wheel, Renew
All models (.4) 6

(G) Ignition Pick-Up Coil, Renew
CJ/Scrambler
Four (.8).... 1.1
Six (.3).... .5
Cherokee/Grand Wagoneer/Truck
Six (.3).... .5
Che/Wag/Comanche
Four (.3).... .5
V-6 (.8).... 1.1
Wrangler
Four & Six (.3) 5

(G) Vacuum Control Unit, Renew
Includes: R&R distributor and reset ignition timing.
CJ/Scrambler
Four (.9).... 1.2
Six (.4).... .6
Cherokee/Grand Wagoneer/Truck
Six (.4).... .6
Che/Wag/Comanche
Four (.4).... .6
V-6 (.9).... 1.2
Wrangler
Four & Six (.9) 1.2

(G) Ignition Cables, Renew
All models (.4) 7

LABOR 3 FUEL SYSTEM 3 LABOR

(Factory Time) — Chilton Time

(G) Fuel Pump, Test
Includes: Disconnect line at carburetor, attach pressure gauge.
All models 3

(G) Carburetor Air Cleaner, Service
All models 3

(G) Carburetor, Adjust (On Truck)
All models 4

(G) Computer Unit (MCU), R&R or Renew
Wrangler
All engs (.3) 4

(G) Carburetor Assembly, Renew
Includes: All necessary adjustments.
Four
150 eng (.5) 8
Six (.8) 1.2
V-6 (.7) 1.1
V-8 (.9) 1.3

(G) Carburetor, R&R and Clean or Recondition
Includes: All necessary adjustments.
Four
150 eng (1.7) 2.5
Six (1.6) 2.4
V-6 (1.5) 2.3
V-8 (1.6) 2.4

(G) Idle Speed Solenoid, Renew
All models (.4) 5

(G) Carburetor Float Level, Adjust
Includes: Renew needle valve and seat if required.
Four-150 eng (.6) 8

(G) Choke Vacuum Diaphragm, Renew
All models (.4) 6

(G) Vacuum Delay Valve, Renew
All models (.2) 3

(G) Electric Choke Relay, Renew
All models (.3) 4

(G) Fuel Pump, Renew
Four
CJ/Scrambler (.5) 7
Wrangler (1.2) 1.6
Six (.5) 7
V-6 (.5) 7
V-8 (.7) 9

(G) Fuel Filter, Renew
All models (.3) 4

(G) Fuel Tank, Renew
CJ/Scrambler (1.0) 1.3
Cherokee/Grand Wagoneer/
Truck (1.4) 1.7
Cke/Wag/Comanche (.8) 1.1
Wrangler (1.0) 1.3

(G) Fuel Gauge (Tank Unit), Renew
CJ/Scrambler (1.3) 1.6
Cherokee/Grand Wagoneer/
Truck (1.2) 1.5
Cke/Wag/Comanche (.7) 1.0
Wrangler (1.1) 1.4

(G) Fuel Gauge (Dash Unit), Renew
CJ/Scrambler (1.3) 1.7
Cherokee/Grand Wagoneer/
Truck (.9) 1.2
Cke/Wag/Comanche (.6) 1.0
Wrangler
hard top (1.7) 2.3
soft top (1.9) 2.6

(G) Intake Manifold and/or Gaskets, Renew
Four
150 eng (2.5) 3.6
Six (1.5) 2.0
V-6 (3.4) 4.9
V-8 (1.5) 2.2
Renew manif add 5

THROTTLE BODY INJECTION

(G) Injection System Electrical Test
All models (.3) 5

(G) Throttle Plate Assy., Renew
Includes: System test.
All models (.7) 1.1

(G) Fuel Injectors, Renew
Includes: System test.
All models-one (.7) 1.0
each adtnl 3

(G) Throttle Body Assy., R&R or Renew
All models (.4) 1.0

(G) Fuel Meter Assembly, Renew
All models (.5) 7

(G) Fuel Pressure Regulator, Renew
All models (.7) 9

(G) Fuel Pressure Regulator, Adjust
All models (.5) 6

(G) Manifold Pressure Sensor, Renew
All models (.3) 4

(G) Wide Open Throttle Switch, Renew
All models (.4) 5

(G) Idle Speed Control Motor, Renew
All models (.4) 6

(G) Manifold Air Temperature Sensor, Renew
All models (.3) 4

(G) Coolant Temperature Sensor, Renew
All models (.4) 7

(G) Throttle Position Sensor, Renew
All models (.5) 8

(G) Electronic Control Module (ECU), Renew
All models (.3) 4

(G) Oxygen Sensor, Renew
All models (.3) 5

DIESEL ENGINE

(G) Turbocharger Assy., R&R or Renew
All models (1.6) 2.5

(G) Intercooler, Renew
All models (.8) 1.2

(G) Fuel Injector, Renew
All models-one (.4) 6
all (1.1) 1.5

(G) Fuel Injection Pump, Renew
All models (3.7) 5.4

(G) Glow Plug Timer, Renew
All models (.2) 4

(G) Glow Plugs, Renew
All models-one (.4) 6
all (.7) 1.1

(G) Injection Timing, Adjust
All models (1.2) 1.5

(G) Intake Manifold and/or Gasket, Renew
All models (.6) 1.1
Renew manif add (.2) 5

LABOR 3A EMISSION CONTROLS 3A LABOR

(Factory Time) — Chilton Time

AIR INJECTION SYSTEM

(G) Air Pump, Renew
CJ/Scrambler
Four (.9) 1.2
Cke/Wag/Comanche
V-6 (.5) 8
All other models
wo/Serpentine belt (.6) 1.0
w/Serpentine belt (.7) 1.1

(G) Exhaust Check Valve, Renew
All models (.4) 5

(G) Air Injection Manifold, Renew
Four (.5) 9
Six
w/V-belt (1.0) 1.6
w/Serpentine belt (1.2) 1.8
V-6-each (.3) 6
V-8-each (.5) 9

(G) Diverter Valve, Renew
Cke/Wag/Comanche
V-6 (.5) 7
All other models (.4) 6

(G) Deceleration Valve, Renew
Cke/Wag/Comanche
Four (.4) 5
All other models (.2) 3

(G) Air Control Valve, Renew
All models (.4) 5

EXHAUST GAS RECIRCULATION

(G) E.G.R. Valve, Renew
All models (.5) 6

FUEL VAPOR RECIRCULATION

(M) P.C.V. Valve, Renew
All models (.3) 3

(M) Charcoal Canister, Renew
Cke/Wag/Comanche (.5) 6
All other models (.3) 4

ELECTRONIC EMISSION CONTROLS

(G) Microprocessor (MCU), Renew
All models (.3) 4

(G) Oxygen Sensor, Renew
All models (.3) 5

(G) Idle Cut-Off Solenoid, Renew
All models (.3) 4

(G) Electric Choke Relay, Renew
All models (.3) 4

(G) Enrichment Actuator, Renew
All models
stepper motor (.4) 6
duty cycle solenoid (.4) 6

LABOR 4 ALTERNATOR AND REGULATOR 4 LABOR

(Factory Time) — Chilton Time

(G) Alternator Circuits, Test
Includes: Test battery, regulator and alternator output.
All models 6

(G) Alternator Assy., Renew
Cke/Wag/Comanche
Four (.4) 6
V-6 (.3) 5
Diesel (1.1) 1.6
All other models (.4) 6
Add circuit test if performed.

(G) Alternator, R&R and Recondition
Cke/Wag/Comanche
Four (1.0) 1.7
V-6 (.8) 1.5
Diesel (2.0) 3.0
All other models (.9) 1.6
Add circuit test if performed.

(G) Alternator Regulator, Renew
Cke/Wag/Comanche
Four (.6) 1.0
V-6 (.7) 1.1
Diesel (1.3) 2.0
All other models (.6) 1.0
Add circuit test if performed.

(G) Voltmeter, Renew
CJ/Scrambler (.5) 9
Wrangler (.5) 9

(G) Ammeter, Renew
Cherokee/Grand Wagoneer/Truck (.8) 1.3

LABOR 5 STARTING SYSTEM 5 LABOR

(Factory Time) — Chilton Time

(G) Starter Draw Test (On Truck)
All models 3

(G) Starter Assy., Renew
All models
Gas (.4) 6
Diesel (2.0) 2.9
Add draw test if performed.

(G) Starter, R&R and Recondition
Includes: Turn down armature.
All models
Gas (1.0) 2.0
Diesel (2.6) 4.0
Renew field coils add 5
Add draw test if performed.

(G) Starter Drive, Renew
Includes: R&R starter.
All models
Gas (.6) 9
Diesel (2.2) 3.2

(G) Starter Solenoid, Renew
Includes: R&R starter.
All models
Gas (.9) 1.2
Diesel (2.5) 3.5

(G) Starter Relay, Renew
All models (.3) 4

(M) Battery Cables, Renew
All models
positive 3
negative 3

(M) Battery Terminals, Clean
All models 3

LABOR 6 BRAKE SYSTEM 6 LABOR

(Factory Time) — Chilton Time

(G) Brake Pedal Free Play, Adjust
All models 4

(G) Bleed Brakes (Four Wheels)
Includes: Fill master cylinder.
All models (.4) 5

(G) Brake Shoes and/or Pads, Renew
Includes: Install new or exchange brake shoes or pads. Adjust service and hand brake. Bleed system.
front-disc (.7) 1.1
rear
semi-float axle (.9) 1.5
full float axle (1.2) 1.9
Resurface disc rotor, add-each 9
Resurface brake drum, add-each 5

(G) Rear Brake Drum, Renew
All models-one (.3) 5
Renew hub add-each 5

(G) Pressure Limiting Valve, Renew
Includes: Bleed system.
All models (1.0) 1.4

Combinations

ADD TO BRAKES, RENEW

(Factory Time) — Chilton Time

(G) RENEW WHEEL CYLINDER
Each 2

(G) REBUILD WHEEL CYLINDER
Each 3

(G) RENEW MASTER CYLINDER
All models 1.0

(G) REBUILD MASTER CYLINDER
All models 1.5

(G) RENEW BRAKE HOSE
Each 3

(G) RENEW REAR WHEEL GREASE SEALS
Semi-floating axle 1.4
Full floating axle 6

(G) REPACK FRONT WHEEL BEARINGS (BOTH WHEELS)
Drum brake 6
Disc brake 8

(G) RENEW BRAKE DRUMS
Each 2

(G) RENEW DISC BRAKE ROTOR
Each 3

(G) CALIPER ASSEMBLY, RENEW
Each 3

(G) CALIPER ASSEMBLY, REBUILD
Each 5

BRAKE HYDRAULIC SYSTEM

(G) Wheel Cylinders, Renew
Includes: Bleed system.
All models-one (.9) 1.3
both (1.5) 2.3

(G) Wheel Cylinders, R&R and Recondition
Includes: Bleed system.
All models-one (.9) 1.6
both (1.5) 2.9

(G) Master Cylinder, Renew
Includes: Bleed system.
CJ/Scrambler (.9) 1.4
Wrangler (.9) 1.4
All other models (.7) 1.2

(G) Master Cylinder, R&R and Rebuild
Includes: Bleed system.
CJ/Scrambler (1.4) 2.0
Wrangler (1.4) 2.0
All other models (1.2) 1.8

(G) Brake Hose, Renew (Flex)
Includes: Bleed system.
All models-one (.6) 9

(G) Brake System, Flush and Refill
All models 1.2

DISC BRAKES

(G) Disc Brake Pads, Renew
Includes: Install new disc brake pads only.
All models (.7) 1.1

(G) Disc Brake Rotor, Renew
Cke/Wag/Comanche/Wrangler
one (.3) 5

LABOR 6 BRAKE SYSTEM 6 LABOR

(Factory Time) — Chilton Time

both (.6) .9
All other models
one (.6) 1.0
both (1.2) 1.8

(G) Caliper Assembly, Renew
Includes: Bleed system.
All models-one (.6) 1.0
both (1.0) 1.8

(G) Caliper Assy., R&R and Recondition
Includes: Bleed system.
All models-one (1.2) 1.5
both (2.2) 2.8

POWER BRAKES

(G) Power Brake Booster, Renew
All models (.6) 1.0

(G) Vacuum Check Valve, Renew
All models (.2) .3

PARKING BRAKE

(G) Parking Brake, Adjust
All models (.3) .4

(G) Parking Brake Lever, Renew
All models (.5) .7

(G) Parking Brake Cables, Renew
All models
primary (.7) 1.0
secondary
semi-float axle (.7) 1.0
full float axle (1.2) 1.5

LABOR 7 COOLING SYSTEM 7 LABOR

(Factory Time) — Chilton Time

(M) Winterize Cooling System
Includes: Run engine to check for leaks, tighten all hose connections. Test radiator and pressure cap, drain radiator and engine block. Add anti-freeze and refill cooling system.
All models .5

(M) Thermostat, Renew
All models (.5) .6

(M) Radiator Assy., R&R or Renew
Includes: Drain and refill cooling system.
Cke/Wag/Comanche
wo/A.C. (.8) 1.2
w/A.C. (1.5) 2.2
All other models (.5) .9

ADD THESE OPERATIONS TO RADIATOR R&R

(G) Boil & Repair 1.5
(G) Rod Clean 1.9
(G) Repair Core 1.3
(G) Renew Tank 1.6
(G) Renew Trans. Oil Cooler 1.9
(G) Recore Radiator 1.7

(M) Radiator Hoses, Renew
All models
upper (.4) .5
lower (.5) .6

(M) Viscous Fan Assembly, Renew
All models (.5) .7

(G) Water Pump, Renew
CJ/Scrambler/Wrangler
Four
150 eng (1.1) 1.7
Six (1.0) 1.5
Cherokee/Grand Wagoneer/Truck
Six (1.0) 1.5
V-8
wo/A.C. (1.3) 2.0
w/A.C. (1.9) 2.8
Cke/Wag/Comanche
Four (1.1) 1.7
V-6 (1.3) 2.0
Diesel (3.0) 4.5

(G) Temperature Gauge (Dash Unit), Renew
CJ/Scrambler (1.3) 1.6
Cke/Wag/Comanche (.6) 1.0
Wrangler
hard top (1.7) 2.3
soft top (1.9) 2.6

(G) Temperature Gauge (Engine Unit), Renew
All models (.3) .4
w/Diesel eng add .1

(G) Water Jacket Expansion Plugs, Renew
each .5
Add time to gain accessibility.

(G) Heater Hoses, Renew
Includes: Drain and refill cooling system.
All models
one or all (.5) .7

(G) Heater Core, R&R or Renew
CJ/Scrambler (1.2) 2.3
Wrangler (1.2) 2.3
Cherokee/Grand Wagoneer/Truck (.8) 1.5
Cke/Wag/Comanche
wo/A.C. (1.7) 3.3
w/A.C. (2.0) 3.9

ADD THESE OPERATIONS TO HEATER CORE R&R

(G) Boil & Repair 1.2
(G) Repair Core .9
(G) Recore 1.2

(G) Heater Water Control Valve, Renew
All models (.4) .5

(G) Temperature Control Head, Renew
Cke/Wag/Comanche (.4) .7
Cherokee/Grand Wagoneer/Truck
1984 (.7) 1.1
1985-88 (.3) .6
All other models (.7) 1.1

(G) Heater Blower Motor, Renew
CJ/Scrambler (1.0) 1.6
Wrangler (1.0) 1.6
All other models (.4) .7

(G) Blower Motor Switch, Renew
CJ/Scrambler/Wrangler
Heater (.3) .5
A.C. (.6) 1.1
Cherokee/Grand Wagoneer/Truck
Heater (.7) 1.2
A.C. (.6) 1.1
Cke/Wag/Comanche (.4) .7

LABOR 8 EXHAUST SYSTEM 8 LABOR

(Factory Time) — Chilton Time

(G) Exhaust Pipe Seal, Renew
Cke/Wag/Comanche (.7) 1.2
All other models (.4) .7

(G) Front Exhaust Pipe, Renew
Cke/Wag/Comanche (.9) 1.3
All other models (.7) 1.1

(G) Rear Exhaust Pipe, Renew
All models (.4) .5

(G) Muffler, Renew
Cke/Wag/Comanche (.9) *1.4
All other models (.6) .9
*Includes R&R tail pipe and converter.

(G) Tail Pipe, Renew
Cke/Wag/Comanche (.9) *1.4
All other models (.6) .8
*Includes R&R tail pipe and converter.

(G) Catalytic Converter, Renew
Cke/Wag/Comanche (.8) 1.2
CJ/Scrambler (.8) 1.2
All other models (.7) 1.1

(G) Manifold Heat Valve (Heat Riser), Renew
All models
V-8 (1.0) 1.5

(G) Exhaust Manifold, Renew
Four
150 eng (2.8) 3.9
Six (1.7) 2.4
V-6-each (.9) 1.4
V-8-each (.9) 1.4
Diesel (2.3) *3.5
*Includes R&R turbo.

LABOR 9 FRONT SUSPENSION 9 LABOR

(Factory Time) Chilton Time

Note: On all front suspension operations alignment charges must be added if performed. Time given does not include alignment.

(M) Wheel, Renew
one 5

(G) Wheels, Balance
one 3
each adtnl 2

(G) Check Alignment of Front End
All models 5
Note: Deduct if alignment is performed.

(G) Toe-In, Adjust
All models (.3) 4

(G) Align Front End
Includes: Adjust front wheel bearings.
All models (1.0) 1.4

(M) Front Wheel Bearings, Clean and Repack or Renew
All models
one side (1.0) 1.2
both sides (1.8) 2.3

(G) Lower Control Arm, Renew
Add alignment charges.
Cke/Wag/Comanche
one side (.4) 7

(G) Upper and Lower Ball Joints, Renew
Add alignment charges.
Cke/Wag/Comanche
one side (.8) 1.2
both sides (1.4) 2.2

(G) Upper Control Arm Bushings, Renew
Add alignment charges.
Cke/Wag/Comanche
in axle housing (.6) 1.0

(G) Front Spring, Renew
CJ/Scrambler/Wrangler
one (.7) 1.0
both (.9) 1.5

Cherokee/Grand Wagoneer/Truck
one (.9) 1.3
both (1.2) 1.9
Cke/Wag/Comanche
one or both (1.3) 2.0

(G) Front Spring Center Bolt, Renew
All models-one (.7) 1.1

(G) Front Spring Shackle Bracket, Renew
All models-one (.5) 8

(G) Front Spring Eye Bushing, Renew
Includes: Renew shackle and bolt.
All models-one (.7) 1.2

(G) Front Spring, R&R and Recondition
CJ/Scrambler/Wrangler
one side (1.8) 2.5
both sides (3.0) 4.4
All other models
one side (1.2) 1.8
both sides (1.8) 2.9

(G) Front Shock Absorbers, Renew
Cke/Wag/Comanche/Wrangler
one (.2) 4
both (.3) 5
All other models
one (.4) 5
both (.5) 7

(G) Front Stabilizer Bar, Renew
All models (.5) 7

(G) Front Stabilizer Bar Bushings, Renew
Cke/Wag/Comanche (.4) 6
All other models (.7) 1.0

4 WHEEL DRIVE FRONT AXLE

(G) Front Differential Cover, Renew or Reseal
All models 6

(G) Front Axle Shaft, R&R or Renew
Cke/Wag/Comanche (.5) 9
Wrangler (.5) 9
All other models (.7) 1.2

Renew shaft joint add-
U-Joint, each (.3) 3
C/V Joint, each (.6) 6
Renew outer oil seal add,
each (.2) 2
Renew C/V Joint boot add (.4) 4

(G) Front Axle Outer Shaft Oil Seals, Renew
All models
w/Select-Trac (1.0) 1.7
Renew outer brg add (.1) 1

(G) Front Axle Bearing and Hub Assy., Renew
Cke/Wag/Comanche
one side (.5) 8
Renew roller brg
and/or seal add (.4) 4

(G) Front Axle Shaft Inner Seals, Renew
All models
one or both (2.7) 3.7

(G) Axle Shift Vacuum Motor, Renew
Cherokee/Grand Wagoneer
Truck (.7) 1.0
All other models (.3) 5

(G) Pinion Shaft Oil Seal, Renew
All models (.9) 1.2

(G) Steering Knuckle, Renew
All models
one side (1.0) 1.7
Renew oil seal add (.2) 2

(G) Steering Spindle and/or Bearing, Renew
All models-one side (.6) 9

(G) Front Axle Assy., R&R or Renew
Cke/Wag/Comanche/Wrangler
2 WD (1.7) 2.5
4 WD (1.9) 2.7
All other models (2.5) 3.4

(G) Front Axle Assy., R&R and Recondition
All models (5.6) 7.8
Renew axle brgs and
seals add (.3) 5

LABOR 10 STEERING LINKAGE 10 LABOR

(Factory Time) Chilton Time

(G) Steering Damper, Renew
All models (.3) 5

(G) Tie Rod Assy., Renew
Does not include reset toe-in.
All models-one (.7) 9

(G) Pitman Arm, Renew
Does not include reset toe-in.
All models (.5) 7

(G) Steering Center Link, Renew
Does not include reset toe-in.
Cke/Wag/Comanche (.5) 8

LABOR 11 STEERING GEAR 11 LABOR

(Factory Time) Chilton Time

(G) Steering Wheel, Renew
All models (.4) 5

(G) Horn Contact, Renew
All models (.4) 5

(G) Pitman Shaft Seal, Renew
All models (.8) 1.2

(G) Flexible Coupling, Renew
All models (.7) 1.0

STANDARD STEERING

(G) Steering Gear, Adjust (On Truck)
All models (.4) 5

(G) Steering Gear, R&R or Renew
All models (.8) 1.2

(G) Steering Gear, R&R and Recondition
Includes: Remove, disassemble, renew necessary parts, reassemble, reinstall and adjust.
All models (1.4) 2.5

POWER STEERING

(G) Power Steering Oil Pressure Check
All models 5

(G) Power Steering Gear, Adjust (On Truck)
All models (.4) 6

(G) Power Steering Gear, R&R or Renew
All models (1.0) 1.7

LABOR 11 STEERING GEAR 11 LABOR

(Factory Time) — Chilton Time

(G) Power Steering Pump, Renew
Cke/Wag/Comanche
Four (1.1) 1.6
V-6 (.6) 1.0
Diesel (.7) 1.2
All other models (1.0) 1.5
Recond pump add (.9) 1.0

(P) Power Steering Gear, R&R and Reconditon
Includes: Remove, disassemble, renew necessary parts, reassemble, reinstall and adjust.
All models (2.2) 3.5

(G) Pump Flow Control Valve, Renew
All models (.3) 7

(G) Pump Reservoir, Renew
All models (1.2) 1.8

(M) Power Steering Hoses, Renew
All models-one (.8) 1.1

LABOR 12 CYLINDER HEAD & VALVE SYSTEM 12 LABOR

(Factory Time) — Chilton Time

GASOLINE ENGINES

(G) Compression Test
Four (.4) 5
Six (.4) 6
V-6 (.6) 7
V-8 (.7) 9

(G) Cylinder Head Gasket, Renew
Includes: Clean carbon.
Four
150 eng (3.8) 5.5
Six (4.3) 5.6
V-6-right side (4.1) 5.8
left side (3.8) 5.4
both sides (4.4) 6.3
V-8-right side (2.8) 4.0
left side (3.7) 5.3
both sides (4.4) 6.3

(G) Cylinder Head, Renew
Includes: Transfer parts as required. Clean carbon.
Four
150 eng (4.2) 6.0
Six (4.2) 6.0
V-8-one side (3.7) 5.3
both sides (5.4) 7.7

(P) Clean Carbon and Grind Valves
Includes: R&R cylinder head(s). Grind valves and seats. Minor tune up.
Four
150 eng (4.9) 6.8
Six (5.2) 7.5
V-6 (5.0) 9.0
V-8 (7.1) 10.0

(G) Rocker Arm Cover Gasket, Renew or Reseal
Four
150 eng (1.0) 1.4
Six (1.5) 1.8
V-6-right side (1.4) 1.9
left side (1.1) 1.5

Combinations

ADD TO VALVE JOB
SEE MACHINE SHOP OPERATIONS

(Factory Time) — Chilton Time

(G) DRAIN, EVACUATE & RECHARGE AIR CONDITIONING SYSTEM
All models (.9) 1.3

(G) ROCKER ARMS, PUSH RODS AND/OR PIVOTS, CLEAN OR RENEW
Six (.6) 8
V-8 (.5) 8

(G) HYDRAULIC VALVE LIFTERS DISASSEMBLE AND CLEAN
Each 2

(G) DISTRIBUTOR, RECONDITION
All models (1.0) 1.4

(G) CARBURETOR, RECONDITION
1 bbl (1.3) 1.6
2 bbl (1.5) 2.1
4 bbl (1.5) 2.1

(P) VALVE GUIDES, REAM OVERSIZE
Each (.1) 2

(Factory Time) — Chilton Time

both sides (2.3) 3.2
V-8-one side (.7) 1.0
both sides (1.0) 1.4

(G) Valve Tappets (Lifters), Renew (All)
Four
150 eng (1.2) 1.8
Six (4.4) 6.0
V-6 (4.1) 5.8
V-8 (2.6) 3.7

(Factory Time) — Chilton Time

(G) Valve Clearance, Adjust
V-6-one side (1.3) 1.8
both sides (2.6) 3.6

(G) Valve Springs and/or Valve Stem Oil Seals, Renew (Head on Truck)
Includes: Renew valve push rods, rocker arms and pivots if required.
Four
one or all cyls (1.7) 2.6
Six
one cyl (1.7) 2.2
all cyls (2.6) 3.7
V-6
all cyls (3.2) 4.6
V-8
one cyl (.7) 1.2
all cyls (2.1) 3.7

DIESEL ENGINE

(G) Compression Test
All models (1.3) 1.8

(G) Cylinder Head Gasket, Renew
Includes: Clean carbon and make all necessary adjustments.
All models (7.4) 10.5

(G) Cylinder Head, Renew
Includes: Transfer parts as required. Make all necessary adjustments.
All models (9.2) 13.0

(P) Clean Carbon and Grind Valves
Includes: R&R cylinder head, grind valves and seats. Make all necessary adjustments.
All models (8.8) 12.5

(G) Valve Cover and/or Gasket, Renew
All models (.6) 1.0

(G) Valve Clearance, Adjust
All models (.8) 1.4

LABOR 13 ENGINE ASSEMBLY & MOUNTS 13 LABOR

(Factory Time) — Chilton Time

GASOLINE ENGINES

(G) Engine Assembly, Remove and Install
Does not include transfer of any parts or equipment.
Four
CJ/Scrambler/Wrangler
150 eng (3.8) 5.4
Cke/Wag/Comanche (5.7) 8.0
Six
w/M.T. (3.5) 5.0
w/A.T. (3.9) 5.5
V-6 (5.7) 8.1
V-8
w/M.T. (3.7) 5.3
w/A.T. (3.9) 5.5
w/A.C. add (.7) 7

(G) Engine Assembly, Renew (Less Head)
Includes: R&R engine assy. Transfer all component parts not supplied with replacement engine. Minor tune up.
Four
CJ/Scrambler/Wrangler
150 eng (6.5) 9.2
Cke/Wag/Comanche (8.4) 11.9
Six
w/M.T. (7.8) 11.1
w/A.T. (8.2) 11.6
V-6 (9.3) 13.2
V-8
w/M.T. (8.9) 12.6
w/A.T. (9.1) 12.9
w/A.C. add (.7) 7

(P) Engine Assembly, R&R and Recondition (Complete)
Includes: Rebore block, remove cylinder top ridge, deglaze cylinder walls, replace pistons, rings, rod and main bearings. Clean carbon, grind valves. Tune engine.
Four
CJ/Scrambler/Wrangler
150 eng (17.5) 24.8
Cke/Wag/Comanche (19.4) 27.5
Six
w/M.T. (18.2) 25.8
w/A.T. (18.6) 26.4
V-6 (19.9) 28.3
V-8
w/M.T. (20.8) 29.5

LABOR 13 ENGINE ASSEMBLY & MOUNTS 13 LABOR

(Factory Time) Chilton Time

w/A.T. (21.0) 29.8
w/A.C. add (.7) 7

(G) Engine Mounts, Renew
Cke/Wag/Comanche
right side (.9) 1.2
left side (.5) 8
All other models
one side (.5) 8

DIESEL ENGINE

(G) Engine Assembly, Remove & Install
Does not include transfer of any parts or equipment.
All models (6.1) 8.7
w/A.C. add (.7) 7

(P) Cylinder Block, Renew
Includes: R&R engine assy. Transfer all component parts not supplied with replacement engine. Make all necessary adjustments.
All models (19.5) 27.6
Renew cyl head add (1.8) 2.4

w/A.C. add (.7) 7

(P) Engine Assy., R&R and Recondition
Includes: Renew cylinder liners, pistons and rings. Renew main and rod bearings. Clean carbon and grind valves. Make all necessary adjustments.
All models (22.6) 32.0
w/A.C. add (.7) 7

(G) Engine Mounts, Renew
All models
right side (.9) 1.2
left side (.5) 8

LABOR 14 PISTONS, RINGS & BEARINGS 14 LABOR

(Factory Time) Chilton Time

GASOLINE ENGINES

(P) Rings, Renew (See Engine Combinations)
Includes: Remove cylinder top ridge, deglaze cylinder walls, replace rod bearings, clean carbon. Minor tune up.
Four
CJ/Scrambler/Wrangler
150 eng (7.4) 10.0
Cke/Wag/Comanche (7.8) 11.0
Six (6.4) 9.9
V-6 (8.6) 12.2
V-8 (8.5) 12.0
w/A.C. add (.7) 7

(P) Piston or Connecting Rod, Renew (One)
Includes: Remove cylinder top ridge, deglaze cylinder wall, replace rod bearing, clean carbon. Minor tune up.
Four
CJ/Scrambler/Wrangler
150 eng (6.7) 9.5
Cke/Wag/Comanche (7.0) 9.9
Six (5.8) 8.2
V-6 (6.6) 9.4
V-8 (6.0) 8.5
w/A.C. add (.7) 7
each adtnl (.3) 4

(P) Connecting Rod Bearings, Renew
Four
CJ/Scrambler/Wrangler
150 eng (2.2) 3.0
Cke/Wag/Comanche (3.0) 4.3
Six (2.2) 3.6
V-6 (3.4) 4.8
V-8 (2.5) 3.6

COMBINATIONS

Add to Engine Work

See Machine Shop Operations

(G) DRAIN, EVACUATE & RECHARGE AIR CONDITIONING SYSTEM
All models (.9) 1.3

(G) ROCKER ARMS, PUSH RODS AND/OR PIVOTS, CLEAN OR RENEW
Four (.4) 7
Six (.6) 8
V-8 (.5) 8

(G) HYDRAULIC VALVE LIFTERS, DISASSEMBLE & CLEAN
Each 2

(G) DISTRIBUTOR, RECONDITION
All models (1.0) 1.4

(G) CARBURETOR, RECONDITION
1 bbl (1.3) 1.6
2 bbl (1.5) 2.1
4 bbl (1.5) 2.1

(G) DEGLAZE CYLINDER WALLS
Four (.7) 1.0
Six (.9) 1.3
V-8 (1.2) 1.5

(G) REMOVE CYLINDER TOP RIDGE
Each (.1) 1

(G) TIMING CHAIN, RENEW (COVER REMOVED)
All models (.4) 6

(G) MAIN BEARINGS, RENEW (PAN REMOVED)
Four (.7) 1.2
Six (.9) 1.5
V-8 (.7) 1.2

(G) PLASTIGAUGE BEARINGS
Each (.1) 1

(G) OIL PUMP RECONDITION
Six (.2) 4

(M) OIL FILTER ELEMENT, RENEW
All models (.3) 3

DIESEL ENGINE

(P) Pistons and Liners, Renew
Includes: R&R cylinder head and oil pan. Renew pistons, rings and cylinder liners. Make all necessary adjustments.
All models (12.5) 17.7
w/A.C. add (.3) 3

(P) Connecting Rod Bearings, Renew
All models (2.9) 4.1

LABOR 15 CRANKSHAFT & DAMPER 15 LABOR

(Factory Time) Chilton Time

GASOLINE ENGINES

(P) Crankshaft and Main Bearings, Renew
Includes: R&R engine assembly.
Four
CJ/Scrambler/Wrangler
150 eng (5.6) 8.0
Cke/Wag/Comanche (7.1) 10.0
Six
w/M.T. (6.0) 8.5
w/A.T. (6.4) 9.0
V-6 (7.2) 10.2
V-8
w/M.T. (6.6) 9.4
w/A.T. (6.8) 9.6
w/A.C. add (.7) 7

(G) Rear Main Bearing Oil Seals, Renew
Four (2.9) 4.1
Six (1.6) 2.5
V-6
split lip
May '84 & earlier (2.9) 4.3
full circle
May '84 & later (8.5) *12.0
wide 1 piece seal
1985-88 (3.0) 4.5
V-8 (1.6) 2.5
*w/A.C. add (.7) 7

DIESEL ENGINE

(P) Crankshaft and Main Bearings, Renew
Includes: R&R engine assembly.
All models (14.8) 21.0
w/A.C. add (.7) 7

(G) Rear Main Bearing Oil Seal, Renew
All models (2.9) 4.2

(G) Crankshaft Front Oil Seal, Renew
All models (2.0) 2.9

LABOR 16 CAMSHAFT & TIMING GEARS 16 LABOR

(Factory Time) Chilton Time

GASOLINE ENGINES

(G) Timing Cover Oil Seal, Renew
Four
150 eng (.9) 1.5
Six (.9) 1.5
V-6 (.8) 1.4
V-8 (.9) 1.5
w/A.C. add (.3) 3

(G) Timing Cover and/or Gasket, Renew
Four
150 eng (1.2) 1.7
Six (1.4) 2.0
V-6 (1.9) 2.7
V-8 (3.2) 4.5
w/A.C. add (.3) 3

(G) Timing Chain, Renew
Four
150 eng (1.5) 2.0
Six (1.7) 2.5
V-6 (2.2) 3.2
V-8 (3.5) 5.0
w/A.C. add (.3) 3

(G) Camshaft, Renew
Four (3.4) 4.8
Six (6.0) 8.5
V-6 (5.4) 7.7
V-8 (4.9) 7.1
w/A.C. add (.3) 3

DIESEL ENGINE

(G) Timing Belt Cover, R&R or Renew
All models (1.6) 2.3

(G) Timing Belt, Renew
All models (1.9) 2.7
Renew tensioner add (.1) 1

(G) Camshaft Front Oil Seal, Renew
All models (2.2) 3.1

(G) Camshaft, Renew
All models (2.5) 3.5

LABOR 17 ENGINE OILING SYSTEM 17 LABOR

(Factory Time) Chilton Time

(G) Oil Pan and/or Gasket, Renew
Cke/Wag/Comanche
All engs (2.3) 3.3
All other models
All engs (1.2) 1.7

(P) Pressure Test Engine Bearings (Pan Off)
All models 1.0

(G) Oil Pump, Renew
Cke/Wag/Comanche
All engs (2.4) 3.4
All other models
All engs (1.4) 1.9

(G) Oil Pump, R&R and Recondition
Cke/Wag/Comanche
All engs (2.7) 3.8
All other models
All engs (1.8) 2.6

(G) Oil Pressure Gauge (Dash), Renew
CJ/Scrambler (1.3) 1.7
Cherokee/Grand Wagoneer/
Truck (.8) 1.2
Cke/Wag/Comanche (.6) 1.0
Wrangler (.5) 9

(G) Oil Pressure Gauge (Engine), Renew
All models (.3) 4

(M) Oil Filter Element, Renew
All models (.2) 3

DIESEL ENGINE

(G) Oil Pan and/or Gasket, Renew
All models (2.5) 3.5

(P) Pressure Test Engine Bearings (Pan Off)
All models 1.0

(G) Oil Pump, Renew
All models (2.7) 3.8

(G) Oil Pump, R&R and Recondition
All models (3.2) 4.5

(M) Oil Filter Element, Renew
All models (.2) 3

LABOR 18 CLUTCH & FLYWHEEL 18 LABOR

(Factory Time) Chilton Time

(G) Clutch Pedal Free Play, Adjust
All models (.3) 4

(G) Clutch Master Cylinder, Renew
Includes: Bleed system.
All models (1.0) 1.4

(G) Clutch Slave Cylinder, Renew
Includes: Bleed system.
Wrangler (2.6) *3.3
All other models (.7) 1.1
*Includes R&R trans.

(G) Clutch Reservoir, Renew
All models (.3) 5

(G) Clutch Assembly, Renew
Includes: R&R trans. Renew T.O. brg, clutch plate and disc. Make all necessary adjustments.
CJ/Scrambler (2.7) 3.7
Wrangler (2.7) 3.6
Cherokee/Grand Wagoneer/
Truck (3.4) 4.7
Cke/Wag/Comanche
2 WD (1.9) 2.6
4 WD (2.9) 4.0
Diesel (3.0) 4.2
Renew f/wheel add (.3) 3
Renew ring gear add (.3) 3
Renew pilot bush add (.2) 2
Renew T.O. brg add (.2) 2

LABOR 19 STANDARD TRANSMISSION 19 LABOR

(Factory Time) Chilton Time

(G) Transmission and Transfer Case, Remove & Reinstall (As A Unit)
CJ/Scrambler (2.7) 3.4
Wrangler (2.0) 2.7
Cherokee/Grand Wagoneer/
Truck (3.4) 4.3
Cke/Wag/Comanche
2 WD (1.9) 2.3
4 WD (2.9) 3.7
Diesel (3.0) 3.9
Renew front seal add 2

(G) Transmission Assy., Recondition (Off Truck)
Note: Add this time to removal and installation operation to obtain R&R and Recondition.
4 Speed
T-4 (2.3) 3.2
AX-4 (1.9) 2.6
T-18A, T-176 (2.3) 3.2
5 Speed
T-5 (2.6) 3.6
AX-5 (2.1) 2.9
BA-10 (2.1) 2.9

(G) Transmission Cover Gasket, Renew
CJ/Scrambler
T-176 (.8) 1.2
Cherokee/Grand Wagoneer
T-176 (1.0) 1.5
Truck
T-176 (1.1) 1.6

(G) Transmission Rear Oil Seal, Renew
Includes: R&R transfer case if required.
CJ/Scrambler (1.6) 2.2
Wrangler (1.6) 2.2
Cherokee/Grand Wagoneer (1.9) 2.6
Truck
Six (1.9) 2.6
V-8 (1.5) 2.0
Cke/Wag/Comanche
w/Command-Trac (1.3) 1.7
w/Selec-Trac (1.6) 2.2
w/2 WD (.4) 7

(G) Speedometer Driven Gear and/or Seal, Renew
All models (.3) 5

(G) Transmission Mounts, Renew
CJ/Scrambler (.5) 7
Wrangler (.5) 7

LABOR 19 STANDARD TRANSMISSION 19 LABOR

(Factory Time) Chilton Time

Cherokee/Grand Wagoneer
Rear Support
Six (.8) 1.1
V-8 (.4) 6
Cke/Wag/Comanche (.6) 9

TRANSFER CASE

(G) Transfer Case Assy., Remove & Reinstall
CJ/Scrambler (1.1) 1.9
Cherokee/Grand Wagoneer/Truck
Six (1.4) 2.1
V-8 (1.0) 1.7
Selec-Trac 229 (1.8) 2.5
Cke/Wag/Comanche/Wrangler
Command Trac (1.1) 1.9
Selec-Trac (1.4) 2.1
Renew assy add (.3) 5

(G) Transfer Case Assy., Recondition (Off Truck)
Note: Add this time to removal and installation operation to obtain R&R and Recondition.
CJ/Scrambler (2.6) 3.5
Cherokee/Grand Wagoneer/Truck
wo/Selec-Trac 229 (3.0) 3.9
w/Selec-Trac 229 (2.8) 3.7
Cke/Wag/Comanche/Wrangler
Command Trac (1.7) 2.2
Selec-Trac 229 (2.8) 3.7

(G) Output Shaft Flange, R&R or Renew (Front or Rear)
All models (.6) 8
Renew shaft seal add (.1) 2

(G) Rear Bearing Retainer, Renew
All models (1.0) 1.4

(G) Transfer Case Bottom Cover and/or Gasket, Renew
CJ/Scrambler (.8) 1.1

(G) Front Axle Shift Switch, Renew
All models (.3) 5

(G) Transfer Case Shift Lever, Renew
CJ/Scrambler (1.0) 1.4
Cke/Wag/Comanche/Wrangler
w/M.T. (1.1) 1.5
w/A.T. (.6) 9
Recond lever add (.5) 5

(G) Vacuum Tube Assembly, Renew
All models (1.4) 2.0

LABOR 21 SHIFT LINKAGE 21 LABOR

(Factory Time) Chilton Time

(G) Gearshift Lever, Renew
Cke/Wag/Comanche
w/M.T. (.6) 8
w/A.T. (.7) 9
All other models
w/M.T. (.6) 8
w/A.T. (.4) 6

(G) Transfer Case Shifter Assy., R&R or Renew
CJ/Scrambler (1.1) 1.6
All other models
w/M.T. (1.1) 1.6
w/A.T. (.4) 8

LABOR 23 AUTOMATIC TRANSMISSION 23 LABOR

(Factory Time) Chilton Time

JEEP–MODEL 727

ON CAR SERVICES

(G) Drain & Refill Unit
All models 8

(G) Oil Pressure Check
All models 6

(G) Check Unit For Oil Leaks
Includes: Clean and dry outside of case and run unit to determine point of leak.
All models 9

(G) Neutral Safety Switch, Renew
1984-88 (.3) 5

(G) Oil Cooler Lines, Renew
1984-88-one (.4) 6
both (.5) 8

(G) Extension Housing, R&R or Renew
CJ Series
1984-88 (1.1) 1.6
WAG-CKE-TRK
1984-88-Six (1.4) 1.9
V-8 (1.0) 1.5
Renew output shaft brg add (.1) 2

(G) Oil Pan Gasket, Renew
1984-88 (.5) 8

(G) Oil Filter, Renew
1984-88 (.6) 9

(G) Valve Body Assembly, Renew
Includes: R&R oil pan.
1984-88 (.7) 1.2

(P) Valve Body, R&R and Recondition
Includes: R&R oil pan and filter. Disassemble clean, inspect, free all valves. Replace parts as required.
1984-88 (1.7) 2.8

CHILTON'S AUTOMATIC TRANSMISSION TUNE-UP

1. Check engine performance
2. Check condition of transmission oil
3. Check transmission, oil cooler and oil cooler lines for external leaks
4. Remove oil pan, clean or renew screen or filter
5. Torque valve body
6. Adjust bands
7. Clean oil pan and install pan with new gasket
8. Check modulator and hose
9. Install new transmission oil to proper level
10. Adjust manual and throttle linkage
11. Road test

All models 1.5
Charge for parts used

(Factory Time) Chilton Time

(G) Low and Reverse Band, Adjust
Includes: R&R oil pan.
1984-88 (.6) 1.0

(G) Throttle Valve Lever Shaft Seal, Renew
Includes: R&R oil pan.
1984-88 (.6) 9

(G) Kickdown Servo, Renew or Recondition
Includes: R&R oil pan.
1984-88 (.9) 1.5

(G) Accumulator Piston, Renew or Recondition
Includes: R&R oil pan.
1984-88 (.6) 1.1

(G) Low and Reverse Servo, Renew or Recondition
Includes: R&R oil pan.
1984-88 (.8) 1.4

(G) Throttle and Regulator Valves, Adjust
Includes: R&R oil pan.
1984-88 (.6) 1.0

(G) Throttle Valve Linkage, Adjust
Includes: R&R oil pan.
1984-88 (.6) 1.0

(G) Kickdown Band, Adjust
Includes: R&R oil pan.
1984-88 (.6) 1.0

SERVICES REQUIRING R&R

(G) Transmission and Transfer Case, R&R or Renew
1984-88 (3.9) 5.0
Renew assy add 5

(P) Transmission and Converter, R&R and Recondition
Includes: Disassemble trans completely, including valve body. Clean and inspect all parts. Renew parts as required. Reassemble and test.
1984-88 (8.7) 11.7
Clean and pressure test converter add 7

(G) Transmission Assembly, Reseal
Includes: R&R trans and renew all seals and gaskets.
1984-88 .... 6.5

(Factory Time) Chilton Time

(G) Torque Converter, Renew
Includes: R&R trans and transfer case.
1984-88 (3.5) 4.7

(G) Converter Drive Plate, Renew
Includes: R&R trans and transfer case.
1984-88 (4.1) 5.2

(G) Front Pump Assembly, Renew or Recondition
Includes: R&R trans and transfer case.
1984-88 (4.2) 5.5

(G) Front Pump Oil Seal, Renew
Includes: R&R trans and transfer case.
1984-88 (4.1) 5.2

JEEP–MODEL 904 & 999-AW-4

ON CAR SERVICES

(G) Drain & Refill Unit
All models 8

(G) Oil Pressure Check
All models 6

(G) Check Unit For Oil Leaks
Includes: Clean and dry outside of case and run unit to determine point of leak.
All models 9

(G) Neutral Safety Switch, Renew
1984-88
904-999 (.3) 5
AW-4 (.5) 7

(G) Oil Cooler Lines, Renew
1984-88–one (.4) 6
both (.5) 8

(G) Auxiliary Oil Cooler Assy., Renew
All models (.6) 1.0

(G) Oil Pan Gasket, Renew
1984-88 (.6) 8

(G) Oil Filter, Renew
1984-88 (.7) 9

(G) Valve Body Assembly, Renew
Includes: R&R oil pan.
1984-88 (.9) 1.2

(P) Valve Body, R&R and Recondition
Includes: R&R oil pan and filter. Disassemble, clean, inspect, free all valves. Replace parts as required.
1984-88 (1.9) 2.8

(G) Throttle Valve Linkage, Adjust
1984-88 (.2) 3

SERVICES REQUIRING R&R

(G) Transmission Assembly, Remove & Install
904-999
CJ/Scrambler (2.1) 2.8
Wrangler (2.1) 2.8
Cherokee/Grand Wagoneer/
Truck (3.9) 5.3
Cke/Wag/Comanche
2 WD (1.6) 2.2
4 WD
Four (2.2) 3.0
V-6 (2.8) 3.8
Diesel (3.2) 4.4
AW-4
2WD (1.6) 2.5
4WD (2.8) 3.9
Renew assy add (.5) 5

(P) Transmission and Converter, R&R and Recondition
Includes: Disassemble trans completely, including valve body. Clean and inspect all parts. Renew all parts as required.
CJ/Scrambler (6.9) 9.6
Wrangler (6.9) 9.6
Cherokee/Grand Wagoneer/
Truck (8.7) 12.1
Cke/Wag/Comanche
2 WD (6.4) 8.9
4 WD
Four (7.0) 9.8
V-6 (7.6) 10.6
Diesel (8.0) 11.2
Clean and test conv add 5

(G) Transmission Assembly, Reseal
Includes: R&R trans and renew all gaskets and seals.
CJ/Scrambler/Wrangler 5.8
Cherokee/Grand Wagoneer/
Truck 8.3
Cke/Wag/Comanche
2 WD 5.2
4 WD
Four 6.0
V-6 .... 6.8
Diesel 7.4

(G) Torque Converter, Renew
Includes: R&R trans.
CJ/Scrambler (2.3) 3.1
Wrangler (2.3) 3.1
Cherokee/Grand Wagoneer/
Truck (4.1) 5.6
Cke/Wag/Comanche
2 WD (1.8) 2.5
4 WD (2.4) 3.3
Diesel (3.4) 4.7
Renew drive plate add (.2) 3

(G) Front Pump Oil Seal, Renew
Includes: R&R trans.
CJ/Scrambler (2.7) 3.7
Wrangler (2.6) 3.7
Cherokee/Grand Wagoneer/
Truck (3.9) 5.4
Cke/Wag/Comanche
2 WD (2.2) 3.0
4 WD (2.8) 3.9
Diesel (3.8) 5.3

AMC–MODEL 904 & 998

ON CAR SERVICES

(G) Drain & Refill Unit
All models 8

(G) Oil Pressure Check
All models 6

(G) Check Unit For Oil Leaks
Includes: Clean and dry outside of case and run unit to determine point of leak.
All models 9

(G) Neutral Safety Switch, Renew
1984-88 (.6) 1.0

(G) Oil Cooler Lines, Renew
1984-88–one (.4) 6
both (.5) 8

(G) Transmission Auxiliary Oil Cooler, Renew
1984-88 (.6) 1.0

(G) Extension Housing, R&R or Renew
1984-88 (1.3) 2.0
Renew output shaft brg add (.1) 1
Renew oil seal add (.1) 1
Renew bushing add (.1) 1

(G) Extension Housing Oil Seal, Renew
1984-88 (1.2) 1.7

(G) Governor, R&R and Recondition
Includes: R&R extension housing.
1984-88 (1.6) 2.4

(G) Oil Pan Gasket, Renew
1984-88 (.6) 8

(G) Oil Filter, Renew
1984-88 (.7) 9

(G) Valve Body Assembly, Renew
Includes: R&R oil pan.
1984-88 (.9) 1.2

(P) Valve Body, R&R and Recondition
Includes: R&R oil pan and filter. Disassemble, clean, inspect, free all valves. Replace parts as required.
1984-88 (1.9) 2.8

(G) Low and Reverse Band, Adjust
Includes: R&R oil pan.
1984-88 (.6) 1.0

(G) Throttle Valve Lever Shaft Seal, Renew
Includes: R&R oil pan.
1984-88 (.6) 9

(G) Kickdown Servo, Renew or Recondition
Includes: R&R oil pan.
1984-88 (.9) 1.5

(G) Accumulator Piston, Renew or Recondition
Includes: R&R oil pan.
1984-88 (.6) 1.1

(G) Low and Reverse Servo, Renew or Recondition
Includes: R&R oil pan.
1984-88 (.8) 1.4

(G) Parking Brake Sprag, Renew
Includes: R&R extension housing.
1984-88 (1.3) 2.2

(G) Throttle and Regulator Valves, Adjust
Includes: R&R oil pan.
1984-88 (.6) 1.0

(G) Throttle Valve Linkage, Adjust
Includes: R&R oil pan.
1984-88 (.6) 1.0

(G) Kickdown Band, Adjust
Includes: R&R oil pan.
1984-88 (.6) 1.0

SERVICES REQUIRING R&R

(G) Transmission, R&R or Renew
Four–1984-88 (2.8) 4.0
Six–1984-88 (3.0) 4.2
Renew trans add (.2) 3

(G) Transmission Assembly, Reseal
Includes: R&R trans and renew all seals and gaskets.
Four–1984-88 .... 6.5
Six–1984-88 .... 6.7

(P) Transmission and Converter, R&R and Recondition
Four–1984-88 (7.6) 11.8
Six–1984-88 (7.8) 12.0
Clean and pressure check converter add (.5) 7

(G) Converter Drive Plate, Renew
Includes: R&R transmission.
Four–1984-88 (3.2) 4.4
Six–1984-88 (3.4) 4.6

LABOR 23 AUTOMATIC TRANSMISSION 23 LABOR

(Factory Time) Chilton Time

(G) Torque Converter, Renew
Includes: R&R transmission.
Four-1984-88 (3.0) 4.5
Six-1984-88 (3.2) 4.7

(G) Front Pump Oil Seal, Renew
Includes: R&R transmission.
Four-1984-88 (3.5) 4.7
Six-1984-88 (3.7) 4.9

(G) Front Oil Pump, Renew or Recondition
Includes: R&R transmission.
Four-1984-88 (3.1) 4.8
Six-1984-88 (3.3) 5.0

(G) Front Clutch, Recondition
Includes: R&R transmission. Disassemble, clean, inspect and reassemble.
Four-1984-88 (4.9) 7.0
Six-1984-88 (5.1) 7.2

(G) Rear Clutch, Recondition
Includes: R&R transmission. Disassemble, clean, inspect and reassemble.
Four-1984-88 (4.6) 6.4
Six-1984-88 (4.8) 6.6

(G) Overrunning Clutch, Recondition
Includes: R&R transmission. Disassemble, clean, inspect and reassemble.
Four-1984-88 (4.7) 6.5
Six-1984-88 (4.9) 6.7

(G) Planetary Gear Set, Recondition
Includes: R&R transmission. Disassemble, clean, inspect and reassemble.
Four-1984-88 (4.8) 7.0
Six-1984-88 (5.0) 7.2

(G) Front or Rear Servo, Recondition
Includes: R&R transmission. Disassemble, clean, inspect and reassemble.
Four-1984-88 (4.7) 6.5
Six-1984-88 (4.9) 6.7

LABOR 25 U-JOINTS & DRIVESHAFT 25 LABOR

(Factory Time) Chilton Time

(G) Propeller Shaft, R&R or Renew
CJ/Scrambler/Wrangler
front (.5) 7
rear (.6) 8
Cke/Wag/Comanche
front (.6) 8
rear (.4) 6
All other models
front (.7) 9
rear (.6) 8
Recond U-joint add
single carden (.4) 5
double joint (1.1) 1.5

LABOR 26 DRIVE AXLE 26 LABOR

(Factory Time) Chilton Time

(M) Differential, Drain & Refill
All models 6

(G) Inspection Cover Gasket, Renew or Reseal
All models 6

(G) Pinion Shaft Oil Seal, Renew
All models (1.0) 1.2

(G) Axle Shaft Bearings, Renew
CJ/Scrambler
right side (1.8) 2.4
left side (1.4) 1.8
both sides (2.0) 2.7
All other models
semi-float axle
one side (1.0) 1.3
both sides (1.7) 2.3
full float axle
each side (.4) 6

(G) Axle Shaft Oil Seal, Renew (Outer)
semi-float axle
one side (.7) 9
both sides (1.1) 1.5
full float axle
each side (.4) 6

(G) Axle Shaft Oil Seal, Renew (Inner & Outer)
CJ/Scrambler
right side (1.8) 2.4
left side (1.4) 1.8
both sides (2.0) 2.7

(G) Axle Shaft, Renew
CJ/Scrambler
right side (1.6) 2.2
left side (1.2) 1.6
both sides (1.7) 2.3
All other models
semi-float axle
one side (.5) 8
both sides (.8) 1.2
full float axle
one side (.3) 5
both sides (.4) 7

(G) Rear Axle Assy., R&R or Renew
Cherokee/Grand Wagoneer/Truck (2.3) 3.2
All other models (3.1) 4.3

(P) Rear Axle Assembly, R&R and Recondition (Complete)
All models (4.0) 5.5

(P) Differential Case, R&R and Recondition
Includes: Renew side bearings, gears and thrust washers.
All models (2.7) 3.9

(G) Rear Axle Housing Assy., Renew
CJ/Scrambler (6.3) 8.7
All other models (5.7) 7.9

LABOR 27 REAR SUSPENSION 27 LABOR

(Factory Time) Chilton Time

(G) Rear Spring Shackle, Renew (One)
Cke/Wag/Comanche (.7) 1.0

(G) Rear Springs, R&R and Recondition
CJ/Scrambler/Wrangler
one (1.8) 2.4
both (3.1) 4.2
All other models
one (1.3) 1.8
both (1.9) 2.6

(G) Rear Spring Center Bolt, Renew
All models-one (.7) 1.0

(G) Rear Spring Eye Bushing, Renew
Includes: Renew shackle and pivot bolt.
All models-one side (.6) 9
both sides (.7) 1.2

(G) Rear Shock Absorbers, Renew
Cke/Wag/Comanche/Wrangler
one (.2) 4
both (.3) 5
All other models
one (.4) 5
both (.5) 7

(G) Rear Stabilizer Bar, Renew
Cke/Wag/Comanche (.5) 8

LABOR 28 AIR CONDITIONING 28 LABOR

(Factory Time) Chilton Time

Note: If more than one item requires replacement where evacuation and discharging the system is already included in the operation, deduct 1.0 hour for each additional item to the time listed.

(G) Drain, Evacuate and Recharge System
All models (.8) 1.0

(G) Refrigerant, Add (Partial Charge)
All models (.5) 6

(G) Compressor Drive Belt, Renew
All models
V-Belt (.3) 4
Serpentine (.5) 6

(G) Compressor Assembly, Renew
Includes: Transfer parts as required. Evacuate and charge system.
V-8 engs (2.0) 3.0
All other engs (1.0) 2.0
Recond comp add (1.8) 2.5

(G) Compressor Clutch and/or Pulley, Renew
Does not include R&R compressor.
All models (.4) 6

(G) Condenser Assembly, Renew
Includes: Evacuate and charge system.
Cke/Wag/Comanche (1.8) 2.5
All other models (1.4) 2.0

(G) Expansion Valve, Renew
Includes: Evacuate and charge system.
All models (1.1) 1.7

(G) Evaporator Core, Renew
Includes: Evacuate and charge system.
CJ/Scrambler (1.6) 2.9
Wrangler (1.6) 2.9
Cherokee/Grand Wagoneer/
Truck (1.5) 2.7
Cke/Wag/Comanche (2.1) 3.9

(G) A.C. Control Module, Renew
Cherokee/Grand Wagoneer/
Truck (.2) 4

(G) A.C. Control Assembly, Renew
Cke/Wag/Comanche (.4) 6
Cherokee/Grand Wagoneer/
Truck
1984 (.7) 1.1
1985-88 (.3) 6
Renew potentiometer add (.1) 2

(G) Evaporator Fan Motor, Renew
Does not include evacuate and charge A.C. system.
CJ/Scrambler (.6) 1.0
Wrangler (.6) 1.0
All other models (.4) 6

(G) Receiver Drier Assembly, Renew
Includes: Evacuate and charge system.
CJ/Scrambler (1.2) 1.7
Cherokee/Grand Wagoneer/
Truck/Wrangler (1.4) 2.0
Cke/Wag/Comanche (1.8) 2.5

(G) A.C. Low Pressure Switch, Renew
All models (.3) 5

(G) Air Conditioning Hoses, Renew
Includes: Evacuate and charge system.
All models-one 1.7
each adtnl 3

LABOR 29 LOCKS, HINGES & WIND. REGULATORS 29 LABOR

(Factory Time) Chilton Time

(G) Hood Lock, Renew
All models (.2) 4

(G) Hood Release Cable, Renew
All models (.3) 6

(G) Hood Hinge, Renew
All models-one (.4) 5
both (.6) 7

(G) Door Lock Cylinder, Renew (Front or Rear)
All models (.6) 8
Recode cyl add (.3) 3

(G) Door Handle (Outside), Renew (Front or Rear)
CJ/Scrambler (.4) 7
Wrangler (.4) 7
Cherokee/Grand Wagoneer/
Truck (.6) 9
Cke/Wag/Comanche (.4) 7

(G) Front Door Window Regulator (Manual), Renew
Cke/Wag/Comanche (.9) 1.5
All other models (.6) 1.0

(G) Front Door Window Regulator (Electric), Renew
Cke/Wag/Comanche (1.1) 1.7
All other models (.7) 1.2

(G) Lock Striker Plate, Renew
All models (.2) 2

(G) Rear Door Window Regulator, Renew
Cherokee/Grand Wagoneer
manual (.7) 1.2
power (.9) 1.5
Cke/Wag/Comanche
manual (.9) 1.5
power (1.1) 1.7

(G) Rear Compartment Lid Lock Cylinder, Renew
All models (.3) 4
Recode cyl add (.3) 3

LABOR 30 HEAD AND PARKING LAMPS 30 LABOR

(Factory Time) Chilton Time

(G) Aim Headlamps
two 4
four 6

(M) Headlamp Sealed Beam Bulb, Renew
All models-one 3
each adtnl 2

(M) Park and Turn Signal Lamp Lens or Bulb, Renew
All models-one (.3) 4

(M) Park and Turn Signal Lamp Assy., Renew
All models-one (.4) 5

(M) Tail Lamp Lens or Bulb, Renew
All models-one (.3) 4

(M) Tail Lamp Assembly, Renew
Cherokee/Grand Wagoneer/
Truck-one (.5) 6
All other models-one (.4) 5

(M) License Lamp Assembly, Renew
All models-one (.3) 4

(M) Side Marker Lamp Assembly, Renew
All models-one (.3) 4

LABOR 31 WINDSHIELD WIPER & SPEEDOMETER 31 LABOR

(Factory Time) Chilton Time

(G) Windshield Wiper Motor, Renew
Cke/Wag/Comanche (.4) 6
All other models (.6) 9

(G) Wiper Timer/Governor, Renew
All models (.3) 5

(G) Rear Window Wiper Motor, Renew
Cke/Wag/Comanche (.3) 5

(G) Wiper Linkage, Renew
Cherokee/Grand Wagoneer/
Truck (1.1) 1.7
CJ/Scrambler (.6) 9
Wrangler (.6) 9
Cke/Wag/Comanche (.4) 7

(G) Windshield Washer Pump, Renew
Cke/Wag/Comanche (.2) 3
All other models (.4) 5

(G) Rear Window Washer Pump, Renew
Cke/Wag/Comanche (.2) 3

(G) Wiper Switch, Renew (Front or Rear)
Wrangler (.8) 1.1

LABOR 31 WINDSHIELD WIPER & SPEEDOMETER 31 LABOR

(Factory Time) Chilton Time

Cke/Wag/Comanche (.7) 1.1
All other models (.4) 7

(G) Speedometer Head, R&R or Renew
CJ/Scrambler (1.2) 1.8
Cherokee/Grand Wagoneer/Truck (.8) 1.2
Cke/Wag/Comanche (.6) 1.0
Wrangler
hard top (1.8) 2.4
soft top (2.0) 2.7
Reset odometer add 2

(G) Speedometer Cable, Renew
All models
one or two piece
cable and core (.4) 7
one piece cable and core (.6) 1.0

(G) Radio, R&R
All models (.7) ....

(G) Rear Window Defogger Switch, Renew
All models (.4) 6

(G) Liftgate Wiper Switch, Renew
Cke/Wag/Comanche (.4) 6

LABOR 32 LIGHT SWITCHES & WIRING 32 LABOR

(Factory Time) Chilton Time

(G) Turn Signal Switch, Renew
Cke/Wag/Comanche (.6) 1.0
All other models (.8) 1.1

(M) Turn Signal or Hazard Warning Flasher, Renew
All models (.2) 3

(G) Hazard Warning Switch, Renew
All models (.8) 1.1

(G) Headlamp Dimmer Switch, Renew
All models (.3) 4

(G) Headlamp Switch, Renew
All models (.4) 6

(G) Stoplight Switch, Renew
All models (.3) 4

(G) Back-Up Lamp or Neutral Switch, Renew
All models
w/M.T. (.5) 6
w/A.T. (.4) 5

(G) Parking Brake Switch, Renew
All models (.3) 4

(G) Horn, Renew
All models-one (.3) 4
each adtnl 2

(G) Horn Relay, Renew
All models (.3) 4

LABOR 34 CRUISE CONTROL 34 LABOR

(Factory Time) Chilton Time

(G) Cruise Control Switch, Renew
Cke/Wag/Comanche (.7) 1.1
Wrangler (.7) 1.1
All other models (.5) 9

(G) Cruise Control Speed Sensor, Renew
All models (.4) 6

(G) Cruise Control Regulator, Renew
Wrangler (.4) 6
Cke/Wag/Comanche (.3) 4
All other models (.5) 7

(G) Cruise Control Chain/Cable, Renew
All models (.4) 5

(G) Cruise Control Vacuum Bleed Switch, Renew
All models (.3) 5

(G) Cruise Control Servo, Renew
All models (.5) 7

(G) Cruise Control Brake Release Switch, Renew (Vacuum Dump)
All models (.4) 6

(G) Cruise Control Wiring Harness, Renew
All models (.5) 9

Courier Pick-Ups

GROUP INDEX

ALPHABETICAL INDEX

LABOR 1 TUNE UP 1 LABOR

(Factory Time) Chilton Time

Compression Test
All models .9

Engine Tune Up, (Minor)
Includes: Clean or renew spark plugs. Renew ignition points and condenser. Set ignition timing. Set carburetor idle mixture and idle speed. Service carburetor air cleaner.
All models 1.5

Engine Tune Up, (Electronic Ignition)
Includes: Test battery and clean connections. Tighten manifold and carburetor mounting bolts. Check engine compression, clean and adjust or renew spark plugs. Test resistance of spark plug cables. Inspect distributor cap and rotor. Adjust air gap. Check vacuum advance operation. Reset ignition timing. Adjust idle mixture and idle speed. Service air cleaner. Inspect and adjust drive belts. Inspect choke operation and adjust or free up. Check operation of EGR valve.
All models 2.0

LABOR 2 IGNITION SYSTEM 2 LABOR

(Factory Time) Chilton Time

Spark Plugs, Clean and Reset or Renew
All models .7

Ignition Timing, Reset
All models .3

Distributor Points and Condenser, Renew
All models .8

Distributor, Renew
Includes: Reset ignition timing.
All models .8

Distributor Cap, Renew
All models .7

Ignition Coil, Renew
All models .8

Ignition Cables, Renew
All models .8

Ignition Switch, Renew
All models .6

Ignition Modulator Assembly, Renew
All models .4

Distributor Armature, Renew
All models .6

Distributor Stator, Renew
Includes: R&R armature.
All models .8

LABOR 3 FUEL SYSTEM 3 LABOR

(Factory Time) Chilton Time

Fuel Pump, Test
Includes: Disconnect line at carburetor, attach pressure gauge.
All models .3

Carburetor, Adjust (On Truck)
All models .3

Carburetor Air Cleaner, Service
All models .2

Carburetor, Renew
Includes: All necessary adjustments.
All models .8

Carburetor, R&R and Clean or Recondition
Includes: All necessary adjustments.
All models 2.7

Fuel Pump, Renew
All models .9
Add pump test if performed.

Fuel Tank, Renew
Includes: Transfer tank gauge unit.
All models 1.4

Fuel Gauge (Tank), Renew
Includes: Drain and refill tank.
All models .1.3

Fuel Gauge (Dash), Renew
All models .9

Intake Manifold or Gaskets, Renew
1800cc-2000cc engs 2.0
2300cc eng 1.5
Renew manif add .5

LABOR 3A EMISSION CONTROLS 3A LABOR

(Factory Time) Chilton Time

Thermactor Air Pump, Renew
All models .7

Charcoal Canister, Renew
All models .5

Deacceleration Valve, Renew
All models .3

E.G.R. Valve, Renew
All models .5

Crankcase Ventilation Valve, Renew
All models .4

LABOR 4 ALTERNATOR AND REGULATOR 4 LABOR

(Factory Time) Chilton Time

Alternator Circuits, Test
Includes: Test battery, regulator and alternator output.
All models .6

Alternator, Renew
All models .9

Alternator Ring Bearing, Renew
All models 1.1

Alternator, R&R and Recondition
Includes: Complete disassembly, replacement of parts as required. Test validity of rotor fields, stator and diodes.
All models 2.3
Circuit test add .6

Alternator Front Bearing or End Plate, Renew
All models 1.2

Alternator Regulator, Renew
All models .6
Circuit test add .6

Ammeter, Renew
All models .9

Instrument Cluster Printed Circuit, Renew
All models 1.3

LABOR 5 STARTING SYSTEM 5 LABOR

(Factory Time) Chilton Time

Starter Draw Test (On Truck)
All models 3

Starter, Renew
1800cc-2000cc engs 1.3
2300cc eng 8
Add draw test if performed.

Starter, R&R and Recondition
Includes: Turn down armature.
1800cc-2000cc engs 2.5
2300cc eng 1.8

Starter Drive, Renew
Includes: R&R starter.
1800cc-2000cc engs 1.6
2300cc eng 1.1

Neutral Safety Switch, Renew
All models 5

Battery Cables, Renew
All models
positive 5
negative 4

LABOR 6 BRAKE SYSTEM 6 LABOR

(Factory Time) Chilton Time

Brake Pedal Free Play, Adjust
All models 4

Brakes, Adjust (Minor)
Includes: Adjust brakes, fill master cylinder.
two wheels 4
four wheels 7

Bleed Brakes (Four Wheels)
Includes: Fill master cylinder.
All models 6

Brake Shoes, Renew
Includes: Install new or exchange brake shoes. Adjust service and hand brake. Bleed system.
All models-front 1.5
rear 1.5
all four wheels 2.9
Resurface brake drum, add-each 5

Brake Shoes and/or Pads, Renew
Includes: Install new or exchange brake shoes or pads. Adjust service and hand brake. Bleed system.
All models
front-disc 9
rear-drum 1.5
all four wheels 2.3
Resurface disc brake rotor, add-each 9
Resurface brake drum, add-each 5

Brake Drum, Renew
All models-front-one 6
rear-one 6

Brake Differential Valve, Renew
Includes: Transfer switch and bleed sysytem.
All models 1.2

Brake Pressure Warning Lamp Switch, Renew
All models 6

BRAKE HYDRAULIC SYSTEM

Wheel Cylinder, Renew
Includes: Bleed complete system.
All models
Front
one 1.4
both-one side 1.6
all-both sides 3.0
Rear
one 1.6
both-one side 1.8
all-both sides 3.2

COMBINATIONS

Add to Brakes, Renew

(Chilton Time)

RENEW WHEEL CYLINDER
Each 2

REBUILD WHEEL CYLINDER
Each 3

RENEW BRAKE HOSE
Each 3

RENEW MASTER CYLINDER
All models 1.0

REBUILD MASTER CYLINDER
All models 1.5

REBUILD CALIPER ASSEMBLY
Each 3

REPACK FRONT WHEEL BEARINGS (BOTH WHEELS)
Drum brakes 4
Disc brakes 6

RENEW REAR WHEEL GREASE SEALS
Each 2

RENEW BRAKE DRUM
Each 1

RENEW DISC BRAKE ROTOR
Each 3

(Factory Time) Chilton Time

Wheel Cylinder, R&R and Rebuild
Includes: Hone cylinder and bleed complete system.
All models
Front
one 1.7
both-one side 2.1
all-both sides 3.8
Rear
one 1.9
both-one side 2.3
all-both sides 4.0

Master Cylinder, Renew
Includes: Bleed complete system.
All models 1.3

Master Cylinder, R&R and Rebuild
Includes: Hone cylinder and bleed complete system.
All models 1.9

Brake Hose, Renew
Includes: Bleed system.
All models
front-one 7
both 1.0
rear-one 1.0

DISC BRAKES

Disc Brake Pads, Renew
Includes: Install new disc brake pads only.
All models 9

Caliper Assembly, Renew
Includes: Bleed system.
All models-one 9
both 1.5

Caliper Assembly, R&R and Rebuild
Includes: Bleed system.
All models-one 1.2
both 2.0

Disc Brake Rotor, Renew
Includes: Renew wheel bearings and seals.
All models-one 8
both 1.3

POWER BRAKES

Brake Booster Assembly, Renew
All models 1.0

PARKING BRAKE

Parking Brake, Adjust
All models 3

Parking Brake Control Assy., Renew
Includes: Adjust.
All models 8

Parking Brake Cables, Renew
All models
rear-one 1.1
both 1.7

LABOR 7 COOLING SYSTEM 7 LABOR

(Factory Time) Chilton Time

Winterize Cooling System
Includes: Run engine to check for leaks, tighten all hose connections. Test radiator and pressure cap, drain radiator and engine block. Add anti-freeze and refill system.
All models 5

Thermostat, Renew
All models 8

Radiator Assembly, R&R or Renew
Includes: Drain and refill cooling system.
All models 1.0

Radiator Hoses, Renew
All models-upper 6
lower 9
both 1.2

ADD THESE OPERATIONS TO RADIATOR R&R
Boil & Repair 1.5
Rod Clean 1.9
Repair Core 1.3
Renew Tank 1.6
Renew Trans. Oil Cooler 1.9
Recore Radiator 1.7

Drive Belt, Renew
All models-one 3
each adtnl 1

Water Pump, Renew
Includes: Drain and refill cooling system.
All models
wo/Therm or A.C. 2.2
w/Therm and A.C. 2.5

Fan Blade, Renew
All models 5

Heater Core, R&R or Renew
All models 2.0

ADD THESE OPERATIONS TO HEATER CORE R&R
Boil & Repair 1.2
Repair Core 9
Recore 1.2

Heater Hoses, Renew
All models-each 4

Heater Water Control Valve, Renew
All models 9

Heater Blower Motor, Renew
All models 2.0

Heater Temperature Control Assy., Renew
All models 1.4

Heater Blower Motor Switch, Renew
All models 1.0

LABOR 8 EXHAUST SYSTEM 8 LABOR

(Factory Time) Chilton Time

Muffler, Renew
All models 9

Catalytic Converter, Renew
All models 1.0

Exhaust Manifold, Renew
1800cc-2000cc engs 1.5
2300cc engs 1.7

Exhaust Pipe, Renew
All models 1.0

Muffler and Exhaust Pipe, Renew
All models 1.2

LABOR 9 FRONT SUSPENSION 9 LABOR

(Factory Time) Chilton Time

Note: On all front suspension operatons alignment charges must be added if performed. Time given does not include alignment.

Wheel, Renew
one 5

Wheels, Rotate (All)
All models 5

Wheel, Balance (On Truck)
one 4
each adtnl 2

Check Alignment of Front End
All models 5
Note: Deduct if alignment is performed.

Toe-In, Adjust
All models 6

Caster, Camber and Toe-In, Adjust
Includes: Adjust front wheel bearings.
All models 1.8

Front Wheel Grease Seals, Renew
Conventional Brakes
one wheel 6
both wheels 9
Disc Brakes
one wheel 7
both wheels 9

Front Wheel Bearings and Cups, Renew
Includes: Repack bearings.
Conventional Brakes
one wheel 8
both wheels 1.4
Disc Brakes
one wheel 9
both wheels 1.5

Front Shock Absorber, Renew
All models-one 5
both 8

Front Spindle Assembly, Renew
Add alignment charges.
All models-one 1.9
both 3.2

Upper Control Arm Assy., Renew
Add alignment charges.
All models-one 1.9
both 2.9

Upper Control Arm Shaft or Bushings, Renew
Add alignment charges.
All models-one side 2.3
both sides 3.3

Lower Control Arm Assy., Renew
Add alignment charges.
All models-one side 2.2
both sides 3.5

Front Spring, Renew
All models-one 1.4
both 2.5

Front Stabilizer Bar or Bushings, Renew
All models 9

LABOR 10 STEERING LINKAGE 10 LABOR

(Factory Time) Chilton Time

Tie Rods or Tie Rod Ends, Renew
Includes: Reset toe-in.
All models-one 1.0
two 1.2
all 1.6

Drag Link, Renew
All models 9

Sector Rod, Renew
Includes: Check toe-in.
All models 1.4

Idler Arm Assembly, Renew
All models 1.3

LABOR 11 STEERING GEAR 11 LABOR

(Factory Time) Chilton Time

Steering Wheel, Renew
All models 4

Upper Mast Jacket Bearing, Renew
All models 7

Steering Gear Sector Arm, Renew
All models 8

Steering Gear, Adjust (Off Truck)
Includes: Adjust bearing preload and mesh.
All models
wo/A.C. ... 3.5
w/A.C. ... 5.2

Steering Gear, R&R and Renew
All models
wo/A.C. ... 3.1
w/A.C. ... 4.8

Steering Gear, R&R and Recondition
Includes: Disassemble, renew necessary parts, reassemble and adjust.
All models
wo/A.C. ... 4.5
w/A.C. ... 6.2

LABOR 12 CYLINDER HEAD & VALVE SYSTEM 12 LABOR

(Factory Time) Chilton Time

Compression Test
All models 9

Cylinder Head Gasket, Renew
Includes: Check cylinder head and block flatness. Clean carbon and make all necessary adjustments.
1800cc-2000cc engs ... 6.0
2300cc eng ... 4.5
w/A.C. add 7

Cylinder Head, Renew
Includes: Transfer all components, clean carbon. Reface valves, check valve spring tension, assembled height and valve head runout.
1800cc-2000cc engs ... 9.0
2300cc eng ... 7.0
w/A.C. add 7

Clean Carbon and Grind Valves
Includes: R&R cylinder head, check valve spring tension, valve seat and head runout. Check stem to guide clearance and spring assembled height. Minor tune up.
1800cc-2000cc engs ... 10.0
2300cc eng ... 8.0
w/A.C. add 7

Valve Spring or Valve Stem Oil Seals, Renew
1800cc-2000cc engs
one ... 6.3
each adtnl 2
2300cc eng
one ... 1.2
all ... 2.3

Rocker Arm Cover Gasket, Renew
1800cc-2000cc engs 7
2300cc eng ... 1.0

Valve Tappets, Adjust
1800cc-2000cc engs ... 1.2

Rocker Arm, Renew
1800cc-2000cc engs
one 9
all ... 1.2
2300cc eng
one ... 1.2
all ... 1.5

LABOR 13 ENGINE ASSEMBLY & MOUNTS 13 LABOR

(Factory Time) Chilton Time

Note: All engine operations listed in this group are for assemblies as supplied by the original equipment manufacturer. Time to replace assemblies from independent rebuilders may vary.

Engine Assembly, Remove & Install
Does not include transfer of any parts or equipment.
1800cc-2000cc engs ... 5.5
2300cc eng
w/M.T. ... 4.6
w/A.T. ... 4.9

Cylinder Block, Renew
Includes: R&R engine assy. Transfer all component parts, renew rings and bearings. Clean carbon, grind valves. Tune engine.
1800cc-2000cc engs ... 19.8
2300cc eng
w/M.T. ... 18.8
w/A.T. ... 19.1

Engine Assembly, R&R and Recondition
Includes: Rebore block, install new pistons, rings, rod and main bearings. Clean carbon, grind valves. Tune engine.
1800cc-2000cc engs ... 26.6
2300cc eng
w/M.T. ... 25.6
w/A.T. ... 25.9

Cylinder Assembly (w/All Internal Parts Less Head and Oil Pan), Renew
Includes: R&R engine assy. Transfer all component parts not supplied with replacement engine. Clean carbon, grind valves. Tune engine.
1800cc-2000cc engs ... 15.3
2300cc eng
w/M.T. ... 14.3
w/A.T. ... 14.6

Engine Mounts, Renew
Front
1800cc-2000cc engs
right side ... 1.6
left side ... 1.7
both sides ... 2.0
2300cc eng
one 9
both ... 1.2
w/A.C. add 4

Rear
All models 8

LABOR 14 PISTONS, RINGS & BEARINGS 14 LABOR

(Factory Time) Chilton Time

Pistons or Connecting Rods, Renew
Includes: R&R oil pan and cylinder head. Remove cylinder top ridge and deglaze cylinder walls. Clean carbon from head and engine block. Minor tune up.
1800cc-2000cc engs
one ... 10.5
all ... 12.0
2300cc eng
one ... 8.7
all ... 10.2
w/A.C. add 7

Connecting Rod Bearings, Renew
1800cc-2000cc engs ... 3.7
2300cc eng
w/M.T. ... 3.9
w/A.T. ... 6.3

Piston Rings, Renew
Includes: R&R oil pan and cylinder head. Remove cylinder top ridge and deglaze cylinder walls. Clean carbon from head and engine block. Minor tune up.
1800cc-2000cc engs
one ... 11.0
all ... 13.5
2300cc eng
one ... 9.2
all ... 11.7
w/A.C. add 7

LABOR 14 PISTONS, RINGS & BEARINGS 14 LABOR

COMBINATIONS

Add to Engine Work

	Chilton Time
DRAIN, EVACUATE & RECHARGE AIR CONDITIONING SYSTEM	
All models	1.5
HYDRAULIC VALVE LIFTERS, DISASSEMBLE AND CLEAN	
Each	.2
DISTRIBUTOR, RECONDITION	
All models	1.0
CARBURETOR, RECONDITION	
All models	1.4
DEGLAZE CYLINDER WALLS	
Each	.1
REMOVE CYLINDER TOP RIDGE	
Each	.1
PLASTIGAUGE BEARINGS	
Each	.1
MAIN BEARINGS, RENEW	
All models	2.5
OIL PUMP, RECONDITION	
All models	.5
OIL FILTER ELEMENT, RENEW	
All models	.3

LABOR 15 CRANKSHAFT & DAMPER 15 LABOR

(Factory Time)	Chilton Time
Crankshaft and Main Bearings, Renew	
Includes: R&R engine, check all bearing clearances.	
1800cc-2000cc engs	10.2
2300cc eng	
w/M.T.	9.4
w/A.T.	9.7
Main Bearings, Renew	
Includes: Check all bearing clearances.	
1800cc-2000cc engs	5.2
2300cc eng	
w/M.T.	5.4
w/A.T.	7.8
Main and Rod Bearings, Renew	
Includes: Check all bearing clearances.	
1800cc-2000cc engs	6.4
2300cc eng	
w/M.T.	5.6
w/A.T.	9.0
Rear Main Bearing Oil Seals, Renew (Upper & Lower)	
1800cc-2000cc engs	3.0
2300 cc eng	
w/M.T.	3.9
w/A.T.	6.3
Vibration Damper, Renew	
1800cc-2000cc engs	1.6
2300cc eng	1.5
Crankshaft Front Oil Seal, Renew	
Note: R&R of front cover not required.	
1800cc-2000cc engs	1.9
2300cc eng	
camshaft seal	1.7
auxiliary shaft seal	2.2
crankshaft seal	2.3
w/A.C. add	.4

LABOR 16 CAMSHAFT & TIMING GEARS 16 LABOR

(Factory Time)	Chilton Time
Timing Case Seal and Gaskets, Renew	
1800cc-2000cc engs	5.0
2300cc eng	3.8
w/A.C. add	.4
Timing Chain or Sprockets, Renew	
Includes: Reset timing.	
1800cc-2000cc engs	8.0
w/A.C. add	.4
Timing Belt, Renew	
2300cc eng	2.0
Camshaft, Renew	
1800cc-2000cc engs	5.4
2300cc eng	4.2
w/A.C. add	.4
Camshaft Bearings, Renew	
1800cc-2000cc engs	6.4
2300cc eng	5.2
w/A.C. add	.4

LABOR 17 ENGINE OILING SYSTEM 17 LABOR

(Factory Time)	Chilton Time
Oil Pan or Gasket, Renew	
1800cc-2000cc engs	2.5
2300cc eng	
w/M.T.	2.7
w/A.T.	5.1
Pressure Test Engine Bearings (Pan Off)	
All models	1.0
Oil Pump, Renew	
1800cc-2000cc engs	2.7
2300cc eng	
w/M.T.	2.9
w/A.T.	5.3
Oil Pump, R&R and Recondition	
1800cc-2000cc engs	3.3
2300cc eng	
w/M.T.	3.5
w/A.T.	5.9
Oil Pressure Gauge (Engine), Renew	
All models	.6
Oil Pressure Gauge (Dash), Renew	
All models	1.0
Oil Filter Element, Renew	
All models	.3

LABOR 18 CLUTCH & FLYWHEEL 18 LABOR

(Factory Time) Chilton Time

Clutch Pedal Free Play, Adjust
All models 4

Bleed Clutch Hydraulic System
All models 5

Clutch Slave Cylinder, Renew
Includes: Bleed system.
4 speed 1.1
5 speed 1.0

Clutch Slave Cylinder, R&R and Recondition
Includes: Bleed system.
4 speed 1.3
5 speed 1.2

Clutch Master Cylinder, Renew
Includes: Bleed system.
4 speed 1.2
5 speed 1.1

Clutch Master Cylinder, R&R and Recondition
Includes: Bleed system.
4 speed 1.5
5 speed 1.4

Clutch Release Bearing, Renew
Includes: R&R trans and adjust free play.
4 speed 2.5
5 speed 2.6

Clutch Assembly, Renew
Includes: R&R trans and adjust free play.
4 speed 2.7
5 speed 2.8

Flywheel, Renew
Includes: R&R trans and adjust free play.
4 speed 2.9
5 speed 3.0
Renew ring gear add 4

LABOR 19 STANDARD TRANSMISSION 19 LABOR

(Factory Time) Chilton Time

Transmission Assy., R&R or Renew
4 speed 2.4
5 speed 2.5

Transmission Assy., R&R and Recondition
Includes: Complete disassembly, clean and inspect or renew all parts. Install new gaskets and seals.
4 speed 5.5
5 speed 6.8

Transmission Input Shaft Gasket, Renew
Includes: R&R transmission.
4 speed 2.9
5 speed 3.0

Speedometer Driven Gear, Renew
All models 6

Extension Housing Seal or Bushing, Renew
Includes: R&R driveshaft.
4 speed 1.2
5 speed 1.5
w/Coupling shaft add 2

LABOR 21 SHIFT LINKAGE 21 LABOR

(Factory Time) Chilton Time

Gear Selector Lever, Renew
4 speed 6
5 speed 7
automatic 9

Manual Linkage, Adjust (Auto Trans)
All models 4

Throttle Linkage, Adjust (Auto Trans)
Includes: Adjust dashpot and idle speed.
All models 5

LABOR 23 AUTOMATIC TRANSMISSION 23 LABOR

(Factory Time) Chilton Time

ON CAR SERVICES

Drain & Refill Unit
All models 8

Oil Pressure Check
All models 5

Check Unit For Oil Leaks
Includes: Clean and dry outside of case and run unit to determine point of leak.
All models 9

Neutral Safety Switch, Renew
All models 5

Linkage, Adjust
manual 4
throttle 5

Front Band, Adjust
All models 1.0

Extension Housing Bushing or Seal, Renew
Includes: R&R driveshaft.
wo/Coupling shaft 1.1
w/Coupling shaft 1.2

Oil Pan Gasket, Renew
All models 9

Valve Body Assembly, Renew
Includes: R&R oil pan.
All models 1.8

Valve Body Assy., R&R and Recondition
Includes: R&R oil pan and replace filter. Disassemble, clean, inspect, free all valves. Replace parts as required.
All models 2.9

Front Servo, R&R and Recondition
Includes: R&R oil pan.
All models 1.4

SERVICES REQUIRING R&R

Transmission Assembly, R&R or Renew
Includes: R&R trans and converter assy. Drain and refill unit. Adjust linkage.
1800cc-2000cc engs 3.8
2300cc eng 4.0

Front Pump Oil Seal, Renew
Includes: R&R trans.
1800cc-2000cc engs 4.0
2300cc eng 4.2

Transmission and Converter, R&R and Recondition
Includes: Disassemble trans including valve body, clean, inspect and replace parts as required.
1800cc-2000cc engs 10.2
2300cc eng 10.4
Clean and check converter add 5
Flush oil cooler and lines add 2

Front Pump Assy., R&R and Recondition
Includes: R&R trans.
1800cc-2000cc engs 4.9
2300cc eng 5.1

Flywheel and Ring Gear Assy., Renew
Includes: R&R trans.
1800cc-2000cc engs 4.1
2300cc eng 4.3

Front and Rear Bands, Renew
Includes: R&R trans.
1800cc-2000cc engs 4.8
2300cc engs 5.0

LABOR 25 U-JOINTS & DRIVESHAFT 25 LABOR

	(Factory Time)	Chilton Time
Drive Shaft, R&R or Renew		
wo/Coupling shaft		.6
w/Coupling shaft		.7
Universal Joints, Renew or Recondition		
Includes: R&R driveshaft.		
All models		
one		1.0
two		1.4
all		1.7
Center Bearing, Renew		
All models		1.1
Coupling Shaft, Renew		
All models		1.5

LABOR 26 REAR AXLE 26 LABOR

	(Factory Time)	Chilton Time
Real Axle Shaft and/or Bearing, Renew		
Includes: Renew oil seal.		
All models-one		1.9
both		2.8
Real Wheel Inner Oil Seal, Renew		
All models-one		1.3
both		1.8
Pinion Shaft Oil Seal, Renew		
All models		.9
Differential Carrier Assy., Remove & Install		
Includes: R&R axle shafts, drain and refill axle, renew housing gasket.		
All models		3.8
w/Coupling shaft add		.2
Differential Carrier Assy., R&R and Recondition		
Includes: Disassemble, clean and renew all parts. Drain and refill axle, replace axle seals and housing gasket.		
All models		7.0
w/Coupling shaft add		.2
Ring and Pinion Set, Renew		
Includes: R&R carrier, drain and refill axle. Renew inner oil seals and housing gasket.		
All models		6.0
w/Coupling shaft add		.2

LABOR 27 REAR SUSPENSION 27 LABOR

	(Factory Time)	Chilton Time
Rear Spring, Renew		
All models-one		1.3
both		2.1
Rear Spring Shackle and/or Bushings, Renew		
All models-one side		.8
both sides		1.2
Rear Spring Front Eye Bushings, Renew		
All models-one side		1.0
both sides		1.5
Rear Shock Absorbers, Renew		
All models-one		.5
both		.7

LABOR 28 AIR CONDITIONING 28 LABOR

Note: If more than one item requires replacement where evacuation and discharging the system is already included in the operation, deduct 1.0 hour for each additional item to the times listed.

	(Factory Time)	Chilton Time
Drain, Evacuate and Recharge System		
Includes: Check for leaks.		
All models		1.5
Flush Refrigerant System, Complete		
To be used in conjunction with component replacement which could contaminate system.		
All models		1.3
Pressure Test System		
All models		.6
Compressor Belt, Renew		
All models		.5
Compressor Assembly, Renew		
Includes: Evacuate and charge system.		
All models		2.4
Compressor Pulley, Renew		
All models		.6
Compressor Shaft Seal Kit, Renew		
Includes: Evacuate and charge system.		
All models		2.0
Compressor Valve Plate, Renew		
Includes: Evacuate and charge system.		
All models		2.2
Compressor Clutch Pulley Bearing, Renew		
All models		1.0
Evaporator Thermostatic Switch, Renew		
All models		1.1
Condenser Assembly, Renew		
Includes: Evacuate and charge system.		
All models		2.0
Expansion Valve, Renew		
Includes: Evacuate and charge system.		
All models		2.8
Evaporator Core, Renew		
Includes: Renew or transfer valve. Evacuate and charge system.		
All models		3.2
Dehydrator Receiver Tank, Renew		
Includes: Evacuate and charge system.		
All models		1.4
Blower Motor, Renew		
All models		1.2
Blower Motor Switch, Renew		
All models		1.2
Air Conditioning Hoses, Renew		
Includes: Evacuate and charge system.		
All models		
Dehydrator to Evap		2.1
Evaporator to Comp		2.2
Compressor to Cond		1.5

LABOR 29 LOCKS, HINGES & WIND. REGULATORS 29 LABOR

	(Factory Time)	Chilton Time
Hood Latch Assembly, Renew		
All models		.7
Hood Hinge, Renew		
All models-one		.4
Front Door Latch Assy., Renew		
All models-one		.6
Lock Striker Plate, Renew		
All models		.4
Door and Ignition Lock Set, Renew		
All models		1.2

LABOR 29 LOCKS, HINGES & WIND. REGULATORS 29 LABOR

	(Factory Time)	Chilton Time
Front Door Handle (Outside), Renew		
All models		.6
Front Door Window Regulator, Renew		
All models		1.0
Tail Gate Hinge, Renew		
All models-one		.6

LABOR 30 HEAD AND PARKING LAMPS 30 LABOR

	(Factory Time)	Chilton Time
Aim Headlamps		
All models		.4
Headlamp Sealed Beam Bulb, Renew		
All models-one		.3
Parking Lamp Lens or Bulb, Renew		
All models		.2
Side Marker Lamp Lens or Bulb, Renew		
All models		.2
Tail Lamp Lens or Bulb, Renew		
All models		.4
License Lamp Lens or Bulb, Renew		
All models		.3

LABOR 31 WINDSHIELD WIPER & SPEEDOMETER 31 LABOR

	(Factory Time)	Chilton Time
Windshield Wiper Motor, Renew		
All models		.8
Windshield Wiper Switch, Renew		
All models		.9
Windshield Washer Pump, Renew		
All models		.5
Speedometer Head, R&R or Renew		
All models		1.0
Speedometer Cable and Casing, Renew		
All models		.8
Radio, R&R		
All models		1.0

LABOR 32 LIGHT SWITCHES & WIRING 32 LABOR

	(Factory Time)	Chilton Time
Stop Light Switch, Renew		
All models		.4
Turn Signal Switch, Renew		
All models		.9
Back-Up Lamp Switch, Renew		
All models		.5
Headlamp Switch, Renew		
All models		.9
Headlamp Dimmer Switch, Renew		
All models		.9
Emergency Flasher Switch, Renew		
All models		.9
Turn Signal or Hazard Warning Flasher, Renew		
All models		.4
Horn, Renew		
All models		.4
Horn Relay, Renew		
All models		.4

GROUP INDEX

ALPHABETICAL INDEX

LABOR 1 TUNE UP 1 LABOR

(Factory Time) Chilton Time

Compression Test
All models .6

Engine Tune Up, (Electronic Ignition)
Includes: Test battery and clean connections. Check engine compression, clean and adjust or renew spark plugs. Test resistance of spark plug cables. Inspect distributor cap and rotor. Set ignition timing. Check vacuum advance operation. Inspect and adjust all drive belts. Set carburetor idle mixture and idle speed. Check operation of EGR valve.
Truck-Montero 1.5
Van-Wagon 1.7

LABOR 2 IGNITION SYSTEM 2 LABOR

(Factory Time) Chilton Time

GASOLINE ENGINES

Spark Plugs, Clean and Reset or Renew
All models .5

Ignition Timing, Reset
All models .4

Distributor Assy., Renew
Includes: Reset ignition timing.
Truck-Montero .9
Van-Wagon 1.0

Distributor, R&R and Recondition
Includes: Reset ignition timing.
Truck-Montero 1.5
Van-Wagon 1.6

Distributor Reluctor, Renew
Includes: R&R distributor and reset ignition timing.
Truck-Montero 1.2
Van-Wagon 1.3

Vacuum Control Unit, Renew
Includes: R&R distributor and reset ignition timing.
Truck-Montero 1.1
Van-Wagon 1.2

Distributor Cap and/or Rotor, Renew
All models .4

Electronic Ignition Control Unit, Renew
All models .7

Ignition Coil, Renew
Truck .6
Montero .5
Van-Wagon .6

Ballast Resistor, Renew
All models .4

Ignition Cables, Renew
All models .4

Ignition Switch, Renew
All models .7

DIESEL ENGINE

Glow Plugs, Renew
All models
one or all .5

Glow Plug Relay, Renew
All models .4

Glow Plug Control Unit, Renew
All models .4

LABOR 3 FUEL SYSTEM 3 LABOR

(Factory Time) Chilton Time

GASOLINE ENGINES

Fuel Pump, Test
Includes: Disconnect line at carburetor, attach pressure gauge.
All models .3

Carburetor, Adjust (On Truck)
All models .6

Carburetor Air Cleaner, Service
All models .2

Carburetor Assy., Renew
Includes: All necessary adjustments.
All models 1.5

Carburetor, R&R and Clean or Recondition
Includes: All necessary adjustments.
All models 2.9

Accelerator Pump, Renew
All models .6

Coasting Air Valve, Renew
All models .4

Air Switching Valve, Renew
All models .4

Jet Air Control Valve, Renew
All models .6

Enrichment Body Assembly, Renew
All models .4

Vacuum Throttle Opener, Renew
All models .8

Fuel Cut-Off Solenoid, Renew
All models .4

Carburetor Sub-EGR Valve, Renew
1983-86 .7

Dash Pot, Renew
All models .4

Throttle Position Sensor, Renew
All models .3

Fuel Filter, Renew
All models .4

Mechanical Fuel Pump, Renew
All models .8

Fuel Tank, Renew
Montero 1.6
Truck
1983-86 1.6
1987 .8
Van-Wagon 1.4

Fuel Gauge (Tank Unit), Renew
Montero .8
Truck
1983-86 1.5
1987 .7
Van-Wagon .6

Fuel Gauge (Dash Unit), Renew
Montero 1.2
Truck
1983-86 1.2
1987 .6
Van-Wagon .9

Intake Manifold and/or Gasket, Renew
Truck-Montero 4.1
Van-Wagon *2.1
*Renew manif add .6

DIESEL ENGINE

Injection Pump Timing, Adjust
All models .6

Fuel Injection Pump Assy., Renew
All models 2.0

Injection Nozzles, R&R or Renew
All models-one .6
each adtnl .4
Clean or recond add-each .3

High Pressure Fuel Lines, Renew
All models-one .6
each adtnl .3

Fuel Pump, Renew
All models .8

Turbocharger Assy., R&R or Renew
Includes: Renew gasket.
All models 1.5
Recond add 1.0

FUEL INJECTION

Idle Speed Control Servo, Renew
Van-Wagon .6

Throttle Body, Renew
Van-Wagon .8

Fuel Injectors, Renew
Van-Wagon
one or all .9

Surge Tank, Renew
Van-Wagon .6

Throttle Position Sensor, Renew
Van-Wagon .6

Fuel Pressure Regulator, Renew
Van-Wagon .4

Electric Fuel Pump, Renew (In Tank)
Van-Wagon 1.5

LABOR 3A EMISSION CONTROLS 3A LABOR

(Factory Time)	Chilton Time
PCV Valve, Renew	
All models	.2
Fuel Vapor Canister, Renew	
All models	.3
Fuel Vapor Separator, Renew (One)	
All models	1.4
Purge Control Valve, Renew	
All models	.3
E.G.R. Valve, Renew	
All models	
Gas or Diesel	.5
E.G.R. Coolant Valve, Renew	
All models	.5
Vacuum Time Delay Solenoid, Renew	
All models	.4
High Altitude Compensator, Renew	
All models	.6
E.G.R. Vacuum Reducer Valve, Renew	
All models	
Diesel	.4
E.G.R. Control Valve, Renew	
All models	
Diesel	.4
Vacuum Regulator Valve, Renew	
All models	
Diesel	.4
Oxygen Sensor, Renew	
Truck	.4
Montero-Van-Wagon	.5

LABOR 4 ALTERNATOR AND REGULATOR 4 LABOR

(Factory Time)	Chilton Time
Alternator Circuits, Test	
Includes: Test battery, regulator and alternator output.	
All models	.6
Alternator Assy., Renew	
Includes: Circuit test. Transfer pulley if required.	
Truck	1.4
Montero-Van-Wagon	1.2
Alternator, R&R and Recondition	
Includes: Complete disassembly, inspect, test, replace parts as required, reassemble.	
Truck	2.4
Montero-Van-Wagon	2.2
Alternator Gauge, Renew	
All models	.7
Alternator Front Bearing, Renew	
Includes: R&R alternator, separate end frames.	
All models	1.1
Renew rear brg add	.2
Voltage Regulator, Test and Renew	
All models	
internal type	1.6

LABOR 5 STARTING SYSTEM 5 LABOR

(Factory Time)	Chilton Time
Starter Draw Test (On Truck)	
All models	.3
Starter Assy., Renew	
Includes: Test relay, starter solenoid and amperage draw.	
All models	1.1
Starter, R&R and Recondition	
Includes: Test relay, starter solenoid and amperage draw. Turn down armature.	
All models	2.3
Renew field coils add	.5
Starter Drive, Renew	
Includes: R&R starter.	
All models	1.2
Starter Solenoid, Renew	
Includes: R&R starter.	
All models	1.2
Neutral Safety and/or Back-Up Lamp Switch, Renew	
All models	.4
Battery Cables, Renew	
All models	
positive	.4
negative	.4

LABOR 6 BRAKE SYSTEM 6 LABOR

(Factory Time)	Chilton Time
Brake Pedal Free Play, Adjust	
All models	.3
Brakes, Adjust (Minor)	
Includes: Adjust brake shoes, fill master cylinder.	
two wheels	.4
Bleed Brakes (Four Wheels)	
Includes: Fill master cylinder.	
All models	.5
Brake Shoes and/or Pads, Renew	
Includes: Install new or exchange brake shoes or pads. Adjust service and hand brake. Bleed system.	
All models	
front-disc	.9
rear-drum	1.5
all four wheels	2.3
Resurface disc rotor add-each	.9
Resurface brake drum add-each	.5
Rear Brake Drum, Renew (One)	
All models	.4
BRAKE HYDRAULIC SYSTEM	
Wheel Cylinder, Renew	
Includes: Bleed brake system.	
Van-Wagon-one	1.0
both	1.9
All other models-one	.9
both	1.7
Wheel Cylinder, R&R and Rebuild	
Includes: Bleed brake system.	
Van-Wagon-one	1.3
both	2.5
All other models-one	1.2
both	2.3
Master Cylinder, Renew	
Includes: Bleed brake system.	
Truck-Montero	.9
Van-Wagon	1.4
Master Cylinder, R&R and Rebuild	
Includes: Bleed brake system.	
Truck-Montero	1.6
Van-Wagon	2.1
Master Cylinder Reservoir, Renew	
Includes: Bleed brake system.	
All models	1.0
Brake Hose (Flexible), Renew	
Includes: Bleed system.	
All models-one	.6
each adtnl	.3
Brake System, Flush and Refill	
All models	1.2
DISC BRAKES	
Disc Brake Pads, Renew	
Includes: Install new disc brake pads only.	
All models	.9
Resurface disc rotor add-each	.9
Caliper Assembly, Renew	
Includes: Bleed brake system.	
Van-Wagon-one	1.0
both	1.9
All other models-one	.8
both	1.5

LABOR 6 BRAKE SYSTEM 6 LABOR

	(Factory Time)	Chilton Time
Caliper Assy., R&R and Recondition		
Includes: Bleed brake system.		
Van-Wagon-one		1.5
both		2.9
All other models-one		1.3
both		2.5
Disc Brake Rotor, Renew		
2 WD models		.6
4 WD models		1.2
Front Disc Brake Hub, Renew		
2 WD models		.8
4 WD models		1.2
Brake System Combination Valve, Renew		
Includes: Bleed brake system.		
All models		1.0
Load Sensing Proportioning Valve, Renew		
Includes: Adjust valve and bleed brake system.		
4 WD models		1.0

COMBINATIONS

Add to Brakes, Renew

RENEW WHEEL CYLINDER	
Each	.2
REBUILD WHEEL CYLINDER	
Each	.3
RENEW BRAKE HOSE	
Each	.3
RENEW MASTER CYLINDER	
All models	.7
REBUILD MASTER CYLINDER	
All models	1.4
REBUILD CALIPER ASSEMBLY	
Each	.5
RENEW DISC BRAKE ROTOR	
Each	.3
CLEAN AND REPACK FRONT WHEEL BEARINGS (BOTH WHEELS)	
All models	.6
RENEW BRAKE DRUM	
Each	.1
RENEW DISC BRAKE ROTOR STUDS	
Each	.1

POWER BRAKES

	(Factory Time)	Chilton Time
Power Brake Unit, Renew		
Truck-Montero		1.1
Van-Wagon		2.5
Power Brake Check Valve, Renew		
All models		.3

PARKING BRAKE

	(Factory Time)	Chilton Time
Parking Brake, Adjust		
All models		.3
Parking Brake Cable, Renew		
Front		
All models		.8
Rear		
Truck-Montero-each		1.0
Van-Wagon-each		1.8
Parking Brake Control, Renew		
All models		.7
Parking Brake Warning Lamp Switch, Renew		
All models		.6

LABOR 7 COOLING SYSTEM 7 LABOR

	(Factory Time)	Chilton Time
Winterize Cooling System		
Includes: Run engine to check for leaks, tighten all hose connections. Test radiator and pressure cap, drain radiator and engine block. Add anti-freeze and refill system.		
All models		.5
Thermostat, Renew		
Includes: Drain and refill cooling system.		
All models		.5
Radiator Assy., R&R or Renew		
Includes: Drain and refill cooling system.		
Truck-Montero		.7
Van-Wagon		1.2
w/A.T. add		.2
ADD THESE OPERATIONS TO RADIATOR R&R		
Boil & Repair		1.5
Rod Clean		1.9
Repair Core		1.3
Renew Tank		1.6
Renew Trans. Oil Cooler		1.9
Recore Radiator		1.7
Drive Belt, Adjust		
All models-one		.2
each adtnl		.1
Drive Belt, Renew		
All models-one		.3
each adtnl		.1
Fluid Fan Drive Unit, Renew		
All models		.5
w/A.C. add		.1
Radiator Hoses, Renew		
Upper		.3
Lower		
Truck-Montero		.4
Van-Wagon		.8

	(Factory Time)	Chilton Time
Water Pump and/or Gasket, Renew		
Includes: Drain and refill cooling system.		
Truck-Montero		
Gas		1.4
Diesel		1.7
Van-Wagon		2.0
w/A.C. add		.3
w/P.S. add		.2
Engine Oil Cooler, Renew		
All models		.7
Temperature Gauge (Dash Unit), Renew		
Truck-Montero		
1983-86		1.2
1987		.5
Van-Wagon		.9
Temperature Gauge Sending Unit, Renew		
All models		.4
Water Jacket Expansion Plugs, Renew (Cylinder Block)		
Right side		
front		1.2
center or rear		1.2
Left side		
upper front		1.3
lower front		1.4
rear		3.0
Rear of Engine		3.5
Heater Hose, Renew		
1983-86		1.0
1987		.8
Front Heater Water Valve, Renew		
Truck		.6
Montero		3.5
Front Heater Blower Motor Switch, Renew		
Truck-Montero		1.2
Van-Wagon		.8

	(Factory Time)	Chilton Time
Front Heater Blower Motor, Renew		
Truck		1.0
Montero-Van-Wagon		.6
Front Heater Blower Motor Resistor, Renew		
Truck		.6
Montero-Van-Wagon		.5
Front Heater Core, R&R or Renew		
Truck		
1983-86		1.7
1987		2.3
Montero-Van-Wagon		3.5
ADD THESE OPERATIONS TO HEATER CORE R&R		
Boil & Repair		1.2
Repair Core		.9
Recore		1.2
Rear Heater Core, R&R or Renew		
Montero		1.5
Van-Wagon		1.1
Rear Heater Water Valve, Renew		
Montero		1.5
Rear Heater Blower Motor, Renew		
Montero		1.5
Van-Wagon		.5
Rear Heater Blower Motor Resistor, Renew		
Van-Wagon		.5
Rear Heater Switch, Renew		
Van-Wagon		.4

LABOR 8 EXHAUST SYSTEM 8 LABOR

(Factory Time) Chilton Time

Front Exhaust Pipe, Renew
All models 7

Center Exhaust Pipe, Renew
All models 7

Tail Pipe, Renew
All models 6

Muffler, Renew
All models 6

Catalytic Converter, Renew
Manif Mount
2 WD 1.0
4 WD 1.2
Ex Mount
All models 8

Exhaust Manifold and/or Gasket, Renew
All models
Gas 1.2
Diesel 2.0

LABOR 9 FRONT SUSPENSION 9 LABOR

(Factory Time) Chilton Time

Note: On all front suspension operations alignment charges must be added if performed. Time given does not include alignment.

Wheel, Renew
one 5

Wheels, Rotate (All)
All models 5

Wheel, Balance
one 3
each adtnl 2

Toe-In, Adjust
All models 6

Align Front End
Includes: Adjust caster, camber and toe. Adjust front wheel bearings.
All models 1.5

Front Wheel Bearings and Cups, Renew
Includes: Renew dust seal.
All models
one side 8
both sides 1.5

Front Wheel Grease Seal, Renew
All models-one side 8

Steering Knuckle, Renew (One)
2 WD models 1.6
4 WD models 1.8
Renew tie rod, add
each 3
Renew whl brgs, add
each side 5

Lower Control Arm, Renew (One)
Includes: Reset toe-in.
2 WD models 2.1
4 WD models 1.6

Lower Control Arm Bushings, Renew (One Side)
Add alignment charges.
2 WD models 2.0
4 WD models 1.7

Lower Ball Joint or Ball Socket, Renew (One Side)
Add alignment charges.
2 WD models 1.8
4 WD models 1.3

Lower Control Arm Strut, Renew (One Side)
Add alignment charges.
2 WD models 1.0

Upper Control Arm, Renew (One)
Includes: Alignment charges.
Truck-Montero 2.5
Van-Wagon 2.0

Upper Ball Joint or Ball Socket, Renew (One Side)
Add alignment charges.
2 WD models 1.5
4 WD models 1.6

Front Shock Absorbers, Renew
All models-one 7
both 1.1

Front Sway Bar, Renew
Truck-Montero 1.5
Van-Wagon 1.2

Front Sway Bar Link and/or Bushings, Renew
All models-one side 5

Front Torsion Bars, Renew
2 WD models
one side 1.0
both sides 1.8
4 WD models
one side 5
both sides 8

Torsion Bar Anchor or Adjusting Bolt, Renew
4 WD models
each 6

Front Coil Springs, Renew
2 WD models-one 1.9
both 3.5

4 WHEEL DRIVE FRONT AXLE

Front Differential, Drain & Refill
All models 6

Front Axle Housing Cover or Gasket, Renew
All models 6

Drive Pinion Oil Seal, Renew
All models 8

Front Axle Propeller Shaft Flange, Renew
All models 6

Front Axle Shaft, Renew (One)
Includes: Renew outer wheel bearings if required.
All models
outer-w/Joint 2.0
inner 1.6

Drive Shaft Boot, Renew (One)
Includes: Clean and lubricate C/V joint.
All models 1.9

Front Wheel Drive Shaft, Renew (w/M.T. or A.T.)
All models-one 1.6
both 3.0

Inner C.V. Joint, Renew
All models-one 1.8

Locking Hub Assy., Renew or Recondition
All models-one 9
both 1.7

Front Propeller Shaft, Renew
All models
transfer case to ft axle 6

Differential Side Bearings, Renew
Includes: R&R ring gear and pinion, renew axle housing oil seals and adjust bearing preload and backlash.
All models 4.9

Differential Side Gears, Renew
Includes: Renew axle housing oil seals if required.
All models 4.7

Differential Case, Renew
Includes: R&R ring gear and pinion, renew bearings and gears, renew pinion and axle housing seals. Adjust backlash.
All models 5.1

Ring Gear and Pinion Set, Renew
Includes: Renew pinion bearing, side bearings and all seals. Adjust bearing preload and backlash.
All models 5.6
Renew diff case add 2

Front Axle Housing, Renew
Includes: Renew oil seals. Transfer axle shafts, differential and brake assemblies.
All models 5.7

LABOR 10 STEERING LINKAGE 10 LABOR

(Factory Time) Chilton Time

Tie Rod End, Renew
Includes: Reset toe-in.
Truck-Montero 1.0
Van-Wagon 1.3

Steering Wheel, Renew
All models 4

Steering Center Link, Renew
Add alignment charges.
All models 6

LABOR 10 STEERING LINKAGE 10 LABOR

(Factory Time) Chilton Time

Idler Arm, Renew
All models 6

Pitman Arm, Renew
Truck-Montero 6

Steering Column Flex Coupling, Renew
Truck 1.3

LABOR 11 STEERING GEAR 11 LABOR

(Factory Time) Chilton Time

STANDARD STEERING

Steering Gear, Adjust (On Truck)
All models 5

Sector Shaft Oil Seal, Renew
Truck 8

Steering Gear Assy., R&R or Renew
Truck 1.0
Van-Wagon 1.4

Steering Gear Assy., R&R and Recondition
Includes: Disassemble, renew necessary parts, reassemble and adjust.
Truck 1.9
Van-Wagon 2.9

POWER STEERING

Power Steering Drive Belt, Renew
All models 3

Power Steering Gear, R&R or Renew
All models 2.0

Power Steering Gear, R&R and Recondition
Includes: Disassemble, renew necessary parts, reassemble and adjust.
All models 2.7

Steering Gear Sector Shaft, Adjust
All models 6

Sector Shaft Oil Seals, Renew (Inner and Outer)
All models 2.1

Gear Control Valve Assy., Renew
All models 3.1

Power Steering Pump, Renew
All models 1.0

Power Steering Pump, R&R and Recondition
All models 1.9

Pump Flow Control Valve, Clean and Test or Renew
All models 9

Pump Reservoir, Renew
Includes: Renew seals.
All models 6

Pump Drive Shaft Oil Seal, Renew
All models 1.6

Power Steering Hoses, Renew
All models
pressure 9
return 9
supply 4

LABOR 12 CYLINDER HEAD & VALVE SYSTEM 12 LABOR

(Factory Time) Chilton Time

GASOLINE ENGINE

Compression Test
All models 6

Cylinder Head Gasket, Renew
Includes: Clean carbon, minor tune up.
All models 3.6

Cylinder Head, Renew
Includes: Reface and adjust valves, clean carbon. Minor tune up.
All models 8.9

Clean Carbon and Grind Valves
Includes: R&R cylinder head, reface valves and seats. Tune engine.
All models
2.0L eng 5.6
2.6L eng 7.2

Cylinder Head Cover Gasket, Renew
All models 6

Valve Rocker Arms and/or Shaft, Renew
Includes: Renew shaft if required.
All models
one shaft 1.4
both shafts 2.3

Jet Valve, Renew (One or All)
All models 2.1

Valve Springs and/or Valve Stem Oil Seals, Renew
All models
2.0L eng
one cyl 1.3
all cyls 3.0
2.6L eng
one cyl 5.6
all cyls 6.0

Valve Clearance, Adjust
All models 1.5

Valve Lash Adjustors, Renew
All models 1.5

DIESEL ENGINE

Compression Test
All models 6

Cylinder Head Gasket, Renew
Includes: Clean carbon. Make all necessary adjustments.
All models 3.5

Cylinder Head, Renew
Includes: Reface and adjust valves, clean carbon. Make all necessary adjustmets.
All models 6.2

Clean Carbon and Grind Valves
Includes: R&R cylinder head. Reface valves and seats. Make all necessary adjustments.
All models 5.5

Cylinder Head Cover Gasket, Renew
All models 6

Valve Rocker Arms, Renew
All models 1.1

Valve Springs and/or Valve Stem Oil Seals, Renew (All)
All models 4.2

Valve Clearance, Adjust
All models 1.5

LABOR 13 ENGINE ASSEMBLY & MOUNTS 13 LABOR

(Factory Time) Chilton Time

GASOLINE ENGINE

Note: All engine operations listed in this group are for assemblies as supplied by the original equipment manufacturer. Time to replace assemblies from independent rebuilders may vary.

Engine Assembly, Remove & Install
Does not include transfer of any parts or equipment.
All models 8.0
w/A.C. add 2
w/P.S. add 3

Short Engine Assembly, Renew (w/All Internal Parts Less Head and Oil Pan)
Includes: R&R engine assy. Transfer all necessary parts not supplied with replacement engine. Clean carbon, grind valves. Minor tune up.
All models 18.2
w/A.C. add 2
w/P.S. add 3

Engine Assy., R&R and Recondition (Complete)
Includes: Rebore block, install new pistons, rings, rod and main bearings. Clean carbon, grind valves. Tune engine.
All models 26.0
w/A.C. add 2
w/P.S. add 3

LABOR 13 ENGINE ASSEMBLY & MOUNTS 13 LABOR

(Factory Time) Chilton Time

Engine Support, Renew
All models-one 7
both 1.1

DIESEL ENGINE

Engine Assembly, Remove & Install
Does not include transfer of any parts or equipment.
All models 5.1
w/A.C. add 6

Short Engine Assembly, Renew (w/All Internal Parts Less Head and Oil Pan)
Includes: R&R engine assy. Transfer all necessary parts not supplied with replacement engine. Clean carbon, grind valves. Make all necessary adjustments.
All models 14.7
w/A.C. add 6

Engine Mount, Renew
All models-one 5
both 7

LABOR 14 PISTONS, RINGS & BEARINGS 14 LABOR

(Factory Time) Chilton Time

GASOLINE ENGINE

Rings, Renew (All)
Includes: Replace connecting rod bearings, deglaze cylinder walls, remove cylinder top ridge. Clean carbon from cylinder head. Minor tune up.
All models 7.5
w/P.S. add 3

Pistons or Connecting Rods, Renew
Includes: Replace connecting rod bearings, deglaze cylinder walls, remove cylinder top ridge, clean carbon from cylinder head. Minor tune up.
All models 8.7
w/P.S. add 3

Connecting Rod Bearings, Renew (All)
All models 4.0

DIESEL ENGINE

Rings, Renew (All)
Includes: Replace connecting rod bearings, deglaze cylinder walls, remove cylinder top ridge, clean carbon from cylinder head. Make all necessary adjustments.
All models 7.1

COMBINATIONS

Add to Engine Work

(Chilton Time)

DRAIN, EVACUATE & RECHARGE AIR CONDITIONING SYSTEM
All models 1.0

DISTRIBUTOR, RECONDITION
All models 1.0

CARBURETOR, RECONDITION
All models 1.6

DEGLAZE CYLINDER WALLS
Each 1

REMOVE CYLINDER TOP RIDGE
Each 1

OIL FILTER ELEMENT, RENEW
All models 2

CYLINDER HEAD, R&R (ENGINE REMOVED)
All models 1.0

RECONDITION CYLINDER HEAD (HEAD REMOVED)
All models 2.5

CONNECTING ROD, RENEW (ENGINE DISASSEMBLED)
Each 4

PLASTIGAUGE BEARINGS
Each 1

ROD BEARINGS, RENEW (PAN REMOVED)
All models 1.2

Pistons or Connecting Rods, Renew (All)
Includes: Replace connecting rod bearings, deglaze cylinder walls, remove cylinder top ridge, replace piston rings. Clean carbon from cylinder head. Make all necessary adjustments.
All models 8.3

Connecting Rod Bearings, Renew (All)
All models 3.1

LABOR 15 CRANKSHAFT & DAMPER 15 LABOR

(Factory Time) Chilton Time

GASOLINE ENGINE

Crankshaft and Main Bearings, Renew
Includes: R&R engine assembly.
All models 17.3
w/A.C. add 1.0

Main Bearings, Renew
Includes: R&R engine.
All models 17.3
w/A.C. add 1.0

Main and Rod Bearings, Renew
Includes: R&R engine.
All models 18.5
w/A.C. add 1.0

Crankshaft Pulley, Renew
All models 6
w/A.C. add 1

Rear Main Bearing Oil Seal, Renew (Complete)
All models
w/M.T. 3.5
w/A.T. 3.8
4X4 add 6

DIESEL ENGINE

Crankshaft and Main Bearings, Renew
Includes: R&R engine assembly.
All models 7.7
w/A.C. add 6

Main Bearings, Renew
All models 3.4

Main and Rod Bearings, Renew
All models 4.6

Crankshaft Pulley, Renew
All models 6
w/A.C. add 1
w/P.S. add 1

Crankshaft Front Oil Seal, Renew
All models 1.7
w/A.C. add 6

LABOR 16 CAMSHAFT & TIMING GEARS 16 LABOR

(Factory Time) Chilton Time

GASOLINE ENGINE

Camshaft, Renew
Includes: Renew valve lifters and adjust valve clearance.
All models
2.0L eng 2.1
2.6L eng 3.0

Camshaft Oil Seal, Renew
All models 2.0

Timing Belt, Renew
Truck-Montero 2.1
Van-Wagon 3.5
w/A.C. add 3
w/P.S. add 2

Timing Chain Tensioner, Renew
Includes: Renew cover oil seal.
All models 5.2
w/A.C. add 7

Timing Belt Tensioner, Renew
Truck-Montero 2.1
Van-Wagon 3.5

LABOR 16 CAMSHAFT & TIMING GEARS 16 LABOR

(Factory Time)	Chilton Time
Timing Chain, Renew	
All models	
cam drive	5.4
silent shaft drive	4.9
w/A.C. add	.7
Timing Chain or Belt Case/Cover Gasket, Renew	
Includes: Renew oil seal.	
All models	
2.6L eng	4.3
2.0L eng	
upper-outer	.4
upper-inner	.8
lower-outer	1.4
lower-inner	1.8
w/A.C. add	.7
Timing Chain Case/Cover Oil Seal, Renew	
All models	2.3
w/A.C. add	.7
Silent Shaft Oil Seal, Renew	
All models	4.4
w/A.C. add	.5
w/P.S. add	.2
Silent Shaft, Renew	
All models	
2.6L eng	
right	7.7
left	7.2
both	8.1
2.0L eng	
right	6.4
left	6.8
both	7.4
w/A.C. add	.7
w/P.S. add	.1

DIESEL ENGINE

(Factory Time)	Chilton Time
Timing Belt Cover, Renew	
All models	
upper	.3
lower	1.0
Timing Belt, Renew	
All models	
cam drive	1.6
silent shaft drive	1.8
w/A.C. add	.6
Timing Belt Tensioner, Renew	
All models	
cam drive	1.7
silent shaft drive	1.9
w/A.C. add	.6
Camshaft, Renew	
All models	2.0
Silent Shaft, Renew	
All models	
right side	2.5
left side	4.0
both sides	4.5
w/A.C. add	.6
Silent Shaft Oil Seal, Renew	
All models	1.9
w/A.C. add	.6

LABOR 17 ENGINE OILING SYSTEM 17 LABOR

GASOLINE ENGINE

(Factory Time)	Chilton Time
Oil Pan and/or Gasket, Renew	
Truck-Montero	1.5
Van-Wagon	1.7
Pressure Test Engine Bearings (Pan Off)	
All models	1.0
Oil Pump, Renew	
Truck-Montero	5.0
Van-Wagon	7.2
Oil Pressure Gauge (Dash), Renew	
Truck	.6
Oil Pressure Sending Unit, Renew	
All models	.5
Oil Filter Element, Renew	
All models	.3

DIESEL ENGINE

(Factory Time)	Chilton Time
Oil Pan and/or Gasket, Renew	
All models	1.6
Oil Pump, Renew	
All models	3.4
Oil Filter Element, Renew	
All models	.3

LABOR 18 CLUTCH & FLYWHEEL 18 LABOR

(Factory Time)	Chilton Time
Clutch Cable, Adjust	
All models	.4
Clutch Release Cable, Renew	
All models	.5
Clutch Slave Cylinder, Renew	
Includes: Bleed system.	
All models	1.0
Clutch Master Cylinder, Renew	
Includes: Bleed system.	
All models	1.0
Clutch Release Bearing, Renew	
All models	
2 WD	3.6
4 WD	4.1
Renew fork add	.3
Clutch Assembly, Renew	
All models	
2 WD	3.9
4 WD	4.4
Flywheel, Renew	
All models	
2 WD	4.2
4 WD	4.7
Renew ring gear add	.4

LABOR 19 STANDARD TRANSMISSION 19 LABOR

(Factory Time)	Chilton Time
Transmission Assy., R&R or Renew	
All models	
4 spd	3.7
5 spd	3.7
Renew assy add	.6
4X4 add	.6
Transmission Assy., R&R and Recondition	
Includes: Disassemble, clean and inspect or renew all parts. Install all new gaskets and seals.	
All models	
4 spd	6.7
5 spd	9.0
4X4 add	.6
Extension Housing Oil Seal, Renew	
5 Spd models	.7

TRANSFER CASE

(Factory Time)	Chilton Time
Transfer Case Adaptor Gasket, Renew	
All models	4.1
Transfer Case Shift Lever Boot, Renew	
All models	.5
Transfer Case Shifter, Renew	
All models	.8
Rear Output Shaft Housing, Renew	
All models	1.0
Rear Output Shaft Seal, Renew	
All models	.6
Front Output Rear Bearing Gasket, Renew	
All models	.4
Speedometer Drive Pinion, Renew	
All models	.3
Transfer Case Assy., Remove & Install	
All models	6.5
Renew assy add	.8
Renew rear housing add	1.9
Renew front housing add	2.8
Renew drive chain add	2.5
Transfer Case Assy., R&R and Recondition (Complete)	
All models	9.5

LABOR 23 AUTOMATIC TRANSMISSION 23 LABOR

(Factory Time) Chilton Time

3 SPEED

ON CAR SERVICES

Drain & Refill Unit
All models.......... .8

Oil Pressure Check
All models.......... .9

Check Unit for Oil Leaks
Includes: Clean and dry outside of case and run unit to determine point of leak.
All models.......... .9

Neutral Safety Switch, Renew
All models.......... .4

Throttle Linkage, Adjust
All models.......... .4

Throttle Valve Lever Shaft Seal, Renew
All models.......... .6

Valve Body Manual Lever Shaft Seal, Renew
All models.......... 1.0

Kickdown Band, Adjust (External)
All models.......... .5

Extension Housing Oil Seal, Renew
All models.......... .8

Governor Assy., Renew or Recondition
Includes: R&R extension housing and renew bearing.
All models.......... 2.4

Governor Support and Parking Gear, Renew
Includes: R&R extension housing and renew bearing.
All models.......... 2.4

Parking Lock Sprag, Renew
Includes: R&R extension housing.
All models.......... 2.2

Oil Pan and/or Gasket, Renew
All models.......... .7

Bands, Adjust
Includes: R&R oil pan.
All models
kickdown.......... 1.2
reverse.......... 1.2

Valve Body Assy., Renew
Includes: R&R oil pan and renew filter.
All models.......... 1.5

Valve Body Assy., R&R and Recondition
Includes: R&R oil pan and renew filter. Disassemble, clean, inspect, free all valves. Replace parts as required.
All models.......... 3.0

SERVICES REQUIRING R&R

Transmission Assy., R&R or Renew
All models.......... 3.5
Renew assy add.......... .6
4X4 add.......... .6

Transmission Assy., R&R and Recondition (Complete)
All models.......... 9.0
Flush cooler lines add.......... .2
4X4 add.......... .6

Transmission Assembly, Reseal
Includes: R&R trans and renew all gaskets and seals.
All models.......... 6.0
4X4 add.......... .6

Torque Converter, Renew
Includes: R&R transmission.
All models.......... 3.6
4X4 add.......... .6

Front Pump Oil Seal, Renew
Includes: R&R transmission.
All models.......... 3.6
4X4 add.......... .6

Front Pump Assy., Renew
Includes: R&R transmission.
All models.......... 4.2
4X4 add.......... .6

4 SPEED

ON CAR SERVICES

Drain and Refill Unit
All models.......... 1.5

Oil Pressure Check
All models.......... .9

Check Unit for Oil Leaks
Includes: Clean and dry outside of case and run unit to determine point of leak.
All models.......... .9

Throttle Linkage, Adjust
All models.......... .3

Gearshift Control Cable, Renew
All models.......... .8

Extension Housing Oil Seal, Renew
All models.......... .7

Throttle Cable, Renew
All models.......... 2.3

Extension Housing Gasket, Renew
4X2 models.......... 1.7
4X4 models.......... 2.4

Governor Assembly, Renew
Includes: R&R extension housing.
4X2 models.......... 2.2
4X4 models.......... 3.0

Transmission Solenoid Valve, Renew
All models.......... 1.8

Oil Pan Gasket, Renew
All models.......... 1.5

SERVICES REQUIRING R&R

Transmission Assy., R&R or Renew
4X2 models.......... 3.2
4X4 models.......... 5.6
Van-Wagon.......... 2.0
Renew assy add.......... .6

Transmission Assy., R&R and Recondition (Complete)
4X2 models.......... 9.5
4X4 models.......... 12.0
Van-Wagon.......... 8.6

Transmission Assembly, Reseal
Includes: R&R trans and renew all gaskets and seals.
4X2 models.......... 6.0
4X4 models.......... 8.4
Van-Wagon.......... 5.5

Torque Converter, Renew
Includes: R&R transmission.
4X2 models.......... 3.6
4X4 models.......... 5.8
Van-Wagon.......... 2.2

Front Pump Oil Seal, Renew
Includes: R&R transmission.
4X2 models.......... 3.5
4X4 models.......... 5.7
Van-Wagon.......... 2.5

Front Pump Assy., Renew
Includes: R&R transmission.
4X2 models.......... 4.0
4X4 models.......... 6.4
Van-Wagon.......... 2.3

LABOR 25 U-JOINTS & DRIVESHAFT 25 LABOR

(Factory Time) Chilton Time

Drive Shaft Center Bearing, Renew
All models.......... 1.3

Drive Shaft Assy., R&R or Renew
Trans to Rear Axle
Truck-Montero.......... .8
Van-Wagon.......... .5
Center Brg to Rear Axle
Truck.......... 1.2
Transfer Case to Front Axle
Truck-Montero.......... .6
Trans to Center Brg
Truck.......... 1.6

Universal Joints, R&R and Recondition
2 Joint Type
one.......... 1.0
3 Joint Type
one.......... 1.1
all.......... 2.8

LABOR 26 DRIVE AXLE 26 LABOR

(Factory Time) Chilton Time

REAR DIFFERENTIAL

Axle Shaft or Bearing, Renew (One)
All models.......... 2.1

Axle Shaft Oil Seal, Renew (One)
All models.......... 1.3

Differential Carrier Gasket, Renew
All models.......... 2.9

Differential Side Bearings, Renew
Includes: Adjust backlash and renew axle shaft oil seals.
All models.......... 4.3

LABOR 26 DRIVE AXLE 26 LABOR

(Factory Time) Chilton Time

Differential Side Gears, Renew
Includes: Adjust backlash and renew axle shaft oil seal.
All models.......... 4.8

Ring Gear and Pinion Set, Renew
Includes: Renew axle shaft oil seals and pinion bearings.
All models.......... 5.5

Pinion Shaft Oil Seal, Renew
All models.......... 1.0

FRONT DIFFERENTIAL

Front Differential, Drain & Refill
All models.......... .6

Front Axle Housing Cover or Gasket, Renew
All models.......... .6

Drive Pinion Oil Seal, Renew
All models.......... .8

Front Axle Propeller Shaft Flange, Renew
All models.......... .6

Front Axle Shaft, Renew (One)
Includes: Renew outer wheel bearings if required.
All models
outer-w/Joint.......... 2.0
inner.......... 1.6

Drive Shaft Boot, Renew (One)
Includes: Clean and lubricate C/V joint.
All models.......... 1.9

Drive Shaft C.V. Joint, Renew
All models.......... 1.8

Front Propeller Shaft, Renew
All models
transfer case to ft axle.......... .6

Differential Side Bearings, Renew
Includes: R&R ring gear and pinion, renew axle housing oil seals and adjust bearing preload and backlash.
All models.......... 4.9

Differential Side Gears, Renew
Includes: Renew axle housing oil seals if required.
All models.......... 4.7

Differential Case, Renew
Includes: R&R ring gear and pinion, renew bearings and gears, renew pinion and axle housing seals. Adjust backlash.
All models.......... 5.1

Ring Gear and Pinion Set, Renew
Includes: Renew pinion bearing, side bearings and all seals. Adjust bearing preload and backlash.
All models.......... 5.6
Renew diff case add.......... .2

Front Axle Housing, Renew
Includes: Renew oil seals. Transfer axle shafts, differential and brake assemblies.
All models.......... 5.7

LABOR 27 REAR SUSPENSION 27 LABOR

(Factory Time) Chilton Time

Rear Shock Absorbers, Renew
All models-one.......... .4
both.......... .6

Rear Springs, Renew (w/Bushings)
All models-one.......... 1.1
both.......... 2.0

Rear Spring Front Eye Bushing, Renew
All models-one.......... 1.0

Rear Spring Shackle and/or Bushing, Renew
All models.......... .9

LABOR 28 AIR CONDITIONING 28 LABOR

(Factory Time) Chilton Time

Note: If more than one item requires replacement where evacuation and discharging the system is already included in the operation, deduct 1.0 hour for each additional item to the times listed.

Drain, Evacuate, Leak Test & Charge System
All models.......... 1.0

Flush Refrigerant System, Complete
To be used in conjunction with component replacement which could contaminate system.
All models.......... 1.3

Partial Charge System
All models.......... .6

Compressor Belt, Renew
All models.......... .4

Compressor Assembly, Renew
Includes: Pressure test and charge system.
Truck.......... 2.5
Montero.......... 2.0
Van-Wagon.......... 2.2

Compressor-Crankshaft Seal, Renew
Includes: Pressure test and charge system.
Truck.......... 3.2
Montero-Van-Wagon.......... 2.3

Compressor Clutch Assy., Renew
Truck.......... 2.8
Montero-Van-Wagon.......... 2.3

Expansion Valve, Renew
Includes: Pressure test and charge system.
Truck-Montero.......... 4.0
Van-Wagon
front.......... 2.8
rear.......... 2.0

Receiver Drier, Renew
Includes: Pressure test and charge system.
Truck-Montero.......... 1.5
Van-Wagon.......... 1.3

High Pressure Cut-Off Switch, Renew
Includes: Pressure test and charge system.
All models
1984 & earlier.......... 1.5
1985 & later.......... 1.2

Condenser Assembly, Renew
Includes: Pressure test and charge system.
Truck.......... 2.0
Montero.......... 1.6
Van-Wagon.......... 1.4

Evaporator Core, Renew
Includes: Pressure test and charge system.
Truck-Montero.......... 3.9
Van-Wagon
front.......... 3.5
rear.......... 2.0

Air Conditioning Switch, Renew
Truck
1983-86.......... 1.2
1987.......... 1.0
Montero.......... 1.2
Van
front.......... .6
rear.......... .5

A.C. Blower Motor Switch, Renew
Truck-Montero.......... 1.2
Van.......... .7

A.C. Blower Motor, Renew
Truck
1983-86.......... 1.0
1987.......... .6
Montero.......... .6
Van
front.......... .6
rear.......... .5

A.C. Blower Motor Resistor, Renew
Truck
1983-86.......... .7
1987.......... .6
Montero.......... .6
Van
front.......... .6
rear.......... .5

Air Conditioning Hoses, Renew
Includes: Pressure test and charge system.
All models-one.......... 1.7
each adtnl.......... .5

LABOR 29 LOCKS, HINGES & WIND. REGULATORS 29 LABOR

(Factory Time) Chilton Time

Hood Hinge, Renew (One)
Does not include painting.
Truck 8

Hood Release Cable, Renew
All models 9

Lock Striker Plate, Renew
All models 3

Door Lock Remote Control, Renew
Truck-Montero 6
Van-Wagon 8

Door Handle (Outside), Renew
All models 6

Front Door Window Regulator, Renew
All models
manual 9
electric 1.0

LABOR 30 HEAD AND PARKING LAMPS 30 LABOR

(Factory Time) Chilton Time

Aim Headlamps
All models 4

Head Lamp Sealed Beam Bulb, Renew
Does not include aiming.
All models 3

License Lamp Assembly, Renew
All models 3

Park and Turn Signal Lamp Assy., Renew
All models 3

Tail, Stop and Turn Signal Lamp Assy., Renew
All models 3

Side Marker Lamp Assy., Renew
All models 4

LABOR 31 WINDSHIELD WIPER & SPEEDOMETER 31 LABOR

(Factory Time) Chilton Time

Windshield Wiper Motor, Renew
All models 7

Windshield Wiper and Washer Switch, Renew
All models 8

Windshield Washer Pump, Renew
All models 5

Windshield Wiper Link Assy., Renew
Truck-Montero 7
Van-Wagon 2.3

Speedometer Head, R&R or Renew
All models 1.2

Speedometer Cable and Casing, Renew
All models 9

Speedometer Cable (Inner), Renew or Lubricate
All models 4

Rear Window Wiper Motor, Renew
Van-Wagon 6

Rear Window Wiper Switch, Renew
Van-Wagon 4

Rear Window Washer Pump, Renew
Van-Wagon 4

Radio, R&R
Truck
1983-86 .... 1.0
1987 5
Montero 1.1
Van-Wagon 6

LABOR 32 LIGHT SWITCHES & WIRING 32 LABOR

(Factory Time) Chilton Time

Headlamp Switch, Renew
All models 6

Back-Up Lamp Switch, Renew (w/Manual Trans)
All models 4

Neutral Safety and/or Back-Up Lamp Switch, Renew
All models 4

Stop Lamp Switch, Renew
All models 4
w/Cruise control add 1

Parking Brake Warning Lamp Switch, Renew
All models 6

Hazard Warning Switch, Renew
All models 4

Column Switch Assy., Renew
Truck-Montero 9
Van-Wagon 8

Turn Signal or Hazard Warning Flasher, Renew
All models 3

Turn Signal, Washer/Wiper Lever Assy., Renew
All models 8

Horn, Renew
Truck-Montero-one 3
Van-Wagon 5

Horn Switch, Renew
All models 4

LABOR 34 CRUISE CONTROL 34 LABOR

(Factory Time) Chilton Time

Speed Control Vacuum Pump, Renew
Truck 1.0

Speed Control Vacuum Switch, Renew
Truck 3

Speed Control Clutch Release Switch, Renew
Truck 5

Speed Control Control Unit, Renew
Truck 4

Speed Control Actuator, Renew
Truck 9

Speed Control Vacuum Hoses, Renew
Truck 4

Dodge D50 • Ram 50 • Raider

GROUP INDEX

ALPHABETICAL INDEX

LABOR 1 TUNE UP 1 LABOR

(Factory Time) Chilton Time

Compression Test
All models.. .6

Engine Tune Up, (Electronic Ignition)
Includes: Test battery and clean connections. Tighten manifold and carburetor mounting bolts. Check engine compression, clean and adjust or renew spark plugs. Test resistance of spark plug cables. Inspect distributor cap and rotor. Adjust air gap. Check vacuum advance operation. Reset ignition timing. Adjust idle mixture and idle speed. Service air cleaner. Inspect and adjust drive belts. Inspect choke operation and adjust or free up. Check operation of EGR valve.
All models.. 1.5

LABOR 2 IGNITION SYSTEM 2 LABOR

(Factory Time) Chilton Time

Spark Plugs, Clean and Reset or Renew
All models.. .5

Ignition Timing, Reset
All models.. .4

Distributor, Renew
Includes: Reset ignition timing.
All models.. .6

Distributor Reluctor, Renew
Includes: R&R distributor and reset ignition timing and dwell.
All models.. 1.0

Vacuum Control Unit, Renew
Includes: R&R distributor and reset ignition timing and dwell.
All models.. .9

Pick-Up Set, Renew
Includes: R&R distributor and reset ignition timing.
All models.. 1.1

Ignitor Set, Renew
Includes: R&R distributor and reset ignition timing.
All models.. 1.0

Distributor Cap and/or Rotor, Renew
All models.. .4

Electronic Ignition Control Unit, Renew
All models.. .8

Ignition Cables, Renew
All models.. .5

Ignition Coil, Renew
All models.. .6

Ignition Switch, Renew
All models.. .7

Electronic Ignition Ballast Resistor, Renew
All models.. .3

DIESEL ENGINE

Glow Plugs, Renew
All models
one or all.. .5

Glow Plug Relay, Renew
All models.. .4

Glow Plug Control Unit, Renew
All models.. .4

LABOR 3 FUEL SYSTEM 3 LABOR

(Factory Time) Chilton Time

GASOLINE ENGINES

Fuel Pump, Test
Includes: Disconnect line at carburetor, attach pressure gauge.
All models.. .3

Carburetor Air Cleaner, Service
All models.. .2

Carburetor, Adjust (On Truck)
All models.. .6

Automatic Choke Cover/Float Chamber, Renew
All models.. 1.5

Dash Pot, Renew
(w/Manual Trans)
All models.. .4

Engine Speed Sensor, Renew
All models.. .6

Accelerator Pump, Renew
All models.. .5

Needle Valve and Seat, Renew
Includes: Renew float, reset idle speed.
All models.. 1.7

Enrichment Body Assembly, Renew
All models.. 1.5

Vacuum Throttle Opener, Renew
All models.. .8

Fuel Cut-Off Solenoid, Renew
All models.. .4

Carburetor Sub-EGR Valve, Renew
All models.. .7

Fuel Filter, Renew
All models.. .4

Carburetor, Renew
Includes: All necessary adjustments.
All models.. 1.5

Carburetor, R&R and Clean or Recondition
Includes: All necessary adjustments.
All models.. 2.9

Fuel Pump, Renew
All models.. .8
Add pump test if performed.

Fuel Tank, Renew
Includes: Drain and refill tank.
All models.. 1.5

Fuel Gauge (Dash), Renew
All models.. 1.2

Fuel Gauge (Tank), Renew
All models.. 1.4

Intake Manifold or Gasket, Renew
All models.. 4.1

DIESEL ENGINE

Injection Pump Timing, Adjust
All models.. .6

Fuel Injection Pump Assy., Renew
All models.. 2.0

Injection Nozzles, R&R or Renew
All models-one.. .6
each adtnl.. .4
Clean or recond add-each.. .3

Fuel Filter Bleed Pump, Renew
All models.. .4

Fuel Temperature Sensor, Renew
All models.. .7

Water Level Sensor, Renew
All models.. .7

Turbocharger Assy., R&R or Renew
Includes: Renew gasket.
All models.. 1.5

Intake and Exhaust Manifold Gaskets, Renew
All models.. 1.8

LABOR 3A EMISSION CONTROLS 3A LABOR

(Factory Time) Chilton Time

Fuel Vapor Canister, Renew
All models.. .3

Fuel Vapor Separator, Renew
All models-one or both.. 1.4

E.G.R. Valve, Renew
All models.. .5

LABOR 3A EMISSION CONTROLS 3A LABOR

(Factory Time) Chilton Time

Coolant Control Valve (CCEGR), Renew
All models .5

Pulse Air Feeder, Renew
All models 1.2

Aspirator, Renew
All models .4

Pulse Air Feeder or Aspirator Tube, Renew
All models 1.0

P.C.V. Valve, Renew
All models .2

Oxygen Sensor, Renew
All models .6

High Altitude Compensator, Renew
All models .6

LABOR 4 ALTERNATOR AND REGULATOR 4 LABOR

(Factory Time) Chilton Time

Alternator Circuits, Test
Includes: Test battery, regulator and alternator output.
All models .6

Alternator, Renew
Includes: Transfer pulley if required.
All models 1.4

Add circuit test if performed.

Alternator, R&R and Recondition
Includes: Test and disassemble.
All models 2.5

Alternator, R&R and Renew Bearings
All models 1.7

Voltage Regulator, Test and Renew
All models 1.6

Alternator Gauge, Renew
All models .7

Instrument Cluster Voltage Limiter, Renew
All models .9

LABOR 5 STARTING SYSTEM 5 LABOR

(Factory Time) Chilton Time

Starter Draw Test (On Truck)
All models .3

Starter, Renew
Includes: Test starter relay, starter solenoid and amperage draw.
All models 1.1

Starter, R&R and Recondition
Includes: Test starter relay, starter solenoid and amperage draw. Turn down armature.
All models 2.3
Renew field coils add .5

Starter Solenoid, Renew
Includes: R&R starter.
All models 1.2

Starter Drive, Renew
Includes: R&R starter.
All models 1.3

Battery Cables, Renew
All models-each .4

LABOR 6 BRAKE SYSTEM 6 LABOR

(Factory Time) Chilton Time

Brakes, Adjust (Minor)
Includes: Adjust brake shoes, fill master cylinder.
two wheels .4

Bleed Brakes (Four Wheels)
Includes: Fill master cylinder.
All models .6

Brake Shoes and/or Pads, Renew
Includes: Install new or exchange brake shoes or pads. Adjust service and hand brake. Bleed system.
front-disc .9
rear-drum 1.4
all four wheels 2.2
Resurface disc rotor, add-each .9
Resurface brake drum, add-each .5

Brake Drum, Renew (One)
All models .4

BRAKE HYDRAULIC SYSTEM

Wheel Cylinder, Renew
Includes: Bleed system.
All models-one .9
both 1.7

Wheel Cylinder, R&R and Rebuild
Includes: Hone cylinder and bleed system.
All models-one 1.2
both 2.3

Master Cylinder, Renew
Includes: Bleed system.
All models 1.0

COMBINATIONS

Add to Brakes, Renew

	Chilton Time
RENEW WHEEL CYLINDER Each	.2
REBUILD WHEEL CYLINDER Each	.3
REBUILD CALIPER ASSEMBLY Each	.5
RENEW MASTER CYLINDER All models	.6
REBUILD MASTER CYLINDER All models	.6
RENEW BRAKE HOSE Each	.3
RENEW REAR WHEEL INNER OIL SEAL Each	.3
REPACK FRONT WHEEL BEARINGS (BOTH WHEELS) All models	.6
RENEW DISC BRAKE ROTOR Each	.3
DISC BRAKE ROTOR STUDS, RENEW Each	.1

Master Cylinder, R&R and Rebuild
Includes: Hone cylinder and bleed system.
All models 1.6

Brake Hose, Renew (Flex)
Includes: Bleed system.
All models-each .6

Brake System Combination Valve, Renew
Includes: Bleed system.
All models 1.2

POWER BRAKES

Power Brake Unit, Rrnew
All models 1.1

Check Valve, Renew
All models .2

DISC BRAKES

Disc Brake Pads, Renew
Includes: Install new disc brake pads only.
All models .9

LABOR 6 BRAKE SYSTEM 6 LABOR

(Factory Time)	Chilton Time
Disc Brake Rotor, Renew (Disc Only)	
All models-one	1.0
both	1.9
Disc Brake Hub Assy., Renew	
Includes: Renew inner and outer bearings if required.	
All models-one	1.3
both	2.5
Caliper Assembly, Renew	
Includes: Bleed system.	
All models-one	.8
both	1.5
Caliper Assy., R&R and Recondition	
Includes: Bleed system.	
All models-one	1.3
both	2.5
PARKING BRAKE	
Parking Brake, Adjust	
All models	.3
Parking Brake Control, Renew	
All models	.7
Parking Brake Cable, Renew	
All models-one	1.0
Parking Brake Warning Lamp Switch, Renew	
All models	.3

LABOR 7 COOLING SYSTEM 7 LABOR

(Factory Time)	Chilton Time
Winterize Cooling System	
Includes: Run engine to check for leaks, tighten all hose connections. Test radiator and pressure cap, drain radiator and engine block. Add anti-freeze and refill system.	
All models	.5
Thermostat, Renew	
All models	.5
Radiator Assembly, R&R or Renew	
Includes: Drain and refill cooling system.	
All models	.7
w/A.T. add	.2
ADD THESE OPERATIONS TO RADIATOR R&R	
Boil & Repair	1.5
Rod Clean	1.9
Repair Core	1.3
Renew Tank	1.6
Renew Trans. Oil Cooler	1.9
Recore Radiator	1.7
Radiator Hoses, Renew	
upper	.3
lower	.4
both	.6
Water Pump, Renew	
All models	
Gas	
chain drive	1.4
belt drive	2.0
Diesel	1.7
w/P.S. add	.4
Fan Blades, Renew	
All models	.5
w/A.C. add	.2
w/P.S. add	.1
Fan and Alternator Belt, Renew	
All models	.3
Fan and Alternator Belt, Adjust	
All models	.2
Fluid Fan Drive Unit, Renew	
All models	.6
w/A.C. add	.2
w/P.S. add	.1
Temperature Gauge (Dash Unit), Renew	
All models	1.2
Temperature Gauge (Engine Unit), Renew	
All models	.4
Transmission Auxiliary Oil Cooler, Renew	
All models	1.0
Heater Core, R&R or Renew	
All models	1.7
ADD THESE OPERATIONS TO HEATER CORE R&R	
Boil & Repair	1.2
Repair Core	.9
Recore	1.2
Heater Water Valve, Renew	
All models	.9
w/A.C. add	.1
Heater Control Assembly, Renew	
All models	.9
Heater Blower Motor Switch, Renew	
All models	.6
Heater Blower Motor, Renew	
All models	1.0
Heater Blower Motor Resistor, Renew	
All models	.4

LABOR 8 EXHAUST SYSTEM 8 LABOR

(Factory Time)	Chilton Time
Muffler, Renew	
All models	.6
Exhaust Pipe, Renew	
All models	.7
Catalytic Converter, Renew	
All models	1.0
Exhaust Manifold or Gasket, Renew	
All models-Gas	1.2
Diesel	1.8

LABOR 9 FRONT SUSPENSION 9 LABOR

Note: On all front suspension operations alignment charges must be added if performed. Time given does not include alignment.

(Factory Time)	Chilton Time
Wheel, Renew	
one	.5
Wheels, Rotate (All)	
All models	.5
Wheels, Balance	
one	.3
each adtnl	.2
Toe-In, Adjust	
All models	.6
Align Front End	
Includes: Adjust front wheel bearings.	
All models	1.4
Front Wheel Bearings, Clean and Repack (Both Wheels)	
All models	1.2
Front Wheel Bearings and Cups, Renew	
Includes: Renew dust seal.	
All models-one side	.8
both sides	1.5
Renew axle shaft outer seal & brg add	.7
Steering Knuckle, Renew	
Add alignment charges.	
4X2 models-one	1.6
both	3.0
4X4 models-one	1.8
both	3.5
Steering Knuckle Arm, Renew	
4X2 models-one	1.0
both	1.8
4X4 models-one	1.5
both	2.9

LABOR 9 FRONT SUSPENSION 9 LABOR

(Factory Time) Chilton Time

Lower Control Arm Assy., Renew
Add alignment charges.
4X2 models-one 2.1
both 4.0
4X4 models-one 1.6
both 3.0

Lower Ball Joint, Renew
Add alignment charges.
4X2 models-one 1.8
both 3.5
4X4 models-one 1.3
both 2.5

Lower Control Arm Strut Bar or Bushings, Renew
All models-one side 9
both sides 1.5

Lower Control Arm Bushings, Renew
Add alignment charges.
4X2 models-one side 2.0
both sides 3.7
4X4 models-one side 1.7
both sides 3.3

Upper Control Arm Assy., Renew
Includes: Align front end.
All models-one 2.5
both 4.3

Upper Ball Joint, Renew
Add alignment charges.
4X2 models-one 1.5
both 2.8
4X4 models-one 1.6
both 3.0

Front Coil Spring, Renew
All models-one 1.9
both 3.5

Front Shock Absorbers, Renew
All models-one 7
both 1.1

Front Sway Bar, Renew
All models 1.5

Front Sway Bar Bushings, Renew
All models-one or all 5

Front Torsion Bars, Renew
All models-one 5
both 8

Torsion Bar Anchor/Adjusting Bolt, Renew
All models-one 6
both 1.0

4 WHEEL DRIVE FRONT AXLE

Front Differential, Drain & Refill
All models 6

Front Axle Housing Cover or Gasket, Renew
All models 6

Drive Pinion Oil Seal, Renew
All models 8

Front Axle Propeller Shaft Flange, Renew
All models 6

Front Axle Shaft, Renew (One)
Includes: Renew outer wheel bearings if required.
All models
outer-w/Joint 2.0
inner 1.6

Drive Shaft Boot, Renew (One)
Includes: Clean and lubricate C/V joint.
All models 1.9

Locking Hub Assy., Renew or Recondition
All models-each 5

Drive Shaft C.V. Joint, Renew
All models-inner 1.8

Front Propeller Shaft, Renew
All models
transfer case to ft axle 6

Differential Side Bearings, Renew
Includes: R&R ring gear and pinion, renew axle housing oil seals and adjust bearing preload and backlash.
All models 4.9

Differential Side Gears, Renew
Includes: Renew axle housing oil seals if required.
All models 4.7

Differential Case, Renew
Includes: R&R ring gear and pinion, renew bearings and gears, renew pinion and axle housing seals. Adjust backlash.
All models 5.1

Ring Gear and Pinion Set, Renew
Includes: Renew pinion bearing, side bearings and all seals. Adjust bearing preload and backlash.
All models 5.6
Renew diff case add 2

Front Axle Housing, Renew
Includes: Renew oil seals. Transfer axle shafts, differential and brake assemblies.
All models 5.7

LABOR 10 STEERING LINKAGE 10 LABOR

(Factory Time) Chilton Time

Tie Rods or Tie Rod Ends, Renew
Includes: Reset toe-in.
All models-one side 1.0
both sides 1.7

Idler Arm, Renew
All models 5

Center Link (Relay Rod), Renew
All models 6

Pitman Arm, Renew
All models 6

LABOR 11 STEERING GEAR 11 LABOR

(Factory Time) Chilton Time

STANDARD STEERING

Steering Wheel, Renew
All models 5

Horn Contact Ring or Cable, Renew
All models 4

Steering Column Flex Coupling, Renew
All models 1.3
w/P.S. add 3

Steering Column Mast Jacket, Renew
Does not include painting.
All models 1.5

Steering Column Upper Mast Jacket Bearing, Renew
All models 1.6

Steering Gear, Adjust (On Truck)
All models 5

Steering Gear Assy., R&R or Renew
All models 1.0

Steering Gear, R&R and Recondition
Includes: Disassemble, renew parts as required, reassemble and adjust.
All models 1.9

Sector Shaft Oil Seal, Renew
All models 8

POWER STEERING

Power Steering Pump Pressure Check
All models 5

Pump Drive Belt, Renew
All models 3

Power Steering Gear, R&R or Renew
All models 2.0

Power Steering Gear, R&R and Recondition
Includes: Disassemble, renew all parts as required, reassemble and adjust.
All models 2.7

Steering Gear Sector Shaft, Adjust
All models 6

Sector Shaft Oil Seals, Renew
Includes: Renew inner and outer seals.
All models 2.1

Gear Control Valve Assy., Renew
All models 3.1

Power Steering Pump, Test and Renew
Includes: Transfer or renew pulley as required.
All models 1.0

Power Steering Pump, R&R and Recondition
All models 1.9

Pump Flow Control Valve, Test and Clean or Renew
All models 9

Power Steering Pump Reservoir, Renew
Includes: Renew seals.
All models 6

LABOR 11 STEERING GEAR 11 LABOR

(Factory Time) Chilton Time

Pump Drive Shaft Oil Seal, Renew
All models.......... 1.6

Power Steering Hoses, Renew
All models
pressure.......... .9
return.......... .9
supply.......... .4

LABOR 12 CYLINDER HEAD & VALVE SYSTEM 12 LABOR

(Factory Time) Chilton Time

GASOLINE ENGINE

Compression Test
All models.......... .6

Cylinder Head Gasket, Renew
Includes: Clean carbon. Minor tune up.
All models.......... 3.5

Cylinder Head, Renew
Includes: Reface and adjust valves, clean carbon. Minor tune up.
All models.......... 6.5

Clean Carbon and Grind Valves
Includes: R&R cylinder head, reface valves and seats. Minor tune up.
All models.......... 6.2

Jet Valve, Renew
All models-one or all.......... 1.1

Cylinder Head Cover Gasket, Renew
All models.......... .6

Valve Rocker Arms, Renew
All models
all-one side.......... 1.4
all-both sides.......... 2.3

Valve Tappets, Renew (Lifters)
All models
2.6L eng-one or all.......... 1.1

Valve Springs or Valve Stem Oil Seals, Renew (Head on Car)
All models-one cyl.......... 1.3
all cyls.......... 3.0

Valve Clearance, Adjust
All models.......... 1.5

DIESEL ENGINE

Compression Test
All models.......... .6

Cylinder Head Gasket, Renew
Includes: Clean carbon. Make all necessary adjustments.
All models.......... 3.5

Cylinder Head, Renew
Includes: Reface and adjust valves, clean carbon. Make all necessary adjustments.
All models.......... 6.2

Clean Carbon and Grind Valves
Includes: R&R cylinder head, reface valves and seats. Make all necessary adjustments.
All models.......... 5.5

Cylinder Head Cover Gasket, Renew
All models.......... .6

Valve Rocker Arms, Renew
All models.......... 1.1

Valve Springs and/or Valve Stem Oil Seals, Renew (All)
All models.......... 4.2

Valve Clearance, Adjust
All models.......... 1.5

LABOR 13 ENGINE ASSEMBLY & MOUNTS 13 LABOR

(Factory Time) Chilton Time

GASOLINE ENGINES

Note: All engine operations listed in this group are for assemblies as supplied by the original equipment manufacturer. Time to replace assemblies from independent rebuilders may vary.

Engine Assembly, Remove and Install
Does not include transfer of any parts or equipment.
All models.......... 5.9
w/A.C. add.......... .6
4X4 add.......... 1.7

Short Engine Assembly, Renew (w/All Internal Parts Less Head and Oil Pan)
Includes: R&R engine, transfer all necessary parts not supplied with replacement engine. Clean carbon, grind valves. Minor tune up.
All models.......... 15.1
w/A.C. add.......... .6
4X4 add.......... 1.7

Engine Assy., R&R and Recondition
Includes: Rebore block, install new pistons, pins, rings, rod and main bearings. Clean carbon, grind valves. Tune engine.
All models.......... 20.8
w/A.C. add.......... .6
4X4 add.......... 1.7

Engine Mounts, Renew
All models-front.......... .7
rear.......... .6

DIESEL ENGINE

Engine Assembly, Remove and Install
Does not include transfer of any parts or equipment.
All models.......... 5.1
w/A.C. add.......... .6

Short Engine Assembly, Renew (w/All Internal Parts Less Cyl. Head and Oil Pan)
Includes: R&R engine assy. Transfer all necessary parts not supplied with replacement engine. Clean carbon, grind valves. Make all necessary adjustments.
All models.......... 14.7
w/A.C. add.......... .6

Engine Mounts, Renew
All models-one.......... .5
both.......... .7

LABOR 14 PISTONS, RINGS & BEARINGS 14 LABOR

(Factory Time) Chilton Time

GASOLINE ENGINES

Rings, Renew
Includes: Replace connecting rod bearings, deglaze cylinder walls, remove cylinder top ridge, clean carbon from cylinder head. Minor tune up.
4X2 models.......... 8.5
4X4 models.......... 10.4

Connecting Rod Bearings, Renew
4X2 models.......... 3.0
4X4 models.......... 4.9

Pistons or Connecting Rods, Renew
Includes: Replace connecting rod bearings, deglaze cylinder walls, remove cylinder top ridge, replace piston rings. Clean carbon from cylinder head. Minor tune up.
4X2 models.......... 9.7
4X4 models.......... 11.6

LABOR 14 PISTONS, RINGS & BEARINGS 14 LABOR

(Factory Time) Chilton Time

DIESEL ENGINE

Rings, Renew

Includes: Replace connecting rod bearings, deglaze cylinder walls, remove cylinder top ridge, clean carbon from cylinder head. Make all necessary adjustments.

	Chilton Time
All models	7.1

Pistons or Connecting Rods, Renew

Includes: Replace connecting rod bearings, deglaze cylinder walls, remove cylinder top ridge, replace piston rings. Clean carbon from cylinder head. Make all necessary adjustments.

	Chilton Time
All models	8.3

Connecting Rod Bearings, Renew

	Chilton Time
All models	3.1

COMBINATIONS

Add to Engine Work

	Chilton Time
DRAIN, EVACUATE & RECHARGE AIR CONDITIONING SYSTEM	
All models	1.4
DISTRIBUTOR, RECONDITION	
All models	1.0
CARBURETOR, RECONDITION	
All models	1.6
DEGLAZE CYLINDER WALLS	
Each	.1
REMOVE CYLINDER TOP RIDGE	
Each	.1
RECONDITION CYLINDER HEAD (HEAD REMOVED)	
All models	2.5
MAIN BEARINGS, RENEW (PAN REMOVED)	
All models	1.5
PLASTIGAUGE BEARINGS	
Each	.1
RENEW OIL PUMP	
All models	1.7
OIL FILTER ELEMENT, RENEW	
All models	.2

LABOR 15 CRANKSHAFT & DAMPER 15 LABOR

(Factory Time) Chilton Time

GASOLINE ENGINES

Crankshaft and Main Bearings, Renew

Includes: R&R engine assembly.

	Chilton Time
All models	12.0
4X4 add	1.7
w/A.C. add	.6

Main Bearings, Renew

Includes: Replace pan gasket and oil seals, plastigauge all bearings.

	Chilton Time
4X2 models	5.5
4X4 models	7.8

Main and Rod Bearings, Renew

Includes: Replace pan gasket and oil seals, plastigauge all bearings.

	Chilton Time
4X2 models	6.7
4X4 models	9.0

Crankshaft Rear Main Oil Seal, Renew (Complete)

	Chilton Time
All models	
w/M.T.	3.5
w/A.T.	4.0
4X4 add	1.7

Crankshaft Front Oil Seal, Renew

	Chilton Time
All models	
2.0L eng	1.9
w/A.C. add	.6
w/P.S. add	.1

Crankshaft Pulley, Renew

	Chilton Time
All models	.6
w/A.C. add	.2
w/P.S. add	.1

DIESEL ENGINE

Crankshaft and Main Bearings, Renew

Includes: R&R engine assembly.

	Chilton Time
All models	10.5
w/A.C. add	.6

Main Bearings, Renew

Includes: Plastigauge all bearings.

	Chilton Time
All models	3.4

Main and Rod Bearings, Renew

Includes: Plastigauge all bearings.

	Chilton Time
All models	4.6

Crankshaft Pulley, Renew

	Chilton Time
All models	.6
w/A.C. add	.1
w/P.S. add	.1

Crankshaft Front Oil Seal, Renew

	Chilton Time
All models	1.7
w/A.C. add	.6

LABOR 16 CAMSHAFT & TIMING GEARS 16 LABOR

(Factory Time) Chilton Time

GASOLINE ENGINES

Timing Belt, Renew

	Chilton Time
All models	
cam drive	1.7
shaft drive	1.8
w/P.S. add	.1
w/A.C. add	.6

Timing Belt Tensioner, Renew

	Chilton Time
All models	
cam drive	1.8
shaft drive	1.9
w/P.S. add	.1
w/A.C. add	.6

Timing Belt Cover, Renew

	Chilton Time
All models	
upper	.3
lower	1.0
w/A.C. add	.6

Timing Chain Cover Gasket, Renew

	Chilton Time
All models	4.4
Renew timing chain guide add-each	.2
w/A.C. add	.6

Timing Chain, Renew

Includes: Renew cover oil seal.

	Chilton Time
All models	
cam drive	5.4
silent shaft drive	4.9
w/A.C. add	.6

Timing Chain Tensioner, Renew

Includes: Renew cover oil seal.

	Chilton Time
All models	5.5
w/A.C. add	.6

Timing Chain Cover Oil Seal, Renew

	Chilton Time
All models	1.1
w/A.C. add	.6

Camshaft, Renew

	Chilton Time
All models	3.0

Camshaft Sprocket, Renew

Includes: Renew crankshaft gear and timing chain if required.

	Chilton Time
All models	
chain driven	5.0
belt driven	1.8
w/A.C. add	.6

Silent Shaft or Bearings, Renew

	Chilton Time
All models	
chain drive	
right	5.3
left	4.9
both	5.5
belt drive	
one	4.0
all	4.2
Renew shaft brg add	
each	.2
w/A.C. add	.6

DIESEL ENGINE

Timing Belt Cover, Renew

	Chilton Time
All models	
upper	.3
lower	1.0

Timing Belt, Renew

	Chilton Time
All models	
cam drive	1.6
silent shaft drive	1.8
w/A.C. add	.6

LABOR 16 CAMSHAFT & TIMING GEARS 16 LABOR

(Factory Time) Chilton Time

Timing Belt Tensioner, Renew
All models
cam drive 1.7
silent shaft drive 1.9
w/A.C. add 6

Camshaft, Renew
All models 2.0

Silent Shaft, Renew
All models
right side 2.5
left side 4.0
both sides 4.5
w/A.C. add 6

Silent Shaft Oil Seal, Renew
All models 1.9
w/A.C. add 6

LABOR 17 ENGINE OILING SYSTEM 17 LABOR

(Factory Time) Chilton Time

GASOLINE ENGINES

Oil Pan or Gasket, Renew
4X2 models 1.5
4X4 models 3.6

Pressure Test Engine Bearings (Pan Off)
All models 1.0

Oil Pump, Renew
4X2 models 4.5
4X4 models 7.4

Oil Pump, R&R and Recondition
4X2 models 4.7
4X4 models 7.6

Oil Pressure Sending Unit, Renew
All models 5

Oil Pressure Gauge, Renew
All models 6

Oil Filter Element, Renew
All models 3

DIESEL ENGINE

Oil Pan and/or Gasket, Renew
All models 1.6

Oil Pump, Renew
All models 3.4

Oil Filter Element, Renew
All models 3

LABOR 18 CLUTCH & FLYWHEEL 18 LABOR

(Factory Time) Chilton Time

Clutch Pedal Free Play, Adjust
All models 4

Clutch Release Cable, Renew
All models 5

Clutch Slave Cylinder, Renew
Includes: Bleed system.
All models 7

Clutch Master Cylinder, Renew
Includes: Bleed system.
All models 1.0

Clutch Assembly, Renew
Includes: R&R trans and adjust clutch pedal free play.
All models
4X2 .... 3.0
4X4 .... 5.3
Renew input shaft seal add 2

Clutch Release Bearing, Renew
Includes: R&R trans and adjust clutch pedal free play.
All models
4X2 .... 2.8
4X4 .... 4.7
Renew clutch fork add 2

Flywheel, Renew
Includes: R&R transmission.
All models
4X2 .... 3.3
4X4 .... 5.6
Renew ring gear add 4

LABOR 19 STANDARD TRANSMISSION 19 LABOR

(Factory Time) Chilton Time

Transmission Assembly, R&R or Renew
All models
4X2 .... 2.7
4X4 .... 5.0
Renew trans add 6

Transmission Assy., R&R and Recondition
Includes: Complete disassembly, clean and inspect or renew all parts. Install new gaskets and seals.
All models
4 Speed
4X2 .... 5.6
4X4 .... 8.0
5 Speed
4X2 .... 8.7
4X4 .... 11.0

Speedometer Driven Pinion, Renew
Includes: Renew oil seal.
All models 4

Extension Housing Oil Seal, Renew
5 Speed 7

TRANSFER CASE

Transfer Case Assy., Remove & Reinstall
All models 3.9
Renew assy add 8

Transfer Case, R&R and Recondition
All models 6.9

Transfer Case Drive Chain, Renew
All models 6.4

LABOR 21 SHIFT LINKAGE 21 LABOR

(Factory Time) Chilton Time

STANDARD

Gearshift Lever, Renew
All models 6

Gearshift Lever Boot, Renew
All models 3

AUTOMATIC

Shift Linkage, Adjust
All models 4

Throttle Linkage, Adjust
All models 3

Gearshift Lever, Renew
All models 7

Gear Selector Indicator Assy., Renew
All models 6

LABOR 23 AUTOMATIC TRANSMISSION 23 LABOR

(Factory Time) Chilton Time

ON CAR SERVICES

Drain & Refill Unit
All models........ 1.0

Oil Pressure Check
All models........ .9

Check Unit For Oil Leaks
Includes: Clean and dry outside of case and run unit to determine point of leak.
All models........ .9

Neutral Safety Switch, Renew
All models........ .4

Throttle Linkage, Adjust
All models........ .3

Throttle Valve Lever Shaft Seal, Renew
All models........ .6

Valve Body Manual Level Shaft Seal, Renew
All models........ 1.0

Extension Housing Oil Seal, Renew
All models........ .9

Extension Housing Gasket, Renew
All models........ 2.0
Renew bushing add........ .3

Governor Assy., Renew or Recondition
Includes: R&R extension housing.
All models........ 2.4

Parking Lock Sprag, Renew
Includes: R&R extension housing.
All models........ 2.2

Oil Pan Gasket, Renew
All models........ .8

Oil Filter, Renew
All models........ 1.0

Accumulator Piston, Renew or Recondition
Includes: R&R oil pan.
All models........ 1.6

Servo's, Renew or Recondition
Includes: R&R oil pan and adjust band.
All models
kickdown........ 1.5
reverse........ 1.4

Valve Body Assembly, Renew
Includes: R&R oil pan.
All models........ 1.5

Valve Body Assy., R&R and Recondition
Includes: R&R oil pan and replace filter. Disassemble, clean, inspect, free all valves. Replace parts as required.
All models........ 3.0

Bands, Adjust
Includes: R&R oil pan.
All models
kickdown........ 1.2
reverse........ 1.2
both........ 1.9

SERVICES REQUIRING R&R

Transmission Assembly, R&R or Renew
Includes: Drain and refill unit.
All models
4X2........ 3.2
4X4........ 5.6
Renew trans add........ .6
Flush converter and cooler lines add........ .7

Transmission Assembly, Reseal
Includes: R&R trans and renew all seals and gaskets.
All models
4X2........ 6.0
4X4........ 8.4

Transmission and Converter, R&R and Recondition
Includes: Disassemble trans including valve body, clean, inspect and replace all parts as required.
All models
4X2........ 9.5
4X4........ 12.0

Torque Converter or Drive Plate, Renew
Includes: R&R trans.
All models
4X2........ 3.6
4X4........ 5.8

Front Pump Assy., and/or Bushing, Renew
Includes: R&R trans.
All models
4X2........ 4.0
4X4........ 6.4

Front Pump Oil Seal, Renew
Includes: R&R trans.
All models
4X2........ 3.5
4X4........ 5.8

LABOR 25 U-JOINTS & DRIVESHAFT 25 LABOR

(Factory Time) Chilton Time

Driveshaft, Renew
All models
trans to rear........ .8
center brg to rear........ 1.2
transfer case to ft. axle........ .8
transfer case to rear axle........ .7
trans to center brg........ 1.6

Universal Joints, Renew
Single Piece Shaft
trans to rear axle........ .9
transfer case to rear axle........ .8
at front axle........ .9
Two Piece Shaft
trans to center brg........ 1.0
center brg to rear axle........ 1.0
at rear axle........ 1.0

Center Bearing, Renew
All models........ 1.3

LABOR 26 DRIVE AXLE 26 LABOR

(Factory Time) Chilton Time

REAR DIFFERENTIAL

Axle Shaft and/or Bearing, Renew
Includes: Renew oil seal.
All models-one........ 2.1
both........ 3.0

Axle Shaft Oil Seal, Renew
All models-one........ 1.3
both........ 2.4

Axle Shaft Wheel Mounting Studs, Renew
All models-one........ .5
each adtnl........ .1

Pinion Shaft Oil Seal, Renew
All models........ .7

Differential Carrier Gasket, Renew
All models........ 2.9

Differential Carrier Assy., R&R or Renew
All models........ 3.3

Differential Side Bearings, Renew
Includes: Renew pinion oil seal and adjust backlash.
All models........ 4.3

Differential Side Gears, Renew
Includes: Renew axle shaft oil seals.
All models........ 4.8

Ring Gear and Pinion Set, Renew
Includes: Renew axle shaft and pinion seals. Make all necessary adjustments.
All models........ 5.5

Rear Axle Housing, Renew
Includes: Renew pinion oil seal, inner and outer axle shaft seals and gaskets. Bleed brakes.
All models........ 4.1

FRONT DIFFERENTIAL

Front Axle Housing Cover, Renew or Reseal
All models........ .6

Drive Pinion Oil Seal, Renew
All models........ .8

Drive Axle Shaft, Renew
All models
outer........ 2.0
inner........ 1.6

Driveshaft Boot, Renew
All models-one side........ 1.9

Driveshaft C/V Joint, Renew
All models-inner........ 1.8

Differential Side Bearings, Renew
All models........ 4.9

Ring Gear and Pinion Set, Renew
All models........ 5.6
Renew diff case add........ .2

LABOR 27 REAR SUSPENSION 27 LABOR

(Factory Time) Chilton Time

Rear Spring, Renew
All models-one........ 1.1
both........ 2.0

Rear Spring Front Eye Bushing, Renew
All models-one........ 1.0
both........ 1.8

Rear Spring Shackle or Bushing, Renew
All models-one side........ .9
both sides........ 1.5

Rear Shock Absorbers, Renew
All models-one........ .4
both........ .6

LABOR 28 AIR CONDITIONING 28 LABOR

(Factory Time) Chilton Time

Note: If more than one item requires replacement where evacuation and discharging the system is already included in the operation, deduct 1.0 hour for each additional item to the times listed.

Drain, Evacuate, Leak Test & Charge System
All models........ 1.0

Flush Refrigerant System, Complete
To be used in conjunction with component replacement which could contaminate system.
All models........ 1.3

Partial Charge
Includes: Leak test.
All models........ .6

Compressor Belt, Renew
All models........ .3

Compressor Assembly, Renew
Includes: Pressure test and charge system.
All models........ 3.0

Compressor Clutch Assy., Renew
All models........ .6

Expansion Valve, Renew
Includes: Pressure test and charge system.
All models........ 3.1
Renew receiver drier add........ .2

Receiver-Drier, Renew
Includes: Add partial charge, leak test and charge system.
All models........ 1.5

High Pressure Cut-Off Switch, Renew
All models........ .4

Thermostatic Control Clutch Cycling Switch, Renew
All models........ 1.0

Condenser Assembly, Renew
Includes: Add partial charge, leak test and charge system.
All models........ 2.3
Renew receiver drier add........ .2

Water Valve, Renew (With Air Conditioning)
All models........ 1.0

Temperature Control Assy., Renew
All models........ 1.5

Blower Motor Switch, Renew
All models........ .6

Blower Motor, Renew
All models........ 1.6

Blower Motor Resistor, Renew
All models........ 1.1

Evaporator Core, Renew
Includes: Add partial charge, leak test and charge system.
All models........ 3.9

Air Conditioning Hoses, Renew
Includes: Add partial charge, leak test and charge system.
All models-suction........ 1.7
discharge........ 1.7
Renew receiver drier add........ .2

LABOR 29 LOCKS, HINGES & WIND. REGULATORS 29 LABOR

(Factory Time) Chilton Time

Hood Hinge, Renew (One)
Does not include painting.
All models........ .8

Hood Latch, Renew
All models........ .6

Hood Lock Release Cable, Renew
All models........ .9

Door Lock Remote Control, Renew
All models........ .6

Lock Striker Plate, Renew
All models........ .3

Door Handle (Outside), Renew
All models........ .5

Door and Ignition Lock Cylinders, Renew
Includes: R&R both door lock cylinders and ignition lock to renew or recode.
All models........ 1.5

Window Regulator, Renew
All models-one........ .9

LABOR 30 HEAD AND PARKING LAMPS 30 LABOR

(Factory Time) Chilton Time

Aim Headlamps
All models........ .4

Head Lamp Sealed Beam Bulb, Renew
All models-each........ .3

Parking Lamp Lens or Bulb, Renew
All models........ .3

Tail Lamp Lens or Bulb, Renew
All models........ .3

Side Marker Lamp Assy., Renew
All models........ .4

License Lamp Assembly, Renew
All models........ .3

LABOR 31 WINDSHIELD WIPER & SPEEDOMETER 31 LABOR

(Factory Time) Chilton Time

Windshield Wiper Motor, Renew
All models........ .7

Wiper Switch, Renew
All models........ .4

Washer Pump, Renew
All models
front........ .5
rear........ .6

Windshield Wiper Linkage, Renew
All models........ .8

Speedometer Head, R&R or Renew
Does not include reset odometer.
All models........ 1.2

Speedometer Cable and Casing, Renew
All models........ .9

Speedometer Cable (Inner), Renew or Lubricate
All models........ .4

Speedometer Driven Pinion, Renew
Includes: Renew oil seal.
All models........ .4

Radio, R&R
All models........ .5

LABOR 32 LIGHT SWITCHES & WIRING 32 LABOR

	(Factory Time)	Chilton Time
Headlamp Switch, Renew		
All models		.4
Headlamp Dimmer Switch, Renew		
All models		.4
Horn Switch, Renew		
All models		.4
Neutral Safety (w/Back-Up Lamp) Switch, Renew		
All models		.4
Parking Brake Warning Lamp Switch, Renew		
All models		.3
Stop Light Switch, Renew		
All models		.3
Combination Switch (Turn Signal/Dimmer), Renew		
All models		1.0
Turn Signal, Washer/Wiper Lever Assy., Renew		
All models		.9
Turn Signal or Hazard Warning Flasher, Renew		
All models		.3
Horn, Renew		
All models		.3

LABOR 34 CRUISE CONTROL 34 LABOR

	(Factory Time)	Chilton Time
Speed Control Servo/Motor Assy., Renew		
All models		.7
Speed Control Valve Body, Renew		
All models		.5
Speed Control Clutch Safety Cut-Out Switch, Renew		
All models		.5
Speed Control and Turn Signal Lever Switch, Renew		
All models		.4
Speed Control Vacuum Actuator, Renew		
All models		.3
Speed Control Module, Renew		
All models		.3

GROUP INDEX

ALPHABETICAL INDEX

LABOR 1 TUNE UP 1 LABOR

	(Factory Time)	Chilton Time
Compression Test		
All models		.6
Engine Tune Up, (Electronic Ignition)		
Includes: Test battery and clean connections. Tighten manifold and carburetor mounting bolts. Check engine compression, clean and adjust or renew spark plugs. Test resistance of spark plug cables. Inspect distributor cap and rotor. Check vacuum advance operation. Reset ignition timing. Adjust idle mixture and idle speed. Service air cleaner. Inspect and adjust drive belts. Inspect choke operation and adjust or free up. Check operation of EGR valve.		
All models		1.5

LABOR 2 IGNITION SYSTEM 2 LABOR

	(Factory Time)	Chilton Time
GASOLINE ENGINE		
Spark Plugs, Clean and Reset or Renew		
All models		.5
Ignition Timing, Reset		
All models		.4
Distributor, Renew		
Includes: Reset ignition timing.		
All models		.6
Distributor Cap and/or Rotor, Renew		
All models		.4
Ignition Coil, Renew		
Includes: Test coil.		
All models		.4
Renew igniter add		.1
Vacuum Control Unit, Renew		
Includes: Reset ignition timing and dwell.		
All models		.7
Ignition Cables, Renew		
All models		.4
Ignition Switch, Renew		
All models		.5
Ignition Switch Lock Cylinder, Renew		
Includes: Recode cylinder.		
All models		1.0
DIESEL ENGINE		
Glow Plugs, Renew		
All models-one		.5
all		.8
Glow Plug Control Switch, Renew		
All models		.3
Coolant Fast Idle Temperature Switch, Renew		
All models		.3
Glow Plug Relay, Renew		
All models-one		.3

LABOR 3 FUEL SYSTEM 3 LABOR

	(Factory Time)	Chilton Time
GASOLINE ENGINE		
Fuel Pump, Test		
Includes: Disconnect line at carburetor, attach pressure gauge.		
All models		.3
Carburetor Air Cleaner, Service		
All models		.2
Air Cleaner Vacuum Motor, Renew		
All models		.4
Air Cleaner Temperature Sensor, Renew		
All models		.5
Carburetor, Adjust (On Truck)		
Includes: Adjust curb and fast idle speed, choke and choke vacuum break adjustments.		
All models		.5
Choke Assembly, Renew		
All models		.8
Float or Needle Valve and Seat, Renew		
All models		1.0
Carburetor, Renew		
Includes: All necessary adjustments.		
All models		1.1
Carburetor, R&R and Clean or Recondition		
Includes: All necessary adjustments.		
All models		2.9
Anti-Dieseling or Idle Stop Solenoid, Renew		
All models		.6
Fuel Gauge (Dash), Renew		
P/up		1.0
Trooper		.7
Fuel Gauge (Tank), Renew		
Includes: Drain and refill tank.		
All models		.7
Fuel Tank, Renew		
Includes: Drain and refill tank.		
All models		1.7
Fuel Pump, Renew		
All models		.9
Add pump test if performed.		
Fuel Pump Relay, Renew		
All models		.3
Intake Manifold or Gasket, Renew		
All models		1.5
Renew manif add		.5
DIESEL ENGINE		
Air Cleaner, Service		
All models		.3
Idle Speed, Adjust		
All models		.3
Injection Pump Timing, Adjust		
All models		.9
w/A.C. add		.2
w/Turbo add		.7
Vacuum Pump, Renew		
All models		.6
Recond pump add		.4
Vacuum Pump Valve, Renew		
All models		.5
High Pressure Fuel Lines, Renew		
All models-one		.5
all		.9
Fuel Injection Nozzles and/or Seals, Renew		
All models-one		.6
all		1.0
Clean nozzles add-each		.2
Fuel Injection Pump, Renew		
All models		3.5
w/A.C. add		.3
w/Turbo add		.7
Intake Manifold or Gasket, Renew		
All models		.8
w/A.C. add		.2
w/P.S. add		.1
w/Turbo add		.2
TURBOCHARGER		
Turbocharger Assy., R&R or Renew		
All models		2.4
Turbocharger Wastegate Actuator, Renew		
All models		.4

LABOR 3A EMISSION CONTROLS 3A LABOR

(Factory Time) Chilton Time

CLOSED LOOP EMISSION CONTROL

Oxygen Sensor, Renew
All models 5

Coolant Temperature Sensor, Renew
All models 4

Electronic Control Module, Renew
All models 8

Idle and Wide Open Throttle Switch, Renew
All models 5

Solenoid and Vacuum Regulator Assy., Renew
All models 4

Barometric Switch, Renew
All models 3

CRS SYSTEM

Engine Speed Sensor, Renew
All models 4

Accelerator Switch, Renew
All models 4

Clutch Switch, Renew
All models 4

Neutral Switch, Renew
All models 5

(Factory Time) Chilton Time

AIR INJECTION SYSTEM

Air Pump, Renew
All models 8

Air Manifold Check Valve, Renew
All models 4

Air Injection Manifold, Renew
All models 1.2

Air Switching Valve, Renew
All models 4

Mixture Control Valve, Renew
All models 6

Vacuum Switching Valve, Renew
All models 4

EGR SYSTEM

EGR Valve, Renew
All models 8

Thermal Vacuum Valve, Renew
All models 4

Back Pressure Tranducer, Renew
All models 5

EFE SYSTEM

EFE Heater, Renew
All models 1.1

EFE Temperature Switch, Renew
All models 4

(Factory Time) Chilton Time

EVAPORATIVE EMISSIONS

Charcoal Canister, Renew
All models 4

Fuel Vapor Separator, Renew
All models 4

Check and Relief Valve, Renew
All models 3

HEATED AIR INLET SYSTEM

Air Cleaner Vacuum Motor, Renew
All models 4

Air Cleaner Temperature Sensor, Renew
All models 5

Idle Compensator, Renew
All models 5

DIESEL EMISSION CONTROLS

EGR Controller, Renew
All models 4

EGR Valve or Gasket, Renew
All models 6

Vacuum Switching Valve, Renew
All models 4

Thermal Vacuum Valve, Renew
All models 4

Vacuum Regulator Valve, Renew
All models 3

LABOR 4 ALTERNATOR AND REGULATOR 4 LABOR

(Factory Time) Chilton Time

Alternator Circuits, Test
Includes: Test battery, regulator and alternator output.
All models 5

Alternator, Renew
Includes: Transfer pulley and fan.
All models
Gas 7
Diesel 1.0
Add circuit test if performed.

(Factory Time) Chilton Time

Alternator, R&R and Recondition
Includes: Complete disassembly, inspect, test, replace parts as required, reassemble.
All models
Gas 2.2
Diesel 2.5

Alternator Bearings, Renew
Includes: R&R alternator, separate end frames.
All models
Gas 1.0

(Factory Time) Chilton Time

Diesel 1.6

Voltage Regulator, Test and Renew
All models
External 6
Internal 1.7

Voltmeter, Renew
P/up 4

LABOR 5 STARTING SYSTEM 5 LABOR

(Factory Time) Chilton Time

Starter Draw Test (On Truck)
All models 3

Starter, Renew
All models 9
Add draw test if performed.

Starter, R&R and Recondition
All models 2.3
Renew field coils add 4
Add draw test if performed.

(Factory Time) Chilton Time

Starter Drive, Renew
Includes: R&R starter.
All models 1.2

Starter Solenoid, Renew
Includes: R&R starter.
All models 1.2

(Factory Time) Chilton Time

Starter Relay, Renew
All models 3

Battery Cables, Renew
All models-each 4

Battery Terminals, Clean
All models 3

LABOR 6 BRAKE SYSTEM 6 LABOR

(Factory Time) Chilton Time

Brake Pedal Free Play, Adjust
All models 3

Bleed Brakes (Four Wheels)
Includes: Fill master cylinder.
All models 6

(Factory Time) Chilton Time

Brakes, Adjust (Minor)
Includes: Adjust brake shoes and fill master cylinder.
two wheels 4
four wheels 7

(Factory Time) Chilton Time

Free Up or Renew Brake Self Adjusting Units
one 7
each adtnl 4

Brake Combination Valve, Renew
All models 7

LABOR 6 BRAKE SYSTEM 6 LABOR

(Factory Time) Chilton Time

Brake Shoes, Renew

Includes: Install new or exchange brake shoes, adjust service and hand brake. Bleed system.

front	1.3
rear	1.7
all four wheels	2.9
Resurface brake drum, add-each	.5

Brake Shoes and/or Pads, Renew

Includes: Install new or exchange brake shoes or pads, adjust service and hand brake. Bleed system.

front-disc	.8
rear-drum	1.7
all four wheels	2.3
Resurface brake rotor, add-each	.9
Resurface brake drum, add-each	.5

Brake Drum, Renew

front-one	.7
rear-one	.5

BRAKE HYDRAULIC SYSTEM

Wheel Cylinder, Renew

Includes: Bleed system.

front-one	.9
both	1.8
rear-one	.9
both	1.8
all four wheels	3.5

Wheel Cylinder, R&R and Rebuild

Includes: Bleed system.

front-one	1.2
both	2.4
rear-one	1.2
both	2.4
all four wheels	4.7

Master Cylinder, Renew

Includes: Bleed system.

All models	.9

COMBINATIONS

Add to Brakes, Renew

	Chilton Time
RENEW WHEEL CYLINDER	
Each	.2
REBUILD WHEEL CYLINDER	
Each	.3
REBUILD CALIPER ASSEMBLY	
Each	.5
RENEW MASTER CYLINDER	
All models	.5
REBUILD MASTER CYLINDER	
All models	.8
RENEW BRAKE HOSE	
Each	.3
REPACK FRONT WHEEL BEARINGS (BOTH WHEELS)	
Drum brakes	.4
Disc brakes	.6
RENEW BRAKE DRUM	
Each	.1
RENEW DISC BRAKE ROTOR	
Each	.4

(Factory Time) Chilton Time

Master Cylinder, R&R and Rebuild

Includes: Hone cylinder and bleed system.

All models	1.5

Brake Hose, Renew

Includes: Bleed system.

front-one	.7
both	1.1
rear	.8

DISC BRAKES

Disc Brake Pads, Renew

Includes: Install new disc brake pads only.

front-disc	.8

Caliper Assembly, Renew

Includes: Bleed system.

All models-one	1.0
both	1.7

Caliper Assy., R&R and Recondition

Includes: Bleed system.

All models-one	1.5
both	2.7

Disc Brake Rotor, Renew

All models-one	1.2
both	2.1

POWER BRAKES

Power Brake Cylinder, Renew

All models	1.0

Power Brake Cylinder, R&R and Recondition

All models	2.0

Check Valve, Renew

All models	.3

PARKING BRAKE

Parking Brake, Adjust

All models	.5

Parking Brake Control, Renew

All models	.8

Parking Brake Cables, Renew

front	1.1
rear-both	2.0
center	.9

LABOR 7 COOLING SYSTEM 7 LABOR

(Factory Time) Chilton Time

Winterize Cooling System

Includes: Run engine to check for leaks, tighten all hose connections. Test radiator and pressure cap, drain radiator and engine block. Add anti-freeze and refill system.

All models	.5

Thermostat, Renew

All models	
Gas	.5
Diesel	.8

Radiator Assy., R&R or Renew

Includes: Drain and refill cooling system.

All models	.9

ADD THESE OPERATIONS TO RADIATOR R&R

Boil & Repair	1.5
Rod Clean	1.9
Repair Core	1.3
Renew Tank	1.6
Renew Trans. Oil Cooler	1.9
Recore Radiator	1.7

Radiator Hoses, Renew

All models-each	.4

Fan Blade, Renew

All models	.5

Fan Clutch, Renew

All models	.6

Drive Belt, Renew

All models-one	.3
each adtnl	.1

Drive Belt, Adjust

All models-one	.2
each adtnl	.1

Water Pump, Renew

All models	
Gas	
1.8-2.0L engs	1.4
2.3L eng	4.0
Diesel	1.2
w/A.C. add	.3
w/P.S. add	.3
w/A.T. add	.2

Water Jacket Expansion Plugs, Renew (Side of Block)

each	.5

Note: If necessary to R&R any component to gain access to plug, add appropriate time.

Temperature Gauge (Dash Unit), Renew

P/up	1.0
Trooper	.7

Temperature Gauge (Engine Unit), Renew

All models	.5

Heater Core, R&R or Renew

All models	5.5

ADD THESE OPERATIONS TO HEATER CORE R&R

Boil & Repair	1.2
Repair Core	.9
Recore	1.2

Heater Blower Motor, Renew

All models	1.8

Blower Motor Resistor, Renew

All models	.4

Temperature Control Assy., Renew

All models	.7

Heater Hose, Renew

All models	.4

LABOR 8 EXHAUST SYSTEM 8 LABOR

(Factory Time) — Chilton Time

Muffler, Renew
All models 8

Exhaust Pipe Packing, Renew
All models 1.0

Front Exhaust Pipe, Renew
All models 1.0

Catalytic Converter, Renew
All models 1.1

Catalytic Converter Catalyst, Renew
All models 9

Intermediate Exhaust Pipe, Renew
All models 8

Tail Pipe, Renew
All models 7

Exhaust Manifold or Gasket, Renew
All models
Gas
1981 .... 1.9
1982-88 .... 1.0
Diesel *1.2
*w/A.C. add 2
*w/P.S. add 1
*w/Turbo add 2

LABOR 9 FRONT SUSPENSION 9 LABOR

(Factory Time) — Chilton Time

Note: On all front suspension operations alignment charges must be added if performed. Time given does not include alignment.

Wheel, Renew
one 5

Wheels, Rotate (All)
All models 5

Wheel, Balance
one 3
each adntl 2

Check Alignment of Front End
All models 5
Note: Deduct if alignment is performed.

Toe-In, Adjust
All models 6

Align Front End
All models 1.4

Front Wheel Grease Seals, Renew
4x2 models
one 5
both 8
4x4 models
one 6
both 1.0

Front Wheel Bearings and Cups, Renew (Inner & Outer)
4x2 models
one side 8
both sides 1.5
4x4 models
one side 2.4
both sides 4.4

Front Shock Absorbers, Renew
All models-one 5
both 7

Front Strut Bar or Bushing, Renew
All models-one 4
both 7
Renew bushing add 3

Front Stabilizer Bar, Renew
All models 5
Renew bushings add 3

Steering Knuckle Assy., Renew
Add alignment charges.
4x2 models
one 1.2
both 2.1
4x4 models
one 1.4
both 2.5
Rebuild knuckle add-each 5

Upper Ball Joints, Renew
Add alignment charges.
4x2 models
one 1.0
both 1.7

Lower Ball Joints, Renew
Add alignment charges.
4x2 models
one 1.0
both 1.7

Front Torsion Bar, Renew
All models-one 8
both 1.2

Upper Control Arm Assy., Renew
Add alignment charges.
4x2 models
one 1.2
both 2.0
4x4 models
one 1.2
both 1.9
Renew bushings add, each 2

Lower Control Arm Assy., Renew
Add alignment charges.
4x2 models
one 2.5
both 4.5
4x4 models
one 1.6
both 2.8
Renew bushings add-each 3

Locking Hub Cam and/or Clutch Assy., Renew
auto lock-one 6
manual lock-one 9

LABOR 10 STEERING LINKAGE 10 LABOR

(Factory Time) — Chilton Time

Relay Rod, Renew
Includes: Reset toe-in.
All models 1.4

Pitman Arm, Renew
All models 6

Tie Rod or Tie Rod End, Renew
Includes: Reset toe-in.
All models-one side 1.0
both sides 1.4

Idler Arm, Renew
All models 7

Center Tie Rod Assy., Renew
Includes: Reset toe-in.
All models 1.2

LABOR 11 STEERING GEAR 11 LABOR

(Factory Time) — Chilton Time

STANDARD STEERING

Steering Wheel, Renew
All models 4

Flexible Coupling, Renew
All models 6

Steering Column, R&R or Renew
All models 1.3

Steering Gear, Adjust (On Truck)
All models 6

Steering Gear, R&R or Renew
All models 1.1

Steering Gear, R&R and Recondition
Includes: Disassemble, renew necessary parts, reassemble and adjust.
All models 2.8

POWER STEERING

Trouble Shoot Power Steering
Includes: Test pump and system pressure. Check pounds pull on steering wheel and check for leaks.
All models 5

Power Steering Gear, Adjust (On Truck)
All models 6

Pump Drive Belt, Renew
All models 3

Power Steering Gear, R&R or Renew
All models 1.5

LABOR 11 STEERING GEAR 11 LABOR

(Factory Time) Chilton Time

Power Steering Gear, R&R and Recondition
Includes: Disassemble, renew necessary parts, reassemble and adjust.
All models........ 2.7

Power Steering Pump, R&R or Renew
All models........ .9

Power Steering Pump, R&R and Recondition
All models........ 1.6

Power Steering Reservoir, Renew
All models........ .4

Pump Shaft Oil Seal, Renew
All models........ 1.0

Power Steering Hoses, Renew
All models
pressure........ .6
return........ .5

LABOR 12 CYLINDER HEAD & VALVE SYSTEM 12 LABOR

(Factory Time) Chilton Time

GASOLINE ENGINE

Compression Test
All models........ .6

Cylinder Head Gasket, Renew
Includes: Clean carbon and make all necessary adjustments.
All models........ 4.2
w/A.C. add........ .3
w/P.S. add........ .3

Cylinder Head, Renew
Includes: Transfer all component parts, reface valves, clean carbon, make all necessary adjustments.
All models........ 5.8
w/A.C. add........ .3
w/P.S. add........ .3

Clean Carbon and Grind Valves
Includes: R&R cylinder head, grind valves and seats. Minor tune up.
All models........ 6.9
w/A.C. add........ .3
w/P.S. add........ .3

Rocker Arm Cover or Gasket, Renew
All models........ .6

Rocker Arms, Renew
All models-one cyl........ 1.3
all cyls........ 1.6

Rocker Arm Shafts, Renew (One or Both)
All models........ 1.2

Valve Spring and/or Valve Stem Oil Seals, Renew (Head on Car)
All models-one cyl........ 1.5
each adtnl cyl........ .3
If nec to R&R head add........ 3.0

Valves, Adjust
All models........ 1.0

DIESEL ENGINE

Compression Test
All models........ 1.0

Cylinder Head Gasket, Renew
Includes: Clean carbon and make all necessary adjustments.
All models........ 4.4
w/A.C. add........ .3
w/P.S. add........ .2
w/Turbo add........ .7

Cylinder Head, Renew
Includes: Transfer parts as required. Make all necessary adjustments.
All models........ 5.0
w/A.C. add........ .3
w/P.S. add........ .2
w/Turbo add........ .7

Clean Carbon and Grind Valves
Includes: R&R cylinder head, reface valves and seats. Make all necessary adjustments.
All models........ 5.7
w/A.C. add........ .3
w/P.S. add........ .2
w/Turbo add........ .7

Rocker Arm Cover and/or Gasket, Renew
All models........ .6

Rocker Arms and/or Push Rods, Renew
All models-one cyl........ 1.3
all cyls........ 1.6

Rocker Arm Shaft, Renew
All models
one or both........ 1.2

Valve Clearance, Adjust
All models........ 1.0

Valve Springs and/or Valve Stem Oil Seals, Renew (Head on Truck)
All models
one cyl........ 1.5
each adtnl cyl........ .3
If necc to R&R head add........ 3.0

Valve Lifters, Renew (All)
Includes: R&R engine assy.
4X2 models........ 10.9
4X4 models........ 11.9

LABOR 13 ENGINE ASSEMBLY & MOUNTS 13 LABOR

(Factory Time) Chilton Time

GASOLINE ENGINE

Note: All engine operations listed in this group are for assemblies as supplied by the original equipment manufacturer. Time to replace assemblies from independent rebuilders may vary.

Engine Assembly, Remove & Install
Does not include transfer of any parts or equipment.
P/up........ *6.0
Trooper........ 7.0
w/A.C. add........ .3
w/P.S. add........ .3
w/A.T. add........ .2
*4X4 add........ 1.0

Cylinder Block, Renew (w/All Internal Parts Less Head and Oil Pan)
Includes: R&R engine assy., transfer all component parts not supplied with replacement engine, clean carbon, grind valves. Tune engine.
P/up........ *13.2
Trooper........ 14.2
w/A.C. add........ .3
w/P.S. add........ .3
w/A.T. add........ .2
*4X4 add........ 1.0

Engine Assy., R&R and Recondition
Includes: Rebore block, install new pistons, rings, rod and main bearings, clean carbon, grind valves. Tune engine.
P/up........ *24.3
Trooper........ 25.3
w/A.C. add........ .3
w/P.S. add........ .3
w/A.T. add........ .2
*4X4 add........ 1.0

Engine Mounts, Renew
Front
one........ .7
both........ 1.0
Rear........ .7

DIESEL ENGINE

Engine Assembly, Remove & Install
Does not include transfer of any parts or equipment.
4X2 models........ 7.4
4X4 models........ 8.8
w/A.T. add........ .3
w/A.C. add........ .3
w/P.S. add........ .3
w/Turbo add........ .2

Engine Assembly, Renew (Partial)
Includes: R&R engine assy. Transfer all component parts not supplied with replacement engine. Clean carbon, grind valves. Make all necessary adjustments.
4X2 models........ 16.0
4X4 models........ 17.4
w/A.T. add........ .3
w/A.C. add........ .3
w/P.S. add........ .3
w/Turbo add........ .7

Engine Assy., R&R and Recondition
Includes: Install new pistons, pins, rings, rod and main bearings. Clean carbon, grind valves. Make all necessary adjustments.
4X2 models........ 27.3
4X4 models........ 28.7
w/A.T. add........ .3
w/A.C. add........ .3
w/P.S. add........ .3
w/Turbo add........ .7

Engine Mounts, Renew
Front-one........ .7
both........ 1.0
Rear........ .7

LABOR 14 PISTONS, RINGS & BEARINGS 14 LABOR

(Factory Time) Chilton Time

GASOLINE ENGINE

Piston Rings, Renew (All)

Includes: Remove cylinder top ridge, deglaze cylinder walls. Clean piston and ring grooves. Minor tune up.

	Chilton Time
P/up	*10.5
Trooper	11.5
w/A.C. add	.3
w/P.S. add	.3
w/A.T. add	.3
*4X4 add	1.0

Pistons or Connecting Rods, Renew (All)

Includes: Remove cylinder top ridge, deglaze cylinder walls. Minor tune up.

	Chilton Time
P/up	*11.7
Trooper	12.7
w/A.C. add	.3
w/P.S. add	.3
w/A.T. add	.3
*4X4 add	1.0

Connecting Rod Bearings, Renew (All)

	Chilton Time
P/up	*7.7
Trooper	8.7
w/A.C. add	.3
w/P.S. add	.3
w/A.T. add	.3
*4X4 add	1.0

COMBINATIONS

Add to Engine Work

	Chilton Time
DRAIN, EVACUATE & RECHARGE AIR CONDITIONING SYSTEM	
All models	1.5
CARBURETOR, RECONDITION	
All models	1.2
REMOVE CYLINDER TOP RIDGE	
Each	.1
DEGLAZE CYLINDER WALLS	
Each	.1
RECONDITION CYLINDER HEAD (HEAD REMOVED)	
All models	2.9
VALVE GUIDES, RENEW	
Each	.2
OIL FILTER ELEMENT, RENEW	
All models	.4

(Factory Time) Chilton Time

DIESEL ENGINE

Piston Rings, Renew (All)

Includes: Remove cylinder top ridge, deglaze cylinder walls, clean piston and ring grooves. Make all necessary adjustments.

	Chilton Time
4X2 models	10.1
4X4 models	11.1
w/A.C. add	.3
w/P.S. add	.3
w/A.T. add	.3
w/Turbo add	.7

Pistons or Connecting Rods, Renew (All)

Includes: Remove cylinder top ridge, deglaze cylinder walls. Make all necessary adjustments.

	Chilton Time
4X2 models	11.3
4X4 models	12.3
w/A.C. add	.3
w/P.S. add	.3
w/A.T. add	.3
w/Turbo add	.7

Connecting Rod Bearings, Renew (All)

	Chilton Time
4X2 models	8.7
4X4 models	9.7
w/A.C. add	.3
w/P.S. add	.3
w/A.T. add	.3
w/Turbo add	.7

LABOR 15 CRANKSHAFT & DAMPER 15 LABOR

(Factory Time) Chilton Time

GASOLINE ENGINE

Crankshaft and Main Bearings, Renew

Includes: R&R engine assy., and cylinder head. Plastigauge all bearings.

	Chilton Time
P/up	*9.9
Trooper	10.9
w/A.C. add	.8
w/P.S. add	.3
w/A.T. add	.3
*4X4 add	1.0

Main and Rod Bearings, Renew

Includes: R&R engine assy. Plastigauge all bearings.

	Chilton Time
P/up	*11.1
Trooper	12.1
w/P.S. add	.3
w/A.T. add	.3
*4X4 add	1.0

Rear Main Bearing Oil Seal, Renew

Includes: R&R transmission.

	Chilton Time
P/up	*3.8
Trooper	4.8
A.T. add	.2
*4X4 add	1.0

Crankshaft Pulley, Renew

	Chilton Time
All models	1.5
w/A.C. add	.1
w/P.S. add	.1

Crankshaft Front Oil Seal, Renew

	Chilton Time
All models	2.3

DIESEL ENGINE

Crankshaft and Main Bearings, Renew

Includes: R&R engine assy. Check all bearing clearances.

	Chilton Time
4X2 models	9.3
4X4 models	10.0
w/A.C. add	.8
w/P.S. add	.3
w/A.T. add	.3
w/Turbo add	.7

Main Bearings, Renew

Includes: R&R engine assy.

	Chilton Time
4X2 models	11.4
4X4 models	12.1
w/A.C. add	.8
w/P.S. add	.3
w/A.T. add	.3
w/Turbo add	.7

Main and Rod Bearings, Renew

Includes: R&R engine assy.

	Chilton Time
4X2 models	12.6
4X4 models	13.3
w/A.C. add	.8
w/P.S. add	.3
w/A.T. add	.3
w/Turbo add	.7

Rear Main Bearing Oil Seal, Renew

Includes: R&R trans.

	Chilton Time
4X2 models	3.8
4X4 models	4.5
w/A.T. add	.3

Crankshaft Pulley or Damper, Renew

	Chilton Time
All models	1.5
w/A.C. or P.S. add	.2

Crankshaft Front Oil Seal, Renew

	Chilton Time
All models	3.5

LABOR 16 CAMSHAFT & TIMING GEARS 16 LABOR

(Factory Time) Chilton Time

GASOLINE ENGINE

Timing Chain Cover and/or Gasket, Renew

Includes: R&R engine, renew cover oil seal.

1.8-2.0L engs

	Chilton Time
P/up	10.5
Trooper	11.5
w/A.C. add	.3
w/A.T. add	.3
w/P.S. add	.3
4X4 add	1.0

Timing Chain, Renew

Includes: R&R engine, renew cover oil seal.

1.8-2.0L engs

	Chilton Time
P/up	11.6
Trooper	12.6
w/A.C. add	.3
w/A.T. add	.3
w/P.S. add	.3
4X4 add	1.0

Camshaft, Renew

	Chilton Time
All models	1.5

Timing Belt Cover, R&R or Renew

Includes: Renew front cover oil seal.

2.3L eng

	Chilton Time
All models	3.2
w/A.C. add	.3
w/A.T. add	.3
w/P.S. add	.3

LABOR 16 CAMSHAFT & TIMING GEARS 16 LABOR

(Factory Time) Chilton Time

Timing Belt, Renew
Includes: R&R front cover, renew cover oil seal.
2.3L eng
All models 3.5
w/A.C. add .3
w/A.T. add .3
w/P.S. add .3

DIESEL ENGINE

Timing Cover and/or Oil Seal, Renew
Includes: R&R pulleys and renew timing belt.
All models 3.2

Camshaft, Renew
Includes: R&R engine assy.
4X2 models 10.9
4X4 models 11.6
w/A.C. add .8
w/P.S. add .3
w/A.T. add .3

Timing Belt, Renew
Includes: R&R pulley housing.
All models 2.8
Renew tensioner add .2

Timing Gears, Renew
Includes: Renew crankshaft and/or camshaft gears.
All models 4.2

LABOR 17 ENGINE OILING SYSTEM 17 LABOR

(Factory Time) Chilton Time

GASOLINE ENGINE

Oil Pan or Gasket, Renew (Except 4X4 w/2.3L eng)
Includes: R&R engine assy.
P/up *6.5
Trooper 7.5
w/A.C. add .3
w/P.S. add .3
w/A.T. add .3
*4X4 add 1.0

Pressure Test Engine Bearings (Pan Off)
All models 1.0

Oil Pump, Renew (Except 4X4 w/2.3L eng)
Includes: R&R engine assy.
P/up *6.7
Trooper 7.7
w/A.C. add .8
w/P.S. add .3
w/A.T. add .3
*4X4 add 1.0

Oil Pan or Gasket, Renew (4X4 w/2.3L eng)
All models .8

Oil Pump, Renew (4X4 w/2.3L eng)
Includes: R&R timing belt cover and timing belt.
All models 3.9
w/A.C. add .3
w/A.T. add .3
w/P.S. add .3

Oil Pressure Sending Unit, Renew
All models .5

Oil Filter Element, Renew
All models .4

DIESEL ENGINE

Oil Pan or Gasket, Renew
Includes: R&R engine assy.
4X2 models 7.8
4X4 models 8.8
w/A.C. add .3
w/P.S. add .3
w/A.T. add .3
w/Turbo add .7

Pressure Test Engine Bearings (Pan Off)
All models 1.0

Oil Pump, Renew
Includes: R&R engine assy.
4X2 models 8.0
4X4 models 9.0
w/A.C. add .3
w/P.S. add .3
w/A.T. add .3
w/Turbo add .7

Oil Pressure Sending Unit, Renew
All models .4

Oil Filter Element, Renew
All models .3

LABOR 18 CLUTCH & FLYWHEEL 18 LABOR

(Factory Time) Chilton Time

Clutch Pedal Free Play, Adjust
All models .3

Clutch Hydraulic System, Bleed
All models .3

Clutch Control Cable, Renew
Includes: Adjust cable.
All models 1.0

Clutch Master Cylinder, Renew
Includes: Bleed system.
All models 1.0

Clutch Slave Cylinder, Renew
Includes: Bleed system.
All models .6

Clutch Master Cylinder, R&R and Recondition
Includes: Bleed system.
both sides 2.0
All models 1.5

Clutch Slave Cylinder, R&R and Recondition
Includes: Bleed system.
All models 1.0

Clutch Assembly, Renew
Includes: R&R trans and adjust linkage.
4X2 models 3.3
4X4 models 4.3

Clutch Release Bearing, Fork and/or Ball Stud, Renew
Includes: R&R trans and adjust linkage.
4X2 models 3.0
4X4 models 4.0

Flywheel, Renew
Includes: R&R trans.
4X2 models 3.6
4X4 models 4.6
Renew ring gear add .5

LABOR 19 STANDARD TRANSMISSION 19 LABOR

(Factory Time) Chilton Time

Transmission Assy., R&R or Renew
4X2 models 2.7
4X4 models 3.7
Renew trans add .5

Transmission Assy., R&R and Recondition
Includes: Complete disassembly, clean and inspect or renew all parts. Install new gaskets and seals.
4X2 models 6.0
4X4 models 7.0

Extension Housing Oil Seal, Renew
All models .7

Speedometer Drive Gear, Renew
Includes: R&R and disassemble trans.
4X2 models 3.0
4X4 models 4.0

Speedometer Driven Gear, Renew
All models .5

TRANSFER CASE

Transfer Case Lever and/or Boot, Renew
All models .4

LABOR 19 STANDARD TRANSMISSION 19 LABOR

(Factory Time) Chilton Time

Rear Cover and/or Gasket, Renew
All models 5

Transfer Case Assy, and/or Gasket, Renew
All models 1.0

Transfer Case Assy., R&R and Recondition
All models 3.6

LABOR 21 SHIFT LINKAGE 21 LABOR

(Factory Time) Chilton Time

STANDARD

Gearshift Control Lever, Renew
All models 5
w/Console add 1

Transfer Case Control Lever, Renew
All models 5

AUTOMATIC

Shift Linkage, Adjust
Includes: Adjust linkage and neutral safety switch.
All models 6

Shift Control Lever, Renew
All models 5

Shift Control Assembly, Renew
All models 1.0

Shift Control Rods, Renew
All models 7

Shift Control Rods, Adjust
All models 3

LABOR 23 AUTOMATIC TRANSMISSION 23 LABOR

(Factory Time) Chilton Time

THM-200

ON TRUCK SERVICES

Drain & Refill Unit
All models 7

Oil Pressure Check
All models 5

Check Unit for Oil Leaks
Includes: Clean and dry outside of case, run unit to determine point of leak.
All models 9

Linkage Adjust
Includes: Adjust neutral safety switch, indicator needle and detent rod, cable or switch.
All models 6

Shift Control Rod, Adjust
All models 5

Detent Cable, Adjust
All models 3

Detent Cable, Renew
Includes: Adjust.
All models 7

Speedometer Driven Gear and/or Oil Seal, Renew
All models 5

Governor Assy., R&R or Renew
All models 1.0

Governor Assy., R&R and Recondition
All models 1.6
Renew governor gear add 3

Extension Housing Rear Oil Seal, Renew
Includes: R&R driveshaft.
All models 8

Oil Pan Gasket, Renew
Includes: Clean oil pan and service screen.
All models 9

Parking Pawl, Renew
Includes: R&R oil pan.
All models 1.9

Intermediate Servo, Renew
Includes: Renew cover and 'O' rings.
All models 9

Intermediate Accumulator, Renew
Includes: R&R oil pan, valve body and accumulator.
All models 1.7

Pressure Regulator Valve, Renew
Includes: R&R oil pan.
All models 1.5

Valve Body Assy., R&R or Renew
Includes: R&R oil pan and filter.
All models 1.7

Valve Body Assy., R&R and Recondition
Includes: R&R oil pan and filter. Disassemble, clean, inspect, free all valves. Replace parts as required.
All models 2.8

SERVICES REQUIRING R&R

Transmission Assy., R&R or Renew
All models 3.8
Leak check converter add 4
Renew trans add 5

Transmission and Converter Assy., R&R and Recondition
Includes: Drain and pressure test converter, recondition all assemblies. Make all necessary adjustments.
All models 10.7

Transmission Assy., Reseal
Includes: R&R trans. Renew all seals and gaskets.
All models 6.0

Front Pump Seal, Renew
Includes: R&R trans.
All models 3.9

Flywheel (Flexplate), Renew
Includes: R&R trans.
All models 4.0

Converter Assy., Renew
Includes: R&R trans, pressure check converter and check end play.
All models 4.4

Front Oil Pump, Renew
Includes: R&R trans, converter and pump seal.
All models 4.6
Recond pump add 9

AW-55

ON TRUCK SERVICES

Drain & Refill Unit
All models 7

Oil Pressure Check
All models 5

Check Unit for Oil Leaks
Includes: Clean and dry outside of case and run unit to determine point of leak.
All models 9

Neutral Safety Switch, Renew
All models 5
w/Console add 1

Extension Housing and/or Gasket, Renew
All models 2.2

Extension Housing Oil Seal, Renew
All models 8

Governor Assy., Renew
Includes: R&R extension housing.
All models 2.4

Oil Pan and/or Gasket, Renew
All models 6

Valve Body Assy., Renew
Includes: R&R oil pan.
All models 1.5

Valve Body Assy., R&R and Recondition
Includes: R&R oil pan and filter. Dissassemble, clean, inspect, free all valves. Replace parts as required.
All models 3.0

Throttle Valve and Kick Down Cam, Renew
Includes: R&R oil pan.
All models 1.2

Speedometer Driven Gear, Renew
All models 5

Manual Valve Lever and/or Seal, Renew
All models 3.7

Parking Pawl, Renew
All models 3.7

SERVICES REQUIRING R&R

Transmission Assy., R&R or Renew
All models 3.8
Long bed add 2
Renew trans add 5

Transmission and Converter Assy., R&R and Recondition
Includes: Drain and pressure test converter, recondition all assemblies. Make all necessary adjustments.
All models 10.5
Long bed add 2

LABOR 23 AUTOMATIC TRANSMISSION 23 LABOR

	(Factory Time)	Chilton Time
Torque Converter, Renew		
Includes: R&R trans.		
All models		4.0
Long bed add		.2
Front Pump Assy., Renew		
Includes: R&R trans.		
All models		4.2
Renew front seal add		.2
Long bed add		.2
Flywheel (Flexplate), Renew		
Includes: R&R trans.		
All models		4.0
Long bed add		.2

LABOR 25 U-JOINTS & DRIVESHAFT 25 LABOR

	(Factory Time)	Chilton Time
Drive Shaft, Renew		
One piece shaft		.5
Two piece shaft		
front		.7
rear		.5
Center Bearing, Renew		
All models		.9
Universal Joint, Renew		
Includes: Disconnect driveshaft.		
All models-one		.8
each adtnl		.4

LABOR 26 DRIVE AXLE 26 LABOR

	(Factory Time)	Chilton Time
REAR DIFFERENTIAL ASSY.		
Axle Shaft Assy., Renew		
All models-one		1.3
both		2.4
Axle Shaft Bearing and/or Oil Seal, Renew		
All models-one		1.2
both		2.3
Axle Tube Oil Seal, Renew		
All models-one		1.2
both		2.2
Pinion Shaft Oil Seal, Renew		
All models		.9
Differential Carrier Case, Renew		
Includes: R&R carrier and renew case.		
All models		4.3
Ring Gear and Pinion Set, Renew		
All models		5.1
Renew pinion brgs add		.4
Renew side brgs add		.6
Pinion Gear Bearings, Renew		
All models		5.5
Side Carrier Bearings, Renew		
All models		3.5
Side Carrier and Pinion Bearings, Renew		
All models		3.2
Rear Axle Housing, Renew		
All models		5.2
Differential Carrier Assy., Renew		
All models		2.8
Rear Axle Housing Cover Gasket, Renew		
All models		2.5
FRONT DIFFERENTIAL ASSY		
Front Axle Shaft Oil Seal, Renew		
All models-one		1.2
both		2.3
Front Axle Shaft Bearing, Renew		
Includes: Renew oil seal.		
All models-one		1.3
both		2.5
Front Axle Shaft Assy., R&R or Renew		
All models		
one or both		4.6
Renew shaft assy add-each		.3
Renew inner shaft add-each		.5
Renew outer shaft add-each		.4
Renew shaft boot(s) add-each		.4
Repack outer joint add-each		.4
Renew D.O. Joint add-each		.4
Renew inner seal add-each		.2
Front Pinion Shaft Oil Seal, Renew		
All models		.9
Front Differential Carrier Assy., R&R or Renew Gasket		
All models		5.6
w/Skid plate add		.3
Front Pinion Shafts and/or Side and Pinion Gears, Renew		
Includes: R&R front carrier assy.		
All models		7.4
w/Skid plate add		.3
Side Bearings, Renew		
Includes: R&R front carrier assy.		
All models		6.3
w/Skid plate add		.3
Pinion Bearings, Renew		
Includes: R&R front carrier assy.		
All models		6.9
w/Skid plate add		.3
Ring Gear and Pinion Assy., Renew		
Includes: R&R front carrier assy.		
All models		7.7
w/Skid plate add		.3

LABOR 27 REAR SUSPENSION 27 LABOR

	(Factory Time)	Chilton Time
Rear Spring, Renew		
All models-one		1.0
both		1.8
Renew bushings add-each		.3
Rear Shock Absorbers, Renew		
All models-one		.5
both		.7
Rear Spring Shackle, Renew		
All models-one		.6
both		1.0
Renew bushings add-each		.2

LABOR 28 AIR CONDITIONING 28 LABOR

Note: If more than one item requires replacement where evacuation and discharging the system is already included in the operation, deduct 1.0 hour for each additional item to the times listed.

	(Factory Time)	Chilton Time
Drain, Evacuate and Recharge System		
All models		1.0
Flush Refrigerant System, Complete		
To be used in conjunction with component replacement which could contaminate system.		
All models		1.3
Leak Check		
Includes: Check all lines and connections.		
All models		.5
Compressor Belt, Renew		
All models		.3
Compressor Assembly, Renew		
Includes: Transfer parts as required. Evacuate and charge system.		
All models		2.0

LABOR 28 AIR CONDITIONING 28 LABOR

(Factory Time)	Chilton Time
Refrigerant, Add (Partial Charge)	
All models	.6
Compressor Assy., R&R and Recondition	
Includes: Completely disassemble compressor. Clean, inspect and renew all parts as required. Evacuate and charge system.	
All models	3.5
Clutch Hub and Drive Plate, Renew	
All models	1.4
Compressor Pulley and/or Bearing, Renew	
All models	1.6
Compressor Shaft Seal Kit, Renew	
Includes: Evacuate and charge system.	
All models	1.7
Receiver-Dehydrator, Renew	
Includes: Evacuate and charge system.	
All models	1.8
Expansion Valve, Renew	
Includes: Evacuate and charge system.	
All models	5.0
Evaporator Core, Renew	
Includes: Evacuate and charge system.	
All models	5.0
Condenser Assembly, Renew	
Includes: Evacuate and charge system.	
All models	2.9
Blower Motor, Renew	
All models	1.8
Blower Motor Resistor, Renew	
All models	.4
Temperature Control Unit, Renew	
All models	.7
Air Conditioning Hoses, Renew	
Includes: Evacuate and charge system.	
All models-one	1.7
each adtnl	.5

LABOR 29 LOCKS, HINGES & WIND. REGULATORS 29 LABOR

(Factory Time)	Chilton Time
Window Regulator, Renew	
All models	.9
Door Handle (Outside), Renew	
All models	.5
Door Lock Assembly, Renew	
All models	.8
Door Lock Cylinder Assy., Renew	
All models	.5
Recode cyl add	.3
Lock Striker Plate, Renew	
All models	.3
Hood Hinge, Renew (One)	
All models	.4
Hood Latch Assembly, Renew	
All models	.4
Hood Release Cable, Renew	
All models	.6

LABOR 30 HEAD AND PARKING LAMPS 30 LABOR

(Factory Time)	Chilton Time
Aim Headlamps	
All models	.4
Headlamp Sealed Beam Bulb, Renew	
All models-each	.5
Turn Signal or Parking Lamp Lens or Bulb, Renew	
All models	.3
Side Marker Lamp Lens or Bulb, Renew	
All models	.3
Tail or Stop Lamp Lens or Bulb, Renew	
All models	.3
License Lamp Assembly, Renew	
All models	.2

LABOR 31 WINDSHIELD WIPER & SPEEDOMETER 31 LABOR

(Factory Time)	Chilton Time
Windshield Wiper Motor, Renew	
All models	.9
Wiper Transmission Assy., Renew	
All models	1.5
Windshield Washer Pump, Renew	
All models	.5
Rear Window Wiper and Washer Switch, Renew	
Trooper	.5
Rear Window Wiper Motor, Renew	
Trooper	.9
Rear Window Washer Motor, Renew	
Trooper	.3
Speedometer Head, R&R or Renew	
P/up	1.0
Trooper	.7
Speedometer Cable and Casing, Renew	
All models	.8
Speedometer Cable (Inner), Renew or Lubricate	
All models	.6
Radio, R&R	
All models	.5

LABOR 32 LIGHT SWITCHES & WIRING 32 LABOR

(Factory Time)	Chilton Time
Headlamp Switch, Renew	
All models	.4
Headlamp Dimmer Switch, Renew	
All models	.6
Combination Switch Assy., Renew	
All models	.9
Parking Brake Lamp Switch, Renew	
All models	.3
Stop Light Switch, Renew	
All models	.3
Starter Safety Switch, Renew	
All models	.4
Back-Up Lamp Switch, Renew	
All models-w/M.T.	.3
w/A.T.	.4
Turn Signal and Hazard Warning Switch Assy., Renew	
All models	.7
Horn Assembly, Renew	
All models-each	.2
Horn Relay, Renew	
All models	.3
Turn Signal or Hazard Warning Flasher, Renew	
All models	.3

Mazda Trucks

GROUP INDEX

ALPHABETICAL INDEX

LABOR 1 TUNE UP 1 LABOR

	(Factory Time)	Chilton Time
Compression Test		
All models		.5
Engine Tune Up, (Minor)		
Includes: Clean or renew spark plugs, renew ignition points and condenser, set ignition timing, set carburetor idle mixture and idle speed. Service carburetor air cleaner.		
B2000 models		1.9
Engine Tune Up, (Electronic Ignition)		
Includes: Test battery and clean connections. Tighten manifold and carburetor mounting bolts. Check engine compression, clean and adjust or renew spark plugs. Test resistance of spark plug cables. Inspect distributor cap and rotor. Check vacuum advance operation. Reset ignition timing. Change fuel filter. Inspect and adjust drive belts. Check operation of EGR valve.		
All models		1.5

LABOR 2 IGNITION SYSTEM 2 LABOR

	(Factory Time)	Chilton Time
GASOLINE ENGINES		
Spark Plugs, Clean and Reset or Renew		
B2000 models		.5
Ignition Timing, Reset		
B2000 models		.3
Distributor, Renew		
Includes: Reset ignition timing.		
B2000 models		.8
Distributor, R&R and Recondition		
Includes: Reset ignition timing.		
B2000 models		1.9
Vacuum Control Unit, Renew		
Includes: R&R distributor cap.		
All models		.5
Pick-Up Coil, Renew		
B2000 models		1.1
Ignition Coils, Renew		
All models-one		.3
both		.4
Ignition Cables, Renew		
All models		.4
Distributor Cap and/or Rotor, Renew		
All models		.3
Ignition Switch, Renew		
B2000-B2200 models		1.0
Igniter Set, Renew		
B2000 models		1.1
DIESEL ENGINE		
Glow Plugs, Renew		
B2200 models-one		.4
all		.6
Glow Plug Relay, Renew		
B2200 models		.3
Glow Plug Control Unit, Renew		
B2200 models		.4

LABOR 3 FUEL SYSTEM 3 LABOR

	(Factory Time)	Chilton Time
GASOLINE ENGINES		
Fuel Pump, Test		
Includes: Disconnect fuel line, attach pressure gauge.		
All models		.3
Air Cleaner, Service		
All models		.2
Carburetor, Adjust (On Truck)		
Includes: Adjust engine idle speed and mixture.		
1981-84		.4
Carburetor, Adjust		
Includes: R&R carburetor.		
1986		1.7
Float Level, Adjust		
1986		1.5
Carburetor, Renew		
Includes: All necessary adjustments.		
1981-84		1.4
1986		1.7
Carburetor, R&R and Clean or Recondition		
Includes: All necessary adjustments.		
1981-84		2.5
1986		2.8
Fuel Filter, Renew		
All models		.3
Fuel Pump, Renew		
1981-84		1.0
1986		.5
Add pump test if performed.		
Fuel Tank, Renew		
Includes: Drain and refill tank. Transfer sending unit.		
B2000 models		1.2
Fuel Gauge (Dash Unit), Renew		
1981-84		1.2
1986		1.1
Fuel Gauge (Tank Unit), Renew		
Includes: R&R fuel tank.		
B2000 models		1.1
Intake Manifold or Gasket, Renew		
1981-84		1.6
1986		2.0
Renew manif add		.5
DIESEL ENGINE		
Injection Pump and/or Gasket, Renew		
B2200 models		1.8
Injection Pump, R&R and Recondition		
B2200 models		4.5
Governor Cover and/or Seal Ring, Renew		
B2200 models		.6
Governor Assembly, Renew		
B2200 models		2.6
Load Limiter, Renew		
B2200 models		2.9
Distributor Head Assy., and/or 'O' Ring, Renew		
B2200 models		3.5
Fuel Injection Nozzles, Renew		
B2200 models-one		.5
all		1.5
Fuel Filter, Renew		
B2200 models		.5
Fuel Gauge (Dash Unit), Renew		
B2200 models		1.4
Fuel Gauge (Tank Unit), Renew		
Includes: R&R fuel tank.		
B2200 models		1.1
Fuel Tank, Renew		
Includes: Drain and refill tank.		
B2200 models		1.4
Intake Manifold Gasket, Renew		
B2200 models		1.9
Renew manif add		.4

LABOR 3A EMISSION CONTROLS 3A LABOR

	(Factory Time)	Chilton Time
Air Pump, Renew		
1981-84		.7
Air Pump Drive Belt, Renew		
1981-84		.3
Anti-After Burn Valve, Renew		
1981-84		.4

LABOR 3A EMISSION CONTROLS 3A LABOR

	(Factory Time)	Chilton Time
Positive Crankcase Ventilation Valve, Renew		
All models		.2
Air Control Valve, Renew		
1981-84		.4
Air Cleaner Control Valve, Renew		
1986		.4
Hot Idle Compensator, Renew		
1986		.4
Altitude Compensator, Renew		
All models		.4
E.G.R. Control Valve, Renew		
1981-84		1.0
1986		.6
Air Manifold, Renew		
All models		.6
Air Injection Nozzles, Renew (All)		
All models		.6
Charcoal Canister or Filter, Renew		
All models		.2

LABOR 4 ALTERNATOR AND REGULATOR 4 LABOR

	(Factory Time)	Chilton Time
Alternator Circuits, Test		
Includes: Test battery, regulator and alternator output.		
All models		.4
Alternator Drive Belt, Renew		
All models		.4
Alternator, Renew		
B2200 models		1.1
All other models		.6
Add circuit test if performed.&..6		
Alternator, R&R and Recondition		
Includes: Disassemble, clean and test all parts. Renew parts as required, reassemble.		
B2200 models		2.5
All other models		2.0
Alternator Bearings, Renew		
Includes: R&R alternator, separate end frames.		
B2200 models-front		1.6
rear		2.0
All other models-front		.9
rear		1.5
Voltage Regulator, Test and Renew		
All models-external		.4
internal		2.0

LABOR 5 STARTING SYSTEM 5 LABOR

	(Factory Time)	Chilton Time
Starter Draw Test (On Truck)		
All models		.3
Starter, Renew		
B2000 models		
1981-84		1.0
1986		.7
B2200 models		.8
Add draw test if performed.		
Starter, R&R and Recondition		
Includes: Turn down armature.		
B2000 models		
1981-84		2.5
1986		2.2
B2200 models		2.5
Magnetic Switch (Solenoid), Renew		
Includes: R&R starter.		
B2000 models		
1981-84		1.2
1986		.9
B2200 models		1.1
Starter Drive, Renew		
Includes: R&R starter.		
B2000 models		
1981-84		1.9
1986		1.6
B2200 models		1.8
Battery Cables, Renew		
B2000 models		
positive		.6
negative		.2
B2200 models		
positive		.5
negative		.2

LABOR 6 BRAKE SYSTEM 6 LABOR

	(Factory Time)	Chilton Time
Brakes, Adjust (Minor)		
Includes: Fill master cylinder.		
two wheels		.4
four wheels		.6
Bleed Brakes (Four Wheels)		
Includes: Fill master cylinder.		
All models		.6
Brake Pedal Free Play, Adjust		
All models		.3
Brake Shoes and/or Pads, Renew		
Includes: Install new or exchange brake shoes or pads. Adjust service and hand brake. Bleed system.		
All models		
front-disc		.8
rear-drum		1.2
all four wheels		1.9
Resurface brake rotor, add-each		.9
Resurface brake drum, add-each		.5
Rear Brake Drum, Renew		
All models-one		.6
both		.9
BRAKE HYDRAULIC SYSTEM		
Wheel Cylinders, Renew		
Includes: Bleed system.		
All models-one		1.0
both		1.9
Wheel Cylinders, R&R and Rebuild		
Includes: Bleed system.		
All models-one		1.2
both		2.3
Master Cylinder, Renew		
Includes: Bleed system.		
All models		1.3
Master Cylinder, R&R and Rebuild		
Includes: Bleed system.		
All models		1.8
Brake Hose, Renew (Flex)		
Includes: Bleed system.		
All models-front-one		.6
rear-one		.6
DISC BRAKES		
Disc Brake Pads, Renew		
Includes: Install new disc brake pads only.		
All models-front		.8
Resurface brake rotor, add-each		.9
Caliper Assembly, Renew		
Includes: Bleed system.		
All models-one		1.0
both		1.5
Caliper Assy., R&R and Recondition		
Includes: Bleed system.		
All models-one		1.4
both		2.3
Disc Brake Rotor, Renew		
All models-one		1.1
both		1.8
Proportioning Valve, Renew		
Includes: Bleed system.		
All models		1.1

LABOR 6 BRAKE SYSTEM 6 LABOR

(Factory Time) Chilton Time

POWER BRAKES

Power Brake Unit, Renew
Includes: R&R master cylinder and bleed system.
All models 1.4

Power Brake Unit, R&R and Recondition
Includes: R&R master cylinder and bleed system.
All models 1.7

Vacuum Check Valve, Renew
All models .2

PARKING BRAKE

Parking Brake, Adjust
All models .3

Parking Brake Control, Renew
All models .6

Parking Brake Cables, Renew
Includes: Adjust cables.
All models-front 1.0
rear-one 1.1
both 1.7

COMBINATIONS

Add to Brakes, Renew

Chilton Time

WHEEL CYLINDER, RENEW
Each .3

WHEEL CYLINDER, REBUILD
Each .4

CALIPER ASSEMBLY, REBUILD
Each .4

MASTER CYLINDER, REBUILD
All models .4

BRAKE HOSE, RENEW
Each .3

FRONT WHEEL BEARINGS, CLEAN AND REPACK (BOTH WHEELS)
Drum Brakes .4
Disc Brakes .6

DISC BRAKE ROTOR, RENEW
Each .3

BRAKE DRUM, RENEW
Each .1

LABOR 7 COOLING SYSTEM 7 LABOR

(Factory Time) Chilton Time

Winterize Cooling System
Includes: Run engine to check for leaks, tighten all hose connections. Test radiator and pressure cap, drain radiator and engine block. Add anti-freeze and refill system.
All models .5

Thermostat, Renew
B2000 models
1981-84 .4
1986 .7
B2200 models .5

Radiator Assy., R&R or Renew
Includes: Drain and refill cooling system.
B2000 models
1981-84 .9
1986 1.2
B2200 models 1.1
w/A.T. add .2

ADD THESE OPERATIONS TO RADIATOR R&R

Boil & Repair 1.5
Rod Clean 1.9
Repair Core 1.3
Renew Tank 1.6
Renew Trans. Oil Cooler 1.9
Recore Radiator 1.7

(Factory Time) Chilton Time

Radiator Hoses, Renew
All models
upper .4
lower .4

Fan Belt, Renew
All models .3

Fan Blade and/or Pulley, Renew
1981-84 .5

Cooling Fan or Drive Assy., Renew
All models .6

Water Pump Assy., Renew
Includes: R&R radiator, drain and refill cooling system.
B2000 models
1981-84 1.3
1986 2.5
B2200 models 1.5

Cooling System Hoses, Renew
All models-each .3

Temperature Gauge (Dash Unit), Renew
B2000 models 1.2
B2200 models 1.4

Temperature Gauge (Engine Unit), Renew
All models .3

(Factory Time) Chilton Time

Heater Control Assembly, Renew
B2000-B2200 models 1.7

Heater Blower Motor, Renew
1981-84 1.7
1986 1.0

Heater Water Valve, Renew
All models .5

Heater Core, R&R or Renew
1981-84 1.9
1986 4.5

ADD THESE OPERATIONS TO HEATER CORE R&R

Boil & Repair 1.2
Repair Core .9
Recore 1.2

Heater Hoses, Renew
All models-one side .6
both sides 1.0

Heater Blower Motor Switch, Renew
1981-84 1.8

Heater Blower Motor Resistor, Renew
1986 .5

LABOR 8 EXHAUST SYSTEM 8 LABOR

(Factory Time) Chilton Time

Front Exhaust Pipe, Renew
1981-84 1.0
1986 .9

Center Exhaust Pipe, Renew
All models .9

Pre-Muffler, Renew
B2000 models 1.3

(Factory Time) Chilton Time

Monolith Converter, Renew
1981-84 1.0
1986 1.5

Muffler, Renew
1981-84 .9
1986 .8

(Factory Time) Chilton Time

Tail Pipe, Renew
1986 .5

Catalytic Converter, Renew
1981-84 1.0
1986 .7

Exhaust Manifold or Gaskets, Renew
1981-84 1.5
1986 1.5

LABOR 9 FRONT SUSPENSION 9 LABOR

(Factory Time)	Chilton Time
Wheel, Renew	
one	.5
Wheels, Balance	
one	.3
each adtnl	.2
Wheels, Rotate (All)	
All models	.5
Toe-In, Adjust	
All models	.6
Caster, Camber and Toe-In, Check and Adjust	
All models	2.0
Front Wheel Bearings, Clean and Repack	
All models-one side	.8
both sides	1.5
Front Wheel Bearings, Renew	
All models-one side	.9
both sides	1.7
Front Hub Oil Seal, Renew	
All models-one side	.7
both sides	1.3
Front Hub Assy., Renew	
All models-one	1.1
both	2.0
Front Shock Absorbers or Rubber Bushings, Renew	
All models-one	.6
both	.9
Front Coil Springs, Renew	
All models-one side	1.4
both sides	2.6
Upper Control Arm and/or Bushings, Renew	
Includes: Align front end.	
All models-one side	2.5
both sides	4.0
Lower Control Arm and/or Bushings, Renew	
Includes: Align front end.	
All models-one side	3.0
both sides	5.4
Ball Joints, Renew (Upper or Lower)	
Add alignment charges.	
All models-one	.9
both-one side	1.5
all-both sides	2.9
Front Stabilizer Bar and/or Bushings, Renew	
All models	.8
Steering Knuckles, Renew	
Includes: Align front end.	
All models-one side	2.4
both sides	4.0
Torsion Rods and/or Bushings, Renew	
Includes: Reset car height.	
1986-one side	1.0
both sides	1.9
Torsion Bar Spring, Renew	
Includes: Reset car height.	
1986-one side	1.1
both sides	1.5
Torsion Arm, Renew	
Includes: Reset car height.	
1986-one side	1.1
both sides	1.6

LABOR 10 STEERING LINKAGE 10 LABOR

(Factory Time)	Chilton Time
Tie Rod, Renew	
Includes: Reset toe-in.	
All models-one side	.7
both sides	1.1
Renew seal add-each	.1
Tie Rod End, Renew	
Includes: Reset toe-in.	
All models-one side	1.0
both sides	1.5
Pitman Arm, Renew	
All models	.8
Center Link, Renew	
Includes: Reset toe-in.	
All models	1.2
Idler Arm Assembly, Renew	
All models	.8
Renew bushing add	.2
Steering Knuckle Arms, Renew	
Includes: Reset toe-in.	
All models-one side	1.1
both sides	1.8

LABOR 11 STEERING GEAR 11 LABOR

STANDARD STEERING

(Factory Time)	Chilton Time
Horn Button, Renew	
All models	.3
Steering Wheel, Renew	
All models	.4
Steering Column Support Bushing, Renew	
All models	.9
Steering Column Mast Jacket, Renew	
1981-84	1.5
Steering Gear, Adjust (On Truck)	
All models	.5
Steering Gear, R&R or Renew	
1981-84	2.5
1986	.9
Steering Gear, R&R and Recondition	
Includes: Disassemble, renew necessary parts, reassemble and adjust.	
1981-84	4.0
1986	2.0
Steering Gear Side Cover Gasket, Renew (On Truck)	
Includes: Adjust steering gear.	
1981-84	1.1
1986	.5
Sector Shaft and/or Oil Seal, Renew	
Includes: Disconnect center link. R&R pitman arm and side cover.	
1981-84	2.0
1986	1.1

POWER STEERING

(Factory Time)	Chilton Time
Power Steering Gear, R&R or Renew	
1986	1.1
Power Steering Gear, R&R and Recondition	
1986	2.4
Power Steering Pump, R&R or Renew	
1986	
wo/A.C.	1.2
w/A.C.	1.9
Power Steering Pump, R&R and Recondition	
1986	
wo/A.C.	2.0
w/A.C.	2.7
Power Steering Hoses, Renew	
1986	
Pressure hose	
wo/A.C.	.8
w/A.C.	1.3
Return hose	.8
Return pipes	
each	.6

LABOR 12 CYLINDER HEAD & VALVE SYSTEM 12 LABOR

GASOLINE ENGINES

(Factory Time)	Chilton Time
Compression Test	
All models	.5
Rocker Arm Cover Gasket, Renew	
All models	.5
Valves, Adjust	
All models	1.0

LABOR 12 CYLINDER HEAD & VALVE SYSTEM 12 LABOR

(Factory Time) Chilton Time

Cylinder Head Gasket, Renew
Includes: Clean carbon. Make all necessary adjustments.
1981-84 .... 6.0
1986 .... 6.5

Cylinder Head, Renew
Includes: Clean carbon. Transfer parts as required. Reface valves. Make all necessary adjustments.
1981-84 .... 9.8
1986 .... 11.3

Clean Carbon and Grind Valves
Includes: R&R cylinder head, clean carbon, reface valves and seats. Minor tune up.
1981-84 .... 9.0
1986 .... 12.5

Rocker Arm(s) or Shaft(s), Renew (One or All)
1981-84 .... 1.7
1986 .... 2.6

Valve Springs and/or Valve Stem Oil Seals, Renew
Includes: R&R cylinder head.
1981-84 .... 6.5

Valve Springs and/or Valve Stem Oil Seals, Renew (Head on Truck)
1986 .... 5.0

Cylinder Head Oil Seals, Renew
Includes: R&R valve cover.
All models 7

Cylinder Head, Retorque
All models 1.3

DIESEL ENGINE

Compression Test
B2200 models 1.4

Cylinder Head Gasket, Renew
Includes: Clean carbon. Make all necessary adjustments.
B2200 models 6.7

Cylinder Head, Renew
Includes: Clean carbon. Transfer parts as required. Reface valves. Make all necessary adjustments.
B2200 models 9.8

Clean Carbon and Grind Valves
Includes: R&R cylinder head, clean carbon, reface valves and seats. Make all necessary adjustments.
B2200 models 9.5

Rocker Arm Cover Gasket, Renew
B2200 models 5

Valve Push Rods, Renew (One or All)
B2200 models 2.3

Rocker Arms or Shaft, Renew (One or All)
B2200 models 2.1

Valve Tappets, Renew
Includes: R&R engine and trans.
B2200 models 6.0

Valve Springs and/or Valve Stem Oil Seals, Renew
Includes: R&R cylinder head.
B2200 models-one cyl 7.0
all cyls 8.2

Valve Clearance, Adjust
B2200 models 1.0

LABOR 13 ENGINE ASSEMBLY & MOUNTS 13 LABOR

(Factory Time) Chilton Time

GASOLINE ENGINES

Note: All engine operations listed in this group are for assemblies as supplied by the original equipment manufacturer. Time to replace assemblies from independent rebuilders may vary.

Engine Assembly, Remove and Install
Does not include transfer of any parts or equipment.
1981-84 .... 6.0
1986 .... 5.6
w/A.C. & P.S. add 4

Cylinder Assy. (Short Block), Renew
Includes: R&R engine assy. Transfer all component parts not supplied with replacement engine. Minor tune up.
1981-84 .... 14.8
1986 .... 14.4
w/A.C. & P.S. add 4

Engine Assy., R&R and Recondition
Includes: Install new pistons, pins, rings, rod and main bearings. Clean carbon, grind valves. Tune engine.
1981-84 .... 22.4
1986 .... 21.9
w/A.C. & P.S. add 4

Engine Mounts, Renew
All models-front-one 5
both 8
rear 6

DIESEL ENGINE

Engine Assembly, Remove and Install
Does not include transfer of any parts or equipment.
B2200 models 4.8

Cylinder Assembly, Renew (Short Block)
Includes: R&R engine assy. Transfer all component parts not supplied with replacement engine. Make all necessary adjustments.
B2200 models 21.2
Renew cyl liners add 8

Engine Assy., R&R and Recondition
Includes: Install new pistons, pins, rings, rod and main bearings. Clean carbon, grind valves. Make all necessary adjustments.
B2200 models 26.0

Engine Mounts, Renew
B2200 models
front-one 6
both 1.0

LABOR 14 PISTONS, RINGS & BEARINGS 14 LABOR

(Factory Time) Chilton Time

GASOLINE ENGINES

Rings, Renew (All)
Includes: Remove cylinder top ridge, deglaze cylinder walls. Clean carbon from cylinder head. Minor tune up.
1981-84 .... 10.6
1986 .... 11.6

Pistons or Connecting Rods, Renew
Includes: Remove cylinder top ridge, deglaze cylinder walls. Clean carbon from cylinder head. Replace rod bearings. Minor tune up.
1981-84 .... 11.8
1986 .... 12.8

Connecting Rod Bearings, Renew
Includes: R&R oil pan.
1981-84 .... 3.2
1986 .... 4.5

COMBINATIONS

	Chilton Time		Chilton Time
DISTRIBUTOR, RECONDITION		**PLASTIGAUGE BEARINGS**	
All models	1.0	Each	.1
CARBURETOR, RECONDITION		**REMOVE CYLINDER TOP RIDGE**	
All models	1.4	Each	.1
OIL PUMP, RECONDITION		**DEGLAZE CYLINDER WALLS**	
All models	.4	Each	.1
WATER PUMP, RECONDITION		**OIL FILTER ELEMENT, RENEW**	
All models	1.0	All models	.3

LABOR 14 PISTONS, RINGS & BEARINGS 14 LABOR

(Factory Time) Chilton Time

DIESEL ENGINE

Rings, Renew (All)
Includes: Remove cylinder top ridge, deglaze cylinder walls. Clean carbon from cylinder head. Make all necessary adjustments.
B2200 models 11.5

Pistons or Connecting Rods, Renew
Includes: Remove cylinder top ridge, deglaze cylinder walls. Clean carbon from cylinder head. Make all necessary adjustments.
B2200 models 12.7

Connecting Rod Bearings, Renew
Includes: R&R oil pan.
B2200 models 3.2

LABOR 15 CRANKSHAFT & DAMPER 15 LABOR

(Factory Time) Chilton Time

GASOLINE ENGINES

Crankshaft and Main Bearings, Renew
Includes: R&R engine assy. Check all bearing clearances.
1981-84 .... 17.2
1986 .... 19.6

Crankshaft Rear Oil Seal, Renew
Includes: R&R transmission.
1981-84 .... 4.7
1986 .... 4.0

Main Bearing Cap Side Seals, Renew
Includes: R&R oil pan and main bearing cap.
1981-84 .... 2.6

Crankshaft Pulley, Renew
1981-84 9
1986 7

DIESEL ENGINE

Crankshaft and Main Bearings, Renew
Includes: R&R engine assy. Check all bearing clearances.
B2200 models 19.7

Crankshaft Front Oil Seal, Renew
B2200 models 2.2

Crankshaft Rear Oil Seal, Renew
Includes: R&R trans.
B2200 models 3.1

Crankshaft Pulley, Renew
B2200 models 2.0

LABOR 16 CAMSHAFT & TIMING GEARS 16 LABOR

(Factory Time) Chilton Time

GASOLINE ENGINES

Timing Chain Cover Gaskets, Renew
Includes: R&R cylinder head, radiator, water and air pumps.
1981-84 .... 7.0
Renew cover add 5

Timing Chain and/or Sprockets, Renew
Includes: R&R front cover.
1981-84 .... 7.5

Timing Chain Tensioner, Renew
Includes: Reset ignition timing.
1981-84 .... 1.7

Vibration Damper and/or Chain Guide, Renew
Includes: R&R front cover.
1981-84 .... 7.3

Camshaft and/or Bearings, Renew
Includes: Adjust valve clearance and reset ignition timing.
1981-84 .... 3.2

Timing Belt Cover and/or Gasket, Renew
1986
upper 6
lower 1.4

Timing Belt Cover Oil Seal, Renew
1986 .... 2.0

Timing Belt Pulley (Crank Sprocket), Renew
Includes: R&R timing belt.
1986 .... 3.2

Timing Belt, Renew
1986 .... 3.0

Timing Belt Tensioner, Renew
1986 .... 1.5

Camshaft Pulley (Sprocket), Renew
1986 .... 1.9

Camshaft, Renew
1986 .... 3.6

DIESEL ENGINE

Timing Case Cover and/or Gasket, Renew
B2200 models 3.0

Timing Gear, Renew
Includes: Renew idler gear and/or bushing.
B2200 models 4.0

Timing Gear Case Assy., and/or Gasket, Renew
Includes: R&R injection pump and idler gear. R&R cam gear and oil pan. Reset injection timing.
B2200 models 5.5

Camshaft, Renew
Includes: Renew thrust plate and cam sprocket. Adjust valve clearance and injection timing.
B2200 models 6.0

LABOR 17 ENGINE OILING SYSTEM 17 LABOR

(Factory Time) Chilton Time

GASOLINE ENGINES

Oil Pan and/or Gasket, Renew
1981-84 .... 2.0
1986 .... 2.6

Pressure Test Engine Bearings (Pan Off)
All models 1.0

Oil Pump Sprockets and/or Chain, Renew
Includes: R&R front cover.
1981-84 .... 7.4

Oil Pump, Renew
1981-84 .... 2.3
1986 .... 4.0

Oil Pump, R&R and Recondition
1981-84 .... 2.7
1986 .... 4.3

Oil Pressure Switch, Renew
All models 4

Oil Filter Element, Renew
All models 3

DIESEL ENGINE

Oil Pan and/or Gasket, Renew
B2200 models 2.0

Pressure Test Engine Bearings (Pan Off)
B2200 models 1.0

Oil Pump, Renew
Includes: R&R oil pan.
B2200 models 2.3

Oil Pump, R&R and Recondition
Includes: R&R oil pan.
B2200 models 2.6

LABOR 18 CLUTCH & FLYWHEEL 18 LABOR

	(Factory Time)	Chilton Time
Clutch Pedal Free Play, Adjust		
All models		.3
Bleed Clutch Hydraulic System		
All models		.3
Clutch Master Cylinder, Renew		
Includes: Bleed system.		
All models		.6
Clutch Master Cylinder, R&R and Recondition		
Includes: Bleed system.		
All models		1.0
Clutch Slave Cylinder, Renew		
Includes: Bleed system.		
All models		.5
Clutch Slave Cylinder, R&R and Recondition		
Includes: Bleed system.		
All models		.7
Clutch Release Bearing and/or Fork, Renew		
Includes: R&R trans and adjust clutch pedal free play.		
B2000 models		
1981-84		3.2
1986		3.6
B2200 models		2.6
Clutch Assembly, Renew		
Includes: R&R trans and adjust clutch pedal free play.		
B2000 models		
1981-84		3.5
1986		3.9
B2200 models		2.9
Flywheel, Renew		
Includes: R&R trans and clutch. Adjust clutch pedal free play.		
B2000 models		
1981-84		3.8
1986		4.2
B2200 models		3.2
Renew ring gear add		.4
Renew pilot brg add		.2

LABOR 19 STANDARD TRANSMISSION 19 LABOR

	(Factory Time)	Chilton Time
Transmission Assembly, Remove & Install		
B2000 models		3.3
B2200 models		2.5
Transmission Assy., R&R and Recondition		
Includes: Clean and inspect all parts. Install all new parts as required. Install new gaskets and seals.		
B2000 models		
4 Speed		8.0
5 Speed		9.0
B2200 models		
5 Speed		7.5
Extension Housing and/or Gasket, Renew		
Includes: R&R trans on Rotary Pick-Up models.		
B2000 models		2.7
B2200 models		2.4
Extension Housing Oil Seal, Renew		
B2000 models		.8
Speedometer Driven Gear, Renew		
All models		.5

LABOR 21 SHIFT LINKAGE 21 LABOR

	(Factory Time)	Chilton Time
STANDARD		
Gear Shift Lever, Renew		
All models		.4
Gear Shift Housing, Renew		
All models		.7
AUTOMATIC		
Shift Linkage, Adjust		
All models		.4
Selector Lever, Renew		
All models		.8

LABOR 23 AUTOMATIC TRANSMISSION 23 LABOR

	(Factory Time)	Chilton Time
ON CAR SERVICES		
Drain & Refill Unit		
All models		.8
Pressure Check		
All models		.8
Check Unit For Oil Leaks		
Includes: Clean and dry outside of case and run unit to determine point of leak.		
All models		.9
Vacuum Control Unit, Renew		
All models		.5
Kickdown Switch, Renew		
All models		.4
Downshift Solenoid, Renew		
All models		.9
Neutral Safety Switch, Renew		
All models		.5
Oil Pan Gasket, Renew		
All models		.8
Valve Body Assembly, Renew		
Includes: R&R oil pan.		
All models		1.7
Valve Body Assy., R&R and Recondition		
Includes: R&R oil pan, clean, inspect, free all valves. Replace parts as required.		
All models		3.0
Speedometer Driven Gear, Renew		
All models		.5
SERVICES REQUIRING R&R		
Transmission Assembly, Remove & Install		
Includes: Drain and refill unit, adjust linkage. Road test.		
1981-84		3.6
Transmission Assy., R&R and Recondition		
Includes: Disassemble complete unit, renew or recondition all parts. Reassemble, make all necessary adjustments. Road test.		
1981-84		10.2
Extension Housing Gasket, Renew		
Includes: R&R transmission.		
1981-84		4.3
Governor Assembly, Renew		
Includes: R&R trans and extension housing.		
1981-84		4.5
Recond governor add		.4
Front Pump Oil Seal, Renew		
Includes: R&R transmission.		
1981-84		4.9
Torque Converter, Renew		
Includes: R&R transmission.		
1981-84		3.6
Drive Plate (Flywheel), Renew		
Includes: R&R transmission.		
1981-84		4.0

LABOR 25 U-JOINTS & DRIVESHAFT 25 LABOR

(Factory Time) Chilton Time

Driveshaft, Renew
All models .7

Universal Joints, Renew or Recondition
Includes: R&R driveshaft.
1981-84
one 1.2
two 1.5
three 1.9
1986
one 1.3

Center Bearing or Seals, Renew
Includes: R&R driveshaft.
All models 1.5

LABOR 26 DRIVE AXLE 26 LABOR

(Factory Time) Chilton Time

Differential, Drain & Refill
All models .6

Axle Shaft Assembly, Renew
Includes: Renew outer oil seals. Bleed rear brake lines.
1981-84-one 1.7
both 3.0
1986-one side 1.5
both sides 2.6

Rear Axle Inner Oil Seals, Renew
Includes: R&R axle shafts. Bleed rear brake lines.
1981-84-one side 1.4
both sides 2.5
1986-one side 1.2
both sides 2.2

Rear Axle Bearings and/or Bearing Housing, Renew
Includes: R&R axle shafts, renew oil seals. Bleed rear brake lines.
1981-84-one side 1.8
both sides 3.2
1986-one side 1.6
both sides 2.8

Pinion Shaft Oil Seal, Renew
All models 1.0

Differential Carrier Assy., Remove & Install
Includes: R&R axle shafts, disconnect brake lines and parking brake cable. Bleed rear brake lines.
All models 3.0

Differential Carrier Assy., R&R and Recondition
Includes: R&R axle shafts. Disconnect brake lines and parking brake cable. Recondition carrier assy. Make all necessary adjustments. Bleed rear brake lines.
All models 6.0

Rear Axle Housing, R&R or Renew
Includes: Disconnect all attaching parts. Transfer carrier assy. Make all necessary adjustments. Bleed rear brake lines.
All models 5.5

LABOR 27 REAR SUSPENSION 27 LABOR

(Factory Time) Chilton Time

Rear Shock Absorbers or Rubber Bushings, Renew
All models-one .6
both .9

Rear Springs, Renew
All models-one 1.3
both 2.1
Recond spring add, each .5

Rear Spring Shackles or Bushings, Renew
All models-one side .6
both sides 1.0

LABOR 29 LOCKS, HINGES & WIND. REGULATORS 29 LABOR

(Factory Time) Chilton Time

Hood Hinge, Renew
All models-one .3
both .5

Hood Lock, Renew
All models .3

Hood Release Cable, Renew
All models .6

Lock Striker Plate, Renew
All models .2

Door Lock Assembly, Renew
Includes: R&R trim panel.
All models .7

Door Lock Cylinder, Renew
All models .6
Recode cyl add .3

Door Window Regulator, Renew
Includes: R&R trim panel.
All models 1.0

LABOR 30 HEAD AND PARKING LAMPS 30 LABOR

(Factory Time) Chilton Time

Aim Headlamps
All models-one side .4
both sides .6

Headlamp Sealed Beam Bulb, Renew
All models-one side .6
both sides .8

Front Turn Signal Lamp Lens or Bulb, Renew
All models .2

Side Marker Lamp Lens or Bulb, Renew
All models .2

Rear Combination Lamp Lens or Bulb, Renew
All models-each .3

License Lamp Assembly, Renew
All models-each .2

LABOR 31 WINDSHIELD WIPER & SPEEDOMETER 31 LABOR

(Factory Time) Chilton Time

Windshield Wiper Motor, Renew
All models .6

Windshield Wiper Motor, R&R and Recondition
All models 1.2

Wiper Link, Renew
All models .7

LABOR 31 WINDSHIELD WIPER & SPEEDOMETER 31 LABOR

	(Factory Time)	Chilton Time
Wiper and Washer Switch, Renew		
1986		.9
Washer Motor, Renew		
All models		.3
Speedometer Cable, Renew		
All models		.8
Speedometer Head, R&R or Renew		
B2000 models		
1981-84		1.2
1986		1.1
B2200 models		1.4

LABOR 32 LIGHT SWITCHES & WIRING 32 LABOR

	(Factory Time)	Chilton Time
Combination Switch Assy., Renew		
All models		.9
Turn Signal or Hazard Flasher, Renew		
All models		.3
Headlamp Switch, Renew		
All models		.4
Back-Up Lamp Switch, Renew		
All models-w/4 spd		.4
w/5 spd		.9
Stop Lamp Switch, Renew		
All models		.4
Parking Brake Lamp Switch, Renew		
All models		.3
Horn Relay, Renew		
All models		.2
Horns, Renew		
All models-one		.3
both		.4

LABOR 34 CRUISE CONTROL 34 LABOR

	(Factory Time)	Chilton Time
Cruise Control Switch, Renew		
1986		.9
Cruise Control Actuator, Renew		
1986		.6
Cruise Control Cut-Out Switch, Renew		
1986		.4
Electronic Control Unit, Renew		
1986		.8

Nissan/Datsun Trucks

GROUP INDEX

ALPHABETICAL INDEX

LABOR 1 TUNE UP 1 LABOR

(Factory Time) Chilton Time

Compression Test
Four.. .7
V-6.. .9

Engine Tune Up, (Electronic Ignition)
Includes: Test battery and clean connections. Tighten manifold and carburetor mounting bolts. Check engine compression, clean and adjust or renew spark plugs. Test resistance of spark plug cables. Inspect distributor cap and rotor. Adjust air gap. Check vacuum advance operation. Reset ignition timing. Adjust idle mixture and idle speed. Service air cleaner. Inspect and adjust drive belts. Inspect choke operation and adjust or free up. Check operation of E.G.R. valve.
Four.. 2.4
V-6.. 3.0
w/A.C. add.. .4

LABOR 2 IGNITION SYSTEM 2 LABOR

(Factory Time) Chilton Time

GASOLINE ENGINES

Spark Plugs, Clean and Reset or Renew
All models
Four.. .6
V-6.. .8
w/A.C. add.. .4

Ignition Timing, Reset
All models.. .3

Distributor, Renew
Includes: Reset ignition timing.
All models
Four.. .6
V-6.. .7

Distributor, R&R and Recondition
Includes: Reset ignition timing.
All models
Four.. 1.7
V-6.. 1.8

Distributor Reluctor and/or Pick-Up Coil, Renew
Includes: Reset ignition timing.
All models.. .7

Distributor Cap and/or Rotor, Renew
All models.. .5

Vacuum Control Unit, Renew
All models.. .6

Transistorized Ignition Control Unit, Renew
Does not include test.
All models.. .6
w/A.C. add.. .2

Integrated Circuit Ignition Unit, Renew
All models.. .6

Ignition Coil Power Transistor, Renew
All models.. .4

Spark Plug Cables, Renew
All models
Four.. .5
V-6.. .6

Ignition Switch, Renew
All models.. .6

Steering Lock Assembly, Renew
Includes: R&R ignition switch.
All models.. 1.2

DIESEL ENGINE

Glow Plugs, Renew
All models.. .6

After Glow Timer, Renew
All models.. .4

Glow Plug Relay, Renew
All models.. .4

LABOR 3 FUEL SYSTEM 3 LABOR

(Factory Time) Chilton Time

GASOLINE ENGINE

Fuel Pump, Test
Includes: Disconnect fuel line, attach pressure gauge.
All models.. .3

Carburetor Air Cleaner, Service
All models.. .3

Air Cleaner Vacuum Motor, Renew
All models.. .5

Air Cleaner Temperature Sensor, Renew
All models.. .5

Anti-Dieseling Solenoid, Renew (Dash Pot)
All models.. .6

Fuel Shut-Off Vacuum Switch, Renew
All models.. .4

Automatic Choke Relay, Renew
All models.. .6

Needle Valve and Seat, Renew
Includes: Renew and/or reset float.
All models.. .8

Carburetor, Renew
Includes: All necessary adjustments.
All models.. 1.2

Carburetor, R&R and Recondition
Includes: All necessary adjustments.
All models.. 3.0

Electric Fuel Pump, Renew
D21 models.. 1.3
720 models.. .7
Recond pump add.. .4

Electric Fuel Pump Control Unit, Renew
All models.. .4

Mechanical Fuel Pump, Renew
All models.. .5

Fuel Tank, Renew
Includes: Drain and refill tank.
D21 models.. 1.2
720 models.. .9

Fuel Gauge (Tank Unit), Renew
D21 models.. 1.4
720 models.. 1.0

Fuel Gauge (Dash Unit), Renew
D21 models.. .7
720 models.. 1.5

Intake and Exhaust Manifold and/or Gaskets, Renew
Four
D21 models.. 2.0
720 models.. 2.5
V-6.. 3.5
Renew exhaust manif or gskt add
D21 models.. 1.0
720 models.. .7

FUEL INJECTION

Fuel Injection Unit, R&R or Renew
All models.. .8
Renew injectors add.. .2

Fuel Pressure Regulator, Renew
All models.. .6

Air Flow Meter, Renew
All models.. .6

Throttle Sensor, Renew
All models.. .7

Solenoid Valve, Renew
All models.. .6

Electronic Control Unit, Renew
All models.. .5

Fuel Pump Relay, Renew
All models.. .5

Mixture Heater Relay, Renew
All models.. .4

Coolant Temperature Sensor, Renew
All models.. .5

DIESEL ENGINE

Air Cleaner, Service
All models.. .3

Injection Pump Timing, Adjust
All models.. 1.0

Primary Fuel Filter, Renew
All models.. .4

Air Control Valves, Renew
All models.. .3

Injection Pump Controller, Renew
All models.. .6

Control Relay, Renew
All models.. .3

Automatic Timer, Renew
All models.. 1.0

LABOR 3 FUEL SYSTEM 3 LABOR

	(Factory Time)	Chilton Time
Altitude Compensator, Renew		
All models		.5
Fuel Injection Nozzles, Renew		
All models		1.2
Clean and test add-each		.2
Fuel Supply Pump, Renew		
Includes: Bleed fuel system.		
All models		.5
Fuel Injection Pump, Renew		
Includes: R&R timing cover and automatic timer.		
All models		1.8
Vacuum Pump, Renew		
All models		.7
Recond add		.4
Fuel Supply Pump, R&R and Recondition		
Includes: Bleed fuel system.		
All models		1.5
Intake Manifold and/or Gasket, Renew		
All models		1.5
Renew manif add		.5

LABOR 3A EMISSION CONTROLS 3A LABOR

	(Factory Time)	Chilton Time
GASOLINE ENGINE		
POSITIVE CRANKCASE VENTILATION SYSTEM		
P.C.V. Valve, Renew		
All models		.5
BOOST CONTROLLED DECELERATION DEVICE (B.C.D.D.)		
B.C.D.D. Assembly, Renew		
All models		.6
B.C.D.D. Control Valve Assy., Renew		
All models		.4
ALTITUDE COMPENSATOR		
Altitude Compensator, Renew		
All models		.5
TRANSMISSION CONTROLLED VACUUM ADVANCE SYSTEM		
Vacuum Valve or Solenoid, Renew		
All models		.7
Top Detecting Switch, Renew		
All models		.7
SPARK TIMING CONTROL		
Vacuum Solenoid Valve, Renew		
All models		.4
Thermal Vacuum Valve, Renew		
All models		.4
Spark Delay Valve, Renew		
All models		.3
Vacuum Control Valve, Renew		
All models		.4
DETONATION CONTROL SYSTEM		
Fuel Cut-Off Solenoid, Renew		
All models		.5
Throttle Valve Switch, Renew		
All models		.5
Fuel Shut-Off Clutch Switch, Renew		
All models		.4
Fuel Shut-Off Vacuum Switch, Renew		
All models		.3
Detonation Sensor, Renew		
All models		.6
Detonation Control Unit, Renew		
All models		.4
EVAPORATIVE EMISSION CONTROL SYSTEM		
Vapor/Liquid Separator, Renew		
All models		.8
Charcoal Canister, Renew		
All models		.3
Canister Filter, Renew		
All models		.4
AIR INJECTION SYSTEM		
Air Pump Assembly, Renew		
All models		.7
Air Pump Drive Belt, Renew		
All models		.6
w/A.C. add		.3
Anti-Backfire Valve, Renew		
All models		.5
Air Control Valve, Renew		
All models		.5
Air Control Solenoid Valve, Renew		
All models		.5
E.C.C. SYSTEM		
E.C.C. Control Unit, Renew		
All models		.5
E.C.C. Relay, Renew		
All models		.4
Air-Fuel Control Solenoid, Renew		
All models		1.2
EXHAUST GAS RECIRCULATION SYSTEM		
E.G.R. Valve, Renew		
All models		.6
E.G.R. Solenoid Valve, Renew		
All models		.3
E.G.R. Thermal Vacuum Valve, Renew		
All models		.8
Back Pressure Transducer, Renew		
All models		.5
Oxygen Sensor, Renew		
All models		.5
DIESEL ENGINE		
Venturi Vacuum Transducer Valve, Renew		
All models		.4
Vacuum Amplifier, Renew		
All models		.5
Check Valve, Renew		
All models		.3
Thermal Vacuum Valve, Renew		
All models		.6
Venturi Assembly, Renew		
All models		.6
Venturi Assy., R&R and Recondition		
All models		1.1
E.G.R. Control Valve, Renew		
All models		.6

LABOR 4 ALTERNATOR AND REGULATOR 4 LABOR

	(Factory Time)	Chilton Time
Alternator Circuits, Test		
Includes: Test battery, regulator and alternator output.		
All models		.6
Alternator Assembly, Renew		
All models		.9
Add circuit test if performed.		
Alternator, R&R and Recondition		
Includes: Complete disassembly, inspect, test, replace parts as required, reassemble.		
All models		2.5
Alternator Bearings, Renew		
Includes: R&R alternator.		
All models		1.3
Voltage Regulator, Test and Renew		
All models		1.3
Ammeter or Voltmeter, Renew		
D21 models		.7
720 models		1.5

LABOR 5 STARTING SYSTEM 5 LABOR

	(Factory Time)	Chilton Time
Starter Draw Test (On Truck)		
All models		.3
Starter, Renew		
All models		.8
Add draw test if performed.		
Starter, R&R and Recondition		
Includes: Turn down armature.		
All models		2.5
Renew field coils add		.5
Add draw test if performed.		
Starter Solenoid, Renew		
Includes: R&R starter.		
All models		1.0
Starter Drive, Renew		
Includes: R&R starter.		
All models		1.1
Starter Relay, Renew		
D21 models		.4
Ignition Switch, Renew		
All models		.6
Battery Cables, Renew		
All models-each		.4

LABOR 6 BRAKE SYSTEM 6 LABOR

	(Factory Time)	Chilton Time
Brake Pedal Free Play, Adjust		
All models		.3
Bleed Brakes (Four Wheels)		
Includes: Fill master cylinder.		
All models		1.0
Brake Shoes, Renew		
Includes: Install new or exchange brake shoes, Adjust service and hand brake. Bleed system.		
All models		
front		1.4
rear		2.2
w/Single rear whls		2.2
w/Dual rear whls		3.0
Resurface brake drum add-each		.5
Brake Drum, Renew (One)		
All models		.7
w/Dual rear whls add		.5

COMBINATIONS

Add to Brakes, Renew

	Chilton Time
RENEW WHEEL CYLINDER	
Each	.3
REBUILD WHEEL CYLINDER	
Each	.4
REBUILD CALIPER ASSEMBLY	
Each	.4
RENEW MASTER CYLINDER	
All models	.5
REBUILD MASTER CYLINDER	
All models	1.0
RENEW BRAKE HOSE	
Each	.3
RENEW BRAKE DRUM	
Each	.1
RENEW DISC BRAKE ROTOR	
Each	.2
REPACK FRONT WHEEL BEARINGS (BOTH WHEELS)	
Drum brakes	.3
Disc brakes	.6

BRAKE HYDRAULIC SYSTEM

	(Factory Time)	Chilton Time
Wheel Cylinder, Renew		
Includes: Bleed system.		
Front		
all models-one		.9
both		1.7
Rear		
w/Single rear whls		
one		.9
both		1.7
w/Dual rear whls		
one		1.9
both		3.6
Wheel Cylinder, R&R and Rebuild		
Includes: Bleed system.		
Front		
all models-one		1.1
both		2.0
Rear		
w/Single rear whls		
one		1.1
both		2.0
w/Dual rear whls		
one		2.0
both		3.8
Master Cylinder, Renew		
Includes: Bleed system.		
All models		.8
Master Cylinder, R&R and Rebuild		
Includes: Bleed system.		
All models		1.5
Brake Hose, Renew (Flex)		
Includes: Bleed system.		
All models-one		.6
Proportioning Valve, Renew		
Includes: Bleed system.		
All models		.7

DISC BRAKES

	(Factory Time)	Chilton Time
Disc Brake Pads, Renew		
Includes: Install new disc brake pads only.		
All models		.8
Caliper Assembly, Renew		
Includes: Bleed system.		
1981-82		
2 WD-one		1.1
both		2.0
4 WD-one		1.2
both		2.2
1983-88		
2 WD-one		.8
both		1.5
4 WD		
Nissan-one		.8
both		1.5
Datsun-one		1.9
both		3.7
Recond caliper add, each		.4
Disc Brake Rotor, Renew		
1981-82		
2 WD-one		1.1
both		2.0
4 WD-one		1.2
both		2.2
1983-88		
2 WD-one		.8
both		1.5
4 WD		
Nissan-one		.8
both		1.5
Datsun-one		1.9
both		3.7
Resurface rotor add-each		.9

POWER BRAKES

	(Factory Time)	Chilton Time
Power Brake Booster, Renew		
Includes: Bleed system.		
All models		1.0
Brake Booster Check Valve, Renew		
All models		.3
Vacuum Pump, R&R or Renew		
All models		.7
Recond pump add		.4

PARKING BRAKE

	(Factory Time)	Chilton Time
Parking Brake, Adjust		
All models		.4
Parking Brake Control, Renew		
All models		.7
Parking Brake Equalizer, Renew		
All models		.6
Parking Brake Cable, Renew (One)		
Includes: Adjust cable.		
All models		.6

LABOR 7 COOLING SYSTEM 7 LABOR

(Factory Time)	Chilton Time
Winterize Cooling System	
Includes: Run engine to check for leaks, tighten all hose connections. Test radiator and pressure cap, drain radiator and engine block. Add anti-freeze and refill system.	
All models	.5
Thermostat, Renew	
All models	
Four	.5
V-6	1.3
Radiator Assembly, R&R or Renew	
Includes: Drain and refill coolant.	
D21 models	.8
720 models	1.0
ADD THESE OPERATIONS TO RADIATOR R&R	
Boil & Repair	1.5
Rod Clean	1.9
Repair Core	1.3
Renew Tank	1.6
Renew Trans. Oil Cooler	1.9
Recore Radiator	1.7
Radiator Hoses, Renew	
All models-each	.4

(Factory Time)	Chilton Time
Drive Belt, Renew	
All models	.5
Drive Belts, Adjust	
All models	.4
Coolant Temperature Sensor, Renew	
All models	
Four	.4
V-6	.8
Fluid Fan Coupling, Renew	
2 WD models	.9
4 WD models	1.3
Temperature Gauge Sending Unit, Renew	
All models	.4
Temperature Gauge (Dash Unit), Renew	
D21 models	.7
720 models	1.5
Water Pump, Renew	
Includes: R&R radiator, Drain and refill coolant.	
All models	
Gas	
Four	1.5
V-6	2.5
Diesel	1.2
w/A.C. or P.S. add	.2

(Factory Time)	Chilton Time
Fan Blade or Pulley, Renew	
D21 models	.7
720 models	1.0
Heater Core, R&R or Renew	
D21 models	*4.5
720 models	2.7
*w/A.C. add	2.5
ADD THESE OPERATIONS TO HEATER CORE R&R	
Boil & Repair	1.2
Repair Core	.9
Recore	1.2
Heater Blower Motor Assy., Renew	
D21 models	1.2
720 models	.5
Heater Hoses, Renew (All)	
D21 models	2.5
720 models-wo/A.C.	.8
w/A.C.	1.9
Heater Temperature Control Assy., Renew	
D21 models	1.4
720 models	1.0
Blower Motor Switch, Renew	
D21 models	1.6
720 models	1.2
Blower Motor Resistor, Renew	
All models	.4

LABOR 8 EXHAUST SYSTEM 8 LABOR

(Factory Time)	Chilton Time
Front Exhaust Pipe, Renew	
All models	1.3
Muffler and Rear Pipe, Renew	
All models	.9
Intermediate Exhaust Pipe, Renew	
All models	1.0

(Factory Time)	Chilton Time
Catalytic Converter, Renew	
All models	1.2
E.F.E. Valve (Heat Riser), Renew	
All models	1.3
Intake and Exhaust Manifolds and/or Gaskets, Renew	
Four	
D21 models	2.0

(Factory Time)	Chilton Time
720 models	2.5
V-6	3.5
Renew exhaust manif or gskt add	
D21 models	1.0
720 models	.7
Diesel	
All models	1.3
Renew manif. add	.4

LABOR 9 FRONT SUSPENSION 9 LABOR

(Factory Time)	Chilton Time
Note: On all front suspension operations alignment charges must be added if performed. Time given does not include alignment.	
Wheel, Renew	
one	.5
Wheels, Rotate (All)	
All models	.5
Wheel, Balance	
one	.3
each adtnl	.2
Toe-In, Adjust	
All models	.6
Align Front End	
Includes: Adjust front wheel bearings.	
All models	1.5
Steering Knuckle Spindle, Renew	
Add alignment charges.	
All models-one	2.1
both	4.0
Front Wheel Hub, Renew	
Includes: Renew bearings and seals.	
All models-one	1.5
both	2.9

(Factory Time)	Chilton Time
Upper Ball Joint, Renew	
Add alignment charges.	
All models-one side	1.0
both sides	1.9
Lower Ball Joint, Renew	
Add alignment charges.	
All models-one side	1.1
both sides	2.0
Steering Knuckle Arm, Renew	
All models-one	.6
both	1.0
Upper Control Arm Assy., Renew	
Add alignment charges.	
All models-one side	1.6
both sides	3.0
Renew bushings add-each side	.4
Lower Control Arm Assy., Renew	
Add alignment charges.	
All models-one side	1.6
both sides	3.0
Renew bushings add-each side	.4
Front Torsion Bar, Renew	
All models	
one side	1.2

(Factory Time)	Chilton Time
both sides	1.9
Front Stabilizer Bar and Bushings, Renew	
All models	.9
Front Shock Absorbers or Rubber Bushings, Renew	
All models-one	.5
both	.8
4 WHEEL DRIVE FRONT AXLE	
Steering Knuckle Spindle, Renew	
Add alignment charges.	
All models-one	2.1
both	4.0
Front Wheel Hub Assy., Renew	
Includes: Renew bearings and seals.	
Nissan models	
one side	.9
both sides	1.7
Datsun models	
one side	1.9
both sides	3.7
Front Drive Shafts, Renew	
All models-one side	1.4
both sides	2.7

LABOR 9 FRONT SUSPENSION 9 LABOR

	(Factory Time)	Chilton Time
Front Drive Shaft Boot, Renew		
All models-one		2.0
both		3.9
Free-Running Hubs, Renew		
All models-one side		.5
both sides		.8
Upper Ball Joint, Renew		
Add alignment charges.		
All models-one side		1.0
both sides		1.9
Steering Knuckle Arms, Renew		
Add alignment charges.		
All models-one side		.6
both sides		1.0

LABOR 10 STEERING LINKAGE 10 LABOR

	(Factory Time)	Chilton Time
Cross Rod Assembly, Renew		
Includes: Reset toe-in.		
All models		1.0
Idler Arm Assembly, Renew		
Includes: Reset toe-in.		
All models		.8
Tie Rod or Tie Rod Ends, Renew		
Includes: Reset toe-in.		
All models-one side		.8
both sides		1.5
Pitman Arm, Renew		
Includes: Reset toe-in.		
All models		.8
Steering Damper, Renew		
4 WD models		.6

LABOR 11 STEERING GEAR 11 LABOR

	(Factory Time)	Chilton Time
STANDARD STEERING		
Steering Gear, Adjust (On Truck)		
All models		.5
Steering Gear Assy., R&R or Renew		
All models		1.2
Sector Shaft and/or Oil Seal, Renew		
Includes: R&R steering gear and make all necessary adjustments.		
All models		1.7
Steering Gear Assy., R&R and Recondition		
Includes: Disassemble, renew necessary parts, reassemble and adjust.		
All models		3.0
Steering Column Upper Bushing, Renew		
All models		1.4
Steering Column Flex Coupler, Renew		
All models		.6
Steering Column Lock Assy., Renew		
All models		1.2
POWER STEERING		
Power Steering Pump Drive Belt, Adjust		
All models		.3
Power Steering Pump Drive Belt, Renew		
All models		.4
Power Steering Gear, Renew		
All models		1.8
Power Steering Pump, Renew		
D21 models		.9
720 models		1.7
Power Steering Pump, R&R and Recondition		
D21 models		2.0
720 models		2.7
Sector Shaft Oil Seals, Renew		
All models		2.2
Power Steering Hoses, Renew		
D21 models		.6
720 models		1.1

LABOR 12 CYLINDER HEAD & VALVE SYSTEM 12 LABOR

	(Factory Time)	Chilton Time
GASOLINE ENGINES		
Compression Test		
Four		.7
V-6		.9
Cylinder Head Gasket, Renew		
Includes: Clean carbon and make all necessary adjustments.		
Four		4.4
V-6		
right side		7.6
left side		8.1
both sides		10.0
w/A.C. add		.2
w/P.S. add		.3
Clean Carbon and Grind Valves		
Includes: R&R cylinder heads. Reface valves and seats. Clean carbon and make all necessary adjustments.		
Four		8.9
V-6		17.6
w/A.C. add		.2
w/P.S. add		.3
Cylinder Head, Renew		
Includes: R&R cylinder head, transfer all necessary component parts. Clean carbon, grind valves. Make all necessary adjustments.		
Four		9.4
V-6		
right side		8.6
left side		9.1
both sides		19.6
w/A.C. add		.2
w/P.S. add		.3
Rocker Arm Cover Gasket, Renew		
Four		.6
V-6-one side		.7
both sides		1.0
Valve Springs or Valve Stem Oil Seals, Renew (Head On Truck)		
Four-all		3.3
V-6-one side		2.0
both sides		3.0
Valve Rocker Arm Pivots, Springs and Arms, Renew (All)		
Four		1.2
Valve Rocker Arms/Shafts and/or Lifters, Renew		
V-6-one side		1.2
both sides		2.0
Valve Clearance, Adjust		
Four		1.0
DIESEL ENGINE		
Compression Test		
All models		1.4
Cylinder Head Gasket, Renew		
Includes: Clean carbon. Make all necessary adjustments.		
All models		3.4
w/A.C. add		.4
Cylinder Head, Renew		
Includes: Clean carbon. Transfer parts as required. Reface valves. Make all necessary adjustments.		
All models		5.3
w/A.C. add		.4

LABOR 12 CYLINDER HEAD & VALVE SYSTEM 12 LABOR

(Factory Time) Chilton Time

Clean Carbon and Grind Valves

Includes: R&R cylinder head. Recondition valves and seats. Make all necessary adjustments.

	Chilton Time
All models	7.2
w/A.C. add	.4

Rocker Arm Cover or Gasket, Renew

All models	.6

Valve Springs and/or Valve Stem Oil Seals, Renew (Head on Truck)

All models-one cyl	1.0
each adtnl cyl	.3

Valve Push Rods, Renew

All models	1.3
w/A.C. add	.4

Valve Rocker Arm Assy., Renew

All models	1.4

LABOR 13 ENGINE ASSEMBLY & MOUNTS 13 LABOR

(Factory Time) Chilton Time

GASOLINE ENGINES

Note: All engine operations listed in this group are for assemblies as supplied by the original equipment manufacturer. Time to replace assemblies from independent rebuilders may vary.

Engine Assembly, Remove & Install

Does not include transfer of any parts or equipment.

Four	
D21 models	
4X2	7.1
4X4	9.1
720 models	
4X2	7.8
4X4	10.4
V-6	
4X2	7.4
4X4	10.5
w/A.C. or P.S. add	.4

Cylinder Assy. (Short Block), Renew

Includes: R&R engine assy. Transfer all component parts not supplied with replacement engine. Tune engine.

Four	
D21 models	
4X2	9.7
4X4	11.8
720 models	
4X2	11.0
4X4	13.9
V-6	
4X2	10.0
4X4	15.5
w/A.C. or P.S. add	.4

Engine Assy., R&R and Recondition

Includes: Rebore block, install new pistons, pins, rings, rod and main bearings. Clean carbon, grind valves. Tune engine.

Four	
D21 models	
4X2	21.3
4X4	27.3
720 models	
4X2	23.4
4X4	31.2
V-6	
4X2	22.2
4X4	31.5
w/A.C. or P.S. add	.4

Engine Mounts, Renew

Front	
All models	1.0
Rear	
2 WD	.8
4 WD	
D21 models	.8
720 models	1.0

DIESEL ENGINE

Engine Assembly, Remove & Install

Does not include transfer of any parts or equipment.

All models	5.9
w/A.C. add	.4
w/P.S. add	.3

Cylinder Block, Renew

Includes: R&R engine assy. Transfer all component parts not supplied with replacement engine. Clean carbon, grind valves. Make all necessary adjustments.

All models	16.6
w/A.C. add	.4
w/P.S. add	.3

Short Block Assy., Renew

Includes: R&R engine assy. Transfer all component parts not supplied with replacement engine. Clean carbon, grind valves. Make all necessary adjustments.

All models	13.3
w/A.C. add	.4
w/P.S. add	.3

Engine Assy., R&R and Recondition

Includes: Install new pistons, rings, pins, rod and main bearings. Renew cylinder liners. Clean carbon, grind valves. Make all necessary adjustments.

All models	25.0
w/A.C. add	.4

Engine Mounts, Renew

All models-front	1.0
rear	.8

LABOR 14 PISTONS, RINGS & BEARINGS 14 LABOR

(Factory Time) Chilton Time

GASOLINE ENGINES

Pistons or Connecting Rods, Renew (All)

Includes: R&R cylinder head and oil pan on all models. Remove cylinder top ridge and deglaze cylinder walls. Renew piston rings and rod bearings.

Four	
D21 models	
4X2 models	11.8
4X4 models	14.2
720 models	
4X2 models	9.1
4X4 models	13.7
V-6	
4X2	12.1
4X4	14.5
w/A.C. add	1.0
w/P.S. add	.3

Connecting Rod Bearings, Renew

Includes: R&R oil pan on all models. R&R engine assy. on 4X4 models.

4X2	2.5
4X4	
D21 models	6.9
720 models	10.5
w/A.C. add	1.0
w/P.S. add	.3

COMBINATIONS

Add to Engine Work

DRAIN, EVACUATE & RECHARGE AIR CONDITIONING SYSTEM	
All models	1.0
DISTRIBUTOR, RECONDITION	
All models	.9
CARBURETOR, RECONDITION	
All models	2.5
VALVE GUIDE OR SEAT, RENEW	
Each	.5
OIL PUMP DRIVING GEAR, RENEW	
All models	.2
DEGLAZE CYLINDER WALLS	
Each	.1
REMOVE CYLINDER TOP RIDGE	
Each	.1
PLASTIGAUGE BEARINGS	
Each	.1
OIL FILTER ELEMENT, RENEW	
All models	.3

DIESEL ENGINE

Pistons or Connecting Rods, Renew (All)

Includes: R&R cylinder head and oil pan.

All models	9.9

LABOR 14 PISTONS, RINGS & BEARINGS 14 LABOR

	(Factory Time)	Chilton Time
Renew cyl liner add each		.3
w/A.C. add		.2

Piston Rings, Renew (All)
Includes: R&R cylinder head and oil pan.

	(Factory Time)	Chilton Time
All models		8.7
Renew cyl liner add each		.3
w/A.C. add		.2

Connecting Rod Bearings, Renew
Includes: R&R oil pan.

	(Factory Time)	Chilton Time
All models		2.7

LABOR 15 CRANKSHAFT & DAMPER 15 LABOR

GASOLINE ENGINES

Crankshaft and Main Bearings, Renew
Includes: R&R engine assy. Plastigauge all bearing clearances.

	(Factory Time)	Chilton Time
Four		
D21 models		
4X2		9.5
4X4		11.8
720 models		
4X2		11.1
4X4		13.3
V-6		
4X2		8.9
4X4		19.5
w/A.C. or P.S. add		.4

Crankshaft Rear Main Oil Seal, Renew

	(Factory Time)	Chilton Time
Four		
D21 models		
4X2		12.4
4X4		14.7
720 models		
4X2		5.0
4X4		8.2
V-6		
4X2		12.7
4X4		15.0
w/A.C. or P.S. add		.4

Crankshaft Pulley, Renew
Includes: R&R radiator.

	(Factory Time)	Chilton Time
All models		1.4
Renew front crankshaft seal add		.2
w/A.C. add		.2

DIESEL ENGINE

Crankshaft and Main Bearings, Renew
Includes: R&R engine assembly. Plastigauge all bearing clearances.

	(Factory Time)	Chilton Time
All models		10.8
w/A.C. add		.4
w/P.S. add		.3

Crankshaft Rear Main Bearing Oil Seal, Renew
Includes: R&R engine and trans, where required.

	(Factory Time)	Chilton Time
All models		
SD 22 eng		13.0
SD 25 eng		6.3
w/A.C. add		.4
w/P.S. add		.3

Crankshaft Pulley, Renew
Includes: R&R radiator assy.

	(Factory Time)	Chilton Time
All models		1.0
w/A.C. add		.2

Crankshaft Front Oil Seal, Renew
Includes: R&R radiator assy.

	(Factory Time)	Chilton Time
All models		1.4
w/A.C. add		.2

LABOR 16 CAMSHAFT & TIMING GEARS 16 LABOR

GASOLINE ENGINES

Timing Chain Cover or Gasket, Renew
Includes: R&R radiator, loosen oil pan on all models.

	(Factory Time)	Chilton Time
720 models		
4X2		5.0
4X4		5.7
w/P.S. add		.2
w/A.C. add		.2

Timing Chain, Crankshaft and Cam Sprockets, Renew

	(Factory Time)	Chilton Time
720 models		
4X2		5.5
4X4		6.2
w/P.S. add		.2
w/A.C. add		.2

Camshaft and Lifters, Renew

	(Factory Time)	Chilton Time
Four		3.4

Camshaft Sprocket or Gear, Renew

	(Factory Time)	Chilton Time
Four		1.0

Timing Belt Cover and/or Gasket, Renew

	(Factory Time)	Chilton Time
Four		4.0
Renew timing belt add		.2
Renew cam or crank gears add		.4

Camshafts, Renew

	(Factory Time)	Chilton Time
V-6-right side		8.8
left side		9.3

Camshaft Oil Seals, Renew

	(Factory Time)	Chilton Time
V-6		4.8

DIESEL ENGINE

Timing Gear Cover or Gasket, Renew

	(Factory Time)	Chilton Time
All models		.7
Renew inj. pump drive gear add		.4
w/A.C. add		.2

Engine Front Cover, Renew

	(Factory Time)	Chilton Time
All models		2.9
w/A.C. add		.2

Crankshaft and Timing Gears, Renew

	(Factory Time)	Chilton Time
All models		3.4
w/A.C. add		.2

Camshaft and Lifters, Renew
Includes: R&R engine assembly.

	(Factory Time)	Chilton Time
All models		8.5
Renew cam bushings add		1.0
w/A.C. add		.4

LABOR 17 ENGINE OILING SYSTEM 17 LABOR

GASOLINE ENGINES

Oil Pan and/or Gasket, Renew
Includes: R&R engine assy. on 4X4 models, where required.

	(Factory Time)	Chilton Time
Four		
D21 models		
4X2		1.6
4X4		5.9
720 models		
4X2		1.6
4X4		9.5
V-6		
4X2		1.8
4X4		3.2
w/A.C. or P.S. add		.4

Oil Pump Assembly, Renew

	(Factory Time)	Chilton Time
Four		
D21 models		
4X2		1.3
4X4		2.1
720 models		
4X2		1.1
4X4		1.9
V-6		
4X2		11.4
4X4		12.3
Recond oil pump add		.4

Oil Pump Regulator or Relief Valve, Renew

	(Factory Time)	Chilton Time
All models		.6

Oil Pressure Gauge (Dash Unit), Renew

	(Factory Time)	Chilton Time
D21 models		.7
720 models		1.5

Oil Pressure Sending Unit, Renew

	(Factory Time)	Chilton Time
All models		.5

LABOR 17 ENGINE OILING SYSTEM 17 LABOR

(Factory Time) Chilton Time

Oil Filter Element, Renew
All models 4

DIESEL ENGINE

Oil Pan and/or Gasket, Renew
All models 1.5

Oil Pump, Renew
All models 1.7

Oil Pump, R&R and Recondition
All models 2.1

Oil Pump Regulator or Relief Valve, Renew
All models 6

Oil Filter Element, Renew
All models 4

LABOR 18 CLUTCH & FLYWHEEL 18 LABOR

(Factory Time) Chilton Time

Clutch Pedal Free Play, Adjust
All models 3

Bleed Clutch Hydraulic System
All models 4

Clutch Damper, Renew
Includes: Bleed system.
All models 6

Clutch Damper, R&R and Recondition
Includes: Bleed system.
All models 9

Clutch Master Cylinder, Renew
Includes: Bleed system.
All models 9

Clutch Master Cylinder, R&R and Recondition
Includes: Bleed system.
All models 1.5

Clutch Slave Cylinder, Renew
Includes: Bleed system.
All models 7

Clutch Slave Cylinder, R&R and Recondition
Includes: Bleed system.
All models 1.0

Clutch Assembly, Renew
Includes: R&R trans.
D21 models
4X2 .... 3.7
4X4 .... 6.6
720 models
4X2 .... 4.1
4X4 .... 7.0
Renew pilot brg add 3

Clutch Release Bearing, Renew
Includes: R&R trans.
D21 models
4X2 .... 3.5
4X4 .... 6.4
720 models
4X2 .... 4.0
4X4 .... 6.8

Flywheel, Renew
Includes: R&R trans.
D21 models
4X2 .... 4.0
4X4 .... 6.9
720 models
4X2 .... 4.4
4X4 .... 7.4
Renew ring gear add 5
Renew rear main seal add 3

LABOR 19 STANDARD TRANSMISSION 19 LABOR

(Factory Time) Chilton Time

Transmission Assy., R&R or Renew
D21 models
4X2 .... 3.4
4X4 .... 6.2
720 models
4X2 .... 3.5
4X4 .... 6.6
Renew front cover, gasket or seal add 4

Rear Extension Housing and/or Gasket, Renew
Includes: R&R trans.
D21 models
4X2 .... 4.3
4X4 .... 6.7
720 models
4X2 .... 4.0
4X4 .... 6.8

Extension Housing Oil Seal, Renew With 2 Joint Drive Shaft
All models
4X2 8
4X4 .... 2.4

Speedometer Pinion, Renew
All models 4

Transmission Assy., R&R and Recondition
Includes: Completely disassemble, clean, inspect, renew all parts as required. Install all new gaskets and seals.
4 Speed
720 models 10.9
5 Speed
D21 models
4X2 .... 6.6
4X4 .... 9.6
720 models
4X2 .... 7.1
4X4 .... 10.5

TRANSFER CASE

720 MODELS

Transfer Case Assembly, Remove & Install
720 models 1.7

Transfer Case Housings, Renew
Includes: R&R transfer case assy.
720 models 3.6

Companion Flanges, Renew (Front or Rear)
720 models 7

Transmission Side Flange, Renew
Includes: R&R transfer case assy.
720 models 2.0

Speedometer Drive Gear, Renew
Includes: Renew rear drive shaft oil seal.
720 models 1.2

Front or Rear Cover Oil Seals, Renew
Includes: R&R companion flange.
720 models 9

Transfer Case Front Cover, R&R or Renew
Includes: R&R transfer case assy.
720 models 3.4

Transfer Case Front Oil Seal, Renew
Includes: R&R transfer case assy.
720 models 2.0

Transfer Case Assy., R&R and Recondition
Includes: Complete disassembly, clean, inspect, renew all parts as required. Install all new gaskets and seals.
720 models 4.5

Transfer Case Mount and Insulator, Renew
Includes: Disconnect transfer case as required.
720 models 1.6

D21 MODELS

Transfer Case Assy., R&R or Renew
D21 models 4.5

Transfer Case Assy., R&R and Recondition
D21 models 8.6

Transfer Case Front Cover, Renew
D21 models 4.7
Renew front case add 4

Rear or Center Case Oil Seals, Renew
D21 models 8

Transfer Case Front Cover Oil Seal, Renew
D21 models 5.4

Speedometer Driven Gear, Renew
D21 models 4

Companion Flange, Renew
D21 models 6

Transfer Case Drive Chain, Renew
D21 models 2.0

LABOR 23 AUTOMATIC TRANSMISSION 23 LABOR

(Factory Time) Chilton Time

ON TRUCK SERVICES

Drain & Refill Unit
All models .8

Oil Pressure Check
All models .7

Check Unit For Oil Leaks
Includes: Clean and dry outside of case and run unit to determine point of leak.
All models .9

Vacuum Diaphragm Assy., Renew
All models .5

Kickdown Switch, Renew
All models .5

Downshift Solenoid, Renew
All models .8

Neutral Safety Switch, Renew
All models .6

Speedometer Pinion, Renew
Includes: Renew oil seal.
All models .5

Overdrive Cancel Solenoid, Renew
All models .6

Overdrive Indicator Switch, Renew
All models .6

Overdrive Cancel/Power Switch, Renew
All models .6

Lock-Up Solenoid, Renew
All models .6

Extension Housing Oil Seal, Renew
With 2 Joint Drive Shaft
All models 1.0
With 3 Joint Drive Shaft
All models 1.1

Oil Pan Gasket, Renew
All models .8

Valve Body Assembly, Renew
Includes: R&R oil pan.
All models 1.7

Valve Body Assy., R&R and Recondition
Includes: R&R oil pan. Clean, inspect, free all valves. Replace parts as required.
All models 3.0

SERVICES REQUIRING R&R

Transmission and Torque Converter Assy., R&R
Includes: Drain and refill unit.
All models 4.0

Transmission and Torque Converter Assy., R&R and Recondition
Includes: Completely disassemble trans, including valve body. Clean, inspect, replace all parts as required. Make all necessary adjustments. Road test.
All models 14.4
Pressure check add .8

Torque Converter, Renew
Includes: R&R trans.
All models 4.2
Renew flywheel add .4

Governor Assy., R&R or Renew
Includes: R&R trans.
All models 4.7
Recond gover add .4

Front Oil Pump, Renew or Recondition
Includes: R&R trans. Renew pump seals and gaskets.
All models 4.8

LABOR 25 U-JOINTS & DRIVESHAFT 25 LABOR

(Factory Time) Chilton Time

Driveshaft, Renew
2 Joint Shaft
All models .5
3 Joint Shaft
All models .6

Universal Joint, Renew or Recondition (One)
Includes: R&R driveshaft.
2 Joint Shaft
All models .9
3 Joint Shaft
All models 1.0

Center Bearing, Renew
Includes: R&R driveshaft.
All models 1.0

LABOR 26 DRIVE AXLE 26 LABOR

(Factory Time) Chilton Time

REAR DIFFERENTIAL ASSY.

Rear Axle Shaft and/or Bearing, Renew
Includes: Renew oil seal.
With Single Rear Whls
one side 1.4
both sides 2.7
With Dual Rear Whls
one side .6
both sides 1.2

Rear Wheel Hub Assy., Renew
With Dual Rear Wheels
All models-one 1.0
both 1.9

Axle Shaft Oil Seal, Renew
All models-one .9
both 1.7

Drive Pinion Oil Seal, Renew
All models
Four 5.3
V-6 1.3

Rear Differential Carrier Assy., Remove and Install
All models 2.5

Ring Gear and Pinion Set, Renew
Includes: R&R carrier assy. and make all necessary adjustments.
All models 5.3

Differential Side Bearings, Renew
Includes: R&R carrier assy. and make all necessary adjustments.
All models 3.6

Rear Differential Carrier Assy., R&R and Recondition
All models 6.8

FRONT DIFFERENTIAL

Differential, Drain & Refill
All models 1.1

Rear Cover Gasket, Renew
All models 1.1

Differential Assy., Remove & Install
D21 models 4.5
720 models 1.5

Differential Assy., R&R and Recondition
D21 models 8.6
720 models 6.0

Ring and Pinion Set, Renew
Includes: R&R differential.
D21 models 7.5
720 models 5.0

Side Flange or Oil Seals, Renew
All models-one 1.6
both 3.1

Drive Pinion Oil Seal, Renew
All models 1.7

Front Drive Shaft Assy., R&R or Renew
All models .6
Renew U-Joint add-each .3

Primary Drive Shaft, Renew
All models .8
Renew U-Joint add-each .3

Front Wheel Hub Assy., Renew
Includes: Renew bearings and seals.
Nissan models
one side .9
both sides 1.7
Datsun models
one side 1.9
both sides 3.7

Front Drive Axle Assy., Renew
720 models-one 1.4
both 2.7

Front Drive Shaft Boot, Renew
All models-one 2.0
both 3.9

DUAL WHEEL DIFFERENTIAL

Drain & Refill Unit
All models .6

Rear Cover Gasket, Renew
All models .6

Drive Pinion Oil Seal, Renew
Includes: R&R carrier assy.
All models 5.3

LABOR 26 DRIVE AXLE 26 LABOR

(Factory Time) Chilton Time

Differential Side Bearings and Seals, Renew
All models.................................... 5.3

Ring Gear and Pinion Set, Renew
All models.................................... 7.1
Renew pinion gears add.................... .5

LABOR 27 REAR SUSPENSION 27 LABOR

(Factory Time) Chilton Time

Rear Leaf Spring, Renew
All models-one.................................... 1.8
both.................................... 3.5

Rear Spring Shackle and/or Bushings, Renew
With Single Rear Whls
All models-one side.................... .6
both sides.................................... 1.1
With Dual Rear Whls
All models-one side.................... .9
both sides.................................... 1.7

Rear Spring Front Eye Mount and/or Bushings, Renew
All models-one side.................... 1.0
both sides.................................... 1.9

Rear Shock Absorber or Rubber Bushing, Renew
D21 models-one.................................... .5
both.................................... .7
720 models-one.................................... .7
both.................................... 1.1

LABOR 28 AIR CONDITIONING 28 LABOR

(Factory Time) Chilton Time

Note: If more than one item requires replacement where evacuation and discharging the system is already included in the operation, deduct 1.0 hour for each additional item to the times listed.

Drain, Evacuate & Recharge System
All models.................................... 1.0

Flush Refrigerant System, Complete
To be used in conjunction with component replacement which could contaminate system.
All models.................................... 1.3

Compressor Drive Belt, Renew
All models.................................... .7

Compressor Assembly, Renew
Includes: Transfer parts as required. Evacuate and charge system.
D21 models.................................... 2.3
720 models.................................... 2.5

Compressor Shaft Seal, Renew
Includes: R&R compressor. Evacuate and charge system.
D21 models.................................... 3.0
720 models.................................... 3.2

Compressor Assembly, R&R and Recondition
Includes: Completely disassemble compressor. Clean, inspect and renew all parts as required. Evacuate and charge system.
D21 models.................................... 3.6
720 models.................................... 3.8

Compressor Relay, Renew
All models.................................... .5

Expansion Valve, Renew
Includes: R&R evaporate. Evacuate and charge system.
D21 models.................................... 3.6
720 models.................................... 2.4

Blower Motor, Renew
D21 models.................................... 2.5
720 models.................................... .5

A.C. Temperature Control Assy., Renew
D21 models.................................... 1.4
720 models.................................... 1.0
Renew fan switch add.................... .2

Evaporator Assembly, Renew
Includes: Evacuate and charge system.
D21 models.................................... 3.6
720 models.................................... 2.4

Receiver-Drier Assembly, Renew
Includes: Evacuate and charge system.
All models.................................... 1.8

Condenser Assembly, Renew
Includes: Evacuate and charge system.
D21 models.................................... 2.0
720 models.................................... 2.4

Air Conditioning Hoses, Renew
Includes: Evacuate and charge system.
All models-one.................................... 1.9
each adtnl.................................... .5

LABOR 29 LOCKS, HINGES & WIND. REGULATORS 29 LABOR

(Factory Time) Chilton Time

Hood Hinge, Renew (One)
All models.................................... .6

Hood Lock, Renew
All models.................................... .6

Hood Release Control Assy., Renew
All models.................................... .7

Door Window Regulator, Renew
Includes: R&R window glass.
D21 models.................................... 1.5
720 models.................................... 1.3

Door Handle (Outside), Renew
D21 models.................................... .6
720 models.................................... .8

Door Lock Assembly, Renew (One)
D21 models.................................... .7
720 models.................................... .9

Door Lock Remote Control Rod, Renew (One)
D21 models.................................... .6
720 models.................................... .8

Door Lock Cylinder, Renew (One)
All models.................................... .5

Lock Striker Plate, Renew
All models.................................... .4

LABOR 30 HEAD AND PARKING LAMPS 30 LABOR

(Factory Time) Chilton Time

Aim Headlamps
two.................................... .4
four.................................... .6

Headlamp Sealed Beam Bulb, Renew (One)
All models.................................... .3

Turn Signal or Parking Lamp Lens or Bulb, Renew
All models-each.................................... .3

Stop and Tail Lamp Lens or Bulb, Renew
All models-each.................................... .3

Side Marker Lamp Lens or Bulb, Renew
All models-each.................................... .3

Back-Up Lamp Assembly, Renew
All models-each.................................... .3

Rear Combination Lamp Assy., Renew
All models-each.................................... .4

License Lamp Assembly, Renew
All models.................................... .3

LABOR 31 WINDSHIELD WIPER & SPEEDOMETER 31 LABOR

	(Factory Time)	Chilton Time
Windshield Wiper Motor, Renew		
All models		.7
Windshield Wiper Rods or Pivots, Renew		
All models		.8
Intermittent Wiper Amplifier, Renew		
All models		.4
720 models		1.5
Speedometer Cable and Casing, Renew		
D21 models		.9
720 models		.7
Radio, R&R		
D21 models		1.0
720 models		1.5
Windshield Washer Motor, Renew		
All models		.4
Windshield Wiper/Washer Switch, Renew		
All models		.6
Speedometer Head, R&R or Renew		
D21 models		.7

LABOR 32 LIGHT SWITCHES & WIRING 32 LABOR

	(Factory Time)	Chilton Time
Turn Signal-Dimmer Switch, Assy., Renew		
All models		.9
Hazard Warning Switch, Renew		
All models		.6
Wiper/Washer Switch Assy., Renew		
All models		.6
Headlamp Switch, Renew		
All models		.6
Combination Switch Assy., Renew		
All models		.9
Stop Lamp Switch, Renew		
All models		.5
Back-Up Lamp Switch, Renew (w/Manual Trans.)		
All models		.5
Parking Brake Switch, Renew		
All models		.4
Turn Signal or Hazard Warning Flasher Unit, Renew		
All models		.3
Horn Assembly, Renew		
All models-one		.3
Horn Relay, Renew		
All models		.5

LABOR 34 CRUISE CONTROL 34 LABOR

	(Factory Time)	Chilton Time
Cruise Control Circuits, Test		
All models		1.0
Cruise Control Cable, Renew		
All models		.6
Actuator Assembly, Renew		
All models		.5
Solenoid or Servo Valve, Renew		
All models		.5
Cruise Control Speed Switch, Renew (Sensor)		
All models		1.2
Cruise Control Master Switch, Renew		
All models		.5
Controller Assembly, Renew		
All models		.6
Cruise Control Clutch Switch, Renew		
All models		.4
Cruise Control Stop Switch, Renew		
All models		.4
Cruise Control Relay, Renew		
All models		.6

Suzuki Samuri

GROUP INDEX

ALPHABETICAL INDEX

LABOR 1 TUNE UP 1 LABOR

(Factory Time) Chilton Time

Compression Test
All models .6

Engine Tune Up, (Electronic Ignition)
Includes: Test battery and clean connections. Tighten manifold and carburetor mounting bolts. Check engine compression, clean and adjust or renew spark plugs. Test resistance of spark plug cables. Inspect distributor cap and rotor. Check vacuum advance operation. Reset ignition timing. Adjust idle mixture and idle speed. Service air cleaner. Inspect and adjust drive belts. Inspect choke operation and adjust or free up. Check operation of EGR valve.
All models 1.5

LABOR 2 IGNITION SYSTEM 2 LABOR

(Factory Time) Chilton Time

Spark Plugs, Clean and Reset or Renew
All models .5

Ignition Timing, Reset
All models .4

Distributor, Renew
Includes: Reset ignition timing.
All models .8

Distributor Cap and/or Rotor, Renew
All models .3

Ignition Coil, Renew
Includes: Test coil.
All models .4

Vacuum Control Unit, Renew
Includes: Reset ignition timing.
All models 1.1

Igniter Assembly, Renew
All models 1.1

Ignition Cables, Renew
All models .4

Ignition Switch Lock Cylinder, Renew
All models 1.2

LABOR 3 FUEL SYSTEM 3 LABOR

(Factory Time) Chilton Time

Fuel Pump, Test
Includes: Disconnect line at carburetor, attach pressure gauge.
All models .3

Carburetor Air Cleaner, Service
All models .2

Air Cleaner Vacuum Motor, Renew
All models .4

Air Cleaner Temperature Sensor, Renew
All models .5

Choke Assembly, Renew
Includes: R&R carburetor.
All models 2.2

Carburetor, Renew
Includes: All necessary adjustments.
All models 2.0

Fuel Gauge (Tank), Renew
All models 1.5

Fuel Tank, Renew
Includes: Drain and refill tank.
All models 1.5

Fuel Pump, Renew
All models .6

Intake Manifold or Gasket, Renew
All models 3.0
Renew manif add .5

LABOR 3A EMISSION CONTROLS 3A LABOR

(Factory Time) Chilton Time

Emission Control Computer, Renew
All models .5

Oxygen Sensor, Renew
All models .5

Coolant Temperature Sensor, Renew
All models .4

Solenoid and Vacuum Regulator Assy., Renew
All models .5

PCV Valve, Renew
All models .3

Vacuum Delay Valve, Renew
All models .3

Vacuum Switching Valve, Renew
All models .3

Mixture Control Valve, Renew
All models .3

EGR Valve, Renew
All models .6

EGR Modulator Valve, Renew
All models .3

Charcoal Canister, Renew
All models .3

Fuel Vapor Separator, Renew
All models .4

Hot Idle Compensator, Renew
All models .4

LABOR 4 ALTERNATOR AND REGULATOR 4 LABOR

(Factory Time) Chilton Time

Alternator Assy., Renew
Includes: Transfer pulley or fan.
All models 1.0
Add circuit test if performed.

Alternator Bearings, Renew
Includes: R&R alternator, separate end frames.
All models 1.2

Alternator Circuits, Test
Includes: Test battery, regulator and alternator output.
All models .5

Alternator, R&R and Recondition
Includes: Complete disassembly, inspect, test, replace parts as required, reassemble.
All models 2.5

Voltage Regulator, Test and Renew
All models 1.3

LABOR 5 STARTING SYSTEM 5 LABOR

(Factory Time) Chilton Time

Starter Draw Test (On Truck)
All models 3

Starter Assy., Renew
All models 6
Add draw test if performed.

Starter, R&R and Recondition
Includes: Turn down armature.
All models 2.1
Renew field coils add 5

Starter Drive, Renew
Includes: R&R starter.
All models 1.0

Starter Solenoid, Renew
Includes: R&R starter.
All models 9

Battery Cables, Renew
All models-each 4

Battery Terminals, Clean
All models 3

LABOR 6 BRAKE SYSTEM 6 LABOR

(Factory Time) Chilton Time

Brake Pedal Free Play, Adjust
All models 3

Brakes, Adjust (Minor)
Includes: Adjust brake shoes and fill master cylinder.
All models 4

Bleed Brakes (Four Wheels)
Includes: Fill master cylinder.
All models 6

Brake Shoes and/or Pads, Renew
Includes: Install new or exchange brake shoes or pads, adjust service and hand brake. Bleed system.
All models
front-disc 1.1
rear-drum 1.7
all four wheels 2.6
Resurface brake rotor, add-each 9
Resurface brake drum, add-each 5

Brake Proportioning Valve, Renew
Includes: Bleed system.
All models 1.3

BRAKE HYDRAULIC SYSTEM

Wheel Cylinders, Renew
Includes: Bleed system.
All models-one 1.7
both 2.7

Wheel Cylinders, R&R and Rebuild
Includes: Bleed system.
All models-one 1.9
both 3.1

COMBINATIONS

RENEW WHEEL CYLINDER
Each 2

REBUILD WHEEL CYLINDER
Each 3

REBUILD CALIPER ASSEMBLY
Each 5

RENEW MASTER CYLINDER
All models 5

REBUILD MASTER CYLINDER
All models 8

RENEW BRAKE HOSE
Each 3

REPACK FRONT WHEEL BEARINGS (BOTH WHEELS)
All models 6

RENEW BRAKE DRUM
Each 1

RENEW DISC BRAKE ROTOR
Each 2

(Factory Time) Chilton Time

Master Cylinder, Renew
Includes: Bleed system.
All models 9

Master Cylinder, R&R and Rebuild
Includes: Bleed system.
All models 1.3

(Factory Time) Chilton Time

DISC BRAKES

Disc Brake Pads, Renew
Includes: Install new disc brake pads only.
All models 1.1

Caliper Assy., Renew
Includes: Bleed system.
All models-one 1.2
both 1.8

Caliper Assy., R&R and Recondition
Includes: Bleed system.
All models-one 1.7
both 2.8

Disc Brake Rotor, Renew
All models-one 1.0
both 1.7

POWER BRAKES

Power Brake Cylinder, Renew
All models 1.4

Power Brake Cylinder, R&R and Recondition
All models 2.0

Vacuum Check Valve, Renew
All models 3

PARKING BRAKE

Parking Brake, Adjust
All models 5

Parking Brake Lever Assy., Renew
All models 5

Parking Brake Cables, Renew
All models-each 9

LABOR 7 COOLING SYSTEM 7 LABOR

(Factory Time) Chilton Time

Winterize Cooling System
Includes: Run engine to check for leaks, tighten all hose connections. Test radiator and pressure cap, drain radiator and engine block. Add anti-freeze and refill system.
All models 5

Thermostat, Renew
All models 4

Radiator Assy., R&R or Renew
Includes: Drain and refill cooling system.
All models 1.4
w/A.C. add 7

ADD THESE OPERATIONS TO RADIATOR R&R

Boil & Repair 1.5
Rod Clean 1.9
Repair Core 1.3
Renew Tank 1.6
Renew Trans. Oil Cooler 1.9
Recore Radiator 1.7

(Factory Time) Chilton Time

Radiator Hoses, Renew
All models-each 6

Fan Blades or Clutch Assy., Renew
All models 1.0

Water Pump Drive Belt, Renew
All models 6

Water Pump Drive Belt, Adjust
All models 3

Cooling Fan and/or Motor, Renew
All models 8

Water Pump By-Pass Hose, Renew
All models 5

Water Pump, Renew
Includes: Drain and refill cooling system.
All models 3.1

Water Jacket Expansion Plugs, Renew (Side of Block)
each 5

(Factory Time) Chilton Time

Note: If necessary to R&R any component to gain access to plug, add appropriate time.

Heater Water Control Valve, Renew
All models 8

Temperature Gauge Sending Unit, Renew
All models 5

Heater Core, R&R or Renew
Includes: Drain and refill cooling system.
All models 4.5

ADD THESE OPERATIONS TO HEATER CORE R&R

Boil & Repair 1.2
Repair Core 9
Recore 1.2

Heater Blower Motor, Renew
All models 4.0

Heater Blower Motor Resistor, Renew
All models 4.0

LABOR 7 COOLING SYSTEM 7 LABOR

	(Factory Time)	Chilton Time
Heater Blower Motor Switch, Renew		
All models		1.0
Temperature Control Assy., Renew		
All models		3.2
Heater Hoses, Renew		
All models		.4

LABOR 8 EXHAUST SYSTEM 8 LABOR

	(Factory Time)	Chilton Time
Muffler, Renew		
All models		.8
Front Exhaust Pipe, Renew		
All models		.9
Catalytic Converter, Renew		
All models		1.0
Exhaust Manifold and/or Gasket, Renew		
All models		1.3
w/A.C. add		.5

LABOR 9 FRONT SUSPENSION 9 LABOR

Note: On all front suspension operations alignment charges must be added if performed. Time given does not include alignment.

	(Factory Time)	Chilton Time
Wheel, Renew		
one		.5
Wheels, Rotate (All)		
All models		.5
Wheels, Balance		
one		.3
each adtnl		.2
Check Alignment of Front End		
All models		.5
Note: Deduct if alignment is performed.		
Toe-In, Adjust		
All models		.6
Align Front End		
All models		1.4
Front Shock Absorbers, Renew		
All models-one		.5
both		.8
Front Stabilizer Bar, Renew		
All models		1.0
Front Spring, Renew		
All models-one		1.3
both		2.5
Recond spring add-each		.5
Front Stabilizer Bar Bushings, Renew		
All models-one		.4
both		.5
Spring Shackle Bushings, Renew		
All models		
front-one side		.6
both sides		.9
rear-one side		.8
both sides		1.5
4 WHEEL DRIVE FRONT AXLE		
Axle Shaft Assy., R&R or Renew		
All models		1.9
Axle Shaft Oil Seal, Renew		
All models-one side		2.0
both sides		3.1
Front Spindle Assy., Renew		
All models-one side		1.7
both sides		2.6
Renew bushing add-each		.1
Front Wheel Hub, Renew		
All models-one		1.4
both		2.1
Renew oil seal add-each		.1
Renew hub brg add-each		.1
Steering Knuckle, Renew		
All models-one		3.9
Steering Knuckle Pivot (King Pin), Renew		
All models-one side		1.9
both sides		3.4
Steering Knuckle Bearings, Renew		
All models-one side		3.4
both		6.0
Steering Knuckle Retainer Oil Seals, Renew		
All models-one side		.9
both sides		1.4
Locking Hub, Renew or Recondition		
All models-one		.4
both		.7

LABOR 10 STEERING LINKAGE 10 LABOR

	(Factory Time)	Chilton Time
Tie Rod or Tie Rod End, Renew		
Includes: Reset toe-in.		
All models-one		1.2
each adtnl		.3
Pitman Arm, Renew		
All models		1.2
Center Tie Rod Assy., Renew		
Includes: Reset toe-in.		
All models		1.2
Steering Damper, Renew		
All models		.4

LABOR 11 STEERING GEAR 11 LABOR

	(Factory Time)	Chilton Time
STANDARD STEERING		
Steering Wheel, Renew		
All models		.4
Flexible Coupling, Renew		
All models		.6
Steering Column, R&R or Renew		
All models		1.4
Steering Gear, Renew		
All models		1.3

LABOR 12 CYLINDER HEAD & VALVE SYSTEM 12 LABOR

	(Factory Time)	Chilton Time
Compression Test		
All models		.6
Cylinder Head Gasket, Renew		
Includes: Clean carbon and make all necessary adjustments.		
All models		4.5
w/A.C. add		.4
Cylinder Head, Renew		
Includes: Transfer all component parts, reface valves, clean carbon, make all necessary adjustments.		
All models		7.5
w/A.C. add		.5
Clean Carbon and Grind Valves		
Includes: R&R cylinder head, grind valves and seats. Minor tune up.		
All models		5.7
w/A.C. add		.4
Rocker Arm Cover Gasket, Renew		
All models		.5
Rocker Arms, Renew (All)		
All models		3.2
w/A.C. add		.8
Rocker Arm Shafts, Renew		
All models		3.2
w/A.C. add		.8
Valve Springs and/or Valve Stem Oil Seals, Renew		
All models-one cyl		5.3
all cyls		6.3
w/A.C. add		.4
Valve Clearance, Adjust		
All models		1.0

LABOR 13 ENGINE ASSEMBLY & MOUNTS 13 LABOR

Note: All engine operations listed in this group are for assemblies as supplied by the original equipment manufacturer. Time to replace assemblies from independent rebuilders may vary.

	(Factory Time)	Chilton Time
Engine Assembly, Remove & Install		
Does not include transfer of any parts or equipment.		
All models		5.0
w/A.C. add		1.0
Cylinder Block, Renew (w/All Internal Parts Less Head and Oil Pan)		
Includes: R&R engine assy., transfer all component parts not supplied with replacement engine. Clean carbon, grind valves. Tune engine.		
All models		13.5
w/A.C. add		1.0
Engine Assy., R&R and Recondition		
Includes: Rebore block, install new pistons, pins, rings, rod and main bearings. Clean carbon, grind valves. Tune engine.		
All models		23.8
w/A.C. add		1.0
Engine Mounts, Renew		
All models		
Front		
one		.8
both		1.2
Rear		.7

LABOR 14 PISTONS, RINGS & BEARINGS 14 LABOR

	(Factory Time)	Chilton Time
Piston Rings, Renew (All)		
Includes: Remove cylinder top ridge, deglaze cylinder walls. Clean piston and ring grooves. Minor tune up.		
All models-one cyl		6.3
all cyls		7.1
Pistons or Connecting Rods, Renew		
Includes: Remove cylinder top ridge, deglaze cylinder walls. Minor tune up.		
All models-one cyl		6.6
all cyls		8.3
Connecting Rod Bearings, Renew (All)		
All models		2.7

COMBINATIONS

	Chilton Time
DRAIN, EVACUATE & RECHARGE AIR CONDITIONING SYSTEM	
All models	1.0
CARBURETOR, RECONDITION	
All models	1.2
REMOVE CYLINDER TOP RIDGE	
Each	.1
DEGLAZE CYLINDER WALLS	
Each	.1
RECONDITION CYLINDER HEAD (HEAD REMOVED)	
All models	1.5
VALVE GUIDES, RENEW	
Each	.2
OIL FILTER ELEMENT, RENEW	
All models	.3

LABOR 15 CRANKSHAFT & DAMPER 15 LABOR

	(Factory Time)	Chilton Time
Crankshaft and Main Bearings, Renew		
Includes: R&R engine assy. Check all bearing clearances.		
All models		11.2
w/A.C. add		.8
Main and Rod Bearings, Renew		
Includes: R&R engine assy. Check all bearing clearances.		
All models		12.8
w/A.C. add		.8
Rear Main Oil Seal, Renew		
All models		5.3
Crankshaft Pulley, Renew		
All models		.9
Crankshaft Front Oil Seal, Renew		
All models		5.4
w/A.C. add		.6

LABOR 16 CAMSHAFT & TIMING GEARS 16 LABOR

	(Factory Time)	Chilton Time
Camshaft and/or Oil Seal, Renew		
All models		5.0
Timing Belt Covers, R&R or Renew		
All models		
inner		3.2
outer		2.1
Timing Belt and/or Tensioner, Renew		
All models		3.0

LABOR 17 ENGINE OILING SYSTEM 17 LABOR

	(Factory Time)	Chilton Time
Oil Pan and/or Gasket, Renew		
All models		1.7
Engine Oil Pump, Renew (Front Cover)		
All models		5.4
w/A.C. add		.6
Oil Pressure Sending Unit, Renew		
All models		.4
w/A.C. add		.2
Oil Filter Element, Renew		
All models		.4

LABOR 18 CLUTCH & FLYWHEEL 18 LABOR

	(Factory Time)	Chilton Time
Clutch Pedal Free Play, Adjust		
All models		.3
Clutch Release Arm, Renew		
All models		.6
Clutch Release Bearing, Renew		
Includes: R&R trans and adjust linkage.		
All models		3.2
Clutch Assembly, Renew		
Includes: R&R trans and adjust linkage.		
All models		3.5
Flywheel, Renew		
Includes: R&R trans and adjust linkage.		
All models		3.8

LABOR 19 STANDARD TRANSMISSION 19 LABOR

	(Factory Time)	Chilton Time
Transmission Assy., R&R or Renew		
All models		3.2
Transmission Assy., R&R and Recondition		
Includes: Complete disassembly, clean and inspect all parts. Renew parts as required. Install new gaskets and seals.		
All models		6.5
Extension Housing Oil Seal, Renew		
All models		3.0
Speedometer Driven Gear, Renew		
All models		.5
TRANSFER CASE		
Transfer Case Lever and/or Boot, Renew		
All models		.8
4 Wheel Drive Switch, Renew		
All models		.5
Transfer Case U-Joint Flange, Renew		
All models		.9
Renew oil seal add		.1
Transfer Case Assy., R&R and Recondition		
All models		4.5

LABOR 25 U-JOINTS & DRIVESHAFT 25 LABOR

	(Factory Time)	Chilton Time
Drive Shaft, Renew		
All models		
front		.9
center		.9
rear		.9
Universal Joint, Renew or Recondition		
Includes: Disconnect drive shaft.		
All models-one		1.2
each adtnl		.5

LABOR 26 DRIVE AXLE 26 LABOR

	(Factory Time)	Chilton Time
REAR DIFFERENTIAL		
Rear Axle Shaft, Renew		
All models-one		2.2
both		3.3
Axle Shaft Bearing and/or Oil Seal, Renew		
All models-one		2.2
both		3.3
Pinion Shaft Oil Seal, Renew		
All models		1.0
Ring Gear and Pinion Set, Renew		
All models		6.0
Renew pinion brgs add		.4
Renew side brgs add		.6
Rear Axle Housing, Renew		
All models		4.9
FRONT DIFFERENTIAL ASSY		
Front Axle Housing, Renew		
All models		7.5
Ring Gear and Pinion Set, Renew		
Includes: R&R front carrier assy.		
All models		7.0

LABOR 27 REAR SUSPENSION 27 LABOR

	(Factory Time)	Chilton Time
Rear Spring, Renew		
All models-one		1.3
both		2.5
Recond spring add-each		.5
Rear Spring Front Eye Bushings, Renew		
All models-one side		.8
both side		1.4
Rear Spring Shackle, Renew		
All models-one		.6
both		.8
Rear Shock Absorbers, Renew		
All models-one		.5
both		.8

LABOR 28 AIR CONDITIONING 28 LABOR

(Factory Time) Chilton Time

Note: If more than one item requires replacement where evacuation and discharging the system is already included in the operation, deduct 1.0 hour for each additional item to the times listed.

Drain, Evacuate and Recharge System
All models.................................... 1.0

Flush Refrigerant System, Complete
To be used in conjunction with component replacement which could contaminate system.
All models.................................... 1.3

Leak Check
Includes: Check all lines and connections.
All models.................................... .5

Refrigerant, Add (Partial Charge)
All models.................................... .6

Compressor Drive Belt, Renew
All models.................................... .3

Compressor Assembly, Renew
Includes: Transfer parts as required. Evacuate and charge system.
All models.................................... 2.0

Compressor Clutch Assembly, Renew
Includes: R&R compressor. Evacuate and charge system.
All models.................................... 2.0

Compressor Shaft Seal Kit, Renew
Includes: Evacuate and charge system.
All models.................................... 2.5

Receiver–Dehydrator, Renew
Includes: Evacuate and charge system.
All models.................................... 1.4

Expansion Valve, Renew
Includes: Evacuate and charge system.
All models.................................... 3.5

Evaporator Core, Renew
Includes: Evacuate and charge system.
All models.................................... 3.5

Condensor Assembly, Renew
Includes: Evacuate and charge system.
All models.................................... 2.1

Blower Motor Resistor, Renew
All models.................................... .4

Air Conditioning Hoses, Renew
Includes: Evacuate and charge system.
All models-one.................................... 1.7
each adtnl.................................... .5

LABOR 29 LOCKS, HINGES & WIND. REGULATORS 29 LABOR

(Factory Time) Chilton Time

Hood Rlease Cable, Renew
All models
wo/A.C.................................... .6
w/A.C.................................... 3.0

Hood Latch Assembly, Renew
All models.................................... .4

Hood Hinge, Renew (One)
All models.................................... .4

Lock Striker Plate, Renew
All models.................................... .3

Door Handle (Outside), Renew
All models.................................... .5

Door Lock Assembly, Renew
All models.................................... 1.0

Door Lock Cylinder Assy., Renew
All models.................................... .7
Recode cyl add.................................... .3

Door Window Regulator, Renew
All models.................................... .9

LABOR 30 HEAD AND PARKING LAMPS 30 LABOR

(Factory Time) Chilton Time

Aim Headlamps
All models.................................... .4

Headlamp Sealed Beam Bulb, Renew
All models.................................... .5

Side Marker Lamp Lens or Bulb, Renew
All models.................................... .3

Turn Signal or Parking Lamp Lens or Bulb, Renew
All models.................................... .3

Tail or Stop Lamp Lens or Bulb, Renew
All models.................................... .3

Rear Combination Lamp Assy., Renew
All models-each.................................... .4

LABOR 31 WINDSHIELD WIPER & SPEEDOMETER 31 LABOR

(Factory Time) Chilton Time

Windshield Washer Pump, Renew
All models.................................... .3

Speedometer Head, R&R or Renew
All models.................................... 1.0

Windshield Wiper Motor, Renew
All models
soft top.................................... 1.1
hardtop.................................... 2.9

Wiper Transmission Assy., Renew
All models
soft top.................................... 1.3
hardtop.................................... 3.2

Speedometer Cable and Casing, Renew
All models.................................... .9

Radio, R&R
All models.................................... 1.0

LABOR 32 LIGHT SWITCHES & WIRING 32 LABOR

(Factory Time) Chilton Time

Headlamp Switch, Renew
All models.................................... .5

Combination Switch, Renew
All models.................................... 1.2

Parking Brake Warning Lamp Switch, Renew
All models.................................... .4

Stop Light Switch, Renew
All models.................................... .4

Starter Safety Switch, Renew
All models.................................... .5

Back-Up Lamp Switch, Renew
All models.................................... .5

Turn Signal or Hazard Warning Flasher, Renew
All models.................................... .2

Horn Assembly, Renew
All models.................................... .2

GROUP INDEX

ALPHABETICAL INDEX

LABOR 1 TUNE UP 1 LABOR

(Factory Time) Chilton Time

Compression Test
Van 7
All other models 6

Engine Tune Up, (Electronic Ignition)
Includes: Test battery and clean connections. Tighten manifold mounting bolts. Check engine compression, clean and adjust or renew spark plugs. Test resistance of spark plug cables. Inspect distributor cap and rotor. Check vacuum advance operation. Reset ignition timing. Adjust idle mixture and idle speed. Service air cleaner. Inspect and adjust drive belts. Inspect choke operation and adjust or free up. Check operation of EGR valve.
Van 2.3
All other models 1.5
Adjust valves add
Four 5
Six 8

LABOR 2 IGNITION SYSTEM 2 LABOR

(Factory Time) Chilton Time

Spark Plugs, Clean and Reset or Renew
Van 6
All other models 5

Ignition Timing, Reset
Van 1.0
All other models 4

Distributor Assy., Renew
Includes: Reset ignition timing.
Van 1.4
All other models 8

Distributor Assy., R&R and Recondition
Includes: Reset ignition timing.
Van 2.0
All other models 1.3

Distributor Cap and/or Rotor, Renew
Van 1.0
All other models 4

Vacuum Advance Unit, Renew
Includes: Reset ignition timing.
Van 1.1
All other models 5

Signal Generator Assy., Renew
Van 1.9
All other models 7

Spark Plug Cables, Renew
Van 5
All other models 4

Ignition Coil or Igniter, Renew
Van 1.7
All other models 4

Ignition Switch, Renew
Van 7
All other models 6

LABOR 3 FUEL SYSTEM 3 LABOR

(Factory Time) Chilton Time

Fuel Pump, Test
Includes: Disconnect line at carburetor, attach pressure gauge.
All models 3

Carburetor Air Cleaner, Service
All models 2

Carburetor Idle Speed, Adjust
All models 4

Float Level, Adjust
All models 1.0

Carburetor Assembly, Renew
Includes: All necessary adjustments.
All models 1.5

Carburetor, R&R and Clean or Recondition
Includes: All necessary adjustments.
All models 3.0

Needle Valve and Seat, Renew
Includes: Reset float level.
All models 1.5

Fuel Pump, Renew
All models
mechanical 6
electric 1.0

Fuel Tank, Renew
Includes: Drain and refill tank.
Van 1.3
P/up-4 Runner 1.9
Land Cruiser
H/T 2.5
Wagon 2.3

Fuel Gauge (Dash Unit), Renew
Van 9
All other models 8

Fuel Gauge (Tank Unit), Renew
Van 1.2
P/up-4 Runner 2.0
Land Cruiser
H/T 1.0
Wagon 5

Intake Manifold Gasket, Renew
Van 3.7
P/up-4 Runner 1.8
w/Fuel inj or E.F.I. add 1.0
Land Cruiser 2.3

Intake and Exhaust Manifold Gaskets, Renew
Land Cruiser 4.0

ELECTRONIC FUEL INJECTION

Throttle Body and/or Gasket, Renew
All models 1.4

Electric Fuel Pump, Renew
All models 1.0

Fuel Filter, Renew
All models 9

Fuel Injection Computer, Renew
All models 9

Water Temperature Sensor, Renew
Van 1.2
All other models 1.1

Start Injector Time Switch, Renew
Van 1.2
All other models 1.1

Oxygen Sensor, Renew
Van 8
All other models 1.1

Air Flow Meter, Renew
Van 1.1
All other models 1.2

Fuel Pressure Regulator, Renew
All models 1.4

Fuel Injectors, Renew (All)
Van 4.0
All other models 3.2

Cold Start Injector Assy., Renew
Van 7
All other models 6

Air Valve Assembly, Renew
Van 2.4
All other models 1.2

Intake Manifold and/or Gasket, Renew
Van 3.7
All other models 3.4

DIESEL ENGINE

Air Cleaner, Service
All models 2

Glow Plugs, Renew
All models-one 4
all 8

Glow Plug Relay, Renew
All models 5

Starter Relay, Renew
All models 4

Fuel Injection Pump, R&R or Renew
P/up 4.0
Land Cruiser
H/T 2.0
Wagon 3.2

Fuel Injection Pump, R&R and Recondition
P/up 9.1
Land Cruiser
H/T 6.1
Wagon 8.0

Delivery Valve and/or Gasket, Renew
P/up 1.3
Land Cruiser
H/T 1.4
Wagon 2.2

Fuel Injection Nozzles, Renew (All)
All models 1.3

LABOR 3 FUEL SYSTEM 3 LABOR

(Factory Time)	Chilton Time
Fuel Injection Lines, Renew	
All models-one	.5
each adtnl	.2
Fuel Filter, Renew	
All models	.4
Fuel Tank, Renew	
All models	1.9
Fuel Gauge (Tank), Renew	
All models	1.9
Intake Manifold and/or Gasket, Renew	
All models	1.7
TURBOCHARGER	
Turbocharger Assembly, Renew	
All models	
Gas	2.9
Diesel	1.5
Turbo to Exhaust Manifold Gasket, Renew	
All models	
Gas	2.5
Diesel	1.2

LABOR 3A EMISSION CONTROLS 3A LABOR

(Factory Time)	Chilton Time
POSITIVE CRANKCASE VENTILATION SYSTEM	
PCV Valve, Renew	
All models	.3
AIR INJECTION SYSTEM	
Air Pump, Renew	
P/up	.6
Land Cruiser	.7
Air Pump Drive Belt, Renew	
P/up	.4
Land Cruiser	.5
Air Injection Manifold, Renew	
P/up	1.3
Land Cruiser	.6
Air Injection Check Valve, Renew	
P/up	1.4
Land Cruiser	.4
Air By-Pass Valve, Renew	
Land Cruiser	.4
Air Switching Valve, Renew	
P/up	.4
Air Control Valve, Renew	
P/up	1.0
1983 & earlier	1.0
1984 & later	.6
Land Cruiser	.7
EXHAUST GAS RECIRCULATION SYSTEM	
E.G.R. Valve, Renew	
P/up	.6
Land Cruiser	.5
E.G.R. Vacuum Modulator Valve, Renew	
P/up	.3
Thermo Sensor, Renew	
Land Cruiser	.3
COMBUSTION SYSTEM	
Vacuum Switching Valve, Renew	
All models	.3
Thermo Sensor, Renew	
All models	.7
Throttle Positioner, Renew	
All models	.4
Computer, Renew	
All models	.5
Vacuum Control Valve, Renew	
All models	.3
Vacuum Transmitting Valve, Renew	
All models	.3
Bimetal Vacuum Switching Valve, Renew	
All models	.9
Mixture Control Valve, Renew	
All models	.4
Check Valve, Renew	
All models	.3
Vacuum Switch, Renew	
All models	.4
High Altitude Compensator Valve, Renew	
All models	.3
Charcoal Canister, Renew	
All models	.3

LABOR 4 ALTERNATOR AND REGULATOR 4 LABOR

(Factory Time)	Chilton Time
Alternator Circuits, Test	
Includes: Test battery, regulator and alternator output.	
All models	.3
Alternator Assembly, Renew	
P/up-4 Runner	•1.0
All other models	1.1
•w/Diesel eng add	.1
Add circuit test if performed.	
Alternator Assy., R&R and Recondition	
Includes: Disassemble, clean and test. Renew parts as required, reassemble.	
P/up-4 Runner	•2.0
All other models	2.3
•w/Diesel eng add	.3
Alternator Bearing, Renew	
P/up-4 Runner	•1.4
All other models	1.6
•w/Diesel eng add	.2
Voltage Regulator, Test and Renew	
All models-external	.5
internal	1.5
Ammeter, Renew	
All models	.8

LABOR 5 STARTING SYSTEM 5 LABOR

(Factory Time)	Chilton Time
Starter Draw Test (On Truck)	
All models	.3
Starter Assembly, Renew	
All models	.7
Add draw test if performed.	
Starter Assy., R&R and Recondition	
Includes: Turn down armature.	
All models	2.0
Renew field coils add	.5
Add draw test if performed.	
Starter Solenoid, Renew	
Includes: R&R starter.	
All models	.8
REDUCTION TYPE	
Starter Assembly, Renew	
All models	.7
Add draw test if performed.	
Starter Assy., R&R and Recondition	
Includes: Turn down armature.	
All models	1.5
Starter Solenoid, Renew	
Includes: R&R starter.	
All models	.9
Battery Cables, Renew	
Van	
each	.6
All other models	
positive	.4
negative	.3

LABOR 6 BRAKE SYSTEM 6 LABOR

(Factory Time) Chilton Time

Bleed Brakes

Includes: Fill master cylinder.

	Chilton Time
two wheels	.6
four wheels	1.0

Brakes, Adjust (Minor)

two wheels	.4
four wheels	.7

Brake Shoes, Renew

Includes: Install new or exchange brake shoes. Adjust service and hand brake. Bleed system.

Van	2.5
All other models	2.0
w/Dual whls add	1.0
Resurface brake drum add-each	.5

Rear Brake Drum, Renew (One)

Van	1.5
All other models	1.2
w/Dual whls add	.5

BRAKE HYDRAULIC SYSTEM

Wheel Cylinders, Renew

Includes: Bleed system.

Van-one side	1.9
All other models one side	1.5
w/Dual whls add	.5

Wheel Cylinders, R&R and Rebuild

Includes: Bleed system.

Van-one side	2.3
All other models one side	1.9
w/Dual whls add	.5

Master Cylinder, Renew

Includes: Bleed system.

Van	2.2
All other models	1.8

Master Cylinder, R&R and Rebuild

Includes: Bleed system.

Van	2.6
All other models	2.2

Brake Hose, Renew (Flex)

Includes: Bleed system.

All models front-one	.8
All models rear-one	.9

COMBINATIONS

Add to Brakes, Renew

	Chilton Time
RENEW WHEEL CYLINDER one side	.2
REBUILD WHEEL CYLINDER One side	.4
REBUILD MASTER CYLINDER All models	.5
REBUILD CALIPER ASSEMBLY Each	.4
RENEW BRAKE HOSE Each	.3
RENEW BRAKE DRUM 2WD	.2
4WD	.4
RENEW DISC BRAKE ROTOR 2WD	.2
4WD	.4

(Factory Time) Chilton Time

Load Sensing Proportioning Valve, Renew

Includes: Bleed system.

Van	1.6
All other models	1.9

Brake System, Flush and Refill

All models	1.2

DISC BRAKES

Disc Brake Pads, Renew

Includes: Install new disc brake pads only.

Van-P/up-4 Runner	1.1
Land Cruiser	1.3

Disc Brake Rotor, Renew (One)

Van	1.4
P/up-4 Runner 2WD	1.5
P/up-4 Runner 4WD	1.8
Land Cruiser	2.2

Caliper Assembly, Renew (One)

Includes: Bleed system.

Van	1.2
P/up-4 Runner	1.3
Land Cruiser	1.4

Caliper Assy., R&R and Rebuild (One)

Includes: Bleed system.

Van	1.6
P/up-4 Runner	1.7
Land Cruiser	1.8

Proportioning and By-Pass Valve, Renew

Includes: Bleed system.

All models	1.1

POWER BRAKES

Brake Booster Assembly, Renew

Includes: Bleed system.

Van	3.0
P/up-4 Runner	2.5
Land Cruiser	2.2

Brake Booster, R&R and Recondition

Includes: Bleed system.

Van	3.6
P/up-4 Runner	3.1
Land Cruiser	2.9

Vacuum Check Valve, Renew

Van-P/up-4 Runner	.4
Land Cruiser	.5

Vacuum Pump, Renew (w/Diesel eng)

All models	.7
Recond pump add	.4

PARKING BRAKE

Parking Brake, Adjust

All models	.3

Parking Brake Control, Renew

All models	.7

Parking Brake Cables, Renew

Front

All models	1.0

Rear

Van	1.9
All other models	1.3

LABOR 7 COOLING SYSTEM 7 LABOR

(Factory Time) Chilton Time

Winterize Cooling System

Includes: Run engine to check for leaks, tighten all hose connections. Test radiator and pressure cap, drain radiator and engine block. Add anti-freeze and refill system.

All models	.5

Thermostat, Renew

Van	1.0
All other models	.6

Radiator Assy., R&R or Renew

Includes: Drain and refill cooling system.

Van	1.8
P/up-4 Runner	1.2
Land Cruiser	1.4

ADD THESE OPERATIONS TO RADIATOR R&R

Boil & Repair	1.5
Rod Clean	1.9
Repair Core	1.3
Renew Tank	1.6
Renew Trans. Oil Cooler	1.9
Recore Radiator	1.7

Radiator Hoses, Renew

UPPER

Van	1.1
P/up-4 Runner	.5
Land Cruiser	.5

LOWER

All models	.8

By-Pass Hose, Renew

P/up-4 Runner	.9
Land Cruiser	.5

Fan Blades or Fluid Coupling, Renew

Van	1.5
All other models	.6

Fan Belt, Renew

Van	.6
All other models	.4

Fan Belt, Adjust

All models	.3

Water Pump, Renew

Van	2.3
All other models Gas	1.4
All other models Diesel	2.1

Temperature Gauge (Dash Unit), Renew

Van	1.2
P/up-4 Runner	1.0
Land Cruiser	1.1

Temperature Gauge Sending Unit, Renew

All models	.6

Heater Blower Motor, Renew

Van	1.4
P/up-4 Runner	.9
Land Cruiser H/T	.9
Land Cruiser Wagon	.5

Heater Core, R&R or Renew

Van	2.4
P/up-4 Runner	2.1
Land Cruiser H/T	3.0
Land Cruiser Wagon	3.6

LABOR 7 COOLING SYSTEM 7 LABOR

(Factory Time)	Chilton Time
ADD THESE OPERATIONS TO HEATER CORE R&R	
Boil & Repair	1.2
Repair Core	.9
Recore	1.2
Heater Control Assembly, Renew	
Van	.8
P/up-4 Runner	.9
Land Cruiser	
H/T	1.2
Wagon	.9
Heater Blower Motor Resistor, Renew	
Van	.8
All other models	.4
Heater Water Valve, Renew	
Van	1.2
P/up-4 Runner	.6
Land Cruiser	.9
Heater Hose, Renew (One)	
Van	1.2
P/up-4 Runner	.5
Land Cruiser	.7

LABOR 8 EXHAUST SYSTEM 8 LABOR

(Factory Time)	Chilton Time
Muffler and Tail Pipe Assy., Renew	
Van	1.0
All other models	.6
Front Exhaust Pipe, Renew	
Van	1.0
P/up-4 Runner	.6
Land Cruiser	
H/T	.9
Wagon	.6
Intermediate Pipe, Renew	
Land Cruiser	.9
Catalytic Converter, Renew	
Van	1.0
P/up-4 Runner	.8
Exhaust Manifold or Gasket, Renew	
Van	3.6
All other models	
Gas	1.3
Diesel	1.7
Intake and Exhaust Manifold or Gaskets, Renew	
P/up-4 Runner	
Gas	1.7
Diesel	1.8
Land Cruiser	
H/T	1.9
Wagon	2.2
w/E.F.I. or Turbo add	1.0

LABOR 9 FRONT SUSPENSION 9 LABOR

(Factory Time)	Chilton Time
Note: On all front suspension operations alignment charges must be added if performed. Time given does not include alignment.	
Wheel, Renew (One)	
All models	.5
Wheels, Rotate (All)	
All models	.5
Wheels, Balance	
one	.3
each adtnl	.2
Toe-In, Adjust	
All models	.4
Align Front End	
All models	1.4
CONTROL ARM SUSPENSION	
Upper Control Arm Assy., Renew (One Side)	
Add alignment charges.	
Van	2.8
P/up-4 Runner	
4X2	2.3
4X4	2.7
Upper Control Arm Shaft and Bushings, Renew (One Side)	
Add alignment charges.	
Van	3.1
P/up-4 Runner	
4X2	2.6
4X4	3.3
Lower Control Arm Assy., Renew (One)	
Add alignment charges.	
Van	2.3
P/up-4 Runner	
4X2	3.2
4X4	2.4
Torsion Bar, Renew (One Side)	
Van	.8
P/up-4 Runner	
4X2	1.2
4X4	1.3
Front Shock Absorbers, Renew	
Van-one	.5
both	.7
P/up-4 Runner	
one	.8
both	1.0
Upper Ball Joint, Renew (One Side)	
Add alignment charges.	
Van	1.8
P/up-4 Runner	
4X2	2.2
4X4	2.7
Lower Ball Joint, Renew (One Side)	
Add alignment charges.	
Van	1.7
P/up-4 Runner	2.3
Front Axle Hub, Renew (One Side)	
Van	1.5
P/up-4 Runner	
4X2	1.4
4X4	2.4
Front Wheel Bearings, Renew (One Side)	
Van	1.3
P/up-4 Runner	
4X2	1.3
4X4	1.9
Front Wheel Grease Seals, Renew (One Side)	
Van	1.0
P/up-4 Runner	
4X2	.8
4X4	1.9
Steering Knuckle, Renew	
Add alignment charges.	
Van	2.2
P/up-4 Runner	
4X2	3.2
4X4	3.4
LEAF SPRING SUSPENSION	
Front Spring, Renew (One)	
All models	1.5
Front Spring, R&R and Recondition (One)	
All models	2.0
Front Spring Shackle Assy., Renew (One Side)	
All models	.8
Front Shock Absorber, Renew (One Side)	
All models	.6
4 WHEEL DRIVE FRONT AXLE	
Front Axle, Hub, Renew (One)	
P/up	2.4
Land Cruiser	2.2
Front Hub Oil Seal, Renew (One Side)	
P/up	1.9
Land Cruiser	1.6
Front Hub Bearings, Renew (One Side)	
P/up	1.9
Land Cruiser	1.7
Steering Knuckle, Renew (One)	
Add alignment charges.	
P/up	3.4
Land Cruiser	3.0
Renew brg add	.2
Front Drive Shaft, Renew	
All models	1.9
Front Drive Shaft Boot, Renew	
All models	2.4

LABOR 10 STEERING LINKAGE 10 LABOR

(Factory Time)	Chilton Time
Pitman Arm, Renew	
All models	.9
Idler Arm, Renew	
Van	.9
All other models	1.0
Tie Rod, Renew (One Side)	
Land Cruiser	
1986	2.0
All other models	1.1
Tie Rod End, Renew (One Side)	
Land Cruiser	
1986	1.4
All other models	1.2
Center Arm Bracket, Renew	
Van	1.0
Recond add	.5
Steering Damper, Renew	
All models	.8

LABOR 11 STEERING GEAR 11 LABOR

(Factory Time)	Chilton Time
Horn Button or Contact Plate, Renew	
All models	.5
Steering Wheel, Renew	
All models	.4
Upper Mast Jacket Bearing, Renew	
Van-Land Cruiser	1.7
All other models	1.2
Flex Coupling, Renew	
All models	
wo/Tilt whl	1.2
w/Tilt whl	.6

MANUAL STEERING

WORM & SECTOR TYPE

(Factory Time)	Chilton Time
Steering Gear, Adjust (On Truck)	
All models	.5
Steering Gear, R&R or Renew	
Van	1.0
P/up-4 Runner	1.2
Land Cruiser	1.4
Steering Gear, R&R and Recondition	
Includes: Disassemble, renew parts as required, reassemble and adjust.	
Van	1.8
P/up-4 Runner	2.0
Land Cruiser	2.5

RACK & PINION TYPE

(Factory Time)	Chilton Time
Manual Rack and Pinion Assy., R&R or Renew	
Van	1.6
Manual Rack and Pinion Assy., R&R and Recondition	
Van	3.1
Steering Rack End, Renew (One Side)	
Van	1.8
Steering Rack End Boot, Renew (One Side)	
Van	1.3
Tie Rod End, Renew	
Van-manual or power	1.2

POWER STEERING

WORM & SECTOR TYPE

(Factory Time)	Chilton Time
Power Steering Pump Drive Belt, Renew	
Van	1.5
All other models	.5
Power Steering Gear, R&R or Renew	
Van	1.6
All other models	2.0
Power Steering Pump, Renew	
Land Cruiser-H/T	2.0
Van	1.7
All other models	1.5
Power Steering Pump, R&R and Recondition	
Land Cruiser-H/T	3.4
Van	2.7
All other models	2.5
Power Steering Hoses, Renew	
Pressure	
Van	1.6
All other models	1.1
Return	
Van	2.3
Land Cruiser	1.1
All other models	.5

RACK & PINION TYPE

(Factory Time)	Chilton Time
Power Steering Pump Drive Belt, Renew	
Van	1.5
Power Rack and Pinion Assy., R&R or Renew	
Van	2.3
Power Rack and Pinion Assy., R&R and Reseal	
Van	3.6
Power Steering Rack End Boot, Renew (One Side)	
Van	1.3
Power Steering Pump, Renew	
Van	1.7
Power Steering Pump, R&R and Recondition	
Van	2.9
Power Steering Hoses, Renew	
Van	
Pressure	1.6
Return	2.3

LABOR 12 CYLINDER HEAD & VALVE SYSTEM 12 LABOR

GASOLINE ENGINES

(Factory Time)	Chilton Time
Compression Test	
Van	.7
All other models	.6
Cylinder Head Gasket, Renew	
Includes: Clean carbon. Make all necessary adjustments.	
Van	5.6
P/up-4 Runner	
wo/F.I.	4.7
w/F.I.	5.5
w/Turbo	6.5
Land Cruiser	
H/T	4.3
Wagon	5.1
w/P.S. add	.5
Cylinder Head, Renew	
Includes: R&R cylinder head. Reface valves and seats. Make all necessary adjustments.	
Van	7.7
P/up-4 Runner	
wo/F.I.	7.3
w/F.I.	8.2
w/Turbo	9.3
Land Cruiser	
H/T	7.0
Wagon	8.6
w/P.S. add	.5
Clean Carbon and Grind Valves	
Includes: R&R cylinder head. Reface valves and seats. Make all necessary adjustments.	
Van	8.0
P/up-4 Runner	
wo/F.I.	8.7
w/F.I.	9.7
w/Turbo	10.8
Land Cruiser	
H/T	8.3
Wagon	10.3
w/P.S. add	.5
Cylinder Head Cover Gasket, Renew	
Van	.8
P/up-4 Runner	.9
Land Cruiser	.7
Valve Springs and/or Valve Stem Oil Seals, Renew (All)	
Van	6.2
P/up-4 Runner	
wo/F.I.	5.5
w/F.I.	6.5
w/Turbo	7.5
Land Cruiser	
H/T	5.5
Wagon	6.0
w/P.S. add	.5
Valve Push Rods, Renew (All)	
Van	1.0
Land Cruiser	1.5
Valve Lifters, Renew (All)	
Van	1.1
Land Cruiser	
H/T	3.2
Wagon	2.3

LABOR 12 CYLINDER HEAD & VALVE SYSTEM 12 LABOR

(Factory Time) Chilton Time

Rocker Arms, Shafts and Supports, Renew (All)

	Chilton Time
Van	1.5
P/up-4 Runner	2.3
Land Cruiser	
H/T	2.0
Wagon	2.3

Valve Clearance, Adjust

All models	1.5

DIESEL ENGINE

Compression Test

All models	1.0

Cylinder Head Gasket, Renew

Includes: Clean carbon. Make all necessary adjustments.

All models	6.0
w/Turbo add	.5

Cylinder Head, Renew

Includes: Transfer parts as required. Clean carbon. Make all necessary adjustments.

All models	8.5
w/Turbo add	.5

Clean Carbon and Grind Valves

Includes: R&R cylinder head. Resurface valves and seats. Make all necessary adjustments.

All models	9.8
w/Turbo add	.5

Cylinder Head Cover Gasket, Renew

All models	.7
w/Turbo add	.2

Valve Springs and/or Valve Stem Oil Seals, Renew (All)

Includes: R&R cylinder head.

All models	7.0
w/Turbo add	.5

Valve Rocker Arms and/or Shafts, Renew (All)

All models	2.5
w/Turbo add	.2

Valve Clearance, Adjust

All models	1.5
w/Turbo add	.2

LABOR 13 ENGINE ASSEMBLY & MOUNTS 13 LABOR

(Factory Time) Chilton Time

GASOLINE ENGINES

Note: All engine operations listed in this group are for assemblies as supplied by the original equipment manufacturer. Time to replace assemblies from independent rebuilders may vary.

Engine Assembly, Remove & Install

Does not include transfer of any parts or equipment.

	Chilton Time
Van	6.4
P/up-4 Runner	
4X2	
wo/F.I.	5.2
w/F.I.	6.0
4X4	
wo/F.I.	7.3
w/F.I.	7.7
Land Cruiser	5.5
w/A.C. add	.7
w/P.S. add	.7

Cylinder Assy., (Short Block), Renew

Includes: R&R engine assy. Transfer all component parts not supplied with replacement engine. Tune up.

Van	15.2
P/up-4 Runner	
4X2	
wo/F.I.	10.2
w/F.I.	11.0
4X4	
wo/F.I.	12.3
w/F.I.	12.7
Land Cruiser	14.0
w/A.C. add	.7
w/P.S. add	.7

Engine Assy., R&R and Recondition

Includes: Install new pistons, pins, rings, rod and main bearings. Clean carbon, grind valves. Tune engine.

Van	21.0
P/up-4 Runner	
4X2	
wo/F.I.	20.4
w/F.I.	21.3
4X4	
wo/F.I.	22.4
w/F.I.	23.2
Land Cruiser	26.6
w/A.C. add	.7
w/P.S. add	.7

Engine Mounts, Renew

Front-one side

Van	.8
P/up-4 Runner	.6
Land Cruiser	.7

Rear

Van	.9
P/up-4 Runner	.7
Land Cruiser	.9

DIESEL ENGINE

Engine Assembly, Remove & Install

Does not include transfer of any parts or equipment.

All models	
4X2	5.6
4X4	6.8
w/A.C. add	.7
w/P.S. add	.7
w/Turbo add	.2

Cylinder Assembly, Renew (Short Block)

Includes: R&R engine assy. Transfer all component parts not supplied with replacement engine. Clean carbon, grind valves. Make all necessary adjustments.

All models	
4X2	13.9
4X4	15.1
w/A.C. add	.7
w/P.S. add	.7
w/Turbo add	.2

Engine Assembly, R&R and Recondition

Includes: Install new pistons, pins and rings. Renew cylinder liners and seals. Renew main and connecting rod bearings. Clean carbon, grind valves. Make all necessary adjustments.

All models	
4X2	20.2
4X4	22.6
w/A.C. add	.7
w/P.S. add	.7
w/Turbo add	.2

Front Engine Mount, Renew

All models-one side	.5

Rear Engine Mount, Renew

All models	.6

LABOR 14 PISTONS, RINGS & BEARINGS 14 LABOR

(Factory Time) Chilton Time

GASOLINE ENGINES

Pistons or Connecting Rods, Renew (All)

Includes: R&R cylinder head and oil pan. Clean carbon. Make all necessary adjustments.

	Chilton Time
Van	8.9
P/up-4 Runner	
wo/F.I.	8.5
w/F.I.	9.3
w/Turbo	10.3
Land Cruiser	
H/T	7.9
Wagon	9.7
w/P.S. add	.5

Piston Rings, Renew (All)

Includes: R&R cylinder head and oil pan. Clean carbon. Make all necessary adjustments.

Van	9.5
P/up-4 Runner	
wo/F.I.	9.2
w/F.I.	10.1
w/Turbo	11.1
Land Cruiser	
H/T	8.3
Wagon	10.4
w/P.S. add	.5

Connecting Rod Bearings, Renew

Includes: R&R oil pan.

Van	3.0
P/up-4 Runner	3.7
Land Cruiser	3.5

DIESEL ENGINE

Piston Rings, Renew (All)

Includes: R&R cylinder head and oil pan.

All models	10.5
w/Turbo add	.2

Pistons or Connecting Rods, Renew (All)

Includes: R&R cylinder head and oil pan.

All models	11.7
w/Turbo add	.2

Connecting Rod Bearings, Renew

All models	3.7

LABOR 14 PISTONS, RINGS & BEARINGS 14 LABOR

COMBINATIONS

Add to Engine Work

	Chilton Time
DRAIN, EVACUATE & RECHARGE AIR CONDITIONING SYSTEM	
All models	1.0
CARBURETOR, RECONDITION	
All models	1.5
WATER PUMP, RECONDITION	
All models	.5
CYLINDER HEAD, RECONDITION (HEAD REMOVED)	
P/up	3.5
Land Cruiser	4.5
OIL PUMP, RECONDITION	
Van	.4
All other models	1.0
VALVE GUIDES, RENEW (ALL) (CYL HEAD STRIPPED)	
Van	1.0
All other models	1.6
PLASTIGAUGE BEARINGS	
Each	.1
REMOVE CYLINDER TOP RIDGE	
Each	.1
DEGLAZE CYLINDER WALLS	
Each	.1
OIL FILTER ELEMENT, RENEW	
All models	.3

LABOR 15 CRANKSHAFT & DAMPER 15 LABOR

(Factory Time) — Chilton Time

GASOLINE ENGINES

Crankshaft and Main Bearings, Renew

Includes: R&R engine assembly.

	Chilton Time
Van	15.8
P/up-4 Runner	
4X2	
wo/F.I.	11.3
w/F.I.	12.3
4X4	
wo/F.I.	13.4
w/F.I.	14.0
Land Cruiser	15.5
w/A.C. add	.7
w/P.S. add	.7

Crankshaft Pulley, Renew

	Chilton Time
Van	1.7
P/up-4 Runner	1.5
Land Cruiser	
H/T	1.0
Wagon	1.5
w/A.C. add	.2
w/P.S. add	.2

Crankshaft Front Oil Seal, Renew

	Chilton Time
Van	1.8
P/up-4 Runner	1.6
Land Cruiser	1.3
w/A.C. add	.2
w/P.S. add	.2

Crankshaft Rear Oil Seal, Renew

	Chilton Time
Van	
w/M.T.	3.6
w/A.T.	3.2
P/up-4 Runner	
4X2	
w/M.T.	4.8
w/A.T.	5.2
4X4	
w/M.T.	5.8
w/A.T.	6.2
Land Cruiser	
w/M.T.	5.0
w/A.T.	7.5

DIESEL ENGINE

Crankshaft and Main Bearings, Renew

Includes: R&R engine assembly.

	Chilton Time
All models	
4X2	12.6
4X4	13.9
w/A.C. add	.7
w/P.S. add	.7
w/Turbo add	.5

Crankshaft Pulley, Renew

	Chilton Time
All models	.8
w/A.C. add	.1
w/P.S. add	.1

Crankshaft Front Oil Seal, Renew

	Chilton Time
All models	5.5
w/A.C. add	.1
w/P.S. add	.1

Crankshaft Rear Oil Seal, Renew

Includes: R&R transmission.

	Chilton Time
All models	
4X2	4.2
4X4	5.2

LABOR 16 CAMSHAFT & TIMING GEARS 16 LABOR

(Factory Time) — Chilton Time

GASOLINE ENGINES

Timing Chain Cover and/or Gasket, Renew

	Chilton Time
Van	1.5
P/up-4 Runner	
wo/F.I.	7.4
w/F.I.	8.2
Land Cruiser	1.8
w/A.C. add	.7
w/P.S. add	.5

Timing Chain or Tensioner, Renew

Includes: All necessary adjustments.

	Chilton Time
Van	2.7
P/up-4 Runner	
wo/F.I.	7.9
w/F.I.	8.7
w/A.C. add	.7
w/P.S. add	.5

Camshaft Gear or Sprocket, Renew

Includes: All necessary adjustments.

	Chilton Time
Van	2.7
P/up-4 Runner	1.1
Land Cruiser	
H/T	4.7
Wagon	4.1
w/A.C. add	.1
w/P.S. add	.1

Crankshaft Gear or Sprocket, Renew

Includes: All necessary adjustments.

	Chilton Time
Van	2.7
P/up-4 Runner	
wo/F.I.	6.2
w/F.I.	7.0
Land Cruiser	1.9
w/A.C. add	.3
w/P.S. add	.5

Camshaft, Renew

Includes: All necessary adjustments.

	Chilton Time
Van	4.7
P/up-4 Runner	2.8
Land Cruiser	
H/T	4.7
Wagon	6.6

DIESEL ENGINE

Camshaft, Renew

	Chilton Time
All models	4.1
w/A.C. add	.7
w/Turbo add	.2

Camshaft Timing Gear or Sprocket, Renew

	Chilton Time
All models	1.5
Renew crank gear add	.3
w/A.C. add	.7

LABOR 16 CAMSHAFT & TIMING GEARS 16 LABOR

	(Factory Time)	Chilton Time
Timing Belt and/or Idler, Renew		
All models		1.5
w/A.C. add		.7
Timing Gear Cover and/or Gasket, Renew		
All models		1.7
w/A.C. add		.7
w/P.S. add		.1

LABOR 17 ENGINE OILING SYSTEM 17 LABOR

	(Factory Time)	Chilton Time
GASOLINE ENGINES		
Oil Pan and/or Gasket, Renew		
Van		2.3
P/up-4 Runner		2.3
Land Cruiser		
H/T		2.0
Wagon		2.3
Pressure Test Engine Bearings (Pan Off)		
All models		1.0
Oil Pump, Renew		
Van		2.5
P/up-4 Runner		2.5
Land Cruiser		
H/T		6.5
Wagon		7.4
Oil Pump, R&R and Recondition		
Van		2.7
P/up-4 Runner		2.7
Land Cruiser		
H/T		6.7
Wagon		7.6
Oil Pressure Sending Unit, Renew		
All models		.5
Oil Pressure Gauge (Dash Unit), Renew		
All models		.8
Oil Filter Element, Renew		
All models		.3
DIESEL ENGINE		
Oil Pan and/or Gasket, Renew		
All models		2.5
Pressure Test Engine Bearings (Pan Off)		
All models		1.0
Oil Pump, Renew		
All models		5.3
Oil Cooler Assembly, Renew		
All models		1.9
Oil Pressure Sending Unit, Renew		
All models		.3
Oil Filter Element, Renew		
All models		.3

LABOR 18 CLUTCH & FLYWHEEL 18 LABOR

	(Factory Time)	Chilton Time
Bleed Clutch Hydraulic System		
All models		.4
Clutch Master Cylinder, Renew		
Includes: Bleed system.		
Van		1.5
All other models		1.0
Clutch Master Cylinder, R&R and Recondition		
Includes: Bleed system.		
Van		1.8
All other models		1.3
Clutch Slave Cylinder, Renew		
Includes: Bleed system.		
All models		.9
Clutch Slave Cylinder, R&R and Recondition		
Includes: Bleed system.		
All models		1.2
Clutch Assembly, Renew		
Van		3.3
P/up-4 Runner		
4X2		4.2
4X4		5.5
Land Cruiser		4.5
Renew throw out brg add		.1
Renew pilot brg add		.1
Flywheel, Renew		
Van		3.7
P/up-4 Runner		
4X2		4.7
4X4		5.8
Land Cruiser		5.3

LABOR 19 STANDARD TRANSMISSION 19 LABOR

	(Factory Time)	Chilton Time
4 SPEED		
Transmission Assy., Remove & Install		
All models		
Gas		4.1
Diesel		4.0
Transmission Assy., R&R and Recondition		
Includes: Complete disassembly, clean and inspect or renew all parts. Install new gaskets and seals.		
All models		
Gas		7.7
Diesel		9.3
Extension Housing Gasket, Renew		
All models		
Gas		2.9
Diesel		1.8
Extension Housing Rear Oil Seal, Renew		
All models		
Gas		1.3
Diesel		1.0
Rear Engine Mount, Renew		
All models		.6
Speedometer Driven Gear, Renew		
Land Cruiser		.6
All other models		.5
5 SPEED		
Transmission Assy., Remove & Install		
Van		3.0
P/up-4 Runner		
4X2		3.9
4X4		5.2
Land Cruiser		
H/T		7.4
Wagon		6.9
Transmission Assy., R&R and Recondition		
Includes: Complete disassembly, clean and inspect or renew all parts. Install new gaskets and seals.		
Van		8.6
P/up-4 Runner		
4X2		
Gas		7.9
Diesel		9.5
4X4		9.9
Land Cruiser		
H/T		12.1
Wagon		11.5
Extension Housing Gasket, Renew		
Van		1.8
P/up-4 Runner		2.7
Extension Housing Rear Oil Seal, Renew		
Van		1.0
P/up-4 Runner		1.4

LABOR 20 TRANSFER CASE 20 LABOR

	(Factory Time)	Chilton Time
Transfer Case Assy., Remove & Install		
P/up-4 Runner		
4X2		5.4
4X4		9.3
Land Cruiser		5.9
Transfer Case Assy., R&R and Recondition		
P/up-4 Runner		
4X2		8.1
4X4		14.3
Land Cruiser		8.9
Front Driveshaft Oil Seal, Renew		
P/up-4 Runner		
4X2		1.2
4X4		8.7
Land Cruiser		
H/T		1.5
Wagon		1.3
Output Shaft Bearing Retainer and/or Oil Seal, Renew		
P/up-4 Runner		
4X2		1.1
4X4		2.5
Land Cruiser		
H/T		1.5
Wagon		1.6

LABOR 21 SHIFT LINKAGE 21 LABOR

	(Factory Time)	Chilton Time
STANDARD		
Gear Shift Lever, Renew		
Van		.6
P/up-4 Runner		.7
Land Cruiser-H/T		.6
Sta Wagon		.9
Gearshift Lever Retainer, Renew		
All models		.8
AUTOMATIC		
Selector Lever, Renew		
Van		.6
P/up-4 Runner		
4X2		1.1
4X4		1.6
Land Cruiser		.8
Selector Lever Boot and/or Retainer, Renew		
P/up-4 Runner		
4X2		.8
4X4		1.8
Selector Lever Indicator Bulb, Renew		
All models		
4X2		.5
4X4		.7

LABOR 23 AUTOMATIC TRANSMISSION 23 LABOR

	(Factory Time)	Chilton Time
A-30		
ON CAR SERVICES		
Drain & Refill Unit		
All models		.8
Check Unit For Oil Leaks		
Includes: Clean and dry outside of case and run unit to determine point of leak.		
All models		.9
Oil Pressure Test		
All models		1.0
Throttle Rod or Cable, Adjust		
All models		.4
Throttle Valve Lever Seal, Renew		
All models		1.9
Parking Lock Rod, Renew		
All models		.6
Extension Housing Rear Oil Seal, Renew		
All models		1.3
Extension Housing Gasket, Renew		
All models		2.7
Governor Assembly, Renew		
Includes: R&R extension housing.		
All models		2.9
Oil Pan or Gasket, Renew		
All models		1.2
Valve Body Assembly, Renew		
Includes: R&R oil pan.		
All models		2.5
Valve Body Assy., R&R and Recondition		
Includes: R&R oil pan. Disassemble, clean, inspect, free all valves. Replace parts as required.		
All models		3.5
SERVICES REQUIRING R&R		
Transmission Assembly, Renew		
All models		4.7
Torque Converter, Renew		
Includes: R&R transmission.		
All models		4.9
Transmission Assy., R&R and Recondition		
Includes: Complete disassembly, including valve body. Clean and inspect or renew all parts. Reassemble, make all necessary adjustments.		
All models		11.0
Front Pump Oil Seal, Renew		
Includes: R&R transmission.		
All models		5.1
Flywheel and Drive Plate, Renew		
Includes: R&R transmission.		
All models		5.1
A-40–A430–A340E–A340H		
ON CAR SERVICES		
Drain and Refill Unit		
All models		.8
Check Unit For Oil Leaks		
Includes: Clean and dry outside of case and run unit to determine point of leak.		
All models		.9
Oil Pressure Test		
All models		1.5
Throttle Rod or Cable, Adjust		
All models		.4
Manual Valve Lever Shaft Seal, Renew		
Van		2.5
P/up-4 Runner		
4X2		5.9
4X4		6.6
Land Cruiser		3.1
Throttle Cable, Renew		
Van-P/up		2.1
Land Cruiser		3.4
Extension Housing Rear Oil Seal, Renew		
Van-P/up		1.1
Extension Housing Gasket, Renew		
Van		2.5
P/up		2.9
Speedometer Cable and Casing, Renew		
Van-P/up		1.1
Land Cruiser		
H/T		.7
Wagon		1.0
Governor Assembly, Renew		
Van-P/up		3.1
Land Cruiser		7.4
SERVICES REQUIRING R&R		
Transmission Assy., R&R or Renew		
Van		4.2
P/up-4 Runner		
4X2		4.9
4X4		5.9
Land Cruiser		7.3
Transmission Assy., R&R and Recondition		
Includes: Complete disassembly, including valve body. Clean and inspect or renew all parts. Reassemble and adjust.		
Van		16.3
P/up-4 Runner		
4X2		13.3
4X4		19.2
Land Cruiser		20.7
Torque Converter, Renew		
Includes: R&R trans.		
Van		5.1
P/up-4 Runner		
4X2		5.0
4X4		6.1
Land Cruiser		7.4
Front Pump Oil Seal, Renew		
Includes: R&R trans.		
Van		5.0
P/up-4 Runner		
4X2		4.9
4X4		5.4
Land Cruiser		7.5
Transfer Case, R&R and Recondition		
Includes: R&R transmission.		
Van-4 Runner		10.7
Land Cruiser		10.0

LABOR 25 U-JOINTS & DRIVESHAFT 25 LABO

(Factory Time) Chilton Time

Rear Driveshaft, R&R or Renew
Van .8
All other models 1.1

Intermediate Driveshaft, R&R or Renew
P/up-4 Runner 1.0

Universal Spider Joint, Renew or Rebuild (One)
Van 1.3
All other models 1.8

U-Joint Yoke, Renew
Van 1.0
P/up-4 Runner 1.3
Land Cruiser 1.6

Center Bearing, Renew
P/up-4 Runner 1.7

LABOR 26 DRIVE AXLE 26 LABOR

(Factory Time) Chilton Time

REAR DIFFERENTIAL ASSEMBLY

Rear Axle Shaft, Renew (One)
Van 1.6
P/up-4 Runner
w/Single rear whls 1.7
w/Dual rear whls .7
Land Cruiser 1.8

Rear Axle Shaft Bearing, Renew (One Side)
Van 1.5
P/up-4 Runner
w/Single rear whls 1.7
w/Dual rear whls 2.0
Land Cruiser 1.7

Rear Axle Shaft Oil Seal, Renew (One Side)
Van 1.0
P/up-4 Runner
w/Single rear whls 1.5
w/Dual rear whls .7
Land Cruiser 1.4

Differential Rear Cover Gasket, Renew
Land Cruiser .9

Pinion Shaft Oil Seal, Renew
Van 1.0
P/up-4 Runner 1.7
Land Cruiser
H/T 1.5
Wagon 1.0

Differential Carrier Assy., R&R or Renew Gasket
Van 2.6
P/up-4 Runner
w/Single rear whls 2.6
w/Dual rear whls 2.5
Land Cruiser 3.1

Differential Carrier Assy., R&R and Recondition
Van 6.0
P/up-4 Runner
w/Single rear whls 6.6
w/Dual rear whls 5.7
Land Cruiser 6.9

Ring Gear and Pinion Set, Renew
Van 5.5
P/up-4 Runner
w/Single rear whls 6.1
w/Dual rear whls 5.2
Land Cruiser 6.4

Differential Side Bearings, Renew (Both Sides)
Van 3.5
P/up-4 Runner
w/Single rear whls 3.7
w/Dual rear whls 3.1
Land Cruiser 4.1

FRONT DIFFERENTIAL ASSEMBLY

Front Axle Inner Shaft, Renew (One)
P/up-4 Runner 1.9
Land Cruiser 2.0

Universal Joint Flange, Renew
P/up-4 Runner 1.9
Land Cruiser .9

Pinion Shaft Oil Seal, Renew
P/up-4 Runner 1.9
Land Cruiser
H/T 1.5
Wagon 1.0

Differential Carrier Assy., R&R or Renew Gasket
P/up-4 Runner 3.2
Land Cruiser 4.9

Ring Gear and Pinion Set, Renew
P/up-4 Runner 7.9
Land Cruiser
H/T 8.1
Wagon 7.4

Differential Side Bearings, Renew
All models 5.9

Pinion Bearings, Renew
P/up-4 Runner 7.1
Land Cruiser 6.7

Front Differential Assy., R&R and Recondition
P/up-4 Runner 8.7
Land Cruiser 8.3

Front Drive Shaft, Renew
All models 1.9

Front Drive Shaft Boot, Renew
All models 2.4

LABOR 27 REAR SUSPENSION 27 LABOR

(Factory Time) Chilton Time

LEAF TYPE

Rear Leaf Spring, Renew (One)
Van 1.2
All other models 1.4

Rear Leaf Spring, R&R and Recondition
Van 1.7
All other models 1.9

Rear Spring Shackle, Renew (One Side)
All models .8

Rear Shock Absorbers, Renew
All models-one .5
both .7

LINK TYPE

Lower Control Arm, Renew (One)
Van .7

Rear Coil Spring, Renew (One)
Van .7

Rear Shock Absorbers, Renew
Van-one .7
both .9

LABOR 28 AIR CONDITIONING 28 LABOR

(Factory Time) Chilton Time

FACTORY INSTALLED SYSTEM

Note: If more than one item requires replacement where evacuation and discharging the system is already included in the operation, deduct 1.0 hour for each additional item to the times listed.

Flush Refrigerant System, Complete
To be used in conjunction with component replacement which could contaminate system.
All models 1.3

Drain, Evacuate & Recharge System
All models 1.0

Compressor Drive Belt, Renew
Van 1.0
All other models .5

Compressor Assembly, Renew
Includes: Transfer parts as required. Evacuate and charge system.
Van 2.3
All other models 1.7

Condenser Assembly, Renew
Includes: Evacuate and charge system.
Van 2.4
All other models 1.7

Receiver-Drier, Renew
Includes: Evacuate and charge system.
Van 2.0
All other models 1.4

LABOR 28 AIR CONDITIONING 28 LABOR

(Factory Time) Chilton Time

Compressor Clutch Assembly, Renew
- Van 2.4
- P/up-Runner
  - Gas 1.0
  - Diesel 1.8
- Land Cruiser 7

Expansion Valve, Renew
Includes: Evacuate and charge system.
- Van 3.0
- All other models 2.1

Evaporator Coil, Renew
Includes: Evacuate and charge system.
- Van 3.0
- All other models 2.3

Pressure Cut Off Switch, Renew
Includes: Evacuate and charge system.
- Van 2.9
- All other models 1.8

A.C. Blower Motor, Renew
- Van 3.7

DEALER INSTALLED SYSTEM

Drain, Evacuate & Recharge System
- All models 1.0

Compressor Drive Belt, Renew
- All models 6

Compressor Assembly, Renew
Includes: Transfer parts as required. Evacuate and charge system.
- All models 2.0

Compressor Clutch Assy., or Bearing, Renew
- All models 9

Condenser Assembly, Renew
Includes: Evacuate and charge system.
- All models 1.9

Receiver-Drier, Renew
Includes: Evacuate and charge system.
- All models 1.4

Expansion Valve, Renew
Includes: Evacuate and charge system.
- All models 1.7

Evaporator Coil, Renew
Includes: Evacuate and charge system.
- All models 2.3

Blower Motor, Renew
- All models 2.0

Blower Motor Resistor, Renew
- All models 2.2

LABOR 29 LOCKS, HINGES & WIND. REGULATORS 29 LABOR

(Factory Time) Chilton Time

Hood Hinges, Renew (Both)
- All models 8

Hood Lock, Renew
- All models 4

Hood Release Cable, Renew
- All models 8

Front Door Lock Assy., Renew (One Side)
- All models 6

Rear Door Lock Assy., Renew
- All models 8

Lock Striker Plate, Renew
- All models 3

Door Handle (Outside), Renew
- All models-front 6
- rear 7

Door Window Regulator, Renew
- All models-front 8
- rear 9
- w/Pwr windows add 2

Tail Gate Lock Assy., Renew
- All models 5

Tail Gate Window Regulator, Renew
- Land Cruiser 1.0

LABOR 30 HEAD AND PARKING LAMPS 30 LABOR

(Factory Time) Chilton Time

Aim Headlamps
- two 4
- four 6

Headlamp Sealed Beam Bulb, Renew
- All models 6

Turn Signal Lamp Lens or Bulb, Renew
- All models 3

Parking Lamp Lens or Bulb, Renew
- All models 3

Side Marker Lamp Lens or Bulb, Renew
- All models 4

Back-Up Lamp Lens or Bulb, Renew
- All models 4

Rear Combination Lamp Lens or Bulb, Renew
- All models 4

License Lamp Lens or Bulb, Renew
- All models 3

LABOR 31 WINDSHIELD WIPER & SPEEDOMETER 31 LABOR

(Factory Time) Chilton Time

Windshield Wiper Motor, Renew
- Van 2.7
- All other models 1.5

Wiper Link Assy., Renew
- Van 2.8
- Land Cruiser-H/T 1.0
- All other models 7

Washer Motor and Pump Assy., Renew
- Van 7
- All other models 4

Speedometer Head, R&R or Renew
- Van 1.1
- All other models 9

Speedometer Cable and Casing, Renew (w/Manual Trans.)
- Van P/up-4 Runner 1.1
- Land Cruiser-H/T 7
  - Wagon 1.0

Windshield Wiper Switch Assy., Renew
- Van 1.1
- P/up-4 Runner 8
- Land Cruiser
  - H/T 1.0
  - Wagon 5

Rear Window Wiper Switch, Renew
- All models 4

Rear Window Wiper Motor, Renew
- Van 6
- P/up-4 Runner 7
- Land Cruiser
  - H/T 9
  - Wagon 5

Rear Window Washer Motor and Pump, Renew
- Van 1.0
- P/up-4 Runner 3
- Land Cruiser
  - H/T 5
  - Wagon 4

Radio, R&R
- Van 6
- All other models 5

LABOR 32 LIGHT SWITCHES & WIRING 32 LABOR

(Factory Time)	Chilton Time
Stop Light Switch, Renew	
All models	.4
Back-Up Lamp Switch, Renew	
Van-P/up-4 Runner	.5
Land Cruiser	
H/T	.5
Wagon	1.0
Neutral Safety Switch, Renew	
All models	.7
Turn Signal Switch Assy., Renew	
Van	.9
P/up-4 Runner	.7
Land Cruiser	.8
Turn Signal Flasher, Renew	
All models	.3
Hazard Warning Switch, Renew	
Van	1.0
Land Cruiser	1.0
Parking Brake Warning Lamp Switch, Renew	
Van-P/up-4 Runner	.4
Land Cruiser	.5
Headlamp Switch, Renew	
Van	1.1
P/up-4 Runner	.8
Land Cruiser	1.0
Horns, Renew	
All models	.4

LABOR 34 CRUISE CONTROL 34 LABOR

(Factory Time)	Chilton Time
Cruise Control Computer, Renew	
Van	.9
P/up	.6
Cruise Control Switch, Renew	
Van	.4
P/up	.5
Cruise Control Actuator, Renew	
Van	.8
P/up	.6

Volkswagen Rabbit Pick-Ups

GROUP INDEX

ALPHABETICAL INDEX

LABOR 1 TUNE UP 1 LABOR

(Factory Time) Chilton Time

Compression Test
All models 6

Engine Tune Up, (Minor)
Includes: Clean or renew spark plugs, test compression. Adjust valve clearance. Renew ignition points and condenser, set ignition timing and dwell. Set carburetor idle mixture and speed. Adjust drive belts. Service carburetor air cleaner.
All models 2.5

Engine Tune Up, (Electronic Ignition)
Includes: Test battery and clean connections. Tighten manifold mounting bolts. Check engine compression, clean and adjust or renew spark plugs. Inspect distributor cap and rotor. Check vacuum advance operation. Reset ignition timing. Adjust idle mixture and idle speed. Service air cleaner. Inspect crankcase ventilation system. Inspect and adjust drive belts. Inspect choke operation and adjust or free up. Check operation of EGR valve.
All models 1.5

LABOR 2 IGNITION SYSTEM 2 LABOR

(Factory Time) Chilton Time

POINT TYPE IGNITION

Spark Plugs, Clean and Reset or Renew
All models 5

Ignition Timing, Reset
All models 4

Distributor, Renew
Includes: Reset ignition timing and dwell.
All models 8

Ignition Points and Condenser, Renew
Includes: Reset ignition timing and dwell.
All models 1.0

Distributor Cap, Renew
All models 3

Vacuum Advance Unit, Renew
Includes: R&R distributor, reset ignition timing and dwell.
All models 9

Ignition Cables, Renew
All models 4

Ignition Coil, Renew
All models 4

Ignition Switch, Renew
All models 1.0

ELECTRONIC IGNITION

Control Unit, Renew
All models 5

Pick-Up Coil, Renew (Hall Generator)
All models 6

DIESEL IGNITION COMPONENTS

Glow Plugs, Renew
All models-one 5
all 8

Glow Plug Relay, Renew
All models 5

LABOR 3 FUEL SYSTEM 3 LABOR

(Factory Time) Chilton Time

Fuel Pump, Test
Includes: Attach pressure gauge.
All models 3

Fuel Tank, Renew
Includes: Drain and refill tank, transfer sending unit.
All models 1.0

Fuel Gauge (Tank Unit), Renew
All models 1.1

Fuel Gauge (Dash Unit), Renew
All models 6

Mechanical Fuel Pump, Renew
All models 6

Electric Fuel Pump, Renew
All models 7

Carburetor, Renew
Includes: All necessary adjustments.
All models 1.2

Carburetor, R&R and Clean or Recondition
Includes: All necessary adjustments.
All models 2.9

Intake Manifold or Gasket, Renew
All models 2.0

CONTINUOUS INJECTION SYSTEM

Bleed System
All models 3

Fuel Injectors, Renew
All models-one 3
all 5
Clean and test add, each 2

Throttle Valve Housing and/or Gasket, Renew
All models 8

Warm-Up Regulator, Renew
All models 3

Cold Start Valve, Renew
All models 4

Oxygen Sensor, Renew
All models 5

Electronic Control Unit, Renew
All models 6

Voltage Supply Relay, Renew
All models 5

Frequency Valve, Renew
All models 3

Thermo Time Switch, Renew
All models 5

Auxiliary Air Regulator, Renew
All models 5

Deceleration Valve, Renew
All models 5

Fuel Distributor, Renew
All models 1.2

Pressure Regulator, Renew
All models 4

Air Flow Sensor Assy., Renew
All models 9

Micro Switch, Renew
All models 9

Intake Manifold Gasket, Renew
All models 1.4

Pressure Relief Valve, Renew
All models 3

DIESEL FUEL INJECTION

Idle Speed, Adjust
All models 5

Cold Start Cable, Renew
All models 6

Air Cleaner, Service
All models 3

Injection Pump, R&R or Renew
All models 2.7
w/Turbo add 7
w/A.C. add 5

Injection Timing, Check and Adjust
All models 1.0

Fuel Injection Lines, Renew
All models-one 4
all 8

Fuel Injectors, Renew
All models-one 5
all 1.0
Clean and test add, each 3

Fuel Shut-Off Valve, Renew
All models 4

Injection Pump Sprocket, Renew
Includes: Adjust injection pump timing.
All models 1.8

Intake Manifold or Gasket, Renew
All models 1.4

TURBOCHARGER

Turbocharger Assy., R&R or Renew
All models 3.0

Wastegate Actuator, Renew
All models 9

LABOR 3A EMISSION CONTROLS 3A LABOR

(Factory Time) Chilton Time

PCV Valve, Renew
All models 3

EXHAUST GAS RECIRCULATION SYSTEM

E.G.R. Valve, Renew
All models 6

E.G.R. Delay Valve, Renew
All models 3

E.G.R. Filter, Renew
Includes: R&R E.G.R. valve.
All models 7

AIR INJECTION SYSTEM

Air Pump, Renew
All models 7

Air Pump Drive Belt, Renew
All models 3

Air Pump Filter, Renew
All models 3

Anti-Backfire Valve, Renew
All models 3

Diverter or Check Valve, Renew
All models 3

Charcoal Filter, Renew
All models 3

LABOR 4 ALTERNATOR AND REGULATOR 4 LABOR

(Factory Time) Chilton Time

Alternator Circuits, Test
Includes: Test battery, regulator and alternator output.
All models 6

Alternator Assembly, Renew
All models 1.1
w/Turbo add 7
w/A.C. add 8
Add circuit test if performed.

Alternator, R&R and Recondition
Includes: Disassemble, clean and inspect all parts. Renew parts as required. Reassemble and test.
All models 2.3
w/Turbo add 7
w/A.C. add 8

Voltage Regulator, Test and Renew
All models 7

LABOR 5 STARTING SYSTEM 5 LABOR

(Factory Time) Chilton Time

Starter Draw Test (On Car)
All models 3

Starter Assembly, Renew
All models
w/M.T. 9
w/A.T. 1.2
w/Diesel eng 1.0
w/Turbo Diesel 1.2
Add draw test if performed.

Starter, R&R and Recondition
Includes: Turn down armature.
All models
w/M.T. 2.7
w/A.T. 3.6
w/Diesel eng 3.0
w/Turbo Diesel 3.2

Starter Solenoid, Renew
Includes: R&R starter.
All models
w/M.T. 1.1
w/A.T. 1.4
w/Diesel eng 1.2
w/Turbo Diesel 1.4

Starter Drive, Renew
Includes: R&R starter.
All models
w/M.T. 1.4
w/A.T. 1.7
w/Diesel eng 1.5
w/Turbo Diesel 1.7

Starter/Ignition Switch, Renew
All models 1.0

Battery Cables, Renew
All models-each 3

LABOR 6 BRAKE SYSTEM 6 LABOR

(Factory Time) Chilton Time

Bleed Brakes (Four Wheels)
Includes: Fill master cylinder.
All models 5

Brakes, Adjust (Minor)
Includes: Adjust service and emergency brake. Fill master cylinder.
All models 7

Brake Shoes, Renew
Includes: Install new or exchange brake shoes. Adjust service and hand brake. Bleed system.
All models
front 1.3
rear 1.5
all four wheels 2.7
Resurface brake drum, add-each 5

Brake Shoes and/or Pads, Renew
Includes: Install new or exchange brake shoes or pads. Adjust service and hand brake. Bleed system.
All models
front-disc 8
rear-drum 1.5
all four wheels 2.2
Resurface brake rotor, add-each 9
Resurface brake drum, add-each 5

COMBINATIONS
Add to Brakes, Renew

Chilton Time

RENEW WHEEL CYLINDER
Each 2

REBUILD WHEEL CYLINDER
Each 3

REBUILD MASTER CYLINDER
All models 6

REBUILD CALIPER ASSEMBLY
Each 5

RENEW BRAKE HOSE
Each 3

RENEW BRAKE DRUM
Each 1

RENEW DISC BRAKE ROTOR
Each 2

Brake Drums, Renew
Includes: Readjust brakes.
All models
front-one 5
rear-one 7

BRAKE HYDRAULIC SYSTEM

Wheel Cylinder, Renew
Includes: Bleed system.
All models
front-one 1.2
both 2.2
rear-one 1.3
both 2.4
all four wheels 4.2

Wheel Cylinder, R&R and Rebuild
Includes: Bleed system.
All models
front-one 1.5
both 2.8
rear-one 1.6
both 3.0
all four wheels 5.4

Master Cylinder, Renew
Includes: Bleed system.
All models 1.3

Master Cylinder, R&R and Rebuild
Includes: Bleed system.
All models 1.9

Brake System, Flush and Refill
All models 1.2

LABOR 6 BRAKE SYSTEM 6 LABOR

(Factory Time) Chilton Time

Brake Hose, Renew
Includes: Bleed system.
All models-one 8

DISC BRAKES

Disc Brake Pads, Renew
Includes: Install new disc brake pads only.
All models 8

Caliper Assembly, Renew
Includes: Bleed system.
All models-one 1.0
both 1.8

Caliper Assy., R&R and Rebuild
Includes: Bleed system.
All models-one 1.5
both 2.8

Disc Brake Rotor, Renew
All models-one 7
both 1.2

Brake Pressure Regulator Valve, Renew
Includes: Bleed system.
All models 1.2

POWER BRAKES

Power Brake Booster, Renew
Includes: Bleed brake system.
All models 2.1

Vacuum Check Valve, Renew
All models 3

Vacuum Pump, Renew (w/Diesel Engine)
All models 7
Recond pump add 4

PARKING BRAKE

Parking Brake, Adjust
All models 3

Parking Brake Lever Assy., Renew
All models 6

Parking Brake Cable, Renew
All models-one side 1.4
both sides 2.1

LABOR 7 COOLING SYSTEM 7 LABOR

(Factory Time) Chilton Time

Winterize Cooling System
Includes: Run engine to check for leaks, tighten all hose connections. Test radiator and pressure cap, drain radiator and engine block. Add anti-freeze and refill system.
All models 5

Thermostat, Renew
Includes: Drain and refill coolant.
All models 6
w/Turbo add 5

Radiator Assembly, R&R or Renew
Includes: Drain and refill coolant.
All models 1.2

ADD THESE OPERATIONS TO RADIATOR R&R

Boil & Repair 1.5
Rod Clean 1.9
Repair Core 1.3
Renew Tank 1.6
Renew Trans. Oil Cooler 1.9
Recore Radiator 1.7

Electric Fan Motor, Renew
All models 5

Electric Fan Thermo Switch, Renew
All models 5

Water Pump, Renew
Includes: Drain and refill coolant.
All models
Gas 1.7
Diesel 1.8
w/A.C. add 1.5
w/Turbo add 6

Drive Belt, Renew
All models-one 3

Radiator Hoses, Renew
All models-one 5
both 6

Temperature Gauge Sending Unit, Renew
All models 3

Temperature Gauge (Dash Unit), Renew
All models 7

Heater Control Valve, Renew
Includes: Drain and refill coolant.
All models 5

Heater Core, R&R or Renew
All models *4.0
*Includes: Evacuate and charge A.C. system.

ADD THESE OPERATIONS TO HEATER CORE R&R

Boil & Repair 1.2
Repair Core 9
Recore 1.2

Heater Hoses, Renew
All models-one 6
both 9

Heater Blower Motor, Renew
All models 1.9

Blower Motor Switch, Renew
All models 4

LABOR 8 EXHAUST SYSTEM 8 LABOR

(Factory Time) Chilton Time

Front Exhaust Pipe, Renew
All models 1.5

Rear Muffler, Renew
Includes: R&R heat shield, if required.
All models 7

Catalytic Converter, Renew
Includes: R&R heat shield and temperature sensor.
All models 1.0

Exhaust Manifold or Gasket, Renew
All models
Gas engine 1.8
Diesel engine 1.3
Turbo Diesel eng 3.7

LABOR 9 FRONT SUSPENSION 9 LABOR

(Factory Time) Chilton Time

Note: On all front suspension operations alignment charges must be added if performed. Time given does not include alignment.

Wheel, Renew (One)
All models 5

Wheels, Rotate (All)
All models 5

Wheels, Balance
one 3
each adtnl 2

Check Alignment of Front End
All models 5
Note: Deduct if alignment is performed.

Toe-In, Adjust
All models 6

Align Front End
Includes: Adjust toe angle and camber.
All models 1.5

Lower Control Arm Assy., Renew
Add alignment charges.
All models
w/M.T.-one 8
both 1.4
w/A.T.-one 1.2
both 1.8

Renew ball joint add 4
Renew bushings add-each side 4

LABOR 9 FRONT SUSPENSION 9 LABOR

(Factory Time) Chilton Time

C.V. Joint, Renew
Includes: R&R front driveshaft.
All models
inner-one 1.6
outer-one 1.5
inner & outer-one side 2.3

C.V. Joint Boots, Renew
Includes: R&R axle shaft.
All models-one 1.3
both-one side 1.5
all-both sides 2.9

Steering Knuckle, Renew
Add alignment charges.
All models
one side 2.1
both sides 3.5

Front Wheel Bearings, Renew
Add alignment charges.
All models
one side 2.1
both sides 4.0

Front Strut Assy., R&R or Renew
Add alignment charges.
All models
one 9
both 1.7

Front Strut Shock Absorbers, Renew
Add alignment charges.
All models
one 1.4
both 2.5

Front Coil Springs, Renew
Add alignment charges.
All models
one 1.3
both 2.4

Front Stabilizer Bar and/or Bushings, Renew
All models 5
w/Turbo add 4

LABOR 11 STEERING GEAR 11 LABOR

(Factory Time) Chilton Time

STANDARD STEERING

Steering Wheel, Renew
All models 3

Upper Mast Jacket Bearing, Renew
All models 9

Steering Gear Assy., R&R or Renew
Add alignment charges.
All models 1.9

Tie Rods, Renew
Add alignment charges.
All models
one 5
both 8

Tie Rod End, Renew
Add alignment charges.
All models-each 5

POWER STEERING

Power Steering Gear Assy., R&R or Renew
All models 2.7

Power Steering Pump, Renew
All models 1.2

Tie Rod End Boot, Renew (One)
All models 1.2

Power Steering Hoses, Renew
All models
pressure 1.1
return 8

LABOR 12 CYLINDER HEAD & VALVE SYSTEM 12 LABOR

(Factory Time) Chilton Time

GASOLINE ENGINES

Compression Test
All models 6

Cylinder Head Gasket, Renew
Includes: Clean carbon. Make all necessary adjustments.
All models 4.7
w/A.C. add 8

Cylinder Head, Renew (Exchange)
Includes: Transfer all parts as required. Make all necessary adjustments.
All models 5.0
w/A.C. add 8

Clean Carbon and Grind Valves
Includes: R&R cylinder head. Reface all valves and seats. Make all necessary adjustments.
All models 9.7
w/A.C. add 8

Cam Followers, Renew
Includes: R&R timing belt and camshaft. Reset valve clearance and timing.
All models&.2.4

Valve Springs, Renew (Head on Car)
Includes: R&R timing belt, camshaft and cam followers. Reset valve clearance and timing.
All models 3.0

Valve Stem Oil Seals, Renew (Head on Car)
Includes: R&R timing belt, camshaft, cam followers and valve springs. Reset valve clearance and timing.
All models 3.0

Valve Clearance, Adjust
All models 1.0

Cylinder Head Bolts, Retorque
All models 8

Valve Cover Gasket, Renew
All models 4

DIESEL ENGINE

Compression Test
All models 1.1

Cylinder Head Gasket, Renew
Includes: Clean carbon. Make all necessary adjustments.
All models 4.8

Cylinder Head, Renew
Includes: Transfer all parts as required. Make all necessary adjustments.
All models 5.2
w/Turbo add 1.5

Clean Carbon and Grind Valves
Includes: R&R cylinder head. Reface all valves and seats. Make all necessary adjustments.
All models 10.0

Cam Followers, Renew
Includes: R&R timing belt and camshaft. Reset valve clearance and timing.
All models 2.4
w/Turbo add 4

Valve Springs, Renew (Head on Car)
Includes: R&R timing belt, camshaft and cam followers. Reset valve clearance and timing.
All models 3.4

Valve Stem Oil Seals, Renew (Head on Car)
Includes: R&R timing belt, camshaft, cam followers and valve springs. Reset valve clearance and timing.
All models 3.4

Valve Clearance, Adjust
All models 1.0

Cylinder Head Bolts, Retorque
All models 8

Valve Cover Gasket, Renew
All models 4

LABOR 13 ENGINE ASSEMBLY & MOUNTS 13 LABOR

(Factory Time) Chilton Time

GASOLINE ENGINES

Engine Assembly, Remove & Install

Does not include transfer of any parts or equipment. Includes: R&R engine and trans as a unit where required.

All models	6.5
w/A.C. add	.8

Cylinder Assy. (Short Block), Renew

Includes: R&R engine assy. Transfer all component parts not supplied with replacement engine. Clean carbon, grind valves. Make all necessary adjustments.

All models	17.0
w/A.C. add	.8

Cylinder Block, Renew

Includes: R&R engine assy. Transfer all component parts not supplied with replacement engine. Clean carbon, grind valves. Make all necessary adjustments.

All models	21.0
w/A.C. add	.8

Engine Mounts, Renew

All models	
front-center	.5
right side	2.0
rear-each	.4

DIESEL ENGINE

Engine Assembly, Remove & Install

Does not include transfer of any parts or equipment.

Includes: R&R engine and trans as a unit where required.

All models	6.5
w/A.C. add	.8

Cylinder Assy. (Short Block), Renew

Includes: R&R engine assy. Transfer all component parts not supplied with replacement engine. Clean carbon, grind valves. Make all necessary adjustments.

All models	17.0
w/A.C. add	.8

Cylinder Block, Renew

Includes: R&R engine assy. Transfer all component parts not supplied with replacement engine. Clean carbon, grind valves. Make all necessary adjustments.

All models	21.0
w/A.C. add	.8

Engine Mounts, Renew

All models	
front-center	.5
right side	1.7
rear-each	.4

Right Engine/Injection Pump Mount, Renew

All models	3.6

LABOR 14 PISTONS, RINGS & BEARINGS 14 LABOR

(Factory Time) Chilton Time

GASOLINE ENGINES

Pistons and Connecting Rods, Renew

Includes: R&R cylinder head and oil pan.

All models	7.0

Piston Rings, Renew

Includes: R&R cylinder head and oil pan.

All models	7.5

Connecting Rod Bearings, Renew

Includes: R&R oil pan.

All models	3.2

COMBINATIONS

Add to Engine Work

	Chilton Time
DRAIN, EVACUATE & RECHARGE AIR CONDITIONING SYSTEM All models	1.5
CARBURETOR, RECONDITION All models	1.6
VALVE GUIDES, RENEW Each	.2
DEGLAZE CYLINDER WALLS Each	.1
REMOVE CYLINDER TOP RIDGE Each	.1
PLASTIGAUGE BEARINGS Each	.1
CAMSHAFT, RENEW (CYLINDER HEAD REMOVED) All models	1.2
RECONDITION CYLINDER HEAD (HEAD REMOVED) All models	3.5
OIL FILTER ELEMENT, RENEW All models	.3

DIESEL ENGINE

Pistons and Connecting Rods, Renew

Includes: R&R cylinder head and oil pan.

All models	7.0
w/Turbo add	1.0

Piston Rings, Renew

Includes: R&R cylinder head and oil pan.

All models	8.2
w/Turbo add	1.0

Connecting Rod Bearings, Renew

Includes: R&R oil pan.

All models	3.2

LABOR 15 CRANKSHAFT & DAMPER 15 LABOR

(Factory Time) Chilton Time

GASOLINE ENGINES

Crankshaft and Main Bearings, Renew

Includes: R&R engine assembly.

All models	10.0
w/A.C. add	.8

Crankshaft Rear Oil Seal, Renew

Includes: R&R transmission.

All models	
w/M.T.	5.2
w/A.T.	6.1

Crankshaft Front Oil Seal, Renew

Includes: R&R belts and crankshaft pulley, intermediate shaft sprocket. Reset valve timing.

All models	1.9

Crankshaft Pulley, Renew

All models	.5

DIESEL ENGINE

Crankshaft and Main Bearings, Renew

Includes: R&R engine assembly.

All models	11.1
w/A.C. add	.8

Crankshaft Rear Oil Seal, Renew

Includes: R&R transmission.

All models	
w/M.T.	5.2
w/A.T.	6.1

Crankshaft Front Oil Seal, Renew

Includes: R&R belts and crankshaft pulley, intermediate shaft sprocket. Reset injection timing.

All models	1.9
w/Turbo add	1.4

Crankshaft Pulley, Renew

All models	.5

LABOR 16 CAMSHAFT & TIMING GEARS 16 LABOR

(Factory Time) Chilton Time

GASOLINE ENGINES

Camshaft, Renew
Includes: Renew cam follower disc if required. Reset valve timing.
All models.......... 2.4

Camshaft Sprocket and/or Oil Seal, Renew
Includes: R&R front cover and belt. Reset valve timing.
All models.......... 1.6

Timing (Spur) Belt, Renew
Includes: Reset valve timing.
All models.......... 1.8

Intermediate Shaft Sprocket or Oil Seal, Renew
Includes: R&R front cover and belts. Reset valve timing.
All models.......... 2.4

Timing (Spur) Belt Cover, Renew
All models.......... .6

Timing (Spur) Belt Pulley/Tensioner, Renew
Includes: R&R timing cover and belt. Reset valve timing.
All models.......... 1.5

DIESEL ENGINE

Camshaft, Renew
Includes: Renew cam follower disc if required. Reset valve timing.
All models.......... 3.0

Camshaft Oil Seal, Renew
Includes: R&R front cover and belt. Reset injection timing.
All models.......... 1.9

Timing (Spur) Belt, Renew
Includes: R&R front cover. Reset valve and injection pump timing.
All models.......... 2.4
w/Turbo add.......... .9

Intermediate Shaft Sprocket or Oil Seal, Renew
Includes: R&R front cover and belt. Reset valve timing.
All models.......... 3.0
w/Turbo add.......... .3

Timing (Spur) Belt Cover, Renew
All models.......... .6

Timing (Spur) Belt Pulley/Tensioner, Renew
Includes: R&R timing cover and belt. Reset valve timing.
All models.......... 1.5
w/Turbo add.......... .3

LABOR 17 ENGINE OILING SYSTEM 17 LABOR

(Factory Time) Chilton Time

GASOLINE ENGINES

Oil Pan or Gasket, Renew
All models.......... 1.5

Pressure Test Engine Bearings (Pan Off)
All models.......... 1.0

Oil Pump, Renew
Includes: R&R oil pan.
All models.......... 1.8

Oil Pressure Switch, Renew
All models.......... .4

Oil Temperature Gauge, Renew
All models.......... .6

Oil Filter Element, Renew
All models.......... .3

DIESEL ENGINE

Oil Pan or Gasket, Renew
All models.......... 1.5
w/Turbo add.......... .6

Pressure Test Engine Bearings (Pan Off)
All models.......... 1.0

Oil Pump, Renew
Includes: R&R oil pan.
All models.......... 1.8
w/Turbo add.......... .6

Oil Pressure Switch, Renew
All models.......... .4

Oil Temperature Gauge, Renew
All models.......... .6

Oil Filter Element, Renew
All models.......... .3

LABOR 18 CLUTCH & FLYWHEEL 18 LABOR

(Factory Time) Chilton Time

Clutch Pedal Free Play, Adjust
All models.......... .3

Clutch Cable, Renew
Includes: Adjust free play.
All models.......... .6

Clutch Release Bearing, Renew
Includes: R&R trans and adjust clutch pedal free play, where required.
All models.......... .7
w/Turbo Diesel add.......... .6

Clutch Assembly, Renew
Includes: R&R trans and adjust clutch pedal free play.
All models.......... 5.1
w/Turbo Diesel add.......... .6

Flywheel, Renew
Includes: R&R transmission.
All models.......... 4.9
w/Turbo Diesel add.......... .6
Renew ring gear add.......... .4

LABOR 19 STANDARD TRANSMISSION 19 LABOR

(Factory Time) Chilton Time

Transmission Assy., Remove & Install
All models.......... 4.0
w/Turbo Diesel add.......... .6

Transmission Assy., R&R and Recondition
Includes: Disassemble trans completely. Clean, inspect or renew all parts. Install new gaskets and seals.
All models.......... 8.1
5 spd add.......... .5
Renew front pinion brgs add.......... .8
w/Turbo Diesel add.......... .6

Speedometer Drive Gear, Renew
All models.......... .5

Transmission Mounts, Renew
All models
left.......... .3
center.......... .6

LABOR 21 SHIFT LINKAGE 21 LABOR

	(Factory Time)	Chilton Time
STANDARD TRANSMISSION		
Gearshift Lever, Renew		
All models		.6
Shift Linkage, Adjust		
4-speed		.4
5-speed		.5
Gearshift Tube, Renew		
Includes: Adjustment.		
All models		1.3
AUTOMATIC TRANSMISSION		
Selector Cable, Adjust		
All models		.4
Selector Lever, Renew		
All models		1.0

LABOR 23 AUTOMATIC TRANSMISSION 23 LABOR

	(Factory Time)	Chilton Time
ON CAR SERVICES		
Drain & Refill Unit		
All models		.8
Performance Test		
Includes: Inspect fluid level, perform stall speed and pressure test.		
All models		1.0
Check Unit for Oil Leaks		
Includes: Clean and dry outside of case and run unit to determine point of leak.		
All models		.9
Neutral Safety Switch, Renew		
All models		.4
Oil Pan Gasket, Renew		
Includes: Clean pan and pump strainer.		
All models		.9
Governor, Renew		
All models		.5
Valve Body Assembly, Renew		
Includes: R&R oil pan.		
All models		1.4
Valve Body Assy., R&R and Recondition		
Includes: R&R oil pan and clean pan and strainer. Disassemble, clean, inspect and free up all valves. Replace parts as required.		
All models		2.5
Vacuum Modulator, Renew		
All models		.6
Kickdown Switch, Renew		
All models		.9
Electro Magnet, Renew		
Includes: R&R oil pan and valve body.		
All models		2.0
Transmission Mounts, Renew		
All models		
left		.3
center		.6
SERVICES REQUIRING R&R		
Transmission Assembly, Remove & Install		
All models		4.9
Transmission Assy., R&R and Recondition		
Includes: Disassemble trans, including valve body. Clean, inspect and renew all parts as required.		
All models		9.4
Torque Converter, Renew		
Includes: R&R transmission.		
All models		5.1
Renew seal add		.4
Renew bushing add		.2

LABOR 26 DRIVE AXLE 26 LABOR

	(Factory Time)	Chilton Time
Final Drive Axle Shaft Assy., R&R or Renew		
All models-one side		.9
both sides		1.5
C.V. Joint Boots, Renew		
Includes: R&R axle shaft.		
All models-one		1.3
both-one side		1.5
all-both sides		2.9
Final Drive Oil Seal or Flange, Renew (One)		
Includes: R&R axle shaft.		
All models		
w/M.T.		1.2
w/A.T.		
left side		2.1
right side		1.2
SERVICES REQUIRING R&R WITH MANUAL TRANS.		
Ring Gear and Pinion, Renew		
Includes: Adjust bearing preload.		
All models		10.5
Differential Housing Bearings, Renew		
Includes: Adjust bearing preload.		
All models		6.0
SERVICES REQUIRING R&R WITH AUTOMATIC TRANS.		
Differential Case, Renew		
Includes: All necessary adjustments.		
All models		11.5
Pinion Bearings, Renew		
Includes: Adjust bearing preload.		
All models		10.0
Ring Gear and Pinion, Renew		
Includes: Adjust bearing preload.		
All models		9.0
Differential Housing Bearings, Renew		
Includes: Adjust bearing preload.		
All models		6.0
Pinion Oil Seal, Renew		
All models		
front or rear		6.4

LABOR 27 REAR SUSPENSION 27 LABOR

	(Factory Time)	Chilton Time
Check Front and Rear Axle Alignment		
Add alignement charges.		
All models		1.0
Rear Wheel Bearings, Renew		
All models-one side		1.4
both sides		2.5
Rear Wheel Bearing Oil Seal, Renew		
All models-one side		.6
Rear Stub Axle, Renew		
All models-one		1.4
both		2.5
Rear Leaf Springs, Renew		
All models-each		1.1
Rear Shock Absorbers, Renew		
All models-each		.3
Rear Sway Bar, Renew		
All models		.6
Renew bushings add		.3

LABOR 28 AIR CONDITIONING 28 LABOR

(Factory Time) Chilton Time

Note: If more than one item requires replacement where evacuation and discharging the system is already included in the operation, deduct 1.0 hour for each additional item to the times listed.

Drain, Evacuate & Recharge System
Includes: Leak check.
All models.. 1.5

Leak Check
Includes: Check all lines and connections.
All models.. .8

Compressor Drive Belt, Renew
All models-Gas 9
Diesel.. .8

Compressor Assembly, Renew
Includes: Transfer parts as required. Evacuate and charge system.
All models
Gas.. 3.0
Diesel.. 2.4

Compressor Clutch Coil, Renew
All models
Gas 1.2
Diesel... 1.1

Compressor Front Seal, Renew
Includes: R&R compressor and clutch assy. Evacuate and charge system.
All models
Gas 3.1
Diesel... 2.5

Condenser Assembly, Renew
Includes: Evacuate and charge system.
All models
large condenser.......................... 2.1
small condenser.......................... 2.0

Receiver-Drier, Renew
Includes: Evacuate and charge system.
All models.. 1.7

Evaporator Coil, Renew
Includes: R&R evaporator. Evacuate and charge system.
All models
factory system 3.7
recirculating system..................... 3.0

Blower Motor, Renew
All models.. 1.5

Expansion Valve, Renew
Includes: Evacuate and charge system.
All models
factory system *2.7
recirculating system..................... *3.6

*Requires R&R evaporator.

Air Conditioning Hoses, Renew
Includes: Evacuate and charge system.
All models
Discharge hose
All systems.............................. 1.6
Suction hose
All systems.............................. 1.6

LABOR 29 LOCKS, HINGES & WIND. REGULATORS 29 LABOR

(Factory Time) Chilton Time

Hood Hinge, Renew (One)
Includes: R&R hood where required.
All models.. 1.1

Hood Lock, Renew
All models.. .5

Hood Release Cable, Renew
All models.. .9

Door Handle (Outer), Renew
Includes: R&R trim panel.
All models-front.............................. .7
rear 4

Front Door Lock Cylinder, Renew
Includes: R&R trim panel and door handle.
All models.. .4

Door Lock Assy., Renew (Front or Rear)
Includes: R&R trim panel.
All models.. .6

Lock Striker Pin, Renew
All models.. .2

Door Lock Remote Control, Renew (Front or Rear)
Includes: R&R trim panel.
All models.. .6

Window Regulator, Renew (Front or Rear)
Includes: R&R trim panel.
All models.. 1.2

Rear Lid Lock Cylinder, Renew
All models.. .4

LABOR 30 HEAD AND PARKING LAMPS 30 LABOR

(Factory Time) Chilton Time

Aim Headlamps
All models.. .4

Headlamp Sealed Beam Bulb, Renew
Includes: Aim headlamp.
All models-one 4

Parking Lamp Lens or Bulb, Renew
All models.. .3

Tail or Stop Lamp Lens or Bulb, Renew
All models.. .3

License Plate Lamp, Renew
All models.. .2

Side Marker Lamp Lens or Bulb, Renew
All models.. .2

LABOR 31 WINDSHIELD WIPER & SPEEDOMETER 31 LABOR

Windshield Wiper Motor, Renew
All models.. .8

Windshield Wiper/Washer Switch Assy., Renew
All models.. .5

Wiper/Washer Relay, Renew
All models.. .4

Wiper Linkage, Renew
All models.. 1.0

Rear Window Wiper Switch, Renew
All models.. .4

Rear Window Wiper Motor, Renew
All models.. 1.2

Windshield Washer Pump, Renew
All models.. .4

Speedometer Head, R&R or Renew
All models.. .6

Speedometer Cable and Casing, Renew
All models
upper.. 1.1
lower 5

Speedometer Drive Gear, Renew
All models.. .5

Radio, R&R
All models.. .7

LABOR 32 LIGHT SWITCHES & WIRING 32 LABOR

Headlamp Switch, Renew
All models.. .5

Brake Light Switches, Renew (One or Both)
Includes: Bleed brakes.
All models.. 1.0

Turn Signal/Dimmer Switch Assy., Renew
All models.. .9

Emergency Flasher Switch, Renew
All models.. .5

Back-Up Light Switch, Renew
All models
w/M.T. 5
w/A.T.. .6

Turn Signal/Emergency Flasher Relay, Renew
All models.. .3

Horns, Renew
All models-each 2

Turn Signal Switch, Renew
All models.. .8

GENERAL CONVERSION TABLE

Multiply By	To Convert	To	
		Length	—
2.54	Inches	Centimeters	.3937
25.4	Inches	Millimeters	.03937
30.48	Feet	Centimeters	.0328
.304	Feet	Meters	3.28
.914	Yards	Meters	1.094
1.609	Miles	Kilometers	.621
		Volume	
.473	Pints	Liters	2.11
.946	Quarts	Liters	1.06
3.785	Gallons	Liters	.264
.016	Cubic inches	Liters	61.02
16.39	Cubic inches	Cubic cms.	.061
28.3	Cubic feet	Liters	.0353
		Mass (Weight)	
28.35	Ounces	Grams	.035
.4536	Pounds	Kilograms	2.20
		Area	
.645	Square inches	Square cms.	.155
.836	Square yds.	Square meters	1.196
		Force	
4.448	Pounds	Newtons	.225
.138	Ft./lbs.	Kilogram/meters	7.23
1.36	Ft./lbs.	Newton-meters	.737
.112	In./lbs.	Newton-meters	8.844
		Pressure	
.068	Psi	Atmospheres	14.7
6.89	Psi	Kilopascals	.145
		Other	
1.104	Horsepower (DIN)	Horsepower (SAE)	.9861
.746	Horsepower (SAE)	Kilowatts (KW)	1.34
1.60	Mph	Km/h	.625
.425	Mpg	Km/1	2.35
—	**To obtain**	**From**	**Multiply by**

TAP DRILL SIZES

NATIONAL COARSE OR U.S.S.						NATIONAL FINE OR S.A.E.					
Screw & Tap Size	Threads Per Inch	Use Drill Number	Screw & Tap Size	Threads Per Inch	Use Drill Number	Screw & Tap Size	Threads Per Inch	Use Drill Number	Screw & Tap Size	Threads Per Inch	Use Drill Number
No. 5	40	39	1/2	13	27/64	No. 5	44	37	1/2	20	29/64
No. 6	32	36	9/16	12	31/64	No. 6	40	33	9/16	18	33/64
No. 8	32	29	5/8	11	17/32	No. 8	36	29	5/8	18	37/64
No. 10	24	25	3/4	10	21/32	No. 10	32	21	3/4	16	11/16
No. 12	24	17	7/8	9	49/64	No. 12	28	15	7/8	14	13/16
1/4	20	8	1	8	7/8	1/4	28	3	1 1/8	12	1 3/64
5/16	18	F	1 1/8	7	63/64	5/16	24	1	1 1/4	12	1 11/64
3/8	16	5/16	1 1/4	7	1 7/64	3/8	24	Q	1 1/2	12	1 27/64
7/16	14	U	1 1/2	6	1 11/32	7/16	20	W			

TAP DRILL SIZES

NATIONAL COARSE OR U.S.S.

Screw & Tap Size	Threads Per Inch	Use Drill Number
No. 5	40	39
No. 6	32	36
No. 8	32	29
No. 10	24	25
No. 12	24	17
1/4	20	8
5/16	18	F
3/8	16	5/16
7/16	14	U
1/2	13	27/64
9/16	12	31/64
5/8	11	17/32
3/4	10	21/32
7/8	9	49/64
1	8	7/8
1 1/8	7	63/64
1 1/4	7	1 7/64
1 1/2	6	1 11/32

NATIONAL FINE OR S.A.E.

Screw & Tap Size	Threads Per Inch	Use Drill Number
No. 5	44	37
No. 6	40	33
No. 8	36	29
No. 10	32	21
No. 12	28	15
1/4	28	3
5/16	24	1
3/8	24	Q
7/16	20	W
1/2	20	29/64
9/16	18	33/64
5/8	18	37/64
3/4	16	11/16
7/8	14	13/16
1 1/8	12	1 3/64
1 1/4	12	1 11/64
1 1/2	12	1 27/64

DECIMAL EQUIVALENT SIZE OF THE NUMBER DRILLS

Drill No.	Decimal Equivalent	Drill No.	Decimal Equivalent	Drill No.	Decimal Equivalent
80	.0135	53	.0595	26	.1470
79	.0145	52	.0635	25	.1495
78	.0160	51	.0670	24	.1520
77	.0180	50	.0700	23	.1540
76	.0200	49	.0730	22	.1570
75	.0210	48	.0760	21	.1590
74	.0225	47	.0785	20	.1610
73	.0240	46	.0810	19	.1660
72	.0250	45	.0820	18	.1695
71	.0260	44	.0860	17	.1730
70	.0280	43	.0890	16	.1770
69	.0292	42	.0935	15	.1800
68	.0310	41	.0960	14	.1820
67	.0320	40	.0980	13	.1850
66	.0330	39	.0995	12	.1890
65	.0350	38	.1015	11	.1910
64	.0360	37	.1040	10	.1935
63	.0370	36	.1065	9	.1960
62	.0380	35	.1100	8	.1990
61	.0390	34	.1110	7	.2010
60	.0400	33	.1130	6	.2040
59	.0410	32	.1160	5	.2055
58	.0420	31	.1200	4	.2090
57	.0430	30	.1285	3	.2130
56	.0465	29	.1360	2	.2210
55	.0520	28	.1405	1	.2280
54	.0550	27	.1440		

DECIMAL EQUIVALENT SIZE OF THE LETTER DRILLS

Letter Drill	Decimal Equivalent	Letter Drill	Decimal Equivalent	Letter Drill	Decimal Equivalent
A	.234	J	.277	S	.348
B	.238	K	.281	T	.358
C	.242	L	.290	U	.368
D	.246	M	.295	V	.377
E	.250	N	.302	W	.386
F	.257	O	.316	X	.397
G	.261	P	.323	Y	.404
H	.266	Q	.332	Z	.413
I	.272	R	.339		

DECIMAL EQUIVALENTS OF THE COMMON FRACTIONS

1/64 = .0156
1/32 = .0313
3/64 = .0469
1/16 = .0625
5/64 = .0781
3/32 = .0938
7/64 = .1094
1/8 = .1250
9/64 = .1406
5/32 = .1563
11/64 = .1719
3/16 = .1875
13/64 = .2031
7/32 = .2188
15/64 = .2344
1/4 = .2500
17/64 = .2656
9/32 = .2813
19/64 = .2969
5/16 = .3125
21/64 = .3281
11/32 = .3438
23/64 = .3594
3/8 = .3750
25/64 = .3906
13/32 = .4063
27/64 = .4219
7/16 = .4375
29/64 = .4531
15/32 = .4688
31/64 = .4844
1/2 = .5000
33/64 = .5156
17/32 = .5313
35/64 = .5469
9/16 = .5625
37/64 = .5781
19/32 = .5938
39/64 = .6094
5/8 = .6250
41/64 = .6406
21/32 = .6563
43/64 = .6719
11/16 = .6875
45/64 = .7031
23/32 = .7188
47/64 = .7344
3/4 = .7500
49/64 = .7656
25/32 = .7813
51/64 = .7969
13/16 = .8125
53/64 = .8281
27/32 = .8438
55/64 = .8594
7/8 = .8750
57/64 = .8906
29/32 = .9063
59/64 = .9219
15/16 = .9375
61/64 = .9531
31/32 = .9688
63/64 = .9844